THE COMPANION BIBLE

THE COMPANION BIBLE

The Authorized Version of 1611
with
the Structures
and
Critical, Explanatory,
and Suggestive Notes
and with
198 Appendixes

"When thou goest, it shall lead thee;
When thou sleepest, it shall keep thee;
And when thou awakest, it shall talk with thee."
(Proverbs 6:22)

kregel
PUBLICATIONS
Grand Rapids, MI 49501

The Companion Bible was originally released in six parts, beginning in 1910. E. W. Bullinger's notes throughout the text give valuable insights into the original Hebrew and Greek languages, alternate translations, explanations of figures of speech, cross-references, detailed outlines of each book, and 198 appendices.

Publisher's Disclaimer: This volume is printed from the original typesetting. Therefore, there are incidences of broken type, typographical errors, and charts that are sometimes difficult to read. This is the nature of this classic volume, and these elements are not considered defects within the publisher's control.

The Companion Bible
The Authorized Version of 1611 (KJV)

Originally published in 1922
Notes and appendixes by E. W. Bullinger

ISBN 978-0-8254-2099-3 Enlarged type hardcover
ISBN 978-0-8254-2203-4 Burgundy hardcover
ISBN 978-0-8254-2180-8 Burgundy hardcover, indexed
ISBN 978-0-8254-2288-1 Burgundy bonded leather
ISBN 978-0-8254-2179-2 Burgundy bonded leather, indexed
ISBN 978-0-8254-2177-8 Black bonded leather
ISBN 978-0-8254-2178-5 Black bonded leather, indexed
ISBN 978-0-8254-2237-9 Black genuine leather
ISBN 978-0-8254-2240-9 Black genuine leather, indexed

20 21 22 23 24 / 18 17 16 15 14

Printed in South Korea

CONTENTS.

PREFACE.

THE COMPANION BIBLE is a new Edition of the English Bible. Published originally in six Parts, it is now presented in one Volume, and the description which follows shows that the Work is a self-explanatory Bible designed for the general use of all English readers throughout the world.

It has an amount of information (much of it hitherto inaccessible to the ordinary English reader) in its wide margins not to be found in any edition of the A.V. extant. Its position, in these respects, is unique.

In size and weight, and type and paper, as well as price, it will compare favourably with all existing editions.

It is called THE COMPANION BIBLE because its wide margin is intended to be a Companion to the Text; and the whole is designed as the Companion of all readers of the Bible.

The human element is excluded, as far as possible, so that the reader may realize that the pervading object of the book is not merely to enable him to interpret the Bible, but to make the Bible the interpreter of God's Word, and Will, to him.

To the same end this Edition is not associated with the name of any man; so that its usefulness may neither be influenced nor limited by any such consideration; but that it may commend itself, on its own merits, to the whole English-speaking race.

It is NOT A NEW Translation.

It is NOT AN AMENDED Translation.

It is NOT A COMMENTARY.

THE TEXT.

The Text is that of the Authorized Version of 1611 as published by the Revisers in their "Parallel Bible" in 1886.

There are NO ALTERATIONS in the Text beyond what can be effected by a variation in the character of the TYPE. Hence, there is nothing that affects the ear when reading it aloud; but only that which meets the eye in order to call attention to important facts and truths.

All ancient readings and new and amended renderings are confined to the margin; which, for this purpose, extends to one-half the width of the page.

There are no minute English or Greek "superior" letters to confuse the Text; or to perplex the reader when searching for the corresponding number or letter in the margin.

PREFACE.

THE TYPES EMPLOYED IN THE TEXT.

1. These distinguish ALL the Divine Names and Titles. (See Ap. 4.)
2. All pronouns used for the above have their initials indicated by capital letters.
3. The pronouns, &c., emphasized in the Original are in special type.
4. Attention is given to the capital and small letters in other cases where they affect interpretation.
5. The words spoken or cited are placed within quotation marks.
6. Where the Hebrew Text is written in separate lines, these lines are preserved by being presented in the same way in the present Edition.
7. In the Book of Psalms, the Titles will be printed so as to present the super-scriptions and sub-scriptions as brought to light and demonstrated by Dr. J. W. Thirtle.
8. In the New Testament, all *quotations* from the Old Testament will also be specially indicated.
9. Proper Names with their pronunciation, &c., are included in a special Appendix, No. 52.

The chapters and verses of the Authorized Version are retained; but spaces are introduced to mark them off into paragraphs; so that the advantages of both Verses and Paragraphs are retained. These paragraphs are not divided according to the usual Paragraph Bibles, but according to the Structures (see page viii), which are given in the right-hand margin; while the corresponding Index-letters are repeated in the left-hand margin, by the side of the Text with the number of the page where they may be found; so that the subjects of the various Paragraphs (or Members) may be seen at a glance, and be intelligently followed.

The other figures in the left-hand margin are the B.C. dates.

THE MARGIN.

A small circle (°) against a word or words in the Text calls attention to the same word or words which are REPEATED in the right-hand margin, with the number of the verse to which they belong.

In order to save repetition, and economize valuable space in the margin, words in the Text on which a note has already been given in a preceding verse in the same chapter, and to which the same note applies, are marked with the number of the verse in which such note is given.

When these words are referred to there will be found no "views" expressed, but only facts which are incontrovertible, and information which is indispensable.

Where references are given, these are not merely to PARALLEL PASSAGES, or to the same ENGLISH words, which are often as unnecessary as they are misleading; but only to those passages which explain the words in the Original, and which throw light upon their truth and teaching.

If an amended rendering is suggested in the margin, and several references follow, then the reader knows that he has before him ALL the occurrences of such words in the Original. Where there is "&c." at the end of such references, then he will know that the Hebrew or Greek word in question occurs too many times for all the passages to be given; but that a sufficient number is selected as evidence in favour of such amended rendering. Thus the reader will be able to judge for himself as to the accuracy of what is suggested: and the Bible becomes its own interpreter.

The Marginal Notes.

1. In the **Old Testament** all the important readings will be given[1] according to Dr. C. D. Ginsburg's *Massoretico-Critical Text* of the Hebrew Bible[2].

2. In the **New Testament** all the important readings will be given according to the evidence of the great textual critics, Griesbach, Lachmann, Tischendorf, Tregelles, Alford, Westcott and Hort, and the Revisers' Greek Text.

3. There are no words in Hebrew or Greek characters to burden or hinder the English reader. But a complete system of *Transliteration*, generally approved by Oriental Scholars (see p. x), will enable him readily to put back all such words into the Original characters with ease and accuracy. The Hebrew words are given not in the Inflection found in the Text, but in the root-form in which they will be looked for in Lexicons.

4. All important emendations are given—
   (*a*) Whether required by the above readings,
   (*b*) Or demanded for the sake of uniformity in translation,
   (*c*) Or, where the current renderings are inadequate and open to amendment[3]: not otherwise, or merely for the sake of giving an alternative.

5. The facts and phenomena treasured up in the *Massōrah* are for the first time presented in connection with the A. V.[2] (see Ap. 30).

6. All Figures of Speech are noted, and their bearing on interpretation[1]. These are the Holy Spirit's own markings, calling attention to what is *emphatic*, and worthy of our deepest attention (see Ap. 6).

7. The spiritual significance of Numbers is pointed out[1] (see Ap. 10).

8. The principal synonymous words in the Original are distinguished, especially those bearing on sin, atonement, and psychology.

9. The first occurrences of important words and expressions are duly noted[1].

10. The most recent Archæological discoveries in Assyria, Egypt, &c., are included.

11. Eastern manners and customs are explained, as they throw light on the Scriptures.

12. The meanings of Proper Names of persons or places are given where these are suggestive.

13. Money and Coins, Weights and Measures, are referred in every case to Appendix 51.

14. Chronology is dealt with on Biblical lines, which proceed on *durations* rather than *dates*. These are adhered to as given in the Bible itself, and are not adapted or made to conform to any system. This transforms a dry study into a subject of deepest interest. The various Charts and Tables are given in Appendix 50.

15. The Structures of the Books are given, and all their parts: which are the surest guide to their interpretation, and the strongest proof of their inspiration[1]. (See p. viii.)

[1] This is the first time that these have been presented in connection with the Authorized Version.
[2] These were inaccessible to the past generation of Commentators and Translators.
[3] By copying out the A. V., and substituting these amended renderings, the student may make *his own* new Revised Version.

The marginal notes do not record every POSSIBLE Reading or Emendation, as these would only load the pages with a mass of needless matter. Only those new readings and renderings are given which will remove difficulties from the Text, enlighten the eyes, inform the mind, affect the conscience, instruct the head, and influence the life.

Several of the above points are, for the first time, placed within the reach of the ordinary English reader.

THE STRUCTURES

referred to on p. vii make THE COMPANION BIBLE an unique edition, and require a special notice.

They give, not a mere *Analysis* evolved from the Text by human ingenuity, but a *Symmetrical Exhibition* of the Word itself, which may be discerned by the humblest reader of the Sacred Text, and seen to be one of the most important evidences of the Divine Inspiration of its words.

For these Structures constitute a remarkable phenomenon peculiar to Divine Revelation; and are not found outside it in any other form of known literature.

This distinguishing feature is caused by the *repetition of subjects* which reappear[1], either in alternation or introversion, or a combination of both in many divers manners.

This repetition is called "Correspondence", which may be by way of similarity of contrast; synthetic or antithetic.

The subjects of the various Members are indicated by letters, which are quite arbitrary and are used only for convenience. The subject of one Member is marked by a letter in Roman type, while the repetition of it is marked by the same letter in Italic type. These are always in line (vertically), one with the other.

When the alphabet is exhausted, it is repeated, as often as may be necessary.

The Structure of the whole book is given at the commencement of each book; and all the succeeding Structures are the expansion of this.

Each Structure is referred back to the page containing the larger Member, of which it is an expansion or development.

The large Members forming a telescopic view of the whole book are thus expanded, divided, and subdivided, until chapters and paragraphs, and even verses and sentences, are seen to form part of a wondrous whole, giving a microscopic view of its manifold details, and showing forth the fact, that while the works of the LORD are great and perfect, the WORD of the LORD is the greatest of His works, and is "perfect" also (Psalm 19. 7).

THE APPENDIXES

contain a large amount of information bearing on the various questions raised by the phenomena of the Sacred Text.

Those issued with each of the four volumes pertain principally to such volumes. But in the complete Bible they will all be placed together at the end.

The number of those which are given with the Pentateuch may be out of proportion to the total number, because those issued with Genesis are needed not only for that book, but many of them (such as the Chronological Tables, &c.) contain information that will be required and referred to throughout the Bible.

The order of the Appendixes is determined for the most part by the order in which the subjects are raised in the Text of the Bible.

[1] It is this repetition which has made possible the system of Bible-marking known by some as "Railways."

EXPLANATIONS.

References. Where there is no name of a book in the margin, the reference is always to the same book, and all the References in the margin are to *The Companion Bible*, not to any Edition of the A. V., or R. V.

Superior Figures, in the Text, always refer to the verse, so numbered, in the same chapter.

The repetition of the same subject in a note is sometimes indicated by its initial (capital) letter.

The figures in the left-hand margin relate to two separate matters. Those in brackets, with a " p ", refer to the number of the page on which the corresponding letter and member will be found. The number of the page so indicated holds good until another page number is given.

The other figures refer to the B. C. dates.

THE TRANSLITERATION OF HEBREW WORDS.

With the aid of the following Table, any English reader who knows the Hebrew alphabet can put back the English letters into the Hebrew characters, by noting the exact equivalents:—

Consonants.

b = בּ (*Beth*).*
d = דּ (*Daleth*).*
g = גּ (*Gimel*).*
h = ה (*He*).
ḥ = ח (*Cheth*), sometimes *ch*.
k = כּ (*Kaph*).* Final = ך.
ḳ = ק (*Koph*).
l = ל (*Lamed*).
m = מ (*Mem*). Final = ם.
n = נ (*Nun*). Final = ן.
p = פּ (*Pē*).*
ph = פ ,, Final = ף.
r = ר (*Resh*).
ș = ס (*Samech*).
s = שׂ (*Sin*).
sh = שׁ (*Shin*).
ṭ = ט (*Teth*).
t = תּ (*Tau*).*
th = ת ,,
v = וּ (*Vau* or *Vav*).
w = ו ,,
y = י (*Yod* or '*Jot*').
z = ז (*Zayin*).
ẓ = צ (*Ẓaddi*). Final = ץ.

Vowels.

' = א (*Aleph*).
' = ע (*Ayin*).
a = ַ (*Pathaḥ*). 'a = אַ; 'a = עַ.
ă = ֲ (*Ḥateph pathaḥ*). 'ă = אֲ; 'ă = עֲ.
ā = ָ (*Ḳamez*). 'ā = אָ; 'ā = עָ.

e = ֶ (*S^e^gol*). 'e = אֶ; 'e = עֶ.
ĕ = ֱ (*Ḥateph S^e^gol*). 'ĕ = אֱ; 'ĕ = עֱ.
ē = ֵ (*Ẓērē*). 'ē = אֵ; 'ē = עֵ.
^e^ = ְ (*Sh^e^vah*).

i = ִ (*Ḥirek*). 'i = אִ; 'i = עִ.
ī = ִי (*Ḥirek*) long. 'ī = אִי; 'ī = עִי.

o = ֹ (*Ḥolem*). 'o = אֹ; 'o = עֹ.
ŏ = ֳ (*Ḥateph ḳamez*). 'ŏ = אֳ; 'ŏ = עֳ.
ō = וֹ (*Ḥolem*) long.

u = ֻ (*Ḳibbuẓ*). 'ŭ = אֻ; 'ŭ = עֻ.
ū = וּ (*Shureḳ*).

The six consonants marked with an asterisk (*) have a dot (*Dagesh*) within them, when placed at the beginning of a word; but not when they are situated in any other

TRANSLITERATION OF HEBREW WORDS (*cont.*).

part of the word (except when the letter in question is to be doubled, in which case it is doubled in the English).

As an example of the application of the above principles, the following is the first verse in the Hebrew Bible, the Hebrew being read from right to left:—

[1] B^{e}rē'shīth [2] bār'ā [3] 'ĕlohīm [4] ēth [5] hashshāmayim [6] v^{e}ēth [7] hā'ārez.

בְּרֵאשִׁית [1] בָּרָא [2] אֱלֹהִים [3] אֵת [4] הַשָּׁמַיִם [5] וְאֵת [6] הָאָרֶץ [7] ׃

All Hebrew words are given, not in the Inflection which occurs in the Text, but in the root-form which will be looked for in the Lexicon.

ABBREVIATIONS.

Abim. = Abimelech.
abt. = about.
Acc. = Accusative Case.
acc. = according to, *or* accordingly.
Acct. = Account.
A. D. = Anno Domini.
Adj. = Adjective.
aff. = affirmation.
agst. = against.
A. M. = Anno Mundi.
Ant. = Antiquities.
Ap. = Appendix.
App. = Apposition.
Appl. = Application.
Arab. = Arabic Version of portions of the Hebrew Old Testament about 900 A. D.
Aram. = Aramaean, or ancient Chaldee translation about 200 A. D.
Art. = the Definite Article "the", when emphatic.
A. S. = Anglo-Saxon.
A. V. = Authorized Version.

Bab. = Babylonian.
B. C. = Before Christ.
bec. = because.
beg. = beginning.

Ch. = Chapter.
Chald. = Chaldee language.
cld. = could.
Cod. = Codex, Codices=MSS.
coll. = collective.
com. = commandment.
comp. = compare.
conj. = Conjunction.
cov. = covenant.
cp. = compare.

diff. = different.
Diod. Sic. = Diodorus Siculus (second half of first century A. D.).
Div. = Divine.

E. = East.
Ed. *or* Edn. = Edition.
Emph. = Emphasis: emphasise: emphatic.
Eng. = English.
Esp. = Especially.

fem. = feminine.
Fig. = Figure of Speech.
follg. = following.
freq. = frequently.
fulf. = fulfilled, *or* fulfilment.

Gb. = Ginsburg.
Gen. = Genitive.
genl. = general.
Gr. = Greek.

Heb. = Hebrew.

Imp. = Imperative Mood.
Imperf. = Imperfect Tense.
Ind. = Indicative Mood.
Int. = Introduction.

Jeh. = Jehovah.
Jer. = Jerome.
Jon. = The Targum of Jonathan ben Uzziel; a Chaldee or Aramaean paraphrase on certain Old Testament books: not so ancient or valuable as that of Onkelos. About 30 B. C.

Lat. = Latin.
Lit. = Literal, literally.

Marg. = Margin.
Masc. = Masculine.
MS. = Manuscript, *or* Codex.
MSS. = Manuscripts, *or* Codices.

N. .... = North.
Neg. .... = Negative.
No. .... = Number.
N. T. .... = New Testament.

Occ. .... = occurs, occurrence.
Onk. .... = The Targum of Onkelos: a Chaldee paraphrase of certain Old Testament books: older and more faithful than that of Jonathan (see "Jon." above). Date about third century B.C. in Babylonia.
opp. .... = opposite.
Orth. .... = Orthography.
O. T. .... = Old Testament.

p. .... = page.
par. .... = particular.
Part. .... = Participle.
Pent. .... = Pentateuch.
pers. .... = person.
Phil. .... = Philadelphus.
pl. .... = plural.
pos. .... = positive.
pp. .... = pages.
Prep. .... = Preposition.
prob. .... = probably.
Prof. .... = Professor.
Pron. .... = Pronoun.

q.v. .... = which see.

R. .... = reading.
Rab. .... = Rabbinic.
ref. .... = referring to, reference.
R.V. .... = Revised Version.

S. .... = South.
Sam. .... = Samaritan Pentateuch. Very ancient. Supposed to have come down from the Ten Tribes at least as early as fourth century B. C., and earlier than the Septuagint.
Sept. .... = Septuagint Version of the Hebrew Old Testament in Greek. Made in Alexandria the third or second century B. C. Valuable, because made from MSS. older than any now extant.
sig. .... = significance.
sing. .... = singular.
Sir. .... = Sirach.
symb. .... = symbolic.
Syr. .... = Syriac Version, made from the Hebrew for Christian use before the fourth century A. D.

Targ. .... = Targum.
Theoc. .... = Theocritus.
trs. .... = translate.

v. .... = verse.
vv. .... = verses.
var. .... = various.
vol. .... = volume.
V. R. .... = various reading.
Vulg. .... = The Vulgate, or Latin Version of the Bible, made by Jerome about close of fourth century A. D., and authorised by the Council of Trent, 1545–1563.

W. .... = West.
wild. .... = wilderness.
wisd. .... = wisdom.

GENESIS.

THE STRUCTURE OF THE BOOK AS A WHOLE.

(*Division*).

A1 | **1. 1 — 2. 3.** THE INTRODUCTION.

A2 | **2. 4 — 50. 26.** THE ELEVEN "GENERATIONS"*.

Gen. 1. 1 — 2. 3. (A1 above) THE INTRODUCTION.

(*Alternation.*)

A1 | **A** | 1. 1. "THE WORLD THAT THEN WAS" (2 Pet. 3. 6). ITS CREATION IN ETERNITY PAST

B | 1. 2-. ITS END. RUIN.

A | 1. -2-31. "THE HEAVENS AND THE EARTH WHICH ARE NOW" (2 Pet. 3. 7). THEIR CREATION IN TIME PRESENT. (THE SIX DAYS.)

B | 2. 1-3. THEIR END. BLESSING.

Gen. 2. 4 — 50. 26. (A2 above) THE ELEVEN "GENERATIONS"*.

(*Extended Alternation with Introversion.*)

A2 | **C** | **E** | "THE HEAVENS AND THE EARTH" (2. 4 — 4. 26)

F | ADAM (5. 1 — 6. 8)

G | NOAH (6. 9 — 9. 29) — MANKIND IN GENERAL.

H | THE SONS OF NOAH (10. 1 — 11. 9)

I | SHEM (11. 10 — 11. 26)

D | TERAH (11. 27 — 25. 11).

C | *E* | ISHMAEL (25. 12-18)

F | ISAAC (25. 19 — 35. 29)

G | ESAU (36. 1-8) — THE CHOSEN PEOPLE.

H | THE SONS OF ESAU (36. 9-43)

I | JACOB (37. 1 — 50. 26)

---

* There are 14 altogether in the Bible:	
The above in Genesis	11
The Generations of Aaron and Moses (Num. 3. 1)	1
The Generations of Pharez (Ruth 4. 18-22)	1
	— 13
† The Book of the Generations of Jesus Christ (Matt. 1. 1)	1
	14

---

† This latter needed to complete the number of spiritual perfection (2 × 7 = 14). See Ap. 10.

THE °FIRST °BOOK OF °MOSES,

CALLED

°GENESIS.

A1 A (p. 1) 1 IN the beginning °God °created °the heaven
and the earth.

B 2 °And °the earth °was °without form, and
void; and darkness °*was* upon the °face of the
deep.

A a And °the Spirit of God moved upon the °face of
(p. 3) the waters.

4004 3 And [1]God °said, "Let there °be light:" and
there °was light.

4 And [1]God °saw the light, that *it was* °good:
and [1]God °divided the light from the darkness.

5 And [1]God °called the light Day, and the
darkness He °called Night. And the °evening
and the morning were the °first °day.

b 6 And [1]God [3]said, "Let there be a °firmament
in the midst of the waters, and let it divide the
waters from the waters."

7 And [1]God °made the [6]firmament, and
[4]divided the waters which *were* under the
firmament from the waters which *were* above
the firmament: and it was so.

8 And [1]God [5]called the [6]firmament °Heaven.
And the [5]evening and the morning were the
second [5]day.

First Book. For its relation to the other books of the Pentateuch as well as to the Hebrew Canon of O.T., see Ap. 1. **Book.** See Ap. 47.

Moses. Ascribed to him, Mark 10. 2-8, &c.; see Ap. 2.

Genesis. No part of Hebrew Title, which is simply *Berēshīth*, "in [the] beginning", because the book of all beginnings. Genesis is Greek = generation, creation. For its being complementary to the Apocalypse, see Ap. 3.

1 "THE WORLD THAT THEN WAS" (2 Pet. 3. 5, 6). See Structure, p. 1. Creation in eternity past, to which all Fossils and "Remains" belong.

God. Heb. *Elohim*, pl. First occurrence connects it with creation, and denotes, by usage, the Creator in relation to His creatures. See Ap. 4. The Heb. accent *Athnach* places the emphasis, and gives pause, on "God" as being Himself the great worker, separating the Worker from His work.

created (sing.). Occurs 6 times in this Introduction. Other acts 46 times. See Ap. 5. Perfection implied. Deut. 32. 4. 2 Sam. 22. 31. Job 38. 7. Ps. 111; 147. 3-5. Prov. 3. 19. Ecc. 3. 11-14. [Even the Greek *Cosmos* = ornament. Ex. 33. 4-6. Isa. 49. 18. Jer. 4. 30. Eze. 7. 20. 1 Pet. 3. 3.]

the heaven and the earth. With Heb. Particle *'eth* before each, emphasising the Article "the", and thus distinguishing both from 2. 1. "Heavens" in Heb. always in pl. See note on Deut. 4. 26.

2 And. Note the Fig. *Polysyndeton* (Ap. 6), by which, in the 34 verses of this Introduction, each one of 102 separate acts are emphasised; and the important word "God" in *v.* 1 is carried like a lamp through the whole of this Introduction (1. 1—2. 3). **the earth.** Fig. *Anadiplosis.* See Ap. 6. **was** = *became.* See Gen. 2. 7; 4. 3; 9. 15; 19. 26. Ex. 32. 1. Deut. 27. 9. 2 Sam. 7. 24, &c. Also rendered *came to pass*, Gen. 4. 14; 22. 1; 23. 1; 27. 1. Josh. 4. 1; 5. 1. 1 Kings 13. 32. Isa. 14. 24, &c. Also rendered *be* (in the sense of *become*), *v.* 3, &c., and where the verb "to be" is not in italic type. Hence, Ex. 3. 1, kept = *became* keeper, quit = *become* men, &c. See Ap. 7. **without form** = *waste.* Heb. *tohū vā bohū.* Fig. *Paronomasia.* Ap. 6. Not created *tohū* (Isa. 45. 18), but became *tohū* (Gen. 1. 2. 2 Pet. 3. 5, 6). "An enemy hath done this" (Matt. 13. 25, 28, 39. Cp. 1 Cor. 14. 33). See Ap. 8. **was.** This is in italic type, because no verb "to be" in Heb. (see Ap. 7). In like manner man became a ruin (Gen. 3. Ps. 14. 1-3; 51. 5; 53. 1-3. Ecc. 7. 20. Rom. 7. 18). **face.** Fig. *Pleonasm.* Ap. 6.

1. -2-31 (*A*, p. 1). "THE HEAVENS AND EARTH WHICH ARE NOW" (*Extended Alternation*).

A | a | -2-5. Darkness and Light. Night and Day — 1st Day.
b | 6-8. Waters. Division between them. — 2nd Day.
c | 9-13. Earth. Fruit from it. — 3rd Day.
a | 14-19. Day and Night. Sun and Moon. — 4th Day.
b | 20-23. Waters. Life from them. — 5th Day.
c | 24-31. Earth. Life from it. — 6th Day.

-2 the Spirit of God moved (see Ap. 9) = The beginning of "the heavens and earth which are now" (2 Pet. 3. 7). It is even so in the New Creation. The Spirit moves (John 3. 3-8. Rom. 8. 5, 9, 14. Gal. 4. 29. 2 Cor. 5. 17, 18). **3 God said** (occurs 10 times in Introduction). This begins each day: 3rd day twice; 6th day four times. The second act is also of God (1 Pet. 1. 23-25). Ap. 5. **be light** = become light (as in *v.* 2), not the verb "to be". Light not located till 4th day. **was** = became, as in *v.* 2. It is even so in the New Creation: His Word enters and gives light (Ps. 119. 130. 2 Cor. 4. 6). **4 saw.** Occurs 7 times in Introduction. Ap. 5. **good** = beautiful (Ecc. 3. 11). **divided.** Occurs twice. Ap. 5. Each day's work called "good", except the 2nd, because nothing created on that day: only division made. **5 called.** Occurs 5 times. Ap. 5. **evening . . . morning.** Fig. *Synecdoche* (of the Part), Ap. 6. Put for a full day. The beginning and end of anything is put for the whole of it. Cp. Ecc. 3. 11; 10. 13; 11. 6. Ps. 92. 2. Isa. 41. 4; 44. 6; 48. 12. Rev. 1. 8, 11, 17; 2. 8; 21. 6; 22. 13. **first.** For spiritual significance see Ap. 10. **first day** = day one. The word "day" may refer to a prolonged period when used without any qualifying words. But when qualified with a numeral (cardinal or ordinal) it is defined and limited by it to a day of 24 hours. It is further limited here by its boundaries "evening and morning", as well as by the 7th day. Cp. Ex. 20. 9, 11. See Ap 11. **6 firmament** = expanse. Something spread out. **7 made.** Occurs 7 times. Ap. 5. **8 Heaven** = Heb. high, lofty.

c (p. 3) 9 And [1]God [3]said, "Let the waters under the heaven be gathered together unto one place, and let the dry *land* appear:" and it was so.

10 And [1]God [5]called the [9]dry *land* Earth; and the gathering together of the waters [5]called He Seas: and [1]God [4]saw that *it was* [4]good.

11 And [1]God [3]said, "Let the earth bring forth grass, the herb yielding seed, *and* the fruit tree yielding fruit °after his kind, whose °seed *is* in itself, upon the earth:" and it was so.

12 And the earth brought forth grass, *and* herb yielding seed [11]after his kind, and the tree yielding fruit, whose seed *was* in itself, [11]after his kind: and [1]God [4]saw that *it was* [4]good.

13 And the [5]evening and the morning were the °third [5]day.

a 14 And [1]God [3]said, "Let there be °lights in the firmament of the heaven to divide the day from the night; and let them be for °signs, and for °seasons, and for days, and years:

15 And let them be for lights in the firmament of the heaven to give light upon the earth:" and it was so.

16 And [1]God [7]made °two great [14]lights; the greater light to rule the day, and the lesser light to rule the night: *He made* °the stars also.

17 And [1]God set them in the firmament of the heaven to give light upon the earth,

18 And to rule over the day and over the night, and to divide the light from the darkness: and [1]God [4]saw that *it was* [4]good.

19 And the [5]evening and the morning were the °fourth [5]day.

b 20 And [1]God [3]said, "Let the waters bring forth abundantly the moving creature that hath °life, and fowl *that* may fly above the earth in the open firmament of heaven."

21 And [1]God [1]created great °whales, and every living °creature that moveth, which the waters brought forth abundantly, [11]after their kind, and every winged fowl [11]after his kind: and [1]God [4]saw that *it was* [4]good.

22 And [1]God °blessed them, saying, "Be fruitful, and multiply, and fill the waters in the seas, and let fowl multiply in the earth."

23 And the °evening and the morning were the °fifth [5]day.

c 24 And [1]God [3]said, "Let the earth bring forth the living °creature [11]after his kind, cattle, and creeping thing, and beast of the earth [11]after his kind:" and it was so.

25 And [1]God [7]made the beast of the earth [11]after his kind, and cattle [11]after their kind, and every thing that creepeth upon the earth [11]after his kind: and [1]God [4]saw that *it was* [4]good.

26 And [1]God [3]said, °"Let Us make °man in Our °image, after Our likeness: °and let them have dominion over the fish of the sea, and over the fowl of the air, and over the cattle, and over all the earth, and over every creeping thing that creepeth upon the earth."

4004 27 So °God °created °man in His °*own* °image, in the °image of God °created He °him; male and female created He °them.

11 after his kind. Occurs 10 times (*vv.* 11, 12, 12, 21, 21, 24, 24, 25, 25, 25). See Ap. 10. Evolution has no answer to this.

seed is in itself. Heb. *seeding seed.* Fig. *Polyptōton,* Ap. 6. First the herb, then seed. First tree, then fruit.

13 third day = day three.

14 lights. Heb. *m'aōr* = lightholders or luminaries (Ex. 25. 6; 27. 20; 35. 14, &c. Cp. *v.* 3).

signs. Heb. *'ōth* = things to come (Jer. 10. 2).

seasons. Heb. *mō'ēd,* appointed times (from *y'ed,* to appoint). Occurs only 3 more times in Gen. See 17. 21; 18. 14; 21. 2.

16 two = the two.

the stars also. See Ap. 12.

19 fourth day = day four. See note on *v.* 5.

20 life = soul. Heb. *nephesh,* as in *vv.* 21, 24, 30; 2. 7, 19; 9. 4, 5, 5, 10, 12, 15, 16. Lev. 11. 46, &c. See Ap. 13.

21 whales = great sea-creatures.

creature = soul. Heb. *nephesh.* Cp. *v.* 20 and Ap. 13.

22 blessed. See on *v.* 1. Note the threefold blessing at Creation (1. 22, 28; 2. 3).

23 evening . . . morning. See on *v.* 5.

fifth. The No. of grace (Ap. 10). No blessing till the 5th day, when there was living soul to bless.

fifth day, or "day five". See note on *v.* 5.

24 creature = soul. Heb. *nephesh.* See Ap. 13.

26 Let us. The Divine *purpose* is here stated. The Divine *act* not described till 2. 7, 21–24.

man. Heb. *'ādām* (no Art.) = mankind.

image . . . likeness. Fig. *Hendiadys.* Ap. 6. One thing, not two = "In the likeness of our image", viz. of *Elohim* (not Jehovah), the 2nd person, who had taken creature form in order to *create* (Col. 1. 15. Heb. 1. 3. Rev. 3. 14; cp. Prov. 8. 22–31, and 1 Cor. 11. 3–11). Refers only to outward *form,* not to attributes. So He afterward took *human* form in order to *redeem* (John 1. 14). Cp. Rev. 4. 11 with 5. 9. In any case the "image and likeness" is physical, not moral. Man fell and is a moral ruin, but some physical likeness to *'ĕlohim* still remains. Cp. Gen. 9. 6. 1 Cor. 11. 7. Jas. 3. 9. No indication that that similitude was ever lost. Gen. 5. 3. See note on 3. 7.

and. Note Fig. *Polysyndeton* (Ap. 6) here, and throughout the Introduction (see *v.* 2), emphasising the Divine *purpose.*

27 God. The Heb. accent (*Paṣeḳ*) places the emphasis on God, the Carrier-out of His *purpose.*

created: i. e., when He did create. The description of the act postponed till 2. 7, 21–24. See note on *v.*26. The *Tosephta* (contemporary with the *Mishna,* about A. D. 200) translate *Sanhedrin,* viii. 7: "Why was man created last? That the heretics might not say there was a companion with Him in the work": i.e. lest man should have claimed a share in it.

man. Here the Heb. *'ādām* has the art., and the demonstrative Heb. *'eth,* to indicate that the man Adam created in 2. 7 was the "man" here purposed.

own. Wrongly supplied by A. V. and R. V.

image. Fig. *Anadiplosis* (Ap. 6) for emph.

him. Emphasised by Heb. accent (*Athnach*).

them. Emph. Here, in purpose. But, Gen. 2. 7, 21–24, in historical act and fact.

28 them. Emph. Fig. *Prolepsis* (Ap. 6). The actual building of Eve not till 2. 20–23.

replenish = fill, as 1. 22 and nearly every occurrence.

have dominion. Cp. Ps. 8. Heb. 2. 6–8. "But now . . . not yet."

28 [2]And [1]God [22]blessed [27]them, and [1]God [3]said unto °them, "Be fruitful, and multiply, and °replenish the earth, and subdue it: and °have dominion over the fish of the sea, and over the fowl of the air, and over every living thing that moveth upon the earth."

29 And [1]God [3]said, "Behold, I have given you every herb °bearing seed, which *is* upon the face of all the earth, and every tree, in the which *is* the fruit of a tree °yielding seed; to you it shall be °for meat.
30 And to every beast of the earth, and to every fowl of the air, and to every thing that creepeth upon the earth, wherein *there is* °life, °*I have given* every green herb for meat:" and it was so.
31 And [1]God [4]saw every thing that He had made, and, behold, *it was* very [4]good. And the [5]evening and the morning were °the sixth [23]day.

B (p. 1) 2 Thus °the heavens and the earth were finished, and all the host of them.
2 And on the °seventh °day °God ended His work which He had °made; and He °rested on the seventh day from all His work which He had °made.
3 And [2]God [22]blessed the seventh [5]day, and sanctified it: because that in it He had [2]rested from all His work which God °created and [2]made.

A (p. 5) 4 These *are* THE °GENERATIONS OF THE HEAVENS AND OF THE EARTH when they were created, °in the day that the °LORD God made the earth and the heavens,
5 And °every plant of the field before it was in the earth, and every herb of the field before it grew:
B a °for the [4]LORD God had not caused it to rain upon the earth, and *there was* not a man to till the ground.
b 6 °But there went up a °mist from the earth, and watered the whole face of the ground.
c 7 And the [4]LORD God °formed °man *of* the dust of the ground, and breathed into his nostrils the °breath °of life; and °man became a living °soul.
C d 8 (And the [4]LORD God planted a °garden °eastward in °Eden; and there He put [7]the man whom He had formed.
e 9 And out of the ground made the [4]LORD God to grow every tree that is pleasant to the sight, and good for food; the °tree of life also in the °midst of the garden, and the tree of °knowledge of °good and evil.
D 10 And a °river went out of Eden to water the

29 bearing seed . . . yielding seed. Heb. "seeding seed". Fig. *Polyptōton* (Ap. 6) for emph.
for meat. Not flesh till after the Flood (9. 3).
30 life = soul. Heb. *nephesh*. Cp. *v.* 20; 2. 7 and Ap. 13.
I have given. Fig. *Ellipsis* (Ap. 6. iii. a) correctly supplied from *v.* 29.
31 the sixth day. Here, with Art. "the"; unlike the other five days. Six, the No. of man. See Ap. 10.

2. 1 the heavens and the earth = "which are now" (2 Pet. 3. 7), see Structure on p. 1. Hence without Heb. Particle *'eth*. See note on 1. 1 and Deut. 4. 26.
2 seventh. Sam. and Sept. read "sixth", which is evidently correct. **day.** See on ch. 1. 5.
God ended. See on 1. 1 and Ap. 5.
made. See note on 1. 7.
rested. From achievement; man rests from fatigue.
3 created. See note on 1. 1.
The Introduction (1. 1—2. 3) is the summary: 2. 4-25 gives the details of ch. 1: ch. 2. 9-14 coming historically between *vv.* 12 and 13 of ch. 1.

2. 4—4. 26 (E, p. 1). "THE GENERATIONS OF THE HEAVENS AND OF THE EARTH."

J[1] | 2. 4-25. BEFORE the Fall. Man in Probation.
J[2] | 3. 1-24. The FALL of Man.
J[3] | 4. 1-26. AFTER the Fall. Man in Ruin.

2. 4-25 (J[1], above). MAN BEFORE THE FALL.
(Introversion and Extended Alternation.)

J[1] A | 2. 4, 5-. The earth for man and woman.
B | a | -5. For the ground, no man.
b | 6. The ground and vegetable creation.
c | 7. The formation of man.
C | d | 8. The Garden.
e | 9. The Trees.
D | 10-14. The Rivers.
C | *d* | 15. The Garden.
e | 16, 17. The Trees.
B | *a* | 18. For the man, no woman.
b | 19, 20-. The ground and animate creation.
c | -20-23. The formation of woman.
A | 24, 25. Man and woman for the earth.

4 generations = Family history. For the 14 in Bible, see the structure of the Book as a whole (p. 1). These are the Divine divisions, in which there is no trace of the Elohistic and Jehovistic theories. It should be seen here if anywhere. But note: there is only one in which *Elohim* is used (No. 1); only one to which *Jehovah* is peculiar (No. 10): five have both titles (Nos. 3, 4, 7, 9, 12). Four have neither title (Nos. 6, 8, 10, 11). All the speakers use "Jehovah" except the Nachash, Abimelech (to Abram, not to Isaac), sons of Heth, Pharaoh (of Joseph), Joseph's brethren, Joseph himself.
in the day = when. See on *v.* 17 and Ap. 18. Cp. 1. 5; 3. 17.
LORD God = First occ. See Ap. 4, and note above.
5 every plant, &c. This is an expansion of ch. 1. 11, 12, giving details.
for. Three reasons why plants in ground "before they grew": (1) no rain; (2) no man; (3) no mist: see *v.* 6.

6 But = and. **mist** = no mist . . . to water. The last of two or three negatives not necessary. Must be supplied by Fig. *Ellipsis* (Ap. 6. iii a), as in Deut. 33. 6. 1 Sam. 2. 3. Ps. 9. 18; 38. 1; 75. 5. Prov. 24. 12; 25. 27. Isa. 38. 18, &c. **7 formed.** As a potter. Isa. 64. 8. **man.** Heb. *'eth-'Hā'ādhām* (with art. and particle = "this same man Adam". See Ap. 14). **breath.** Heb. *neshāmāh*. See Ap. 16. **of.** Gen. of Apposition (Ap. 17) = "breath [that is] life". **soul.** Heb. *nephesh*. See "life", 1. 20, and Ap. 13. Cp. 7. 22. **8-14** Fig. *Parecbasis*. Ap 6. **8 garden.** This garden may be additional to 1. 11, 12; 2. 4, 5-. That creation concerns the "plants of the *field*" (1st occ.). This may have been a special planting, and lost when the garden and Eden were lost. Note the three gardens: (1) Eden, death *in* sin; (2) Gethsemane, death *for* sin; (3) Sepulchre, death *to* sin. **eastward in Eden** = "in Eden, eastward". **Eden.** In the cuneiform texts = the plain of Babylonia, known in the Accado-Sumerian as *edin* = "the fertile plain", called by its inhabitants *Edinu*. In Heb. *'ēden*, Sept. *paradise*. Occ. 2. 8, 10, 15; 3. 23, 24; 4. 16. Isa. 51. 3. Ezek. 28. 13; 31. 9, 16, 18, 18; 36. 35. Joel 2. 3. **9 tree of life.** Gen. of cause (Ap. 17) = the Tree supporting and continuing the life which had been imparted. Cp. 3. 22. Hence "the bread of life", John 6. 48, 51, 53. **midst.** Cp. Rev. 2. 7. **knowledge** = sense or perception (Gen. 12. 12. Song 6. 11. Isa. 59. 8). **good and evil.** See on *v.* 17. **10 river** = the Persian Gulf, known as such to the Accadians, in which the river became four mouths (or heads) at spots where they flowed into the source which received and fed them.

garden; and from thence it was parted, and became into four heads.

11 The name of the first *is* °Pison: that *is* it which °compasseth the whole land of °Havilah, where *there is* gold;

12 And the gold of that land *is* good: there *is* bdellium and the °onyx stone.

13 And the name of the second river *is* °Gihon: the same *is* it that compasseth the whole land of °Ethiopia.

14 And the name of the third river *is* °Hiddekel: that *is* it which goeth toward the east of °Assyria. And the fourth river *is* °Euphrates.

C d (p. 5) 15 And the [4]LORD God took °the man, and put him into the garden of Eden to dress it and to °keep it.)

e 16 And the [4]LORD God commanded °the man, saying, "Of every tree of the garden thou mayest °freely eat:

17 But of the °tree of the [9]knowledge of °good and evil, thou shalt not eat of it: for °in the day that thou eatest thereof °thou shalt surely die."

B a 18 And the [4]LORD God said, "*It is* not good that [16]the man should be alone; I will make him an help °meet for him."

b 19 And out of the °ground the [4]LORD God formed every beast of the field, and every fowl of the air; and brought *them* unto Adam to see what he would call them: and whatsoever Adam called every living °creature, that *was* the name thereof.

20 And Adam gave names to all cattle, and to the fowl of the air, and to every beast of the field;

c but for Adam there was not found an help [18]meet for him.

21 And the [4]LORD God caused a deep sleep to fall upon Adam, and he slept: and He took one of his ribs, and closed up the flesh instead thereof;

22 And the rib, which the [4]LORD God had taken from [16]man, made He a °woman, and brought her unto the [16]man.

23 And Adam said, "This *is* now bone of my bones, and flesh of my flesh: she shall be called [22]Woman, because she was taken out of °Man."

A 24 °Therefore shall [23]a man leave his father and his mother, and shall cleave unto his wife: and they shall be one flesh.

25 And they were both °naked, [16]the man and his wife, and were not ashamed.

J[2] E (p. 7) **3** Now the °serpent was more °subtil than any °beast of the field which °the LORD God had made. °And he said unto the woman,

11 Pison = the river W. of the Euphrates, called *Pallukat* in reign of Nabonidos, last king of Babylonia, or the Pallakopas Canal.

compasseth. The Pallukat or Pison encircled the N. borders of the great sandy desert which stretched westward to the mountain chains of Midian and Sinai.

Havilah = the region of Sand. Indicated in 25. 18. 1 Sam. 15. 7. Shur would be the E. end of Havilah, the W. of this region. Connected with Ophir in 10. 29.

12 onyx. Heb. *shoham*, identified with Assyr. *samtu*, from that region.

13 Gihon = the river E. of the Tigris. The modern *Kerkhah*, and ancient *Khoaspes*, rising in the mountains of the *Kassi*. *Kas* has been confused with the Heb. *Cush*. It is not the African Cush or **Ethiopia**, but the Accadian *Kạs*.

14 Hiddekel = Accadian for the Tigris, which was *Idiqla*, or *Idiqlat* = "the encircling".

Assyria. Heb. *Hashshur* (*Asshur*). This is not Assyria, but the city of *Assur*, the primitive capital of Assyria (which lay E. and W. of the Tigris).

Euphrates. Heb. = *phᵉrāth*. The Greek Euphrates comes from the old Persian *Ufratū*, and this from *Purat* or *Puratu* = the river. Sometimes *Pura-nun* = the great river.

15 the man. Heb. *'eth-hā'ādhām* = this same man Adam. See Ap. 14. i.

keep = keep safe, preserve. Same Heb. as 3. 24; 17. 9, 10; 18. 19, &c.

16 the man. Heb. *hā'ādhām* (with art.) = the man Adam. See Ap. 14. i.

freely. Heb. "Eating thou mayest eat". Fig. *Polyptōton* (Ap. 6) for emphasis (see note on 26. 28). Here rightly marked by "freely". Toned down by Eve in ch. 3. 2.

17 tree. Note the three trees: "Knowledge" (2. 9), man's Ruin; "the Cross" (Acts 10. 39; 5. 30. 1 Pet. 2. 24), man's Redemption; "the Tree of Life" (2. 9. Rev. 2. 7; 22. 2), man's Regeneration.

good and evil. See on "knowledge", *v.* 9. Obedience proving what was "good" (Deut. 6. 24), disobedience revealing what was "evil" (Rom. 3. 20).

in the day = when. See Ap. 18. Cp. 2. 4. 1 Kings 2. 37. Ezek. 36. 33, &c.

thou shalt surely die. Heb. "dying thou shalt die". Fig. *Polyptōton*, for emph. (Ap. 6). Cp. 20. 7; 26. 11. **Ex.** 19. 12; 21. 12, 15, 16, 17; 31. 14, 15. **Lev.** 20. 2, 9, 10, 11, 12, 13, 15, 16, 27; 24. 16, 17; 27. 29. **Num.** 15. 35; 26. 65; 35. 16, 17, 18, 21, 31. **Judg.** 13. 22; 15. 13; 21. 5. 1 Sam. 14. 39, 44; 22. 16. 2 Sam. 12. 14. 1 Kings 2. 37, 42. 2 Kings 1. 4, 6, 16; 8. 10. **Jer.** 26. 8, 19; 38. 15. Ezek. 3. 18; 18. 13; 33. 8, 14. See note on ch. 26. 28 for the emphasis of this Figure exhibited in other ways; and cp. esp. note on Num. 26. 65. Here marked by the word "surely", as in *v.* 16 by the word "freely". This certainty changed by Eve in 3. 3 into a contingency.

18 meet = as his counterpart.

19 ground: giving the details of 1. 24.

creature = soul. Heb. *nephesh*. See ch. 1. 20 and Ap. 13.

22 woman. Heb *'ishah*, fem. of *'ish* (Ap. 14) = female.

23 Man. Heb. *'ish*. Ap. 14. ii.

24 Therefore, &c., quoted Matt. 19. 5, &c. 1 Cor. 6. 16. Eph. 5. 31.

25 naked. Heb. *'ārūm*, a Homonym. The same spelling as word rendered "subtil" in 3. 1.

3. 1-24 For Structure see next page.

1 serpent. Heb. *Nachash*, a shining one. See note on Num. 21. 6, 9. The old serpent (2 Cor. 11. 3) transformed as "an angel of light" (= a glorious angel, 2 Cor. 11. 14). Cp. Ezek. 28, 14, 17, connected with "cherub" (Ezek. 28. 13, 14, 16), and contrasted with it here in *v.* 24. See Ap. 19. **subtil** = wise. Heb. *'ārūm*, a Homonym. Same as 2. 25; here = wise (as Job 5. 12; 15. 5. Prov. 12. 16, 23; 13. 16; 14. 8, 15, 18; 22. 3; 27. 12). Cp. Ezek. 28. 12, 13, 17. If the *Ellipsis* (Ap. 6. iii. 1) be supplied from the preceding context, 3. 1 will then read on from 2. 25, thus: "they were both naked (*'arum*), the man and his wife, and [knowing only good, 2. 17] were not ashamed [before God]. But the *Nachash* was more wise (*'arum*) than any living being of the field which Jehovah Elohim had made, and [knowing evil, and not ashamed (2. 25) to question the truth of God's word] he said unto the woman," &c. **beast** = living creature or being; same as *Zōon* in Rev. 4. 6-9; 5. 6, 8, 14, &c. **And.** Note the Fig. *Polysyndeton* (Ap. 6) throughout this chapter emphasising each detail. **the LORD God.** See note on 2. 4.

°"Yea, hath °God said, 'Ye shall not eat of every tree of the garden'?"
2 And the woman said unto the serpent, "We °may eat of the fruit of the trees of the garden:
3 But of the fruit of the tree which *is* in the midst of the garden, [1]God hath said, 'Ye shall not eat of it, °neither shall ye touch it, °lest ye die.'"
4 And the serpent said unto the woman, °"Ye shall not surely die:
5 For [1]God doth know that in the day ye eat thereof, then your eyes shall be opened, and °ye shall be as gods, [17]knowing good and evil."

F (p. 7) 6 And when the woman saw that the tree *was* °good for food, and that it *was* °pleasant to the eyes, and a tree to be desired to °make *one* wise, she took of the fruit thereof, and did eat, and °gave also unto her husband °with her; and he did eat.

G f 7 And the eyes of them both were opened, and they °knew that they *were* naked;

g and they sewed °fig leaves together, and made themselves °aprons.

H 8 And they heard the °voice of the [1]LORD [1]God walking in the garden in the °cool of the day: and Adam and his wife °hid themselves from the presence of the [1]LORD [1]God amongst the trees of the garden.
9 And the [1]LORD [1]God called unto Adam, and said unto him, °"Where *art* thou?"
10 And he said, "I heard Thy voice in the garden, and I was afraid, because I *was* [25]naked; and I hid myself."
11 And He said, "Who told thee that thou *wast* naked? Hast thou eaten of the tree, whereof I commanded thee that thou shouldest not eat?"
12 And °the man said, °"The woman whom °Thou gavest *to be* with me, she gave me of the tree, and I did eat."

I 13 And the [1]LORD [1]God said unto the woman, "What *is* this *that* thou hast done?" And the woman said, °"The serpent beguiled me, and I did eat."

K 14 And the [1]LORD [1]God °said unto the serpent, "Because thou hast done this, thou *art* cursed above all cattle, and above every beast of the field; °upon thy belly shalt thou go, and °dust shalt thou eat all the days of thy life:

K 15 And I will put enmity between thee and the woman, and between thy seed and her Seed; °It shall bruise thy °head, and thou shalt bruise His °heel."

I 16 Unto the woman He said, "I will °greatly

3. 1-24 (J[2], p. 5). THE FALL.
(*Introversion and Alternation.*)

J[2] E | 1-5. The *Nachash*: procuring man's death, in Adam.
F | 6. The Tree of knowledge. Eating of it.
G | f | 7-. Effect on both: the man and the woman.
g | -7. Human provision: man-made aprons.
H | 8-12. God's enquiry of the man.
I | 13. God's enquiry of the woman.
K | 14. Sentence on the *Nachash*.
K | 15. Promise of the Seed.
I | 16. God's sentence on the woman.
H | 17-19. God's sentence on the man.
G | *f* | 20. Effect on both: the man and the woman.
g | 21. Divine provision: God-made coats.
F | 22-24-. The Tree of Life. Expulsion from it.
E | -24. The *Cherubim*: preserving man's life, in Christ.

Not allegory: but literal history, emphasised by Figures of Speech.

Yea, hath God said = Can it be that God hath said. Not a Q., but Figure *Erotēsis* (Ap. 6) for emph. Opposition to God's Word is Satan's sphere of activity. This is Satan's first utterance in Scripture. **God** = *Elohim*. Ap. 4.

2 may eat. Misquoted from 2. 16 by not repeating the emphatic Figure *Polyptōton* (Ap. 6), and thus omitting the emph. "freely".

3 neither shall ye touch it. This sentence is added. Cp. 2. 16, 17.

lest ye die. Misquoted from 2. 16, 17, by not repeating the emphatic Figure *Polyptōton* (Ap. 6), thus changing the emph. preserved in the word "surely".

4 Ye shall not surely die = Satan's second utterance. Contradiction of God's Word in 2. 17. This has become the foundation of Spiritism and Traditional belief as to death. See note on 2. 17.

5 ye shall be as gods = be as God, Heb. *Elohim*. This is the foundation of Satan's second lie: "The immanence of God in man."

6 good for food. See 1 John 2. 16, "Lust of the flesh". Cp. Matt. 4. 3.

pleasant to the eyes. See 1 John 2. 16, "Lust of the eyes". Cp. Matt. 4. 5.

make one wise. See 1 John 2. 16, "Boastful of life". Cp. Matt. 4. 8. **gave.** See 1 Tim. 2. 14.

with her. Therefore Adam present. Cp. "Ye", *vv.* 4, 5.

7 knew. Fig. *Metonymy* (of Subj.). Ap. 6. They knew before, but their knowledge now received a new meaning. Adam becomes "naked" by losing something of *Elohim's* glorious likeness. Rom. 8. 3 may refer to this.

fig leaves. The man-made covering contrasted, in the structure, with the God-made clothing (*v.* 21).

aprons. Heb. word occurs only here.

8 voice = sound. (Ecc. 7. 6 = crackling.) Here = footsteps, as in 2 Sam. 5. 24. 1 Kings 14. 6. 2 Kings 6. 32.

cool. Heb. *ruach*. Ap. 9.

hid themselves. No "quest for God" in fallen man. Cp. 4. 14. Luke 15. 13. Eph. 2. 13. Jer. 23. 24.

9 Where art thou? The 1st Q. in O. T. comes from God to the sinner. Cp. 1st Q. in N. T. of the seeking sinner, "Where is He?" (Matt. 2. 2).

12 the man. Heb. *Hā'ādhām* = the man Adam. Ap. 14.

the woman. Characteristic of fallen man (Job 31. 33, hence Deut. 13. 6). **Thou gavest.** Implying blame to Jehovah as well as to his wife. **13 The serpent.** See note on *v.* 1 and Ap. 19; and cp. 2 Cor 11. 3, 14. **14 said.** God asks the serpent no question. There is no parley. Sentence at once pronounced. **upon thy belly, &c.** Fig. of speech. See Ap. 19. The words imply the utmost humiliation, as in Ps. 44. 25. **dust, &c.** Fig. of utter defeat, as in Ps. 72. 9. See Ap. 19. **15 it,** i. e. Christ. The corruption of this in the Vulgate into "she" lies at the root of Mariolatry: the verb in sing. masc. shows that *zer'a* (seed) is here to be taken in singular, with Sept., i. e. *Christ*; see note on Gen 17. 7; 21. 12, and Gal. 3. 16. **head ... heel.** See Ap. 19. No more literal than 1 Cor. 11. 8, or Ps. 41. 9, and John 13. 18. They denote the temporary sufferings of the Seed, and the complete destruction of Satan and his works (Heb. 2. 14. 1 John 3. 8). Heel = lower part. Head = vital part. This is the first great promise and prophecy. Note its position in the centre of Structure above. **16 greatly multiply.** Heb. "multiplying I will multiply". Fig. *Polyptōton* (Ap. 6). Emph. preserved in word "greatly". Cp. *v.* 4, and see note on 26. 28.

multiply thy sorrow and thy conception; °in
sorrow thou shalt bring forth °children; and
thy desire *shall be* °to thy husband, and he
shall rule over thee."
H (p.7) 17 And unto Adam He said, "Because thou
hast hearkened unto the voice of thy wife, and
hast eaten of the tree, of which I commanded
thee, saying, 'Thou shalt not eat of it:' °cursed
is the ground for thy sake; in sorrow shalt
thou eat *of* it all the days of thy life;
18 °Thorns also and thistles shall it bring
forth to thee; and thou shalt eat the herb of
the °field;
19 In the sweat of thy °face shalt thou eat
°bread, till thou return unto the ground; for
out of it wast thou taken: for °dust thou *art*,
and unto dust shalt thou return."
G f 20 And Adam called his wife's name °Eve;
because she was the mother of °all living.
g 21 Unto Adam also and to his wife did the
LORD God make °coats °of skins, and clothed
them.
F 22 And [1]the LORD [1]God said, °"Behold, the
°man is become as one of Us, to know °good and
evil: and now, lest he put forth his hand, and
take also of the tree of life, and eat, and °live
for ever:—" °
23 °Therefore [1]the LORD [1]God sent him forth
from the garden of Eden, to till the ground
from whence he was taken.
24 So He °drove out the [22]man;
E and He °placed at the east of the garden of
Eden °Cherubims, and °a flaming sword which
turned °every way, to °keep the way of the
°tree of life.

J[3] L (p. 8) **4** And Adam knew Eve his wife; and she
conceived, and bare °Cain, and said,
"I have gotten °a man from the LORD."
2 And she again bare his brother °Abel. And
Abel was a keeper of sheep, but Cain was a
tiller of the ground.
3 And °in process of time it came to pass,
that Cain brought of the fruit of the °ground
an °offering unto [1]the °LORD.
4 And Abel, he also °brought of the °firstlings
of his flock and of the fat thereof. And [1]the
LORD had °respect unto Abel and to his
[3]offering:
5 But unto Cain and to his [3]offering He had
not respect. And Cain was very wroth, and
his countenance fell.
6 And [1]the LORD said unto Cain, °"Why art
thou wroth? and °why is thy countenance
fallen?

in sorrow. Cp. 1 Tim. 2. 14, 15.

children. Heb. = sons; but daughters included by context.

to = subject to.

17 cursed. Nature affected. Rom. 8. 19–23.

18 Thorns. The sign of the curse. What else was brought forth is not stated; but the word may include all kinds of noxious insects, &c., as well as poisonous weeds.

field. Not the fruit of Paradise.

19 face = whole body. Fig. *Synecdoche* (of Part). Ap. 6.

bread = all kinds of food. Fig. *Synecdoche* (of Species). Ap. 6.

dust. This is literal. See Gen. 2. 7. Ps. 103. 14. Ecc. 12. 7. 1 Cor. 15. 47. Note the emph. by *Introversion*—

| return.
| it = (dust).
| dust.
| return.

20 Eve = Heb. *Chavvah* = *Life, Life-spring*. Showing that he believed God. *The name* "Eve" occ. 4 times: here; 4. 1; 2 Cor. 11. 3; and 1 Tim. 2. 13.

all = all who should live after her. Fig. *Synecdoche* (of Genus), Ap. 6.

21 coats. Cp. the structure, p. 7, *v.* –7.

of skins = skin. Omitted in the Codex "Severus". See Ap. 34.

22 Behold. Fig. *Asterismos* (Ap. 6).

man. Heb. the man, Adam.

good. Heb. *tōv* = general good. Cp. Gen. 1. 4, 10, 12, 18, 21, 25; 6. 2. Deut. 1. 25; 3. 25. Judg. 8. 2. Est. 1. 11. Prov. 8. 11. Ecc. 7. 14; 11. 7. Verse ends with Fig. *Aposiopēsis* = Sudden silence (Ap. 6), emphasising the result as being unspeakable.

live for ever clearly shows the nature of man.

23 Therefore: the object is self-evident.

24 drove out. Note the failure of man under every dispensation.

placed. Heb *shākan*, *to place in a tabernacle*, hence *to dwell*. The Cherubim placed later in the tents of Shem, 9. 26, 27. Cp. 4. 3, 7, 14, 16.

Cherubim. See Ap. 41. 1 Sam. 4. 4. Ps. 80. 1; 99. 1.

a = should be "the".

every way, not *nāṭah* (aside), *ṣāvav* (about), *ṣūg* (back), *pānah* (toward), but *haphak* (every way), effectually preserving the way.

keep. See note on Gen. 2. 15 = *preserve*, so that man should not "live for ever" in his fallen condition, but only in Christ, 1 John 5. 11, 12.

tree of life. See note on 2. 9.

4. 1–26 (J[3], p. 5). **AFTER THE FALL.**
(*Alternation*)

J[3] | L | 1–16. Adam's sons: Cain and Abel.
  M | 17–24. Cain's son: Enoch.
 L | 25. Adam's son: Seth.
  M | 26. Seth's son: Enos.

1 Cain = *acquisition*.

a man. Heb. *'ish*. (See Ap. 14. ii.) Lit. "a man, even Jehovah". R.V. "with the help of", in italics. Heb. *'ish 'eth Jehovah*. Cp. Luke 2. 11.

2 Abel = transitoriness.

3 in process of time. Heb. *at* [*the*] *end of days.* The time as well as place and offering probably appointed. **ground.** The product of the curse. Cp. 3. 17. **offering, &c.** = a sacrifice unto Jehovah. Most religious, but his own "way" (Jude 11); but not first-fruits as Abel's. Heb. *minchah.* See Ap. 43. II. iii. **LORD** = Jehovah. Note, the sacrifices both brought to Jehovah as the covenant God; not to *Elohim*, the Creator. See Ap. 4. **4 brought**: "by faith", Heb. 11. 4, which came by hearing the word of God (Rom. 10. 17). **firstlings . . . and the fat, &c.** Fig. *Hendiadys*, Ap. 6 = "the firstlings, and the fattest ones too." **respect**: by accepting it by fire Divinely sent, Lev. 9. 24. Judg. 6. 21. 1 Kings 18. 38. 1 Chron. 21. 26. 2 Chron. 7. 1; and cp. Ps. 20. 3, and Heb. 11. 4.

Fig. *Antimetabole* (Ap. 6) {
had respect.
 his offerings.
 his offerings.
had not respect.

6 Why. . .? Fig. *Erotēsis* for emph. (Ap. 6).

7 If thou doest well, shalt thou not be accepted? and °if thou doest not well, °sin °lieth at the door. And unto thee °*shall be* his desire, °and thou shalt rule over him."

8 And Cain °talked with Abel his brother: and it came to pass, when they were in the field, that Cain rose up against Abel his brother, and °slew him.

9 And [1]the LORD said unto Cain, "Where *is* Abel thy brother?" And he said, "I know not: *Am* I my brother's keeper?"

10 And He said, "What hast thou done? the voice of thy brother's °blood crieth unto Me from the ground.

11 And now *art* thou cursed °from the earth, which hath opened her mouth to receive thy brother's blood from thy hand;

12 When thou tillest the ground, it shall not henceforth yield unto thee her °strength; a fugitive and a vagabond shalt thou be in the earth."

13 And Cain said unto [1]the LORD, "My °punishment *is* greater than I can bear.

14 °Behold, Thou hast driven me out this day from the face of the °earth; and from Thy face shall I be °hid; and I shall be a fugitive and a vagabond in the earth; and it shall come to pass, *that* °every one that findeth me shall slay me."

15 And [1]the LORD said unto him, "°Therefore whosoever slayeth Cain, vengeance shall be taken on him sevenfold." And [1]the LORD set a mark °upon Cain, lest any finding him should kill him.

16 And Cain went out from the °presence of [1]the LORD, and dwelt in the land of °Nod, on the east of Eden.

M (p. 8) **17** And Cain knew his wife; and she conceived, and bare °Enoch: and he builded a °city, and called the name of the city, after the name of his son, Enoch.

18 And unto Enoch was born °Irad: and Irad begat Mehujael: and Mehujael begat Methusael: and Methusael begat °Lamech.

19 And Lamech took unto him °two wives: the name of the one *was* Adah, and the name of the other Zillah.

20 And Adah bare °Jabal: he was the father of such as dwell in tents, °and *of such as have* cattle.

21 And his brother's name *was* °Jubal: he was the father of all such as handle the harp and °organ.

22 And Zillah, she also bare °Tubal-cain, an instructer of every artificer in brass and iron: and the sister of Tubal-cain *was* °Naamah.

23 And Lamech said unto his wives,
"Adah and Zillah, °Hear my voice;
Ye wives of Lamech, °hearken unto my speech:
For °I have slain a man to my wounding,
And a young man to my hurt.

24 If Cain shall be avenged sevenfold,
Truly °Lamech seventy and sevenfold."

L **25** And Adam knew his wife again; and she bare a son, and called his name °Seth: "For °God," *said she,* "hath appointed me another °seed instead of Abel, whom Cain slew."

M **26** And to Seth, to him also there was born a son; and he called his name °Enos: then

---

7 if. The Heb. Accent (*Pashta*) puts the emphasis on the 1st "well" and on this 2nd "if", to mark the solemn and important alternative.

sin = sin offering. Heb. *chat'a.* See Ap. 43. v. The word "offering" is actually added in Ex. 30. 10. Lev. 4. 3; 6. 25; 8. 2. Ps. 40. 6. Cp. 2 Cor. 5. 21. Eph. 5. 2.

lieth. Lieth is masc. Sin offering is fem. So that the Heb. reads "at the entrance [a male] is lying, a sin offering".

shall be. Supply "is" instead.

and thou shalt rule. Cp. 3. 16.

8 talked = said. Heb. = (*'amār*) to say, which must be followed by the words spoken (not so *dābar*, which means to speak absolutely). What Cain said is preserved in the Sam. Pent., Sept., Syr., Vulg., Targ. Jer., and MSS., viz. "Let us go into the field." MSS., which have not the words, have a hiatus.

slew: 1 John 3. 12. "Religion" is and ever has been the greatest cause of blood-shedding.

10 blood. Heb. "bloods", denoting his posterity Matt. 23. 35.

11 from the earth. The Heb. accent (*athnach*, after "cursed" suggests "more than the ground" (3. 17).

12 strength = *Metonymy* (of the Cause). Ap. 6. Strength put for that which it produces.

13 punishment = iniquity. Heb. *'aven.* See Ap. 44. iii. For "my punishment", &c., read "Is mine iniquity too great to be forgiven?" with Sept., Vulg., Syr., Arabic, Targ. of Onk., Sam. Pent., and Greek and Latin Fathers.

14 Behold. Fig. *Asterismos* (Ap. 6).

earth. Heb. ground.

hid. Cp. note on 3. 8.

every one = any one. Cp. *v.* 15.

15 Therefore = not so (with Sept.). This is emphasised by the Heb. accent (*Pashta*).

upon = set a sign for Cain, *i. e.* gave him a pledge; same word as 1. 14; 9. 12, 13, 17 (token). See also Ex. 4. 8, 9, 17, 28, 30; 12. 13. Ezek. 20. 12, 20.

16 presence, &c., i. e. the Tabernacle placed by God for His worship (3. 24), whither offerings were brought (4. 3, 4).

Nod = wandering. Cp. *v.* 12 = the *Manda* of the Cuneiform Inscriptions = the land of the Nomads.

17 Enoch = Teaching or Initiation. Cain's posterity (*vv.* 16-24) comes in "the Generations of the heavens and the earth" (see Structure, p. 5). See Ap. 20. This seed was begotten after the slaying of Abel.

city. A city has been discovered beneath the brick platform on which Nipur, in South Babylonia, was built.

18 Irad = city of witness.

Lamech = powerful, 7th from Adam in Cain's line.

19 two. The first polygamist.

20 Jabal = flowing.

and = the Fig. *Zeugma.* (Ap. 6.) Supplied here by the italics.

21 Jubal = joyful sound.

organ. Heb. *'ūgab.* The well-known "Pan's pipe".

22 Tubal-cain = flowing from Cain.

Naamah = pleasant. See Ruth 1. 19, 20.

23 Hear . . . hearken. Refers to Gen. 3. 17. Lamech was in greater danger than Adam. Adam had only one wife, Lamech had two. Hear *my* voice, emph. on "my".

I have = continuous present. May be rendered thus:

"I can kill a man for wounding me,
And a young man for hurting me."

24 Lamech. Supply *Ellipsis* (Ap. 6), "shall be avenged".

25 Seth = substituted. Fig. *Paronomasia* (Ap 6). *Shēth* (Seth) . . . *Shēth* (appointed).

God = Elohim.

seed = son, by Fig. *Metonymy* (of Cause). (Ap. 6.)

26 Enos = frail, incurable.

°began men to call upon the name of the
LORD.

5 This *is* THE °BOOK OF THE GENE-
F A RATIONS OF ADAM. °In the day that
°God created °man, in the likeness of °God
(p. 10) made He °him;
2 Male and female created He °them; and
blessed them, and called their name Adam, [1]in
the day when they were created.

B 3 And Adam lived an hundred and thirty
3874 years, and begat *a son* in his °own likeness,
after his image; and called his name °Seth:
4 And °the days of Adam after he had begotten Seth were eight hundred years: and he
°begat sons and daughters:
5 And all the days that Adam lived were nine
hundred and thirty years: and he died.

C 6 And Seth lived an hundred and five years,
3769 and begat °Enos:
7 And Seth lived after he begat Enos eight
hundred and seven years, and begat sons and
daughters:
8 And all the days of Seth were nine hundred
and twelve years: and he died.

3679 9 And Enos lived ninety years, and begat
°Cainan:
10 And Enos lived after he begat Cainan
eight hundred and fifteen years, and begat sons
and daughters:
11 And all the days of Enos were nine hundred and five years: and he died.

3609 12 And Cainan lived seventy years, and begat
°Mahalaleel:
13 And Cainan lived after he begat Mahalaleel eight hundred and forty years, and begat
sons and daughters:
14 And all the days of Cainan were nine
hundred and ten years: and he died.

3544 15 And Mahalaleel lived sixty and five years,
and begat °Jared:
16 And Mahalaleel lived after he begat Jared
eight hundred and thirty years, and begat sons
and daughters:
17 And all the days of Mahalaleel were
eight hundred ninety and five years: and he
died.

3382 18 And Jared lived an hundred sixty and two
years, and he begat °Enoch:
19 And Jared lived after he begat Enoch eight
hundred years, and begat sons and daughters:
20 And all the days of Jared were nine hundred sixty and two years: and he died.

3317 21 And Enoch lived sixty and five years, and
begat °Methuselah:
22 And Enoch °walked with [1]God after he
begat Methuselah three hundred years, and
begat sons and daughters:
23 And all the days of Enoch were three
hundred sixty and five years:
3017 24 And Enoch walked with [1]God: and he *was*
not; for [1]God °took him.

25 And Methuselah lived an hundred eighty
3130 and seven years, and begat °Lamech:
26 And Methuselah lived after he begat Lamech seven hundred eighty and two years, and
begat sons and daughters:

began. Not began to worship: for Abel worshipped, and others, doubtless, long before. But here: "began to call upon [their gods] by the name of Jehovah," or "began profanely to call upon the name of the Lord" (see Ap. 21). Enos, though the son of Seth, is included here because he went in "the way of Cain".

5. 1—6. 8 (**F**, p. 1). "THE BOOK OF THE GENERATIONS OF ADAM" (*Extended Alternation*).

A | 5. 1, 2. Unfallen Adam: a "son of God" (Luke 3. 38).
B | 5. 3-5. Fallen Adam, and his years. The total 930, and the first 130.
C | 5. 6-27. The progeny of Adam, and their deaths.
D | 5. 28-32. Noah, and his promise of "comfort".
A | 6. 1, 2. The fallen angels: "sons of God" (see Ap. 23).
B | 6. 3. Fallen Adam, and his years. The total 930, and the last 120.
C | 6. 4-7. The progeny of the fallen angels, and their threatened destruction. The *Nephīlim* (see Ap. 25).
D | 6. 8. Noah, and his possession of "grace".

1 book of the generation. Only here and Matt. 1. 1: "the second man" and "last Adam".
In the day. See ch. 2. 17 and Ap. 18. **God** = Elohim.
man. Art. not needed = the man Adam. Ap. 14. i.
him. Emph. reference to Adam.
2 them, i. e. Adam and Eve, going back to 1. 27; 2. 7.
3 own. Adam *created* in God's likeness. All his descendants *begotten* in Adam's likeness, after his Fall. See Ps. 51. 5. Rom. 5. 12-19.
Seth. Refers back to 4. 25, and develops his line.
4 the days of Adam. None of these particulars are given of Cain's line. Not even of their deaths.
begat. If Adam begat after Seth, so doubtless others after Cain and Abel.
6 Enos. See 4. 26.
9 Cainan = Heb. a possession.
12 Mahalaleel = praise of God.
15 Jared = descent.
18 Enoch = teaching, or initiation.
21 Methuselah = when he is dead it shall be sent, i. e. the Deluge.
22 walked = walked to and fro; why not literally as with Adam before the Fall? 2. 19; 3. 8.
24 took him. See Heb. 11. 5. Translated without dying: as Elijah was, 2 Kings 2. 9. Enoch was "the seventh from Adam" (Jude 14). He prophesied "by faith". Therefore Divinely instructed, Rom. 10. 17.
25 Lamech (powerful).
29 Noah = rest, comfort, or consolation. 8. 21.
comfort us concerning = give us rest from.
work: should be *works* (with Sam., Sept., Syr., &c.).
work and toil = grievous toil, or trouble, "*works*" ref. prob. to the evil deeds going on around. See 6. 3, and cp. Ex. 23. 24. Lev. 18. 3. Mic. 6. 16. Ecc. 4. 3. Job 33. 17. Prob. Fig. *Hendiadys* (Ap. 6), for emph. = toilsome labour.
the LORD. Heb. Jehovah. Ap. 4.

27 And all the days of Methuselah were nine
hundred sixty and nine years: and he died.

28 And Lamech lived an hundred eighty and D
two years, and begat a son:
29 And he called his name °Noah, saying, (p. 10)
"This *same* shall °comfort us concerning our 2948
°work and °toil of our hands, because of the
ground which °the LORD hath cursed."
30 And Lamech lived after he begat Noah five
hundred ninety and five years, and begat sons
and daughters:
31 And all the days of Lamech were seven
hundred seventy and seven years: and he
died.

2446 32 And Noah was °five hundred years old:
and Noah °begat °Shem, Ham, and Japheth.

A (p. 10) 6 And it came to pass, when °men began to
multiply on the face of the °earth, and
daughters were born unto °them,
2 That °the sons of °God saw the daughters
of °men that °they *were* fair; and they took
them °wives of all which they chose.
B 3 And the [6]LORD said, "My °spirit shall not
always °strive with °man, for that °he °also
°*is* flesh: °yet his days shall be an °hundred
3194 and twenty years."
C 4 There were °giants in the earth in °those
days; and °also after that, when the [2]sons of
God came in unto the daughters of men, and
they bare *children* to them, the same *became*
mighty men which *were* of old, men of °renown.
5 And °GOD saw that the °wickedness of
man *was* °great in the earth, and *that* every
imagination of the thoughts of his heart *was*
only evil continually.
6 And it °repented the °LORD that He had
made man on the earth, and it grieved Him at
His heart.
7 And the [6]LORD said, "I will °destroy man
whom I have created from the face of the
earth; both man, and beast, and the creeping
thing, and the fowls of the air; for it [6]repenteth
Me that I have made them."
D 8 But Noah found grace in the eyes of the
[6]LORD.

G A (p. 11) 9 THESE *are* °THE GENERATIONS OF
NOAH: Noah was a just °man *and* °perfect
in °his generations, *and* Noah °walked with
[2]God.
B 10 And Noah begat °three sons, Shem, Ham,
and Japheth.
C 11 The earth also was °corrupt before [2]God,
and the earth was filled with °violence.
12 And [2]God looked upon the earth, and, behold,
it was corrupt; for °all flesh had corrupted
his way upon the earth.
13 And °God said unto Noah, "The end of
all flesh is come before Me; for the earth is
filled with violence through them; and, behold,
I will destroy them with the earth.

D 14 Make thee an °ark °of gopher wood; °rooms
shalt thou make in the ark, and shalt °pitch it
within and without °with pitch.
15 And this *is the fashion* which thou shalt
make it *of*: The length of the ark *shall be*
three hundred °cubits, the breadth of it fifty
cubits, and the height of it thirty cubits.

32 five. See chronology of Patriarchs. Ap. 22.
begat. See 6. 10 below.
Shem, Ham, and Japheth. Named in inverted order. Japheth was the elder (10. 21), Shem the youngest, and, as in other cases, the youngest chosen for the blessing. Cp. the inversion of the order in 10. 1, with 2, 6, and 21, and see 11. 10 and note on 9. 24; 10. 1.

6. 1 The Chronology having been brought up to Noah's days, the History takes us back (not forward).
men = sing. with art. = *the man Adam*. See Ap. 14. i.
earth = Heb. *h'adāmāh*, *ground*.
them: i. e. to Adam and Eve, as in Gen. 1. 27 and 5. 2
2 the sons of God = angels. See Ap. 23, 25, and 26.
God = *ha-Elohim* = the Creator.
men: in contrast with angels. Heb. *ha-'ādhām*, sing. *the man Adam*. See Ap. 14. i.
they: emph. **wives** = women. 2. 22.
3 spirit. Heb. *ruach*. See Ap. 9.
strive = remain in, with Sept., Arab., Syr., and Vulg.; occ. only here.
man: with art., as in *vv.* 1 and 2 = the man Adam, Ap. 14. i.
he: emphatic, i. e. the man Adam.
also: i. e. the man Adam also, as well as the others. (Not "men"; if so, as well as—what?)
is flesh. If taken as a verb, then it = "in their erring". Heb. *shāgāg*. Ap. 44. xii. Adam had become like the others.
yet his days = yet Adam's days. See Ap. 24.
120 years: this fixes the date A.M. 930 − 120 = 810. The B.C. date being 3194, as given.
4 giants = *Nephīlim*. See Ap. 25.
those days = "the days of Noah."
also after that = after their destruction by the Flood, as well as before it. There was another irruption, the result being like those "of old". See notes on 12. 6 and 13. 7; also Ap. 23 and 25.
renown. Heb. the men of name. The "heroes" of the Greek mythology. The remains of primitive truth, corrupted in transmission.
5 GOD = Jehovah. Ap. 4.
wickedness = lewdness, moral depravity. Ap. 44. viii.
great = multiplied. Very emphatic.
6 repented = the Fig. *Anthropopatheia*. Ap. 6.
LORD = Jehovah, in His covenant relation with mankind.
7 destroy = wipe off, blot out.

6. 9—9. 29 (**G**, p. 1). THE GENERATIONS OF NOAH (*Introversion*).

A | 6. 9. Noah before the Flood.
B | 6. 11. Noah's Family.
C | 6. 11-13. The Earth corrupt.
D | 6. 14-22. The making of the Ark.
E | 7. 1-24. Noah entering the Ark.
E | 8. 1-19. Noah leaving the Ark.
D | 8. 20. The building of the Altar.
C | 8. 21—9. 17. The Earth replenished.
B | 9. 18-27. Noah's Family.
A | 9. 28, 29. Noah after the Flood.

9 the generations. Heb. *tōldoth* = family history.
man = Heb. *'ish*. See Ap. 14. ii.
perfect. Heb. *tāmīm*, *without blemish* as to breed or pedigree. See Ap. 26. All flesh corrupted but Noah's family. See *vv.* 11, 12.
his generations: his contemporaries. Heb. *dōr* (not *tōledoth*, as at beginning of the verse). See note on 7. 1.
walked. Same as ch. 5. 22, 24. Heb. = walked habitually. **10 three sons.** See 9. 18; 10. 1; and 1 Chron. 1. 4. See note on 5. 32. **11 corrupt**: destroyed by being debased. **violence**: the Fig. *Metonymy*. Ap. 6. **12 all flesh.** Noah's family the only exception. The Fig. *Synecdoche* (of the Part), Ap. 6. **13 God** = the Creator in connection with the two beasts for preservation (*vv.* 13, 22, and 7. 9). Jehovah in ch. 7. 1, in connection with the *seven clean* for sacrifice. See note on *v.* 19. **14 ark.** Heb. *tēbāh* = a floating [building] (not *'ārōn*, a chest). So in Ex. 2. 2, 3. **of.** Gen. of material. Ap. 17. **rooms** = nests. **pitch it** = coat it. Heb. *kāphar*, to cover: the only word for "atonement" in O.T. So that it is only atonement that can keep the waters of judgment from us. **with pitch** = Heb. *kopher* = resin (not "pitch" or bitumen, which is *zepheth*, Ex. 2. 3. Isa. 34. 9, 9). Fig. *Paranomasia* (Ap. 6). **15 cubit.** The latest approximation gives 17·5 inches. But this is the "profane" cubit. The sacred cubit was probably about 25 inches.

16 A °window shalt thou make to the ark, and in a cubit shalt thou finish it above; and the door of the ark shalt thou set in the side thereof; *with* lower, second, and third *stories* shalt thou make it.

17 And, °behold, °I, even I, do bring °a flood of waters upon the earth, to destroy °all flesh, wherein *is* the °breath of °life, from under heaven; *and* every thing that *is* in the earth shall °die.

18 But with thee will I establish My °covenant; °and thou shalt come into the ark, thou, and thy sons, and thy wife, and thy sons' wives with thee.

19 And of every living thing of all flesh, °two of every *sort* shalt thou bring into the ark, to keep *them* alive with thee; they shall be male and female.

20 Of fowls after their kind, and of cattle after their kind, °of every creeping thing of the °earth after his kind, two of every *sort* shall come unto thee, to keep *them* alive.

21 And take thou unto thee of all food that is eaten, and thou shalt gather *it* to thee; and it shall be for food for thee, and for them."

22 °Thus did Noah; according to all that [2]God commanded him, so did he.

E
(p. 11) **7** And the °LORD said unto Noah, "Come thou and all thy °house into the ark; for thee have I seen righteous before Me in this °generation.

2 Of every °clean beast thou shalt take to thee by sevens, the male and his female: and of beasts that *are* not clean by °two, the male and his female.

3 Of fowls also of the air by sevens, the male and the female; to keep seed alive upon the face of all the earth.

4 For yet °seven days, and I will cause it to rain upon the earth °forty days and forty nights; and every living substance that I have made will I °destroy from off the face of the °earth."

2348 5 And Noah did according unto all that [1]the LORD commanded him.

6 And Noah *was* six hundred years old when the flood of waters was upon the earth.

7 °And Noah went in, and his sons, and his wife, and his sons' wives with him, into the ark, because of the waters of the flood.

8 Of clean beasts, and of beasts that *are* not clean, and of fowls, and of every thing that creepeth upon the earth,

9 There went in two and two unto Noah into the ark, the male and the female, °as God had commanded Noah.

10 And it came to pass after seven days, that the waters of the flood were upon the earth.

11 In the six hundredth year of Noah's life, in the second month, the seventeenth day of the month, the same day were all the fountains of the great °deep broken up, and the °windows of heaven were opened.

12 And the rain was upon the earth forty days and forty nights.

13 In the selfsame day °entered Noah, [7]and Shem, and Ham, and Japheth, the sons of Noah, and Noah's wife, and the three wives of his sons with them, into the ark;

14 They, and every beast after his kind, and all the cattle after their kind, and every creeping thing that creepeth upon the earth after his kind, and every fowl after his kind, every bird of every °sort.

15 And they went in unto Noah into the ark, two and two of all flesh, wherein *is* the °breath of life.

16 And they that went in, went in male and female of all flesh, as °God had commanded him: and the °LORD shut him in.

17 And the flood was forty days upon the earth; and the waters increased, and bare up the ark, and it was lift up above the earth.

18 And the waters prevailed, and were increased greatly upon the earth; and the ark went upon the face of the waters.

---

16 window. Heb. = a place for light (7. 11; 8. 6).
17 behold. Fig. *Asterismos*. Ap. 6.
I, even I. Fig. *Epizeuxis*. Ap. 6.
a flood. Heb. *mabbūl*. Limited to this account of the Deluge, and Ps. 29. 10, which therefore refers to it. The Babylonian tablets of the Epic of Gilgames are the traditional accounts of primitive truths, corrupted in transmission. The inspired account here corrects the imaginary accretions which had gathered round it.
all flesh. Fig. *Synecdoche* (of part), Ap. 6, put here for every kind of being.
breath. Heb. *ruach* = spirit. See Ap. 9.
life. Heb. *chaiyīm*, pl. for all kinds and manifestations.
die = cease to breathe, expire.
18 covenant. First occurrence of the word.
and. Note the *Polysyndeton* (Ap. 6) emph. the assurance given to each.
19 two. For preservation of species. In contrast with the "seven" (7. 2) clean animals, which were for sacrifice. Hence here it is *Elohim* (*vv.* 13, 22, and 7. 9) as the Creator; while in ch. 7 it is Jehovah in His covenant-relation. See Ap. 4.
20 of. Sam., Onk., Jon., Sept., and Syr. read "and of".
earth = ground.
22 Thus. See Heb. 11. 17.
7. 1 LORD = Jehovah in His covenant-relation with Noah, and in connection with the seven clean beasts for sacrifice. See note on 6. 12, 19.
house = household. *Metonymy* (of subject). Ap. 6.
generation. Heb. *dōr*, as in 6. 9 = those who were then alive: Noah's contemporaries.
2 clean. For sacrifice Lev. 1. 2, 10, 14, &c., sevens. For propagation cp. 6. 19.
two. See note on 6. 19 and 12.
4 seven days. The number of spiritual perfection (Ap. 10). All the Flood dates are Sabbaths except one (8. 5).
forty. The number of probation (Ap. 10).
destroy = wipe out, blot out.
earth. Heb. *'adāmāh* = ground.
7 And. Note the Fig. *Polysyndeton* (Ap. 6) in verses 7, 8, and 13, as in 6. 18.
9 as God = according as *Elohim*. Cp. 6. 13.
11 deep. Heb. *t^ehōm* = the waters of the abyss, as in Gen. 1. 2; 49. 25. Deut. 33. 13. Ps. 104. 6.
windows. Not *challōn*, a small aperture (8. 6), or *zohar*, an opening for light (6. 16), but *'ărubāh*, lattice or net-work, not glass. Here "floodgates". Only here, and 8. 2. 2 Kings 7. 2, 19. Ecc. 12. 3. Isa. 24. 18; 60. 8. Hos. 13. 3. Mal. 3. 10.
13 entered, i. e. the eight persons of 1 Pet. 3. 20.
14 sort. Heb. wing: put by *Metonymy* (of Adjunct), Ap. 6, for every kind.
15 breath. Heb. *ruach*. See note on 6. 17, and Ap. 9.
16 God = Elohim, the Creator.
LORD = Jehovah, Noah's Covenant-God. See Ap. 4.

19 °And the waters prevailed °exceedingly upon the earth; and all the high hills, that *were* under the whole heaven, were covered.
20 Fifteen cubits upward did the waters prevail; and the mountains were covered.
21 °And all flesh °died that moved upon the earth, both of fowl, and of cattle, and of beast, and of every creeping thing that creepeth upon the earth, and every man:
22 All in whose nostrils *was* the °breath °of life, of all that *was* in the dry *land*, [21] died.
23 And every °living substance was °destroyed which was upon the face of the ground, both man, and cattle, and the creeping things, and the fowl of the heaven; and they were °destroyed from the earth: and °Noah only remained *alive*, and they that *were* with him in the ark.
24 And the waters prevailed upon the earth an hundred and fifty days.

E (p. 11) **8** And °God °remembered Noah, and every living thing, and all the cattle that *was* with him in the ark: and °God made a °wind to pass over the earth, and the waters asswaged;
2 The fountains also of the deep and the °windows of heaven were stopped, and the rain from heaven was restrained;
3 And the waters returned from off the earth continually: and after the end of the hundred and fifty days the waters were abated.
4 And the ark °rested in the seventh month, on the seventeenth day of the month, upon the mountains of Ararat.
5 And the waters decreased continually until the tenth month: in the tenth *month*, on the first *day* of the month, were the tops of the mountains seen.
6 And it came to pass at the end of forty days, that Noah opened the °window of the ark which he had made:
7 And he sent forth a °raven, which went forth to and fro, until the waters were dried up from off the earth.
8 Also he sent forth a °dove from him, to see if the waters were abated from off the face of the ground;
9 But the dove found no rest for the sole of her foot, and she returned unto him into the ark, for the waters *were* on the face of the whole earth: then he put forth his hand, and took her, and pulled her in unto him into the ark.
10 And he stayed yet other °seven days; and again he sent forth the dove out of the ark;
11 And the dove came in to him in the evening; and, lo, in her mouth *was* an °olive leaf pluckt off: so Noah knew that the waters were abated from off the earth.
12 And he stayed yet other °seven days; and sent forth the dove; which returned not again unto him any more.
13 And it came to pass in the °six hundredth and first year, in °the first *month*, the first *day* of the month, the waters were dried up from off the earth: and Noah removed the covering of the ark, and looked, and, behold, the face of the ground was dry.
14 And in the second month, on the °seven and twentieth day of the month, was the earth dried.

19 And the waters. Fig. *Anadiplosis* (Ap. 6) for emphasis.
exceedingly. The Flood universal. Fig. *Epizeuxis* (*greatly greatly*). See Ap. 6.
21 And. Note the *Polysyndeton* (Ap. 6) in *vv.* 21-23, solemnly emphasising the complete extinction of life. Many other examples in this narrative to emph. its complete details. Heaps of animals and birds found together, mostly on hills. Bones not gnawed or exposed to the weather. There is also a break—and a fresh beginning—in Egyptian monuments.
died = ceased to breathe.
22 breath = *nᵉshāmāh*. Ap. 16.
of life. Heb. of the spirit (*ruach*, Ap. 9), of life (Heb. *chay*).
23 living substance = standing thing.
destroyed. Heb. wiped out.
Noah. See 1 Pet. 3. 20. 2 Pet. 2. 5.

8. 1 God = Heb. *'Elohim* = the Creator, because every living creature is included. Cp. 7. 16.
remembered. Fig. *Anthropopatheia.* See Ap. 6.
wind. Heb. *ruach.* See Ap. 9.
2 windows. Heb. *'ărubboth.* See note on 7. 11.
4 rested. Saturday, the Sabbath Day. Cp. 7. 4.
5 first day. Tuesday. (The only day named that is not a Sabbath.)
6 window. Heb. *challon* = a small aperture. Cp. 7. 11 (not 8. 2). Same as Josh. 2. 18, 21. 1 Kings 6. 4. Ezek. 40. 16; 41. 16, 26.
7 raven: an unclean bird. Lev. 11. 15. Deut. 14. 14.
8 dove: a clean bird. Deut. 14. 11.
10 seven = the seven. Another Sabbath, 18th day of 11th month.
11 olive leaf. Heb. a newly-sprouted olive leaf.
12 seven. Saturday, 25th day of 11th month.
13 six hundredth and first year: i. e. of Noah's life.
the first month, the first day. Six important dates in Bible: (1) Here, the drying up of the waters (8. 13); (2) The setting up of Tabernacle by Moses (Ex. 40. 2); (3) The sanctification of cleansed-up Temple by Hezekiah (2 Chron. 29. 17); (4) The going up of Ezra (7. 9); (5) The giving up of strange wives (Ezra 10. 17); (6) The offering up of a bullock in Ezekiel's future Temple (Ezek. 45. 18).
14 twenty-seventh day of second month. Completing one solar year from 7. 11.
15 God. *Elohim*, the Creator, speaking from without. Cp. 7. 16 and 8. 1.
16 Go forth. Heb. *zē*. But in ch. 7. 1, Jehovah (from within), "Come thou". Heb. *b'o.* Cp. 7. 1.
17 Bring forth. *Elohim*, speaking from without.
20 altar. The first mentioned in Scripture.

15 And °God spake unto Noah, saying,
16 "°Go forth of the ark, thou, and thy wife, and thy sons, and thy sons' wives with thee.
17 °Bring forth with thee every living thing that *is* with thee, of all flesh, *both* of fowl, and of cattle, and of every creeping thing that creepeth upon the earth; that they may breed abundantly in the earth, and be fruitful, and multiply upon the earth."
18 And Noah went forth, and his sons, and his wife, and his sons' wives with him: 2347
19 Every beast, every creeping thing, and every fowl, *and* whatsoever creepeth upon the earth, after their kinds, went forth out of the ark.
20 And Noah builded an °altar unto [21] the LORD; and took of every clean beast, and of D (p. 11)

every clean fowl, and °offered °burnt offerings on the altar.

C F (p. 14) 21 And °the LORD °smelled a sweet °savour; and °the LORD said °in His heart, "I will not again curse the ground any more for man's sake; °for the imagination of man's heart *is* evil from his youth; neither will I again smite any more every thing living, as I have done.

22 °While the earth remaineth, seedtime °and harvest, and cold and heat, and summer and winter, and day and night shall not cease."

G a **9** And °God blessed Noah and his sons, and said unto them, "Be fruitful, and multiply, and °replenish the earth.

b 2 And the °fear of you and the °dread of you shall be upon every °beast of the earth, and upon every fowl of the air, upon all that moveth *upon* the °earth, and upon all the fishes of the sea; into your hand are they delivered.

c 3 °Every moving thing that liveth shall be meat for you; even as the green herb have I given you °all things.

4 But flesh with the °life thereof, *which is* the °blood thereof, shall ye not eat.

G c 5 And surely your blood °of your °lives will I require; at the °hand of every [2]beast will I require it, and at the hand of man; at the hand of every man's brother will I require the [4]life of man.

b 6 Whoso sheddeth man's blood, by man shall his blood be shed: for in the °image of God made He man.

a 7 And **you**, be ye fruitful, and multiply; bring forth abundantly in the earth, and multiply therein."

F 8 And [1]God spake unto Noah, and to his sons with him, saying,

9 "And °**I**, °behold, I establish My °covenant with you, and with your seed after you;

10 And with every living °creature that *is* with you, of the fowl, of the cattle, and of every [2]beast of the earth with you; from all that go out of the ark, to every beast of the earth.

11 And I will establish My covenant with you; neither shall all flesh be cut off any more by the waters of a flood; neither shall there any more be a flood to destroy the earth."

12 And [1]God said, "This *is* the °token of the covenant which **I** make between Me and you and every living [10]creature that *is* with you, for perpetual generations:

13 I do °set My bow in the cloud, and it shall be for a token of a covenant between Me and the earth.

14 And it shall come to pass, when I bring a cloud over the earth, °that the bow shall be seen in the cloud:

15 And I will °remember My covenant, which *is* between Me and you and every living [10]creature of all flesh; and the waters shall no more become a flood to destroy all flesh.

16 And the bow shall be in the cloud; and I will look upon it, that I may [15]remember the °everlasting covenant between [1]God and every living [10]creature of all flesh that *is* upon the earth."

offered. Heb. *'ālāh.* Ap. 43. I. vi.
burnt offerings. Heb. *'ōlāh.* Ap. 43. II. ii.

8. 21—9. 17 (*C*, p. 11). THE EARTH REPLENISHED (*Double Introversion*).

C | F | 8. 21, 22. God's covenant with the earth.
 G | a | 9. 1. Fruitfulness committed to man.
 b | 9. 2. Power committed to man.
 c | 9. 3. Change in Ordinance (nourishment).
 G | *c* | 9. 4, 5. Change in Ordinance (punishment).
 b | 9. 6. Power committed to man.
 a | 9. 7. Fruitfulness committed to man.
 (a–a: **God's blessing for Noah.**)
 F | 9. 8–17. God's covenant with Noah.

21 the LORD = Jehovah, in covenant-relationship.
smelled a sweet savour. Heb. "smelled a smell". Fig. *Polyptōton* (Ap. 6).
savour. First occ. Heb. *nīḥoaḥ*, found only in this connection = rest, acquiescence.
in His heart. Fig. *Anthropopatheia* (Ap. 6), in condescension, and for emphasis.
for = although, as in Ex. 13. 17. 2 Sam. 23. 5. Ps. 49. 18. Hab. 3. 17.
22 While. Jehovah's covenant with Noah was unconditional in connection with the earth; as with Abraham, to give him the land (ch. 15), and with David, to give him the throne (2 Sam. 7).
and. Note the Fig. *Polysyndeton* (Ap. 6) seven times in this verse, to emphasise the completeness and perfection of the Covenant (Ap. 10). Eight things named in 4 pairs of opposites.

9. 1 God. Heb. *'ĕlohīm*, the Creator, because in connection with creation (*v.* 2) and the earth.
replenish = fill, as in 6. 11.
2 fear . . . dread. Fig. *Synonymia* (Ap. 6).
beast = living thing, as in 3. 1.
earth. Heb. *'ădhāmah* = the ground.
3 Every . . . all. Fig. *Epanadiplosis* (Ap. 6), for emphasis. Same word in Heb.
4 life = soul. Heb. *nephesh.* See Ap. 13.
blood. This is the essence and foundation of the doctrine of substitution and atonement = "life for life". "The wages of sin is death" (Rom. 6. 23), and "without shedding of blood [and thus giving up the life] is no remission" (Heb. 9. 22).
5 of. Gen. of Apposition (Ap. 17) = "blood, [that is] your lives".
lives = souls. Plural of Heb. *nephesh.* See Ap. 13.
hand of every beast. Fig. *Prosopopœia* (Ap. 6).
6 image of God. Heb. image of *'elohim* (Ap. 4). See note on 1. 26, and 3. 7. See Ap. 15 for the Laws before Sinai.
9 I, behold, I. Fig. *Epizeuxis* (Ap. 6) for emphasis.
behold. Fig. *Asterismos* (Ap. 6) for emphasis.
covenant. Mentioned seven times in *vv.* 9–17 (*F*).
10 creature = soul. Heb. *nephesh.* So rendered in 1. 21, 24; 2. 19; 9. 10, 12, 15, 16. Lev. 11. 46, &c. See Ap. 13.
12 token, or sign; then so associated with the bow.
13 set. Heb. grant. Not then first seen as a phenomenon, but then first assigned as a token.
14 that. Heb. = and [when]. See *v.* 13.
15 remember. Fig. *Anthropopatheia* (Ap. 6).
16 everlasting covenant. This expression occurs thirteen times in O.T. and once in N.T., making fourteen in all. Gen. 9. 16; 17. 13, 19. Lev. 24. 8. 2 Sam. 23. 5. 1 Chron. 16. 17. Ps. 105. 10. Isa. 24. 5; 55. 3; 61. 8. Jer. 32. 40. Ezek. 37. 26, and Heb. 13. 20.

17 And [1]God said unto Noah, "This *is* the token of the covenant, which I have established between Me and all flesh that *is* upon the earth."

B (p. 11) 18 And the sons of Noah, that went forth of the ark, were Shem, and Ham, and Japheth: and Ham *is* the father of Canaan.

19 These *are* the three sons of Noah: and of them was the whole earth overspread.

20 And Noah °began *to be* an °husbandman, and he planted a vineyard:

21 And he drank of the °wine, and was drunken; and he was uncovered within his tent.

22 And Ham, the father of Canaan, saw the nakedness of his father, and told his two brethren without.

23 And Shem and Japheth took a garment, and laid *it* upon both their shoulders, and went backward, and covered the nakedness of their father; and their faces *were* backward, and they saw not their father's nakedness.

24 And Noah °awoke from his wine, and knew what his °younger son had done unto him.

25 And he said, "°Cursed *be* Canaan; a °servant of servants shall he be unto his brethren."

26 And he said, "°Blessed *be* °the LORD [1] God of Shem; and Canaan shall be his servant.

27 [1] God shall °enlarge Japheth, and he shall °dwell in the °tents of Shem; and Canaan shall be his servant."

A 28 And Noah lived after the flood three hundred and fifty years.

1998 29 And all the days of Noah were nine hundred and fifty years: and he died.

A^1 B C D (p. 15) **10** Now these *are* THE GENERATIONS OF THE SONS OF NOAH, °Shem, °Ham, and °Japheth: and unto them were sons born after the flood.

D 2 The sons of Japheth; °Gomer, and °Magog, and °Madai, and °Javan, and °Tubal, and °Meshech, and °Tiras.

3 And the sons of [2] Gomer; Ashkenaz, and Riphath, and Togarmah.

4 And the sons of Javan; °Elishah, and °Tarshish, °Kittim, and °Dodanim.

5 By these were the °isles of the Gentiles divided °in their lands; every one after his tongue, after their families, in their nations.

C 6 And the sons of Ham; °Cush, and °Mizraim, and °Phut, and °Canaan.

7 And the sons of Cush; Seba, and Havilah, and Sabtah, and Raamah, and Sabtechah: and the sons of Raamah; Sheba, and Dedan.

about 2185 8 And Cush begat °Nimrod: he began to be a °mighty one in the earth.

9 He was a mighty °hunter before the LORD: wherefore °it is said, "Even as Nimrod the mighty hunter °before the LORD."

10 And the beginning of his kingdom was

20 began to be = was. Heb. idiom. Cp. Luke 12. 1. Matt. 26. 37. Mark 10. 41. Luke 3. 23. Mark 11. 15.

husbandman. Heb. *man of the ground*, i. e. giving himself to tillage. Cp. "man of war" = a soldier (Josh. 5. 4); "man of blood" = a murderer (2 Sam. 16. 7); "man of cattle" = a shepherd or grazier (Gen. 46. 32); "man of words" = eloquent (Ex. 4. 10).

21 wine: first occ. Heb. *yayin*. See Ap. 27.

24 awoke. Sept. *eknēpho*, only here 1 Sam. 25. 37. Hab. 2. 7, 19; and Joel 1. 5. In N. T. only 1 Cor. 15. 34, means very much awake, awake to wisdom.

younger = than Japheth, not Shem. See notes on 5. 32; 10. 1.

25 Cursed. Fulf. in Book of Joshua.

servant of servants. Fig. *Polyptōton* (Ap. 6).

26 Blessed. Fulf. in Shem being in the line of the promised seed, and in the overthrow of Canaanites.

the LORD. Heb. Jehovah. Ap. 4.

27 enlarge Japheth. Fig. *Paronomasia* (Ap. 6). *Yapht le-yephth.* Fulf. in increase of Western nations.

dwell: as in a Tabernacle (Gen. 3. 24, q. v.), i. e. worship the God of Shem: Israel's God, Heb. *shākan*. See Ap. 40. Gentiles to be blessed in Shem. The Eunuch (Ham) Acts 8. Saul (Shem) Acts 9. Cornelius (Japheth) Acts 10. See note on Gen. 11. 9.

tents. Heb. *'ohel* (Ap. 40). Prob. pl. of majesty, the Great Tent or Tabernacle of Shem, who would thus be the "Priest of the most High God". See note on 14. 18.

10. 1 — 11. 9 (**H**, p. 1). THE GENERATIONS OF THE SONS OF NOAH (*Division*).

A^1 | 10. 1-32. The Nations divided in the Earth.
A^2 | 11. 1-9. The Nations scattered abroad on the Earth.
Chs. 10 and 11. Fig. *Hysterologia* (Ap. 6), by which the dispersion of the nations (ch. 10) is put before the cause of it (ch. 11).

10. 1-32 (A^1, above). NATIONS DIVIDED. (*Introversion.*)

A^1 B | 1-. Shem.
C | -1-. Ham.
D | -1. Japheth.
D | 2-5. The sons of Japheth.
C | 6-20. The sons of Ham.
B | 21-32. The sons of Shem.

1 Shem. Note the *Asyndeton* (Ap. 6) here, and contrast the *Polysyndeton* of 7. 13. This order in 5. 32; 6. 10; 7. 13; 9. 18. 1 Chron. 1. 4.

Japheth, the eldest, 1 Chron. 1. 5. Gen. 10. 21.

Ham, second, Gen. 9. 24. "Younger" than Japheth.

Shem, the youngest. Cp. 5. 32 and 11. 10. Last here (in Introversion) because his history is to be continued. Japheth = enlargement. Ham = Heat, Black. Shem = Name or Renown.

2 Gomer. In Assyrian *Gimirrā* (the Kimmerians of Herodotus). Progenitor of the Celts.

Magog. Associated with Gomer in Ezek. 38. 2, 6.

Madai. First seen on Assyrian monuments B.C. 840, and called *Amadā* = the Kurdish tribes E. of Assyria.

Javan = the *Ionians* of the cuneiform inscriptions, and the Tel-el-Amarna tablets. Greeks first known by this name. **Tubal** = the Tabali.

Meshech = the Muskā of the Assyrian Mon. E. Asia Minor. **Tiras** = Thracians.

4 Elishah = Egyptian *Alasia* (the Cilician coast).

Tarshish is probably Tarsus.

Kittim = Kition in Cyprus. See note on Num. 24. 24. **Dodanim** = Rodanim (1 Chron. 1. 7) with Sam. and Sept. **5 isles** = coast-lands (Isa. 42. 15). **in their** = these were the sons of Japheth in their, &c. For these fourfold divisions cp. 10. 5, 20, 31. Rev. 5. 9; 7. 9; 10. 11; 11. 9; 13. 7; 14. 6; 17. 15; ten occurrences (Ap. 10). N.B. — In Rev. 13. 7 all critical texts add "and people". N.B. — The same divisions seen in Israel. In Gen. "families"; in Ex. "tongue"; in Num. "nation"; in Deut. the "land" (in Lev. the Sanctuary as being apart from the Earth). **6 Cush** = Ethiopia, S. of Egypt. **Mizraim** = Egypt, became the name of Egypt = "the two Matsors". One *Matsor* was country of the Delta within the great wall of defence called "Shur"; the other was Egypt proper. See notes on Isa. 19. 6 and 37. 25. **Phut:** cp. Jer. 46. 9. Ezek. 27. 10; 30. 5; 38. 5. Nah. 3. 9. **Canaan** became a province of Egypt, as shown by the Tel el-Amarna tablets. **8 Nimrod:** from Heb. *Marad, to rebel.* 1st pers. pl., Jussive, "*We will rebel*", or, "Come, let us rebel". See Ap. 28. **mighty one** = a hero. N.B.—From Ham; not from Shem. **9 hunter.** Cp. Jer. 16. 16. **it is said.** A later proverb of Semitic origin, as Jehovah was not known in Babylonia. **before** = in defiance of (6. 11).

°Babel, and Erech, and Accad, and Calneh, in the land of °Shinar.

11 Out of that land °went forth Asshur, and builded °Nineveh (and °the city Rehoboth) and Calah,

12 And Resen between Nineveh and Calah: the same *is* a °great city.

13 And [6]Mizraim begat °Ludim, and Anamim, and Lehabim, and Naphtuhim,

14 And Pathrusim, and Casluhim, (out of whom came °Philistim,) and Caphtorim.

15 And Canaan begat °Sidon his firstborn, and °Heth,

16 And the °Jebusite, and the Amorite, and the Girgasite,

17 And the Hivite, and the Arkite, and the Sinite,

18 And the Arvadite, and the Zemarite, and the Hamathite: and afterward were the families of the Canaanites spread abroad.

19 And the border of the Canaanites was from Sidon, as thou comest to Gerar, unto Gaza; as thou goest, unto Sodom, and Gomorrah, and Admah, and Zeboim, even unto Lasha.

20 These *are* the sons of Ham, after their families, after their °tongues, in their countries, *and* in their nations.

B 21 Unto °Shem also, the father of all the
(p. 15) children of Eber, the brother of Japheth °the elder, even to him were *children* born.

22 The children of Shem; °Elam, and Asshur, and Arphaxad, and Lud, and Aram.

23 And the children of Aram; °Uz, and Hul, and Gether, and Mash.

24 And Arphaxad begat Salah; and Salah begat °Eber.

25 And unto Eber were born two sons: the name of one *was* °Peleg; for in his days was the earth °divided; and his brother's name *was* Joktan.

26 And Joktan begat Almodad, and Sheleph, and Hazarmaveth, and Jerah,

27 And Hadoram, and Uzal, and Diklah,

28 And Obal, and Abimael, and Sheba,

29 And Ophir, and Havilah, and Jobab: all these *were* the sons of Joktan.

30 And their dwelling was from Mesha, as thou goest unto Sephar a mount of the east.

31 These *are* the sons of Shem, after their °families, after their tongues, in their lands, after their nations.

32 These *are* the families of the sons of Noah, after their generations, in their nations: and by these were the nations °divided in the earth after the flood.

A² E a **11** And the whole °earth was of one °lan-
(p. 16) guage, and of one speech.

b 2 And it came to pass, as they journeyed °from the east, that they found a plain in the land of °Shinar; and they dwelt there.

F 3 And they °said one to another, "Go to, let us make brick, and °burn them throughly."

10 Babel. In Semitic Babylonian = *Bab-ili* = "the gate of the god", cp. 11. 9.

Shinar = Babylonia, and is to be distinguished from Assyria (Isa. 11. 11).

11 went forth: Targ. of Onk. says: "he [Nimrod] went forth into Asshur" (i. e. invaded it).

Nineveh. The competitor of Babylon as the capital of Assyria.

the city Rehoboth = better, "the city boulevards", in parenthesis.

12 great: i. e. the four cities Nineveh, Rehoboth, Calah, and Resen. Resen had ceased to be a great city in the time of Sennacherib.

13 Ludim = the Lydians, cp. Jer. 46. 9. Ezek. 27. 10; 30. 5.

14 Philistim: hence the name of Palestine. Cp. Amos 9. 7. Jer. 47. 4. The parenthesis in this verse should come after Caphtorim as these gave the name Philistine. The five cities of the Philistines (Gaza, Ashkelon, Ashdod, Ekron, and Gath) were on the confines of Egypt (Deut. 2. 23).

15 Sidon = the oldest Canaanite city.

Heth = the Hittites.

16 Jebusite. The founders of Jebus; afterward Jerusalem. The Citadel was afterward Zion, S. of Moriah, 2 Sam. 5. 6-9. Cp. Ezek. 16. 3, 45, which explains the connection of the Jebusite here, with the Amorite and Hittite, *v.* 15.

20 tongues. See *v.* 5.

21 Shem: comes last (acc. to the Structure, which is an Introversion) because his "Generations" occupy the rest of the book. Hence when mentioned with the other two, Shem the youngest comes first. See note 5. 32; 9. 24; 10. 1.

the elder, see 5. 32.

22 Elam = the mountainous district E. of Babylonia.

23 Uz: the country of the Sabeans and Chaldeans. See Job 1. 15, 17, and Teman near Petra (Job 2. 11).

24 Eber. Whence the name Hebrews (Gen. 14. 13) = beyond. The people coming from and beyond the "Flood", i. e. the Euphrates, to Canaan (Josh. 24. 2, 3, 14, 15).

25 Peleg = division. His generations reserved till 11. 10-27.

divided. Heb. *pālag, to cleave.* In *vv.* 5, 32, *pārad*, to break off. In Deut. 32. 8 it is *nāḥal*, to divide for an inheritance.

31 families, &c. Note the thrice-repeated fourfold division in *vv.* 5, 20. See Ap. 10.

32 divided: i. e. in judgment. Cp. *v.* 25. Here *pārad* = *disruption* in judgment. God's division (*v.* 25) included Zion. Man's disruption included Babylon (11. 2, 9).

11. 1-9 (A², p. 15). THE NATIONS SCATTERED.
(*Introversion and Alternation.*)

A² E | a | 1. Unity.
      | b | 2. Shinar.
      F | 3, 4. The Tower. Man's building.
      F | 5. The Tower. God's inspection.
E | *a* | 6, 7. Unity.
      | *b* | 8, 9. Babel.

1 earth = people of the earth. Fig. *Metonymy* (of Subject). Ap. 6; "earth" put for inhabitants.

language. Heb. "lip". Fig. *Metonymy* (of cause), Ap. 6; lip put for language.

The chapter begins with man's attempt to unify mankind, and ends with God's new provision to unify all in blessing with Abraham's seed.

2 from the east = eastward.

Shinar = Babylonia.

3 said. Sin with their tongues punished in the same manner (*v.* 7).

burn, &c. Heb. brick bricks, and burn a burning. Fig. *Polyptōton.* Ap. 6, emphasising their determination. Burning in fire, not waiting for sun. See note on "brick-kiln", 2 Sam. 12. 31.

And they had brick for stone, and °slime had they for morter.

4 And they said, "Go to, let us build us a city and a tower, whose top °*may reach* unto heaven; and let us make us °a name, lest we be scattered abroad upon the face of the whole earth."

F (p. 16) **5 And the LORD °came down to see the city and the tower, which the children of men builded.**

E a **6 And the LORD said, * Behold, the people *is* one, and they have all one language; and this they begin to do: and now nothing will be restrained from them, which they have imagined to do.**

7 °Go to, let Us go down, and there confound their language, that they may not understand one another's speech."

b **8 So the LORD °scattered them abroad from**
1946 **thence upon the face of all the earth: and they left off to build the city.**

9 Therefore is the name of it called °Babel; because the LORD did there confound the language of all the earth: and from thence did the LORD °scatter them abroad upon the face of all the earth.

I (p. 1) **10 These *are* THE GENERATIONS OF SHEM: Shem *was* an hundred years old, and**
2346 **begat Arphaxad two years after the flood:**

11 And °Shem lived after he begat Arphaxad five hundred years, and begat sons and daughters.

2311 **12 And Arphaxad lived five and thirty years, and begat °Salah:**

13 And Arphaxad lived after he begat Salah four hundred and three years, and begat sons and daughters.

2281 **14 And Salah lived thirty years, and begat Eber:**

15 And Salah lived after he begat Eber four hundred and three years, and begat sons and daughters.

2247 **16 And °Eber lived four and thirty years, and begat °Peleg:**

17 And Eber lived after he begat °Peleg four hundred and thirty years, and begat sons and daughters.

2217 **18 And Peleg lived thirty years, and begat Reu:**

19 And Peleg lived after he begat Reu two hundred and nine years, and begat sons and daughters.

2185 **20 And Reu lived two and thirty years, and begat °Serug:**

21 And Reu lived after he begat Serug two hundred and seven years, and begat sons and daughters.

2155 **22 And Serug lived thirty years, and begat Nahor:**

23 And Serug lived after he begat Nahor two hundred years, and begat sons and daughters.

2126 **24 And Nahor lived nine and twenty years, and begat °Terah:**

25 And Nahor lived after he begat Terah an hundred and nineteen years, and begat sons and daughters.

slime = bitumen. So tenacious to-day that detachment almost impossible. Cp. the slime of Babel with the jewels of Zion (Rev. 21. 19).

4 may reach. No *Ellipsis* here. Heb. "and its top with the heavens", i. e. with the Zodiac depicted on it, as in ancient temples of Denderah and Esneh in Egypt.

a name. Manifesting independence of God. Nimrod being the rebel leader. See 10. 8-10, and cp. 12. 2.

5 came down. Fig. *Anthropopatheia* (Ap. 6).

7 Go to, let Us go down. This is always in judgment (cp. 18. 21. Ex. 3. 8). Here in contrast with *v.* 4, to man's "Go to, let us go up". Fig. *Anthropopatheia*, Ap. 6. See *v.* 5.

8 scattered. Sept. same word as in Acts 8. 1 (Isa. 8. 9). This was to preserve the revelation contained in the Zodiac and the constellations.

9 Babel. Heb. = confusion. Cp. Job 5. 12, another application of the Hebrew word.

scatter. Sept. same word as in Acts 8. 1. Result of which was the conversion of the Ethiopian (Acts 8. 26), of HAM. Saul (Acts 9), of SHEM. Cornelius (Acts 10), of JAPHETH.

Tongues confounded in *judgment* (Gen. 11. 9). Given in *grace* (Acts 2. 4). United in *glory* (Rev. 7. 9).

11. 10-26 (I, p. 1). THE GENERATIONS OF SHEM.

11 Shem. A return to the main purpose of the Book. See note on 5. 32.

12 Salah. Luke 3. 36 says Cainan, but this was probably a gloss from Sept., and crept into the text. No second Cainan in Heb. text here or elsewhere. Cp. 1 Chron. 1. 18.

16 Eber. See above, 10. 24.

Peleg born (10. 25) 14 years before *v.* 9.

17 Peleg. See above, 10. 25 (Luke 3. 35, Phalec).

20 Serug born (Luke 3. 35, Saruch).

24 Terah. Name prob. = traveller.

11. 27—25. 11 (D, p. 1). THE GENERATIONS OF TERAH. Introduction (11. 27-30). See Ap. 29.

(*Repeated Alternation.*)

A[1] | 11. 31—22. 19. Abram's history: From his Call, to his Trial. (Isaac's birth.)
  B[1] | 22. 20-24. The Posterity of Nahor.
A[2] | 23, 24. Abram's history. His old age. (Isaac's marriage.)
  B[2] | 25. 1-4. The Posterity of Keturah.
A[3] | 25. 5-11. Abram's history. Death. (Isaac's inheritance.)

27 Generations of Terah. The centre of the eleven. See page 1 and Ap. 29.

Abram the youngest comes first (born 1996). Cp. Shem (10. 21), Jacob (25. 23; 27. 15), Ephraim (48. 20).

28 before his father. The first death so recorded.

Ur = the *Uru* or "city" of the cuneiform texts. Now = Mugheir on W. bank of Euphrates.

29 Iscah. See Ap. 29.

26 And [24]Terah lived seventy years, and begat Abram, Nahor, and Haran. 2056

27 Now these *are* THE °GENERATIONS OF TERAH: Terah begat °Abram, Nahor, and Haran; and Haran begat Lot. **D** (p. 1)

28 And Haran died °before his father Terah in the land of his nativity, in °Ur of the Chaldees.

29 And Abram and Nahor took them wives: the name of Abram's wife *was* Sarai; and the name of Nahor's wife, Milcah, the daughter of Haran, the father of Milcah, and the father of °Iscah.

30 But Sarai was barren; she *had* no child.

A[1] C (p. 18) 31 And °Terah took Abram his son, and Lot
the son of Haran his son's son, and Sarai his
°daughter in law, his son Abram's wife; and
°they went forth with them from °Ur of the
Chaldees, to go into the land of Canaan; and
they came unto °Haran, and °dwelt there.
32 And the days of Terah were two hundred
1921 and five years: and Terah °died in °Haran.

12 Now the °LORD had said unto Abram,
"°Get thee out of thy country, and from
thy °kindred, and from thy father's house, unto
a land that I will °shew thee:
2 °And °I will make of thee a great nation,
and I will bless thee, and make thy name great;
and thou shalt be a blessing:
3 And I will bless them that bless thee, and
curse him that curseth thee: and in °thee shall
all families of the earth be blessed."

D 4 So Abram departed, as [1]the LORD had spoken
unto him; and Lot went with him: and Abram
was °seventy and five years old when he departed out of Haran.
5 And Abram took Sarai his wife, and Lot his
brother's son, and all their substance that they
had gathered, and the °souls that they had
1921 gotten in Haran; and they went forth to go
into the land of Canaan; and into the land of
Canaan °they came.
6 And Abram passed through the land unto
the place of °Sichem, unto the plain of Moreh.
(And the °Canaanite °*was* °then in the land.)
7 And [1]the LORD appeared unto Abram, and
said, "Unto thy seed will I give this land:"
and there builded he an °altar unto [1]the LORD,
Who appeared unto him.
8 And he removed from thence unto a mountain on the east of °Beth-el, and pitched his
tent, *having* Beth-el on the west, and Hai on
the east: and there he builded an °altar unto
[1]the LORD, and called upon the name of [1]the
LORD.
9 And Abram journeyed, going on still toward the °south.

E a 10 And there was a °famine in the land: and
Abram went °down into Egypt to sojourn
there; for the famine *was* grievous in the land.

11. 31 — 22. 19 (A[1], p. 17). ABRAM'S HISTORY. (Call to Trial). (*Introversions and Alternations.*)

A[1] | C | 11. 31 — 12. 3. Abram's Call. Promise of Seed.
D | 12. 4-9. Sojourn in Canaan.
E | a | 12. 10-20. Sojourn in Egypt. Denial of Sarai.
b | c | 13. 1-13. Separation of Lot.
d | 13. 14-18. Manifestation of the Land.
F | 14. 1-24. War on Sodom. Rescue of Lot by Abram.
G | e[1] | 15. Covenant made.
f[1] | 16. Sarai's Policy.
e[2] | 17. 1-14. Covenant repeated.
f[2] | 17. 15-27. Sarah's blessing.
e[3] | 18. 1-15. Covenant renewed.
F | 18. 16—19. 38. Destruction of Sodom. Rescue of Lot by angels.
E | *a* | 20. 1-18. Sojourn in Gerar. Denial of Sarah.
b | *d* | 21. 1-8. Manifestation of the Seed.
c | 21 9-21. Separation of Ishmael.
D | 21. 22-34. Sojourn in Gerar.
C | 22. 1-19. Abraham's Trial. Blessing of Seed.

31 Terah took. Terah being 200 and Abram 70. Cp. 15. 7. Josh. 24. 3. Neh. 9. 7. Acts 7. 2-4. Heb. 11. 8.
daughter in law = daughter by another wife. See Ap. 29.
they. Others beside those named. Cp. 24. 10, 15; 29. 10.
Ur = a city of great pretensions. Recent excavations show luxury and attainments. Abraham no nomad. See note on 11. 28.
Haran. Not the *Haran* of *v.* 26 above; but Charran (Acts 7. 2, 4), the frontier town of Bab. Empire, devoted to the worship of the Moon-god.
dwelt. Till he died (*v.* 32).
32 died in Haran (Charran). With this Acts 7. 4 agrees. Not seeing this, the Massorites wrongly marked *v.* 32 with an inverted *Nun* (נ) as being a dislocation of the Text.

12. 1 LORD = Jehovah, "The God of Glory" of Acts 7. 2. Fig. *Enallage* = *The Glorious God*, in contrast with idols (Josh. 24. 2).
Get thee out = Go for thyself, i. e. whatever others may do. Death had broken the link of nature's tie, which hindered Abram's obedience. **kindred.** Leaving Nahor and his family (except Lot), 24. 4, 10-15; 25. 20; 28. 7-10. **shew.** See Heb. 11. 8. **2 And.** Note the Fig. *Polysyndeton* (Ap. 6). **I will.** Note this sevenfold promise with the sevenfold blessing in Ex. 6. 4-8 (Ap. 10). **3 thee.** To Abraham personally. See note on 50. 24. **4 seventy and five.** The Law was 430 years "after" this (Ex. 12. 40. Gal. 3. 17). Abram 100 when Isaac born, and 105 when Isaac recognised as his "seed" (Gen. 21. 12). This 25 + 5 explains the 400 years of Gen. 15. 13 and Acts 7. 6. See note on 15. 13. **5 souls.** Heb. pl. of *nephesh* = souls. See Ap. 13. **they came.** This time: not when they had started from Chaldea (11. 31). **6 Sichem.** The place of Abram's first altar and Christ's first mission (John 4). Also of Jacob's altar (33. 18). **Canaanite . . . then in the land.** It is evident that from Terah's and Abraham's call, Satan knew the line by which "the seed of the woman" (3. 15) was coming into the world. In ch. 6 he aimed at the whole human race. Now he aims at Abraham and his land. Here is the second explanation of the words "after that" in 6. 4. He pre-occupies the territory ready to dispute the advance. The Canaanite "was then" = "being already" there (cp. 13. 7). The progeny of the later attempt to corrupt the race had to be destroyed by the sword of Israel, as those "in the days of Noah" had been by the Flood. See Ap. 23 and 25. **was** = being. **then** = already. **7 altar.** See note on Sichem, *v.* 6. **8 Beth-el.** An ancient Canaanite sacred pillar, doubtless here from previous times, called Luz (28. 19; 35. 6; 48. 3. Josh. 16. 2; 18. 13. Judg. 1. 23). Cp. Judg. 1. 26. When Moses wrote he used the later name. **altar.** Between Beth-el and Ai would probably be Gerizim and Ebal, which were already or thus became sacred places. Cp. Deut. 27. 2, 12 and Josh. 8. 9, 30. **9 south.** Heb. the *Negeb* or hill country S. of Judah (cp. 13. 1, 3). The Egyptian texts mention the Negeb. Towns taken by Shishak are mentioned as being there, e. g. Jerahmeel, Gerar, Kadesh, and Gaza. **10 famine.** Satan's attempt (thus early) to destroy Abraham's seed, through Sarah. See Ap. 23. Thirteen (Ap. 10) famines recorded, 12. 10; 26. 1; 41. 54. Ruth 1. 1. 2 Sam. 21. 1. 1 Kings 18. 2. 2 Kings 4. 38; 7. 4; 25. 3. Neh. 5. 3. Jer. 14. 1. Luke 15. 14. Acts 11. 28. **down.** Always "down" to Egypt! Cp. Isa. 30. 2; 31. 1.

11 And it came to pass, when he was come near to enter into Egypt, that he said unto Sarai his wife, "Behold now, I know that thou *art* a fair woman to look upon:

12 Therefore it shall come to pass, when the Egyptians shall °see thee, that they shall say, 'This *is* his wife:' and they will °kill me, but they will save thee alive.

13 Say, I pray thee, thou *art* my °sister: that it may be well with me for thy sake; and °my soul shall live because of thee."

14 And it came to pass, that, when Abram was come into Egypt, the Egyptians beheld the woman that she *was* very fair.

15 The princes also of °Pharaoh saw her, and commended her before Pharaoh: and the woman was taken into Pharaoh's house.

16 And he entreated Abram well for her sake: °and he had °sheep, and oxen, and he asses, and menservants, and maidservants, and she asses, and camels.

17 And the °LORD plagued Pharaoh and his house with great plagues because of Sarai Abram's wife.

18 And Pharaoh called Abram, and said, °"What *is* this *that* thou hast done unto me? °why didst thou not tell me that she *was* thy wife?

19 [18] Why saidst thou, 'She *is* my [13] sister?' so I might have taken her to me to wife: now therefore behold thy wife, take *her*, and go thy way."

20 °And Pharaoh commanded *his* men concerning him: and they sent him away, and his wife, and all that he had.

E b c (p. 18) **13** And Abram went °up out of Egypt, he, and his wife, and all that he had, and Lot with him, into the °south.

2 And Abram *was* very rich in cattle, in °silver, and in gold.

3 And he went on his journeys from the [1] south even to Beth-el, unto the place where his °tent had been °at the beginning, °between Beth-el and Hai;

4 Unto the place of the °altar, which he had made there °at the first: and there Abram called on the name of [10] the LORD.

5 And Lot also, which went with Abram, had flocks, and herds, and °tents.

6 And the land was not able to bear °them, that they might dwell together: for their substance was great, so that they could not dwell together.

7 And there was a °strife between the herdmen of Abram's cattle and the herdmen of Lot's cattle: (and the °Canaanite and the °Perizzite °dwelled °then °in the land).

8 And Abram said unto Lot, "Let there be no strife, I pray thee, between me and thee, and between my herdmen and thy herdmen; for we *be* °brethren.

9 °*Is* not the whole land before thee? separate thyself, I pray thee, from me: if °*thou wilt take* the left hand, then I will go to the right; or if *thou depart* to the right hand, then I will go to the left."

10 And Lot lifted up his eyes, and beheld all the plain of Jordan, that it *was* °well watered every where, before °the LORD destroyed °Sodom and °Gomorrah, *even* as the garden of °the LORD, like the land of Egypt, as thou comest unto Zoar.

11 Then Lot °chose him all the plain of Jordan; and Lot journeyed east: and they separated themselves the one from the other.

12 Abram dwelled in the land of Canaan, and Lot dwelled in the °cities of the plain, and pitched *his* tent °toward Sodom.

---

12 see thee. In Egypt the women went unveiled.
kill me. Satan's next assault, working on Abraham's fear. If God had not interfered (*v.* 17), where would His promise have been? (3. 15; 12. 7; 13. 15, &c.). See Ap. 23 and 25.
13 sister. See note on 20. 12 and Ap. 29.
my soul = I, myself. Heb. *nephesh.* See Ap. 13. Fig. *Synecdoche* (of Part), Ap. 6.
15 Pharaoh = the official title of all kings of Egypt, like Kaiser, Czar, &c.
16 and. Note the Fig. *Polysyndeton.* See Ap. 6, emph. each class of property. All these pictured on the Monuments in Egypt.
sheep, &c. No *horses* in Egypt till 18th Dynasty.
17 LORD. Divine intervention necessary. Ap. 23, 25.
18 What? Why? Fig. *Erotesis.* Ap. 6.
20 And. Note the Fig. *Polysyndeton.* See Ap. 6.

13. 1 up = Palestine an ascent from Egypt.
south = Heb. *the Negeb,* S. of Judea, N. from Egypt. Cp. 11. 9.
2 silver, and in gold: scarce in Palestine, but plentiful in Egypt.
3 tent: shows him a stranger.
at the beginning: very significant. No altar for Abram in Egypt.
between Beth-el and Hai. Prob Ebal or Gerizim. See note on 12. 8.
4 altar: shows him to be a worshipper.
at the first. No worship in Egypt. See note *v.* 3.
5 tents. Fig. *Metonymy* (of Subject): "tents" put for the dwellers therein.
6 them. Those two. For signification of the No. 2, see Ap. 10.
7 strife. The first step in Lot's downward course. Note Lot's six downward steps: *v* 7, "strife"; *v.* 10, "beheld"; *v.* 11, "chose"; *v.* 12, "pitched toward"; ch. 14. 12, "dwelt in": 19. 1, "sat in its gate", as a ruler and citizen. See Ap. 10.
Canaanite and Perizzite. See on 12. 6. These were the *Nephilim.* See Ap. 23, 25.
dwelled. Heb. were dwelling.
then = already. See note on 12. 6.
in the land. Occupying it in advance, and spreading later to "the giant cities of Bashan".
8 brethren. Put by *Synecdoche* (of Species), for relatives. Ap. 6.
9 Is not the whole land, &c. Fig. *Erotesis.* Ap. 6.
thou wilt take. Fig. *Complex Ellipsis.* See Ap. 6.
10 well watered. Great contrast with Palestine after the famine; and likeness to the fertility of Egypt. **the LORD.** Heb. Jehovah. Ap. 4.
Sodom = flaming, burning.
Gomorrah = people of fear: already mixed up in the sins of the *Nephilim.* 2 Pet. 2. 4. Jude 6.
11 chose. Lot lifted up his own eyes (*v.* 10), and made his own choice. Cp. Abram, *v* 14.
12 cities = one of the cities. Fig. *Synecdoche* (of the Whole). See Ap. 6. Or "among the cities". Cp. *v.* 18.
toward Sodom. See note on *v.* 7.

13 (But the men of Sodom *were* °wicked and sinners before [10] the LORD exceedingly.)

E b d (p. 18) 14 And [10] the LORD said unto Abram, after that Lot was separated from him, °"Lift up now thine eyes, and °look from the place where thou art northward, and southward, and eastward, and westward:

15 For all the land which thou seest, °to thee will I give it, and to thy seed °for ever.

16 And I will make thy seed as the °dust of the earth: so that if a man can number the dust of the earth, *then* shall thy seed also be numbered.

17 Arise, walk through the land in the length of it and in the breadth of it; for I will give it unto °thee."

18 Then Abram removed *his* tent, and came and dwelt in the °plain of Mamre, which *is* in °Hebron, and built there an altar unto [10] the LORD.

F **14** And it °came to pass °in the days of °Amraphel king of Shinar, °Arioch king of Ellasar, °Chedorlaomer king of Elam, and °Tidal king of °nations;

2 *That these* made war with Bera king of Sodom, and with Birsha king of Gomorrah, Shinab king of Admah, and Shemeber king of Zeboiim, and the king of Bela, which is °Zoar.

3 All these were joined together in the °vale of °Siddim, which is the salt sea.

4 °Twelve years they °served Chedorlaomer, and in the °thirteenth year they rebelled.

5 And in the fourteenth year came Chedorlaomer, and the kings that *were* with him, and smote the °Rephaims in Ashteroth Karnaim, and the °Zuzims in Ham, and the °Emims in Shaveh Kiriathaim,

6 And the °Horites in their mount Seir, unto El-paran, which *is* by the wilderness.

7 And they returned, and came to °En-mishpat, which *is* Kadesh, and smote °all the country of the Amalekites, and also the Amorites, that dwelt in Hazezon-tamar.

8 And there went out the king of Sodom, and the king of Gomorrah, and the king of Admah, and the king of Zeboiim, and the king of Bela (the same *is* °Zoar;) and they joined battle with them in the [3] vale of [3] Siddim;

9 With [1] Chedorlaomer the king of Elam, and with Tidal king of nations, and Amraphel king of Shinar, and Arioch king of Ellasar; °four kings with five.

10 And the vale of [3] Siddim *was full of* °slimepits; and the kings of Sodom and Gomorrah fled, and fell there; and they that remained fled to the mountain.

11 And they took all the goods of Sodom and Gomorrah, and all their victuals, and went their way.

12 And they took Lot, Abram's brother's son, °who dwelt in Sodom, and his goods, and departed.

13 And there came one that had escaped, and told Abram the °Hebrew; for °he dwelt in the plain of Mamre the Amorite, brother of Eshcol, and brother of Aner: and °these *were* confederate with Abram.

13 A parenthetical statement to show the nature of Lot's choice. Fig. *Parenthesis.* Ap. 6.

wicked and sinners = very wicked sinners. Fig. *Hendiadys.* See Ap. 6, and Ap. 44, viii and xiii.

14 Lift up. God chose for Abraham; strictly topographical. See note *v.* 11.

look. Note Abraham's four "looks": 13. 14 (earth); 15. 5 (heaven); 18. 2 (Jehovah); 22. 13 (a substitute).

15 to thee. Repeated to Isaac (26. 3), and to Jacob (28. 13; 35. 12). See note on 50. 24.

for ever. Hence Israel is "the everlasting nation", Isa. 44. 7. "To thee" ensures resurrection. Cp. Ex. 3. 6 and Matt. 22. 23-33.

16 dust. Fig. *Parœmia.* Ap. 6. In ch. 15. 5, as the "stars", marking the two parties in Israel: the earthly and heavenly (Heb. 11. 9-16); *partakers of* "the heavenly calling" (Heb. 3. 1).

17 thee. See note on 50. 24.

18 plain = among the oaks belonging to Mamre, brother of Eshcol and Aner (14. 13).

Hebron, a later name used here. See notes on 23. 2 and Num. 13. 22.

14. 1 came to pass in the days of. Heb. *v'yahi bēmeyi*: occurs 6 times (see Ap. 10); always marks a time of trouble ending in blessing. Cp. Ruth 1. 1. Isa. 7. 1. Jer. 1. 3. Est. 1. 1. 2 Sam. 21. 1 (cp. *v.* 14).

in the days. Dated in the reign of a king of Babylon: the united forces led by a king of Elam. The Assyrian tablets show that Elam had conquered and overrun Babylonia. Amraphel reigned in N. (Shinar); Eri-Aku (Arioch), an Elamite prince, in the S. at Larsa (Ellasar). All the names here are found on one tablet.

Amraphel = *Khammurabi* of the Tablets. Ammurapi is Amraphel transliterated.

Arioch = *Eri-aku* of the Tablets, in which it is found that his mother was sister to Chedorlaomer.

Chedorlaomer = the *Kudur-Lahgumal* of the Tablets.

Tidal = the *Tudghula* of the Tablets.

nations. The Tablet says "he assembled the *Umman-manda*", or the barbarian tribes of the Kurdish mountains, and that he "did evil" to the land of Bel. The Assyrian tablets are therefore shown to be correct by their agreement with Genesis.

2 Zoar. Cp. *v.* 8 and 19. 22.

3 vale. Afterward, the Salt (or Dead Sea), when Moses wrote.

Siddim = the Siddim.

4 Twelve. The No. of Government. See Ap. 10.

served = had served. *v.* 4 goes back to the events leading up to the present war with Sodom.

thirteenth. The first occ. Hence the No. of Rebellion. See Ap. 10.

5 Rephaim = a branch of the *Nephilim.* See Ap. 25. Superhuman beings, so called after one Rapha: as the *Anakim* after Anak. See 15. 20. Deut. 2. 11, 20, 21; 3. 11, 13. Josh. 12. 4; 13. 12; 15. 8; 17. 15; 18. 16. See notes on 6. 4; 12. 6; 13. 7; 14. 5; 15. 20, 21.

Zuzims in Ham, same as Zam-zummim in Cuneiform writing. Cp. Deut. 2. 20.

Emim. Cp. Deut. 2. 10.

6 Horites. Deut. 2. 12.

7 En-mishpat = the spring of judgment. Not yet Kadesh = the Sanctuary.

all the country. Heb. "the whole field", put by *Synecdoche* (of the Part), Ap. 6, for country.

8 takes up the present war with Sodom.

Zoar. Cp. *v.* 2 and 19. 22.

9 four kings with five. See the No. 9, the number of Judgment. See Ap. 10.

10 slimepits = pits of bitumen, still a feature of the shores of the Dead Sea.

12 who dwelt: emph. to call attention to ch. 13. 12. See note. Heb. *HE* (Lot), *being a dweller in Sodom.*

13 Hebrew. So called from *'Eber* (11. 14. Cp. 10. 21; 39. 14; 41. 12. Num. 24. 24), from *'ābar*, "to pass on" = "he who passed over from beyond" (Gr. *hyper*), i. e. beyond the Euphrates (Josh. 24. 2). **he**: emph. in contrast with Lot. **these**: emph. = *these also* having a covenant with Abram. See 13. 17.

14 And when Abram heard that his brother was taken captive, he armed his °trained *servants*, born in his own house, °three hundred and eighteen, and pursued *them* unto °Dan.

15 And he divided himself against them, °he and his servants, by night, and smote them, and pursued them unto Hobah, which *is* on the left hand of Damascus.

16 And he brought back all the goods, °and also brought again his brother Lot, and his goods, and the women also, and the people.

17 And the king of Sodom went out to meet him after his return from the slaughter of Chedorlaomer, and of the kings that *were* with him, at the valley of Shaveh, which *is* the °king's dale.

(18 And °Melchizedek king of °Salem brought forth bread and °wine: and he *was* the °priest of the °MOST HIGH GOD.

19 And he blessed him, and said, "Blessed *be* Abram of the [18]MOST HIGH GOD, possessor of heaven and earth:

20 And blessed be the [18]MOST HIGH GOD, Which hath delivered thine enemies into thy hand." And °he gave °him tithes of all.)

21 And the king of Sodom said unto Abram, "Give me the °persons, and take the goods to thyself."

22 And Abram said to the king of Sodom, "I have °lift up mine hand unto the LORD, the [18]MOST HIGH GOD, the possessor of heaven and earth,

23 That °I will not *take* from a thread even to a shoelatchet, and that I will not take any thing that *is* thine, lest thou shouldest say, 'I have made Abram rich:'

24 Save only that which the young men have eaten, and the portion of the men which went with me, Aner, Eshcol, and Mamre; let them take their portion."

G e1 g1 (p. 22) **15** After these things °the word of the LORD came unto Abram in °a vision, saying, "Fear not, Abram: °I *am* thy shield, *and* thy exceeding great reward."

h1 2 And Abram said, °"Lord GOD, what wilt Thou give me, seeing I °go childless, and the steward of my house *is* this Eliezer of Damascus?"

3 And Abram said, °"Behold, to me Thou hast given no seed: and, °lo, one born in my house is mine °heir."

g2 4 And, [3]behold, the word of [1]the LORD *came* unto him, saying, "This shall not be thine heir; but he that shall come forth out of thine own bowels shall be thine heir."

5 And He brought him forth abroad, and said, °"Look °now toward heaven, and tell the °stars, if thou be able to °number them:" and He said unto him, "So shall thy seed be."

h2 6 And he °believed in [1]the LORD; and He °counted it to him for °righteousness.

14 trained = initiated or instructed, prob. in the worship of Jehovah. Cp. 12. 5; 15. 2; 18. 19; 24. 12-29; and Prov. 22. 6 (same word).

318 = a multiple of 6, the No. of "man". See Ap. 10.

Dan. Not the Dan of Judges 18. 29, but a city in N. of Palestine long before the Danites changed the name of Laish.

15 he and his servants. Note the emphasis on "he".

16 and. Note the Fig. *Polysyndeton*. See Ap. 6.

17 king's dale = the king of Salem mentioned in next verse. The name still retained in 2 Sam. 18. 18.

18 Note the parenthetical clause (18-20), which interrupts in order to interpret.

Melchizedek = *King of righteousness*, or by Fig. *Enallage* (Ap. 6), *righteous king*. In History, Gen. 14. In Prophecy, Ps. 110. In Fulfilment, Heb. 7. This might be Shem in type, Christ in antitype.

Salem. Called, on the bricks of the ruins of an ancient city in S. of Palestine, *Uru-Salim = the city of Salim*. The Tablets show that Palestine was at this time in possession of Egypt, and the Tablets are letters to the Pharaohs Amenophis III and IV. One is from *Ebed-Tob*, the successor of Melchizedek. Three times he says "not my father, not my mother installed me in this place but the Mighty King" (cp. Heb. 7. 1-4), i. e. he did not inherit by succession, but by the gift and "the arm of the Mighty King" (the deity).

wine. Same as 9. 20-24. See Ap. 27. i.

priest. Yet no sacrifices. Hence a type of Him to Whom all shall bow (Ps. 110. 4), and pay their tithes and bring their gifts (Ps. 72). See note on 9. 27.

MOST HIGH GOD. Heb. *El Elyon*, so *vv.* 19, 20, 22. See Ap. 4. First occ. of this title. Cp. 1st occ. in N.T. (Luke 1. 76) "Highest", in relation to the *earth*. See also Deut. 32. 8 (cp. Acts 17. 26). Ps. 8; 9. 18, 27; and note on Num. 24. 16.

20 he. Fig. *Ellipsis* = Abram (see Ap. 6).

him = Melchizedek.

21 persons = Heb. *nephesh, souls.* Ap. 13. Fig. *Synecdoche* (of the Part). See Ap. 6.

22 lift up mine hand = *I swear*. Cp. Ex. 6. 8. Ps. 106. 26. Isa. 3. 7 margin. Fig. *Metonymy* (of Adjunct). See Ap. 6.

23 I will not take. The blessing of Melchizedek, and the bread and wine, prepared him for this great renunciation.

15. 1-21 (G e1, p. 18). THE COVENANT MADE.
The Seed and The Land.
[For Structure see next page.]

1 the word of the LORD. First occ. of this expression is with the prep. *'el*, unto, implying action of a person; or, at least, articulate speech.

a vision = the vision. Occurs only 4 times (here, Num. 24. 4, 16; Ezra 13. 7).

I am thy shield. Manifested in 14. 13-16 and 17-24. Cp. John 8. 56. The Incarnate Christ is Faith's shield (Eph. 6. 16).

2 Lord GOD. Heb. *Adonai Jehovah.* See Ap. 4. First occ., relating to blessing in the earth.

go = am going on.

3 Behold . . . lo. Fig. *Asterismos* (Ap. 6).

heir. Heb. *inherits me.* Fig. *Metonymy* (of Subject). See Ap. 6. This was strictly in accordance with § 191 of the Code of Khammurabi. See Ap. 15.

5 Look. See note on 13. 14.

now = steadfastly. **stars.** See on 13. 16 = the heavenly calling in Israel (Heb. 3. 1; 11. 9-16). Fig. *Parœmia.* Ap. 6. **number them.** Hence Joab's objection in 2 Sam. 24. 3. **6 believed:** i. e. believed Jehovah = believed what he "heard" (Rom. 10. 17). **counted** = reckoned or imputed. **righteousness.** No art. = as righteousness. This was positive imputed righteousness (because he believed concerning Christ). It was more than forensic righteousness, which was negative or non-imputation of sin (Ps. 32. 1, 2). This was the consequence of the Gospel preached to Abram. (Cp. Gal. 3. 8, and read Rom. 4 and Gal. 3).

g3 7 And He said unto him, "I am [1]the LORD
(p. 22) That brought thee out of Ur of the Chaldees,
to give thee this land to inherit it."
h3 8 And he said, °"Lord GOD, whereby shall I
know that I shall inherit it?"
g4 9 And He said unto him, °"Take Me an
°heifer of three years old, and a she goat of
three years old, and a ram of three years old,
and a turtledove, and a young pigeon."
10 And he took unto him all °these, and
°divided them in the °midst, and laid each
piece one against another: but the birds divided he not.
11 And when the fowls came down upon the
carcases, Abram drove them away.
h4 12 And when the sun was going down, a deep
sleep fell upon °Abram; and, °lo, an horror of
great darkness fell upon him.
13 And He said unto Abram, °"Know of a
surety that °thy seed shall be a stranger in a
land *that is* not theirs, (°and shall serve them;
and they shall afflict them) four hundred years;
14 And also that nation, whom they shall
serve, will I °judge: and afterward shall they
come out with great substance.
15 And thou shalt °go to thy fathers in peace;
thou shalt be buried in a good old age.
16 But in the °fourth generation they shall
come hither again: for the °iniquity of the
Amorites *is* °not yet full."
g5 17 And it came to pass, that, when the sun
went down, and it was dark, °behold a smoking
°furnace, and a burning °lamp that passed
between those pieces.
18 In the same day °the LORD made a covenant with Abram, saying, "Unto thy seed
°have I given °this land, from the river of
Egypt unto the great river, the river Euphrates:
19 The Kenites, and the Kenizzites, and the
Kadmonites,
20 And the °Hittites, and the Perizzites, and
the °Rephaims,
21 And the Amorites, and the Canaanites,
and the Girgashites, and the Jebusites."

G f1 **16** Now Sarai Abram's wife bare him no
(p. 18) children: and she had an °handmaid,
an Egyptian, whose name *was* °Hagar.
2 And Sarai said unto Abram, "Behold now,
[7]the LORD hath restrained me from bearing:
I pray thee, go in unto my maid; it may be
that I may obtain children by her." And Abram
hearkened to the voice of Sarai.
3 And Sarai Abram's wife took Hagar her
maid the Egyptian, after Abram had dwelt
1911 °ten years in the land of Canaan, and gave
her to her husband Abram to be his °wife.
4 And he went in unto Hagar, and she conceived: and when she saw that she had
conceived, her mistress was despised in her
eyes.
5 And Sarai said unto Abram, "My wrong
be upon thee: I have given my maid into thy
bosom; and when she saw that she had conceived, I was despised in her eyes: [7]the LORD
judge between me and °thee."
6 But Abram said unto Sarai, "Behold, thy
maid *is* in thy hand; do to her as it pleaseth

15. 1-21 (G e1, p. 18). THE COVENANT MADE.
The Seed and The Land.
(*Repeated Alternation.*)

e1 | g1 | 1. The Covenant Maker. (The Word of Jehovah.)
h1 | 2, 3. Enquiry. "What wilt Thou give?"
g2 | 4, 5. The Covenant. Announced. (The Seed.)
h2 | 6. Belief.
(The Seed)
g3 | 7. The Covenant Maker. (Jehovah.)
h3 | 8. Enquiry. "Whereby shall I know?"
g4 | 9-11. The Covenant. Prepared.
h4 | 12-16. Answer. "Know of a surety."
g5 | 17-21. The Covenant. Solemnized.
(The Land)

8 Lord GOD. Heb. *Adonai Jehovah.* See *v.* 2 and Ap. 4.
9 Take me = take for me: i. e. an offering for me.
heifer. See Ap. 15.
10 these. Five, the No. of Grace, because Covenant was unconditional. See Ap. 10.
divided. So Covenants were made (Jer. 34. 18-20).
midst, i. e. in half.
12 Abram. Put to sleep so that he should have no part in it, and that the Covenant should be unconditional, in which "God was the one" and only contracting party (Gal. 3. 20). Cp. *v.* 17. Contrast "both", ch. 21. 27.
lo. Fig *Asterismos.* See Ap. 6.
13 Know of a surety. Heb. *knowing thou shalt know.* Fig. *Polyptōton.* See Ap. 6, and note on 26. 28.
thy seed, i. e. Isaac. See note on 21. 12. The 400 years date from Isaac's birth (Acts 7. 6). The 430 from the "promise" or Covenant here made (cp. Gal. 3. 17), and include the whole "sojourning" (Ex. 12. 40).
and shall serve, &c. Fig. *Epitrechon.* See Ap. 6. This is shown by the Structure (*Introversion*).

a | Thy seed shall be a stranger, &c.
b | and shall serve them
b | and they shall afflict them
a | four hundred years.

In a and *a* we have the whole sojourning and duration. In b and *b* the servitude in Egypt (215 years).
14 judge. Put by *Metonymy* (of Cause), Ap. 6, for punish.
15 go to thy fathers = die and be buried. Abram's fathers were idolaters. Josh. 24. 2. Fig. *Euphemism* (Ap. 6).
16 fourth = Levi, Kohath, Amram, Moses; (or Levi), Jochebed (born in Egypt).
iniquity. Heb. *'avōn.* See Ap. 44. iii.
not yet. Another mark of the corruption of the Canaanite nations through the Nephilim and Rephaim.
17 behold. Fig. *Asterismos.* See Ap. 6.
furnace. Symbolic of the affliction of Israel (Deut. 4. 20. 1 Kings 8. 51. Isa. 31. 9. Ezek. 22. 18-22. Jer. 11. 4).
lamp. Symbolic of Israel's deliverance (1 Kings 11. 36; 15. 4. Isa. 62. 1. 2 Sam. 21. 17).
18 the LORD. Not Abram (Gal. 3. 17). See note on *v.* 12.
have. Before this it was "I will". From now it is "I have".
this land. Never yet possessed with these boundaries.
20 Hittites. First occ. See Ex. 32. 2. Josh. 3. 10, &c.
Rephaim. Another link in the chain from 6. 4. Cp. 12. 6; 13. 7; 14. 5; and see Ap. 23, 25.
19, 20, 21 Ten nations. See Ap. 10.

16. 1 handmaid. Not necessarily a slave. Cp 1 Sam. 25. 41.
Hagar = Heb. *Flight.* See *v.* 3.
3 ten. These 10 years to be taken into account in any calculations.
wife. This was strictly in accordance with the enactment of Khammurabi (§ 146) which Abram had brought from Ur. See Ap. 15.
5 thee. Should be "her". See Ap. 31.

thee." And when Sarai °dealt hardly with
her, she fled from her face.
7 And the °angel of °the LORD found her by a
fountain of water in the wilderness, by the
fountain in the way to °Shur.
8 And He said, "Hagar, Sarai's maid, whence
camest thou? and whither wilt thou go?"
And she said, "I flee from the °face of my
mistress Sarai."
9 And the angel of [7]the LORD said unto her,
"Return to thy mistress, and submit thyself
under her hands."
10 And the angel of [7]the LORD said unto her,
"I will multiply thy seed exceedingly, that it
shall not be numbered for multitude."
11 And the angel of [7]the LORD said unto her,
"Behold, thou *art* with child, and shalt bear a
son, and shalt call his name Ishmael; because
the LORD hath heard thy affliction.
12 And he will be a wild man; his hand *will*
be °against every man, and every man's hand
against him; and he shall dwell in the °pre-
sence of all his °brethren."
13 And she called the name of [7]the LORD that
spake unto her, Thou °GOD seest me: for she
°said, "Have I also here °looked after Him
That seeth me?"
14 Wherefore the well was called °Beer-lahai-
roi; behold, *it is* between Kadesh and Bered.
15 And °Hagar bare Abram a son: and
Abram called his son's name, which Hagar
bare, Ishmael.
16 And Abram *was* fourscore and six years
1910 old, when Hagar bare Ishmael to Abram.

e² i k¹ (p. 23) **17** And when Abram was ninety years old
and nine, °the LORD appeared to Abram,
and said unto him, "I *am* the °Almighty
1897 GOD; °walk before Me, and be thou perfect.
2 And I will make My covenant between Me
and thee, and will multiply thee °exceedingly."
l 3 And Abram °fell on his face:
k² and °God talked with him, saying,
4 "As for Me, behold, My covenant *is* with
thee, and thou shalt be a father of °many
nations.
5 Neither shall thy name any more be called
Abram, but thy name shall be °Abraham; for
a father of [4]many nations have I made thee.
6 And I will make thee °exceeding fruitful,
and I will make °nations of thee, and kings
shall come out of thee.
7 And I will establish My °covenant between
Me and thee and °thy seed after thee in their
generations for an °everlasting °covenant, to
be a [3]God unto thee, and to °thy seed after
thee.
8 And I will give unto thee, and to thy seed
after thee, the °land wherein thou art a
stranger, all the land of Canaan, for an [7]ever-
lasting possession; and I will be their [3]God."
j 9 And God said unto Abraham, "Thou shalt
keep My covenant therefore, thou, and °thy
seed after thee in their generations.
10 This *is* My covenant, which ye shall keep,
between Me and you and thy seed after thee;
Every man child among you shall be circumcised.

6 dealt hardly. Heb. afflicted her. The Code of Khammurabi (§ 119) forbade her being sold. Sarah could only lay tasks on her. See Ap. 15.
7 angel of the LORD. First occ. = messenger = 2nd Person, as being *sent*. *Elohim* = as being commissioned *by oath*. **the LORD.** Heb. Jehovah. Ap. 4.
Shur = wall. The nearest way to her native land. Shur was the name of the great fortified wall shutting Egypt off from Palestine, with its *Migdol* or Fort.
8 face = presence. Fig. *Pleonasm*. See Ap. 6.
12 against. True to-day and for over 3,000 years. Cp. 21. 20. Isa. 21. 13. Jer. 3. 2. Ezra 8. 31. Ps. 10. 8, 9.
presence = face, i. e. on the face of the same country.
brethren. Esp. with the Midianites (37. 28), Midian being his half-brother, by Keturah (cp. Judg. 8. 22, 24). Cp. the fulfilment in 25. 18.
13 GOD. Heb. *'ēl*. See Ap. 4.
said. Translate: "Do I see, here, even after the Vision?" i. e. "Do I live, after seeing God?"
looked = Fig. *Metonymy* (of Adjunct), implying living as well as looking. Cp. 32. 30. Judg. 13. 22.
14 Beer-lahai-roi = *the well of living after seeing*.
15 Hagar bare. Through infirmity of Sarah's faith. So the Law (parenthetically) "because of transgression" (Gal. 3. 19). Levitical Law given, as Ishmael was, until Christ the antitype of Isaac should be born (Gal. 4. 1–5, 19, 31).

17. 1–27 (17. 1–14 and 17. 15–27) (e² and f², p. 18).
THE COVENANT REPEATED AND SARAH'S BLESSING (*Alternation and Introversion*).

e² | i | k¹ | 1, 2. Promise of seed to Abram.
l | 3–. Prostration of Abram, and reverence.
k² | –3–8. God's talk with Abram. His seed.
j | 9–14. Circumcision. Command.
f² | *i* | k³ | 15, 16. Promise of seed to Sarah.
l | 17. Prostration of Abraham, and joy.
k⁴ | 18–22. God's talk with Abraham. Sarah's seed.
j | 23–27. Circumcision. Obedience.

1 the LORD. Heb. Jehovah. Ap. 4.
Almighty GOD = *El Shaddai*. First occ. See Ap. 4. This title assures Abram that He Who had called him was almighty to supply all his need. Cp. first occ. in N.T. (2 Cor. 6. 18), which assures us of the same supply.
walk = *continue to walk*.
2 exceedingly. Fig. *Epizeuxis* (*greatly greatly*). Ap. 6.
3 fell. Cp. Mary (John 11. 32) and contrast Martha (John 11. 21).
God = *Elohim*, Creator. Used in this ch. (*vv.* 3, 9, 15, 18, 22, 23) because He *creates* new names (*vv.* 5, 15), a new Sign of Covenant (*vv.* 9–14), and a new thing, from one as good as dead (Heb. 11. 12).
4 many. Emph. Fig. *Antimereia* (of Noun), for emphasis. Ap. 6.
5 Abraham. The fifth letter of Heb. alphabet (ה = H), put in middle of his name = No. 5, *Grace*. See Ap. 10. Abram = exalted father; Abraham = father of a multitude.
6 exceeding. Fig. *Epizeuxis* (*greatly greatly*). Ap. 6.
nations. Abraham was the progenitor not only of Israel, but of Ishmaelites, Midianites, Arabians, &c.
7 covenant: unconditional.
thy seed. Here, the coll. noun *zer'a* is shown to be plural by the words "after thee" (cp. *vv.* 8, 9), and by the pl. pron. "their generations" (*vv.* 7, 9). This is not the verse referred to in Gal. 3. 16, but Gen. 21. 12. See note on 21. 12, where "seed" must be in the sing. because of the verb.
everlasting. Hence Israel so called. Isa. 44. 7 margin.
8 land . . . stranger. Heb. *land of thy sojournings*.
9 thy seed. Still practised by Ishmaelites and others. Non-circumcision was the "reproach" of Egypt (Josh. 5. 9).

11 And ye shall circumcise the flesh of your foreskin; and it shall be a token of the covenant betwixt Me and you.

12 And he that is °eight days old shall be circumcised among you, every man child in your generations, he that is born in the house, or bought with money of any stranger, which *is* not of thy seed.

13 He that is born in thy house, and he that is bought with thy money, must needs be circumcised: and My covenant shall be in your °flesh for an everlasting covenant.

14 And the uncircumcised man child whose flesh of his foreskin is not circumcised, that °soul shall be cut off from his people; he hath broken My covenant."

k[3] 15 And [3]God said unto Abraham, "As for
(p. 23) Sarai thy wife, thou shalt not call her name Sarai, but °Sarah *shall* her name *be*.

16 And I will bless her, and give thee a son also of her: yea, I will bless her, and she shall be *a mother* of nations; °kings of people shall be of her."

l 17 Then Abraham [3]fell upon his face, and °laughed, and said in his heart, °"Shall *a child* be born unto him that is an hundred years old? and shall Sarah, that is ninety years old, bear?"

k[4] 18 And Abraham said unto [3]God, "O that Ishmael °might live before Thee!"

19 And [3]God said, "Sarah thy wife shall bear thee a son indeed; and thou shalt call his name Isaac: and I will establish My covenant with him for an everlasting covenant, °*and* with his seed after him.

20 And as for Ishmael, °I have heard thee: Behold, I have blessed him, and will make him fruitful, and will multiply him °exceedingly; twelve princes shall he beget, and I will make him a great nation.

21 But My covenant will I establish with °Isaac, which Sarah shall bear unto thee at this °set time in the next year."

22 And He left off talking with him, and [3]God went up from Abraham.

j 23 And Abraham took Ishmael his son, and all that were born in his house, and all that were bought with his money, every male among the °men of Abraham's house; and °circumcised the flesh of their foreskin in the selfsame day, as [3]God had said unto him.

24 And Abraham *was* ninety years old and nine, when he was circumcised in the flesh of his foreskin.

25 And Ishmael his son *was* °thirteen years old, when he was circumcised in the flesh of his foreskin.

26 In the selfsame day was Abraham circumcised, and Ishmael his son.

27 And all the men of his house, born in the house, and bought with money of the stranger, were circumcised with him.

e[3] m **18** And °the LORD appeared unto him in the
(p. 24) °plains of Mamre: and he °sat in the tent door in the heat of the day;

2 And he lift up his eyes and °looked, and, °lo, °three men stood by him: and when he saw *them*, he ran to meet them from the tent door, and bowed himself toward the ground,

3 And said, "My °LORD*, if now I have found n
favour in Thy sight, pass not away, I pray (p. 24)
Thee, from Thy servant:

4 Let a little water, I pray you, be fetched, and °wash your feet, and rest yourselves under the tree:

5 And I will fetch a morsel of °bread, and comfort ye your hearts; after that ye shall pass on: for therefore are ye come to your servant." And they said, "So do, as thou hast said."

6 And Abraham hastened into the tent unto

12 eight = the number of Resurrection (Ap. 10); associated here with circumcision, the sign of *death*.

13 flesh. Fig. *Synecdoche*, for the whole person. Ap. 6.

14 soul. Heb. *nephesh*. Ap. 13. Fig. *Synecdoche*, for person. Ap. 6.

15 Sarah. The addition of the 5th letter (ה = H) of Heb. alphabet (the No. of *Grace*, Ap. 10) as in Abraham's case (*v.* 5) and Joshua's (Num. 13. 16). The letter ה (H) is common to both the names of Jehovah and Elohim. Sarai = *princely*; Sarah = *princess*.

16 kings. Sam., Onk., Jon., Sept., and Syr. read "and kings".

17 laughed: for joy. Heb. *was joyful*. Cp. John 8. 56, "rejoiced to see my day . . . and was glad." The laughter of faith, Rom. 4. 19. Sarah did not fall down as Abraham did, *v.* 3.

Shall, &c. Fig. *Erotēsis*. Ap. 6. (Cp. Heb. 11. 12).

18 might live, as though he thought Ishmael was to die: showing his faith in Isaac's birth. This is proved from *v.* 20.

19 and. Sam., Onk., Jon., Sept., Syr. read this "and" in the text.

20 I have heard. Showing the subject of Abraham's prayer.

exceedingly. Fig. *Epizeuxis* (*greatly greatly*). Ap. 6.

21 Isaac. Heb. *laughter*.

set time. See note on 1. 14.

23 men. Heb. pl. of *'ish*, or *'enosh*. See Ap. 14.

circumcised. Hence Ishmaelites and kindred nations still practise the rite.

25 thirteen. Symbolic; and in contrast with Isaac on *eighth* day. See Ap. 10. Ishmaelites and Arabians still circumcise in the 13th year.

18. 1-16 (G e[3], p. 18). THE COVENANT RENEWED (*Introversion*).

e[3] | m | 1, 2. Appearance of Jehovah. (Three men.)
n | 3-8. Their reception by Abraham.
n | 9-15. Their conference with Abraham.
m | 16-. Departure of Jehovah. (Three men.)

1 the LORD. Heb. Jehovah. Ap. 4.

plains = among the oaks of Mamre. Cp. 13. 18; 14. 13; and 18. 8. **sat** = was sitting.

2 looked. See note on 13. 14.

lo. The Fig. *Asterismos*. Ap. 6.

three men. Elohim (Ap. 4) and two angels called men (Heb. *'ish*, pl., Ap. 14) here, and *vv.* 16, 22: but in 19. 1, 15 the two are called "angels". *Three* the No. of Divine perfection (see Ap. 10). When two departed, Elohim (the Divine Presence) remained (*vv.* 16, 22).

3 LORD = Jehovah, not Adonai. See Ap. 32. But plural throughout ch. 19 of the *two*.

4 wash your feet. A common practice to this day; needed from use of sandals and bare feet; cp. 24. 32; 43. 24.

5 bread. Fig. *Synecdoche* (of Species), Ap. 6, put for food in general.

Sarah, and said, "Make ready quickly °three measures of fine meal, knead *it*, and make °cakes upon the hearth."
7 And Abraham °ran unto the herd, and fetcht a calf tender and good, and gave *it* unto a young man; and he hasted to dress it.
8 And he took butter, and milk, and the calf which he had dressed, and set *it* before them; and **he** stood by them under the °tree, and they did °eat.
n 9 And they said unto him, °"Where *is* Sarah
(p. 24) thy wife?" And he said, °"Behold, in the tent."
10 And He said, "I will °certainly return unto thee according to the time of life; and, °lo, Sarah thy wife shall have a son." And Sarah °heard *it* in the tent door, which *was* behind him.
11 Now Abraham and Sarah *were* °old *and* well stricken in age; *and* it ceased to be with Sarah after the manner of women.
12 Therefore Sarah °laughed within herself, saying, °"After I am waxed old shall I have pleasure, °my lord being old also?"
13 And [1]the LORD said unto Abraham, °"Wherefore did Sarah laugh, saying, 'Shall **I** of a surety bear a child, which am old?'
14 °Is any thing too °hard for [3]the LORD? At the °time appointed I will return unto thee, according to the time of life, and Sarah shall have a son."
15 Then Sarah denied, saying, "I laughed not;" for she was afraid. And He said, "Nay; but thou didst laugh."
m 16 And the °men rose up from thence, and °looked toward Sodom:
o q^1 and Abraham went with them to bring them
(p. 25) on the way.
r 17 And [3]the LORD said, °"Shall **I** hide from Abraham that thing which **I** do;
18 Seeing that Abraham °shall surely become a great and mighty nation, and all the °nations of the earth shall be blessed in him?
19 For I know him, °that he will °command his children and his household after him, and they shall keep the way of [3]the LORD, to do justice and judgment; that [3]the LORD may bring upon Abraham that which He hath spoken of him."
20 And [3]the LORD said, "Because the °cry of Sodom and Gomorrah is great, and because their sin is very grievous;
21 °I will go down now, and see whether they have done altogether according to °the cry of it, which is come unto Me; and if not, °I will know."
q^2 22 And °the men turned their faces from thence, and went toward Sodom: but °Abraham stood yet before [3]the LORD.
r 23 And Abraham drew near, and said, "Wilt Thou °also destroy the righteous with the °wicked?
24 °Peradventure there be fifty righteous within the city: wilt Thou also destroy and not spare the place for the fifty righteous that *are* therein?
25 That be far from Thee to do after this manner, to slay the righteous with the [23]wicked: and that the righteous should be as the [23]wicked, that be far from Thee: Shall not the Judge of all the °earth do right?"
26 And [3]the LORD said, "If I find in Sodom fifty righteous within the city, then I will spare all the place for their sakes."
27 And Abraham answered and said, "Be-

6 three measures. Note the No. 3. See *v.* 2 and Ap. 10.
cakes. Evidently unleavened.
7 ran. Such speedy hospitality common in the East.
8 tree. See *v.* 1.
eat. We do not understand this mystery. But we read of "angels' food" (Ps. 78. 25); and that Christ ate after His resurrection (Luke 24. 30, 43. Acts 10. 41).
9 Where, &c. Translate "And as to Sarah thy wife . . . and he [interrupting] said, Lo! [she is] in the tent". See Ap. 31.
10 certainly return. Fig. *Polyptōton* (returning I will return) for emphasis. Ap. 6 and note on 26. 28.
lo! Fig. *Asterismos.* Ap. 6.
heard. Heb. was listening.
11 old. This explains how Rebekah, a granddaughter of Abraham's brother, should be old enough to marry Isaac, Abraham's son.
12 laughed. See note on 17. 17.
After. Fig. *Erotesis.* Ap. 6.
my lord. Heb. *Adon.* See Ap. 4 and cp. 1 Pet. 3. 6.
13 Wherefore? Fig. *Erotesis.* Ap. 6.
14 Is any thing? Fig. *Erotesis.* Ap. 6.
hard = wonderful. A similar question and same Fig. used in Luke 1. 37.
time appointed. See note on 1. 14.
16 men. Heb. pl. of *'īsh*, or *'enosh.* See Ap. 14.
looked = looked down upon. Heb. *shakaph.* 1st occ.

18. -16—19. 38 (*F*, p. 18). DESTRUCTION OF SODOM. (*Alternation.*)

F | o | 18. -16-33. Abraham and Jehovah.
p | 19. 1-26. Lot and the Angels.
o | 19. 27-29. Abraham and Jehovah.
p | 19. 30-38. Lot and his daughters.

18. -16-33 (o, above). ABRAHAM AND JEHOVAH. (*Repeated alternation.*)

o | q^1 | -16. Abraham before Jehovah.
r | 17-21. Announcement of Sodom's destruction.
q^2 | 22. Jehovah before Abraham (see note).
r | 23-32. Intercession for Sodom's preservation.
q^3 | 33. Jehovah's departure. Abraham's return.

17 Shall I hide? Fig. *Erotesis.* Ap. 6. Cp. Amos 3. 7.
18 shall surely become. Heb. "being shall be". Fig. *Polyptōton* (Ap. 6). See note on 26. 28.
nations. Another proof that the mystery (Eph. 3) means more than Gentile blessing. Cp. 22. 18.
19 that = how that.
command. Cp. Ps. 78. 1-8.
20 cry. Fig. *Prosopopœia.* Ap. 6.
21 I will go down = let us now go down. See Gen. 11. 7. Ex. 3. 8, all times of judgment.
the cry. Should be *their outcry*: with Sept., Onk., and ancient reading in MSS. called *Sevir.* See Ap. 34.
I will know. Fig. *Anthropopatheia.* Ap. 6.
22 the men. Prob. the two of 19. 1.
Abraham stood yet before the LORD. The primitive text read "Jehovah stood yet before Abraham." One of the 18 emendations of the Sopherim. See Ap. 33.
23 also = even, or really. Note the 6 petitions in Abraham's prayer, *vv.* 24-32. See Ap. 10.
wicked. Heb. *rasha'.* Ap. 44. x.
24 Peradventure = perhaps.
25 earth. Fig. *Metonymy* (of Subject). Ap. 6. "Earth" put for its inhabitants.

hold now, I have taken upon me to speak
unto [3]the °LORD*, which *am but* °dust and
ashes:
28 Peradventure there shall lack five of the
fifty righteous: wilt Thou destroy all the city
for *lack of* five?" And He said, "If I find
there forty and five, I will not destroy *it*."
29 And he spake unto Him yet again, and
said, "Peradventure there shall be forty found
there." And He said, "I will not do *it* for forty's
sake."
30 And he said *unto Him*, "Oh let not the
[27]LORD* be angry, and I will speak: Peradventure there shall thirty be found there." And
He said, "I will not do *it*, if I find thirty
there."
31 And he said, "Behold now, I have taken
upon me to speak unto the [27]LORD*: Peradventure there shall be twenty found there."
And He said, "I will not destroy *it* for twenty's
sake."
32 And he said, "Oh let not the [27]LORD* be
angry, and I will speak yet but this once: Peradventure ten shall be found there." And He
said, "I will not destroy *it* for ten's sake."

q³ 33 And [3]the LORD °went His way, as soon as
(p. 25) He had left communing with Abraham: and
Abraham returned unto his place.

p s¹ **19** And there came °two angels to °Sodom
(p. 26) at °even; and Lot sat in the °gate of
Sodom: and Lot seeing *them* rose up to meet
them; and he bowed himself with his face
toward the ground;
2 And he said, "Behold now, °my lords, turn
in, I pray you, into your servant's house, and
tarry all night, and wash your feet, and ye
shall rise up early, and go on your ways."
And they said, "Nay; but we will abide °in
the street all night."
3 And he pressed upon them greatly; and
they turned in unto him, and entered into his
house; and he made them a feast, and did bake
unleavened bread, and they did °eat.
4 But before they lay down, the °men of the
city, *even* the men of Sodom, compassed the
house round, both old and young, all the people
from every quarter:
5 And they called unto Lot, and said unto
him, "Where *are* the [4]men which came in to
thee this night? bring them out unto us, that
we may °know *them*."

t¹ 6 And Lot went out at the door unto them,
and shut the door after him,
7 And said, "I pray you, brethren, do not so
°wickedly.
8 Behold now, I have two daughters which
have not °known °man; let me, I pray you,
bring *them* out unto you, and do ye to them as
is good in your eyes: only unto °these [4]men
do nothing; for therefore came they under the
shadow of my °roof."
9 And they said, "Stand back." And they
said *again*, "This one *fellow* came in to sojourn,
and he will needs be a °judge: now will we
deal °worse with thee, than with them." And
they pressed sore upon the man, *even* Lot, and
came near to °break the door.

s 10 But the men put forth their hand, and
pulled Lot into the house to them, and shut to
the door.
11 And they smote the men that *were* at the
door of the house with °blindness, both small
and great: so that they wearied themselves to
find the door.
12 And the men said unto Lot, "Hast thou
here any besides? son in law, °and thy sons,
and thy daughters, and whatsoever thou hast
in the city, bring *them* out of this place:
13 For *we* °will destroy this place, because
the cry of them is waxen great before the
°face of [14]the LORD; and [14]the LORD hath
sent us to destroy it."

14 And Lot went out, and spake unto his sons t²
in law, which married his daughters, and said, (p. 26)
"Up, get you out of this place; for °the LORD

---

27 LORD*. One of the 134 places where the Primitive Text was Jehovah, and the Sopherim changed it to Adonai. These are distinguished in the text by an asterisk, and printed LORD*. See list, Ap. 32.
dust and ashes. Fig. *Meiosis.* Ap. 6. Also *Paronomasia* (*v'ephar 'aphar*). Ap. 6.
dust. Fig. *Metonymy* (of Cause). Ap. 6.
33 went His way. The same as the one who came in *vv.* 1, 2.

19. 1-26 ("p", p. 25). **LOT AND THE ANGELS.**
(*Repeated Alternation.*)

p s¹ | 1-5. *Even.* The Angels. Reception by Lot.
t¹ | 6-9. Lot's remonstrance with Sodomites.
s² | 10-13. *Night.* The Angels. Protection of Lot. Announcement of the destruction of Sodom.
t² | 14. Lot's remonstrance with his family.
s³ | 15-17. *Dawn.* Jehovah merciful to Lot.
t³ | 18-20. Lot's remonstrance with Jehovah.
s⁴ | 21-26. *Sunrise.* Jehovah's acquiescence with Lot. Destruction of Sodom.

1 two. Heb. the two. With art., viz. two of the three, 18. 16.
Sodom = *flaming, burning.*
even. Note emph. on notes of time in the Structure.
gate. The seat of judgment, showing that Lot was a real citizen, *v.* 9; 23. 10, 18; 34. 20, 24. Ruth 4. 1.
2 my lords. Pl. of *Adon.* See Ap. 4.
in the street. Fig. *Peristasis.* Ap. 6.
3 eat. See 18. 8.
4 men. Heb. pl. of *'enosh.* Ap. 14. iii.
5 know. Fig. *Metonymy* (of Cause). Ap. 6.
7 wickedly. Heb. *ra'.* Ap. 44. viii.
8 known. Fig. *Metonymy* (of Cause). Ap. 6.
man. Heb. *'ish.* See Ap. 14. ii.
these. Archaic pron. showing antiquity of Pent.
roof. Fig. *Metalepsis.* Ap. 6. Roof put for house, and house put for protection.
9 judge. See *v.* 1. He sat in Sodom's gate, the seat of the judges. See note on 13. 7.
worse. Heb. *ra'.* Ap. 44. viii.
break = break open, shiver.
11 blindness. Produced by dazzlings of light. Fig. *Heterosis* (of Noun). Ap. 6. Pl. put for sing. only here and 2 Kings 6. 18. 9 instances of people so smitten (see Ap. 10). See 19. 11; 27. 1; 48. 10. Judg. 16. 21. 1 Sam. 4. 15. 1 Kings 14. 4. 2 Kings 6. 18; 25. 7. Acts 13. 11.
12 and. Note the Fig. *Polysyndeton.* Ap. 6.
13 will destroy = are about to destroy.
face. Fig. *Anthropopatheia.* Ap. 6.
14 the LORD. Cp. the "we" of *v.* 13. Heb. Jehovah. Ap. 4.

will destroy this city." But he seemed as °one
that mocked unto his sons in law.
s[3] (p. 26) 15 And when the morning arose, then the
angels hastened Lot, saying, "Arise, take thy
wife, and thy two daughters, which are here;
lest thou be consumed in the °iniquity of the
city."
16 And while he °lingered, the men laid hold
upon his hand, and upon the hand of his wife,
and upon the hand of his two daughters; [14]the
LORD being merciful unto him: and they
brought him forth, and set him without the
city.
17 And it came to pass, when they had
brought them forth abroad, that °He said,
"Escape for thy °life; °look not behind thee,
neither stay thou in all the plain; escape to
the mountain, lest thou be consumed."

t[3] 18 And Lot said unto them, "Oh, not so, my
°LORD*:
19 Behold now, Thy servant hath found grace
in Thy sight, and Thou hast magnified Thy
mercy, which Thou hast shewed unto me in
saving my [17]life; and I cannot escape to the
mountain, lest some evil take me, and I die:
20 Behold now, this city *is* near to flee unto,
and it *is* a little one: Oh, let me escape thither,
°(*is* it not a little one?) and °my soul shall
live."

s[4] 21 And He said unto him, "See, I have accepted °thee concerning this thing °also, that
I will not overthrow this city, for the which
thou hast spoken.
22 Haste thee, escape thither; for I cannot
do any thing till thou be come thither." Therefore the name of the city was called °Zoar.
23 The sun was risen upon the earth when
Lot entered into Zoar.
24 Then °the LORD rained upon Sodom and
upon Gomorrah °brimstone and fire from °the
LORD out of heaven;
25 And He °overthrew those cities, and all
the plain, and all the inhabitants of the cities,
and that which grew upon the ground.
26 But his °wife °looked back from behind
him, and she °became a pillar of salt.

F o (p. 25) 27 And Abraham gat up early in the morning
to the place where he °stood before [14]the LORD:
28 And he °looked toward Sodom and Gomorrah, and toward all the land of the plain,
and beheld, and, °lo, the °smoke of the country
went up as the smoke of a furnace.
29 And it came to pass, when °God destroyed
the cities of the plain, that °God °remembered
Abraham, and sent Lot out of the midst of the
overthrow, when He overthrew the °cities in
the which Lot dwelt.

p 30 And Lot went up out of Zoar, and dwelt
in the mountain, and his two daughters with
him; for he feared to dwell in Zoar: and he
dwelt in a cave, he and his two daughters.
31 And the firstborn said unto the younger,
"Our father *is* old, and *there is* not a °man in
the earth to come in unto us after the manner
of all the earth:
32 Come, let us make our father drink °wine,
and we will lie with him, that we may preserve
seed of our father."

33 And they made their father drink [32]wine
that night: and the firstborn went in, and lay
with her father; and he perceived not when
she lay down, °nor when she arose.
34 And it came to pass on the morrow, that
the firstborn said unto the younger, "Behold,
I lay yesternight with my father: let us make
him drink wine this night also; and go thou
in, *and* lie with him, that we may preserve
seed of our father."
35 And they made their father drink [32]wine
that night also: and the younger arose, and
lay with him; and he perceived not when she
lay down, °nor when she arose.
36 Thus were both the daughters of Lot with
child by their father.

---

one that mocked = talked nonsense. He had looked, and pitched his tent toward Sodom, had dwelt and made his home there, and married his daughters, and sat in its gate as a judge. No wonder he seemed as one that mocked. He chose Sodom (13. 11), and "lingered" in the place of his choice (*v.* 16). See note, 13. 7.

15 iniquity. Fig. *Metonymy* (of Cause). Ap. 6. Cause put for effect = *judgment.* Cp. Ps. 7. 16. See Ap. 44. iii.

16 lingered. See *v.* 14.

17 He. Sept. reads "they".

life = soul. Heb. *nephesh.* See Ap. 13.

look, &c. Fig. *Asyndeton.* Ap. 6. (No ands, but climax.)

18 LORD*. See note on 18. 27.

20 is it not a little one? Fig. *Epitrechon.* Ap. 6.

my soul = myself. Heb. my *nephesh.* Ap. 13.

21 thee. Heb. *thy face.* Fig. *Synecdoche* (of the Part). Ap. 6.

also. Omitted in A.V. 1611.

22 Zoar = *little,* or *smallness.* Cp. 14. 2, 8.

24 the LORD . . . from the LORD. Heb. Jehovah. Repetition very emphatic. Cp. "we", *v.* 13.

brimstone and fire. Fig. *Hendiadys* (Ap. 6) = burning brimstone. Referred to in Deut. 29 23. Isa. 13. 19. Jer. 49. 18. Zeph. 2. 9. Matt. 10. 15. 2 Pet. 2. 6. Jude 7.

25 overthrew. These cities are not in the Dead Sea, but their ruins have been discovered by M. de Saulcy (called to-day *Kharbet-Goumran*), about 4 miles square (*Journey round the Dead Sea*, vol. ii, pp. 42-46).

Note the parallelism (*Alternation*).

a | cities.
  b | plain.
a | cities (inhabitants).
  b | plain (produce).

26 wife. Cp. Luke 17. 32.

looked back: i. e. curiously. Cp. Isa. 63. 5 and *v.* 28. Same word as in *v.* 17.

became. Same word as 1. 2, "the earth became."

27 stood. Cp. note on 18. 22.

28 looked toward. A different word from *v.* 27. Abraham bent forward and looked with awe and grief.

lo. Fig. *Asterismos.* Ap. 6.

smoke. It does not say he saw the cities, but only the smoke.

29 God. Heb. Elohim. Ap. 4.

remembered. Lot's deliverance due to Abraham's prayer. Fig. *Anthropopatheia.* Ap. 6.

cities = the city. Fig. *Heterosis* (of Number). Ap. 6.

31 man. Heb. *'ish.* Ap. 14. ii.

32 wine. Heb. *yayin.* See Ap. 27. i.

33, 35 nor = but. This clause is one marked with the "fifteen extraordinary points" calling attention to the ancient reading = "he *did know* when she arose." See Ap. 31.

37 And the firstborn bare a son, and called his name °Moab: the same *is* the father of the Moabites unto this day.

38 And the younger, she also bare a son, and called his name °Ben-ammi: the same *is* the father of the children of Ammon unto this day.

a H¹ (p. 28) **20** And Abraham journeyed from thence toward the °south country, and dwelled between Kadesh and Shur, and sojourned in Gerar.

2 And Abraham °said of Sarah his wife, "She *is* °my sister:"

H² and °Abimelech king of Gerar sent, and °took Sarah.

u **3** But [17]God came to Abimelech in a °dream by night, and said to him, °"Behold, thou *art but* a dead °man, for the woman which thou hast taken; for she *is* a man's wife."

4 But Abimelech had not come near her: and he said, °"LORD*, wilt Thou slay °also a righteous °nation?

5 Said he not unto me, 'She *is* my sister?' and she, even she herself said, 'He *is* my brother:' in the integrity of my heart and innocency of my hands have I done this."

6 And [17]God said unto him in a dream, "Yea, I know that thou didst this in the integrity of thy heart; for °I also withheld thee from °sinning against Me: therefore suffered I thee not to touch her.

v **7** Now therefore restore the °man *his* wife;

w for he *is* a °prophet, and he shall pray for thee, and thou shalt live: and if thou restore *her* not, know thou that thou shalt surely die, thou, and all that *are* thine."

u **8** Therefore Abimelech rose early in the morning, and called all his servants, and told all these things in their ears: and the °men were sore afraid.

9 Then Abimelech called Abraham, and said unto him, °"What hast thou done unto us? and what have I offended thee, that thou hast brought on me and on my kingdom a great °sin? thou hast done deeds unto me that ought not to be done."

10 And Abimelech said unto Abraham, "What °sawest thou, that thou hast done this thing?"

11 And Abraham said, "Because I °thought, Surely the fear of [17]God *is* not in this place; and they will °slay me for my wife's sake.

12 And yet indeed *she is* my °sister; she *is* the daughter of my father, but not the daughter of my mother; and she became my wife.

13 And it came to pass, when [17]God° caused me to wander from my father's house, that I said unto her, 'This *is* thy °kindness which thou shalt shew unto me; at every place whither we shall come, say of me, "He *is* my brother."'"

v **14** And Abimelech took sheep, °and oxen, and menservants, and womenservants, and gave *them* unto Abraham, and restored him Sarah his wife.

15 And Abimelech said, °"Behold, my land *is* before thee: dwell where it pleaseth thee."

16 And unto Sarah he said, "Behold, I have given thy °brother a thousand *pieces* of silver: behold, he *is* to thee a °covering of the eyes, unto all that *are* with thee, and with all *other*:" thus she was °reproved.

37 Moab. Heb. *from a father.*

38 Ben-ammi. Heb. *son of Ammi* = "the god Am". See on 14. 5 and Deut. 2. 20. Begotten in shame, both had a shameful history. Deut. 23. 3, 4. Cp. Judg. 10. 10; 11. 4, 15. Num. 21. 29. Deut. 2. 19; 3. 16. 2 Chron. 20. 1. Zeph. 2. 8.

20. 1-18 (*E a*, p. 18). ABRAHAM'S SOJOURN IN GERAR.

Introduction { H¹ | Expedient, *vv.* 1, 2-.
H² | Consequences, *v.* -2.

(*Extended Alternation.*)

a | u | 3-6. Dream, &c.
v | 7-. Restoration commanded.
w | -7. Prayer.
u | 8-13. Dream, &c.
v | 14-16. Restoration effected.
w | 17, 18. Prayer.

1 south = the *Negeb.* See 12. 9; 13. 1.

2 said. Abraham's expedient = the next assault on Abraham in the Great Conflict for the destruction of the promised seed of the woman (Gen. 3. 15). See Ap. 23. God had to intervene (*v.* 3), for man could know nothing of it. Abraham's fear shown in *v.* 11.

my sister = half-sister. See note on *v.* 12 and Ap. 29.

Abimelech. Heb. *Father-king.* The official title of the kings of Gerar (cp. 26. 1), like Pharaoh in Egypt.

took. See note on 21. 7. In Sarah's conception God must have renewed her youth, for she nursed Isaac (21. 7).

3 dream. 20 recorded in Scripture (see Ap. 10). 20. 3; 28. 12; 31. 10, 24; 37. 5, 9; 40. 5, 5; 41. 1, 5, 5. Judg. 7. 13. 1 Kings 3. 5. Dan. 2. 3; 4. 5; 7. 1. Matt. 1. 20; 2. 12, 13, 19; 27. 19.

Behold. Fig. *Asterismos.* Ap. 6.

man . . . for. Fig. *Aposiopesis*, or "sudden silence". Ap. 6. We must supply "If thou dost not restore her"; or "I will slay thee". See *vv.* 4 and 7.

4 LORD* = Jehovah. One of the 134 emendations of the Sopherim. See Ap. 32.

also, i. e. as well as Sodom and Gomorrah, ch. 19.

nation. Abimelech evidently expected God to slay the whole nation.

6 I also withheld. Divine intervention needed. Cp. *v.* 2. Note the emphatic pronouns. See Ap. 23.

sinning. See Ap. 44. i.

7 man. Heb. *'îsh.* See Ap. 14. ii.

prophet. First occ., showing that prediction is only a small part of its meaning = God's spokesman. Here, it is *prayer* (cp. Ex. 4. 16 and 7. 1), and prayer is associated with prophesying, i. e. *witnessing* (1 Cor. 11. 5).

8 men. Heb. pl. of *'enosh.* Ap. 14. iii.

9 What. Fig. *Aganactesis.* Ap. 6.

sin. Heb. *chât'a.* See Ap. 44. i.

10 sawest thou = hadst thou seen.

11 thought. Heb. *said*: i. e. said [to myself].

slay me. Showing how his fears were worked upon by the enemy. See *v.* 2.

12 sister. The daughter of Terah by another wife (than Abraham's mother): therefore, Abraham's half-sister. See Ap. 29.

13 caused. The verb is in the plural.

kindness. Fig. *Metonymy* (of Cause). Ap. 6. Kindness put for the kind *deeds* caused by it.

14 and. Fig. *Polysyndeton.* Ap. 6.

15 Behold. Fig. *Asterismos.* Ap. 6.

16 brother. Fig. *Irony.* Ap. 6.

covering, &c. Fig. *Periphrasis.* Ap. 6. Having called Abraham her "brother", he uses this beautiful Figure for her husband. Cp. 24. 65. 1 Cor. 11. 5, &c.

reproved, i. e. by the Irony.

w (p. 28) 17 So Abraham prayed unto °God: and God healed Abimelech, and his wife, and his maid-servants; and they bare *children.*

18 For °the LORD had fast closed up all the wombs of the house of Abimelech, because of Sarah Abraham's wife.

E b d x (p. 29) **21** And °the LORD visited Sarah °as He had °said, and °the LORD did unto Sarah as He had °spoken.

2 For Sarah conceived, and bare Abraham a son in his old age, at the °set time of which °God had spoken to him.

3 And Abraham called the name of his son that was born unto him, whom Sarah bare to him, °Isaac.

y 4 And Abraham circumcised his son Isaac being °eight days old, as God had commanded him.

1896 5 And Abraham was an °hundred years old, when his son Isaac was born unto him.

x 6 And Sarah said, [2]"God hath made me to laugh, *so that* all that hear will laugh with me."

7 And she said, "Who would have said unto Abraham, that Sarah should have given children °suck? for I have born *him* a son in his old age."

y 8 And the child °grew, and was weaned: and Abraham made a great feast the *same* day that Isaac was weaned.

c z 9 And Sarah saw the son of Hagar the Egyptian, which she had born unto Abraham, °mocking.

1891 10 Wherefore she said unto Abraham, °"Cast out this bondwoman and her son: for the son of this bondwoman shall not be heir °with my son, *even* with Isaac."

a 11 And the °thing was very grievous in Abraham's sight because of his son.

b 12 And God said unto Abraham, "Let it not be grievous in thy sight because of the lad, and because of thy bondwoman; in all that Sarah hath said unto thee, hearken unto her voice; for in °Isaac shall °thy seed be called.

13 And also of the son of the bondwoman will I make a nation, because he *is* thy seed."

c 14 And Abraham rose up early in the morning, and took bread, and a °bottle of water, and gave *it* unto Hagar, putting *it* on her shoulder, and the child, and sent her away: and she departed, and wandered in the wilderness of Beer-sheba.

z 15 And the water was spent in the bottle, and she cast the child under one of the shrubs.

a 16 And she went, and sat her down over against *him* a good way off, °as it were a bowshot: for she said, "Let me °not see the death of the child." And she sat over against *him,* and °lift up her voice, and wept.

b 17 And [2]God °heard the voice of the lad; and the angel of [2]God called to Hagar out of heaven, and said unto her, °"What aileth thee, Hagar? fear not; for [2]God hath °heard the voice of the lad where he *is.*

17 God. Heb. *Elohim.* Ap. 4.
18 the LORD. Heb. Jehovah. Ap. 4.

21. 1-8 (*E b d*, p. 18). MANIFESTATION OF SEED. (*Alternation.*)

d | x | 1-3. Isaac's birth and naming.
y | 4, 5. Circumcision.
x | 6, 7. Cause of Isaac's naming.
y | 8. Weaning.

1 the LORD. Heb. Jehovah. Ap. 4.
as = according as.
said. Emphasis on "said" for our faith.
spoken. Fig. *Pleonasm* (Ap. 6), for emphasis.
2 set time = exact time.
God. Heb. Elohim. Ap. 4. Note change of title here, till *v.* 32, because it is Creator and creature. In *v.* 33, *Jehovah,* where it is Covenant relation. In Mary's song both titles united (Luke 1. 46, 47 and cp. *vv.* 37, 38).
3 Isaac. Heb. *Let him laugh.* Cp. 17. 17; 18. 12, 13, 15; 21. 6, 9; 26. 8.
4 eight. The Dominical No. See Ap. 10. Cp. Ishmael, 13th year. **5 hundred.** See Ap. 10.
7 suck. A proof that "God", the Creator, had renewed her youth, showing why Abimelech should have taken her (20. 2). Sarah's Magnificat may be compared with Mary's. The scenes of both near to each other. Mary's words (Luke 1. 54, 55) connect her "mercy" with that shown to "Abraham and his seed".
8 grew. Cp. Luke 2. 40.

21. 9-21 (*E b c*, p. 18). SEPARATION OF ISHMAEL. (*Extended Alternation.*)

c | z | 9, 10. Hagar and Ishmael, in house.
a | 11. Abraham's suffering.
b | 12, 13. God's intervention.
c | 14. Hagar and Ishmael. Wilderness of Beer-sheba.
z | 15. Hagar and Ishmael, out of house.
a | 16. Hagar's suffering.
b | 17-19. God's intervention.
c | 20, 21. Hagar and Ishmael. Wilderness of Paran.

9 mocking. Heb. "laughing" or "chaffing", or "mocking again" (as we say).
10 Cast out, &c. See the Divine interpretation. Gal. 3. 6-29; 4. 22-31; 5. 1-12.
with my son, &c. Heb. idiom "with my son—with Isaac". Cp. Num. 12. 8.
11 thing. Heb. *word.*
12 Isaac . . . thy seed. Here *zer'a* is in the sing. sense, because of the word "Isaac", and because of the sing. verb "it shall be called." *Zer'a* is a collective noun (like Eng. "sheep"), but the context must determine whether it is sing. or pl. It is to this verse Gal. 3. 16 refers; not to 12. 7, where it is indefinite; or 17. 7 where the verb and pronouns show it is plural. See note there, and on Gal. 3. 16; and cp. Rom. 9. 7. Heb. 11. 18. "Thy seed" is therefore "Christ". The difference of the 30 years comes in here: 430 to the Exodus (12. 40) from Gen. 12. 4, when Abraham was 75: 25 thence to Isaac's birth: and now, 5 to his recognition as the seed = 30 years.
14 bottle. Cp. man's provision (a bottle) with God's (a well) (*v.* 19).
16 as it were, &c. Fig. *Epitheton.* Ap. 6.
not see, &c. Fig. *Tapeinosis.* Ap. 6.
lift up her voice = *the boy lifted up his voice and wept.* So Sept. (see *v.* 17).
17 heard. Fig. *Anthropopatheia.* Ap. 6.
What, &c. Fig. *Erotēsis.* Ap. 6.
heard. Fig. *Anthropopatheia.* Ap. 6.

18 Arise, lift up the lad, and hold him in thine hand; for I will make him a great nation."

19 And [2]God opened her eyes, and she saw a

°well of water; and she went, and filled the bottle with water, and gave the lad drink.

c 20 And [2]God was with the lad; and he grew,
(p. 29) and dwelt in the wilderness, and became an archer.

21 And he dwelt in the wilderness of Paran: and his mother took him a wife out of the land of Egypt.

D d 22 And it came to pass at that time, that
(p. 30) Abimelech and Phichol the chief captain of his host spake unto Abraham, saying, [2]"God *is* with thee in all that thou doest:

23 Now therefore swear unto me here by God that thou wilt not deal falsely with me, nor with my son, nor with my son's son: *but* according to the °kindness that I have done unto thee, thou shalt do unto me, and to the land wherein thou hast sojourned."

24 And Abraham said, "I will swear."

e 25 And Abraham reproved Abimelech because of a well of water, which Abimelech's servants had °violently taken away.

26 And Abimelech said, "I °wot not who hath done this thing: neither didst thou tell me, neither yet heard I *of it*, but to day."

f 27 And Abraham took sheep and oxen, and gave them unto Abimelech; and °both of them °made a covenant.

x e 28 And Abraham set seven ewe lambs of the flock by themselves.

29 And Abimelech said unto Abraham, "What *mean* these seven ewe lambs which thou hast set by themselves?"

30 And he said, "For *these* seven ewe lambs shalt thou take of my hand, that they may be a witness unto me, that I have digged this well."

31 Wherefore he called that place °Beer-sheba; because there they sware both of them.

f 32 Thus they made a covenant at Beer-sheba: then Abimelech rose up, and Phichol the chief captain of his host, and they returned into the land of the Philistines.

33 And *Abraham* planted a °grove in Beer-sheba, and called there on the name of [1]the LORD, °the everlasting GOD.

d 34 And Abraham sojourned in the Philistines' land many days.

C g[1] **22** And it came to pass °after these things, that °God did °tempt Abraham, and said unto him, "Abraham:" and he said, °"Behold, *here* I *am*."

abt. 2 And He said, "Take now thy son, thine
1871 only *son* Isaac, whom thou °lovest, and get
or thee into the land of °Moriah; and °offer him
1863 there for a °burnt offering upon one of the mountains which I will tell thee of."

h[1] 3 °And Abraham rose up early in the morning, °and saddled his ass, °and took two of his young men with him, °and Isaac his son, °and clave the wood for the burnt offering, °and rose up, °and went unto the place of which [1]God had told him.

4 Then on °the third day Abraham lifted up his eyes, and saw the place afar off.

5 And Abraham said unto his young men, "Abide ye here with the ass; and °I and the lad will go °yonder and worship, and °come again to you."

6 And Abraham took the wood of the burnt offering, and °laid *it* upon Isaac his son; and he took the °fire in his hand,

---

19 well. Heb. *b^eer*, a well (digged): not *'ayin*, a spring or fountain; or *bōr*, a cistern (hewn).

21. 22-34 (*D*, p. 18). SOJOURN IN GERAR.
(*Introversion and Alternation.*)

D | d | 22-24. Sojourning. Commencement.
x | e | 25, 26. The well taken.
f | 27. Covenant.
x | *e* | 28-31. The well digged.
f | 32, 33. Covenant.
d | 34. Sojourning. Continued.

23 kindness. Fig. *Metonymy* (of Cause). Ap. 6. See 20. 13.

25 violently, &c. Cp. 26. 19, 20. Ex. 2. 17. Judg. 5. 11. This explains Ex. 17. 8, "Then came Amalek", because of *vv.* 1-7.

26 wot not = know not. O. Eng. idiom.

27 both. Not one party as in 15. 10-18. Cp. Gal 3. 20.
made. Heb. *cut*, because of the dividing of the sacrifice. Cp. 15. 10. Jer. 34. 18-20. Eng. concluded or solemnised.

31 Beer-sheba = Heb. *well of the oath*.

33 grove. Heb. *'ēshel* = trees, not *'ăsherāh* (Ap. 42), but the wood for 22. 3 about twenty years later.
the everlasting GOD. This is the Divine definition of Jehovah (LORD), Heb. *'ōlām* = duration, secret and hidden from man. Cp. Ps. 90. 2.

22. 1-19 (*C*, p. 18). ABRAHAM'S TRIAL.
(*Repeated Alternation.*)

C | g[1] | 1, 2. Jehovah. Command.
h[1] | 3-10. Abraham. Journey.
g[2] | 11, 12. Jehovah. 1st call.
h[2] | 13, 14. Abraham. The offering.
g[3] | 15-18. Jehovah. 2nd call.
h[3] | 19. Abraham. Return.

1 God. Heb. Elohim. Ap. 4.
after, i.e. after 40 or 50 years in Canaan.
tempt. Heb. *prove*, so Ex. 15. 25; 16. 4; 20. 20. Deut. 8. 2, 16. Judg. 2. 22; 3. 1, 4. Ecc. 2. 1; 7. 23. 1 Sam. 17. 39. 1 Kings 10. 1. 2 Chron. 9. 1; 33. 31. Ps. 26. 2. Cp. Deut. 4. 34 (assayed). In later usage trial meant *trouble*. Wisd. 3. 5; 11. 10. Sir. 2. 1. Judith 8. 24-27. Luke 8, 13 (cp. Matt. 13. 21). Acts 20. 19. Heb. 2. 18. 1 Pet. 1. 6.
Behold, &c. = behold me.

2 lovest. Note the reference to the Antitype.
Moriah. Heb. = shown or provided by Jah. Cp. 1 Chron. 21. 22; 22. 1. 2 Chron. 3. 1. Christ crucified also on one of these mountains. Matt. 27. 33.
offer. Heb. *'alah*. See Ap. 43. I. vi.
burnt offering. Heb. *'olah*. See Ap. 43. II. ii.

3 and. Note the Fig. *Polysyndeton* (Ap. 6), emphasising the calmness of Abraham's deliberate faith. Each "and" is to be noted, and each act weighed.

4 the third day. No. 3. Symb. of resurrection (Ap. 10). Cp. *v.* 5, "Come again," 1st pers. pl. Exactly 3 days journey from Beer-sheba to Moriah. Gerizim is 2 days' further.

5 I and the lad. This is polite Hebrew, while "the lad and I" would be polite English.
yonder. Heb. *as far as there* (as though pointing).
come again. This was proof of Abraham's faith. 1st pers. plural, "We will come again."

6 laid. Cp. John 19. 17.
fire. Without doubt fire from Abraham's own altar (12. 7; 13. 4, 18; and see note on 21. 33), for God accepted a sacrifice only by fire from heaven. See on 4. 4.

and a knife; and they went °both of them together.

7 And Isaac spake unto Abraham his father, and said, "My father:" and he said, °"Here *am* I, my son." And he said, "Behold the fire and the wood: but where *is* the lamb for a burnt offering?"

8 And Abraham said, "My son, [1]God will °provide °Himself °a lamb for a burnt offering:" so they went [6]both of them together.

9 °And they came to the place which [1]God had told him of; and Abraham built °an altar there, and laid the wood in order, and bound Isaac his son, and laid him on the altar upon the wood.

10 And Abraham stretched forth his hand, and took the knife to slay his son.

g² 11 And the angel of °the LORD called unto him
(p. 30) out of heaven, and said, °"Abraham, Abraham:" and he said, [7]"Here *am* I."

12 And He said, "Lay not thine hand upon the lad, neither do thou any thing unto him: for °now I know that thou fearest [1]God, seeing thou hast not withheld thy son, thine only *son* from Me."

h² 13 And Abraham °lifted up his eyes, and °looked, and °behold behind *him* °a ram caught in °a thicket by his horns: and Abraham went and took the ram, and [2]offered him up for a [2]burnt offering °in the stead of his son.

14 And Abraham called the name of that place °Jehovah-jireh: as it is said *to* this day, °"In the mount of [11]the LORD °it shall be seen."

g³ 15 And the angel of [11]the LORD called unto Abraham out of heaven °the second time,

16 And said, "By Myself have I °sworn, saith [11]the LORD, for because thou hast done this thing, and hast not withheld thy son, thine only *son:*

17 That in °blessing I will bless thee, and in multiplying I will multiply thy seed as the °stars of the heaven, and as the °sand which *is* upon the sea shore; and thy seed shall possess °the gate of his enemies;

18 And in thy seed shall °all the nations of the earth be blessed; because thou hast obeyed My voice."

h³ 19 So Abraham returned unto his young men, and they rose up and went together to Beer-sheba; and Abraham dwelt at Beer-sheba.

B¹ 20 And it came to pass after these things,
(p. 17) that it was told Abraham, saying, "Behold, Milcah, she hath also born children unto thy brother Nahor;

21 Huz his firstborn, and Buz his brother, and Kemuel the father of Aram,

22 And Chesed, and Hazo, and Pildash, and Jidlaph, and Bethuel."

23 And Bethuel begat Rebekah: °these eight Milcah did bear to Nahor, Abraham's brother.

24 And his concubine, whose name *was* Reumah, she bare also Tebah, and Gaham, and Thahash, and °Maachah.

both of them together. Cp. the Father and the Son in the antitype. Emph. by repetition in *v.* 8. John 10. 30; 14. 10, 11; 16. 33. The sinner is not seen in the type; his part is subsequent to this, viz. to believe what the Father and the Son have done for him in substitution. See also Rom. 8. 32. 2 Cor. 5. 19.

7 Here, &c. Heb. Behold me, my son.

8 provide. Heb. *yireh* = God will see or *look out.*

Himself = for Himself.

a lamb. Heb. the lamb.

9, 10 and. Each act is emph. by the Fig. *Polysyndeton* (Ap. 6), and is to be dwelt upon and considered.

9 an altar. Heb. the altar.

11 the LORD. Heb. Jehovah. Ap. 4.

Abraham, Abraham. Fig. *Epizeuxis* (Ap. 6), for emph. Cp. the 10 Duplications: (1) Seven used by God to men: 22. 11; 46. 2. Ex. 3. 4. 1 Sam. 3. 10. Luke 10. 41; 22. 31. Acts 9. 4; (2) Three under other circumstances: Matt. 7. 21, 22 (Luke 6. 46; 13. 25). Matt. 23. 37 (Luke 13. 34). Mark 15. 34 (Matt. 27. 46. Ps. 22. 1).

12 now I know. Fig. *Anthropopatheia.* Ap. 6.

13 lifted up his eyes. Fig. *Pleonasm,* for emph. (Ap. 6).

looked. See note on 13. 14.

behold. Fig. *Asterismos.* Ap. 6.

a ram. Some Cod. (with Sam., Jon., Sept., and Syr.) read "one ram", i. e. a solitary ram.

a thicket. Heb. the thicket.

in the stead. Here is the doctrine of substitution, clearly stated.

14 Jehovah-jireh. Heb. *Jehovah will see,* or provide, as in *v.* 8. See Ap. 4.

In the mount, &c. Fig. *Parœmia.* Ap. 6.

it shall be seen: it will be provided, or "in the mount Jehovah will be seen". So it was in 2 Sam. 24. 25. 1 Chron. 21. 26. 2 Chron. 7. 1-3.

15 the second time. Heb. a second time; the first time was for substitution; the second was for revelation.

16 sworn. This oath is the foundation of Israel's blessings (24. 7; 26. 3; 50. 24. Ex. 13. 5, 11; 33. 1). David's "sure mercies" all grounded on it (Ps. 89. 35; 132. 11. Cp. Luke 1. 73).

17 blessing I will bless = I will surely bless; or, I will richly bless. Fig. *Polyptōton* (Ap. 6), for emphasis.

stars . . . sand, &c. Fig. *Parœmia.* Ap. 6. See note on 13. 16.

the gate. Fig. *Synecdoche* (of the Part), Ap. 6. "Gate" put for the cities.

18 all the nations. Proof that the "Mystery" does not mean blessing of Gentiles as such: but the secret concerning Christ and the church (Eph. 5. 32).

22. 20-24 (B¹, p. 17). THE POSTERITY OF NAHOR.

Introduced here to lead up to Rebekah, the future wife of Isaac. Not proceeding further with Nahor's posterity. See (p. 17) how Abraham's history is broken up into three portions by two posterities, just as Isaac's and Jacob's histories are broken up. See p. 52, and Ap. 29.

23 these eight. Nahor had 12 in all, as Ishmael had (25. 13-16), and as Jacob had (35. 23-27).

24 Maachah. See Deut. 3. 14. Josh. 12. 5. 2 Sam. 10. 6.

23. 1—24. 67 (A², p. 17). ABRAHAM'S HISTORY. (OLD AGE.)

[For Structure see next page.]

1 Sarah. The only woman whose age is mentioned in the Bible. In 22. 23 Rebekah is mentioned: one sun rising before the other sets.

2 Kirjath-arba. See notes on Num. 13. 22, and Ap. 25.

23 And °Sarah was an hundred and seven A² X¹ i
and twenty years old: *these were* the (p. 32)
years of the life of Sarah.
2 And Sarah died in °Kirjath-arba; the same 1859

is °Hebron in the land of Canaan: and Abraham came to mourn for Sarah, and to weep
for her.
k l^1 3 And Abraham stood up from °before his
(p. 32) dead, and spake unto the sons of Heth, saying,
4 °"𝔍 *am* a °stranger and a sojourner with
you: give me a possession of a buryingplace
with you, that I may bury my dead out of my
sight."
m^1 5 And the °children of Heth answered Abraham, saying unto him,
6 "Hear us, my lord: 𝔱𝔥𝔬𝔲 *art* a °mighty
prince among us: in the choice of our sepulchres bury thy dead; none of us shall withhold
from thee his sepulchre, but that thou mayest
bury thy dead."
l^2 7 And Abraham stood up, and bowed himself
to the people of the land, *even* to the children
of Heth.
8 And he communed with them, saying, "If
it be your °mind that I should bury my dead
out of my sight; hear me, and intreat for me
to Ephron the son of Zohar,
9 That he may give me the cave of Machpelah, which he hath, which *is* in the end of
his field; for as much °money as it is worth he
shall give it me for a possession of a °burying-
place amongst you."
m^2 10 And Ephron °dwelt among the children of
Heth: and Ephron the Hittite answered Abraham in the audience of the children of Heth,
even of all that went in at the gate of his city,
saying,
11 "Nay, my lord, hear me: the field °give I
thee, and the cave that *is* therein, I give it
thee; in the presence of the sons of my people
give I it thee: bury thy dead."
l^3 12 And Abraham bowed down himself before
the people of the land.
13 And he spake unto Ephron in the audience
of the people of the land, saying, "But if 𝔱𝔥𝔬𝔲
°*wilt give it*, I pray thee, hear me: I will give
thee money for the field; take *it* of me, and
I will bury my dead there."
m^3 14 And Ephron answered Abraham, saying
unto him,
15 "My lord, hearken unto me: the land *is*
worth four hundred shekels of silver; °what
is 𝔱𝔥𝔞𝔱 betwixt me and thee? bury therefore
thy dead."
16 And Abraham hearkened unto Ephron;
and Abraham weighed to Ephron the silver,
which he had named in the audience of the
sons of Heth, four hundred shekels of silver,
current *money* with the merchant.
17 And the field of Ephron, which *was* in
Machpelah, which *was* before Mamre, the field,
and the cave which *was* therein, and all the
trees that *were* in the field, that *were* in all the
borders round about, were made sure
18 Unto °Abraham for a possession in the
presence of the children of Heth, °before all
that went in at the gate of his city.
i 19 And after this, Abraham buried Sarah his
wife in the cave of the field of Machpelah
before Mamre: the same *is* Hebron in the land
of Canaan.

Hebron. See note on Num. 13. 22.

23. 1—24. 67 (A^2, p. 17). ABRAHAM'S HISTORY. (OLD AGE). (*Division.*)

A^2 | X^1 | 23. 1-20. Death of Sarah.
| X^2 | 24. 1-67. Marriage of Isaac.

23. 1-20 (X^1, above). THE DEATH OF SARAH. (*Alternation.*)

X^1 | i | 23. 1, 2. Death of Sarah.
k | 3-18. Abraham's Treaty for buryingplace.
i | 19. Burial of Sarah.
k | 20. Ratification of Treaty.

23. 3-18 (k, above). ABRAHAM'S TREATY. (*Repeated Alternation.*)

k | l^1 | 3, 4. Request.
m^1 | 5, 6. Grant.
l^2 | 7-9. Request.
m^2 | 10, 11. Grant.
l^3 | 12, 13. Request.
m^3 | 14-18. Purchase.

3 before his dead. Heb. leaning over the face of his dead. Fig. *Pleonasm.* Ap. 6.
4 I am. Cp. "thou art", *v.* 6.
stranger and a sojourner. Cp. 1 Pet. 2. 11. Ps. 39. 12.
5 children. Heb. *sons*, and so elsewhere.
6 mighty prince. Heb. *prince of El.* Gen. of relation (Ap. 17), for Adjective. Cp. Ps. 36. 7; 80. 10.
8 mind = *soul.* Heb. *nephesh.* Ap. 13.
9 money. Heb. silver.
buryingplace. What Jacob bought (33. 19, 20) was for an altar.
10 dwelt. Heb. was sitting there.
11 give I. Heb. have I given. Fig. *Antimereia* (of Verb), past for present, Ap. 6.
13 wilt give. Fig. *Ellipsis.* Ap. 6. Supply "hast given" from *v.* 11.
15 what is that. Fig. *Erotēsis.* Ap. 6.
18 Abraham. This is not the purchase referred to in 33. 19 and Acts 7. 16. 80 years between this purchase and Jacob's. See note on Acts 7. 16.
before all. Some Cod. with Sam. have "even before all".
20 made sure. This was all strictly in conformity with the commercial enactments of the Code of Khammurabi. See Ap. 15.
buryingplace. All that Abraham possessed; but in the faith and hope of resurrection.

24 (X^2, above). THE MARRIAGE OF ISAAC.
[For Structure see next page.]

1 old. About 140 years old.
the LORD. Heb. Jehovah. Ap. 4.
2 eldest servant. Prob. Eleazar of Damascus. 15. 2.
thigh. According to the Midrash and ancient Jewish expositors, a *Euphemism* (Ap. 6) for the organs of generation, as most sacred. According to Ibn Ezra and present Indian custom, *on* the thigh is a token of subjection.
3 God. Heb. Elohim. Ap. 4.

20 And the field, and the cave that *is* therein,
were °made sure unto Abraham for a possession of a °buryingplace by the sons of Heth.

24 And Abraham was °old, *and* well X^2 n o
stricken in age: and °the LORD had (p. 33)
blessed Abraham in all things.
2 And Abraham said unto his °eldest servant 1858
of his house, that ruled over all that he had,
"Put, I pray thee, thy hand under my °thigh;
3 And I will make thee swear by [1]the LORD,

the °God of heaven, and the °God of the earth, that thou shalt not take a wife unto my son of the daughters of the °Canaanites, among whom °I dwell:

4 But thou shalt go unto my country, and to °my kindred, and take a wife unto my son Isaac."

5 And the servant said unto him, "Peradventure the woman will not be willing to follow me unto this land: must I needs bring thy son again unto the land from whence thou camest?"

6 And Abraham said unto him, "Beware thou that thou bring not my son °thither again.

7 [1]The LORD [3]God of °heaven, Which took me from my °father's house, and from the land of my kindred, and Which spake unto me, and That sware unto me, saying, 'Unto thy seed will I give this land;' He shall send His angel before thee, and thou shalt take a wife unto my son from thence.

8 And if the woman will not be willing to follow thee, then thou shalt be clear from this my oath: only bring not my son [6]thither again."

9 And the servant put his hand under the thigh of Abraham his master, and sware to him concerning that matter.

q (p. 33) 10 And the servant took ten camels of the camels of his master, and departed; for all the goods of his master *were* in his hand: and he °arose, and went to °Mesopotamia, unto the city of Nahor.

11 And he made his camels to kneel down without the city by a well of water at the time of the evening, *even* the time that women go out to draw *water*.

r 12 And he said, "O [1]LORD [3]God of my master Abraham, I pray Thee, send me good speed this day, and shew kindness unto my master Abraham.

13 °Behold, I stand *here* by the °well of water; and the daughters of the °men of the city °come out to draw water:

14 And let it come to pass, that the damsel to whom I shall say, 'Let down thy °pitcher, I pray thee, that I may drink;' and she shall say, 'Drink, and °I will give thy camels drink also:' *let the same be* she *that* Thou hast appointed for Thy servant Isaac; and thereby shall I know that Thou hast shewed kindness unto my master."

15 And it came to pass, °before he had done speaking, that, [13]behold, °Rebekah came out, who was °born to °Bethuel, son of Milcah, the wife of Nahor, Abraham's brother, with her pitcher upon her shoulder.

16 And the damsel *was* very fair to look upon, a °virgin, neither had any °man known her: and she went down to the [13]well, and filled her pitcher, and came up.

17 And the servant ran to meet her, and said, "Let me, I pray thee, drink a little water of thy pitcher."

18 And she said, "Drink, my lord:" and she hasted, and let down her pitcher upon her hand, and gave him drink.

19 And when she had done giving him drink, she said, "I will draw *water* for thy camels also, until they have done drinking."

24. 1-67 (X², p. 32). THE MARRIAGE OF ISAAC. (*Division.*)

X² | n¹ | 1-54-. Eleazar's mission and his progress.
   | n² | -54-67. Eleazar's mission and his return.

24. 1-54- (n¹, above). ELEAZAR'S MISSION IN PROGRESS. (*Extended Alternation.*)

n¹ | o | 1. Abraham's blessing and prosperity.
   p | 2-9. Eleazar's oath and commission.
   q | 10, 11. Journey of Eleazar.
   r | 12-21. Prayer of Eleazar. Ans. 15-21.
   s | 22-25. His conference with Rebekah.
   t | 26. His worship of Jehovah.
   u | 27-32. Reception of Eleazar.
   v | 33. Entertainment. Declined.
 o | 34-36. Abraham's blessings and prosperity.
   p | 37-41. Eleazar's oath and commission.
   q | 42-. Journey of Eleazar.
   r | -42-45-. Prayer of Eleazar. Ans. 45-.
   s | -45-47. His conference with Rebekah.
   t | 48. His worship of Jehovah.
   u | 49-53. Reception of Eleazar's message.
   v | 54-. Entertainment. Accepted.

3 Canaanites. Mixed with the *Nephilim.* Ap. 23, 25.

I. Emph. in contrast with the Canaanites. Hence Abraham's horror of mixing the holy seed with that of the *Nephilim.*

4 my kindred. Gentiles thus expressly excluded from this chapter, if regarded as a type. Cp. *vv.* 3, 4, 7, 37, 38. See also 26 35; 27. 46; 28. 1, 8.

6 thither. Cp. Heb. 11. 15.

7 heaven. The Sept. reads: "heaven, and God of the earth." See Ap. 4.

father's house, and from the land of my kindred. The Severus Codex reads: "from my house and from my country," as in *v.* 4. See Ap. 34.

10 arose = mounted.

Mesopotamia Heb. *Aram-naharaim*, i.e. Aram of the two rivers (the Tigris and Euphrates). The country of Haran. 11. 31.

13 Behold. Fig. *Asterismos.* Ap. 6.

well - spring. Heb. *'ayin.* See note on 21. 19.

men. Heb. pl. of *'ish* or *'enosh.* Ap. 14.

come out. Heb. are coming out.

14 pitcher. Still used in Palestine as in John 4. 28.

I will give. A sign requested contrary to the custom. Cp. 29. 10.

15 before he had done speaking. Cp. Isa. 65. 24.

Rebekah. Heb. captivating.

born to Bethuel. See Ap. 29.

Bethuel. Heb. separated of God.

16 virgin. Heb. *bethulah.* Cp. *v.* 43. See note on *v.* 43.

man. Heb. *'ish.* Ap. 14. ii.

21 wondering: or eagerly watching her.

to wit to know.

22 golden. Heb. of gold. Gen. of material. Ap. 17.

earring. Prob. a nose (or "face") ring. See *v.* 47.

20 And she hasted, and emptied her pitcher into the trough, and ran again unto the well to draw *water*, and drew for all his camels.

21 And the [16]man °wondering at her held his peace, °to wit whether [1]the LORD had made his journey prosperous or not.

22 And it came to pass, as the camels had done drinking, that the man took a °golden °earring of half a shekel weight, and two bracelets for her hands of ten *shekels* weight of gold; s (p. 33)

23 And said, "Whose daughter *art* thou? tell me, I pray thee: is there room *in* thy father's house for us to lodge in?"

24 And she said unto him, "I *am* the daughter

of [15] Bethuel the son of Milcah, which she bare unto °Nahor."

25 She said moreover unto him, "We have both straw and provender enough, and room to lodge in."

t 26 And the °man bowed down his head, and
(p. 33) worshipped [1] the LORD.

u 27 And he said, "Blessed *be* [7] the LORD God of my master Abraham, Who hath not left destitute my master of His mercy and His truth: I *being* in the way, [1] the LORD led me to the house of my master's brethren."

28 And the damsel ran, and told *them of* her mother's house these things.

29 And Rebekah had a brother, and his name *was* °Laban: and Laban ran out unto the [26] man, unto the [13] well.

30 And it came to pass, °when he saw the [22] earring and bracelets upon his sister's hands, and when he heard the words of Rebekah his sister, saying, "Thus spake the [26] man unto me;" that he came unto the [26] man; and, behold, he stood by the camels at the [13] well.

31 And °he said, "Come in, thou blessed of [1] the LORD; wherefore standest thou without? for I have prepared the house, and room for the camels."

32 And the [26] man came into the house: and °he ungirded his camels, and gave straw and provender for the camels, and water to wash his feet, and the °men's feet that *were* with him.

v 33 And there was set *meat* before him to eat: but he said, "I will not eat, until I have told mine errand." And he said, "Speak on."

o 34 And he said, "I *am* Abraham's servant.

35 °And [1] the LORD hath blessed my master greatly; and he is become great: and He hath given him flocks, and herds, and silver, and gold, and menservants, and maidservants, and camels, and asses.

36 And Sarah my master's wife bare a son to my master when she was old: and unto him hath he given all that he hath.

p 37 And my master made me swear, saying, 'Thou shalt not take a wife to my son of the daughters of the Canaanites, in whose land I dwell:

38 But thou shalt go unto my father's house, and to my kindred, and take a wife unto my son.'

39 And I said unto my master, 'Peradventure the woman will not follow me.'

40 And he said unto me, [1] 'The LORD, before Whom °I walk, will send His angel with thee, and prosper thy way; and thou shalt take a wife for my son of my kindred, and of my father's house:

41 Then shalt thou be clear from *this* my oath, when thou comest to my kindred; and if they give not thee *one*, thou shalt be clear from my oath.'

q 42 And I came this day unto the [13] well, and °said,

r 'O [7] LORD God of my master Abraham, if now Thou do prosper my way which I go:

43 Behold, I stand by the [13] well of water; and it shall come to pass, that when the °virgin cometh forth to draw *water*, and I say to her, "Give me, I pray thee, a little water of thy pitcher to drink;"

44 And she say to me, "Both drink thou, and I will also draw for thy camels:" *let* the same *be* the woman whom the LORD hath appointed out for my master's son.'

45 And before I had done speaking in mine heart, behold, Rebekah came forth with her pitcher on her shoulder; and she went down unto the [13] well, and drew *water*:

and I said unto her, 'Let me drink, I pray thee.' s

46 And she made haste, and let down her (p. 33)
pitcher from her *shoulder*, and said, 'Drink, and I will give thy camels drink also:' so I drank, and she made the camels drink also.

47 And I asked her, and said, 'Whose daughter *art* thou?' And she said, 'The daughter of Bethuel, Nahor's son, whom Milcah bare unto him:' and I put the earring upon her °face, and the bracelets upon her hands.

48 And I bowed down my head, and worshipped the LORD, and blessed the LORD God t
of my master Abraham, Which had °led me in the right way to take my master's brother's °daughter unto his son.

49 And now if ye will deal kindly and truly u
with my master, tell me: and if not, tell me; that I may turn to the right hand, or to the left."

50 Then Laban and Bethuel answered and said, "The thing proceedeth from the LORD: we cannot speak unto thee bad or good.

51 °Behold, Rebekah *is* before thee, take *her*, and go, and let her be thy master's son's wife, °as the LORD hath spoken."

52 And it came to pass, that, when Abraham's servant heard their words, he wor-

24 Nahor. See Ap. 29. Rebekah his granddaughter; but old enough to marry Isaac, because Sarah was "well stricken in years" when Isaac was born (18. 11, 12). Cp. 24. 36.

26 man. Heb. *'ish.* Ap. 14. ii.

29 Laban. See Ap. 29.

30 when he saw. Characteristic of Laban. Rebekah showed kindness before she saw.

31, 32 he, i. e. Laban.

32 men. Heb. pl. of *'ish*, or *'enosh.* Ap. 14.

35 And. Note the Fig. *Polysyndeton*, Ap. 6, to emphasise all the items which went to make up Abraham's wealth. Twelve "ands" (3 × 4 = 12) = abundance of earthly wealth. See Ap. 10.

40 I walk = I walk habitually. Heb. verb in *Hithpael.*

42 said. Eleazar repeats his prayer from memory, but inexactly. Who could have written the actual words (*vv.* 12–21) but the Holy Inspiring Spirit? He records both the prayer itself and Eleazar's remembrance of it.

43 virgin. Heb. *'almah.* Every *bethulah* is an *'almah*, but every *'almah* is not a *bethulah*: *'almah* occ. 7 times, 24. 43 (first occ.). Ex. 2. 8. Ps. 68. 25. Prov. 30. 19. Song, 1. 3; 6. 8. Isa. 7. 14. *Bethulah* occ. 49 times (Ap. 10).

47 face or nose. Cp. *v.* 22.

48 led me in the right way. Cp. Ps. 107. 7.

daughter. Fig. *Synecdoche* (of the Species), Ap. 6, daughter put for granddaughter.

51 Behold. Fig. *Asterismos.* Ap. 6.

as the LORD hath spoken = according as Jehovah, &c. Laban regards Jehovah as arranging all.

shipped [1]the LORD, *bowing himself* to the
earth.
53 And the servant brought forth jewels of
silver, and jewels of gold, and °raiment, and
gave *them* to Rebekah: he gave also to her
brother and to her mother precious things.
v (p. 33) 54 And they did eat and drink, he and the
°men that *were* with him, and tarried all
night;
n² w (p. 35) and they rose up in the morning, and he said,
x y "Send me away unto my master."
z 55 And her brother and her mother said,
"Let the damsel abide with us *a few* days, at
the least °ten; after that she shall go."
x y 56 And he said unto them, "Hinder me not,
seeing [1]the LORD hath prospered my way; send
me away that I may go to my master."
z 57 And they said, "We will call the damsel,
and enquire at her mouth."
58 And they called Rebekah, and said unto
her, "Wilt thou go with this °man?" And
she said, "I will go."
59 And they sent away Rebekah their sister,
and her nurse, and Abraham's servant, and
his men.
60 And they blessed Rebekah, and said unto
her, "Thou *art* our sister, be thou *the mother*
of thousands of millions, and let thy seed possess the gate of those which hate them."
w 61 And Rebekah arose, and her damsels, and
they rode upon the camels, and followed the
man: and the servant took Rebekah, and
went his way.
62 And Isaac came from the way of the °well
°Lahai-roi; for he dwelt in the south country.
63 And Isaac went out to °meditate in the
field at the eventide: and he lifted up his eyes,
and saw, and, °behold, the camels *were* coming.
64 And Rebekah lifted up her eyes, and when
she saw Isaac, she °lighted off the camel.
65 For she *had* said unto the servant, "What
°man *is* this that walketh in the field to meet
us?" And the servant *had* said, "It *is* my
master:" therefore she took a vail, and covered
herself.
66 And the servant told Isaac all things that
he had done.
1856 67 And Isaac brought her into his mother
Sarah's tent, and took Rebekah, and she became his wife; and he loved her: and Isaac
was °comforted after his mother's *death*.

B² (p. 17) 1846 **25** Then again Abraham took °a wife, and
her name *was* Keturah.
2 And she bare him Zimran, and Jokshan,
and °Medan, and °Midian, and Ishbak, and
Shuah.
3 And Jokshan begat Sheba, and Dedan.
And the sons of Dedan were Asshurim, and
Letushim, and Leummim.
4 And the sons of Midian; Ephah, and Epher,
and Hanoch, and Abidah, and Eldaah. All
°these *were* the children of Keturah.
A³ 5 And Abraham gave all that he had unto
Isaac.

53 raiment: or garments; i. e. changes of raiment.
54 men. Heb. pl. of *'ish* or *'enosh.* Ap. 14. iii.

24. -54-67 (n², p. 33). ELEAZAR'S MISSION AND RETURN. (*Introversion and Alternation*).

n² | w | -54-. The return desired.
x | y | -54. Request for departure made.
z | 55. Departure hindered.
x | *y* | 56. Request for departure renewed.
z | 57-60. Departure expedited.
w | 61-67. The return consummated.

55 ten. Seven days = a week, but ten or a *decad* ($\frac{1}{3}$ of a month) sometimes reckoned as a longer, but strictly defined period. Cp. Ex. 12. 3. Lev. 16. 29.
58 man. Heb. *'ish.* Ap. 14. ii.
62 well = spring. Heb. *b*e*'ēr.* See note on 21. 19.
Lahai-roi. Heb. *the well of life and vision.*
63 meditate. Refers back to the historical context, 23. 19, the death and burial of Sarah, his mother. What follows this digression (of which Isaac as yet knew nothing) in 24. 1-67 shows that Isaac went out, not to "meditate", or "to pray" (A.V. marg.), or "take a walk" (Syr.), or "muster the flocks" (Gesenius), but *to mourn.* This is the meaning of the Heb. *sūach* in Ps. 44. 25. Lam. 3. 20.
behold. Fig. *Asterismos.* Ap. 6.
64 lighted off. Heb. *fell*, or alighted hastily.
65 man. Heb. *'ish.* Ap. 14. ii.
67 comforted after, or consoled himself for.

25. 1-4 (B², p. 17). THE POSTERITY OF KETURAH.
1 This genealogy, and Abraham's death recorded here, because no more is to be said about Abraham. Abraham, however, lived till Jacob was 15. Shem died 1846.
a wife = another, instead of "again".
2 Medan and **Midian** were half-brothers with Ishmael, and they were mixed up together in their dealings. See note on 37. 25, 28, and cp. 16. 12; 17. 20.
4 these = the tares, sown after Isaac, the good seed.
7 175 years. Therefore a sojourner 100 years. Cp. 12. 4.
8 full of. Heb. "satisfied with". Supply "days" (not "years"), with Sam., Onk., Jon., Sept., and Syr.
gathered to his people, an idiomatic *Euphemism* (Ap. 6) for death and burial. Abraham's "people" were idolaters (Josh. 24. 2). See note on 2 Sam. 12. 23.
9 Machpelah. Cp. 23. 9.
10 purchased. Cp. 23. 16.
11 God. Heb. Elohim. Ap. 4.
well. Heb. *b*e*'ēr.* See note on 21. 19.
Lahai-roi. Cp. 16. 14; 24. 62.

6 But unto the sons of the concubines, which Abraham had, Abraham gave gifts, and sent them away from Isaac his son, while he yet lived, eastward, unto the east country.
7 And these *are* the days of the years of Abraham's life which he lived, an °hundred threescore and fifteen years.
8 Then Abraham gave up the ghost, and died in a good old age, an old man, and °full *of years;* and was °gathered to his people.
9 And his sons Isaac and Ishmael buried him in the cave of °Machpelah, in the field of Ephron the son of Zohar the Hittite, which *is* before Mamre;
10 The field which Abraham °purchased of the sons of Heth: there was Abraham buried, and Sarah his wife.
11 And it came to pass after the death of Abraham, that °God blessed his son Isaac; and Isaac dwelt by the °well °Lahai-roi.

C 12 Now these *are* THE GENERATIONS OF
(p. 1) ISHMAEL, Abraham's son, whom Hagar
the Egyptian, Sarah's handmaid, bare unto
Abraham:
13 And these *are* the names of the °sons of
Ishmael, by their names, according to their
generations: the firstborn of Ishmael, Nebajoth; and Kedar, and Adbeel, and Mibsam,
14 And Mishma, and Dumah, and Massa,
15 Hadar, and Tema, Jetur, Naphish, and
Kedemah:
16 These *are* the sons of Ishmael, and these
are their names, by their towns, and by their
castles; twelve princes according to their
nations.
1773 17 And these *are* the years of the life of
Ishmael, an hundred and thirty and seven
years; and he gave up the ghost and died;
and was [8] gathered unto his people.
18 And they dwelt from Havilah unto Shur,
that *is* before Egypt, as thou goest toward
Assyria: *and* he °died in the presence of all
his brethren.

F A 19 And these *are* THE GENERATIONS OF
(p. 36) ISAAC, Abraham's son: Abraham °begat
Isaac:

B a 20 And Isaac was forty years old when he
1856 took Rebekah to wife, the daughter of Bethuel
the Syrian of Padan-aram, the sister to Laban
the Syrian.
21 And Isaac intreated °the LORD for his wife,
because she *was* barren: and the LORD was
intreated of him, and Rebekah his wife conceived.
22 And the children struggled together within
her; and she said, "If *it be* so, why *am* I
thus?" And she went to enquire of [21] the
LORD.
b 23 And [21] the LORD said unto her, "Two
nations *are* in thy womb, and two manner
of people shall be separated from thy bowels;
and *the one* people shall be stronger than
the other people; and the elder shall serve
the younger."
24 And when her days to be delivered were
fulfilled, behold, *there were* twins in her womb.
25 And the first came out red, all over like
an hairy garment; and they called his name
Esau.
26 And after that came his brother out, and
his hand took hold on Esau's °heel; and his
name was called Jacob: and Isaac *was* threescore years old when she bare them.
1836 27 And the boys grew: and Esau was a
°cunning hunter, °a man of the field; and Jacob
was a °plain man, dwelling in tents.
28 And Isaac loved Esau, because he did eat
of *his* °venison: but Rebekah loved Jacob.
c 29 And Jacob °sod °pottage: and Esau came
from the field, and he *was* faint:
30 And Esau said to Jacob, "Feed me, I pray
thee, with that same °red [29] *pottage;* for I *am*
faint:" therefore was his name called °Edom.
31 And Jacob said, "Sell me °this day thy
°birthright."
32 And Esau said, "Behold, I *am* at the point
to die: and what profit shall this [31] birthright
do to °me?"

25. 12-18 (*C*, p. 1). THE GENERATIONS OF ISHMAEL.
(*Alternation.*)

C | A | 12. Ishmael. Birth.
  B | 13-16. His sons. Names and dwelling.
  A | 17. Ishmael. Death.
  B | 18. His sons. Their dwelling.

18 died=had inheritance. Heb. *nāphal*, to fall, esp. as a lot, giving inheritance (Judg. 18. 1. 1 Chron. 1. 20; 26. 14. 2 Chron. 15. 9. Ps. 16. 6 (cp. Josh. 23. 4. Heb. caused the lot to fall). Hence, to dwell with, as in Prov. 1. 14. Cp. Judg. 7. 12, to encamp, *lying along* the ground. Ishmael was to dwell in the presence (Heb. "on the face") of his brethren, i. e. mixed up with them (16. 12). See 37. 25, 28, 36; 39. 1, and cp. Judg. 8. 24 (Midian, being his half-brother (15. 11, 12). *Nāphal* never rendered "die" elsewhere.

25. 19—35. 29 (*F*, p. 1). THE GENERATIONS OF ISAAC (*Introversion and Alternation*).

F | A | 25. 19. The birth of Isaac.
  B | a | 25. 20-22. Marriage with Rebekah.
    b | 25. 23-28. Isaac's two sons.
      C | 25. 29-34. Esau and Jacob.
        D | E | 26. 1. Journey to Gerar.
          F | 26. 2-5. Appearance of Jehovah.
            G | c | 26. 6-11. Isaac's wife.
              d | 26. 12-22. Sep. from Abim.
        D | *E* | 26. 23. Journey to Beer-sheba.
          F | 26. 24, 25. Appearance of Jehovah.
            G | *d* | 26. 26-33. Cov. with Abim.
              c | 26. 34, 35. Esau's wives.
      C | 27. 1—35. 15. Esau and Jacob.
  B | *a* | 35. 16-20. Death of Rachel.
    b | 35. 21-26. Israel's twelve sons.
A | 35. 27-29. The death of Isaac.

19 begat. The same form of the verb as in ch. 5, used of the godly seed.
21 the LORD. Heb. Jehovah. Ap. 4.
26 heel. Heb. *yakob*, whence the name Jacob (*yakob*) heel-catcher: hence, contender.
27 cunning knowing or skilled in.
a man of the field. "The field is the world."
plain - upright or pure. Job 1. 1, 8; 2. 3, &c.
28 venison. Heb. *hunting*. Fig. *Metonymy* (of the Cause), Ap. 6, hunting put for what was caught. Eating was strong in Esau too (*v.* 34). It was "the will of the flesh" which Isaac's faith overcame in ch. 27, for he wished to bless Esau, and he loved his savoury meat. See note on 27. 3, 4. Cp. Heb. 11. 20.
29 sod. Part. of O. Eng. verb *seethe*, to boil.
pottage=anything cooked in a *pot*.
30 red. Heb. red red. Fig. *Epizeuxis* (Ap. 6). (No superlative in Heb.) Fig.=*that delicious red* [food]. Lentiles. See *v.* 34.
Edom=Heb. *red, ruddy*. A reference also to *v.* 25.
31 this day. Heb. "as on this very day." Fig. *Simile.* Ap. 6. Cp. Luke 23. 43.
birthright. Included (1) the Father's blessing and supremacy (which went to Jacob, ch. 27, and Judah, 49. 8. 1 Chron. 5. 1, 2); (2) a double portion (which went to Joseph, ch. 48. 1 Chron. 5. 1, 2); and (3) the Domestic Priesthood (which after going to the first-born of each family was vested in Levi for the whole nation, Num. 3. 6, 12. Cp. Num. 16. 1-3).
32 me. Fig. *Ellipsis* (Ap. 6) = *Brachyology.* The words to be supplied are "I will sell it". A famine accounts for the sale. See 26. 1.

33 And Jacob said, "Swear to me [31]this °day;" and he sware unto him: and he sold his °birthright unto Jacob.

abt. 1812 **34** Then Jacob gave Esau bread and pottage of lentiles; °and he did eat and drink, and rose up, and went his way: thus Esau °despised *his* [31]birthright.

D E (p. 36) **26** And there was a °famine in the land, beside the °first famine that was in the days of Abraham. And Isaac went unto °Abimelech king of the Philistines unto Gerar.

F **2** And °the LORD appeared unto him, and said, °"Go not down into Egypt; dwell in the land which I shall tell thee of:

3 Sojourn in this land, and I will be with thee, and will bless thee; for °unto thee, and unto thy seed, I will give all these countries, and I will perform the oath which I sware unto Abraham thy father;

4 And I will make thy seed to multiply as the °stars of heaven, and will give unto thy seed all these countries; and in thy seed shall all the nations of the earth be blessed;

5 Because that Abraham obeyed °My °voice, and kept My °charge, My °commandments, My °statutes, and My °laws."

G c **6** And Isaac dwelt in Gerar:

7 And the °men of the place asked *him* of his wife; and °he said, "She *is* my °sister:" for he feared to say, "*She is* my wife;" "lest," *said he*, "the °men of the place should kill me for Rebekah;" because she *was* fair to look upon.

8 And it came to pass, when he had been there a long time, that Abimelech king of the Philistines looked out at a window, and saw, and, behold, Isaac *was* °sporting with Rebekah his wife.

9 And Abimelech called Isaac, and said, °"Behold, of a surety she *is* thy wife: and °how saidst thou, 'She *is* my sister?'" And Isaac said unto him, "Because I said, 'Lest I die for her.'"

10 And Abimelech said, °"What *is* this thou hast done unto us? one of the people might lightly have lien with thy wife, and thou shouldest have brought °guiltiness upon us."

11 And Abimelech charged all *his* people, °saying, "He that toucheth this man or his wife shall surely be put to death."

G d **12** Then Isaac sowed in that land, and °received in the same year an hundredfold: and [2]the LORD blessed him.

13 And the man waxed great, and went forward, and grew until he became very great:

14 For he had possession of flocks, and possession of herds, and great °store of servants: and the Philistines envied him.

15 For all the wells which his father's servants had digged in the days of Abraham his father, the Philistines had stopped them, and filled them with earth.

16 And Abimelech said unto Isaac, "Go from us; for thou art much mightier than we."

17 And Isaac departed thence, and pitched his tent in °the valley of Gerar, and dwelt there.

18 And Isaac digged again the wells of water, which they had digged °in the days of Abraham his father; for the Philistines had stopped them after the death of Abraham: and he called °their names after the names by which his father had called them.

19 And Isaac's servants digged in the valley, and found there a °well of °springing water.

20 And the herdmen of Gerar did strive with Isaac's herdmen, saying, "The water *is* ours:" and he called the name of the well °Esek; because they strove with him.

21 And they digged another well, and strove for that also: and he called the name of it °Sitnah.

22 And he removed from thence, and digged another well; and for that they strove not: and he called the name of it °Rehoboth; and

---

33 day. Fig. *Brachyology.* Ap. 6. Supply "that thou wilt sell it".

birthright. The Severus Codex here reads "ware", i. e. Esau treated his birthright as merchandise. See Ap. 34.

34 and. Fig. *Polysyndeton* (Ap. 6). *Four* "ands" marking the deliberateness of Esau's acts, and their solemn significance. He despised *grace.* See Ap. 10.

despised. Hence in Heb. 12. 16 he is called "a profane person".

26 (D E, p. 36). ISAAC'S JOURNEY TO GERAR.

1 famine. Accounts for Esau's despair of living, and hence selling his birthright. 25. 29-34.

first. One of the thirteen famines. See note on 12. 10.

Abimelech = official name. Not the same as ch. 20. 2.

2 the LORD. Heb. Jehovah. Ap. 4.

Go not down (as Abraham did, ch. 12. 10).

3 unto thee. So to each Patriarch: Abraham (13. 15), Jacob (28. 13, &c.), involving resurrection. See note on 50. 24, and cp. Ex. 3. 6 and Matt. 22. 23-33.

4 stars. Fig. *Parœmia.* Ap. 6.

5 My. Repeated 5 times for emph. The No. of Grace. See Ap. 10 and note on John 1. 17.

voice, to be heard and believed (Rom. 10. 17).

charge, to be observed.

commandments, to be obeyed.

statutes, i. e. decrees, to be acknowledged.

laws, i. e. instructions to be followed.

7 men. Heb. pl. of *'ish*, or *'enosh.* Ap. 14.

he said. As Abraham had said (12. 13; 20. 2, 12).

sister. See note on 20. 12.

8 sporting with, or caressing.

9 Behold. Fig. *Asterismos.* Ap. 6.

how . . . ? Fig. *Erotēsis.* Ap. 6.

10 What . . . ? Fig. *Erotēsis.* Ap. 6.

guiltiness. See Ap. 15 and 44. ii.

11 saying. One of the Laws given and observed before Moses. See Ap. 15.

12 received. Heb. found. Fig. *Synecdoche* (of the Species). Ap. 6. Cp. 6. 8. Rom. 4. 1.

14 store = body.

17 the valley. Some distance from the city.

18 in the days of Abraham his father. Isaac a placid character: shown by his obedience (22. 6, 8), his meekness in betrothal (24), his mourning for his mother (24. 63-67; cp. note on *v.* 63), his following in his father's steps to Gerar (20. 1) in denying his wife there (20), his finding an Abimelech and Phichol there, and digging wells there, renewing the oath and renaming the well.

their names. Cp. the four names below and their special meaning.

19 well. Heb. *'ayin.* See note on 21. 19.

springing. Heb. living. See note on 21. 19.

20 Esek. Heb. strife or contention.

21 Sitnah. Heb. opposition.

22 Rehoboth. Heb. roominess.

he said, "For now [2]the LORD hath made room for us, and we shall be fruitful in the land."

D E (p. 36) 23 And he went up from thence to °Beer-sheba.

F 24 And [2]the LORD appeared unto him the same night, and said, "I *am* the °God of Abraham thy father: fear not, for I *am* with thee, and will bless thee, and multiply thy seed for My servant Abraham's sake."

25 And he builded an altar there, and called upon the name of [2]the LORD, and pitched his tent there: and there Isaac's servants digged a well.

G d 26 Then Abimelech went to him from Gerar, and Ahuzzath one of his friends, and °Phichol the chief captain of his army.

27 And Isaac said unto them, "Wherefore come ye to me, seeing ye hate me, and have sent me away from you?"

28 And they said, "We °saw certainly that [2]the LORD was with thee: and we said, 'Let there be now an oath betwixt us, *even* betwixt us and thee, and let us make a covenant with thee;

29 That thou wilt do us no hurt, as we have not °touched thee, and as we have done unto thee nothing but good, and have sent thee away in peace:' thou *art* now the blessed of [2]the LORD."

30 And he made them a feast, and they did eat and drink.

31 And they rose up betimes in the morning, and sware one to another: and Isaac sent them away, and they departed from him in peace.

32 And it came to pass the same day, that Isaac's servants came, and told him concerning the well which they had digged, and said unto him, "We have found water."

33 And he called it °Shebah: °therefore the name of the city *is* Beer-sheba unto this day.

c 34 And Esau was forty years old when he took to wife °Judith the daughter of °Beeri the

1796 °Hittite, and °Bashemath the daughter of Elon the Hittite:

35 Which were a °grief of °mind unto Isaac and to Rebekah.

C J e (p. 38) 1759 **27** And it came to pass, that when Isaac was °old, and his eyes were dim, so that he could not see, he called Esau his eldest son, and said unto him, "My son:" and he said unto him, °"Behold, *here am* I."

2 And he said, [1]"Behold now, I am old, I know not the day of my death:

3 Now therefore take, I pray thee, thy weapons, thy quiver and thy bow, and go out to the field, and °take me *some* venison;

4 And make me savoury meat, °such as I love, and bring *it* to me, that I may eat; that °my soul may °bless thee before I die."

5 And Rebekah °heard when Isaac °spake to Esau his son. And Esau went to the field to hunt *for* [3]venison, *and* to bring *it*.

6 And Rebekah spake unto Jacob her son, saying, [1]"Behold, I heard thy father speak unto Esau thy brother, saying,

7 'Bring me [3]venison, and make me savoury

23 Beer-sheba. Heb. the well of the oath.
24 God. Heb. *Elohim*. Ap. 4.
26 Phichol. Prob. an official military title. Cp. 21. 22.
28 saw certainly. Fig. *Polyptōton* (Ap. 6), for emphasis. Heb. "seeing we saw". Cp. 2. 16 "*freely* eat"; 27. 30 "*scarce* gone out"; 43. 3 "*solemnly* protest"; 43. 7 "asked us *straitly*", "could we *certainly* know"; 43. 20 "came *indeed* down"; Ex. 5. 23 "not delivered us *at all*"; 18. 18 "wilt *surely* wear away"; 21. 5 "shall *plainly* say"; Job 37. 2 "hear *attentively*"; Num. 22. 17, 37 "promote thee to *very great* honour" = honouring I will honour thee; 24. 10 "*altogether* blessed", Heb. "blessing thou hast blessed". Num. 26. 65; 30. 12 "*utterly* destroyed"; 23. 11; 24. 10 "*altogether* blessed".
29 touched. Fig. *Tapeinosis*. Ap. 6. Emphasising the fact that so far from injuring him in any way they had shown him favour.
33 Shebah. Heb. an oath.
therefore. Same name given by Abraham (21. 31). Names were sometimes reimposed for a new reason. Cp. Bethel (28. 18, 19 with 35. 6, 7) and Israel (32. 28 with 35. 10).
34 These names exhibit the Fig. *Polynymia*. Ap. 6.
Judith. She had a second name, Aholibamah (36. 5, 14, 25).
Beeri. His name was also Anah, but he had acquired the name "Beeri" (or the spring-man) from his having discovered the hot springs. See on 36. 24.
Hittite = the general name. See note on 1 Kings 10. 29.
Bashemath had a second name, Adah. The name Bashemath dropped in 36. 2 to avoid confusion with the daughter of Ishmael. In ch. 26 we have general *history*, but in 36 precise *genealogy*.
35 grief. Fig. *Metonymy* (of Effect), Ap. 6, grief put for that which caused it. No wonder it caused "bitterness of spirit" when we remember who the Canaanites were.
mind = spirit. Heb. *ruach*. See Ap. 9.

27. 1—35. 15 (*C*, p. 36). ESAU AND JACOB.
(*Introversion and Alternation.*)

C | H | J | e | 27. 1-40. Deception of father and brother by Jacob and Rebekah.
f | 27. 41. Hatred of Esau.
K | 27. 42—28. 5. Departure of Jacob to Padan-aram.
I | g | 28. 6-9. Esau's wives.
h | 28. 10-22. Jacob's Vision at Bethel.
I | *g* | 29. 1—31. 55. Jacob's wives.
h | 32. 1, 2. Jacob's Vision at Mahanaim.
H | *J* | *f* | 32. 3—33. 17. Reconciliation of Esau.
e | 33. 18—34. 31. Deception of Shechemites by Jacob's sons.
K | 35. 1-15. Return of Jacob to Padan-aram.

1 old. About 137 years (same age as his brother Ishmael died at). He recovered and lived 43 years longer (cp. 35. 28).
Behold. Fig. *Asterismos*. Ap. 6.
3 take me some venison. Heb. hunt me some hunting. Fig. *Polyptōton*, Ap. 6, and *Metonymy* (of Cause), Ap. 6, by which venison, the result of hunting, is put for the hunting itself (from Lat. *venatio*, a hunting). In ch. 25. 29 Esau missed his venison and lost his birthright. Was he now to miss it again and lose his blessing?
4 such as I love. See *vv.* 9, 14 and 25. 28.
my soul = myself. Heb. *nephesh*. Ap. 13.
bless thee. He must have heard that he was to bless Jacob, for it was "by faith" he ultimately did so (Heb. 11. 20); and it came "by hearing" (Rom. 10. 17). "The will of the flesh" made him wish to bless Esau (cp. *v.* 4 with 25. 28). But his faith in the end overcame "the will of the flesh" in him.
5 heard. Heb. was listening.
spake. Heb. was speaking.

meat, that I may eat, and bless thee before
° the LORD before my death.'
8 Now therefore, my son, obey my voice according to that which I command thee.
9 Go now to the flock, and fetch me from
thence two good kids of the goats; and I will
make them savoury meat for thy father, [4]such
as he loveth:
10 And thou shalt bring *it* to thy father, that
he may eat, and that he may bless thee before
his death."
11 And Jacob said to Rebekah his mother,
"Behold, Esau my brother *is* a hairy °man,
and I *am* a smooth °man:
12 My father peradventure will feel me, and I
shall °seem to him as a deceiver; and I shall
bring a curse upon me, and not a blessing."
13 And his mother said unto him, "Upon me
be thy curse, my son: only obey my voice, and
go fetch me *them*."
14 And he went, and fetched, and brought
them to his mother: and his mother made
savoury meat, [4]such as his father loved.
15 And Rebekah took °goodly °raiment of
her eldest son Esau, which *were* with her in
the house, and put them upon Jacob her
younger son:
16 And she put the skins of the kids of the
goats upon his hands, and upon the smooth
of his neck:
17 And she gave the savoury meat and the
bread, which she had prepared, into the hand
of her son Jacob.
18 And he came unto his father, and said,
"My father:" and he said, "Here *am* I; who
art thou, my son?"
19 And Jacob said unto his father, °"I *am*
Esau thy firstborn; I have done according as
thou badest me: arise, I pray thee, sit and eat
of my venison, that °thy soul may bless me."
20 And Isaac said unto his son, "How *is it*
that thou hast found *it* so quickly, my son?"
And he said, "Because [7]the LORD thy °God
brought *it* to me."
21 And Isaac said unto Jacob, "Come near,
I pray thee, that I may feel thee, my son,
whether thou *be* my very son Esau or not."
22 And Jacob went near unto Isaac his father;
and he felt him, and said, "The voice *is* Jacob's
voice, but the hands *are* the hands of Esau."
23 And he discerned him not, because his
hands were hairy, as his brother Esau's hands:
so he blessed him.
24 And he said, "*Art* thou my very son Esau?"
And he said, "I *am*."
25 And he said, "Bring *it* near to me, and I
will eat of my son's [3]venison, that [4]my soul
may bless thee." And he brought *it* near to
him, and he did eat: and he brought him
°wine, and he drank.
26 And his father Isaac said unto him, "Come
near °now, and kiss me, my son."
27 And he came near, and kissed him: and
he smelled the smell of his [15]raiment, and
blessed him, and said, "See, the smell of my
son *is* as the smell of a field which [7]the LORD
hath blessed:
28 Therefore [20]God give thee of the dew of
heaven, and the fatness of the earth, and plenty
of °corn and °wine:
29 Let °people serve thee, and nations bow
down to thee: be lord over thy brethren, and
let thy mother's sons bow down to thee: cursed
be every one that curseth thee, and blessed *be*
he that blesseth thee."
30 And it came to pass, as soon as Isaac had
made an end of blessing Jacob, and Jacob was
yet °scarce gone out from the presence of Isaac
his father, that Esau his brother came in from
his hunting.
31 And he also had made savoury meat, and
brought it unto his father, and said unto his
father, "Let my father arise, and eat of his
son's venison, that [19]thy soul may bless me."
32 And Isaac his father said unto him, "Who
art thou?" And he said, "I *am* thy son, °thy
firstborn Esau."
33 And Isaac °trembled very exceedingly, and
said, "Who? where *is* he that hath taken
venison, and brought *it* me, and I have eaten
of all before thou camest, and have blessed
him? yea, *and* he shall be blessed."
34 And when Esau heard the words of his
father, he cried with a great and exceeding
bitter cry, and said unto his father, "Bless me,
even me also, O my father."
35 And he said, "Thy brother came with
subtilty, and hath taken away thy blessing."
36 And he said, "Is not he rightly named

7 the LORD. Heb. Jehovah. Ap. 4.
11 man. Heb. *'ish.* See Ap. 14. ii.
12 seem. He shrinks, not from the fraud, but from its detection.
15 goodly. Heb. desires. Fig. *Metonymy* (of the Adjunct), Ap. 6, put for the things desired or coveted (2 Chron. 36. 10. Isa. 64. 11. Lam. 1. 10).
raiment. All raiment in the East to this day marks the social rank and position of the wearer. Among the Bedouins, the chief and his eldest son wear a distinctive garment. This accounts for Jacob's desire here, and his act with Joseph (37. 3). Being the garment of the firstborn it doubtless denoted also his official and priestly position. Here, Heb. *beged* (cp. Ex. 28. 2, 4; 35. 19. Lev. 10. 6; 21. 10), used of sacred things. Not the word rendered clothes in Deut. 29. 5. No wonder Esau is called "profane" when he sold this his birthright (Heb. 12. 16).
19 I am. Said perhaps because he had bought the birthright.
thy soul = thou. Heb. *nephesh.* Ap. 13.
20 God. Heb. *Elohim.* Ap. 4.
25 wine = Heb. *yayin.* See Ap. 27. i.
26 now. Not an adv. of time, but an expletive in command, emphasising the solemnity of the command. It must have been at this point that Isaac's faith overcame "the will of the flesh", and made him resolve to bless Jacob, in spite of it.
28 corn. Put by *Metonymy* (of the Cause), Ap. 6, for bread and solid food generally. Cp. Lam. 2. 12.
wine. Heb. *tīrōsh.* See Ap. 27. ii. Usually combined with "corn", as put by *Metonymy* (of the Cause) for all liquids. Ap. 6. **29 people.** Heb. peoples.
30 scarce gone out. Heb. "going was gone". Fig. *Polyptōton,* for emph.; well represented by the word "scarce". See note on 26. 28.
32 thy firstborn. Esau still claims what he had sold.
33 trembled very exceedingly. The Fig. *Polyptōton* (Ap. 6) is thus beautifully rendered. Heb. "trembled a great trembling greatly." See note on 26. 28. This trembling was not from doubt, or from the discovery (now made, *vv.* 26, 27), but on account of the difficulty into which it had brought him with a man of Esau's temperament.

°Jacob? for he hath °supplanted me these two
times: he took away my birthright; and, behold, now he hath taken away my °blessing."
And he said, "Hast thou not reserved a blessing for me?"
37 And Isaac answered and said unto Esau,
°"Behold, I have made him °thy lord, and all
his brethren have I given to him for servants;
and with corn and °wine have I sustained
him: and what shall I do now unto thee, my
son?"
38 And Esau said unto his father, "Hast thou
but one blessing, my father? bless me, *even* me
also, O my father." And Esau lifted up his
voice, and °wept.
39 And Isaac his father answered and said
unto him, °"Behold, thy dwelling shall be °the
fatness of the earth, and of the dew of heaven
from above;
40 And by thy sword shalt thou live, and
shalt °serve thy brother; and it shall come to
pass when thou shalt have the dominion, that
°thou shalt break his yoke from off thy neck."
f 41 And Esau hated Jacob because of the
(p. 38) blessing wherewith his father blessed him:
and Esau said in his heart, "The days of
mourning for my father are °at hand; then
will I slay my brother Jacob."
K 42 And these words of Esau her elder son
were told to Rebekah: and she sent and called
Jacob her younger son, and said unto him,
°"Behold, thy brother Esau, as touching thee,
doth comfort himself, *purposing* to kill thee.
43 Now therefore, my son, obey my voice;
and arise, °flee thou to Laban my brother to
°Haran;
44 And tarry with him °a few days, °until
thy brother's fury turn away;
45 [44]Until thy brother's anger turn away from
thee, and he forget *that* which thou hast done
to him: then I will send, and fetch thee from
thence: °why should I be deprived also of you
°both in one day?"
46 And Rebekah said to Isaac, "I am weary
of my life because of the °daughters of Heth:
if Jacob take a wife of the daughters of Heth,
such as these *which are* of the daughters of
the land, °what good shall my life do me?"
28 And Isaac called Jacob, and °blessed
him, and charged him, and said unto
him, °"Thou shalt not take a wife of the
daughters of Canaan.
2 Arise, go to °Padan-aram, to the house of
Bethuel thy mother's father; and take thee a
wife from thence of the daughters of Laban thy
mother's brother.
3 °And °GOD ALMIGHTY bless thee, and make
thee fruitful, and multiply thee, that thou
mayest be a °multitude of °people;
4 And give thee the blessing of Abraham, to
thee, and to thy seed with thee; that thou
mayest inherit the land °wherein thou art a
stranger, which °God gave unto Abraham."
5 And Isaac sent away Jacob: and he went
to [2]Padan-aram unto Laban, son of Bethuel
the Syrian, the brother of Rebekah, Jacob's
and Esau's mother.
I g 6 When Esau saw that Isaac had blessed
Jacob, °and sent him away to Padan-aram, to
take him a wife from thence; °and that as he
blessed him he gave him a charge, saying,
"Thou shalt not take a wife of the daughters
of °Canaan;"
7 And that Jacob obeyed his father and his
mother, and was gone to Padan-aram;
8 And Esau seeing that the daughters of
[6]Canaan °pleased not Isaac his father;
9 Then went Esau unto Ishmael, and took
unto the wives which he had °Mahalath the

Jacob. See on 25. 26.
supplanted. Jacobed or over-reached me. See note on 25. 26 and 32. 28.
blessing. This "blessing" is the "it" of Heb. 12. 17.
37 Behold. Fig. *Asterismos.* Ap. 6.
thy lord = a mighty man unto thee. See Ap. 14. iv. Fulfilled in 2 Sam. 8. 14.
wine. See note on *v.* 28 above.
38 wept. See Heb. 12. 17, but could not change his father's mind.
39 Behold. Fig. *Asterismos.* Ap. 6.
the fatness of the earth, and of. Heb. of the fatness, &c. The "of", which is omitted in the first clause, is the prep. מִ, which means "from". R.V. marg. *away from.* Cp. Isa. 22. 3. Jer. 48. 33. Lam. 4. 9. Should be "Far from the fatness of the earth shall be thy dwelling, and far from the dew of the heavens," &c. Jacob had already received the blessing "of" the fatness of the earth or the land (*v.* 28). Esau's was to be far from it, in the desert; and so it was.
40 serve. See 1 Sam. 14. 47. 2 Sam. 8. 14. 2 Kings 8. 20, and cp. 1 Kings 22. 47.
thou shalt break. Fulfilled in 2 Kings 8. 20, 22. 2 Chron. 21. 8-10.
41 at hand. Isaac mistaken, *vv.* 1, 2. Esau mistaken here.
42 Behold. Fig. *Asterismos.* Ap. 6.
43 flee thou. Heb. flee for thyself.
Haran. See 11. 31.
44 a few days. Rebekah mistaken, for he was there 20 years. **until.** Fig. *Synonymia.* Ap. 6.
45 why . . ? Fig. *Erotēsis.* Ap. 6.
both. Jacob by Esau's hand, and Esau by the avenger of blood. 9. 6.
46 daughters of Heth. Refers to Esau's wives. 26. 34, 35.
what good. Fig. *Erotēsis*, and Fig. *Aposiopēsis*, Ap. 6, Lit. "Wherefore to me life?" Eng. Idiom, "What good would my life be to me?"

28 1 blessed. This blessing God endorses (*vv.* 13-15), by sending Jacob to Haran, as he had blessed Abraham to bring him from Haran (12. 1-3).
Thou shalt not take. See 24. 3.
2 Padan-aram = the plain of Syria.
3 And. Note the Fig. *Polysyndeton* in *vv.* 3 & 4 (Ap. 6), marking 4 items in blessing. See Ap. 10.
GOD ALMIGHTY. *El Shaddai.* See Ap. 4.
multitude: or convocation. Heb. *kāhal.* First occ. Occurs 123 times: rendered "multitude" 3, "assembly" 17, "congregation" 86, "company" 17. Cp. 49. 6. Ps. 22. 22, 25.
people. Heb. peoples.
4 wherein thou art a stranger. Heb. of thy sojournings.
God. Heb. *Elohim.* Ap. 4.
6 and. Note the Fig. *Polysyndeton* (Ap. 6), emphasising (*vv.* 6-8) the effort of Esau to note what would please his parents.
Canaan. Cp. 24. 3, and remember who these Canaanites were. See note on 12. 6.
8 pleased not. Cp. 26. 35.
9 Mahalath. She had a second name, Bashemath. See ch. 36. 3.

daughter of Ishmael Abraham's son, the sister of Nebajoth, to be his wife.

h (p. 38) 10 °And Jacob went out from Beer-sheba, and went toward Haran.

11 And he lighted upon a certain place, and tarried there all night, because the sun was set; and he took °of the stones of that place, and put *them for* his pillows, and lay down in that place to sleep.

12 And he dreamed, and °behold a °ladder set up on the earth, and the top of it reached to heaven: and behold the angels of God ascending and descending on it.

13 And, [12]behold, °the LORD stood °above it, and said, "I *am* the LORD God of Abraham thy father, and the God of Isaac: the land whereon thou liest, °to thee °will I give it, and to thy seed;

14 And thy seed shall be as the °dust of the earth, and thou shalt spread abroad to the west, and to the east, and to the north, and to the south: and °in thee and in thy seed shall °all the families of the earth be blessed.

15 And, [12]behold, I *am* with thee, and will keep thee in all *places* whither thou goest, and will bring thee again into this land; for °I will not leave thee, until I have done *that* which I have spoken to thee of."

16 And Jacob awaked out of his sleep, and he said, °"Surely [13]the LORD is in °this place; and I knew *it* not."

17 And he was afraid, and said, "How dreadful *is* this place! this *is* none other but °the house of God, and this *is* the gate of heaven."

18 And Jacob rose up early in the morning, and took °the stone that he had put *for* his pillows, and set it up *for* a °pillar, and °poured oil upon the top of it.

19 And he called the name of that place °Beth-el: but the name of that city *was called* Luz at the first.

20 And Jacob °vowed a vow, saying, "If God will be with me, and will keep me in this way that I go, and will give me bread to eat, and raiment to put on,

21 So that I come again to my father's house in peace; then shall [13]the LORD be my God:

22 And °this stone, which I have set *for* a [18]pillar, shall be °God's house: and of all that Thou shalt give me I will surely give the °tenth unto Thee."

I g i1 (p. 41) 29 Then Jacob °went on his journey, and came into the land of the people of the east.

2 And he looked, and °behold a °well in the field, and, lo, there *were* °three flocks of sheep lying by it; for out of that °well they watered the flocks: and a great stone *was* upon the well's mouth.

3 And thither were all the flocks gathered: and they rolled the stone from the [2]well's mouth, and watered the sheep, and put the stone again upon the well's mouth in his place.

4 And Jacob said unto them, "My brethren, whence *be* ye?" And they said, "Of Haran *are* we."

5 And he said unto them, "Know ye Laban the °son of Nahor?" And they said, "We know *him*."

6 And he said unto them, "*Is* he well?" And they said, "*He is* well: and, °behold, Rachel his daughter cometh with the sheep."

10 And. Note the Fig. *Polysyndeton* (Ap. 6), emphasizing the items in *vv.* 10–15.
11 of the stones. Heb. from; i. e. one from among them. Cp. *vv.* 18, 22.
12 behold. Fig. *Asterismos.* Ap. 6.
ladder. Heb. *sullam*, from *salal*, to pile up like terraces; a way cast up, stairway. Occurs only here. Cp. Isa. 35. 8–10; 57. 14; 62. 10.
13 the LORD = Jehovah (Ap. 4).
above it. The Heb. accent (*zark'ā*) emphasizes this as meaning "beside him" (cp. 18. 2, where *'al* is rendered "by"). It is not the angels, but the Divine faithfulness and promise, which mark "this place" (*vv.* 16, 17) and make it "the house of God".
to thee. As He had said to Abraham (13. 15) and to Isaac (26. 3). See note on 50. 24.
will I. Note the "shalls" and "wills" in this and all these repetitions of Jehovah's covenant.
14 dust . . . &c. Fig. *Parœmia.* Ap. 6. See on 15. 5.
in thee. Mark the personal gift, and see note on 17. 7 and 50. 24.
all. This can be fulfilled only in Christ.
I will not leave thee. This promise first made, here, to Jacob for covenant grace; to the People, for journey (Deut. 31. 6); to Joshua, for conflict (Josh. 1. 5, 8); to Solomon, for work (1 Chron. 28. 20); to us, for daily provision (Heb. 13. 5, 6).
16 Surely. Fig. *Ecphonēsis.* Ap. 6.
this place. See on the word "above", *v.* 13.
17 the house of God. This "house" is the place where God meets the unworthy in *grace.* It was so with David (1 Chron. 22. 1). It is so for us. Our "place of worship" is where God manifests Himself to us in grace. "The God of all grace" is emphatically "the God of Jacob" (Ps. 146. 5).
18 the stone. See *v.* 11. Not the so-called "Coronation stone" in London: inasmuch as the heads of the "Geological Survey of Great Britain" unanimously declared that "no stone of that kind was to be found in any part of the Holy Land whence it traditionally comes". Prof. Ramsay also pronounced it as being "not known to occur in Egypt or in the rocks around Bethel".
pillar. Afterwards forbidden. Lev. 26. 1. Deut. 16. 22.
poured oil. A law before Moses. See Ap. 15.
19 Beth-el. Heb. the house of El.
20 vowed a vow = made a solemn vow. Fig. *Polyptōton.* Ap. 6. The first recorded vow.
22 this stone. See *vv.* 11, 18.
God's house. Heb. *Beth-elohim*, not Beth-el.
tenth. See Ap. 15 and cp. 14. 20.

29. 1—31. 55 (*g*, p. 38). **JACOB'S WIVES.**
(*Repeated Alternation.*)

g | i1 | 29. 1–14. Arrival at Padan-aram.
  k1 | 29. 15 — 30. 24. Servitude.
i2 | 30. 25, 26. Return desired.
  k2 | 30. 27 — 31. 16. Service.
i3 | 31. 17–55. Return effected.

1 went, &c. = lifted up his feet. Heb. *Idiom*, Ap. 6.
2 behold. Fig. *Asterismos.* Ap. 6.
well. Heb. *be'ēr.* See note on 21. 19.
three flocks. Cp. *v.* 8.
5 son. Fig. *Synecdoche* (of Species), Ap. 6, put for grandson. Cp. 24. 15. In *v.* 12 Jacob calls himself the "brother" of Laban by the same Fig.
6 behold. Fig. *Asterismos.* Ap. 6.

7 And he said, °"Lo, *it is* yet high day, neither *is it* time that the cattle should be gathered together: water ye the sheep, and go *and* feed *them*."

8 And they said, "We cannot, until all the flocks be gathered together, and *till* they roll the stone from the well's mouth; then we water the sheep."

9 And while he yet spake with them, Rachel came with °her father's sheep: for she kept them.

10 And it came to pass, when Jacob saw Rachel the daughter of Laban his mother's brother, and the sheep of Laban his mother's brother, that Jacob went near, and rolled the stone from the well's mouth, and watered the flock of Laban his mother's brother.

11 And Jacob °kissed Rachel, and lifted up his voice, and wept.

12 And Jacob told Rachel that he *was* her father's °brother, and that he *was* Rebekah's son: and she ran and told her father.

13 And it came to pass, when Laban °heard the tidings of Jacob his sister's son, that he ran to meet him, °and embraced him, and kissed him, and brought him to his house. And he told Laban all these things.

1759 14 And Laban said to him, "Surely thou *art*
my bone and my flesh." And he abode with
him the °space of a month.

k[1] 15 And Laban said unto Jacob, "Because thou
(p. 41) *art* my [12]brother, shouldest thou therefore serve
me for nought? tell me, what *shall* thy wages
be?"

16 And Laban had two daughters: the name of the elder *was* °Leah, and the name of the younger *was* °Rachel.

17 Leah *was* °tender eyed; but Rachel was °beautiful and °well favoured.

18 And Jacob loved Rachel; and said, "I will serve thee seven years for Rachel thy younger daughter."

19 And Laban said, "*It is* better that I give her to thee, than that I should give her to another man: abide with me."

20 And Jacob °served seven years for Rachel; and they seemed unto him *but* a few days, for the love he had to her.

21 And Jacob said unto Laban, "Give *me* my wife, for my days are fulfilled, that I may go in unto her."

22 And Laban gathered together all the men of the place, and made a feast.

23 And it came to pass in the evening, that he took Leah his daughter, and brought her to him; and he went in unto her.

24 And Laban gave unto his daughter Leah °Zilpah his maid *for* an handmaid.

25 And it came to pass, that in the morning, °behold, it *was* Leah: and he said to Laban, "What *is* this thou hast done unto me? did not I serve with thee for Rachel? wherefore then hast thou beguiled me?"

26 And Laban said, "It must not be so done in our country, to give the younger before the firstborn.

27 Fulfil her week, and °we will give thee this also for the service which thou shalt serve with me yet seven other years."

28 And Jacob did so, and fulfilled °her week: and °he gave him Rachel his daughter to wife also.

29 And Laban gave to Rachel his daughter °Bilhah his handmaid to be her maid.

30 And he went in also unto Rachel, and he loved also Rachel more than Leah, and served with him yet seven other years.

31 And when the °LORD saw that Leah *was* °hated, He opened her womb: but Rachel *was* barren.

32 And Leah conceived, and bare a son, and 1751
she called his name °Reuben: for she said,
"Surely the [31]LORD hath looked upon my
affliction; now therefore my husband will love
me."

33 And she conceived again, and bare a son; 1750
and said, "Because the [31]LORD hath °heard
that I *was* hated, He hath therefore given
me this *son* also:" and she called his name
°Simeon.

34 And she conceived again, and bare a son; 1749
and said, "Now this time will my husband be
°joined unto me, because I have born him three
sons:" therefore °was his name called °Levi.

7 Lo. Fig. *Asterismos*, Ap. 6, giving life to the scene.
9 her father's sheep. Shepherds usually slaves, younger sons, or daughters. Cp. David, 1 Sam. 17. 13-15. Ex. 2. 16, 17. Note exception, Gen. 37. 14, and reason.
11 kissed. The Eastern greeting.
12 brother. See on *v.* 5 and Ap. 29.
13 heard the tidings. Fig. *Polyptōton.* Ap. 6. "Heard the hearing."
and. Fig. *Polysyndeton*, Ap. 6, for emphasis.
14 space of a month. Heb. a month of days, i. e., by Fig. *Hypallage* (Ap. 6), the days of a month. Cp. Num. 11. 20.
16 Leah. Heb. weary. **Rachel.** Heb. a ewe.
17 tender = weak.
beautiful = comely in form. Cp. 39. 6.
well favoured = comely in countenance.
20 served. Cp. Hos. 12. 12.
24 Zilpah. See on *v.* 29.
25 behold. Fig. *Asterismos.* Ap. 6. To call attention to the fact that he was deceived, as he had deceived Isaac (ch. 27).
27 we, i. e. I, by Fig. *Heterosis* (of Number). Ap. 6.
28 her, i. e. Leah's week.
he gave him Rachel. A popular mistake to suppose that Jacob did not marry Rachel till the end of the second seven years, for in the first seven were born seven sons: Reuben, Simeon, Levi, Judah, Dan, Naphtali, and Joseph. In the second seven: Gad, Asher, Issachar, Zebulon, and Dinah.
29 Bilhah. This was strictly in accordance with the Code of Khammurabi, § 145. See Ap. 15.
31 LORD. Jehovah used with the five sons (29. 31-35 and 30. 24). Elohim is used with six (30. 2, 6, 17, 18, 20, 23). No title used with Benjamin (35. 16-18). All were in pairs. Two pairs from Leah, one pair from Bilhah, one from Zilpah, one from Leah, one from Rachel.
hated. Fig. *Metonymy* (of Cause), Ap. 6, by which love and hate are put for the esteem or neglect, caused by love and hate = less loved, Deut. 21. 15. Matt. 6. 24. Luke 14. 26.
32 Reuben. Heb. *behold a son.* For the various orders of the 12 tribes, see Ap. 45.
33 heard. Heb. *shām'a* (heard).
Simeon. Heb. *Shimeʿōn* (hearing). Fig. *Paronomasia.* Ap. 6.
34 joined. Heb. *yillaveh* (joined).
was his name called. Heb. she called his name, with Sam. and Sept. Error due to neglected abbreviation in primitive Heb. text. Fig. *Paronomasia.* Ap. 6.
Levi. Heb. *Lēvī* (joiner).

1748 35 And she conceived again, and bare a son:
and she said, "Now will I °praise the [31] LORD:"
therefore she called his name Judah; and °left
bearing.

30 And when Rachel saw that she bare
Jacob no °children, Rachel envied her
sister; and said unto Jacob, "Give me °children,
or else I die."
2 And Jacob's anger was kindled against
Rachel: and he said, "*Am I* in °God's stead,
Who hath withheld from thee the fruit of the
womb?"
3 And she said, "Behold my maid °Bilhah,
go in unto her; and she shall bear upon my
knees, that I may also °have children by her."
4 And she gave him Bilhah her handmaid to
wife: and Jacob went in unto her.
5 And Bilhah conceived, and bare Jacob a
son.
1749 6 And Rachel said, "God hath °judged me,
and hath also heard my voice, and hath given
me a son:" therefore called she his name °Dan.
7 And Bilhah Rachel's maid conceived again,
and bare Jacob a second son.
1748 8 °And Rachel said, "With °great wrestlings have I wrestled with my sister, and I
have prevailed:" and she called his name
°Naphtali.
9 When Leah saw that she had left bearing,
she took °Zilpah her maid, and gave her Jacob
to °wife.
10 And Zilpah Leah's maid bare Jacob a son.
1747 11 And Leah said, °"A troop cometh:" and
she called his name °Gad.
12 And Zilpah Leah's maid bare Jacob a
second son.
1746 13 And Leah said, °"Happy am I, for the
daughters °will call me blessed:" and she
called his name °Asher.
14 And Reuben went in the days of wheat
harvest, and found °mandrakes in the field,
and brought them unto his mother Leah. Then
Rachel said to Leah, "Give me, I pray thee, of
thy son's mandrakes."
15 And she said unto her, "*Is it* a small
matter that thou hast taken my husband? and
wouldest thou take away my son's [14] mandrakes also?" And Rachel said, "Therefore
he shall lie with thee to night for thy son's
mandrakes."
16 And Jacob came out of the field in the
evening, and Leah went out to meet him, and
said, "Thou must come in unto me; for surely
I have hired thee with my son's [14] mandrakes."
And he lay with her that night.
17 And God hearkened unto Leah, and she
conceived, and bare Jacob the fifth son.
18 And Leah said, "God hath given me my
°hire, because I have given my maiden to
my husband:" and she called his name °Is-
sachar.
1745 19 And Leah conceived again, and bare Jacob
the sixth son.
20 And Leah said, "God hath endued me *with*
a good °dowry; now will my husband dwell
with me, because I have born him six sons:"
and she called his name °Zebulun.
21 And afterwards she bare a °daughter, and
called her name °Dinah.
22 And °God remembered Rachel, and God
hearkened to her, and opened her womb.
23 And she conceived, and bare a son; and
said, "God hath taken away my reproach:"
24 And she called his name °Joseph; and
said, °"The LORD °shall add to me another
son."
25 And it came to pass, when Rachel had i[2]
born Joseph, that Jacob said unto Laban, (p. 41)
"Send me away, that I may go unto mine own
place, and to my country.
26 Give *me* my wives and my children, for
whom I have served thee, and let me go: for
thou knowest my service which I have done
thee."
27 And Laban said unto him, "I pray thee, k[2]
if I have found favour in thine eyes, °*tarry:*
for I have learned by °experience that [24] the
LORD hath blessed me for thy sake."

35 praise. Heb. *'ōdeh* (I shall, or, Let me *praise*); *yehūdah* (he shall be praised). Cp. Gen. 49. 8. Fig. *Paronomasia*. Ap. 6.
left: i. e. for a time.

30 1 children. Heb. sons.
2 God's. See note on 29. 31.
3 Bilhah. This was strictly in accordance with the Code of Khammurabi, § 145. See Ap. 15. Cp. 29. 29.
have children. Heb. be builded up. See note above, and cp. 16. 1-3.
6 judged. Heb. *dānannī* (judged).
Dan. Heb. judge. Fig. *Paronomasia*. Ap. 6.
8 And. Fig. *Polysyndeton*, for emphasis. Ap. 6.
great wrestlings have I wrestled. Heb. with wrestlings of *El* (= GOD) i. e. mighty wrestlings. Fig. *Polyptōton*, and *Paronomasia*. Ap. 6.
Naphtali. Heb. my wrestling.
9 Zilpah . . . wife. This was strictly in accordance with the Code of Khammurabi, § 145. Cp. 16. 1-3; 30. 3, 4. See Ap. 15.
11 A troop. Heb. over-run, or, have victory; so the Sept., Syr., Arab., Onk., Vulg.
Gad = Jupiter (of the Babylonians). See Isa. 65. 11 marg., and Josh. 11. 17; 12. 7, where Baal-Gad = the God-Jupiter.
13 Happy. Heb. *be'āshrī* (happy).
will call, &c. Heb. *'ishshrūnī* (sure to call me).
Asher. Heb. *Asher* (happy). Cp. Deut. 33. 24. Fig. *Paronomasia*. Ap. 6.
14 mandrakes. Sept. *mandragora*, the root easily formed, by pinching it, into the shape of a man. Hence its name; also supposed to be and used as a "love-philtre". Arab. = "apples of Satan".
18 hire. Heb. *sekārī* (hire). Fig. *Paronomasia*. (Ap. 6), with Issachar.
Issachar. Heb. there is hire, or, he is wages.
20 dowry = God hath dowered me with a good dowry. Fig. *Polyptōton*. Ap. 6.
Zebulun. Heb. dwelling, or habitation. An Assyrian word, *to honour*, brought out of Ur.
21 daughter. Jacob may have had other daughters not named.
Dinah. Heb. prob. vindication, or, judgment.
22 God remembered. Fig. *Anthropopatheia*. Ap. 6.
22-24 Fig. *Hysterologia*, Ap. 6, for Joseph born after Naphtali, not after Dinah. This Fig. is used to keep Leah's children together.
24 Joseph. Heb. *yōsēph*, may He add.
The LORD. Note the occurrence of Jehovah here in connection with Joseph.
shall add. Heb. *yosēph*, is adding. Fig. *Paronomasia*. Ap. 6.
27 tarry: for. Fig. *Ellipsis*, Ap. 6. ii d, which requires some such supply.
experience = by divination. Heb. *niḥashtī*, from *naḥash* (Gen. 3. 1).

28 And he said, "Appoint me thy wages, and I will give *it*."

29 And he said unto him, "Thou knowest how I have served thee, and how thy cattle was with me.

30 For *it was* little which thou hadst before I *came*, and it is *now* increased unto a multitude; and [24]the LORD hath blessed thee since my coming: and now when shall I °provide for mine own °house also?"

1742 31 And he said, "What shall I give thee?" And Jacob said, "Thou shalt not give me any thing: if thou wilt do this thing for me, I will again feed *and* keep thy flock.

32 I will pass through all thy flock to day, removing from thence all the speckled and spotted cattle, and all the brown cattle among the sheep, and the spotted and speckled among the goats: and *of such* shall be my hire.

33 So shall my righteousness °answer for me °in time to come, when it shall come for my hire before thy face: every one that *is* not speckled and spotted among the goats, and brown among the sheep, that shall be counted stolen with me."

34 And Laban said, "Behold, I would it might be according to thy word."

35 And he removed that day the he goats that were ringstraked and spotted, and all the she goats that were speckled and spotted, *and* every one that had *some* white in it, and all the brown among the sheep, and gave *them* into the hand of his sons.

36 And he set three days' journey betwixt himself and Jacob: and Jacob fed the rest of Laban's flocks.

37 And Jacob took him rods of green poplar, and of the hazel and chesnut tree; and pilled white strakes in them, and made the white appear which *was* in the rods.

38 And he set the rods which he had pilled before the flocks in the gutters in the watering troughs when the flocks came to drink, that they should conceive when they came to drink.

39 And the flocks conceived before the rods, and brought forth cattle ringstraked, speckled, and spotted.

40 And Jacob did separate the lambs, and set the faces of the flocks toward the ringstraked, and all the brown in the flock of Laban; and he put his own flocks by themselves, and put them not unto Laban's cattle.

41 And it came to pass, whensoever the stronger cattle did conceive, that Jacob laid the rods before the eyes of the cattle in the gutters, that they might conceive among the rods.

42 But when the cattle were feeble, he put *them* not in: so the feebler were Laban's, and the stronger Jacob's.

43 And °the man increased °exceedingly, and had much cattle, and maidservants, and menservants, and camels, and asses.

31 And he heard the words of Laban's sons, saying, "Jacob hath taken away all that *was* our father's; and of *that* which *was* our father's hath he gotten all this °glory."

2 And Jacob beheld the countenance of Laban, and, °behold, it *was* not toward him °as before.

3 And °the LORD said unto Jacob, "Return unto the land of thy fathers, and to thy kindred; and I will be with thee."

4 And Jacob sent and called Rachel and Leah to the field unto his flock,

5 And said unto them, "I see your father's countenance, that it *is* not toward me as before; but the God of my father hath been with me.

6 And ye know that with all my power I have served °your father.

7 And your father hath deceived me, and changed my wages ten times; but God °suffered him not to °hurt me.

8 If he said thus, 'The speckled shall be thy wages;' then all the cattle bare speckled: and if he said thus, 'The ringstraked shall be thy hire;' then bare all the cattle ringstraked.

9 Thus God hath taken away the cattle of your father, and given *them* to me.

10 And it came to pass at the time that the cattle conceived, that I lifted up mine eyes, and saw in a dream, and, [2]behold, the rams which leaped upon the cattle *were* ringstraked, speckled, and grisled.

11 And the °angel of God spake unto me in a dream, *saying*, 'Jacob:' And I said, 'Here *am* I.'

12 And he said, 'Lift up now thine eyes, and see, all the rams which leap upon the °cattle *are* ringstraked, speckled, and grisled: for I have seen all that Laban doeth unto thee.

13 I *am* the °GOD of Beth-el, where thou anointedst the pillar, *and* where thou °vowedst a vow unto Me: now arise, get thee out from this land, and return unto the land of thy kindred.'"

14 And Rachel and Leah answered and said unto him, °"*Is there* yet any portion or inheritance for us in our father's house?

15 °Are we not counted of him strangers? for he hath sold us, and hath quite devoured also our money.

30 provide. Heb. the verb *to do*, which by *Metonymy* (of the Cause), Ap. 6, means to provide, or, do for.

house. Fig. *Metonymy* (of Subject), Ap. 6, by which "house" is put for all who dwell in it.

33 answer. By the Fig. *Prosopopœia*, Ap. 6, righteousness is personified.

in time to come. Heb. *to-morrow*. Fig. *Antimereia* (of Adverb), Ap. 6 = some future day.

43 the man. Heb. *ha-'ish*. Ap. 14. ii.

exceedingly. Heb. *m^eōd m^eōd* = greatly greatly. Fig. *Epizeuxis*. Ap. 6.

31. 1 glory. Heb. weight. Fig. *Metonymy* (of Effect), Ap. 6 = wealth, the effect (i. e. the burden or weight) being put for that which caused it.

2 behold. Fig. *Asterismos*. Ap. 6.

as before. Heb. yesterday and the day before. Fig. *Synecdoche* (of the Part), Ap. 6 = aforetime.

3 the LORD = Jehovah (Ap. 4).

6 your father: repeated at beginning of next verse by the Fig. *Anadiplosis*. Ap. 6.

7 suffered him not. Fig. *Idioma*. Ap. 6. Heb. did not give him to do me evil.

hurt. Heb. *rā'a'*. See Ap. 44. viii.

11 angel of God (Heb. *Elohim*). In *v.* 13 called by Himself, "I am the God of Beth-el", El of Beth-el. Cp. 28. 12, 13, and 48. 16.

12 cattle. Cp. Ps. 50. 10.

13 GOD. Heb. *'El*. See Ap. 4.

vowedst a vow. Fig. *Polyptōton*, Ap. 6 = madest a solemn vow.

14 Is there yet, &c.? Fig. *Erotēsis*. Ap. 6.

15 Are we not, &c.? Fig. *Erotēsis*. Ap. 6.

16 For all the riches which God hath taken
from our father, that *is* ours, and our children's: now then, whatsoever God hath said
unto thee, do."

i³ 17 Then Jacob rose up, and set his sons and
(p. 41) his wives upon camels;
18 And he carried away all his cattle, and all
his goods which he had gotten, the cattle of
his getting, which he had gotten in Padan-
aram, for to go to Isaac his father in the land
of Canaan.
19 And Laban went to shear his sheep: and
Rachel had stolen the °images that *were* her
father's.
20 And Jacob stole away °unawares to Laban
the Syrian, in that he told him not that he fled.
1739 21 So he fled with all that he had; and he
rose up, and passed over °the river, and set
his face *toward* the mount °Gilead.
22 And it was told Laban on the third day
that Jacob was fled.
23 And he took his °brethren with him, and
pursued after him seven days' journey; and
they overtook him in the mount Gilead.
24 And God came to Laban the Syrian in a
dream by night, and said unto him, "Take
heed that thou speak not to Jacob either °good
or bad."
25 Then Laban overtook Jacob. Now Jacob
had pitched his tent in the mount: and Laban
with his brethren pitched in the mount of
Gilead.
26 And Laban said to Jacob, °"What hast
thou done, that thou hast stolen away [20]un-
awares to me, and carried away my daughters,
as captives *taken* with the sword?
27 °Wherefore didst thou flee away secretly,
and steal away from me; and didst not tell me,
that I might have sent thee away °with mirth,
and with songs, with tabret, and with harp?
28 And hast not suffered me to kiss my
°sons and my daughters? thou hast now done
foolishly in *so* doing.
29 It is in the power of my °hand to do °you
hurt: but the °God of °your father spake unto
me yesternight, saying, 'Take thou heed that
thou speak not to Jacob either good or bad.'
30 And now, *though* thou wouldest needs
be gone, because thou °sore longedst after thy
father's house, *yet* wherefore hast thou stolen
°my gods?"
31 And Jacob answered and said to Laban,
"Because I was afraid: for I said, Peradventure thou wouldest take by force thy daughters
from me.
32 With whomsoever thou findest thy gods,
°let him not live: before our brethren discern
thou what *is* thine with me, and take *it* to
thee." For Jacob knew not that Rachel had
stolen them.
33 And Laban went into Jacob's tent, and
into Leah's tent, and into the two maidservants' tents; but he found *them* not. Then
went he out of Leah's tent, and entered into
°Rachel's tent.
34 Now °Rachel had taken the [19]images, and
put them in the camel's °furniture, and sat
upon them. And Laban °searched all the tent,
but found *them* not.
35 And she said to her father, "Let it not
displease °my lord that I cannot rise up before
thee; for the °custom of women *is* upon me."
And he searched, but found not the [19]images.
36 And Jacob was wroth, and chode with
Laban: and Jacob answered and said to
Laban, "What *is* my trespass? what *is* my
sin, that thou hast so hotly pursued after me?
37 Whereas thou hast [34]searched all my stuff,
what hast thou found of all thy household
stuff? set *it* here before my brethren and thy
brethren, that they may judge betwixt us both.
38 This °twenty years *have* I *been* with
thee; thy ewes and thy she goats have not
cast their young, and the rams of thy flock
have I not eaten.
39 That which was torn of *beasts* I brought
not unto thee; I bare the loss of it; of °my
hand didst thou require it, *whether* stolen by
day, or stolen by night.
40 °*Thus* I was; in the day the °drought
consumed me, and the frost by night; and
°my sleep departed from mine eyes.

19 images. Heb. *teraphīm*, a kind of household gods, showing that the idolatry of Babylonia still clung to Laban's family, in spite of his protestations in *v.* 29; 30. 27. Cp. *v.* 30; 35. 2.

20 unawares to Laban. Heb. stole the heart. Fig. *Synecdoche* (of the Part), Ap. 6, heart being put for knowledge. Cp. *v.* 27. Rachel stole Laban's idols; and Jacob stole Laban's heart.

21 the river=the Euphrates. Fig. *Synecdoche* (of the Genus). Ap. 6.

Gilead = perpetual fountain. Cp. Num. 32. 1, 39. Deut. 3. 12-16; 34. 1.

23 brethren. Fig. *Synecdoche* (of Species), Ap. 6, one relationship put for a general one.

24 good or bad. Heb. from good to bad.

26 What . . .? Figs. *Erotēsis* and *Aganactēsis.* Ap. 6.

27 Wherefore . . .? Fig. *Erotēsis* (of Expostulation). Ap. 6.

with mirth. Laban adds hypocrisy, covetousness, and avarice, to idolatry.

28 sons. Fig. *Metonymy* (of Species), Ap. 6, sons put for grandsons, &c. Cp. *v.* 55.

29 hand. Fig. *Synecdoche* (of the Part), Ap. 6, hand put for the whole person, "in my power".

you and your are plural.

God of your father. In ch. 30. 27, 30, Laban had spoken of the LORD = Jehovah; now he has sunk so low as to say "your" God, and calls the *teraphim* "my gods".

30 sore longedst. Heb. with longing thou hast longed. Fig. *Polyptōton.* Ap. 6.

my gods. Cp. on *v.* 29.

32 let him not live. This was in strict accordance with the Code of Khammurabi (§ 9), but in contrast with the Mosaic law. See Ap. 15.

33, 34 Rachel. Repeated by the Fig. *Anadiplōsis.* Ap. 6. Heb. "tent of Rachel, and Rachel had taken."

furniture=saddle.

searched=felt [with his hands].

35 my lord. Heb. the eyes of my lord. Fig. *Prosopopœia.* Ap. 6.

custom. Laban's deceit begets deceit.

38 twenty. The No. of disappointed expectancy. See Ap. 10.

39 my hand. Fig. *Synecdoche* (of the Part), Ap. 6, hand put for "me". Cp. *v.* 29.

40 Thus I was. Fig. *Ellipsis* (Ap. 6)="Thus (wherever) I was".

drought=heat. Fig. *Metonymy* (of Effect), Ap. 6, effect put for the burning heat which caused it. Contrast with cold produced by the frost.

my sleep. The Eastern shepherd often away from home for weeks at a time.

41 Thus have I been [38]twenty years in thy house; I served thee fourteen years for thy two daughters, and six years for thy cattle: and thou hast changed my wages ten times.
42 Except the God of my father, the God of Abraham, and °the fear of Isaac, had been °with me, surely thou hadst sent me away now empty. God hath seen mine affliction and the labour of my hands, and rebuked *thee* yesternight."
43 And Laban answered and said unto Jacob, "*These* daughters *are* my daughters, and *these* children *are* my children, and *these* cattle *are* my cattle, and all that thou seest *is* mine: and what can I do this day unto these my daughters, or unto their children which they have born?
44 Now therefore come thou, let us °make a covenant, I and thou; and let it be for a witness between me and thee."
45 And Jacob took a stone, and set it up *for* a °pillar.
46 And Jacob said unto his brethren, "Gather stones;" and they took stones, and made an heap: and they did °eat there upon the heap.
47 And Laban called it °Jegar-sahadutha: but Jacob called it °Galeed.
48 And Laban said, "This heap *is* a witness between me and thee this day." Therefore was the name of it called Galeed;
49 And °Mizpah; for °he said, °"The LORD watch between me and thee, when we are °absent one from another.
50 If thou shalt afflict my daughters, or if thou shalt take *other* wives beside my daughters, no °man *is* with us; see, God *is* witness betwixt me and thee."
51 And Laban said to Jacob, °"Behold this heap, and °behold *this* °pillar, which I have cast betwixt me and thee;
52 This heap *be* witness, and *this* pillar *be* witness, that I will not pass over this heap to thee, and that thou shalt not pass over this heap and this pillar unto me, for harm.
53 The God of Abraham, and the God of Nahor, the God of their father, judge betwixt us." And Jacob sware by [42]the fear of his father Isaac.
54 Then Jacob °offered sacrifice upon the mount, and called his brethren to eat bread: and they did eat bread, and tarried all night in the mount.
55 And early in the morning Laban rose up, and kissed his °sons and his °daughters, and blessed them: and Laban departed, and returned unto his place.

h (p. 38) **32** And Jacob °went on his way, and the °angels of God met him.
2 And when Jacob saw them, he said, "This *is* God's °host:" and he called the name of that place °Mahanaim.

J f l (p. 46) 3 And Jacob sent messengers before him to Esau his brother unto the land of Seir, the country of Edom.
4 And he commanded them, saying, "Thus shall ye speak unto my lord Esau; 'Thy servant Jacob saith thus, 'I have sojourned with Laban, and stayed there until now:
5 And I have oxen, and asses, flocks, and menservants, and womenservants: and I have sent to tell my lord, that I may find grace in thy sight.'"

6 And the messengers returned to Jacob, saying, "We came to thy brother Esau, and also he cometh to meet thee, and four hundred men with him." m (p. 46) 1738

7 Then Jacob was greatly afraid °and distressed: and he divided the people that *was* with him, and the flocks, and herds, and the camels, into °two bands; o

42 the fear. Fig. *Metonymy* (of Adjunct), Ap. 6, fear put for the God Whom Jacob worshipped.
with me = on my side. Ps. 118. 6, 7.
44 make. Heb. cut (Cp. 15. 10, 18) = solemnize.
45 pillar. Cp. 28. 18.
46 eat: i. e. of the covenant sacrifices. Cp. 26. 30. Ex. 24. 5, 11.
47 Jegar-sahadutha. Chaldaic = witness-heap.
Galeed. Heb. same meaning.
49 Mizpah. Heb. watch-tower.
he, i. e. Laban. So that he knew Heb. as well as Chaldee.
the LORD. Laban also uses the name Jehovah. It is used by all the speakers in Gen. except the *Nachash* (ch. 3), Abimelech (when speaking to Abram, not to Isaac), the sons of Heth, Pharaoh, Joseph's brethren, and Joseph himself.
absent. Fig. *Metonymy* (of Adjunct), Ap. 6 = Heb. hidden, put for absent.
50 man. Heb. *'ish*. Ap. 14. ii.
51 Behold. Fig. *Asterismos*. Ap. 6.
pillar. Distinct from the "heap". Cp. *v.* 45, 46.
54 offered sacrifice = killed beasts. Fig. *Metonymy* (of Adjunct). Ap. 6. Cp. Ap. 43. I. iv.
55 sons. Fig. *Synecdoche* (of the Part). Ap. 6. Put for grandsons as well.
daughters. Also for granddaughters.

32. 1, 2. JACOB'S VISION AT MAHANAIM.

The second vision, corresponding with that of Bethel: see 28. 10-22. See the structure on p. 32.

1 went on his way. S. from Galeed and Mizpah.
angels of God. Cp. Ps. 34. 7, to assure him of God's presence with him, and of His protection.
2 host = camp. Heb. *mahăneh* as in *vv.* 8, 21. Cp. Deut. 33. 2. Josh. 5. 14, 15. Ps. 27. 3; 78. 28; 106. 16.
Mahanaim = two camps.

32. 3—33. 17 (*f*, p. 32). **THE RECONCILIATION OF ESAU** (*Introversion and Alternation*).

f | l | 32. 3-5. Reconciliation desired.
  m | 32. 6. Approach of Esau announced.
    n | o | 32. 7, 8. The Present resolved on.
        p | 32. 9-12. Prayer.
    n | *o* | 32. 13-23. The Present prepared.
        p | 32. 24-32. Prayer.
  m | 33. 1-. Approach of Esau seen.
l | 33. -1-17. Reconciliation effected.

7 In n and *n* (*vv.* 7-32) note that Jacob alternately uses means as though there were no such thing as prayer; and then prays as though there were no such things as means. We may *use* means, but not *trust* in them.
and. The Fig. *Polysyndeton* (Ap. 6) shows the care with which he prepared.
two bands = two camps. Same word (and perhaps idea) as in *v.* 2. See note.

8 And said, "If Esau come to the one ²company, and smite it, then the other ²company which is left shall escape."

p 9 And Jacob said, "O God of my father
(p. 46) Abraham, and God of my father Isaac, the LORD Which °saidst unto me, 'Return unto thy country, and to thy kindred, and I will deal well with thee:'

10 °I am not worthy of the least of all the °mercies, and of all the truth, which Thou hast shewed unto Thy servant; for with °my staff I passed over this Jordan; and now I am become two bands.

11 Deliver me, I pray Thee, from the hand of my brother, from the hand of Esau: for I fear him, lest he will come and smite me, *and* the mother °with the children.

12 And Thou °saidst, 'I will surely do thee good, and make thy seed °as the sand of the sea, which cannot be numbered for multitude.'"

o 13 And he lodged there that same night; and took of that which came to his hand a °present for Esau his brother;

14 Two hundred she goats, and twenty he goats, two hundred ewes, and twenty rams,

15 Thirty milch camels with their colts, forty kine, and ten bulls, twenty she asses, and ten foals.

16 And he delivered *them* into the hand of his servants, every drove by themselves; and said unto his servants, "Pass over before me, and put a space betwixt drove and drove."

17 And he commanded the foremost, saying, "When Esau my brother meeteth thee, and asketh thee, saying, 'Whose *art* thou? and whither goest thou? and whose *are* these before thee?'

18 Then thou shalt say, '*They be* thy servant Jacob's; it *is* a present sent unto my lord Esau: and, °behold, also he *is* behind us.'"

19 And so commanded he the second, and the third, and all that followed the droves, saying, "On this manner shall ye speak unto Esau, when ye find him.

20 And say ye moreover, ¹⁸'Behold, thy servant Jacob *is* behind us.'" For he said, "I °will appease him with the ¹³present that goeth before me, and afterward I will see his face; peradventure he will accept °of me."

21 So went the present over before him: and himself lodged that night in the ²company.

22 And he rose up that night, and took his two wives, and his two womenservants, and his eleven sons, and passed over the ford °Jabbok.

23 And he took them, and sent them over the brook, and sent over that he had.

p 24 And Jacob was left alone; and there wrestled °a Man with him until the °breaking of the day.

25 And when He saw that He prevailed not against him, He touched the hollow of his thigh; and the hollow of Jacob's thigh was out of joint, as He wrestled with him.

26 And He said, "Let Me go, for the °day breaketh." And he said, "I will not let Thee go, except Thou bless me."

27 And He said unto him, °"What *is* thy name?" And he said, "Jacob."

28 And He said, "Thy name shall be called no more °Jacob, but °Israel: for as a °prince °hast thou power with God and with °men, and hast °prevailed."

29 And Jacob asked *Him*, and said, "Tell *me*, I pray Thee, Thy name." And He said, "Wherefore *is* it *that* thou dost ask after My name?" And He blessed him there.

30 And Jacob called the name of the place °Peniel: "for I have °seen God face to face, and my °life is preserved."

9 Jacob's first prayer acknowledges both Elohim and Jehovah.

saidst. Cp. *v.* 12 and 31. 13.

10 I am not worthy. Heb. I have proved unworthy. Fig. *Heterosis* (of Tense), Ap. 6. =I have been and am unworthy.

mercies. Fig. *Metonymy* (of Cause). Ap. 6. First occ. of pl.

my staff. Having nothing and deserving nothing but chastisement. Hence, the God who met him there (the God of Bethel) is "the God of Jacob", and is "the God of all grace" (1 Pet. 5. 10): cp. Ps. 146. 5.

11 with. Heb. upon. As though sons slain first and mothers falling on them.

12 saidst. Cp. *v.* 9 and 28. 13-15.

as the sand. Fig. *Parœmia.* Ap. 6. See note on 13. 16.

13 present. See Ap. 43. II, iii.

18 behold. Fig. *Asterismos.* Ap. 6.

20 will appease him. Heb. "cover his face", i. e. hide my offence from him: "face" being put by *Synecdoche* (of the Part), Ap. 6, for himself.

of me. Heb. my face. *Synecdoche* (of the Part), Ap. 6.

22 Jabbok. Heb. pouring out, or emptying.

24 a Man. Heb. *'ish.* Ap. 14. ii. Called "God" (*vv.* 28, 30), an "Angel", and Jehovah Elohim, Hos. 12. 4, 5.

breaking. Heb. going up. Fig. *Antimereia* (of Verb Part. for noun). Ap. 6.

26 day breaketh. Heb. dawn hath ascended.

27 What is thy name? Fig. *Anthropopatheia.* Ap. 6. For He knew his name.

28 Jacob = contender (25. 22). Used of the natural Jacob and his natural seed. Israel used for spiritual Jacob and his spiritual seed.

Israel = "God commands, orders or rules". Man attempts it but always, in the end, fails. Out of some forty Hebrew names compounded with "El" or "Jah", God is always the doer of what the verb means (cp. *Dani*-el, God judges).

prince = commander, orderer. Here used not to dignify but to reproach. Cp. Gen. 12. 15, princes (courtiers); 26. 26, chief of soldiers; 39. 1, officer; 40. 2, chief; 3, jailor; 47. 6, herdsmen; Ex. 1. 11, taskmasters, &c.

hast thou power = hast thou contended. Jacob had contended with Esau in the womb, and thus got his name Jacob, which is referred to here in reproach, not in eulogy.

men. Heb. pl. of *'ish,* or *'ĕnōsh.* Ap. 14.

prevailed = succeeded. He had contended for the birthright and succeeded (25. 29-34). He had contended for the blessing and succeeded (27). He had contended with Laban and succeeded (31). He had contended with "men" and succeeded. Now he contends with God—and fails. Hence his name was changed to Isra-el, *God commands,* to teach him the greatly needed lesson of dependence upon God.

30 Peniel = Heb. God's face.

seen. Cp. 16. 13.

life = soul. Heb. *nephesh.* See Ap. 13.

31 And as he passed over Penuel the sun rose upon him, and ° He ° halted upon his thigh.

32 Therefore the children of Israel eat not *of* the sinew which shrank, which *is* upon the hollow of the thigh, unto this day: because He touched the hollow of Jacob's thigh in the ° sinew that shrank.

m (p. 46) **33** And Jacob lifted up his eyes, and looked, and, behold, Esau came, and with him four hundred ° men.

l And he divided the children unto Leah, and unto Rachel, and unto the two handmaids.

2 And he put the handmaids and their children foremost, and Leah and her children after, and Rachel and Joseph hindermost.

3 And He passed over before them, and bowed himself to the ground seven times, until he came near to his brother.

4 And Esau ran to meet him, and embraced him, and fell on his neck, ° and kissed him: and they wept.

5 And he lifted up his eyes, and saw the women and the children; and said, "Who *are* those with thee?" And he said, "The children which God hath graciously given thy servant."

6 Then the handmaidens came near, they and their children, and they bowed themselves.

7 And Leah also with her children came near, and bowed themselves: and after came Joseph near and Rachel, and they bowed themselves.

8 And he said, "What *meanest* thou by all this drove which I met?" And he said, "*These are* to find grace in the sight of my lord."

9 And Esau said, "I have ° enough, my brother; keep that thou hast unto thyself."

10 And ° Jacob ° said, "Nay, I pray thee, if now I have found grace in thy sight, then receive my present at my hand: for therefore I have seen thy face, as though I had seen the face of God, and thou wast pleased with me.

11 Take, I pray thee, my blessing that is brought to thee; because God hath dealt graciously with me, and because I have ⁹ enough." And he urged him, and he took *it*.

12 And he said, "Let us take our journey, and let us go, and I will go before thee."

13 And he said unto him, "My lord knoweth that the children *are* tender, and the flocks and herds with young *are* with me: and if ° men should overdrive them one day, all the flock will die.

14 Let my lord, I pray thee, pass over before his servant: and I will lead on softly, according as the cattle that goeth before me and the children be able to endure, until I come unto my lord unto Seir."

15 And Esau said, "Let me now leave with thee *some* of the folk that *are* with me." And he said, ° "What needeth it? let me find grace in the sight of my lord."

16 So Esau returned that day on his way unto Seir.

1737 17 And Jacob journeyed to Succoth, and built him an ° house, and made ° booths for his cattle: therefore the name of the place is called Succoth.

J e (p. 38) 18 And Jacob ° came to Shalem, a city of Shechem, which *is* in the land of Canaan, when he came from Padan-aram; and pitched his tent before the city.

1736 19 And he bought a parcel of a field, where he had spread his tent, at the hand of the children of ° Hamor, Shechem's father, for an hundred pieces of money.

20 And he erected there an altar, and called it ° El-elohe-Israel.

1732 **34** And Dinah the ° daughter of Leah, which she bare unto Jacob, went out to see the daughters of the land.

2 And when Shechem the son of Hamor the Hivite, prince of the country, saw her, he took her, and lay with her, and ° defiled her.

3 And ° his soul clave unto Dinah the daughter of Jacob, and he loved the damsel, and spake ° kindly unto the damsel.

4 And Shechem spake unto his father Hamor, saying, "Get me this damsel to wife."

5 And Jacob heard that he had defiled Dinah his daughter: now his sons were with his cattle in the field: and Jacob held his peace until they were come.

---

31 he. Emph. to call attention to the fact that he was not only late, but limping.

halted = limped. The sign that it is God who commands, and has real power to overcome. Typical of the national humiliation required before entering on the blessing.

32 sinew = the ligament of the hip joint.

33. 1 men = Heb. sing. *'īsh* (Ap. 14), as we use the expression "400 foot". When pl., used only of angels.

4 and kissed him. This is one of the Heb. words with "extraordinary points", to show that the Massorites thought it should be omitted. See Ap. 31. It should read, "and fell on his neck and wept"; without kissing. This is the custom in Genesis. Cp. 45. 14; 46. 29.

9 enough = abundance, plenty.

10 Jacob said. Fig. *Ellipsis* (Ap. 6. ii b). Ellipsis should be supplied thus: "Jacob [refused, and] said.

13 men. Sam. and Sept. read "I".

15 What needeth it? Heb. What for? or Why so? Fig. *Erotēsis* and *Ellipsis* (Ap. 6) = Why [have] anything?

17 house. The first we read of a house in connection with the Patriarchs.

booths. Heb. *succoth.* Hence the name. First occ.

18 came to Shalem, a city of Shechem: read, came in peace to the city of Shechem; the Heb. *Shalem* means peace.

19 Hamor. Probably a title, like Abimelech and Pharaoh.

20 El-elohe-Israel—"GOD—the God-of-Israel", but not the place for this altar. Cp. 35. 1.

34. 1—37. 36. JACOB'S TROUBLE IN THE LAND.

At Shechem, Dinah's disgrace, 34. Three burials: Deborah, 35. 8; Rachel (*v.* 20); and Isaac (35. 29). Joseph sold, 37.

34. 1 daughter of Leah. Cp. 30. 21, and own sister of Simeon and Levi, 29. 33, 34.

2 defiled. Heb. humbled.

3 his soul = himself. Fig. *Synecdoche* (of Part). Ap. 6. Heb. *nephesh.*

kindly. Heb. on her heart (as though making an impression on it).

6 And Hamor the father of Shechem went out unto Jacob to commune with him.

7 And the sons of [1]Jacob came out of the field when they heard *it:* and the °men were grieved, and they were very wroth, because he had wrought folly in °Israel in lying with Jacob's daughter; which thing ought not to be done.

8 And Hamor communed with them, saying, "The °soul of my son Shechem longeth for your daughter: I pray you give her him to wife.

9 And make ye marriages with us, *and* give your daughters unto us, and take our daughters unto you.

10 And ye shall dwell with us: and the land shall be before you; dwell and trade ye therein, and get you possessions therein."

11 And Shechem said unto her father and unto her brethren, "Let me find grace in your eyes, and what ye shall say unto me I will give.

12 Ask me never so much dowry and °gift, and I will give according as ye shall say unto me: but give me the damsel to wife."

13 And the sons of Jacob answered Shechem and Hamor his father °deceitfully, and said, because he had defiled Dinah their sister:

14 And they said unto them, "We cannot do this thing, to give our sister to one that is uncircumcised; for that *were* a reproach unto us:

15 But in this will we consent unto you: If ye will be as we *be,* that every male of you be circumcised;

16 Then will we give our daughters unto you, and we will take your daughters to us, and we will dwell with you, and we will become one people.

17 But if ye will not hearken unto us, to be circumcised; then will we take our daughter, and we will be gone."

18 And their words pleased Hamor, and Shechem Hamor's son.

19 And the young man deferred not to do the thing, because he had delight in Jacob's daughter: and he *was* more honourable than all the house of his father.

20 And Hamor and Shechem his son came unto the gate of their city, and communed with the [7]men of their city, saying,

21 "These [7]men *are* peaceable with us; therefore let them dwell in the land, and trade therein; for the land, °behold, *it is* large enough for them; let us take their daughters to us for wives, and let us give them our daughters.

22 Only herein will the [7]men consent unto us for to dwell with us, to be one people, if every male among us be circumcised, as they *are* circumcised.

23 °*Shall* not their cattle and their substance and every beast of theirs *be* ours? only let us consent unto them, and they will dwell with us."

24 And unto Hamor and unto Shechem his son hearkened all that went out of the gate of his city; and every male was circumcised, all that went out of the gate of his city.

25 And it came to pass on the third day, when they were sore, that two of the sons of Jacob, Simeon and Levi, Dinah's brethren, took each °man his sword, and came upon the city boldly, and slew all the males.

7 men. Heb. pl. of *'ish* or *'ĕnōsh.* See Ap. 14. iii.
Israel. The first occ. in a collective sense.
8 soul. Heb. *nephesh.* Ap. 13. Fig. *Synecdoche* (of Part) and *Pleonasm* (Ap. 6), to emphasise the intensity of the longing.
12 gift. The noun put by *Metonymy* for the verb = ask me to give, &c. See Ap. 6.
13 deceitfully. Jacob's character his own scourge. The first and only occ. in Gen.
21 behold. Fig. *Asterismos.* Ap. 6.
23 Shall not, &c. Fig. *Erotēsis.* Ap. 6.
25 man. Heb. *'ish.* See Ap. 14. ii.
26 edge. Heb. mouth. Fig. *Pleonasm.* Ap. 6.
The acts of Jacob and his sons at Shechem may be contrasted with those of Abraham (12. 6), and of Joshua (Josh. 24. 1–27), and of Christ (John 4. 5).
27 The sons. Some MSS. read "And the sons".
28 and. Note the Fig. *Polysyndeton,* Ap. 6, to emphasise each item, in *vv.* 28, 29.
29 wealth. Heb. strength. Fig. *Metonymy* (of Adjunct). Ap. 6. Strength put for the wealth which it acquires.
30 Canaanites. Descendants of the *Nephilim.* See 12. 6 and Ap. 23 and 25.
I . . . I. Fig. *Repetitio,* Ap. 6, to emphasise Jacob's perturbation.
31 Should he . . . ? Fig. *Erotēsis.* Ap. 6.
35. 1 God. Heb. *Elohim.* Ap. 4.
Jacob. See notes on 32. 28; 43. 8; 45. 26, 28.
Beth-el. House of GOD. Heb. *El.* Ap. 4 (28. 19).
when. Cp. 27. 43.
2 Put away. Purification necessary in going up to Beth-el = the house of God.
strange gods. Doubtless part of the spoils taken from the houses of the Shechemites. Cp. *v.* 4, and see 34. 28, 29. **and.** Fig. *Polysyndeton.* Ap. 6.
be clean. First occ. Here and always used of ceremonial cleansing.
3 with me. Cp. 28. 20; 31. 3, 42.

26 And they slew Hamor and Shechem his son with the °edge of the sword, and took Dinah out of Shechem's house, and went out.

27 °The sons of [1]Jacob came upon the slain, and spoiled the city, because they had defiled their sister.

28 They took their sheep, °and their oxen, and their asses, and that which *was* in the city, and that which *was* in the field,

29 And all their °wealth, and all their little ones, and their wives took they captive, and spoiled even all that *was* in the house.

30 And [1]Jacob said to Simeon and Levi, "Ye have troubled me to make me to stink among the inhabitants of the land, among the °Canaanites and the Perizzites: and I *being* few in number, they shall gather themselves together against me, and slay me; and °I shall be destroyed, °I and my house."

31 And they said, °"Should he deal with our sister as with an harlot?"

35 And °God said unto °Jacob, "Arise, go up to °Beth-el, and dwell there: and make there an altar unto °GOD, That appeared unto thee °when thou fleddest from the face of Esau thy brother." K (p. 38) 1731

2 Then Jacob said unto his household, and to all that *were* with him, °"Put away the °strange gods that *are* among you, °and °be clean, °and change your garments:

3 And let us arise, and go up to Beth-el; and I will make there an altar unto GOD, Who answered me in the day of my distress, and was °with me in the way which I went."

4 And they gave unto °Jacob all the [2]strange
gods which *were* in their hand, and *all their*
°earrings which *were* in their ears; and °Jacob
hid them under the oak which *was* by Shechem.

5 And they journeyed: and the terror of °God
was upon the cities that *were* round about
them, and they did not pursue after the sons
of Jacob.

6 So [1]Jacob came to °Luz, which *is* in the
land of Canaan, that *is*, Beth-el, he and all the
people that *were* with him.

7 And he built there an altar, and called the
place °El-Beth-el: because there [5]God °appeared
unto him, when he fled from the face
of °his brother.

8 But °Deborah Rebekah's nurse died, and she
was buried beneath Beth-el under an oak: and
the name of it was called °Allon-bachuth.

9 And [5]God appeared unto [1]Jacob again, when
he came out of Padan-aram, and blessed him.

10 And [5]God said unto him, "Thy name *is*
[1]Jacob: thy name shall not be called any more
Jacob, but °Israel shall be thy name:" and He
called his name °Israel.

11 And [5]God said unto him, "I *am* °GOD
ALMIGHTY: be fruitful and multiply; a nation
and a company of nations shall be of thee, and
°kings shall come out of thy loins;

12 And the land which °I gave Abraham and
Isaac, to thee I will give it, and to thy seed
after thee will I give the land."

13 And [5]God °went up from him in the place
where °He talked with him.

14 And [1]Jacob °set up a pillar in the place
where He talked with him, *even* a pillar of
stone: and he °poured a drink offering thereon,
and he poured oil thereon.

15 And [1]Jacob called the name of the place
where [5]God spake with him, Beth-el.

B a (p. 36) 16 And they journeyed from Beth-el; and
there was but a little way to come to °Ephrath:
and Rachel travailed, and she had hard
labour.

17 And it came to pass, when she was in hard
labour, that the midwife said unto her, "Fear
not; thou shalt have this son also."

18 And it came to pass, as °her soul was °in
departing, (for she died) that she called his
name °Ben-oni: but his father called him
°Benjamin.

1728 19 And Rachel died, and was buried in the
way to Ephrath, which *is* °Beth-lehem.

20 And [1]Jacob [14]set a pillar upon her °grave:
that *is* the pillar of Rachel's grave °unto this day.

b 21 And [10]Israel journeyed, and spread his tent
beyond the tower of Edar.

1728 22 And it came to pass, when [10]Israel dwelt
in that land, that Reuben went and °lay
with Bilhah his father's concubine: and Israel
heard *it*.

Now the sons of Jacob were °twelve:

23 The sons of Leah; Reuben, Jacob's firstborn,
and Simeon, and Levi, and Judah, and
Issachar, and Zebulun:

24 The sons of Rachel; Joseph, and Benjamin:

25 And the sons of Bilhah, Rachel's handmaid;
Dan, and Naphtali:

26 And the sons of Zilpah, Leah's handmaid;
Gad, and Asher: these *are* the sons
of Jacob, which were born to him in Padan-aram.

27 And [1]Jacob °came unto Isaac his father unto A (p. 36)
Mamre, unto the city of Arbah, which *is* Hebron,
where Abraham and Isaac sojourned. 1726

28 And the days of Isaac were an hundred
and fourscore years.

29 And Isaac gave up the ghost, °and died,
and °was gathered unto his people, *being* old

4 Jacob = Supplanter, or Contender. See on 32. 28; 43. 8; 45. 26, 28.
earrings. Showing that the "strange gods" were part of the booty: probably of precious metals.
5 God. Heb. *Elohim*. Ap. 4.
6 Luz. Cp. 28. 19.
7 El-Beth-el = GOD of the House of GOD.
appeared: or revealed Himself.
his brother. Some MSS., with Sam., Jon., Sept., Syr., read "Esau his brother".
8 Deborah Rebekah's nurse. We hear no more of Rebekah from the time Jacob left home (27. 45), not even of her death! Deborah may have come with a message, or she may, on Rebekah's death, have joined his household.
Allon-bachuth. Heb. The oak of weeping.
10 Israel = GOD rules. See note on 32. 28.
11 GOD ALMIGHTY = Heb. *El-Shaddai*, GOD—the all-bountiful or all-sufficient. The title which best accords with the promise here given. Cp. 15. 1.
kings. Fig. *Metonymy* (of Effect). Ap. 6.
12 I gave. Fig. *Metonymy* (of Subject). Ap. 6. = which I promised to give.
13 went up . . . talked. Fig. *Anthropopatheia*. Ap. 6.
He. i. e. God.
14 set up a pillar = Heb. pillared a pillar. Fig. *Polyptōton*. Ap. 6.
poured a drink offering. See Ap. 15. First occurrence of "drink offering": afterward provided for in Lev. 23. 13, 18, 37, and in Num. 15, 5-10. Always "poured out," never drunk. **16 Ephrath.** Heb. fertility.
18 her soul = her life. Heb. *nephesh* (Ap. 13), rendered "life" in 1. 20, 30; 9. 4, 5; 19. 17, 19; 32. 30; 44. 30.
in departing = ebbing away, or failing (42. 28. Song 5. 6); or ending (Ex. 23. 16). In Ezek. 7. 10 rendered "gone forth"; Ex. 23. 26. In Ezek. 26. 18 rendered "departure". **Ben-oni** = Son of my sorrow.
Benjamin = Son of my right hand. The word rendered "sorrow" (*'āvon*) is a *Homonym*, the other meaning being "strength", and is so rendered in Gen. 49. 3. Deut. 21. 17. Job 18. 7, 12 &c. It is rendered "mourning" in Deut. 26. 14. Hos. 9. 4. This *Homonym* is the basis of Jacob's change of Benjamin's name. The A.V. and R.V. both recognize this *Homonym*.
19 Beth-lehem = House of bread.
20 grave. Heb. *ḳeber*, first occ. 23. 4. = A sepulchre, from *ḳabar* to bury. Not *sheol*, which = THE grave. Cp. Ap. 35.
unto this day. Well-known in the days of Samuel. See 1 Sam. 10. 2. **22 lay with.** Cp. 49. 4.
twelve. The number of governmental perfection. See Ap. 10. Fig. *Synecdoche* (of the Whole), Ap. 6. For the various orders of the twelve tribes, see Ap. 45.

27-29 (*A*, p. 36). **The Death of Isaac.**

27 came. It does not follow that Jacob did not often see Isaac. As soon as Isaac was married, Abraham disappears from the history. It is the same with Isaac when Jacob married: and the same with Jacob when Joseph comes into prominence. They do not appear together in the history: but Abraham is described as "dwelling in tabernacles *with Isaac and Jacob*" (Heb. 11. 9).
29 and died. Fig. *Synonymia*, Ap. 6, for great emphasis. They all mean the same thing, repeated in other words, to add solemnity to the event.
was gathered. See note on 49. 33. 2 Sam. 12. 23.

and full of days: and his sons Esau and Jacob
buried him.

G A (p. 51) **36** Now these *are* THE °GENERATIONS OF ESAU, who *is* Edom.

B a 2 Esau took his wives of the daughters of Canaan; °Adah the daughter of Elon the Hittite,
b and °Aholibamah the daughter of Anah the °daughter of Zibeon the Hivite;
c 3 And °Bashemath Ishmael's daughter, sister of Nebajoth.
B a 4 And Adah bare to Esau Eliphaz;
c and Bashemath bare Reuel;
b 5 And Aholibamah bare Jeush, and Jaalam, and Korah: these *are* the sons of Esau, which were born unto him in the land of Canaan.
A 6 And Esau took his wives, °and his sons, and his daughters, and all the °persons of his house, and his cattle, and all his beasts, and all his substance, which he had got in the land of °Canaan; and went into the country from the face of his brother °Jacob.
7 For their riches were more than that they might dwell together; and the land wherein they were strangers could not bear them because of their cattle.
8 Thus dwelt Esau in mount Seir: °Esau *is* Edom.

H A 9 °And these *are* THE GENERATIONS OF ESAU the father of the Edomites IN MOUNT SEIR:
B a^1 10 These *are* the names of Esau's sons; Eliphaz the son of Adah the wife of Esau,
b^1 Reuel the son of Bashemath the wife of Esau.
a^2 11 And the sons of Eliphaz were °Teman, Omar, Zepho, and Gatam, and Kenaz.
12 And Timna was concubine to Eliphaz Esau's son; and she bare to Eliphaz °Amalek: these *were* the °sons of Adah Esau's wife.
b^2 13 And these *are* the sons of Reuel; Nahath, and Zerah, Shammah, and Mizzah: these were the sons of Bashemath Esau's wife.
C 14 And these were the sons of Aholibamah, the daughter of Anah the ²daughter of Zibeon, Esau's wife: and she bare to Esau Jeush, and Jaalam, and Korah.
B a^3 15 These *were* °dukes of the sons of Esau: the sons of Eliphaz the firstborn *son* of Esau; duke Teman, duke Omar, duke Zepho, duke Kenaz,
16 Duke Korah, duke Gatam, *and* duke Amalek: these *are* the dukes *that came* of Eliphaz in the land of Edom; these *were* the sons of Adah.
b^3 17 And these *are* the sons of Reuel Esau's son; duke Nahath, duke Zerah, duke Shammah, duke Mizzah: these *are* the dukes *that came* of Reuel in the land of Edom; these *are* the sons of Bashemath Esau's wife.
C 18 And these *are* the sons of Aholibamah Esau's wife; duke Jeush, duke Jaalam, duke Korah: these *were* the dukes *that came* of Aholibamah the daughter of Anah, Esau's wife.
19 These *are* the sons of Esau, who *is* Edom, and these *are* their dukes.
20 These *are* the sons of Seir the Horite, °who inhabited the land; Lotan, and Shobal, and Zibeon, and Anah,
21 And Dishon, and Ezer, and Dishan: these *are* the dukes of the Horites, the children of Seir in the land of Edom.
22 And the °children of Lotan were Hori and Hemam; and Lotan's sister *was* °Timna.
23 And the children of Shobal *were* these; Alvan, and Manahath, and Ebal, Shepho, and Onam.
24 And these *are* the children of Zibeon; °both Ajah, and Anah: this *was that* Anah

---

36. 1-8 (*G*, p. 1). THE GENERATIONS OF ESAU (IN CANAAN).
(*Introversion and Extended Alternation.*)

G A | 1. Esau. In Canaan.
B | a | 2-. Adah.
b | -2. Aholibamah.
c | 3. Bashemath.
B | *a* | 4-. Adah's son, Eliphaz.
c | -4. Bashemath's son, Reuel.
b | 5. Aholibamah's sons, Jeush, &c.
A | 6-8 Esau. Removal from Canaan.

1 generations. Given here, as no more is to be said about him.
2 Adah. Her second name was Bashemath, 26. 34.
Aholibamah. Her second name was Judith, 26. 34; and her father, Anah, got a second name also from his discovery of the hot springs (see note on "mules", 36. 24). In 26. 34, called Hittite, because Hittite included Hivite.
daughter. Sam., Sept., and Syr. read "son".
3 Bashemath also had a second name, Mahalath, 28. 9.
6 and. Note the Fig. *Polysyndeton*, Ap. 6, pointing with emphasis to each item.
persons = souls, Heb. *nephesh.* Ap. 13.
Canaan. Esau's sons, born in the land went out of it. Jacob's sons, all born out of it and went into it.
Jacob. "Unto Seir" should be added, according to Gb. Heb. Text.
8 Esau is Edom. Should be "Esau, he is Edom".
9 And these. See p. 45.

36. 9-43 (*H*, p. 1). THE GENERATIONS OF ESAU (IN MOUNT SEIR).
(*Introversion and Repeated Alternation.*)

H A | 9. Sons of Esau (Edom).
B | a^1 | 10-. Eliphaz, Adah's son.
b^1 | -10. Reuel, Bashemath's son.
a^2 | 11, 12. Sons of Eliphaz.
b^2 | 13. Sons of Reuel.
C | 14. Jeush, &c., Aholibamah's sons.
B | a^3 | 15, 16. Dukes of Eliphaz (Adah).
b^3 | 17. Dukes of Reuel (Bashemath).
C | 18. Dukes of Jeush (Aholibamah).
A | 20-43. Dukes of Edom, &c.

11 Teman. Whence came Eliphaz the Temanite. Job 2. 11; 15. 1.
12 Amalek. One of Israel's bitterest foes, with whom Jehovah has perpetual war, Ex. 17. 8, 14. Cp. Num. 24. 20. Deut. 25. 17-19. The land of A. so-called by Fig. *Prolepsis* (Ap. 6.), in Gen. 14. 7.
sons. The "sons" of Adah are her son and grandsons.
15 dukes. Heb. chiefs, or, chieftains.
20 who inhabited, &c. The Horites were a branch of the *Nephīlīm.* See Ap. 23 and 25.
22 children = sons.
Timna. Cp. *v.* 12.
24 both. Some codices, with Sam., Sept., and Syr., omit "both".

that °found the °mules in the wilderness, as he fed the asses of Zibeon his father.

25 And the children of Anah *were* these; Dishon, and Aholibamah the daughter of Anah.

26 And these *are* the children of Dishon; Hemdan, and Eshban, and Ithran, and Cheran.

27 The children of Ezer *are* these; Bilhan, and Zaavan, and Akan.

28 The children of Dishan *are* these; Uz, and Aran.

29 These *are* the dukes *that came* of the Horites; duke Lotan, duke Shobal, duke Zibeon, duke Anah,

30 Duke Dishon, duke Ezer, duke Dishan: these *are* the dukes *that came* of Hori, among their dukes in the land of Seir.

31 And these *are* the kings that reigned in the land of Edom, °before there reigned any king over the children of Israel.

32 And Bela the son of Beor reigned in Edom: and the name of his city *was* Dinhabah.

33 And Bela died, and Jobab the son of Zerah of Bozrah reigned in his stead.

34 And Jobab died, and Husham of the land of Temani reigned in his stead.

35 And Husham died, and Hadad the son of Bedad, who smote Midian in the field of Moab, reigned in his stead: and the name of his city *was* Avith.

36 And Hadad died, and Samlah of Masrekah reigned in his stead.

37 And Samlah died, and Saul of Rehoboth *by* °the river reigned in his stead.

38 And Saul died, and Baal-hanan the son of Achbor reigned in his stead.

39 And Baal-hanan the son of Achbor died, and Hadar reigned in his stead: and the name of his city *was* Pau; and his wife's name *was* Mehetabel, the daughter of Matred, the daughter of Mezahab.

40 And these *are* the names of the dukes *that came* of Esau, according to their families, after their places, by their names; duke Timnah, duke Alvah, duke Jetheth,

41 Duke Aholibamah, duke Elah, duke Pinon,

42 Duke Kenaz, duke Teman, duke Mibzar,

43 Duke Magdiel, duke Iram: these *be* the dukes of Edom, according to their habitations in the land of their possession: he *is* Esau the father of the Edomites.

A[1] (p. 52) ° **37** And °Jacob dwelt in the land °wherein his father was a stranger, in the land of Canaan.

B[1] C a 1727 2 These *are* the generations of [1]Jacob. Joseph, *being* seventeen years old, was feeding the flock with his brethren; and the lad *was* with the sons of °Bilhah, and with the sons of °Zilpah, his father's wives: and Joseph brought unto °his father their evil report.

3 Now Israel loved Joseph more than all his children, because he *was* the son of his old age: and he made him a °coat of *many* °colours.

4 And when his brethren saw that their father loved him more than all his °brethren, they hated him, and could not speak peaceably unto him.

b 5 And Joseph °dreamed a dream, and he told *it* his brethren: and they hated him yet the more.

found. Heb. *mātzā*, to happen on, discover (not invent); to find (not find out).
mules. Heb. *hayyēmīm*, hot springs (with Vulg. and Syr.), hence Anah got the name of Beeri from Beer, a well, cp. 26. 34; and to distinguish him from the Anah of *v.* 20.
31 before there reigned. The ref. is to 17. 6 and 35. 11. Deut. 17. 14-20.
37 the river. i.e. the Euphrates.

37. The whole chapter, Fig. *Hysterologia*. Ap. 6.

The last of the eleven Toledoth.

37. 1—50. 26 (I, p. 1). THE GENERATIONS OF JACOB (*Repeated Alternation*).

I | A[1] | 37. 1. JACOB in Canaan.
  B[1] | 37. 2—45. 28. Sons of Jacob. Posterity (Joseph and brethren).
 A[2] | 46. 1-7. JACOB. Removal to Egypt.
  B[2] | 46. 8-27. Sons of Jacob. (Posterity.)
 A[3] | 46. 28—50. 14. JACOB. Settlement and death in Egypt. Removal to Canaan.
  B[3] | 50. 15-26. Sons of Jacob. Posterity (Joseph and brethren).

37. 2—45. 28 (B[1], above). THE SONS OF JACOB: Joseph and his brethren (*Alternation*).

B[1] | C | 37. 2-36. Joseph in Canaan.
  D | 38. 1, 30. His brother (Judah).
 C | 39. 1—41. 57. Joseph in Egypt.
  D | 42. 1—45. 28. His brethren.

37. 2-36 (C, above). JOSEPH IN CANAAN. (*Alternation.*)

C | a | 1-4. With his brethren.
  b | 5-11. His dreams (communicated).
 a | 12-17. Seeking his brethren.
  b | 18-36. His dreams (counteracted).

1 Jacob. See notes on 32. 28; 43. 8; 45. 26, 28.
wherein = of his father's sojournings.
2 Bilhah. i. e. Dan and Naphtali, 30. 6-8.
Zilpah. i. e. Gad and Asher, 30. 10-13.
his. Heb. their.
3 coat: with long sleeves, worn only by the chief and his heir. This the first cause of brothers' enmity. See note on 27. 15 and 25. 31.
colours. Not "pieces". Marking it as priestly or royal. Ex. 28. 4, 39; 39. 1. 2 Sam. 13. 18, 19. Ps. 45. 14.
4 brethren. Heb. sons.
5 dreamed a dream. Fig. *Polyptōton*. Ap. 6. For emphasis = had a significant dream.
7 behold. Fig. *Asterismos*. Ap. 6.
in the field = in the midst of the field.
stood upright. Heb. took its stand, or was set upright.
8 shalt thou, &c. Fig. *Erotēsis*. Ap. 6. Cp. the rejection of Moses, Ex. 2. 14; and of Christ, Luke 19. 14.

6 And he said unto them, "Hear, I pray you, this dream which I have dreamed:

7 For, °behold, we *were* binding sheaves °in the field, and, lo, my sheaf arose, and also °stood upright; and, behold, your sheaves stood round about, and made obeisance to my sheaf."

8 And his brethren said to him, °"Shalt thou indeed reign over us? or shalt thou indeed have dominion over us?" And they hated him yet the more for his dreams, and for his words.

9 And he dreamed yet another dream, and told it his brethren, and said, [7]"Behold, I have dreamed a dream more; and, [7]behold, the sun

and the moon and the °eleven stars °made obeisance to me."

10 And he told *it* to his father, and to his brethren: and his father rebuked him, and said unto him, [5]"What *is* this dream that thou hast dreamed? Shall I and thy mother and thy brethren indeed come to bow down ourselves to thee to the earth?"

11 And his brethren envied him; but his father observed the saying.

a 12 And his brethren went to feed °their father's flock in Shechem.

13 And Israel said unto Joseph, "Do not thy brethren feed °*the flock* in °Shechem? come, and I will send thee unto them." And he said to him, "Here *am I.*"

14 And he said to him, "Go, I pray thee, see whether it be well with thy brethren, and well with the flocks; and bring me word again." So he sent him out of the vale of Hebron, and he came to Shechem.

15 And a certain °man found him, and, behold, *he was* wandering in the field: and the man asked him, saying, "What seekest thou?"

16 And he said, "I seek my brethren: tell me, I pray thee, where they feed [13]*their flocks.*"

17 And the man said, "They are departed hence; for I heard them say, 'Let us go to °Dothan.'" And Joseph went after his brethren, and found them in °Dothan.

b 18 And when they saw him afar off, even before he came near unto them, they °conspired against him to slay him.

19 And they said one to another, °"Behold, this °dreamer cometh.

20 Come now therefore, °and let us slay him, and cast him into some pit, and we will say, 'Some evil beast hath devoured him:' and we shall see what will become of his dreams."

21 And Reuben heard *it*, and he delivered him out of their hands; and said, "Let us not kill °him."

22 And Reuben said unto them, "Shed no blood, *but* cast him into this pit that *is* in the wilderness, and lay no hand upon him;" (°that he might rid him out of their hands, to deliver him to his father again).

23 And it came to pass, when Joseph was come unto his brethren, that they stript Joseph out of his coat, °*his* coat of *many* colours that *was* on him;

24 And they took him, and cast him into a pit: and the pit *was* empty, *there was* no water in it.

25 And they °sat down to eat bread: and they lifted up their eyes and looked, and, °behold, a °company of °Ishmeelites came from Gilead with their camels bearing spicery and balm and myrrh, going to carry *it* down to Egypt.

26 And Judah said unto his brethren, "What profit *is it* if we slay our brother, and conceal his blood?

27 Come, and let us °sell him to the [25]Ishmeelites, and let not our hand be upon him; for he *is* our brother *and* our flesh." And his brethren °were content.

1727 28 Then there passed by °Midianites merchantmen; and °they drew and lifted up Joseph out of the pit, and sold Joseph to the [25]Ishmeelites for °twenty *pieces* of silver: and they brought Joseph into Egypt.

29 And Reuben returned unto the pit; and, [25]behold, Joseph *was* not in the pit; and he rent his clothes.

30 And he returned unto his brethren, and said, "The child *is* not; and I, °whither shall I °go?"

31 And they took Joseph's coat, and °killed a kid of the goats, and dipped the coat in the blood;

32 And they sent the coat of *many* colours, and they brought *it* to their father; and said, "This have we found: know now whether it *be* thy son's coat or no."

33 °And he knew it, and said, "*It is* my son's coat; an evil beast hath devoured him; Joseph is °without doubt rent in pieces."

34 [33]And Jacob rent his clothes, and put sackcloth upon his loins, and mourned for his son many days.

35 [33]And all his sons [34]and °all his daughters

9 eleven stars = the eleven signs of the Zodiac, Joseph being the twelfth. See note on Num. 2. 2.
made obeisance. Cp. 42. 6; 43. 26; 44. 14.
12 their father's flock. One of the fifteen expressions with the extraordinary points (see Ap. 31), indicating a doubtful reading, and suggesting that they had gone to feed themselves and make merry.
13 the flock. With the omission in *v.* 12 these words are unnecessary.
Shechem. Was Jacob afraid after 34. 25-30?
15 man. Heb. *'ish.* See Ap. 14. ii.
17 Dothan. On the high road to Egypt for caravans from the East.
18 conspired. Cp. Matt. 27. 1.
19 Behold. Fig. *Asterismos.* Ap. 6.
dreamer. Heb. master (or lord, *Baal*) of dreams.
20 and. Note the Fig. *Polysyndeton* (Ap. 6), emphasising the deliberateness of their actions.
21 him = his soul. Heb. *nephesh.* Ap. 13.
22 that he might rid him, &c. Fig. *Parenthesis* (Ap. 6), by way of explanation.
23 his coat. See on *v.* 3.
25 sat down. Showing their indifference. Cp. 42. 21 and Matt. 27. 36.
behold. Fig. *Asterismos.* Ap. 6.
company = caravan. There was a well-organized trade in sixteenth dynasty.
Ishmeelites. So 39. 1. In *vv.* 28 and 36 called Midianites. Ishmael was the son of Abraham by Hagar (16. 11, 12); Midian the son of Abraham by Keturah (25. 2). See Judg. 8. 24, 25, where they were mixed together, and were distinguished only by their nose-rings. (Cp. 24. 47; 35. 4, Ex. 32. 2, &c.)
27 sell him. A Judas sold Joseph, and a Judas sold Christ. Slaves were in great demand in Egypt.
were content = hearkened.
28 Midianites. See note on *v.* 25.
they, i. e. Joseph's brethren.
twenty. The number of disappointed expectancy. See Ap. 10.
30 whither. Fig. *Erotēsis.* Ap. 6.
go = go in, as though to hide himself.
31 killed. Heb. *shahath.* See Ap. 42. i, v.
33 And. Note the Fig. *Polysyndeton* (Ap. 6), in *vv.* 33, 34, to emphasise the successive steps in Jacob's grief.
without doubt. Fig. *Polyptōton* (Ap. 6), "tearing he has been torn". Deceived by the blood of a kid, as he had deceived his father with the skin of a kid, 27. 16.
35 all his daughters. See on 30. 21, or it may be *Synecdoche* (of the Part), Ap. 6, put for all his female relatives and granddaughters.

**rose up to comfort him; but he refused to be
comforted; and he said, "For I will go down
into the °grave unto my son mourning." Thus
his father wept for him.
36 And the [23] Midianites sold him into Egypt
unto °Potiphar, an officer of Pharaoh's, *and*
°captain of the guard.**

D °**38** **And it came to pass at that time, that
Judah went down from his brethren,**
(p. 52) **and turned in to a °certain Adullamite, whose
name *was* Hirah.
2 And Judah saw there a daughter of a certain °Canaanite, whose name *was* Shuah; and
he took her, and went in unto her.
3 And she conceived, and bare a son; and °he
called his name Er.
4 And she conceived again, and bare a son;
and she called his name Onan.
5 And she yet again conceived, and bare a
son; and called his name Shelah: and [3] he was
at Chezib, when she bare him.
6 And Judah took a wife for Er his firstborn,
whose name *was* Tamar.
7 And Er, Judah's firstborn, was wicked in the
°sight of the LORD; and the LORD slew him.
8 And Judah said unto Onan, "Go in unto thy
brother's wife, and marry her, and °raise up
seed to thy brother."
9 And Onan knew that the seed should not
be his; and it came to pass, when he went
in unto his brother's wife, that he spilled *it*
on the ground, lest that he should give seed
to his brother.
10 And the thing which he did °displeased the
LORD: wherefore He slew him also.
11 Then said Judah to Tamar his daughter
in law, "Remain a widow at thy father's
house, till Shelah my son be grown:" for he
said, "Lest peradventure °he die also, as his
brethren *did*." And Tamar went and dwelt in
her father's house.
12 And in process of time the daughter of
Shuah Judah's wife died; and Judah was
comforted, and went up unto his sheepshearers
to Timnath, he and his friend Hirah the Adullamite.
13 And it was told Tamar, saying, °"Behold
thy father in law goeth up to Timnath to shear
his sheep."
14 °And she put her widow's garments off
from her, and covered her with a vail, and
wrapped herself, and sat °in an open place,
which *is* by the way to Timnath; for she saw
that Shelah was grown, and she was not given
unto him to wife.
15 When Judah saw her, he thought her
to be an harlot; because she had covered her
face.
16 And he turned unto her by the way, and
said, "Go to, I pray thee, let me come in unto
thee;" (for he knew not that she *was* his
daughter in law.) And she said, "What wilt
thou give me, that thou mayest come in unto
me?"
17 And he said, "I will send *thee* a kid from
the flock." And she said, "Wilt thou give *me*
a pledge, till thou send *it*?"
18 And he said, "What pledge shall I give
thee?" And she said, "Thy signet, °and thy
bracelets, and thy staff that *is* in thine hand."
And he gave *it* her, and came in unto her, and
she conceived by him.
19 And she arose, and went away, and laid by
her vail from her, and put on the garments of
her °widowhood.
20 And Judah sent the kid by the hand of his
friend the Adullamite, to receive *his* pledge from
the woman's hand: but he found her not.
21 Then he asked the °men of that place,
saying, "Where *is* the harlot, that *was* °openly
by the way side?" And they said, "There was
no harlot in this *place*."
22 And he returned to Judah, and said, "I
cannot find her; and also the men of the place
said, *that* there was no harlot in this *place*."
23 And Judah said, "Let her take *it* to her,
lest we be shamed: [13] behold, I sent this kid,
and thou hast not found her."
24 And it came to pass about three months
after, that it was told Judah, saying, "Tamar
thy daughter in law hath played the harlot;
and also, behold, she *is* with child by whoredom." And Judah said, "Bring her forth, and
let her be °burnt."
25 When she *was* brought forth, she sent to
her father in law, saying, "By the °man,
whose these *are*, *am* I with child:" and she
said, "Discern, I pray thee, whose *are* these,
the signet, and bracelets, and staff."
26 And Judah acknowledged *them*, and said,
"She hath been more righteous than I; because**

---

grave. Heb. *Sheōl*, first occ. of word. See Ap. 35.

36 Potiphar = consecrated to *Ra*: one of the gods of lower Egypt.

captain of the guard. Cp. 2 Kings 25. 8, 11, 20: had charge of police, as well as military duties.

38. 1-30 (D, p. 52). JOSEPH'S BROTHER: JUDAH.

The whole Chapter is the Fig. *Parecbasis* (Ap. 6).

1 certain, &c. = a man, an Adullamite. Heb. *'ish.* See Ap. 14. ii.

2 Canaanite. In this was Judah's sin. Cp. 24. 3; 26. 35; 27. 46; 28. 1. Ex. 34. 16. Deut. 7. 3. A warning, and a revelation of the human heart. Note who these Canaanites were! Ap. 23, 25.

3 he, should be "she", with Sept.

7 sight. Heb. eyes. Fig. *Anthropopatheia.* Ap. 6.

8 raise up seed, &c. = a law before Sinai. See Ap. 15. Cp. Deut. 25. 5-9. Ruth 4. 10. Matt. 22. 24. An old and present Eastern law. See Ap. 15.

10 displeased. Heb. was evil in the eyes of Jehovah. Fig. *Anthropopatheia.* Ap. 6.

11 he die also. Judah, an unnatural brother, is punished in his own children.

13 Behold. Fig. *Asterismos.* Ap. 6.

14 And. Note the Fig. *Polysyndeton* (Ap. 6) emphasising the deliberateness of each action.

in an open place. Heb. "in the entrance to Enaim".

18 and. Note the Fig. *Polysyndeton* (Ap. 6) in *vv.* 18 and 19 marking each act.

19 widowhood. *Nine* widows mentioned. See Ap. 10 for significance. Tamar, here. Tekoah, 2 Sam. 14. 5. Hiram's mother, 1 Kings 7. 14. Zeruah, 1 Kings 11. 26. Widow of Zarephath, 1 Kings 17. 9. Poor widow, Mark 12. 42. Anna, Luke 2. 37. Widow of Nain, Luke 7. 12. Importunate, Luke 18. 3.

21 men. Heb. pl. of *'ish*, or, *'enōsh.* See Ap. 14. iii.

openly. Heb. "at Enaim".

24 burnt. This was strictly in accordance with the Code of Khammurabi (§ 157), which was then in force throughout Canaan. See Ap. 15.

25 man. Heb. *'ish.* See Ap. 14. ii.

that I gave her not to Shelah my son." And he knew her again °no more.

27 And it came to pass in the time of her travail, that, [13] behold, twins *were* in her womb.

28 And it came to pass, when she travailed, that *the one* put out *his* hand: and the midwife took and bound upon his hand a scarlet thread, saying, "This came out first."

29 And it came to pass, as he drew back his hand, that, [13] behold, his brother came out: and she said, "How hast thou broken forth? *this* breach *be* upon thee:" therefore his name was called °Pharez.

30 And afterward came out his brother, that had the scarlet thread upon his hand: and his name was called °Zarah.

C E c (p. 55) 1727 **39** And Joseph was brought down to Egypt; and °Potiphar, an officer of Pharaoh, captain of the °guard, an °Egyptian, bought him of the hands of the °Ishmeelites, which had brought him down thither.

2 And the LORD was with Joseph, and he °was a prosperous man; and he was in the house of his master the [1] Egyptian.

d 3 And his master saw that the LORD *was* with him, and that the LORD made all that he did to prosper in his hand.

4 And Joseph found grace in his sight, and he °served him: and he made him overseer over his house, and all *that* he had he put into his °hand.

5 And it came to pass from the time *that* he had made him overseer in his house, and over all that he had, that the LORD blessed the [1] Egyptian's house for Joseph's sake; and the blessing of the LORD was upon all that he had °in the house, and in the field.

6 And °he °left all that he had in Joseph's hand; and °he °knew not ought he had, save the °bread which he did °eat.

e f And Joseph [2] was *a* °goodly *person*, and well favoured.

7 And it came to pass after these things, that his master's °wife cast her eyes upon Joseph; and she said, "Lie with me."

g 8 But °he refused, and said unto his master's wife, °"Behold, my master °wotteth not what *is* with me in the house, and he hath committed all that he hath to my [4] hand;

9 *There is* none greater in this house than I; neither hath he kept back any thing from me but thee, because thou *art* his wife: how then can I do this great °wickedness, and °sin against God?"

10 And it came to pass, as she spake to Joseph day by day, that he hearkened not unto her, to lie by her, *or* to be with her.

f 11 And it came to pass about this time, that *Joseph* °went into the house to do his business; and *there was* none of the °men of the house there within.

12 And she caught him by his °garment, saying, "Lie with me:"

g and he left his garment in her hand, and fled, and got him out.

13 And it came to pass, when she saw that he had left his garment in her hand, and was fled forth,

14 That she called unto the men of her house, and spake unto them, saying, °"See, he hath brought in an Hebrew unto us to mock us; he

---

26 no more. But God remembered her (Matt. 1. 3).

29 Pharez = "breach".

30 Zarah = "a rising of light", "Offspring", or "Dawn". Both Pharez and Zarah, together with their mother Tamar, are in the genealogy of Christ (Matt. 1. 3). This is why this parenthetical chapter is inserted here. It is here by the Fig. *Parecbasis* (Ap. 6). It comes, historically, before chapter 37.

39. 1—41. 57 (*C*, p. 52). JOSEPH IN EGYPT.

C | E[1] | 39. 1—40. 23. His humiliation.
  | E[2] | 41. 1-57. His exaltation.

39. 1—40. 23 (E[1], above). JOSEPH'S HUMILIATION (*Extended Alternation*).

E[1] | c | 39. 1, 2. In Potiphar's house.
  d | 39. 3-6-. Confidence of Potiphar.
  e | 39. -6-18. Chastity of Joseph.
  c | 39. 19, 20. In Prison.
  d | 39. 21-23. Confidence of Jailor.
  e | 40. 1-23. Wisdom of Joseph.

39. 1 Potiphar. See note on 37. 36.

guard = executioners.

Egyptian. This is emphasised three times (*vv.* 1, 2, 5); because recent discoveries show that Egypt was at this time under a new dynasty; and emphasis is put on the fact that Potiphar, though an "Egyptian", was retained in high position.

Ishmeelites. See note on chapter 37. 25.

2 was = came to be. See Gen. 1. 2.

4 served = became his personal servant.

hand. Fig. *Metonymy* (of Cause). Ap. 6. Hand put for care which it takes.

5 in the house, &c. = at home or abroad.

6 he = Potiphar. Fig. *Ellipsis.* Ap. 6. i. a.

left. Heb. *'azab,* a *Homonym.* Its other meaning is "to help". See note on Ex. 23. 5.

knew. Fig. *Metonymy* (of Cause). Ap. 6. Knowing put for caring for.

bread. Fig. *Synecdoche* (of Species). Ap. 6. Bread put for all kinds of food.

eat. He knew and cared for that, as the Egyptians might not eat with Hebrews (43. 32).

39. -6-18 (e, above). THE CHASTITY OF JOSEPH. (*Alternation.*)

e | f | -6, 7. Potiphar's wife. Request.
  g | 8-10. Joseph's Refusal, and Reason.
  f | 11, 12-. Potiphar's wife. Request repeated.
  g | -12-20. Joseph's Flight, and consequences.

goodly, &c. Exactly what is said of his mother, 29. 17.

7 wife. Egyptian women were not secluded as the Syrian women were. This is shown by the Egyptian paintings of the period.

8 he refused. Joseph (now reckoned the first-born, 1 Ch. 5. 2): thus by his chastity shames the unchastity of Reuben the first-born before.

Behold. Fig. *Asterismos.* Ap. 6.

wotteth not = knoweth not. O. Eng. *Idiom.*

9 wickedness. Heb *r'a'a.* See Ap. **44.** viii.

sin. Heb. *chāṭ'ā.* See Ap. **44.** i.

11 went into the house. Pictures of an Egyptian house are extant which show the store-room at the back of the house.

men. Heb. pl. of *'ish* or *'enōsh.* Ap. 14.

12 garment. Heb. *beged.* Cp. 37. 31, 32. That, to cover the sin of his brethren; this, to cover the sin of Potiphar's wife.

14 See. Fig. *Asterismos.* Ap. 6.

came in unto me to lie with me, and I cried with a loud voice:
15 And it came to pass, when he heard that I lifted up my voice and cried, that he left his [12] garment with me, and fled, and got him out."
16 And she laid up his [12] garment by her, until his lord came home.
17 And she spake unto him according to these words, saying, "The Hebrew servant, which thou hast brought unto us, came in unto me to mock me:
18 And it came to pass, as I lifted up my voice and cried, that he left his [12] garment with me, and fled out."
19 And it came to pass, when his master heard the words of his wife, which she spake unto him, saying, °"After this manner did thy servant to me;" that his wrath was kindled.
20 And Joseph's master took him, and put him into the ° prison, a place where the king's prisoners *were* bound: and he was there in the ° prison.

d (p. 55) 21 But the LORD was with Joseph, and shewed him ° mercy, and gave him favour in the sight of the keeper of the prison.
22 And the ° keeper of the prison committed to Joseph's hand all the prisoners that *were* in the prison; and whatsoever they did there, he was the doer *of it*.
23 The [22] keeper of the prison looked not to any thing *that was* under his hand; because the LORD was with him, and *that* which he did, the LORD made *it* to prosper.

h (p. 56) 1717 **40** And it came to pass after these things, *that* the ° butler of the king of Egypt and *his* ° baker had offended their lord the king of Egypt.
2 And Pharaoh was wroth against two *of* his officers, against the chief of the butlers, and against the chief of the bakers.
3 And he put them in ward in the house of the captain of the guard, into the prison, the place where Joseph *was* bound.
4 And the captain of the guard charged Joseph with them, and he served them: and they continued a ° season in ward.
5 And they ° dreamed a dream both of them, each man his dream in one night, each man according to the interpretation of his dream, the [1] butler and the [1] baker of the king of Egypt, which *were* bound in the prison.
6 And Joseph came in unto them in the morning, and looked upon them, and, ° behold, they *were* sad.
7 And he asked Pharaoh's officers that *were* with him in the ward of his lord's house, saying, "Wherefore look ye *so* sadly to day?"
8 And they said unto him, "We have [5] dreamed a dream, and *there is* no interpreter of it." And Joseph said unto them, "*Do* not interpretations *belong* to God? tell me *them*, I pray you."

e i l 9 And the chief [1] butler told his dream to Joseph, and said to him, "In my dream, [6] behold, a vine *was* before me;
10 And in the vine *were* three branches: and it *was* as though it budded, *and* her blossoms shot forth; and the clusters thereof brought forth ripe grapes:
11 And Pharaoh's cup *was* in my hand: and I took the grapes, and ° pressed them into Pharaoh's cup, and I gave the cup into Pharaoh's hand."

12 And Joseph said unto him, "This *is* the interpretation of it: The three branches ° *are* three days: m (p. 56)
13 Yet within three days shall Pharaoh ° lift up thine head, and restore thee unto thy place: and thou shalt deliver Pharaoh's cup into his hand, after the former manner when thou wast his butler.

14 But ° think on me when it shall be well with thee, and shew kindness, I pray thee, unto me, and make mention of me unto Pharaoh, and bring me out of this house: k
15 For indeed I was stolen away out of the land of the Hebrews: and here also have I done nothing that they should put me into the dungeon."

16 When the chief [1] baker saw that the interpretation was good, he said unto Joseph, "I also *was* in my dream, and, behold, *I had* three ° white baskets on my head: i l
17 And in the uppermost basket *there was* of all manner of bakemeats for Pharaoh; and the birds did eat them out of the basket upon my head."

18 And Joseph answered and said, "This *is* m

---

19 After this manner = According to these words.
20 prison = the house of the fortress.
21 mercy = kindness.
22 keeper = governor.

40. 1-23 (*e*, p. 55). THE WISDOM OF JOSEPH.
(*Alternations.*)

h Introd. 1-8. His fellow-prisoners and their dreams.
e | i | l | 9-11. The Butler's dream.
m | 12, 13. Its Interpretation.
k | 14, 15. Joseph's request (made).
i | *l* | 16, 17. The Baker's dream.
m | 18-22. Its Interpretation.
k | 23. Joseph's request (forgotten).

1 butler = the cupbearer. Neh. 1. 11.
baker. A Papyrus, in the National Library, Paris (nineteenth dynasty), gives the name of a similar officer (Djadja), the chief; and mentions "114,064 loaves made in the white fortress". (See *Records of the Past*, vol. ii, p. 126.)
4 season. Heb. days (Gen. 4. 3) = either "some days" (4. 3), or, perhaps, a year.
5 dreamed a dream. Fig. *Polyptōton* (Ap. 6), i. e. had a significant or important dream.
6 behold. Fig. *Asterismos*. Ap. 6.
11 pressed, &c. A religious ceremony, connected with the worship of *Horus*, portrayed in Egyptian paintings. Existence of vines in Egypt has been denied by critics; but now they are seen depicted in paintings. In the cup was honey, or some other liquid, with which the grape juice was mixed.
12 are. Should be "they [are]".
13 lift up thine head = uplift thee, i. e. restore thee to favour. For this was the highest honour that the cupbearer could have.
14 think on me, &c. Cp. Luke 23. 42.
16 white, or, wicker.

the interpretation thereof: The three baskets
° *are* three days:
19 Yet within three days shall Pharaoh lift
up thy head ° from off thee, and shall hang thee
on a tree; and the birds shall eat thy flesh
° from off thee."
20 And it came to pass the third day, *which*
was Pharaoh's ° birthday, that he made a feast
unto all his servants: and he lifted up the
head of the chief butler and of the chief [5] baker
among his servants.
21 And he ° restored the chief butler unto his
butlership again; and he gave the cup into
Pharaoh's hand:
22 But he ° hanged the chief baker: ° as Joseph
had interpreted to them.
k 23 Yet did not the chief butler remember
(p. 56) Joseph, ° but forgat him.

n¹ o **41** And it came to pass at the end of two
full years, that Pharaoh dreamed: and,
(p. 57) ° behold, he stood by ° the river.
1715 2 And, [1] behold, there came up out of the river
° seven well favoured kine and fatfleshed; and
they fed ° in a meadow.
3 And, [1] behold, seven other kine came up
after them out of the [1] river, ill favoured and
leanfleshed; and stood by the *other* kine upon
the brink of the [1] river.
4 And the ill favoured and leanfleshed kine
did eat up the seven well favoured and fat kine.
So Pharaoh awoke.

p 5 And he slept and dreamed the second time:
and, [1] behold, ° seven ears of corn came up upon
one stalk, ° rank and good.
6 And, [1] behold, seven thin ears and blasted
with the ° east wind sprung up after them.
7 And the seven thin ears devoured the seven
rank and full ears. And Pharaoh awoke, and,
behold, *it was* a dream.

q 8 And it came to pass in the morning that his
° spirit was troubled; and he sent and called
for all the ° magicians of Egypt, and all the
wise men thereof: and Pharaoh told them his
dream; but *there was* none that could interpret
them unto Pharaoh.
9 Then spake the chief butler unto Pharaoh,
saying, "I do ° remember my faults this day:
10 Pharaoh was wroth with his servants, and
put me in ward in the captain of the guard's
house, *both* me and the chief baker:
11 And we dreamed a dream in one night, I
and he; we dreamed each ° man according to
the interpretation of his dream.
12 And *there was* there with us a young man,
an Hebrew, servant to the captain of the guard;
and we told him, and he interpreted to us our
dreams; to each man according to his dream
he did interpret.
13 And it came to pass, ° as he interpreted to
us, so it was; me ° he restored unto mine office,
and him ° he hanged."
14 Then Pharaoh sent and called Joseph, and
they ° brought him hastily out of the dungeon:
and he ° shaved *himself*, and changed his raiment,
and came in unto Pharaoh.
15 And Pharaoh said unto Joseph, "I have
° dreamed a dream, and *there is* none that can
interpret it: and I have heard say of thee, *that*
thou canst understand a dream to interpret it."
16 And Joseph answered Pharaoh, saying,
"*It is* not in me: ° God shall give Pharaoh an
answer of peace."

17 And Pharaoh said unto Joseph, "In my o
dream, behold, I stood upon the bank of [1] the
river: (p. 57)
18 And, [1] behold, there came up out of the river
[2] seven kine, fatfleshed and well favoured;
and they fed [2] in a meadow:
19 And, [1] behold, seven other kine came up
after them, poor and very ill favoured and lean-

18 are = "they [are]."
19 from off thee. Contrast this with *v.* 13.
20 birthday. These were observed with great ceremony and state. Critics have *supposed* it to be only a Persian custom. The Rosetta stone contains a decree concerning the keeping of the birthday feast of Ptolemy Epiphanes. Other evidence is also forthcoming.
21 restored. Cp. *v.* 13, and see 41. 13.
22 hanged. Cp. *v.* 19, and see 41. 13.
as = according as.
23 but forgat him. Fig. *Pleonasm.* Ap. 6. Used for great emphasis. Cp. Amos 6. 6.

41. 1-57 (E², p. 55). **JOSEPH'S EXALTATION.**

n¹ | 1-36. Prediction.
n² | 37-57. Fulfilment.

41. 1-36 (n¹, above). **PREDICTION**
(Extended Alternation.)

n¹ o | 1-4. Dream of the kine } dreamt.
p | 5-7. Dream of the ears }
q | 8-16. Interpretation sought.
o | 17-21-. Dream of the kine } related.
p | -21-24. Dream of the ears }
q | 25-36. Interpretation given.

1 behold. Fig. *Asterismos.* Ap. 6.
the river: i.e. the Nile.
2 seven . . . kine. The cow was the emblem of Isis. In the Egyptian "Book of the Dead", Osiris is represented as a bull, accompanied by seven cows. (British Museum.) This was the basis of the dream, and gave it such significance and mystery.
in a meadow = among the rushes, or reeds. *'āḥū*, probably an Egyptian word.
5 seven ears. Unknown to us; but common in Egypt with the *Triticum compositum.* **rank** = fat.
6 east wind. In Egypt the prevailing winds are N. and S.: in Palestine E. and W. The wind here is the *Chamsin* (Heb. *ḳadim*), which is S.E., and is a blighting wind. Hebrews had only the four quarters. Had it said here S., it would have meant nothing, but E. conveys the nature of the wind, especially as evil was supposed to come from the E. and good from the W., as in other countries.
8 spirit. Heb. *ruach.* See Ap. 9.
magicians. Priests were divided into four classes; and five priests chosen from them were the king's councillors.
9 remember = bring to [Pharaoh's] remembrance.
11 man. Heb. *'ish.* See Ap. 14. ii.
13 as = according as.
he restored: he = Joseph. Fig. *Metonymy* (of Subject). Ap. 6. i. e. he declared I should be restored.
he hanged: he = Joseph. Fig. *Metonymy* (of Subject). Ap. 6. = declared he would be hanged.
14 brought him hastily out. Heb. made him run.
shaved. The beard was a disgrace in Egypt; shaving a disgrace in Palestine. Cp. 2 Sam. 10. 4.
15 dreamed a dream. Fig. *Polyptōton.* Ap. 6. = I have had a significant dream.
16 God. Heb. Elohim (Ap. 4).
17 the river = the Nile.

fleshed, such as I never saw in all the land of Egypt for badness:

20 And the lean and the ill favoured kine did eat up the first seven fat kine:

21 And when they had eaten them up, it could not be known that they had eaten them; but they *were* still ill favoured, as at the beginning.

p So I awoke.

(p. 57) 22 And I saw in my dream, and, [1]behold, seven ears came up in one stalk, full and good:

23 And, [1]behold, seven ears, withered, thin, *and* blasted with the east wind, sprung up after them:

24 And the thin ears devoured the seven good ears: and I told *this* unto the magicians; but *there was* none that could declare *it* to me."

25 And Joseph said unto Pharaoh, "The dream of Pharaoh °*is* one: [16]God hath shewed Pharaoh what He *is* about to do.

26 The seven good kine °*are* seven years; and the seven good ears *are* seven years: the dream *is* one.

27 And the seven thin and ill favoured kine that came up after them *are* seven years; and the seven empty ears blasted with the [6]east wind shall be seven years of famine.

28 This *is* the thing which I have spoken unto Pharaoh: What [16]God *is* about to do He sheweth unto Pharaoh.

29 [5]Behold, there come seven years of great plenty throughout all the land of Egypt:

30 And there shall arise after them °seven years of famine; and all the plenty shall be forgotten in the land of Egypt; and the famine shall consume °the land;

31 And the plenty shall not be known in the land by reason of that famine following; for it *shall be* very grievous.

32 And for that the dream was °doubled unto Pharaoh °twice; *it is* because the thing *is* established by [16]God, and [16]God will shortly bring it to pass.

33 Now therefore let Pharaoh look out a °man discreet and wise, and set him over the land of Egypt.

34 Let Pharaoh °do *this*, and let him appoint officers over the land, and take up the fifth part of the land of Egypt in the seven plenteous years.

35 And let them gather all the food of those good years that come, and lay up corn under the hand of Pharaoh, and let them keep food in the cities.

36 And that food shall be for store to the land against the seven years of famine, which shall be in the land of Egypt; that the [30]land perish not through the famine."

n² r¹ 37 And the thing was good in the eyes of

(p. 58) Pharaoh, and in the eyes of all his servants.

38 And Pharaoh said unto his servants, "Can we find *such a one* as this *is*, a [33]man in whom °the spirit of [16]God *is?*"

39 And Pharaoh said unto Joseph, "Forasmuch as [16]God hath shewed thee all this, *there is* none so discreet and wise as thou *art:*

1715 40 Thou shalt be over my house, and according unto thy °word shall all my people °be ruled: only in the throne will I be °greater than thou."

25 is. Heb. "it [is]".
26 are. Heb. "they [are]".
30 seven years. This explains and confirms the hieroglyphic inscription discovered by Wilbour at Sehēl (first cataract). It is referred to in another inscription in the tomb of Baba, at El-Kab, translated by Brugsch (*History of Egypt*, i, 304). In July 1908, Brugsch Bey discovered inscriptions which tell how "for seven successive years the Nile did not overflow, and vegetation withered and failed; that the land was devoid of crops, and that during these years, famine and misery devastated the land of Egypt". The date is given as 1700 B.C., which cannot be earlier, therefore, than the last year of the famine. The last year of the seven years of plenty was in B.C. 1708, according to Ussher (Gen. 41. 53), with which the inscription agrees. See further, Ap. 37.
the land. Fig. *Metonymy* (of Subject). Ap. 6. i.e. the people in the land.
32 doubled. To denote its establishment by God. Cp. Isa. 40. 2; 61. 7. Jer. 16. 18; 17. 18. Zech. 9. 12. Rev. 18. 6.
twice. Fig. *Ellipsis* (Ap. 6) = "[and sent] twice."
33 man. Heb. *'ish.* Ap. 14. ii.
34 do this = take action.

41. 37-56 (n², p. 57). **FULFILMENT.**
(*Repeated Alternation.*)

n² | r¹ | 37-46. Joseph's Exaltation.
| s¹ | 47-49. Dream of ears fulfilled.
| r² | 50-52. Joseph's Fruitfulness.
| s² | 53-56-. Dream of kine fulfilled.
| r³ | -56, 57. Joseph's Authority.

38 the spirit. Heb. *ruach.* Ap. 9. No art. = a Divine spirit or inspiration. Pharaoh knew nothing of Biblical Psychology.
40 word. Heb. mouth. *Metonymy* (of Cause). Ap. 6. Mouth is put for the commands uttered by it.
be ruled. Heb. *nashak,* to bend (as a bow). Fig. *Metonymy* (of Adjunct). Ap. 6. = bend put for submit. See *v.* 43, below, "Bow the knee", and note on "kiss", Ps. 2. 12.
greater. Cp. 45. 8.
41 all. Apepi only recently ruled over all. Before this he had reigned with his father and grandfather. So the Monuments.
42 and. Note the Fig. *Polysyndeton* (Ap. 6) in *vv.* 42 and 43, emphasising each act.
43 they. Some codices, with Sam., Sept., and Syr., read "one".
Bow the knee. This is not Heb. "tender father", as A.V. marg., but Egyptian. *Abrek* = bend or bow the knee. See *v.* 40 above, and Ps. 2. 12. Cp. 45. 8, and John 8. 8 in Coptic N.T. ("stooped down"). A command still used in Egypt to make camels kneel ("*Abrok*"). According to Sayce, *Abrek* is a Sumerian title = "The Seer". This would demand prostration.
45 Zaphnath-paaneah. This, too, is not Heb., but Egyptian. *Zap* = abundance; *nt* (*nath*) = of; *pa* = the; *aneh* = life. The whole name = *abundance of life*, or, *of food for the living.*

41 And Pharaoh said unto Joseph, "See, I have set thee over °all the land of Egypt."

42 And Pharaoh took off his ring from his hand, °and put it upon Joseph's hand, and arrayed him in vestures of fine linen, and put a gold chain about his neck;

43 And he made him to ride in the second chariot which he had; and °they cried before him, °"Bow the knee:" and he made him *ruler* over all the land of Egypt.

44 And Pharaoh said unto Joseph, "I *am* Pharaoh, and without thee shall no man lift up his hand or foot in all the land of Egypt."

45 And Pharaoh called Joseph's name °Zaphnath-paaneah; and he gave him to wife

°Asenath the daughter of °Poti-pherah priest of On. And Joseph went out over *all* the land of Egypt.

46 And Joseph *was* thirty years old when he stood before Pharaoh king of Egypt. And Joseph went out from the presence of Pharaoh, and went throughout all the land of Egypt.

s[1] (p. 58) 47 And in the seven plenteous years the earth brought forth by handfuls.

48 And he gathered up °all the food of the seven years, °which were in the land of Egypt, and laid up the food in the cities: the food of the field, which *was* round about every city, laid he up in the same.

49 And Joseph gathered corn as the °sand of the sea, very much, until he left numbering; for *it was* without number.

r[2] 50 And unto Joseph were born two sons before the years of famine came, which Asenath the daughter of Poti-pherah priest of On bare unto him.

51 And Joseph called the °name of the first-born °Manasseh: "For [16]God," *said he,* "hath made me °forget all my °toil, and all my father's house."

52 And the name of the second called he °Ephraim: "For [16]God hath caused me °to be fruitful in the land of my affliction."

s[2] 53 And the seven years of plenteousness, that °was in the land of Egypt, were ended.

1707 to 1701 54 And the seven years of °dearth began to come, according [30]as Joseph had said: and the dearth was in all lands; but in all the land of Egypt there was bread.

55 And when all the land of Egypt was famished, the people cried to Pharaoh for bread: and Pharaoh said unto all the Egyptians, "Go unto Joseph; what he saith to you, do."

56 And the famine was over all the face of the earth:

r[3] And Joseph opened all the storehouses, and sold unto the Egyptians; and the famine waxed sore in the land of Egypt.

57 And °all countries came into Egypt to Joseph for to buy *corn;* because that the famine was *so* sore in °all lands.

D F t (p. 59) **42** Now when Jacob saw that there was corn in Egypt, Jacob said unto his sons, °"Why do ye look one upon another?"

2 And he said, °"Behold, I have heard that there is corn in Egypt: get you down thither, and buy for us from thence; that we may live, °and not die."

u z 3 And Joseph's ten brethren went down to buy corn °in Egypt.

a 4 But Benjamin, Joseph's brother, Jacob sent not with his brethren; for he said, "Lest peradventure mischief befall him."

v 5 And the sons of Israel came to buy *corn* among those that came: for the famine was in the land of Canaan.

w 6 And Joseph °*was* the governor over the land, *and* he *it was* that sold to all the people of the land: and Joseph's brethren came, and °bowed down themselves before him *with* their faces to the earth.

7 And Joseph saw his brethren, and he knew them, but made himself strange unto them, and spake °roughly unto them; and he said unto them, "Whence come ye?" And they said, "From the land of Canaan to buy food."

8 And Joseph knew his brethren, but they knew not him.

9 And Joseph °remembered the dreams which he dreamed of them, and said unto them, "Ye *are* spies; to see the °nakedness of the land ye are come."

10 And they said unto him, "Nay, my lord, but to buy food are thy servants come.

11 °We *are* all one °man's sons; we *are* true *men,* thy servants are no spies."

Asenath = an Egyptian name.

Poti-pherah. The Egyptian priest of On = "City of the Sun", called in Heb. *Aven* and *Bethshemesh* (Jer. 43. 13), and in Greek *Heliopolis.* It was the university of Old Egypt.

48 all the food. Fig. *Synecdoche* (of the Whole), food put for corn. (Ap. 6).

which were. Sam. and Sept. read "in which there was plenty".

49 sand, &c. Fig. *Parœmia* (Ap. 6).

51 name. Fig. *Pleonasm* (Ap. 6).

Manasseh . . . forget. Fig. *Paronomasia* (Ap. 6). Heb. *M'anash-sheh . . . nashshani.*

toil. Heb. *'amal.* Ap. 44. v.

52 Ephraim . . . to be fruitful. Fig. *Paronomasia* (Ap. 6). *Ephraim . . . hiphrani.*

53 was = came to pass. See note on 1. 2.

54 dearth. One of 13 famines. See note on 12. 10.

57 all countries. Fig. *Metonymy* (of Subject). Ap. 6. i.e. people from all countries.

all lands. Fig. *Synecdoche* (of the Whole). Ap. 6. i.e. all neighbouring lands.

42. 1—45. 28 (*D*, p. 52). JOSEPH'S BRETHREN.
(*Extended Alternation, with Introversion.*)

D | F | t | 42. 1, 2. Commission to buy corn.
u | z | 3. Journey.
a | 4. Benjamin left.
v | 5. Arrival.
w | 6-24. Meeting with Joseph.
x | 25, 26. Dismissal.
y | 27-38. Return.
F | *t* | 43. 1, 2. Commission to buy corn.
u | *a* | 3-15-. Benjamin taken.
z | -15-. Journey.
v | -15. Arrival.
w | 16-34. Meeting with Joseph.
x | 44. 1—45. 24. Dismissal.
y | 45. 25-28. Return.

42. 1 Why . . . ? &c. Fig. *Erotēsis.* Ap. 6. That is what we all too often do when in trouble or difficulty.

2 Behold. Fig. *Asterismos.* Ap. 6.

and not die. Fig. *Pleonasm.* Ap. 6, for emphasis.

3 in Egypt. Some Codices read "from the Egyptians".

6 was. Heb. "he [was]".

bowed down. Cp. 37. 7, 8.

7 roughly. Each step in Joseph's treatment must be noted, all tending to one end: viz.: to bring them back to the pit at Dothan, convict them of their sin, and compel their confession of it. That climax is not reached till verse 21. Judah's words voice it, 44. 18-34.

9 remembered. Cp. 37. 5, 9.

nakedness. Fig. *Prosopopœia.* Ap. 6.

11 We are, &c. Heb. "all of us the sons of one man [are] we".

man's. Heb. *'ish.* Ap. 14. ii.

12 And he said unto them, "Nay, but to see
the [9] nakedness of the land ye are come."
13 And they said, "Thy servants *are* twelve
brethren, °the sons of one [11] man in the land
of Canaan; and, behold, the youngest *is* this
day with our father, and one *is* not."
14 And Joseph said unto them, "That *is it* that
I spake unto you, saying, 'Ye *are* spies:'
15 Hereby ye shall be °proved: By the life of
Pharaoh ye shall not go forth hence, except
your youngest brother come hither.
16 Send one of you, and let him fetch your
brother, and ye shall be kept in prison, that
your words may be proved, whether *there be*
any truth in you: or else by the life of Pharaoh
surely ye *are* spies."
17 And he °put them all together into ward
three days.
18 And Joseph said unto them the third day,
"This do, and °live; *for* I fear °God:
19 If ye *be* true *men*, let one of your brethren
be bound in the house of your prison: go ye,
carry corn for the famine of your houses:
20 But bring your youngest brother unto me;
so shall your words be verified, and ye shall
not die." And they did so.
21 And they said one to another, "We *are*
verily °guilty concerning our brother, in that
we saw the anguish of °his soul, when he besought us, and we would not hear; therefore
is this distress come upon us."
22 And °Reuben answered them, saying,
°"Spake I not unto you, saying, 'Do not °sin
against the child;' and ye would not hear?
therefore, [2] behold, also his blood is required."
23 And they knew not that Joseph °under-
stood *them;* for °he spake unto them by an
interpreter.
24 And he turned himself about from them,
and wept; and returned to them again, and
communed with them, and took from them
°Simeon, and bound him before their eyes.

x (p. 59) 25 Then Joseph commanded to fill their sacks
with corn, and to restore every °man's money
into his sack, and to give them provision for
the way: and thus did he unto them.
26 And they laded their asses with the corn,
and departed thence.

y 27 And as one of them opened his sack to
give his ass provender in the inn, he espied
his money; for, behold, it *was* in his sack's
mouth.
28 And he said unto his brethren, "My money
is restored; and, °lo, *it is* even in my sack:"
and their heart °failed *them*, and they were
afraid, saying one to another, °"What *is* this
that God hath done unto us?"
29 And they came unto Jacob their father
unto the land of Canaan, and told him all that
befell unto them; saying,
30 "The [11] man, *who is* the lord of the land,
spake °roughly to us, and °took us for spies of
the country.
31 And we said unto him, 'We *are* true *men;*
we °are no spies:
32 We *be* twelve brethren, sons of our father;
°one *is* not, and the youngest *is* this day with
our father in the land of Canaan.'
33 And the [11] man, the lord of the country, said
unto us, 'Hereby shall I know that ye *are* true
men; leave one of your brethren *here* with me,
and take °*food for* the famine of your households, and be gone:
34 And bring your youngest brother unto
me: then shall I know that ye *are* no spies,
but *that* ye *are* true *men:* °*so* will I deliver
you your brother, and ye shall traffick in the
land.'"
35 And it came to pass as they emptied their
sacks, that, [28] behold, every [11] man's bundle of
money *was* in his sack: and when *both* they
and their father saw the bundles of money,
they were afraid.
36 And Jacob their father said unto them,
"Me have ye bereaved °*of my children:*
Joseph *is* not, and Simeon *is* not, and ye
will take Benjamin *away:* all these things are
against me."
37 And Reuben spake unto his father, saying,
"Slay my two sons, if I bring him not to thee:
deliver him into my hand, and I will bring him
to thee again."
38 And he said, "My son shall not go down
with you; for his brother is dead, and he is left
alone: if mischief befall him by the way in the
which ye go, °then shall ye °bring down °my
gray hairs with sorrow to °the grave."

43 And the famine *was* sore in the land. F t
2 And it came to pass, when they had (p. 59)
eaten up the corn which they had brought out

13 the sons. Heb. "we [are]". See note on *v.* 11.
15 proved. Joseph, from his high position, could make very strict inquiry.
17 put them . . . into ward. Second step: to alarm.
18 live. Fig. *Heterosis* (of Mood). Ap. 6. Heb. "this do and ye shall live". Imp. for Ind.
God. Heb. Elohim. Ap. 4.
21 guilty. The treatment begins to take effect.
his soul. Heb. *nephesh* (Ap. 13). His anguish emphasised.
22 Reuben. See 37. 21.
Spake. Cp. 37. 21. Fig. *Erotesis.* Ap. 6.
sin. Heb. *chatah.* See Ap. 44. i.
23 understood. Heb. was listening.
he spake, &c.=for the interpreter was between them.
24 Simeon. Probably because his cruel nature (34. 25, cp. 49. 5) made him the deviser of the evil.
25 man's. Heb. *'ish.* Ap. 14. ii. The third step.
28 lo. Fig. *Asterismos.* Ap. 6.
failed them. Heb. "went out". Fig. *Hyperbole* (Ap. 6).
What . . . ? Fig. *Erotēsis.* Ap. 6.
30 roughly. Cp. *v.* 7.
took us for. Or; set us down as.
31 are no spies. Heb. have never proved spies.
32 one is not. Some codices, with Sam. and Syr., read "but the one is not". And this is all they have to say of Gen. 37. 28!
33 food. Aram. and Sept. read "corn".
34 so will I, &c. Some codices, with Sept., Syr., and Vulg., read "and your brother will I deliver up to you".
36 of my children. No *Ellipsis.* These italics unnecessary.
38 then, &c. Fig. *Euphemismos* (Ap. 6), for "then shall ye kill me".
bring down. Fig. *Metonymy* (of Effect), i.e. ye will be the cause of it. Ap. 6.
my gray hairs. Fig. *Metonymy* (of the Adjunct). Ap. 6. i.e. "me in my old age".
the grave. Heb. *Sheōl.* See note on 37. 35 and Ap. 35.

of Egypt, their father said unto them, "Go again, buy us a little food."

u a (p. 59) 3 And Judah spake unto him, saying, "The °man °did solemnly protest unto us, saying, 'Ye shall not see my face, except your brother *be* with you.'
4 If thou wilt send our brother with us, we will go down and buy thee food:
5 But if thou wilt not send *him*, we will not go down: for the [3]man said unto us, 'Ye shall not see my face, except your brother *be* with you.'"
6 And °Israel said, "Wherefore dealt ye *so* °ill with me, *as* to tell the [3]man whether ye had yet a brother?"
7 And they said, "The [3]man °asked us straitly of our state, and of our kindred, saying, '*Is* your father yet alive? have ye *another* brother?' and we told him according to the °tenor of these words: °could we certainly know that he would say, 'Bring your brother down?'"
8 °And Judah said unto [6]Israel his father, "Send the lad with me, and we will arise and go; that we may live, and not die, both we, and thou, *and* also our little ones.
9 I will be surety for him; of my hand shalt thou require him: if I bring him not unto thee, and set him before thee, then let me bear the blame °for ever:
10 For except we had lingered, surely now we had returned this second time."
11 And their father [6]Israel said unto them, "If *it must be* so now, do this; take of the °best fruits in the land in your vessels, and carry down the [3]man a present, a little balm, and a little honey, spices, and myrrh, nuts, and almonds:
12 And take double money in your hand; and the money that was brought again in the mouth of your sacks, carry *it* again in your hand; peradventure it *was* an oversight:
13 Take also your brother, and arise, go again unto the [3]man:
14 And °GOD ALMIGHTY give you °mercy before the [3]man, that he may send away your other brother, and Benjamin. If I be bereaved *of my children*, I am bereaved."
15 And the °men took that present, °and they took double money in their hand, and Benjamin;

u z and rose up, and went down to Egypt,

v and stood before Joseph.

w 16 And when Joseph saw Benjamin with them, he said to the ruler of his °house, "Bring *these* [15]men home, and °slay, and make ready; for *these* men shall dine with me at noon."
17 And the [3]man did °as Joseph bade; and the [3]man brought the [15]men into Joseph's house.
18 And the [15]men were afraid, because they were brought into Joseph's house; and they said, "Because of the money that was returned in our sacks at the first time are we brought in; that he may seek occasion against us, and fall upon us, and take us for bondmen, and our asses."
19 And they came near to the steward of Joseph's house, and they communed with him at the door of the house,
20 And said, "O sir, °we came indeed down at the first time to buy food:
21 And it came to pass, when we came to the inn, that we opened our sacks, and, behold, *every* man's money *was* in the mouth of his sack, our money in full weight: and we have brought it again in our hand.
22 And other money have we brought down in our hands to buy food: we cannot tell who put our money in our sacks."
23 And he said, °"Peace *be* to you, fear not: your °God, and the °God of your father, hath given you °treasure in your sacks: I had your money." And he brought Simeon out unto them.
24 And the [14]man brought the [15]men into Joseph's house, and gave *them* water, and they washed their feet; and he gave their asses provender.
25 And they made ready the present against Joseph came at noon: for they heard that they should eat °bread there.
26 And when Joseph came home, they brought him the present which *was* in their hand into the house, and °bowed themselves to him to the earth.
27 And he asked them of *their* welfare, and

---

43. 3-5. Note the *Introversion* in this Colloquy.

a | 3. Judah's words.
b | 4. Jacob's act.
b | 5-. Jacob's act.
a | -5. Joseph's words.

3 man. Heb. *'ish.* Ap. 14. ii.
did solemnly protest. Heb. "protesting he protested". Fig. *Polyptōton* (Ap. 6). See note on 26. 28.
6 Israel. Note the name. Jacob is used of his weakness (42. 36, &c.), Israel of his resignation to God's will. In this use of the names Jacob and Israel, men might well invent a Jacobite and Israelite authorship, as well as an Elohist and Jehovist theory!
ill. Heb. *R'a'a.* See Ap. 44. viii.
7 asked us straitly. Heb. "asking he asked us". Fig. *Polyptōton* (Ap. 6). See note on *v.* 3 above, and 26. 28.
tenor. Heb. mouth. Fig. *Pleonasm.* Ap. 6.
could we certainly know. Heb. "knowing could we know". Fig. *Polyptōton* (Ap. 6). See note on 26. 28.
8 And. Note the *Polysyndeton* in this verse.
9 for ever. Heb. "all the days".
11 best fruits in the land. Heb. "the praise of the land". Fig. *Metonymy* (of the Cause). Ap. 6. "Praise" put for the choice fruits which called forth the praise.
14 God Almighty. Heb. *El Shaddai.* Ap. 4. VII.
mercy. Fig. *Metonymy* (of Cause). Ap. 6. Mercy put for the favours shown.
15 men. Heb. pl. of *'ish*, or *'enosh.* Ap. 14. iii.
and. Note the Fig. *Polysyndeton* (Ap. 6) in *v.* 15.
16 house. Fig. *Metonymy* (of Subject). Ap. 6. House put for the servants of it.
slay. Heb. "slay a slaying". Fig. *Polyptōton.* Ap. 6. = slay abundantly.
17 as = according as.
20 we came indeed. Heb. "coming down we came down". Fig. *Polyptōton.* Ap. 6. See note on 26. 28.
23 Peace. Fig. *Synecdoche* (of Species). Ap. 6. Peace put for all its blessings.
God. Heb. *Elohim.* Ap. 4.
treasure = hidden or secret treasure.
25 bread. Fig. *Synecdoche* (of Species). Ap. 6. Bread put for all kinds of food.
26 bowed themselves. Some codices, with Sept. and Vulg., add "with their faces". Cp. 37. 7, 8.

said, "*Is* °your father well, the old man of whom ye spake? *Is* he yet alive?"

28 And they answered, "Thy servant our father *is* in good health, he *is* yet alive." And they °bowed down their heads, and made obeisance.

29 And he lifted up his eyes, and saw his brother °Benjamin, his mother's son, and said, "*Is* this your younger brother, of whom ye spake unto me?" And he said, [23]"God be gracious unto thee, my son."

30 And Joseph made haste; for his bowels did yearn upon his brother: and he sought *where* to weep; and he entered into *his* chamber, and °wept there.

31 And he washed his face, and went out, and refrained himself, and said, "Set on [25]bread."

32 And they set on for him by himself, and for them by themselves, and for the Egyptians, which did eat with him, by themselves: because the Egyptians might not eat bread with the Hebrews; for that *is* an abomination unto the Egyptians.

33 And °they sat before him, the °firstborn according to his birthright, and the °youngest according to his youth: and the °men °marvelled one at another.

34 And he °took *and sent* messes unto them from before him: but Benjamin's mess was °five times so much as any of theirs. And they drank, and °were merry with him.

x b d **44** And he commanded the steward of his house, saying, "Fill the °men's sacks
(p. 59) *with* food, as much as they can carry, and put every man's money in his sack's mouth.

2 And put my °cup, the silver cup, in the sack's mouth of the °youngest, and his corn money." And he did according to the word that Joseph had spoken.

e 3 As soon as the morning was light, the men were sent away, they and their asses.

d 4 *And* when they were gone out of the city, *and* not *yet* far off, Joseph said unto his steward, "Up, follow after the [1]men; and when thou dost overtake them, say unto them, °'Wherefore have ye rewarded evil for good?

5 *Is* not this *it* in which my lord drinketh, and whereby indeed he °divineth? ye have done °evil in so doing.'"

6 And he overtook them, and he spake unto them these same words.

7 And they said unto him, "Wherefore saith my lord these words? °God forbid that thy servants should do according to this thing:

8 °Behold, the money, which we found in our sacks' mouths, we brought again unto thee out of the land of Canaan: how then should we steal out of thy lord's house silver or gold?

9 With whomsoever of thy servants it be found, both °let him die, and we also will be my lord's bondmen."

10 And he said, "Now also *let* it *be* according unto your words: he with whom it is found shall be my servant; and ye shall be blameless."

11 Then they speedily took down every °man his sack to the ground, and opened every °man his sack.

12 And he searched, *and* began at the eldest, and left at the youngest: and the [2]cup was found in Benjamin's sack.

13 Then they rent their clothes, and laded every man his ass, and returned to the city. e

14 And Judah and his brethren came to Joseph's house; for he *was* yet there: and they fell before him on the ground. c f

15 And Joseph said unto them, "What deed (p. 62)

---

27 your father . . . the old man = your aged father.
28 bowed down, &c. Cp. ch. 37. 7-10.
29 Benjamin. Now twenty-two, and father of ten sons. Cp. 46. 21.
30 wept. See note on 42. 24.
33 they sat. Egyptian pictures show that it was the custom to sit at meals.
firstborn. Joseph thus showing that he knew their ages and order, and causing them to marvel.
youngest, &c. This was to try them, and see whether they were still "moved with envy". Cp. 37. 4, 8, 11, 18. It was also a type of the coming day, when the true Joseph will be able to do for the scattered and mingled tribes what was done here for the tribal heads. Cp. Zech. 12. 9-14.
men. Heb. pl. of *'ish*, or *'enosh*. Ap. 14. iii.
marvelled [and looked] at one another. Fig. *Ellipsis* (Ap. 6), thus supplied.
34 took and sent, &c. Heb. "lifted liftings". Fig. *Polyptōton* (Ap. 6), for emphasis = sent choice portions.
five times. The number of grace. See Ap. 10, and cp. 41. 34; 45. 22; 47. 2, 24.
were merry. Heb. drank abundantly. Cp. Hag. 1. 6. John 2. 10.

44. 1—45. 20 (*F x*, p. 59). THE DISMISSAL OF JOSEPH'S BRETHREN (*Introversion*).

x | b | 44. 1-13. Feigned Dismissal.
  c | 44. 14-34. Brethren's explanation to Joseph.
  c | 45. 1-16. Joseph's explanation to Brethren.
b | 45. 17-24. Actual Dismissal.

1-14 (b, above). FEIGNED DISMISSAL (*Alternation*).

b | d | 1, 2. The Cup concealed.
  e | 3. The sending away.
d | 4-12. The Cup found.
  e | 13, 14. The return.

15-34 (c, above). THE CUP SOUGHT (*Alternation*).

c | f | 15. Joseph.
  g | 16. Judah.
f | 17. Joseph.
  g | 18-34. Judah.

1 men. Heb. pl. of *'ish*, or *'enosh*. Ap. 14. iii.
2 cup. Heb. *gᵉbiʻa*, out of which wine was poured: distinguishing from the smaller cups from which it was drunk. Jer. 35. 5.
youngest. This was the fourth step to try them, and to prove whether they were the same brethren still, and would treat Benjamin as they had treated Joseph.
4 Wherefore. Fig. *Erotēsis*. Ap. 6. Sept. and Syr. insert "Wherefore then have ye the silver cup?"
5 divineth. This was to confirm their belief that Joseph was an Egyptian. Emphasised by Fig. *Polyptōton* (Ap. 6). Heb. divining he divineth.
evil. Heb. *Rʻaʻa*. See Ap. 44. viii.
7 God forbid. No word for "God" here. Heb. = Far be it from thy servants.
8 Behold. Fig. *Asterismos* (Ap. 6).
9 let him die. This was the penalty in the Code of Khammurabi, with which they were acquainted in Canaan (§ 6); death for stealing from a palace. Property more sacred than life.
11 man. Heb. *'ish*. Ap. 14. ii.

is this that ye have done? wot ye not that such a man as I can certainly divine?"

g (p. 62) 16 And Judah said, °"What shall we say unto my lord? what shall we speak? or how shall we clear ourselves? °God hath found out the °iniquity of thy servants: behold, we *are* my lord's servants, both we, and *he* also with whom the cup is found."

f 17 And he said, [7] "God forbid that I should do so: *but* the man in whose hand the cup is found, he shall be my servant; and as for you, get you up in peace unto your father."

g 18 Then °Judah came near unto him, and said, "Oh my lord, let thy servant, I pray thee, speak a word in my lord's ears, and let not thine anger burn against thy servant: for thou *art* even as Pharaoh.

19 My lord asked his servants, saying, 'Have ye a father, or a brother?'

20 And we said unto my lord, 'We have a father, an old man, and a child of his old age, a little one; and his brother is dead, and he alone is left of his mother, and his father loveth him.'

21 And thou saidst unto thy servants, 'Bring him down unto me, that I may set mine eyes upon him.'

22 And we said unto my lord, 'The lad cannot leave his father: for *if* he should leave his father, *his father* would die.'

23 And thou saidst unto thy servants, 'Except your youngest brother come down with you, ye shall see my face no more.'

24 And it came to pass when we came up unto thy servant my father, we told him the words of my lord.

25 And our father said, 'Go again, *and* buy us a little food.'

26 And we said, 'We cannot go down: if our youngest brother be with us, then will we go down: for we may not see the man's face, except our youngest brother *be* with us.'

27 And thy servant my father said unto us, 'Ye know that my wife bare me two *sons*:

28 And the one went out from me, and °I said, 'Surely he is torn in pieces;' and I saw him not since:

29 And if ye take this also from me, and mischief befall him, ye shall bring down °my gray hairs with sorrow to °the grave.'

30 Now therefore when I come to thy servant my father, and the lad *be* not with us; seeing that his °life is bound up in the lad's °life;

31 It shall come to pass, when he seeth that the lad *is* not °*with us*, that he will die: and thy servants shall bring down [29] the gray hairs of thy servant our father with sorrow to [29] the grave.

32 For thy servant became surety for the lad unto my father, saying, 'If I bring him not unto thee, then I shall bear the blame to my father for ever.'

33 Now therefore, I pray thee, let thy servant abide instead of the lad a bondman to my lord; and let the lad go up with his brethren.

34 For how shall I go up to my father, and the lad *be* not with me? lest peradventure I °see the evil that shall °come on my father."

16 What . . . ? Fig. *Erotēsis* (Ap. 6).

God hath found out. This confession was what Joseph had been labouring to procure. Heb. *Elohim.* Ap. 4.

iniquity. Heb. *'avōn.* See Ap. 44. iii.

18 Judah. He who proposed to sell Joseph and save his life (37. 26, 27), now proposes to remain a bondman for Benjamin. He had already become surety for his safety (43. 8, 9).

28 I said. Here Joseph learned what happened after they had sold him; and how they had deceived their father (37. 31, 32).

29 my gray hairs. Fig. *Metonymy* (of Adjunct). Ap. 6. = "me, in my old age".

the grave. Heb. *Sheōl.* See note on 37. 35, and Ap. 35. The whole phrase is a *Euphemism* (Ap. 6) for "ye will kill me"; so *v.* 31, "he will die".

30 life=soul. Heb. *nephesh.* See Ap. 13.

31 with us. Sam., Sept., and Syr. have the words in the text.

34 see. Put by *Metonymy* (of Cause) (Ap. 6) for the feelings produced by seeing them. Note the *Ellipsis* "see [and grieve over] the evil," &c. See Ap. 6.

come. Heb. find. Evil is thus personified, by Fig. *Prosopopœia* (Ap. 6).

45. 1-16 (*c*, p. 63). THE CUP DISCOVERED.
(*Extended Alternation.*)

c | h | 1. Joseph affected.
  i | 2-. Weeping.
    k | -2. Pharaoh and his house.
  h | 3-13. Joseph revealed.
  i | 14, 15. Weeping.
    k | 16. Pharaoh and his house.

3-13 (*h*, above). **Joseph revealed** (*Introversion*).

h | l | 3, 4. Declaration.
  m | 5. Overruling by God.
    n | 6. Famine.
  m | 7, 8. Overruling by God
l | 9-13. Invitation.

1 man. Heb. *'īsh.* Ap. 14. ii.

2 wept aloud. Heb. gave [forth] his voice in weeping, showing the intensity of feeling. See note on 42. 24.

3 I am Joseph. So the true Joseph will one day reveal Himself, and His brethren will then be troubled indeed, Rev. 1. 7. Matt. 24. 30. Zech. 12. 9-14.

doth, &c. Fig. *Erotēsis* (Ap. 6). For he had just been informed of the fact (43. 28).

4 whom ye sold. Words adopted by Stephen (Acts 7. 9).

5 be not grieved, &c. Cp. Acts 3. 17.

nor angry, &c. Heb. "let not anger kindle in your eyes". Fig. *Prosopopœia.* Ap. 6.

45 Then Joseph could not refrain himself c h
before all them that stood by him; and (p. 63)
he cried, "Cause every °man to go out from me." And there stood no man with him, while Joseph made himself known unto his brethren.

2 And he °wept aloud: i

and the Egyptians and the house of Pharaoh heard. k

3 And Joseph said unto his brethren, °"I *am* Joseph; °doth my father yet live?" And his brethren could not answer him; for they were troubled at his presence. *h* l

4 And Joseph said unto his brethren, "Come near to me, I pray you." And they came near. And he said, "I *am* Joseph your brother, °whom ye sold into Egypt.

5 Now therefore °be not grieved, °nor angry m

with yourselves, that ye sold me hither: for °God did send me before you to °preserve life.

n 6 For these two years *hath* the famine *been*
(p. 63) in the land: and yet *there are* five years, in the which *there shall* neither *be* °earing nor harvest.

m 7 And [5]God sent me before you to [5]preserve you a posterity in the earth, and to save your lives by a great deliverance.

8 So now *it was* not you *that* sent me hither, but °God: and He hath °made me °a father to Pharaoh, and lord of all his house, and a ruler throughout all the land of Egypt.

l 9 Haste ye, and go up to my father, and say unto him, 'Thus saith thy son Joseph, [5]God hath made me lord of all Egypt: come down unto me, tarry not:

10 °And thou shalt dwell in the land of Goshen and thou shalt be near unto me, thou, and thy °children, and thy °children's °children and thy flocks, and thy herds, and all that thou hast:

11 And there will I nourish thee; for yet *there are* five years of famine; lest thou, and thy household, and all that thou hast, come to poverty.'

12 And, °behold, your eyes see, and the eyes of my brother Benjamin, °that *it is* my mouth that speaketh unto you.

13 And ye shall tell my father of all my glory in Egypt, and of all that ye have seen; and ye shall haste and bring down my father hither."

i 14 And he fell upon his brother Benjamin's neck, and [2]wept; and Benjamin wept upon his neck.

15 Moreover he kissed all his brethren, and [2]wept upon them: and after that his brethren talked with him.

k 16 And the fame thereof was heard in Pharaoh's house, saying, "Joseph's brethren are come:" and it pleased Pharaoh well, and his servants.

b 17 And Pharaoh said unto Joseph, "Say unto
(p. 62) thy brethren, 'This do ye; lade your beasts, and go, get you unto the land of Canaan;

18 And take your father and your households, and come unto me: and I will give you the good of the land of Egypt, and °ye shall eat the fat of the land.'

19 °Now thou art commanded, this do ye; take you °wagons out of the land of Egypt for your little ones, and for your wives, and bring your father, and come.

20 Also °regard not your stuff; for the good of all the land of Egypt *is* yours.'"

21 And the [10]children of Israel did so: and Joseph gave them [19]wagons, according to the °commandment of Pharaoh, and gave them provision for the way.

22 To all of them he gave each [1]man changes of raiment; but to Benjamin °he gave three hundred *pieces* of silver, and five changes of raiment.

23 And to his father he sent after this *manner;* ten asses laden with the good things of Egypt, and ten she asses laden with corn and bread and meat for his father by the way.

God did send. So, *v.* 7; 50. 20. Ps. 105. 17. Heb. *Elohim.* Ap. 4.

preserve life. i.e. to preserve you a posterity in the earth (*v.* 7), and hence, to ensure the birth of the true Joseph, and all who have life eternal in Him.

6 earing = ploughing (Anglo-Saxon).

8 God. Heb. *ha Elohim* (with definite article) for emphasis = the Triune God Himself.

made me. The Severus Codex reads "lent me". See Ap. 34.

a father to Pharaoh. This is not the Hebrew *Ab*, "father"; but *Ab en Perao* is an Egyptian title of high office of state. See on 41. 43 = first minister of Pharaoh's household.

10 And. Note the *Polysyndeton* (Ap. 6) in this verse.

children = sons. And so throughout.

12 behold. Fig. *Asterismos.* Ap. 6.

that. Heb. because, showing the *Ellipsis* (Ap. 6, i. e. *Brachyology*); read "Benjamin; because my own mouth is speaking unto you [I cannot speak of all my glory], but ye shall tell my father of all my glory".

19 Now thou art commanded. Sept. and Vulg. read "Thou, therefore, command them".

wagons. Not yet used in Canaan. Those in Egypt depicted as having two wheels.

20 regard not your stuff. Heb. let not your eye pity. Fig. *Prosopopœia.* Ap. 6.

21 commandment. Heb. mouth, put by *Metonymy* (of Cause), Ap. 6, for command given by it.

22 he gave. Cp. 43. 34.

26 Jacob's. Heb. his. Cp. *v.* 28.

fainted = began to cease beating. Cp. Jacob's fainting, with Israel's "strength", *v.* 28.

27 spirit. Heb. *ruach*, put by *Metonymy* (of Cause), Ap. 6, for its manifestations. See Ap. 9.

Jacob. Note this name connected with unbelief (*v.* 26) and weakness, and

28 Israel, which is used in connection with his strength of faith, and act, 46. 1. Cp. Israel's strength, with Jacob's fainting, *v.* 26.

46. 1-7 (A², p. 52). JACOB'S REMOVAL TO EGYPT (*Introversion*).

A² | G | 1. Departure to Beer-sheba and Egypt.
  H | 2-. Divine Manifestation and Call.
   I | -2. Jacob's response.
  H | 3, 4. Divine Manifestation and Promise.
 G | 5-7. Arrival in Egypt from Beer-sheba.

1 offered sacrifices. Heb. *zabach.* Ap. 43. i, iv.

God. Heb. *Elohim.* Ap. 4.

24 So he sent his brethren away, and they departed: and he said unto them, "See that ye fall not out by the way."

25 And they went up out of Egypt, and came y
into the land of Canaan unto Jacob their father, (p. 59)

26 And told him, saying, "Joseph *is* yet alive, and he *is* governor over all the land of Egypt." And °Jacob's heart °fainted, for he believed them not.

27 And they told him all the words of Joseph, which he had said unto them: and when he saw the [19]wagons which Joseph had sent to carry him, the °spirit of °Jacob their father revived:

28 And °Israel said, "*It is* enough; Joseph my son *is* yet alive: I will go and see him before I die."

46 And [28]Israel took his journey with all A² G
that he had, and came to Beer-sheba, (p. 64)
and °offered sacrifices unto the °God of his father Isaac.

II (p. 64) 2 And °God spake unto °Israel in the visions of the night, and said, °"Jacob, Jacob."
I And he said, "Here *am* I."

H 3 And He said, "I *am* °GOD, the [2]God of thy father: °fear not to go down into Egypt; for I will there make of thee a great nation:
4 I will go down with thee into Egypt; and I will also °surely bring thee up *again:* and Joseph shall °put his hand upon thine eyes."

G 1706 5 And [2]Jacob rose up from Beer-sheba: and the °sons of [2]Israel carried [2]Jacob their father, and their little ones, and their wives, in the °wagons which Pharaoh had sent to carry him.
6 And they took their cattle, and their goods, which they had gotten in the land of Canaan, and came into Egypt, [2]Jacob, and all his seed with him:
7 His sons, and his sons' sons with him, his °daughters, and his sons' daughters, and all his seed brought he with him into Egypt.

K^1 L (p. 65) 8 And these *are* °the names of the children of Israel, which came into Egypt, [2]Jacob and his sons: Reuben, Jacob's firstborn.
9 And the sons of Reuben; Hanoch, and Phallu, and Hezron, and Carmi.
10 And the sons of Simeon; Jemuel, and Jamin, and Ohad, and Jachin, and Zohar, and Shaul the son of a Canaanitish woman.
11 And the sons of Levi; Gershon, Kohath, and °Merari.
12 And the sons of Judah; Er, and Onan, and Shelah, and Pharez, and Zarah: °but Er and Onan died in the land of Canaan. And the sons of Pharez were °Hezron and Hamul.
13 And the sons of Issachar; Tola, and Phuvah, and Job, and Shimron.
14 And the sons of Zebulun; Sered, and Elon, and Jahleel.
15 These *be* the sons of Leah, which she bare unto Jacob in Padan-aram, with his daughter Dinah: all the °souls of his sons and his daughters *were* thirty and three.

M 16 And the sons of Gad; Ziphion, and Haggi, Shuni, and Ezbon, Eri, and Arodi, and Areli.
17 And the sons of Asher; Jimnah, and Ishuah, and Isui, and Beriah, and Serah their sister: and the sons of Beriah; Heber, and Malchiel.
18 These *are* the sons of Zilpah, whom Laban gave to Leah his daughter, and these she bare unto Jacob, *even* sixteen [15]souls.

L 19 The sons of Rachel Jacob's wife; Joseph, and Benjamin.
20 And unto Joseph in the land of Egypt were born Manasseh and Ephraim, which Asenath the daughter of Poti-pherah priest of On bare unto him.
21 And the sons of Benjamin *were* Belah, and Becher, and Ashbel, Gera, and Naaman, Ehi, and Rosh, Muppim, and Huppim, and Ard.
22 These *are* the sons of Rachel, which °were born to Jacob: all the [15]souls *were* fourteen.

M 23 And the °sons of Dan; Hushim.
24 And the sons of Naphtali; Jahzeel, and Guni, and Jezer, and Shillem.
25 These *are* the sons of Bilhah, which Laban gave unto Rachel his daughter, and she bare these unto Jacob: all the [15]souls *were* seven.

26 All the [15]souls that came with Jacob into Egypt, (which came °out of his loins), besides Jacob's sons' wives, all the [15]souls *were* °threescore and six; K^2 (p. 65)
27 And the sons of Joseph, which were born

---

2 God. Heb. *Elohim.* Ap. 4.
Israel. See note on 32. 28; 43. 8; 45. 26, 28.
Jacob, Jacob. Fig. *Epizeuxis*, Ap. 6, for emphasis. To remind him of what he was and had been, in contrast to what God would make him. See note on 22. 11.
3 GOD. Heb. *El.* Ap. 4.
fear not, &c. Though Isaac forbidden to go (26. 2), and Abraham warned (15. 13, 14), no need to fear where God goes with Jacob and us.
4 surely bring thee up. Fig. *Polyptōton.* Ap. 6. Cp. 15. 14.
put his hand, &c. i. e. shall close thine eyes in peace.
5 sons of Israel carried Jacob. They now take the ground of faith.
wagons. See note on 45. 19.
7 daughters. Cp. 31. 55 and 46. 15 and 17.

46. 8-27 (B^2, p. 52). THE SONS OF JACOB. POSTERITY.

B^2 | K^1 | 8-25. Severally.
| K^2 | 26, 27. Collectively.

8-25 (K^1, above). THE NAMES. SEVERALLY. (*Alternation.*)

			"into" (*v.* 8) "in" (*v.* 27).
K^1 L	8-15.	Leah	33 = 32 + 1 (Num. 26. 59).
M	16-18.	Zilpah	16 = 16
L	19-22.	Rachel	14 = 11 + 3 (*v.* 27).
M	23-25.	Bilhah	7 = 7
			70 = 66 + 4

8 the names. Cp. the above order with that of 49. 3-27, and see Ap. 45.
11 Merari. Jochebed is to be added, for she "came into" Egypt in her mother (Num. 26. 59).
12 but Er and Onan. These are not to be reckoned.
Hezron and Hamul. These grandsons take their place.
15 souls of his sons. Heb. *nephesh.* Souls put by *Synecdoche* (of the Part) for the persons (Ap. 6). And "of" = the Gen. of Apposition: i. e. "the souls, that is to say, his sons," &c. (Ap. 17).
22 were born. Some codices, with Sam., Onk., Sept., and Syr., read "whom she bare".
23 sons. Fig. *Synecdoche* (of Species). Ap. 6. Only one mentioned; some codices read "son".

26, 27 (K^2, above). THE NAMES. COLLECTIVELY. (*Introversion.*)

K^2 N	26.	The Total that "came into" = 66 (above).	
O	27-.	Born and in Egypt	4
N	-27.	The Total of both	70

26 out of his loins. This is said in order to distinguish the numbers sixty-six and seventy from Stephen's seventy-five, in Acts 7. 14, which includes Jacob as well as "all his *kindred*" (which are not included in the direct descendants of this verse).
These extra nine are made up in part by the five in 1 Ch. 7. 14-20 (Machir, Gilead, Shuthelah, Tahath, Eden, as in Sept.: also here).
threescore and six. See note on 46. 8.

him in Egypt, *were* two [15]souls: all the [15]souls
of the house of [2]Jacob, which came into Egypt,
were °threescore and ten.

A^3 P R^1 (p. 66) 28 And he sent °Judah before him unto
Joseph, to direct his face unto °Goshen; and
they came into the land of Goshen.

S 29 And Joseph made ready his chariot, and
went up to meet [2]Israel his father, to Goshen,
and presented himself unto him; and he
fell on his neck, and wept on his neck a good
while.

30 And [2]Israel said unto Joseph, "Now let me
die, since I have seen thy face, because thou
art yet alive."

T o 31 And Joseph said unto his brethren, and
unto his father's house, "I will go up, and shew
Pharaoh, and say unto him, 'My brethren, and
my father's house, which *were* in the land of
Canaan, are come unto me;

32 And the °men *are* °shepherds, for their
trade hath been to feed cattle; and they have
brought their flocks, and their herds, and all
that they have.'

p 33 And it shall come to pass, when Pharaoh
shall call you, and shall say, 'What *is* your
occupation?'

34 That ye shall say, 'Thy servants' trade
hath been about cattle from our youth even
until now, both we, *and* also our fathers:'
that ye may dwell in the land of [28]Goshen; for
every shepherd *is* an °abomination unto the
Egyptians."

R^2 **47** Then Joseph came and told Pharaoh,
and said, "My father and my brethren,
and their flocks, and their herds, and all that
they have, are come out of the land of Canaan;
and, behold, they *are* in the land of
°Goshen."

T o 2 And he took some of °his brethren, *even* °five
°men, and presented them unto Pharaoh.

p 3 And Pharaoh said unto his brethren, "What
is your occupation?" And they said unto
Pharaoh, "Thy servants *are* shepherds, both
we, *and* also our fathers."

4 They said moreover unto Pharaoh, "For to
sojourn in the land are we come; for thy
servants have no pasture for their flocks; for
the famine *is* sore in the land of Canaan: now
therefore, we pray thee, let thy servants dwell
in the land of [1]Goshen."

5 And Pharaoh spake unto Joseph, saying,
"Thy father and thy brethren are come unto
thee:

6 The land of Egypt *is* before thee; in the
best of the land make thy father and brethren
to dwell; in the land of [1]Goshen let them
dwell: and if thou knowest *any* [2]men of activity
among them, then make them rulers over
my cattle."

S 7 And Joseph brought in °Jacob his father,
and set him before Pharaoh: and Jacob blessed
Pharaoh.

8 And Pharaoh said unto [7]Jacob, °"How old
art thou?"

9 And [7]Jacob said unto Pharaoh, "The °days
of the years of my °pilgrimage *are* °an hundred and thirty years: few and evil have the
days of the years of my life been, and have
not attained unto the days of the years of
the life of my fathers in the days of their
pilgrimage."

10 And °Jacob blessed Pharaoh, and went
out from before Pharaoh.

11 And Joseph placed his father and his brethren, R^3 (p. 66)
and gave them a possession in the land of
Egypt, in the best of the land, in the land of
°Rameses, °as Pharaoh had commanded.

12 And Joseph nourished his father, and his
brethren, and all his father's household, with
bread, according to *their* families.

13 And *there was* no bread in all the land; Q
for the famine *was* very sore, so that the land

---

27 threescore and ten. 7 × 10. See Ap. 10.
These seventy (Ex. 1. 5. Ruth 4. 11) are in contrast with the seventy nations of Gen. 10, and in correspondence with the seventy elders (Ex. 24. 1. Num. 11. 16).

46. 28—50. 13 (A^3, p. 52). JACOB IN EGYPT.
(*Introversion.*)

A^3 | P | 46. 28 — 47. 12. Israelites.
Q | 47. 13–26. Egyptians.
P | 47. 27 — 50. 13. Israelites.

46. 28—47. 12 (P, above). ISRAELITES.

P | R^1 | 46. 28. Jacob's arrival in Goshen accomplished.
X^1 | S | 46. 29, 30. Jacob's meeting with Joseph.
T | o | 46. 31, 32. Presentation planned.
p | 46. 33, 34. Directions given.
R^2 | 47. 1. Jacob's arrival in Goshen announced.
X^2 | *T* | *o* | 47. 2. Presentation made.
p | 47. 3–6. Directions followed.
S | 47. 7–10. Jacob's meeting with Pharaoh.
R^3 | 47. 11, 12. Jacob's settlement in Rameses.

28 Judah. See 44. 18 and cp. 37. 26.
Goshen. The land east of Memphis, suitable for grazing, called "the field of Zoan". Zoan (or Tanis) mentioned in the Inscriptions as containing non-Egyptian inhabitants and Semites.
32 men. Heb. pl. of *'ish*, or *'enōsh*. Ap. 14. iii.
shepherds. See on *v.* 34.
34 abomination. *Metonymy* (of Adjunct). Ap. 6. = an abominable person.
Apepi, the Pharaoh of Joseph, was one of the Hyksos, or shepherd kings. Joseph's advice would commend his brethren to Pharaoh (47. 6), and keep them separate from the Egyptians. It was a *race* prejudice, not a *class* prejudice.

47. 1 Goshen. See on 46. 28.
2 his brethren. Sam., Jon., Sept., Syr. read "the brethren of Joseph".
five. The number of *grace*. See Ap. 10.
men. Heb. pl. of *'ish*, or *'enōsh*. Ap. 14. iii.
7 Jacob. See notes on 32. 28; 43. 8; 45. 26, 28.
8 How old . . . ? Heb. How many are the days? The first question asked in the East to-day.
9 days. Joined with years = Fig. *Pleonasm*. Ap. 6.
pilgrimage = sojournings.
an hundred and thirty years. Joseph being 39; Reuben 46; Simeon 45; Levi 44; Judah 43. Two hundred and fifteen years from Abram's call from Chaldea.
10 Jacob blessed Pharaoh. "The less is blessed of the better" (Heb. 7. 7). Cp. *v.* 2.
11 Rameses. Later name of Goshen. See Ex. 1. 11.
as = according as.

of Egypt and *all* the land of Canaan °fainted by reason of the famine.

14 And Joseph °gathered up all the money that was found in the land of Egypt, and in the land of Canaan, for the corn which they bought: and Joseph brought the money into Pharaoh's house.

15 And when money failed in the land of Egypt, and in the land of Canaan, °all the Egyptians came unto Joseph, and said, "Give us bread: for °why should we die in thy presence? for the money faileth."

16 And Joseph said, "Give your cattle; and I will give °you for your cattle, if money fail."

17 And they brought their cattle unto Joseph: and Joseph gave them bread *in exchange* for horses, and for the flocks, and for the cattle of the herds, and for the asses: and he fed them with bread for all their cattle for that year.

18 When that year was ended, they came unto him the second year, and said unto him, "We will not hide *it* from my lord, how that our money is spent; my lord also hath our herds of cattle; there is not ought left in the sight of my lord, but our bodies, and our lands:

19 [15] Wherefore shall we die before thine eyes, both we and °our land? buy us and our land for bread, and we and our land will be servants unto Pharaoh: and give *us* seed, that we may °live, and not die, that the land be not desolate."

20 And Joseph bought all the land of Egypt for Pharaoh; for the Egyptians sold every °man his field, because the famine prevailed over them: so the land became Pharaoh's.

21 And as for the people, he °removed them to cities from *one* end of the borders of Egypt even to the *other* end thereof.

22 Only the land of the priests bought he not; for the priests had a °portion *assigned them* of Pharaoh, and did eat their °portion which Pharaoh gave them: wherefore they °sold not their lands.

23 Then Joseph said unto the people, °"Behold, I have bought you this day and your land for Pharaoh: °lo, *here is* seed for you, and ye shall sow the land.

24 And it shall come to pass in the increase, that ye shall give the °fifth *part* unto Pharaoh, and four parts shall be your own, for seed of the field, and for your food, and for them of your households, and for food for your little ones."

25 And they said, "Thou hast saved our lives: let us find grace in the sight of my lord, and we will be Pharaoh's servants."

26 And Joseph made it °a law over the land of Egypt unto this day, *that* Pharaoh should have the fifth *part*; except the land of the priests only, *which* became not Pharaoh's.

U (p. 67) 27 And °Israel dwelt in the land of Egypt, in the country of Goshen; and they had possessions therein, and °grew, and multiplied exceedingly.

V 28 And [7] Jacob lived in the land of Egypt seventeen years: so °the whole age of [7] Jacob was an hundred forty and seven years.

W X 29 And the time drew nigh that °Israel must die: and he called his son Joseph, and said unto him, "If now I have found grace in thy sight, put, I pray thee, thy hand under my thigh, and deal kindly and truly with me; bury me not, I pray thee, in Egypt:

30 But I will lie with my fathers, and thou shalt carry me out of Egypt, and bury me in their buryingplace." And he said, "I will do °as thou hast said."

31 And he said, "Swear unto me." And he sware unto him. And °Israel bowed himself upon the bed's head.

---

13 fainted. Fig. *Prosopopœia.* Ap. 6.
14 gathered up: i. e. caused it to be gathered up. Fig. *Metonymy* (of Cause). Ap. 6.
15 all the Egyptians. Heb. all Egypt. Fig. *Metonymy* (of Subject). Ap. 6.
why should we die? Fig. *Erotēsis.* Ap. 6.
16 you. Sam., Jon., and Sept. add "bread".
19 our land. Fig. *Prosopopœia.* Ap. 6.
live, and not die. Fig. *Pleonasm.* Ap. 6.
20 man. Heb. *'ish.* Ap. 14. ii.
21 removed them to cities. Sam., Pent., and Vulg. read, "made them serve as servants"; or, "made them bondmen".
22 portion. Heb. "statute". Fig. *Synecdoche* (of Genus). Ap. 6. Statute is put for the portion allowed by it.
sold not. The reference of Herodotus to this is thus proved to be correct.
23 Behold . . . lo. Fig. *Asterismos.* Ap. 6.
24 fifth part. This is the Turkish law in Palestine to-day, if the landlord supplies cattle and seed. So the terms would not be too onerous.
26 a law. Heb. *chok,* decree.
27 See Structure below.

47. 27—50. 13 (*P*, p. 66). ISRAELITES.
(*Alternation and Introversion.*)

P | Q | U | 47. 27. Jacob's dwelling in Egypt.
V | 47. 28. Years of life (147); and dwelling (17).
W | 47. 29—49. 32. Charges.
Q | *U* | 49. 33—50. 2. Jacob's death in Egypt.
V | 50. 3-14. Days of mourning.

27 Israel. Used here, for the first time, of the nation.
grew, and multiplied, &c. Fulfilling 46. 3, and preparing for Ex. 1. 7 and 12. 37.
28 the whole age. Heb. the days of the years of his life. Fig. *Pleonasm.* Ap. 6.

47. 29—49. 32 (W, above). **Jacob's Charges.**

W | X | 47. 29-31. Charge to Joseph, *re* burial.
Y | 48. 1-20. Blessing of Joseph and his sons.
Z | 48. 21, 22. Assurance of return.
Y | 49. 1-28. Blessing of all his sons.
X | 49. 29-32. Charge to all his sons, *re* burial.

This charge concerning his burial to be distinguished from the charge to all his sons.
29 Israel. Used here of the man Jacob. See notes on *v.* 27; 43. 8; 45. 26, 28.
30 as = according as.
31 Israel bowed himself. Much confusion caused by supposing Heb. 11. 21 refers to this. Mistake made by Ancient Versions and modern commentators. Heb. 11. 21 refers to his blessing of Joseph's sons. This refers to the charge concerning his burial.
It may or may not be bed, or staff.

Y q (p. 68) 48 And it came to pass °after these things, that *one* told Joseph, "Behold, thy father *is* sick:" and he took with him his two sons, Manasseh and Ephraim.

2 And *one* told °Jacob, and said, "Behold, thy son Joseph cometh unto thee:" and °Israel strengthened himself, and °sat upon the bed.

r 3 And [2]Jacob said unto Joseph, °"GOD ALMIGHTY appeared unto me at °Luz in the land of Canaan, and blessed me.

4 And said unto me, °'Behold, I will make thee fruitful, °and multiply thee, and I will make of thee a multitude of people; and will give this land to thy seed after thee *for* an everlasting possession.'

s 5 And now thy two sons, Ephraim and Manasseh, which were born unto thee in the land of Egypt before I came unto thee into Egypt, °*are* mine; as Reuben and Simeon, they shall be mine.

6 And thy issue, which thou begettest after them, shall be thine, *and* shall be called after the name of their brethren in their inheritance.

7 And as for me, when I came from Padan, °Rachel died by me in the land of Canaan in the way, when yet *there was* but a little way to come unto Ephrath: and I buried her there in the way of Ephrath; the same *is* Beth-lehem."

q 8 And [2]Israel beheld Joseph's sons, and said, "Who *are* these?"

9 And Joseph said unto his father, "They *are* my sons, whom °God hath given me in this *place*." And he said, "Bring them, I pray thee, unto me, and I will bless them."

10 Now the eyes of [2]Israel were dim for age, *so that* he could not see. And he brought them near unto him; and he kissed them, and embraced them.

11 And [2]Israel said unto Joseph, "I had not thought to see thy face: and, °lo, [9]God hath shewed me also thy seed."

12 And Joseph brought them out from between his knees, and °he bowed himself with his face to the earth.

r 13 And Joseph took them both, Ephraim in his right hand toward [2]Israel's left hand, and Manasseh in his left hand toward [2]Israel's right hand, and brought *them* near unto him.

14 And [2]Israel stretched out his right hand, and laid *it* upon Ephraim's head, who *was* the younger, and his left hand upon Manasseh's head, °guiding his hands wittingly; for Manasseh *was* the firstborn.

15 And he blessed Joseph, and said, [9]"God, before Whom my fathers Abraham and Isaac did °walk, the [9]God Which fed me all my life long unto this day,

16 °The Angel Which °redeemed me from all evil, bless the lads; and let my name be named on them, and the name of my fathers Abraham and Isaac; and let them °grow into a multitude in the midst of the °earth."

s 17 And when Joseph saw that his father laid his right hand upon the head of Ephraim, it °displeased him: and he held up his father's hand, to remove it from Ephraim's head unto Manasseh's head.

18 And Joseph said unto his father, °"Not so, my father: for this *is* the firstborn; put thy right hand upon his head."

19 And his father °refused, and said, "I know *it*, my son, I know *it*: he also shall become a people, and he also shall be great: but truly his younger brother shall be °greater than he, and his seed shall become a °multitude of nations."

20 And he blessed them that day, saying, "In thee shall [2]Israel bless, saying, [9]'God make thee as Ephraim and as Manasseh:'" and he set Ephraim before Manasseh.

21 And [2]Israel said unto Joseph, [4]"Behold, I die: but [9]God shall be with you, and bring you again unto the land of your fathers. Z (p. 67)

48. 1-20 (Y, p. 67). BLESSING OF JOSEPH AND HIS SONS (*Extended Alternation*).

Y | q | 1, 2. Joseph's sons brought.
  r | 3, 4. Blessing of Jacob.
   s | 5-7. United preference.
  q | 8-12. Joseph's sons presented.
   r | 13-16. Blessing by Jacob.
    s | 17-20. Inverted preference.

1 after these things. The blessing of Joseph's sons took place after Jacob's charge concerning his burial.

2 Jacob . . . Israel. See note on use of these names, 32. 28; 43. 8; 45. 26, 28.

sat upon the bed. This is neither leaning on it nor worshipping. Cp. *v.* 12.

3 GOD ALMIGHTY. Heb. *'El Shaddai.* See Ap. 4.

Luz. Cp. 28. 13, 19; 35. 6.

4 Behold. Fig. *Asterismos.* Ap. 6.

and. Note the Fig. *Polysyndeton* (Ap. 6), to emphasise the four parts of the blessing.

5 are. Heb. they [are] mine. The united preference of Joseph's two sons.

7 Rachel died. Cp. 35. 19.

9 God. Heb. *Elohim*, with art. = God Himself.

11 lo. Fig. *Asterismos.* Ap. 6.

12 he bowed himself. i. e. Jacob worshipped; and, as we know from the Divine addition in Heb. 11. 21, he leaned on his staff = sitting on the (Egyptian) bed (*v.* 2).

14 guiding his hands wittingly (i. e. knowingly). Fig. *Prosopopœia* (Ap. 6). Heb. "making his hands to understand".

15 walk = walk habitually (Heb. *Hithpael*).

16 Note the three titles in *vv.* 15, 16.

The Angel = the creature form of the second person as the messenger of Jehovah (Elohim as consecrated by oath). This form not assumed for the occasion, but for permanent communion with His creatures (Gen. 3. 8; 15. 1; 17. 1; 18. 1, 2; 28. 13; 32. 24, 30. Ex. 23. 20, 21. Num. 22. 21. Josh. 5. 13-15. Prov. 8. 22-31. Mal. 3. 1. Col. 1. 15. Rev. 3. 14).

redeemed. Heb. *g'ãal* = to redeem (by payment of charge). See note on Ex. 6. 6.

grow = swarm as fishes.

earth, or the land.

17 displeased. Heb. was evil in his eyes.

18 Not so, &c. This was Joseph's "will", which Jacob's faith overcame.

19 refused. This is Jacob's faith overcoming "the will of man" (Heb. 11. 21), as Isaac's faith overcame "the will of the flesh", Gen. 27. Heb. 11. 20.

greater. Fulfilled. Cp. Num. 1. 32-35; 2. 18-20. Deut. 33. 17.

multitude = assembly, or convocation. Heb. *kahal,* to call, or muster.

22 Moreover I have given to thee one °portion °above thy brethren, which I took out of the hand of the Amorite with my sword and with my bow."

Y t (p. 69) **49** And °Jacob called unto his sons, and said, "Gather yourselves together, that I may tell you *that* °which shall befall you in °the last days.

2 Gather yourselves together, and hear, ye sons of [1]Jacob; and hearken unto °Israel your father.

u v 3 °Reuben, thou *art* my firstborn, my might, and the beginning of my strength, the excellency of dignity, and the excellency of power:

4 °Unstable as °water, °thou shalt not excel; because thou wentest up to thy father's bed; then defiledst thou *it:* he went up to my couch.

5 Simeon and Levi *are* brethren; instruments of cruelty *are in* their habitations.

6 O °my soul, come not thou into their °secret; °unto their °assembly, mine honour, be not thou united: for in their anger they slew a °man, and in their selfwill they °digged down a wall.

7 Cursed *be* their anger, for *it was* fierce; and their wrath, for it was cruel: I will °divide them in °Jacob, and scatter them in °Israel.

8 °Judah, thou *art he* whom thy brethren shall praise: thy hand *shall be* in the neck of thine enemies; thy father's children shall °bow down before thee.

9 Judah °*is* a lion's whelp: from the prey, my son, thou art gone up: he stooped down, he couched as a °lion, and as an old lion; who shall rouse him up?

10 The °sceptre shall not depart from Judah, nor a °lawgiver °from between his feet, °until Shiloh come; and unto Him *shall* the °gathering of the people *be.*

11 Binding his foal unto the °vine, and his ass's colt unto the choice vine; he washed his garments in °wine, and his clothes in the blood of grapes:

12 His eyes *shall be* red with [11]wine, and his teeth white with milk.

13 Zebulun shall dwell at the haven of the sea; and he *shall be* for an haven of ships; and his border *shall be* unto Zidon.

14 °Issachar *is* a strong ass couching down between two burdens:

15 And he saw that rest *was* good, and the land that *it was* pleasant; and bowed his shoulder to bear, and became a servant unto tribute.

22 portion. Heb. *Shechem*, Gr. *Sychar*, see John 4. 5. Both Abraham and Jacob bought property at Shechem, 23. 18, 19; 33. 18, 19; and here supplemental history tells how Jacob recovered it out of the hand of the Amorite who must have seized it. Fig. *Hysterēsis.* Ap. 6.

above: i.e. the double portion of the firstborn, which Reuben forfeited. Cp. Deut. 21. 17. Cp. 1 Chron. 5. 2. Ezek. 47. 13.

49. 1-28 (*Y*, p. 67). JACOB'S BLESSING OF ALL HIS SONS (*Introversion*).

Y | t | 1, 2. Collectively.
  u | 3-27. Separately. The order of the names.
 t | 28. Collectively.

1 Jacob. See notes on 32. 28; 43. 8; 45. 26, 28.

which shall befall you. This blessing (*v.* 28) is therefore direct prophecy.

the last days. First occ. of fourteen: Gen. 49. 1. Num. 24. 14. Deut. 4. 30; 31. 29. Isa. 2. 2. Jer. 23. 20; 30. 24; 48. 47; 49. 39. Ezek. 38. 16. Dan. 2. 28; 10. 14. Hos. 3. 5. Mic. 4. 1. In ten of these rendered "latter days". A study of these will show that the prophecy (*v.* 1) and "blessing" (*v.* 28) extends to, and embraces the days of Messiah, and His first and second advents.

2 Israel. See notes on 32. 28; 43. 8; 45. 26, 28.

49. 3-27 (u, above). THE ORDER OF THE NAMES. Ap. 45 (*Introversion*).

u | v | 3-15. Leah's six sons. Wife's offspring.
  w | 16-18. Bilhah's son (Dan). } Slave
   x | 19, 20. Zilphah's two sons. } offspring.
  w | 21. Bilhah's son (Naphtali). }
 v | 22-27. Rachel's two sons. Wife's offspring.

3 Reuben. See *v.* 28, cp. 46. 8-25, and Ap. 45.

4 Unstable as water. Fig. *Simile.* Ap. 6. Cp. Num. 16. 1, 2; 32. 1.

water . . . thou. Fig. *Ellipsis* here (Ap. 6. ii b). The word "unstable" = to flow down, and requires the *Ellipsis* to be filled up thus: "Flowing down as water [passes away, so] thou shalt not excel". What thus would pass away is set forth in *v.* 3, and so it came to pass (1 Chron. 5. 1).

6 my soul = myself. Heb. *nephesh.* Ap. 13.

secret = council.

unto. Sam., Jon., Sept., and Syr. insert "and" = "and into".

assembly. Heb. *ḳahal* = Gr. *ecclesia.* See 28. 3.

man. Heb. *'īsh.* Ap. 14. ii.

digged down a wall. Sam. and Sept. read "hamstrung an ox". Cp. 34. 26.

7 divide. Fulfilled, Josh. 19. 1. 1 Chron. 4. 39-43. Lev. 25. 32-34. Levi's turned to blessing later, Ex. 32. 26-29. Deut. 10. 8, 9.

Jacob. First occ. as used of the whole nation.

Israel. See note on 34. 7. Cp. 47. 27.

8 Judah = Praise. Fig. *Paronomasia* (Ap. 6). "*Jehuda, Joducha*".

bow down. Cp. 2 Sam. 5. 1-3 and Ps. 72. 11. Phil. 2. 10.

9 is. Fig. *Metaphor.* Ap. 6. Rest of verse is *Allegory.* Ap. 6.

lion. See note on Num. 2. 32.

10 sceptre. First occ. Put by *Metonymy* (of Adjunct) for Him Who holds it (Ap. 6). Sept. and Targ. read "ruler". See Num. 24. 17. Ps. 45. 6. Zech. 10. 11. **lawgiver.** First occ. Cp. Num. 21. 18. Deut. 33. 21. Ps. 60. 7; 108. 8. Isa. 33. 22. **from between his feet** = from his posterity. Put by Fig. *Euphemy* (Ap. 6). Sept. and Onk. read "from his thighs", i.e. "his seed". Cp. Deut. 28. 57. **until Shiloh come** = until He, Shiloh, comes. So Aq., Sym., Syr. Note the six Pentateuch titles: "Seed" (3. 15), "Shiloh" (49. 10), "Sceptre" (49. 10), "Shepherd" and "Stone" (49. 24), "Star" (Num. 24. 17). **gathering.** Heb. *yiḳhāh* = obedience, submission (not *ḳābaẓ*, as in Jer. 31. 10).

Note the Structure of this verse (*Alternation*).

a | The Sceptre shall not depart from Judah,
 b | Nor a Lawgiver from his seed,
a | Until He, Shiloh, come [Whose right it is, Ez. 21. 27]
 b | And [until] to Him, [the Lawgiver, shall be] the obedience of the peoples.

11 vine. So plentiful in Judah, that people were without care in such matters. **wine.** Heb. *yayin* (Ap. 27). There was more than enough to lavish. **14, 15 Issachar.** Original Orth. = he bringeth reward; referring to birth, 30. 18 (cp. Ps. 24. 5. Ecc. 5. 18. Est. 2. 9, &c.). But here = a hireling. The prophecy is:

"The hireling is the ass (or saddle-bearer) of strangers, | When he saw rest that it was good,
Couching down among the folds; | And the land that it was pleasant:" &c.

He preferred to pay tribute to the Canaanites rather than engage in the struggle to expel them.

w (p. 69) 16 °Dan shall judge his people, as one of the °tribes of Israel.
17 Dan shall be °a serpent by the way, an adder in the path, that biteth the horse °heels, so that his rider shall fall backward.
18 (I have waited for Thy °salvation, O °LORD).

x 19 °Gad, a troop shall °overcome him: but he shall °overcome at the last.
20 °Out of Asher his °bread *shall be* fat, and he shall yield royal dainties.

w 21 Naphtali *is* a hind °let loose: °he giveth °goodly words.

v 22 °Joseph *is* a fruitful bough, *even* a fruitful bough by a well; °*whose* branches run over the wall:
23 The archers have °sorely grieved him, and shot *at him*, and hated him:
24 But his bow abode in strength, and the arms of his hands were made strong by the hands of the mighty °*God* of Jacob; (from thence *is* the Shepherd, the Stone of Israel:)
25 *Even* by the °GOD of thy father, Who shall help thee; and by °the ALMIGHTY, Who shall bless thee with blessings of heaven above, blessings of the deep that lieth under, blessings of the breasts, and of the womb:
26 The blessings of thy father have prevailed above the blessings of my progenitors unto the utmost bound of the everlasting hills: they shall be on the head of Joseph, and on the crown of the head of him that was °separate from his brethren.
27 Benjamin shall °ravin *as* a wolf: in the morning he shall devour the prey, and at night he shall divide the spoil."

t 28 All these *are* the twelve tribes of Israel: and this *is it* that their father spake unto them, and blessed them; every one according to his blessing he blessed them.

X (p. 67) 29 And he charged them, and said unto them, "I am to be °gathered unto my people: bury me °with my fathers in the cave that *is* in the field of Ephron the Hittite,
30 In the cave that *is* in the field of Machpelah, which *is* before Mamre, in the land of Canaan, which Abraham °bought with the field of Ephron the Hittite for a possession of a buryingplace.
31 There they buried °Abraham and Sarah his wife; there they buried Isaac and Rebekah his wife; and there I buried Leah.
32 The purchase of the field and of the cave that *is* therein *was* from the children of Heth."

U 33 And when [1]Jacob had made an end of commanding his sons, he gathered up his feet into the bed, and °yielded up the ghost, and was °gathered unto his people.

1689 **50** And Joseph fell upon his father's face, and °wept upon him, and kissed him.
2 And Joseph commanded his servants the physicians to embalm his father: and the physicians embalmed °Israel.

V 3 And forty days were fulfilled for him; °(for so are fulfilled the days of those which are embalmed): and the Egyptians mourned for him threescore and ten days.

4 And when the days of his mourning were past, °Joseph spake unto the house of Pharaoh, saying, "If now I have found grace in your eyes, speak, I pray you, in the ears of Pharaoh, saying,
5 'My father made me swear, saying, °'Lo, I die: in my grave which I have °digged for me

16 Dan shall judge. Fig. *Paronomasia.* Ap. 6. *Dan Jadīn*, cp. 30. 6. Fulfilled in Judg. 15. 20.
tribes. Heb. sceptres (*v.* 10). Fig. *Metonymy* (of Adjunct). Ap. 6. Put for ruler.
17 a serpent. Beguiling to idolatry. The first tribe to do so. See note on Judg. 18. 30. Hence omitted in Rev. 7. 4 (cp. Deut. 29. 18–21. Lev. 24. 10–16. 1 Kings 12. 30. 2 Kings 10. 29).
heels. Cp. 3. 15. Jer. 8. 16, 17.
18 salvation. Fig. *Metonymy* (of Effect). Ap. 6. Put for Him Who brings deliverance from all the works of the old serpent (Isa. 25. 8, 9. Matt. 24. 13). See Ap. 36.
LORD. Heb. Jehovah. Ap. 4.
19 Gad. Heb. *Gād gedūd.* Fig. *Paronomasia.* Ap. 6.
overcome him = "shall troop (or press) upon him, but he shall press upon their heel".
20 Out of. The Heb. letter "m", which should end *v.* 19, making it "upon their heels", has been wrongly prefixed to the next word, "Asher", *v.* 20, thus making "Asher" begin "Out of", unlike all the others. It should read:

"He shall press upon their heels,
Asher, his bread shall be," &c.

The R.V. rightly keeps the Heb. letter "m" at end of *v.* 19, but repeats it at beginning of *v.* 20, thus translating it twice!
bread. Put for all food. Fig. *Synecdoche* (of Species). Ap. 6.
21 let loose. Emphasis on freedom.
he giveth = he it is that giveth.
goodly words = song of Deborah. Judg. 5. 18.
22 Joseph. Cp. Deut. 33. 13–17.
whose branches run over the wall = branches [it hath] each hath overclimbed a wall.
23 sorely grieved. Cp. Amos 6. 6.
24 God = One.
25 GOD. Heb. *'ēl.* Ap. 4.
the. Should be *'El* = GOD (with Sam., Sept., and Syr.).
26 separate = or set apart. Heb. *nazir*, the consecrated one.
27 ravin, &c. Cp. the Benjamites, Judg. 3. 15. 1 Sam. 11. 6–11; 14. 13–48. Acts 7. 58; 8. 1, 3; 9. 13, 14, 21; 22. 4–8. 1 Tim. 1. 13.
28 The sons collectively. See Ap. 45.
29 gathered unto my people. Fig. *Euphemy.* Put for "death and burial". See *v.* 33. Ap. 6. See note on *v.* 33.
with my fathers. Cp. 23. 9, 10; 47. 30.
30 bought. Cp. 23. 16.
31 Abraham. The five previously buried there form an acrostic of the sixth. Isaac, Sarah, Rebekah, Abraham, Leah = Israel (Heb. 11. 13).
33 yielded up the ghost. The spirit going to God who gave it (Ecc. 12. 7. Num. 16. 22; 27. 16).
gathered unto his people. Refers to body, as the previous gathering (*v.* 33) refers to his feet. See on *v.* 29. He was aged 147.

50. 1 wept. See note on 42. 24.
2 Israel. See notes on 32. 28; 43. 8; 45. 26, 28.
3 for so, &c. Israelites never embalmed. Hence the need of this *parenthetical* explanation. See Ap. 6.
4 Joseph spake. He could not speak before, for, in mourning, Egyptians never shaved, and Joseph, therefore, was not presentable. See on 41. 14.
5 Lo. Fig. *Asterismos.* Ap. 6.
digged. Hence, probably rock-hewn.

in the land of Canaan, there shalt thou bury
me.' Now therefore let me go up, I pray thee,
and bury my father, and I will come again.'"
6 And Pharaoh said, "Go up, and bury thy
father, according as he made thee swear."
7 °And Joseph went up to bury his father:
and with him went up all the servants of Pharaoh, the elders of his house, and all the elders
of the land of Egypt,
8 And all the house of Joseph, and his brethren,
and his father's house: (only their little ones,
and their flocks, and their herds, they left in
the land of Goshen).
9 And there went up with him both chariots
and horsemen: and it was a very great company.
10 And they came to the threshingfloor of
Atad, which *is* beyond Jordan, and there they
mourned with a great and very sore lamentation: and he made a mourning for his father
seven days.
11 And when the inhabitants of the land, the
Canaanites, saw the mourning in the floor of
°Atad, they said, "This *is* a grievous mourning
to the Egyptians:" wherefore the name of it
was called °Abel-mizraim, which *is* beyond
Jordan.
12 And his sons did unto him according as he
commanded them:
13 For °his sons carried him into the land of
Canaan, and °buried him in the cave of the field
of Machpelah, which Abraham °bought with
the field for a possession of a buryingplace of
Ephron the Hittite, before Mamre.
14 And Joseph returned into Egypt, he, and
his brethren, and all that went up with him to
bury his father, after he had buried his father.

B³ A (p. 71) 15 And when Joseph's brethren saw that their
father was dead, they said, "Joseph will peradventure hate us, and will certainly requite
us all the evil which we did unto him."
16 And they sent a messenger unto Joseph,
saying, "Thy father did command before he
died, saying,
17 'So shall ye say unto Joseph, 'Forgive, I
pray thee now, the trespass of thy brethren,
and their sin; for they did unto thee evil:'
and now, we pray thee, forgive the trespass of
the servants of the °God of thy father." And
°Joseph wept when they spake unto him.
18 And his brethren also went and °fell down
before his face; and they said, °"Behold, we
be thy servants."
19 And Joseph said unto them, "Fear not:
for °*am* I in the place of [17] God?
20 But as for you, ye thought evil against me;
but °God meant it unto good, to bring to pass,
as *it is* this day, to save much people °alive.
21 Now therefore fear ye not: I will nourish
you, and your little ones." And he comforted
them, and spake °kindly unto them.

B 22 And Joseph dwelt in Egypt, he, and his
father's house: and Joseph lived an hundred
and ten years.
23 And Joseph saw Ephraim's children of the
third *generation:* the children also of °Machir
the son of Manasseh were °brought up upon
Joseph's knees.

24 And Joseph said unto his brethren, "I die: C
and [17] God will °surely visit you, and bring you
out of this land unto the land which He sware
to °Abraham, to °Isaac, and to °Jacob."
25 And Joseph took an oath of the children of
Israel, saying, [17] "God will [24] surely visit you,
and ye shall °carry up my bones from hence."

26 So Joseph died, *being* an hundred and ten *B*
years old: 1635

and they embalmed him, and he was put in °a *A*
coffin in Egypt.

7-10 And. Note the Fig. *Polysyndeton* (Ap. 6), emphasising each party.

11 Atad. Probably named after the owner, as 2 Sam. 6. 6, "Nachon's"; 2 Sam. 24. 16, "Araunah's".

Abel-mizraim = the mourning of the Egyptians.

13 his sons . . . buried him. See note on Acts 7. 16.

bought. Cp. 23. 16.

15 The final section of Genesis.

50. 15-26 (B³, p. 52). THE SONS OF JACOB.
Joseph and his brethren (*Introversion*).

B³ | A | 15-21. Brethren after Jacob's death.
  B | 22, 23. Joseph's living in Egypt, and age.
   C | 24, 25. Charges.
  B | 26-. Joseph's death in Egypt, and age.
 A | -26. Brethren after Joseph's death.

17 God. Heb. Elohim. Ap. 4.

Joseph wept. See note on 42. 24.

18 fell down. Cp. 37. 7-10.

Behold. Fig. *Asterismos.* Ap. 6.

19 am I, &c. Fig. *Erotēsis* (Ap. 6). Sept. reads "I am in the place of God". The Syr. and Arab. read "I fear God".

20 God meant it, &c. Cp. Ps. 105. 17. Heb. Elohim, Ap. 4.

alive. See on 45. 5.

21 kindly. Heb. spake unto their hearts.

23 Machir. Cp. Num. 26. 29; 32. 39. Josh. 17. 1.

brought up, &c. Heb. born. See 30. 3: *i.e.*, were adopted by him as soon as they were born.

24, 25 (C, above). JOSEPH'S CHARGES.
(*Introversion and Alternation.*)

C | D | 24-. Death approaching.
  E | y | -24. Assurance of return to Canaan.
    z | 25-. Oath.
  E | *y* | -25-. Assurance of return to Canaan.
    z | -25. Oath.
 D | 26. Death experienced.

24 surely visit you. (Ex. 3. 16.) Fig. *Polyptōton.* Ap. 6. Heb. "visiting will visit you"; used for great emphasis. See note on 26. 28. This was the faith of Joseph referred to in Heb. 11. 22. He had "heard" (Rom. 10. 17) and believed what God had said to

Abraham. Gen. 12. 7; 15. 18; 13. 14, 15;

Isaac. 26. 3, 4;

Jacob. 28. 13; 35. 12; 48. 1-4.

All three names are united and discriminated in Ex. 2. 24; 3. 6. Ps. 105. 9, 10. And cp. Ex. 6. 3, 4. Deut. 11. 21. Luke 1. 72, 73, &c.

25 carry up my bones from hence. Which they did. See Ex. 13. 19. Josh. 24. 32. So Jacob had charged them, Gen. 49. 29, 30, and so they had done, Gen. 50. 7-13.

hence. Some codices, with Sam., Sept., Syr., and one printed edition (1494), add "with you".

26 a coffin. Thus the book of Genesis begins with God, and ends with man. It begins with the creation of the heavens above, and ends with "a coffin in Egypt".

EXODUS.

THE STRUCTURE OF THE BOOK AS A WHOLE.

(*Alternation.*)

A | 1. 1—2. 10. THE BONDAGE OF ISRAEL BEGUN.

B | 2. 11—14 31. FREEDOM EFFECTED.

A | 15. 1-21. THE BONDAGE OF ISRAEL ENDED.

B | 15. 22—40. 38. FREEDOM USED

THE SECOND BOOK OF °MOSES,

CALLED

°EXODUS.

A A¹ (p. 73) **1** °Now these *are* the °names of the °children
of Israel, which °came into Egypt; every
°man and his household came with Jacob.
2 °Reuben, Simeon, Levi, and Judah,
3 Issachar, Zebulun, and Benjamin,
4 Dan, and Naphtali, Gad, and Asher.
5 And all the °souls that came out of the loins
of Jacob were °seventy °souls: for Joseph was
in Egypt *already*.
1635 6 And Joseph died, and °all his brethren, and
all that generation.
7 °And the ¹ children of Israel were °fruitful,
and °increased abundantly, and °multiplied,
and waxed °exceeding mighty; and the land
was filled with them.
B¹ 8 Now there °arose up a °new king over
Egypt, which knew not Joseph.
9 And he said unto his people, "Behold, the
people of ¹ the children of Israel *are* more and
mightier than we:
10 Come on, let us °deal wisely with them;
lest they multiply, and it come to pass, that,
when there °falleth out any war, they join also
unto our enemies, and fight against us, and *so*
get them up out of the land."
11 Therefore they did set over them °task-
masters to afflict them with their burdens.
And they built for Pharaoh °treasure cities,
°Pithom and °Raamses.
A² 12 But the more they afflicted them, the more
they °multiplied and grew. And they were
°grieved because of the ¹ children of Israel.
B² 13 And the Egyptians made the ¹ children of
Israel to serve °with rigour:
14 And they made their lives bitter with hard
bondage, in morter, and in brick, and in all
manner of service in the field: all their service,

TITLE, Moses. See Ap. 2.
Exodus. Greek, *The way out*, or *going out*. Heb. *vᵉ'ālleh shᵉmōth* = "these are the names". It is the book of *Redemption* (Ex. 6. 6; 15. 13). Hence the work of redemption is called "Exodus" (Gr. Luke 9. 31, "decease"), and its types are types of Redemption. JAH, the name of the Redeemer, occurs first in Ex. 15. 2, and in the Psalms, in the Exodus book (Ps. 68. 4).

1. 1—2. 10 (A, p. 72). THE BONDAGE OF ISRAEL BEGUN (*Repeated Alternation*).

A | A¹ | 1. 1–7. Israel's sons. Their increase.
B¹ | 1. 8–10. Pharaoh's policy.
A² | 1. 12. Israel's sons. Their increase.
B² | 1. 13–22. Pharaoh's policy.
A³ | 2. 1–10. | Israel's sons. Birth of Moses.

1 Now. The conj. "now" = "and"; thus connecting Ex. closely with Gen.: Lev., Num., and Deut. begin in the same way. Thus the Pentateuch is one book. For the relation of Exodus to the other books of the Pentateuch, see Ap. 1.
names. Thus Redemption is connected with names. Cp. 1. 1–4 with 39. 6, 7, 8–14.
The Name of the Redeemer is published throughout.
He reveals His name: 3. 14, 15; 6. 3; 33. 19; 34. 5–7.
Moses speaks to Pharaoh in His name: 5. 23.
Pharaoh raised up to add glory to it: 9. 16.
Law given in the name of Jehovah: 20. 2.
His name in the Angel: 23. 21.
God knows Moses by his name: 33. 12, 17.
Bezaleel and Aholiab, &c.: 31. 26; 35. 30, 34.
Names of Israel's sons: 1. 1–4; and 28. 9–12, 15–21; 39. 6, 7, 8–14.
children = sons; and so throughout O.T.
came into Egypt. Cp. Gen. 46.
man. Heb. *'ish.* See Ap. 14. ii.
2 Reuben. The order is the six sons of Leah, one of Rachel, two of Bilhah, and two of Zilpah. Note the Introversion of these four.
5 souls. Heb. *nephesh* (Ap. 13).
seventy. See on Gen. 46. 26, Deut. 10. 22, and Acts 7. 14.

6 all. Levi survived him about twenty-three years. Cp. Gen. 50. 26 and Ex. 6. 16. **7 And.** Note the Fig. *Polysyndeton* (Ap. 6), greatly emphasising each particular. Note *five* "ands", the number of grace. See Ap. 10. **fruitful**; as trees. **increased.** Heb. *swarmed*, as fishes. **multiplied.** Cp. Gen. 1. 28. **exceeding.** Fig. *Epizeuxis* (Ap. 6), repeated for emphasis. Heb. *exceedingly*. Fig. *Epizeuxis* (Ap. 6). Note the Fig. *Synonymia* (Ap. 6). **8 arose.** Heb. *kūm*, stood up. Always denotes a standing up in the place of another whom he removed. See Dan. 2. 31, 39, 44; 3. 24. **new king** = a fresh dynasty. "New" here is used in the sense of being quite different from what preceded. See Deut. 32. 17. Judg. 5. 8, and cp. *heteros* in Acts 7. 18, "another" of a *different* kind [not *allos*, another of the *same* kind]. This Pharaoh was of a different race and dynasty, as shown by Josephus, who says "the crown being come into another family" (*Ant.* ii, 9). He was the Assyrian of Isa. 52. 4. See Ap. 37. **10 deal wisely** = diplomatically. The wisdom of Egypt ended in Pharaoh having to bring up, educate, and prepare the very man who was to accomplish what he feared. Cp. Job 5. 13. Prov. 19. 21; 21. 30. Ps. 33. 10, 11. Zoan was the capital of Egypt, and noted for wisdom. But cp. God's comment in Isa. 19. 11, 13; and Ps. 78. 12, 13. **falleth out.** Aram., Sam., and Sept. read "befall us." **11 taskmasters.** Heb. *sārei miṣṣim* is Egyptian for *chiefs of tribute*, allotters and exactors of labour. **treasure cities** = store cities. All now known and named. **Pithom** is the Egyptian *Pa-Tum*, the abode of the god *Tum* = the Greek *Heroöpolis* = city of the store-houses. **Raamses.** Said to be so called because built by Ramases II, but not certain. **12 multiplied and grew** = increasingly multiplied. Fig. *Hendiadys* (Ap. 6). **grieved** = filled with alarm. **13 with rigour** = crushingly.

wherein they made them serve, *was* [13] with rigour.

15 And °the king of Egypt spake to the Hebrew midwives, of which the name of the one *was* Shiphrah, and the name of the other Puah:

16 And he said, "When ye do the office of a midwife to the Hebrew women, and see °*them* upon the °stools; if it *be* a son, then ye shall °kill him: but if it *be* a daughter, then she shall live."

17 But the midwives feared °God, and did not °as [15] the king of Egypt commanded them, but °saved the men children alive.

18 And [15] the king of Egypt called for the midwives, and said unto them, "Why have ye done this thing, and have saved the men children alive?"

19 And the midwives said unto Pharaoh, "Because the Hebrew women *are* not as the Egyptian women; for they *are* lively, and are delivered ere the midwives come in unto them."

20 Therefore °God dealt well with the midwives: and the people multiplied, and waxed very mighty.

21 And it came to pass, because the midwives feared [20] God, that He made them °houses.

22 And Pharaoh charged all his people, saying, "Every son that is °born ye shall cast into the river, and every daughter ye shall °save alive."

A³ c (p. 74) 1571 **2** And there went °a man of the °house of °Levi, and took *to wife* a daughter of Levi.

2 And the woman conceived, and bare °a son: and when she saw him that he *was a* °goodly *child,* she °hid him three months.

3 And when she could not longer hide him, she took for him an °ark of °bulrushes, and daubed it with slime and with pitch, and put the child therein; and she laid *it* in the °flags by the river's brink.

d 4 And his °sister stood afar off, °to wit what would be done to him.

c 5 And the daughter of Pharaoh came down to wash *herself* at the river; and her maidens walked along by the river's side; and when she saw the ark among the flags, she sent her maid to fetch it.

6 And when she had opened *it,* she saw the child: and, behold, °the babe wept. And she had °compassion on him, and said, "This *is one* of the Hebrews' children."

d 7 Then said his sister to Pharaoh's daughter, "Shall I go and call to thee a nurse of the Hebrew women, that she may nurse the child for thee?"

8 And Pharaoh's daughter said to her, "Go." And the maid went and called the child's mother.

9 And Pharaoh's daughter said unto her, "Take this child away, and nurse it for me, and I will give *thee* thy wages." And the woman took the child, and nursed it.

10 And the child grew, and she brought him unto Pharaoh's daughter, and he became °her son. And she called his name °Moses: and she said, "Because I drew him out of the water."

B E¹ 11 And it came to pass in those days, when Moses was °grown, that he went out °unto his brethren, and °looked on their burdens: and he spied °an Egyptian smiting °an Hebrew, one of his brethren.

12 And he looked this way and that way, and when °he saw that *there was* no [1] man, he slew the Egyptian, and hid him in the sand.

15 the king of Egypt. See Ap. 37.

16 them: i.e. the children.

stools. Heb. "two stones". Probably the stone bath in which the children were bathed.

kill him. This was another assault of Satan, to destroy the male children, and so prevent "the seed of the woman" from coming into the world. See Ap. 23. But God intervened by providing the Hebrew midwives, and preserving and preparing Moses.

17 God. Heb. *Eth ha-'Elohim*, very emphatic for the true or triune God.

as = according as.

saved = suffered . . . to live.

20 God. Heb. Elohim. Ap. 4.

21 houses = families or progeny. Fig. *Metonymy* (of Subject). Ap. 6.

22 born. Sam., Onk., Jon., and Vulg. add "to the Hebrews."

save alive = suffer to live.

2. 1-10 (A³, p. 73). ISRAEL'S SONS, MOSES. (*Alternation.*)

A³ | c | 1-3. The child concealed.
  | d | 4. The sister watching.
  | c | 5, 6. The child discovered.
  | *d* | 7-10. The sister interposing.

1 a man. Heb. *'ish*, Ap. 14. ii. = Amram, 6. 16-20.

house = lineage. Fig. *Metonymy* (of Subject), Ap. 6.

Levi. For Genealogy see Ap. 29.

2 a son. Moses was the seventh from Abraham, Abraham the seventh from Heber, Enoch the seventh from Adam. Miriam already born (*v.* 4. Num. 26. 59). Also Aaron (7. 7).

goodly. Heb. *tōv*. Sept. and Acts 7. 20, Heb. 11. 23, *asteios to Theō*, "beautiful to God" = divinely fair.

hid him. This was "by faith" (Heb. 11. 23). Therefore she must have "heard" from God (Rom. 10. 17 and Heb. 11. 7), or it would have been through affection or fancy. All the steps taken (*vv.* 2-4) were the result of believing what she had *heard* from God.

3 ark. Cp. Gen. 6. 14.

bulrushes = papyrus, made by the same Divine instructions as Noah's (Rom. 10. 17).

flags = reeds. Cp. Isa. 18. 2.

4 sister = Miriam. to wit = to know.

6 the babe wept. Heb. a babe weeping.

compassion. In that tear lay the defeat of the enemy, the preservation of the Nation, the faithfulness of Jehovah's word, the bringing to naught "the wisdom of Egypt", and the coming of "the seed of the woman", Gen. 3. 15. Cp. 1. 10 and Job 5. 12, 13. (See Ap. 23.)

10 her son = as her son.

Moses, prob. Egyptian *water-saved*, or Heb. drawn out of the water. No record of his Hebrew name.

2. 11—14. 31 (**B**, p. 72). FREEDOM EFFECTED. (*Repeated Alternation.*)

[For Structure see next page.]

11 grown; and learned in all the wisdom of Egypt, but not yet of God.

unto his brethren. Acts 7. 23, "it came into his heart".

looked on: more than merely saw = regarded with lively sympathy.

an Egyptian = a man (*'ish*), an Egyptian (Ap. 14. ii).

an Hebrew = a man (*'ish*), a Hebrew (Ap. 14. ii).

12 he saw that there was no man: i.e. to help. Cp. same words in Is. 59. 16; 63. 5, and context there.

13 And when he went out the second day, behold, two °men of the Hebrews °strove together: and °he said to him that did the °wrong, "Wherefore smitest thou thy fellow?"
14 And he said, ° "Who made thee °a prince and a judge over us? intendest thou to kill me, as thou killedst the Egyptian?" And Moses °feared, and said, "Surely this thing is known."
1531 15 Now when Pharaoh heard this thing, he sought to slay Moses. But Moses fled from °the face of Pharaoh, and dwelt in the land of Midian: and he sat down by °a well.
16 Now the °priest of Midian had seven daughters: and they came and drew *water*, and filled the troughs to water their father's flock.
17 And the shepherds came and °drove them away: but Moses stood up and °helped them, and watered their flock.
18 And when they came to °Reuel their father, he said, "How *is it that* ye are come so soon to day?"
19 And they said, ° "An Egyptian delivered us out of the hand of the shepherds, and also drew *water* enough for us, and watered the flock."
20 And he said unto his daughters, "And °where *is* he? why *is* it *that* ye have left the man? call him, that he may eat bread."
21 And Moses was °content to dwell with the man: and he gave Moses Zipporah his daughter.
22 And she bare *him* a son, and °he called his name °Gershom: for he said, "I have been a stranger in a strange land."

F^1 (p. 75) 23 And it came to pass in process of time, that °the king of Egypt died: and the °children of Israel °sighed by reason of the bondage, and they °cried, and their °cry came up unto °God by reason of the bondage.
24 And [23]God °heard their °groaning, and [23]God °remembered His covenant °with Abraham, °with Isaac, and °with Jacob.
25 And [23]God °looked upon the [23]children of Israel, and [23]God °had respect unto *them*.

E^2 **3** Now Moses °kept the flock of °Jethro his father in law, the priest of °Midian: and he led the flock to the °backside of the desert, and came to the mountain of °God, *even* to °Horeb.

F^2 g^1 (p. 76) 1491 2 And the °Angel of °the LORD °appeared unto him in a flame of fire out of the midst of a bush: and he looked, and, behold, the °bush burned with fire, and the bush *was* not consumed.

h^1 3 And Moses said, "I will now turn aside, and see this great sight, why the bush is not burnt."

g^2 4 And when [2]the LORD saw that he turned

2. 11 — 14. 31 (**B**, p. 72). FREEDOM EFFECTED.
(*Repeated Alternation.*)

B | E^1 | 2. 11-22. Moses self-sent. Failure and flight.
| F^1 | 2. 23-25. Interposition of Jehovah.
| E^2 | 3. 1. Moses in Midian.
| F^2 | 3. 2—4. 17. Interposition of Jehovah.
| E^3 | 4. 18-20. Moses' departure from Midian.
| F^3 | 4. 21-23. Jehovah's commission to Moses.
| E^4 | 4. 24-26. Moses at Horeb.
| F^4 | 4. 27, 28. Jehovah's commission to Aaron.
| E^5 | 4. 29 — 6. 1. Moses and Aaron in Egypt.
| F^5 | 6. 2-8. Jehovah's revelation of Himself.
| E^6 | 6. 9 — 12. 30. Moses and Aaron in Egypt.
| F^6 | 12. 31 — 14. 31. Jehovah's deliverance of Israel.

13 men. Heb. pl. of *'īsh*, or *'enōsh*. Ap. 14.
strove = striving.
he said. Supposing they would have understood. "But they understood not," Acts 7. 25.
wrong. Heb. *rāsh'ā*, Ap. 44. x.
14 Who made thee . . .? Fig. *Erotēsis* (Ap. 6) for emphasis. Spoken by a Hebrew; cp. Gen. 37. 8. Luke 19. 14.
a prince. Heb., "a man (*'īsh*), a prince".
feared. The "not fearing," in Heb. 11. 27 refers to Ex. 10. 28, 29.
15 the face of. Fig. *Pleonasm* (Ap. 6).
a well. Heb. *b^{e}ēr*. See note on Gen. 21. 19. The well, i.e. of Jethro.
16 priest: or chieftain exercising priestly functions, as Job and Melchizedec. Jethro (3. 1) is called *Reuel* (*v.* 18).
17 drove them away. Probably the only well (*v.* 15); hence cause of contention. Cp. Gen. 21. 25; 26. 15, 18, 20, 21, 22.
helped. Cp. Gen. 29. 10.
18 Reuel. Heb. = friend of God. A true worshipper, 18. 12. Same as Raguel, Num. 10. 29.
19 An Egyptian. Heb. a man (*'īsh*), an Egyptian (Ap. 14. ii).
20 where? . . . why? Fig. *Erotēsis* (Ap. 6).
21 content = well pleased.
22 he. Many codices and a special reading called *sevir* (Ap. 34), read "she".
Gershom. Heb. "a stranger here".
23 the king of Egypt. See Ap. 37.
children = sons.
sighed. Heb. *'ānach*, under pressure of evil.
cried. Heb. *z^e'ak*: with a loud voice, from sorrow or fear.
cry. Heb. *shāv'a*, for help in distress. Note the Fig. *Synonymia* (Ap. 6), to emphasise the greatness of the distress; see also *vv.* 24 and 25.
Can it be that (according to Lightfoot II, 22, Pitman) Pss. 88 and 89 come in here? If so, the latter is a wondrous prophecy, containing "Maschil" = instruction. For Heman and Ethan, see note on 1 Chron. 6. 44, and cp. 1 Kings 4. 31.
God = *Elohim* the Creator in heaven, not yet revealed to them as the Covenant Jehovah.
24 groaning. Heb. *nā'aḳ*, denoting heaviest affliction. Note the Fig. *Synonymia*: **heard . . . remembered . . . looked . . . had respect.** *Anaphora*: **with . . . with . . . with**; see note, Gen. 50. 24, not yet revealed to them as Jehovah. Fig. *Repetitio*. Ap. 6. God, repeated five times. Also the Fig. *Anthropopatheia* (Ap. 6).

3. 1 kept the flock. Forty years, Acts 7. 30. **Jethro** = Reuel, 2. 18. **Midian.** A descendant of Abraham, by Keturah. Moses was called in this land (Arabia); Mahomet also arose there. **backside.** Would be the West side, very fertile. First mention of Desert of Sinai is in connection with feeding a flock! **God.** Heb. Elohim. Ap. 4. **Horeb.** Never used in New Testament. There "the wisdom of Egypt" had to be unlearned and God made known, Isa. 50. 4.

3. 2 — 4. 17. [For Structure see next page.]

2 Angel of the LORD. Heb. Jehovah (Ap. 4). Gen. of App. (Ap. 17): i.e. Jehovah Himself, *v.* 4, then "God" (*v.* 4). Cp. Gen. 18. 1, 13, 17, 20, 22, 33; 19. 1, 24; and cp. Gen. 32. 24, 30 with Hos. 12. 3, 4. **appeared.** Forty years after. **bush burned.** Same lesson as the "furnace" of Gen. 15. 17.

1491 aside to see, ° God called unto him out of the
midst of the bush, and said, ° "Moses, Moses."
And he said, "Here *am* I."
5 And ° He said, "Draw not nigh hither: put
off thy shoes from off thy feet, for the place
whereon thou standest ° *is* ° holy ground."
6 Moreover [5]He said, ° "I *am* the ° God of
thy father, the God of Abraham, the God of
Isaac, and the God of Jacob." And Moses hid
his face; for he was ° afraid to look upon God.
7 And ° the LORD said, ° "I have surely seen
the affliction of My People which *are* in Egypt,
and have heard their cry by reason of their
taskmasters; for I know their sorrows;
8 And I am come down to ° deliver them out
of the hand of the Egyptians, and to bring
them up out of that land unto a ° good land
and a large, unto a land flowing with ° milk
and honey; unto the place of the ° Canaanites,
° and the Hittites, and the Amorites, and the
Perizzites, and the Hivites, and the Jebusites.
9 Now therefore, behold, the cry of the ° children of Israel is come unto Me: and I have
also seen the oppression wherewith the Egyptians oppress them.
10 Come now therefore, and ° I will send thee
unto ° Pharaoh, that thou mayest bring forth
My People the [9]children of Israel out of Egypt."
h^2 11 And Moses said unto [1]God, ° "Who *am* I,
(p. 76) that I should go unto Pharaoh, and that I
should bring forth the [9]children of Israel out of
Egypt?"
g^3 12 And [5]He said, "Certainly ° I will be with
thee; and this *shall be* a token unto thee, that
I have sent thee: When thou hast brought
forth the people out of Egypt, ye shall serve
° God upon this mountain."
h^3 13 And Moses said unto [1]God, "Behold, *when*
I come unto the [9]children of Israel, and shall
say unto them, 'The [1]God of your fathers hath
sent me unto you;' and they shall say to me,
'What *is* His name?' what shall I say unto
them?"
g^4 14 And ° God said unto Moses, ° "I AM THAT
I AM:" and [5]He said, "Thus shalt thou say
unto the [9]children of Israel, ° 'I AM hath sent
me unto you.'"
15 And [14]God said moreover unto Moses, "Thus
shalt thou say unto the [9]children of Israel,
° 'The LORD [1]God of your fathers, the [1]God of
Abraham, the [1]God of Isaac, and the [1]God of
Jacob, hath sent me unto you:' this *is* My
name ° for ever, and this *is* My memorial unto
all generations.

3. 2—4. 17 (F², p. 75). INTERPOSITION OF JEHOVAH (*Repeated Alternation*).

e^2 | g^1 | 3. 2. Vision of the Burning Bush.
  h^1 | 3. 3. Moses' curiosity.
g^2 | 3. 4-10. Divine revelation and commission.
  h^2 | 3. 11. Moses' inquiry "Who am I?"
g^3 | 3. 12. Divine assurance.
  h^3 | 3. 13. Moses' inquiry "Who art Thou?"
g^4 | 3. 14-22. Divine commission.
  h^4 | 4. 1. Moses' doubt.
g^5 | 4. 2-9. Divine assurance.
  h^5 | 4. 10. Moses' inefficiency.
g^6 | 4. 11, 12. Divine power and inspiration.
  h^6 | 4. 13. Moses' request.
g^7 | 4. 14-17. Divine anger and provision.

4 God called. Only here in Exodus. See note on 19. 3. Heb. Elohim. Ap. 4.

Moses, Moses. Fig. *Epizeuxis* (Ap. 6). Cp. Gen. 22. 11.

5 He [God = Elohim] **said.** Occ. four times in Ex. (3. 5, 6, 12, 14). **is.** Heb. "it [is]".

holy. = Separated, or set apart [for God]. Always the rendering of Heb. *ḳodesh* (first occ. here) except Ps. 42. 4, where it is *ḥagag* - holy day; and De. 33. 8, Ps. 16. 2; 86. 2; 89. 19; 145. 17, where it is *ḥasīd* = favour, or grace. *Ḳodesh* must have one identical meaning (as above) in all passages; and does not imply *moral quality* except when used of God Himself. It is rendered "consecrated", "dedicated", "hallowed", "holiness", "saint", and "sanctuary", which are distinguished in the notes under their respective occurrences. **6 I.** Pronoun emphatic.

God = *'Elohim*, the Creator. Note the five-fold repetition. (Ap. 10). Christ founds the doctrine of Resurrection on this verse. See note on Matt. 22. 31, 32.

afraid. Cp. Acts 7. 32.

7 the LORD said = Jehovah said (Heb. *'āmar*, requiring the words spoken). This expression occurs forty-five "sundry times" in Exodus, and in ten "divers manners" (see Ap. 10), and cp. Lev. 1. 1; 5. 14. Num. 3. 40, and see note on 6. 10:—

(1) The LORD said, 3. 7; 33. 21.
(2) To Moses (or to "him"), 4. 2, 4, 6, 11, 19; 6. 1; 7. 1, 14; 9. 22; 10. 1, 12, 21; 11. 1, 9; 14. 26; 16. 4, 28; 17. 5; 19. 9, 10, 24; 24. 12; 32. 7, 9, 33; 33. 1. 17; 34. 1, 27.
(3) To Moses to say unto Aaron, 8. 16.
(4) To Moses to say unto Pharaoh, 4. 21 (cp. 22); 8. 20; 9. 1, 13.
(5) To Moses to rehearse to Joshua, 17. 14.
(6) To Moses to charge the people, 19. 21.
(7) To Moses to speak to the people, 11. 1 (cp. 2).
(8) To Moses to say to the children of Israel, 14. 15; 20 22; 33. 5.
(9) To Moses and unto Aaron, 9. 8; 12. 43.
(10) To Aaron, 4. 27.

I have surely seen. Heb. "seeing I have seen". Fig. *Polyptōton* (Ap. 6); see note on Gen. 26. 28. All begins with God. All is of His grace. Note the five statements in *vv.* 7, 8; and "My People". Cp. Deut. 32. 8, 9. **8 deliver.** Connect this with "serve" in *v.* 12; and connect both with 1 Thess. 1. 9, 10.

good. *Five*-fold description of the land: good, large, milk, honey, place of the nations. See Ap. 10. **milk and honey.** Fig. *Synecdoche* (of Species). Ap. 6. **Canaanites.** Six nations named. The number of man (see Ap. 10). **and.** Note the Fig. *Polysyndeton* (Ap. 6). **9 children** = sons. **10 I will send.** Cp. Acts 7. 23. **Pharaoh.** See Ap. 37. **11 Who am I..?** Fig. *Erotēsis*, in expostulation (Ap. 6) for emphasis. Occupation with self is the cause of all *distrust*. Note these four instances. Cp. 4. 1, 10-12, 13. Very different from the Moses of 2. 11-14. **12 I will be with thee.** Here the meaning of name "Jehovah" is anticipated. **God.** Heb. *eth ha 'Elohim*, very emphatic. God Himself = the Triune God. Cp. "deliver", *v.* 8. **14 God** ['Elohim] **said.** This expression occurs twice in Ex., only here in *vv.* 14 and 15. **I AM THAT I AM.** Heb. *'ehyeh 'asher 'ehyeh.* I will be what I will be (or become). Ap. 48. **I AM.** Heb. *'ehyeh* = I will be (speaking of Himself). **15 The LORD.** Heb. Jehovah = He will be, spoken of by others. See Ap. 4 and cp. Rev. 1. 4, "which is" = continuance in time present; "which was" = continuance in time past; "which is to come" = continuance for ever. The French, "The Eternal", is a much better rendering than LORD, which = Master and Owner. What He will be is left to be filled up according to the needs of those with whom He is in covenant = He Who becometh Saviour, Redeemer, Deliverer, Strengthener, Comforter, &c. **for ever.** He changeth not. Mal. 3. 6. He is therefore Israel's God to-day, as then.

1491 16 Go, and gather the elders of Israel together, and say unto them, '[2]The LORD [1]God of your fathers, the God of Abraham, of Isaac, and of Jacob, appeared unto me, saying, 'I have °surely visited you, and °*seen* that which is done to you in Egypt:

17 And I have said, 'I will bring you up out of the affliction of Egypt unto the land of the [8]Canaanites, [8]and the Hittites, and the Amorites, and the Perizzites, and the Hivites, and the Jebusites, unto a land flowing with [8]milk and honey.'''

18 And they shall hearken to thy voice: and thou shalt come, thou and the elders of Israel, unto the king of Egypt, and ye shall say unto him, 'The [2]LORD [1]God of the Hebrews hath met with us: and now let us go, we beseech thee, three days' journey into the wilderness, that we may °sacrifice to [2]the LORD our [1]God.'

19 And I am sure that the king of Egypt will not let you go, °no, not by a mighty hand.

20 And I will stretch out My hand, and smite Egypt with all My wonders which I will do in the midst thereof: and after that he will let you go.

21 And I will give this people favour in the sight of the Egyptians: and it shall come to pass, that, when ye go, ye shall not go empty:

22 But every woman shall °borrow of her neighbour, and of her that sojourneth in her house, °jewels of silver, and jewels of gold, and raiment: and ye shall put *them* upon your sons, and upon your daughters; and ye shall spoil the Egyptians."

h[1] (p. 76) 4 And Moses answered and said, "But, °behold, °they will not believe me, nor hearken unto my voice: for they will say, °'The LORD hath not appeared unto thee.'"

g[5] 2 And °the LORD said unto him, "What *is* that in thine hand?" And he said, "A rod."

3 And °He said, "Cast it on the ground." And he cast it on the ground, and it became a serpent; and Moses fled from before it.

4 And [1]the LORD said unto Moses, "Put forth thine hand, and take it by the tail." And he put forth his hand, and °caught it, and it became a rod in his hand:

5 "That they may believe that [1]the LORD °God of their fathers, the °God of Abraham, the °God of Isaac, and the °God of Jacob, hath appeared unto thee."

6 And [1]the LORD said furthermore unto him, "Put now thine hand into thy bosom." And he put his hand into his bosom: and when he took it out, behold, his hand *was* °leprous as snow.

7 And [3]He said, "Put thine hand into thy bosom again." And he put his hand into his bosom again; and plucked it out of his bosom, and, behold, it was turned again as his *other* flesh.

8 "And it shall come to pass, if they will not believe thee, neither hearken to the °voice of the first sign, that they will believe the °voice of the latter sign.

3. 16 surely visited you. Fig. *Polyptōton*, "visiting I have visited you" (Ap. 6). Gen. 50. 24, 25.
seen. Ellipsis of the second verb. Fig. *Zeugma* (*Protozeugma*). Ap. 6.
18 sacrifice. Heb. *zabach*. See Ap. 43. I, iv.
19 no, not, &c. Fig. *Epitasis* (Ap. 6).
22 borrow. This is a most unfortunate rendering. Heb. *shā'al*, to ask. Out of 168 occurrences, only six times "borrow", but 162 ask, beg, require, &c. Cp. 11 2; 12. 35, 36. Ps. 2. 8. 1 Sam. 1. 20; 8. 10. Gen. 24. 47, 57; 32. 17; 43. 7. 1 Kings 3. 11.
jewels: or articles. Cp. Gen. 15. 14 and *v.* 21 above.

4. 1 behold. Fig. *Asterismos*. Ap. 6.
they will not = suppose they will not.
The LORD (Heb. Jehovah). Ap. 4.
2 the LORD said. See note on 3. 7, and cp. note on 6. 10.
3 He [Jehovah] said. Occurs nine times in Exodus: 4. 3, 7, 14; 15. 26; 24. 1; 33. 14, 19, 20; 34. 10. Cp. notes on 3. 7 and 6. 10.
4 caught it = stiffened it. Same word as "hardened" Pharaoh's heart.
5 God. Heb. *Elohim*. Ap. 4.
6 leprous. First occ. Nine so afflicted: Ex. 4. 6. Num. 12. 10. 2 Kings 5. 1, 27; 7. 3; 15 5. (2 Chron. 26. 20). Matt. 8. 2; 26. 6. Luke 17. 12. (Ninth case, 21 individuals. Ap. 10.)
8 voice. Fig. *Prosopopœia* (Ap. 6), by which the "sign" is personified.
9 these two signs. See note on 7. 17.
10 my LORD. Should be "Jehovah". One of the 134 places where "Jehovah" in the Primitive Text was altered to "Adonai". Ap. 32.
not eloquent. Heb. "not a man of words" (Heb. *'ĭsh*. Ap. 14. ii). Supposed to contradict Acts 7. 22, but eloquence is no necessary part of "wisdom". With "all the wisdom of the Egyptians" he had not the wisdom needed for his work. The latter had to be learned at "the backside of the desert".
slow. But "mighty". Cp. Acts 7. 22.
11 Who hath made, &c. Fig. *Erotēsis*. Ap. 6.
man = Heb. *'adam*. Ap. 14. i.
12 I will be. Heb. *'ehyeh*. See on 3. 14, 15.
14 Is not Aaron, &c. Fig. *Erotēsis* in Negative affirmation. Ap. 6.

9 And it shall come to pass, if they will not believe also °these two signs, neither hearken unto thy voice, that thou shalt take of the water of the river, and pour *it* upon the dry *land:* and the water which thou takest out of the river shall become blood upon the dry *land*."

10 And Moses said unto [1]the LORD, "O °my LORD*, I *am* °not eloquent, neither heretofore, nor since Thou hast spoken unto Thy servant: but I *am* °slow of speech, and of a °slow tongue." h[5]

11 And [2]the LORD said unto him, °"Who hath made °man's mouth? or Who maketh the dumb, or deaf, or the seeing, or the blind? have not I [1]the LORD? g[6]

12 Now therefore go, and °I will be with thy mouth, and teach thee what thou shalt say."

13 And he said, "O [10]my LORD*, send, I pray Thee, by the hand *of Him Whom* Thou wilt send." h[6]

14 And the anger of [1]the LORD was kindled against Moses, and [3]He said, °"*Is* not Aaron

1491 °the Levite thy brother? I know that He can speak well. And also, behold, He cometh forth to meet thee: and when he seeth thee, he will be glad in his heart.

15 And thou shalt speak unto him, and °put words in his mouth: and °I will be with thy mouth, and with his mouth, and will teach you what ye shall do.

16 And °He shall be °thy spokesman unto the People: and °he shall be, *even* He shall be to thee instead of a mouth, and thou shalt be to him instead of [5]God.

17 And thou shalt take this rod in thine hand, wherewith thou shalt do signs."

E³ (p. 75) 18 And Moses went and returned to Jethro his father in law, and said unto him, "Let me go, I pray thee, and return unto my brethren which *are* in Egypt, and see whether they be yet alive." And Jethro said to Moses, "Go in peace."

19 And °the LORD °said unto Moses in Midian, "Go, return into Egypt: for °all the men °are dead which sought °thy life."

20 And Moses took his wife and his °sons, and set them °upon an ass, and he returned to the land of Egypt: and Moses took the °rod of [5]God in his hand.

F³ 21 And [19]the LORD said unto Moses, "When thou goest to return into Egypt, see that thou do all those wonders before Pharaoh, which I have put in thine hand: but °I will harden his heart, that he shall not let the People go.

22 And thou shalt say unto Pharaoh, °'Thus saith [1]the LORD, 'Israel *is* °My son, *even* My firstborn:

23 And I say unto thee, 'Let My son go, that he may serve Me:' and if thou refuse to let him go, behold, I will slay thy son, *even* thy firstborn.'"

E⁴ 24 And it came to pass °by the way in the inn, that [1]the LORD met him, and sought to kill °him.

25 Then Zipporah took a sharp °stone, and cut off the foreskin of her °son, and cast *it* at his feet, and said, "Surely a °bloody husband *art* thou to me."

26 So °He let °him go: then she said, "A bloody husband *thou art*, because of the circumcision."

F⁴ 27 And [1]the LORD said to °Aaron, "Go into the wilderness to meet Moses." And he went, and °met him in the mount of [5]God, and kissed him.

28 And Moses told Aaron all the words of [1]the LORD Who had sent him, and all the signs which He had commanded him.

E⁵ G (p. 79) 29 And Moses and Aaron went and gathered together all the elders of the °children of Israel:

30 And Aaron spake all the words which [1]the LORD had spoken unto Moses, and did the signs in the sight of the People.

H 31 And °the People believed: and when they heard that [1]the LORD had °visited the [29]children of Israel, and that He had looked upon their affliction, then they bowed their heads and worshipped.

---

the Levite. Why this? Was not Moses a Levite? Is it not to indicate that He whom He would send (*v.* 13) would be of the tribe of Judah?

15 put words (Heb. "the words") **in his mouth.** Cp. Num. 23. 5, 16; 22. 35. Deut. 18. 18. John 17. 8. This is a definition of Divine inspiration.

I will be. Heb. *'ehyeh.* See on 3. 14, 15.

16 he shall be. Fig. *Repetitio* (Ap. 6), for emphasis.

thy spokesman. In ch. 7. 1 = "thy prophet": hence God's prophet is God's spokesman, "the man of God" (Deut. 33. 1. Ps. 90, Title), "God's man" who spoke for God. Qualified only by God's Spirit (Num. 11. 29), and God's Word (2 Tim. 3. 16–4. 4), and by God's making known what is to be spoken (Num. 12. 6).

19 the LORD said. See note on 3. 7, and cp. note on 6. 10.

all. Not merely Pharaoh, but all the court faction.

are dead. The counterpart to Matt. 2. 15 and 20.

thy life = thy soul. Heb. *nephesh.* Ap. 13.

20 sons = Gershom and Eliezer. See on 2. 1.

upon an ass. Still young. So that Moses married after many years in Midian.

rod of God. His own rod is now thus dignified.

21 I will harden = I will embolden. By Heb. idiom active verbs of doing are used of suffering or permitting a thing to be done. Cp. Gen. 31. 7: e. g. Heb. "God did not give him to do me evil". Cp. A.V. Ex. 5. 22. Ps. 16. 10 (give = suffer); Jer. 4. 10 (deceived = suffered to be deceived). So Ezek. 14. 9; 20. 25. Matt. 6. 13; 11. 25 (hid = not revealed); 13. 11. Acts 13. 29 (took him down = permitted). Rom. 9. 18 (hardeneth = suffereth to be). Used six times by Jehovah (9. 12; 10. 1, 20, 27; 11. 10; 14. 8), but not till Pharaoh had done it seven times. Three words used for "harden":—

(1) *ḥāzaḳ* = to brace or tighten up (opp. to relax). Cp. 4. 21; 7. 13, 22; 8. 19; 9. 12, 35; 10. 20, 27; 11. 10; 14. 4, 8, 17 (and once of the Egyptians, 12. 33), thirteen times in all.

(2) *ḳāshah* = to make sharp, hard, severe, cruel. Used twice, 7. 3; 13. 15 (cp. Gen. 49. 7).

(3) *kābēd* = to become heavy (7. 14; 8. 15, 32; 9. 7, 34; 10. 1), six times.

It was in each case God's clemency and forbearing goodness which produced the hardening. That goodness which "leadeth to repentance" (Rom. 2. 4): just as the same sun which softens the wax hardens the clay.

22 Thus saith the LORD [Jehovah]. Occurs in Ex. three times, 4. 22; 7. 17; 9. 1. Lit. "hath said"; as elsewhere.

My son. Cp. Matt. 2. 15.

24 by the way in the inn. A further lesson, not learnt in Egypt or at Horeb. A secret in Moses' life, known only to himself. Moses had neglected to circumcise Eliezer. To save the child's life, Zipporah now performs the rite herself.

him = the son (*v.* 23). Cp. Gen. 17. 14.

25 stone, or knife.

son = Eliezer. Cp. *v.* 20.

bloody husband. Heb. "a husband of bloods" = Gen. of relation, i. e. with rites of blood; alluding to circumcision, which she had tried to evade and avoid.

26 He: i.e., Jehovah.

him = Moses' son Eliezer. Cp. *v.* 24. Gen. 17. 14.

27 Aaron, "Go, &c. Aaron apparently brought up in Pharaoh's house. See 1 Sam. 2. 27, 28.

met him. Cp. the parting at mount Hor, Num. 20. 22–29.

29 children = sons.

31 the People believed. Cp. 4. 1, 8; 3. 18.

visited. See Gen. 50. 24, 25 and Ex. 2. 24, 25. Cp. 6. 6, "redeem", with Luke 1. 68.

G (p. 79) 1491 5 And afterward Moses and Aaron went in, and °told Pharaoh, °"Thus saith °the LORD °God of Israel, °'Let My People go, that they may hold a feast unto Me in the wilderness.'"

2 And Pharaoh said, °"Who *is* °the LORD, that °I should obey His °voice to let °Israel go? °I know not [1]the LORD, neither will °I let Israel go."

3 And they said, "The [1]God of the Hebrews hath °met with us: let us go, we pray thee, three days' journey into the desert, and °sacrifice unto [1]the LORD our [1]God; lest He fall upon us with pestilence, or with the °sword."

H I 4 And °the king of Egypt said unto them, °"Wherefore do ye, Moses and Aaron, °let the people from their works? get you unto your burdens."

5 And [1]Pharaoh said, "Behold, the People of the land now *are* many, and ye make them rest from their burdens."

6 And [1]Pharaoh commanded the same day the °taskmasters of the People, and their °officers, saying,

7 "Ye shall no more give the people °straw to make brick, as heretofore: let them go and gather straw for themselves.

8 And the °tale of the bricks, which they did make heretofore, ye shall lay upon them; ye shall not diminish *ought* °thereof: for they *be* idle; therefore they cry, saying, 'Let us go °*and* [3]sacrifice to our [1]God.'

9 Let there more work be laid upon the men, that they may labour therein; and let them not regard °vain words."

K 10 And the [6]taskmasters of the people went out, and their °officers, and they spake to the People, saying, "Thus saith Pharaoh, 'I will not give you [7]straw.

11 Go ye, get you [7]straw where ye can find it: yet not ought of your work shall be diminished.'"

12 So the People were scattered abroad throughout all the land of Egypt to gather °stubble instead of straw.

13 And the [6]taskmasters hasted *them*, saying, "Fulfil your works, *your* daily tasks, as when there was straw."

14 And the [10]officers of the °children of Israel, which Pharaoh's [6]taskmasters had set over them, were beaten, *and* demanded, "Wherefore have ye not fulfilled your task in making brick both yesterday and to day, as heretofore?"

L 15 Then the [10]officers of the [14]children of Israel came and cried unto Pharaoh, saying, "Wherefore dealest thou thus with thy servants?

16 There is no [7]straw given unto thy servants, and they say to us, 'Make brick:' and, behold, thy servants *are* beaten; but the fault *is* in thine own people."

M 17 But he said, °"Ye *are* idle, *ye are* idle: therefore ye say, 'Let us go *and* do [3]sacrifice to [1]the LORD.'

I 18 Go therefore now, *and* work; for there shall no straw be given you, yet shall ye deliver the [8]tale of bricks."

K 19 And the [10]officers of the [14]children of Israel did see *that* they *were* in evil *case*, after it was said, "Ye shall not minish *ought* from your bricks of your daily task."

L 20 And they met Moses and Aaron, who stood in the way, as they came forth from Pharaoh:

21 And they said unto them, [1]"The LORD look upon you, and judge; because ye have made

4. 29—6. 1 (E[5], p. 75). MOSES AND AARON IN EGYPT (*Alternation*).

E[5] | G | 4. 29, 30. Communication to the elders.
  H | 4. 31. Result—belief and worship.
 G | 5. 1-3. Communication to Pharaoh.
  H | 5. 4—6. 1. Result—unbelief and oppression.

5. 1 told Pharaoh. This was in Zoan (cp. Ps. 78. 12, 43), where Pharaoh had made his palace. It could not have been written in Babylon, for there the kings were not seen, and were hidden behind their ministers. Here, in Egypt, the king was his own minister, and could be easily approached. Cp. 3. 10 and Ap. 37. Note Jehovah's sixfold (Ap. 10) demand and Pharaoh's sixfold objection:—

I. **"Thus saith Jehovah Elohim"** (5. 1).
 (1) "Who is Jehovah?" (5. 2). Q. occ. only here.
II. **"Let My People go"** (5. 1).
 (2) "Go. Sacrifice in the Land" (8. 25).
III. **"We will go three days' journey into the wilderness"** (8. 27).
 (3) "Go", only "not very far away" (8. 28).
IV. **"Let My People go"** (10. 3).
 (4) "Who are they that shall go?" (10. 8).
V. **All must go** (10. 9).
 (5) Not so. Men, but not children or flocks (10. 11).
 (6) Go. Children, but not flocks (10. 24).
VI. **Flocks too: for "we know not . . till"**, &c. (10. 25, 26).

2 Who is the LORD? Fig. *Erotēsis* (Ap. 6). Note the repetition of Pharaoh's "I", answered by Jehovah's "I" eighteen times in ch. 6. 1-8.

voice. Fig. *Metonymy* (of Cause). Ap. 6. Voice put for commands uttered by it.

Israel. Fig. *Metonymy* (of Adjunct). Ap. 6.

3 met with us. Cp. 3. 2-10.

sacrifice. Heb. *zabach.* See Ap. 43. I. iv.

sword. Fig. *Metonymy* (of Cause). Ap. 6.

5. 4—6. 1 (*H*, above). RESULT: UNBELIEF AND OPPRESSION (*Extended Alternation*).

H | I | 5. 4-9. Pharaoh's order given.
  K | 5. 10-14. Evil case.
   L | 5. 15, 16. Complaint: To Pharaoh.
    M | 5. 17. Answer.
 I | 5. 18. Pharaoh's order repeated.
  K | 5. 19. Evil case.
   L | 5. 20-23. Complaints: To Moses, 20, 21. By Moses, 22, 23.
    M | 6. 1. Answer.

4 the king of Egypt. See on *v.* 1, and Ap. 37.

Wherefore. Fig. *Erotēsis.* Ap. 6.

let. A.S. *to hinder.*

6 taskmasters. Cp. 1. 11, Egyptian.

officers: an Egyptian title, scribes, who kept account of work done.

7 straw. *Tebn,* an Egyptian word for chaff, or chopped straw; not our Eng. stubble.

8 tale. A.S. *talu,* a number.

thereof. The suffix is Masc. and refers to the people, "diminish [your exactions] from them."

and. Some codices, with one early printed edition, Onk., and Sept., read "that we may".

9 vain words. Man's estimate of Divine revelation.

10 officers. See on *v.* 6, Hebrews.

12 stubble. Heb. *gash* = reeds. Shown in Egyptian pictures on the monuments.

14 children = sons.

17 Ye are idle. Fig. *Epizeuxis* (Ap. 6) for emphasis.

1491 our savour to be °abhorred in the eyes of Pharaoh, and in the eyes of his servants, to put a sword in their hand to slay us."

22 And Moses returned unto [1]the LORD, and said, °"LORD*, °wherefore hast Thou *so* °evil entreated this People? °why *is* it *that* Thou hast sent me?

23 For since I came to Pharaoh to speak in Thy name, he hath done [22]evil to this People; neither hast Thou °delivered Thy People at all."

M (p. 79) **6** Then °the LORD °said unto Moses, "Now shalt thou see what I will do to Pharaoh: for with a strong hand shall he let them go, and with a strong hand shall he drive them out of his land."

F[5] (p. 75) 2 And °God °spake unto Moses, and said unto him, "*I am* °the LORD:

3 And I appeared unto Abraham, unto Isaac, and unto Jacob, by *the name of* GOD ALMIGHTY, but by My name JEHOVAH was I not °known to them.

4 And °I have also established My covenant with them, to give °them the land of Canaan, the land of their °pilgrimage, wherein they were strangers.

5 And [4]*I* have °also heard the groaning of the °children of Israel, whom the Egyptians keep in bondage; and [4]I have °remembered My covenant.

6 Wherefore say unto the [5]children of Israel, '*I am* [2]the LORD, °and °I will bring you out from under the burdens of the Egyptians, and I will rid you out of their bondage, and I will °redeem you with a stretched out arm, and with great judgments:

7 And I will take you to Me for a People, and I will be to you a [2]God: and ye shall know that *I am* [2]the LORD your [2]God, which bringeth you out from under the burdens of the Egyptians.

8 And I will bring you in unto the land, concerning the which I did °swear to give it to Abraham, to Isaac, and to Jacob; and I will give it you for an heritage: *I am* [2]the LORD.'"

E[6] N[1] a (p. 80) 9 And Moses spake so unto the [5]children of Israel: but they hearkened not unto Moses for anguish of °spirit, and for cruel bondage.

10 And [2]the LORD °spake unto Moses, saying,

11 "Go in, speak unto Pharaoh king of Egypt, that he let the [5]children of Israel go out of his land."

12 And Moses spake before [2]the LORD, saying,

b "Behold, the [5]children of Israel have not hearkened unto me;

b how then shall Pharaoh hear me, who *am* of uncircumcised lips?"

a 13 And [10]the LORD [10]spake unto Moses and unto Aaron, and gave them a charge unto the [5]children of Israel, and unto Pharaoh king of

---

21 abhorred, &c. Heb. "stink in the eyes". Fig. *Catachresis* (Ap. 6) for emphasis.

22 LORD. One of the 134 places where Jehovah in the Primitive Text was altered to Adonai. See Ap. 32.

wherefore..? why..? Fig. *Erotēsis* (Ap. 6). We, like Moses, are full of similar questions, to our sin and sorrow.

evil entreated. Heb. Idiom = suffered to be evil entreated. Heb. *Ra'a*. Ap. 44. viii. See note on 4. 21.

23 delivered Thy People at all. Fig. *Polyptōton* (Ap. 6). Heb. "delivering Thou hast not delivered Thy People". Fig. used for great emphasis. See Gen. 26. 28.

6. 1 the LORD (Heb. Jehovah) **said.** See note on 3. 7, and cp. note on *v.* 10, and see Ap. 4.

2 God spake. Occurs only twice in Exodus: here, and 20. 1. See notes on 3. 7 and 6. 10.

God. Heb. Elohim. Ap. 4.

the LORD = Jehovah. Note the repetition five times in this revelation, *vv.* 2, 3, 6, 7, 8, and see Ap. 10.

3 known. Heb. = perceived or understood. The *name* Jehovah was known as the covenant name; but was not known so as to be understood. The Ellipsis may be better supplied "in [the character of] *El Shaddai*." Cp. 7. 5.

4 I have. Note the three repetitions in *vv.* 4, 5. See Ap. 10.

them = individually (see on Gen. 50. 24). This is why this revelation of Jehovah as "the God of the living" ensures their resurrection. See on ch. 3. 6, and cp. Deut. 11. 21.

pilgrimage. They "sojourned" in Canaan, and they "dwelt" in Egypt.

5 also. Read "I also have:" i.e. as well as thou.

children = sons.

remembered My covenant. All Israel's blessings based on this. See 2. 24.

6 and. Note the Fig. *Polysyndeton* (Ap. 6) in *vv.* 6-8, to emphasise every detail. Cp. Deut. 7. 8.

I will. Note the sevenfold blessing in *vv.* 6-8 and cp. the sevenfold promise in Gen. 12. 2, 3. See Ap. 10.

redeem. Heb. *g'ăal* = to redeem (from charge, by payment). First occ. in connection with Israel. Not *pādāh*. See note on 13. 13.

8 swear. Heb. "I lifted up mine hand". Fig. *Metonymy* (of Adjunct). Ap. 6. Act put for the thing accompanying it: rightly rendered "swear". The Fig. *Anthropopatheia* is also involved in it.

6. 9—12. 30 (E[6], p. 75). MOSES AND AARON IN EGYPT (*Repeated Alternation*).

E[6] N[1] | 6. 9-13. Commission and first results.
  O[1] | 6. 14-27. Moses and Aaron. Gathering the "heads".
 N[2] | 6. 28—7. 5. Commission repeated.
  O[2] | 7. 6, 7. Moses and Aaron. Obedience and age.
 N[3] | 7. 8-13. Commission and credentials.
  O[3] | 7. 14—10. 29. Moses and Aaron. Nine plagues ineffectual.
 N[4] | 11. 1—12. 30. Commission. Tenth plague effectual.

6. 9-13 (N[1], above). COMMISSION AND FIRST RESULTS (*Introversion*).

N[1] a | 9-11. Mission.
  b | 12-. Failure, alleged.
  b | -12. Failure, anticipated.
 a | 13. Mission.

9 spirit. Heb. *ruach*. See Ap. 9.

10 the LORD spake = Jehovah spake (Heb. *dāvar*). This expression occurs in Ex. twenty "sundry times" and in seven "divers manners" (see Ap. 10). Cp. note on 3. 7. Lev. 1. 1. Num. 1. 1:—

(1) To Moses alone, 13. 1; 30. 11, 17, 22, 34; 31. 1; 33. 11; 40. 1.
(2) To Moses to speak to Aaron, 7. 19; 8. 5.
(3) To Moses to speak to the children of Israel, 14. 1; 16. 11 (cp. *v.* 12); 25. 1; 31. 12.
(4) To Moses to speak to Pharaoh, 6. 10 (cp. *v.* 11), 29; 8. 1.
(5) To Moses and unto Aaron, 7. 8.
(6) To Moses and Aaron to speak to the congregation of Israel, 12. 1.
(7) To Moses and Aaron to give a charge to the children of Israel, and unto Pharaoh, 6. 13.

1491 Egypt, to bring the children of Israel out of the land of Egypt.

O^1 (p. 81) 14 These *be* the heads of their fathers' houses: The sons of Reuben the firstborn of Israel; Hanoch, and Pallu, Hezron, and Carmi: these *be* the families of Reuben.

15 And the sons of Simeon; Jemuel, and Jamin, and Ohad, and Jachin, and Zohar, and Shaul the son of a Canaanitish woman: these *are* the families of Simeon.

16 And these *are* the names of the sons of Levi according to their generations; Gershon, and Kohath, and Merari: and the years of
1612 the life of °Levi *were* an hundred thirty and seven years.

17 The sons of Gershon; Libni, and Shimi, according to their families.

18 And the sons of Kohath; Amram, and Izhar, and Hebron, and Uzziel: and the years of the life of Kohath *were* an hundred thirty and three years.

19 And the sons of Merari; Mahali and Mushi: these *are* the families of Levi according to their generations.

20 And Amram took him °Jochebed his father's sister to wife; and she bare him Aaron and Moses: and the years of the life of Amram *were* an hundred and thirty and seven years.

21 And the sons of Izhar; Korah, and Nepheg, and Zichri.

22 And the sons of Uzziel; Mishael, and Elzaphan, and Zithri.

23 And Aaron took him Elisheba, daughter of Amminadab, sister of Naashon, to wife; and she bare him Nadab, and Abihu, Eleazar, and Ithamar.

24 And the sons of Korah; Assir, and °Elkanah, and Abiasaph: these *are* the families of the Korhites.

25 And Eleazar Aaron's son took him *one* of the daughters of Putiel to wife; and she bare him Phinehas: these *are* the heads of the fathers of the Levites according to their families.

26 These *are* that °Aaron and Moses, to whom [1]the LORD said, "Bring out the children of Israel from the land of Egypt according to their armies."

27 These *are* they which spake to °Pharaoh king of Egypt, to bring out the children of Israel from Egypt: these *are* that °Moses and Aaron.

N^2 c 28 And it came to pass on the day *when* [2]the LORD spake unto Moses in the land of Egypt,

29 That °the LORD spake unto Moses, saying, "I *am* [2]the LORD: speak thou unto Pharaoh king of Egypt all that I say unto thee."

d 30 And Moses said before [2]the LORD, "Behold, I *am* of uncircumcised lips, and how shall Pharaoh hearken unto me?"

c **7** And °the LORD °said unto Moses, "See, I have °made thee a °god to Pharaoh: and Aaron thy brother shall be thy °prophet.

2 Thou shalt speak all that I command thee: and Aaron thy brother shall speak unto Pharaoh, that he send the °children of Israel out of his land.

3 And I will °harden Pharaoh's heart, and multiply My signs and My wonders in the land of Egypt.

4 But Pharaoh shall not hearken unto you, that I may lay My hand upon Egypt, and bring forth Mine °armies, °*and* My People the children of Israel, out of the land of Egypt by great judgments.

5 And the Egyptians °shall know that I *am* [2]the LORD, when I stretch forth Mine hand upon Egypt, and bring out the children of Israel from among them."

6 And Moses and Aaron did °as [2]the LORD commanded them, so did they. O^2 (p. 80)

7 And Moses *was* fourscore years old, and Aaron fourscore and three years old, when they spake unto °Pharaoh.

8 And °the LORD spake unto Moses and unto Aaron, saying, N^3

6. 14-27 (O^1, p. 80). MOSES AND AARON: GENEALOGY.

(Choosing the "heads" to speak to Pharaoh.)

O^1 | 14-16. Sons of Israel (Reuben, Simeon, Levi).
| 17-19. Sons of Levi (Gershon, Kohath, Merari).
| 20-27. Sons of Kohath.

14 Moses and Aaron shown to be the crown of the previous pedigrees. They gather the "heads" who are to speak to Pharaoh, *v.* 27.

16 Levi died twenty-three years after Joseph, forty-one years before Moses.

20 Jochebed. See note on Num. 26. 59.

24 Elkanah. The ancestor of Samuel. Cp. 1 Sam. 1. 1-24 and Num. 26. 11, &c.

26 Aaron and Moses. The order according to age and genealogy. Cp. *v.* 27.

27 Pharaoh king of Egypt. See Ap. 37.

Moses and Aaron. The order according to God's choice. Cp. *v.* 26.

6. 28—7. 5 (N^2, p. 80). COMMISSION REPEATED (*Introversion*).

N^2 | c | 6. 28, 29. Mission.
| d | 6. 30. Excuse—ineloquence.
| c | 7. 1-5. Mission.

29 the LORD (Heb. Jehovah) spake. See note on *v.* 10, and cp. note on 3. 7.

7. 1 the LORD (Heb. Jehovah) said. See note on 3. 7, and cp. note on 6. 10.

made = given (as in Eph. 4. 11) as such.

god. i. e. in God's stead. *Elohim* = one appointed by oath. Elohim is thus used of those so given and appointed. Ps. 82. 1, 6. John 10. 34, 35.

prophet. See on 4. 16.

2 children = sons.

3 harden. See note on 4. 21.

4 armies = hosts.

and. No "and" required.

5 shall know: i. e. by a great experience. That was the great object of all these ten plagues; as it will be in the coming day of the judgments described in the Apocalypse. Rev. 16. 5-7.

6 as = according as.

7 Pharaoh. See Ap. 37.

7. 8-13 (N^3, p. 80). COMMISSION AND CREDENTIALS (*Alternation*).

N^3 | e | 8, 9. Command for miracle.
| f | 10. Result. Obedience.
| *e* | 11, 12. Imitation of miracle.
| *f* | 13. Result. Obduracy.

8 the LORD (Heb. Jehovah) spake. See note on 6. 10, and cp. note on 3. 7.

1491 9 "When Pharaoh shall speak unto you, saying, °'Shew a miracle for you:' then thou shalt say unto Aaron, 'Take thy rod, and cast *it* before Pharaoh,' *and* it shall become a °serpent."

10 And Moses and Aaron went in unto Pharaoh, and they did so °as [2]the LORD had commanded: and Aaron cast down his rod before °Pharaoh, and before his servants, and it became a serpent.

11 Then Pharaoh also called the °wise men and the sorcerers: now the magicians of Egypt, they also did in like manner with their enchantments.

12 For they cast down every °man his rod, and they became serpents: but Aaron's °rod °swallowed up their rods.

13 And °He hardened Pharaoh's heart, that he hearkened not unto them; °as [2]the LORD had said.

O^3 P^1 g (p. 82) 14 And °the LORD [1]said unto Moses, "Pharaoh's heart *is* °hardened, he refuseth to let the People go.

15 Get thee unto Pharaoh in the morning; lo, he goeth out unto the water; and thou shalt stand by the river's brink against he come; and the rod which was turned to a °serpent shalt thou take in thine hand.

16 And thou shalt say unto him, '[2]The LORD °God of the Hebrews hath sent me unto thee, saying, 'Let My People go, that they may serve Me in the wilderness:' and, behold, hitherto thou wouldest not hear.

17 °Thus saith [2]the LORD, 'In this thou shalt know that I *am* [2]the LORD:' behold, I will smite with the rod that *is* in mine hand upon the waters which *are* in the °river, and they shall be turned to blood.

18 And the fish that *is* in the river shall die, and the river shall stink; and the Egyptians shall lothe to drink of the water of the river.'"

h 19 And °the LORD °spake unto Moses, "Say unto Aaron, 'Take thy rod, and stretch out thine hand upon the waters of Egypt, upon their °streams, upon their °rivers, and upon their °ponds, and upon all their °pools of water, that they may become blood; and *that* there may be blood throughout all the land of Egypt, both in °*vessels of* wood, and in °*vessels of* stone.'"

20 And Moses and Aaron did so, [10]as [1]the LORD commanded; and he lifted up the rod, and smote the waters that *were* in the °river, in the sight of Pharaoh, and in the sight of his servants; and all the waters that *were* in the °river were turned to blood.

21 And the fish that *was* in the river died; °and the river stank, and the Egyptians could not drink of the water of the river; and there was blood throughout all the land of Egypt.

h 22 And the °magicians of Egypt did so with their enchantments:

g and Pharaoh's heart was °hardened, neither did he hearken unto them; as [1]the LORD had said.

23 And Pharaoh turned and went into his house, neither did he set his heart to this also.

24 And all the Egyptians digged °round about

9 Shew a miracle for you = show us a sign.

serpent. Heb. *thannin* = a crocodile.

10 as = according as.

Pharaoh. Heb. "the face of Pharaoh". Fig. *Pleonasm.* Ap. 6.

11 wise men, &c. Two sets of men mentioned. Pharaoh "called for the wise men, and for the magicians—and these also (the sacred scribes of Egypt) did in like manner with their secret arts".

Two of these named by the Holy Spirit in 2 Tim. 3. 8, "Jannes and Jambres".

12 man. Heb. *'ish.* Ap. 14. ii.

rod. Fig. *Ampliatio* (Ap. 6). The rod still called a rod, though it had become a serpent.

swallowed up: and thus inflicted the first blow on the gods of Egypt. See note on *v.* 20.

13 He hardened. The Heb. here is "Pharaoh's heart was hardened". See on 4. 21.

as = according as.

7. 14—10. 29 (O^3, p. 80). MOSES AND AARON: THE NINE PLAGUES.

(*Extended and Repeated Alternation.*)

O^3 | P^1 | 7. 14-25. First Plague (Blood). Warning.
- Q^1 | 8. 1-15. Second Plague (Frogs). Warning.
  - R^1 | 8. 16-19. Third Plague (Lice). No warning.

P^2 | 8. 20-32. Fourth Plague (Flies). Warning.
- Q^2 | 9. 1-7. Fifth Plague (Murrain). Warning.
  - R^2 | 9. 8-12. Sixth Plague (Boils). No warning.

P^3 | 9. 13-35. Seventh Plague (Hail). Warning.
- Q^3 | 10. 1-20. Eighth Plague (Locusts). Warning.
  - R^3 | 10. 21-27. Ninth Plague (Darkness). No warning.

It will be noticed that the number *nine* is connected with judgment (see Ap. 10), and that the third plague of each three is without warning. To make the symmetry complete, Aaron was used in the infliction of the first three, and Moses of the last three.

7. 14-25 (P^1, above). FIRST PLAGUE (BLOOD).

(*Introversion.*)

P^1 | g | 14-18. Liberation demanded (warning).
- h | 19-21. Plague inflicted.
- *h* | 22-. Plague imitated.

g | -22-25. Liberation refused.

14 the LORD said. See note on 3. 7 and 6. 10.

hardened. See note on 4. 21.

15 serpent. Heb. *nachash.* See note on Gen. 3. 1, and Ap. 19.

16 God. Heb. Elohim. Ap. 6.

17 Thus saith the LORD. See note on 4. 22.

river. Probably the Nile canals.

19 the LORD spake. See note on 6. 10, and cp. note on 3. 7.

streams = canals.

rivers = the seven streams of the Delta.

ponds = lakes where reeds grew.

pools = reservoirs.

vessels of wood, &c. Gen. of material. Fig. *Metonymy* (of Cause). Ap. 6. Heb. "woods and stones", put for [channels] made of wood [and canals] made of stone.

20 river. This first plague was directed against the Nile, an object of worship, which was thus polluted, and became a means of pollution to the people. Cp. 12. 12.

21 and. Note the Fig. *Polysyndeton* in *vv.* 20, 21.

22 magicians . . . did so. Evidently from the water referred to in *v.* 24.

hardened. See note on 4. 21.

24 round about: i. e. on either side of.

1491 the river for water to drink; for they could not drink of the water of the river.
25 And seven days were fulfilled, after that the LORD had smitten the river.

Q[1] i (p. 83) **8** And °the LORD spake unto Moses, "Go unto Pharaoh, and say unto him, 'Thus saith °the LORD, 'Let My People go, that they may serve Me.'
2 And if thou refuse to let *them* go, behold, I will smite all thy borders with °frogs:
3 °And the river shall bring forth frogs abundantly, which shall go up and come into thine house, and into thy °bedchamber, and upon thy bed, and into the house of thy servants, and upon thy people, and into thine ovens, and into thy °kneadingtroughs:
4 And the frogs shall come up both on thee, and upon thy people, and upon all thy servants.'"

k 5 And [1]the LORD spake unto Moses, "Say unto Aaron, 'Stretch forth thine hand with thy rod over the streams, over the rivers, and over the ponds, and cause frogs to come up upon the land of Egypt.'"
6 And Aaron stretched out his hand over the waters of Egypt; and the frogs came up, and covered the land of Egypt.

k 7 And the magicians did so with their enchantments, and brought up frogs upon the land of Egypt.

i 8 Then Pharaoh called for Moses and Aaron, and said, "Intreat [1]the LORD, that He may take away the frogs from me, and from my people; and I will let the People go, that they may do sacrifice unto [1]the LORD."
9 And Moses said unto Pharaoh, °"Glory over me: when shall I intreat for thee, and for thy servants, and for thy people, to destroy the frogs from thee and thy houses, *that* they may remain in the river only?"
10 And he said, "To morrow." And he said, "*Be it* according to thy word: that thou mayest know that *there is* none like unto [1]the LORD our °God.
11 And the frogs shall depart from thee, °and from thy houses, and from thy servants, and from thy people; they shall remain in the river only."
12 And Moses and Aaron went out from Pharaoh: and Moses cried unto [1]the LORD because of the frogs which He had brought against Pharaoh.
13 And [1]the LORD did according to the word of Moses; and the frogs died out of the houses, out of the villages, and out of the fields.
14 And they gathered them together °upon heaps: and the land stank.
15 But when Pharaoh saw that there was respite, he hardened his heart, and hearkened not unto them; °as [1]the LORD had said.

R[1] l 16 And °the LORD said unto Moses, "Say unto Aaron, 'Stretch out thy rod, and smite the dust of the land, that it may become °lice throughout all the land of Egypt.'"

m 17 And they did so; for Aaron stretched out his hand with his rod, and smote the dust of the earth, and it became [16]lice in °man, and in beast; °all the dust of the land became [16]lice throughout all the land of Egypt.

18 And the magicians °did so with their enchantments to bring forth [16]lice, but °they could not: so there were lice upon man, and upon beast. *m*
19 Then the magicians said unto Pharaoh, "This *is* the °finger of [10]God:" *l*
and Pharaoh's heart was hardened, and he hearkened not unto them; °as [1]the LORD had said.

---

8. 1-15 (Q[1], p. 82). SECOND PLAGUE (FROGS).
(*Introversion*).

Q[1] | i | 1-4. Liberation demanded (warning.)
| k | 5, 6. Plague inflicted.
| *k* | 7. Plague imitated.
| *i* | 8-15. Liberation refused.

8. 1 the LORD (Heb. Jehovah) spake. See note on 6. 10, and cp. note on 3. 7.
the LORD=Heb. Jehovah. Ap. 4.
2 frogs. Worshipped as symbol of fecundity.
3 And. Note the *Polysyndeton* (Ap. 6) in *vv.* 3 and 4.
bedchamber. In Palestine beds were mats or couches, and could be moved; but in Egypt there were special bedchambers. These were used later in Palestine (2 Sam. 4. 7).
kneadingtroughs. These are found in every home; none is complete without them.
9 Glory over me. Treat this as part of the following question, which requires this to be rendered: "Explain thyself to me: when shall I," &c.
10 God. Heb. Elohim. Ap. 4.
11 and. Note the Fig. *Polysyndeton* (Ap. 6) emphasising the items, and marking the completeness of the removal.
14 upon heaps. Heb. "heaps, heaps." Fig. *Epizeuxis* (Ap. 6)=in many great heaps.
15 as the LORD had said. Cp. 4. 21.

8. 16-19 (R[1], p. 82). THIRD PLAGUE (LICE).
(*Introversion*).

R[1] | l | 16. Jehovah's command given (no warning).
| m | 17. Plague inflicted.
| *m* | 18, 19–. Imitation abortive.
| *l* | –19. Jehovah's prophecy fulfilled.

16 the LORD (Heb. Jehovah) said. See note on 3. 7, and cp. note on 6. 10.
lice. An Egyptian word=mosquito-gnats. Note that this third plague (like the sixth and ninth) falls without warning.
17 man. Heb. *'adam*, with art.=mankind.
all the dust. A special various reading called *sevir* reads "and all", &c. See Ap. 34. But other codices, with Sept., read, "and in all the dust there came to be".
18 did so. Heb. Idiom, attempted to do so.
they could not. Not because a question of life, for the frogs had life.
God suffered them to do so in the former cases to show the limits of their power; and, by contrast, to show that His power was unlimited.
19 finger. Fig. *Anthropopatheia* (Ap. 6). Note, the Egyptians say "God", not Jehovah.
as the LORD had said. Cp. 4. 21. Jehovah, because in connection with His word.

P² n (p. 84) 1491 20 And °the LORD said unto Moses, "Rise up early in the morning, and stand before Pharaoh; °lo, he cometh forth to the water; and say unto him, 'Thus saith [1]the LORD, 'Let My People go, that they may serve Me.

21 Else, if thou wilt not let My People go, behold, I will send °swarms *of flies* upon thee, °and upon thy servants, and upon thy people, and into thy houses: and the houses of the Egyptians shall be full of swarms *of flies*, and also the ground whereon they *are*.

22 And I will sever in that day the land of Goshen, in which My People dwell, that no swarms *of flies* shall be there; to the end thou mayest know that I *am* [1]the LORD in the midst of the earth.

23 And I will put °a division between My People and thy people: to morrow shall this sign be.'"

o 24 And [1]the LORD did so; and there came a grievous swarm *of flies* into the house of Pharaoh, and °*into* his servants' houses, °and °into all the land of Egypt: °the land was °corrupted by reason of the swarm *of flies*.

o 25 And Pharaoh called for Moses and for Aaron, and said, "Go ye, °sacrifice to your [10]God °in the land."

26 And Moses said, "It is not meet so to do; for we shall [25]sacrifice the °abomination of the Egyptians to [1]the LORD our [10]God: lo, °shall we [25]sacrifice the abomination of the Egyptians before their eyes, and will they not stone us?

27 We will go °three days' journey into the wilderness, and sacrifice to [1]the LORD our [19]God, as °He shall command us."

28 And Pharaoh said, "I will let you go, that ye may [25]sacrifice to [1]the LORD your [10]God in the wilderness; only ye shall °not go very far away: intreat for me."

29 And Moses said, "Behold, I go out from thee, and I will intreat [1]the LORD that the [21]swarms *of flies* may depart from Pharaoh, °from his servants, and from his people, to morrow: but let not Pharaoh deal deceitfully any more in not letting the People go to [25]sacrifice to [1]the LORD."

30 And Moses went out from Pharaoh, and intreated [1]the LORD.

31 And [1]the LORD did according to the word of Moses; and he removed the [21]swarms *of flies* from Pharaoh, [29]from his servants, and from his people; there remained not one.

n 32 And Pharaoh hardened his heart at this time also, neither would he let the People go.

Q² p **9** Then °the LORD °said unto Moses, "Go in unto Pharaoh, and tell him, °'Thus saith °the LORD God of the Hebrews, 'Let My People go, that they may serve Me.

2 For if thou refuse to let *them* go, and wilt hold them still,

3 Behold, the °hand of [1]the LORD is upon thy cattle which *is* °in the field, upon the horses, °upon the asses, upon the camels, upon the oxen, and upon the sheep: *there shall be* a very grievous °murrain.

4 And [1]the LORD shall sever between the cattle of Israel and the cattle of Egypt: and

8. 20-32 (P², p. 82). FOURTH PLAGUE (FLIES).
(*Introversion.*)

P² | n | 20-23. Liberation demanded (warning.)
o | 24. Plague inflicted.
o | 25-31. Plague removed.
n | 32. Liberation refused.

This plague was a severe blow to all idolatrous worship and worshippers. Cleanliness was imperative. For this cause the priests wore linen, and shaved daily. Moreover, it was designed to destroy the worship of Beelzebub, the god of flies, and to manifest his impotence. Cp. 12. 12.

20 the LORD (Heb. Jehovah) **said.** See note on 3. 7, and cp. note on 6. 10.

lo. Fig. *Asterismos* (Ap. 6) for emphasis.

21 swarms of flies. Ellipsis supplied. But should not be thus limited. Heb. root shows that they were *mixed*: all sorts of insects.

and. Note the Fig. *Polysyndeton* (Ap. 6) emphasises the universality of the plague.

23 a division. Heb. *pādāh* = redemption. See notes on 6. 6 and 13. 13. This it is which makes the division between those who are the LORD's people and those who are not. It is the Fig. *Metonymy* (of the Subject), Ap. 6, by which the redemption is put for the judgment which was the sign of it. Cp. Ps. 111. 9; 130. 7.

24 into. This word, in italics, is a special reading called *Sevir*. See Ap. 34.

and. This is omitted in the readings called *Sevir*.

the land. Sam. and Sept. read "and the land".

corrupted = laid waste.

25 sacrifice. Heb. *zabaḥ*. See Ap. 43. I, iv.

in the land. Pharaoh's objection to Jehovah's second demand. Note Moses' reply, and the spiritual lesson as to our worship to-day. See note on 5. 1.

26 abomination. Fig. *Metonymy* (of Adjunct), Ap. 6, put for the act of sacrificing cattle, which was abominated by the Egyptians.

shall, &c. Fig. *Erotēsis* (Ap. 6).

27 three. The number of Divine perfection. See Ap. 10. Jehovah's third demand. See note on 5. 1.

He, &c. Should be "Jehovah hath commanded us." The Heb. word, "He said", should be divided differently: the first letter standing as an abbreviation for "Jehovah".

28 not go very far away. Pharaoh's objection to Jehovah's third demand (*v.* 25). Note the spiritual lesson as to our worship to-day. See note on 5. 1.

29 from. Some codices, with Sam., Sept., and Syr., read "and from".

9. 1-7 (Q², p. 82). FIFTH PLAGUE (MURRAIN).
(*Introversion.*)

Q² | p | 1-5. Liberation demanded (warning).
q | 6. Plague inflicted.
q | 7-. Plague verified.
p | -7. Liberation refused.

The fifth plague was aimed at all kinds of animal worship. Cp. 12. 12.

1 the LORD (Heb. Jehovah) **said.** See note on 3. 7, and cp. note on 6. 10.

Thus saith the LORD God (Heb. Jehovah Elohim) **of the Hebrews.** Occurs only three times, 9. 1, 13 and 10. 3.

3 hand. Fig. *Anthropopatheia* (Ap. 6). Also *Metonymy* (of Cause), "hand" being put for the judgments inflicted by it.

in the field. The cattle, &c., were in the field in the spring and early summer.

upon. Some codices, with Sam., Sept., and Syr., read "and upon".

murrain, or pestilence. See *v.* 15.

1491 there shall nothing die of all *that is* the °children's of Israel.' ' "

5 And [1]the LORD appointed a set time, saying, "To morrow [1]the LORD shall do this thing in the land."

q (p. 84) 6 And [1]the LORD did that thing on the morrow, and °all the cattle of Egypt died: but of the cattle of the [4]children of Israel died not one.

7 And Pharaoh sent, and, behold, there was not one of the cattle of the °Israelites dead.

q And the heart of Pharaoh was °hardened, and
p he did not let the People go.

R² r (p. 85) 8 And [1]the LORD said unto Moses and unto Aaron, "Take to you handfuls of ashes of the furnace, and let Moses sprinkle it toward the heaven in the sight of Pharaoh.

9 And it shall become small dust in all the land of Egypt, and shall be a boil breaking forth *with* blains upon °man, and upon °beast, throughout all the land of Egypt."

s 10 And they took °ashes of the furnace, and stood before Pharaoh; and Moses sprinkled it up toward heaven; and it became a boil breaking forth *with* blains upon man, and upon beast.

s 11 And the magicians could not stand before Moses because of the boils; for the boil was upon the magicians, and upon all the °Egyptians.

r 12 And [1]the LORD [7]hardened the heart of Pharaoh, and he hearkened not unto them; as [1]the LORD had spoken unto Moses.

P³ t 13 And [1]the LORD said unto Moses, "Rise up early in the morning, and stand before Pharaoh, and say unto him, 'Thus saith [1]the LORD [1]God of the Hebrews, 'Let My People go, that they may serve Me.

14 For I will at this time send all My plagues °upon thine heart, and upon thy servants, and upon thy people; that thou mayest know that *there is* none like Me in all the earth.

15 For now I will stretch out My hand, that I may smite thee and thy people with pestilence; and thou shalt be cut off from the earth.

16 And in very deed for this *cause* have I °raised thee up, for to shew *in* thee My power; and that My name may be declared throughout all the earth.

17 °As yet exaltest thou thyself against My People, that thou wilt not let them go?

18 Behold, to morrow about this time I will cause it to rain a very grievous °hail, such as hath not been in Egypt since the foundation thereof even until now.

19 Send therefore now, *and* gather thy cattle, and all that thou hast in the field; *for upon* every man and beast which shall be found in the field, °and shall not be brought home, the hail shall come down upon them, and they shall die.' ' "

u 20 He that feared the word of [1]the LORD among the servants of Pharaoh made his servants and his cattle flee into the houses:

21 And he that regarded not the word of [1]the LORD left his servants and his cattle in the field.

4 children = sons.
6 all the cattle. Fig. *Synecdoche* (of Genus), Ap. 6 = all kinds of cattle.
7 Israelites. Some codices, with Sam., Jon., and Sept., read "sons of Israel".
hardened. See note on 4. 21.

8-12 (R², p. 82). SIXTH PLAGUE (BOILS). (*Introversion*).

R² | r | 8, 9. Jehovah's command (no warning).
 s | 10. Plague inflicted.
 s | 11. Plague not imitated.
 r | 12. Jehovah's hardening (1st occ.).

9 man. Heb. *'adām*, with art. = mankind.
beast. Other than those "in the field", *v.* 3.
10 ashes of the furnace: i. e. one of the altars on which human sacrifices were sometimes offered to propitiate their god *Typhon* (i.e. the Evil Principle). These were doubtless being offered to avert the plagues, and Moses, using the ashes in the same way, produced another plague instead of averting it.
11 Egyptians. Some codices, with Sept., Syr., and Vulg., read "all the land of Egypt".
12 as = according as.

9. 13-35 (P³, p. 82). SEVENTH PLAGUE (HAIL). (*Alternation*).

P³ | t | 13-19. Warning given.
 u | 20, 21. People's regard and disregard.
 t | 22-26. Warning fulfilled.
 u | 27-35. Pharaoh's regard and disregard.

14 upon = into.
16 raised thee up = made thee to stand, i. e., with Sept., "preserved thee" through all the plagues and till the end.
17 As yet . . . ? Fig. *Erotēsis* (Ap. 6).
18 hail. Plague directed against Isis and Osiris. See 12. 12.
19 and shall not be brought home = Fig. *Pleonasm* (Ap. 6).
24 mingled = catching hold of itself like a chain.
25 all the land. Fig. *Synecdoche* (of Genus), Ap. 6, i. e. all parts of it.
27 sinned. Heb. *chāṭ'ā.* See Ap. 44. i.
righteous = the righteous One.
wicked = wicked ones. Heb. *rāsh'a.* See Ap. 44. x.
28 mighty thunderings = Heb. "voices of Elohim" = a strong superlative.

22 And [1]the LORD said unto Moses, "Stretch forth thine hand toward heaven, that there may be hail in all the land of Egypt, upon man, and upon beast, and upon every herb of the field, throughout the land of Egypt." *t*

23 And Moses stretched forth his rod toward heaven: and [1]the LORD sent thunder and hail, and the fire ran along upon the ground; and [1]the LORD rained hail upon the land of Egypt.

24 So there was hail, and fire °mingled with the hail, very grievous, such as there was none like it in all the land of Egypt since it became a nation.

25 And the hail smote throughout °all the land of Egypt all that *was* in the field, both man and beast; and the hail smote every herb of the field, and brake every tree of the field.

26 Only in the land of Goshen, where the children of Israel *were*, was there no hail.

27 And Pharaoh sent, and called for Moses and Aaron, and said unto them, "I have °sinned this time: [1]the LORD *is* °righteous, and I and my people *are* °wicked. *u*

28 Intreat [1]the LORD (for *it is* enough) that there be no *more* °mighty thunderings and

1491 hail; and I will let you go, and ye shall stay no
longer."
29 And Moses said unto him, "As soon as I
am gone out of the city, I will spread abroad
my hands unto [1]the LORD; *and* the thunder
shall cease, neither shall there be any more
hail; that thou mayest know how that the
earth *is* [1]the LORD'S.
30 But as for thee and thy servants, I know
that ye will not yet fear [1]the LORD [1]God."
°31 And the flax and the barley was smitten:
for the barley *was* in the ear, and the flax *was*
°bolled.
32 But the wheat and the rie were not smitten:
for they *were* not grown up.
33 And Moses went out of the city from
Pharaoh, and spread abroad his hands unto
[1]the LORD: and the thunders and hail ceased,
and the rain was not poured upon the earth.
34 And when Pharaoh saw that the rain and
the hail and the thunders were ceased, he
[27]sinned yet more, and [7]hardened his heart, he
and his servants.
35 And the heart of Pharaoh was [7]hardened,
neither would he let the children of Israel go;
as [1]the LORD had °spoken °by Moses.

Q³ v (p. 86) **10** And °the LORD said unto Moses, "Go
in unto Pharaoh: for I have °hardened
his heart, and the heart of his servants, that
I might shew these My signs before him:
2 And that thou mayest tell in the ears of thy
son, and of thy son's son, what things I have
wrought in Egypt, and My signs which I have
done among them; that ye may know how
that I *am* [1]the LORD."
3 And Moses and Aaron came in unto Pharaoh, and said unto him, °"Thus saith [1]the
LORD °God of the Hebrews, 'How long wilt thou
refuse to °humble thyself before Me? °let My
People go, that they may serve Me.
4 Else, if thou refuse to let My People go, behold, to morrow will I bring the °locusts into
thy coast:
5 And they shall cover the °face of the earth,
that one cannot be able to see the earth: and
they shall eat the residue of that which is
escaped, which remaineth unto you from the
hail, and shall eat every tree which groweth
for you out of the field:
6 And they shall fill thy houses, and the
houses of all thy servants, and the houses of
all the Egyptians; which neither thy fathers,
nor thy fathers' fathers have seen, since the
day that they were upon the earth unto this
day.'" And he turned himself, and went out
from Pharaoh.

w 7 And Pharaoh's servants said unto him,
"How long shall °this man be a snare unto
us? let the men go, that they may serve [1]the
LORD their [3]God: knowest thou not yet that
Egypt is destroyed?"
8 And Moses and Aaron were brought again
unto Pharaoh: and he said unto them, "Go,
serve [1]the LORD your [3]God: *but* °who *are*
they that shall go?"
9 And Moses said, °"We will go with our
young and with our old, with our sons and
with our daughters, with our flocks and with
our herds will we go; for we *must hold* a feast
unto [1]the LORD."

31 Note the *Introversion* in this verse.

a | flax
  b | barley
  b | barley
a | flax

These ripened in middle of February or early in March. Israel left early in April.

bolled. A word of Scandinavian origin, like bulged, i. e. swelled, or ripe. But Heb. = blossom, i. e. the capsules formed. True to the seasons in Egypt to this day.

35 spoken. Cp. 4. 21.

by Moses. Lit. by the hand of Moses. Fig. *Metonymy* (of Adjunct): hand being put for instrumentality.

10. 1-20 (Q³, p. 82). EIGHTH PLAGUE (Locusts). (*Simple Alternation*).

Q³ | v | 1-6. Warning given.
  w | 7-11. Reception by Pharaoh's servants (parley).
 v | 12-15. Warning carried out.
  w | 16-20. Reception by Pharaoh (parley).

The eighth plague was directed against the god *Serapis*, who was supposed to protect the land from locusts. They came at Moses' bidding, and retired only at his bidding. Thus the impotence of *Serapis* was manifest.

1 the LORD. Heb. Jehovah. Ap. 4.

the LORD said = Jehovah said. See note on 3. 7 and cp. note on 6. 10.

hardened. See note on 4. 21.

3 Thus saith the LORD God of the Hebrews. Occurs only here and 9. 1, 13.

God. Heb. Elohim. Ap. 4.

humble = depression of spirit rather than softening of heart. "To cry out" as conscious of suffering. A man may be humbled without humbling himself.

let My People go. Jehovah's fourth demand. See note on 5. 1.

4 locusts. Cp. Joel 2. 1-10, and Rev. 9. 3-11.

5 face of the earth. Heb. "eye of the earth". Fig. *Metonymy* (of Effect), eye put for what is seen by it. Ap. 6.

7 this man. Heb. this one. No word for man here in Hebrew text.

8 who are they? Pharaoh's answer to Jehovah's fourth demand in *v.* 3. See note on 5. 1.

9 We will go with our young, &c. Moses knew nothing of forsaking Egypt and leaving the little ones behind. Note the spiritual lesson; and cp. Eph. 6. 4 and Gen. 7. 1.

10 evil. Fig. *Metonymy* (of Effect), Ap. 6, evil put for death, threatened in *v.* 28.

11 men. Heb. pl. of *'ish*, or *'enōsh* (Ap. 14. iii). This was Pharaoh's first objection to Jehovah's fifth demand in 5. 1.

13 wind. Heb. *rūach.* Ap. 9.

10 And he said unto them, "Let [1]the LORD be
so with you, as I will let you go, and your little
ones: look *to it*; for °evil *is* before you.
11 Not so: go now ye *that are* °men, and
serve [1]the LORD; for that ye did desire." And
they were driven out from Pharaoh's presence.

12 And [1]the LORD said unto Moses, "Stretch v
out thine hand over the land of Egypt for the
locusts, that they may come up upon the land
of Egypt, and eat every herb of the land, *even*
all that the hail hath left."
13 And Moses stretched forth his rod over the
land of Egypt, and [1]the LORD brought an east
°wind upon the land all that day, and all *that*
night; *and* when it was morning, the east
°wind brought the locusts.
14 And the locusts went up over all the land
of Egypt, and rested in all the coasts of Egypt:
very grievous *were they*; before them there
were no such locusts as they, neither after them
shall be such.
15 For they covered the [5]face of the whole

1491 °earth, so that the land was darkened; and they did eat every herb of the land, and all the fruit of the trees which the hail had left: and there remained not any green thing in the trees, or in the herbs of the field, through all the land of Egypt.

w
(p. 86) **16 Then Pharaoh called for Moses and Aaron in haste; and he said, "I have °sinned against [1]the LORD your [3]God, and against you.**

17 Now therefore forgive, I pray thee, my sin only this once, and intreat [1]the LORD your [3]God, that He may take away from me this °death only."

18 °And he went out from Pharaoh, and intreated [1]the LORD.

19 And [1]the LORD turned a °mighty strong west [13]wind, which took away the locusts, and cast them into the Red sea; there remained not one locust in all the °coasts of Egypt.

20 But °the LORD [1]hardened Pharaoh's heart, so that he would not let the children of Israel go.

R³ x
(p. 87) **21 And °the LORD °said unto Moses, "Stretch out thine hand toward heaven, that there may be °darkness over the land of Egypt, even darkness *which* may be felt."**

y **22 And Moses stretched forth his hand toward heaven; and there was a thick darkness in all the land of Egypt three days:**

23 They saw not one another, neither rose any from his place for three days: but all the children of Israel had light in their dwellings.

y **24 And Pharaoh called unto Moses, and said, "Go ye, serve [1]the LORD; only °let your flocks and your herds be stayed: let your little ones also go with you."**

25 And Moses said, "Thou must give us also °sacrifices and burnt offerings, that we may °sacrifice unto [1]the LORD our [3]God.

26 Our cattle also shall go with us; there shall not an °hoof be left behind; for thereof must we take to serve [1]the LORD our [3]God; and °we know not with what we must serve [1]the LORD, °until we come thither."

x **27 But [1]the LORD °hardened Pharaoh's heart, and he would not let them go.**

28 And Pharaoh said unto him, °"Get thee from me, take heed to thyself, see my face no more; for in *that* day thou seest my face thou shalt die."

29 And Moses said, "Thou hast spoken well, I will see thy face again °no more."

N⁴ a c **11 (And °the LORD °said unto Moses, "Yet will I bring one plague *more* upon Pharaoh, and upon Egypt; °afterwards he will let you go hence: when he shall let *you* go, he shall surely thrust you out hence altogether.**

d **2 Speak now in the ears of the People, and let every °man °borrow of his neighbour, and every woman of her neighbour, °jewels of silver, and °jewels of gold."**

3 And [1]the LORD gave the People favour in the sight of the Egyptians. Moreover the [2]man Moses *was* very great in the land of Egypt, in the sight of Pharaoh's servants, and in the sight of the people.)

d **4 And Moses said, "Thus saith [1]the LORD, 'About midnight will I go out into the midst of Egypt:**

5 And all the firstborn in the land of Egypt shall die, from the firstborn of Pharaoh that sitteth upon his throne, even unto the firstborn of the maidservant that *is* behind the mill; and all the firstborn of beasts.

6 And there shall be a great cry throughout all the land of Egypt, such as there was none like it, nor shall be like it any more.

---

15 earth = land.

16 sinned. Heb. *chāṭ'ā.* Ap. 44. i.

17 death. Fig. *Metonymy* (of Effect), Ap. 6, death put for the plague which caused it.

18 And he. Some codices, with Sam., Sept., and Syr., read "So Moses".

19 mighty strong. Fig. *Synonymia.* Ap. 6. Locusts are always brought by east wind and carried away by west wind.

coasts = bounds, or borders.

20 the LORD hardened. Again this is stated. Cp. 4. 21.

10. 21–27 (R³, p. 82). NINTH PLAGUE (DARKNESS). (*Introversion*).

R³ | x | 21. Jehovah's command (no warning).
  y | 22, 23. Infliction of Plague.
  y | 24–26. Reception of Plague.
 x | 27–29. Jehovah's hardening.

21 the LORD (Heb. Jehovah) **said.** See note on 3. 7, and cp. note on 6. 10.

darkness. First of four instances of darkness in judgment. Ex. 10. 22. Matt. 27. 45. Jude 13. Rev. 16. 10.

24 let your flocks and your herds be stayed. Pharaoh's second objection to Jehovah's fifth and final demand in 10. 9.

25 sacrifices. Heb. *zebach.* See Ap. 43. II. iv.

sacrifice. Heb. *'asah.* See Ap. 43. I. iii.

26 hoof. Fig. *Synecdoche* (of Part), Ap. 6, "hoof" put for whole animal.

we know not. Note the contrast between the "thou" of *v.* 25 and the "we" of *v.* 26.

until we come thither. Note the spiritual lesson. Not until we leave the world can we have a true conception of Jehovah's requirements: "if any man do His will he shall know of the doctrine" (John 7. 17).

27 hardened. See on 4. 21.

28 Get thee from me. Eleven kings and rulers thus offended. Ex. 10. 28. Num. 24. 11. 1 Kings 13. 4; 22. 27. 2 Kings 5. 12. 2 Chron. 16. 10; 24. 21; 26. 19. Jer. 26. 21; 32. 3. Matt. 14. 3.

29 no more. Moses did not leave Pharaoh's presence till 11. 8. So this is the Fig. *Prolepsis* (Ap. 6).

11. 1–12. 30 (N⁴, p. 80). COMMISSION FOR TENTH PLAGUE (*Introversion*).

N⁴ | a | 11. 1–10. The Tenth Plague threatened.
  b | 12. 1–20. Passover commanded.
  b | 12. 21–28. Passover command communicated.
 a | 12. 29, 30. The Tenth Plague inflicted.

11. 1–10 (a, above). THE TENTH PLAGUE THREATENED (*Introversion*).

a | c | 1. God's word to Moses as to the Tenth Plague.
  d | 2, 3. Direction as to actions (people).
  d | 4–8. Direction as to words (Pharaoh).
 c | 9. God's words to Moses as to result.

1 the LORD (Heb. Jehovah) **said.** See note on 3. 7, and cp. note on 6. 10.

afterwards. Some codices, with Sept., Syr., and Vulg., read "and after".

2 man. Heb. *'ish* (Ap. 14. ii).

borrow = ask. See note on 3. 22.

jewels: or articles, or vessels.

1491 7 But against any of the children of Israel shall not a °dog move his tongue, against man or beast: that ye may know how that [1]the LORD doth put a difference between the Egyptians and Israel.'

8 And all these thy servants shall come down unto me, and bow down themselves unto me, saying, 'Get thee out, and all the People that follow thee:' and after that I will go out." And he went out from Pharaoh in a great anger.

c (p. 87) 9 And [1]the LORD said unto Moses, "Pharaoh shall not hearken unto you; that My wonders may be multiplied in the land of Egypt."

°10 And Moses and Aaron did all these wonders before Pharaoh: and [1]the LORD [7]hardened Pharaoh's heart, so that he would not let the children of Israel go out of his land.

b e (p. 88) **12** And °the LORD spake unto Moses and Aaron in the land of Egypt, saying,

2 "This °month *shall be* unto you the beginning of months: it *shall be* the first month of the year to you.

f g 3 Speak ye unto all the congregation of °Israel, saying, 'In the tenth *day* of this month they shall take to them every °man a °lamb, according to the house of *their* fathers, a lamb for an °house:

4 And if the household be too little for the lamb, let him and his neighbour next unto his house take °*it* according to the number of the °souls; every man according to his °eating shall make your count for the °lamb.

5 Your lamb shall be °without blemish, a male of the first year: ye shall take *it* out from the sheep, or from the goats:

6 And ye shall keep it up until the fourteenth day of the same month: and the whole assembly of the congregation of °Israel shall °kill it °in the evening.

7 And they shall take of the blood, and strike *it* on the two side posts and on the upper door post of the houses, wherein they shall eat it.

8 And they shall eat the flesh in that night, roast with fire, and unleavened bread; *and* with bitter *herbs* they shall eat it.

9 Eat not of it raw, nor °sodden at all °with water, but roast *with* fire; his head with his legs, and with the purtenance thereof.

10 And ye shall let nothing of it remain until the morning; and that which remaineth of it until the morning ye shall burn with fire.

11 And thus shall ye eat it; *with* your °loins girded, your shoes on your feet, and your staff in your hand; and ye shall eat it in haste: it *is* [1]the LORD's passover.

h 12 For I will pass through the land of Egypt this night, and will smite all the firstborn in the land of Egypt, both man and beast; and against all the °gods of Egypt I will execute judgment: °I *am* [1]the LORD.

13 And the °blood shall be to you for a °token upon the houses where ye *are*: and °when I see the blood, I will pass over you, and the plague shall not be upon you to destroy *you*, when I smite the land of Egypt.

f g 14 And this day shall be unto you for a memorial; and ye shall keep it a feast to [1]the LORD throughout your generations; ye shall keep it a feast by an ordinance for ever.

15 Seven days shall ye eat unleavened bread; even the first day ye shall put away °leaven out of your houses: for whosoever eateth leavened bread from the first day °until the seventh day, that [4]soul shall be cut off from Israel.

16 °And in the first day *there shall be* an holy convocation, and in the seventh day there shall

---

7 dog, &c. Fig. *Parœmia* (Ap. 6).

10 This verse is Fig. *Prolepsis*, Ap. 6, as the acts were not done till later.

12. 1-20 (b, p. 87). THE PASSOVER INSTITUTED. (*Introversion and Alternation*).

b | e | 1, 2. The Month.
  f | g | 3-11. The Symbol.
    h | 12, 13. The Signification and Reason.
  f | *g* | 14-17-. The Symbol.
    h | -17. The Signification and Reason.
  e | 18-20. The Month.

1 the LORD (Heb. Jehovah) **spake.** See note on 6. 10, and cp. note on 3. 7.

2 month. Heb. name *Abib*, or "green-ear-month". Becomes the first month, and the fifteenth the ruling date, henceforth. Cp. 13. 4; 23. 15. Deut. 16. 1. Afterward called *Nisan* (Neh. 2. 1. Est. 3. 7). "First", cp. 40. 2, 17. Lev. 23. 5, in place of *Tisri*, which thus became the seventh month.

3 Israel. Some codices, with Sam., Jon., Sept., and Syr., read "of the sons of Israel".

man. Heb. *'ish* (Ap. 14. ii).

lamb. Heb. *seh*, "one of a flock", i.e. a lamb or a kid, *v.* 5. Deut. 14. 4. 2 Chron. 35. 7.

house. Fixed later (by custom) as not less than ten persons.

4 it. *Ellipsis* to be supplied by "the lamb" from verse preceding (Ap. 6. iii. a).

souls. Heb. pl. of *nephesh*. Verse 15, sing. See Ap. 13.

eating. Heb. mouth. Fig. *Metonymy* (of Cause), Ap. 6, mouth put for what is eaten by it.

lamb. Repeated at beginning of next clause in the Fig. *Anadiplosis* (Ap. 6) for emphasis.

5 without blemish. Even as "Christ our Passover".

6 Israel. Some codices, with Sam., Jon., Sept., and Syr., read "of the sons of Israel".

kill. Heb. *shahat*. See Ap. 43. I. v.

in the evening. Heb. between the two evenings, or, according to Lightfoot, between the decline of the sun (after noon) and its setting.

9 sodden = boiled. with = in.

11 loins girded, i.e. the loose flowing garments fastened up with a belt or girdle, making the men ready for action. Cp. Luke 12. 35, 37; 17. 8. Acts 12. 8. 1 Kings 18. 46. 2 Kings 4. 29; 9. 1. Eph. 6. 14.

12 gods, or princes. But see notes on object of the several plagues.

I am the LORD, or I, Jehovah.

13 blood . . . token. The blood was the token for Jehovah. Faith in the fact that it had been sprinkled gave peace to all within. It was (and is) not the *act* of faith which secured, but the *truth* that was believed. If no blood, belief that it was there gave no security. If blood there, doubt as to the fact would destroy peace, but could not destroy the security, because that was grounded on Jehovah's word, and faith consists in "hearing" that. Rom. 10. 17. Heb. 11. 1, marg.

when I see the blood. Not when you feel, or even believe. So the scarlet cord (Josh. 2. 18, 19) was for Joshua to see, not those within the house. Feelings useless apart from faith.

15 leaven = fermented bread. First occ. See Ap. 38.

until. Some codices, with Sam. and Jon., read "and until".

16 And. Some Codices, with Sam. and Syr., omit.

1491 be an holy convocation to you; no manner of work shall be done in them, save *that* which every °man must eat, that only may be done of you.

17 And ye shall observe *the feast of* unleavened bread;

h for in this selfsame day have I brought your
(p. 88) armies out of the land of Egypt: therefore shall ye observe this day in your generations by an ordinance for ever.

e 18 In the first *month,* on the fourteenth day of the month at even, ye shall eat unleavened bread, until the one and twentieth day of the month at even.

19 Seven days shall there be no [15]leaven found in your houses: for whosoever eateth that which is leavened, even that [4]soul shall be cut off from the congregation of Israel, whether he be a stranger, or born in the land.

20 Ye shall eat nothing [15]leavened; in all your habitations °shall ye eat unleavened bread.' "

b i 21 Then Moses called for all the elders of
(p. 89) Israel, and said unto them, "Draw out and take you a lamb according to your families, and °kill the passover.

22 And ye shall take a bunch of hyssop, and dip *it* in the blood that *is* in the bason, and strike the lintel and the two side posts with the blood that *is* in the bason; and none of you shall go out at the door of his house until the morning.

k 23 For [1]the LORD will pass through to smite the Egyptians; and when He seeth the blood upon the lintel, and on the two side posts, [1]the LORD will pass over the door, and will not suffer the destroyer to come in unto your houses to smite *you.*

i 24 And ye shall observe this thing for an ordinance to thee and to thy sons for ever.

k 25 And it shall come to pass, when ye be come to the land which [1]the LORD will give you, according as He hath promised, that ye shall keep this service.

26 And it shall come to pass, when your children shall say unto you, 'What mean ye by this service?'

27 That ye shall say, 'It *is* the sacrifice of [1]the LORD'S passover, Who passed over the houses of the °children of Israel in Egypt, when He smote the Egyptians, and delivered our houses.'" And the People bowed the head and worshipped.

28 And the [27]children of Israel went away, °and did as [1]the LORD had commanded Moses and Aaron, so did they.

a 29 And it came to pass, that °at midnight [1]the LORD °smote all the firstborn in the land of Egypt, from the firstborn of Pharaoh that sat on his throne unto the firstborn of the captive that *was* in the dungeon; and all the firstborn of cattle.

30 And Pharaoh rose up in the night, he, and all his servants, and all the Egyptians; and there was a great cry in Egypt; for *there was* not a house where *there was* not one dead.

F[6] l 31 And he °called for Moses and Aaron by night, and said, "Rise up, *and* get you forth from among my people, both ye and the children of Israel; and go, serve [1]the LORD, as ye have said.

32 Also °take your flocks and your herds, °as ye have said, and be gone; and bless me also."

33 And the Egyptians were urgent upon the People, that they might send them out of the land in haste; for they said, "We *be* all dead *men.*"

34 And the People took their dough before it was leavened, their kneadingtroughs being bound up in their clothes upon their shoulders.

35 And the [27]children of Israel did according to the word of Moses; and they °borrowed of the Egyptians °jewels of silver, and °jewels of gold, and raiment:

36 And [1]the LORD gave the People favour in the sight of the Egyptians, so that they °lent unto them °*such things as they required.* And they spoiled the Egyptians.

37 And the [27]children of Israel journeyed from m
°Rameses to °Succoth, about six hundred thousand on foot *that were* °men, beside children.

38 And °a mixed multitude went up also with

---

man. Heb. *nephesh,* soul (Ap. 13). Cp. *vv.* 4, 15, 19.

20 shall ye eat (repeated). Fig. *Pleonasm* (Ap. 6).

12. 21–28 (*b*, p. 87). THE PASSOVER COMMUNICATED (*Alternation*).

b | i | 21, 22. The Symbol.
  | k | 23. The Signification.
  | *i* | 24. The Symbol.
  | *k* | 25–28. The Signification.

21 kill the passover. Fig. *Metonymy* (of Adjunct), Ap. 6, "Passover" put for the lamb.

27 children = sons.

28 and did. Ten Passovers recorded (see Ap. 10). Ex. 12. 28. Num. 9. 5. Josh. 5. 10. 2 Chron. 30. 13–15. 2 Kings 23. 22 (2 Chron. 35. 1). Ezra 6. 19. Matt 26. 17. Luke 2. 41. John 2. 13; 6. 4.

29 at midnight. On the fourteenth of *Abib.* See 11. 4. **smote.** Cp. 11. 5.

12. 31—14. 31 (F[6], p. 75).
JEHOVAH'S DELIVERANCE OF ISRAEL.
(*Introversion and Alternation.*)

F[6] | l | 12. 31–36. Dismissal, and Spoiling of Egyptians.
  | m | 12. 37–39. Departure from Egypt to Succoth.
  | n | o | 12. 40–42. Fulfilment of prophecy.
  | | p | 12. 43–50. Ordinance of Passover.
  | *n* | *o* | 12. 51—13. 2. Fulfilment of prophecy.
  | | *p* | 13. 3–16. Ordinance of the Phylacteries.
  | *m* | 13. 17–22. Departure from Succoth to Etham.
  | *l* | 14. 1–31. Pursuit, and Destruction of Egyptians.

31 called for, i. e. sent message to.

32 take your flocks. See note on 10. 25, 26, and 5. 1. **as** = according as.

35 borrowed = asked. See note on 3. 22. **jewels.** See note on 11. 2.

36 lent = gladly gave. Heb. verb is in the *Hiphil* mood and = caused them to ask, i. e. the Egyptians pressed them to take.

such things, &c. There is no need for this addition. No Ellipsis in Heb.

37 Rameses. City of the Sun. See note on 1. 11. **Succoth** = booths.

men. Not *'ish,* males, but Heb. *geber,* with art. = the strong men; or, men of military age. Num. 14. 29. See Ap. 14. 4.

38 a mixed multitude = Egyptians. Cp. Num. 11. 4. Neh. 13. 3.

1491 them ; and flocks, and herds, ° *even* very much
cattle.
39 And they baked unleavened cakes of the
dough which they brought forth out of Egypt,
for it was ° not leavened ; because they were
thrust out of Egypt, and could not tarry, neither
had they prepared for themselves any victual.
n o 40 Now the ° sojourning of the [27] children of
(p. 89) ° Israel, (° who dwelt in Egypt), *was* ° four
hundred and thirty years.
1921 41 And it came to pass at the end of the [40] four
to hundred and thirty years, even ° the selfsame
1491 day it came to pass, that all the hosts of [1] the
LORD went out from the land of Egypt.
42 It *is* a night to be ° much observed unto
[1] the LORD for bringing them out from the land
of Egypt : this *is* that night of [1] the LORD to be
observed of all the [27] children of Israel in their
generations.
p 43 And ° the LORD said unto Moses and Aaron,
"This *is* the ordinance of the passover : There
shall no stranger eat thereof :
44 But every [2] man's servant that is ° bought
for money, when thou hast circumcised him,
then shall he eat thereof.
45 A foreigner and an hired servant shall not
eat thereof.
46 In ° one house shall it be eaten ; thou shalt
not carry forth ought of the flesh abroad out of
the house; neither shall ye break a bone thereof.
47 All the congregation of Israel shall keep it.
48 And when a stranger shall sojourn ° with
thee, and will keep the passover to the LORD,
let all his males be circumcised, and then let
him come near and keep it ; and he shall be as
one that is born in the land : for ° no uncircumcised person shall eat thereof.
49 One law shall be to him that is homeborn,
and unto the stranger that sojourneth among
you."
50 Thus did all the [27] children of Israel ; [32] as
[1] the LORD commanded Moses and Aaron, so
did they.
n o 51 And it came to pass the selfsame day, *that*
[1] the LORD did bring the [27] children of Israel out
of the land of Egypt by their ° armies.
13 And ° the LORD spake unto Moses, saying,
2 ° "Sanctify unto Me all the firstborn, whatsoever openeth the womb among the ° children of
Israel, *both* of ° man and of beast : it *is* Mine."
p q 3 And Moses said unto the People, "Remember
(p. 90) this day, in which ye came out from Egypt, out
of the house of bondage; for by strength of hand
[1] the LORD brought you out from this *place* :
there shall no ° leavened bread be eaten.
4 This day came ye out in the month ° Abib.
5 And it shall be when ° the LORD shall bring
thee into the land of the ° Canaanites, ° and the
Hittites, and the Amorites, and the Hivites, and
the Jebusites, which He sware unto thy fathers
to give thee, a land flowing with milk and honey,
that thou shalt keep this service in this month.
r 6 Seven days thou shalt eat unleavened bread,
and in the seventh day *shall be* a feast to [1] the
LORD.
7 Unleavened bread shall be eaten seven days ;
and there shall no [3] leavened bread be seen with

even. Some codices, with Jon., Sept., and Syr., have this word, "even" in the text.

39 not leavened. Bread always unleavened when baked in haste. Cp. Gen. 18. 6.

40 sojourning. Commenced with Gen. 12. 1. Quite a different subject from the *dwelling* in Egypt. See Ap. 50. iii.

Israel = Fig. *Synecdoche* (of the Part), Ap. 6, by which one man's name, Israel, is put for his father and grandfather.

who dwelt in Egypt. Fig. *Epitrechon* (Ap. 6). A form of Parenthesis used to further define the People and connect the two parts of their history.

four hundred and thirty years. There are two reckonings of the sojourning : one starting from the "promise" to Abraham, Ex. 12. 40. Gal. 3. 14, 17 = 430 years ; the other starting from the recognition of his "seed" (Isaac), Gen. 21. 12. See Acts 7. 6 and Gen. 15. 13 = 400 years. N.B. 450 years to Samuel ; 490 to Saul. See Ap. 50. iii, and vii. 7.

This *dwelling* in Egypt was only 215 years (see Ap. 50) ; and is to be distinguished from the "sojourning", which was another 215 years. See note above.

41 the selfsame day : i. e. the fifteenth day of the seventh month. The years of the solar cycle show that it was the day that Abraham left "Ur of the Chaldees".

42 much observed. Heb. *shimmurim*, a night of watchings. Occurs only here.

43 the LORD (Heb. Jehovah) **said.** See note on 3. 7, and cp. note on 6. 10.

44 bought for money. Cp. Gen. 17. 12, 13.

46 one house = the same house. Cp. *v.* 4.

48 with thee. Some codices, with Sam., Jon., Onk., Sept., and Syr., read "with you".

no uncircumcised person shall eat. Were they circumcised during the three days' darkness, and was the command then given, the word against which they did not rebel? (Ps. 105. 28).

51 armies = hosts.

13. 1 the LORD (Heb. Jehovah) **spake.** See note on 6. 10, and cp. note on 3. 7.

2 Sanctify. Fig. *Metonymy* (of Subject). Ap. 6. = Declare that I will sanctify (or set apart), which Moses did in *vv.* 11, 12.

children = sons.

man. Heb. *'ādām.* Ap. 14. i.

13. 3-16 (*p*, p. 89). THE ORDINANCE OF PHYLACTERIES (*Extended Alternation*).

p | q | 3-5. "And it shall be," &c.
  r | 6, 7. Separation of Days.
    s | 8. Thy son's instruction.
      t | 9-. The Sign.
        u | -9, 10. Reason, "For by a strong hand."
  q | 11. "And it shall be," &c.
    r | 12, 13. Separation of First-born.
      s | 14, 15. Thy son's instruction.
        t | 16-. The Token.
          u | -16. Reason, "For by strength of hand."

There are two pairs of Phylacteries, so called (in Greek) from their use = a prayer-fillet or band worn to-day on forehead and hands during prayer. First pair here, Ex. 13. 3-10 and 13. 11-16. Second pair in Deut. 6. 4-9 and 11. 13-21. Cp. the structures in De. 6. 4-9.

3 leavened = fermented.

4 Abib = the month of *green ears.* Jewish tradition says that in this month Abram was called, Isaac was born, Israel delivered from Egypt, and Tabernacle reared up. The Talmud further says : "As in Nisan there had been redemption, so in Nisan there should be redemption" (*Bab.* fol. 11). John's preaching began and the Lord's death occurred in this month.

5 the LORD. Some codices, with Sam., Jon., and Sept., add "thy God".

Canaanites. The Perizzites and Girgashites not included in this list.

and. Note the Fig. *Polysyndeton* in this verse. (Ap. 6.)

1491 thee, neither shall there be leaven seen with
thee in all thy quarters.

s 8 And thou shalt shew thy son in that day,
(p. 90) saying, '*This is done* because of that *which*
[1] the LORD did unto me when I came forth out
of Egypt.'

t 9 And it shall be for a sign unto thee upon thine
hand, and for a memorial between thine eyes,
that [1] the LORD'S law may be in thy mouth:

u for with a strong hand hath [1] the LORD brought
thee out of Egypt.
10 Thou shalt therefore keep this ordinance
in his season from year to year.

q 11 And it shall be when [1] the LORD shall bring
thee into the land of the Canaanites, as He
sware unto thee and to thy fathers, and shall
give it thee,

r 12 That thou shalt set apart unto [1] the LORD
all that openeth the matrix, and every firstling
that cometh of a beast which thou hast; the
males *shall be* [1] the LORD'S.
13 And every firstling of an °ass thou shalt
°redeem with a lamb; and if thou wilt not
°redeem it, then thou shalt break his neck: and
all the firstborn of man among thy children
shalt thou °redeem.

s 14 And it shall be when thy son asketh thee
in time to come, saying, 'What *is* this?' that
thou shalt say unto him, 'By strength of hand
[1] the LORD brought us out from Egypt, from the
house of bondage:
15 And it came to pass, when Pharaoh would
hardly let us go, that [1] the LORD slew all the firstborn in the land of Egypt, both the firstborn of
°man, and the firstborn of beast: therefore I
°sacrifice to [1] the LORD °all that openeth the
matrix, being males; but all the firstborn of
my [2] children I [13] redeem.'

t 16 And it shall be for a °token upon thine hand,
and for frontlets between thine eyes:

u for by strength of hand [1] the LORD brought us
forth out of Egypt."

m v 17 And it came to pass, when Pharaoh had let
(p. 91) the People go, that °God led them not *through*
the way of the land of the Philistines, although
that *was* near; for °God said, "Lest peradventure the People repent when they see war, and
they return to Egypt:"
18 But [17] God led the People about, *through* the
way of the wilderness of the °Red sea: and
the [2] children of Israel went up °harnessed out
of the land of Egypt.

w 19 And Moses took °the bones of Joseph with
him: for he had straitly sworn the [2] children of
Israel, saying, [17] "God will °surely visit you; and
ye shall carry up my bones away hence with
you."

v 20 And they took their journey from Succoth,
and encamped in Etham, in the edge of the
wilderness.
21 And °the LORD went before them by day
in a pillar of a cloud, to lead them the way;
and by night in a pillar of fire, to give them
light; to go by day and night:

13 ass. Fig. *Synecdoche* (of Species), Ap. 6, "ass" put for all animals not offered in sacrifice.

redeem = ransom. Heb. *pādāh* = to redeem (from bondage, by power). First occ. Not *g'āal*. See note on 6. 6.

15 man. Heb. *'adam.* Ap. 14.

sacrifice. Heb. *zabach.* See Ap. 43. I. iv.

all. Ellipsis to be supplied "every [beast]".

16 token. See the Structure on p. 90.

13. 17-22 (*m*, p. 89). **DEPARTURE: SUCCOTH TO ETHAM** (*Introversion*).

m | v | 17, 18. Jehovah's leading.
  w | 19. The bones of Joseph.
 v | 20-22. Jehovah's guidance.

17 God. Heb. Elohim. Ap. 14.

18 Red sea. Heb. *Yam suph* = weedy, or reedy. Eng. "Red" comes from the Greeks reading Edom (whose land it washed) as an appellative instead of a proper name (Esau or Edom = red, Gen. 25. 25). Called "red" from Sept. Dried up fifty miles north of present shore. Will quite dry up at future Exodus. Isa. 11. 15, 16; 19. 5.

harnessed = armed, as Josh. 1. 14. Judg. 7. 11. 1 Chron. 7. 21; or marshalled by fives, as in 2 Kings 1. 9. Isa. 3. 3 (the number of grace, see Ap. 10). To this day five is an evil number in Egypt. Whichever is the meaning, both point to *order* and organization. They were an ordered "host" (12. 41), and not a disorderly rabble.

19 the bones of Joseph. Another evidence of order. Cp. Gen. 50. 25. Joseph's faith exhibited 150 years before. Cp. also Josh. 24. 32 and Acts 7. 15, 16.

surely visit you. See Gen. 50. 25, and cp. note on Gen. 26. 28.

21 the LORD went before them. Cp. 14. 19 and 32. 34, the Angel of Jehovah.

22 took not away. See note on 40. 36-38.

14. 1-31. The next assault by Satan to destroy the whole Nation. See Ap. 23, 25.

14. 1-31 (*l*, p. 89). **PURSUIT AND DESTRUCTION OF ENEMY** (*Extended Alternation*).

l | x | 1-4. Prediction.
  y | 5-9. Fulfilment.
   z | 10-12. Israel troubled.
    a | 13, 14. Salvation promised.
 x | 15-18. Prediction.
  y | 19-23. Fulfilment.
   z | 24, 25. Egyptians troubled.
    a | 26-31. Salvation realized.

1 the LORD (Heb. Jehovah) **spake.** See note on 6. 10, and cp. note on 3. 7. **2 children** = sons.

Migdol. The great fortress on the "Shur" or wall, built to protect Egypt from Asia. The present geography of the Eastern Delta does not, to day, agree with the Biblical record. But its geography in the nineteenth dynasty is well known from papyri, and is in perfect accord with it, as given in Exodus.

3 For. The assault of the enemy foreseen and provided against by Jehovah.

Pharaoh. See Ap. 37.

22 He °took not away the pillar of the cloud
by day, nor the pillar of fire by night, *from*
before the People.

14 And °the LORD spake unto Moses, say- *l* x
ing,
2 "Speak unto the °children of Israel, that
they turn and encamp before Pi-hahiroth,
between °Migdol and the sea, over against
Baal-zephon: before it shall ye encamp by
the sea.
3 °For °Pharaoh will say of the [2] children of
Israel, '*They are* entangled in the land, the wilderness hath shut them in.'

1491 4 And °I will harden Pharaoh's heart, that he shall follow after them; and I will be honoured upon [3]Pharaoh, and upon all his °host; that the Egyptians may know that I *am* [1]the LORD." And they did so.

y (p. 91) 5 And it was °told the king of Egypt that the People fled: and the heart of Pharaoh and of his servants was turned against the People, and they said, °"Why have we done this, that we have let Israel go from serving us?"

6 °And he made ready his chariot, and took his people with him:

7 And he took six hundred chosen chariots, and all the chariots of Egypt, and captains over every one of them.

8 And [1]the LORD [4]hardened the heart of [3]Pharaoh king of Egypt, and he pursued after the [2]children of Israel: and the [2]children of Israel went out with an high hand.

9 But the Egyptians pursued after them, all the °horses *and* chariots of [3]Pharaoh, and his horsemen, and his army, and overtook them encamping by the sea, beside Pi-hahiroth, before Baal-zephon.

z 10 And when [3]Pharaoh drew nigh, the [2]children of Israel lifted up their eyes, and, behold, the Egyptians marched after them; and they were sore afraid: and the [2]children of Israel cried out unto [1]the LORD.

11 And they said unto Moses, °"Because *there were* no graves in Egypt, hast thou taken us away to die in the wilderness? °wherefore hast thou dealt thus with us, to carry us forth out of Egypt?

12 °*Is* not this the word that we did tell thee in Egypt, saying, 'Let us alone, that we may serve the Egyptians'? For *it had been* better for us to serve the Egyptians, than that we should die in the wilderness."

a 13 And Moses said unto the People, "Fear ye not, °stand still, and see the salvation of [1]the LORD, which He will shew to you to day: for the Egyptians whom ye have seen to day, ye shall see them again no more for ever.

14 [1]The LORD shall fight for you, and ye shall hold your peace."

x 15 And °the LORD said unto Moses, °"Wherefore criest thou unto Me? speak unto the [2]children of Israel, that they °go forward:

16 But lift thou up thy rod, and stretch out thine hand over the sea, and divide it: and the [2]children of Israel shall go on dry *ground* through the midst of the sea.

17 And °I, °behold, I will [4]harden the hearts of the Egyptians, and they shall follow them: and I will get Me honour upon Pharaoh, and upon all his host, upon his °chariots, and upon his horsemen.

18 And the Egyptians shall know that I *am* [1]the LORD, when I have gotten Me honour upon Pharaoh, upon his [17]chariots, and upon his horsemen."

y 19 And the Angel of °God, Which went before the camp of Israel, removed and went behind them; and the pillar of the cloud went from before their face, and stood behind them:

20 And it came between the camp of the Egyptians and the camp of Israel; and it was °a cloud and darkness *to them*, but it gave light by night *to these*: so that the one came not near the other all the night.

21 And Moses stretched out his hand over the sea; and [1]the LORD caused the sea to go *back* by a strong east °wind all that night, and made the sea dry *land*, and the waters were divided.

22 And the [2]children of Israel went into the midst of the sea upon the dry *ground*: and the waters *were* a wall unto them on their right hand, and on their left.

23 And the Egyptians pursued, and went in after them to the midst of the sea, *even* all Pharaoh's horses, his chariots, and his horsemen.

24 And it came to pass, that in the morning watch [1]the LORD looked unto the host of the Egyptians through the pillar of fire and of the cloud, and troubled the host of the Egyptians, z

25 And took off their chariot wheels, that they drave them heavily: so that the Egyptians said, "Let us flee from the face of Israel; for [1]the LORD fighteth for them against the Egyptians."

26 And [15]the LORD said unto Moses, "Stretch out thine hand over the sea, that the waters may come again upon the Egyptians, upon their chariots, and upon their horsemen." a

27 And Moses stretched forth his hand over the sea, and the sea returned to his °strength

---

4 I will. Cp. Ps. 103. 7, "His *ways* unto Moses", and in *vv.* 13, 14, "His *acts* unto the sons of Israel".

host=force. Put by Fig. *Metonymy* (of Adjunct) for his army. See Ap. 6.

5 told. On the fourth day. See Ap. 50. iv.

Why . . . ? Fig. *Erotēsis*. See Ap. 6.

6 And. Note the *Polysyndeton* (Ap. 6) in *vv.* 6 and 7.

9 horses. Egypt was noted for chariots, horses, and cavalry, which had been introduced by the eighteenth dynasty.

11 Because . . . ? / **wherefore . . . ?** / **12 Is not . . . ?** } Fig. *Erotēsis*. Ap. 6.

13 stand still, and see. Note importance of this command. Cp. Stand still, and hear, Num. 9. 8. 1 Sam. 9. 27; 12. 7. 2 Chron. 20. 17. Job 37. 14.

15 the LORD (Heb. Jehovah) **said.** See note on 3. 7, and cp. note on 6. 10.

Wherefore . . . ? Fig. *Erotēsis*. Ap. 6. It is also the Fig. *Hysterēsis*; for no mention has been made of Moses' crying to the LORD.

go forward. This was Israel's faith. It was "by faith" in what they *heard* (Rom. 10. 17. Heb. 11. 29).

17 I, behold, I. Fig. *Epizeuxis*, for emphasis. Ap. 6.

behold. Fig. *Asterismos*. Ap. 6.

chariots. Heb. sing. chariot. Note the alternation.

| Pharaoh (sing.).
  | His host (pl.).
| Pharaoh's chariot (sing.).
  | His horsemen (pl.).

19 God. Heb. Elohim: the Creator in relation to His creatures. See Ap. 4.

20 a cloud and darkness. Fig. *Hendiadys* (Ap. 6) =a very dark cloud.

21 wind. Heb. *ruach*. Ap. 9.

27 strength=irresistible might.

1491 when the morning appeared; and the Egyp-
21 tians fled against it; and [1]the LORD overthrew
Abib the Egyptians in the midst of the sea.
28 And the waters returned, and covered the chariots, and the horsemen, *and* all the host of Pharaoh that came into the sea after them; there remained °not so much as one of them.
29 But the [2]children of Israel walked upon dry *land* in the midst of the sea; and the waters *were* a wall unto them on their right hand, and on their left.
22 30 Thus [1]the LORD saved Israel that day out
Abib of the hand of the Egyptians; and Israel saw
Sab. the Egyptians dead upon the sea shore.
31 And Israel saw that great work which [1]the LORD did upon the Egyptians: and the people feared [1]the LORD, and believed [1]the LORD, and °His servant Moses.

A b e (p. 72) **15** °Then sang Moses and the °children of Israel °this song °unto °the LORD, and spake, saying,

f "I will sing unto °the LORD, for He hath triumphed gloriously:
The horse and his rider hath He thrown into the sea.

c 2 °THE LORD *is* my strength and °song,
And He is become my °salvation:
He *is* my °GOD, and I will prepare Him an habitation;
My father's °God, and I will exalt Him.
3 [1]The LORD *is* a °man °of war:
[1]The LORD *is* His name.

d g a 4 Pharaoh's chariots and his host hath He cast into the sea:
His chosen captains also are drowned in the Red sea.
5 The depths have covered them:
They sank into the bottom as a stone.

b c 6 Thy °right hand, O [1]LORD, is become glorious in power:
Thy right hand, O [1]LORD, hath dashed in pieces the enemy.

d 7 And in the greatness of Thine excellency Thou hast overthrown them that rose up against Thee:
Thou sentest forth Thy wrath, *which* consumed them as stubble.
8 And with the °blast of Thy °nostrils the waters were gathered together,
The floods stood upright as an heap,
And the depths were congealed in the heart of the sea.

a 9 The enemy said,
°'I will pursue, I will overtake, I will divide the spoil;
My °lust shall be satisfied upon them;
I will draw my sword, my hand shall destroy them.'

d 10 Thou didst blow with Thy °wind, the sea covered them:
They sank as °lead in the mighty waters.
11 °Who *is* like unto Thee, O [1]LORD, among the °gods?

---

28 not so much as one of them. This implies that Pharaoh himself did not escape. Cp. 15. 9, 10. Ps. 106. 11; 136. 15. His body may have been washed up on the shore, cp. *v.* 30, and "also" in 15. 4.

31 His servant Moses. First occ. See the five, Ex. 14. 31. Josh. 9. 24; 11. 15. 1 Kings 8. 56. Ps. 105. 26, and cp. notes on Num. 12. 7. Deut. 35. 5. 1 Kings 8. 53. Neh. 10. 29.

15. 1 Moses began and ended his wilderness career with a song. Cp. Deut. 32, which is "the" song referred to in Rev. 15. 3.
The structure gives the scope:—

15. 1-21 (*A*, p. 72). THE BONDAGE OF ISRAEL ENDED. THE SONGS OF MOSES AND MIRIAM.
(*Introversion and Alternation.*)

A | b | e | 1-. Singers: Moses and the men } Moses' Song.
f | -1. The Theme.
c | 2, 3. Praise.
d | g | 4-12. Overthrow of Pharaoh. } The Song itself.
h | 13. Israel's guidance.
d | *g* | 14-16. Overthrow of Egyptians.
h | 17. Israel's settlement.
c | 18, 19. Praise.
b | *e* | 20. Singers: Miriam and women. } Miriam's Song.
f | 21. The Theme.

The song proper occupies *vv.* 4-17. It is preceded and followed by praise with introduction and conclusion.

1 Then sang. There was no singing in Egypt, only sighing and groaning (2. 23, 24). **children** = sons.
this song. Note the ten Songs of Praise: (1) Ex. 15. 1-19. (2) Num. 21. 17, 18. (3) Deut. 32. 1-43. (4) Judg. 5. 1-31. (5) 1 Sam. 2. 1-10. (6) 2 Sam. 22. 1-51. (7) Luke 1. 46-55. (8) Luke 1. 68-79. (9) Luke 2. 29-32. (10) Rev. 14. 3.
unto the LORD. Jehovah is the sole theme: and should be the theme of our praise. Note the "Thee" and "Thou", and contrast the "We" of Num. 13. 33, and the result, *weeping*, in 14. 1. It begins with Redemption, and ends with glory. No "praise" short of this.
the LORD. Heb. Jehovah. Ap. 4.

2 THE LORD = Heb. JAH, the Eternal, inhabiting eternity. See Ap. 4. The first occ. of this Title: connects it with Redemption.
song. Some codices, with Sam. and Onk., read "and my song". Fig. *Metonymy* (of Adjunct). Ap. 6. = "He of Whom I sing".
salvation. Cp. Ps. 118. 14, 21.
GOD. Heb. El. See Ap. 4.
God. Heb. Elohim. Ap. 4.

3 man. Heb. *'īsh.* See Ap. 14.
of war. This is what He is out of Christ; and to those who are not the subjects of His redeeming power.

4-12 (g, above). OVERTHROW OF PHARAOH.
(*Alternation and Introversion.*)

g | a | 4, 5. The Enemy overthrown.
b | c | 6. Thy right hand.
d | 7, 8. Thou, Thee, Thy.
a | 9. The Enemy's words.
b | *d* | 10, 11. Thou, Thy, Thee.
c | 12. Thy right hand.

6 right hand. Fig. *Anthropopatheia.* Ap. 6.

8 blast. Heb. *rūach.* See Ap. 9.
nostrils. Fig. *Anthropopatheia.* See Ap. 6.

9 I will pursue. Note the Fig. *Asyndeton* (Ap. 6), in *vv.* 9 and 10. No "ands": to hasten on to the grand climax—"they sank as lead" (*v.* 10).
lust. Heb. *nephesh* = soul. See Ap. 13.

10 wind. Heb. *rūach.* Ap. 9.
lead. First occ.

11 Who is like unto Thee? This is ever the saints' noblest praise. Emphasised by the Fig. *Erotēsis.* (Ap. 6). Cp. Deut. 33. 26, 27. 1 Sam. 2. 2. 1 Ch. 17. 20. Ps. 35. 10; 71. 19; 73. 25; 86. 8; 89. 6, 8; 113. 5. **gods** = mighty ones, as in *v.* 15. Heb. *ēlīm.* See note on 22. 8.

1491 °Who *is* like Thee, glorious in holiness,
°Fearful *in* praises, doing wonders?

c 12 Thou stretchedst out Thy right hand,
(p. 93) The earth swallowed them.
h 13 Thou in Thy °mercy hast led forth the People *which* Thou hast °redeemed:
Thou hast guided *them* in Thy strength unto Thy holy habitation.

g x 14 The °people °shall hear, *and* be afraid:
(p. 94) Sorrow shall take hold on the inhabitants of
y Palestina.
z 15 Then the °dukes of Edom shall be amazed;
z The mighty men of Moab, trembling shall take hold upon them;
y All the inhabitants of Canaan shall melt away.
x 16 Fear and dread shall fall upon them;
By the greatness of Thine arm they shall be *as* still as a stone;
°Till Thy People pass over, O [1]LORD,
°Till the People pass over, *which* Thou hast purchased.

h 17 Thou shalt bring them in, and °plant them in the mountain of Thine inheritance,
In the °place, O [1]LORD, *which* Thou hast made for Thee to dwell in,
In the Sanctuary, °O LORD*, *which* Thy hands have established.

c 18 [1]The LORD shall reign for ever and ever.
19 For the horse of Pharaoh went in with his chariots and with his horsemen into the sea, and [1]the LORD brought again the waters of the sea upon them; but the [1]children of Israel went on dry *land* in the midst of the sea."

b e 20 And °Miriam the °prophetess, the sister of Aaron, took °a timbrel in her hand; and all the women went out after her with °timbrels and with dances.

f 21 And Miriam answered them,
"Sing ye to the LORD, for He hath triumphed gloriously;
The horse and his rider hath He thrown into the sea."

B S i[1] 22 So Moses brought Israel from the Red sea,
(p. 95) and they went out into the wilderness of
25 °Shur; and they went three days in the wil-
Abib derness, and found no water.

k[1] l[1] 23 And when they came to °Marah, they could not drink of the waters of Marah, for they *were* bitter: therefore the name of it was called Marah.

m[1] 24 And the People °murmured against Moses, saying, "What shall we drink?"

l[2] 25 And he cried unto [1]the LORD; and [1]the LORD shewed him a °tree, *which* when he had cast into the waters, the waters were made sweet:

m[2] There °He made for them a statute and an ordinance, and there °He proved them,

Fearful in praises: i.e. to be revered in praising Him for His wondrous acts.
13 mercy = loving-kindness, or grace. N.B. Led forth in mercy, redeemed in grace, guided by strength.
redeemed. Heb. *g'āal.* See notes on 6. 6 and 13. 13. Exodus the book of Redemption. See Title.

14-16. (*g*, p. 93). OVERTHROW OF EGYPTIANS. (*Introversion.*)

g | x | 14-. The peoples: "hear and fear."
y | -14. Palestine.
z | 15-. Edom.
z | -15-. Moab.
y | -15. Canaan.
x | 16. "Them": "fear and dread."

14 people = peoples: no Art. (cp. Gen. 49. 16, first occ.).
shall hear. Cp. Josh. 2. 9-11. **15 dukes** = chiefs.
16 Till Thy People, &c. Note Fig. *Epizeuxis.* Ap. 6.
17 plant. The word used by God throughout of settling His People. Jer. 18. 9. Amos 9. 15. Rom. 6. 5. 1 Cor. 3. 6-10. **place** = appointed place.
O LORD. One of the 134 places where Jehovah was altered, by the Sopherim, to Adonai. Ap. 32.
20 Miriam. Heb. form of Mary.
prophetess. First occ. **a** = the.
timbrels = drum. Heb. *toph*, rendered "tabret" (Gen. 31. 27. 1 Sam. 10. 5; 18. 6. 2 Sam. 6. 5. Isa. 5. 12; 24. 8; 30. 32. Jer. 31. 4. Ezek. 28. 13), "timbrel" (Ex. 15. 20. Judg. 11. 34. 2 Sam. 6. 5. 1 Ch. 13. 8. Job 21. 12. Ps. 81. 2; 149. 3; 150. 4).

15. 22—40. 38 (*B*, p. 72). FREEDOM USED. (*Introversion, with Simple and Repeated Alternation.*)

B | S | 15. 22—19. 2. Journeyings to Sinai.
U | X[1] | 19. 3-6. Ascent I: Proclamation of Covenant.
Y[1] | 19. 7, 8-. Descent.
X[2] | 19. -8-13. Ascent II: Preparation of People.
Y[2] | 19. 14-19. Descent.
X[3] | 19. 20-24. Ascent III: Setting of bounds.
Y[3] | 19. 25. Descent.
V | 20. 1—24. 8. GIVING OF THE LAW.
T | *U* | X[4] | 24. 9—32. 14. Ascent IV: First 40 days (De. 9. 9) and 1st Tables.
Y[4] | 32. 15-30. Descent. Breaking of Tables.
X[5] | 32. 31-33. Ascent V: Manifestation of glory.
Y[5] | 32. 34—34. 3. Descent.
X[6] | 34. 4-28. Ascent VI: Second 40 days (De. 10. 10) and 2nd Tables.
Y[6] | 34. 29—35. 3. Descent.
V | 35. 4—40. 35. MAKING OF TABERNACLE.
S | 40. 36-38. Journeyings from Sinai.

Note the journeyings, at the extremes; with the six ascents and descents of Moses, separated by the two principal subjects of the book: the giving of the Law and the making of the Tabernacle.
In Ch. 24 the fourth ascent is given as consisting of several stages.

15. 22—19. 2 [For Structure see next page].
22 Shur. Name given from the great wall built to protect Egypt from Asia, with its great *Migdol*, or fortress. See note on 14. 2.
23 Marah = Bitter. The Divine principle in the training of God's People. Foreshown in Abraham's furnace and lamp; Marah before Elim; wilderness before Canaan; cross before crown; worse before better (John 2. 10); suffering before glory (Luke 24. 26, 46. 2 Tim. 2. 11, 12; cp. Rom. 8. 17. 18. 2 Cor. 4. 17, 18. Jas. 1. 12. Rev. 2. 10. 1 Pet. 1. 11; 4. 13; 5. 1, 10, 11. Heb. 12. 11. Ps. 126. 6; 66. 10-13. John 12. 24. Matt. 5. 4. John 16. 20, 22). **24 murmured.** The first murmuring after leaving Egypt. Note seven others: 16. 2; 17. 2, 3; Num. 11. 33, 34; 14. 2; 16. 41; 21. 5. Josh. 9. 18, and cp. 1 Cor. 10. 10. **25 tree.** The Cross is the Divine provision for every trial: See Olney Hymns, i. 13. Jehovah showed it. **He**: i.e. Jehovah.

1491 **26** °And said, "If thou wilt °diligently hearken to the voice of [1]the LORD thy [2]God, and wilt do that which is right in His sight, and wilt give ear to His commandments, and keep all His statutes, I will put none of these diseases upon thee, which I have brought upon the Egyptians: for I *am* °the LORD That healeth thee."

l^3 (p. 95) 27 Abib 2nd Sab. **27** And they came to Elim, where °*were* °twelve wells of water, °and °threescore and °ten palm trees: and they encamped there by the waters.

i^2 15 Ziph k^2 n **16** And they took their °journey from Elim, and all the congregation of the °children of Israel came unto the wilderness of °Sin, which *is* between Elim and °Sinai, on the °fifteenth day of the second month after their departing out of the land of Egypt.

2 And the whole congregation of the [1]children of Israel °murmured against Moses and Aaron in the wilderness:

3 And the [1]children of Israel said unto them, "Would *to God* we had died by the hand of °the LORD in the land of Egypt, when we sat by the flesh pots, *and* when we did eat °bread to the full; for ye have brought us forth into this wilderness, to kill this whole assembly with hunger."

o **4** Then °said [3]the LORD unto Moses, °"Behold, I will rain [3]bread from heaven for you; and the People shall go out and gather a certain rate every day, that I may prove them, whether they will walk in My law, or no.

5 And it shall come to pass, that on the sixth day they shall prepare *that* which they bring in; and it shall be twice as much as they gather daily."

p **6** And Moses and Aaron said unto all the [1]children of Israel, "At even, then ye shall know that [3]the LORD hath brought you out from the land of Egypt:

7 And in the morning, then ye shall see the glory of [3]the LORD; for that He heareth your murmurings against [3]the LORD: and °what *are* we, that ye murmur against us?"

8 And Moses said, "*This shall be*, when [3]the LORD shall give you in the evening flesh to eat, and in the morning bread to the full; for that [3]the LORD heareth your °murmurings which ye murmur against Him: and what *are* we? your murmurings *are* not against us, but against [3]the LORD."

p **9** And Moses spake unto Aaron, "Say unto all the congregation of the [1]children of Israel, 'Come near before [3]the LORD: for He hath heard your murmurings.'"

10 And it came to pass, as Aaron spake unto the whole congregation of the [1]children of Israel, that they looked toward the wilderness, and, [4]behold, the glory of [3]the LORD appeared in the cloud.

o q **11** And °the LORD spake unto Moses, saying,

12 "I have heard the murmurings of the [1]children of Israel: speak unto them, saying, 'At even ye shall eat flesh, and in the morning ye shall be filled with bread; and ye shall know that I *am* [3]the LORD your °God.'"

15. 22—19. 2 (S, p. 94). JOURNEYINGS TO SINAI (*Repeated Alternation*).

S | i^1 | 15. 22. From Egypt to Wilderness of Shur.
  k^1 | 15. 23-27. Events in Wilderness of Shur.
i^2 | 16. 1. From Shur to Wilderness of Sin.
  k^2 | 16. 2-36. Events in Wilderness of Sin.
i^3 | 17. 1-. From Wilderness of Sin to Rephidim.
  k^3 | 17. -1—18. 22. Events at Rephidim.
i^4 | 19. 1, 2. From Rephidim to Wilderness of Sinai.

15. 23-27 (k^1, above). EVENTS IN WILDERNESS OF SHUR (*Repeated Alternation*).

k^1 | l^1 | 23. Marah's bitter water.
  m^1 | 24. Murmuring of people.
l^2 | 25-. Marah's sweet water.
  m^2 | -25, 26. Ordinance of God.
l^3 | 27. Elim's wells of water.

26 And [He, Jehovah] **said.** See note on 4. 3.
diligently hearken. Fig. *Polyptōton* (Ap. 6). Heb. "if an hearkening thou hearken".
the LORD That healeth thee. *Jehovah rophe'ekā*, one of the Jehovah titles. See Ap. 4.
27 were. Supply *Ellipsis*, "they found", instead of "were". Cp. Num. 21. 16-18. The scene at Rephidim (ch. 17) after the thirty-nine years was because they expected God to provide for them still.
twelve . . . threescore . . . ten. See Ap. 10.

16. 1-36 (k^2, above). EVENTS IN WILDERNESS OF SIN (*Introversion*).

k^2 | n | 2-3. Murmuring of people.
  o | 4, 5. Promise of Jehovah made.
    p | 6-8. Promise repeated by Moses.
    p | 9, 10. Promise fulfilled through Moses.
  o | 11-31. Promise of Jehovah fulfilled.
n | 32-36. Memorial of Jehovah.

1 journey. The Egyptian kings of twelfth dynasty worked copper and turquoise mines in peninsula of Sinai. Afterward disused until eighteenth dynasty. Old roads left. See Ap. 50. vii. 2, on the forty years' wandering; and note on Num. 33. 1.
children = sons.
Sin. Heb. a bush.
Sinai = Bush of Jehovah. Sinai mentioned thirty-one times in Pentateuch, only four times in rest of Old Testament (Judg. 5. 5. Neh. 9. 13. Ps. 68. 8, 17); in New Testament four times (Acts 7. 30, 38. Gal. 4. 24, 25).
fifteenth day. See Ap. 50. vii. 3.
2 murmured. Murmurings mentioned eight times in these verses: viz. 2, 7, 7, 8, 8, 8, 9, 12.
3 the LORD. Heb. Jehovah. Ap. 4.
bread. Fig. *Synecdoche* (of Part), put for all kinds of food (Ap. 6), not for water, because of 15. 27.
4 said the LORD. See notes on 3. 7 and 6. 10.
Behold. Fig. *Asterismos.* Ap. 6.
7 what . . . ? Fig. *Erotēsis.* Ap. 6.
8 murmurings which ye murmur. Fig. *Polyptōton.* Ap. 6. = your wicked or terrible murmurings.

16. 11-31 (*o*, above). PROMISE OF JEHOVAH FULFILLED (*Extended Alternation*).

o | q | 11, 12. Promise of Jehovah.
  r | 13, 14. Giving of the food.
    s | 15. Name: "Manna."
q | 16-. Command of Jehovah.
  r | -16-30. Gathering of the food.
    s | 31. Name: "Manna."

11 the LORD spake. See note on 6. 10, and cp. note on 3. 7.
12 God. Heb. Elohim. Ap. 4.

1491 13 And it came to pass, that at even the quails
r came up, and covered the camp: and in the
(p. 95) morning the dew lay round about the °host.
14 And when the dew that lay was gone up,
[4]behold, upon the face of the wilderness *there*
lay a °small °round thing, *as* °small as the
hoar frost on the ground.

s 15 And when the °children of Israel saw *it*,
they said one to another, °"It *is* manna:" for
they °wist not what °it *was*. And Moses said
unto them, °"This *is* the bread which [3]the LORD
hath given you to eat.

q 16 This *is* the thing which [3]the LORD hath
commanded,

r t[1] Gather of it every °man according to his
(p. 96) eating, an [36]omer °for every man, *according to*
the number of your °persons; take ye every
°man for *them* which *are* in his tents."

u[1] 17 And the [1]children of Israel did so, and
gathered, some more, some less.
18 And when they did mete *it* with an [36]omer,
he that gathered much had nothing over, and
he that gathered little had no lack; they
gathered every man according to his eating.

t[2] 19 And Moses said, "Let no man leave of it
till the morning."

u[2] 20 Notwithstanding they hearkened not unto
Moses; but some of them left of it until the
morning, and it bred worms, and stank: and
Moses was wroth with them.
21 And they gathered it every morning, every
man according to his eating: and when the
sun waxed hot, °it melted.
19 22 And it came to pass, *that* on the sixth day
Ziph they gathered twice as much bread, two
[36]omers for one *man:* and all the rulers of the
congregation came and told Moses.

t[3] 23 And he said unto them, "This *is that* which
[3]the LORD hath said, 'To morrow *is* the °rest of
the holy sabbath unto [3]the LORD: bake *that*
which ye will bake *to day*, and seethe that ye
will seethe; and that which remaineth over
lay up for you to be kept until the morning.'"

u[3] 24 And they laid it up till the morning, °as
Moses bade: and it did not stink, neither was
there any worm therein.

t[4] 25 And Moses said, "Eat that to day; for
to day *is* a sabbath unto [3]the LORD: to day ye
shall not find it in the field.
26 Six days ye shall gather it; but on the
seventh day, *which is* the sabbath, in it there
shall be none."

u[4] 27 And it came to pass, *that* there went out
20 *some* of the People on the seventh day for to
Ziph gather, and they found none.
6th 28 And °the LORD said unto Moses, °"How
Sab. long refuse ye to keep My commandments and
My laws?
29 °See, for that [3]the LORD hath given you
the sabbath, therefore He giveth you on the
sixth day the bread of two days; abide ye
every man in his place, let no man go out of
his place on the °seventh day."
30 So the People rested on the [29]seventh day.
s
(p. 95) 31 And °the house of Israel called the name
thereof °Manna: and it *was* like coriander
seed, white; and the taste of it *was* like
°wafers *made* with honey.

32 And Moses said, "This *is* the thing which n
[3]the LORD commandeth, Fill an °omer of it to
be kept for your generations; that they may
see the bread wherewith I have fed you in the
wilderness, when I brought you forth from the
land of Egypt."
33 And Moses said unto Aaron, "Take °a
pot, and put an [32]omer full of manna therein,
and lay it up before [3]the LORD, to be kept for
your generations."
34 As [3]the LORD commanded Moses, so Aaron
laid it up before °the Testimony, to be kept.

---

13 host = camp.
14 small = thin.
round thing = flakey.
15 "It is manna". Heb. *man-hu* = "What is that? for they knew not what 'that' was". See on *v.* 31.
wist = knew. From Anglo-Saxon, *witan*, to know.
it = that. **This** = that.

16. 16-30 (*r*, p. 95). THE GATHERING OF THE FOOD (*Repeated Alternation*).

r | t[1] | -16. Directions (Positive).
  | u[1] | 17, 18. Obedience.
  | t[2] | 19. Directions (Negative).
  | u[2] | 20-22. Disobedience.
  | t[3] | 23. Directions (Sabbath).
  | u[3] | 24. Obedience.
  | t[4] | 25, 26. Directions (Sabbath).
  | u[4] | 27-30. Disobedience.

16 man. Heb. *'ish.* See Ap. 14. ii.
for every man = for every skull. Fig. *Synecdoche* (of Part). Ap. 6. Skull put for person, as we say "per head".
persons. Heb. *nephesh.* Ap. 13.
21 it melted. See note on Num. 14. 9.
23 rest of the [holy] sabbath. Heb. "a sabbath of sabbaths". Occurs seven times (see Ap. 10). *Four* times of the weekly sabbath (Ex. 16. 23; 31. 15; 35. 2. Lev. 23. 3). *Twice* of the Day of Atonement (Lev. 16. 31; 23. 32). *Once* of the sabbath of years (Lev. 25. 4).
24 as = according to what.
28 the LORD said. See note on 3. 7, and cp. note on 6. 10.
How long . . . ? Fig. *Erotēsis.* Ap. 6.
29 See. Fig. *Asterismos.* Ap. 6.
seventh day. See Ap. 50. vii. 3.
31 the house of Israel. (First occurrence.) The *Massorah* (Ap. 30) contains a list of all the occurrences of this expression. There are fourteen occurrences of this expression before the division of the nation into two kingdoms: Ex. 16. 31; 40. 38. Lev. 10. 6; 17. 3. Num. 20. 29. Josh. 21. 45. 1 Sam. 7. 2, 3. 2 Sam. 1. 12; 6. 5, 15; 12. 8; 16. 3. Ruth 4. 11 (cp. Ex. 19. 3, note). "The house of Judah" also occurs four times. See its first occ., 2 Sam. 2. 4. See note on 1 Kings 12. 17.
Manna. Heb. "What is that?" Seven characteristics:—
1. Small = thin, *v.* 14 (Antitype, Phil. 2. 6-8).
2. Round = flakey, *v.* 14.
3. White, *v.* 31.
4. Sweet, *v.* 31 (Ps. 119. 103. Jer. 15. 16).
5. Hard, Num. 11. 8.
6. Melted, Num. 14. 9.
7. From heaven (daily), *v.* 13. See note on Matt. 6. 11.

wafers = flat-cake.
32 omer. See Ap. 51. III. iii.
33 a = one.
34 the Testimony = the Ark. Fig. *Hysterologia.* Ap. 6. The ark not yet made.

1491 35 And the [1]children of Israel °did eat manna
°forty years, °until they came to a land inhabited; they °did eat manna, °until they
came unto the borders of the land of Canaan.
36 Now °an omer *is* the tenth *part* of an
ephah.

k^3 v^1 (p. 97) 21st Ziph **17** And all the congregation of the °children
of Israel journeyed from the wilderness
of °Sin, after their journeys, according to the
°commandment of °the LORD, and pitched in
°Rephidim: and *there was* no water for the
People to drink.
2 Wherefore the People did °chide with Moses,
and said, "Give us water that we may drink."
And Moses said unto them, °"Why chide ye
with me? °wherefore do ye °tempt [1]the LORD?"
3 And the People thirsted there for water;
and the People murmured against Moses, and
said, "Wherefore *is* this *that* thou hast brought
us up out of Egypt, to kill °us and our [1]chil-
dren and our cattle with thirst?"
w^1 4 And Moses cried unto [1]the LORD, saying,
"What shall I do unto this People? °they be
almost ready to stone me."
x^1 5 And °the LORD said unto Moses, "Go on
before the People, and take with thee of the
elders of Israel; and thy rod, wherewith thou
smotest the River, take in thine hand, and go.
6 °Behold, °I will stand before thee there
upon the °rock in °Horeb; and thou shalt
°smite the °rock, and there shall come °water
out of it, that the People may drink." And
Moses did so in the sight of the elders of Israel.
y^1 (p. 97) 7 And he called the name of the place
°Massah, and °Meribah, because of the chiding
of the [1]children of Israel, and because they
°tempted [1]the LORD, saying, "Is [1]the LORD
among us, or not?"
v^2 5th Sivan 8 °Then came °Amalek, and fought with
Israel in Rephidim.
w^2 9 And Moses said unto °Joshua, "Choose us
out °men, and go out, °fight with Amalek:
to morrow I will stand on the top of the hill
with the rod of °God in mine hand."
x^2 10 So Joshua did °as Moses had said to him,
and fought with Amalek: and °Moses, °Aaron,
and °Hur went up to the top of the hill.
11 And it came to pass, °when Moses held up
his °hand, that Israel prevailed: and when he
let down his hand, Amalek prevailed.
12 But Moses' hands *were* °heavy; and they
took a stone, and put *it* under him, and he sat
thereon; and Aaron and Hur stayed up his
hands, the one on the one side, and the other

35 did eat manna. The repetition (for emphasis) is the Fig. *Epibole* (Ap. 6).
forty years. Cp. Josh. 5. 6, 11, 12. Fig. *Hysterologia* (Ap. 6), a prior mention of a subsequent event.
until they came. Given on 16th Ziph, B.C. 1491, ceased 16th Ziph, B.C. 1451 = 39 years 11 months. See Josh. 5. 12. See Ap. 50. vii. 3, 4.
36 an omer is the tenth part of an ephah. This is not to be confused with Ezek. 45. 11, "an ephah is the tenth part of an homer". They are two different words: in Ex. 16. 36 it is *'omer*, in Ezek. 45. 11 it is *ḥomer*. See note on Lev. 27. 16, and Ap. 51. III. 3.

17. 1—18. 27 (k^3, p. 95). EVENTS AT REPHIDIM.
(*Extended and Repeated Alternation.*)

k^3 | v^1 | 17. 1-3. Coming of Israel & chiding of People.
w^1 | 4. Moses and Jehovah.
x^1 | 5, 6. Giving of water by Jehovah.
y^1 | 7. Memorial of Massah and Meribah.
v^2 | 8. Coming of Amalek and fighting with Israel.
w^2 | 9. Moses and Joshua.
x^2 | 10-13. Giving of victory by Jehovah.
y^2 | 14-16. Memorial of victory.
v^3 | 18. 1-5. Coming of Jethro and message to Moses.
w^3 | 6-12. Moses and Jethro.
x^3 | 13-16. Giving of judgment by Moses.
y^3 | 17-27. Memorial of Jethro's visit.

1 children = sons.
Sin. Heb. Bush.
commandment. Heb. "mouth". Fig. *Metonymy* (of Cause). Ap. 6. Mouth put for what is spoken by it.
the LORD. Heb. Jehovah. Ap. 4.
Rephidim = reclining places. Two stations omitted here. Cp. 17. 1. Num. 33. 12-14.
2 chide. Murmuring was good policy. They would not "dig" (as at B^{e}ēr and Elim)—to "beg" they were not ashamed. "Give us water." See note on 15. 24.
Why chide . . . ? Fig. *Erotēsis*. Ap. 6.
wherefore. Some codices, with Sam., Jon., Sept., and Syr., read "And why".
tempt = put to the proof. Heb. from *nāṣāh*, to smell, hence, to try. Fig. *Anthropopatheia*. Ap. 6.
3 us. Heb. **me**. Fig. *Heterosis* (of Number). Ap. 6.
4 they be almost ready. Heb. "yet a little and they will". Moses, David, Jeremiah, Stephen, Paul, and the Lord Jesus suffered from stoning or its threatening
5 the LORD (Heb. Jehovah) **said.** See note on 3. 7, and cp. note on 6. 10.
6 Behold. Fig. *Asterismos*. Ap. 6.
I will stand. Fig. *Anthropopatheia*. Ap. 6.
rock: a type of Christ. Frequently referred to (Deut. 32. 4, 15, 18, 31, 37. 1 Sam. 2. 2. Ps. 18. 2). Rock of life (Deut. 32. 18): Salvation (2 Sam. 22. 47, &c.): Refuge (Ps. 27. 5; 62. 6, 7): Rest and refreshment (Isa. 32. 2).
Horeb. Cp. 3. 1.
smite. Smitten only once. Cp. Isa. 53. 4. Zech. 13. 7. Jehovah on the Rock = God in Christ (2 Cor. 5. 19). No water till smitten (Ps. 78. 20. John 7. 38, 39; 12. 24).
water. Water from the rock. Fire out of the rock (Judg. 6. 21). Honey from the rock (Ps. 81. 16). Oil from the rock (Deut. 32. 13).
7 Massah = Temptation. Tempting of God.
Meribah = Strife. Striving with Moses.
tempted. Fig. *Anthropopatheia*. Ap. 6. (i.e. tempting Jehovah to cut them off). **8 Then came Amalek.** See on Gen. 21. 25 and Judg. 5. 11. Amalek came to fight for the water. Cp. Deut. 25. 17, 18. Amalek came behind and attacked the rear, and he "feared not God", Deut. 25. 8. **Amalek,** Fig. *Synecdoche* (of Part), Ap. 6, put for Amalekites. At Rephidim, they got water plus Amalek; at Meribah, water plus Edom. **9 Joshua.** First occ. (250 times in all). Heb. *Jehoshua*. Now fifty-three years of age. Hence a bondman in Egypt. Twenty-seven years younger than Moses. See Ap. 50. iv and vii. 1. **men.** Heb. pl. of *'īsh* or *'enōsh*. Ap. 14. **fight.** There was a large population in the peninsula at this time. A wilderness, a place of pasture, not a desert. **God.** Heb. Elohim. Ap. 4. **10 as** = according as. **Moses** (prophet), **Aaron** (priest), **Hur** (royal tribe, Judah). **Hur.** Heb. noble or well-born. The son of Caleb, the son of Hezron, the son of Pharez, the son of Judah (1 Chron. 2. 3, 4, 5, 18, 19). Josephus makes him the husband of Miriam and grandfather of Bezaleel (Ex. 31. 2; 35. 30; 38. 22). **11 when** = according as. **hand.** Sam. and Sept. read "hands". Cp. *v.* 12. **12 heavy** = weary.

1491 on the other side; and his hands were steady until the going down of the sun.

13 And Joshua discomfited Amalek and his people with the °edge of the °sword.

y2 (p. 97) 14 And °the LORD said unto Moses, °"Write this *for* a memorial °in a book, and rehearse *it* in the ears of Joshua: for I will utterly °put out the remembrance of Amalek from under heaven."

15 And Moses built an altar, and called the name of it °Jehovah-nissi:

16 For he said, "Because the °LORD °hath sworn *that* [1]the LORD *will have* war with Amalek from generation to generation."

v3 (**18** °When °Jethro, the priest of Midian, Moses' father in law, heard of all that °God had done for Moses, and for Israel His People, *and* that °the LORD had brought Israel out of °Egypt;

2 Then Jethro, Moses' father in law, took Zipporah, Moses' wife, after he had °sent her back,

3 And her two sons; of which the name of the one *was* °Gershom; for he said, "I have been an alien in a strange land:"

4 And the name of the other *was* °Eliezer; "for the [1]God of my father," *said he,* "*was* mine help, and delivered me from the sword of Pharaoh:"

5 And Jethro, Moses' father in law, came with his sons and his wife unto Moses into the wilderness, where he encamped at the mount of [1]God:

w3 6 And he said unto Moses, °"I thy father in law Jethro am come unto thee, and thy wife, and her two sons with her."

7 And Moses went out to meet his father in law, and did obeisance, and kissed him; and they asked each other of *their* welfare; and they came into the tent.

8 And Moses told his father in law all that [1]the LORD had done unto Pharaoh and to the Egyptians for Israel's sake, *and* all the travail that had come upon them by the way, and *how* [1]the LORD delivered them.

9 And Jethro rejoiced for all the goodness which [1]the LORD had done to Israel, whom He had delivered out of the hand of the Egyptians.

10 And Jethro said, °"Blessed *be* [1]the LORD, Who hath delivered you out of the °hand of the Egyptians, and out of the °hand of Pharaoh, Who hath delivered the People from under the °hand of the Egyptians.

11 Now I know that [1]the LORD *is* °greater than all gods: for in the thing wherein they dealt proudly *He was* above them."

12 And Jethro, Moses' father in law, took a burnt offering and sacrifices for [1]God: and Aaron came, and all the elders of Israel, to eat bread with Moses' father in law before [1]God.

x3 13 And it came to pass on the morrow, that Moses sat to judge the People: and the People stood by Moses from the morning °unto the evening.

14 And when Moses' father in law saw all that he did to the People, he said, "What *is* this thing that thou doest to the People? why sittest thou thyself alone, and all the People stand by thee from morning [13]unto even?"

15 And Moses said unto his father in law, "Because the People come unto me to enquire of [1]God:

16 When they have a matter, they come unto me; and I judge between one and another, and I do make *them* know the °statutes of [1]God, and His laws."

17 And Moses' father in law said unto him, "The thing that thou doest *is* not good. y3

18 Thou °wilt surely wear away, both thou, and this People that *is* with thee: for this thing *is* too heavy for thee; thou art not able to perform it thyself alone.

19 Hearken now unto my voice, I will give thee counsel, and [1]God shall be with thee: Be thou for the People to [1]God-ward, that thou mayest bring the causes unto [1]God:

---

13 edge. Heb. mouth. Fig. *Prosopopœia.* Ap. 6.
sword in the Plain: Rod of God on the mount (*v.* 9): Jehovah above all (*v.* 6).
14 the LORD (Heb. Jehovah) **said.** See notes on 3. 7 and 6. 10.
Write. First occurrence. The tablets found at Lachish and Tel-el-Amarna show that writing of a high order was fully developed before the time of Moses.
in a book. Heb. "in the book" (*bassēpher*). This writing afterward ordered for "the Book of the Law" (24. 4, 7). See Ap. 47, where the history of that Book is traced from this passage to Malachi.
put out = blot out. Cp. Deut. 25. 19. Num. 24. 20.
15 Jehovah-nissi = "Jehovah [is] my banner." One of the Jehovah titles. Ap. 4.
16 LORD = Jah. See Ap. 4.
hath sworn. The margins of A.V. and R.V. show the perplexity caused by the *Ellipsis* of the verb. "Surely the hand [lifted up] upon the banner of Jah [is to swear]: for the war of Jehovah against Amalek is to be from generation to generation". So it was. It was carried on by Ehud (Judg. 3. 13–15), Barak (Judg. 5. 14), Gideon (Judg. 6. 3; 7. 12–14), Saul (1 Sam. 15. 2–9, cp. *v.* 11), Samuel (1 Sam. 15. 32, 33), David (1 Sam. 27. 8; 30. 1, 17; 2 Sam. 8. 12), Simeonites (1 Chron. 4. 42, 43), and Mordecai (Est. 3. 1–6; 9. 7–10).

18. 1 When. This chapter is a *parenthesis* (Ap. 6). Introduced here because Jethro, though he lived among the Amalekites, yet was not under their curse (17. 14–16). The event occurred between *vv.* 10 and 11 of Num. 10. Jethro's counsel was given, and taken, when Israel was ready to depart from Sinai (Deut. 1. 7–14).
Jethro. Cp. 3. 1. Probably a descendant of Abraham by Keturah, and not, therefore, an idolater. Cp. *v.* 12 and context.
God. Heb. Elohim. Ap. 4.
the LORD. Heb. Jehovah. Ap. 4.
Egypt. A reading (*Sevir*) reads "land of Egypt". See Ap. 34.
2 sent her back. Probably at Ex. 4. 26.
3 Gershom = a stranger.
4 Eliezer = God [is] my helper.
6 I. The Sam., Sept., and Syr. read "Lo", or "Behold": in which case we must read instead of "he", *v.* 6, "and one said unto Moses, 'Behold, thy father-in-law cometh'", &c.
10 Blessed. Fig. *Benedictio.* Ap. 6.
hand. Thrice put for "power" by Fig. *Metonymy* (of Cause). Ap. 6.
11 greater. Fig. *Anthropopatheia.* Ap. 6. Magnitude attributed to God.
13 unto. Some codices, with one early printed edition, Sam., and Syr., read "even until".
16 statutes of God. Those before Sinai. See Ap. 15.
18 wilt surely wear away. Fig. *Polyptōton* (Ap. 6), "a wearing thou wilt wear". See note on Gen. 26. 28.

1491 20 And thou shalt teach them °ordinances and laws, and shalt shew them the way wherein they must walk, and the work that they must do.
21 Moreover thou shalt provide out of all the People able °men, such as fear [1]God, men of truth, hating covetousness; and place *such* over them, °*to be* rulers of thousands, *and* rulers of hundreds, °rulers of fifties, and rulers of tens:
22 And let them judge the People at all seasons: and it shall be, *that* every great matter they shall bring unto thee, but every small matter they shall judge: so shall it be easier for thyself, and they shall bear *the burden* with thee.
23 If thou shalt do this thing, and [1]God command thee *so,* then thou shalt be able to endure, and all this People shall also go to their place in peace."
24 So Moses hearkened to the voice of his father in law, and did all that he had said.
25 And Moses chose able men out of all Israel, and made them heads over the People, rulers of thousands, rulers of hundreds, rulers of fifties, and rulers of tens.
26 And they judged the People at all seasons: the hard causes they brought unto Moses, but every small matter they judged themselves.
27 And Moses let his father in law depart; and he went his way into his own land.)

k[3] **19** In the °third month, when the °children
(p. 95) of Israel were gone forth out of the land
15th of Egypt, the same day came they *into* the
Sivan wilderness of Sinai.
2 For they were departed from Rephidim, and were come *to* the desert of Sinai, and had pitched in the wilderness; and there Israel camped before the mount.

T U X[1] 3 And Moses °went up unto °God, and °the
(p. 94) LORD °called unto him out of the mountain,
16th saying, "Thus shalt thou say to the house of
Sivan Jacob, and tell the °children of Israel;
4 'Ye have seen what I did unto the Egyptians, and *how* °I bare you on eagles' wings, and brought you unto Myself.
5 Now therefore, if ye will obey My voice indeed, and keep My covenant, then ye shall be a °peculiar treasure unto Me above all °people: for °all the earth *is* Mine:
6 And ye shall be unto Me a °kingdom of priests, and an holy nation.' These *are* the words which thou shalt speak unto the [1]children of Israel."

Y[1] 7 And Moses °came and called for the elders of the People, and laid before their faces all these words which [3]the LORD commanded him.
8 And all the People answered together, and said, "All that [3]the LORD hath spoken we will do."

X[2] And Moses °returned the words of the People
17th unto [3]the LORD.
Sivan 9 And °the LORD said unto Moses, °"Lo, I come unto thee in a thick cloud, that the People may hear when I °speak with thee, and °believe thee for ever." And Moses told the words of the People unto [3]the LORD.
10 And [9]the LORD said unto Moses, "Go unto the People, and sanctify them to day and to morrow, and let them wash their clothes,
11 And be ready against the third day: for the third day [3]the LORD will come down in the sight of all the People upon mount Sinai.
12 And thou shalt set bounds unto the People round about, saying, 'Take heed to yourselves,

---

20 ordinances and laws. Heb. "the Ordinances and (or, even) the Laws".

21 men. Heb. pl. of *'ish,* or *'enōsh.* Ap. 14.

to be. Supply "as" for *Ellipsis* (Ap. 6).

rulers. Some codices, with Sam., Sept., and Syr., read "and rulers".

19. 1 third month. Ap. 50. vii. 3. Fifty days from Rameses, vii. 1, 2.

children = sons.

3 went up unto God: Moses' first ascent. From the Structures T, U, and *U* (p. 85), it will be seen that we have here the first occurrence of this expression, and the first of the six ascents and descents of Moses to receive and give His laws and ordinances. The following is a summary:—

ASCENTS.		DESCENTS.
19. 3-6.	First.	19. 7, 8-.
19. -8-13.	Second.	19. 14-19.
19. 20-24.	Third.	19. 25.
24. 9—32. 14.	Fourth.	32. 15-30.
32. 31-33.	Fifth.	32. 34-34. 3.
34. 4-28.	Sixth.	34. 29-35.

Note that the two sets of three each are marked off by the two great events: the giving of the Law, and the setting up of the Tabernacle; while the fourth and sixth ascents are marked by the giving of the first and second tables (See Ap. 10).

The fourth and sixth ascents are the fullest, and receive special expansion. See above X[4] (p. 94), 20. 21—24. 2, and X[5] (p. 94), 24. 9—32. 15.

God. Heb. *ha-'Elohim.* See Ap. 4.

the LORD (Heb. Jehovah) **called.** The only occ. of this expression in Exodus. In 3. 4, it is "God (Elohim) called".

children of Israel. A reading called *Sevīr* reads "house of Israel". See Ap. 34.

4 I bare you, &c. Cp. Deut. 32. 11, 12.

5 peculiar treasure = a treasure acquired for a possession. Cp. 1 Chron. 29. 3. Ecc. 2. 8. 1 Pet. 2. 9. Heb. *segullāh.* First occ. Eight times: 19. 5, and Deut. 7. 6; 14. 2; 26. 18. Ps. 135. 4. Mal. 3. 17, where it is used of Israel; and in 1 Chron. 29. 3 and Ecc. 7. 8, where it is used of purchased and personal property. It denotes a treasure *reserved* for one's self. The Lat. *sigillo,* to *seal up,* is from this Heb. word. Cp. Matt. 13. 44.

people = peoples. God's People are:—
A separated People. Ex. 33. 16.
A People of inheritance. Deut. 4. 20.
A special People. Deut. 7. 6.
A purchased People. Ex. 15. 16; Ps. 74. 2.
A holy People. Deut. 7. 6; 14. 1.
A redeemed People. Ex. 15. 13.
A sanctified People. Isa. 63. 18.

all the earth is Mine. Cp. Ps. 24. 1; 50. 12.

6 kingdom of priests. Not the genitive of character (Ap. 17), which would be priestly kingdom. But by the Fig. *Antiptosis* (Ap. 6) = "a royal priesthood", as explained in 1 Pet. 2. 9. The whole nation being a priest with respect to other nations, as the tribe of Levi for Israel. Now in abeyance, because Israel did not fulfil the condition in *v.* 5. But in the future it will be realised (Isa. 61. 6; 66. 21).

7 came. Moses' first descent. See note on 19. 3.

8 returned. Moses' second ascent, *vv.* -8-13. See note on 19. 3.

9 the LORD said. See note on 3. 7, and cp. note on 6. 10. **Lo.** Fig. *Asterismos.* Ap. 6.

speak . . . believe. Cp. Rom. 10. 17. "Faith cometh by hearing".

1491 *that ye* go *not* up into the mount, or touch the border of it: whosoever toucheth the mount shall be °surely put to death:

13 There shall not an hand touch °it, but he shall °surely be stoned, or shot through; whether *it be* beast or man, it shall not live:' when the trumpet soundeth long, they shall come up to the mount."

Y[2] (p. 94) 14 And Moses °went down from the mount unto the People, and sanctified the People; and they washed their clothes.

18th Sivan 15 And he said unto the People, "Be ready against the third day: come not at *your* wives."

19th Sivan 16 And it came to pass on the third day in the morning, that there were thunders and lightnings, and a thick cloud upon the mount, and the voice of the trumpet exceeding loud; so that all the People that *was* in the camp trembled.

17 And Moses brought forth the People out of the camp to meet with [3]God; and they stood at the nether part of the mount.

18 And mount Sinai was altogether on a smoke, because [3]the LORD descended upon it in fire: and the smoke thereof ascended as the smoke of a furnace, and the whole °mount quaked greatly.

19 And when the voice of the trumpet sounded long, and waxed louder and louder, Moses spake, and [3]God °answered him by a voice.

X[3] 20 And [3]the LORD came down upon mount Sinai, °on the top of the mount: and [3]the LORD called Moses *up* to the top of the mount; and Moses °went up.

21 And [9]the LORD said unto Moses, "Go down, charge the People, lest they break through unto [3]the LORD to gaze, and many of them perish.

22 And let the priests also, which come near to [3]the LORD, sanctify themselves, lest [3]the LORD break forth upon them."

23 And Moses said unto [3]the LORD, "The People cannot come up to mount Sinai: for Thou chargedst us, saying, 'Set bounds about the mount, and sanctify it.'"

24 And [9]the LORD said unto him, "Away, get thee down, and thou shalt come up, thou, and Aaron with thee: but let not the °priests and the People break through to come up unto [3]the LORD, lest He break forth upon them."

Y[3] 25 So Moses °went down unto the People, and °spake unto them.

V a A (p. 100) **20** And °God spake °all these words, °saying,

(I.) 2 °"*I am* °the LORD thy God, Which have brought thee out of the land of Egypt, out of the house of bondage.

3 Thou shalt have no other gods °before Me.

B (II.) 4 Thou shalt not °make unto thee any °graven image, or any likeness *of any thing* that *is* in heaven above, or that *is* in the earth beneath, or that *is* in the water under the earth:

12 surely put to death. Fig. *Polyptōton*. Ap. 6. "A dying he shall die." See note on Gen. 2. 17.

13 it = him: i. e. not arrested or seized lest trespass on mount incurred.

surely be stoned. Fig. *Polyptōton* (Ap. 6). Cp. Gen. 26. 28.

14 went down. Moses' second descent, *vv.* 14–19. See note on 19. 3.

19 answered him by a voice. Heb. denotes repeated speaking, and thus tells us how the next and following chapters were given to Moses.

20 on = to.

went up. Moses' third ascent.

24 priests. See Ap. 15. The firstborn were priests.

25 went down. Moses' third descent. See note on 19. 3.

spake. Fig. *Ellipsis* (Ap. 6): i. e. "repeated [these things] to the People".

20. 1—24. 8 (V, p. 94). THE GIVING OF THE LAW (*Introversion and Repeated Alternation*).

V | a | 20. 1–17. The Covenant stated. "The ten words."
b | 20. 18–21. People "afar off." Moses draws near.
c | 20. 22—23. 33. General Laws.
b | 24. 1, 2. People "afar off." Moses to draw near.
a | 24. 3–8. The Covenant made.

20. 1–17 (a, above). THE COVENANT STATED. "THE TEN WORDS" (*Introversion*).

a | A | 2, 3. Commands I and II = THOUGHT.
B | 4–6. Command III = WORD.
C | 7–12. Commands IV and V = DEED.
} "THE LORD THY GOD."
C | 13–15. Commands VI, VII, and VIII—DEED.
B | 16. Command IX—WORD.
A | 17. Command X = THOUGHT.
} "THOU."

Here, the three subjects, Thought, Word, and Deed, are repeated in the second table in inverse order.

The law given in Arabia. The same country witnessed the giving of Mahomet's Law.

The moral law given in public at Horeb. Cp. Mal. 4. 4.

The ceremonial law given to Moses in the Tabernacle.

The judicial law given at sundry times; neither so public and solemn as the former, nor so private as the latter.

20. 1 God spake. Heb. Elohim: hence of universal application. Cp. Heb. 1. 1. Deut. 4. 12. Heb. 12. 26; &c., &c. Not Jehovah, for this title would have limited the law to Israel. See Ap. 4, and note on 6. 2.

all these words. It has been asserted that there are three strata of laws in the Pentateuch:—

(1) The Prophetic code. Ex. 20—23 and 34. 17–26.
(2) The Priest code. Rest of Ex., Lev., and Num.
(3) The Deuteronomy code.

But the *Structures* of these books, displayed above, show that these were all in perfect order, spoken "at sundry times and in divers manners."

The Ten Commandments divided by Christ into two [tables], Duty to God and Neighbour (Matt. 22. 37–40). Divided by man into four and six. By Roman Catholics (in their Catechism) the second is joined to the first, and the tenth is divided into two. But this is impossible: see the Structure of Com. X on *v.* 17, p. 101.

The Structure of the whole divides them into 5 + 5, the number of Grace. See Ap. 10, and cp. John 1. 17, "the law was given by Moses, but grace and truth came by Jesus Christ", which, by the Fig. *Hendiadys* (Ap. 6) = "true grace". For there was grace in the law, seeing no other nation was favoured with it. Moreover, the first five are linked together by the words "the LORD thy God", the second five by the word "Thou".

saying. The Ten Commandments begin, therefore, with *v.* 2. See Ap. 39.

2 I am, &c. = "I, Jehovah [am] thy God (Heb. Elohim)." This must go with Com. I, or we should not have the Ap. 4. **2 the LORD** (Heb. Jehovah) **thy God.** five repetitions of it in the first five. **3 before Me** = before My face. **4 make.** The making is equally forbidden as the worshipping. **graven image.** Heb. *pesel*, a sculpture. First occ.

1491 5 Thou shalt not bow down thyself to them,
nor serve them: for I ²the LORD thy ¹God *am* a
°jealous °GOD, °visiting the °iniquity of the
fathers upon the °children unto the third and
fourth *generation* of them that hate Me;
6 And shewing mercy unto thousands of them
that love Me, and keep My commandments.

B (p. 100) (III.) 7 Thou shalt not °take the name of ²the
LORD thy ¹God in vain; for ²the LORD will °not
hold him guiltless that taketh His name in
vain.

C (IV.) 8 °Remember the sabbath day, to keep
it holy.
9 Six days shalt thou °labour, and do all thy
work:
10 But the seventh day *is* the sabbath of ²the
LORD thy ¹God: *in it* thou shalt not do °any
work, thou, °nor thy son, nor thy daughter,
°thy manservant, nor thy maidservant, nor
thy cattle, nor thy stranger that *is* within thy
°gates:
11 For *in* six days ²the LORD °made °heaven
and earth, °the sea, and all that in them *is*, and
rested the seventh day: wherefore ²the LORD
blessed the sabbath day, and hallowed it.

(V.) 12 °Honour thy father and thy mother:
that thy days may be long upon the land
which ²the LORD thy ¹God giveth thee.

C (VI.) 13 Thou shalt not kill.

(VII.) 14 Thou shalt not commit adultery.

(VIII.) 15 Thou shalt not steal.

B (IX.) 16 Thou shalt not bear false witness
against thy neighbour.

A (°X.) 17 Thou shalt not covet thy neighbour's
house, thou shalt not covet thy neighbour's
wife, ¹⁰nor his manservant, nor his maidservant, nor his ox, nor his ass, nor any thing that
is thy neighbour's."

b 18 And all the People °saw the thunderings,
°and the lightnings, and the noise of the
trumpet, and the mountain smoking: and
when the People saw *it*, they removed, and
stood afar off.
19 And they said unto Moses, °"Speak thou
with us, and we will hear: but let not ¹God
speak with us, lest we die."
20 And Moses said unto the People, "Fear
not: for ¹God is come °to prove you, and °that
His fear may be before your faces, that ye °sin
not."
21 And the People stood °afar off,

c D¹ (p. 102) and Moses °drew near unto the thick darkness where ¹God *was*.
22 And °the LORD said unto Moses, "Thus
thou shalt say unto the ⁵children of Israel, 'Ye
have seen that I have talked with you from
heaven.
23 Ye shall not make with Me gods of silver,
neither shall ye make unto you gods of gold.

5 jealous = zealous. Fig. *Anthropopatheia*. Ap. 6. Cp. Deut. 4. 24. Heb. 12. 29.
GOD = El. See Ap. 4.
visiting = charging. This burden of God's revelation of Himself reappears in Ex. 34. 6, 7. Num. 14. 18. Deut. 5. 9, 10. The punishment being not lengthened in vengeance, but distributed in mercy over the third and fourth, so that the whole weight falls not on the first or second.
iniquity. Heb. *'āvōn*. Ap. 44. iii.
children = sons.
7 take the name . . . in vain. Much more important than the mere mispronunciation of the Name.
not hold him guiltless. Fig. *Tapeinosis*. Ap. 6.
8 Remember. Because already hallowed, and command given. See Ap. 15, and notes on Gen. 8. 5, 10, 12, 14. The Babylonians had a seventh-day rest, doubtless from Gen. 2. 2, 3: not this from Babylonians. Note the Structure of this longest Commandment:—

20. 8-11 (C, p. 100). THE FOURTH COMMANDMENT (*Introversion and Simple Alternation*).

C | D | 8. To be remembered and kept by man. } Man (command).
  E | x | 9. The six days for man's work.
    y | 10. Seventh for man's rest.
  E | *x* | 11-. Six days for Jehovah's work.
    y | -11-. Seventh for Jehovah's rest. } God (reason).
  D | -11. Sabbath blessed and hallowed by Jehovah.

9 labour. The Heb. accent (*zarka*) marks this word for emphasis: implying that the fourth Commandment is twofold, and no seventh-day rest can be really enjoyed without, or apart from, the six days of labour.
10 any. Fig. *Synecdoche* (of Genus). Ap. 6. i. e. not any forbidden work. Cp. Lev. 23. 7, 8. Num. 28. 18.
nor. Note the Fig. *Paradiastolē* (Ap. 6), for emphasis.
thy manservant. Some codices, with three early printed editions and Jon., read "nor thy manservant".
gates. Put by *Metonymy* (of Adjunct), Ap. 6, for cities.
11 made = took to make.
heaven and earth. See note on Deut. 4. 26.
the sea. Sam., Onk., Jon., Sept., and Syr. read "and the sea".
12 Honour. This completes the first five, and ends with "promise" (Eph. 6. 2). These five, that relate to *piety*, are thus separated from the five that relate to *probity*. The first and fifth begin and end the five with honour to God, and to our parents whom He honours. They have nothing to do with our "neighbours".
17 The Structure of Commandment X shows that it cannot be divided, except as follows:—

(*A*, p. 100.) THE TENTH COMMANDMENT. (*Introversion.*)

A | c | Thy *neighbour's* house (General).
  d | Wife, servant, maid (human) } (Particular).
  d | Ox and ass (animal)
  c | Anything that is thy *neighbour's* (General).

18 saw. Fig. *Zeugma*. Ap. 6 (here, *Protozeugma*), the one verb "saw" used for two things, but appropriate only for one. Emphasis on "saw".
and. Note Fig. *Polysyndeton* (Ap. 6).
19 Speak thou, &c. From Deut. 5. 28 and 18. 17 we learn that on that very day God promised to send "Him that speaketh from heaven" (18. 15-18).
20 to prove: i. e. for the purpose of proving.
that = in order that.
sin. Heb. *chat'a*. See Ap. 44. i.
21 afar off. Note the difference between law and grace. (Eph. 2. 13).
drew near. Moses' fourth ascent. See note on 19. 3.

20. 22—23. 33 (c, p. 102). GENERAL LAWS (*Repeated Alternation*).
[For Structure see next page.]

22 the LORD [Heb. Jehovah] **said.** See note on 3. 7, and cp. note on 6. 10.

1491 24 An altar ° of earth thou shalt make unto Me, and shalt ° sacrifice thereon thy burnt offerings, and thy peace offerings, thy sheep, and thine oxen: ° in all places where I record My name I will come unto thee, and I will bless thee.

25 And if thou wilt make Me an altar of stone, thou shalt ° not build it of ° hewn stone: for if thou lift up thy ° tool upon it, thou hast polluted it.

26 Neither shalt thou go up ° by steps unto Mine altar, that thy nakedness be not discovered thereon.'

E¹ e g (p. 102) **21** Now these *are* the judgments which thou shalt set before them.

2 If thou buy an Hebrew servant, six years he shall serve: and in the seventh he shall go out free for nothing.

3 If he came in ° by himself, he shall go out by himself: if he were married, then his wife shall go out with him.

4 If his master have given him a wife, and she have born him sons or daughters; the wife and her children shall be her master's, and he shall go out by himself.

5 And if the servant ° shall plainly say, 'I love my master, my wife, and my ° children; I will not go out free:'

6 Then his master shall bring him unto ° the judges; he shall also bring him to the door, or unto the door post; and his master shall ° bore his ear through with an aul; and he shall serve him ° for ever.

7 And if ° a man sell his daughter to be a maidservant, she shall not go out as the menservants do.

8 If she please not her master, who hath betrothed her to himself, then shall he let her be redeemed: to sell her unto a strange ° nation he shall have no ° power, seeing he hath dealt deceitfully with her.

9 And if he have betrothed her unto his son, he shall deal with her after the manner of daughters.

10 If he take him another *wife*; her food, her raiment, and her duty of marriage, shall he not diminish.

11 And if he do not these three unto her, then shall she go out free without money.

h i 12 He that smiteth ° a man, so that he die, shall be surely put to death.

13 And if a man lie not in wait, but ° God ° deliver *him* into his hand; then I will appoint thee a place whither he shall flee.

14 But if a man come presumptuously upon his neighbour, to slay him with ° guile; thou shalt take him from mine altar, that he may die.

j 15 And he that ° smiteth his father, or his mother, shall be surely put to death.

g 16 And he that stealeth ° a man, and selleth him, or if he be found in his hand, he shall surely be put to death.

h j 17 And he that ° curseth his father, or his mother, shall be surely put to death.

m 18 And if ° men strive together, and ° one smite ° another with a stone, or with *his* fist, and he die not, but keepeth *his* bed:

20. -21—23. 33 (c, p. 100). GENERAL LAWS. (*Repeated Alternation*).

c | D¹ | 20. -21-26. God: Worship (Canaanites and Commands).
E¹ | 21. 1—22. 17. Man (Persons and Property).
D² | 22. 18-20. God: Worship (Witchcraft).
E² | 22. 21-28. Man (Oppression and Property).
D³ | 22. 29-31. God: Worship (Offerings).
E³ | 23. 1-9. Man (Falsehood and Oppression).
D⁴ | 23. 10-19-. God: Worship (Sabbaths and Feasts).
E⁴ | 23. -19. Man (Treatment of Animals).
D⁵ | 23. 20-33. God: Worship (Canaanites and Commands).

24 of earth . . . in all places. Shiloh was the first place, Jer. 7. 12; Bethel, 1 Sam. 10. 3; then Zion, Ps. 78. 68. "Where'er we seek Thee Thou art found".

sacrifice. Heb. *zabach.* Ap. 43. I. iv.

25 not . . . hewn stone. No human handiwork to be used in approaching God in worship.

tool. Man's work, in this sphere, pollutes.

26 by steps. Only exposes nakedness. "*I* will come unto *thee*" (*v.* 24) is the essence of worship. *Our* approach is quite secondary. Whether by "tool" or "steps", it either pollutes the Divine or exposes the human.

21. 1—22. 17 (E¹, above). MAN: PERSONS AND PROPERTY (*Introversion*).

E¹ | e | 21. 1-32. Persons.
f | 21. 33—22. 15. Property.
e | 22. 16, 17. Persons.

21. 1-32 (e, above). LAWS RELATING TO PERSONS (*Alternation and Introversion*).

e | g | 1-11. Servitude.
h | i | 12-14. Violence.
j | 15. Parents (Smiting).
g | 16. Servitude.
h | *j* | 17. Parents (Cursing).
i | 18-32. Violence.

Chapters 21-23 are an expansion of chapter 20.

3 by himself. Heb. "with his body". Fig. *Synecdoche* (of Part). Ap. 6.

5 shall plainly say. Heb. "saying shall say". Fig. *Polyptōton* (Ap. 6) for emphasis. See note on Gen. 26. 28.

children = sons.

6 the judges. See note on 22. 9.

bore his ear. Hence a symbol of obedience and perpetual servitude. Cp. Ps. 40. 6. Isa. 48. 8; 50. 5; and see note on Heb. 10. 5.

for ever. Fig. *Synecdoche* (of Whole). Ap. 6. All time put for limited time;—"for life", or till the jubilee, Lev. 25. 13, 28, 40, 41.

7 a man. Heb. *'īsh.* See Ap. 14.

8 nation = people.

power = authority.

13 God [Heb. Elohim] **deliver.** Heb. idiom, by which God is said to do what He allows to be done.

deliver. Heb. permit him to meet, or come.

14 guile . . . thou. Fig. *Ellipsis* (Ap. 6); between these two words, supply: "and then seek refuge at Mine altar".

15 smiteth. Here and elsewhere in this chapter (except *v.* 26), to smite to death, or seriously.

16 a man. (Heb. *'īsh.* Ap. 14.) Aram. and Sept. add "of the sons of Israel".

17 curseth, or revileth. Cp. Matt. 15. 4. Mark 7. 10.

18-32 (*i*, above). VIOLENCE: RELATING TO PERSONS (*Extended Alternation*).

[For Structure see next page.]

18 men. Heb. pl. of *'īsh*, or *'enōsh.* See Ap. 14. ii.

one. Heb. *'īsh.* Ap. 14. ii.

another = his neighbour.

1491 19 If he rise again, and walk abroad upon his staff, then shall he that smote *him* be quit: only he shall pay *for* the loss of his time, and shall cause *him* to be thoroughly healed.

n 20 And if [7]a man smite his servant, or his
(p. 103) maid, with a rod, and he die under his hand; he shall be surely °punished.

21 Notwithstanding, if he continue a day or two, he shall not be [20]punished: for he *is* his °money.

o 22 If [18]men strive, and hurt a woman with °child, so that her fruit depart *from her*, and yet no mischief follow: he shall be surely °punished, according as the woman's husband will lay upon him; and he shall pay as the judges *determine*.

m 23 And if *any* mischief follow, then thou shalt give °life for °life,

24 °Eye for eye, tooth for tooth, hand for hand, foot for foot,

25 Burning for burning, wound for wound, stripe for stripe.

n 26 And if [7]a man smite the eye of his servant, or the eye of his maid, that it perish; he shall let him °go free for his eye's sake.

27 And if he °smite out his manservant's tooth, or his maidservant's tooth; he shall let him [26]go free for his tooth's sake.

o 28 If an ox gore a [7]man or a woman, that they die: then the ox shall be surely stoned, and his flesh shall not be eaten; but the owner of the ox *shall be* quit.

29 But if the ox were wont to push with his horn in time past, and it hath been testified to his owner, and he hath not kept him in, but that he hath killed a man or a woman; the ox shall be stoned, and his owner also shall be put to death.

30 If there be laid on him a sum of money, then he shall give for the °ransom of his [23]life whatsoever is laid upon him.

31 Whether he have gored a son, or have gored a daughter, according to this judgment shall it be done unto him.

32 If the ox shall push a manservant or a maidservant; he shall give unto their master thirty °shekels of silver, and the ox shall be stoned.

f p 33 And if a man shall open a pit, or if a man shall dig a pit, and not cover it, and an ox or an ass fall therein;

34 The owner of the pit shall make *it* good, *and* give money unto the owner of them; and the dead *beast* shall be his.

35 And if one man's ox hurt another's, that he die; then they shall sell the live ox, and divide the money of it; and the dead *ox* also they shall divide.

36 Or if it be known that the ox hath used to push in time past, and his owner hath not kept him in; he shall surely pay ox for ox; and the dead shall be his own.

q **22** If °a man shall steal an ox, or a sheep, and kill it, or sell it; he shall restore five oxen for an ox, and °four sheep for a sheep.

2 If a thief be °found breaking up, and be smitten that he die, *there shall* no blood *be shed* for him.

18-32 (*i*, p. 102). VIOLENCE: RELATING TO PERSONS (*Extended Alternation*).

i | m | 21. 18, 19. Man.
  n | 20, 21. Servants.
   o | 22. Men and women.
 m | 23-25. Man.
  n | 26, 27. Servants.
   o | 28-32. Men and women.

20 punished = avenged.
21 money. Fig. *Metonymy* (of Cause), Ap. 6, money put for the servant who earns it.
22 child . . . so. Fig. *Ellipsis* (Ap. 6); supply "who intervenes".
punished = amerced, or fined. The laws of Khammurabi distinguished between three classes (§§ 209, 211, 213). Here it is *any* woman. See Ap. 15.
23 life = soul. Heb. *nephesh*. See Ap. 13.
24-25 Eye for eye, &c. *Lex talionis*, eight particulars for completeness (Ap. 10), seven in separate category (*vv.* 24, 25). These laws made prisons unnecessary, and prevented crime.
26 go free. By Code of Khammurabi, the master was compensated, § 199 (see Ap. 15). Cp. Deut. 4. 8.
27 smite. Not the same word as elsewhere in this chapter.
30 ransom. Implying that death-penalties were in certain cases commutable. Cp. 30. 12 and Ps. 49. 8.
32 shekels. See Ap. 51. I.

21. 33—**22.** 15 (f, p. 102). LAWS AS TO PROPERTY (*Alternation*).

f | p | 21. 33-36. Carelessness (Pit. Oxen).
  q | 22. 1-5. Dishonesty (Theft).
 p | 22. 6. Carelessness (Fire).
  q | 22. 7-15. Dishonesty (Trusts).

22. 1 a man. Heb. *'ish* (Ap. 14).
four sheep. So David judged, 2 Sam. 12. 6.
2 found: i. e. caught in the act of.
3 If the sun, &c. Therefore killed after he had got away, and in cold blood.
5 field .. of. Between these two words the Sam. and Sept. have "he shall surely make restitution out of his own field according to the yield thereof; and if the whole field be eaten". This is not due to *Ellipsis* but to *Homœoteleuton* (Ap. 6), by which, in transcribing, the eye of the copyist went back (in error) to the latter of the like endings of two sentences, and thus omitted the intervening words between "field" and "field".

3 (°If the sun be risen upon him, *there shall be* blood *shed* for him); *for* he should make full restitution; if he have nothing, then he shall be sold for his theft.

4 If the theft be certainly found in his hand alive, whether it be ox, or ass, or sheep; he shall restore double.

5 If a [1]man shall cause a field or vineyard to be eaten, and shall put in his beast, and shall feed in another man's °field; °of the best of his own field, and of the best of his own vineyard, shall he make restitution.

6 If fire break out, and catch in thorns, so *p*
that the stacks of corn, or the standing corn, or the field, be consumed *therewith;* he that kindled the fire shall surely make restitution.

7 If a man shall deliver unto his neighbour *q*
money or stuff to keep, and it be stolen out of the man's house; if the thief be found, let him pay double.

8 If the thief be not found, then the master of the house shall be brought unto the [9]judges, *to see* whether he have put his hand unto his neighbour's goods.

1491 9 For all manner of °trespass, *whether it be* for ox, for ass, for sheep, for raiment, *or* for any manner of lost thing, which *another* challengeth to be his, the cause of both parties shall come °before the judges; *and* whom the judges shall condemn, he shall pay double unto his neighbour.

10 If [1]a man deliver unto his neighbour an ass, or an ox, or a sheep, or any beast, to keep; and it die, or be hurt, or driven away, °no man seeing *it:*

11 *Then* shall an oath of °the LORD be between them both, that he hath not put his hand unto his neighbour's goods; and the owner of it shall accept *thereof,* and he shall not make *it* good.

12 And if it be stolen from him, he shall make restitution unto the owner thereof.

13 If it be torn in pieces, *then* let him bring °it *for* witness, *and* he shall not make good that which was torn.

14 And if [1]a man borrow *ought* of his neighbour, and it be hurt, or die, the owner thereof *being* not with it, he shall surely make *it* good.

15 *But* if the owner thereof *be* with it, he shall not make *it* good: if it *be* an hired *thing,* it came for his hire.

e (p. 102) 16 And if [1]a man entice a maid that is not betrothed, and lie with her, he shall surely endow her to be his wife.

17 If her father utterly refuse to give her unto him, he shall pay money according to the °dowry of virgins.

D² 18 Thou shalt not suffer a °witch to live.

19 Whosoever lieth with a beast shall surely be put to death.

20 He that °sacrificeth unto *any* god, save unto [11]the LORD only, he shall be utterly destroyed.

E² 21 Thou shalt neither vex a stranger, nor oppress him: for ye were strangers in the land of Egypt.

22 Ye shall not afflict any °widow, or fatherless child.

23 If thou afflict them in any wise, and they cry at all unto Me, I will surely hear their cry;

24 And My wrath shall wax hot, and I will kill you with the sword; and your wives shall be widows, and your children fatherless.

25 If thou lend money to *any of* My People *that is* poor by thee, thou shalt not be to him as an usurer, neither shalt thou lay upon him usury.

26 If thou at all take thy neighbour's °raiment to pledge, thou shalt deliver it unto him by that the sun goeth down:

°27 For that *is* his covering only, it *is* his raiment for his skin: wherein shall he sleep? and it shall come to pass, when he crieth unto Me, that I will hear; for I *am* gracious.

28 Thou shalt not revile [8]the gods, nor °curse the ruler of thy People.

D³ 29 Thou shalt not delay *to offer* the first of thy °ripe fruits, and of thy °liquors: the firstborn of thy sons shalt thou °give unto Me.

30 Likewise shalt thou do with thine oxen, *and* with thy sheep: seven days it shall be with his dam; on the eighth day thou shalt give it Me.

31 And ye shall be holy °men unto Me: neither shall ye eat *any* flesh *that is* torn of beasts in the field; ye shall cast it to the dogs.

23 Thou shalt not °raise a false report: put not thine hand with °the wicked to be an unrighteous witness. E³ r t (p. 104)

2 Thou shalt not follow a multitude to *do* °evil; neither shalt thou °speak in a cause to °decline after many to wrest *judgment:*

3 Neither shalt thou °countenance a poor man in his cause. u

4 If thou meet thine enemy's °ox or his ass going astray, thou shalt surely bring it back to him again. s

5 If thou see the ass of him that hateth thee lying under his burden, and wouldest

---

9 trespass = rebellion. Heb. *Pāsh'a.* Ap. 44. ix.
before the judges. Heb. *ha-'ĕlohim* = "gods". See Ap. 4, and note on ch. 21. 6. Or, before God (the judges representing Him), and acting in His stead, according to Rom. 13. 1-6. See this usage (with the Article), 21. 6; 22. 8, 28. See ch. 18. 15-19; and cp. Ps. 82. 1, 6. John 10. 34, 35.
10 no man = no one.
11 the LORD. Heb. Jehovah. Ap. 4.
13 it. Fig. *Synecdoche* (of the Whole). Ap. 6. i. e. bring one of the pieces. Cp. Gen. 31. 39; and Amos 3. 12.
17 dowry = 50 shekels. Deut. 22. 29. See Ap. 51. II.
18 witch or spiritist. Medium to or from, from root to *mutter,* as to some demon. Cp. Lev. 19. 26, 31; 20. 27. Deut. 18. 9-14. This enactment shows the reality of intercourse with evil spirits (angels) and demons.
20 sacrificeth. Heb. *zabach.* Ap. 43. I. iv.
22 widow, or fatherless. Fig. *Synecdoche* (of Species), Ap. 6, put for all kinds of helpless ones.
26 raiment = mantle. Raiment by day, and sole covering at night. Cp. 12. 34. Deut. 24. 12, 13. Judg. 4. 18. Amos 2. 8.
27 According to the *Massorah* (Ap. 30) this is the middle of the 1,209 verses of Exodus.
28 curse. Cp. Ecc. 10. 20. Acts 23. 5. 2 Pet. 2. 10. Jude 8.
29 ripe fruits, and . . . liquors = thy corn and wine and oil. Fig. *Synecdoche* (of Species). Ap. 6.
give. On the eighth day.
31 men. Heb. pl. of *'ish* or *'enōsh.* Ap. 14.

23. 1-9 (E³, p. 102). LAWS AS TO MAN.
(*Alternation and Introversion.*)

E³ | r | t | 1, 2. Falsehood.
       u | 3. Cause of poor man.
     s | 4, 5. Enemy. Assistance.
   | r | u | 6. Cause of poor man.
       t | 7, 8. Falsehood.
     s | 9. Stranger. Oppression.

1 raise = utter, or take up. Same as 20. 7.
the wicked = a wicked one. Heb. *rāsh'ā.* Ap. 44. x.
2 evil = injury. Heb. *r'a'a.* See Ap. 44. viii.
speak = testify.
decline = "turn away [and follow]". Fig. *Ellipsis* (Ap. 6. iii. a).
3 countenance = prefer, or favour.
4 ox or his ass. Fig. *Synecdoche* (of Species), Ap. 6, put for any kind of beast of burden.

1491 forbear to ° help him, thou shalt ° surely help with him.

r u 6 Thou shalt not wrest the judgment of thy poor in his cause.

t 7 Keep thee far from a false matter; and the innocent and righteous slay thou not: for I will not justify the ° wicked.

8 And thou shalt take no gift: for the gift ° blindeth the ° wise, and ° perverteth the words of the righteous.

s 9 Also thou shalt not oppress a stranger: for ye know the ° heart of a stranger, seeing ye were strangers in the land of Egypt.

D[4] v (p. 105) 10 And six years thou shalt sow thy land, and shalt gather in the ° fruits thereof:

11 But the seventh *year* thou shalt let it rest and lie still; that the poor of thy people may eat: and what they leave the beasts of the field shall eat. In like manner thou shalt deal with thy vineyard, ° *and* with thy oliveyard.

12 Six days thou shalt do thy work, and on the seventh day thou shalt rest: that thine ox and thine ass may rest, and the son of thy handmaid, and the stranger, may be ° refreshed.

w 13 And in all *things* that I have said unto you ° be circumspect: and ° make no mention of the name of other gods, neither let it be heard out of thy mouth.

14 ° Three times thou shalt keep a feast unto Me in the year.

v 15 Thou shalt keep the feast of unleavened bread: (thou shalt eat unleavened bread seven days, ° as I commanded thee, in the time appointed of the ° month Abib; for in it thou camest out from Egypt: and none shall ° appear before Me ° empty:)

16 And the feast of harvest, the firstfruits of thy labours, which thou hast sown in the field: and the feast of ingathering, *which is* in the end of the year, when thou hast gathered in thy labours out of the field.

17 Three times in the year all thy males shall appear ° before ° THE Lord GOD.

w 18 Thou shalt not ° offer the blood of My ° sacrifice with leavened bread; neither shall the fat of My ° sacrifice remain until the morning.

19 The first of the firstfruits of thy land thou shalt bring into the house of ° the LORD thy ° God.

E[4] Thou shalt not seethe a kid in his ° mother's milk.

D[5] x[1] 20 ° Behold, I send ° an angel before thee, to keep thee in the way, and to bring thee into the place which I have prepared.

y[1] 21 Beware of him, and obey his voice, provoke him not; for he will not pardon your ° transgressions: for ° My name *is* in him.

22 But if thou shalt indeed obey his voice, and do all that I speak; then I will be an enemy unto thine enemies, and an adversary unto thine adversaries.

x[2] 23 For [20] Mine angel shall go before thee,

5 help. Heb. *Homonym.* *'azab* two words:—
(1) *'āzab* = to leave, or forsake.
(2) *'āzab* = to help, or restore (hence strengthen, or fortify).
No. 1 in Gen. 2. 24; 39. 6. Neh. 5. 10. Ps. 49. 10. Mal. 4. 1. But here it should be No. 2 (as in Neh. 3. 8. Deut. 32. 36. 1 Kings 14. 10. 2 Kings 14. 26. Jer. 49. 25).

surely help with him. Fig. *Polyptōton* (Ap. 6), "helping shalt help him", or, supplying the *Ellipsis*, "surely help him [to unload]".

7 wicked = a wicked one. Heb. *rāsh'a.* Ap. 44. x.

8 blindeth . . . perverteth: i. e. causeth these acts, or sins. Fig. *Metonymy* (of Effect), Ap. 6.

wise. Heb. seeing = the most clear-sighted.

9 heart = soul. Heb. *nephesh.* Ap. 13.

23. 10-19-. (D[4], p. 102). GOD: LAWS OF HIS WORSHIP (*Alternation*).

D[4] | v | 10-12. Time. Six and seven of years and days.
w | 13. False worship (Positive and Negative).
v | 14-17. Time. Three feasts in year.
w | 18, 19-. True worship (Negative and Positive).

10 fruits. Heb. harvest.

11 and. Some codices, with Sam. and Sept., have this in text; it need not, therefore, be in italics.

12 refreshed. Heb. verbal form of *nephesh* (soul) = quickened, have new life put in, renewed, or revived.

13 be circumspect = take heed.

make no mention, &c. A command often disobeyed, especially in house of Saul. Cp. "Baal", 1 Chron. 8. 33; 9. 39; 12. 5; 14. 7; 27. 28. Hence the importance of the prophecy as to the future in Hos. 2. 16, 17.

14 Three times. No. of Divine perfection. Ap. 10.

15 as = according as.

month Abib. See Ap. 51. III. iv.

appear before Me. This is the current Heb. text: but this, and ten other passages were altered by the Sopherim (only in the pointing). Ap. 33. The primitive text read (and ought to be) "see My face". They did not know that "face" was used by Fig. *Synecdoche* (of Part), Ap. 6, for the person "Me", and they thought it too anthropomorphitic. See note on 34. 20.

empty = empty-handed.

17 before = Heb. "before the face of".

THE Lord GOD = Heb. *ha-'adōn Jehovah.* See Ap. 4.

18 offer. Heb. "slay", requiring the supply of the *Ellipsis*, ii. d (Ap. 6) = "slay [and pour out]". See Ap. 43. I. iv.

sacrifice. Heb. "feast", put by *Metonymy* (of Adjunct for "festal sacrifice" (Ap. 6).

19 the LORD. Heb. Jehovah. Ap. 4.

God. Heb. Elohim. Ap. 4.

mother's: i. e. in the milk of its dam. Repeated, 34. 26 and Deut. 14. 21. For similar consideration cp. Deut. 22. 6. Lev. 22. 28.

23. 20-33 (D[5], p. 102). GOD: WORSHIP (CANAANITES AND COMMANDS).
(*Repeated Alternation.*)

D[5] | x[1] | 20. Promise: I will.
y[1] | 21, 22. Command: Thou shalt.
x[2] | 23. Promise: I will.
y[2] | 24, 25-. Command: Thou shalt not.
x[3] | -25-31. Promise: I will.
y[3] | 32, 33. Command: Thou shalt.

20 Behold. Fig. *Asterismos* (Ap. 6) for emphasis.

an angel. It is Elohim speaking, therefore, who can it be but Micha-el? Cp. Dan. 10. 13, 21; 12. 1. Jude 9; and see Mal. 3. 1; Is. 63. 9.

21 transgressions = Heb. *pāsh'a.* Ap. 44. ix.

My name. Cp. Jer. 23. 26. Col. 2. 9.

1491 and bring thee in unto the Amorites, and the
Hittites, and the Perizzites, and the Canaanites, °the Hivites, and the Jebusites: and I
will cut °them off.

y[2] 24 Thou shalt not bow down to their gods,
(p. 105) nor serve them, nor do after their works: but
thou shalt utterly overthrow them, and quite
break down their °images.
25 And ye shall serve [19]the LORD your [19]God,
and He shall bless thy °bread, and thy water;

x[1] and I will take sickness away from the midst
of thee.
26 There shall nothing cast their young, nor
be barren, in thy land: the number of thy
days I will fulfil.
27 I will send °My fear before thee, and will
destroy all the people to whom thou shalt
come, and I will make all thine enemies turn
their backs unto thee.
28 And I will send °hornets before thee,
which shall drive out the Hivite, the Canaanite, and the Hittite, from before thee.
29 I will not drive them out from before
thee in one year; lest the land become desolate, and the beast of the field multiply
against thee.
30 By little and little I will drive them out
from before thee, until thou be increased, and
inherit the land.
31 And I will set thy bounds from the Red
sea even unto the °sea of the Philistines, and
°from the desert unto °the river: for I will
deliver °the inhabitants of the land into your
hand; and thou shalt drive them out before
thee.

y[3] 32 Thou shalt make no covenant with them,
nor with their gods.
33 They shall not dwell in thy land, lest
they make thee °sin against Me: for if thou
serve their gods, it will surely be a snare
unto thee."

b **24** And °He said unto Moses, "Come up
(p. 100) unto °the LORD, thou, and Aaron, °Na-
dab, and Abihu, and °seventy of the elders of
Israel; and worship ye °afar off.
2 And Moses alone shall come °near [1]the
LORD: but they shall not come nigh; neither
shall the People go up with him."

a 3 And Moses °came and told the People °all
the words of [1]the LORD, and °all the judgments: and all the People answered with one
voice, and said, "All the words which [1]the
LORD hath said will we do."
4 And Moses °wrote all the words of [1]the
LORD, and rose up early in the morning,
and builded an altar under °the hill, and
twelve pillars, according to the twelve tribes
of Israel.
5 And he sent °young men of the °children of
Israel, which °offered °burnt offerings, and
°sacrificed °peace offerings of oxen unto [1]the
LORD.
6 And Moses took half of the blood, and put
it in basons; and half of the blood he sprinkled
°on the altar.
7 And he took the book of the covenant, and
read in the audience of the People: and they
said, "All that [1]the LORD hath said will we do,
and °be obedient."
8 And Moses took °the blood, and sprinkled
it on °the People, and said, °"Behold the blood
of the covenant, which [1]the LORD hath made
with you concerning all these words."

9 Then °went up Moses, and Aaron, Nadab, X[4] F
and Abihu, and seventy of the elders of Israel: (p. 94)
10 And °they saw the °God of Israel: and
there was °under His feet as it were a paved
work of a sapphire stone, and as it were the
body of heaven in *his* clearness.

the Hivites. Some codices, with Sam., Onk., and one early printed edition, read "and the Hivites".
them = the six nations. See Ap. 10.
24 images = sacred pillars or statues. 24. 4; 34. 13. See note on Ex. 26. 1.
25 bread, and thy water. Fig. *Synecdoche* (of Species), Ap. 6, put for all kinds of food and drink.
27 My fear = a terror of me.
28 hornets. Cp. Deut. 7. 20. Josh. 24. 12.
31 sea of the Philistines = the Mediterranean or "Great Sea".
from the desert = the desert of Shur.
the river = the Euphrates.
the inhabitants. Some codices, with Jon. and one early printed edition, read "all the inhabitants".
33 sin. Heb. *chāt'ā*. See Ap. 44. i.

24. 1 He (Elohim of 20. 1) **said.** See note on 4. 3.
the LORD. Heb. Jehovah. Ap. 4.
Nadab, and Abihu. Aaron's eldest two sons.
seventy. See Ap. 10.
afar off. See note on 20. 21. **2 near** = near unto.
3 came. Moses' fourth descent. See note on 19. 3.
all the words. (1) The Ten Commandments. Ex. 20. 1–17. (2) **all the judgments**, chaps. 21–23.
4 wrote. See note on Ex. 17. 14, and Ap. 47.
the hill = the mountain.
5 young men. The whole nation as yet were priests, represented in the fathers and elder sons. Probably the redeemed firstborn from all the tribes.
children = sons.
offered. Heb. *'ālah*. See Ap. 43. I. vi.
burnt offerings. Heb. *'ōlah*. See Ap. 43. II. ii.
sacrificed. Heb. *zabach*. Ap. 43. I. iv.
peace offerings. Heb. *shelem*. Ap. 43. II. iv.
5-8 This is the subject of Heb. 9. 15–23, where "testament" should be rendered *covenant*, and the word "men", which is not in the text, should be "over the dead sacrifices" referred to here. (Gr. *epi nekrois.*)
6 on the altar. This was pledging Jehovah to this conditional covenant. See Heb. 9. 19, where the book also is said to be sprinkled.
7 be obedient. Connect this with the sprinkling of the blood in next verse; and connect both with 1 Pet. 1. 2.
8 the blood = the other half of the blood. Fig. *Synecdoche* (of the Part), Ap. 6. See Heb. 9. 20.
the People. Thus pledging them to their part of the covenant, which was thereby made conditional; unlike that with Abraham in Gen. 15, which was unconditional.
Behold. Fig. *Asterismos* (Ap. 6).

24. 9—32. 14 (X[4], p. 94). THE FOURTH ASCENT. THE MAKING OF THE TABERNACLE.
(*Introversion and Repeated Alternation.*)
[For Structure see next page.]

9 went up. Moses' fourth ascent. See note on 19. 3.
10 they saw. Heb. *ḥāzāh*, to see with the mental eye, or in vision (Isa. 1. 1; 2. 1; 13. 1. Ezek. 13. 7. Amos 1. 1. Mic. 1. 1. Hab. 1. 1. Num. 24. 4, 16). Hence, to discern, observe, contemplate, understand. Job 34. 32. Ps. 46. 8. Prov. 22. 29; 24. 32; 29. 20. Ps. 62. 2.
God. Heb. Elohim. Ap. 4.
under. Was this seen from beneath?

1491 11 And upon the nobles of the [5]children of
Israel °He laid not His hand: also [10]they saw
[10]God, and did °eat and drink.

G (p. 107) 12 And °the LORD said unto Moses, "Come
up to Me into the mount, and be there: and
I will give thee tables of stone, and °a law,
and °commandments which I have °written;
that thou mayest teach them."

13 And Moses rose up, and his minister Joshua:
and Moses went up into the mount of [10]God.

14 And he said unto the elders, "Tarry ye
here for us, until we come again unto you:
and, behold, Aaron and Hur *are* with you:
if any man have any matters to do, let him
come unto them."

H z 15 And Moses went up into the mount,
a b and °a cloud covered the mount.

c 16 And the glory of [1]the LORD abode upon
mount Sinai,

a b and the cloud covered it °six days:

and the seventh day he called unto Moses out
of the midst of the cloud.

c 17 And the sight of the glory of [1]the LORD
was like devouring fire on the top of the mount
in the eyes of the [5]children of Israel.

z 18 And Moses °went into the midst of the cloud,
and gat him up into the mount: and Moses
was in the mount forty days and forty nights.

J K[1] **25** And °the LORD spake unto Moses,
saying,

2 "Speak unto the °children of Israel, that
they bring Me an °offering: of every °man
that giveth it willingly with his heart ye shall
take My °offering.

3 °And this *is* the [2]offering which ye shall
take of them; °gold, and silver, and °brass,

4 And blue, and °purple, and scarlet, and
fine linen, and goats' *hair*,

5 And rams' skins dyed red, and badgers'
skins, and °shittim wood,

6 Oil for °the light, spices for anointing oil,
and for sweet incense,

7 Onyx stones, and stones to be set in the
ephod, and in the breastplate.

8 And let them make Me a °sanctuary; that
I may dwell among them.

9 According to all that I shew thee, *after*
the °pattern of the °tabernacle, and the
pattern of all the instruments thereof, even
so shall ye make *it*.

L[1] M[1] 10 And they shall make an °ark *of* shittim
wood: two °cubits and a half *shall be* the
length thereof, and a °cubit and a half the
breadth thereof, and a °cubit and a half the
height thereof.

11 And thou shalt overlay it with pure
gold, within and without shalt thou over-

24. 9—32. 14 (X[4], p. 94). THE FOURTH ASCENT
THE MAKING OF THE TABERNACLE.
(*Introversion and Repeated Alternation.*)

X[4] | F | 24. 9-11. The worship of the Seventy Elders.
 G | 24. 12-14. The Tables promised.
 H | 24. 15-18. The six days and the seventh.
 J | K[1] | 25. 1-9. Materials.
 L[1] | 25. 10—27. 21. Furniture. (The Tabernacle.)
 K[2] | 28. 1—29. 46. Priests.
 L[2] | 30. 1-11. Furniture.
 K[3] | 30. 12-16. Worshippers.
 L[3] | 30. 17-38. Furniture.
 K[4] | 31. 1-6. Artificers.
 L[4] | 31. 7-11. Furniture.
 H | 31. 12-17. The six days and the seventh.
 G | 31. 18. The Tables given.
 F | 32. 1-14. The idolatry of the People.

11 He laid not His hand = put not forth His hand [in vengeance]. Cp. Ex. 3. 20; 33. 22.
eat and drink. Fig. *Metonymy* (of Adjunct), Ap. 6, put for living, i. e. though they were favoured with this vision, they yet lived.
12 the LORD [Heb. Jehovah] **said.** See note on 3. 7, and cp. note on 6. 10. **a** = the.
commandments = the commandment.
written. See note on 17. 14, and Ap. 47.

24. 15-18 (H, above). THE SIX DAYS AND THE SEVENTH (*Introversion and Alternation*).

H | z | 15-. Ascent of Moses.
 a | b | -15. The cloud.
 c | 16-. The glory.
 a | *b* | -16. The cloud.
 c | 17. The glory.
 z | 18. Ascent of Moses.

15 a cloud = the cloud.
16 six days. See Ap. 50. vii. 1, 2, 3.
18 went into. On 20-25th and 26th of SIVAN The fourth Sabbath.
25. 1 the LORD [Heb. Jehovah] **spake.** See notes on 3. 7 and 6. 10.
2 children = sons.
offering = heave offering. Ap. 43. II. viii.
man. Heb. *'ish.* Ap. 14.
3 And. Note the Fig. *Polysyndeton* (Ap. 6) in *vv.* 3-5. Fifteen objects (*vv.* 3-7), 3 × 5. All numbers connected with the Tabernacle are multiples of 5. See Ap. 10.
gold, &c. No iron in the tabernacle.
brass. A mixture of copper and zinc was unknown then. Probably copper, or bronze (a mixture of copper and tin).
4 purple, &c. These colours connected with the crucifixion. Matt. 27. 28. John 19. 2. White mentioned last. So in Rev. 19. 13, 14. **5 shittim** = acacia.
6 the light = the light-holder, as in Gen. 1. 14.
8 sanctuary. Heb. *kodesh.* See note on 3. 5.
9 pattern. Cp. Heb. 8. 5. Not a plan, but a model. The reality is in heaven. So with the temple, later. 1 Chron. 28. 11-19. With the utmost exactitude certain representative measurements given. Nine others, vital to construction, but not for significance, not given. Probably these Divine silences were to make any unauthorised structures impossible. These nine were: (1) Thickness of sides and bottom of ark; (2) thickness of mercy seat and details of cherubim; (3) thickness of table; (4) dimensions of lampstand; (5) thickness of boards; (6) middle-bar dimensions; (7) size, &c., of rams' skins; (8) ditto badgers' skins; (9) all thicknesses of brazen altar (the third dimension). **tabernacle.** Heb. *mishkan.* First occ. See Ap. 40. Cp. *v.* 8.

25. 10—27. 21 (L[1], p. 96). THE FURNITURE OF THE TABERNACLE (*Alternation*).
[For Structure see next page.]

Note, in "M" we have furniture, for the worship, within; and in "N" the protection without. **10 ark.** Note the order in which these things were made, and the lesson arising therefrom. God begins from within; man from without, Matt. 15. 16-20. Here the work begins with the ark and ends with the gate 25. 10-26. 37. So with the four great offerings. So with His work in the heart of the saved sinner. *We* begin from the "gate" and with the "sin-offering". God begins with the "ark" and the "burnt-offering".
10 cubits. See Ap. 51. III. ii.

1491 lay it, and shalt make °upon it a °crown of gold round about.

12 And thou shalt cast four rings of gold for it, and put *them* in the four corners thereof; and two rings *shall be* in the one °side of it, and two rings in the other °side of it.

13 And thou shalt make staves *of* shittim wood, and overlay them with gold.

14 And thou shalt put the staves into the rings by the [12]sides of the ark, that the ark may be borne with them.

15 The staves shall be in the rings of the ark: they shall not be taken from it.

16 And thou shalt put into the ark °the testimony which I shall give thee.

17 And thou shalt make a °mercy seat *of* °pure gold: two cubits and a half *shall be* the length thereof, and a cubit and a half the breadth thereof.

18 And thou shalt make two °cherubims *of* gold, *of* beaten work shalt thou make them, in the two ends of the mercy seat.

19 And make one cherub on the one end, and the other cherub on the other end: °*even* of the mercy seat shall °ye make the cherubims on the two ends thereof.

20 And the cherubims shall stretch forth *their* wings on high, covering the mercy seat with their wings, and their faces *shall look* one to another; °toward the mercy seat shall the faces of the cherubims be.

21 And thou shalt put the mercy seat above upon the ark; and in the ark thou shalt put the testimony that I shall give thee.

22 And there °I will meet with thee, and I will commune with thee from above the mercy seat, from between the two cherubims which *are* upon °the ark of the testimony, of all *things* which I will give thee in commandment unto the [2]children of Israel.

23 Thou shalt also make a table *of* shittim wood: two cubits *shall be* the length thereof, and a cubit the breadth thereof, and a cubit and a half the height thereof.

24 And thou shalt overlay it with pure gold, and make thereto a °crown of gold round about.

25 And thou shalt make unto it a border of an °hand breadth round about, and thou shalt make a golden crown to the border thereof round about.

26 And thou shalt make for it four rings of gold, and put the rings in the four corners that *are* on the four feet thereof.

27 Over against the border shall the rings be for places of the staves to bear the table.

28 And thou shalt make the staves *of* shittim wood, and overlay them with gold, that the table may be borne with them.

29 And thou shalt make the dishes thereof, and spoons thereof, and covers thereof, and bowls thereof, °to cover withal: *of* pure gold shalt thou make them.

30 And thou shalt set upon the table °shewbread before °Me alway.

31 And thou shalt make a °candlestick *of* pure gold: *of* beaten work °shall the candlestick be made: his shaft, and his branches, his bowls, his °knops, and his flowers, shall be of the same.

25. 10—27. 21 (L[1], p. 107). THE FURNITURE OF THE TABERNACLE (*Repeated Alternation*).

L[1] | M[1] | 25. 10-22. The Ark.
| 23-30. The Table.
| 31-40. The Lampstand. } Contents.
N | 26. 1-6. The Curtains.
| 7-14. The Coverings.
| 15-30. The Boards.
| 31-35. The Vail.
| 36, 37. The Hangings for Door. } Construction.
M[2] | 27. 1-8. The Altar of Burnt Offering. Contents.
N | 9-19. Hangings for Court. Construction.
M[3] | 20, 21. Oil for the Lamp. Contents.

11 upon it. Some codices, with Sam., Sept., and Syr., read "thereto".

crown. See note on *v.* 24.

12 side. Heb. *ẕēl'a*, rib. See note on *v.* 32.

16 the testimony. Heb. *'ēdūth* = witness, from *'ūd*, to bear witness, give testimony. The two tables so called because they bore witness to, and were evidences of the covenant made, and of its future extension. 1 Tim. 2. 6, "the testimony in its own season" (= "all", without distinction).

17 mercy seat = propitiatory cover (Heb. *kapporeth* = cover). By Fig. *Metonymy* (Ap. 6) *cover* put for the propitiation made through the blood sprinkled thereon. It therefore denotes propitiation. Cp. Heb. 9. 5. Hence the meaning, God's "propitiatory gift", as in Papyri. Cp. Rom. 3. 25.

pure gold. Not overlaid, because propitiation is a Divine work throughout.

18 cherubims. Pl. of Heb. cherub. Fig. *Metonymy* here put for *representation* of the celestial beings, of which we know nothing. They are a reality, there, and representative of creation, symbolical of blessing for all creation. These (in *v.* 18) were not the cherubims themselves, but representations of them. See Gen. 3. 24: but no "sword", because of the blood of propitiation. Occurs seven times in *vv.* 17-22.

19 even of = out of.

ye. Some codices, Hillel, Sam., Sept., and Syr., read "thou".

20 toward. Looking toward the blood of propitiation. Cp. Ex. 12. 13 and Josh. 2. 18-21. See especially Ex. 37. 9.

22 I will meet. Heb. meet as by appointment, and this, in the appointed place and way: "there". Cp. 23. 14-17; 29. 42, 43, 45, 46; 34. 22-24; 40. 34, 35.

the ark of the testimony. It has seven names:—
Ark of the covenant of Jehovah, Num. 10. 33.
Ark of Adonai Jehovah, 1 Kings 2. 26.
Ark of Jehovah, Josh. 3. 13.
Ark of Elohim, 1 Sam. 3. 3.
The holy ark, 2 Chron. 35. 3.
The ark of Thy strength, Ps. 132. 8.

24 crown of gold. Note the three "crowns":—
(1) Ark (25. 11), *the crown of the Law.* The atoning blood between it, and the cherubim its executant.
(2) Altar of incense (30. 3), *the crown of the priesthood.* Its incense fired only by the fire from the altar of burnt offering.
(3) Table of shewbread (25. 24), *the crown of the kingdom.* The twelve tribes symbolised by the twelve loaves.

25 hand breadth. See Ap. 51. III. 2.

29 to cover = to pour out.

30 shewbread. Heb. bread of faces; faces being put for *presence* by Fig. *Metonymy* (of Adjunct), Ap. 6, denoting the Divine presence in which the bread stood, and from Whom all supplies, material and spiritual, came. First occ.

Me. Heb. "My face." So that here we have the Fig. *Paronomasia*, "*panīm lᵉphanai*" (Ap. 6).

31 candlestick = lampstand.

shall . . . be made. Some codices, with Sam., Jon., Sept., and Syr., read "shalt thou make".

knops = knobs.

1491 32 And six branches shall come out of the °sides of it; three branches of the candlestick out of the one °side, and three branches of the candlestick out of the other °side:

33 °Three bowls made like unto almonds, *with* a knop and a flower in one branch; and three bowls made like almonds in the other branch, *with* a knop and a flower: so in the six branches that come out of the candlestick.

34 And in the candlestick *shall be* [33]four bowls made like unto almonds, *with* their knops and their flowers.

35 And *there shall be* a knop under two branches of the same, and a knop under two branches of the same, and a knop under two branches of the same, according to the six branches that proceed out of the candlestick.

36 Their knops and their branches shall be of the same: all it *shall be* one beaten work *of* pure gold.

37 And thou shalt make the seven lamps thereof: and they shall light the lamps thereof, that they may give light over against °it.

38 And the °tongs thereof, and the snuffdishes thereof, *shall be of* pure gold.

39 *Of* a °talent of pure gold °shall he make it, with all these vessels.

40 And look that thou make *them* after their °pattern, which was shewed thee in the mount.

N
(p. 108) **26** Moreover thou shalt make the °tabernacle *with* °ten curtains *of* fine twined linen, and blue, and purple, and scarlet: *with* cherubims °of cunning work shalt thou make them.

2 The length of one curtain *shall be* eight and twenty °cubits, and the breadth of one curtain four °cubits: and every one of the curtains shall have one measure.

3 The five curtains shall be °coupled together one to another; and *other* five curtains *shall be* coupled one to another.

4 And thou shalt make loops of blue upon the edge of the one curtain from the selvedge in the coupling; and likewise shalt thou make in the uttermost edge of *another* curtain, in the coupling of the second.

5 Fifty loops shalt thou make in the one curtain, and fifty loops shalt thou make in the edge of the curtain that *is* in the coupling of the second; that the loops may take hold one of another.

6 And thou shalt make fifty °taches of gold, and couple the curtains together with the taches: and it shall be one [1]tabernacle.

7 And thou shalt make °curtains *of* goats' *hair* to be a °covering upon the °tabernacle: eleven curtains shalt thou °make.

8 The length of one curtain *shall be* thirty cubits, and the breadth of one curtain four cubits: and the eleven curtains *shall be all* of one measure.

9 And thou shalt couple five curtains by themselves, and six curtains by themselves, and shalt double the sixth curtain in the forefront of the tabernacle.

10 And thou shalt make fifty loops on the edge of the one curtain *that is* outmost in the coupling, and fifty loops in the edge of the curtain which coupleth the second.

32 sides. There are seventeen Heb. words translated "side", important in this technical description. Here it is the ordinary word for "side", *ẓad*.
33 Three. Note connection with **four**, *v.* 34, making seven. See Ap. 10.
37 it. Heb. the face of it. Fig. *Prosopopœia* (Ap. 6).
38 tongs = snuffers (but no extinguishers).
39 talent. See Ap. 51. II.
shall he. The reading called *Sevir* (see Ap. 34) reads "shalt thou"; so some codices, with Sam., Sept., and Syr.
40 pattern. See note on Heb. 8. 5, and cp. 1 Ch. 28. 11, 12, 18, 19.

26. 1 tabernacle. Heb. *mishkān*, the place of God's presence or habitation. Cp. *v.* 7. See Ap. 40.
ten. See Ap. 10.
of cunning work = the work of a skilful weaver. Probably working both sides alike, whereas the embroiderer worked only one side.
2 cubits. See Ap. 51. III. ii.
3 coupled together. Like the five commandments on the two tables. See on Ex. 20. 1.
6 taches = hooks.
7 curtains. These were for the upper covering forming the tent.
covering = Heb. *'ohel*, tent (Ap. 40).
tabernacle. Heb. *mishkān* = dwelling place (Ap. 40).
make. Heb. adds "them", as being distinct from the former.
11 brass. See note on 25. 3.
tent. Heb. *'ohel*, tent (Ap. 40).
12 tabernacle. Heb. *mishkān* (Ap. 40).
13 side. Heb. *ẓad.* See note on 25. 32.

15-30. THE BOARDS.

18 side = Heb. *pē'āh* = region.
20 side. Heb. *ẓēl'ā* = rib.
21 silver. See note on "brass", 27. 17.

11 And thou shalt make fifty taches of °brass, and put the taches into the loops, and couple the °tent together, that it may be one.

12 And the remnant that remaineth of the curtains of the tent, the half curtain that remaineth, shall hang over the backside of the °tabernacle.

13 And a cubit on the one °side, and a cubit on the other side of that which remaineth in the length of the curtains of the tent, it shall hang over the sides of the [12]tabernacle on this side and on that side, to cover it.

14 And thou shalt make a covering for the [11]tent *of* rams' skins dyed red, and a covering above *of* badgers' skins.

15 And thou shalt make boards for the tabernacle *of* shittim wood standing up.

16 Ten cubits *shall be* the length of a board, and a cubit and a half *shall be* the breadth of one board.

17 Two tenons *shall there be* in one board, set in order one against another: thus shalt thou make for all the boards of the tabernacle.

18 And thou shalt make the boards for the tabernacle, twenty boards on the south °side southward.

19 And thou shalt make forty sockets of silver under the twenty boards; two sockets under one board for his two tenons, and two sockets under another board for his two tenons.

20 And for the second °side of the tabernacle on the north [18]side *there shall be* twenty boards:

21 And their forty sockets *of* °silver; two

1491 sockets under one board, and two sockets under another board.

22 And for the °sides of the tabernacle westward thou shalt make six boards.

23 And two boards shalt thou make for the corners of the tabernacle in the two [22]sides.

24 °And they shall be coupled together beneath, and they shall be coupled together above the head of it unto one ring: thus shall it be for them both; they shall be for the two corners.

25 And they shall be eight boards, and their sockets *of* silver, sixteen sockets; two sockets under one board, and two sockets under another board.

26 And thou shalt make °bars *of* shittim wood; five for the boards of the one °side of the tabernacle,

27 And five [26]bars for the boards of the other [26]side of the tabernacle, and five °bars for the boards of the [26]side of the tabernacle, for the two [22]sides westward.

28 And the middle bar in the midst of the boards °shall reach from end to end.

29 And thou shalt overlay the boards with gold, and make their rings *of* gold *for* places for the bars: and thou shalt overlay the [26]bars with gold.

30 And thou shalt °rear up the tabernacle according to the °fashion thereof which was shewed thee in the mount.

31 And thou shalt make a °vail *of* blue, and purple, and scarlet, and fine twined linen of cunning work: with cherubims °shall it be made:

32 And thou shalt hang it upon four pillars of shittim *wood* overlaid with gold: their hooks *shall be of* gold, upon the four sockets of silver.

33 And thou shalt hang up the [31]vail under the taches, that thou mayest bring in thither °within the vail the ark of the testimony: and the vail shall divide unto you between °the holy *place* and °the most holy.

34 And thou shalt put the mercy seat upon the ark of the testimony in the most holy *place*.

35 And thou shalt set the table without the vail, and the °candlestick over against the table on the [26]side of the tabernacle toward the south: and thou shalt put the table on the north [26]side.

36 And thou shalt make an °hanging for the °door of the tent, *of* blue, and purple, and scarlet, and fine twined linen, wrought with needlework.

37 And thou shalt make for the hanging five pillars *of* shittim *wood*, and overlay them with gold, *and* their °hooks *shall be of* gold: and thou shalt cast five sockets of °brass for them.

M²
(p. 108) **27** And thou shalt make an altar *of* °shittim wood, five °cubits long, and five cubits broad; the altar shall be foursquare: and the height thereof *shall be* three cubits.

2 And thou shalt make the horns of it upon the four corners thereof: his horns shall be of the same: and thou shalt overlay it with °brass.

3 And thou shalt make his pans to receive his ashes, and his shovels, and his basons, and

22 sides. Heb. *yarkāh* = hinder side.
24 And they shall be. So some codices, and Sam.; but Heb. text reads, "that they may be."
26 bars. Heb. *beriaḥ*, from *bāraḥ*, to pass, or shoot.
side. Heb. *zēl'ā* = rib.
27 bars. This is omitted in Severus Codex (Ap. 34).
28 shall reach = passing, or shooting.
30 rear up = erect, or put together.
fashion = regulation, or manner.

31-35. THE VAIL OF THE HOLY PLACE.

31 vail. Heb. *pāroketh* (not *māṣak*, as in *v.* 36), means *to separate*. Cp. Heb. 6. 19; 9. 3. Matt. 27. 51. Mark 15. 38. Luke 23. 45.
shall it be made. The *Sevir* (Ap. 34) reading is "shalt thou make it", with other codices, Sam., Sept., Syr., and Vulg.
33 within the vail. See Heb. 9. 3, 8, 24, 25.
the holy place. See note on 3. 5. Heb. 9. 11, 12.
the most holy. Heb. "holy of holies." Fig. *Polyptōton* (Ap. 6). See note on Ex. 3. 5.
35 candlestick = lampstand.

36, 37. THE HANGING FOR THE DOOR.

36 hanging. Heb. *māṣak*, a covering to hide (cp. *v.* 31) not the *pāroketh* of *v.* 31. No cherubim woven on this; and sockets of pillars of brass, instead of gold or silver. See note on *v.* 17.
36 door = entrance.
37 hooks = pegs, pins, or nails.
brass. See note on *v.* 17, and 25. 3.

27. 1-8 (M², p. 108). ALTAR OF BURNT OFFERING.

1 shittim wood. Acacia wood.
cubits. See Ap. 51. III. 2.
2 brass, or copper. Perhaps bronze. See 25. 3.
5 compass of the altar. Probably the margin or place where the priests stood. The "place" of 2 Chron. 30. 16. A raised position from which the sacrificing priest is said to "come down", Lev. 9. 22.
7 the staves. Heb. its staves.
8 as. Heb. according as.

9-19 (*N*. p. 108). THE HANGINGS OF THE COURTS.

9 tabernacle. Heb. *mishkān*. See Ap. 40.
south side southward. Fig. *Polyptōton*. Ap. 6.
side. Heb. *pē'ah*, quarter or region.

his fleshhooks, and his firepans: all the vessels thereof thou shalt make *of* [2]brass.

4 And thou shalt make for it a grate of network *of* [2]brass; and upon the net shalt thou make four brasen rings in the four corners thereof.

5 And thou shalt put it under the °compass of the altar beneath, that the net may be even to the midst of the altar.

6 And thou shalt make staves for the altar, staves *of* shittim wood, and overlay them with [2]brass.

7 And °the staves shall be put into the rings, and the staves shall be upon the two [26]sides of the altar, to bear it.

8 Hollow with boards shalt thou make it: °as it was shewed thee in the mount, so shall they make *it*.

9 And thou shalt make the court of the °tabernacle: for the °south °side southward *there shall be* hangings for the court *of* fine twined linen of an hundred [1]cubits long for one °side: N

10 And the twenty pillars thereof and their

1491 twenty sockets *shall be of* °brass; the °hooks
of the pillars and their [17]fillets *shall be of* silver.
11 And likewise for the north [9]side in length
there shall be hangings of an hundred *cubits*
long, and his twenty pillars and their twenty
sockets *of* brass; the hooks of the pillars and
their [10]fillets *of* silver.
12 And *for* the breadth of the court on the
west °side *shall be* hangings of fifty [1]cubits:
their pillars ten, and their sockets ten.
13 And the breadth of the court on the east
[12]side eastward *shall be* fifty [1]cubits.
14 The hangings of one °side *of the gate*
shall be fifteen cubits: their pillars three, and
their sockets three.
15 And on the other [14]side *shall be* hangings
fifteen *cubits*: their pillars three, and their
sockets three.
16 And for the gate of the court *shall be* an
hanging of twenty [1]cubits, *of* blue, and purple,
and scarlet, and fine twined linen, wrought
with needlework: *and* their pillars *shall be*
four, and their sockets four.
17 All the pillars round about the court *shall*
be °filleted with silver; their [10]hooks *shall be*
of silver, and their sockets *of* [10]brass.
18 The length of the court *shall be* an hundred [1]cubits, and the breadth fifty °every where,
and the height five [1]cubits *of* fine twined linen,
and their sockets *of* [10]brass.
19 All the vessels of the °tabernacle in all the
service thereof, and all the pins thereof, and all
the pins of the court, *shall be of* brass.
M³ 20 And thou shalt command the °children of Is-
(p. 108) rael, that they bring thee °pure oil olive beaten
for °the light, to cause the lamp °to burn always.
21 In the °tabernacle of the congregation
without the vail, which *is* before °the testimony, Aaron and his sons shall order it from
evening to morning before °the LORD: *it shall*
be a statute for ever unto their generations on
the behalf of the [20]children of Israel.

K² O **28** And °take thou unto thee °Aaron thy
(p. 111) brother, and his sons with him, °from
among the °children of Israel, that he may
°minister unto Me in the priest's office, *even*
Aaron, Nadab and Abihu, Eleazar and Ithamar,
Aaron's sons.

P d 2 And thou shalt make °holy garments for
Aaron thy brother °for glory and for beauty.
3 And thou shalt speak unto all *that are* wise
hearted, °whom I have filled with the °spirit of
wisdom, that they may make Aaron's garments
to [41]consecrate him, that he may [1]minister unto
Me in the priest's office.
4 And these *are* the °garments which they
shall make; a breastplate, °and an ephod, and
a robe, and a broidered coat, a mitre, and a
girdle: and they shall make holy garments for
Aaron thy brother, and his sons, that he may
[1]minister unto Me in the priest's office.
5 And they shall take gold, and blue, and
purple, and scarlet, and fine linen.

e f 6 And they shall make the °ephod *of* gold, *of*
blue, and *of* purple, *of* scarlet, and fine twined
linen, with °cunning work.
7 It shall have the two shoulderpieces thereof
joined at the two edges thereof; and *so* it shall
be joined together.
8 And the °curious girdle of the ephod, which
is upon it, shall be of the same, according to
the work thereof; *even of* °gold, *of* blue, and
purple, and scarlet, and fine twined linen.
9 And thou shalt take °two onyx °stones, and

10 brass. All other sockets (of boards) in "silver" (26. 19; denoting redemption). The sockets of these pillars (the way of access) of "brass" (denoting judgment in righteousness). Cp. the brazen Altar and Laver.
hooks = pegs, pins, or nails.
12 side. Heb. *pē'ah* = quarter, region.
14 side. Heb. *kāthēph* = shoulder.
17 filleted with = connected with rods.
18 every where = by fifty.
19 tabernacle. Heb. *mishkān*. See Ap. 40.
20 children = sons.
pure oil. This is without measure. See on John 3. 34
the light = the light-holder. Cp. Gen. 1. 14.
to burn always: i. e. a perpetual light.
21 tabernacle = tent. Heb. *'ohel*. Ap. 40.
the testimony. Cp. 26. 33.
the LORD. Heb. Jehovah. Ap. 4.

28. 1—29. 46 (K², p. 107). THE CONSECRATION OF THE PRIESTS (*Introversion and Alternation*).

K² | O | 28. 1. Aaron and sons (Denomination).
  P | d | 28. 2-5. Garments (General).
    e | 28. 6-38. Garments (Aaron's).
  P | *d* | 28. 39. Garments (General).
    e | 28. 40-43. Garments (Aaron's sons).
O | 29. 1-46. Aaron and sons (Consecration).

1 take thou. Heb. = bring thou near.
Aaron. Five named (Aaron and his four sons). Ap. 10.
from among = from the midst of. Cp. Deut. 18. 15, 18 (Prophet).
children = sons.
minister unto Me. This was the one object here; and the same when Christ was transfigured, and so consecrated for His office of Priest. See notes on *v.* 2 below.
2 holy garments. Heb. garments of holiness. See Ap. 17: emphasis on "holy". See note on 3. 5.
for glory and for beauty. Sept., τιμὴ καὶ δόξα (*timē kai doxa*), same as Heb. 2. 9 and 2 Pet. 1. 17. With which Christ was clothed and crowned for the same purpose when He was consecrated priest (Matt. 17. 1-8. Mark 9. 1-10. Luke 9. 28-36) "to minister unto Me in the priest's office."
3 whom I have filled. This agrees with the Severus Codex (Ap. 34), "I have filled them". See 35. 30-36. 7.
spirit. Heb. *ruach*. Ap. 9.
4 garments. In this *v.* and *v.* 39 general. See Structure above.
and. Note the Fig. *Polysyndeton*, Ap. 6.

6-38 (e, above). THE GARMENTS OF AARON. (*Alternation.*)

e | f | 6-14. The Ephod and its girdle.
  g | 15-30. The Breastplate.
  f | 31-35. The Ephod and its robe.
  g | 36-38. The Mitre-plate.

Aaron's garments described first. There were in all *eight*: (1) the mitre (with its plate); (2) the breastplate; (3) the ephod; (4) the robe of the ephod; (5) the turban; (6) the girdle; (7) the drawers; (8) the coat. *Eight* is the Dominical number, or number of the Lord See Ap. 10.
6 ephod. From Heb. *'aphad*, to bind on, because it held the breastplate in its place. See *v.* 28. Worn by Aaron the priest, Samuel the prophet (1 Sam. 2. 18), and David the king (2 Sam. 6. 14), Christ combining all three offices.
cunning work = work of a skilful weaver.
8 curious = embroidered.
gold. Note the number five in these items. Ap. 10.
9 two . . . stones, with six names on each: the names collectively, on the shoulders, the place of strength. The names on the breastplate, one on each stone (individually) on the heart, the place of love, *vv.* 15-21.

1491 °grave on them the names of the [1]children of Israel:

10 Six of their names on one stone, and *the other* six names of the rest on the other stone, °according to their birth.

11 With the work of an engraver in stone, *like* the engravings of a signet, shalt thou engrave the two stones with the names of the [1]children of Israel: thou shalt make them to be set in °ouches of gold.

12 And thou shalt put the two stones upon the shoulders of the ephod *for* stones of memorial unto the [1]children of Israel: and Aaron shall bear their names before °the LORD upon his two shoulders for a memorial.

13 And thou shalt make [11]ouches *of* gold;

14 And two chains *of* pure gold at the ends; *of* wreathen work shalt thou make them, and fasten the wreathen chains to the [13]ouches.

g (p. 111) **15** And thou shalt make the °breastplate of °judgment with °cunning work; after the work of the ephod thou shalt make it; *of* gold, *of* blue, and *of* purple, and *of* scarlet, and *of* fine twined linen, shalt thou make it.

16 Foursquare it shall be *being* doubled; a °span *shall be* the length thereof, and a °span *shall be* the breadth thereof.

17 And thou shalt set in it settings of stones, *even* °four rows of stones: *the first* row *shall be* a sardius, a topaz, and a carbuncle: *this shall be* the first row.

18 And the second row *shall be* an emerald, a sapphire, and a diamond.

19 And the third row a ligure, an agate, and an amethyst.

20 And the fourth row a beryl, and an onyx, and a jasper: they shall be set in gold in their inclosings.

21 And the stones shall be with °the names of the [1]children of Israel, twelve, according to their names, *like* the [9]engravings of a signet; every one with his name shall they be according to °the twelve tribes.

22 And thou shalt make upon the breastplate chains at the ends *of* wreathen work *of* pure gold.

23 And thou shalt make upon the breastplate two rings of gold, and shalt put the two rings on the two ends of the breastplate.

24 And thou shalt put the two wreathen *chains* of gold in the two rings *which are* on the ends of the breastplate.

25 And *the other* two ends of the two wreathen *chains* thou shalt fasten in the two [11]ouches, and put *them* on the shoulderpieces of the ephod before it.

26 And thou shalt make two rings of gold, and thou shalt put them upon the two ends of the breastplate in the border thereof, which *is* in the °side of the ephod inward.

27 And two *other* rings of gold thou shalt make, and shalt put them on the two °sides of the ephod underneath, toward the forepart thereof, over against the *other* coupling thereof, above the [8]curious girdle of the ephod.

28 And they shall bind the breastplate by the rings thereof unto the rings of the ephod with a lace of blue, that *it* may be above the curious girdle of the ephod, and that the breastplate be not loosed from the ephod.

grave. Note the three gravings connected with the heart (*v.* 9), the shoulder (*v.* 21), and the head (*v.* 36).

10 according to their birth. Here, on the shoulders (the place of strength), all were borne up alike; but over the heart (the place of love) the order was "according to the tribes" as God chose them, *v.* 21.

11 ouches = sockets for precious stones.

12 the LORD. Heb. Jehovah. Ap. 4.

15 breastplate of judgment. Genitive of relation, or Fig. *Metonymy* (of Adjunct), Ap. 6, by which judgment is put for "giving judicial decision". See note on *v.* 30.

cunning = skilful. See note on 26. 1.

16 span. See Ap. 51. III. 2.

17 four rows. Three in each row, 3 × 4 = 12, as 3 + 4 = 7. See Ap. 10.

21 the names. Order according to the "twelve tribes" as God chose them. They were individual here, because over the heart, the place of love: one name on each stone.

the twelve tribes. Order not given here. In *v.* 10 according to the order of *birth.* Here, perhaps, according to Num. 2. See Ap. 45.

26 side = opposite side. Heb. *'ēver.*

27 sides = shoulders. Heb. *kāthēph.*

29 upon his heart. The place of love. See notes on *vv.* 9, 10, and 21, and note the repetition of the word heart for emphasis.

30 Urim and Thummim. No command of God to *make* these. Only told to put (*nathan*, to give) them in the breastplate, i. e. into the *bag* of the breastplate (cp. *v.* 26 and 16, also ch. 39. 9 and 19). This bag was a doubled part, and the Urim and Thummim were probably two precious stones which were drawn out as a lot to give Jehovah's judgment. "The lot is cast into the lap (Heb. bosom); but the whole judgment thereof is of the LORD" (Prov. 16. 33). Bosom here is put for the clothing or covering over it (cp. Ex. 4. 6, 7. Ruth 4. 16. *Chēk* (bosom) = any hollow thing, as of a chariot, 1 Kings 22. 35). The Heb. *Urim* and *Thummim* mean "lights" and "perfections". Probably these are the plurals of majesty, the sing. "light" (being put by *Metonymy* for what is brought to light, i. e. *guilt*), and "perfection" (put by *Metonymy* for moral perfection, i. e. *innocence*). Thus, these two placed in the "bag", and one drawn out, would give the judicial decision (the name connected with the breastplate, cp. *v.* 15, above), which would be "of the LORD". Hence, the breastplate itself was known as "the breastplate of *judgment*" (*v.* 15), because, by that, Jehovah's judgment was obtained whenever it was needed. Hence, when the land was divided "by lot" (Num. 26. 55, &c.), Eleazar, the high priest, must be present (Num. 34. 17 (cp. 27. 21). Josh. 17. 4). When he would decide it the lot "came up" (Josh. 18. 11); "came forth" (Josh. 19. 1); "came out" (Josh. 19. 17): i. e. "out", or "forth" from the bag of the ephod.

In Ezra 2. 61-63 & Neh. 7. 63-65, no judgment could be given unless the high priest was present with the breastplate, with its bag, with the lots of Urim and Thummim, which gave Jehovah's decision, "guilty" or "innocent", "yes" or "no". The Heb. for lot is always *gōrāl* = a stone, except in Deut. 32. 9, 1 Chron. 16. 18 and Ps. 105. 11, where it is = *ḥēbel* = a measuring line, put by *Metonymy* for the inheritance so measured. In Josh 13. 6; 23. 4. Ezek. 45. 1; 47. 22; 48. 29, it is *nāphal*, to fall, put by *Metonymy* for the inheritance which falls to one from any cause. See all the passages where the Urim and Thummim are mentioned: Ex. 28. 30. Lev. 8. 8. Deut. 33. 8. Num. 27. 21. 1 Sam. 28. 6. Ezra 2. 63. Neh. 7. 65, and cp. especially the notes on Num. 26. 55, and 1 Sam. 14 41.

29 And Aaron shall bear the names of the [1]children of Israel in the [15]breastplate [15]of judgment °upon his heart, when he goeth in unto the holy *place*, for a memorial before [12]the LORD continually.

30 And thou shalt put in the [15]breastplate of [15]judgment the °Urim and the °Thummim;

1491 and they shall be upon Aaron's heart, when
he goeth in before [12]the LORD: and Aaron shall
bear the judgment of the [1]children of Israel
upon his heart before [12]the LORD continually.

f (p. 111) 31 And thou shalt make the robe of the ephod
all *of* blue.
32 And there shall be an °hole in the top of
it, in the midst thereof: it shall have a binding
of woven work round about the hole of it, as it
were the hole of an °habergeon, that it be not
rent.
33 And *beneath* upon the °hem of it thou
shalt make °pomegranates *of* blue, and *of*
purple, and *of* scarlet, round about the hem
thereof; and bells of gold between them round
about:
34 °A golden bell and a pomegranate, a
golden bell and a [33]pomegranate, upon the
hem of the robe round about.
35 And it shall be upon Aaron to minister:
and his sound shall be heard when he goeth in
unto the holy *place* before [12]the LORD, and
when he cometh out, that he die not.

g 36 And thou shalt make a plate *of* pure gold,
and [9]grave upon it, *like* the engravings of a
signet, °HOLINESS TO [12]THE LORD.
37 And thou shalt put it on a blue lace, that
it may be upon °the mitre; upon the forefront
of the mitre it shall be.
38 And it shall be upon Aaron's forehead,
that Aaron may °bear the °iniquity of the
°holy things, which the [1]children of Israel
shall hallow in all their holy gifts; and it
shall be always upon °his forehead, that °they
may be accepted before [12]the LORD.

P d 39 And thou shalt embroider the coat of fine
linen, and thou shalt make the mitre *of* fine
linen, and thou shalt °make the girdle *of*
needlework.

e 40 And for Aaron's sons thou shalt make
coats, and thou shalt make for them girdles,
and °bonnets shalt thou make for them, [2]for
glory and for beauty.
41 And thou shalt put them upon Aaron thy
brother, and his sons with him; and shalt
anoint them, and °consecrate them, and sanctify
them, that they may [1]minister unto Me in the
priest's office.
42 And thou shalt make them °linen breeches
to cover their nakedness; from the loins even
unto the thighs they shall reach:
43 And they shall be upon Aaron, and upon
his sons, when they come in unto the °taber-
nacle of the congregation, or when they come
near unto the altar to minister in the holy
place; that they bear not [38]iniquity, and die:
it shall be a statute for ever unto him and his
seed after him.

O Q (p. 113) **29** And this *is* the thing that thou shalt do
unto them to hallow them, to °minister
unto Me in the priest's office: Take one young
bullock, and two rams °without blemish,
2 And unleavened bread, and °cakes unleavened tempered with oil, and wafers unleavened
anointed with oil: *of* wheaten flour shalt thou
make them.
3 And thou shalt put them into one basket,
and bring them in the basket, with the bullock
and the two rams.
4 And Aaron and his sons thou shalt bring
unto the door of the °tabernacle of the congregation, and shalt °wash them with water.
5 And thou shalt take the garments, and put
upon Aaron the coat, and the robe of the °ephod,
and the °ephod, and the breastplate, and gird
him with the °curious girdle of the ephod:
6 And thou shalt put the mitre upon his head,
and put the holy crown upon the mitre.
7 Then shalt thou take the anointing oil, and
pour *it* upon his head, and anoint him.
8 And thou shalt bring his sons, and put coats
upon them.
9 And thou shalt gird them with girdles, Aaron
and his sons, and put the [40]bonnets on them:
and the priest's office shall be theirs for a perpetual statute: and thou shalt °consecrate
Aaron and his sons.
10 And thou shalt cause a bullock to be Q²
brought before the [4]tabernacle of the congre-

32 hole in the top of it, in the midst. To enable the hand of the High Priest to be put into the bag to draw out the Urim or Thummim. Cp. *vv.* 16 and 26, also 39. 9, 19. See also the note on *v.* 30.
habergeon = coat of mail.
33 hem = skirts.
pomegranates. See note on Num. 13. 23.
34 Note the Fig. *Epizeuxis* (Ap. 6), "a golden bell and a pomegranate", instead of saying "alternately".
36 HOLINESS TO THE LORD. This is one of the few places where the A.V. uses large capital letters (see Ap. 48). Here it was worn only on the forehead of the high priest; but in Millennial days it will be worn even on the bells of the horses, Zech. 14. 20, 21. Cp. Rev. 19. 11-14; 14. 20.
37 the mitre = tiara, or turban. Heb. *miznepheth*, from *zanaph*, to wind round.
38 bear = bear away, carry off. Lev. 10. 17. Ps. 32. 1. Isa. 33. 24. iniquity. Heb. *'avōn.* Ap. 44. iii.
holy. See note on 3. 5.
his . . . they. Note these words. Christ is our Representative, we are holy in Him, and this "always".
39 make. The making deferred to ch. 39. See *v.* 3.
40 bonnets = caps.
41 consecrate them = instal them. Heb. fill their hand, "hand" being put by *Metonymy* (of Adjunct), Ap. 6, for the authority and official power given to them. Cp. Lat. *mandare.*
42 linen. Priests were *effendi* (Lev. 6. 10. 1 Sam. 2. 18; 22. 18). Prophets were *fellahin*, and wore coarse clothing (2 Kings 1. 8. Zech. 13. 4. Matt. 3. 4).
43 tabernacle = tent. Heb. *'ohel.* Ap. 40.

29. 1-46 (*O*, p. 111). THE CONSECRATION OF THE PRIESTS (*Repeated Alternation*).

O Q¹ | 1-3. Sacrifices.
R¹ | 4-9. Aaron and his sons.
Q² | 10-28. Sacrifices.
R² | 29, 30. Aaron and his sons.
Q³ | 31-34. Sacrifices.
R³ | 35. Aaron and his sons.
Q⁴ | 36-46. Sacrifices.

1 minister. See note on 28. 1.
without blemish. This, with bread "without leaven" (*v.* 2), shows the inner meaning of "leaven".
2 cakes = pierced cakes.
4 tabernacle = tent. Heb. *'ohel.* Ap. 40.
wash. Heb. *rāchaz* = one of the ceremonial washings referred to in Heb. 6. 2, and rendered "baptisms".
5 ephod. See note on 28. 6.
curious = embroidered.
9 consecrate. See note on 28. 41.

1491 gation: and Aaron and his sons shall put their hands upon the head of the bullock.

11 And thou shalt kill the bullock before [41]the LORD, *by* the door of the [4]tabernacle of the congregation.

12 And thou shalt take of the blood of the bullock, and put *it* upon the horns of the altar with thy finger, and pour all the blood beside the bottom of the altar.

13 And thou shalt take all the fat that covereth the inwards, and the °caul *that is* above the liver, and the two kidneys, and the fat that *is* upon them, and burn *them* upon the altar.

14 But the flesh of the bullock, and his skin, and his dung, shalt thou burn with fire °without the camp: it *is* a °sin offering.

15 Thou shalt also take one ram; and Aaron and his sons shall put their hands upon the head of the ram.

16 And thou shalt slay the ram, and thou shalt take his blood, and sprinkle *it* round about upon the altar.

17 And thou shalt cut the ram in pieces, and wash the inwards of him, and his legs, and put *them* unto his pieces, and unto his head.

18 And thou shalt burn the whole ram upon the altar: it *is* a burnt offering unto [11]the LORD: it *is* a °sweet savour, an offering made by fire unto [11]the LORD.

19 And thou shalt take the other ram; and Aaron and his sons shall put their hands upon the head of the ram.

20 Then shalt thou kill the ram, and take of his blood, °and put *it* upon the tip of the right ear of °Aaron, and upon the tip of the right ear of his sons, and upon the thumb of their right hand, and upon the great toe of their right foot, and sprinkle the blood upon the altar round about.

21 And thou shalt take of the blood that *is* upon the altar, and of the anointing oil, and sprinkle *it* upon Aaron, and upon his garments, and upon his sons, and upon the garments of his sons with him: and he shall be hallowed, and his garments, and his sons, and his sons' garments with him.

22 Also thou shalt take of the ram the fat and the rump, and the fat that covereth the inwards, and the caul *above* the liver, and the two kidneys, and the fat that *is* upon them, and the right shoulder; for it *is* a ram of consecration:

23 And one loaf of bread, and one cake of oiled bread, and one wafer out of the basket of the unleavened bread that *is* before [11]the LORD:

24 And thou shalt put all in the hands of Aaron, and in the hands of his sons; and shalt wave them *for* a wave offering before [11]the LORD.

25 And thou shalt receive them of their hands, and burn *them* upon the altar for a burnt offering, for a sweet savour before [11]the LORD: it *is* an offering made by fire unto [11]the LORD.

26 And thou shalt take the breast of the ram of Aaron's consecration, and wave it *for* a wave offering before [11]the LORD: and it shall be thy part.

27 And thou shalt sanctify the breast of the °wave offering, and the shoulder of the °heave offering, which is waved, and which is heaved up, of the ram of the consecration, *even* of *that* which *is* for Aaron, and of *that* which is for his sons:

28 And it shall be Aaron's and his sons' by a statute for ever from the °children of Israel: for it *is* an heave offering: and it shall be an heave offering from the °children of Israel of the sacrifice of their peace offerings, *even* their heave offering unto [11]the LORD.

29 And the holy garments of Aaron shall be his sons' after him, to be anointed therein, and to be consecrated in them. R[2] (p. 113)

30 *And* that son that is priest in his stead shall put them on seven days, when he cometh into the [4]tabernacle of the congregation to minister in the °holy *place*.

31 And thou shalt take the ram of the consecration, and seethe his flesh in the [30]holy place. Q[3]

32 And Aaron and his sons shall °eat the flesh of the ram, and the bread that *is* in the basket, *by* the door of the [4]tabernacle of the congregation.

33 And they shall [32]eat those things wherewith the °atonement was made, to °consecrate *and* to sanctify them: but a stranger shall not eat *thereof*, because they *are* holy.

34 And if ought of the flesh of the consecrations, or of the bread, remain unto the morning, then thou shalt burn the remainder with fire: it shall not be eaten, because it *is* holy.

35 And thus shalt thou do unto Aaron, and to his sons, according to all *things* which I have commanded thee: seven days shalt thou [33]consecrate them. R[3]

36 And thou shalt °offer every day a bullock *for* a [14]sin offering for [33]atonement: and thou shalt cleanse the altar, when thou hast made Q[4]

13 caul = the *omentum*, not the midriff.
14 without the camp. Cp. Heb. 13. 11-13. An unholy camp was unfit for a holy sin offering.
sin offering. Heb. sin, put (as in Gen. 4. 7) by Fig. *Metonymy* (of Subject), Ap. 6, for sin offering. See Ap. 43. II. v.
18 sweet savour. Heb. "savour of rest", i. e. complacency or satisfaction. See note on Gen. 8. 21.
20 and. Note the Fig. *Polysyndeton* (Ap. 6), calling our attention to the several parts touched by the atoning blood. All were consecrated, and each one is singled out and emphasised by the several "and".
Aaron. The Antitype, Christ, so anointed and set apart "on the holy mount" (2 Pet. 1. 16-18). See notes on 28. 1, 2. Cp. Ps. 45. 7. Heb. 1. 9. Note "thy fellows", but "above" them, infinitely "above".
27 wave offering. Turned to the four quarters of the earth. See Ap. 43. II. ix.
heave offering. Lifted up to heaven for Jehovah only. See Ap. 43. II. viii.
28 children = sons. **30 holy.** See note on 3. 5.
32 eat, &c. This explains John 6. 33. In Ex. 29 this was literal, but in our case it must perforce be purely and wholly spiritual. Cp. the eating of *v.* 33 and the burning of *v.* 34 with the eating and burning of the Paschal Lamb, Ex. 12. 10, 11.
33 atonement. The first occurrence of the English word. The Heb. *kāphar*, to cover, gives the essential meaning, as shown in its first occurrence, Gen. 6. 14, where it is rendered "pitch [it]". See notes on Gen. 32. 20. Ps. 32. 1. Hence used of the mercy-seat. See note on 25. 17. The English "at-one-ment" has no connection whatever with the Heb. word *kāphar*.
consecrate. See on 28. 41.
36 offer. Heb. *'āsah*. See Ap. 43. I. iii.

1491 an [33]atonement °for it, and thou shalt anoint it, to sanctify it.

37 Seven days thou shalt make an [33]atonement for the altar, and sanctify it; and it shall be an altar most °holy: whatsoever toucheth the altar shall be °holy.

38 Now this *is that* which thou shalt [36]offer upon the altar; two lambs of the first year °day by day °continually.

39 The one lamb thou shalt [36]offer in the morning; and °the other lamb thou shalt [36]offer °at even:

40 And with the one lamb a tenth deal of flour mingled with the fourth part of an °hin of beaten oil; and the fourth part of an °hin of °wine *for* a drink offering.

41 And the other lamb thou shalt [36]offer [39]at even, and shalt do thereto according to the °meat offering of the morning, and according to the drink offering thereof, for a [18]sweet savour, an offering made by fire unto °the LORD.

42 *This shall be* a [38]continual burnt offering throughout your generations *at* the door of the [4]tabernacle of the congregation before [41]the LORD: where I will °meet °you, to speak there unto thee.

43 And there I will [42]meet with the [28]children of Israel, and °*the tabernacle* shall be sanctified by My glory.

44 And I will sanctify the [4]tabernacle of the congregation, and the altar: I will sanctify also both Aaron and his sons, to minister to Me in the priest's office.

45 And I will dwell among the [28]children of Israel, and will be their °God.

46 And they shall know that I *am* [41]the LORD their [45]God, That brought them forth out of the land of Egypt, °that I may dwell °among them: I *am* [41]the LORD their [45]God.

L² (p. 107) **30** And thou shalt make an altar to burn incense upon: *of* shittim wood shalt thou make it.

2 A °cubit *shall be* the length thereof, and a °cubit the breadth thereof; foursquare shall it be: and two °cubits *shall be* the height thereof: the horns thereof *shall be* of the same.

3 And thou shalt overlay it with pure gold, the top thereof, and the °sides thereof round about, and the horns thereof; and thou shalt make unto it a °crown of gold round about.

4 And two golden rings shalt thou make to it under the crown of it, by the two corners thereof, upon the two °sides of it shalt thou make *it;* and they shall be for places for the staves to bear it withal.

5 And thou shalt make the staves *of* shittim wood, and overlay them with gold.

6 And thou shalt put it before the vail that *is* by the ark of the testimony, before the °mercy seat that *is* over the testimony, where I will meet with thee.

7 And Aaron shall °burn thereon °sweet incense every morning: when he dresseth the lamps, he shall °burn incense upon it.

8 And when Aaron lighteth the lamps °at even, he shall [7]burn incense upon it, a perpetual incense before °the LORD throughout your generations.

9 Ye shall °offer no °strange incense thereon,

for it = upon it. **37 holy.** See note on 3. 5.
38 day by day continually. See the Divine comment on this. Heb. 9. 9; 10. 1, 2.
39 the other = the second.
at even = Heb. between the two evenings = at dusk. Ex. 12. 6; 16. 12; 30. 8.
40 hin. See Ap. 51. III. 3.
wine. Heb. *yayin* (see Ap. 27).
41 meat = meal.
the LORD = Jehovah. Ap. 4. II.
42 meet = meet by appointment. See note on 25. 22.
you. Some codices, with Sam. and Sept., read "thee".
43 the tabernacle. Supply Ellipsis with "it" (Ap. 6).
45 God. Heb. Elohim. Ap. 4.
46 that I may dwell. This was the object in bringing them forth from Egypt. **among** = in the midst.

30. 1-11 (L², p. 107). FURNITURE: ALTAR OF INCENSE.

2 cubit. See Ap. 51. III. 2.
3 sides. Heb. *kīr, a wall*, or side.
crown of gold. See note on 25. 24.
4 sides. Heb. *ẓad*, side.
6 mercy seat. See note on 25. 17.
7 burn: with fire taken from the brasen altar of atonement, implying that there could be no acceptable worship except on the ground of atonement made. All other fire was "strange fire", and all other worship strange worship, and therefore unacceptable.
sweet incense. Heb. incense of spices.
8 at even. See note on 29. 39.
the LORD. Heb. Jehovah. Ap. 4.
9 offer. Heb. *'ālah.* See Ap. 43. I. vi.
strange incense = incense different from and other than that which God had prescribed. See note on Lev. 10. 1. **meat** = meal.
10 once in a year, viz. the tenth day of the seventh month. Lev. 16. 18, 29, 30. Num. 29. 7.
sin offering. See note on 29. 14.
holy. See note on 3. 5.
11 the LORD spake. See note on 6. 10 and 3. 7.
12 children = sons.
man. Heb. *'īsh.* See Ap. 14. II.
ransom. Heb. *kāpher* = covering, hence atonement. See note on 29. 33.
his soul = himself. Heb. *nephesh.* See Ap. 13. The acknowledgement of Ezek. 18. 4.
13 shekel of the sanctuary. See Ap. 51. II. Cp. Matt. 17. 24.
gerah, a measure of weight. See Ap. 51. II.
offering. Heb. *terūmāh.* See Ap. 43. II. viii.

nor burnt sacrifice, nor °meat offering; neither shall ye pour drink offering thereon.

10 And Aaron shall make an atonement upon the horns of it °once in a year with the blood of the °sin offering of atonements: °once in the year shall he make atonement upon it throughout your generations: it *is* most °holy unto [8]the LORD."

11 And °the LORD spake unto Moses, saying,

12 "When thou takest the sum of the °children K³
of Israel after their number, then shall they give every °man a °ransom for °his soul unto [8]the LORD, when thou numberest them; that there be no plague among them, when *thou* numberest them.

13 This they shall give, every one that passeth among them that are numbered, half a shekel after the °shekel of the sanctuary: (a shekel *is* twenty °gerahs:) an half shekel *shall be* [8]the °offering of the LORD.

14 Every one that passeth among them that are numbered, from twenty years old and above, shall give an [13]offering unto [8]the LORD.

1491 15 °The rich shall not give more, and the poor shall not give less than half a [13]shekel, when *they* give an °offering unto [8]the LORD, to make an °atonement for your [12]souls.

16 And thou shalt take the [15]atonement money of the [12]children of Israel, and shalt appoint it for the service of the °tabernacle of the congregation; that it may be a memorial unto the [12]children of Israel before [8]the LORD, to make an [15]atonement for your [12]souls."

L³ (p. 107) 17 And [11]the LORD spake unto Moses, saying,

18 "Thou shalt also make °a laver *of* brass, and his °foot *also of* brass, to wash *withal*: and thou shalt put it between the [16]tabernacle of the congregation and the altar, and thou shalt put water therein.

19 For Aaron and his sons shall wash their hands and their feet thereat:

20 When they go into the [16]tabernacle of the congregation, they shall wash with water, that they die not; or when they come near to the altar to minister, to °burn offering made by fire unto [8]the LORD:

21 So they shall wash their hands and their feet, that they die not: and it shall be a statute for ever to them, *even* to him and to his seed throughout their generations."

22 Moreover [11]the LORD spake unto Moses, saying,

23 "Take thou also unto thee principal spices, of pure °myrrh five hundred *shekels*, and of sweet cinnamon half so much, *even* two hundred and fifty *shekels*, and of °sweet calamus two hundred and fifty *shekels*,

24 And of °cassia five hundred *shekels*, after the [13]shekel of the sanctuary, and of oil olive an °hin:

25 And thou shalt make it an oil of holy ointment, an ointment compound after the art of the apothecary: it shall be an holy anointing oil.

26 And thou shalt anoint the [16]tabernacle of the congregation therewith, and the ark of the testimony,

27 And the table and all his vessels, and the candlestick and his vessels, and the altar of incense,

28 And the altar of burnt offering with all his vessels, and the [18]laver and his foot.

29 And thou shalt sanctify them, that they may be most holy: whatsoever toucheth them shall be holy.

30 And thou shalt anoint Aaron and his sons, and °consecrate them, that *they* may minister unto Me in the priest's office.

31 And thou shalt speak unto the [12]children of Israel, saying, 'This shall be an holy anointing oil unto Me throughout your generations.

32 Upon °man's °flesh shall it not be poured, neither shall ye make *any other* like it, after the composition of it: it *is* holy, *and* it shall be holy unto you.

33 Whosoever compoundeth *any* like it, or whosoever putteth *any* of it upon a stranger, shall even be cut off from his people.'"

34 And °the LORD said unto Moses, "Take unto thee °sweet spices, stacte, and °onycha, and galbanum; *these* °sweet spices with pure frankincense: of each shall there be °a like *weight*:

35 And thou shalt make it a perfume, a confection after the art of the apothecary, °tempered together, °pure *and* holy:

36 And thou shalt beat *some* of it very small, and put of it before the testimony in the [16]tabernacle of the congregation, where I will meet with thee: it shall be unto you most holy.

37 And *as for* the perfume which thou shalt make, ye shall not make to yourselves according to the composition thereof: it shall be unto thee holy for [8]the LORD.

38 Whosoever shall make like unto that, to smell thereto, shall even be cut off from his people."

31 And °the LORD spake unto Moses, saying, K⁴ S (p. 116)

2 °"See, °I have called by name Bezaleel

---

15 The rich = the rich one. "There is no difference" in the matter of atonement, Acts 10. 34. Rom. 3. 22, 23; 10. 12. Then, all Israel without *exception*: but now "all" without *distinction*.

offering. Heb. heave offering. See on 29. 27, and cp. Ap. 43. II. viii.

atonement. See note on 29. 33.

16 tabernacle = tent. Heb. *'ohel.* Ap. 40.

18 a laver of brass. Probably copper or bronze. See note on 25. 3.

The laver comes after the altar; the altar is for sinners; the laver is for priests = cleansing for worship. Not included in Ex. 25-28, but *added* here after atonement. John 13. 10 is the Divine antitype.

foot. Heb. base.

20 burn offering made by fire. Heb. to burn as incense. See Ap. 43. viii.

23 myrrh = gum of Arabian thorny shrubs.

sweet calamus = lemon grass of India.

24 cassia = the bark of a kind of Indian cinnamon.

hin. See Ap. 51. III. 3.

30 consecrate. See note on 28. 41.

32 man's. Heb *'adām*, human kind. See Ap. 14.

flesh. The oil is the type of the Holy Spirit. His work not to act on the flesh, but to give holy spirit (*pneuma hagion*). Cp. John 3. 6.

34 the LORD [Jehovah] **said.** See note on 3. 7 and cp. 6. 10.

sweet spices. Five in number. Cp. Ap. 10.

onycha = a sweet-smelling shell found on the shores of the Red Sea and Indian Ocean.

a like weight. Typical of the perfect proportion of all the excellencies of Christ.

35 tempered together. Perfect in its parts; perfect in its whole. So in the Antitype.

pure and holy. Typical of the holiness and unimaginable purity of Christ.

31. 1-6 (K⁴, p. 107). **THE ARTIFICERS.**
(*Extended Alternation.*)

K⁴ | S | 1, 2. The principal, Bezaleel.
  T | 3. His qualification.
   U | 4, 5. His work.
 S | 6-. His subordinates, Aholiab and others.
  T | -6-. Their qualification.
   U | -6. Their work (= L⁴, *vv.* 7-11).

1 the LORD [Heb. Jehovah] **spake.** See note on 6. 10, and cp. note on 3. 7.

2 See. Fig. *Asterismos* (Ap. 6), to call our attention to the importance of this member.

I have called. Note the qualifications in T and *T*: "I have filled", "I have given", "I have put", &c. Cp. John 3. 27. No Tubal-Cain could instruct these artificers.

1491 26 Sivan to 7 Abib the son of Uri, the son of Hur, of the tribe of Judah:

3 And I have filled him with the °spirit of °God, in wisdom, °and in understanding, and in knowledge, and in all manner of workmanship,

4 To °devise cunning works, to work in gold, and in silver, and in brass,

5 And in cutting of stones, to set *them*, and in carving of timber, to work in all manner of workmanship.

6 And I, °behold, I have given with him Aholiab, the son of Ahisamach, of the tribe of Dan: and in the hearts of all that are wise hearted °I have put wisdom, that they may make all that I have commanded thee;

L4 (p. 107) 7 The °tabernacle of the congregation, °and the ark of the testimony, and the mercy seat that *is* thereupon, and all the furniture of the °tabernacle,

8 And the table and his furniture, and the pure candlestick with all his furniture, and the altar of incense,

9 And the altar of burnt offering with all his furniture, and the laver and his foot,

10 And the cloths of service, and the holy garments for Aaron the priest, and the garments of his sons, to minister in the priest's office,

11 And the anointing oil, and sweet incense for the holy *place:* according to all that I have commanded thee shall they do."

H 12 And [1]the LORD spake unto Moses, saying,

13 "Speak thou also unto the °children of Israel, saying, 'Verily °My sabbaths ye shall keep: for it *is* a sign between Me and °you throughout your generations; that *ye* may know that I *am* [1]the LORD That doth sanctify you.

14 Ye shall keep the sabbath therefore; for it *is* holy unto you: every one that defileth it shall surely be put to death: for whosoever doeth *any* work therein, that °soul shall be cut off from among his people.

15 Six days may work be done; but in the seventh *is* the °sabbath of rest, holy to [1]the LORD: whosoever doeth *any* work in the sabbath day, he shall surely be put to death.'

16 Wherefore the [13]children of Israel shall keep the sabbath, to observe the sabbath throughout their generations, *for* a perpetual covenant.

17 It *is* °a sign between Me and the [13]children of Israel for ever: for *in* six days [1]the LORD made °heaven and earth, and on the seventh day He rested, and was °refreshed."

G 18 And He gave unto Moses, when He had made an end of communing with him upon mount Sinai, °two tables of testimony, tables of °stone, °written with the °finger of [3]God.

F V f (p. 117) 32 And when the People saw that Moses °delayed to come down °out of the mount, the People gathered themselves together unto Aaron, and said unto him, "Up, °make us gods, which shall go before us; for *as for* this Moses, the °man that brought us up out of the land of Egypt, we °wot not what is become of him."

2 And Aaron said unto them, "Break off the golden earrings, which *are* in the ears of your wives, of your sons, and of your daughters, and bring *them* unto me." g

3 And °all the People brake off the golden earrings which *were* in their ears, and brought °*them* unto Aaron. W h

4 And he received [3]*them* at their hand, and

3 spirit. Heb. *rūach*. Ap. 9. Put by Fig. *Metonymy* (of Cause) for the gifts of the Holy Spirit

God. Heb. Elohim = the Creator. Ap. 4.

and. Note the Fig. *Polysyndeton* (Ap. 6) in verses 3-5, emphasising the *four* particulars and details.

4 devise. Note the 5 and the 7 (see Ap. 10). See note on 26. 1.

Cunning works.
  Gold, silver, brass, stones, timber. } 5 } 7
All workmanship.

6 behold. Fig. *Asterismos* (Ap. 6) for emphasis. Note also the "I" emphasised.

I have put, &c. See note on *v.* 2.

7 tabernacle = tent. Heb. *'ohel*. Ap. 40.

and. Note the Fig. *Polysyndeton* (Ap. 6), emphasising twelve things to be made in *vv.* 7-11.

13 children = sons.

My sabbaths. Another special reference to this in connection with any special position in which Israel might be placed. (1) The manna, ch. 16; (2) the giving of the law, ch. 20; (3) the making of the Tabernacle, ch. 31.

you. Israel, not the church of God.

14 soul. Heb. *nephesh* (Ap. 13).

15 sabbath of rest. Heb. "sabbath of sabbatizing". See note on 16. 23.

17 a sign: that Jehovah is our God—that Christ is LORD.

heaven and earth. One of thirteen occurrences. See note on Deut. 4. 26.

refreshed. Heb. = verbal form of *nephesh* (Ap. 13). Fig. *Anthropopatheia* (Ap. 6). See note on 23. 12.

18 two tables. These *first* tables were "the work of God" (32. 16; 24. 12).

stone. Sing. The *second* tables were hewn by Moses (34. 1-4, and stones in pl.). Both written by God.

written. See note on 17. 14.

finger. Fig. *Anthropopatheia* (Ap. 6).

32. 1-14 (*F*, p. 107). THE IDOLATRY OF THE PEOPLE (*Introversion and Alternation*).

F | V | f | 1. Request of the People.
    g | 2. Aaron's answer.
      W | h | 3, 4-. Idolatry purposed.
          i | -4. Jehovah's rejection.
      W | *h* | 5, 6. Idolatry practised.
          i | 7-10. Jehovah's wrath.
  V | *f* | 11-13. Request of Moses.
      g | 14. Jehovah's answer.

1 delayed = put them to shame by his not coming down. Cp. Ps. 44. 7; 53. 5; 119. 31. **out of** = from.

make us gods. The great sin of to-day (1 Cor. 10. 7, 11). Made now not of materials; but made by imagination; and worshipped by the senses.

man. Heb. *'ish*, Ap. 14. ii. **wot not** = know not.

3 all = the greater part. Fig. *Synecdoche* (of Genus), Ap. 6.

them. The *Ellipsis* (Ap. 6) should be supplied by the word "it": i. e. the gold (*v.* 3).

1491 fashioned it with a graving tool, after he had
26 made it a molten °calf:
Sivan and they said, °"These *be* thy gods, O Israel,
to 7 which brought thee up out of the land of
Abib Egypt."
i
W h 5 And when Aaron saw *it,* he built an altar
(p. 117) before it; and Aaron made proclamation, and
said, "To morrow *is* °a feast to °the LORD."
6 And they rose up early on the morrow,
and °offered °burnt offerings, and brought
peace offerings; and the people sat down to
°eat and to drink, and rose up °to play.

i 7 And °the LORD said unto Moses, "Go, get
thee down; for °thy people, which °thou
broughtest out of the land of Egypt, have
corrupted *themselves:*
8 They have turned aside quickly out of
the way which I commanded them: they
have made them a molten calf, and have
worshipped it, and have °sacrificed thereunto, and said, 'These *be* thy gods, O Israel,
which have brought thee up out of the land
of Egypt.'"
9 And [7]the LORD said unto Moses, "I have
seen this people, and, °behold, it *is* a stiffnecked people:
10 Now therefore let Me alone, that My
wrath may wax hot against them, and that
I may consume them: and I will make of thee
a great nation."

V f 11 And Moses besought °the LORD his °God,
and said, [5]"LORD, why doth Thy wrath wax
hot against °Thy people, which °Thou hast
brought forth out of the land of Egypt with
great power, and with a mighty hand?
12 °Wherefore should the Egyptians speak,
and say, 'For °mischief did He bring them
out, to slay them in the mountains, and to
consume them from the face of the earth?'
Turn from Thy fierce wrath, and °repent of
this °evil against Thy people.
13 Remember Abraham, Isaac, and °Israel,
Thy servants, to whom Thou °swarest by
Thine own Self, and saidst unto them, 'I will
multiply your seed °as the stars of heaven,
and all this land that I have spoken of will
I give unto your seed, and they shall inherit
it for ever.'"

g 14 And [5]the LORD [12]repented of the [12]evil
which He °thought to do unto His people.

Y⁴ X j 15 And Moses turned, and °went down from
(p. 118) the mount, and °the two tables of the testi-
7 Abib mony *were* in his hand: the tables *were*
written on both their sides; on the one side
and on the other *were* they written.
16 And °the tables *were* the work of [3]God,
and °the writing *was* °the writing of [3]God,
graven upon °the tables.

k l 17 And when Joshua heard the noise of the
people as they shouted, he said unto Moses,
"*There is* a noise of war in the camp."

m 18 And he said, "*It is* not the voice of
them that °shout for mastery, neither *is it*
the voice of *them that* °cry for being overcome: *but* the noise of *them that* °sing do
I hear."

4 calf. The chief Egyptian god, with which they were familiar in Egypt.

These be thy gods. Expounded in Neh. 9. 18 as meaning "This is thy god". Cp. Ps. 106. 19-21.

5 a feast to the LORD. All done under cover of "religion".

the LORD. Heb. Jehovah. Ap. 4.

6 offered. Heb. *'ālah.* See Ap. 43. I. vi.

burnt offerings. Heb. pl. of *'ālah.* See Ap. 43. II. ii.

eat and to drink. Fig. *Ellipsis* (Ap. 6), i. e. to eat [the sacrifices] and to drink [the libations].

to play = to make sport. Cp. *v.* 19. So 1 Cor. 10. 7. to dance: i. e. lasciviously. This was part of idolatrous worship.

7 the LORD [Heb. Jehovah] **said.** See note on 3. 7, and cp. note on 6. 10.

thy . . thou. As though disowning them. Cp. Moses' grand faith, in his reply, *v.* 11.

8 sacrificed. Heb. *zabach.* Ap. 43. I. iv.

9 behold. Fig. *Asterismos* (Ap. 6).

11 the LORD. Heb. "the face of Jehovah": i. e. before, or in the presence of Jehovah.

God. Heb. Elohim. Ap. 4.

Thy . . . Thou. This is the reply of Moses. He knows they were not "cast off" (Rom. 11. 2), but only "cast aside" (Rom. 11. 15) for a little moment. See notes on Rom. 11. 2, 15.

12 Wherefore . . . ? Fig. *Erotēsis* (Ap. 6).

mischief, or wrong-doing. Heb. *r'ā'a.* Ap. 44. viii.

repent. Fig. *Anthropopatheia* (Ap. 6).

evil. Heb. *r'ā'a.* Ap. 44. viii.

13 Israel. Not Jacob, because this is the language of highest faith.

swarest. Fig. *Anthropopatheia* (Ap. 6). Cp. Heb. 6 13, 17. Gen. 22. 16-18.

as the stars. Fig. *Parœmia* (Ap. 6).

14 thought to do. Heb. which He spake of doing.

32. 15-30 (Y⁴, p. 94). THE FOURTH DESCENT.

Y⁴ | X | 15-24. The Sin of the People.
   | Z | 25-30. The Judgment of the People.

15-24 (X, above). THE SIN OF THE PEOPLE.
(*Alternations.*)

X | j | 15, 16. The Tables carried.
  | k | l | 17. Moses and Joshua.
  | | m | 18. Answer of Moses.
  | *j* | 19, 20. Tables broken.
  | *k* | *l* | 21. Moses and Aaron.
  | | *m* | 22-24. Answer of Aaron.

15 went down. Moses' fourth descent. See note on 19. 3 (the fifth ascent was in 24. 9).

the two tables. See on 31. 18.

16 the tables . . the tables. Fig. *Epanadiplosis* (Ap. 6), emphasising the importance of the statement.

the writing . . the writing. Fig. *Epizeuxis.* Ap. 6. The two figures together greatly emphasising the verse as a whole; and, combined = another Fig. *Anadiplosis* (Ap. 6), viz. "tables", "writings"—;—"writings", "tables" = the solemn or important writing. See note on 17. 14.

18 shout . . . cry . . . sing. The same word in Hebrew.

19 dancing. Cp. *v.* 6. As in the worship of Apis.

20 burnt. A secret known to the Egyptians.

19 And it came to pass, as soon as he came *j*
nigh unto the camp, that he saw the calf, and
the °dancing: and Moses' anger waxed hot,
and he cast the tables out of his hands, and
brake them beneath the mount.
20 And he took the calf which they had
made, and °burnt *it* in the fire, and ground

1491 7 Abib *it* to powder, and strawed *it* upon the °water,
and made the °children of Israel drink *of it.*

k l (p. 118) 21 And Moses said unto Aaron, "What did this People unto thee, that thou hast brought so great a °sin upon them?"

m 22 And Aaron said, "Let not the anger of my lord wax hot: thou knowest the People, that they °*are set* on mischief.

23 For they said unto me, 'Make us gods, which shall go before us: for *as for* this Moses, the °man that brought us up out of the land of Egypt, we °wot not what is become of him.'

24 And I said unto them, 'Whosoever hath any gold, let them break *it* off.' So they gave *it* me: then I cast it into the fire, and there came out this calf."

Z n (p. 119) 25 And when Moses saw that the People *were* naked; (for Aaron had made them naked unto *their* shame among their enemies:)

o p 26 Then Moses stood in the gate of the camp, and said, °"Who *is* on [5]the LORD'S side? *let him come* unto me."

q And °all the sons of Levi gathered themselves together unto him.

o p 27 And he said unto them, "Thus saith [5]the LORD [11]God of Israel, 'Put every [23]man his sword by his °side, *and* go in and out from gate to gate throughout the camp, and slay every [23]man his brother, and every man his companion, and every [23]man his neighbour.'"

q 28 And the °children of Levi did according to the word of Moses: and there fell of the People that day about °three thousand [23]men.

n 29 For Moses had said, °"Consecrate yourselves to day to the LORD, even every man upon his son, and upon his brother; that He may bestow upon you a blessing this day."

8 Abib 30 And it came to pass on the morrow, that Moses said unto the People, "Ye have °sinned a great [21]sin: and now I will go up unto [5]the LORD; peradventure I shall make an atonement for your °sin."

X[5] A[1] 9 Abib Sab. 31 And Moses °returned unto [5]the LORD, and said, "Oh, this People have [21]sinned a great [21]sin, and have made them gods of gold.

32 Yet now, if Thou wilt forgive their °sin—; and if not, blot me, I pray Thee, out of °Thy book which Thou hast written."

33 And [7]the LORD said unto Moses, "Whosoever hath [21]sinned against Me, °him will I blot out of My book.

B r 34 Therefore now go, lead the People unto *the place* of which I have spoken unto thee:

s °behold, °Mine angel shall go before thee: nevertheless in the day °when I visit I will visit their [21]sin upon them."

A[2] 35 And the LORD °plagued the People, because they made the calf, which Aaron made.

B r **33** And °the LORD said unto Moses, "Depart, *and* go up hence, thou and the People which thou hast brought up out of the land of Egypt, unto the land which I sware unto Abraham, to Isaac, and to Jacob, saying, 'Unto thy seed will I give it:'

2 And I will send an angel before thee; and I will drive out the Canaanite, °the Amorite, and the Hittite, and the Perizzite, °the Hivite, and the Jebusite: *s*

3 Unto a land flowing with °milk and honey: for I will not go up in the midst of thee; for thou *art* a stiffnecked People: lest I consume thee in the way." A[3]

---

water. Cp. Deut. 9. 21. Ex. 17. 6.
children = sons.
21 sin. Heb. *chat'a.* Ap. 44. i.
22 are set: or, supply the Ellipsis "are ready for".
23 man. Heb. *'ish,* Ap. 14. ii.
wot = know.

25-30 (Z, p. 118). THE JUDGMENT OF THE PEOPLE (*Introversion and Simple Alternation*).

Z | n | 25. Idolatry.
  o | p | 26-. Call of Moses.
     q | -26. Levites' response.
  o | *p* | 27. Command of Moses.
     q | 28. Levites' obedience.
  n | 29, 30. Atonement.

26 Who . . . ? &c. Fig. *Erotēsis* (Ap. 6).
all. Fig. *Synecdoche* (of Genus), Ap. 6, i. e. all who had not joined in the idolatry. Cp. Deut. 33. 9.
27 side = thigh.
28 children = sons.
three thousand men. These 3,000 were the "men" slain by "the sons of Levi." The 23,000 of 1 Cor. 10. 8 includes those who died of the "plague" which followed. See verse 35, below.
29 Consecrate. See note on 28. 41.

32. 31—33. 3 (X[5], p. 94). MOSES' FIFTH ASCENT (*Alternations*).

X[5] | A[1] | 32. 31-33. The Sin and its consequences.
  B | r | 32. 34-. Command to depart.
     s | 32. -34. Angel's guidance promised.
  A[2] | 32. 35. The Sin and its consequences.
  B | *r* | 33. 1. Command to depart.
     s | 33. 2, 3-. Angel's guidance promised.
  A[3] | 33. -3. The Sin and its consequences.

31 returned. Moses' fifth ascent. See note on 19. 3.
32 sin—. Fig. *Aposiopēsis* (Ap. 6), to emphasise the unspeakableness of the sin.
Thy book. Fig. *Anthropopatheia* (Ap. 6). Cp. Ps. 69. 28. Isa. 4. 3.
33 him. Under the Law, the sinner blotted out: under grace, sin blotted out.
34 behold. A special reading (Severus Codex, Ap. 34) has "and behold". See Ap. 34.
Mine angel. Probably an inferior angel, not that of Ex. 23. 20, 21.
when I visit. Fig. *Polyptōton* (Ap. 6). Lit. "when I visit I will visit". See note on Gen. 26. 28 and 50. 24, 25. This is to emphasise the fact that there is such a thing as postponed judgment. Cp. 34. 7. Num. 14. 33. Ezek. 18. 1-3. Matt. 23. 32-36.
35 plagued. See note on *v.* 28 above.

33. 1 the LORD [Heb. Jehovah] **said.** See note on 3. 7, and cp. note on 6. 10.
2 the. Some codices, with Sam., Syr., and Onk., read "and the".
3 milk and honey = all kinds of good things. Fig. *Synecdoche* (of Species), Ap. 6.

Y⁵ C (p. 120) 4 And when the People °heard these evil tidings, they mourned: and no °man did put on him his ornaments.

1491 5 For [1]the LORD had said unto Moses, "Say unto the °children of Israel, 'Ye *are* a °stiffnecked People: I will come up into the midst of thee in a moment, and consume thee: therefore now put off thy ornaments from thee, that I may know what to do unto thee.'"

6 And the [5]children of Israel stripped themselves of their ornaments by the mount Horeb.

D 10-15 Abib 7 And Moses took the °tabernacle, and pitched it °without the camp, afar off from the camp, and called it the °Tabernacle of the congregation. And it came to pass, *that* every one which sought [1]the LORD went out unto the °tabernacle of the congregation, which *was* °without the camp.

8 And it came to pass, when Moses went out unto the [7]tabernacle, *that* all the People rose up, and stood every °man *at* his tent door, and looked after Moses, until he was gone into the [7]tabernacle.

9 And it came to pass, as Moses entered into the [7]tabernacle, the cloudy pillar descended, and stood *at* the door of the [7]tabernacle, and *the LORD* talked with Moses.

10 And all the People saw the cloudy pillar stand *at* the [7]tabernacle door: and all the People rose up and worshipped, every man *in* his tent door.

11 And °the LORD spake unto Moses °face to face, as a man speaketh unto his friend. And he turned again into the camp: but his °servant °Joshua, the son of Nun, a young man, departed not out of the [7]tabernacle.

D t¹ 12 And Moses said unto the LORD, "See, Thou sayest unto me, 'Bring up this People:' and Thou hast not let me know °whom Thou wilt send with me. Yet Thou hast said, 'I know thee °by name, and thou hast also °found grace in My sight.'

13 Now therefore, I pray Thee, if I have found grace in Thy sight, shew me now °Thy way, that I may know Thee, that I may find grace in Thy sight: and consider that this nation *is* Thy People."

u¹ 14 And °He said, °"My presence shall go *with thee*, and I will give thee rest."

t² 15 And °he said unto Him, "If Thy presence go not *with me*, carry us not up hence.

16 For °wherein shall it be known here that I and Thy People have found grace in Thy sight? *is it* not in that Thou goest with us? °so shall we be separated, I and Thy People, from all the people that *are* upon the face of the °earth."

u² 17 And [1]the LORD said unto Moses, "I will do this thing also that thou hast spoken: for thou hast found grace in My sight, and I know thee by name."

t³ 18 And °he said, "I beseech thee, shew me Thy glory."

u³ 19 And [14]He said, "I will make all My °goodness pass before thee, and °I will proclaim the name of [1]the LORD before thee; and will be gracious to whom I will be gracious, and will shew mercy on whom I will shew mercy."

20 And [14]He said, "Thou canst not °see My face: for there shall no °man see Me, and live."

33. 4–34. 4- (Y⁵, p. 94). MOSES' FIFTH DESCENT (*Introversion*).

Y⁵ | C | 33. 4-6. Stripping of ornaments.
 D | 33. 7-11. Jehovah. Removal.
 D | 33. 12-23. Jehovah. Manifestation.
 C | 34. 1-4-. Making of the (second) Tables.

4 heard. This shows Moses had descended again.
man. Heb. *'ish* (Ap. 14).
5 children = sons.
stiffnecked People. These have to be humbled; but an afflicted people is an object for Divine favour Cp. ch. 2. 24, 25; 3. 7; 4. 31.
7 tabernacle = tent; eleven times called tent; Heb. *'ohel.* Not *the* tabernacle, for this was not yet made, but a different building altogether, called "the tent of assembly" (see Ap. 40).
without the camp. In presence of corporate failure God withdraws Himself. Typical of our own day. Those who seek Him must "go forth to Him." Cp. Heb. 13. 13.
8 man. Heb. *'ish.* See Ap. 14.
11 the LORD spake. See note on 6. 10, and cp. note on 3. 7.
face to face. To emphasise the communion in the presence of corporate failure; this must ever be individual and personal.
servant = personal attendant, as in 24. 13. Heb. *n'ar*, rendered "servant". 2 Sam. 19. 17. 2 Kings 5. 20. Neh. 5. 10, &c. = assistant.
Joshua. See 17. 9. He had not been in the camp; and when Moses went out Joshua remained in the tent.

12-23 (*D*, above). MANIFESTATION OF JEHOVAH (*Repeated Alternation*).

D | t¹ | 12, 13. Request (Positive).
 u¹ | 14. Answer—Presence.
 t² | 15, 16. Request (Negative).
 u² | 17. Answer—Grace.
 t³ | 18. Request (Positive).
 u³ | 19-23. Answer—Goodness.

12 whom. As promised in 32. 34.
by name. Cp. Isa. 43. 1; 49. 1. In the presence of corporate failure all is individual, cp. 2 Tim. 2. 19. (In 1 Tim. we see corporate rule, in 2 Tim. we see corporate ruin. Hence, 2 Tim. is individual throughout).
found grace: or, favour. All is of grace, cp. 34. 9, &c. Noah (Gen. 6. 8); Abraham (Gen. 18. 3); Moses (34. 9), &c.
13 Thy way. Different from Thy works. Cp. Ps. 103. 7. "Ways" are esoteric, "acts" are exoteric; we must go "outside the camp" to learn the "ways" of Jehovah.
14 He [Jehovah] **said.** See note on 3. 7, and cp. 6. 10.
My presence. If this verse be punctuated as a question, then we can understand verse 15, "Shall My presence go with thee, and shall I lead thee into rest?" as much as to say, How can My presence go with thee after this rejection of Me?
15 he = Moses.
16 wherein . . . ? Fig. *Erotēsis* (Ap. 6).
so shall we be: or, "and by our being".
earth. Heb. *'ădāmāh*, ground.
18 he = Moses.
19 goodness. The glory could not have been endured; *grace* comes first, *glory* is reserved for the future.
I will proclaim the name. This is done in 34. 5-7.
20 see My face. Cp. notes on 23. 15 and 34. 20.
man. Heb. *'ādām.* Ap. 14. i.

1491 21 And [1]the LORD said, "Behold, *there is*
a place by Me, and thou shalt stand upon
°a rock:
22 And it shall come to pass, while My glory
passeth by, that I will put thee in °a clift of
the rock, and will cover thee with °My hand
while I pass by:
23 And I will take away Mine hand, and
thou shalt see My back parts: but My face
shall not be seen."
34 °And °the LORD said unto Moses,
°"Hew thee two tables of stone like
unto the first: and I will °write upon *these*
tables the words that were in the first tables,
which thou brakest.
2 And be ready in the morning, and come
up in the morning unto mount Sinai, and
present thyself there to Me in the top of the
mount.
3 And no °man shall come up with thee,
neither let any °man be seen throughout all
the mount; neither let the flocks nor herds
feed before that mount."
4 And he hewed two tables of stone like unto
the first;
X^6 E and Moses rose up early in the morning, and
(p. 121) °went up unto mount Sinai, °as [1]the LORD
16 had commanded him, and took in his hand
Abib the two tables of stone.
Sab. 5 And [1]the LORD descended in the cloud, and
F stood with him there, and °proclaimed the
name of [1]the LORD.
6 And [1]the LORD passed by before him, and
[5]proclaimed, [1]"The LORD, [1]The LORD °GOD,
merciful and gracious, °longsuffering, and
abundant in °goodness and °truth,
7 Keeping °mercy for thousands, °forgiving
°iniquity and °transgression and °sin, and
That will °by no means clear *the guilty;*
visiting the °iniquity of the fathers upon
the children, and upon the children's children, °unto the third and to the fourth *generation.*"

G 8 And Moses made haste, and bowed his
head toward the earth, and °worshipped.
9 And he said, "If now I have found grace
in Thy sight, O °Lord, let °my Lord, I pray
Thee, go among us; °for it *is* a stiffnecked
People; and pardon our [7]iniquity and our [7]sin,
and take us for Thine inheritance."

F H K^1 10 And °He said, °"Behold, I make °a
covenant: before all thy People I will do
marvels, such as have not been done in all
the earth, nor in any nation: and all the
People among which thou *art* shall see the
work of [1]the LORD: for it *is* a terrible thing
that I will do with thee.
11 Observe thou that which I command
thee this day: behold, I drive out before thee
the Amorite, and the Canaanite, and the
Hittite, and the Perizzite, and the Hivite,
and the Jebusite.
K^2 12 Take heed to thyself, lest thou make a
covenant with the inhabitants of the land
whither thou goest, lest °it be for a snare in
the midst of thee:
13 But ye shall destroy their altars, break
their °images, and cut down their °groves:

21 a rock=the rock.
22 a clift=the clift or hollow.
My hand. Fig. *Anthropopatheia* (Ap. 6).

34. 1 And. Moses must have descended for the fifth time. See note on 19. 3.
the LORD. Heb. Jehovah. Ap. 4.
the LORD said. See note on 3. 7, and cp. note on 6. 10.
Hew thee. Moses makes these second tables; Jehovah made the first. See on 31. 18.
write. See note on 17. 14 and Ap. 47.
3 man. Heb. *'ish.* See Ap. 14.

34. 4-28 (X^6, p. 94). MOSES' SIXTH ASCENT. (*Introversion.*)

X^6 | E | -4. The new Tables taken up by Moses.
F | 5-7. The Proclamation of Jehovah.
G | 8, 9. The worship and prayer of Moses.
F | 10-26. The Commandments of Jehovah.
E | 27, 28. The Tables written by Jehovah.

4 went up. Moses' sixth and last ascent. See note on 19. 3.
as=according as.
5 proclaimed. As promised in 33. 19.
6 GOD. Heb. El. See Ap. 4.
longsuffering=slow to anger.
goodness=lovingkindness, or grace.
truth=faithfulness.
7 mercy=lovingkindness, or grace.
forgiving=bearing away.
iniquity=perverseness. Heb. *'āvāh.* Ap. 44. iv.
transgression=rebellion. Heb. *pash'a.* Ap. 44. ix.
sin. Heb. *chāt'a.* See Ap. 44. i.
by no means clear the guilty. Not even Christ, when our sins were imputed to Him: therefore, all now in Him are "cleared", Fig. *Polyptōton* (Ap. 6). Heb. "clearing will not clear", emphasis on "by no means".
unto the third and to the fourth generation. This refrain recurs in whole or in part in Ex. 20. 5. Cp. also Num. 14. 18. Deut. 5. 9. Neh. 9. 17. Ps. 103. 8. Jer. 9. 24; 30. 11; 46. 28; Dan. 9. 4. Nah. 1. 3. The visiting spread over in mercy, not extended in wrath.
8 worshipped. This is ever the effect of the manifestation of Jehovah in grace. Cp. 2 Sam. 7. 18.
9 Lord . . . my Lord. Heb. *Adonai, Adonai.* But this is one of the 134 places where Jehovah was altered to Adonai by the Sopherim. See Ap. 32.
for, &c. The moment Jehovah speaks of grace, Moses turns the very charge of Jehovah, in 33. 5, into a plea and ground for His presence.

10-26 (*F*, above). COVENANT AND LAWS OF JEHOVAH (*Division*).

F | H^1 | 10-17. The Covenant of Jehovah remade.
H^2 | 18-26. The Commandments of Jehovah repeated.

10-17 (H^1, above). THE COVENANT OF JEHOVAH REMADE.

H^1 | K^1 | 10, 11. Jehovah the only true God.
K^2 | 12-17. No other gods.

10 He [Jehovah] **said.** See note on 3. 7, and cp. 6. 10.
Behold. Fig. *Asterismos* (Ap. 6) for emphasis.
a covenant of marvels. This covenant finds its complete fulfilment in the Apocalypse.
12 it=they.
13 images=sacred pillars. Cp. 23. 24; 24. 4, and note on Lev. 26. 1.
groves=Heb. *'ăshērāh.* First occurrence out of forty: always rendered "groves", but denotes a phallic image, worshipped by libidinous rites and lascivious practices. See Ap. 42.

1491 14 For thou shalt worship no other god: for [1]the LORD, Whose name *is* Jealous, °*is* a jealous °GOD:

15 Lest thou make a covenant with the inhabitants of the land, and they go a whoring after their gods, and do °sacrifice unto their gods, and *one* call thee, and thou eat of his °sacrifice;

16 And thou take of their daughters unto thy sons, and their daughters go a whoring after their gods, and make thy sons go a whoring after their gods.

17 Thou shalt make thee no molten gods.

H² M v (p. 122) 18 The feast of unleavened bread shalt thou keep. Seven days thou shalt eat unleavened bread, °as I commanded thee, in the °time of the month °Abib: for in the month °Abib thou camest out from Egypt.

w 19 All that openeth the matrix *is* Mine; and every firstling among thy cattle, *whether* ox or sheep, *that is male*.

20 But the firstling of an ass thou shalt °redeem with a lamb: and if thou °redeem *him* not, then shalt thou break his neck. All the firstborn of thy sons thou shalt °redeem. And none shall °appear before Me °empty.

N 21 Six days thou shalt work, but on the seventh day thou shalt rest: in °earing time and in harvest thou shalt rest.

M v 22 And thou shalt observe the feast of weeks, of the firstfruits of wheat harvest, and the feast of ingathering at the year's end.

23 °Thrice in the year shall all your men-children [20]appear before THE °Lord GOD, the God of Israel.

24 For I will cast out the nations before thee, and enlarge thy borders: neither shall any man desire thy land, when thou shalt go up to [20]appear before [1]the LORD thy °God thrice in the year.

25 Thou shalt not °offer the blood of My sacrifice with leaven; neither shall the sacrifice of the feast of the passover be left unto the morning.

w 26 The first of the firstfruits of thy land thou shalt bring unto the house of [1]the LORD thy [24]God. Thou shalt not seethe a kid in his mother's milk."

E (p. 121) 27 And [1]the LORD said unto Moses, °"Write thou these words: for after the tenor of these words I have made a covenant with thee and with Israel."

16 Abib to 26 Elul 28 And he was there with [1]the LORD forty days and forty nights; he did neither eat bread, nor drink water. And °He [27]wrote upon the °tables the words of the covenant, the ten commandments.

Y⁶ X¹ (p. 122) 26 Elul 29 And it came to pass, when Moses °came down from mount Sinai (with the two [28]tables of testimony in Moses' hand, when he came down from the mount), that Moses °wist not that the skin of his face °shone °while He talked with him.

30 And when Aaron and all the °children of Israel saw Moses, behold, the skin of his face shone; and they were °afraid to come nigh him.

14 is = "he [is]". GOD = Heb. El. Ap. 4.
15 sacrifice. Heb. *zabaḥ*. Ap. 43. I. iv.

18-26 (H², p. 121). THE COMMANDMENTS OF JEHOVAH REPEATED.
(*Introversion and Alternation.*)

H² | M | v | 18. The one Feast. No leaven.
| | w | 19, 20. The Firstborn. Liberality.
| N | 21. The Sabbath.
| *M* | *v* | 22-25. The three Feasts. No leaven.
| | *w* | 26. The Firstfruits. Kindliness.

18 as. Some codices, with Sam., Onk., Jon., Sept., Syr., and Vulg., read "according as".
time = appointed time.
Abib. See note on 13. 4, and Ap. 51. III. 4.
20 redeem. Heb. *pādāh*. See note on 6. 6. and 13. 13.
appear before Me. This is an alteration (in pointing) made by the Sopherim to soften the Fig. *Anthropopatheia* (Ap. 6) of the primitive text, which was "see My face". See note on 23. 15, and compare the other passages where this change is made, viz. 34. 20, 23, 24. Deut. 16. 16; 31. 11. Ps. 11. 7; 17. 15; 42. 2. Isa. 1. 12; 38. 11. In this, therefore, there is no contradiction of 33. 20.
empty = empty-handed.
21 earing = ploughing. From A.S. *erian*, Lat. *arare*.
23 Thrice = the number of Divine perfection. (Ap. 10.)
Lord GOD, the God. Heb. the *'Adōn, Jehovah Elohim*. Ap. 4.
24 God. Heb. Elohim. Ap. 4.
25 offer = slay. Heb. *zābach*. Supply *Ellipsis* (Ap. 6. ii. c), "slay [and pour out]". See Ap. 43. I. iv.
27 Write thou. See note on 17. 14 and Ap. 47.
28 He = Jehovah. See *v.* 1. tables. See on 31. 18.

34. 29—35. 3 (Y⁶, p. 94). MOSES' SIXTH DESCENT. (*Division.*)

Y⁶ | X¹ | 34. 29-35. Conclusion of the ascents.
| X² | 35. 1-3. Preparation for the work.

Two episodes, concluding the ascents and descents preparatory to the other great event of this section (Ex. 15. 22—40. 38), viz. the setting up of the Tabernacle, and the command that none of the work was to be done on the Sabbath.

29 came down. Moses' sixth and last descent. Cp. 19. 3.
wist not = knew not. Cp. Moses: unconscious moral strength for testimony.
Samson: unconscious weakness for unfaithfulness (Judg. 16. 20).
Peter: unconscious deliverance for service (Acts 12. 9).
shone = radiated, or was glorious, i. e. reflected as a mirror the Divine glory, see 2 Cor. 3. 7; and cp. 1 Cor. 15. 41. Rev. 18. 1. Matt. 17. 2. Acts 6. 15.
The Vulg. mistook the Heb. word *kāran* = to radiate, for *keren*, a beam or horn of light (see Hab. 3. 4 and note on the subscription to Ps. 21). Hence the traditional paintings of Moses with two horns.
while, &c. = through his having spoken with him. This interprets 1 John 3. 2. Cp. Matt. 17. 2, and the "till" of *v.* 33, and the "until" of *v.* 35.
30 children = sons.
afraid. See Ex. 20. 18-21.
32 gave them, &c. Charged them with.
34 went in: i. e. into the tent.

31 And Moses called unto them; and Aaron and all the rulers of the congregation returned unto him: and Moses talked with them.

32 And afterward all the [30]children of Israel came nigh: and he °gave them in commandment all that [1]the LORD had spoken with him in mount Sinai.

33 And *till* Moses had done speaking with them, he put a vail on his face.

34 But when Moses °went in before [1]the

1491 **LORD to speak with Him, °he took the vail off, until he came out. And he came out, and spake unto the [30] children of Israel *that* which he was commanded.**

35 And the [30] children of Israel saw the face of Moses, that the skin of Moses' face shone: and Moses put the vail upon his face °again, until he went in to speak with Him.

X² (p. 122) **35 And Moses gathered all the congregation of the °children of Israel together, and said unto them, "These *are* the words which °the LORD hath commanded, that *ye* should do them.**

2 Six days shall work be done, but on the seventh day there shall be to you an holy day, a °sabbath of rest to [1] the LORD: whosoever doeth work therein shall be put to death.

3 Ye shall kindle no fire throughout your habitations upon the sabbath day."

V O (p. 123) **4 And Moses spake unto all the congregation of the [1] children of Israel, saying, "This *is* the thing which [1] the LORD °commanded, saying,**

5 'Take ye from among you °an offering unto [1] the LORD: whosoever *is* of a °willing heart, let him bring it, °an offering of [1] the LORD; gold, and silver, and brass,

6 And blue, and purple, and scarlet, and fine linen, and goats' *hair*,

7 And rams' skins dyed red, and badgers' skins, and °shittim wood,

8 And oil for the light, and spices for anointing oil, and for the sweet incense,

9 And onyx stones, and stones to be set for the ephod, and for the breastplate.

P **10 And every °wise hearted among you shall come, and make all that [1] the LORD hath commanded;**

Q **11 °The tabernacle, his tent, and his covering, his taches, and his boards, his bars, his pillars, and his sockets,**

12 The ark, and the staves thereof, *with* the mercy seat, and the vail of the covering,

13 The table, and his staves, and all his vessels, and the shewbread,

14 The candlestick also for the light, and his furniture, and his lamps, with the oil for the light,

15 And the incense altar, and his staves, and the anointing oil, and the sweet incense, and the hanging for the °door at the entering in of the tabernacle,

16 The altar of burnt offering, with his brasen grate, his staves, and all his vessels, the laver and his foot,

17 The hangings of the court, his pillars, and their sockets, and the hanging for the °door of the court,

18 The pins of the tabernacle, and the pins of the court, and their cords,

19 The cloths of service, to do service in the holy *place*, the holy garments for Aaron the priest, and the garments of his sons, to minister in the priest's office.'"

O **20 And all the congregation of the [1] children of Israel departed from the presence of Moses.**

21 And °they came, every one whose °heart stirred him up, and every one whom his °spirit made willing, *and* they brought °the [1] LORD'S offering to the work of the °tabernacle of the congregation, and for all His service, and for the holy garments.

22 And [21] they came, both °men and women, as many as were [5] willing hearted, *and* brought bracelets, °and earrings, and rings, and tablets, all jewels of gold: and every °man that offered °*offered* an offering of gold unto [1] the LORD.

23 And every °man, with whom was found blue, °and purple, and scarlet, and fine °linen, and goats' *hair*, and red skins of rams, and badgers' skins, brought *them*.

24 Every one that did °offer an offering of

---

he took the vail off. And, when Israel turns thus to Jehovah, He will take the vail from their heart, as Moses did from his face, 2 Cor. 3. 16. We, now, are "not as Moses", *v.* 13.

35 again. So 2 Cor. 3. 13. Greek = kept putting a vail on his face" (imperfect tense). They could not see "the end of the Law", which is Christ. Rom. 10. 4.

35. 1-3 Before the work commences, they are reminded of the commandment as to the six days and the seventh, even in the making of the Tabernacle.

children = sons.

the LORD. Heb. Jehovah. Ap. 4.

2 sabbath of rest. Heb. "sabbath of sabbatizing". See note on 16. 23.

35. 4—40. 33 (*V*, p. 94). THE MAKING OF THE TABERNACLE (*Extended Alternation*).

V | O | 35. 4-9. Free-will offerings required.
  P | 35. 10. Artificers called for.
   Q | 35. 11-19. The work described.
 O | 35. 20-29. Free-will offerings given.
  P | 35. 30—36. 7. Artificers fitted.
   Q | 36. 8—40. 33. The work executed.

4 commanded. See 25. 1, &c.

5 an offering. Note the Fig. *Polysyndeton* (Ap. 6), emphasising the 15 (3 × 5) articles in *vv.* 5-9 (Ap. 10). Heb. = heave offering. See note on 29. 27, and Ap. 43. II. viii.

willing heart. Note the "willing" hearted, 35. 5, 22, 29; the "wise" hearted, 35. 10, 25, 35; 36. 1, 2, 8; and the "stirred" heart, 35. 21, 26; 36. 2.

10 wise hearted. See note on *v.* 5.

11 Note the 42 items enumerated in *vv.* 11-19.

15 door = entrance (Heb. *petach*).

17 door = gate (Heb. *sha'ar*).

21 they came. Sam. and Sept. read "they brought in".

heart stirred. See note on *v.* 5.

spirit. Heb. *rūach.* See Ap. 9.

the LORD'S offering = the heave offering of Jehovah. See note on 29. 27, and cp. Ap. 43. II. viii.

tabernacle = tent. Heb. *'ohel.* Ap. 40.

22 men. Heb. pl. of *'īsh*, or *'enōsh.* Ap. 14.

and. Note the Fig. *Polysyndeton* (Ap. 6), to emphasise the number four.

man = every one.

offered an offering. Fig. *Polyptōton* (Ap. 6). Heb. *tenūphah*, a wave offering. See note on 29. 27, and Ap. 43. II. ix.

23 man. Heb. *'īsh.* See Ap. 14. ii.

and. Note the Fig. *Polysyndeton* (Ap. 6), to emphasise the seven items divided into three and four. See Ap. 10.

linen. Egypt noted for it. The thread was dyed before being woven.

24 offer, &c. = "heave a heave offering". See 29. 27. Fig. *Polyptōton* (Ap. 6).

1491 silver and brass brought [21]the LORD'S offering: and every [22]man, with whom was found
shittim wood for any work of the service,
brought *it*.
25 And all the °women that were [10]wise
hearted did spin with their hands, and
brought that which they had spun, *both* of
blue, °and of purple, *and* of scarlet, and of
fine linen.
26 And all the women whose [21]heart stirred
them up in wisdom spun goats' *hair*.
27 And the rulers brought onyx stones, and
stones to be set, for the ephod, and for the
breastplate;
28 °And spice, and oil for the light, and for
the anointing oil, and for the sweet incense.
29 The [1]children of Israel brought a willing
°offering unto [1]the LORD, every [23]man and
woman, whose heart made them [5]willing to
bring for all manner of work, which [1]the
LORD had commanded to be made by the
hand of Moses.

P R¹ a¹ (p. 124) 30 And Moses said unto the [1]children of
Israel, "See, [1]the LORD hath °called by name
Bezaleel the son of Uri, the son of Hur, of the
tribe of Judah;

b¹ 31 And He hath filled him with the °spirit
of °God, in wisdom, in understanding, and
in knowledge, and in all manner of workmanship;

c¹ 32 °And to devise curious works, to work in
gold, °and in silver, and in brass,
33 And in the cutting of stones, to set *them*,
and in carving of wood, to make any manner
of °cunning work.

a² 34 And He hath put in his heart that he
may teach, *both* he, and Aholiab, the son of
Ahisamach, of the tribe of Dan.

b² 35 Them hath He filled with [10]wisdom of heart,
c² to °work all manner of work, of the engraver,
and of the [33]cunning workman, and of the embroiderer, in blue, and in purple, °in scarlet,
and in fine linen, and of the weaver, *even* of
them that do any work, and of those that
devise [33]cunning work."

a³ **36** Then wrought Bezaleel and Aholiab,
1 Tisri and every °wise hearted man, in whom
7th °the LORD put wisdom and understanding to
month. know how to work all manner of work for
the service of the sanctuary, according to all
that °the LORD had commanded.

b³ 2 And Moses called Bezaleel and Aholiab,
and every [1]wise hearted °man, in whose heart
[1]the LORD had put wisdom, *even* every one
whose °heart stirred him up to come unto the
work to do it:
3 And they received of Moses all the °offer-
ing, which the °children of Israel had brought
for the work of the service of the sanctuary,
to make it *withal*. And they brought yet unto
him °free offerings every morning.

c³ 4 And all the wise men, that wrought all the
work of the sanctuary, came every [2]man from
his work which they made;
5 And they spake unto Moses, saying, "The
People bring much more than enough for the
service of the work, which [1]the LORD commanded to make."
6 And Moses gave commandment, and they
caused it to be proclaimed throughout the
camp, saying, "Let neither man nor woman
make any more work for the [3]offering of the
sanctuary." So the People were restrained
from bringing.
7 For the stuff they had was sufficient for all
the work to make it, and too much.

8 And every [1]wise hearted man among them Q S U
that wrought the work of the °tabernacle
made ten °curtains *of* °fine twined linen, and

25 women. In Egypt the women did the dyeing and spinning; the men did the weaving and embroidering.
and. Note the Fig. *Polysyndeton* (Ap. 6), to emphasise the four items.
28 And. Note the Fig. *Polysyndeton* (Ap. 6), to emphasise the four items.
29 offering. Heb. *n^edābā*. See Ap. 43. II. vii.

35. 30—36. 7 (*P*, p. 123). THE ARTIFICERS FITTED (*Extended Alternation, Repeated*).

P | R¹ | a¹ | 35. 30. Bezaleel called.
b¹ | 35. 31. Bezaleel filled.
c¹ | 35. 32, 33. His gifts.
R² | a² | 35. 34. Aholiab called.
b² | 35. 35-. Aholiab filled.
c² | 35. -35. His gifts.
R³ | a³ | 36. 1. Bezaleel, Aholiab, and companions.
b³ | 36. 2. Their filling.
c³ | 36. 3-7. Their and the people's gifts.

30 called by name. Cp. 31. 2. This, in Exodus, the book of the names. See note on 1. 1.
31 spirit. Heb. *rūach*. Ap. 9.
God. Heb. Elohim, the Creator. Ap. 4.
32 And to devise. This "and" is omitted in Sept.
and in silver. Note the Fig. *Polysyndeton* (Ap. 6), to emphasise the items in *vv.* 32, 33.
33 cunning work = skilful work. See note on 26. 1.
35 work all. Some codices, one early printed edition, and Sam. read "work in all".
in scarlet. Some codices, Sam., Onk., one early printed edition, Jon., and Syr. read "and in scarlet".

36. 1 wise hearted. See note on 35. 5.
the LORD. Heb. Jehovah. Ap. 4.
2 man. Heb. *'ish* (Ap. 14. ii).
heart stirred. See note on 35. 5.
3 offering = Heb. *t^erūmāh* = heave offering. See note on 29. 27, and Ap. 43. II. viii.
free offerings. Heb. *n^edābāh*. Ap. 43. II. vii.

36. 8—40. 33 (*Q*, p. 123). THE WORK CARRIED OUT (*Alternation*).

Q | S | 36. 8—39. 42. The Tabernacle made.
T | 39. 43. Approbation and blessing. Moses.
S | 40. 1-33. The Tabernacle set up.
T | 40. 34. Approbation and blessing. Jehovah.

36. 8—39. 42 (S, above). THE TABERNACLE MADE (*Alternation*).

S | U | 36. 8—37. 28. The Tabernacle (twelve items).
V | 37. 29. Its service.
U | 38. 1-20. The Tabernacle (three items).
V | 38. 21—39. 31. Its service.

8-13 curtains (26. 1), fifteen in all (with the ark in the centre), divided into twelve (U) and three (*U*).
8 tabernacle. Heb. *mishkan*. See Ap. 40.
fine twined linen. See 35. 23.

1491 1st Eth. to 1st Abib. 6th mth.

blue, and purple, and scarlet: *with* cherubims of °cunning work made he them.

9 The length of one curtain *was* twenty and eight °cubits, and the breadth of one curtain four °cubits: the curtains *were* all of one size.

10 And he coupled the five curtains one unto another: and *the other* five curtains he coupled one unto another.

11 And he made loops of blue on the edge of one curtain from the selvedge in the coupling: likewise he made in the uttermost °side of *another* curtain, in the coupling of the second.

12 Fifty loops made he in one curtain, and fifty loops made he in the edge of the curtain which *was* in the coupling of the second: the loops held one *curtain* to another.

13 And he made fifty °taches of gold, and coupled the curtains one unto another with the taches: so it became one °tabernacle.

14 And he made curtains *of* goats' *hair* for the tent over the [13]tabernacle: eleven curtains he made them.

15 The length of one curtain *was* thirty [9]cubits, and four [9]cubits *was* the breadth of one curtain: the eleven curtains *were* of one size.

16 And he coupled five curtains by themselves, and six curtains by themselves.

17 And he made fifty loops upon the uttermost edge of the curtain in the coupling, and fifty loops made he upon the edge of the curtain which coupleth the second.

18 And he made fifty [13]taches *of* °brass to couple the tent together, that it might be one.

19 And he made a covering for the tent *of* rams' skins dyed red, and a covering *of* badgers' skins above *that*.

20 And he made boards for the [13]tabernacle *of* shittim wood, standing up.

21 The length of a board *was* ten [9]cubits, and the breadth of a board one [9]cubit and a half.

22 One board had two tenons, equally distant one from another: thus did he make for all the boards of the [13]tabernacle.

23 And he made boards for the [13]tabernacle; twenty boards for the south °side southward:

24 And forty °sockets of silver he made under the twenty boards; two sockets under one board for his two tenons, and two sockets under another board for his two tenons.

25 And for the other °side of the [13]tabernacle, *which is* toward the north corner, he made twenty boards,

26 And their forty [24]sockets of silver; two sockets under one board, and two sockets under another board.

27 And for the °sides of the [13]tabernacle westward he made six boards.

28 And two boards made he for the corners of the [13]tabernacle in the two [27]sides.

29 And they were coupled beneath, and coupled together °at the head thereof, to one ring: thus he did to both of them in both the corners.

30 And there were eight boards; and their sockets *were* sixteen [24]sockets of silver, under every board two sockets.

31 And he made bars of shittim wood; five for the boards of the one [25]side of the [13]tabernacle,

32 And five bars for the boards of the other [25]side of the [13]tabernacle, and five bars for the °boards of the [13]tabernacle for the [27]sides westward.

33 And he made the middle bar to shoot through the boards from the one end to the other.

34 And he overlaid the boards with gold, and made their rings *of* gold *to be* °places for the bars, and overlaid the bars with gold.

35 And he made a vail *of* blue, and purple, and scarlet, and fine twined linen: *with* cherubims made he it of [8]cunning work.

36 And he made thereunto four pillars *of* shittim *wood*, and overlaid them with gold: their hooks *were of* gold; and he cast for them four [24]sockets of silver.

37 And he made an hanging for the °tabernacle °door *of* blue, and purple, and scarlet, and fine twined linen, of needlework;

38 And the five pillars of it with their hooks: and he overlaid their chapiters and their °fillets with gold: but their five °sockets *were of* °brass.

37 And Bezaleel made the °ark *of* °shittim wood: two °cubits and a half *was* the length of it, and a °cubit and a half the breadth of it, and a °cubit and a half the height of it:

2 And he overlaid it with pure gold within and without, and made a °crown of gold to it round about.

3 And he cast for it four rings of gold, *to be*

---

cunning work. See note on 26. 1.
9 cubits. See Ap. 51. III. 2.
11 side. Heb. *sāphāh* = edge.
13 taches. Hooks, pins, or clasps. In Eastern tents, curtains not sewn together, but pinned with wooden pins. Here made of gold.
tabernacle = habitation. Heb. *mishkān*. Ap. 40.

14 THE COVERING OF THE TENT.

18 brass. See note on 25. 3.

20-30 THE BOARDS.

23 side. Heb. *pe'āh*, quarter or part.
24 sockets of silver. See note on 27. 10.
25 side. Heb. *zēl'ā* = rib, or corresponding side.
27 sides. Heb. *yārēk* = hinder side.
29 at. Some codices, with Sam. and Onk., read "upon".

31-34 THE BARS.

32 boards of the tabernacle. Some codices, with Sam., Onk., and Jon., read "boards of the side of the tabernacle". Cp. 26. 27. **34 places** = receptacles.

37, 38 THE HANGING FOR THE ENTRANCE.

37 tabernacle = tent. Heb. *'ohel*. Ap. 40.
door = entrance. Heb. *pitath*.
38 fillets = cross or connecting rods.
sockets . . . brass. See note on 27. 10.

37. 1-5 THE ARK. Occupying the central position of the fifteen here described (Ex. 25. 10).

1 ark. See note on 24. 22. shittim = acacia.
cubit. See Ap. 51. III. 2.
2 crown = rim. See note on 25. 24.

1491 1st Eth. set by the four corners of it; even two rings upon the one ° side of it, and two rings upon the other ° side of it.

4 And he made staves *of* shittim wood, and
to 1st Abib. overlaid them with gold.

5 And he put the staves into the rings by the [3] sides of the [1] ark, to bear the ark.

6 And he made the ° mercy seat *of* pure gold: two [1] cubits and a half *was* the length thereof, and one [1] cubit and a half the breadth thereof.

7 And he made two ° cherubims *of* gold, beaten out of one piece made he them, on the two ends of the mercy seat;

8 One cherub ° on the end on this side, and another cherub ° on the *other* end on that side: out of the mercy seat made he the cherubims on the two ends thereof.

9 And the [7] cherubims spread out *their* wings on high, *and* covered with their wings over the [6] mercy seat, with their faces one to another; *even* to the mercy seatward were the faces of the [7] cherubims.

10 And he made the table *of* shittim wood: two [1] cubits *was* the length thereof, and a [1] cubit the breadth thereof, and a [1] cubit and a half the height thereof:

11 And he overlaid it with pure gold, and made thereunto a [2] crown of gold round about.

12 Also he made thereunto a border of an ° handbreadth round about; and made a [2] crown of gold for the border thereof round about.

13 And he cast for it four rings of gold, and put the rings upon the four corners that *were* in the four feet thereof.

14 Over against the border were the rings, the ° places for the staves to bear the table.

15 And he made the staves *of* shittim wood, and overlaid them with gold, to bear the table.

16 And he made the vessels which *were* upon the table, his dishes, and his ° spoons, and his bowls, and his ° covers ° to cover withal, *of* pure gold.

17 And he made the candlestick *of* pure gold: *of* beaten work made he the candlestick; his shaft, and his branch, his bowls, his knops, and his flowers, were of the same:

18 And six branches going out of the ° sides thereof; three branches of the candlestick out of the one ° side thereof, and three branches of the candlestick out of the other ° side thereof:

19 Three bowls made after the fashion of almonds in one branch, a ° knop and a flower; and three bowls made like almonds in another branch, a ° knop and a flower: so throughout the six branches going out of the candlestick.

20 And in the candlestick *were* four bowls made like almonds, his knops, and his flowers:

21 And a [19] knop under two branches of the same, and a knop under two branches of the same, and a knop under two branches of the same, according to the six branches going out of it.

22 Their [19] knops and their branches were of the same: all of it *was* one beaten work *of* pure gold.

23 And he made his seven lamps, and his ° snuffers, and his snuffdishes, *of* pure gold.

24 *Of* a ° talent of pure gold made he it, and all the vessels thereof.

25 And he made the incense altar *of* shittim wood: the length of it *was* a [1] cubit, and the breadth of it a [1] cubit; *it was* foursquare; and two [1] cubits *was* the height of it; the horns thereof were of the same.

26 And he overlaid it with pure gold, *both* the top of it, and the ° sides thereof round about, and the horns of it: also he made unto it a [2] crown of gold round about.

27 And he made two rings of gold for it under the crown thereof, by the two corners of it, upon the two ° sides thereof, to be places for the staves to bear it withal.

28 And he made the staves *of* shittim wood, and overlaid them with gold.

29 And he made the holy anointing oil, and V (p. 124)
the pure incense of sweet spices, according to the work of the apothecary.

38 And he made the altar of burnt offer- U
ing *of* shittim wood: five ° cubits *was* the length thereof, and five ° cubits the breadth thereof; *it was* foursquare; and three ° cubits the height thereof.

2 And he made the horns thereof on the four corners of it; the horns thereof were of the same: and he overlaid it with ° brass.

3 And he made all the vessels of the altar, the pots, and the shovels, and the basons, *and* the fleshhooks, and the firepans: all the vessels thereof made he *of* brass.

---

3 side. Heb. *ẓēl'ā* = rib, one of two corresponding sides.

6-9 THE MERCY SEAT AND CHERUBIMS.

6 mercy seat = propitiatory. See note on 25. 17

7 cherubims. See note on 25. 18, and Ap. 41.

8 on = out of.

10-15 THE TABLE.

12 handbreadth. See Ap. 51. III. 2.

14 places = receptacles.

16 THE VESSELS OF THE TABLE.

16 spoons = pans.
covers = bowls.
to cover = to pour.

17-24 THE LAMPSTAND.

18 side = Heb. *tzad*.

19 knop = knob.

23 snuffers. These were provided, but no extinguisher.

24 talent. See Ap. 51. II. vi.

25-29 THE ALTAR OF INCENSE (see 30. 1).

26 sides. Heb. *kīr* = walls.

27 sides = opposite sides. Heb. *'eber*.

29 (V, p. 124). THE SERVICE OF THE TABERNACLE. (The oil and the incense, see 30. 35.)

38. 1-7 (*U*, p. 124). THE ALTAR OF BURNT OFFERING. (Cp. chapter 27. 1.)

1 cubits. See Ap. 51. III. 2.

2 brass. See note on 25. 3.

1491 4 And he made for the altar a brasen grate
1st of network under the compass thereof beneath
Eth. unto the midst of it.
5 And he cast four rings for the four ends
to 1st of the grate of [2]brass, *to be* places for the
Abib. staves.

6 And he made the staves *of* shittim wood, and overlaid them with [2]brass.

7 And he put the staves into the rings on the °sides of the altar, to bear it withal; he made the altar hollow with boards.

8 And he made the laver *of* brass, and the foot of it *of* brass, of the °lookingglasses of *the women* °assembling, which assembled *at* the °door of the °tabernacle of the congregation.

9 And he made the court: on the south °side southward the hangings of the court *were of* fine twined linen, an hundred [1]cubits:

10 Their pillars *were* twenty, and their brasen °sockets twenty; the hooks of the pillars and their °fillets *were of* silver.

11 And for the north [9]side *the hangings were* an hundred [1]cubits, their pillars *were* twenty, and their sockets of °brass twenty; the hooks of the pillars and their [10]fillets *of* silver.

12 And for the west [9]side *were* hangings of fifty [1]cubits, their pillars ten, and their sockets ten; the hooks of the pillars and their [10]fillets *of* silver.

13 And for the east [9]side eastward fifty [1]cubits.

14 The hangings of the one °side *of the gate were* fifteen [1]cubits; their pillars three, and their sockets three.

15 And for the other [14]side of the court gate, on this hand and that hand, *were* hangings of fifteen [1]cubits; their pillars three, and their sockets three.

16 All the hangings of the court round about *were* of °fine twined linen.

17 And the sockets for the pillars *were of* [10]brass; the hooks of the pillars and their [10]fillets *of* silver; and the overlaying of their chapiters *of* silver; and all the pillars of the court *were* filleted with silver.

18 And the hanging for the gate of the court *was* needlework, *of* blue, and purple, and scarlet, and fine twined linen: and twenty [1]cubits *was* the length, and the height in the breadth *was* five [1]cubits, answerable to the hangings of the court.

19 And their pillars *were* four, and their [10]sockets *of* brass four; their hooks *of* silver, and the overlaying of their chapiters and their [10]fillets *of* silver.

20 And all the pins of the °tabernacle, and of the court round about, *were of* [11]brass.

V d 21 This is the sum of the [20]tabernacle, *even*
(p. 127) of the [20]tabernacle of testimony, as it was °counted, according to the commandment of Moses, *for* the service of the Levites, by the hand of Ithamar, son to Aaron the priest.

e 22 And °Bezaleel the son of Uri, the son of Hur, of the tribe of Judah, made all that °the LORD commanded Moses.

23 And with him *was* Aholiab, son of Ahisamach, of the tribe of Dan, an engraver, and a °cunning workman, and an embroiderer in blue, and in purple, and in scarlet, and fine linen.

24 All the gold that was occupied for the work in all the work of the holy *place*, even the gold of the °offering, was twenty and nine °talents, and seven hundred and thirty °shekels, after the °shekel of the sanctuary. *d*

25 And the silver of °them that were numbered of the congregation *was* an hundred [24]talents, and a thousand seven hundred and threescore and fifteen [24]shekels, after the [24]shekel of the sanctuary:

26 A °bekah for every °man, *that is*, half a [24]shekel, after the [24]shekel of the sanctuary, for every one that went to be numbered, from twenty years old and upward, for six hundred thousand and three thousand and five hundred and fifty *men*.

27 And of the hundred [24]talents of silver were cast the sockets of the sanctuary, and the sockets of the vail; an °hundred sockets of the hundred [24]talents, a [24]talent for a socket.

28 And of the thousand seven hundred seventy and five *shekels* he made hooks for the pillars, and overlaid their °chapiters, °and filleted them.

29 And the [2]brass of the [24]offering *was* seventy [24]talents, and two thousand and four hundred [24]shekels.

30 And therewith he made the sockets to the °door of the [8]tabernacle of the congregation,

---

7 sides. Heb *ẓēlʻā* = rib, or side of the altar.

8 THE LAVER. (Ex. 30. 18.)

8 lookingglasses = mirrors of polished metal. Cp. 2 Cor. 3. 18.

assembling = doing service, or worshipping according to Egyptian practice. By using these for the laver this practice was abolished. Cp. Num. 4. 23 (same word), and see Luke 2. 37. door = entrance.

tabernacle = tent. Heb. *'ohel*. See Ap. 40.

9-20 THE HANGINGS OF THE COURT.

9 side. Heb. *pē'āh*, region, or quarter.

10 sockets. See note on 27. 10.

fillets = connecting rods.

11 brass. See note on 25. 3.

14 side = shoulder. Heb. *kātheph*.

16 fine twined linen. See note on 35. 23.

20 tabernacle. Heb. *mishkān*. See Ap. 40.

38. 21—39. 31 (*V*, p. 124). THE SERVICE OF THE TABERNACLE (*Alternation*).

V | d | 38. 21. Computation.
    e | 38. 22, 23. Artificers.
d | 38. 24-31. Computation.
    e | 39. 1-31. Garments.

21 counted = accounted.

22 Bezaleel. Cp. 31. 2 and 35. 30—36. 7.

the LORD. Heb. Jehovah. Ap. 4.

23 cunning workman. See note on 26. 1.

24 offering = wave offering. Heb. *t^enuphah*. See 29. 27, and Ap. 43. II. ix.

talents. See Ap. 51. II. vi.

shekel. See Ap. 51. II. v.

25 them that were numbered. The sanctuary was thus made (in part) out of the redemption money.

26 bekah. See Ap. 51. II. i. man = poll.

27 hundred. See Ap. 10.

28 chapiters = capitals.

and filleted them = and united them with connecting rods.

30 door = entrance.

1491 and the brasen altar, and the brasen grate for
1st it, and all the vessels of the altar,
Eth. 31 And the sockets of the court round about, and the sockets of the court gate, and all the
to 1st pins of the [20]tabernacle, and all the pins of
Abib. the court round about.

e (p. 127) **39** And of the blue, and purple, and scarlet, they made cloths of service, to do service in the °holy *place*, and made the holy garments for Aaron; °as °the LORD commanded Moses.

2 And he made the °ephod *of* gold, blue, and purple, and scarlet, and °fine twined linen.

3 And they did beat the gold into thin plates, and cut *it into* °wires, to work *it* in the blue, and in the purple, and in the scarlet, and in the fine linen, *with* °cunning work.

4 They made shoulderpieces for it, to couple *it* together: by the two edges was it coupled together.

5 And the curious °girdle of his ephod, that *was* upon it, °*was* of the same, according to the work thereof; *of* gold, blue, and purple, and scarlet, and fine twined linen; [1]as [1]the LORD commanded Moses.

6 And they wrought onyx stones inclosed in ouches of gold, graven, as signets are graven, with the names of the °children of Israel.

7 And he put them on the shoulders of the ephod, *that they should be* stones for a memorial to the [6]children of Israel; [1]as [1]the LORD commanded Moses.

8 And he made the °breastplate *of* °cunning work, like the work of the ephod; *of* gold, blue, and purple, and scarlet, and fine twined linen.

9 It was foursquare; they made the breastplate double: a °span *was* the length thereof, and a °span the breadth thereof, *being* doubled.

10 And they set in it four rows of stones: *the first* row *was* a sardius, a topaz, and a carbuncle: this *was* the first row.

11 And the second row, an emerald, a sapphire, and a diamond.

12 And the third row, a ligure, an agate, and an amethyst.

13 And the fourth row, a beryl, an onyx, and a jasper: *they were* inclosed in ouches of gold in their inclosings.

14 And the stones *were* according to the names of the [6]children of Israel, twelve, according to their names, *like* the engravings of a signet, every °one with his name, according to the °twelve tribes.

15 And they made upon the breastplate °chains at the ends, *of* wreathen work *of* pure gold.

16 And they made two ouches *of* gold, and two gold rings; and put the two rings in the two ends of the breastplate.

17 And they put the two wreathen chains of gold in the two rings on the ends of the breastplate.

18 And the two ends of the two wreathen chains they fastened in the two ouches, and put them on the shoulderpieces of the ephod, before it.

19 And they made two rings of gold, and put *them* on the two ends of the breastplate, upon the border of it, which *was* on the side of the ephod inward.

20 And they made two *other* golden rings, and put them on the two °sides of the ephod underneath, toward the forepart of it, over against the *other* coupling thereof, above the curious girdle of the ephod.

21 And they did bind the breastplate by his rings unto the rings of the ephod with a lace of blue, that it might be above the curious girdle of the ephod, and that the breastplate might not be loosed from the ephod; °as [1]the LORD commanded Moses.

22 And he made the °robe of the ephod *of* woven work, all *of* blue.

23 And *there was* an hole in the midst of the robe, as the hole of an °habergeon, *with* a band round about the hole, that it should not rend.

24 And they made upon the hems of the robe °pomegranates *of* blue, and purple, and scarlet, *and* °twined *linen*.

25 And they made bells *of* pure gold, and put the bells between the [24]pomegranates upon the hem of the robe, round about between the pomegranates;

26 A bell and a [24]pomegranate, a bell and a pomegranate, round about the hem of the robe to minister *in;* [1]as [1]the LORD commanded Moses.

27 And they made °coats *of* fine linen *of* woven work for Aaron, and for his sons,

28 And a °mitre *of* fine linen, and °goodly bonnets *of* fine linen, and linen breeches *of* fine twined linen,

29 And a girdle *of* fine twined linen, and

---

39. 1 holy. See note on 3. 5.
as = according as. Note this in each of the sevenfold repetition of the words "as the LORD commanded Moses" in this record of the *completion* of the work: and again in the work of the *setting up* of the tabernacle, ch. 40. Thus in 39. 1, 5, 7, 21, 26, 29, and 31; and in 40. 19, 21, 23, 25, 27, 29, and 32, the former is followed by the blessing of Moses, and the latter by the blessing of Jehovah. See the Structure "Q", p. 124.
the LORD. Heb. Jehovah. Ap. 4.
2 ephod. See note on 28. 6.
fine twined linen. See note on 35. 23.
3 wires = threads, or cords. **cunning** = skilful.
5 girdle. See note on 28. 8. **was** = "it [was]".
6 children = sons.
8 breastplate. See 28. 15–21. Always used of the Aaronic breastplate except Lev. 8. 8.
cunning work = work of a skilful deviser. See note on 26. 1.
9 span. Ap. 51. III. ii.
14 one = Heb. *'ish*, man. See Ap. 14.
twelve tribes. The names according to the tribes. On the shoulders according to their births. See Ap. 45.
15 chains. See 28. 22–30.
20 sides. Heb. *kātheph* = shoulders.
21 as, &c. See note on *v.* 1.
22 robe. See 28. 31–35.
23 habergeon = coat of mail. From O. French *haubere* = neck defence.
24 pomegranates. See note on Num. 13. 23.
twined. Some codices, with Sam., Sept., and Syr., read "fine twined linen".
27 coats. See 28. 39–43. **28 mitre** = turban.
goodly bonnets = ornamental tiaras or turban ornaments. See Isa. 61. 10 and Ezek. 24. 17.

1491 blue, and purple, and scarlet, *of* needlework;
[1]as [1]the LORD commanded Moses.
30 And they made the plate of the holy
crown *of* pure gold, and °wrote upon it a
writing, *like to* the engravings of a signet,
°HOLINESS TO [1]THE LORD.
31 And they tied unto it a lace of blue, to
fasten *it* on high upon the [8]mitre; [1]as [1]the
LORD commanded Moses.

32 Thus was all the work of the °tabernacle
of the tent of the congregation finished: °and
the [6]children of Israel did according to all that
[1]the LORD commanded Moses, so did they.
33 °And they brought the [32]tabernacle unto
Moses, the tent, and all his furniture, his
°taches, his boards, his bars, and his pillars,
and his sockets,
34 And the covering of rams' skins dyed
red, and the covering of badgers' skins, and
the vail of the covering,
35 °The ark of the testimony, and the staves
thereof, and the °mercy seat,
36 °The table, °*and* all the vessels thereof,
and the shewbread,
37 °The pure candlestick, °*with* the lamps
thereof, *even with* the lamps to be set in
order, and all the vessels thereof, and the oil
for light,
38 And the golden altar, and the anointing
oil, and the sweet incense, and the hanging
for the °tabernacle °door,
39 °The brasen altar, and his grate of
°brass, °his staves, and all his vessels, the
laver and his foot,
40 °The hangings of the court, °his pillars,
and his sockets, and the hanging for the court
gate, °his cords, and his pins, and all the
°vessels of the service of the [32]tabernacle, for
the tent of the congregation,
41 °The cloths of service to do service in
the holy *place*, and the holy garments for
Aaron the priest, and his sons' garments, to
minister in the priest's office.
42 According to all that [1]the LORD commanded Moses, so the [6]children of Israel made
all the work.
T (p. 124) 43 And Moses did look upon all the work,
and, behold, they had done it [1]as [1]the LORD
had commanded, even so had they done it:
and Moses blessed them.

S f (p. 129) **40** And °the LORD spake unto Moses,
saying,
2 "On °the first day of the °first month
g shalt thou set up the °tabernacle of the °tent
of the congregation.
h 3 And thou shalt put therein the °ark of
the testimony, and °cover the °ark with the
vail.
4 And thou shalt bring in the table, and
°set in order the things that are to be set in
order upon it; and thou shalt bring in the
candlestick, and °light the lamps thereof.
5 And thou shalt set the altar of gold
for the incense before the ark of the testimony, and put the hanging of the °door to
the [2]tabernacle.
6 And thou shalt set the altar of the burnt

30 wrote. See note on 17. 14.
HOLINESS, &c. See on 28. 36-38.
32 tabernacle. Heb. *mishkān*, habitation (Ap. 40).
and the children of Israel did, &c. Read "thus did the children of Israel, according", &c.
33 And. Note the Fig. *Polysyndeton* (Ap. 6) in *vv.* 33-41 emphasising each separate detail, and impressing the fact that nothing was omitted. Thirty-six "ands" in nine verses.
taches = hooks, clasps, or pins, 36. 13.
35 The ark. Some codices, with Sam., Onk., Jon., and Syr., read "And the ark".
mercy seat. See note on 25. 17.
36 The table. Some codices, with Onk., read "And the table".
and. Some codices, with Sam., Onk., and Syr., read "and all".
37 The pure. Some codices, with Jon. and Syr., read "And the pure".
with. Some codices, with Sam., Onk., Jon., and Syr., read "and the lamps".
38 tabernacle. Heb. *'ohel*, tent. Ap. 40.
door = entrance.
39 The. Some codices, with Jon. and Syr., read "And the".
brass. See note on 25. 3.
his. Some codices, with Onk. and Syr., read "and his".
40 The. Some codices, with Sam., Onk., Jon., Syr., and Vulg., read "And the".
his. Some codices, with Sam., Onk., Jon., Syr., and Vulg., read "and his".
vessels = utensils, or furniture.
41 The. Some codices, with Sam., Onk., and Syr., read "And the".

40. 1-33 (*S*, p. 124). **THE TABERNACLE SET UP** (*Extended Alternation*).

S | f | 1, 2-. The date.
  g | -2. The Tabernacle set up.
    h | 3-8. The placing of the furniture.
      i | 9-16. Consecration.
  f | 17-. The date.
  g | -17-19. The Tabernacle set up.
    h | 20-33-. The placing of the furniture.
      i | -33. Completion.

1 the LORD (Heb. Jehovah) **spake.** See note on 6. 10, and cp. note on 3. 7.
2 the first day of the first month. Six events in Scripture on this day. See note on Gen. 8. 13.
first month. On the fourteenth day the first Passover was kept (Num. 9. 1-3). On the *first* day of the *second* month they were numbered (Num. 1. 1, 2): (50 days between Ex. 40. 17 and Num. 10. 11). In the interval comes the book of Leviticus, and Num. chaps. 1. 1-10. 10. On the twentieth day of the second month the Tabernacle was taken down, and the journey began from Sinai to Canaan (Num. 10. 11). See Ap. 50. vii. 3.
tabernacle. = habitation. Heb. *mishkān*, Ap. 40.
tent. Heb. *'ohel.* Ap. 40.
3 ark. See note on Ex. 25. 22.
cover = screen.
ark. Some codices, with Sam. and Jon., read "ark and the mercy seat".
4 set in order: i. e. in two piles, six loaves in each pile, answering to the stones on the shoulders of the High Priest. There was a golden dish at the bottom of each, and another reversed on the top, with a golden bowl of frankincense on the top. Cp. 25. 23-30.
light = set up, or mount.
5 door = entrance.

1491 offering before the [5]door of the [2]tabernacle of the tent of the congregation.

7 And thou shalt set the laver between the [2]tent of the congregation and the altar, and shalt put water therein.

8 And thou shalt set up the court round about, and hang up the hanging at the court gate.

i (p. 129) 9 And thou shalt take the anointing oil, and °anoint the [2]tabernacle, and all that *is* therein, and shalt °hallow it, and all the °vessels thereof: and it shall be °holy.

10 And thou shalt anoint the altar of the burnt offering, and all his vessels, and sanctify the altar: and it shall be an altar °most holy.

11 And thou shalt anoint the laver and his °foot, and sanctify it.

12 And thou shalt bring Aaron and his sons unto the [5]door of the °tabernacle of the congregation, and °wash them °with water.

13 And thou shalt put upon Aaron the holy garments, and °anoint him, and sanctify him; that he may minister unto Me in the priest's office.

14 And thou shalt bring his sons, and °clothe them with coats:

15 And thou shalt anoint them, °as thou didst anoint their father, that they may minister unto Me in the priest's office: for their anointing shall surely be an everlasting priesthood throughout their generations."

16 Thus did Moses: according to all that [1]the LORD commanded him, so did he.

f 17 And it came to pass in the [2]first month
1492 in the second year, on the first *day* of the month, *that* the [2]tabernacle was reared up.

g 18 And Moses reared up the [2]tabernacle, and fastened his sockets, and set up the boards thereof, and put in the bars thereof, and reared up his pillars.

19 And he spread abroad the tent over the [2]tabernacle, and put the covering of the tent above upon it; °as [1]the LORD commanded Moses.

h 20 And he took and put the testimony into the ark, and set the staves on the ark, and put the °mercy seat above upon the ark:

21 And he brought the ark into the [2]tabernacle, and set up the vail of the covering, and covered the ark of the testimony; [19]as [1]the LORD commanded Moses.

22 And he put the table in the tent of the congregation, upon the °side of the [2]tabernacle northward, without the vail.

23 And he set the bread in order upon it before [1]the LORD; [19]as [1]the LORD had commanded Moses.

24 And he put the candlestick in the [2]tent of the congregation, over against the table, on the [22]side of the [2]tabernacle southward.

25 And he lighted the lamps before [1]the LORD; [19]as [1]the LORD commanded Moses.

26 And he put the golden altar in the tent of the congregation before the vail:

27 And he burnt sweet incense thereon; [19]as [1]the LORD commanded Moses.

28 And he set up the hanging *at* the [5]door of the [2]tabernacle.

9 anoint. Cp. 30. 22-29.
hallow . . . holy. See note on "holy", 3. 5.
vessels = furniture.
10 most holy. Heb. holiness of holinesses. Fig. *Polyptōton* (Ap. 6) for emphasis.
11 foot = base.
12 tabernacle = tent. Heb. *'ohel* (Ap. 40).
wash = bathe. Cp. 29. 1-4.
with, or in.
13 anoint him. Cp. 29. 5-7.
14 clothe. Cp. 29. 8, 9.
15 as = according as.
19 as = according as. See note on 39. 1, and note the seven occurrences of the expression "as Jehovah commanded Moses" in this chapter as in chapter 39.
20 mercy seat. See note on 25. 17.
22 side. Heb. *yārēk* = the opposite side.
29 burnt offering. Heb. *'ōlah.* See Ap. 43. II. ii.
31 washed. The ceremonial cleansings or "baptisms" (Heb. 6. 2), always performed by the persons themselves.
33 the work. Some codices, with Sam., Sept., and Vulg., read "all the work".

34, 35 THE APPROBATION AND BLESSING OF JEHOVAH,
Corresponding with that of Moses in 39. 43.
(See the Structure Q on p. 123).

36 when the cloud, &c. This continued till Moses' death, when the ark (which till then was carried in the midst of the host) took its place and went "before them". See Josh. 3. 3-6, 11.
children = sons.
journeys = journeyings. Lit. settings forward.
38 on it: i.e. in the cloud.
house of Israel. See note on 16. 31.

29 And he put the altar of °burnt offering *by* the [5]door of the [2]tabernacle of the tent of the congregation, and offered upon it the °burnt offering and the meat offering; [19]as [1]the LORD commanded Moses.

30 And he set the laver between the tent of the congregation and the altar, and put water there, to wash *withal.*

31 And Moses and Aaron and his sons °washed their hands and their feet thereat:

32 When they went into the tent of the congregation, and when they came near unto the altar, they washed; [19]as [1]the LORD commanded Moses.

33 And he reared up the court round about the [2]tabernacle and the altar, and set up the hanging of the court gate.

So Moses finished °the work. i

34 Then a cloud covered the tent of the congregation, and the glory of [1]the LORD filled the tabernacle. T (p. 124)

35 And Moses was not able to enter into the tent of the congregation, because the cloud abode thereon, and the glory of [1]the LORD filled the [2]tabernacle.

36 And °when the cloud was taken up from over the [2]tabernacle, the °children of Israel went onward in all their °journeys: S (p. 94)

37 But if the cloud were not taken up, then they journeyed not till the day that it was taken up.

38 For the cloud of [1]the LORD *was* upon the tabernacle by day, and fire was °on it by night, in the sight of all the °house of Israel, throughout all their [36]journeys.

LEVITICUS.

THE STRUCTURE OF THE BOOK AS A WHOLE.

(Repeated Alternation and Introversion).

A[1] | 1. 1—7. 38. THE OFFERINGS AND THEIR LAWS.

B[1] | **D** | 8. 1—10. 20. PRIESTHOOD.

| **E** | 11. 1—15 33. CEREMONIAL LAWS (PROMULGATION).

C | 16. 1-34. ISRAEL'S FAST (DAY OF ATONEMENT).

A[2] | 17. 1-16. THE OFFERINGS AND THEIR REQUIREMENTS.

B[2] | *E* | 18. 1—20. 27. CEREMONIAL LAWS (PENALTIES).

| *D* | 21. 1—22. 33. PRIESTHOOD.

C | 23. 1—25. 55. JEHOVAH'S FEASTS.

A[3] | 26. 1—27. 34. THE OFFERERS AND THEIR CHARGES.

THE THIRD BOOK OF °MOSES,

CALLED

°LEVITICUS.

A[1] D 1 °AND °the LORD °called unto Moses, and
(p. 131) °spake unto him °out of the °tabernacle
1490 of the congregation, saying,
2 "Speak unto the °children of Israel, and
°say unto them, 'If any °man of you bring
an °offering unto [1]the LORD, ye shall bring
your °offering of the cattle, *even* of the herd,
and of the flock.

E 3 If his offering *be* a °burnt sacrifice of the
herd, let him offer a °male °without blemish:
he shall offer it of °his own voluntary will at
the door of the [1]tabernacle of the congregation
before [1]the LORD.
4 °And he shall °put his hand upon the
head of the burnt offering; and it shall be
accepted for him to °make atonement for
him.
5 And °he shall kill the bullock before [1]the
LORD: and °the priests, Aaron's sons, shall
bring the blood, and °sprinkle the blood round
about upon the altar that *is by* the °door of
the [1]tabernacle of the congregation.
6 And [5]he shall °flay the burnt offering, and
°cut it into his pieces.
7 And the sons of Aaron the °priest shall
put fire upon the altar, and lay the °wood in
order upon the fire:

TITLE, Moses. See Ap. 2.
Leviticus. From the Sept. and Vulg., because thought to be pertaining to the Levites.
The Heb. name = *vayyikra*, being the first word = "And He called".
Leviticus, therefore, is the Book relating to worship: for only those whom God thus *calls* does He seek to worship Him. John 4. 23, and cp. Ps. 65. 4: "Blessed is the man whom Thou *choosest*, and causest to approach unto Thee, that he may dwell in Thy courts."
All its types relate to *worship*, as those of Exodus relate to Redemption.
The Holy Spirit is not once named, though referred to in all the other books of the Pentateuch, because all here relates to Christ; and it is the Spirit's work to glorify Christ (John 16. 14).
The whole of Lev., and Num. 1-10. 10, come between the first day of the first month and the twentieth day of the second month (cp. Num. 10. 11), on the hypothesis that Israel would forthwith advance and enter the land.

1. 1—7. 38 (A[1], p. 131). **THE OFFERINGS AND THEIR LAWS.**
(*Introversion and Extended Alternation.*)

[For Structure see next page.]

1 AND. This connects Lev. very closely with Ex., as Ex. is linked with Genesis.
the LORD. Heb. Jehovah, Whose glory filled the tabernacle, Ex. 40. 35.
No other book contains so many words of Jehovah: "Jehovah spake", thirty-six times (see note on 5. 14); "I am Jehovah", twenty-one times; "I am Jehovah your God", twenty-one times; "I (Jehovah) am", three times; "I, Jehovah, do", twice. **called.** The last letter of this word (in Heb.) is minuscular, i. e. smaller than the others. This calling is in contrast with the thunders from Sinai. **spake.** See note on 5. 14. **out of the tabernacle of the congregation.** Heb. out of the tent of assembly: Heb. *'ohel.* See Ap. 40, not *mishkān*, therefore before 1491. There are four such calls: (1) from the burning bush (Ex. 3. 4); (2) and (3) from Sinai (Ex. 19. 3, 20); and here. **2 children** = sons. **say.** Cp. note on Jer. 7. 22, 23. **man.** Heb. *'ādām* (Ap. 14), i. e. a descendant of Adam, not the priests. **offering.** Heb. *ḳorbān*, admittance, entrance, or access offering. See Ap. 43. II. i. All the offerings were what God had first given to man; only such can be accepted by Him.

3-17 (E, p. 134). **THE BURNT OFFERING.**

3 Jehovah begins with the burnt offering and ends with the sin offering: we, in our approach, begin with the sin offering and end with the burnt offering. **burnt sacrifice.** Heb. *'olāh.* See Ap. 43. II. ii. **male.** A female permitted in some other offerings, but not here, because of the type. Christ not the sinbearer here, as in ch. 4. **without blemish.** Heb. *tamīm*, said of all sacrifices, and the same of Noah, Gen. 6. 9. **his own voluntary will.** Not the same as a freewill offering. This not a freewill offering. Heb. here = "to be accepted for him", i. e. in his stead. Cp. *v.* 4. Cp. Ex. 28. 38. Lev. 19. 5; 22. 19, 20, 29; 23. 11. There was a double transfer: the unworthiness of the offerer was transferred to the victim; and the acceptableness of the offering was transferred to the offerer. This is confined to the burnt offerings and peace offerings; never with the sin offerings. **4 And.** Note the Fig. *Polysyndeton* (Ap. 6) in *vv.* 4-9. **put.** Heb. lean, place, or press. It could not be done by proxy. This was all that the sinner could do. It was for God to accept. **make atonement.** Heb. *kāphar*, to cover the sinner and his sin, so that neither is seen. See note on Ex. 29. 33. No such thing as progress in justification. **5 he.** The sacrificer himself killed: the priest received the blood. **the priests, Aaron's sons.** Heb. = the sons of Aaron, the priests. Occurs seven times: Lev. 1. 5, 8, 11; 2. 2; 3. 2. Num. 10. 8. Josh. 21. 19. **sprinkle** = dash. Heb. throw or jerk. **door** = entrance. **6 flay** = have it flayed. Skin not offered with burnt offering, only with the sin offering. **cut it . . . pieces.** To show that all was without blemish. **7 priest.** Some codices, with Sam., Onk., Sept., and Syr., read plural, "priests". **wood** = logs. No other fuel might be used.

1490 8 And [5]the priests, Aaron's sons, shall lay
the parts, the head, and the fat, °in order
upon the wood that *is* on the fire which *is*
upon the altar:
9 But his inwards and his legs shall °he
°wash in water: and the priest shall °burn
all on the altar, *to be* a [3]burnt sacrifice, an
°offering made by fire, of a °sweet savour
unto [1]the LORD.

10 And if his [2]offering *be* of the flocks,
namely, of the sheep, or of the goats, for a
[3]burnt sacrifice; he shall bring it a male
without blemish.
11 And [5]he shall kill it on the side of the
altar northward before [1]the LORD: and [5]the
priests, Aaron's sons, shall [5]sprinkle his blood
round about upon the altar.
12 And [5]he shall [6]cut it into his pieces, with
his head and his fat: and the priest shall lay
them in order on the wood that *is* on the fire
which *is* upon the altar:
13 But [5]he shall [9]wash the inwards and the
legs with water: and the priest shall bring *it*
all, and [9]burn *it* upon the altar: it *is* a [3]burnt
sacrifice, an [9]offering made by fire, of a [9]sweet
savour unto [1]the LORD.

14 And if the [3]burnt sacrifice for his offering to [1]the LORD *be* of fowls, then he shall
bring his [2]offering of turtledoves, or of young
pigeons.
15 And °the priest shall bring it unto the
altar, and wring off his head, and burn *it* on
the altar; and the blood thereof shall be
wrung out at the side of the altar:
16 And he shall pluck away his crop with
his °feathers, and cast it beside the altar on
the east part, by the place of the ashes:
17 And he shall cleave it with the wings
thereof, *but* shall not divide *it* asunder: and
the priest shall [9]burn it upon the altar, upon
the wood that *is* upon the fire: it *is* a [3]burnt
sacrifice, an [9]offering made by fire, of a [9]sweet
savour unto [1]the LORD.

F (p. 134) 2 And when °any will °offer °a °meat
offering unto °the LORD, °his offering
shall be *of* °fine flour; and he shall pour °oil
upon it, and put °frankincense thereon:
2 And he shall bring it to °Aaron's sons the
priests: and he shall take thereout his handful of the flour thereof, and of the oil thereof,
with all the frankincense thereof; and the
priest shall °burn the °memorial of it upon
the altar, *to be* an °offering made by fire, of
a °sweet savour unto [1]the LORD:
3 And the remnant of the [1]meat offering
shall be Aaron's and his sons': *it is* a thing
°most holy of the [2]offerings of [1]the LORD
made by fire.

4 And if thou bring an °oblation of a [1]meat
offering °baken in the oven, *it shall be* unleavened cakes of [1]fine flour mingled with oil,
or unleavened wafers anointed with oil.
5 And if thy [4]oblation *be* a [1]meat offering
baken in a °pan, it shall be *of* [1]fine flour unleavened, mingled with oil.
6 Thou shalt part it in pieces, and pour oil
thereon: it *is* a [1]meat offering.
7 And if thy [4]oblation *be* a [1]meat offering
baken in the fryingpan, it shall be made *of*
[1]fine flour with oil.
8 And thou shalt bring the [1]meat offering
that is made of these things unto [1]the LORD:
and when it is presented unto the priest, he
shall bring it unto the altar.
9 And the priest shall take from the [1]meat

1. 1—7. 38 (A[1], p. 131). THE OFFERINGS AND THEIR LAWS.
(*Introversion and Extended Alternation.*)

A[1] | D | 1. 1, 2. Introduction (General).
x | E | 1. 3-17. Burnt Offerings.
F | 2. 1-16. Meal Offerings.
G | a | 3 1-17. Peace Offerings.
b | 4. 1—6. 7. Sin Offerings.
(The Offerings.)

x | *E* | 6. 8-13. Burnt Offerings.
F | 6. 14-23. Meal Offerings.
G | *b* | 6. 24—7. 10. Sin Offerings.
a | 7. 11-34. Peace Offerings.
(The *Law* of the Offerings.)
D | 7. 35-38. Conclusion (Particular).

8 in order. Because with the future Antitype all was to be in order.
9 he. Sam., Sept., and Vulg. read "they".
wash. To render the sacrifice like the Antitype. Cp. Eph. 5. 26, all in order of God's word.
burn. Heb. *ḳāṭar.* See Ap. 43. I. vii.
offering. Heb. *'ishsheh.* Ap. 43. II. xi.
sweet savour=a savour of satisfaction. Cp. Gen. 8. 21.
15 the priest. To make up for the humble offering, the priest did this instead of the offerer.
16 feathers, or filth.

2. 1-16 (F). THE MEAL OFFERING.

1 any=soul. Heb. *nephesh,* as in 4. 2. See Ap. 13.
offer. Heb. *ḳārab.* See Ap. 43. I. i.
a=an approach offering of. Heb. *ḳorbān.* See Ap. 43. II. i.
meat offering. Better, "an oblation of a meal offering". Heb. *minchah.* See Ap. 43. II. iii.
the LORD. Heb. Jehovah. Ap. 4.
his offering. Heb. his *ḳorbān.* See Ap. 43. II. i.
fine flour. Not merely ground, but perfect and ready, no unevenness. So with the life of the Antitype, "the Man Christ Jesus". Flour is to the wheat what blood is to the body; and *pneuma* is to the resurrection body.
oil. Flour mixed with oil, and then oil poured on it. So Christ's life permeated and actuated by the Holy Spirit.
frankincense. This ascended to God as a sweet savour.
2 Aaron's sons. See on 1. 5.
burn. Heb. *ḳāṭar.* See Ap. 43. I. vii.
memorial: i. e. to remind. Cp. Ps. 20. 3. Acts 10. 4.
offering. Heb. *'ishsheh.* Ap. 43. II. xi.
sweet savour. See note on 1. 9.
3 most holy. Two classes of seven holy things: three holy, four most holy. (1) Holy=thank offerings, 23. 20. Num. 6. 20. Firstborn, Num. 18. 17. Firstfruits, 2. 12. (2) The most holy=The incense, Ex. 30. 36. Shewbread, 24. 9. Sin and trespass offering, 6. 25-29; 7. 1, 6; 14. 13, &c. And the Meal offering, here.
4 oblation=present. Heb. *ḳorbān.* See Ap. 43. II. i. The only word rendered oblation, except Isa. 40. 20. Ezek. 44. 30; 45. 1, 6, 7, 13, 16; 48. 9, 10, 12, 18, 20, 21, where it is Heb. *t^erūmah* (heave offering). See Ap. 43. II. viii. and Dan. 2. 46; 9. 21, 27, where it is Heb. *minchah.* Ap. 43. II. iii.
baken. Type of the sufferings and trials of the Antitype, "tried as by fire".
5 pan=a flat plate or griddle. Cp. Ezek. 4. 3.

1490 offering a memorial thereof, and shall [2]burn *it* upon the altar: *it is* an [2]offering made by fire, of a [2]sweet savour unto [1]the LORD.

10 And that which is left of the [1]meat offering *shall be* Aaron's and his sons': *it is* a thing most holy of the [2]offerings of [1]the LORD made by fire.

11 No meat offering, which ye shall bring unto [1]the LORD, shall be made with °leaven: for ye shall burn no leaven, nor any °honey, in any [2]offering of [1]the LORD made by fire.

12 As for the [4]oblation of the firstfruits, ye shall [1]offer them unto [1]the LORD: but they shall not be °burnt on the altar for a sweet savour.

13 And every [4]oblation of thy [1]meat offering shalt thou season with °salt; neither shalt thou suffer the °salt of the covenant of thy °God to be lacking from thy [1]meat offering: with all thine °offerings thou shalt [1]offer salt.

14 And if thou [1]offer a [1]meat offering of thy firstfruits unto [1]the LORD, thou shalt offer for the [1]meat offering of thy firstfruits green ears of corn dried by the fire, *even* corn °beaten out of full ears.

15 And thou shalt put [1]oil upon it, and lay frankincense thereon: it *is* a [1]meat offering.

16 And the priest shall [2]burn the memorial of it, *part* of the [14]beaten corn thereof, and *part* of the oil thereof, with all the frankincense thereof: *it is* an [2]offering made by fire unto [1]the LORD.

G a (p. 134) **3** And if his °oblation *be* a °sacrifice of °peace offering, if he °offer *it* of the herd; whether *it be* a male or °female, he shall offer it without blemish before °the LORD.

2 And he shall lay his hand upon the head of his °offering, and kill it *at* the °door of the °tabernacle of the congregation: and °Aaron's sons the priests shall sprinkle the blood upon the altar round about.

3 And °he shall [1]offer of the [1]sacrifice of the [1]peace offering an °offering made by fire unto [1]the LORD; the fat that covereth the inwards, and all the fat that *is* upon the inwards,

4 And the two kidneys, and the fat that *is* on them, which *is* by the flanks, and the caul above the liver, with the kidneys, it shall he take away.

5 And Aaron's sons shall °burn it on the altar upon the burnt sacrifice, which *is* upon the wood that *is* on the fire: *it is* an [2]offering made by fire, of a °sweet savour unto [1]the LORD.

6 And if his °offering for a °sacrifice of °peace offering unto [1]the LORD *be* of the flock; male or female, he shall offer it without blemish.

7 If he °offer a °lamb for his [6]offering, then shall he °offer it before [1]the LORD.

8 And he shall lay his hand upon the head of his offering, and kill it before the [2]tabernacle of the congregation: and Aaron's sons shall sprinkle the blood thereof round about upon the altar.

11 leaven. See Ap. 38.

honey. Leaven is fermentation, and honey or any sweet liquor is the cause of it. These two things forbidden because there was no error or corruption in the Antitype. All was Divine perfection. Nothing therefore which answers to leaven may be in our sacrifice of praise now.

12 burnt. Heb. *'ālah* = ascend. See Ap. 43. I. vi.

13 salt. First occurrence. Salt was, and is, the great antiseptic, preventing fermentation. As leaven and honey were forbidden in sacrifices, so salt is prescribed, because, when partaken of by the two parties, it made the covenant inviolable.

salt of the covenant. See note on Num. 18. 19. 2 Chron. 13. 5. Salt denotes an indissoluble alliance. In Ezra 4. 14 = obligations of loyalty.

God. Heb. Elohim. Ap. 4.

offerings. Heb. *minchah*. Ap. 43. II. ii.

14 beaten. Same type as baken, *v.* 4.

3. 1-17 (G, a). THE PEACE OFFERING.

1 oblation. Heb. *ḳorbān*. See on 2. 4 and Ap. 43. II. i.

sacrifice. Heb. *zebach*. See Ap. 43. II. xii.

peace offering. Heb. *shelem*. Ap. 43. II. iv.

offer it = bring near. Heb. *ḳārab*. Ap. 43. I. i.

female. The burnt offering must be a male. 1. 3, 10.

the LORD. Heb. Jehovah. Ap. 4.

2 offering. Heb. *ḳorbān*. Ap. 43. II. i.

door = entrance.

tabernacle of the congregation = tent (*'ohel*) of meeting or assembly. Ap. 40.

Aaron's sons. See note on 1. 5.

3 he = the offerer, not the priest.

offering. Heb. *'ishsheh*. Ap. 43. II. xi.

5 burn = burn as incense. Heb. *ḳāṭar*. Ap. 43. I. vii.

sweet savour = savour of satisfaction. See note on Gen. 8. 21.

6 offering. Heb. *ḳorbān*. Ap. 43. II. i.

sacrifice. Heb. *zebach*. Ap. 43. II. xii.

peace offering. Heb. *shelem*. Ap. 43. II. iv.

7 offer = bring. Heb. *ḳārab*. Ap. 43. I. i.

lamb: better "sheep", as in 1. 10; 7. 23; 22. 19, 27, &c.

9 offering made by fire. Heb. *'isseh*. Ap. 43. II. xi.

whole rump = the fat tail entire. 7. 3; 8. 25; 9. 19. Ex. 29. 22.

11 food. Heb. "bread", put by Fig. *Synecdoche* (of Species), Ap. 6, for food in general. Cp. 21. 6, 8, 17, 21, 22. Num. 28. 2.

9 And he shall [7]offer of the sacrifice of the [6]peace offering an °offering made by fire unto [1]the LORD; the fat thereof, *and* the °whole rump, it shall he take off hard by the backbone; and the fat that covereth the inwards, and all the fat that *is* upon the inwards,

10 And the two kidneys, and the fat that *is* upon them, which *is* by the flanks, and the caul above the liver, with the kidneys, it shall he take away.

11 And the priest shall [5]burn it upon the altar: *it is* the °food of the [9]offering made by fire unto [1]the LORD.

12 And if his [6]offering *be* a goat, then he shall [7]offer it before [1]the LORD.

13 And he shall lay his hand upon the head of it, and kill it before the [8]tabernacle of the congregation: and the sons of Aaron shall sprinkle the blood thereof upon the altar round about.

14 And he shall [7]offer thereof his [6]offering, *even* an [9]offering made by fire unto [1]the

1490 LORD; the fat that covereth the inwards, and all the fat that *is* upon the inwards,

15 And the two kidneys, and the fat that *is* upon them, which *is* by the flanks, and the caul above the liver, with the kidneys, it shall he take away.

16 And the priest shall [11]burn them upon the altar: *it is* the food of the [9]offering made by fire for a °sweet savour: all the fat *is* [1]the LORD'S.

17 *It shall be* °a perpetual statute for your generations throughout all your dwellings, that ye eat neither fat nor blood.'"

G b (p. 134) 4 And °the LORD °spake unto Moses, saying,

2 "Speak unto the °children of Israel, saying, 'If a °soul shall °sin through °ignorance against any of the commandments of [1]the LORD *concerning* °*things* which ought not to be done, and shall do against any of them:

3 If °the priest that is anointed °do sin according to °the sin of the people; then let him bring for °his sin, which he hath °sinned, a young bullock without blemish unto [1]the LORD for a °sin offering.

4 And he shall bring the bullock unto the °door of the °tabernacle of the congregation before [1]the LORD; and shall lay his hand upon the bullock's head, and kill the bullock before [1]the LORD.

5 And the [3]priest that is anointed shall take of the bullock's blood, and bring it to the [4]tabernacle of the congregation:

6 And the priest shall dip his finger in the blood, and °sprinkle of the blood °seven times before [1]the LORD, °before the °vail of the sanctuary.

7 And the priest shall put *some* of the blood upon the horns of the altar of sweet incense °before [1]the LORD, which *is* in the [4]tabernacle of the congregation; and shall pour °all the blood of the bullock at the bottom of the altar of the burnt offering, which *is at* the [4]door of the [4]tabernacle of the congregation.

8 And he shall take off from it all the °fat of the bullock for the sin offering; the fat that covereth the inwards, and all the fat that *is* upon the inwards,

9 And the two kidneys, and the fat that *is* upon them, which *is* by the flanks, and the °caul above the liver, with the kidneys, it shall he take away,

10 °As it was taken off from the bullock of the sacrifice of peace offerings: and the priest shall °burn them upon the altar of the burnt offering.

11 And the skin of the bullock, and all his flesh, with his head, and with his legs, and his inwards, and his dung,

12 Even the whole bullock shall °he carry forth °without the camp unto a clean place, where the ashes are poured out, and °burn him on the °wood with fire: where the ashes are poured out shall he be [10]burnt.

13 And if the whole °congregation of Israel °sin through ignorance, and the thing be hid from the eyes of the assembly, and they have done °*somewhat against* any of the commandments of [1]the LORD °*concerning things* which should not be done, and are guilty;

14 When the °sin, which they have °sinned against it, is known, then the congregation shall °offer a young bullock °for the sin, and bring him before the [4]tabernacle of the congregation.

15 And the elders of the congregation shall lay their hands upon the head of the bullock

16 sweet savour. A savour of satisfaction. Some codices, with Sam. and Sept., add "unto Jehovah".

17 a perpetual statute, &c. Heb. "a statute for ever, throughout your generations, in all your dwellings". This important phrase occurs only four times, Lev. 3. 17; 23. 14, 21 (inverted), 31.

4. 1—6. 7 (G b, p. 134). THE SIN AND TRESPASS OFFERINGS.

1 the LORD. Heb. Jehovah. Ap. 4.

spake. Introducing new class: *non savour* offerings. The sweet savour offerings introduced by the word "called". See note on 5. 14.

2 children. Heb. sons.

soul. Heb. *nephesh.* See Ap. 13. Not as in the burnt offering; no voluntary offering here.

sin. Heb. *chāṭ'ā.* Ap. 44. i.

ignorance. If man cannot *know* what sin is, how can he know how to put it away? If he know not his own sin, how can he know or put away that of others?

3 the priest that is anointed. This phrase is confined to Lev. (4. 3, 5, 16; 6. 22) four times. In other portions of the Pentateuch it is "high priest" or "great priest" (Lev. 21. 10. Num. 35. 25, 28, and in Josh. 20. 6), after this it is "chief priest" (2 Kings 25. 18. 2 Chron. 19. 11; 26. 20; 31. 10. Ezra 7. 5. Hag. and Zech.)

do sin. Heb. *chāṭ'ā.* Ap. 44. i.

the sin. Heb. *'āshām.* See Ap. 44. ii.

his sin . . . sinned. Heb. *chāṭ'ā.* Ap. 44. i.

sin offering. Heb. *chāṭ'ā.* See Ap. 43. II. v. "Offering" not in Heb.; rightly supplied here, as it should be in Gen. 4. 7.

4 door=entrance.

tabernacle of the congregation=tent of assembly.

6 sprinkle. Heb. throw, or splash.

seven times. The number of spiritual perfection. See Ap. 10.

before. Not in the Hebrew. On vail or floor. Explanatory of previous sentence. Or, may=before the LORD, by Fig. *Metonymy* (Ap. 6.)

vail. Type of the perfect humanity of Christ. No avail for purposes of atonement without blood. We are saved by His death, not by His life (Eph. 2. 13).

7 before. A various reading called *Sevir* has "which is before". See Ap. 34.

all=all the remaining blood.

8 fat=the best or choicest part, 3. 3.

9 caul, or the network.

10 As=according as.

burn. Heb. *sāraph.* See Ap. 43. I. viii; and note that it is not the word used for burning incense, which is *kāṭar.* Ap. 43. I. vii.

12 he carry forth=cause to be carried. Cp. *v.* 14.

without the camp. Cp. Heb. 13. 11, 12. See note on Ex. 29. 14.

wood=logs. Any wood allowed, such as straw or stubble. Not so with the other offerings.

13 congregation=assembly. Not the same word as in *v.* 14.

sin. Heb. *shāgāh.* See Ap. 44. xii. See 1 Sam. 14. 32.

somewhat, &c., and **concerning, &c.** These two *Ellipses* rightly supplied. See Ap. 6.

14 sin . . . sinned. Heb. *chāṭ'ā.* Ap. 44. i.

offer=cause to be offered. Cp. *v.* 12.

for the sin=as a sin offering. See Ap. 43. II. v.

1490 before [1] the LORD: and the bullock shall be killed before [1] the LORD.

16 And the [3] priest that is anointed shall bring of the bullock's blood to the [14] tabernacle of the congregation:

17 And the priest shall dip his finger *in some* of the blood, and sprinkle ° *it* seven times before [1] the LORD, *even* ° before the vail.

18 And he shall put *some* of the blood upon the horns of the altar which *is* before [1] the LORD, that *is* in the [14] tabernacle of the congregation, and shall pour out all the blood at the bottom of the altar of the burnt offering, which *is at* the ° door of the [14] tabernacle of the congregation.

19 And he shall take all his fat from him, and ° burn *it* upon the altar.

20 And he shall do with the bullock ° as he did with the bullock for a [3] sin offering, so shall he do with this: and the priest shall ° make an atonement for them, and it shall be forgiven them.

21 And he shall carry forth the bullock without the camp, and burn him ° as he burned the first bullock: it *is* a [3] sin offering for the congregation.

22 When a ° ruler hath ° sinned, and done *somewhat* through ignorance *against* any of the commandments of [1] the LORD his ° God *concerning things* which should not be done, and is ° guilty;

23 Or if his ° sin, wherein he hath [22] sinned, come to his knowledge; he shall bring his offering, a kid of the goats, a ° male without blemish:

24 And he shall lay his hand upon the head of the goat, and kill it in the place where they kill the burnt offering before [1] the LORD: it *is* a [3] sin offering.

25 And the priest shall take of the blood of the [3] sin offering with his finger, and put *it* upon the horns of the altar of burnt offering, and shall pour out his blood at the bottom of the altar of burnt offering.

26 And he shall burn all his fat upon the altar, as the fat of the sacrifice of peace offerings: and the priest shall [20] make an atonement for him as concerning his [23] sin, and it shall be forgiven him.

27 And if any ° one of the common People [23] sin through ignorance, while he doeth *somewhat against* any of the commandments of [1] the LORD *concerning things* which ought not to be done, and ° be guilty;

28 Or if his [23] sin, which he hath [22] sinned, come to his knowledge: then he shall bring his offering, a kid of the goats, a ° female without blemish, for his [23] sin which he hath sinned.

29 And he shall lay his hand upon the head of the [3] sin offering, and slay the [3] sin offering ° in the place of the burnt offering.

30 And the priest shall take of the blood thereof with his finger, and put *it* upon the horns of the altar of burnt offering, and shall pour out all the blood thereof at the bottom of the altar.

31 And he shall take away all the fat thereof, as the fat is taken away from off the sacrifice of peace offerings; and the priest shall [19] burn *it* upon the altar for a ° sweet savour unto [1] the LORD; and the priest shall [20] make an atonement for him, and it shall be forgiven him.

32 And if he bring ° a lamb for a [23] sin ° offering, he shall bring it a female without blemish.

33 And he shall lay his hand upon the head of the [3] sin offering, and slay it for a [3] sin offering in the place where they kill the burnt offering.

34 And the priest shall take ° of the blood of the [3] sin offering with his finger, and put *it* upon the horns of the altar of burnt offering, and shall pour out all the blood thereof at the bottom of the altar:

35 And he shall take away all the fat thereof, as the fat of the lamb is taken away from the ° sacrifice of the peace offerings; and the priest shall burn them upon the altar, ° according to the ° offerings made by fire unto [1] the LORD: and the priest shall [20] make an atonement for his [32] sin that he hath committed, and it shall be forgiven him.

---

17 it. Read "the blood", with Sam., as in *v.* 6.
before the vail. See note on 4. 6.
18 door=entrance.
19 burn. Heb. *ḳāṭar*, to burn as incense, not as in *v.* 12. See Ap. 43. I. vii.
20 as=according as.
make an atonement. See note on 1. 4 and Ex. 29. 33.
21 as he burned=according as he burned. Heb. *sāraph*, as in *v.* 12. See Ap. 43. I. vii.
22 ruler. Heb. word is used of a king (1 Kings 11. 34. Ezek. 34. 24; 46. 2), the head of a tribe (Num. 1. 16, 46; 34. 18), but as the words "his God" are used here, and are absent (in *vv.* 2, 13, 27), it denotes one whom God appoints and to whom the ruler is responsible.
sinned. Heb. *chāt'ā.* See Ap. 44. i.
God. Heb. Elohim. Ap. 4.
guilty=should become aware of his inadvertences.
23 sin. Heb. *chāṭ'ā.* Ap. 44. i.
male: for ruler, female for one of the people, *v.* 28. Cp. 5. 13.
27 one=soul. Heb. *nephesh.* See Ap. 13.
be guilty=acknowledges his guilt, as in *v.* 22.
28 female for one of the People, male for "ruler", *v.* 22. Cp. 5. 13.
29 in the place: i.e. where the burnt offering is wont to be slain.
31 sweet savour. This is added here because of the burning of the fat. It is not said of the sin offering of the high priest, the ruler, or the congregation (cp. *vv.* 10, 19, 26), though used in the burnt offerings (1. 9, 13), and peace offerings (3. 5, 16). The sweet savour here, in this connection, exalts the offering of the humblest person.
32 a lamb = a sheep, cp. 3. 7. Ritual same as the goat, but treated separately because of the fat tail.
offering. Heb. *ḳorbān.* Ap. 43. II. i. Lit. "an offering for his sin [offering]".
34 of the blood of the sin offering. A reading of the Severus Codex is "from its blood", as in *v.* 30.
35 sacrifice. Heb. *zebach.* Ap. 43. I. iv.
according to=upon.
offerings made by fire. Heb. *'ishsheh.* Ap. 43. II. xi.

1490 **5** And if a °soul °sin, °and hear the voice of °swearing, and °*is* a witness, whether he hath seen or known *of it;* if he do not utter *it*, then he shall bear his °iniquity.

2 Or if a [1]soul touch any unclean thing, whether *it be* a carcase of an unclean beast, or a carcase of unclean cattle, or the carcase of unclean creeping things, and *if* it °be hidden from him; he also shall be unclean, and guilty.

3 Or if he touch the uncleanness of °man, whatsoever uncleanness *it be* that a man shall be defiled withal, and it [2]be hid from him; when he knoweth *of it,* then he shall be guilty.

4 Or if a [1]soul swear, °pronouncing with *his* lips to do °evil, or to do °good, whatsoever *it be* that a [3]man shall pronounce with an oath, and it be [2]hid from him; when he knoweth *of it,* then he shall be guilty in one of these.

5 And it shall be, when he shall be guilty in one of these *things,* that he shall confess that he hath °sinned in that *thing:*

6 And he shall bring °his trespass offering unto °the LORD for his °sin which he hath [5]sinned, a female from the flock, a lamb or a kid of the goats, for a sin offering; and the priest shall °make an atonement for him concerning his °sin.

7 And if he be not able to bring a lamb, then he shall bring for his °trespass, which he hath committed, two turtledoves, or two young pigeons, unto [6]the LORD; one for a sin offering, and the other for a burnt offering.

8 And he shall bring them unto the priest, who shall offer *that* which *is* for the sin offering first, and wring off his head from his neck, but shall not divide *it* asunder:

9 And he shall sprinkle of the blood of the sin offering upon the side of the altar; and the rest of the blood shall be wrung out at the bottom of the altar: it *is* a sin offering.

10 And he shall offer the second *for* a burnt offering, according to the °manner: and the priest shall make an atonement for him for his [6]sin which he hath sinned, and it shall be forgiven him.

11 But if he be not able to bring two turtledoves, or two young pigeons, then he that [5]sinned shall bring for his °offering the tenth part of an ephah of fine flour for a sin offering; he shall put no oil upon it, neither shall he put *any* frankincense thereon: for it *is* a °sin offering.

12 Then shall he bring it to the priest, and the priest shall take his handful of it, *even* °a memorial thereof, and °burn *it* on the altar, °according to the °offerings made by fire unto [6]the LORD: it *is* a sin offering.

13 And the priest shall make an atonement for him as touching his [6]sin that he hath [5]sinned in °one of these, and it shall be forgiven him: °and *the remnant* shall be the priest's, as a meat offering.'"

14 And [6]the LORD °spake unto Moses, saying,

15 "If a [1]soul commit a °trespass, and [5]sin through ignorance, in the °holy things of [6]the LORD; then he shall bring °for his trespass unto [6]the LORD a ram without blemish out of the flocks, with thy °estimation by

5. 1 soul = a person. Heb. *nephesh*. Ap. 13.
sin. Heb. *chāṭ'ā*. Ap. 44. i.
and hear = because he heard.
swearing = adjuration.
is = "he [is]".
iniquity = perverseness. Heb. *'āvāh*. Ap. 44. iv. Put here by Fig. *Metonymy* (of Cause) for the punishment due to it. Ap. 6.

2 be hidden: i. e. if he forget his uncleanness. This clause "and if", &c., is omitted in the Sept. and included in *v.* 3.

3 man. Heb. *'ādām*. See Ap. 14.

4 pronouncing with his lips = speaking heedlessly.
evil. Heb. *rā'a'*. Ap. 44. viii.
evil . . . good. Fig. *Synecdoche* (of the Whole), to include all human actions. Cp. Gen. 24. 50; 31. 29. Num. 24. 13.

5 sinned. Heb. *chāṭ'ā*. Ap. 44. i.

6 his trespass offering = as his trespass offering. Heb. *'āshām*. Ap. 43. II. vi.
the LORD. Heb. Jehovah. Ap. 4.
sin. Heb. *chāṭ'ā*. Ap. 44. i.
make an atonement. See note on Ex. 26. 33.

7 trespass. Heb. *'āshām*. Ap. 44. ii.

10 manner. See note on 1. 14, &c.

11 offering. Heb. *ḳorbān*. Ap. 43. II. i. For the poor only a little flour. Cp. 4. 23 and 28. All equally forgiven. Cp. 4. 26, 31 and 5. 13.
sin offering: and not a *minchah*, 2. 11.

12 a memorial thereof = a memorial portion.
burn = burn as incense. Heb. *ḳāṭar*. Ap. 43. I. vii.
according to = upon.
offerings made by fire. Heb. *'ishsheh*. Ap. 43. II. xi.

13 one of these. Specified in *vv.* 1–4 above. Cp. *v.* 5.
and the remnant: better "and it shall belong to the priest".

14 spake. This formula denotes another communication made at a different time, and gives a further development of the laws of the trespass offering.
Note that in this book Jehovah "spake" at thirty-five "sundry times", and in ten "divers manners" (see Ap. 10):—

(1) To Moses alone (5. 14; 6. 1, 19; 8. 1; 14. 1; 22. 26; 23. 26).
(2) To Moses, to speak to Aaron alone (16. 1).
(3) To Moses, to speak to "Aaron and his sons" (6. 8, 24; 22. 1).
(4) To Moses, to speak to "the priests, the sons of Aaron" (21. 1).
(5) To Moses, to speak to "Aaron and his sons, and to all the children of Israel" (17. 1; 21. 16 (cp. *v.* 24); 22. 17).
(6) To Moses, to speak to "the children of Israel" (1. 1; 4. 1; 7. 22, 28; 12. 1; 18. 1; 20. 1; 23. 1, 9, 23; 24. 1, 13; 25. 1; 27. 1).
(7) To Moses, to speak "to all the congregation of the children of Israel" (19. 1).
(8) To Moses and Aaron conjointly (13. 1; 14. 33).
(9) To Moses and Aaron, to speak to "the children of Israel" (11. 1; 15. 1).
(10) To Aaron alone (10. 8).

The reasons for these distinctions will be seen from the respective contexts.

15 trespass. Heb. *mā'al*, to act covertly; to be faithless, especially in covenant matters, either with God (Lev. 26. 40. Num. 31. 16. Deut. 32. 51, &c.) or between husband and wife (Num. 5. 12, 27). Not the same word as in *vv.* 6, 7, 15, 16, and below in this verse.
holy things, &c., such as firstfruits, firstborn, &c. Ex. 28. 38. See note on Ex. 3. 5.
estimation = valuation. Made here by Moses, transferred by him to the priests. See 27. 8, 12. Num. 18. 16.

1490 °shekels of silver, after the °shekel of the sanctuary, [15]for a trespass offering:

16 And he shall make amends for the °harm that he hath done in the holy thing, and shall °add the fifth part thereto, and give it unto the priest: and the priest shall [6]make an atonement for him with the ram of the trespass offering, and it shall be forgiven him.

17 And if a [1]soul [1]sin, and commit °any of these things which are forbidden to be done by the commandments of [6]the LORD; though he °wist *it* not, yet is he guilty, and shall bear his °iniquity.

18 And he shall bring a ram without blemish out of the flock, with thy [15]estimation, for a trespass offering, unto the priest: and the priest shall [6]make an atonement for him concerning his ignorance wherein he °erred and [17]wist *it* not, and it shall be forgiven him.

19 It *is* a [6]trespass offering: he hath certainly °trespassed against [6]the LORD."

6 And °the LORD °spake unto Moses, saying,

2 "If a °soul °sin, and commit a °trespass against [1]the LORD, and lie unto his neighbour in that which was °delivered him to keep, or °in fellowship, or in a thing taken away by violence, or hath deceived his neighbour;

3 Or have found that which was lost, and lieth concerning it, and sweareth falsely; in any of all these that a °man doeth, sinning therein:

4 Then it shall be, because he hath [17]sinned, and is guilty, that he shall restore that which he took violently away, or the thing which he hath deceitfully gotten, or that which was [2]delivered him to keep, or the lost thing which he found,

5 Or all that about which he hath sworn falsely; he shall even restore it in the principal, and shall °add the °fifth part more thereto, *and* give it unto him to whom it appertaineth, °in the day of his trespass offering.

6 And he shall bring his trespass offering unto [1]the LORD, a ram without blemish out of the flock, with thy °estimation, for a trespass offering, unto the priest:

7 And the priest shall make an atonement for him before [1]the LORD: and it shall be forgiven him for any thing of all that he hath done in trespassing therein."

x E (p. 134) 8 And [1]the LORD [1]spake unto Moses, saying,

9 "Command Aaron and his sons, saying, 'This *is* the law of the burnt offering: It *is* the burnt offering, because of the °burning upon the altar all night unto the morning, and the fire of the altar shall be °burning in it.

10 And the priest shall put on his °linen garment, and his linen breeches shall he put upon his flesh, and take up the ashes which the fire hath consumed °with the burnt offering on the altar, and he shall put them beside the altar.

11 And he shall put off his garments, and put on other garments, and carry forth the ashes without the camp unto a clean place.

12 And the fire upon the altar shall be [9]burning in it; it shall not be put out: and the priest shall °burn wood on it °every morning, and lay the burnt offering in order upon it; and he shall °burn thereon the fat of the peace offerings.

13 °The fire shall ever be [9]burning upon the altar; it shall never go out.

14 And this *is* °the law of the meat offering: the sons of Aaron shall offer it before [1]the LORD, before the altar. F

---

shekels. See Ap. 51. II.

16 harm that he hath done. Heb. *chāṭā'*. Ap. 44. i.

add. In trespass in holy things sacrifice comes first (5. 15) and addition afterwards. In human affairs the addition comes first (6. 5) and sacrifice follows (6. 7).

17 any = any one of these things specified in *v.* 15.

wist it not = knew it not. This effectually disposes of the fallacy that it is only *sincerity* that matters. Note the repetition of the words in *vv.* 17–19 to emphasise this.

iniquity. Heb. *'āvāh*. Ap. 44. iv.

18 erred. Heb. *shāgag*. Ap. 44. xii.

19 trespassed. Heb. *'āshām*. Ap. 44. ii. Cp. *v.* 17.

6. 1 the LORD. Heb. Jehovah. Ap. 4.

spake. Cp. 5. 14. 6. 1–7 belongs to ch. 5, according to the Structure (p. 134). See note on 5. 14.

2 soul = person. Heb. *nephesh* (Ap. 13).

sin. Heb. *chāṭā'*. Ap. 44. i.

trespass. Heb. *mā'al*. Ap. 44. xi. All sin is viewed as "against Jehovah". Cp. Ps. 51. 4.

delivered him to keep = a deposit. Otherwise treasure was generally hidden in the ground. Isa. 45. 3. Prov. 2. 4. Job. 3. 21.

in fellowship = in pledge. Heb. giving the hand, put by Fig. *Metonymy* (of the Adjunct) for pledging. Ap. 6.

3 man. Heb *'ādām*. Ap. 14.

5 add. See note on 5. 16.

fifth part = twenty per cent. Zacchæus gave much more (Luke 19. 8).

in the day = when. See Ap. 18.

6. 8–13 (*E*, p. 134). **THE LAW OF THE BURNT OFFERING.**

Note the order of the "offerings", and their "laws".

In the former (God's side), "peace" made, comes in centre.

In the latter, "sin" comes before "peace" experienced. See note on 7. 11.

6 estimation. See note on 5. 15.

9 burning = kept burning. Heb. *yākad*, to burn as an ordinary culinary fire.

10 linen garment. See 8. 13. Ex. 28. 4, 40; 29. 5–10.

with the burnt offering. Abbreviation of Heb. word = "the offerings of Jehovah" (so Sam., Sept., and Vulg., and some codices).

12 burn [wood]. Heb. *b'ā'ar*, burn as fuel, consume.

every morning. Heb. morning by morning. Fig. *Epizeuxis*. Ap. 6.

burn = burn as incense. Heb. *kātar*. Ap. 43. I. vii.

13 The fire. This fire was originally from heaven (9. 24), supernatural fire. Only this fire could be used to set fire to the incense on the golden altar. So only those who have atonement can pray or worship. Ever burning until rekindled by a special descent. [This is the origin of the perpetual light in Roman Catholic worship.] It was preserved till the destruction of the temple by Nebuchadnezzar; was one of the five things lacking in the second temple.

14–23 (*F*, p. 134). **THE LAW OF THE MEAL OFFERING.**

14 the law. In 2. 1–3 we have the directions. In 6. 14–18 we have the law, and additional directions.

1490 **15** And °he shall take of it his handful, of
the flour of the meat offering, and of the oil
thereof, and all the frankincense which *is*
upon the meat offering, and shall °burn *it*
upon the altar *for* a sweet savour, *even* the
°memorial of it, unto [1]the LORD.
16 And the remainder thereof shall Aaron
and his sons eat: °with unleavened bread shall
it be eaten in the °holy place; in the court of
the °tabernacle of the congregation they shall
eat it.
17 It shall not be baken with leaven. I have
given it *unto them for* their portion of My
°offerings made by fire; it *is* most [16]holy, as *is*
the sin offering, and as the trespass offering.
18 °All the males among the children of Aaron
shall eat of it. *It shall be* a statute for ever in
your generations concerning the [17]offerings
of [1]the LORD made by fire: every one that
toucheth them shall be [16]holy.' "
19 And [1]the LORD [1]spake unto Moses, saying,
(**20** "This *is* the °offering of Aaron and of his
sons, which they shall °offer unto [1]the LORD °in
the day when he is anointed; the tenth part
of an °ephah of fine flour for a meat offering
perpetual, half of it in the morning, and half
thereof at night.
21 In a pan it shall be made with oil;
°*and when it is* baken, thou shalt bring it in:
and the baken pieces of the meat offering
shalt thou offer *for* a °sweet savour unto
[1]the LORD.
22 And °the priest of his sons that is
anointed in his stead shall offer it: *it is* a
statute for ever unto [1]the LORD; it shall be
°wholly burnt.
23 For every meat offering for the priest
shall be wholly burnt: it shall not be eaten.")
G b (p. 134) **24** And [1]the LORD [1]spake unto Moses, saying,
25 "Speak unto Aaron and to his sons,
saying, 'This *is* the law of the °sin °offering:
In the place where the burnt offering is killed
shall the °sin °offering be killed before [1]the
LORD: it *is* °most holy.
26 The priest that offereth it for sin °shall
eat it: in the holy place shall it be eaten,
in the court of the [16]tabernacle of the congregation.
27 Whatsoever shall touch the flesh thereof
shall be holy: and when there is sprinkled
of the blood thereof upon any garment, thou
shalt wash that whereon it was sprinkled
in the holy place.
28 But the earthen vessel wherein it is
sodden shall be broken: and if it be sodden
in a brasen pot, it shall be both scoured,
and rinsed in water.
29 All the males among the priests shall
eat thereof: it *is* most holy.
30 °And °no sin offering, whereof *any* of the
blood is brought into the [16]tabernacle of the
congregation °to reconcile *withal* in the holy
place, °shall be eaten: it shall be burnt in
the fire.
7 Likewise this *is* the law of the trespass
offering: it *is* °most holy.
2 °In the place where they kill the burnt
offering shall °they kill the trespass offering:
and the blood thereof shall he sprinkle round
about upon the altar.
3 And he shall °offer of it all the fat thereof;
the rump, and the fat that covereth the
inwards,
4 And the two kidneys, and the fat that *is*
on them, which *is* by the flanks, and the
caul *that is* above the liver, with the kidneys,
it shall he take away:
5 And the priest shall °burn them upon the

15 he: i. e. one of the sons whose turn it was.
burn: as incense. Heb. *ḳāṭar*. Ap. 43. I. vii.
memorial = memorial portion. See note on 2. 2.
16 with unleavened bread shall it be eaten. Heb. "unleavened shall it be eaten"; there is no "with" in the Heb. Cp. 10. 12.
holy. See note on Ex. 3. 5.
tabernacle = tent. Heb. *'ohel*. Ap. 40.
17 offerings made by fire. Heb. *'ishsheh*. Ap. 43. II. xi.
18 All the males = every male.
20 offering. Heb. *ḳorbān*. Ap. 43. II. i. This is explained in Heb. 7. 27. Note the *Parenthesis* (Ap. 6) concerning Aaron.
offer. Heb. *ḳārab*. Ap. 43. I. i.
in the day = when. See Gen. 2. 4, 17 and Ap. 8; and cp. 8. 35; 9. 1.
ephah. See Ap. 51. III. 3.
21 and when, &c. Better, "thou shalt bring it in well kneaded".
sweet savour = savour of satisfaction. See note on 1. 9 and Gen. 8. 21.
22 the priest . . . anointed. See on 4. 3.
wholly burnt. Because the priest did not eat his own.

6. 24–7. 10 (*G*, *b*, p. 134). THE LAW OF THE SIN OFFERING.

25–30 THE LAW OF THE SIN OFFERING.

25 sin = Heb. *chāṭ'ā*, and implies offering as in Gen. 4. 7.
offering. This word not in the Heb. text, but the Ellipsis is rightly supplied, and should be in Gen. 4. 7
most holy. This comes out in the "law" of the sin offering, because of the Antitype. See note on Ex. 3. 5.
26 shall eat it. Because blood *not* taken within the holy place. Cp. 10. 16–20, and see 7. 6. This explains Heb. 13. 11.
30 And = But.
no sin offering . . . shall be eaten. Because the blood *was* taken into the holy place. Cp. Lev. 10. 16–20. In this case it was to be wholly burnt, 4. 26. This explains Heb. 13. 11.
There were eight offerings to be eaten by the priests in the precincts of the holy place:—
(1) The flesh of the sin offering (4. 26; 6. 26).
(2) The flesh of the trespass offering (7. 6).
(3) The peace offering of the congregation (7. 14, 15).
(4) The remainder of the *'omer* (2. 3–10).
(5) The meal offering of the Israelites (2. 3–10).
(6) The two loaves (13. 19, 20; 23. 20).
(7) The shewbread (23. 9).
(8) The leper's log of oil (14. 10–13).
to reconcile = to make atonement for. See note on Ex. 29. 33.

7. 1–10 (*G*, *b*, above). THE LAW OF THE TRESPASS OFFERING. (Supplementing ch. 5. 1–13.)

1 most holy. See note on 6. 25 and Ex. 3. 5.
2 In the place. i. e. on the north side. Cp. 1. 11.
they = the people who bring them.
3 offer = bring near. Heb. *ḳārab*. Ap. 43. I. i. For these regulations see 3. 3, 4, 8, 9.
5 burn: i. e. as incense. Heb. *ḳāṭar*. Ap. 43. I. vii. See ch. 4. 26, 31.

1490 **altar *for* an offering made by fire unto °the LORD: it *is* a [1]trespass offering.**

6 Every male among the priests shall eat thereof: it shall be eaten in the °holy place: it *is* [1]most holy.

7 As the sin offering *is,* so *is* the [1]trespass offering: *there is* °one law for them: the priest that °maketh atonement therewith shall have *it.*

8 And the priest that [3]offereth any °man's burnt offering, *even* the priest shall have to himself the skin of the burnt offering which he hath [3]offered.

9 And all the °meat offering that is baken in the oven, and all that is dressed in the fryingpan, and in the pan, shall be °the priest's that [3]offereth it.

10 And every [9]meat offering, mingled with oil, and dry, shall all the sons of Aaron have, one *as much* as another.

G a (p. 134) **11 And this *is* °the law of the sacrifice of peace offerings, which °he shall offer unto [5]the LORD.**

12 If he [3]offer it for a °thanksgiving, then he shall [3]offer with the °sacrifice of thanksgiving unleavened cakes mingled with oil, and unleavened wafers anointed with oil, and cakes mingled with oil, of fine flour, fried.

13 Besides the cakes, he shall [3]offer *for* his °offering leavened bread with the sacrifice of thanksgiving of his °peace offerings.

14 And of it he shall [3]offer one out of the whole °oblation *for* an heave offering unto [5]the LORD, *and* it shall be the priest's that sprinkleth the blood of the [13]peace offerings.

15 And the flesh of the [12]sacrifice of his [13]peace offerings for thanksgiving shall be eaten the °same day that it is [3]offered; he shall not leave any of it until the morning.

16 But if the [12]sacrifice of his [13]offering *be* a vow, or a voluntary offering, it shall be eaten the [15]same day that he [3]offereth his [12]sacrifice: and on the morrow also the remainder of it shall be eaten:

17 But the remainder of the flesh of the [12]sacrifice on the third day shall be °burnt with fire.

18 And if *any* of the flesh of the [12]sacrifice of his peace offerings be eaten at all on the third day, it shall not be accepted, neither shall it be imputed unto him that [12]offereth it: it shall be an abomination, and the °soul that eateth of it shall bear his °iniquity.

19 And the flesh that toucheth any unclean *thing* shall not be eaten; it shall be [17]burnt with fire: and as for the flesh, all that be clean shall eat °thereof.

20 But the [18]soul that eateth *of* the flesh of the [12]sacrifice of [13]peace offerings, that *pertain* unto [5]the LORD, having his °uncleanness upon him, even that [18]soul shall be °cut off from °his people.

21 Moreover the [18]soul that shall touch any unclean *thing, as* the uncleanness of °man, or *any* unclean beast, or any °abominable unclean *thing,* and eat of the flesh of the sacrifice of [13]peace offerings, which *pertain* unto [5]the LORD, even that [18]soul shall be [20]cut off from his people.'"

22 And [5]the LORD °spake unto Moses, saying,

23 °"Speak unto the °children of Israel, saying, 'Ye shall eat °no manner of fat, of ox, or of sheep, or of goat.

24 And the fat of the beast that dieth of itself, and the fat of that which is torn with beasts, may be used in any °other use: but ye shall in no wise eat of it.

25 For whosoever eateth [24]the fat of the beast, of which °men [3]offer an °offering made by fire unto [5]the LORD, even the [18]soul that eateth *it* shall be [20]cut off from his people.

26 Moreover ye shall eat no manner of blood, *whether it be* of fowl or of beast, in any of your dwellings.

27 Whatsoever [18]soul *it be* that eateth any

---

the LORD. Heb. Jehovah. Ap. 4.
6 holy place, or court. Cp. 6. 26. See note on Ex. 3. 5.
7 one law. See 6. 27, 28.
maketh atonement. See note on Ex. 29. 33.
8 man's. Heb. *'ish.* Ap. 14.
9 meat offering. Heb. *minḥah.* Ap. 43, II. 3.
the priest's. Except the memorial part, 2. 4–10. Cp. 1 Cor. 9. 13, 14. Gal. 6. 6 is based on this principle.

11–34 (*G, a,* p. 134). THE LAW OF THE PEACE OFFERING.

11 the law: i.e. specific and fuller directions given to the *priests,* additional to those given to the *People* in 3. 1–15. So in the law of the sin offering (6. 24–30, cp. with 4. 24–31); the law of the trespass offering (7. 1–10, cp. with 5. 1–13).
It will be noted from the Structure (on p. 134) that the peace offering comes before the sin offerings; but here, in "the LAW" of the offerings, the peace offerings comes last. This is because it has to do with the communion of the offerer; and this follows at the end of all, to show that this communion is based on, and must flow from, a full knowledge of all that which the types foreshow. Not until we have done with our sins and ourselves can we delight in Christ. See note on 6. 8. Cp. Col. 1. 12–14. **he** = one.
12 thanksgiving for special mercies received, as enumerated in Ps. 107. This is the sacrifice alluded to in Heb. 13. 15.
sacrifice. Heb. *zabaḥ.* Ap. 43. II. xii.
13 offering. Heb. *ḳorbān.* Ap. 43. II. i.
peace offerings. Heb. *shelem.* Ap. 43. II. iv.
14 oblation. Heb. *ḳorbān.* Ap. 43. II. i.
15 same day. In second temple, limited to midnight.
17 burnt. Heb. *sāraph.* Ap. 43. I. viii.
18 soul. Heb. *nephesh.* See Ap. 13. Put by Fig. *Synecdoche* (of the Part) for the person (Ap. 6).
iniquity. Heb. *'āvāh.* Ap. 44. iv. Put by Fig. *Metonymy* (of the Cause) for punishment.
19 thereof. Heb. "the flesh". Fig. *Epanadiplosis* (Ap. 6) for emphasis of the verse as a whole.
20 uncleanness. See 11. 8–44; 15. 1–33.
cut off, &c. This phrase, variously translated, occurs (in Hebrew) six times in Leviticus: 7. 20, 21, 25, 27; 19. 8; 23. 29. Cp. the other phrase, ". . . from My presence". See 22. 3.
his = her in Heb. Fem. to agree with Heb *nephesh,* soul.
21 man. Heb. *'ādām.* Ap. 14.
abominable unclean thing = anything an abomination to Jehovah. Some codices, with Sam., Onk., and Syr., have "unclean reptiles".
22 spake. Indicating explanations and restrictions in *vv.* 22–27, additional to those given in ch. 3. 17.
23 Speak. Used only of the non-savour offering. See note on 5. 14. ("Jehovah called and spake *re* the sweet savour offering", 1. 1.)
children = sons.
no manner of fat: i.e. of beeves, sheep, or goats.
24 other use: e.g. making candles, &c.
25 men. Should be in italics.
offering made by fire. Heb. *'ishsheh.* Ap. 43. II. xi.

1490 manner of blood, even that [18]soul shall be [20]cut off from his people.' "

28 And [5]the LORD °spake unto Moses, saying,

29 [3]"Speak unto the [23]children of Israel, saying, 'He that [13]offereth the [13]sacrifice of his [13]peace offerings unto [5]the LORD shall bring his [14]oblation unto [1]the LORD of the sacrifice of his peace offerings.

30 °His own hands shall bring the [25]offerings of [5]the LORD made by fire, the fat with the breast, it shall he bring, that the breast may be waved *for* a °wave offering before [5]the LORD.

31 And the priest shall burn the fat upon the altar: but the breast shall be Aaron's and his sons'.

32 And the right shoulder shall ye give unto the priest *for* an °heave offering of the [12]sacrifices of your peace offerings.

33 He among the sons of Aaron, that [13]offereth the blood of the peace offerings, and the fat, shall have the right shoulder for *his* part.

34 For the °wave °breast and the °heave °shoulder have I taken of the [29]children of Israel from off the sacrifices of their peace offerings, and have given them unto Aaron the priest and unto his sons by a statute °for ever from among the [23]children of Israel.

D (p. 134) 35 This °*is the portion* of the anointing of Aaron, and of the anointing of his sons, out of the °offerings of [5]the LORD made by fire, in the day *when* he presented them to minister unto [5]the LORD in the priest's office;

36 Which [5]the LORD commanded to be given them of the [23]children of Israel, in the day that He anointed them, *by* a statute for ever throughout their generations.

37 This *is* °the law of the °burnt offering, of the °meat offering, and of the °sin offering, and of the °trespass offering, and of the °consecrations, and of the sacrifice of the [13]peace offerings;

38 Which [5]the LORD °commanded Moses in mount Sinai, in the day that He commanded the [23]children of Israel to offer their [14]oblations unto [5]the LORD, in the wilderness of Sinai.' "

DA H¹ c (p. 142) **8** °And °the LORD °spake unto Moses, saying,

2 "Take Aaron and his sons with him, and the garments, and the anointing oil, and a bullock for the sin offering, and two rams, and a basket of unleavened bread;

3 And gather thou all the congregation together unto the °door of the °tabernacle of the congregation."

d e 4 And Moses did °as [1]the LORD commanded him; and the assembly was gathered together unto the door of the [3]tabernacle of the congregation.

5 And Moses said unto the congregation, "°This *is* the thing which [1]the LORD commanded to be done."

6 And Moses brought Aaron and his sons, and °washed them with water.

7 And he put upon him the coat, and girded him with °the girdle, and clothed him with the robe, and put the ephod upon him, and he girded him with the curious girdle of the ephod, and bound *it* unto him therewith.

8 And he put the breastplate upon him: °also he put in the breastplate °the Urim and the Thummim.

9 And he put the °mitre upon his head; also upon the mitre, *even* upon his forefront, did he put the °golden plate, the °holy crown; as [1]the LORD commanded Moses.

---

28 spake. See note on 5. 14.
30 His own hands: i. e. the owner or offerer.
wave offering. See note on Ex. 29. 27.
32 heave offering. See note on Ex. 29. 27.
34 See notes on *vv.* 30, 32.
for ever: i. e. as long as the priesthood lasts.
35 is the portion of. Supply the Ellipsis (Ap. 6) better, thus: This [is what pertaineth to].
offerings . . . made by fire. Heb. *'ishsheh.* Ap. 43. II. xi.
37 the law. Verses 37 and 38 sum up chapters 1–8.
burnt offering (1. 3–17 and 6. 8–13).
meat offering (2. 1–16 and 6. 14–18).
sin offering (4. 1–35 and 6. 24–30).
trespass offering (5. 1–13 and 5. 14–19 and 6. 1–7 and 7. 1–10).
consecrations (6. 19–23).
peace offerings (3. 1–17 and 7. 11–21, 28–36).
38 commanded. Subject to "If" in Lev. 1. 2.

8. 1—10. 20 (D, A, p. 131). PRIESTHOOD.
(Division.)

A | H¹ | 8. 1–36. Consecration.
A | H² | 9. 1–24. Ministration.
A | H³ | 10. 1–20. Transgression.

8. 1–36 (H¹, above). CONSECRATION.
(Alternation.)

H¹ | c | 1–3. Command.
H¹ | d | 4–30. Obedience.
H¹ | *c* | 31–35. Command.
H¹ | *d* | 36. Obedience.

8. 1 And. Note the Fig. *Polysyndeton* throughout the chapter for emphasising each particular act (Ap. 6).
the LORD. Heb. Jehovah. Ap. 4.
spake. Indicating a new subject. See note on 5. 14. The ritual is prescribed in Ex. 28. 1–43 and 29. 1–37. Now the appointment to the priestly office resumes the instructions broken off in Exodus.
3 door = entrance.
tabernacle = tent. Heb. *'ohel.* Ap. 40.

4–30 (d, above). OBEDIENCE.
(Alternation.)

d | e | 4–9. Investiture of Aaron.
d | f | 10–12. Anointing of Tabernacle and Aaron.
d | *e* | 13. Investiture of Aaron's sons.
d | *f* | 14–30. Offerings for Aaron and his sons.

4 as = according as.
5 This is the thing. See Ex. 28. 1–43; 29. 1–37; now made known to the People.
6 washed = the "divers washings" of Heb. 6. 2. After this, all ceremonial washings done by the persons for themselves. These are rendered "baptisms" in Sept. of Lev. 11. 25, 40; 17. 15, 16; 14. 8; 15. 8, 13, 16, 21, 22, 27. Extended to "clothes", Lev. 11. 25, &c.
7 the girdle. Not the band of the ephod called the "curious girdle", but the one of needlework, ch. 16. 4 and Ex. 28. 39.
8 also. Thus distinguishing these two stones from the twelve stones, which were quite distinct. Cp. Ex. 25. 7.
the Urim and the Thummim. See note on Ex. 28. 30.
9 mitre = turban or tiara. See Ex. 28. 36–38.
golden plate, or crown. Ex. 28. 36, &c.
holy. See note on Ex. 3. 5.

f 1490 (p. 142) 10 And Moses took the °anointing oil, and anointed the °tabernacle and all that *was* therein, and °sanctified them.

11 And he sprinkled thereof upon the altar seven times, and anointed °the altar and all his vessels, both the laver and his °foot, to [10]sanctify them.

12 And he °poured of the anointing oil upon Aaron's head, and anointed him, to sanctify him.

e 13 And Moses brought °Aaron's sons, and put coats upon them, and girded them with girdles, and °put bonnets upon them; [4]as [1]the LORD commanded Moses.

f 14 And he brought the bullock for the °sin offering: and Aaron and his sons laid their hands upon the head of the bullock for the °sin offering.

15 And he slew *it;* and Moses took the blood, and put *it* upon the horns of the altar round about with his finger, and purified the altar, and poured the blood at the bottom of the altar, and [10]sanctified it, to make reconciliation upon it.

16 And he took all the fat that *was* upon the inwards, and the caul *above* the liver, and the two kidneys, and their fat, and Moses °burned *it* upon the altar.

17 But the bullock, and his hide, his flesh, and his dung, he °burnt with fire °without the camp; [4]as [1]the LORD commanded Moses.

18 And he °brought the ram for the burnt offering: and Aaron and his sons laid their hands upon the head of the ram.

19 And he killed *it;* and Moses °sprinkled the blood upon the altar round about.

20 And he cut the ram into °pieces; and Moses °burnt the head, and the pieces, and the fat.

21 And he °washed the inwards and the legs in water; and Moses burnt the whole ram upon the altar: it *was* a burnt sacrifice for a °sweet savour, *and* an offering made by fire unto [1]the LORD; [4]as [1]the LORD commanded Moses.

22 And he brought °the other ram, the ram of consecration: and Aaron and his sons laid their hands upon the head of the ram.

23 And he °slew *it;* and Moses took of the blood of it, and °put *it* upon the tip of Aaron's right ear, and upon the thumb of his right hand, and upon the great toe of his right foot.

24 And he brought Aaron's sons, and Moses put of the blood upon the tip of their right ear, and upon the thumbs of their right hands, and upon the great toes of their right feet: and Moses sprinkled the blood upon the altar round about.

25 And °he took the fat, and °the rump, and all the fat that *was* upon the inwards, and the caul *above* the liver, and the two kidneys, and their fat, and the right shoulder:

26 And out of the basket of unleavened bread, that *was* before [1]the LORD, he took one unleavened cake, and °a cake of oiled bread, and one wafer, and put *them* on the fat, and upon the right shoulder:

27 And he put all upon Aaron's hands, and upon his sons' hands, and °waved them *for* a wave offering before [1]the LORD.

28 And Moses took them from off their hands, and [20]burnt *them* on the altar upon the burnt offering: they *were* °consecrations for a sweet savour: it *is* an offering made by fire unto [1]the LORD.

29 And Moses took the breast, and [27]waved it *for* a wave offering before [1]the LORD: *for* of the ram of consecration it was Moses' part; [4]as [1]the LORD commanded Moses.

30 And Moses took of the anointing oil, and of the blood which *was* upon the altar, and sprinkled *it* upon Aaron, °*and* upon his garments, and upon his sons, and upon his sons' garments with him; and sanctified Aaron, °*and* his garments, and his sons, and his sons' garments with him.

31 And Moses said unto Aaron and to his sons, "Boil the flesh *at* the °door of the °tabernacle of the congregation: and there eat it with the bread that *is* in the basket of consecrations, °as I commanded, saying, 'Aaron and his sons shall eat it.' c

32 And that which remaineth of the flesh and of the bread shall ye [17]burn with fire.

33 And ye shall not go out of the door of the [31]tabernacle of the congregation *in*

---

10 anointing oil. See Ex. 30. 26–30; 40. 9–11, and cp. Ex. 30. 23–25.
tabernacle. Heb. *mishkān.* Ap. 40.
sanctified=set them apart. Ex. 29. 37; 30. 29–30.
11 the altar. Cp. Matt. 23. 19.
foot=base.
12 poured. Not touched with the finger, as in the case of the common priests, but profusely poured. See Ps. 133. 2.
13 Aaron's sons. These could not be invested till after Aaron. Cp. John 17. 19.
put. Heb.=bound.
14 sin offering. Heb. *chātā.* Ap. 43. II. 5.
16 burned: as incense. Heb. *ḳāṭar.* Ap. 43. I. vii.
17 burnt. Heb. *sāraph.* Ap. 43. I. viii.
without the camp. Cp. Ex. 29. 14. Lev. 4. 12, 18, 21; 6. 11; 16. 27. John 19. 17, 18. Acts 7. 58.
18 brought. See Ex. 29. 15–18.
19 sprinkled=cast. Not the same word as *v.* 15.
20 pieces=its pieces.
burnt: i. e. as incense. Heb. *ḳāṭar.* Ap. 43. I. vii.
21 washed. See note on *v.* 6.
sweet savour=savour of satisfaction. See note on 1. 9, and Gen. 8. 21.
22 the other ram. Mentioned in *v.* 2. See Ex. 29. 19–24.
23 slew. Same word as "killed", *v.* 15, 19.
put it: on ear, thumb, and toe, to point out the hearkening, the working, and the walking.
25 he took. Ex. 29. 22–25.
the rump=the fat tail. See 3. 9. Cp. Ex. 29. 22.
26 a=one.
27 waved. Cp. note on Ex. 29. 27.
28 consecrations. Cp. 6. 19–23.
30 and upon. Some codices, with Sam., Onk., Lisbon Pentateuch (1491), Jon., Sept., Syr., and Vulg., have this "and" in the text.
and. Many authorities have this "and" in the text.
31 door=entrance.
tabernacle=tent (*'ohel*). Ap. 40.
as I commanded. Sam. Sept., Syr., and Vulg. read "as I have been commanded".

1490 °seven days, until the days of your °consecration be at an end: for °seven days shall He °consecrate you.

34 As °He hath done this day, *so* [1]the LORD hath commanded to do, to °make an atonement for you.

1-7 Abib **35** Therefore shall ye abide *at* the door of the [31]tabernacle of the congregation day and night seven days, and keep the charge of [1]the LORD, that ye die not: for so I am commanded."

d **36** So Aaron and his sons did all things which [1]the LORD commanded by °the hand of Moses.

H² e¹ (p. 144) 8th Abib **9** And it came to pass on the °eighth day, *that* Moses called Aaron and his sons, and the elders of Israel;

2 And he said unto Aaron, "Take thee a young calf for a °sin offering, and a ram for a burnt offering, without blemish, and °offer *them* °before °the LORD.

3 And unto the °children of Israel °thou shalt speak, saying, 'Take ye a kid of the goats for a [2]sin offering; and a calf and a lamb, *both* of the first year, without blemish, for a burnt offering;

4 Also a bullock and a ram for °peace offerings, to sacrifice before [2]the LORD; and a meat offering mingled with oil:

f¹ for to day [2]the LORD will °appear unto you.'"

e² **5** And they brought *that* which Moses commanded before the °tabernacle of the congregation: and all the congregation drew near and stood before [2]the LORD.

6 And Moses said, "This *is* the thing which [2]the LORD commanded that ye should do:

f² and the glory of [2]the LORD shall appear unto you."

e³ **7** And Moses °said unto Aaron, "Go unto the altar, and °offer °thy [2]sin offering, and thy burnt offering, and °make an atonement for thyself, and for the People: and °offer the °offering of the People, and °make an atonement for them; °as [2]the LORD commanded."

8 Aaron therefore went unto the altar, and slew °the calf of the [2]sin offering, which *was* for himself.

9 And the sons of Aaron brought the blood unto him: and he dipped his finger in the blood, and put *it* upon the horns of the altar, and poured out the blood at the bottom of the altar:

10 But the fat, and the kidneys, and the caul above the liver of the [2]sin offering, he °burnt upon the altar; [7]as [2]the LORD commanded Moses.

11 And the flesh and the hide he °burnt with fire without the camp.

12 And he slew the burnt offering; and Aaron's sons °presented unto him the blood, which he sprinkled round about upon the altar.

13 And they [12]presented the burnt offering unto him, with the pieces thereof, and the head: and he [10]burnt *them* upon the altar.

14 And he did wash the inwards and the legs, and [10]burnt *them* upon the burnt offering on the altar.

15 And he brought °the People's offering, and took the goat, which *was* the [2]sin offering for the People, and slew it, and °offered it for [2]sin, °as the first.

16 And he brought the burnt offering, and [7]offered it according to the °manner.

17 And he brought the meat offering, and °took an handful thereof, and [10]burnt *it* upon the altar, beside the burnt sacrifice of the morning.

18 He slew also the bullock and the ram *for* a sacrifice of [4]peace offerings, which *was* for the People: and Aaron's sons [12]presented unto him the blood, which he sprinkled upon the altar round about,

---

33 seven days. Aaron consecrated on the eighth day, after waiting seven days.
consecration = setting apart.
consecrate. See note on Ex. 28. 41.
34 He hath done = hath been done.
make an atonement. See note on Ex. 29. 33.
36 the hand. Put by Fig. *Metonymy* (of the Cause) for what is performed by it (Ap. 6). Hence a common idiom for instrumentality or agency; esp. writing.

9. 1-24 (H², p. 142). MINISTRATION.
(*Repeated Alternation.*)

H²
- e¹ | 1-4-. Command.
  - f¹ | -4. Appearing of Jehovah promised.
- e² | 5, 6-. Obedience.
  - f² | -6. Appearing of glory promised.
- e³ | 7-23-. Command and obedience.
  - f³ | -23, 24. Appearing of the glory of Jehovah.

1 eighth day: i. e. the day following the seven days of consecration (8. 33, 35).
2 sin offering. Heb. *chāṭ'ā.* Ap. 43. II. v.
offer. Heb. *ḳarab.* Ap. 43. I. i.
before the LORD = before the door of the tent of meeting (1. 5, 11).
the LORD. Heb. Jehovah. Ap. 4.
3 children. Heb. sons.
thou shalt speak. Aaron now to give the orders about the sacrifices.
4 peace offerings. Heb. *shelem.* Ap. 43. II. iv.
appear: i. e. manifest Himself in a special manner.
5 tabernacle = tent. Heb. *'ohel.* Ap. 40.
7 said unto Aaron. Showing that Aaron did not take this honour upon himself. Heb. 5. 4, 5.
offer = prepare. Heb. *'āsāh.* Ap. 43. I. iii.
thy sin offering. Ancient Jewish interpretation refers this "calf" (*v.* 8) to the sin of the golden calf. The People's share in that sin is referred to in *v.* 15. Cp. Ex. 32. 35: "they made (Ex. 32. 1) the calf which Aaron made" (*v.* 4).
make an atonement. See note on Ex. 29. 33. Cp. Ex. 28. 41.
offering. Heb. *ḳorbān.* Ap. 43. II. i.
as = according as.
8 the calf. See note on *v.* 7. Aaron slew this himself, like any other offerer, as it was for his *own* sin (1. 5).
10 burnt: i. e. as incense. Heb. *ḳāṭar.* Ap. 43. I. vii.
11 burnt. Heb. *sāraph.* Ap. 43. I. viii.
12 presented = cause to be delivered. *Hiphil* of *māẓ'a* only here, *vv.* 13, 18. 2 Sam. 3. 8. Job 34. 11; 37. 13. Zech. 11. 6.
15 the People's offering. See note on *v.* 7.
offered. Heb. *chāṭ'ā* (verb), to offer a sin offering. Ap. 43. II. v.
as the first. See *v.* 8. He accordingly burnt it "without the camp", for which he was reproved by Moses (10. 16-20).
16 manner = ordinance, or regulation. Cp. the same word in 5. 10.
17 took an handful thereof. Heb. filled his hand therefrom, i. e. installed himself therewith. Here we have the Divine explanation of consecration. Cp. Ex. 28. 41.

1490 19 And the fat of the bullock and of the ram, the °rump, and that which covereth *the inwards*, and the kidneys, and the caul *above* the liver:

20 And they put the fat upon the breasts, and he [10]burnt the fat upon the altar:

21 And the breasts and the right shoulder Aaron waved *for* a °wave offering before [2]the LORD; °as Moses commanded.

22 And Aaron lifted up his hand toward the People, and °blessed them, and °came down from offering of the [2]sin offering, and the burnt offering, and peace offerings.

23 And Moses and Aaron went into the [5]tabernacle of the congregation, and came out, and °blessed the People:

f[3] (p. 144) and the °glory of [2]the LORD appeared unto all the People.

24 And there °came a fire out from before [2]the LORD, and consumed upon the altar the burnt offering and the fat: *which* when all the people saw, they °shouted, and fell on their faces.

H[3] g (p. 145) **10** And Nadab and Abihu, the sons of Aaron, took either of them his censer, and put fire therein, and put incense thereon, and °offered °strange fire before °the LORD, which He °commanded them not.

8th Abib 2 And there went out fire °from [1]the LORD, and °devoured them, and they °died before [1]the LORD.

3 Then Moses said unto Aaron, °"This *is it* that [1]the LORD spake, saying, °'I will be sanctified in them that come nigh Me, and before all the people °I will be glorified.'" And Aaron °held his peace.

4 And Moses called Mishael and Elzaphan, the °sons of Uzziel the uncle of Aaron, and said unto them, "Come near, carry your brethren from before the sanctuary °out of the camp."

5 So they went near, and carried them in their coats out of the camp; °as Moses had said.

6 And Moses said °unto Aaron, and °unto Eleazar and unto Ithamar, his sons, "Uncover not your heads, neither °rend your clothes; °lest ye die, and lest wrath come upon all the °people: °but let your brethren, the °whole house of Israel, bewail the °burning which [1]the LORD hath kindled.

7 And ye shall not go out from the °door of the °tabernacle of the congregation, lest ye die: for the anointing oil of [1]the LORD *is* upon you." And they did according to the word of Moses.

h 8 And [1]the LORD °spake unto Aaron, saying,

19 rump. Heb. "the fat tail".

21 wave offering. See note on Ex. 29. 27.

as Moses commanded. Some codices, with Sam., Jon., and Sept., read "as Jehovah commanded Moses".

22 blessed them: i.e. according to the precept in Num. 6. 24-26. Cp. Deut. 10. 8; 21. 5.

came down. Does not imply "steps", which were forbidden (Ex. 20. 26). Probably = the margin or edge. See note on Ex. 27. 5.

23 blessed the People. This joint blessing is given in the Chaldee version of the Pentateuch, thus: "May the word of Jehovah accept your sacrifice with favour, and remit and pardon your sins."

glory of the LORD. According to the promise in *v.* 4. See the Structure, p. 144.

24 came a fire. See note on 10. 2, and cp. 1 Chron. 21. 26 and Gen. 4. 4. Judg. 6. 20, 21. 1 Kings 18. 38. 2 Chron. 7. 1, 2. See Lev. 6. 13.

shouted. Cp. 2 Chron. 7. 3.

10. 1-20 (H[3], p. 144). **TRANSGRESSION.**
(*Introversion.*)

H[3] | g | 1-7. Disobedience (positive sin).
  h | 8-11. Command (as to holy and unclean).
  h | 12-15. Command (as to meal offering).
g | 16-20. Disobedience (negative failure).

1 offered = brought near. Heb. *ḳārab*. Ap. 43. I. i.

strange fire: i.e. fire other than that Jehovah had commanded, required, and given from heaven (1. 7; 6. 12; 9. 24; 16. 12. Cp. Ex. 30. 9). It was of their own kindling: so is all that is offered to God in worship to-day. If so, according to John 4. 23, 24, it is "strange fire", and deserves the same judgment!

All worship that is not kindled by the Holy Spirit is "strange", and is of the flesh. Cp. John 3. 6 and 6. 63. It "profiteth nothing", and "God has no respect to it" (Gen. 4. 4, 5. Heb. 11. 4).

The incense of prayer and worship on the golden altar in the holy place was kindled by fire taken from the brazen altar in the outer court, on which atonement was made (see Lev. 16. 12, 13 and Rev. 8. 5): only those, therefore, whose sin is atoned for can worship. Compare the "strange incense", Ex. 30. 9.

the LORD. Heb. Jehovah. Ap. 4.

commanded them not. Negative. The introduction of anything "strange", where *all* is ordered by God, is abomination in His sight; and calls for, and calls down, His judgment. Thus the first recorded individual use of incense began in *disobedience* (10. 1), and the last ended in *unbelief* (Luke 1. 10, 18, 20).

2 from = from before.

devoured them = slew them; for they were not consumed, as is shown in verses 4 and 5.

Note the three fires here: (1) the fire of true worship (9. 24); (2) the strange fire of false worship (10. 1); (3) the devouring fire of judgment (10. 2).

died before the LORD: i.e. in the court of the sanctuary, where their sin had been committed.

3 This is it, &c., in contrast with *v.* 1. The positive opposed to the negative. Note the emphasis on "This" = this and nothing else: this very thing. Disobedience here is vital; this is why "judgment must begin at the house of God": 1 Pet. 4. 17, yea "the time is come".

I will. Note this double "I will": and compare it with the "must" of John 4. 24. Cp. John 3. 7, 14.

All worship which has not Christ for its object, the glory of Jehovah for its end, and the Holy Spirit for its power, will be rejected and judged. **held his peace:** in solemn submission to God's judgment on his two sons, just struck dead so soon after their anointing, installation, and investiture. Cp. 8. 13. **4 sons of Uzziel.** Izhar and Hebron. The older uncles were passed over because of their probable sympathy with their nephews Nadab and Abihu (Num. 16. 5, 7, 8). **out** = to without. Burials took place in the open fields. Cp. Gen. 23. 9, 17. Matt. 27. 52, 53. Luke 7. 12. **5 as** = according as. **6 unto** (Heb. *'ĕl*) **Aaron** **unto** (= to Heb. *l*) Eleazar, &c. **rend.** Heb. *pāram*, only here, 14. 45, and 21. 10. **lest ye die, and lest wrath come** = and so ye will not (Heb. *'al*) die, and wrath will not (Heb. *l'o*) come. **people** = assembly. **but let, &c.** = but your brethren . . . will bewail. **whole house of Israel.** See note on Ex. 16. 31. **burning.** Heb. *sāraph.* See Ap. 43. I. viii. **7 door** = entrance. **tabernacle of the congregation** = "tent (Heb. *'ohel*) of meeting". Ap. 40. **8 spake.** The only time to Aaron alone. See note on 5. 14.

1490 9 "Do not drink °wine nor °strong drink,
thou, nor thy sons with thee, °when ye go
into the [7]tabernacle of the congregation, lest
ye die: *it shall be* a statute for ever throughout your generations:
10 And that ye may put difference between
°holy and unholy, and between unclean and
clean;
11 And that ye may °teach the °children of
Israel all the statutes which [1]the LORD hath
spoken unto them by the hand of Moses."

h (p. 145) 12 And Moses spake unto Aaron, and unto
Eleazar and unto Ithamar, his sons that were
left, "Take the meat offering that remaineth
of the °offerings of [1]the LORD °made by fire,
and eat it °without leaven °beside the altar:
for it *is* most [10]holy:
13 And ye shall eat it in the [10]holy place,
because it *is* °thy due, and thy sons' due, of
the °sacrifices of [1]the LORD [12]made by fire: for
so I am commanded.
14 And the °wave breast and °heave
shoulder shall ye eat in a clean place; thou,
and thy sons, and °thy daughters with thee:
for *they be* thy due, and thy sons' due, *which*
are given out of the sacrifices of peace offerings of the [11]children of Israel.
15 The [14]heave shoulder and the [14]wave
breast shall they bring with the offerings
made by fire of the fat, to wave *it for* a wave
offering before [1]the LORD; and it shall be
thine, and thy sons' with thee, by a statute for
ever; [5]as [1]the LORD hath commanded."

g 16 And Moses diligently sought the goat of the
sin offering, and, behold, it was °burnt: and he
was angry with Eleazar and Ithamar, the sons
of Aaron *which were* left *alive*, saying,
17 °"Wherefore have ye not eaten the °sin
offering in the [10]holy place, seeing it *is* most
[10]holy, and *God* hath given it you °to bear the
°iniquity of the congregation, to °make atonement for them before [1]the LORD?
18 °Behold, the blood of it was not brought
in within the [10]holy *place*: ye should indeed
have eaten it in the [10]holy *place*, as I commanded."
19 And Aaron said unto Moses, "Behold,
this day have they offered their [17]sin offering and their burnt offering before [1]the
LORD; and such things have befallen me:
and *if* I had eaten the [17]sin offering to day,
should it have been accepted in the sight of
[1]the LORD?"
20 And when Moses heard *that*, he was
content.

J[1] K[1] i[1] (p. 146) **11** And °the LORD °spake unto Moses and
to Aaron, saying unto them,
2 "Speak unto the °children of Israel, saying, °'These *are* the °beasts which ye shall
eat among all the °beasts that *are* on the
earth.
3 Whatsoever °parteth the hoof, and is
clovenfooted, *and* cheweth the cud, among the
beasts, that shall ye eat.
4 Nevertheless these shall ye °not eat of
them that chew the cud, or of them that
divide the hoof: *as* the camel, because he
cheweth the cud, but divideth not the hoof;
he *is* unclean unto you.

9 wine. Heb. *yayin.* See Ap. 27. i.
strong drink. Heb. *shēkār.* Ap. 27. iv. Does this law follow here, because it was intoxication which led to the sin of Nadab and Abihu?
when ye go. Cp. Ezek. 44. 21. The exception implies the rule. Nothing may be done to excite or stimulate the flesh in the sanctuary: neither drink within, nor music without, nor sensuous surroundings. The old nature must not be stimulated by moving scenes or mere human eloquence. All "must" be of the Spirit. John 4. 24.
10 holy. See note on Ex. 3. 5.
11 teach. This was a special part of the priests' work. See note on Deut. 33. 10.
children. Heb. sons.
12 offerings. Heb. pl. of *ķārbān.* Ap. 43. II. i.
made by fire. Heb. *'ishsheh.* Ap. 43. II. xi.
without leaven. See Ap. 38.
beside the altar: in the outer court. Cp. *v.* 2 and 6. 20.
13 thy due = thy statute. Notwithstanding the failure in *vv.* 1–7.
sacrifices. Heb. pl. of *zābaḥ.* Ap. 43. II. xii.
14 wave . . . heave. See note on Ex. 29. 27.
thy daughters. Note this: as well as sons. We must distinguish the privileges confined to males; others are common to all alike. The daughters could not eat of the "sin offering" (*v.* 17), but could eat of the "meal offering" (*v.* 14).
16 burnt. Heb. *sāraph.* Ap. 43. I. viii.
17 Wherefore . . . ? Fig. *Erotēsis* (Ap. 6) to call attention to ch. 6. 26.
sin. Heb. *chāṭ'ā.* Ap. 43. II. v. and 44. i.
to bear = to bear away, or remove. Cp. Gen. 50. 17. Ex. 32. 32. Ps. 32. 1, 5. Matt. 8. 17. So here, the Chald., Syr., and Sept. render it "take away" or "remove". The A.V. follows the Vulgate here.
iniquity. Heb. *ā'vah.* Ap. 44. iv.
make atonement. See note on Ex. 29. 33.
18 Behold. Fig. *Asterismos* (Ap. 6), to emphasise the distinction laid down in ch. 6. 26, 30; 10. 17. Cp. 4. 5, 16; 6. 23, 30.

11. 1–15. 33 (**E**, p. 131). CEREMONIAL LAWS. (*Division.*)

E | J[1] | 11. 1–47. Food and defilement.
| J[2] | 12. 1–8. Child-bearing.
| J[3] | 13. 1—14. 57. Leprosy.
| J[4] | 15. 1–33. Issues.

11. 1–47 (J[1] above). FOOD AND DEFILEMENT. (*Division.*)

J[1] | K[1] | 1–23. Food.
| K[2] | 24–47. Defilement.

1–3 (K[1] above). FOOD. (*Division.*)

K[1] | i[1] | 1–8. Beasts (pos., 1–3; neg., 4–8).
| i[2] | 9–12. Water animals (pos., 9; neg., 10–12).
| i[3] | 13–19. Flying animals.
| i[4] | 20–23. Creeping or swarming animals (neg., 20; pos., 21, 22; neg., 23).

1 the LORD. Heb. Jehovah. Ap. 4.
spake. See note on 5. 14.
2 children. Heb. sons.
These. Heb. this. Fig. *Heterosis* (of Number), sing. for plural. (Ap. 6.)
beasts = living creatures.
beasts = animals. Heb. *b^ehēmāh.* The Heb. division of animal kingdom was: (1) Land animals; (2) water animals; (3) birds of the air; (4) swarming animals. Deut. 14. 4, 5 enumerates ten clean animals.
3 parteth the hoof. Cp. Deut. 14. 6.
4 not eat. These laws are not arbitrary. Food plays a chief part in health and sickness. It is our *wisdom* to obey these laws now, as far as possible. All are based on the preservation and health of the race. Some for sanitary reasons. Some from peculiarities of climate. Some for separating from other peoples.

1490 5 And the °coney, because he cheweth the
cud, but divideth not the hoof; he *is* unclean
unto you.
6 And the °hare, because he cheweth the
cud, but divideth not the hoof; he *is* unclean
unto you.
7 And the swine, though he divide the hoof,
and be clovenfooted, yet he cheweth not the
cud; he *is* unclean to you.
8 Of their flesh shall ye not eat, and their
carcase shall ye not touch; they *are* unclean
to you.

i² 9 These shall ye eat of all that *are* in the
(p. 146) waters: whatsoever hath fins and scales in
the waters, in the seas, and in the rivers, them
shall ye eat.

10 And all that have not fins and scales
in the seas, and in the rivers, of all that
move in the waters, and of any living °thing
which *is* in the waters, they *shall be* an
abomination unto you:
11 They shall be even an abomination unto
you; ye shall not eat of their flesh, but ye
shall have their carcases in abomination.
12 Whatsoever hath no fins nor scales in
the waters, that *shall be* an abomination unto
you.

i³ 13 And these *are they which* ye shall have in
abomination among the °fowls; they shall not
be eaten, they *are* an abomination: the °eagle,
and the °ossifrage, and the °ospray,
14 And the °vulture, and the °kite after his
kind;
15 Every °raven after his kind;
16 And the owl, and the night hawk, and the
°cuckow, and the hawk after his kind,
17 And the °little owl, and the °cormorant,
and the °great owl,
18 And the °swan, and the °pelican, and the
°gier eagle,
19 And the °stork, the °heron after her kind,
and the °lapwing, and the °bat.

i⁴ 20 All fowls that creep, going upon *all* four,
shall be an abomination unto you.
21 Yet these may ye eat of every flying
creeping thing that goeth upon *all* four, which
have legs above their feet, to leap withal upon
the earth;
22 *Even* °these of them ye may eat; the
°locust after his kind, and the °bald locust
after his kind, and the °beetle after his kind,
and the °grasshopper after his kind.
23 But all *other* flying creeping things,
which have four feet, *shall be* an abomination
unto you.

K² j 24 And for these ye shall be unclean: who-
(p. 147) soever toucheth the carcase of them shall be
unclean until the even.
25 And whosoever beareth *ought* of the carcase of them shall wash his clothes, and be
unclean until the even.

k 26 *The carcases* of every beast which
divideth the hoof, and *is* not clovenfooted,
nor cheweth the cud, *are* unclean unto you:
every one that toucheth them shall be unclean.

5 coney = the old English name for rabbit.
6 hare. Only here, and Deut. 14. 7. Heb. *'arnebeth*, not yet identified.
10 thing = soul. Heb. *nephesh*. Ap. 13.
13 fowls = flying things; very difficult to identify the *English* names.
eagle: or vulture.
ossifrage. A rendering of the Heb. "bone-breaker", from taking their prey up in the air and dropping it on a rock to break it.
ospray: or sea eagle.
14 vulture: or kite.
kite = falcon.
15 raven, or black birds of all kinds.
16 cuckow. Probably = sea-gull.
17 little owl, or simply "owl". Only here, Deut. 14. 16, and Ps. 102. 6.
cormorant: or the "darter".
great owl = Heb. "night-bird".
18 swan, not our swan: it is variously rendered "ibis", "bat", "heron", and "pelican".
pelican: or vomiting pelican.
gier eagle: or little vulture. Heb. "the merciful".
19 stork. Heb. *chăsîdah*, "the pious": rendered "stork" in Job 39. 13 (marg.). Ps. 104. 17. Jer. 8. 7. Zech. 5. 9.
heron. Heb. *'ănāphāh*, "the cruel".
lapwing. Better, the hoopoe, a dirty bird.
bat. A vile creature and symbol of evil (Isa. 2. 20): comes last as a link between two classes, quadrupeds and birds.
22 these: being all "after his kind", are probably four different species of the same, viz.:
locust = swarming locust.
bald locust = devouring locust.
beetle = *chargol* (or wingless) locust.
grasshopper = *chārgāb* locust, Nu. 13. 33. 2 Chron. 7. 13. Ecc. 12. 5. Is. 40. 22.
27 beasts = living creatures. See note on *v.* 2.

24—47 (K², 146). **DEFILEMENT** (*Alternation*).

K² | j | 24, 25. Command.
| k | 26–43. Clean and unclean.
| *j* | 44, 45. Command.
| *k* | 46, 47. Clean and unclean.

29 weasel. Heb. *choled* = the glider or slipper, occ. only here.
mouse. Heb. *'akbār* = the corn destroyer. 1 Sam. 6. 4, 5, 11, 18. Isa. 66. 17.
tortoise. Heb. *zāb* = the inflated, Num. 5. 27; probably = toad.
30 ferret = hedgehog. Heb. *'ănākāh*, only here.
lizard: or wall-lizard.
snail. Heb. *chomet*, Ps. 58. 8 = *shabbel*.
31 unclean. Better, "most unclean"; so in *v.* 29.
when they be dead. Cp. *v.* 24.

27 And whatsoever goeth upon his paws,
among all manner of °beasts that go on *all*
four, those *are* unclean unto you: whoso
toucheth their carcase shall be unclean until
the even.
28 And he that beareth the carcase of them
shall wash his clothes, and be unclean until
the even: they *are* unclean unto you.
29 These also *shall be* unclean unto you
among the creeping things that creep upon
the earth; the °weasel, and the °mouse, and
the °tortoise after his kind,
30 And the °ferret, and the chameleon, and
the °lizard, and the °snail, and the mole.
31 These *are* °unclean to you among all
that creep: whosoever doth touch them,
°when they be dead, shall be unclean until
the even.
32 And upon whatsoever *any* of them, when

1490 they are dead, doth fall, it shall be unclean; whether *it be* any vessel of wood, or raiment, or skin, or sack, whatsoever vessel *it be*, wherein *any* work is done, it must be put into water, and it shall be unclean until the even; so it shall be cleansed.

33 And every earthen vessel, whereinto *any* of them falleth, whatsoever *is* in it shall be unclean; and ye shall break it.

34 Of all °meat which may be eaten, *that* on which *such* water cometh shall be unclean: and all drink that may be drunk in every *such* vessel shall be unclean.

35 And every *thing* whereupon *any part* of their carcase falleth shall be unclean; *whether it be* oven, or ranges for pots, they shall be broken down: *for* they *are* unclean, and shall be unclean unto you.

36 Nevertheless a fountain or pit, *wherein there is* °plenty of water, shall be clean: but °that which toucheth their carcase shall be unclean.

37 And if *any part* of their carcase fall upon any sowing seed which is to be sown, it *shall be* clean.

38 But if *any* water be put upon the seed, and *any part* of their carcase fall thereon, it *shall be* unclean unto you.

39 And if any beast, of which ye may eat, die; he that toucheth the carcase thereof shall be unclean until the even.

40 And °he that eateth of the carcase of it shall wash his clothes, and be unclean until the even: he also that beareth the carcase of it shall wash his clothes, and be unclean until the even.

41 And every creeping thing that creepeth upon the earth *shall be* an abomination; it shall not be eaten.

42 Whatsoever goeth upon the belly, and whatsoever goeth upon *all* four, or whatsoever hath °more feet among all creeping things that creep upon the earth, them ye shall not eat; for they *are* an abomination.

43 Ye shall not make °your selves °abominable with any creeping thing that creepeth, neither shall ye make yourselves unclean with them, that ye should be defiled thereby.

j (p. 147) 44 For I *am* [1] the LORD your °God: ye shall therefore sanctify °yourselves, and ye shall be holy; °for I *am* holy: neither shall ye defile yourselves with any manner of creeping thing that creepeth upon the earth.

45 For I *am* [1] the LORD °that bringeth you up out of the land of Egypt, to be your [44] God: ye shall therefore be °holy, for I *am* °holy.

k 46 °This *is* the law of the °beasts, and of the fowl, and of every living °creature that moveth in the waters, and of every °creature that creepeth upon the earth:

47 To °make a difference between the unclean and the clean, and between the [27] beast that may be eaten and the [27] beast that °may not be eaten.'"

L¹ l (p. 148) **12** And °the LORD °spake unto Moses, saying,

2 "Speak unto the °children of Israel, saying, 'If a woman have conceived seed, and born a man child:

then she shall be unclean °seven days; °according to the days of the separation for her infirmity shall she be unclean. n

3 And in the eighth day the flesh of his foreskin shall be °circumcised.

4 And she shall then continue in the blood of her purifying °three and thirty days; she shall touch no °hallowed thing, nor come into the sanctuary, until the days of her purifying be fulfilled. o

5 But if she bear a maid child, m

then she shall be unclean two weeks, as in her separation: n

---

34 meat = food. Fig. *Synecdoche* (of the Part), one kind put for all kinds of food. Ap. 6.

36 plenty. Heb. = "a gathering together".

that which = he who.

40 he that eateth: i.e. ignorantly: otherwise, wilfully, it was the death penalty. Num. 15. 30. Deut. 14. 21.

42 more = many.

43 your selves = your souls. Heb. pl. of *nephesh.* Ap. 13.

abominable. Only here and 7. 21; 11. 10-13, 20, 23, 41, 42, and Isa. 66. 17. Ezek. 8. 10. The phrase occurs only once more, in ch. 20. 25, where it is used of souls.

44 God. Heb. Elohim. Ap. 4.

yourselves = your souls. Heb. pl. of *nephesh.* Ap. 13.

for I am holy. Cp. 1 Pet. 1. 15, 16; and see ch. 20. 7, 8.

45 that bringeth you up, &c. This wondrous redemption is repeatedly appealed to, to magnify Jehovah's grace and Israel's ingratitude. Cp. Deut. 8. 14; 13. 10; 20. 1. Josh. 24. 17. Judg. 2. 12, &c.

holy. See note on Ex. 3. 5.

46 This is the law of the beasts, &c. A recapitulation of the four classes. See structure of verses 1-23 (p. 146). There it was land, water, flying, and swarming. Here it is land animals, flying, water animals, and swarming. Cp. the summary of the sacrificial law, 7. 37, 38.

beasts. Heb. pl. of *bᵉhēmah.* See note on *v.* 27.

creature = soul. Heb. *nephesh.* Ap. 13.

47 make a difference: or, put, &c. Same word as in 10. 10.

may not be eaten. See 20. 25, and cp. Acts 10. 11-16.

12. 1—8 (J², p. 146). CHILD-BEARING.

(Division.)

J² | L¹ | 1-5. Ordinances.
   | L² | 6-8. Offerings.

12. 1—5 (L¹, above). ORDINANCES.

(Extended alternation.)

L¹ | l | 1, 2-. Man child.
   | m | -2, 3. Separation (seven days) } Forty
   | n | 4. Continuance (thirty-three days) } days.
   | *l* | 5-. Maid child.
   | *m* | -5-. Separation (fourteen days) } Eighty
   | *n* | -5. Continuance (sixty-six days) } days.

1 the LORD. Heb. Jehovah. Ap. 4.

spake. See note on 5. 14.

2 children. Heb. sons.

seven days. See note on *v.* 5.

according to the days. Cp. 15. 19.

3 circumcised. See note on "leprosy", 13. 2.

4 three and thirty. Half the period of maid child. See *v.* 5 (7 + 33 = 40. See Ap. 10).

hallowed. Heb. *ḳādesh.* See note on Ex. 3. 5.

n and she shall continue in the blood of her
(p. 148) °purifying °threescore and six days.

1490 6 And when the days of her purifying are
L[2] fulfilled, for a son, or for a daughter, °she
shall bring a lamb of the first year for a burnt
offering, and a young pigeon, or a turtledove,
for a °sin offering, unto the °door of the
°tabernacle of the congregation, unto the
priest:
7 Who shall °offer it before [1]the LORD, and
°make an atonement for her; and she shall
be cleansed from the °issue of her blood. This
is the law for her that hath born a male or
a female.
8 And if she be not able to bring a lamb,
then she shall bring °two turtles, or two
young pigeons; the one for the burnt offering,
and the other for a [6]sin offering: and the
priest shall [7]make an atonement for her, and
she shall be clean.' "

J[3] M **13** And °the LORD °spake unto Moses and
(p. 149) Aaron, saying,
2 "When a °man shall have in the skin of
his flesh a rising, a scab, or bright spot, and
it be in the skin of his flesh *like* °the plague
of °leprosy; then he shall be brought unto
Aaron the priest, or unto one of his sons the
priests:
3 And the priest shall look on the plague
in the skin of the flesh: and *when* the hair
in the plague is turned white, and the plague
in sight *be* deeper than the skin of his flesh,
it *is* a plague of leprosy: and the priest shall
look on him, and °pronounce him unclean.
4 If the bright spot *be* white in the skin of
his flesh, and in sight *be* not deeper than the
skin, and the hair thereof be not turned white;
then the priest shall shut up *him that hath*
the °plague seven days:
5 And the priest shall look on him the
seventh day: and, °behold, *if* the plague in
°his sight be at a stay, *and* the plague spread
not in the skin; then the priest shall shut
him up seven days more:
6 And the priest shall look on him again the
seventh day: and, [5]behold, *if* the plague *be*
somewhat dark, *and* the plague °spread not
in the skin, the priest shall [3]pronounce him
clean: it *is but* a scab: and he shall wash
his clothes, and be clean.
7 But if the scab spread much abroad in
the skin, after that he hath been seen of
the priest for his cleansing, he shall be seen
of the priest again:
8 And *if* the priest see that, [5]behold, the
scab spreadeth in the skin, then the priest
shall [3]pronounce him unclean: it *is* a leprosy.

9 When the plague of leprosy is in a [2]man,
then he shall be brought unto the priest;
10 And the priest shall see *him*: and, [5]behold,
if the rising *be* °white in the skin, and it have
turned the hair white, and *there be* °quick
raw flesh in the rising;
11 It *is* an old leprosy in the skin of his flesh,
and the priest shall pronounce him unclean,
and °shall not shut him up: for he °*is* unclean.
12 And if a leprosy °break out abroad in the
skin, and the leprosy cover all the skin of
him that hath the plague from his head even
to his foot, wheresoever the priest looketh;
13 Then the priest shall consider: and,
[5]behold, *if* the leprosy have covered all his
flesh, he shall pronounce *him* clean *that hath*
the plague: it is all turned white: he *is* clean.

5 purifying = purification, i.e. pure blood as distinct from the other.
threescore and six days. Double that after a man child. See *v.* 4 (14 + 66 = 80). This ordinance was not on account of any disparity between the sexes, but was in order to regulate them, so that the birth-rate of females might not be in too great excess, as it otherwise would have been, and is, where this ordinance is not known or observed.

6—8 (L[2], p. 148). OFFERINGS.

6 she shall bring. As Mary did. Luke 2. 22-24.
sin. Heb. *'chāṭ'ā.* Ap. 44. i.
door = entrance.
tabernacle = tent. Heb. *'ohel.* Ap. 40.
7 offer it = bring it near. Heb. *ḳārab.* Ap. 43. I. i.
make. Sam., Sept., and Syr. read, "and the priest shall make", as in *v.* 8.
make an atonement. See note on Ex. 29. 33.
issue = fount.
8 two turtles. See Luke 2. 22, 24, and cp. 2 Cor. 8. 9.

13. 1—14. 57 (J[3], p. 146). LEPROSY.
(*Alternations.*)

J[3] | M | 13. 1-46. Leprosy in man.
  N | o | 13. 47-57. In a garment.
    p | 13. 58. Cleansing of garment.
    q | 13. 59. Law for garment.
 M | 14. 1-32. Law of Leprosy.
  N | *o* | 14. 33-47. In a house.
    p | 14. 48-53. Cleansing of house.
    q | 14. 54-57. Law for all cases.

1 the LORD. Heb. Jehovah. Ap. 4.
spake. See note on 5. 14.
2 man. Heb. *'ādām.* Ap. 14.
the plague = spot: mark too weak for person, though suited for house (14. 34): "plague" and "stroke" would be too strong in every case.
leprosy. Heb. *ẓār'āth*, from *ẓār'a*, to *strike down*, a leper being one stricken of God. One of the four points which Christ endorses Leviticus as being written by Moses:
1. Circumcision, 12. 3 (John 7. 22, 23).
2. Law of leper, 14. 3-32 (Matt. 8. 4).
3. The shewbread, 24. 5-9 (Matt. 12. 4).
4. Death penalty for cursing parents, 20. 9 (Mark 7. 10).
Leprosy is the type of what man *is* by nature. (All the offerings relate to what man has *done* or *not* done.) It has reference to the evil "in" him (*v.* 2, 9), not to the outcome of it. See note on *v.* 45.
3 pronounce. Heb. "shall make him". Fig. *Metonymy* (of Subject) = pronounce or declare him to be. Ap. 6. Cp. Ezek. 43. 3, &c.
4 plague = plagued person. Heb. "shut up the plague". Fig. *Metonymy* (of Adjunct). Ap. 6. The meaning is supplied in italics.
5 behold. Fig. *Asterismos.* (Ap. 6.)
his sight = its appearance.
6 spread. This is the criterion here for persons, as for houses and garments (cp. *v.* 55, & 14. 44, 48). This is the criterion for our judgment of the antitype—"sin"—our old nature, to which our attention is called by the Fig. *Asterismos*, "Behold" (see Ap. 6).
10 white. See note on *v.* 30. **quick** = living.
11 shall not: or, need not.
is: i.e. is undoubtedly, no further proof being needed.
12 break out abroad = cometh quite out. Type of the sinner confessing his totality of evil—then he is clean, 1 John 1. 9, 10.

1490 14 But °when raw flesh appeareth in him, he shall be unclean.

15 And the priest shall see the raw flesh, and [3]pronounce him to be unclean: *for* the raw flesh °*is* unclean: it *is* a leprosy.

16 Or if the raw flesh turn again, and be changed unto white, he shall come unto the priest;

17 And the priest shall see him: and, [5]behold, *if* the plague be turned into white; then the priest shall [3]pronounce *him* clean *that hath* the plague: he *is* clean.

18 The flesh also, in which, *even* in the skin thereof, was a boil, and is healed,

19 And in the place of the boil there be a white rising, or a bright spot, white, and somewhat reddish, and it be shewed to the priest;

20 And if, when the priest seeth it, [5]behold, it *be* in sight lower than the skin, and the hair thereof be turned white; the priest shall [3]pronounce him unclean: it *is* a [2]plague of leprosy broken out of the boil.

21 But if the priest look on it, and, [5]behold, *there be* no white hairs therein, and *if* it *be* not lower than the skin, but °*be* °somewhat dark; then the priest shall shut him up seven days:

22 And if it spread much abroad in the skin, then the priest shall [3]pronounce him unclean: it *is* a plague.

23 But if the bright spot stay in his place, *and* spread not, it *is* a burning boil; and the priest shall [3]pronounce him clean.

24 Or if there be *any* flesh, in the skin whereof *there is* a hot burning, and the [10]quick *flesh* that burneth have a white bright spot, somewhat reddish, or white;

25 Then the priest shall look upon it: and, [5]behold, *if* the hair in the bright spot be turned white, and it *be in* sight deeper than the skin; it *is* a leprosy broken out of the burning: wherefore the priest shall [3]pronounce him unclean: it *is* the [2]plague of leprosy.

26 But if the priest look on it, and, [5]behold, *there be* no white hair in the bright spot, and it *be* no lower than the *other* skin, but [21]*be* [21]somewhat dark; then the priest shall shut him up seven days:

27 And the priest shall look upon him the seventh day: *and* if it be spread much abroad in the skin, then the priest shall [3]pronounce him unclean: it *is* the plague of leprosy.

28 And if the bright spot stay in his place, *and* spread not in the skin, but it *be* somewhat dark; it *is* a rising of the burning, and the priest shall [3]pronounce him clean: for it *is* an inflammation of the burning.

29 If a °man or woman have a °plague upon the head or the beard;

30 Then the priest shall see the [29]plague: and, [5]behold, if it *be* in sight deeper than the skin; *and there be* in it a yellow °thin hair; then the priest shall [3]pronounce him unclean: it *is* a dry °scall, °*even* a leprosy upon the head or beard.

31 And if the priest look on the [2]plague of the [30]scall, and, [5]behold, it *be* not in sight deeper than the skin, and *that there is* no black hair in it; then the priest shall shut up *him that hath* the plague of the [30]scall seven days:

32 And in the seventh day the priest shall look on the plague: and, [5]behold, *if* the [30]scall spread not, and there be in it no yellow hair, and the [30]scall *be* not in sight deeper than the skin;

33 He shall be shaven, but the [30]scall shall he not shave; and the priest shall shut up *him that hath* the [30]scall seven days more:

34 And in the seventh day the priest shall look on the [30]scall: and, [5]behold, *if* the [30]scall be not spread in the skin, nor *be* in sight deeper than the skin; then the priest shall [3]pronounce him clean: and he shall wash his clothes, and be clean.

35 But if the [30]scall spread much in the skin after his cleansing;

36 Then the priest shall look on him: and, [5]behold, if the [30]scall be spread in the skin, the priest shall not seek for yellow hair; he *is* unclean.

37 But if the [30]scall be in [5]his sight at a stay, and *that* there is black hair grown up therein; the [30]scall is healed, he *is* clean: and the priest shall [3]pronounce him clean.

38 If a [29]man also or a [29]woman have in the skin of their flesh bright spots, *even* white bright spots;

39 Then the priest shall look: and, [5]behold, *if* the bright spots in the skin of their flesh *be* °darkish white; it *is* a freckled spot *that* groweth in the skin; he *is* clean.

40 And the man whose hair is fallen off his head, he *is* bald; *yet is* he clean.

41 And he that hath his hair fallen off from the part of his head toward his face, he *is* forehead bald: *yet is* he clean.

42 And if there be in the bald head, or bald forehead, a white reddish sore; it *is* a leprosy sprung up in his bald head, or his bald forehead.

43 Then the priest shall look upon it: and, behold, *if* the rising of the sore *be* white reddish in his bald head, or in his bald forehead, as the leprosy appeareth in the skin of the flesh;

44 He is a leprous man, he *is* unclean: the priest shall [3]pronounce him utterly unclean; his plague *is* in his head.

45 And the leper in whom [2]the plague *is*, his clothes shall be °rent, and his head bare,

14 when. Heb. "in the day", same as Gen. 2. 17; see Ap. 18.
15 is = it [is].
21 be = it [be].
somewhat dark = faint.
29 man or woman = *'ish* or *'ishah*. See Ap. 14.
plague: better, "spot". See note on *v.* 2.
30 thin = short. An infallible sign of leprosy. A long hair, even though "yellow", no sign. In other parts of the body the hairs would be short and white. Cp. *v.* 10. scall = scab.
even = it [is].
39 darkish white = faintish, or dead white; a harmless eruption, or "tetter".
45 rent. See note on 10. 6.

1490 and he shall put a °covering upon his upper
lip, and shall cry, °'Unclean, unclean.'
46 All the days wherein the plague *shall be*
in him he shall be defiled; he *is* unclean: he
shall dwell alone; °without the camp *shall*
his habitation *be*.
N o 47 The °garment also that the plague of
(p. 149) leprosy is in, *whether it be* a woollen garment,
or a linen garment;
48 Whether *it be* in the °warp, or °woof; of
linen, or of woollen; whether in a skin, or
in any thing made of skin;
49 And if the plague be greenish or reddish
in the garment, or in the skin, either in the
[48]warp, or in the [48]woof, or in any thing of skin;
it *is* a plague of leprosy, and shall be shewed
unto the priest:
50 And the priest shall look upon the plague,
and shut up *it that hath* the plague seven
days:
51 And he shall look on the plague on the
seventh day: if the plague be spread in the
garment, either in the [48]warp, or in the [48]woof,
or in a skin, *or* in any work that is made
of skin; the plague *is* a °fretting leprosy;
it *is* unclean.
52 He shall therefore burn that garment,
whether [48]warp or [48]woof, in woollen or in linen,
or any thing of skin, wherein the plague is:
for it *is* a [51]fretting leprosy; it shall be °burnt
in the fire.

53 And if the priest shall look, and, [5]behold,
the plague be not spread in the garment,
either in the [48]warp, or in the [48]woof, or in any
thing of skin;
54 Then the priest shall command that they
wash *the thing* wherein the plague *is*, and
he shall shut it up seven days more:
55 And the priest shall look on the plague,
after that it is washed: and, [5]behold, *if* the
plague have not changed his °colour, and the
plague be not spread; it *is* unclean; thou
shalt burn it in the fire; it *is* fret inward,
whether it *be* bare within or without.

56 And if the priest look, and, [5]behold, the
plague *be* [21]somewhat dark after the washing
of it; then he shall rend it out of the garment,
or out of the skin, or out of the [48]warp, or out
of the [48]woof:
57 And if it appear still in the garment,
either in the [48]warp, or in the [48]woof, or in any
thing of skin; it *is* a spreading *plague:* thou
shalt [52]burn that wherein the plague *is* with
fire.

p 58 And the garment, either [48]warp, or [48]woof,
or whatsoever thing of skin *it be*, which thou
shalt wash, if the plague be departed from
them, then it shall be washed the second time,
and shall be clean.

q 59 This *is* the law of the plague of leprosy
in a garment of woollen or linen, either in
the [48]warp, or [48]woof, or any thing of skins,
to [3]pronounce it clean, or to [3]pronounce it
unclean."

M **14** And °the LORD °spake unto Moses,
saying,
2 "This shall be °the law of the leper °in
the day of his cleansing: He °shall be °brought
unto the priest:
3 And the priest shall go forth out of the
camp; and the priest shall look, and, °behold,
if the plague of leprosy be healed in
the leper;
4 Then shall the priest command to take
for him that °is to be cleansed two °birds
alive *and* clean, and °cedar wood, and °scarlet,
and °hyssop:
5 And the priest shall command that one of
the birds be killed in an earthen vessel over
°running water:
6 °As for the living bird, he shall take it,
and the cedar wood, and the scarlet, and the
hyssop, and shall dip them and the living bird
in the blood of the bird *that was* killed over
the [5]running water:
7 And he shall sprinkle upon him that is to
be cleansed from the leprosy °seven times,

covering = muffler.
'Unclean, unclean.' Fig. *Epizeuxis*, Ap. 6, to emphasise the *condition*. Leprosy is the great type of sin: and teaches that the sinner is not only lost and ruined on account of what he has *done*, but on account of what he *is*. The former needed atonement to procure *judicial* righteousness, but the latter requires a Divine act and cleansing to give him an *imputed* righteousness. The former we have through Christ's atonement, the latter we have from God in Christ. It is not enough to confess what we "have done" or "left undone"; there must be also the confession "there is no health in us". Cp. Isa. 6. 5. Job 40. 4; 42. 6. Ps. 51. 5. Luke 5. 8, &c.

46 without the camp. Num 5. 2; 12. 10-15.

47 garment. Type of habits and ways seen by others. Cp. Jude 23.

48 warp. A.S. *wearpen*, to cast or throw = the longitudinal lines in the loom, through which the shuttle passes. Heb. *shāthah*, to drink in. So called because of its *drinking in* the thread thrown by the shuttle.

woof. A.S. to weave in. Heb *'ārab*, to intermingle. Hence used of what is mingled or woven in by the shuttle.

51 fretting = rankling, only of what is malignant: occurs only here, *v.* 52; 14. 14, and Ezek. 28. 24.

52 burnt. Heb. *sāraph.* Ap. 43. I. viii.

55 colour = appearance. Heb. eye. Fig. *Metonymy* (of Adjunct), Ap. 6: eye put for appearance.

14. 1-57 (M, N, p. 149). **THE LAW OF LEPROSY.**

1 the LORD. Heb. Jehovah. Ap. 4.

spake. This was delivered to Moses alone, who was to communicate these regulations to Aaron and his sons; while the rules by which the plague was to be discerned were given to both Moses and Aaron. Thus the position of Moses as the great lawgiver was upheld and secured. See note on 5. 14.

2 the law of the leper: provides for his cleansing.

in the day = when. Cp. Gen. 2. 17, and see Ap. 18.

shall be brought unto the priest. Cp. Matt. 8. 2. Mark 1. 40. Luke 5. 12; 17. 13.

brought. The leper could do nothing. He must be "brought". The priest must go forth to him (*v.* 3).

3 behold. Fig. *Asterismos.* Ap. 6.

4 is to be cleansed = him that is cleansing himself.

birds, or sparrows.

cedar wood, and scarlet, and hyssop. Hence the ancient tradition that the highest tree and the lowest herb give the leper purity, because *pride* was the cause of the plague, and *humility* is the necessary condition of its cure. These three were used also with the red heifer (Num. 19. 6). Cp. Heb. 9. 19. Ps. 51. 7.

5 running. Heb. living, i. e. not stagnant.

6 As. Some codices, with Sam., Sept., Syr., and Vulg., read "and as".

7 seven times. Cp. 4. 6. 2 Kings 5. 10, 14. Ap. 10.

1490 and shall °pronounce him clean, and shall let the living bird loose °into the open field.

8 And he that [4]is to be cleansed shall °wash his clothes, and shave off all his hair, and °wash himself in water, that he may be clean: and after that he shall come into the camp, and shall tarry abroad out of his tent [7]seven days.

9 But it shall be on the °seventh day, that he shall shave all his hair off his head and his beard and his eyebrows, even all his hair he shall shave off: and he shall wash his clothes, also he shall °wash his flesh in water, and he shall be clean.

10 And on the °eighth day he shall take two he lambs without blemish, and one ewe lamb of the first year without blemish, and three tenth °deals of fine flour *for* a °meat offering, mingled with oil, and one °log of oil.

11 And the priest that maketh *him* clean shall °present the man that is to be made clean, and those things, before [1]the LORD, *at* the °door of the °tabernacle of the congregation:

12 And the priest shall take one he lamb, and °offer him for a °trespass offering, and the [10]log of oil, and wave them *for* a °wave offering before [1]the LORD:

13 And he shall slay the lamb in the place where he shall kill the sin offering and the burnt offering, in the holy place: for as the °sin offering *is* the priest's, *so is* the [12]trespass offering: it *is* most °holy:

14 And the priest shall take *some* of the blood of the [12]trespass offering, and the priest shall put *it* upon the tip of the right ear of him that is to be cleansed, and upon the thumb of his right hand, and upon the great toe of his right foot:

15 And the priest shall take *some* of the [10]log of oil, and pour *it* into the palm of his own left hand:

16 And the priest shall dip his right finger in the oil that *is* in his left hand, and shall sprinkle of the oil with his finger seven times before [1]the LORD:

17 And of the rest of the oil that *is* in his hand shall the priest put upon the tip of the right ear of him that is to be cleansed, and upon the thumb of his right hand, and upon the great toe of his right foot, upon the blood of the [12]trespass offering:

18 And the remnant of the oil that *is* in the priest's hand he shall pour upon °the head of him that is to be cleansed: and the priest shall °make an atonement for him before [1]the LORD.

19 And the priest shall °offer the [13]sin offering, and [18]make an atonement for him that is to be cleansed from his uncleanness; and afterward he shall kill the burnt offering:

20 And the priest shall offer the burnt offering and the meat offering upon the altar: and the priest shall [18]make an atonement for him, and he shall be clean.

21 And if he *be* °poor, and °cannot get so much; then he shall take one lamb *for* a [12]trespass offering to be waved, to [18]make an atonement for him, and one tenth [10]deal of fine flour mingled with oil for a meat offering, and a [10]log of oil;

22 And two turtledoves, or two young pigeons, such as he is able to get; and the one shall be a [13]sin offering, and the other a burnt offering.

23 And he shall bring them on the eighth day for his cleansing unto the priest, unto the °door of the [11]tabernacle of the congregation, before [1]the LORD.

24 And °the priest shall take the lamb of the [12]trespass offering, and the [10]log of oil, and the priest shall wave them *for* a [12]wave offering before [1]the LORD:

25 And he shall kill the lamb of the [12]trespass offering, and the priest shall take *some* of the blood of the [12]trespass offering, and put *it* upon the tip of the right ear of him that is to be cleansed, and upon the thumb of his right hand, and upon the great toe of his right foot:

26 And the priest shall pour of the oil into the palm of his own left hand:

27 And the priest shall sprinkle with his right finger *some* of the oil that *is* in his left hand seven times before [1]the LORD:

28 And the priest shall put of the oil that *is* in his hand upon the tip of the right ear of him that is to be cleansed, and upon the thumb of his right hand, and upon the great toe of his right foot, upon the place of the blood of the [12]trespass offering:

29 And the rest of the oil that *is* in the priest's hand he shall put upon the head of

pronounce him clean = Heb. make him clean. Fig. *Metonymy* (of Adjunct), Ap. 6. = declare him to be clean.

into the open field. Heb. "over the face of the field". Fig. *Prosopopœia*. Ap. 6.

8 wash = bathe.

9 seventh day. He was clean on the first day, now he enters into the enjoyment of it himself.

wash his flesh in water = bathe his body. Flesh put by Fig. *Synecdoche* (of Part), Ap 6, for his body, as in Ecc. 2. 3. Isa. 10. 8. Ezek. 10. 12. Occurs eight times in Leviticus (14. 9; 15. 13, 16; 16. 4, 24, 26, 28; 22. 6), and is rendered in three different ways in A.V. But a peculiar ritual phrase should obviously be rendered by the same English phrase. This is to be distinguished from "himself" in 14. 8; 15. 5, 6, 7, 8, 10, 11, 16, 18, 21, 22, 27; 17. 15.

10 eighth day. Now, all the offerings are introduced, but the trespass offering comes first (*v.* 12).

deals. See Ap. 51. III. 3.

meat offering. Heb. *minḥāh.* Ap. 43. II. 3.

log. See Ap. 51. III. 3.

11 present the man = cause the man to stand. All is done *for* the leper, he can do nothing.

door = entrance.

tabernacle = tent. Heb. *'ohel.* See Ap. 40.

12 offer = bring him near. Heb. *ḳārab.* Ap. 43. I. i.

trespass offering. Heb. *'āsām.* Ap. 43. II. vi.

wave offering. See note on Ex. 29. 27.

13 sin. Heb. *chāṭ'ā.* Ap. 44. i.

holy. See note on Ex. 3. 5.

18 the head. Note how all the members of the body are in turn cleansed. All is forgiven. Ps. 103. 3. Col. 1. 14; 2. 13. Eph. 1. 7.

make an atonement. See note on Ex. 29. 33.

19 offer. Heb. *'āsāh.* Ap. 43. I. 3.

21 poor. The Divine consideration is again shown here. Cp. 5. 7, 11; 12. 8.

cannot get. Heb. "his hand reach not". Translated in *v.* 22.

23 door = entrance.

24 the priest shall take, &c. The ritual as imposing for the poor as for the rich.

1490 him that is to be cleansed, to [18]make an atonement for him before [1]the LORD.

30 And he shall [19]offer the one of the turtledoves, or of the young pigeons, such as he can get;

31 *Even* such as he is able to get, the one *for* a [13]sin offering, and the other *for* a burnt offering, with the meat offering: and the priest shall [18]make an atonement for him that is to be cleansed before [1]the LORD.

32 This *is* the law *of him* in whom *is* the plague of leprosy, whose hand is not able to get *that which pertaineth* to his cleansing."

N p 33 And [1]the LORD °spake unto Moses and
(p. 149) unto Aaron, saying,

34 °"When ye be come into the land of Canaan, which I give to you for a possession, and I put the °plague of leprosy in a house of the land of your possession;

35 And he that owneth the house shall come and tell the priest, saying, 'It seemeth to me *there is* as it were a [34]plague in the house:'

36 Then the priest shall command that they empty the house, °before the priest go *into it* to see the [34]plague, that all that *is* in the house be not made unclean: and afterward the priest shall go in to see the house:

37 And he shall look on the [34]plague, and, behold, *if* the [34]plague *be* in the walls of the house with °hollow strakes, greenish or reddish, which in sight *are* lower °than the wall;

38 Then the priest shall go out of the house to the [23]door of the house, and shut up the house seven days:

39 And the priest shall come again °the seventh day, and shall look: and, behold, *if* the [34]plague be °spread in the walls of the house;

40 Then the priest shall command that °they take away the stones in which the [34]plague *is*, and °they shall cast them into an unclean place without the city:

41 And he shall cause the house to be scraped within round about, and they shall pour out the dust that they scrape off without the city into an unclean place:

42 And they shall take other stones, and put *them* in the place of those stones; and °he shall take other morter, and shall plaister the house.

43 And if the [34]plague come again, and break out in the house, after that he hath taken away the stones, and after he hath scraped the house, and after it is plaistered;

44 Then the priest shall come and look, and, °behold, *if* the plague be °spread in the house, it *is* a °fretting leprosy in the house: it *is* unclean.

45 And he shall break down the house, the stones of it, and the timber thereof, and all the morter of the house; and he shall carry *them* forth out of the city into an unclean place.

46 Moreover he that goeth into the house all the while that it is shut up shall be unclean until the even.

47 And he that lieth in the house shall wash his clothes; and he that eateth in the house shall wash his clothes.

48 And if the priest °shall come in, and look *upon it*, °and, behold, the [34]plague hath not [44]spread in the house, after the house was plaistered: then the priest shall [7]pronounce the house clean, because the plague is healed. p

49 °And he shall take to °cleanse the house two birds, and cedar wood, and scarlet, and hyssop:

50 And he shall kill the one of the birds in an earthen vessel over [5]running water:

51 And he shall take the cedar wood, and the hyssop, and the scarlet, and the living bird, and dip them in the blood of the slain bird, and in the [5]running water, and sprinkle the house seven times:

52 And he shall [49]cleanse the house with the blood of the bird, and with the running water, and with the living bird, and with the

33-53 (*p q*, p. 149). LEPROSY IN A HOUSE.

33 spake. See note on 5. 14. The law of cleansing persons addressed to Moses alone; that about houses, &c., addressed to Aaron as well.

34 When ye be come, &c. Here we have the first of four prospective laws, having no immediate bearing. See 19. 23; 23. 10; 25. 2. Hence it is separated from the law for leprous men and garments, in the form of an appendix.

plague. House leprosy is here represented as being supernatural. This was peculiar to Palestine and to houses of Israelites. The Targum of Jonathan renders this: "And if there be a man who buildeth his house with stolen goods, then I will put", &c.

36 before, &c. This law was most benign in its intention.

37 hollow strakes = sunken places.

than the wall = Fig. *Ellipsis*, Ap. 6. ii. a. = "deeper than [the surface of] the wall".

39 the seventh day = on the seventh day. Note the frequency of this number throughout, and see Ap. 10.

spread. This is a bad sign in noting the presence and workings of our inward corruption.

40 they. Of the verbs in these three verses, note that two are in the singular, viz. *v.* 42, "he shall take", and "he shall plaister". Hence the authorities of the second temple interpreted the plural of the owners of the "party-wall", and the singular of the owner of the affected house.

42 he. See note on *v.* 40.

44 behold. Fig. *Asterismos.* Ap. 6.

spread. The same criterion as in the case of men and garments. See note on *v.* 37 and 13. 6.

fretting = rankling. See note on 13. 51.

48 shall come. Heb. "coming in shall come in." Fig. *Polyptōton.* (Ap. 6.) = shall actually come in.

49 And. Note the Fig. *Polysyndeton* (Ap. 6) in *vv.* 48-53.

cleanse = cleanse from sin.

51, 52. Note the emphasis put upon this ceremony by the Structure (an *Introversion*). Note also the Fig. *Polysyndeton.* (Ap. 6.)

s | 51-. Cedar wood, hyssop, and scarlet.
  t | -51-. And the living bird.
    u | -51-. Blood of the bird and running water.
      v | -51. The house.
      v | 52-. The house.
    u | -52-. Blood of the bird and running water.
  t | -52-. And the living bird.
s | -52. Cedar wood, hyssop, and scarlet.

1490 cedar wood, and with the hyssop, and with the scarlet:

53 But he shall let go the living bird out of the city into the open fields, and [18]make an atonement for the house: and it shall be clean.

q (p. 149) **54 This *is* the law for all manner of plague of leprosy, and scall,**

55 And for the leprosy of a garment, and of a house,

56 And for a rising, and for a scab, and for a bright spot:

57 °To teach °when *it is* unclean, and °when *it is* clean: this *is* the law of leprosy."

J[4] O (p. 154) **15 And °the LORD °spake unto Moses and to Aaron, saying,**

2 "Speak unto the °children of Israel, and say unto them, 'When any °man hath a running issue out of his °flesh, *because of* his issue he *is* unclean.

3 And this shall be his uncleanness in his issue: whether his [2]flesh run with his issue, or his flesh be stopped from his issue, it *is* his uncleanness.

4 Every bed, whereon he lieth that hath the issue, is unclean: and every °thing, whereon he sitteth, shall be unclean.

5 And whosoever toucheth his bed shall wash his clothes, and °bathe *himself* in water, and be unclean until the even.

6 And he that sitteth on *any* thing whereon he sat that hath the issue shall wash his clothes, and [5]bathe *himself* in water, and be unclean until the even.

7 And he that toucheth the flesh of him that hath the issue shall wash his clothes, and [5]bathe *himself* in water, and be unclean until the even.

8 And if he that hath the issue °spit upon him that is clean; then he shall wash his clothes, and [5]bathe *himself* in °water, and be unclean until the even.

9 And what °saddle soever he rideth upon that hath the issue shall be °unclean.

10 And whosoever toucheth any thing that was under him shall be unclean until the even: and he that beareth *any of* those things shall wash his clothes, and [5]bathe *himself* in water, and be unclean until the even.

11 And whomsoever he toucheth that hath the issue, and hath not rinsed his hands in water, he shall wash his clothes, and [5]bathe *himself* in water, and be unclean until the even.

12 And the vessel of earth, that he toucheth which hath the issue, shall be broken: and every vessel of wood shall be °rinsed in water.

P **13 And when he that hath an issue is cleansed of his issue; then he shall number to himself seven days for his cleansing, and wash his clothes, and [5]bathe his flesh in °running water, and shall be clean.**

14 And on the eighth day he shall take to him two turtledoves, or two young pigeons, and come before [1]the LORD unto the °door of the °tabernacle of the congregation, and give them unto the priest:

15 And the priest shall °offer them, the one *for* a °sin offering, and the other *for* a burnt offering; and the priest shall °make an atonement for him before [1]the LORD for his issue.

16 And if any °man's seed of copulation go out from him, then he shall °wash all his flesh in water, and be unclean until the even.

17 And every garment, and every skin, whereon is the seed of copulation, shall be washed with water, and be unclean until the even.

18 The woman also with whom man shall lie *with* seed of copulation, they shall *both* [5]bathe *themselves* in water, and be unclean until the even.

19 And if a woman have an issue, *and* her issue in her [2]flesh be blood, she shall be put apart seven days: and whosoever toucheth her shall be unclean until the even. O

20 And every thing that she lieth upon

54—57 (*r*, p. 136). The recapitulation of the law, corresponding with "r", 13. 59 (p. 136), summing up chapters 13 and 14.

57 To teach. Some codices, with Sam., Sept., and Syr., read "and to", thus preserving the Fig. *Polysyndeton* (Ap. 6) in this member *r* (*vv.* 54–57) without a break. Eight "ands" in all.

when. Heb. "in the day". Cp. Gen. 2. 17, and see Ap. 18.

15 (J[4], p. 146). ISSUES.

(*Alternation.*)

J[4] | O | 1–12. Men.
  P | 13–18. Their cleansing.
 O | 19–27. Women.
  P | 28–33. Their cleansing.

1 the LORD. Heb. Jehovah. Ap. 4.

spake. See note on 5. 14.

2 children = sons.

man. Heb. *'îsh.* See Ap. 14.

flesh. Fig. *Synecdoche* (of Whole). Ap. 6. = any part of his flesh.

4 thing = piece of furniture, vessel, or article.

5 bathe. See note on 14. 5.

8 spit upon him. A common practice among oriental nations to express insult or contempt (Num. 12. 14. Deut. 25. 9. Job 30. 10. Isa. 50. 6. Matt. 26. 67.

water. The Severus Codex has "running water", as in *v.* 13. (See Ap. 34.)

9 saddle = carriage. Occ. only here and 1 Kings 4. 26, where it is rendered "chariot", and Song 3. 9. The seat in a palanquin. The fem. form occurs forty-four times, and is always rendered "chariot".

unclean. The Sept. adds "until evening", as in every other case. See *vv.* 5, 6, 7, 8, 10, 11. But in these verses *persons* are referred to. In *v.* 9 it is a *thing.*

12 rinsed = washed or baptized. This is what is referred to in Mark 7. 4.

13 running. Heb. living, not stagnant. See 14. 5.

14 door = entrance.

tabernacle of the congregation. Heb. tent (*'ohel*) of meeting. See Ap. 40.

15 offer = prepare. Heb. *'āsāh.* Ap. 43. I. iii.

sin. Heb. *chāṭ'ā.* Ap. 44. i.

make an atonement. See note on Ex. 29. 33.

16 man's. Heb. *'îsh.* See Ap. 14. iii.

wash = bathe. Here, with *ĕth kol* added, meaning all his body, to distinguish it from the word "flesh", which is thus probably used in this section by the Fig. *Euphemy* (Ap. 6) for private parts. Cp. 15. 5–8, 10, 11, 18, 21, 22, 27, where the A.V. has inserted "himself" in italics. See further note on 14. 9.

1490 in her separation shall be unclean: every thing also that she sitteth upon shall be unclean.

21 And whosoever toucheth her bed shall wash his clothes, and [5] bathe *himself* in water, and be unclean until the even.

22 And whosoever toucheth any thing that she sat upon shall wash his clothes, and [5] bathe *himself* in water, and be unclean until the even.

23 And if it *be* on *her* bed, or on any thing whereon she sitteth, when he toucheth it, he shall be unclean until the even.

24 And if any °man lie with her at all, and her °flowers be upon him, he shall be unclean seven days; and all the bed whereon he lieth shall be unclean.

25 And if a woman have an issue of her blood many days out of the time of her separation, or if it run beyond the time of her separation; all the days of the issue of her uncleanness shall be as the days of her separation: she *shall be* unclean.

26 Every bed whereon she lieth all the days of her issue shall be unto her as the bed of her separation: and whatsoever she sitteth upon shall be unclean, as the uncleanness of her separation.

27 And whosoever toucheth those things shall be unclean, and shall wash his clothes, and [5] bathe *himself* in water, and be unclean until the even.

P (p. 154) 28 But if she be cleansed of her issue, then she shall number to herself seven days, and after that she shall be clean.

29 And on the eighth day she shall take unto her two °turtles, or two young pigeons, and bring them unto the priest, to the [14] door of the [14] tabernacle of the congregation.

30 And the priest shall [15] offer the one *for* a sin offering, and the other *for* a burnt offering; and the priest shall [15] make an atonement for her before [1] the LORD for the issue of her uncleanness.

31 Thus shall °ye separate the [2] children of Israel from their uncleanness; that they die not in their uncleanness, when they defile My °tabernacle that *is* among them.

32 °This *is* the law of him that hath an issue, and *of him* whose seed goeth from him, °and is defiled therewith;

33 And of her that is sick of her [24] flowers, and of him that hath an issue, of the man, and of the woman, and of him that lieth with her that is unclean.' "

C Q (p. 155) **16** And °the LORD °spake unto Moses after the death of the two sons of Aaron, when they °offered before °the LORD, and died;

2 And [1] the LORD said unto Moses, "Speak unto Aaron thy brother, that he come not at °all times into the °holy *place* within the vail before the °mercy seat, which *is* upon the ark; that he die not: for °I will appear in the cloud upon the °mercy seat.

R 3 °Thus shall Aaron come into the holy *place:* with a young bullock for a °sin offering, and a ram for a burnt offering.

24 man. Heb. *'ish.* Ap. 14. **flowers** = uncleanness.

29 turtles = turtle-doves.

31 ye = Moses and Aaron.

tabernacle. Heb. *mishkān,* dwelling-place.

32 This is the law. *vv.* 32, 33 are a summary of the contents of the chapter, though the order (as in other cases) is varied. **and** = to be.

16. 1–34 (C, p. 131). ISRAEL'S FAST.
(THE DAY OF ATONEMENT.)
(*Introversion.*)

C | Q | 1, 2. Times for entering within the Vail (Neg.).
  R | 3. For himself alone.
   S | 4. Garments put on.
    T[1] | 5. Two goats and ram (people).
     U[1] | 6. For himself (bullock).
    T[2] | 7–10. Two goats (people).
     U[2] | 11–14. For himself (bullock).
    T[3] | 15–22. Two goats (people).
   S | 23. Garments changed.
  R | 24–28. For himself and people.
 Q | 29–34. Time for entering within the Vail (Pos.).

1 the LORD. Heb. Jehovah. Ap. 4.

spake. See note on 5. 14.

offered = brought near. Heb. *ḳārab.* Ap. 43. I. i. Onk., Jon., Sept., Syr., and Vulg., add "strange fire", as in 10. 1.

2 all times = any time: i.e. just at any time.

holy place = sanctuary or holy of holies. In this chapter "holy" is used for "holy of holies" without this adjunct. See *vv* 3, 16, 17, 20, 23, 27. Cp. note on Ex. 3. 5.

mercy seat. Fig. *Antemereia* (of Noun), Ap. 6, noun, "mercy", used as adjective. See note on Ex. 25. 17.

I will appear = I am wont to appear. See Ex. 25. 22.

3 Thus = with this.

sin. Heb. *chāṭ'ā.* Ap. 44. i.

4 wash = bathe. See note on 14. 9.

5 children = sons. **kids.** Heb. shaggy he-goats.

6 offer = bring near. Heb. *ḳārab.* Ap. 43. I. i.

make an atonement. See note on Ex. 29. 33.

7 door = entrance.

tabernacle of the congregation = tent (*'ohel*) of meeting.

8 for the scapegoat. Heb. for *'Azāzēl.* This "for" looks like a personality answering to "for Jehovah". If it be the Evil one who is meant, then it is for his defiance. For in *v.* 10 atonement is made for this goat, and he is to go free. Where there is atonement there must be forgiveness. See note on *v.* 22 below.

4 He shall put on the [2] holy linen coat, and he shall have the linen breeches upon his flesh, and shall be girded with a linen girdle, and with the linen mitre shall he be attired: these *are* [2] holy garments; therefore shall he °wash his flesh in water, and *so* put them on. S

5 And he shall take of the congregation of the °children of Israel two °kids of the goats for a [3] sin offering, and one ram for a burnt offering. T[1]

6 And Aaron shall °offer his bullock of the [3] sin offering, which *is* for himself, and °make an atonement for himself, and for his house. U[1]

7 And he shall take the two goats, and present them before [1] the LORD *at* the °door of the °tabernacle of the congregation. T[2]

8 And Aaron shall cast lots upon the two goats; one lot for [1] the LORD, and the other lot °for the scapegoat.

9 And Aaron shall bring the goat upon

1490 which [1]the LORD'S lot °fell, and °offer him *for* a [3]sin offering.

10 But the goat, on which the lot [9]fell °to be the [8]scapegoat, shall be °presented alive before [1]the LORD, to [6]make an atonement °with him, *and* to let him go for a [8]scapegoat into the °wilderness.

U² (p. 155) 11 And Aaron shall bring the bullock of the [3]sin offering, which *is* for himself, and shall [6]make an atonement for himself, and for his house, and shall kill the bullock of the [3]sin offering which *is* for himself:

12 And he shall take a censer full of burning coals of °fire from off the altar before [1]the LORD, and his hands full of sweet incense beaten small, and bring *it* within the vail:

13 And he shall put the incense upon the [12]fire before [1]the LORD, that the cloud of the incense may cover the [2]mercy seat that *is* upon the testimony, that he die not:

14 And he shall take of the blood of the bullock, and sprinkle *it* with his finger upon the [2]mercy seat eastward; and before °the [2]mercy seat shall he sprinkle of the blood with his finger seven times.

T³ 15 Then shall he kill the goat of the [3]sin offering, that *is* for the people, and bring his blood within the vail, and do with that blood °as he did with the blood of the bullock, and sprinkle it upon the [2]mercy seat, and before the [2]mercy seat:

16 And he shall [6]make an atonement for the [2]holy *place*, because of the uncleanness of the [5]children of Israel, and because of their [21]transgressions in all their [3]sins: and so shall he do for the [7]tabernacle of the congregation, that remaineth among them in the midst of their uncleanness.

17 And there shall be no °man in the [7]tabernacle of the congregation when he goeth in to [6]make an atonement in the [2]holy *place*, until he come out, and have [6]made an atonement for himself, and for his household, and for all the congregation of Israel.

18 And he shall go out unto the altar that *is* before [1]the LORD, and [6]make an atonement for it; and shall take of the blood of the bullock, and of the blood of the goat, and put *it* upon the horns of the altar round about.

19 And he shall sprinkle of the blood upon it with his finger seven times, and cleanse it, and °hallow it from the uncleanness of the [5]children of Israel.

20 And when he hath made an end of °reconciling the [2]holy *place*, and the [7]tabernacle of the congregation, and the altar, he shall bring the live goat:

21 And Aaron shall lay °both his hands upon the head of the °live goat, and confess over him °all the °iniquities of the [5]children of Israel, and °all their °transgressions in °all their [3]sins, putting them upon the head of the goat, and shall send *him* away by the hand of °a fit man into the [10]wilderness:

22 And the goat °shall bear upon him °all their [21]iniquities unto a °land not inhabited: and he shall °let go the goat in the [21]wilderness.

S 23 And Aaron shall come into the [7]tabernacle of the congregation, and shall put off the linen garments, which he put on when he went into the [2]holy *place*, and shall leave them there:

R 24 And he shall [4]wash his flesh with water in the [2]holy place, and put on his garments, and come forth, and offer his burnt offering, and the burnt offering of the people, and [6]make an atonement for himself, and for the people.

9 fell. Heb. "came up": i.e. out of the bag containing the Urim and Thummim. No other means of taking Jehovah's lot, or judgment. (See note on Ex. 28. 30.)

offer = "make him [sin]". (2 Cor. 5. 21.) Heb. *'āsāh*. Ap. 43. I. iii.

10 to be the scapegoat. Heb. "to be for *'Azāzēl*" (see *vv.* 8 and 22).

presented = made to stand.

with him. Heb. "for him". See *vv.* 16, 18. The scapegoat was not used to make atonement, but atonement was made *for* it. Hence he was to be "let go" free. See *v.* 22.

wilderness: or desert, symbol of abode of all evil things (Isa. 13. 21; 34. 14. Matt. 12. 43. Luke 8. 27; 11. 24. Rev. 18. 2). *'Azāzēl* probably the personification of all that is "great and terrible" there (Deut. 1. 19; 8. 15. Jer. 2. 6).

12 fire. Only fire from the brazen altar of burnt offering, where atonement had been made, could be used for kindling the incense on the golden altar in the holy place. See note on 10. 1. All other fire was "strange fire". See note on 10. 1, 7.

15 as = according as.

17 man = *'ādam*. Ap. 14. i.e. no human being. This effectually disposes of all priestly pretensions now, while the Antitype is "within the vail". See Heb. 4. 14; 6. 20; 9. 24.

19 hallow. See note on Ex. 3. 5.

20 reconciling = making atonement. See note on Ex. 29. 33.

21 both his hands. This for solemnity; and only here, on this occasion.

live goat. The two goats complete the one type of Christ. One could not, for He was "put to death as to the flesh", but made alive [again] as to the spirit", i.e. in resurrection (1 Pet. 3. 17. 1 Cor. 15. 45). He was "*made* sin" for us, that we might *become* divinely righteous in Him" (2 Cor. 5. 21).

all. Note the four "alls" in *vv.* 21, 22. Fig. *Repetitio* (Ap. 6) to emphasise the completeness of our deliverance from sins, and their entire removal.

iniquities. Heb. *'avah*. Ap. 44. iv.

transgressions. Heb. *pāsh'a*. Ap. 44. ix.

a fit man. The phrase occurs only here.

22 shall bear = shall bear away, as Isa. 53. 4.

land not inhabited. Heb. "a land cut off".

let go. This is the point of the type. The live goat was sent away, not in judgment or atonement, but in peace and at liberty. "All" had already been atoned for in the death of the other goat (*v.* 10). Now he was free to go into the land of forgetfulness, where their "sins and iniquities are remembered no more" (Isa. 43. 25. Jer. 31. 34). The scapegoat goes forth to *'Azāzēl*, all enemies thus personified (Heb. 2. 14), proclaiming, "Who is he that condemneth?" (Rom. 8. 33, 34). Not in fear of death, but saying, "Who dares to kill me?" It is the lesson, over again, of the "two birds" in ch. 14. 51-53, applied to the whole nation.

It is a type of those who are "risen with Christ" (Col. 3. 1), i.e. made alive again in His resurrection life.

Tradition treats this second goat as loaded with sin and sent out to destruction; whereas "all" is "atoned" for and is therefore "forgiven" and liberty enjoyed before it was sent away.

1490 25 And the fat of the [3]sin offering shall he °burn upon the altar.

26 And °he that let go the goat for the [8]scapegoat shall wash his clothes, and [4]bathe his flesh in water, and afterward come into the camp.

27 And the bullock *for* the [3]sin offering, and the goat *for* the [3]sin offering, whose blood was brought in to [6]make atonement in the [2]holy *place*, shall *one* carry forth °without the camp; and they shall °burn in the fire their skins, and their flesh, and their dung.

28 And he that [27]burneth them shall wash his clothes, and [4]bathe his flesh in water, and afterward he shall come into the camp.

Q (p. 155) 29 And *this* shall be a statute for ever unto you: *that* in the seventh month, on the tenth *day* of the month, ye shall °afflict your °souls, and °do no work at all, *whether it be* one of your own country, or a stranger that sojourneth among you:

30 For on that day shall *the priest* [6]make an atonement for you, to cleanse you, *that* ye may be clean from all your [3]sins before [1]the LORD.

31 It *shall be* a °sabbath of rest unto you, and ye shall [29]afflict your [29]souls, by a statute for ever.

32 And the priest, whom he shall anoint, and whom he shall °consecrate to minister in the priest's office in his father's stead, shall make the atonement, and shall put on the linen clothes, *even* the °holy garments:

33 And he shall [6]make an atonement for the [2]holy sanctuary, and he shall [6]make an atonement for the [7]tabernacle of the congregation, and for the altar, and he shall [6]make an atonement for the priests, and for all the people of the congregation.

34 And this shall be an everlasting statute unto you, to [6]make an atonement for the [5]children of Israel for all their [2]sins once a year." And he did °as [1]the LORD commanded Moses.

A[2] w[1] (p. 157) **17** And °the LORD °spake unto Moses, saying,

2 "Speak unto Aaron, and unto his sons, °and unto all the °children of Israel, and say unto them; 'This *is* the thing which [1]the LORD hath commanded, saying,

3 °'What man soever *there be* of the house of Israel, that °killeth an ox, or lamb, or goat, in the camp, or that killeth *it* out of the camp,

4 And bringeth it not unto the door of the °tabernacle of the congregation, to °offer an °offering unto [1]the LORD before the °tabernacle of [1]the LORD; blood shall be imputed unto that man; he hath shed blood; and that man shall be cut off from among his people:'

5 To the end that the [2]children of Israel may bring their sacrifices, which they °offer in the open field, even that they may bring them unto [1]the LORD, unto the °door of the [4]tabernacle of the congregation, unto the priest, and °offer them *for* peace offerings unto [1]the LORD.

25 burn = burn as incense. Heb. *ḳāṭar*. Ap. 43. I. vii. Cp. *v.* 27.
26 he that let go = he that leadeth away the goat to, or for, *'Azāzēl*, *v.* 10.
27 without the camp. Cp. 6. 11. Heb. 13. 11.
burn. Heb. *sāraph*. Ap. 43. I. viii.
29 afflict = fast. See Isa. 58. 3, 5, 10.
souls. Heb. *nephesh*. Ap. 13.
do no work at all. Heb. "no manner of work". This legal expression occurs five times (Ap. 10) in the Pentateuch, but is differently rendered. See 23. 3, 28, 31. Num. 29. 7. Work on the Sabbath day incurred stoning: on this day, excommunication.
31 sabbath of rest. Heb. "sabbath of sabbatizing". See note on Ex. 16. 23. = "Most holy sabbath", Fig. *Polyptōton* or *Enallage*. Ap. 6.
32 consecrate. See note on Ex. 28. 41. Lev. 9. 17.
holy. See note on Ex. 3. 5.
34 as = according as.

17. 1-16 (A[2], p. 131). THE OFFERINGS AND THEIR REQUIREMENTS (*Division*).

A[2] | w[1] | 17. 1-9. The appointed place.
| w[2] | 17. 10-16. The appointed food.

1—9. UNLAWFUL PLACES.

1 the LORD. Heb. Jehovah. Ap. 4.
spake. See note on 5. 14.
2 and unto all the children of Israel. First occurrence of this phrase: see note on Lev. 5. 14, marking the solemnity of the charge, and the subject.
children. Heb. sons.
3 What man soever = Heb. *'ish 'ish*.
killeth [in sacrifice]. The Fig. ***Ellipsis*** (Ap. 6. ii. d) must be thus supplied. For, although the word is Heb. *shāchaṭ* (Ap. 43. I. v.) and not *zabach* (Ap. 43. I. iv.), the context (*vv.* 5, 7-9) shows that only ***sacrifices*** in unlawful places are being treated of. There is no contradiction, therefore, of Deut. 12. 15, 21, where the context shows equally clearly that only ***food*** is in question. Cp. *v.* 5.
4 tabernacle. Heb. *mishkān*. Ap. 40.
offer = bring near. Heb. *ḳārab*. Ap. 43. I.
offering = Heb. *ḳorbān*. Ap. 43. II. i.
tabernacle = tent. Heb. *'ohel*. Ap. 40.
5 offer = slay in sacrifice. Heb. *zābāch*. Ap. 43. I. iv., thus showing the correct supply of the ***ellipsis*** in *v.* 3.
door = entrance.
6 burn = burn as incense. Heb. *ḳāṭar*. Ap. 43. I. vii.
sweet savour. See note on 1. 9.
7 no more: implies that they had done so in Egypt to the goat image "Pan". Cp. Josh. 24. 14. Ezek. 20. 7; 23. 3, &c., and especially 2 Chron. 11. 15.
offer = slay in sacrifice. Heb. *zābāch*. Ap. 43. I. iv.
devils. Heb. *sā'īr*. (Only here and 2 Chron. 11. 15, "devils". In Isa. 13. 21; 34. 14 rendered "satyrs" = an imaginary demon: half-goat, half-man. Sept. = demons:) from Heb. root, meaning *to shudder*. From this "Pan" came the "satyrs", "fauns", and woodland gods of Greece and Rome, and also the "devil" of Christendom.

6 And the priest shall sprinkle the blood upon the altar of [1]the LORD *at* the [5]door of the [4]tabernacle of the congregation, and °burn the fat for a °sweet savour unto [1]the LORD.

7 And they shall °no more °offer their sacrifices unto °devils, after whom they have gone a whoring. This shall be a statute for ever unto them throughout their generations."

1490 8 And thou shalt say unto them, "Whatsoever °man *there be* of the house of Israel, or of the strangers which sojourn among you, that °offereth a burnt offering or sacrifice,

9 And bringeth it not unto the [5]door of the [4]tabernacle of the congregation, to °offer it unto [1]the LORD; even that [8]man shall be cut off from among his people.

W[2] (p. 157) 10 And whatsoever [8]man *there be* of the house of Israel, or of the strangers that sojourn among you, that eateth any manner of blood; I will even set my face against that °soul that eateth blood, and will cut him off from among his people.

11 °For the °life of the flesh *is* in the blood: and I have given it to you upon the altar to °make an atonement for your °souls: for it *is* the blood *that* °maketh an atonement for the °soul.

12 °Therefore I said unto the [2]children of Israel, 'No [10]soul of you shall eat blood, neither shall any stranger that sojourneth among you eat blood.'

13 And whatsoever man *there be* of the [2]children of Israel, or of the strangers that sojourn among you, °which hunteth and catcheth any beast or fowl that may be eaten; he shall even pour out the blood thereof, and cover it with dust.

14 For *it is* the [11]life of all flesh; the blood of it *is* for the [11]life thereof: therefore I said unto the [2]children of Israel, 'Ye shall eat the blood of no manner of flesh: for the [11]life of all flesh *is* the blood thereof: whosoever eateth it shall be cut off.'

15 And every [10]soul that eateth that which died *of itself*, or that which was torn *with beasts, whether it be* one of your own country, or a stranger, he shall both wash his clothes, and °bathe *himself* in water, and be unclean until the even: then shall he be clean.

16 But if he wash *them* not, nor bathe his flesh; then he shall bear his °iniquity."

E x[1] (p. 158) **18** And °the LORD °spake unto Moses, saying,

2 "Speak unto the °children of Israel, and say unto them, 'I am [1]the LORD your °God.

3 After °the doings of the land of Egypt, wherein ye dwelt, shall ye not do: and after °the doings of the land of Canaan, whither I bring you, shall ye not do: neither shall ye walk in their °ordinances.

4 Ye shall do My °judgments, and keep Mine [3]ordinances, to walk therein: I *am* [1]the LORD your [2]God.

5 Ye shall therefore keep My statutes, and My [4]judgments: °which if a man do, he shall °live in them: I *am* [1]the LORD.

6 °None of you shall approach to any that is °near of kin to him, to uncover *their* nakedness: I *am* [1]the LORD.

7 The nakedness of thy °father, or the nakedness of thy mother, shalt thou not uncover: she *is* thy mother; thou shalt not uncover her nakedness.

8 The nakedness of thy °father's wife shalt thou not uncover: it *is* thy father's nakedness.

8 man. Heb. *'īsh*. Ap. 14.
offereth = offereth up. Heb. *'ālāh*. Ap. 43. I. vi.
9 offer = prepare. Heb. *'āsāh*. Ap. 43. I. iii.

10-16 (W[2], p. 157). THE APPOINTED FOOD.

10 soul = Heb. *nephesh*. Ap. 13.
11 For. This verse, with Luke 24. 39, 1 Cor. 15. 50, and Heb. 13. 20, forms a strong chain of truth against the "Mass".
life = soul. Heb. *nephesh*. Ap. 13.
make an atonement. See note on Ex. 29. 33.
soul. Heb. *nephesh*, because the soul is the life. Thus a life is substituted for a life. Hence Heb. 9. 22.
12 Therefore. Hence Acts 15. 20, 29; 21. 25.
13 which hunteth = which shall hunt any hunting. Fig. *Polyptōton*, Ap. 6, a necessity with Israel, not sport; for extermination (Ex. 23. 29) and for food (Gen. 25. 27. Prov. 12. 27). Cp. 1 Sam. 14. 32-34 and Ezek. 33. 25.
15 bathe. See note on 14. 9. The rigour of this law seen from 1 Sam. 14. 32-35.
16 iniquity. Heb. *'āvāh*. Ap. 44. iv.

18. 1—20. 27 (E, p. 131). CEREMONIAL LAWS (PENALTIES) (*Division*).

E		
	x[1]	18. 1-18. Unlawful connections.
	x[2]	18. 19-30. Unlawful lusts.
	x[3]	19. 1-37. Unlawful practices.
	x[4]	20. 1-27. Unlawful defilements.

18. 1-18 (x[1], above). UNLAWFUL CONNECTIONS.

1 the LORD. Heb. Jehovah. Ap. 4.
spake. See note on 5. 14. **2** children. Heb. sons.
God. Heb. Elohim. Ap. 4.
3 the doings: i. e. all the abominable practices of the Canaanitish nations (*v.* 27), for which they were cut off, Rom. 1. 23-29. ordinances = statutes.
4 judgments = regulations.
5 which, &c. = "which, if the man (Heb. *'ādām*, Ap. 14) shall do them, he shall also live by them".
live = "live again" in resurrection life (Rev. 20. 5). The Chald. paraphrase = "shall live by them to life eternal". Sol. Jarchi, "live in the world that is to come". Cp. the other passages where "live" is used in this sense: Ezek. 13. 21; 20. 11. Luke 10. 28. Rom. 10. 5. Gal. 3. 12. Neh. 9. 29. Hab. 2. 4. Rom. 1. 17. Heb. 10. 38, &c. In this sense the verb is used more often than is generally thought. Cp. Isa. 26. 19; 38. 16; 55. 3. Ezek. 18. 19; 33. 19; 37. 3, 5, 6, 14. Hos. 6. 2. Amos 5. 4, &c. The spiritual authorities of the second temple so interpreted the phrase. Thus "eternal life", by faith, is set in contrast with eternal life by works.
6 None of you. Heb. "Man, man, ye shall not approach"; should be "No man (Heb. *'īsh*. Ap. 14) whatsoever shall approach". Emphasised by Fig. *Epizeuxis*. See Ap. 6.
The absence of the words "of the house of Israel", as in 17. 3, 8, 13, shows that the strangers are included in this law.
near of kin. Heb. "the remainder of his flesh" (Gen. 2. 23), i. e. by the Fig. *Polyptōton*, Ap. 6, "his *own* flesh (or relatives)". Cp. *vv.* 12, 13, 17. For emphasis.
7 father. See Gen. 19. 31-38.
8 father's wife. See Gen. 35. 22. 2 Sam. 16. 20-23. 1 Kings 2. 17, and 1 Cor. 5. 1-5.
9 sister. See Gen. 20. 12. 2 Sam. 13. 12, 16, 20.
11 father's wife. In Heb. always means one's "stepmother" (see *v.* 8; 20. 11).

9 The nakedness of thy °sister, the daughter of thy father, or daughter of thy mother, *whether she be* born at home, or born abroad, *even* their nakedness thou shalt not uncover.

10 The nakedness of thy son's daughter, or of thy daughter's daughter, *even* their nakedness thou shalt not uncover: for theirs *is* thine own nakedness.

11 The nakedness of thy °father's wife's

1490 daughter, begotten of thy father, she *is* thy sister, thou shalt not uncover her nakedness.

12 Thou shalt not uncover the nakedness of thy °father's sister: °she *is* thy father's near kinswoman.

13 Thou shalt not uncover the nakedness of thy mother's sister: for she *is* thy mother's near kinswoman.

14 Thou shalt not uncover the nakedness of thy father's brother, °thou shalt not approach to his wife: she *is* thine aunt.

15 Thou shalt not uncover the nakedness of thy daughter in law: she *is* thy son's wife; thou shalt not uncover her nakedness.

16 Thou shalt not uncover the nakedness of thy brother's wife: it *is* thy brother's nakedness.

17 Thou shalt not uncover the nakedness of a woman and her daughter, neither shalt thou take her son's daughter, or her daughter's daughter, to uncover her nakedness; *for* they *are* her near kinswomen: it *is* °wickedness.

18 Neither shalt thou take a wife to her sister, to vex *her*, to uncover her nakedness, beside the other in her life *time*.

x² 19 Also thou shalt not approach unto a
(p. 159) woman to uncover her nakedness, as long as she is put apart for her uncleanness.

20 Moreover thou shalt not lie carnally with thy neighbour's wife, to defile thyself with her.

21 And thou shalt not let any of thy °seed °pass through *the fire* to °Molech, neither shalt thou profane the name of thy ²God: I *am* ¹the LORD.

22 Thou shalt not lie with mankind, °as with womankind: it *is* °abomination.

23 Neither shalt thou lie with °any beast to defile thyself therewith: neither shall any woman stand before a beast to lie down thereto: it *is* confusion.

24 Defile not ye yourselves in any of these things: for in all these the nations are defiled which I cast out before you:

25 And the land is defiled: therefore I do visit the °iniquity thereof upon it, and the land itself °vomiteth out her inhabitants.

26 °Ye shall therefore keep My statutes and My judgments, and shall not commit *any* of these ²²abominations; *neither* any of your own nation, nor any stranger that sojourneth among you:

27 (°For all these ²²abominations have the °men of the land done, which *were* before you, and the land is defiled;)

28 That the land °spue not you out also, when ye defile it, °as it spued out the nations that *were* before you.

29 For whosoever shall commit any of these ²²abominations, even the °souls that commit *them* shall be cut off from among their people.

30 Therefore shall ye °keep Mine ordinance, that *ye* commit not *any one* of these ²²abominable °customs, which were committed before you, and that ye defile not yourselves therein: °I *am* ¹the LORD your ²God.'"

12 father's sister. See Ex. 6. 20.
she. Some codices, with Sept., Syr., and Vulg., read "for she".
14 thou. Some codices, with Sam., Jon., Sept., and Syr., read "and thou".
17 wickedness=lewdness. Heb. *zimmah.* Ap. 44. xiii.

19-30 (x², p. 158). UNLAWFUL LUSTS.
(*Repeated Alternation.*)

x² | y¹ | 19-24-. Commands.
  z¹ | -24, 25. Reason.
 y² | 26. Command.
  z² | 27-29. Reason.
 y³ | 30. Command.

21 seed=children.
pass through, &c. Heb. "pass to Molech", i. e. into his arms, from which it passed through the fire to him.
Molech. Always has the article (except 1 Kings 11. 7, which is probably a copyist's omission) denoting *the* king, or the king-idol (see *v.* 21; 20. 2, 3, 4, 5. See *seq.* 2 Kings 23. 10. Jer. 32. 35).
The Massorites pointed it *Molech*, to assimilate it to "shameful thing", but omitted to do so in Isa. 30. 33 and 57. 9, which they left *melech*=king. It should read Molech in these two passages also.
22 as. Referring to the sin of Sodom (whence its name), Gen. 19. 5. Cp. 20. 13. Judg. 19. 22. 1 Kings 14. 24.
abomination=a thing to be abhorred.
23 any beast. This was part of the religious worship of the Egyptians.
25 iniquity. Heb. *'āvāh.* Ap. 44. iv.
vomiteth. Fig. *Prosopopœia*, Ap. 6. Cp. "spued", *v.* 28. From the beginning, the earth has shared the consequences of man's guilt (Gen. 3. 17. Rom. 8. 19-22). Since it yields no fruit when man yields no obedience; and defiled when man is defiled (Deut. 11. 17). Is blessed when man is blessed (Lev. 25. 19; 26. 4. Deut. 32. 43). Mourns when man sins (Isa. 24. 4, 5). Glad when God avenges His People (Ps. 96. 11-13).
26 Ye. In some codices, with Sam., Sept., Syr., and Vulg., this "Ye" has no emphasis.
27 For, &c. These "doings" are specially legislated against, because these were the corruptions pertaining to the origin and character of the *Nephilim* (Ap. 25). These formed the nations of Canaan, and this was why they had to be destroyed by the sword of Israel, as those in the days of Noah had to be destroyed by the Flood. Verses 24 and 25 are emphasised by the other way of putting the facts.
men. Heb. pl. of *'enōsh.* Ap. 14.
28 spue=vomit of *v.* 25. **as**=according as. Cp. *v.* 25.
29 souls. Heb. pl. of *nephesh.* Ap. 13.
30 keep Mine ordinance. This is the Fig. *Polyptōton* (Ap. 6)="observe my observance", but, Eng. keep my charge.
customs=statutes: because they were legal enactments of the land, cp. *v.* 3. The word is rendered "statutes" in Deut. 6. 24; 16. 12; and 26. 16.
I am the LORD your God. This body of laws (ch. 18) is emphasised and solemnized by beginning and ending with the same expression. Fig. *Epanadiplosis.* See Ap. 6.

19. 1-37 (x³, p. 158). UNLAWFUL PRACTICES.
(*Repeated Alternation.*)

x³ | W¹ | 1-8. Sundry commands and prohibitions.
  X | 9, 10. Gleanings.
 W² | 11-22. Sundry commands and prohibitions.
  X | 23-25. Firstfruits.
 W³ | 26-37. Sundry commands and prohibitions.

1 the LORD. Heb. Jehovah. Ap. 4.
spake. See note on 5. 14.
2 all the congregation, &c. Only here in Leviticus, and once more in the Pentateuch (Ex. 12. 3).
children. Heb. sons.

x³ 19 And °the LORD °spake unto Moses, saying,
2 "Speak unto °all the congregation of the °children of Israel, and say unto them, 'Ye

1490 shall be °holy: for °I [1]the LORD your °God *am* °holy.

3 Ye shall fear every °man his mother, and his father, and keep My sabbaths: [2]I *am* [1]the LORD your [2]God.

4 Turn ye not unto °idols, nor make to yourselves molten gods: I *am* [1]the LORD your [2]God.

5 And if ye °offer a sacrifice of peace offerings unto [1]the LORD, ye shall offer it °at your own will.

6 It shall be eaten the same day ye offer it, and on the morrow: and if ought remain until the third day, it shall be °burnt in the fire.

7 And if it be eaten at all on the third day, it *is* abominable; it shall not be accepted.

8 Therefore *every one* that eateth it shall bear his °iniquity, because he hath profaned the °hallowed thing of [1]the LORD: and that °soul shall be °cut off from among his people.

X (p. 159) 9 And when ye reap the harvest of your land, thou shalt not wholly reap the corners of thy field, neither shalt thou gather the gleanings of thy harvest.

10 And thou shalt not glean thy vineyard, neither shalt thou gather *every* grape of thy vineyard; thou shalt leave *them* for the poor and stranger: I *am* [1]the LORD your [2]God.

W[2] 11 Ye shall not steal, neither deal falsely, neither lie one to another.

12 And ye shall not swear by My name falsely, neither shalt thou profane the name of thy [2]God: I *am* [1]the LORD.

13 Thou shalt not defraud thy neighbour, neither rob *him:* °the °wages of him that is hired shall not abide with thee all night until the morning.

14 Thou shalt not curse the deaf, nor put a stumblingblock before the blind, but shalt fear thy [2]God: I *am* [1]the LORD.

15 Ye shall do no unrighteousness in judgment: thou shalt not respect the person of the poor, nor honour the person of the mighty: *but* in righteousness shalt thou judge thy neighbour.

16 Thou shalt not go up and down *as* a °talebearer among thy people: neither shalt thou stand against the blood of thy neighbour: I *am* [1]the LORD.

17 Thou shalt not hate thy brother in thine heart: thou shalt in any wise rebuke thy neighbour, and not °suffer °sin °upon him.

18 Thou shalt not avenge, nor bear any grudge against the [2]children of thy people, but °thou shalt love thy °neighbour as thyself: I *am* [1]the LORD.

19 Ye shall keep My statutes. Thou shalt not let thy cattle gender with a °diverse kind: thou shalt not sow thy field with °mingled seed: neither shall a garment °mingled of linen and woollen come upon thee.

20 And whosoever lieth carnally with a woman, that *is* a bondmaid, betrothed to an husband, and not at all °redeemed, nor freedom given her; she shall be scourged; they shall not be put to death, because she was °not free.

21 And he shall bring his °trespass offering unto [1]the LORD, unto the °door of the °tabernacle of the congregation, *even* a ram for a [21]trespass offering.

22 And the priest shall °make an atonement for him with the ram of the [21]trespass offering before [1]the LORD for his [17]sin which he °hath done: and the [17]sin which he hath done shall be forgiven him.

23 And °when ye shall come into the land, X
and shall have planted all manner of trees for food, then ye shall count the fruit thereof as °uncircumcised: three years shall it be as °uncircumcised unto you: it shall not be eaten of.

24 But in the fourth year all the fruit

---

holy = set apart. See note on Ex. 3. 5.

I the LORD, &c. There are fifteen groups in this body of laws (ch. 19), seven ending with the longer formula, "I am the LORD your God" (23, 4, 10, 25, 31, 34, 36), and eight with the shorter formula "I am the LORD" (12, 14, 16, 18, 28, 30, 32, 37).

God. Heb. Elohim. Ap. 4.

3 man. Heb. *'îsh.* Ap. 14. ii.

4 idols = Heb. *'ĕlîlîm.* See Lev. 26. 1.

5 offer = slay for sacrifice. Heb. *zâbach.* Ap. 43. I. iv.

at your own will. Heb. = "for your acceptance", or "that ye may be accepted".

6 burnt = burnt up. Heb. *sâraph.* Ap. 43. I. viii.

8 iniquity. Heb. *'âvâh.* Ap. 44. iv.

hallowed = set apart. See note on. 12. 4.

soul = person. Heb. *nephesh.* Ap. 13.

cut off. See note on 7. 20.

9, 10 (X, p. 159). GLEANINGS. (Cp. Ruth 2. 14–16.)

11–22 (W[2], p. 159). SUNDRY COMMANDS AND PROHIBITIONS.

13 the. Some codices, with Sam., Jon., and Sept., read "and the".

wages. Heb. "work". Put by Fig. *Metonymy* (of Cause), Ap. 6, for wages earned by it. Note the Divine care for the labourer (Deut. 24. 14, 15. Jer. 22. 13. Mal. 3. 5. Jas. 5. 4).

16 talebearer. A solemn warning here. Rendered "slandering" in Jer. 6. 28; 9. 4. Ezek. 22. 9 (margin). (Cp. 1 Sam. 22. 9–18.)

17 suffer: or countenance him in his sin; or, lest on his account thou bear sin. This is the Divine method, and the best.

sin. Heb. *châṭ'â.* Ap. 44. i. **upon him** = in him.

18 thou shalt love. See Matt. 7. 12; 22. 39, 40. Luke 6. 31; 10. 27.

neighbour. Not merely one who is "near", but any one with whom one has dealings. This is the point of Luke 10. 29. Cp. John 4. 9.

19 diverse kind. Everything created "after his kind". See note on Gen. 1. 11; a deep, moral, and spiritual lesson is contained in this prohibition.

mingled. Another lesson here as to mingling the clean and unclean, human and Divine, flesh and spirit, &c. This law relates only to "seeds" which are used for food and actually eaten. Cp. Luke 13. 6.

20 redeemed = set free (by power). Heb. *pâdah.* See note on Ex. 13. 13.

not free. Otherwise death. Deut. 22. 24.

21 trespass. Heb. *'âsâm.* Ap. 44. ii.

door = entrance.

tabernacle = tent. Heb *'ohel.*

22 make an atonement. See note on Ex. 29. 33.

hath done = hath sinned. Heb. *châṭâ'.* Ap. 44. i.

23 when ye shall come. The second of four prospective laws. See note on 14. 34. Cp. 19. 23; 23. 10; 25.

uncircumcised: or, uncovenanted. Fig. *Prosopopœia.* Ap. 6.

1490 thereof shall be °holy to praise [1]the LORD *withal*.

25 And in the fifth year shall ye eat of the fruit thereof, that it may yield unto you the increase thereof: I *am* [1]the LORD your [2]God.

W[3] (p. 159) 26 Ye shall not eat *any thing* with the blood: neither shall ye use enchantment, nor °observe times.

27 Ye shall °not round the corners of your heads, neither shalt thou mar the °corners of thy beard.

28 Ye shall not make any °cuttings in your flesh for °the dead, nor print any marks upon you: °I *am* the LORD.

29 Do not °prostitute thy daughter, to cause her to be a whore; lest the land fall to whoredom, and the land become full of °wickedness.

30 Ye shall keep My sabbaths, and reverence My sanctuary: I *am* the LORD.

31 Regard not them that have °familiar spirits, neither seek after °wizards, to be defiled by them: I *am* [1]the LORD your [2]God.

32 Thou shalt rise up before the hoary head, and honour the face of the old man, and °fear thy [2]God: I *am* [1]the LORD.

33 And if a stranger sojourn with °thee in your land, ye shall not °vex him.

34 °*But* the stranger that dwelleth with you shall be °unto you as one born among you, and thou shalt love him °as thyself; for °ye were strangers in the land of Egypt: I *am* [1]the LORD your [2]God.

35 Ye shall do no unrighteousness in judgment, in °meteyard, in °weight, or in °measure.

36 °Just balances, just weights, a just °ephah, and a just °hin, shall ye have: I *am* [1]the LORD your [2]God, Which brought you out of the land of Egypt.

37 Therefore shall ye observe all My statutes, and all My judgments, and do them: I *am* [1]the LORD.'"

x[4] Y (p. 161) **20** And °the LORD °spake unto Moses, saying,

2 °"Again, thou shalt say to the °children of Israel, 'Whosoever *he be* of the °children of Israel, or of the strangers that sojourn in Israel, that giveth *any* of his seed unto °Molech; he shall surely be put to death: the people of the land shall stone him with stones.

3 And I will set My face against that °man, and will cut him off from among his people; because he hath given of his seed unto [2]Molech, to defile My sanctuary, and to profane My °holy name.

4 And if the people of the land do any ways hide their eyes from °the [3]man, when he giveth of his seed unto [2]Molech, and kill him not:

5 Then I will set My face against that man, and against his °family, and will cut him off,

24 holy to praise. Heb. "holiness of praises". "Praises" in pl. Fig. *Heterōsis* (of Number), Ap. 6, for emphasis, and noun, "holiness", put for adj. by Fig. *Antimereia* (of Noun), Ap. 6, for emphasis = "for a sacred and great praise unto Jehovah".

26 observe times: i. e. watch clouds, or days, for good or ill luck, e. g. not commencing a journey on a Friday. See note on *v.* 31 below.

27 not round the corners of your heads: i. e. to cut round, so as to have a tuft of hair, like the Canaanitish priests. Cp. Jer. 9. 26; 25. 23; 49. 32.

corners of thy beard = whiskers, as Egyptians did. Cp. Gen. 41. 14.

28 cuttings. A practice in Canaanitish heathen worship. Cp. 21. 5. Deut. 14. 1. 1 Kings 18. 28. Jer. 48. 37.

the dead = a dead soul. Heb. *nephesh* (Ap. 13). Thus there is such a thing as "a dead soul" as well as a "living soul" (Gen. 2. 7); so also in 21. 1; 22. 4. Num. 5. 2; 6. 11. *Nephesh* is incorrectly rendered "body" in 21. 11. Num. 6. 6; 19. 11, 13; and "dead body" in Num. 9. 6, 7, 10. Hag. 2. 13. In all these passages the Heb. *nephesh* (soul) is thus rendered, and yet it is rendered "life" in 17. 14 and elsewhere.

I am the LORD. Some codices, with Onk., Sept., and Syr., add "your God".

29 prostitute thy daughter. The common practice, as a religious act, by the Canaanite and other ancient forms of idolatry.

wickedness = lewdness. Heb. *zimmāh*. Ap. 44. xiii.

31 familiar spirits. These are evil spirits personating dead human beings, and attaching themselves only to "mediums" and those who give up their will to them. A dread reality is provided against by these enactments. Cp. 20. 27. Deut. 18. 10–12. 1 Chron. 10. 13–14. Isa. 8. 19. The Heb. *'ōb*, borrowed from an Akkadian word, *ubi* = a charm, used of one who was mistress of the spell, or spirit. Isa. 29. 4. See Acts 16. 16, where it is defined as "a spirit of *Python*" (= Pythius Apollo), i. e. the devil.

wizards = knowing ones: those having occult knowledge.

32 fear thy. Perhaps an *Ellipsis* (Ap. 6), "fear [a visitation from] thy God". Cp. 25. 17, 36, 43.

33 thee. Some codices, with Sam., Onk., Jon., Sept., Syr., and Vulg., read "you". **vex** = oppress.

34 But. This is better omitted.

unto you. A.V., 1611, omitted these words.

as thyself. Cp. *v.* 18.

ye were strangers. Occurs four times in the Pentateuch: Ex. 22. 21; 23. 9. Lev. 19. 34. Deut. 10. 19.

35 meteyard = measures of length or dimension.

weight = measures of weight.

measure = measures of capacity.

36 Just balances = Heb. balances of justice. Genitive of character. So with the other measures in this verse. Cp. Deut. 25. 13–16. Prov. 11. 1; 16. 11; 20. 10, 23.

ephah . . . hin. See Ap. 51. III. 3.

20. 1–27 (x[4], p. 158). UNLAWFUL DEFILEMENTS (*Introversion*).

x[4] | Y | 1–6. Molech and witchcraft.
  Z | 7. Sanctification.
    A | 8. Charge as to obedience.
      B | 9. Death penalty: cursing parents.
      B | 10–21. Death penalty: criminal connections.
    A | 22–25. Charge as to obedience.
  Z | 26. Sanctification.
Y | 27. Witchcraft.

1 the LORD. Heb. Jehovah. Ap. 4.

spake. See note on 5. 14.

2 Again. See Lev. 18. 21. This is so serious that it must be repeated. There, only a command; here, the penalty. **children.** Heb. sons.

Molech. The king-idol. See note on 18. 21, where this law follows that on incest; while here it precedes it. **3 man.** Heb. *'īsh*. Ap. 14. iii. **holy.** See note on Ex. 3. 5. **4 the** = that. **5 family.** Cp. Ezek. 18. 2, and note the contrast. Jer. 31. 29.

1490 and all that go a whoring after him, to commit whoredom with [2]Molech, from among their People.

6 And the °soul that turneth after such as have °familiar spirits, and after °wizards, to go a whoring after them, I will even set My face against that °soul, and will cut him off from among his People.

Z (p. 161) 7 Sanctify yourselves therefore, and be ye [3]holy: for I *am* °the LORD your God.

A 8 And ye shall keep My statutes, and do them: I *am* °the LORD Which sanctify you.

B 9 For °every one that curseth his father or his mother shall be surely put to death: he hath cursed his father or his mother; his °blood *shall be* upon him.

B 10 And the [3]man that committeth adultery with *another* man's wife, *even he* that committeth adultery with his neighbour's wife, the adulterer and the adulteress shall surely be put to death.

11 And the [3]man that lieth with his °father's wife hath uncovered his father's nakedness: both of them shall surely be put to death; their [9]blood *shall be* upon them.

12 And if a [3]man lie with his °daughter in law, both of them shall surely be put to death: they have wrought confusion; their [9]blood *shall be* upon them.

13 If a [3]man also lie with °mankind, as he lieth with a woman, both of them have committed an °abomination: they shall surely be put to death; their [9]blood *shall be* upon them.

14 And if a [3]man take a °wife and her mother, it *is* °wickedness: they shall be °burnt with fire, both he and they; that there be no °wickedness among you.

15 And if a [3]man lie with a °beast, he shall surely be put to death: and ye shall slay the beast.

16 And if a woman approach unto any beast, and lie down thereto, thou shalt kill the woman, and the beast: they shall surely be put to death; their [9]blood *shall be* upon them.

17 And if a [3]man shall take his °sister, his father's daughter, or his mother's daughter, and see her nakedness, and she see his nakedness; it *is* a [14]wicked thing; and they shall be cut off in the °sight of their People: he hath uncovered his sister's nakedness; he shall bear his °iniquity.

18 And if a [3]man shall lie with a woman having her °sickness, and shall uncover her nakedness; he hath discovered her fountain, and she hath uncovered the fountain of her blood: and both of them shall be cut off from among their People.

19 And thou shalt not uncover the nakedness of thy mother's sister, nor of thy father's sister: for he uncovereth his near kin: they shall bear their [17]iniquity.

20 And if a [3]man shall lie with his uncle's wife, he hath uncovered his uncle's nakedness: they shall bear their °sin; they shall die childless.

21 And if a [3]man shall take his brother's wife, it *is* an unclean thing: he hath uncovered his brother's nakedness; they shall be childless.

6 soul. Heb. *nephesh*. Ap. 13.
familiar spirits. See note on 19. 31.
wizards. See note on 19. 31.
7 the LORD [Heb. Jehovah] **your God** [Heb. Elohim]. Some codices, with Sam. and Sept., read "I am holy, Jehovah your God".
8 the LORD Which sanctify you=*Jehovah Mĕkaddishkem*, one of the Jehovah titles. See Ap. 4.
9 every one. Heb. *'īsh 'īsh*. Ap. 14. ii.
blood. Fig. *Metalepsis*, Ap. 6, "bloods", put by Fig. *Metonymy* (of Adjunct) for guilt, and "guilt" put by Fig. *Metonymy* (of Cause) for penalty.
11 father's wife. See 18. 8.
12 daughter in law. See 18. 15.
13 mankind. Heb. "male". See 18. 22.
abomination. See note on 18. 22.
14 wife and her mother. See ch. 18. 17.
wickedness=disgraceful thing. Heb. *chesed* (Ap. 44. xiv). *Chesed* is a *Homonym*: i. e. another word, spelt the same. It means (1) *mercy, grace, goodness* (Gen. 24. 12. 2 Sam. 7. 15. 1 Chron. 19. 2. 2 Chron. 6. 14. Job 37. 13. Ps. 103. 4, 8, 11, &c. But here (2) it is *chesed*, a *disgraceful* or *reproachful* thing. It is so taken here and in Prov. 14. 34.
burnt=burnt up: i.e. in judgment. Heb. *sāraph*. Ap. 43. I. viii. **15 beast.** See 18. 23.
17 sister. See 18. 9.
sight of their People. A special penalty is attached to this disgraceful thing.
iniquity=perverseness. Heb. *'āvōn*. Ap. 44. iii.
18 sickness. See 15. 24; 18. 19.
20 sin=penalty. Put by Fig. *Metonymy* (of Cause). Ap. 6.
22 spue. Cp. 18. 28, where it is rendered "vomit".
23 manners=statutes. It was this that brought down the judgment of extermination. No other remedy would do. These nations were descended from the *nephīlīm* (see Ap. 25), who like those who were destroyed by the Flood, were "after that" (Gen. 6. 4) to be destroyed by the sword of Israel.
nation. Some codices, with Sam., Onk., Sept., Syr., and Vulg., read "nations" (pl.).
25 difference=separation, as in verse 24. Cp. 10. 10; 11. 47. **souls.** Heb. pl. of *nephesh*. Ap. 13.
26 severed=separated, as in verses 24 and 25.
27 familiar spirit. See note on 19. 31.

22 Ye shall therefore keep all My statutes, and all My judgments, and do them: that the land, whither I bring you to dwell therein, °spue you not out. A

23 And ye shall not walk in the °manners of the °nation, which I cast out before you: for they committed all these things, and therefore I abhorred them.

24 But I have said unto you, Ye shall inherit their land, and I will give it unto you to possess it, a land that floweth with milk and honey: I *am* [1]the LORD your [7]God, Which have separated you from *other* people.

25 Ye shall therefore put °difference between clean beasts and unclean, and between unclean fowls and clean: and ye shall not make your °souls abominable by beast, or by fowl, or by any manner of living thing that creepeth on the ground, which I have separated from you as unclean.

26 And ye shall be [3]holy unto Me: for I [1]the LORD *am* holy, and have °severed you from *other* people, that ye should be Mine. Z

27 A [3]man also or woman that hath a °familiar spirit, or that is a wizard, shall Y

1490 surely be put to death: they shall stone them
with stones: their [9]blood *shall be* upon
them.' "

D G a (p. 163) 21 And °the LORD °said unto Moses,
"Speak unto °the priests the sons of
Aaron, and say unto them, 'There shall none
be defiled for °the dead among his people:
2 But for his °kin, that is near unto him,
that is, for his mother, and for his father,
and for his son, and for his daughter, and
for his brother,
3 And for his sister a virgin, that is nigh
unto him, which hath had no husband; for
her may he be defiled.
4 *But* he shall not °defile himself, *being*
°a chief man among his people, to profane
himself.
5 They shall not make baldness upon their
head, neither shall they °shave off °the corner
of their beard, nor make any cuttings in their
flesh.

b 6 They shall be °holy unto their °God, and
not profane the name of their °God: for the
°offerings of [1]the LORD made by fire, *and*
the °bread °of their °God, they do °offer:
therefore they shall be °holy.

J c 7 They shall not take a wife *that is* a whore,
or profane; neither shall they take a woman
put away from her husband:

d for he *is* [6]holy unto his [6]God.
8 Thou shalt sanctify him therefore;

for he [6]offereth the °bread of thy [6]God: he
shall be [6]holy unto thee: for °I [1]the LORD,
Which sanctify you, *am* [6]holy.

H 9 And the daughter of any priest, if she
profane herself by playing the whore, she
profaneth her father: she shall be °burnt
with fire.

G a 10 And *he that is* the °high priest among
his brethren, upon whose head the anointing
oil was poured, and that is °consecrated to
put on the garments, shall not uncover his
head, nor °rend his clothes;
11 Neither shall he go in to any °dead body:
nor defile himself for his father, or for his
mother;
12 Neither shall he go out of the sanctuary,
nor profane the sanctuary of his [6]God; for
the °crown of the anointing oil of his [6]God *is*
upon him:

b I *am* [1]the LORD.

J c 13 And he shall take a wife in her virginity.
14 A widow, or a divorced woman, or profane, *or* an harlot, these shall he not take:
but he shall take a virgin of his own people
to wife.
15 Neither shall he profane his seed among
his people:

d for [8]I [1]the LORD do sanctify him.' "

E 16 And [1]the LORD °spake unto Moses, saying,
17 "Speak unto Aaron, saying, 'Whosoever
he be of thy seed in their °generations that
hath *any* blemish, let him not approach to
[6]offer the [6]bread [6]of his [6]God.

18 For whatsoever man *he be* that hath a
blemish, he shall not approach: a blind man,
or a lame, or he that hath a °flat nose, or
°any thing superfluous,
19 Or a °man that is brokenfooted, or broken-
handed,

21. 1—22. 31 (*D*, p. 131). PRIESTHOOD.
(*Division.*)

D | C¹ | 21. 1—22. 16. Persons.
| C² | 22. 17-33. Offerings.

21. 1—22. 16 (C¹, above). PERSONS.
(*Introversion.*)

C¹ | D | 21. 1-15. Defilements (mourning).
| E | 21. 16-24. Blemishes.
| *D* | 22. 1-16. Defilements (uncleanness).

21. 1-15 (D, above). DEFILEMENTS (MOURNING).
(*Introversion and Alternation.*)

D | F | G | a | 1-5. Relations.
| | | b | 6. Reason.
| | J | c | 7-. Wife.
| | | d | -7, 8. Reason.
| H | 9. Daughter.
| *F* | *G* | *a* | 10-12-. Parents.
| | | *b* | -12. Reason.
| | *J* | *c* | 13-15-. Wife.
| | | *d* | -15. Reason.

1 the LORD. Heb. Jehovah. Ap. 4.
said. See note on 5. 14.
the priests the sons of Aaron. Occurs only here. In all the other seven passages it is in Heb. "the sons of Aaron, the priests". See Lev. 1. 5.
the dead = a dead soul. Heb. *nephesh.* See Ap. 13, and note on 19. 28.
2 kin = flesh.
4 defile himself [for his wife]. Fig. *Ellipsis.* Ap. 6.
a chief = a lord, or leader. Heb. *bā'al.* Supply Fig. *Ellipsis* (Ap. 6) [a priest].
5 shave. Forbidden to the Israelites; but in Egypt a disgrace not to shave. See Gen. 41. 14. 2 Sam. 10. 4, 5.
the corner of their beard = their whiskers.
6 holy = set apart, or separate. See note on Ex. 3. 5. Here, a singular noun = a separated set.
God. Heb. Elohim. Ap. 4.
offerings = Heb. *'ishsheh.* Ap. 43. II. xi.
bread = food of all kinds. Put by Fig. *Synecdoche* (of Species). Ap. 6. See note on 3. 11.
of their God. Genitive of relation. Ap. 17.
offer = bring near. Heb. *ḳārab.* Ap. 43. I. i.
holy. See note on Ex. 3. 5.
8 I the LORD, Which, &c. = Jehovah title. See note on 20. 8, and Ap. 4.
9 burnt = burnt up. Heb. *sāraph.* Ap. 43. I. viii.
10 high priest. See note on 4. 3.
consecrated. See note on Ex. 28. 41. Lev. 9. 17.
rend. See notes on 10. 6; 13. 45.
11 dead body = dead soul. Heb. "dead *nephesh*". The opposite of "living soul" in Gen. 2. 7. See note on 19. 28, and Ap. 13.
12 crown = consecration: i. e. = Nazariteship.

16—24 (E, above). BLEMISHES.

16 spake. See note on 5. 14.
17 generations = posterity.
18 flat = any deformity (of the nose).
any thing superfluous = any thing over long or excessive. Cp. 22. 23.
19 man. Heb. *'ish.* Ap. 14. ii.

1490 20 Or crookbackt, or a dwarf, or that hath a °blemish in his eye, or be scurvy, or scabbed, or hath his stones broken;

21 No man that hath a blemish of the seed of Aaron the priest shall come nigh to offer the offerings of [1]the LORD made by fire: he hath a blemish; he shall not come nigh to offer the [17]bread of his [6]God.

22 He shall eat the bread of his [6]God, *both* of the most [6]holy, and of the [6]holy.

23 Only he shall not go in unto the vail, nor come nigh unto the altar, because he hath a blemish; that he profane not My sanctuaries: for [8]I [1]the LORD do sanctify them.'"

24 And Moses told *it* unto Aaron, and to his sons, and unto all the °children of Israel.

D e[1] (p. 164) **22** And °the LORD °spake unto Moses, saying,

2 "Speak unto Aaron and to his sons, that they separate themselves °from the °holy things of the °children of Israel, and that they profane not My °holy name *in those things* which they °hallow unto Me:

f[1] I *am* [1]the LORD.

e[2] 3 Say unto them, 'Whosoever *he be* of all your seed among your generations, that goeth unto the holy things, which the [2]children of Israel [2]hallow unto [1]the LORD, having his uncleanness upon him, that °soul shall be °cut off from My presence:

f[2] I *am* [1]the LORD.

e[3] 4 What °man soever of the seed of Aaron *is* a leper, or hath a running issue; he shall not eat of the [2]holy things, until he be clean. And whoso toucheth any thing *that is* unclean *by* °the dead, or a man whose °seed goeth from him;

5 Or whosoever toucheth any creeping thing, whereby he may be made unclean, or a °man of whom he may take uncleanness, whatsoever uncleanness he hath;

6 The °soul which hath touched any such shall be unclean until even, and shall not eat of the [2]holy things, unless he °wash his flesh with water.

7 And when the sun is down, he shall be clean, and shall afterward eat of the [2]holy things; because it *is* his food.

8 That which dieth of itself, or is torn *with beasts*, he shall not eat to defile himself therewith:

f[3] I *am* [1]the LORD.

e[4] 9 They shall therefore °keep Mine °ordinance, lest they bear °sin for it, and die therefore, if they profane it: I [1]the LORD do sanctify them.

10 There shall no stranger eat *of* the [2]holy thing: a sojourner of the priest, or an hired servant, shall not eat *of* the [2]holy thing.

11 But if the priest buy *any* °soul with his money, °he shall eat of it, and he that is born in his house: they shall eat of his °meat.

12 If the priest's daughter also be *married* unto °a stranger, she may not eat of an °offering of the [2]holy things.

20 blemish in his eye = defective vision, or cataract.
24 children. Heb. sons.

22. 1—16 (*D*, p. 163). DEFILEMENTS (UNCLEANNESS). (*Repeated Alternation.*)

D e[1] | 1, 2-. General.
  f[1] | -2. Reason.
 e[2] | 3-. Uncleanness.
  f[2] | -3. Reason.
 e[3] | 4-8-. Leprous, &c.
  f[3] | -8. Reason.
 e[4] | 9-16-. Strangers.
  f[4] | -16. Reason.

1 the LORD. Heb. Jehovah. Ap. 4.
spake. See note on 5. 14.
2 from. When subject to the following disabilities.
holy. See note on Ex. 3. 5.
children. Heb. sons.
hallow. See note on 12. 4.
3 soul. Heb. *nephesh.* Ap. 13. Here rendered "soul", but in 21. 11 inaccurately rendered "body". See note on 19. 28.
cut off from My presence. Occurs only here in the Pentateuch; elsewhere, "cut off from his people". See note on 7. 20. Accounted for here by the seriousness of the offence.
4 man. Heb. *'ish.* Ap. 14. ii.
the dead. Heb. *nephesh* (Ap. 13), rendered "soul" in preceding verse. Heb = "a dead soul". Cp. *v.* 11.
seed goeth. See 15. 16.
5 man. Heb. *'ādām.* Ap. 14. 1.
6 soul. Heb. *nephesh.* (Ap. 13.) Here again rendered soul. See *vv.* 3, 4; 21. 11, and note on 19. 28.
wash = bathe. See note on 14. 9.
9 keep Mine ordinance = observe my observance. Fig. *Polyptōton,* Ap. 6, for emphasis. Cp. 18. 30.
ordinance = charge.
sin = penalty. Put by Fig. *Metonymy* (of Cause). Ap. 6.
11 soul. Heb. *nephesh* (Ap. 13). Here put by Fig. *Synecdoche* (of Part), Ap. 6, for "any person", i. e. a heathen slave.
he = the slave so bought. Emphatic.
meat = Fig. *Metonymy* (of Species), for any kind of food. Ap. 6.
12 a stranger = a man (Heb. *'ish.* Ap. 14. ii.), i. e. an Israelite, but not of Aaron's seed (Num. 16. 40).
offering = heave offering. Heb. *terūmah.* Ap. 43. II. viii. **14** man. Heb. *'ish.* Ap. 14. ii.
unwittingly: i.e. through ignorance. See 4. 2, 22, 27; 5. 15, 18.
15 offer = offer up, as a heave offering. Heb. *rūm.* Ap. 43. I. ix.
16 iniquity = penalty. Put by Fig. *Metonymy* (of Cause). Ap. 6. Heb. *'āvōn.* Ap. 44. iii.
trespass. Heb. *'āsām.* Ap. 44. ii.
I the LORD do sanctify. A Jehovah title. See note on 21. 8, and Ap. 4.

13 But if the priest's daughter be a widow, or divorced, and have no child, and is returned unto her father's house, as in her youth, she shall eat of her father's meat: but there shall no stranger eat thereof.

14 And if a °man eat *of* the [2]holy thing °unwittingly, then he shall put the fifth *part* thereof unto it, and shall give *it* unto the priest with the [2]holy thing.

15 And they shall not profane the [2]holy things of the [3]children of Israel, which they °offer unto [1]the LORD;

16 Or suffer them to bear the °iniquity of °trespass, when they eat their [2]holy things: for °I [1]the LORD do sanctify them.'" f[4]

C² K 17 And [1]the LORD [1]spake unto Moses, say-
(p. 165) ing,
1490 18 "Speak unto Aaron, and to his sons, and unto all the [3]children of Israel, and say unto them,

L °'Whatsoever *he be* of the house of Israel, or of the strangers in Israel, that will °offer his °oblation for all his vows, and for all his °freewill offerings, which they will °offer unto [1]the LORD for a burnt offering;

19 *Ye shall offer* °at your own will a male without blemish, of the beeves, of the sheep, or of the goats.

20 *But* whatsoever hath a blemish, *that* shall ye not [18]offer: for it shall not be acceptable for you.

21 And whosoever [18]offereth a sacrifice of peace offerings unto [1]the LORD to accomplish *his* vow, or a freewill offering in beeves or sheep, it shall be perfect to be accepted; there shall be no blemish therein.

M 22 Blind, or broken, or maimed, or having a wen, or scurvy, or scabbed, ye shall not [18]offer these unto [1]the LORD, nor make an °offering by fire of them upon the altar unto [1]the LORD.

23 Either a bullock or a lamb that hath any thing superfluous or lacking in his parts, that mayest thou °offer *for* a freewill offering; but for a vow it shall not be accepted.

24 Ye shall not [18]offer unto [1]the LORD that which is bruised, or crushed, or broken, or cut; neither shall ye make *any offering thereof* in your land.

25 Neither from a stranger's hand shall ye [18]offer the °bread °of your °God of any of these; because their corruption *is* in them, *and* blemishes *be* in them: they shall not be accepted for you.'"

M 26 And [1]the LORD [1]spake unto Moses, saying,

27 "When a bullock, or a sheep, or a goat, is brought forth, then it shall be seven days under the dam; and from the eighth day and thenceforth it shall be accepted for an °offering made by fire unto [1]the LORD.

28 And *whether it be* °cow or ewe, ye shall not kill it and her young both in one day.

L 29 And when ye will °offer a sacrifice of thanksgiving unto [1]the LORD, offer *it* [19]at your own will.

30 On the same day it shall be eaten up; ye shall leave none of it until the morrow: I *am* [1]the LORD.

K 31 Therefore shall ye keep My commandments, and do them: I *am* [1]the LORD.

32 Neither shall ye profane My °holy name; but I will be °hallowed among the [3]children of Israel: [16]I *am* [1]the LORD Which °hallow you,

33 That °brought you out of the land of Egypt, to be your [25]God: I *am* [1]the LORD."

P R T¹ **23** And °the LORD °spake unto Moses, saying,

2 "Speak unto the °children of Israel, and say unto them, '*Concerning* the °feasts of [1]the LORD, which ye shall °proclaim *to be* °holy °convocations, *even* these *are* My feasts.

3 Six days shall work be done: but the seventh day *is* the °sabbath of rest, an [2]holy [2]convocation; ye shall do no work *therein*: it *is* the sabbath of [1]the LORD in all your dwellings. U¹

17—33 (C², p. 163). OFFERINGS.
(*Introversion*).

C² | K | 17, 18-. General charge.
  L | -18-21. Burnt offerings and Peace offerings.
   M | 22-25. Offerings; their perfection.
   M | 26-28. Offerings; their age.
  L | 29, 30. Meal offering.
 K | 31-33. General charge.

18 Whatsoever=what man soever. Heb. *'ish 'ish*. Ap. 14. ii.
offer=bring near. Heb. *ḳārab*. Ap. 43. I. i.
oblation=Heb. *ḳorbān*. Ap. 43. II. i. Translated "offering", 3. 7, 14; 7. 12; 17. 4, &c.
freewill offerings. Cp. Ps. 40. 8. John 10. 17, 18; 17. 4. Phil. 2. 7, 8.
19 at your own will=for your acceptance. So rendered in *vv.* 20, 21, 25, 27: see note on 1. 3. For this kind of offering, see note on 7. 15, 16.
22 offering. Heb. *'ishsheh*. Ap. 43. II. xi.
23 offer=prepare. Heb. *'āsāh*. Ap. 43. I. iii.
25 bread=food. Fig. *Synecdoche* (of Species), put for all kinds of food. Ap. 6.
of. Genitive of relation. Ap. 17.
God. Heb. Elohim. Ap. 4.
27 offering=approach offering. Heb. *ḳorbān*. Ap. 43. II. i.
28 cow. Heb. *shōr*, rendered "cow" only here and Num. 18. 17.
29 offer a sacrifice=kill [an offering] as a sacrifice. Ap. 43. I. iv., and II. xii.
32 holy=set apart. See note on Ex. 3. 5.
hallowed . . . hallow=set apart. See note on Ex. 3. 5.
33 brought you out. See note on 11. 45.

23. 1—26. 3 (*C*, p. 131). JEHOVAH'S FEASTS.
(*Introversion*).

C | N | P | 23. 1-44. Weekly and annual.
   Q | 24. 1-9. Repetitions from Exodus.
  O | 24. 10-23. Episode of blasphemer.
 N | *P* | 25. 1-55. Sabbatic and jubilee.
   Q | 26. 1, 2. Repetitions from Exodus.

23. 1—44 (P, above). WEEKLY AND ANNUAL FEASTS (*Introversions and Repeated Alternation*).

P | R | T¹ | 1, 2. General charge.
   U¹ | 3. Seventh day (sabbath rest).
  T² | 4. General charge.
   S | V¹ | 5-8. Passover.
     W¹ | 9-14. Unleavened bread.
    V² | 15-21. Pentecost.
     W² | 22. Harvest.
    V³ | 23-25. Trumpets.
     W³ | 26-32. Atonement.
    V⁴ | 33-36. Tabernacles.
 R | T³ | 37, 38. General charge.
   U² | 39-43. Seventh month. (Booths.)
  T⁴ | 44. General charge.

1 the LORD. Heb. Jehovah. Ap. 4.
spake. See note on 5. 14. **2 children.** Heb. sons.
feasts of the LORD. This was their primal name; but in the day of Christ's rejection they had become "feasts of the Jews". John 5. 1; 2. 13; 6. 4; 11. 55.
proclaim. Cause to be [publicly] heard. Occurs outside the Pentateuch only in Nehemiah.
holy. See note on Ex. 3. 5.
convocation=a calling together, assembly.
3 sabbath of rest. See note on Ex. 16. 23.

T[2] (p. 165) 1490 4 °These *are* the °feasts of [1]the LORD, *even* [2]holy [2]convocations, which ye shall [2]proclaim in their seasons.

V[1] 5 In the fourteenth *day* of the °first month °at even *is* °the LORD'S passover.

6 And on the fifteenth day of the same month *is* the feast of °unleavened bread unto [1]the LORD: seven days ye must eat unleavened bread.

7 In the first day ye shall have an [2]holy [2]convocation: ye shall do no °servile work therein.

8 But ye shall °offer an °offering made by fire unto [1]the LORD seven days: °in the seventh day *is* an [2]holy [2]convocation: ye shall do no [7]servile work *therein*.'"

W[1] 9 And [1]the LORD [1]spake unto Moses, saying,

10 "Speak unto the [2]children of Israel, and say unto them, °'When ye be come into the land which I give unto you, and shall reap the harvest thereof, then ye shall bring a °sheaf of the firstfruits of your harvest unto the priest:

11 And he shall °wave the sheaf before [1]the LORD, to be accepted for you: on the morrow after the sabbath the priest shall wave it.

12 And ye shall °offer °that day when ye wave the sheaf an he lamb without blemish of the first year for a burnt offering unto [1]the LORD.

13 And the meat offering thereof *shall be* two °tenth deals of fine flour mingled with oil, an [8]offering made by fire unto [1]the LORD *for* a °sweet savour: and the drink offering thereof *shall be* of °wine, the fourth *part* of an °hin.

14 And ye shall eat neither bread, nor parched corn, nor green ears, until the selfsame day that ye have brought an °offering unto your °God: *it shall be* a °statute for ever throughout your generations in all your dwellings.

V[2] 15 And ye shall count unto you from the morrow after the sabbath, from the day that ye brought the sheaf of the [11]wave offering; °seven sabbaths shall be complete:

16 Even unto the morrow after the seventh sabbath shall ye number °fifty days; and ye shall [8]offer a new °meat offering unto [1]the LORD.

17 Ye shall bring out of your habitations two wave loaves of two tenth deals: they shall be of fine flour; they shall be baken °with leaven; *they are* the firstfruits unto [1]the LORD.

18 And ye shall [8]offer with the bread seven lambs without blemish of the first year, and one young bullock, and two rams: they shall be *for* a burnt offering unto [1]the LORD, with their meat offering, and their drink offerings, *even* an [8]offering made by fire, of [13]sweet savour unto [1]the LORD.

19 Then ye shall °sacrifice one kid of the goats for a sin offering, and two lambs of the first year for a sacrifice of peace offerings.

20 And the priest shall [11]wave them with the bread of the firstfruits *for* a wave offering before [1]the LORD, with the two lambs: they shall be [2]holy to [1]the LORD for the priest.

21 And ye shall [2]proclaim on the selfsame day, *that* it may be an [2]holy [2]convocation unto you: ye shall do no [7]servile work *therein: it shall be* [14]a statute for ever in all your dwellings throughout your generations.

W[2] 22 And when ye reap the °harvest of your land, thou shalt not make clean riddance of the corners of thy field when thou reapest, neither shalt thou gather any gleaning of thy harvest: thou shalt leave them unto the poor, and to the stranger: I *am* [1]the LORD your [14]God.'"

V[3] 23 And [1]the LORD [1]spake unto Moses, saying,

24 "Speak unto the [2]children of Israel, saying, 'In the seventh month, in the first *day* of the month, shall ye have a sabbath, a memorial of blowing of trumpets, an [2]holy [2]convocation.

---

4 These are the feasts: thus marking the sabbath offering as distinct.
feasts = Heb. appointed seasons.
feasts of the LORD. This was their true character. But in our Lord's day they had degenerated into "feasts of the Jews" (John 2. 13; 5. 1; 6. 4; 11. 55).
5 first month: called in Pentateuch "Abib" (Ex. 13. 4; 23. 15; 34. 18. Deut. 16. 1); and "Nisan" in later books (Neh. 2. 1. Est. 3. 7) = about beginning of April.
at even: any time from sunset of one day till sunrise of the second day. Heb. "between the evenings".
the LORD'S [Heb. Jehovah's] **passover.** This is the first of the Feasts; Tabernacles is the seventh. First, redemption; last, rest. Redemption is the title to rest.
6 unleavened. Note the exception in *v.* 17, and see note there.
7 servile = laborious.
8 offer = bring near. Heb. *ḳārab.* Ap. 43. I.
offering. Heb. *'ishsheh.* Ap. 43. II. xi.
in. Some codices, with Sam., Sept., Syr., and Vulg., read "and on (or in)".
10 When ye be come. See note on 14. 34.
sheaf. The Antitype is Christ, the firstfruits. 1 Cor. 15. 23.
11 wave. See note on Ex. 29. 27.
12 offer = prepare. Heb. *'āsāh.* Ap. 43. I. iii.
that day. All these offerings were without leaven. Cp. *v.* 17.
13 tenth deals. See Ap. 51. III. 3.
sweet savour = savour of satisfaction. See note on Gen. 8. 21.
wine. Heb. *yayin.* Ap. 27. 1.
hin. See Ap. 51. III. 3.
14 offering. Heb. *ḳorbān.* See Ap. 43. II. i.
God. Heb. Elohim. Ap. 4.
statute for ever. See *v.* 21; 3. 17; 6. 18, 22; 7. 34; 10. 9, 15; 24. 8, 9. Ex. 12. 14; 29. 28; 30. 21. Num. 18. 8, 11, 19. Jer. 5. 22, &c.
15 seven sabbaths = seven weeks. Cp. Luke 18. 12. Matt. 28. 1. Hence the name "feast of weeks" in Old Testament. Ex. 34. 22. Deut. 16. 10, 16. 2 Chron. 8. 13.
16 fifty days. Hence the name Pentecost. Acts 2. 1; 20. 16. 1 Cor. 16. 8.
meat offering = meal offering. See note on 2. 1.
17 with leaven. This great exception is made because the antitype is not Christ but human kind, and not without sin. "They that are Christ's", 1 Cor. 15. 23. Cp. *vv.* 6 and 10 above.
19 sacrifice = prepare; same as "offer" in *v.* 12.
22 harvest. In the Antitype = "the end" or the remainder. 1 Cor. 15. 24.

1490 25 Ye shall do no [7]servile work *therein:*
but ye shall [8]offer an [8]offering made by fire
unto [1]the LORD.'"

W[3] 26 And [1]the LORD [1]spake unto Moses, say-
(p. 165) ing,
27 "Also on the tenth *day* of this seventh
month *there shall be* a day of °atonement: it
shall be an [2]holy [2]convocation unto you; and
ye shall °afflict °your souls, and [25]offer an
offering made by fire unto [1]the LORD.
28 And ye shall do no work in that same
day: for it *is* a day of [27]atonement, to make
an [27]atonement for you before [1]the LORD your
[14]God.
29 For whatsoever °soul *it be* that shall not
be °afflicted in that same day, he shall be °cut
off from among his people.
30 And whatsoever [29]soul *it be* that doeth
any work in that same day, the same °soul
will I destroy from among his people.
31 Ye shall do no manner of °work: *it shall
be* a [14]statute for ever throughout your generations in all your dwellings.
32 It *shall be* unto you a sabbath of rest,
and ye shall [27]afflict [27]your souls: in the ninth
day of the month at even, from even unto
even, shall ye °celebrate your sabbath."

V[4] 33 And [1]the LORD [1]spake unto Moses, saying,
34 "Speak unto the [2]children of Israel, saying, 'The fifteenth day of this seventh month
shall be the feast of °tabernacles *for* seven
days unto [1]the LORD.
35 On the first day *shall be* an [2]holy [2]convo-
cation: ye shall do no °servile work *therein.*
36 Seven days ye shall [8]offer [8]an offering
made by fire unto [1]the LORD: °on the eighth
day shall be an [2]holy [2]convocation unto you;
and ye shall [25]offer an [25]offering made by fire
unto [1]the LORD: it *is* a solemn assembly; *and*
ye shall do no [7]servile work *therein.*

T[3] 37 °These *are* the feasts of [1]the LORD, which
ye shall [2]proclaim *to be* [2]holy [2]convocations,
to [36]offer an offering made by fire unto [1]the
LORD, a burnt offering, and a meat offering,
a sacrifice, and drink offerings, every thing
upon his day:
38 Beside the °sabbaths of [1]the LORD, and
beside your gifts, and beside all your vows,
and beside all your freewill offerings, which
ye give unto [1]the LORD.

U 39 Also in the fifteenth day of the seventh
month, when ye have gathered in the fruit
of the land, ye shall keep a °feast unto [1]the
LORD seven days: on the first day *shall be*
a sabbath, and on the eighth day *shall be*
a sabbath.
40 And ye shall take you on the first day
the boughs of goodly trees, branches of palm
trees, and the boughs of thick trees, and
willows of the brook; and ye shall rejoice
°before [1]the LORD your [14]God seven days.
41 And ye shall keep it a [39]feast unto [1]the
LORD seven days in the year. *It shall be* a
statute for ever °in your generations: ye shall
celebrate it in the seventh month.
42 Ye shall dwell °in booths seven days;
all that are Israelites born shall dwell °in
booths:

27 atonement. See note on Ex. 29. 33.
afflict=humble.
your souls=yourselves. Heb. *nephesh.* Ap. 13.
29 soul=person. Heb. *nephesh.* Ap. 13.
afflicted=humbled. Put by Fig. *Metonymy* (of the Adjunct), for the outward sign of it. Ap. 6.
cut off. See note on 7. 20.
31 work. Some codices, with Sam., Syr., and Vulg., add "therefore".
32 celebrate your sabbath. See note on Ex. 16. 23.
34 tabernacles=booths. Heb. *sukkōth*=a lodge in a garden. Is. 1. 8, "cottage".
35 servile=laborious.
36 on. Some codices, with Sam., Sept., Syr., and Vulg., read "and on".
37 These are the feasts of the LORD: viz. the above-mentioned festivals. See Structure "S" (23. 1, p. 165).
38 sabbaths. Put by Fig. *Metonymy* (of the Adjunct), Ap. 6, for the sacrifices offered on the sabbath. See note on 25. 6.
39 feast=festival.
40 before the LORD. Heb. before the face of Jehovah (Ap. 4). Fig. *Pleonasm.* Ap. 6.=in the presence of.
41 in=throughout.
42 in booths. In Heb., the verse begins and ends with these words, for emphasis, by the Fig. *Epanadiplosis.* Ap. 6.
44 declared: according to verse 2.
feasts=appointed seasons.

24. 1—9 (Q, p. 165). REPETITIONS FROM EXODUS.

1 the LORD. Heb. Jehovah. Ap. 4.
spake. See note on 5. 14.
2 Command. Only twice, here and in 6. 9, is the word "command" used for communicating.
children. Heb. sons.
the light=the light-bearer or lamp-stand. Cp. Ex. 27. 20, 21.
3 of. Genitive of relation.=the vail relating to the testimony or ark of the covenant, i. e. the vail that is *before* it.
tabernacle=tent. Heb. *'ōhel.* Ap. 40.
Aaron. Some codices, with Sam. and Onk., add "and his sons", as in *v.* 9.
statute for ever. See 23. 14, and note on 3. 17.
4 candlestick=light-holder as *v.* 2 above, and Gen. 1. 14, &c. The word "pure" here=purified or ceremonially cleansed: i. e. not for common uses.

43 That your generations may know that
I made the [2]children of Israel to dwell in
booths, when I brought them out of the land of
Egypt: I *am* [1]the LORD your [14]God.'"
44 And Moses °declared unto the [2]children T[4]
of Israel the °feasts of [1]the LORD.

24 And °the LORD °spake unto Moses, Q
saying,
2 °"Command the °children of Israel, that
they bring unto thee pure oil olive beaten
for °the light, to cause the lamps to burn
continually.
3 Without the vail °of the testimony, in the
°tabernacle of the congregation, shall °Aaron
order it from the evening unto the morning
before [1]the LORD continually: *it shall be* a
°statute for ever in your generations.
4 He shall order the lamps upon the pure
°candlestick before [1]the LORD continually.

1490 5 And thou shalt take fine flour, and bake twelve cakes thereof: °two °tenth deals shall be in one cake.

6 And thou shalt set them in two °rows, six on a °row, upon the °pure table °before [1]the LORD.

7 And thou shalt put pure frankincense upon *each* [6]row, that it may be on the bread for a memorial, *even* an °offering made by fire unto [1]the LORD.

8 °Every sabbath he shall set it in order before [1]the LORD continually, *being taken* from the [2]children of Israel by an everlasting covenant.

9 And it shall be Aaron's and his sons'; and they shall °eat it in the °holy place: for it *is* most °holy unto him of the [7]offerings of [1]the LORD made by fire by a perpetual statute."

O (p. 165) 10 And the son of an Israelitish woman, whose father *was* an Egyptian, went out among the [2]children of Israel: and this son of the Israelitish *woman* and °a man of Israel °strove together in the camp;

11 And the Israelitish woman's son °blasphemed °the name *of the LORD*, and cursed. And they brought him unto Moses: (and his mother's name *was* Shelomith, the daughter of Dibri, of the tribe of °Dan:)

12 And they put him in ward, that the mind of [1]the LORD might be shewed them.

13 And [1]the LORD [1]spake unto Moses, saying,

14 "Bring forth him that hath cursed without the camp; and let all that heard *him* °lay their hands upon his head, and let all the congregation °stone him.

15 And thou shalt speak unto the [2]children of Israel, saying, 'Whosoever curseth his °God shall °bear his °sin.

16 And he that blasphemeth the name of [1]the LORD, he shall surely be put to death, *and* all the congregation shall certainly stone him: as well the stranger, as he that is born in the land, when he [11]blasphemeth the name *of the LORD*, shall be put to death.

17 And he that killeth °any °man shall surely be put to death.

18 And he that killeth °a beast shall make it good; °beast for °beast.

19 And if a °man cause a blemish in his neighbour; °as he hath done, so shall it be done to him;

20 Breach for breach, eye for eye, tooth for tooth: [19]as he hath caused a blemish in a °man, so shall it be done to him *again*.

21 And he that killeth a beast, he shall restore it: and he that killeth a [20]man, he shall be put to death.

22 Ye shall have one °manner of law, as well for the stranger, as for one of your own country: for I *am* [1]the LORD your [15]God.'"

23 And Moses spake to the [2]children of Israel, that they should bring forth him that had cursed out of the camp, and [14]stone him with stones. And the [2]children of Israel did [19]as [1]the LORD commanded Moses.

5 two. Only one required for the ordinary meal offering (Ex. 29. 40. Num. 15. 4; 28. 9, 13, &c.).

tenth deals. See Ap. 51. III. 3.

6 rows = piles. **row** = pile.

pure = purified or ceremonially cleansed. Cp. *v.* 4.

before the LORD: i. e. in the holy place. Hence called "the table of the presence" (Num. 4. 7), and the cakes called "the bread of the presence" (Ex. 25. 30; 35. 13; 39. 36). The word "shewbread" taken from the Vulgate, and Luther, does not correctly represent the Hebrew name. The use of this word quite hides the Hebrew expression "bread of ordering" (set in order), "the sets of bread", "the table set in order", in 1 Chron. 9. 32; 23. 29. 2 Chron. 13. 11. Neh. 10. 33; and the table in 2 Chron. 29. 18. These Hebrew expressions are based on and derived from this verse.

7 offering. Heb. *'ishsheh.* Ap. 43. II. xi.

8 Every sabbath. Heb. "on the day of the sabbath, on the day of the sabbath", Fig. *Epizeuxis.* Ap. 6. = on the holy sabbath day. Cp. 1 Chron. 9. 32.

9 eat it in the holy place. Eight things were thus consumed by the priests. See note on 7. 9.

holy. See note on Ex. 3. 5.

10—23 (O, p. 165). EPISODE OF THE BLASPHEMER.

10 a man of Israel. Heb. a man (*'ish*, Ap. 14. ii.) an Israelite. Jewish tradition says he was a Danite.

strove together. Cp. Ex. 2. 13. The Chald. version says the semi-Egyptian strove to encamp in the tribe of Dan.

11 blasphemed, &c. Cp. Gen. 4. 24. Hence the use of "the name" instead of "Jehovah".

the name, or supply *Ellipsis* (Ap. 6. iii. a) from *v.* 16.

Dan, another sad blot on this tribe.

14 lay their hands upon. Done only in the case of a blasphemer.

stone him. Nine persons stoned (see Ap. 10):

- The blasphemer, Lev. 24. 14.
- The sabbath-breaker, Num. 15. 36.
- Achan, Josh. 7. 25.
- Abimelech, Judg. 9. 53.
- Adoram, 1 Kings 12. 18 (2 Chron. 10. 18).
- Naboth, 1 Kings 21. 13.
- Zechariah, 2 Chron. 24. 21.
- Stephen, Acts 7. 58.
- Paul, Acts 14. 19 (2 Cor. 11. 25).

15 God. Heb. Elohim. Ap. 4.

bear his sin. Fig. *Metonymy* (of the Cause). Ap. 6 "sin" (*chāṭ'ā*, Ap. 44. i.) being put for its penalty.

17 any man = the soul (Heb. *nephesh.* Ap. 13) of a man. Heb. *'ādām.* Ap. 14. i.

18 a beast = the soul (Heb. *nephesh.* Ap. 13).

beast for beast = soul for soul (Heb. *nephesh.* Ap. 13).

19 man. Heb. *'ish.* Ap. 14. ii. **as** = according as.

20 man. Heb. *'ādām.* Ap. 14. i.

22 manner of law = rule or regulation. Heb. *mishpāṭ* = judgment.

25. 1-55 (*P*, p. 165). SABBATIC AND JUBILEE YEARS (*Alternation*).

P | X | 1, 2. The sabbatic year.
  Y | 3-7. The six years.
X | 8-13. The jubilee year.
  Y | 14-55. The forty-nine years.

1 the LORD. Heb. Jehovah. Ap. 4.

spake. See note on 5. 14.

mount Sinai. See note in title "Leviticus"; not out of the tabernacle.

2 children. Heb. sons.

When, &c. See note on 14. 34.

keep a sabbath. Heb. sabbath a sabbatizing. Fig. *Polyptōton.* Ap. 6. For emphasis = keep a sacred sabbath.

N P x (p. 168) 25 And °the LORD °spake unto Moses in °mount Sinai, saying,

2 "Speak unto the °children of Israel, and say unto them, °'When ye come into the land which I give you, then shall the land °keep a sabbath unto [1]the LORD.

1490 3 Six years thou shalt sow thy field, and six
Y years thou shalt prune thy vineyard, and
(p. 168) gather in the fruit thereof;
1st Sab. 4 But in the seventh year shall be a °sab-
year, bath of rest unto the land, a sabbath for [1]the
1444- LORD: thou shalt neither sow thy field, nor
1443 prune thy vineyard.
5 That which groweth of its own accord
of thy harvest thou shalt not reap, neither
gather the grapes of thy vine °undressed: *for*
it is a year of [4]rest unto the land.
6 And the °sabbath of the land shall be
meat for you; for thee, and for thy servant,
and for thy maid, and for thy hired servant,
and for thy stranger that sojourneth with
thee,
7 And for thy cattle, and for the beast that
are in thy land, shall all the °increase thereof
be meat.

X 8 And thou shalt number °seven sabbaths
of years unto thee, seven times seven years;
and the space of the seven sabbaths of years
shall be unto thee forty and nine years.
9 Then shalt thou cause the °trumpet of
the jubile to sound on the tenth *day* of the
seventh month, in the day of °atonement
shall ye make the trumpet sound throughout
all your land.
1st Jub., 10 And ye shall °hallow the fiftieth year, and
1401- °proclaim liberty throughout *all* the land unto
1400 all the inhabitants thereof: it shall be a jubile
unto you; and ye shall return every man unto
his possession, and ye shall return every man
unto his family.
11 A jubile shall that fiftieth year be unto
you: ye shall not sow, neither reap that
which groweth of itself in it, nor gather *the*
grapes in it of thy vine undressed.
12 For it *is* the jubile; it shall be °holy unto
you: ye shall eat the [7]increase thereof out of
the field.
13 In the year of this jubile ye shall return
every °man unto his possession.

Y z[1] 14 And if thou sell ought unto thy neigh-
(p. 169) bour, or buyest *ought* of thy neighbour's hand,
ye shall not °oppress one another:
15 °According to the number of years after
the jubile thou shalt buy of thy neighbour,
and according unto the number of years of the
fruits he shall sell unto thee:
16 [15]According to the multitude of years
thou shalt [36]increase the price thereof, and
according to the fewness of years thou shalt
diminish the price of it: for *according* to the
number *of the years* of the fruits doth he sell
unto thee.
17 Ye shall not therefore oppress one another; but thou shalt fear thy °God: for I
am [1]the LORD your °God.
18 Wherefore ye shall do My statutes, and
keep My judgments, and do them; and ye shall
dwell in the land in °safety.
19 And the land shall yield her fruit, and
ye shall eat your fill, and dwell therein in
safety.

A[1] 20 And if ye shall say, °'What shall we eat
the seventh year? °behold, we shall not sow,
nor gather in our [20]increase:'
21 Then I will command My blessing upon
you in the sixth year, and it shall bring forth
fruit for three years.
22 And ye shall sow the eighth year, and eat
yet of old fruit until the ninth year; until her
fruits come in ye shall eat *of* the old *store*.

23 The land shall not be sold °for ever: Z[2]
for °the land *is* Mine; for ye *are* strangers
and sojourners with Me.
24 And in all the land of your possession ye
shall °grant a °redemption for the land.

25 °If thy brother be °waxen poor, and hath A[2]
sold away *some* of his possession, and if °any
of his kin come to °redeem it, then shall he
°redeem that which his brother sold.
26 And if the [13]man have °none to [25]redeem
it, and himself be able to [25]redeem it;

3—7 (Y, p. 168). THE SIX YEARS.

4 sabbath of rest. See note on Ex. 16. 23.

5 undressed = unpruned.

6 sabbath. Put by Fig. *Metonymy* (of the Adjunct), Ap. 6, for the fruits of the seventh year.

7 increase = gain or profit. Heb. *tᵉbû'âh.* So in *vv.* 12, 20; not in *vv.* 16, 36, 37.

8—13 (*X*, p. 168). THE JUBILEE YEAR.

8 seven sabbaths of years. 7 × 7 = 49. See Ap. 10.

9 trumpet = a curved horn of *jubilee*, i.e. of loud or joyful sound. Heb. *yôbēl.* First jubilee; the last at the Nativity (the 29th).

atonement. See note on Ex. 29. 33.

10 hallow = set apart. Heb. *châdash.* See note on Ex. 3. 5. **proclaim** = cause public notice to be given.

12 holy. See note on Ex. 3. 5.

13 man. Heb *'îsh.* Ap. 14. ii.

14—55 (*Y*, p. 168). THE FORTY-NINE YEARS.
(*Repeated Alternation.*)

Y | Z[1] | 14–19. Goods.
 A[1] | 20–22. Case of want.
Z[2] | 23, 24. Land.
 A[2] | 25–28. Case of poverty.
Z[3] | 29–34. Houses.
 A[3] | 35. Case of poverty.
Z[4] | 36–38. Money.
 A[4] | 39–41. Cases of poverty.
Z[5] | 42–46. Bondage.
 A[5] | 47–55. Cases of poverty.

14—19 (Z[1], above). PARTING WITH GOODS.

14 oppress = overreach.

15 According = in proportion. The estimation of value regulated by nearness of the jubilee. So our estimation of value of earthly things governed by our sense of the nearness of Christ's coming.)

17 God. Heb. Elohim. Ap. 4.

18 safety = confidence.

20—22 (A[1], above). CASE OF WANT.

20 What . . . ? Fig. *Erotēsis.* Ap. 6. (A lesson for us. God's "I will" the answer to our "What?").
behold. Fig. *Asterismos.* Ap. 6.

23, 24 (Z[2], above). PARTING WITH LAND.

23 for ever. Fig. *Synecdoche* (of the Whole), Ap. 6, as we say "in perpetuity" = absolutely or beyond recovery.
the land is Mine. Cp. Ex. 15. 17; Isa. 14. 8, 25; Jer. 2. 7; Ps. 10. 16; 78. 54. **24 grant** = give.
redemption = repurchase. Heb. *g'âal.* See note on Ex. 6. 6.

25—28 (A[2], above). CASE OF POVERTY.

25 If. Some codices, with Sam., Sept., and Syr., read "And if". **waxen poor** = brought low.
any of his kin = his *goël*, or redeemer, next of kin. See note on Ex. 6. 6.
redeem = Heb. *g'âal*, buy back. See note on Ex. 6. 6.
26 none to redeem it = no redeemer.

1490 27 Then let him count the years of the sale thereof, and restore the overplus unto the [26]man to whom he sold it; that he may return unto his possession.

28 But if he be not able to restore *it* to him, then that which is sold shall remain in the hand of him that hath bought it until the year of jubile: and in the jubile it shall go out, and he shall °return unto his possession.

Z[3] (p. 169) 29 And if a man sell a dwelling house in a walled city, then he may [25]redeem it °within a whole year after it is sold; *within* a full year may he [24]redeem it.

30 And if it be not [25]redeemed [29]within the space of a full year, then the house that *is* in °the walled city shall be established [23]for ever to him that bought it throughout his generations: it shall not go out in the jubile.

31 But the houses of the villages which have no wall round about them shall be counted as the fields of the country: they may be [25]redeemed, and they shall go out in the jubile.

32 Notwithstanding °the cities of the Levites, *and* the houses of the cities of their possession, may the Levites [25]redeem at any time.

33 And °if a man purchase of the Levites, then the house that was sold, and the city of his possession, shall go out in *the year of* jubile: for the houses of the cities of the Levites *are* their possession among the [2]children of Israel.

34 But the field of the suburbs of their cities may not be sold; for it *is* °their perpetual possession.

A[3] 35 And if thy brother be [25]waxen poor, and °fallen in decay with thee; then thou shalt relieve him: *yea, though he be* a stranger, or a sojourner; that he may live with thee.

Z[4] 36 Take thou no °usury of him, or °increase: but fear thy [17]God; that thy brother may live with thee.

37 Thou shalt not give him thy money upon [36]usury, nor lend him thy victuals for [36]increase.

38 I *am* [1]the LORD your [17]God, Which brought you forth out of the land of Egypt, to give you the land of Canaan, °*and* to be your [17]God.

A[4] 39 And if thy brother *that dwelleth* by thee be [25]waxen poor, and be °sold unto thee; thou shalt not compel him to serve as a bondservant:

40 *But* as an hired servant, *and* as a sojourner, he shall be with thee, *and* shall serve thee unto the year of jubile:

41 And *then* shall he depart from thee, *both* he and his [2]children with him, and shall return unto his own family, and unto the possession of his fathers shall he return.

Z[5] 42 For they *are* My servants, which I °brought forth out of the land of Egypt: they shall not be sold °as bondmen.

43 Thou shalt not rule over him with rigour; but shalt fear thy [17]God.

44 Both thy bondmen, and thy bondmaids, which thou shalt have, *shall be* of the heathen that are round about you; of them shall ye buy bondmen and bondmaids.

45 Moreover of the [2]children of the strangers that do sojourn among you, of them shall ye buy, and of their families that *are* with you, which they begat in your land: and they shall be your possession.

46 And ye shall take them as an inheritance for your [2]children after you, to inherit *them for* a possession; they shall be your bondmen [23]for ever: but over your brethren the [2]children of Israel, ye shall not rule one over another with rigour.

47 And if a sojourner or stranger wax rich by thee, and thy brother *that dwelleth* by him wax poor, and sell himself unto the stranger *or* sojourner by thee, or to the stock of the stranger's family: A[5]

48 After that he is sold he may be [24]redeemed again; one of his brethren may [25]redeem him:

49 Either his uncle, or his uncle's son, may [25]redeem him, or *any* that is nigh of kin unto him of his family °may [25]redeem him; or if he be able, he may [25]redeem himself.

28 return. The twelve loaves of ch. 24 were a witness as to the People; the jubilee (ch. 25) as to the Land.

29—34 (Z[3], p. 169). PARTING WITH A HOUSE.

29 within a whole year = within days, "days" being put by Fig. *Synecdoche* (of the Part), for a whole year of days. Ap. 6.

30 the walled city = a city that hath walls.

32 the cities of the Levites. Cp. the forty-eight cities, Num. 35. 1-8. Josh. 21. 1-8.

33 if a man purchase of the Levites. Should be "if one of the Levites should not redeem".

34 their. Some codices, with Onk., have "your".

35 (A[3], p. 169). CASE OF POVERTY.

35 fallen in decay = "his hands have become shaky" or become feeble.

36—38 (Z[4], p. 169). MONEY OR USURY.

36 usury (Heb. *nāshak*), is a charge on *money*. **increase** (Heb. *tarbith* or *marbith*) is a charge on *goods*. See notes on *v.* 7 and 26. 4. These were the definitions of the authorities of the second temple.

38 and to be your God. Jehovah became their God, by giving them Canaan. Cp. 26. 45.

39—41 (A[4], p. 169). CASE OF POVERTY.

39 sold, as in 2 Kings 4. 1.

42—46 (Z[5], p. 169). BONDAGE.

42 brought forth. Note the four occurrences of this expression in these two chapters: 26. 13, brought out to be free men (in relation to the Egyptians); 25. 42 (in relation to fellow-Israelites); 25. 38, to be inheritors; and 25. 55, to be Jehovah's servants.

as bondmen. Heb. "with the sale of a bondman": i.e. as "bondmen [are sold]".

47—55 (A[5], p. 169). CASE OF POVERTY.

49 may redeem. Cp. Neh. 5. 8.

1490 **50** And he shall reckon with him that bought him from the year that he was sold to him unto the year of jubile: and the price of his sale shall be according unto the number of years, according to the time of an hired servant shall it be with him.

51 If *there be* yet many years *behind*, according unto them he shall give again the price of his [24] redemption out of the money that he was bought for.

52 And if there remain but few years unto the year of jubile, then he shall count with him, *and* according unto his years shall he give him again the price of his [24] redemption.

53 *And* as a yearly hired servant shall he be with him: *and the other* shall not rule with rigour over him in thy sight.

54 And if he be not [25] redeemed in these *years*, then he shall go out in the year of jubile, *both* he, and his [2] children with him.

55 For unto Me the [2] children of Israel *are* servants; they *are* My servants whom I brought forth out of the land of Egypt: I *am* [1] the LORD your [17] God.

Q (p. 165) **26** °Ye shall make you no °idols nor °graven image, neither rear you up a °standing image, neither shall ye set up *any* °image of stone in your land, to bow down unto it: for I *am* °the LORD your °God.

2 °Ye shall keep My sabbaths, and reverence My sanctuary: I *am* [1] the LORD.

B[1] C E (p. 171) **3** °If ye walk in My statutes, and keep My commandments, and do them;

F **4** °Then I will give you °rain in due season, and the land shall yield her °increase, and the trees of the field shall yield their fruit.

5 And your threshing shall reach unto the vintage, and the vintage shall reach unto the sowing time: and ye shall eat your bread to the full, and dwell in your land safely.

6 And I will give °peace in the land, and ye shall lie down, and none shall make *you* afraid: and I will °rid evil beasts out of the land, neither shall the sword go through your land.

7 And ye shall chase your °enemies, and they shall fall before you by the sword.

8 And °five of you shall chase an hundred, and an hundred of you shall put ten thousand to flight: and your enemies shall fall before you by the sword.

9 For I will °have respect unto you, and make you fruitful, and multiply you, and establish My covenant with you.

10 And ye shall eat old store, and bring forth the old because of the new.

11 And I will set My °tabernacle among you: and °My soul shall not abhor you.

12 And I will °walk among you, and will be your [1] God, and ye shall be My people.

13 I *am* [1] the LORD your [1] God, which brought you forth out of the land of Egypt, that ye should not be their bondmen; and I have °broken the bands of your yoke, and made you go °upright.

D G[1] **14** But if ye will not hearken unto Me, and will not do all these commandments;

26. 1, 2 (*Q*, p. 165). REPETITIONS FROM EXODUS.

1, 2 Ye refers to any Israelites sold to heathen masters, who hence were in danger of being tempted to idolatry, while in this servitude.

idols = non-entities.. Heb. *'ĕlīlīm* = clay or terra cotta "gods". Cp. 1 Cor. 8. 4. Occurs only once more in Pentateuch, Lev. 19. 4.

graven image. Heb. *pesel*, an idol of wood or stone.

standing image. Heb. *Mazzēbāh*, a sacred pillar. In Gen. always "pillar". Cp. *v.* 30.

image of stone. Heb. *maskīth*, a sculptured or painted stone. Cp. *v.* 30.

the LORD. Heb. Jehovah. Ap. 4.

God. Heb. Elohim. Ap. 4.

26. 3—27. 34 (**A**[3], p. 131). THE OFFERERS AND THEIR CHARGES IN MOUNT SINAI (*Division*).

A[3] | B[1] | 26. 3-46. Jehovah's charge to the offerers.
| B[2] | 27. 1-34. The offerers' vows to Jehovah.

26. 3—46 (B[1], above). JEHOVAH'S CHARGE.
(*Introversion, and Repeated Alternation.*)

B[1] | C | E | 3. The People. Obedience.
F | 4-13. Blessings.
D | G[1] | 14, 15. Disobedience.
H[1] | 16, 17. Punishment.
G[2] | 18-. Disobedience.
H[2] | -18-20. Punishment.
G[3] | 21-. Disobedience.
H[3] | -21, 22. Punishment.
G[4] | 23. Disobedience.
H[4] | 24-26. Punishment.
G[5] | 27. Disobedience.
H[5] | 28-39. Punishment.
C | *E* | 40, 41. The People. Repentance.
F | 42-46. Blessings.

3 (E, above). OBEDIENCE.
(*Introversion.*)

3 If . . . Then. Note the four occurrences of "If" and "Then" in this chapter.

4—13 (F, above). BLESSINGS.

a | 3, 4. Obedience. Consequence.
b | 23, 24. Disobedience.
b | 27, 28. Disobedience.
a | 40, 42. Obedience. Confession.

4 Then. See note on "If", *v.* 3 above.

rain. Heb. rains: i.e. the early and latter rains. Deut. 11. 14; 28. 12. Jer. 14. 22. Deut. 32. 2. Ps. 72. 6.

increase = produce, sustenance. Heb *ybûl*. See notes on 25. 7 and 36.

6 peace, or prosperity.

rid evil beasts. Cp. Ezek. 34. 25, 28.

7 enemies = foes. First occurrence in Leviticus.

8 five. See Ap. 10, this promise enlarged in Deut. 32. 30. Josh. 23. 10. Cp. 2 Sam. 23. 8, 18. 1 Chron. 11. 11, 18. Isa. 30. 17.

9 have respect = turn unto you, as rendered in Ezek. 46. 9; the only other place where this form occurs.

11 tabernacle = habitation. Heb. *mishkān*. Ap. 40.

My soul = Myself, or *I*. Fig. *Anthropopatheia*. Ap. 6.

12 walk. Fig. *Anthropopatheia*, Ap. 6; or, literally, as in Eden. See Gen. 3. 8. Ap. 4. Quoted 2 Cor. 6. 16.

13 broken = broken in pieces. Heb. *shābar*, as in *vv.* 19, 26; not *pārar*, as in *vv.* 15, 24.

upright. The yoke makes the wearer stoop.

14, 15 (G[1], above). DISOBEDIENCE.

The above structure (D, above) shows God's fivefold *threatening* for disobedience. We have the fivefold *execution* in Isa. 5. 25; 9. 12, 17, 21; 10. 4; and His fivefold *lamentation* in Amos 4. 6-12.

1490 15 And if ye shall despise My statutes, or if °your soul abhor My judgments, so that ye will not do all My commandments, *but* that ye °break My covenant:

H1 (p. 171) 16 I also will do this unto you; I will even appoint over you terror, consumption, and the °burning ague, that shall °consume the eyes, and cause sorrow of °heart: and ye shall sow your seed in vain, for your enemies shall eat it.

17 And I will set My °face against you, and ye shall be slain before your enemies: they that hate you shall °reign over you; and ye shall flee when none pursueth you.

18 And if ye will not yet for all this hearken unto Me,

H2 then I will punish you seven times more for your °sins.

19 And I will [13]break the pride °of your power; and I will make your heaven as iron, and your earth as brass:

20 And your strength shall be spent in vain: for your land shall not yield her [4]increase, neither shall the trees °of the land yield their fruits.

G3 21 And if ye walk °contrary unto Me, and will not hearken unto Me;

H3 I will bring seven times more plagues upon you according to your [18]sins.

22 I will also send °wild beasts among you, which shall rob you of your children, and destroy your cattle, and make you few in number; and your *high* ways shall be desolate.

G4 23 And if ye will not be reformed by Me by these things, but will walk [21]contrary unto Me;

H4 24 Then will I also [12]walk [21]contrary unto you, and will punish you yet seven times for your [18]sins.

25 °And I will bring a sword upon you, that shall avenge the quarrel of *My* covenant: and when ye are °gathered together within your cities, I will send the pestilence among you; and ye shall be delivered into the hand of the enemy.

26 *And* when I have [13]broken °the staff of your bread, °ten women shall bake your bread in one oven, and they shall deliver *you* your bread again by weight: and ye shall eat, and not be satisfied.

G5 27 And if ye will not for all this hearken unto Me, but [12]walk [21]contrary unto Me;

H5 28 Then I will [12]walk [21]contrary unto you also in fury; and I, even I, will chastise you seven times for your [18]sins.

29 And ye shall eat the flesh of your sons, and the flesh of your daughters shall ye eat.

30 And I will destroy your °high places, and cut down your °images, and cast your carcases upon the °carcases of your °idols, and °My soul shall abhor you.

31 And I will make your cities waste, and bring your °sanctuaries unto desolation, and I will not °smell the savour of your sweet °odours.

32 And °I will bring the land into desolation: and your enemies which dwell therein shall be astonished at it.

33 And I will scatter you among the °heathen, and will draw out a sword after you: and your land shall be desolate, and your cities waste.

15 your soul = you (emphatic). Heb. *nephesh*. Ap. 13.
break = violate. Heb. *pārar*, break asunder, as in *v.* 46; not *shābar*, as in *vv.* 13, 19, 26.

16, 17 (H1, p. 171). PUNISHMENT.

16 burning ague. Probably = fever.
consume the eyes = causing the sight to fail.
heart = soul. Heb. *nephesh*. Ap. 13.
17 face. Fig. *Anthropopatheia*. Ap. 6.
reign = rule.

18- (G2, p. 171). DISOBEDIENCE.

-18-20 (H2, p. 171). PUNISHMENT.

18 sins. Heb. pl. of *'āvōn*. Ap. 44. iii.
19 of. Genitive of cause, the power being the cause of the pride = your great pride. Cp. Ezek. 30. 6. So Ezek. 24. 21, where the sense is lost in A.V. by the rendering "the excellency of your strength".
20 of the land. Some codices, with Sam. and Sept., read "of the field".

21- (G3, p. 171). DISOBEDIENCE.

21 contrary. First occurrence, and only in this chapter (seven times).

-21, 22 (H3, p. 171). PUNISHMENT.

22 wild beasts. These abounded in Palestine. (Deut. 32. 24. 2 Kings 17. 25. Isa. 13. 21, 22. Ezek. 14. 15, &c.)

23 (G4, p. 171). DISOBEDIENCE.

24—26 (H4, p. 171). PUNISHMENT.

25 And I = I also.
gathered together = withdrawn or escaped to (cp. Jer. 21. 6-9. Ezek. 5. 12; 7. 15).
26 broken the staff of your bread. Fig. *Metalepsis* (Ap. 6), bread being put for the support it gives, and staff which it is; and the breaking of the staff put for the cutting off the supply. Cp. Is. 3. 1. Ezek. 4. 16; 5. 16; 14. 13. Ps. 105. 16.
ten. Supply *Ellipsis* (Ap. 6) by supplying the word "then" = then ten: i.e. one oven shall be sufficient for ten families. Cp. 2 Kings 6. 28, 29.

27 (G5, p. 171). DISOBEDIENCE.

28—39 (H5, p. 171). PUNISHMENT.

30 high places: used for idolatrous worship (Num. 22. 41; 33. 52. Deut. 12. 2. Josh. 13. 17 (margin). Thus showing the helplessness of the gods worshipped.
images. Heb. *ḥammānīm*, sun-idols. Cp. *v.* 1. 2 Chron. 34. 4. This was prophetic.
carcases. Fig. *Catachresis*. Ap. 6. Another prophecy. See 2 Kings 23. 20. 2 Chron. 34. 5.
idols = logs of wood. Heb. *gillūlīm*, trunks, blocks, used in derision for idols. Also derived from *galal* = dung, or detestable thing. First occurrence; frequently in Ezekiel.
My soul. Heb. *nephesh*. Ap. 13. Fig. *Anthropopatheia*. Ap. 6. This is the converse of verse 11.
31 sanctuaries, or holy places. Some codices, with one printed edition, Sam., and Syr., read the singular "sanctuary".
smell. Fig. *Anthropopatheia*. Ap. 6.
odours. Cp. Isa. 11. 3 (margin).
32 I. Emphatic = I myself.
33 heathen = nations.

1490 34 Then shall the land °enjoy her sabbaths, as long as it lieth desolate, and ye *be* in your enemies' land; *even* then shall the land rest, and °enjoy her sabbaths.

35 As long as it lieth desolate it shall °rest; because it did not °rest in your sabbaths, when ye dwelt upon it.

36 And upon them that are left *alive* of you I will send a faintness into their hearts in the lands of their enemies; and the sound of a shaken leaf shall chase them; and they shall flee, as fleeing from a sword; and they shall fall when none pursueth.

37 And they shall fall one upon another, as it were before a sword, when none pursueth: and ye shall have no power to stand before your enemies.

38 And ye shall perish among the heathen, and the land of your enemies shall eat you up.

39 And they that are left of you shall pine away in their °iniquity in your enemies' lands; and also in the °iniquities of their fathers shall they pine away with them.

C E (p. 171) 40 °If they shall confess their [39]iniquity, and the [39]iniquity of their fathers, with their °trespass which they °trespassed against Me, and that also they have walked [21]contrary unto Me;

41 And *that* I also have °walked [21]contrary unto them, and have brought them into the land of their enemies; if then their uncircumcised hearts be humbled, and they then accept of the punishment of their [39]iniquity:

F 42 Then will I remember My covenant with °Jacob, and also My covenant with Isaac, and also My covenant with Abraham will I remember; and I will remember the land.

43 The land also shall be left of them, and shall enjoy her sabbaths, while she lieth desolate without them: and they shall accept of the punishment of their [41]iniquity: because, even because they despised My judgments, and because °their soul abhorred My statutes.

44 And yet for all that, °when they be in the land of their enemies, I will not cast them away, neither will I abhor them, to destroy them utterly, and to break My covenant with them: for I *am* [1]the LORD their [1]God.

45 But I will for their sakes remember the covenant of their ancestors, whom I brought forth out of the land of Egypt in the sight of the [33]heathen, that I might be their [1]God: °I *am* [1]the LORD.

46 These *are* the statutes and judgments and laws, which [1]the LORD made between Him and the °children of Israel °in mount Sinai by the hand of Moses."

B² J (p. 173) 27 And °the LORD °spake unto Moses, saying,

2 "Speak unto the °children of Israel, and say unto them,

K L¹ c¹ 'When a °man shall °make a singular vow, the °persons *shall be* for [1]the LORD by thy estimation.

3 And thy estimation shall be of the male from twenty years old even unto sixty years old, even thy estimation shall be fifty shekels of silver, after the °shekel of the sanctuary.

4 And if it *be* a female, then thy estimation shall be thirty [3]shekels.

5 And if *it be* from five years old even unto twenty years old, then thy estimation shall be of the male twenty [3]shekels, and for the female ten [3]shekels.

6 And if *it be* from a month old even unto five years old, then thy estimation shall be of the male five [3]shekels of silver, and for the female thy estimation *shall be* three [3]shekels of silver.

7 And if *it be* from sixty years old and above; if *it be* a male, then thy estimation shall be fifteen [3]shekels, and for the female ten [3]shekels.

8 But if he be poorer than thy estimation, then he shall present himself before the priest, and the priest shall value him; according to his ability that vowed shall the priest value him. d¹

9 And if *it be* a beast, whereof °men M¹ e¹

34 enjoy. Fig. *Prosopopatheia*. Ap. 6. Cp. 18. 25.
35 rest. Fig. *Prosopopatheia*. Ap. 6. Cp. Jer. 34. 17. 2 Chron. 36. 21.
39 iniquity = perversity. Heb. *'āvāh*. Ap. 44. iv.

40-41 (E, p. 156). REPENTANCE.

40 If they shall confess. This is the one abiding condition for national blessing and restoration.
trespass . . . trespassed. Heb. *mā'al*. Ap. 44. xi.
41 walked. Fig. *Anthropopatheia*. Ap. 6.
42 Jacob. This is the only place where the order of the three Patriarchs is inverted.
43 their soul = they. Heb. *nephesh*. Ap. 13.
44 when, &c. Cp. Deut. 4. 31. 2 Kings 13. 23. Rom. 11. 1, 2, 28, 29.
I am the LORD. Cp. Ps. 144. 15; 33. 12.
46 children. Heb. sons.
in mount Sinai: thus concluding with the words with which this section began in 25. 1.

27. (B², p. 171). THEIR VOWS TO JEHOVAH.

B² | J | 1. Jehovah's command to Moses.
  K | L¹ | c¹ | 2-7. Ability } Personalty.
      d¹ | 8. Inability }
    M¹ | e¹ | 9, 10. Clean } Beasts.
      f¹ | 11-13. Unclean }
  L² | c² | 14, 15. Houses } Property.
      d² | 16-25. Fields }
    M² | e² | 26. Clean } Beasts.
      f² | 27. Unclean }
  L³ | c³ | 28, 29. Devoted } Property.
      d³ | 30-33. Tithes }
J | 34. Jehovah's command to Moses.

1 the LORD. Heb. Jehovah. Ap. 4.
spake. See note on 5. 14.
2 children = sons.
man = Heb. *'ish*. Ap. 14. ii.
make a singular vow = make a *special* vow. Heb. "separate a vow" because a vow was separated into negative or positive, restraining or promising, i.e., "binding" or "loosing".
persons = souls. Heb. *nephesh*. Ap. 13.

3-7 (c¹, above). ABILITY (PERSONS).

3 shekels. See Ap. 51. II.
4 it = that soul. Cp. note on *v.* 2.

9, 10 (e¹, above). CLEAN BEASTS.

9 men. Some codices, with Sam., read "one".

1490 bring an °offering unto [1]the LORD, all that
any man giveth of such unto [1]the LORD
shall be °holy.
10 He shall not °alter it, nor °change it, a good
for a bad, or a bad for a good: and if he shall
at all change beast for beast, then it and the
exchange thereof shall be [9]holy.
f¹ 11 And if *it be* any unclean beast, of which
(p. 173) they do not °offer a °sacrifice unto [1]the
LORD, then he shall °present the beast before
the priest:
12 And the priest shall value it, whether it
be good or bad: °as thou valuest it, *who art*
the priest, so shall it be.
13 But if he will °at all °redeem it, then he
shall add a fifth *part* thereof unto thy estimation.
L² c² 14 And when a °man shall °sanctify °his
house *to be* [9]holy unto [1]the LORD, then the
priest shall estimate it, whether it be good
or bad: as the priest shall estimate it, so
shall it stand.
15 And if he that [14]sanctified it will redeem
his house, then he shall add the fifth *part*
of the money of thy estimation unto it, and
it shall be his.
d² 16 And if a [14]man shall [14]sanctify unto [1]the
LORD *some part* of a field of his possession,
then thy estimation shall be according to the
seed thereof: an °homer of barley seed *shall*
be valued at fifty [3]shekels of silver.
17 °If he [14]sanctify his field from the year
of jubile, according to thy estimation it shall
stand.
18 But if he [14]sanctify his field after the jubile,
then the priest shall reckon unto him the
money according to the years that remain,
even unto the year of the jubile, and it shall
be abated from thy estimation.
19 And if he that [14]sanctified the field will in
any wise redeem it, then he shall add the
fifth *part* of the money of thy estimation unto
it, and it shall be assured to him.
20 And if he will not redeem the field, or if
he have sold the field to another [14]man, it
shall not be redeemed any more.
21 But the field, when it goeth out in the
jubile, shall be [9]holy unto [1]the LORD, as a
field °devoted; the possession thereof shall be
the priest's.
22 And if *a man* sanctify unto [1]the LORD
a field which he hath bought, which *is* not
of the fields of his possession;
23 Then the priest shall reckon unto him
the worth of thy estimation, *even* unto the
year of the jubile: and he shall give thine
°estimation in that day, *as* a [9]holy thing unto
[1]the LORD.
24 In the year of the jubile the field shall
return unto him of whom it was bought, *even*
to him to whom the possession of the land
did belong.
25 And all thy estimations shall be according to the [3]shekel of the sanctuary: twenty
gerahs shall be the [3]shekel.
M² e² 26 °Only the firstling of the beasts, which
should be [1]the LORD'S firstling, no [14]man
shall sanctify it; whether *it be* ox, or sheep:
it *is* [1]the LORD'S.

27 And if *it be* of an unclean beast, then he f²
shall redeem *it* according to thine estimation,
and shall add a fifth *part* of it thereto: or if it
be not redeemed, then it shall be sold according to thy estimation.
28 °Notwithstanding no [21]devoted thing, that L³ c³
a °man shall [21]devote unto [1]the LORD of all
that he hath, *both* of °man and beast, and
of the field of his possession, shall be sold
or redeemed: every [21]devoted thing °*is* most
[9]holy unto [1]the LORD.
29 None [21]devoted, which shall be [21]devoted
of men, shall be redeemed; *but* shall surely be
put to death.
30 And all the tithe of the land, *whether* of d³
the seed of the land, °*or* of the fruit of the tree,
is [1]the LORD'S: *it is* [9]holy unto [1]the LORD.

offering. Heb. *korbān.* Ap. 43. II. i.
holy. See note on Ex. 3. 5.
10 alter. Heb. *mālaph*, to change for the better. Cp. Ps. 55. 19.
change. Heb. *mūr*, to change for the worse: note the *Introversion.*

g | alter (bad for good).
h | change (good for bad).
h | good for bad.
g | bad for good.

11-13 (f¹, p. 173). UNCLEAN BEASTS.

11 offer = bring near. Heb. *karab.* Ap. 43. I. i.
sacrifice = Heb. *korbān.* Ap. 43. II. i.
present = make it stand, as in *v.* 8.
12 as thou, &c. = as thou, O priest, valuest it so, &c.
13 at all redeem it. Fig. *Polyptōton* (Ap. 6). Heb. "redeeming he will redeem it". Well translated by "at all". See note on Gen. 26. 28. Heb. *gā'al.* See note on Ex. 6. 6.

14, 15 (c², p. 173). HOUSES.

14 man. Heb. *'īsh.* Ap. 14. ii.
sanctify = set apart. Heb. *kādash.* See note on "holy", Ex. 3. 5.
his: i.e. his own house, and what was therein.

16-25 (d², p. 173). FIELDS.

16 homer. Heb. *hōmer*, as in Num. 11. 32. Is. 5. 10. Ezek. 45. 11, 13, 14. Hos. 3. 2. To be distinguished from *'omer*, in Ex. 16. 16, 18, 22, 32, 33, 36. See Ap. 51. III. 3.
17 If. Some codices, with Sam., Sept., and Syr., read "And if".
21 devoted. Heb. *haram*, denotes a total and complete separation, which does not admit of redemption. First occ. of *haram.* It is rendered "devoted" only in this chapter (six times) and once in Num. 18. 14.
23 estimation = valuation.

26 (e², p. 173). CLEAN BEASTS.

26 Only = nevertheless. Rendered in v. 28, "notwithstanding".

27 (f², p. 173). UNCLEAN BEASTS.

28, 29 (c³, p. 173). DEVOTED THINGS.

28 Notwithstanding. See note on *v.* 26.
man = *'ādām.* Ap. 14. i.
is = it [is].

30-33 (d³, p. 173). TITHES.

30 or. Some codices, with Sam., Jon., Sept., Syr., and Vulg., have this "or" in the text.

1490 **31** And if a °man will at all redeem *ought*
of his tithes, he shall add thereto the fifth
part thereof.
32 And concerning the tithe of the herd,
or of the flock, *even* of whatsoever °passeth
under the rod, the tenth shall be [9]holy unto
[1]the LORD.
33 He shall not search whether it be good
or bad, neither shall he change it: and if
he change it at all, then both it and the
change thereof shall be [9]holy; it shall not be
redeemed.'"
J (p. 173) **34** These *are* the commandments, which
[1]the LORD commanded Moses for the [2]chil-
dren of Israel °in mount Sinai.

31 man. Heb. *'ish.* Ap. 14. ii.

32 passeth under the rod. The custom of counting was for the animals to pass through a small opening, and to be counted with the rod as they passed. Every tenth one was to be taken and marked; and not to be chosen (*v.* 33). This custom is referred to in Ezek. 20. 37, i.e. once more claimed and marked as belonging to Jehovah.

34 (*J*, p. 173). JEHOVAH'S COMMAND TO MOSES.

34 in mount Sinai. Cp. note on 1. 1.

NUMBERS.

THE STRUCTURE OF THE BOOK AS A WHOLE.

(Repeated Alternation.)

A[1] | 1. 1—4. 49. NUMERATION AND ORDER. ENCAMPMENT AND SERVICE.

B[1] | 5. 1—9. 23. LAWS AND EVENTS.

A[2] | 10. 1-36. JOURNEYINGS AND ORDER. MARCH.

B[2] | 11. 1—25. 18. EVENTS AND LAWS.

A[3] | 26. 1—27. 11. NUMERATION AND ORDER. INHERITANCE.

B[3] | 27. 12—31. 54. EVENTS AND LAWS.

A[4] | 32. 1—36. 12. JOURNEYINGS AND ORDER. DIVISION OF LAND.

EPILOGUE. 36. 13.

THE FOURTH BOOK OF °MOSES,

CALLED

°NUMBERS.

A¹ A a c (p. 176) 1490 **1** °AND °the LORD spake unto Moses in the
1 wilderness of °Sinai, in the °tabernacle of
the congregation, on the first *day* of the
second month, in the second year after they
were °come out of the land of Egypt, saying,
2 °"Take ye the °sum of all the °congre-
gation of the °children of Israel, after their
families, by the house of their fathers, with
the number of *their* names, every male by
their °polls;
3 From twenty years old and upward, all
that are able to go forth to war in Israel:
°thou and Aaron shall number them by their
armies.
4 And with you there shall be a °man of
°every tribe; every one head of the house
of his fathers.
5 And °these *are* the names of the °men that
shall stand with you: of *the tribe of* Reuben;
Elizur the son of Shedeur.
6 Of Simeon; Shelumiel the son of Zurishaddai.
7 Of Judah; °Nahshon the son of Amminadab.

TITLE, Moses. See Ap. 2.

Numbers. Translation of Greek name in Sept. given by man according to his idea of contents.

Heb. Title = *B^emidbar* = "in the wilderness", because it records what took place there; the numberings (1-3 and 26) being only two of the events. It is the book of the sojournings, the fourth book of the Pentateuch (see Ap. 10 and Deut. 1. 1).

Four is the number of the earth: hence the types of Numbers, the fourth book, are wilderness types (cp. the fourth book of the Psalms, 90-106). Its types of Christ, the Son of Man on earth, are *four*:—

(1) Bread of life, 11. 7-9 (John 6. 57, 58).
(2) Water of life, 20. 11 (1 Cor. 10. 4).
(3) Lifted up, 21. 9 (John 3. 14, 15).
(4) The coming star out of Jacob, 24. 17 (Luke 1. 78. 2 Pet. 1. 19. Rev. 2. 28; 22. 16).

1. 1—4. 49 (**A¹**, p. 176). NUMERATION AND ORDER OF SERVICE, &c. (*Alternation*).

A¹ | A | 1. 1-54. Numeration. The nation.
| B | 2. 1-34. Order of its encampment.
| A | 3. 1-51. Numeration. The Levites.
| B | 4. 1-49. Order of their service.

1. 1-54. [For Structure see next page.]

1 AND. Numbers begins with "And", as all the books of the Pentateuch do. It is therefore one whole in five sections, rather than separate books. **the LORD spake** = Jehovah (the Covenant God) spake to His own People. He spake fifty-six "sundry times" (7 × 8) in Numbers, and in thirteen "divers manners" (twelve to Moses, once to Aaron), and four times indefinite:—

(1) To Moses alone (1. 1, 48; 3. 5, 11, 14, 44; 4. 21; 7. 4; 8. 5, 23; 10. 1; 11. 25; 13. 1; 16. 44; 25. 10, 16; 26. 52; 27. 6; 31. 1, 25; 34. 16.
(2) To Moses, to speak to Aaron (8. 1).
(3) To Moses, to speak to Aaron and his sons (6. 22).
(4) To Moses, to speak to Eleazar, the son of Aaron the priest (16. 36).
(5) To Moses, to speak to the Levites (18. 25).
(6) To Moses, to speak to the congregation (16. 23).
(7) To Moses, to speak to the children of Israel (5. 1, 5, 11; 6. 1; 9. 1 (cp. *v.* 4), 9; 15. 1, 17, 37; 17. 1; 28. 1 (cp. *v.* 2); 33. 50; 34. 1; 35. 1, 9).
(8) To Moses, to speak to the rock (20. 7).
(9) To Moses and Aaron (2. 1; 4. 1, 17; 14. 26; 16. 20; 20. 12, 23).
(10) To Moses and Aaron, to speak to the children of Israel (19. 1).
(11) To Moses and Aaron and Miriam (12. 4).
(12) To Moses and Eleazar (26. 1).
(13) To Aaron (18. 8). (*v.* 20 should be "said".)
(14) Jehovah spake (indefinite) (1. 19; 3. 1; 14. 35; 27. 23).

For "the LORD said", see note on 3. 40 (sixteen times, making seventy-two in all).

Sinai. To which they had come on the third month after the exodus (Ex. 19. 1), and where they abode till the twentieth day of the second month of the second year (Num. 10. 11). The numbering (ch. 1) began on the first day of that month (*v.* 18). **tabernacle** = tent (Heb. *'ohel*). See Ap. 40. **come** = gone.

2 Take ye. Cp. Ex. 30. 11, 12; 38. 25. In Exodus, moral law (prophet); Leviticus, ritual law (priest); Numbers, commonwealth law (king). **sum.** Three numberings. Ex. 30. 11, 12 (cp. 38. 25, 26); here; and 26. **congregation.** See note on Gen. 28. 3. **children** = sons. Heb. *bānīm*, from *bānāh*, to build, because the family thus built up. Cp. Gen. 30. 3. Ruth 4. 11. So throughout. **polls.** Edition of 1611 = poll. Fig. *Synecdoche* (of Part), Ap. 6, skull or head put for person. **3 thou and Aaron.** In second numbering it is Moses and Eleazar, 26. 1. **4 man.** Heb. *'ish.* See Ap. 14. ii. **every tribe.** Hence twelve, and, with Moses and Aaron, fourteen. So the twelve apostles, with Paul and Barnabas = fourteen.

5 these are the names. The order here = five sons of Leah, three of Rachel, one of Bilhah, two of Zilpah, and one of Bilhah. See Ap. 45 for other orders of the names. **men.** Heb. pl. of *'ish*, or *'enōsh.* See Ap. 14.

7 Nahshon. In the line of the promised seed, the father of Salmon (husband of Rahab of Jericho), progenitor of Boaz of Bethlehem (husband of Ruth). Cp. Ruth 4. 18-22. Matt. 1. 4, 5. Luke 3. 32.

1490 8 Of Issachar; Nethaneel the son of Zuar.
9 Of Zebulun; Eliab the son of Helon.
10 Of the [2]children of Joseph: of Ephraim; Elishama the son of Ammihud: of Manasseh; Gamaliel the son of Pedahzur.
11 Of Benjamin; Abidan the son of Gideoni.
12 Of Dan; Ahiezer the son of Ammishaddai.
13 Of Asher; Pagiel the son of Ocran.
14 Of Gad; Eliasaph the son of Deuel.
15 Of Naphtali; Ahira the son of Enan."
16 These *were* the renowned of the congregation, princes of the tribes of their fathers, heads of thousands in Israel.

d 17 And Moses and Aaron took these [5]men
(p. 178) which are expressed by *their* names:
18 And they assembled all the [2]congregation together on the [1]first *day* of the second month, and they declared their pedigrees after their families, by the house of their fathers, according to the number of the names, from twenty years old and upward, by their [2]polls.
19 °As [1]the LORD commanded Moses, so he numbered them in the °wilderness of Sinai.
20 And the [2]children of °Reuben, Israel's °eldest son, by their generations, after their families, by the house of their fathers, according to the number of the names, by their [2]polls, every male from twenty years old and upward, all that were able to go forth to war;
21 Those that were numbered of them, *even* of the tribe of Reuben, *were* forty and six thousand and five hundred.

22 Of the [2]children of °Simeon, by their generations, after their families, by the house of their fathers, °those that were numbered of them, according to the number of the names, by their polls, every male from twenty years old and upward, all that were able to go forth to war;
23 Those that were numbered of them, *even* of the tribe of Simeon, *were* fifty and nine thousand and three hundred.

24 Of the [2]children of °Gad, by their generations, after their families, by the house of their fathers, according to the number of the names, from twenty years old and upward, all that were able to go forth to war;
25 Those that were numbered of them, *even* of the tribe of Gad, *were* forty and five thousand six hundred and °fifty.

26 Of the [2]children of °Judah, by their generations, after their families, by the house of their fathers, according to the number of the names, from twenty years old and upward, all that were able to go forth to war;
27 Those that were numbered of them, *even* of the tribe of Judah, *were* threescore and fourteen thousand and six hundred.

28 Of the [2]children of Issachar, by their generations, after their families, by the house of their fathers, according to the number of the names, from twenty years old and upward, all that were able to go forth to war;
29 Those that were numbered of them, *even* of the tribe of Issachar, *were* fifty and four thousand and four hundred.

30 Of the [2]children of Zebulun, by their generations, after their families, by the house of their fathers, according to the number of the names, from twenty years old and upward, all that were able to go forth to war;
31 Those that were numbered of them, *even* of the tribe of Zebulun, *were* fifty and seven thousand and four hundred.

32 Of the [2]children of °Joseph, *namely*, of the [2]children of °Ephraim, by their generations, after their families, by the house of their fathers, according to the number of the names, from twenty years old and upward, all that were able to go forth to war;
33 Those that were numbered of them, *even* of the tribe of Ephraim, *were* forty thousand and five hundred.

34 Of the [2]children of °Manasseh, by their generations, after their families, by the house of their fathers, according to the number of the names, from twenty years old and upward, all that were able to go forth to war;
35 Those that were numbered of them, *even* of the tribe of Manasseh, *were* thirty and two thousand and two hundred.

36 Of the [2]children of Benjamin, by their generations, after their families, by the house of their fathers, according to the number of the names, from twenty years old and upward, all that were able to go forth to war;
37 Those that were numbered of them, *even* of the tribe of Benjamin, *were* thirty and five thousand and four hundred.

1. 1-54 (A, p. 177). NUMERATION: THE NATION AND LEVITES (*Introversion and Alternation*).

A | a | c | 1-16. Command
A | a | d | 17-46. Obedience } Nation.
A | b | 47. Exception.
A | *a* | *c* | 48-53. Command
A | *a* | *d* | 54. Obedience } Levites.

19 As = according as.
wilderness of Sinai (*v.* 1), to distinguish it from the second, which was in the plains of Moab.
20 Reuben. Lost his dignity in Gen. 49. 3, 4; not many in number here.
eldest son. See Ap. 45.
22 Simeon was greatly diminished by sin in Num. 26. 4, and Moses does not mention him in Deut. 33.
Those that were numbered of them. Some codices, with two early printed editions, Onk., Jon., Sept., and Syr., omit this clause. Cp. *vv.* 20, 24, 26, &c.
24 Gad takes the place of Levi here.
25 fifty. Gad is the only one who has "tens", all the others "hundreds". In the case of the firstborn (3. 43) we have not only tens but units.
26 Judah. His number is greatest (Gen. 49. 8).
32 Joseph. "The fruitful vine" (Gen. 49. 22) has two tribes (not merely "families"). Thus Joseph has "the double portion" (1 Chron. 5. 1, 2).
Ephraim. Blessed first (Gen. 48. 19, 20), is here named first, and is increased more than Manasseh (Deut. 33. 17). But in journeyings his numbers were diminished by 8,000. See 26. 37, and cp. 1 Chron. 7. 20-22.
34 Manasseh. The lowest in number. See Gen. 48. 19. Increased by 20,500 in journeying, 26. 34, 37 (cp. Job 12. 23).

1490 38 Of the [2]children of Dan, by their generations, after their families, by the house of their fathers, according to the number of the names, from twenty years old and upward, all that were able to go forth to war;

39 Those that were numbered of them, *even* of the tribe of Dan, *were* threescore and two thousand and seven hundred.

40 Of the [2]children of Asher, by their generations, after their families, by the house of their fathers, according to the number of the names, from twenty years old and upward, all that were able to go forth to war;

41 Those that were numbered of them, *even* of the tribe of Asher, *were* forty and one thousand and five hundred.

42 °Of the [2]children of Naphtali, throughout their generations, after their families, by the house of their fathers, according to the number of the names, from twenty years old and upward, all that were able to go forth to war;

43 Those that were numbered of them, *even* of the tribe of Naphtali, *were* fifty and three thousand and four hundred.

44 These *are* those that were numbered, which Moses and Aaron numbered, and the princes of Israel, *being* °twelve °men: each one was for the house of his fathers.

45 So were all those that were numbered of the [2]children of Israel, by the house of their fathers, from twenty years old and upward, all that were able to go forth to war in Israel;

46 Even °all they that were numbered were six hundred thousand and three thousand and five hundred and fifty.

b (p. 178) 47 But the °Levites after the tribe of their fathers were not numbered among them.

c 48 For [1]the LORD had °spoken unto Moses, saying,

49 "Only thou shalt not number the tribe of Levi, neither take the sum of them among the [2]children of Israel:

50 But thou shalt appoint the Levites over the °tabernacle of testimony, and over all the vessels thereof, and over all things that *belong* to it: they shall bear the °tabernacle, and all the vessels thereof; and they shall minister unto it, and shall encamp round about the °tabernacle.

51 And when the [50]tabernacle setteth forward, the Levites shall take it down: and when the [50]tabernacle is to be pitched, the Levites shall set it up: and the stranger that cometh nigh shall be °put to death.

52 And the [2]children of Israel shall pitch their tents, every [44]man by his own °camp, and every man by his own standard, throughout their hosts.

53 But the Levites shall °pitch round about the [50]tabernacle of testimony, °that there be no wrath upon the congregation of the [2]children of Israel: and the Levites shall keep the charge of the [50]tabernacle of testimony."

d 54 And the [2]children of Israel did according to all that [1]the LORD commanded Moses, so did they.

42 Of the children. So in A.V., and R.V., but not in Heb. text, though it is so in some codices, Sam., Sept., Syr., and Vulg. Some Jewish commentators explain it as being only "the sons", because Naphtali had more daughters than sons, and in Gen. 49. 21 is likened to a female (hind). Hence in 26. 64 it is said, the "men" died (but the women multiplied).

44 twelve men: one man for one tribe (*v.* 4).

men. Heb. *'ish.* Ap. 14. ii.

46 all they. The number in Ex. 12. 37 is not "exaggerated", as the number here had increased since then; moreover, the numbers here coincide with the numbers of the half-shekels, which had been contributed by them in Ex. 30. 14 and 38. 25, 26, before the tabernacle was set up. Cp. Ex. 38. 25 with 40. 17.

47 Levites not numbered here with the nation, but separately in 3. 14-29.

48 spoken. See note on 1. 1.

50 tabernacle = habitation. Heb. *mishkān.* See Ap. 40.

51 put to death. Probably by Jehovah. Cp. 1 Chron. 13. 10,

52 camp: to be set forth in detail in member B, below.

53 pitch = encamp.

that there be no wrath: i.e. no judgment from God. "wrath" put by Fig. *Metonymy* (of Cause) for the judgment inflicted. Ap. 6. Heb. *kāzaph.* First occurrence.

2. 1-34 (B, p. 177). ORDER OF ENCAMPMENT.
(*Introversion and Repeated Alternation.*)

B | e | 1, 2. Command.
  f[1] | 3, 4. Judah / 5, 6. Issachar / 7, 8. Zebulon } East.
   g[1] | 9. Total.
  f[2] | 10, 11. Reuben / 12, 13. Simeon / 14, 15. Gad } South.
   g[2] | 16. Total.
    h[1] | 17. Levites.
  f[3] | 18, 19. Ephraim / 20, 21. Manasseh / 22, 23. Benjamin } West.
   g[3] | 24. Total.
  f[4] | 25, 26. Dan / 27, 28. Asher / 29-31. Naphtali } North.
   g[4] | 32. Total.
    h[2] | 33. Levites.
 e | 34. Obedience.

1 the LORD [Heb. Jehovah] **spake.** See note on 1. 1.

2 man. Heb. *'ish.* See Ap. 14. ii.

children = sons. See note on 1. 2.

pitch = encamp.

standard. Heb. *degel.*

ensign. Each standard is said to have had as its "sign" one of the twelve constellations (see note on Gen. 1. 16, and Ap. 12. Heb. *'ōth*) depicted on it. One standard, with its sign on it for each tribe. Hence called "ensign". See notes on the tribes below, from the Targum of Jonathan.

far off = over against. Same as Ps. 38. 12, yet so as to be in view. Cp. 2 Kings 2. 7. Deut. 32. 52. Gen. 21. 16.

tabernacle = tent. Heb. *'ohel.* See Ap. 40.

2 And °the LORD °spake unto Moses and unto Aaron, saying, B e (p. 179)

2 "Every °man of the °children of Israel shall °pitch by his own °standard, with the °ensign of their father's house: °far off about the °tabernacle of the congregation shall they pitch.

f[1] 3 And on the °east side toward the rising
(p. 179) of the sun shall they of the standard of the
1490 °camp of °Judah pitch throughout their armies: and Nahshon the son of Amminadab *shall be* captain of the [2]children of Judah."

4 And his host, and those that were numbered of them, *were* threescore and fourteen thousand and six hundred.

f[2] 5 "And those that do pitch next unto him *shall be* the tribe of °Issachar: and Nethaneel the son of Zuar *shall be* captain of the [2]children of Issachar."

6 And his host, and those that were numbered thereof, *were* fifty and four thousand and four hundred.

f[3] 7 °"*Then* the tribe of °Zebulun: and Eliab the son of Helon *shall be* captain of the [2]children of Zebulun."

8 And his host, and those that were numbered thereof, *were* fifty and seven thousand and four hundred.

g[1] 9 All that were numbered in the camp of Judah *were* an hundred thousand and fourscore thousand and six thousand and four hundred, throughout their armies. "These shall first set forth.

f[4] 10 On the °south side *shall be* the standard of the [3]camp of °Reuben according to their armies: and the captain of the [2]children of Reuben *shall be* Elizur the son of Shedeur."

11 And his host, and those that were numbered thereof, *were* forty and six thousand and five hundred.

f[5] 12 "And those which pitch by him *shall be* the tribe of °Simeon: and the captain of the [2]children of Simeon *shall be* Shelumiel the son of Zurishaddai."

13 And his host, and those that were numbered of them, *were* fifty and nine thousand and three hundred.

f[6] 14 "Then the tribe of Gad: and the captain of the sons of °Gad *shall be* Eliasaph the son of °Reuel."

15 And his host, and those that were numbered of them, *were* forty and five thousand and six hundred and fifty.

g[2] 16 All that were numbered in the [3]camp of Reuben *were* an hundred thousand and fifty and one thousand and four hundred and fifty, throughout their armies. "And they shall set forth in the second rank.

h[1] 17 Then the °tabernacle of the congregation shall set forward with the [16]camp of the °Levites in the midst of the camp: °as they encamp, so shall they set forward, every man in his place by their standards.

f[3] 18 On the °west side *shall be* the standard of the [16]camp of °Ephraim according to their armies: and the captain of the sons of Ephraim *shall be* Elishama the son of Ammihud."

19 And his host, and those that were numbered of them, *were* forty thousand and five hundred.

3 east. The order proceeds according to the course of the sun: east, south, west, north.

camp. Each camp composed of three tribes. Cp. *vv.* 3, 10, 17, 18, 25, 32.

Judah. The sign, a lion (Gen. 49. 9. Ezek. 1. 10. Rev. 4. 7). The standard, the colours of the three stones of the second row, Ex. 28. 18. For the order, see Ap. 45.

5 Issachar, brother of Judah (same mother, Leah). Gen. 35. 23. Sign on standard = Cancer.

7 Then. This word, according to some codices, with Sam., should not be in italics. Cp. *vv.* 14, 22, 29.

Zebulun, brother of Judah (same mother, Leah). Gen. 35. 23. Sign on standard = Virgo.

10 south. See note on "east", *v.* 3.

Reuben. The centre of the south side, with standard in the colours of stones of first row of Ex. 28. 17; and sign, a man (Gen. 30. 14) = Aquarius in Zodiac.

12 Simeon, the brother of Reuben (same mother, Leah). Gen. 35. 23. Sign = Pisces.

14 Gad, brother of Reuben (same mother, Leah). Gen. 35. 23. Sign = Aries.

Reuel. Some codices, with one early printed edition, Onk., Jon., and Vulg., have "Deuel", as in ch. 1. 14; 7. 42; 10. 20; the ר (Resh, R) being mistaken for ד (Daleth, D). Probably called, indifferently, by either name.

17 tabernacle of the congregation. See note on *v.* 2. This was in centre. So is the tent of the chief of the tribe to this day. The manner of its being carried is shewn in ch. 10. 17, &c.

Levites. The order of the Levites' camping is shown in ch. 3, their marching in ch. 10. Their sign was Libra, or more anciently the "altar".

as = according as.

18 west. See note on *v.* 3. Heb. = sea, that being west.

Ephraim. The centre on the west side. The colours of the stones in fourth row of Ex. 28. 20. The sign, an ox (Deut. 33. 17. Ezek. 1. 10. Rev. 4. 7). In the Zodiac, Ephraim and Manasseh are the two horns of Taurus, the bull. Ephraim, the younger, bears the standard, according to the blessing in Gen. 48. 14–20.

20 Manasseh, brother of Ephraim by same mother (Gen. 41. 51, 52). Sign, see *v.* 18.

22 Benjamin, sons of Rachel, all on west side. Sign, Gemini.

25 Dan. The centre on the north side. Colours of standard same as those of the third row of stones in Ex. 28. 19. Sign, the eagle (substituted for the serpent of Gen. 49. 17). Cp. Ezek. 1. 10. Rev. 4. 7.

20 "And by him *shall be* the tribe of °Manasseh: and the captain of the children of Manasseh *shall be* Gamaliel the son of Pedahzur."

21 And his host, and those that were numbered of them, *were* thirty and two thousand and two hundred.

22 "Then the tribe of °Benjamin: and the captain of the sons of Benjamin *shall be* Abidan the son of Gideoni."

23 And his host, and those that were numbered of them, *were* thirty and five thousand and four hundred.

24 All that were numbered of the camp of g[3]
Ephraim *were* an hundred thousand and eight thousand and an hundred, throughout their armies. "And they shall go forward in the third rank.

25 The standard of the [16]camp of °Dan *shall* f[4]

1490 *be* on the °north side by their armies: and the captain of the [2]children of Dan *shall be* Ahiezer the son of Ammishaddai."
26 And his host, and those that were numbered of them, *were* threescore and two thousand and seven hundred.
27 "And those that encamp by him *shall be* the tribe of °Asher: and the captain of the [2]children of Asher *shall be* Pagiel the son of Ocran."
28 And his host, and those that were numbered of them, *were* forty and one thousand and five hundred.
29 "Then the tribe of °Naphtali: and the captain of the [2]children of Naphtali *shall be* Ahira the son of Enan."
30 And his host, and those that were numbered of them, *were* fifty and three thousand and four hundred.
31 All they that were numbered in the camp of Dan *were* an hundred thousand and fifty and seven thousand and six hundred. "They shall go hindmost with their standards."
g[4] (p. 179) 32 These *are* those which were numbered of the [2]children of Israel by the house of their fathers: all those that were numbered of °the camps throughout their hosts *were* six hundred thousand and three thousand and five hundred and fifty.

h[2] 33 But the Levites were not numbered among the [2]children of Israel; as [1]the LORD commanded Moses.
34 And the [2]children of Israel did according to all that [1]the LORD commanded Moses: so they pitched by their standards, and so they set forward, every one after their families, according to the house of their fathers.

A i (p. 181) **3** These also *are* the °generations of Aaron and Moses in the day *that* °the LORD °spake with Moses in mount Sinai.
2 And these *are* the names of the sons of Aaron; Nadab the firstborn, and Abihu, Eleazar, and Ithamar.
3 °These *are* the names of the sons of Aaron, the priests which were anointed, °whom he °consecrated to minister in the priest's office.
4 (And Nadab and Abihu °died before [1]the LORD, when they offered strange fire before [1]the LORD, in the wilderness of Sinai, and they had no °children: and Eleazar and Ithamar ministered in the priest's office in the sight of Aaron their father.)
k 5 And [1]the LORD [1]spake unto Moses, saying,
6 "Bring the tribe of Levi near, and °present them before Aaron the priest, that they may minister unto him.
7 And they shall keep his charge, and the charge of the whole congregation before the °tabernacle of the congregation, to do the service of °the tabernacle.
8 And they shall keep all the °instruments of the [7]tabernacle of the congregation, and the charge of the [4]children of °Israel, to do the service of [7]the tabernacle.

north. See note on *v.* 3.
27 Asher, the son of the other handmaid Zilpah, put with Dan and Naphtali, the sons of Bilhah. His sign was Sagittarius, the Archer.
29 Naphtali. His sign was Capricornus, the goat. Cp. Gen. 49. 21.
32 the camps. See note on *v.* 3, and Ap. 45. They may be thus set forth :—

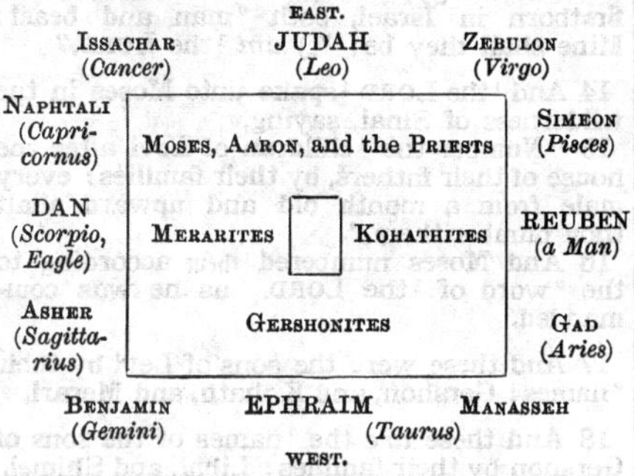

3. 1-51 (*A*, p. 177). **NUMERATION OF THE LEVITES.**

A | i | 1-4. Priests. Their "generations."
| k | 5-9. Levites. Given out of the whole congregation.
| *i* | 10. Priests. Their appointment.
| *k* | 11-51. Levites. Substituted for the rest of congregation.

1 generations. The twelfth occurrence (eleven in Genesis (see p. 1), one here, one in Ruth 4. 18-22, one in Matt. 1. 1, fourteen (2 × 7, see Ap. 10) in all.
the LORD = Jehovah, Israel's Covenant God. See Ap. 4.
spake. See note on 1. 1.
3 These. Some codices, with one early printed edition, Sam., Onk., and Syr., read "And these".
whom he consecrated. See note on Ex. 28. 41.
4 died before the LORD. This parenthetical statement is an undesigned coincidence referring to Lev. 10. 1-7. Cp. Num. 26. 61, and 1 Chron. 24. 2.
children = sons.
6 present = cause it to stand.
7 tabernacle = tent. Heb. *'ohel.* See Ap. 40.
the tabernacle. Heb. *mishkān.* Ap. 40.
8 instruments = vessels or furniture.
Israel. The whole nation was responsible for this charge, but Levi was taken in substitution for the firstborn. Cp. *vv.* 38, 41, and cp. 8. 16. Ex. 13. 11-16.
9 wholly given. Heb. "given, given". Fig. *Epizeuxis* (Ap. 6), for emphasis. Hence called *nᵉthūnim* = given ones.

11-51 [For Structure see next page].

9 And thou shalt give the Levites unto Aaron and to his sons: they *are* °wholly given unto him out of the [4]children of Israel.
10 And thou shalt appoint Aaron and his sons, and they shall wait on their priest's office: and the stranger that cometh nigh shall be put to death." *i*
11 And [1]the LORD [1]spake unto Moses, saying, *k* l (p. 182)

1490 12 "And I, °behold, I have taken the Levites from among the [4]children of Israel instead of all the firstborn that openeth the matrix among the [4]children of Israel: therefore the Levites shall be Mine;

13 Because all the firstborn *are* Mine; *for* on the day that I smote all the firstborn in the land of Egypt I °hallowed unto Me all the firstborn in Israel, both °man and beast: Mine shall they be: °I *am* [1]the LORD."

m (p. 182) 14 And [1]the LORD [1]spake unto Moses in the wilderness of Sinai, saying,

15 "Number the [4]children of Levi after the house of their fathers, by their families: every male from a month old and upward shalt thou number them."

16 And Moses numbered them according to the °word of [1]the LORD, °as he was commanded.

17 And these were the sons of Levi by their °names; Gershon, and Kohath, and Merari.

18 And these *are* the °names of the sons of Gershon by their families; Libni, and Shimei.

19 And the sons of Kohath by their families; Amram, and Izehar, Hebron, and Uzziel.

20 And the sons of Merari by their families; Mahli, and Mushi. These *are* the families of the Levites according to the house of their fathers.

21 Of Gershon *was* the family of the Libnites, and the family of the Shimites: these *are* the families of the Gershonites.

22 Those that were numbered of them, according to the number of all the males, from a month old and upward, *even* those that were numbered of them *were* seven thousand and five hundred.

23 The families of the Gershonites shall pitch behind [7]the tabernacle westward.

24 And the chief of the house of the father of the Gershonites *shall be* Eliasaph the son of Lael.

25 And the charge of the sons of Gershon in the [7]tabernacle of the congregation *shall be* the [7]tabernacle, and the tent, °the covering thereof, and the hanging for the °door of the [7]tabernacle of the congregation,

26 And the hangings of the court, and the curtain for the door of the court, which *is* by [7]the tabernacle, and by the altar round about, and the cords of it for all the service thereof.

27 And of Kohath *was* the family of the Amramites, and the family of the Izeharites, and the family of the Hebronites, and the family of the Uzzielites: these *are* the families of the Kohathites.

28 In the number of all the males, from a month old and upward, *were* eight thousand and six hundred, keeping the charge of the sanctuary.

29 The families of the sons of Kohath shall pitch on the side of [7]the tabernacle southward.

30 And the chief of the house of the father of the families of the Kohathites *shall be* Elizaphan the son of Uzziel.

31 And their charge *shall be* the ark, and the table, and the °candlestick, and the altars, and the vessels of the sanctuary wherewith they minister, and the hanging, and all the service thereof.

32 And Eleazar the son of Aaron the priest *shall be* °chief over the chief of the Levites, *and have* the oversight of them that keep the charge of the sanctuary.

33 Of °Merari *was* the family of the Mahlites, and the family of the Mushites: these *are* the families of °Merari.

34 And those that were numbered of them, according to the number of all the males, from a month old and upward, *were* six thousand and two hundred.

35 And the chief of the house of the father of the families of Merari *was* Zuriel the son of Abihail: *these* shall pitch on the side of [7]the tabernacle northward.

36 And *under* the custody and charge of the sons of Merari *shall be* the boards of [7]the tabernacle, °and the bars thereof, and the pillars thereof, and the sockets thereof, and all the vessels thereof, and all that serveth thereto,

37 And the pillars of the court round about, and their sockets, and their pins, and their cords.

38 But those that encamp before the [7]tabernacle toward the east, *even* before [7]the tabernacle of the congregation eastward, *shall be* Moses, and Aaron and his sons, keeping the charge of the sanctuary for the °charge of the [4]children of Israel; and the stranger that cometh nigh shall be put to death.

39 All that were numbered of the Levites,

11-51 (*k*, p. 181). **LEVITES SUBSTITUTED FOR THE FIRSTBORN** (*Introversion*).

k | l | 11-13. Substitution of Levites for firstborn.
  m | 14-39. Numbering of substitutes.
  m | 40-43. Numbering of firstborn.
  l | 44-51. Substitution of Levites for firstborn.

12 behold. Fig. *Asterismos* (Ap. 6), for emphasis.

13 hallowed = separated. See note on "holy", Ex. 3. 5.

man. Heb. *'ādām*. See Ap. 14. i.

I am the LORD. This is the reason for this act of sovereignty. Cp. Ex. 12. 29, 30; 13. 2. The interpretation of Heb. 12. 23 depends on this ordinance. Note the emphatic "I", *v.* 12, and the Fig. *Asterismos* there.

16 word. Heb. "mouth", put by Fig. *Metonymy* (of Cause), Ap. 6, for words spoken by it.

as = according as.

17 names. Substituted by name here because redeemed by name. Ex. 1. 1.

25 the. Some codices, with Sam., Onk., Sept., Syr., and Vulg., read "and the"

door = entrance.

31 candlestick = lampstand.

32 chief over the chief. Heb. = "chief of the chief". Fig. *Polyptōton* (Ap. 6), being a kind of *Enallage* (Ap. 6).

33 Merari. Fig. *Epanadiplōsis* (Ap. 6), the verse beginning and ending with the same word.

36 and. Note the Fig. *Polysyndeton* in *vv.* 36, 37 (Ap. 6), to emphasise each item mentioned.

38 charge of the children of Israel. The whole nation responsible. Cp. *vv.* 8 and 41, 45.

1490 which Moses °and Aaron numbered at the °commandment of [1]the LORD, throughout their families, all the males from a month old and upward, *were* twenty and two thousand.

m (p. 182) 40 And [1]the LORD °said unto Moses, "Number all the firstborn of the males of the [4]children of Israel from a month old and upward, and take the number of their names.

41 And thou shalt take the Levites for Me ([13]I *am* [1]the LORD) instead of all the firstborn among the [4]children of Israel; and the cattle of the Levites instead of all the firstlings among the cattle of the [4]children of Israel."

42 And Moses numbered, °as [1]the LORD commanded Him, all the firstborn among the [4]children of Israel.

43 And all the firstborn males by the number of names, from a month old and upward, of those that were numbered of them, were twenty and two thousand two hundred and threescore and thirteen.

l 44 And [1]the LORD [1]spake unto Moses, saying,

45 "Take the Levites °instead of all the firstborn among the [4]children of Israel, and the cattle of the Levites instead of their cattle; and the Levites shall be Mine: [41]I *am* [1]the LORD.

46 And for those that are to be °redeemed of the two hundred and threescore and thirteen of the firstborn of the [4]children of Israel, which are °more than the Levites;

47 Thou shalt even take five °shekels apiece by the poll, after the °shekel of the sanctuary shalt thou take *them:* (the °shekel *is* twenty °gerahs:)

48 And thou shalt give the money, wherewith the odd number of them is to be [46]redeemed, unto Aaron and to his sons."

49 And Moses took the redemption money °of them that were over and above them that were [46]redeemed by the Levites:

50 Of the firstborn of the [4]children of Israel took he the money; °a thousand three hundred and threescore and five *shekels*, after the [47]shekel of the sanctuary:

51 And Moses gave the money of them that were [46]redeemed unto Aaron and to his sons, according to the [16]word of [1]the LORD, [42]as [1]the LORD commanded Moses.

B n p¹ (p. 183) **4** And °the LORD °spake unto Moses and unto Aaron, saying,

2 "Take the sum of the sons of Kohath from among the sons of Levi, after their families, by the house of their fathers,

3 From °thirty years old and upward even until fifty years old, °all that enter into the host, to do the work in the °tabernacle of the congregation.

r¹ 4 This *shall be* the service of the sons of Kohath in the [3]tabernacle of the congregation, *about* the °most holy things:

5 °And when the camp setteth forward, Aaron shall come, and his sons, and they shall take down the covering vail, and cover the ark of testimony with it:

39 and Aaron. These two words are dotted in the Hebrew. See Ap. 31. The command was given to Moses alone (*vv.* 14, 15), and was carried out by him alone (*v.* 16). As Aaron took part, according to 1. 3, 4, and 4. 41, 45, 46, his name was included here by some ancient copyist; and later scribes *dotted* the words rather than leave them out.

commandment. Heb. "mouth", put for what was spoken by it by Fig. *Metonymy* (of Cause), Ap. 6.

40 the LORD said = Jehovah said. Heb. *'āmar* (not *dāvar*, spake). *'āmar* is followed by the words spoken, *dāvar* is not. This expression, Jehovah said, occurs eighteen "sundry times" and in five "divers manners" in this book of Numbers. Cp. note on 1. 1

(1) To Moses (alone), 3. 40; 7. 11; 11. 16, 23; 12. 14; 14. 11; 15. 35; 17. 10; 21. 8, 34; 25. 4; 27. 12, 18.
(2) To Aaron, 18. 1.
(3) To Balaam, 23. 5, 16.
(4) He said, 12. 6.
(5) I Jehovah have said, 14. 35.

With the fifty-six times "Jehovah spake" (see 1. 1), these eighteen make seventy-four times, and sixteen manners. See note on 22. 9, for "God said" (four times, making seventy-eight in all).

42 as = according as

45 instead. This substitution is the subject of this large member.

46 redeemed = bought back. Heb. *g'āal.* See note on Ex. 6. 8

more = over and above: 273 (= 13 × 21). Ap. 10.
The firstborn males were 22,273 } difference 273.
The Levites were 22,000 }

47 shekels. See Ap. 51. II.

gerahs. See Ap. 51. II.

49 of = from.

50 a thousand, &c. = 1365 (= 13 × 105), being 5 × 273, i.e. five shekels apiece, *v.* 47. See Ap. 10.

4. 1-49 (*B*, p. 177). LEVITES: THE ORDER OF THEIR SERVICE.
(*Introversion.*)

B | n | 1-33. Command (given).
  | o | 34-45. Obedience.
  | *n* | 46-49. Command (completed).

1-33 (n, above). THE COMMAND (GIVEN).
(*Repeated Alternation.*)

n | p¹ | q¹ | 1-3. Kohathites. Age.
  | | r¹ | 4-20. Their service.
  | p² | q² | 21-23. Gershonites. Age.
  | | r² | 24-28. Their service.
  | p³ | q³ | 29, 30. Merarites. Age.
  | | r³ | 31-33. Their service.

1 the LORD. Heb. Jehovah. Ap. 4.

spake. See note on 1. 1.

3 thirty. This thirty pertains to their *numbering.* The age twenty-five pertains to their *service.* So that there was a probationary five years. Changed (by Divine direction given to David) in 1 Chron. 23. 23, 24, 27 to twenty. Cp. 2 Chron. 31. 17.

all that enter into the host. This expression occurs five times in this chapter, *vv.* 3, 30, 35, 39, 43.

tabernacle of the congregation = "tent of meeting". Heb. *'ohel.* See Ap. 40.

4 most holy = the holiest. Heb. holiness of holinesses. See note on Ex. 3. 5.

5 And. Note the Fig. *Polysyndeton* (Ap. 6), here and in following verses, to emphasise each particular in *vv.* 5-15.

1490 6 And shall put thereon the covering of badgers' skins, and shall spread over *it* a cloth wholly of blue, and shall put in the staves thereof.

7 And upon the °table of shewbread they shall spread a cloth of blue, and put thereon the °dishes, and the °spoons, and the °bowls, and °covers °to cover withal: and the °continual bread shall be thereon:

8 And they shall spread upon them a cloth of scarlet, and cover the same with a covering of badgers' skins, and shall put in the staves thereof.

9 And they shall take a cloth of blue, and cover the °candlestick of the light, and his lamps, and his tongs, and his snuffdishes, and all the oil vessels thereof, wherewith they minister unto it:

10 And they shall put it and all the vessels thereof within a covering of badgers' skins, and shall put *it* upon a °bar.

11 And upon the golden altar they shall spread a cloth of blue, and cover it with a covering of badgers' skins, and shall put to the staves thereof:

12 And they shall take all the instruments of ministry, wherewith they minister in the sanctuary, and put *them* in a cloth of blue, and cover them with a covering of badgers' skins, and shall put *them* on a bar:

13 And they shall take away the ashes from the altar, and spread a purple cloth thereon:

14 And they shall put upon it all the vessels thereof, wherewith they minister about it, *even* the censers, °the °fleshhooks, °and the shovels, and the °basons, all the vessels of the altar; and they shall spread upon it a covering of badgers' skins, and put to the staves of it.

15 And when Aaron and his sons have made an end of covering the sanctuary, and all the vessels of the sanctuary, as the camp is to set forward; after that, the sons of Kohath shall come to bear *it:* but they shall not touch *any* °holy thing, lest they die. These *things are* the burden of the sons of Kohath in the [3]tabernacle of the congregation.

16 And to the office of Eleazar the son of Aaron the priest *pertaineth* the oil for the °light, and the sweet incense, and the daily meat offering, and the anointing oil, *and* the oversight of all the °tabernacle, and of all that therein *is*, in the sanctuary, and in the vessels thereof."

17 And [1]the LORD [1]spake unto Moses and unto Aaron, saying,

18 "Cut ye not off the tribe of the families of the Kohathites from among the Levites:

19 But thus do unto them, that they may live, and not die, when they approach unto the most [15]holy things: Aaron and his sons shall go in, and appoint them °every one to his service and to his burden:

20 But they shall not go in °to see when the [15]holy things are covered, lest they die."

q² 21 And [1]the LORD [1]spake unto Moses, say-
(p. 183) ing,

22 "Take also the sum of the sons of Gershon, throughout the houses of their fathers, by their families;

7 table of shewbread. See Ex. 25. 30 and Lev. 24. 6.
dishes. In chap. 4 rendered "charger" throughout.
spoons = dishes. **bowls** = pans.
covers = bowls. **to cover** = to pour.
continual. Cp. Lev. 24. 8.
9 candlestick = light-holder, as in Gen. 1. 14.
10 bar = pole. Cp. 13. 23.
14 the. Some codices, with Sam., Onk., Jon., Sept., Syr., and Vulg., read "and the". See note on *v.* 5 above. **fleshhooks**: or forks.
and. Note the Fig. *Polysyndeton* (Ap. 6), emphasising each separate item.
basons: or sprinkling-bowls.
15 holy. See note on Ex. 3. 5.
16 light = candlestick. See on *v.* 9 above.
tabernacle = habitation. Heb. *mishkān*. Ap. 40
19 every one = each to his own work. No confusion.
20 to see. Cp. Ex. 19. 21. 1 Sam. 6. 19.
23 perform the service. Heb. war the warfare. Fig *Polyptōton* (Ap. 6), for emphasis = do the important or solemn work.
25 door = entrance.
27 appointment. Heb. "mouth", put for what is said or bidden by it. Fig. *Metonymy* (of Cause). Ap. 6.
30 do the work. Heb. "serve the service". Fig. *Polyptōton* (Ap. 6), for emphasis = perform the solemn service.

23 From [3]thirty years old and upward until fifty years old shalt thou number them; all that enter in to °perform the service, to do the work in the [3]tabernacle of the congregation.

24 This *is* the service of the families of the r²
Gershonites, to serve, and for burdens:

25 And they shall bear the curtains of the [16]tabernacle, and the [3]tabernacle of the congregation, his covering, and the covering of the badgers' skins that *is* above upon it, and the hanging for the °door of the [3]tabernacle of the congregation,

26 And the hangings of the court, and the hanging for the [25]door of the gate of the court, which *is* by the [16]tabernacle and by the altar round about, and their cords, and all the instruments of their service, and all that is made for them: so shall they serve.

27 At the °appointment of Aaron and his sons shall be all the service of the sons of the Gershonites, in all their burdens, and in all their service: and ye shall appoint unto them in charge all their burdens.

28 This *is* the service of the families of the sons of Gershon in the [3]tabernacle of the congregation: and their charge *shall be* under the hand of Ithamar the son of Aaron the priest.

29 As for the sons of Merari, thou shalt q³
number them after their families, by the house of their fathers;

30 From [3]thirty years old and upward even unto fifty years old shalt thou number them, every one that entereth into the service, to °do the work of the [3]tabernacle of the congregation.

31 And this *is* the charge of their burden, r³
according to all their service in the [3]tabernacle of the congregation; the boards of the [16]tabernacle, and the bars thereof, and the pillars thereof, and sockets thereof,

32 And the pillars of the court round about, and their sockets, and their pins, and their

1490 cords, with all their instruments, and with all their service: and by name ye shall reckon °the instruments of the charge of their burden.

33 This *is* the service of the families of the sons of Merari, according to all their service, in the [3]tabernacle of the congregation, under the hand of Ithamar the son of Aaron the priest."

o s^1 t^1 (p. 185) 34 And Moses and Aaron and the chief of the congregation numbered the sons of the Kohathites after their families, and after the house of their fathers,

u^1 35 From [3]thirty years old and upward even unto fifty years old, every one that entereth into the service, for the work in the [3]tabernacle of the congregation:

w^1 36 And those that were numbered of them by their families were two thousand seven hundred and fifty.

37 These *were* they that were numbered of the families of the Kohathites, all that might do service in the [3]tabernacle of the congregation, which Moses and Aaron did number

x^1 according to the °commandment of [1]the LORD by the °hand of Moses.

t^2 38 And those that were numbered of the sons of Gershon, throughout their families, and by the house of their fathers,

u^2 39 From [3]thirty years old and upward even unto fifty years old, every one that entereth into the service, for the work in the [3]tabernacle of the congregation,

w^2 40 Even those that were numbered of them, throughout their families, by the house of their fathers, were two thousand and six hundred and thirty.

41 These *are* they that were numbered of the families of the sons of Gershon, of all that might do service in the [3]tabernacle of the congregation, whom Moses and Aaron did number

x^2 according to the [37]commandment of [1]the LORD.

t^3 42 And those that were numbered of the families of the sons of Merari, throughout their families, by the house of their fathers,

u^3 43 From [3]thirty years old and upward even unto fifty years old, every one that entereth into the service, for the work in the [3]tabernacle of the congregation,

w^3 44 Even those that were numbered of them after their families, were three thousand and two hundred.

45 These *be* those that were numbered of the families of the sons of Merari, whom Moses and Aaron numbered

x^3 according to the word of [1]the LORD by the [37]hand of Moses.

n t^4 46 All those that were numbered of the Levites, whom Moses and Aaron and the chief of Israel numbered, after their families, and after the house of their fathers,

47 From [3]thirty years old and upward even unto fifty years old, every one that came to °do the service of the ministry, and the service of the burden in the [3]tabernacle of the congregation, u^4

48 Even those that were numbered of them, were eight thousand and five hundred and fourscore. w^4

49 According to the °commandment of [1]the LORD they were numbered by the °hand of Moses, °every one according to his service, and according to his burden: thus were they numbered of him, as [1]the LORD commanded Moses. x^4

5 And °the LORD °spake unto Moses, saying, C a c^1 d^1 (p. 186)

2 "Command the °children of Israel, that they put out of the camp every leper, and

---

32 the instruments of. Instead of these words some codices, with Sam., Jon., and Sept., read "all", i.e. "all the charge".

34–45 (o, p. 183). OBEDIENCE.
(*Repeated and Extended Alternation.*)

o | s^1 | t^1 | 34. KOHATHITES. Numeration.
| | | u^1 | 35. Age and service.
| | | w^1 | 36, 37–. Number.
| | | x^1 | –37. According to the commandment.
| s^2 | t^2 | 38. GERSHONITES. Numeration.
| | | u^2 | 39. Age and service.
| | | w^2 | 40, 41–. Number.
| | | x^2 | –41. According to the commandment.
| s^3 | t^3 | 42. MERARITES. Numeration.
| | | u^3 | 43. Age and service.
| | | w^3 | 44, 45–. Number.
| | | x^3 | –45. According to the commandment.

37 commandment. Heb. "mouth". Fig. *Metonymy* (of Cause), Ap. 6, put for words spoken by it.
hand. Fig. *Metonymy* (of Cause), Ap. 6, "hand" put for ministry performed by Moses.

46–49 (*n*, p. 183). COMMAND (COMPLETED).
(*Extended Alternation.*)

n | t^4 | 46. Numeration.
| u^4 | 47. Age and service.
| w^4 | 48. Number.
| x^4 | 49. According to the commandment.
(Compare the above with "o", above.)

47 do the service. Heb. "serve the service". Fig. *Polyptōton* (Ap. 6), for emphasis = do the solemn or important service.

49 commandment. Heb. "mouth", put for what is said by Fig. *Metonymy* (of Cause). Ap. 6.
hand. Put by Fig. *Metonymy* (of Cause), Ap. 6, for ministry performed by it.
every one. Heb. *'īsh 'īsh.* See Ap. 14. ii.

5. 1—9. 23 [For Structures see next page].

1 the LORD. Heb. Jehovah. Ap. 4.
spake. See note on 1. 1.
2 children = sons. See note on 1. 2.

1490 every one that hath an issue, and whosoever
is defiled by °the dead:
3 Both male and female shall ye °put out,
without the camp shall ye put them; that
they defile not their camps, in the midst
whereof I dwell."
4 And the [2]children of Israel did so, and
put them out without the camp: °as [1]the
LORD spake unto Moses, so did the [2]children
of Israel.

d[2] (p. 186) 5 And [1]the LORD [1]spake unto Moses, saying,
6 "Speak unto the [2]children of Israel, When
a °man or woman shall commit any °sin that
°men commit, to do a °trespass against [1]the
LORD, and that °person be guilty;
7 Then they shall confess their [6]sin which
they have done: and he shall °recompense his
°trespass with the principal thereof, and add
unto it the fifth *part* thereof, and give *it* unto
him against whom he hath °trespassed.
8 But if the man have no °kinsman to [7]recompense the [7]trespass unto, let the [7]trespass
be [7]recompensed unto [1]the LORD, *even* to the
priest; beside the ram of the °atonement,
whereby an °atonement shall be made for
him.
9 And every °offering of all the °holy things
of the [2]children of Israel, which they bring
unto the priest, shall be his.
10 And every [6]man's °hallowed things shall
be his: °whatsoever any [6]man giveth the
priest, it shall be °his."

d[3] e[1] 11 And [1]the LORD [1]spake unto Moses, saying,
12 "Speak unto the [2]children of Israel, and
say unto them, 'If any [6]man's wife go aside,
and commit a [7]trespass against him,
13 And a [6]man lie with her carnally, and it
be hid from the eyes of her husband, and be
kept close, and she be defiled, and *there be* no
witness against her, neither she be taken *with
the manner;*
14 And °the spirit of jealousy come upon
him, and he be jealous of his wife, and she be
defiled:

f[1] or if °the spirit of jealousy come upon him,
and he be jealous of his wife, and she be not
defiled:

e[2] 15 Then shall the man bring his wife unto
the priest, and he shall bring her °offering
for her, the tenth *part* of an °ephah of °barley
meal; he shall pour no oil upon it, nor put
frankincense thereon; for it *is* an °offering
of jealousy, an °offering of memorial, bringing
°iniquity to remembrance.
16 And the priest shall bring her near, and
set her before [1]the LORD:
17 And the priest shall take °holy water in
an earthen vessel; and of the dust that is in
the floor of the °tabernacle the priest shall
take, and put *it* into the water:
18 And the priest shall set the woman before
[1]the LORD, and uncover the woman's head,
and put the [15]offering of memorial in her
hands, which *is* the [15]jealousy offering: and
the priest shall have in his hand the °bitter
water that causeth the °curse:
19 And the priest shall charge her by an oath,
and say unto the woman, 'If no man have
lain with thee, and if thou hast not gone
aside to uncleanness *with another* instead of
thy husband, be thou free from this bitter
water that causeth the curse:

5. 1—9. 23 (**B**[1], p. 176). LAWS AND EVENTS.
(*Alternation and Introversion.*)

B[1] | C | a | 5. 1—6. 21. Laws for the People (Leprosy, &c.).
| | b | 6. 22-27. Laws for the priests (Blessing, &c.).
| D | 7. 1-89. Event (dedication of altar).
| *C* | *b* | 8. 1-26. Laws for priests and Levites.
| | *a* | 9. 1-14. Laws for People (Passover).
| *D* | 9. 15-23. Event (erection of tabernacle).

5. 1—6. 21 (a, above). LAWS FOR THE PEOPLE.

a | c[1] | 5. 1-31. Necessary laws.
| c[2] | 6. 1-21. Voluntary laws.

5. 1—31 (c[1], above). NECESSARY LAWS.

c[1] | d[1] | 1-4. Leprosy.
| d[2] | 5-10. Trespass.
| d[3] | 11-31. Jealousy.

the dead = the soul. Heb. *nephesh*. See Ap. 13. Cp. ch. 6. 6. Lev. 21. 1. Num. 19. 11. See note on Lev. 19. 28. Touching a dead man, rendered the one who touched unclean seven days (19. 11); touching other dead creatures, rendered unclean only till the evening (Lev. 11. 27, 39, 40).
3 put out, without the camp. Cp. 12. 14, 15.
4 as = according as.
6 man. Heb. *'ish*. See Ap. 14. ii.
sin. Heb. *chāṭ'a*. Ap. 44. i.
men. Heb. *'ādām*. See Ap. 14. i.
trespass. Heb. *mā'al*. Ap. 44. xi.
person = soul. Heb. *nephesh*. (Ap. 13.)
7 recompense = return back.
trespass. Heb. *'āsham*. Ap. 44. ii.
8 kinsman. Heb. *goēl*, redeemer. See note on Ex. 6. 6.
atonement. See note on Ex. 29. 33.
9 offering = heave offering. Heb. *t^erūmah*. See Ap. 43. viii., and note on Ex. 29. 27.
holy = separated. See note on Ex. 3. 5.
10 hallowed = separated. See note on "holy", Ex. 3. 5.
whatsoever. Some codices, with one printed edition, Sam., Sept., Syr., and Vulg., read "and whatsoever".
his: i.e. the priest's.

11-31 (d[3], above). JEALOUSY (*Repeated Alternation*).

d[3] | e[1] | 11-14-. Guilt } Case.
| f[1] | -14. Innocence }
| e[2] | 15-27. Guilt } Trial and proof.
| f[2] | 28. Innocence }
| e[3] | 29. Guilt } Case.
| f[3] | 30, 31. Innocence }

14 the spirit of jealousy = a jealous motion or affection of the mind. Here, Heb. *rūach* (Ap. 9) is put for the feelings, &c., as in Isa. 11. 2. Eph. 1. 17. Hos. 4. 12.
15 offering. Heb. *ḳorbān*, approach-offering. See Ap. 43. II. i.
ephah. See Ap. 51. III. 3.
barley. No other grain, and no other measure. Cp. Lev. 2. 1.
offering: i.e. of jealousy. Heb. *minchah* (Ap. 43. II. iii.), meal offering.
offering: i.e. of memorial. i.e. causing iniquity to be remembered.
iniquity. Heb. *'āvāh*. Ap. 44. iv.
17 holy = separated: taken from the laver. See note on Ex. 3. 5.
tabernacle. Heb. *mishkān*. Ap. 40.
18 bitter water. Heb. water of bitters, Genitive of cause: i.e., causing bitterness of spirit. Cp. Ps. 109. 18. Prov. 5. 4. Bitter = *ham'ārīm*.
curse. Fig. *Paronomasia* (Ap. 6). Heb. *ham'ārīm*.

1490 **20 But if thou hast gone aside *to another***
instead of thy husband, and if thou be defiled,
and some man have lain with thee beside
thine husband:'
21 Then the priest shall °charge the woman
with an oath of cursing, and the priest shall
say unto the woman, [1]'The LORD make thee
a curse and an oath among thy people, when
[1]the LORD doth make thy thigh to rot, and
thy belly to swell;
22 And this water that causeth the curse
shall go into thy bowels, to make *thy* belly to
swell, and *thy* thigh to [21]rot:' And the woman
shall say, °'Amen, amen.'
23 And the priest shall write these curses in
a book, and he shall blot *them* out with the
bitter water:
24 And he shall cause the woman to drink
the bitter water that causeth the curse: and
the water that causeth the curse shall enter
into her, *and* °*become* bitter.
25 Then the priest shall take the jealousy
°offering out of the woman's hand, and shall
°wave the °offering before [1]the LORD, and
°offer it upon the altar:
26 And the priest shall take an handful of
the offering, *even* the °memorial thereof, and
°burn *it* upon the altar, and afterward shall
cause the woman to drink the water.
27 And when he hath made her to drink the
water, then it shall come to pass, *that*, if she
be defiled, and have done [12]trespass against
her husband, that the water that causeth
the curse shall enter into her, *and* [24]*become*
bitter, and her belly shall swell, and her
thigh shall rot: and the woman shall be a
curse among her People.

f² **28 And if the woman be not defiled, but °be**
(p. 186) **clean; then she shall be free, and shall con-**
ceive seed.

e³ **29 This *is* the law of jealousies, when a wife**
goeth aside *to another* instead of her husband,
and is defiled;

f³ **30 Or when [14]the spirit of jealousy cometh**
upon him, and he be jealous over his wife,
and shall set the woman before [1]the LORD,
and the priest shall execute upon her all this
law.
31 Then shall the man be guiltless from
°iniquity, and this woman shall °bear her
iniquity.'"

c² g **6 And °the LORD °spake unto Moses, say-**
(p. 187) **ing,**
2 "Speak unto the °children of Israel,
and say unto them, 'When either °man or
°woman shall separate *themselves* to °vow
a vow of °a Nazarite, to separate *themselves*
unto [1]the LORD:

h **3 He shall separate *himself* from °wine and**
°strong drink, and shall drink no vinegar of
°wine, or vinegar of °strong drink, neither
shall he drink any °liquor of grapes, nor eat
°moist grapes, or dried.
4 All the days of his °separation shall he eat
nothing that is made of the °vine tree, from
the kernels even to the husk.
5 All the days of the vow of his [4]separation
there shall no rasor come upon his head:
until the days be fulfilled, in the which he
separateth *himself* unto [1]the LORD, he shall
be holy, *and* shall let the locks of the hair of
his head grow.
6 All the days that he separateth *himself*
unto [1]the LORD he shall °come at °no dead
body.
7 He shall not make himself unclean for his
father, or for his mother, for his brother, or for
his sister, when they die: because the °conse-
cration of his °God *is* upon his head.
8 All the days of his [4]separation he *is* holy
unto [1]the LORD.

9 And if any man die very suddenly by him, g
and he hath defiled the [7]head of his [7]conse-
cration; then he shall shave his head in the
day of his cleansing, on the seventh day shall
he shave it.
10 And on the eighth day he shall bring
two °turtles, or two young pigeons, to the
priest, to the °door of the °tabernacle of the
congregation:

21 charge, &c. This ordeal was provided for in the Laws of Khammurabi, §§ 131, 132. See Ap. 15.
22 Amen. A Hebrew word, transferred to the Greek = verily, truly so. If one adjured another and he replied "Amen", it was thereby considered as confirmed by an oath. Cp. 2 Cor. 1. 20.
24 become bitter = turn to bitterness.
25 offering. Heb. *minchah*, gift or meal offering. See Ap. 43. II. iii.
wave. See note on Ex. 29. 27.
offer it = bring it. Heb. *ḳārab*. Ap. 43. I. i.
26 memorial. The handful (Lev. 2. 2) so-called.
burn. Heb. *ḳaṭar*. See Ap. 43. I. vii.
28 be. Heb. she be.
31 iniquity. Heb. *'āvah*. Ap. 44. iv.
bear her iniquity = bear the punishment of it. Fig. *Metonymy* (of Cause), Ap. 6. Cp. Lev. 20. 17, 19, 20. Ezek. 4. 4, 5. See Ap. 44. iv.

6. 1-21 (c², p. 186). VOLUNTARY (NAZARITE VOW) (*Alternation*).

c² | g | 1, 2. The vow made.
  h | 3-8. Observances during separation.
 g | 9-12. Vow interrupted.
  h | 13-21. Observances at close of separation.

Note the order in these laws: (1) separation, 6. 1-12; (2) worship, 6. 13-21; (3) blessing, 6. 22-27; (4) service, 7. 1-89.

1 the LORD. Heb. Jehovah. Ap. 4.
spake. See note on 1. 1.
2 children = sons.
man. Heb. *'īsh*. See Ap. 14. ii.
woman. Either could be a Nazarite.
vow a vow. Fig. *Polyptōton* (Ap. 6), for emphasis = make a special vow. Cp. Acts 18. 18; 21. 23.
a Nazarite = one separate, from Heb. *nazīr*, to separate. Cp. Gen. 49. 26. Judg. 13. 5, 7. Lam. 4. 7.
3 wine. Heb. *yayin*. See Ap. 27. i.
strong drink. Heb. *shēkār*. See Ap. 27. iv.
liquor of grapes = mashed grapes.
moist = green or "fresh".
4 separation = Nazariteship.
vine tree = grape vine.
6 come at = come near.
no dead body = no dead soul. Heb. *nephesh*. See Ap. 13, and note on Lev. 19. 28.
7 consecration = separation, or Nazariteship.
God. Heb. Elohim. Ap. 4.
10 turtles = turtle-doves.
door = entrance.
tabernacle of the congregation = tent of assembly. See Ap. 40.

1490 **11** And the priest shall °offer the one for a sin offering, and the other for a burnt offering, and make an °atonement for him, for that he sinned by the °dead, and shall °hallow his head that same day.

12 And he shall °consecrate unto [1] the LORD the days of his °separation, and shall bring a lamb of the first year for a °trespass offering: but the days that were before shall °be lost, because his °separation was defiled.

h (p. 187) **13** And this *is* the law of °the Nazarite, when the days of his [12] separation are fulfilled: he shall be brought unto the [10] door of the [10] tabernacle of the congregation:

14 And he shall °offer his °offering unto [1] the LORD, one he lamb of the first year without blemish for a burnt offering, and one ewe lamb of the first year without blemish for a °sin offering, and one ram without blemish for peace offerings,

15 And a basket of unleavened bread, °cakes of fine flour mingled with oil, and wafers of unleavened bread anointed with oil, and their °meat offering, and their drink offerings.

16 And the priest shall bring *them* before [1] the LORD, and shall offer his [14] sin offering, and his burnt offering:

17 And he shall offer the ram *for* a sacrifice of peace offerings unto [1] the LORD, with the basket of unleavened bread: the priest shall [11] offer also his [15] meat offering, and his drink offering.

18 And [13] the Nazarite shall shave the head of his [12] separation *at* the [10] door of the [10] tabernacle of the congregation, and shall take the hair of the head of his [12] separation, and put *it* in the fire which *is* under the °sacrifice of the peace offerings.

19 And the priest shall take the °sodden shoulder of the ram, and one unleavened cake out of the basket, and one unleavened wafer, and shall put *them* upon the hands of the Nazarite, after *the hair of* his [12] separation is shaven:

20 And the priest shall wave them *for* a °wave offering before [1] the LORD: this *is* °holy for the priest, with the wave breast and heave shoulder: and after that [13] the Nazarite may drink wine.

21 This *is* the law of [13] the Nazarite who hath vowed, *and of* his offering unto [1] the LORD for his [12] separation, °beside *that* that his hand shall get: according to the vow which he vowed, so he must do after the law of his [12] separation.' "

C b (p. 186) **22** And [1] the LORD [1] spake unto Moses, saying,

23 "Speak unto °Aaron and unto his sons, saying, 'On this wise ye shall °bless the [2] children of Israel, saying unto them,

24 °'The LORD bless thee, and keep thee:

25 °The LORD make His °face shine upon thee, and be gracious unto thee:

26 °The LORD lift up His °countenance upon thee, and give thee °peace.'

27 And they shall put My name upon the [2] children of Israel; and I will bless them."

D E (p. 188) **7** And it came to pass on the day that Moses had fully set up the °tabernacle, and had anointed it, and sanctified it, and all the instruments thereof, both the altar and all the vessels thereof, and had anointed them, and sanctified them;

2 That °the princes of Israel, heads of the house of their fathers, who *were* the princes of the tribes, and were over them that were numbered, °offered:

3 And they °brought their °offering before °the LORD, six covered wagons, and twelve oxen; a wagon for two of the princes, and for each one an ox: and they brought them before the tabernacle.

4 And [3] the LORD °spake unto Moses, saying, i k (p. 189)

5 "Take *it* of them, that they may be to

---

11 offer = prepare. See Ap. 43. I. iii.
atonement. See note on Ex. 29. 33.
dead = soul. Heb. *nephesh* (Ap. 13): i.e. the dead person.
hallow his head: i.e. by beginning anew the days of his vow (*v.* 9), during which the hair must grow, as in *v.* 5. See note on "holy", Ex. 3. 5.
12 consecrate = separate.
separation = Nazariteship.
trespass offering. See Ap. 43. II. vi.
be lost. Heb. fall, i.e. not be counted.
13 the Nazarite = the one separate.
14 offer = bring near. Heb. *ḳārab.* See Ap. 43. I. i.
offering = approach offering. Ap. 43. II. i.
sin offering. See Ap. 43. II. v.
15 cakes = pierced cakes.
meat offering = meal or gift offering. Ap. 43. II. iii.
18 sacrifice. Ap. 43. I. iv. and II. xii.; cp. Acts 21. 26, 27.
19 sodden = boiled.
20 wave offering. See note on Ex. 29. 27.
holy. See note on Ex. 3. 5.
21 beside, &c.: i.e., if able, he might voluntarily make an addition thereto.

22-27 (b, p. 186). THE PRIESTS' LAW. BLESSING.

A triple blessing of three members, from Father, Son, and Holy Spirit. See Ap. 10.
23 Aaron and unto his sons. Cp. Deut. 21. 5. 1 Chron. 23. 13.
bless. Deut. 10. 8.
24 The LORD = Jehovah the Father, the *source* of all blessing. Cp. Eph. 1. 3. Heb. 10. 7.
25 The LORD = Jehovah the Son, the *channel* of all blessing, Eph. 1. 3. Cp. Acts 3. 26. Heb. 10. 10.
face: put by Fig. *Metonymy* (of Adjunct), for whole Person. Ap. 6. Also Fig. *Anthropopatheia.*
26 The LORD = Jehovah the Spirit, the *witness* of all blessing. Cp. Heb. 10. 7, 10, 15.
countenance: same as "face" in *v.* 25: this is the token of Divine favour and delight. Cp. Job 29. 24. Ps. 4. 6, and the result *v.* 7.
peace = rest or security.

7. 1-89 (D, p. 186). DEDICATION OF THE ALTAR (*Alternation*).

D | E | 1-3. Offerings of the princes.
  | F | 4-9. Arrangement.
  | *E* | 10. Offerings of the princes.
  | *F* | 11-89. Arrangement.

1 tabernacle = habitation. Heb. *mishkān.* Cp. Ex. 40. 18. See Ap. 40.
2 the princes. Though their offerings were the same as the others, yet each is recorded separately.
offered = brought near. Heb. *ḳārab.* Ap. 43. I. i.
3 brought. Same as "offered", *v.* 2.
offering = approach offering. Heb. *ḳorbān.* Ap. 43. II. i.
the LORD. Heb. Jehovah. Ap. 4.

4-9 [For Structure see next page].

4 spake. See note on 1. 1.

1490 °do the service of the °tabernacle of the congregation;
l (p. 189) and thou shalt give them unto the Levites, to every °man according to his service."

k 6 And Moses took the wagons and the oxen,
l and gave them unto the Levites.

7 Two wagons and four oxen he gave unto the sons of Gershon, according to their service:

8 And four wagons and eight oxen he gave unto the sons of Merari, according unto their service, under the hand of Ithamar the son of Aaron the priest.

9 But unto the sons of Kohath he gave none: because the service of the sanctuary belonging unto them *was that* they should bear upon their shoulders.

E (p. 188) 10 And the princes [2]offered for dedicating of the altar in the day that it was anointed, even the princes [2]offered their [3]offering before the altar.

F m[1] (p. 189) 11 And [3]the LORD °said unto Moses, "They shall [3]offer their [3]offering, each prince on his day, for the dedicating of the altar."

m[2] 12 And he that [2]offered his [3]offering the first day was Nahshon the son of Amminadab, of the °tribe of Judah:

13 And his [3]offering *was* one silver charger, the weight thereof *was* an hundred and thirty *shekels*, one silver bowl of seventy °shekels, after the shekel of the sanctuary; both of them *were* full of fine flour mingled with oil for a °meat offering:

14 One spoon of ten *shekels* of gold, full of incense:

15 One young bullock, one ram, one lamb of the first year, for a burnt offering:

16 °One kid of the goats for a sin offering:

17 And for a sacrifice of peace offerings, two oxen, five rams, five he goats, five lambs of the first year: this *was* the [3]offering of Nahshon the son of Amminadab.

18 On the second day Nethaneel the son of Zuar, prince of Issachar, did offer:

19 He [2]offered *for* his [3]offering one silver charger, the weight whereof *was* an hundred and thirty *shekels*, one silver bowl of seventy [13]shekels, after the shekel of the sanctuary; both of them full of fine flour mingled with oil for a meat offering:

20 One spoon of gold of ten *shekels*, full of incense:

21 One young bullock, one ram, one lamb of the first year, for a burnt offering:

22 [16]One kid of the goats for a sin offering:

23 And for a sacrifice of peace offerings, two oxen, five rams, five he goats, five lambs of the first year: this *was* the [3]offering of Nethaneel the son of Zuar.

24 On the third day Eliab the son of Helon, prince of the children of Zebulun, *did offer*:

25 His [3]offering *was* one silver charger, the weight whereof *was* an hundred and thirty *shekels*, one silver bowl of seventy [13]shekels, after the shekel of the sanctuary; both of them full of fine flour mingled with oil for a meat offering:

26 One golden spoon of ten *shekels*, full of incense:

27 One young bullock, one ram, one lamb of the first year, for a burnt offering:

28 [16]One kid of the goats for a sin offering:

29 And for a sacrifice of peace offerings, two oxen, five rams, five he goats, five lambs of the first year: this *was* the [3]offering of Eliab the son of Helon.

30 On the fourth day Elizur the son of Shedeur, prince of the °children of Reuben, *did offer*:

31 His [3]offering *was* one silver charger of the weight of an hundred and thirty *shekels*, one silver bowl of seventy [13]shekels, after the shekel of the sanctuary; both of them full of fine flour mingled with oil for a meat offering:

32 One golden spoon of ten *shekels*, full of incense:

33 One young bullock, one ram, one lamb of the first year, for a burnt offering:

34 [16]One kid of the goats for a sin offering:

35 And for a sacrifice of peace offerings, two oxen, five rams, five he goats, five lambs of the first year: this *was* the [3]offering of Elizur the son of Shedeur.

36 On the fifth day Shelumiel the son of Zurishaddai, prince of the [30]children of Simeon, *did offer*:

37 His [3]offering *was* one silver charger, the weight whereof *was* an hundred and thirty *shekels*, one silver bowl of seventy [13]shekels, after the [13]shekel of the sanctuary; both of them full of fine flour mingled with oil for a meat offering:

38 One golden spoon of ten *shekels*, full of incense:

39 One young bullock, one ram, one lamb of the first year, for a burnt offering:

4-9 (F, p. 188). ARRANGEMENT.
(Alternation.)

F | i | k | 4, 5-. Acceptance } Command.
  | | l | -5. Distribution }
  | i | k | 6-. Acceptance } Obedience.
  | | l | -6-9. Distribution }

5 do the service. Heb. serve the service. Fig. *Polyptōton* (Ap. 6), for emphasis = perform the solemn service.

tabernacle of the congregation = tent of assembly. See Ap. 40.

man. Heb. *'ish.* See Ap. 14. ii.

11-89 (*F*, p. 188). ARRANGEMENT.
(Division.)

F | m[1] | 11. Command.
   | m[2] | 12-89. Obedience.

11 said. See note on 3. 40.

12 tribe. The order is the same as in ch. 2. See Ap. 45.

13 shekels. See Ap. 51. II.

meat offering = gift offering. See Ap. 43. II. iii.

16 One. Some codices, with Sam., Sept., Syr., and Vulg., read "And one".

30 children = sons.

1490 **40** °One kid of the goats for a °sin offering:
41 And for a sacrifice of peace offerings, two oxen, five rams, five he goats, five lambs of the first year: this *was* the [3]offering of Shelumiel the son of Zurishaddai.

42 On the sixth day Eliasaph the son of °Deuel, prince of the [30]children of Gad, *offered:*
43 His [3]offering *was* one silver charger of the weight of an hundred and thirty *shekels,* a silver bowl of seventy [13]shekels, after the shekel of the sanctuary; both of them full of fine flour mingled with oil for a meat offering:
44 One golden spoon of ten *shekels,* full of incense:
45 One young bullock, one ram, one lamb of the first year, for a burnt offering:
46 One kid of the goats for a sin offering:
47 And for a sacrifice of peace offerings, two oxen, five rams, five he goats, five lambs of the first year: this *was* the [3]offering of Eliasaph the son of Deuel.

48 On the seventh day Elishama the son of Ammihud, prince of the [30]children of Ephraim, *offered:*
49 His [3]offering *was* one silver charger, the weight whereof *was* an hundred and thirty *shekels,* one silver bowl of seventy [13]shekels, after the shekel of the sanctuary; both of them full of fine flour mingled with oil for a meat offering:
50 One golden spoon of ten *shekels,* full of incense:
51 One young bullock, one ram, one lamb of the first year, for a burnt offering:
52 [40]One kid of the goats for a sin offering:
53 And for a sacrifice of peace offerings, two oxen, five rams, five he goats, five lambs of the first year: this *was* the [3]offering of Elishama the son of Ammihud.

54 On the eighth day *offered* Gamaliel the son of Pedahzur, prince of the [30]children of Manasseh:
55 His [3]offering *was* one silver charger of the weight of an hundred and thirty *shekels,* one silver bowl of seventy [13]shekels, after the shekel of the sanctuary; both of them full of fine flour mingled with oil for a meat offering:
56 One golden spoon of ten *shekels,* full of incense:
57 One young bullock, one ram, one lamb of the first year, for a burnt offering:
58 One kid of the goats for a sin offering:
59 And for a sacrifice of peace offerings, two oxen, five rams, five he goats, five lambs of the first year: this *was* the [3]offering of Gamaliel the son of Pedahzur.

60 On the ninth day Abidan the son of Gideoni, prince of the [30]children of Benjamin, *offered:*
61 His [3]offering *was* one silver charger, the weight whereof *was* an hundred and thirty *shekels,* one silver bowl of seventy [13]shekels, after the shekel of the sanctuary; both of them full of fine flour mingled with oil for a meat offering:
62 One golden spoon of ten *shekels,* full of incense:
63 One young bullock, one ram, one lamb of the first year, for a burnt offering:
64 [40]One kid of the goats for a sin offering:
65 And for a sacrifice of peace offerings, two oxen, five rams, five he goats, five lambs of the first year: this *was* the [3]offering of Abidan the son of Gideoni.

66 On the tenth day Ahiezer the son of Ammishaddai, prince of the [30]children of Dan, *offered:*
67 His [3]offering *was* one silver charger, the weight whereof *was* an hundred and thirty *shekels,* one silver bowl of seventy [13]shekels, after the shekel of the sanctuary; both of them full of fine flour mingled with oil for a meat offering:
68 One golden spoon of ten *shekels,* full of incense:
69 One young bullock, one ram, one lamb of the first year, for a burnt offering:
70 [40]One kid of the goats for a sin offering:
71 And for a sacrifice of peace offerings, two oxen, five rams, five he goats, five lambs of the first year: this *was* the [3]offering of Ahiezer the son of Ammishaddai.

72 On the eleventh day Pagiel the son of Ocran, prince of the [30]children of Asher, *offered:*
73 His [3]offering *was* one silver charger, the weight whereof *was* an hundred and thirty *shekels,* one silver bowl of seventy [13]shekels, after the shekel of the sanctuary; both of them full of fine flour mingled with oil for a meat offering:
74 One golden spoon of ten *shekels,* full of incense:
75 One young bullock, one ram, one lamb of the first year, for a burnt offering:
76 [40]One kid of the goats for a sin offering:
77 And for a sacrifice of peace offerings, two oxen, five rams, five he goats, five lambs of the first year: this *was* the [3]offering of Pagiel the son of Ocran.

78 On the twelfth day Ahira the son of Enan, prince of the [30]children of Naphtali, *offered:*
79 His [3]offering *was* one silver charger, the weight whereof *was* an hundred and thirty *shekels,* one silver bowl of seventy [13]shekels, after the shekel of the sanctuary; both of them full of fine flour mingled with oil for a meat offering:
80 One golden spoon of ten *shekels,* full of incense:
81 One young bullock, one ram, one lamb of the first year, for a burnt offering:
82 [40]One kid of the goats for a sin offering:
83 And for a °sacrifice of peace offerings, two oxen, five rams, five he goats, five lambs of the first year: this *was* the [3]offering of Ahira the son of Enan.

---

40 One. Some codices, with Sam., Sept., Syr., and Vulg., read "And one".
sin. Heb. *chāṭ'a.* Ap. 44. i.
42 Deuel = Deguel, in ch. 2. 14 = Reguel. See note there, and cp. 1. 14.
83 sacrifice. Heb. *zābaḥ.* Ap. 43. xii.

1490 **84** This *was* the dedication of the altar, °in
the day when it was anointed, by the princes
of Israel: twelve chargers of silver, twelve
silver bowls, twelve spoons of gold:
85 Each charger of silver *weighing* an hundred and thirty *shekels*, each bowl seventy:
all the silver vessels *weighed* two thousand
and four hundred *shekels*, after the [13]shekel
of the sanctuary:
86 The golden spoons *were* twelve, full of
incense, *weighing* ten *shekels* apiece, after the
[13]shekel of the sanctuary: all the gold of the
spoons *was* an hundred and twenty *shekels*.
87 All the oxen for the burnt offering *were*
twelve bullocks, the rams twelve, the lambs
of the first year twelve, with their meat
offering: and the kids of the goats for sin
offering twelve.
88 And all the oxen for the [83]sacrifice of the
peace offerings *were* twenty and four bullocks,
the rams sixty, the he goats sixty, the lambs
of the first year sixty. This *was* the dedication of the altar, after that it was anointed.
89 And when Moses was gone into the
°tabernacle of the congregation to speak
°with Him, then he heard the voice of One
speaking unto him from off the °mercy seat
that *was* upon the ark of testimony, from
between the two cherubims: and He spake
unto him.

b n[1] (p. 191) **8** And °the LORD °spake unto Moses, saying,
2 "Speak unto Aaron, and say unto him,
'When thou lightest the lamps, the seven
lamps shall give light over against °the
°candlestick.'"
3 And Aaron did so; he lighted the lamps
thereof over against the [2]candlestick, °as [1]the
LORD commanded Moses.
4 And this work of the [2]candlestick *was of*
beaten gold, °unto the shaft thereof, unto the
flowers thereof, *was* beaten work: according
unto the pattern which [1]the LORD had shewed
Moses, so he made the [2]candlestick.

o[1] **5** And [1]the LORD [1]spake unto Moses, saying,
6 "Take the Levites from among the °chil-
dren of Israel, and cleanse them.
7 And thus shalt thou do unto them, to
cleanse them: Sprinkle °water of purifying
upon them, and let them shave all their flesh,
and let them wash their clothes, and *so* make
themselves clean.
8 Then let them take a young bullock with
his °meat offering, *even* fine flour mingled
with oil, and another young bullock shalt
thou take for a °sin offering.
9 And thou shalt bring the Levites before
the °tabernacle of the congregation: and thou
shalt gather the whole assembly of the [6]chil-
dren of Israel together:
10 And thou shalt bring the Levites before
[1]the LORD: and the [6]children of Israel shall
put their hands upon the Levites:
11 And Aaron shall °offer the Levites before
[1]the LORD *for* an °offering of the [6]children of
Israel, that they may °execute the service of
[1]the LORD.
12 And °the Levites shall lay their hands
upon the heads of the bullocks: and thou shalt

84 in the day: i.e. in the twelve days. See Ap. 18.
89 tabernacle of the congregation. Heb. tent of meeting. See Ap. 40.
with Him: i.e. with Jehovah. Cp. *v.* 11.
mercy seat. See note on Ex. 25. 17.

8. 1-26 (*C b*, p. 186). LAWS FOR THE PRIESTS AND LEVITES (*Repeated Alternation*).

b | n[1] | 1-4. Service of Aaron.
| o[1] | 5-14. Levites' purification. Command.
| n[2] | 15-19. Service of Levites.
| o[2] | 20, 21. Levites' purification. Obedience.
| n[3] | 22-26. Service of Levites.

1 the LORD. Heb. Jehovah. Ap. 4.
spake. See note on 1. 1.
2 the=the face of the.
candlestick=light-holder (as in Gen. 1. 14), or lampstand. Cp. Ex. 25. 31-39; 37. 17-24.
3 as=according as.
4 unto. Some codices, with Sam., Onk. MS., and Jon., read "and unto".
6 children=sons.
7 water of purifying=sin water: i.e., water prepared as in ch. 19.
8 meat offering. See Ap. 43. II. iii.
sin offering. See Ap. 43. II. v.
9 tabernacle of the congregation=tent of meeting. Ap. 40.
11 offer. Heb. wave. See note on Ex. 29. 27.
offering. Heb. wave offering. See Ap. 43. II. ix.
execute the service. Fig. *Polyptōton* (Ap. 6). Heb. "serve the service"=perform the solemn service.
12 the Levites. Fig. *Epanadiplōsis* (Ap. 6), the verse beginning and ending with the same word.
offer=prepare. Heb. *'āsāh*. Ap. 43. I. iii.
atonement. See note on Ex. 29. 33.
14 Mine. Cp. 3. 45.
15 offer them for an offering=wave them for a wave offering. See Ex. 29. 27.
17 For. Cp. Ex. 13. 2. Num. 3. 13.
man. Heb. *'ādām*. See Ap. 14. i.
on the day. See Ap. 18.

°offer the one *for* a sin offering, and the other
for a burnt offering, unto [1]the LORD, to make
an °atonement for °the Levites.
13 And thou shalt set the Levites before
Aaron, and before his sons, and offer them *for*
an offering unto [1]the LORD.
14 Thus shalt thou separate the Levites
from among the [6]children of Israel: and the
Levites shall be °Mine.
15 And after that shall the Levites go in to n[2]
do the service of the [9]tabernacle of the congregation: and thou shalt cleanse them, and
°offer them *for* an offering.
16 For they *are* wholly given unto Me from
among the [6]children of Israel; instead of such
as open every womb, *even instead of* the
firstborn of all the [6]children of Israel, have I
taken them unto Me.
17 °For all the firstborn of the [6]children of
Israel *are* Mine, *both* °man and beast: °on the
day that I smote every firstborn in the land of
Egypt I sanctified them for Myself.
18 And I have taken the Levites for all the
firstborn of the [6]children of Israel.
19 And I have given the Levites *as* a gift
to Aaron and to his sons from among the
[6]children of Israel, to [15]do the service of

1490 the [6]children of Israel in the [9]tabernacle of the congregation, and to make an [12]atonement for the [6]children of Israel: that there be no plague among the [6]children of Israel, when the [6]children of Israel come nigh unto the sanctuary."

o² (p. 191) **20** And Moses, and Aaron, and all the congregation of the [6]children of Israel, did to the Levites according unto all that [1]the LORD commanded Moses concerning the Levites, so did the [6]children of Israel unto them.

21 And the Levites were purified, and they washed their clothes; and Aaron [11]offered them *as* an [11]offering before [1]the LORD; and Aaron made an [12]atonement for them to cleanse them.

n³ **22** And after that went the Levites in to do their service in the [9]tabernacle of the congregation before Aaron, and before his sons: °as [1]the LORD had commanded Moses concerning the Levites, so did they unto them.

23 And [1]the LORD [1]spake unto Moses, saying,

24 "This *is it* that *belongeth* unto the Levites: from °twenty and five years old and upward they shall go in °to wait upon the service of the [9]tabernacle of the congregation:

25 And °from the age of fifty years they shall cease waiting upon the service *thereof*, and shall serve no more:

26 But shall minister with their brethren in the [9]tabernacle of the congregation, to keep the charge, and shall do no service." Thus shalt thou do unto the Levites touching their charge."

a p (p. 191) **9** And °the LORD °spake unto Moses in the wilderness of Sinai, in the °first month of the second year after they were come out of the land of Egypt, saying,

2 "Let the °children of Israel also keep the passover at his appointed season.

3 In the fourteenth day of this month, at even, ye shall keep it in his appointed season: according to all the rites of it, and according to all the ceremonies thereof, shall ye keep it."

q **4** And Moses spake unto the [2]children of Israel, that they should keep the passover.

14th Abib. **5** And they °kept the passover on the fourteenth day of the first month at even in the wilderness of Sinai: according to all that [1]the LORD commanded Moses, so did the [2]children of Israel.

q **6** And there were certain °men, who were defiled °by the dead °body of a °man, that they could not keep the passover on that day: and they came before Moses and before Aaron on that day:

7 And those [6]men said unto him, "We *are* defiled by the dead body of a [6]man: wherefore are we kept back, that we may not offer an offering of [1]the LORD in his appointed season among the [2]children of Israel?"

8 And Moses said unto them, "Stand still, and I will hear what [1]the LORD will command concerning you."

p **9** And [1]the LORD [1]spake unto Moses, saying,

10 "Speak unto the [2]children of Israel, saying, 'If °any man of you or of your posterity shall be unclean by reason of a dead °body, or *be* in a journey °afar off, yet he shall keep the passover unto [1]the LORD.

11 The fourteenth day of the °second month at even they shall keep it, *and* eat it with unleavened bread and bitter *herbs*. 14th Ziph.

12 They shall leave none of it unto the morning, nor break any bone of it: according to all the ordinances of the passover they shall keep it.

13 But the °man that *is* clean, and is not in a journey, and forbeareth to keep the passover, even the same °soul shall be cut off from among his people: because he brought not the °offering of [1]the LORD in his appointed season, that [6]man shall bear his sin.

14 And if a stranger shall sojourn among you, and will keep the passover unto [1]the LORD; according to the ordinance of the passover, and according to the manner thereof, so shall he do: ye shall have one ordinance, both for the stranger, and for him that was born in the land.'"

---

22 as = according as.

24 twenty and five years old. This was the commencement of a five years' probation. The age, thirty, was the age of their numbering. See note on 4. 3.

to wait, &c. Fig. *Polyptōton* (Ap. 6), as in *vv.* 11, 15, 19. Lit. war the warfare.

25 from the age, &c. Observe the gracious care of Jehovah.

9. 1-14 (*a*, p. 186). LAWS FOR THE PEOPLE. (*Introversion.*)

a | p | 1–3. Command. Passover.
 q | 4, 5. Obedience rendered.
 q | 6–8. Obedience hindered.
 p | 9–14. Command. Second passover.

1 the LORD. Heb. Jehovah. Ap. 4.

spake. See note on 1. 1. During the week of Aaron's consecration, Abib 1–8.

first month, &c. Therefore before the numbering which was on the first day of the second month (1. 1, 2). The observance mentioned here in connection with the second passover, a month later (*vv.* 6–11).

2 children = sons.

5 kept the passover: the second of ten recorded. See note on Ex. 12. 18, 28. Lev. 23. 5. Num. 28. 16. Deut. 16. 2, and cp. 7. 89—9. 14.

6 men. Heb. pl. of *'īsh* or *'enōsh*, Ap. 14. ii. Probably Mishael and Elizaphan, who had buried Nadab and Abihu (Lev. 10. 1–4); they were thus rendered unclean, and could not keep the passover (Num. 19. 11; 5. 2).

by = for touching.

body = soul. Heb. *nephesh*. Ap. 13.

man. Heb. *'ādām*. Ap. 14. i.

10 any man. Heb. *'īsh, 'īsh*. Ap. 14. ii.

body = soul. Heb. *nephesh*. Ap. 13.

afar off. In Heb. MSS. dotted, to show these words are to be omitted. See Ap. 31. Distance not limited.

11 second month. Therefore a month later than the appointed day (*v.* 1).

13 man. Heb. *'enōsh*. Ap. 14. iii.

soul. Heb. *nephesh*. Ap. 13.

offering = approach offering. Heb. *ḳorbān*. Ap. 43. II. i.

D G (p. 193) 1490 15 And on the day that the °tabernacle °was reared up the cloud covered the °tabernacle, *namely*, the tent of the testimony:

H^1 and at even there °was upon the °tabernacle as it were the appearance of fire, until the morning.

G^2 16 So it was alway:

H^2 the cloud covered it *by day*, and the appearance of fire by night.

G^3 17 And when the cloud was taken up from the °tabernacle, then after that the [2]children of Israel journeyed: and in the place where the cloud abode, there the [2]children of Israel pitched their tents.

H^3 18 °At the °commandment of [1]the LORD the [2]children of Israel journeyed, and at the °commandment of [1]the LORD they pitched:

G^4 as long as the cloud abode upon the [15]tabernacle they rested in their tents.
19 And when the cloud tarried long upon the [15]tabernacle many days, then the [2]children of Israel kept the charge of [1]the LORD, and journeyed not.
20 And *so* it was, when the cloud [15]was °a few days upon the [15]tabernacle;

H^4 °according to the [18]commandment of [1]the LORD they abode in their tents, and according to the [18]commandment of [1]the LORD they journeyed.

G^5 21 And *so* it was, when the cloud abode from even unto the morning, and *that* the cloud was taken up in the morning, then they journeyed: whether *it was* by day or by night that the cloud was taken up, they journeyed.
22 Or *whether it were* two days, or a month, or a year, that the cloud tarried upon the [15]tabernacle, remaining thereon, the [2]children of Israel °abode in their tents, and journeyed not: but when it was taken up, they journeyed.

H^5 23 °At the commandment of [1]the LORD they rested in the tents, and at the commandment of [1]the LORD they journeyed: they kept the charge of [1]the LORD, at the commandment of [1]the LORD by the °hand of Moses.

I^1 **10** And °the LORD °spake unto Moses, saying,
2 "Make thee °two °trumpets of silver; °of a whole piece shalt thou make them: that thou mayest °use them for the calling of the °assembly, and for the journeying of the camps.
3 And when they shall blow with them, all the [2]assembly shall assemble themselves to thee at the °door of the °tabernacle of the congregation.
4 And if they blow *but* with one *trumpet*, then the princes, *which are* heads of the thousands of Israel, shall gather themselves unto thee.
5 When ye °blow an alarm, then the camps that lie on the east parts shall go forward.
6 When ye blow an alarm the second time, then the camps that lie on the south side shall take their journey: they shall blow an alarm for their journeys.
7 But when the °congregation is to be gathered together, ye shall blow, but ye shall not sound an alarm.
8 And the °sons of Aaron, the priests, shall blow with the trumpets; and they shall be to you for an ordinance for ever throughout your generations.
9 And if ye go to war in your land against the enemy that oppresseth you, then ye shall blow an alarm with the trumpets; and ye shall be remembered before [1]the LORD your °God, and ye shall be saved from your enemies.

---

9. 15-23 (*D*, p. 186). EVENT. ERECTION OF TABERNACLE (*Repeated Alternation*).

D | G^1 | 15-. Time: "on the day".
  H^1 | -15. Event—Cloud and fire.
 G^2 | 16-. Time: "alway".
  H^2 | -16. Event—Cloud and fire.
 G^3 | 17. Time: when cloud taken up.
  H^3 | 18-. Event—They journeyed.
 G^4 | -18-20-. Time: alternations.
  H^4 | -20. Event—Command to journey.
 G^5 | 21, 22. Time: alternations.
  H^5 | 23. Event—Command to rest.

15 tabernacle = habitation. Heb. *mishkān*. Ap. 40.
was = came to be: i. e. remained.
17 tabernacle = tent. Heb. *'ohel*. Ap. 40.
18 At the, &c. Fig. *Epibole*. Ap. 6, repeated.
commandment. Heb. mouth. Fig. *Metonymy* (of Cause), Ap. 6; mouth put for command given by it.
20 a few days. Heb. "days of number"; i. e. days easily counted.
according to, &c. Fig. *Mesarchia*, Ap. 6 (twice).
22 abode. Cp. Ex. 40. 34-38.
23 At the commandment, &c. Fig. *Epibole* Ap. 6.
hand = mediation, or ministry; "hand" put by Fig *Metonymy* (of Cause), Ap. 6.

10. 1-36 (A^2, p. 176). JOURNEYINGS AND ORDER (MARCH) (*Repeated Alternation*).

A^2 | I^1 | 1-10. Journey. Preparation.
  K^1 | 11. Removal of cloud.
 I^2 | 12-16. Journey. Commenced.
  K^2 | 17. Removal of tabernacle.
 I^3 | 18-28. Journey. Order.
  K^3 | 29-32. Removal of Hobab.
 I^4 | 33. Journey. Progress.
  K^4 | 34. Removal of cloud.
 I^5 | 35. Journey. Commenced.
  K^5 | 36. Rest of cloud.

1 the LORD. Heb. Jehovah. Ap. 4.
spake. See note on 1. 1.
2 two: here only two. Later, 120 (2 Chron. 5. 12).
trumpets. These were of two principal kinds: those called *chăzoẓ'rah*, made of silver, and straight; the other, *shōphār*, a horn. These must be distinguished. The other words are *yōbēl*, a jubilee horn (Ex. 19. 16); and *tākō'a*, the blast of a trumpet (Ezek. 7. 14).
of a whole piece = of beaten work.
use them: for four purposes: (1) assembly; (2) journeying; (3) for war; (4) for the feasts.
assembly = whole congregation: i e. in its civil character.
3 door = entrance.
tabernacle of the congregation = tent of meeting. Ap. 40.
5 blow. Heb. *teru'ah* = a prolonged blowing.
7 congregation = assembly = a portion only, in its military character.
8 sons. Cp. Lev. 1. 5.
9 God. Heb. Elohim. Ap. 4.

1490 10 Also in the day of your gladness, and in your °solemn days, and in the beginnings of your months, ye shall blow with the trumpets over your burnt offerings, and over the sacrifices of your peace offerings; that they may be to you for a memorial before your God: I *am* [1]the LORD your [9]God."

K[1] (p. 193) 20th Ziph 11 And it came to pass on the °twentieth *day* of the second month, in the second year, that the cloud was taken up from off the °tabernacle of the testimony.

I[2] 12 And the °children of Israel °took their journeys out of the wilderness of Sinai; and the cloud rested in the wilderness of Paran.

13 And they first took their journey according to the °commandment of [1]the LORD by the hand of Moses.

14 In °the first *place* went the standard of the °camp of the [12]children of Judah according to their armies: and over his host *was* °Nahshon the son of Amminadab.

15 And over the host of the tribe of the [12]children of Issachar *was* Nethaneel the son of Zuar.

16 And over the host of the tribe of the [12]children of Zebulun *was* Eliab the son of Helon.

K[2] 17 And the [11]tabernacle was taken down; and the sons of Gershon and the sons of Merari set forward, bearing the [11]tabernacle.

I[3] 18 And the standard of the camp of Reuben set forward according to their armies: and over his host *was* Elizur the son of Shedeur.

19 And over the host of the tribe of the [12]children of Simeon *was* Shelumiel the son of Zurishaddai.

20 And over the host of the tribe of the [12]children of Gad *was* Eliasaph the son of °Deuel.

21 And the Kohathites set forward, bearing the sanctuary: and °*the other* did set up the [11]tabernacle against they came.

22 And the standard of the camp of the [12]children of Ephraim set forward according to their armies: and over his host *was* Elishama the son of Ammihud.

23 And over the host of the tribe of the [12]children of Manasseh *was* Gamaliel the son of Pedahzur.

24 And over the host of the tribe of the [12]children of Benjamin *was* Abidan the son of Gideoni.

25 And the standard of the camp of the [12]children of Dan set forward, *which was* the rereward of all the camps throughout their hosts: and over his host *was* Ahiezer the son of Ammishaddai.

26 And over the host of the tribe of the [12]children of Asher *was* Pagiel the son of Ocran.

27 And over the host of the tribe of the [12]children of Naphtali *was* Ahira the son of Enan.

28 Thus *were* the journeyings of the [12]children of Israel according to their armies, when they set forward.

29 And Moses said unto Hobab, the son of °Raguel the Midianite, Moses' father in law, "We are journeying unto the place of which [1]the LORD said, I will give it you: come thou with us, and we will do thee good: for [1]the LORD hath spoken good concerning Israel."

30 And he said unto him, "I will not go; but I will depart to mine own land, and to my kindred."

31 And he said, "Leave us not, I pray thee; forasmuch as thou knowest how we are to encamp in the wilderness, and thou mayest be to us instead of eyes.

32 And it shall be, if thou go with us, yea, it shall be, that what goodness [1]the LORD shall do unto us, the same will we do unto thee."

33 And they departed from the °mount of [1]the LORD °three days' journey: and the ark of the covenant of [1]the LORD went before them in the three days' journey, to search out a resting place for them. 20 to 23 Ziph Sabb.

34 And the cloud of [1]the LORD *was* upon them by day, when they went out of the camp.

35 °And it came to pass, when the ark set forward, that Moses said, °"Rise up, [1]LORD, and let Thine enemies be scattered; and let them that hate Thee flee before Thee."

36 And when it rested, he said, °"Return, O [1]LORD, unto the many thousands of Israel."

10 solemn days = appointed seasons.

Between *vv.* 10 and 11 comes in the account of Jethro, Ex. 18. See Deut. 1. 7–14, where the choosing of judges takes place after Horeb, but is recorded in Ex. 18 before Horeb. See note on Ex. 18.

11 twentieth day, &c. See Ap. 50. vii. 3.

tabernacle = habitation. Heb. *mishkān*. Ap. 40.

12 children = sons.

took their journeys. Heb. idiom, "journeyed for their journeyings" = set forward. On 20th of Ziph, 1490, and ended 10th Abib 1451. Lasted 38 years and 15 days.

13 commandment. Heb. mouth. Fig. *Metonymy* (of Cause), Ap. 6; "mouth" put for what is spoken by it.

14 the first place. For the order of the twelve tribes, see Ap. 45.

camp. Note distinction between "camp" and "host". Cp. 2. 3.

Nahshon. Cp. 1. 7; 2. 3.

20 Deuel, called also Reuel, 2. 14.

21 the other: i.e. the Gershonites and Merarites. See *v.* 17.

29 Raguel, called also Reuel (Ex. 2. 18).

33 mount of the LORD = mountain of Jehovah: because His glory had there been revealed.

three days. From 20–23 Ziph. Ap. 50. VII. 3.

34 Read this verse after *v.* 36. See following note.

35, 36. These two verses are marked Heb. MSS. by "inverted *Nūns*", i.e. the Heb. letter נ (*n*) inverted and used as brackets, to show that *vv.* 35 and 36 are thus enclosed to show that *v.* 34 should follow *v.* 36.

This is shown by the Structure:—

33 | The setting forth of the ark.
35 | "Rise up, O Jehovah" } Words spoken.
36 | "Return, O Jehovah" }
34 | The setting forth of the cloud.

There are eight of these inverted *nūns*. See notes on Ps. 107. 23–28.

Rise up. A beautiful prayer. Cp. Ps. 3. 7; 7. 6; 10. 12; 17. 13; 44. 26; 68. 1.

36 Return. Either, Return, O Jehovah; or, Cause to return. Cp. Deut. 30. 3. Ps. 14. 7; 126. 1. The former better. Cp. Ex. 33. 14–16.

u **11** And *when* the People °complained, °it
(p. 195) displeased °the LORD: and °the LORD
1490 heard *it;* and His anger was kindled;
v and °the fire of °the LORD burnt among them,
and consumed *them that were* in the uttermost
parts of the camp.
2 And the People cried unto Moses; and
when Moses prayed unto [1]the LORD, the fire
was quenched.
3 And °he called the name of °the place
°Taberah: because the fire of [1]the LORD
burnt among them.
w[1] y[1] 4 And the mixt °multitude that *was* among
them °fell a lusting: and the °children of
Israel also wept again, and said, °"Who
shall give us flesh to eat?
5 We remember °the fish, which we did eat
in Egypt °freely; the cucumbers, °and the
melons, °and the leeks, °and the onions, °and
the garlick:
6 But now °our soul *is* dried away: *there is*
nothing at all, beside this manna, *before* our
eyes."
7 And the °manna *was* as coriander seed,
and the °colour thereof as the °colour of
bdellium.
8 *And* the People went about, and gathered
it, and ground *it* in mills, or beat *it* in a
mortar, and baked *it* in pans, and made cakes
of it: and the taste of it was as the taste of
fresh oil.
9 And when the °dew fell upon the camp in
the night, the manna fell upon it.
z[1] 10 Then Moses heard the People weep
throughout their families, every °man in the
°door of his tent: and the anger of [1]the LORD
was kindled greatly; °Moses also was displeased.
11 And Moses said unto [1]the LORD,
°"Wherefore hast Thou afflicted Thy servant? and °wherefore have I not found
favour in Thy sight, that Thou layest the
burden of all this People upon me?
12 Have I conceived all this People? have I
begotten them, that Thou shouldest say unto
me, 'Carry them in thy °bosom,' °as a nursing
father beareth the sucking child, unto the land
which Thou swarest unto their fathers?
13 °Whence should I have flesh to give unto
all this People? for they weep unto me, saying, 'Give us flesh, that we may eat.'
14 I am not able to bear all this People alone,
because °*it is* too heavy for me.
15 And if Thou deal thus with me, kill me,
I pray Thee, out of hand, if I have found
favour in Thy sight; and let me not see °my
°wretchedness."
x[1] 16 And [1]the LORD °said unto Moses, "Gather
unto me seventy [10]men of the elders of Israel,
whom thou knowest °to be the elders of the
People, and officers over them; and bring them

11. 1—25. 18 (**B**², p. 176). EVENTS AND LAWS.
(*Repeated Alternation.*)

B² | L¹ | 11. 1—14. 45. Events—Murmurings and journeyings.
M¹ | 15. 1-41. Laws for the People.
L² | 16. 1—17. 13. Events—Rebellion of Korah.
M² | 18. 1—19. 22. Laws for priests and People.
L³ | 20. 1—25. 18. Events—Journeyings and murmurings.

11. 1—14. 45 (L¹, above). EVENTS.

L¹ | N¹ | 11. 1—12. 16. Murmurings.
N² | 13. 1—14. 45. The spies.

11. 1—12. 16 (N¹, above). MURMURINGS AND JOURNEYINGS (*Alternation*).

N¹ | r | 11. 1-34. Murmurings of People.
s | 11. 35. To Hazeroth.
r | 12. 1-15. Murmurings of Miriam and Aaron.
s | 12. 16. To Paran.

11. 1—34 (r. above). MURMURINGS OF PEOPLE.
(*Alternation.*)

r | u | 1-. Complaint.
v | -1-3. Plague—Taberah.
u | 4-33-. Murmuring.
v. | -33, 34. Plague—Kibroth-hattaavah.

1 complained. Heb. were as complainers, Ps. 78. 19. In this word another inverted *nūn* (נ, *n*), to mark the fact of the People's turning back in their hearts. See note on 10. 35.
it displeased the LORD. Heb. "was evil in the ears of Jehovah". Some codices, with Onk., Jon., Sept., and Syr., read "eyes" instead of "ears".
the LORD. Heb. Jehovah. Ap. 4. II.
the fire. Those before the Law not punished, Ex. 14. 11-15; 15. 24-26; 16. 2-4, 9, 20, 27, 28; 17. 2-4. Punished after Law given. Ex. 32. 27-35. Cp. Rom. 4. 15.
3 he called: i. e. Moses called.
the place = that place.
Taberah. Heb. "burning".

4-34 (*u*, p. 195). MURMURING AND PLAGUE.
(*Repeated Alternation.*)

u | w¹ | y¹ | 4-9. Flesh: lusting for it.
z¹ | 10-15. Complaint of Moses.
x¹ | 16, 17. Elders. Command.
w² | y² | 18-20. Flesh: promise of it.
z² | 21-23. Complaint of Moses.
x² | 24-30. Elders. Obedience.
v | w³ | y³ | 31-32. Flesh: given.
z³ | 33. Wrath of Jehovah.

4 multitude = camp followers. See Ex. 12. 38.
fell a lusting. Heb. Fig. *Polyptōton.* Ap. 6. = "lusted a lusting", emphatic for lusted exceedingly. Ps. 106. 14; 78. 18-20.
children = sons.
Who shall give? Fig. *Erotēsis* (Ap. 6).
5 the fish. Six items given of Egypt's food: seven of Canaan's, in Deut. 8. 8. See Ap. 10.
freely = gratuitously.
and. Note Fig. *Polysyndeton* in this verse (Ap. 6), to emphasise the six items. See *v.* 8.
6 our soul is. Heb. *nephesh* = we [are]. Ap. 13.
7 manna. Cp. John 6. 31-33. 1 Cor. 10. 3.
colour. Heb. "eye", put by Fig. *Metonymy* (of Adjunct), Ap. 6, for that which it distinguishes. Ex. 16. 14, 31.

9 dew fell. Manna between the two dews, cp. Ex. 16. 13, 14. **10 man.** Heb. *'ish.* Ap. 14. ii. **door** = entrance. **Moses also was displeased** = it was evil in Moses' eyes, as in *v.* 1. **11 Wherefore, &c.** Fig. *Erotēsis.* Ap. 6. **12 bosom.** Fig. *Anthropopatheia.* Ap. 6. **as** = even as. **13 Whence, &c.** Fig. *Erotēsis.* Ap. 6. **14 it is** = the burden is. The *Ellipsis* to be supplied according to Ap. 6. II. 4. **15 my wretchedness.** Should be "thy evil", evil being put by Fig. *Metonymy* (of Cause), Ap. 6. One of the eighteen emendations of the Sopherim. See Ap. 33. **wretchedness.** Heb. *rā'a'.* See Ap. 44. viii., put by Fig. *Metonymy* (of Cause), Ap. 6, for punishment due, see above. **16 said.** See note on 3. 40. **to be** = "that [they] be".

1490 unto the °tabernacle of the congregation, that they may stand there with thee.

17 And I will come down and talk with thee there: and I will °take of the °spirit which *is* upon thee, and will put *it* upon them; and they shall bear the burden of the People with thee, that thou bear *it* not thyself alone.

y[2] (p. 195) 18 And say thou unto the People, °'Sanctify yourselves against to morrow, and ye shall eat flesh: for ye have wept in the ears of [1]the LORD, saying, 'Who shall give us flesh to eat? for *it was* well with us in Egypt:' therefore [1]the LORD will give you flesh, and ye shall eat.

19 Ye shall not eat one day, °nor two days, nor five days, neither ten days, nor twenty days;

20 *But* even a °whole month, until it come out at your nostrils, and it be loathsome unto you: because that ye have despised [1]the LORD Which *is* among you, and have wept before Him, saying, 'Why came we forth out of Egypt?'''

z[2] 21 And Moses said, "The People, among whom I *am, are* six hundred thousand footmen; and Thou hast said, I will give °them flesh, that they may eat a whole month.

22 Shall the flocks and the herds be slain for them, to suffice them? or shall all the fish of the sea be gathered together for them, to suffice them?"

23 And [1]the LORD [16]said unto Moses, °"Is [1]the LORD'S °hand waxed short? thou shalt see now whether My word shall come to pass unto thee or not."

x[2] 24 And Moses went out, and told the People the words of [1]the LORD, and gathered the seventy [10]men of the elders of the °People, and set them round about the °tabernacle.

25 And [1]the LORD came down in a cloud, and °spake unto him, and [17]took of the [17]spirit that *was* upon him, and gave *it* unto the seventy elders: and it came to pass, *that*, when the [17]spirit rested upon them, they prophesied, and °did not cease.

26 But there remained two *of the* °men in the camp, the name of the one *was* Eldad, and the name of the other Medad: and the [17]spirit rested upon them; and they *were* of °them that were °written, but °went not out unto the [24]tabernacle: and they prophesied °in the camp.

27 And there ran °a young man, and told Moses, and said, "Eldad and Medad do prophesy in the camp."

28 And Joshua the son of Nun, the servant of Moses, *one* of his young men, answered and said, "My lord Moses, forbid them."

29 And Moses said unto him, °"Enviest thou for my sake? °would God that all [1]the LORD'S people were prophets, *and* that [1]the LORD would °put His [17]spirit upon them!"

30 And Moses gat him into the camp, he and the elders of Israel.

y[3] 31 And there went forth a °wind from [1]the LORD, and brought quails from the sea, and let *them* °fall by the camp, as it were °a day's journey on this side, and as it were °a day's journey on the other side, round about the camp, and as it were two °cubits °*high* upon the face of the earth.

32 And the People stood up all that day, and all *that* night, and all the next day, and they gathered the quails: he that gathered least gathered ten °homers: and they spread *them* all abroad for themselves round about the camp.

33 And while the °flesh *was* yet between their teeth, ere it was chewed, the wrath of [1]the LORD was kindled against the People, z[3]
and [1]the LORD smote the People with a very great plague. v

34 And he called the name of that place °Kibroth-hattaavah: because there they buried the People that lusted.

35 *And* the People journeyed from Kibroth-hattaavah unto Hazeroth; and abode at Hazeroth. s

tabernacle = tent. Heb. *'ohel.* Ap. 40.

17 take of = withdraw.

spirit. Heb. *rūach,* spirit, put by Fig. *Metonymy* (of Cause), Ap. 6, for the gifts and manifestations of the Holy Spirit. Cp. 1 Cor. 12. 4. See Ap. 9.

18 sanctify = separate. See note on "holy". Ex. 3. 5.

19 nor. Fig. *Paradiastolē,* Ap. 6, for emphasis.

20 whole month = a month of days.

21 them. Some codices have a reading called *Sevīr* (Ap. 34), which reads "unto you".

23 Is . . . ? &c. Fig. *Erotēsis.* Ap. 6.

hand. Put by Fig. *Metonymy* (of Cause), Ap. 6, for power exercised by it.

24 People. Some codices, with Jon. and Vulg., read "Israel".

tabernacle. Heb. *'ōhel,* tent. See Ap. 40.

25 spake. See note on 1. 1.

did not cease. So the Vulg.; but Heb. = "did not add" (so Sept. and Syr.), i. e. did not add any more, or again, after that day. Cp. Ex. 11. 6. Deut. 5. 22. Job. 38. 11. 1 Sam. 19. 24.

26 men. Heb. pl. of *'īsh* or *'enōsh.* Ap. 14.

them = the seventy.

written = enrolled. See note on Ex. 17. 14.

went not out. Cp. 1 Sam. 10. 22.

in the camp. Cp. Ps. 139. 7.

27 a. Heb. the, viz. the young man, to be described later.

29 Enviest thou . . . ? Fig. *Erotēsis.* Ap. 6. Art thou jealous for me?

would God. "God" should be in italics. Fig. *Œonismos.* Ap. 6.

put His spirit. This is the definition of a true prophet. Cp. *v.* 17, and 12. 6.

31 wind. Heb. *rūach.* Ap. 9.

fall. Cp. Ps. 78. 27, 28.

a day's journey. See Ap. 51. III. 4.

cubits. See Ap. 51. III. 2.

high upon. Heb. = "above"; i.e. "[flying] above", so that they could be easily caught. It does not say "deep".

32 homers. See Lev. 27. 16, and Ap. 51. III. 3.

33 flesh. Cp. Ps. 78. 27-31.

34 Kibroth-hattaavah. Heb. graves of lust.

r a b (p. 197) 1490 **12** And °Miriam and Aaron spake against Moses because of the °Ethiopian woman whom he had married: for he had married an Ethiopian woman.

2 And they said, °"Hath °the LORD indeed spoken only by Moses? hath He not spoken also by us?" And °the LORD heard *it*.

3 (Now the °man Moses *was* °very meek, above all the °men which *were* upon the face of the earth.)

c d e 4 And [2]the LORD °spake suddenly unto Moses, and unto Aaron, and unto Miriam, "Come out ye three unto the °tabernacle of the congregation." And they three came out.

5 And [2]the LORD came down in the pillar of the cloud, and stood *in* the °door of the [4]tabernacle, and called Aaron and Miriam: and they both came forth.

f 6 And °He °said, "Hear now My words: °If there be a prophet among you, *I* [2]the LORD will °make Myself known unto him in a vision, *and* will speak unto him in a dream.

7 °My servant Moses *is* °not so, °who *is* faithful in all Mine house.

8 With him will I speak °mouth to mouth, even °apparently, and °not in dark speeches; and the °similitude of [2]the LORD shall he behold: wherefore then were ye not afraid to speak °against [7]My servant Moses?"

e 9 And the anger of [2]the LORD was °kindled against them; and °He departed.

10 And the cloud departed from off the [4]tabernacle;

f and, behold, Miriam *became* °leprous, *white* as snow: and Aaron looked upon Miriam, and, °behold, *she was* leprous.

b 11 And Aaron said unto Moses, "Alas, my lord, I beseech thee, lay not the °sin upon us, wherein we have done foolishly, and wherein we have °sinned.

12 Let her not be as one °dead, of whom °the flesh is half consumed when he cometh out of °his mother's womb."

c 13 And Moses cried unto [2]the LORD, saying, "Heal her now, O °GOD, I beseech Thee."

14 And [2]the LORD [6]said unto Moses, "If her father had but °spit in her face, should she not be ashamed °seven days? let her be shut out from the camp seven days, and after that let her be °received in *again*."

15 And Miriam was shut out from the camp seven days: and the People journeyed not till Miriam was °brought in *again*.

s (p. 195) 16 And afterward the People removed from Hazeroth, and pitched in the wilderness of Paran.

P (p. 198) **13** And °the LORD °spake unto Moses, saying,

2 °"Send thou °men, that they may °search the land of °Canaan, which *I* give unto the

12. 1-15 (*r*, p. 195). MURMURINGS OF MIRIAM AND AARON (*Alternation*).

r | a | b | 1-3. Murmuring.
    c | 4-10. Punishment inflicted.
  a | *b* | 11, 12. Confession.
    c | 13-15. Punishment removed.

1 Miriam. Named first to show she was first in the rebellion. See *v.* 10. Cp. Gen. 3. 3.

Ethiopian=Zipporah. Heb. *Cushite.* Arabia was in the land of Cush: or Zipporah (Ex. 2. 21) may have been of Cushite nationality, though territorially a Midianite.

2 Hath . . .? Fig. *Erotēsis.* Ap. 6.

the LORD. Heb. Jehovah. Ap. 4.

3 man. Heb. *'īsh.* Ap. 14. ii.

verymeek=patient. First occurrence. Heb. *'ānāh*=to endure with submission what might be evaded: in contrast with Heb. *'ănī*=to bear what cannot be avoided.

men. Heb. *'adām.* Ap. 14.

4-10 (c, above). PUNISHMENT INFLICTED. (*Alternation.*)

c | d | e | 4, 5. Cloud. Descent.
      f | 6-8. Rebuke.
  d | *e* | 9, 10-. Cloud. Departure.
      f | -10. Judgment.

4 spake. See note on 1. 1.

tabernacle=tent. Heb. *'ohel.* See Ap. 40.

5 door=entrance.

6 He: i.e. Jehovah.

said. See note on 3. 40.

If there be=should there be; i.e. when ye have your prophet.

make Myself known. This also essential to a prophet. Cp. 11. 29.

7 My servant Moses. First occurrence. Occurs six times. See Num. 12. 7, 8. Josh. 1. 2, 7. 2 Kings 21. 8. Mal. 4. 4.

not so: i.e. much greater. Cp. *v.* 8.

who is faithful. Cp. Heb. 3. 2, or, Faithful is he, &c.

8 mouth to mouth. Cp. Gen. 45. 12. 2 John 12. 3 John 14. See also Ex. 33. 11. Deut. 34. 10. Fig. *Anthropopatheia.* Ap. 6. **apparently**=plainly.

not, &c.=Fig. *Pleonasm.* Ap. 6.

similitude: i.e. likeness or image. This must be understood in harmony with Ex. 33. 20, 23. Cp. Deut. 4. 12, 15. John 1. 18. 1 Tim. 6. 16. Cp. Col. 1. 15.

against, &c. Heb. "against my servant, against Moses." Cp. idiom in Gen. 21. 10 and note.

9 kindled: with instant result.

He: i.e. Jehovah.

10 leprous. See note on Ex. 4. 6.

behold. Fig. *Asterismos.* Ap. 6. ="there she was—leprous!" abruptness of language reveals the excitement produced.

11 sin . . . sinned. Heb. *chāṭ'ā.* Ap. 44. i.

12 dead=stillborn.

the flesh. The Primitive Text read "our flesh". This is one of the eighteen emendations of the Sopherim (see Ap. 33), to avoid what was supposed to be derogatory to Aaron.

his mother's. The Primitive Text read "our mother's" (see above note): thus it is made impersonal.

13 GOD=El.=God, the mighty God. See Ap. 4. iv.

spit in her face=treat with contempt: so the idiom is used in Syr. and Arabic to-day. Heb. "had spitted a spitting." Fig. *Polyptōton* (Ap. 6), for emphasis. Cp. Job 30. 10.

seven days. Cp. Lev. 13. 4, 5, 21, 26.

received in. *Homonym 'āsaph* (1) to heal or recover, here, 2 Kings 5. 6. Ps. 27. 10; (2) to snatch away or destroy, Ps. 26. 9. Jer. 16. 5. **15 brought**=received, *v.* 14.

13. 1—14. 45 [For Structures see next page].

1 the LORD. Heb. Jehovah. Ap. 4. **spake.** See note on 1. 1. **2 Send thou.** This was spoken in consequence of People's request. Cp. Deut. 1. 19-22, and "we will" of *v.* 22. This was walking by "sight." **men.** Heb. pl. of *'īsh* or *'enōsh.* Ap. 14. ii. **search,** for Jehovah had told them about it. See Deut. 8. 7-9. Cp. 1 Sam. 8. 6, 22, and Hos. 13. 11. Jehovah already espied it. Ezek. 20. 6. **Canaan.** Cp. Deut. 7. 1. The land of the seven mighty nations. See App. 23 and 25.

1490 °children of Israel: of every tribe of their fathers shall ye send a °man, every one a °ruler among them."

3 And Moses °by the °commandment of [1] the LORD sent them from the wilderness of Paran: all those men *were* °heads of the [2] children of Israel.

Q a (p. 198) 4 And these *were* their °names: of the tribe of Reuben, Shammua the son of Zaccur.

5 Of the tribe of Simeon, Shaphat the son of Hori.

6 Of the tribe of Judah, Caleb the son of Jephunneh.

7 Of the tribe of Issachar, Igal the son of Joseph.

8 Of the tribe of Ephraim, °Oshea the son of °Nun.

9 Of the tribe of Benjamin, Palti the son of Raphu.

10 Of the tribe of Zebulun, Gaddiel the son of Sodi.

11 Of the tribe of Joseph, *namely,* of the tribe of Manasseh, Gaddi the son of Susi.

12 Of the tribe of Dan, Ammiel the son of Gemalli.

13 Of the tribe of Asher, °Sethur the son of Michael.

14 Of the tribe of Naphtali, Nahbi the son of Vophsi.

15 Of the tribe of Gad, Geuel the son of Machi.

16 These *are* the °names of the men which Moses sent to spy out the land. And Moses called [8] Oshea the son of Nun °Jehoshua.

b 17 And Moses sent them to spy out the land of Canaan, and said unto them, "Get you up this *way* °southward, and go up into the mountain:

18 And see the land, what it *is;* and the people that dwelleth therein, whether they *be* strong or weak, few or many;

19 And what the land *is* that they dwell in, whether it *be* good or bad; and what cities *they be* that they dwell in, whether in °tents, or in strong holds;

20 And what the land *is,* whether it *be* fat or lean, whether there be wood therein, or not. And be ye of good courage, and bring of the fruit of the land." Now the time *was* the time of the firstripe grapes.

Q a 21 So they °went up, and searched the land from the wilderness of Zin unto Rehob, as men come to Hamath.

22 And they ascended by the °south, and came unto °Hebron; where °Ahiman, Sheshai, and Talmai, the °children of Anak, *were.* (Now Hebron was °built °seven years before °Zoan in Egypt.)

23 °And they came unto the brook of Eshcol, and cut down from thence a branch with one cluster of °grapes, °and they bare it between two upon a staff; °and *they brought* of the °pomegranates, °and of the °figs.

24 The place was called the °brook °Eshcol, because of the °cluster of grapes which the [2] children of Israel cut down from thence.

13. 1—14. 45 (N^2, p. 195). THE SPIES (*Division*).

N^2 | O^1 | 13. 1—14. 38. The Expedition.
| O^2 | 14. 39-45. The Episode.

13. 1—14. 38 (O^1, above). THE EXPEDITION.
(*Introversion and Alternation.*)

O^1 | P | 13. 1-3. Command of Jehovah.
Q | a | 13. 4-16. Selection of spies.
b | 13. 17-20. Directions to spies.
Q | *a* | 13. 21-25. Searching of the spies.
b | 13. 26—14. 10-. Report and reception.
P | 14. -10-38. Provocation of Jehovah.

children = sons.

man. Heb. *'ish.* See Ap. 14. ii. = a great or chief man. Cp. Isa. 5. 15.

ruler: or prince. This made the rebellion so serious.

3 by the commandment of the LORD. Cp. Deut. 1. 19-22.

commandment. Heb. "mouth". Fig. *Metonymy* (of Cause), Ap. 6, put for what is spoken by the mouth.

heads = captains over thousands. Ex. 18. 25.

4 names. For the order of the tribes here, see Ap. 45.

8 Oshea = salvation. Cp. *v.* 16. See note on *v.* 16.

Nun. 1 Chron. 7. 27, "Non".

13 Sethur = hidden, or mystical: by Gematria = 666 (Ap. 10). Probably marking the ringleader of the Provocation.

16 names. Levi not named. No inheritance in the land.

Jehoshua. Name occurs over 250 times; see the first, Ex. 17. 9. Sometimes Jeshua (Neh. 8. 17). Greek, *Jesus* (Matt. 1. 21. Acts 7. 45. Heb. 4. 8). In Deut. 32. 44 called Hoshea again: *Hōshea* = saviour, or salvation. *Je,* prefixed = he by whom Jehovah will save.

17 southward. For first nine miles, on account of the roads, then by the mountain passes eastward.

19 tents = camps.

21 went up. In the month Ab (our July).

22 south = the *Negeb.* Cp. Gen. 12. 9; 13. 1.

Hebron. Ancient name, Kirjath-arba (or stronghold of Arba) (Gen. 23. 2, 19), because built by Anak and the sons of Arba. Josh. 14. 15; 15. 13. The Tel-el-Amarna Tablets show that certain bands of Hittite condottieri are called "*Khabiri*", or "allies" (hence the name Hebron, which means "confederacy", or friendship, which is not met with till Ramases II), captured Kirjath-Arba. Ebed-Tob, king of Jerusalem (see note on Gen. 14. 18), in his letters to Pharaoh frequently mentions these *Khabiri* (or confederates of Amorites and Hittites). God's confederacy with His people in Christ was "*before* the foundation of the world". Before Zoan the city of the wise was known.

Ahiman. Driven out by Caleb. Josh. 15. 13, 14. Slain by Judah. Judg. 1. 10.

children of Anak = home-born persons: usually of slaves. These were the result of a second irruption of the fallen angels. See Gen. 6. 4, "after that". These are called "Nephilim" in *v.* 33. See Ap. 23 and 25. The name "Anak" occurs here, and *vv.* 28, 33. Deut. 9. 2. Josh. 15. 14.

built: i.e. rebuilt (*bānāh* frequently has this meaning). Cp. Josh. 6. 26. 1 Kings 16. 34. 2 Kings 14. 22. Isa. 44. 28. Amos 9. 14.

seven years before Zoan in Egypt. Built by the first kings of the nineteenth dynasty (see Ap. 37). Ramases II made it his capital, cp. Isa. 30. 4 (and is the first to mention Hebron). Zoan was the scene of the Exodus (see Ps. 78. 12, 13), and "the house of bondage"

Zoan. See note on Ex. 1. 10.

23 And. Note the Fig. *Polysyndeton* (Ap. 6), calling attention to each of the three items.

grapes, &c. No mere accident that these three were brought. These symbolical of the "fruit" of our Land, even of Him Who is the true Vine. *He* comes *first.*

pomegranates. His *worship* comes next (largely used symbolically in tabernacle and temple, see Ex. 27, 28, and 29 and 2 Chron. 3 and 4). **figs.** The common support of life in the East, next to bread. These symbolise the common duties of life. (The grapes and pomegranates its luxuries and spiritual privileges).

24 brook: or valley. **Eshcol** = cluster. **cluster.** Heb. *'eshcōl.*

1490 25 And they returned from searching of the land after °forty days.

b c d[1] (p. 199) 26 And they went and came to Moses, and to Aaron, and to all the congregation of the [2]children of Israel, unto the wilderness of Paran, to °Kadesh; and brought back word unto them, and unto all the congregation, and shewed them the fruit of the land.

27 And they told him, and said, "We came unto the land whither thou sentest us, and surely it floweth with milk and honey; and this *is* the fruit of it.

28 °Nevertheless the people *be* strong that dwell in the land, and the cities *are* walled, *and* °very great: and moreover °we saw the [22]children of Anak there.

29 The Amalekites dwell in the land of the south: and the Hittites, and the Jebusites, and the Amorites, dwell in the mountains: and the Canaanites dwell by the sea, and by the coast of Jordan."

e[1] 30 And °Caleb °stilled the People before Moses, and said, "Let us go up at once, and possess it; for we are °well able to overcome it."

d[2] 31 But the °men that went up with him said, "We be °not able to go up against the people; for °they *are* stronger than we."

32 And they °brought up an evil report of the land which they had searched unto the [2]children of Israel, saying, "The land, through which we have gone to search it, *is* a land that eateth up the inhabitants thereof; and all the people that °we saw in it *are* men of a great stature.

33 And there [32]we saw the °giants, the sons of Anak, *which come* of the °giants: and we were in our own °sight as °grasshoppers, and so we were in their sight."

d[3] **14** And all the congregation °lifted up their voice, and °cried; and the People wept that night.

2 And all the °children of Israel murmured against Moses and against Aaron: and the whole congregation said unto them, °"Would God that we had died in the land of Egypt! or °would God we had died in this wilderness!

3 And °wherefore hath °the LORD brought us unto this land, to fall by the sword, that our wives and our children should be a prey? °were it not better for us to return into Egypt?"

4 And they said one to another, "Let us make a °captain, and let us return into Egypt."

5 Then Moses and Aaron fell on their faces before all the assembly of the congregation of the [2]children of Israel.

c[2] 6 And °Joshua the son of Nun, and Caleb the son of Jephunneh, *which were* of them that searched the land, rent their clothes:

7 And they spake unto all the company of the [2]children of Israel, saying, "The land, which we passed through to search it, *is* an °exceeding good land.

8 °If [3]the LORD delight in us, then He will bring us into this land, and give it us; a land which floweth with milk and honey.

9 Only rebel not ye against [3]the LORD, neither fear ye the people of the land; for they *are* bread for us: their °defence is departed from them, and [3]the LORD *is* with us: fear them not."

10 But all the congregation bade stone them with stones. d[4]

25 **forty.** The number of Probation. See Ap. 10. At the end of Elul (our August), exactly six months from setting up of the Tabernacle. See Ap. 50. VII. 3.

13. 26—14. 10- (*b*, p. 198). REPORT AND RECEPTION (*Introversion*).

b | c | d[1] | 13. 26-29. Evil report } Report
  e[1] | 13. 30. Action of Caleb
  d[2] | 13. 31-33. Evil report
c | d[3] | 14. 1-5. The congregation } Reception.
  e[2] | 14. 6-9. Joshua and Caleb
  d[4] | 14. 10-. The congregation

26 **Kadesh** = Kadesh-barnea. Deut. 1. 19.

28 **Nevertheless.** In spite of the evidence produced. This is the conclusion of *sight*, not of faith. Note the words "we saw", *vv.* 28, 32, 33.

very great. Great in size as well as in wickedness, abnormal, superhuman. See Ap. 23 and 25.

we saw. This was "walking by sight, not by faith", 2 Cor. 5. 7.

30 **Caleb** = whole-hearted.

stilled = silenced.

well able = the conclusion of faith.

31 **men.** Heb. pl. of *'ish* or *'enōsh*. Ap. 14. ii.

not able = the conclusion of sight.

they are stronger than we = the conclusion of unbelief, which always leaves God out.

32 **brought up an evil report** = sent forth a slander. Cp. 14. 37.

we saw. The language of unbelief.

33 **giants.** Heb. *nephilim*. Those mentioned in Gen. 6. 4 were all destroyed in the Flood; these came from a second irruption of fallen angels, "after that": i. e. after "those days" = the days of Noah. See Gen. 6. 4, and Ap. 23 and 25. See note on *v.* 22.

sight. It is all "sight" where there is no faith 2 Cor. 5. 7.

grasshoppers: or locusts.

14. **1** **lifted up their voice.** Heb. idiom "lifted up and gave their voice". Gen. 21. 16. Ps. 18. 13. Jer. 2. 15. Ps. 104. 12; 77. 18. Hab. 3. 10.

cried = cried aloud. What a contrast to Ex. 15. 1, "Then sang". Cp. Ex. 15. 13-17, and note 1 Cor. 10. 11.

2 **children** = sons.

Would God. Fig. *Œonismus*. Ap. 6.

3 **wherefore.** Fig. *Erotēsis*. Ap. 6.

the LORD. Heb. Jehovah. Ap. 4.

were it not . . . ? Fig. *Erotēsis*. Ap. 6.

4 **captain.** At Horeb they made a "calf"; at Kadesh they would make a "captain". Two notable occasions.

6 **Joshua . . . and Caleb.** Only *two* out of twelve; only two out of the whole congregation. Let us heed the lesson, and take courage. 1 Cor. 10. 11.

7 **exceeding.** Heb. "very, very". Fig. *Epizeuxis*. Ap. 6.

8 **If the LORD delight in us.** This is the secret of all blessing. Deut. 10. 15. 2 Sam. 15. 25, 26; 22. 20. 1 Kings 10. 9. Ps. 22. 8; 147. 10, 11. Isa. 62. 4.

9 **defence.** Heb. = shadow. Note Fig. *Ellipsis* (Ap. 6. i. 2). Lit. "they [are] like our bread (= manna), their shadow hath turned aside from off them". The manna when out of the shade melted, though hard (cp. 11. 8 and Ex. 16. 21): so the hearts of their enemies would melt away, not having Jehovah for their shadow, or defence. Cp. Ex. 15. 15. Josh. 2. 9, 11. Isa. 13. 7; 19. 1. Ezek. 21. 7.

P R f (p. 200) 1490 And the glory of [3]the LORD appeared in the °tabernacle of the congregation before all the [2]children of Israel.

11 And [3]the LORD °said unto Moses, °"How long will this People provoke Me? and °how long will it be ere they believe Me, for all the signs which I have shewed among them?

g 12 I will smite them with the pestilence, and disinherit them, and will make of thee a greater nation and mightier than they."

S h 13 And Moses said unto [3]the LORD, "Then the Egyptians shall hear *it*, (for Thou broughtest up this People in Thy might °from among them;)

14 And they will tell *it* to the inhabitants of this land: *for* they have heard that Thou [3]LORD *art* among this People, that Thou [3]LORD art seen °face to face, and *that* °Thy cloud standeth over them, and *that* Thou goest before them, by day time in a pillar of a cloud, and in a pillar of fire by night.

15 Now *if* Thou shalt kill *all* this People as one °man, then the nations which have heard the fame of Thee will speak, saying,

16 'Because [3]the LORD was not able to bring this People into the land which He sware unto them, therefore He hath slain them in the wilderness.'

17 And now, I beseech Thee, let the power of °my LORD* be great, according as Thou hast spoken, saying,

18 °'The LORD *is* longsuffering, and of great °mercy, forgiving °iniquity and °transgression, and by no means clearing *the guilty*, visiting the °iniquity of the fathers upon the [2]children unto the third and fourth *generation*.'

19 Pardon, I beseech Thee, the [18]iniquity of this People according unto the greatness of Thy [18]mercy, and as Thou hast forgiven this people, from Egypt even until now."

i 20 And [3]the LORD said, "I have pardoned according to thy word:

h 21 But *as* truly °*as* I live, °all the earth shall be filled with the glory of [3]the LORD.

22 Because all those °men which have seen My glory, and My miracles, which I did in Egypt and in the wilderness, and have tempted Me now these °ten times, and have not hearkened to My voice;

23 Surely they shall not see the land which I sware unto their fathers, neither shall any of them that provoked Me see it:

i 24 But My servant Caleb, because he had °another °spirit with him, and hath followed Me fully, him will I bring into the land whereinto he went; and his seed shall possess it."

25 (Now the Amalekites and the Canaanites dwelt in the valley.) "To morrow turn you, and get you into the wilderness by the way of the Red sea."

f 26 And [3]the LORD spake unto Moses and unto Aaron, saying,

27 °"How long °*shall I bear with* this evil congregation, which murmur against Me? I have heard the murmurings of the [2]children of Israel, which they murmur against Me.

g k m 28 Say unto them, '*As truly* [21]*as* I live, saith [3]the LORD, °as ye have spoken in Mine ears, °so will I do to you:

29 Your carcases shall fall in this wilderness;

and all that were °numbered of you, according n
to your whole number, from twenty years old and upward, which have murmured against Me,

---

-10-38 (*P*, p. 198). PROVOCATION OF JEHOVAH. (*Introversion and Alternation.*)

P R | f | -10, 11. Reproach: "How long?"
  g | 12. Threatening. General.
   S | 13-25. Moses and Jehovah.
 R | *f* | 26, 27. Reproach: "How long?"
  g | 28-38. Threatening. Particular.

10 tabernacle = tent. Heb. *'ohel.* See Ap. 40.

11 said. See note on 3. 40.

How long . . . ? = to what *point.* Cp. *v.* 27. Fig. *Erotēsis.* Ap. 6.

13-25 (S, above). MOSES AND JEHOVAH (*Alternation.*)

S | h | 13-19. Intercession to enter land.
  i | 20. Exception. Pardon for the people.
 h | 21-23. Refusal. None of that generation to enter.
  i | 24. Exception. Entrance for Caleb and Joshua.

13 from among. Fig. *Pleonasm* (Ap. 6). = "out of the midst of".

14 face to face. Heb. eye to eye.

Thy cloud. Cp Ex. 13. 21.

15 man. Heb. *'īsh.* Ap. 14. ii.

17 my LORD = Jehovah. One of the 134 alterations of the Sopherim. See Ap. 32. Many codices, and first printed edition, read "Jehovah".

18 The LORD = Jehovah. Quoted from Ex. 34. 6; 20. 5 and 34. 7.

mercy = lovingkindness, or grace.

iniquity. Heb. *'āvāh.* Ap. 44. iv.

transgression. Heb. *pāsh'a.* Ap. 44. ix. Some codices, with Sam., Jon., and Sept., read "transgression and sin", as in Ex. 34. 7.

21 as I live. Heb. "assuredly I live; and all the earth", &c. Cp. Ezek. 18. 3; 20. 33. Rom. 14. 11.

all the earth. First occurrence of this expression. Cp. Isa. 6. 3; 11. 9. Ps. 72. 19. Hab. 2. 14. Note the unconditional covenant.

22 men. Heb. pl. of *'īsh* or *'enōsh.* Ap. 14.

ten times. Not a "round" number:—

(1) At Red Sea (Ex. 14. 11, 12).
(2) At Marah (Ex. 15. 23, 24).
(3) Wilderness of Sin (Ex. 16. 2).
(4, 5) Twice about manna (Ex. 16. 20, 27).
(6) At Rephidim (Ex. 17. 1-3).
(7) At Horeb (golden calf) (Ex. 32).
(8) At Taberah (Num. 11. 1).
(9) At Kibroth Hattaavah (Num. 11. 4).
(10) Here, at Kadesh (Num. 14. 2).

24 another = different. Cp. Phil. 3. 15, "otherwise". Cp. Eph. 4. 23.

spirit. Heb. *rūach.* Spirit put for motions of the mind and character (Ap. 9).

27 How long . . . ? = to what *time.* Cp. *v.* 11. Fig. *Erotēsis.* Ap. 6.

shall I bear with. Fig. *Ellipsis.* Ap. 6. ii. 2.

28-38 (*g*, above). THREATENING. (*Alternations.*)

g | k | m | 28, 29-. Fall in wilderness.
   n | -29. Age above twenty years.
    l | 30, 31. Exception—Caleb and Joshua.
 k | *m* | 32. Fall in wilderness.
   n | 33-37. Time—Forty years.
    l | 38. Exception—Joshua and Caleb.

28 as = according as . . . so will I do. Ps. 95. 11. Num. 26. 65; 32. 11. Deut. 1. 35. Heb. 3. 17, 18.

29 numbered. Cp. 1. 45 and 26. 63-65.

l (p. 200) 1490 30 Doubtless ye shall not come into the land, *concerning* which °I sware to make you dwell therein, save Caleb the son of Jephunneh, and Joshua the son of Nun.

31 But your little ones, which °ye said should be a prey, them will I bring in, and they shall °know the land which ye have despised.

m 32 But *as for* you, your carcases, they shall fall in this wilderness.

n From 15 Ab 1491 to 15 Abib 1451 33 And your [2]children shall °wander in the wilderness forty years, and bear your °whoredoms, until your carcases be wasted in the wilderness.

34 After the number of the days in which ye searched the land, *even* °forty days, °each day for a year, shall ye bear your [18]iniquities, *even* forty years, and ye shall know My °breach of promise.'

35 I [3]the LORD have °said, I will surely do it unto all this evil congregation, that are gathered together against Me: in this wilderness they shall be consumed, and there they °shall die."

36 And the °men, which Moses sent to search the land, who returned, and made all the congregation to murmur against him, by bringing up a slander upon the land,

37 Even those [36]men that did [32]bring up the evil report upon the land, died by the plague before [3]the LORD.

l 38 But Joshua the son of Nun, and Caleb the son of Jephunneh, *which were* of the men that went to search the land, lived *still*.

O² o (p. 201) 39 And Moses told these sayings unto all the [2]children of Israel: and the People mourned greatly.

p 27 Ab 1490 40 And they rose up early in the morning, and gat them up into the top of the mountain, saying, °"Lo, we *be here*, and will go up unto the place which [3]the LORD hath promised: for we have °sinned."

q 41 And Moses said, "Wherefore now do ye transgress the °commandment of [3]the LORD? but it shall not prosper.

42 Go not up, for [3]the LORD *is* not among you; that ye be not smitten before your enemies.

43 For the Amalekites and the Canaanites *are* there before you, and ye shall fall by the sword: because ye are turned away from [3]the LORD, therefore [3]the LORD will not be with you."

p 44 But they °presumed to go up unto the hill top: nevertheless the ark of the covenant of [3]the LORD, and Moses, departed not out of the camp.

o 45 Then the Amalekites came down, and the Canaanites which dwelt in that hill, and smote them, and discomfited them, *even* unto °Hormah.

M¹ r t 1490 1452 15 And °the LORD °spake unto Moses, saying,

2 "Speak unto the °children of Israel, and say unto them, 'When ye be come °into the land of your habitations, which I give unto you,

u w 3 And will make an °offering by fire unto [1]the LORD, a °burnt offering, or a °sacrifice in performing a vow, or in a °freewill offering,

30 I sware. Heb. I lifted up my hand. Fig. *Metonymy* (of Adjunct), Ap. 6, put for swearing. Cp. *v.* 21. Deut. 32. 40, &c.

31 ye said. *v.* 3. Cp. Deut. 1. 39.

know = get to know, and enjoy. Sept. = shall inherit.

33 wander = be wanderers.

whoredoms. Put by Fig. *Metonymy* (of Cause), Ap. 6, for the punishment they produced, all caused by idolatry. Cp. Jer. 3. 9. Ezek. 16. 15-17. Ex. 34. 15, 16. Lev. 17. 7.

34 forty days. See Ap. 10. The number of Probation. See also Ap. 50. VII. 2.

each day for a year. No universal law here: "day" means day, and "year" means year. See Ap. 11.

breach = "my breach of promise (cp. *vv.* 42 and 43) [with which ye charge me] meaneth". Cp. Deut. 31. 16, 17. Zech. 11. 10. Rom. 11. 22; also Job 33. 10.

35 said. See note on 3. 40. Said on 26 Ab (fifth month, second year). The whole period is contained in chs. 15—19; 33. 19-36, inclusive. See Ap. 50. VII. 3.

shall die. Aaron died on first day of fifth month of fortieth year, 20. 28; 33. 38. The second numbering took place after that.

36 men. Heb. pl. of *'īsh* or *'enōsh.* Ap. 14. These ten men died by a special plague at the time. Cp. 1 Chron. 13. 10. 2 Sam 6. 7. Cp. *v.* 37 here.

39-45 (O², p. 198). **THE EPISODE.**
(*Introversion.*)

O² o | 39. Mourning.
  p | 40. Presumption.
    q | 41-43. Prohibition.
  p | 44. Presumption.
o | 45. Discomfiture.

40 Lo. Fig. *Asterismos.* Ap. 6.

sinned. Heb. *chāṭā.* Ap. 44. i.

41 commandment. Heb. "mouth". Put by Fig. *Metonymy* (of Cause), Ap. 6, for the word spoken by it.

44 presumed to go up = were presumptuous to go up. Cp. idiom, 35. 31. Gen. 2. 3; 31. 27. Deut. 1. 42, 43.

45 Hormah = destruction.

15. 1-41 (M¹, p. 195). **LAWS FOR THE PEOPLE.**
(*Introversion.*)

M¹ r | 1-29. Laws *re* Offerings.
  s | 30, 31. Presumptuous sins. Cut off.
  s | 32-36. Presumptuous sin. Stoned.
r | 37-41. Laws *re* Dress.

1-29 (r, above). **LAWS *RE* OFFERINGS.**
(*Extended Alternation, and Introversion.*)

r t | 1, 2. Place. The land.
  u | w | 3. Purposes.
    x | 4-12. Offerings (Burnt).
      v | 13-16. Unity of law.
t | 17, 18. Place. The land.
  u | *x* | 19-21. Offerings (Meal).
    w | 22-28. Purpose.
      v | 29. Unity of law.

1 the LORD. Heb. Jehovah. Ap. 4.

spake. See note on 1. 1. **2 children** = sons.

into the land. Note that the turning away from the land does not affect Jehovah's purpose to bring them in.

3 offering. Heb. *'ishsheh.* Ap. 43. II. xi.

burnt offering. Heb. *'ōlah.* Ap. 43. II. ii.

sacrifice. Heb. *zebach.* Ap. 43. II. xii.

freewill offering. Heb. *nedābāh.* Ap. 43. II. vii.

or in your °solemn feasts, to make a °sweet savour unto [1]the LORD, of the herd, or of the flock:

x (p. 201) 4 Then shall he that °offereth his °offering unto [1]the LORD bring a meat offering of a °tenth deal of flour mingled with the fourth *part* of an °hin of oil.

5 And the fourth *part* of an [4]hin of wine for a drink offering shalt thou prepare with the burnt offering or °sacrifice, for one lamb.

6 Or for a ram, thou shalt prepare *for* a °meat offering two tenth deals of flour mingled with the third *part* of an [4]hin of oil.

7 And for a drink offering thou shalt °offer the third *part* of an [4]hin of wine, *for* a [3]sweet savour unto [1]the LORD.

8 And when thou preparest a bullock *for* a burnt offering, or *for* a sacrifice in performing a vow, or peace offerings unto [1]the LORD:

9 Then shall he bring with a bullock a meat offering of three [4]tenth deals of flour mingled with half an [4]hin of oil.

10 And thou shalt bring for a drink offering half an [4]hin of wine, *for* an [3]offering made by fire, of a [3]sweet savour unto [1]the LORD.

11 Thus shall it be done for one bullock, or for one ram, or for a lamb, or a kid.

12 According to the number that ye shall prepare, so shall ye do to every one according to their number.

v 13 All that are born of the country shall do these things after this manner, in offering an [3]offering made by fire, of a [3]sweet savour unto [1]the LORD.

14 And if a stranger sojourn with you, or whosoever *be* among you in your generations, and will °offer an [3]offering made by fire, of a [3]sweet savour unto [1]the LORD; °as ye do, so °he shall do.

15 One ordinance *shall be both* for you of the °congregation, and also for the stranger that sojourneth *with you,* an ordinance for ever in your generations: as ye *are,* so shall the stranger be before [1]the LORD.

16 One law and one °manner shall be for you, and for the stranger that sojourneth with you.' "

t 17 And [1]the LORD [1]spake unto Moses, saying,

18 "Speak unto the [2]children of Israel, and say unto them, 'When ye come into the land whither I bring you,

x 19 Then it shall be, that, when ye eat of the bread of the land, ye shall offer up an heave offering unto [1]the LORD.

20 Ye shall offer up a °cake of the first of your dough *for* an °heave offering: as *ye do* the heave offering of the threshingfloor, so shall ye heave it.

21 Of the first of your dough ye shall give unto [1]the LORD an heave offering in your °generations.

w 22 And if ye have erred, and not observed all these commandments, which [1]the LORD hath spoken unto Moses,

23 *Even* all that [1]the LORD hath commanded you by the hand of Moses, from the day that [1]the LORD commanded *Moses,* and henceforward among your generations;

24 Then it shall be, if *ought* be committed by ignorance without the knowledge of the congregation, that all the congregation shall [14]offer one young bullock for a burnt offering, for a [3]sweet savour unto [1]the LORD, with his meat offering, and his drink offering, according to the [16]manner, and one kid of the goats for a sin offering.

25 And the priest shall make an °atonement for all the congregation of the [2]children of Israel, and it shall be forgiven them; for it *is* ignorance: and they shall bring their [4]offering, a °sacrifice made by fire unto [1]the LORD, and their sin offering before [1]the LORD, for their ignorance:

26 And it shall be forgiven °all the congregation of the [2]children of Israel, and the stranger that sojourneth among them; seeing all the People *were* in ignorance.

27 And if any °soul °sin through ignorance, then he shall bring a she goat of the first year for a sin offering.

28 And the priest shall make an [25]atonement for the [27]soul that °sinneth ignorantly, when he [27]sinneth by ignorance before [1]the LORD, to make an [25]atonement for him; and it shall be forgiven him.

29 Ye shall have one law for him that °sinneth through ignorance, *both for* him that is born among the [2]children of Israel, and for the stranger that sojourneth among them. v

30 But the [27]soul that doeth *ought* °presumptuously, *whether he be* born in the land, or a stranger, the same reproacheth [1]the LORD; and that [27]soul shall be cut off from among his people. s

31 Because he hath despised the word of [1]the LORD, and hath broken His commandment, that [27]soul shall utterly be cut off; his °iniquity *shall be* upon him.' "

solemn feasts = appointed seasons.
sweet savour. See note on Lev. 1. 9.
4 offereth = bringeth near. Ap. 43. I. i.
offering = approach-offering. Ap. 43. II. i.
tenth deal. / **hin.** } See Ap. 51. III. 3.
5 sacrifice. Probably peace-offerings. Ap. 43. II. xii.
6 meat offering. Ap. 43. II. iii.
7 offer = bring near. Heb. *ḳārab.* Ap. 43. I. i.
14 offer = prepare. Heb. *'āsāh.* Ap. 43. I. iii.
as = according as. **he** = the stranger.
15 congregation = assembly.
16 manner. Heb. judgment, or ordinance.
20 cake = pierced cake.
heave offering. See note on Ex. 29. 27.
21 generations. Severus Codex reads this as singular. See Ap. 34.
25 atonement. See note on Ex. 29. 33.
sacrifice made by fire. Heb. *'ishsheh.* Ap. 43. II. xi.
26 all = the whole.
27 soul = person. Heb. *nephesh* See Ap. 13. Cp. *vv.* 28, 30.
sin. Heb. *chāṭ'ā.* Ap 44. i.
28 sinneth. Heb. *shāgag.* Ap. 44. xii.
29 sinneth. Heb. *'āsāh.* Ap. 44. ii.
30 presumptuously. Heb. with a high hand.
31 iniquity. Heb. *'āvāh.* Ap. 44. iv. Put here by Fig. *Metonymy* (of Cause), Ap. 6, for the punishment produced by it.

s y^1 (p. 203) 1490 1452 32 And ° while the [2] children of Israel were in the wilderness, they found a ° man ° that gathered sticks upon the sabbath day.

33 And they that found him gathering sticks brought him unto Moses and Aaron, and unto all the congregation.

34 And they put him in ward, because it was not ° declared ° what should be done to him.

y^2 35 And [1] the LORD ° said unto Moses, "The man shall be surely put to death: all the congregation shall stone him with stones without the camp."

36 And all the congregation brought him without the camp, and stoned him with stones, and he died; ° as [1] the LORD commanded Moses.

r (p. 201) 37 And [1] the LORD [1] spake unto Moses, saying,

38 "Speak unto the [2] children of Israel, and bid them that they make them ° fringes in the borders of their garments throughout their generations, and that they put upon the ° fringe of the borders a ribband of blue:

39 And it shall be unto you for a [38] fringe, that ye may look upon it, and remember all the commandments of [1] the LORD, and do them; and that ye seek not after your own heart and your own eyes, after which ye use to go a whoring:

40 That ye may remember, and do all My commandments, and be ° holy unto your ° God.

41 I *am* [1] the ° LORD your [40] God, which brought you out of the land of Egypt, to be your [40] God: I *am* the ° LORD your [40] God."

L^2 f l (p. 203) **16** ° Now ° Korah, the son of Izhar, the son of Kohath, the son of Levi, and Dathan and Abiram, the sons of Eliab, and On, the son of Peleth, ° sons of Reuben, took ° *men*:

2 And they rose up before Moses, with certain of the ° children of Israel, two hundred and fifty princes of the ° assembly, famous in the ° congregation, ° men of renown:

3 And they gathered themselves together against Moses and against Aaron, and said unto them, "*Ye take* too much upon you, seeing all the ° congregation *are* ° holy, every one of them, and ° the LORD *is* among them: wherefore then lift ye up yourselves above the [2] congregation of the LORD?"

m 4 And when Moses heard *it*, he fell upon his face:

n 5 And he spake unto Korah and unto all his company, saying, "Even to morrow [3] the LORD will shew who *are* His, and *who is* [3] holy; and will cause *him* to come near unto Him: even *him* whom He hath chosen will He cause to come near unto Him.

6 This do; Take you censers, Korah, and all his company;

7 And put fire therein, and put incense in them before [3] the LORD to morrow: and it shall be *that* the ° man whom [3] the LORD doth choose, he *shall be* [3] holy: *ye take* too much upon you, ye sons of Levi."

8 And Moses said unto Korah, "Hear, I pray you, ye sons of Levi:

9 ° *Seemeth it but* a small thing unto you,

32-36 (*s*, p. 201). PRESUMPTUOUS SIN.
(*Division.*)

s | y^1 | 32-34. The sin.
  | y^2 | 35, 36. The punishment.

32 while. Only three events recorded during the Punishment wanderings: (1) The Sabbath breaker (15. 32-36); (2) The usurpation of Korah (16. 1—17. 13); and (3) The red heifer (19. 1-10).

man. Heb. *'ish.* Ap. 14. ii.

that gathered = gathering.

34 declared. Heb. *pārash,* make known. This is the meaning of Gr. *sunkrino,* rendered "comparing" in 1 Cor. 2. 13.

what should be done to him: i. e. what death he should die. It had been made known that he was to die, but not in what manner. Ex. 31. 15; 35. 2.

35, 36 (y^2, above). THE PUNISHMENT.
(*Introversion.*)

y^2 | a | And the LORD said unto Moses.
  b | The man shall surely be put to death.
    c | They shall stone him with stones.
      d | Without the camp . . .
      d | Without the camp.
    c | They stoned him with stones.
  b | And he died.
a | As the LORD commanded Moses.

35 said. See note on 3. 40.

36 as = according as.

38 fringes. Heb. *ẓiẓith,* a fringe, as in Deut. 22. 12. Occurs only four times: here, *vv.* 38, 39, and Ezek. 8. 3 (*lock* [of hair]) = a fringe where the threads hang down, like a lock of hair.

40 holy. See note on Ex. 3. 5.

God. Heb. *Elohim.* Ap. 4. i.

41 the LORD your God. Fig. *Epanadiplosis.* Ap. 6. The word "Jehovah" beginning and ending the verse, to emphasise it.

16. 1—17. 13 (L^2, p. 195). EVENTS: REBELLION OF KORAH (*Extended Alternation*).

L^2 | e | f | 16. 1-19-. Sin of Korah and company.
      g | 16. -19. Glory of Jehovah manifested.
        h | 16. 20-35. Punishment.
          i | 16. 36-40. Memorial—Censers.
  e | *f* | 16. 41. Sin of the congregation.
      g | 16. 42, 43. Glory of Jehovah manifested.
        h | 16. 44-50. Punishment.
          i | 17. 1-13. Memorial—Rods.

1-19- (f, above). THE SIN OF KORAH.
(*Introversion and Extended Alternation.*)

f | j | l | 1-3. Conspirators' sin.
      m | 4. Moses' prostration.
        n | 5-11. Address to Korah, &c.
          k | 12-. Message to Dathan and Abiram.
  j | *l* | -12-14. Conspirators' reply.
      m | 15. Moses' prayer.
        n | 16-19-. Address to Korah, &c.

1 Now. See note on "while", 15. 32.

Korah. First cousin to Moses and Aaron. 6. 8. 1 Chron. 6. 2, 3. These three associated, because encamped together on south side. Cp. 2. 10 and 3. 29. See p. 181.

sons. Some codices, with Sam. and Sept., read "son".

men. This word necessitated through A.V. and R.V. misplacing the verb "took", which should be after Levi. "Korah took Dathan . . . and Abiram . . . and On, the son of Peleth, the son of Reuben". See below.

2 children = sons.

assembly = appointed assembly.

congregation = assembly. Heb. *'ēdah.*

men. Heb. pl. of *'ish* or *'enōsh.* Ap. 14.

3 congregation = appointed assembly. Heb. *'ēdah.*

holy. See note on Ex. 3. 5.

the LORD. Heb. Jehovah. Ap. 4.

congregation = assembly.

7 man. Heb. *'ish.* Ap. 14.

9 Seemeth it . . . ? Fig. *Erotēsis.* Ap. 6.

1490 that the °God of Israel hath separated you
1452 from the congregation of Israel, to bring you
near to Himself to do the service of the
°tabernacle of [3]the LORD, and to stand before
the congregation to minister unto them?
10 And He hath brought thee near *to Him*,
and all thy brethren the sons of Levi with
thee: and seek ye the priesthood also?
11 For which cause *both* thou and all thy
company *are* gathered together against [3]the
LORD: °and what *is* Aaron, that ye murmur
against him?"

k (p. 203) 12 And Moses sent to call Dathan and
Abiram, the sons of Eliab:

l which said, "We will not come up:
13 °*Is it* a small thing that thou hast brought
us up out of a land that floweth with milk and
honey, to kill us in the wilderness, except thou
make thyself altogether a prince over us?
14 Moreover thou hast not brought us into
a land that floweth with milk and honey, or
given us inheritance of fields and vineyards:
wilt thou °put out the eyes of these men?
we will not come up."

m 15 And Moses was very wroth, and said unto
[3]the LORD, "Respect not thou their °offering:
I have not taken one ass from them, neither
have I hurt one of them."

n 16 And Moses said unto Korah, "Be thou
and all thy company before [3]the LORD, thou,
and they, and Aaron, to morrow:
17 And take every man his censer, and put
incense in them, and bring ye before [3]the
LORD every man his censer, two hundred
and fifty censers; thou also, and Aaron, each
of you his censer."
18 And they took every man his censer, and
put °fire in them, and laid incense thereon,
and stood in the °door of the °tabernacle of
the [3]congregation °with Moses and Aaron.
19 And Korah gathered all the congregation
against them unto the [18]door of the [18]taber-
nacle of the [3]congregation:

g and the glory of [3]the LORD appeared unto all
the [3]congregation.

h o (p. 204) 20 And [3]the LORD °spake unto Moses and
unto Aaron, saying,
21 "Separate yourselves from among this
congregation, that I may consume them in a
moment."
22 And they fell upon their faces, and said,
°"O GOD, the °God of the °spirits of all flesh,
shall one °man °sin, and wilt Thou be wroth
with all the congregation?"

p 23 And [3]the LORD [20]spake unto Moses, saying,
24 "Speak unto the [3]congregation, saying,
'Get you up from about the °tabernacle of
Korah, Dathan, and Abiram.'"
25 And Moses rose up and went unto Dathan
and Abiram; and the elders of Israel followed
him.
26 And he spake unto the [3]congregation,
saying, "Depart, I pray you, from the tents
of these °wicked °men, and touch nothing of
theirs, lest ye be consumed in all their [22]sins."
27 So °they gat up from the [24]tabernacle

God. Heb. Elohim. Ap. 4.
tabernacle = Heb. *mishkān*, habitation. Ap. 40.
11 and what is Aaron? = "and Aaron, who is he"? Fig. *Erotēsis*. Ap. 6.
13 Is it . . . ? Fig. *Erotēsis*. Ap. 6.
14 put out = bore out.
15 offering = gift offering. Ap. 43. II. iii.
18 fire. Note three kinds of fire here, *v.* 18 = strange fire; *v.* 35, judicial fire; *v.* 46, sacrificial fire. Cp. Lev. 9. 24 and 10. 1, 2.
door = entrance.
tabernacle = tent. Heb. *'ohel*. Ap. 40.

20-35 (h, p. 203). PUNISHMENT.
(*Introversion.*)

h	o	20-22. Conspirators. Threat to consume.
	p	23-27. Message to the People.
	p	28-30. Message to conspirators.
	o	31-35. Conspirators. Threat carried out.

20 spake. See note on 1. 1.
22 O GOD = O *'Ēl*. Ap. 4. IV.
God = Elohim. Ap. 4. I.
spirits. Heb. pl. of *rūach*. Ap. 9.
man. Heb. *'īsh*. Ap. 14. ii.
sin. Heb. *chāṭ'ā*. Ap. 44. i.
24 tabernacle. Heb. *mishkān*, habitation in sing. here = the habitation of each, separately; in *v.* 26 plural, "tents".
26 wicked. Heb. *rāsh'a*. Ap. 44. x.
men. Heb. pl. of *'īsh* or *'enōsh*. Ap. 14.
27 they = and Korah and his sons among them. Cp. 26. 11.
27 door = entrance.
their sons: i.e. the sons of Dathan and Abiram, not of Korah. Cp. ch. 26. 11. Ps. 106. 17. See note on *v.* 32.
28 I have not done them. Fig. *Ellipsis*. Ap. 6. i. 4.
29 men. Heb. *'ādām*. Ap. 14. i.
30 make a new thing. Heb. "create a creation". Fig. *Polyptōton*. Ap. 6, for emphasis, throwing light on Gen. 1. 1. Cp. Isa. 45. 7; 48. 6, 7.
them: Dathan and Abiram. Cp. *v.* 27. Korah's sons had obeyed the command, cp. 26. 11.
quick = alive.
pit = *Sheōl*, see *v.* 33 and Ap. 35.
32 men: Heb. *'ādām*. Ap. 14. These did not include Korah's sons. Cp. 26. 11.

of Korah, Dathan, and Abiram, on every side:
and Dathan and Abiram came out, and stood
in the °door of their tents, and their wives,
and °their sons, and their little children.

28 And Moses said, "Hereby ye shall know *p*
that [3]the LORD hath sent me to do all these
works; for °*I have* not *done them* of mine
own mind.
29 If these men die the common death of all
°men, or if they be visited after the visitation
of all °men; *then* [3]the LORD hath not sent me.
30 But if [3]the LORD °make a new thing, and
the earth open her mouth, and swallow them
up, with all that *appertain* unto °them, and
they go down °quick into the °pit; then ye
shall understand that these men have provoked [3]the LORD."

31 And it came to pass, as he had made an *o*
end of speaking all these words, that the
ground clave asunder that *was* under them:
32 And the earth opened her mouth, and
swallowed them up, and their houses, and all
the °men that *appertained* unto Korah, and
all *their* goods.

1490 33 They, and all that *appertained* to them,
1452 went down [30]alive into the °pit, and the earth closed upon them: and they perished from among the [2]congregation.

34 And all Israel that *were* round about them fled at the cry of them: for they said, "Lest the earth swallow us up *also*."

35 And there came out a fire from [3]the LORD, and consumed the °two hundred and fifty °men that offered incense.

i 36 And [3]the LORD [3]spake unto Moses, say-
(p. 203) ing,

37 "Speak unto Eleazar the son of Aaron the priest, that he take up the censers out of the °burning, and scatter thou °the fire yonder; for they are °hallowed.

38 The censers of these °sinners against their own °souls, let them make them broad plates *for* a covering of the altar: for they °offered them before [3]the LORD, therefore they are [37]hallowed: and they shall be a sign unto the [2]children of Israel."

39 And Eleazar the priest took the brasen censers, wherewith they that were burnt had [38]offered; and they were made broad *plates for* a covering of the altar:

40 *To be* a °memorial unto the [2]children of Israel, that no stranger, which *is* not of the seed of Aaron, come near to °offer incense before [3]the LORD; that he be not as Korah, and as his company: °as [3]the LORD said °to him by the hand of Moses.

e f 41 But on the morrow all the [2]congregation of the [2]children of Israel murmured against Moses and against Aaron, saying, "Ye have killed the People of [3]the LORD."

g 42 And it came to pass, when the [2]congregation was gathered against Moses and against Aaron, that they looked toward the °tabernacle of the [2]congregation: and, °behold, the cloud covered it, and the glory of [3]the LORD appeared.

43 And Moses and Aaron came before the [42]tabernacle of the [2]congregation.

h 44 And [3]the LORD [20]spake unto Moses, saying,

45 "Get you up from among this [2]congregation, that I may consume them as in a moment." And they fell upon their faces.

46 And Moses said unto Aaron, "Take a censer, and put fire therein from off the altar, and put on incense, and go quickly unto the congregation, and make an °atonement for them: for there is wrath gone out °from [3]the LORD; the plague is begun."

47 And Aaron took [40]as Moses commanded, and ran into the midst of the [2]congregation; and, behold, the plague was begun among the People: and he put on incense, and made an [46]atonement for the People.

48 And he stood between the dead and °the living; and the plague was stayed.

49 Now they that died in the plague were °fourteen thousand and seven hundred, beside them that died about the matter of Korah.

50 And Aaron returned unto Moses unto the °door of the [42]tabernacle of the [2]congregation: and the plague was stayed.

33 pit = Heb. *sheōl* = the grave, not "a" grave, but all graves viewed as one. See Ap. 35. They went alive, with all their cattle, tents, and goods. All sank into the earth.

35 two hundred and fifty. Plus the 14,700 of *v.* 49

men. Heb. pl. of *'īsh* or *'enōsh.* Ap. 14. ii.

36 spake. See note on 1. 1.

37 burning. Heb. *sāraph.* See Ap. 43. I. viii, i.e from among those that were burnt.

the fire. Cp. *v.* 7, not accepted by Jehovah.

hallowed = set apart. See note on "holy". Ex. 3. 5.

38 sinners. See Ap. 44. i.

souls = their own selves. Heb. *nephesh.* Ap. 13.

their own. Cp. Gen. 19. 17 and Prov. 20. 2.

offered. Heb. brought near. Ap. 43. I. i.

40 memorial. Cp. ch. 17. 10, 1 Cor. 10. 11, and see Structure, p 203. Hence history rehearsed in Deut. 11. 6-8. Note the two memorials added to the tabernacle through Korah's rebellion (see the Structure, p. 203), the plates (i, 36-40) and Aaron's rod (*i*, 17. 1-13).

offer = burn. Heb. *kātar.* Ap. 43. I. vii.

as = according as.

to him, or with regard thereto.

42 tabernacle = tent. Heb. *'ohel.* Ap. 40.

behold. Fig. *Asterismos.* Ap. 6.

46 atonement. See note on Ex. 29. 33.

from = from before.

48 the = Heb. between the.

49 fourteen thousand and seven hundred. This, with the 250 of *v.* 35 = 14,950 (= 13 × 1,150). See Ap. 10 for significance of the number 13.

50 door = entrance.

17. 1-13 (*i*, p. 203). MEMORIAL (THE RODS).
(*Alternations.*)

i | q | s | 1-4. Commandment.
  t | 5. Intention announced.
 r | u | 6, 7. Obedience.
  v | 8, 9. Intention. Effected.
 q | *s* | 10-. Commandment.
  t | -10. Intention. Predicted.
 r | *u* | 11. Obedience.
  v | 12, 13. Intention. Accomplished.

1 the LORD. Heb. Jehovah. Ap. 4.

spake. See note on 1. 1.

2 children = sons.

man's. Heb. *'īsh.* Ap. 14. ii.

4 tabernacle = tent. Heb. *'ohel.* See Ap. 40.

testimony = the ark of the covenant. Cp. Ex. 25. 16

you. Some codices, with Sam., Sept., and Vulg., read "thee".

17 And °the LORD °spake unto Moses, saying, *i q s*
(p. 205)

2 "Speak unto the °children of Israel, and take of every one of them a rod according to the house of *their* fathers, of all their princes according to the house of their fathers twelve rods: write thou every °man's name upon his rod.

3 And thou shalt write Aaron's name upon the rod of Levi: for one rod *shall be* for the head of the house of their fathers.

4 And thou shalt lay them up in the °tabernacle of the congregation before the °testimony, where I will meet with °you.

5 And it shall come to pass, *that* the [2]man's rod, whom I shall choose, shall blossom: and *t*
I will make to cease from Me the murmurings of the [2]children of Israel, whereby they murmur against you."

6 And Moses spake unto the [2]children of *r u*
Israel, and every one of their princes gave

1490 him a rod apiece, for each prince one, ac-
1452 cording to their fathers' houses, *even* twelve
rods: and the rod of Aaron *was* among their
rods.
7 And Moses °laid up the rods before [1]the
LORD in the °tabernacle of witness.

v (p. 205) 8 And it came to pass, that on the morrow
Moses went into the [7]tabernacle of witness;
and, °behold, the rod of Aaron for the house
of Levi was budded, and brought forth buds,
and bloomed blossoms, and yielded almonds.
9 And Moses brought out all the rods from
before [1]the LORD unto all the [2]children of
Israel: and they looked, and took every man
his rod.

q s 10 And [1]the LORD °said unto Moses, "Bring
Aaron's rod again before the °testimony, to be
kept for a token against the °rebels;

t and thou shalt quite °take away their murmurings from Me, that they die not."

r u 11 And Moses did *so:* as [1]the LORD commanded him, so did he.

v 12 And the [2]children of Israel spake unto
Moses, saying, "Behold, we die, °we perish,
we all perish.
13 Whosoever cometh any thing near unto
the °tabernacle of [1]the LORD shall °die: shall
we be consumed with dying?"

T¹ U¹ w¹ (p. 206) **18** And °the LORD °said unto °Aaron,
"Thou and thy sons and thy father's
house with thee shall bear the °iniquity of the
sanctuary: and thou and thy sons with thee
shall bear the °iniquity of your priesthood.

x¹ 2 And thy brethren also of the °tribe of
°Levi, the °tribe of thy father, bring thou
with thee, that they may be °joined unto thee,
and minister unto thee: but thou and thy sons
with thee *shall minister* before the °taber-
nacle of witness.
3 And they shall keep thy charge, and the
charge of all the [2]tabernacle: only they shall
not come nigh the vessels of the sanctuary
and the altar, that neither they, nor ye also,
die.
4 And they shall be joined unto thee, and
keep the charge of the [2]tabernacle of the congregation, for all the service of the [2]tabernacle:
and a stranger shall not come nigh unto you.

w² 5 And ye shall keep the charge of the sanctuary, and the charge of the altar: that there
be no wrath any more upon the °children of
Israel.

x² 6 And I, °behold, I have taken your
brethren the Levites from among the [5]chil-
dren of Israel: to you *they are* given *as* a
gift for [1]the LORD, to °do the service of the
[2]tabernacle of the congregation.

w³ 7 Therefore thou and thy sons with thee
shall keep your priest's office for every thing
of the altar, and within the vail; and ye shall
serve: I have given your priest's office *unto
you as* a service of gift: and the stranger that
cometh nigh shall be put to death."

U² 8 And [1]the LORD °spake unto Aaron,
[6]"Behold, I also have given thee the charge
of Mine heave offerings of all the °hallowed
things of the [5]children of Israel; unto thee
have I given them by reason of °the anointing,
and to thy sons, by an ordinance for ever.
9 This shall be thine of the most °holy
things, *reserved* from the fire: every °obla-
tion of theirs, every meat offering of theirs,
and every sin offering of theirs, and every
trespass offering of theirs, which they shall
render unto Me, °*shall be* most °holy for thee
and for thy sons.
10 In the most [9]holy *place* shalt thou eat it;
every male shall eat it: it shall be [9]holy unto
thee.

---

7 laid up the rods. Korah's rebellion added two things to the tabernacle: Aaron's rod within, brazen plates without (16. 39, 40).
tabernacle of witness = tent of (or containing) the testimony (i. e. the ark, and the two tables). Ap. 40. See note on Ex. 25. 22.
8 behold. Fig. *Asterismos.* Ap. 6.
10 said. See note on 3. 40.
testimony = the ark of the covenant, as in *v.* 4.
rebels. Heb. sons of rebellion. Genitive of character = rebellious ones. Ap. 17.
take away = assuage, or, abate, as in *v.* 5. Cp. Gen. 8. 1.
12 we perish, we all perish. Fig. *Epizeuxis* (Ap. 6), to enhance the alarm of the People.
13 tabernacle = habitation. Heb. *mishkān.* Ap. 40.
die . . . dying. Fig. *Epizeuxis* (Ap. 6), as in *v.* 12, to emphasise alarm.

18. 1—19. 22 (M², p. 195). LAWS FOR PRIESTS AND PEOPLE (*Division*).

M² | T¹ | 18. 1-32. Laws for Priests and Levites.
| T² | 19. 1-22. Laws for People.

18. 1—32 (T¹, above). LAWS FOR PRIESTS AND LEVITES (*Division*).

T¹ | U¹ | 1-7. Priests and their offices.
| U² | 8-19. Priests and their dues. Generally.
| U³ | 20-24. Priests and their inheritance.
| U⁴ | 25-32. Priests and their dues. From the Levites.

1-7 (U¹, above). PRIESTS AND THEIR OFFICES.

U¹ | w¹ | 1. Priests.
| x¹ | 2-4. Levites.
| w² | 5. Priests.
| x² | 6. Levites.
| w³ | 7. Priests.

1 the LORD. Heb. Jehovah. Ap. 4.
said. See note on 3. 40.
Aaron. Jehovah "spoke" again to Aaron in *vv.* 8 and 20.
iniquity. Heb. *'āvāh.* Ap. 44. iv.
2 tribe = *matteh* = staff.
Levi . . . joined. Fig. *Paronomasia.* Ap. 6. Heb. *Levi . . . v'yillāvū.*
tribe = *shēbet* = rod.
tabernacle = tent. Heb. *'ohel.* Ap. 40.
5 children = sons.
6 behold. Fig. *Asterismos.* Ap. 6.
do the service. Heb. serve the service. Fig. *Polyptōton.* Ap. 6, i.e. perform the solemn service.
8 spake. See note on 1. 1.
hallowed = holy. See note on "holy", Ex. 3. 5.
the anointing. Put by Fig. *Metonymy* (of Adjunct), Ap. 6, for the priesthood associated with it.
9 holy. See note on Ex. 3. 5.
oblation. Heb. approach-offering. See Ap. 43. II. i.
shall be. Heb. "it [shall be]".

1490 11 And this *is* thine; the heave offering of
1452 their gift, with all the wave offerings of the [5]children of Israel: I have given them unto thee, and to thy sons and to thy daughters with thee, by a statute for ever: every one that is clean in thy house shall eat of it.

12 All the best of the oil, and all the best of the °wine, and of the wheat, the firstfruits of them which they shall offer unto [1]the LORD, them have I given thee.

13 *And* whatsoever is first ripe in °the land, which they shall bring unto [1]the LORD, shall be thine; every one that is clean in thine house shall eat *of* it.

14 °Every thing °devoted in Israel shall be thine.

15 Every thing that openeth °the matrix in all flesh, which they bring unto [1]the LORD, *whether it be* of °men or beasts, shall be thine: nevertheless the firstborn of °man shalt thou surely °redeem, and the firstling of unclean beasts shalt thou °redeem.

16 And those that are to be [15]redeemed from a month old shalt thou redeem, according to thine estimation, for the money of five °shekels, after the °shekel of the sanctuary, °which *is* twenty °gerahs.

17 But the firstling of a cow, or the firstling of a sheep, or the firstling of a goat, thou shalt not [15]redeem; they *are* [9]holy: °thou shalt sprinkle their blood upon the altar, and shalt °burn their fat *for* an offering made by fire, for a °sweet savour unto [1]the LORD.

18 And the flesh of them shall be thine, as the wave breast and as the right shoulder are thine.

19 All the heave offerings of the [9]holy things, which the [5]children of Israel °offer unto [1]the LORD, have I given thee, and thy sons and thy daughters with thee, by a statute for ever: it *is* a °covenant of salt for ever before [1]the LORD unto thee and to thy seed with thee."

U³ y (p. 207) 20 And [1]the LORD [8]spake unto Aaron, "Thou shalt have no inheritance in their land, neither shalt thou have any part among them:

z I *am* thy part and thine inheritance among the [5]children of Israel.

z 21 And, [6]behold, I have given the [5]children of Levi all the tenth in Israel °for an inheritance, °for their service which they serve, *even* the service of the [2]tabernacle of the congregation.

22 Neither must the [5]children of Israel henceforth come nigh the [2]tabernacle of the congregation, lest they bear °sin, and die.

23 But the Levites shall [6]do the service of the [2]tabernacle of the congregation, and they shall bear their [1]iniquity: *it shall be* a statute for ever throughout your generations, that among the [5]children of Israel they have no inheritance.

24 But the tithes of the [5]children of Israel, which they [19]offer *as* an heave offering unto [1]the LORD, I have given to the Levites to inherit: therefore I have said unto them, Among the [5]children of Israel they shall have no inheritance."

25 And [1]the LORD [8]spake unto Moses, saying, y

26 "Thus speak unto the Levites, and say unto them, 'When ye take of the [5]children of Israel the tithes which I have given you from them for your inheritance, then ye shall offer up an heave offering of it for [1]the LORD, *even* a tenth *part* of the tithe.

27 And *this* your heave offering shall be reckoned unto you, as though *it were* the corn °of the threshingfloor, and as the fulness of the winepress.

28 Thus ye also shall [19]offer an heave offering unto [1]the LORD of all your tithes, which ye receive of the [5]children of Israel; and ye shall give thereof [1]the LORD'S heave offering to Aaron the priest.

29 Out of all your gifts ye shall [19]offer every heave offering of [1]the LORD, of all the best thereof, *even* the [8]hallowed part thereof out of it.'

30 Therefore thou shalt say unto them, 'When ye have heaved the best thereof from it, then it shall be counted unto the Levites as the increase of the threshingfloor, and as the increase of the winepress.

31 And ye shall eat it in every place, ye and your households: for it *is* your reward for

---

12 wine. Heb. *tīrōsh.* See Ap. 27. ii.
13 the = their.
14 Every thing. See Lev. 27. 28.
devoted. See note on Lev. 27. 1.
15 the matrix. See 3. 13. Ex. 13. 2; 34. 19. Lev. 27. 26.
men . . . man = Heb. *'ādām.* Ap. 14. I.
redeem. Heb. *pādāh.* See note on Ex. 6. 6.
16 shekels . . . shekel. See Ap. 51. II.
which = it. Cp. 3. 47. Ex. 30. 13. Lev. 27. 25.
gerahs. See Ap. 51. III. 3.
17 thou. Some codices, with Sam., Sept., Jon., Onk., and Syr., read "but thou".
burn = burn as incense. See Ap. 43. I. vii.
sweet savour. See note on Lev. 1. 9.
19 offer = heave up as a heave offering. See note on Ex. 29. 27.
covenant of salt. Heb. covenant = *b^erīth,* from *bārāh, to cut;* hence, *to eat.* As salt was scarce and precious, and used with all eating, so it was put, by Fig. *Metonymy* (of Adjunct), Ap. 6, for eating, just as the breaking of bread was. See Isa. 58. 7 (A.V. "deal"); Jer. 16. 7 (A.V. "tear"). Lam. 4. 4. Ezek. 18. 7 (A.V. "given"). Hence, when wages were paid in kind, by finding the worker in food, "salt" was put (by Fig. *Metonymy*) for wages generally; so that a worker was spoken of as being worth, or not worth, his "salt". "A covenant of salt" was therefore a covenant made by sacrifice, which was first *cut* in two (Gen. 15. 10-18. Jer. 34. 18, 19) and then *eaten,* thus solemnising an inviolable covenant.

20-32 (U³, p. 206). PRIESTS AND THEIR INHERITANCE (*Introversion*).

U³ | y | 20-. Negative. Not the land.
| z | -20. Positive. Jehovah.
| z | 21-24. Positive. The tenth.
| y | 25-32. Negative. Not the tenth of the tenth.

21 for = instead of.
22 sin. Heb. *chāṭāh.* Ap. 44. i.
27 of = from.

1490 your service in the [3]tabernacle of the con-
1452 gregation.

32 And ye shall bear no [22]sin by reason of it, when ye have heaved from it the best of it: neither shall ye pollute the [9]holy things of the [5]children of Israel, lest ye die.'"

T² V
(p. 208)
19 And °the LORD °spake unto Moses and unto Aaron, saying,

2 "This *is* the °ordinance of the law which [1]the LORD hath commanded, saying, 'Speak unto the °children of Israel, that they °bring thee °a red heifer °without spot, wherein *is* °no blemish, *and* upon which never came yoke:

3 And ye shall give her unto Eleazar the priest, that he may bring her forth °without the camp, and *one* shall slay her before his face:

4 And Eleazar the priest shall take of her blood with his finger, and sprinkle of her blood directly before the °tabernacle of the congregation seven times:

5 And *one* shall °burn the heifer in his sight; her skin, and her flesh, and her blood, with her dung, shall he burn:

6 And the priest shall take cedar wood, and hyssop, and scarlet, and cast *it* into the midst of the burning of the heifer.

7 Then the priest shall wash his clothes, and he shall bathe his flesh in water, and afterward he shall come into the camp, and the priest shall be unclean until the even.

8 And he that burneth her shall wash his clothes °in water, and bathe his flesh in water, and shall be unclean until the even.

9 And a °man *that is* clean shall gather up the ashes of the heifer, and lay *them* up [3]without the camp in a clean place, and it shall be kept for the congregation of the [2]children of Israel for a water of separation: it *is* a purification for °sin.

10 And he that gathereth the ashes of the heifer shall wash his clothes, and be unclean until the even:

W and it shall be unto the [2]children of Israel, and unto the stranger that sojourneth among them, for a statute for ever.

V a 11 He that toucheth the dead °body of any °man shall be unclean seven days.

12 He shall purify himself with it on the °third day, and on the °seventh day he shall be clean: but if he purify not himself the third day, then °the seventh day he shall not be clean.

b 13 Whosoever toucheth the dead °body of any man that is dead, and purifieth not himself, defileth the °tabernacle of [1]the LORD; and that °soul shall be cut off from Israel: because the water of separation was not sprinkled upon him, he shall be unclean; his uncleanness *is* yet upon him.

a 14 This *is* the law, when a man dieth in a tent: all that come into the tent, and all that *is* in the tent, shall be unclean seven days.

15 And every open vessel, which hath no covering bound upon it, °*is* unclean.

19. 1-22 (T², p. 206). LAWS FOR THE PEOPLE. (Water of separation: The red heifer.) (*Alternation.*)

T² V | 1-10-. Preparation of the water.
 W | -10. A statute for ever.
 V | 11-20. Use of the water.
 W | 21, 22. A statute for ever.

1 the LORD. Heb. Jehovah. Ap. 4.

spake. See note on 1. 1.

2 ordinance = statute. The whole clause = Fig. *Pleonasm* (Ap. 6), for emphasising the lesson of the red heifer.

children = sons.

bring = take. This is the third of three events recorded during the punishment wanderings. See note on "while", 15. 32.

a red heifer. Christ, the Antitype.

without spot = without defect. Cp. the Antitype. Heb. 9. 14.

no blemish. Cp. 1 Pet. 1. 19.

3 without the camp. Cp. the Antitype. Heb. 13. 12.

4 tabernacle = tent. Heb. *'ohel.* Ap. 40.

5 burn. Heb. *sāraph.* See Ap. 43. I. viii.

8 in water. Some codices, with Sept., Syr., and Vulg., omit these words. Cp. Lev. 16. 28.

9 man. Heb. *'ish.* Ap. 14. ii. Cp. the antitype, Joseph of Arimathea. Matt. 27. 57-60. Luke 23. 50-53. John 19. 38-42.

sin. See Ap. 44. i.

11-20 (*V*, above). USE OF THE WATER. (*Alternation.*)

V | a | 11, 12. Purification.
 b | 13. Threatening.
 a | 14-19. Purification.
 b | 20. Threatening.

11 body = soul. Heb. *nephesh.* Lit. "the dead *nephesh* of". Ap. 13.

man = Heb. *'ādām.* Ap. 14. i.

12 third . . . seventh. Cp. the Antitype. Heb. 9. 14. The numbers significant. See Ap. 10.

the = on the.

13 body = soul. Heb. *nephesh.* Ap. 13.

tabernacle = habitation. Heb. *mishkān.* See Ap. 40.

soul. Heb. *nephesh* (Ap. 13). Cp. *vv.* 11 and 13.

15 is = "it [is]".

16 dead body. Heb. *b^emēth*, no word for body = one dead, as in *v.* 18, not *vv.* 11 and 13.

17 ashes = dust.

sin. See Ap. 44. i.

running = living. Not stagnant.

18 person = Heb. *'ish.* Ap. 14. ii.

persons = souls. Heb. *nephesh.* Ap. 13.

19 wash. The common rite. See Lev. 11. 25; 14. 8, 9, &c.

himself = his flesh, as in Lev. 15. 16.

16 And whosoever toucheth one that is slain with a sword in the open fields, or a °dead body, or a bone of a man, or a grave, shall be unclean seven days.

17 And for an unclean *person* they shall take of the °ashes of the [5]burnt heifer of purification for [9]sin, and °running water shall be put thereto in a vessel:

18 And a clean °person shall take hyssop, and dip *it* in the water, and sprinkle *it* upon the tent, and upon all the vessels, and upon the °persons that were there, and upon him that touched a bone, or one slain, or one dead, or a grave:

19 And the clean *person* shall sprinkle upon the unclean on the third day, and on the seventh day: and on the seventh day he shall purify himself, and °wash his clothes, and bathe °himself in water, and shall be clean at even.

20 But the man that shall be unclean, and *b*

1490 shall not purify himself, that °soul shall be
1453 cut off from among the congregation, because he hath defiled the sanctuary of [1]the
LORD: the water of separation hath not been
sprinkled upon him; he *is* unclean.

W (p. 208) 21 And it shall be a perpetual statute unto
them, that he that sprinkleth the water of
separation shall wash his clothes; and he
that toucheth the water of separation shall
be unclean until even.
22 And whatsoever the unclean *person*
toucheth shall be unclean; and the [20]soul
that toucheth *it* shall be unclean until even.'"

L^3 A^1 c^1 (p. 209) 1452 1st Abib
20 °Then came the °children of Israel,
even the whole congregation, into the
desert of Zin in the first month:

d^1 f °and the People abode in °Kadesh; and
°Miriam died there, and was buried there.
2 And there was no water for the congregation: and they gathered themselves together
against Moses and against Aaron.
3 And the People chode with Moses, and
spake, saying, °"Would °God that we had
died °when our brethren died before °the
LORD!
4 And °why have ye brought up the °congregation of [3]the LORD into this wilderness,
that we and our cattle should die there?
5 And °wherefore have ye made us to come
up out of Egypt, to bring us in unto this °evil
place? it *is* no place of seed, °or of °figs, or of
°vines, or of °pomegranates; neither *is* there
any water to drink."

i 6 And Moses and Aaron went from the
presence of the assembly unto the °door of
the °tabernacle of the congregation, and they
fell upon their faces: and the glory of [3]the
LORD appeared unto them.

g 7 And [3]the LORD °spake unto Moses, saying,
8 "Take °the rod, and gather thou the
°assembly together, thou, and Aaron thy
brother, and °speak ye unto the rock before
their eyes; and it shall give forth his water,
and thou shalt bring forth to them water out
of the rock: so thou shalt give the congregation and their beasts drink."

f i 9 And Moses took the rod from before [3]the
LORD, °as He commanded him.
10 And Moses and Aaron gathered the [4]congregation together before the rock, and he
°said unto them, "Hear now, ye rebels;
°must we fetch you water out of this rock?"
11 And Moses lifted up his hand, and with
°his rod he °smote the rock °twice: and the
water came out abundantly, and the congregation °drank, and their beasts *also*.

f h 12 And [3]the LORD [7]spake unto Moses and
Aaron, "Because ye °believed Me not, to
sanctify °Me °in the eyes of the [1]children

20 soul = person. Heb. *nephesh*. Used of "living souls" and "dead souls". Cp. *vv.* 11, 13 (where it is rendered "any", and "body" respectively). See Ap. 13.

20. 1—25. 18 (L^3, p. 180). EVENTS: JOURNEYINGS AND MURMURINGS.
(*Repeated and Extended Alternations.*)

L^3 A^1 | c^1 | 20. 1-. To Desert of Zin.
d^1 | 20. -1-13. Events—Death of Miriam, and murmuring.
e^1 | 20. 14-21. Opposition of Edom (Edomites).
A^2 | c^2 | 20. 22. To Mount Hor.
d^2 | 20. 23-29. Event—Death of Aaron.
e^2 | 21. 1-3. Opposition of Arad (Canaanites).
A^3 | c^3 | 21. 4-. To compass land of Edom.
d^3 | 21. -4, 5. Event—Murmuring.
e^3 | 21. 6-9. Opposition of God. Fiery serpents.
A^4 | c^4 | 21. 10-16-. To Oboth and Arnon.
d^4 | 21. -16-20. Event—Giving of water.
e^4 | 21. 21-31. Opposition of Sihon (Amorites).
A^5 | c^5 | 21. 32-. To Jaazer.
d^5 | 21. -32. Event—Taking of villages, &c.
e^5 | 21. 33-35. Opposition of Og (Bashan).
A^6 | c^6 | 22. 1. To Plains of Moab.
d^6 | 22. 2-4. Event—Fear of Moab.
e^6 | 22. 5—25. 18. Opposition of Balak (Moabites).

1 Then came. This was in the first month of the fortieth year after Exodus. Cp. 20. 28 with 33. 38 and Deut. 2. 1-7. A gap of 37½ years between the spies (13, 14) and this chapter. This blank should be carefully noted. See note on 14. 34, and Ap. 50. vii. 3.
children = sons.
and. Note the Fig. *Polysyndeton* throughout this chapter. The old nation dead. History of new nation begins here, and each event singled out and emphasised.
Kadesh. The second time in eventful Kadesh. No history since the first time—all a blank, except a list of journeyings in ch. 33.
Miriam: died early in fortieth year; Aaron in the fifth month. Cp. *vv.* 23-29 with *vv.* 33, 38.

-1-13 (d^1, above). EVENTS: MIRIAM'S DEATH, &c.
(*Introversion.*)

d^1 | f | h | 2-5. Contention of People. Chiding with Moses.
i | 6. Action of Moses and Aaron.
g | 7, 8. Command of Jehovah.
f | i | 9-11. Action of Moses and Aaron.
h | 12, 13. Contention of people. Sentence on Moses and Aaron.

3 Would God. Fig. *Œonismos* (Ap. 6). No Heb. for "God" here. **when.** Cp. 11. 33.
the LORD. Heb. Jehovah. Ap. 4.
4 why have ye . . . ? Sept. reads, "why hast thou?" Fig. *Erotēsis* (Ap. 6).
congregation = assembly.
5 wherefore . . . ? Fig. *Erotēsis*. Ap. 6.
evil. See Ap. 44. viii.
or of. Note Fig. *Paradiastole*, Ap. 6, to emphasise the three items: figs, vines, and pomegranates.
figs, vines, . . . pomegranates. See note on 13. 23.
6 door = entrance.
tabernacle = tent. Heb. *'ohel*. See Ap. 40.
7 spake. See note on 1. 1.
8 the rod. Cp. 17. 5. Some think (from *v.* 9) the rod "from before the testimony", as in 17. 10; but *v.* 11 it is "his rod". **assembly** = congregation. **speak ye unto the rock.** Not "smite" as in *v.* 11. **9 as** = according as. **10 said.** He spoke to the People instead of to the rock. **must we . . . ?** Fig. *Erotēsis*. Ap. 6. **11 his**: i. e. Moses' tribal rod. Cp. *v.* 8. **smote.** Instead of speaking. **twice.** Showing the heat of his feeling. **drank.** Cp. 1 Cor. 10. 4, and see note there. **12 believed Me not.** So Moses entered not in, because of unbelief. **Me.** Hence called "rebellion" in *v.* 24 and 27. 14. Cp. Deut. 32. 51. Cp. "we" in *v.* 10. **in the eyes, &c.** His complaint in 11. 21-23 was not public.

1452 of Israel, therefore ye shall not bring this
[4]congregation into the land which I have
given them."

13 This *is* the water of °Meribah; because the
[1]children of Israel strove with [3]the LORD, and
°He was sanctified in them.

e[1] j 14 And Moses sent messengers from Kadesh
(p. 210) unto the king of Edom, "Thus saith thy
brother Israel, 'Thou knowest all the travel
that hath °befallen us:

15 How our fathers went down into Egypt,
and we have dwelt in Egypt a long time; and
the Egyptians vexed us, and our fathers:

16 And when we cried unto [3]the LORD, He
heard our voice, and sent an Angel, and hath
brought us forth out of Egypt: and, °behold,
we *are* in Kadesh, a city in the uttermost of
thy border:

17 Let us pass, I pray thee, through thy
country: we will not pass through the fields,
or through the vineyards, neither will we
drink *of* the water of the °wells: we will go
by the king's *high* way, we will not turn to
the right hand nor to the left, until we have
passed thy borders.'"

k 18 And Edom said unto him, "Thou shalt
not pass °by me, lest I come out against thee
with the sword."

j 19 And the [1]children of Israel said unto him,
"We will go by the high way: and if I and
my cattle drink of thy water, then I will pay
for it: I will only, °without *doing* any thing
else, go through on my feet."

k 20 And he said, "Thou shalt not go
through." And Edom came out against him
with much people, and with a strong hand.

21 Thus Edom refused to give Israel passage
through his border: wherefore Israel °turned
away from him.

A[2] c[2] 22 And the [1]children of Israel, *even* the
(p. 209) whole congregation, journeyed from °Kadesh,
and came unto mount °Hor.

d[2] l 23 And [3]the LORD [1]spake unto Moses and
(p. 210) Aaron in mount Hor, by the coast of the land
of Edom, saying,

24 "Aaron shall be °gathered unto his
people: for he shall not enter into the land
which I have given unto the [1]children of
Israel, because ye rebelled against my °word
at the water of Meribah.

25 Take Aaron and Eleazar his son, and
bring them up unto mount Hor:

26 And strip Aaron of his garments, and
put them upon Eleazar his son: and Aaron
shall be gathered °*unto his people*, and shall
die there."

m 27 And Moses did °as [3]the LORD commanded: and they went up into mount Hor
in the sight of all the congregation.

28 And Moses stripped Aaron of his garments, and put them upon Eleazar his son;
and Aaron died there in the °top of the
mount: and Moses and Eleazar came down
from the mount.

l 29 And when all the congregation °saw that
Aaron was °dead,

13 Meribah = contention. Ps. 106. 32, &c.

He was sanctified = He hallowed Himself. See note on "holy", Ex. 3. 5. Cp. Ezek. 38. 23.

20. 14-21 (e[1], p. 209). OPPOSITION OF EDOM. (*Alternation.*)

e[1] | j | 14-17. Request.
| k | 18. Refusal.
| *j* | 19. Request.
| *k* | 20, 21. Refusal.

14 befallen us = "found us". Fig. *Prosopopœia*. Ap. 6.

16 behold. Fig. *Asterismos* (Ap. 6), to emphasise the importance of the place. See notes on *v.* 1.

17 wells. Heb. *b^{e}'ēr*. See note on Gen. 21. 19.

18 by me = through me. "Me" put by Fig. *Metonymy* (of Adjunct), Ap. 6, for "my country".

19 without doing any thing else. Heb. "without a word": i. e. without [saying] a word. Fig. *Ellipsis*. Ap. 6.

21 turned away. Cp. Judg. 11. 18. Deut. 2. 4, 5.

22 Kadesh. See notes on *v.* 1, and cp. 33. 37.

Hor. Cp. 33. 37.

23-26 (d[2], p. 209). EVENT: THE DEATH OF AARON (*Alternation*).

d[2] | l | 23-26. Moses.
| m | 27, 28. His obedience.
| *l* | 29-. The congregation.
| *m* | -29. Their mourning.

24 gathered. Fig. *Euphemismos* (Ap. 6) for dying = die, and be buried as all his fathers were, *Sheōl* being *the* grave. See Ap. 35. Cp. Gen. 25. 8. Ps. 26. 9. Acts 13. 36.

word. Heb. "mouth". Put by Fig. *Metonymy* (of Cause), Ap. 6, for what was spoken by it. Cp. *v.* 12.

26 unto his people. Fig. *Ellipsis*, supplied from *v.* 24. See Ap. 6. iii. 1.

27 as = according as.

28 top of the mount. Cp. Gen. 8. 4; 22. 2. Ex. 19. Matt. 5. 1. Ezek. 40. 2. Rev. 21. 10. Deut. 34. 1-5. Matt. 17. 1-3.

29 saw. Heb. *rā'ah*, to perceive, understand. Cp. Gen. 16. 13; 42. 1. Ex. 20. 18.

dead. The death of Aaron coincides with the end of the wanderings.

the house of Israel. See note on Ex. 16. 31; one of the thirteen occurrences of the expression before the division of the two kingdoms; and cp. note on 1 Kings 12. 17.

21. 1-3 (e[2], p. 209). OPPOSITION OF ARAD. (*Introversion.*)

e[2] | n | 1. Aggression of Arad.
| o | 2. Vow made.
| *o* | 3-. Vow heard.
| *n* | -3. Destruction of Arad.

1 Arad. Cp. Josh. 12. 14.

south = the *Negeb*. See Gen. 12. 9; 13. 1, 3; 24. 62. Num. 13. 17.

came = was entering.

way of the spies. 13. 21, &c. = "the way of the *Atharim*". Sept. so renders it, as a proper name; probably the name of the caravan route.

they mourned for Aaron thirty days, *even* all m
°the house of Israel.

21 And *when* king °Arad the Canaanite, e[2] n
which dwelt in the °south, heard tell
that Israel °came by the °way of the spies;
then he fought against Israel, and took *some*
of them prisoners.

o 2 And Israel °vowed a vow unto °the LORD,
(p. 210) and said, "If Thou °wilt indeed deliver this
1452 people into my hand, then I will utterly
destroy their cities."

o 3 And [2]the LORD hearkened to the voice of
Israel, and delivered up the °Canaanites;

n and they utterly destroyed them °and their
cities: and he called the name of the place
°Hormah.

c^3 4 And they journeyed from mount Hor by
(p. 209) the way of the Red sea, to compass the land
of Edom:

d^3 and the °soul of the People was much °dis-
couraged because of the way.
5 And the People spake against °God, and
against Moses, °"Wherefore have ye brought
us up out of Egypt to die in the wilderness?
for *there is* no bread, neither *is there any*
water; and °our soul loatheth this light
bread."

e^3 p 6 And [2]the LORD sent °fiery serpents
(p. 211) among the People, and they bit the People;
and much people of Israel died.

q 7 Therefore the People came to Moses, and
said, "We have °sinned, for we have spoken
against [2]the LORD, and against thee; pray
unto [2]the LORD, that He take away the
serpents from us." And Moses prayed for
the People.

p 8 And [2]the LORD °said unto Moses, "Make
thee a [6]fiery serpent, and set it upon a pole:
and it shall come to pass, that every one that
is bitten, when he looketh upon it, shall live."

q 9 And Moses made a °serpent of brass, and
put it upon a pole, and it came to pass, that
if a °serpent had bitten any man, when he
beheld the °serpent of brass, °he lived.

A^4 c^4 10 And the °children of Israel set forward,
(p. 209) and pitched in Oboth.
11 And they journeyed from Oboth, and
pitched at Ije-abarim, in the wilderness
which *is* before Moab, toward the sunrising.
12 From thence they removed, and pitched
in the valley of Zared.
13 From thence they removed, and pitched
on the other side of Arnon, which *is* in the
wilderness that cometh out of the °coasts of
the Amorites: for Arnon *is* the border of
Moab, between Moab and the Amorites.
14 Wherefore it is said in the book °of the
wars of [2]the LORD,

"What He did in °the Red sea,
And in °the brooks of Arnon,
15 And at the stream of the brooks that
goeth down to the dwelling of Ar,
And lieth upon the border of Moab."

16 And from thence °*they went* to Beer:

d^4 that *is* the well whereof [2]the LORD °spake
unto Moses, "Gather the People together,
and I will give them water."
17 Then Israel sang °this song,

"Spring up, O well;
Sing ye unto it:
18 The princes digged the well,
The nobles of the People digged it,
By *the direction of* the lawgiver, with
their staves."

And from the wilderness °*they went* to Mattanah:
19 And from Mattanah to Nahaliel: and
from Nahaliel to Bamoth:
20 And from Bamoth *in* the valley, that *is*
in the °country of Moab, to the top of Pisgah,
which looketh toward °Jeshimon.

---

2 vowed a vow. Fig. *Polyptōton* (Ap. 6), for emphasis = made a solemn vow.

the LORD. Heb. Jehovah. Ap. 4.

wilt indeed deliver = same Fig. *Polyptōton* (Ap. 6), only here it is translated and emphatically expressed by the word "indeed". Heb. = "a delivering Thou wilt deliver".

3 Canaanites. The Sept. and Sam. add "into his (i. e. Israel's) hand".

and their cities. These destroyed after Israel came into the land. Cp. Josh. 12. 14. Judg. 1. 16, 17.

Hormah = utter destruction.

4 soul. Heb. *nephesh* (Ap. 13).

discouraged = grieved or impatient.

5 God = *Elohim.* They had lost sight of the covenant God, Jehovah. Cp. Ap. 4. I. II.

Wherefore . . . ? Fig. *Erotēsis.* Ap. 6.

our soul = we. Heb. *nephesh.* Ap. 13.

6-9 (e^3, p. 209). THE FIERY SERPENTS.

e^3 | p | 6. Fiery serpents.
  q | 7. Prayer made.
 p | 8. The brazen serpent.
  q | 9. Prayer answered.

6 fiery serpents = burning. Heb. *nacheshīm sarāphīm.* Fig. *Metonymy* (of Effect), Ap. 6, because the effect of the bite was a burning sensation. Heb. *sārāph* (see Ap. 43. I. viii). The *Seraphim* so called in Isa. 6. 2, because they were *burning* ones: hence the name for these serpents. In the same way *nāchāsh, shining* one, is also used for serpents, because they are shining ones in appearance. See Gen. 3. 1, and cp. Ap. 19.

7 sinned. See Ap. 44. i.

8 said. See note on 3. 40.

9 serpent = Heb. *nāchāsh,* a *shining* thing of brass, as in Deut. 8. 15. 2 Kings 18. 4, &c.: so that *nāchāsh* is synonymous with *sārāph,* and both words are thus used of serpents.

he lived. Cp. John 3. 14, 15.

10 children = sons. **13 coasts** = border.

14 of the wars of the LORD. This may *commence* the quotation, thus: "the wars of Jehovah [were with] Eth-Vāhēb by the Red sea (or with a whirlwind. Heb. *Supha.* Cp. Amos 1. 14. Isa. 66. 15. Nah 1. 3. Jer. 4. 13) and by the brooks of Arnon". Eth-Vāhēb may be the proper name of the king of the Amorites, who took Heshbon, as in *v.* 26.

the Red sea. Heb. *Suphah,* a city situated as described here, and in Deut. 1. 1. Cp. 1 Kings 9. 26.

the brooks of Arnon = the outpouring of the torrents.

16 they went. This *Ellipsis* is wrongly supplied. It should be "from thence toward Beer". No mention is made of Beer in the list of journeys in ch. 33.

spake. See note on 1. 1.

17 this song. See note on Ex. 15. 1.

18 they went. No mention is made of any of these places in the itinerary in ch. 33. Why not supply "[the waters or streams] went" into all these places? See *v.* 16. The Structure shows the scope of this member to be an "event"; "journeys" are the subject of the preceding member. Cp. note on Ex. 15. 27.

Note the *Alternation,* which gives the interpretation:

The princes digged the well;
 The nobles of the people digged it,
With the lawgiver
 [They digged it] with their staves.

20 country = field.

Jeshimon = the wilderness.

e^4 r (p. 212) 1452 21 And Israel sent messengers unto Sihon king of the Amorites, saying,
22 "Let me pass through thy land: we will not turn into the fields, or into the vineyards; we will not drink *of* the waters of the well: *but* we will go along by the king's *high* way, until we be past thy borders."

s 23 And Sihon °would not suffer Israel to pass through his border: but Sihon gathered all his people together, and went out against Israel into the wilderness: and he came to Jahaz, and fought against Israel.

r 24 And Israel smote him with the edge of the sword, and possessed his land from Arnon unto Jabbok, even unto the [10]children of Ammon: for the border of the [10]children of Ammon *was* strong.

s t 25 And Israel took all these cities: and Israel dwelt in all the cities of the Amorites, in Heshbon, and in all the °villages thereof.

u 26 For Heshbon *was* the city of Sihon the king of the Amorites, who had fought against the former king of Moab, and taken all his land out of his hand, even unto Arnon.

u 27 Wherefore they that speak in °proverbs say,

"Come into Heshbon,
Let the city of Sihon be built and prepared:
28 For there is a fire gone out of Heshbon,
A flame from the city of Sihon:
It hath consumed Ar of Moab,
And °the lords of the °high places of Arnon.
29 Woe to thee, Moab!
Thou art undone, O people of Chemosh:
He hath given his sons that escaped,
And his daughters, into captivity
Unto Sihon king of the Amorites.
30 °We have shot at them;
Heshbon is perished even unto Dibon,
And °we have laid them waste even unto Nophah,
Which *reacheth* unto Medeba."

t 31 Thus Israel dwelt in the land of the Amorites.

c^5 32 And Moses sent to spy out Jaazer,
(p. 209) d^5 and they took the villages thereof, and drove out the Amorites that *were* there.

e^5 33 And they turned and went up by the way of Bashan: and Og the king of Bashan went out against them, he, and all his people, to the battle at Edrei.
34 And [2]the LORD [8]said unto Moses, "Fear him not: for I have delivered him into thy hand, and all his people, and his land; and °thou shalt do to him as thou didst unto Sihon king of the Amorites, which dwelt at Heshbon."
35 So they smote him, and his sons, and all his people, until there was none left him alive: and they possessed his land.

c^6 (p. 213) **22** And the °children of Israel set forward, and pitched in the °plains of Moab on this side Jordan *by* Jericho.

d^6 2 And Balak the son of Zippor saw all that Israel had °done to the Amorites.
3 And Moab was sore afraid of the People, because they *were* many: and Moab was distressed because of the [1]children of Israel.
4 And Moab said unto the elders of Midian "Now shall this company lick up °all *that are* round about us, as the ox licketh up the grass of the field." And Balak the son of Zippor *was* king of the Moabites at that time.

5 He sent messengers therefore unto °Balaam the son of °Beor to °Pethor, which *is* by the river of the land of the children of °his people, e^6 v^1 x

---

21-31 (e^4, p. 209). OPPOSITION OF SIHON. (*Alternation.*)

e^4 | r | 21, 22. Israel's demand.
| s | 23. Sihon's denial.
| *s* | 24. Sihon. Defeat.
| *r* | 25-31. Israel. Dwelling.

23 would not suffer. Fig. *Tapeinosis*, Ap. 6, much more being meant, even armed opposition.

25-31 (*s*, above). POSSESSION. (*Introversion.*)

s | t | 25. Dwelling. Particular.
| u | 26. Doings.
| *u* | 27-30. Sayings.
| *t* | 31. Dwelling. General.

25 villages = Heb. daughters. Fig. *Prosopopœia* Ap. 6.

27-30 (*u*, above). SAYINGS. (*Introversion.*)

u | a | 27, 28. The Amorites. Their boasting.
| b | 29-. The calamities of Moab.
| *b* | -29. The captivity of Moab.
| *a* | 30. The Amorites. Their destruction.

27 proverbs. Heb. poems.
28 the lords. Heb. *Baalim.*
high places. Cp. 22. 41 and Jer. 48. 35.
30 We = Israel.
we have laid, &c., to end of verse. These two clauses are affected by the "extraordinary points" (see Ap. 31), which necessitates the following rendering of *v.* 30:—

"We have shot them down:
Heshbon is destroyed even unto Dibon,
The women also even unto Nopha,
And the men even unto Medeba."

34 thou shalt do, &c. Cp. Ps. 135. 11.

22. 1 children = sons.
plains of Moab: i. e. which had belonged to Moab.
2 done to the Amorites. Cp. 21. 35.
4 all that are round about us: Heb. all our circuits. Fig. *Metonymy* (of Subject). Ap. 6.

22. 5—25. 18 [For Structures see next page].

5 Balaam. So written after the Greek. In Heb. his name is *Bil'am.* Cp. Josh. 13. 22 and 24. 9, 10. 2 Pet. 2. 15, 16. He was a spiritist or medium. He is identified by Sayce with Bela, Gen. 36. 31, 32, where Moses incorporates a list of Edomite kings. According to the Tel-el-Amarna tablets he was a Hittite chieftain, who established a kingdom for himself: and he died fighting against Israel by the side of his Midianite allies (31. 8. Jos. 13. 22).
Beor. Heb. = *Be'ōr.* In 1 Pet. 2. 15 called Bosor. The Heb. letter ע (ayin = 'ō), often pronounced "s" by Greeks.
Pethor. A city in Aram (23. 7) or Mesopotamia (Deut. 23. 4).
his people: i. e. whom he had banded together and led. Some codices, with Sam., Syr., and Vulg., read "sons of Ammon".

1452 to call him, saying, °"Behold, there is a People come out from Egypt: °behold, they cover the °face of the earth, and they °abide over against me:

6 Come now therefore, I pray thee, °curse me this People; for they *are* too mighty for me: peradventure I shall prevail, *that* we may smite them, and *that* I may drive them out of the land: for I °wot that he whom thou blessest *is* blessed, and he whom thou °cursest is °cursed."

y (p. 213) 7 And the elders of Moab and the elders of Midian departed with the °rewards of divination in their hand; and they came unto Balaam, and spake unto him the words of Balak.

z 8 And he said unto them, "Lodge here this night, and I will bring you word again, as °the LORD shall speak unto me:" and the princes of Moab abode with Balaam.

9 And °God came unto Balaam, and °said, "What men *are* these with thee?"

10 And Balaam said unto [9]God, "Balak the son of Zippor, king of Moab, hath sent unto me, *saying*,

11 [5]'Behold, °*there is* a People come out of Egypt, which covereth the face of the earth: come °now, °curse me them; °peradventure I shall be able to overcome them, and drive them out.'"

a 12 And [9]God said unto Balaam, "Thou shalt °not go with them; °thou shalt not [6]curse the people: for they *are* blessed."

13 And °Balaam rose up in the morning, and °said unto the princes of Balak, "Get you into your land: for [8]the LORD refuseth to give me leave to go with you."

14 And the princes of Moab rose up, and °they went unto Balak, and °said, "Balaam refuseth to come with us."

x 15 And Balak sent yet again princes, more, and more honourable than they.

y 16 And they came to Balaam, and said to him, "Thus saith Balak the son of Zippor, 'Let nothing, I pray thee, hinder thee from coming unto me:

17 For I will °promote thee unto very great honour, and I will do whatsoever thou sayest unto me: come therefore, I pray thee, [11]curse me this People.'"

z 18 And Balaam answered and said unto the servants of Balak, "If Balak would give me his house full of silver and gold, I cannot go beyond the word of [8]the LORD my [9]God, to do less or more.

19 Now therefore, I pray you, tarry ye also here this night, that I may know what [8]the LORD will say unto me more."

a 20 And [9]God came unto Balaam at night, and said unto him, °"If the men come to call thee, rise up, *and* go with them; but yet the word which I shall say unto thee, that shalt thou do."

w^1 b 21 And Balaam rose up in the morning, and saddled his ass, and °went with the princes of Moab.

22. 5—25. 18 (e^6, p. 209). OPPOSITION OF BALAK (*Repeated Alternation*).

e^6 | v^1 | 22. 5-20. Balak's messages to Balaam.
  w^1 | 22. 21-35. Balaam's journey.
 v^2 | 22. 36-40. Balak's reception of Balaam.
  w^2 | 22. 41—24. 25. Balaam's four prophecies.
 v^3 | 25. 1-18. Balak's teaching by Balaam. See 31. 16. Rev. 2. 14.

These *five* members are each expanded below.

22. 5-20 (v^1, above). BALAK'S MESSAGES TO BALAAM (*Extended Alternation*).

v^1 | x | 5, 6. FIRST message.
 y | 7. Delivered.
  z | 8-11. Received.
   a | 12-14. Forbidden by God (absolutely).
 x | 15. SECOND message.
  y | 16, 17. Delivered.
   z | 18, 19. Received.
    a | 20. Permitted by God (conditionally).

5 Behold. Fig. *Asterismos*. Ap. 6.
behold. For this second word some codices, with Sam., Onk., Jon., Sept., and Syr., read "and behold".
face. Heb "eye". Fig. *Metonymy* (of Adjunct), Ap. 6; also Fig. *Prosopopœia*. Ap. 6.
abide = sit, i. e. ready for war, having subdued the Amorites, ch. 21, cp. Job 38. 40. Ps. 10. 8; 17. 12.
6 curse. Heb. *'ārar*. To wish or speak evil against, as to *effect* rather than as to the act.
wot = know.
7 rewards of divination. Heb. "divinations". Fig. *Metonymy* (of Effect), Ap. 6, put for the money which procures it. Cp. 2 Pet. 2. 15.
8 the LORD. Heb. Jehovah. Ap. 4. II.
9 God . . . said. Note the change to *'Elohim*.
said. Only four times: in *vv.* 9, 12, 20: in connection with Balaam. See Ap. 4, and notes on 1. 1; 3. 40.
11 there is a People. Heb. = the People.
now. Some codices, with Sam., Jon., and Sept., read "now therefore".
curse. Heb. *ḳābab*, to pierce with words. Note that this word is found only in Balak's and Balaam's mouths. Here, first occurrence, and later in seven other places. See note on 23. 8.
peradventure = perhaps.
12 not go. This is absolute. Cp. *v.* 20, where the permission is conditional. See Structure above.
thou shalt not curse. A special various reading called *Sevir* (see Ap. 34), with Sam., Jon., Sept., Syr., and Vulg., read "neither shalt thou".
13 Balaam . . . said. Note what he suppressed.
14 they . . . said. Note what they suppressed.
17 promote thee unto very great honour. Fig. *Polyptōton* (Ap. 6), for the emphasis rightly shown in the translation. Heb. an honouring I will honour thee. See note on Gen. 26. 28.
20 If the men come to call thee. This was the condition with which Balaam did not comply. See *v.* 21.

22. 21—35 (w^1, above). BALAAM'S JOURNEY. (*Introversion, with Repeated and Extended Alternation.*)

w^1 | b | 21. Journey commenced.
 c | 22-. Anger of God.
  d | e^1 | f^1 | -22. The angel.
     g^1 | 23-. The ass.
      h^1 | -23. Balaam.
   e^2 | f^2 | 24. The angel.
     g^2 | 25-. The ass.
      h^2 | -25. Balaam.
   e^3 | f^3 | 26. The angel.
     g^3 | 27-. The ass.
      h^3 | -27. Balaam.
 c | 28-35-. Rebuke of Jehovah.
 b | -35. Journey completed.

21 went. Without waiting for the condition given by the LORD in *v.* 20. Hence God's anger. See *v.* 22.

c (p. 213) 1452 22 And °God's anger was kindled because he °went: and the Angel of [8]the LORD °stood in the way for an adversary against him.

d e[1] f[1] Now he was riding upon his ass, and his two servants *were* with him.

g[1] 23 And the ass saw the Angel of [8]the LORD standing in the way, and °His sword drawn in His hand: and the ass turned aside °out of the way, and went into the field:

h[1] and Balaam smote the ass, to turn her into the way.

f[2] 24 But the Angel of [8]the LORD stood in a °path of the vineyards, a °wall *being* on this side, and a °wall on that side.

g' 25 And when the ass saw the Angel of [8]the LORD, she thrust herself unto the wall, and crushed Balaam's foot against the wall:

h and he smote her again.

f 26 And the Angel of [8]the LORD went further, and stood in a °narrow place, where *was* no way to turn either to the right hand or to the left.

g' 27 And when the ass saw the Angel of [8]the LORD, she fell down under Balaam:

h[3] and Balaam's anger was kindled, and he smote the ass with a staff.

c i (p. 214) 28 And [8]the LORD °opened the mouth of the ass, and she said unto Balaam,

k l "What have I done unto thee, that thou hast smitten me these three times?"

m 29 And Balaam said unto the ass, "Because thou hast mocked me: I would there were a sword in mine hand, for now would I kill thee."

l 30 And the ass said unto Balaam, "*Am* not I thine ass, upon which thou hast ridden ever since *I was* thine unto this day? was I ever wont to do so unto thee?"

m And he said, "Nay."

i 31 Then [8]the LORD °opened the eyes of Balaam, and he saw the Angel of [8]the LORD standing in the way, and His sword drawn in His hand: and he bowed down his head, and fell flat on his face.

k n 32 And the Angel of [8]the LORD °said unto him, °"Wherefore hast thou smitten thine ass these three times? °behold, I went out °to withstand thee, because *thy* way is °perverse before Me:

33 And the ass saw Me, and turned from Me these three times: unless she had turned from Me, surely now also I had slain °thee, and saved °her alive."

o 34 And Balaam said unto the Angel of [8]the LORD, "I have °sinned; for I knew not that Thou stoodest in the way against me: now therefore, if it displease Thee, I will get me back again."

n 35 And the Angel of [8]the LORD [32]said unto Balaam, °"Go with the °men: but °only the word that I shall speak unto thee, that thou shalt speak."

22 God's anger. Note *'Elohim*, not Jehovah.
went = was really going. Emphasised to show that even this condition was not meant as a condition, but was to be taken rather as irony. It shows also Balaam's determination to go, whether or no.
stood = stationed himself.

23 His sword drawn. As in 1 Chron. 21. 16. Balaam was going to have Israel killed with the sword.

24 path = a narrow or hollow way. Heb. *mish'ōl.* Occurs only here.
wall. Especially the wall of a vineyard. Cp. Isa. 5. 5.

26 narrow. Heb. *ẓārar.* Occurs only here, Prov. 23. 27, and Isa. 28. 20.

28-35 (c, p. 213). THE REBUKE OF JEHOVAH.
(*Alternation and Introversion.*)

c | i | 28-. By the ass. Ass's mouth opened.
  k | l | -28. The ass.
    m | 29. Balaam.
   l | 30-. The ass.
    m | -30. Balaam.
 i | 31. By the angel. Balaam's eyes opened.
  k | n | 32, 33. The angel.
    o | 34. Balaam.
   n | 35-. The angel.

28 opened the mouth, &c. Heb. *pātaḥ.* Cp. *v.* 31. This was Jehovah's work (as in *v.* 31). But how could Satan open the mouth of the serpent, which has no organs of speech? See Gen. 3. 1, &c., and Ap. 19.

31 opened = uncover. Heb. *gālah.* Cp. *v.* 28.

32 said. See note on 3. 40.
Wherefore . . . ? Fig. *Erotēsis.* Ap. 6.
behold. Fig. *Asterismos.* Ap. 6.
to withstand = to be an adversary, as in *v.* 22.
perverse. Heb. *'ăvil.* Occurs only here and Job 16. 11 (ungodly).

33 thee . . . her. Note the emphasis on these pronouns.

34 sinned. Heb. *chaṭa.* Ap. 44. i.

35 Go. Jehovah now overrules the evil for Israel's good.
men = Heb. pl. of *'īsh*, or *'enōsh.* Ap. 14. II.
only the word. Permission limited.

36-40 (v[2], p. 213). BALAK'S RECEPTION OF BALAAM (*First Day*).

v[2] | p | 36. Meeting (at frontier).
  q | 37, 38. Greetings.
 p | 39. Accompanying (to Kirjath-huzoth).
  q | 40. Offering.

36 coast = border.

37 Did I not earnestly send. Fig. *Polyptōton* (Ap. 6), Heb. "a sending did I not send". See note on Gen. 26. 28.
am I not able . . . ? Vain boast! Fig. *Erotēsis.* Ap. 6.

38 Lo. Fig. *Asterismos* (Ap. 6).
have I . . . ? Fig. *Erotēsis* (Ap. 6).
God = *'Elōhim.* Not Jehovah. Note this, and see Ap. 4.

So Balaam went with the princes of Balak. b (p. 213)

36 And when Balak heard that Balaam was come, he went out to meet him unto a city of Moab, which *is* in the border of Arnon, which *is* in the utmost °coast. v[2] p (p. 214)

37 And Balak said unto Balaam, °"Did I not earnestly send unto thee to call thee? wherefore camest thou not unto me? °am I not able indeed to promote thee to honour?" q

38 And Balaam said unto Balak, °"Lo, I am come unto thee: °have I now any power at all to say any thing? the word that °God putteth in my mouth, that shall I speak."

39 And Balaam went with Balak, and they came unto Kirjath-huzoth. *p*

q (p. 214) 1452 40 And Balak °offered oxen and sheep, and sent to Balaam, and to the princes that *were* with him.

w^2 t^1 u (p. 215) 41 And it came to pass on the morrow, that Balak took Balaam, and brought him up into the high places of Baal, that thence he might see °the utmost *part* of the People.

v **23** And Balaam said unto Balak, "Build me here seven altars, and prepare me here seven oxen and seven rams."

2 And Balak did °as Balaam had spoken; and Balak and Balaam °offered on *every* altar a bullock and a ram.

w 3 And Balaam said unto Balak, "Stand by thy burnt offering, and I will go: peradventure °the LORD will come to °meet me: and whatsoever He sheweth me I will tell thee." And °he went to an high place.

x 4 And °God °met Balaam: and he said unto Him, "I have prepared seven altars, and I have [2]offered upon *every* altar a bullock and a ram."

5 And [3]the LORD °put a word in Balaam's mouth, and °said, "Return unto Balak, and thus thou shalt speak."

y 6 And he returned unto him, and, °lo, he stood by his burnt sacrifice, he, and all the princes of Moab.

z c 7 And he took up his parable, and said,
"Balak the king of Moab hath brought me from Aram,
Out of the mountains of the east, *saying*,
'Come, °curse me Jacob, and come, defy Israel.'

d 8 °How shall I °curse, whom °GOD hath not °cursed?
Or how shall I °defy, *whom* [3]the LORD hath not °defied?

d 9 For from the top of the rocks I see him,
And from the hills I behold him:
[6]Lo, the People shall dwell alone,
And shall °not be reckoned among the nations.
10 °Who can count the dust of Jacob,
And °the number of the fourth *part* of Israel?

c Let °me die the death of the °righteous,
And let my °last end be like his!"

a 11 And Balak said unto Balaam, "What hast thou done unto me? I took thee to °curse mine enemies, and, behold, thou hast blessed *them* altogether."

b 12 And he answered and said, "Must I not take heed to speak that which [3]the LORD hath [5]put in my mouth?"

u 13 And Balak said unto him, "Come, I pray thee, with me unto another place, from whence thou mayest see them: thou shalt see but the utmost part of them, and shalt not see them all: and [11]curse me them from thence."

14 And he brought him into the field of Zophim, to the top of Pisgah, and built seven altars, and [2]offered a bullock and a ram on *every* altar. *v*

15 And he said unto Balak, "Stand here by thy °burnt offering, while I [3]meet *the* LORD yonder." *w*

16 And the [3]LORD [4]met Balaam, and [5]put a word in his mouth, and [5]said, "Go again unto Balak, and say thus." *x*

17 And when he came to him, °behold, he stood by his burnt offering, and the princes of *y*

---

40 offered. Heb. *zabach*, to slay. See Ap. 43. I. iv.

22. 41—24. 25 (w^2, p. 213). BALAAM'S PROPHECIES (*Second Day*): (*Division*).

w^2 | t^1 | 22. 41 — 23. 26. With enchantments.
| t^2 | 23. 27 — 24. 25. Without enchantments.

22. 41—23. 26 (t^1, above). WITH ENCHANTMENTS (*Extended Alternation*).

t^1 u | 22. 41. FIRST station: high places.
v | 23. 1, 2. Altars and offerings.
w | 3. Balaam goes to meet Jehovah.
x | 4, 5. Word put in Balaam's mouth.
y | 6. Return and station.
z | 7-10. His FIRST Parable.
a | 11. Balak's expostulation.
b | 12. Balaam's answer.
u | 23. 13, 14-. SECOND station: Zophim.
v | -14. Altars and offerings.
w | 15. Balaam goes to meet Jehovah.
x | 16. Word put in Balaam's mouth.
y | 17. Return and station.
z | 18-24. His SECOND Parable.
a | 25. Balak's expostulation.
b | 26. Balaam's answer.

41 the utmost part = the extremity of the camp.

23. 2 as = according to what.
offered = offered up. Heb. *'ālāh*. See Ap. 43. I. vi.
3 the LORD. Heb. Jehovah. See Ap. 4. II.
meet: in a neutral sense. Heb. *ḳār'ā*.
he went. Heb. he went solitary. Cp. 24. 1.
4 God. Heb. *'Elohim*. See Ap. 4. I.
met: in a hostile sense. Heb. *kārah*.
5 put a word. This is inspiration.
said. See note on 3. 40.
6 lo. Fig. *Asterismos* (Ap. 6).

7-10 (z, above). BALAAM'S FIRST PARABLE. (*Introversion.*)

z | c | 7. Balak's wish.
d | 8. Israel immune from man's cursing.
d | 9, 10-. Israel excluded from man's reckoning.
c | -10. Balaam's wish.

7 curse. Heb. *'ārar*. See notes on 22. 6 and 11.
8 How . . .? Fig. *Erotēsis*. Ap. 6.
curse = revile. Heb. *naḳab*.
GOD = Heb. *'Ēl* = the mighty God. See Ap. 4. IV.
cursed. Heb. *ḳabab* = to pierce with words.
defy . . . defied. Heb. *zā'am* = to be enraged with.
9 not be reckoned. Therefore cannot be in the judgment of Matt. 25, or confused with "the Gentiles, or with the church of God". 1 Cor. 10. 32.
10 Who can count . . .? Fig. *Erotēsis*. Ap. 6.
the number of = Who can number? Fig. *Erotēsis* (Ap. 6). So with Sam. and Sept. The word "number" is thought by Ginsburg to be an abbreviation of two words = "Who can number?"
me die = my soul die. Heb. *nephesh*. See Ap. 13.
righteous = upright. To die the death of the righteous one must have the righteousness of the righteous.
last end = latter end, i. e. issue or reward.
11 curse. Heb. *ḳabab*. See note on 22. 11.
15 burnt offering. Some codices, one early printed edition, with Sam. and Syr., read "offerings" (*plural*).
17 behold. Fig. *Asterismos* (Ap. 6).

1452 Moab with him. And Balak said unto him, "What hath the [3]LORD spoken?"

e f[1] (p. 216) 18 And he took up his parable, and said,
"Rise up, Balak, and hear;
Hearken unto me, thou son of Zippor:
19 [8]GOD *is* not a man, that He should lie;
Neither the son of man, that He should repent:
°Hath He said, and shall He not do *it*?
Or °hath He spoken, and shall He not make it good?

f[2] 20 [17]Behold, I have received *commandment* to bless: and °He hath blessed;
And I cannot reverse it.

e[2] g i 21 He hath not beheld °iniquity in Jacob,
Neither hath He seen °perverseness in Israel:

k [3]The LORD his [4]God *is* with him,
And the shout of a king *is* among them.

h 22 [8]GOD brought them out of Egypt;
He hath as it were the °strength of an °unicorn.

i 23 Surely *there is* no enchantment against Jacob,
Neither *is there* any divination against Israel:

k According to this time it shall be said of Jacob and of Israel,
'What hath [8]GOD wrought!'

h 24 [20]Behold, the people shall rise up as a great lion,
And lift up himself as a young lion:
He shall not lie down until he eat *of* the prey,
And drink the blood of the slain."

a (p. 215) 25 And Balak said unto Balaam, "Neither [11]curse them at all, nor bless them at all."

b 26 But Balaam answered and said unto Balak, "Told not I thee, saying, 'All that [3]the LORD speaketh, that I must do?'"

t[2] l (p. 216) 27 And Balak said unto Balaam, "Come, I pray thee, I will bring thee unto another place; peradventure it will please [4]God that thou mayest [11]curse me them from thence."
28 And Balak brought Balaam unto the top of Peor, that looketh toward °Jeshimon.

m 29 And Balaam said unto Balak, "Build me here seven altars, and prepare me here seven bullocks and seven rams."
30 And Balak did [2]as Balaam had said, and °offered a bullock and a ram on *every* altar.

n **24** And when Balaam saw that it °pleased °the LORD to bless Israel, he went not, as at °other times, °to seek for enchantments, but he set his face toward the wilderness.

o 2 And Balaam lifted up his eyes, and he saw Israel abiding *in his tents* °according to their tribes; and °the Spirit of °God came °upon him.

p q 3 °And he took up his parable, and said,
"Balaam the son of Beor hath said,
And °the man °whose eyes are °open hath said:
4 He hath said, which heard the words °of °GOD,

18-24 (*z*, p. 215). BALAAM'S SECOND PARABLE. (*Division.*)

z | e[1] | 18-20. God's immutable purpose.
| e[2] | 21-24. Israel's immutable privileges.

18-20 (e[1], above). GOD'S IMMUTABLE PURPOSE. (*Division.*)

e[1] | f[1] | 18, 19. God's nature unchangeable.
| f[2] | 20. God's Word irreversible.

19 Hath He said. Fig. *Erotēsis.* Ap. 6.

20 He hath blessed. Sam. and Sept. read "I will bless".

21 iniquity. Heb. *'āvōn*, trespass. Ap. 44. III.
perverseness. Heb. *'āmāl.* Ap. 44. v.

21-24 (e[2], above). ISRAEL'S IMMUTABLE PRIVILEGES (*Extended Alternation*).

e[2] | g | i | 21-. Negative. Absence of iniquity.
| k | -21, 22-. Positive. Presence of God.
| h | -22. STRENGTH (Simile: Buffalo).
| *g* | *i* | 23-. Negative. Powerlessness of enemies.
| *k* | -23. Positive. Power of God.
| *h* | 24. VICTORY (Simile: Lion).

22 strength = heights or heaps of. Heb. *tō'āpōth.* Only here, 24. 8, Job 22. 25 (plenty), and Ps. 95. 4 (= heights).
unicorn. This word is from the Sept. The Heb. is *r[e]ēm.* Supposed to be the rhinoceros, buffalo, or antelope: always rendered "unicorn" in A.V.

23. 27—24. 25 (t[2], p. 215). WITHOUT ENCHANTMENTS.
(*Extended Alternation.* Corresponding with t[1], p. 215.)

t[2] | l | 23. 27, 28. Station: Peor.
| m | 23. 29, 30. Offerings.
| n | 24. 1. Non-departure.
| o | 24. 2. Spirit upon Balaam.
| p | 24. 3-25. His Third and Fourth Parables.

28 Jeshimon. See note on 21. 20.
30 offered = offered up. Heb. *'ālāh.* Ap. 43. II. ii.

24. 1 pleased the LORD. Heb. was good in the eyes of Jehovah.
the LORD. Heb. Jehovah. Ap. 4.
other times. Cp. 23. 3, 15, and see Structure (t[1], p. 215).
to seek for enchantments = to meet with familiar spirits (Deut. 18. 10, 14). Heb. *n[e]chashīm*, from *nachash*, a serpent. Cp. Gen. 3. 1, and see Ap. 19.
2 according to their tribes. Cp. ch. 2.
the spirit of God (Heb. *'Elohim*). This expression occurs eight times outside the books of Samuel (Gen. 1. 2; 41. 38. Ex. 31. 3; 35. 31. Num. 24. 2. Ezek. 11. 24. 2 Chron. 15. 1; 24. 20). In all other places it is "the spirit of Jehovah".
Spirit. Heb. *rūach.* Ap. 9.
upon. Always "upon" (not "in") in Old Testament.

3-25 (p, above). BALAAM'S THIRD AND FOURTH PARABLES (*Alternation and Introversion*).

p | q | 3-9. Balaam's THIRD Parable.
| r | s | 10, 11. Balak's anger.
| t | 12-14. Balaam's answer.
| *q* | 15-24. Balaam's FOURTH Parable.
| *r* | *t* | 25-. Balaam's return.
| *s* | -25. Balak's departure.

3-9 [For Structure see next page].

3 And he took up his parable. Cp. 23. 7, 18.
the man = the strong or mighty man. Heb. *geber.* See Ap. 14. IV.
whose eyes are. Heb. "whose eye is".
open. Heb. *shātham, to close*, i. e. "the man with closed eye", i. e. in an ecstasy; closed, but seeing.
4 of. Genitive of origin = words from God.
GOD = the mighty God. Heb. *'Ēl.* Ap. 4. iv.

1452 Which saw the vision of ° the ALMIGHTY,
° *Falling into a trance*, but having his eyes
[3]open:

u[1] (p. 217) 5 ° 'How goodly are thy tents, O ° Jacob,
° *And* thy tabernacles, O ° Israel!
6 As the valleys are they spread forth,
As gardens by the river's side,
° As the trees of lign aloes which [1]the LORD hath planted,
And as cedar trees beside the waters.
7 He shall ° pour the water out of his buckets,
v And his seed *shall be* in many waters,
And his king shall be higher than Agag,
And his kingdom shall be exalted.
u[2] 8 [4]GOD brought ° him forth out of Egypt;
He hath as it were the strength of an ° unicorn:
v[2] He shall eat up the nations his enemies, and shall break their bones,
And pierce *them* through with his arrows.
u[3] 9 ° He couched, he lay down as a lion,
And as a great lion: who shall stir him up?
v[3] Blessed *is* he that blesseth thee,
And ° cursed *is* he that ° curseth thee.'"

r s (p. 216) 10 And ° Balak's anger was kindled against
Balaam, and he smote his hands together:
and Balak said unto Balaam, "I called thee
to ° curse mine enemies, and, ° behold, thou
hast ° altogether blessed *them* these three
times.
11 Therefore now flee thou to thy place:
I thought to ° promote thee unto great honour;
but, ° lo, [1]the LORD hath kept thee back from
honour."
t 12 And Balaam said unto Balak, "Spake I
not also to thy messengers which thou sentest
unto me, saying,
13 'If Balak would give me his house full of
silver and gold, I cannot go beyond the commandment of [1]the LORD, to do *either* good or
bad of mine own mind; *but* what [1]the LORD
saith, that will I speak?'
14 And now, [10]behold, I go unto my people:
come *therefore, and* I will advertise thee
what this People shall do to thy People in
° the latter days."

q w[1] (p. 217) 15 And he took up his parable, and said,
"Balaam the son of Beor hath said,
And [3]the man whose eyes are [3]open hath said:
16 He hath said, which heard the words of [4]GOD,
And knew the knowledge of the ° Most High,
Which saw the vision of the [4]ALMIGHTY,
[4]Falling *into a trance*, but having his eyes [3]open:
w[2] x 17 'I shall see Him, ° but not now:
I shall behold Him, ° but not nigh:
There shall come a ° Star out of [5]Jacob,
And a ° Sceptre shall rise out of [5]Israel,
y And shall smite the ° corners of Moab,
And ° destroy all the children of ° Sheth.
18 And Edom shall be a possession,

3-9 ("q", p. 216). BALAAM'S THIRD PARABLE.
(*Repeated Alternation.*)

q | 3, 4. Introduction.
u[1] | 5-7-. Goodliness (Simile: Valleys, Gardens, Trees).
v[1] | -7. EXALTATION.
u[2] | 8-. Strength (Simile: Buffalo).
v[2] | -8. VICTORY.
u[3] | 9-. Security (Simile: Lions).
v[3] | -9. BLESSING.

the ALMIGHTY = Shaddai, the All-bountiful or All-sufficient. See Ap. 4. VII.

falling into a trance. The *Ellipsis* better supplied = "falling [to the ground]".

5 How goodly. Fig. *Thaumasmos.* Ap. 6. This is only in "the vision of the Almighty".

Jacob. Fig. *Metonymy* (of Adjunct), put for posterity (Ap. 6).

And. This not to be in italics, according to some codices, with Sam., Jon., Syr., and Vulg.

Israel. See note on "Jacob", *v.* 5.

6 As the trees of lign aloes, &c. Some codices, with Jon., Sept., and Syr., read "as tents which Jehovah hath pitched".

7 pour the water. This refers to Millennial blessings. See Ezek. 47 and Zech. 14.

8 him. Some codices, with Onk., Jon., and Syr., read "them". Cp. 23. 22.

unicorn. See note on 23. 22.

9 He couched, &c. Cp. Gen. 49. 9.

cursed . . . curseth. Heb. *'ārar*, execrate, chiefly as to its effect. See notes on 22. 11; 23. 8.

10 Balak's anger. See note on Ex. 10. 28.

curse = to pierce with words. Heb. *ḳābab.* See note on 22. 11.

behold. Fig. *Asterismos.* Ap. 6.

altogether blessed. Heb. "a blessing thou hast blessed". Fig. *Polyptōton.* Ap. 6. See note on Gen. 26. 28.

11 promote thee unto great honour. See note on 22. 17, 37.

lo. Fig. *Asterismos.* Ap. 6.

14 the latter days = the end of the days, denoting a definite period. Cp. Gen. 49. 1. Deut. 4. 30. Isa. 2. 2. Jer. 23. 20; 30. 24; 48. 47; 49. 39. Ezek. 38. 16. Dan. 10. 14. Hos. 3. 5. Mic. 4. 1.

15-24 ("*q*", p. 216). BALAAM'S FOURTH PARABLE (*Division*).

q | w[1] | 15, 16. Introduction.
w[2] | 17-19. Israel.
w[3] | 20-24. The nations.

16 Most High. Heb. *Elyōn*, the High One over all the earth. See note on first occurrence, Gen. 14. 18. The Old Testament usage of this title is always in connection with dominion in the earth. Ap. 4.

17-19 (w[1], above). ISRAEL.
(*Introversion.*)

w[1] | x | 17-. The Star out of Jacob.
y | -17, 18. His enemies.
x | 19. The Messiah out of Jacob.

17 but not. Heb. Who is not.

Star. Heb. *ḳōkāb* = Messiah. See Luke 1. 78. 2 Pet. 1. 19. Rev. 2. 28; 22. 16, and cp. Matt. 2. 2.

Sceptre. See note on Gen. 49. 10, and cp. Ps. 2.

corners = quarters.

destroy = subdue.

Sheth = Seth, i. e. all men, for all are now descendants of Sheth through Noah.

1452 Seir also shall be a possession for his enemies;
And Israel shall do valiantly.
x (p. 217) 19 °Out of Jacob shall come He that shall have dominion,
And shall destroy him that remaineth of the city.'"
w[3] 20 And when he looked on Amalek, he took up his parable, and said,
"Amalek *was* °the first of the nations;
But his latter end °*shall be* that he perish for ever."
21 And he looked on the °Kenites, and took up his parable, and said,
"Strong is thy dwellingplace,
And thou puttest thy °nest in a rock.
22 Nevertheless the [21]Kenite shall be wasted,
Until Asshur shall carry thee away captive."
23 And he °took up his parable, and said,
"Alas, who shall °live when [4]GOD doeth this!
24 And ships *shall come* from the coast of °Chittim,
And shall °afflict °Asshur, and shall °afflict °Eber,
And °he also shall perish for ever."
r t (p. 216) 25 And Balaam rose up, and went and returned to his place: and Balak also went
s his way.

z[1] a (p. 218) **25** And Israel °abode in °Shittim, and the people began to commit whoredom °with the daughters of Moab.
2 And °they called the People unto the sacrifices of °their gods: and the People did eat, and bowed down to °their gods.
3 And Israel °joined himself unto °Baal-peor:
a and the °anger of °the LORD was kindled against Israel.
4 And [3]the LORD °said unto Moses, "Take all the °heads of the People, and °hang them up before [3]the LORD against the sun, that the fierce anger of [3]the LORD may be turned away from Israel."
5 And Moses said unto the judges of Israel, "Slay ye every one his °men that were [3]joined unto Baal-peor."
a 6 And, °behold, one of the °children of Israel came and brought unto his brethren a Midianitish woman in the sight of Moses, and in the sight of all the congregation of the °children of Israel, °who *were* weeping *before* the °door of the °tabernacle of the congregation.
b 7 And when °Phinehas, the son of Eleazar, the son of Aaron the priest, saw *it*, he rose up from among the congregation, and took a javelin in his hand;
8 And he went after the °man of Israel into the °tent, and thrust both of them through, the °man of Israel, and the woman through her °belly. So the plague was stayed from the [6]children of Israel.
9 And those that died in the plague were °twenty and four thousand.
z[2] c 10 And [3]the LORD °spake unto Moses, saying,

19 Out of Jacob. In Heb. there is the *Ellipsis* of the *Participle* (Ap. 6); "shall come" is implied and should be repeated from the previous clause. R.V. is literal.
20 the first: i. e. the first that warred against Israel. Ex. 17. 8. Not the first in time or importance.
shall be, &c. = "[shall be] destruction". Cp. Ex. 17. 16.
21 Kenites. With the word "nest" forms the Fig. *Paronomasia* (Ap. 6). Heb. *bēn ḳain*. **nest.** Heb. *ḳēn*.
23 took up. This is not a fifth parable, but part of the fourth. **live** = survive.
24 Chittim. A son of Javan, son of Japheth. Gen. 10. 4.
Probably Cyprus, including north coast-line of Mediterranean, spelt Kittim in Gen. 10. 4 and 1 Chron. 1. 7.
afflict = humble.
Asshur = Assyrians. **Eber** = the Hebrews.
he also: i. e. who sends the ships and humbled Asshur and Heber.

25. 1-18 (v[3], p. 213). **BALAK'S TEACHING BY BALAAM** (Cp. 31. 16 with Rev. 2. 14). (*Division.*)

v[3] | z[1] | 1-9. Balak's teaching and its results.
| z[2] | 10-18. Jehovah's action and its results.

1-9 (z[1], above). **BALAK'S TEACHING AND ITS RESULTS** (*Alternation*).

z[1] | a | 1-3-. Sin of the People.
| b | -3-5. Punishment enjoined.
| *a* | 6. Sin of the people.
| *b* | 7-9. Punishment executed.

1 abode: i. e. till after Moses' death. Cp. Josh. 2. 1; 3. 1, and see Mic. 6. 5.
Shittim. Called Abel-shittim in 33. 49.
with = to (Heb. *'el*). Requiring the supply of the *Ellipsis* "to join themselves to", from *v.* 3.
2 they: i. e. the daughters of Moab.
their. Feminine pronoun.
3 joined = yoked.
Baal-peor. Baal = Lord; Peor was the mountain on which he was worshipped (25. 18. Josh. 22. 17). Baal was a Moabitish idol, and those who called (*v.* 2) the Israelites were the prostitutes necessary for his worship by others. Cp. Hos. 9. 10. Jer. 11. 13. *Peōr* also means "opening", and may have relation to this "worship".
anger of the LORD (Heb. Jehovah). Cp. Ps. 106. 28, 29.
4 said. See note on 3. 40.
heads: i. e. chiefs or princes of the People. The number not stated here, but must have been 1,000, and included in the 24,000 of *v.* 9, and excluded in 1 Cor. 10. 8. The 23,000 mentioned in 1 Cor. 10. 8 "fell in one day": the day of the plague, *vv.* 9. 18. And those who were hanged prior to that (*vv.* 4, 5) are not included.
hang them up: i. e. impaled or nailed to a stake, as in crucifixion (Vulg. renders it "crucify", which means the same thing).
5 men. Heb. pl. of *'ish*, or *'enōsh*. Ap. 14.
6 behold. Fig. *Asterismos*. Ap. 6.
children = sons. **who** = and they.
door = entrance. Heb. *'ohel*. Ap. 40.
tabernacle = tent.
7 Phinehas. Cp. Ps. 106. 30.
8 man. Heb. *'īsh*. Ap. 14. ii.
tent. Heb. *ḳubbāh*, a high and vaulted pleasure tent, used in the worship of Baal. Occurs only here.
belly. Heb. *ḳobāh*, the part between the ribs and loins. Occurs only here, for the Fig. *Paronomasia* (Ap. 6).
9 twenty and four thousand. This includes the 1,000 previously "hanged" (*vv.* 4, 5), as well as those who died of the "plague". These must have been 23,000 of 1 Cor. 10. 8, which "fell in one day".

10-18 (z[2], above). **JEHOVAH'S ACTION AND ITS RESULTS** (*Division*).

z[2] | c | 10-13. Phinehas and his reward.
| c | 14-18. Midianites and their wiles.

10 spake. See note on 1. 1.

1452 11 "Phinehas, the son of Eleazar, the son of Aaron the priest, hath turned My wrath away from the [6]children of Israel, while he was zealous for My sake among them, that I consumed not the [6]children of Israel in My jealousy.

12 Wherefore say, [6]'Behold, I give unto him My covenant of peace:

13 And °he shall have it, and his seed after him, *even* the covenant of an °everlasting priesthood; because he was zealous for his °God, and made an °atonement for the [6]children of Israel.'"

c (p. 218) 14 Now the name of the Israelite that was slain, *even* that was slain with the Midianitish woman, *was* Zimri, the son of Salu, a prince of a chief house among the Simeonites.

15 And the name of the Midianitish woman that was slain *was* Cozbi, the daughter of Zur; he *was* head over a °people, *and* of a chief house in Midian.

16 And [3]the LORD [10]spake unto Moses, saying,

17 °"Vex the Midianites, and smite them:

18 For they vex you with their °wiles, wherewith they have beguiled you in the matter of Peor, and in the matter of Cozbi, the daughter of a prince of Midian, their sister, which was slain in the °day of the plague for Peor's sake."

A[3] A c (p. 219) **26** And it came to pass °after the plague, that °the LORD °spake unto Moses and unto Eleazar the son of Aaron the priest, saying,

2 °"Take the sum of all the congregation of the °children of Israel, from twenty years old and upward, throughout °their fathers' house, all that are able to go to war in Israel."

3 And Moses and Eleazar the priest spake with them in the plains of Moab by Jordan *near* Jericho, saying,

4 °"*Take the sum of the People,* from twenty years old and upward; °as [1]the LORD commanded Moses and the [2]children of Israel, which went forth out of the land of Egypt."

d[1] 5 °Reuben, the eldest son of Israel: the [2]children of Reuben; Hanoch, *of whom cometh* the °family of the Hanochites: of Pallu, the family of the Palluites:

6 °Of Hezron, the family of the Hezronites: of Carmi, the family of the Carmites.

7 These *are* the [5]families of the Reubenites: and they that were numbered of them were °forty and three thousand and seven hundred and thirty.

8 And the °sons of Pallu; Eliab.

9 And the sons of Eliab; Nemuel, and Dathan, and Abiram. This *is that* Dathan and Abiram, °*which were* famous in the congregation, who °strove against Moses and against Aaron in the company of Korah, when they strove against [1]the LORD:

(10 °And the earth opened her mouth, and swallowed them up together with Korah, when that company died, what time the fire devoured two hundred and fifty men: and they became a °sign.)

13 he shall have it. See Ps. 106. 30, 31 and Mal. 2. 4, 5. Cp. 1 Chron. 6. 4-15. 1 Sam. 22. 18. 1 Kings 2. 27 with 1 Sam. 14. 17. Also 1 Chron. 6. 4-15. Ezra was of his line (Ezra 7. 1, 5).

everlasting priesthood. Restored to Phinehas, and remained with him, after Eli.

God. Heb. Elohim. Ap. 4.

atonement. See note on Ex. 29. 33.

15 people = clan or tribe. Heb. *'ummoth.* Occurs only here, Gen. 25. 16 and Ps. 117. 1.

17 Vex. Cp. ch. 31.

18 wiles = seductions. Heb. *nĕkal.* Occurs only here.

day: i. e. the "one day" of 1 Cor. 10. 8.

26. 1—27. 11 (**A**[3], p. 176). NUMERATION AND ORDER: INHERITANCE (*Alternation*).

A[3] | A | 26. 1-51. The People.
B | 26. 52-62. Their inheritance.
A | 26. 63-65. The People.
B | 27. 1-11. Their inheritance.

1-51 (A, above). THE PEOPLE.
(*Introversion and Division.*)

A | c | 1-4. Command to number.
d[1] | 5-11. Reuben.
12-14. Simeon.
15-18. Gad.
d[2] | 19-22. Judah.
23-25. Issachar.
26, 27. Zebulun.
d[3] | 28-34. Manasseh.
35-37. Ephraim.
38-41. Benjamin.
d[4] | 42, 43. Dan.
44-47. Asher.
48-50. Naphtali.
c | 51. The total number.

1 after the plague. Cp. 25. 9.

the LORD. Heb. Jehovah. Ap. 4.

spake. See note on 1. 1.

2 Take the sum. For the order of the tribes see Ap. 45. Moses received them by number, Ex. 38. 26; so now, when preparing to die, he delivers them over by number. This was the third numbering.

children = sons.

their fathers' house: i. e. the families. These shown here to be forty-seven. In Gen. 46 they are fifty-two; so five are extinct (one of Simeon, one of Asher, and three of Benjamin).

4 Take the sum of the people. This correctly supplies the Ellipsis from *v.* 2. See **Fig. *Ellipsis*,** Ap. 6. iii. 1.

as = according to what.

5 Reuben. Cp. Gen. 46. 8. Ex. 6. 14. The order is the same as in 1. 20, except that Ephraim and Manasseh are reversed. See Ap. 45.

family. See note on "house", *v.* 2, and throughout the chapter.

6 Of Hezron = To Hezron [pertained], and so throughout. Cp. *vv.* 12, 13, 15, 16, 17, 20, 21, 23, 24, 26, 28, 29, 30, 31, 32.

7 forty and three, &c. = 43,730 In Num. 1. 21 = 46,500, decrease of 2,770. This is an undesigned evidence of accuracy: an uninspired writer would have made an increase.

8 sons. A special reading of MS. called *Sevir* reads "son". See Ap. 34.

9 which were famous, &c. Heb. "the called of the congregation". No Ellipsis.

strove = struggled. Heb. *nāzāh.* Cp. Ex. 2. 13. Lev. 24. 10. 2 Sam. 14. 6. Cp. 16. 2, 3.

10 And the earth. This tenth verse is a *Parenthesis.* See Ap. 6.

sign: i. e. a warning.

1452 11 Notwithstanding °the children of Korah died not.

12 The sons of Simeon after their [5]families: [6]of Nemuel, the [5]family of the Nemuelites: [6]of Jamin, the family of the Jaminites: [6]of Jachin, the family of the Jachinites:

13 [6]Of Zerah, the family of the Zarhites: [6]of Shaul, the family of the Shaulites.

14 These *are* the [5]families of the Simeonites, °twenty and two thousand and two hundred.

15 The [2]children of Gad after their families: [6]of Zephon, the family of the Zephonites: [6]of Haggi, the family of the Haggites: [6]of Shuni, the family of the Shunites:

16 [6]Of Ozni, the family of the Oznites: [6]of Eri, the family of the Erites:

17 Of Arod, the family of the Arodites: of Areli, the family of the Arelites.

18 These *are* the families of the [2]children of Gad according to those that were numbered of them, °forty thousand and five hundred.

d² 19 The sons of Judah *were* Er and Onan:
(p. 219) and Er and Onan died in the land of Canaan.

20 And the sons of Judah after their families were; [6]of Shelah, the family of the Shelanites: [6]of Pharez, the family of the Pharzites: [6]of Zerah, the family of the Zarhites.

21 And the sons of Pharez were; [6]of Hezron, the family of the Hezronites: [6]of Hamul, the family of the Hamulites.

22 These *are* the [5]families of Judah according to those that were numbered of them, °threescore and sixteen thousand and five hundred.

23 °*Of* the sons of Issachar after their families: °*of* Tola, the family of the Tolaites: [6]of Pua, the family of the Punites:

24 [6]Of Jashub, the family of the Jashubites: [6]of Shimron, the family of the Shimronites.

25 These *are* the families of Issachar according to those that were numbered of them, °threescore and four thousand and three hundred.

26 [23]*Of* the sons of Zebulun after their families: of Sered, the family of the Sardites: [6]of Elon, the family of the Elonites: [6]of Jahleel, the family of the Jahleelites.

27 These *are* the [5]families of the Zebulunites according to those that were numbered of them, °threescore thousand and five hundred.

d³ 28 The sons of Joseph after their families *were* °Manasseh and Ephraim.

29 [23]Of the sons of [28]Manasseh: [6]of Machir, the family of the Machirites: and Machir begat Gilead: [6]of Gilead *come* the family of the Gileadites.

30 These *are* the sons of °Gilead: [6]*of* °Jeezer, the family of the Jeezerites: [6]of Helek, the family of the Helekites:

31 And [6]*of* Asriel, the family of the Asrielites: and *of* Shechem, the family of the Shechemites:

32 And [6]*of* Shemida, the family of the Shemidaites: and [6]*of* Hepher, the family of the Hepherites.

33 °And Zelophehad the son of Hepher had no sons, but °daughters: and the names of the daughters of Zelophehad *were* Mahlah, and Noah, Hoglah, Milcah, and Tirzah.

34 These *are* the [5]families of Manasseh, and those that were numbered of them, °fifty and two thousand and seven hundred.

35 These *are* the sons of Ephraim after their families: [6]of Shuthelah, the family of the Shuthalhites: [6]of Becher, the family of the Bachrites: [6]of Tahan, the family of the Tahanites.

36 °And these *are* the sons of Shuthelah: of °Eran, the family of the °Eranites.

37 These *are* the [5]families of the sons of Ephraim according to those that were numbered of them, °thirty and two thousand and five hundred. These *are* the sons of Joseph after their families.

38 The sons of Benjamin after their families: [6]of Bela, the family of the Belaites: [6]of Ashbel, the family of the Ashbelites: [6]of Ahiram, the family of the Ahiramites:

39 [6]Of Shupham, the family of the Shuphamites: [6]of Hupham, the family of the Huphamites.

40 And the sons of Bela were Ard and

11 the children of Korah died not. Cp. 16. 32, 35. They were Assir, Elkanah, and Abiasaph (Ex. 6. 24). Their descendants were prominent in the Temple-worship (1 Chron. 6. 22-38). Of them came Samuel (cp. 1 Chron. 6. 33, 4 with 1 Sam. 1. 20) and Heman (cp. 1 Chron. 6. 33 with 25. 4, 6). Two groups of Psalms are associated with them (42-49 and 84-88).

14 twenty and two, &c. In Num. 1. 23 = 59,300, decrease 37,100.

18 forty thousand, &c. = 40,500. In Num. 2. 15 = 45,650, decrease 5,150.

22 threescore, &c. = 76,500. In Num. 2. 4 = 74,600, increase 1,900.

23 Of. This word is not needed.

of Tola. Should be "to Tola [pertained]", as in *v.* 6. The word "to" or "unto" is read in some codices with Sam. and Sept.

25 threescore, &c. = 64,300. In Num. 2. 6 = 54,400, increase 9,900.

27 threescore, &c. = 60,500. In Num. 2. 8 = 57,400, increase 3,100.

28 Manasseh comes before Ephraim here, because the tribe had increased. In Num. 2. 18, 20 Ephraim comes first, because he was the standard-bearer, and because of the blessing (Gen. 48. 14).

30 Gilead. Cp. 32. 39, 40 and Josh. 17. 1.

Jeezer. In Josh. 17. 2, Abiezer. Only this tribe, and Judah (*v.* 21) had great-grandsons as "heads". Cp. Gen. 50. 23.

33 And = Now.

daughters. Cp. 27. 1; 36. 1-12; and Josh. 17. 3, 4. Their names are written Mahlah, Noah, Hoglah, Milcah (some codices, with Sept., Syr., and Vulg., read "and Milcah"), and Tirzah.

34 fifty and two, &c. = 52,700. In Num. 2. 21 = 32,200, increase 20,500.

36 And. Some codices, with Sam., Jon., and Sept., omit "And".

Eran . . . Eranites. Some codices, with Sam., Sept., and Syr., have "Edan . . . Edanites", the letters ד (*Daleth*) and ר (*Resh*) being easily mistaken.

37 thirty and two, &c. = 32,500. In Num. 2. 19 = 40,500, decrease 7,500.

1452 **Naaman: ° *of Ard*, the family of the Ardites: *and* [6]of Naaman, the family of the Naamites.**
41 These *are* the sons of Benjamin after their [5]families: and they that were numbered of them *were* ° forty and five thousand and six hundred.

d[4] (p. 219) **42 These *are* the sons of Dan after their families: of Shuham, the family of the Shuhamites. These *are* the families of Dan after their families.**
43 All the [5]families of the Shuhamites, according to those that were numbered of them, *were* ° threescore and four thousand and four hundred.

44 *Of* the ° children of Asher after their families: [6]of Jimna, the family of the Jimnites: [6]of Jesui, the family of the Jesuites: [6]of Beriah, the family of the Beriites.
45 [6]Of the sons of Beriah: [6]of Heber, the family of the Heberites: [6]of Malchiel, the family of the Malchielites.
46 And the name of the daughter of Asher *was* Sarah.
47 These *are* the [5]families of the sons of Asher according to those that were numbered of them; *who were* ° fifty and three thousand and four hundred.

48 *Of* the sons of Naphtali after their families: [6]of Jahzeel, the family of the Jahzeelites: [6]of Guni, the family of the Gunites:
49 [6]Of Jezer, the family of the Jezerites: [6]of Shillem, the family of the Shillemites.
50 These *are* the families of Naphtali according to their families: and they that were numbered of them *were* ° forty and five thousand and four hundred.

51 These *were* the numbered of the [2]children of Israel, ° six hundred thousand and a thousand seven hundred and thirty.

B e[1] (p. 221) **52 And [1]the LORD [1]spake unto Moses, saying,**
53 "Unto these the land shall be divided for an inheritance according to the number of names.
54 To ° many thou shalt give the more inheritance, and to ° few thou shalt give the less inheritance: to every one shall his inheritance be given according to those that were numbered of him.
55 Notwithstanding the land shall be divided ° by lot: according to the names of the tribes of their fathers they shall inherit.
56 According to ° the lot shall the possession thereof be divided between many and few."

e[2] **57 And these *are* they that were numbered of the Levites after their ° families: of Gershon, the family of the Gershonites: ot Kohath, the family of the Kohathites: of Merari, the family of the Merarites.**
58 These *are* the [5]families of the Levites: the family of the Libnites, the family of the Hebronites, the family of the Mahlites, the family of the Mushites, the family of the Korathites. And Kohath begat Amram.
59 And the name of Amram's wife *was* ° Jochebed, the daughter of Levi, whom *her mother* ° bare to Levi in Egypt: and she bare unto Amram Aaron and Moses, and Miriam their sister.
60 And unto Aaron was born Nadab, and Abihu, Eleazar, and Ithamar.
61 And ° Nadab and Abihu died, when they offered strange fire before [1]the LORD.
62 And those that were numbered of them were twenty and three thousand, all males from a month old and upward: for they were not numbered among the [2]children of Israel, because there was no inheritance given them among the [2]children of Israel.

63 These *are* they that were numbered by Moses and Eleazar the priest, who numbered *A* (p 219)

40 of Ard. Ellipsis (Ap. 6) should be supplied thus: "[to Ard] pertained".
41 forty and five, &c. = 45,600. In Num. 2. 23 = 35,400, increase 10,200.
43 threescore and four, &c. = 64,400. In Num. 2. 26 = 62,700. Decrease = 1,700.
44 children = sons.
47 fifty and three, &c. = 53,400. In Num. 2. 28 = 41,500, increase 11,900.
50 forty and five, &c. = 45,400. In Num. 2. 30 = 53,400, decrease 8,000.
51 The total number, accomplishing the command, *v.* 2. See the Structure, p. 219.
six hundred, &c. = 601,730. In Num. 2. 32 = 603,550, total decrease 1,820. In Egypt they increased like fishes, Ex. 1. 7, now they decrease. Cp. Ps. 78. 17-33.
Seven tribes increased (Judah, Issachar, Zebulun, Manasseh, Benjamin, Dan, Asher), total 59,200, beside the 1,000 Levites.
Five tribes decreased (Reuben, Simeon, Gad, Ephraim, and Naphtali), total 61,020.
LEAH, increase: in Judah 1,900, Issachar 9,900, Zebulun 3,100, Levi 1,000; and decrease in Reuben 2,770, Simeon 37,100. Total decrease 23,970.
RACHEL, increase: in Manasseh 20,500, Benjamin 10,200; and decrease in Ephraim 8,000; total increase 22,700.
ZILPAH, increase: in Asher 11,900; and decrease in Gad 5,150; total increase 6,750.
BILHAH, increase: in Dan 1,700; and decrease in Naphtali 8,000; total decrease 6,300.
So, in the four camps: East camp, all increased; South camp, all decreased; West camp, Benjamin and Manasseh increased, Ephraim decreased; North camp, Dan and Asher increased, Naphtali decreased.
On the whole, cp. Job 12. 9, 10, 14, 23.

52-62 (B, p. 200). THEIR INHERITANCE.

B | e[1] | 52-56. Inheritance by number.
  | e[2] | 57-62. Levi no inheritance.

54 many = the greater number.
few = the smaller number.
55 by = "upon": i. e. "contingently upon" (see *v.* 56). By Eleazar (34. 17), because, as high priest, he had the Urim and Thummim, which were the lots cast. The high priest must be present for the lot to speak, and give Jehovah's decision (Josh. 17. 4). Cp. Ezra 2. 61-63. Neh. 7. 63-65. The lot "came up" (Josh. 18. 11); "came forth" (Josh. 19. 1); "came out" (Josh. 19. 17) of the bag (containing the Urim and Thummin) which was in or behind the breastplate. See note on Ex. 28. 30, and cp. Prov. 16. 33; 18. 18.
56 the lot = Heb. "the mouth of the lot", as though the "lot" spoke and was personified, by the Fig. *Prosopopœia* (Ap. 6). See on *v.* 55.
59 Jochebed. Cp. Ex. 2. 1 and 6. 20.
bare to Levi in Egypt. This explains apparent discrepancy between her age and that of Amram. See Ap. 50. III.
61 Nadab. Cp. Lev. 10. 2. Num. 3. 4. 1 Chron. 24. 2.

1452 the [2]children of Israel in the plains of Moab by Jordan *near* Jericho.

64 But among these there was not a man of them whom Moses and Aaron the priest numbered, when they numbered the [2]children of Israel in the wilderness of Sinai.

65 For [1]the LORD had °said of them, "They °shall surely die in the wilderness." And there was not left a man of them, °save Caleb the son of Jephunneh, and Joshua the son of Nun.

B f (p. 222) **27** Then came the °daughters of Zelophehad, the son of Hepher, the son of Gilead, the son of Machir, the son of Manasseh, of the families of Manasseh the son of Joseph: and these *are* the names of his °daughters; Mahlah, Noah, and Hoglah, and Milcah, and Tirzah.

2 And they stood before Moses, and before Eleazar the priest, and before the princes and all the congregation, *by* the °door of the °tabernacle of the congregation, saying,

3 "Our father °died in the wilderness, and he was not in the company of them that gathered themselves together against °the LORD in the company of Korah; but died in his own °sin, and had no sons.

4 °Why should the name of our father be done away from among his family, because he hath no son? Give unto us *therefore* a possession among the brethren of our father."

g 5 And Moses brought their cause before [3]the LORD.

f 6 And [3]the LORD °spake unto Moses, saying,

7 "The daughters of Zelophehad speak right: thou °shalt surely give them a possession of an inheritance among their father's brethren; and thou shalt cause the inheritance of their father to pass unto them.

g 8 And thou shalt speak unto the °children of Israel, saying, 'If a man die, and have no son, then ye shall cause his inheritance to pass unto his daughter.

9 And if he have no daughter, then ye shall give his inheritance unto his brethren.

10 And if he have no brethren, then ye shall give his inheritance unto his father's brethren.

11 And if his father have no brethren, then ye shall give his inheritance °unto his kinsman that is next to him of his family, and he shall possess it: and it shall be unto the [8]children of Israel °a statute of judgment, °as [3]the LORD commanded Moses.'"

B³ A i 12 And [3]the LORD °said unto Moses, "Get thee up into this mount Abarim, and see the land which I have given unto the [8]children of Israel.

13 And when thou hast seen it, thou also shalt be gathered unto thy People, [11]as °Aaron thy brother was gathered.

14 For ye °rebelled against °My commandment in the desert of Zin, in the strife of the congregation, to sanctify Me at the water before their eyes: that *is* the °water of Meribah in Kadesh in the wilderness of Zin."

k 15 And Moses spake unto [3]the LORD, saying,

16 "Let [3]the LORD, the °God of the °spirits of all flesh, °set a °man over the congregation,

17 Which may °go out before them, and which may °go in before them, and which may lead them out, and which may bring them in; that the congregation of [3]the LORD be not as sheep which have no shepherd."

18 And [3]the LORD °said unto Moses, "Take i

---

65 said. Forty years before. Cp. ch. 14. 28–33.
shall surely die. Heb. "a dying they will die". Fig. *Polyptōton* (Ap. 6). See note on Gen. 2. 17; 26. 28.
save Caleb, &c. Cp. 14. 24, 30, 38. The whole congregation therefore composed of men over twenty, and none older than sixty.

27. 1-11 (*B*, p. 219). INHERITANCE: THE DAUGHTERS OF ZELOPHEHAD. (*Alternation.*)

B | f | 1–4. Their plea.
  g | 5. Reference to Jehovah.
 f | 6, 7. Answer to plea.
  g | 8–11. Statute of Jehovah.

1 daughters. Cp. 26. 33. Josh. 17. 3.
2 door = entrance.
tabernacle = tent. Heb. *'ohel*. Ap. 40.
3 died. Cp. 26. 64, 65.
the LORD. Heb. Jehovah. Ap. 4.
sin. Heb. *chăṭ'ā*. Ap. 44. i.
4 Why . . . ? Fig. *Erotēsis*. Ap. 6.
6 spake. See note on 1. 1.
7 shalt surely give. Heb. "a giving thou shalt give". Fig. *Polyptōton* (Ap. 6), for emphasis. See note on Gen. 26. 28. This command obeyed in Josh. 17. 4.
8 children = sons.
11 unto his kinsman. Cp. note on Lev. 18. 6.
a statute of judgment: or, regulative statute. Cp. 35. 29.
as = according to what.
12 the LORD said = Jehovah said. See note on 3. 40.

27. 12–31. 54 (B³, p. 176). EVENTS AND LAWS (*Introversion*).

B³ | A | 27. 12–23. Event: Moses' successor appointed.
  B | 28. 1—29. 40. Laws as to offerings (necessary).
  B | 30. 1–16. Laws as to vows (voluntary).
 A | 31. 1–54. Event: Moses' vengeance on Midian.

27. 12–23 (A, above). EVENT: MOSES' SUCCESSOR (*Alternation*).

A | h | i | 12–14. Warning to Moses.
   k | 15–17. Response of Moses.
 h | *i* | 18–21. Appointment of Joshua.
   k | 22, 23. Obedience.

13 Aaron. Cp. 20. 24.
14 rebelled. Cp. 20. 24.
My commandment. Heb. "My mouth". Fig. *Metonymy* (of Cause), Ap. 6, "mouth" put for what is spoken by it.
water. Cp. Ex. 17. 7. Of another Meribah.
16 God = Elohim. God, the Creator of men and the spirits of men (Gen. 2. 7), Who giveth the spirit to man, and takes it to Himself again (Ecc. 12. 7), and Who giveth all the gifts of the Spirit (1 Cor. 14. 12).
spirits. Plural of Heb. *rūach*. See Ap. 9.
set = or visit: i. e. provide and appoint.
man. Heb. *'īsh*. See Ap. 14. ii.
17 go out . . . go in. Fig. *Synecdoche* (of Species), Ap. 6, put for life in general, especially all official movements, and actions.
18 said. See note on 3. 40.

1452 thee °Joshua the son of Nun, a man in whom *is* the °spirit, and lay thine hand upon him;

19 And [16]set him before °Eleazar the priest, and before all the congregation; and give him a charge in their sight.

20 And thou shalt put *some* of thine honour upon him, that all the congregation of the [8]children of Israel may be obedient.

21 And °he shall stand before [19]Eleazar the priest, who shall ask °*counsel* °for him °after the °judgment of °Urim before [3]the LORD: °at his °word shall they [17]go out, and at his °word they shall [17]come in, *both* he, and all the [8]children of Israel with him, even all the congregation."

k (p. 222) 22 And Moses did [13]as [3]the LORD commanded him: and he took Joshua, and [16]set him before Eleazar the priest, and before all the congregation:

23 And he laid his hands upon him, and gave him a charge, as [3]the LORD °commanded °by the hand of Moses.

B l (p. 223) 28 And °the LORD °spake unto Moses, saying,

m 2 "Command the °children of Israel, and say unto them, 'My °offering, *and* My °bread for My sacrifices made by fire, *for* a °sweet savour unto Me, shall ye observe to °offer unto Me in their °due season.'

n o1 3 And thou shalt say unto them, 'This *is* the offering made by fire which ye shall offer unto [1]the LORD; two lambs of the first year °without spot day by day, *for* a continual burnt offering.

4 The one lamb shalt thou °offer in the morning, and the other lamb shalt thou °offer °at even;

5 And a tenth *part* of an °ephah of flour for a °meat offering, mingled with the fourth *part* of an °hin of beaten oil.

6 *It is* a continual burnt offering, which was ordained in mount Sinai for a [2]sweet savour, a sacrifice made by fire unto [1]the LORD.

7 And the drink offering thereof *shall be* the fourth *part* of an [5]hin for the one lamb: in the °holy *place* shalt thou cause the °strong wine to be poured unto [1]the LORD *for* a drink offering.

8 And the other lamb shalt thou [4]offer at even: as the [5]meat offering of the morning, and as the drink offering thereof, thou shalt offer *it*, a sacrifice made by fire, of a [2]sweet savour unto the LORD.

o2 9 And on the sabbath day two lambs of the first year [3]without spot, and two tenth deals of flour *for* a [5]meat offering, mingled with oil, and the drink offering thereof:

10 *This is* the burnt offering of every sabbath, °beside the continual burnt offering, and his drink offering.

o3 11 And in the beginnings of your months ye shall °offer a burnt offering unto [1]the LORD; two young bullocks, and one ram, seven lambs of the first year [3]without spot;

12 And three °tenth deals of flour *for* a meat offering, mingled with oil, for one bullock; and two °tenth deals of flour *for* a [5]meat offering, mingled with oil, for one ram;

13 And a several [12]tenth deal of flour mingled with oil *for* a [5]meat offering unto one lamb; *for* a burnt offering of a [2]sweet savour, a sacrifice made by fire unto [1]the LORD.

14 And their drink offerings shall be half an [5]hin of °wine unto a bullock, and the third *part* of an [5]hin unto a ram, and a fourth *part* of an [5]hin unto a lamb: this *is* the burnt offering of every month throughout the months of the year.

Joshua. See note on Ex. 17. 9.

spirit. Heb. *rūach* (Ap. 9). Put here by the Fig. *Metonymy* (of Cause), Ap. 6, for the gifts of the Holy Spirit: here, a spirit of "wisdom" (Deut. 34. 9).

19 Eleazar the priest: because he had the breast-plate with Urim and Thummim, and could alone give Joshua the decision or "judgment" of Jehovah.

21 he shall stand = take his stand. Heb. *'āmad*, as *v.* 2.

counsel. Supply *Ellipsis* with the word "judgment" from next clause (Ap. 6. iii. 1).

for = by. **after** = for.

judgment = decision.

Urim = the Urim. See note on Ex. 28. 30.

at his word = at the mouth: i. e. of the Urim.

word = commandment or instruction, "word" put by Fig. *Metonymy* (of Adjunct), Ap. 6, for what is spoken by the mouth.

23 commanded = spake. See note on 1. 1.

by the hand. Fig. *Metonymy* (of Cause), Ap. 6: i. e. by the instrumentality or agency of the hand.

28. 1—29. 40 (B, p. 222). LAWS AS TO OFFERINGS (*Introversion*).

B | l | 28. 1. Command given.
  m | 28. 2. General specification.
   n | 28. 3-31. Particular: as to offerings.
   n | 29. 1-38. Particular: as to seventh month.
  m | 29. 39. General summary.
 l | 29. 40. Command communicated.

28. 1 the LORD. Heb. Jehovah. Ap. 4.

spake. See note on 1. 1.

2 children = sons.

offering = approach offering Heb. *korbān*. Ap. 43. II. i.

bread. Fig. *Synecdoche* (of Species), Ap. 6, put for all kinds of food.

sweet savour. See note on Lev. 1. 9.

offer = bring near. Heb. *kārab*. Ap. 43. I. i.

due season = appointed time. Heb. *mō'ēd*. See note on Gen. 1. 14.

3-31 (n, above). PARTICULAR: AS TO OFFERINGS (*Division*).

n | o1 | 3-8. Daily.
  o2 | 9, 10. Sabbatic.
  o3 | 11-15. Monthly.
  o4 | 16-25. Paschal.
  o5 | 26-31. Firstfruits.

3 without spot. Heb. *tāmīm*, without blemish. See Ap. 26.

4 offer = prepare. Heb. *'āsāh*. Ap. 43. I. iii.

at even = between the evenings.

5 ephah. See Ap. 51. III. 3.

meat offering. Heb. *minchah* = meal or gift offering. Ap. 43. II. iii.

hin. See Ap. 51. III. 3.

7 holy. See note on Ex. 3. 5.

strong wine. Heb. *shēkar*. Ap. 27. iv.

10 beside = over and above.

11 offer = bring near. Heb. *kārav*. Ap. 43. I. i.

12 tenth deals. See Ap. 51. III. 3.

14 wine. Heb. *yayin*. Ap. 27. 1.

1452 **15** And one kid of the goats for a °sin
offering unto [1]the LORD shall be [4]offered,
beside the continual burnt offering, and his
drink offering.

o[4] (p. 223) **16** And in the °fourteenth day of the °first
month *is* the passover of [1]the LORD.
14 Abib **17** And in the fifteenth day of this month *is*
the feast: seven days shall unleavened bread
15 Abib be eaten.
18 In the [16]first day *shall be* an [5]holy convocation; ye shall do no manner of servile work
therein:
19 But ye shall [2]offer a sacrifice made by
fire *for* a burnt offering unto [1]the LORD; two
young bullocks, and one ram, and seven lambs
of the first year: they shall be unto you
without blemish:
20 And their [5]meat offering *shall be of* flour
mingled with oil: three [12]tenth deals shall ye
[4]offer for a bullock, and two [12]tenth deals for
a ram;
21 A several [12]tenth deal shalt thou offer for
every lamb, throughout the seven lambs:
22 And one goat *for* a sin offering, to make
an °atonement for you.
23 Ye shall offer these °beside the burnt
offering in the morning, which *is* for a continual burnt offering.
24 After this manner ye shall [2]offer daily,
throughout the seven days, the meat of the
sacrifice made by fire, of a [2]sweet savour unto
[1]the LORD: it shall be [2]offered [10]beside the
continual burnt offering, and his drink
offering.
25 And on the seventh day ye shall have
an [5]holy convocation; ye shall do no servile
work.

o[5] **26** Also °in the day of the firstfruits, when
ye bring a new [5]meat offering unto [1]the LORD,
°after your weeks *be out,* ye shall have an
[5]holy convocation; ye shall do no servile
work:
27 But ye shall [11]offer the burnt offering for
a [2]sweet savour unto [1]the LORD; two young
bullocks, °one ram, seven lambs of the first
year;
28 And their [5]meat offering of flour mingled
with oil, three [12]tenth deals unto one bullock,
°two [12]tenth deals unto one ram,
29 A several [12]tenth deal unto one lamb,
throughout the seven lambs;
30 °*And* one kid of the goats, to make an
[22]atonement for you.
31 Ye shall [4]offer *them* [23]beside the continual
burnt offering, and his meat offering, (they
shall be unto you without blemish) and their
drink offerings.

n p[1] (p. 224) **29** And in the °seventh month, on the
first *day* of the month, ye shall have
1st Tisri an °holy convocation; ye shall do no °servile
work: it is a day of °blowing the trumpets
unto you.
2 And ye shall °offer a burnt offering for a
°sweet savour unto °the LORD; one young
bullock, one ram, *and* seven lambs of the
first year °without blemish:
3 And their °meat offering *shall be of* flour
mingled with oil, three °tenth deals for a
bullock, *and* two °tenth deals for a ram,
4 And one [3]tenth deal for one lamb, throughout the seven lambs:
5 And one kid of the goats *for* a °sin offering,
to make an °atonement for you:
6 °Beside the burnt offering of the month,
and his [3]meat offering, and the daily burnt
offering, and his meat offering, and their
drink offerings, according unto their °manner,
for a sweet savour, a sacrifice made by fire
unto [2]the LORD.

7 And ye shall have on the tenth *day* of this p[2]
seventh month an [1]holy convocation; and ye
shall afflict your °souls: ye shall not do any
work *therein:*
8 But ye shall °offer a burnt offering unto the
LORD *for* a [2]sweet savour; one young bullock,
one ram, *and* seven lambs of the first year;
they shall be unto you [2]without blemish:
9 And their [3]meat offering *shall be of* flour
mingled with oil, three [3]tenth deals to a
bullock, *and* two [3]tenth deals to one ram,
10 °A several [3]tenth deal for one lamb,
throughout the seven lambs:
11 °One kid of the goats *for* a [5]sin offering;

---

15 sin offering. Heb. *chăṭ'ā.* Ap. 43. II. v.
16 fourteenth. Cp. Ex. 12. 2, 14, 18. Lev. 23. 5.
first. Cp. Lev. 23. 7.
22 atonement. See note on Ex. 29. 33.
23 beside = in addition to, as in *v.* 31 (not "upon", as in *vv.* 10 and 24).
26 in the day = at the time. See Ap. 18.
after your weeks be out = on the eve of your weeks.
27 one. Some codices, with one early printed edition, Sam., Jon., and Syr., read "and one".
28 two. Some codices, with one early printed edition, Sam., Sept., and Syr., read "and two".
30 And. This word, "and", is read in some codices, with Sam., Sept., Syr., and Vulg.

29. 1-38 (*n*, p. 223). PARTICULAR: *re* SEVENTH MONTH (*Division*).

n	p[1]	1-6.	First day. Seventh month.
	p[2]	7-11.	Tenth day.
	p[3]	12-16.	Fifteenth day.
	p[4]	17-19.	Second day.
	p[5]	20-22.	Third day.
	p[6]	23-25.	Fourth day.
	p[7]	26-28.	Fifth day.
	p[8]	29-31.	Sixth day.
	p[9]	32-34.	Seventh day.
	p[10]	35-38.	Eighth day.

1 seventh month. Heb. name Tisri not known in Scripture (our Sept.-Oct.). The old civil year went out (Ex. 23. 16; 34. 22), known as Ethanim (1 Kings 8. 2). Tisri = the first month of civil year. Nisan, or Abib = the first month of sacred year.
holy. See note on Ex. 3. 5. servile = laborious.
blowing the trumpets. Cp. Lev. 23. 24.
2 offer = prepare. Heb. *'āsāh.* Ap. 43. I. iii.
sweet savour. See note on Lev. 1. 9.
the LORD. Heb. Jehovah. Ap. 4.
without blemish = physically perfect. See Ap. 26.
3 meat offering. See Ap. 43. II. iii.
tenth deals. See Ap. 51. III. 3.
5 sin offering. See Ap. 43. II. v.
atonement. See note on Ex. 29. 33.
6 Beside = in addition to. See note on 28. 23.
manner = ordinance, or regulation.
7 souls. Plural of Heb. *nephesh.* See Ap. 13.
8 offer = bring near. Heb. *ḳārav.* Ap. 43. I. i.
10 A several tenth. Heb. "a tenth, a tenth" = a tenth severally, i. e. to each.
11 One. Some codices, with Sam., Sept., Syr., and Vulg., read "And one".

1452 [6]beside °the [11]sin offering of [5]atonement, and the continual burnt offering, and the meat offering of it, and their drink offerings.

p[3] (p. 224) 15th. Tisri 12 And on the °fifteenth day of °the seventh month ye shall have an [1]holy convocation; ye shall do no [1]servile work, and ye shall keep a feast unto [2]the LORD seven days:
13 And ye shall [8]offer a burnt offering, a sacrifice made by fire, of a [2]sweet savour unto [2]the LORD; thirteen young bullocks, two rams, *and* fourteen lambs of the first year; they shall be without blemish:
14 And their meat offering *shall be of* flour mingled with oil, three [3]tenth deals unto every bullock of the thirteen bullocks, two [3]tenth deals to each ram of the two rams,
15 And °a several [3]tenth deal to each lamb of the fourteen lambs:
16 And one kid of the goats *for* a sin offering; [11]beside the continual burnt offering, °his meat offering, and his drink offering.

p[4] 16th Tisri 17 And on the second day °*ye shall offer* twelve young bullocks, two rams, fourteen lambs of the first year [2]without spot:
18 And their meat offering and their drink offerings for the bullocks, for the rams, and for the lambs, *shall be* according to their number, after the [6]manner:
19 And one kid of the goats *for* a [11]sin offering; [6]beside the continual burnt offering, and the meat offering thereof, and their drink offerings.

p[5] 17th Tisri 20 And on the third day eleven bullocks, two rams, fourteen lambs of the first year [2]without blemish;
21 And their meat offering and their drink offerings for the bullocks, for the rams, and for the lambs, *shall be* according to their number, after the [6]manner:
22 And [11]one goat *for* a [11]sin offering; [6]beside the continual burnt offering, and his meat offering, and his drink offering.

p[6] 18th Tisri 23 And on the fourth day ten bullocks, two rams, *and* fourteen lambs of the first year [2]without blemish:
24 °Their meat offering and their drink offerings for the bullocks, for the rams, and for the lambs, *shall be* according to their number, after the [6]manner:
25 And one kid of the goats *for* a [11]sin offering; [6]beside the continual burnt offering, °his meat offering, and his drink offering.

p[7] 19th Tisri 26 And on the fifth day nine bullocks, two rams, *and* fourteen lambs of the first year [2]without spot:
27 And their meat offering and their drink offerings for the bullocks, for the rams, and for the lambs, *shall be* according to their number, after the [6]manner:
28 And one goat *for* a [11]sin offering; [6]beside the continual burnt offering, and his meat offering, and his drink offering.

p[8] 20th Tisri 29 And on the sixth day eight bullocks, two rams, *and* fourteen lambs of the first year without blemish:
30 And their meat offering and their drink offerings for the bullocks, for the rams, and for the lambs, *shall be* according to their number, after the [6]manner:
31 And one goat *for* a [11]sin offering; [6]beside the continual burnt offering, °his meat offering, and his °drink offering.

p[9] 21st Tisri 32 And on the seventh day seven bullocks, two rams, *and* fourteen lambs of the first year [2]without blemish:
33 And their meat offering and their drink offerings for the bullocks, for the rams, and for the lambs, *shall be* according to their number, after the [6]manner:
34 And one goat *for* a [11]sin offering; [6]beside the continual burnt offering, °his meat offering, and his [31]drink offering.

p[10] 22nd Tisri 35 On the eighth day ye shall have a °solemn assembly: ye shall do no [1]servile work *therein*:
36 But ye shall [8]offer a burnt offering, a sacrifice made by fire, of a [2]sweet savour unto [2]the LORD: one bullock, one ram, seven lambs of the first year [2]without blemish:
37 °Their meat offering and their drink offerings for the bullock, for the ram, and for the lambs, *shall be* according to their number, after the [6]manner:
38 And one goat *for* a [11]sin offering; [6]beside the continual burnt offering, and his meat offering, and his drink offering.

m (p. 223) 39 These *things* ye shall do unto [2]the LORD in your °set feasts, beside your vows, and your freewill offerings, for your burnt offerings, and for your meat offerings, and for your drink offerings, and for your peace offerings.' "

l 40 And Moses told the °children of Israel according to all that [2]the LORD commanded Moses.

the sin offering of atonement. This was the great offering of the day of atonement. Lev. 16.
12 fifteenth day. The Feast of Tabernacles.
the seventh month. Some codices, with Sam., Sept., Syr., and Vulg., read "this month".
15 a several tenth. As in *v.* 10, but the second word "tenth" has the extraordinary points (Ap. 31) omitting the word, making it like *v.* 4, instead of like *v.* 10.
16 his meat offering = the meal offering thereof. Some codices, with Sam., Sept., Syr., and Vulg., read "and the", or "and his".
17 ye shall offer. The Ellipsis (Ap. 6) is correctly supplied from preceding verses (*vv.* 2, 8, 13).
24 Their. Some codices, with one early printed edition, Sam., Sept., and Syr., read "And their".
25 his. See note on *v.* 16. Some codices, with Sam., Onk., Syr., and Vulg., read "and his".
31 his. See note on *v.* 16. Some codices, with one early printed edition, Sam., Onk., and Syr., read "and his".
drink offering. Some codices have this in the plural.
35 solemn assembly. Cp. Lev. 23. 36.
37 Their. Some codices, with Sam., Syr., and Vulg., read "With their".
39 set feasts = appointed seasons. See note on 28. 2 and Gen. 1. 14.
40 children = sons.

B q (p. 226) 1452 **30** And Moses spake unto the °heads of the tribes concerning the °children of Israel, saying, "This *is* the thing which °the LORD hath commanded.

2 If a °man °vow a vow unto [1]the LORD, or swear an oath to bind his °soul with a bond; he shall not °break his word, he shall do according to all that proceedeth out of his mouth.

r s **3** If a woman also [2]vow a vow unto [1]the LORD, °and °bind *herself* by a bond, *being* in her father's house in her youth;

4 And her father hear her vow, and her bond wherewith she hath bound her [2]soul, and her father shall hold his peace at her: then all her vows °shall stand, and every bond wherewith she hath bound her [2]soul °shall stand.

5 But if her father disallow her in the day that he heareth; not any of her vows, or of her bonds wherewith she hath bound her [2]soul, shall stand: and [1]the LORD shall forgive her, because her father disallowed her.

t **6** And if she had at all an husband, when she vowed, or uttered ought out of her lips, wherewith she bound her [2]soul;

7 And her husband heard *it*, and held his peace at her in the day that he heard *it*: then °her vows [4]shall stand, and her bonds wherewith she bound her [2]soul [4]shall stand.

8 But if her husband disallowed her on the day that he heard *it*; then he shall make her vow which she vowed, and that which she uttered with her lips, wherewith she bound her [2]soul, of none effect: and [1]the LORD shall forgive her.

s **9** But every vow of a widow, and of her that is °divorced, wherewith they have bound their [2]souls, [4]shall stand against her.

t **10** And if she vowed in her husband's house, or bound her [2]soul by a bond with an oath;

11 And her husband heard *it*, and held his peace at her, *and* disallowed her not: then all her vows shall stand, and every bond wherewith she bound her [2]soul [4]shall stand.

12 But if her husband °hath utterly made them void on the day he heard *them; then* whatsoever proceeded out of her lips concerning her vows, or concerning the bond of her [2]soul, shall not stand: her husband hath made them void; and [1]the LORD shall forgive her.

13 Every vow, and every binding oath to afflict the [2]soul, her husband may establish it, or her husband may make it void.

14 But if her husband °altogether hold his peace at her from day to day; then he establisheth all her vows, or all her bonds, which *are* upon her: he confirmeth them, because he held his peace at her in the day that he heard *them*.

15 But if he shall any ways make them void after that he hath heard *them;* then he shall bear her °iniquity."

q **16** These *are* the statutes, which [1]the LORD commanded Moses, between a [2]man and his wife, between the father and his daughter, *being yet* in her youth in her father's house.

30. 1-16 (*B*, p. 222). LAWS AS TO VOWS. (*Introversion.*)

B | q | 1, 2. Vows made by men.
  r | 3-15. Vows made by women.
 q | 16. Vows made by men and women.

1 heads = rulers or princes.
children = sons.
the LORD. Heb. Jehovah. Ap. 4.
2 man. Heb. *'ish.* Ap. 14. ii.
vow a vow. Fig. *Polyptōton* (Ap. 6) = make a solemn promise.
soul. Heb. *nephesh* (Ap. 13), used in this chapter twelve times for the whole (responsible) person.
break = Heb. profane.

3-15 (r, above). VOWS MADE BY WOMEN. (*Alternation.*)

r | s | 3-5. Virgin.
  t | 6-8. Wife.
 s | 9. Widow (or Divorcee).
  t | 10-15. Wife.

3 and = or.
bind . . . a bond. Fig. *Polyptōton* (Ap. 6) = make a solemn bond.
4 shall stand = abideth firm. Cp. Gen. 23. 17, 20. Ps. 19. 7. Isa. 14. 24; 40. 8. Jer. 44. 29.
7 her. Some codices, with Sam., Sept., Syr., and Vulg., read "all her", as in *v.* 4.
9 divorced. Heb. "put away [from her husband]". Cp. Lev. 21. 7.
12 hath utterly made them void. Fig. *Polyptōton* (Ap. 6). Heb. "a making void he hath made them void". Fig. well represented by the word "utterly". See note on Gen. 26. 28.
14 altogether, &c. Heb. "a holding his peace, he held his peace". Fig. *Polyptōton* (Ap. 6), well translated by "altogether".
15 iniquity. Put by Fig. *Metonymy* (of Cause), Ap. 6, for the punishment occasioned by it. Heb. *'āvah.* Ap. 44. iv.

31. 1-54 (*A*, p. 222). EVENT: MOSES' VENGEANCE ON MIDIANITES (*Alternation*).

A | u | 1-4. Commands.
  v | 5-13. Obedience.
 u | 14-30. Commands (14-20 by Moses; 21-24 by Eleazar; 25-30 by Jehovah).
  v | 31-54. Obedience.

1 the LORD. Heb. Jehovah. Ap. 4.
spake. See note on 1. 1.
2 Avenge. Heb. revenge the revengement. Fig. *Polyptōton* (Ap. 6). = execute due vengeance.
children = sons.
afterward. Sam., Jon., Sept., Syr., and Vulg. read "and afterward".
be gathered, &c. Cp. 27. 13.
3 avenge the LORD of Midian = render the vengeance of Jehovah upon Midian. Cp. ch. 25. 17.

31 And °the LORD °spake unto Moses, saying, A u

2 °"Avenge the °children of Israel of °the Midianites: °afterward shalt thou °be gathered unto thy people."

3 And Moses spake unto the People, saying, "Arm some of yourselves unto the war, and let them go against [2]the Midianites, and °avenge [1]the LORD of Midian.

4 Of every tribe a thousand, throughout all the tribes of Israel, shall ye send to the war."

v 5 So there were delivered out of the thou-
(p. 226) sands of Israel, a thousand of *every* tribe,
1452 twelve thousand °armed for war.

6 And Moses sent them to the war, a thousand of *every* tribe, them and °Phinehas the son of Eleazar the priest, to the war, with the holy °instruments, and the °trumpets to blow in his hand.

7 And they warred against the Midianites, °as [1]the LORD commanded Moses; and they slew all the males.

8 And they slew the kings of Midian, beside the rest of them that were slain; *namely*, °Evi, and Rekem, and Zur, and Hur, and Reba, °five kings of Midian: °Balaam also the son of Beor they °slew with the sword.

9 And the [2]children of Israel took *all* the women of Midian captives, and their little ones, and took the spoil of all their cattle, and all their flocks, and all their goods.

10 And they °burnt all their cities wherein they dwelt, and all their goodly °castles, with fire.

11 And they took all the spoil, and all the °prey, *both* of °men and of beasts.

12 And they brought the °captives, and the prey, and the spoil, unto Moses, and Eleazar the priest, and unto °the congregation of the [2]children of Israel, unto the camp at the plains of Moab, which *are* by Jordan *near* Jericho.

13 And Moses, and Eleazar the priest, and all the princes of the congregation, went forth to °meet them without the camp.

u 14 And Moses was °wroth with the officers of the host, *with* the captains over thousands, and captains over hundreds, which came from the °battle.

15 And Moses said unto them, "Have ye saved all the women alive?

16 Behold, °these caused the [2]children of Israel, through the °counsel of Balaam, to commit °trespass against [1]the LORD in the matter of Peor, and there was a plague among the congregation of [1]the LORD.

17 Now therefore kill every male among the little ones, and kill every woman that hath known °man by lying with °him.

18 But all the women children, that have not known a man by lying with him, keep alive for yourselves.

19 And do ye abide without the camp seven days: whosoever hath killed any °person, and whosoever hath touched any slain, purify *both* yourselves and your [12]captives on the third day, and on the seventh day.

20 And purify all *your* raiment, and all that is made of skins, and all work of goats' *hair*, and all things made of wood."

21 And Eleazar the priest said unto the °men of war which °went to the battle, "This *is* the °ordinance of the law which [1]the LORD commanded Moses;

22 Only the gold, and the silver, °the brass, °the °iron, °the tin, and the lead,

23 Every thing that may abide the fire, ye shall make *it* go through the fire, and it shall be clean: nevertheless it shall be purified with the °water of separation: and all that abideth not the fire ye shall make go through the water.

24 And ye shall wash your clothes on the seventh day, and ye shall be clean, and afterward ye shall come into the camp."

25 And [1]the LORD °spake unto Moses, saying,

26 "Take the sum of the prey that was taken, *both* of °man and of beast, thou, and Eleazar the priest, and the chief fathers of the congregation:

27 And divide the prey into two parts; between them that took the war upon them, who went out to battle, and between all the congregation:

28 And levy a °tribute unto [1]the LORD of the [21]men of war which went out to battle: one °soul of five hundred, *both* of the °persons, and of the beeves, and of the asses, and of the sheep:

29 Take *it* of their half, and °give *it* unto Eleazar the priest, *for* an heave offering of [1]the LORD.

30 And of the [2]children of Israel's half, thou shalt take one portion of fifty, of the [28]persons, °of the beeves, °of the asses, and of the flocks, of all manner of beasts, and give them unto the Levites, which keep the charge of the °tabernacle of [1]the LORD."

---

5 armed = assigned to or for, &c.
6 Phinehas. Cp. 25. 7-15.
instruments = vessels.
trumpets = alarm trumpets, which were also prayer trumpets. Cp. 10. 9, 10. **7 as** = according as.
8 Evi. Cp. Josh. 13. 21.
five kings: called princes or dukes of Sihon, Josh. 13. 21. **Balaam.** Cp. Josh. 13. 22.
slew. Balaam thus did not "die the death of the righteous". Cp. 23. 10.
10 burnt = burnt up, or down. Heb. *sārăph.* Ap. 43. I. viii. The same judgment is in store for spiritual fornication. Rev. 17. 16; 18. 8.
castles = fortified places.
11 prey = booty. Heb. *malḳōah.* First occurrence. Always used of animated prey.
men. Heb. *'ādām.* Ap. 14. I.
12 captives. Heb. captivity.
the. Some codices, with Sam., Jon., Sept., Syr., and Vulg., read "all the".
13 meet them: as Melchizedek met Abram (Gen. 14. 17).
14 wroth. Moses meek in his own matters, but not in Jehovah's. In these there was a "godly jealousy".
battle. Heb. battle of the war = "the [battle] array (or host) of the war", or martial host.
16 these. Cp. 25. 2.
counsel = word, or doctrine (Rev. 2. 14).
trespass = Heb. *mā'al.* Cp. Ap. 44. xi.
17 man. Heb. *'īsh* (Ap. 14. II). **him** = male.
19 person = soul. Heb. *nephesh* (Ap. 13).
21 men. Heb. pl. of *'īsh*, or *'enōsh.* Ap. 14.
went = came, or had come. **ordinance** = statute.
22 the. Some codices, with Sam., Jon., Sept., Syr., and Vulg., read "and the" in each of these three instances, making the Fig. *Polysyndeton* (Ap. 6).
iron. Found in Egypt as early as 2800 B.C.
23 water of separation. See ch. 19.
25 spake. See note on 1. 1.
26 man. Heb *'ādām.* Ap. 14. I.
28 tribute = computed value, assigned to Jehovah. Heb. *mekes.* Occurs only in this chapter.
soul. Heb. *nephesh.* Ap. 13.
persons = men. Heb. *'ādām.* Ap. 14. I.
29 give it. An extra portion in addition to Deut. 18. 1, 2 and Num. 18. 19. So Abram, Gen. 14. 20.
30 of the. Some codices, with Sam., Jon., Sept., Syr., and Vulg., read "and of the".
tabernacle = habitation. Heb. *mishkān.* Ap. 40.

v
(p. 226)
1452 31 And Moses and Eleazar the priest did °as the LORD commanded Moses.

32 And the booty, *being* the rest of the prey which the [28]men of war had caught, was six hundred thousand and seventy thousand and five thousand sheep,

33 And threescore and twelve thousand beeves,

34 And threescore and one thousand asses,

35 And thirty and two thousand °persons in all, of women that had not known °man by lying with him.

36 And the half, *which was* the portion of them that went out °to war, was in number three hundred thousand and seven and thirty thousand and five hundred sheep:

37 And [1]the LORD'S [28]tribute of the sheep was six hundred and threescore and fifteen.

38 And the beeves *were* thirty and six thousand; of which [1]the LORD'S [28]tribute *was* threescore and twelve.

39 And the asses *were* thirty thousand and five hundred; of which [1]the LORD'S [28]tribute *was* threescore and one.

40 °And the °persons *were* sixteen thousand; of which [1]the LORD'S [28]tribute *was* thirty °and two °persons.

41 And Moses gave the [28]tribute, *which was* [1]the LORD'S heave offering, unto Eleazar the priest, [31]as [1]the LORD commanded Moses.

42 And of the [2]children of Israel's half, which Moses divided from the [21]men that warred,

43 (Now the half *that pertained unto* the congregation was three hundred thousand and thirty thousand *and* seven thousand and five hundred sheep,

44 And thirty and six thousand beeves,

45 And thirty thousand asses and five hundred,

46 And sixteen thousand [40]persons;)

47 Even of the [2]children of Israel's half, Moses took one portion of fifty, *both* of [26]man and of beast, and °gave them unto the Levites, which kept the charge of the [30]tabernacle of [1]the LORD; [31]as [1]the LORD commanded Moses.

48 And the officers which *were* over thousands of the host, the captains of thousands, and captains of hundreds, came near unto Moses:

49 And they said unto Moses, "Thy servants have taken the sum of the [21]men of war which *are* under our charge, and there lacketh not one [17]man of us.

50 We have therefore brought an °oblation for [1]the LORD, what every man hath gotten, of °jewels of gold, chains, and bracelets, rings, earrings, and tablets, to make an °atonement for our °souls before [1]the LORD."

51 And Moses and Eleazar the priest took the gold of them, *even* all wrought [50]jewels.

52 And all the gold of the °offering that they °offered up to [1]the LORD, of the captains of thousands, and of the captains of hundreds, was sixteen thousand seven hundred and fifty °shekels.

53 (*For* the [21]men of war had taken spoil, every man for himself.)

54 And Moses and Eleazar the priest took the gold of the captains of thousands and of hundreds, and brought it into the °tabernacle of the congregation, *for* a memorial for the [2]children of Israel before [1]the LORD.

31 as = according as.
33 beeves. Old English (from the French), for oxen.
35 persons. Heb. pl. of *nephesh*. Ap. 13. III. note man = male.
36 to war = to, or, for the host.
40 And the persons. Fig. *Epanadiplōsis*. Ap. 6.
persons = souls. Heb. *nephesh* (pl.). Ap. 13. Lit. soul of man (Ap. 14. I).
47 gave them. See 1 Chron. 9. 2. Heb. *nāthan*, to give. Hence their name, "Nethinim."
50 oblation. This was voluntary. The levy in *v.* 25, &c., was commanded. See Lev. 2. 4.
jewels = instruments or vessels.
atonement. See note on Ex. 29. 33.
souls. Heb. pl. of *nephesh*. Ap. 13.
52 offering = heave offering. See Ap. 43. II. viii., and note on Ex. 29. 27.
offered up = heaved.
shekels. See Ap. 51. II.
54 tabernacle = tent. Heb. *'ohel*. See Ap. 40.

32. 1—36. 13 (**A^4**, p. 176). DIVISION OF LAND: JOURNEYINGS AND ORDER (SETTLEMENT). (*Introversion.*)

A^4 | B | 32. 1-42. Division: East of Jordan.
  C | 33. 1-49. Journeyings.
 B | 33. 50—36. 13. Division: West of Jordan.

32. 1-42 (B, above). DIVISION: EAST OF JORDAN (*Repeated Alternation*).

B | w^1 | 1-5. Petition of Reuben and Gad.
  x^1 | 6-15. Expostulation of Moses.
 w^2 | 16-19. Stipulation of Reuben and Gad.
  x^2 | 20-24. Reply of Moses.
 w^3 | 25-27. Stipulation of Reuben and Gad.
  x^3 | 28-30. Condition of Moses.
 w^4 | 31, 32. Compliance of Reuben and Gad.
  x^4 | 33-42. Compliance of Moses.

1 children = sons.
cattle. In Heb. this verse begins and ends with the word "cattle". Fig. *Epanadiplōsis* (Ap. 6), to emphasise the first cause of this division.
behold. Fig. *Asterismos* (Ap. 6), to strengthen the emphasis.
3 Ataroth, &c. These were the places in the countries of Sihon and Og, on the east of Jordan. Cp. Josh. 16. 2, 5, 7.
Dibon. Cp. 21. 30. Josh. 13. 9, 17.
Nimrah. Called Beth-nimrah, *v.* 36, and Nimrim. Isa. 15. 6. Cp. Josh. 13. 27.
Heshbon. 21. 26. Josh. 13. 17.
Shebam. Called Shibmah, *v.* 38. Cp. Josh. 13. 19. Isa. 16. 8, 9. Jer. 48. 32.
Beon. Called Baal-meon, *v.* 38; Beth-meon, Jer. 48. 23; and Beth-baal-meon, Josh. 13. 17.
4 the LORD. Heb. Jehovah. Ap. 4.
is. Heb "it [is]".

32 Now the °children of Reuben and the children of Gad had a very great multitude of °cattle: and when they saw the land of Jazer, and the land of Gilead, that, °behold, the place *was* a place for °cattle; B w^1 (p. 228)

2 The [1]children of Gad and the children of Reuben came and spake unto Moses, and to Eleazar the priest, and unto the princes of the congregation, saying,

3 °"Ataroth, and °Dibon, and Jazer, and °Nimrah, and °Heshbon, and Elealeh, and °Shebam, and Nebo, and °Beon,

4 *Even* the country which °the LORD smote before the congregation of Israel, °*is* a land for cattle, and thy servants have cattle:"

5 "Wherefore," said they, "if we have found grace in thy sight, let this land be given unto

1452 thy servants for a possession, *and* bring us not over Jordan."

x[1] (p. 228) 6 And Moses said unto the [1]children of Gad and to the [1]children of Reuben, "Shall your brethren go to war, and shall ye sit here?

7 And wherefore discourage ye the heart of the [1]children of Israel from going over into the land which [4]the LORD hath given them?

8 Thus did your fathers, when I sent them from Kadesh-barnea to see the land.

9 For when they went up unto the valley of °Eshcol, and saw the land, they discouraged the heart of the [1]children of Israel, that they should not go into the land which [4]the LORD had given them.

10 And [4]the LORD'S anger was kindled °the same time, and He sware, saying,

11 'Surely none of the °men that came up out of Egypt, from twenty years old and upward, shall see the land which I sware °unto Abraham, unto Isaac, and unto Jacob; because they have not wholly followed Me:

12 Save Caleb the son of Jephunneh the Kenezite, and Joshua the son of Nun: for they have wholly followed [4]the LORD.'

13 And [4]the LORD'S anger was kindled against Israel, and He made them wander in the wilderness forty years, until all °the generation, that had done °evil in the sight of [4]the LORD, was consumed.

14 And, °behold, ye are risen up in your fathers' stead, an °increase of °sinful men, to augment yet the fierce anger of [4]the LORD toward Israel.

15 For if ye turn away from after Him, He will yet again °leave them in the wilderness; and ye shall destroy all this People."

w[2] 16 And they came near unto him, and said, "We will build sheepfolds here for our cattle, and cities for our little ones:

17 But we ourselves will go ready armed before the [1]children of Israel, until we have brought them unto their place: and our little ones shall dwell in the fenced cities because of the inhabitants of the land.

18 We °will not return unto our houses, until the [1]children of Israel have inherited every °man his inheritance.

19 For we will not inherit with them on yonder side Jordan, or forward; because our inheritance is fallen to us on this side Jordan eastward."

x[2] 20 And Moses said unto them, "If ye will do this thing, if ye will go armed before [4]the LORD to war,

21 And will go all of you armed over Jordan before [4]the LORD, until He hath driven out His enemies from before Him,

22 And the land be subdued before [4]the LORD: then afterward ye shall return, and be guiltless before [4]the LORD, and before Israel; and this land shall be your possession before [4]the LORD.

23 But if ye will not do so, [14]behold, ye have sinned against [4]the LORD: and be sure your sin will find you out.

24 Build you cities for your little ones, and folds for your sheep; and do that which hath proceeded out of your mouth."

25 And the [1]children of Gad and the [1]children of Reuben °spake unto Moses, saying, "Thy servants will do °as my lord commandeth. w[3]

26 Our little ones, our wives, our flocks, and all our cattle, shall be there in the cities of Gilead:

27 But thy servants °will pass over, every man armed for war, before [4]the LORD to battle, as my lord saith."

28 So concerning them Moses commanded Eleazar the priest, and Joshua the son of Nun, and the chief fathers of the tribes of the [1]children of Israel: x[3]

29 And Moses said unto them, "If the [1]children of Gad and the [1]children of Reuben will pass with you over Jordan, °every man armed to battle, before [4]the LORD, and the land shall be subdued before you; then ye shall give them the land of Gilead for a possession:

30 But if they will not pass over with you °armed, °they shall have possessions among you in the land of Canaan."

31 And the [1]children of Gad and the [1]children of Reuben answered, saying, "As [4]the LORD hath said unto thy servants, so will we do. w[4]

32 We will pass over armed before [4]the LORD into the land of Canaan, that the possession of our inheritance on this side Jordan *may be* ours."

33 And °Moses gave unto them, *even* to the [1]children of Gad, x[4] y (p. 230)

and to the [1]children of Reuben, z

and unto half the tribe of Manasseh the son of Joseph, the kingdom of Sihon king of the Amorites, and the kingdom of Og king a

---

9 Eshcol. Cp. 13. 23, 24.
10 the same time. Heb. "on that day".
11 men. Heb. pl. of *'ish* or *'enōsh*. Ap. 14.
unto Abraham, &c. All three mentioned together here as equally subjects of the oath of Jehovah. Cp. Gen. 50. 24.
13 the generation: or, the men of that generation.
evil. Heb. *rā'a'*. Ap. 44. VIII.
14 behold. Fig. *Asterismos* (Ap. 6), to emphasise what follows.
increase = a crew, multitude, or brood.
sinful. Heb. *chāṭā*. Ap. 44. i.
15 leave them: or leave them behind.
18 will not return. Promise fulfilled (Josh. 22. 3, 4).
man. Heb. *'ish* (Ap. 14).
25 spake. Heb. text reads sing., "he spake", and by Fig. *Heterōsis* (of Number), Ap. 6, might be translated plural, "they spake". But "they spake" is the actual reading in several codices: Sam., Jon., Onk., Sept., Syr., and Vulg. It is also the *Sevīr* reading. See Ap. 34.
as = according as.
27 will pass over. Cp. Josh. 4. 12.
29 every man = all.
30 armed . . . they. Between these two words the Sept. has "to do battle before Jehovah, then shall ye bring over their baggage, and their wives, and their cattle earlier than you into the land of Canaan; so shall" (they have possession), &c.

32. 33-42 [For Structure see next page].
33 Moses gave. Cp. Deut. 3. 12. Josh. 13. 8; 22. 4.

1452 of Bashan, the land, with the cities thereof
in the °coasts, *even* the cities of the country
round about.

y 34 And the [1]children of Gad built Dibon, and
(p. 230) Ataroth, and Aroer,
35 And Atroth, Shophan, and Jaazer, and
Jogbehah,
36 And Beth-nimrah, and Beth-haran, fenced
cities: and folds for sheep.

z 37 And the [1]children of Reuben built Heshbon,
and Elealeh, and Kirjathaim,
38 And Nebo, and Baal-meon, (their names
being changed,) and Shibmah: and gave
other names unto the cities which they
builded.

a 39 And the [1]children of Machir the son of
Manasseh went to Gilead, and took it, and dispossessed
the Amorite which *was* in it.
40 And Moses gave Gilead unto Machir the
son of Manasseh; and he dwelt therein.
41 And °Jair the son of Manasseh went
and took the small towns thereof, and called
them °Havoth-°jair.
42 And Nobah went and took Kenath, and
the °villages thereof, and called it Nobah,
after his own name.

C b¹ **33** These *are* the °journeys of the °children
of Israel, which went forth out of
the land of Egypt with their armies under the
hand of Moses and Aaron.
2 And Moses °wrote their goings out according
to their journeys by the °commandment
of °the LORD: and these *are* their journeys
according to their goings out.
15th 3 And they departed from Rameses in the
Abib first month, on the fifteenth day of the first
1491 month; on the morrow after the passover the
[1]children of Israel went out with an high hand
in the sight of all °the Egyptians.
4 For °the Egyptians buried all *their* firstborn,
which [2]the LORD had smitten among
them: °upon their gods also [2]the LORD executed
judgments.
5 And the [1]children of Israel removed from
Rameses, and pitched in Succoth.
6 And they departed from Succoth, and
pitched in Etham, which *is* in the edge of the
wilderness.
7 And they removed from Etham, and
turned again unto Pi-hahiroth, which *is*
before Baal-zephon: and they pitched before
Migdol.
8 And they departed from °before Pi-hahiroth,
and passed through the midst of the
sea into the wilderness, and went three days'
journey in the wilderness of Etham, and
pitched in Marah.
9 And they removed from Marah, and came
unto °Elim: and in Elim *were* twelve fountains
of water, and threescore and ten palm trees;
and they pitched there.
10 And they removed from Elim, and encamped
°by the Red sea.
11 And they removed from the Red sea, and
encamped in the °wilderness of Sin.
12 And they took their journey out of the
wilderness of Sin, and encamped in °Dophkah.
13 And they departed from Dophkah, and
encamped in °Alush.

32. 33-42 (x⁴, p. 228). COMPLIANCE OF MOSES (GRANT TO THE TWO-AND-A-HALF TRIBES).
(*Extended Alternation.*)

x⁴ | y | 33-. Gad
| z | -33-. Reuben } Distribution.
| a | -33. Half Manasseh
| y | 34-36. Gad
| z | 37, 38. Reuben } Possession.
| a | 39-42. Half Manasseh

coasts = borders, or confines.

41 Jair. In the Heb. this verse begins and ends with the word "Jair". Fig. *Epanadiplosis* (Ap. 6).
Havoth = the encampments, or tent villages (of Jair).

42 villages. Heb. daughters; depending on the mother or metropolitan city. Fig. *Prosopopœia* (Ap. 6).

33. 1-49 (C, p. 228). JOURNEYINGS.
(*Division.*)

C | b¹ | 1-15. *First* Period. Rameses to Sinai. Twelve stations.
| b² | 16, 17. *Second* Period. Sinai to Rithmah (= Kadesh) (first time). Three stations.
| b³ | 18-36. *Third* Period. Rithmah to Kadesh (second time). Eighteen stations. 38 years. No history.
| b⁴ | 37-49. *Fourth* Period. Kadesh (second time) to Plains of Moab. 40th year. Ten stations.

33. 1-15 (b¹, above). FIRST PERIOD.

1 journeys. Heb. pullings up: i. e. of the tent-pegs, or the breakings up of the camps.
children = sons.

2 wrote. See note on Ex. 17. 14, and Ap. 47.
commandment. Heb. "mouth", put by Fig. *Metonymy* (of Cause) for what is spoken by it (Ap. 6).
the LORD. Heb. Jehovah. Ap. 4.

3, 4 the Egyptians: repeated = Fig. *Anadiplosis* (Ap. 6).

4 upon their gods. Cp. Ex. 12. 12; 18. 8, 11.

8 before Pi-hahiroth. Heb. text and R.V. = "before Hahiroth"; but this differs from the other two occurrences of the name (Ex. 14. 2, 9), in all three of which it is *Pi-hahiroth.* A special various reading called *Sevīr* (Ap. 34) has the full name Pi-hahiroth in this verse. The A.V. has kept the Pi as well, and made it "before Pi-". It should, perhaps, read here, as in every other case in this chapter, "from Pi-hahiroth".

9 Elim. Cp. Ex. 15. 27; 16. 1.

10 by the Red sea. Not named before.

11 wilderness of Sin. Ex. 16. 1, 2.

12 Dophkah. Not named before.

13 Alush. Not named before.

14 Rephidim. Cp. Ex. 17.

15 wilderness of Sinai. Cp. Ex. 19. 1. Acts 7. 38.

33. 16-17 (b², above). SECOND PERIOD.

16 Kibroth-hattaavah. Cp. 11. 4-34.

17 Hazeroth. Cp. Num. 11. 35.

33. 18-36 (b³, above). THIRD PERIOD (NO HISTORY).

18 Rithmah. Cp. 13. 1-3. Whence the spies went to view the land: means "Juniper": well named for the evil tongues of the spies. Cp. Ps. 120. 3, 4.

14 And they removed from Alush, and encamped
at °Rephidim, where was no water
for the people to drink.
15 And they departed from Rephidim, and
pitched in the °wilderness of Sinai.

16 And they removed from the desert of b²
Sinai, and pitched at °Kibroth-hattaavah.
17 And they departed from Kibroth-hattaavah,
and encamped at °Hazeroth.

18 And they departed from Hazeroth, and b³
pitched in °Rithmah.

1490 to 1452 19 And they departed from Rithmah, and pitched at ° Rimmon-parez.
20 And they departed from Rimmon-parez, and pitched in ° Libnah.
21 And they removed from Libnah, and pitched at ° Rissah.
22 And they journeyed from Rissah, and pitched in Kehelathah.
23 And they went from Kehelathah, and pitched in mount Shapher.
24 And they removed from mount Shapher, and encamped in Haradah.
25 And they removed from Haradah, and pitched in Makheloth.
26 And they removed from Makheloth, and encamped at Tahath.
27 And they departed from Tahath, and pitched at Tarah.
28 And they removed from Tarah, and pitched in Mithcah.
29 And they went from Mithcah, and pitched in Hashmonah.
30 And they departed from Hashmonah, and encamped at Moseroth.
31 And they departed from Moseroth, and pitched in Bene-jaakan.
32 And they removed from Bene-jaakan, and encamped at Hor-hagidgad.
33 And they went from Hor-hagidgad, and pitched in ° Jotbathah.
34 And they removed from Jotbathah, and encamped at Ebronah.
35 And they departed from Ebronah, and encamped at ° Ezion-gaber.
36 And they removed from Ezion-gaber, and pitched in the wilderness of Zin, which *is* Kadesh.

b⁴ (p. 230) 37 And they removed from Kadesh, and pitched in mount Hor, in the edge of the land of Edom.
1st Abib 38 And Aaron the priest went up into mount Hor at the ²commandment of ²the LORD, and died there, in the °fortieth year after the ¹children of Israel were come out of the land of Egypt, in the first *day* of the fifth month.
39 And Aaron *was* an hundred and twenty and three years old when he ° died in ° mount Hor.
40 And ° king Arad the Canaanite, which dwelt in the south in the land of Canaan, heard of the coming of the ¹children of Israel.
41 And they departed from mount Hor, and pitched in Zalmonah.
42 And they departed from Zalmonah, and pitched in Punon.
43 And they departed from Punon, and pitched in Oboth.
44 And they departed from Oboth, and pitched in ° Ije-abarim, in the border of Moab.
45 And they departed from Iim, and pitched in ° Dibon-gad.
46 And they removed from Dibon-gad, and encamped in Almon-diblathaim.
47 And they removed from Almon-diblathaim, and pitched in the mountains of Abarim, before ° Nebo.
48 And they departed from the mountains of Abarim, and pitched in the plains of Moab by Jordan *near* Jericho.
49 And they pitched by Jordan, from Beth-jesimoth *even* unto Abel-shittim in the plains of Moab.

B c (p. 231) 50 And ² the LORD ° spake unto Moses in the plains of Moab by Jordan *near* Jericho, saying,
d e¹ f 51 "Speak unto the ¹children of Israel, and say unto them, 'When ye are passed over Jordan into the land of Canaan;
52 Then ye shall ° drive out all the inhabitants of the land from before you, and destroy all their pictures, and destroy all their molten images, and quite pluck down all their high places:
53 And ye shall dispossess *the* ° *inhabitants of* the land, and dwell therein:
g for I have given you the land to possess it.
h 54 And ° ye shall divide the land by lot for an inheritance among your families: *and* to the more ye shall give the more inheritance,

---

19 Rimmon-parez. Not named before.
20 Libnah. Perhaps the Laban of Deut. 1. 1.
21 Rissah. Not elsewhere mentioned.
33 Jotbathah. Cp. Deut. 10. 7.
35 Ezion-gaber. Cp. Deut. 2. 8. Edom's seaport on the Red Sea.

33. 37-49 (b⁴, p. 230). FOURTH PERIOD.

38 fortieth year. The number of Probation (Ap. 10).
39 died. Cp. 20. 24, 26, &c., born 1575 B. C.
mount Hor. Cp. 21. 4.
40 king Arad. Cp. 21. 1-3.
44 Ije-abarim = heaps, or ruins, of Abarim. "Iim", *v.* 45, probably an abbreviation.
45 Dibon-gad = Dibon of the tribe of Gad. Cp. Num. 21. 30. So called because it was appropriated by Gad (32. 34); and to distinguish it from another Dibon given to Reuben (Josh. 13. 15, 17).
47 Nebo. Where Moses died. Deut. 32. 49, 50; 34. 1, 5.

33. 50—36. 12 (*B*, p. 228). DIVISION WEST OF JORDAN (*Alternation*).

B | c | 33. 50. The Plains of Moab.
  d | 33. 51—34. 29. The Land of Canaan.
  c | 35. 1. The Plains of Moab.
  d | 35. 2—36. 12. The Land of Canaan.

50 spake. See note on 1. 1.

33. 51—34. 29 (d, above). THE LAND OF CANAAN (*Division*).

d | e¹ | 33. 51—34. 15. The Division.
  e² | 34. 16-29. The Dividers.

33. 51—34. 15 (e¹, above). THE DIVISION. (*Extended Alternation.*)

e¹ | f | 33. 51-53-. Command—Expulsion.
  g | 33. -53. Possession.
  h | 33. 54. Division.
  f | 33. 55-. Disobedience—Non-expulsion.
  g | 33. -55, 56. Punishment.
  h | 34. 1-15. Division.

52 drive out. This was one of the great purposes for which the sword of Israel was raised up. Cp. Deut. 7. 1, 2. Ex. 23. 33. See App. 23 and 25.
53 inhabitants of the land. Fig. *Ellipsis* (Ap. 6) correctly supplied. Heb. "land" is put by Fig. *Metonymy* (of Subject), Ap. 6, for the inhabitants.
54 ye shall divide. Cp. 26. 53.

1452 and to the fewer ye shall give the less inheritance: every man's *inheritance* shall be in the place where his lot falleth; according to the tribes of your fathers ye shall inherit.

f 55 But if ye will °not drive out the inhabitants of the land from before you;

g then it shall come to pass, that those which ye let remain of them *shall be* °pricks in your eyes, and thorns in your sides, and shall vex you in the land wherein ye dwell.

56 Moreover it shall come to pass, *that* I shall do unto you, as I thought to do unto them.'"

h **34** And °the LORD °spake unto Moses, saying,

2 "Command the °children of Israel, and say unto them, °'When ye come into the land of Canaan; (this *is* the land that shall fall unto you for an inheritance, *even* the land of Canaan with the °coasts thereof:)

3 Then your °south quarter shall be from the wilderness of Zin along by the coast of Edom, and your south border shall be the outmost coast of the °salt sea eastward:

4 And your border shall turn from the south to the ascent of °Akrabbim, and pass on to Zin: and the °going forth thereof shall be from the south to Kadesh-barnea, and shall go on to Hazar-addar, and pass on to Azmon:

5 And the border shall fetch a compass from Azmon unto the °river of Egypt, and the goings out of it shall be at the sea.

6 And *as for* the western border, ye shall even have the great sea for a border: this shall be your west border.

7 And this shall be your north border: from the °great sea ye shall °point out for you °mount Hor:

8 From mount Hor ye shall [7]point out *your border* unto the entrance of °Hamath; and the goings forth of the border shall be to Zedad:

9 And the border shall go on to Ziphron, and the goings out of it shall be at Hazar-enan: this shall be your north border.

10 And ye shall [7]point out your east border from Hazar-enan to Shepham:

11 And the coast shall go down from Shepham to °Riblah, on the east side of Ain; and the border shall descend, and shall reach unto the side of the sea of °Chinnereth eastward:

12 And the border shall go down to Jordan, and the goings out of it shall be at the salt sea: this shall be your land with the coasts thereof round about.'"

13 And Moses commanded the [2]children of Israel, saying, "This *is* the land which ye shall inherit by lot, which [1]the LORD commanded to give unto the nine tribes, and to the half tribe:

14 °For the tribe of the [2]children of Reuben according to the house of their fathers, and the tribe of the [2]children of Gad according to the house of their fathers, have received *their inheritance;* and half the tribe of Manasseh have received their inheritance:

15 The two tribes and the half tribe have received their inheritance on this side Jordan *near* Jericho eastward, toward the sunrising."

16 And [1]the LORD [1]spake unto Moses, saying, e[2] (p. 231)

17 °"These *are* the names of the °men which shall divide the land unto you: °Eleazar the priest, and Joshua the son of Nun.

18 And ye shall take one prince of every tribe, to divide the land by inheritance.

19 And the names of the men *are* these: Of the tribe of Judah, °Caleb the son of Jephunneh.

20 And of the tribe of the [2]children of Simeon, Shemuel the son of Ammihud.

21 Of the tribe of Benjamin, Elidad the son of Chislon.

22 And the prince of the tribe of the [2]children of Dan, Bukki the son of Jogli.

23 The prince of the [2]children of Joseph, for the tribe of the [2]children of Manasseh, Hanniel the son of Ephod.

24 And the prince of the tribe of the [2]children of Ephraim, Kemuel the son of Shiphtan.

25 And the prince of the tribe of the [2]children of Zebulun, Elizaphan the son of Parnach.

---

55 not drive out. Alas! they did not. Cp. Josh. 13. 13; 15. 63; 16. 10. Judg. 1. 19, 21, 28, 29, 30–36; 2. 1–5. See Ap. 25.

pricks. Cp. Josh. 23. 13. =for pricks. Cp. Ezek. 28. 24. Judg. 2. 3.

34. 1 the LORD. Heb. Jehovah. Ap. 4.
spake. See note on 1. 1.
2 children=sons.
When ye come. After the final command (above) follow instructions as to the quiet possession of the land thus cleared of enemies.
coasts=borders, or confines.
3 south quarter. Cp. Josh. 15. 1. Begins at east corner.
salt sea. So *v.* 12.
4 Akrabbim=Maaleh-akrabbim. Josh. 15. 3. =the ascent of scorpions. Cp. Deut. 8. 15.
going forth=ascending. Cp. Josh. 15. 3
5 river. Heb. *nachal*, a wady; not *nahar*, a river. Here used of "Sihor", and called the river of Egypt. Cp. Gen. 15. 18, where it is *nahar*=the Nile.
7 great sea: i. e. the Mediterranean, a modern name for the Great Sea.
point out=mark out or claim. Heb. *tā'āh.* Occurs only here.
mount Hor. Not the mount Hor where Aaron died, which was in the south corner of Edom (33. 37, 38), but another, in the north, mount Hermon, a spur of the Lebanon (Josh. 13. 5). Hermon had several names. Cp. Deut. 3. 9; 4. 48.
8 Hamath. In Amos 6. 2 called "Hamath the great", mentioned as in the north border.
11 Riblah. A city in Hamath, where God executed His judgment on two kings of Judah and others (2 Kings 23. 33; 25. 6, 20, 21. Jer. 39. 5, 6).
Chinnereth. Cp. Josh. 12. 3; 13. 27. In New Testament "the sea of Galilee" and "sea of Tiberias" (John 6. 1); also "the lake of Gennesaret" (Luke 5. 1).
14 For the tribe. Cp. 32. 33. Josh. 14. 2, 3.
17 These are the names. Cp. 13. 2–16. See Ap. 45.
men. Heb. pl. of *'īsh* or *'enōsh.* Ap. 14.
Eleazar. Because he was the high priest, and had the breastplate with the lots, the "Urim and Thummim." See notes on Ex. 28. 30 and Num. 26. 55. Josh. 17. 4. See also Num. 27. 21.
19 Caleb. The only one of the spies, beside Joshua, left, ch. 13. 6, 30, and cp. 14. 24. Josh. 14. 6, &c.

1452 26 And the prince of the tribe of the [3]children of Issachar, Paltiel the son of Azzan.

27 And the prince of the tribe of the [2]children of Asher, Ahihud the son of Shelomi.

28 And the prince of the tribe of the [2]children of Naphtali, Pedahel the son of Ammihud."

29 °These *are they* whom [1]the LORD commanded to divide the inheritance unto the [2]children of Israel in the land of Canaan.

c (p. 231) **35** And °the LORD °spake unto Moses in the plains of Moab by Jordan *near* Jericho, saying,

d i k (p. 233) 2 "Command the °children of Israel, °that they give unto the Levites of the inheritance of their possession cities to dwell in; and ye shall give *also* unto the Levites suburbs for the cities round about them.

3 And the cities shall they have to dwell in; and the °suburbs of them shall be for their cattle, and for their goods, and for all their beasts.

4 And the suburbs of the cities, which ye shall give unto the Levites, *shall reach* from the wall of the city and outward a thousand °cubits round about.

5 And ye shall measure from without the city on the east side two thousand [4]cubits, and on the south side two thousand [4]cubits, and on the west side two thousand [4]cubits, and on the north side two thousand [4]cubits; and the city *shall be* in the midst: this shall be °to them the suburbs of the cities.

i l 6 And among the cities which ye shall give unto the Levites *there shall be* °six cities for refuge, which ye shall appoint for the manslayer,

k that he may flee thither: and to them ye shall add forty and two cities.

7 *So* all the cities which ye shall give to the Levites *shall be* °forty and eight cities: *them shall ye give* with their suburbs.

8 And the cities which ye shall give *shall be* of the possession of the [2]children of Israel: from *them that have* many ye shall give many; but from *them that have* few ye shall give few: every one shall give of his cities unto the Levites °according to his inheritance which he inheriteth."

l m 9 And [1]the LORD [1]spake unto Moses, saying,

10 "Speak unto the [2]children of Israel, and say unto them, °'When *ye* be come over Jordan into the land of Canaan;

11 Then ye shall appoint you cities to be cities of refuge for you;

n that the slayer may flee thither, which killeth any °person °at unawares.

12 And they shall be unto you cities for refuge from the °avenger; that the manslayer die not, until he stand before the congregation in judgment.

m 13 And of these cities which ye shall give six cities shall ye have for refuge.

14 Ye shall give °three cities on this side Jordan, °and three cities shall ye give in the land of Canaan, *which* shall be cities of refuge.

15 These six cities shall be a refuge, *both* for the [2]children of Israel, and for the stranger, and for the sojourner among them:

n o (p. 234) that every one that killeth any °person unawares may flee thither.

p 16 And if he smite him with an instrument

---

29 These. See the order of the tribes in Ap. 45.

35. 1 the LORD. Heb. Jehovah. Ap. 4.

spake. See note on 1. 1.

35. 2—36. 12 (*d*, p. 231). **THE LAND OF CANAAN** (*Division*).

d | i[1] | 35. 2-34. Levitical cities.
   | i[2] | 36. 1-12. Heiresses.

2-34 (i[1], above). **THE LEVITICAL CITIES.** (*Alternation.*)

i[1] | k | 2-5. Levitical cities: description.
   | l | 6-. Cities of refuge: number (6).
   | *k* | -6-8. Levitical cities: number (48).
   | *l* | 9-34. Cities of refuge: description.

In this Structure the cities are given in Alternation; their number in an Introversion.

2 children = sons.

that they give. Jehovah gives to the Nation; the Nation gives to the Levites.

3 suburbs = pasture grounds.

4 cubits. See Ap. 51. III. 2.

5 to them. A special various reading called *Sevîr* (Ap. 34) reads "to you", with which agree some codices, Sam., Jon., Sept., Syr., and one early printed edition.

6 six cities. See Deut. 4. 41. Josh. 20. 2, 7, 8; 21. 3.

7 forty and eight cities. Cp. Josh. 21. 41. So was Gen 49. 5, 7 fulfilled, that Levi should be "divided in Jacob and scattered in Israel". At first a curse, but changed to a blessing on account of Ex. 32. 26, 29.

8 according to his inheritance. Nine from Judah and Simeon; four from Benjamin; four from Ephraim; four from Dan; two from the half of Manasseh; two from the other half; four from Issachar; four from Asher; three from Naphtali; four from Zebulon; four from Reuben; four from Gad. Cp. Josh. 21. 9, 16, &c.

9-34 (*l*, above). **CITIES OF REFUGE: DESCRIPTION** (*Alternation*).

l | m | 9-11-. The cities (general).
   | n | -11, 12. Purpose.
   | *m* | 13-15-. The cities (particular).
   | *n* | -15-34. Purpose.

10 When ye be come. Cp. Deut. 19. 2. Josh. 20. 2.

11 person = soul. Heb. *nephesh.* Ap. 13.

at unawares = by misadventure.

12 avenger. Heb. *Goël*, to redeem, to ransom. First occurrence is Gen. 48. 16; next, Ex. 6. 6; 15. 13. *Goël*, when used in this connection, means to avenge bloodshed, as here; both were the duties of the next of kin, the kinsman. Our *Goël* not only redeems us from all evil, but avenges us of all our enemies. Rom. 8. 31-34.

14 three cities = Bezer, Ramoth, Golan (Deut. 4. 41-43).

and three = Kedesh, Shechem, Hebron (Josh. 20. 7). These were placed in due order, east and west, in two ranks:

Hebron over against Bezer.
Shechem over against Ramoth.
Kedesh over against Golan.

If the Lord enlarged their land, they were to add three more (Deut. 19. 8, 9).

-15-34 [For Structure see next page].

15 person = soul. Heb. *nephesh.* Ap. 13.

1452 of iron, so that he die, he *is* a murderer: the
murderer shall surely be put to death.
17 And if he smite him with throwing a
stone, wherewith he may die, and he die, he
is a murderer: the murderer shall surely be
put to death.
18 Or *if* he smite him with an hand weapon
of wood, wherewith he may die, and he die,
he *is* a murderer: the [16]murderer shall surely
be put to death.
19 The °revenger of blood himself shall slay
the [16]murderer: when he meeteth him, he
shall slay him.
20 But if he thrust him °of hatred, or hurl
at him by °laying of wait, that he die;
21 Or in enmity smite him with his hand,
that he die: he that smote *him* shall surely be
put to death; *for* he *is* a [16]murderer: the
[19]revenger of blood shall slay the murderer,
when he meeteth him.

n o 22 But if he thrust him suddenly °without
(p. 234) enmity, or have cast upon him any thing
without [20]laying of wait,
23 Or with any stone, wherewith a man
may die, seeing *him* not, and cast *it* upon
him, that he die, and °*was* not his enemy,
neither sought his harm:
24 Then the congregation shall judge
between the slayer and the [19]revenger of
blood according to these judgments:
25 And the congregation shall deliver the
slayer out of the hand of the [19]revenger of
blood, and the congregation shall restore him
to the city of his refuge, whither he was fled:
and he shall abide in it unto the death of the
high priest, which was anointed with the holy
oil.

p q 26 But if the slayer shall at any time come
without the border of the city of his refuge,
whither he was fled;
27 And the [19]revenger of blood find him
without the borders of the city of his refuge,
and the [19]revenger of blood kill the slayer;
he shall not be guilty of blood:
28 Because he should have remained in the
city of his refuge until the death of the high
priest: but after the death of the high priest
the slayer shall return into the land of his
possession.

r 29 So these *things* shall be for a °statute of
judgment unto you throughout your generations
in all your °dwellings.

q 30 Whoso killeth any °person, the [16]murderer
shall be put to death by the °mouth
of witnesses: but one witness shall not
testify against any °person *to cause him* to
die.
31 Moreover ye shall take °no satisfaction
for the °life of a [16]murderer, °which *is* guilty
of death: but he shall be surely put to death.
32 And ye shall take [31]no satisfaction for
him that is fled to the city of his refuge, that
he should come again to dwell in the land,
until the death of the °priest.

r 33 So ye shall not pollute the land °wherein
ye *are*: for °blood it defileth the land: and the
land cannot be cleansed of the blood that is
shed therein, but by the blood of °him that
shed it.
34 °Defile not therefore the land which ye
shall inhabit, °wherein I dwell: for I [1]the
LORD dwell °among the [2]children of Israel.'"

36 And the °chief fathers of the families i² s
of the °children of Gilead, the son of
Machir, the son of Manasseh, of the families
of the °sons of Joseph, came near, and spake
before Moses, and before the princes, the
°chief fathers of the °children of Israel:

2 And they said, °"The LORD commanded t
°my lord to give the land for an inheritance
by lot to the [1]children of Israel: and °my lord

-15-34 (*n*, p. 233). PURPOSE.
(*Alternation.*)

n | o | -15. Positive.
| p | 16-21. Negative.
| *o* | 22-25. Positive.
| *p* | 26-34. Negative.

19 revenger of blood. See note on *v.* 12.
20 of hatred. Deut. 19. 11, 12.
laying of wait=fixing the eyes upon. Heb. *ẓedīyyah.* Occurs only here and *v.* 22.
22 without enmity. Cp. Ex. 21. 13.
23 was not his enemy. Heb. "he not [being] his enemy".

26-34 (*p*, above). NEGATIVE PURPOSE.
(*Alternation.*)

p | q | 26-28. Negative.
| r | 29. Purpose secured.
| *q* | 30-32. Negative.
| *r* | 33, 34. Purpose secured.

29 statute of judgment=a regulative ordinance. Cp. 27. 11.
dwellings=dwelling-places.
30 person=soul. Heb. *nephesh.* Ap. 13.
mouth. Put by Fig. *Metonymy* (of Cause), Ap. 6, for the *evidence* given by it.
31 no satisfaction=no ransom. Cp. Ps. 49. 7. Only God can redeem (*v.* 15).
life=soul. Heb. *nephesh.* Ap. 13.
which is guilty of death=if he has unlawfully caused death: "guilty" being put by Fig. *Metonymy* (of Effect), Ap. 6, for the crime which has caused it. Heb. "wicked, to die".
32 priest: i. e. the high priest. Some codices, with Sam., Sept., and Syr., read it so, as in *v.* 28.
33 wherein ye are. Some codices, with Sam., Syr., and Vulg., read "wherein ye are dwelling".
blood: i. e. blood unlawfully shed.
him that shed it. Cp. Gen. 9. 6.
34 Defile not=Defile thou not. Some codices, with Sam., Onk., Jon., Sept., Syr., and Vulg., read "Defile ye not".
wherein=in the midst of which.
among=in the midst of.

36. 1-12 (i², p. 233). HEIRESSES.
(*Alternation.*)

i² | s | 1. Applicants.
| t | 2-4. Plea.
| *s* | 5. Applicants.
| *t* | 6-12. Response.

1 chief fathers=heads.
sons. A special various reading called *Sevīr* (Ap. 34), with Syr., reads "son", as in *v.* 12.
children=sons.
2 The LORD. Heb. Jehovah. Ap. 4.
my lord=Moses, to whom the commandment was given. 26. 52, 53, &c.; 27. 6, 7.

1452 was commanded by the LORD to give the inheritance of Zelophehad our brother unto his daughters.

3 And if they be married to any of the sons of the *other* tribes of the [1]children of Israel, then shall their inheritance be taken from the inheritance of our fathers, and shall be put to the inheritance of the tribe whereunto they are received: so shall it be taken from the lot of our inheritance.

4 And when the °jubile of the [1]children of Israel shall be, then shall their inheritance be put unto the inheritance of the tribe whereunto they are received: so shall their inheritance be taken away from the inheritance of the tribe of our fathers."

s (p. 234) 5 And Moses commanded the [1]children of Israel according to the °word of [2]the LORD, saying, "The tribe of the sons of Joseph hath said well.

t 6 This *is* the thing which [2]the LORD doth command concerning the daughters of Zelophehad, saying, 'Let them marry to whom they think best; only to the family of the tribe of their father shall they marry.

7 So shall not the inheritance of the [1]children of Israel remove from tribe to tribe: for every one of the [1]children of Israel shall °keep himself to the inheritance of the tribe of his fathers.

8 And every daughter, that possesseth an inheritance in any tribe of the [1]children of Israel, shall be wife unto one of the family of the tribe of her father, that the [1]children of Israel may enjoy every °man the inheritance of his fathers.

9 Neither shall the inheritance remove from *one* tribe to another tribe; but every one of the tribes of the [1]children of Israel shall keep himself to his own inheritance.' "

10 Even as [2]the LORD commanded Moses, so did the daughters of Zelophehad:

11 For Mahlah, Tirzah, and Hoglah, and Milcah, and Noah, the daughters of Zelophehad, were married unto their father's brothers' sons:

12 *And* they were married into the families of the sons of Manasseh the son of Joseph, and their inheritance remained in the tribe of the family of their father.

13 °These *are* the commandments and the judgments, which [2]the LORD commanded by the hand of Moses unto the [1]children of Israel in the plains of Moab by Jordan *near* Jericho. Epilogue (p. 176)

---

4 jubile. Cp. Lev. 25.

5 word. Heb. mouth. Put by Fig. *Metonymy* (of Cause), Ap. 6, for what is spoken by it.

7 keep himself=cleave.

8 man. Heb. *'ish.* Ap. 14. II.

13 These. This verse forms the closing Epilogue to the whole book of Numbers.

DEUTERONOMY.

THE STRUCTURE OF THE BOOK AS A WHOLE.

A | 1. 1-5. INTRODUCTION.

B | **C** | 1. 6—32. 47. THE TRIBES. THEIR ADMINISTRATION.

D | 32. 48-52. MOSES. HIS DEATH ANNOUNCED.

B | ***C*** | 33. 1-29. THE TRIBES. THEIR BLESSING.

D | 34. 1-7. MOSES. HIS DEATH ACCOMPLISHED.

A | 34. 8-12. CONCLUSION.

THE FIFTH BOOK OF °MOSES,

°CALLED

°DEUTERONOMY.

A (p. 236) **1** °**THESE** ***be*** °**the words which Moses spake**
unto °all Israel on °this side Jordan in the
wilderness, in °the plain over against the °Red
sea**, between Paran, and Tophel, and Laban,**
and Hazeroth, and Dizahab.
2 (*There are* °eleven days' *journey* from
Horeb by the way of mount °Seir unto °Kadesh-
barnea.)
1st Sebat 1452 **3 And it came to pass in the °fortieth year,**
in the eleventh month, on the first *day* of the
month, *that* Moses spake unto the °children of
Israel, °according unto all that °the LORD had
given him in commandment unto them;
4 After he had slain Sihon the king of the
Amorites, which dwelt in Heshbon, °and Og
the king of Bashan, which dwelt at Astaroth
°in Edrei;
5 On [1]this side Jordan, in the land of Moab,
°began Moses to °declare this °law, saying,
C E G e (p. 238) **6 °"The LORD our °God °spake unto us in**
°Horeb, saying, 'Ye have dwelt long enough in
this mount:
7 °Turn you, and take your journey, and go
to the mount of the Amorites, and unto all *the*
***places* nigh thereunto, in [1]the plain, in the**
hills, and in the °vale, and in the °south, and
by the sea side, to the land of the Canaanites,
and unto Lebanon, unto the great °river, °the
river Euphrates.
8 °Behold, I have set the land before you: go
in and possess the land which [3]the LORD
sware unto your fathers, °Abraham, Isaac, and
Jacob, to give unto them and to their seed after
them.'
f h[1] **9 And °I spake unto you at that time, saying,**
'I am not able to bear you myself alone:
10 [3]The LORD your [6]God hath °multiplied
you, and, behold, ye *are* this day as the stars
of heaven for multitude.'
11 ([3]The LORD [6]God of your fathers make
you a thousand times so many more as ye *are*,
and bless you, °as He hath °promised you!)

TITLE. Moses. See Ap. 2 and 47.

Called: by the Sept. translators, and from them by Jerome, in the Vulgate.

Deuteronomy = Second Law, from 17. 18, where "copy of the law" is so rendered from Rabbinic *mishneh*, a doubling.

Hebrew Title = *Hadd[e]bārīm* = "the words". It is the fifth book, concluding the five books of the Pentateuch (see Ap. 10). No scroll of the Pentateuch ever seen with more than these five. See Ap. 46 and 47.

The whole history of the book took place in the eleventh month of the fortieth year. Only the last fifteen chapters of Numbers refer to the time of Deut.

1 These. Note the ten (see Ap. 10) addresses by Moses:—

1. 1. 6—4. 40	6. 29. 2—30. 20
2. 5. 1—10. 5	7. 31. 2-6
3. 10. 10—12. 32	8. 32. 1-43
4. 13. 1—26. 19	9. 32. 44-47
5. 27. 1—28. 68	10. 33. 2-29

the words = *Hadd[e]bārīm.* See note above.

all Israel. Cp. 5. 1. Mode given by God, Ex. 3. 16; 4. 29. Lev. 24. 14. "All" used by Fig. *Synecdoche* (Ap. 6) to signify a national gathering of any size (1 Sam. 7. 3; 12. 1, 19. 1 Kings 8. 2, 14, 22, 55, 62; 12. 12, 16, 18, &c.).

this side Jordan = across Jordan, a neutral term, expression to be determined by context. Num. 22. 1.

the plain. Heb. *'Arābāh* = name of vale from Jordan to gulf of Akabah.

Red sea = *Ṣūph*, name of a place. Omit "sea". See Num. 33. 48, 49, 50; 35. 1; 36. 13.

2 eleven days': i.e. going direct. **Seir** = Edom.

Kadesh-barnea. See Num. 32. 8.

3 fortieth. The number of Probation. See Ap. 10. First month, Miriam died, Num. 20. 1; fifth month, Aaron died, Num. 33. 38; at the end, Moses died on 29 Sebat, 1452; for the thirty days' mourning end with last day of the fortieth year (29 Adar, 1452). See Ap. 50, vii. 3, 4. **children** = sons.

according unto, &c. Always thus. Cp. 2 Pet. 1. 20, 21.

the LORD. Heb. Jehovah. Ap. 4.

4 and Og. Fig. *Ellipsis* (Ap. 6. iii. 1) = "and [had slain] Og". Cp. Num. 21. 34, 35.

in Edrei. Some codices, with Sept., Syr., and Vulg., read "and in". Cp. Josh. 12. 4.

5 began = undertook with will. Heb *yā'al.* First occurrence Gen 18. 27, 31.

declare. Heb. *bā'ar*, make plain, show sense, set forth, especially in writing. Occurs only here and 27. 8, and Hab. 2. 2. **law** = *tōrah* = instruction.

1. 6—32. 47. [For Structures see next page.]

6 The LORD our God = *Jehovah 'ĕloheīnū.* Two titles of later date do *not* occur in Deut.: "The LORD of hosts" (Samuel) and "the Holy One of Israel" (Isaiah). **spake.** Jehovah spake only here to "us". His speaking to others, see 2. 1. Jehovah "said", see 2. 9. Jehovah "commanded", see 4. 14. **Horeb.** Twentieth day of second month. Num. 10. 11-13. **7 Turn you** = Face about. Note the Fig. *Polyonymia* (Ap. 6) in this verse. Heb. *pānāh*, set one's face; start. **vale.** Heb. *Shephelah* = Philistia. **south.** Heb. *Negeb*, the hill country south of Judea. See note on "South", Gen. 12. 9; 13. 1. **river.** Heb. *nāhār*, a flood, not *naḥal*, a wady. Cp. Gen. 15. 18. **the river.** Fig. *Anadiplosis.* Ap. 6. **8 Behold.** Fig. *Asterismos* (Ap. 6). **Abraham.** Gen. 15. 18; 17. 7, 8; 24. 7; 26. 3, &c. This promise mentioned twenty-seven times in Deut., but unintelligible without Genesis.

1. 9-45. [For Structure see next page.]

9 I spake. See Ex. 18. 17, 18. Num. 11. 14. **10 multiplied.** Cp. 10. 22. **11 as** = according as. **promised.** See Gen. 12. 2; 22. 17, &c.

1452 12 °'How can I myself alone bear your °cumbrance, and your burden, and your strife?
13 Take you wise °men, and understanding, and known among your °tribes, and I will make them rulers over you.'
14 And ye answered me, and said, 'The thing which thou hast spoken *is* good *for us* to do.'
15 So °I took the °chief of your tribes, wise °men, and known, and made them heads over you, captains over thousands, and captains over hundreds, and captains over fifties, and captains over tens, and officers among your tribes.
16 And I charged your judges at that time, saying, 'Hear *the causes* between your brethren, and judge righteously between *every* [15]man and his brother, and the stranger *that is* with him.
17 Ye shall not °respect °persons in °judgment; *but* ye shall hear the small as well as the great; ye shall not be afraid of the face of man; for the judgment °*is* [6]God's: and the cause that is too hard for you, bring *it* unto me, and I will hear it.'
18 And I commanded you at that time all the things which ye should do.
i[1] (p. 238) 19 And when we departed from Horeb, we went through all that great and terrible °wilderness, which ye saw by the way of the mountain of the Amorites, °as [3]the LORD our [6]God commanded us; and we came to °Kadesh-barnea.
20 And I said unto you, 'Ye are come unto the mountain of the °Amorites, which [3]the LORD our [6]God doth give unto us.
h[2] 21 °Behold, [3]the LORD thy [6]God hath set the land before thee: go up *and* possess *it*, as [3]the LORD [6]God of thy fathers hath said unto thee; °fear not, neither be discouraged.'
22 And ye came near unto me °every one of you, and said, °'We will send °men before us, and they shall search us out the land, and bring us word again by what way we must go up, and into what cities we shall come.'
23 And the saying pleased me well: and I took twelve men of you, one of a tribe:
24 And they turned and went up into the mountain, and came unto the valley of °Eshcol, and searched it out.
25 And they took of the fruit of the land in their hands, and brought *it* down unto us, and brought us word again, and said, '*It is* a °good land which [3]the LORD our [6]God doth give us.'
i[2] 26 Notwithstanding ye would not go up, but rebelled against the °commandment of [3]the LORD your [6]God:
27 And ye °murmured in your tents, and said, 'Because [3]the LORD hated us, He hath brought us forth out of the land of Egypt, to deliver us into the hand of the °Amorites, to °destroy us.

1. 6—32. 47 (**C**, p. 236). THE TRIBES. THEIR ADMINISTRATION.
(*Alternation and Introversion.*)

C | E | G | 1. 6—3. 29. Possession East of Jordan. Retrospective.
H | a | 4. 1—5. 33. Injunctions in Horeb. Retrospective.
b | 6. 1—11. 25. Injunctions on entry. Prospective.
J | c | 11. 26–28. Blessings and curses.
d | 11. 29–32. Gerizim and Ebal.
F | 12. 1—27. 10. Laws IN the Land.
E | *J* | *d* | 27. 11–26. Gerizim and Ebal.
c | 28. 1–68. Blessings and curses.
H | *a* | 29. 1–17. Injunctions *plus* Horeb. Retrospective.
b | 29. 18—30. 20. Injunctions *re* Dispersion. Prospective.
G | 31. 1–8. Possession West of Jordan. Prospective.
F | 31. 9—32. 47. Laws and Song: IN and OUT of the Land.

1. 6—3. 29 (G, above). POSSESSION EAST OF JORDAN: RETROSPECTIVE (*Extended Alternation*).

G | K | e | 1. 6–8. Command to go up
f | 1. 9–45. Disobedience rehearsed
g | 1. 46. Abode in Kadesh
} Before the forty years.
K | *e* | 2. 1–3. Command to go up
f | 2. 4—3. 28. Obedience rehearsed
g | 3. 29. Abode in Beth-peor
} After the forty years.

9–45 (f, above). DISOBEDIENCE REHEARSED.
(*Repeated Alternation.*)

f | h[1] | 9–18. Appointment of judges, &c.
i[1] | 19–21. Command to go up.
h[2] | 22–25. Appointment of spies.
i[2] | 26–33. Disobedience.
h[3] | 34–45. Appointment of judgment.

12 How. See note on Lam. 1. 1.
cumbrance. Heb. *ṭorah*, only here and Isa. 1. 14 (trouble).
13 men. Heb. pl. of *'īsh* or *'ĕnōsh*. Ap. 14.
tribes. Heb. *shēbeṭ*, tribe, according to historical or political corporation; always this word in Deut. Where "tribe" is genealogical or geographical elsewhere it is *matteh*.
15 I took. Cp. Ex. 18. 21–26.
chief. Heb. *sar*. Cp. Gen. 32. 28.
men. Heb. *'īsh*. Ap. 14. II.
17 respect = recognise.
persons. Heb. faces. Fig. *Synecdoche* (of Part), Ap. 6, put for persons. Cp. Lev. 19. 15.
judgment. Heb. the judgment: i. e. suited to each case. Cp. Ex. 18. 26.
is God's = it [is] God's.
19 wilderness = desert. Cp. Num. 10. 11–36; 11. 5; 12. 16; 13 26; and ch. 8. 15.
as = according as.
Kadesh-barnea. Cp. Num. 32. 8. A place of solemn import in Israel's history.
20 Amorites = descendants of the *Nephīlīm*. See Ap. 25.
21 Behold. Fig. *Asterismos*. Ap. 6.
fear not, &c. Cp. 31. 6, 8. Josh. 1. 9; 8. 1; 10. 25. 1 Chron. 22. 13; 28. 20. 2 Chron. 20. 15, 17; 32. 7. Jer. 23. 4; 30. 10.

22 every one, &c. = all of you. See note on *v.* 1. **We will send, &c.** Proposal came from people, and is here charged home against them. Jehovah assented, and this assent appears in the history. Num. 13. 1–3. **men.** Heb. pl. of *'īsh*, or *'ĕnōsh*. Ap. 14. **24 Eshcol** = a cluster of grapes. Num. 13. 22–25. **25 good land.** Cp. Num. 13. 27. **26 commandment.** Heb. mouth. Put by Fig. *Metonymy* (of Cause), Ap. 6, for the word spoken by it. So *v.* 43. Ex. 17. 1. Gen. 24. 57, &c. **27 murmured.** Heb. *rāgan*, to rebel. Only here, Ps. 106. 25, and Isa. 29. 24. **Amorites.** The Severus codex reads "the Amorite" (sing.). See Ap. 34. **destroy** = exterminate. Heb. *shāmad*.

1452 28 Whither shall we go up? °our brethren have discouraged our °heart, saying, 'The people *is* greater and °taller than we; the cities *are* great and °walled up to heaven; and moreover we have seen the sons of the °Anakims there.'

29 Then I said unto you, 'Dread not, neither be afraid of them.

30 [3]The LORD your [6]God which goeth before you, He shall fight for you, according to all that He did for you in Egypt before your eyes;

31 And in the wilderness, where thou hast seen how that [3]the LORD thy [6]God bare thee, [19]as a man doth bear his °son, in all the way that ye went, until ye came into this place.'

32 Yet in this thing ye did not believe °the LORD your [6]God,

33 Who went in the way before you, to search you out °a place to pitch °your tents *in*, °in fire by night, to shew you by what way ye should go, and in a cloud by day.

h[3] (p. 238) 34 And [3]the LORD heard the voice of your words, and °was wroth, and sware, saying,

35 'Surely there shall not one of these [22]men of this evil generation see that good land, which I sware to give unto your fathers,

36 Save °Caleb the son of Jephunneh; he shall see it, and to him will I give the land that he hath trodden upon, and to his °children, because he hath wholly followed [3]the LORD.'

37 ° (Also [3]the LORD was °angry with me for your sakes, saying, 'Thou also shalt not go in thither.

38 *But* °Joshua the son of Nun, which standeth before thee, he shall go in thither: encourage him: for he shall cause Israel to inherit it.')

39 'Moreover °your little ones, which ye said should be a prey, and your [36]children, which in that day had no knowledge between good and evil, they shall go in thither, and unto them will I give it, and they shall possess it.

40 But *as for* you, [7]turn you, and take your journey into the wilderness by the way of the °Red sea.'

41 Then ye °answered and said unto me, 'We have °sinned against [3]the LORD, °we will go up and fight, according to all that [3]the LORD our [6]God commanded us.' And when ye had girded on every man his weapons of war, ye were °ready to go up into the hill.

42 And [3]the LORD said unto me, 'Say unto them, 'Go not up, neither fight; for I *am* not among you; lest ye be smitten before your enemies.'

43 So I spake unto you; and ye would not hear, but °rebelled against the °commandment of [3]the LORD, and went presumptuously up into the hill.

27 Ab. 1490 44 And the °Amorites, which dwelt in that mountain, came out against you, and chased you, as °bees do, and °destroyed you in Seir, *even* unto Hormah.

45 And ye returned and wept before [3]the LORD; but [3]the LORD would not hearken to your voice, nor give ear unto you.

28 our brethren = our own brethren. Cp. Num. 13. 28.
heart. Some codices, with one early printed edition, read "hearts" (pl.).
taller = greater. Some codices, with Sam. and Sept., read "more in number".
walled, &c. Fig. *Hyperbole*. Ap. 6.
Anakims. First occurrence; elsewhere, 2. 10, 11, 21; 9. 2. Josh. 11. 21, 22; 14. 12, 15. See Ap. 25. For "sons of Anak", see note on Num. 13. 22.
31 son. See Num. 11. 11, 12, and cp. Isa. 63. 9 and Acts 13. 18.
32 the LORD. Heb. "in the LORD" (= Jehovah).
33 a place. See Ex. 15. 17. Num. 10. 33. Josh. 3. 3, 4. Ezek. 20. 6.
your tents. Not only your inheritance, but the halting-place for daily journeying thither. Both were and are Jehovah's choice for His People.
in fire by night. See Ex. 13. 21, 22. Num. 10. 33, 34.
34 was wroth. See Num. 14. 20-35 and Ps. 95. 8-11.
36 Caleb. Cp. Num. 14. 23, 24. Josh. 14. 9. Judg. 1. 20.
children = sons.
37 This and the next verse are put in a Parenthesis (Ap. 6). **angry.** See Num. 20. 12.
38 Joshua. Num. 14. 30.
39 your little ones. Num. 14. 31.
40 turn you = start. Num. 14. 25.
Red sea = eastern arm. The gulf of Akabah. Cp. *v.* 1.
41 answered and said. Idiom. Ap. 6. In this idiom the word "answered" receives its meaning from the context. Here it = confessed, or repented and said.
sinned. Heb. *chāṭā*. Ap. 44. I.
we will go up. Cp. Num. 14. 40-42.
ready. Heb. *hūn*. Occurs only here: = rash, or presumptuous.
43 rebelled. Num. 14. 44, 45.
commandment. Heb. mouth. Fig. *Metonymy* (of Cause), Ap. 6, put for what is uttered by it, as in *v.* 26.
44 Amorites. Cp. Num. 14. 43. See Ap. 25.
bees. Heb. with art. "the bees". Art. of species.
destroyed you = beat you down. Heb. *kathath.*
46 abode in Kadesh. This is not a summary of the thirty-eight years' wandering, but of what happened before then. How solemn the word "abode" when the command had been "go up".

2. 1 turned = faced about. Cp. 1. 7.
as = according as.
the LORD spake. Jehovah spake at nine "sundry times" and in three "divers manners":
1. To me (Moses), 2. 1, 2, 17; 9. 13; 32. 48.
2. To you, 4. 12, 15; 10. 4.
3. To all your assembly, 5. 22.

spake = said, as in 1. 42. Cp. Num. 21. 4.
many days. These are distinguished from those mentioned in 1. 46. Those were resting in disobedience, these were journeying in obedience.

2. 4—3. 28. [For Structure see next page.]

4 pass through = cross the border. Num. 20. 4, 14-17. Judg. 11. 17. **children** = sons.

46 So ye °abode in Kadesh many days, according unto the days that ye abode *there*. g

2 Then we °turned, and took our journey into the wilderness by the way of the Red sea, °as °the LORD °spake unto me: and we compassed mount Seir °many days. K e

2 And [1]the LORD [1]spake unto me, saying,

3 'Ye have compassed this mountain long enough: [1]turn you northward.

4 And command thou the People, saying, f L[1] k[1] (p. 240)
'Ye *are* to °pass through the coast of your brethren the °children of Esau, which dwell in Seir; and they shall be afraid of you: take ye good heed unto yourselves therefore:

l¹ **5 Meddle not with them; for I will not give**
(p. 240) **you of their land, no, not so much as a foot**
1452 **breadth; °because I have given mount Seir unto Esau *for* °a possession.**

6 Ye shall buy °meat of them for money, that ye may eat; and ye shall also buy water of them for money, that ye may drink.

7 For °the LORD thy °God hath blessed thee in all the works of thy °hand: He knoweth thy walking through this great wilderness: these °forty years °the LORD thy °God *hath been* with thee; thou hast lacked °nothing.' '

8 And when we °passed by from our brethren the [4]children of Esau, which dwelt in Seir, through the way of the plain °from Elath, and from Ezion-gaber, we turned and °passed by the way of the °wilderness of Moab.

9 And °the LORD said unto me, °'Distress not the Moabites, neither contend with them in battle: for I will not give thee of their land *for* a possession; because I have given Ar unto the [4]children of Lot *for* a possession.'

m¹ **10 The °Emims dwelt therein in times past,**
(p. 240) **a people great, and many, and tall, as the °Anakims;**

11 Which also were accounted °giants, as the Anakims; but the Moabites call them Emims.

12 The °Horims also dwelt in Seir beforetime; but the children of Esau succeeded them, when they had °destroyed them from before them, and dwelt in their °stead; [1]as Israel did unto the land of his °possession, which [1]the LORD °gave unto them.

L² k² **13 °'Now rise up,' *said I,* 'and get you over the °brook Zered.' And we went over the brook Zered.**

14 And the space in which we came from Kadesh-barnea, until we were come over the brook Zered, *was* °thirty and eight years; until all the generation of the men of war were wasted out from among the host, [1]as [1]the LORD sware unto them.

15 For indeed the hand of [1]the LORD was against them, to °destroy them from among the host, until they were consumed.

16 So it came to pass, when all the men of war were consumed and dead from among the People,

17 That [1]the LORD [1]spake unto me, saying,

18 'Thou art to pass over through Ar, the coast of Moab, this day:

l² **19 And *when* thou comest nigh over against the [4]children of °Ammon, distress them not, nor meddle with them: for I will not give thee of the land of the [4]children of Ammon *any* possession; because I have given it unto the [4]children of Lot *for* a possession.'**

m² **20 (That also was accounted a land of [11]giants: [11]giants dwelt therein in old time; and the Ammonites call them °Zamzummims;**

21 A people great, and many, and tall, as the °Anakims; but [1]the LORD [12]destroyed them before them; and they succeeded them, and dwelt in their stead:

22 As He did to the [4]children of Esau, which dwelt in Seir, when He °destroyed the Horims from before them; and they succeeded them, and dwelt in their stead even unto this day:

23 And the °Avims which dwelt in Hazerim

2. 4—3. 28 (*f*, p. 238). OBEDIENCE REHEARSED.
(*Extended and Repeated Alternation.*)

f | L¹ | k¹ | 2. 4. Passage through Edom.
l¹ | 2. 5-9. Command as to Edom and Moab.
m¹ | 2. 10-12. Former inhabitants and Moab.
L² | k² | 2. 13-18. Passage over Zered.
l² | 2. 19. Command as to Ammon.
m² | 2. 20-33. Former inhabitants and Ammon.
L³ | k³ | 2. -24-. Passage over Arnon.
l³ | 2. -24-29. Command as to Amorites.
m³ | 2. 30—3. 28. Former inhabitants and Israel.

5 because, &c. Cp. Gen. 32. 3; 33. 6-8; 36. 8. Josh. 24. 4.

a possession. Heb. *yārash* (because given). Also in *vv.* 9, 12, and 3. 19, 20, &c.; in Deut. not *'āhaz* (because seized), as in other books; though *'āhaz* is used in ch. 32. 49.

6 meat. Put by Fig. *Synecdoche* (Ap. 6) for all kinds of food.

7 the LORD thy God. Jehovah thy Elohim = the triune God.

hand. Some codices, with some early printed editions, and Sam., Jon., Sept., Syr., and Vulg., read "hands".

forty years. Cp. Neh. 9. 21.

nothing. Heb. "not a word": i. e. of what Jehovah had promised. Cp. 8. 2-4.

8 passed by. Cp. Num. 20. 21; 21. 11-13. 2 Chron. 20. 10.

from Elath, &c. Gulf of Akabah. Cp. Num. 33. 35, 35, and 1 Kings 9. 26.

wilderness of Moab. See the route, Judg. 11. 16-18.

9 the LORD [Heb. Jehovah] **said unto me** (or Moses). Occurs thirteen times in Deut.: 2. 9, 31; 3. 2, 26; 4. 10; 5. 28; 9. 12; 10. 1, 11; 18. 17; 31. 2, 14, 16; 34. 4.

Distress not, &c. God judged both (2 Chron. 20. 1-25. Amos 1. 13-15).

10 Emims = terrible ones (Gen. 14. 5). A race of the *Nephīlīm*. See Ap. 25.

Anakims. See on 1. 28, and Ap. 25.

11 giants. Heb. *Rephaïm*, another name for the *Nephīlīm*, from one Rapha. See Ap. 25. Connected with *healing*, and with Egypt (Gen. 50. 2). See Ap. 23.

12 Horims. Another race or name of the *Nephīlīm*. See Ap. 25. Cp. Gen. 14. 6. See Ap. 25.

destroyed = exterminated. Heb. *shāmad*.

stead = room. These are the Canaanites with whom Satan had preoccupied the land to thwart God's purpose in Abraham. Cp. Gen. 12. 6; 13. 7, and see Ap. 25. All these had to be destroyed, as the *Nephīlīm* were destroyed by the Flood. Cp. Gen. 6. 4, which tells of a later irruption. See Gen. 14. 5.

possession . . . gave. See ch. 3. 20, and note on *v.* 5.

13 Now. Some codices, with Sam. and Sept., read "Now therefore".

brook Zered, which flows into the Arnon, the frontier between Moab and Ammon. Num. 21. 13.

14 thirty and eight years. Cp. the antitype of Israel in the flesh, John 5. 5.

15 destroy = shake off. Heb. *hāmam*.

19 Ammon. See Gen. 19. 36-38, and cp. Judg. 11. 15.

20 Zamzummims. A name given them by the Ammonites = noisy ones. See *vv.* 10-12, and Ap. 25.

21 Anakims. See note on 1. 28, and Ap. 25.

22 destroyed = exterminated. Heb. *shāmad*.

23 Avims. Another name for these *Nephīlīm*. Josh. 13. 3. (Ap. 25.)

1452 *even* unto °Azzah, the °Caphtorims, which came forth out of Caphtor, [22]destroyed them, and dwelt in their stead.)

k^3 (p. 240) 24 'Rise ye up, °take your journey, and pass over the river Arnon: behold, I have given into thine hand Sihon the Amorite, king of Heshbon, and his land:

l^3 begin to possess *it*, and contend with him in battle.

25 This day will I begin to °put the dread of thee and the fear of thee upon the nations *that are* under the whole heaven, who shall hear report of thee, and shall tremble, and be in anguish because of thee.'

26 And I °sent messengers out of the wilderness of °Kedemoth unto Sihon king of Heshbon with words of peace, saying,

27 'Let me pass through thy land: I will go along by the high way, I will neither turn unto the right hand nor to the left.

28 Thou °shalt sell me [6]meat for money, that I may eat; and give me water for money, that I may drink: only I will pass through on my feet;

29 (°As the [4]children of Esau which dwell in Seir, and the Moabites which dwell in Ar, did unto me;) until I shall pass over Jordan into the land which [1]the LORD our [7]God giveth us.'

m^3 M^1 (p. 241) 30 But °Sihon king of Heshbon would not let us pass by him: for [1]the LORD thy [7]God °hardened his °spirit, and made his heart obstinate, that He might deliver him into thy hand, as *appeareth* this day.

31 And [1]the LORD [9]said unto me, °'Behold, I have begun to give Sihon and his land before thee: begin to possess, that thou mayest inherit his land.'

32 Then Sihon °came out against us, he and all his people, to fight at Jahaz.

33 And [1]the LORD our [7]God delivered him before us; and we smote him, and his °sons, and all his people.

34 And we took all his cities at that time, and utterly °destroyed the °men, and the women, and the little ones, of every city, we left none to remain:

35 Only the cattle we took for °a prey unto ourselves, and the spoil of the cities which we took.

36 From °Aroer, which *is* by the brink of the river of Arnon, and *from* °the city that *is* by the river, even unto Gilead, there was not one city too strong for us: [1]the LORD our [7]God °delivered all unto us:

37 Only unto the land of the [4]children of Ammon thou camest not, *nor* unto any place of the river Jabbok, nor unto the cities in the mountains, nor unto whatsoever [1]the LORD our [7]God forbad us.

M^2 n **3** Then we turned, and went up the way to °Bashan: and Og the king of Bashan °came out against us, he and all his People, to battle at Edrei.

2 And °the LORD °said unto me, 'Fear him not: for I will deliver him, and all his People, and his land, into thy °hand; and thou shalt do unto him °as thou didst unto Sihon king of the Amorites, which dwelt at Heshbon.'

3 So [2]the LORD our °God °delivered into our hands Og also, the king of Bashan, and all his people: and we smote him until none was left to him remaining. o

4 And we took all his cities at that time, there was not a city which we took not from them, °threescore cities, all the °region of °Argob, the kingdom of Og in Bashan.

Azzah = Gaza. Gen. 10. 19. 1 Sam. 6. 17. Cp. 1 Kings 4. 24. Jer. 25. 20. Acts 8. 26.

Caphtorims. Another name, for those that came out of Caphtor. Gen. 10. 14. Amos 9. 7. Jer. 47. 4. Sometimes identified with Crete, or the Delta.

24 take your journey. Cp. Num. 21. 13.

25 put the dread. Fulfilment of Ex. 15. 14, 15. Cp. Josh. 2. 9, 10.

26 sent messengers. Num. 21. 21, 22. Judg. 11. 19.

Kedemoth. Cp. Num. 21. 21-24. Afterward a Levitical city (Josh. 13. 18; 21. 37. 1 Chron. 6. 64, 79).

28 shalt sell. Edom refused to let Israel pass through, but did sell, as here stated. Cp. Num. 20. 17-21. Moab, too, "sold", but did not meet as a friend (23. 4, where *ḳāram* means to offer unasked). Cp. Isa. 21. 17.

29 As = According as.

2. 30—3. 29 (m^3, p. 241). FORMER INHABITANTS (*Division*).

m^3 | M^1 | 2. 30-37. Conquest of Sihon.
| M^2 | 3. 1-29. Conquest of Og.

30 Sihon . . . would not. Cp. Num. 21. 23. Judg. 11. 20.

God = Elohim, acting as the Creator with a creature. See Ap. 4.

hardened. Heb. *ḳāshāh.* See note on Ex. 4. 21.

spirit = Heb. *rūach.* See Ap. 9.

31 Behold. Fig. *Asterismos.* Ap. 6.

32 came out. Sihon was the aggressor. Num. 21. 23. Judg. 11. 20.

33 sons. So read, but written in Heb. text "son" (sing.).

34 destroyed = devoted to destruction. Heb. *ḥāram.* Cp. 3. 6; 7. 2; 20. 17.

men. Heb. *m^{e}thim.* See Ap. 14. v.

35 a prey. For the law governing this see Num. 31.

36 Aroer. Num. 32. 34. The name is on the Moabite Stone. See Ap. 54.

the city: i. e. Ar of Moab. Num. 21. 15.

delivered. Cp. Judg. 11. 21, 22, 26. "For His mercy endureth for ever", Ps. 136. 18-22.

3. 1-29 (M^2, above). THE CONQUEST OF OG. (*Introversion.*)

M^2 | n | 1, 2. Command of Jehovah's.
| o | 3-11. Land. Conquest.
| o | 12-17. Land. Division { Manasseh, 12-15. Reuben, 16, 17.
| n | 18-29. Commands of Moses.

1 Bashan. Cp. Num. 21. 33, 34.

came out. Og was the aggressor. Num. 21. 33.

2 the LORD. Heb. Jehovah. Ap. 4.

said. See note on 2. 9.

hand. Some codices, with three early printed editions, Sept., and Vulg., read "hands".

as = according as.

3 God. Heb. Elohim. Ap. 4. I.

delivered. Cp. 2. 36.

4 threescore cities. They can all be seen, and counted to-day. (See Dr. Porter's *Giant Cities of Bashan.*)

region. Heb. = "cord". Put by Fig. *Metonymy* (of Cause), Ap. 6, for the region marked out by it.

Argob. Cp. 1 Kings 4. 13. Ps. 136. 18-22.

1452 5 All these ° cities *were* fenced with high
walls, gates, and bars; beside unwalled towns
a great many.
6 And we utterly ° destroyed them, as we did
unto Sihon king of Heshbon, utterly ° destroying the ° men, ° women, and children, of every
city.
7 But all the cattle, and the ° spoil of the
cities, we took for a prey to ourselves.
8 And we took at that time out of the hand
of the two kings of the Amorites the land that
was ° on this side Jordan, from the river of
Arnon ° unto mount ° Hermon;
9 (° *Which* Hermon the Sidonians call ° Sirion;
and the Amorites call it ° Shenir;)
10 All the cities of the plain, and all ° Gilead,
and all Bashan, unto Salchah and Edrei, cities
of the kingdom of Og in Bashan.
11 (For only Og king of Bashan remained of
the remnant of ° giants; ° behold, his ° bedstead
was a bedstead of ° iron; ° *is* it not in ° Rabbath
of the ° children of Ammon? nine ° cubits *was*
the length thereof, and four ° cubits the breadth
of it, after the ° cubit of a ° man.)

o 12 And this land, *which* we possessed ° at
(p. 241) that time, from Aroer, which *is* by the river
Arnon, and half mount Gilead, and the cities
thereof, gave I unto the Reubenites and to the
Gadites.
13 And the rest of Gilead, and all Bashan,
being the kingdom of Og, gave I unto the half
tribe of Manasseh; all the region of Argob,
with all Bashan, which was called the land of
[11] giants.
14 (Jair the son of Manasseh took all the
country of Argob unto the ° coasts of Geshuri
and Maachathi; and called them after his own
name, ° Bashan-havoth-jair, ° unto this day.)
15 And I gave Gilead unto Machir.
16 And unto the Reubenites and unto the
Gadites I gave from Gilead even unto the river
Arnon half the valley, and the border even
unto the river Jabbok, *which is* the border of
the [11] children of Ammon;
17 The plain also, and Jordan, and the [14] coast
thereof, from ° Chinnereth even unto the sea
of ° the plain, *even* the salt sea, under ° Ashdoth-
pisgah eastward.

n p 18 And ° I commanded you at that time, saying,
(p. 242) [2]'The LORD your [3] God hath given you this
land to possess it: ye shall pass over armed
before your brethren the [11] children of Israel, all
that are ° meet for the war.
19 But your wives, and your little ones, and
your cattle, (*for* I know that ye have much
cattle,) shall abide in your cities which I have
given you;
20 Until [2] the LORD have given rest unto your
brethren, as well as unto you, and *until* they
also possess the land which [2] the LORD your
[3] God hath given them beyond Jordan: and
then shall ye ° return every man unto his
possession, which I have given you.'

q 21 And [18] I commanded Joshua at that time,
saying, 'Thine eyes have seen all that [2] the
LORD your [3] God hath done unto these two
kings: so shall [2] the LORD do unto all the
kingdoms whither thou passest.
22 Ye shall ° not fear them: for [2] the LORD
your [3] God He shall fight for you.'

23 And I besought [2] the LORD at that time, p
saying,
24 'O ° Lord GOD, Thou hast begun to shew
Thy servant Thy greatness, and Thy mighty

5 cities. See note on *v.* 4.
6 destroyed . . . destroying = devoted to destruction. Heb. *ḥāram*. Cp. 7. 2.
men. Heb. *m^ethim* = adult males. Ap. 14. v.
women. Some codices, with Jon., Sept., Syr., and Vulg., read "and the women".
7 spoil. For laws regulating this, see Num. 31.
8 on this side = across, a neutral term. See note on 1. 1.
unto. Some codices, with Sam., Sept., and Syr., read "and (or even) unto".
Hermon = high mountain.
9 Which. Note these topographical parentheses, *vv.* 9, 11, 14, cp. 2. 20-23, 29.
Sirion = breastplate.
Shenir = coat of mail.
10 Gilead = the rough country.
11 giants. Heb. "*Rephaim*", descendants of one Rapha, a branch of the *Nephīlīm*. See Ap. 25.
behold. A special various reading called *Sevīr* (see Ap. 34) reads "and behold".
bedstead = bed or couch, but not the usual word which is *mishkāb*. It is *'eres*, and is exactly the same measurement as the tomb of Marduk in Babylon. The mythological significance of *'eres* (Bab. *irsu*) is nuptial bed, or funeral couch. Probably = tomb.
iron. Probably basalt.
is it not . . . ? Fig. *Erotēsis* (Ap. 6), for emphasis.
Rabbath was the capital of Ammon, where the temple of Milchom was: and where Og's tomb would naturally be.
children = sons.
cubits. See Ap. 51. III. 2.
cubit of a man = a common cubit = a man's forearm.
man. Heb. *'ish*. Ap. 14. II.
12 at that time. Cp. Num. 32. 33; 21. 24. Josh. 12. 1-6; 13. 8-12, 15-32.
14 coasts = borders.
Bashan-havoth-jair = the villages (or cluster of villages) of Jair in Bashan. Heb. *Havoth* = towns, used only of Jair's. Cp. Num. 32. 41. Josh. 13. 30. Judg. 10. 4. 1 Kings 4. 13. 1 Chron. 2. 23.
unto this day: unto the time of writing. Here the time mentioned is from Num. 21 to the eleventh month of the fortieth year (Deut. 1. 3).
17 Chinnereth. Afterward called Gennesaret, cp. Num. 34. 11. Josh. 19. 35. So called from its shape, *kinnōr*, a harp.
the plain. Heb. *'Arābāh*. See 1. 1.
Ashdoth-pisgah = the springs of Pisgah. Note the Fig. *Polyonymia* (Ap. 6) in this verse.

18-28 (*n*, p. 241). COMMANDS OF MOSES.
(*Alternation.*)

n | p | 18-20. Manasseh and Reuben to go over.
  q | 21, 22. Charge to Joshua.
 p | 23-27. Moses not to go over.
  q | 28, 29. Charge to Joshua.

18 I commanded. See Num. 32. 20-24.
meet for the war. Heb. = sons of valour. Fig. *Antimereia* (of Noun), Ap. 6 = valiant men. Emphasis on valiant. Cp. 2 Sam. 2. 7. 1 Kings 1. 52.
20 return. Cp. Josh. 22. 4.
22 not fear. Cp. 1. 29, 30. Ex. 14. 13, 14.
24 Lord GOD = *Adonai Jehovah*. See Ap. 4. This prayer not mentioned elsewhere.

1452 °hand: for what °GOD *is there* in heaven or
in earth, that can do according to Thy works,
and according to Thy might?
25 I pray Thee, let me go over, and see °the
good land that *is* beyond Jordan, that goodly
mountain, and Lebanon.'
26 But [2]the LORD was °wroth with me for
your sakes, and would not hear me: and [2]the
LORD °said unto me, 'Let it suffice thee; speak
no more unto Me of this matter.
27 Get thee up into the top of Pisgah, and lift
up thine eyes °westward, °and northward, and
southward, and eastward, and behold *it* with
thine eyes: for thou shalt °not go over this
Jordan.
q (p. 242) 28 But °charge Joshua, and encourage him,
and strengthen him: for he shall go over before
this People, and he shall cause them to inherit
the land which thou shalt see.'
29 So we abode in the valley over against
°Beth-peor.

a N t (p. 243) **4** Now therefore hearken, O Israel, unto the
°statutes and unto the °judgments, which
I °teach you, °for to do *them*,
u that ye may live, and go in and possess the
land which °the LORD °God of your fathers
giveth you.
v 2 °Ye shall not add unto the word which I
command you, neither shall ye diminish *ought*
from it, that ye may keep the commandments
of [1]the LORD your [1]God which I command you.
w 3 Your eyes have seen what [1]the LORD did
because of Baal-peor: for all the °men that
followed °Baal-peor, [1]the LORD thy [1]God hath
°destroyed them from among you.
4 But ye that did cleave unto [1]the LORD your
[1]God *are* alive every one of you this day.
t 5 °Behold, I have taught you [1]statutes and
[1]judgments, even as the LORD my [1]God commanded me,
u that ye should do so in the land whither ye go
to possess it.
v 6 Keep therefore and do *them*;
w for this *is* your wisdom and your °understanding in the sight of the nations, which shall
hear all these statutes, and say, 'Surely this
great nation *is* a wise and °understanding
People.'
7 For °what nation *is there so* great, who *hath*
[7]God *so* °nigh unto them, as [1]the LORD our
[1]God *is* in all *things that* we call upon Him
for?
8 And [7]what nation *is there so* great, that
hath [1]statutes and [1]judgments °*so* righteous
as all this law, which I set before you this
day?
O r x 9 Only °take heed to thyself, and keep °thy
soul diligently, lest thou forget the things
which thine eyes have seen, and lest they
depart from thy heart all the days of thy life:
but teach them thy sons, and thy sons' sons;
10 °*Specially* the day that thou stoodest
before [1]the LORD thy [1]God in °Horeb, when

hand. Fig. *Metonymy* (of Cause), Ap. 6, put for works wrought by the hand.

GOD. Heb *'El.* = God as the omnipotent One. See Ap. 4. IV.

25 the good land. Cp. Ps. 106. 24. Num. 13. 27.

26 wroth. See Num. 20. 12.

said. See note on 2. 9.

27 westward, &c. The points of the compass here are seaward, darkness-ward, Teman-ward, and sunrise-ward. Teman-ward (i. e. south of Edom) first used for south in Ex. 26. 18. See Num. 27. 12.

and. Note the Fig. *Polysyndeton,* Ap. 6, emphasising the extent of the view.

not go over. Cp. Num. 27. 13.

28 charge Joshua. Cp. Num. 27. 18, 19.

29 Beth-peor = the house (or temple) of Peor, where Baal was worshipped (Num. 23. 28; 25. 3. Deut. 4. 3. Here Moses was buried (Deut. 34. 6). It was a Moabite holy place (Num. 25. 18; 31. 16. Josh. 22. 17). Allotted to Reuben (Josh. 13. 20).

4. 1—5. 33 (a, p. 238). INJUNCTIONS IN HOREB: RETROSPECTIVE (*Introversion and Alternation*).

a | N | 4. 1-8. Statutes announced.
  O | r | 4. 9-20. Warnings against idolatry.
      s | 4. 21, 22. Moses (Death announced).
  O | r | 4. 23-40. Warnings against idolatry.
      s | 4. 41-43. Moses (Cities of Refuge severed).
  N | 4. 44 — 5. 33. Statutes recited.

4. 1-8 (N, above). STATUTES ANNOUNCED. (*Extended alternation.*)

N | t | 1-. Statutes: Hearken.
      u | -1. Object.
        v | 2. Injunction.
          w | 3, 4. Motive (from experience).
    t | 5-. Statutes: Behold.
      u | -5. Object.
        v | 6-. Injunction.
          w | -6-8. Motive (from privilege).

1 statutes = ordinances: Godward. Ex. 12. 24, 43; 30. 21. Heb. 9. 1.

judgments = duties and punishments, manward. First occurrence in plural in Ex. 21. 1. The two often united. See 5. 1; 6. 1; 12. 1. Mal. 4. 4, &c.

teach. Heb. *lāmad* (whence "Talmud") = to cause to learn. First occurrence.

for to do. Old English idiom: modern idiom = to do.

the LORD God = Jehovah 'Elohim.

2 Ye shall not add. Cp. ch. 12. 32. Prov. 30. 5, 6. Jer. 23. 28; 26. 2. Ezek. 2. 5, 7. Rev. 22. 18, 19.

3 men. Heb. *'ish.* See Ap. 14. II.

Baal-peor. See note on 3. 29 and Num. 25. 1-5, 9. Ps. 106. 28. Hos. 9. 10. 1 Cor. 10. 8.

destroyed = exterminated. Heb. *shmadh.*

5 Behold. Fig. *Asterismos.* Ap. 6.

6 understanding = discernment.

understanding = discerning.

7 what . . . ? Fig. *Erotēsis.* Ap. 6.

God = a god, or gods. Heb. 'Elohim. Ap. 4. I.

nigh = nigh to help. Cp. Ps. 32. 9; 34. 18; 119. 151; 145. 18. Neh. 13. 4.

8 so righteous. See Ap. 15. Cp. 2 Sam. 7. 23.

9-20 (r, above). WARNINGS AGAINST IDOLATRY. (*Alternation.*)

r | x | 9-13. Law at Horeb. No similitude.
    y | 14. Intention—Command.
  x | 15-19. Law at Horeb. No similitude.
    y | 20. Intention—Act.

9 take heed. Note the three occurrences in this chapter (*vv.* 9, 15, 23).

thy soul = thyself. Heb. thy *nephesh,* cp. yourselves, *v.* 15. Ap. 13.

10 Specially. Fig. *Ellipsis.* Ap. 6. Might be supplied by the word "Remember". **Horeb.** Occurs three times before Deut. (viz. Ex. 3. 1; 17. 6; 33. 6). Sinai is the general word, but occurs only once in Deut. (33. 2).

1452 [1]the LORD °said unto me, 'Gather Me the People together, and I will make them hear My words, that they may learn to fear Me all the days that they shall live upon the earth, and *that* they may teach their children.'

11 And ye came near and stood under the mountain; and the mountain burned with fire unto the midst of heaven, with darkness, clouds, and °thick darkness.

12 And [1]the LORD °spake unto you out of the midst of the fire: ye heard the voice of the words, but °saw no °similitude; only *ye heard* a voice.

13 And He declared unto you His covenant, which He commanded you to perform, °*even* ten commandments; and He °wrote them upon two tables of stone.

y (p. 243) 14 And [1]the LORD commanded °me at that time to teach you [1]statutes and [1]judgments, that ye might do them in the land whither ye go over to possess it.

x 15 Take ye therefore good heed unto °yourselves; for ye saw no manner of [12]similitude on the day *that* [1]the LORD [12]spake unto you in Horeb out of the midst of the fire:

16 Lest ye corrupt *yourselves,* and make you a °graven image, the [12]similitude of any °figure, the °likeness of male or female,

17 The likeness of any beast that *is* on the earth, the likeness of any winged fowl that flieth in the air,

18 The likeness of any thing that creepeth on the ground, the likeness of any fish that *is* in the waters beneath the earth:

19 And lest thou lift up thine eyes unto heaven, and when thou seest the sun, and the moon, and the stars, *even* all the °host of heaven, shouldest be driven to worship them, and serve them, which [1]the LORD thy [1]God hath divided unto all nations under the whole heaven.

y 20 But [1]the LORD hath taken you, and brought you forth out of the °iron furnace, *even* out of Egypt, °to be unto Him a People of inheritance, as *ye are* this day.

s 21 Furthermore [1]the LORD was °angry with me for your sakes, and sware that I should not go over Jordan, and that I should not go in unto that good land, which [1]the LORD thy [1]God giveth thee *for* an inheritance:

22 But I must die in this land, I must not go over Jordan: but ye shall go over, and possess that good land.

r a (p. 244) 23 Take heed unto yourselves, lest ye forget the covenant of [1]the LORD your [1]God, which He made with you, and make you a [16]graven image, *or* the [16]likeness of any *thing,* which [1]the LORD thy [1]God hath °forbidden thee.

24 (For [1]the LORD thy [1]God *is* °a consuming fire, *even* a jealous °GOD.)

25 When thou shalt beget °children, and °children's °children, and ye shall have remained long in the land, and shall corrupt *yourselves,* and make a graven image, *or* the [23]likeness of any *thing,* and shall do °evil in the sight of [1]the LORD thy [1]God, to provoke Him to anger:

b 26 °I call °heaven and earth to witness against you °this day, that ye shall soon utterly perish from off the land whereunto ye go over Jordan to possess it; ye shall not prolong *your* days upon it, but shall utterly be °destroyed.

27 And [1]the LORD shall °scatter you among the °nations, and ye shall be left few in number among the °heathen, whither [1]the LORD shall lead you.

---

said. See note on 2. 9.

11 thick darkness. See Ex. 20. 21, and cp. Heb. *'ărāphel.* 2 Sam. 22. 10. 1 Kings 8. 12. Ps. 97. 2.

12 spake. See note on 2. 1.

saw. Fig. *Zeugma.* Ap. 6. i.: by which one verb "saw" is used with two objects and suits only the first. A second verb "heard" must be supplied: cp. Ex. 3. 16. 2 Kings 11. 12. 1 Tim. 4. 3. It is for the purpose of calling attention to the emphasis thus put on the verb "saw"; an idol being that which is *seen.*

similitude = appearance of form, or likeness.

13 even ten. Heb. the ten.

wrote. See note on Ex. 17. 14; only here and 10. 4 in Deut. See also Ap. 47.

14 me. Emphasis on "me" to call attention to the mediation of Moses.

15 yourselves = your souls. Heb. *nephesh.* See *v.* 9 above and Ap. 13.

16 graven image. Heb. *peṣel* = a sculpture (Ex. 20. 4).

figure. Heb. *semel* = only here, 2 Chron. 33. 7, 15, and Ezek. 8. 3, 5.

likeness = form. Heb. *tablinith* = model.

19 host of heaven: sun, moon, and stars. This sin foreknown. 2 Kings 17. 18; 23. 4. Cp. Amos 5. 26 with Acts 7. 42, 43.

20 iron furnace. Cp. Gen. 15. 17. Ex. 3. 2, 3. 1 Kings 8. 51-53. Jer. 11. 4.

to be, &c. Cp. Ex. 19. 5. Deut. 9. 29; 32. 9.

21 angry. Cp. 1. 37; 3. 2.

23-40 (*r*, p. 243). WARNINGS AGAINST IDOLATRY (*Alternation*).

r | a | 23-25. Sin.
  b | 26-28. Threatening—Dispersion.
 a | 29, 30. Repentance.
  b | 31-40. Promise. Reason.

23 forbidden thee. Heb. *zivvah,* a Homonym = to command, and to forbid. Here it = forbid, also in Judg. 13. 14, where it is wrongly rendered "command".

24 a consuming fire. Fig. *Anthropopatheia.* Ap. 6. Cp. Ex. 24. 17. Heb. 12. 29.

GOD. Heb. *'Ēl.* See Ap. 4.

children = sons.

25 evil. Heb. *rā'a'.* Ap. 44. viii.

26 I call. Fig. *Deasis.* Ap. 6. Cp. 31. 28.

heaven and earth = the heavens and the earth (always plural and with Heb. particle *'eth,* except Gen. 2. 1. See note on 1. 1). One of the thirteen occurrences of the Heb. expressions noted in the Massorah. Gen. 1. 1. Ex. 20. 11; 31. 17. Deut. 4. 26; 30. 19; 31. 28. 2 Kings 19. 15. 2 Chron. 2. 12. Isa. 37. 16. Jer. 23. 24; 32. 17. Hag. 2. 6, 21.

this day. A solemn idiom, used for great emphasis. Occurs forty-two times (see Ap. 10) in this book: 4. 26, 39, 40; 5. 1; 6. 6; 7. 11; 8. 1, 11, 19; 9. 1, 3; 10. 13; 11. 2, 8, 13, 26, 27, 28, 32; 13. 18; 15. 5, 15; 19. 9; 26. 3, 16, 17, 18; 27. 1, 4, 10; 28. 1, 13, 14, 15; 30. 2, 8, 11, 15, 16, 18, 19; 32. 46. It is this Old Testament idiom in Luke 23. 43.

destroyed = exterminated. Heb. *shmad.*

27 scatter. Heb. *pūẓ* = disperse. See Gen. 10. 18; 11. 4, 9, not used in Lev. 26. 33, but is used in Jer. 30. 11, and frequently: also in Ezek. Cp. Deut. 28. 64, and Ezek. 20. 23.

nations = peoples.

heathen = nations.

1452 **28 And there ye shall °serve gods, the work of °men's hands, wood and stone, which neither see, nor hear, nor eat, nor smell.**

a **29 But if from thence °thou shalt °seek [1]the LORD thy [1]God, thou shalt find *Him*, if thou °seek Him with all thy heart and with all thy °soul.**

30 When thou art in tribulation, and all these things are come upon thee, *even* in °the latter days, if thou turn to [1]the LORD thy [1]God, and shalt be obedient unto His voice;

b **31 (For [1]the LORD thy [1]God *is* a merciful [24]GOD); °He will not forsake thee, neither [26]destroy thee, nor forget the covenant of thy fathers which He sware unto them.**

32 For ask now of °the days that are past, which were before thee, since the day that [1]God °created °man upon the earth, and *ask* from the one side of heaven unto the other, whether there hath been *any such thing* as this great thing *is*, or hath been heard like it?

33 °Did *ever* people hear the voice of °God speaking out of the midst of the fire, °as thou hast heard, and live?

34 Or °hath °God assayed to go *and* take Him a nation °from the midst of *another* nation, by °temptations, by signs, °and by wonders, and by °war, and by a mighty hand, and by a stretched out arm, and by great terrors, according to all that [1]the LORD your [1]God did for you in Egypt before your eyes?

35 Unto thee it was shewed, that thou mightest know that [1]the LORD °He *is* [1]God; *there is* none else beside Him.

36 Out of heaven He made thee to hear His voice, that He might instruct thee: and upon earth He shewed thee His great fire; and thou heardest His words out of the midst of the fire.

37 And °because He loved thy fathers, therefore He chose their seed after them, and brought thee out in His sight with His mighty power out of Egypt;

38 To drive out nations from before thee greater and mightier than thou *art*, to bring thee in, to give thee their land *for* an inheritance, as *it is* this day.

39 Know therefore [26]this day, and consider *it* in thine heart, that [1]the LORD He *is* °God in heaven above, and upon the earth beneath: *there is* none else.

40 Thou shalt keep therefore His [1]statutes, and His commandments, which I command thee [26]this day, that it may go well with thee, and with thy children after thee, and that thou mayest prolong *thy* days upon the earth, which [1]the LORD thy [1]God giveth thee, °for ever."

s **41 °Then °Moses °severed three cities on**
(p. 243) **this side Jordan toward the sunrising;**

42 That the slayer might flee thither, which should kill his neighbour unawares, and °hated him not in times past; and that fleeing unto one of these cities he might live:

43 *Namely*, Bezer in the wilderness, in the plain country, of the Reubenites; and Ramoth in Gilead, of the Gadites; and Golan in Bashan, of the Manassites.

44 And °this *is* the law which Moses set N c
before the °children of Israel:

45 These *are* the °testimonies, and the °statutes, and the °judgments, which Moses spake unto the [44]children of Israel, after they came forth out of Egypt,

46 On this side Jordan, in the valley over against Beth-peor, in the land of Sihon king of the Amorites, who dwelt at Heshbon, whom Moses and the [44]children of Israel °smote, after they were come forth out of Egypt:

47 And they possessed his land, and the land °of Og king of Bashan, two kings of the

---

28 serve gods. Cp. Dan 5. 23. Rev. 9. 20.
men's. Heb. *'ādām*. Ap. 14. I.
29 thou shalt. This agrees with the Sam. Text., but the printed Heb. Text has "ye shall".
seek. Cp. Lev. 26. 40. Jer. 29. 13, &c.
soul. Heb. *nephesh*. See Ap. 13.
30 the latter days = the end of the days.
31 He will not forsake. First occurrence of this promise. Repeated in 31. 6 for the journey. Repeated to Joshua for conflict, Josh. 1. 5, 6; to Solomon for work, 1 Chron. 28. 20; to us for daily provision and comfort, Heb. 13. 5, 6.
32 the days. Fig. *Metonymy* (of Adjunct), Ap. 6, put for the events which took place in them.
created (sing.). These two words occur together three times (Gen. 1. 1; 2. 3, and here).
man = Heb. *'ādām*. Ap. 14. I.
33 Did . . . ? Fig. *Erotēsis*. Ap. 6.
God: or, a god.
as = according as.
34 hath . . . ? Fig. *Erotēsis*. Ap. 6.
God: or, a god.
from the midst. Here we have the whole of Exodus, cp. Jer. 32. 21.
temptations = trials, or, provings.
and. Note the Fig. *Polysyndeton* (Ap. 6), in this verse.
war = fightings. Ex. 14. 25.
35 He is God. Cp. 1 Kings 18. 39. Isa. 45. 21.
37 because. Cp. 7. 7; 9. 5; 10. 15.
39 God. Heb. *hā-'ĕlohīm* = the God.
40 for ever = all the days: i. e. for all time.
41 Then. Emphatic, marking the end of his first address.
Moses. Change to third person, not because it is now editorial, but because the first direct address is ended. See note on 1. 1.
severed = separated. Cp. Ex. 21. 13. Num. 35. 6-29.
42 hated = he hated.

4. 44—5. 32 (*N*, p. 243). **STATUTES RECITED.** (*Alternation.*)

N | c | 4. 44—5. 4. The Law. General.
| d | 5. 5. Mediation of Moses.
| c | 5. 6-21. The Law. Particular.
| *d* | 5. 22-33. Mediation of Moses.

44 this: i. e. which hereafter followeth. The commencement of the new section according to the Structure.
children = sons.
45 testimonies. Heb. *'ūd*, to say again and again, hence, testifyings, affirmations, &c.
statutes, and the judgments. See note on 4. 1.
46 smote. Cp. Num. 21. 24. Deut. 1. 4.
47 of Og. Cp. Num. 21. 33. Deut. 3. 3.

1452 Amorites, which *were* on this side Jordan toward the sunrising;

48 From Aroer, which *is* by the bank of the river Arnon, even unto mount °Sion, which *is* Hermon,

49 And all the plain °on this side Jordan eastward, even unto the sea of the plain, under the springs of Pisgah.

5 And °Moses called all Israel, and said unto them, "Hear, O Israel, the °statutes and [1]judgments which I speak in your ears °this day, that ye may learn them, and °keep, and do them.

2 °The LORD our °God °made a covenant with us in Horeb.

3 [2]The LORD [2]made not this covenant with °our fathers, but with °us, °*even* us, who *are* all of us here alive this day.

4 [2]The LORD °talked with you face to face in the mount out of the midst of the fire,

d 5 °(I stood between [2]the LORD and you at that time, to shew you the word of [2]the LORD: for ye were afraid by reason of the fire, and went not up into the mount;) °saying,

c 6 'I *am* [2]the LORD thy [2]God, Which brought thee out of the land of Egypt, from the house of °bondage.

7 Thou shalt have none other gods before Me.

8 Thou shalt not make thee *any* °graven image, *or* any °likeness *of any thing* that *is* in heaven above, or that *is* in the earth beneath, or that *is* in the waters beneath the earth:

9 Thou shalt not bow down thyself unto them, nor serve them: for I [2]the LORD thy [2]God *am* a jealous °GOD, visiting the °iniquity of the fathers upon the children unto the third and fourth *generation* of them that hate Me,

10 And shewing °mercy unto thousands of them that love Me and keep My commandments.

11 Thou shalt not take the name of [2]the LORD thy [2]God in vain: for [2]the LORD will not hold *him* guiltless that taketh His name in vain.

12 Keep the sabbath day to sanctify it, °(as [2]the LORD thy [2]God hath commanded thee).

13 Six days thou shalt °labour, and do all thy work:

14 But the seventh day *is* the sabbath of [2]the LORD thy [2]God: *in it* thou shalt not do any work, thou, nor thy son, nor thy daughter, nor thy manservant, nor thy maidservant, nor thine ox, nor thine ass, nor any of thy cattle, nor thy stranger that *is* within thy gates; that thy manservant and thy maidservant may rest as well as thou.

15 (°And remember that thou wast a servant in the land of Egypt, and *that* [2]the LORD thy [2]God brought thee out thence °through a mighty hand and by a stretched out arm: therefore [2]the LORD thy [2]God commanded thee to keep the sabbath day.)

16 Honour thy father and thy mother, as [2]the LORD thy [2]God hath commanded thee; that thy days may be prolonged, and that it may go well with thee, in the land which [2]the LORD thy [2]God giveth thee.

17 Thou shalt not kill.

18 Neither shalt thou commit adultery.

19 Neither shalt thou steal.

20 Neither shalt thou bear false witness against thy neighbour.

21 Neither shalt thou desire thy neighbour's wife, neither shalt thou covet thy neighbour's house, his field, °or his manservant, or his maidservant, °his ox, or his ass, or any *thing* that *is* thy neighbour's.'

22 These words [2]the LORD °spake unto all d
your assembly in the mount out of the midst (p. 245)
of the fire, of the cloud, and of the thick darkness, with a great voice: and He added no more. And He °wrote them °in two tables of stone, and delivered them unto me.

23 And it came to pass, when ye heard the voice out of the midst of the darkness, (for the mountain did burn with fire,) that ye came near unto me, *even* all the heads of your tribes, and your elders;

24 And ye said, °'Behold, [2]the LORD our [2]God hath shewed us His glory and His greatness, and we have heard His voice out of the midst of the fire: we have seen this day that [2]God doth talk with °man, and he liveth.

25 Now therefore °why should we die? for this great fire will consume us: if we hear the voice of [2]the LORD our [2]God any more, then we shall die.

48 Sion. Written for Sirion. See Deut. 3. 9.
49 on this side = across: a neutral term. Cp. 1. 1.

5. 1 Moses called. Here begins his second address. See note on 1. 1.
statutes and judgments. See note on 4. 1.
this day. See note on 4. 26.
keep, and do = observe to do.
2 The LORD our God. *Jehovah our 'Elohim.*
made. Heb. cut, because covenants were made by cutting the sacrifice in twain and passing between the parts. See Gen. 15. 10. Jer. 34. 18, 19. Heb. 9. 16, 17. Gal. 3. 20, the latter referring to the one of the two necessary parties to a covenant.
3 our fathers = our fathers only.
us, even us. Fig. *Epizeuxis*, Ap. 6, well rendered.
4 talked. Cp. Ex. 19. 19, 20.
5 I stood. Cp. Ex. 20. 19.
saying. Cp. Ex. 20. 1-17.
6 bondage = Heb. servants, put for servitude.
8 graven image. Heb. *pesel*, a sculpture. First occurrence is Ex. 20. 4. See note on 4. 16.
likeness = form.
9 GOD. Heb. *'El.* See Ap. 4. IV.
iniquity. Heb. *'āvāh.* Ap. 44. iv.
10 mercy = kindness.
12 as = according as.
13 labour. This word is emphasised by the Heb. accent *zarḳā*, to show that the fourth Commandment is twofold, and that the one day's rest cannot be enjoyed without the preceding six days of labour.
15 And remember. A parenthetical break in Moses' recital, in view of their shortly having servants of their own. **through** = by.
21 or. Fig. *Paradiastole.* Ap. 6.
his ox. Some codices, with Sept. and Syr., read "or his ox".
22 spake. See note on 2. 1.
wrote. See note on Ex. 17. 14; and Ap. 47.
in = on.
24 Behold. Fig. *Asterismos.* Ap. 6.
man. Heb. *'ādām.* Ap. 14. I.
25 why. . . ? Fig. *Erotēsis.* Ap. 6.

1452 26 For °who *is there of* all flesh, that hath
heard the voice of °the living [2]God speaking
out of the midst of the fire, as we *have*, and
lived?
27 Go thou near, and hear all that [2]the LORD
our [2]God shall say: and speak thou unto us
all that [2]the LORD our [2]God shall speak unto
thee; and we will hear *it*, and do *it*.'
28 And [2]the LORD heard the voice of your
words, when ye spake unto me; and [2]the
LORD °said unto me, 'I have heard the voice
of the words of this people, which they have
spoken unto thee: they have well said all
that they have spoken.
29 °O that there were such an heart in
them, that they would fear Me, and keep all
My [31]commandments °always, that it might
be well with them, and with their children
for ever!
30 Go say to them, 'Get you into your tents
again.'
31 But as for thee, stand thou here by Me,
and I will speak unto thee all the °command-
ments, and the °statutes, and the °judgments,
which thou shalt teach them, that they may
do *them* in the land which I give them to
possess it.'
32 Ye shall observe to do therefore [12]as [2]the
LORD your [2]God hath commanded you: ye
shall not turn aside to the right hand or to
the left.
33 Ye shall walk in all the ways which [2]the
LORD your [2]God hath commanded you, that
ye may live, and *that it may be* well with
you, and *that* ye may prolong *your* days in
the land which ye shall possess.

O (p. 247) 6 Now °these *are* the °commandments,
the °statutes, and the °judgments, which
°the LORD your °God commanded to teach
you, that ye might do *them* in the land whither
ye °go to possess it:
2 That thou mightest fear [1]the LORD thy
[1]God, to keep all His [1]statutes and His [1]com-
mandments, which I command thee, thou,
and thy son, and thy son's son, all the days
of thy life; and that thy days may be prolonged.
3 °Hear therefore, O Israel, and °observe to
do *it*; that it may be well with thee, and that
ye may increase mightily, °as [1]the LORD [1]God
of thy fathers hath promised thee, in °the land
that floweth with milk and honey.

P e 4 °Hear, O Israel: [1]The LORD our [1]God *is*
°one [1]LORD:
5 And thou shalt °love [1]the LORD thy [1]God
with all thine heart, and with all thy °soul,
and with all thy might.

f 6 And these words, which I command thee
°this day, shall be in thine heart:

g i 7 And thou shalt °teach them diligently
unto thy children, and shalt talk of them
when thou sittest in thine house, and when
thou walkest by the way, and when thou
liest down, and when thou risest up.

k 8 And thou shalt °bind them for a sign upon

26 who . . . ? Fig. *Erotēsis*. Ap. 6.
the living God. Both plurals. First occurrence of this title, always in contrast with idols, latent or expressed. Cp. Acts 14. 15. 1 Thess. 1. 9, &c.
28 said. See note on 2. 9.
29 O that, &c. Fig. *Œonismos*. Ap. 6.
always = every day, or all the days.
31 commandments. Heb. pl. "all the commandment", i. e. this whole Law.
statutes, and the judgments. See note on 4. 1.

6. 1—11. 25 (b, p. 219). INJUNCTIONS ON ENTRY INTO LAND (*Introversion and Alternations*).

b | O | 6. 1-3. Conditions of blessing.
P | e | 6. 4, 5. "Hear, O Israel." (PHYLACTERY.)
f | 6. 6. "These words" (heart).
g | i | 6. 7. "Thou shalt teach."
k | 6. 8. "Thou shalt bind."
h | 6. 9. "Thou shalt write."
Q^1 | l^1 | 6. 10—7. 26. Warnings.
m^1 | 8. 1-9. Command to remember.
Q^2 | l^2 | 8. 10-20. Warnings.
m^2 | 9. 1-. Command to hear.
Q^3 | l^3 | 9. -1—10. 11. Warnings.
m^3 | 10. 12—11. 12. Command to obey.
P | *e* | 11. 13-17. "Ye shall hear." (PHYLACTERY.)
f | 11. 18-. "These my words" (heart).
g | *k* | 11. -18. "Bind them."
i | 11. 19. "Ye shall teach them."
h | 11. 20, 21. "Thou shalt write."
O | 11. 22-25. Conditions of blessing.

1 these are. Heb. "this is".
commandments. See note on 5. 31.
statutes, and the judgments. See note on 4. 1.
the LORD. Heb. Jehovah. Ap. 4. II.
God. Heb. *Elohim*. Ap. 4. I.
go. Heb. pass over.
3 Hear . . . observe. Note the Fig. *Paronomasia* (Ap. 6), used for emphasis: *vᵉshāmā'tā . . . vᵉshāmārtā*. May be Englished "*Hear . . . Heed*".
as = according as.
the land, &c. Cp. Gen. 17. 8. Ex. 3. 8, 17; 13. 5; 33. 3. Num. 13. 27; 14, 8; 16. 13, 14. Josh. 5. 6. Jer. 11. 5; 32. 22. Ezek. 20. 6, 15.
4 Hear. In the Heb. text this word (*shām'a*) has the last letter majuscular (i. e. larger than the others) as also the last letter of the last word (*'echād*), to emphasise "the first and great commandment" (Matt. 22. 38. Mark 12. 29, 30). These two letters taken together make *'ed* = "a witness", because God is a witness and looketh on the heart (1 Sam. 16. 7).
In Heb. *shᵉm'a yisrāēl yᵉhōvā ĕlhēynū yᵉhōvā echād* = "Hear, O Israel, Jehovah (the Self and ever existing One), our Elohim is one Jehovah".
one. Heb. *'ehād* = a compound unity (Lat. *unus*), one made up of others: Gen. 1. 5, one of seven; 2. 11, one of four; 2. 21, one of twenty-four; 2. 24, one made up of two; 3. 22, one of the Trinity: 49. 16, one of twelve; Num. 13. 23, one of a cluster. So Ps. 34. 20, &c. It is not *yāhīd*, which is (Lat.) *unicus*, unique—a single, or only one, occurs twelve times: Gen. 22. 2, 12, 16. Judg. 11. 34. Ps. 22. 20; 25. 16; 35. 17; 68. 6. Prov. 4. 3. Jer. 6. 26. Amos 8. 10. Zech. 12. 10. Heb. of all other words for "one" is *'echād*.

4-9 One of the four Phylacteries. Ex. 13. 1-10; 13. 11-16. Deut. 6. 4-9; 11. 13-21. See note on Ex. 13. 1. Compare the Structures of the second pair (above).
5 love. The Law founded on love.
soul. Heb. *nephesh*. See Ap. 13.
6 this day. See note on 4. 26.
7 teach. Heb. "sharpen" or "whet" = rub them in by repetition.
8 bind. Still practised by orthodox Jews.

1452 thine °hand, and they shall be °as °frontlets
between thine eyes.
h 9 And thou shalt °write them upon the
(p. 247) °posts of thy house, and on thy gates.

$Q\ l^1\ o^1$ 10 And it shall be, when [1]the LORD thy
[1]God shall have brought thee into the land
which He sware unto thy fathers, to
°Abraham, to Isaac, and to Jacob, to give
thee great and goodly cities, which thou
buildedst not,
11 And houses full of all good *things*, which
thou filledst not, and wells digged, which thou
diggedst not, vineyards and olive trees, which
thou plantedst not; when thou shalt have
eaten and be full;

p^1 12 *Then* beware lest thou forget the °LORD,
(p. 248) Which brought thee forth out of the land of
Egypt, from the house of °bondage.
13 °Thou shalt fear [1]the LORD thy [1]God,
and serve Him, and shalt swear by His
name.
14 Ye shall not go after other gods, of the
gods of the people which *are* round about
you;
15 (For [1]the LORD thy [1]God *is* a jealous
°GOD among you) lest the anger of [1]the LORD
thy [1]God be kindled against thee, and °de-
stroy thee from off the face of the °earth.
16 °Ye shall not °tempt [1]the LORD your
[1]God, °as ye tempted *Him* in Massah.
17 Ye shall diligently keep the [1]command-
ments of [1]the LORD your [1]God, and His
testimonies, and His [1]statutes, which He hath
commanded thee.
18 And thou shalt do *that which is* right and
good in the sight of [1]the LORD:
q^1 that it may be well with thee, and that thou
mayest go in and possess the good land which
[1]the LORD sware unto thy fathers,
19 To cast out all thine enemies from before
thee, as [1]the LORD hath spoken.

$n^2\ o^2$ 20 *And* when thy son asketh thee °in time
to come, saying, 'What *mean* the testimonies,
and the [1]statutes, and the [1]judgments, which
[1]the LORD our [1]God hath commanded you?'
p^2 21 Then thou shalt say unto thy son, 'We
were Pharaoh's bondmen in Egypt; and [1]the
LORD brought us out of Egypt with a mighty
hand:
22 And [1]the LORD shewed signs and
wonders, great and °sore, upon Egypt, upon
Pharaoh, and upon all his household, before
our eyes:
23 And He brought us out from thence,
q^2 that He might bring us in, to give us the land
which He sware unto our fathers.
24 And [1]the LORD commanded us to do all
these [1]statutes, to fear [1]the LORD our [1]God,
for our good °always, that He might preserve
us alive, as *it is* at this day.
25 And it shall be °our righteousness, if we
observe to do all these [1]commandments before
[1]the LORD our [1]God, [16]as He hath commanded
us.'

o^3 7 When °the LORD thy °God shall bring
thee into the land whither thou goest to

hand. Some codices, with Sam., read pl. "hands".
as = for.
frontlets. Gr. phylacteries = guards or watch-posts.
9 write. See note on Ex. 17. 4 and Ap. 47.
posts = door-posts. Heb. *m^{e}zūzāh*. Used to-day, for cases containing the Phylactery.

6. 10—7. 26 (l^1, p. 247). **WARNINGS. PROSPECTIVE.**
(*Repeated and Extended Alternations.*)

l^1 | n^1 | o^1 | 6. 10, 11. Hypothesis. Possession.
p^1 | 6. 12-18-. Warning. Forgetfulness.
q^1 | 6. -18, 19. Reason: "that."
n^2 | o^2 | 6. 20. Hypothesis. Inquiry of son.
p^2 | 6. 21-23-. Direction as to answer.
q^2 | 6. -23-25. Reason: "that."
n^3 | o^3 | 7. 1, 2-. Hypothesis. Possession.
p^3 | 7. -2-5. Injunction. Destroy.
q^3 | 7. 6-11. Reason: "For."
n^4 | o^4 | 7. 12-. Hypothesis. Obedience.
q^4 | 7. -12-15. Blessing: "that."
p^4 | 7. 16. Injunction. Not to spare.
n^5 | o^5 | 7. 17. Hypothesis. Inability.
p^5 | 7. 18-21-. Injunction. Not to fear.
q^5 | 7. -21-26. Reason: "for."

10 Abraham, &c. Note inclusion of all three patriarchs. See note on 1. 8.
12 LORD = Jehovah. Some codices, with Sam., Jon., Sept., Syr., add "thy God".
bondage. Heb. bondmen, put by Fig. *Metonymy* (of Adjunct), Ap. 6, for their bondage.
13 Thou shalt fear. Read this verse as follows, and preserve the emphasis on "Him", and the Fig. *Polysyndeton*, Ap. 6:—
"Jehovah, thy Elohim, Him shalt thou reverence,
And Him shalt thou serve,
And by His Name shalt thou swear."
15 GOD. Heb. *'Ēl*. See Ap. 4, and note parenthesis (Ap. 6).
destroy = cut off: exterminate. Heb. *shāmad*.
earth. Heb. *'ădāmāh*, ground, cultivated land.
16 Ye, &c. Quoted by the Lord to Satan, and changed to sing. by adaptation. See Matt. 4. 7.
tempt = try: by questioning Jehovah's presence. This was the point in Matt. 4. 7.
as = according as. Cp. Ex. 17. 2-7.
20 in time to come. Heb. "to-morrow". Definite date put for indefinite.
22 sore. Heb. *r'a* = inflicted evil, not moral. Cp. Jer. 18. 11. Amos 3. 6, and see note on Isa. 45. 7.
24 always = for all time. Heb. all the days.
25 our righteousness. This is superseded by Rom. 10. 4, 5. Gal. 3. 12. That true then: this true now. No discrepancy if the Dispensations are rightly divided according to 2 Tim. 2. 15.

7. 1 the LORD thy God = *Jehovah* thy *Elohim*.
nations. Ten altogether are mentioned by name, here seven only. Other lists name six. Girgashites generally omitted. In the days of Ezra (9. 1) five were still in the land. In the Tel-el-Amarna Tablets eight are named.
2 destroy them = devote them to destruction. Heb. *ḥāram*. Cp. Ex. 23. 24; 34. 12-17, and see note on *v.* 16.

possess it, and hath cast out many °nations
before thee, the Hittites, and the Girgashites,
and the Amorites, and the Canaanites, and
the Perizzites, and the Hivites, and the
Jebusites, seven nations greater and mightier
than thou;
2 And when [1]the LORD thy [1]God shall deliver
them before thee;
thou shalt smite them, *and* utterly °destroy p^3

1452 them; thou shalt make no covenant with them, nor shew mercy unto them:

3 Neither shalt thou make marriages with them; thy daughter thou shalt not give unto his son, nor his daughter shalt thou take unto thy son.

4 For they will turn away thy son from following °Me, that °they may serve other gods: so will the anger of [1]the LORD be kindled against you, and °destroy thee suddenly.

5 °But thus shall ye deal with them; ye shall °destroy their altars, and °break down their images, and cut down their groves, and °burn their °graven images with fire.

q[3] (p. 248) **6** For thou *art* an °holy people unto [1]the LORD thy [1]God: [1]the LORD thy [1]God hath °chosen thee to be a °special people unto Himself, above all °people that *are* upon the face of the °earth.

7 [1]The LORD did not set his °love upon you, nor choose you, because ye were more in number than any people; for ye *were* the fewest of all people:

8 But because [1]the LORD °loved you, and because He would keep the oath which He had sworn unto your fathers, hath [1]the LORD brought you out with a mighty hand, and redeemed you out of the house of °bondmen, from the hand of Pharaoh king of Egypt.

9 Know therefore that [1]the LORD thy [1]God, He *is* [1]God, the faithful °GOD, Which keepeth covenant and °mercy with them that [8]love Him and keep His °commandments to a thousand generations;

10 And repayeth them that hate Him to their face, to °destroy them: °He will not be slack to him that hateth Him, He will repay him to his face.

11 Thou shalt therefore keep the commandments, °and the °statutes, and the °judgments, which I command thee °this day, to do them.

o[4] **12** Wherefore it shall come to pass, if ye hearken to these [11]judgments, and keep, and do them,

q[4] that [1]the LORD thy [1]God shall keep unto thee the covenant and the mercy which He sware unto thy fathers:

13 [11]And He will [8]love thee, and bless thee, and multiply thee: He will also bless the fruit of thy womb, [11]and the fruit of thy land, thy corn, [11]and thy °wine, and thine oil, the °increase of thy kine, and the °flocks of thy sheep, in the land which He sware unto thy fathers to give thee.

14 Thou shalt be blessed above all [6]people: there shall not be male or female °barren among you, or among your cattle.

15 And [1]the LORD will take away from thee all sickness, and will put none of the evil °diseases of Egypt, which thou knowest, upon thee; but will lay them upon all *them* that hate thee.

p[4] **16** And thou °shalt consume all the people which [1]the LORD thy [1]God shall deliver thee; thine eye shall have no pity upon them: neither shalt thou serve their gods; for that *will be* a snare unto thee.

17 If thou shalt say in thine heart, 'These nations *are* more than I; °how can I dispossess them?' o[5]

18 Thou shalt not be afraid of them: *but* shalt well remember what [1]the LORD thy [1]God did unto Pharaoh, and unto all Egypt; p[5]

19 The great °temptations which thine eyes saw, °and the signs, and the wonders, and the mighty hand, and the stretched out arm, whereby [1]the LORD thy [1]God brought thee out: so shall [1]the LORD thy [1]God do unto all the people of whom thou art afraid.

20 Moreover [1]the LORD thy [1]God will send the °hornet among them, until they that are left, and hide themselves from thee, be [10]destroyed.

21 Thou shalt not be affrighted at them:
for [1]the LORD thy [1]God *is* among you, a °mighty [9]GOD and °terrible. q[5]

---

4 Me. The very words of Jehovah introduced.
they. Some codices, with Sam., Syr., and Vulg., read "he".
destroy = cut off. Heb. *shāmad.*
5 But = But rather, or, Verily.
destroy = break down. Heb. *nāthaz.*
break down = break into fragments. Heb. *shābab.*
burn = burn up. See Ap. 43. I. viii.
graven images = sculptures.
6 holy. See note on Ex. 3. 5.
chosen. This is the word emphasised by the Heb. accent (*paseḳ*), "thee hath Jehovah chosen". This is the basis of all else that is here stated.
special = peculiar. See note on Ex. 19. 5, or "His people as a treasure". Cp. 26. 18. 1 Pet. 2. 9.
people. Heb. Peoples. **earth** = ground.
7 love = affection. Heb. *ḥāshaḳ*, a love which joins one to what is loved = to set one's love upon.
8 loved. Heb. *'āhab*, love in its highest sense, love that delights in its object.
bondmen. Cp. 5. 6, and Ex. 20. 2.
9 GOD = *'El*, the great and mighty God. See Ap. 4. iv.
mercy = lovingkindness, or grace.
commandments. Heb. text written singular, but read plural.
10 destroy = cause them to perish. Heb. *'ābad.*
He. Some codices with one early printed edition, Jon., Onk., Sept., and Vulg., read "and He".
11 and. Note the Fig. *Polysyndeton* (Ap. 6).
statutes, and the judgments. See note on 4. 1.
this day. See note on 4. 26.
13 wine. Heb. *tīrōsh.* See Ap. 27. II.
increase. Heb. *sheger*, only here, 28. 4, 18, 51, and Ex. 13. 12 ("cometh of") in the sense of multiplying by generation.
flocks. Only here, and Deut. 28. 4, 18, 51. These three words are peculiar to Deut.
14 barren. Cp. Ex. 23. 26.
15 diseases. Some codices, with one early printed edition, Sept and Vulg., read "disease". Cp. Ex. 23. 22, 25.
16 shalt consume. This command never fully obeyed. Cp. Ezra 9. 1, and see Ex. 23. 24, 32; 34. 12-17.
17 how . . .? Fig. *Erotēsis* (Ap. 6).
19 temptations = trials, as manifested in Jehovah's wonderful works.
and. Note the Fig. *Polysyndeton* (Ap. 6).
20 hornet = a fierce kind of wasp. May be taken literally or by Fig. *Metonymy* (of Cause), for the terror caused by it. Cp. Ex. 23. 27, and Deut. 2. 25. Or, by Fig. *Metonymy* (of Adjunct), for Egypt; the hornet being the royal symbol. Occurs three times. Ex. 23. 28 and Deut. 7. 20, prophecy, and once fulfilment, Josh. 24. 12.
21 mighty = great. **terrible** = to be feared.

1452 22 And [1]the LORD thy [1]God will put out those nations °before thee by °little and little: thou mayest not consume them at once, lest the beasts of the field increase upon thee.

23 But [1]the LORD thy [1]God shall deliver them unto thee, and shall °destroy them with a mighty °destruction, until they be °destroyed.

24 And He shall deliver their kings into thine hand, and thou shalt [23]destroy their name from under heaven: there shall no °man be able to stand before thee, until thou have [23]destroyed them.

25 The graven images of their gods shall ye °burn with fire: thou shalt not desire the silver or gold *that is* on them, nor take *it* unto thee, lest thou be snared therein: for it *is* an abomination to [1]the LORD thy [1]God.

26 Neither shalt thou bring an abomination into thine house, lest thou be °a cursed thing like it: *but* thou shalt utterly detest it, and thou shalt utterly abhor it; for it *is* °a cursed thing.

Q[1] m[1] r (p. 250) **8** All the °commandments which I command thee °this day shall ye observe to do, that ye may live, and multiply, and go in and possess the land which °the LORD sware unto your fathers.

s 2 And thou shalt remember all the way which [1]the LORD thy °God led thee these °forty years in the wilderness, to humble thee, *and* to prove thee, °to know what *was* in thine heart, whether thou wouldest keep His °commandments, or no.

3 And He humbled thee, and suffered thee to hunger, and fed thee with °manna, which thou knewest not, neither did thy fathers know; that He might make thee know that °man doth not live °by °bread only, but °by every *word* that proceedeth out of the °mouth of [1]the LORD doth man live.

4 °Thy raiment waxed not old upon thee, neither did thy foot swell, these forty years.

5 Thou shalt also consider in thine heart, that, °as °a man °chasteneth °his son, *so* [1]the LORD thy [2]God chasteneth thee.

r 6 Therefore thou shalt keep the commandments of [1]the LORD thy [2]God, to walk in His ways, and to fear Him.

s 7 For [1]the LORD thy [2]God bringeth thee into a good land, a land of brooks of water, of fountains and depths that spring out of valleys and °hills;

8 A land of wheat, and barley, and °vines, and fig trees, and pomegranates; a land of oil olive, and honey;

9 A land wherein thou shalt eat bread without °scarceness, thou shalt not lack any *thing* in it; a land whose stones *are* iron, and out of whose hills thou mayest dig °brass.

Q[2] l[2] t[1] 10 When thou hast eaten and art full, then thou shalt bless [1]the LORD thy [2]God for the good land which He hath given thee.

u[1] 11 Beware that thou °forget not [1]the LORD thy [2]God, in not keeping His commandments, and His °judgments, and His °statutes, which I command thee [1]this day:

22 before thee. Heb. "before thy face".
little by little: referring to all the nations of Canaan. (Ex. 23. 29, 30). Cp. 9. 3, "quickly", which refers to Israel and the "sons of Anak" (9. 2).
23 destroy = discomfit. Heb. *hūm*, to put in consternation.
destruction = discomfiture.
destroyed = exterminated. Heb. *shāmad*. Cp. *v.* 26.
24 man. Heb. *'ish*. See Ap. 14.
25 burn = burn up. See Ap. 43. I. viii.
26 a cursed thing. Heb. a thing devoted to destruction; cp. 13. 17. Josh. 6. 18. Isa. 34. 5; 43. 28 Mal. 4. 6. Heb. *ḥērem*. Cp. other words in *vv.* 23, 24.

8. 1-9 (m[1], p. 247). COMMAND TO REMEMBER.
(*Alternation.*)

m[1] | r | 1. Command (particular).
  s | 2-5. Motives. Preservation.
  r | 6. Command.
  s | 7-9. Motives. Provision.

1 commandments. Heb. sing. = every commandment.
this day. See note on 4. 26.
the LORD = Jehovah. Ap. 4. II.
2 God = Heb. 'Elohim. Ap. 4. I.
forty. The number of Probation. See Ap. 10.
to know = get to know. Fig. *Anthropopatheia*. Ap. 6.
commandments. Written in Heb. text plural, but read singular, cp. 6. 25 = the whole Law regarded as one great command.
3 manna. See note on Ex. 16. 31.
man. Heb. *'ādām*. This verse quoted by Christ. Matt. 4. 4. Luke 4. 4.
by. Fig. Ellipsis (Ap. 6) = "by [eating] bread".
bread = food, by Fig. *Synecdoche* (of Species), Ap. 6.
by every. Fig. *Ellipsis* (Ap. 6) = "by [keeping] every word": or by obeying.
mouth. Fig. *Anthropopatheia*. Ap. 6.
4 Thy raiment. Cp. 29. 5. Neh. 9. 20, 21. Not mentioned in Ex., Lev., or Num.
5 as = according as.
a man. Heb. *'ish*. Ap. 14. II.
chasteneth = correcteth, applicable to instruction as well as chastisement. 2 Sam. 7. 14. Ps. 89. 32. Prov. 3. 12.
his son. Cp. Prov. 3. 12 and Heb. 12. 5, 6.
7 hills = mountains.
8 vines. All three (fig, olive, and vine) mentioned in this verse. See notes on Judg 9. 8-12.
9 scarceness. Heb. *miskēnuth* = poverty, misery; occurs only here.
brass = bronze, or copper.

10-20 (l[2], p. 247). WARNINGS; PROSPECTIVE.
(*Repeated Alternation.*)

l[2] | t[1] | 10. Hypothesis: "When thou hast eaten."
  u[1] | 11. Warning. Forgetfulness.
  t[2] | 12, 13. Hypothesis: "When thou hast eaten."
  u[2] | 14-16. Warning. Forgetfulness.
  t[3] | 17. Hypothesis: "If thou say."
  u[3] | 18. Warning. Memory.
  t[4] | 19-. Hypothesis: "If thou forget."
  u[4] | -19-21. Warning. Destruction.

11 forget. Note the emphasis put on this by the Structure, as in the whole book. Cp. Judg. 3. 7. Hos. 13. 6.
judgments, and . . . statutes. See note on 4. 1.
12 and. Note the Fig. *Polysyndeton* (Ap. 6), in *vv.* 12 and 13.

12 Lest *when* thou hast eaten °and art full, and hast built goodly houses, and dwelt *therein;* t[2]

13 And *when* thy herds and thy flocks multiply, and thy silver and thy gold is multiplied, and all that thou hast is multiplied;

u[2] (p. 250) 1452 14 Then thine heart be lifted up, and thou [11]forget [1]the LORD thy [2]God, Which brought thee forth out of the land of Egypt, from the house of °bondage;

15 Who led thee through that great and terrible °wilderness, *wherein were* fiery °serpents, and scorpions, and °drought, where *there was* no water; °Who brought thee forth water out of the rock of flint;

16 Who fed thee in the wilderness with [3]manna, which thy fathers knew not, that He might humble thee, and that He might prove thee, to do thee good at thy latter end;

t[3] 17 And thou say in thine heart, 'My power and the might of *mine* hand hath gotten me this °wealth.'

u[3] 18 But thou shalt remember [1]the LORD thy [2]God: for *it is* He that giveth thee power to get [17]wealth, that He may establish His covenant which He sware unto thy fathers, as *it is* this day.

t[4] 19 And it shall be, if thou do at all forget [1]the LORD thy [2]God, and walk after other gods, and serve them, and worship them,

u[4] I testify against you [1]this day that ye shall surely perish.

20 As the nations which [1]the LORD °destroyeth before your face, so shall ye perish; because ye would not be obedient unto the voice of [1]the LORD your [2]God.

m[2] (p. 247) l[3] v[1] w (p. 251) **9** Hear, O Israel:

Thou *art* to pass over Jordan °this day, to go in to possess °nations greater and mightier than thyself, cities great and fenced up to heaven,

2 A People great and tall, the °children of the °Anakims, whom thou knowest, and *of whom* thou hast heard *say*, 'Who can stand before the °children of Anak!'

x 3 Understand therefore [1]this day,

y z[1] that °the LORD thy °God *is* He which goeth over before thee; *as* a °consuming fire He °shall destroy them, and He shall bring them down before thy face: so shalt thou drive them out, °and destroy them °quickly, °as °the LORD hath said unto thee.

a 4 Speak not thou in thine heart, after that [3]the LORD thy [3]God hath cast them out from before thee, saying, 'For my righteousness [3]the LORD hath brought me in to possess this land:'

z[2] but for the °wickedness of these nations [3]the LORD doth drive them out from before thee.

a 5 °Not for thy righteousness, or for the uprightness of thine heart, dost thou go to possess their land:

z[3] but for the [4]wickedness of these nations [3]the LORD thy [3]God doth drive them out from before thee, and that He may perform the word which [3]the LORD sware unto °thy fathers, Abraham, Isaac, and Jacob.

x 6 Understand therefore,

w that [3]the LORD thy [3]God giveth thee not this good land to possess it for thy righteousness; for thou *art* a stiffnecked People.

7 Remember, *and* forget not, how thou provokedst [3]the LORD thy [3]God to wrath in the v[2] b[1]

---

14 bondage = bondmen, put by Fig. *Metonymy* (of Adjunct), Ap. 6.

15 wilderness = desert, cp. 1. 19.

serpents. Heb. *nachash.*

drought. Heb. *ẓimm'ōn.* Only here and Ps. 107. 33, and Isa. 35. 7.

Who brought. Cp. Ps. 114. 8.

17 wealth. Heb. = strength, put by Fig. *Metonymy* (of Adjunct) for the wealth it procures. Ap. 6.

20 destroyeth. Heb. *'ābad,* cause to perish.

9. 1—10. 11 (l[3], p. 247). WARNINGS.
(*Division.*)

l[3] | v[1] | 9. 1-6. Prospective.
| v[2] | 9. 7—10. 11. Retrospective.

9. 1-6 (v[1], above). WARNINGS; PROSPECTIVE.
(*Introversion and Repeated Alternation.*)

v[1] | w | 1, 2. Possession given by Jehovah.
x | 3-. "Understand therefore."
y | z[1] | -3. Jehovah going before.
a | 4-. Warning (negative).
z[2] | -4. Jehovah driving out.
a | 5-. Warning (negative).
z[3] | -5. Jehovah driving out.
x | 6-. "Understand therefore."
w | -6. Possession given by Jehovah.

1 this day: i. e. it is declared this day that, &c. Fig. *Metonymy* (of Subject), Ap. 6, where the action is put for the declaration concerning it. Punctuate thus: "Hear, O Israel this day", &c. See note on 4. 26.

nations. Put by Fig. *Metonymy* (of Subject), Ap. 6, for the countries inhabited by them.

2 children = sons.

Anakims. The descendants of Anak; the progeny of the second irruption of fallen angels (see Gen. 6. 4 and Ap. 25, and cp. Josh. 11. 22.

3 the LORD thy God = Jehovah thy 'Elohim. Ap. 4.

consuming fire. Fig. *Anthropopatheia.* Ap. 6.

shall destroy. Heb. *shāmad,* exterminate.

and destroy. Heb. *'ābad,* cause to perish.

quickly. See note on 7. 22.

as = according as. See Ex. 23. 29, 30. Moab subdued (Judg. 3. 30); Midian subdued (Judg. 8. 28); Ammon subdued (Judg. 11. 33); Philistines subdued (1 Sam. 7. 13). Cp. Neh. 9. 24.

4 wickedness. Heb. *rāsh'a.* Ap. 44. x.

5 Not. Cp. Tit. 3. 5. Rom. 11. 6. 2 Tim. 1. 9.

thy fathers. All three named in connection with the oath.

9. 7—10. 11 (v[2], above). RETROSPECTIVE WARNINGS (*Repeated Alternation*).

v[2] | b[1] | 9. 7, 8. People. Provocation.
c[1] | 9. 9-11. Moses. Ascent of Mount.
b[2] | 9. 12-14. People. Provocation.
c[2] | 9. 15. Moses. Descent. Tables carried.
b[3] | 9. 16. People. Provocation.
c[3] | 9. 17. Moses. Tables broken.
b[4] | 9. 18, 19-. People. Provocation.
c[4] | 9. -19-21. Moses. Intercession.
b[5] | 9. 22-24. People. Provocation.
c[5] | 9. 25—10. 5. Moses. Intercession and second Tables.
b[6] | 10. 6-11. People. Journeying.

1452 wilderness: from the day that thou didst
depart out of the land of Egypt, until °ye
came unto this place, ye have been rebellious
against [3]the LORD.
8 Also in Horeb ye provoked [3]the LORD to
wrath, so that [3]the LORD was angry with you
to have °destroyed you.

c1 9 When I was gone up into the mount to
(p. 251) receive the tables of stone, *even* the tables
of the covenant which [3]the LORD made with
you, then I abode in the mount °forty days
and forty nights, I neither did eat bread nor
drink water:
10 And [3]the LORD delivered unto me two
tables of stone °written with the finger of
[3]God; and on them *was written* according
to all the words, which [3]the LORD spake
with you in the mount out of the midst of
the fire in the day of the assembly.
11 And it came to pass at the end of forty
days and forty nights, *that* [3]the LORD gave
me the two tables of stone, *even* the tables of
the covenant.

b2 12 And [3]the LORD °said unto me, 'Arise,
get thee down quickly from hence; for thy
People which thou hast brought forth out of
Egypt have corrupted *themselves;* they are
quickly turned aside out of the way which
I commanded them; they have made them
a molten image.'
13 Furthermore [3]the LORD °spake unto me,
saying, 'I have seen this People, and, °behold,
it *is* a stiffnecked People:
14 °Let Me alone, that I may [8]destroy them,
and blot out their name from under heaven:
and I will make of thee a nation mightier and
greater than they.'

c2 15 So °I turned and came down from the
mount, and the mount burned with fire: and
the two tables of the covenant *were* in my
two hands.

b3 16 And I looked, and, °behold, ye had °sinned
against [3]the LORD your [3]God, *and* had made
you a molten calf: ye had turned aside quickly
out of the way which [3]the LORD had commanded you.

c3 17 And °I took the two tables, and cast them
out of my two hands, and brake them before
your eyes.

b4 18 And I fell down before [3]the LORD, as at
the first, forty days and forty nights: I did
neither eat bread, nor drink water, because
of all your [16]sins which ye [16]sinned, in doing
°wickedly in the sight of [3]the LORD, to
provoke Him to anger.
19 For I was °afraid of the anger and hot
displeasure, wherewith [3]the LORD was wroth
against you to [8]destroy you.

c4 But [3]the LORD hearkened unto me at that
time also.
20 And [3]the LORD was very angry with
Aaron to have [8]destroyed him: and I prayed
for Aaron also the same time.
21 And I took your sin, the calf which ye
had made, and °burnt it with fire, and stamped
it, *and* ground *it* very small, *even* until it was
as small as dust: and I cast the dust thereof
into the brook that °descended out of the
mount.

22 °(And at °Taberah, and at °Massah, and b5
at °Kibroth-hattaavah, ye provoked [3]the
LORD to wrath.
23 Likewise when [3]the LORD sent you from
Kadesh-barnea, saying, 'Go up and possess
the land which I have given you;' then ye
rebelled against the °commandment of [3]the
LORD your [3]God, and ye believed Him not,
nor hearkened to His voice.
24 Ye have been rebellious against [3]the
LORD from the day that I knew you.)

25 Thus I fell down before [3]the LORD forty c5
days and forty nights, as I fell down *at the
first;* because [3]the LORD had said He would
[8]destroy you.
26 °I prayed therefore unto [3]the LORD, and
said, 'O °Lord °GOD, [8]destroy not Thy
People and Thine inheritance, which Thou
hast redeemed through Thy greatness, which
Thou hast brought forth out of Egypt with
a mighty hand.
27 Remember Thy servants, Abraham, Isaac,
and Jacob; look not unto the °stubbornness
of this people, nor to their °wickedness, nor
to their [16]sin:
28 Lest the land whence thou broughtest us
out say, 'Because [3]the LORD was not able to
bring them into the land which He promised
them, and because He hated them, He hath
brought them out to slay them in the wilderness.'
29 Yet they *are* Thy People and Thine
inheritance, which Thou broughtest out by
Thy mighty power and by Thy stretched
out arm.'

7 ye came. So some codices, with Sam., Sept., and Syr.; but Heb. text reads "thou camest".
8 destroyed. Heb. *shāmad,* exterminate, or cut off.
9 forty days. Ex. 24. 18; 34. 28. See Ap. 10.
10 written. See note on Ex. 17. 14 and Ap. 47.
12 said. See note on 2. 9, and cp. Ex. 32. 7, 8.
13 spake. See note on 2. 1.
behold. Fig. *Asterismos.* Ap. 6.
14 Let Me alone. Cp. Ps. 46. 10, where it is rendered "Be still".
15 I turned. Cp. Ex. 32. 15.
16 behold. Fig. *Asterismos.* Ap. 6.
sinned. Heb. *chāṭ'ā.* See Ap. 44. i.
17 I took. Cp. Ex. 32. 19.
18 wickedly. Heb. *rā'a',* the wicked thing: i. e. idolatry. See Ap. 44. viii.
19 afraid = alarmed.
21 burnt it = burnt it up. Heb. *sārāph.* Ap. 43. I. viii.
descended. Cp. Ex. 32. 20, which is here explained.
22 And, &c. Note the Parenthesis of *vv.* 22–24.
Taberah. Cp. Num. 11. 1–3.
Massah. Cp. Ex. 17. 7.
Kibroth-hattaavah. Cp. Num. 11. 34.
23 commandment. Heb. mouth. Put by Fig. *Metonymy* (of Cause), for what is spoken by it. Ap. 6.
26 I prayed. Cp. Ex. 32. 11–13.
Lord GOD = Adonai Jehovah. God's ownership emphasised by this title. See Ap. 4. viii. 2.
27 stubbornness = obduracy, or obstinacy.
wickedness. Heb. *rāsh'a.* See Ap. 44. x.

1452 **10** At that time °the LORD °said unto me, 'Hew thee two tables of stone like unto the first, and come up unto Me into the mount, and make thee an °ark of wood.
2 And I will °write on the tables the words that were in the first tables which thou °brakest, and thou shalt put them in the ark.'
3 And I made an [1]ark *of* shittim wood, and hewed two tables of stone like unto the first, and went up into the mount, having the two tables in mine hand.
4 And He [2]wrote on the tables, according to the first [2]writing, the ten °commandments, which [1]the LORD °spake °unto you in the mount out of the midst of the fire in the day of the °assembly: and [1]the LORD gave them unto me.
5 And I turned myself and came down from the mount, and put the tables in the ark which I had made; and there they be, °as [1]the LORD commanded me.
b[6] (p. 251) 6 (And the °children of Israel took their journey from °Beeroth of the children of Jaakan to Mosera: there Aaron died, and there he was buried; and Eleazar his son ministered in the priest's office in his stead.
7 From thence they journeyed unto Gudgodah; and from Gudgodah to Jotbath, a land of rivers of waters.)
8 At that time [1]the LORD °separated the tribe of °Levi, to bear the ark of the covenant of [1]the LORD, to °stand before [1]the LORD to minister unto Him, and to bless in His name, unto this day.
9 Wherefore Levi hath no part nor inheritance with his brethren; [1]the LORD °*is* his inheritance, according as [1]the LORD thy °God promised him.
10 And I °stayed in the mount, according to the first time, forty days and forty nights; and [1]the LORD hearkened unto me at that time also, °*and* [1]the LORD would not °destroy thee.
11 And [1]the LORD [1]said unto me, 'Arise, °take *thy* journey before the people, that they may go in and possess the land, which I sware unto their fathers to give unto them.'
m[3] d (p. 253) 12 And now, Israel, °what doth [1]the LORD thy [9]God require of thee, but to fear [1]the LORD thy [9]God, to walk in all His ways, and to love Him, and to serve [1]the LORD thy [9]God with all thy heart and with all thy °soul,
13 To keep the commandments of [1]the LORD, and His °statutes, which I command thee °this day
e f for thy good?
g k 14 °Behold, the heaven and the °heaven of heavens *is* [1]the LORD'S thy [9]God, the earth *also*, with all that therein *is*.
l 15 Only [1]the LORD had a delight in thy fathers to love them, and He chose their seed after them, *even* you above all °people, as *it is* this day.
i 16 °Circumcise therefore the foreskin of your heart, and be no more stiffnecked.
h k 17 For °the LORD your °God °*is* °God of °gods, and °Lord of °lords, a great °GOD,

10. 1 the LORD = Jehovah. Ap. 4. I.
said. See note on 2. 9.
ark. First used of Joseph's coffin (Gen. 50. 26); used of money-box (2 Kings 12. 9). Not the ark of the covenant made later, but a temporary box.
2 write. See note on Ex. 17. 14, and Ap. 47.
brakest = breakedst in pieces, or smashed.
4 commandments = words. Cp. Ex. 34. 4, 28.
spake. See note on 2. 1.
unto. Some codices, with Sam., Onk., and Jon., read "with".
assembly. Heb. *kāhal*, convocation of called-out people.
5 as = according as.
6 children = sons.
Beeroth, &c. = the wells of the sons of Jaakan. Cp. Num. 20. 22–29; 33. 31–38.
8 separated. Cp. Num. 3. 5–12.
Levi. (1) On account of loyalty. Ex. 32. 26, and Deut. 33. 8. (2) After revolt of Korah, &c. Num. 16; 17. (3) After the sin of People with Moabites. Num. 25. 6–13. Ps. 106. 30. Mal. 2. 4, 5; 3. 3.
stand = serve. Fig. *Metonymy* (of Adjunct), Ap. 6, put for all service and ministration.
9 is. Heb. "he [is]".
God. Heb. Elohim. Ap. 4. I.
10 stayed. Cp. Ex. 34. 28.
and. Some codices, with Sam., Sept., Syr., and Vulg., read "therefore".
destroy. Heb. *shāhath* = infliction of judgments.
11 take thy journey. Cp. Num. 10. 11.

10. 12—11. 12 (m[3], p. 227). COMMAND TO OBEY (*Alternation and Introversion*).

m[3] d | 10. 12, 13-. To fear and love Him.
 e | f | 10. -13. Intention: "for thy good."
  g | 10. 14–19. Motives and reasons.
d | 10. 20, 21. To fear and praise Him.
 e | *g* | 10. 22—11. 8-. Motives and reasons.
  f | 11. -8–12. Intention: "that ye may be strong."

12 what . . . ? Fig. *Erotēsis.* Ap. 6. Cp. Mic. 6. 8. Hos. 12. 6. Josh. 22. 5. 1 Sam. 15. 22.
soul. Heb. *nephesh.* Ap. 13.
statutes. See note on 4. 1.
13 this day. See note on 4. 26.

14–19 (g, above). MOTIVES AND REASONS. (*Alternations.*)

g | h | k | 14. Jehovah. Power unchallengeable.
  l | 15. Jehovah. Love without cause.
 i | 16. Reason. Circumcision of heart.
h | *k* | 17. Jehovah. Power irresistible.
  l | 18. Jehovah. Judgment impartial.
 i | 19. Reason. Love to others required.

14 Behold. Fig. *Asterismos.* Ap. 6.
heaven of heavens. Fig. *Polyptōton.* Ap. 6. = the highest heavens.
15 people. Heb. peoples.
16 Circumcise. Here charged as a duty. In 30. 6 promised as a future blessing. Cp. Lev. 26. 41. Jer. 6. 10. Acts 7. 51. Circumcision mentioned after Ex. 12. 48 only in Josh. 5. 3–7 and Jer. 9. 25. Uncircumcision of Gentiles shows that circumcision was practised. Cp. Isa. 52. 1. Jer. 9. 25, 26. Ezek. 31. 18.
17 the LORD your God = Jehovah your 'Elohim (Ap. 4).
is. Heb. "he [is]".
God = '*Elohē*. Ap. 4.
gods = '*Elohim*. Ap. 4. I. Cp. Josh. 22. 22. Dan. 2. 47.
Lord = Adonai. Ap. 4. viii. 2.
lords = Adonim. Ap. 4. viii. 3.
GOD = '*El*. See Ap. 4. iv.

1452 a mighty, and a °terrible, Which regardeth not
persons, nor °taketh reward:

l (p. 253) 18 He doth execute the judgment of the
°fatherless and widow, and loveth the
stranger, in giving him food and raiment.

i 19 °Love ye therefore the °stranger: for ye
were strangers in the land of Egypt.

d 20 Thou shalt fear [1]the LORD thy [9]God;
°Him shalt thou serve, and to Him shalt thou
°cleave, and swear by His name.
21 He *is* thy °praise, and He *is* thy [9]God, that
hath done for thee these °great and terrible
things, which thine eyes have seen.

g m (p. 254) 22 Thy fathers °went down into Egypt with
°threescore and ten °persons; and now [1]the
LORD thy [9]God hath made thee °as the stars
of heaven for multitude.

n **11** Therefore thou shalt love °the LORD thy
°God, °and keep His charge, and His
°statutes, and His °judgments, and His commandments, alway.

m 2 And know ye °this day: for *I speak* not
with your children which have not known,
and which have not seen the chastisement
of [1]the LORD your [1]God, His greatness, °His
mighty hand, °and His stretched out arm,
3 And His miracles, and His °acts, which
He did in the midst of Egypt unto Pharaoh
the king of Egypt, and unto all his land;
4 And what He did unto the army of Egypt,
unto their horses, and to their chariots; how
He made the water of the Red sea to overflow
them as they pursued °after you, and *how*
[1]the LORD hath °destroyed them unto this
day;
5 And what He did unto you in the °wilder-
ness, until ye came into this place;
6 And what He did unto °Dathan and
Abiram, the sons of Eliab, the son of Reuben:
how the earth opened her mouth, and swallowed them up, and their households, and
their tents, and all the °substance that *was*
in their possession, in the midst of all Israel:
7 But your eyes have seen all the great [3]acts
of [1]the LORD which He did.

n 8 Therefore shall ye keep all the °command-
ments which I command you [2]this day,

f (p. 253) that ye may be strong, and go in and possess
the land, whither ye °go to possess it;
9 And that ye may prolong *your* days °in
the land, which [1]the LORD sware unto your
fathers to give unto them and to their seed,
a land that floweth with milk and honey.
10 For the land, whither thou goest in to
possess it, °*is* not °as the land of Egypt, from
whence ye came out, where thou sowedst thy
seed, and °wateredst *it* with thy °foot, as a
garden of herbs:
11 But the land, whither ye °go to possess it,
is a land of hills and valleys, *and* °drinketh
water of the rain of heaven:
12 A land which [1]the LORD thy [1]God careth
for: the °eyes of [1]the LORD thy [1]God *are*
always upon it, from the beginning of the
year even unto the end of the year.

P e (p. 247) 13 And it shall come to pass, if ye shall
hearken diligently unto My commandments
which I command you [2]this day, to love [1]the
LORD your [1]God, and to serve Him with all
your heart and with all your °soul,
14 That I will give *you* the rain of your land
in his due season, the °first rain and the °latter
rain, that thou mayest gather in thy corn, and
thy °wine, and thine oil.
15 And I will send grass in thy fields for
thy cattle, that thou mayest eat and be full.
16 Take heed to yourselves, that your heart

---

terrible = to be feared.
taketh reward = accepteth a bribe. 2 Chron. 19. 7. Acts 10. 34. Rom. 2. 11. 1 Pet. 1. 17.
18 fatherless, &c. Cp. Ps. 68. 5; 146. 9. Fig. *Synecdoche* (of Species), Ap. 6, put for all the afflicted.
19 Love ye, &c. Cp. Lev. 19. 34.
stranger = sojourner.
20 Him. Some codices, with Sam., Onk., Jon., Sept., Syr., and Vulg., read "and Him".
cleave. Cp. Josh. 23. 8. 2 Kings 17. 36.
21 praise = song of praise.
great. Cp. 2 Sam. 7. 23.

10. 22—11. 8- (*g*, above). MOTIVES AND REASONS (*Alternation.*)

g | m | 10. 22. Fulfilment of promises to the fathers.
  n | 11. 1. Therefore, love and obey.
 m | 11. 2-7. Fulfilment of judgment to enemies.
  n | 11. 8-. Therefore, obey.

22 went down. Cp. Gen. 46. 27. Ex. 1. 5.
threescore and ten. See notes on Gen. 46. 27. Acts 7. 14.
persons = souls. Heb. pl. of *nephesh.* Ap. 13.
as the stars. Cp. Gen. 22. 17; 26. 4. Ex. 32. 13. 1 Chron. 27. 23. Neh. 9. 23. Fig. *Paroemia.* Ap. 6.

11. 1 the LORD. Heb. Jehovah. Ap. 4. II.
God. Heb. Elohim. Ap. 4. I.
and. Note the Fig. *Polysyndeton* in this verse. Ap. 6.
statutes, and . . . judgments. See note on 4. 1.
2 this day. See note on 4. 26.
His. Some codices, with one early printed edition, Sam., Jon., Sept., Syr., and Vulg., read "and His".
and. Note the Fig. *Polysyndeton* (Ap. 6) in *vv.* 2, 3.
3 acts. Cp. Ps. 103. 7, as distinguished from His "ways" shown only to Moses.
4 after you. One important codex, quoting others, reads "after them".
destroyed = caused to perish. Cp. Ex. 14. 28.
5 wilderness. Cp. Ex. 15. Num. 32.
6 Dathan and Abiram. Cp. Num. 16.
substance = living things.
8 commandments. See note on 6. 1, 25; 7. 11.
go = are going over.
9 in the land = on the ground.
10 is not = "it [is] not".
as the land of Egypt. Rain very rare in Egypt. Cp. Zech. 14. 18.
wateredst . . . foot. Referring to the system of irrigation, by which the water was turned into different channels by the foot.
11 go = are going.
drinketh = drinketh continually.
12 eyes. Fig. *Anthropopatheia.* Ap. 6.

13-21 One of the *Phylacteries.* See note on 6. 4-9.
soul. Heb. *nephesh.* See Ap. 13.
14 first rain = "early rain". Falling middle of October to January, preparing ground for seeds. First occurrence of these rains.
latter rain. Falling in March and April, bringing on the harvest. Cp. Lev. 26. 3, 4. Joel 2. 23. Jer. 5. 24. Zech. 10. 1. James 5. 7.
wine. Heb. *tîrôsh*, new wine. See Ap. 27. ii.

1452 be not deceived, and ye turn aside, and serve
other gods, and worship them;
17 And *then* [1]the LORD's wrath be kindled
against you, and He °shut up the heaven,
that there be no rain, and that the land yield
not her fruit; and *lest* ye perish quickly from
off the good °land which [1]the LORD giveth
you.

f 18 Therefore shall ye lay up these My words
(p. 247) in your heart and in your [12]soul,

g k and bind them for a sign upon your hand,
that they may be °as frontlets between your
eyes.

i 19 And ye shall teach them your children,
speaking of them when thou sittest in thine
house, and when thou walkest by the way,
when thou liest down, and when thou risest up.

h 20 And thou shalt °write them upon the
door posts of thine house, and upon thy gates:
21 That your days may be multiplied, and
the days of your children, [9]in the land which
[1]the LORD sware unto your fathers to give
them, as the days of heaven upon the earth.

O 22 For if ye shall diligently keep all these
commandments which I °command you, to
do them, to love [1]the LORD your [1]God, to
walk in all His ways, and to cleave unto
Him;
23 Then will [1]the LORD drive out all these
nations from before you, and ye shall possess
greater nations and mightier than yourselves.
24 °Every place whereon the soles of your
feet shall tread shall be yours: from the
wilderness and Lebanon, °from the °river,
the river Euphrates, even unto the uttermost
sea shall your °coast be.
25 There shall no °man be able to stand
before you: *for* [1]the LORD your [1]God shall
lay the fear of you and the dread of you upon
all the land that ye shall tread upon, °as He
hath said unto you.

J o 26 °Behold, I set before you [2]this day a
(p. 255) blessing and a curse;

p q 27 °A blessing, if ye obey the commandments of [1]the LORD your [1]God, which I
command you [2]this day:

r 28 And °a curse, if ye will not obey the
commandments of [1]the LORD your [1]God, but
turn aside out of the way which I command
you [2]this day, to go after other gods, which
ye have not known.

s 29 And it shall come to pass, when [1]the
LORD thy [1]God hath brought thee in unto
the land whither thou goest to possess it,

p q that thou shalt put the blessing upon mount
°Gerizim,

r and the curse upon mount °Ebal.

s 30 °*Are* they not on the °other side Jordan,
by the way where the sun goeth down, in the
land of the Canaanites, which dwell in the
°champaign over against °Gilgal, °beside the
plains of °Moreh?
31 For ye shall pass over Jordan to go in to
possess the land which [1]the LORD your [1]God
giveth you, and ye shall possess it, and dwell
therein.

32 And ye shall observe to do all the [1]statutes *o*
and judgments which I set before you [2]this
day.

12 These *are* the °statutes and judgments, F R t
which ye shall observe to do in the
land, which °the LORD °God of thy fathers
giveth thee to possess it, all the days that ye
live upon the °earth.

---

17 shut up. The power of the Creator thus manifested. Cp. 1 Kings 8. 35. Jas. 5. 17.
land=ground. Heb. *'ădāmāh.*
18 as=for.
20 write. See note on Ex. 17. 14, and Ap. 47.
22 command. Some codices, with Sam., Sept., and Syr., read "command this day". Cp. the idiom of Luke 23. 43.
24 Every place. Cp. Josh. 1. 3-5; 23. 5. Ex. 23. 31.
from. Some codices, with Sam., Sept., and Syr., read "and from".
river. Heb. *nāhār,* a flood, not *naḥal,* a Wady. Some codices, with Sept. and Vulg., read "great river".
coast=border.
25 man. Heb. *'īsh.* See Ap. 14. ii.
as=according as.

26-32 (J, p. 238). BLESSINGS AND CURSES.
(*Introversion and Extended Alternation.*)

J | o | 26. This day. The blessing and the curse.
  p | q | 27. The blessing.
    r | 28. The curse.
      s | 29-. The place: "In the land."
  p | *q* | -29-. The blessing (Gerizim).
    r | -29. The curse (Ebal).
      s | 30, 31. The place: "In the land."
  o | 32. This day. Statutes and judgments.

26 Behold. Fig. *Asterismos.* Ap. 6.
27 A blessing=the blessing.
28 a curse=the curse.
29 Gerizim. North of Shechem. Cp. Josh. 8. 33, 34, and see Deut. 27. 12.
Ebal. South of Shechem. Both mounts here named for first time. Not mentioned after Judges.
30 Are they not . . . ? Fig. *Erotēsis.* Ap. 6.
other side. These particulars connect this place with the rehearsing of the law to Abraham. Cp. Gen. 12. 6.
champaign=plain. Heb *'ărābāh.* Cp. 1. 1.
Gilgal=enclosure. Not the Gilgal near Jericho.
beside=near. Hence thirty miles from the Gilgal of Josh. 5. 9.
Moreh. Cp. Gen. 12. 6, 7; 35. 4.

12. 1—27. 10 (F, p. 219). LAWS IN THE LAND.
(*Introversions and Alternations.*)

F R | t | 12. 1. These statutes.
  u | 12. 2—14. 29. Sacred places and meats.
    S[1] | 15. 1—16. 17. Ecclesiastical laws (Sabbath, &c.).
      T | v | 16. 18—17. 13. Laws. Civil.
        w | 17. 14-20. The KING.
    S[2] | 18. 1-8. Laws. Ecclesiastical (Levites, &c.).
      T | *w* | 18. 9-22. The PROPHET.
        v | 19. 1—25. 19. Laws. Civil.
    S[3] | 26. 1-15. Laws. Ecclesiastical (Firstfruits).
R | *t* | 26. 16-19. These statutes.
  u | 27. 1-10. Sacred places and worship.

1 statutes and judgments. See note on 4. 1.
the LORD. Heb. Jehovah. Ap. 4. II.
God. Heb. Elohim. Ap. 4. I.
earth=ground. Heb. *'ădāmāh.*

u U[1] x (p. 256) 1452 2 Ye shall utterly destroy all the places, wherein the nations which ye shall possess served their gods, upon the high mountains, and upon the hills, and under every °green tree:

3 And ye shall overthrow their altars, and °break their °pillars, and burn their °groves with fire; and ye shall hew down the °graven images of their gods, and °destroy the names of them out of that place.

y a 4 Ye shall not do so unto [1]the LORD your [1]God.

b 5 But unto °the place which [1]the LORD your [1]God shall choose out of all your tribes to put His name there, *even* unto His habitation shall ye seek, and thither thou shalt come:

6 And thither ye shall bring your burnt offerings, °and your sacrifices, and your tithes, and heave offerings of your hand, and your vows, and your freewill offerings, and the firstlings of your herds and of your flocks:

7 And there ye shall eat before [1]the LORD your [1]God, and ye shall rejoice in all that ye °put your hand unto, ye and your households, wherein [1]the LORD thy [1]God hath blessed thee.

8 Ye shall not do after all *the things* that we do here this day, °every man whatsoever *is* right in his own eyes.

9 For ye are not as yet come to the °rest and to the inheritance, which [1]the LORD your [1]God giveth you.

10 But *when* ye go over Jordan, and dwell in the land which [1]the LORD your [1]God giveth you to inherit, and *when* He giveth you [9]rest from all your enemies round about, so that ye dwell in safety;

11 Then there shall be °a place which [1]the LORD your [1]God shall choose to cause His name to dwell there; thither shall ye bring all that I command you; your burnt offerings, and your sacrifices, your tithes, and the heave offering of your hand, and all your choice vows which ye vow unto [1]the LORD:

12 And ye shall °rejoice before [1]the LORD your [1]God, ye, and your sons, and your daughters, and your menservants, and your maidservants, and the Levite that *is* within your °gates; forasmuch as he hath no part nor inheritance °with you.

13 Take heed to thyself that thou offer not thy burnt offerings in every place that thou seest:

14 But in the place which [1]the LORD shall choose in one of thy tribes, there thou shalt offer thy burnt offerings, and there thou shalt do all that I command thee.

e 15 Notwithstanding thou mayest kill and eat flesh in all thy gates, whatsoever °thy soul °lusteth after, according to the blessing of [1]the LORD thy [1]God which He hath given thee: the unclean and the clean may eat thereof, as of the roebuck, and as of the hart.

f 16 Only ye shall not eat the blood; ye shall pour it upon the earth as water.

d 17 Thou mayest not eat within thy gates the tithe of thy corn, or of thy °wine, or of thy oil, or the firstlings of thy herds or of thy flock, nor any of thy vows which thou vowest, nor thy freewill offerings, or heave offering of thine °hand:

18 But thou must eat them before [1]the LORD thy [1]God in the place which [1]the LORD thy [1]God shall choose, thou, °and thy son, and thy daughter, and thy manservant, and thy maidservant, and the Levite that *is* within thy gates: and thou shalt rejoice before [1]the LORD thy [1]God in all that thou puttest thine hands unto.

19 Take heed to thyself that thou forsake not the Levite °as long as thou livest upon the [1]earth.

20 When [1]the LORD thy [1]God shall enlarge thy border, °as He hath promised thee, and c e

---

12. 2—14. 29 (u, p. 255). SACRED PLACES AND MEATS (*Division*).

u | U[1] | 12. 2–32. Places.
| U[2] | 13. 1–18. Idolatry.
| U[3] | 14. 1–29. Meats.

12. 2–32 (U[1], above). SACRED PLACES. (*Alternation.*)

U[1] | x | 2, 3. False gods. Destruction of places.
| y | 4–28. Jehovah: "Not so."
| *x* | 29, 30. False gods. Destruction of worship.
| *y* | 31, 32. Jehovah: "Not so."

2 green. Heb. *z'anan.* First occurrence.

3 break = smash.

pillars. These "menhirs" constantly dug up to-day.

groves = Heb. *'ashērah.* See Ap. 42.

graven images = sculptures, as in 7. 25.

destroy = cause to perish. Heb. *'ābad.* Cp. Ex. 23. 24; 34. 13. Judg. 2. 2; 6. 28. 2 Kings 10. 19; 11. 1. Ezek. 6. 3.

4–28 (y, above). JEHOVAH: "NOT SO." (*Introversion and Alternation.*)

y | a | 4. Command. General (negative).
| b | 5–14. Restrictions.
| c | e | 15. Exception.
| | f | 16. Prohibition of foods.
| d | 17–19. Tenths.
| *c* | *e* | 20–22. Exceptions.
| | *f* | 23–25. Prohibition of foods.
| *b* | 26, 27. Restrictions.
| *a* | 28. Commands. General (positive).

5 the place. Only in the Land could these laws be carried out. See the Structure above. Cp. Ex 20. 24.

6 and. Note the Fig. *Polysyndeton* (Ap. 6) in *vv.* 6, 7.

7 put your hand unto. Fig. *Metonymy* (of Adjunct), Ap. 6, hand used for all works done by it.

8 every man. Heb. *'ish.* See Ap. 14. ii.

9 rest. Cp. Josh. 23. 1. Deut. 25. 19. 1 Kings 8. 56.

11 a place. The ark of the covenant would be the place until the temple was built.

12 rejoice. Cp. Lev. 23. 40.

gates. Fig. *Synecdoche* (of Part), put for the whole city.

with you. Cp. 10. 8, 9. Num. 3. 11–13.

15 thy soul = thyself. Heb. *nephesh.* See Ap. 13.

lusteth after = longeth for.

17 wine. Heb. *tīrōsh.* Ap. 27. ii.

hand. Some codices, with Sam., Jon., Sept., Syr., and Vulg., read "hands" (pl.).

18 and. Note the Fig. *Polysyndeton* in this verse.

19 as long as thou livest. Heb. = all the days.

20 as = according as.

1452 thou shalt say, I will eat flesh, because °thy soul longeth to eat flesh; thou mayest eat flesh, whatsoever °thy soul lusteth after.

21 If the place which [1]the LORD thy [1]God hath chosen to put His name there be too far from thee, then thou shalt °kill of thy herd and of thy flock, which [1]the LORD hath given thee, as I have commanded thee, and thou shalt eat in thy gates whatsoever [20]thy soul lusteth after.

22 Even as the roebuck and the hart is eaten, so thou shalt eat them: the unclean and the clean shall eat *of* them alike.

f (p. 256) 23 Only be sure that thou eat not the blood: for °the blood *is* °the life; and thou mayest not eat °the life with the flesh.

24 °Thou shalt not eat it; thou shalt pour it upon the earth as water.

25 [24]Thou shalt not eat it; that it may go well with thee, and with thy children after thee, when thou shalt do *that which is* right in the sight of [1]the LORD.

b 26 Only thy holy things which thou hast, and thy vows, thou shalt take, and go unto the place which [1]the LORD shall choose:

27 And thou shalt °offer thy burnt offerings, the flesh and the blood, upon the altar of [1]the LORD thy [1]God: and the blood of thy sacrifices shall be poured out upon the altar of [1]the LORD thy [1]God, and thou shalt eat the flesh.

a 28 Observe and hear all these words which I command thee, that it may go well with thee, and with thy children after thee for ever, when thou doest *that which is* good and right in the sight of [1]the LORD thy [1]God.

x 29 When [1]the LORD thy [1]God shall cut off the nations from before thee, whither thou goest to possess them, and thou succeedest them, and dwellest in their land;

30 Take heed to thyself that thou be not snared by following them, after that they be destroyed from before thee; and that thou enquire not after their gods, saying, °'How did these nations serve their gods? even so will I do likewise.'

y 31 Thou shalt not do so unto [1]the LORD thy [1]God: for every abomination to [1]the LORD, which He hateth, have they done unto their gods; for even their sons and their daughters they have °burnt in the fire to their gods.

32 °What thing soever I command you, observe to do it: thou shalt not add thereto, nor diminish from it.

V[1] g[1] (p. 257) **13** °If there arise among you a prophet, or a dreamer of dreams,

h[1] and giveth thee a sign or a wonder,

2 And the sign or the wonder come to pass, whereof he spake unto thee, saying, 'Let us go after other gods,' which thou hast not known, and let us serve them;

i[1] 3 Thou shalt not hearken unto the words of that prophet, or that dreamer of dreams: for °the LORD your °God °proveth you. to know whether ye love °the LORD your °God with all your heart and with all °your soul.

4 Ye shall walk after [3]the LORD your [3]God, °and fear Him, and keep His commandments, and obey His voice, and ye shall serve Him, and °cleave unto Him.

5 And that prophet, or that dreamer of dreams, shall be put to death; because he hath spoken to turn *you* away from [3]the LORD your [3]God, Which brought you out of the land of Egypt, and redeemed you out of the house of °bondage, to thrust thee out of the way which [3]the LORD thy [3]God commanded thee to walk in. k[1]

°So shalt thou °put °the evil away from the midst of thee. l[1]

6 If thy brother, the son of thy mother, or thy son, or thy daughter, or the wife of thy bosom, or thy friend, which *is* as thine °own soul, °entice thee °secretly, V[2] g[2]

---

thy soul = thyself. Heb. *nephesh*. Ap. 13.

21 kill = kill in sacrifice. Ap. 43. I. iv. Cp. 1 Sam. 16. 5 ("sacrifice").

23 the blood is the life. Heb. "the blood it [is] the soul". Heb. *nephesh*. Ap. 13. Cp. Lev. 17. 11, 14, and *v.* 16 above.

the life = the soul. Heb. *nephesh*. Ap. 13.

24 Thou shalt not eat it. Repeated in *v.* 25. Fig. *Anaphora* (Ap. 6), for emphasis.

27 offer = prepare. See Ap. 43. I. iii.

30 How . . . ? Fig. *Erotēsis*. Ap. 6.

31 burnt = burnt up. See Ap. 43. I. viii.

32 What, &c. Close of third address. See note on 1. 1.

13. 1-18 (U[2], p. 256). IDOLATRY.
(*Extended and Repeated Alternations.*)

U[2] V[1] | g[1] | 1-. The instigator. False prophet.
h[1] | -1, 2. Seduction.
i[1] | 3, 4. Prohibition.
k[1] | 5-. Punishment.
l[1] | -5. Evil removed.
V[2] | g[2] | 6-. Instigator. A brother.
h[2] | -6, 7. Seduction.
i[2] | 8. Prohibition.
k[2] | 9, 10. Punishment.
l[2] | 11. Evil removed.
V[3] | g[3] | 12. Instigator. A city.
h[3] | 13. Seduction.
i[3] | 14. Inquiry.
k[3] | 15, 16. Destruction.
l[3] | 17, 18. Evil removed.

1 If, &c. Beginning of Moses' fourth address. See note on 1. 1.

3 the LORD. Heb. Jehovah. Ap. 4.

God. Heb. Elohim. Ap. 4.

proveth: i. e. suffereth you to be proved. Heb. idiom, which speaks of doing what one allows to be done.

your soul = yourself. Heb. *nephesh*. Ap. 13.

4 and. Note the Fig. *Polysyndeton* (Ap. 6), to emphasise each item.

cleave. Cp. 10. 20.

5 bondage = bondmen. See note on 5. 6.

So shalt thou put . . . away. This expression occurs eleven times in this book: 13. 5; 17. 7, 12; 19. 13, 19; 21. 9, 21; 22. 21, 22, 24; 24. 7.

put . . . away. Heb. *bā'ar*, to burn up in order to clear out.

the evil = the wicked thing. Heb. *rā'a'*. Ap. 44. viii.

6 own soul = own self. Heb. *nephesh*. Ap. 13.

entice . . . secretly. Both (Heb.) words used here for the first time.

h2 saying, 'Let us go and serve other gods,'
(p. 257) which thou hast not known, thou, nor thy
1452 fathers;

7 *Namely*, of the gods of the people which *are* round about you, nigh unto thee, or far off from thee, from the *one* end of the earth even unto the *other* end of the earth;

i2 8 Thou shalt not consent unto him, nor hearken unto him; neither shall thine °eye pity him, neither shalt thou spare, neither shalt thou conceal him:

k2 9 But thou shalt surely kill him; thine hand shall be first upon him to put him to death, and afterwards the hand of all the people.

10 And thou shalt stone him with stones, that he die; because he hath sought to thrust thee away from [3]the LORD thy [3]God, Which brought thee out of the land of Egypt, from the house of [5]bondage.

l2 11 And all Israel shall hear, and fear, and shall do no more any such °wickedness as this is among you.

V3 g3 12 If thou shalt hear *say* in one of thy cities, which [3]the LORD thy [3]God °hath given thee to dwell there, saying,

h3 13 '*Certain* °men, the °children of °Belial, are gone out from among you, and have withdrawn the inhabitants of their city, saying, 'Let us go and serve other gods,' which ye have not known;'

i3 14 Then shalt thou enquire, and make search, and ask °diligently; and, °behold, *if it be* truth, *and* the thing certain, *that* such abomination is wrought among you;

k3 15 Thou shalt surely smite the inhabitants of that city with the °edge of the sword, °destroying it utterly, and all that *is* therein, and the cattle thereof, with the °edge of the sword.

16 And thou shalt gather all the spoil of it into the midst of the street thereof, and shalt °burn with fire the city, and all the spoil thereof every whit, for [3]the LORD thy [3]God: and it shall be an °heap for ever; it shall not be built again.

l3 17 And there shall cleave nought of the °cursed thing to thine hand: that [3]the LORD may turn from the fierceness of His anger, and shew thee mercy, and have compassion upon thee, and multiply thee, °as He hath sworn unto thy fathers;

18 When thou shalt hearken to the voice of [3]the LORD thy [3]God, to keep all His commandments which I command thee °this day, to do *that which is* right in the eyes of [3]the LORD thy [3]God.

U3 W
(p. 258) **14** Ye *are* the children of °the LORD your °God: °ye shall not cut yourselves, nor make any baldness between your eyes for °the dead.

2 For thou *art* an °holy people unto [1]the LORD thy [1]God, and °the LORD hath chosen thee to be a °peculiar people unto Himself, above all the nations that *are* upon °the earth.

X m o1 3 Thou shalt not eat any abominable thing.

8 eye. Fig. *Prosopopœia.* Ap. 6.
11 wickedness. Heb. *rā'ā'.* Ap. 44. viii.
12 hath given=giveth.
13 men. Heb. pl. of *'īsh* or *'enōsh.* Ap. 14.
children=sons.
Belial. First occurrence. A word denoting all that is wicked and worthless; hopeless, as to character and destiny. Put by Fig. *Metonymy*, Ap. 6, for the Evil One as the instigator of all the uncleanness of heathenism. Cp. 2 Cor. 6. 15.
14 diligently=thoroughly. Occurs only here and 17. 4; 19. 18. **behold.** Fig. *Asterismos.* Ap. 6.
15 destroying=exterminating. Heb. *ḥāram.*
edge. Heb. "mouth". Put by Fig. *Metonymy* (of Subject), Ap. 6, for edge.
16 burn=burn up. Heb. *sāraph.* Ap. 43. I. viii.
heap for ever. Cp. Josh. 8. 28.
17 cursed=devoted [to destruction]. Cp. Josh. 6. 18; 7. 1. **as**=according as.
18 this day. See note on 4. 26.

14. 1-29 (U3, p. 256). MEATS.
(*Introversion and Alternation.*)

U3 | W | 1, 2. Jehovah thy *'Elohim.* Choosing.
X | m | 3-21. Meats (negative and positive).
n | 22, 23. Tithes.
X | *m* | 24-26. Meats (positive).
n | 27-29-. Tithes.
W | -29. Jehovah thy *'Elohim.* Blessing.

1 the LORD. Heb. Jehovah. Ap. 4. II.
God. Heb. Elohim. Ap. 4. I.
ye shall not, &c. Cp. Lev. 19. 27, 28; 21. 5. Jer. 16. 6; 41. 5; 47. 5.
the dead=dead people (not dead bodies). No art. in Sept. Cp. 28. 26 with art., and rendered rightly "carcase".
2 holy. See note on Ex. 3. 5.
the LORD. (Heb. Jehovah.) Some codices, with Sam., Jon., Sept., and Syr., add "thy God".
peculiar=as a treasure. See note on Ex. 19. 5. Cp. Deut. 7. 6.
the earth=the face of the soil. Fig. *Pleonasm.* Ap. 6. Heb. *'ădāmāh.*

3-21 (m, above). MEATS.
(*Enumeration.*)

m | o1 | 3-8. Beasts.
o2 | 9, 10. Fish.
o3 | 11-20. Birds.
o4 | 21-. What dieth of itself.
o5 | -21. Kid.

4 These. There are eleven animals named in Deuteronomy which are not included in Leviticus and Numbers. More names known after forty years from Egypt. Cp. Lev. 11.
5 roebuck=gazelle (R.V.).
fallow deer=roebuck.
pygarg=mountain goat.
wild ox=antelope (R.V.).
chamois=mountain sheep (R.V.).
6 parteth the hoof. Cp. Lev. 11. 2, 8.
cleaveth the cleft. Fig. *Polyptōton.* Ap. 6.

4 °These *are* the beasts which ye shall eat: the ox, the sheep, and the goat,

5 The hart, and the °roebuck, and the °fallow deer, and the wild goat, and the °pygarg, and the °wild ox, and the °chamois.

6 And every beast that °parteth the hoof, and °cleaveth the cleft into two claws, *and* cheweth the cud among the beasts, that ye shall eat.

7 Nevertheless these ye shall not eat of them that chew the cud, or of them that divide the cloven hoof; *as* the camel, and the hare, and

1452 the °coney: for they chew the cud, but divide not the hoof; *therefore* they *are* unclean unto you.

8 And the swine, because it divideth the hoof, yet cheweth not the cud, it *is* unclean unto you: ye shall not eat of their flesh, nor touch their dead carcase.

o[2] 9 °These ye shall eat of all that *are* in the waters: all that have fins and scales shall ye eat:

10 And whatsoever hath not fins and scales ye may not eat; it *is* unclean unto you.

o[3] 11 *Of* all clean birds ye shall eat.

(p. 258) 12 But °these *are they* of which ye shall not eat: the eagle, and the °ossifrage, and the ospray,

13 And the °glede, and the °kite, and the °vulture after his kind,

14 And every raven after his kind,

15 And the °owl, and the night hawk, and the °cuckow, and the hawk after his kind,

16 The little owl, and the great owl, and the °swan,

17 And the pelican, and the °gier eagle, and the cormorant,

18 And the stork, and the °heron after her kind, and the °lapwing, and the bat.

19 And every °creeping thing that flieth °*is* unclean unto you: °they shall not be eaten.

20 *But of* all clean fowls ye may eat.

o[4] 21 Ye shall not eat *of* any thing that °dieth of itself: thou shalt give it unto the stranger that *is* in thy gates, that he may eat it; or thou mayest sell it unto an alien: for thou *art* an [2]holy people unto [1]the LORD thy [1]God.

o[5] Thou shalt not °seethe a kid in his mother's milk.

X n 22 Thou shalt truly °tithe all the increase of thy seed, that the field bringeth forth year by year.

23 And thou shalt °eat before [1]the LORD thy [1]God, in the place which He shall choose °to place His name there, the tithe of thy corn, of thy °wine, and of thine oil, and the °firstlings of thy herds and of thy flocks; that thou mayest learn to fear [1]the LORD thy [1]God always.

m 24 And if the way be too long for thee, so that thou art not able to carry it; *or* if the place be too far from thee, which [1]the LORD thy [1]God shall choose to set His name there, when [1]the LORD thy [1]God hath blessed thee:

25 Then shalt thou °turn *it* into money, and bind up the money in thine hand, and shalt go unto the place which [1]the LORD thy [1]God shall choose:

26 And thou shalt bestow that money for whatsoever °thy soul °lusteth after, for oxen, or for sheep, or for °wine, or for °strong drink, or for whatsoever °thy soul °desireth: and thou shalt eat there before [1]the LORD thy [1]God, and thou shalt rejoice, thou, and thine household,

n 27 And °the Levite that *is* within thy gates; thou shalt not forsake him; for he hath no part nor inheritance with thee.

28 At the end of three years thou shalt bring forth all the tithe of thine increase the same year, and shalt lay *it* up within thy gates:

29 And the Levite, (because he hath no part nor inheritance with thee,) and the stranger, and the fatherless, and the widow, which *are* within thy gates, shall come, and shall eat and be satisfied;

that [1]the LORD thy [1]God may bless thee in all the work of thine hand which thou doest. W

15 At the end of *every* °seven years thou shalt make a °release. Y[1] p[1] r (p. 260)

2 And this *is* the manner of the [1]release: Every creditor that lendeth *ought* unto his neighbour shall release *it;* he shall not exact *it* of his neighbour, or of his brother; because it is called °the LORD'S [1]release.

3 Of a foreigner thou mayest exact *it again:* but *that* which is thine with thy brother thine hand shall [1]release;

4 °Save when there shall be no poor among you;

---

7 coney. Heb. *shaphan.* R.V. margin, called "Hyrax Syriacus", or rock-badger.
9 These. Cp. Lev. 11. 9-12.
12 these. Cp. Lev. 11. 13-20.
ossifrage = gier eagle (R.V.).
13 glede. Probably = vulture.
kite = falcon (R.V.).
vulture = kite (R.V.).
15 owl = ostrich (R.V.).
cuckow = seamew (R.V.): i. e. sea-gull.
16 swan = horned owl (R.V.).
17 gier eagle = vulture (R.V.) or bittern.
18 heron. Very doubtful; probably = parrot.
lapwing = hoopoe (R.V.).
19 creeping thing = swarming creature: i. e. rapidly multiplying. Cp. Gen. 1. 20, 21; 7. 21; 8. 17; 9. 7. Ex. 8. 3. Lev. 11. 29, &c.
is. Heb. "it [is]".
they. A special reading, called *Sevîr*, reads, "it". See Ap. 34.
21 dieth, &c. Cp. Ex. 22. 31. Lev. 11. 39; 17. 15; 22. 8. Ezek. 4. 14.
seethe = boil. Cp. Ex. 23. 19; 34. 26.
22 tithe. Cp. Lev. 27. 30. Num. 18. 24, 30. Deut. 12. 6; 14. 28; 26. 12.
23 eat. Tithes were eaten. Amos 4. 4.
to place = to make a habitation.
wine. Heb. *tîrôsh.* See Ap. 27. ii.
firstlings. Cp. Gen. 4. 4. Ex. 13. 11-15; 23. 19. Lev. 27. 26. Num. 18. 15-17, and Neh. 10. 36.
25 turn it into money: as in Matt. 21. 12. Mark 11. 15. Luke 19. 45, and John 2. 14, 15.
26 thy soul = thyself. Heb. *nephesh.* Ap. 13.
lusteth after = longeth for.
wine. Heb. *yayin.* Ap. 27. I.
strong drink = *shēkār.* See Ap. 27. iv.
desireth = asketh of thee.
27 the Levite. Cp. 12. 19.

15. 1—16. 17 [For Structures see next page].
1 seven years = when the seventh year has arrived. Cp. Ex. 23. 10, 11. Lev. 25. 3, 4.
release. Cp. Ex. 23. 10, 11. Lev. 25. 6, 7. In Ex. and Lev. rest for the land. In Deut. release for the debtor. The noun, *shāmaṭ*, only here and 31. 10. The verb, only in Ex. 23. 11 = to let lie down.
2 the LORD'S. Heb. Jehovah. Ap. 4. II.
4 Save when. This rendering not in any ancient version. A.V. margin has "that there be no poor", &c. R.V. = howbeit. Cp. *v.* 11, shall never cease: i. e. or die from your neglect; which would be the case if these laws were not carried out.

s for [2]the LORD shall greatly bless thee in the
(p. 260) land which [2]the LORD thy °God giveth thee
1452 *for* an inheritance to possess it:

r 5 Only if thou carefully hearken unto the voice of [2]the LORD thy [4]God, to observe to do all these commandments which I command thee °this day.

s 6 For [2]the LORD thy [4]God blesseth thee, °as He promised thee: and thou shalt °lend unto many nations, but thou shalt not borrow; and thou shalt °reign over many nations, but they shall not °reign over thee.

q[1] t v 7 If there be among you a poor man of one of thy brethren within any of thy gates in thy land

w which [2]the LORD thy [4]God giveth thee,

u x thou shalt not harden thine heart, nor shut thine hand from thy poor brother:

y 8 But thou shalt open thine hand wide unto him, and shalt surely lend him sufficient for his need, *in that* which he wanteth.

u x 9 Beware that there be not a °thought in thy °wicked heart, saying, 'The seventh year, the year of [1]release, is at hand;' and thine eye be evil against thy poor brother, and thou givest him nought; and he cry unto [2]the LORD against thee, and it be °sin unto thee.

y 10 Thou shalt surely give him, and thine heart shall not be grieved when thou givest unto him: because that for this thing [2]the LORD thy [4]God shall bless thee in all thy works, and in all that thou puttest thine hand unto.

v 11 For the poor shall °never cease out of the land:

w therefore I command thee, saying, 'Thou shalt open thine hand wide unto thy brother, to thy poor, and to thy needy, in thy land.'

p[2] 12 *And* if thy °brother, an °Hebrew man, or an Hebrew woman, be sold unto thee, and serve thee six years; then in the seventh year thou shalt let him go free from thee.

13 And when thou sendest him out free from thee, thou shalt not let him go away empty:

14 Thou shalt furnish him liberally out of thy flock, and out of thy °floor, and out of thy winepress: *of that* wherewith [2]the LORD thy [4]God hath blessed thee thou shalt give unto him.

15 And thou shalt remember that thou wast a bondman in the land of Egypt, and [2]the LORD thy [4]God redeemed thee: therefore I command thee this thing [5]to day.

q[2] 16 And it shall be, °if he say unto thee, 'I will not go away from thee;' because he loveth thee and thine house, because he is well with thee:

17 Then thou shalt take an °aul, and thrust *it* through his ear unto the door, and he shall be thy servant °for ever. And also unto thy maidservant thou shalt do likewise.

p[3] 18 It shall not seem hard unto thee, when thou sendest him away free from thee; for he hath been worth a °double hired servant *to* thee, in serving thee six years: and [2]the LORD thy [4]God shall bless thee in all that thou doest.

19 °All the firstling males that come of thy herd and of thy flock thou shalt sanctify unto [2]the LORD thy [4]God: Y[2] a b

thou shalt do no work with the firstling of thy bullock, nor shear the firstling of thy sheep. c

---

15. 1–16. 17 (S[1], p. 256). LAWS: ECCLESIASTICAL (*Enumeration*).

S[1] | Y[1] | 15. 1–18. Sabbatical year.
Y[2] | 15. 19–23. Firstlings.
Y[3] | 16. 1–17. Three feasts.

15. 1–18 (Y[1], above). SABBATICAL YEAR. (*Repeated Alternation.*)

Y[1] | p[1] | 1–6. Release.
q[1] | 7–11. Hypothetical case.
p[2] | 12–15. Release.
q[2] | 16, 17. Hypothetical case.
p[3] | 18. Release.

1–6 (p[1], above). RELEASE. (*Alternation.*)

p[1] | r | 1–4–. Command.
s | –4. Reason. Blessing.
r | 5. Obedience.
s | 6. Reason. Blessing.

God. Heb. Elohim. Ap. 4.
5 this day. See note on 4. 26.
6 as = according as.
lend = lend in pledge.
reign = rule.

7–11 (q[1], above). HYPOTHETICAL CASE, POVERTY (*Introversion and Alternation*).

q[1] | t | v | 7–. Case of poverty.
w | –7–. Thy land.
u | x | –7. Warning.
y | 8. Command.
u | *x* | 9. Warning.
y | 10. Command.
t | *v* | 11–. Cases of poverty.
w | –11. Thy land.

9 thought = word (= thought expressed).
wicked heart = heart of Belial.
sin = Heb. *chāṭā*. See Ap. 44. i.
11 never cease. See note on *v.* 4.
12 brother. Supply the Ellipsis (Ap. 6) by adding "[or thy sister]".
Hebrew man. Cp. Ex. 21. 2. Jer. 34. 13, 14.
14 floor = threshing-floor.
16 if he say. Cp. Ex. 21. 5, 6.
17 aul. Only here, and Ex. 21. 6.
for ever. Fig. *Synecdoche* (of the Whole), Ap. 6, whole time put for part of time.
18 double. Fig. *Metonymy* (of Subject), put for that which is more than one. Ap. 6.

19–23 (Y[2], above). FIRSTLINGS. (*Extended Alternation.*)

Y[2] | a | b | 19–. Without blemish.
c | –19. Prohibition. Not worked.
d | 20. Eating (positive).
a | *b* | 21–. Without blemish.
c | –21. Prohibition. Not sacrificed.
d | 22, 23. Eating (negative).

19 All, &c. Cp. Ex. 34. 19, 20.

d (p. 260) 1452 20 Thou shalt eat *it* before [2]the LORD thy [4]God year by year in the place which [2]the LORD shall choose, thou and thy household.

b 21 And if there be *any* °blemish therein, *as if it be* lame, or blind, *or have* any ill blemish,
c thou shalt not sacrifice it unto [2]the LORD thy [4]God.

d 22 Thou shalt eat it within thy gates: the unclean and the clean *person shall eat it* alike, as the roebuck, and as the hart.
23 Only °thou shalt not eat the blood thereof; thou shalt pour it upon the ground as water.

e[1] f[1] g (p. 261) **16** °Observe the month of °Abib, and keep the passover unto °the LORD thy °God: for in the month of Abib °the LORD thy °God brought thee forth out of Egypt by night.

h i 2 Thou shalt therefore sacrifice the passover unto [1]the LORD thy [1]God, of the flock and the herd, in the place which [1]the LORD shall choose °to place His name there.

k 3 Thou shalt eat no leavened bread with it; seven days shalt thou eat unleavened bread therewith, *even* the °bread of affliction; for thou camest forth out of the land of Egypt °in haste: that thou mayest remember the day when thou camest forth out of the land of Egypt all the days of thy life.
4 And there shall be no °leavened bread seen with thee in all thy coast seven days; neither shall there *any thing* of the flesh, which thou sacrificedst the first day at even, remain all night until the morning.

h i 5 Thou mayest not sacrifice the passover within any of thy °gates, which [1]the LORD thy [1]God giveth thee:
6 But at the place which [1]the LORD thy [1]God shall choose [2]to place His name in, there thou shalt sacrifice the passover at even, at the going down of the sun, at the season that thou camest forth out of Egypt.

k 7 And thou shalt °roast and eat *it* in the place which [1]the LORD thy [1]God shall choose: and thou shalt turn in the morning, and go unto thy tents.

g 8 Six days thou shalt eat unleavened bread: and on the °seventh day *shall be* a solemn assembly to [1]the LORD thy [1]God: thou shalt do no work *therein*.

f[2] l n 9 Seven weeks shalt thou number unto thee: begin to number the seven weeks from *such time as* thou beginnest *to put* the sickle to the °corn.

o 10 And thou shalt keep the feast of weeks unto [1]the LORD thy [1]God with a tribute of a freewill offering of thine hand,
m which thou shalt give *unto the LORD thy God*, according as [1]the LORD thy [1]God hath blessed thee:

m 11 °And thou shalt rejoice before [1]the LORD thy [1]God, thou, and thy son, and thy daughter, and thy manservant, and thy maidservant, and the Levite that *is* within thy gates, and the stranger, and the fatherless, and the widow, that *are* among you, in the place which [1]the LORD thy [1]God hath chosen [6]to place His name there.

12 And thou shalt remember that thou wast a bondman °in Egypt: *l n*
and thou shalt observe and do these statutes. o

13 Thou shalt observe the feast of tabernacles seven days, f[3] p q (p. 262)

---

21 blemish. Cp. Lev. 22. 20-22. Mal. 1. 8.
23 thou. Some codices, with Onk., Jon., Sept., and Syr., read "ye".

16. 1-17 (Y[3], p. 260). THREE FEASTS. (*Division.*)

Y[3] | e[1] | 1-15. Particular.
| e[2] | 16, 17. General.

1-15 (e[1], above). PARTICULAR (FEASTS). (*Enumeration.*)

e[1] | f[1] | 1-8. Passover.
| f[2] | 9-12. Weeks.
| f[3] | 13-15. Tabernacles.

1-8 (f[1], above). PASSOVER (FEAST). (*Introversion and Alternation.*)

f[1] | g | 1. The feast. Ordinance.
h | i | 2. The chosen place (positive).
k | 3, 4. The manner.
h | *i* | 5, 6. The chosen place (negative).
k | 7. The manner.
g | 8. The feast. Ordinance.

1 Observe. Cp. Ex. 13. 3, 4. Lev. 23. 5, 6. Num. 28. 16.
Abib is Egyptian and means "green ears". Cp. Ex. 9. 31. Lev. 2. 14. Not found again after this passage. "Nisan" substituted for it.
the LORD. Heb. Jehovah. Ap. 4. II.
God. Heb. Elohim. Ap. 4. I.
2 to place = to make a habitation for.
3 bread of affliction. Fig. *Metonymy* (of Subject) = bread which is the symbol of their affliction in Egypt.
in haste. Not the reason given in Ex. 12. 17 for the Exodus. But here the reason why the bread was unleavened. There was no time for it to "rise" by fermentation.
4 leavened = fermented. Cp. Ex. 13. 7; 12. 18-20.
5 gates. Fig. *Synecdoche* (of Part), Ap. 6, put for the cities themselves. Note the Introversion of the lines of this member (*i*), *vv.* 5, 6.
7 roast = cook.
8 seventh day. Cp. Ex. 12. 16; 13. 6.
9 corn = standing corn.

9-12 (f[2], above). WEEKS (FEAST). (*Introversion and Alternation.*)

f[2] | l | n | 9. Command. "Thou shalt remember".
o | 10-. Feast. "Thou shalt keep".
m | -10. Offering of gift. "Thou shalt give".
m | 11. Offering of praise. "Thou shalt rejoice".
l | *n* | 12-. Command. "Thou shalt remember".
o | -12. Feast. "Thou shalt observe".

11 And. Note the Fig. *Polysyndeton* in this verse. See Ap. 6.
12 in Egypt. Some codices, with Sam. and Sept., have "in the land of Egypt".

13-15 [For Structure see next page].

r (p. 262) 1452 after that thou hast gathered in thy °corn and thy °wine:

s 14 °And thou shalt rejoice in thy feast, thou, and thy son, and thy daughter, and thy manservant, and thy maidservant, and the Levite, the stranger, and the fatherless, and the widow, that *are* within thy gates.

p q 15 Seven days shalt thou keep a solemn feast unto [1]the LORD thy [1]God

r in the place which [1]the LORD shall choose:

s because [1]the LORD thy [1]God shall bless thee in all thine increase, and in all the works of thine hands, therefore thou shalt surely rejoice.

Y[3] e[2] (p. 261) 16 Three times in a year shall all thy males °appear before [1]the LORD thy [1]God in the place which He shall choose; in the feast of unleavened bread, and in the feast of weeks, and in the feast of tabernacles: and they shall not °appear before [1]the LORD empty:

17 Every °man *shall give* as he is able, according to the blessing of [1]the LORD thy [1]God which He hath given thee.

v A (p. 262) 18 Judges and officers shalt thou make thee in all thy [5]gates, which [1]the LORD thy [1]God giveth thee, throughout thy tribes: and they shall judge the people with just judgment.

19 Thou shalt not wrest judgment; °thou shalt not respect persons, neither take a °gift: for a °gift doth blind the eyes of the wise, and pervert the words of the righteous.

20 That which is °altogether just shalt thou follow, that thou mayest live, and inherit the land which [1]the LORD thy [1]God giveth thee.

B 21 Thou shalt not plant thee a °grove of any trees near unto the altar of [1]the LORD thy [1]God, which thou shalt make thee.

22 Neither shalt thou set thee up *any* °image; which [1]the LORD thy [1]God hateth.

B **17** Thou shalt not sacrifice unto °the LORD thy °God *any* bullock, or sheep, wherein is blemish, *or* any evilfavouredness: for that *is* an abomination unto °the LORD thy °God.

t v w 2 If there be found among you, within any of thy gates which [1]the LORD thy [1]God giveth thee, °man or woman,

x that hath wrought °wickedness in the sight of [1]the LORD thy [1]God, in °transgressing His covenant,

3 And hath gone and served other gods, and worshipped them, either the sun, or moon, or any of the host of heaven, which I have °not commanded;

y 4 And it be told thee, and thou hast heard *of it*, and enquired °diligently, and, °behold, *it be* true, *and* the thing certain, *that* such abomination is wrought in Israel:

w 5 Then shalt thou bring forth that man or that woman,

x which have committed that [2]wicked thing, unto thy gates, *even* that man or that woman, and shalt stone them with stones, till they die.

6 At the °mouth of °two witnesses, or three witnesses, shall he that is worthy of death be put to death; *but* at the mouth of one witness he shall not be put to death. y

7 The hands of the witnesses shall be first upon him to put him to death, and afterward the hands of all the people. So thou shalt °put the evil away from among you.

8 If there arise a matter too hard for thee in judgment, between blood and blood, °between t a (p. 263)

13-15 (f[3], p. 261). TABERNACLES (FEAST).
(*Extended Alternation.*)

f[3] | p | q | 13-. The feast. Seven days.
    r | -13. Time.
    s | 14. Rejoicing. Command.
  p | *q* | 15-. The feast. Seven days.
    r | -15-. Place.
    s | -15. Rejoicing. Reason.

13 corn = threshing-floor; wine = winepress } Put by Fig. *Metonymy* (of Adjunct), Ap. 6, for what is produced from them.
14 And. Note the Fig. *Polysyndeton*. Ap. 6.
16 appear. See note on Ex. 23. 15, 17.
17 man. Heb. *'ish*. See Ap. 14. II.

16. 18—17. 13 (v, p. 255). LAWS. CIVIL.
(*Introversion.*)

v | A | 16. 18-20. Judges. Appointment.
  B | 16. 21, 22. Illegal acts.
  B | 17. 1. Illegal offerings.
  A | 17. 2-13. Judges. Duties.

19 thou shalt not. A special reading, known as *Sevîr*, has "neither shalt thou". See Ap. 34.
gift = bribe.
20 altogether just. This is the rendering of the Fig. *Epizeuxis* (Ap. 6). Heb. "just, just", i. e. perfectly just.
21 grove. Heb. *'ăshêrāh*. See Ap. 42. Here in the fem. gender.
22 image = pillar.

17. 2-13 (*A*, above). JUDGES. DUTIES.
(*Alternation.*)

A | t | 2-7-. Law. Simple cases.
  u | -7. Intention. Removal of evil.
  t | 8-12. Law. Difficult cases.
  u | 13. Intention. Removal of evil.

2-7 (t, above). LAW. SIMPLE CASES.
(*Extended Alternation.*)

t | v | w | 2-. Criminals.
    x | -2, 3. Crime. Commission.
    y | 4. Proof.
  v | *w* | 5-. Criminals.
    x | -5. Crime. Punishment.
    y | 6, 7-. Proof.

1 the LORD. Heb. Jehovah. Ap. 4. II.
God. Heb. Elohim. Ap. 4. I.
2 man. Heb. *'ish*. Ap. 14. II.
wickedness. Heb. *rā'a'*. Ap. 44. viii.
transgressing. Heb. *'ābar*. Ap. 44. VII.
3 not commanded. Equally authoritative in matters of faith and worship to-day.
4 diligently. See note on 13. 14.
behold. Fig. *Asterismos*. Ap. 6.
6 mouth. Fig. *Metonymy* (of Cause), put for the witness borne by it. Ap. 6.
two. Cp. Num. 35. 30, and see Matt. 18. 16. 2 Cor. 13. 1. 1 Tim. 5. 19.
7 put the evil away. See note on 13. 5.

8-12 [For Structure see next page].

8 between. Some codices, with Sam., Jon., Sept., and Syr., read "or between".

1452 plea and plea, and between °stroke and stroke, *being* matters of controversy within thy gates:

b (p. 263) then shalt thou arise, and get thee up into the place which [1]the LORD thy [1]God shall choose;
9 And thou shalt come unto °the priests the Levites, and unto the judge that shall be in those days, and enquire; and they shall shew thee the sentence of judgment:
10 °And thou shalt do according to the sentence, which they of that place which [1]the LORD shall choose shall shew thee; and thou shalt observe to do according to all that they inform thee:
11 According to the sentence of the law which °they shall teach thee, and according to the judgment which they shall tell thee, thou shalt do: thou shalt not decline from the sentence which they shall shew thee, *to* the right hand, nor *to* the left.

a 12 And the [2]man that will do presumptuously, and will not hearken unto the priest that standeth to minister there before [1]the LORD thy [1]God, or unto the judge,

b even that [2]man shall die: and thou shalt [7]put away the evil from Israel.
13 And all the people shall hear, and fear, and do no more presumptuously.

w c 14 When thou art come unto the land which [1]the LORD thy [1]God giveth thee, and shalt possess it, and shalt dwell therein, °and shalt say, 'I will set a king over me, like as all the nations that *are* about me;'

d 15 Thou shalt in any wise set *him* king over thee, whom [1]the LORD thy [1]God shall choose: *one* from among thy brethren shalt thou set king over thee: thou mayest not set a °stranger over thee, which *is* not thy brother.

e 16 But he shall not multiply horses to himself, nor cause the people to return to Egypt, to the end that he should multiply horses: forasmuch as [1]the LORD hath said unto you, 'Ye shall henceforth return no more that way.'
17 Neither shall he multiply °wives to himself, that his heart turn not away: neither shall he greatly multiply to himself silver and gold.

e 18 And it shall be, when he sitteth upon the throne of his kingdom,

d that he shall °write him a copy of this law °in a book out of *that which is* before [9]the priests the Levites:

c 19 And it shall be with him, and he shall read therein all the days of his life: that he may learn to fear [1]the LORD his [1]God, to keep all the words of this law and these statutes, to do them:
20 That his heart be not lifted up above his brethren, and that he °turn not aside from the commandment, *to* the right hand, or *to* the left: to the end that he may prolong *his* days in his kingdom, he, and his children, in the midst of Israel.

S² f¹ **18** The priests the Levites, *and* all the tribe of Levi, shall have no part nor inheritance with Israel: they shall eat the offerings of °the LORD made by fire, and His inheritance.
2 Therefore shall they have no inheritance among their brethren: [1]the LORD °*is* their inheritance, as He hath said unto them.

3 And this shall be the °priest's due from the people, from them that °offer a sacrifice, whether *it be* ox or sheep; and they shall give unto the priest the shoulder, and the two cheeks, and the maw. f²
4 The firstfruit *also* of thy corn, of thy °wine, and of thine oil, and the first of the fleece of thy sheep, shalt thou give him.
5 For [1]the LORD thy °God hath chosen him out of all thy tribes, to stand to minister in the name of [1]the LORD, him and his sons for ever.
6 And if °a Levite come from any of thy gates out of all Israel, where he sojourned, and come with all the desire of °his mind unto the place which [1]the LORD shall choose;

---

17. 8-12 (*t*, above). LAW. DIFFICULT CASES. (*Alternation.*)

t | a | 8-. Cases. Difficult.
  | b | -8-11. Process and sentence.
  | *a* | 12-. Cases. Presumptuous.
  | *b* | -12, 13. Punishment—Death.

stroke = punishment. Fig. *Synecdoche* (of Species), Ap. 6.

9 the priests the Levites. First occurrence of this expression. Occurs six times in Deut.; elsewhere in Josh. 3. 31; 8. 33. 2 Chron. 30. 27. Neh. 11. 20. Isa. 66. 21. Jer. 33. 21. Ezek. 44. 15. The expression refers to the Levitical priests as distinct from the Tribal priests (or Levites).

10 This is the middle verse of Deut.

11 they shall teach thee. This was the great duty of the Priests. See 33. 10. Lev. 10. 11. Ezra 7. 10. Jer. 18. 18. Hag. 2. 11, 12. Mal. 2. 7.

14 and shalt say. A prophetic contingency provided for. Cp. Gen. 36. 31.

14-20 (w, p. 255). THE KING. (*Introversion.*)

w | c | 14. If a king desired.
  | d | 15. Jehovah's choice: his credential.
  | e | 16, 17. Commands (negative).
  | *e* | 18-. Command (positive).
  | *d* | -18. Jehovah's law: his study.
  | *c* | 19, 20. The king desirable.

15 stranger = foreigner.

17 wives. Cp. 1 Kings 11. 1-3.

18 write. See note on Ex. 17. 14 and Ap. 47.

in a book. See Ap. 47.

20 turn not aside. See 28. 14. 2 Kings 22. 2. Josh. 1. 7; 23. 6.

18. 1-8 (S², p. 255). LAWS ECCLESIASTICAL: THE LEVITES (*Division*).

S² | f¹ | 1, 2. General (negative and positive, alternately).
   | f² | 3-8. Particular.

1 the LORD. Heb. Jehovah. Ap. 4. II.

2 is. Heb. "he [is]".

3 priest's due = priest's custom. Cp. 1 Sam. 2. 13, 28, 29. Lev. 7. 33, 34. Num. 18. 8-14.

offer = sacrifice. See Ap. 43. I. iv.

4 wine. Heb. *tīrōsh.* Ap. 27. ii.

5 God. Heb. Elohim. Ap. 4. I.

6 a Levite: i. e. a Tribal Levite who devoted himself to the Aaronic service. Cp. Lev. 25. 33.

his mind = his soul. Heb. *nephesh.* Ap. 13.

1452 7 Then he shall minister in the name of [1]the LORD his [5]God, as all his brethren the Levites *do*, which stand there before [1]the LORD.

8 They shall have like portions to eat, beside that which cometh of the sale of his patrimony.

w C g (p. 264) 9 When thou art come into the land which [1]the LORD thy [5]God giveth thee, thou shalt not learn to do after the °abominations of those nations.

10 There shall not be found among you *any one* that maketh his son or his daughter to pass through the fire, *or* that useth divination, *or* an observer of times, °or an enchanter, or a witch,

11 Or a charmer, or a consulter with °familiar spirits, or a wizard, or a °necromancer.

h 12 For all that do these things *are* an abomination unto °the LORD: and because of these abominations [1]the LORD thy [5]God doth drive them out from before thee.

g 13 Thou shalt be °perfect with [1]the LORD thy [5]God.

h 14 For these nations, which thou shalt possess, hearkened unto observers of times, and unto diviners: but as for thee, [1]the LORD thy [5]God hath not suffered thee so *to do*.

D i 15 [1]The LORD thy [5]God °will raise up unto thee a Prophet from the midst of thee, of thy brethren, like unto me;

k unto Him ye shall °hearken;

16 According to all that thou desiredst of [1]the LORD thy [5]God in Horeb in the day of the assembly, saying, 'Let me not hear again the voice of [1]the LORD my [5]God, neither let me see this great fire any more, that I die not.'

17 And [1]the LORD °said unto me, 'They have well *spoken that* which they have spoken.

D i 18 °I will raise them up °a Prophet from among their brethren, like unto thee, and °will put My words in His mouth; and He shall speak unto them all that I shall command Him.

k 19 And it shall come to pass, *that* whosoever will not [15]hearken unto My words which He shall speak in My name, °I will require *it* of him.

C l 20 But the prophet, which shall presume to speak a word in My name, which I have not commanded him to speak, or that shall speak in the name of other gods,

m even that prophet shall die.'

l 21 And if thou say in thine heart, °'How shall we know the word which [1]the LORD hath not spoken?'

22 When a prophet speaketh in the name of [1]the LORD, if the thing follow not, nor come to pass, that *is* the thing which [1]the LORD hath not spoken, *but* the prophet hath spoken it presumptuously:

m thou shalt not be afraid of him.

v n p E **19** °When °the LORD thy °God hath cut off the nations, whose land °the LORD thy °God giveth thee, and thou °succeedest them, and dwellest in their cities, and in their houses;

F 2 Thou shalt separate °three cities for thee in the midst of thy land, which [1]the LORD thy [1]God giveth thee to possess it.

3 Thou shalt prepare thee a way, and divide

---

18. 9-22 (w, p. 255). THE PROPHET.
(*Introversion and Alternations.*)

w C g | 9-11. Command. Jehovah thy God
h | 12. Reason. Abomination
g | 13. Command. Jehovah thy God
h | 14. Reason. Hearkening
(False prophet: heathen.)

D i | 15-. "Like unto Moses"
k | -15-17. Hearken. Command (positive)
D *i* | 18. "Like unto Moses"
k | 19. Hearken. Command (negative)
(THE PROPHET.)

C l | 20-. Presumptuous prophet. Utterance
m | -20. Not to live (negative)
l | 21, 22-. Presumptuous prophet. Testimony
m | -22. Not to be feared (negative)
(False prophet: Israel.)

9 abominations. See Ap. 42.
10 or. Note the Fig. *Paradiastole*. Ap. 6.
11 familiar spirits. See note on Lev. 19. 31.
necromancer = a seeker unto the dead; a medium.
12 the LORD (Heb. Jehovah). Some codices, with Sam., Sept., and Syr., add "thy God".
13 perfect = devoted, or single-hearted.
15 will raise up. Note the transition, and the Structure above.
hearken. Cp. Matt. 17. 5. Acts 3. 22, 23.
17 said. See note on 2. 9. This was said before leaving Horeb, so that "the Prophet like unto Moses" was promised at Sinai!
18 I will raise. Cp. John 6. 14. Acts 3. 22; 7. 37.
a Prophet (Deut. 18. 18), a Priest (Ps. 110. 4), a King (Zech. 6. 13).
will put My words, &c. Cp. John 12. 48, 49, and note John 3. 34; 7. 16; 8. 28, 47; 12. 49; 14. 10, 24; 17. 8.
19 I will require it. Cp. John 12. 48, and Heb. 4. 12, where "discerner" means "able to judge" (Gr. *kritikos*). That "Word" is the "critic" (or judge), and will judge all other "critics".
21 How shall we know . . . ? Cp. Jer. 28. 9.

19. 1—25. 19 (*v*, p. 235). LAWS: CIVIL.
(*Alternation.*)

v | n | 19. 1-21. Israel.
o | 20. 1-20. The nations. War.
n | 21. 1—25. 16. Israel.
o | 25. 17-19. The nations. War.

19. 1-21 (n, above). ISRAEL.
(*Introversion.*)

n | p | 1-13. Persons. Manslayer.
q | 14. Property. Landmarks.
p | 15-21. Persons. Witnesses.

1-13 (p, above). PERSONS: MANSLAYER.
(*Extended Alternations and Introversions.*)

p | E | 1. Prospective. "When."
F | 2, 3-. Cities. Separation of three.
G | r[1] | -3. Purpose.
s[1] | 4, 5-. Case of ignorance.
s[1] | -5. Provision. Flight.
r[1] | 6, 7. Purpose.
E | 8, 9-. Prospective. "If."
F | -9. Cities. Addition of three.
G | r[2] | 10. Purpose.
s[2] | 11. Case of intention.
s[2] | 12, 13-. Provision. Death.
r[2] | -13. Purpose.

19. 1 When. Cp. Num. 35. 10, 11.
the LORD. Heb. Jehovah. Ap. 4. II.
God. Heb. Elohim. Ap. 4. I.
succeedest = dispossessest.
2 three cities. Cp. Num. 35. 14.

1452 the °coasts of thy land, which [1]the LORD thy
[1]God giveth thee to inherit, into three parts,
G r[1] (p. 264) that every slayer may flee thither.

s[1] 4 And this *is* the case of the slayer, which
shall flee thither, that he may live: Whoso
killeth his neighbour °ignorantly, whom he
hated not in time past;
5 °As when a man goeth into the wood with
his neighbour to hew wood, and his hand
fetcheth a stroke with the axe to cut down the
tree, and the °head slippeth from the °helve,
and lighteth upon his neighbour, that he die;
s[1] he shall flee unto one of those cities, and live:
r[1] 6 Lest the °avenger of the blood pursue the
slayer, while his heart is hot, and overtake
him, because the way is long, and °slay him;
whereas he *was* not worthy of death, inasmuch as he hated him not in time past.
7 Wherefore I command thee, saying, 'Thou
shalt separate three cities for thee.

E 8 And if [1]the LORD thy [1]God enlarge thy
[3]coast, °as He hath sworn unto thy fathers,
and give thee all the land which He promised
to give unto thy fathers;
9 If thou shalt keep all these commandments
to do them, which I command thee °this day,
to love [1]the LORD thy [1]God, and to walk ever
in His ways;
F then shalt thou °add three cities more for
thee, beside these three:
G r[2] 10 That innocent blood be not shed in thy
land, which [1]the LORD thy [1]God giveth thee
for an inheritance, and *so* °blood be upon thee.
s[2] 11 But if any °man °hate his neighbour, and
lie in wait for him, and rise up against him,
and °smite him mortally that he die, and
fleeth into one of these cities:
s[2] 12 Then the elders of his city shall send and
fetch him thence, and deliver him into the hand
of the [6]avenger of °blood, that he may die.
13 Thine eye shall not pity him, but thou
shalt °put away *the guilt of* innocent blood
from Israel,
r[2] that it may go well with thee.'
q 14 Thou shalt °not remove thy neighbour's
°landmark, which they of old time have set
in thine inheritance, which thou shalt inherit
in the land that [1]the LORD thy [1]God giveth
thee to possess it.
p t (p. 265) 15 °One witness shall not rise up against
a [11]man for any °iniquity, or for any °sin, in
any sin that he sinneth:
u at the mouth of two witnesses, or at the
mouth of three witnesses, shall the matter
be established.
t 16 If °a false witness rise up against [11]any man
to testify against him *that which is* wrong;
u 17 Then both the men, between whom the
controversy *is*, shall stand before [1]the LORD,
°before the priests and the judges, which
shall be in those days;
18 And the judges shall make °diligent
inquisition: and, °behold, *if* the witness *be*
a false witness, *and* hath testified falsely
against his brother;
19 Then shall ye do unto him, [8]as he had
thought to have done unto his brother: so
shalt thou [13]put the evil away from among you.
20 And those which remain shall hear, and
fear, and shall henceforth commit no more
any such °evil among you.
21 And thine °eye shall not pity; *but* °life
shall go for °life, eye for eye, tooth for tooth,
hand for hand, foot for foot.

20 When thou goest out to battle against H[1] t[1]
thine °enemies, and seest horses, and
chariots, *and* a people more than thou, be not

---

3 coasts = borders, or confines.
4 ignorantly. Cp. Ex. 21. 12.
5 As when. Fig. *Synecdoche* (of Species), Ap. 6, one example put for every kind. **head.** Heb. = iron. **helve** = handle. Heb. = wood, which may mean the handle or the tree. **6 avenger** = kinsman avenger. **slay him** = slay his soul. Heb. *nephesh* (Ap. 13), i. e. take his life. **8 as** = according as.
9 this day. See note on 4. 26.
add. Done by Joshua, ch. 20. 7, 8.
10 blood = guilt. Fig. *Metonymy* (of Cause), the blood shed put for guilt incurred.
11 man. Heb. *'ish.* Ap. 14. II. Case of presumption. **hate.** Cp. Ex. 21. 14.
smite him mortally = smite his soul. Heb. *nephesh* (Ap. 13) = take his life. Cp. *v.* 6.
12 blood = murder. Fig. *Metonymy* (of Cause), Ap. 6. Cp. *v.* 10. **13 put away, &c.** See note on 13. 5.
14 not remove. Cp. 27. 17. Hos. 5. 10. Prov. 22. 28. **landmark.** Not to be removed: but "'stumbling-blocks' to be taken out of the way". Lev. 19. 14. Isa. 57. 14. Rom. 14. 13.

15-21 (*p*, p. 264). PERSONS: WITNESSES.
(*Alternation.*)

p | t | 15-. True witness. One insufficient.
  u | -15. Direction. Two or three necessary.
  t | 16. False witness. One insufficient.
  u | 17-21. Direction (Trial, 17, 18; Penalty, 19-21).

15 One witness. Cp. 17. 6.
iniquity. See Ap. 44. iv.
sin. See Ap. 44. i.
16 a false witness. Cp. Ex. 23. 1, and Deut. 19. 16.
17 before. Some codices, with Sam., Sept., and Syr., read "even before".
18 diligent. See note on 13. 14.
behold. Fig. *Asterismos.* Ap. 6.
20 evil. See Ap. 44. viii.
21 eye. Fig. *Prosopopœia* (Ap. 6).
life = soul. Heb. *nephesh.* Ap. 13. Cp. Ex. 21. 23-25.

20. 1-20 (o, p. 264). THE NATIONS: WAR.
(*Extended and Repeated Alternation.*)

o | H[1] | t[1] | 1. War.
  u[1] | 2-8. Enemy. Proclamation.
  v[1] | 9. Action as to leaders.
H[2] | t[2] | 10-. War.
  u[2] | -10, 11. Enemy. Proclamation to city.
  v[2] | 12. Action. Siege.
H[3] | t[3] | 13-. War.
  u[3] | -13, 14. Enemy. Treatment.
  v[3] | 15. Action towards distant cities.
H[4] | t[4] | 16-. War. Canaanite nations.
  u[4] | -16, 17. Enemy. Treatment.
  v[4] | 18. Action towards them.
H[5] | t[5] | 19-. War. Any siege.
  u[5] | -19. Treatment as to trees.
  v[5] | 20. Action as to other trees.

20. 1 enemies. Heb. text has sing., but some codices, with Sam., Onk., Syr., and Vulg., read the plural, as A.V.

1452 afraid of them: for °the LORD thy °God *is* with thee, Which brought thee up out of the land of Egypt.

u[1] (p. 265) 2 And it shall be, when ye are come nigh unto the battle, that the priest shall approach and speak unto the people,

3 And shall say unto them, 'Hear, O Israel, ye approach this day unto battle against your enemies: let not your hearts °faint, fear not, and do not °tremble, neither be ye terrified because of them;

4 For [1]the LORD your [1]God *is* He that goeth with you, °to fight for you against your enemies, to save you.'

5 And the officers shall speak unto the people, saying, 'What °man *is there* that hath built a new house, and hath not dedicated it? let him go and return to his house, lest he die in the battle, and another man dedicate it.

6 And °what man *is he* that hath planted a vineyard, and hath not *yet* eaten of it? let him *also* go and return unto his house, lest he die in the battle, and another man eat of it.

7 And [6]what man *is there* that hath betrothed a wife, and hath not taken her? let him go and return unto his house, lest he die in the battle, and another man take her.'

8 And the officers shall speak further unto the people, and they shall say, [6]'What man *is there that is* fearful and fainthearted? let him go and return unto his house, lest his brethren's heart °faint as well as his heart.'

v[1] 9 And it shall be, when the officers have made an end of speaking unto the people, that they shall make captains of the armies to lead the people.

H[2] t[2] 10 When thou comest nigh unto a city to fight against it,

u[2] then °proclaim peace unto it.

11 And it shall be, if it make thee answer of peace, and open unto thee, then it shall be, *that* all the people *that is* found therein shall be tributaries unto thee, and they shall serve thee.

v[2] 12 And if it will make no peace with thee, but will make war against thee, then thou shalt besiege it:

H[3] t[3] 13 And when [1]the LORD thy [1]God hath delivered it into thine hands,

u[3] thou shalt smite every male thereof with the edge of the sword:

14 But the women, and the little ones, and the cattle, and all that is in the city, *even* all the °spoil thereof, shalt thou °take unto thyself; and thou shalt eat the spoil of thine enemies, which [1]the LORD thy [1]God hath given thee.

v[3] 15 Thus shalt thou do unto all the cities *which are* very far off from thee, which *are* not of the cities of these nations.

H[4] t[4] 16 But of the cities of these people, which

the LORD. Heb. Jehovah. Ap. 4. II.
God. Heb. Elohim. Ap. 4. I.
3 faint. This and the following three words = Fig. *Synonymia.* Ap. 6.
tremble = be excited. (Heb. = make haste.)
4 to fight for you. Cp. Ex. 14. 25, Ps. 3. 8; 35. 1.
5 man. Heb *'ish.* Ap. 14. II.
6 what. Fig. *Erotēsis.*
8 faint = melt.
10 proclaim peace: i. e. if it belong not to the Canaanites. Cp. Matt. 10. 12, 13.
14 spoil . . . take = take as a prey. These two words, "spoil" and "prey", occur in the name Maher-shalal-hash-baz. Isa. 8. 1.
16 breatheth. Heb. *n^eshāmāh* = that hath breath. See Ap. 16.
17 utterly destroy. Because descendants of the *Nephīlīm.* Ap. 25. Cp. ch. 7. 1, 2.
namely. Only six mentioned here.
as = according as.
18 That = to the intent that.
sin. Idolatry was, and still is, the great sin. Cp. Gal. 5. 20.
19 man's. Heb. *'ādām.* Ap. 14. I.

21. 1—25. 16 (*n*, p. 264). **ISRAEL.**
(*Repeated Alternation.*)

n J[1] | 21. 1—22. 8. Persons and property.
K[1] | 22. 9, 10. Sowing and ploughing.
J[2] | 22. 11—23. 23. Persons.
K[2] | 23. 24, 25. Vineyards and cornfields.
J[3] | 24. 1–18. Persons.
K[3] | 24. 19–22. Harvests.
J[4] | 25. 1–3. Persons.
K[4] | 25. 4. Threshing.
J[5] | 25. 5–16. Persons and property.

1 the LORD. Heb. Jehovah. Ap. 4.
God. Heb. Elohim. Ap. 4.
lying = fallen down.

[1]the LORD thy [1]God doth give thee *for* an inheritance,

thou shalt save alive nothing that °breatheth: u[4]

17 But thou shalt °utterly destroy them; °*namely*, the Hittites, and the Amorites, the Canaanites, and the Perizzites, the Hivites, and the Jebusites; °as [1]the LORD thy [1]God hath commanded thee:

18 °That they teach you not to do after all their abominations, which they have done unto their gods; so should ye °sin against [1]the LORD your [1]God. v[4]

19 When thou shalt besiege a city a long time, in making war against it to take it, H[5] t[5]

thou shalt not destroy the trees thereof by forcing an axe against them: for thou mayest eat of them, and thou shalt not cut them down (for the tree of the field *is* °man's *life*) to employ *them* in the siege: u[5]

20 Only the trees which thou knowest that they *be* not trees for meat, thou shalt destroy and cut them down; and thou shalt build bulwarks against the city that maketh war with thee, until it be subdued. v[5]

21 If *one* be found slain in the land which °the LORD thy °God giveth thee to possess it, °lying in the field, *and* it be not known who hath slain him: L[1] w z (p. 267)

a b c (p. 267) 1452 2 Then thy elders and thy judges shall come forth, and they shall measure unto the cities which *are* round about him that is slain:

d 3 And it shall be, *that* the city *which is* next unto the slain man,

e even the elders of that city shall take an heifer, which hath not been wrought with, *and* which hath not drawn in the yoke;
4 And the elders of that city shall bring down the heifer unto a °rough valley, which is neither °eared nor sown, and shall °strike off the heifer's neck there in the valley:

a b c 5 And °the priests the sons of Levi shall come near; for them [1]the LORD thy [1]God hath chosen to minister unto Him, and to bless in the name of [1]the LORD; and by their °word shall every controversy and every °stroke be °*tried:*

d 6 And all the elders of that city, *that are* next unto the slain *man*, shall wash their hands over the heifer that is beheaded in the valley:

e 7 And they shall answer and say, 'Our hands have not shed this blood, neither have our eyes seen *it*.
8 °Be merciful, O [1]LORD, unto Thy people Israel, whom Thou hast redeemed, and lay not °innocent blood unto Thy people of Israel's charge.' And the blood °shall be forgiven them.

z 9 So shalt thou °put away the °*guilt of* [8]innocent blood from among you, when thou shalt do *that which is* right in the sight of [1]the LORD.

L[1] x y[1] 10 When thou goest forth to war against thine enemies, and [1]the LORD thy [1]God hath delivered them into thine °hands, and thou hast taken them captive,
11 And seest among the captives a beautiful woman, and hast a desire unto her, that thou wouldest have her to thy wife;
12 Then thou shalt bring her home to thine house; and she shall shave her head, and pare her nails;
13 And she shall put the °raiment of her captivity from off her, and shall remain in thine house, and bewail her father and her mother °a full month: and after that thou shalt go in unto her, and be her °husband, and she shall be thy wife.
14 And it shall be, if thou have no delight in her, then thou shalt let her go °whither she will; but thou shalt not sell her at all for money, thou shalt not °make merchandise of her, because thou hast humbled her.

y[2] f 15 °If a °man have two wives, one beloved, and another hated, and they have born him children, *both* the beloved and the hated; and *if* the firstborn son be hers that was hated:

g 16 Then it shall be, °when he maketh his sons to inherit *that* which he hath,

f *that* he may not make the son of the beloved firstborn before the son of the hated, *which is indeed* the firstborn:
17 But he shall acknowledge the son of the hated *for* the firstborn,

g by giving him a double portion of all that he

21. 1—22. 8 (J[1], p. 266). PERSONS AND PROPERTY (*Division*).

J[1] | L[1] | 21. 1-23. Persons.
| L[2] | 22. 1-8-. Property.

21. 1-23 (L[1], above). PERSONS. (*Introversion and Enumeration.*)

L[1] | w | 1-9. Crime. Dead body found slain.
| x | y[1] | 10-14. Captives.
| | y[2] | 15-17. Two wives. } Living Persons.
| | y[3] | 18-21. Rebellious son.
| *w* | 22, 23. Crime. Dead body, hanged.

1-9 (w, above). CRIME. DEAD BODY FOUND SLAIN (*Introversion, and Alternations*).

w | z | 1. The guilt incurred.
a | b | c | 2. Elders and Judges.
| | d | 3-. City next to crime.
| | e | -3, 4. Elders of that city.
a | *b* | *c* | 5. Priests, the sons of Levi.
| | *d* | 6. City next to crime.
| | *e* | 7, 8. Elders of that city.
z | 9. The guilt put away.

4 rough valley = ravine, or rough gully.
eared = ploughed. Old English idiom.
strike off = behead, or break the neck.
5 the priests the sons of Levi. See note on 17. 9.
word. Heb. mouth. Put by Fig. *Metonymy* (of Cause), Ap. 6, for what is uttered by it.
stroke = punishment. Fig. *Synecdoche* (of Species), Ap. 6. Cp. 17. 8.
tried. Better to supply "settled", or "decided".
8 Be merciful = Be propitious, or make expiation or atonement.
innocent blood. Put by Fig. *Synecdoche* (of Species), for the guilt which shed it. See Ap. 6.
shall be = shall assuredly be.
9 put away, &c. See note on 13. 5.
guilt of innocent blood = blood-guiltiness, blood being put for guilt. See note on *v.* 8.
10 hands. Heb. text reads "hand"; but some codices, with Jon., Sept., and Syr., read "hands", as A.V.
13 raiment of her captivity = mantle in which she was taken captive. "Of" = Genitive of relation (see Ap. 17).
a full month. Heb. = a moon of days.
husband. Heb. Baal, or lord. Cp. first occurrence of verb, Gen. 20. 3.
14 whither she will = according to her soul. Heb. *nephesh.* See Ap. 13.
make merchandise. Heb. *'āmar.* In this sense, only here and 24. 7.

15-17 (y[2], above). TWO WIVES. (*Alternation.*)

y[2] | f | 15. Firstborn } Case.
| g | 16-. Inheritance }
| *f* | -16, 17-. Firstborn } Prohibition.
| *g* | -17. Inheritance }

15 If. Cp. 1 Sam. 1. 2. 2 Chron. 24. 3.
man. Heb. *'ish.* See Ap. 14. II.
16 when. Heb. in the day. See Ap. 18.

1452 hath: for °he *is* the beginning of his °strength;
the right of the firstborn *is* °his.

y³ h (p. 268) 18 If a man have a °stubborn and °rebellious
son, which will not obey the voice of his
father, or the voice of his mother, and *that*,
when they have chastened him, will not
hearken unto them:

i 19 Then shall his father and his mother
lay hold on him, and bring him out unto the
elders of his city, and unto °the gate of his
place;
20 And they shall say unto the elders of
his city, 'This our son *is* [18]stubborn and
[18]rebellious, he will not obey our voice;
he is a °glutton, and a drunkard.'

i 21 And all the °men of his city shall stone
him with stones, that he die:

h so shalt thou [9]put evil away from among you;
and all Israel shall hear, and fear.

w (p. 267) 22 And if [15]a man have committed a sin
worthy of death, and he be to be put to death,
and thou °hang him on °a tree:
23 His body shall not remain all night upon
the tree, but thou shalt in any wise bury him
that day; (for he that is hanged *is* °accursed
of [1]God;) that thy °land be not defiled, which
[1]the LORD thy [1]God giveth thee *for* an inheritance.

L² k (p. 268) **22** Thou shalt °not see thy brother's ox
or his sheep go astray, and hide thyself
from them: thou shalt in any case bring
them again unto thy brother.
2 And if thy brother *be* not nigh unto thee,
or if thou know him not, then thou shalt bring
it unto thine own house, and it shall be with
thee until thy brother seek after it, and thou
shalt restore it to him again.
3 In like manner shalt thou do with his ass;
and so shalt thou do with his raiment; and
with all lost thing of thy brother's, which he
hath lost, and thou hast found, shalt thou do
likewise: thou mayest not hide thyself.
4 Thou shalt [1]not see thy brother's ass or
his ox fall down by the way, and hide thyself
from them: thou shalt surely °help him to
lift *them* up again.

l 5 The woman shall not wear °that which
pertaineth unto a °man, neither shall a man
put on a °woman's garment: for all that do
so *are* abomination unto °the LORD thy °God.

k 6 If a bird's nest chance to be before thee in
the way in any tree, or on the ground, *whether
they be* young ones, or eggs, and the dam
sitting upon the young, or upon the eggs,
thou shalt not take the dam with the °young:
7 *But* thou shalt in any wise let the dam go,
and take the young to thee; that it may be
well with thee, and *that* thou mayest prolong
thy days.

l 8 When thou buildest a new house, then
thou shalt make a °battlement for thy roof,
that thou bring not blood upon thine house,
if any man fall from thence.

K¹ (p. 266) 9 Thou shalt not sow thy vineyard with
°divers seeds: lest the fruit of thy seed which
thou hast sown, and the fruit of thy vineyard,
be defiled.
10 Thou shalt not plow with an °ox and an
ass together.

J² m¹ (p. 268) 11 Thou shalt not wear a garment of [9]divers
sorts, *as* of °woollen and linen together.
12 Thou shalt make thee °fringes upon the
four °quarters of thy vesture, wherewith thou
coverest *thyself*.

17 he. Cp Gen. 49. 3.
strength. Heb. *'ōvōn.* *Homonym* = strength, here and Gen. 49. 3 and Job 31. 25 (A.V. "wealth"); but = suffering, &c., in Gen. 35. 18 (marg.). Deut. 26. 14, and Hos. 9. 4.
his. Some codices, with Sam., Onk., Sept., Syr., and Vulg., read "his therefore".

21. 18-21 (y³, p. 267). **REBELLIOUS SON.**
(*Introversion.*)

y³ | h | 18. Evil case.
  i | 19, 20. Prosecution.
  i | 21-. Penalty.
 h | -21. Evil put away.

18 stubborn = rebellious.
rebellious = refractory.
19 the gate: i. e. the place of judgment.
20 glutton, &c. Cp. Matt. 11. 19.
21 men. Heb. pl. of *'īsh*, or *'enōsh.* Ap. 14.
22 hang = hang up: i. e. after putting to death, not to put to death by hanging.
a tree = timber: i. e. a wooden stake. Cp. Josh. 8. 29; 10. 26, 27. Gal. 3. 13.
23 accursed = a curse. Cp. Num. 25. 4. 2 Sam. 21. 6.
land = soil. Heb. *'ădāmāh.*

22. 1-8 (L², p. 267). **PROPERTY.**
(*Alternation.*)

L² | k | 1-4. Lost. (Animals, astray.)
  l | 5. Dress.
 k | 6, 7. Found. (Birds.)
  l | 8. Dwellings.

1 not see. Cp. Ex. 23. 4, 5.
4 help. See note on Ex. 23. 5.
5 that which: i.e. any article of ornament or apparel.
man = *geber.* See Ap. 14. III.
woman's garment. Generally red, and eschewed by men.
the LORD. Heb. Jehovah. Ap. 4. II.
God. Heb. Elohim. Ap. 4. I.
6 young. A special various reading called *Sevīr* (Ap. 34) reads "their laying nest": i. e. before all the eggs are laid.
8 battlement: i. e. a low wall about three feet high running round the flat roof.
9 divers = two kinds. Cp. Lev. 19. 19.
10 ox and an ass. One clean, the other unclean; one tall, the other short, therefore cruel under the same yoke.

22. 11—23. 25 (J², p. 267). **PERSONS.**
(*Repeated Alternation.*)

J² | m¹ | 22. 11, 12. Men.
  n¹ | 22. 13-30. Women.
 m² | 23. 1-16. Men.
  n² | 23. 17, 18. Women.
 m³ | 23. 19-23. Men.

11 woollen and linen. One animal, the other vegetable. Linen used of Divine righteousness (Rev. 19. 8), and not to be mixed with animal or fleshly labour.
12 fringes = twisted cords. In Matt. 23. 5 the Greek is *craspeda*, because hanging like locks of hair. Not the same as Num. 15. 38, which was ordained to distinguish Israel from the nations.
quarters. Heb. "wings".

n[1] o[1] 13 If any °man take a wife, and go in unto
(p. 269) her, and hate her,
1452 14 And give occasions of speech against her, and bring up an evil name upon her, and say, 'I took this woman, and when I came to her, I found her not a maid:'

15 Then shall the father of the damsel, and her mother, take and bring forth *the tokens of* the damsel's °virginity unto the elders of the city in the gate:

16 And the damsel's father shall say unto the elders, 'I gave my daughter unto this man to wife, and he hateth her;

17 And, °lo, he hath given occasions of speech °*against her*, saying, 'I found not thy daughter a maid;' and yet these *are the tokens of* my daughter's [15]virginity.' And they shall spread the cloth before the elders of the city.

18 And the elders of that city shall take that man and chastise him;

19 And they shall °amerce him in an hundred *shekels* of silver, and give *them* unto the father of the damsel, because he hath brought up an evil name upon a virgin of Israel: and she shall be his wife; he may not put her away all his days.

20 But if this thing be true, *and the tokens of* [15]virginity be not found for the damsel:

21 Then they shall bring out the damsel to the °door of her father's house, and the °men of her city shall stone her with stones that she die: because she hath wrought folly in Israel, to play the whore in her father's house: so shalt thou °put evil away from among you.

o[2] 22 If a man be found lying with a woman married to an husband, then they shall both of them die, *both* the man that lay with the woman, and the woman: so shalt thou [21]put away evil from Israel.

23 If a damsel *that is* a virgin be °betrothed unto an husband, and a man find her in the city, and lie with her;

24 Then ye shall bring them both out unto the gate of that city, and ye shall stone them with stones that they die; the damsel, because she cried not, *being* in the city; and the man, because he hath humbled his neighbour's °wife: so thou shalt [21]put away evil from among you.

25 But if a [13]man find a betrothed damsel in the field, and the man force her, and lie with her: then the man only that lay with her shall die:

26 But unto the damsel thou shalt do nothing; *there is* in the damsel no sin *worthy* of death: for °as when a man riseth against his neighbour, and slayeth °him, even so *is* this matter:

27 For he found her in the field, *and* the betrothed damsel cried, and *there was* none to save her.

28 If a [13]man find a damsel *that is* a virgin, which is not betrothed, and lay hold on her, and lie with her, and they be found;

29 Then the [25]man that lay with her shall give unto the damsel's father fifty *shekels* of silver, and she shall be his wife; because he hath humbled her, he may not put her away all his days.

22. 13-30 (n[1], p. 268). WOMEN. (*Division.*)

n[1] | o[1] | 13-21. Wives.
  | o[2] | 22-30. Violations.

13 man. Heb. *'îsh.* Ap. 14. II.

15 virginity. The Fig. *Metonymy* (of Subject), Ap. 6, explained by these words, "the tokens of".

17 lo. Fig. *Asterismos.* Ap. 6.

against her. These words are not in Heb. text, but are contained in some codices, with Sam., Sept., Syr., and Vulg.

19 amerce him=fine him. Old English.

21 door=entrance.

men. Heb. pl. of *'îsh*, or *'enôsh.* Ap. 14.

put evil away. See note on 13. 5.

23 betrothed. This, taken with "wife" (*v.* 24) explains Matt. 1. 19, 20.

24 wife. See note on *v.* 23, above.

26 as=according as.

him=his soul. Heb. *nephesh* (Ap. 13).

30 skirt. Put by Fig. *Euphemy* (Ap. 6), for nakedness. Cp. Lev. 18. 7, 8; 20. 11.

23. 1-16 (m[2], p. 246). MEN. (*Enumeration.*)

m[2] | p[1] | 1-8. Congregation (exclusions).
  | p[2] | 9-14. Camp (cleanness).
  | p[3] | 15, 16. Home (slave).

1 congregation=assembly.

the LORD=Heb. Jehovah. Ap. 4. II.

3 Moabite. Heb. masc. Therefore not excluding Ruth the Moabitess. Matt. 1. 5. Cp. Ruth 1. 14-16.

4 they hired. Cp. Num. 22. 5. Jude 11. Neh. 13. 1, 2.

Mesopotamia. Heb.=Aram-Naharaim, i. e. "Syria of the two rivers".

5 God. Heb. Elohim. Ap. 4. I.

7 Thou. Some codices, with Sam., Onk., Syr., Vulg., read "But thou".

thy brother. The posterity of Esau. Gen. 25. 25-30. Obad. 10, 12. Num. 20. 14.

30 A [25]man shall not take his father's wife, nor discover his father's °skirt.

23 He that is wounded in the stones, or hath his privy member cut off, shall not enter into the °congregation of °the LORD. m[2] p[1]

2 A bastard shall not enter into the congregation of [1]the LORD; even to his tenth generation shall he not enter into the [1]congregation of [1]the LORD.

3 An Ammonite or °Moabite shall not enter into the congregation of [1]the LORD; even to their tenth generation shall they not enter into the [1]congregation of [1]the LORD for ever:

4 Because they met you not with bread and with water in the way, when ye came forth out of Egypt; and because °they hired against thee Balaam the son of Beor of Pethor of °Mesopotamia, to curse thee.

5 Nevertheless [1]the LORD thy °God would not hearken unto Balaam; but [1]the LORD thy °God turned the curse into a blessing unto thee, because [1]the LORD thy °God loved thee.

6 Thou shalt not seek their peace nor their prosperity all thy days for ever.

7 °Thou shalt not abhor an Edomite; for he *is* °thy brother: thou shalt not abhor an Egyptian; because thou wast a stranger in his land.

8 The children that are begotten of them

1452 °shall enter into the [1]congregation of [1]the LORD in their third generation.

p² (p. 269) 9 When the host goeth forth against thine enemies, then keep thee from every wicked thing.

10 If there be among you any °man, that is not clean by reason of uncleanness that chanceth him by night, then shall he go abroad out of the camp, he shall not come within the camp:

11 But it shall be, when evening cometh on, he shall °wash *himself* with water: and when the sun is down, he shall come into the camp *again*.

12 Thou shalt have a place also without the camp, whither thou shalt go forth abroad:

13 And thou shalt have a °paddle upon thy °weapon; and it shall be, when thou °wilt ease thyself abroad, thou shalt dig therewith, and shalt turn back and cover that which cometh from thee:

14 For [1]the LORD thy [5]God °walketh in the midst of thy camp, to deliver thee, and to give up thine enemies before thee; therefore shall thy °camp be °holy: that He see no unclean thing in thee, and turn away from thee.

p³ 15 Thou shalt not deliver unto his master the servant which is escaped from his master unto thee:

16 He shall dwell with thee, *even* among you, in that place which he shall choose in one of thy gates, where it liketh him best: thou shalt not oppress him.

n² a (p. 270) 17 There shall be no °whore of the daughters of Israel,

b nor a °sodomite of the sons of Israel.

a 18 Thou shalt not bring the hire of a °whore,

b or the price of a °dog, into the house of [1]the LORD thy [5]God for any vow: for even both these *are* abomination unto [1]the LORD thy [5]God.

m³ q¹ 19 Thou shalt not lend upon °usury to thy brother; usury of money, usury of victuals, usury of any thing that is lent upon usury:

20 Unto a stranger thou mayest lend upon usury; but unto thy brother thou shalt not lend upon usury: that [1]the LORD thy [5]God may bless thee in all that thou settest thine hand to in the land whither thou goest to possess it.

q² 21 When thou shalt °vow a vow unto [1]the LORD thy [5]God, thou shalt not slack to pay it: for [1]the LORD thy [5]God will surely require it of thee; and it would be °sin in thee.

22 But if thou shalt forbear to vow, it shall be no [21]sin in thee.

23 That which is gone out of thy lips thou shalt keep and perform; *even* a freewill offering, according as thou hast vowed unto [1]the LORD thy [5]God, which thou hast promised with thy mouth.

K² r s 24 When thou comest into thy neighbour's vineyard,

t then thou mayest eat grapes thy fill °at thine own pleasure;

u but thou shalt not put *any* in thy vessel.

25 When thou comest into the °standing corn of thy neighbour, *r s*

then thou mayest pluck the ears with thine hand; *t*

but thou shalt not move a sickle unto thy neighbour's standing corn. *u*

24 When a °man hath taken a wife, and married her, and it come to pass that she find no favour in his eyes, because he hath found some uncleanness in her: then let him °write her a bill of divorcement, and give *it* in her hand, and send her out of his house. J³ M¹ v¹ (p. 271)

---

8 shall enter into the congregation, &c. The Massorah (Ap. 30) quotes the Babylonian Codex, which reads "shall enter unto you in the assembly of Jehovah", by reading *lākem*, "unto you," instead of the second *lākem* which the R.V. ignores, and the A.V. paraphrases. The present Heb. text reads "shall enter unto them", which can only mean unto the Edomite and Egyptian, which is incongruous. The reading of the Babylonian Codex makes all clear.

9 wicked. See Ap 44 viii

10 man. Heb. *'īsh.* Ap. 14. II.

11 wash himself with water. See note on Lev. 14. 9.

13 paddle = blade. **weapon** = staff.

wilt ease. Heb. sit down. Beautiful *Euphemy* (Ap. 6), when dealing with physical uncleanness, but plain speaking when dealing with moral uncleanness.

14 walketh. Fig. *Anthropopatheia.* Ap. 6. Cp. Gen. 3. 8. Lev. 26. 12.

camp. Some codices, with Sam., Sept., Syr., and Vulg., read "camps".

holy = separated. See note on Ex. 3. 5.

23. 17, 18 (n², p. 268). WOMEN.

n² | a | 17–. Whore (*Kᵉdēshāh*).
  b | –17. Sodomite.
  a | 18–. Whore (*Zōnah*).
  b | –18. Dog.

17 whore = sodomitess. Heb. means one consecrated as such in connection with heathen worship. Hence her name *ḳᵉdēshāh*, a separated one. Cp. 1 Kings 14. 24; 15. 12; 22. 46. Job 36. 14 ("unclean" = temple women). Hos. 4. 14. The Laws of Khammurabi refer to these (§§ 181, 187, 192).

sodomite. First occurrence. See above note.

18 whore = a prostitute. Heb. *zōnah*, different from *v.* 17.

dog. Heb. *keleb*; but here, probably = *priest* (of the above orgies), same as Arabic *kaleb.*

19-23 (m³, p. 268). MEN (*Division*).

m³ | q¹ | 19, 20. Usury.
  q² | 21-23. Vows.

19 usury. Cp. Ex. 22. 25. Lev. 25. 35-37.

21 vow a vow. Fig. *Polyptōton* (Ap. 6) = make a solemn vow. Cp. Num. 30. 2.

sin. See Ap 44. i.

23. 24, 25 (K², p. 266). VINEYARDS AND CORNFIELDS (*Extended Alternation*).

K² | r | s | 24–. Vineyard
    t | –24–. Permission } Vineyard.
    u | –24. Prohibition
  r | *s* | 25–. Cornfields
    t | –25–. Permission } Cornfields.
    u | –25. Prohibition

24 at thine own pleasure = as thy soul [desireth]. Heb. *nephesh.* Ap. 13.

25 standing corn. Cp. Matt. 12. 1.

24. 1 man. Heb. *'īsh.* Ap. 14. II. Cp. Matt. 5. 31; 19. 7, 8.

write. See note on Ex. 17. 14 and Ap. 47. Cp. Matt. 5. 31.

1452 2 And when she is departed out of his house, she may go and be another man's *wife*.

3 And *if* the latter husband hate her, and write her a bill of divorcement, and giveth *it* in her hand, and sendeth her out of his house; or if the latter husband die, which took her *to be* his wife;

4 Her former husband, which sent her away, °may not take her again to be his wife, after that she is defiled; for that *is* abomination before °the LORD: and thou shalt not cause the land to °sin, which °the LORD thy °God giveth thee *for* an inheritance.

w[1] (p. 271) 5 °When a man hath taken a new wife, he shall not go out to war, neither shall he be charged with any business: *but* he shall be free at home one year, and shall cheer up his wife which he hath taken.

x[1] 6 No man shall take the nether or the upper °millstone to °pledge: for he taketh *a man's* °life to °pledge.

M[2] v[2] 7 If a [1]man be found stealing °any of his brethren of the children of Israel, and maketh merchandise of °him, or selleth him; then that thief shall die; and thou shalt °put evil away from among you.

w[2] 8 Take heed in the plague of leprosy, that thou observe diligently, and do according to all that the priests the Levites shall teach you: °as I commanded them, *so* ye shall observe to do.

9 Remember what [4]the LORD thy [4]God did unto °Miriam by the way, after that ye were come forth out of Egypt.

x[2] 10 When thou dost °lend thy °brother any thing, thou shalt not go into his house to fetch his °pledge.

11 Thou shalt stand abroad, and the man to whom thou dost lend shall bring out the [10]pledge abroad unto thee.

12 And if the man *be* poor, thou shalt not sleep with his [10]pledge:

13 In any case thou shalt deliver him the [10]pledge again when the sun goeth down, that he may sleep in his own °raiment, and bless thee: and it shall be righteousness unto thee before [4]the LORD thy [4]God.

M[3] v[3] 14 Thou shalt not °oppress an hired servant *that is* poor and needy, *whether he be* of thy brethren, or of thy strangers that *are* in thy land within thy gates:

15 At his day thou shalt give *him* his hire, neither shall °the sun go down upon it; for he *is* poor, °and setteth °his heart upon it: lest he cry against thee unto [4]the LORD, and it be [4]sin unto thee.

w[3] 16 The fathers shall not be put to death °for the children, neither shall the children be put to death for the fathers: every man shall be put to death for his own [4]sin.

x[3] 17 Thou shalt not pervert the judgment of the stranger, *nor* of the °fatherless; nor take a widow's raiment to °pledge:

18 But thou shalt remember that thou wast a bondman °in Egypt, and [4]the LORD thy [4]God redeemed thee thence: therefore I command thee to do this thing.

24. 1-18 (J[3], p. 244). PERSONS.
(*Extended and Repeated Alternations.*)

J[3] | M[1] | v[1] | 1-4. Divorce.
w[1] | 5. Remarriage.
x[1] | 6. Pledge.
M[2] | v[2] | 7. Slavery.
w[2] | 8, 9. Leprosy.
x[2] | 10-13. Pledge.
M[3] | v[3] | 14, 15. Service.
w[3] | 16. Punishments.
x[3] | 17, 18. Pledge.

4 may not take her again. Cp. Jer. 3. 1. Isa. 50. 1.
sin. See Ap. 44. i.
the LORD. Heb. Jehovah. Ap. 4. II.
God. Heb. Elohim. Ap. 4. I.
5 When, &c. Cp. 20. 7.
6 millstone. Hand-mills found in every house. Corn ground daily.
pledge. Heb. *kabal* = something tied up with a cord, hence the term bond (= bound); cp. Ex. 22. 26: transferred to the person so bound. Cp. *v.* 10-13.
life = soul. Heb. *nephesh.* Ap. 13.
7 any = a soul. Heb. *nephesh.* Ap. 13. Cp. Ex. 21. 16.
him. A special various reading called *Sevīr* (Ap. 34), reads "her", fem. to agree with *nephesh*; or else a female in contrast with the "him" in next sentence.
put evil away. See note on 13. 5.
8 as = according as. But a special various reading called *Sevīr* (Ap. 34) reads "which", or "for that".
9 Miriam. Cp. Num. 12. 10.
10 lend. Cp. Ex. 22. 25-27.
brother = neighbour.
pledge. Heb. *'ăbōṭ.* = a security. Not the same word in *vv.* 10, 11, 12, 13 as in *vv.* 6 and 17.
13 raiment = the mantle given to this day; not only for debt, but as a token that a business promise will be kept.
14 oppress = defraud. Cp. Lev. 19. 13.
15 the sun go down. Cp. Jas. 5. 4.
and setteth = and he lifteth up.
his heart = his soul. Heb. *nephesh.* Ap. 13.
16 for the children. This is Jehovah's law for man. His own right of judgment remains. Cp. 2 Kings 14. 6. 2 Chron. 25. 4.
17 fatherless. Some codices, with Jon. and Sept., read "or the widow".
pledge. Not Heb. *'ăbōṭ* as *v.* 10-13, but *kabal*, as in *v.* 6.
18 in Egypt. Some codices, with one early printed edition, Onk., and Sept., read "in the land of Egypt", as in *v.* 22.

19-22 (K[3], p. 244). HARVESTS.
(*Extended and Repeated Alternations.*)

K[3] | N[1] | y[1] | 19-. Harvest. Wheat.
z[1] | -19-. Prohibition.
a[1] | -19. Reason.
N[2] | y[2] | 20-. Harvest. Olives.
z[2] | -20-. Prohibition.
a[2] | -20. Reason.
N[3] | y[3] | 21-. Harvest. Grapes.
z[3] | -21-. Prohibition.
a[3] | -21. Reason.

19 harvest, put for "corn" by Fig. *Metonymy* (of Adjunct). See Ap. 6.
stranger . . . fatherless . . . widow. Not the tramp, or ne'er-do-well, or the drunkard. And in kind, not money.

19 When thou cuttest down thine °harvest in thy field, and hast forgot a sheaf in the field, K[3] N[1] y[1]
thou shalt not go again to fetch it: it shall be for the °stranger, for the °fatherless, and for the °widow: z[1]
that [4]the LORD thy [4]God may bless thee in all the work of thine hands. a[1]

y^2 (p. 271) 1452 20 When thou beatest thine olive tree,
z^2 thou shalt not go over the boughs again:
a^2 it shall be for the [19]stranger, for the fatherless, and for the widow.
y^3 21 When thou gatherest the grapes of thy vineyard,
z^3 thou shalt not glean *it* afterward:
a^3 it shall be for the [19]stranger, for the fatherless, and for the widow.
22 And thou shalt remember that thou wast a bondman in the land of Egypt: therefore I command thee to do this thing.

J^4 (p. 266) **25** If there be a controversy between °men, and they come unto judgment, that *the judges* may judge them; then they °shall justify the righteous, and condemn the °wicked.
2 And it shall be, if the wicked man *be* worthy to be beaten, that the judge shall cause him to lie down, and to be beaten before his face, according to his fault, by a certain number.
3 °Forty stripes he may give him, *and* not exceed: lest, *if* he should exceed, and beat him above these with many stripes, then thy brother should seem °vile unto thee.
K^4 4 Thou shalt °not muzzle the ox when he treadeth out *the corn*.
b O^1 d^1 (p. 272) 5 °If brethren dwell together, and one of them die, and have no child,
e^1 the wife of the dead shall not marry without unto a °stranger: her husband's brother shall go in unto her, and take her to him to wife, and perform the duty of an husband's brother unto her.
f^1 6 And it shall be, *that* the firstborn which she beareth shall succeed in the name of his brother *which is* dead, that his name be not °put out of Israel.
O^2 d^2 7 And if the °man like not to take his brother's wife,
e^2 then let his brother's wife go up to the gate unto the elders, and say, 'My husband's brother refuseth to raise up unto his brother a name in Israel, he will not perform the duty of my husband's brother.'
f^2 8 Then the elders of his city shall call him, and speak unto him:
O^3 d^3 and *if* he stand *to it*, and say, 'I like not to take her;'
e^3 9 Then shall his brother's wife come unto him °in the presence of the elders, and °loose his °shoe from off his foot, and spit in his face, and shall answer and say, 'So shall it be done unto that man that will not build up his brother's house.'
f^3 10 And his name shall be called in Israel, The house of him that hath his shoe loosed.
c 11 When [1]men strive together one with another, and the wife of the one draweth near for to deliver her husband out of the hand of him that smiteth him, and putteth forth her hand, and taketh him by the secrets:
12 Then thou shalt cut off her hand, thine eye shall not pity *her*.
13 Thou shalt not have in thy bag °divers weights, a great and a small. *b*
14 Thou shalt not have in thine house °divers measures, a great and a small.
15 *But* thou shalt have a perfect and just weight, a perfect and just measure shalt thou have: that thy days may be lengthened °in the land which °the LORD thy [15]God giveth thee.
16 For all that do such things, *and* all that do unrighteously, *are* an abomination unto [15]the LORD thy God.
17 °Remember what °Amalek did unto thee by the way, when ye were come forth out of Egypt; o (p. 264)
18 How he met thee by the way, and smote the hindmost of thee, *even* all *that were* feeble behind thee, when thou *wast* faint and weary; and he feared not [15]God.

25. 1-3 (J^4, see p. 266). PERSONS.

1 men. Heb. pl. of *'ish*, or *'enōsh*. Ap. 14.
shall justify. Cp. 16. 18; 17. 8. Ex. 23. 7. Prov. 17. 15.
wicked. Heb. *rāsh'a*. See Ap. 44. x.
3 Forty stripes. To ensure obedience to this law, tradition made the stripes 39, and gave three strokes with a thong of thirteen cords. Cp. 2 Cor. 11. 24.
vile = mean, or lightly esteemed.

4 (K^4, p. 266). THRESHING.

4 not muzzle. Animals generally muzzled in the East. Cp. 1 Cor. 9. 9. 1 Tim. 5. 18.

5-16 (J^5, p. 266). PERSONS AND PROPERTY. (*Introversion*.)

J^5 | b | 5-10. Injustice *re* Seed.
  c | 11, 12. Unfairness *re* Striving.
| *b* | 13-16. Injustice *re* Dealing.

5-10 (b, above). INJUSTICE *re* SEED. (*Repeated and Extended Alternation*.)

b O^1 | d^1 | 5-. Case. Refusal.
  e^1 | -5. Command.
    f^1 | 6. Result. Succession.
O^2 | d^2 | 7-. Case. Refusal.
  e^2 | -7. Declaration.
    f^2 | 8-. Result. Remonstrance.
O^3 | d^3 | -8. Case. Persistence.
  e^3 | 9. Action.
    f^3 | 10. Result. Stigma.

5 If brethren, &c. Cp. Gen. 38. 8. Ruth 4. 5, &c. Matt. 22. 24. Mark 12. 19. Luke 20. 28.
stranger = foreigner.
6 put out = blotted out.
7 man. Heb. *'ish*. Ap. 14. II. Cp. Ruth 3. 12, 13; 4. 5, 6.
9 in the presence, &c. Ruth 4. 11.
loose his shoe. Cp. Ruth 4. 7, 8.
shoe = sandal.
13 divers weights. Heb. a stone and a stone. Put by Fig. *Metonymy* (of Cause), for any weight. Ap. 6.
14 divers measures. Heb. an ephah and an ephah. Cp. Lev. 19. 35, 36. Prov. 11. 1; 20. 10. See Ap. 51. III. 3.
15 in the land = on the soil or ground.
the LORD. Heb. Jehovah. Ap. 4.
God. Heb. Elohim. Ap. 4.
17 Remember. Cp. Ex. 17. 8-16. An event ordered to be written down.
Amalek. Name of a man, put for his posterity, by Fig. *Metonymy* (of Adjunct), Ap. 6.

1452 19 Therefore it shall be, when [15]the LORD
thy [15]God hath given thee rest from all thine
enemies round about, in the land which [15]the
LORD thy [15]God giveth thee *for* an inheritance
to possess it, *that* thou shalt °blot out the °re-
membrance of °Amalek from under heaven;
thou shalt not forget *it*.

P[1] Q g (p. 273) **26** And it shall be, when thou *art* come
in unto the °land which °the LORD °thy
God giveth thee *for* an inheritance, and
possessest it, and dwellest therein;
h 2 That thou shalt take of the first of all the
fruit of the °earth, which thou shalt bring of
thy land that [1]the LORD thy [1]God giveth thee,
and shalt put *it* in a °basket, and shalt go unto
the place which [1]the LORD thy [1]God shall
choose °to place His name there.
3 And thou shalt go unto the priest that shall
be in those days, and say unto him, 'I °profess
°this day unto [1]the LORD thy [1]God, that I am
come unto the country which [1]the LORD sware
unto our fathers for to give us.'
4 And the priest shall take the [2]basket out of
thine hand, and set it down before the altar
of [1]the LORD thy [1]God.
5 And thou shalt °speak and say before [1]the
LORD thy [1]God,
R i 'A °Syrian °ready to perish *was* my father,
and he went down into Egypt, and sojourned
there with a few, and became there a nation,
great, °mighty, and populous:
k 6 And the Egyptians evil entreated us, and
afflicted us, and laid upon us hard bondage:
l 7 And when °we cried unto [1]the LORD [1]God
of our fathers,
l [1]the LORD heard our voice, and looked on our
affliction, and our labour, and our oppression:
k 8 And [1]the LORD brought us forth out of
Egypt with a mighty hand, and with an outstretched arm, and with great terribleness,
and with signs, and with wonders:
i 9 And He hath brought us into this place,
and hath given us this land, *even* a land that
floweth with milk and honey.
h 10 And now, °behold, I have brought the
firstfruits of the °land, which Thou, O [1]LORD,
hast given me.' And thou shalt set it before
[1]the LORD thy [1]God, and worship before [1]the
LORD thy [1]God:
g 11 And thou shalt rejoice in every good *thing*
which [1]the LORD thy [1]God hath given unto
thee, and unto thine house, thou, and the
Levite, and the stranger that *is* among you.
P[2] m 12 When thou hast made an end of °tithing
all the tithes of thine increase the third year
which is the year of tithing,
n and hast given *it* unto the Levite, the stranger,
the fatherless, and the widow, that they may
eat within thy gates, and be filled;
13 Then thou shalt say before [1]the LORD
thy [1]God, 'I have brought away the °hallowed
things out of *mine* house, and also have given
them unto the Levite, and unto the stranger,
to the fatherless, and to the widow, according
to all Thy commandments which Thou hast
commanded me: I have not °transgressed Thy
commandments, neither have I forgotten *them*:
14 I have not eaten thereof in my °mourning, *n*
neither have I taken away *ought* thereof for
any unclean *use*, nor given *ought* thereof °for
the dead: *but* I have hearkened to the voice
of [1]the LORD my [1]God, *and* have done according to all that Thou hast commanded me.
15 Look down from Thy °holy habitation, *m*
from heaven, and bless Thy people Israel, and

19 blot out. Fulfilled in the time of Esther in 462 B.C. See Ap. 50. vii. 5.
remembrance. Heb. *zekar*, not *zākar*, males; as Joab seems to have understood it in 1 Kings 11. 15, 16.
Amalek. Cp. 1 Sam. 15. 2, 3. Num. 24. 20.

26. 1-15 (S[3], p. 255). LAWS: ECCLESIASTICAL. (*Division.*)

S[3] | P[1] | 1-11. Basket of firstfruits.
| P[2] | 12-15. Tithes.

1-11 (P[1], above). BASKET OF FIRSTFRUITS. (*Introversions.*)

P[1] | Q | g | 1. Inheritance possessed.
h | 2-5-. Command.
R | i | -5. Unworthiness of grace.
k | 6. Egypt. Bondage.
l | 7-. Cry made.
R | *l* | -7. Cry heard.
k | 8. Egypt. Deliverance.
i | 9. Grace for the unworthy.
Q | *h* | 10. Obedience.
g | 11. Inheritance enjoyed.

1 land. Heb *'erez*=Canaan.
the LORD. Heb. Jehovah. Ap. 4. II.
thy God=thy Elohim. Ap. 4. I. This was omitted in A.V. of 1611.
2 earth. Heb.=ground or soil, *'ădāmāh*, as in Ex. 23. 19; 34. 26. Lev. 2. 12; 23. 10. Num. 15. 20, 21. Deut. 18. 4. Prov. 3. 9, 10.
basket. Heb *men'e* (woven), only here and 28. 5, 17.
to place=to cause to dwell.
3 profess=declare.
this day. See note on 4. 26.
5 speak and say. Note the idiom, generally rendered "answer and say", where the first verb must always be rendered according to the context. Here "confess and say".
Syrian=an Aramaean: *i.e.* Jacob.
ready to perish=perishing. Gen. 42. 1, 2.
mighty. Some codices, with Sam., Onk., Jon., and Sept., read "and mighty". Note the Fig. *Polysyndeton* (Ap. 6), thus produced.
7 we cried. See Ex. 2. 23-25; 3. 7, &c. Ps. 107. 6, and cp. Josh. 24. 7. Judg. 4. 3; 10. 12. 2 Chron. 13. 14. Neh. 9. 27 and Ps. 107. 8, 28.
10 behold. Fig. *Asterismos.* Ap. 6.
land. Heb. *'ădāmāh*=ground or soil, as in references on "earth" in *v.* 2.

12-15 (P[2], above). TITHES (*Introversion*).

P[2] | m | 12-. Tithes gathered.
n | -12, 13. Duly appropriated (positive).
n | 14. Duly appropriated (negative).
m | 15. Prayer offered.

12 tithing all the tithes. Fig. *Polyptōton* (Ap. 6)=carefully and completely tithed thy increase. Cp. 14. 28, 29.
13 hallowed=holy. See note on Ex. 3. 5.
transgressed=passed over. Heb. *'ābar.* Ap. 44. vii.
14 mourning. Heb. *'āvōn*, a Homonym: here=suffering, or sorrow (as in Gen. 35. 18 (marg.), and Hos. 9. 4), but=might in Gen. 49. 3. Deut. 21. 17. Job 31. 25.
for the dead. Probably=defilement for touching a dead body. **15 holy.** See note on Ex. 3. 5.

1452 the [10]land which Thou hast given us, °as Thou swarest unto our fathers, a [1]land that floweth with milk and honey.'

R t o (p. 274) 16 [3]This day [1]the LORD thy [1]God hath commanded thee to do these °statutes and judgments: thou shalt therefore keep and do them with all thine heart, and with all thy °soul.

p 17 Thou hast °avouched [1]the LORD [3]this day to be thy [1]God, °and to walk in His ways, and to keep His [16]statutes, and His commandments, and His [16]judgments, and to hearken unto His voice:

p 18 And [1]the LORD hath avouched thee [3]this day to be His °peculiar people, as He hath promised thee, and that *thou* shouldest keep all His commandments;

19 And to make thee high above all nations which He hath made, in praise, and in name, and in honour;

o and that thou mayest be an [15]holy people unto [1]the LORD thy [1]God, °as He hath spoken."

u q **27** °And Moses with the elders of Israel commanded the people, saying, "Keep all the commandments which I command you °this day.

r s 2 And it shall be °on the day when ye shall pass over Jordan unto the land which °the LORD thy °God giveth thee,

t that thou shalt set thee up great °stones, and plaister them with °plaister:

3 And thou shalt °write upon them all the words of °this law, when thou art passed over, that thou mayest go in unto the land which [2]the LORD thy [2]God giveth thee, a land that floweth with milk and honey; °as [2]the LORD [2]God of thy fathers hath promised thee.

r s 4 Therefore it shall be when ye be gone over Jordan,

t *that* ye shall set up these [2]stones, which I command you [1]this day, °in mount Ebal, and thou shalt plaister them with [2]plaister.

5 And there shalt thou build an altar unto [2]the LORD thy [2]God, an altar of [2]stones: thou shalt not lift up *any* °iron *tool* upon them.

6 Thou shalt build the altar of [2]the LORD thy [2]God of whole stones: and thou shalt offer burnt offerings thereon unto [2]the LORD thy [2]God:

7 And thou shalt offer peace offerings, and shalt eat there, and rejoice before [2]the LORD thy [2]God.

8 And thou shalt [3]write upon the stones all the words of this law °very plainly."

q 9 And Moses and the priests the Levites spake unto all Israel, saying, °"Take heed, and hearken, O Israel; [1]this day thou art become the people of [2]the LORD thy [2]God.

10 Thou shalt therefore obey the voice of [2]the LORD thy [2]God, and do His °commandments and His statutes, which I command thee [1]this day."

d S[1] u 11 And Moses charged the people the same day, saying,

15 as = according as.

a land. Heb. *'erez*, the land of Canaan.

26. 16-19 (*R*, *t*, p. 265). THESE STATUTES. (*Introversion.*)

t | o | 16. Command.
  p | 17. Jehovah avouched by people.
  p | 18, 19-. People avouched by Jehovah.
 o | -19. Purpose.

16 statutes and judgments. See note on 4. 1.

soul. Heb. *nephesh*. Ap. 13.

17 avouched = avowed.

and. Note Fig. *Polysyndeton* (Ap. 6) in *vv.* 17-19.

18 peculiar = as a treasure. Cp. 7. 6, and see note on Ex. 19. 5.

19 as = according as. This is the end of the fourth address. See note on 1. 1.

27. 1-10 (*R*, *u*, p. 255). SACRED PLACES. (*Introversion and Alternation.*)

u | q | 1. Command.
  r | s | 2-. Passage of Jordan.
    t | -2, 3. Sacred stones.
  r | *s* | 4-. Passage of Jordan.
    t | -4-8. Sacred stones.
 q | 9, 10. Command.

1 And Moses. This is the beginning of the fifth address. See note on 1. 1.

this day. See note on 4. 26.

2 on the day = in the day, or, when. See Ap. 18.

the LORD. Heb. Jehovah. Ap. 4. II.

God. Heb. Elohim. Ap. 4. I.

stones: i.e. rough and unhewn. Cp. Ex. 20. 25.

plaister = gypsum. A hard white cement.

3 write. See note on Ex. 17. 14. Cp. Josh. 8. 30-32.

this law: i.e. which follows, viz. the blessings and curses.

as = according as.

4 in mount Ebal. The stones, therefore, carried thither from Jordan. Ebal = heaps.

5 iron. Probably a technical name for a chisel, as we now associate it with a laundry or a prison.

8 very plainly. A useful hint for us = plainly and well.

9 Take heed = keep silence, or, take note.

10 commandments. In Hebrew text written singular, but read plural, as here.

27. 11-26 (*d*, p. 238). GERIZIM AND EBAL. (*Division.*)

d | S[1] | 11-13. Arrangement of tribes.
 | S[2] | 14-26. Curses.

11-13 (S[1], above). ARRANGEMENT OF TRIBES. (*Alternation.*)

S[1] | u | 11, 12-. On Gerizim to bless.
  v | -12. Tribes detailed.
  u | 13-. On Ebal to curse.
  v | -13. Tribes detailed.

12 Simeon. For order of tribes see Ap. 45.

12 "These shall stand upon mount Gerizim to bless the people, when ye are come over Jordan;

°Simeon, and Levi, and Judah, and Issachar, and Joseph, and Benjamin: v

13 And these shall stand upon mount Ebal to curse; *u*

Reuben, Gad, and Asher, and Zebulun, Dan, and Naphtali. *v*

S² 14 And the Levites shall °speak, and say
(p. 274) unto all the °men of Israel with a loud voice,
1452 15 °'Cursed *be* the man that maketh °*any*
graven or molten image, an abomination unto [2]the LORD, the work of the hands of the craftsman, and putteth *it* in *a* secret *place.*' And all the people shall answer and say, °'Amen.'

16 'Cursed *be* he that °setteth light by his father or his mother.' And all the people shall say, 'Amen.'

17 'Cursed *be* he that °removeth his neighbour's landmark.' And all the people shall say, 'Amen.'

18 'Cursed *be* he that maketh °the blind to wander out of the way.' And all the people shall say, 'Amen.'

19 'Cursed *be* he that perverteth the judgment of the °stranger, fatherless, and widow.' And all the people shall say, 'Amen.'

20 'Cursed *be* he that °lieth with his father's wife; because he uncovereth his father's skirt.' And all the people shall say, 'Amen.'

21 'Cursed *be* he that lieth with any manner of °beast.' And all the people shall say, 'Amen.'

22 'Cursed *be* he that lieth with °his sister, the daughter of his father, or the daughter of his mother.' And all the people shall say, 'Amen.'

23 'Cursed *be* he that lieth with his °mother in law.' And all the people shall say, 'Amen.'

24 'Cursed *be* he that °smiteth his neighbour secretly.' And all the people shall say, 'Amen.'

25 'Cursed *be* he that taketh °reward to slay an innocent °person.' And all the people shall say, 'Amen.'

26 'Cursed *be* he that °confirmeth not °*all* the words of this law to do them.' And all the people shall say, 'Amen.'

T¹ w **28** And it shall come to pass, if thou shalt
(p. 275) hearken diligently unto the voice of °the LORD thy °God, to observe °*and* to do all His commandments which I command thee °this day,

x that °the LORD thy °God will set thee on high °above all nations of the earth:
2 And all °these blessings shall come on thee, and overtake thee,

w if thou shalt hearken unto the voice of [1]the LORD thy [1]God.

x 3 °Blessed *shalt* thou *be* in the city, and blessed *shalt* thou *be* in the field.

4 Blessed *shall be* the fruit of thy body, and the fruit of thy ground, and the fruit of thy cattle, the increase of thy kine, and the flocks of thy sheep.

5 Blessed *shall be* thy °basket and thy °store.

6 Blessed *shalt* thou *be* when thou °comest in, and blessed *shalt* thou *be* when thou goest out.

7 [1]The LORD shall cause thine enemies that rise up against thee to be smitten before thy face: they shall come out against thee one way, and flee before thee seven ways.

8 [1]The LORD shall command the blessing upon thee in thy °storehouses, and in all that thou °settest thine °hand unto; and He shall bless thee in the land which [1]the LORD thy [1]God giveth thee.

9 [1]The LORD shall establish thee an °holy people unto Himself, °as He hath sworn unto thee, if thou shalt keep the commandments of [1]the LORD thy [1]God, and walk in His ways.

10 And all °people of the earth shall see that thou art called by the name of [1]the LORD; and they shall be afraid of thee.

11 And [1]the LORD shall make thee plenteous °in goods, in the fruit of thy body, and in the

14 speak, and say. Note idiom, usually rendered in New Testament "answer and say". The first verb is to be rendered according to the context. Here = "curse and say".

men. Heb. pl. of *'ish* or *'enōsh.* Ap. 13.

15 Cursed. Fig. *Anaphora.* See Ap. 6. "Cursed" twelve times.

any graven = a sculpture. Cp. 4. 23. Lev. 19. 4.

Amen. Note the Fig. *Epistrophe* (see Ap. 6), each clause ending with the same word "Amen."

16 setteth light. Cp. Ex. 21. 17. Lev. 19. 3.

17 removeth. Cp. 19. 14.

18 the blind. Cp. Lev. 19. 14.

19 stranger = foreigner. These three put by Fig. *Synecdoche* (of Species) for all kinds of afflicted. Ap. 6. Cp. 24. 17. Ex. 22. 21, 22. Jer. 22. 3.

20 lieth. Cp. 22. 30. Lev. 18. 8; 20. 11.

21 beast. Cp. Ex. 22. 19. Lev. 18. 23; 20. 15.

22 his sister. Cp. Lev. 18. 9; 20. 17.

23 mother in law. Cp. Lev. 18. 17; 20. 14.

24 smiteth. Cp. Ex. 21. 12.

25 reward = bribe. Cp. 10. 17; 16. 19. Ex. 23. 7, 8. Ps. 15. 5.

person = soul. Heb. *nephesh.* Ap. 13.

26 confirmeth not. Cp. 28. 1, 15. Jer. 11. 3-5. Gal. 3. 10.

all. Some codices, with Sam. and Sept., have this "all" in the text.

28. 1-68 (*c*, p. 238). BLESSINGS AND CURSES. (*Division.*)

c | T¹ | 1-14. Blessings.
  | T² | 15-68. Curses.

1-14 (T¹, above). BLESSINGS (*Alternation*).

T¹ | w | 1-. Obedience.
   | x | -1, 2-. Blessings (general).
   | *w* | -2. Obedience.
   | *x* | 3-14. Blessings (particular).

1 the LORD. Heb. Jehovah. Ap. 4. II.

God. Heb. Elohim. Ap. 4. I.

and to do. No "and" in Hebrew text, but it is read in some codices with Sam., Jon., Sept., Syr., and Vulg.

this day. See note on 4. 26.

above all nations. See 26. 19.

2 these blessings. Fig. *Hypotyposis.* Ap. 6.

3 Blessed. Fig. *Anaphora.* Ap. 6. "Blessed" six times. Cp. note on "Cursed", 27. 15.

5 basket. Put by Fig. *Metonymy* (of Subject) for its contents. Ap. 6. Cp. 26. 2, 4.

store = kneading-troughs, put for the dough in them.

6 comest in. Cp. Ps. 121. 8.

8 storehouses = barns. Heb. *'āsam.* Occurs only here and Prov. 3. 10.

settest thine hand = lettest thine hand go forth. Put by Fig. *Metonymy* (of Cause) for all that is wrought by it. Ap. 6.

hand. Some codices, with three early printed editions, Sam., Jon., Vulg., read "hands".

9 holy. See note on Ex. 3. 5. **as** = according as.

10 people = Peoples.

11 in goods = for good; or, in that which is good.

1452 fruit of thy cattle, and in the fruit of °thy ground, °in the land which [1]the LORD sware unto thy fathers to give thee.

12 [1]The LORD shall open unto thee His good treasure, the heaven to give the rain unto thy land in his °season, and to bless all the work of thine °hand: and thou shalt °lend unto many nations, and thou shalt not borrow.

13 And [1]the LORD shall make thee °the head, and not the tail; and thou shalt be °above only, and thou shalt not be beneath; if that thou hearken unto the commandments of [1]the LORD thy [1]God, which I command thee [1]this day, to observe and to do *them:*

14 And thou shalt not °go aside from any of the words which I command thee [1]this day, *to* the right hand, or *to* the left, to go after other gods to serve them.

T^2 y (p. 276) 15 But it shall come to pass, if thou wilt not hearken unto the voice of [1]the LORD thy [1]God, to observe to do all His commandments and His °statutes which I command thee [1]this day;

z that all °these curses shall come upon thee, and overtake thee:

16 Cursed *shalt* thou *be* in the city, and cursed *shalt* thou *be* in the field.

17 Cursed *shall be* thy [5]basket and thy [5]store.

18 Cursed *shall be* the fruit of thy body, and the fruit of thy land, the increase of thy kine, and the flocks of thy sheep.

19 Cursed *shalt* thou *be* when thou comest in, and cursed *shalt* thou *be* when thou goest out.

20 [1]The LORD shall send upon thee cursing, vexation, and rebuke, in all that thou settest thine hand unto for to do, until thou be destroyed, and until thou perish quickly; because of the °wickedness of thy doings, whereby thou hast forsaken Me.

21 [1]The LORD shall make the °pestilence cleave unto thee, until He have consumed thee from off the °land, whither thou goest to possess it.

22 [1]The LORD shall smite thee with a °consumption, and with a °fever, and with an °inflammation, and with an °extreme burning, and with the sword, and with blasting, and with mildew; and they shall pursue thee until thou perish.

23 And thy heaven that *is* over thy head shall be brass, and the earth that *is* under thee *shall be* iron.

24 [1]The LORD shall make the rain of thy land powder and dust: from heaven shall it come down upon thee, until thou be destroyed.

25 [1]The LORD °shall cause thee to be smitten before thine enemies: thou shalt go out one way against them, and flee seven ways before them: and shalt be removed into all the kingdoms of the earth.

26 And °thy carcase shall be meat °unto all fowls of the air, and unto the beasts of the earth, and no man shall °fray *them* away.

27 [1]The LORD will smite thee with the °botch of Egypt, and with the °emerods, and with the °scab, and with the °itch, whereof thou canst not be healed.

28 [1]The LORD shall smite thee with madness, and blindness, and astonishment of heart:

29 And thou shalt grope at noonday, [9]as the blind gropeth in darkness, and thou shalt not prosper in thy ways: and thou shalt be only oppressed and spoiled evermore, and no man shall save *thee.*

30 Thou shalt betroth a wife, and another man shall °lie with her: thou shalt build an house, and thou shalt not dwell therein: thou shalt plant a vineyard, and shalt not gather the grapes thereof.

31 Thine ox *shall be* slain before thine eyes, and thou shalt not eat thereof: thine ass *shall be* violently taken away from before thy face, and shall not be restored to thee: thy sheep *shall be* given unto thine enemies, and thou shalt have none to rescue *them.*

32 Thy sons and thy daughters *shall be* given unto another people, and thine eyes shall look, and fail *with longing* for them all the day long: and *there shall be* no °might in thine °hand.

33 The fruit of thy land, and all thy °labours, shall a nation which thou knowest not eat up;

thy ground = thy soil.
in the land = on the soil. Heb *'ădāmāh.*
12 season. Cp. 11. 14.
hand. Some codices, with two early printed editions, Sam., Jon., Sept., Syr., and Vulg., read "hands".
lend. Cp. 15. 6 and Prov. 22. 7.
13 the head, and not the tail. Fig. *Pleonasm* (Ap. 6) for great emphasis.
above . . . and not beneath. Fig. *Pleonasm.* See note above.
14 go aside. Cp. 17. 11, 20. Prov. 4. 27.

28. 15-68 (T^2, p. 275). CURSES (*Alternation*).

T^2 | y | 15-. Disobedience.
| z | -15-57. Curses.
| *y* | 58. Disobedience.
| *z* | 59-68. Curses.

15 statutes. See note on 4. 1.
these curses. Fig. *Hypotyposis.* Ap. 6.
20 wickedness. Heb. *rā'a'.* Ap. 44. viii.
21 pestilence. Probably true Oriental plague.
land = soil. Heb. *'ădāmāh.*
22 consumption. Probably phthisis.
fever. Probably a continued fever of some kind.
inflammation. Probably the rigor and heat of malarial intermittent fever.
extreme burning. Probably prickly-heat.
25 shall cause. Note the fulfilment of *vv.* 25, 37, 46, 48, 49, 50, 52, 62, reaching down to the present day.
26 thy carcase. Sept. *hoi nekroi,* with article, denoting corpses as distinct from the people who are dead.
unto all fowls. Some codices, with Sam., Onk., Sept., and Syr., read "for the bird".
fray = frighten (Old English).
27 botch = elephantiasis.
emerods = Old English spelling of modern Hæmorrhoids, or "piles". Written "posteriors" in Hebrew text, but read "tumours" by way of Fig. *Euphemism.*
scab = aggravated psoriasis.
itch = prurigo.
30 lie with. Heb. *Euphemism* for "ravish".
32 might = power. Heb. *'ēl.* Ap. 4. iv.
hand. Some codices, with three early printed editions and Syr., read plural, "hands".
33 labours. Put by Fig. *Metonymy* (of Cause) for the result or fruit of them. Ap. 6.

1452 and thou shalt be only oppressed and crushed alway:

34 So that thou shalt be mad for the sight of thine eyes which thou shalt see.

35 [1]The LORD shall smite thee in the knees, and in the legs, with a sore botch that cannot be healed, from the sole of thy foot unto the top of thy head.

36 [1]The LORD shall bring thee, and thy king which thou shalt set over thee, unto a nation which neither thou nor thy fathers have known; and there shalt thou serve other gods, wood and stone.

37 And thou shalt become an astonishment, a proverb, and a byword, among all °nations whither [1]the LORD shall lead thee.

38 Thou shalt carry much seed out into the field, and shalt gather *but* little in; for the °locust shall consume it.

39 Thou shalt plant vineyards, and dress *them,* but shalt neither drink *of* the wine, nor gather *the grapes;* for the worms shall eat them.

40 Thou shalt have olive trees throughout all thy °coasts, but thou shalt not anoint *thyself* with the oil; for thine olive shall cast *his fruit.*

41 Thou shalt beget sons and daughters, but thou shalt not enjoy them; for they shall go into captivity.

42 All thy trees and fruit of thy land shall the °locust °consume.

43 The stranger that *is* within thee shall get up above thee °very high; and thou shalt come down °very low.

44 He shall lend to thee, and thou shalt not lend to him: he shall be the head, and thou shalt be the tail.

45 Moreover all these curses shall come upon thee, and shall pursue thee, and overtake thee, till thou be destroyed; because thou hearkenedst not unto the voice of [1]the LORD thy [1]God, to keep His commandments and His °statutes which He commanded thee:

46 And they shall be upon thee for a sign and for a wonder, and upon thy seed °for ever.

47 Because thou servedst not [1]the LORD thy [1]God with joyfulness, and with gladness of heart, for the abundance of all *things;*

48 Therefore shalt thou serve thine enemies which [1]the LORD shall send against thee, in hunger, and in thirst, and in nakedness, and in want of all *things:* and he shall put a °yoke of iron upon thy neck, until he have destroyed thee.

49 [1]The LORD shall bring a nation against °thee from far, from the end of the earth, *as swift* °as the eagle flieth; a nation whose tongue thou shalt not °understand;

50 A nation °of fierce countenance, which shall not regard the person of the old, nor shew favour to the young:

51 And he shall eat the fruit of thy cattle, and the fruit of thy land, until thou be destroyed: which *also* shall not leave thee *either* corn, °wine, or oil, *or* the increase of thy kine, or flocks of thy sheep, until he have destroyed thee.

52 And he shall besiege thee in all thy gates, until thy high and fenced walls come down, wherein thou trustedst, throughout all thy land: and he shall besiege thee in all thy gates throughout all thy land, which [1]the LORD thy [1]God hath given thee.

53 And thou shalt °eat the fruit of thine own body, the flesh of thy sons and of thy daughters, which [1]the LORD thy [1]God hath given thee, in the siege, and in the straitness, wherewith thine enemies shall distress thee:

54 *So that* the °man *that is* tender among you, and very delicate, his eye shall be evil toward his brother, and toward the wife of his bosom, and toward the remnant of his children which he shall leave:

55 So that he will not give to any of them of the flesh of his children whom he shall eat: because he hath nothing left him in the siege, and in the straitness, wherewith thine enemies shall distress thee in all thy gates.

56 The tender and delicate woman among you, which would not °adventure to set the sole of her foot upon the ground for delicateness and tenderness, her eye shall be evil toward the husband of her bosom, and toward her son, and toward her daughter,

57 And toward her young one that cometh out from between her feet, and toward her children which she shall bear: for she shall eat them for want of all *things* secretly in the siege and straitness, wherewith thine enemy shall distress thee in thy gates.

58 If thou wilt not observe to do all the words of this law that are °written in °this book, that thou mayest fear this glorious and fearful °name, °THE LORD THY GOD; *y* (p. 276)

37 nations = peoples. Cp. 1 Kings 9. 8. Ps. **44.** 13, 14.
38 locust. Heb. *'arbeh.* Used of the Egyptian plague. Ex. 10. 4, &c. Cp. *v.* 42.
40 coasts = borders, or confines.
42 locust = grasshopper. Heb. *ẓelāẓal,* from noise of its wings.
consume. Heb. possess.
43 very high. Heb. "high, high". Fig. *Epizeuxis.* Ap. 6.
very low. Heb. "low, low". Fig. *Epizeuxis.* Ap. 6. Cp. the Fig. Isa. 26. 3, &c.
45 statutes. See note on **4.** 1.
46 for ever. Fig. *Synecdoche* (of Whole). Ap. 6. The whole of time put for a part of it.
48 yoke of iron. Put by Fig. *Metonymy* (of Adjunct) (Ap. 6) for a heavy yoke or a grievous bondage.
49 thee. The judgments that follow are for "the Jew first", but also for the Gentile. Cp. Isa. 13. 9. Rom. 2. 7-10.
as = according as.
understand. Heb. "hear". Put by Fig. *Metonymy* (of Adjunct) for understanding. Ap. 6.
50 of fierce countenance. Heb. = strong of face: "strong" put by Fig. *Metonymy* (of Adjunct) for boldness or fierceness. Cp. Isa. 5. 26-29. Jer. 5. 15-17.
51 wine. Heb. *tīrōsh.* See Ap. 27. II. Some codices, with Sam. and Syr., read "or new wine".
53 eat. Cp. Jer. 19. 9.
54 man. Heb. *'īsh.* Ap. 14. II.
56 adventure. Old English idiom for "venture to go".
58 written. See note on Ex. **17.** 14.
this book. See Ap. 47, and cp. *v.* 61 below.
name. Put by Fig. *Metonymy* (of Adjunct) for Him who bears it. Ap. 6.
THE LORD THY GOD = Jehovah thy Elohim. For words in large capitals in A.V. and R.V. see Ap. 48.

z (p. 276) 1452 **59** Then [1]the LORD will make thy plagues wonderful, and the plagues of thy seed, *even* great plagues, and of long continuance, and sore sicknesses, and of long continuance.

60 Moreover He will bring upon thee all the diseases of Egypt, which thou wast afraid of; and they shall cleave unto thee.

61 Also every sickness, and every plague, which *is* not [58]written in °the book of this law, them will [1]the LORD bring upon thee, until thou be destroyed.

62 And ye shall be left few in number, whereas ye were as the stars of heaven for multitude; because thou wouldest not obey the voice of [1]the LORD thy [1]God.

63 And it shall come to pass, *that* [49]as [1]the LORD rejoiced over you to do you good, and to multiply you; so [1]the LORD will rejoice over you to destroy you, and to bring you to nought; and ye shall be plucked from off the land whither thou goest to possess it.

64 And [1]the LORD shall scatter thee among °all people, from the one end of the earth even unto the other; and there thou shalt serve other gods, which neither thou nor thy fathers have known, *even* wood and stone.

65 And among these nations shalt thou find no ease, neither shall the sole of thy foot have rest: but [1]the LORD shall give thee there a trembling heart, and failing of eyes, and sorrow of °mind:

66 And thy life shall hang in doubt before thee; and thou shalt °fear day and night, and shalt have none assurance of thy life:

67 In the morning thou shalt say, °'Would God it were even!' and at even thou shalt say, °'Would God it were morning!' for the fear of thine heart wherewith thou shalt fear, and for the sight of thine eyes which thou shalt see.

68 And [1]the LORD shall bring thee °into Egypt again with °ships, by the way whereof I spake unto thee, 'Thou shalt see it no more again:' and there ye shall be °sold unto your enemies for bondmen and bondwomen, and no man shall °buy *you*."

a U (p. 278) **29** These *are* the words of the °covenant, which °the LORD commanded Moses to make with the °children of Israel in the land of Moab, beside the covenant which He made with them in Horeb.

W b **2** And °Moses called unto all Israel, and said unto them, "Ye have seen all that [1]the LORD did before your eyes in the land of Egypt unto Pharaoh, and unto all his servants, and unto all his land;

3 The great temptations which thine eyes have seen, the signs, and those great miracles:

4 Yet [1]the LORD hath not given you an heart to perceive, and eyes to see, and ears to hear, unto this day.

c **5** And I have led you forty years in the wilderness: your clothes are °not waxen old upon you, and thy shoe is not waxen old upon thy foot.

6 Ye have not eaten bread, neither have ye drunk °wine or °strong drink: that ye might know that I *am* [1]the LORD your °God.

61 the book of this law = this book of the law. Cp. *v.* 58. Deut. 29. 21; 30. 10. 2 Kings 22. 13, and Ap. 47.
64 all people = all kinds of peoples. Put by Fig. *Synecdoche* (of Genus). Ap. 6.
65 mind. Heb. *nephesh*, soul. Ap. 13.
66 fear. Heb. *Homonym*: *pāḥad*, to fear, here and Job 23. 15; but = rejoice, Isa. 60. 5 (cp. A.V. and R.V.). Hos. 3. 5.
67 Would God. Fig. *Euche*. Ap. 6.
68 into Egypt. So Hos. 8. 13; 9. 3. May be put by Fig. *Metonymy* for servitude.
ships. Second occurrence in O. T. See Gen. 49. 13.
sold = put up for sale.
buy you. This is the end of Moses' fifth address. See note on 1. 6.

29. 1-17 (*a*, p. 238). **INJUNCTIONS** *plus* **HOREB. RETROSPECTIVE.**
(*Alternation and Introversion.*)

a | U | 1. Command.
  | W | b | 2-4. Egypt. Retrospective.
  | | c | 5-8. Past days (wilderness).
  | *U* | 9. Command.
  | *W* | *c* | 10-15. This day.
  | | *b* | 16, 17. Egypt. Retrospective.

1 covenant. See 2 Kings 23. 2, 3.
the LORD. Heb. Jehovah. Ap. 4. II.
children = sons.
2 Moses called. This begins his sixth address. See note on 1. 1.
5 not waxen old. See ch. 8. 4, and Neh. 9. 21.
6 wine. Heb. *yāyin*. See Ap. 27. I.
strong drink. Heb. *shēkār*. See Ap. 27. iv.
God. Heb. Elohim. Ap. 4. I.
9 Keep. Cp. 1 Kings 2. 3. Ps. 1. 3.
10 men. Heb. pl. of *'īsh* or *'enōsh*. See Ap. 14.
12 maketh = confirmeth.
13 to Abraham, &c. All three Patriarchs named. See note on Gen. 50. 24.

7 And when ye came unto this place, Sihon the king of Heshbon, and Og the king of Bashan, came out against us unto battle, and we smote them:

8 And we took their land, and gave it for an inheritance unto the Reubenites, and to the Gadites, and to the half tribe of Manasseh.

9 °Keep therefore the words of this covenant, and do them, that ye may prosper in all that ye do. U

10 Ye stand this day all of you before [1]the LORD your [6]God; your captains of your tribes, your elders, and your officers, *with* all the °men of Israel, W c

11 Your little ones, your wives, and thy stranger that *is* in thy camp, from the hewer of thy wood unto the drawer of thy water:

12 That thou shouldest enter into covenant with [1]the LORD thy [6]God, and into His oath, which [1]the LORD thy [6]God °maketh with thee this day:

13 That He may establish thee to day for a people unto Himself, and *that* He may be unto thee a [6]God, as He hath said unto thee, and as He hath sworn unto thy fathers, °to Abraham, to Isaac, and to Jacob.

14 Neither with you only do I [12]make this covenant and this oath;

15 But with *him* that standeth here with us this day before [1]the LORD our [6]God, and also with *him* that *is* not here with us this day:

16 (For ye know how we have dwelt in the land of Egypt; and how we came through the nations which ye passed by; b

1452 17 And ye have seen their abominations, and their °idols, wood and stone, silver and gold, which *were* among them:)

b X d (p. 279) 18 Lest there should be among you man, or woman, or family, or °tribe, whose heart turneth away this day from [1]the LORD our [6]God, to go *and* serve the gods of these nations; lest there should be among you a root that beareth gall and wormwood;

19 And it come to pass, when he heareth the words of this curse, that he bless himself in his heart, saying, 'I shall have peace, though I walk in the imagination of mine heart, to add drunkenness to thirst:'

20 [1]The LORD will not spare him, but then the anger of [1]the LORD and His jealousy shall °smoke against that man, and all the curses that are °written in this book shall lie upon him, and [1]the LORD shall °blot out his name from under heaven.

21 And [1]the LORD shall separate him unto °evil out of all the tribes of Israel, according to all the curses of the covenant that are [20]written in this book of the law:

e 22 So that the generation to come of your children that shall rise up after you, and the stranger that shall come from a far land, shall say, when they see the plagues of that land, and the sicknesses which [1]the LORD hath laid upon it;

23 *And that* the whole land thereof *is* brimstone, and salt, *and* burning, *that* it is not sown, nor beareth, nor any grass groweth therein, like the overthrow of Sodom, and Gomorrah, Admah, and Zeboim, which [1]the LORD overthrew in His anger, and in His wrath:

24 Even all nations shall say, 'Wherefore hath [1]the LORD done thus unto this land? °what *meaneth* the heat of this great anger?'

25 Then men shall say, 'Because they have forsaken the covenant of [1]the LORD [6]God of their fathers, which He made with them when He brought them forth out of the land of Egypt:

26 For they went and served other gods, and worshipped them, gods whom they knew not, and *whom* He had not °given unto them:

27 And the anger of [1]the LORD was kindled against this land, to bring upon it all the curses that are [21]written in this book:

28 And [1]the LORD rooted them out of their land in anger, and in wrath, and in great indignation, and cast them into another land, as *it is* this day.'

Y f 29 The °secret *things belong* unto [1]the LORD our [6]God: but those *things which are* revealed *belong* unto us and to our children for ever,

g that *we* may do all the words of this law.

X d **30** And it shall come to pass, when all these things are come upon thee, the blessing and the curse, which I have set before thee, and thou shalt call *them* to mind among all the nations, whither °the LORD thy °God hath driven thee,

2 And shalt return unto [1]the LORD thy [1]God, and shalt obey His voice according to all that I command thee °this day, thou and thy children, with all thine heart, and with all thy °soul;

3 That then [1]the LORD thy [1]God will °turn thy captivity, and have compassion upon thee, and will return and gather thee from all the °nations, whither [1]the LORD thy [1]God hath scattered thee. e

4 If *any* of thine be driven out unto the outmost *parts* of heaven, from thence will [1]the LORD thy [1]God gather thee, and from thence will He fetch thee:

5 And [1]the LORD thy [1]God will bring thee into the land which thy fathers possessed, and thou shalt possess it; and He will do thee good, and multiply thee above thy fathers.

6 And [1]the LORD thy [1]God °will circumcise thine heart, and the heart of thy seed, to love [1]the LORD thy [1]God with all thine heart, and with all thy [2]soul, that thou mayest live.

7 And [1]the LORD thy [1]God will put all these curses upon thine enemies, and on them that hate thee, which persecuted thee.

8 And °thou shalt return and obey the voice

---

17 idols = either as manufactured, or derived from *gālāl* = dung = rotten, or detestable.

29. 18 — 30. 20 (*b*, p. 238). INJUNCTIONS ON DISPERSION. PROSPECTIVE (*Alternations*).

b | X | d | 29. 18-21. Apostasy of persons.
  | e | 29. 22-28. Land. Judgment on.
  | Y | f | 29. 29-. The word of Jehovah. Revealed.
  | g | 29. -29. Object: that we may do.
  | X | *d* | 30. 1, 2. Repentance of people.
  | *e* | 30. 3-10. Land. Return to.
  | *Y* | *f* | 30. 11-14. The word of Jehovah. Plain.
  | *g* | 30. 15-20. Object: that they may do.

18 tribe. Dan and Ephraim not named in Rev. 7. Cp. Judg. 17 Ephraim, and 18, Dan. See Ap. 45.

20 smoke. Fig. *Anthropopatheia*. Ap. 6.

written. See note on Ex. 17. 14, and Ap. 47.

blot out. See note on *v.* 18 above.

21 evil. See Ap. 44. viii.

24 what. Some codices, with one early printed edition, Sept., and Syr., read "and what".

26 given = divided.

29 secret. The italics in A.V. (put in roman type in R.V.) show that the Hebrew was not clear to the translators. They make good sense in English, but this is not the sense of the Hebrew text. The words rendered "unto the LORD our God" have the extraordinary points (Ap. 31) to show that they form no part of the text, and should come out. The meaning, then, is:

"The secret things, even the revealed things, [belong] to us and our children for ever, that we may do all the words of this law"; i.e. the revealed things, and the secret things which have not been, but will yet be revealed.

30. 1 the LORD. Heb. Jehovah. Ap. 4. II.

God. Heb. Elohim. Ap. 4. I.

2 this day. See note on 4. 26.

soul. Heb. *nephesh*. Ap. 13.

3 turn thy captivity. Fig. *Paronomasia*. Ap. 6. Heb. *v*e*shāb . . . eth-sh*e*būthkā*. Cp. Amos 9. 14, 15. Jer. 30. 3. Idiom for relief from any trouble. Cp. Job 42. 10.

nations = peoples.

6 will circumcise. Cp. 10. 16. Jer. 32. 39. Ezek. 11. 19; 36. 26.

8 thou shalt return. Cp. Hos. 6. 1; 14. 1.

1452 of °the LORD, and do all His commandments
which I command thee [2]this day.
9 And [1]the LORD thy [1]God will make thee
plenteous in every work of thine °hand, in
the fruit of thy body, and in the fruit of thy
cattle, and in the fruit of thy land, for good:
for [1]the LORD will again °rejoice over thee
for good, °as He rejoiced over thy fathers:
10 If thou shalt hearken unto the voice of
[1]the LORD thy [1]God, to keep His commandments and His °statutes which are written in
°this book of the law, *and* if thou turn unto
[1]the LORD thy [1]God with all thine heart, and
with all thy [2]soul.

f h (p. 280) 11 For this commandment which I command
thee [2]this day, it *is* °not hidden from thee,

i neither *is* it far off.

k 12 It *is* not in heaven, that thou shouldest
say, 'Who shall go up for us to heaven, and
bring it unto us, that we may hear it, and do
it?'

k 13 Neither *is* it beyond the sea, that thou
shouldest say, 'Who shall go over the °sea
for us, and bring it unto us, that we may hear
it, and do it?'

i 14 But the word *is* very nigh unto thee,

h in thy mouth, and in thy heart, that thou
mayest do it.

g l 15 °See, I have set before thee [2]this day °life
and good, and death and °evil;
16 °In that I command thee [2]this day to love
[1]the LORD thy [1]God, to walk in His ways,
and to keep His commandments and His
[10]statutes and His judgments,

m that thou mayest live and multiply: and [1]the
LORD thy [1]God shall bless thee in the land
whither thou goest to possess it.
17 But if thine heart turn away, so that thou
wilt not hear, but shalt be drawn away, and
worship other gods, and serve them;
18 I °denounce unto you [2]this day, that ye
shall surely perish, *and that* ye shall not
prolong *your* days upon the land, whither
thou passest over Jordan to go to possess it.

l 19 °I call °heaven and earth °to record [2]this
day against you, *that* I have set before you
life and death, blessing and cursing: therefore
choose life, that both thou and thy seed may
live:

m 20 That thou mayest love [1]the LORD thy
[1]God, *and* that thou mayest obey His voice,
and that thou mayest cleave unto Him: for
He *is* thy life, and the length of thy days: that
thou mayest dwell °in the land which [1]the
LORD sware unto °thy fathers, to Abraham,
to Isaac, and to Jacob, to give °them."

G n **31** And Moses went and spake °these
words unto all Israel.
2 And he said unto them, "I *am* an hundred
and twenty years old this day; I can no more
go out and come in: also °the LORD hath said
unto me, 'Thou shalt not go over this Jordan.'
3 °The LORD thy °God, He will go over
before thee,

and He will destroy these nations from before
thee, and thou shalt possess them: o p

and Joshua, he shall go over before thee, °as
°the LORD hath said. q

the LORD = Jehovah. Some codices, with Sam., Onk., Sept., Syr., and Vulg., add "thy Elohim".

9 hand. Some codices, with three early printed editions, Sam., Onk., Sept., and Vulg., read plural 'hands'.

rejoice. Fig. *Anthropopatheia.* Ap. 6. Cp. 28. 63. Jer. 32. 41. **as** = according as.

10 statutes. See note on 4. 1.

this book of the law. See Ap. 47, and cp. 2 Kings 22. 8; 23. 25. See note on Ex. 17. 14.

30. 11-14 (*f*, p. 279). THE WORD OF JEHOVAH (PLAIN) (*Introversion*).

f | h | 11-. Not hidden.
  i | -11. Distance. Not far off.
   k | 12. Not in heaven. Hear and do.
   k | 13. Not over seas. Hear and do.
  i | 14-. Distance. Very nigh.
 h | -14. Not hidden. In mouth and heart.

11 not hidden = not too wonderful. Cp. Rom. 10. 6, &c.

13 sea. Cp. Rom. 10. 7.

30. 15-20 (*g*, p. 279). OBJECT: THAT THEY MAY CHOOSE (*Alternation*).

g | l | 15, 16-. Life and good, &c.
  m | -16-18. Object.
 l | 19. Life and good, &c.
  m | 20. Object.

15 See = Behold. Fig. *Asterismos.* Ap. 6.

life and good, and death and evil. Fig. *Metonymy* (of Effect). Ap. 6. Put for the good things which end in life, and evil things which end in death. Cp. Amos 5. 14. **evil.** See Ap. 44. viii.

16 In that. The Sept. reads, "For thou must keep the commandments of Jehovah thy God which", instead of "In that". So that this clause apparently was in the MS. from which the Sept. was translated.

18 denounce = declare.

19 I call. Fig. *Deasis*, or, *Obtestatio.* Ap. 6.

heaven and earth = the heavens and the earth. One of thirteen occurrences. See note on 4. 26.

to record = to witness.

20 in the land = on the soil. Heb. *'ădāmāh.*

thy fathers. All three Patriarchs are named. See note on Gen. 50. 24.

them. This is the end of the sixth address. See note on 1. 1.

31. 1-8 (*G*, p. 238). POSSESSION WEST OF JORDAN (*Introversion and Alternation*).

G | n | 1-3-. Jehovah to go before.
  o | p | -3-. Jehovah to act.
    q | -3. Joshua.
  o | *p* | 4-6. Jehovah to act.
    q | 7. Joshua.
 n | 8. Jehovah to go before.

1 these words. The Massorah itself, with Onk., Sept., Syr., and Vulg., read "all these words". This is the beginning of the seventh address, which ends with *v.* 6.

2 the LORD. Heb. Jehovah. Ap. 4. II.

3 the LORD = Jehovah. Note the Fig. *Epanadiplōsis* (Ap. 6) in this verse, which in the Hebrew text begins and ends with "Jehovah".

God. Heb. Elohim. Ap. 4. I.

as = according as. Cp. the references to past statements: 2. 9; 3. 28. Ex. 23. 20, 23; 33. 2. Num. 27. 15-23.

o p (p. 280) 1452 4 °And [2]the LORD shall do unto them [3]as He did to Sihon and to Og, kings of the Amorites, and unto the land of them, whom He destroyed.

5 [4]And [2]the LORD shall give them up before your face, that ye may do unto them according unto all the commandments which I have commanded you.

6 °Be strong and of a good courage, fear not, nor be afraid of them: for [2]the LORD thy [3]God, He *it is* that doth go with thee; °He will not fail thee, nor forsake thee.

q 7 And °Moses called unto Joshua, and said unto him in the sight of all Israel, [6]'Be strong and of a good courage: for thou must °go with this people unto the land which [2]the LORD hath sworn unto their fathers to give them; and thou shalt cause them to inherit it.

n 8 And [2]the LORD, He *it is* that doth go before thee; He will be with thee, [6]He will not fail thee, neither forsake thee: fear not, neither be dismayed.' "

r t[1] (p. 281) 9 And Moses °wrote this law, and delivered it unto °the priests the sons of Levi, which bare the ark of the covenant of [2]the LORD, and unto all the elders of Israel.

10 And Moses commanded them, saying, °"At the end of *every* seven years, in the °solemnity of the °year of release, in the feast of °tabernacles,

11 When all Israel is come °to appear before [2]the LORD thy [3]God in the place which He shall choose, thou shalt °read this law before all Israel in their hearing.

12 Gather the people together, °men, and women, and °children, and thy stranger that *is* within thy gates, that they may hear, and that they may learn, and fear [2]the LORD your [3]God, and observe to do all the words of this law:

13 And *that* their °children, which have not known *any thing*, may hear, and learn to fear [2]the LORD °your [3]God, °as long as ye live in the land whither ye go over Jordan to possess it."

u[1] 14 And [2]the LORD °said unto Moses, °"Behold, thy days approach that thou must die: call Joshua, and present yourselves in the °tabernacle of the congregation, that I may give him a charge." And Moses and Joshua went, and presented themselves in the °tabernacle of the congregation.

15 And [2]the LORD appeared in the [14]tabernacle in a °pillar of a cloud: and the pillar of the cloud stood over the °door of the [14]tabernacle.

16 And [2]the LORD said unto Moses, [14]"Behold, thou °shalt sleep with thy fathers; and this people will rise up, and °go a whoring after the gods of the strangers of the land, whither they go *to be* among them, and will forsake Me, and break My covenant which I have made with them.

17 Then My anger °shall be kindled against them in that day, and I will forsake them, and I will °hide My face from them, and they shall be devoured, and many °evils and troubles shall °befall them; so that they will say in that day, °'Are not these °evils come upon us, because our [3]God *is* not among us?'

4 And the LORD (Heb. Jehovah). Note Fig. *Anadiplosis* (Ap. 6) in *vv.* 4, 5, each beginning with these words.

6 Be strong, &c. Cp. *vv.* 7, 23. Josh. 1. 6, 9, 18; 10. 25. 1 Chron. 22. 13; 28. 20. 2 Chron. 32. 7. Isa. 35. 3, 4.

He will not fail, &c. Cp. 4. 31. Josh. 1. 5. 1 Chron. 28. 20. See note on 4. 31.

This is the end of Moses' seventh address.

7 go with=bring in.

31. 9—32. 47 (*F*, p. 238). LAWS AND SONG: IN AND OUT OF THE LAND (*Introversion*).

F | r | 31. 9-30. Laws *re* the Song.
s | 32. 1-43. The Song itself.
r | 32. 44-47. Laws *re* the Song.

9-30 (r, above). LAWS *re* THE SONG. (*Repeated Alternation.*)

r | t[1] | 9-13. Laws written and read.
u[1] | 14-18. Charge to Moses and Joshua.
t[2] | 19. Song to be written.
u[2] | 20, 21. Charge to People.
t[3] | 22. Song written.
u[3] | 23. Charge to Joshua.
t[4] | 24. Song written.
u[4] | 25-29. Charge to Levites.
t[5] | 30. Song recited.

9 wrote. See note on Ex. 17. 14, and Ap. 47.

the priests, &c.=the Kohathites. Num. 4. 1-15.

10 At the end, &c. Cp. 15. 1.

solemnity=appointed time. Heb. *mō'ed.*

year of release. So called in 15. 9. The "release" is referred to in 15. 1, 2, 3. The noun "release" occurs only in these two passages. The verb occurs in Ex. 23. 11. **tabernacles**=booths.

11 to appear. See note on Ex. 23. 15 and 34. 20.

read this law. Cp. 16. 13-15, and see Neh. 8. 1-18.

12 men. Heb. pl. of *'ish* or *'enōsh.* Ap. 14.

children=little ones.

13 children=sons.

your God. A special various reading called *Sevīr* (Ap. 34), with some codices and four early printed editions, read "their God".

as long as=all the days.

14 said. See note on 2. 9.

Behold. Fig. *Asterismos.* Ap. 6.

tabernacle=tent. Heb. *'ohel.* Ap. 40. The only reference to it in Deuteronomy.

15 pillar of a cloud. The only reference to it in Deuteronomy. **door**=entrance.

16 shalt sleep with thy fathers=shalt lie down to sleep. A beautiful *Euphemism* (Ap. 6) for death. This is the first occurrence. It is used alike of good people and evil: of Ahab as well as David; of all the kings, even Jehoiakim, who had no burial. See 2 Sam. 7. 12. 1 Kings 1. 21; 2. 10; 11. 21, 43; 14. 20, 31; 15. 8, 24; 16. 6, 28; 22. 40, 50. 2 Kings 8. 24; 10. 35; 13. 9, 13; 14. 16, 22, 29; 15. 7, 22, 38; 16. 20; 20. 21; 21. 18; 24. 6. 2 Chron. 9. 31; 12. 16; 14. 1; 16. 13; 21. 1; 26. 2, 23; 27. 9; 28. 27; 32. 33; 33. 20.

go a whoring. The constant idiom for idolatry.

17 shall be kindled. Cp. 2 Kings 22. 17. Hos. 5. 3-6. Mic. 3. 4.

hide My face. Some codices, with Sam., Onk., Jon., Sept., and Syr., add "from them". Cp. 32. 20. Isa. 8. 17; 54. 8; 59. 2; 64. 7. See also Gen. 4. 14.

evils. See Ap. 44. viii.

befall=find. Fig. *Prosopopœia* (Ap. 6).

Are not . . . ? &c. Should be "Have not these evils found me out, because my God is not in my midst?"

18 And I will surely [17]hide My face in that day for all the evils which they shall have wrought, in that they are turned unto other gods.

t2 19 Now therefore [9]write ye °this song for
(p. 281) you, and °teach it the [13]children of Israel:
1452 put it in their mouths, that this song may be
a witness for Me against the [13]children of
Israel.
u2 20 For when I shall have brought them
°into the land which I sware unto their
fathers, that floweth with milk and honey;
and they shall have eaten and filled themselves,
and waxen fat; then will they turn
unto other gods, and serve them, and provoke
Me, and break My covenant.
21 And it shall come to pass, when many
[17]evils and troubles are [17]befallen them, that
°this song shall °testify against them as a
witness; for it shall °not be forgotten out of
the mouths of their seed: for I know their
imagination which they go about, even now,
before I have brought them into the land
which °I sware."
t3 22 Moses therefore [9]wrote °this song the
same day, and taught it the [19]children of
Israel.
u3 23 And °He gave Joshua the son of Nun
a charge, and said, °"Be strong and of a good
courage: for thou shalt bring the [19]children of
Israel into the land which I sware unto them:
and I will be with thee."
t4 24 And it came to pass, when Moses had
made an end of [9]writing the words of this
law °in a book, until they were finished,
u4 25 That Moses commanded [9]the Levites,
which bare the ark of the covenant of [2]the
LORD, saying,
26 "Take °this book of the law, and put it
°in the side of the ark of the covenant of [2]the
LORD your [2]God, that it may be there for a
witness against thee.
27 For I know thy rebellion, and thy stiff
neck: °behold, while I am yet alive with you
this day, ye have been rebellious against [2]the
LORD; and how much more after my death?
28 Gather unto me all the elders of your
tribes, and your officers, that I may speak
these words in their ears, and call °heaven
and earth to record against them.
29 For °I know that after my death ye will
utterly corrupt *yourselves*, and turn aside
from the way which I have commanded you;
and [17]evil [17]will befall you in °the latter days;
because ye will do [17]evil in the sight of [2]the
LORD, to provoke Him to anger through °the
work of your hands."
t5 30 And °Moses spake in the ears of all the
°congregation of Israel the words of °this
song, until they were ended.

A 32 °"Give ear, O ye heavens, and I will
(p. 283) speak;
And hear, O earth, the words of my mouth.
2 My °doctrine shall drop as the rain,
°My speech shall distil °as the dew,
As the small rain upon the tender herb,
And as the °showers upon the grass:
3 Because I will publish the name of °the
LORD:
Ascribe ye greatness unto our °God.
4 *He is* the °Rock, His work *is* perfect:
For all His ways *are* judgment:
A °GOD of truth and without °iniquity,
Just and right *is* He.
5 °They have corrupted themselves, their
°spot *is* not *the spot* of his °children:
They are a perverse and crooked generation.
6 °Do ye thus requite [3]the LORD,
O foolish People and unwise?
Is not He thy Father *that* hath bought
thee?
Hath He not made thee, and established
thee?

19 this song. First reference to the "Song of Moses". See ch. 32. The last in Rev. 15. 3.
teach it. To be both written and taught. Cp. *v.* 22.
20 into the land = on to the soil. Heb. *'ădāmāh.*
21 this song. Second mention of this song.
testify against = answer them to their face.
not be forgotten. This song quoted and referred to more than any other part of Pentateuch.
I sware. The Sam., Sept., and Syr. add "unto their fathers".
22 this song. The third reference to it.
23 He: i.e. Jehovah.
Be strong. See note on *v.* 6.
24 in a book. See Ap. 47. This was the "book" found by Hilkiah. 2 Kings 22. 8. 2 Chron. 34. 14.
25 the Levites = Kohathites, *v.* 9. Cp. Num. 3. 31, 32. 2 Sam. 15. 24.
26 this book of the law. See the effect of finding it by Jeremiah's father, 2 Kings 22. 8, and note the references to it in *vv.* 13, 16, 17 (Deut. 29. 25–27), *v.* 19 (Deut. 28. 36, 37, 45, words used). Cp. also 2 Kings 23. 1–3 with Deut. 29. 1; and *v.* 21 with Deut. 16. 1–8; and *v.* 24 with Deut. 18. 10, 11 ("put away" occurs only in Deut.); and *v.* 25 with Deut. 30. 10. **in**, or by.
27 behold. Fig. *Asterismos.* Ap. 6.
28 heaven and earth. One of the thirteen occurrences. See note on 4. 26.
29 I know. Cp. Acts 20. 28, 29.
the latter days. Cp. Gen. 49. 1 (Num. 24. 14). Used by Moses, 4. 30. Found also in Jer. 23. 20; 48. 47; 49. 39. Ezek. 38. 16. Hos. 3. 5. Mic. 4. 1.
the work, &c., viz., idolatry and other evils.
30 Moses spake. Beginning of his eighth address.
this song. The fourth reference to it. It is the key to the Apocalypse, Rev. 15. 3. See note on Ex. 15. 1.

32. 1-43 [For Structure see next page].

1 Give ear. Fig. *Apostrophe.* Ap. 6. Cp. Isa. 1. 2.
2 doctrine. Heb. *lekaḥ.* First occurrence. = good teaching.
My speech = the words of my mouth.
as the dew. Cp. Mic. 5. 7.
showers. First occurrence. Heb. *r^ebîbim.* Elsewhere: Ps. 65. 10; 72. 6. Jer. 3. 3; 14. 22. Mic. 5. 7.
3 the LORD = Jehovah. See Ap. 4. II.
God = Elohim. See Ap. 4. I.
4 Rock. Omit "He is", and read "The Rock, His work is perfect". Used of Jehovah in this song five times (the number of Grace. See Ap. 10), *vv.* 4, 15, 18, 30, 31. Used twice in irony (Ap. 6), *vv.* 31, 37. Cp. 2 Sam. 22. 31, 32.
GOD = Heb. *'ēl.* See Ap. 4. IV.
iniquity. See Ap. 44. vi.
5 They have, &c. The Nom., "generation", is put last by Fig. *Hyperbaton* (Ap. 6), for emphasis, in contrast with "the Rock" of *v.* 4, which is there put first. Cp. *v.* 20. Render the verse thus:
"A perverse and crooked generation hath corrupted itself:
[To be] no sons of His is their blemish."
spot = blemish. **children** = sons.
6 Do . . . ? Fig. *Erotēsis.* Ap. 6.

B (p. 283) 1452 7 Remember the days °of old,
Consider the years of many generations:
Ask thy father, and he will shew thee;
Thy elders, and they will tell thee.
8 °When the °MOST HIGH °divided to the nations their inheritance,
When He separated the sons of Adam,
He set the bounds of the °People
According to the number of the [5]children of Israel.
9 For [3]the LORD'S portion *is* His People;
Jacob *is* the °lot of His inheritance.
10 He found °him in a desert land,
And in the waste howling wilderness;
He led him about, He instructed him,
He kept him as the °apple of His eye.
11 As an eagle °stirreth up her °nest,
Fluttereth over her young,
Spreadeth abroad her °wings, taketh them,
Beareth them on her °wings:
12 *So* [3]the LORD alone did lead °him,
And *there was* no strange °GOD with him.
13 He made him ride on the high places of the earth,
°That he might eat the °increase of the fields;
And He made him to suck °honey out of the °rock,
And °oil out of the °flinty rock;
14 Butter of kine, and milk of sheep,
With fat of lambs,
And rams of the breed of °Bashan, and goats,
With the °fat of kidneys of wheat;
And thou didst drink the °pure °blood of the grape.

C 15 But °Jeshurun waxed fat, and °kicked:
°Thou art waxen fat, thou art grown thick, thou art covered *with fatness;*
Then he forsook °GOD *Which* made him,
And lightly esteemed the °Rock of his salvation.
16 °They provoked Him to °jealousy with °strange *gods,*

32. 1-43 (s, p. 281). THE SONG OF MOSES.
(*Introversion.*)

s | A | 1-6. Call to hear: and the reason. The publishing of Jehovah's name: His perfect work and righteous ways.
B | 7-14. The goodness and bounty of Jehovah to Israel. (Period of the Pentateuch.)
C | 15-19. Israel's evil return for that goodness. Their pride: forsaking of God; despising the Rock of their Salvation; moving Him to anger. (Period, past history. The Historical books.)
D | 20. Divine reflections on the period while Israel is "*Lo Ammi*" (not my people). (Period of Minor Prophets, especially Hosea.)
E | 21. Jehovah's provocation of Israel. (Period of Acts and present Dispensation.)
E | 22-25. Jehovah's threatening of judgment on Israel in the great tribulation.
D | 26-33. Divine reflections on the period while Israel is scattered. (Hosea.)
C | 34-38. Israel's evil return for Jehovah's goodness. Their helpless condition moving Him to pity. He not forsaking them. Their rock useless. (Period of present history.)
B | 39-42. The judgments of Jehovah. (The period of the Apocalypse.)
A | 43. Call to rejoice: and the reason. The publishing of Jehovah's Kingdom. Vengeance on Israel's enemies. Mercy for His "Land" and for His "People". (Fulfilment of all prophecy.)

7 of old, or, the days of long ago. Cp. Ps. 77. 5.
8 When, &c., i.e. He foreknew His purposes concerning Israel. See Gen. 10. 32. This was 200 years before Abraham.
MOST HIGH = *'elyōn*. See Ap. 4.
divided. As an inheritance. Cp. *v.* 9. Heb. *nāḥal* = to possess. See note on *v.* 9. Not Heb. *pālag* (Gen. 10. 25), which = to cleave by disruption, or *pārar* (Gen. 10. 5, 32), which = to divide by breaking off. (See note Ap. 50. I.)
People = Peoples.
9 lot = line. Fig. *Metonymy* (of Cause), Ap. 6, because the inheritance was allotted by a cord or line. Cp. 1 Chron. 16. 18. Ps. 16. 6; 19. 4. Mic. 2. 5.
10 him: i.e. Jacob. Emphasis on "him" marked by Fig. *Epistrophe* (Ap. 6), by which each clause ends with the same word. Here (in Heb.) "him".

"In a desert land He found HIM,
In the waste howling wilderness, about, He led HIM,
He instructed HIM,
As the apple of His eye He kept HIM."

apple. First occurrence of Heb. *bābah*, used of the small round dark pupil of the eye. Heb. = hole, gate, or door of the eye. Cp. Ps. 17. 8. See note on Zech. 2. 8. Called "pupil" from Latin *pupilla* = a little girl. **11 stirreth up** = fluttereth. Same word as Gen. 1. 2. **nest.** Put by Fig. *Metonymy* (of Subject), Ap. 6, for the young in it. Cp. Ex. 19. 4. Isa. 63. 9. **wings.** Heb. *kānaph*: in which lie the *feathers*. **wings.** Heb. *'ēber*: in which lie the *strength*. We may read *vv.* 11, 12 thus:

"As an eagle that stirreth up her nest,
That fluttereth over her young,
[So] He spread abroad His wings; He took him;
He bare him on His pinions:
Jehovah alone did lead him,
And [there was] no strange god with him."

12 him. Note Fig. *Epistrophe* (Ap. 6), each line ending with same word "him" in Hebrew and English for emphasis, as *v.* 10. **GOD.** Heb. *'ēl.* (See Ap. 4. IV.) **13 That he might eat.** Sam. and Sept. read "caused him to eat". Hebrew text reads "And he did eat". **increase.** Heb. *nūb*, fruit from land. First occurrence. **honey . . . oil.** Put by Fig. *Synecdoche* (of Species) for all delicious things. **rock.** Heb. *sel'a* = a rock, as a fortress, immovable. **flinty rock.** Heb. *ẓūr* = rock *in situ*, sharp and precipitous. Hence a refuge and security. **14 Bashan.** Confirming the promise of *v.* 13 as to high or mountainous places. **fat of kidneys** = white of the kernels. **pure** = unmixed. **blood.** Put by Fig. *Metonymy* (of Adjunct) for red juice, blood of grapes. Fig. *Catachresis.* Ap. 6. **15 Jeshurun** = the Upright One. First occurrence. Put by Fig. *Metonymy* (of Adjunct), Ap. 6, for the ideal Israel (cp. 33. 5, 26. Isa. 44. 2) as chosen by God. **kicked** = trampled under foot. Hence, to contemn. Heb. *bā'aṭ*. First occurrence. **Thou.** Note the Fig. *Anaphora* in this verse (Ap. 6). **GOD** = *Eloah.* The God in respect of worship. First occurrence. Ap. 4. V. **Rock.** Heb. *ẓūr*, as in *v.* 13. **16** Note the *Introversion* of these four lines:

"They provoked Him to jealousy
with foreign gods:
with abominations
They provoked Him to anger."

From this, "abominations" generally means idols.
jealousy. Fig. *Anthropopatheia.* Ap. 6. Cp. Ps. 78. 58.
strange = foreign.

1452 With abominations provoked they Him
to anger.
17 They sacrificed unto °devils, not to
°GOD;
To °gods whom they knew not,
To °new *gods that* came °newly up,
Whom your fathers °feared not.
18 Of the [15]Rock *That* begat thee thou art
unmindful,
And hast forgotten [3]GOD That formed
thee.
19 And when [3]the LORD saw *it*, He °ab-
horred *them*,
Because of the provoking °of His sons,
and of His daughters.

D (p. 283) 20 And He said, 'I will °hide My face from
them,
I will see what their end *shall be:*
For they *are* a very °froward generation,
Children in whom *is* no faith.

E 21 They have moved Me to [16]jealousy with
that which is °not GOD;
They have °provoked Me to anger with
their vanities:
And I will move them to jealousy with
those which are °not a People;
I will provoke them to anger with a
foolish nation.

E 22 For a fire is kindled in Mine anger,
And shall burn unto the lowest °hell,
And shall consume the earth with her
increase,
And °set on fire the foundations of the
mountains.
23 I will heap °mischiefs upon them;
I will spend Mine °arrows upon them.
24 *They shall be* burnt with hunger,
And devoured with °burning heat,
And with bitter destruction:
I will also send the teeth of beasts upon
them,
With the poison of °serpents of the dust.
25 The sword without,
And terror °within,
Shall °destroy both the young man and
the virgin,
The suckling *also* with the °man of gray
hairs.

D 26 I said, I would °scatter them into
corners,
I would make the remembrance of them
to cease from among °men:
27 Were it not that °I feared the wrath of
the enemy,
Lest their adversaries should °behave
themselves strangely,
And lest they should say, 'Our hand *is*
high,
And °the LORD hath not done all this.'
28 For they *are* a nation void of °counsel,
Neither *is there any* understanding in
them.
29 °O that they were wise, *that* they understood this,
That they would consider their latter end!
30 How should °one chase a thousand,
And two put ten thousand to flight,
Except their [15]Rock had sold them,
And [3]the LORD had shut them up?
31 °For their [15]rock *is* not as our [15]Rock,
Even our enemies themselves *being* judges.
32 For their vine *is* of the vine of Sodom,
And of the fields of Gomorrah:
Their grapes *are* grapes of gall,
Their clusters *are* bitter:
33 Their °wine *is* the poison of dragons,
And the cruel venom of asps.

34 °*Is* not this laid up in store with Me, C
And sealed up among My treasures?
35 °To Me *belongeth* vengeance, and recompence;

17 devils = demons. Heb. *shēd*. First occurrence. Cp. Ps. 106. 37. 1 Cor. 10. 20.
GOD = *'eloah*. See Ap. 4.
gods = *'elohim*. Ap. 4. I.
new = recent, lately. Heb. *kārob*, as in Judg. 5. 8.
newly = recently.
feared = trembled at. Heb. *sā'ar*. Not *gūr*, reverence.
19 abhorred. Cp. Ps. 106. 40.
of. Gen. of origin = the provocation produced by the conduct of His People.
20 hide My face. See note on 31. 17.
froward = perverse. Heb. *hăphakpak*. First occ.
21 Note the *alternation* of the four lines, marked by "jealousy, anger, jealousy, anger".
not GOD = no *'ēl*. Ap. 4. IV.
provoked. Cp. Rom. 10. 19.
not a People = no People. Cp. Rom. 10. 19; 11. 11. See Ap. 35.
22 hell = *sh'eōl*.
set on fire. Heb. *lāhaṭ*. First occurrence.
23 mischiefs. See Ap. 44. viii.
arrows. Fig. *Anthropopatheia*. Ap. 6. They are named in *v.* 24.
24 burning heat. Heb. *resheph*. First occ. = fever.
serpents. Heb. *zāḥal* = to crawl or creep. First occ.
25 within = from the inner chambers.
destroy = bereave.
man. Heb. *'īsh*. Ap. 14. II.
26 scatter them into corners = disperse them, scatter as with the wind. The verb *pā'ah* occurs only here. The Severus Codex (Ap. 34) divides the one word *'aph'ēyḥem* (disperse them) into the three words *'aph, 'ēy, ḥem*, "[I said] in anger, Where are they?"
men. Heb. *'ĕnōsh* = mortals. Ap. 14. III.
27 I feared. Fig. *Anthropopatheia* (Ap. 6).
behave themselves strangely = mistake it. Heb. *nākar*, a *Homonym* with three meanings: (1) to mistake, Deut. 32. 27; (2) to acknowledge, Job 34. 19; (3) to deliver. 1 Sam. 23. 7. Both A.V. and R.V. miss the first (R.V. = misdeem), admit the second and third (though the R.V. margin suggests "alienated" for "delivered").
the LORD = Jehovah. Note the five Divine Titles in this song. Ap. 4.
28 counsel = deliberation. Heb. *yā'aẓ*.
29 O that. Fig. *Œonismos*. Ap. 6. Cp. Ps. 81. 13, 14.
30 one chase, &c. Cp. Lev. 26. 8. Josh. 23. 10. 2 Chron. 24. 24. Isa. 30. 17.
31 For, &c. Cp. 1 Sam. 2. 2, and note on *v.* 4, above.
33 wine. Heb. *yayīn*. See Ap. 27. i.
34 Is not this. Fig. *Erotēsis*. Ap. 6.
35 To Me. Hebrew text is *lī* = "to Me", but Dr. Ginsburg thinks it is an abbreviation for *līyom*, "for the day", as seems evident from Sam., Onk., and Sept., and from agreeing with the next line. So that *vv.* 34, 35 will read:
"Is not this laid up in store with Me,
Sealed up in My treasures?
For the day of vengeance and recompence,
For the time when their foot shall slip?"
This shows that the *Ellipsis* is wrongly supplied in the A.V.; and that the R.V. misses the point

1452 Their foot shall slide in *due* time:
For the day of their calamity *is* at hand,
And the things that shall come upon them make haste.
36 For [3]the LORD shall °judge His People,
And repent Himself for His servants,
When He seeth that *their* °power is gone,
And *there is* none °shut up, or left.
37 And He shall say, °'Where *are* their gods,
Their [15]rock in whom they °trusted,
38 Which did eat the fat of their sacrifices,
And drank the [33]wine of their drink offerings?
Let them rise up and help you,
°*And* be your protection.'

B (p. 283) 39 See now that °I, *even* I, *am* He,
And *there is* no god with Me:
°I kill, and I make alive;
°I wound, and I heal:
Neither *is there any* that can deliver out of My hand.
40 For °I lift up My hand to heaven,
And say, I live for ever.
41 If I whet My glittering °sword,
And Mine hand take hold on °judgment;
I will render vengeance to Mine enemies,
And will reward them that hate Me.
42 I will make Mine °arrows °drunk with blood,
And My [41]sword shall °devour flesh;
And that with the blood of the slain and of the captives,
°From the beginning of revenges upon the enemy.

A 43 °Rejoice, O ye °nations, *with* His people:
For He will avenge the blood of His servants,
And will render vengeance to His adversaries,
And will °be merciful unto His °land, *and* to His °people."

r (p. 281) 44 And Moses came and spake all the words of °this song in the ears of the people, he, and °Hoshea the son of Nun.
45 And Moses made an end of speaking all these words to all Israel:
46 And he said unto them, °"Set your hearts unto all °the words which I testify among you °this day, which ye shall command your children to observe °to do, all the words of this law.
47 For it *is* not a vain thing for you; because it *is* your life: and through this thing ye shall prolong *your* days °in the land, whither ye go over Jordan to possess it."

D (p. 236) 48 And [3]the LORD °spake unto Moses that selfsame day, saying,
49 "Get thee up into this mountain Abarim, *unto* mount Nebo, which *is* in the land of Moab, that *is* over against Jericho; and behold the land of Canaan, which I give unto the °children of Israel for a possession:
50 And °die in the mount whither thou goest up, and °be gathered unto thy people; °as Aaron thy brother died in mount Hor, and was gathered unto his people:
51 °Because ye °trespassed against Me among the children of Israel at the waters of Meribah-Kadesh, in the wilderness of Zin; because ye sanctified Me not in the midst of the [49]children of Israel.
52 Yet thou shalt see the land before *thee;* but thou shalt not go thither unto the land which I give the [49]children of Israel."

36 judge = vindicate. Cp. Lev. 26. 25. Judg. 2. 18. Ps. 7. 8; 135. 14. Jer. 51. 6.
power. Heb. "hand". Put by Fig. *Metonymy* (of Adjunct), Ap. 6, for power contained in it.
shut up, or left. Heb. *'āzab*, is a *Homonym*, with two meanings: (1) to leave, or forsake, Gen. 2. 24; 39. 6. Neh. 5. 10. Ps. 49. 10. Mal. 4. 1. (2) To help, restore, strengthen, shut in, or fortify, as in Ex. 23. 5. 1 Kings 14. 10. 2 Kings 14. 26. Neh. 3. 8. Jer. 49. 25. See the notes on these passages. Hence, here, *v.* 36 = defended and protected. Note the perplexity manifested in the margins of A.V. and R.V.
37 Where . . . ? Fig. *Erotēsis.* Ap. 6.
trusted. Heb. *ḥaṣa.* See Ap. 69.
38 And be. Sam., Onk., Sept., Syr., and Vulg. read "Let them be".
39 I, even I, am He. Cp. Isa. 44. 8.
I kill. Cp. 1 Sam. 2. 6. 2 Kings 5. 7.
I wound. Cp. Job 5. 18. Hos. 6. 1.
40 I lift up My hand = I swear. The lifting of the hand being put by Fig. *Metonymy* (of Adjunct), Ap. 6, for the thing signified by it.
41 sword. Fig. *Anthropopatheia.* Ap. 6. Cp. Rev. 19. 15.
judgment = justice, or retribution. Cp. Isa. 1. 24.
42 arrows. Fig. *Prosopopatheia.* Ap. 6.
drunk = devour. Fig. *Prosopopœia.* Ap. 6.
From the beginning = from [the flesh] of the chief leader of. Note the alternation:
"I will make Mine arrows drunk with blood,
And My sword shall devour much flesh;
With the blood of the slain and of the captives,
With [the flesh] of the chief leader of the enemy."
Cp. Rev. 19. 17–21, to which this refers. See also Ezek. 39. 17–20.
43 Rejoice. Fig. *Pœanismos.* Ap. 6. The song began with *Apostrophe*, Ap. 6, and thus ends, with the same Figure, Moses' eighth address. See note on 1. 6.
nations. Cp. Ps. 67. 1–7.
be merciful = be propitious. Cp. Joel 2. 18. Rom. 15. 9.
land . . . people = the two great subjects of the song and of the Old Testament.
44 this song. This is the fifth and last contextual reference to "the Song of Moses".
Hoshea = the old spelling of Joshua. Later it was "Jeshua" (Ezra 2. 2). This was adopted by the Sept., and ultimately became "Jesus".
46 Set your hearts. Moses' ninth address. See note on 1. 6.
the words. Not merely the Word of God as a whole, but the "words" of which it is made up. Cp. Jer. 15. 16. John 17. 8, 14, 17.
this day. See note on 4. 26.
to do. Some codices, with one early printed edition, Sam., Sept., Jon., and Syr., read "and to do".
47 in the land = on the soil. The end of Moses' ninth address. See note on 1. 1.
48 spake. See note on 2. 1.
49 children = sons.
50 die . . . be gathered. Fig. *Heterōsis* (of Mood), Ap. 6. Imperative for Indicative. Cp. Gen. 25. 8, 17.
as Aaron = according as Aaron. Cp. Num. 20. 24; 27. 12–14.
51 Because. Cp. Num. 20. 12.
trespassed. Heb. *mā'al.* Ap. 44. xi.

B C F (p. 286) 1452 **33** And °this *is* the °blessing, wherewith Moses °the man of °God blessed the °children of Israel before his death.

G 2 And he said,
°"The LORD °came from Sinai,
And °rose up from Seir unto them;
He °shined forth from mount Paran,
And He °came with ten thousands of °saints:
From His right hand *went* a fiery °law for them.
3 Yea, He °loved the people;
All His [2]saints *are* in Thy °hand:
And °they sat down at Thy °feet;
Every one °shall receive of Thy words."
4 Moses commanded us a law,
Even the inheritance of the °congregation of Jacob.
5 And °He was king in °Jeshurun,
When the heads of the people *and* the tribes of Israel °were gathered together.
v[1] 6 "Let °Reuben °live, and not die;
And °let *not* his °men be few."
v[2] 7 And this *is the blessing* of °Judah: and he said,
"Hear, [2]LORD, the voice of Judah,
And bring him unto his people:
Let his hands be sufficient for him;
And °be Thou an help *to him* from his enemies."
v[3] 8 And of Levi he said,
"*Let* Thy °Thummim and Thy °Urim *be* with °Thy holy one,
Whom Thou didst prove at Massah,
And with whom Thou didst strive at the waters of Meribah;
9 Who said unto his father and to his mother, 'I have not seen him;'
Neither did he acknowledge his brethren,
°Nor knew his own °children:
For they have observed Thy °word,
And kept Thy covenant.
10 They shall °teach Jacob Thy judgments, and Israel Thy law:
They shall put incense °before Thee, and whole burnt sacrifice upon Thine altar.
11 Bless, [2]LORD, his substance,
And accept the work of his hands:
Smite through the loins of them that rise against him,
And of them that hate him, that they rise not again."
v 12 °*And* of Benjamin he said,
"The beloved of [2]the LORD shall dwell in safety °by Him;
And the LORD shall cover him all the day long,
And he shall dwell between His shoulders."
v[5] 13 And of Joseph he said,
°"Blessed of [2]the LORD *be* his land,
For the precious things of heaven,
For the dew, °and for the deep that coucheth beneath,
14 And for the precious fruits *brought forth* by the sun,
And for the precious things put forth by the °moon,
15 And for the chief things of the °ancient mountains,

33. 1-29 (*C*, p. 236). THE BLESSING OF THE TRIBES (*Introversion and Numeration*).

C | F | 1. Introduction.
  G | 2-5. Israel, collectively, with Jehovah king.
    H | v[1] | 6. Reuben.
      v[2] | 7. Judah.
      v[3] | 8-11. Levi.
      v[4] | 12. Benjamin.
      v[5] | 13-17. Joseph.
      v[6] | 18, 19. Zebulun and Issachar.
      v[7] | 20, 21. Gad.
      v[8] | 22. Dan.
      v[9] | 23. Naphtali.
      v[10] | 24, 25. Asher.
  G | 26, 27. Israel, collectively, with Jehovah king.
F | 28, 29. Conclusion.

1 this. Moses' tenth (and last) address. See note on 1. 1.
blessing. To be distinguished from the Song.
the man of God. First occurrence. See Ap. 49.
God. Heb. Elohim. Ap. 4. I.
children = sons.
2 The LORD = Jehovah. Ap. 4.
came. Heb. *bō'*, to come, or enter on business. Cp. Hab. 3. 3.
rose up. Heb. *zārah*, to break forth as light.
shined forth. Heb. *yāph'a*, to shine forth in glory.
came. Heb. *'āthāh*, to come with speed. Cp. *maran-athah* = the LORD cometh, 1 Cor. 16. 22.
saints = holy ones, i. e. angels. Cp. Ps. 68. 17. Acts 7. 53. Gal. 3. 19. Hab. 2. 2. Jude 14. And see note on Ex. 3. 5.
law. Heb. *dath*, an edict, or mandate. Imperial mandate.
3 loved. Heb. "loveth". *Chābab*, used only here, and only of Jehovah's love to Israel.
hand . . . feet. Fig. *Anthropopatheia*. Ap. 6.
they sat down. Fig. *Synecdoche* (of Part). Ap. 6. Put for teaching thus received.
shall receive = bore, or carried away.
4 congregation = assembly.
5 He = Jehovah, from *v.* 2. See the Structure G, above.
Jeshurun. See note on 32. 15.
were gathered together = gathered themselves together.
6 Reuben. For the order of the tribes see Ap. 45.
live, and not die. Fig. *Pleonasm* (Ap. 6) for emphasis, reversing Gen. 49. 3, 4.
let not. The word "not" is rightly repeated from preceding clause, to supply the Fig. *Ellipsis* (Ap. 6).
men. Heb. *m^ethīm*, men as opposed to women and children. Ap. 14. V.
7 Judah. Fig. *Synecdoche* (of Part), Ap. 6, including Simeon; for their inheritance and blessing were one. Josh. 19. 1. Judg. 1. 3. **be** = become.
8 Thummim . . . Urim. See note on Ex. 28. 30. Num. 26. 55.
Thy holy one = Thy man (*'īsh*, Ap. 14. II.) of loving-kindness, or gracious One = the High Priest who was of the tribe of Levi. See note on Ex. 3. 5.
9 Nor knew. Fig. *Metonymy* (of Cause), put for not caring for. Ap. 6.
children = sons. Written in Hebrew text "son", but read "sons". **word** = sayings.
10 teach. This was the great work of the priests. Cp. Lev. 10. 11. Deut. 17. 9, 10. Ezra 7. 10. Jer. 18. 18. Hag. 2. 11. Mal. 2. 7.
before Thee = to Thy nose. Fig. *Anthropopatheia*. Ap. 6.
12 And of. This "and" is contained in some codices, with Sam., Sept., and Syr.
by Him. Sam. and Sept. omit "by Him".
13 Blessed. Cp. Gen. 49. 25.
and. Note the Fig. *Polysyndeton* in *vv.* 14-18. Ap. 6.
14 moon. Put by Fig. *Metonymy* (of Adjunct) for months. Ap. 6.
15 ancient mountains = mountains of old. Cp *v.* 27.

1452 And for the precious things of the °lasting
hills,
16 And for the precious things of the earth
and fulness thereof,
And *for* the good will of Him That dwelt in
°the bush:
Let *the blessing* come upon the head of
Joseph,
And upon the top of the head of him *that*
was °separated from his brethren.
17 His glory *is like* the firstling of his
bullock,
And his °horns *are like* the °horns of °unicorns:
With them he shall push the °people
together to the ends of the °earth:
And they *are* the ten thousands of Ephraim,
And they *are* the thousands of Manasseh."

v6 (p. 286) 18 And of Zebulun he said,
"Rejoice, Zebulun, in thy going out;
And, Issachar, in thy tents.
19 They shall call the [17]people unto the
mountain;
There they shall offer sacrifices of
righteousness:
For they shall suck *of* the abundance of
the seas,
And *of* °treasures hid in the sand."

v7 20 And of Gad he said,
"Blessed *be* He That enlargeth Gad:
He dwelleth as a lion,
And teareth the arm °with the crown of
the head.
21 And he provided the first part for himself,
Because there, °*in* a portion of the lawgiver,
°*was he* °seated;
And he came with the heads of the people,
He executed the justice of [2]the LORD, and
His judgments with Israel."

v8 22 And of °Dan he said,
"Dan *is* a lion's whelp:
He shall leap from Bashan."

v9 23 And of °Naphtali he said,
"O Naphtali, satisfied with favour,
And full with the blessing of [2]the LORD:
Possess thou the west and the south."

v10 24 And of °Asher he said,
"*Let* Asher *be* blessed with children;
Let him be acceptable to his brethren,
And let him °dip his foot in oil.
25 Thy °shoes *shall be* iron and brass;
And °as thy °days, *so shall* thy °strength
be."

G 26 *There is* °none like unto the °GOD of
°Jeshurun,
"*Who* °rideth upon the heaven in thy help,
And in His excellency on the sky.
27 The eternal [1]God *is thy* °refuge,
And underneath *are* the everlasting °arms:
And He shall thrust out the enemy from
before thee;
And shall say, 'Destroy *them*.'

F 28 °Israel then shall °dwell in safety
alone:
The °fountain of °Jacob *shall be* upon
a land of corn and °wine;
Also his heavens shall drop down dew.
29 Happy *art* thou, °O Israel:

Who *is* like unto thee, O people °saved by
[2]the LORD,
The shield of thy help,
And who *is* the sword of thy excellency!
And thine enemies °shall be found liars
unto thee;
And thou shalt tread upon their °high
places."

34 And Moses went up from the plains of
Moab unto the mountain of Nebo, to the
top of Pisgah, that *is* over against Jericho. *D* J x (p. 287)

---

lasting = everlasting. Cp. Gen. 49. 26.

16 the bush. Cp. Ex. 3. 2. The word occurs only in these two places.

separated. Cp. Gen. 49. 26.

17 horns. Put by Fig. *Metonymy* (of Subject), Ap. 6, for Ephraim and Manasseh.

unicorns. See note on Num. 23. 22.

people = peoples.

earth, or land.

19 treasures hid in the sand = hidden treasures of the sand: amber, agate, jet, pearls, glass, &c.

20 with = likewise, or, yea.

21 in. Omit.

was he seated = was reserved.

22 Dan. Cp. Gen. 49. 16-18.

23 Naphtali. Cp. Gen. 49. 21, and Josh. 19. 32-39.

24 Asher. Cp. Gen. 49. 20.

dip his foot in oil. Oil found there when water failed. See 1 Kings 17. 9, and cp. Josh. 19. 24-28.

25 shoes = under thy shoes, as A.V. margin, i.e. above the ground, olives and oil; beneath, iron and copper. Refers to rich ores.

as thy days = as the length of thy days (not "day", as often quoted).

strength = sufficiency, or security, as in a fold.

26 none like. See note on Ex. 15. 11.

GOD. Heb. *'El.* See Ap. 4.

Jeshurun = Upright, i.e. the ideal Israel (cp. *v.* 29) as the "upright" nation, possessing all these laws. See note on first occurrence, 32. 15.

rideth. Cp. Ps. 68. 4, 33.

27 refuge = abode. Ps. 90. 1; 91. 9. Or,
"Above is the everlasting God
And beneath are His everlasting arms."

arms. Put by Fig. *Metonymy* (of Subject), Ap. 6, for the strength which is in them. Also Fig. *Anthropopatheia.* Ap. 6.

28 Israel . . . Jacob. The name of a man put by Fig. *Metonymy* (of Cause) for his posterity. Ap. 6. Note the name, "Israel" connected with Divine safety, and "Jacob" with earthly substance.

dwell . . . alone. Cp. Num. 23. 9. Jer. 23. 6.

fountain, or eye . . . [shall look] upon.

wine. See Ap. 27. ii. Heb. *tirosh.*

29 O Israel. The ideal nation, viewed as Jeshurun the upright. See note on 32. 15.

saved by the LORD. This their greatest glory.

shall be found liars = shall submit themselves. Cp. 2 Sam. 22. 45. Ps. 66. 3.

high places. The end of Moses' tenth (and last) address. See note on 1. 1.

34. 1-7 (*D*, p. 236). MOSES' DEATH AND BURIAL.
(*Introversion and Alternation.*)

D | J | x | 1-. His ascent.
| | y | -1-4. His eye caused to see.
| K | 5. His death.
| *K* | 6. His burial.
| *J* | *x* | 7-. His age.
| | *y* | -7. His eye not dim.

This chapter is editorial and historical. Always part of the Pentateuch. Probably by Joshua, Samuel, or School of the Prophets. See Ap. 47.

1452 And °the LORD °shewed him all the land of
y Gilead, unto °Dan,
(p. 287) 2 And all Naphtali, and the land of Ephraim,
and Manasseh, and all the land of Judah, unto
the °utmost sea,
3 And the °south, and the plain of the valley
of Jericho, the city of palm trees, unto Zoar.
4 And [1]the LORD °said unto him, "This *is*
the land which °I sware °unto Abraham, unto
Isaac, and unto Jacob, saying, 'I will give it
unto thy seed:' I have caused thee to see *it*
with thine eyes, but thou shalt not go over
thither."

K 5 So °Moses the servant of [1]the LORD died
there in the land of Moab, according to the
°word of [1]the LORD.

K 6 And °He buried him in a valley in the land
of Moab, over against Beth-peor: but no °man
knoweth of his sepulchre unto this day.

Jx 7 And Moses *was* °an hundred and twenty
years old when he died:
y his eye was not dim, nor his °natural force
abated.

A L 8 And the °children of Israel wept for Moses
(p. 288) in the plains of Moab °thirty days: so the days
of weeping *and* mourning for Moses were
ended.

M 9 And °Joshua the son of Nun was full of
the °spirit of wisdom; for Moses had laid his
hands upon him:
M and the [8]children of Israel hearkened unto
him, and did °as [1]the LORD commanded Moses.

L 10 And there arose not °a prophet since in
Israel like unto Moses, whom [1]the LORD knew
°face to face,
11 In all the signs and the wonders, which
[1]the LORD sent him to do in the land of
Egypt to Pharaoh, and to all his servants,
and to all his land,
12 And in all that mighty hand, and in all
the great terror which Moses shewed in the
sight of all Israel.

1 the LORD. Heb. Jehovah. Cp. Ap. 4. II.
shewed him = caused him to see. Cp. Matt. 4. 8. Luke 4. 5.
Dan. Cp. Gen. 14. 14. Not Judg. 18. 29.
2 utmost sea. Called "the great sea". See Joel 2. 20, and Zech. 14. 8, where A.V. and R.V. not correct.
3 south = the "Negeb". See note on Gen. 12. 8, 9; 13. 3, &c.
4 said. See note on 2. 9.
I sware. See Gen. 12. 7; 13. 17; and cp. Deut. 3. 27.
unto Abraham. All three Patriarchs named.
5 Moses the servant of the LORD. First occurrence. Occurs eighteen times. See Josh. 1. 1, 13, 15; 8. 31, 33; 11. 12; 12. 6, 6; 13. 8; 14. 7; 18. 7; 22. 2, 4, 5. 2 Kings 18. 12. 2 Chron. 1. 3; 24. 6; and cp. Heb. 3. 1-6. Cp. for other variations of Moses as a servant, Ex. 14. 31. Num. 12. 7. 1 Kings 8. 53. 1 Chron. 6. 49.
word. Heb. mouth. Fig. *Metonymy* (of Cause), Ap. 6, put for what is spoken by it.
6 He buried him = Jehovah buried Moses. Said of no other. Hence, when raised for the Transfiguration, Satan, who has the power of death (Heb. 2. 14), "contended" with Michael about his body, Jude 9. So God has buried the Law for those who, being "in Christ", have died and are dead to the Law. Cp. Rom. 6. 2, 6-8; 7. 1-5, 6 (margin).
man. Heb. *'ish.* Ap. 14. II.
an hundred and twenty years old. Moses died the youngest of any of his kindred, *e.g.* Levi was 137, Kohath 133, Amram 137, Aaron 123, Miriam 126 or more.
natural force = moisture, or freshness.

34. 8-12 (*A*, p. 236). CONCLUSION (*Introversion*).

A | L | 8. Moses. Mourned.
  | M | 9-. Joshua. Qualified.
  | *M* | -9. Joshua. Obeyed.
  | *L* | 10-12. Moses. Praised.

8 children = sons.
thirty days. The mourning lasted from thirtieth day of the eleventh month (Sebat) till the twenty-ninth (and last) day of the twelfth month (Adar). See Ap. 51. III. 5. Thus the forty years were completed: from 1st Abib, 1491. See Ap. 50. VII. 4.
9 Joshua. Cp. Num. 27. 23.
spirit. Heb. *rūach.* Ap. 9.
as = according as.
10 a prophet. Fig. *Synecdoche* (of Genus). Ap. 6. A common name put for a proper name, Moses being the prophet. Ap. 6.
face to face. Fig. *Anthropopatheia.* Ap. 6. Cp. 5. 4, 5.

JOSHUA.

THE STRUCTURE OF THE BOOK AS A WHOLE.

(Introversion.)

A | 1. 1-18. JOSHUA ENTERING ON HIS WORK.

B | 2. 1—7. 26. JORDAN. EVENTS CONNECTED THEREWITH.

C | 8. 1.—12. 24. THE LAND. CONQUEST.

C | 13. 1—21. 45. THE LAND. DIVISION.

B | 22. 1-34. JORDAN. EVENTS CONNECTED THEREWITH.

A | 23. 1—24. 28. JOSHUA ENDING HIS WORK.

EPILOGUE to the whole Book (24. 29-33).

For the relation of JOSHUA to the Pentateuch, see note on Title (p. 291).
For the relation of JOSHUA to the Earlier and Later Prophets, see Ap. 1.
For the relation of JOSHUA to the Earlier Prophets, see below.

x | JOSHUA. Israel's settlement in the LAND; under JOSHUA and PRIESTS.
y | JUDGES. Israel's *failure* under PRIESTS.
x | SAMUEL. Israel's settlement in the LAND; under SAMUEL and KINGS.
y | KINGS. Israel's *failure* under KINGS.

THE

BOOK OF °JOSHUA.

A A (p. 289) 1451 **1** ° Now ° after the death of ° Moses the servant of ° the LORD it came to pass, that
° the LORD spake unto Joshua the son of Nun,
Moses' ° minister, saying,

B a **2** ° "Moses My servant ° is dead; now therefore arise, go over this Jordan, thou, and all
this People, unto the land which ° I do give to
them, *even* to the ° children of Israel.
3 Every place that the sole of your foot shall
tread upon, that have I given unto you, ° as I
° said unto Moses.
4 ° From the wilderness and this Lebanon
even unto the great river, the river Euphrates,
all the land of the Hittites, and unto the great
sea toward the going down of the sun, shall be
your ° coast.

b **5** There shall not any ° man be able to stand
before thee all the days of thy life: as I was
with Moses, *so* ° I will be with thee: I WILL ° NOT
FAIL THEE, NOR FORSAKE THEE.
6 Be strong and of a good courage: for unto
this people shalt ° thou divide for an inheritance the land, which I sware unto their
fathers to give them.
7 Only be thou strong and very courageous,
that thou mayest ° observe to do according to
all the law, which Moses My servant commanded thee: turn not from it *to* the right
hand or *to* the left, that thou mayest ° prosper
whithersoever thou goest.
8 ° This book of the law shall not depart
out of thy ° mouth; but thou shalt ° meditate
therein day and night, that thou mayest [7] observe to do according to all that is written
therein: for then thou shalt make thy ° way
prosperous, and then thou shalt have good
success.
9 ° Have not I commanded thee? Be strong
and of a good courage; be not afraid, neither
be thou dismayed: for [1] the LORD thy ° God *is*
° with thee whithersoever thou goest."

B b **10** Then Joshua commanded the officers of
the People, saying,
11 "Pass through the host, and command the
People, saying, 'Prepare you victuals; for
° within three days ye shall pass over this

TITLE, Joshua. Heb. *Jehoshua'* = "Jehovah the Saviour". In Greek "Jesus". See Acts 7. 45. Heb. 4. 8, and Matt. 1. 18.

The great subject is the LAND, as that of the Pentateuch was the PEOPLE.

1. 1-18 (A, p. 289). JOSHUA ENTERING ON HIS WORK. (*Introversion, Double.*)

A | A | 1. Joshua. Appointment over the People.
  B | a | 2-4. History rehearsed. (Jehovah's Promises.)
      b | 5-9. Admonition (Jehovah to Joshua).
  B | *b* | 10, 11. Admonition (Joshua to People).
      a | 12-15. History rehearsed. (Reubenites' Promises.)
  A | 16-18. Joshua. Obedience of the People.

1 Now. Heb. "And". Linked on to Pentateuch as the books of Pentateuch are thus linked on to each other; and as the four books of earlier Prophets are linked on to Joshua. See Ap. 1. Joshua not necessarily the author, but doubtless is so, as asserted by Talmud. Book referred to in Old and New Testament: Judg. 18. 31. 1 Sam. 1. 3, 9, 24; 3. 21. Ps. 44. 2, 3; 68. 12, 13; 78. 54, 55; 114. 1-8. Isa. 28. 1. Hab. 3. 11-13. Acts 7. 45; 13. 19. Heb. 11. 32. Jas. 2. 25.

No MS. of the five books yet found with Joshua bound up with them, making a sixth (or a so-called and hitherto unheard of "Hexateuch").

after the death of Moses, in the eleventh month of fortieth year. Cp. Deut. 1. 3, 38; 34. 5, 9, and see Ap. 50. v, vii, viii. Cp. the beginning of the Book of Judges.

Moses the servant of the LORD. See note on Deut. 34. 5, and cp. Heb. 3. 5.

the LORD. Heb. Jehovah. Ap. 4.

the LORD spake = Jehovah spake. When Moses is dead. Moses is a type of Law, Joshua of the Messiah. The Law is "until Christ", Gal. 3. 24.

Jehovah spake at four sundry times, and in three divers manners:
To Joshua, 1. 1; 4. 1.
To Joshua to command the priests, 4. 15.
To Joshua to speak to the sons of Israel, 20. 1.

minister. Cp. Ex. 24. 13. Num. 11. 28. Deut. 1. 38.

2 Moses My servant. See note on Num. 12. 7, 8.

is dead. Cp. John 1. 17. Rom. 7. 1-6.

I do give = I, even I, am giving.

children = sons.

3 as = according as. Cp. Deut. 11. 24.

said unto Moses. Cp. Deut. 11. 24. Josh. 14. 9.

4 From. For these boundaries, cp. Gen. 15. 18. Ex 23. 31. Num. 34. 3-12. Deut. 11. 24.

coast = border or boundary.

5 man. Heb. *'ish.* See Ap. 14. II. **I will be.** Heb. *'ehyeh.* Cp. Ex. 3. 14, part of title Jehovah. **not fail thee.** This promise first made to Jacob, Gen. 28. 15. Passed on by Moses, Deut. 31. 6. See note on Deut. 4. 31. **6 thou.** Emphatic. This is the great subject of the book. **7 observe** = take heed. Some codices, with two early printed editions, Sept., Syr., and Vulg., read "observe and do". **prosper** = deal wisely. **8 This book of the law:** i. e. the five books referred to as one throughout the Old Testament. See Ap. 47. **mouth.** Put by Fig. *Metonymy* (of Cause), for what is spoken by it (Ap. 6), i. e. Joshua is to continually speak of it. **meditate** = talk to thyself. Cp. Ps. 1. 2 = audible musing. **way.** Some codices, with one early printed edition, read "ways". **9 Have not I?** Fig. *Erotēsis* (Ap. 6), for emphasis. **God.** Heb. Elohim. Ap. 4. **with thee.** Cp. Ex. 3. 12. **11 within three days** = after three days. Spoken 6th or 7th of Abib. Cp. 4. 19. Spies probably already sent (2. 16, 22; 3. 1, 2).

1451 Jordan, to go in to possess the land, which
[1]the LORD your [9]God giveth you to possess
it.'"

a (p. 291) 12 And to the Reubenites, and to the Gadites,
and to half the tribe of Manasseh, spake
Joshua, saying,
13 "Remember °the word which [1]Moses the
servant of [1]the LORD commanded you, saying,
[1]'The LORD your [9]God hath given you rest,
and hath given you this land.'
14 Your wives, °your little ones, and your
cattle, shall remain in the land which Moses
gave you on this side Jordan; but ye shall
pass before your brethren °armed, all the
mighty men of valour, and help them;
15 Until [1]the LORD have given your brethren
rest, as *He hath given* you, and they also have
possessed the land which the LORD your [9]God
giveth °them: then ye shall return unto the
land of your possession, and enjoy it, which
[1]Moses the [1]LORD'S [1]servant gave you on
this side Jordan toward the sunrising."

A c (p. 292) 16 And they answered Joshua, saying, °"All
that thou commandest us we will do, and
whithersoever thou sendest us, we will go.
17 According as we hearkened unto Moses
in all things, so will we hearken unto thee:
d only [1]the LORD thy [9]God °be with thee, as
He was with Moses.

c 18 Whosoever *he be* that °doth rebel against
thy °commandment, and will not hearken
unto thy words in all that thou °commandest
him, he shall be put to death:

d only be strong and of a good courage."

B C e **2** And °Joshua the son of Nun °sent out of
Shittim two °men to spy secretly, saying,
"Go °view the land, even °Jericho."
f g And they went, and °came into an °harlot's
house, named °Rahab, and lodged there.

h 2 And it was told the king of Jericho, saying,
°"Behold, there came [1]men in hither to night
of the °children of Israel to search out the
country."
3 And the king of Jericho sent unto Rahab,
saying, "Bring forth the [1]men that are come
to thee, which are entered into thine house:
for they be come to search out °all the
country."
4 And the woman took the two [1]men, and
hid them, and said thus, "There came men
unto me, but I °wist not whence they *were*:
5 And it came to pass *about the time* of shutting of the gate, when it was dark, that the
[1]men went out: °whither the men went I
°wot not: pursue after them quickly; for ye
shall overtake them."
6 But she had brought them up to the roof
of the house, and hid them with the °stalks
of flax, which she had laid in order upon the
roof.
7 And the [1]men pursued after them the way
to Jordan unto the fords: and as soon as they
which pursued after them were gone out, they
shut the gate.

g i k 8 And before they were laid down, she came
up unto them upon the roof;

13 the word. Cp. Num. 32. 20-24.
14 your. Some codices, with Sept., Syr., and Vulg., read "and your". Hence note Fig. *Polysyndeton* (Ap. 6).
armed. Heb. = marshalled by fives (see Ap. 10). Cp. Ex. 13. 18, where it is rendered "harnessed".
15 them. A special various reading called *Sevīr* (Ap. 34) reads "you", as in next clause, with many codices, and three early printed editions.

16-18 (*A*, p. 291). JOSHUA. OBEDIENCE OF PEOPLE. (*Alternation.*)

A | c | 16, 17-. Whatsoever. Positive.
  | d | -17. Only. Jehovah "be with thee".
  | c | 18-. Whatsoever. Negative.
  | d | -18. Only. "Be strong."

16 All = whatsoever, as in *v.* 18.
17 be with thee. Cp. Ex. 3. 14.
18 doth = shall.
commandment. Heb. "mouth", put by Fig. *Metonymy* (of Cause), for what is uttered by it. See Ap. 6.
commandest = shalt command.

2. 1—7. 26 (**B**, p. 289). JORDAN. EVENTS CONNECTED THEREWITH. (*Alternation.*)

B | C | 2. 1-24. Joshua's two spies.
  | D | 3. 1—5. 12. Jordan. The passage of it.
  | *C* | 5. 13-15. Jehovah's one Captain.
  | *D* | 6. 1—7. 26. Jericho. The taking of it.

2. 1-24 (C, above). JOSHUA'S TWO SPIES. (*Alternation.*)

C | e | 1-. Their mission.
  | f | -1-22. Events. Their happening.
  | *e* | 23-. Their return.
  | *f* | -23, 24. Events. Their narration.

-1-22 (f, above). EVENTS. THEIR HAPPENING. (*Alternation.*)

f | g | -1. The Spies. Their Arrival.
  | h | 2-7. Search of king.
  | *g* | 8-22-. The Spies. Their Entertainment.
  | *h* | -22. Search of king.

1 Joshua. He had been one of the twelve spies himself. Num. 13. 8, 16.
sent = had sent. See 1. 11. Cp. 1. 2.
men. Heb. pl. of *'īsh* or *'ěnōsh.* See Ap. 14.
view. Some codices, with one early printed edition, Sept., and Vulg., read "and view".
Jericho. In Num. eleven times *Y^e^rěchō.* Here *Y^e^richō.* Showing difference of authorship.
came. The Sept. preserves the primitive text by adding "to Jericho and came". Omitted by Fig. *Homœoteleuton.* See Ap. 6.
harlot's. Word to be taken in usual sense.
Rahab. See Matt. 1. 5. Heb. 11. 31. Jas. 2. 25.
2 Behold. Fig. *Asterismos.* Ap. 6.
children = sons.
3 all. Some codices, with Sept. and Syr., omit "all".
4 wist not. Anglo-Saxon for "knew not". It is *this record* that is inspired, not the act and words of Rahab.
5 whither. Some codices, with one early printed edition, read "and whither".
wot. Anglo-Saxon "know".
6 stalks of flax. Heb. = flax of stalks. Fig. *Hypallage,* Ap. 6. Flax now ripe: just before the Passover. Cp. Ex. 9. 31 with Josh. 4. 19; 5. 10.

8-22- (*g*, above). ENTERTAINMENT OF SPIES. (*Extended Alternation.*)

g | i | k | 8-14. Treaty with Rahab.
  | | l | 15. Dismissal of Spies.
  | | m | 16. Advice given.
  | *i* | *k* | 17-21-. Treaty with Rahab.
  | | *l* | -21. Dismissal of Spies.
  | | *m* | 22-. Advice taken.

1451 9 And she said unto the men, ° "I know that
° the LORD hath given you the land, and that
your terror is fallen upon us, and that all
the inhabitants of the land ° faint because
of you.
10 For we have ° heard how [9] the LORD
° dried up the water of the Red sea for you,
when ye came out of Egypt; and what ye did
unto the two kings of the Amorites, that *were*
on the ° other side Jordan, Sihon and Og,
whom ye utterly destroyed.
11 And as soon as we had heard *these things*,
our hearts did ° melt, neither did there ° remain
any more ° courage in ° any man, because
of you: for [9] the LORD your ° God, he *is* ° God
in heaven above, and in earth beneath.
12 Now therefore, I pray you, swear unto me
by [9] the LORD, since I have shewed you kindness,
that ye will also shew kindness unto my
father's house, ° and give me a true token:
13 And *that* ye will save alive my father,
and my mother, and my brethren, and my
sisters, and all that they have, and deliver
our ° lives from death."
14 And the [1] men answered her, "Our [13] life
for yours, if ° ye utter not this our business.
And it shall be, when [9] the LORD hath given us
the land, that we will deal ° kindly and truly
with thee."

l (p. 292) 15 Then she let them down by a ° cord
through the window: for her house *was* ° upon
the town wall, and she dwelt ° upon the wall.

m 16 And she said unto them, "Get you to the
mountain, lest the pursuers meet you; and
hide yourselves there three days, until the
pursuers be returned: and afterward may ye
go your way."

k 17 And the [1] men said unto her, "We *will be*
blameless of this thine oath which thou hast
made us swear.
18 ° Behold, *when* we come into the land,
thou shalt bind this ° line of scarlet thread in
the window which thou didst let us down
° by: and thou shalt ° bring thy father, and
thy mother, and thy brethren, and all thy
father's household, ° home unto thee.
19 And it shall be, *that* whosoever shall go
out of the doors of thy house into the street,
his blood *shall be* upon his head, and we *will be*
guiltless: and whosoever shall be with thee
in the house, his blood *shall be* on our head, if
any hand be upon him.
20 And if thou utter this our business, then
we will be quit of thine oath which thou hast
made us to swear."
21 And she said, "According unto your
words, so *be* it."

l And she sent them away, and they departed:
and she bound the scarlet line in the
window.

m 22 And they went, and came unto the mountain,
and abode there three days, until the
pursuers were returned:

h and the pursuers sought *them* throughout all
the way, but found *them* not.

9 I know. Faith's conclusion, from what she had heard, *vv.* 10, 11. Corresponds with Sarah's "she judged" in Heb. 11. 11.
the LORD. Heb. Jehovah. Ap. 4. II.
faint. Heb. = have melted. Cp. *v.* 11.
10 heard. This is the "ground" (Heb. 11. 1) of faith. Cp. Rom. 10. 17.
dried up. Cp. Ex. 14. 21.
other side. This written in the Land. Cp. Num. 21. 31.
11 melt. Cp. Ex. 15. 14, 15. Prophecy fulfilled.
remain. Heb. = rise up.
courage. Heb. *rūach*, spirit. See Ap. 9.
any man. Heb. *'ish.* See Ap. 14. II.
God. Heb. Elohim. Ap. 4. I.
12 and. Note the Fig. *Polysyndeton* (Ap. 6) here and *v.* 13, showing the earnestness of the appeal.
13 lives. Heb. "souls". See Ap. 13.
14 ye. Some codices, with one early printed edition, and Vulg., read "thou".
kindly and truly = in lovingkindness and faithfulness. Perhaps Fig. *Hendiadys* (Ap. 6), "in true lovingkindness".
15 cord = the rope. Cp. Sept. here with Acts 9. 25, and 2 Cor. 11. 33. Cp. 1 Cor. 11. 10.
upon the town wall = [built] into the *ḥōmah*; i. e. the outer or lower wall.
upon the wall = in the *ḳir*; i. e. the inner or higher wall.
18 Behold. Fig. *Asterismos.* Ap. 6.
line. Heb. "hope", put by Fig. *Metonymy* (of Adjunct), Ap. 6, for the line which was the token of it.
by = through: referring to the window. Cp. *v.* 21.
bring = gather.
home = unto the house. The "line" was outside, for Joshua to see; not for the inmates. Cp. Ex. 12. 13, "When I see, &c." So the ground of our assurance is not experience within, but the token without.

3. 1—5. 12 (D, p. 292). JORDAN. THE PASSAGE OF IT. (*Division.*)

D | E¹ | 3. 1—4. 24. Event. The Passage.
  | E² | 5. 1-12. Event. After the Passage.

3. 1—4. 24 (E¹, above). EVENT. THE PASSAGE. (*Extended Alternation.*)

E¹ | F | n | 3. 1-6. The Ark going before.
   | | o | 3. 7. Joshua magnified. (Promise.)
   | | p | 3. 8. Commands to Priests.
   | | q | r | 3. 9-17. Cutting off of the waters.
   | | | s | 4. 1-10. Memorial.
   | *F* | *n* | 4. 11-13. The Ark going before.
   | | *o* | 4. 14. Joshua magnified. (Performance.)
   | | *p* | 4. 15-17. Commands to Priests.
   | | *q* | *r* | 4. 18, 19. Return of the waters.
   | | | *s* | 4. 20-24. Memorial.

1 early in the morning: i. e. after the command in 1. 2.
children = sons.
2 after = at the end of.
host = camp.

23 So the two [1] men returned, and descended e
from the mountain, and passed over, and came (p. 292)
to Joshua the son of Nun, 5th or 6th Abib

and told him all *things* that befell them: f
24 And they said unto Joshua, "Truly [9] the
LORD hath delivered into our hands all the
land; for even all the inhabitants of the
country do [9] faint because of us."

3 And Joshua rose ° early in the morning; E¹ F n
and they removed from Shittim, and came (p. 293)
to Jordan, he and all the ° children of Israel, 10th
and lodged there before they passed over. Abib
2 And it came to pass ° after three days, that
the officers went through the ° host;

1451 3 And they commanded the People, saying, "When ye see °the ark of the covenant of °the LORD your °God, and the priests °the Levites °bearing it, then ye shall remove from your place, and go after it.

4 Yet there shall be °a space between you and it, about two thousand °cubits by measure: come not near unto it, that ye may know the way by which ye must go: for ye have not passed *this* way heretofore."

5 And Joshua said unto the People, "Sanctify yourselves: for to morrow [3]the LORD will do wonders among you."

6 And Joshua spake unto the priests, saying, "Take up [3]the ark of the covenant, and pass over before the People." And they took up [3]the ark of the covenant, and went before the People.

o (p. 293) 7 And °the LORD said unto Joshua, "This day will I begin to magnify thee in the sight of all Israel, that they may know that, °as I was with Moses, *so* I will be with thee.

p 8 And thou shalt command the priests that bear the ark of the covenant, saying, 'When ye are come to the brink of the water of Jordan, ye shall stand still in Jordan.'"

r t v (p. 294) 9 And Joshua said unto the [1]children of Israel, "Come hither, and hear the words of [3]the LORD your [3]God."

10 And Joshua said, "Hereby ye shall know that the °living °GOD *is* among you, and *that* He will without fail drive out from before you the Canaanites, °and the Hittites, and the Hivites, and the Perizzites, and the Girgashites, and the Amorites, and the Jebusites.

11 °Behold, the ark of the covenant of °the Lord of all the earth passeth over before you into Jordan.

12 Now therefore take you °twelve °men out of the tribes of Israel, out of every tribe a man.

w 13 And it shall come to pass, as soon as the soles of the feet of the priests that bear the ark of °the LORD, [11]the Lord of all the earth, shall rest in the waters of Jordan, *that* the waters of Jordan shall be °cut off *from* the waters that come down from above; and they shall stand upon °an heap."

v 14 And it came to pass, when the People removed from their tents, to pass over Jordan, and the priests bearing the [3]ark of the covenant before the People;

w 15 And as they that [3]bare the ark were come unto Jordan, and the feet of the priests that bare [3]the ark were dipped in the brim of the water, (°for Jordan °overfloweth all his °banks all the time of °harvest,)

16 That the waters which came down from above stood *and* rose up upon an heap very far from the city °Adam, that *is* beside °Zaretan: and those that came down toward the °sea of the plain, *even* the °salt sea, failed, *and* were cut off: and °the People passed over right against Jericho.

u 17 And the priests that bare [3]the ark of the covenant of [3]the LORD stood firm on dry ground in the midst of Jordan, and °all the Israelites passed over on dry ground, until all the People °were passed clean over Jordan.

4 And it came to pass, when all the People °were clean passed over Jordan, that °the LORD °spake unto Joshua, saying, s t z[1] (p. 295)

3. 9—4. 10 (r, p. 293). CUTTING OFF, AND MEMORIAL. (*Alternation.*)

r | t | 3. 9-16. The cutting off.
  u | 3. 17. Priests' feet standing firm.
  t | 4. 1-9. The Memorial.
  u | 4. 10. Priests' feet standing firm.

3. 9-16 (t, above). THE CUTTING OFF. (*Alternation.*)

t | v | 3. 9-12. Ark going before.
  w | 13. Prediction. Waters.
  v | 14. Ark going before.
  w | 15, 16. Fulfilment. Waters.

3 the ark. Not the cloud, but the ark; as from Sinai. Cp. Num. 10. 33.

the LORD your God = Jehovah your Elohim. Ap. 4.

the Levites. Some codices, with three early printed editions, Sept., and Syr., read "and the Levites".

bearing it. Supply the Ellipsis (Ap. 6. III) by adding "[going before]" from next clause.

4 a space. This is very significant. Cp. Ex. 19. 12, 13, 22. Lev. 10. 3.

cubits. See Ap. 51. III. 2. About 1½ miles.

7 the LORD (Heb. Jehovah) **said unto Joshua** (or him), at nine sundry times: 3. 7; 5. 2; 6. 2; 7. 10; 8. 1, 18; 10. 8; 11. 6; 13. 1. **as** = according as.

10 living. This title always has a latent reference to idols. Here, to the gods of the idolatrous nations named.

GOD. Heb. *'el.* Ap. 4. IV.

and. Note the Fig. *Polysyndeton* (Ap. 6), to emphasise the seven nations.

11 Behold. Fig. *Asterismos.* Ap. 6.

the Lord of all the earth. Heb. the *Adōn* of all the earth. A title connected with sovereignty in the earth. Cp. 3. 11, 13. Zech. 6. 5, the only three occurrences of this full title. See Ap. 4. VIII. (1); and cp. Ps. 97. 5. Mic. 4. 13. Zech. 4. 14.

12 twelve. The number of governmental perfection. See Ap. 10. **men.** Heb. *'ish.* See Ap. 14. II.

13 the LORD. Heb. Jehovah. Ap. 4. II.

cut off. Three times: here, for Israel; 2 Kings 2. 8, for Elijah; and 2 Kings 2. 14, for Elisha.

an heap = one heap. Cp. Ps. 114. 3.

15 for. Note the parenthesis.

overfloweth. So to the present day.

banks. Heb. found only four times in O.T.; here, 4. 18. 1 Chron. 12. 15. Isa. 8. 7. All but the last, of the Jordan.

harvest = barley harvest. Cp. note on 2. 6.

16 Adam. The waters were divided at (or near) the city "Adam", and they were heaped up at (or near) "Zaretan", another city far off from "Adam".

Zaretan: in the land of Manasseh. Called Zartanah in 1 Kings 4. 12. The brazen vessels of the temple were cast there in the plain of Jordan (1 Kings 7. 46).

sea of the plain: i. e. the Dead Sea.

salt sea. Fig. *Polyonymia.* Ap. 6.

the People passed over. A way cleft through the sea (Ex. 14), through the river (Josh. 3), and in the future through the air (Phil. 3. 14. 1 Thess. 4. 17).

17 all the Israelites: better = all Israel.

were passed clean over = finished passing over.

4. 1-9 [For Structure see next page].

1 were clean passed over = were finished passing over.

the LORD. Heb. Jehovah. Ap. 4. II.

spake. See note on 1. 1.

1451 2 "Take you twelve ° men out of the People,
out of every tribe a ° man,
a^1 (p. 295) 3 And command ye them, saying,

'Take you hence out of the midst of Jordan,
out of the place where the priests' feet stood
firm, twelve stones, and ye shall carry them
over with you,

y^1 and leave them in the lodging place, where ye
shall lodge this night.'"

z^2 4 Then Joshua called the twelve [2]men, whom
he had prepared of the ° children of Israel, out
of every tribe a man:

a^2 5 And Joshua said unto them, "Pass over
° before the ark of [1]the LORD your ° God into
the midst of Jordan, and take ye up every man
of you a stone upon his shoulder, according
unto the number of the tribes of the [4]children
of Israel:

y^2 6 That this may be a sign among you, *that*
when your [4]children ask ° *their fathers* in time
to come, saying, 'What *mean* ye by these
stones?'
7 Then ye shall answer them, 'That the
waters of Jordan were cut off before the ark
of the covenant of [1]the LORD; when it passed
over Jordan, the waters of Jordan were cut
off:' and these stones shall be for a memorial
unto the [4]children of Israel for ever."

a^3 8 And the [4]children of Israel did so ° as
Joshua commanded, and ° took up twelve
stones out of the midst of Jordan, ° as [1]the
LORD spake unto Joshua,

z^3 according to the number of the tribes of the
[4]children of Israel, and carried them over with
them

y^3 unto the place where they lodged, and laid
them down ° there.
9 And Joshua set up ° twelve stones in the
midst of Jordan, in the place where the feet of
the priests which bare the ark of the covenant
stood: and they are there unto this day.

u (p. 294) 10 For the priests which bare the ark stood
in the midst of Jordan, until every thing was
finished that [1]the LORD commanded Joshua
to speak unto the People, according to all that
Moses commanded Joshua: and the People
hasted and passed over.

F n (p. 293) 11 And it came to pass, when all the People
[1]were clean passed over, that the ark of [1]the
LORD passed over, and the priests, in the
presence of the People.
12 And the [4]children of ° Reuben, and the
[4]children of Gad, and half the tribe of Manasseh, passed over ° armed before the [4]children
of Israel, [8]as Moses spake unto them:
13 About forty thousand ° prepared for war
passed over before [1]the LORD unto battle, to
the plains of Jericho.

o 14 ° On that day [1]the LORD magnified Joshua
in the sight of all Israel; and they feared him,
[8]as they feared Moses, all the days of his life.

p 15 And [1]the LORD [1]spake unto Joshua,
saying,

4. 1-9 (*t*, p. 294). THE MEMORIAL.
(*Repeated Alternation and Introversion.*)

t | x^1 | z^1 | 1, 2. Twelve men.
a^1 | 3-. Twelve stones.
y^1 | -3. The Place.
x^2 | z^2 | 4. Twelve men.
a^2 | 5. Twelve stones.
y^2 | 6, 7. The Memorial.
x^3 | a^3 | 8-. Twelve stones.
z^3 | -8-. Twelve men.
y^3 | -8, 9. The Place.

2 men. Pl. of *'ish* or *'ĕnōsh.* See Ap. 14.
man. Heb. *'ish.* Ap. 14. II.
4 children = sons.
5 before = in the presence of.
God. Heb. Elohim. Ap. 4. I.
6 their fathers. These words are read in some codices, with four early printed editions, as in *v.* 21.
8 as = according as.
took up. Four things said of these memorial stones in *vv.* 8 and 9: (1) taken up; (2) carried over; (3) laid down; (4) set up.
there. See note on 8. 30.
9 twelve. Sept. has "other twelve". There were two twelves.
12 Reuben. Cp. Num. 32. 27. Cp. 1. 12.
armed = by fives. Cp. 6. 7, 9. These formed the van.
13 prepared for war = ready armed.
14 On that day. Cp. 3. 7.
20 took out. Cp. *vv.* 8, 9.
23 which He dried up. Ex. 14. 21.
24 People = Peoples.

16 "Command the priests that bear the ark
of the testimony, that they come up out of
Jordan."
17 Joshua therefore commanded the priests,
saying, "Come ye up out of Jordan."

18 And it came to pass, when the priests that *q r*
bare the ark of the covenant of [1]the LORD
were come up out of the midst of Jordan, *and*
the soles of the priests' feet were lifted up unto
the dry land, that the waters of Jordan returned unto their place, and flowed over all
his banks, as *they did* before.
19 And the People came up out of Jordan 10th
on the tenth *day* of the first month, and Abib
encamped in Gilgal, in the east border of
Jericho.

20 And those twelve stones, which they *s*
° took out of Jordan, did Joshua pitch in
Gilgal.
21 And he spake unto the [4]children of Israel,
saying, "When your [4]children shall ask their
fathers in time to come, saying, 'What *mean*
these stones?'
22 Then ye shall let your [4]children know,
saying, 'Israel came over this Jordan on dry
land.
23 For [1]the LORD your [5]God dried up the
waters of Jordan from before you, until ye
were passed over, as [1]the LORD your [5]God
did to the Red sea, ° which He dried up from
before us, until we were gone over:
24 That all the ° People of the earth might
know the hand of [1]the LORD, that it *is* mighty:
that ye might fear [1]the LORD your [5]God for
ever.'"

E[2] (p. 293) 1451
5 And it came to pass, when all the kings of the Amorites, which *were* on the side of Jordan westward, and all the kings of the Canaanites, which *were* by the sea, heard that °the LORD had dried up the waters of Jordan from before the °children of Israel, until °we were passed over, that their heart °melted, neither was there °spirit in them any more, because of the °children of Israel.

2 At that time [1]the LORD °said unto Joshua, "Make thee sharp knives, and circumcise °again the [1]children of Israel °the second time."

3 And Joshua made him sharp knives, and circumcised the [1]children of Israel at the hill of the foreskins.

4 And this *is* the cause why Joshua did circumcise: All the People that came out of Egypt, *that were* males, *even* all the °men of war, died in the wilderness by the way, after they came out of Egypt.

5 Now all the People that came out were circumcised: but all the People *that were* born in the wilderness by the way as they came forth out of Egypt, *them* they had not circumcised.

6 For the [1]children of Israel walked forty years in the wilderness, till all the °People *that were* [4]men of war, which came out of Egypt, were consumed, because they °obeyed not the voice of [1]the LORD: unto whom [1]the LORD sware that He would not shew them the land, which [1]the LORD sware unto their fathers that He would give us, a land that floweth with milk and honey.

7 And their [1]children, *whom* He raised up in their stead, them Joshua circumcised: for they were uncircumcised, because they had not circumcised them by the way.

11th–13th Abib
8 And it came to pass, when they had done circumcising all the [6]People, that they °abode in their places in the camp, till they were whole.

9 And [1]the LORD said unto Joshua, "This day have I °rolled away the reproach of Egypt from off you." Wherefore the name of the place is called °Gilgal unto this day.

14th Abib
10 And the [1]children of Israel encamped in Gilgal, and °kept the passover on the fourteenth day of the month at even in the plains of Jericho.

11 And they did eat of the old corn of the land on °the morrow after the passover, unleavened cakes, and parched *corn* in the selfsame day.

16th Abib
12 And the manna ceased on the morrow after they had eaten of the old corn of the land; neither had the [1]children of Israel manna any more; but they did eat of the °fruit of the land of Canaan that year.

C b[1] (p. 296)
13 And it came to pass, °when Joshua was by Jericho, that he lifted up his eyes and looked, and, behold, there stood °a Man over against him with His sword drawn in His hand:

c[1]
and Joshua went unto Him, and said unto Him, "*Art* Thou for us, or for our adversaries?"

b[2]
14 And He said, "Nay; but *as* °Captain of the °host of [1]the LORD am I now come."

c[2]
And Joshua fell on his face to the earth, and did °worship, and said unto Him, "What saith °my Lord unto His servant?"

b[3]
15 And the Captain of [1]the LORD'S host said unto Joshua, °"Loose thy shoe from off thy foot; for the place whereon thou standest °*is* holy."

c[3]
And Joshua did so.

D G[1] H[1] d (p. 297)
6 Now Jericho °was straitly shut up because of the °children of Israel: none went out, and none came in.

---

1 the LORD. Heb. Jehovah. Ap. 4. II.
children = sons.
we. So written, but read "they". Some codices have "they", both written and read, with three early printed editions, Sept., Syr., and Vulg.
melted. See note on 2. 9, 11.
spirit. Heb. *rūach.* Ap. 9.
2 said. See note on 3. 7.
again . . . the second time. Not repeated as an act on the *person*, but on the *nation* on a second occasion (cp. for this usage Isa. 11. 11 and Jude 5), implying that the rite was performed in Egypt. See *vv.* 4–7.
4 men. Heb. pl. of *'īsh* or *'ĕnōsh.* Ap. 14. II.
6 People = nation. Some codices, with two early printed editions, read "generation".
obeyed not = hearkened not unto.
8 abode. 11th to 13th Abib.
9 rolled away = Heb. *gallōthī.* Hence **Gilgal** = rolling.
10 kept the passover. Some codices, with two early printed editions, and MS. of Aramaic, add "in the first [month]". The second of the ten Passovers recorded. See note on Ex. 12. 28.
11 the morrow. Feast of unleavened bread ended 21st Abib at even, exactly forty years from Ex. 12. 41.
12 fruit = produce.

13–15 (*C*, p. 292). **JEHOVAH'S ONE CAPTAIN.** (*Repeated Alternation.*)

C | b[1] | 13–. The Captain. Vision.
   c[1] | –13. Joshua. Question asked.
 b[2] | 14–. The Captain. Revelation.
   c[2] | –14. Joshua. Worship accepted.
 b[3] | 15–. The Captain. Direction.
   c[3] | –15. Joshua. Obedience given.

13 when. Between 15th and 21st Abib.
a Man. Heb. *'īsh.* Ap. 14. II.
14 Captain, or Prince.
host = Israel as Jehovah's host. Cp. Ex. 12. 41.
worship. Therefore Divine. Cp. Rev. 19. 10; 22. 9.
my Lord = *Adonai.* Ap. 4. VIII (2).
15 Loose thy shoe. Cp. Ex. 3. 5. The origin of a solemn Eastern custom of reverence observed to this day. Cp. Ex. 3. 5.
is holy. Heb. "it [is] holy". See note on Ex. 3. 5.

6. 1—7. 26 (*D*, p. 292). **JERICHO: THE TAKING OF IT.** (*Division.*)

D | G[1] | 6. 1–27. The Taking of Jericho.
 | G[2] | 7. 1–26. The Trespass of Achan.

6. 1–27 (G[1], above). **THE TAKING OF JERICHO.** (*Division.*)

G[1] | H[1] | 1–19. The City Given.
 | H[2] | 20–27. The City Taken.

6. 1–19 [For Structure see next page].

1 was straitly shut up. Heb. "was shutting up and was shut up". Fig. *Polyptōton* (Ap. 6) for emphasis, thus beautifully rendered. See note on Gen. 26. 28.
children = sons.

1451 2 And °the LORD °said unto Joshua, °"See, °I have given into thine hand Jericho, and the king thereof, *and* the mighty °men of valour.

e f (p. 297) 3 And ye shall compass the city, all *ye* men of war, *and* go round about the city once. Thus shalt thou do six days.

4 And seven priests shall bear before the ark seven trumpets of °rams' horns: and °the seventh day ye shall compass the city seven times, and the priests shall blow with the trumpets.

g 5 And it shall come to pass, that when they make a long *blast* with the [4]ram's horn, *and* when ye hear the sound of the trumpet, all the people shall shout with a great shout; and the wall of the city shall fall down °flat, and the People shall ascend up °every man straight before him."

e f 6 And Joshua the son of Nun called the priests, and said unto them, "Take up the ark of the covenant, and let seven priests bear seven trumpets of [4]rams' horns before the ark of [2]the LORD."

7 And °he said unto the People, "Pass on, and compass the city, and let him that is armed pass on before the ark of [2]the LORD."

8 And it came to pass, when Joshua had spoken unto the People, that the seven priests bearing the seven trumpets of [4]rams' horns passed on °before [2]the LORD, and blew with the trumpets: and the ark of the covenant of [2]the LORD followed them.

9 And the armed men °went before the priests that blew with the trumpets, and the °rereward °came after the ark, *the priests* °going on, and blowing with the trumpets.

10 And Joshua had commanded the People, saying, "Ye shall not shout, nor °make any noise with your voice, neither shall *any* word proceed out of your mouth, until the day I bid you shout; then shall ye shout."

22nd Abib 11 So the ark of [2]the LORD compassed the city, going about *it* once: and they came into the camp, and lodged in the camp.

12 And Joshua rose early in the morning, and the priests took up the ark of [2]the LORD.

13 And seven priests bearing seven trumpets of [4]rams' horns before the ark of [2]the LORD went on continually, and blew with the trumpets: and the armed men went before them; but the [9]rereward came after the ark of [2]the LORD, *the priests* going on, and blowing with the trumpets.

28th Abib 14 And the second day they compassed the city once, and returned into the camp: so they did six days.

15 And it came to pass on the seventh day, that they rose early about the dawning of the day, and compassed the city after the same manner seven times: only on that day they compassed the city seven times.

g 16 And it came to pass at °the seventh time, when the priests blew with the trumpets, Joshua said unto the People, "Shout;

d for [2]the LORD hath given you the city.

6. 1-19 (H[1], p. 296). THE CITY GIVEN.
(Introversion and Alternation.)

H[1] | d | 1, 2. The City given.
| e | f | 3, 4. Encompassing.
| | g | 5. Promise.
| *e* | *f* | 6-15. Encompassing.
| | *g* | 16-. Promise.
| *d* | -16-19. The City. Exceptions in Gift.

2 the LORD. Heb. Jehovah. Ap. 4. II.
said. This is the continuation of the Captain's words, 5. 15. See note on 3. 7.
See. Fig. *Asterismos.* Ap. 6.
I have given. It was Jehovah's to give.
men. Heb. pl. of *'ish* or *'ĕnōsh.* Ap. 14. II.
4 rams' horns = trumpets of Jubilee, of long sound. Ex. 19. 13.
the seventh day = on the seventh day.
5 flat = under it. Probably into the ground. Cp. 11. 13. Jer. 49. 2. See note on *v.* 20.
every man = Heb. *'ish.* Ap. 14. II.
7 he. In Heb. text written "they", but read "he". In some codices, with five early printed editions, both written and read "he".
8 before. Some codices, with five early printed editions, and Aram., Syr., and Vulg., add "the ark of".
9 went = marching.
rereward = the main or central body. Cp. Num. 10. 25.
came = marched.
going = marching.
10 make = cause your voice to be heard.
16 the seventh time. Cp. Heb. 11. 30.
17 accursed = devoted. Probably because this was the "first-fruit" of conquest. Num. 31. 54. Cp. *v.* 19.
she hid. Cp. 2. 4.
18 trouble it. A warning of Achan's sin (7. 25).
19 vessels = utensils, or weapons.
are. Heb. = "they are".
consecrated = holy. See note on Ex. 3. 5.

20-27 (H[2], p. 296). THE CITY TAKEN.
(Introversion and Alternation.)

H[2] | h | 20. The city taken.
| i | k | 21. The city destroyed.
| | l | 22, 23. Exception. Rahab.
| *i* | *k* | 24-. The city burned.
| | *l* | -24, 25. Exception. Rahab, &c.
| *h* | 26, 27. The city cursed.

20 flat = under itself. Cp. *v.* 5. Jericho was thrice built, and thrice destroyed; so that the city of Joshua's

17 And the city shall be °accursed, *even* it, and all that *are* therein, to [2]the LORD: only Rahab the harlot shall live, she and all that *are* with her in the house, because °she hid the messengers that we sent.

18 And ye, in any wise keep *yourselves* from the accursed thing, lest ye make *yourselves* accursed, when ye take of the [17]accursed thing, and make the camp of Israel a curse, and °trouble it.

19 But all the silver, and gold, and °vessels of brass and iron, °*are* °consecrated unto [2]the LORD: they shall come into the treasury of [2]the LORD."

20 So the People shouted when *the priests* H[2] h
blew with the trumpets: and it came to pass, when the People heard the sound of the trumpet, and the People shouted with a great shout, that the wall fell down °flat, so that the

1451 People went up into the city, [5]every man straight before him, and they took the city.

i k (p. 297) 21 And they utterly °destroyed all that *was* in the city, both man and woman, young and old, and ox, and sheep, and ass, °with the edge of the sword.

l 22 But Joshua had said unto the two men that had spied out the country, "Go into the harlot's house, and bring out thence the woman, and °all that she hath, °as ye sware unto her."

23 And the young men that were spies went in, °and brought out Rahab, and her father, and her mother, and her brethren, and all that she had; and they brought out all her kindred, and left them without the camp of Israel.

i k 24 And they burnt the city with fire, and all that *was* therein:

l only the silver, [23]and the gold, and the vessels of brass and of iron, they put into the treasury of the house of [2]the LORD.

25 [23]And Joshua saved °Rahab the harlot alive, [24]and her father's household, and all that she had; and she dwelleth °in Israel *even* °unto this day; because she hid the messengers, which Joshua sent to spy out Jericho.

h 26 And Joshua adjured *them* at that time, saying, "Cursed *be* the °man before [2]the LORD, that riseth up and °buildeth this city Jericho: °he shall lay the foundation thereof °in his firstborn, and in his youngest *son* shall he set up the gates of it."

27 So [2]the LORD was with Joshua; and his fame was *noised* throughout all the country.

G^2 J (p. 298) **7** But the °children of Israel committed °a trespass in the °accursed thing: for °Achan, the son of Carmi, the son of Zabdi, the son of Zerah, of the tribe of Judah, °took of the °accursed thing: and the anger of °the LORD was kindled against the °children of Israel.

K m 2 And Joshua sent °men from Jericho to °Ai, which *is* beside °Beth-aven, on the east side of °Beth-el, and spake unto them, saying, "Go up and view the country." And the men went up and viewed Ai.

n 3 And they returned to Joshua, and said unto him, "Let not all the People °go up; but let about two or three thousand °men go up and smite Ai; *and* make not all the People to labour thither; for they *are but* few."

n 4 So there went up thither of the People about three thousand [3]men: and they fled before the men of Ai.

5 And the [2]men of Ai smote of them about thirty and six men: for they chased them *from* before the gate *even* unto Shebarim, and smote them in the going down: wherefore the hearts of the People °melted, and became as water.

m 6 And Joshua rent his clothes, and fell to the earth upon his face before the ark of [1]the LORD until the eventide, he and the elders of Israel, and put dust upon their heads.

7 And Joshua said, °"Alas, O °Lord °GOD, °wherefore hast Thou at all brought this people over Jordan, to deliver us into the hand of the Amorites, to destroy us? °would to God we had been content, and dwelt on the other side Jordan!

---

time has not yet been reached by recent excavations. The city, rebuilt by Hiel in Ahab's reign (822–790 B.C.), was captured by the Herodians (3 B.C.) and rebuilt by Archelaus (A.D. 2). This was the Jericho of our Lord's day, which was destroyed by Vespasian, A.D. 68.

21 destroyed = devoted [to destruction]. Fig. *Ellipsis* (Ap. 6), to be thus supplied.

with the edge = according to the mouth. "Mouth" by Fig. *Metonymy* (of Cause), Ap. 6 = without quarter.

22 all that she hath = all her household, *v.* 17.

as = according as. Cp. 2. 14. Heb. 11. 31.

23 and. Note the Fig. *Polysyndeton* in *vv.* 23–25. Ap. 6.

25 Rahab. Cp. Matt. 1. 5. Married to Salmon, in the line of the Messiah.

in = in the midst of.

unto this day. Written therefore during her lifetime.

26 man. Heb. *'ish.* Ap. 14. II.

buildeth this city: i.e. its walls and gates (*v.* 26), for Joshua himself gave it to the Benjamites, 18. 12. Cp. 2 Sam. 10. 5. See note on *v.* 20.

he shall lay. Prophecy fulfilled in Hiel the Beth-elite. 1 Kings 16. 34.

in = in [the death of] his firstborn.

7. 1–26 (G^2, p. 296). THE TRESPASS OF ACHAN. (*Introversion.*)

G^2 | J | 1. Achan's trespass committed. Jericho.
  K | 2–9. Consequence. Defeat at Ai.
  K | 10–12. Cause of defeat explained.
J | 13–26. Achan's trespass to be put away. Achor.

1 children = sons.

a trespass = a treachery, unfaithfulness. Heb. *ma'al.* Ap. 43. xi. Cp. Lev. 6. 2. Deut. 32. 51. 1 Chron. 5. 25: breach of faith or trust.

accursed = devoted. Cp. 6. 17, &c.

Achan = Troubler; called Achar, 1 Chron. 2. 7.

took. Sept. has *enosphisanto* = took for themselves, i.e. sacrilege. Same word as in Acts 5. 1, 2 of Ananias and Sapphira.

the LORD. Heb. Jehovah. Ap. 4. II.

2–9 (K, above). CONSEQUENCE. DEFEAT AT AI. (*Introversion.*)

K | m | 2. Joshua's mission.
  n | 3. Advice given. Report.
  n | 4, 5. Advice taken. Result.
m | 6–9. Joshua's mourning.

2 men. Heb. pl. of *'ish* or *'ĕnōsh.* Ap. 14.

Ai. Near Beth-el. Cp. Gen. 12. 8; 13. 3.

Beth-aven = House of vanity.

Beth-el = House of God. Cp. Gen. 28. 19.

3 go up = go toilingly thither.

men = Heb. *'ish.* Ap. 14. II.

5 melted = became as water. Fig. *Hyperbolē.* Ap. 6.

7 Alas. Fig. *Ecphōnēsis.* Ap. 6.

Lord GOD = Adonai Jehovah. See Ap. 4. II, VIII (2), and X.

wherefore . . . ? Fig. *Erotēsis.* Ap. 6.

would to God. Heb. "would that". No "to God" in Heb. text.

1451 8 °O LORD*, what shall I say, when Israel °turneth their backs before their enemies!

9 For the Canaanites and all the inhabitants of the land shall hear *of it*, and shall environ us round, and cut off our name from the earth: and °what wilt Thou do unto Thy great name?"

K (p. 298) 10 And [1]the LORD °said unto Joshua, "Get thee up; [7]wherefore liest thou thus upon thy face?

11 Israel hath sinned, °and they have also transgressed My covenant which I commanded them: °for they have even taken of the [1]accursed thing, and have also stolen, and dissembled also, and they have put *it* even among their own stuff.

12 Therefore the [1]children of Israel could not stand before their enemies, *but* turned *their* backs before their enemies, because they were [1]accursed: neither will I be with you any more, except ye destroy the [1]accursed from among you.

J o q (p. 299) 13 Up, sanctify the People, and say, 'Sanctify yourselves against to morrow: for thus saith [1]the LORD °God of Israel, '*There is* an [1]accursed thing in the midst of thee, O Israel: thou canst not stand before thine enemies, until ye take away the [1]accursed thing from among you.

14 In the morning therefore ye shall be brought according to your tribes: and it shall be, *that* the tribe which [1]the LORD °taketh shall come according to the families *thereof;* and the family which [1]the LORD shall take shall come by households; and the household which [1]the LORD shall take shall come °man by °man.

15 And it shall be, *that* he that is [14]taken with the [13]accursed thing shall be °burnt with fire, he and all that he hath: because he hath transgressed the covenant of [1]the LORD, and because he hath wrought folly in Israel.'' "

r 16 So Joshua rose up early in the morning, and brought Israel by their tribes; and the tribe of Judah was taken:

17 And he brought the °family of Judah; and he took the family of the Zarhites: and he brought the family of the Zarhites °man by man; and Zabdi was taken:

18 And he brought his household [17]man by man; and Achan, the son of Carmi, the son of Zabdi, the son of Zerah, of the tribe of Judah, was taken.

p 19 And Joshua said unto Achan, "My son, °give, I pray thee, glory to [1]the LORD [13]God of Israel, and make confession unto Him; and tell me now what thou hast done; hide *it* not from me."

20 And Achan answered Joshua, and said, "Indeed I have sinned against [1]the LORD [13]God of Israel, and thus and thus have I done:

21 When I saw among the spoils °a goodly °Babylonish garment, and two hundred °shekels of silver, and a °wedge of gold of fifty °shekels weight, then I coveted them, and took them; and, °behold, they *are* hid in the earth in the midst of my tent, and the silver under °it."

p 22 So Joshua sent messengers, and they ran unto the tent; and, [21]behold, *it was* hid in his tent, and the silver under [21]it.

23 And they took them out of °the midst of the tent, and brought them unto Joshua, and unto all the [1]children of Israel, and laid them out before [1]the LORD.

24 And Joshua, and all Israel with him, took Achan the °son of Zerah, °and the silver, and the garment, and the [21]wedge of gold, and his sons, and his daughters, and his oxen, and his asses, and his sheep, and his tent, and all that he had: and they brought them unto the valley of Achor.

25 And Joshua said, °"Why hast thou °troubled us? [1]the LORD shall °trouble thee this day." And all Israel stoned him with stones, and [15]burned them with fire, after they had °stoned them with stones. o r

26 And they raised over him a great heap of stones unto this day.

8 O LORD*. Heb. O Adonai; but this is one of the 134 places altered from Jehovah to Adonai by the *Sōpherīm.*

turneth = hath [once] turned.

9 what . . . ? Fig. *Erotēsis.* Ap. 6.

10 said. See note on 3. 7.

11 and. Note the Fig. *Polysyndeton.* Ap. 6.

for = and. All these "ands" might be well rendered "moreover".

10-13. There is a minute correspondence between *vv.* 10-12 and 13, an *Extended Alternation* of five members each, for which we have no space; also between *vv.* 14 and 16-18.

13-26 (*J*, p. 298). ACHAN'S TRESPASS PUT AWAY. (*Introversions.*)

J | o | q | 13-15. The trouble to be removed.
  | | r | 16-18. The troubler to be discovered.
  | | | p | 19-21. Joshua and Achan. Conviction.
  | | | *p* | 22-24. Joshua and Achan. Proof.
  | *o* | *r* | 25, 26-. The troubler stoned.
  | | *q* | -26. The trouble removed.

13 God. Heb. Elohim. Ap. 4. I.

14 taketh = taketh [by lot], i.e. by the *Urim* and *Thummim.* See note on Ex. 28. 30 and Num. 26. 55. The *Urim* stone bringing to "light" the guilty, and the *Thummim* declaring the "perfection" or innocence.

man = *geber.* Ap. 14. IV.

15 burnt = burnt up, but not necessarily alive. Heb. *sārăph.* See Ap. 43. I. viii.

17 family. Some codices, with Sept. and Vulg., read pl. "families".

man by man. Some codices, with two early printed editions, Syr., and Vulg., read "by their households".

19 give . . . glory to the LORD. All the Vulgate versions corrupt this passage by omitting "to Him". The Portuguese version of Figuerado changes "Him" to "me".

21 a = one.

Babylonish. Heb. = "of Shinar", i.e. of Babylonia.

shekels. See Ap. 51. II.

wedge = bar. Heb. tongue: put by Fig. *Metonymy* (of Adjunct) for a coin of this shape (Ap. 6).

behold. Fig. *Asterismos* (Ap. 6).

it. Fem. Probably referring to the garment.

23 the midst. Fig. *Pleonasm* (Ap. 6).

24 son of Zerah. Put by Fig. *Synecdochē* (of Species) for great-grandson. Ap. 6.

and. Note the Fig. *Polysyndeton* (Ap. 6), emphasising each particular.

25 Why . . . ? Fig. *Erotēsis* (Ap. 6).

troubled . . . trouble. Heb. *Achored . . . Achor.*

stoned them: i.e. the people, not the property.

q So [1]the **LORD** turned from °the fierceness of
(p. 299) His anger. Wherefore the name of that place
1451 was called, The valley of [24]Achor, unto this
day.

C L Q **8** And °the **LORD** °said unto Joshua, "Fear
(p. 300) not, neither be thou dismayed: take all
the People of war with thee, and arise, go up
to Ai: °see, I have given into thy hand the
king of Ai, °and his People, and his city, and
his land:
2 And thou shalt do to Ai and her king as
thou didst unto °Jericho and her king: only
the spoil thereof, and °the cattle thereof, shall
ye take for a prey unto yourselves: lay thee
an ambush for the city behind it."

R s 3 So Joshua arose, and all the People of war,
to go up against Ai: and Joshua chose out
thirty thousand mighty men of valour, and
sent them away by night.
4 And he commanded them, saying, °"Behold,
ye shall lie in wait against the city, *even* behind
the city: go not very far from the city, but be
ye all ready:

t 5 And I, and all the People that *are* with me,
will approach unto the city: and it shall come
to pass, when they come out against us, as at
the first, that we will flee before them,

u 6 (For they will come out after us) till we
have drawn them from the city; for they will
say, 'They flee before us, as at the first:'
therefore we will flee before them.

v 7 Then ye shall rise up from the ambush, and
seize upon the city: for [1]the **LORD** your °God
will deliver it into your °hand.
8 And it shall be, when ye have taken the
city, *that* ye shall set the city on fire: according to the commandment of [1]the **LORD** shall
ye do. °See, I have commanded you."

S 9 Joshua therefore sent them forth: and they
went to lie in ambush, and abode °between
Beth-el and Ai, on the west side of Ai: but
Joshua lodged that night among the People.
10 And Joshua rose up early in the morning,
and °numbered the People, and went up, he
and the elders of Israel, before the People to Ai.
11 And all the People, *even the people* of war
that *were* with him, went up, and drew nigh,
and came before the city, and pitched on the
north side of Ai: now *there was* a valley
between them and Ai.
12 And he took about five thousand men,
and set them to lie in ambush between Beth-el
and Ai, on the west side °of the city.
13 And when they had set the People, *even*
all the host that *was* on the north of the city,
and their liers in wait on the west of the city,
Joshua °went that night into the midst of the
valley.

R s 14 And it came to pass, when the king of Ai
saw *it*, that they hasted and rose up early, and
the °men of the city went out against Israel to
battle, he and all his People, at a time appointed,
before the plain; but he °wist not that *there
were* liers in ambush against him behind the
city.

26 the fierceness. Fig. *Anthropopatheia* (Ap. 6).

8. 1—12. 24 (**C**, p. 289). CONQUEST OF THE LAND. (*Introversion and Alternation.*)

C | L | 8. 1-29. Conquest of Ai.
  M | O | 8. 30-35. Joshua's obedience.
    P | 9. 1-27. League with Gibeonites.
      N | 10. 1-43. Confederacy against Gibeonites by Adoni-zedec.
      N | 11. 1-17. Confederacy against Israel by Jabin.
  M | *O* | 11. 18. Joshua's obedience.
    P | 11. 19, 20. League with Gibeonites.
L | 11. 21—12. 24. Conquest of other cities.

8. 1-29 (L, above). CONQUEST OF AI. (*Introversion and Extended Alternation.*)

L | Q | 1, 2. The Promise.
  R | s | 3, 4. The Ambush.
    t | 5. The Residue and Decoy
    u | 6. The Pursuit
    v | 7, 8. Seizure of City
    } Command.
      S | 9-13. Arrangement.
  R | *s* | 14. The Ambush.
    t | 15. The Residue and Decoy
    u | 16, 17. The Pursuit
    v | 18-22. Seizure of City
    } Obedience.
Q | 23-29. The Performance.

1 the **LORD**. Heb. Jehovah. Ap. 4. II.
said. See note on 3. 7.
see. Fig. *Asterismos* (Ap. 6).
and. Note the Fig. *Polysyndeton* (Ap. 6) emphasising each particular.
2 Jericho. Cp. 6. 21. the cattle. Cp. Deut. 20. 14.
4 Behold. Fig. *Asterismos*. Ap. 6.
7 God. Heb. Elohim. Ap. 4. I.
hand. Put by Fig. *Metonymy* (of Cause) for the power which is in it (Ap. 6). Cp. *v.* 20, where it is rendered "power".
8 See. Fig. *Asterismos*. Ap. 6.
9 between Beth-el and Ai. The place of Abraham's altar, Gen. 12. 8: so that the place where the promise of the Land was made, is the place where it began to be fulfilled. Abraham had come down from Sichem: Joshua goes up to Sichem, and builds his altar on the same spot where Abraham had built his. Cp. Gen. 12. 6-8 with Josh. 8. 30-35 and Deut. 11. 30.
10 numbered = inspected or mustered.
12 of the city. Another school of Massorites read "of Ai", with many codices and Aramaic.
13 went. Some codices, with three early printed editions, read "lodged in".
14 men. Heb. pl. of *'ish* or *'ĕnōsh*. Ap. 14.
wist not = knew not. Anglo-Saxon *witan*, to know.
15 made as if they were beaten. The only form of the verb in the Heb. Bible.
16 in Ai. Some codices read "in the city".
17 man. Heb. *'ish*. Ap. 14. II.
18 spear = a short javelin. First occurrence of Heb. *kīdōn*.

15 And Joshua and all Israel °made as if they *t*
were beaten before them, and fled by the way
of the wilderness.

16 And all the People that *were* °in Ai were *u*
called together to pursue after them: and they
pursued after Joshua, and were drawn away
from the city.
17 And there was not a °man left in Ai or
Beth-el, that went not out after Israel: and
they left the city open, and pursued after
Israel.

18 And [1]the **LORD** [1]said unto Joshua, *v*
"Stretch out the °spear that *is* in thy hand
toward Ai; for I will give it into thine hand."

1451 **And Joshua stretched out the °spear that *he***
***had* in his hand toward the city.**
19 And the ambush arose quickly out of
their place, and they ran as soon as he had
stretched out his hand: and they entered into
the city, and took it, and hasted and set the
city on fire.
20 And when the men of Ai looked behind
them, they saw, and, °behold, the smoke of
the city ascended up to heaven, and they had
no °power to flee this way or that way: and
the People that fled to the wilderness turned
back upon the °pursuers.
21 And when Joshua and all Israel saw that
the ambush had taken the city, and that the
smoke of the city ascended, then they turned
again, and slew the men of Ai.
22 And the other issued out of the city
against them; so they were in the midst of
Israel, some on this side, and some on that
side: and they smote them, so that they °let
none °of them remain or escape.

Q w (p. 301) **23 And the king of Ai they took alive, and**
brought him to Joshua.

x **24 And it came to pass, when Israel had**
made an end of slaying all the inhabitants of
Ai in the field, in the wilderness wherein they
chased them, and when they were all fallen on
the edge of the sword, until they were °con-
sumed, that all the Israelites returned unto Ai,
and smote it with the edge of the sword.
25 And *so* it was, *that* all that fell that day,
both of men and women, *were* twelve thou-
sand, *even* all the men of Ai.
26 For Joshua drew not his hand back,
wherewith he stretched out the [18]spear, until
he had utterly °destroyed all the inhabitants
of Ai.

y **27 Only °the cattle and the spoil of that city**
Israel took for a prey unto themselves, ac-
cording unto the word of [1]the LORD which
He °commanded Joshua.

x **28 And Joshua burnt Ai, and made it an**
°heap for ever, *even* a desolation unto this
day.

w **29 And the king of Ai he hanged on a tree**
until eventide: and °as soon as the sun was
down, Joshua commanded that they should
take his carcase down from the tree, and cast
it at the entering of the gate of the city, and
raise thereon a great heap of stones, °*that*
***remaineth* unto this day.**

O a **30 Then Joshua built an altar unto [1]the LORD**
[7]God of Israel in mount Ebal,
31 As °Moses the servant of [1]the LORD com-
manded the °children of Israel, °as it is written
in the °Book of the Law of Moses, an altar of
°whole stones, over which no man hath lift up
***any* iron: and they offered thereon burnt offer-**
ings unto [1]the LORD, and sacrificed peace
offerings.

b **32 And °he wrote there upon the stones °a**
copy of the law of Moses, which he wrote in
the presence of the [31]children of Israel.

b **33 And all Israel, and their elders, °and**
officers, and their judges, stood on this side
the ark and on that side before the priests the
Levites, which bare the ark of the covenant of
[1]the LORD, as well the stranger, as he that
was born among them; half of them over
against mount Gerizim, and half of them over
against mount Ebal; [31]as Moses the servant
of [1]the LORD had commanded °before, that
they should bless the People of Israel.
34 And afterward he read all the words of
the law, the blessings and cursings, according
to all that is written in the [31]Book of the Law.

35 There was not a word of all that Moses *a*
commanded, which Joshua read not before all
°the congregation of Israel, with the women,
and the little ones, and the strangers that
°were conversant among them.

9 And it came to pass, when all the kings P c (p. 302)
which *were* on this side Jordan, in the
hills, and in the valleys, and in all the coasts
of the great sea over against Lebanon, the
Hittite, and the Amorite, °the Canaanite, °the
Perizzite, the Hivite, and the Jebusite, heard
thereof;

---

20 behold. Fig. *Asterismos.* Ap. 6.
power. Heb. hands. Put by Fig. *Metonymy* (of Cause), for the power put forth by them (Ap. 6).
pursuers = the pursuing force (sing.).
22 let none. Cp. Deut. 7. 2.
of them. One Massoretic reading is remain "to him".

23-29 (*Q*, p. 300). THE PERFORMANCE.
(*Introversion.*)

Q | w | 23. The king.
  x | 24-26. The city.
    y | 27. The spoil.
  x | 28. The city.
w | 29. The king.

24 consumed = spent.
26 destroyed = devoted.
27 the cattle. Cp. Num. 31. 22-28.
commanded Joshua. Cp. *v.* 2.
28 heap. Its only name to-day is "Tell" = the Heap.
29 as soon as. Cp. Deut. 21. 22, 23 and Josh. 10. 27.
that remaineth. Fig. *Parenthesis* (relative). Ap. 6.

30-35 (O, p. 300). JOSHUA'S OBEDIENCE.
(*Introversion.*)

O | a | 30, 31. Moses's command.
  b | 32. Words written.
  b | 33, 34. Words read.
a | 35. Moses's command.

31 Moses the servant of the LORD. See note on Deut. 34. 5.
children = sons.
as = according as.
Book of the Law. See note on Ex. 17. 14; 24. 4; and Ap. 47. So that Joshua had a copy of Deuteronomy.
whole stones. Cp. Ex. 20. 25. Deut. 27. 5.
32 he wrote. See note on Ex. 17. 14.
a copy = duplicate.
33 and officers. Some codices, with Aram. and Syr., read "and their officers".
before = at the first.
35 the congregation = assembly (as mustered).
were conversant. Heb. walked.

9. 1-27 [For Structure see next page].

1 the Canaanite, the Perizzite. Some codices, with two early printed editions, read "and the Canaanite and the Perizzite".

1451 2 That they gathered themselves together,
to fight with Joshua and with Israel, with one
°accord.

d e[1] 3 And when the °inhabitants of °Gibeon
(p. 302) heard °what Joshua had done unto Jericho
and to Ai,
4 °They did work wilily, and went and °made
as if they had been ambassadors, and took old
sacks upon their asses, and wine °bottles, old,
and rent, and bound up;
5 And old shoes and °clouted upon their feet,
and old garments upon them; and all the
bread of their provision was dry *and* °mouldy.

f[1] 6 And they went to Joshua unto the camp at
Gilgal, and said unto him, and to the °men of
Israel, "We be come from a far country: now
therefore make ye a league with us."
7 And the men of Israel said unto the Hivites,
"Peradventure ye dwell among us; and how
shall we make a league with you?"
8 And they said unto Joshua, "We *are* thy
servants." And Joshua said unto them, "Who
are ye? and from whence come ye?"

e[2] 9 And they said unto him, "From a very far
country thy servants are come because of the
name of °the LORD thy °God: for we have
heard the fame of Him, and all that He did in
Egypt,
10 And all that He did to the two kings of
the Amorites, that *were* beyond Jordan, to
Sihon king of Heshbon, and to Og king of
Bashan, which *was* at Ashtaroth.
11 Wherefore our elders and all the inhabitants of our country spake to us, saying,
'Take victuals °with you for the journey,
and go to meet them, and say unto them, 'We
are your servants:''

f[2] therefore now make ye a league with us.

e[3] 12 This our bread we took hot *for* our provision out of our houses on the day we came
forth to go unto you; but now, °behold, it is
dry, and it is mouldy:
13 And these [4]bottles of wine, which we
filled, *were* new; and, behold, they be rent:
and these our garments and our shoes are become old by reason of the very long journey."

f[3] 14 And °the men °took of their victuals, and
°asked not *counsel* at the °mouth of [9]the
LORD.
15 And Joshua made peace with them, and
°made a league with them, to let them live:
and the princes of the congregation sware
unto them.

e[4] 16 And it came to pass at the end of three
days after they had made a league with them,
that they heard that they *were* their neighbours, and *that* they dwelt among them.
17 And the °children of Israel journeyed, and
came unto their cities on the third day. Now
their cities *were* Gibeon, and Chephirah, and
Beeroth, and Kirjath-jearim.

f[4] 18 And the [17]children of Israel smote them
not, because the princes of the congregation
had sworn unto them by [9]the LORD [9]God of
Israel. And all the congregation murmured
against the princes.

9. 1-27 (P, p. 300). **LEAGUE WITH THE GIBEONITES.**

(*Introversion and Repeated Alternation.*)

P c | 1, 2. What Joshua had done. Cause.
  d e[1] | 3-5. Deception proposed.
    f[1] | 6-8. League proposed.
  e[2] | 9-11-. Deception carried out.
    f[2] | -11. League proposed.
  e[3] | 12, 13. Deception successful.
    f[3] | 14, 15. League made.
  e[4] | 16, 17. Deception discovered.
    f[4] | 18. League questioned.
  e[5] | 19-21. Deception compounded.
c | 22-27. What Joshua did. Consequence.

2 accord. Heb. "mouth": put by Fig. *Metonymy* (of Cause), Ap. 6, for what is said by it: i.e. one consent.

3 inhabitants. The Gibeonites were Hivites (*v.* 7), condemned to extermination as mixed with the descendants of the *Nephīlīm* (Ap. 25). Ex. 23. 32; 34. 12-15. Num. 33. 51-56. Deut. 7. 1, 2; 20. 16. They were aware of this. Hence their mission; by which they exposed themselves to the enmity of the other nations (10. 1-4).

Gibeon = High place. About six and a half miles from Beth-el, eight miles north-north-west of Jerusalem.

what. Some codices, with Sept. and Vulg., read "all that".

4 They = They too.

made as if they had been ambassadors. Some codices, with Aram., Sept., Syr., and Vulg., read "furnished themselves with provisions", as in *vv.* 11 and 12.

bottles = skins: i.e. wine-skins.

5 clouted = patched. (Anglo-Saxon, *clút.*)

mouldy = become crumbly.

6 men. Heb. *'ish.* Ap. 14. II.

9 the LORD. Heb. Jehovah. Ap. 4. II.

God. Heb. Elohim. Ap. 4. I.

11 with you. Heb. = in your hand.

12 behold. Fig. *Asterismos.* Ap. 6.

14 the men. Heb. pl. of *'ish* or *'ĕnōsh.* Ap. 14.

took of their victuals. Probably tasted, or partook of their food; or, ate with them = a token of friendship.

asked not: i.e. by "Urim and Thummim". Cp. Ex. 28. 30, note.

mouth. Put by Fig. *Metonymy* (of Cause), Ap. 6, for the counsel given by the mouth.

15 made a league = solemnised a covenant.

17 children = sons.

21 be = become.

promised. Cp. *v.* 15.

22-27. Note the expansion of P c (an *Alternation*).

x | 22. The question of Joshua.
  y | 23. The sentence of Joshua. "Now therefore," &c.
x | 24. Reply to question by Gibeonites.
  y | 25-27. The sentence submitted to. "Now behold," &c.

19 But all the princes said unto all the con- e[5]
gregation, "We have sworn unto them by [9]the
LORD [9]God of Israel: now therefore we may
not touch them.
20 This we will do to them; we will even let
them live, lest wrath be upon us, because of the
oath which we sware unto them."
21 And the princes said unto them, "Let
them live; but let them °be hewers of wood
and drawers of water unto all the congregation;" as the princes had °promised them.

22 And Joshua called for them, and he spake P c
unto them, saying, "Wherefore have ye beguiled us, saying, 'We *are* very far from you;'
when ye dwell among us?

1451 23 Now therefore ye *are* cursed, and there shall none of you be freed from being bondmen, and hewers of wood and drawers of water for the house of my [9]God."

24 And they answered Joshua, and said, "Because it was certainly told thy servants, how that [9]the LORD thy [9]God °commanded His servant Moses to give you all the land, and to destroy all the inhabitants of the land from before you, therefore we were sore afraid of °our lives because of you, and have done this thing.

25 And now, [12]behold, we *are* in thine hand: as it seemeth good and right unto thee to do unto us, do."

26 And so did he unto them, and delivered them out of the hand of the [17]children of Israel, that they slew them not.

27 And Joshua made them that day hewers of wood and drawers of water for the congregation, and for the altar of [9]the °LORD, °even unto this day, °in the place which He should choose.

N T (p. 303) **10** Now it came to pass, when Adoni-zedec king of °Jerusalem had heard how Joshua had °taken Ai, and had utterly destroyed it; °as he had done to Jericho and her king, so he had done to Ai and her king; and how the inhabitants of Gibeon had made peace with Israel, and were among them;

2 That they feared greatly, because Gibeon *was* a great city, as one of the royal cities, and because it *was* greater than Ai, and all the °men thereof *were* mighty.

U g 3 Wherefore Adoni-zedec king of Jerusalem sent unto Hoham king of Hebron, and unto Piram king of Jarmuth, and unto Japhia king of Lachish, and unto Debir king of Eglon, saying,

4 "Come up unto me, and help me, that we may smite Gibeon:

h for it hath made peace with Joshua and with the °children of Israel."

i 5 Therefore the five kings of the Amorites, the king of Jerusalem, the king of Hebron, the king of Jarmuth, the king of Lachish, the king of Eglon, gathered themselves together, and went up, they and all their hosts, and encamped before Gibeon, and made war against it.

g 6 And the men of Gibeon sent unto Joshua to the camp to Gilgal, saying, "Slack not thy °hand from thy servants; come up to us quickly, and save us, and help us:

h for all the kings of the Amorites that dwell in the °mountains are gathered together against us."

i j 7 So Joshua ascended from Gilgal, he, and all the people of war with him, and all the mighty men of valour.

k 8 And °the LORD °said unto Joshua, "Fear them not: for I have delivered them into thine °hand; °there shall not a °man of them stand before thee."

j 9 Joshua therefore came unto them suddenly, *and* went up from Gilgal all night.

24 commanded. Cp. Deut. 7. 1-5.
our lives = our souls. Heb. *Nephesh*. See Ap. 13.
27 LORD. There is an *Homœoteleuton* (Ap. 6) here, preserved in the Sept.; a scribe going back to the former of the two words "LORD"; and reading "the altar of Jehovah [and the inhabitants of Gibeon became hewers of wood and drawers of water for the altar of Jehovah]", even unto this day, &c.
even. Supply Fig. *Ellipsis* (Ap. 6), thus = "[as they are] even".
in = for.

10. 1–11. 17 (N *N*, p. 300). CONFEDERACY AGAINST GIBEONITES.
(*Extended Alternation.*)

N | T | 10. 1, 2. Confederacy against Gibeon, Adoni-zedec.
U | 10. 3-27. Kings.
V | 10. 28-39. Cities.
W | 40-43. Territory.
N | *T* | 11. 1-. Confederacy against Israel.
U | 11. -1-9. Kings.
V | 11. 10-14. Cities.
W | 11. 15-17. Territory.

1 Jerusalem = vision of peace. First occ. is connected with war, and next mention is siege and fire (Judg. 1. 8); called Jebus (Judg. 19. 10-11). Assigned by Joshua to Benjamin (Josh. 18. 28).
taken Ai. Cp. 8. 23-29.
as = according as.
2 men. Heb. pl. of *'ish* or *'ĕnōsh*. Ap. 14.

3-27 (U, above). KINGS.
(*Extended Alternation.*)

U | g | 3, 4-. Message of Adoni-zedec to the kings.
h | -4. Reason.
i | 5. Enemies' assemblage for war.
g | 6-. Message of Gibeonites to Joshua.
h | -6. Reason.
i | 7-27. Israel's assemblage for war.

4 children = sons.
6 hand. So some codices, with two early printed editions; but Heb. text has "hands".
mountains = hill country.

7-27 (*i*, above). ISRAEL'S ASSEMBLAGE FOR WAR. (*Alternation.*)

i | j | 7. March.
k | 8. Promise.
j | 9. March.
k | 10-27. Performance.

8 the LORD. Heb. Jehovah. Ap. 4. II.
said. See note on 3. 7.
hand. Written plural, but read singular in Heb. text. In some codices and six early printed editions, "hand" both written and read. Other codices, with Sept., Syr., and Vulg., read "hands".
there. Some codices, with two early printed editions, read "and not", i.e. "and there shall not", &c., or "and not a man".
man. Heb. *'īsh*. Ap. 14. II.

10-27 [For Structures see next page].

10 Beth-horon = the Upper Beth-horon, which stood at the head of the Pass to the coast.
Azekah. Near Shochoh, where Goliath afterwards opposed Israel (1 Sam. 17. 1).

10 And [8]the LORD discomfited them before Israel; and slew them with a great slaughter at Gibeon, and chased them along the way that goeth up to °Beth-horon, and smote them to °Azekah, and unto Makkedah. *k* l¹ m¹ (p. 304)

m^2 (p. 304) 1451 11 And it came to pass, as they fled from before Israel, *and* were in the going down to Beth-horon, that [8]the LORD cast down great stones from °heaven upon them unto Azekah, and they died: *they were* more which died with hailstones than *they* whom the [4]children of Israel slew with the sword.

m^3 12 Then spake Joshua to [8]the LORD in the day when [8]the LORD delivered up the Amorites before the [4]children of °Israel, and he said in the sight of Israel,

°"Sun, °stand thou still °upon Gibeon;
And thou, Moon, in the valley of Ajalon."

13 And the sun °stood still, and the moon stayed,
Until the People had avenged themselves upon their enemies.

Is not this written in °the book of Jasher? So the [12]sun °stood still in the midst of [11]heaven, and hasted not to go down about a whole day.

14 And there was no day like that before it or after it, that [8]the LORD hearkened unto the voice of a [8]man: for [8]the LORD fought for Israel.

l^2 n p 15 And Joshua returned, and all Israel with him, unto the camp to Gilgal.

q 16 But these five kings fled, and hid themselves in a cave at Makkedah.

17 And it was told Joshua, saying, "The five kings are found hid in a cave at Makkedah."

18 And Joshua said, "Roll great stones upon the mouth of the cave, and set °men by it for to keep them:

o 19 And stay ye not, *but* pursue after your enemies, and smite the hindmost of them; suffer them not to enter into their cities: for [8]the LORD your °God hath delivered them into your hand."

20 And it came to pass, when Joshua and the [4]children of Israel had made an end of slaying them with a very great slaughter, till they were consumed, that the rest *which* remained of them entered into fenced cities.

p 21 And all the people returned to the camp to Joshua at Makkedah in peace: none moved his tongue against any of the [4]children of Israel.

q 22 Then said Joshua, "Open the mouth of the cave, and bring out those five kings unto me out of the cave."

23 And they did so, and brought forth those five kings unto him out of the cave, the king of Jerusalem, the king of Hebron, the king of Jarmuth, the king of Lachish, *and* the king of Eglon.

24 And it came to pass, when they brought out those kings unto Joshua, that Joshua called for all the °men of Israel, and said unto the captains of the °men of war which went with him, "Come near, put your feet upon the necks of °these kings." And they came near, and put their feet upon the necks of them.

25 And Joshua said unto them, "Fear not, nor be dismayed, °be strong and of good courage: for thus shall [8]the LORD do to all your enemies against whom ye fight."

26 And afterward Joshua smote them, and slew them, and hanged them on five trees: and they were hanging upon the trees until the evening.

27 And it came to pass at the time of the going down of the sun, *that* Joshua commanded, and they °took them down off the trees, and cast them into the cave wherein they had been hid, and laid great stones in the cave's mouth, *which remain* until this very day.

28 And that day Joshua took Makkedah, and smote it with the edge of the sword, and the king thereof he utterly destroyed, °them, and all the °souls that *were* therein; he let V r^1 (p. 305)

10-27 (*k*, p. 303). PERFORMANCE. (*Division.*)

k | l^1 | 10-14. By Jehovah before the Flight.
  | l^2 | 15-27. By Joshua after the Flight.

10-14 (l^1, above). BY JEHOVAH BEFORE THE FLIGHT. (*Division.*)

l^1 | m^1 | 10. By the sword of Israel.
  | m^2 | 11. By hailstones from the clouds.
  | m^3 | 12-14. By the sun in the heavens.

11 heaven = the heavens; i.e. the clouds.

12 Israel. Here the Sept. supplies the words omitted by *Homœoteleuton* (Ap. 6) of the word "Israel, [when He destroyed them in Gibeon, and they were destroyed before the sons of] Israel".

Sun = the sun itself, because of what is said in the next verse.

stand thou still. Hab. 3. 11. This is not the only miracle in connection with the sun. See shadow going back (2 Kings 20. 11. Isa. 38. 8). Going down at noon (Amos 8. 9). No more going down (Isa. 60. 20). Darkened (Isa. 13. 10. Ezek. 32. 7. Joel 2. 10, 31; 3. 15. Matt. 24. 29. Rev. 6. 12; 8. 12; 9. 2; 16. 8). Miracle to be again performed (Luke 23. 44, 45). His motion described (Ps. 19. 4-6).

upon = in, as in next line.

13 stood still = waited silently.

the book of Jasher. Why may not this be "the book of the Upright", another name for Israel, like Jeshurun? See note on Deut. 32. 15. It is so in Arabic and Syriac. It is mentioned in 2 Sam. 1. 18. In the Targum it is "the book of the Law". Josephus appeals to it as a book in the temple, which probably perished with it. Two spurious books so called, A. D. 1394 and 1625.

15-27 (l^2, above). BY JOSHUA AFTER THE FLIGHT. (*Introversion and Alternation.*)

l^2 | n | p | 15. Return to camp at Gilgal.
  | q | 16-18. Five kings shut up.
  | o | 19, 20. Pursuit of hosts.
  | *n* | *p* | 21. Return to camp at Makkedah.
  | *q* | 22-27. Five kings brought out.

18 men. Pl. of *'ish* or *'ĕnōsh*. Ap. 14.

19 God. Heb. Elohim. Ap. 4. I.

24 men. Pl. of *'ish*. Ap. 14. II.

these kings. Some codices, with three early printed editions, read "these five kings".

25 be strong, &c. See note on Deut. 31. 6.

27 took them down. Cp. Deut. 21. 22, 23.

28-39 [For Structure see next page].

28 souls. Pl. of *nephesh*. Ap. 14. Seven times in this chapter: *v.* 40 puts "all that breathed" instead.

1451 none remain: and he did to the king of Makkedah ° as he did unto the king of Jericho.

s[1] (p. 305) 29 Then Joshua passed from Makkedah, and all Israel with him, unto ° Libnah, and fought against Libnah:

r[2] 30 And [8] the LORD delivered it also, and the king thereof, into the hand of Israel; and he smote it with the ° edge of the sword, and all the [28] souls that *were* therein; he let none remain in it; but did unto the king thereof [28] as he did unto the king of Jericho.

s[2] 31 And Joshua passed from Libnah, and all Israel with him, unto ° Lachish, and encamped against it, and fought against it:

r[3] 32 And [8] the LORD delivered [31] Lachish into the hand of Israel, which took it ° on the second day, and smote it with the edge of the sword, and all the [28] souls that *were* therein, according to all that he had done to Libnah.
33 Then Horam king of ° Gezer came up to help Lachish; and Joshua smote him and his people, until he had left him none remaining.

s[3] 34 And from Lachish Joshua passed unto ° Eglon, and all Israel with him; and they encamped against it, and fought against it:

r[4] 35 And they took it on that day, and smote it with the edge of the sword, and all the [28] souls that *were* therein he utterly destroyed that day, according to all that he had done to Lachish.

s[4] 36 And Joshua went up from Eglon, and all Israel with him, unto ° Hebron; and they fought against it:

r[5] 37 And they took it, and smote it with the edge of the sword, and the king thereof, and all the cities thereof, and all the [28] souls that *were* therein; he left none remaining, according to all that he had done to Eglon; but destroyed it utterly, and all the [28] souls that *were* therein.

s[5] 38 And Joshua returned, and all Israel with him, to ° Debir; and fought against it:

r[6] 39 And he took it, and the king thereof, and all the cities thereof; and they smote them with the edge of the sword, and utterly destroyed all the [28] souls that *were* therein; he left none remaining: as he had done to Hebron, so he did to Debir, and to the king thereof; [28] as he had done also to Libnah, and to her king.

W (p. 303) 40 So Joshua smote all the ° country of the hills, and of the south, and of the vale, and of the springs, and all their kings: he left none remaining, but utterly destroyed all that ° breathed, [28] as [8] the LORD [19] God of Israel ° commanded.
41 And Joshua smote them from ° Kadesh-barnea even unto Gaza, and all the country of Goshen, even unto Gibeon.
42 And all these kings and their land did Joshua take at one time, because [8] the LORD [19] God of Israel ° fought for Israel.
43 And Joshua returned, and all Israel with him, unto the camp to Gilgal.

28-39 (V, p. 303). CITIES OF THE KINGS. (*Repeated Alternation.*)

V | r[1] | 28. Makkedah taken.
s[1] | 29. Advance to Libnah.
r[2] | 30. Libnah taken.
s[2] | 31. Advance to Lachish.
r[3] | 32, 33. Lachish taken.
s[3] | 34. Advance to Eglon.
r[4] | 35. Eglon taken.
s[4] | 36. Advance to Hebron.
r[5] | 37. Hebron taken.
s[5] | 38. Advance to Debir.
r[6] | 39. Debir taken.

as = according as.
29 Libnah. Afterward one of the cities of the priests. Josh. 21. 13. See note on 2 Chron. 21. 10.
30 edge = mouth. Fig. *Pleonasm*. Ap. 6.
31 Lachish. Destroyed and rebuilt seven times. A strong city, as shown by recent explorations.
32 on the second day. A most significant statement. In 2 Kings 18. 17. 2 Chron. 32. 9, Sennacherib besieged it; yet when Rabshakeh returned from Jerusalem he found the siege raised (2 Kings 19. 8). Similar proof of its strength given in Jer. 34. 7.
33 Gezer. See note on 1 Kings 9. 16, 17.
34 Eglon, about two miles east of Lachish, now *Ajlan*.
36 Hebron, before called *Kirjath-arba*, Judg. 1. 10. Some Canaanites afterwards returned here, Judg. 1. 9-11.
38 Debir = Oracle: south of Hebron. Called *Kirjath-sepher* = Book Town (15. 15. Judg. 1. 11), and *Kirjath-sannah* = Precept Town (15. 49).
40 country of the hills = the land of the hill country.
breathed = had *n^eshāmāh*. Ap. 16.
commanded. Cp. Deut. 20. 16, 17.
41 Kadesh-barnea. This verse describes Joshua's conquests West, South, and North.
42 fought for Israel. For the reason, see Ap. 23 and 25.

11. -1-9 (*U*, p. 303). KINGS. (*Extended Alternation.*)

U | t | u | -1-5. Kings' assemblage.
v | 6-. Promise of Jehovah. Given.
w | -6. Command to Joshua.
t | *u* | 7. Kings smitten.
v | 8. Promise of Jehovah. Fulfilled.
w | 9. Obedience of Joshua.

1 when Jabin . . . heard. Note the stages: (1) Jericho, unresisting; (2) Ai, a sortie; (3) Gibeon, confederacy; (4) Jabin, aggressive.
Hazor. Celebrated in Judg. 4. 2, 17.
2 of the mountains = in the hill country.
of the plains = in the low country.
Chinneroth. Cp. Num. 34. 11. Deut. 3. 17. Afterward called Lake of Gennesareth, Sea of Galilee, and Sea of Tiberias (Matt. 4. 14-18, 23).
borders = uplands. Used only in connection with Dor. Heb. *nāphāh*. Cp. 12. 23 "coast", and 1 Kings 4. 11 "region".
west = sea, or coast.

11 And it came to pass, ° when Jabin king of ° Hazor had heard *those things*, T
that he sent to Jobab king of Madon, and to the king of Shimron, and to the king of Achshaph, U
2 And to the kings that *were* on the north ° of the mountains, and ° of the plains south of ° Chinneroth, and in the valley, and in the ° borders of Dor on the ° west,
3 *And to* the Canaanite on the east and on the west, and *to* the Amorite, and the Hittite, and the Perizzite, and the Jebusite in the

1451 mountains, and *to* the Hivite under Hermon in
to the land of ° Mizpeh.
1444 4 And ° they went out, they and all their
hosts with them, much people, even ° as the
sand that *is* upon the sea shore in multitude,
with horses and chariots very many.

5 And when all these kings were ° met together, they came and pitched together at the waters of Merom, to fight against Israel.

v (p. 305) 6 And ° the LORD ° said unto Joshua, "Be not afraid because of them: for to morrow about this time will I deliver them up all slain before Israel:

w thou shalt ° hough their horses, and burn their chariots with fire."

t u 7 So Joshua came, and all the people of war with him, against them by the waters of Merom suddenly; and they fell upon them.

v 8 And [6] the LORD delivered them into the hand of Israel, who smote them, and chased them unto great Zidon, and unto ° Misrephoth-maim, and unto the valley of Mizpeh eastward; and they smote them, until they left them none remaining.

w 9 And Joshua did unto them ° as [6] the LORD bade him: he houghed their horses, and burnt their chariots with fire.

V Y x (p. 306) 10 And Joshua at that time turned back, and took Hazor, and smote the king thereof with the sword: for Hazor beforetime was the head of all those kingdoms.

y 11 And they smote all the ° souls that *were* therein with the ° edge of the sword, utterly destroying *them:* there was not any left to ° breathe:

z and he burnt Hazor with fire.

Z 12 And all the cities of those kings, and all the kings of them, did Joshua take, and smote them with the [11] edge of the sword, *and* he utterly destroyed them, ° as ° Moses the servant of [6] the LORD commanded.

z 13 But *as for* the cities that stood still in their strength, Israel burned none of them, save Hazor only; *that* did Joshua burn.

Y x 14 And all the spoil of these cities, and the cattle, the ° children of Israel took for a prey unto themselves;

y but every ° man they smote with the edge of the sword, until they had destroyed them, neither left they any to [11] breathe.

Z 15 ° As [6] the LORD commanded Moses his servant, ° so did Moses command Joshua, and ° so did Joshua; he left nothing undone of all that [6] the LORD commanded Moses.

W (p. 303) 16 So Joshua took all that land, ° the hills, and all the south country, and all the land of Goshen, and the valley, and the plain, and the mountain of Israel, and the ° valley of the same;

17 *Even* from the mount Halak, that goeth up to Seir, even unto Baal-gad in the valley of Lebanon under mount Hermon: and all their kings he took, and smote them, and slew them.

3 Mizpeh = Watch-tower.
4 they went out, &c. Cp. *v.* 4 with Rev. 20. 8, 9.
as, &c. Fig. *Parœmia.* Ap. 6.
5 met together: i. e. by appointment. Cp. Amos 3. 3.
6 the LORD. Heb. Jehovah. Ap. 4. II.
said. See note on 3. 7.
hough = sever the hamstring.
8 Misrephoth-maim. Salt, or glass, works.
9 as = according as.

10-15 (*V*, p. 303). CITIES. (*Involved Introversion and Alternation.*)

V | X | Y | x | 10. Hazor taken.
y | 11-. Inhabitants slain.
z | -11. Hazor burned.
Z | 12. Moses's command.
z | 13. Cities not burned.
X | *Y* | *x* | 14-. Spoil taken.
y | -14. Inhabitants slain.
Z | 15. Moses's command.

11 souls. Heb. pl. of *nephesh.* Ap. 13.
edge. Heb. mouth. Fig. *Pleonasm.* Ap. 6.
breathe. Heb. *n^e shāmāh.* Ap. 16.
12 as = according as. Cp. Num. 33. 52. Deut. 7. 2; 20. 16, 17. See also Structure, *vv.* 15, &c.
Moses the servant of the LORD. See note on Deut. 34. 5.
14 children = sons.
man. Heb. *'ādām.* Ap. 14. I.
15 As = according as. Cp. Ex. 34. 11.
so. Cp. Deut. 7. 2.
16 the hills = the hill country.
valley = the low country.
18 a long time = many days.
20 of the LORD. Because they were the descendants of the *Nephīlīm*; and it was as necessary for the Sword to destroy these, as the Flood those.

11. 21—12. 24 (*L*, p. 300). CONQUEST OF OTHER KINGS. (*Alternation.*)

L | c[1] | 11. 21—12. 1. General.
d | 12. 2-6. Particular (East of Jordan).
c[2] | 12. 7, 8. General.
d | 12. 9-24-. Particular (West of Jordan).
c[3] | 12. -24. General.

21 Anakims = the descendants of the second incursion of evil angels (Gen. 6. 4) through one, Anak. See Ap. 23 and 25, and notes on Num. 13. 22 and Deut. 1. 28.
mountains = hill country.
from Anab. Some codices, with two early printed editions, Sept., Syr., and Vulg., read "and from Anab".

18 Joshua made war ° a long time with all those kings. *O* (p. 300)

19 There was not a city that made peace with the [14] children of Israel, save the Hivites the inhabitants of Gibeon: all *other* they took in battle. *P*

20 For it was ° of [6] the LORD to harden their hearts, that they should come against Israel in battle, that He might destroy them utterly, *and* that they might have no favour, but that He might destroy them, as [6] the LORD commanded Moses.

21 And at that time came Joshua, and cut off the ° Anakims from the ° mountains, from Hebron, from Debir, ° from Anab, and from all the ° mountains of Judah, and from all the ° mountains of Israel: Joshua destroyed them utterly with their cities. *L* c[1] (p. 306)

22 There was none of the [21] Anakims left in the land of the [14] children of Israel: only in Gaza, in Gath, and in Ashdod, there remained.

1451 to 1444 23 So Joshua took the whole Land, according to all that [6]the LORD said unto Moses; and Joshua gave it for an inheritance unto Israel °according to their divisions by their tribes. And the Land rested from war.

12 Now these *are* the kings of the Land, which the °children of Israel smote, and possessed their Land on the other side Jordan toward the rising of the sun, from the river Arnon unto mount Hermon, and all the plain on the east:

d (p. 306) 2 °Sihon king of the Amorites, who dwelt in Heshbon, *and* ruled from Aroer, which *is* upon the bank of the river Arnon, and from the middle of the river, and from half Gilead, even unto the river Jabbok, *which is* the border of the [1]children of Ammon;

3 And from the plain to the sea of °Chinneroth on the east, and unto the sea of the plain, *even* the salt sea on the east, the way to Beth-jeshimoth; and from the south, under Ashdoth-pisgah:

4 And the °coast of Og king of Bashan (*which was* of the remnant of the °giants) that dwelt at Ashtaroth and at Edrei,

5 And reigned in mount Hermon, and in Salcah, and in all Bashan, unto the border of the Geshurites and the Maachathites, and half Gilead, the border of Sihon king of Heshbon.

6 Them did °Moses the servant of °the LORD and the [1]children of Israel smite: and °Moses the servant of °the LORD gave it *for* a possession unto the Reubenites, and the Gadites, and the half tribe of Manasseh.

c² 7 And these *are* the kings of the country which Joshua and the [1]children of Israel smote on this side Jordan on the west, from Baal-gad in the valley of Lebanon even unto the mount Halak, that goeth up to Seir; which Joshua gave unto the tribes of Israel *for* a possession °according to their divisions;

8 In the °mountains, and in the valleys, and in the plains, and in the springs, and in the wilderness, and in the south country; the Hittites, the Amorites, and the Canaanites, the Perizzites, the Hivites, and the Jebusites:

d 9 The king of °Jericho, °one;
The king of °Ai, which *is* beside Beth-el, one;
10 The king of °Jerusalem, one;
The king of Hebron, one;
11 The king of Jarmuth, one;
The king of Lachish, one;
12 The king of Eglon, one;
The king of °Gezer, one;
13 The king of °Debir, one;
The king of Geder, one;
14 The king of Hormah, one;
The king of °Arad, one;
15 The king of °Libnah, one;
The king of Adullam, one;
16 The king of °Makkedah, one;
The king of Beth-el, one;
17 The king of Tappuah, one;
The king of Hepher, one;
18 The king of Aphek, one;
The king of Lasharon, one;
19 The king of Madon, one;
The king of °Hazor, one;
20 The king of Shimron-meron, one;
The king of Achshaph, one;
21 The king of Taanach, one;
The king of Megiddo, one;
22 The king of Kedesh, one;
The king of Jokneam of Carmel, one;
23 The king of Dor in the °coast of Dor, one;
The king of the nations of Gilgal, one;
24 The king of Tirzah, one;
All the kings thirty and one. c³

13 Now Joshua was °old *and* stricken in years; and °the LORD °said unto him, "Thou art old *and* stricken in years, and there remaineth yet very much land to be possessed. *C* A (p. 307)

2 This *is* the land that yet remaineth: all the °borders of the Philistines, and all Geshuri, B E¹ F

---

23 according to. Cp. Num. 26. 53. But some codices, with seven early printed editions, Sept., and Syr., read "in their portions".

12. 1 children = sons.
2 Sihon. Cp. Num. 21. 23, 24. Deut. 3. 6.
3 Chinneroth. See note on 11. 2.
4 coast = border, or confines.
giants. Heb. *Rephaim.* Another branch of the *Nephīlīm,* called so after one, *Rapha*; as the *Anakim* after *Anak.* See Ap. 23 and 25.
6 Moses the servant of the LORD. See note on Deut. 34. 5.
the LORD. Heb. Jehovah. Ap. 4.
7 according to their. Some codices, with five early printed editions, and Syr., read "in their".
8 mountains = hill country.
9 Jericho. Cp. 6. 2.
one. These names (*vv.* 9-24) are written thus in the Hebrew MSS. and printed editions.
Ai. Cp. 8. 29.
10 Jerusalem. Cp. 10. 23.
12 Gezer. Cp. 10. 33; and see note on 1 Kings 9. 16, 17.
13 Debir. Cp. 10. 38.
14 Arad. Cp. Num. 21. 1-3.
15 Libnah. Cp. 10. 30.
16 Makkedah. Cp. 10. 28.
19 Hazor. Cp. 11. 10.
23 coast. See note on "borders", 11. 2.

13. 1—21. 45 (*C*, p. 289). DIVISION OF THE LAND. (*Introversion and Alternation.*)

C | A | 13. 1. Jehovah's gifts. Unpossessed.
B | C | 13. 2—17. 18. Civil. Unallotted land.
D | 18. 1. Sacred. Tabernacle in Shiloh.
B | *C* | 18. 2—19. 51. Civil. Unappropriated cities.
D | 20. 1—21. 42. Sacred. Cities.
A | 21. 43-45. Jehovah's gifts. Possessed.

1 old and stricken in years. Fig. *Synonymia.* Ap. 6. Joshua now in his 101st year (1544).
the LORD. Heb. Jehovah. Ap. 4.
said. See note on 3. 7.

13. 2—17. 18 (C, above). CIVIL. UNALLOTTED LAND. (*Division.*)

C | E¹ | 13. 2—14. 5. By Moses.
E² | 14. 6—17. 18. By Joshua.

13. 2—14. 5 (E¹, above). BY MOSES. (*Alternation.*)

E¹ | F | 13. 2-7. Command as to the 9½ tribes.
G | 13. 8-33. East of Jordan.
F | 14. 1, 2. Obedience as to the 9½ tribes.
G | 14. 3-5. East of Jordan.

2 borders = circuit. Heb. *gᵉlīlah*, a rare word.

1544 3 From °Sihor, which *is* before Egypt, even
to unto the borders of Ekron northward, *which*
1543 is counted to the Canaanite: five °lords of
the Philistines; the Gazathites, and the Ashdothites, the Eshkalonites, °the Gittites, and the Ekronites; also the Avites:
4 °From the south, all the land of the Canaanites, and Mearah that *is* beside the Sidonians, unto Aphek, to the borders of the Amorites:
5 And the land of the Giblites, and all Lebanon, toward the sunrising, from Baal-gad under mount Hermon unto °the entering into Hamath.
6 All the inhabitants of the hill country from Lebanon unto Misrephoth-maim, *and* all the Sidonians, them will I drive out from before the °children of Israel: only divide thou it by lot unto the Israelites for an inheritance, °as I have commanded thee.
7 Now therefore divide this land for an inheritance unto the nine tribes, and the half tribe of °Manasseh,

G a 8 With whom the Reubenites and the Gadites
(p. 308) have received their inheritance, which °Moses
gave them, beyond Jordan eastward, °*even* as °Moses the servant of [1] the LORD gave them;
9 From Aroer, that *is* upon the bank of the river Arnon, and the city that *is* in the midst of the river, and all the plain of Medeba unto Dibon;
10 And all the cities of Sihon king of the Amorites, which reigned in Heshbon, unto the border of the [6] children of Ammon;
11 And Gilead, and the border of the Geshurites and Maachathites, and all mount Hermon, and all Bashan unto Salcah;
12 All the kingdom of Og in Bashan, which reigned in Ashtaroth and in Edrei, who remained of the remnant of the °giants: for these did Moses smite, and cast them out."
13 Nevertheless the [6] children of Israel expelled not the Geshurites, nor the Maachathites: but the Geshurites and the Maachathites dwell among the Israelites until this day.

b 14 Only unto the tribe of Levi he gave none
inheritance; the sacrifices of [1] the LORD °God of Israel made by fire *are* their inheritance, as He said unto them.

a 15 And Moses gave unto the tribe of the [6] children of Reuben *inheritance* according to their families.
16 And their °coast was from Aroer, that *is* on the bank of the river Arnon, and the city that *is* in the midst of the river, and all the plain °by Medeba;
17 Heshbon, and all her cities that *are* in the plain; Dibon, and Bamoth-baal, and Beth-baal-meon,
18 And Jahaza, and Kedemoth, and Mephaath,
19 And Kirjathaim, and Sibmah, and °Zareth-shahar in the mount of the valley,
20 And Beth-peor, and Ashdoth-pisgah, and Beth-jeshimoth,
21 And all the cities of the plain, and all the kingdom of Sihon king of the Amorites, which reigned in Heshbon, whom Moses smote with the princes of Midian, Evi, and Rekem, and Zur, and Hur, and Reba, *which were* °dukes of Sihon, dwelling in the country.
22 °Balaam also the son of Beor, the soothsayer, did the [6] children of Israel slay with the sword among them that were slain by them.
23 And the border of the [6] children of Reuben was Jordan, and the border *thereof*. This *was* the inheritance of the [6] children of Reuben after their families, the cities and the villages thereof.
24 And Moses gave *inheritance* unto the tribe of Gad, *even* unto the [6] children of Gad according to their families.
25 And their [16] coast was Jazer, and all the cities of Gilead, and half the land of the [6] children of Ammon, unto Aroer that *is* before Rabbah;
26 °And from Heshbon unto Ramath-mizpeh, and Betonim; and from Mahanaim unto the border of Debir;
27 And in the valley, Beth-aram, and Beth-nimrah, and Succoth, and Zaphon, the rest of the kingdom of Sihon king of Heshbon, Jordan and *his* border, *even* unto the edge of the sea of Chinnereth on the other side Jordan eastward.
28 This *is* the inheritance of the [6] children of Gad after their families, the cities, and their villages.
29 And Moses gave *inheritance* unto the

3 Sihor. Heb. "the Sihor".
lords. Heb. *ṣeren*, a prince; first occurrence. Used only of the Philistine princes. Josh. 13. 3. Judg. 3. 3; 16. 5, 8, 18, 18, 23, 27, 30. 1 Sam. 5. 8, 11; 6. 4, 4, 12, 16, 18; 7. 7; 29. 2, 6, 7. 1 Chron. 12. 19.
the Gittites. Some codices, with three early printed editions, Sept., and Syr., read "and the."
4 From=on. The Syr. punctuates *vv.* 3 and 4, thus: "also the Avites on the south".
5 the entering into=the pass of.
6 children=sons.
as=according as.
7 Manasseh. The Sept. adds, "from the Jordan to the Great Sea westward thou shalt give it: the Great Sea shall be the boundary; and to the two tribes, and to the half tribe of Manasseh".

8-33 (G, p. 307). EAST OF JORDAN.
(*Alternation.*)

G | a | 8-13. General.
  b | 14. Exception. Tribe of Levi.
  a | 15-32. General.
  b | 33. Exception. Tribe of Levi.

8 Moses gave. Cp. Num. 32. 33. Deut. 3. 13. Josh. 22. 4.
even as. So a special reading called *Sevīr* (Ap. 34), but Heb. text reads "as".
Moses the servant of the LORD. See note on Deut. 34. 5.
12 giants. Heb. *Rephaim.* See note on 12. 4.
14 God. Heb. Elohim. Ap. 4. I.
16 coast=border.
by. A special various reading called *Sevīr* (Ap. 34) reads "as far as", with some codices, and three early printed editions, Aram., Syr., and Sept.
19 Zareth-shahar=light of the dawn, because it catches the rays of the rising sun. Cp. Subscription to Ps. 22.
21 dukes=anointed [leaders], called kings in Num. 31. 8.
22 Balaam. Cp. Num. 22. 5; 24. 3, 15; 31. 8. Deut. 23. 4.
26 And. This is the middle verse of this book.

1444 half tribe of Manasseh: and *this* was *the pos-*
1443 *session* of the half tribe of the [6]children of
Manasseh by their families.

30 °And their [25]coast was from Mahanaim,
°all Bashan, all the kingdom of Og king of
Bashan, and all the °towns of Jair, which *are*
in Bashan, threescore cities:

31 And half Gilead, and Ashtaroth, and
Edrei, cities of the kingdom of Og in Bashan,
were pertaining unto the [6]children of Machir
the son of Manasseh, *even* to the one half of
the [6]children of °Machir by their families.

32 These *are the countries* which Moses did
distribute for inheritance in the plains of
Moab, on the other side Jordan, by Jericho,
eastward.

b 33 But unto the tribe of Levi Moses gave not
(p. 308) *any* inheritance: [1]the LORD [14]God of Israel
°*was* their inheritance, °as He said unto them.

F **14** And these *are the countries* which the
°children of Israel inherited in the land
of Canaan, which °Eleazar the priest, and
Joshua the son of Nun, and the heads of the
fathers of the tribes of the °children of Israel,
distributed for inheritance to them.

2 °By lot *was* their inheritance, °as °the
LORD commanded by the hand of Moses, °for
the nine tribes, and *for* the half tribe.

G 3 For Moses had given the inheritance of two
tribes and an half tribe on the other side
Jordan: but unto the Levites he gave none
inheritance among them.

4 For the [1]children of Joseph were two tribes,
Manasseh and Ephraim: therefore they gave
no part unto the Levites in the land, save
cities to dwell *in*, with their suburbs for their
cattle and for their substance.

5 °As [2]the LORD commanded Moses, so the
[1]children of Israel did, and they °divided the
land.

E^2 H^1 c^1 6 Then the [1]children of Judah came unto
(p. 309) Joshua in Gilgal: and Caleb the son of Jephunneh the Kenezite said unto him,

d "Thou knowest the thing that [2]the LORD said
unto Moses the man of °God concerning me
°and thee in Kadesh-barnea.

7 Forty years old *was* I when °Moses the
servant of [2]the LORD sent me from Kadesh-
barnea to espy out the land; and I brought
him word again °as *it was* °in mine heart.

8 Nevertheless my brethren that went up
with me made the heart of the People melt:
but I wholly followed [2]the LORD my [6]God.

9 And °Moses sware on that day, saying,
'Surely the Land whereon thy feet have
trodden shall be thine inheritance, and thy
children's for ever, because thou hast wholly
followed [2]the LORD my [6]God.'

10 And now, °behold, [2]the LORD hath kept
me alive, as He said, these °forty and five years,
even since [2]the LORD spake this word unto
Moses, while *the children of* Israel wandered
in the wilderness: and now, °lo, I *am* this
day fourscore and five years old.

11 As yet I *am as* strong this day as *I was* in
the day that Moses sent me: as my strength
was then, even so *is* my strength now, for
war, both to go out, and to come in.

12 Now therefore give me this mountain,
whereof [2]the LORD spake in that day; for
thou heardest in that day how the °Anakims
were there, and *that* the cities *were* great *and*
fenced: if so be [2]the LORD *will be* with me,
then I shall be able to drive them out, [7]as
[2]the LORD said."

13 And Joshua blessed him, and gave unto
Caleb the son of Jephunneh Hebron for an
inheritance.

14 °Hebron therefore °became the inheritance
of Caleb the son of Jephunneh the Kenezite
unto this day, because that he wholly followed
[2]the LORD [6]God of Israel.

15 And the name of Hebron before *was* °Kir-
jath-arba; *which Arba was* a great man
among the [12]Anakims. And the land °had rest
from war.

---

30 And their. Some codices in the margin read "and all their".
all. Some codices, with one early printed edition, and Sept., read "and all".
towns = villages. Heb. Havoth Jair. Cp. Deut. 3. 14. Heb. daughters. Fig. *Prosopopœia* (Ap. 6).
31 Machir. Cp. Num. 32. 39.
33 was. Lit. "He [was]".
as = according as. Cp. Num. 18. 20.

14. 1 children = sons.
Eleazar the priest now acts with Joshua, because the land is to be divided by lot (*v.* 2); and he alone has the lot, i. e. the Urim and Thummim by which the lots were drawn from the bag behind the breastplate. See notes on Ex. 28. 30. Num. 26. 55.
2 By lot. See note on *v.* 1.
as = according as, but a special various reading called *Sevir*, reads "which".
the LORD. Heb. Jehovah. Ap. 4. II.
for. Instead of "for", some codices, with one early printed edition, and Syr., read "to be given to".
5 As = according as. Cp. Num. 35. 2. Josh. 14. 2-5.
divided = "divided [by lot]". Fig. *Ellipsis*. Ap. 6.

14. 6—17. 18 (E^2, p. 307). **BY JOSHUA.**
(*Division.*)

E^2 | H^1 | 14. 6—15. 63. Judah.
 | H^2 | 16. 1—17. 18. Joseph.

14. 6—15. 63 (H^1, above). **JUDAH.**
(*Alternation.*)

H^1 c^1 | 14. 6-. The Tribe.
 d | 14. -6-15. Caleb.
 c^2 | 15. 1-12. The Tribe.
 d | 15. 13-19. Caleb.
 c^3 | 15. 20-63. The Tribe.

6 God. Heb. Elohim. Ap. 4. I.
and thee. Supply the Fig. *Ellipsis* (Ap. 6) thus: "and [concerning] thee".
7 Moses the servant of the LORD. See note on Deut. 34. 5. **as** = according as.
in = with: i. e. "in accordance with my heart".
9 Moses sware. Cp. Deut. 1. 34, 36 (cp. Judg. 1. 20).
10 behold. Fig. *Asterismos.* Ap. 6.
forty and five. See note on Ap. 50. III (p. 53).
lo. Fig. *Asterismos.* Ap. 6.
12 Anakims. See note on Num. 13. 22. Deut. 1. 28, and Ap. 23 and 25.
14 Hebron . . . became. Cp. 21. 12.
15 Kirjath-arba. Arba was the great man among the Anakims. See Ap. 23 and 25. Heb. "city of Arba, he [was] the greatest man", &c.
had rest. During the first Sabbatic year. See Ap. 50. IV (p. 53).

c² **15** *This* then was °the lot of the tribe of
(p. 309) the °children of Judah by their families;
1444 *even* to the border of Edom the wilderness of
1443 Zin southward *was* the uttermost part of the
south coast.

2 And their south border was from the shore of the salt sea, from the bay that looketh southward:

3 And it went out to the south side to Maaleh-acrabbim, and passed along to Zin, and ascended up on the south side unto Kadesh-barnea, and passed along to Hezron, and went up to Adar, and °fetched a compass to Karkaa:

4 *From thence* it passed toward Azmon, and went out unto the river of Egypt; and the goings out of that coast were at the sea: this shall be your south °coast.

5 And the east border *was* the salt sea, *even* unto the end of Jordan. And *their* border in the north quarter *was* from the °bay of the sea at the uttermost part of Jordan:

6 And the border went up to Beth-hogla, and passed along by the north of Beth-arabah; and the border went up to the stone of Bohan the son of Reuben:

7 And the border went up toward Debir from the valley of Achor, and so northward, looking toward Gilgal, that *is* before the going up to Adummim, which *is* on the south side of the river: and the border passed toward the waters of En-shemesh, and the goings out thereof were at En-rogel:

8 And the border went up by the valley of the son of Hinnom unto the south side of the Jebusite; the same *is* Jerusalem: and the border went up to the top of the mountain that *lieth* before the valley of °Hinnom westward, which *is* at the end of the valley of the °giants northward:

9 And the border was drawn from the top of the hill unto the fountain of the water of Nephtoah, and went out to the cities of mount Ephron; and the border was drawn to Baalah, which *is* Kirjath-jearim:

10 And the border compassed from Baalah westward unto mount Seir, and passed along unto the side of mount Jearim, which *is* Chesalon, on the north side, and went down to Beth-shemesh, and passed on to Timnah:

11 And the border went out unto the °side of Ekron northward: and the border was drawn to Shicron, and passed along to mount Baalah, and went out unto Jabneel; and the goings out of the border were at the sea.

12 And the west border *was* to the great sea, and the [4]coast *thereof*. This *is* the coast of the [1]children of Judah round about according to their families.

d 13 And unto Caleb the son of Jephunneh he gave a part among the [1]children of Judah, according to the commandment of °the LORD to Joshua, *even* the city of °Arba the father of Anak, which *city is* Hebron.

14 And °Caleb drove thence the three sons of Anak, Sheshai, and Ahiman, and Talmai, the [1]children of Anak.

15 And he went up thence to the inhabitants of °Debir: and the name of Debir before *was* °Kirjath-sepher.

16 And Caleb said, "He that smiteth [15]Kirjath-sepher, and taketh it, to him will I give Achsah my daughter to wife."

17 And Othniel the son of Kenaz, the brother of Caleb, took it: and he gave him Achsah his daughter to wife.

18 And it came to pass, as she came *unto him*, that she moved him to ask of her father a field: and °she lighted off *her* ass; and Caleb said unto her, °"What wouldest thou?"

19 Who answered, "Give me °a blessing; for thou hast given me a south land; give me also °springs of water." And °he gave her the upper springs, and the nether springs.

20 This *is* the inheritance of the tribe of the c³
[1]children of Judah according to their families.

21 And the uttermost cities of the tribe of the [1]children of Judah toward the coast of Edom southward were Kabzeel, and Eder, and Jagur,

22 And Kinah, and Dimonah, and Adadah,

23 And Kedesh, and Hazor, and Ithnan,

24 Ziph, and Telem, and Bealoth,

25 And °Hazor, Hadattah, and Kerioth, *and* Hezron, which *is* °Hazor,

26 Amam, and Shema, and Moladah,

27 And Hazar-gaddah, and Heshmon, and Beth-palet,

28 And Hazar-shual, and Beer-sheba, and Bizjothjah,

29 Baalah, and Iim, and Azem,

30 And Eltolad, and Chesil, and Hormah,

31 And Ziklag, and Madmannah, and Sansannah,

32 And Lebaoth, and Shilhim, °and Ain, and Rimmon: all the cities *are* twenty and nine, with their villages:

33 *And* in the valley, Eshtaol, and Zoreah, and Ashnah,

34 And Zanoah, and En-gannim, Tappuah, and Enam,

35 Jarmuth, and Adullam, Socoh, and Azekah,

15. 1 the lot. See note on 14. 1.
children = sons.
3 fetched a compass. English idiom. Heb. turned about. Cp. Acts 28. 13.
4 coast = border or boundary.
5 bay = tongue.
8 Hinnom. Some codices, with three early printed editions, and Syr., read "the sons of Hinnom".
giants = the *Rephaim*. See note on 12. 4.
11 side, or slope, or shoulder.
13 the LORD. Heb. Jehovah. Ap. 4. II.
Arba. Cp. note on 14. 15.
14 Caleb drove thence. Cp. Judg. 1. 10. It seems that some evidently returned and repossessed it.
15 Debir = Place of the Oracle.
Kirjath-sepher = Book Town.
18 she lighted off. Cp. Gen. 24. 64. 1 Sam. 25. 23.
What wouldest thou? Lit. "What to thee?" = "What aileth thee?"
19 a blessing = a present. Cp. Judg. 1. 15. 1 Sam. 25. 27.
springs of water. Fig. *Metonymy* (of Adjunct), i. e. land containing them (Ap. 6).
he. Some codices, with four early printed editions, Sept., Syr., and Vulg., read "Caleb".
25 Hazor. Fig. *Epanadiplosis* (Ap. 6).
32 and Ain, and Rimmon: should be "and En-Rimmon".

1444 36 And Sharaim, and Adithaim, and Gederah,
1443 and Gederothaim; fourteen cities with their villages:
37 Zenan, and Hadashah, and Migdal-gad,
38 And Dilean, and Mizpeh, and Joktheel,
39 Lachish, and Bozkath, and Eglon,
40 And Cabbon, and Lahmam, and Kithlish,
41 And Gederoth, Beth-dagon, and Naamah, and Makkedah; sixteen cities with their villages:
42 Libnah, and Ether, and Ashan,
43 And Jiphtah, and Ashnah, and Nezib,
44 And Keilah, and Achzib, and Mareshah; nine cities with their villages:
45 Ekron, with her towns and her villages:
46 °From Ekron even unto the sea, all that *lay* near Ashdod, with their villages:
47 Ashdod with her towns and her villages, Gaza with her towns and her villages, unto the river of Egypt, and the great sea, and the border *thereof:*
48 And in °the mountains, Shamir, and Jattir, and Socoh,
49 And Dannah, and Kirjath-sannah, which *is* Debir,
50 And Anab, and Eshtemoh, and Anim,
51 And Goshen, and Holon, and Giloh; eleven cities with their villages:
52 Arab, and Dumah, and Eshean,
53 And Janum, and Beth-tappuah, and Aphekah,
54 And Humtah, and °Kirjath-arba, which *is* Hebron, and Zior; nine cities with their villages:
55 Maon, Carmel, and Ziph, and Juttah,
56 And Jezreel, and Jokdeam, and Zanoah,
57 Cain, Gibeah, and Timnah; ten cities with their villages:
58 Halhul, Beth-zur, and Gedor,
59 And Maarath, and Beth-anoth, and Eltekon; six cities with their villages:
60 Kirjath-baal, which *is* Kirjath-jearim, and Rabbah; two cities with their villages:
61 In the wilderness, Beth-arabah, Middin, and Secacah,
62 And Nibshan, and the city of Salt, and En-gedi; six cities with their villages:
63 As for the Jebusites the inhabitants of Jerusalem, the [1]children of °Judah could not drive them out: but the Jebusites dwell with the [1]children of Judah at Jerusalem unto this day.

H^2 J^1 (p. 311) **16** And °the lot of the °children of Joseph °fell from Jordan by Jericho, unto the water of Jericho on the east, to the wilderness that goeth up from Jericho throughout mount Beth-el,
2 And goeth out from °Beth-el to Luz, and passeth along unto the borders °of Archi to Ataroth,
3 And goeth down westward to the coast of Japhleti, unto the coast of Beth-horon the nether, and to Gezer: and the goings out thereof are at the sea.
4 So the [1]children of Joseph, Manasseh and Ephraim, took their inheritance.
J^2 e 5 And °the border of the [1]children of Ephraim according to their families °was *thus:* even the border of their inheritance on the east side was Ataroth-addar, unto Beth-horon the upper;
6 And the border went out toward the sea to Michmethah on the north side; and the border went about eastward unto Taanath-shiloh, and passed by it on the east to Janohah;
7 And it went down from Janohah to Ataroth, and to Naarath, and came to Jericho, and went out at Jordan.
8 The border went out from Tappuah westward unto the river Kanah; and the goings out thereof were at the sea. This *is* the inheritance of the tribe of the [1]children of Ephraim by their families.
9 And the separate cities for the [1]children of Ephraim *were* among the inheritance of the [1]children of Manasseh, all the cities with their villages.

10 And they °drave not out the Canaanites f
that dwelt in °Gezer: but the Canaanites dwell among the Ephraimites unto this day, and serve under tribute.

17 There was also °a lot for the tribe of e g^1
Manasseh; for he *was* the °firstborn of Joseph; *to wit,* for Machir the firstborn of

---

46 From. Some codices, with four early printed editions, read "and from".

48 the mountains = the hill country.

54 Kirjath-arba. Cp. 14. 15 and 15. 13.

63 Judah could not, &c. Cp. Judg. 1. 8. Caleb succeeded at Hebron. Not until David's day was this thoroughly accomplished (2 Sam. 5. 3, 6, 7).

16. 1—17. 18 (H^2, p. 309). JOSEPH.
(*Division.*)

H^2 | J^1 | 16. 1-4. Collectively.
| J^2 | 16. 5—17. 18. Severally.

1 the lot. See note on 14. 1.
children = sons.
fell = came forth, i. e. from the bag behind the High Priest's breastplate, the Thummim meaning "Yes". See notes on Ex. 28. 30 and Num. 26. 55.

2 Beth-el to Luz. Cp. Gen. 28. 19 and Judg. 1. 26: the "Mount" Beth-el of *v.* 1.
of Archi = the Archite. Cp. 2 Sam. 15. 32; 16. 16.

16. 5—17. 18 (J^2, above). SEVERALLY.
(*Alternation.*)

J^2 | e | 16. 5-9. Ephraim. Possessed.
f | 16. 10. Unexpelled.
e | 17. 1-11. Manasseh. Possessed.
f | 17. 12-18. Unexpelled.

5 the border, or boundary. Note the Fig. *Topographia* (Ap. 6), in *vv.* 5 and 6.
was thus = turned out to be.

10 drave not out . . . Gezer. Gross disobedience to the repeated command of Jehovah. Cp. Ex. 23. 31. Deut. 7. 2, &c. See note on 1 Kings 9. 16, 17.

17. 1-11 (*e*, above). MANASSEH. POSSESSED.
(*Repeated Alternation.*)

e | g^1 | 1, 2. Manasseh. East and West of Jordan.
h^1 | 3, 4. Daughters of Zelophehad.
g^2 | 5. Manasseh. West of Jordan.
h^2 | 6-. Daughters of Zelophehad.
g^3 | -6-11. Manasseh. West and East of Jordan.

1 a lot = the lot. Cp. 16. 1, above.
firstborn of Joseph. Gen. 41. 51; 46. 20; 50. 23. Num. 32. 39.

1444 Manasseh, the father of Gilead: because he
1443 was a °man of war, therefore he had Gilead
and Bashan.
2 There was also *a lot* for the rest of the
°children of Manasseh by their families; for
the °children of Abiezer, and for the °children
of Helek, and for the °children of Asriel, and
for the °children of Shechem, and for the °chil-
dren of Hepher, and for the °children of Shemida: these *were* the male °children of Manasseh the son of Joseph by their families.
h[1] (p. 311) 3 But °Zelophehad, the son of Hepher, the
son of Gilead, the son of Machir, the son of
Manasseh, had no sons, °but daughters: and
these *are* the names of his daughters, Mahlah,
and Noah, Hoglah, °Milcah, and Tirzah.
4 And they came near before °Eleazar the
priest, and before Joshua the son of Nun, and
before the princes, saying, °"The LORD commanded °Moses to give us an inheritance
among our brethren." Therefore according
to the commandment of °the LORD he gave
them an inheritance among the brethren of
their father.
g[2] 5 And °there fell ten portions to Manasseh,
beside the land of Gilead and Bashan, which
were on the other side Jordan;
h[2] 6 Because the daughters of Manasseh had an
inheritance among his sons:
g[3] and the rest of Manasseh's sons had the land
of Gilead.
7 And the coast of Manasseh was from Asher
to Michmethah, that *lieth* before Shechem;
and the border went along on the right hand
unto the inhabitants of En-tappuah.
8 *Now* Manasseh had the land of Tappuah:
but Tappuah on the border of Manasseh
belonged to the [2]children of Ephraim;
9 And the coast descended unto the river
Kanah, southward of the river: these cities
of Ephraim *are* among the cities of Manasseh:
the coast of Manasseh also *was* on the north
side of the river, and the °outgoings of it were
at the sea:
10 Southward *it was* Ephraim's, and northward *it was* Manasseh's, and the sea is his
border; and they met together in Asher on the
north, and in Issachar on the east.
11 And Manasseh had in Issachar and in
Asher Beth-shean and her °towns, and Ibleam
and her °towns, and the inhabitants of Dor and
her °towns, and the inhabitants of En-dor
and her °towns, and the inhabitants of Taanach and her °towns, and the inhabitants of
Megiddo and her °towns, *even* three countries.
f 12 Yet the [2]children of Manasseh °could not
drive out *the inhabitants of* those cities; but
the Canaanites would dwell in that land.
13 Yet it came to pass, when the [2]children of
Israel were waxen strong, that they put the
Canaanites to tribute; but did not utterly
drive them out.
14 And the °children of Joseph spake unto
Joshua, saying, "Why hast thou given me
but one lot and one °portion to inherit, seeing
I *am* a great People, °forasmuch as [4]the LORD
hath blessed me hitherto?"
15 And Joshua answered them, "If thou *be*
a great People, *then* get thee up to the wood

man = Heb. *'ish*. Ap. 14. II.
2 children = sons.
3 Zelophehad. Cp. Num. 26. 33; 27. 1; 36. 2.
but = but [only]: or "but [he had]".
Milcah. Some codices, with three early printed editions, Sept., Syr., and Vulg., read "and Milcah".
4 Eleazar the priest. His presence necessary for the casting of lots, with the Urim and Thummim. See notes on Ex. 28. 30, and Num. 26. 55.
The LORD. Heb. Jehovah. Ap. 4. II.
Moses. Some codices, with three early printed editions, Sept., and Vulg., read "by the hand of Moses": "hand" being put by Fig. *Metonymy* (of Cause), for what is done by it (Ap. 6).
5 there fell: i. e. by lot. Cp. *v.* 1, and note.
9 outgoings = utmost limits. English idiom.
11 towns = Heb. daughters. Fig. *Prosopopœia* (Ap. 6) = villages.
12 could not drive out. Cp. 15. 63; 16. 10; and see Ex. 23. 31. Deut. 7. 2, &c.
14 children of Joseph = sons of Joseph, i. e. Manasseh. Note their selfishness, so well reproved by Joshua (*vv.* 15–18), who was of that tribe himself.
portion. Heb. "line", put by Fig. *Metonymy* (of Cause), for the territory marked out by it (Ap. 6).
forasmuch = to such a degree.
15 cut down = carve out, or create as in Gen. 1. 1.
giants. Heb. *Rephaim*. See note on Num. 13. 22. Deut. 1. 28, and Ap. 23 and 25.

18. 2—19. 51 (*B*, p. 307). CIVIL. UNINHERITED CITIES (THE SEVEN TRIBES). (*Introversion.*)

B | K | 18. 2, 3. Survey proposed.
  L | 18. 4–6. Directions.
  L | 18. 7. Exceptions.
 K | 18. 8—19. 51. Survey executed.

1 children = sons.
Shiloh = tranquillity or rest. Cp. Gen. 49. 10; eight times in this book. See 18. 1, 8, 9, 10; 19. 51; 21. 2; 22. 9, 12. See note on Judg. 18. 31.
tabernacle. Heb. *'ohel* = tent (Ap. 40). It remained here (Judg. 21. 12. 1 Sam. 1. 3; 3. 3) till the Philistines took the ark (1 Sam. 4. 11). In the days of Saul it was at Nob (of Benjamin, 1 Sam. 21. 1; 22. 19), and at Gibeon at beginning of Solomon's reign (1 Kings 3. 5. 2 Chron. 1. 3). Cp. Ps. 78. 60, 67, 68. Jer. 7. 12.

country, and °cut down for thyself there in
the land of the Perizzites and of the °giants,
if mount Ephraim be too narrow for thee."
16 And the [2]children of Joseph said, "The hill
is not enough for us: and all the Canaanites
that dwell in the land of the valley have
chariots of iron, *both they* who *are* of Beth-
shean and her [11]towns, and *they* who *are* of
the valley of Jezreel."
17 And Joshua spake unto the house of
Joseph, *even* to Ephraim and to Manasseh,
saying, "Thou *art* a great People, and hast
great power: thou shalt not have one lot *only*:
18 But the mountain shall be thine; for it *is*
a wood, and thou shalt cut it down: and the
outgoings of it shall be thine: for thou shalt
drive out the Canaanites, though they have
iron chariots, *and* though they *be* strong."

18 And the whole congregation of the D
°children of Israel assembled together
at °Shiloh, and set up the °tabernacle of the
congregation there. And the land was subdued before them.
2 And there remained among the [1]children of *B* K (p. 312)

1444 Israel seven tribes, which had not yet received
to their inheritance.
1443 3 And Joshua said unto the [1]children of Israel, "How long *are* ye slack to go to possess the land, which °the LORD °God of your fathers hath given you?

L (p. 312) 4 Give out from among you three °men for *each* tribe: and I will send them, and they shall rise, and °go through the Land, and describe it according to the inheritance of them; and they shall come *again* to me.
5 And they shall °divide it into seven parts: Judah shall abide in their °coast on the south, and the house of Joseph shall abide in their °coasts on the north.
6 Ye shall therefore °describe the Land *into* seven parts, and bring °*the description* hither to me, that I may cast lots for you here before [3]the LORD our [3]God.

L 7 But the Levites have no part among you; for the priesthood of [3]the LORD *is* their inheritance: and Gad, and Reuben, and half the tribe of Manasseh, have received their inheritance beyond Jordan on the east, which °Moses the servant of [3]the LORD gave them."

K M (p. 313) 8 And the men arose, and went away: and Joshua charged them that went to [6]describe the Land, saying, "Go and °walk through the Land, and describe it, and come again to me, that I may here cast lots for you before [3]the LORD in [1]Shiloh."
9 And the [4]men went and passed through the Land, and described it by cities into seven parts °in a book, and came *again* to Joshua to the host at [1]Shiloh.

N 10 And °Joshua cast lots for them in [1]Shiloh before [3]the LORD: and there Joshua divided the Land unto the [1]children of Israel °according to their divisions.

M l[1] 11 And the lot of the tribe of the [1]children of Benjamin came up according to their families: and the [5]coast of their lot °came forth between the [1]children of Judah and the [1]children of Joseph.
12 And their border on the north side was from Jordan; and the border went up to the side of Jericho on the north side, and went up through the °mountains westward; and the goings out thereof were at the wilderness of Beth-aven.
13 And the border went over from thence toward Luz, to the side of Luz, which *is* Beth-el, southward; and the border descended to Ataroth-adar, near the hill that *lieth* on the south side of the nether Beth-horon.
14 And the border was drawn *thence*, and compassed the corner of the sea southward, from the hill that *lieth* before Beth-horon southward; and the goings out thereof were at Kirjath-baal, which *is* Kirjath-jearim, a city of the [1]children of Judah: this *was* the west quarter.
15 And the south quarter *was* from the end of Kirjath-jearim, and the border went out on the west, and went out to the well of waters of Nephtoah:
16 And the border came down to the end of the mountain that *lieth* before the valley of the son of Hinnom, *and* which *is* in the valley of the °giants on the north, and descended to the valley of Hinnom, to the side of Jebusi on the south, and descended to En-rogel,
17 And was drawn from the north, and went forth to En-shemesh, and went forth toward Geliloth, which *is* over against the going up of Adummim, and descended to the stone of Bohan the son of Reuben,
18 And passed along toward the side over against °Arabah northward, and went down unto Arabah:
19 And the border passed along to the side of Beth-hoglah northward: and the outgoings of the border were at the north bay of the salt sea at the south end of Jordan: this *was* the south coast.
20 And Jordan was the border of it on the east side. This *was* the inheritance of the [1]children of Benjamin, by the [5]coasts thereof round about, according to their families.
21 Now the cities of the tribe of the [1]children of Benjamin according to their families were Jericho, and Beth-hoglah, and the valley of Keziz,

---

3 the LORD, God = *Jehovah Elohim.* Ap. 4. I, II.
4 men. Heb. pl. of *'ish* or *'ĕnōsh.* Ap. 14.
go through = walk to and fro.
5 divide it. Tracing the boundaries by the ravines, it is said that there is some resemblance in outline to the tribal signs, as given in notes on Num. 2.
coast = boundary; put by Fig. *Metonymy* (of Adjunct) for territory. Ap. 6.
6 describe = map out.
the description. The Fig. *Ellipsis* (Ap. 6) here may be filled in by saying "the surveys or maps".
7 Moses the servant of the LORD. See note on first occurrence, Deut. 34. 5.

18. 8—19. 51 (*K*, p. 312). SURVEY EXECUTED. (*Alternation.*)

K M | 18. 8, 9. Joshua's survey of land.
N | 18. 10. The division by lot.
M | 18. 11—19. 50. Joshua's allotment of land.
N | 19. 51. The division by lot.

8 walk. See note on "go", *v.* 4.
9 in a book. See note on Ex. 17. 14 and Ap. 47.
10 Joshua cast lots. He directing Eleazar the priest, without whom no lot could be cast. See note on Ex. 28. 30. Num. 26. 55.
according to. Some codices, with five early printed editions, read "in their portions".

18. 11—19. 50 (*M*, above). JOSHUA'S ALLOTMENT. (*Divisions.*)

M l[1] | 18. 11-28. Benjamin.
l[2] | 19. 1-9. Simeon.
l[3] | 19. 10-16. Zebulun.
l[4] | 19. 17-23. Issachar.
l[5] | 19. 24-31. Asher.
l[6] | 19. 32-39. Naphtali.
l[7] | 19. 40-48. Dan.
l[8] | 19. 49, 50. Joshua.

11 came forth. i. e. from the bag containing the Urim and Thummim. See note on Ex. 28. 30. Num. 26. 55.
12 mountains = hill country.
16 giants. Heb. *Rephaim.* See note on Num. 13. 22. Deut. 1. 28. Also Ap. 23 and 25.
18 Arabah. See note on Deut. 1. 1.

1444 22 And Beth-arabah, and Zemaraim, and
to Beth-el,
1443 23 And Avim, and Parah, and Ophrah,
24 And Chephar-haammonai, and Ophni,
and Gaba; twelve cities with their villages:
25 Gibeon, and Ramah, and Beeroth,
26 And Mizpeh, and Chephirah, and Mozah,
27 And Rekem, and Irpeel, and Taralah,
28 And Zelah, Eleph, and Jebusi, which *is*
Jerusalem, Gibeath, *and* Kirjath; fourteen
cities with their villages. This *is* the inheritance of the [1] children of Benjamin according to
their families.

1² **19** And the second ° lot came forth to
(p. 313) Simeon, *even* for the tribe of the ° children of Simeon according to their families:
and their inheritance was within the inheritance of the ° children of Judah.
2 And they had in their inheritance Beer-
sheba, and Sheba, and Moladah,
3 And Hazar-shual, and Balah, and Azem,
4 And Eltolad, and Bethul, and Hormah,
5 And Ziklag, and Beth-marcaboth, and
Hazar-susah,
6 And Beth-lebaoth, and Sharuhen; thirteen
cities and their villages:
7 Ain, Remmon, and Ether, and Ashan; four
cities and their villages:
8 And all the villages that *were* round about
these cities to Baalath-beer, Ramath of the
south. This *is* the inheritance of the tribe of
the [1] children of Simeon according to their
families.
9 Out of the portion of the [1] children of Judah
was the inheritance of the [1] children of Simeon:
for the part of the [1] children of Judah was too
much for them: therefore the [1] children of
Simeon had their inheritance within the inheritance of them.

1³ 10 And the third lot ° came up for the [1] children of Zebulun according to their families:
and the border of their inheritance was unto
Sarid:
11 And their border went up toward the
sea, and Maralah, and reached to Dabbasheth,
and reached to the river that *is* before Jokneam;
12 And turned from Sarid eastward toward
the sunrising unto the border of Chisloth-
tabor, and then goeth out to Daberath, and
goeth up to Japhia,
13 And from thence passeth on along on
the east to Gittah-hepher, to Ittah-kazin, and
goeth out to Remmon-methoar to Neah;
14 And the border compasseth it on the north
side to Hannathon: and the outgoings thereof
are in the valley of Jiphthah-el:
15 And Kattath, and Nahallal, and Shimron,
and Idalah, and Beth-lehem: twelve cities
with their villages.
16 This *is* the inheritance of ° the [1] children
of Zebulun according to their families, these
cities with their villages.

1⁴ 17 *And* the fourth lot ° came out to Issachar,
for the [1] children of Issachar according to their
families.
18 And their border was toward Jezreel, and
Chesulloth, and Shunem,

19. 1 lot came forth. See note on Ex. 28. 30. Num. 26. 55.
children. Heb. sons.
10 came up. i.e. out of the bag. See *v.* 1.
16 the children of Zebulun = the sons of Zebulun. Some codices, with Sept. and Vulg., read "the tribe of the sons of Zebulun".
17 came out. See note on *vv.* 1 and 10.
22 coast = boundary.
33 outgoings = utmost limits.
35 Chinnereth. In New Testament called Gennesareth. Cp. Num. 34. 11. Deut. 3. 17. Josh. 11. 2; 13. 27.

19 And Haphraim, and Shihon, and Anaha-
rath,
20 And Rabbith, and Kishion, and Abez,
21 And Remeth, and En-gannim, and En-
haddah, and Beth-pazzez;
22 And the ° coast reacheth to Tabor, and
Shahazimah, and Beth-shemesh; and the outgoings of their border were at Jordan: sixteen
cities with their villages.
23 This *is* the inheritance of the tribe of the
[1] children of Issachar according to their families, the cities and their villages.

24 And the fifth lot [17] came out for the tribe 1⁵
of the [1] children of Asher according to their
families.
25 And their border was Helkath, and Hali,
and Beten, and Achshaph,
26 And Alammelech, and Amad, and Mi-
sheal; and reacheth to Carmel westward, and
to Shihor-libnath;
27 And turneth toward the sunrising to Beth-
dagon, and reacheth to Zebulun, and to the
valley of Jiphthah-el toward the north side of
Beth-emek, and Neiel, and goeth out to Cabul
on the left hand,
28 And Hebron, and Rehob, and Hammon,
and Kanah, *even* unto great Zidon;
29 And *then* the coast turneth to Ramah,
and to the strong city Tyre; and the coast
turneth to Hosah; and the outgoings thereof
are at the sea from the coast to Achzib:
30 Ummah also, and Aphek, and Rehob:
twenty and two cities with their villages.
31 This *is* the inheritance of the tribe of the
[1] children of Asher according to their families,
these cities with their villages.

32 The sixth lot [1] came out to the [1] children of 1⁶
Naphtali, *even* for the [1] children of Naphtali
according to their families.
33 And their [22] coast was from Heleph, from
Allon to Zaanannim, and Adami, Nekeb, and
Jabneel, unto Lakum; and the ° outgoings
thereof were at Jordan:
34 And *then* the [33] coast turneth westward to
Aznoth-tabor, and goeth out from thence to
Hukkok, and reacheth to Zebulun on the
south side, and reacheth to Asher on the west
side, and to Judah upon Jordan toward the
sunrising.
35 And the fenced cities *are* Ziddim, Zer, and
Hammath, Rakkath, and ° Chinnereth,
36 And Adamah, and Ramah, and Hazor,
37 And Kedesh, and Edrei, and En-hazor,
38 And Iron, and Migdal-el, Horem, and
Beth-anath, and Beth-shemesh; nineteen cities
with their villages.

1444 39 This *is* the inheritance of the tribe of
to the [1]children of Naphtali according to their
1443 families, the cities and their villages.

l7 40 *And* the seventh lot [17]came out for the
(p. 313) tribe of the [1]children of Dan according to their
families.
41 And the [33]coast of their inheritance was
Zorah, and Eshtaol, and Ir-shemesh,
42 And Shaalabbin, and Ajalon, and Jethlah,
43 And Elon, and Thimnathah, and Ekron,
44 And Eltekeh, and Gibbethon, and Baalath,
45 And Jehud, and Bene-berak, and Gath-
rimmon,
46 And Me-jarkon, and Rakkon, with the
border before Japho.
47 And the [33]coast of the [1]children of Dan
went out *too little* for them: therefore the
[1]children of Dan went up to fight against
Leshem, and took it, and smote it with the
edge of the sword, and possessed it, and dwelt
therein, and called Leshem, Dan, after the
name of Dan their father.
48 This *is* the inheritance of the tribe of the
[1]children of Dan according to their families,
these cities with their villages.

l8 49 When they had made an end of dividing
the Land for inheritance by their [33]coasts,
the [1]children of Israel gave an inheritance to
Joshua the son of Nun among them:
50 According to the °word of °the LORD they
gave him the city which he asked, *even* Timnath-serah in mount Ephraim: and he °built
the city, and dwelt therein.

N 51 These *are* the inheritances, which Eleazar
the priest, and Joshua the son of Nun, and
the heads of the fathers of the tribes of the
[1]children of Israel, divided for an inheritance
by lot in °Shiloh before [50]the LORD, at the door
of the °tabernacle of the congregation. So
they made an end of dividing the country.

D O[1] m 20 °The LORD also °spake unto Joshua,
(p. 315) saying,
2 "Speak to the °children of Israel, saying,
'Appoint out for you cities of refuge, whereof
I spake unto you by the hand of Moses:

n 3 That the slayer that °killeth *any* person
unawares *and* °unwittingly may flee thither:
and they shall be your refuge from the avenger
of blood.
4 And when he that doth flee unto one of
those cities shall stand at the entering of the
gate of the city, and shall declare his cause in
the ears of the elders of that city, they shall
take him into the city unto them, and give him
a place, that he may dwell among them.
5 And if the avenger of blood pursue after
him, then they shall not deliver the slayer up
into his hand; because he smote his neighbour
unwittingly, and hated him not beforetime.
6 And he shall dwell in that city, °until he
stand before the congregation for judgment,
and until the death of the high priest that
shall be in those days: then shall the slayer
return, and come unto his own city, and unto
his own house, unto the city from whence he
fled.'"

50 word. Heb. = mouth. Put by Fig. *Metonymy* (of Cause) for what is spoken by it. Ap. 6.
the LORD. Heb. Jehovah. Ap. 4.
built = rebuilt.
51 Shiloh. See note on 18. 1.
tabernacle = tent. See Ap. 40.

20. 1—21. 42 (*D*, p. 307). SACRED. CITIES.
(*Division.*)

D | O[1] | 20. 1-9. Cities of Refuge.
| O[2] | 21. 1-42. Cities of the Levites.

20. 1-9 (O[1], above). CITIES OF REFUGE.
(*Alternation.*)

O[1] | m | 1, 2. Command.
| n | 3-6. Intention.
| *m* | 7-9-. Obedience.
| *n* | -9. Intention.

1 The LORD. Heb. Jehovah. Ap. 4. II.
spake. See note on 1. 1.
2 children = sons.
3 killeth any person = smiteth a soul. Heb. *nephesh.* See Ap. 13. Lit. a killer, smiting a soul.
unwittingly = unknowingly (Anglo-Saxon).
6 until. The cities of refuge, being cities of the priests, bore the sin of the manslayer. What the high priest was to the Levites, the Levites were to the nation. On the Day of Atonement, therefore, all the sins of the nation came into his hand. On his death he was freed from the Law (Rom. 6. 7; 7. 1-4), and those whom he represented were freed also. Cp. Rom. 5. 9-11. Heb. 7. 23-25 for the contrast.
7 appointed = separated, and thus sanctified.
9 killeth any person = "smiteth a soul". Heb. *nephesh.* See Ap. 13.

21. 1-42 (O[2], above). CITIES OF THE LEVITES.
(*Introversion.*)

O[2] | P | 1, 2. Levites. Application made.
| Q | 3. Cities granted. Collectively.
| *Q* | 4-40. Cities granted. Severally.
| *P* | 41, 42. Levites. Application granted.

1 Eleazar the priest. See note on 14. 1.
children = sons.

7 And they °appointed Kedesh in Galilee in m
mount Naphtali, and Shechem in mount Ephraim, and Kirjath-arba, which *is* Hebron, in
the mountain of Judah.
8 And on the other side Jordan by Jericho
eastward, they assigned Bezer in the wilderness upon the plain out of the tribe of Reuben,
and Ramoth in Gilead out of the tribe of
Gad, and Golan in Bashan out of the tribe of
Manasseh.
9 These were the cities appointed for all the
[2]children of Israel, and for the stranger that
sojourneth among them,
that whosoever °killeth *any* person at unawares n
might flee thither, and not die by the hand of
the avenger of blood, until he stood before the
congregation.

21 Then came near the heads of the fathers O[2] P
of the Levites unto °Eleazar the priest,
and unto Joshua the son of Nun, and unto the
heads of the fathers of the tribes of the °chil-
dren of Israel;

1444 to 1443 2 And they spake unto them at °Shiloh in the land of Canaan, saying, °"The LORD commanded by the °hand of Moses to give us cities to dwell in, with the °suburbs thereof for our cattle."

Q (p. 315) 3 And the [1] children of Israel gave unto the Levites out of their inheritance, at the commandment of °the LORD, these cities and their [2] suburbs.

Q o p (p. 316) 4 And the lot °came out for the families of the Kohathites: and the [1] children of Aaron the priest, *which were* of the Levites, had by lot out of the tribe of Judah, and out of the tribe of Simeon, and out of the tribe of Benjamin, thirteen cities.

5 And the rest of the [1] children of Kohath *had* by lot out of the families of the tribe of Ephraim, and out of the tribe of Dan, and out of the half tribe of Manasseh, ten cities.

q 6 And the [1] children of Gershon *had* by lot out of the families of the tribe of Issachar, and out of the tribe of Asher, and out of the tribe of Naphtali, and out of the half tribe of Manasseh in Bashan, thirteen cities.

r 7 The [1] children of Merari by their families *had* out of the tribe of Reuben, and out of the tribe of Gad, and out of the tribe of Zebulun, twelve cities.

8 And the [1] children of Israel gave by lot unto the Levites these cities with their [2] suburbs, °as [3] the LORD commanded by the hand of Moses.

o p 9 And they gave out of the tribe of the [1] children of Judah, and out of the tribe of the [1] children of Simeon, these cities which are *here* mentioned by name,

10 Which the [1] children of Aaron, *being* of the families of the Kohathites, *who were* of the [1] children of Levi, had: for theirs was the first lot.

11 And they gave them the city of °Arba the father of Anak, which *city is* Hebron, in the hill *country* of Judah, with the [2] suburbs thereof round about it.

12 But the fields of the city, and the villages thereof, gave they to °Caleb the son of Jephunneh for his possession.

13 Thus they gave to the [1] children of Aaron the priest Hebron with her [2] suburbs, *to be* a city of refuge for the slayer; and Libnah with her [2] suburbs,

14 And Jattir with her [2] suburbs, and Eshtemoa with her [2] suburbs,

15 And °Holon with her [2] suburbs, and Debir with her [2] suburbs,

16 And Ain with her [2] suburbs, and Juttah with her [2] suburbs, *and* °Beth-shemesh with her [2] suburbs; nine cities out of those two tribes.

17 And out of the tribe of Benjamin, Gibeon with her [2] suburbs, Geba with her [2] suburbs,

18 °Anathoth with her [2] suburbs, and Almon with her [2] suburbs; four cities.

19 All the cities of the [1] children of Aaron, the priests, *were* thirteen cities with their [2] suburbs.

20 And the families of the [1] children of Kohath, the Levites which remained of the [1] children of Kohath, even they had the cities of their lot out of the tribe of Ephraim.

21 For they gave them Shechem with her [2] suburbs °in mount Ephraim, *to be* a city of refuge for the slayer; and Gezer with her [2] suburbs,

22 And Kibzaim with her [2] suburbs, and Beth-horon with her [2] suburbs; four cities.

23 And out of the tribe of Dan, Elteketh with her [2] suburbs, °Gibbethon with her [2] suburbs,

24 °Aijalon with her [2] suburbs, Gath-rimmon with her [2] suburbs; four cities.

25 And out of the half tribe of Manasseh, Tanach with her [2] suburbs, and Gath-rimmon with her [2] suburbs; two cities.

26 All the cities *were* ten with their [2] suburbs for the families of the [1] children of Kohath that remained.

27 And unto the [1] children of Gershon, of the families of the Levites, out of the *other* half tribe of Manasseh *they gave* Golan in Bashan with her [2] suburbs, *to be* a city of refuge for the slayer; and Beesh-terah with her [2] suburbs; two cities. q

28 And out of the tribe of Issachar, Kishon with her [2] suburbs, Dabareh with her [2] suburbs,

29 Jarmuth with her [2] suburbs, °En-gannim with her [2] suburbs; four cities.

30 And out of the tribe of Asher, Mishal with her [2] suburbs, Abdon with her [2] suburbs,

31 °Helkath with her [2] suburbs, and Rehob with her [2] suburbs; four cities.

---

2 Shiloh. See note on 18. 1.

The LORD commanded = Jehovah commanded. Cp. Num. 35. 1-4. Lev. 25. 33.

hand. Put by Fig. *Metonymy* (of Cause) for what is effected by it.

suburbs = common lands, or pasture lands; and so throughout the chapter, fifty-seven times.

3 the LORD. Heb. Jehovah. Ap. 4.

4-40 (Q, p. 315). CITIES GRANTED. SEVERALLY. (*Extended Alternation.*)

Q | o | p | 4, 5. Kohath
 q | 6. Gershon } Severally.
 r | 7, 8. Merari
o | p | 9-26. Kohath
 q | 27-33. Gershon } In detail, and sum.
 r | 34-40. Merari

4 came out. i. e. out of the bag containing the Urim and Thummim. See note on Ex. 28. 30. Num. 26. 55.

8 as the LORD. According as Jehovah.

11 Arba. Cp. 14. 12-15. 1 Chron. 6. 55.

12 Caleb. Cp. 14. 14. 1 Chron. 6. 56.

15 Holon. In 1 Chron. 6. 58 = Hilon.

16 Beth-shemesh. Some codices, with four early printed editions, Sept., Syr., and Vulg., read "and Beth-shemesh".

18 Anathoth. Some codices, with Sept., Syr., and Vulg., read "and Anathoth".

21 in mount = in the hill country of.

23 Gibbethon. Some codices, with three early printed editions, Sept., Syr., and Vulg., read "and Gibbethon".

24 Aijalon. Some codices, with two early printed editions, Sept., Syr., and Vulg., read "and Aijalon".

29 En-gannim. Some codices, with one early printed edition, Sept., Syr., and Vulg., read "and En-gannim".

31 Helkath. Some codices, with two early printed editions, Sept., Syr., and Vulg., read "and Helkath".

1444 to 1443 32 And out of the tribe of Naphtali, Kedesh in Galilee with her [2]suburbs, *to be* a city of refuge for the slayer; and Hammoth-dor with her [2]suburbs, and Kartan with her [2]suburbs; three cities.
33 All the cities of the Gershonites according to their families *were* thirteen cities with their [2]suburbs.

r (p. 316) 34 And unto the families of the [1]children of
Merari, the rest of the Levites, out of the tribe of Zebulun, Jokneam with her [2]suburbs, and °Kartah with her [2]suburbs,
35 Dimnah with her [2]suburbs, Nahalal with her [2]suburbs; four cities.
36 °And out of the tribe of °Reuben, °Bezer with her [2]suburbs, °and Jahazah with her [2]suburbs,
37 °Kedemoth with her [2]suburbs, and Mephaath with her [2]suburbs; four cities.
38 And out of the tribe of Gad, Ramoth in Gilead with her [2]suburbs, *to be* a city of refuge for the slayer; and Mahanaim with her [2]suburbs,
39 Heshbon with her [2]suburbs, Jazer with her [2]suburbs; four cities in all.
40 So all the cities for the [1]children of Merari by their families, which were remaining of the families of the Levites, were *by* their lot twelve cities.

O[2] P (p. 315) 41 All the cities of the Levites within the possession of the [1]children of Israel *were* forty and eight cities with their [2]suburbs.
42 These cities were every one with their [2]suburbs round about them: thus *were* all these cities.

A (p. 307) 43 And [2]the LORD gave unto Israel all the Land which He sware to give unto their fathers; and they possessed it, and dwelt therein.
44 And [2]the LORD gave them rest round about, according to all that He sware unto their fathers: and there stood not a °man of all their enemies before them; [3]the LORD delivered all their enemies into their hand.
45 There failed not ought of any good thing which [2]the LORD had spoken unto the house of Israel; all came to pass.

B B a (p. 317) **22** Then Joshua called the Reubenites, and the Gadites, and the half tribe of Manasseh,

b 2 And said unto them, "Ye have kept all that °Moses the servant of °the LORD commanded you, and have obeyed my voice in all that I commanded you:
3 Ye have not left your brethren these many days unto this day, but have kept the charge of the commandment of [2]the LORD your °God.
4 And now [2]the LORD your [3]God hath given rest unto your brethren, °as He promised °them: therefore now return ye, and get you unto your tents, *and* unto the Land of your possession, which [2]Moses the servant of [2]the LORD gave you on the other side Jordan.
5 But take diligent heed to do the commandment and the Law, which [2]Moses the servant of [2]the LORD charged you, to love [2]the LORD your [3]God, °and to walk in all His ways, and to keep His commandments, and to cleave unto

34 Kartah. Some codices, with five early printed editions, Aram., and Vulg., read "and Kartah".
36 And out of the tribe of Reuben. See note on *v.* 38.
Reuben. Some codices, with one early printed edition, add "a city of refuge for the manslayer".
Bezer. Some codices, with Sept. and Vulg., add "in the desert".
and Jahazah. Some codices omit this "and".
37 Kedemoth. Some codices, with six early printed editions, and Sept., read "and Kedemoth".
38 By an *Homœoteleuton* (Ap. 6) some scribe, writing as far as "four cities" at end of *v.* 35, went back with his eye to the same words at the end of *v.* 37, and so omitted, by an accident, the two verses 36 and 37, and continued at *v.* 38, which commences with the same words which end *v.* 35. Hence they are not contained in the current text of the Hebrew Bible. The A.V. puts these verses in, however, without a note; the R.V. also, but with a note. The two verses are contained in all the early printed Hebrew Bibles, the Sept. and Vulg., and very many codices. They were first omitted by Jacob ben Chayim (1524, 1525), and the current Hebrew printed texts have followed him.
44 man. Heb. *'ish.* Ap. 14. II.

22. 1-34 (*B*, p. 289). JORDAN. EVENTS CONNECTED THEREWITH. (*Division.*)

B | A[1] | 1-9. West of Jordan.
  | A[2] | 10-34. East of Jordan.

1-9 (A[1], above). WEST OF JORDAN. (*Alternation.*)

A[1] | B | a | 1. Two and a half tribes. Called.
  | | b | 2-6. Their charge.
  | *B* | *a* | 7-. The half tribe. Allotted.
  | | *b* | -7-9. Their dismission and return.

2 Moses the servant of the LORD. See note on Deut. 34. 5.
the LORD. Heb. Jehovah. Ap. 4. II.
3 God. Heb. Elohim. Ap. 4. I.
4 as=according as.
them. A special various reading called *Sevir* (Ap. 34), with many codices and two early printed editions, reads "to you".
5 and. Note the Fig. *Polysyndeton* (Ap. 6) in this verse.
soul. Heb. *nephesh.* Ap. 13.
8 divide=share.
9 children=sons.
Shiloh. See note on 18. 1.

Him, and to serve Him with all your heart and with all your °soul."
6 So Joshua blessed them, and sent them away: and they went unto their tents.

7 Now to the *one* half of the tribe of Manasseh Moses had given *possession* in Bashan: but unto the *other* half thereof gave Joshua among their brethren on this side Jordan westward. *B a*
And when Joshua sent them away also unto their tents, then he blessed them, *b*
8 And he spake unto them, saying, "Return with much riches unto your tents, [5]and with very much cattle, with silver, and with gold, and with brass, and with iron, and with very much raiment: °divide the spoil of your enemies with your brethren."
9 And the °children of Reuben and the °children of Gad and the half tribe of Manasseh returned, and departed from the °children of Israel out of °Shiloh, which *is* in the land of

1443 Canaan, to go unto the country of Gilead, to the Land of their possession, whereof they were possessed, according to the °word of [2]the LORD by the hand of Moses.

A[2] c 10 And when they came unto the °borders of
(p. 318) Jordan, that *are* in the land of Canaan, the
[9]children of Reuben and the [9]children of Gad and the half tribe of Manasseh built there an altar by Jordan, a great altar °to see to.

d 11 And the [9]children of Israel heard say, °"Behold, the [9]children of Reuben and the [9]children of Gad and the half tribe of Manasseh have built an altar °over against the land of Canaan, in the borders of Jordan, °at the passage of the [9]children of Israel."

12 And when the [9]children of Israel heard *of it*, the whole congregation of the [9]children of Israel gathered themselves together at [9]Shiloh, to go up to war against them.

e 13 And the [9]children of Israel sent unto the
1442 [9]children of Reuben, and to the [9]children of
Gad, and to the half tribe of Manasseh, into the land of Gilead, Phinehas the son of Eleazar the priest,

14 And with him ten princes, of each chief house a prince throughout all the tribes of Israel; and each one *was* an head of the house of their fathers among the thousands of Israel.

f g 15 And they came unto the [9]children of Reuben, and to the [9]children of Gad, and to the half tribe of Manasseh, unto the land of Gilead, and they spake with them, saying,

16 "Thus saith the whole congregation of [2]the LORD, 'What °trespass *is* this that ye have committed against the [3]God of Israel, to turn away this day from following [2]the LORD, in that ye have builded you an altar, that ye might rebel this day against [2]the LORD?

h 17 *Is* the °iniquity of °Peor too little for us, from which we are not cleansed until this day, although there was a plague in the congregation of [2]the LORD,

g 18 But that ye must turn away this day from following [2]the LORD? and it will be, *seeing* ye rebel to day against [2]the LORD, that to morrow He will be wroth with the whole congregation of Israel.

19 Notwithstanding, if the Land of your possession *be* unclean, *then* pass ye over unto the land of the possession of [2]the LORD, wherein [2]the LORD'S °tabernacle dwelleth, and take possession among us: but rebel not against [2]the LORD, nor rebel against us, in building you an altar beside the altar of [2]the LORD our [3]God.

h 20 Did not Achan the son of Zerah commit a [16]trespass in the accursed thing, and wrath fell on all the congregation of Israel? and that man perished not alone in his [17]iniquity.'"

f i l 21 Then the [9]children of Reuben and the [9]children of Gad and the half tribe of Manasseh answered, and said unto the heads of the thousands of Israel,

22 °"The LORD GOD of gods, °the LORD GOD of gods, He knoweth, and Israel he shall know; if *it be* in rebellion, or if in °transgression against [2]the LORD, (°save us not this day,)

word. Heb. "mouth", put by Fig. *Metonymy* (of Cause), Ap. 6, for what was spoken by it.

10-34 (A[2], p. 317). EAST OF JORDAN. (*Introversion.*)

A[2] c | 10. The altar erected.
  d | 11, 12. Offence. War proposed
    e | 13, 14. Mission of Phinehas.
      f | 15-20. Expostulation.
      f | 21-29. Explanation.
    e | 30-32. Approbation of Phinehas.
  d | 33. Offence removed. War averted.
c | 34. The altar named.

10 borders = windings or bendings.
to see to = to look at, i. e. in appearance.
11 Behold. Fig. *Asterismos* (Ap. 6).
over against = in front of, i. e. on the east side of Jordan. at the passage of = beyond, or opposite to.

15-20 (f, above). EXPOSTULATION. (*Alternation.*)

f | g | 15, 16. Trespass pointed out.
    h | 17. Example of Peor adduced.
  g | 18, 19. Rebellion pointed out.
    h | 20. Example of Achan adduced.

16 trespass. Heb. *chāṭā'*. Ap. 44. i.
17 iniquity = perverseness. Heb. *'āvāh*. Ap. 44. iv.
Peor. Cp. Num. 25. 3, 4.
19 tabernacle. Habitation. Heb. *mishkān*. Ap. 40.

21-29 (*f*, above). EXPLANATION. (*Introversion and Alternation.*)

f | i | l | 21, 22. Rebellion disclaimed.
        m | 23. Offerings disclaimed.
      k | 24-27. Real purpose: a witness.
      k | 28. Real purpose: a pattern.
  i | *l* | 29-. Rebellion disclaimed.
        m | -29. Offerings disclaimed.

22 The LORD GOD of gods. Heb. El Elohim Jehovah. Fig. *Epizeuxis* (Ap. 6).
transgression. Heb. *mā'al*. Ap. 44. xi.
save us not this day. Note the Fig. *Parenthesis*. Ap. 6.
23 offer = offer up. See Ap. 43. I. vi.
offer = make ready. Ap. 43. I. iii.
24 What have ye . . . ? Fig. *Erotēsis*. Ap. 6.
27 a witness. Cp. Gen. 31. 48, and see *v.* 34 below, and ch. 24. 27.

23 That we have built us an altar to turn from following [2]the LORD, or if to °offer thereon burnt offering or meat offering, or if to °offer peace offerings thereon, let [2]the LORD Himself require *it*; m

24 And if we have not *rather* done it for fear of *this* thing, saying, 'In time to come your [9]children might speak unto our [9]children, saying, °"What have ye to do with [2]the LORD [3]God of Israel?"' k

25 For [2]the LORD hath made Jordan a border between us and you, ye [9]children of Reuben and [9]children of Gad; ye have no part in [2]the LORD: so shall your [9]children make our [9]children cease from fearing [2]the LORD.

26 Therefore we said, 'Let us now prepare to build us an altar,' not for burnt offering, nor for sacrifice:

27 But *that* it *may be* °a witness between us, and you, and our generations after us, that we might do the service of [2]the LORD before Him with our burnt offerings, and with our sacrifices, and with our peace offerings; that your [9]children may not say to our [9]children in time to come, 'Ye have no part in [2]the LORD.'

28 Therefore said we, that it shall be, when *k*

1442 they should *so* say to us or to our generations in time to come, that we may say *again*, °'Behold the °pattern of the altar of [2]the LORD, which our fathers made, not for burnt offerings, nor for sacrifices; but it *is* a witness between us °and you.'

i l (p. 318) 29 °God forbid that we should rebel against [2]the LORD, and turn this day from following [2]the LORD,

m to build an altar for burnt offerings, for meat offerings, or for sacrifices, beside the altar of [2]the LORD our [3]God that *is* before His [19]tabernacle."

e 30 And when Phinehas the priest, and the princes of the congregation and heads of the thousands of Israel which *were* with him, heard the words that the [9]children of Reuben and the [9]children of Gad and the [9]children of Manasseh spake, °it pleased them.

31 And Phinehas the son of Eleazar the priest said unto the [9]children of Reuben, and to the [9]children of Gad, and to the [9]children of Manasseh, "This day we perceive that [2]the LORD *is* among us, because ye have not committed this [16]trespass against [2]the LORD: now ye have delivered the [9]children of Israel out of the hand of [2]the LORD."

32 And Phinehas the son of Eleazar the priest, and the princes, returned from the [9]children of Reuben, and from the [9]children of Gad, out of the land of Gilead, unto the land of Canaan, to the [9]children of Israel, and brought them word again.

d 33 And the thing pleased the [9]children of Israel; and the [9]children of Israel blessed [3]God, and did not intend to go up against them in battle, to destroy the Land wherein the [9]children of Reuben and Gad dwelt.

c 34 And the [9]children of Reuben and the [9]children of Gad called the altar °*Ed:* for it *shall be* a witness between us that [2]the LORD *is* °God.

A C (p. 319) **23** And it came to pass °a long time after that °the LORD had given rest unto Israel from all their enemies round about, that Joshua waxed °old *and* stricken in age.

D E n 2 And Joshua °called for all Israel, *and* for their elders, °and for their heads, and for their judges, and for their officers, and said unto them, "I am [1]old *and* stricken in age:

o 3 And ye have seen all that [1]the LORD your °God hath done unto all these nations because of you; for [1]the LORD your °God *is* He That hath fought for you.

p 4 °Behold, I have divided unto you by lot these nations that remain, to be an inheritance for your tribes, from Jordan, with all the nations that I have cut off, even unto the great sea westward.

F q 5 And [1]the LORD your [3]God, He shall expel them from before you, and drive them from out of your sight; and ye shall possess their land, °as [1]the LORD your [3]God hath promised unto you.

28 Behold = behold ye. Not the Fig. *Asterismos*.
pattern = construction.
and you. Note Fig. *Ellipsis*, "and [between] you." Ap. 6.
29 God forbid = far be it from us.
30 it pleased them. Heb. "was good in their eyes".
34 Ed. Heb. *'ed*, "a witness." This, and the verb "shall be", not in the received Hebrew text. (Some codices have it.) Lit. "called the altar. A witness it is, &c."
God = the God. Heb. *hā-'Elohim*. Ap. 4. I.

23. 1—24. 28 (*A*, p. 289). JOSHUA ENDING HIS WORK. (*Alternation.*)

A | C | 23. 1. Time. Israel at rest.
  D | 23. 2-16. Address to Israel.
 C | 24. 1. Place. Assembling of Israel.
  D | 24. 2-28. Address to Israel.

1 a long time after. Eight years. See Ap. 50. IV, p. 53. the LORD. Heb. Jehovah. Ap. 4. II.
old and stricken in age. Aged 102. Cp. 13. 1. Fig. *Pleonasm*. Ap. 6. Heb. "old and advanced in (or come into) the days".

2-16 (D, above). ADDRESS TO ISRAEL.
(*Introversion, with Extended and Simple Alternation.*)

D | E | n | 2. Advancing age.
  o | 3. Appeal to Jehovah's faithfulness.
  p | 4. Division of the land. Accomplished.
 F | q | 5. Promise.
  r | 6-8. Exhortation.
 F | *q* | 9, 10. Promise.
  r | 11-13. Exhortation.
E | *n* | 14-. Approaching death.
  o | -14. Appeal to Jehovah's goodness.
  p | 15, 16. Forfeiture of land. Possible.

2 called. Probably at Shiloh.
and. Note the Fig. *Polysyndeton*. Ap. 6.
3 God. Heb. Elohim. Ap. 4. I.
4 Behold. Fig. *Asterismos*. Ap. 6.
5 as = according as.

6-8 (r, above). EXHORTATION. (*Introversion.*)

r | s | 6. To observe the Law of Moses.
  t | 7-. Warning against Canaanites.
  t | -7. Command against their idolatry.
 s | 8. To cleave to Jehovah.

6 the Book of the Law. See note on Ex. 17. 14, and Ap. 47.
that ye turn not. Cp. Deut. 5. 32; 28. 14.
9 man. Heb. *'ish*. Ap. 14. II.
10 for. The Hebrew accent (*Legarmeh*) puts the pause or emphasis on this word, as calling attention to the basis of all blessing and success.

6 Be ye therefore very courageous to keep and to do all that is written in °the Book of the Law of Moses, °that ye turn not aside therefrom *to* the right hand or *to* the left; r s

7 That ye come not among these nations, these that remain among you; t

neither make mention of the name of their gods, nor cause to swear *by them*, neither serve them, nor bow yourselves unto them: *t*

8 But cleave unto [1]the LORD your [3]God, [5]as ye have done unto this day. *s*

9 For [1]the LORD hath driven out from before you great nations and strong: but *as for* you, no °man hath been able to stand before you unto this day. *F q*

10 One man of you shall chase a thousand: °for [1]the LORD your [3]God, He *it is* that fighteth for you, as He hath promised you.

r u (p. 320) 1442 11 Take good heed therefore unto your °selves, that ye love [1]the LORD your [3]God.

v 12 °Else if ye do in any wise go back, and cleave unto the remnant of these nations, *even* these that remain among you, and shall make marriages with them, and go in unto them, and they to you:

v 13 Know for a certainty that [1]the LORD your [3]God will no more drive out °*any of* these nations from before you; but °they shall be snares and traps unto you, and scourges in your sides, and thorns in your eyes, until ye perish from off

u this good land which [1]the LORD your [3]God hath given you.

E n (p. 319) 14 And, °behold, this day I *am* going the way of all the earth:

o and ye know in all your hearts and in all your °souls, that not one °thing hath failed of all °the good things which [1]the LORD your [3]God spake concerning you; all are come to pass unto you, *and* not one °thing hath failed thereof.

p 15 Therefore it shall come to pass, *that* as all good [14]things are come upon you, which [1]the LORD your [3]God promised you; so shall [1]the LORD bring upon you all °evil [14]things, until He have destroyed you from off this good Land which [1]the LORD your [3]God hath given you.

16 When ye have transgressed the covenant of [1]the LORD your [3]God, which He commanded you, and have gone and served other gods, and bowed yourselves to them; then shall the anger of [1]the LORD be kindled against you, and ye shall perish quickly from off the good Land which He hath given unto you."

D w (p. 320) 1435 to 1434 **24** And Joshua gathered all the tribes of Israel to Shechem, and called for the elders of Israel, and for their heads, and for their judges, and for their officers; and they presented themselves before °God.

x G[1] 2 And Joshua said unto all the People, °"Thus °saith °the LORD °God of Israel, 'Your fathers dwelt on the other side of the °flood in old time, *even* Terah, the father of Abraham, and the father of Nachor: and they served other gods.

3 And °I took your father Abraham from the other side of the [2]flood, and led him throughout all the land of Canaan, and multiplied his seed, °and gave him Isaac.

4 And I gave unto Isaac °Jacob and Esau: and I gave unto °Esau mount Seir, to possess it; °but Jacob and his °children went down into Egypt.

5 °I sent Moses also and Aaron, and I plagued Egypt, according to that which I did among them: and afterward I brought you out.

6 And I brought your fathers out of °Egypt: and ye came unto the sea; and the Egyptians pursued after your fathers with chariots and horsemen unto the Red sea.

7 And when they cried unto [2]the LORD, He put °darkness between you °and the Egyptians, and brought the sea upon them, and covered them; and your eyes °have seen what I °have done in Egypt: and ye dwelt in the wilderness a long season.

8 And I brought you into the Land of the Amorites, which dwelt on the other side Jordan; and °they fought with you: and I gave them into your hand, that ye might possess their Land; and I destroyed them from before you.

9 Then Balak the son of Zippor, king of Moab, arose and warred against Israel, and °sent and called Balaam the son of Beor to curse you:

10 But I would not hearken unto Balaam;

11-13 (*r*, p. 319). EXHORTATION. (*Introversion.*)

r | u | 11. Jehovah your God. Love to be given Him.
  | v | 12. Warning against Canaanites. Alliances.
  | v | 13-. Warning against Canaanites. Consequences.
  | u | -13. Jehovah your God. Land given by Him.

11 selves = souls. Heb. *nephesh*. Ap. 13.

12 Else. The Hebrew accent (*Legarmeh*) puts the pause or emphasis on this word, as marking the solemn alternative.

13 any of these. Some codices, with four early printed editions, read "all these".

they shall be. Cp. Ex. 23. 33. Num. 33. 55. Deut. 7. 16.

14 behold, this day I, &c. Punctuate "behold this day, I am, &c." Joshua lived 8 years longer. Cp. Deut. 4. 16. **souls.** Heb. *nephesh*. Ap. 13.

thing = word. Cp. 21. 45.

the good things = the good words.

15 evil things = the evils threatened.

24. 1-28 (*D*, p. 319). ADDRESS TO ELDERS (*Introversion.*)

D | w | 1. Assemblage of elders.
  | x | 2-24. Covenant made.
  | x | 25-27. Covenant ratified.
  | w | 28. Dismissal of People.

1 God. Heb. *hā-'Ĕlohim*, the God. Ap. 4. I. Cp. 22. 34.

2-24 (x, above). COVENANT MADE. (*Repeated Alternation.*)

x | G[1] | 2-15. Joshua. History and exhortations.
  | H[1] | 16-18. People. Assent.
  | G[2] | 19, 20. Joshua. Alternatives.
  | H[2] | 21. People. Assent affirmed.
  | G[3] | 22-. Joshua. Appeal.
  | H[3] | -22. People. Assent.
  | G[4] | 23. Joshua. Exhortation.
  | H[4] | 24. People. Promise.

2 Thus saith the LORD. A supplementary revelation by the Spirit of God, who knows all (Heb. Jehovah).

saith = hath said.

the LORD God. Heb. Jehovah Elohim. Ap. 4. I, II.

flood = the river Euphrates.

3 I took. Gen. 11. 31—12. 1.

and gave. Gen. 21. 1-3.

4 Jacob and Esau. Cp. Gen. 25. 25, 26.

Esau. Cp. Gen. 36. 8. Deut. 2. 5.

but Jacob. Cp. Gen. 46. 6. **children** = sons.

5 I sent. Cp. Ex. 3. 10; 4. 14-16.

6 Egypt. After this word the Sept. preserves a sentence omitted by Fig. *Homœoteleuton*: "And they became there a great, populous, and mighty people, and were afflicted by Egypt"; the scribe's eye going back to this preceding word Egypt and continuing from there. **the Red sea.** Cp. Ex. 14. 9.

7 darkness. Heb. *'ophēlāh*, thick and intense darkness. Occ. only here.

and the. Note Fig. *Ellipsis* (Ap. 6) = "and [between] the".

have seen = saw. **have done** = did.

8 they fought. Cp. Num. 21. 32.

9 sent. Cp. Num. 22. 5. Deut. 23. 4.

1435 to 1434 therefore he blessed you still: so I delivered
you out of his hand.
11 And ye went over Jordan, and came unto
Jericho: and the °men of Jericho fought against
you, the Amorites, and the Perizzites, and the
Canaanites, and the Hittites, and the Girgashites, the Hivites, and the Jebusites; and I delivered them into your hand.
12 And I sent the hornet before you, which
drave them out from before you, *even* the °two
kings of the Amorites; *but* not with thy sword,
nor with thy bow.
13 And I have given you a land for which ye
did not labour, and cities which ye built not,
and ye dwell in them; of the vineyards and
oliveyards which ye planted not do ye eat.'
14 Now therefore fear [2]the LORD, and serve
Him in sincerity and in truth: and put away
the gods which your fathers served on the
other side of the flood, °and in Egypt; and
serve ye [2]the LORD.
15 And if it seem evil unto you to serve [2]the
LORD, choose you this day whom ye will serve;
whether the gods which your fathers served
that *were* on the other side of the flood, or the
gods of the Amorites, in whose land ye dwell:
but as for me and my house, we will serve [2]the
LORD."

H[1] (p. 320) 16 And the People answered and said, °"God
forbid that we should forsake [2]the LORD, to
serve other gods;
17 For [2]the LORD our [2]God, °He *it is* that
brought us up and our fathers out of the land
of Egypt, from the house of bondage, and
which did those great signs in our sight, and
preserved us in all the way wherein we went,
and among all the °people through whom we
passed:
18 And [2]the LORD drave out from before us all
the [17]people, even the Amorites which dwelt
in the land: *therefore* will we also serve [2]the
LORD; for He *is* our [2]God."

G[2] 19 And Joshua said unto the People, °"Ye
cannot serve [2]the LORD: for He *is* an °holy
[2]God; He *is* a jealous °GOD; He will not forgive your transgressions nor your °sins.
20 If ye forsake [2]the LORD, and serve strange
gods, °then He will turn and do you hurt, and
consume you, after that He hath done you good."

H[2] 21 And the People said unto Joshua, "Nay;
but we will serve [2]the LORD."

G[3] 22 And Joshua said unto the People, "Ye
are witnesses against yourselves that ye have
chosen you [2]the LORD, to serve Him."

H[3] And they said, "*We are* witnesses."

G[4] 23 "Now therefore put away," *said he*, "the
°strange gods which *are* among you, and incline
your heart unto [2]the LORD [2]God of Israel."

H[4] 24 And the People said unto Joshua, [2]"The
LORD our [2]God will we serve, and His voice
will we obey."

x 25 So Joshua °made a covenant with the
People that day, and set them a statute and an
ordinance in Shechem.
26 And Joshua wrote these words in °the
Book of the Law of [2]God, and took a great
stone, and set it up there under °an oak, that
was by the sanctuary of [2]the LORD.
27 And Joshua said unto all the People,
°"Behold, this stone shall be a witness unto
us; for °it hath heard all the words of [2]the
LORD which He spake unto us: it shall be
therefore a witness unto you, lest ye deny
your [2]God."

28 So Joshua let the People depart, °every *w*
man unto his inheritance.

29 And it came to pass after these things, that X y (p. 321) Epilogue 1434
Joshua the son of Nun, the servant of [2]the
LORD, °died, *being* an hundred and ten years old.
30 And they buried him in the border of his
inheritance in Timnath-serah, which *is* in
°mount Ephraim, on the north side of the
hill of °Gaash.

31 And Israel served [2]the LORD all the days z
of Joshua, and °all the days of the elders that
overlived Joshua, and which had known all
the °works of [2]the LORD, that He had done for
Israel.

11 men = lords or rulers. Heb. *ba'al.*
12 two kings. Promise began to be fulfilled here. See Ex. 23. 28. Deut. 7. 20.
14 and in Egypt. So that they were idolaters there. Cp. Ezek. 23. 8. Three systems of idolatry referred to in *vv.* 14, 15: Chaldean, Egyptian, and Canaanite.
16 God forbid = Far be it from us.
17 He. The italics not needed. There is a Fig. *Homœoteleuton* (Ap. 6), which the Sept. supplies: "He [is God. He] brought us up", &c. The scribe's eye went back to the latter "He".
people = peoples.
19 Ye cannot serve. The Ellipsis must be supplied by adding from *v.* 14. "Unless ye put away your idols". See Ap. 6. iii. 1.
holy. See note on Ex. 6. 5.
GOD. Heb. El. Ap. 4. IV.
sins. Ap. 44. i. **20 then.** Cp. 23. 15.
23 strange gods = strangers' (or foreigners') gods.
25 made a covenant: i. e. by sacrifice. Cp. Jer. 34. 18, 19.
26 the Book of the Law. See note on Ex. 17. 14 and Ap. 47. **an** = the.
27 Behold. Fig. *Asterismos.* Ap. 6.
it hath heard. Fig. *Prosopopœia.* Ap. 6.
28 every man. Heb. *'ish.* Ap. 14. II.

24. 29-33 (p. 289). EPILOGUE.

X | y | 29, 30. Death and burial of Joshua.
| z | 31. Obedience to Jehovah's command.
| z | 32. Obedience to Joseph's command.
| y | 33. Death of Eleazar.

29 died. In 1434, after living seventeen years in the Land. Ap. 50. IV, p. 53.
30 mount = the hill country.
Gaash. The Sept. adds here: "And they placed with him in the tomb in which they buried him the knives of stone with which he circumcised the sons of Israel in Gilgal, when he brought them out of Egypt, as the LORD appointed them; and there they are until this day."
31 all the days. The expression is not necessarily a long period. In 11. 18 it = seven years; in 23. 1 = within ten years; here it = three years. See Ap. 50. IV, p. 53.
works = work.

z (p. 321) 1434 **32 And ° the bones of Joseph, which the [4] children of Israel brought up out of Egypt, buried they in ° Shechem, in a parcel of ground which ° Jacob bought of the sons of Hamor the father of Shechem for an hundred pieces of silver: and it became the inheritance of the [4] children of Joseph.**

y **33 And ° Eleazar the son of Aaron died; and they buried him in a hill *that pertained to* Phinehas his son, which was given him in [30] mount ° Ephraim.**

32 the bones of Joseph. Cp. Gen. 50. 25. Heb. 11. 22.

Shechem. Where God first appeared to Abraham in Canaan (Gen. 12. 6), and where he built his first altar (Gen. 12. 6, 7).

Jacob bought. Cp. Gen. 33. 19. Not Acts 7. 16, nor Gen. 23, which was quite a different transaction.

33 Eleazar. He dies and is succeeded by his son Phinehas. Cp. Judg. 20. 28. Phinehas had been acting as deputy High Priest as far back as 1444; ten or twelve years before his father died. Cp. 22. 13-32.

Ephraim. The Sept. adds here: "In that day the sons of Israel took the ark of God, and carried it about among them; and Phinees exercised the priest's office in the room of Eleazar his father, till he died, and he was buried in his own place Gabaar. But the sons of Israel departed every one to their place, and to their own city. And the sons of Israel worshipped Astarte (i.e. the Ashērah; see Ap. 42) and Astarōth, and the gods of the nations round about them; and the LORD delivered them into the hands of Eglōm king of Mōab, and he ruled over them eighteen years".

JUDGES.

THE STRUCTURE OF THE BOOK AS A WHOLE.

(*Alternation and Introversion.*)

A | **C** | 1. 1—2. 5. ISRAEL AND OTHER PEOPLES. AGGRESSIONS.

D | 2. 6—8. 35. GOVERNMENT.

B | 9. 1-57. INTERNAL DISORDERS.

A | ***D*** | 10. 1—16. 31. GOVERNMENT.

C | 17. 1—18. 31. ISRAEL AND OTHER PEOPLES. AGGRESSIONS.

B | 19. 1—21. 25. INTERNAL DISORDERS.

THE

BOOK OF °JUDGES.

A a c 1 °Now after the death of °Joshua it came to
(p. 325) pass, that the °children of Israel °asked
1434 °the LORD, saying, °"Who shall go up for us
against the Canaanites first, to fight against
them?"
2 And [1]the LORD said, "Judah shall go up
°behold, I have delivered the land into his
hand."
3 And Judah said unto Simeon his brother,
"Come up with me into my lot, that we may
fight against the Canaanites; and I likewise
will go with thee into thy lot." So Simeon
went with him.
4 And Judah went up; and [1]the LORD delivered the Canaanites and the Perizzites into
their hand: and they slew of them in Bezek
ten thousand °men.

d 5 And they found °Adoni-bezek in Bezek:
and they fought against him, and they slew
the Canaanites and the Perizzites.
6 But Adoni-bezek fled; and they pursued
after him, and caught him, and °cut off his
thumbs and his great toes.
7 And Adoni-bezek said, "Threescore and
ten kings, having their thumbs and their great
toes cut off, °gathered *their meat* under my
table: °as I have done, so °God hath requited
me." And they brought him to Jerusalem,
and there he died.
8 Now the [1]children of Judah had fought
against °Jerusalem, and had °taken it, and
smitten it with the edge of the sword, and set
the city on fire.

b e 9 And afterward the [1]children of Judah went
down to fight against the Canaanites, that
dwelt in the °mountain, and in the °south,
and in the °valley.

f 10 And Judah went against the Canaanites
that dwelt in Hebron: (°now the name of
°Hebron before *was* °Kirjath-arba:) and they
slew °Sheshai, and Ahiman, and Talmai.

a c 11 And from thence he went against the inhabitants of Debir: and the name of °Debir
before *was* °Kirjath-sepher:

d 12 And Caleb said, "He that smiteth Kirjath-sepher, and taketh it, to him will I give Achsah
my daughter to wife."
13 And °Othniel the son of Kenaz, Caleb's
younger brother, took it: and he gave him
Achsah his daughter to wife.

TITLE, Judges. The Heb. name is *Shôph^e^tîm* = rulers; from verb *to put right and then rule.* Not Judges, as modern English. For origin and description of name, cp. 2. 7–19. In Sept. = *kritai*; Latin, *Liber Judicum.* The office peculiar to Israel. The book records the history of thirteen Judges (twelve called of God and one a usurper), whose names by Gematria make a multiple of eight and thirteen (see Ap. 10); six "evil" doings (see note on 2. 11); six oppressors and oppressions (see note on 2. 14); and six deliverances (see note on 2. 16).

1. 1–2. 5 (C, p. 323). CONQUESTS. ISRAEL AND OTHER NATIONS. (*Alternation.*)

C | A | 1. 1–20. By the tribe of Judah.
  | B | 1. 21. Unexpelled inhabitants.
  | *A* | 1. 22–26. By the house of Joseph.
  | *B* | 1. 27–2. 5. Unexpelled inhabitants.

1–20 (A, above). BY THE TRIBE OF JUDAH. (*Alternations.*)

A | a | c | 1–4. Judah.
  | | d | 5–8. Conquest. Jerusalem.
  | b | e | 9. Judah.
  | | f | 10. Conquest. Hebron.
  | *a* | *c* | 11. Judah.
  | | *d* | 12–16. Conquest. Debir.
  | *b* | *e* | 17. Judah.
  | | *f* | 18–20. Conquest. Hebron.

1 Now = And. Commencing with the same word as the preceding books; thus connecting them all together. The book of Joshua = the inheritance possessed: Judges = the inheritance despised. Records the failure of the People, and the faithfulness of Jehovah. The Epilogue (21. 25) gives the key to the whole book. See note on 17. 6.

Joshua. Cp. Josh. 24. 29. **children** = sons.

asked = enquired: i. e. by Urim and Thummim, as in 18. 5; 20. 18. See note on Ex. 28. 30. Num. 26. 55.

the LORD. Heb. Jehovah. Ap. 4. II.

Who . . . ? All had been commanded. Deut. 20. 17. Josh. 10. 40.

2 behold. Fig. *Asterismos* (Ap. 6). Some codices, with three early printed editions, read "and behold".

4 men. Heb. *'ish.* Ap. 14. II.

5 Adoni-bezek = Lord of Bezek. Bezek was seventeen miles south of Shechem. Cp. 1 Sam. 11. 8. Cp. Josh. 15. 13–19.

6 cut off. As he had done to others. See *v.* 7.

7 gathered. i. e. [the pieces].

as = according as.

God. Heb. Elohim. Ap. 4. I.

8 Jerusalem. The first occurrence is in Josh. 10. 1, in connection with Adoni-zedek's fear of its being "utterly destroyed" like Ai. Here, in *v.* 8, we have a picture of its future history in miniature. See Ap. 53. The *Tel-el-Amarna* tablets contain a long correspondence with Egypt about 1400 B.C.

taken it. The citadel not taken till 2 Sam. 5. 6–9, by David.

---

9 mountain = hill country. **south.** Heb. *Negeb.* **valley** = lowlands. **10 now.** Note the Fig. *Parenthesis* (Ap. 6), and cp. with *v.* 17. **Hebron.** Cp. Num. 13. 22. Josh. 14. 13. **Kirjath-arba.** Cp. Gen. 23. 2. Josh. 14. 15; 20. 7. **Sheshai.** These are sons of Anak. Cp. *v.* 20.
11 Debir . . . Kirjath-sepher. See note on Josh. 11. 21 and 15. 49. **13 Othniel.** Mentioned only here; and 3. 9–11. Josh. 15. 17; and 1 Chron. 4. 13.

1434 to 1431 14 And it came to pass, when she came °*to him,* that she moved him to ask of her father °a field: and she lighted from off *her* ass; and Caleb said unto her, °"What wilt thou?"

15 And she said unto him, "Give me a blessing: for thou hast given me a south land; give me also springs of water." And Caleb gave her the upper springs and the nether springs.

16 And the [1]children of the °Kenite, Moses' father in law, went up out of the city of °palm trees with the [1]children of Judah into the wilderness of Judah, which *lieth* in the south of Arad; and they went and dwelt among °the People.

b e (p. 325) 17 And Judah went with Simeon his brother, and they slew the Canaanites that inhabited Zephath, and utterly °destroyed it. (And the name of the city was called °Hormah.)

f 18 Also Judah °took Gaza with the °coast thereof, and Askelon with the °coast thereof, and Ekron with the °coast thereof.

19 And [1]the LORD was with Judah; and °he drave out *the inhabitants of* the °mountain; but could not drive out the inhabitants of the °valley, because they had °chariots of iron.

20 And they gave Hebron unto Caleb, °as Moses said: and he expelled thence the °three sons of Anak.

B 21 And the [1]children of Benjamin °did not drive out the Jebusites that inhabited Jerusalem; but the Jebusites dwell with the [1]children of Benjamin in Jerusalem unto this day.

A g i (p. 326) 22 And the house of Joseph, they also went up against Beth-el: and [1]the LORD *was* with them.

23 And the house of Joseph sent to descry Beth-el.

k (Now the name of the city before *was* °Luz.)

h 24 And the °spies saw a man come forth out of the city, and they said unto him,

h "Shew us, we pray thee, the entrance into the city, and we will shew thee mercy."

g i 25 And when he shewed them the entrance into the city, they smote the city with the edge of the sword; but they let go the man and all his family.

k 26 And the man went into the land of the °Hittites, and built a city, and called the name thereof Luz: which *is* the name thereof unto this day.

C[1] l n 27 °Neither did Manasseh °drive out *the inhabitants of* Beth-shean and her towns, °nor Taanach and her towns, nor the inhabitants of Dor and her towns, nor the inhabitants of Ibleam and her towns, nor the inhabitants of Megiddo and her towns: but the Canaanites would dwell in that land.

o 28 And it came to pass, when Israel was strong, that they put the Canaanites to tribute, and did not utterly drive them out.

m p 29 [27]Neither did Ephraim [27]drive out the Canaanites that °dwelt in Gezer; but the Canaanites °dwelt in Gezer among them.

30 Neither did Zebulun [27]drive out the inhabitants of Kitron, nor the inhabitants of Nahalol;

but the Canaanites dwelt among them, and became tributaries. q

31 Neither did Asher [27]drive out the inhabitants of Accho, nor the inhabitants of Zidon, nor of Ahlab, nor of Achzib, nor of Helbah, nor of Aphik, nor of Rehob: *m p*

32 But the Asherites °dwelt among the

---

14 to him. Supply Fig. *Ellipsis* with "home".
a = the.
What wilt thou? or, What aileth thee? Josh. 15. 18, 19.

16 Kenite. A non-Israelite race (Gen. 15. 19. Num. 24. 21, &c. 1 Sam. 27. 10; 30. 29). See Saul's correspondence with them (1 Sam. 15. 6). One branch in the north (4. 11).
palm trees: i.e. Jericho, 3. 13. Deut. 34. 3.
the People: i.e. Israel.

17 destroyed = devoted.
Hormah = utter destruction.

18 took Gaza, &c. These were wholly or partially retaken by the enemy, cp. 14. 19; 16. 1. 1 Sam. 5. 10. Perhaps this accounts for the Sept. reading, "Judah too did not inherit".
coast = border.

19 he drave out = he possessed. (Omit italics.)
mountain = hill country. valley = lowlands.
chariots of iron. Cp. 4. 3.

20 as = according as. Cp. Num. 14. 24. Josh. 14. 13; 15. 13.
three sons of Anak. See their names in *v.* 10 and Ap. 23 and 25.

21 did not drive out. Cp. Josh. 15. 63; 18. 28. 2 Sam. 5. 6–10.

22–26 (*A*, p. 325). BY THE HOUSE OF JOSEPH.
(*Introversion and Alternation.*)

A g | i | 22, 23–. Beth-el besieged.
  | k | –23. Name explained.
  h | 24–. Spies. Mission.
  h | –24. Spies. Action.
g | *i* | 25. Beth-el taken.
  | *k* | 26. Name explained.

23 Luz. Cp. Gen. 28. 19, and see Josh. 16. 1, 2. Luz and Beth-el not two cities.

24 spies = sentries.

26 Hittites. A nation north of Syria, mentioned on Egyptian inscriptions from 1500 B.C.

1. 27—2. 5 (*B*, p. 325). UNEXPELLED INHABITANTS. (*Division.*)

B | C[1] | 1. 17–36. Non-expulsion. The sin.
  | C[2] | 2. 1–5. Non-expulsion. The punishment.

27–36 (C[1], above). NON-EXPULSION. SIN.
(*Introversion and Alternation.*)

C[1] | l | n | 27. Manasseh.
  | o | 28. Made them tributaries.
  m | p | 29, 30–. Ephraim and Zebulun.
  | q | –30. Made them tributaries.
  m | *p* | 31–33–. Asher and Naphtali.
  | *q* | –33. Made them tributaries.
l | *n* | 34, 35–. Dan.
  | *o* | –35, 36. Made them tributaries.

27 Neither ... nor. Note the Fig. *Paradiastolē* (Ap. 6) in *vv.* 29–33. Emphasising the unfaithfulness and disobedience, the cause of all subsequent trouble.
drive out = possess.

29 dwelt: i.e. in friendly relations. Ps. 133. 1. 2 Kings 4. 13. See note on 1 Kings 9. 16, 17.

32 dwelt among = dwelt in the inside, as in the heart or bowels of the Canaanites; *vv.* 27–30 are very different.

1434 Canaanites, the inhabitants of the land: for
to they did not drive them out.
1431 33 Neither did Naphtali [27]drive out the inhabitants of Beth-shemesh, nor the inhabitants
of Beth-anath; but he [32]dwelt among the
Canaanites, the inhabitants of the land:

q nevertheless the inhabitants of Beth-shemesh
(p. 326) and of Beth-anath became tributaries unto
them.

l n 34 And the Amorites forced the [1]children of
Dan into the mountain: for they would not
suffer them to come down to the valley:
35 But the Amorites would dwell in mount
Heres in Aijalon, and in Shaalbim:

o yet the °hand of the house of Joseph prevailed,
so that they became tributaries.
36 And the °coast of the Amorites *was* from
the going up to Akrabbim, from the rock, and
upward.

C² r **2** And °an °Angel of °the LORD came up
(p. 327) from Gilgal to °Bochim, and said, "I made
1434 you to go up out of Egypt, and have brought
to you unto the land which I sware unto your
1100 fathers; and °I said, 'I will never break My
covenant with you.
2 And °ye shall make no league with the inhabitants of this land; °ye shall throw down
their altars:' but ye have not obeyed My
voice: °why have ye done this?

s 3 Wherefore I also said, 'I will not drive them
out from before you; but they shall °be *as
thorns* in your sides, and their gods shall be
a snare unto you.'"

r 4 And it came to pass, when the Angel of
[1]the LORD spake these words unto all the
°children of Israel, that the people lifted up
their voice, and wept.

s 5 And they called the name of that place
[1]Bochim: and they sacrificed there unto [1]the
LORD.

D¹ t 6 And when Joshua had °let the People go,
the [4]children of Israel went every °man unto
his inheritance to possess the land.

u 7 And the People served [1]the LORD all the
days of Joshua, and all the days of the elders
that outlived Joshua, °who had seen all the
great °works of [1]the LORD, that He did for
Israel.

t 8 And Joshua the son of Nun, the servant of
1434 [1]the LORD, died, *being* an hundred and ten
years old.
9 And they buried him in the border of his
inheritance in °Timnath-heres, in the °mount
of Ephraim, on the north side of the hill
Gaash.
10 And also all that generation were gathered unto their fathers:

u and there arose another generation after them,
which °knew not [1]the LORD, nor yet the
[7]works which He had done for Israel.

D² E¹ v 11 And the [4]children of Israel did °evil in the
sight of [1]the LORD, and served Baalim:

12 And they °forsook [1]the LORD °God of
their fathers, Which brought them out of the
land of Egypt, and followed other gods, of the
gods of the °people that *were* round about
them, and bowed themselves unto them, and
provoked [1]the LORD to anger.

35 hand. Fig. *Metonymy* (of Cause), Ap. 6, by which the hand is put for the power exerted by it.
36 coast = border or boundary.

2. 1-5 (C², p. 326). NON-EXPULSION. PUNISHMENT. (*Alternation.*)

C² | r | 1, 2. Expostulation. Cause. Disobedience.
  s | 3. Threatening.
 r | 4. Expostulation. Effect. Weeping.
  s | 5. Worship.

Chapter 2 gives a summary of events from 3. 1—16. 31. The period it covers is therefore 1434–1100, i. e. 334 years.
1 an Angel = the Angel or Captain of Jehovah's host, Who had appeared to Joshua in Gilgal. Josh. 5. 13-15.
the LORD. Heb. Jehovah. Ap. 4. II.
Bochim = weepers. **I said.** Cp. Gen. 17. 7.
2 ye shall make no league. Cp. Ex. 23. 32. Deut. 7. 2, 5, &c.
ye shall throw down. Cp. Ex. 34. 12, 13. Deut. 12. 3.
why . . . ? Fig. *Erotēsis* (Ap. 6). Or, "what [is] this [that] ye have done?"
3 be as thorns in your sides. Some codices read "be adversaries to you". Cp. Num. 33. 55. Josh. 23. 13.
4 children = sons.

2. 6—8. 32 (D, p. 323). GOVERNMENT. (*Division.*)

D | D¹ | 2. 6-10. Antecedent.
 D² | 2. 11—8. 32. Subsequent.

2. 6-10 (D¹, above). ANTECEDENT. (*Alternation.*)

D¹ | t | 6. Joshua's life.
  u | 7. Predecessors. Knowledge. Obedience.
 t | 8-10-. Joshua's death.
  u | -10. Successors. Ignorance. Disobedience.

6 let the People go. Cp. Josh. 24. 28-31.
man. Heb. *'ish.* Ap. 14. II.
7 who. Some codices, with two early printed editions, Syr., and Vulg., read "and who".
works = work.
9 Timnath-heres. Some codices, with Syr. and Vulg., read "Timnath-serah". Cp. Josh. 19. 50; 24. 30.
mount = hill country.
10 knew not. Fig. *Metonymy* (of Cause). Ap. 6. Put for obeyed not or cared not for.

2. 11—8. 32 (D², above). SUBSEQUENT. (*Division.*)

D² | E¹ | 2. 11—3. 4. The People and their Apostasies.
 E² | 3. 5—8. 32. The oppressors and Deliverers.

2. 11—3. 4 (E¹, above). THE PEOPLE AND THEIR APOSTASIES. (*Extended Alternation.*)

E¹ | v | 2. 11-13. Evil committed.
  w | 2. 14-. Anger of Jehovah.
   x | 2. -14, 15. Punishment. Sold to enemies.
 v | 2. 16-19. Evil repeated.
  w | 2. 20-. Anger of Jehovah.
   x | 2. -20—3. 4. Punishment. Proved by enemies.

11 evil = the evil. Heb. *rā'a'.* See Ap. 44. viii. Six "evil" doings recorded in this book (Ap. 10): 3. 7, 12; 4. 1; 6. 1; 10. 6; 13. 1.
12 forsook. Religion is not a gradual evolution to what is higher, but a declension to what is lower. See note on Josh. 24. 14.
God. Heb. Elohim. Ap. 4. I.
people = peoples.

1434 to 1100 13 And they [12]forsook [1]the LORD, and served Baal and °Ashtaroth.
w (p. 327) 14 And the anger of [1]the LORD was hot against Israel,
x and He delivered them into the hands of °spoilers that spoiled them, and He sold them into the hands of their °enemies round about, so that they could not any longer stand before their enemies.
15 Whithersoever they went out, the hand of [1]the LORD was against them for °evil, as [1]the LORD had said, and °as [1]the LORD had sworn unto them: and they were greatly distressed.
v y (p. 328) 16 Nevertheless [1]the LORD raised up °judges,
z which °delivered them out of the hand of those that spoiled them.
a 17 And yet they would not hearken unto their judges, but they went a whoring after other gods, and bowed themselves unto them: they turned quickly out of the way which their fathers walked in, obeying the commandments of [1]the LORD; *but* they did not so.
y 18 And when [1]the LORD raised them up judges,
z then [1]the LORD was with the judge, and [16]delivered them out of the hand of their enemies °all the days of the judge: for it repented [1]the LORD because of their groanings by reason of them that oppressed them and vexed them.
a 19 And it came to pass, °when the judge was dead, *that* they returned, and corrupted *themselves* more than their fathers, in following other gods to serve them, and to bow down unto them; they ceased not from their own doings, nor from their stubborn way.
w (p. 327) 20 And the anger of [1]the LORD was hot against Israel; and He said,
x b¹ (p. 328) "Because that this °people hath °transgressed My covenant which I commanded their fathers, and have not hearkened unto My voice;
21 I also will not henceforth drive out any from before them of the nations which Joshua left when he died:
c¹ 22 That through them I may prove Israel, whether they will keep the way of [1]the LORD to walk °therein, as their fathers did keep *it*, or not."
b² 23 Therefore [1]the LORD left those nations, without °driving them out hastily; neither delivered He them into the hand of Joshua.

c² 1434 to 1431 3 Now these *are* the nations which °the LORD left, to prove Israel by them, *even* as many *of Israel* as had not known all the wars of Canaan;
2 Only that the generations of the °children of Israel might know, to teach them war, at the least such as before knew nothing thereof;
b³ 3 *Namely*, °five lords of the Philistines, and all the Canaanites, and the Sidonians, and the Hivites that dwelt in mount Lebanon, from mount Baal-hermon unto the °entering in of Hamath.
c³ 4 And they were to prove Israel by them, to know whether they would hearken unto the commandments of [1]the LORD, which He commanded their fathers by the hand of Moses.

5 And the [2]children of Israel °dwelt among the Canaanites, Hittites, and Amorites, and Perizzites, and Hivites, and Jebusites: E² F d

13 Ashtaroth. The special evil of Canaanite nations. Name derived from the *Ashērah* (see Ap. 42). The *Ashērah* was idolatry of the most revolting form of immorality under the guise of religion. All virtue surrendered. The "going a whoring" is more than a figure of speech. See Ex. 34. 13. Deut. 7. 5; 12. 3; 16. 21. Note all the occurrences of *'Ashtārōth*: Deut. 1. 4. Josh. 9. 10; 12. 4; 13. 12, 31. Judg. 2. 13; 10. 6. 1 Sam. 7. 3, 4; 12. 10; 31. 10.

14 spoilers . . . enemies. *Six* oppressors and servitudes named: Judg. 3. 8, 12; 4. 2; 6. 1; 10. 7; 13. 1.

15 evil. Heb. *rā'a'*. Ap. 44. viii.
as = according as. Cp. Lev. 26. Deut. 28.

16–19 (*v*, p. 327). EVIL REPEATED.
(*Extended Alternation.*)

v | y | 16–. Judges raised up.
  z | –16. Deliverance.
  a | 17. Apostasy.
  y | 18–. Judges raised up.
  z | –18. Deliverance.
  a | 19. Apostasy.

16 judges. This word gives the name to the book = one who put right what was wrong; hence, a ruler.
delivered = saved. Six deliverances: 3. 9, 15; 4. 23; 8. 28; 11. 33; 16. 30.

18 all the days, &c. This raises the question as to Deborah's call. See note on 4. 4.

19 when. Cp. 3. 12.

2. 20—3. 4 (*x*, p. 327). PUNISHMENT. PROVING.
(*Repeated Alternation.*)

x | b¹ | 2. –20, 21. Non-expulsion.
  c¹ | 2. 22. Trial.
  b² | 2. 23. Non-expulsion.
  c² | 3. 1, 2. Trial.
  b³ | 3. 3. Non-expulsion.
  c³ | 3. 4. Trial.

20 people = nation.
transgressed. Heb. *'ābar*. Ap. 44. vii.

22 therein. A special various reading called *Sevīr* (Ap. 34), with some codices, Sept., and Vulg., read "in it": i. e. in Jehovah's way.

23 driving them out = dispossessing.

3. 1 the LORD. Heb. Jehovah. Ap. 4. II.
2 children = sons.
3 five lords. See note on Josh. 13. 2-6.
entering in = pass.

3. 5—8. 32 (E², p. 327). OPPRESSORS AND DELIVERERS. (*Introversion.*)

E² | F | 3. 5-11. Chushan-rishathaim. (Othniel.)
  G | 3. 12-30. Eglon. (Ehud.)
  H | 3. 31. Shamgar. (Philistines.)
  G | 4. 1—5. 31. Jabin. (Barak.)
  F | 6. 1—8. 35. Midian. (Gideon.)

3. 5-11 (F, above). CHUSHAN-RISHATHAIM, AND OTHNIEL. (*Extended Alternation.*)

F | d | 5-7. Evil committed.
  e | 8–. Oppressor. (Chushan-rishathaim.)
  f | –8. Servitude. Eight years.
  d | 9–. Evil repented of.
  e | –9, 10. Deliverer. (Othniel.)
  f | 11. Rest. Forty years.

5 dwelt among. Not the Canaanites dwelling in Israel, but Israel dwelling among the Canaanites, who were to be exterminated. Ex. 3. 8, 17; 23. 23-28. Deut. 7. 1-5.

6 And they °took their daughters to be their wives, and gave their daughters to their sons, and served their gods.
7 And the [2]children of Israel did °evil in the sight of [1]the LORD, and forgat [1]the LORD their °God, and served Baalim and °the groves.

e (p. 328) 8 Therefore the anger of [1]the LORD was hot against Israel,

f 1431 to 1423 and He °sold them into the hand of Chushan-rishathaim king of Mesopotamia: and the [2]children of Israel served Chushan-rishathaim eight years.

d 9 And when the [2]children of Israel cried unto [1]the LORD,

e [1]the LORD raised up a °deliverer to the [2]children of Israel, who °delivered them, *even* °Othniel the son of Kenaz, Caleb's younger brother.
10 And °the Spirit of [1]the LORD came upon him, and he judged Israel, and went out to war: and [1]the LORD delivered Chushan-rishathaim king of Mesopotamia into his hand; and his hand prevailed against Chushan-rishathaim.

f 1423 to 1383 11 And the land °had rest forty years. And Othniel the son of Kenaz died.

G g (p. 329) 12 And the [2]children of Israel did [7]evil again in the sight of [1]the LORD:

h and [1]the LORD strengthened Eglon the king of Moab against Israel, because they had done evil in the sight of [1]the LORD.
13 And he gathered unto him the [2]children of Ammon and °Amalek, and went and smote Israel, and possessed the city of °palm trees.

i 1383 to 1365 14 So the [2]children of Israel served Eglon the king of Moab eighteen years.

g 15 But when the [2]children of Israel cried unto [1]the LORD,

h [1]the LORD raised them up a [9]deliverer, Ehud the son of Gera, a Benjamite, a man lefthanded:

j[1] k[1] l and by him the [2]children of Israel sent a present unto Eglon the king of Moab.

m 16 But Ehud made him a dagger which had two edges, of a °cubit length; and he did gird it under his raiment upon his right thigh.

l 17 And he brought the °present unto Eglon king of Moab: and Eglon *was* a very fat °man.
18 And when he had made an end to °offer the present, he sent away the people that bare the [17]present.

k[2] n 19 But he himself turned again from the °quarries °that *were* by Gilgal, and said, "I have a secret °errand unto thee, O king:" who said, "Keep silence." And all that stood by him went out from him.
20 And Ehud came unto him; and he was sitting in a °summer parlour, which he had for himself alone. And Ehud said, "I have a °message from °God unto thee." And he arose out of *his* °seat.

o 21 And Ehud put forth °his left hand, and took the dagger from his right thigh, and thrust it into his belly:
22 And the °haft also went in after the blade; and the fat closed upon the blade, so that he could not draw the dagger out of his belly; and the dirt came out.

23 Then Ehud went forth through the porch, and shut the doors of the [20]parlour upon him, and locked them. n

6 took their daughters, contrary to Jehovah's express command. Ex. 34. 16. Deut. 7. 3.
7 evil. Heb. "the evil"; i. e. the special evil (idolatry) which had been forbidden as such. See Ap. 44. viii. **God.** Heb. Elohim. Ap. 4. I.
the groves = *Asherim.* Ap. 42. See note on Ex. 34. 13.
8 sold. Cp. 2. 14. 490 years since Abraham left Mesopotamia. See Ap. 50. IV.
9 deliverer = saviour.
delivered = saved. Cp. Luke 1. 68–70.
Othniel. Cp. Josh. 15. 16, 17.
10 the Spirit of the LORD. Of Jehovah, Ap. 4. II, not *Elohim.* The spirit (Heb. *rūach,* Ap. 9) of Jehovah bestowing *gifts* rather than power or might (Gen. 1. 2). Cp. Isa. 11. 2; 61. 1.
11 had rest. Repeated four times: 3. 11, 30; 5. 31; 8. 28, to prevent the periods of rest and servitude being "telescoped". See Ap. 50. I, Introduction.

12–30 (G, p. 328). EGLON. (EHUD.)
(Extended Alternation.)

G | g | 12–. Evil committed.
  h | –12, 13. Oppressor. (Eglon.)
   i | 14. Servitude. Eighteen years.
 g | 15–. Evil repented of.
  h | –15–30–. Deliverer. (Ehud.)
   i | –30. Rest. Eighty years.

13 Amalek. See note on Ex. 17. 16.
palm trees. Cp. Deut. 34. 3.

–15–30 (*h*, above). DELIVERER. (EHUD.)
(Division.)

h | j[1] | –15–26. Assassination of Eglon.
  j[2] | 27–30. Slaughter of Moabites.

–15–26 (j[1], above). ASSASSINATION OF EGLON.
(Division and Introversion.)

j[1] | k[1] | l | –15. Present sent.
     m | 16. Dagger prepared.
    l | 17, 18. Present brought.
  k[2] | n | 19, 20. Interview sought.
     o | 21, 22. Dagger used.
    n | 23–26. Interview ended.

16 cubit. Occurs only here = a cut. Sept. *spithamē,* a dirk, about 9 inches long.
17 present = admittance-offering. Heb. *ḳorban.* Ap. 43. II. i.
man. Heb. *'ish.* Ap. 14.
18 offer = bring near. Heb. *ḳārab.* Ap. 43. I. i.
19 quarries = graven images. So Sept., Vulg., and Targum, here and *v.* 26. Heb. *p^esīlim.* Deut. 7. 5, 25; 12. 3. 2 Kings 17. 41. Ps. 78. 58, &c.
that were by Gilgal. Heb. the same [as] at Gilgal.
errand. Heb. word. See note on "message", *v.* 20.
20 summer parlour. Cooling room. Occurs only here and *v.* 24.
message = word; put by Fig. *Metonymy* (of Subject) for what is meant by it: here it is the "errand" of *v.* 19.
God = Elohim. Ap. 4. I. The Creator to the creature; not Jehovah (the Covenant God) to His servant.
seat = throne.
21 his left hand. Note the seven weak things in this book, illustrating 1 Cor. 1. 27. 2 Cor. 12. 9: left hand (3. 21); ox goad (3. 31); a woman (4. 4); a nail (4. 21); piece of a millstone (9. 53); pitcher and trumpet (7. 20); jawbone of an ass (15. 16). So in later times. Luther (a miner's son), Calvin (a cooper's son), Zwingle (a shepherd's son), Melancthon (an armourer's son), John Knox (a plain burgess's son).
22 haft = handle. Heb. *nizzab,* occurs only here.

24 When he was gone out, his servants came;
and when they saw that, °behold, the doors of
the parlour *were* locked, they said, "Surely he
°covereth his feet in his [20] summer chamber."
25 And they tarried till they were ashamed:
and, [24] behold, he opened not the doors of the
parlour; therefore they took °a key, and
opened *them:* and, [24] behold, their lord *was*
fallen down dead on the earth.
26 And Ehud escaped while they tarried, and
°passed °beyond the °quarries, and escaped
unto Seirath.

j[2] (p. 329) 27 And it came to pass, when he was come,
that he blew a trumpet in the mountain of
Ephraim, and the [2] children of Israel went down
with him from °the mount, and he before them.
28 And he said unto them, "Follow after
me: for [1] the LORD hath delivered your enemies the Moabites into your hand." And they
went down after him, and took the fords of
Jordan toward Moab, and suffered not a °man
to pass over.
29 And they slew of Moab at that time about
ten thousand [28] men, all lusty, and all [28] men of
valour; and there escaped not a [28] man.
30 So Moab was subdued that day under the
hand of Israel.

i And the land [11] had rest fourscore °years.

1365 to 1285

H (p. 328) 31 And after him was °Shamgar the son
of Anath, which slew of the Philistines six
hundred men with °an ox goad: and he also
delivered Israel.

G J[1] p (p. 330) **4** And the °children of Israel again did °evil
in the sight of °the LORD, when Ehud was
dead.

q 2 And [1] the LORD sold them into the hand of
°Jabin king of Canaan, that reigned in Hazor;
the captain of whose host *was* Sisera, °which
dwelt in Harosheth of the Gentiles.

p 3 And the [1] children of Israel cried unto [1] the
LORD: for he had nine hundred chariots of iron;

q and °twenty years he mightily oppressed the
1285 to 1265 [1] children of Israel.

J[2] K 4 And Deborah, °a prophetess, the wife of
Lapidoth, °she judged Israel °at that time.
5 And she °dwelt under the palm tree of
Deborah between Ramah and Beth-el in
mount Ephraim: and the [1] children of Israel
came up to her for judgment.

L M 6 And she sent and called Barak the son of
Abinoam out of Kedesh-naphtali, and said
unto him, °"Hath not [1] the LORD °God of
Israel commanded, *saying,* 'Go and draw
toward mount Tabor, and take with thee ten
thousand °men of the [1] children of Naphtali
and of the [1] children of Zebulun?

N r 7 And I will draw unto thee to the °river
Kishon Sisera, the captain of Jabin's army,
with his chariots and his multitude;

s and I will deliver him into thine °hand.'"

t 8 And Barak said unto her, "If thou wilt go
with me, then I will go: but if thou wilt not go
with me, *then* I will not go."

9 And she said, "I will surely go with thee:
notwithstanding the journey that thou takest
shall not be for thine honour; for [1] the LORD
shall sell Sisera into the hand of a woman."

24 behold. Fig. *Asterismos.* Ap. 6.
covereth his feet. Fig. *Euphemism* for act performed while stooping, and causing feet to be covered.
25 a key = the key.
26 passed = he passed.
beyond = by.
quarries = the graven images of Ehud. Cp. *v.* 19.
27 the mount = the hill country.
28 man. Heb. *'īsh.* Ap. 14. II.
30 years. The Sept. adds "until he died".
31 Shamgar. Cp. 5. 6-8.
an ox goad. See note on 3. 21. No weapons. Cp 5. 8. 1 Sam. 13. 19-22.

4. 1—5. 31 (*G*, p. 329). JABIN. (DEBORAH.)
(*Division.*)

G | J[1] | 4. 1-3. Oppression by Jabin.
  | J[2] | 4. 4—5. 31. Deliverance by Barak.

1-3 (J[1], above). OPPRESSION BY JABIN.
(*Alternation.*)

J[1] | p | 1. Evil wrought.
     | q | 2. Oppression.
     | *p* | 3-. Evil repented of.
     | *q* | -3. Oppression.

1 children = sons.
evil = the evil: i. e. idolatry. See Ap. 44. viii.
the LORD. Heb. Jehovah. Ap. 4.
2 Jabin. Another king. Cp. Josh. 11. 1-10.
which = and he.
3 twenty years. A long time to wait for deliverance.

4. 4—5. 31 (J[2], above). DELIVERANCE BY DEBORAH. (*Alternation.*)

J[2] | K | 4. 4, 5. Deliverer raised up.
     | L | 4. 6-24. Deliverance.
     | *K* | 5. 1-31-. Deliverers' song.
     | *L* | 5. -31. Rest.

4 a prophetess. Not therefore a "judge" in the strict sense of the title. Like Miriam, Ex. 15. 20; Huldah, 2 Kings 22. 14. Cp. her prophecy in *vv.* 7, 9.
she. Some codices, with two early printed editions, read "and she". Note the two women connected with Barak, Deborah and Jael, *vv.* 17-21. See note on *v.* 17, and cp. 5. 7, 11, 24, 30.
at that time. Yet Israel was "mightily oppressed", contrary to 2. 18. The words "she judged" state a fact: but do they imply a Divine appointment to the office? She was "a prophetess", but was she "a judge" in the proper sense of the word?
5 dwelt = sat [as judge]: near where her namesake, Rebekah's nurse, died. Gen. 35. 8.

6-24 (L, above). DELIVERANCE.
(*Introversion and Extended Alternation.*)

L | M | 6. Command given by Jehovah.
  | N | r | 7-. Place of battle.
  | | s | -7. Victory promised.
  | | t | 8, 9. Instruments. Barak and a woman.
  | *N* | *r* | 10-13. Place of battle.
  | | *s* | 14-16. Victory. Promise fulfilled.
  | | *t* | 17-22. Instruments. Barak and a woman.
  | *M* | 23, 24. Victory given by Jehovah.

6 Hath not . . . ? Fig. *Erotēsis.* Ap. 6.
God. Heb. Elohim. Ap. 4.
men. Heb. *'īsh* or *'ĕnōsh.* Ap. 14.
7 river Kishon. Cp. Ps. 83. 9, 10.
hand. Some codices, with two early printed editions, Sept., and Syr., read "hands".

And Deborah arose, and went with Barak to Kedesh.

N r (p. 330) 10 And Barak °called Zebulun and Naphtali to Kedesh; and he went up with ten thousand [6]men at his feet: and Deborah went up with him.

11 Now Heber the Kenite, *which was* of the children of °Hobab the father in law of Moses, had severed himself from the Kenites, and pitched his tent °unto the plain of Zaanaim, which *is* by Kedesh.

12 And they shewed Sisera that Barak the son of Abinoam was gone up to mount Tabor.

13 And Sisera °gathered together all his chariots, *even* nine hundred chariots of iron, and all the people that *were* with him, from Harosheth of the Gentiles unto the river of Kishon.

s 14 And Deborah said unto Barak, "Up; for this *is* the day in which [1]the LORD hath delivered Sisera into thine hand: °is not [1]the LORD gone out before thee?" So Barak went down from mount Tabor, and ten thousand men after him.

15 And °the LORD discomfited Sisera, and all *his* chariots, and all *his* host, with the edge of the sword before Barak; so that Sisera lighted down off *his* chariot, and fled away on his feet.

16 But Barak pursued after the chariots, and after the host, unto Harosheth of the Gentiles: and all the host of Sisera fell °upon the edge of the sword; *and* there was °not a man left.

t u (p. 331) 17 Howbeit Sisera fled away on his feet to °the tent of Jael the wife of Heber the °Kenite: for *there was* peace between Jabin the king of Hazor and the house of Heber the Kenite.

v 18 And Jael went out to meet Sisera, and said unto him, "Turn in, my lord, turn in to me; fear not."

w And when he had turned in unto her into the tent, she covered him with a °mantle.

19 And he said unto her, "Give me, I pray thee, a little water to drink; for I am thirsty." And she opened a °bottle of °milk, and gave him drink, and covered him.

20 Again he said unto her, "Stand in the °door of the tent, and it shall be, when °any man doth come and enquire of thee, and say, 'Is there °any man here?' that thou shalt say, °'No.'"

x 21 Then Jael Heber's wife took a °nail of the tent, and took an hammer in her hand, and went softly unto him, and smote the °nail into his temples, and fastened it into the ground: for he was fast asleep and weary. °So he died.

u 22 And, °behold, as Barak pursued Sisera,

v Jael came out to meet him, and said unto him,

w "Come, and I will shew thee the man whom thou seekest."

x And when he came into her *tent*, behold, Sisera lay dead, and the [21]nail *was* in his temples.

M (p. 330) 23 So [6]God subdued on that day Jabin the king of Canaan before the [1]children of Israel.

24 And the hand of the [1]children of Israel °prospered, and prevailed against Jabin the king of Canaan, until they had destroyed Jabin king of Canaan.

10 called: i.e. by proclamation.
11 Hobab. Cp. Num. 10. 29.
unto the plain. Or, at the oak. Josh. 19. 33.
13 gathered: i.e. by proclamation. Cp. *v.* 10.
14 is not . . . ? Fig. *Erotēsis.* Ap. 6.
15 the LORD discomfited = Jehovah discomfited. Cp. Ps. 83. 9. The word implies supernatural phenomena. Cp. 5. 20–22. Ex. 14. 24. Josh. 10. 10. 2 Sam. 22. 15. Ps. 18. 15.
16 upon = by.
not a man. Heb. not so much as one.

17-22 (*t*, p. 330). INSTRUMENT. A WOMAN.
(*Extended Alternation.*)

t u | 17. Flight of Sisera.
  v | 18-. Jael meeting Sisera.
    w | -18-20. Concealment.
      x | 21. Sisera slain.
u | 22-. Pursuit by Barak.
  v | -22-. Jael meeting Barak.
    w | -22-. Discovery.
      x | -22. Sisera dead.

17 the tent of Jael. Note, not of Heber: the woman's tent, which itself brought Sisera under the death penalty. But there is nothing to apologise for here. The Author and Giver of life came on Jael as on Ehud, and enabled her to save the daughters of Israel from a fate worse than death. Cp. 5. 7, 11, 24, 30.
Kenite. Cp. *v.* 11.
18 mantle = rug. Heb. *s*[e]*mîkāh* occurs only here.
19 bottle = skin.
milk. Rendered "butter" in 5. 25; probably = buttermilk, much used in the East.
20 door = entrance.
any man. Heb. *'ish.* Ap. 14. II.
No = there is not.
21 nail of the tent = a tent peg. Constantly tents are taken down and put up by the women to the present day.
So he died. The first of ten recorded deaths at the hands of women: Sisera (Judg. 4. 21); Abimelech (Judg. 9. 53. 2 Sam. 11. 21); Sheba (2 Sam. 20. 22); the harlot's child (1 Kings 3. 19); prophets (1 Kings 18. 4); Naboth (1 Kings 21. 9, 10); a son by his mother (2 Kings 6. 29); seed royal (2 Kings 11. 1. 2 Chron. 22. 10); Haman's sons (Est. 9. 13, 14); John Baptist (Matt. 14. 8).
22 behold. Fig. *Asterismos.* Ap. 6.
24 prospered. Fig. *Polyptōton.* Ap. 6. Heb. going on went on. R.V. = prevailed more and more.

5. 1-31- (*K*, p. 330). THE DELIVERERS' SONG.
(*Introversions.*)

K | O | 1, 2-. Praise to Jehovah. Avenging of Israel.
  P | y | -2, 3. Israel. People's voluntary service.
    z | 4-8. Contrasted states of the country
  y | 9. Israel. Leaders' voluntary service.
    Q | 10, 11. Contrasted states of the country.
    Q | 12-18. Contrasted conduct of tribes.
  P | a | 19-22. Enemy. Battle and defeat.
    b | 23-27. Contrasted succour for Israel.
    a | 28-30. Enemy. Presumption and defeat.
O | 31-. Praise to Jehovah. Avenging of Israel.

1 Then sang. No singing till after victory. Cp. Ex. 15. 1. Only weeping before. Cp. 2. 4 with Ex. 2 23, 24. See note on Ex. 15. 1 for the ten songs.
2 the LORD. Heb. Jehovah. Ap. 4. II.

5 °Then sang Deborah and Barak the son of Abinoam on that day, saying, K O

2 "Praise ye °the LORD for the avenging of Israel,

When the People willingly offered themselves. P y

3 Hear, O ye kings; give ear, O ye princes;
°I, *even* I, will sing unto [2]the LORD;
I will sing *praise* to [2]the LORD °God of Israel.

z (p. 331) 4 [2]LORD, °when Thou wentest out of Seir,
When Thou marchedst out of the field of Edom,
The earth trembled, and the heavens °dropped,
The clouds also °dropped water.
5 °The mountains melted from before [2]the LORD,
Even that Sinai from before [2]the LORD [3]God of Israel.
6 In the days of °Shamgar the son of Anath,
In the days of Jael, °the highways were unoccupied,
And the travellers walked through byways.
7 °*The inhabitants of* the villages °ceased, they °ceased in Israel,
Until that °I Deborah arose,
That °I arose a mother in Israel.
8 They chose °new gods;
Then *was* war in the gates:
°Was there a shield or spear seen
Among forty thousand in Israel?

y 9 My heart °*is* toward the governors of Israel,
That offered themselves willingly among the People.
Bless ye [2]the LORD.

Q 10 Speak, ye that ride on white asses,
Ye that sit in judgment,
And walk by the way.
11 °*They that are delivered* from the noise of archers in °the places of drawing water,
There shall they rehearse the righteous acts of [2]the LORD,
Even the righteous acts *toward* [7]*the inhabitants* of his villages in Israel:
Then shall the People of [2]the LORD go down to the gates.

Q c (p. 332) 12 °Awake, awake, Deborah:
°Awake, awake, utter a song:
Arise, Barak, and °lead thy captivity captive, thou son of Abinoam.
13 °Then He made him that remaineth have dominion over the nobles among the people:
[2]The LORD made me have dominion over the mighty.
14 Out of Ephraim °*was there* °a root of them against Amalek;
After thee, Benjamin, among thy people;
Out of Machir came down governors,
And out of Zebulun they that °handle the °pen of the °writer.
15 °And the princes of Issachar *were* with Deborah;
°Even Issachar, and also Barak:
°He was sent on foot into the valley.

d °For the divisions of Reuben
There were great thoughts of heart.
16 °Why abodest thou among the sheepfolds,
To hear the bleatings of the flocks?

3 I, even I. Fig. *Epizeuxis*. Ap. 6.
God. Heb. Elohim. Ap. 4. I.
4 when. Cp. Ex. 19. 18. dropped = dripped.
5 The mountains melted = from the mountains flowed down streams.
6 Shamgar. Cp. 3. 31.
the highways, &c. = the highways were closed.
7 The inhabitants. Why not supply the Fig. *Ellipsis* (Ap. 6) by the words "the women", considering the objects of Jabin's oppression? see notes on 4. 4, 17; 5. 7, 11, 24, 30.
ceased = ceased [to be]. Same word as "unoccupied" in *v.* 6. I arose. Fig. *Epizeuxis*. Ap. 6.
8 new gods. Cp. Deut. 32. 16.
Was there . . . ? Fig. *Erotēsis*. Ap. 6.
9 is toward. Supply "saith to", instead of "is". The next clause gives the words spoken.
11 the places of drawing water: i. e. where the women were to be found. See notes on 4. 4, 17; 5. 7, 30. Cp. Gen. 24. 11. Ex. 2. 15-19.
Translate *v.* 11 thus:—
Instead of the shouting of the archers among the wells,
There they laud the righteous acts of Jehovah,
The righteous acts of His rule over Israel.
Then the People of Jehovah hastened to the gates.

12-18 (*Q*, p. 331). CONTRASTED CONDUCT OF TRIBES. (*Introversion.*)

Q | c | 12-15-. Warriors.
  d | -15-17. Absentees.
 c | 18. Warriors.

12 Awake, awake. Fig. *Epizeuxis*. Ap. 6.
lead thy captivity captive = lead thy captives captive; "captivity" put by Fig. *Metonymy* (of Subject) for the persons made captive = lead captive thy captive train.
13 Some codices and Sept. divide the two lines thus:—
Then came down a remnant of the nobles,
And the People of Jehovah [came down] with me against the mighty ones.
14 was there. Supply Fig. *Ellipsis* thus: "came down", from *vv.* 13 and 15.
a root, &c. = whose root was in Amalek. Cp. 12. 15. Or, according to Sept., "they who rooted them out in Amalek."
handle = draw, in the sense of numbering, enrolling, or mustering, as in 4. 6.
pen = rod (used in numbering). Lev. 27. 32. Ezek. 20. 37. Nowhere else rendered pen.
writer = numberer. Heb. *sāphar*, translated scribe. Cp. 2 Kings 25. 19. 2 Chron. 26. 11.
15 And = But. Even = Yea.
He was sent, &c. = into the valley they rushed at his feet. For = among.
16 Why . . . ? Fig. *Erotēsis*. Ap. 6.
17 breaches = creeks or bays.
18 lives = souls. Heb. *nephesh*. See Ap. 13.
19 gain = plunder.

[15]For the divisions of Reuben
There were great searchings of heart.
17 Gilead abode beyond Jordan:
And [16]why did Dan remain in ships?
Asher continued on the sea shore,
And abode in his °breaches.

18 Zebulun and Naphtali *were* a people *that* jeoparded their °lives unto the death in the high places of the field. c

19 The kings came *and* fought, P a (p. 331)
Then fought the kings of Canaan
In Taanach by the waters of Megiddo;
They took no °gain of money.

20 They fought from heaven;
The stars in their courses °fought against Sisera.
21 The °river of °Kishon °swept them away,
That ancient river, the river Kishon.
O my °soul, thou hast trodden down strength.
22 Then were the horsehoofs broken
By the means of °the pransings, the pransings of their mighty ones.
b e (p. 333) 23 'Curse ye Meroz,' said the Angel of [2]the LORD,
'Curse ye bitterly the inhabitants thereof;
f Because they came not to the help of [2]the LORD,
To the help of [2]the LORD against the mighty.'
e 24 °Blessed above women shall Jael
The wife of Heber the Kenite be,
Blessed shall she be above women in the tent.
f 25 He asked water, *and* she gave *him* milk;
She brought forth °butter in a lordly dish.
26 She put her hand to the nail,
And her right hand to the workmen's hammer;
And with the hammer she smote Sisera, she smote off his head,
When she had pierced and stricken through his temples.
27 °At her feet °he bowed, he fell, he lay down:
At her feet °he bowed, he fell:
Where he bowed, there he fell down °dead.
a 28 °The mother of Sisera looked out at °a window, and cried through the lattice,
'Why is his chariot *so* long in coming?
Why tarry the wheels of his chariots?'
29 Her °wise ladies answered her,
Yea, she °returned answer to herself,
30 °'Have they not °sped? °have they *not* divided the prey;
°To every °man a °damsel *or* two;
To Sisera a prey of divers colours,
A prey of divers colours of needlework,
Of divers colours of needlework on both sides,
Meet for the necks of *them that take* the °spoil?'
o 31 °So let all Thine enemies perish, O [2]LORD:
But *let* them that love Him *be* as the sun when he goeth forth in his might."
L (p. 330) 1265-1225 And the land °had rest forty years.

F R[1] g (p. 333) **6** And the °children of Israel did °evil in the sight of °the LORD:
h and °the LORD delivered them into the hand of Midian
i seven years.
1225-1218 *h* 2 And the hand of Midian prevailed against Israel: *and* because of the Midianites the [1]children of Israel made them the dens which *are* in the mountains, and caves, °and strong holds.
3 And *so* it was, when Israel had sown, that
the Midianites came up, and the Amalekites, and the [1]children of the east, even they came up against them;
4 And they encamped against them, and destroyed the increase of the earth, till thou come unto Gaza, and left no sustenance for Israel, neither sheep, nor ox, nor ass.
5 For they came up with their cattle and their tents, and they came as °grasshoppers for multitude; *for* both they and their camels were without number: and they entered into the land to destroy it.
6 And Israel was greatly impoverished because of the Midianites;
and the [1]children of Israel cried unto [1]the LORD. *g*
7 And it came to pass, when the [1]children of Israel cried unto [1]the LORD because of the Midianites,
8 That [1]the LORD sent °a prophet unto the

20 fought. Fig. *Prosopopœia*. Ap. 6. Cp. Josh. 10. 11.
21 river = torrent.
Kishon. Rising in Mount Tabor and running into the Mediterranean near Mount Carmel.
swept. Swollen by the heavy rains (*v.* 4).
soul. Heb. *nephesh*. Ap. 13.
22 the pransings. Fig. *Epizeuxis*. Ap. 6.

23-27 (*b*, p. 331). CONTRASTED SUCCOUR FOR ISRAEL. (*Alternation*.)

b | e | 23-. Curse.
f | -23. Reason.
e | 24. Blessing.
f | 25-27. Reason.

24 Blessed above women. Cp. Luke 1. 28 "among". See notes on 4. 4, 17; 5. 7, 11, 30.
25 butter. See note on 4. 19.
27 At her feet. Note the Fig. *Asyndeton*. Ap. 6.
he bowed, he fell. Fig. *Epibolē*. Ap. 6.
dead = destroyed.
28 The mother. A woman active on each side, with other women involved (*v.* 30). a = the.
30 Have . . . ? Fig. *Erotēsis*. Ap. 6.
sped = found; i. e. the damsels they were fighting for: and while doing so they were defeated by a woman.
To every man = to every head of a man; "head" put by Fig. *Synecdoche* (of the Part), Ap. 6, for the whole person.
man. Heb. *geber* (Ap. 14. IV) = a strong man.
damsel. Heb. womb. Put by Fig. *Synecdoche* (of the Part) for the whole person, to emphasise the motive underneath. This was the one object of Jabin's oppression. See notes on 4. 4, 17; 5. 7, 11, 24.
spoil. Fig. *Aposiopesis*. Ap. 6.
31 So. Fig. *Epiphonēma*. Ap. 6.
had rest. See note on 3. 11.

6. 1—8. 35 (*F*, p. 328). MIDIAN. (GIDEON.) (*Division*.)

F | R[1] | 6. 1-10. Midian.
R[2] | 6. 11—8. 35. Gideon.

6. 1-10 (R[1], above). MIDIAN. (*Introversion*.)

R[1] | g | 1-. The evil wrought.
h | -1-. The oppressor.
i | -1. Servitude (seven years)
h | 2-6-. The oppression.
g | -6-10. The evil repented of.

1 children = sons.
evil. Heb. *rā'a'*. Ap. 44. viii.
the LORD. Heb. Jehovah. Ap. 4. II.
2 and = the. **5** grasshoppers = locusts.
8 a prophet. Heb. "a man (*'ish*, Ap. 14. II) a prophet".

1219 [1]children of Israel, which said unto them,
1218 "'Thus saith [1]the LORD °God of Israel, I
brought you up °from Egypt, and brought you
forth out of the house of °bondage;
9 And I delivered you out of the hand of the
Egyptians, and out of the hand of all that
oppressed you, and drave them out from before
you, and gave you their land;
10 And I said unto you, 'I *am* [1]the LORD
your [8]God; fear not the gods of the Amorites,
in whose land ye dwell:' but ye have not
obeyed My voice.'"

S^1 j o^1 (p. 334) 11 And there came an Angel of [1]the LORD,
and sat under °an oak which *was* in Ophrah,
that *pertained* unto °Joash the Abi-ezrite:
p^1 and his son °Gideon threshed wheat °by the
winepress, to hide *it* from the Midianites.
o^2 12 And the °Angel of [1]the LORD appeared
unto him, and said unto him, [1]"The LORD *is*
with thee, thou °mighty man of valour."
p^2 13 And Gideon said unto Him, "Oh °my Lord,
if [1]the LORD be with us, why then is all this
befallen us? and where *be* all His miracles
which our fathers told us of, saying, 'Did not
[1]the LORD bring us up from Egypt?' but now
[1]the LORD hath forsaken us, and delivered us
into the hands of the Midianites."
o^3 14 And [1]the LORD looked upon him, and said,
"Go in this °thy might, and thou shalt save
Israel from the hand of the Midianites: have
not I sent thee?"
p^3 15 And he said unto Him, "Oh °my LORD*,
wherewith shall I save Israel? °behold, my
°family *is* °poor in Manasseh, and I *am* the
least in my father's house."
o^4 16 And [1]the LORD said unto him, "Surely
°I will be with thee, and thou shalt smite the
Midianites as one °man."
k^1 q^1 (p. 335) 17 And he said unto Him, "If now I have
found grace in Thy sight, then shew me a sign
that °Thou talkest with me.
18 Depart not hence, I pray Thee, until I come
unto Thee, and bring forth my °present, and
set *it* before Thee."
r^1 And He said, "I will tarry until thou come
again."
q^2 19 And Gideon went in, and made ready a
°kid, and °unleavened cakes of an °ephah of
flour: the flesh he put in °a basket, and he put
the broth in °a pot, and brought *it* out unto
Him under the oak, and presented *it*.
r^2 20 And the Angel of °God said unto him,
"Take the flesh and the unleavened cakes,
and lay *them* upon °this rock, and pour out the
broth." And he did so.
21 Then the Angel of [1]the LORD put forth
the end of the staff that *was* in His hand, and
touched the flesh and the unleavened cakes;
and there °rose up °fire out of the rock, and
consumed the flesh and the unleavened cakes.
Then the Angel of [1]the LORD departed out of
his sight.
q^3 22 And when Gideon perceived that He *was*
an Angel of [1]the LORD, Gideon said, "Alas,

God. Heb. Elohim. Ap. 4. I.
from Egypt. Some codices, with Sept. and Syr., read "from the land of Egypt".
bondage. Heb. bondmen. Fig. *Metonymy* (of Adjunct). Ap. 6.

6. 11—8. 35 (R^2, p. 333). GIDEON. (*Repeated Alternation.*)

R^2 | S^1 | 6. 11—7. 18. The Deliverer. Raised up.
T^1 | 7. 19—8. 23. Deliverance.
S^2 | 8. 24-27. The Deliverer. Rewarded.
T^2 | 8. 28. Rest (forty years).
S^3 | 8. 29-35. The Deliverer. Forgotten.

6. 11—7. 18 (S^1, above). THE DELIVERER. RAISED UP. (*Extended Alternation, with Introversion.*)

S^1 | U | j | 6. 11-16. Angel of Jehovah. Message to Gideon.
k | 6. 17-24. Sign. Fire.
l | 6. 25-27. Command.
V | m | 6. 28-32. Obedience of Gideon.
n | 6. 33. Midianites.
U | *j* | 6. 34, 35. Spirit of Jehovah. Message to tribes.
k | 6. 36-40. Signs. Fleece.
l | 7. 1-11. Directions.
V | *n* | 7. 12-14. Midianites.
m | 7. 15-18. Obedience of Gideon.

6. 11-16 (j, above). ANGEL OF JEHOVAH. MESSAGE, &c. (*Repeated Alternation.*)

j | o^1 | 11-. Angel. Place.
p^1 | -11. Gideon. Employment.
o^2 | 12. Angel. Encouragement.
p^2 | 13. Gideon. Complaint.
o^3 | 14. Angel. Mission.
p^3 | 15. Gideon. Question.
o^4 | 16. Angel. Answer.

11 an oak = the oak, as being well known.
Joash = Jehovah gave.
Gideon = cutter down.
by the winepress = in the winepress. Shows the straits of the people. Cp. *vv.* 2-6. Threshing-floor exposed, winepress sunk in ground.
12 Angel of the LORD = angel of Jehovah; i. e. the Covenant God "with" His servant (Gideon). Cp. *v.* 20 = angel of Elohim, the Creator working a miracle for His creature.
mighty man. Heb. *gibbōr*. Adj. of Ap. 14. IV.
13 my Lord = *Adonai*. Ap. 4. VIII (2).
14 thy might. His might lay in the knowledge of Jehovah's strength (*v.* 13) and his own weakness.
15 my LORD*. This is one of the 134 places where the primitive text "Jehovah" has been altered to "Adonai". See Ap. 32.
behold. Fig. *Asterismos*. Ap. 6.
family = thousand (1 Sam. 10. 19).
poor = the meanest.
16 I will be with thee. Cp. Ex. 3. 12. Isa. 7. 14. Matt. 1. 23. **man.** Heb. *'ish*. Ap. 14. II.

17-24 [For Structure see next page].

17 Thou talkest. Supply Fig. *Ellipsis* (Ap. 6) thus: "Thou [art Jehovah Who] talkest".
18 present = Heb. *minḥah*. Ap. 43. II. iii.
19 kid = kid of the goats.
unleavened. For offering: quickly made.
ephah. See Ap. 51. III. 3.
a basket = the tray. Heb. *sal*, always connected with royalty, or sacrifice. **a pot** = the pot.
20 God = Elohim. See note on *v.* 12, above.
this = you.
21 rose up fire. This fire was the token of Jehovah's acceptance. See note on "respect", Gen. 4. 4.
fire = the fire.

1219 **° O Lord ° GOD! ° for because I have seen an**
1218 **Angel of [1]the LORD face to face."**
r^3 (p. 335) **23 And [1]the LORD said unto him, "Peace *be***
unto thee; fear not: thou shalt not die."
q^4 **24 Then Gideon built an altar there unto**
[1]the LORD, and called it ° Jehovah-shalom:
unto this day it *is* yet in Ophrah of the Abi-
ezrites.

l (p. 334) **25 And it came to pass the same night, that**
[1]the LORD said unto him, "Take thy father's
young bullock, ° even the second bullock of
seven years old, and throw down the altar of
Baal that thy father hath, and cut down ° the
grove that *is* by it:
26 And build an altar unto [1]the LORD thy
[8]God upon the top of this ° rock, in the ° ordered
place, and take the second bullock, and ° offer
a burnt sacrifice with the wood of the grove
which thou shalt cut down."
27 Then Gideon took ten ° men of his serv-
ants, and did ° as [1]the LORD had said unto
him: and *so* it was, because he feared his
father's household, and the men of the city,
that he could not do *it* by day, that he did *it* by
night.

V m **28 And when the men of the city arose early**
in the morning, [15]behold, the altar of Baal was
cast down, and the grove was cut down that
***was* by it, and the second bullock was [26]offered**
upon the altar *that was* built.
29 And they said one to another, "Who hath
done this thing?" And when they enquired
and asked, they said, "Gideon the son of Joash
hath done this thing."
30 Then the men of the city said unto Joash,
"Bring out thy son, that he may die: because
he hath cast down the altar of Baal, and be-
cause he hath cut down [25]the grove that *was*
by it."
31 And Joash said unto all that stood against
him, "Will ye plead for Baal? will ye save
him? he that will plead for him, let him be put
to death whilst *it is yet* morning: if he *be* a
god, let him plead for himself, because *one*
hath cast down his altar."
32 Therefore on that day he called him
° Jerubbaal, saying, "Let Baal plead against
him, because he hath thrown down his altar."
n **33 Then all the Midianites and the Ama-**
lekites and the children of the east were
gathered together, and went over, and pitched
in the valley of Jezreel.

U j **34 But the ° Spirit of [1]the LORD ° came upon**
Gideon, and he blew a trumpet; and Abi-ezer
was ° gathered after him.
35 And he sent messengers throughout all
Manasseh; who also was [34]gathered after him:
and he sent messengers unto Asher, and unto
Zebulun, and unto Naphtali; and they came
up to meet them.

k s (p. 335) **36 And Gideon said unto ° God, "If Thou wilt**
save Israel by mine hand, [27]as Thou hast said,
37 [15]Behold, I will put a fleece of wool in the
° floor; *and* if the dew be on the fleece only,
and *it be* dry upon all the earth *beside*, then
shall I know that Thou wilt save Israel by
mine hand, as Thou hast said."

17-24 (k, p. 334). SIGN. FIRE. (*Repeated Alternation.*)

k^1 | q^1 | 17, 18-. Gideon. Request.
r^1 | -18. Angel. Compliance.
q^2 | 19. Gideon. Offering.
r^2 | 20, 21. Angel. Acceptance.
q^3 | 22. Gideon. Fear.
r^3 | 23. Angel. Assurance.
q^4 | 24. Gideon. Worship.

22 O Lord GOD = O Adonai Jehovah. Ap. 4. II, VIII (2).
for because = forasmuch as.
24 Jehovah-shalom. Jehovah [gives] peace. One of the Jehovah titles. See Ap. 4. II.
25 even, or "and".
the grove = the *'ashērah*. See Ex. 34. 13. Ap. 42.
26 rock = strong place.
ordered place, or due order.
offer. See Ap. 43. I. vi.
27 men. Heb. pl. of *'ĕnōsh*. Ap. 14. III.
as = according as.
32 Jerubbaal = Let Baal plead. 1 Sam. 12. 11. 2 Sam. 11. 21. **34 Spirit** = Heb. *rūach*. See Ap. 9.
came upon = clothed (1 Chron. 12. 18. 2 Chron. 24. 20). Heb. *labash*, to put on so as to fill.
gathered: gathered by proclamation.

36-40 (*k*, p. 334). SIGN. FLEECE. (*Alternation.*)

k | s | 36, 37. Request.
t | 38. Compliance.
s | 39. Request.
t | 40. Compliance.

36 God. See note on *v.* 12.
37 floor = threshing-floor.
39 God = *hā-'Ĕlohim*. The God. Ap. 4. I.

7. 1-11 (*l*, p. 334). DIRECTION.
(*Introversion and Repeated Alternation.*)

l | u | 1. Gideon. Obedience.
v | w^1 | 2, 3-. Jehovah's objection.
x^1 | -3. Result.
w^2 | 4. Jehovah's objection.
x^2 | 5, 6. Result.
w^3 | 7. Jehovah's selection.
x^3 | 8. Result.
u | 9-11. Gideon. Command.

1 host = camp.
2 the LORD. Heb. Jehovah. Ap. 4. II.

38 And it was so: for he rose up early on the t
morrow, and thrust the fleece together, and
wringed the dew out of the fleece, a bowl full
of water.

39 And Gideon said unto ° God, "Let not s
Thine anger be hot against me, and I will
speak but this once: let me prove, I pray
Thee, but this once with the fleece; let it now
be dry only upon the fleece, and upon all the
ground let there be dew."

40 And [8]God did so that night: for it was *t*
dry upon the fleece only, and there was dew
on all the ground.

7 Then Jerubbaal, who *is* Gideon, and all *l* u
the People that *were* with him, rose up
early, and pitched beside the well of Harod:
so that the ° host of the Midianites were on the
north side of them, by the hill of Moreh, in the
valley.

2 And ° the LORD said unto Gideon, "The v w^1
People that *are* with thee *are* too many for
Me to give the Midianites into their hands,

1219 °lest Israel vaunt themselves against Me, say-
1218 ing, 'Mine own hand hath saved me.'
3 Now therefore go to, proclaim in the ears of the People, saying, 'Whosoever *is* fearful and afraid, let him return and depart early from °mount Gilead.' "

x¹ (p. 335) And there returned of the People °twenty and two thousand; and there remained ten thousand.

w² 4 And [2]the LORD said unto Gideon, "The People *are* yet *too* many; bring them down unto the water, and I will try them for thee there: and it shall be, *that* of whom I say unto thee, 'This shall go with thee,' the same shall go with thee; and of whomsoever I say unto thee, 'This shall not go with thee,' the same shall not go."

x² 5 So he brought down the People unto the water: and [2]the LORD said unto Gideon, "Every one that °lappeth of the water with his tongue, °as a dog lappeth, him shalt thou set by himself; likewise every one that boweth down upon his knees to drink."

6 And the number of them that lapped, *putting* their hand to their mouth, were three hundred °men: but all the rest of the People bowed down upon their knees to drink water.

w³ 7 And [2]the LORD said unto Gideon, "By the three hundred [6]men that lapped will I save you, and deliver the Midianites into thine hand: and let all the *other* People go [6]every man unto his place."

x³ 8 So °the People took victuals in their hand, and their trumpets: and he sent all *the rest of* Israel [6]every man unto his tent, and retained those three hundred [6]men: and the [1]host of Midian was beneath him in the valley.

u 9 And it came to pass the same night, that [2]the LORD said unto him, "Arise, get thee down unto the [1]host; for I have delivered it into thine hand.

10 But if thou fear to go down, go thou with Phurah thy servant down to the [1]host:

11 And thou shalt hear what they say; and afterward shall thine hands be strengthened to go down unto the [1]host." Then went he down with Phurah his servant unto the outside of the armed men that *were* in the [1]host.

V n (p. 334) 12 And the Midianites and the °Amalekites and all the °children of the east lay along in the valley like °grasshoppers for multitude; and their camels *were* without number, °as the sand by the sea side for multitude.

13 And when Gideon was come, °behold, *there was* a [6]man that told °a dream unto his fellow, and said, °"Behold, I dreamed a dream, and, °lo, a cake of barley bread tumbled into the host of Midian, and came unto a tent, and smote it that it fell, and overturned it, that the tent lay along."

14 And his fellow answered and said, "This *is* nothing else save the sword of Gideon the son of Joash, a [6]man of Israel: *for* into his hand hath °God delivered Midian, and all the [1]host."

m 15 And it was *so*, when Gideon heard the telling of the dream, and the interpretation thereof, that he worshipped, and returned into the [1]host of Israel, and said, "Arise; for [2]the LORD hath delivered into your hand the [1]host of Midian."

16 And he divided the three hundred [6]men *into* three companies, and he put a trumpet in every man's hand, with empty pitchers, and °lamps within the pitchers.

17 And he said unto them, "Look on me, and do likewise: and, behold, when I come to the outside of the camp, it shall be *that*, as I do, so shall ye do.

18 When I blow with a trumpet, I and all that *are* with me, then blow ye the trumpets also on every side of all the camp, and say, °'*The sword* of [2]the LORD, and of Gideon.'"

19 So Gideon, and the hundred [6]men that *were* with him, came unto the outside of the camp in the beginning of the middle watch; and they had but newly set the watch: and they blew the trumpets, and brake the pitchers that *were* in their hands. T¹ y (p. 336)

20 And the three companies blew the trumpets, and brake the pitchers, and held the lamps in their left hands, and the trumpets in their right hands to blow *withal*: and they

lest, &c. This is the real reason of this direction.

3 mount Gilead. What was more natural than that the half tribe of Manasseh on the west side of Jordan should so name a mount in *their* tribe in compliment to the famous mount on the east side? (Gen. 31. 21-25; 37. 25. Num. 32. 1, 40. Deut. 3. 15. Josh. 17. 1). Gideon was of that tribe. Probably "the wood of Ephraim", on east side; so named here out of compliment to the half tribe on west side (2 Sam. 18. 6).

twenty = probably 20 + 2,000 = 2,020. Cp. 12. 6. 1 Sam. 6. 19. If there remained 10,000, there must have been 10,000 + 2,020 = 12,020; and, as only 300 remained, 9,700 must have gone away at the second testing. Only 1,000 of each tribe = 12,000, sent out to fight in Num. 31. 4, 5.

5 lappeth: i. e. without kneeling down as idolaters were accustomed to do (1 Kings 19. 18. 2 Chron. 29. 9. See note on Est. 3. 2. **as** = according as.

6 men. Heb. *'ish.* Ap. 14. II.

8 the People. So the 300 are called.

12 Amalekites. See note on Ex. 17. 16.

children = sons.

grasshoppers = locusts.

as the sand, &c. Fig. *Parœmia.* Ap. 6.

13 behold . . . Behold . . . lo. Fig. *Asterismos* (three times). Ap. 6.

a dream. See note on Gen. 20. 3.

14 God = *hā-'Ĕlohim* here (= the God), because in connection with Midianites, His creatures. Not Jehovah. Ap. 4. I, II.

16 lamps = torches, which smoulder till waved in the air.

18 The sword. These words are supplied by Fig. *Ellipsis* from *v.* 20. But some codices, with Aram. and Syr., read these words in the text. Lit. "For Jehovah and for Gideon".

7. 19—8. 23 (T¹, p. 334). DELIVERANCE.
(Alternation and Introversion.)

T¹ | y | 7. 19, 20. The assault.
  z | a | 7. 21, 22. Midianite host. Flight.
    b | 7. 23. Pursuit by Naphtali.
  y | 7. 24, 25. The victory.
  z | b | 8. 1-12. Pursuit by Gideon.
    a | 8. 13-23. Midianite kings. Capture.

1219 cried, "The sword °of [2]the LORD, and of
1218 Gideon."
z a 21 And they stood [6]every man in his place
(p. 336) round about the camp: and all the [1]host ran,
and cried, and fled.
22 And the three hundred blew the trumpets,
and [2]the LORD set [6]every man's sword against
his fellow, even throughout all the [1]host: and
the [1]host fled to Beth-shittah in Zererath, *and*
to the border of Abel-meholah, unto Tabbath.

b 23 And the [6]men of Israel gathered themselves together out of Naphtali, and out of
Asher, and out of all Manasseh, and pursued
after the Midianites.

y 24 And Gideon sent messengers throughout
all °mount Ephraim, saying, "Come down
against the Midianites, and take before them
the waters unto Beth-barah and Jordan."
Then all the [6]men of Ephraim gathered themselves together, and took the waters unto
Beth-barah and Jordan.
25 And they took °two princes of the Midianites, Oreb and Zeeb; and they slew Oreb upon
the rock Oreb, and Zeeb they slew at the
winepress of Zeeb, and pursued Midian, and
brought the heads of Oreb and Zeeb to Gideon
on the other side Jordan.

z b c **8** And the °men of Ephraim said unto him,
(p. 337) °"Why hast thou served us thus, that
thou calledest us not, when thou wentest to
fight with the Midianites?" And they did
°chide with him sharply.
2 And he said unto them, °"What have
I done now in comparison of you? °*Is* not
the gleaning of the grapes of Ephraim better
than the vintage of Abiezer?
3 °God hath delivered into your hands the
princes of Midian, Oreb and Zeeb: and what
was I able to do in comparison of you?" Then
their °anger was abated toward him, when he
had said that.

d e g 4 And Gideon came to Jordan, *and* passed
over, he, and the three hundred [1]men that *were*
with him, faint, yet pursuing *them*.
5 And he said unto the °men of Succoth,
"Give, I pray you, loaves of bread unto the
people that follow me; for they *be* faint, and
I am pursuing after Zebah and Zalmunna,
kings of Midian."
6 And the princes of Succoth said, "*Are* the
hands of Zebah and Zalmunna now in thine
hand, that we should give bread unto thine
army?"
7 And Gideon said, "Therefore when °the
LORD hath delivered Zebah and Zalmunna
into mine hand, then I will tear your flesh
with the thorns of the wilderness and with
briers."

h 8 And he went up thence to Penuel, and spake
unto them likewise: and the [5]men of Penuel
answered him as the [5]men of Succoth had
answered *him*.
9 And he spake also unto the [5]men of Penuel,
saying, "When I come again in peace, I will
break down this tower."

f 10 Now Zebah and Zalmunna *were* in
Karkor, and their °hosts with them, about
fifteen thousand *men*, all that were left of all
the [1]hosts of the °children of the east: for
there fell an hundred and twenty thousand
[5]men that drew sword.
11 And Gideon went up by the way of them
that dwelt in tents on the east of Nobah and
Jogbehah, and smote the °host: for the °host
was secure.
12 And when Zebah and Zalmunna fled, he
pursued after them, and took the two kings of
Midian, Zebah and Zalmunna, and discomfited
all the [1]host.

13 And Gideon the son of Joash returned from *d e g*
battle before the sun *was up*,
14 And caught a young man of the [5]men of
Succoth, and enquired of him: and he described
unto him the princes of Succoth, and the elders
thereof, *even* threescore and seventeen [1]men.
15 And he came unto the [5]men of Succoth,
and said, "Behold Zebah and Zalmunna, with
whom ye did upbraid me, saying, °'*Are* the
hands of Zebah and Zalmunna now in thine
hand, that we should give bread unto thy [5]men
that are weary?'"
16 And he took the elders of the city, and
thorns of the wilderness and briers, and with
them he taught the [5]men of Succoth.

17 And he beat down the tower of Penuel, *h*
and slew the [5]men of the city.

18 Then said he unto Zebah and Zalmunna, *f*
"What manner of [5]men *were they* whom ye
slew at Tabor?" And they answered, "As
thou *art*, so *were* they; each one resembled
the [10]children of °a king."
19 And he said, "They *were* my brethren,
even the sons of my mother: *as* [7]the LORD
liveth, if ye had saved them alive, I would not
slay you."

---

20 of the LORD = of Jehovah. Lit. "A sword for Jehovah and Gideon."
24 mount = hill country.
25 two princes. Cp. Ps. 83. 11. Isa. 10. 26.

8. 1-23 (*z*, p. 336). PURSUIT AND CAPTURE.
(*Introversion and Alternation.*)

z | c | 1-3. Men of Ephraim, and Gideon.
  d | e | g | 4-7. Succoth. Colloquy.
      h | 8, 9. Penuel. Colloquy.
    f | 10-12. Kings taken.
  d | *e* | *g* | 13-16. Succoth. Retribution.
      h | 17. Penuel. Retribution.
    f | 18-21. Kings slain.
c | 22, 23. Men of Israel, and Gideon.

1 men. Heb. *'ish.* Ap. 14. II.
Why . . . ? Fig. *Erotēsis.* Ap. 6.
chide. This was the beginning of the strife which ended in the division of the kingdom (1 Kings 12).
2 What . . . ? Is not . . . ? Fig. *Erotēsis.* Ap. 6.
3 God = Elohim delivered His creatures; not Jehovah the Covenant-God. Ap. 4. I, II.
anger. Heb. *rūach,* spirit (Ap. 9). Put by Fig. *Metonymy* (of Cause) for the angry manifestations of it.
5 men = folk. Heb. *'ĕnōsh.* Ap. 14.
7 the LORD. Heb. Jehovah. Ap. 4.
10 hosts = camps.
children. Heb. sons.
11 host = camp.
15 Are . . . ? Fig. *Erotēsis.* Ap. 6.
18 a = the.

1219 20 And he said unto Jether his firstborn,
1218 "Up, *and* slay them." But the youth drew not his sword: for he feared, because he *was* yet a youth.

21 Then Zebah and Zalmunna said, "Rise thou, and fall upon us: for as the [1]man *is, so is* his strength." And Gideon arose, and slew Zebah and Zalmunna, and took away the °ornaments that *were* on their camels' necks.

c (p. 337) 22 Then the [1]men of Israel said unto Gideon, "Rule thou over us, both thou, and thy son, and thy son's son also: for thou hast delivered us from the hand of Midian."

23 And Gideon said unto them, "I will not rule over you, neither shall my son rule over you: [7]the LORD shall rule over you."

S² (p. 334) 24 And Gideon said unto them, "I would desire a request of you, that ye would give me [1]every man the °earrings of his prey." (For they had golden earrings, °because they *were* Ishmaelites.)

25 And they answered, "We will willingly give *them*." And they spread [18]a garment, and did cast therein [1]every man the earrings of his prey.

26 And the weight of the golden [24]earrings that he requested was a thousand and seven hundred *shekels* of gold; beside ornaments, and collars, and purple raiment that *was* on the kings of Midian, and beside the chains that *were* about their camels' necks.

27 And Gideon made an °ephod thereof, and put it in his city, *even* in Ophrah: and all Israel went thither a whoring after it: which thing became a snare unto Gideon, and to his house.

T² 28 Thus was Midian subdued before the
1218 °children of Israel, so that they °lifted up
1178 their heads no more. And the country °was in quietness forty years in the days of Gideon.

S³ 29 And Jerubbaal the son of Joash went and dwelt in his own house.

30 And Gideon had threescore and ten sons of his body begotten: for he had many wives.

31 And his concubine that *was* in Shechem, she also bare him a son, whose name he called Abimelech.

32 And Gideon the son of Joash died in a good old age, and was buried in the sepulchre of Joash his father, in Ophrah of the Abi-ezrites.

33 And it came to pass, as soon as Gideon was dead, that the [18]children of Israel turned again, and went a whoring after Baalim, and made Baal-berith their god.

34 And the [18]children of Israel remembered not [7]the LORD their [3]God, Who had delivered them out of the hands of all their enemies on every side:

35 Neither shewed they kindness to the house of Jerubbaal, *namely*, Gideon, according to all the goodness which he had shewed unto Israel.

B A (p. 338) **9** And Abimelech the son of Jerubbaal went to Shechem unto his mother's °brethren, and communed with them, and with all the family of the house of his mother's father, saying,

2 "Speak, I pray you, in the ears of all the °men of Shechem, 'Whether *is* better for you, either that all the sons of Jerubbaal, *which are* threescore and ten °persons, reign over you, or that one reign over you? remember also that I *am* your bone and your flesh.'"

3 And his mother's brethren spake of him in the ears of all the °men of Shechem all these words: and their hearts inclined to follow Abimelech; for they said, "He *is* our brother."

4 And they gave him threescore and ten *pieces* of silver out of the house of Baal-berith, wherewith Abimelech hired vain and °light °persons, which followed him.

5 And he went unto his father's house at Ophrah, and slew his brethren the sons of Jerubbaal, *being* threescore and ten [2]persons, upon one stone: notwithstanding yet Jotham the youngest son of Jerubbaal was left; for he hid himself.

6 And all the [2]men of Shechem gathered together, and all the house of Millo, and went, and made Abimelech king, by the °plain °of the pillar that *was* in Shechem.

7 And when they told *it* to Jotham, he went and stood in the top of mount Gerizim, and lifted up his voice, and cried, and said unto B c (p. 339)

---

21 ornaments = crescent-shaped ornaments used still on necks of horses and camels.

24 earrings. Heb. *Nezem.* Any ring worn in ear or nose = a nose ring in Gen. 24. 47. Prov. 11. 22. Isa. 3. 21. Ezek. 16. 12; and "earring" in Gen. 35. 4 and Ex. 32. 2. Other passages doubtful (*v.* 25. Job 42. 11. Prov. 25. 12. Hos. 2. 13).

because. This parenthetical remark solves the difficulty of Gen. 37. 25, 28, 36, and 39. 1. Ishmael and Midian were half-brothers, sons of Abraham by Hagar and Keturah (Gen. 16. 11, 12; 25. 1, 2). All Midianites were Ishmaelites, but all Ishmaelites were not Midianites.

27 ephod. Probably the priests were lax in restoring the worship of the true God. So that Gideon would have meant well and desired to judge well. Cp. 17. 5, where Micah made another. The reason given being that "there was no king, and every man did what was right in his own eyes", 17. 6; and 18. 5, where it was used to "ask counsel"; and for the same reason, 18. 1.

28 children = sons.

lifted up their heads no more = made no more attempts to vex.

was in quietness. See note on 3. 11.

9. 1-57 (B, p. 323). INTERNAL DISORDERS.

(*Introversion.*)

B | A | 1-6. Abimelech's usurpation.
 | B | 7-21. Action of Jotham.
 | *B* | 22-55. Action of God.
 | *A* | 56, 57. Abimelech's usurpation avenged.

1 brethren. Put by Fig. *Synecdoche* (of Species) for other relatives. Ap. 6.

2 men = masters, lords, or owners. Heb. *baalīm.*

persons = Heb. *'īsh.* Ap. 14. II.

3 men. Heb. *'īsh.* Ap. 14. II.

4 light = rash.

persons. Heb. *'ěnōsh.* Ap. 14. III.

6 plain = oak.

of the pillar. Gen. of Apposition (Ap. 6) = that is to say, the pillar made of oak. See Josh. 24. 26. Cp. Gen. 28. 18, 22; 31. 13, 45; 35. 14, 20. 2 Sam. 18. 18.

7-21 [For Structure see next page].

1178 them, "Hearken unto me, ye [2]men of Shechem, that ° God may hearken unto you.

d (p. 339) 8 ° The trees ° went forth *on a time* to anoint a king over them; and they said unto ° the olive tree, 'Reign thou over us.'

9 But the olive tree said unto them, 'Should I leave my fatness, wherewith by me they ° honour [7]God and ° man, and ° go to be promoted over the trees?'

10 And the trees said to ° the fig tree, 'Come thou, *and* reign over us.'

11 But the fig tree said unto them, 'Should I ° forsake my sweetness, and my good fruit, and go to be promoted over the trees?'

12 Then said the trees unto ° the vine, 'Come thou, *and* reign over us.'

13 And the vine said unto them, 'Should I ° leave my ° wine, which cheereth [7]God and [9]man, and go to be promoted over the trees?'

14 Then said all the trees unto ° the bramble, 'Come thou, *and* reign over us.'

15 And the bramble said unto the trees, 'If in truth ye anoint me king over you, *then* come *and* ° put your trust in my shadow: and if not, let fire come out of the bramble, and devour the cedars of Lebanon.'

d 16 Now therefore, if ye have done truly and sincerely, in that ye have made Abimelech king, and if ye have dealt well with Jerubbaal and his house, and have done unto him according to the deserving of his hands;

17 ° (For my father fought for you, and adventured his ° life far, and delivered you out of the hand of Midian:

18 And ye are risen up against my father's house this day, and have slain his sons, threescore and ten [2]persons, upon one stone, and have made Abimelech, the son of his maidservant, king over the [2]men of Shechem, because he *is* your brother;)

19 If ye then have dealt truly and sincerely with Jerubbaal and with his house this day, *then* rejoice ye in Abimelech, and let him also rejoice in you:

20 But if not, let fire come out from Abimelech, and devour the [2]men of Shechem, and the house of Millo; and let fire come out from the [3]men of Shechem, and from the house of Millo, and devour Abimelech."

c 21 And Jotham ran away, and fled, and went to Beer, and dwelt there, for fear of Abimelech his brother.

C[1] D 22 When Abimelech had ° reigned ° three years over Israel,

1178 to 1176 23 Then ° God sent ° an evil spirit between Abimelech and the [2]men of Shechem; and the [2]men of Shechem dealt treacherously with Abimelech:

E F 24 That the cruelty *done* to the threescore and ten sons of Jerubbaal might come, and their blood be laid upon Abimelech their brother, which slew them;

G and upon the [2]men of Shechem, which aided him in the killing of his brethren.

C[2] H[1] e 25 And the [2]men of Shechem set liers in wait for him in the top of the mountains, and they robbed all that came along that way by them: and it was told Abimelech.

7-21 (B, p. 338). ACTION OF JOTHAM.
(*Introversion.*)

B | c | 7. Jotham's coming forth.
  d | 8-15. Parable given.
  d | 16-20. Parable interpreted.
 c | 21. Jotham's fleeing away.

7 God. Heb. Elohim. Ap. 4. I. Not Jehovah in covenant.

8 The trees. This is pure allegory (Ap. 6). The *interpretation* is local and historical. The *application* is dispensational.

went forth. Verb, duplicated by Fig. *Polyptōton* (Ap. 6). Very emphatic = "a going forth they went forth", or went forth with great earnestness of purpose

the olive tree = Israel's *religious* privileges. Rom. 11.

9 honour. Cp. Ex. 27. 20, 21. Lev. 2. 1. The *interpretation* of these three—"honour", &c.—is clear from the context. An *application* may be made as to what should be seen in Israel and in ourselves.

man. Heb. *'ĕnōsh.* Ap. 14. III.

go = march about, instead of fulfilling my mission.

10 the fig tree. Israel's *national* privileges (Matt. 21. 19, 20. Mark 11. 13, 20, 21. Luke 13. 6-9).

11 forsake. Same Heb. as "leave" in *vv.* 9 and 13.

12 the vine = Israel's *spiritual* privileges (Isa. 5. John 15).

13 leave. Same Heb. as "forsake" (*v.* 11).

wine = new wine. Heb. *tīrōsh.* Ap. 27. II.

14 the bramble. This is prophetic of the false nation under the rule of Antichrist, which will devour the nation as foreshown in *v.* 20.

15 put your trust = flee for refuge. Heb. *ḥaṣah.* Ap. 69. ii.

17 Note the parenthesis of *vv.* 17, 18.

life = soul. Heb. *nephesh.* Ap. 13.

22-55 (*B*, p. 338). ACTION OF GOD.
(*Alternation and Introversion.*)

B | C[1] | D | 22, 23. Evil spirit sent out. } Purpose.
    E | F | 24-. Against Abimelech. } Purpose.
      G | -24. Against Shechemites. } Purpose.
 C[2] | *D* | 25-41. Evil spirit in operation. } Accomplishment.
    E | *G* | 42-49. Against Shechemites. } Accomplishment.
      F | 50-55. Against Abimelech. } Accomplishment.

22 reigned = exercised power over. Heb. *sūr.* Occurs only here, and Hos. 8. 4; 12. 4.

three years. A usurpation, and therefore not included in *Anno Dei* reckoning. See Ap. 50. 4. They are concurrent with Tola's first three.

23 God = Elohim. Not Jehovah. Ap. 4. I, II.

an evil spirit = an evil *rūacḥ.* Ap. 9.

25-55 (C[2], above). EVIL SPIRIT IN OPERATION.
(*Alternations.*)

C[2] | H[1] | e | 25. Shechemites.
      f | 26-. Gaal.
     e | -26, 27. Shechemites.
      f | 28, 29. Gaal.
       J[1] | 30-33. Zebul. Conspiracy.
   H[2] | g | 34. Abimelech.
      h | 35-. Gaal.
     g | -35. Abimelech.
      h | 36-38. Gaal.
       J[2] | 39-41. Zebul. Flight.
   H[3] | i | 42-45. Shechemites.
      k | 46-49. Tower of Shechem.
     i | 50. Thebez.
      k | 51-55. Tower of Thebez.

26 And Gaal the son of Ebed came with his brethren, and went over to Shechem: f

and the [2]men of Shechem put their confidence in him. *e*

27 And they went out into the fields, and

1176 gathered their vineyards, and trode *the grapes*,
and made merry, and went into the house of
their god, and did eat and drink, and cursed
Abimelech.

f 28 And Gaal the son of Ebed said, ° "Who *is*
(p. 339) Abimelech, and ° who *is* ° Shechem, that we
should serve him? ° *is* not *he* the son of Jerubbaal? and Zebul his officer? serve the ° men
of Hamor the father of Shechem: for ° why
should we serve him?
29 And ° would to God this people were under
my hand! then would I remove Abimelech."
° And he said to Abimelech, "Increase thine
army, and come out."

J[1] 30 And when Zebul the ruler of the city
heard the words of Gaal the son of Ebed, his
anger was kindled.
31 And he sent messengers unto Abimelech
° privily, saying, ° "Behold, Gaal the son of
Ebed and his brethren be come to Shechem;
and, ° behold, they fortify the city against thee.
32 Now therefore up by night, thou and the
people that *is* with thee, and lie in wait in the
field:
33 And it shall be, *that* in the morning, as
soon as the sun is up, thou shalt rise early,
and set upon the city: and, behold, *when* he
and the people that *is* with him come out
against thee, then mayest thou do to them ° as
thou shalt find occasion."

H[2] g 34 And Abimelech rose up, and all the people
that *were* with him, by night, and they laid
wait against Shechem in four companies.

h 35 And Gaal the son of Ebed went out, and
stood in the entering of the gate of the city:

g and Abimelech rose up, and the people that
were with him, from lying in wait.

h 36 And when Gaal saw the people, he said to
Zebul, [31] "Behold, there come people down from
the top of the mountains." And Zebul said
unto him, "Thou seest the shadow of the
mountains as *if they were* [28] men."
37 And Gaal spake again and said, "See there
come people down by the middle of the land,
and another company come along by the ° plain
of Meonenim."
38 Then said Zebul unto him, ° "Where *is*
now thy mouth, wherewith thou saidst, ° 'Who
is Abimelech, that we should serve him?' ° *is*
not this the people that thou hast despised?
go out, I pray ° now, and fight with them."

J[2] 39 And Gaal went out before the [2] men of
Shechem, and fought with Abimelech.
40 And Abimelech chased him, and he fled
before him, and many were overthrown *and*
wounded, *even* unto the entering of the gate.
41 And Abimelech ° dwelt at Arumah: and
Zebul thrust out Gaal and his brethren, that
they should not dwell in Shechem.

H[3] i 42 And it came to pass on the morrow, that
(p. 339) the people went out into the field; and they
told Abimelech.
43 And he took the people, and divided them
into three companies, and laid wait in the
field, and looked, and, [31] behold, the people

28 Who . . . ? who . . . ? Fig. *Erotēsis*. Ap. 6.
Shechem. Some codices, with Sept., read "the son of Shechem".
is not . . . ? why . . . ? Fig. *Erotēsis*. Ap. 6.
men. Heb. *'ĕnōsh*. Ap. 14.
29 would to God = would that. Fig. *Ecphōnēsis*. Ap. 6.
And he said. The Sept. reads "and say".
31 privily = deceitfully or craftily.
Behold. Fig. *Asterismos*. Ap. 6.
33 as = according as.
37 plain = oak.
38 Where . . . ? Who . . . ? is not . . . ? Fig. *Erotēsis*. Ap. 6.
now. A special various reading called *Sevīr* has "thou" (emphatic) instead of "now" = I pray thee, *thou*, &c.
41 dwelt = waited, or sat down.
44 ran = rushed.

46-49 (k, p. 339). THE TOWER OF SHECHEM.
51-55 (*k*, p. 339). THE TOWER OF THEBEZ.
(*Extended Alternation and Introversion.*)

H[3] | k | l | 46, 47. Refuge.
  m | o | 48. Brushwood.
    p | 49-. Burning.
   n | -49. Deaths. Shechemites.
 k | *l* | 51. Refuge.
  m | *p* | 52. Burning.
    o | 53. Millstone.
   n | 54, 55. Death. Abimelech.

46 Berith = covenant = a sanctuary.
48 trees = brushwood.

were come forth out of the city; and he rose
up against them, and smote them.
44 And Abimelech, and the company that
was with him, rushed forward, and stood in
the entering of the gate of the city: and the
two *other* companies ° ran upon all *the people*
that *were* in the fields, and slew them.
45 And Abimelech fought against the city all
that day; and he took the city, and slew the
people that *was* therein, and beat down the
city, and sowed it with salt.

46 And when all the [2] men of the tower of k l
Shechem heard *that*, they entered into an hold (p. 340)
of the house of the god ° Berith.
47 And it was told Abimelech, that all the
[2] men of the tower of Shechem were gathered
together.

48 And Abimelech gat him up to mount Zal- m o
mon, he and all the people that *were* with him;
and Abimelech took an axe in his hand, and
cut down a bough from the ° trees, and took it,
and laid *it* on his shoulder, and said unto the
people that *were* with him, "What ye have
seen me do, make haste, *and* do as I *have done*."

49 And all the people likewise cut down p
[3] every man his bough, and followed Abimelech, and put *them* to the hold, and set the
hold on fire upon them;

so that all the [28] men of the tower of Shechem n
died also, about a thousand [3] men and women.

50 Then went Abimelech to Thebez, and *F i*
encamped against Thebez, and took it. (p. 339)

51 But there was a strong tower within the *k l*
city, and thither fled all the [28] men and women, (p. 340)

1176 and all they of the city, and shut *it* to them,
and gat them up to the top of the tower.
m p (p. 340) 52 And Abimelech came unto the tower, and
fought against it, and went °hard unto the
door of the tower to burn it with fire.
o 53 And a certain woman cast °a piece of a
millstone upon Abimelech's head, and °all to
brake his skull.
n 54 Then he called hastily unto the young
man his armourbearer, and said unto him,
"Draw thy sword, and slay me, that men say
not of me, °'A woman slew him.'" And his
young man thrust him through, and he died.
55 And when the °men of Israel saw that Abimelech was dead, they departed every man
unto his place.
A (p. 338) 56 Thus [7]God °rendered the °wickedness of
Abimelech, which he did unto his father, in
slaying his seventy brethren:
57 And all the evil of the [9]men of Shechem
did [7]God [56]render upon their heads: and upon
them came the curse of Jotham the son of
Jerubbaal.

D A (p. 341) **10** And after Abimelech there arose to °de-
fend Israel Tola the son of Puah, the
1178 son of Dodo, a °man of Issachar; and he dwelt
to in Shamir in °mount Ephraim.
1155 2 And he judged Israel °twenty and three
years, and died, and was buried in Shamir.
1155 3 And after him arose Jair, a Gileadite, and
to judged Israel °twenty and two years.
1151 4 And he had thirty sons that rode on thirty
ass colts, and they had thirty cities, which are
called Havoth-jair unto this day, which *are* in
the land of Gilead.
5 And Jair died, and was buried in Camon.
B C 6 And the °children of Israel did °evil °again
in the sight of °the LORD, and served Baalim,
and °Ashtaroth, and the °gods of Syria, and
the °gods of Zidon, and the °gods of Moab,
and the gods of the °children of Ammon,
and the °gods of the Philistines, and forsook
°the LORD, and served not Him.
D 7 And the anger of [6]the LORD was hot
against Israel, and He sold them into the
hands of the Philistines, and into the hands
of the [6]children of Ammon.
E 8 And that year they °vexed and oppressed
the [6]children of Israel: eighteen years, all the
[6]children of Israel that *were* on the other side
Jordan in the land of the Amorites, which *is* in
Gilead.
9 Moreover the [6]children of Ammon passed
over Jordan to fight also against Judah, and
against Benjamin, and against the house of
Ephraim; so that Israel was sore distressed.
C a 10 And the [6]children of Israel cried unto [6]the
LORD, saying, "We have sinned against Thee,
both because we have forsaken °our God, and
also served Baalim."
b 11 And [6]the LORD said unto the [6]children
of Israel, °"*Did* not *I deliver you* from the
Egyptians, and from the Amorites, from the
[6]children of Ammon, and from the Philistines?
12 The Zidonians also, and the Amalekites,
and the °Maonites, did oppress you; and ye cried
to Me, and I delivered you out of their hand.
13 °Yet ye have forsaken Me, and served other
gods: wherefore I will deliver you no more.
14 °Go and cry unto the gods which °ye
have chosen; let them deliver you in the time
of your tribulation."
15 And the [6]children of Israel said unto [6]the a
LORD, "We have sinned: do Thou unto us
whatsoever seemeth good unto Thee; deliver
us only, we pray Thee, this day."
16 And they put away the °strange gods
from among them, and served [6]the LORD:
and °His soul was grieved for the misery of b
Israel.

52 hard = close.
53 a piece of a = an upper.
all to brake = altogether brake. (Obsolete.)
54 A woman slew. See note on 4. 21.
55 men. Heb. *'ish.* Ap. 14. II.
56 rendered = requited. Heb. brought back.
wickedness. Heb. *rā'a'.* Ap. 44. viii.

10. 1—16. 31 (*D*, p. 323). GOVERNMENT. (*Alternation.*)

D | A | 10. 1-5. Judges. (Tola and Jair.)
B | 10. 6—12. 7. Ammonites and Jephthah.
A | 12. 8-15. Judges. (Ibzan, Elon, Abdon.)
B | 13. 1—16. 31. Philistines and Samson.

1 defend = save or deliver.
man. Heb. *'ish.* Ap. 4. II.
mount = hill country.
2 twenty, &c. See note on 9. 22.
3 twenty. See note, Ap. 50. IV, p. 55.

10. 6—12. 7 (B, above). AMMONITES AND JEPHTHAH. (*Extended Alternation.*)

B | C | 10. 6. The evil wrought.
D | 10. 7. Selling to Philistines and Ammonites.
E | 10. 8, 9. Oppression (eighteen years).
C | 10. 10-16. The evil repented of.
D | 10. 17—12. 6. Deliverance by Jephthah.
E | 12. 7. Government by Jephthah (six years).

6 children = sons.
evil. Heb. *rā'a'.* Ap. 44. viii.
again. Cp. 2. 11; 3. 7; 4. 1; 6. 1; 13. 1.
the LORD. Heb. Jehovah. Ap. 4. II.
Ashtaroth, pl. = the Ashtoreths. Cp. 2. 11-13.
gods of Syria. Gen. 35. 3-6.
gods of Zidon. 1 Kings 11. 5 (Baal, Astarte).
gods of Moab. 11. 24 (Chemosh). 1 Kings 11. 33 (Milcom or Molech).
gods of the Philistines: e.g. Dagon (16. 23).
8 vexed and oppressed = brake and crushed. See note on *v.* 3, above.

10-16 (*C*, above). THE EVIL REPENTED OF. (*Alternation.*)

C | a | 10. Confession.
b | 11-14. Reproach.
a | 15, 16-. Confession.
b | -16. Pity.

10 our God. Heb. *Elohim* (Ap. 4. I). Some codices, with Aram., Sept., and Vulg., read "Jehovah our God".
11 Did not I . . . ? Fig. *Erotēsis.* Ap. 6.
12 Maonites. Cp. 2 Chron. 26. 7, 8. A mixture of Moabites and Ammonites = the two words combined.
13 Yet. Cp. Deut. 32. 15. Jer. 2. 13.
14 Go. Fig. *Eironeia* (Divine *Irony*). Ap. 6.
ye have chosen. Cp. Deut. 32. 37, 38. Jer. 2. 28.
16 strange gods = gods of strangers or foreigners.
His soul = He (emph.). Heb. *nephesh* (Ap. 13). Attributed by Fig. *Anthropopatheia* to God (Ap. 6).

D F[1] G[1] (p. 342) 1152 17 Then the [6]children of Ammon were °gathered together, and encamped in Gilead. And the [6]children of Israel assembled themselves together, and encamped in Mizpeh.

H[1] c[1] 18 And the people *and* princes of Gilead said one to another, "What °man *is he* that will begin to fight against the [6]children of Ammon? he shall be head over all the inhabitants of Gilead."

d[1] **11** Now °Jephthah the °Gileadite was a mighty °man of valour, and he *was* the son of an harlot: and Gilead begat Jephthah.

2 And Gilead's wife bare him sons; and his wife's sons grew up, and they thrust out Jephthah, and said unto him, "Thou shalt not inherit in our father's house; for thou *art* the son of a °strange woman."

3 Then Jephthah fled °from his brethren, and dwelt in the land of °Tob: and there were gathered °vain °men to Jephthah, and went out with him.

F[2] G[2] 4 And it came to pass in process of time, that the °children of Ammon made war against Israel.

H[2] c[2] 1151 5 And it was so, that when the [4]children of Ammon made war against Israel, the elders of Gilead went to fetch Jephthah out of the land of Tob:

6 And they said unto Jephthah, "Come, and be our captain, that we may fight with the [4]children of Ammon."

d[2] 7 And Jephthah said unto the elders of Gilead, "Did not ye hate me, and expel me out of my father's house? and why are ye come unto me now when ye are in distress?"

8 And the elders of Gilead said unto Jephthah, "Therefore we turn again to thee now, that thou mayest go with us, and fight against the [4]children of Ammon, and be our head over all the inhabitants of Gilead."

9 And Jephthah said unto the elders of Gilead, "If ye bring me home again to fight against the [4]children of Ammon, and °the LORD deliver them before me, shall I be your head?"

10 And the elders of Gilead said unto Jephthah, [9]"The LORD °be witness between us, if we do not so according to thy words."

11 Then Jephthah went °with the elders of Gilead, and the people made him head and captain over them: and Jephthah uttered all his words °before [9]the LORD °in Mizpeh.

F[3] G[3] e 12 And Jephthah sent messengers unto the king of the [4]children of Ammon, saying, °"What hast thou to do with me, that thou art come against me to fight in my land?"

f 13 And the king of the [4]children of Ammon answered unto the messengers of Jephthah, "Because Israel took away my land, when they came up out of Egypt, from Arnon even unto Jabbok, and unto Jordan: now therefore restore those *lands* again peaceably."

e 14 And Jephthah sent messengers again unto the king of the [4]children of Ammon:

15 °And said unto him, "Thus saith Jephthah, 'Israel took not away the land of Moab, nor the land of the [4]children of Ammon:

16 But when Israel came up from Egypt, and walked through the wilderness unto the Red sea, and came to Kadesh;

17 Then Israel sent messengers unto the king of Edom, saying, 'Let °me, I pray thee, pass through thy land:' but the king of Edom would not hearken *thereto*. And in like manner they sent unto the king of Moab: but he would not *consent*: and Israel abode in Kadesh.

18 Then they °went along through the wilderness, and compassed the land of Edom, and the land of Moab, and came by the east side of the land of Moab, and pitched on the other side of Arnon, °but came not within the border of Moab: for Arnon *was* the border of Moab.

---

17 gathered = gathered by proclamation. Note the extended alternation in this verse "children, gathered, encamped".

18 man. Heb. *'ish.* Ap. 14. II.

10. 17—12. 6 (*D*, p. 341). DELIVERANCE BY JEPHTHAH. (*Repeated Alternations.*)

D | F[1] | G[1] | 10. 17. Ammonite invasion.
  H[1] | c[1] | 10. 18. A Leader needed.
  d[1] | 11. 1-3. Leader rejected.
F[2] | G[2] | 11. 4. Ammonite war.
  H[2] | c[2] | 11. 5, 6. Jephthah called.
  d[2] | 11. 7-11. Jephthah appointed.
F[3] | G[3] | 11. 12-28. Ammonite negotiation.
  H[3] | c[3] | 11. 29. Jephthah inspired.
  d[3] | 11. 30, 31. Jephthah's vow made.
F[4] | G[4] | 11. 32, 33. Ammonite defeat.
  H[4] | c[4] | 11. 34-. Jephthah's return.
  d[4] | 11. -34-40. Jephthah's vow performed.
F[5] | G[5] | 12. 1. Ephraimite dispute.
  H[5] | c[5] | 12. 2, 3. Jephthah's answer.
  d[5] | 12. 4-6. Jephthah's action.

11. 1 Jephthah = He will deliver. Note the Fig. *Epanadiplōsis* (Ap. 6), to call attention to the facts of this verse, introducing Jephthah. All was irregular: no king, no judge, no priest.

Gileadite = son of the man Gilead.

man. Heb. *gibbōr.* Ap. 14. IV.

2 strange = foreign.

3 from. Heb. "from the face of". Fig. *Pleonasm.* Ap. 6.

Tob = fruitful land. East of Syria.

vain = unemployed, or bankrupt.

men. Heb. pl. of *'ĕnōsh.* Ap. 14. III.

4 children = sons.

9 the LORD. Heb. Jehovah. Ap. 4. II.

10 be witness = be a hearer.

11 with. Some codices, with three early printed editions, read "unto".

before the LORD = in the presence of Jehovah.

in Mizpeh. Cp. 10. 17.

12-28 (G[3], above). AMMONITE NEGOTIATION. (*Alternation.*)

G[3] | e | 12. First message.
  f | 13. King's answer.
  e | 14-27. Second message.
  f | 28. King's obstinacy.

12 What . . . ? Fig. *Erotēsis.* Ap. 6.

15 And said. A special reading (*Sevir*, Ap. 34) and some codices read "and they said". Heb. text = he.

17 me. Most codices, with Syr., read "us" as in *v.* 19. Cp. Num. 20. 14.

18 went along = went on.

but came not. Cp. Num. 21. 13, 24.

1151 19 And °Israel sent messengers unto Sihon king of the Amorites, the king of Heshbon; and Israel said unto him, 'Let °us pass, we pray thee, through thy land into my place.'

20 But Sihon °trusted not Israel to pass through his °coast: but Sihon gathered all his people together, and pitched in Jahaz, and fought against Israel.

21 And [9]the LORD °God of Israel delivered Sihon and all his people into the hand of Israel, and they smote them: so Israel possessed all the land of the Amorites, the inhabitants of that country.

22 And they possessed all the [20]coasts of the Amorites, from Arnon even unto Jabbok, and from the wilderness even unto Jordan.

23 So now [9]the LORD [21]God of Israel hath dispossessed the Amorites from before His People Israel, and °shouldest thou possess °it?

24 °Wilt not thou possess that which Chemosh thy god giveth thee to possess? So whomsoever [9]the LORD our [21]God shall drive out from before us, them will we possess.

25 And now °*art* thou any thing better than Balak the son of Zippor, king of Moab? did he ever strive against Israel, or did he ever fight against them,

26 While Israel dwelt in Heshbon and her towns, and in Aroer and her towns, and in all the cities that *be* along by the [20]coasts of Arnon, °three hundred years? why therefore did ye not recover *them* within that time?

27 Wherefore I have not °sinned against thee, but thou doest me wrong to war against me: [9]the LORD the Judge be judge this day between the [4]children of Israel and the [4]children of Ammon.'"

f (p. 342) 28 Howbeit the king of the [4]children of Ammon hearkened not unto the words of Jephthah which he sent him.

H^3 c^3 29 Then °the Spirit of [9]the LORD came upon Jephthah, and he passed over Gilead, and Manasseh, and passed over Mizpeh of Gilead, and from Mizpeh of Gilead he passed over °*unto* the [4]children of Ammon.

d^3 30 And Jephthah °vowed a vow unto [9]the LORD, and said, "If thou shalt without fail deliver the [4]children of Ammon into mine hands,

31 Then it shall be, that °whatsoever cometh forth of the doors of my house to meet me, when I return in peace from the [4]children of Ammon, shall surely be [9]the LORD'S, °and I will offer it up for a burnt offering."

F^1 G^4 32 So Jephthah passed over unto the [4]children of Ammon to fight against them; and [9]the LORD delivered them into his hands.

33 And he smote them from Aroer, even till thou come to Minnith, *even* twenty cities, and unto the plain of the vineyards, with a very great slaughter. Thus the [4]children of Ammon were subdued before the [4]children of Israel.

H^4 c^4 34 And Jephthah came to Mizpeh unto his house,

d^4 g (p. 343) and, °behold, his daughter came out to meet him with °timbrels and with dances: and she *was his* only child; °beside her he had neither son nor daughter.

35 And it came to pass, when he saw her, that he rent his clothes, and said, °"Alas, my daughter! thou hast brought me very low, and thou art one of them that trouble me: for I have °opened my mouth unto [9]the LORD, and I cannot go back."

36 And she said unto him, "My father, *if* thou hast [35]opened thy mouth unto [9]the LORD, do to me according to that which hath proceeded out of thy mouth; forasmuch as [9]the LORD hath taken vengeance for thee of thine enemies, *even* of the [4]children of Ammon."

h 37 And she said unto her father, "Let this thing be done for me: let me alone two months, that I may °go up and down upon the mountains, and bewail my virginity, I and my fellows."

38 And he said, "Go." And he sent her away

---

19 Israel sent. Cp. Deut. 2. 26.
us. Cp. *v.* 17 and Deut. 2. 27.
20 trusted = stayed or rested on. See Ap. 69.
coast = border.
21 God. Heb. Elohim. Ap. 4. I.
23 shouldest thou . . . ? Fig. *Erotēsis.* Ap. 6.
it = him: i. e. Israel. Being *masc.* (in Heb.), cannot refer to the land of *v.* 21; and *sing.*, so that it cannot refer to coasts of *v.* 22.
24 Wilt not thou . . . ? Fig. *Erotēsis.* Ap. 6. Jephthah does not recognise Chemosh as a god. The emphasis is on "thy" and "our", and is the argument *a fortiori*: and, taking them on their own ground, it is the *argumentum ad hominem.*
25 art thou . . . ? Fig. *Erotēsis.* Ap. 6. Cp. Num. 22. 2. Deut. 23. 4. Josh. 24. 9.
26 three hundred years. Not a "round number". See Ap. 50. IV, p. 54.
27 sinned. Heb. *chātā'.* Ap. 44. i.
29 the Spirit. Heb. *rūach* (fem.). See Ap. 9.
unto. This word is read in the text of some codices with Aram., Syr., and Vulg.
30 vowed a vow. Fig *Polyptōton* (Ap. 6) = made a solemn vow. See notes on Lev. 27. 1-8.
31 whatsoever. This is *masculine.* But the issuer from his house was *feminine.* Thus his rash vow was impossible of fulfilment, and was to be repented of.
and = or. The Heb. ו (*Vav*) is a connective Particle, and is rendered in many different ways. It is also used as a *disjunctive*, and is often rendered "or" (or, with a negative, "nor"). See Gen. 41. 44. Ex. 20. 4; 21. 15, 17, 18. Num. 16. 14; 22. 26 (R. V. "nor"); Deut. 3. 24. 2 Sam. 3. 29. 1 Kings 18. 10, 27. With a negative = "nor", "neither". Ex. 20. 17. Deut. 7. 25. 2 Sam. 1. 21. Ps. 26. 9. Prov. 6. 4; 30. 3, &c. See note on "but", 1 Kings 2. 9. Here, Jephthah's vow consisted of two parts: (1) He would either dedicate it to Jehovah (according to Lev. 27); or (2) if unsuitable for this, he would offer it as a burnt offering. He performed his vow, and dedicated his daughter to Jehovah by a perpetual virginity (*vv.* 36, 39, 40); but he did not offer her as a burnt offering, because it was forbidden by Jehovah, and could not be accepted by Him (Lev. 18. 21; 20. 2-5).

11. -34-40 (d^4, p. 342). THE VOW PERFORMED.
(*Alternation.*)

d^4 | g | -34-36. Performance.
  h | 37, 38. Suspension.
  g | 39-. Performance.
  h | -39, 40. Commemoration.

34 behold. Fig. *Asterismos.* Ap. 6.
timbrels = drums. See note on Ex. 15. 20.
beside her. Fig. *Pleonasm.* Ap. 6. The fact is stated in two ways, in order to emphasise it.
35 Alas! Fig. *Ecphōnēsis.* Ap. 6.
opened my mouth. Hebraism for making a formal, prepared, and solemn statement.
37 go up and down = wander about.

1151 *for* two months: and she went with her companions, and bewailed her virginity upon the mountains.

g (p. 343) 39 And it came to pass at the end of two months, that she returned unto her father, who °did with her *according* to his [30]vow which he had vowed: °and she knew no °man.

h °And it was a custom in Israel,
40 *That* the daughters of Israel went yearly °to lament the daughter of Jephthah the Gileadite °four days in a year.

F⁵ G⁵ (p. 342) **12** And the °men of Ephraim gathered themselves together, and went northward, and said unto Jephthah, "Wherefore passedst thou over to fight against the °children of Ammon, and didst not call us to go with thee? we will burn thine house upon thee with fire."

H⁵ c⁵ 2 And Jephthah said unto them, "I and my people were at great strife with the [1]children of Ammon; and when I called you, ye delivered me not out of their hands.
3 And when I saw that ye delivered *me* not, I put °my life in my hands, and passed over against the [1]children of Ammon, and °the LORD delivered them into my hand: wherefore then are ye come up unto me this day, to fight against me?"

d⁵ 4 Then Jephthah gathered together all the °men of Gilead, and fought with Ephraim: and the °men of Gilead smote Ephraim, because they said, "Ye Gileadites *are* fugitives of Ephraim among the Ephraimites, °*and* among the Manassites."
5 And the Gileadites took the °passages of Jordan before the Ephraimites: and it was *so,* that when those Ephraimites which were escaped said, "Let me go over;" that the [4]men of Gilead said unto him, "*Art* thou an Ephraimite?" If he said, "Nay;"
6 Then said they unto him, "Say now 'Shibboleth:'" and he said "Sibboleth:" for he could not °frame to pronounce *it* right. Then they took him, and slew him at the passages of Jordan: and there fell at that time of the Ephraimites °forty and two thousand.

E (p. 341) 1151-1145 7 And Jephthah °judged Israel six years. Then died Jephthah the Gileadite, and was °buried in *one of* the cities of Gilead.

A i¹ j¹ (p. 344) 8 And after him Ibzan of Beth-lehem judged Israel.
9 And he had thirty sons, and thirty daughters, *whom* he sent abroad, and took in thirty daughters from abroad for his sons.

k¹ 1145-1138 And he judged Israel seven years.

l¹ 10 Then died Ibzan, and was buried at Beth-lehem.

i² j² 11 And after him Elon, a Zebulonite, judged Israel;

k² 1138-1128 and he judged Israel ten years.

l² 12 And Elon the Zebulonite died, and was buried in Aijalon in the country of Zebulun.

i³ j³ 1128-1120 13 And after him Abdon the son of Hillel, a Pirathonite, judged Israel.

14 And he had forty sons and thirty °nephews, that rode on threescore and ten ass colts:

and he judged Israel eight years. k³ 1128-112

15 And Abdon the son of Hillel the Pirathonite died, and was buried in Pirathon in the land of Ephraim, in the °mount of the Amalekites. l³

13 And the °children of Israel °did °evil again in the sight of °the LORD; B J

and °the LORD delivered them into the hand of the Philistines °forty years. K

---

39 did with her according to his vow which he had vowed = He did not offer her as a burnt offering; for Jehovah could not accept *that.* Therefore Jephthah must have *dedicated* her to the LORD by a perpetual virginity. Such a vow was provided for in Lev. 27. See note on *v.* 31.

and she knew no man. This is conclusive. It has nothing to do with a sacrificial death, but it has to do with a dedicated life to Jehovah. Thus was Jephthah's vow fulfilled. **man.** Heb. *'ish.* Ap. 14. II.

And it was = and it became.

40 to lament = to rehearse with, as in 5. 11; to celebrate [her dedication] in praises.

four days in a year. Thus annually her friends "went", evidently to Jephthah's daughter, to rehearse with her this great event of her life: not of her death.

12. 1 men. Heb. *'ish* or *'enosh.* Ap. 14.

children = sons.

3 my life = my soul. Heb. *nephesh.* Ap. 13. II.

the LORD. Heb. Jehovah. Ap. 4. II.

4 men. Heb. *'ish.* Ap. 14. II.

and. This "and" is read in the text in some codices, with two early printed editions, Sept., Syr., and Vulg.

5 passages = fords.

6 frame = take heed, give attention.

forty and two thousand = 40 + 2,000 = 2,040. The *whole* tribe numbered only 32,500 at previous census (Num. 26. 37; see note on 7. 3), and that was less than the first numbering (Num. 1. 33). Only 1,000 from each tribe formed the army. Num. 31. 4, 5.

7 judged. First, deliverance; then rule.

buried in one of the cities. City unnamed. Memory not honoured, though mentioned in Heb. 11. 32; yet the last name in that list.

8-15 (*A*, p. 341). **JUDGES (IBZAN, ELON, ABDON).** (*Extended Alternation.*)

A | i¹ | j¹ | 8, 9-. Ibzan.
k¹ | -9. Government (seven years).
l¹ | 10. Death.
i² | j² | 11-. Elon.
k² | -11. Government (ten years).
l² | 12. Death.
i³ | j³ | 13, 14-. Abdon.
k³ | -14. Government (eight years).
l³ | 15. Death.

14 nephews = grandsons.

15 mount = hill country.

13. 1—16. 31 (*B*, p. 341). **PHILISTINES AND SAMSON.** (*Alternation.*)

B | J | 13. 1-. Delivered to oppressors.
K | 13. -1. Time of servitude (forty years).
J | 13. 2—16. 31-. Delivered by Samson.
K | 16. -31. Time of government (twenty years).

1 children = sons.

did evil again = Heb. added to commit.

evil. Heb. *ra'a'.* Ap. 44. viii.

the LORD. Heb. Jehovah. Ap. 4.

forty years. 1120-1080.

J L m¹ n (p. 345) 1120-1100 2 And there was a certain °man of Zorah,
of the family of the Danites, whose name *was*
Manoah;
o and his wife *was* barren, and bare not.
o 3 And °the Angel of [1]the LORD appeared unto
the woman, and said unto her, °"Behold now,
thou *art* barren, and bearest not: but thou
shalt conceive, and bear a son.
4 Now therefore beware, I pray thee, and
°drink not wine nor strong drink, and eat not
any unclean *thing*:
5 For, °lo, thou shalt conceive, and bear
a son; and no rasor shall come on his head:
for °the child shall be °a Nazarite unto °God
from the womb: and he shall begin to deliver
Israel out of the hand of the Philistines."
n 6 Then the woman came and told her
husband, saying, °"A Man of °God came unto
me, and His °countenance *was* like the
°countenance of an Angel of °God, very
°terrible: but I asked Him not whence He
was, neither told He me His name:
7 But He said unto me, [3]'Behold, thou shalt
conceive, and bear a son; and now drink no
wine nor strong drink, neither eat any unclean *thing*: for [5]the child shall be [5]a Nazarite
to [6]God from the womb to the day of his
death.'"
m² p 8 Then Manoah intreated [1]the LORD, and said,
q "O °my LORD,* let the [6]Man of [6]God Which
thou didst send come again unto us, and
teach us what we shall do unto [5]the child
that shall be born."
p 9 And °God hearkened to the voice of
Manoah; and the Angel of [6]God °came again
unto the woman as she sat in the field: but
Manoah her husband *was* not with her.
10 °And the woman made haste, and ran,
and shewed her husband, and said unto him,
[3]"Behold, [6]the Man hath appeared unto me,
That came unto me the *other* day."
11 And Manoah arose, and went after his
wife, and came to [6]the Man, and said unto
Him, "*Art* Thou [6]the Man That spakest unto
the woman?" And He said, "*I am*."
q 12 And Manoah said, "Now °let Thy words
come to pass. °How shall we order [5]the child,
and °*how* shall we do unto him?"
13 And [3]the Angel of [1]the LORD said unto
Manoah, "Of all that I said unto the woman
let her beware.
14 She may not eat of any *thing* that cometh
of the vine, neither let her drink wine or
strong drink, nor eat any unclean *thing*: all
that I °commanded her let her observe."
m³ r 15 And Manoah said unto the Angel of [1]the
LORD, "I pray Thee, let us detain Thee, until
we shall have made ready °a kid for Thee."
16 And the Angel of [1]the LORD said unto
Manoah, "Though thou detain Me, I will not
eat of thy °bread: and if thou wilt °offer
a burnt offering, thou must °offer it unto [1]the
LORD."
s t For Manoah knew not that He *was* an Angel
of [1]the LORD.
u 17 And Manoah said unto the Angel of [1]the
LORD, "What *is* Thy name, that when Thy
sayings come to pass we may do Thee
honour?"

13. 2—16. 31- (*J*, p. 344). DELIVERED BY SAMSON. (*Introversion*.)

J | L | 13. 2-21. Promise. A deliverer.
M | 13. 22, 23. Parents. Fear, and Cheer.
M | 13. 24, 25. Child. Growth, and Power.
L | 14. 1—16. 31-. Promise fulfilled. Deliverer.

13. 2-21 (L, above). PROMISE. A DELIVERER. (*Division*.)

L | m¹ | 2-7. First appearance of Angel.
m² | 8-14. Second appearance of Angel.
m³ | 15-21. Detention of Angel.

13. 2-7 (m¹, above). FIRST APPEARANCE OF ANGEL. (*Introversion*.)

m¹ | n | 2-. Manoah, alone.
o | -2. His wife, alone.
o | 3-5. His wife, and Angel.
n | 6, 7. Manoah, and wife.

2 man. Heb. *'ish.* Ap. 4. II.

3 the Angel = Messenger. From *vv.* 18, 19, 22, the same that appeared to Gideon (6. 12).

Behold. Fig. *Asterismos.* Ap. 6.

4 drink. Cp. Num. 6. 2, 3.

5 lo. Fig. *Asterismos.* Ap. 6.

the child. Heb. *na'ar.*

a Nazarite unto God = one separate unto Elohim.

6 A Man. Heb. *'ish.* Ap. 14. II. This was according to the woman's apprehension.

God. Heb. Elohim. Ap. 4. I.

countenance = appearance.

terrible = awe-inspiring.

8-14 (m², above). SECOND APPEARANCE OF ANGEL. (*Alternation*.)

m² | p | 8-. Reappearance intreated.
q | -8. Direction sought.
p | 9-11. Reappearance vouchsafed.
q | 12-14. Direction given.

8 my LORD* = *'Adonai.* Should be "Jehovah". This is one of the 134 changes indicated in the *Massōrah.* Ap. 32.

9 God = The God: *hā-'Elohim.* Ap. 4. I.

came. Some codices, with three early printed editions, read "appeared".

10 And. Note the Fig. *Polysyndeton* (Ap. 6) in this verse.

12 How shall we order the child, and how shall we do unto him? Heb. "What shall be the rule of (Gen. of relation = concerning) the boy, and what shall be his work?"

14 commanded = forbade. The verb *zivvāh* is a Homonym here and Deut. 4. 23, where it is correctly rendered "forbid". Elsewhere "command".

15-21 (m³, above). DETENTION OF THE ANGEL. (*Alternation and Introversion*.)

m³ | r | 15, 16-. Invitation of Manoah.
s | t | -16. Manoah's ignorance.
u | 17, 18. Angel's name. "Wonderful."
r | 19-. Offering of Manoah.
s | *u* | -19-21-. Angel's action. "Wonderful."
t | -21. Manoah's knowledge.

15 a kid = a kid of the goats.

16 bread. Fig. *Synecdoche* (of Species). Ap. 6. Put for all kinds of food.

offer = prepare. Ap. 43. I. iii.

offer it = cause it to ascend. Ap. 43. I. vi.

1120 to 1100 18 And the Angel of [1]the LORD said unto him, "Why askest thou thus after My name, seeing it *is* °secret?"

r (p. 345) 19 So Manoah took [15]a kid with a meat offering, and [16]offered *it* upon a rock unto [1]the LORD:

s u and *the Angel* did °wonderously; (and Manoah and his wife looked on).

20 For it came to pass, when °the flame went up toward heaven from off °the altar, that the Angel of [1]the LORD ascended in the flame of the altar. And Manoah and his wife looked on *it*, and fell on their faces to the ground.

21 But the Angel of [1]the LORD did no more appear to Manoah and to his wife.

t u Then Manoah knew that He *was* an Angel of [1]the LORD.

M 22 And Manoah said unto his wife, "We shall surely die, because we have seen [6]God."

23 But his wife said unto him, "If [1]the LORD were pleased to kill us, He would not have °received a burnt offering and a meat offering at our hands, neither would He have shewed us all these *things*, nor would as at this time have told us *such things* as these."

M 24 And the woman bare a son, and °called his name Samson: and [5]the child °grew, and [1]the LORD blessed him.

25 And °the Spirit of [1]the LORD °began to °move him °at times in °the camp of Dan between Zorah and °Eshtaol.

L A P¹ v (p. 346) **14** And Samson went down to Timnath, and saw a woman in Timnath of the daughters of the Philistines.

2 And he came up, and told his father and his mother, and said, "I have seen a woman in Timnath of the daughters of the Philistines: now therefore get her for me to wife."

3 Then his father and his mother said unto him, "*Is there* never a woman among the daughters of thy brethren, or among all my People, that thou goest to °take a wife of the uncircumcised Philistines?" And Samson said unto his father, "Get her for me; for she °pleaseth me well."

4 But his father and his mother knew not that it *was* of °the LORD, that he sought an °occasion against the Philistines: for at that time the Philistines had dominion over Israel.

w 5 Then went Samson down, and his father and his mother, to Timnath, and came to the vineyards of Timnath: and, °behold, °a young lion roared °against him.

6 And °the Spirit of [4]the LORD came mightily upon him, and he rent him as he would have rent a kid, and *he had* nothing in his hand:

x but he told not his father or his mother what he had done.

v 7 And he went down, and talked with the woman; and she pleased Samson well.

w 8 And after a time he returned to take her, and he turned aside to see the carcase of the lion: and, [5]behold, *there was* a swarm of bees and honey in the carcase of the lion.

9 And he took thereof in his hands, and went on eating, and came to his father and mother, and he gave them, and they did eat:

but he told not them that he had taken the honey out of the carcase of the lion. *x*

10 So his father went down unto the woman: and Samson made there a feast; for so used the young men to do. P² y

11 And it came to pass, °when they saw him,

18 secret. Heb. wonderful. Same as Isa. 9. 6.
19 wonderously = a wonderful thing.
20 the flame went up. See note on Gen. 4. 4.
the altar. The rock is deemed the altar.
23 received. It is the acceptance of our Substitute by God which saves, not our acceptance of Him. This was sound reasoning.
24 called his name = called him. Fig. *Pleonasm*. Ap. 6.
grew. Israel waited twenty years for deliverance. Cp. 15. 20; 16. 31.
25 the Spirit. Heb. *rūach*. Ap. 9.
began. They had yet to wait. Cp. 15. 20.
move him = stir him with trouble. See Gen. 41. 8. Ps. 77. 3. Dan. 2. 1, 3.
at times = to and fro.
the camp of Dan, where Israel lay in a fortified place. Cp. 18. 12.
Eshtaol. On the borders of Judah.

14. 1—16. 31- (*L*, p. 345). PROMISE FULFILLED.
(*Alternation and Introversion.*)

L | N | A | 14. 1-20. Marriage.
  B | 15. 1-19. Slaughter, in life.
  O | 15. 20. Government, twenty years.
  N | *A* | 16. 1-20. Harlots.
  B | 16. 21-31-. Slaughter, in death.

1-20 (N, above). MARRIAGE.
(*Division.*)

N | P¹ | 1-9. Proposals.
  P² | 10-20. Feast.

1-9 (P¹, above). PROPOSALS.
(*Extended Alternations.*)

P¹ | v | 1-4. Wife.
  w | 5, 6-. Lion. Rent.
  x | -6. Concealment.
  v | 7. Wife.
  w | 8, 9-. Lion. Honey in it.
  x | -9. Concealment.

3 take a wife of, &c. An unlawful connection. Cp. Ex. 34. 16. Deut. 7. 3, with Josh. 23. 12.
pleaseth me well. Heb. is right in mine eyes.
4 the LORD. Heb. Jehovah. Ap. 4. II.
occasion = opportunity.
5 behold. Fig. *Asterismos*. Ap. 6.
a young lion. Lions once abounded in Palestine. Hence names *Lebaoth* (Josh. 15. 32; 19. 6). *Arieh* (2 Kings 15. 25). *Laish* (Judg. 18. 7). See also 1 Sam. 17. 36. 1 Kings 13. 24, &c.).
against him = at meeting him.
6 the Spirit. Heb. *rūach*. Ap. 9.

10-20 (P², above). THE FEAST.
(*Introversion and Alternation.*)

P² | y | 10, 11. Wife and companions.
  z | 12, 13. Conditions proposed.
  a | b | 14. Riddle put forth.
  c | 15-17. Wife's deceit.
  a | *b* | 18-. Riddle solved.
  c | -18. Wife's deceit.
  z | 19. Conditions fulfilled.
  y | 20. Wife and companions.

11 when they saw him: i. e. saw what sort of man he was. Note emphasis on "him".

1120 to 1100 that they brought thirty companions to be with him.

z (p. 346) 12 And Samson said unto them, °"I will now put forth a riddle unto you: if ye can certainly declare it me within the seven days of the feast, and find *it* out, then I will give you thirty °sheets and thirty change of garments:
13 But if ye cannot declare *it* me, then shall ye give me thirty [12]sheets and thirty change of garments." And they said unto him, "Put forth thy riddle, that we may hear it."

a b 14 And he said unto them,
°"Out of the eater came forth meat,
And out of the strong came forth sweetness."
And they could not in three days expound the riddle.

c 15 And it came to pass on the °seventh day, that they said unto Samson's wife, "Entice thy husband, that he may declare unto us the riddle, lest we burn thee and thy father's house with fire: have ye called us to take that we have? °*is it* not *so?*"
16 And Samson's wife wept before him, and said, "Thou dost but hate me, and lovest me not: thou hast put forth a riddle unto the °children of my people, and hast not told *it* me." And he said unto her, [5]"Behold, I have not told *it* my father nor my mother, and shall I tell *it* thee?"
17 And she wept before him the seven days, while their feast lasted: and it came to pass on the seventh day, that he told her, because she lay sore upon him: and she told the riddle to the [16]children of her people.

a b 18 And the °men of the city said unto him on the seventh day before the sun went down,
°"What *is* sweeter than honey?
And what *is* stronger than a lion?"
And he said unto them,

c °"If ye had not plowed with my heifer,
Ye had not found out my riddle."

z 19 And [6]the Spirit of [4]the LORD came upon him, and he went down to Ashkelon, and slew thirty °men of them, and took their spoil, and gave change of garments unto them which expounded the riddle. And his anger was kindled, and he went up to his father's house.

y 20 But Samson's wife was *given* to his companion, whom he had used as °his friend.

B Q[1] d (p. 347) **15** But it came to pass within a while after, in the time of wheat harvest, that Samson visited his wife with a °kid; and he said, °"I will go in to my wife into the chamber." But her father would not suffer him to go in.
2 And her father said, "I verily thought that thou hadst utterly hated her; therefore I gave her to thy companion: *is* not her younger sister fairer than she? take her, I pray thee, instead of her."

e 3 And Samson said °concerning them, °"Now shall I be more blameless than the Philistines, though I do them a displeasure."
4 And Samson went and caught three hundred °foxes, and took °firebrands, and turned tail to tail, and put a firebrand in the midst between two tails.
5 And when he had set the brands on fire, he let *them* go into the standing corn of the Philistines, and burnt up both the shocks, and also the standing corn, with the vineyards *and* olives.

d 6 Then the Philistines said, "Who hath done this?" And they answered, "Samson, the son in law of the Timnite, because he had taken his wife, and given her to his companion." And the Philistines came up, and °burnt her and her father with fire.

e 7 And Samson said unto them, "Though ye have done °this, yet will I be avenged of you, and after that I will cease."
8 And he smote them hip and thigh with a great slaughter:

Q[2] f h and he °went down and dwelt in the °top of the rock Etam.

---

12 I will = Let me.
sheets = linen wraps, or shirts.
14 Out of. Fig. *Ænigma*. Ap. 6.
15 seventh. The Sept. reads "fourth".
is it not so? The italics reveal the uncertainty of A.V. Many codices read "hither", which yields better sense. Heb. text reads simply "not".
16 children = sons.
18 men. Heb. pl. of *'ĕnōsh*. Ap. 14. III.
What . . . ? Fig. *Anteisagogē*. Ap. 6.
If. Fig. *Parœmia*. Ap. 6.
19 men. Heb. *'īsh*. Ap. 14. II.
20 his friend. This was strictly in accordance with the laws of Khammurabi, §§ 159, 163, 164.

15. 1-19 (B, p. 346). SLAUGHTER, IN LIFE. (*Division*.)

B | Q[1] | 1-8. First slaughter.
  | Q[2] | 9-19. Second slaughter.

1-8 (Q[1], above). FIRST SLAUGHTER. (*Alternation*.)

Q[1] | d | 1, 2. Wife refused.
     | e | 3-5. Retribution. Burning.
     | *d* | 6. Wife burnt.
     | *e* | 7, 8-. Retribution. Slaughter.

1 kid = kid of the goats.
I will go in = Let me come in.
3 concerning = to.
Now = this once.
4 foxes = jackals. These go in packs, foxes go alone.
firebrands = torches.
6 burnt her and her father. Some codices, with one early printed edition, Sept., and Syr., read "burned the house of her father".
7 this = like [this]: i. e. on this wise.

-8-19 (Q[2], above). SECOND SLAUGHTER. (*Alternation*.)

Q[2] | f | -8-16. Expected retaliation.
     | g | 17. Meaning of place. *Ramath-lehi*.
     | *f* | 18, 19-. Expected retaliation.
     | *g* | -19. Meaning of place. *En-hakkore*.

-8-16 (f, above). EXPECTED RETALIATION. (*Alternation*.)

f | h | -8. Etam. Samson there.
  | i | 9. Philistines. Camp at Lehi.
  | *h* | 10-13. Etam. Mission to Samson.
  | *i* | 14-16. Philistines. Slaughter at Lehi.

8 went down. Some codices, with one early printed edition, and Syr., read "went".
top = cleft.

i (p. 347) 1120-1100 9 Then the Philistines went up, and ° pitched
in Judah, and spread themselves in Lehi.
h 10 And the ° men of Judah said, "Why are
ye come up against us?" And they answered,
"To bind Samson are we come up, to do to
him ° as he hath done to us."
11 Then three thousand men of Judah went
to the [8] top of the rock Etam, and said to
Samson, "Knowest thou not that the Philistines *are* rulers over us? what *is* this *that*
thou hast done unto us?" And he said unto
them, [10] "As they did unto me, so have I done
unto them."
12 And they said unto him, "We are come
down to bind thee, that we may deliver thee
into the hand of the Philistines." And Samson
said unto them, "Swear unto me, that ye will
not fall upon me yourselves."
13 And they spake unto him, saying, "No;
but we will bind thee fast, and deliver thee
into their hand: but surely we will not kill
thee." And they bound him with two new
cords, and brought him up from the rock.
i 14 *And* when he came unto Lehi, the Philistines shouted ° against him: and ° the Spirit of
° the LORD came mightily upon him, and the
cords that *were* upon his arms became as flax
that was burnt with fire, and his bands loosed
from off his hands.
15 And he found a new ° jawbone of an ass,
and put forth his hand, and took it, and slew
a thousand [10] men therewith.
16 And Samson said,
°"With the jawbone of an ass,
Heaps upon heaps,
With the jaw of an ass
Have I slain a thousand [10] men."
g 17 And it came to pass, when he had made
an end of speaking, that he cast away the
jawbone out of his hand, and called that place
° Ramath-lehi.
f 18 And he was sore athirst, and called on
[14] the LORD, and said, "Thou hast given this
great deliverance into the hand of Thy servant: and now shall I die for thirst, and fall
into the hand of the uncircumcised?"
19 But ° God ° clave an hollow place that *was*
in the jaw, and there came water thereout;
and when he had drunk, his ° spirit came again,
and he revived:
g wherefore he called the name thereof ° En-
hakkore, which *is* in Lehi unto this day.
O 20 And he judged Israel in the days of the
(p. 346) 1120-1100 Philistines ° twenty years.

A j[1] k (p. 348) **16** ° Then went Samson to ° Gaza, and saw
there ° an harlot, and went in unto her.
l 2 *And it was told* the Gazites, saying,
"Samson is come hither." And they compassed *him* in, and laid wait for him all night
in the gate of the city,
l and were quiet all the night, saying, "In the
morning, when it is day, we shall kill him."
k 3 And Samson lay till midnight, and arose
at midnight, and ° took the doors of the gate
of the city, and the two posts, and went away
with them, bar and all, and put *them* upon his
shoulders, and carried them up to the top of
° an hill that *is* ° before Hebron.
4 And it came to pass afterward, that he j[2] m
loved a woman in the valley of Sorek, whose
name *was* Delilah.
5 And the ° lords of the Philistines came up n
unto her, and said unto her, "Entice him, and
see wherein his great strength *lieth*, and by
what *means* we may prevail against him, that
we may bind him to ° afflict him: and we will
give thee every one of us ° eleven hundred
pieces of silver."

9 pitched = camped.
10 men. Heb. *'ish.* Ap. 14. II.
as = according as.
14 against = at meeting him, or to meet him.
the Spirit. Heb. *rūach.* Ap. 9. No art. here.
the LORD. Heb. Jehovah. Ap. 4. II.
15 jawbone of an ass. One of the seven "weak things" in Judges. See note on 3. 21.
16 With. Note the *alternation* of four lines. Another pointing of the second line given in Sept. is, *chāmōr chămartīm* = "destroying I destroyed them", which by Fig. *Polyptōton* (Ap. 6) = I utterly destroyed them. There is also the Fig. *Antanaclasis* (Ap. 6) in the words *chāmōr*, "ass", and "destroyed".
17 Ramath-lehi = the uplifting of the jawbone.
19 God. Heb. *Elohim.* Ap. 4. I. Not Jehovah. A sign of distant or withdrawn relationship. In 13. 24, 25, and 14. 4, 6, we have Jehovah, but not again in Samson's history till he is humbled, 16. 20; then he prays to Jehovah, *v.* 28.
clave an hollow place that was in the jaw = clave open the hollow that is in Lehi.
spirit = courage. Heb. *rūach.* Ap. 9.
En-hakkore = the Caller's Fount.
20 twenty. See note on 13. 24.

16. 1-20 (*A*, p. 346). HARLOTS.
(*Division.*)

A | j[1] | 1-3. In Gaza.
  | j[2] | 4-20. In Sorek.

1-3 (j[1], above). IN GAZA.
(*Introversion.*)

j[1] | k | 1. Samson. Harlot of Gaza.
  | l | 2-. Information given. } Gazites.
  | *l* | -2. Expectation roused. } Gazites.
  | *k* | 3. Samson. Gates of Gaza.

1 Then = and.
Gaza. About thirty-five miles south of his native place.
an harlot. He could rend a lion, but not his lusts. He could break his bonds, but not his habits. He could conquer the Philistines, but not his passions. Now *Ghuzzeh.*
3 took the doors: i.e. unhinged both leaves. Cp. Isa. 45. 1. **an hill** = the hill.
before = over against.

4-20 (j[2], above). IN SOREK. (*Introversion.*)

j[2] | m | 4. Samson. Gaza to Sorek.
  | n | 5. Delilah's bribe.
  | *n* | 6-20. Delilah's snares.
  | *m* | 21-31-. Samson. Sorek to Gaza.

5 lords. See note on Josh. 13. 3.
afflict = humble.
eleven hundred. One of the two occurrences of this number. Eleven = the number of *defective administration* (= 12 − 1. See Ap. 10). Cp. 17. 2, where similar want of rule is seen. This 1,100 ruined them politically; the other (17. 2) ruined them religiously.

n o^1 p^1 q^1 (p. 349) 1120 to 1100 **6 And Delilah said to Samson, "Tell me,**
I pray thee, wherein thy great strength *lieth,*
and wherewith thou mightest be bound to
afflict thee."

r^1 **7 And Samson said unto her, "If they bind**
me with seven °green withs that were never
dried, then shall I be weak, and be as another
°man."

s^1 **8 Then the lords of the Philistines brought**
up to her seven green [7]withs which had not
been dried, and she bound him with them.

t^1 **9 Now *there were* men lying in wait, abiding**
with her in the chamber. And she said unto
him, "The Philistines *be* upon thee, Samson."
And he °brake the [7]withs, °as a thread of
°tow is broken when it °toucheth the fire. So
his strength was not known.

p^2 q^2 **10 And Delilah said unto Samson, °"Behold,**
thou hast mocked me, and told me lies: now
tell me, I pray thee, wherewith thou mightest
be bound."

r^2 **11 And he said unto her, "If they bind me**
fast with new ropes that never were occupied,
then shall I be weak, and be as another
[7]man."

s^2 **12 Delilah therefore took new ropes, and**
bound him therewith, and said unto him,
"The Philistines *be* upon thee, Samson."
And *there were* liers in wait abiding in the
chamber.

t^2 **And he [9]brake them from off his arms like**
a thread.

p^3 q^3 **13 And Delilah said unto Samson, "Hitherto**
thou hast mocked me, and told me lies: °tell
me wherewith thou mightest be bound."

r^3 **And he said unto her, "If thou weavest the**
seven locks of my head °with the web."

s^3 **14 And she fastened *it* with the pin, and said**
unto him, "The Philistines *be* upon thee,
Samson."

t^3 **And he awaked °out of his sleep, and went**
away with the pin of the beam, and with the
web.

o^2 u **15 And she said unto him, °"How canst thou**
say, 'I love thee,' when thine heart *is* not
with me? thou hast mocked me these three
times, and hast not told me wherein thy great
strength *lieth.*"
16 And it came to pass, when she pressed
him daily with her words, and urged him, *so*
that his °soul was °vexed °unto death;
17 That he told her all his heart, and said
unto her, "There hath not come a rasor upon
mine head; for *I have been* °a Nazarite unto
°God from my mother's womb: if I be shaven,
then my strength will go from me, and I shall
become weak, and be like any *other* [7]man."
18 And when Delilah saw that he had told
her all his heart, she sent and called for the
[5]lords of the Philistines, saying, "Come up this
once, for he hath shewed me all his heart."
Then the [5]lords of the Philistines came up unto
her, and brought money in their hand.

v **19 And she made him sleep upon her knees;**
and she called for a °man, and she caused him
to shave off the seven locks of his head; and
she began to afflict him, and his strength went
from him.

20 And she said, "The Philistines *be* upon *v*
thee, Samson." And he awoke out of his
sleep, and said, "I will go out as at other
times before, and shake myself."

And *He* °wist not that °the LORD was de- *u*
parted from him.

---

16. 6-20 (*n*, p. 348). DELILAH'S SNARES.
(*Division.*)

n | o^1 | 6-14. Delilah's attempts. Failure.
| o^2 | 15-20. Delilah's attempts. Success.

6-14 (o^1, above). DELILAH'S FAILURE.
(*Repeated and Extended Alternation.*)

o^1 | p^1 | q^1 | 6. Binding.
r^1 | 7. Means. Green withs.
s^1 | 8. Used.
t^1 | 9. Broken.
p^2 | q^2 | 10. Binding.
r^2 | 11. Means. New ropes.
s^2 | 12-. Used.
t^2 | -12. Broken.
p^3 | q^3 | 13-. Binding.
r^3 | -13. Means. Web and pin.
s^3 | 14-. Used.
t^3 | -14. Carried away.

7 green withs = green twigs. Anglo-Saxon, a willow, because of its twining and flexibility.
man. Heb. *'ādām.* Ap. 14. I.
9 brake = snapped.
as = according as.
tow. Old English. Coarse flax or hemp for spinning or twining. Occurs only here and Isa. 1. 31. Very inflammable.
toucheth = smelleth (before it toucheth).
10 Behold. Fig. *Asterismos.* Ap. 6.
13 tell me. Some codices, with one early printed edition, and Sept. add "I pray thee".
with the web. Note the *Homœoteleuton.* In the primitive text these words were probably followed by "and fasten them with a pin". For the Sept. adds "I shall be as another man. And it came to pass that when he was asleep that Delilah took the seven locks of his head and wove them with the web, and she fastened them with a pin". Ginsburg suggests that some ancient scribe, in copying the first words, "fasten them with a pin", carried his eye back to these last words, and omitted the whole of this clause, which has been preserved in the Sept.
14 out of his sleep: i.e. the sleep mentioned in the *Homœoteleuton* above.

15-20 (o^2, above). DELILAH'S SUCCESS.
(*Introversion.*)

o^2 | u | 15-18. Strength. Secret given.
v | 19. Sleeping.
v | 20-. Waking.
u | -20. Strength. Secret gone.

15 How ...? Fig. *Erotēsis.* Ap. 6.
16 soul. Heb. *nephesh.* Ap. 13.
vexed. Became impatient, or grieved.
unto death = to make him die.
17 a Nazarite unto God = separate unto God.
God. Heb. Elohim. Ap. 4. I.
19 man. Heb. *'īsh.* Ap. 14. II.
20 wist not = knew not. See note on Ex. 34. 29.
the LORD. Heb. Jehovah. Ap. 4. II. Since 14. 6, only *'Elohim.* See note on 15. 19.

B *m* w (p. 350) 1120-1100 21 But the Philistines took him, and put out his eyes, and brought him down to Gaza, and bound him with °fetters of brass;

x and he did °grind in the prison house.

y 22 Howbeit the hair of his head began to grow again after he was shaven.

z 23 Then the [5] lords of the Philistines gathered them together for to °offer a great sacrifice unto Dagon their god, and °to rejoice: for they said, "Our god hath delivered Samson our enemy into our hand."

24 And when the people saw him, they praised their god: for they said, "Our god hath delivered into our hands our enemy, and the destroyer of our country, which slew many of us."

z 25 And it came to pass, when their hearts were merry, that they said, "Call for Samson, that he may °make us sport." And they called for Samson out of the prison house; and he made °them sport: and they set him between the pillars.

26 And Samson said unto the lad that held him by the hand, °"Suffer me that I may feel the pillars whereupon the house standeth, that I may lean upon them."

27 Now the house was full of °men and women; and all the lords of the Philistines *were* there; and *there were* upon the roof about three thousand °men and women, that beheld while Samson made sport.

y 28 And Samson called unto [20] the LORD, and said, "O °Lord °GOD, remember me, I pray Thee, and strengthen me, I pray Thee, only this once, O [17] God, that I may be at once avenged of the Philistines for my two eyes."

x 29 And Samson took hold of °the two middle pillars upon which the house stood, and on which it was borne up, of the one with his right hand, and of the other with his left.

30 And Samson said, "Let °me die with the Philistines." And he bowed himself with *all his* might; and the house fell upon the lords, and upon all the people that *were* therein. So the dead which he slew at his death were more than *they* which he slew in his life.

w 31 Then °his brethren and all the house of his father came down, and took him, and brought *him* °up, and buried him °between Zorah and Eshtaol in the buryingplace of Manoah his father.

K (p. 344) 1120-1100 And he °judged Israel twenty years.

C A[1] a (p. 350) **17** And there was a °man of °mount Ephraim, whose name *was* Micah.

2 And he said unto his mother, "The °eleven hundred *shekels* of silver that were °taken from thee, about which thou cursedst, and spakest of also in mine ears, °behold, the silver *is* with me; I took it." And his mother said, "Blessed *be thou* of °the LORD, my son."

3 And when he had restored the eleven hundred *shekels* of silver to his mother, his mother said, "I had °wholly dedicated the silver unto [2] the LORD from my hand for my son, to make a graven image and a molten image: now therefore I will restore it unto thee."

4 Yet he restored the °money unto his mother; and his mother took two hundred

---

21 fetters of brass. Heb. "two brasses". Put by Fig. *Metonymy* (of Cause), for the two fetters made of brass. Ap. 6.

grind. The work of women and slaves. Denotes the condition to which he was reduced. Cp. Ex. 11. 5. Isa. 47. 2.

16. 21-31 (*B*, p. 346). **SLAUGHTER IN DEATH.** (*Introversion.*)

B | w | 21-. Servitude.
  x | -21. Prison-house. Labour.
   y | 22. Hair growing.
    z | 23, 24. Festival.
    z | 25-27. Sport.
   y | 28. Strength restored.
  x | 29, 30. Prison-house. Destruction.
 w | 31-. Burial.

23 offer. Heb. "slay". See Ap. 43. I. v.

to rejoice. Fig. *Antimereia* (of Noun). Ap. 6. Noun "rejoicing", put for verb "to rejoice" = for a rejoicing.

25 make us sport. Some codices, with one early printed edition, Sept., Syr., and Vulg., read "make sport before us".

them sport = sport before them.

26 Suffer me that = Let me alone that, &c.

27 men. Heb. *'ish* or *'enōsh*. Ap. 14.

28 Lord GOD = Adonai Jehovah. Ap. 4. VIII (2) and II.

29 the two middle pillars. Recent excavations at Gaza have laid bare two smooth stone bases close together in the centre, on (not in) which these two pillars stood. On these the main beams rested, and by which the whole house was sustained. Samson had only to pull these pillars out of the perpendicular, to effect his object.

30 me = my soul. Heb. *nephesh.* Ap. 13.

31 his brethren. Probably his parents were now dead.

up: i.e. from Gaza, *v.* 21.

between Zorah and Eshtaol. Where the Spirit had first come upon him, 13. 25.

judged Israel. But he only *began* to deliver Israel. See 13. 5.

17. 1—18. 31 (*C*, p. 323). **ISRAEL AND OTHER PEOPLES. AGGRESSIONS.** (*Division.*)

C | A[1] | 17. 1—18. 1-. The idolatry of Micah.
  | A[2] | 18. -1-31. Aggression of Danites.

17. 1—18. 1- (A[1], above). **IDOLATRY OF MICAH.** (*Extended Alternation.*)

A[1] | a | 17. 1-4. Micah's house. Fabrication of image.
  b | 17. 5. Consecration of his son.
   c | 17. 6. "No king".
 a | 17. 7-11. Micah's house. Arrival of Levite.
  b | 17. 12, 13. Consecration of Levite.
   c | 18. 1-. "No king".

1 man. Heb. *'ish.* Ap. 14. II.

mount = hill country of Ephraim, where Joshua dwelt and was buried (Josh. 24. 30).

2 eleven hundred. See note on 16. 5.

taken. Idolatry in Israel commenced with dishonesty.

behold. Fig. *Asterismos.* Ap. 6.

the LORD. Heb. Jehovah. Ap. 4. II.

3 wholly dedicated. Fig. *Polyptōton* (Ap. 6). Heb. "dedicating I had dedicated it".

4 money = silver (*v.* 2).

1423 to 1383 *shekels* of silver, and gave them to the founder, who made thereof [3]a graven image and a molten image: and they were in the house of Micah.

b (p. 350) 5 And the [1]man Micah had an °house of gods, and made an °ephod, and teraphim, and °consecrated one of his sons, who became °his priest.

c 6 In those days *there was* °no king in Israel, *but* [1]every man did *that which was* right in his own eyes.

a 7 And there was °a young man out of °Beth-lehem-judah of the family of Judah, who *was* a Levite, and he sojourned there.

8 And the man departed out of the city from [7]Beth-lehem-judah °to sojourn where he could find *a place:* and he came to [1]mount Ephraim to the house of Micah, as he journeyed.

9 And Micah said unto him, "Whence comest thou?" And he said unto him, "I *am* a Levite of Beth-lehem-judah, and I go [8]to sojourn where I may find *a place.*"

10 And Micah said unto him, "Dwell with me, and be unto me a father and a priest, and I will give thee ten *shekels* of silver by the year, and a suit of apparel, and thy victuals." So the Levite went in.

11 And the Levite was content to dwell with the [1]man; and [7]the young man was unto him as one of his sons.

b 12 And Micah [5]consecrated the Levite; and [7]the young man became °his priest, and was in the house of Micah.

13 Then said Micah, "Now know I that [2]the LORD will °do me good, seeing I have a Levite to *my* priest."

c **18** In °those days *there was* °no king in Israel:

A² d (p. 351) and in those days the tribe of the °Danites sought them an inheritance to dwell in; for unto that day *all their* inheritance had not fallen unto them among the tribes of Israel.

e f 2 And the °children of Dan sent of their family five °men from their °coasts, °men of valour, from Zorah, and from Eshtaol, to spy out the land, and to search it; and they said unto them, "Go, search the land:" who when they came to °mount Ephraim, to the house of Micah, they lodged there.

3 When they *were* by the house of Micah, they knew the voice of °the young man the Levite: and they turned in thither, and said unto him, "Who brought thee hither? and what °makest thou in this *place?* and what hast thou here?"

4 And he said unto them, "Thus and thus dealeth Micah with me, and hath hired me, and I am his priest."

5 And they said unto him, °"Ask counsel, we pray thee, of °God, that we may know whether our way which we go shall be prosperous."

6 And the priest said unto them, "Go in peace: before °the LORD *is* your way wherein ye go."

g 7 Then the five [2]men departed, and came to °Laish, and saw the people that *were* therein, how they dwelt careless, after the manner of the Zidonians, °quiet and secure; and *there was* no magistrate in the land, that might put *them* to shame in *any* thing; and they *were* far from the Zidonians, and had no business with *any* °man.

8 And they came unto their brethren to Zorah and Eshtaol: and their brethren said unto them, "What *say* ye?"

9 And they said, "Arise, that we may go up against them: for we have seen the land, and, °behold, it *is* very good: and *are* ye still? be not slothful to go, *and* to enter to possess the land.

10 When ye go, ye shall come unto a people secure, and to a large land: for [5]God hath given it into your hands; a place where *there is* no want of any thing that *is* in the earth."

---

5 house of gods. The true house of God was neglected, and as hard to find as it is to-day (21. 19); and, when found, dancing was the prominent feature, not sacrifice or worship (21. 21-23).
ephod. In imitation of Aaron's. Ex. 25. 7; 28. 4.
consecrated. See note on Ex. 28. 41. Lev. 9. 17.
his priest. Not Jehovah's, but "made with hands".
6 no king. First occurrence of four, see 18. 1; 19. 1; 21. 25. Two conform to the structure here; and two in chs. 19. 1, and 21. 25.
7 a young man. See note on 18. 30.
Beth-lehem-Judah. To distinguish it from Beth-lehem in Zebulun (Josh. 19. 15).
8 to sojourn. True worship neglected. Priests and Levites unemployed. Idolaters busy making idols and dancing.
12 his priest. Not Jehovah's; see on *v.* 5.
13 do me good. The "good" (as in all such cases) never came. For Micah is afterward robbed both of his idols and his priest.

18. -1-31 (A², p. 350). AGGRESSION OF DANITES.
(*Introversion and Alternation.*)

A² | d | -1. Danites. Inheritance.
  e | f | 2-6. Mission of spies.
     g | 7-10. Security of Laish.
  e | f | 11-26. Expedition of Danites.
     g | 27-29. Conquest of Laish.
 d | 30, 31. Danites. Idolatry.

1 those days. Chs. 17—21 thought by some to record earlier events in the days of Othniel by Fig. *Hysterēsis* (Ap. 6). See note on 17. 1, and Structure.
no king. No true "house of God" religiously (17. 5), leads to "no king" nationally (18. 1); and nationally to apostasy. See note on *v.* 6, above.
Danites. See note on Gen. 49. 17.
2 children = sons.
men. Heb. pl. of *'ĕnōsh.* Ap. 14. III.
coasts = borders.
men of valour = sons of valour.
mount = hill country of.
3 the young man. Cp. 17. 7.
makest = doest.
5 Ask counsel. By the use of the ephod. See 17. 5.
God. Heb. Elohim. Ap. 4. I. Not Jehovah. Ap. 4. II.
6 the LORD. Heb. Jehovah. Ap. 4. II.
7 Laish. Called Leshem. Josh. 19. 47.
quiet and secure. Probably arising from the enervating effects of malaria now endemic there. If so, it may be identified with *Tel-el-kadi* in the fever-ridden district at the head of the Jordan.
man = Heb. *'ādām.* Ap. 14. I.
9 behold. Fig. *Asterismos.* Ap. 6.

e f h
(p. 352)
1423
to
1383

11 And there went from thence of the family of the ¹ Danites, out of Zorah and out of Eshtaol, six hundred ° men ° appointed with weapons of war.

12 And they went up, and pitched in Kirjath-jearim, in Judah: wherefore they called that place ° Mahaneh-dan unto this day: ⁹ behold, *it is* behind Kirjath-jearim.

13 And they passed thence unto ² mount Ephraim, and came unto the house of Micah.

i 14 Then answered the five ² men that went to spy out the country of Laish, and said unto their brethren, ° " Do ye know that there is in these houses an ephod, and teraphim, and a graven image, and a molten image? now therefore consider what ye have to do."

15 And they turned thitherward, and came to the house of ³ the young man the Levite, *even* unto the house of Micah, and saluted him.

16 And the six hundred ¹¹ men ¹¹ appointed with their weapons of war, which *were* of the ² children of Dan, stood by the entering of the gate.

17 And the five ² men that went to spy out the land went up, *and* came in thither, *and* took the graven image, and the ephod, and the teraphim, and the molten image: and the priest stood in the entering of the gate with the six hundred ¹¹ men *that were* ¹¹ appointed with weapons of war.

18 And these went into Micah's house, and fetched the carved image, ° the ephod, and the teraphim, and the molten image. Then said the priest unto them, " What do ye?"

19 And they said unto him, " Hold thy peace, ° lay thine hand upon thy mouth, and go with us, and be to us a father and a priest: *is it* ° better for thee to be a priest unto the house of one man, or that thou be a priest unto a tribe and a family in Israel?"

20 And the priest's heart was glad, and he took the ephod, ° and the teraphim, and the graven image, and went in the midst of the people.

h 21 So they turned and departed, and put the little ones and the cattle and the ° carriage before them.

i 22 *And* when they were a good way from the house of Micah, ⁵ the men that *were* in the houses near to Micah's house were gathered together, and overtook the ² children of ¹ Dan.

23 And they cried unto the ² children of ¹ Dan. And they turned their faces, and said unto Micah, " What aileth thee, ° that thou comest with such a company?"

24 And he said, " Ye have taken away my gods which I made, and the priest, and ye are gone away: and what have I more? and what *is* this *that* ye say unto me, ' What aileth thee?'"

25 And the ² children of ¹ Dan said unto him, " Let not thy voice be heard among us, lest angry fellows run upon thee, and thou lose thy ° life, with the ° lives of thy household."

26 And the ² children of ¹ Dan went their way: and when Micah saw that they *were* too strong for him, he turned and went back unto his house.

18. 11-26 (*f*, p. 351). EXPEDITION OF DANITES.
(*Alternation*.)

f | h | 11-13. Expedition.
  | i | 14-20. Interview with Levite.
  | h | 21. Expedition.
  | i | 22-26. Interview with Micah.

11 men. Heb. ʾ*ish*. Ap. 14. II.
appointed = girded.
12 Mahaneh-dan = camp of Dan (13. 25).
14 Do ye know ... ? Fig. *Erotêsis*. Ap. 6.
18 the ephod. Sept. reads "and the ephod". Cp. *v.* 17. The Heb. text has "the carved image of the ephod".
19 lay thine hand, &c. Put by Fig. *Metonymy* (of Adjunct) for "be silent". Ap. 6.
better. Man's priest soon gets promotion.
20 and. Note the Fig. *Polysyndeton*. Ap. 6.
21 carriage = goods. Put by Fig. *Metonymy* (of Adjunct) for things carried.
23 that thou comest, &c. Heb. "that thou hast called thyself out".
25 life = soul. Heb. *nephesh*. Ap. 13.
lives = souls. Heb. *nephesh*. Ap. 13.
27 unto. Some codices, with one early printed edition, and Sept. read "as far as".
28 business = dealings.
29 after the name. Cp. Josh. 19.
30 set up. On account of this, Dan is not named in Rev. 7, and Ephraim is there merged in Joseph.
Manasseh. This word is one of the four that has a suspended letter. Here the letter (נ), *nun* (n), is written partly in the line and partly above the line, to show that originally it formed no part of the word, but was put in to make it spell "Manasseh" instead of "Moses". Jonathan was the grandson of Moses (his contemporary Phinehas, the grandson of Aaron, being mentioned in 20. 28). This was done for two reasons: (1) to spare the honour of Moses' memory and name; (2) to put the sin upon one who committed so gross a sin. The Talmud gives this latter as the reason. Jonathan's name is omitted in 1 Chron. 23. 15, 16, and 26. 24. The Chald. paraphrase says that "Shebuel", there substituted, is meant for Jonathan after his repentance and restoration. Shebuel = " he returned to God". The A.V. follows Sept. and Chald. by putting "Manasseh" in the text; R.V. follows Vulg., and those codices and early editions which have "n" suspended, by putting "Moses" in the text and "Manasseh" in the margin.

27 And they took *the things* which Micah had made, and the priest which he had, and came ° unto Laish, unto a people *that were* at quiet and secure: and they smote them with the edge of the sword, and burnt the city with fire. *g* (p. 351)

28 And *there was* no deliverer, because it *was* far from Zidon, and they had no ° business with *any* ⁷ man; and it was in the valley that *lieth* by Beth-rehob. And they built a city, and dwelt therein.

29 And they called the name of the city ¹ Dan, ° after the name of ¹ Dan their father, who was born unto Israel: howbeit the name of the city *was* Laish at the first.

30 And the children of ¹ Dan ° set up the graven image: and Jonathan, the son of Gershom, the son of ° Manasseh, he and his sons were priests to the tribe of Dan until the day of the captivity of the land. *d*

31 And they ³⁰ set them up Micah's graven

1423 to 1383 image, which he made, all the time that °the house of °God was in °Shiloh.

B A (p. 353) **19** And it came to pass °in those days, when *there was* °no king in Israel,

C a that there was °a certain Levite sojourning on the side of °mount Ephraim, who took to him a concubine out of Beth-lehem-judah.

2 And his concubine played the whore against him, and went away from him unto her father's house to Beth-lehem-judah, and was there °four whole months.

3 And her husband arose, and went after her, to speak °friendly unto her, *and* to bring her again, having his servant with him, and a couple of asses: and she brought him into her father's house: and when the father of the damsel saw him, he rejoiced to meet him.

4 And his father in law, the damsel's father, retained him; and he abode with him three days: so they did eat and drink, and lodged there.

5 And it came to pass on the fourth day, when they arose early in the morning, that he rose up to depart: and the damsel's father said unto his son in law, "Comfort thine heart with a morsel of bread, and afterward go your way."

6 And they sat down, and did eat and drink both of them together: for the damsel's father had said unto the °man, "Be content, I pray thee, and tarry all night, and let thine heart be merry."

7 And when the [6]man rose up to depart, his father in law urged him: therefore he lodged there again.

8 And he arose early in the morning on the fifth day to depart: and the damsel's father said, "Comfort thine heart, I pray thee." And they tarried until afternoon, and they did eat both of them.

9 And when the [6]man rose up to depart, he, and his concubine, and his servant, his father in law, the damsel's father, said unto him, °"Behold, now the day draweth toward evening, I pray you tarry all night: behold, the day groweth to an end, lodge here, that thine heart may be merry; and to morrow get you early on your way, that thou mayest go home."

b 10 But the [6]man would not tarry that night, but he rose up and departed, and came over against °Jebus, which *is* Jerusalem; and *there were* with him two asses saddled, his concubine also *was* with him.

11 *And* when they *were* by [10]Jebus, the day was far spent; and the servant said unto his master, "Come, I pray thee, and let us turn in into this city of the Jebusites, and lodge in it."

12 And his master said unto him, "We will not turn aside hither into the city of a stranger, that *is* not of the °children of Israel; we will pass over to °Gibeah."

13 And he said unto his servant, "Come, and let us draw near to one of these places to lodge all night, in Gibeah, or in Ramah."

14 And they passed on and went their way; and the sun went down upon them *when they were* by Gibeah, which *belongeth* to Benjamin.

31 the house of God: i.e. the Tabernacle of Moses, but not recognised as the house of Jehovah, the Covenant God.

God. Heb. *hā-'Ĕlohim* = the [true] God. Ap. 4.

Shiloh. First of five occurrences in Judges, cp. 21. 12, 19, 21, 21. For the eight occurrences in Joshua see note on Josh. 18. 1.

19. 1—21. 25 (*B*, p. 323). INTERNAL DISORDERS. (*Introversion and Alternation.*)

B | A | 19. 1-. "No king".
| B | C | 19. -1-28. The Provocation.
| | D | 19. 29—20. 11. Resentment.
| *B* | *C* | 20. 12-46. The civil war.
| | *D* | 20. 47—21. 24. The Regret.
| *A* | 21. 25. "No king".

19. -1-28 (C, above). THE PROVOCATION. (*Alternation.*)

C | a | -1-9. At father-in-law's house.
| b | 10-15. Journey.
| *a* | 16-26. At old man's house.
| *b* | 27, 28. Journey.

1 in those days. In the same days as ch. 18. 1. Soon after the death of Joshua. Fig. *Hysterologia.* Ap. 6.

no king. See note on 18. 1.

a certain Levite. The house of God neglected. Priests and Levites unemployed and wandering about. Cp. 17. 7.

mount = the hill country of.

2 four whole months. Heb. "days, four months", so some think = "a year and four months".

3 friendly. Heb. "to her heart" = affectionately.

6 man. Heb. *'ish.* Ap. 14. II.

9 Behold. Fig. *Asterismos.* Ap. 6.

10 Jebus. At that time still occupied by Canaanites. See Josh. 10. 1; 15. 63.

12 children = sons.

Gibeah. City of Benjamin; later, the residence of Saul (1 Sam. 10. 26; 11. 4).

15 street = open place.

16 men. Heb. *'ěnōsh.* Ap. 14. III.

18 going. His direction was towards mount Ephraim, not to Shiloh!

the house of the LORD. So Micah's temple was already called. Cp. 18. 31.

the LORD. Heb. Jehovah. Ap. 4. II.

19 servants. Some codices, with three early printed editions, Aram., and Syr., read "servant" (Singular).

15 And they turned aside thither, to go in *and* to lodge in Gibeah: and when he went in, he sat him down in a °street of the city: for *there was* no [6]man that took them into his house to lodging.

16 And, [9]behold, there came an old [6]man from his work out of the field at even, which *was* also of mount Ephraim; and he sojourned in Gibeah: but the °men of the place *were* Benjamites. *a*

17 And when he had lifted up his eyes, he saw a wayfaring [6]man in the street of the city: and the old [6]man said, "Whither goest thou? and whence comest thou?"

18 And he said unto him, "We *are* passing from Beth-lehem-judah toward the side of mount Ephraim; from thence *am* I: and I went to Beth-lehem-judah, but I *am now* °going to °the house of °the LORD; and there *is* no [6]man that receiveth me to house.

19 Yet there is both straw and provender for our asses; and there is bread and wine also for me, and for thy handmaid, and for the young man *which is* with thy °servants: *there is* no want of any thing."

20 And the old [6]man said, "Peace *be* with

1423 to 1383 thee; howsoever *let* all thy wants *lie* upon me; only lodge not in the street."

21 So he brought him into his house, and gave provender unto the asses: and they washed their feet, and did eat and drink.

22 *Now* as they were making their hearts merry, [9]behold, the [16]men of the city, certain °sons of Belial, beset the house round about, *and* beat at the °door, and spake to the master of the house, the old [6]man, saying, "Bring forth the [16]man that came into thine house, that we may know him."

23 And °the [6]man, the master of the house, went out unto them, and said unto them, "Nay, my brethren, *nay*, I pray you, do not *so* °wickedly; seeing that this [6]man is come into mine house, do not this folly.

24 °Behold, *here is* my daughter a maiden, and his concubine; them I will bring out now, and humble ye them, and do with them what seemeth good unto you: but unto this [6]man do not so vile a thing."

25 But the [16]men would not hearken to him: so the [6]man took his concubine, and brought her forth unto them; and they knew her, and abused her all the night until the morning: and when the day began to spring, they let her go.

26 Then came the woman in the dawning of the day, and fell down at the °door of the [6]man's house where her lord *was*, till it was light.

b (p. 353) 27 And her lord rose up in the morning, and opened the doors of the house, and went out to go his way: and, [24]behold, the woman his concubine was fallen down *at* the door of the house, and her hands *were* upon the threshold.

28 And he said unto her, "Up, and let us be going." But none answered. Then the man took her *up* upon °an ass, and the man rose up, and gat him unto his place.

D c (p. 354) 29 And when he was come into his house, he took a knife, and laid hold on his concubine, and divided her, *together* with her bones, into twelve pieces, and sent her into all the °coasts of Israel.

30 And it was so, that all that saw it said, "There was °no such deed done nor seen from the day that the [12]children of Israel came up out of the land of Egypt unto this day: consider of it, take advice, and speak *your minds*."

d **20** °Then all the °children of Israel went out, and the congregation was gathered together °as one °man, from Dan even to Beer-sheba, with the land of Gilead, unto °the LORD in Mizpeh.

2 And the chief of all the people, *even* of all the tribes of Israel, presented themselves in the assembly of the people of °God, four hundred thousand footmen that drew sword.

3 (°Now the [1]children of Benjamin heard that the [1]children of Israel were gone up to °Mizpeh.) Then said the [1]children of Israel, "Tell *us*, how was this °wickedness?"

c 4 And °the Levite, the husband of the woman that was slain, answered and said, "I came into Gibeah that *belongeth* to Benjamin, I and my concubine, to lodge.

22 sons of Belial = worthless scoundrels, sons of the devil.

door. Like Sodom (Gen. 19. 4), a sign of the moral corruption which follows apostasy and accompanies idolatry.

23 the man. Another Lot in another Sodom.

wickedly. Heb. *rā'a'*. Ap. 44. viii.

24 Behold. Fig. *Asterismos*. Ap. 6.

26 door = entrance. **28 an** = the.

19. 29—20. 11 (D, p. 353). **RESENTMENT.**
(*Alternation.*)

D | c | 19. 29, 30. Message to tribes.
  | d | 20. 1-3. Unanimity.
  | c | 20. 4-7. Recital to tribes.
  | *d* | 20. 8-11. Unanimity.

29 coasts = borders.

30 no such deed done. "The days of Gibeah" became proverbial. Cp. Hos. 9. 9; 10. 9.

20. 1 Then. These chapters (20, 21), by Fig. *Hysterologia* (Ap. 6), describe events which took place soon after Joshua's death. See notes on 18. 1 and 19. 1.

children = sons.

as one man. All this excitement, unanimity, and bloodshed about an injury done to a woman; no sense of the evil of idolatry and sin against God, recorded in ch. 19. **man.** Heb. *'ish*. Ap. 14. II.

the LORD. Heb. Jehovah. Ap. 4. II.

2 God. Heb. *hā-'Elohim* = the [true] God. Ap. 14. See note on 18. 31.

3 Now. Note the Fig. *Parenthesis* in this verse. Ap. 6.

Mizpeh on the south-west border of Benjamin, not Mizpeh on the east of Jordan (10. 17; 11. 11, 29).

wickedness. Heb. *rā'a'*. Ap. 44. viii.

4 the Levite. Heb. = "the man, the Levite".

5 men = masters or head-men.

7 Behold. Fig. *Asterismos*. Ap. 6.

10 men. Heb. *'ěnōsh*. Ap. 14. III.

11 men. Heb. *'ish*. Ap. 14. II.

12-46 [For Structures see next page].

5 And the °men of Gibeah rose against me, and beset the house round about upon me by night, *and* thought to have slain me: and my concubine have they forced, that she is dead.

6 And I took my concubine, and cut her in pieces, and sent her throughout all the country of the inheritance of Israel: for they have committed lewdness and folly in Israel.

7 °Behold, ye *are* all [1]children of Israel; give here your advice and counsel."

8 And all the people arose as one [1]man, *d*
saying, "We will not any *of us* go to his tent, neither will we any *of us* turn into his house.

9 But now this *shall be* the thing which we will do to Gibeah; *we will go up* by lot against it;

10 And we will take ten °men of an hundred throughout all the tribes of Israel, and an hundred of a thousand, and a thousand out of ten thousand, to fetch victual for the People, that they may do, when they come to Gibeah of Benjamin, according to all the folly that they have wrought in Israel."

11 So all the °men of Israel were gathered against the city, knit together as one [1]man.

12 And the tribes of Israel sent [10]men through *C* E e (p. 355)
all the tribe of Benjamin, saying, "What [3]wickedness *is* this that is done among you?

f (p. 355) 1423 to 1383 13 Now therefore deliver *us* the [10]men, the [1]children of Belial, which *are* in Gibeah, that we may put them to death, and put away evil from Israel."

f But the [1]children of Benjamin would not hearken to the voice of their brethren the [1]children of Israel:

e 14 But the [1]children of Benjamin gathered themselves together out of the cities unto Gibeah, to go out to battle against the [1]children of Israel.

F 15 And the [1]children of Benjamin were numbered at that time out of the cities twenty and six thousand °men that drew sword, beside the inhabitants of Gibeah, which were numbered seven hundred chosen °men.

16 Among all this people *there were* seven hundred chosen men °lefthanded; every one could sling stones at an °hair °*breadth*, and not °miss.

F 17 And the [15]men of Israel, beside Benjamin, were numbered four hundred thousand men that drew sword: all these *were* men of war.

G[1] g i 18 And the [1]children of Israel arose, and went up to the house of °God, and asked counsel of °God, and said, "Which of us shall go up first to the battle against the [1]children of Benjamin?" And [1]the LORD said, "Judah *shall go up* first."

k 19 And the [1]children of Israel rose up in the morning, and encamped against Gibeah.

20 And the men of Israel went out to battle against Benjamin; and the men of Israel put themselves in array to fight against them at Gibeah.

h 21 And the [1]children of Benjamin came forth out of Gibeah, and destroyed down to the ground of the Israelites that day twenty and two thousand men.

g k 22 And the People the [15]men of Israel encouraged themselves, and set their battle again in array in the place where they put themselves in array the first day.

i 23 (°And the [1]children of Israel went up and wept °before [1]the LORD until even, and °asked counsel of [1]the LORD, saying, "Shall I go up again to battle against the children of Benjamin my brother?" And [1]the LORD said, "Go up against him.")

h 24 And the [1]children of Israel came near against the [1]children of Benjamin the second day.

25 And Benjamin went forth against them out of Gibeah the second day, and destroyed down to the ground of the [1]children of Israel again eighteen thousand men; all these drew the sword.

G[2] H[1] 26 Then all the [1]children of Israel, and all the People, went up, and came unto °the house of [18]God, and wept, and sat there before [1]the LORD, and fasted that day until even, and °offered burnt offerings and peace offerings before [1]the LORD.

27 And the [1]children of Israel enquired of [1]the LORD, (for the ark of the covenant of [26]God *was* there in those days,

28 And °Phinehas, the son of Eleazar, the son of °Aaron, stood before it in those days,) saying, "Shall I yet again go out to battle against the [1]children of Benjamin my brother, or shall I cease?" And [1]the LORD said, "Go up; for to morrow I will deliver them into thine hand."

29 And Israel set liers in wait round about Gibeah. H[2] J l (p. 356)

30 And the [1]children of Israel went up against the [1]children of Benjamin on the third day, and put themselves in array against Gibeah, as at other times. m

---

20. 12-46 (*C*, p. 353). THE CIVIL WAR. (*Introversion.*)

C | E | 12-14. Negotiations.
  F | 15, 16. Army of Benjamites.
  F | 17. Army of Israelites.
  E | 18-46. Hostilities.

12-14 (E, above). NEGOTIATIONS. (*Introversion.*)

E | e | 12. Expostulation.
  f | 13-. Requisition.
  f | -13. Refusal.
  e | 14. Preparation.

15 men. Heb. *'ish.* Ap. 14. II.

16 lefthanded. Heb. lame, or bound, in his right hand.

hair breadth = a hair. No *Ellipsis*, omit "breadth".

miss. Heb. *chāṭā'.* See Ap. 44. i.

18-46 (*E*, above). HOSTILITIES. (*Division.*)

E | G[1] | 18-25. Unsuccessful.
  G[2] | 26-46. Successful.

18-25 (G[1], above). UNSUCCESSFUL. (*Alternation and Introversion.*)

G[1] | g | i | 18. Inquiry.
  k | 19, 20. Array.
  h | 21. Slain of Israel (22,000).
  g | *k* | 22. Array.
  i | 23. Inquiry.
  h | 24, 25. Slain of Israel (18,000).

18 God. Heb. Elohim. Ap. 4.

23 And. Note the Fig. *Parenthesis.* Ap. 6.

before the LORD. At Shiloh (18. 31).

asked counsel. By Phinehas, with Urim and Thummim. Cp. *v.* 28, and see notes on Ex. 28. 30. Num. 26. 55.

26-46 (G[2], above). SUCCESSFUL. (*Division.*)

G[2] | H[1] | 26-28. Promise.
  H[2] | 29-46. Fulfilment.

26 the house of God. Not to be rendered "Beth-el" as in Sept., Syr., &c.; for the house of God was in Shiloh (18. 31), also the camp of Israel (21. 12).

offered = offered up. See Ap. 43. I. vi.

28 Phinehas. The grandson of Aaron, the contemporary of Jonathan the grandson of Moses (18. 30). This is the only mention of the high priest throughout the book.

Aaron. Some codices, with Syr., add "the priest".

29-46 [For Structures see next page].

n (p. 356) 1423 to 1383 31 And the [1] children of Benjamin went out against the People, *and* were drawn away from the city; and they began to smite of the People, *and* kill, as at other times, in the highways, of which one goeth up to °the house of [18] God, and the other to Gibeah in the field, about thirty [15] men of Israel.

32 And the children of Benjamin said, "They *are* smitten down before us, as at the first."

m But the [1] children of Israel said, "Let us flee, and draw them from the city unto the highways."

33 And all the [15] men of Israel rose up out of their place, and put themselves in array at Baal-tamar:

l and the liers in wait of Israel came forth out of their places, *even* out of the °meadows of Gibeah.

K o 34 And there came against Gibeah ten thousand chosen [15] men out of all Israel, and the battle was sore:

p but they knew not that °evil *was* near them.

q 35 And [1] the LORD smote Benjamin before Israel: and the [1] children of Israel destroyed of the Benjamites that day twenty and five thousand and an hundred [15] men: all these drew the sword.

p 36 So the [1] children of Benjamin saw that they were smitten: for the [15] men of Israel gave place to the Benjamites, because they °trusted unto the liers in wait which they had set beside Gibeah.

o 37 And the liers in wait hasted, and rushed upon Gibeah; and the liers in wait °drew *themselves* along, and smote all the city with the edge of the sword.

J r 38 Now there was an appointed sign between the [15] men of Israel and the liers in wait, that they should make a great flame with smoke rise up out of the city.

s 39 And when the [15] men of Israel retired in the battle, Benjamin began to smite *and* kill of the [15] men of Israel about thirty persons: for they said, "Surely they are smitten down before us, as *in* the first battle."

r 40 But when the flame began to arise up out of the city with a pillar of smoke, the Benjamites looked behind them, and, °behold, the flame of °the city ascended up to heaven.

s 41 And when the [15] men of Israel turned again, the [15] men of Benjamin were amazed: for they saw that [34] evil was come upon them.

K t 42 Therefore they turned *their backs* before the [15] men of Israel unto the way of the wilderness; but the battle overtook them;

u and them which *came* out of the cities they destroyed in the midst of them.

43 *Thus* they inclosed the Benjamites round about, *and* chased them, *and* trode them down with ease °over against Gibeah toward the sunrising.

44 And there fell of Benjamin eighteen thousand [15] men; all these *were* [15] men of valour.

20. 29-46 (H[2], p. 355). **FULFILMENT.**
(*Alternation.*)

H[2] | J | 29-33. Ambuscade.
  K | 34-37. Defeat.
 J | 38-41. Ambuscade.
  K | 42-46. Defeat.

29-33 (J, above). **AMBUSCADE.**
(*Introversion.*)

J | l | 29. Ambuscade.
  m | 30. Array.
   n | 31, 32-. Slain of Israel (thirty).
  m | -32, 33-. Pretended flight.
 l | -33. Ambuscade.

31 the house of God = Beth-el. Here it denotes Beth-el. One of the three cities mentioned.

33 meadows. Probably = forest.

34-37 (K, above). **DEFEAT.**
(*Introversion.*)

K | o | 34-. Attack by ambuscade.
  p | -34. Danger unknown.
   q | 35. Slain of Benjamites (25,000).
  p | 36. Danger known.
 o | 37. Attack by ambuscade.

34 evil. Heb. *rā'a'*. Ap. 44. viii.

36 trusted. Confided or placed hope in. Heb. *bāṭah*. Ap. 69. I.

37 drew themselves along = marched forward.

38-41 (*J*, above). **AMBUSCADE.**
(*Alternation.*)

J | r | 38. Signal arranged.
  s | 39. Slain of Israel.
 r | 40. Signal given.
  s | 41. Amazement of Benjamites.

40 behold. Fig. *Asterismos*. Ap. 6.

the city = the whole city, or the holocaust of the city.

42-46 (*K*, above). **DEFEAT.**
(*Alternation.*)

K | t | 42-. Flight.
  u | -42-44. Slain of Benjamites.
 t | 45-. Flight.
  u | -45, 46. Slain of Benjamites.

43 over against = as far as over against.

47—21. 24 (*D*, p. 353). **REGRET.**
(*Alternation and Introversion.*)

D | v | 20. 47. The 600 fugitives (Rimmon).
  w | x | 20. 48. Destruction of others.
   y | 21. 1-12. First expedient.
 v | 21. 13-15. The 600 fugitives (Rimmon).
  w | *y* | 21. 16-23-. Second expedient.
   x | 21. -23, 24. Reparation.

47 six hundred. Cp. 21. 13.

45 And they turned and fled toward the wilderness unto the rock of Rimmon: *t*

and they gleaned of them in the highways five thousand [15] men; and pursued hard after them unto Gidom, and slew two thousand [15] men of them. *u*

46 So that all which fell that day of Benjamin were twenty and five thousand [15] men that drew the sword; all these *were* [15] men of valour.

47 But °six hundred [15] men turned and fled to the wilderness unto the rock Rimmon, and abode in the rock Rimmon four months. *D* v

48 And the [15] men of Israel turned again w x

1423 upon the [1]children of Benjamin, and smote
to them with the edge of the sword, as well °the
1383 men of *every* city, as the beast, and all that
came to hand: also they set on fire all the cities
that they came to.

y z b **21** Now the °men of Israel °had sworn in
(p. 357) Mizpeh, saying, "There shall not any
of us give his daughter unto Benjamin to
wife."

c **2** And the people came to °the house of
°God, and abode there till even before °God,
and lifted up their voices, and °wept sore;
3 And said, "O °LORD °God of Israel, why
is this come to pass in Israel, that there should
be to day one tribe lacking in Israel?"
4 And it came to pass on the morrow, that
the People rose early, and built there an altar,
and °offered burnt offerings and peace offerings.

a **5** And the °children of Israel said, "Who *is*
there among all the tribes of Israel that came
not up with the °congregation unto [3]the
LORD?" For they had made a great oath
concerning him that came not up to [3]the LORD
to Mizpeh, saying, "He shall surely be put to
death."

z c **6** And the [5]children of Israel repented them
for Benjamin their brother, and said, "There
is one tribe cut off from Israel this day.

b **7** How shall we do for wives for them that
remain, seeing we have sworn by [3]the LORD
that we will not give them of our daughters to
wives?"

a **8** And they said, "What one *is there* of the
tribes of Israel that came not up to Mizpeh to
[3]the LORD?" And, °behold, there came none
to the camp from Jabesh-gilead to the assembly.
9 For the People were numbered, and, [8]be-
hold, *there were* none of the inhabitants of
Jabesh-gilead there.
10 And the congregation sent thither twelve
thousand [1]men of the valiantest, and commanded them, saying, "Go and smite the inhabitants of Jabesh-gilead with the edge of
the sword, with the women and the °chil-
dren.
11 And this *is* the thing that ye shall do, Ye
shall utterly destroy every male, and every
woman that hath lain by °man."
12 And they found among the inhabitants of
Jabesh-gilead four hundred °young °virgins,
that had known no man by lying with any
male: and they brought them unto the camp to
°Shiloh, which *is* in the land of Canaan.

v **13** And the whole congregation sent *some* to
speak to the [1]children of Benjamin that *were*
in the rock Rimmon, and to °call peaceably
unto them.
14 And Benjamin came again at that time;
and they gave them wives which they had
saved alive of the women of Jabesh-gilead:
and yet so they sufficed them not.
15 And the People repented them for Benjamin, because that [3]the LORD had made a
breach in the tribes of Israel.

v y d[1] e **16** Then the elders of the congregation said,
"How shall we do for wives for them that
remain, seeing the women are destroyed out
of Benjamin?"
17 And they said, "*There must be* an inheritance for them that be escaped of Benjamin,
that a tribe be not destroyed out of Israel.

18 Howbeit we may not give them wives of f
our daughters: for the [5]children of Israel have
sworn, saying, 'Cursed *be* he that giveth a
wife to Benjamin.'"

19 Then they said, [8]"Behold, *there is* °a *e*
feast of [3]the LORD in [12]Shiloh °yearly *in a*
place which *is* on the °north side of Beth-el,
on the east side of the highway that goeth
up from Beth-el to Shechem, and on the south
of °Lebonah."

20 Therefore they commanded the [5]children d[2] g

---

48 the men = every one.

21. 1-12 (y, p. 356). FIRST EXPEDIENT.
(Alternation and Introversion.)

y | z | b | 1. Oath.
  c | 2-4. Sorrow.
  a | 5. Absentees. Inquiry.
z | *c* | 6. Sorrow.
  b | 7. Oath.
  a | 8-12. Absentees. Punishment.

1 men. Heb. *'ish.* Ap. 14. II.
had sworn: i. e. before the fighting of ch. 20.
2 the house of God. Probably Shiloh, cp. *v.* 12 and 18. 31.
God. Heb. *hā-'Elohim,* "the [true] God". Ap. 4. I.
wept sore. Fig. *Polyptōton* (Ap. 6), "wept a great weeping". See note on Gen. 26. 28. Benjamin is indeed, now, "a son of sorrow" (*Ben-oni,* a son of sorrow, Gen. 35. 18).
3 LORD God = *Jehovah Elohim.* Ap. 4. I, II.
4 offered. Heb. *'ālāh.* Ap. 43. I. vi.
5 children = sons.
congregation = military assembly.
8 behold. Fig. *Asterismos.* Ap. 6.
10 children = little children. Heb. *ṭaph.* Cp. 13. 5.
11 man = male. Heb. *zākār.*
12 young virgins. Heb. young women, virgins.
virgins. Heb. *bethūlāh.*
Shiloh. See note on 18. 31.
13 call peaceably = proclaim peace.

16-23- (*y*, p. 356). SECOND EXPEDIENT.
(Division and Introversions.)

y | d[1] | e | 16, 17. Deficiency. Inquiry.
  f | 18. Prevention.
  e | 19. Deficiency. Supply.
d[2] | g | 20, 21. Advice given.
  h | 22. Conciliation.
  g | 23-. Advice taken.

19 a feast of the LORD. Some codices, with two early printed editions, read "a feast to Jehovah".
yearly. The three feasts had come down to one. Apostasy was the cause of all their internal disorders.
north side, &c. Shiloh and the house of Jehovah were so neglected that these minute instructions were necessary to enable an Israelite to find it. We have the same difficulty to-day; and when we find it we too often find, not the sacrifice of praise and thanksgiving, but what answers to that which we find in *v.* 21.
Lebonah. A.V. 1611 reads "Lebanon" by an error. Modern "Lubban", about 3½ miles north-west of Shiloh.

1423 of Benjamin, saying, "Go and lie in wait in the
to vineyards;
1383 **21** And see, and, [8]behold, if the daughters of
[12]Shiloh come out to °dance in dances, then
come ye out of the vineyards, and catch you
every °man his wife of the daughters of
[12]Shiloh, and go to the land of Benjamin.

h **22** And it shall be, when their fathers or
their brethren come unto us to complain, that
we will say unto them, 'Be favourable unto
them for our sakes: because we reserved not
to each man his wife in the war: for ye did not
give unto them °at this time, *that* ye should be
guilty.'"

g **23** And the [5]children of Benjamin did so, and
took *them* wives, according to their number, of
them that danced, whom they caught:

x and they went and returned unto their inheritance, and °repaired the cities, and dwelt in
them.

21 dance in dances. This is what "religion" had come to in those days of apostasy, by which we must judge it.

man. Heb. *'ish.* Ap. 14. II.

22 at this time, &c.: i.e. "at the time when ye would have incurred guilt [by so doing]".

23 repaired=rebuilt, or built up.

25 no king. Note the structural arrangement of the four occurrences of this expression. See note on 18. 1.

did=did continually. This is the Divine summing up of the whole book, by way of Epilogue. All the evil follows as the result of the disobedience in 1. 27-36.

24 And the [5]children of Israel departed
thence at that time, [21]every man to his tribe
and to his family, and they went out from
thence [21]every man to his inheritance.

25 In those days *there was* °no king in A
Israel: [21]every man °did *that which was* right
in his own eyes.

RUTH.

THE STRUCTURE OF THE BOOK AS A WHOLE.

A | 1. 1-18. ELIMELECH'S FAMILY. THE DEPRESSION.

B | 1. 19-22. SYMPATHY WITH NAOMI. IN GRIEF.

C | 2. 1-23. BOAZ AND RUTH.

C | 3. 1—4. 13. RUTH AND BOAZ.

B | 4. 14-17. SYMPATHY WITH NAOMI. IN JOY.

A | 4. 18-22. ELIMELECH'S FAMILY. THE UPLIFTING.

THE
°BOOK OF °RUTH.

A A[1] (p. 361) about 1336 1 °Now it came to pass in the days °when the judges ruled, that there was °a famine in the land. And a certain °man of Beth-lehem-judah went to sojourn in the °country of Moab, he, and his wife, and his two sons.

2 And the name of the [1]man *was* °Elimelech, and the name of his wife °Naomi, and the name of his two sons °Mahlon and °Chilion, °Ephrathites of Beth-lehem-judah. And they came into the [1]country of Moab, and continued there.

3 And Elimelech Naomi's husband died; and she was left, and her two sons.

B[1] 4 And they °took them wives of the women of Moab; the name of the one *was* °Orpah, and the name of the other °Ruth: and they
1336 to 1326 dwelled there about ten years.
5 And Mahlon and Chilion died also both of them; and the woman was °left of her two sons and her husband.

A[2] 6 Then she arose with her daughters in law, that she might °return from the [1]country of Moab: for she had heard in the [1]country of Moab how that °the LORD had °visited His People in giving them bread.

7 Wherefore she went forth out of the place where she was, and her two daughters in law with her; and they went on the way to return unto the land of Judah.

B[2] a[1] 8 And Naomi said unto her two daughters in law, "Go, return each to her mother's house: [6]the LORD deal kindly with you, °as ye have dealt with the dead, and with me.

9 [6]The LORD grant you that ye may find °rest, each *of you* in the house of her husband." Then she kissed them;

b[1] and they lifted up their voice, and wept.

10 And they said unto her, "Surely °we will return with thee unto thy People."

a[2] 11 And Naomi said, "Turn again, my daughters: °why will ye go with me? *are* there yet *any more* sons in my womb, that they may be your husbands?

12 Turn again, my daughters, go *your way*; for I am too old to have an husband. If I °should say, I have hope, *if* I should have an husband also to night, and should also bear sons;

13 °Would ye tarry for them till they were grown? °would ye stay for them from having husbands? nay, my daughters; for it grieveth me much for your sakes that the hand of [6]the LORD is gone out against me."

b[2] 14 And they lifted up their voice, and wept again: and Orpah kissed her mother in law; but Ruth clave unto her.

TITLE, Book. For its place in the Hebrew Canon, see Ap. 1. The second of the five *Megillōth*, or Scrolls. Read at the Feast of Pentecost. Their order determined by the order of the feasts. Written as being necessary for the link it affords in the Genealogy of David and Christ "the son of David", Matt. 1. 5–16. Placed in the Canon after Judges by the Sept. Followed by all the versions.

Ruth. Two books with names of women: Ruth, a Gentile, marries a Hebrew husband; Esther, a Jewess, marries a Gentile husband. Two tokens that Gentiles, as such, were to be blessed only through Abraham's seed, according to Gen. 12. 3; 18. 18; 22. 18; 26. 4. Ps. 72. 17. Acts 3. 25.

1. 1–18 (A, p. 359). ELIMELECH'S FAMILY. THE DEPRESSION. (*Alternation.*)

A | A[1] | 1–3. Departure from Beth-lehem.
B[1] | 4, 5. Daughters-in-law. Bereavement.
A[2] | 6, 7. Departure for Beth-lehem.
B[2] | 8–18. Daughters-in-law. Colloquy.

1 Now it came to pass in the days. Occurs five times. Always denotes impending trouble, followed by happy deliverance. Cp. Gen. 14. 1. Est. 1. 1. Isa. 7. 1. Jer. 1. 3.

when the judges ruled. Doubtless, in the early days, before the sin of Judg. 1 developed the later internal disorders, and outward oppressions.

a famine. See note on Gen. 12. 10.

man. Heb. *'ish.* Ap. 14. II.

country = fields.

2 Elimelech = My God is king.

Naomi = My pleasant one.

Mahlon = Sick. **Chilion** = Pining.

Ephrathites. Ephrath was the ancient name of Beth-lehem, where Rachel was buried (Gen. 35. 19; 48. 7).

4 took them wives. Canaanitish wives forbidden (Deut. 7. 3, &c.), but not Moabitish wives; though a Moabite man might not enter the congregation of Jehovah. See note, Deut. 23. 3.

Orpah = Hind or Fawn.

Ruth = Beauty. Wife of Mahlon the elder.

5 left = left survivor.

6 return. This was in 1326, the year before the second jubilee (1325–1324). See Ap. 50. IV, p. 54.

the LORD. Heb. Jehovah. Ap. 4. II.

visited. Cp. Ex. 4. 31. Ps. 132. 15. Luke 1. 68.

8–18 (B[2], above). DAUGHTERS-IN-LAW. COLLOQUY. (*Repeated Alternation.*)

B[2] | a[1] | 8, 9–. Advice to leave her.
b[1] | –9, 10. Reception. Refusal of both.
a[2] | 11–13. Advice to leave her.
b[2] | 14. Reception. Refusal of Ruth.
a[3] | 15. Advice to leave her.
b[3] | 16–18. Reception. Resolve of Ruth.

8 as = according as.

9 rest. Cp. 3. 1. A characteristic word in this Book.

10 we will return with thee. This liberty was allowed by the laws of Khammurabi, §§ 171–173 and 177.

11 why . . .? Fig. *Erotēsis.* Ap. 6.

12 should say = should have said.

13 Would . . .? Fig. *Erotēsis.* Ap. 6.

a[3] (p. 361) 1326 15 And she said, ° "Behold, thy sister in law is gone back unto her People, and unto her gods: return thou after thy sister in law."

b[3] 16 And Ruth said, "Intreat me not to leave thee, *or* to return from following after thee: for whither thou goest, I will go; and where thou lodgest, I will lodge: thy People *shall be* my People, and thy ° God my ° God:

17 Where thou diest, will I die, and there will I be buried: [6]the LORD do so to me, and more also, *if ought* but death part thee and me."

18 When she saw that she was stedfastly minded to go with her, then she left speaking unto her.

B C (p. 362) 19 So they two went until they came to ° Beth-lehem.

D And it came to pass, when they were come to Beth-lehem, that all the city was moved about them, and they said, "*Is* this Naomi?"

D 20 And she said unto ° them, "Call me not Naomi, call me Mara: for ° the ALMIGHTY hath dealt very bitterly with me.

21 I went out full, and [6]the LORD hath brought me home again empty: why *then* call ye me Naomi, seeing [6]the LORD hath testified against me, and [20]the ALMIGHTY hath afflicted me?"

C 22 So [20]Naomi returned, and Ruth ° the Moabitess, her daughter in law, with her, which returned out of the country of Moab: and they came to Beth-lehem in the beginning of ° barley harvest.

C c **2** And Naomi had a kinsman of her husband's, a mighty ° man of wealth, of the family of Elimelech; and his name *was* Boaz.

d e 2 And Ruth ° the Moabitess said unto Naomi, "Let me now go to the field, and glean ears of corn after *him* in whose sight I shall find grace." And she said unto her, "Go, my daughter."

f 3 And she went, and came, and ° gleaned in the field after the reapers: and her ° hap was to light on a part of the field *belonging* unto Boaz, who *was* of the kindred of Elimelech.

g 4 And, ° behold, Boaz came from Beth-lehem, and said unto the reapers, ° "The LORD *be* with you." And ° they answered him, ° "The LORD bless thee."

5 Then said Boaz unto his servant that was set over the reapers, "Whose damsel *is* this?"

6 And the servant that was set over the reapers answered and said, "It *is* [2]the Moabitish damsel that came back with Naomi out of the country of Moab:

7 And she said, 'I pray you, let me glean and gather after the reapers among the sheaves:' so she came, and hath continued even ° from the morning until now, that she tarried a little in the house."

8 Then said Boaz unto Ruth, ° "Hearest thou not, my daughter? Go not to glean in another field, neither go from hence, but abide here ° fast by my maidens:

15 Behold. Fig. *Asterismos*. Ap. 6.
16 God. Heb. Elohim. Ap. 4.

19-22 (B, p. 359). SYMPATHY WITH NAOMI. IN GRIEF. (*Introversion.*)

B | C | 19-. Beth-lehem. Arrival.
  D | -19. Sympathy given.
  D | 20, 21. Sympathy needed.
 C | 22. Beth-lehem. Settlement.

19 Beth-lehem = House of bread.
20 them. Fem., and the verb "call" is fem. also, so that Naomi was addressing the women.
the ALMIGHTY = *Shaddai*. See Ap. 4.
22 the Moabitess. So called five times. In Deut. 23. 3, it is masculine, and does not affect Ruth.
barley harvest. Therefore at the Passover.

2. 1-23 (C, p. 359). BOAZ AND RUTH. (*Introversion and Extended Alternation.*)

C | c | 1. Boaz. His kindred.
 d | e | 2. Ruth. Purpose.
   f | 3. Departure.
    g | 4-16. Colloquy. Boaz and Ruth.
 d | *e* | 17. Ruth. Performance.
   f | 18. Return.
    g | 19-22. Colloquy. Naomi and Ruth.
 c | 23. Boaz. His maidens.

1 man. Heb. *'ish*. Ap. 14. II.
2 the Moabitess. See note on 1. 4, 22.
3 gleaned. Cp. Lev. 19. 9, 10; 23. 22. Deut. 24. 19.
hap. From Anglo-Saxon, good luck=happy. Heb. "her chance chanced". Fig. *Polyptōton*. Ap. 6.
4 behold. Fig. *Asterismos*. Ap. 6.
The LORD. Heb. Jehovah. Ap. 4. II.
they answered. This tells of a time of peace, prosperity, and quiet.
7 from the morning = all the morning.
8 Hearest thou not . . . ? Fig. *Erotēsis*. Ap. 6.
fast. Anglo-Saxon = steadfast: i. e. cleave to.
10 take knowledge. Fig. *Metonymy* (of Cause), put for "caring for". Ap. 6.
stranger = foreigner.
12 work . . . reward . . . trust. Note the order of these three words for a spiritual application.
God. Heb. Elohim. Ap. 4. I.
wings. By Fig. *Anthropopatheia* (Ap. 6) attributed to Jehovah; denoting His tender care.
trust = flee for refuge. Heb. *ḥaṣah*. Ap. 69. II.

9 *Let* thine eyes *be* on the field that they do reap, and go thou after them: have I not charged the young men that they shall not touch thee? and when thou art athirst, go unto the vessels, and drink of *that* which the young men have drawn."

10 Then she fell on her face, and bowed herself to the ground, and said unto him, "Why have I found grace in thine eyes, that thou shouldest ° take knowledge of me, seeing I *am* a ° stranger?"

11 And Boaz answered and said unto her, "It hath fully been shewed me, all that thou hast done unto thy mother in law since the death of thine husband: and *how* thou hast left thy father and thy mother, and the land of thy nativity, and art come unto a People which thou knewest not heretofore.

12 [4]The LORD recompense thy ° work, and a full ° reward be given thee of [4]the LORD ° God of Israel, under Whose ° wings thou art come to ° trust."

13 Then she said, "Let me find favour in thy

1326 sight, my lord; for that thou hast comforted
me, and for that thou hast spoken °friendly
unto thine handmaid, °though 𝕴 be not like
unto one of thine handmaidens."
14 And Boaz said unto her, "At mealtime
come thou hither, and eat of the bread, and dip
thy morsel in the vinegar." And she sat
beside the reapers: and he reached her parched
corn, and she did eat, and was sufficed, and
°left.
15 And when she was risen up to glean, Boaz
commanded his young men, saying, "Let her
glean even among the sheaves, and reproach
her not:
16 And let fall also *some* of the handfuls °of
purpose for her, and leave *them*, that she may
glean *them*, and rebuke her not."
d e 17 So she gleaned in the field until even, and
(p. 362) beat out that she had gleaned: and it was
about an °ephah of barley.
f 18 And she took *it* up, and went into the
city: and her mother in law saw what she
had gleaned: and she brought forth, and
gave to her that she had reserved after she
was sufficed.
g 19 And her mother in law said unto her,
"Where hast thou gleaned to day? and where
wroughtest thou? blessed be he that did [10]take
knowledge of thee." And she shewed her
mother in law with whom she had wrought,
and said, "The [1]man's name with whom I
wrought to day *is* Boaz."
20 And Naomi said unto her daughter in law,
"Blessed *be* 𝔥𝔢 of [4]the LORD, Who hath not left
off His °kindness to the living and to the dead."
And Naomi said unto her, "The [19]man *is* near
of kin unto us, °one of our next kinsmen."
21 And Ruth °the Moabitess said, "He said
unto me also, 'Thou shalt keep [8]fast by my
young men, until they have ended all my harvest.'"
22 And Naomi said unto Ruth her daughter
in law, "*It is* good, my daughter, that thou go
out with his maidens, that they meet thee not
in any other field."
c 23 So she kept fast by the maidens of Boaz
to glean unto the end of barley harvest °and
of wheat harvest; and °dwelt with her mother
in law.

C E **3** Then Naomi her mother in law said unto
(p. 363) her, "My daughter, °shall I not seek °rest
for thee, that it may be well with thee?
2 And now *is* not Boaz of our kindred, with
whose maidens thou wast? °Behold, °𝔥𝔢 winnoweth barley to night in the threshingfloor.
3 Wash thyself therefore, and anoint thee,
and put thy raiment upon thee, and get thee
down to the floor: *but* make not thyself known
unto the °man, until he shall have done eating
and drinking.
4 And it shall be, when he lieth down, that
thou shalt mark the place where he shall lie,
and thou shalt go in, and uncover his feet, and
lay thee down; and 𝔥𝔢 will tell thee what thou
shalt do."
5 And she said unto her, "All that thou sayest
°unto me I will do."

13 friendly = to the heart.
though I be not. Or, Oh that I might be.
14 left = left thereof remaining.
16 of purpose = on purpose.
17 ephah. See Ap. 51. III. 3.
20 kindness = lovingkindness.
one of = "𝔥𝔢 [is]".
21 the Moabitess. See note on 1. 4, 22.
23 and of wheat harvest. Therefore near the Feast of Pentecost. This is why this book is read at that feast. See note on title.
dwelt with. Some codices read "returned unto". Vulg. commences the next chapter with this sentence.

3. 1–4. 13 (*C*, p. 359). **RUTH AND BOAZ.**
(*Introversion.*)

C | E | 3. 1-12. Claim of kinsman. Asserted.
  F | 3. 13. Promise made.
  F | 3. 14-18. Promise waited for.
  E | 4. 1-13. Claim of kinsman. Fulfilled.

1 shall I not . . . ? Fig. *Erotēsis.* Ap. 6.
rest. See 1. 9.
2 Behold. Fig. *Asterismos.* Ap. 6.
he winnoweth. This was, and is to-day, the master's work. His servants plowed, sowed, and reaped.
3 man. Heb. *'īsh.* Ap. 14. II.
5 unto me. Some codices, with Sept. and Vulg., omit these words.
9 thy skirt = wing (with Sept. and Vulg.). Other codices, with two early printed editions, read "wings". "Wing" put by Fig. *Metonymy* (of Cause) for protective care. Ap. 6.
10 the LORD. Heb. Jehovah. Ap. 4. II.
11 thou requirest = thou shalt say. Some codices, with Aram., Syr., and Vulg., add "unto me".
city. Heb. gate, put by Fig. *Synecdoche* (of Part) for the people assembling there.

6 And she went down unto the floor, and
did according to all that her mother in law
bade her.
7 And when Boaz had eaten and drunk, and
his heart was merry, he went to lie down at
the end of the heap of corn: and she came
softly, and uncovered his feet, and laid her
down.
8 And it came to pass at midnight, that the
[3]man was afraid, and turned himself: and,
[2]behold, a woman lay at his feet.
9 And he said, "Who *art* 𝔱𝔥𝔬𝔲?" And she
answered, "𝕴 *am* Ruth thine handmaid:
spread therefore °thy skirt over thine handmaid; for 𝔱𝔥𝔬𝔲 *art* a near kinsman."
10 And he said, "Blessed *be* 𝔱𝔥𝔬𝔲 of °the
LORD, my daughter: *for* thou hast shewed
more kindness in the latter end than at the
beginning, inasmuch as thou followedst not
young men, whether poor or rich.
11 And now, my daughter, fear not; I will do
to thee all that °thou requirest: for all the
°city of my People doth know that 𝔱𝔥𝔬𝔲 *art*
a virtuous woman.
12 And now it is true that 𝕴 *am thy* near
kinsman: howbeit there is a kinsman nearer
than I.
13 Tarry this night, and it shall be in the F
morning, *that* if he will perform unto thee the
part of a kinsman, well; let him do the kinsman's part: but if he will not do the part of
a kinsman to thee, then will 𝕴 do the part of
a kinsman to thee, *as* [10]the LORD liveth: lie
down until the morning."

F (p. 363) 1326 14 And she lay at his feet until the morning: and she rose up before °one could know another. And he said, "Let it not be known that a woman came into the floor."

15 Also he said, "Bring the °vail that *thou hast* upon thee, and hold it." And when she held it, he measured six *measures* of barley, and laid *it* on her: and °she went into the city.

16 And when she came to her mother in law, she said, "Who *art* thou, my daughter?" And she told her all that the [3]man had done to her.

17 And she said, "These six *measures* of barley gave he me; for he said to me, 'Go not empty unto thy mother in law.'"

18 Then said she, "Sit still, my daughter, until thou know how the matter will fall: for the [3]man will not be in rest, until he have finished the thing this day."

E h (p. 364) **4** Then went Boaz up to the gate, and sat him down there: and, °behold, °the kinsman of whom Boaz spake came by; unto whom he said, °"Ho, such a one! turn aside, sit down here." And he turned aside, and sat down.

2 And he took ten °men of the elders of the city, and said, "Sit ye down here." And they sat down.

3 And he said unto [1]the kinsman, "Naomi, that is come again out of the °country of Moab, selleth °a parcel of land, which *was* our brother Elimelech's:

4 And I thought to advertise thee, saying, 'Buy *it* °before the inhabitants, and before the elders of my People. If thou wilt °redeem *it*, °redeem *it:* but if °thou wilt not °redeem *it, then* tell me, that I may know: for *there is* none to °redeem *it* beside thee; and I *am* after thee.'" And he said, "I will °redeem *it*."

5 Then said Boaz, "What day thou buyest the field of the hand of Naomi, thou must buy *it* also of Ruth the Moabitess, the wife of the dead, to raise up the name of the dead upon his inheritance."

6 And [1]the kinsman said, "I cannot [4]redeem *it* for myself, lest I mar mine own inheritance: [4]redeem thou my right to thyself; for I cannot [4]redeem *it*."

7 Now this *was the manner* in former time in Israel concerning [4]redeeming and concerning changing, for to confirm all things; °a man plucked off his shoe, and gave *it* to his neighbour: and this *was* a testimony in Israel.

8 Therefore [1]the kinsman said unto Boaz, "Buy *it* for thee." So he °drew off his shoe.

9 And Boaz said unto the elders, and *unto* all the People, "Ye *are* witnesses this day, that I have bought all that *was* Elimelech's, and all that *was* Chilion's and Mahlon's, of the hand of Naomi.

10 Moreover Ruth the Moabitess, the wife of Mahlon, have I purchased to be my wife, to raise up the name of the dead upon his inheritance, that the name of the dead be not cut off from among his brethren, and °from the gate of his place: ye *are* witnesses this day."

11 And all the People that *were* in the gate, and the elders, said, "*We are* witnesses.

i °The LORD make the woman that is come into thine house like Rachel and like Leah, which two did build the house of Israel: and do thou worthily in Ephratah, and °be famous in Bethlehem:

12 And let thy house be like the house of °Pharez, whom Tamar bare unto Judah, of the seed which [11]the LORD shall give thee of this young woman."

13 So Boaz took Ruth, and she was his wife: h
and when he went in unto her, [11]the LORD 1325
gave her conception, and she °bare a son.

14 And the women said unto Naomi, "Blessed B k
be [11]the LORD, Which hath not left thee this (p. 364)
day without a [1]kinsman, that his name may be famous in Israel.

15 And he shall be unto thee a restorer of *thy* °life, and a nourisher of thine old age: for thy daughter in law, which loveth thee, which is better to thee than seven sons, hath born him."

16 And Naomi took the child, and laid it in l
her bosom, and became nurse unto it.

17 And the women her neighbours gave it k
a name, saying, "There is a son born to Naomi;"

and they called his name Obed: he *is* the father A m
of Jesse, the father of David.

---

14 one = a man. Heb. *'ish*. Ap. 14. II.

15 vail = mantle or cloak, worn by all peasants; only the town-women veiling the face. Cp. Isa. 3. 23.

she went = he went. The verb is masculine. Some codices, with Syr. and Vulg., read "she".

4. 1-13 (*E*, p. 363). CLAIM OF KINSMAN. FULFILLED. (*Introversion*.)

E | h | 1-11-. In detail.
  i | -11, 12. Prayer.
  h | 13. In sum.

1 behold. Fig. *Asterismos*. Ap. 6.

the kinsman. Heb. *Goel* = the next of kin, who has the right of redemption. See notes on Ex. 6. 6, and 13. 13.

Ho. Fig. *Exclamatio*. Ap. 6.

2 men. Heb. *'ĕnōsh*. Ap. 14. III.

3 country = fields.

a parcel of land = the parcel of the field.

4 before the inhabitants = in the presence of such as are seated here.

redeem. Heb. *gā'al*, to redeem by purchase. See Ex. 6. 6, and cp. 13. 13.

thou. Heb. text has "he". But a special various reading called *Sevīr* (Ap. 34), and some codices, with Aram., Sept., Syr., and Vulg., read "thou", which the A.V. seems to have followed.

7 a man. Heb. *'īsh*. Ap. 14. II. A custom that grew up outside the Law.

8 drew = plucked.

10 from the gate = from the people of his city, "gate" being put by Fig. *Synecdoche* (of Part) for the people wont to assemble there. Ap. 6.

11 The LORD. Heb. Jehovah. Ap. 4. II.

be famous = proclaim a name.

12 Pharez. Cp. Gen. 38. 29. 1 Chron. 2. 4. Matt. 1. 3.

13 bare a son. In the second jubilee year (1325-1324).

14-17- (*B*, p. 359). SYMPATHY WITH NAOMI. IN JOY. (*Introversion*.)

B | k | 14, 15. Blessing by women.
  l | 16. Naomi's joy.
  k | 17-. Naming by women.

15 life = soul. Heb. *nephesh*. Ap. 13.

-17-22 [For Structure see next page].

n 18 Now °these *are* the generations of °Pha-
1325 rez: Pharez begat Hezron,
19 And °Hezron begat Ram, and °Ram begat Amminadab,
20 And Amminadab begat °Nahshon, and Nahshon begat °Salmon,
21 And Salmon begat °Boaz, and Boaz begat Obed,
m 22 And Obed begat Jesse, and Jesse begat David.

-17-22 (*A*, p. 359). ELIMELECH'S FAMILY. THE UPLIFTING. (*Introversion.*)

A | m | -17. Obed, Jesse, and David.
  n | 18-21. The generations of Pharez.
 m | 22. Obed, Jesse, and David.

18 these are the generations. The thirteenth occurrence, out of fourteen given in the Bible. The last in O.T. See note on p. 1.

Pharez. The son of Judah. See Ap. 29. Gen. 38. 29. 1 Chron. 2. 4. Matt. 1. 3. Luke 3. 33. See note below.

19 Hezron. Cp. Gen. 46. 12.

Ram. Cp. 1 Chron. 2. 9.

20 Nahshon. Prince of Israel in the wilderness (1 Chron. 2. 10). Cp. Num. 1. 7; 7. 12; 10. 14.

Salmon. Married Rahab (Matt. 1. 5). Nephew of Aaron. **21 Boaz.** Married Ruth. Cp. *v.* 13.

THE GENERATIONS OF PHAREZ.*

Judah = Thamar
|
Pharez
|
Hezron
|
Aram
|
Amminadab
|
Elisheba — Nahshon
|
Salmon
(nephew of Aaron, m. Rahab)
|
Boaz
(married Ruth)
|
Obed
|
Jesse
|
David

* NOTE ON "THE GENERATIONS OF PHAREZ".

If SALMON married RAHAB in the year of the entry into the land (1451 B.C.); and the birth of DAVID was in 990 B.C.; then, according to the above Table of Generations, the period of 461 years is covered by only *four* lives; viz. SALMON, BOAZ, OBED, and JESSE.

The inference therefore seems clear that, as in a *Royal* line it is not necessary to include *every* link (as it is in the case of an ordinary man), certain names are omitted in this pedigree, in order that "the generations of PHAREZ" may be reckoned as ten generations, to accord with the principle which we observe from ADAM to ZEDEKIAH (viz. ADAM to NOAH, ten; SHEM to ABRAHAM, ten; SOLOMON to ZEDEKIAH, twice ten). So here PHAREZ to DAVID is given in ten generations.

We see the same principle at work in other Tables of our LORD's ancestry, names are omitted in order to make uniform reckonings.

For example, in Matt. 1. 1-17 we have three counts of "fourteen generations"; see notes there. In *v.* 1 we have the whole given in *two* links (DAVID and ABRAHAM). Ruth herself is omitted in *v.* 17, above.

1 AND 2 SAMUEL.

THE STRUCTURE OF THE TWO BOOKS * AS A WHOLE.

THE WHOLE.

(Division.)

A[1] | 1 Sam. **1. 1 — 7. 17.** RULE UNDER THE JUDGES.

A[2] | 1 Sam. **8. 1** — 2 Sam. **24. 25.** RULE UNDER THE KINGS.

---

1 Sam. **8. 1** — 2 Sam. **24. 25** (**A**[2], above). RULE UNDER THE KINGS.

(Division.)

A[2] | **B**[1] | 1 Sam. 8. 1—2 Sam. 1. 27. KING SAUL.

| **B**[2] | 2 Sam. 2. 1—24. 25. KING DAVID.

---

2 Sam. **2. 1 — 24. 25** (**B**[2], above). KING DAVID.

(Division.)

B[2] | **C**[1] | 2 Sam. 2. 1—4. 12. KINGDOM DIVIDED.

| **C**[2] | 2 Sam. 5. 1—24. 25. KINGDOM UNITED.

---

* It is necessary that the two books should be treated as one; because, in the Hebrew Canon (as given in the MSS. and early printed editions of the Hebrew text) the two are, and always have been, presented and reckoned as one book.

They were first divided, and treated as two, by the Septuagint Translators (cent. 3 B.C.). And this division has been followed in all subsequent versions.

Probably, scrolls were more or less equal in length; and, as Greek requires at least one-third more space than Hebrew, one scroll was filled before the translation of the one long book of fifty-five chapters was completed. Hence, the poor division. Of the thirty-four *Sedarim* (or cycles for public reading), the twentieth begins with 1 Sam. 30. 25 and ends with 2 Sam. 2. 6, showing no break in the text.

The same applies to the two so-called Books of Kings; for Kings also made a long book of forty-seven chapters, and came to be divided in the same way, the four being numbered respectively the "First, Second, Third, and Fourth Book of the Kingdoms"[1]; and, in the Vulgate, "of the Kings". In no Hebrew MS. or early printed edition is the book found divided into two. The thirty-five divisions, called *Sedarim*, are numbered throughout without regard to any division: the nineteenth beginning with 1 Kings 22. 43 and ending with 2 Kings 2. 14. This division must have been governed by the exigencies of the parchment, or the break would not have been made in the midst of the reign of Ahaziah and the ministry of Elijah.

The one book, Chronicles, consisting of sixty-five chapters, came under the same treatment. There are twenty-five *Sedarim* (or cycles for public reading), of which the eleventh begins with 1 Chron. 28. 10 and ends with 2 Chron. 2. 2, showing no break in the text. For the division of the book Ezra-Nehemiah, see notes on p. 616.

[1] The Structure of these four "BOOKS OF THE KINGDOMS" may be exhibited thus:

X | Y | 2 Sam. 2. 1—4. 12. The Divided Kingdom.

| Z | 2 Sam. 5. 1—24. 25. The United Kingdom.

| *Z* | 1 Kings 1. 1—12. 15. The United Kingdom.

| *Y* | 1 Kings 12. 16—2 Kings 25. 38. The Divided Kingdom.

THE °FIRST BOOK OF °SAMUEL,

°OTHERWISE CALLED,

THE FIRST BOOK OF THE KINGS.

A^1 A C^1 (p. 367) about 1064 to 1061
1 Now there was a certain man of Ramathaim-zophim, of °mount Ephraim, and his name *was* °Elkanah, the son of Jeroham, the son of Elihu, the son of Tohu, the son of Zuph, an Ephrathite:

2 And he had two wives; the name of the one *was* °Hannah, and the name of the other °Peninnah: and Peninnah had °children, but Hannah had no °children.

3 And this man went up out of his city °yearly to worship and to sacrifice unto °the LORD of hosts in °Shiloh.

D^1 And the two sons of Eli, Hophni and Phinehas, the priests of °the LORD, *were* there.

E 4 And when the °time was that Elkanah offered, he gave to Peninnah his wife, and to all her sons and her daughters, portions:

5 But unto Hannah he gave a °worthy portion; for he loved Hannah: (but [3]the LORD had shut up her womb.)

6 And her adversary also provoked her sore, for to make her fret, because [3]the LORD had shut up her womb.

7 And *as* he did so year by year, when she went up to the house of [3]the LORD, so she provoked her; therefore she wept, and did not eat.

F a 1061 8 Then said Elkanah her husband to her, "Hannah, °why weepest thou? and °why eatest thou not? and °why is thy heart grieved? *am* not I °better to thee °than ten sons?"

9 So Hannah rose up after they had eaten in Shiloh, and after they had drunk. Now Eli the priest sat upon °a seat by °a post of °the temple of [3]the LORD.

TITLE, First Book of Samuel. See note on p. 366. For its place in the Heb. canon, see Ap. 1.

Samuel. The books follow on Judges, and yet hold a peculiar place of their own, looking backward and forward. Heb. *Shᵉmū'ēl* = Asked of God, or God-heard, and the impression of this is left on the books (chs. 8, 9, 16, and 2 Sam. 7). As to authorship, cp. 1 Chron. 29. 29, which shows that the prophets kept up the national records, which accounts for such passages as 1 Sam. 27. 6. In the Books of Samuel and Kings events are viewed from the human and exoteric standpoint, while in Chronicles the same events are viewed from the Divine and esoteric standpoint. Examples of these abound. (See Ap. 56.)

otherwise called. See note on p. 366. For the parallel passages in the Book of Chronicles, see Ap. 56.

1. 1—7. 17 (A^1, p. 366). RULE UNDER JUDGES. (*Alternation.*)

A^1
- A | 1. 1—4. 1-. The provocation of Israel.
  - B | 4. -1—7. 2-. Subjection by Philistines.
- *A* | 7. -2-6. The repentance of Israel.
  - *B* | 7. 7-17. Deliverance from Philistines.

1. 1—4. 1- (A, above). PROVOCATION OF ISRAEL. (*Repeated Alternation.*)

A
- C^1 | 1. 1-3-. Elkanah and family.
  - D^1 | 1. -3. The sons of Eli.
- C^2 | 1. 4—2. 11. Elkanah and family.
  - D^2 | 2. 12-17. The sons of Eli.
- C^3 | 2. 18-21. Elkanah and family.
  - D^3 | 2. 22-25. The sons of Eli.
- C^4 | 2. 26. Elkanah's son, Samuel.
  - D^4 | 2. 27-36. Eli and his sons.
- C^5 | 3. 1-10. Elkanah's son, Samuel.
  - D^5 | 3. 11-18. Eli and his sons.
- C^6 | 3. 19—4. 1-. Elkanah's son, Samuel.

1 mount = hill country of.

Elkanah = Acquired by God, i. e. perhaps in exchange for firstborn (Num. 3. 13, 45), a son of Korah. See Ex. 6. 24. **2 Hannah** = Grace. **Peninnah** = Pearl. Note the Fig. *Antimetabole*. Ap. 6. **children** = offspring. Heb. *yālad*. **3 yearly.** Heb. "from days to days". Fig. *Synecdoche* (of Part), Ap. 6, to emphasise the regularity. **the LORD of hosts** = Jehovah Sabaioth, one of the Jehovah-titles. The first of 281 occurrences. Denotes the God of Israel as the Lord of all the hosts of heaven and earth. See Ap. 4. II. This title specially characterises this book. **Shiloh.** Where the Tabernacle and Ark were. Josh. 18. 1; 19. 51; 22. 9. Judg. 18. 31. **the LORD.** Heb. Jehovah. Ap. 4. II.

1. 4—2. 11 (C^2, above). ELKANAH AND FAMILY. (*Introversion and Alternation.*)

C^2
- E | 1. 4-7. Hannah and her adversary.
  - F | a | 1. 8-10. Prayer offered.
    - b | 1. 11. Vow made.
  - *F* | *a* | 1. 12-20. Prayer answered.
    - *b* | 1. 21-28. Vow fulfilled.
- *E* | 2. 1-11. Hannah and Jehovah.

4 time = day. Punctuality thus emphasised. **5 worthy** = double. **8 why . . . ?** Fig. *Erotēsis.* Ap. 6. Cp. John 20. 13, 15. **better . . . than ten sons.** Probably a *Parœmia* (Ap. 6). It is so to-day among the Arabs: such a woman being called *moonejeba* = ennobled. **9 a seat** = the seat. First occurrence. Cp. Zech. 6. 13. **a post** = door post, or side post. **the temple** = palace. Heb. *heykal*. Seven mentioned in Scripture: (1) The Tabernacle, 1 Sam. 1. 9; (2) Solomon's, 1 Kings 6. 5, 17; (3) Zerubbabel's, Ezra 4. 1, 2; (4) Herod's, John 2. 20; (5) The future one of 2 Thess. 2. 4; (6) The millennial temple of Ezek. 41. 1; and (7) the heavenly temple of Rev. 21. 3, 22. Also seven references to believers as a temple in N. T.: 1 Cor. 3. 9-17; 6. 19. 2 Cor. 6. 16. Eph. 2. 20, 21. Heb. 3. 6. 1 Pet. 2. 5; 4. 17.

1061 10 And she *was* in bitterness of °soul, and prayed unto [3]the LORD, and wept sore.

b (p. 367) 11 And she °vowed a vow, and said, "O [3]LORD of hosts, if Thou wilt indeed look on the affliction of Thine handmaid, and °remember me, and not forget Thine handmaid, but wilt give unto Thine handmaid a man child, then I will give him unto [3]the LORD all the days of his life, and there shall °no razor come upon his head."

F a 12 And it came to pass, as she continued praying before [3]the LORD, that Eli marked her mouth.
13 Now Hannah, she spake in her heart; only her lips moved, but her voice was not heard: therefore Eli thought she had been drunken.
14 And Eli said unto her, °"How long wilt thou be drunken? put away thy wine from thee."
15 And Hannah answered and said, "No, my lord, I *am* a woman of a sorrowful °spirit: I have drunk neither wine nor strong drink, but have poured out my [10]soul before [3]the LORD.
16 Count not thine handmaid for a daughter of Belial: for out of the abundance of my complaint and grief have I spoken hitherto."
17 Then Eli answered and said, "Go in peace: and the °God of Israel grant *thee* thy petition that thou hast asked of Him."
18 And she said, "Let thine handmaid find grace in thy sight." So the woman went her way, and did eat, and her countenance was no more *sad*.
19 And they rose up in the morning early, and worshipped before [3]the LORD, and returned, and came to their house to °Ramah: and Elkanah knew Hannah his wife; and [3]the LORD °remembered her.
20 Wherefore it came to pass, when the time was come about after Hannah had conceived,
1060 that she °bare a son, and called his name °Samuel, *saying*, "Because I have asked him of [3]the LORD."

b c[1] (p. 368) 21 And the °man Elkanah, and all his house, went up to °offer unto [3]the LORD the yearly sacrifice, and his vow.

d[1] 22 But Hannah went not up; for she said unto her husband, "*I will not go up* until the °child be weaned, and *then* I will bring him, that he may appear before [3]the LORD, and there abide °for ever."
23 And Elkanah her husband said unto her, "Do what seemeth thee good; tarry until thou have weaned him; only [3]the LORD establish
1055 His word." So the woman abode, and gave her son suck until she weaned him.

c[2] 24 And when she had °weaned him, she
1048 took him up with her, with °three bullocks, and one °ephah of flour, and °a bottle of wine, and brought him unto the house of [3]the LORD in Shiloh: (°and the [22]child *was* young).
25 And they slew °a bullock, and brought the [22]child to Eli.

d[2] 26 And she said, "Oh my lord, *as* °thy soul liveth, my lord, I *am* the woman that stood by thee here, praying unto [3]the LORD.

27 For this [22]child I prayed; and [3]the LORD hath given me my petition which I asked of Him:
28 Therefore also I have lent him to °the LORD; as long as he liveth he shall be lent to °the LORD."

And he worshipped °the LORD there. c[3]

2 And Hannah prayed, and said, *E* e[1] (p. 369)
"My heart rejoiceth in °the LORD,
°Mine horn is exalted in °the LORD:
My mouth is enlarged over mine enemies;
Because I rejoice in Thy salvation.

---

10 soul. Heb. *nephesh*. Ap. 13.
11 vowed a vow = made a solemn vow. Fig. *Polyptōton*. Ap. 6. See note on Gen. 26. 28.
remember me, and not forget. Fig. *Pleonasm* (Ap. 6) for great emphasis.
no razor. See Num. 6. 5. Judg. 13. 5; 16. 17.
14 How long . . . ? Fig. *Erotēsis*. Ap. 6.
15 spirit. Heb. *rūach*. Ap. 9.
17 God. Heb. Elohim. Ap. 4. I.
19 Ramah. Hence this was Samuel's residence.
remembered. Fig. *Anthropopatheia*. Ap. 6.
20 bare a son. Thus Samuel was a descendant of Korah. See Ex. 6. 24.
Samuel. See note on Title, p. 367.

21-28 (*b*, p. 367). **VOW FULFILLED.**
(Repeated Alternation.)

b | c[1] | 21. Worship.
d[1] | 22, 23. Presentation postponed.
c[2] | 24, 25. Worship.
d[2] | 26-28-. Presentation made.
c[3] | -28. Worship.

21 man. Heb. *'īsh*. Ap. 14. II.
offer = sacrifice. Ap. 43. I. iv.
22 child = young child.
for ever. Fig. *Synecdoche* (of Whole), Ap. 6. The whole put for a portion; i. e. as long as he lives. Put literally in *v*. 28.
24 weaned. From 2 Macc. 7. 27 it has been inferred that the time of weaning included the periods of nourishment and up-bringing, which would bring Samuel to the age of at least twelve years. Cp. Isaac's weaning at the age of five years, and see Gen. 21. 8.
three bullocks. Sept. and Syr. read "a bullock of three years". Cp. *v*. 25, and Gen. 15. 9.
ephah. See Ap. 51. III. 3.
a bottle = a skin bottle.
and the child was young. Heb. *v[e]hannar nā'ar*. Fig. *Paronomasia* (Ap. 6) = "now the boy was a child". Note also the Fig. *Parenthesis*. Ap. 6.
25 a = the.
26 thy soul = thyself. Heb. *nephesh*. Ap. 13.
28 the LORD = Jehovah. Punctuate thus, "to Jehovah as long as he liveth. He shall be", &c. Note the Fig. *Paronomasia* (Ap. 6) in *vv*. 27, 28. "Jehovah hath given me my petition (*sh[e]'ēlāthī*) which I asked of Him (*shā'altī*): therefore also I have lent him (*hishiltīhū*) to Jehovah."

2. 1-11 [For Structure see next page].

1 the LORD. Heb. Jehovah. Ap. 4. II.
Mine horn. First occurrence. Part of head-dress over which the veil is thrown hanging over the shoulders; mothers making it more perpendicular. This is now fast becoming extinct. Cp. 2 Sam. 22. 3. Ps. 75. 4. Luke 1. 69.
the LORD. Heb. Jehovah (Ap. 4. II). Some codices, with two early printed editions, read "My God". Ap. 4. I. Cp. *v*. 17.

about 1048 2 *There is* °none °holy as [1]the LORD:
For *there is* none beside Thee:
Neither *is there* °any rock like our °God.

f1 (p. 369) 3 Talk no more so °exceeding proudly;
Let °*not* arrogancy come out of your mouth:

e2 For [1]the LORD *is* a °GOD of knowledge,
And by Him actions are weighed.

f2 4 The bows of the mighty men *are* broken,
And they that stumbled are girded with strength.
5 *They that were* full have hired out themselves for bread;
And *they that were* hungry ceased:
So that the barren hath born seven;
And she that hath many °children is waxed feeble.

e3 6 [1]The LORD killeth, and maketh alive:
He bringeth down to °the grave, and bringeth up.
7 [1]The LORD maketh poor, and maketh rich:
He bringeth low, and lifteth up.
8 He raiseth up °the poor out of the dust,
And lifteth up the beggar from the dunghill,
To set *them* among princes,
And to make them inherit the throne of glory:
For the °pillars of the earth *are* [1]the LORD'S,
And He hath set the world upon them.
9 He will keep the feet of His saints,
And the °wicked shall be silent in darkness;
For by strength shall no °man prevail.

f3 10 The adversaries of [1]the LORD shall be broken to pieces;
°Out of heaven shall He thunder upon them:
[1]The LORD shall judge the ends of the earth;

e4 And He shall give strength unto °His king,
And exalt [1]the horn of °His °Anointed."

11 And Elkanah went to Ramah to his house. And the °child did minister unto [1]the LORD before Eli the priest.

D2 12 Now the sons of Eli *were* sons of Belial; they knew not [1]the LORD.
13 And the priests' custom with the people *was, that,* when any [9]man °offered sacrifice, the priest's servant came, while the flesh was °in seething, with a fleshhook of three teeth in his hand;
14 And he struck *it* into the pan, or kettle, or caldron, or pot; all that the fleshhook brought up the priest °took for himself. So they did in Shiloh unto all the Israelites that came thither.
15 Also before °they burnt the fat, the priests' servant came, and said to the [13]man that sacrificed, °"Give flesh to roast for the priest; for he will not have °sodden flesh of thee, but raw."
16 And *if* any [13]man said unto him, "Let them not fail to °burn the fat °presently, and *then* take *as much* as °thy soul desireth;" then he would answer °him, "*Nay;* but thou shalt give *it me* now: and if not, I will take *it* by force."
17 Wherefore the °sin of the young men was very great before [1]the LORD: for °men abhorred the offering of [1]the LORD.

18 But Samuel ministered before [1]the LORD, *being* a [11]child, girded with °a linen ephod. C3 g

19 Moreover his mother made him a little coat, and brought *it* to him from year to year, when she came up with her husband to [13]offer the yearly sacrifice. h i

20 And Eli blessed Elkanah and his wife, and k

---

2. 1-11 (*E*, p. 367). HANNAH AND JEHOVAH.
(*Repeated Alternation.*)

E | e1 | 1, 2. Jehovah. Holiness.
  f1 | 3-. Enemies. Pride broken.
 e2 | -3. Jehovah. Knowledge.
  f2 | 4, 5. Enemies. Weapons broken.
 e3 | 6-9. Jehovah. Grace.
  f3 | 10-. Enemies. Themselves broken.
 e4 | -10. Jehovah. Grace.

2 none holy. This is the cry of all His saints. See note on Ex. 15. 11. **holy.** See note on Ex. 3. 5.
any rock. Cp. Deut. 32. 4. 2 Sam. 22. 32.
God. Heb. Elohim. Ap. 4.
3 exceeding proudly. This is the true rendering of the Fig. *Epizeuxis* (Ap. 6). Heb. "proudly, proudly".
not. The latter of two or more negatives not necessary in Heb. An Ellipsis must be supplied, as here. See note on Gen. 2. 6.
GOD = *El.* Ap. 4. IV.
5 children = sons.
6 the grave. Heb. *sh^eōl.* Ap. 35.
8 the poor: i. e. the oppressed. Cp. Ps. 113. 7.
pillars. Heb. *māzūk* = that which is set fast. Occurs only here and 14. 5, where it is rendered "situate".
9 wicked = lawless. See Ap. 44. x.
man. Heb. *'īsh.* Ap. 14. II.
10 Out of heaven. See 7. 10.
His king. First occurrence. Cp. Ps. 2. 6.
His Anointed = His Messiah. The first occurrence as used of Christ. So Sept. and Vulg.
Anointed. Sept. reads "Christos" = Christ.
11 child = youth.
13 offered. Heb. *zābāh.* Ap. 43. I. iv.
in seething = boiling.
14 took for himself. Robbing the offerers of their own portion. See Lev. 7. 31-35. Deut. 18. 3.
15 they: i.e. not the offerer, but the priest for him.
Give flesh. This was contrary to Lev. 3. 16; 7. 23, 25, 30, 31. **sodden** = boiled.
16 burn (as incense). See Ap. 43. I. vii.
presently = now, immediately, without delay, at once. This English meaning is now obsolete.
thy soul = thou (emph.). Heb. *nephesh.* Ap. 13.
him, Nay. "Nay" is to be read, instead of "him". In some codices, with three early printed editions, Sept., Syr., and Vulg.
17 sin. Heb. *chāta'.* Ap. 44. i.
men. Heb. *'ĕnōsh.* Ap. 14. III.

18-21 (C3, p. 367). ELKANAH AND FAMILY.
(*Introversion and Alternation.*)

C3 | g | 18. Samuel. Ministration.
 h | i | 19. Parents' yearly visit.
  k | 20-. Eli's blessing.
 h | *i* | -20. Parents' return.
  k | 21-. Jehovah's visitation.
 g | -21. Samuel. Growth.

18 a linen ephod. Not the High Priest's, but a simple linen robe of the ordinary priests and Levites and others. 1 Sam. 22. 18. 2 Sam. 6. 14. Cp. Ex. 28. 42. Lev. 6. 10.

1048 to 1044 said, [1]"The LORD give thee seed of this woman for the °loan which is lent to [1] the LORD."

h i (p. 369) And they went unto their own home.

k 21 And [1]the LORD visited Hannah, so that she conceived, and bare three sons and two daughters.

g And the [11]child Samuel grew before [1]the LORD.

D3 (p. 367) 22 Now Eli was very old, and heard all that his sons did unto all Israel; and how they lay with the women that assembled *at* the °door of the °tabernacle of the congregation.
23 And he said unto them, °"Why do ye such things? for I hear of your °evil dealings °by all this People.
24 Nay, my sons; °for *it is* no good report that I hear: ye make [1]the LORD'S People °to transgress.
25 If one [13]man [17]sin against another, °the judge shall judge him: but if a [13]man [17]sin against [1]the LORD, °who shall intreat for him?" Notwithstanding they hearkened not unto the voice of their father, because [1]the LORD would slay them.

C4 26 And the [11]child Samuel grew on, and was in favour both with [1]the LORD, and also with [13]men.

D4 l1 (p. 370) 27 And there came a °man of [2]God unto Eli, and said unto him, "Thus saith [1]the LORD, °'Did I plainly °appear unto the house of thy father, when °they °were in Egypt in Pharaoh's house?
28 And [27]did I choose him out of all the tribes of Israel *to be* My priest, °to offer upon Mine altar, to °burn incense, to wear an ephod before Me? and [27]did I give unto the house of °thy father all the offerings made by fire of the °children of Israel?

m1 29 Wherefore °kick ye at My sacrifice and at Mine °offering, which I have commanded *in My* habitation; and honourest thy sons above Me, to make yourselves fat with the chiefest of all the °offerings of Israel My People?'

l2 30 Wherefore [1]the LORD [2]God of Israel saith, 'I said indeed *that* thy house, and the house of thy father, should walk before Me for ever:'

m2 but now [1]the LORD saith, 'Be it far from Me; for them that honour Me I will honour, and they that despise Me shall be lightly esteemed.
31 °Behold, the days come, that I will cut off thine °arm, and the °arm of thy father's house, that there shall not be an old man in thine house.
32 And thou shalt °see an enemy *in my* habitation, in all *the wealth* which *God* shall give Israel: and there shall not be an old man in thine house for ever.
33 And the [13]man of thine, *whom* I shall not cut off from Mine altar, *shall be* to consume °thine eyes, and to °grieve °thine °heart: and all the increase of °thine house shall die °in the flower of their age.
34 And this *shall be* a sign unto thee, that shall come upon thy two sons, on Hophni and Phinehas; in one day they shall °die both of them.

l3 35 And I will raise Me up a faithful priest, *that* shall do according to *that* which *is* in Mine heart and in My °mind: and I will build him a sure house; and he shall walk before Mine anointed for ever.
36 And it shall come to pass, *that* every one that is left in thine house shall come *and* crouch °to him for a piece of silver and a morsel of bread, and shall say, 'Put me, I pray thee, into one of the priests' offices, that I may eat a piece of bread.'"

C5 n (p. 371) **3** And the °child Samuel ministered unto °the LORD before Eli. And the word of °the LORD °was °precious in those days; *there was* no open vision.

---

20 loan which is lent = the great gift. Fig. *Polyptōton*, for emphasis. Ap. 6.
22 door = entrance.
tabernacle = tent of meeting.
23 Why . . . ? Fig. *Erotēsis*. Ap. 6.
evil. Heb. *rāʿaʿ*. Ap. 44. viii. by = from.
24 for. Heb. has the disjunctive accent on this word (Great *Telīsha*), emphasising the guilt of Hophni and Phinehas as (1) a public scandal (*v.* 23); (2) a cause of stumbling (*v.* 24); (3) a sin against Jehovah (*v.* 25).
to transgress, or cry out. Heb. *ʿābar*. Ap. 44. vii.
25 the judge = God. Heb. Elohim. Ap. 4. I.
who . . . ? Fig. *Erotēsis*. Ap. 6.

2. 27-36 (D4, p. 367). ELI AND HIS SONS.
(*Repeated Alternation.*)

D4 | l1 | 27, 28. Election of priestly order.
m1 | 29. Provocation of Eli's sons.
l2 | 30-. Election of Eli.
m2 | -30-34. Rejection of Eli's sons.
l3 | 35, 36. Election of Samuel.

27 man of God: i.e. a prophet. See Deut. 33. 1 and Ap. 49. Cp. Judg. 13. 6.
Did I plainly . . . ? = I did indeed, with Sept., Aram., and Syr.
appear = reveal Myself.
they. Aaron as well as Moses was in Pharaoh's house. See note on Ex. 4. 27.
were. Sept. reads "were servants". Cp. Deut. 5. 6.
28 to offer. See Ap. 43. I. vi.
burn incense. See Ap. 43. I. vii.
thy father: i.e. Aaron. Ex. 29. 27, 28. Lev. 10. 14.
children = sons.
29 kick. Cp. Deut. 32. 15; its only other occurrence.
offering = gift offerings. See Ap. 43. II. iii.
31 Behold. Fig. *Asterismos*. Ap. 6.
arm = seed.
32 see an enemy. Cp. Ps. 78. 60-64.
33 thine. Sept. reads "his".
grieve. Heb. *'ādab*. Occurs only here.
heart = soul. Heb. *nephesh*. Ap. 13.
in the flower of their age. Sept. reads "with the sword of men".
34 die both. See 4. 11.
35 mind = soul. Heb. *nephesh*. Ap. 13.
36 to him: i.e. to the Anointed [king] of *v.* 10: already pointing to the High Priest as being no longer the judge, but subordinate to the king.

3. 1-10 [For Structure see next page].

1 child = youth. Heb. *naʿar*.
the LORD. Heb. Jehovah. Ap. 4. II.
was = had come to be.
precious. Heb. *yāḳar* = heavy (in price). Note the five precious things in Old Testament: the word of God (3. 1, its first occurrence); redemption (Ps. 49. 8); the death of His saints (Ps. 72. 14; 116. 15); the lips of knowledge (Prov. 20. 15); the thoughts of God (Ps. 139. 17). See note on the five in New Testament (Matt. 26. 7).

o p[1] (p. 371) 1044 to 1040 2 And it came to pass at that time, when Eli *was* laid down in his place, and his eyes began to wax dim, *that* he could not ° see;

3 And ere the ° lamp of ° God went out in ° the temple of [1] the LORD, where the ark of ° God *was*, and Samuel was laid down *to sleep;*

4 That [1] the LORD called Samuel: and he answered, ° "Here *am* I."

5 And he ran unto Eli, and said, "Here *am* I; for thou calledest me." And he said, "I called not; lie down again." And he went and lay down.

p[2] 6 And [1] the LORD called yet again, "Samuel." And Samuel arose and went to Eli, and said, "Here *am* I; for thou didst call me." And he answered, "I called not, my son; lie down again."

n 7 Now Samuel did not yet know [1] the LORD, neither was the word of [1] the LORD yet revealed unto him.

o p[3] 8 And [1] the LORD called Samuel again the third time. And he arose and went to Eli, and said, [4] "Here *am* I; for thou didst call me." And Eli perceived that [1] the LORD had called the [1] child.

9 Therefore Eli said unto Samuel, "Go, lie down: and it shall be, if He call thee, that thou shalt say, 'Speak, [1] LORD; for Thy servant heareth.'" So Samuel went and lay down in his place.

p[4] 10 And [1] the LORD came, and stood, and called as at other times, ° "Samuel, Samuel." Then Samuel answered, "Speak; for Thy servant heareth."

D[5] q[1] 11 And [1] the LORD said to Samuel, ° "Behold, I will do a thing in Israel, at which both the ears of every one that heareth it shall ° tingle.

12 In that day I will perform against Eli all *things* which I have spoken concerning his house: when I begin, I will also make an end.

13 For I have told him that I will judge his house for ever for the ° iniquity which he knoweth; because his sons ° made themselves vile, and he restrained them not.

14 And therefore I have sworn unto the house of Eli, that the [13] iniquity of Eli's house shall not be purged with sacrifice nor offering for ever."

r[1] 15 And Samuel lay until the ° morning, and opened the doors of the house of [1] the LORD. And Samuel feared to shew Eli the vision.

q[2] 16 Then Eli called Samuel, and said, "Samuel, my son." And he answered, "Here *am* I."

17 And he said, "What *is* the ° thing that *the* LORD hath said unto thee? I pray thee hide *it* not from me: [3] God do so to thee, and more also, if thou hide *any* thing from me of all the things that He said unto thee."

r[2] 18 And Samuel told him ° every whit, and hid nothing from him.

q[3] And he said, "It *is* [1] the LORD: let Him do what seemeth Him good."

C[6] s 19 And Samuel grew, and [1] the LORD was with him, and did let none of his words fall to the ground.

t 20 And all Israel from Dan even to Beer-sheba knew that Samuel *was* ° established *to be* a prophet of [1] the LORD.

3. 1-10 (C[5], p. 367). ELKANAH'S SON, SAMUEL (*Alternation.*)

C[5] | n | 1. Samuel, and the word of Jehovah.
o | p[1] | 2-5. His first call.
p[2] | 6. His second call.
n | 7. Samuel, and the word of Jehovah.
o | p[3] | 8, 9. His third call.
p[4] | 10. His fourth call.

2 see = see clearly.
3 lamp of God = the seven-branched candlestick.
God. Heb. Elohim. Ap. 4.
the temple: i. e. the tabernacle. See note on 1. 9.
4 Here am I = Behold me.
10 Samuel, Samuel. Fig. *Epizeuxis*. Ap. 6. See note on Gen. 22. 11 for the ten reduplications.

11-18 (D[5], p. 367). ELI AND HIS SONS. (*Repeated Alternation.*)

D[5] | q[1] | 11-14. Eli. Threatening.
r[1] | 15. Samuel's fear.
q[2] | 16, 17. Eli. Demand.
r[2] | 18-. Samuel. Compliance.
q[3] | -18. Eli. Submission.

11 Behold. Fig. *Asterismos*. Ap. 6.
tingle. Cp. 2 Kings 21. 12. Jer. 19. 3.
13 iniquity. Heb. *'āvāh*.
made themselves vile. This is one of the eighteen emendations of the *Sōpherīm*, on their own confession. See Ap. 33. By omitting one letter they changed this, from a mistaken sense of reverence. The primitive text, preserved in the Sept., stood, "his sons cursed God".
15 morning. The copyist's eye, in going back to this word, went to the word at the end of the next sentence, and thus omitted "and rose early in the morning". These words are preserved in the Sept.
17 thing = word.
18 every whit = every particle. Anglo-Saxon, *wiht*. Every bit. Heb. "all the words".

3. 19—4. 1- (C[6], p. 367). ELKANAH'S SON, SAMUEL. (*Alternation.*)

C[6] | s | 3. 19. Samuel. Jehovah with him.
t | 3. 20. Israel. Acknowledgment.
s | 3. 21. Samuel. Jehovah's revelation to him.
t | 4. 1-. Israel. Submission.

20 established, &c. Samuel was the first of "the prophets" and last of the judges, preparing the way for the change of government.
21 by. Or, according to.

4. -1—7. 2 (B, p. 367). SUBJECTION BY PHILISTINES. (*Extended Alternation.*)

B | u | 4. -1-. Israel in camp of war.
v | 4. -1. Philistines.
w | 4. 2. First battle, and result.
u | 4. 3-5. Israel in camp of war.
v | 4. 6-9. Philistines.
w | 4. 10—7. 2. Second battle, and result.

1 came. Cp. Acts 3. 24. Heb. 11. 32.
Eben-ezer = Stone of help. So called in anticipation of Samuel's victory twenty years later (7. 12).
Aphek = Fortress. Josh. 15. 53.

21 And [1] the LORD appeared again in Shiloh: for [1] the LORD revealed Himself to Samuel in Shiloh ° by the word of [1] the LORD. s

4 And the word of Samuel ° came to all Israel. *t*

Now Israel went out against the Philistines to battle, and pitched beside ° Eben-ezer: u

and the Philistines pitched in ° Aphek. v

w 2 And the Philistines put themselves in array
(p. 371) against Israel: and when they joined battle,
1040 Israel was smitten before the Philistines: and they slew of the army in the field about four thousand °men.

u 3 And when the People were come into the camp, the elders of Israel said, °"Wherefore hath °the LORD smitten us to day before the Philistines? Let us fetch the ark of the covenant of °the LORD out of Shiloh unto us, that, when it cometh among us, it may save us out of the hand of our °enemies."

4 So the People sent to °Shiloh, that they might bring from thence the ark of the covenant of °the LORD of hosts, which dwelleth *between* the cherubims: and the two sons of Eli, Hophni and Phinehas, *were* there with the ark of the covenant of °God.

5 And when the ark of the covenant of [1] the LORD came into the camp, all Israel °shouted with a great °shout, so that the earth rang again.

v 6 And when the Philistines heard the °noise of the shout, they said, "What °*meaneth* the noise of this great shout in the camp of the Hebrews?" And they understood that the ark of [3] the LORD was come into the camp.

7 And the Philistines were afraid, for they said, [4] "God is come into the camp." And they said, °"Woe unto us! for there hath not been such a thing heretofore.

8 [7] Woe unto us! °who shall deliver us out of the hand of these mighty Gods? these *are* °the Gods that smote the Egyptians with all the plagues in the wilderness.

9 Be strong, and °quit yourselves like °men, O ye Philistines, that ye be not servants unto the Hebrews, °as they have been to you: °quit yourselves like °men, and fight."

w G 10 And the Philistines fought, and Israel was
(p. 372) smitten, and they fled °every man into his tent: and there was a very great slaughter; for there fell of Israel thirty thousand footmen.

H 11 And the ark of [4] God was taken; and the two sons of Eli, Hophni and Phinehas, were slain.

G x[1] 12 And there ran a °man of Benjamin out of the army, and came to Shiloh the same day with his clothes rent, and with earth upon his head.

y[1] 13 And when he came, °lo, Eli sat upon °a seat by the wayside watching: for his heart trembled for the ark of °God.

x[2] And when the [12] man came into the city, and told *it*, all the city cried out.

y[2] 14 And when Eli heard the noise of the crying, he said, "What *meaneth* the °noise of this tumult?"

x[3] And the [12] man came in hastily, and told Eli.

y[3] 15 Now Eli was ninety and eight years old; and his eyes °were dim, that he °could not see.

16 And the [12] man said unto Eli, "I *am* he that came out of the army, and I fled to day out of the army." And he said, "What is there done, my son?"

17 And the messenger answered and said, "Israel is fled before the Philistines, °and there hath been also a great slaughter among the People, and thy two sons also, Hophni and Phinehas, are dead, and the ark of [13] God is taken."

2 men. Heb. *'ish*. Ap. 14. II.
3 Wherefore . . . ? Fig. *Erotēsis*. Ap. 6.
the LORD. Heb. Jehovah. Ap. 4. II.
enemies. Some codices, with four early printed editions, read "enemy".
4 Shiloh. See note on 1. 3.
the LORD of hosts. See note on 1. 3.
God = *Elohim*. Ap. 4. I. Marking His relation to His creatures.
5 shouted . . . shout. Fig. *Polyptōton*. Ap. 6. See note on Gen. 26. 28.
6 noise of the shout. Fig. *Pleonasm*. Ap. 6. Cp. *v.* 14.
meaneth = is. Cp. Matt. 9. 13; 26. 26, 28.
7 Woe unto us! Fig. *Anaphora* (Ap. 6), repeated in *v.* 8.
8 who . . . ? Fig. *Erotēsis*. Ap. 6.
the Gods = the Gods themselves.
9 quit yourselves like = the Heb. verb *hāyāh*, to become; as "was" should be rendered in Gen. 1. 2.
men. Heb. *'īsh* or *'ĕnōsh*. Ap. 14.
as = according as.

4. 10—7. 2 (*w*, p. 371). SECOND BATTLE AND RESULT. (*Alternation*.)

w | G | 4. 10. Israel. Defeat.
  H | 4. 11. Ark taken by Philistines.
 G | 4. 12-22. Israel. Report of defeat.
  H | 5. 1—7. 2. Ark in captivity to Philistines.

10 every man. Heb. *'ish*. Ap. 14.

12-22 (*G*, above). ISRAEL. REPORT OF DEFEAT. (*Repeated Alternation*.)

G | x[1] | 12. Fugitive comes to Shiloh.
  y[1] | 13-. Eli's fear for Ark.
 x[2] | -13. Fugitive comes to people.
  y[2] | 14-. Eli's alarm for Ark.
 x[3] | -14. Fugitive comes to Eli.
  y[3] | 15-18. Eli's death.
 x[4] | 19-. Tidings come to son's wife.
  y[4] | -19-22. Her death.

12 man. Heb. *'ish*. Ap. 14. II.
13 lo. Fig. *Asterismos*. Ap. 6. a = the.
God. Heb. with Art. = the God. Ap. 14. I.
14 noise of this tumult. Fig. *Pleonasm*. Ap. 6.
15 were dim = were set, as in 1 Kings 14. 4.
could not see. One of the nine cases of blindness. See note on Gen. 19. 11.
17 and. Note the Fig. *Polysyndeton* in *v.* 17.
19 came = came suddenly. 20 about = at.
21 I-chabod = Where is the glory?
because of. Some codices add "the death of". Cp. *v.* 19.

18 And it came to pass, when he made mention of the ark of [13] God, that he fell from off the seat backward by the side of the gate, and his neck brake, and he died: for he was an old [12] man, and heavy. And he had judged Israel forty years.

19 And his daughter in law, Phinehas' wife, x[4]
was with child, *near* to be delivered: and when she heard the tidings that the ark of [13] God was taken, and that her father in law and her husband were dead,

she bowed herself and travailed; for her pains y[4]
°came upon her.

20 And °about the time of her death the women that stood by her said unto her, "Fear not; for thou hast born a son." But she answered not, neither did she regard *it*.

21 And she named the child °I-chabod, saying, "The glory is departed from Israel: because the ark of [13] God was taken, and °because of her father in law and her husband."

22 And she said, "The glory is departed from Israel: for the ark of [13] God is taken."

H J a (p. 373) 1040 **5** And the Philistines took the ark of °God, and brought it from °Eben-ezer unto °Ashdod.

2 When the Philistines took the ark of ¹God, they brought it into the house of °Dagon, and set it by Dagon.

3 And when they of Ashdod arose early on °the morrow, °behold, Dagon *was* fallen upon his face to the earth before the ark of °the LORD. And they took Dagon, and set him in his place again.

4 And when they arose early on the morrow morning, ³behold, Dagon *was* fallen upon his face to the ground before the ark of ³the LORD; and the head of Dagon and both the palms of his hands *were* cut off upon the threshold; °only *the stump of* °Dagon was left to him.

5 Therefore neither the priests of Dagon, nor any that come into Dagon's house, tread on the threshold of Dagon in Ashdod unto this day.

6 But the °hand of ³the LORD was heavy upon them of Ashdod, and He destroyed them, and smote them with °emerods, *even* Ashdod and the coasts thereof.

7 And when the °men of Ashdod saw that *it was* so, they said, "The ark of the ¹God of Israel shall not abide with us: for His hand is sore upon us, and upon Dagon our god."

8 They sent therefore and gathered all the °lords of the Philistines unto them, and said, "What shall we do with the ark of the ¹God of Israel?" And they answered, "Let the ark of the ¹God of Israel be carried about unto Gath." And they carried the ark of the ¹God of Israel about *thither*.

9 And it was *so*, that, after they had carried it about, the hand of ³the LORD was against the city with a very great destruction: and He smote the ⁷men of the city, both small and great, and they had ⁶emerods in their secret parts.

10 Therefore they sent the ark of ¹God to Ekron. And it came to pass, as the ark of ¹God came to Ekron, that the Ekronites cried out, saying, "They have brought about the ark of the ¹God of Israel to us, to slay us and our people."

11 So they sent and gathered together all the ⁸lords of the Philistines, and said, "Send away the ark of the ¹God of Israel, and let it go again to his own place, that it slay us not, and our people:" for there was a deadly destruction throughout all the city; the ⁶hand of ¹God was very heavy there.

12 And the ⁷men that died not were smitten with the ⁶emerods: and the cry of the city went up to heaven.

b **6** And the ark of °the LORD was in the country of the Philistines seven months.

K M e g 2 And the Philistines called for the priests and the diviners, saying, "What shall we do to the ark of ¹the LORD? tell us wherewith we shall send it to his place."

h 3 And they said, "If ye send away the ark of the °God of Israel, send it not empty; but in any wise return Him a trespass offering: then ye shall be healed, and it shall be known to you why His hand is not removed from you."

5. 1—7. 2 (*H*, p. 372). ARK IN CAPTIVITY TO PHILISTINES. (*Introversion and Alternation.*)

H | J | a | 5. 1–:2. Captivity in Philistia.
  b | 6. 1. Duration. Seven months.
 K | 6. 2–16. Removal to Beth-shemesh.
  L | 6. 17, 18. Lords of Philistines.
 K | 6. 19, 20. Judgment at Beth-shemesh.
J | *a* | 6. 21—7. 1. Captivity of Ark ended.
  b | 7. 2–. Duration. Twenty years.

5. 1-12 (a, above). CAPTIVITY IN PHILISTIA. (*Repeated Alternation.*)

a | c¹ | 1. From Eben-ezer to Ashdod.
 d¹ | 2-6. Judgment on Ashdodites.
c² | 7, 8. From Ashdod to Gath.
 d² | 9. Judgment on Gathites.
c³ | 10–. From Gath to Ekron.
 d³ | –10-12. Judgment on Ekronites.

1 God. Heb. Elohim. See Ap. 4. I.

Eben-ezer. Cp. 4. 1; 7. 12.

Ashdod = fortified. Now Esdud. Cp. Josh. 13. 3. See note on Gen. 10. 14.

2 Dagon = great fish.

3 the morrow. Sept. adds "and entered into the house of Dagon, they looked and" behold, &c.

behold. Fig. *Asterismos.* Ap. 6.

the LORD. Heb. Jehovah, in contrast with Dagon. Ap. 4. II.

4 only . . . Dagon. The hands and feet being gone, only Dagon (the fish part) remained.

6 hand. Put by Fig. *Metonymy* (of Cause), Ap. 6, for the judgments inflicted by it.

emerods. See note on Deut. 28. 27.

7 men. Heb. *'ĕnōsh.* Ap. 14. III.

8 lords = princes. See note on Josh. 13. 3.

6. 1 the LORD. Heb. Jehovah. Ap. 4. The Ark now gets its own Divine title.

6. 2-16 (K, above). REMOVAL TO BETH-SHEMESH. (*Alternation.*)

K | M | 2-12–. Dismissal of Ark.
 N | –12. Lords of Philistines following.
M | 13-15. Reception of Ark.
 N | 16. Lords of Philistines returning.

2-12– (M, above). DISMISSAL OF ARK. (*Alternation.*)

M | e | 2-8. Consultation of Philistines.
 f | 9. Test suggested.
e | 10, 11. Consultation. Result.
 f | 12–. Test applied.

2-8 (e, above). CONSULTATION OF PHILISTINES. (*Alternation.*)

e | g | 2. Questions. What? Wherewith?
 h | 3. Answer. Trespass offering.
g | 4–. Question. What?
 h | –4-8. Answer. A new cart.

3 God. Heb. Elohim. Ap. 4. I.

4 emerods. See note on 5. 6; i.e. models of them in gold; of which, modern "votive offerings" are the lineal descendants. Cp. *v.* 5.

lords. See note on Josh. 13. 3.

4 Then said they, "What *shall be* the trespass offering which we shall return to Him?" *g*

They answered, "Five golden °emerods, and five golden mice, *according to* the number of the °lords of the Philistines: for one plague *was* on you all, and on your °lords. *h*

5 Wherefore ye shall make images of your emerods, and images of your mice that mar the

1040 land; and ye shall give glory unto the [3]God of
Israel: peradventure He will lighten His °hand
from off you, and from off your gods, and from
off your land.

6 Wherefore then do ye harden your hearts,
°as the Egyptians and Pharaoh hardened their
hearts? when He had wrought wonderfully
among them, did they not let the people go,
and they departed?

7 Now therefore make °a new cart, and take
two milch kine, on which there hath come no
yoke, and tie the kine to the cart, and bring
their calves home from them:

8 And take the ark of [1]the LORD, and lay it
upon the cart; and put the jewels of gold,
which ye return Him *for* a trespass offering,
in a coffer by the side thereof; and send it
away, that it may go.

f 9 And see, if °it goeth up by the way of his
(p. 373) own °coast to °Beth-shemesh, *then* He hath
done us °this great °evil: but if not, then we
shall know that *it is* not His hand *that* smote
us; it *was* a chance *that* happened to us."

e 10 And °the men did so; and took two milch
kine, and tied them to the cart, and shut up
their calves at home:

11 And they laid the ark of [1]the LORD upon
the cart, and the coffer with the mice of gold
and the images of their [4]emerods.

f 12 And the kine took the straight way to the
way of [9]Beth-shemesh, *and* went along the
highway, lowing as they went, and turned not
aside *to* the right hand or *to* the left;

N and the [4]lords of the Philistines went after
them unto the border of Beth-shemesh.

M 13 And *they of* [9]Beth-shemesh *were* reaping
their wheat harvest in the valley: and they
lifted up their eyes, and saw the ark, and rejoiced to see *it*.

14 And the cart came into the field of Joshua,
a Beth-shemite, and stood there, where *there*
was a great stone: and they clave the wood
of the cart, and °offered the kine a burnt offering unto [1]the LORD.

15 And the Levites took down the ark of [1]the
LORD, and the coffer that *was* with it, wherein
the jewels of gold *were*, and put *them* on the
great stone: and the [10]men of Beth-shemesh
[14]offered burnt offerings and °sacrificed sacrifices the same day unto [1]the LORD.

N 16 And when the five [12]lords of the Philistines
had seen *it*, they returned to Ekron the same
day.

L 17 And these *are* the golden [11]emerods which
the Philistines returned *for* a trespass offering
unto [1]the LORD; for °Ashdod one, for Gaza
one, for Askelon one, for Gath one, for Ekron
one;

18 And the golden mice, *according to* the
number of all the cities of the Philistines
belonging to the five [4]lords, *both* of fenced
cities, and of country villages, even unto the
great *stone of* Abel, whereon they set down
the ark of [1]the LORD: *which stone remaineth*
unto this day in the field of Joshua, the Beth-
shemite.

K 19 And He smote the [10]men of Beth-shemesh,
because they had looked into the ark of [1]the
LORD, even He smote of the People °fifty
thousand and threescore and ten °men: and
the People lamented, because [1]the LORD had
smitten *many* of the People with a great
°slaughter.

20 And the [10]men of Beth-shemesh said,
°"Who is able to stand before this °holy
[1]LORD [3]God? and to whom shall °he go up
from us?"

21 And they sent messengers to the inhabit- *J a*
ants of Kirjath-jearim, saying, "The Philis- (p. 373)
tines have brought again the ark of [1]the
LORD; come ye down, *and* fetch it up to you."

7 And the °men of Kirjath-jearim came,
and fetched up the ark of °the LORD, and
brought it into the house of °Abinadab °in the
hill, and sanctified Eleazar his son to keep the
ark of °the LORD.

2 And it came to pass, while the ark abode in *b*
Kirjath-jearim, that the °time was long; for 1040 to
it was twenty years: 1020

and all the house of Israel lamented after *A* i
[1]the LORD. (p. 375)

5 hand. See note on 5. 6.
6 as=according as.
7 a new cart. This was done in ignorance of God's requirement (Num. 4. 15; 7. 9; 10. 21). They could not have complied with the Law, even if they had known it; hence, no judgment fell on them. But contrast David's "new cart", and see note on 2 Sam. 6. 3.
9 it: i. e. the "ark", which is masc.; not the "cart", which is fem.
coast=border, or boundary.
Beth-shemesh=House of the sun, now *Ain Shems*, on the borders of Judah and Dan. Cp. Josh. 15. 10.
this. Some codices, with three early printed editions, read "all this".
evil. Heb. *rā'a'*. Ap. 44. viii.
10 the men. Heb. *'ĕnōsh*. Ap. 14. III.
14 offered=offered up. Ap. 43. I. vi.
15 sacrificed sacrifices=made great sacrifices. Fig. *Polyptōton*. Ap. 6. See note on Gen. 26. 28.
17 Ashdod one. See note on Gen. 10. 14.
19 fifty thousand and threescore and ten men=50,070. This number being out of all proportion to the size of Beth-shemesh, has led to various readings. Some codices omit 50,000. The Syr. and Arabic versions read "five" instead of fifty. Josephus reads "seventy". The Heb. text reads "seventy men two fifties and one thousand"=70+100+1,000=1,170.
men. Heb. *'ish*. Ap. 14. II.
slaughter=smiting, making the Fig. *Polyptōton*. Ap. 6.
20 Who . . .? Fig. *Erotēsis*. Ap. 6.
holy. See note on Ex. 3. 5.
he=it: i. e. the ark. See note on *v.* 9.

7. 1 men. Heb. *'ĕnōsh*. Ap. 14. III.
the LORD. Heb. Jehovah. Ap. 4. II.
Abinadab. Some codices, with one early printed edition, Aram., Sept., and Syr., add "which is".
in the hill. Or, in Gibeah.

7. 2-6 [For Structure see next page].

2 time was long. Ark remained with Philistines seven months (6. 1); sent from Ekron to Kirjath-jearim in 1040, and remained there twenty years (ch. 7). From the capture (in 1040) to its entry into Zion (in 950) was eighty-nine years (2 Sam. 7. 17).

1020 **3** And Samuel spake unto all the house of Israel, saying, "If ye do return unto [1]the LORD with all your hearts, *then* put away the strange gods and Ashtaroth from among you, and prepare your hearts unto [1]the LORD, and serve Him only: and He will deliver you out of the hand of the Philistines."

4 Then the °children of Israel did put away Baalim and Ashtaroth, and served [1]the LORD only.

5 And Samuel said, "Gather all Israel to Mizpeh, and I will pray for you unto [1]the LORD."

6 And they gathered together to Mizpeh, and drew water, and poured *it* out before [1]the LORD, and fasted on that day, and said there, "We have °sinned against [1]the LORD."

k (p. 375) And Samuel judged the [4]children of Israel in Mizpeh.

B i **7** And when the Philistines heard that the [4]children of Israel were gathered together to Mizpeh, the °lords of the Philistines went up against Israel. And when the [4]children of Israel heard *it*, they were afraid of the Philistines.

8 And the [4]children of Israel said to Samuel, "Cease not to cry unto [1]the LORD our °God for us, that He will save us out of the hand of the Philistines."

9 And °Samuel took a sucking lamb, and °offered *it for* a burnt offering wholly unto [1]the LORD: and Samuel cried unto [1]the LORD for Israel; and [1]the LORD heard him.

10 And as Samuel was [9]offering up the burnt offering, the Philistines drew near to battle against Israel: but [1]the LORD °thundered with a great thunder on that day upon the Philistines, and discomfited them; and they were smitten before Israel.

11 And the [1]men of Israel went out of Mizpeh, and pursued the Philistines, and smote them, until *they came* under Beth-car.

12 Then Samuel took a stone, and set *it* between Mizpeh and Shen, and called the name of it Eben-ezer, saying, "Hitherto hath [1]the LORD helped us."

13 So the Philistines were subdued, and they came no more into the °coast of Israel: and the hand of [1]the LORD was against the Philistines all the days of Samuel.

14 And the cities which the Philistines had taken from Israel were restored to Israel, from Ekron even unto Gath; and the [13]coasts thereof did Israel deliver out of the hands of the Philistines. And there was peace between Israel and the Amorites.

k **15** And Samuel judged Israel all the days of his life.

16 And he went from year to year in circuit to Beth-el, and Gilgal, and Mizpeh, and judged Israel in all those places.

17 And his return *was* to Ramah; for °there *was* his house; and there he judged Israel; and there he built an °altar unto [1]the LORD.

B[1] Q T n **8** And it came to pass, when Samuel was °old, that he made his sons judges over Israel.

2 Now the name of his firstborn was Joel; and the name of his second, Abiah: *they were* judges in Beer-sheba.

3 And his sons walked not in his ways, but °turned aside after lucre, and °took bribes, and perverted judgment.

4 Then all the elders of Israel gathered themselves together, and came to Samuel unto Ramah,

5 And said unto him, °"Behold, thou art old, and thy sons walk not in thy ways: now

---

7. -2-6 (*A*, p. 367). REPENTANCE OF ISRAEL.

7. 7-17 (*B*, p. 367). DELIVERANCE FROM PHILISTINES. (*Alternation.*)

A | i | -2-6-. Israel. Repentance.
  k | -6. Government of Samuel. Place.
B | *i* | 7-14. Israel. Recovery.
  k | 15-17. Government of Samuel. Time.

4 children = sons.
6 sinned. Heb. *chāṭā'*. Ap. 44. I.
7 lords. See note on Josh. 13. 3.
8 God. Heb. Elohim. Ap. 4.
9 Samuel took. Samuel was a Levite, and according to 1 Chron. 23. 27-32 could do this; though according to Num. 18. 3 he could not have acted in the holy place.
offered = offered up. See Ap. 43. I. vi.
10 thundered with a great thunder. Fig. *Polyptōton.* Ap. 6.
13 coast = border, or boundary.
17 there was his house. Cp. 1. 19, &c.
altar. Shiloh forsaken, and Ark separated from Tabernacle. There was no chosen "place".

1 Sam. **8. 1**—2 Sam. **1. 27** (**B**[1], p. 366). KING SAUL. (*Alternation.*)

B[1] | O | 1 Sam. 8. 1—12. 25. Choice of SAUL.
  P | 1 Sam. 13. 1—15. 35. Provocation of Saul. Rejection threatened.
O | 1 Sam. 16. 1—27. 4. Choice of DAVID.
  P | 1 Sam. 27. 5—2 Sam. 1. 27. Provocation of Saul. Rejection carried out.

8. 1—12. 25 (O, above). CHOICE OF SAUL. (*Introversion.*)

O | Q | 8. 1—10. 26. Settlement of Kingdom.
  R | 10. 27. Men of Belial.
    S | 11. 1-11. Aggression of Nahash.
  R | 11. 12, 13. Men of Belial.
Q | 11. 14—12. 25. Inauguration of Kingdom.

8. 1—10. 26 (Q, above). SETTLEMENT OF SAUL'S KINGDOM. (*Alternation.*)

Q | T | 8. 1-22-. King desired.
  U | 8. -22. Dismissal of People to cities.
T | 9. 1—10. 25-. King given.
  U | 10. -25, 26. Dismissal of People to homes.

8. 1-22- (T, above). KING DESIRED. (*Introversion and Alternation.*)

T | l | n | 1-5. Desire expressed.
    o | 6-9-. Compliance.
      m | -9. Warning. (General.)
      m | 10-18. Warning. (Particular.)
  l | *n* | 19, 20. Desire persisted in.
    o | 21, 22-. Compliance.

1 old. From 28. 3 he predeceased Saul by about two years. Consequently he acted for thirty-eight years after Saul's anointing (i.e. 1000-962 B.C.). When he anointed David he would be about eighty-six; and lived to about the age of Eli, ninety-eight years.
3 turned aside, &c.: i.e. stooped to extortion.
took bribes: contrary to Deut. 16. 19.
5 Behold. Fig. *Asterismos.* Ap. 6.

1004 °make us a king to judge us like all the na-
to tions."
1000 6 But the thing °displeased Samuel, when
o they said, "Give us a king to judge us." And
(p. 375) Samuel prayed unto °the LORD.
7 And [6]the LORD said unto Samuel, "Hearken unto the voice of the People in all that they say unto thee: for they have not rejected thee, but they have rejected Me, that I should not reign over them.
8 According to all the works which they have done since the day that I brought them up out of Egypt even unto this day, wherewith they have forsaken Me, and served other gods, so do they also unto thee.
9 Now therefore hearken unto their voice:

m howbeit yet protest solemnly unto them, and shew them the manner of the king that shall reign over them."

m 10 And Samuel told all the words of [6]the LORD unto the People that asked of him a king.
11 And he said, °"This will be the manner of the king that shall reign over you: He will take your sons, and appoint *them* for himself, for his chariots, and *to be* his horsemen; and *some* shall run before his chariots.
12 And he will appoint him captains over thousands, and captains over fifties; and *will set them* to °ear his ground, and to reap his harvest, and to make his instruments of war, and instruments of his chariots.
13 And he will take your daughters *to be* confectionaries, and *to be* cooks, and *to be* bakers.
14 And he will take your fields, and your vineyards, and your oliveyards, *even* the best *of them*, and give *them* to his servants.
15 And he will take the tenth of your seed, and of °your vineyards, and give to his officers, and to his servants.
16 And he will take your menservants, and your maidservants, and your goodliest °young men, and your asses, and put *them* to his work.
17 He will take the tenth of your sheep: and ye shall be his servants.
18 And ye shall cry out in that day because of your king which ye shall have chosen you; and [6]the LORD will not °hear you in that day."

n 19 Nevertheless the People refused to obey the voice of Samuel; and they said, "Nay; but we will have a king over us;
20 That we also may be like all the nations; and that our king may judge us, and go out before us, and fight our battles."

o 21 And Samuel heard all the words of the people, and he rehearsed them in °the ears of [6]the LORD.
22 And [6]the LORD said to Samuel, "Hearken unto their voice, and make them a king."

U And Samuel said unto the °men of Israel, "Go ye every °man unto his city."

T W¹ (p. 376) **9** Now there was a °man of Benjamin, whose name *was* °Kish, the son of Abiel, the son of Zeror, the son of Bechorath, the son of Aphiah, °a Benjamite, a °mighty man of power.
2 And he had a son, whose name *was* °Saul, a choice young man, and a goodly: and *there* *was* not among the °children of Israel a goodlier person than he: from his shoulders and upward *he was* higher than any of the people.

3 And the asses of Kish Saul's father were °lost. X¹ Y¹ p¹

And Kish said to Saul his son, "Take now one of the °servants with thee, and arise, go seek the asses." q¹

4 And °he passed through °mount Ephraim, and passed through the land of Shalisha, but they found *them* not: then they passed through the land of Shalim, and *there they were* not: and °he passed through the land of the Benjamites, but they found *them* not. r¹

5 *And* when they were come to the land of Zuph, Saul said to his [3]servant that *was* with him, "Come, and let us return; lest my father Y² p²

---

make us a king. Cp. Hos. 13. 10, 11. Acts 13. 20, 21. Note the words "gave judges" and "desired a king". The Hebrew monarchy thus began with the choosing of Saul, and ended with the choosing of Cæsar.
6 displeased = was evil in the eyes of: i.e. evil, in not waiting for God's time and for God's king, as promised. Gen. 17. 6, 16; 35. 11; 49. 10. Num. 24. 17. Deut. 17. 14-20.
the LORD. Heb. Jehovah. Ap. 4. II.
11 This will be, &c. Fulfilled, 14. 52.
12 ear=plough (Anglo-Saxon, *erian*).
15 your vineyards. Cp. 1 Kings 21. 7.
16 young men. Sept. reads "oxen".
18 hear = answer.
21 the ears. Fig. *Anthropopatheia*. Ap. 6.
22 men. Heb. *'ĕnôsh*. Ap. 14. III.
man. Heb. *'îsh*. Ap. 14. II.

9. 1—10. 25- (*T*, p. 375). KING GIVEN.
(*Repeated Alternation.*)

T | W^1 | 9. 1, 2. King designated.
  X^1 | 9. 3-14. Asses lost.
 W^2 | 9. 15—10. 13. King sought.
  X^2 | 10. 14-16. Asses found.
 W^3 | 10. 17-25-. King appointed.

1 man. Heb. *'îsh*. Ap. 14. II.
Kish. Cp. 14. 51. 1 Chron. 8. 33; 9. 39. For the difficulties of the genealogy, see note on 1 Chron. 8. 33.
a Benjamite. As was Saul of Tarsus (Phil. 3. 5).
mighty man. Heb. *gibbōr*. Ap. 14. IV.
2 Saul. Many points of resemblance and contrast with Saul of Tarsus. Name = Asked for: i. e. by man.
children = sons.

9. 3-14 (X^1, above). ASSES LOST.
(*Extended Alternation.*)

X^1 | Y^1 | p^1 | 3-. Kish. Asses lost.
   q^1 | -3. His command.
    r^1 | 4. Obeyed by Saul.
 Y^2 | p^2 | 5. Saul's servant.
   q^2 | 6-10-. His advice.
    r^2 | -10. Taken by Saul.
 Y^3 | p^3 | 11. Maidens of the city.
   q^3 | 12, 13. Their advice.
    r^3 | 14. Taken by Saul.

3 lost. Contrast David, who had charge of his father's "sheep", and "*kept* them" (16. 11); with Saul, who *lost* his father's "asses" (9. 3).
servants = young men. Tradition says "Doeg". Cp. 21. 7.
4 he. Some codices, with Sept. and Vulg., read "they", as in *v.* 6.
mount = the hill country of.

1000 leave *caring* for the asses, and °take thought for us."

q^2 s (p. 377) 6 And he said unto him, °"[6] Behold now, *there is* in this city a °man of °God, and *he is* an honourable °man; all that he saith cometh surely to pass: now let us go thither; peradventure he can shew us our way that we should go."

t 7 Then said Saul to his servant, "But, [6]behold, *if* we go, what shall we bring the [6]man? for the bread is spent in our vessels, and *there is* not a °present to bring to the [6]man of [6]God: what have we?"

s 8 And the servant answered Saul again, and said, [6]"Behold, I have here at hand the fourth part of a °shekel of silver: °*that* will I give to the [6]man of [6]God, to tell us our way."

9 (°Beforetime in Israel, when a [1]man went to enquire of [6]God, thus he spake, "Come, and let us go to the °seer:" for *he that is* now *called* a °Prophet was beforetime called a °Seer.)

t 10 Then said Saul to his servant, "Well said; come, °let us go."

r^2 So they went unto the city where the [6]man of [6]God *was.*

p^3 (p. 376) 11 *And* as they went °up the hill to the city, they found young maidens going out to draw water, and said unto them, "Is the [9]seer here?"

q^3 12 And they answered them, and said, "He is; [6]behold, *he is* before you: make haste now, for he came to day to the city; for *there is* a sacrifice °of the People to day in °the high place:

13 As soon as ye be come into the city, ye shall straightway find him, before he go up to [12]the high place to eat: for the People will not eat until he come, because he doth bless the sacrifice; *and* afterwards they eat that be bidden. Now therefore get you up; for about this time ye shall find him."

r^3 14 And they went up into the city: *and* when they were come into the city, [6]behold, Samuel came °out against them, for to go up to the high place.

W^2 A (p. 377) 15 Now °the LORD had °told Samuel in his ear °a day before Saul came, saying,

16 "To morrow about this time I will send thee a [6]man out of the land of Benjamin, and thou shalt anoint him *to be* °captain over My People Israel, that he may save My People out of the hand of the Philistines: for I have looked upon °My People, because their cry is come unto Me."

17 And when Samuel saw Saul, [15]the LORD said unto him, [6]"Behold the [6]man whom I spake to thee of! this same shall °reign over My People."

B u 18 Then Saul drew near to Samuel °in the gate, and said, "Tell me, I pray thee, where the seer's house *is.*"

v 19 And Samuel answered Saul, and said, "I *am* the seer: go up before me unto the high place; for ye shall eat with me to day, and to morrow I will let thee go, and will tell thee all that *is* in thine heart.

20 And as for thine asses that were lost three days ago, set not thy °mind on them; for they are found. And on whom *is* all the desire of Israel? *Is it* not on thee, and on all thy father's house?"

21 And Saul answered and said, °"*Am* not I a Benjamite, of °the smallest of the tribes of Israel? and my family the least of all the families of the tribe of Benjamin? wherefore then speakest thou °so to me?" *v*

---

take thought = be anxious. Cp. Matt. 6. 25, 27, 28, 31, 34.

9. 6-10- (q^2, p. 376). SERVANT'S ADVICE. (*Alternation.*)

q^2 | s | 6. The man of God. Statement.
  t | 7. Objection.
 s | 8, 9. The man of God. Explanation.
  t | 10-. Assent.

6 Behold. Fig. *Asterismos.* Ap. 6.

man of God = God's man: i.e. a prophet, because God's spokesman. See Ap. 49. (Heb. *'ish* and Elohim.)

man. Heb. *'ish.* Ap. 14. II.

God. Heb. Elohim. Ap. 4. I. Lit. "the God".

7 present. Heb. *teshurah.* Occurs only here. It is from *shūr*, to behold. Hence, that which procures and secures an interview, or sight of the person sought.

8 shekel. See Ap. 51. II.

that will I give. Sept. reads "which thou canst give".

9 Beforetime. Note the parenthesis.

seer. Heb. *ro'eh*=a seer of visions. Another name for seer was *chozeh*, which referred rather to spiritual apprehension of what was seen. In 1 Chron. 29. 29 all three words occur in the same verse.

Prophet. Heb. *nab'ī* = one who spoke for or was moved by God.

10 let. Some codices, with one early printed edition, and Sept., read "and let".

11 up the hill=by the ascent of.

12 of=by. Gen. of Instrument. See Ap. 17.

the high place. In Num. 21. 19 = Bamoth-Baal. Shiloh was now forsaken. No "place" within the meaning of Deut. 12. Cp. 1 Sam. 7. 10, 17.

14 out against=opposite, so as to meet them.

9. 15—10. 13 (W^2, p. 376). KING SOUGHT. (*Alternation.*)

W^2 | A | 9. 15-17. The anointing. Command.
  B | 9. 18-27. Reception by Samuel.
 A | 10. 1. The anointing. Obedience.
  B | 10. 2-13. Directions by Samuel.

15 the LORD. Heb. Jehovah. Ap. 4. II.

told Samuel in his ear=opened or uncovered the ear of Samuel. **a**=one.

16 captain=leader.

My people. Aram. and Syr. read "the oppression". In that case the Fig. *Ellipsis* should be supplied after it, "of My People" being implied.

17 reign=control, restrain, or rule.

18-27 (B, above). RECEPTION BY SAMUEL. (*Introversion.*)

B | u | 18. Meeting of Samuel with Saul.
  v | 19, 20. Samuel's answer to Saul.
  v | 21. Saul's answer to Samuel.
 u | 22-27. Communication of Samuel.

18 in the gate. Heb. "in the midst of the gate": i.e. the open place near the gate where judgment was given.

20 mind. Heb. "heart"="do not regard them".

21 Am not I . . . ? Fig. *Erotēsis.* Ap. 6.

the smallest. Very true, since the events recorded in Judg. 20. 35.

so to me=according to this word.

u 22 And Samuel took Saul and his servant,
(p. 377) and brought them into the parlour, and made
1000 them sit in the chiefest place among them
that were bidden, which *were* about thirty
persons.
23 And Samuel said unto the cook, "Bring
the portion which I gave thee, of which I said
unto thee, 'Set it by thee.'"
24 And the cook took up the shoulder, and
that which *was* upon it, and set *it* before Saul.
And *Samuel* said, [6]"Behold that which is
°left! set *it* before thee, *and* eat: for unto this
time hath it been kept for thee since I said,
'I have invited the People.'" So Saul did eat
with Samuel that day.
25 And when they were come down from the
high place into the city, *Samuel* communed
with Saul upon the top of the house.
26 And they arose early: and it came to pass
about the spring of the day, that Samuel called
Saul to the top of the house, saying, "Up, that
I may send thee away." And Saul arose, and
they went out both of them, he and Samuel,
abroad.
27 *And* as they were going down to the end of
the city, Samuel said to Saul, "Bid the servant
pass on before us," (and he passed on,) "but
stand thou still a while, that I may shew thee
°the word of °God."

A **10** Then Samuel took °a vial of oil, and
poured *it* upon his head, and kissed
him, and said, °"*Is it* not because °the LORD
hath anointed thee *to be* °captain over His
inheritance?

B w 2 When thou art departed from me to day,
(p. 378) then °thou shalt find two °men by °Rachel's
sepulchre in the border of Benjamin at Zelzah;
and they will say unto thee, 'The asses which
thou wentest to seek are found: and, °lo, thy
father hath left the care of the asses, and
sorroweth for you, saying, 'What shall I do
for my son?''
3 Then shalt thou go on forward from thence,
and thou shalt come to the °plain of Tabor,
and there shall meet thee three [2]men going up
to °God to °Beth-el, one °carrying three kids,
and another carrying three loaves of bread,
and another carrying a bottle of wine:
4 And they will °salute thee, and give thee
two *loaves* of bread; which thou shalt receive
of their hands.
5 After that thou shalt come to the hill of
[3]God, where *is* °the garrison of the Philistines: and it shall come to pass, when thou
art come thither to the city, that thou shalt
meet °a company of prophets coming down
from the high place with a °psaltery, and a
°tabret, and a °pipe, and a harp, before them;
and they shall °prophesy:
6 And °the Spirit of [1]the LORD will come
upon thee, and thou shalt prophesy with them,
and shalt be turned into another °man.
x 7 And let it be, when these signs are come
unto thee, *that* thou do as °occasion serve
thee; for [3]God *is* with thee.
x 8 And °thou shalt go down before me to
Gilgal; and, °behold, I will come down unto
thee, to °offer burnt offerings, *and* to °sacri-
fice sacrifices of peace offerings: seven days
shalt thou tarry, till I come to thee, and shew
thee what thou shalt do."

24 left! = reserved.
27 the word of God. First occurrence of this expression. "Word of Jehovah" frequent from Gen. 15. 1.
God = Elohim. Ap. 4. I. Creation relationship.

10. 1 a vial = flask. Not "the".
Is it not . . . ? Fig. *Erotēsis*. Ap. 6.
the LORD. Heb. Jehovah. Ap. 4. Note the Jehovah relationship. Here is another *Homœoteleuton*, which is preserved in the Sept. and Vulg., "the LORD [and thou shalt rule among the people of Jehovah, and thou shalt save them out of the hand of their enemies, and this shall be a sign unto thee, that] the LORD hath, &c. The eye of some ancient scribe evidently went back to the latter of these two words "the LORD" and accidentally omitted the words between them.
captain: "a" captain; not "the".

10. 2-13 (*B*, p. 377). DIRECTIONS BY SAMUEL.
(*Introversion.*)

B | w | 2-6. Signs given.
x | 7. Command.
x | 8. Appointment.
w | 9-13. Signs fulfilled.

2 thou shalt find. Three signs given (cp. Mark 14. 3) to indicate the coming change.
men. Heb. *'ĕnōsh*. Ap. 14. III.
Rachel's sepulchre. Cp. Gen. 35. 20.
lo. Fig. *Asterismos*. Ap. 6.
3 plain = oak, or terebinth; growing generally alone, becomes a conspicuous landmark.
God. Heb. Elohim. Ap. 4. I.
Beth-el = House of God. Evidently a place of worship, in the absence of any "place", according to Deut. 12. 5, &c. Cp. Ex. 20. 24.
carrying. Probably their firstfruits. Cp. 2 Kings 4. 42.
4 salute. Heb. ask after thy peace.
5 the garrison. So the Sept., Aram., and Syr., but Heb. text has pl.
a company of prophets. The first occurrence of this expression. Probably a school established by Samuel (cp. Acts 3. 24; 13. 20). The head of such school called "father" (cp. 10. 12; 19. 20), or "master" (2 Kings 2. 3). Such communities found later at Beth-el, Jericho, Gilgal (2 Kings 2. 3, 5; 4. 38); and probably here at Gibeah and Ramah (cp. Naioth, 19. 18, 20).
psaltery = viol. A stringed instrument, same as lute. Cp. 2 Sam. 6. 5. 1 Kings 10. 12. 1 Chron. 16. 5. Isa. 5. 12; 14. 11. Amos 5. 23; 6. 5.
tabret = drum. Heb. *toph*. Cp. 18. 6. 2 Sam. 6. 5. Isa. 5. 12; 24. 8; 30. 32. Jer. 31. 4. Ezek. 28. 13. See note on "timbrel" (Ex. 15. 20).
pipe = a plain reed, single or double, played like modern flute. Note pl. in the Subscription of Ps. 5 (*Companion Bible*).
prophesy. Not necessarily "foretell", but speak in the name of the Lord.
6 the Spirit. Heb. *rūach*. Ap. 9.
man. Heb. *'īsh*. Ap. 14. II.
7 occasion serve thee = thy hand shall find.
8 thou shalt go down. This was the beginning of organised rising against the Philistines. All directed by God through Samuel; not by Saul.
behold. Fig. *Asterismos*. Ap. 6.
offer = offer up. Ap. 43. I. vi.
sacrifice = slay. Ap. 43. I. iv. Note the Fig. *Polysyndeton* in *v.* 8. Ap. 6.

w (p. 378) 1000 9 And it was *so*, that when he had turned his back to go from Samuel, [3]God gave him °another heart: and all those signs came to pass that day.

10 And when they came thither to the hill, [8]behold, a company of prophets met him; and [6]the Spirit of [3]God came upon him, and he prophesied among them.

11 And it came to pass, when all that knew him beforetime saw that, [8]behold, he prophesied among the prophets, then the People said one to another, °"What *is* this *that* is come unto the son of Kish? *Is* Saul also among the prophets?"

12 And one °of the same place answered and said, "But who *is* their father?" Therefore it became a proverb, °"*Is* Saul also among the prophets?"

13 And when he had made an end of prophesying, he came to the high place.

X^2 (p. 376) 14 And Saul's uncle said unto him and to his servant, "Whither went ye?" And he said, "To seek the asses: and when we saw that *they were* no where, we came to Samuel."

15 And Saul's uncle said, "Tell me, I pray thee, what Samuel said unto you."

16 And Saul said unto his uncle, "He told us plainly that the asses were found." But of the matter of the kingdom, whereof Samuel spake, he told him not.

W^3 y^1 (p. 379) 17 And Samuel called the People together unto [1]the LORD to Mizpeh;

z^1 18 And said unto the °children of Israel, °"Thus saith [1]the LORD [3]God of Israel, 'I brought up Israel out of Egypt, and delivered you out of the hand of the Egyptians, and out of the hand of all kingdoms, *and* of them that oppressed you:

19 And ye have this day rejected your [3]God, Who Himself saved you out of all your adversities and your tribulations; and ye have said unto Him, °'*Nay*, but set a king over us.'

y^2 Now therefore present yourselves °before [1]the LORD by your tribes, and by your thousands.'"

z^2 20 And when Samuel had caused all the tribes of Israel to come near, the tribe of Benjamin °was taken.

21 When he had caused the tribe of Benjamin to come near by their families, the family of Matri was taken, °and Saul the son of Kish was taken: and when they sought him, he could not be found.

22 Therefore they °enquired of [1]the LORD further, if the °man should yet come thither. And [1]the LORD answered, [8]"Behold, he hath hid himself among the stuff."

23 And they ran and fetched him thence: and when he stood among the People, he was higher than any of the People from his shoulders and upward.

24 And Samuel said to all the People, °"See ye him whom [1]the LORD hath chosen, that *there is* none like him among all the People?"

y^3 And all the People shouted, and said, °"God save the king."

z^3 25 Then Samuel told the People the manner of the kingdom, and °wrote *it* in a book, and laid *it* up before [1]the LORD.

And Samuel sent all the people away, every [22]man to his house. U (p. 375)

26 And Saul also went home to Gibeah; and there went with him a band of men, whose hearts [3]God had °touched.

27 But the [18]children of Belial said, °"How shall this man save us?" And they despised him, and brought him no presents. But °he held his peace.

11

Then Nahash the Ammonite came up, and encamped against Jabesh-gilead: S a^1 (p. 379)

and all °the men of Jabesh said unto Nahash, "Make a covenant with us, and we will serve thee." b^1

---

9 another = different.

11 What . . . ? Fig. *Erotēsis*. Ap. 6.

12 of the same place = from thence.

Is Saul . . . ? Origin of this *Parœmia*. Ap. 6.

10. 17-25 (W³, p. 376). KING APPOINTED.
(*Repeated Alternation.*)

W³ | y^1 | 17. People assembled. *En masse.*
z^1 | 18, 19-. Samuel's remonstrance.
y^2 | -19. People presented. By tribes.
z^2 | 20-24-. Samuel. Lots cast.
y^3 | -24. People. Approbation.
z^3 | 25-. Samuel. Confirmation.

18 children = sons.

Thus saith the LORD. This rehearsal is to show that they had sinned, although He was giving a king. Their sin was not in asking, but in forestalling Jehovah's already expressed purpose to give them a king (see Deut. 17. 15 and cp. Gen. 49. 10).

19 Nay. Some codices, with one early printed edition, Sept., Syr., and Vulg., have this word in the text.

before the LORD = before Jehovah: i. e. in Mizpeh, *v.* 17.

20 was taken: i. e. by lot, by the Urim and Thummim. See note on Ex. 28. 30.

21 and Saul. Sept. reads "and [when he had brought near the family of Matri man by man] Saul". Cp. Josh. 7. 17.

22 enquired: i. e. by the High Priest. No priest mentioned between chapters 4 and 14, a period of forty years.

man. Heb. *'ish.* Ap. 14. II.

24 See . . . ? Fig. *Erotēsis.* Ap. 6.

God save the king. Heb. Let the king live. An idiom which includes the desire that he might have everything that makes life worth living, including also eternal life.

25 wrote it in a book. Heb. the book: viz. the book kept before the Lord; even the scriptures of truth. See Ex. 17. 14 and Ap. 47.

26 touched = moved.

27 How . . . ? Fig. *Erotēsis.* Ap. 6.

he held his peace = he was as one that was deaf.

11. 1-11 (S, p. 375). AGGRESSION OF NAHASH.
(*Repeated Alternation.*)

S | a^1 | 1-. Aggression of Nahash.
b^1 | -1. Men of Jabesh-gilead. Message to Nahash.
a^2 | 2. Ultimatum of Nahash.
b^2 | 3, 4. Men of Jabesh-gilead. Message to Saul.
a^3 | 5-9. Ultimatum of Nahash.
b^3 | 10. Men of Jabesh-gilead. Reply to Nahash.
a^4 | 11. Defeat of Nahash.

1 the men. Heb. *'ĕnōsh.* Ap. 14. II. Those who had not obeyed the summons of Judg. 21. 8 were extinguished, and their daughters given to remnant of Benjamin. This gave them a claim on Saul, who was a Benjamite.

a^{2} (p. 379) 2 And Nahash the Ammonite answered them, "On this *condition* will I make °*a covenant* with you, that I may thrust out all your °right eyes, and lay it *for* a reproach upon all Israel."

b^{2} 3 And the elders of Jabesh said unto him, "Give us °seven days' respite, that we may send messengers unto all the °coasts of Israel: and then, if *there be* no °man to save us, we will come out to thee."

4 Then came the messengers to Gibeah of Saul, and told the tidings in the ears of the people: and all the people lifted up their voices, and wept.

a^{3} 5 And, °behold, Saul came after the herd out of the field; and Saul said, "What *aileth* the people that they weep?" And they told him the tidings of the [1]men of Jabesh.

6 And °the Spirit of °God °came upon Saul when he heard those tidings, and his anger was kindled greatly.

7 And he took a yoke of oxen, and °hewed them in pieces, and sent *them* throughout all the coasts of Israel by the hands of °messengers, saying, "Whosoever cometh not forth after Saul and after Samuel, so shall it be done unto his oxen." And the fear of °the LORD fell on the People, and they came out °with one consent.

8 And when he numbered them in Bezek, the °children of Israel were three hundred thousand, and the °men of Judah thirty thousand.

9 And they said unto the messengers that came, "Thus shall ye say unto the [1]men of Jabesh-gilead, 'To morrow, by *that time* the sun be hot, ye shall have °help.'" And the messengers came and shewed *it* to the [1]men of Jabesh; and they were glad.

b^{3} 10 Therefore the [1]men of Jabesh said, "To morrow we will come out unto you, and ye shall do with us all that seemeth good unto you."

a^{4} 11 And it was *so* on the morrow, that Saul put the People in three companies; and they came into the midst of the °host in the morning watch, and slew the Ammonites until the heat of the day: and it came to pass, that they which remained were scattered, so that two of them were not left together.

R 12 And the People said unto Samuel, "Who *is* he that said, 'Shall Saul reign over us?' bring the [1]men, that we may put them to death."

13 And Saul said, "There shall not a [8]man be put to death this day: for to day [7]the LORD hath wrought salvation in Israel."

Q D^{1} (p. 380) 14 Then said Samuel to the People, "Come, and let us go to Gilgal, and renew the kingdom there."

15 And all the People went to Gilgal; and there they made Saul king before [7]the LORD in Gilgal; and there they °sacrificed sacrifices of peace offerings before [7]the LORD; and there Saul and all the [1]men of Israel rejoiced greatly.

D^{2} E^{1} c^{1} **12** And Samuel said unto all Israel, °"Behold, I have hearkened unto your voice in all that ye said unto me, and have made a king over you.

2 And now, [1]behold, the king walketh before you:

2 a covenant. Some codices, with Sept., Syr., and Vulg., read this word in the text, which already implies it.

right eyes. As the shield covered the left eye, the right was necessary for seeing. The loss of it incapacitated men from fighting.

3 seven days. A very short respite.

coasts = borders.

man to save us = saviour.

5 behold. Fig. *Asterismos.* Ap. 6.

6 the Spirit. Heb. *rūach.* Ap. 9.

God. Some codices, with Aram., Sept., and Vulg., read "Jehovah". Cp. Ap. 4. II.

came = came mightily. Same word as in 10. 6, 10.

7 hewed. Always used of dividing what is already dead, and mostly of sacrifices.

messengers = the messengers.

the LORD. Heb. Jehovah. Ap. 4. II.

with one consent. Heb. as one man. Heb. *'īsh.* Ap. 14. II.

8 children = sons.

men. Heb. *'īsh.* Ap. 14. II.

9 help = salvation, or deliverance.

11 host = camp.

11. 14—12. 25 (Q, p. 375). INAUGURATION OF KINGDOM. (*Division.*)

Q | D^{1} | 11. 14, 15. People assembled.
  | D^{2} | 12. 1-25. People addressed.

15 sacrificed sacrifices. Fig. *Polyptōton.* Ap. 6. For emphasis. See Ap. 43. I. iv.

12. 1-25 (D^{2}, above). PEOPLE ADDRESSED.
(*Introversions and Alternations.*)

D^{2} | E^{1} | c^{1} | 1, 2-. The king presented. Desired.
  d^{1} | e | -2-5. Samuel's past administration.
  f | 6-12. Remonstrance.
  c^{2} | 13. The king presented. Given.
E^{2} | c^{3} | 14, 15. The king presented. Conditions.
  d^{2} | f | 16-22. Remonstrance.
  e | 23. Samuel's future action.
  c^{4} | 24, 25. The king presented. Conditions.

1 Behold. Fig. *Asterismos.* Ap. 6.

3 the LORD. Heb. Jehovah. Ap. 4. II.

whom. Some codices, with three early printed editions, read "or whom", thus preserving the Fig. *Paradiastole* (Ap. 6) throughout *vv.* 3 and 4.

4 man's. Heb. *'īsh.* Ap. 14. II.

and I am old and grayheaded; and, [1]behold, my sons *are* with you: and I have walked before you from my childhood unto this day. d^{1} e

3 [1]Behold, here I *am*: witness against me before °the LORD, and before His anointed: whose ox have I taken? or whose ass have I taken? or whom have I defrauded? °whom have I oppressed? or of whose hand have I received *any* bribe to blind mine eyes therewith? and I will restore it you."

4 And they said, "Thou hast not defrauded us, nor oppressed us, neither hast thou taken ought of any °man's hand."

5 And he said unto them, [3]"The LORD *is* witness against you, and His anointed *is* witness this day, that ye have not found ought in my hand." And they answered, "*He is* witness."

6 And Samuel said unto the People, "*It is* [3]the LORD That advanced Moses and Aaron, and that brought your fathers up out of the land of Egypt. f

7 Now therefore stand still, that I may reason with you before [3]the LORD of all the right-

1000 eous acts of [3]the LORD, which He did to you
and to your fathers.
8 When °Jacob was come into Egypt, and
your fathers cried unto [3]the LORD, then [3]the
LORD °sent Moses and Aaron, which brought
forth your fathers out of Egypt, and °made
them dwell in this place.
9 And when they forgat [3]the LORD their
°God, He sold them into the hand of Sisera,
captain of the host °of Hazor, and into the
hand of the Philistines, and into the hand of
the king of Moab, and they fought against them.
10 And they cried unto [3]the LORD, and said,
'We have °sinned, because we have forsaken
[3]the LORD, and have served Baalim and Ashtaroth: but now deliver us out of the hand of
our enemies, and we will serve Thee.'
11 And [3]the LORD sent Jerubbaal, °and Bedan, and Jephthah, °and Samuel, and delivered
you out of the hand of your enemies on every
side, and ye dwelled safe.
12 And when °ye saw that Nahash the king
of the °children of Ammon came against you,
ye said unto me, 'Nay; but a king shall reign
over us:' when [3]the LORD your [9]God *was*
your king.

c² (p. 380) 13 Now therefore behold the king whom ye
have chosen, °*and* whom ye have desired! and,
behold, [3]the LORD hath set a king over you.

E² c³ 14 If ye will fear [3]the LORD, and serve Him,
and obey His voice, and not rebel against the
commandment of [3]the LORD, then shall both
ye and also the king that reigneth over you
continue following [3]the LORD your [9]God:
15 But if ye will not obey the voice of [3]the
LORD, but rebel against the commandment of
[3]the LORD, then shall the hand of [3]the LORD
be against you, °as *it was* against your fathers.

d² *f* 16 Now therefore stand and see this great
thing, which [3]the LORD will do before your eyes.
17 *Is it* not wheat harvest to day? I will call
unto [3]the LORD, and He shall °send thunder
and rain; that ye may perceive and see that
your °wickedness *is* great, which ye have done
in the sight of [3]the LORD, in asking you a
king."
18 So Samuel called unto [3]the LORD; and
[3]the LORD sent thunder and rain that day:
and all the People greatly feared [3]the LORD
and Samuel.
19 And all the People said unto Samuel,
°"Pray for thy servants unto [3]the LORD thy
[9]God, that we die not: for we have added unto
all our [10]sins *this* °evil, to ask us a king."
20 And Samuel said unto the people, "Fear
not: ye have done all this [17]wickedness: yet
turn not aside from following [3]the LORD, but
serve [3]the LORD with all your heart;
21 And turn ye not aside: for *then should
ye go* after vain *things*, which cannot profit
nor deliver; for they *are* °vain.
22 For [3]THE LORD °WILL NOT FORSAKE HIS PEOPLE
for His great name's sake: because it
hath pleased [3]the LORD to make you °His
People.

e 23 Moreover as for me, [9]God forbid that I
should sin against [3]the LORD in ceasing to
pray for you: but I will teach you the good
and the right way:

8 Jacob. Cp. Gen. 46. 5, 6.
sent. Cp. Ex. 4. 16.
made = He caused. So Aram., Sept., Syr., and Vulg.
9 God. Heb. Elohim. Ap. 4. I.
of Hazor. Sept. reads "of Jabin king of".
10 sinned. Heb. *chāṭā'*. Ap. 44. i.
11 and Bedan. The Sept., Syr., and Arab. read "and Barak" (the names being much alike in Hebrew).
and Samuel. The Peshito (or Revised Syr.) reads "and Samson". But, if "Samuel", these are not Samuel's words, but Jehovah's in Samuel's mouth.
12 ye saw. Fig. *Hysterēsis*, or *Hysterologia* (Ap. 6), by which a prior event is recorded later.
children = sons.
13 and. Some codices, with three early printed editions, Syr., and Vulg., read "for".
15 as, &c. Sept. reads "and against your king".
17 send. It had to be sent, for rain in harvest was most exceptional; and would be regarded as sent in judgment. Cp. Prov. 26. 1.
wickedness. Heb. *rā'a'*. Ap. 44. viii.
19 Pray. Moses and Samuel specially named as intercessors. Ps. 99. 6. Jer. 15. 1.
evil. Same word as "wickedness" above.
22 will not forsake. Cp. Gen. 28. 15. Josh. 1. 5. Quoted in Rom. 11. 1, 2.
His People = a People for Himself.

13. 1—15. 35 (P, p. 375). PROVOCATION OF SAUL. (*Alternation.*)

P | F | 13. 1, 2. The levies of Saul.
  G | 13. 3—14. 46. War with Philistines.
  F | 14. 47–52. The levies of Saul.
  G | 15. 1–35. War with Amalek.

13. 3—14. 46 (G, above). WAR WITH PHILISTINES. (*Division.*)

G | H¹ | 13. 3–22. First aggression of Jonathan.
  | H² | 13. 23—14. 46. Second aggression of Jonathan.

13. 3–22 (H¹, above). FIRST AGGRESSION OF JONATHAN.
(*Introversion and Extended Alternation.*)

H¹ J¹ | g | 3, 4. Saul's assemblage of Israel.
  h | j | 5–. The Philistines. Number.
    k | –5. Encampment at Michmash.
  i | 6, 7. Israel. Distress.
  K | 8. Delay of Samuel.
  K | 9–15–. Sin of Saul.
J² | *g* | –15, 16–. Saul's assemblage of Israel.
  h | *k* | –16. Encampment at Michmash.
    j | 17, 18. The Philistines. Number.
  i | 19–22. Israel. Disarmament.

2 men. Sept. reads this word in text.
mount = hill country.
every man. Heb. *'ish*. Ap. 14. II.
3 Jonathan. See note on 18. 1.

24 Only fear [3]the LORD, and serve Him in c⁴
truth with all your heart: for consider how
great *things* He hath done for you.
25 But if ye shall still do wickedly, ye shall
be consumed, both ye and your king."

13 Saul reigned one year; and when he P F (p. 381)
had reigned two years over Israel, 1000 to
2 Saul chose him three thousand °*men* of 998
Israel; *whereof* two thousand were with Saul
in Michmash and in °mount Beth-el, and a
thousand were with Jonathan in Gibeah of
Benjamin: and the rest of the people he sent
°every man to his tent.

3 And °Jonathan smote the garrison of the H¹ J¹ g
Philistines that *was* in Geba, and the Philis-

998 to 974 tines heard *of it*. And Saul blew the trumpet throughout all the land, saying, "Let the Hebrews hear."

4 And all Israel heard say *that* Saul had smitten a garrison of the Philistines, and *that* Israel also was had in abomination with the Philistines. And the people were called together after Saul to °Gilgal.

h j (p. 381) 5 And the Philistines gathered themselves together to fight with Israel, °thirty thousand chariots, and °six thousand horsemen, and people °as the sand which *is* on the sea shore in multitude:

k and they came up, and pitched in Michmash, eastward from Beth-aven.

i 6 When the °men of Israel saw that they were in a strait, (for the People were °distressed,) then the People did hide themselves in caves, °and in thickets, and in rocks, and in high places, and in pits.

7 And *some of* °the Hebrews went over Jordan to the land of Gad and Gilead. As for Saul, he *was* yet in Gilgal, and all the People followed him trembling.

K 8 And he tarried seven days, according to the set time that Samuel °*had appointed:* but Samuel came not to Gilgal; and the People were scattered from him.

K 9 And Saul said, "Bring hither a burnt offering to me, and peace offerings." And he °offered the burnt offering.

10 And it came to pass, that as soon as he had made an end of [9]offering the burnt offering, °behold, Samuel came; and Saul went out to meet him, that he might °salute him.

11 And Samuel said, "What hast thou done?" And Saul said, "Because I saw that the People were scattered from me, [6] and *that* thou camest not within the days appointed, and *that* the Philistines gathered themselves together at Michmash;

12 Therefore said I, 'The Philistines will come down now upon me to Gilgal, and I have not made supplication unto °the LORD:' I forced myself therefore, and [9] offered °a burnt offering."

13 And Samuel said to Saul, "Thou hast done foolishly: °thou hast not kept the commandment of [12] the LORD thy °God, which He commanded thee: for now would [12] the LORD have established °thy kingdom upon Israel for ever.

14 But now thy kingdom shall not continue: [12] the LORD hath sought Him A °MAN AFTER HIS °OWN HEART, and [12] the LORD hath commanded him *to be* °captain over His People, because thou hast not kept *that* which [12] the LORD commanded thee."

15 And Samuel arose, and gat him up from °Gilgal unto Gibeah of Benjamin.

J² *g* And Saul numbered the People *that were* °present with him, about six hundred °men.

16 And Saul, and Jonathan his son, and the People *that were* present with them, abode in °Gibeah of Benjamin:

h k but the Philistines encamped in Michmash.

17 And the spoilers came out of the camp of the Philistines in three companies: one company turned unto the way *that leadeth* to Ophrah, unto the land of Shual: *j*

18 And another company turned the way *to* Beth-horon: and another company turned *to* the way of the border that looketh to the valley of Zeboim toward the wilderness.

19 Now there was °no smith found throughout all the °land of Israel: for the Philistines said, "Lest the Hebrews make *them* swords or spears:" *i*

20 But all the Israelites went down to the Philistines, to sharpen every [14] man his share, and his °coulter, and his axe, and his °mattock.

21 Yet they had a file for the [20] mattocks, and for the [20] coulters, and for the forks, and for the axes, and to sharpen the goads.

22 So it came to pass in the day of battle, that there was neither sword nor spear found in the hand of any of the People that *were* with Saul and Jonathan: but °with Saul and with Jonathan his son was there found.

---

4 Gilgal. In the plain of Jordan, east of Jericho, good for water, remote from Philistines, and connected with sacred memories.

5 thirty thousand . . . six, &c. Multiples of six. See Ap. 10.

as the sand, &c. Fig. *Parœmia.* Ap. 6.

6 men. Heb. *'īsh.* Ap. 14. II.

distressed = pressed : i. e. into Saul's service.

and. Note the Fig. *Polysyndeton.* Ap. 6.

7 the Hebrews went over. Fig. *Paronomasia* (Ap. 6), *'ibrīm 'abrū.*

8 had appointed. Some codices, with three early printed editions, Aram., and Sept., read "said". Some codices read "appointed".

9 offered = offered up. See Ap. 43. I. vi.

10 behold. Fig. *Asterismos.* Ap. 6.

salute = bless.

12 the LORD. Heb. Jehovah. Ap. 4. II.

a = the.

13 thou hast not. Some codices, with three early printed editions, and Vulg., read "and hast". Some codices, with Sept. and Syr., read "because thou hast".

God. Heb. Elohim. Ap. 4. I.

thy kingdom. This possible only with God as sovereign.

14 man, &c. Heb. *'īsh.* Ap. 14. II. Quoted in Acts 13. 22.

own heart = his own pleasure. Cp. Ps. 89. 20, 21.

captain = leader, or representative.

15 Gilgal. The Sept. preserves a *Homœoteleuton* here, adding after "Gilgal [and the rest of the people went up after Saul to meet the army when they arrived from] Gilgal"; the eye of the scribe going back to this last "Gilgal" instead of to the one in *v.* 15.

present = found.

men. Heb. *'īsh.* Ap. 14. II.

16 Gibeah. Probably the Geba of *v.* 3.

19 no smith. This explains why Ehud had to make his own dagger (Judg. 3. 16); why Shamgar had only an ox-goad (Judg. 3. 31); why Samson "had nothing in his hand" (Judg. 14. 5, 6); and why "not a shield or spear among 40,000 in Israel" (Judg. 5. 8). In other days we read of how many "drew sword".

land. Some codices read "bounds".

20 coulter. Anglo-Saxon = a *culter*; hence, a ploughshare.

mattock = a kind of pickaxe, with broad instead of pointed ends.

22 with Saul = with those who were with Saul and Jonathan : a picked force.

H² L l (p. 383) 998-974 23 And the ° garrison of the Philistines went out to the ° passage of Michmash.

m **14** Now it came to pass upon ° a day, that Jonathan the son of Saul said unto the young man that bare his armour, "Come, and let us go over to the Philistines' garrison, that *is* on the other side." But he told not his father.

n 2 And Saul tarried in the uttermost part of Gibeah under ° a pomegranate tree which *is* in ° Migron: and the People that *were* with him *were* about six hundred ° men;
3 And ° Ahiah, the son of Ahitub, ° I-chabod's brother, the son of Phinehas, the son of Eli, ° the LORD'S priest in Shiloh, ° wearing an ephod. And the people knew not that Jonathan was gone.

l 4 And between the passages, by which Jonathan sought to go over unto the Philistines' garrison, *there was* a ° sharp rock on the one side, and a ° sharp rock on the other side: ° and the name of the one *was* ° Bozez, and the name of the other ° Seneh.
5 The forefront of the one ° *was* situate northward over against ° Michmash, and the other southward over against ° Gibeah.

m 6 And Jonathan said to the young man that bare his armour, "Come, and let us go over unto the garrison of these uncircumcised: it may be that ° the LORD will work for us: for *there is* no restraint to [3]the LORD to save by many or by few."
7 And his armourbearer said unto him, "Do all that *is* in thine heart: turn thee; ° behold, I *am* with thee according to thy heart."
8 Then said Jonathan, [7]"Behold, we will pass over unto *these* ° men, and we will discover ourselves unto them.
9 If they say thus unto us, ° 'Tarry until we come to you;' then we will stand still in our place, and will not go up unto them.
10 But if they say thus, 'Come up unto us;' then we will go up: for [3]the LORD hath delivered them into our ° hand: and this *shall be* a sign unto us."
11 And both of them discovered themselves unto the garrison of the Philistines: and the Philistines said, [7]"Behold, ° the Hebrews come forth out of the holes where they had hid themselves."
12 And the [8]men of the garrison answered Jonathan and his armourbearer, and said, "Come up to us, and we will ° shew you a thing." And Jonathan said unto his armourbearer, "Come up after me: for [3]the LORD hath delivered them into the hand of Israel."
13 And Jonathan climbed up upon his hands and upon his feet, and his armourbearer after him: and they fell before Jonathan; and his armourbearer slew after him.
14 And that first slaughter, which Jonathan and his armourbearer made, was about twenty men, within as it were an half ° acre of land, *which* a yoke *of oxen might plow*.
15 And there was trembling in the ° host, in the field, and among all the people: the garrison, and the spoilers, they also ° trembled, and

13. 23—14. 46 (H², p. 381). SECOND AGGRESSION OF JONATHAN. (*Introversion.*)

H² | L | 13. 23—14. 19. Jonathan's success.
M | 14. 20-23. Saul's success.
L | 14. 24-46. Jonathan's sin.

13. 23—14. 19 (L, above). JONATHAN'S SUCCESS. (*Extended Alternation.*)

L | l | 13. 23. Garrison of Philistines. Place.
m | 14. 1. Attack proposed.
n | 14. 2, 3. Army of Saul.
l | 14. 4, 5. Garrison of Philistines. Description.
m | 14. 6-15. Attack carried out.
n | 14. 16-19. Army of Saul.

23 garrison = post, or permanent camp.
passage = pass.

14. 1 a day: i. e. a certain day.
2 a pomegranate tree = the pomegranate tree: i. e. the well-known one.
Migron. North of Gilgal.
men. Heb. *'īsh.* Ap. 14. II.
3 Ahiah (= brother or friend of Jehovah). As Ahimelech (brother or friend of the king) was also the son of *Ahitub*, therefore Ahiah and Ahimelech were brothers, and the latter succeeded the former (22. 11).
I-chabod's. Cp. 4. 21.
the LORD'S. Heb. Jehovah. Ap. 4. II.
wearing an ephod. See note on *v.* 18.
4 sharp rock = a crag. Heb. *sela'.* See notes on Ex. 17. 6. Ps. 18. 1, 2.
and. Some codices, with two early printed editions, Sept., Syr., and Vulg., omit this "and".
Bozez = Shining.
Seneh = Sharp, or pointed. Heb. = thorn.
5 was situate. Heb. *māẓūḳ*, only here, and 2. 8 = the sharp crag, or pillar of *v.* 4.
Michmash. Nine miles from Jerusalem.
Gibeah = Geba.
6 the LORD (Jehovah) **will work.** Note the language of faith. Cp. 2 Chron. 14. 11.
7 behold. Fig. *Asterismos.* Ap. 6.
8 men. Heb. *'ĕnōsh.* Ap. 14. III.
9 Tarry = keep quiet.
10 hand. Some codices, with two early printed editions, Sept., and Vulg., read "hands".
11 the Hebrews. Cp. *v.* 21.
12 shew you a thing = tell you something.
14 acre. Heb. = furrow, or a furrow's length. The Fig. *Ellipsis* (Ap. 6) is supplied, but the words "in a day" might be added for completeness at end of verse. This is the standard measure throughout the Turkish empire, called a *deunum* = 40 *arshuns.*
15 host = camp.
trembled = were panic-stricken. Cp. 2 Sam. 5. 24. 2 Kings 7. 6; 19. 7.
a very great trembling = a preternatural trembling. Heb. a trembling from Elohim. Ap. 4. I.
16 and they went on beating down, &c. Heb. hither and thither. A supposed *Ellipsis* is unnecessarily supplied. Read "melted away hither and thither", with Sept. and Syr.

the earth quaked: so it was ° a very great trembling.

16 And the watchmen of Saul in Gibeah of Benjamin looked; and, [7]behold, the multitude melted away, ° and they went on beating down *one another*. n
17 Then said Saul unto the People that *were* with him, "Number now, and see who is gone from us." And when they had numbered, [7]behold, Jonathan and his armourbearer *were* not *there*.
18 And Saul said unto Ahiah, "Bring hither

998 to 974 °the ark of °God." For the ark of °God was at that time with the °children of Israel.

19 And it came to pass, while Saul °talked unto the priest, that the noise that *was* in the [15]host of the Philistines went on and increased: and Saul said unto the priest, °"Withdraw thine °hand."

M o (p. 384) 20 And Saul and all the People that *were* with him °assembled themselves, and they came to the battle:

p and, behold, °every man's sword was against his fellow, *and there was* a very great discomfiture.

o 21 Moreover °the Hebrews *that* were with the Philistines before that time, which went up with them into the camp *from the country* round about, even they also °*turned* to be with the Israelites that *were* with Saul and Jonathan.

22 Likewise all the [2]men of Israel which had hid themselves in °mount Ephraim, *when* they heard that the Philistines fled, even they also followed hard after them in the battle.

p 23 So °the LORD saved Israel that day: and the battle passed over °unto °Beth-aven.

L q N[1] s 24 And the [2]men of Israel were distressed that day: for Saul had adjured the People, saying, "Cursed *be* the [2]man that eateth *any* °food until evening, that I may be avenged on mine enemies." So none of the People tasted *any* food.

25 And all *they of* the land came to a wood; and there was honey upon °the ground.

26 And when the People were come into the wood, °behold, the honey dropped; but no [2]man put his hand to his mouth: for the People feared the oath.

t 27 But Jonathan heard not when his father charged the People with the oath: wherefore he put forth the end of the rod that *was* in his hand, and dipped it in °an honeycomb, and put his hand to his mouth; and his eyes were enlightened.

28 Then answered one of the People, and said, "Thy father °straitly charged the People with an oath, saying, 'Cursed *be* the [2]man that eateth *any* food this day.'"

s And the People were °faint.

t 29 Then said Jonathan, "My father hath troubled the °land: see, I pray you, how mine eyes have been enlightened, because I tasted a little of this honey.

30 °How much more, if haply the People had eaten freely to day of the spoil of their enemies which they found? for had there not been now a much greater slaughter among the Philistines?"

N[2] u (p. 385) 31 And they smote the Philistines that day from Michmash to Aijalon:

v and the People were very faint.

18 the ark of God. The word rendered "bring" (*nāgash*) inappropriate for the Ark, which was at Kirjath-jearim (Judg. 20. 27, and cp. 2 Sam. 11. 11; 15. 24). The Sept. reads "the ephod, for he bare the ephod at that time before Israel". Cp. *v.* 3. The context shows that inquiry of the LORD by Urim and Thummim was in Saul's mind. See *v.* 18 and note on Ex. 28. 30, and cp. 1 Sam. 23. 6, 9; 30. 7, 8, where the same word is used for "bring".

God. Heb. Elohim. Ap. 4. I. Lit. "the God".

children = sons.

19 talked: i. e. concerning the inquiry proposed.

Withdraw: i. e. from the ephod = Stop!

hand. Some codices, with three early printed editions, and Sept., read "hands".

14. 20-23 (M, p. 383). SAUL'S SUCCESS. (*Alternation.*)

M | o | 20-. Assemblage.
p | -20. Mutual slaughter of enemies.
o | 21, 22. Assemblage.
p | 23. Salvation of Israel.

20 assembled themselves = were assembled (by proclamation).

every man's. Heb. *'ish.* Ap. 14.

21 the Hebrews. Called so in distinction from the foreigners among whom they lived; referring to language rather than nationality. Cp. *v.* 11.

turned. Sept. and Vulg. read "turned round".

22 mount = hill country of.

23 the LORD (Jehovah) **saved**: according to Jonathan's faith.

unto. Some codices, with Aram. and Vulg., read "as far as".

Beth-aven. The Sept. adds: "and all the people with Saul were about 10,000 men: and the battle extended itself to every city in the mount Ephraim. And Saul committed a great trespass of ignorance on that day."

24-46 (*L*, p. 383). JONATHAN'S SIN. (*Alternation.*)

L | q | 24-35. Sin committed.
r | 36-. Pursuit proposed by Saul.
q | -36-45. Sin discovered.
r | 46. Pursuit abandoned by Saul.

24-35 (q, above). SIN COMMITTED. (*Division.*)

q | N[1] | 24-30. By Jonathan.
N[2] | 31-35. By the people.

24-30 (N[1], above). BY JONATHAN. (*Alternation.*)

N[1] | s | 24-26. The people distressed.
t | 27, 28-. Jonathan ignorant.
s | -28. The people faint.
t | 29, 30. Jonathan troubled.

24 food. Heb. "bread", put by Fig. *Synecdoche* (of Species), Ap. 6, for all kinds of food.

25 the ground. Heb. "the face (i. e. surface) of the ground". Fig. *Pleonasm.* Ap. 6.

26 behold. Fig. *Asterismos.*

27 an honeycomb. The Heb. *ya'ar* never means honeycomb, but "a wood". It is rendered "forest" thirty-eight times, "wood" nineteen times, "honeycomb" only here and Song 5. 1. It points to a dense growing wood or thicket; and it has been suggested that it was the *cannabis indica*, or hemp plant, producing the Eastern intoxicant *hashish.* This would produce an effect on the eyes, though it would *subsequently* dull the senses. Song 5. 1 would read "I have eaten my cannabis with my honey". The Sept. and Vulg. did not understand either passage, and the latter misled with "honeycomb" (*favum*). **28 straitly** = strictly. **faint** = weary. **29 land** = people. Fig. *Metonymy* (of Subject), Ap. 6. **30 How...?** Fig. *Erotēsis.* Ap. 6.

31-35 [For Structure see next page].

998 to 974 32 And the People flew upon the spoil, and took sheep, and oxen, and calves, and slew *them* on the ground: and the People did eat *them* with the blood.

33 Then they told Saul, saying, [26] "Behold, the People ° sin against [3] the LORD, in that they eat with the blood." And he said, "Ye have ° transgressed:

v roll a great stone unto me ° this day."

(p. 385) 34 And Saul said, "Disperse yourselves among the people, and say unto them, 'Bring me hither [20] every man his ox, and [20] every man his sheep, and slay *them* here, and eat; and [33] sin not against [3] the LORD in eating with the blood.'" And all the People brought [20] every man ° his ox with him that night, and slew *them* there.

u 35 And Saul built an altar unto [3] the LORD: the same was the first altar that he built unto [3] the LORD.

r (p. 384) 36 And Saul said, "Let us go down after the Philistines by night, and spoil them until the morning light, and let us not leave a man of them." And they said, "Do whatsoever seemeth good unto thee."

q Then said the priest, "Let us draw near hither unto [18] God."

37 And Saul asked counsel of [18] God, "Shall I go down after the Philistines? wilt Thou deliver them into the hand of Israel?" But He answered him not that day.

38 And Saul said, "Draw ye near hither, all the chief of the People: and know and see wherein this [33] sin hath been this day.

39 For, *as* [3] the LORD liveth, Which saveth Israel, though it be in Jonathan my son, he shall surely die." But *there was* not a [20] man among all the People *that* answered him.

40 Then said he unto all Israel, "Be ye on one side, and I and Jonathan my son will be on the other side." And the People said unto Saul, "Do what seemeth good unto thee."

41 Therefore Saul said unto ° the LORD [18] God of Israel, ° "Give a perfect *lot*." And Saul and Jonathan were taken: but the People escaped.

42 And Saul said, "Cast *lots* between me and Jonathan my son." And Jonathan was taken.

43 Then Saul said to Jonathan, "Tell me what thou hast done." And Jonathan told him, and said, "I did but taste a little honey with the end of the rod that *was* in mine hand, *and*, ° lo, I must die."

44 And Saul answered, [18] "God ° do so and more also: for thou shalt surely die, Jonathan."

45 And the People said unto Saul, "Shall Jonathan die, who hath wrought this great salvation in Israel? [18] God forbid: *as* [3] the LORD liveth, there shall ° not one hair of his head fall to the ground; for he hath wrought with [18] God this day." So the People ° rescued Jonathan, that he died not.

46 Then Saul went up from following the Philistines: and the Philistines went to their own place.

F w y (p. 385) 47 So Saul took the kingdom over Israel, ° and fought against all his enemies on every side, against Moab, and against the ° children of Ammon, and against Edom, and against the kings of Zobah, and against the Philistines: and whithersoever he turned himself, ° he vexed *them*.

48 And he gathered ° an host, and smote the Amalekites, and delivered Israel out of the hands of them that spoiled them.

49 Now the sons of Saul were Jonathan, and z
° Ishui, and Melchi-shua: and the names of his two daughters *were these;* the name of the firstborn Merab, and the name of the younger Michal:

50 And the name of Saul's wife *was* Ahinoam, the daughter of Ahimaaz:

and the name of the captain of his host *was* x
Abner, the son of Ner, Saul's uncle.

51 And ° Kish *was* the father of Saul; and Ner w z
the father of Abner *was* the son of Abiel.

52 And there was sore war against the Phi- y
listines all the days of Saul: and when Saul

---

14. 31-35 (N², p. 384). SIN OF THE PEOPLE.
(*Introversion.*)

N² | u | 31-. Victory.
  v | -31-33-. Sin.
  v | -33, 34. Remedy.
 u | 35. Altar.

33 sin. Heb. *chāṭā'*. Ap. 44. i.

transgressed = dealt treacherously.

this day. Sept. reads "here".

34 his ox with him. Sept. reads "what was in his hand".

41 the LORD = Jehovah. Punctuate thus: "Saul said unto Jehovah: 'O God of Israel'", &c.

Give a perfect lot = Give perfections: i.e. *Thummim.* See Ex. 28. 30. There is evidently a *Homœoteleuton* (Ap. 6) here. The scribes, having written the word "Israel", went forward to the word "Israel" a line or two farther on, and omitted the words between, which are preserved in two ancient versions, older than any Heb. MS. extant. These omitted words are enclosed within brackets below, in the translation given of the Sept. version:—"LORD God of Israel, [Why hast thou not answered Thy servant this day? Is the iniquity in me, or in Jonathan my son? LORD God of Israel, Give clear [manifestation, i.e. *Urim*]; and if [the lot] should declare this, give, I pray Thee, to Thy People Israel, give, I pray, holiness" (i.e. *Thummim*, a perfect lot). The Heb. (unpointed) *thamīm* (perfect) would thus have been *Thummim.*

43 lo. Fig. *Asterismos.* Ap. 6.

44 do so. Some codices, with three early printed editions, Aram., Sept., Syr., and Vulg., add "unto me".

45 not one hair, &c. Fig. *Parœmia.* Ap. 6.

rescued. Heb. *pādāh* = redeemed. See note on Ex. 6. 6 and 13. 13. Perhaps a victim was offered in his stead.

47-52 (*F*, p. 381). THE LEVIES OF SAUL.
(*Introversions.*)

F | w | y | 47, 48. Wars.
   z | 49, 50-. Family.
    x | -50. Abner. Chief captain.
  w | *z* | 51. Kindred.
   y | 52. Wars.

47 and. Note the Fig. *Polysyndeton* (Ap. 6) in *vv.* 47, 48.

children = sons.

he vexed them = he put them to the worse. But Sept. reads "he was victorious".

48 an host. Heb. "power". Fig. *Metonymy* (of Adjunct), Ap. 6, put for the army which manifested the power. Or it may be rendered "he wrought mightily".

49 Ishui. Called Abinadab in 31. 2.

51 Kish was the father of Saul. For the difficulties of this genealogy, see note on 1 Chron. 8. 33.

998-974 saw any strong °man, or any °valiant man,
°he took him unto him.

G a c (p. 386) **15** Samuel also said unto Saul, °"The LORD
sent me to anoint thee *to be* king over
His People, over Israel: now therefore hearken
thou unto the voice of the words of °the LORD.

d 2 Thus saith °the LORD of hosts, °'I remember
that which Amalek did to Israel, °how he laid
wait for him in the way, when he came up
from Egypt.

e 3 °Now go and smite °Amalek, and °utterly
destroy all that they have, and spare them
not; but slay both °man and woman, infant
and suckling, ox and sheep, camel and ass.'"

b 4 And Saul gathered the People together,
and numbered them in °Telaim, two hundred
thousand footmen, and ten thousand °men of
Judah.

b 5 And Saul came to a city of Amalek, and
laid wait in the valley.

a c 6 And Saul said unto the °Kenites, °"Go, depart, get you down from among the Amalekites,
lest I destroy you with them:

d for ye shewed kindness to all the °children of
Israel, when they came up out of Egypt."
So the Kenites departed from among the
Amalekites.

e O 7 And Saul smote the Amalekites °from
Havilah *until* thou comest to Shur, that *is*
over against Egypt.
8 And he took Agag the king of the [3]Amalek-
ites alive, and [3]utterly destroyed all the people
with the edge of the sword.
9 But Saul and the People spared Agag, °and
the best of the sheep, and of the oxen, and of
the fatlings, and the lambs, and all *that was*
good, and would not [3]utterly destroy them:
but °every thing *that was* vile and refuse, that
they destroyed utterly.

P f 10 Then came the word of [1]the LORD unto
Samuel, saying,
11 °"It repenteth Me that I have set up Saul
to be king: for he is turned back from following Me, and hath not performed My commandments."

g And it grieved Samuel; and he cried unto [1]the
LORD all night.

h 12 And when Samuel rose early to meet Saul
in the morning, it was told Samuel, saying,
"Saul came to Carmel, and, °behold, he set
him up a °place, and is gone about, and passed
°on, and gone down to Gilgal."
13 And Samuel came to Saul:

Q[1] R[1] i[1] and Saul said unto him, "Blessed *be* thou of
[1]the LORD: °I have performed the command-
ment of [1]the LORD."

k[1] 14 And Samuel said, "What *meaneth* then
this bleating of the sheep in mine ears, and the
lowing of the oxen which I hear?"

i[1] 15 And Saul said, "They have brought them
from the Amalekites: for the people spared
the best of the sheep and of the oxen, to sacrifice unto [1]the LORD thy °God; and the rest we
have [3]utterly destroyed."

16 Then Samuel said unto Saul, "Stay, and S[1]
I will tell thee what [1]the LORD hath said to me
this night." And he said unto him, "Say on."
17 And Samuel said, "When thou *wast* little

---

52 man. Heb. *'ish.* Ap. 14. II.
valiant man. Heb. son of valour.
he took him. As Samuel had said (8. 11, 16).

15. 1-35 (*G*, p. 381). WAR WITH AMALEKITES.
(*Introversion and extended Alternation.*)

G | a | c | 1. Saul's call by Samuel.
      d | 2. Amalekites' crime against Israel.
         e | 3. Command to smite Amalek.
    b | 4. Saul's army.
    b | 5. Saul's strategy.
  a | *c* | 6-. Saul's call to the Kenites.
      d | -6. The Kenites' kindness to Israel.
         e | 7-35. Disobedience of Saul.

1 The LORD. Heb. Jehovah. Ap. 4. II.
2 the LORD of hosts. See note on 1. 3.
I remember. Fig. *Anthropopatheia.* Ap. 6.
how he laid wait. Cp. Ex. 17. 8.
3 Now go. Some codices, with Aram., Sept., and Vulg., read "now therefore go".
Amalek. Cp. Ex. 17. 16. Num. 24. 20.
utterly destroy = devote to destruction.
man. Heb. *'ish.* Ap. 14. II.
4 Telaim. Probably Telem (Josh. 15. 24).
men. Heb. *'ish.* Ap. 14. II.
6 Kenites. Said to be the same as the Rechabites.
Go, depart. Note the Fig. *Asyndeton* in *v.* 6.
children = sons.

7-35 (*e*, above). DISOBEDIENCE OF SAUL.
(*Alternation and Introversion.*)

e | O | 7-9. Saul's sin.
    P | f | 10, 11-. Repentance of Jehovah.
        g | -11. Sorrow of Samuel.
          h | 12, 13-. Journey to Saul.
  O | -13-33. Saul's reproof.
    P | *h* | 34, 35-. Departure from Saul.
        g | -35-. Sorrow of Samuel.
      f | -35. Repentance of Jehovah.

7 from. Supply Fig. *Ellipsis* (Ap. 6) thus: "[that dwell] from Havilah," &c.
9 and. Note the Fig. *Polysyndeton* (Ap. 6) in this verse.
every thing that was vile = all the stock that was worthless.
11 It repenteth Me. Fig. *Anthropopatheia.* Ap. 6.
12 behold. Fig. *Asterismos.* Ap. 6.
place. Heb. a hand. Either to mark his claim to the place, or a monument, as in 2 Sam. 18. 18.
on = over.
13 I have performed. See *v.* 11.

-13-33 (*O*, above). SAUL'S REPROOF.
(*Division.*)

O | Q[1] | -13-31. By Samuel's word.
    | Q[2] | 32, 33. By Samuel's action.

-13-31 (Q[1], above). BY SAMUEL'S WORD.
(*Alternations and Introversions.*)

Q[1] | R[1] | i[1] | -13. Saul's self-commendation.
         k[1] | 14. Samuel's condemnation.
       i[1] | 15. Saul's self-justification.
           S[1] | 16-19. Message from Jehovah.
     R[2] | i[2] | 20, 21. Saul's self-justification.
         k[2] | 22, 23. Samuel's refutation.
       i[2] | 24, 25. Saul's confession.
           S[2] | 26-29. Sentence of Jehovah.
     R[3] | i[3] | 30. Saul's confession and request.
         k[3] | 31-. Samuel's compliance.
       i[3] | -31. Saul's worship.

15 God. Heb. Elohim. Ap. 4. I.

998 in thine own sight, *wast* thou not *made* the
to head of the tribes of Israel, and [1]the LORD
974 anointed thee king over Israel?
18 And [1]the LORD sent thee on a journey, and said, 'Go and utterly destroy the °sinners the Amalekites, and fight against them until °they be consumed.'
19 Wherefore then didst thou not °obey the voice of [1]the LORD, but didst fly upon the spoil, and didst °evil in the sight of [1]the LORD?"

R[2] i[2] (p. 386) 20 And Saul said unto Samuel, "Yea, I have °obeyed the voice of [1]the LORD, and have gone the way which [1]the LORD sent me, and have brought Agag the king of Amalek, and have utterly destroyed the Amalekites.
21 But the People took of the spoil, sheep and oxen, the chief of the things which should have been utterly destroyed, to sacrifice unto [1]the LORD thy [15]God in Gilgal."

k[2] 22 And Samuel said, "Hath [1]the LORD *as great* delight in burnt offerings and sacrifices, as in obeying the voice of [1]the LORD? [12]Behold, °to obey *is* better than sacrifice, *and* °to hearken than the fat of rams.
23 For rebellion *is as* the °sin of °witchcraft, and stubbornness *is as* °iniquity and idolatry. Because thou hast rejected the word of [1]the LORD, He hath also rejected thee from *being* king."

i[2] 24 And Saul said unto Samuel, "I have [23]sinned: for I have °transgressed the °commandment of [1]the LORD, and thy °words: because I feared the People, and [20]obeyed their voice.
25 Now therefore, I pray thee, pardon my [23]sin, and turn again with me, that I may worship [1]the LORD."

S[2] 26 And Samuel said unto Saul, "I will not return with thee: for thou hast rejected the word of [1]the LORD, and [1]the LORD hath rejected thee from being king over Israel."
27 And as Samuel turned about to go away, °he laid hold upon the skirt of °his mantle, and it rent.
28 And Samuel said unto him, [1]"The LORD hath rent the kingdom of Israel from thee this day, and hath given it to a neighbour of thine, *that is* better than thou.
29 And also °the °Strength of Israel will not lie nor °repent: for He *is* not °a man, that He should °repent."

R[3] i[3] 30 Then he said, "I have [23]sinned: *yet* honour me now, I pray thee, before the elders of my People, and before Israel, and turn again with me, that I may worship [1]the LORD thy [15]God."

k[3] 31 So Samuel turned again after Saul;

i[3] and Saul worshipped [1]the LORD.

Q[2] 32 Then said Samuel, "Bring ye hither to me Agag the king of the Amalekites." And Agag came unto him °delicately. And Agag said, "Surely the bitterness of death is past."
33 And Samuel said, °"As thy sword hath made women childless, so shall thy mother be childless among women." And Samuel °hewed °Agag in pieces before [1]the LORD in Gilgal.

34 Then Samuel went to Ramah; and Saul went up to his house to Gibeah of Saul. P h
35 And Samuel came °no more to see Saul until the day of his death:

nevertheless °Samuel mourned for Saul: g

and [1]the LORD [29]repented that He had made Saul king over Israel. f

16 And °the LORD said unto Samuel, "How long wilt thou mourn for Saul, seeing °I have rejected him from reigning over Israel? fill thine horn with oil, and go, I will send thee to Jesse the Beth-lehemite: for °I have provided Me a king among his sons." O T[1] l (p. 387) 974

---

18 sinners. Heb. *chātā'*. Ap. 44. i.
they be consumed = they have consumed them. Some codices, with Aram., Sept., and Syr., read "thou have consumed them".
19 obey = hearken to.
evil = the evil. Heb. *rā'a'*. Ap. 44. viii.
20 obeyed = hearkened.
22 to obey = to hearken to.
to hearken = to give heed.
23 sin. Heb. *chātā'*. Ap. 44. i.
witchcraft = divination or necromancy; i. e. dealings with spirits.
iniquity. Heb. *'āven*. Ap. 44. iii.
24 transgressed. Heb. *'abar*. Ap. 44. vii.
commandment. Heb. "mouth", put by Fig. *Metonymy* (of Cause), Ap. 6, for what is spoken by it.
words. Some codices, with one early printed edition, read "word".
27 he = Saul.
his = Samuel's. Cp. 1 Kings 11. 30, 31.
29 the Strength = the Eternal One. First occurrence. Heb. *nezah*. A Divine title.
repent: i. e. as God, though He is said to do so by the Fig. *Anthropopatheia*. Ap. 6.
a man. Heb. *'ādām*. Ap. 14. I.
32 delicately = in fetters (Job 38. 31). Sept. has "trembling"; Vulg. has "sleek and trembling".
33 As = according as.
hewed: i. e. commanded him to be hewed or cut asunder after death. Verb occurs only here.
Agag. See note on Amalek (Ex. 17. 16, and cp. *v.* 3).
35 no more. Cp. 16. 1, 14; 19. 23.
Samuel mourned: i. e. as for one dead. We do not read that Saul mourned for himself.

16. 1—27. 4 (*O*, p. 375). CHOICE OF DAVID.
(*Division.*)

O | T[1] | 16. 1-13. David's call and anointing by God.
  | T[2] | 16. 14-23. Episode. Inserted here to show the contrast between David and Saul.
  | T[3] | 17. 1—27. 4. David opposed by Saul. An earlier episode (17. 1—18. 9), see p. 389.

16. 1-13 (T[1], above). DAVID'S CALL.
(*Alternation.*)

T[1] | l | 1-3. Jehovah's provision of David.
  | m | 4, 5. Samuel's arrival.
  | *l* | 6-12. Jehovah's choice of David.
  | *m* | 13. Samuel's anointing.

1 the LORD. Heb. Jehovah. Ap. 4.
I have rejected. Note here Jehovah's sovereignty.
I have provided. Note Jehovah's sovereignty in this choice of the youngest. It is *this choice* that makes David the "man after Jehovah's heart"; not David's personal character or conduct.

974 2 And Samuel said, “How can I go? if Saul
hear *it*, he will kill me.” And [1]the LORD said,
“Take an heifer °with thee, and say, ‘I am
come to sacrifice to [1]the LORD.’
3 And call Jesse to the sacrifice, and I will
shew thee what thou shalt do: and thou shalt
anoint unto Me *him* whom I name unto thee.”
m 4 And Samuel did that which [1]the LORD
(p. 387) spake, and came to °Beth-lehem. And the
elders of the town trembled at his coming, and
°said, “Comest thou peaceably?”
5 And he said, “Peaceably: I am come to
sacrifice unto [1]the LORD: sanctify yourselves,
and come with me to the sacrifice.” And he
sanctified °Jesse and his sons, and called them
to the sacrifice.
l 6 And it came to pass, when they were come,
that he looked on Eliab, and said, “Surely [1]the
LORD'S anointed *is* before Him.”
7 But [1]the LORD said unto Samuel, “Look
not on his countenance, or on the height of his
stature; because I have refused him: for °*the*
LORD seeth not as °man °seeth; for °man
°looketh on the outward appearance, but [1]the
LORD °looketh on the °heart.”
8 Then Jesse called Abinadab, and made him
pass before Samuel. And he said, “Neither
hath [1]the LORD chosen this.”
9 °Then Jesse made °Shammah to pass by.
And he said, “Neither hath [1]the LORD chosen
this.”
10 °Again, Jesse made °seven of his sons to
pass before Samuel. And Samuel said unto
Jesse, [1]“The LORD hath not chosen these.”
11 And Samuel said unto Jesse, °“Are here
all *thy* °children?” And he said, “There remaineth yet the °youngest, and, °behold, °he
keepeth the sheep.” And Samuel said unto
Jesse, “Send and fetch him: for we will not
sit °down till he come hither.”
12 And he sent, and brought him in. Now
he *was* ruddy, °*and* withal of a beautiful countenance, and °goodly to look to. And [1]the
LORD said, “Arise, anoint him: for this *is* he.”
m 13 Then Samuel took the horn of oil, and
°anointed him in the midst of his brethren:
and °the Spirit of [1]the LORD came upon °David
from that day forward. So Samuel rose up,
and went to Ramah.
T² n 14 °But [13]the Spirit of [1]the LORD departed
(p. 388) from Saul, and an °evil °spirit from [1]the LORD
°troubled him.
15 And Saul's servants said unto him, [11]“Behold now, an [14]evil [14]spirit from °God troubleth
thee.
16 Let our lord now command thy servants,
which are before thee, to seek out a °man,
who is a °cunning player on an °harp:
p and it shall come to pass, when the [14]evil
[14]spirit from [15]God is upon thee, that he shall
play with his hand, and thou shalt be well.”
o 17 And Saul said unto his servants, “Provide
me now a [16]man that can play well, and bring
him to me.”
18 Then answered one of the °servants, and
said, [11]“Behold, I have seen a son of Jesse the
Beth-lehemite, *that is* [16]cunning in playing,
°and a mighty valiant [16]man, and a [16]man of
war, and prudent in °matters, and a comely
person, and [1]the LORD *is* with him.”
19 Wherefore Saul sent messengers unto
Jesse, and said, “Send me David thy son,
which *is* with the sheep.”
20 And Jesse took an ass *laden* with bread,
and a °bottle °of °wine, and a kid, and sent
them by David his son unto Saul.

2 with thee = in thine hand.
4 Beth-lehem = house of bread.
said. Heb. text reads verb in sing., requiring “he, or one, said”. In this case it is the Fig. *Heterōsis* (of Number), Ap. 6. But several codices, the *Sevîr* (Ap. 34), Targ., Sept., Syr., Vulg., and the two earliest printed editions, read “they said”.
5 Jesse and his sons. He had eight sons and two daughters, Zeruiah (mother of Abishai, Joab, and Asahel) and Abigail (mother of Amasa). David is the eighth here (*vv.* 10, 11), but called the seventh in 1 Chron. 2. 15. One son must have died shortly after this, or been the son of a concubine, or died without issue and so not reckoned in the genealogy. Samuel is *history*, Chronicles is *genealogy*.
7 the LORD seeth. These words correctly supply the *Ellipsis* (Ap. 6. III. 1), from the Sept.
man = *'ādām*. Ap. 14. I. **seeth** = looketh to.
looketh on = looketh to.
heart. Cp. 1 Chron. 28. 9. Ps. 7. 9. Jer. 11. 20; 17. 10; 20. 12.
9 Then = and.
Shammah. Probably = Shimeah. 2 Sam. 13. 3; 21. 21.
10 Again = So. **seven.** See note on *v.* 5.
11 Are here all thy children? Heb. “Have the young men finished [passing by]?” This correctly supplies the Fig. *Ellipsis*. Ap. 6. Heb. *na'ar* = young men.
youngest = least. See note on *v.* 5.
behold. Fig. *Asterismos*. Ap. 6.
he keepeth. Saul lost his father's asses (9. 3, 4, 20).
down = round.
12 and withal of a beautiful, &c. = a stripling (17. 56), with handsome eyes.
goodly to look to = with, or of, noble mien.
13 anointed him. Three anointings of David: (1) by Samuel, here; (2) by “men of Judah” (2 Sam. 2. 4); and (3) by “the elders of Israel” (2 Sam. 5. 3).
the Spirit. Heb. = *rūach*. Ap. 9.
David = beloved.

16. 14-23 (T², p. 387). THE LATER EPISODE.
(*Introversion*.)

T² | n | 14, 15. Evil spirit troubling Saul.
  o | 16-. Harper recommended.
    p | -16. Recovery promised.
  o | 17-22. Harper successful.
n | 23. Evil spirit departing from Saul.

14 But. This marks and introduces the later episode, placed here in order to bring out and connect the contrast of the Spirit's departing from Saul and coming on David. See notes on 17. 1 and 18. 12.
evil: always. Heb. *rā'a'* (Ap. 44. viii), in this connection. **spirit.** Heb. *rūach*. Ap. 9.
troubled = terrified.
15 God. Heb. Elohim (Ap. 4. I). Saul's servants not in communion with Jehovah, the Covenant God. Ap. 4. II.
16 man. Heb. *'ish*. Ap. 14. II.
cunning = skilful.
harp = *kinnor*. An instrument of many strings.
18 servants. Not the same word as in *vv.* 15-17, but “young men” as in 14. 1. Perhaps Saul's bodyguard; possibly fellow-pupils of Samuel at Naioth.
and. Note Fig. *Polysyndeton* (Ap. 6) in these verses.
matters = speech.
20 bottle = skin-bottle.
of. Gen. of contents. Ap. 17.
wine. Heb. *yayin*. See Ap. 27. I.

974 21 And David came to Saul, and stood before him: and °he loved °him greatly; and he became his armourbearer.

22 And Saul sent to Jesse, saying, "Let David, I pray thee, stand before me; for he hath found favour in my sight."

n (p. 388) 23 And it came to pass, when the *evil* [14] spirit from [15] God was upon Saul, that David took an harp, and played with his hand: so Saul was refreshed, and was well, and the evil [14] spirit departed from him.

U X q (p. 389) **17** °Now the Philistines gathered together their armies to battle, and were gathered together at Shochoh, which *belongeth* to Judah, and pitched between Shochoh and Azekah, in Ephes-dammim.

2 And Saul and the °men of Israel were gathered together, and pitched °by the valley of Elah, and set the battle in array against the Philistines.

3 And the Philistines stood on a mountain on the one side, and Israel stood on a mountain on the other side: and *there was* a valley between them.

r Z s 4 And there went out a °champion out of the camp of the Philistines, named Goliath, of Gath, whose height *was* °six °cubits and a °span.

5 °And *he had* an helmet of brass upon his head, and he *was* armed with a coat of mail; and the weight of the coat *was* five thousand °shekels of brass.

6 And *he had* greaves of brass upon his legs, and a °target of brass between his shoulders.

7 And the staff of his spear *was* like a weaver's beam; and his spear's head *weighed* [4] six hundred [7] shekels of iron: and one bearing a °shield went before him.

t 8 And he stood and cried unto the armies of Israel, and said unto them, "Why are ye come out to set *your* battle in array? *am* not I a Philistine, and ye servants to Saul? choose you a °man for you, and let him come down to me.

9 If he be able to fight with me, and to kill me, then will we be your servants: but if I prevail against him, and kill him, then shall ye be our servants, and serve us."

10 And the Philistine said, "I defy the armies of Israel this day; give me a [8] man, that we may fight together."

u 11 When Saul and all Israel heard those words of the Philistine, they were dismayed, and °greatly afraid.

A B (p. 390) 12 Now David *was* the son of that Ephrathite of Beth-lehem-judah, whose name *was* Jesse; and he had °eight sons: and the [8] man went among °men °*for* an old [8] man in the days of Saul.

21 he = Saul.
him = David.

17. 1–27. 4 (T[3], p. 387). DAVID OPPOSED BY SAUL. (*Extended Alternation.*)

T[3] | U | 17. 1—18. 9. War with the Philistines.
V | 18. 10, 11. Evil spirit incites Saul against David.
W | 18. 12—19. 7. Saul's hostility to David.
U | 19. 8. War with the Philistines.
V | 19. 9—20. 1–. Evil spirit incites Saul against David.
W | 20. –1—27. 4. Saul's hostility to David.

17. 1—18. 9 (U, above). WAR WITH PHILISTINES. (*Alternation.*)

U | X | 17. 1–54. Battle with Philistines.
Y | 17. 55—18. 5. Favour of Saul to David.
X | 18. 6, 7. Battle won. Praise for victory.
Y | 18. 8, 9. Disfavour of Saul to David.

17. 1–54 (X, above). BATTLE WITH PHILISTINES. (*Introversion.*)

X | q | 1–3. The two armies. Arrayed.
r | 4–40–. Defiance of Goliath.
r | –40–51–. Combat with Goliath.
q | –51–54. The two armies. Flight and pursuit.

1 Now. Ch. 17. 1 reads on chronologically from 16. 13 (see note on 16. 14). An author's right is claimed for placing the later episode here (16. 14, 23), in order to connect and contrast the two spirits with Saul and David. The canonical order alternates David's call and Saul's. See notes on 16. 14; 18. 12.

Canonical Order.
| 16. 1–13. David's call by God.
| 16. 14–23. Saul. Spirit departing.
| 17. 1—18. 4. David's call by Saul.
| 18. 5–30. Saul. Spirit departing.

The chronological order is clear on the face of the text for all who will see it.

Chronological Order.
| 16. 1–13. David's call by Jehovah.
| 17. 1—18. 4. David's exploits.
| 16. 14–23. David's call by Saul.
| 18. 5–30. David's exploits.

2 men. Heb. *'ish.* Ap. 14. II.
by = in. About sixteen miles south-west of Jerusalem.

4–40– (r, above). DEFIANCE OF GOLIATH. (*Introversion.*)

r | Z | s | 4–7. Goliath's armour.
t | 8–10. Goliath's challenge.
u | 11. Israel's fear.
A | 12–31. David's mission.
Z | *u* | 32–. Saul's encouragement.
t | –32–37. Goliath's challenge accepted.
s | 38–40. David's armour.

4 champion. Heb. *'ish-habbēnayim* = "the man between the two [hosts]", or, the duellist. This accords with the subscription of Psalm 8 (see note there). *Mūth-labbēn* = the death of the man between; i. e. the death of the champion (Goliath) which Ps. 8 celebrates. Ps. 144, which has the same words, "What is man", has for its title in Sept. "A Psalm of David concerning Goliath" (cp. Ps. 8. 4 with 144. 3). See *v.* 23.

six. Note this number "6" stamped like a "hall-mark" on this "man" (as on Nebuchadnezzar, Dan. 3). Cp. the six pieces of armour, *vv.* 5–7.

cubits. See Ap. 51. III. 2. **span.** See Ap. 51. III. 2. **5 And.** Note the Fig. *Polysyndeton* in *vv.* 5–7. Ap. 6. Note the six pieces of armour thus emphasised; and see Ap. 10. **6 target.** Heb. *kedōn*, a small shield. Translated "shield" in *v.* 45. **7 shield.** Heb. *zinnah*, a shield of the largest size, covering the whole body. Same word in *v.* 41, not *vv.* 6 and 45. **8 man.** Heb. *'ish.* Ap. 14. II. **11 greatly afraid** = feared exceedingly. Cp. *v.* 24. **12 eight sons.** David was now between sixteen and seventeen years old. See note on 16. 5. **men.** Heb. *'ĕnōsh.* Ap. 14. III. **for an old man.** Sept. and Syr. read "was old", advanced in years.

12–30 [For Structure see next page].

C v x (p. 390) 974 13 And the three eldest sons of Jesse went *and* followed Saul to the battle: and the names of his three sons that went to the battle *were* Eliab the firstborn, and next unto him Abinadab, and the third Shammah.

y 14 And David °*was* the youngest:

x and the three eldest followed Saul.

y 15 But David went and returned from Saul to feed his father's sheep at Beth-lehem.

w 16 And the Philistine drew near morning and evening, and presented himself °forty days.

B z[1] 17 And Jesse said unto David his son, "Take now for thy brethren an °ephah of this parched *corn,* and these ten loaves, and run to the camp to thy brethren;

18 And carry these ten cheeses unto the captain of *their* thousand, and look how thy brethren fare, and take °their pledge."

z[2] 19 Now Saul, and they, and all the [8]men of Israel, *were* in the valley of Elah, fighting with the Philistines.

20 And David rose up early in the morning, and left the sheep with a keeper, and took, and went, °as Jesse had commanded him; and he came to the trench, as the host was going forth to the °fight, and shouted for the battle.

21 For Israel and the Philistines had put the battle in array, army against army.

22 And David left his °carriage in the hand of the keeper of the °carriage, and ran into the army, and came and saluted his brethren.

C w 23 And as he talked with them, °behold, there came up the [4]champion, the Philistine of Gath, Goliath by name, out of the °armies of the Philistines, and spake according to the same words: and David heard *them.*

24 And all the °men of Israel, when they saw the °man, fled from him, and °were sore afraid.

v a 25 And the [24]men of Israel said, "Have ye seen this [24]man that is come up? surely to defy Israel is he come up: and it shall be, *that* the [24]man who killeth him, the king will enrich him with great riches, °and will give him his daughter, and make his father's house free in Israel."

b d 26 And David spake to the °men that stood by him, saying, "What shall be done to the [8]man that killeth this Philistine, and taketh away the reproach from Israel? for who *is* this uncircumcised Philistine, that he should °defy the armies of the living °God?"

e 27 And the people answered him after this manner, saying, "So shall it be done to the [8]man that killeth him."

c 28 And Eliab his eldest brother heard when he spake unto the [12]men; and Eliab's anger was kindled against David, and he said, "Why camest thou down hither? and with whom hast thou left those few sheep in the wilderness? I know thy pride, and the naughtiness of thine heart; for thou art come down that thou mightest see the battle."

c 29 And David said, "What have I now done? *Is there* not a cause?"

17. 12-31 (A, p. 389). DAVID'S MISSION.
(*Alternation and Introversion.*)

A | B | 12. House of Jesse.
C | v | 13-15. The army.
w | 16. Goliath's challenge.
B | 17-22. Message of Jesse.
C | *w* | 23, 24. Goliath's challenge.
v | 25-31. The army.

13-15 (v, above). THE ARMY.
(*Alternation.*)

v | x | 13. The eldest three.
y | 14-. David.
x | -14. The eldest three.
y | 15. David.

14 was = he [was].
16 forty. The number significant of probation. Ap. 10.

17-22 (*B*, above). MESSAGE OF JESSE.
(*Division.*)

B | z[1] | 17, 18. Command.
z[2] | 19-22. Obedience.

17 ephah. See Ap. 51. III. 3.
18 their pledge: i. e. a token from them of their welfare = a message or letter, or a lock of hair. Cp. Gen. 37. 13, 14, 32, 33.
20 as = according as.
fight = place of battle.
22 carriage = baggage: i. e. goods carried.
23 behold. Fig. *Asterismos.* Ap. 6.
armies = ranks.
24 men. Heb. *'īsh.* Ap. 14. II.
man. Heb. *'īsh.* Ap. 14. II.
were sore afraid = feared exceedingly. Cp. *v.* 11.

25-31 (*v*, above). THE ARMY.
(*Introversion and Alternation.*)

v | a | 25. The king's reward.
b | d | 26. David. Inquiry.
e | 27. People. Answer.
c | 28. Eliab's reproof of David.
c | 29. David's reply to Eliab.
b | *d* | 30-. David. Inquiry.
e | -30. People. Answer.
a | 31. The king's mission.

25 and. Note the Fig. *Polysyndeton.* Ap. 6.
26 men. Heb. *'ĕnōsh.* Ap. 14. III.
defy = reproach.
God. Heb. Elohim. Ap. 4. I. "Living", always in contrast with idols.
30 manner = word.
32 Let no man's heart fail. Sept. reads "Let not the heart of my lord fail".
man's. Heb. *'ādām.* Ap. 14. I.

30 And he turned from him toward another, and spake after the same °manner: *b d*

and the people answered him again after the former manner. *e*

31 And when the words were heard which David spake, they rehearsed *them* before Saul: and he sent for him. *a*

32 And David said to Saul, °"Let no °man's heart fail because of him; *Z u* (p. 389)

thy servant will go and fight with this Philistine." *t*

33 And Saul said to David, "Thou art not able to go against this Philistine to fight with him: for thou *art but* a youth, and he a [8]man of war from his youth."

974 34 And David said unto Saul, "Thy servant °kept °his father's sheep, °and there came a lion, and a bear, and took a lamb out of the flock:

35 And I went out after him, and smote him, and delivered *it* out of his mouth: and when he arose against me, I caught *him* by his °beard, and smote him, and slew him.

36 Thy servant slew both the lion and the bear: and this uncircumcised Philistine shall be as one of °them, seeing he hath °defied the armies of the °living °God."

37 David said moreover, °"The LORD That delivered me out of the °paw of the lion, and out of the °paw of the bear, He will deliver me out of the °hand of this Philistine." And Saul said unto David, "Go, and °the LORD be with thee."

s (p. 389) 38 And Saul armed David with his armour, and he put an helmet of brass upon his head; also he armed him with a coat of mail.

39 And David girded his sword upon his armour, and he °assayed to go; for he had not proved *it*. And David said unto Saul, "I cannot go with these; for I have not proved *them*." And David put them off him.

40 And he took his °staff in his hand, and chose him five smooth stones out of the brook, and put them in a shepherd's bag which he had, even in a scrip; and his sling *was* in his hand:

r f (p. 391) and he drew near to the Philistine.

41 And the Philistine came on and drew near unto David; and the [8] man that bare the shield *went* before him.

g h¹ 42 And when the Philistine looked about, and saw David, he disdained him: for he was *but* a youth, and °ruddy, and of a fair countenance.

43 And the Philistine said unto David, "*Am* I a °dog, that thou comest to me with staves?" And the Philistine cursed David by his °gods.

44 And the Philistine said to David, "Come to me, and I will give thy flesh unto the fowls of the air, and to the beasts of the °field."

h² 45 Then said David to the Philistine, "Thou comest to me with a sword, and with a spear, and with a °shield; but I come to thee in the name of °the LORD of hosts, the [26]God of the armies of Israel, Whom thou hast [36] defied.

46 This day will [37] the LORD deliver thee into mine hand; °and I will smite thee, and take thine head from thee; and I will °give the carcases of the host of the Philistines this day unto the fowls of the air, and to the wild beasts of the earth; that all the earth may know °that there is a [26] God in Israel.

47 And all this °assembly shall know that [37] the LORD saveth not with sword and spear: for the battle *is* [37] the LORD'S, and He will give you into our [37] hands."

f 48 And it came to pass, when the Philistine arose, and came and drew nigh to meet David, that David hasted, and ran toward the army to meet the Philistine.

g 49 And David put his hand in his bag, and took thence a stone, and slang *it*, and smote the Philistine in his forehead, that the stone sunk into his forehead; and he fell upon his face to the earth.

50 So David prevailed over the Philistine with a sling and with a stone, and smote the Philistine, and slew him; but *there was* no sword in the hand of David.

51 Therefore David ran, and stood upon the Philistine, and took his sword, and °drew it out of the sheath thereof, and slew him, and cut off his head therewith.

And when the Philistines saw their °champion was dead, they fled. *q* (p. 389)

52 And the [12]men of Israel and of Judah arose, and shouted, and pursued the Philistines, until thou come to °the valley, and to the gates of Ekron. And the °wounded of the Philistines fell down by the way to Shaaraim, even unto Gath, and unto Ekron.

53 And the °children of Israel returned from

---

34 kept = was keeping. Cp. 16. 11.
his. Some codices, quoted in the *Massōrah*, read "my".
and. Note the Fig. *Polysyndeton* (Ap. 6) in *vv.* 34-36.
35 beard = mane, or throat.
36 them. The Sept. adds "them" and reads "[Shall I not go and smite him, and turn aside reproach to-day from Israel? For who is this uncircumcised Philistine] that he hath", &c.
defied = reproached.
living God. Both these words in pl. in Heb. Cp. *v.* 26.
37 The LORD = Jehovah. Ap. 4. II.
paw . . . hand. Put by Fig. *Metonymy* (of Cause) for power put forth by it. Ap. 6.
39 assayed = tried, or, was content to start: assay = French *essayer*.
40 staff = club, one of the three equipments of the Eastern shepherd: crook for the sheep's help, club for sheep's defence, and the bag for himself.

17. -40-51- (*r*, p. 389). **COMBAT WITH GOLIATH.**
(*Alternation.*)

r | f | -40, 41. Approach.
  | g | 42-47. Colloquy.
  | *f* | 48. Approach.
  | *g* | 49-51-. Conflict.

42-47 (g, above). **COLLOQUY.**
(*Division.*)

g | h¹ | 42-44. Goliath.
  | h² | 45-47. David.

42 ruddy. Cp. 16. 12, 13.
dog. No stronger term of contempt. 2 Kings 8. 13. Matt. 15. 26.
gods = god, as in Judg. 16. 23.
44 field. Some codices, with Aram., Sept., and Vulg., read "earth".
45 shield. See note on "target", *v.* 6.
the LORD of hosts. See note on 1. 3.
46 and. Note the Fig. *Polysyndeton* in *vv.* 46, 47.
give. Sept. reads "give [thy limbs and] the carcasses", &c.
that there is a God in Israel = that Israel hath a God.
47 assembly = assembled host. Cp. Num. 22. 4, "company".
51 drew it out; showing that Goliath had not deigned to do so.
champion. Heb. *gibbōr* = mighty man. Ap. 14. IV. Not the same word as in *vv.* 4 and 23.
52 the valley. Sept. reads "entrance into Gath".
wounded = stricken, or slain.
53 children = sons.

chasing after the Philistines, and they spoiled their ° tents.

54 And David took the head of the Philistine, and brought it to ° Jerusalem; but he put his armour in his tent.

Y **55 And when Saul saw David go forth against**
(p. 389) **the Philistine, he said unto Abner, the captain of the host, "Abner, ° whose son *is* this youth?" And Abner said, "*As* ° thy soul liveth, O king, I cannot tell."**

56 And the king said, "Inquire thou [55] whose son the stripling *is*."

57 And as David returned from the slaughter of the Philistine, Abner took him, and brought him before Saul with the head of the Philistine in his hand.

58 And Saul said to him, [55] "Whose son *art* thou, *thou* young man?" And David answered, "*I am* the son of thy servant Jesse the Bethlehemite."

18 And it came to pass, when he had made an end of speaking unto Saul, that the ° soul of ° Jonathan was knit with the ° soul of David, and Jonathan loved him as his own ° soul.

2 And Saul took him that day, and would let him go no more home to his father's house.

3 Then Jonathan and David ° made a covenant, because he loved him as his own [1] soul.

4 And Jonathan stripped himself of the robe that *was* upon him, ° and gave it to David, and his garments, even to his sword, and to his bow, and to his girdle.

5 And David went out whithersoever Saul sent him, *and* behaved himself wisely: and Saul set him over the ° men of war, and he was accepted in the sight of all the People, and also in the sight of Saul's servants.

X **6 And it came to pass as they came, when David was returned from the slaughter of the ° Philistine, that the women came out of all cities of Israel, singing and ° dancing, to meet king Saul, with ° tabrets, with joy, and with instruments of musick.**

7 And the women answered *one another* as they played, and said,

"Saul hath slain his thousands,
And David his ten thousands."

Y **8 And Saul was very wroth, and ° the saying displeased him; and he said, "They have ascribed unto David ten thousands, and to me they have ascribed *but* thousands: and *what* can he have more but the kingdom?"**

9 And Saul eyed David from that day and forward.

V **10 And it came to pass on the morrow, that the ° evil ° spirit from ° God came upon Saul, and he prophesied in the midst of the house: and David played with his hand, as at other times: and *there was* a javelin in Saul's hand.**

11 And Saul ° cast the javelin; for he said, "I will smite David even to the wall *with it*." And David avoided out of his presence twice.

i^1 j **12 And Saul was ° afraid of David,**
(p. 392) **because ° the LORD was with him, ° and was**
k **departed from Saul.**
l **13 Therefore Saul removed him from him, and made him his captain over a thousand; and he went out and came in before the People.**

14 And David behaved himself wisely in all his ways; and [12] the LORD *was* with him. *l*

15 Wherefore when Saul saw that he behaved himself very wisely, *k*
he was ° afraid of him. *j*

tents = camps.

54 Jerusalem. Jerusalem (west of Moriah) had been taken by Judah, who dwelt there. The Jebusites were still holding Jebus, or Zion, the mount immediately south of Moriah. Cp. Josh. 15. 63. Judg. 1. 7, 8. Zion was taken later by David. See 2 Sam. 5. 7, and Ap. 68.

55 whose son . . . ? Though Saul had just had an interview with David, he did not know his father, whom he had promised (*v.* 25) to make free in Israel. Note in all these passages (*vv.* 55, 56, 58) Saul's inquiry is not about David, but about David's father.

thy soul = thyself (emph.). Heb. *nephesh*. Ap. 13.

18. 1 soul. Heb. *nephesh*. Ap. 13.

Jonathan. At this time he was about forty; and about fifty-three or fifty-four when he died. He would be about twenty-four years older than David, and his love was maternal in character. Ish-bosheth, Saul's second son, was forty at his father's death (2 Sam. 2. 10).

3 made = solemnised.

4 and. Mark the Fig. *Polysyndeton* (Ap. 6) in *vv.* 4, 5.

5 men. Heb. *'ĕnōsh*. Ap. 14. III.

6 Philistine. A.V. and R.V. marg. "Philistines".

dancing. A great celebration. Twice referred to later (21. 11; 29. 5). Cp. subscription of Ps. 52, which is *maḥălath* = "the great dancing".

A | 1-5. David's apostrophe to Goliath and Doeg.
  B | 6, 7. The righteous onlookers.
A | 8, 9. David's praise to God.

tabrets. Heb. *toph* = drums of various sizes.

8 the = this.

10 evil. See note on 16. 16.

spirit. Heb. *rūach*. Ap. 9.

God. Heb. Elohim. Ap. 4. I.

11 cast the javelin. Another attempt of Satan to thwart Jehovah's purpose in Gen. 3. 15, and prevent the "seed of the woman" from coming into the world. See Ap. 23 and 25, and the Structure of "*V*" (19. 9–20. 1-), p. 394.

18. 12—19. 7 (W, p. 389). **HOSTILITY TO DAVID.**
(*Alternation.*)

W | E | 18. 12-16. Saul's fear of David.
    F | 18. 17-27. Machinations against David.
  E | 18. 28-30. Saul's fear of David.
    F | 19. 1-7. Aggressions against David.

12-16 (E, above). **SAUL'S FEAR OF DAVID.**
(*Division.*)

E | i^1 | 12-15. Saul's fear.
  | i^2 | 16. The People's love.

12-15 (i^1, above). **SAUL'S FEAR.** (*Introversion.*)

i^1 | j | 12-. Fear.
  k | -12. Reason.
    l | 13. Promotion.
    l | 14. Propriety.
  k | 15-. Reason.
j | -15. Fear.

12 afraid. Heb. *yārē'* = apprehensive. Cp. *v.* 15.

the LORD. Heb. Jehovah. Ap. 4. II.

and was departed. Ch. 16. 14-23 comes in here, chronologically. It is placed after 16. 1-13 by Fig. *Hysterologia* (Ap. 6) in order to lay bare to us the secret workings underneath the history. See notes on 16. 14; 17. 1.

15 afraid. Heb. *nūr* = shrank from, sore afraid; stronger than *v.* 12.

i² (p. 392)
16 But all Israel and Judah loved David, because he went out and came in before them.

972
F m¹ (p. 393)
17 And Saul said to David, °"Behold my elder daughter Merab, her will I give thee to wife: only be thou °valiant for me, and fight [12]the LORD'S battles." For Saul said, °"Let not mine hand be upon him, but let the hand of the Philistines be upon him."

18 And David said unto Saul, "Who *am* I? and what *is* my life, *or* my father's family in Israel, that I should be son in law to the king?"

19 But it came to pass at the time when Merab Saul's daughter should have been given to David, that she °was given unto Adriel the Meholathite to wife.

m²
20 And Michal Saul's daughter loved David: and they told Saul, and the thing pleased him.

21 And Saul said, "I will give him her, that she may be a snare to him, and that the hand of the Philistines may be against him." Wherefore Saul said to David, "Thou shalt this day be my son in law in *the one of* the twain."

22 And Saul commanded his servants, *saying*, "Commune with David secretly, and say, [17]'Behold, the king hath delight in thee, and all his servants love thee: now therefore be the king's son in law.'"

23 And Saul's servants spake those words in the ears of David. And David said, "Seemeth it to you *a* light *thing* to be a king's son in law, seeing that I *am* a poor °man, and lightly esteemed?"

24 And the servants of Saul told him, saying, "On this manner spake David."

25 And Saul said, "Thus shall ye say to David, 'The king desireth not any dowry, but an hundred foreskins of the Philistines, to be avenged of the king's enemies.'" But Saul thought to make David fall by the hand of the Philistines.

26 And when his servants told David these words, it pleased David well to be the king's son in law: and the days were not expired.

27 Wherefore David arose and went, he and °his men, and slew of the Philistines two hundred °men; and David brought their foreskins, and °they gave them in full tale to the king, that he might be the king's son in law. And Saul gave him Michal his daughter to wife.

E (p. 392)
28 And Saul saw and knew that [12]the LORD *was* with David, and *that* °Michal Saul's daughter loved him.

29 And Saul was yet the more [12]afraid of David; and Saul became David's enemy continually.

30 Then the princes of the Philistines went forth: and it came to pass, °after they went forth, *that* David behaved himself more wisely than all the servants of Saul; so that his name was much set by.

F n¹ (p. 393)
19 And Saul spake to Jonathan his son, and to all his servants, that they should kill David.

o¹
2 But Jonathan Saul's son delighted much in David: and Jonathan told David, saying, "Saul my father seeketh to kill thee: now

18. 17-27 (F, p. 392). MACHINATIONS AGAINST DAVID. (*Division.*)

F | m¹ | 17-19. By means of Merab.
  | m² | 20-27. By means of Michal.

17 Behold. Fig. *Asterismos.* Ap. 6.
valiant. Heb. son of valour.
Let not mine hand, &c. Cp. David and Uriah. 2 Sam. 11. 15.
19 was given = had (already) been given. This is the key to 20. 30.
23 man. Heb. *'ish.* Ap. 14. II.
27 his men. Heb. *'ĕnōsh.* Ap. 14. III.
men. Heb. *'ish.* Ap. 14. II.
they: i. e. Saul's servants. Sept. and Vulg. read "he".
28 Michal Saul's daughter. Sept. reads "all Israel", accounting for his greater fear (*v.* 29).
30 after = whenever; or, as often as.

19. 1-7 (*F*, p. 392). AGGRESSIONS AGAINST DAVID. (*Repeated Alternation.*)

F | n¹ | 1. Saul and David. Resolve to kill David.
  o¹ | 2, 3. David and Jonathan.
  n² | 4-6. Saul and Jonathan.
  o² | 7-. David and Jonathan.
  n³ | -7. Saul and David. Reconciliation.

2 until = in, or against.
3 what I see, &c. = "I shall see what [he replies] and shall tell thee". Fig. *Ellipsis.* Ap. 6.
4 sin. Heb. *chāṭā'.* Ap. 44. i.
5 life = soul. Heb. *nephesh.* Ap. 13.
the LORD. Heb. Jehovah. Ap. 4.

19. 9—20. 1- [For Structure see next page].

9 evil. See note on 16. 16.
spirit. Heb. *rūach.* Ap. 9.

therefore, I pray thee, take heed to thyself °until the morning, and abide in a secret *place*, and hide thyself:

3 And I will go out and stand beside my father in the field where thou *art*, and I will commune with my father of thee; and °what I see, that I will tell thee."

4 And Jonathan spake good of David unto Saul his father, and said unto him, "Let not the king °sin against his servant, against David; because he hath not °sinned against thee, and because his works *have been* to thee-ward very good: n²

5 For he did put his °life in his hand, and slew the Philistine, and °the LORD wrought a great salvation for all Israel: thou sawest *it*, and didst rejoice: wherefore then wilt thou [4]sin against innocent blood, to slay David without a cause?"

6 And Saul hearkened unto the voice of Jonathan: and Saul sware, "*As* [5]the LORD liveth, he shall not be slain."

7 And Jonathan called David, and Jonathan shewed him all those things. o²

And Jonathan brought David to Saul, and he was in his presence, as in times past. n³

8 And there was war again: and David went out, and fought with the Philistines, and slew them with a great slaughter; and they fled from him. *U* (p. 389)

9 And the °evil °spirit from [5]the LORD was upon Saul, as he sat in his house with his javelin in his hand: and David played with *his* hand. *V* G¹ p¹ (p. 394)

972-970 10 And °Saul sought to smite David °even to
the wall with the javelin;
q^1 (p. 394) but he slipped away out of Saul's presence,
and he smote the javelin into the wall:
r^1 and David fled, and escaped that night.
H^1 s^1 11 Saul also sent messengers unto David's
house, to watch him, and to slay him in the
morning:
t^1 and Michal David's wife told him, saying, "If
thou °save not thy [5]life to night, to morrow
thou shalt be slain."
12 So Michal let David down through a window:
and he went, and fled, and escaped.
13 And Michal took an °image, and laid *it* in
the bed, and put a pillow of goats' *hair* for
his bolster, and covered *it* with a cloth.
s^2 14 And when Saul sent messengers to take
David,
t^2 she said "He *is* sick."
s^3 15 And Saul sent the messengers *again* to see
David, saying, "Bring him up to me in the bed,
that I may slay him."
t^3 16 And when the messengers were come in,
behold, *there was* an [13]image in the bed, with
a pillow of goats' *hair* for his bolster.
G^2 p^2 17 And Saul said unto Michal, "Why hast
thou deceived me so, and sent away mine
enemy, that he is escaped?"
q^2 And Michal answered Saul, "He said unto me,
'Let me go; °why should I kill thee?'"
r^2 18 So David fled, and escaped, and came to
Samuel to Ramah, and told him all that Saul
had done to him. And he and Samuel went
and dwelt in Naioth.
H^2 s^4 19 And it was told Saul, saying, °"Behold,
David *is* at Naioth in Ramah."
20 And Saul sent messengers to take David:
t^4 and when they saw the °company of the prophets
prophesying, and Samuel standing *as* °appointed
over them, the Spirit of °God was upon
the messengers of Saul, and they also prophesied.
s^5 21 And when it was told Saul, he sent other
messengers,
t^5 and they prophesied likewise.
s^6 And Saul sent messengers again the third time,
t^6 and they prophesied also.
G^3 p^3 22 Then went he also to Ramah, and came to a
great well that *is* in Sechu: and he asked and
said, "Where *are* Samuel and David?" And °*one*
said, [19]"Behold, *they be* at Naioth in Ramah."
23 And he went °thither to Naioth in Ramah:
q^3 and the [20]Spirit of [20]God was upon him also,
and he went on, and prophesied, until he
came to Naioth in Ramah.
24 And he stripped off his °clothes also, and
prophesied before Samuel in like manner, and
lay down °naked all that day and all that
night. Wherefore they say, °"*Is* Saul also
among the prophets?"

r^3 **20** And David fled from Naioth in Ramah,
W I K^1 y and came and said before Jonathan, "What
have I done? what *is* mine °iniquity? and
what *is* my °sin before thy father, that he
seeketh °my life?"

19. 9—20. 1– (*V*, p. 389). EVIL SPIRIT INCITES SAUL. (*Repeated and Extended Alternation.*)

V | G^1 | p^1 | 9, 10–. Saul's first attempt. } Personal (I).
| q^1 | –10–. Failure. } Thwarted by
| r^1 | –10. David's escape. } David.
H^1 | s^1 | 11–. Saul's second attempt.
| t^1 | –11-13. Failure. Michal's rescue.
| s^2 | 14–. Saul's third attempt.
| t^2 | –14. Failure. Michal's ruse.
| s^3 | 15. Saul's fourth attempt.
| t^3 | 16. Failure. Michal's deception.
} Messengers: three attempts thwarted by human agency.
G^2 | p^2 | 17–. Saul's fifth attempt. } Personal (II).
| q^2 | –17. Failure. } Thwarted
| r^2 | 18. David's escape. } by David.
H^2 | s^4 | 19, 20–. Saul's sixth attempt.
| t^4 | –20. Failure. Spirit of God.
| s^5 | 21–. Saul's seventh attempt.
| t^5 | –21–. Failure. Spirit of God.
| s^6 | –21–. Saul's eighth attempt.
| t^6 | –21. Failure. Spirit of God.
} Messengers: three attempts thwarted by Divine agency.
G^3 | p^3 | 22, 23–. Saul's ninth attempt. } Personal (III).
| q^3 | –23, 24. Failure. } Thwarted by
| r^3 | 20. 1–. David's escape. } God.

10 Saul sought. Note the nine attempts on David's life; three personally by Saul, and six by his messengers (nine being the number of judgment, Ap. 10). See note on 18. 11, and Ap. 23 and 25.
even to, or, even [to pin him] to.
11 save not thy life = save not thy soul: i.e. deliver not thyself. Heb. *nephesh*. Ap. 13.
13 image = teraphim.
17 why . . . ? Fig. *Erotēsis*. Ap. 6.
19 Behold. Fig. *Asterismos*. Ap. 6.
20 company. Cp. 10. 5. 2 Kings 2. 3-5; 5. 22. College for instruction of prophets, priests having failed in their duty as teachers. Deut. 17. 11; 33. 10.
appointed over. Samuel the head here. Elisha in 2 Kings 2. 15. **God.** Heb. Elohim. Ap. 4. I.
22 one. A special various reading (*Sevīr*) reads "they". See Ap. 34. **23 thither.** Sept. reads "thence".
24 clothes: i.e. his robes, or armour, or both.
naked. Cp. 18. 4: i.e. stripped of outer garments.
Is Saul . . . ? Fig. *Parœmia*. Ap. 6.

20. –1—27. 4 (*W*, p. 389). HOSTILITY TO DAVID. (*Alternation.*)

W | I | 20. –1-42. Visit of David to Jonathan. Covenant.
| J | 21. 1—23. 15. Saul's pursuit of David.
| *I* | 23. 16-18. Visit of Jonathan to David. Covenant.
| *J* | 23. 19—27. 4. Saul's pursuit of David.

20. –1-42 (H, above). VISIT OF DAVID TO JONATHAN. (*Division.*)

I | K^1 | –1-4. David's peril.
| K^2 | 5-42. David's expedients.

1-4 (K^1, above). DAVID'S PERIL. (*Alternation.*)

K^1 | y | –1. David's complaint.
| z | 2. Jonathan's reassurance.
| *y* | 3. David's plea.
| *z* | 4. Jonathan's promise.

1 iniquity. Heb. *'āvāh*. Ap. 44. iv.
sin. Heb. *chātā'*. Ap. 44. i.
my life = my soul. Heb. *nephesh*. Ap. 13. "Me" emphatic.

z 2 And he said unto him, "God forbid; thou
(p. 394) shalt not die: °behold, my father will do
970 nothing either great or small, but that he will
shew it me: and why should my father hide
this thing from me? it *is* not *so*."

y 3 And David sware moreover, and said, "Thy
father certainly knoweth that I have found
grace in thine eyes; and he saith, 'Let not
Jonathan know this, lest he be grieved:' but
truly *as* °the LORD liveth, and *as* °thy soul
liveth, *there is* but a °step between me and
death."

z 4 Then said Jonathan unto David, "Whatsoever [3] thy soul desireth, I will even do *it* for
thee."

K[2] L[1] a[1] 5 And David said unto Jonathan, [2]"Behold,
(p. 395) to morrow *is* the new moon, and I °should
not fail to sit with the king at meat: but let
me go, that I may hide myself in the field °unto
the third *day* at even.
6 If thy father at all miss me, then say, 'David
earnestly asked *leave* of me that he might run
to Beth-lehem his city: for *there is* a yearly
sacrifice there for all the family.'
7 If he say thus, '*It is* well;' thy servant shall
have peace: but if he be very wroth, *then* be
sure that °evil is determined by him.
8 Therefore thou shalt deal kindly with thy
servant; for thou hast brought thy servant
into a covenant of [3] the LORD with thee: notwithstanding, if there be in me [1] iniquity, slay
me thyself; for why shouldest thou bring me
to thy father?"
9 And Jonathan said, "Far be it from thee:
for if I knew certainly that [7] evil were determined by my father to come upon thee, then
would not I tell it thee?"

b[1] 10 Then said David to Jonathan, "Who shall
tell me? or what *if* thy father answer thee
roughly?"

c[1] 11 And Jonathan said unto David, "Come,
and let us go out into the field." And they
went out both of them into the field.
12 And Jonathan said unto David, °"O [3] LORD
°God of Israel, when I have sounded my father
about to morrow any time, *or* [5] the third *day*,
and, [2] behold, *if there be* good toward David,
and I then send not unto thee, and shew it thee;
13 [3] The LORD do so and much more to
Jonathan: but if it please my father *to do*
thee [7] evil, then I will shew it thee, and send
thee away, that thou mayest go in peace: and
[3] the LORD be with thee, °as He hath been with
my father.
14 And thou shalt not only while yet I live
shew me the kindness of [3] the LORD, that I die
not:
15 But *also* thou shalt not cut off thy kindness from my house for ever: no, not when
[3] the LORD hath cut off the enemies of David
every one from °the face of the earth."
16 So Jonathan °made *a covenant* with the
house of David, *saying*, "Let [3] the LORD even
require *it* at the hand of David's enemies."
17 °And Jonathan caused David to swear
again, because he loved him: for he loved him
as he loved his own °soul.

L[2] a[2] 18 Then Jonathan said to David, "To morrow

2 behold. Fig. *Asterismos*. Ap. 6.
3 the LORD. Heb. Jehovah. Ap. 4. II.
thy soul = thou. Heb. *nephesh*. Ap. 13.
step = stride. Heb. *pesa'*. Occ. only here.

20. 5-42 (K[2], p. 394). DAVID'S EXPEDIENTS
(*Repeated and Extended Alternation.*)

K[2] | L[1] | a[1] | 5-9. Expedient. David's.
b[1] | 10. Signal desired.
c[1] | 11-17. Covenant made.
L[2] | a[2] | 18, 19. Expedient. Jonathan's.
b[2] | 20-22. Signal arranged.
c[2] | 23. Covenant asserted.
L[3] | a[3] | 24-34. Expedient carried out.
b[3] | 35-41. Signal given.
c[3] | 42. Covenant reasserted.

5 should not fail to sit. Sept. reads "shall not sit".
unto the third day at even. Sept. reads "until the evening". Cp. *v.* 12.
7 evil. Heb. *rā'a'*. Ap. 44. viii.
12 O LORD God of Israel. Syr. reads "Jehovah, God of Israel, [be] witness that I will sound", &c.
God. Heb. Elohim. Ap. 4. I.
13 as = according as.
15 the face of. Fig. *Pleonasm*. Ap. 6.
16 made = solemnised.
17 And Jonathan caused David to swear again. Sept. reads "And again Jonathan sware unto David".
soul. Heb. *nephesh*. Ap. 13.
19 when the business was in hand: i. e. the day when Jonathan arranged for David to overhear Saul's murderous intention (19. 2, 3), and when Jonathan devoted himself to the business of David's safety.
stone Ezel. Sept. reads "the side of this mound".
24 meat. Put by Fig. *Synecdoche* (of Species), Ap. 6, for all kinds of food.
26 not any thing: i. e. "nothing [concerning David's absence] that day".

is the new moon: and thou shalt be missed,
because thy seat will be empty.
19 And *when* thou hast stayed three days,
then thou shalt go down quickly, and come to
the place where thou didst hide thyself °when
the business was *in hand*, and shalt remain by
the °stone Ezel.

20 And I will shoot three arrows on the side b[2]
thereof, as though I shot at a mark.
21 And, [2] behold, I will send a lad, *saying*,
'Go, find out the arrows.' If I expressly say
unto the lad, 'Behold, the arrows *are* on this
side of thee, take them;' then come thou: for
there is peace to thee, and no hurt; *as* [3] the
LORD liveth.
22 But if I say thus unto the young man,
'Behold, the arrows *are* beyond thee;' go
thy way: for [3] the LORD hath sent thee away.

23 And *as touching* the matter which thou c[2]
and I have spoken of, [2] behold, [3] the LORD *be*
between thee and me for ever."

24 So David hid himself in the field: and when L[3] a[3]
the new moon was come, the king sat him down
to eat °meat.
25 And the king sat upon his seat, as at other
times, *even* upon a seat by the wall: and Jonathan arose, and Abner sat by Saul's side, and
David's place was empty.
26 Nevertheless Saul spake °not any thing
that day: for he thought, Something hath befallen him, he *is* not clean; surely he *is* not clean.

970 27 And it came to pass on the morrow, *which*
was the second *day* of the month, that David's
place was empty: and Saul said unto Jonathan
his son, "Wherefore cometh not the son of
Jesse to [24]meat, neither yesterday, nor to day?"
28 And Jonathan answered Saul, "David
earnestly asked *leave* of me *to go* to Beth-
lehem:
29 And he said, 'Let me go, I pray thee; for
our family hath a sacrifice in the city; and my
brother, he hath commanded me *to be there*:
and now, if I have found favour in thine eyes,
let me get away, I pray thee, and see my brethren.' Therefore he cometh not unto the king's
table."
30 Then Saul's anger was kindled against
Jonathan, and he said unto him, °"Thou son
of the perverse rebellious *woman*, do not I
know that thou hast chosen the son of Jesse to
thine own confusion, and unto the confusion
of thy mother's nakedness?
31 For as long as the son of Jesse liveth upon
the ground, thou shalt not be established, nor
thy kingdom. Wherefore now send and fetch
him unto me, for he °shall surely die."
32 And Jonathan answered Saul his father,
and said unto him, "Wherefore shall he be
slain? what hath he done?"
33 And Saul cast a javelin at him to smite
him: whereby Jonathan knew that it was
determined of his father to slay David.
34 So Jonathan arose from the table in fierce
anger, and did eat no meat the second day of
the month: for he was grieved for David, because his father had done him shame.

b³ (p. 395) 35 And it came to pass in the morning,
that Jonathan went out into the field at the
time appointed with David, and a little lad
with him.
36 And he said unto his lad, "Run, find out
now the arrows which I shoot." *And* as the
lad ran, he shot an arrow beyond him.
37 And when the lad was come to the place
of the arrow which Jonathan had shot, Jonathan cried after the lad, and said, "*Is* not the
arrow beyond thee?"
38 And Jonathan cried after the lad, "Make
speed, haste, stay not." And Jonathan's lad
gathered up the arrows, and came to his master.
39 But the lad knew not any thing: only
Jonathan and David knew the matter.
40 And Jonathan gave his °artillery unto
his lad, and said unto him, "Go, carry *them* to
the city."
41 *And* as soon as the lad was gone, David
arose °out of *a place* toward the south, and
fell on his face to the ground, and bowed himself three times: and they kissed one another,
and wept one with another, until David exceeded.

c³ 42 And Jonathan said to David, "Go in peace,
forasmuch as we have sworn both of us in the
name of [3]the LORD, saying, [3]'The LORD be
between me and thee, and between my seed
and thy seed for ever.'" And he arose and
departed: and Jonathan went into the city.

J M d¹ (p. 396) 21 Then came David to Nob to °Ahimelech
the priest: and Ahimelech was afraid
at the meeting of David, and said unto him,
"Why *art* thou alone, and no °man with
thee?"

e¹ 2 And David said unto Ahimelech the priest,
"The king hath commanded me a business,
and hath said unto me, 'Let no [1]man know
any thing of the business whereabout I send
thee, and what I have commanded thee:' and
I have appointed *my* servants to such and
such a place.
3 Now therefore what is under thine hand?
give *me* five *loaves of* bread in mine hand, or
what there is present."

d² 4 And the priest answered David, and said,
"*There is* no °common bread under mine
hand, but there is °hallowed bread; if the
young men have °kept themselves at least
from women."
5 And David answered the priest, and said
unto him, "Of a truth women *have been* kept
from us about these three days, since I came
out, and the °vessels of the young men are
°holy, and *the bread is* in a manner [4]common,
°yea, though it were sanctified this day in
the °vessel."
6 So the priest gave him [4]hallowed *bread*:
for there was no bread there but the shewbread, that was taken from before °the LORD,
to put hot bread in the day when it was taken
away.

30 Thou son of the perverse rebellious woman = a son of rebellious perversity: i.e. a rebel like David. Cp. note on 18. 19.

31 shall surely die = the son of death: i.e. doomed to die.

40 artillery = weapons. Word extended from Latin *ars* = art. The oldest art was ploughing, but the chief weapon in the art of war has usurped to itself this word.

41 out of a place toward the south. Sept. reads "from beside the mound": i.e. Ezel, in *v.* 19.

21. 1–23. 15 (J, p. 394). PURSUIT OF DAVID.
(*Extended Alternation.*)

J | M | 21. 1-9. Nob. Priest's help given.
  N | 21. 10-15. Philistines. David's flight to Achish.
   O | 22. 1-5. Places of refuge. Adullam.
 M | 22. 6-23. Nob. Priests slaughtered.
  N | 23. 1-13. Philistines. Relief of Keilah.
   O | 23. 14, 15. Place of refuge. Desert of Ziph.

21. 1–9 (M, above). PRIEST'S HELP GIVEN.
(*Repeated Alternation.*)

M | d¹ | 1. Ahimelech's fear.
  e¹ | 2, 3. "Let no man know".
 d² | 4-6. Ahimelech's help.
  e² | 7. Doeg knows.
 d³ | 8, 9. Ahimelech's gift.

1 Ahimelech. So called here and in 22. 9, 11, 14, 16, 20. See note on 14. 3 and Mark 2. 26.
man. Heb. *'ish.* Ap. 14. II.

4 common: i.e. or unhallowed.
hallowed = holy. See note on Ex. 3. 5.
kept. And thus ceremonially clean, to eat such bread.

5 vessels = wallets. Cp. 17. 40. Word not used in O.T. in the N.T. sense of 2 Tim. 2. 21, 1 Thess. 4. 4, &c.
holy. See note on Ex. 3. 5. Cp. "hallowed", *v.* 4.
yea, though it were sanctified this day in the vessel = and the more so, when to-day [there are other loaves] to be hallowed in respect of their vessels.

6 the LORD. Heb. Jehovah. Ap. 4. II.

e[2] (p. 396) 969 7 Now a certain [1]man of the servants of Saul
was there that day, °detained before [6]the
LORD; and his name *was* Doeg, an Edomite,
the chiefest of the herdmen that *belonged* to
Saul.

d[3] 8 And David said unto Ahimelech, "And is
there not here under thine hand spear or
sword? for I have neither brought my sword
nor my weapons with me, because the king's
business required haste."

9 And the priest said, "The sword of Goliath
the Philistine, whom thou slewest in the valley
of Elah, °behold, it *is here* wrapped in a cloth
behind the ephod: if thou wilt take that, take
it: for *there is* no other save that here." And
David said, "*There is* none like that; give
it me."

N f 10 And David arose, and fled that day °for
fear of Saul, and went to Achish the king of
Gath.

g 11 And the servants of Achish said unto him,
°"*Is* not this David the king of the land?
°did they not sing one to another of him in
dances, saying,
'Saul hath slain his thousands,
And David his ten thousands?'"

g 12 And David laid up these words in his
heart, and was sore afraid of °Achish the king
of Gath.
13 And he °changed his behaviour before
them, and feigned himself mad in their hands,
and °scrabbled on the doors of the gate, and let
his spittle fall down upon his beard.

f 14 Then said Achish unto his servants, °"Lo,
ye see the [1]man is mad: °wherefore *then* have
ye brought °him to me?
15 °Have I need of mad [1]men, that ye have
brought this *fellow* to play the mad [1]man in
my presence? °shall this *fellow* come into my
house?"

O 968 **22** David therefore departed thence, and
escaped to the cave °Adullam: and
when his brethren and all his father's house
heard *it*, they went down thither to him.
2 And every °one *that was* in distress, and
every °one that *was* in debt, and every °one
that was °discontented, gathered themselves
unto him; and he became a °captain over
them: and there were with him about four
hundred °men.
3 And David went thence to Mizpeh of Moab:
and he said unto the king of Moab, "Let my
father and my mother, I pray thee, °come
forth, *and be* with you, till I know what °God
will do for me."
4 And he brought them before the king of
Moab: and they dwelt with him all the while
that David was in the °hold.
5 And the prophet Gad said unto David,
"Abide not in the hold; depart, and get thee
into the land of Judah." Then David departed, and came into the forest of Hareth.

M h (p. 397) 6 When Saul heard that David was discovered, and the °men that *were* with him,
(°now Saul abode in Gibeah under a tree °in
Ramah, having his spear in his hand, and all
his servants *were* standing about him;)

7 detained, &c. Probably from some ceremonial reason. Cp. "shut up" (Jer. 36. 5), or a "vow" (Acts 21. 23-27), or "uncleanness" (Lev. 13. 4, 11, 21).
9 behold. Fig. *Asterismos*. Ap. 6.

21. 10-15 (N, p. 396). PHILISTINES. DAVID'S FLIGHT. (*Introversion.*)

N | f | 10. Achish. Arrival of David.
  g | 11. David's fear.
  g | 12, 13. David's simulation.
 f | 14, 15. Achish. Deception by David.

10 for fear of Saul = from the face of Saul.
11 Is not this. Cp. 18. 7 and 29. 5.
did they not . . . ? Fig. *Erotēsis*. Ap. 6. Cp. 18. 7 and 29. 5.
12 Achish. See subscription of Ps. 55 (*Comp. Bible*). (Not superscription of Ps. 56 as in A.V.)
13 changed, &c. See title of Ps. 34 (*Comp. Bible*).
scrabbled on. Sept. reads "struck against".
14 Lo. Fig. *Asterismos*. Ap. 6.
wherefore . . . ? Fig. *Erotēsis*. Ap. 6.
him = the man (*v.* 1).
15 Have I . . . ? shall this . . . ? Fig. *Erotēsis*. Ap. 6.

22. 1 Adullam. See title of Ps. 57 (*Comp. Bible*).
2 one = man. Heb. *'īsh*. Ap. 14. II.
discontented = bitter of soul. Heb. *nephesh*. Ap. 13. Cp. Judg. 18. 25, "angry": i. e. embittered.
captain = chief, leader, or prince.
men. Heb. *'īsh*. Ap. 14. II.
3 come forth. Syr. and Vulg. read "dwell". No Ellipsis then to be supplied.
God. Heb. Elohim. Ap. 4. I.
4 hold = stronghold, or fortified camp. First occ.

6-23 (*M*, p. 396). NOB. PRIESTS SLAUGHTERED. (*Introversion.*)

M | h | 6-8. Saul's threatening of Benjamites.
  i | 9, 10. Doeg informs against David.
   k | 11-19. Ahimelech slain by Saul.
   k | 20, 21. Abiathar's escape to David.
  i | 22. Doeg suspected by David.
 h | 23. David's assurance to Abiathar.

6 men. Heb. *'ěnōsh*. Ap. 14. III.
now Saul. Note the Fig. *Parenthesis*. Ap. 6.
in Ramah. Or, in the high place.
8 is sorry for = taketh pity upon.
9 Then, &c.: *vv.* 9-16, by the Fig. *Hysterēsis* (Ap. 6), give details not contained in former narration (21. 1-9).
10 the LORD. Heb. Jehovah. Ap. 4. II.

7 Then Saul said unto his servants that stood
about him, "Hear now, ye Benjamites; will
the son of Jesse give every one of you fields
and vineyards, *and* make you all captains of
thousands, and captains of hundreds;
8 That all of you have conspired against me,
and *there is* none that sheweth me that my
son hath made a league with the son of Jesse,
and *there is* none of you that °is sorry for me,
or sheweth unto me that my son hath stirred
up my servant against me, to lie in wait, as at
this day?"

9 °Then answered Doeg the Edomite, which i
was set over the servants of Saul, and said, "I
saw the son of Jesse coming to Nob, to Ahimelech the son of Ahitub.
10 And he enquired of °the LORD for him,
and gave him victuals, and gave him the sword
of Goliath the Philistine."

11 Then the king sent to call Ahimelech the k
priest, the son of Ahitub, and all his father's
house, the priests that *were* in Nob: and they
came all of them to the king.

968 to 967 12 And Saul said, "Hear now, thou son of Ahitub." And he answered, "Here I *am*, my lord."

13 And Saul said unto him, "Why have ye conspired against me, thou and the son of Jesse, in that thou hast given him bread, and a sword, and hast enquired of [3]God for him, that he should rise against me, to lie in wait, as at this day?"

14 Then Ahimelech answered the king, and said, "And who *is so* faithful among all thy servants as David, which is the king's son in law, and °goeth at thy bidding, and is honourable in thine house?

15 °Did I then begin to enquire of [3]God for him? be it far from me: let not the king impute *any* thing unto his servant, °*nor* to all the house of my father: for thy servant knew nothing of all this, less or more."

16 And the king said, "Thou shalt surely die, Ahimelech, thou, and all thy father's house."

17 And the king said unto the °footmen that stood about him, "Turn, and slay the priests of [10]the LORD; because their °hand also *is* with David, and because they knew °when he fled, and did not shew it to me." But the servants of the king would not put forth their hand to fall upon the priests of [10]the LORD.

18 And the king said to Doeg, "Turn thou, and fall upon the priests." And Doeg the Edomite turned, and he fell upon the priests, and °slew on that day fourscore and five °persons that did wear a linen ephod.

19 And Nob, the city of the priests, smote he with the edge of the sword, both [2]men and women, children and sucklings, and oxen, and asses, and sheep, with the edge of the sword.

k (p. 397) 20 And one of the sons of Ahimelech the son of Ahitub, named °Abiathar, escaped, and fled after David.

21 And Abiathar shewed David that Saul had slain [10]the LORD'S priests.

i 22 And David said unto Abiathar, "I knew *it* that day, when Doeg the Edomite *was* there, that he would surely tell Saul: °I have occasioned *the death* of °all the persons of thy father's house.

h 23 Abide thou with me, fear not: for he that seeketh my °life seeketh thy °life: but with me thou *shalt be* in safeguard."

N P (p. 398) 966 **23** Then they told David, saying, °"Behold, the Philistines fight against Keilah, and they rob the threshingfloors."

Q l 2 Therefore David enquired of °the LORD, saying, "Shall I go and smite these Philistines?" And °the LORD said unto David, "Go, and smite the Philistines, and save Keilah."

m 3 And David's °men said unto him, [1]"Behold, we be afraid here in Judah: how much more then if we come to Keilah against the armies of the Philistines?"

l 4 Then David enquired of [2]the LORD yet again. And [2]the LORD answered him and said, "Arise, go down to Keilah; for I will deliver the Philistines into thine °hand."

14 goeth at thy bidding: or, cometh near for audience. Sept. reads "is captain over thy bodyguard".
15 Did I . . .? Fig. *Erotēsis*. Ap. 6.
nor. This word is read in the text of Sept. and Syr.
17 footmen = runners.
hand. Put by Fig. *Metonymy* (of Cause) for the help given by it. Ap. 6.
when he fled = that he was fleeing.
18 slew. Thus partly fulfilling 2. 31; 3. 12, on Eli's house.
persons. Heb. *'ish*. Ap. 14. II.
20 Abiathar, escaped. Saul thus caused the transfer of the High Priest, with the Urim and Thummim, to David.
22 I have occasioned, &c.: i.e. involved. A mark of David's characteristic tenderness.
all the persons = every soul. Heb. *nephesh*. Ap. 13.
23 life = soul. Heb. *nephesh*. Ap. 13.

23. 1-13 (*N*, p. 396). PHILISTINES. RELIEF OF KEILAH. (*Alternations.*)

N | P | 1. Keilah. Assault by Philistines.
  Q | l | 2. David's inquiries.
    m | 3. David and his men.
  l | 4. David's inquiries.
    m | 5-. David and his men.
P | -5. Keilah. Delivered by David.
  Q | n | 6. David and Abiathar.
    o | 7, 8. Information given to Saul.
  n | 9-13-. David and Abiathar.
    o | -13. Information given to Saul.

1 Behold. Fig. *Asterismos*. Ap. 6.
2 the LORD. Heb. Jehovah. Ap. 4. II.
3 men. Heb. *'ĕnōsh*. Ap. 14. III.
4 hand. Some codices, with one early printed edition, Sept., and Syr., read "hands".
6 fled. Cp. 22. 20. This verse is the Fig. *Hysterēsis*. Ap. 6.
7 God. Heb. Elohim. Ap. 4. I.
delivered. Heb. *nākar*. A homonym. Cp. Deut. 32. 27, "behave strangely"; Job 34. 19, regard or acknowledge. Here = to deliver.
9 secretly practised = contrived.
11 men = masters, or lords. Heb. *bă'ālim*.
as = according as.

5 So David and his [3]men went to Keilah, and fought with the Philistines, m
and brought away their cattle, and smote them with a great slaughter. So David saved the inhabitants of Keilah. P

6 And it came to pass, when Abiathar the son of Ahimelech °fled to David to Keilah, *that* he came down *with* an ephod in his hand. Q n

7 And it was told Saul that David was come to Keilah. And Saul said, °"God hath °delivered him into mine hand; for he is shut in, by entering into a town that hath gates and bars." o

8 And Saul called all the people together to war, to go down to Keilah, to besiege David and his [3]men.

9 And David knew that Saul °secretly practised mischief against him; and he said to Abiathar the priest, "Bring hither the ephod." n

10 Then said David, "O [2]LORD [7]God of Israel, Thy servant hath certainly heard that Saul seeketh to come to Keilah, to destroy the city for my sake.

11 Will the °men of Keilah deliver me up into his hand? will Saul come down, °as Thy servant hath heard? O [2]LORD [7]God of Israel,

966 to 964 I beseech Thee, tell Thy servant." And [2]the LORD said, "He will come down."

12 Then said David, "Will the [11]men of Keilah deliver me and my [3]men into the hand of Saul?" And [2]the LORD said, "They will deliver *thee* up."

13 Then David and his [3]men, *which were* about six hundred, arose and departed out of Keilah, and went whithersoever they could go.

o (p. 398) And it was told Saul that David was escaped from Keilah; and he forbare to go forth.

O (p. 396) 14 And David abode in the wilderness in strong holds, and remained in a °mountain in the wilderness of Ziph. And Saul sought him every day, but [7]God delivered him not into his hand.

15 And David saw that Saul was come out to seek his °life: and David *was* in the wilderness of Ziph in a wood.

I (p. 394) 16 And Jonathan Saul's son arose, and went to David into the wood, and strengthened his hand in [7]God.

17 And he said unto him, "Fear not: for the hand of Saul my father shall not find thee; and thou shalt be king over Israel, and I shall be next unto thee; and that also Saul my father knoweth."

18 And they two made a °covenant before [2]the LORD: and David abode in the wood, and Jonathan went to his house.

J R (p. 399) 19 Then came up °the Ziphites to Saul to Gibeah, saying, "Doth not David hide himself with us in strong holds in the wood, in the hill of Hachilah, which *is* on the south of Jeshimon?

20 Now therefore, O king, come down according to all the desire of thy °soul to come down; and our part *shall be* to deliver him into the king's hand."

21 And Saul said, "Blessed *be* ye of [2]the LORD; for ye have compassion on me.

22 Go, I pray you, °prepare yet, and know and see his place where his °haunt is, *and* who hath seen him there: for it is told me *that* he dealeth very subtilly.

23 See therefore, and °take knowledge of all the lurking places where he hideth himself, and come ye again to me with the certainty, and I will go with you: and it shall come to pass, if he be in the land, that I will search him out throughout all the thousands of Judah."

24 And they arose, and went to Ziph before Saul: but David and his [3]men *were* in °the wilderness of Maon, in the plain on the south of Jeshimon.

25 Saul also and his [3]men went to °seek *him.* And they told David: wherefore he came down °into a rock, and abode in the wilderness of Maon. And when Saul heard *that,* he pursued after David in the wilderness of Maon.

26 And °Saul went on this side of the mountain, and David and his [3]men on that side of the mountain: and David made haste to get away °for fear of Saul; for Saul and his [3]men compassed David and his [3]men round about to take them.

S 27 But there came a messenger unto Saul, saying, "Haste thee, and come; for the Philistines have invaded the land."

14 mountain = hill country.
15 life = soul. Heb. *nephesh.* Ap. 13.
18 covenant. Some codices, with two early printed editions, add "in a wood".

23. 19—27. 4 (*J*, p. 394). PURSUIT OF DAVID.
(*Alternation.*)

J | R | 23. 19-26. Place of refuge.
  | S | 23. 27, 28. Philistines.
  | *R* | 23. 29—26. 25. Places of refuge.
  | *S* | 27. 1-4. Philistines.

19 the Ziphites. See title of Ps. 54 (*Comp. Bible*).
20 soul. Heb. *nephesh.* Ap. 13.
22 prepare. Some codices, with two early printed editions, read "and prepare".
haunt = track, or trail.
23 take knowledge of = get to know.
24 the wilderness = a wild forest or park-like country. Carmel of Judah. Not Carmel of Manasseh.
25 seek him. Some codices, with one early printed edition (marg.), read "seek David".
into a rock = from the rock.
26 Saul. Some codices, with one early printed edition (marg.), add "and his men".
for fear of Saul = from the face of Saul.
28 Sela-hammahlekoth = the cliff of divisions or separations. Now Wady *Malaky,* where two forces could be inaccessible the one to the other, and yet within sight and hearing.

23. 29—26. 25 (*R*, above). PLACES OF REFUGE.
(*Introversion.*)

R | T | 23. 29—24. 22. Desert of En-gedi.
  | U | 25. 1-. Trouble. Death of Samuel.
  | *U* | 25. -1-44. Trouble. Action of Nabal.
  | *T* | 26. 1-25. Desert of Ziph.

23. 29—24. 22 (T, above). DESERT OF EN-GEDI.
(*Introversion and Alternation.*)

T | p | 23. 29—24. 1. Information brought to Saul.
  | q | r | 24. 2. Search by Saul.
  | | s | 24. 3-7. Proof obtained by David.
  | *q* | *r* | 24. 8. Sight by Saul.
  | | *s* | 24. 9-22-. Proof exhibited by David.
  | *p* | 24. -22-. Separation from Saul.

1 Behold. Fig. *Asterismos.* Ap. 6.
2 men. Heb. *'ish.* Ap. 14. II.
his men. Heb. *'ĕnōsh.* Ap. 14. III.
3 to cover his feet. Fig. *Euphemism.* Ap. 6. Fig. *Metonymy* (of Adjunct), Ap. 6: i. e. to stoop, and so cause feet to be covered by the robe.

28 Wherefore Saul returned from pursuing after David, and went against the Philistines: therefore they called that place °Sela-hammahlekoth.

29 And David went up from thence, and dwelt in strong holds at En-gedi. R T p

24 And it came to pass, when Saul was returned from following the Philistines, that it was told him, saying, °"Behold, David *is* in the wilderness of En-gedi." 964

2 Then Saul took three thousand chosen °men out of all Israel, and went to seek David and °his men upon the rocks of the wild goats. q r

3 And he came to the sheepcotes by the way, where *was* a cave; and Saul went in °to cover his feet: and David and [2]his men remained in the sides of the cave. s

964 4 And the °men of David said unto him,
[1]“Behold the day of which °the LORD said
unto thee, [1]‘Behold, I will deliver thine
enemy into thine hand, that thou mayest do
to him °as it shall seem good °unto thee.’”
Then David arose, and cut off the °skirt of
Saul's robe privily.
5 And it came to pass afterward, that David's
heart smote him, because he had cut off °Saul's
skirt.
6 And he said unto his [4]men, [4]“The LORD
forbid that I should do this thing unto my
°master, [4]the LORD'S anointed, to stretch forth
mine hand against him, seeing he *is* the anointed
of [4]the LORD.”
7 So David stayed his servants with these
words, and suffered them not to rise against
Saul. But Saul rose up out of the cave, and
went on *his* way.
q r 8 David also arose afterward, and went out
(p. 399) of the cave, and cried after Saul, saying, “My
lord the king.” And when Saul looked behind
him, David stooped with his face to the earth,
and bowed himself.
s V[1] t 9 And David said to Saul, “Wherefore hearest
(p. 400) thou °men's words, saying, [1]‘Behold, David
seeketh thy hurt?’
10 [1]Behold, this day thine eyes have seen
how that [4]the LORD had delivered thee to day
into mine hand in the cave: and *some* bade
me kill thee: but *mine eye* spared thee; and
I said, ‘I will not put forth mine hand against
my lord; for he *is* [4]the LORD'S anointed.’
11 Moreover, my father, see, yea, see the
[4]skirt of thy robe in my hand: for in that I
cut off the [4]skirt of thy robe, and killed thee
not, know thou and see that *there is* neither
°evil nor °transgression in mine hand, and I
have not °sinned against thee; yet thou huntest my °soul to take it.
u 12 [4]The LORD judge between me and thee,
and [4]the LORD avenge me of thee: but mine
hand shall not be upon thee.
13 As saith the proverb of the ancients,
°‘Wickedness °proceedeth from the wicked:’
but mine hand shall not be upon thee.
t 14 After whom is the king of Israel come out?
after whom dost thou pursue? after °a dead
dog, after °a flea.
u 15 [4]The LORD therefore be judge, and judge
between me [12]and thee, and see, and plead my
cause, and °deliver me out of thine hand.”
V[2] v 16 And it came to pass, when David had made
an end of speaking these words unto Saul, that
Saul said, “*Is* this thy voice, my son David?”
And Saul lifted up his voice, and wept.
w x 17 And he said to David, “Thou *art* more
righteous than I: for thou hast rewarded me
good, whereas I have rewarded thee [11]evil.
18 And thou hast shewed this day how that
thou hast dealt well with me: forasmuch as
when [4]the LORD had delivered me into thine
hand, thou killedst me not.
19 For °if a °man find his enemy, will he let
him go well away?
y wherefore [4]the LORD reward thee good for
that thou hast done unto me this day.

4 men. Heb. *'ĕnōsh.* Ap. 14. III.
the LORD. Heb. Jehovah. Ap. 4. II.
as = according as.
unto thee = in thine eyes.
skirt = corner, or wing.
5 Saul's skirt = the lappet of Saul's robe.
6 master. Heb. *'Adōnī,* my lord. Ap. 4. IV.

24. 9-22- (*s*, p. 399). PROOF EXHIBITED.
(*Division.*)

s | V[1] | 9-15. Remonstrance of David.
| V[2] | 16-22-. Reconciliation of Saul.

9-15 (V[1], above). REMONSTRANCE OF DAVID.
(*Alternation.*)

V[1] | t | 9-11. Expostulation with Saul.
| u | 12, 13. Appeal to Jehovah.
| *t* | 14. Expostulation with Saul.
| *u* | 15. Appeal to Jehovah.

9 men's. Heb. *'ādām.* Ap. 14. I.
11 evil. Heb. *rā'a'.* Ap. 44. viii.
transgression. Heb. *pāsha'.* Ap. 44. ix.
sinned. Heb. *chāṭā'.* Ap. 44. i.
soul. Heb. *nephesh.* Ap. 13.
13 Wickedness = lawlessness. Heb. *rā'a'.* See Ap. 44. viii. Cp. “evil”, *v.* 11.
proceedeth. Fig. *Parœmia.*
14 a dead dog, &c. Fig. *Meiosis.* Ap. 6.
a flea. Heb. a single flea.
15 deliver = judge, or justly deliver.

16-22- (V[2], above). RECONCILIATION OF SAUL.
(*Introversion and Alternation.*)

V[2] | v | 16. Recognition of David by Saul.
| w | x | 17-19-. Acknowledgment of David's act.
| | y | -19. Blessing.
| *w* | *x* | 20. Acknowledgment of Jehovah's will.
| | *y* | 21, 22-. Oath.
| *v* | -22. Separation of David and Saul.

19 if . . . ? Fig. *Erotēsis.* Ap. 6.
man. Heb. *'īsh.* Ap. 14. II.
20 behold. Fig. *Asterismos.* Ap. 6.
22 hold = stronghold.

25. -1-44 [For Structure see next page].

1 lamented. As for a second Moses. Cp. Jer. 15. 1.
in = by, or near.
down. Topography here is most exact. It is a continuous descent to the *Negeb* for more than a day's journey.

20 And now, °behold, I know well that thou *w x*
shalt surely be king, and that the kingdom of
Israel shall be established in thine hand.
21 Swear now therefore unto me by [4]the *y*
LORD, that thou wilt not cut off my seed after
me, and that thou wilt not destroy my name
out of my father's house.”
22 And David sware unto Saul.

And Saul went home; *p*

but David and his [4]men gat them up unto the (p. 399)
°hold. *v*
(p. 400)

25 And Samuel died; and all the Israelites U
were gathered together, and °lamented (p. 399)
him, and buried him °in his house at Ramah.
And David arose, and went °down to the wil- *U*
derness of Paran.

U X a 2 And *there was* a °man in Maon, whose °pos-
(p. 401) sessions *were* in Carmel; and the °man *was*
962 very great, and he had three thousand sheep, and a thousand goats: and he was shearing his sheep in Carmel.

3 Now the name of °the [2]man *was* °Nabal; and the name of his wife Abigail: and *she was* a woman of good understanding, and of a beautiful countenance: but the [2]man *was* churlish and evil in his doings; and he *was* °of the house of Caleb.

4 And David heard in the wilderness that Nabal did shear his sheep.

b e 5 And David sent out ten young men, and David said unto the young men, "Get you up to Carmel, and go to Nabal, and greet him in my name:

6 And thus shall ye say to °him that liveth *in prosperity*, 'Peace *be* both to thee, and peace *be* to thine house, and peace *be* unto all that thou hast.

7 And now I have heard that thou hast shearers: now thy shepherds which were with us, we hurt them not, neither was there ought missing unto them, all the while they were in Carmel.

8 Ask thy young men, and they will shew thee. Wherefore let the young men find favour in thine eyes: for we come in a good day: give, I pray thee, whatsoever cometh to thine hand unto thy °servants, and to thy son David.' "

f 9 And when David's young men came, they spake to Nabal according to all those words in the name of David, and ceased.

e 10 And Nabal answered David's servants, and said, "Who *is* David? and who *is* the son of Jesse? there be many servants now a days that break away every [2]man from his master.

11 Shall I then take my bread, and my °water, and my flesh that I have killed for my shearers, and give *it* unto °men, whom I know not whence they *be?*"

f 12 So David's young men turned their way, and went again, and came and told him all those sayings.

Y 13 And David said unto his [11]men, "Gird ye on every [2]man his sword." And they girded on every [2]man his sword; and David also girded on his sword: and there went up after David about four hundred [2]men; and two hundred abode by the °stuff.

Z c 14 But one of the young men told Abigail, Nabal's wife, saying, °"Behold, David sent messengers out of the wilderness to salute our master; and he °railed on them.

15 But the [11]men *were* very good unto us, and we were not hurt, neither missed we any thing, as long as we were conversant with them, when we were in the fields:

16 They were a wall unto us both by night and day, all the while we were with them keeping the sheep.

17 Now therefore know and consider what thou wilt do; for °evil is determined against our master, and against all his household: for he *is such* a son of Belial, that *a man* cannot speak to him."

25. -1-44 (*U*, p. 399). ACTION OF NABAL.
(*Introversions and Alternations.*)

U | W | -1. David. Personal. Other dwelling.
X | a | 2-4. Nabal's wealth.
b | 5-12. David's message to Nabal.
Y | 13. Resentment of David.
Z | c | 14-17. Report of David to Abigail.
d | 18-20. Abigail's present prepared.
Y | 21, 22. Resentment of David.
Z | *d* | 23-31. Abigail's present presented.
c | 32-35. Answer of David to Abigail.
X | *a* | 36-38. Nabal's death.
b | 39-42. David's message to Abigail.
W | 43, 44. David. Personal. Other wives.

2 man. Heb. *'ish.* Ap. 14. II.
possessions were: or, business [was].
3 the man. Note the introversion of the four lines of this verse:

x | Nabal.
y | Abigail.
y | Abigail.
x | Nabal.

Nabal = foolish.
of the house of Caleb = a Calebite. But Sept., Syr., and Arab. have translated the word "cynical".

5-12 (b, above). DAVID'S MESSAGE TO NABAL.
(*Alternation.*)

b | e | 5-8. Message of David.
f | 9. Delivery by young men.
e | 10, 11. Reply to David.
f | 12. Report by young men.

6 him that liveth = the *bon vivant.*
8 servants. Some codices, with one early printed edition, read "servant".
11 water. Sept. reads "wine".
men. Heb. *'ěnōsh.* Ap. 14. III.
13 stuff = baggage.
14 Behold. Fig. *Asterismos.* Ap. 6.
railed on them = flew at them, or stormed at them.
17 evil. Heb. *rā'a'.* Ap. 44. viii.
18 and. Note the Fig. *Polysyndeton* (Ap. 6), emphasising Abigail's thought and care, as well as rapidity.
measures. See Ap. 51. III. 3.
22 God. Heb. Elohim. Ap. 4. I.
any, &c. = any male.

18 Then Abigail made haste, °and took two hundred loaves, and two bottles of wine, and five sheep ready dressed, and five °measures of parched *corn*, and an hundred clusters of raisins, and two hundred cakes of figs, and laid *them* on asses. d

19 And she said unto her servants, "Go on before me; [14]behold, I come after you." But she told not her husband Nabal.

20 And it was *so, as* she rode on the ass, that she came down by the covert of the hill, and, [14]behold, David and his [11]men came down against her; and she met them.

21 Now David had said, "Surely in vain have I kept all that this *fellow* hath in the wilderness, so that nothing was missed of all that *pertained* unto him: and he hath requited me [17]evil for good. *Y*

22 So and more also do °God unto the enemies of David, if I leave of all that *pertain* to him by the morning light °any that pisseth against the wall."

Z d (p. 401) 962 23 And when Abigail saw David, she hasted, and lighted off the ass, and fell before David on her face, and bowed herself to the ground,

24 And fell at his feet, and said, "Upon me, my lord, *upon* me *let this* °iniquity *be:* and let thine handmaid, I pray thee, speak in thine audience, and hear the words of thine handmaid.

25 Let not my lord, I pray thee, regard this [2]man of Belial, *even* Nabal: for as his name *is*, so *is* he; Nabal *is* his name, and folly *is* with him: but I thine handmaid saw not the young men of my lord, whom thou didst send.

26 Now therefore, my lord, *as* °the LORD liveth, and *as* thy °soul liveth, seeing °the LORD hath withholden thee from °coming to *shed* blood, and from °avenging thyself with thine own hand, now let thine enemies, and they that seek [17]evil to my lord, be as Nabal.

27 And now this °blessing which thine handmaid hath °brought unto my lord, let it even be given unto the young men that follow my lord.

28 I pray thee, forgive the °trespass of thine handmaid: for [26]the LORD will certainly make my lord a sure house; because my lord fighteth the battles of [26]the LORD, and [17]evil hath not been found in thee *all* thy days.

29 Yet a °man is risen to pursue thee, and to seek thy [26]soul: but the [26]soul of my lord shall be bound in the °bundle of life with [26]the LORD thy [22]God; and the [26]souls of thine enemies, them shall He °sling out, *as out* of the middle of a sling.

30 And it shall come to pass, when [26]the LORD shall have done to my lord according to all the good that He hath spoken concerning thee, and shall have appointed thee ruler over Israel;

31 That this shall be no grief unto thee, nor offence of heart unto my lord, either that thou hast °shed blood causeless, or that my lord hath °avenged himself: but when [26]the LORD shall have dealt well with my lord, then remember thine handmaid."

c 32 And David said to Abigail, "Blessed *be* [26]the LORD [22]God of Israel, Which sent thee this day to meet me:

33 And blessed *be* thy °advice, and blessed *be* thou, which hast kept me this day from [26]coming to *shed* blood, and from [31]avenging myself with mine own hand.

34 For in very deed, *as* [26]the LORD [22]God of Israel liveth, Which hath kept me back from hurting thee, except thou hadst hasted and come to meet me, surely there had not been left unto Nabal by the morning light [22]any that pisseth against the wall."

35 So David received of her hand *that* which she had brought him, and said unto her, "Go up in peace to thine house; see, I have hearkened to thy voice, and have °accepted thy person."

X a 36 And Abigail came to Nabal; and, °behold, he held a °feast in his house, like the feast of a king; and Nabal's heart *was* merry within him, for he *was* very drunken: wherefore she told him nothing, less or more, until the morning light.

37 But it came to pass in the morning, when the wine was gone out of Nabal, and his wife had told him these things, that his °heart died within him, and he became *as* a stone.

24 iniquity. Heb. ʻāvah. Ap. 44. iv.
26 the LORD. Heb. Jehovah. Ap. 4. II.
soul. Heb. *nephesh*. Ap. 13.
coming to shed blood = wading in blood (as we say). Cp. *v.* 26.
avenging = saving.
27 blessing = present.
brought. Verb is masc.; and is so when women act in masc. way, and fem. when men act in fem. way.
28 trespass. Heb. *pāshaʻ*. Ap. 44. ix.
29 man. Heb. *'ādām*. Ap. 14. I.
bundle of life = bag (as in 17. 40, 49) of the living.
sling out: i. e. like the stones in David's sling.
31 shed blood causeless = shed innocent blood. Fig. *Antimereia* (of Adverb). Ap. 6.
avenged = saved.
33 advice = good taste.
35 accepted thy person = uplifted thy face.
36 behold. Fig. *Asterismos*. Ap. 6.
feast = banquet or drinking feast. Cp. 2 Sam. 13. 28.
37 heart died. Fig. *Hyperbolē*. Ap. 6.
39 wickedness. Heb. *raʻaʻ*. Ap. 44. viii.
41 wash the feet, &c. This was and is the most menial service.
42 went. See note on "brought", *v.* 27.
44 Michal. Cp. 2 Sam. 3. 14, 15.

26. 1-25 (*T*, p. 399). DESERT OF ZIPH.
(*Introversion and Alternation.*)

T | A | 1. Information given.
  B | g | 2-4. Search by Saul.
    h | 5-13. Camp. Proof obtained.
  B | *g* | 14. Search by Saul.
    h | 15-25-. Camp. Proof exhibited.
  A | -25. Separation made.

2 men. Heb. *'īsh*. Ap. 14. II.

38 And it came to pass about ten days *after*, that [26]the LORD smote Nabal, that he died.

39 And when David heard that Nabal was dead, he said, "Blessed *be* [26]the LORD, That hath pleaded the cause of my reproach from the hand of Nabal, and hath kept His servant from [17]evil: for [26]the LORD hath returned the °wickedness of Nabal upon his own head." And David sent and communed with Abigail, to take her to him to wife. b

40 And when the servants of David were come to Abigail to Carmel, they spake unto her, saying, "David sent us unto thee, to take thee to him to wife."

41 And she arose, and bowed herself on *her* face to the earth, and said, [36]"Behold, *let* thine handmaid *be* a servant to °wash the feet of the servants of my lord."

42 And Abigail hasted, and arose, and rode upon an ass, with five damsels of hers that °went after her; and she went after the messengers of David, and became his wife.

43 David also took Ahinoam of Jezreel; and they were also both of them his wives. W

44 But Saul had given °Michal his daughter, David's wife, to Phalti the son of Laish, which *was* of Gallim.

26 And the Ziphites came unto Saul to Gibeah, saying, "Doth not David hide himself in the hill of Hachilah, *which is* before Jeshimon?" T A (p. 402)

2 Then Saul arose, and went down to the wilderness of Ziph, having three thousand chosen °men of Israel with him, to seek David in the wilderness of Ziph. B g

962 3 And Saul pitched in the hill of Hachilah, which *is* before Jeshimon, by the way. But David abode in the wilderness, and he saw that Saul came after him into the wilderness.

4 David therefore sent out spies, and understood that Saul was come in very deed.

h (p. 402) 5 And David arose, and came to the place where Saul had pitched: and David beheld the place where Saul lay, and Abner the son of Ner, the captain of his host: and Saul lay in the °trench, and the People pitched round about him.

6 Then answered David and said to Ahimelech the Hittite, and to Abishai the son of Zeruiah, brother to Joab, saying, "Who will go down with me to Saul to the camp?" And Abishai said, "I will go down with thee."

7 So David and Abishai came to the People by night: and, behold, Saul lay sleeping within the 5 trench, and his °spear stuck in the ground at his °bolster: but Abner and the People lay round about him.

8 Then said Abishai to David, °"God hath delivered thine enemy into thine hand this day: now therefore °let me smite him, I pray thee, with the spear even to the earth at once, and I will not *smite* him the second time."

9 And David said to Abishai, °"Destroy him not: for who can stretch forth his hand against °the LORD'S anointed, and be guiltless?"

10 David said furthermore, "*As* 9 the LORD liveth, 9 the LORD shall smite him; or his day shall come to die; or he shall descend into battle, and perish.

11 9 The LORD forbid that I should stretch forth mine hand against 9 the LORD'S anointed: but, I pray thee, take thou now the spear that *is* at his bolster, and the °cruse of water, and let us go."

12 So David took the spear and the cruse of water from Saul's bolster; and they gat them away, and °no man saw *it*, nor knew *it*, neither awaked: for they *were* all asleep; because a deep sleep from 9 the LORD was fallen upon them.

13 Then David went over to the other side, and stood on the top of an hill afar off; a great space *being* between them:

B g 14 And David cried to the People, and to Abner the son of Ner, saying, "Answerest thou not, Abner?" Then Abner answered and said, "Who *art* thou *that* criest to the king?"

h i[1] (p. 403) 15 And David said to Abner, "*Art* not thou a *valiant* °man? and who *is* like to thee in Israel? wherefore then hast thou °not kept thy lord the king? for there came one of the People in to destroy the king thy lord.

16 This thing *is* not good that thou hast done. *As* 9 the LORD liveth, ye *are* worthy to die, because ye have °not kept your master, 9 the LORD'S anointed. And now see where the king's spear *is*, and the cruse of water that *was* at his bolster."

i[2] k[1] 17 And Saul °knew David's voice, and said, "*Is* this thy voice, my son David?"

l[1] And David said, "*It is* my voice, my lord, O king."

18 And he said, "Wherefore doth my lord thus pursue after his servant? for what have I done? or what °evil *is* in mine hand?

19 Now therefore, I pray thee, let my lord the king hear the words of his servant. If 9 the LORD have stirred thee up against me, let Him accept an °offering: but if *they be* the °children of °men, cursed *be* they before 9 the LORD; for they have driven me out this day from abiding in the inheritance of 9 the LORD, saying, 'Go, °serve other gods.'

20 Now therefore, let not my blood fall to the earth before the face of 9 the LORD: for the king of Israel is come out to seek °a flea, as when one doth hunt a partridge in the mountains."

21 Then said Saul, "I have °sinned: return, my son David: for I will no more do thee harm, because my °soul was precious in thine eyes this day: behold, I have played the fool, and have °erred exceedingly." k[2]

22 And David answered and said, 7 "Behold the king's spear! and let one of the young men come over and fetch it. l[2]

23 °The LORD render to every 15 man his righteousness and his faithfulness: for 9 the LORD delivered thee into *my* hand to day, but I would not stretch forth mine hand against °the LORD'S anointed.

24 And, 7 behold, as thy °life was much set by this day in mine eyes, so let my °life be much set by in the eyes of 9 the LORD, and let Him deliver me out of all tribulation."

---

5 trench, or, barricade.

7 spear. This is still the mark of the chief's tent. Cp. 18. 10. bolster = head.

8 God. Heb. Elohim. Ap. 4. I.

let me smite him. Note Abishai's character. 2 Sam. 16. 9; 19. 21.

9 Destroy . . . not. See Deut. 9. 26, the subscriptions of Pss. 56, 57, 58, 74, and Ap. 65.

the LORD'S. Heb. Jehovah. Ap. 4. II.

11 cruse, or, flask.

12 no man = no one.

15-25 (*h*, p. 402). PROOF EXHIBITED. (*Division.*)

h | i[1] | 15, 16. Remonstrance with Abner.
  | i[2] | 17-25. Reconciliation with Saul.

15 man. Heb. *'īsh.* Ap. 14. II.

not. Heb. *'el.* (Hypothetical.)

16 not. Heb. *'al.* (Absolute.)

17-25 (i[2], above). RECONCILIATION WITH SAUL. (*Repeated Alternation.*)

i[2] | k[1] | 17-. Saul's recognition of David.
  | l[1] | -17-20. David's remonstrance.
  | k[2] | 21. Saul's acknowledgment.
  | l[2] | 22-24. David's remonstrance.
  | k[3] | 25-. Saul's blessing.

17 knew = recognised.

18 evil. Heb. *rā'a'.* Ap. 44. viii.

19 offering. See Ap. 43. II. iii.

children = sons.

men. Heb. *'ādām.* Ap. 14. I.

serve other gods. David was being driven from God's altar.

20 a flea = one flea.

21 sinned. Heb. *chāṭā'.* Ap. 44. i.

soul = life. Heb. *nephesh.* Ap. 13.

erred. Heb. *shāgāh.* Ap. 44. xii.

23 The LORD = Jehovah. Note the Fig. *Epanadiplōsis.* Ap. 6.

24 life = soul. Heb. *nephesh.* Ap. 13.

k³ (p. 403) 962 25 Then Saul said to David, "Blessed *be* thou, my son David: thou shalt both do great *things*, and also shalt still prevail."

A (p. 402) So David went on his way, and Saul returned to his place.

J S (p. 399) **27** And David said °in his heart, °"I shall now perish one day by the hand of Saul: *there is* nothing better for me than that I should speedily escape into the land of the Philistines; and Saul shall despair of me, to seek me any more in any °coast of Israel: so shall I escape out of his hand."

2 And David arose, and he passed over with the six hundred °men that *were* with him unto Achish, the son of Maoch, king of Gath.

3 And David dwelt with Achish at Gath, he and his ²men, every °man with his household, *even* David with his two wives, Ahinoam the Jezreelitess, and Abigail the Carmelitess, °Nabal's wife.

4 And it was told Saul that David was fled to Gath: and he sought no more again for him.

E m¹ (p. 404) 5 And David said unto Achish, "If I have now found grace in thine eyes, let them give me a place in some town in the country, that I may dwell there: for why should thy servant dwell in the royal city with thee?"

6 Then Achish gave him Ziklag that day: wherefore °Ziklag pertaineth unto the kings of Judah unto this day.

7 And the time that David dwelt in the °country of the Philistines was a full year

961 and four months.

n¹ 8 And David and his ³men went up, and invaded the Geshurites, and the Gezrites, and the Amalekites: for those *nations were* of old the inhabitants of the land, as thou goest to Shur, even unto the land of Egypt.

9 °And David smote the land, and left neither ³man nor woman alive, and took away the sheep, and the oxen, and the asses, and the camels, and the apparel, and returned, and came to Achish.

m² 10 And Achish said, °"Whither have ye made a °road to day?" And David said, "Against the °south of Judah, and against the south of the Jerahmeelites, and against the south of the Kenites."

n² 11 And David saved neither ³man nor woman alive, to bring *tidings* to Gath, saying, "Lest they should tell on us, saying, 'So did David, and so *will be* his manner all the while he dwelleth in the country of the Philistines.'"

m³ 12 And Achish believed David, saying, "He hath made his °People Israel utterly to abhor him; therefore he shall be my servant for ever."

F 960 **28** And it came to pass in those days, that the Philistines gathered their armies together for warfare, to fight with Israel. And Achish said unto David, "Know thou assuredly, that thou shalt go out with me to battle, thou and thy °men."

2 And David said to Achish, °"Surely thou shalt know what thy servant can do." And Achish said to David, "Therefore will I make thee °keeper of mine head for ever."

D o¹ 3 Now Samuel was dead, and all Israel had lamented him, and buried him °in Ramah, even in his own city. And Saul had put away those that °had familiar spirits, and the °wizards, out of the land.

p q 4 And the Philistines gathered themselves

---

1 in his heart = to himself.
I shall now perish. This lack of faith acted with disastrous results to David. It put him in a false position; shook the People's confidence in him; delayed his own election; and led to divisions in the kingdom.
coast = border.
2 men. Heb. *'ĕnōsh*. Ap. 14. III.
3 man. Heb. *'ish*. Ap. 14. II.
Nabal's wife. See note on 30. 5.

27. 5—2 Sam. **1. 27** (*P*, p. 375). THE PROVOCATION OF SAUL. REJECTION CARRIED OUT. (*Alternation and Introversion.*)

P | C | E | 27. 5-12. Ziklag. Possessed by David.
  F | 28. 1, 2. Philistines and David.
  D | 28. 3-25. Saul's sin.
C | *F* | 29. 1-11. Philistines and David.
  E | 30. 1-31. Ziklag. Repossessed by David.
  D | 31. 1—2 Sam. 1. 27. Saul's death.

5-12 (E, above). ZIKLAG. DAVID'S POSSESSION OF. (*Repeated Alternation.*)

E | m¹ | 5-7. David and Achish. Gift.
  n¹ | 8, 9. David. Invasion of aborigines.
 m² | 10. Achish and David. Deception.
  n² | 11. David. Extermination.
 m³ | 12. Achish and David. Deception.

6 Ziklag. An outpost which protected Gath.
7 country. Heb. "field". Put by Fig. *Synecdoche* (of Part) for country. Ap. 6.
9 And. Note the Fig. *Polysyndeton* (Ap. 6) in *v.* 9.
10 Whither. Some codices, with Sept. and Vulg., read "against whom".
road = raid.
south. Heb. the *Negeb* or hill country south of Judah.
12 People Israel = Israel's People.

28. 1 men. Heb. *'ĕnōsh*. Ap. 14. III.
2 Surely = Therefore; which Achish repeats in his reply.
keeper of mine head: i.e. captain of my bodyguard.

3-25 (D, above). SAUL'S SIN. (*Repeated Alternation, and Introversion.*)

D | o¹ | 3. Familiar spirits. Owner put away.
 p | q | 4, 5. Saul's fear. (Of Philistines.)
  r | 6. No answer from Jehovah.
 o² | 7-14. Familiar spirit. Woman sought.
 p | *r* | 15-19. Answer from familiar spirit.
  q | 20. Saul's fear. (Of Jehovah.)
 o³ | 21-25. Familiar spirit. Woman spared.

3 in Ramah, &c. Heb. "in Ramah and in his own city". Fig. *Hendiadys* (Ap. 6) = in his own city, Ramah.
had familiar spirits. Familiar spirits are demons pretending to be dead persons; hence the word "necromancy". See notes on Lev. 19. 31 and Isa. 8. 19.
wizards = wise, cunning, or knowing ones.

960 together, and came and pitched in Shunem: and Saul gathered all Israel together, and they pitched in Gilboa.

5 And when Saul saw the host of the Philistines, he was afraid, and his heart greatly trembled.

r 6 And when Saul °enquired of °the LORD, °the LORD °answered him not, neither by dreams, nor by °Urim, nor by prophets.

o² 7 Then said Saul unto his servants, "Seek me °a woman that °hath a [3] familiar spirit, that I may go to her, and °enquire of her." And his servants said to him, °"Behold, *there is* a woman that hath a [3] familiar spirit at En-dor."

8 And Saul disguised himself, and put on other raiment, and he went, and two [1] men with him, and they came to the woman by night: and he said, "I pray thee, divine unto me °by the familiar spirit, and bring me *him* up, whom I shall name unto thee."

9 And the woman said unto him, [7] "Behold, thou knowest what Saul hath done, how he hath cut off those that have [3] familiar spirits, and the wizards, out of the land: wherefore then layest thou a snare for my °life, to cause me to die?"

10 And Saul sware to her by [6] the LORD, saying, "*As* [6] the LORD liveth, there shall no punishment happen to thee for this thing."

11 Then said the woman, "Whom shall I bring °up unto thee?" And he said, "Bring me °up Samuel."

12 And when the woman °saw Samuel, °she cried with a loud voice: and the woman spake to Saul, saying, "Why hast thou deceived me? for °thou *art* Saul."

13 And the king said unto her, "Be not afraid: for what sawest thou?" And the woman said unto Saul, "I saw °gods ascending °out of the earth."

14 And he said unto her, "What form *is* he of?" And she said, "An old °man cometh [11] up; and he *is* covered with a °mantle." And Saul °perceived that it *was* Samuel, and he °stooped with *his* face to the ground, and bowed himself.

p r 15 And °Samuel said to Saul, "Why hast thou °disquieted °me, to bring me [11] up?" And Saul answered, "I am sore distressed; for the Philistines make war against me, and °God is departed from me, and answereth me °no more, neither °by prophets, nor by dreams: therefore I have called thee, that thou mayest make known unto me what I shall do."

16 °Then said Samuel, "Wherefore then dost thou ask of me, seeing [6] the LORD is departed from thee, and is °become thine enemy?

17 And [6] the LORD hath done to him, °as He spake °by me: for [6] the LORD hath rent the kingdom out of thine hand, and given it to thy neighbour, *even* to David:

18 Because thou °obeyedst not the voice of [6] the LORD, nor executedst His fierce °wrath upon Amalek, therefore hath [6] the LORD done this thing unto thee this day.

19 Moreover [6] the LORD will also deliver Israel with thee into the hand of the Philistines: and to morrow *shalt* thou and thy sons *be* °with me: [6] the LORD also shall deliver the host of Israel into the hand of the Philistines."

20 Then Saul °fell straightway all along on q
the earth, and was sore afraid, because of the words of Samuel: and there was no strength in him; for he had eaten no °bread all the day, nor all the night.

21 And the woman came unto Saul, and saw o³
that he was sore troubled, and said unto him,

6 enquired = asked. Heb. *shā'āl*, to ask. Not *dārash*, "to seek out". See note on *v.* 7, and 1 Chron. 10. 13, 14.
the LORD. Heb. Jehovah. Ap. 4.
answered him not. Not likely therefore to answer now by a way He had forbidden. Samuel had been dead two years.
Urim. See note on Ex. 28. 30. Num. 26. 55. It must have been an ephod of his own making, as Abiathar the High Priest was with David. Saul makes no mention of this in *v.* 15.
7 a woman. Answering to the modern "mediums".
hath = owneth, possesses as mistress. See note on Lev. 19. 31.
enquire = seek out. Heb. *dārash*, a deeper meaning than *v.* 6. See note above. Cp. 1 Chron. 10. 13, 14.
Behold. Fig. *Asterismos.* Ap. 6.
8 by the familiar spirit. Hence called necromancy.
9 life = soul. Heb. *nephesh.* Ap. 13.
11 up. Note: not down, or forth. Cp. *v.* 13.
12 saw Samuel. Or the materialisation of a deceiving spirit personating Samuel, as is done by "mediums" to-day.
she cried, &c. Evidently surprised, and getting more than she expected.
thou art Saul. How should she know this but by a communication from the spirit.
13 gods. Pl. of *Elohim.* Either "a god" or a spirit manifestation.
out of the earth. Not down, or forth, as in John 11. 43, 44.
14 man. Heb. *'īsh.* Ap. 14. II. Not a spirit.
mantle. If a spirit, why a mantle? Samuel's spirit was with God (Ecc. 12. 7). And if Samuel's body, it would be with "grave-clothes" (John 11. 44).
perceived = understood: i. e. from what the medium said. He *saw* nothing.
stooped = did obeisance.
15 Samuel said: i. e. the spirit personating Samuel said. Just as it is done in the present day by the medium: never directly.
disquieted. If Samuel, then it shows he was "quiet" before. **me.** Not my spirit.
God. Heb. Elohim. Ap. 4. I.
no more. Therefore certainly not by means which He had expressly forbidden. See Lev. 19. 31; 20. 6, 27. Deut. 18. 10, 13, &c.
by prophets. Saul omits the reference to "Urim" because it would remind him of the murder of the priests (22. 18, 19). See note on *v.* 6.
16 Then said Samuel. Jehovah might have sent "a lying spirit", and given by it a true message, just as He did in 2 Chron. 18. 19-22. Nothing was said but what was well known before.
become thine enemy. The Sept. reads "and hath come to be with thy neighbour". Cp. *v.* 17 and 15. 28.
17 as = according as. **by me** = by my hand.
18 obeyedst not = hearkenedst not to.
wrath. Put by Fig. *Metonymy* (of Cause), Ap. 6, for the judgment in consequence of it.
19 with me: i. e. with the dead.
20 fell straightway = remained motionless. Cp. Acts 9. 7, where "stood speechless" = remained speechless. See Acts 26. 14. The two passages together = fell, and remained so.
bread = food. Fig. *Synecdoche* (of Species). Ap. 6.

960 °"Behold, thine handmaid hath [18]obeyed thy voice, and I have put my [9]life in my hand, and have hearkened unto thy words which thou spakest unto me.

22 Now therefore, I pray thee, hearken thou also unto the voice of thine handmaid, and let me set a morsel of bread before thee; and eat, that thou mayest have strength, when thou goest on thy way."

23 But he refused, and said, "I will not eat." But his servants, together with the woman, compelled him; and he hearkened unto their voice. So he arose from the earth, and sat upon the bed.

24 And the woman had a fat calf in the °house; and she hasted, and killed it, and took flour, and kneaded *it*, and did bake unleavened bread thereof:

25 And she brought *it* before Saul, and before his servants; and they did eat. Then they rose up, and went away that night.

F s **29** Now the Philistines gathered together all their armies to Aphek: and the Israelites pitched by a fountain which *is* in Jezreel.

2 And the °lords of the Philistines passed on by hundreds, and by thousands:

t but David and his °men passed on in the rereward with Achish.

s 3 Then said the princes of the Philistines, "What *do* these Hebrews *here?*" And Achish said unto the princes of the Philistines, "*Is* not this David, the servant of Saul the king of Israel, which hath been with me these days, or these years, and I have found no fault in him since he °fell °*unto me* unto this day?"

4 And the princes of the Philistines were wroth with him; and the princes of the Philistines said unto him, "Make this °fellow return, that he may go again to his place which thou hast appointed him, and let him not go down with us to battle, lest in the battle he be an adversary to us: for wherewith should he reconcile himself unto his master? °*should it* not *be* with the heads of these [2]men?

5 *Is* not this David, of whom they sang one to another in dances, saying,

'Saul slew his thousands,
And David his ten thousands?'"

6 Then Achish called David, and said unto him, "Surely, *as* °the LORD liveth, thou hast been upright, and thy going out and thy coming in with me in the host *is* good in my sight: for I have not found °evil in thee since the day of thy coming unto me unto this day: nevertheless °the [2]lords favour thee not.

7 Wherefore now return, and go in peace, that thou displease not the [2]lords of the Philistines."

8 And David said unto Achish, "But what have I done? and what hast thou found in thy servant so long as I have been °with thee unto this day, that I may not go fight against the enemies of my lord the king?"

9 And Achish answered and said to David, "I know that thou *art* good in my sight, as °an angel of °God: notwithstanding the princes of the Philistines have said, 'He shall not go up with us to the battle.'

21 Behold. Fig. *Asterismos*. Ap. 6.
24 house=shed.

29. 1-11 (*F*, p. 404). **PHILISTINES AND DAVID.**
(*Alternation.*)

F | s | 1, 2-. Philistines. Assembly.
  | t | -2. David's junction.
  | *s* | 3-10. Philistines. Objection.
  | *t* | 11. David's return.

2 lords=princes; *vv.* 3, 4, &c. See note on Josh. 13. 3.
men. Heb. *'ĕnōsh*. Ap. 14. III.
3 fell=fell away; or, departed.
unto me. These words are in the text of Sept. and Vulg.
4 fellow. Heb. *'ish*. Ap. 14. II.
should . . . ? Fig. *Erotēsis*. Ap. 6.
6 the LORD. Heb. Jehovah. Ap. 4. II.
evil. Heb. *rā'a'*. Ap. 44. viii.
the lords favour thee not="thou art not good in the eyes of the princes". See *v.* 1.
8 with thee=before thee.
9 an angel=a messenger.
God. Heb. Elohim. Ap. 4. I.
10 with thy master's servants. Sept. reads "thou, and the servants of thy lord". Probably the Manassites named in 1 Chron. 12. 19, 20, who deserted to David.
with thee. The Sept. adds "and depart unto the place where I appointed you, and entertain no evil thought in thy heart; for thou art good in my sight".
11 and his men=he and his men, as in *v.* 2.

30. 1-31 (*E*, p. 404). **ZIKLAG REPOSSESSED.**
(*Introversion and Alternation.*)

E | G | 1-6-. Ziklag. Taken.
  | H | u | -6-8. Jehovah's promise. Made.
  | | v | 9, 10. Division of forces.
  | J | 11-16. Colloquy with Egyptian.
  | *H* | *u* | 17-20. Jehovah's promise. Kept.
  | | *v* | 21-25. Junction of forces.
  | *G* | 26-31. Ziklag. Retaken.

1 men. Heb. *'ĕnōsh*. Ap. 14. III.
the south=the *Negeb*. The hill-country S. of Judah.
burned=burned up. See Ap. 43. I. viii.
2 the women captives, that were therein. Sept. reads "the women, and all who were therein".
3 and. Note the Fig. *Polysyndeton* (Ap. 6) in this verse.
burned=burning.

10 Wherefore now rise up early in the morning °with thy master's servants that are come °with thee: and as soon as ye be up early in the morning, and have light, depart."

11 So David °and his °men rose up early to depart in the morning, to return into the land of the Philistines. And the Philistines went up to Jezreel. t

30 And it came to pass, when David and his °men were come to Ziklag on the third day, that the Amalekites had invaded °the south, and Ziklag, and smitten Ziklag, and °burned it with fire; E G

2 And had taken °the women captives, that *were* therein: they slew not any, either great or small, but carried *them* away, and went on their way.

3 So David and his [1]men came to the city, °and, behold, *it was* °burned with fire; and their wives, and their sons, and their daughters, were taken captives.

960 **4** Then David and the People that *were* with him lifted up their voice and wept, until they had no more power to weep.

5 And David's two wives were taken captives, Ahinoam the Jezreelitess, and Abigail °the wife of Nabal the Carmelite.

6 And David was greatly distressed; for the People spake of stoning him, because the °soul of all the People was °grieved, °every man for his sons and for his daughters:

H u but David °encouraged himself in °the LORD his °God.

7 And David said to Abiathar the priest, Ahimelech's son, "I pray thee, bring me hither the ephod." And °Abiathar brought thither the ephod to David.

8 And David enquired at [6]the LORD, saying, "Shall I pursue after this troop? shall I overtake them?" And He answered him, "Pursue: for thou shalt surely overtake *them*, and without fail recover *all*."

v **9** So David went, he and the six hundred °men that *were* with him, and came to the brook Besor, where those that were left behind stayed.

10 But David pursued, he and four hundred [9]men: for two hundred abode behind, which were so faint that they could not go over the brook Besor.

J **11** And they found an Egyptian in the field, and brought him to David, and gave him bread, and he did eat; and they made him drink water;

12 And they gave him a piece of a cake of figs, and two clusters of raisins: and when he had eaten, his °spirit came again to him: for he had eaten no bread, nor drunk *any* water, °three days and three nights.

13 And David said unto him, "To whom *belongest* thou? and whence *art* thou?" And he said, "I *am* a young man of Egypt, servant to an Amalekite; and my master left me, because three days agone I fell sick.

14 We made an invasion *upon* the south of the °Cherethites, and upon *the coast* which *belongeth* to Judah, and upon the south of Caleb; and we burned Ziklag with fire."

15 And David said to him, "Canst thou bring me down to this company?" And he said, "Swear unto me by [6]God, that thou wilt neither kill me, nor deliver me into the hands of my master, and I will bring thee down to this °company."

16 And when he had brought him down, °behold, *they were* spread abroad upon all the °earth, eating and drinking, and dancing, because of all the great spoil that they had taken out of the land of the Philistines, and out of the land of Judah.

H u **17** And David smote them from °the twilight even unto the evening of the next day: and there escaped not a °man of them, save four hundred young [9]men, which rode upon camels, and fled.

18 And David recovered all that the Amalekites had carried away: and David rescued his two wives.

19 And there was nothing lacking to them, neither small nor great, neither sons nor daughters, neither spoil, nor any *thing* that they had taken to them: David recovered all.

20 And David took all the flocks and the herds, *which* they °drave before those *other* °cattle, and said, "This *is* David's spoil."

21 And David came to the two hundred [1]men, which were so faint that they could not follow David, whom they had made also to abide at the brook Besor: and they went forth to meet David, and to meet the People that *were* with him: and when David came near to the People, °he saluted them. *v*

22 Then answered all the wicked [17]men and *men* of Belial, of those that went with David, and said, "Because they went not with us, we will not give them *ought* of the spoil that we have recovered, save to every [17]man his wife and his °children, that they may lead *them* away, and depart."

23 Then said David, "Ye shall not do so, my brethren, with that which [6]the LORD hath given us, Who hath preserved us, and delivered the [15]company that came against us into our hand.

24 For who will hearken unto you in this matter? but as his part *is* that goeth down to the battle, so *shall* his part *be* that tarrieth by the stuff: they shall part alike."

25 °And it was *so* from that day forward, that he made it a statute and an ordinance for Israel unto this day.

26 And when David came to Ziklag, he sent of the spoil unto the elders of Judah, *even* to his friends, saying, [16]"Behold a °present for you of the spoil of the enemies of [6]the LORD;" *G*

5 the wife. The Fig. *Ampliatio* (Ap. 6), by which Abigail is still called the wife of Nabal, though he was dead. Cp. 27. 3; 2 Sam. 3. 3. Those ignorant of Figures of Speech would call this a "discrepancy".
6 soul. Heb. *nephesh.* Ap. 13.
grieved = embittered.
every man. Heb. *'ish.* Ap. 14. II.
encouraged = strengthened.
the LORD. Heb. Jehovah. Ap. 4. II.
God. Heb. Elohim. Ap. 4. I.
7 Abiathar. He had the ephod, with David. Zadok, who was with Saul, had it not.
9 men. Heb. *'ish.* Ap. 14. II.
12 spirit. Heb. *rūach.* Ap. 9.
three days and three nights. Fig. *Idioma*, by which a part of a day is reckoned as a whole day. See 2 Sam. 1. 1, 2, and cp. Est. 4. 16. Jonah 1. 17. Matt. 12. 40.
14 Cherethites. Probably a clan of Philistines, *v.* 16.
15 company = troop, as *v.* 8.
16 behold. Fig. *Asterismos.* Ap. 6.
earth = surrounding land.
17 the twilight = the morning. Heb. *nesheph*, a Homonym: meaning (1) *darkness*, 2 Kings 7. 5, 7. Job 24. 15. Prov. 7. 9. Isa. 5. 11; 21. 4; 59. 10. Jer. 13. 16; (2) *daylight*, 1 Sam. 30. 17. Job 7. 4. Ps. 119. 147.
man. Heb. *'ish.* Ap. 14. II.
20 drave = drave in triumph.
cattle = spoils. Heb. acquisition, or substance.
21 he saluted them. Sept. reads "they inquired of his welfare".
22 children = sons.
25 And it was so. The 20th *Seder* begins here, and ends with 2 Sam. 2. 6. See note on p. 366.
26 present. All these places south of Hebron were protected by David, and these presents were a return for their support.

960 27 To *them* which *were* in Beth-el, and to *them* which *were* in south Ramoth, and to *them* which *were* in Jattir,

28 And to *them* which *were* in Aroer, and to *them* which *were* in Siphmoth, and to *them* which *were* in Eshtemoa,

29 And to *them* which *were* in Rachal, and to *them* which *were* in the cities of the Jerahmeelites, and to *them* which *were* in the cities of the Kenites,

30 And to *them* which *were* in Hormah, and to *them* which *were* in Chor-ashan, and to *them* which *were* in Athach,

31 And to *them* which *were* in °Hebron, and to all the places where David himself and his [1]men were wont to °haunt.

D K[1] w[1] **31** Now the Philistines fought against Israel: and the °men of Israel fled from before the Philistines, and fell down slain in mount Gilboa.

2 And the Philistines followed hard upon Saul and upon his sons; and the Philistines slew Jonathan, and °Abinadab, and Melchi-shua, Saul's sons.

3 And the battle went sore against Saul, and the archers hit him; and he was °sore wounded of the archers.

x 4 Then said Saul unto his armourbearer, "Draw thy sword, and thrust me through therewith; lest these uncircumcised come and thrust me through, and °abuse me." But his armourbearer would not; for he was sore afraid. Therefore Saul took a sword, and fell upon it.

5 And when his armourbearer saw that Saul was dead, he fell likewise upon his sword, and died with him.

6 °So Saul died, and his three sons, and his armourbearer, °and all his [1]men, that same day together.

w[2] 7 And when the [1]men of Israel that *were* on the other side of the valley, and *they* that *were* on the other side Jordan, saw that the [1]men of Israel fled, and that Saul and his sons were dead, they forsook the cities, and fled; and the Philistines came and dwelt in them.

x 8 And it came to pass on the morrow, when the Philistines came to strip the slain, that they found Saul and his three sons fallen in mount Gilboa.

9 And they cut off his head, and stripped off his armour, and sent into the land of the Philistines round about, to publish *it in* the house of their idols, and among the people.

10 And they put his armour in the house of Ashtaroth: and they fastened °his body to the wall of °Beth-shan.

11 And when the inhabitants of Jabesh-gilead heard of that which the Philistines had done °to Saul; w[3]

12 All the valiant °men arose, and went all night, and took the body of Saul and the bodies of his sons from the wall of [10]Beth-shan, and came to Jabesh, and burnt them there.

13 And they took their bones, and buried *them* under a tree at Jabesh, and fasted seven days.

31 Hebron. Caleb's lot: the *Negeb*. Cp. 27. 10.
haunt = frequent.

1 Sam. **31. 1**—2 Sam. **1. 27** (*D*, p. 404). SAUL'S DEATH. (*Division*.)

D | K[1] | 1 Sam. 31. 1–13. The battle.
| K[2] | 2 Sam. 1. 1–27. Report of the battle.

31. 1–13 (K[1], above). THE BATTLE. (*Repeated Alternation*.)

K[1] | w[1] | 1–3. Israel. Defeat.
x | 4–6. Saul's death.
w[2] | 7. Israel. Flight.
x | 8–10. Saul. Indignities.
w[3] | 11–13. Israel. Rescue of bodies.

1 men. Heb. *'ĕnōsh*. Ap. 14. III.
2 Abinadab. Called Ishui (14. 49).
3 sore wounded = in sore anguish.
4 abuse = insult.
6 So Saul died. Cp. 1 Chron. 10. 13, 14. Here, history from human standpoint; in Chronicles, God's standpoint, and reasons of the history. See notes on 1 Chron. 10. 13, and Ap. 55. If Saul was thirty years of age when anointed, he would now be seventy; and Jonathan fifty-three or fifty-four. See note on 13. 1.
and. Some codices, with two early printed editions, Syr., and Vulg., read "yea, and".
10 his body. This is additional to 1 Chron. 10. 10; and "his head", there, is additional to 1 Sam. 31. 10. The two books and accounts are independent, supplementary, and complementary by Fig. *Hysterēsis* (Ap. 6). See Ap. 55.
Beth-shan. It had remained Canaanite, and therefore friendly to Philistines (Judg. 1. 27).
11 to = about. **12** men. Heb. *'īsh*. Ap. 14. II.

THE °SECOND BOOK OF SAMUEL,

OTHERWISE CALLED,

THE SECOND BOOK OF THE KINGS.

K[2] y **1** Now it came to pass after the death of Saul, when David was returned from °the slaughter of the Amalekites, and David had abode two days in °Ziklag;

2 It came even to pass on °the third day, that, °behold, a °man came out of the camp from Saul with his clothes rent, and earth upon his head: and *so* it was, when he came to David, that he fell to the earth, and did obeisance.

3 And David said unto him, "From whence comest thou?" And he said unto him, "Out of the camp of Israel am I escaped."

TITLE, Second Book. See note on First Book, p. 366.

2 Sam. **1. 1–27** (K[2], above). REPORT OF BATTLE. (*Alternation*.)

K[2] | y | 1–10. Amalekite's report.
z | 11, 12. The lamentation of David.
y | 13–16. Amalekite's execution.
z | 17–27. The lamentation of "the Bow".

1 the slaughter. Cp. 1 Sam. 30. 17.
Ziklag. Cp. 1 Sam. 27. 6.
2 the third day. See note on 1 Sam. 30. 12.
behold. Fig. *Asterismos*. Ap. 6.
man. Heb. *'īsh*. Ap. 14. II.

960 4 And David said unto him, "How went the
matter? I pray thee, tell me." And °he
answered, "That the People are fled from the
battle, and many of the People also are fallen
and dead; and Saul and Jonathan his son are
dead also."
5 And David said unto the young man that
told him, "How knowest thou that Saul and
Jonathan his son be dead?"
6 And the young man that told him said,
"As I happened by chance upon mount Gilboa,
°behold, Saul leaned upon his spear; and, °lo,
the chariots and horsemen followed hard after
him.
7 And when he looked behind him, he saw
me, and called unto me. And I answered,
'Here *am* I.'
8 And he said unto me, 'Who *art* thou?' And
I answered him, 'I *am* an °Amalekite.'
9 °He said unto me again, 'Stand, I pray thee,
upon me, and slay me: for anguish is come
upon me, because my °life *is* yet whole in me.'
10 So I stood upon him, and slew him, because I was sure that he could not live after
that he was °fallen: and I took the crown that
was upon his head, and the bracelet that *was*
on his arm, and have brought them hither unto
my lord."

z (p. 408) 11 Then David took hold on his clothes, and
rent them; and likewise all the °men that
were with him:
12 And they mourned, and wept, and fasted
until even, for Saul, and for Jonathan his son,
and for the People of °the LORD, and for the
house of Israel; because they were fallen by
the sword.

y 13 And David said unto the young man that
told him, "Whence *art* thou?" And he answered, "I *am* the son of a stranger, an
[8] Amalekite."
14 And David said unto him, "How wast thou
not afraid to stretch forth thine hand to destroy
[12] the LORD'S anointed?"
15 And David called one of the young men,
and said, "Go near, *and* fall upon him." And
he smote him that he died.
16 And David said unto him, °"Thy blood *be*
upon °thy head; for thy mouth hath testified
against thee, saying, 'I have slain [12] the LORD'S
anointed.'"

L^1 (p. 409) 17 And David lamented with this lamentation
over Saul and over Jonathan his son:

L^2 18 (Also he bade them teach the °children of
Judah °*the use of* °the bow: °behold, *it is*
°written in the book of Jasher.)

z a^1 19 "The °beauty of Israel is slain upon thy
high places:

b^1 How are the mighty fallen!

a^2 20 Tell *it* not in Gath,
Publish *it* not in the streets of Askelon;
Lest the daughters of the Philistines rejoice,
Lest the daughters of the uncircumcised triumph.
21 Ye mountains of Gilboa, *let there be* no dew,
Neither *let there be* rain, upon you,
Nor fields of offerings:
For there the shield of the mighty is vilely cast away,
°The shield of Saul, *as though he had* not been anointed with oil.

22 From the blood of the slain, b^2
From the fat of the mighty,
The bow of Jonathan turned not back,
And the sword of Saul returned not empty.
23 Saul and Jonathan *were* lovely and pleasant in their lives,
And in their death they were not divided:
They were °swifter than eagles,
They were °stronger than lions.

24 Ye daughters of Israel, weep over Saul, a^3
Who clothed you in scarlet, with *other* delights,
Who put on ornaments of gold upon your apparel.

25 How are the mighty fallen in the midst of the battle! b^3

O Jonathan, *thou wast* slain in thine high places. a^4

---

4 he answered. He thought he brought news which would be welcomed.
6 behold . . . lo. Fig. *Asterismos.* Ap. 6.
8 Amalekite. Thus Saul was dishonoured by one whom his disobedience spared. Cp. 1 Sam. 15. 3 and Ex. 17. 16.
9 He said. His whole story was a fabrication. See the facts in 1 Sam. 31. 4, 5.
life=soul. Heb. *nephesh.* Ap. 13.
10 fallen: i. e. upon his own sword (1 Sam. 31. 4).
11 men. Heb. *'ĕnōsh.* Ap. 14. III.
12 the LORD. Heb. Jehovah. Ap. 4. II.
16 Thy blood. Cp. *v.* 10.
thy head=thyself. Fig. *Synecdoche* (of Part). Ap. 6.

1. 17-27 (*z*, p. 408). **THE LAMENTATION OF "THE BOW".** (*Repeated Alternation.*)

Title | L^1 | 17. The Lament.
Title | L^2 | 18. The Lamentation.

z | a^1 | 19-. Apostrophe (sing.). Saul.
  b^1 | -19. Lamentation (pl.). Saul and Jonathan.
a^2 | 20, 21. Apostrophe (sing.). Saul.
  b^2 | 22, 23. Celebration (pl.). Saul and Jonathan.
a^3 | 24. Apostrophe (sing.). Saul.
  b^3 | 25-. Lamentation (pl.). Saul and Jonathan.
a^4 | -25, 26. Apostrophe (sing.). Jonathan.
  b^4 | 27. Lamentation (pl.). Saul and Jonathan.

18 children=sons.
the use of. The *Ellipsis* is wrongly supplied. The word "Lamentation" should be repeated from *v.* 17; "The Bow" being the *subject* of the Lamentation (*v.* 22).
the bow. This is the name of the Lamentation, because it is mentioned in *v.* 22; and it is what the tribe of Saul and Jonathan (Benjamin) was noted for (cp. 1 Chron. 8. 40; 12. 2. 2 Chron. 14. 8; 17. 17). For a similar reason the scripture (Ex. 3) about "The Bush" is so called in Mark 12. 26. Luke 20. 37.
behold. Fig. *Asterismos.* Ap. 6.
written, &c. In the Book of Jasher (or The Upright One)="Thy hart, Israel, lies slain", &c.
19 beauty=gazelle. Symbolic of beauty and grace.
21 The shield of Saul. Omit the italics that follow, and supply instead "the weapon of one anointed with oil", the Heb. *kelī* "weapons" being read instead of *belī* in the first edition of the *Hebrew Bible*, 1488, and the Syr. and Arabic Versions and Chaldee paraphrase.
23 swifter . . . stronger. Fig. *Hyperbolē.* Ap. 6.

960 **26** I am distressed for thee, my brother
Jonathan:
Very pleasant hast thou been unto me:
Thy love to me was wonderful,
Passing the love of women.

b4 **27** °How are the mighty fallen,
(p. 409) And the weapons of war perished!"

A c **2** And it came to pass after this, that David
(p. 410) °enquired of °the LORD, saying, "Shall
I go up into any of the cities of Judah?" And °the LORD said unto him, "Go up." And David said, "Whither shall I go up?" And He said, "Unto Hebron."

2 So David went up thither, and his two wives also, Ahinoam the Jezreelitess, and Abigail °Nabal's wife the Carmelite.

3 And his °men that *were* with him did David bring up, every °man with his household: and they dwelt in the cities of Hebron.

d e **4** And the [3]men of Judah came, and there they °anointed David king over the house of Judah.

f And they told David, saying, *That* "the [3]men of Jabesh-gilead *were they* that buried Saul."

5 And David sent messengers unto the [3]men of Jabesh-gilead, and said unto them, "Blessed *be* ye of [1]the LORD, that ye have shewed this kindness unto your lord, *even* unto Saul, and have buried him.

6 And now [1]the LORD shew kindness and truth unto you: and I also will requite you this kindness, because ye have done this thing.

7 Therefore now let your hands be strengthened, and be ye °valiant: for your master Saul is dead, and also the house of Judah have anointed me king over them."

d e **8** But Abner the son of Ner, captain of Saul's host, took °Ish-bosheth the son of Saul, and brought him over to Mahanaim;

9 And made him king over Gilead, °and over the Ashurites, and over Jezreel, and over Ephraim, and over Benjamin, and over all Israel.

960 **10** Ish-bosheth Saul's son *was* forty years
to old when he began to reign over Israel, and
958 reigned two years.

f But the house of Judah followed David.

c **11** And the time that David was king in Hebron over the house of Judah was seven years and six months.

B g **12** And Abner the son of Ner, and the servants of Ish-bosheth the son of Saul, went out from Mahanaim to Gibeon.

13 And Joab the son of Zeruiah, and the servants of David, went out, and met together by the pool of °Gibeon: and they sat down, the one on the one side of the pool, and the other on the other side of the pool.

14 And Abner said to Joab, "Let the °young men now arise, and °play before us." And Joab said, "Let them arise."

h **15** Then there arose and went over by number twelve of Benjamin, °which *pertained* to Ish-bosheth the son of Saul, and twelve of the servants of David.

27 **How, &c.** Render: "How [is it that] mighty ones have fallen, and weapons of war have perished".

2 Sam. **2. 1—24. 25** (**B2**, p. 366). KING DAVID.
(Division.)

B2 | C1 | 2. 1—4. 12. The Kingdom. Divided.
| C2 | 5. 1—24. 25. The Kingdom. United.

2. 1—4. 12 (C1, above). KINGDOM DIVIDED.
(Alternation.)

C1 | A | 2. 1-11. Followers. Accessions.
| B | 2. 12-32. Conflicts. Military.
| *A* | 3. 1-39. Followers. Defections.
| *B* | 4. 1-12. Conflicts. Personal.

2. 1-11 (A, above). FOLLOWERS. ACCESSIONS.
(Introversion and Alternation.)

A | c | 1-3. David goes to Hebron.
| d | e | 4-. David anointed over house of Judah.
| | f | -4-7. Those who followed David.
| *d* | *e* | 8-10-. Ish-bosheth anointed over Israel.
| | *f* | -10. Those who followed David.
| *c* | 11. David reigns in Hebron.

1 enquired. Probably by Urim and Thummim, in the breastplate of Abiathar the High Priest, who was with David (1 Sam. 22. 20).

the LORD. Heb. Jehovah. Ap. 4. II.

3 men. Heb. *'ĕnōsh.* Ap. 14. III.

man. Heb. *'īsh.* Ap. 14. II.

4 anointed David. Aged thirty years. See note on 1 Sam. 16. 13.

6 The 20th *Seder* ends here. See note on p. 366.

7 valiant = sons of valour.

8 Ish-bosheth = man of shame: i. e. the idol "Baal". In 1 Chron. 8. 33 = Esh-baal.

9 and. Note the Fig. *Polysyndeton* (Ap. 6) in *v.* 9.

12-32 (B, above). CONFLICTS. MILITARY.
(Extended Alternation.)

B | g | 12-14. Abner and Joab. Colloquy.
| h | 15-17. Conflict ensues.
| i | 18-25. Pursuit. Asahel's death.
| *g* | 26, 27. Abner and Joab. Colloquy.
| *h* | 28. Conflict ended.
| *i* | 29-32. Return. Asahel's burial.

13 Gibeon. Abner's city, in Benjamin (1 Chron. 8. 29, 30; 9. 35, 36).

14 young men = common soldiers.

play = make sport.

15 which pertained. Sept. and Syr. read "pertaining".

18 as a wild roe = as one of the gazelles which are in the field.

16 And they caught every one his fellow by the head, and *thrust* his sword in his fellow's side; so they fell down together: wherefore that place was called Helkath-hazzurim, which *is* in Gibeon.

17 And there was a very sore battle that day; and Abner was beaten, and the [3]men of Israel, before the servants of David.

18 And there were three sons of Zeruiah there, i
Joab, and Abishai, and Asahel: and Asahel *was as* light of foot °as a wild roe.

19 And Asahel pursued after Abner; and in going he turned not to the right hand nor to the left from following Abner.

20 Then Abner looked behind him, and said, "*Art* thou Asahel?" And he answered, "I *am*."

21 And Abner said to him, "Turn thee aside to thy right hand or to thy left, and lay thee hold on one of the young men, and take thee

960 his armour." But Asahel would not turn aside
from following of him.
22 And Abner said again to Asahel, "Turn
thee aside from following me: wherefore
should I smite thee to the ground? how
then should I hold up my face to Joab thy
brother?"
23 Howbeit he refused to turn aside: wherefore Abner with the hinder end of the spear
smote him under the fifth *rib*, that the spear
came out behind him; and he fell down there,
and died in the same place: and it came to
pass, *that* as many as came to the place where
Asahel fell down and died °stood still.
24 Joab also and Abishai pursued after Abner:
and the sun went down when they were come
to the hill of Ammah, that *lieth* before Giah by
the way of the wilderness of Gibeon.
25 And the °children of Benjamin gathered
themselves together after Abner, and became
one troop, and stood on the top of an hill.

g (p. 410) 26 Then Abner called to Joab, and said,
"Shall the sword devour for ever? knowest
thou not that it will be bitterness in the latter
end? how long shall it be then, ere thou
bid the People return from following their
brethren?"
27 And Joab said, "*As* °God liveth, unless
thou hadst °spoken, surely then in the morning the People had gone up every one from
following his brother."

h 28 So Joab blew a trumpet, and all the people
stood still, and pursued after Israel no more,
neither fought they any more.

i 29 And Abner and his [3] men walked all that
night through the plain, and passed over Jordan, and went through all °Bithron, and they
came to Mahanaim.
30 And Joab returned from following Abner:
and when he had gathered all the People together, there lacked of David's servants nineteen [3] men and Asahel.
31 But the servants of David had smitten of
Benjamin, and of Abner's [3] men, *so that* three
hundred and threescore °men died.
32 And they took up Asahel, and buried him
in the sepulchre of his father, which *was in*
Beth-lehem. And Joab and his [3] men went all
night, and they came to Hebron at break of day.

A j (p. 411) 3 Now there was long war between the
house of °Saul and the house of David:
but David waxed stronger and stronger,
k and the house of Saul waxed weaker and
weaker.
l 2 And unto David were sons born in Hebron:
and his firstborn was Amnon, of Ahinoam the
Jezreelitess;
3 And his second, Chileab, of Abigail the °wife
of Nabal the Carmelite; and the third, °Absa-
lom the son of Maacah the daughter of Talmai
king of Geshur;
4 And the fourth, Adonijah the son of Haggith; and the fifth, Shephatiah the son of
Abital;
5 And the sixth, Ithream, by Eglah °David's
wife. These were born to David in Hebron.
k m 6 And it came to pass, while there was war
between the house of Saul [1] and the house of
David, that Abner made himself strong for the
house of Saul.

7 And Saul had a concubine, whose name n
was Rizpah, the daughter of Aiah: and °*Ish-
bosheth* said to Abner, "Wherefore hast thou
gone in unto my father's concubine?"

8 Then was Abner very wroth for the words m
of Ish-bosheth, and said, "*Am* I a dog's head,
which against Judah do shew kindness this
day unto the house of Saul thy father, to his
brethren, and to his friends, and have not
delivered thee into the hand of David, that
thou chargest me to day with a °fault concerning this woman?
9 So do °God to Abner, and more also, except,
°as °the LORD hath sworn to David, even so
I do to him;
10 To translate the kingdom from the house
of Saul, and to set up the throne of David over
Israel and over Judah, from Dan even to Beer-
sheba."

11 And he could not answer Abner a word n
again, because he feared him.

12 And Abner sent messengers to David on j o
his behalf, saying, "Whose *is* the land?"

---

23 stood still: i. e. with horror at the sight.
25 children = sons.
27 God. Heb. Elohim. Ap. 4. I (with Art.).
spoken. Supply the *Ellipsis* (Ap. 6) thus: "spoken [the words which caused the provocation], surely". Cp. *v.* 14.
29 Bithron = the ravine.
31 men. Heb. *'ish.* Ap. 14. II.

3. 1-39 (*A*, p. 410). FOLLOWERS. DEFECTIONS.
(*Introversion.*)

A | j | 1-. House of David.
k | -1. House of Saul.
l | 2-5. Sons of David.
k | 6-11. House of Saul.
j | 12-39. House of David.

1 Saul. Note the Fig. *Antimetabolē* (Ap. 6) in this verse, and the Introversion of the subjects of this chapter.
3 wife of Nabal. Figs. *Epitheton* and *Ampliatio* (Ap. 6), by which Abigail is still so called by way of explanation. See note on 1 Sam. 30. 5.
Absalom. Born in the Jubilee year, 958-957. Hence his name.
5 David's wife. Probably added, parenthetically, to indicate his *first* wife.

6-11 (*k*, above). HOUSE OF SAUL.
(*Alternation.*)

k | m | 6. Abner Strong.
n | 7. Ish-bosheth. Wrath with Abner.
m | 8-10. Abner. Wrath.
n | 11. Ish-bosheth. Fear of Abner.

7 Ish-bosheth. Ellipsis. But some codices, with three early printed editions, read "the name".
8 fault. Heb. *'āven*, iniquity. See Ap. 44. iii.
9 God. Heb. Elohim. Ap. 4. I.
as = according as.
the LORD. Heb. Jehovah. Ap. 4. II.

12-39 (*j*, above). HOUSE OF DAVID.
(*Alternation.*)

j | o | 12. Abner's overtures to David.
p | 13-16. Return of Michal to David.
o | 17-19. Abner's overtures to Israel.
p | 20-39. Return of Abner to David.

960 to 953 saying *also*, "Make thy °league with me, and,
°behold, my °hand *shall be* with thee, to bring
about all Israel unto thee."

p (p. 411) 13 And he said, °"Well; I will make a
[12]league with thee: but one thing I require of
thee, that is, Thou shalt not see my face,
except thou first bring Michal Saul's daughter, when thou comest to see my face."
14 And David sent messengers to Ish-bosheth
Saul's son, saying, "Deliver *me* my wife
Michal, which I espoused to me for an hundred
foreskins of the Philistines."
15 And Ish-bosheth sent, and took her from
°*her* husband, *even* from °Phaltiel the son of
Laish.
16 And her husband went with her °along
weeping behind her to Bahurim. Then said
Abner unto him, "Go, return." And he returned.

o 17 And Abner had communication with the
elders of Israel, saying, "Ye sought for David
in times past *to be* king over you:
18 Now then °do *it*: for [9]the LORD hath spoken
of David, saying, 'By the hand of My servant
David I will save My people Israel out of the
hand of the Philistines, and out of the hand of
all their enemies.'"
19 And Abner also spake in the ears of Benjamin: and Abner went also to speak in the
ears of David in Hebron all that seemed good
to Israel, and that seemed good to the whole
house of Benjamin.

p q (p. 412) 20 So Abner came to David to Hebron, and
twenty °men with him. And David made
Abner and the °men that *were* with him a
feast.

r t 21 And Abner said unto David, "I will arise
and go, and will gather all Israel unto my
lord the king, that they may make a [12]league
with thee, and that thou mayest reign over
all that °thine heart desireth." And David
°sent Abner away; and he went in peace.

u 22 And, [12]behold, the servants of David and
Joab came from °*pursuing* a troop, and brought
in a great spoil with them: but Abner *was* not
with David in Hebron; for he had [21]sent him
away, and he was gone in peace.
23 When Joab and all the host that *was* with
him were come, they told Joab, saying, "Abner
the son of Ner came to the king, and he hath
sent him away, and he is gone in peace."

t 24 Then Joab came to the king, and said,
°"What hast thou done? [12]behold, Abner came
unto thee; °why *is it that* thou hast [21]sent him
away, and he is quite gone?
25 Thou knowest Abner the son of Ner, that
he came to deceive thee, and to know thy going
out and thy coming in, and to know all that
thou doest."

u 26 And when Joab was come out from David,
he sent messengers after Abner, which brought
him again from the well of Sirah: but David
knew *it* not.

s v 27 And when Abner was returned to Hebron,
Joab took him aside in the gate to speak with
him quietly, and smote him there under the
fifth *rib*, that he died, for the blood of Asahel
his brother.

28 And afterward when David heard *it*, he w
said, "I and my kingdom *are* guiltless before
[9]the LORD for ever from the °blood of Abner
the son of Ner:
29 Let it °rest on the head of Joab, and on all
his father's house; and let there not fail from
the house of Joab one that hath an issue, °or
that is a leper, °or that leaneth on a staff, °or
that °falleth on the sword, °or that lacketh
bread."

30 So Joab and Abishai his brother slew *v*
Abner, because he had slain their brother
Asahel at °Gibeon in the battle.

31 And David said to Joab, and to all the *w*
People that *were* with him, "Rend your clothes,
and gird you with sackcloth, and mourn before
Abner." And king David *himself* followed the
°bier.
32 And they buried Abner in Hebron: and the
king lifted up his voice, and wept at the grave
of Abner; and all the People wept.

---

12 league = covenant.
behold. Fig. *Asterismos*. Ap. 6.
hand. Fig. *Metonymy* (of Cause), Ap. 6. Hand put for help given by it.
13 Well = Good!
15 her. Aram., Sept., Syr., and Vulg. read "her" in the text.
Phaltiel. Same as Phalti (1 Sam. 25. 44).
16 along weeping = weeping as he went.
18 do it = act.

20-39 (*p*, p. 411). RETURN OF ABNER TO DAVID.
(*Extended Alternation.*)

p | q | 20. Feasting.
  r | 21-26. Treatment of Abner.
   s | 27-34. Death of Abner. Joab guilty.
 q | 35, 36. Fasting.
  r | 37. Treatment of Abner.
   s | 38, 39. Death of Abner. David innocent.

20 men. Heb. *'ĕnōsh*. Ap. 14. III.

21-26 (r, above). TREATMENT OF ABNER.
(*Alternation.*)

r | t | 21. David and Abner.
  u | 22, 23. Return of Joab.
 t | 24, 25. David and Joab.
  u | 26. Return of Abner.

21 thine heart = thy soul. Heb. *nephesh*. Ap. 13.
sent Abner away = let Abner go.
22 pursuing a troop = making a raid.
24 What . . . ? . . . why . . . ? Fig. *Erotēsis*. Ap. 6.

27-34 (s, above). DEATH OF ABNER.
(*Alternation.*)

s | v | 27. Retaliation of Joab.
  w | 28, 29. David's imprecation.
 v | 30. Retaliation of Joab.
  w | 31-34. David's lamentation.

28 blood. Heb. = bloods. Fig. *Heterōsis* (of Number) = much or noble blood. (Ap. 6).
29 rest = recoil. **or.** See note on Judg. 11. 31.
falleth on the sword. Fig. *Periphrasis* (Ap. 6) for death by executioner; or, in war: commonly used where guilt of some kind is involved.
30 Gibeon. Cp. 2. 13.
31 bier. Heb. *mittah*, a bed; see 4. 7, and cp. Ex. 8. 3. The poor man's couch by day was his bed by night, and sometimes his bier.

960 to 953 33 And the king lamented over Abner, and said,
°"Died Abner as °a fool dieth?
34 Thy hands *were* °not bound, nor thy feet put into °fetters:
As a man falleth before °wicked men, *so* fellest thou."
And all the People wept again over him.

q 35 And when all the People came to cause David to eat °meat while it was yet day, David sware, saying, "So do [9] God to me, and more also, if I taste bread, or ought else, till the sun be down."
36 And all the People took notice *of it*, and it °pleased them: as whatsoever the king did pleased all the People.

r 37 For all the People and all Israel understood that day that it was not of the king to slay Abner the son of Ner.

s 38 And the king said unto his servants, °"Know ye not that there is a prince and a great man fallen this day in Israel?
39 And I *am* this day weak, though anointed king; and these [20] men the sons of Zeruiah *be* too hard for me: [9] the LORD °shall reward the doer of °evil according to his °wickedness."

B C x **4** And when Saul's son heard that Abner was dead in Hebron, his hands were feeble, and all the Israelites were troubled.

y 2 And Saul's son had two °men *that were* captains of bands: the name of the one *was* Baanah, and the name of the other Rechab, the sons of Rimmon a °Beerothite, of the °children of Benjamin: (° for Beeroth also was reckoned to Benjamin:
3 And the Beerothites fled to Gittaim, and were sojourners there until this day.)

D 4 And Jonathan, Saul's son, had a son *that was* °lame of *his* feet. He was five years old when the tidings came °of Saul and Jonathan out of Jezreel, and his nurse took him up, and fled: and it came to pass, as she made haste to flee, that he fell, and became lame. And his name *was* Mephibosheth.

C x 5 And the sons of Rimmon the Beerothite, Rechab and Baanah, went, and came about the heat of the day to the house of Ish-bosheth, who lay on a bed at noon.
6 °And they came thither into the midst of the house, *as though* they would have fetched wheat; and they smote him under the fifth *rib*: and Rechab and Baanah his brother escaped.
7 For when they came into the house, he lay on his °bed in his bedchamber, and they smote him, and slew him, and beheaded him, and took his head, and gat them away through the plain all night.
8 And they brought the head of Ish-bosheth unto David to Hebron, and said to the king, "Behold the head of Ish-bosheth the son of Saul thine enemy, which sought thy °life; and °the LORD hath avenged my lord the king this day of Saul, and of his seed."

y 9 And David answered Rechab and Baanah his brother, the sons of Rimmon the Beerothite, and said unto them, "*As* [8] the LORD liveth, Who hath redeemed my °soul out of all adversity,
10 When one told me, saying, °'Behold, Saul is dead,' thinking to have brought good tidings, I took hold of him, and slew him in Ziklag, who *thought* that I would have given him a reward for his tidings:
11 How much more, when wicked [2] men have slain a righteous °person in his own house upon his bed? shall I not therefore now °require his blood of your hand, and take you away from the °earth?"
12 And David commanded his young men, and they slew them, and cut off their hands and their feet, and hanged *them* up over the pool in Hebron. But they took the head of Ish-bosheth, and buried *it* in the °sepulchre of Abner in Hebron.

5 Then came all the tribes of Israel to David unto Hebron, and spake, saying, °"Behold, we *are* thy bone and thy flesh. E N a

33 Died . . .? Fig. *Erotēsis*. Ap. 6.
a fool dieth: i. e. running into needless danger.
34 not bound: i. e. as a malefactor. Cp. 1 Sam. 25. 25, 26.
fetters. Heb. = brass, put by Fig. *Metonymy* (of Cause) for fetters made of it. Ap. 6.
wicked men = "sons of *'avlāh*". Ap. 44. vi.
35 meat. Put by Fig. *Synecdoche* (of Species) for food in general.
36 pleased them = was good in their eyes.
38 Know ye . . .? Fig. *Erotēsis*. Ap. 6.
39 shall reward. Cp. 1 Kings 2. 5, 6.
evil. Heb. *rā'a'*. Ap. 44. viii.
wickedness. Heb. *rā'a'*. Ap. 44. viii.

4. 1-12 (*B*, p. 410). CONFLICTS. PERSONAL. (*Introversion and Alternation.*)

B | C | x | 1. Ish-bosheth's weakness.
| | y | 2, 3. His two captains. Description.
| D | 4. Mephibosheth.
C | x | 5-8. Ish-bosheth's murder.
| y | 9-12. His two captains. Execution.

2 men. Heb. *'ĕnōsh*. Ap. 14. III.
Beerothite. Near Gibeon (Josh. 18. 25), now *El Bīreh*, 6 miles north of Jerusalem, one of the Hivite towns possessed by Benjamin.
children = sons.
for. Note Fig. *Parenthesis*. Ap. 6.
4 lame of his feet. Cp. state of sinner by nature.
of Saul: i.e. of the death of Saul, &c.: *v.* 4 is introduced here to explain the ease with which David's accession was accomplished, Mephibosheth being unable to succeed his father or avenge the death of Ish-bosheth.
6 And they came thither. Or, "Thither, into the interior of the house, came wheat-fetchers, and they smote", &c.
7 bed. Cp. 3. 31.
8 life = soul. Heb. *nephesh*. Ap. 13.
the LORD. Heb. Jehovah. Ap. 4. II.
9 soul. Heb. *nephesh*. Ap. 13.
10 Behold. Fig. *Asterismos*. Ap. 6.
11 person. Heb. *'īsh*. Ap. 14. II.
require = exact the penalty for.
earth = land.
12 sepulchre. Cp. 3. 32.

5. 1—24. 25 [For Structures see next page].

1 Behold. Fig. *Asterismos*. Ap. 6.

2 Also in time past, when Saul was king over us, thou wast he that leddest out and broughtest in Israel: and °the LORD said to thee, 'Thou shalt °feed My people Israel, and thou shalt be a captain over Israel.'"
3 So all the elders of Israel came to the king to Hebron; and king David °made a league with them in Hebron before [2]the LORD: and they °anointed David king over Israel.

b 4 David *was* thirty years old when he began
960 to reign, *and* he reigned forty years.
to 5 In Hebron he reigned over Judah seven
920 years and six months: and in Jerusalem he reigned thirty and three years over all Israel and Judah.

c 6 And the king and his °men went to Jerusalem unto the Jebusites, the inhabitants of the land: which spake unto David, °saying, "Except thou take away the blind and the lame, thou shalt not come in hither:" thinking, David cannot come in hither.
7 Nevertheless David took °the strong hold of °Zion: the same *is* °the City of David.
8 And David said on that day, "Whosoever getteth up °to the gutter, and smiteth the Jebusites, and the lame and the blind, *that are* hated of David's °soul, °*he shall be chief and captain.*" °Wherefore they said, "The blind and the lame shall not come into the house."

O d 9 So David dwelt in the °fort, and called it [7]the city of David. And David built °round about from °Millo and inward.

e 10 And David °went on, and grew great, and °the LORD God of hosts *was* with him.

O d 11 And °Hiram king of °Tyre sent messengers to David, and cedar trees, and carpenters, and masons: and they built David an house.

e 12 And David perceived that [2]the LORD had established him king over Israel,

N a and that He had exalted his kingdom for His People Israel's sake.

b 13 And David took *him* more concubines and wives °out of Jerusalem, after he was come from Hebron: and there were yet sons and daughters born to David.
14 And these *be* the names of those that were born unto him in Jerusalem; Shammuah, and Shobab, and Nathan, and Solomon,
15 Ibhar also, and Elishua, and Nepheg, and Japhia,
16 And Elishama, and °Eliada, and Eliphalet.

c f 17 But when the Philistines heard that they
953 had anointed David king over Israel, all the Philistines came up to °seek David; and David heard *of it,* and went down to the °hold.
18 The Philistines also came and spread themselves in the valley of °Rephaim.

5. 1—24. 25 (C^2, p. 410). KINGDOM UNITED.
(*Introversion with Alternations.*)

C^2 | E | 5. 1-25. David's accession over Israel.
F | H | 6. 1—7. 29. Worship.
J | 8. 1-14. David's mighty acts.
G | K | 8. 15-18. David's officers.
L | 9. 1—10. 5. David's kindness.
M | 10. 6—20. 22. Wars and events.
G | *K* | 20. 23-26. David's officers.
L | 21. 1-14. David's zeal.
M | 21. 15-22. Wars and events.
F | *H* | 22. 1—23. 7. Worship.
J | 23. 8-39. David's mighty men.
E | 24. 1-25. David's sin. Numbering Israel.

5. 1-25 (E, above). DAVID'S ACCESSION.
(*Extended and Simple Alternations.*)

E | N | a | 1-3. King anointed.
b | 4, 5. Hebron. Reign.
c | 6-8. Jebusites expelled.
O | d | 9. City of David.
e | 10. Greatness of king.
O | *d* | 11. House of David.
e | 12-. Establishment of king.
N | *a* | -12. Kingdom exalted.
b | 13-16. Hebron. Family.
c | 17-25. Philistines vanquished.

2 the LORD. Heb. Jehovah. Ap. 4. II.
feed = feed as a shepherd.
3 made a league = solemnised a covenant.
anointed David. See note on 1 Sam. 16. 13.
6 men. Heb. *'ĕnōsh.* Ap. 14. III.
saying. What they said must be rendered thus: "Thou shalt not come in hither, for the blind and the lame shall drive thee away [by saying] 'David shall not come in hither.'"
7 the strong hold of Zion: i.e. the hill of Ophel, immediately south of Moriah.
Zion. First occurrence. Occurs 154 times in O.T. (7 × 22, Ap. 10); used later (especially in prophecy) of the whole city. See Ap. 68.
the City of David. Which is on Jebus, therefore, and not on the west side. First occurrence. Occurs forty times in O.T. Used of Zion five times (2 Sam. 5. 7, 9. 1 Kings 8. 1. 1 Chron. 11. 5. 2 Chron. 5. 2).
8 to the gutter = by (or through) the *ẓinnōr*, a rock-cut passage from the lower Gihon or En-Rogel (now the Virgin's Fount on east of Ophel), leading up into the city and supplying water. Discovered by Sir Charles Warren. Cp. note on Neh. 2. 13, &c.
soul. Heb. *nephesh.* Ap. 13.
he shall be chief and captain. These words are supplied from 1 Chron. 11. 6, which tells that Joab got up the *ẓinnōr* first. Probably revealed to him (or to David) by Araunah, who (though a Jebusite) was not slain, but is found, later on, owning property quite near (24. 16). Josephus says Araunah was a friend of David's.
Wherefore = Because.
9 fort = the "strong hold" of *v.* 7. Citadel.
round about = the wall, which was continued by Solomon (1 Kings 9. 15, 24; 11. 27), afterward by Hezekiah (2 Chron. 32. 5), and extended by Manasseh (2 Chron. 33. 14).
Millo = the Millo, or the filling up: i. e. of the valley between Moriah and Jebus.
10 went on = went on and on.
the LORD God of hosts = Jehovah *Elohim ẓebaiōth.* Ap. 4. See note on 1 Sam. 1. 3.

11 Hiram. Not the Hiram of 1 Kings 9. 11, which was sixty years later. Josephus says he was his father. Cp. 2 Chron. 2. 13. 1 Kings 5. 1. **Tyre.** Israel had no war with Phœnicians. Asher failed to expel them (Judg. 1. 31). **13 out of.** Perhaps this should read "into", as in 1 Chron. 14. 3. But both accounts are independent and complementary. **16 Eliada** = Another name, Beeliada. See note on 1 Chron. 14. 7.

17-25 [For Structure see next page].

17 seek. Cp. 1 Sam. 26. 2. **hold.** Probably Adullam. 1 Sam. 22. 1. Not Zion, because he went "down" to it. **18 Rephaim.** The descendants of the Nephilim through one "Rapha". See Ap. 23 and 25. Cp. 1 Chron. 11. 15.

g 19 And David enquired of °the LORD, saying,
(p. 415) "Shall I go up to the Philistines? wilt Thou
953 deliver them into mine hand?" And °the LORD
said unto David, "Go up: for I will doubtless
deliver the Philistines into thine hand."

h 20 And David came to Baal-perazim, and
David smote them there, and said, [2]"The LORD
hath °broken forth upon mine enemies before
me, as the breach of waters." Therefore he
called the name of that place Baal-perazim.
21 And there they left their images, and
David and his [6]men burned them.

f 22 And the Philistines came up yet again,
952 and spread themselves in the valley of [18]Rephaim.

g 23 And when David enquired of [2]the LORD,
he said, "Thou shalt not go up; *but* fetch a
compass behind them, and come upon them
over against the mulberry trees.
24 And let it be, when thou hearest the sound
of a going in the tops of the mulberry trees,
that then thou shalt bestir thyself: for then
shall [2]the LORD go out before thee, to smite
the host of the Philistines."

h 25 And David did so, °as [2]the LORD had
commanded him; and smote the Philistines
from °Geba until thou come to Gazer.

H P[1] i 6 Again, David gathered together all *the*
chosen *men* of Israel, thirty thousand.
2 And David arose, and went with all the
people that *were* with him from °Baale of
Judah, to bring up from thence the ark of
°God, °whose name is called by the name
of °the LORD of hosts That dwelleth *between*
the cherubims.
3 And they set the ark of [2]God upon °a new
cart, and brought it out of the house of Abinadab
that *was* in Gibeah: and Uzzah and Ahio,
the sons of Abinadab, drave the new cart.
4 And they brought it out of the house of
Abinadab which *was* at Gibeah, accompanying
the ark of [2]God: and Ahio went before the
ark.

k 5 And David and all the house of Israel
played before °the LORD on all manner of °*instruments
made of* fir wood, even on harps,
and on psalteries, and on °timbrels, and on
cornets, and on °cymbals.

l 6 And when they came to °Nachon's threshingfloor,
Uzzah put forth °*his hand* to the ark
of [2]God, and took hold of it; for the oxen
shook *it*.
7 And the anger of [5]the LORD was kindled
against Uzzah; and [2]God smote him there for
his °error; and there he died by the ark of
[2]God.
8 And David was displeased, because [5]the
LORD had °made a breach upon Uzzah: and
he called the name of the place Perez-uzzah
to this day.

m 9 And David was afraid of [5]the LORD that
day, and said, "How shall the ark of [5]the
LORD come to me?"
10 So David would not remove the ark of
[5]the LORD unto him into the city of David:
but David carried it aside into the house of
Obed-edom the Gittite.
11 And the ark of [5]the LORD continued in the
house of Obed-edom the Gittite three months:

5. 17-25 (*c*, p. 414). PHILISTINES VANQUISHED.
(*Extended Alternation.*)

c | f | 17, 18. Positions of Philistines.
  g | 19. Inquiry of Jehovah.
    h | 20, 21. Defeat.
| *f* | 22. Position of Philistines.
  g | 23, 24. Inquiry of Jehovah.
    h | 25. Defeat.

19 the LORD. Heb. Jehovah (Ap. 4. II). See note on 1 Chron. 14. 10.
20 broken forth. Fig. *Anthropopatheia.* Ap. 6.
25 as = according as.
Geba. Abbreviation for "Gibeon". Cp. Sept., and 1 Chron. 14. 16.

6. 1—7. 29 (H, p. 414). WORSHIP.
(*Division.*)

H | P[1] | 6. 1-23. The Ark of Jehovah.
  | P[2] | 7. 1-29. The House of Jehovah.

6. 1-23 (P[1], above). THE ARK OF JEHOVAH.
(*Extended Alternation.*)

P[1] | i | 1-4. Removal of Ark from Gibeah.
  k | 5. Music.
    l | 6-8. Sin of Uzzah.
      m | 9-11-. Carried aside.
        n | -11, 12-. Blessing.
| *i* | -12, 13. Removal of Ark from house of Obed-edom.
  k | 14, 15. Dancing.
    l | 16. Offence of Michal.
      m | 17. Carried in.
        n | 18-23. Blessing, &c.

2 Baale. The old Canaanite name of Kirjath-jearim. Cp. 1 Sam. 6. 21; 7. 2. 1 Chron. 13. 6.
God. Heb. Elohim. Ap. 4. I.
whose name is called by the name. Some codices, with Aram. and Vulg., read "whereupon is called the name", &c.
the LORD of hosts. Heb. Jehovah Sebaioth. One of the Jehovah titles. Ap. 4. II. Cp. 5. 10, and see note on 1 Sam. 1. 3.
3 a new cart. This was contrary to the Divinely prescribed law (Num. 4. 15; 7. 9; 10. 21. Deut. 10. 8. Josh. 3. 14. 2 Sam. 15. 24. 1 Chron. 13. 7; 15. 2, &c.). When the Philistines did it in ignorance (1 Sam. 6. 7) no judgment fell on them, because the Law of Moses was not delivered to them. But David should have known: hence judgment came. The solemn lesson is that anything introduced into the worship of God contrary to His requirements is deserving of His judgments. This includes all that is contrary to John 4. 24, and all that is of the flesh, which "profiteth nothing" (John 6. 63). All this is like David's "new cart" and is sin in God's sight. See note on 1 Sam. 6. 7, and cp. 1 Sam. 15. 22.
5 the LORD. Heb. Jehovah. Ap. 4.
instruments made of fir wood. The Sept. reads "with all boldness and with songs". See *v.* 14 and 1 Chron. 13. 8. According to Heb. text "fir woods", put by Fig. *Metonymy* (of Material) for instruments made from it. Ap. 6.
timbrels = drums. See note on Ex. 15. 20.
cymbals = timbrels, or tambourines. Heb. *zilzilim.* See note on 1 Chron. 13. 8.
6 Nachon's. Same as Chidon (1 Chron. 13. 9).
his hand. These words are contained in the Aram., Sept., Syr., and Vulg.
7 error = negligence.
8 made a breach = broke forth. Fig. *Anthropopatheia.* Ap. 6.

n and [5]the LORD blessed Obed-edom, and all his
(p. 415) household.
952 12 And it was told king David, saying, [5]"The
LORD hath blessed the house of Obed-edom,
and all that °*pertaineth* unto him, because of
the ark of [2]God."

i So David went and °brought up the ark of
[2]God from the house of Obed-edom into the city
of David with gladness.
13 And it was *so*, that when they that bare
the ark of [5]the LORD had gone °six paces, he
sacrificed oxen and fatlings.

k 14 And David °danced before [5]the LORD with
all *his* might; and David *was* girded with °a
linen ephod.
15 So David and all the house of Israel
brought up the ark of [5]the LORD with shouting,
and with the sound of the trumpet.

l 16 And as the ark of [5]the LORD came into
the city of David, Michal Saul's daughter
looked through a window, and saw king David
°leaping and dancing before [5]the LORD;
and she despised him in her heart.

m 17 And they brought in the ark of [5]the LORD,
951 and set it in his place, in the midst of the
Sab. °tabernacle that David had pitched for it: and
year David °offered burnt offerings and °peace
offerings before [5]the LORD.

n o^1 18 And as soon as David had made an end of
(p. 416) [17]offering burnt offerings and [17]peace offerings,
he blessed the People in the name of [2]the LORD
of hosts.
19 And he dealt among all the People, *even*
among the whole multitude of Israel, as well
to the women as °men, to °every one a cake of
bread, and a °good piece *of flesh*, and a °flagon
of wine.

p^1 So all the People departed °every one to his
house.

o^2 20 Then David returned to bless his household.

p^2 And Michal the °daughter of Saul came out
to meet David, and said, "How glorious was
the king of Israel to day, who °uncovered
himself to day in the eyes of the handmaids
of his servants, as one of the vain fellows
shamelessly °uncovereth himself!"

o^3 21 And David said unto Michal, °"*It was*
before [5]the LORD, Which chose me before
thy father, and before all his house, to appoint
me ruler over the People of [5]the LORD, over
Israel: therefore will I play before [5]the LORD.
22 And I will yet be more vile than thus, and
will be base in mine own sight: and of the
maidservants which thou hast spoken of, of
them shall I be had in honour."

p^3 23 Therefore Michal the [20]daughter of Saul
had no child unto the day of her death.

P² Q **7** And it °came to pass, when °the king sat
950 in his house, and °the LORD had given
to him rest round about from all his enemies;
948 2 That the king said unto °Nathan the prophet,
°"See now, I dwell in an house °of
cedar, but the ark of °God dwelleth within
°curtains."

3 And °Nathan said to the king, "Go, °do all R
that *is* in thine heart; for [1]the LORD *is* with
thee."

4 And it came to pass °that night, that the R q

---

12 pertaineth. A.V. (1611) reads "pertained".
brought up the ark. Cp. 1 Chron. 15. 3.
13 six paces. See Ap. 51. III. 1. Cp. 1 Chron. 15. 26.
14 danced. This explains the subscription of Ps. 87 (not the title of 88, see note there), *Mahalath Leannoth* = dancing with shoutings. Cp. 1 Chron. 15. 25-29. See Ap. 65.
a linen ephod. Cp. Aaron (Ex. 28. 6) and Samuel (1 Sam. 2. 18).
16 leaping and dancing. See note on *v.* 14.
17 tabernacle = *'ohel*, tent. Not the Tabernacle of Moses, which was at Gibeon, cp. 1 Chron. 16. 39 (Ap. 40), but the tent David had prepared on Zion (7. 1-3). Cp. Ps. 132. 3-5.
offered = offered up. Ap. 43. I. 6.
peace offerings, which were for thanksgiving.

6. 18-23 (*n*, p. 415). **BLESSING.**
(*Repeated Alternation.*)

n | o^1 | 18, 19-. Blessing of the People.
  | p^1 | -19. Return of the People.
  | o^2 | 20-. Blessing of the household.
  | p^2 | -20. Return of David. Reproach.
  | o^3 | 21, 22. Blessing from Jehovah.
  | p^3 | 23. No return to Michal.

19 men . . . every one. Heb. *'ish.* Ap. 14.
good piece of flesh. Note, "of flesh" is in italics, following the Vulgate. Translate, "a measure [of wine]".
flagon of wine. Omit "flagon of wine", and render "a cake of raisins".
20 daughter of Saul. Note this. It does not say "the wife of David".
uncovered = disrobed, referring to his royal robes.
21 It was. Omit these words and supply *Ellipsis* by adding, with Sept., "Before Jehovah [did I dance]".

7. 1-29 (P², p. 415). **THE HOUSE OF JEHOVAH.**
(*Introversion.*)

P² | Q | 1, 2. David before himself. ("Who I am.")
   | R | 3. Reply of Nathan.
   | *R* | 4-17. Reply of Jehovah.
   | *Q* | 18-29. David before Jehovah. ("Who am I?")

1 came to pass. This chapter takes its place with Gen. 15. It is the unconditional Covenant with David, to give him the *Throne*; as that was with Abraham, to give him the *Land*.
the king. Thus now dignified.
the LORD. Heb. Jehovah. Ap. 4. II.
2 Nathan. The first occurrence of his name. Cp. 1 Chron. 29. 29. An important figure in David's reign, and associated with his son Solomon (*vv.* 12, 13; 12. 25. 1 Kings 1. 10-45).
See now. Fig. *Asterismos.* Ap. 6.
of. Genitive of Material. Ap. 17.
God. Heb. Elohim. Ap. 4.
curtains. Put by Fig. *Metonymy* (of Cause) for the tent formed by them. Cp. 6. 17.
3 Nathan said. Not from Jehovah, as in *v.* 5, but from himself: and said what was wrong.
do all that, &c. This is seldom safe advice.

4-17 [For Structure see next page].

4 that night. After these words all the MSS. have a hiatus, marking a solemn pause, and pointing back to the corresponding night of Gen. 15. 12-17, thus connecting the two great unconditional Covenants. See note on *v.* 1.

word of [1]the LORD came unto Nathan, saying,

r (p. 417) 950-948 5 "Go and tell °My servant David, 'Thus saith [1]the LORD, 'Shalt thou build Me an house for Me to dwell in?

s 6 Whereas I have not dwelt in *any* house since the time that I brought up the °children of Israel out of Egypt, even to this day, but have °walked in a tent °and in a °tabernacle.

7 In all *the places* wherein I have walked with all the [6]children of Israel spake I a word with any of the °tribes of Israel, whom I commanded to feed My People Israel, saying, 'Why build ye not Me an house of cedar?'''

s 8 Now therefore so shalt thou say unto My servant David, 'Thus saith °the LORD of hosts, °'I took thee from the sheepcote, from following the sheep, to be ruler over My People, °over Israel:

9 And I was with thee whithersoever thou wentest, and have cut off all thine enemies out of thy sight, and °have made thee a great name, like unto the name of the great *men* that *are* in the earth.

10 Moreover I will appoint a place for My People Israel, and will plant them, that they may dwell in a place of their own, and move no more; neither shall the [6]children of °wickedness afflict them any more, as beforetime,

11 And as since the time that I commanded judges *to be* over My People Israel, and have caused thee to rest from all thine enemies. Also [1]the LORD telleth thee that °He will make thee an °house.

12 And when thy days be fulfilled, and thou shalt °sleep with thy fathers, I will set up thy seed after thee, which shall proceed out of thy bowels, and I will establish his kingdom.

r 13 He shall build an house for My name, and I will stablish the throne of his kingdom for ever.

14 I will be °his Father, and he shall be °My son. If he commit °iniquity, I will chasten him with the rod of °men, and with the stripes of the [6]children of °men:

15 But My °mercy shall not depart away from him, °as I took *it* from Saul, whom I put away before thee.

16 And thine house and thy kingdom shall be established for ever before °thee: thy throne shall be established for ever.'''"

q 17 According to all these words, and according to all this vision, so did Nathan speak unto David.

Q S t 18 °Then went king David in, and °sat before [1]the LORD, and he said, °"Who *am* I, °O Lord °GOD? and what *is* my house, that Thou hast brought me hitherto?

u 19 And this was yet a small thing in Thy sight, [18]O Lord [18]GOD; but Thou hast spoken also of Thy servant's house for a great while to come. And *is* this the °manner of °man, [18]O Lord [18]GOD?

v 20 And what can David say more unto Thee? for Thou, [18]Lord [18]GOD, knowest Thy servant.

21 For Thy word's sake, and according to Thine own heart, hast Thou done all these great things, to make Thy servant know *them*. *u*

7. 4-17 (*R*, p. 416). REPLY OF JEHOVAH. (*Introversion.*)

R | q | 4. Word of Jehovah to Nathan for David.
  r | 5. "Shalt thou build?" (Negative). David.
   s | 6, 7. Jehovah's condescension.
   s | 8-12. Jehovah's grace.
  r | 13-16. "He shall build" (Positive). Solomon.
 q | 17. Word of Jehovah for Nathan to David.

5 My servant. Note the repetition of this word throughout this chapter. See note on *v.* 18.

6 children = sons.

walked = have been walking [habitually].

and in a tabernacle = as my habitation. Heb. *mishkan.* Ap. 40.

7 tribes, or "judges", as in 1 Chron. 17. 6.

8 the LORD of hosts. Heb. Jehovah Sebaioth. Ap. 4. II. One of the Jehovah titles. Cp. 5. 10; 6. 2, and see note on 1 Sam. 1. 3.

I took. Cp. 1 Sam. 16. 11, 12. Ps. 78. 70, 71.

over. Some codices, with one early printed edition, Syr., and Vulg., omit this second "over".

9 have made = I will assuredly make.

10 wickedness. Heb. *'āmāl.* Ap. 44. v.

11 He. Heb. Jehovah. Ap. 4. II.

house. Put by Fig. *Metonymy* (of Subject), Ap. 6, for household or family: i. e. a line of succession.

12 sleep with thy fathers. Fig. *Euphemism* (Ap. 6), put for "die". See note on Deut. 31. 16.

14 his Father = to him for a Father.

My son = to Me for a son.

iniquity. Heb. *'āvāh.* Ap. 44. iv.

men. Heb. *'ĕnōsh.* Ap. 14. III. Ps. 89. 31, 32.

men. Heb. *'ādām.* Ap. 14. I.

15 mercy = lovingkindness.

as = according as.

16 thee. Some cod., with Sept. and Syr., read "Me".

18-29 (*Q*, p. 416). DAVID BEFORE JEHOVAH. (*Introversion.*)

Q | S | 18-22. David. Thanksgiving for himself.
  T | 23, 24. For Israel.
 S | 25-29. David. Prayer for his house.

18-22 (S, above). DAVID. THANKSGIVING FOR HIMSELF. (*Introversion.*)

S | t | 18. Self-abasement. "Who am I?"
  u | 19. Acknowledgment of benefits.
   v | 20. Inability to praise aright.
  u | 21. Acknowledgment of benefits.
 t | 22. Divine exaltation. "Thou art great."

18 Then. It is grace that really humbles.

sat before the LORD. Very different from sitting before one's self, as in *v.* 1.

Who am I . . . ? Fig. *Erotēsis.* Ap. 6. Cp. *v.* 1. When David sat in his own house he sat before himself. See Structure, p. 416, "Q" and "*Q*".

O Lord GOD = O Adonai Jehovah. Adonai because (1) David is the servant and He the master; (2) because this title has to do with lordship in the earth. Ap. 4. VIII (2). Cp. *vv.* 19 (twice), 20, 28, 29, six times in this chapter.

19 manner = *Torah* or Law.

man. Heb. *ha-adam* = the man. "And is this the law of the man?" i. e. the Man of Ps. 8. 5, 6, who is to have dominion over all the earth, embracing all the world in the scope of this blessing in connection with the Messiah. This is an exclamation of greatest surprise and wonder of this revelation concerning David's son and David's Lord.

t (p. 417) 950-948 22 °Wherefore Thou art great, °O LORD God: for *there is* none like Thee, neither *is there any* [2]God beside Thee, according to all that we have heard with our ears.

T 23 And °what one nation in the earth *is* like Thy People, *even* °like Israel, whom [2]God went to °redeem for a People to Himself, and to make Him a name, and to do for you great things and terrible, for Thy land, before thy People, which thou °redeemedst to Thee from Egypt, *from* the nations and their gods?

24 For Thou hast confirmed to Thyself Thy people Israel *to be* a people unto Thee for ever: and Thou, [1]LORD, art become their [2]God.

S w (p. 418) 25 And now, [22]O LORD [22]God, the word that Thou hast spoken concerning Thy servant, and concerning his house, establish *it* for ever, and do °as Thou hast said.

26 And let Thy name be magnified for ever, saying, [8]The LORD of hosts *is* the [2]God over Israel: and let the house of Thy servant David be established before Thee.

x 27 For Thou, O [8]LORD of hosts, [2]God of Israel, hast revealed to Thy servant, saying, 'I will build thee an house:' therefore hath Thy servant °found in his heart to pray this prayer unto Thee.

x 28 And now, [18]O Lord [18]GOD, Thou *art* that [2]God, and Thy words be °true, and Thou hast promised this goodness unto Thy servant:

w 29 Therefore now let it please Thee to bless the house of Thy servant, that it may continue for ever before Thee: for Thou, [18]O Lord [18]GOD, hast spoken *it*: and with Thy blessing let the house of Thy servant be blessed for ever."

J a 948 **8** And after this it came to pass, that David smote the Philistines, and °subdued them: and David took °Metheg-ammah out of the hand of the Philistines.

2 And he °smote Moab, and °measured °them with a °line, °casting them down to the ground; even with two °lines °measured he °to put to death, and with one full °line to keep alive. And *so* the Moabites became David's servants, *and* brought gifts.

3 David smote also °Hadadezer, the son of Rehob, king of °Zobah, as he went to °recover his °border at the river °Euphrates.

4 And David took from him a thousand *chariots*, and °seven hundred horsemen, and twenty thousand footmen: and David houghed all the chariot *horses*, but reserved of them *for* an hundred chariots.

5 And when the Syrians of Damascus came to succour [3]Hadadezer king of Zobah, David slew of the Syrians two and twenty thousand °men.

b 6 Then David put garrisons in Syria of Damascus:

c and the Syrians became servants to David, *and* brought °gifts.

d And °the LORD preserved David whithersoever he went.

7 And David took the °shields of gold that were on the servants of [3]Hadadezer, and brought them to Jerusalem. *a*

8 And from Betah, and from Berothai, cities

22 Wherefore Thou art great. Fig. *Metonymy* (of Subject), Ap. 6 = wherefore I will declare and praise Thee as great.

O LORD God = O Jehovah Elohim. Note the change, because it is not now in connection with *the earth*, but what He is in Himself.

23 what . . . ? Fig. *Erotēsis*. Ap. 6.

like Israel. Some codices, with Sept., Syr., and Vulg., read "like Thy People Israel".

redeem. Heb. *pādāh*. See notes on Ex. 13. 13 and 6. 6.

7. 25-29 (*S*, p. 417). DAVID. PRAYER FOR HIS HOUSE. (*Introversion.*)

S | w | 25, 26. Prayer. Establishment.
x | 27. Divine revelation. } Praise.
x | 28. Divine promise. }
w | 29. Prayer. Continuance.

25 as = according as.

27 found = taken heart, become emboldened.

28 true = truth.

8. 1-14 (J, p. 414). DAVID'S MIGHTY ACTS. (*Extended Alternation.*)

J | a | 1-5. Conquests.
b | 6-. Garrisons in Syria.
c | -6-. Subjection of Syrians.
d | -6. Preservation of David.
a | 7-13. Conquests.
b | 14-. Garrisons in Syria.
c | -14-. Subjection of Edomites.
d | -14. Preservation of David.

1 subdued. While David was victorious over enemies without, he was defeated by enemies within. See chs. 11 and 12.

Metheg-ammah. 1 Chron. 18. 1 gives us the meaning, and shows that Metheg = bridle or reins, is put by Fig. *Metonymy* (of Cause), Ap. 6, for power or government, and Ammah = mother-city: i. e. "Gath and her daughters (i. e. towns)" (1 Chron. 18. 1).

2 smote Moab. Thus fulfilling Num. 24. 17.

measured = allotted, or divided by lot. See note on "line", below: i. e. David divided into two companies those who were to be spared and those who were not.

them = the territory. Put by Fig. *Metonymy* (of Subject), Ap. 6, for their territory.

line. Line, put by Fig. *Metonymy* (of Cause), Ap. 6, for dividing or allotting what was measured with it. Deut. 3. 4, 13 (region); 32. 8, 9. Josh. 17. 6, 14. Ps. 19. 4. Amos 7. 17. Mic. 2. 5. 2 Cor. 10. 16.

casting them = casting down the cities. See note on "them", above, and cp. 1 Chron. 18. 2 = "made them his servants", or vassals.

to put to death. These were soldiers in arms, not inhabitants.

3 Hadadezer. Some codices, with four early printed editions, Sept., Syr., and Vulg., read "Hadarezer" (cp. 1 Chron. 18. 3, 5). Some divide and make it two words.

Zobah. See Ps. 60 (title), and cp. 1 Sam. 14. 47.

recover. Heb. cause his hand to cover: "hand" put by Fig. *Metonymy* (of Cause), Ap. 6, for possessing.

border = boundary. 1 Chron. 18. 2, "establish his dominion there".

Euphrates. Cp. 1 Chron. 18. 3 and Gen. 15. 18.

4 seven hundred. 1 Chron. 18. 4 = 7,000; but Heb. ז = 7 and ן = 700, are easily mistaken one for the other. See note on 1 Kings 4. 26.

5 men. Heb. *'īsh*. Ap. 14. II.

6 gifts: i. e. tribute.

the LORD. Heb. Jehovah. Ap. 4. II.

7 shields. Sept. reads "bracelets".

948 of [3]Hadadezer, king David took exceeding much brass.
9 When °Toi king of Hamath heard that David had smitten all the host of [3]Hadadezer,
10 Then [9]Toi sent °Joram his son unto king David, to salute him, and to bless him, because he had fought against [3]Hadadezer, and smitten him: for [3]Hadadezer °had wars with [9]Toi. And °*Joram* brought °with him vessels of silver, and vessels of gold, and vessels of brass:
11 Which also king David did dedicate unto [6]the LORD, with the silver and gold that he had dedicated of all nations which he subdued;
12 Of °Syria, °and of Moab, and of the °children of Ammon, and of the Philistines, and of °Amalek, and of the spoil of [3]Hadadezer, son of Rehob, king of [3]Zobah.
13 And David °gat *him* a name when he returned from °smiting of the Syrians in the valley of salt, *being* °eighteen thousand *men*.

b (p. 418) 14 And he put °garrisons in Edom; throughout all Edom put he garrisons,

c and all they of Edom became David's servants.

d And [6]the LORD preserved David whithersoever he went.

K e (p. 419) 15 And David reigned over all Israel; and David executed judgment and justice unto all his People.

f 16 And Joab the son of Zeruiah *was* over the host;

g and Jehoshaphat the son of Ahilud *was* °recorder;

h 17 And °Zadok the son of Ahitub, and °Ahimelech the son of °Abiathar, *were* the priests;

g and Seraiah *was* °the scribe;

f 18 And °Benaiah the son of Jehoiada *was over* both the °Cherethites and the °Pelethites;

e and David's sons were chief rulers.

M[1] N[1] i **9** And David said, "Is there yet any that is left of the house of Saul, that I may shew him °kindness for Jonathan's sake?"
2 And *there was* of the house of Saul a servant whose name *was* Ziba. And when they had called him unto David, the king said unto him, "*Art* thou Ziba?" And he said, "Thy servant *is he*."
3 And the king said, "*Is* there not yet °any of the house of Saul, that I may shew the [1]kindness of °God unto him?"

k And Ziba said unto the king, "Jonathan hath yet a son, *which is* °lame on *his* feet."

i 4 And the king said unto him, "Where *is* he?"

k And Ziba said unto the king, °"Behold, he *is* in the house of Machir, the son of Ammiel, in °Lo-debar."

N[2] l (p. 420) 5 Then king David °sent, and fetched him out of the house of Machir, the son of Ammiel, from [4]Lo-debar.

---

9 Toi. Sept. and Vulg. read "Tou" throughout. Cp. 1 Chron. 18. 9. He was a Hittite king.

10 Joram. Sept. reads "Hadoram". Cp. 1 Chron. 18. 10.

had wars with. Heb. = "was a man (*'ish*, Ap. 14. II) of wars with." **with him.** Heb. in his hand.

12 Syria. Some codices, with Sept. and Syr., read "Edom".

and. Note the Fig. *Polysyndeton.* Ap. 6.

children = sons. **Amalek.** See note on Ex. 17. 16.

13 gat him = made himself.

smiting = his smiting. This is David's exploit. In 1 Chron. 18. 3, 12 it is Abishai's command, while in title of Ps. 60 it is Joab's share in the campaign (1 Kings 11. 16).

eighteen thousand. This is the total. Joab's share was 12,000, and took six months longer. Cp. 1 Kings 11. 15, 16.

14 garrisons, or political residents.

8. 15-18 (K, p. 414). DAVID'S OFFICERS. (*Introversion.*)

K | e | 15. David. King.
  f | 16-. Chief captain.
   g | -16. Recorder.
    h | 17-. Priests.
   g | -17. Scribe.
  f | 18-. Captain.
 e | -18. David's sons.

16 recorder = remembrancer.

17 Zadok. Probably served at Gibeon. Cp. 1 Chron. 18. 16.

Ahimelech the son of Abiathar. Named after his grandfather (1 Sam. 21. 1; 22. 9, 16).

Abiathar. Probably served at Jerusalem.

the scribe. The first occurrence of this title. Heb. *ṣōphīr*, a counter. Individual scribes held high positions as associates of the High Priests, and of the commander-in-chief. They were amanuenses, registrars, accountants (2 Kings 12. 10); adjutants (2 Kings 25. 19); secretaries of state (2 Sam. 8. 17. Isa. 33. 18). First occurrence as a class or caste (1 Chron. 2. 55); a branch of the Levites (2 Chron. 34. 13). When Priests, who should have been teachers of the Law (Deut. 17. 11; 33. 10), became absorbed in ritual, the Scribes became custodians. Ezra was an ideal priest and scribe.

18 Benaiah. Cp. 23. 20.

Cherethites . . . Pelethites. David's body-guard.

Here ends the *prosperous* part of David's reign.

9. 1—10. 5 (L, p. 414). DAVID'S KINDNESS. (*Division.*)

L | M[1] | 9. 1-13. To Mephibosheth. (Son of Jonathan.)
  | M[2] | 10. 1-5. To Hanun. (Son of Nahash.)

1-13 (M[1], above). KINDNESS TO MEPHIBOSHETH. (*Division.*)

M[1] | N[1] | 1-4. Mephibosheth. Sought.
   | N[2] | 5-13. Mephibosheth. Found.

1-4 (N[1], above). MEPHIBOSHETH. SOUGHT. (*Alternation.*)

N[1] | i | 1-3-. Inquiry of David. "Who?"
   k | -3. Ziba's answer. Person. Mephibosheth.
   i | 4-. Inquiry of David. "Where?"
   k | -4. Ziba's answer. Place. Lo-debar.

1 kindness = grace, favour, or lovingkindness.

3 any = a man. Heb. *'ish.* Ap. 14. II.

God. Heb. Elohim. Ap. 4. I. **lame.** Cp. 4. 4.

4 Behold. Fig. *Asterismos.* Ap. 6.

Lo-debar = no pasture. Where the sinner is until found by God's free grace.

5-13 [For Structure see next page].

5 sent, and fetched. This is the action of grace towards the "lost" sinner. Cp. Luke 15. 4, 5, 8, 9.

948 6 Now when °Mephibosheth, the son of Jonathan, the son of Saul, was come unto David, he fell on his face, and did reverence. And David said, "Mephibosheth." And he answered, "Behold thy servant!"

m (p. 420) 7 And David said unto him, "Fear not: for I will surely shew thee [1]kindness for Jonathan °thy father's sake, and will restore thee all the land of °Saul thy father; and thou shalt eat bread at my table continually."

8 And he bowed himself, and said, °"What *is* thy servant, that thou shouldest look upon such °a dead dog as °I *am?*"

m 9 Then the king called to Ziba, Saul's servant, and said unto him, "I have given unto thy master's son all that pertained to Saul and to all his house.

10 Thou therefore, and thy sons, and thy servants, shall till the land for him, and thou shalt bring in *the fruits,* that thy master's son may have food to eat: but Mephibosheth thy master's son shall eat bread alway at my table." Now Ziba had fifteen sons and twenty servants.

11 Then said Ziba unto the king, "According to all that my lord the king hath commanded his servant, so shall thy servant do." "As for Mephibosheth," *said the king,* "he shall eat at my table, as one of the king's sons."

12 And Mephibosheth had a young son, whose name *was* Micha. And all that dwelt in the house of Ziba *were* servants unto °Mephibosheth.

l 13 So Mephibosheth dwelt in Jerusalem: for he did eat continually at the king's table; and °was lame on both his feet.

M² n¹ 948 to 942 **10** And it came to pass after this, that the king of the °children of Ammon died, and Hanun his son reigned in his stead.

2 Then said David, "I will shew °kindness unto Hanun the son of Nahash, °as his father shewed kindness unto me."

o And David sent to comfort him by the hand of his servants for his father. And David's servants came into the land of the [1]children of Ammon.

n² 3 And the princes of the [1]children of Ammon said unto Hanun their lord, "Thinkest thou that David doth honour thy father, that he hath sent comforters unto thee? hath not David *rather* sent his servants unto thee, to °search °the city, and to spy it out, and to overthrow it?"

o 4 Wherefore Hanun took David's servants, and shaved off the one half of their beards, and cut off their garments in the middle, *even* to their buttocks, and sent them away.

n³ 5 When they told *it* unto David, he sent to meet them, because the °men were greatly ashamed: and the king said, "Tarry at Jericho until your beards be grown, and *then* return."

O¹ p 6 And when the [1]children of Ammon saw that they stank before David, the [1]children of Ammon sent and hired the Syrians of Beth-rehob, and the Syrians of Zoba, twenty thousand footmen, and of king Maacah a thousand °men, and of °Ish-tob twelve thousand °men.

7 And when David heard of *it,* he sent Joab, and all the host of the mighty men.

8 And the children of Ammon came out, and put the battle in array at the entering in of the gate: and the Syrians of Zoba, and of Rehob, and [6]Ish-tob, and Maacah, *were* by themselves in the field.

9 When Joab saw that the front of the battle was against him before and behind, he chose of all the choice *men* of Israel, and put *them* in array against the Syrians:

10 And the rest of the People he delivered into the hand of Abishai his brother, that he might put *them* in array against the [1]children of Ammon.

11 And he said, "If the Syrians be too strong for me, then thou shalt help me: but if the

9. 5-13 (N², p. 419). MEPHIBOSHETH. FOUND.
(*Introversion.*)

N² | l | 5, 6. Mephibosheth comes to Jerusalem.
  m | 7, 8. David's promise made.
  m | 9-12. David's promise fulfilled.
l | 13. Mephibosheth dwells in Jerusalem.

6 Mephibosheth. Born in 965 (4. 4). Now seventeen, and father of a young son (*v.* 12).

7 thy father's sake. So with God's grace to us; not for the sake of the lost one.

Saul thy father = Saul thy grandfather.

8 What . . . ? Fig. *Erotēsis.* Ap. 6.

a dead dog. Self-abasement is ever the result of grace shown.

I am. So the sinner is concerned about what he *is,* rather than what he has *done.* Cp. Isa. 6. 5. Luke 5. 8.

12 Mephibosheth. Note the Fig. *Epanadiplosis* (Ap. 6) in this verse: being repeated at the beginning of the next verse.

was – he was.

10. 1-5 (M², p. 419). KINDNESS TO HANUN.
(*Repeated Alternation.*)

M² | n¹ | 1, 2-. David's purpose. Formed.
  o | -2. Servants sent.
 n² | 3. David's purpose. Suspected.
  o | 4. Servants insulted.
 n³ | 5. David's purpose. Defeated.

1 children = sons.

2 kindness = lovingkindness, or grace. Cp. 9. 1.

as = according as.

3 search = explore.

the city. Some codices, with one early printed edition, read "the land". Cp. 1 Chron. 19. 3.

5 men. Heb *'ěnōsh.* Ap. 14. III.

10. 6—20. 22 (M, p. 414). WARS AND EVENTS.
(*Division.*)

M | O¹ | 10. 6-19. First and second wars.
 O² | 11. 1—20. 22. Third war, and events.

10. 6-19 (O¹, above). FIRST AND SECOND WARS.
(*Repeated Alternation.*)

O¹ | p | 6-12. Armies arrayed. } First
 q | 13, 14-. Fight and flight. Ammon. } with
 r | -14. Return of Joab. Peace. } Ammon.
 p | 15-17-. Armies arrayed. } Second
 q | -17, 18. Fight and flight. Syrians. } with
 r | 19. Submission of enemies. Peace. } Syrians.

6 men. Heb. *'īsh.* Ap. 14. II.

Ish-tob = men of Tob.

948 [1]children of Ammon be too strong for thee, then
to I will come and help thee.
942 12 Be of good courage, and let us °play the
men for our People, and for the cities of our
°God: and °the LORD do that which seemeth
Him good."

q 13 And Joab drew nigh, and the People that
(p. 420) *were* with him, unto the battle against the
Syrians: and they fled before him.
14 And when the [1]children of Ammon saw
that the Syrians were fled, then fled they also
before Abishai, and entered into the city.

r So Joab returned from the [1]children of Ammon,
and came to Jerusalem.

p 15 And when the Syrians saw that they were
smitten before Israel, they gathered themselves
together.
16 And Hadarezer sent, and brought out the
Syrians that *were* beyond the °river: and they
came to Helam; and °Shobach the captain of
the host of Hadarezer *went* before them.
17 And when it was told David, he gathered
all Israel together, and passed over Jordan,
and came to Helam.

q And the Syrians set themselves in array
against David, and fought with him.
18 And the Syrians fled before Israel; and
David slew *the men of* °seven hundred chariots
of the Syrians, and forty thousand horsemen,
and smote Shobach the captain of their host,
who died there.

r 19 And when all the kings *that were* servants
to Hadarezer saw that they were smitten before
Israel, they made peace with Israel, and served
them. So the Syrians feared to help the [1]children of Ammon any more.

O^2 P **11** And it came to pass, after the year was
(p. 421) expired, °at the time when kings go forth
942 *to battle,* that David sent Joab, and his servants with him, and all Israel; and they destroyed the °children of Ammon, and besieged
°Rabbah.

Q R^1 °But David tarried still at Jerusalem.
2 And it came to pass in an eveningtide, that
David arose from off his bed, and walked upon
the roof of the king's house: and from the roof
he saw a woman °washing herself; and the
woman *was* very beautiful to look upon.
3 And David sent and enquired after the
woman. And *one* said, "*Is* not this °Bath-sheba, the daughter of °Eliam, the wife of
°Uriah the Hittite?"
4 And David sent messengers, and took her;
and she came in unto him, and he lay with
her; °for she was °purified from her uncleanness: and she returned unto her house.
5 And the woman conceived, and °sent and
told David, and said, "I *am* with child."

S^1 T V 6 And David sent to Joab, *saying,* "Send me
Uriah the Hittite." And Joab sent Uriah to
David.

W 7 And when Uriah was come unto him, David
demanded *of him* how Joab did, and how the
people did, and how the war prospered.

12 play the men = Be strong and let us put forth our strength. Heb. *ḥozak*.
God. Heb. Elohim. Ap. 4. I.
the LORD. Heb. Jehovah. Ap. 4. II.
16 river: i. e. the Euphrates.
Shobach. Another name, Shophach (1 Chron. 19. 16).
18 seven hundred. 1 Chron. 19. 18 = 7,000. But Heb. ז = 7 and ז = 7,000, probably a scribe's infirmity. Cp. 8. 4 and 1 Chron. 18. 4.

11. 1—20. 22 (O^2, p. 420). THIRD WAR, AND EVENTS. (*Alternation.*)

O^2 | P | 11. 1-. Rabbah. Besieged.
  Q | 11. -1—12. 25. David's sin. Committed.
  P | 12. 26-31. Rabbah. Captured.
  Q | 13. 1—20. 22. David's sin. Punished.

1 at the time, &c.: i. e. the next spring.
children = sons.
Rabbah. The capital of Ammon (Deut. 3. 11. Josh. 13. 25).

11. -1—12. 25 (Q, above). DAVID'S SIN. (*Repeated Alternation and Introversion.*)

Q | R^1 | 11. -1-5. David and Bath-sheba.
  S^1 | T | 11. 6-24. David and Uriah.
    U | 11. 25. Displeasure of Joab.
  R^2 | 11. 26, 27-. David and Bath-sheba.
  S^2 | *U* | 11. -27. Displeasure of Jehovah.
    T | 12. 1-14. David and Nathan.
  R^3 | 12. 15-25. David and Bath-sheba's child.

But David tarried. Note contrast with "kings" going forth, above, and this word "But".
2 washing = bathing. Probably in the court below.
3 Bath-sheba. Called Bath-shua, 1 Chron. 3. 5.
Eliam. Called "Ammiel", 1 Chron. 3. 5. The son of Ahithophel (23. 34).
Uriah. One of David's faithful soldiers (23. 39). Married the daughter of Eliam (11. 3), who was the son of Ahithophel (23. 34). This relationship probably led to Ahithophel's disloyalty (15. 12).
4 for = and when.
purified. Cp. Lev. 15. 18. It is possible to be more punctilious about the ceremonial Law than the moral Law.
5 sent and told: that David might shield her from the death penalty (Lev. 20. 10).

6-24 (T, above). DAVID AND URIAH. (*Alternation.*)

T | V | 6. Message to Joab.
  W | 7-13. Uriah's reception.
  V | 14, 15. Letter to Joab.
  W | 16-24. Uriah's death.

9 door = entrance.
11 thy soul = thou (emph.). Heb. *nephesh*. Ap. 13.

8 And David said to Uriah, "Go down to thy
house, and wash thy feet." And Uriah departed out of the king's house, and there followed him a mess *of meat* from the king.
9 But Uriah slept at the °door of the king's
house with all the servants of his lord, and
went not down to his house.
10 And when they had told David, saying,
"Uriah went not down unto his house," David
said unto Uriah, "Camest thou not from *thy*
journey? why *then* didst thou not go down
unto thine house?"
11 And Uriah said unto David, "The ark, and
Israel, and Judah, abide in tents; and my lord
Joab, and the servants of my lord, are encamped in the open fields; shall I then go
into mine house, to eat and to drink, and to
lie with my wife? *as* thou livest, and *as* °thy
soul liveth, I will not do this thing."
12 And David said to Uriah, "Tarry here to

942 day also, and to morrow I will let thee depart." So Uriah abode in Jerusalem that day, and the morrow.

13 And when David had called him, he did eat and drink before him; and he made him drunk: and at even he went out to lie on his bed with the servants of his lord, but went not down to his house.

V (p. 421) 14 And it came to pass in the morning, that David wrote a letter to Joab, and sent *it* by the hand of Uriah.

15 And he wrote in the letter, saying, "Set ye Uriah in the forefront of the hottest battle, and retire ye from him, that he may be smitten, and die."

$W\ s^1$ (p. 422) 16 And it came to pass, when Joab observed the city, that he assigned Uriah unto a place where he knew that valiant °men *were*.

17 And the °men of the city went out, and fought with Joab: and there fell *some* of the People of the servants of David;

t^1 and Uriah the Hittite died also.

s^2 18 Then Joab sent and told David all the things concerning the war;

19 And charged the messenger, saying, "When thou hast made an end of telling the matters of the war unto the king,

20 And if so be that the king's wrath arise, and he say unto thee, 'Wherefore approached ye so nigh unto the city when ye did fight? knew ye not that they would shoot °from the wall?

21 Who smote Abimelech the son of °Jerubbesheth? did not °a woman cast a °piece of a °millstone upon him from the wall, that he died in Thebez? why went ye nigh the wall?' then say thou,

t^2 'Thy servant Uriah the Hittite is dead also.'"

s^3 22 So the messenger went, and came and shewed David all that Joab had sent him for.

23 And the messenger said unto David, "Surely the [17]men prevailed against us, and came out unto us into the field, and we were upon them even unto the °entering of the gate.

24 And the shooters shot [20]from off the wall upon thy servants; and *some* of the king's servants be dead,

t^3 and thy servant Uriah the Hittite is dead also."

U (p. 421) 25 Then David said unto the messenger, "Thus shalt thou say unto Joab, 'Let not this thing °displease thee, for the sword devoureth °one as well as another: make thy battle more strong against the city, and overthrow it:' and encourage thou him."

R^2 26 And when the wife of Uriah heard that Uriah her husband was dead, she °mourned for her husband.

941 27 And when the mourning was past, David °sent and fetched her to his house, and she became his wife, and bare him a son.

$S^2\ U$ But the thing that David had done [25]displeased °the LORD.

11. 16-24 (*W*, p. 421). URIAH'S DEATH.
(*Repeated Alternation.*)

W | s^1 | 16, 17-. Joab. Obedience.
  t^1 | -17. Death of Uriah.
 s^2 | 18-21-. Joab. Message sent.
  t^2 | -21. Death of Uriah.
 s^3 | 22-24-. Joab. Message delivered.
  t^3 | -24. Death of Uriah.

16 men. Heb. *'îsh.* Ap. 14. II.
17 men. Heb. *'ĕnôsh.* Ap. 14. III.
20 from = from off, as in *v.* 24.
21 Jerubbesheth (Judg. 9. 1) = Jerubbaal. **Baal** = lord, **Bosheth** = shame; changed by Holy Ghost here to suit his idolatry (Judg. 8. 27), and now David's sin.
a woman, one of the ten deaths caused by a woman. See note, Judg. 4. 21. **piece** = upper piece.
millstone. One of the "despised" things used. See note on Judg. 3. 21; 9. 53.
23 entering = entrance.
25 displease thee = be evil in thine eyes. This event put David in Joab's power, which Joab freely used. David was not tongue-tied in 3. 29; but from now he had to endure Joab's insolence, being too suspicious to trust him, and too weak to dismiss him. Cp. 14. 19; 19. 7. 1 Kings 2. 5, 32, 33.
one as well as another = now this one, now that one.
26 mourned = made lamentations.
27 sent. Not till nine months after.
the LORD. Heb. Jehovah. Ap. 4. II.

12. 1-14 (*T*, p. 421). DAVID AND NATHAN.
(*Repeated Alternation.*)

T | u^1 | 1-4. Parable. Propounded.
  v^1 | 5, 6. David's anger.
 u^2 | 7-9. Parable. Applied.
  v^2 | 10-12. David's judgment.
 u^3 | 13-. Parable. Effect.
  v^3 | -13, 14. David's forgiveness.

1 the LORD. Heb. Jehovah. Ap. 4. II.
sent. See 11. 27.
Nathan. Sept. and Syr. read "Nathan the prophet".
he came. Cp. title of Ps. 51.
men. Heb. *'îsh.* Ap. 14. II.
3 meat = morsel.
5 shall surely die. Heb. is a son of death = liable to die.
6 fourfold. Cp. Ex. 22. 1. Sept. reads "sevenfold".

12 And °the LORD °sent °Nathan unto David. And °he came unto him, and said unto him, "There were two °men in one city; the one rich, and the other poor. *T* u^1 (p. 422)

2 The rich *man* had exceeding many flocks and herds:

3 But the poor *man* had nothing, save one little ewe lamb, which he had bought and nourished up: and it grew up together with him, and with his children; it did eat of his own °meat, and drank of his own cup, and lay in his bosom, and was unto him as a daughter.

4 And there came a traveller unto the rich [1]man, and he spared to take of his own flock and of his own herd, to dress for the wayfaring [1]man that was come unto him; but took the poor [1]man's lamb, and dressed it for the [1]man that was come to him."

5 And David's anger was greatly kindled against the [1]man; and he said to Nathan, "*As* [1]the LORD liveth, the [1]man that hath done this *thing* °shall surely die: v^1

6 And he shall restore the lamb °fourfold, because he did this thing, and because he had no pity."

u^2 7 And Nathan said to David, ° "Thou *art* the
(p. 422) [1]man. Thus saith [1]the LORD °God of Israel,
941 'I °anointed thee king over Israel, and I delivered thee out of the hand of Saul;
8 And I gave thee thy master's house, and
thy master's wives into thy bosom, and gave
thee the house of Israel and of Judah; and if
that had been too little, I would moreover have
given unto thee such and such things.
9 Wherefore hast thou despised the commandment of [1]the LORD, to do °evil in His
sight? °thou hast killed Uriah the Hittite
with the sword, and hast taken his wife *to
be* thy wife, and hast slain him with the sword
of the °children of Ammon.

v^2 10 Now therefore °the sword shall °never
depart from thine house; because thou hast
despised Me, and hast taken the wife of Uriah
the Hittite to be thy wife.'
11 Thus saith [1]the LORD, °'Behold, I will
raise up °evil against thee out of °thine own
house, and I will take thy wives before thine
eyes, and give *them* unto thy neighbour, and
he shall lie with thy wives in the sight of this
sun.
12 For °thou didst *it* secretly: but I will do
this thing before all Israel, and before the
sun.'"

u^3 13 And David said unto Nathan, °"I have
°sinned against [1]the LORD."

v^3 And Nathan said unto David, [1]"The LORD
also °hath put away thy °sin; °thou shalt not
die.
14 Howbeit, because by this deed °thou hast
given great occasion to the enemies of [1]the
LORD to blaspheme, the child also *that is* born
unto thee shall surely die."

R^3 w^1 x^1 15 And Nathan departed unto his house.
(p. 423) And [1]the LORD struck the child that Uriah's
wife bare unto David, and it was very sick.

y^1 16 David therefore besought [7]God for the
child; °and David °fasted, and went in, and
°lay all night upon the earth.

z^1 17 And the elders of his house arose, *and
went* to him, to raise him up from the earth:
but he would not, neither did he eat bread with
them.

w^2 x^2 18 And it came to pass on the seventh day,
that the child died. And the servants of
David feared to tell him that the child was
dead: for they said, [11]"Behold, while the child
was yet alive, we spake unto him, and he
would not hearken unto our voice: how will
he then vex himself, if we tell him that the
child is dead?"
19 But when David saw that his servants
whispered, David perceived that the child was
dead: therefore David said unto his servants,
"Is the child dead?" And they said, "He is
dead."

y^2 20 Then David arose from the earth, and
washed, and anointed *himself*, and changed
his apparel, and came into the house of [1]the
LORD, and worshipped:

z^2 then he came to his own house; and when he
required, they set bread before him, and he
did eat.

21 Then said his servants unto him, "What w^3 x^3
thing *is* this that thou hast done? thou didst
fast and weep for the child, *while it was* alive;
but when the child was dead, thou didst rise
and eat bread."

22 And he said, "While the child was yet y^3
alive, I fasted and wept: for I said, °'Who can
tell *whether* °GOD will be gracious to me, that
the child may live?'

7 Thou art the man. Many means used to produce conviction: God's greatness (Job 42. 1-6); God's glory (Isa. 6. 5); God's power (Luke 5. 8); a famine (Luke 15. 14, 18); a parable (2 Sam. 12. 1-13), &c.

God. Heb. Elohim. Ap. 4. I.

anointed thee. 1 Sam. 16. 13.

9 evil. Heb. *rā'a'.* Ap. 44. viii, with Art.

thou hast killed. Not Joab, or the Ammonites.

children = sons.

10 the sword. Put by Fig. *Metonymy* (of Adjunct), Ap. 6, for manifested hostility.

never. Fig. *Synecdoche* (of the Whole), Ap. 6, put for a part of time: i. e. lifetime.

11 Behold. Fig. *Asterismos.* Ap. 6.

evil. Heb. *rā'a'.* Ap. 44. viii. See the Structure of 13. 1—20. 22 (*Q*, p. 424).

thine own house. Disgraced by one son (13. 14), banished by another (15. 19), revolted against by a third (1 Kings 2), bearded by his servant, betrayed by his friends, deserted by his People, bereaved of his children.

12 thou. See note on *v.* 9.

13 I have sinned. Ps. 51 is the expansion of this.

sinned . . . sin. Heb. *chāṭā'.* Ap. 44. i.

hath put away. Divine forgiveness instantly follows the sinner's confession (1 John 1. 9). Cp. Job 42. 6, 8, 10. Isa. 6. 5, 6, "then flew". Luke 15. 18, 20, "his father ran", &c.

thou, &c. Some codices, with two early printed editions, read "and (or therefore) thou wilt not die".

14 thou hast given great occasion, &c. This is noted in the *Massōrah* (Ap. 30) as one of the emendations of the *Sōpherīm* (Ap. 33), who altered the primitive text out of a mistaken reverence for David and Jehovah. The original reading was "thou hast greatly blasphemed Jehovah".

12. 15-25 (R^3, p. 421). **DAVID AND THE CHILD.**
(*Repeated and Extended Alternation.*)

R^3 | w^1 | x^1 | 15. Child stricken.
| | y^1 | 16. David's intercession.
| | z^1 | 17. Abstinence.
| w^2 | x^2 | 18, 19. Child's death.
| | y^2 | 20-. David's worship.
| | z^2 | -20. Eating.
| w^3 | x^3 | 21. Child's death. Inquiry.
| | y^3 | 22. David's weeping.
| | z^3 | 23. Abstinence given up.

24, 25. EPILOGUE.

16 and. Note the Fig. *Polysyndeton* in this verse. Ap. 6.

fasted. Heb. *fasted* a fast = made a strict fast. Fig. *Polyptōton.* Ap. 6.

lay all night upon the earth: as a penitent, with Ps. 51 for his utterance. Note his *sitting* before Jehovah as a worshipper, and his utterance (2 Sam. 7. 18-29); and his *standing* as a servant (1 Chron. 28. 2), and his utterance and service (1 Chron. 28. 3—29. 21).

22 Who can tell . . .? Fig. *Erotēsis.* Ap. 6.

GOD = Jehovah. Ap. 4. II.

z³ 23 But now he is dead, wherefore should I
(p. 423) fast? can I bring him back again? °I shall
941 go to him, but he shall not return to me."
Epilogue 24 °And David comforted Bath-sheba his wife,
and went in unto her, and lay with her: and
940 she bare a son, and °he called his name °Solo-
mon: and [1] the LORD loved him.
25 [21] And He sent by the hand of Nathan the
prophet; and °He called his name °Jedidiah,
°because of [1] the LORD.
P X¹ 26 And Joab fought against Rabbah of the
(p. 424) [9] children of Ammon, and took the royal city.
27 And Joab sent messengers to David, and
said, "I have fought against Rabbah, and
have taken the °city of waters.
28 Now therefore gather the rest of the People together, and encamp against the city, and
take it: lest I take the city, and it be called
after my name."
X² 29 And David gathered all the People together,
and went to Rabbah, and fought against it, and
took it.
30 And he took °their king's crown from off
his head, the weight whereof *was* a °talent of
gold with the precious stones: and it was *set*
on David's head. And he brought forth the
spoil of the city in great abundance.
31 [24] And he brought forth the people that
were therein, and °put *them* °under saws, and
°under harrows of iron, and °under axes of
iron, and made them °pass through the °brick-
kiln: and °thus did he unto all the cities of
the [9] children of Ammon. So David and all the
people returned unto Jerusalem.

Q Y¹ A **13** And it came to pass °after this, that
938 °Absalom the son of David had a fair
sister, whose name *was* Tamar; and °Amnon
the son of David loved her.
2 And Amnon was so vexed, that he fell sick
for his sister Tamar; for she *was* a virgin; and
Amnon thought it hard for him to do any thing
to her.

23 I shall go to him = I shall die and be buried (cp. *v.* 19): i. e. I shall go to the (not "a") grave (*Sheōl*). On the use of this Fig. *Euphemy* (Ap. 6) as denoting death and burial, see Gen. 15. 15 (cp. Josh. 24. 2, 14, 15, Abraham's "fathers" being *idolaters*); 25. 8, 17; 35. 29; 49. 29, 33. Num. 20. 26; 27. 13; 31. 2. Deut. 31. 16; 32. 50. Judg. 2. 10. 1 Sam. 28. 19 (note "thou and thy sons"). 2 Kings 22. 20. 1 Chron. 17. 11. 2 Chron. 34. 28. Acts 13. 36.

24 And. Note the Fig. *Polysyndeton* in *vv.* 24–27. Ap. 6.

he. Some codices, with Syr. and Vulg., read "she", in contrast with "he" in next verse.

Solomon = Pacific or Peaceable. Cp. 7. 13.

25 He: i. e. Jehovah, by the hand of Nathan, in contrast with Bath-sheba. See note on *v.* 24.

Jedidiah = beloved of Jah. See note on Ps. 127. 2.

because of the LORD = for Jehovah's sake.

12. 26–31 (*P*, p. 421). RABBAH. CAPTURED. (*Division.*)

P | X¹ | 26–28. Rabbah and Joab.
  | X² | 29–31. Rabbah and David.

27 city of waters. Fig. *Hypallagē.* Ap. 6 = waters of the city: i. e. the lower waters or town, cutting off the citadel, which David came and took.

30 their king's crown = the crown of Milcom, with Sept. Cp. 1 Chron. 20. 2. Jer. 49. 1, 3. Amos 1. 15. Zeph. 1. 5 (*Comp. Bible*).

talent. See Ap. 51. II.

31 put = appointed, appointed over, set, &c. Heb. *sūm* (Gen. 2. 8; 45. 8, 9; 47. 6. Ex. 2. 14; 5. 14. 1 Sam. 8. 11; 2 Sam. 7. 10. 2 Kings 10. 24. Ps. 78. 5; 81. 5. Hos. 1. 11, &c.).

under = with, especially to work *with.* Heb. letter ב (*Beth*), prefixed as prep. = *in, within, with.* When the prep. "under" = beneath, then it is either part of a verb or one of four distinct words: *'ēl* (2 Sam. 2. 23); *mattāh* (1 Chron. 27. 23); *tᵉhoth'* (Jer. 10. 11. Dan. 4. 12, 21; 7. 27, "under the heavens"); *tahath* (Dan. 4. 14, "under a tree"). *Beth,* when translated "under", is only in the sense of *within* (as "under (or within the shelter of) the wing", or "under (or within) the earth"). Otherwise, used with a tool or weapon or instrument, it always means "with". See "with an axe" (Deut. 19. 5. Jer. 10. 3); "with axes" (Jer. 46. 22. Ezek. 26. 9. Ps. 74. 6); "with nails and with hammers" (Jer. 10. 4); "with an ox-goad" (Judg. 3. 31); "with mattock" (Isa. 7. 25); "with sword and with bow" (Gen. 48. 22. Josh. 24. 12. 2 Kings 6. 22); "with a graving tool" (Ex. 32. 4), &c.

pass through = pass by or before. Heb. *'ābar,* as in Ezek. 37. 2; 46. 21. Deut. 2. 30. Ex. 33. 19. 1 Sam. 16. 8, 9, 10, &c.

brickkiln = brick-work; hence, brick pavement or paved area (R.V. marg.). Not brickkiln; no brickkilns in Palestine. All bricks there are sun-dried. Only once spoken of as burnt—as being a strange thing (Gen. 11. 3, and marg.). Heb. *malbēn,* occurs only here, Jer. 43. 9, and Nah. 3. 14, the former at "entry" of royal palace, the latter said to be "fortified". Both out of the question, and quite incongruous for a brickkiln. The very paved area of Jer. 43. 9 was discovered at *Tahpanhes* by Flinders Petrie in 1886, where Nebuchadnezzar did exactly what David did here and in ch. 8. 2 and 1 Chron. 20. 3.

thus did he: i. e. as in 8. 2, with Moab, so here; he caused the captives to pass by before him, he seated on a pavement of brick-work, or paved area, where he appointed them to the various departments of labour for which they were suited. Cp. Jer. 43. 9–11. These were the "strangers" (i. e. foreigners) and the "abundance of workmen" referred to in 1 Chron. 22. 2, 15. Cp. Deut. 29. 11. Josh. 9. 27. See notes on 1 Kings 5. 13; 9. 15, 21, 22.

13. 1—20. 22 (*Q*, p. 421). DAVID'S SIN. PUNISHED. (*Division.*)

Q | Y¹ | 13. 1—14. 33. Amnon's sin.
  | Y² | 15. 1—19. 43. Absalom's rebellion.
  | Y³ | 20. 1–22. Sheba's revolt.

13. 1—14. 33- (Y¹, above). AMNON'S SIN. (*Introversion and Extended Alternation.*)

Y¹ | A | 13. 1–4. Amnon's desire for sister's love.
  B | a | 13. 5–10. Stratagem. } Amnon's sin.
    b | 13. 11–18. Crime.
    c | 13. 19–22. Emotions.
  B | *a* | 13. 23–27. Stratagem. } Absalom's revenge.
    b | 13. 28, 29–. Crime.
    c | 13. -29—14. 27. Commotions.
  A | 14. 28–33. Absalom's desire for father's love.

1 after this: i. e. 938. David, 53; Amnon, 22; Absalom, 20; Tamar, 15; Solomon, 2.

Absalom. Son of Maacah, daughter of king of Geshur (see note on 3. 3).

Amnon. Son of Ahinoam (3. 2).

938 3 But Amnon had a friend, whose name *was* Jonadab, the son of °Shimeah David's brother: and Jonadab *was* a very °subtil °man.

4 And he said unto him, "Why *art* thou, *being* the king's son, lean from day to day? wilt thou not tell me?" And Amnon said unto him, "I love Tamar, my brother Absalom's sister."

B a (p. 424) 5 And Jonadab said unto him, "Lay thee down on thy bed, and °make thyself sick: and when thy father cometh to see thee, say unto him, 'I pray thee, let my sister Tamar come, and give me meat, and dress the °meat in my sight, that I may see *it*, and eat *it* at her hand.'"

6 So Amnon lay down, and [5]made himself sick: and when the king was come to see him, Amnon said unto the king, "I pray thee, let Tamar my sister come, and make me a couple of °cakes in my sight, that I may eat at her hand."

7 Then David sent home to Tamar, saying, "Go now to thy brother Amnon's house, and dress him [5]meat."

8 So Tamar went to her brother Amnon's house; and he was laid down. And she took °flour, and kneaded *it*, and made [6]cakes in his sight, and did bake the [6]cakes.

9 And she took °a pan, and °poured *them* out before him; but he refused to eat. And Amnon said, "Have out all °men from me." And they went out every °man from him.

10 And Amnon said unto Tamar, "Bring the meat into the chamber, that I may eat of thine hand." And Tamar took the [6]cakes which she had made, and brought *them* into the chamber to Amnon her brother.

b 11 And when she had brought *them* unto him to eat, he took hold of her, and said unto her, "Come lie with me, my sister."

12 And she answered him, "Nay, my brother, do not °force me; for no such thing ought to be done in Israel: do not thou this folly.

13 And I, whither shall I cause my shame to go? and as for thee, thou shalt be as one of the fools in Israel. Now therefore, I pray thee, speak unto the king; for he will not withhold me from thee."

14 Howbeit he would not hearken unto her voice: but, being stronger than she, forced her, and lay with her.

15 Then Amnon hated her exceedingly; so that the hatred wherewith he hated her *was* greater than the love wherewith he had loved her. And Amnon said unto her, "Arise, be gone."

16 And she said unto him, "*There is* °no cause: this °evil in sending me away *is* greater than the other that thou didst unto me." But he would not hearken unto her.

17 Then he called his servant that ministered unto him, and said, "Put now this *woman* out from me, and bolt the door after her."

18 And *she had* a garment of °divers colours upon her: for with such robes were the king's daughters *that were* virgins apparelled. Then his servant brought her out, and bolted the door after her.

c d (p. 425) 19 And Tamar put ashes on her head, and rent her garment of divers colours that *was* on her, and °laid her hand on her head, and went on crying.

20 And Absalom her brother said unto her, e
"Hath Amnon thy brother been with thee? but hold now thy peace, my sister: he *is* thy brother; regard not this thing." So Tamar remained °desolate in her brother Absalom's house.

21 But when king David heard of all these d
things, he was very wroth.

22 And Absalom spake unto his brother e
Amnon neither good nor bad: for Absalom hated Amnon, because he had forced his sister Tamar.

23 And it came to pass after two full years, B a
that Absalom had sheepshearers in Baal-hazor, (p. 424)
which *is* beside Ephraim: and Absalom invited all the king's sons.

24 And Absalom came to the king, and said, °"Behold now, thy servant hath sheepshearers; let the king, I beseech thee, and his servants go with thy servant."

25 And the king said to Absalom, "Nay, my son, let us not all now go, lest we be °chargeable unto thee." And he pressed him: howbeit he would not go, but blessed him.

26 Then said Absalom, "If not, I pray thee, let my brother Amnon go with us." And the king said unto him, "Why should he go with thee?"

27 But Absalom pressed him, that he let Amnon and all the king's sons go °with him.

28 Now Absalom had commanded his serv- b
ants, saying, "Mark ye now when Amnon's heart is merry with wine, and when I say unto you, 'Smite Amnon;' then kill him, fear not: have not I commanded you? be courageous, and be °valiant."

29 And the servants of Absalom did unto Amnon °as Absalom had commanded.

3 Shimeah = Shammah (1 Sam. 16. 9).
subtil = wise. **man.** Heb. *'ish*. Ap. 14. II.
5 make = feign.
meat = heart-shaped cakes. Occurs only here and in *vv.* 6, 7, 8, 10. **6 cakes.** See note on "meat", *v.* 5.
8 flour = dough, or paste.
9 a pan = the pan. Occurs only here.
poured = put down. **men.** Heb. *'ish*. Ap. 14. II.
12 force = humble.
16 no cause. Heb. *'al*. "[Give] no ground for talk".
evil. Heb. *rā'a'*. Ap. 44. viii.
18 divers colours = a long tunic with sleeves.

13. 19-22 (c, p. 424). **EMOTIONS.**
(*Alternations.*)

c | d | 19. Grief of Tamar.
  e | 20. Absalom's dissimulation.
  d | 21. Anger of David.
  e | 22. Absalom's hatred.

19 laid her hand. Fig. *Metonymy* (of Adjunct), Ap. 6, put for "grieved".
20 desolate. Heb. "remained and [remained] desolate". Cp. 1 Tim. 5. 5.
24 Behold. Fig. *Asterismos*. Ap. 6.
25 chargeable = burdensome.
27 with him. The Sept. and Vulg. add here "and Absalom made a banquet, like the banquet of a king". Cp. 1 Sam. 25. 36.
28 valiant = sons of valour. **29 as** = according as.

c C^1 f^1 (p. 426) 938 Then all the king's sons arose, and every [3]man gat him up upon his °mule, and fled.

g^1 30 And it came to pass, while they were in the way, that tidings came to David, saying, "Absalom hath slain all the king's sons, and there is not one of them left."

31 Then the king arose, and tare his garments, and lay on the earth; and all his servants stood by °with their clothes rent.

32 And Jonadab, the son of [3]Shimeah David's brother, answered and said, "Let not my lord suppose *that* they have slain all the young men the king's sons; for Amnon only is dead: for by the appointment of Absalom this hath been determined from the day that he forced his sister Tamar.

33 Now therefore let not my lord the king take the thing to his heart, to think that all the king's sons are dead: for Amnon only is dead."

f^2 34 But Absalom fled.

g^2 And the young man that kept the watch °lifted up his eyes, and looked, and, [24]behold, there came much people by the way of the hill side behind him.

35 And Jonadab said unto the king, [24]"Behold, the king's sons come: [29]as thy servant said, so it is."

36 And it came to pass, as soon as he had made an end of speaking, that, [24]behold, the king's sons came, and lifted up their voice and wept: and the king also and all his servants °wept very sore.

f^3 37 But Absalom fled, and went to Talmai, the son of °Ammihud, king of Geshur. And °*David* mourned for his son every day.

938-936 38 So Absalom fled, and went to Geshur, and was there three years.

g^3 39 And °*the soul of* king David longed to go forth unto Absalom: for he was comforted concerning Amnon, seeing he was dead.

C^2 D **14** Now Joab the son of Zeruiah perceived that the king's heart *was* toward Absalom.

E 2 And Joab sent to °Tekoah, and fetched thence a wise woman, and said unto her, "I pray thee, feign thyself to be a mourner, and put on now mourning apparel, and anoint not thyself with oil, but be as a woman that had a long time mourned for the dead:

3 And come to the king, and speak on this manner unto him." So Joab put the words in her mouth.

F h^1 4 And when the woman of Tekoah °spake to the king, she fell on her face to the ground, and did obeisance, and said, "Help, O king."

i^1 5 And the king said unto her, "What aileth thee?"

h^2 And she answered, "I *am* indeed °a widow woman, and °mine husband is dead.

6 And thy handmaid had two sons, and they two strove together in the field, and *there was* none to part them, but the one smote the other, and slew him.

13. -29—14. 27 (*c*, p. 424). COMMOTIONS. (*Division.*)

c | C^1 | 13. -29-39. Absalom's flight.
  | C^2 | 14. 1-33. Absalom's recall.

-29-39 (C^1, above). ABSALOM'S FLIGHT. (*Repeated Alternation.*)

C^1 | f^1 | -29. Flight of king's sons.
  | g^1 | 30-33. David. Anxiety.
  | f^2 | 34-. Flight of Absalom.
  | g^2 | -34-36. David. Mourning.
  | f^3 | 37, 38. Flight of Absalom.
  | g^3 | 39. David. Comforted.

mule. First occurrence. Not Gen. 36. 24. See note there.

31 with their clothes rent = and rent their garments.

36 wept very sore. Fig. *Polyptōton* (Ap. 6) = "wept with a great weeping".

37 Ammihud, or Ammihur.

David. Sept. reads "David the king".

39 the soul of king David. The Aram. reads "the soul (*nephesh*) of the king". Cp. the omission of *nephesh* in Ps. 16. 2.

14. 1-33 (C^2, above). ABSALOM'S RECALL. (*Introversion.*)

C^2 | D | 1. David's heart toward Absalom.
  | E | 2, 3. Joab's stratagem planned.
  | F | 4-11. Parable. Put forth.
  | *F* | 12-17. Parable. Applied.
  | *E* | 18-20. Joab's stratagem discovered.
  | *D* | 21-33. David's recall of Absalom.

2 Tekoah. On the edge of the hill country of Judah, south-east of Beth-lehem, about seven miles from Jerusalem (cp. Jer. 6. 1). Abounding in caverns. The abode of Amos.

4-11 (F, above). PARABLE. PUT FORTH. (*Repeated Alternation.*)

F | h^1 | 4. Woman's importunity.
  | i^1 | 5-. King's response.
  | h^2 | -5-7. Woman's grievance.
  | i^2 | 8. King's assurance.
  | h^3 | 9. Woman's importunity.
  | i^3 | 10. King's assurance.
  | h^4 | 11-. Woman's grievance.
  | i^4 | -11. King's assurance.

4 spake to the king. Many codices, with three early printed editions, Sept., Syr., and Vulg., read "came in unto the king".

5 a widow. One of nine widows specially mentioned. See note on Gen. 38. 19.

mine husband is dead. Fig. *Synonymia.* Ap. 6.

7 behold. Fig. *Asterismos.* Ap. 6.

life = soul. Heb. *nephesh.* Ap. 13.

9 iniquity. Heb. *'āvāh.* See Ap. 44. iv.

7 And, °behold, the whole family is risen against thine handmaid, and they said, 'Deliver him that smote his brother, that we may kill him, for the °life of his brother whom he slew; and we will destroy the heir also: and so they shall quench my coal which is left, and shall not leave to my husband *neither* name nor remainder upon the earth.'"

8 And the king said unto the woman, "Go to thine house, and I will give charge concerning thee." i^2

9 And the woman of Tekoah said unto the king, "My lord, O king, the °iniquity *be* on me, h^3

936 and on my father's house: and the king and his throne *be* guiltless."

i[3] (p. 426) 10 And the king said, "Whosoever saith *ought* unto thee, bring him to me, and he shall not touch thee any more."

h[4] 11 Then said she, "I pray thee, let the king °remember °the LORD thy °God, that thou wouldest not suffer the °revengers of blood to destroy any more, lest they destroy my son."

i[4] And he said, "*As* °the LORD liveth, there shall °not one hair of thy son fall to the earth."

F 12 Then the woman said, "Let thine handmaid, I pray thee, speak *one* word unto my lord the king." And he said, "Say on."

13 And the woman said, "Wherefore then hast thou thought such a thing against the People of [11]God? for the king doth speak this thing as one which is faulty, in that the king doth not fetch home again his banished.

14 For we must needs die, and *are* as water spilt on the ground, which cannot be gathered up again; neither doth [11]God respect *any* °person: yet doth He devise means, that His banished be not expelled from Him.

15 Now therefore that I am come to speak of this thing unto my lord the king, *it is* because the People have made me afraid: and thy handmaid said, 'I will now speak unto the king; it may be that the king will perform the request of his handmaid.

16 For the king will hear, to deliver his handmaid out of the hand of the °man *that would* destroy me and my son together out of the inheritance of [11]God.'

17 Then thine handmaid said, 'The word of my lord the king shall now be comfortable: for as an angel of [11]God, so *is* my lord the king to discern good and bad: therefore [11]the LORD thy [11]God will be with thee.'"

E 18 Then the king answered and said unto the woman, "Hide not from me, I pray thee, the thing that I shall ask thee." And the woman said, "Let my lord the king now speak."

19 And the king said, "*Is not* the °hand of Joab with thee in all this?" And the woman answered and said, "*As* thy °soul liveth, my lord the king, °none can turn to the right hand or to the left from ought that my lord the king hath spoken: for thy servant Joab, he bade me, and he put all these words in the mouth of thine handmaid:

20 °To fetch about this form of speech hath thy servant Joab done this thing: and my lord *is* wise, according to the wisdom of an angel of [11]God, to know all *things* that *are* in the earth."

D G[1] (p. 427) 21 And the king said unto Joab, °"Behold now, °I have done this thing: go therefore, bring the young man Absalom again."

H j 22 And Joab fell to the ground on his face, and bowed himself, and °thanked the king: and Joab said, "To day thy servant knoweth that I have found grace in thy sight, my lord, O king, in that the king hath fulfilled the request of his servant."

k 23 So Joab arose and went to Geshur, and brought Absalom to Jerusalem.

G[2] 936 24 And the king said, "Let him turn to his own house, and let him not see my face." So Absalom returned to his own house, and saw not the king's face.

25 But in all Israel there was [19]none to be so much praised as Absalom for his beauty: from the sole of his foot even to the crown of his head there was no blemish in him.

26 And when he polled his head, (°for it was at every year's end that he polled *it*: because *the hair* was heavy on him, therefore he polled it:) he weighed the hair of his head at two hundred shekels after the °king's weight.

27 And unto Absalom there were born °three sons, and one daughter, whose name *was* Tamar: she was a woman of a fair countenance.

H k 936-935 28 So Absalom dwelt two full years in Jerusalem, and saw not the king's face.

j 29 Therefore Absalom sent for Joab, to have sent him to the king; but he would not come to him: and when he sent again the second time, he would not come.

30 Therefore he said unto his servants, "See, Joab's field is near mine, and he hath barley there; go and set it on fire." And Absalom's servants set the field on fire.

31 Then Joab arose, and came to Absalom unto *his* house, and said unto him, "Wherefore have thy servants set my field on fire?"

32 And Absalom answered Joab, [21]"Behold, I sent unto thee, saying, 'Come hither, that I may send thee to the king, to say, 'Wherefore am I come from Geshur? *it had been* good for me *to have been* there still: now therefore let me see the king's face; and if there be *any* [9]iniquity in me, let him kill me.'"

---

11 remember = recall to mind: i. e. take an oath.
the LORD. Heb. Jehovah. Ap. 4. II.
God. Heb. Elohim. Ap. 4. I.
revengers = avengers, or next of kin. Heb. *gā'al.* See note on Ex. 6. 6, and cp. Num. 35. 19, 21, 24, 25, 27.
not one hair, &c. Fig. *Parœmia.* Ap. 6.
14 person = soul. Heb. *nephesh.* Ap. 13.
16 man. Heb. *'īsh.* Ap. 14. II.
19 hand = work, or handiwork. Put by Fig. *Metonymy* (of Cause), Ap. 6, for what is wrought by it.
soul. Heb. *nephesh.* Ap. 13.
none = no man. Heb. *'īsh.* Ap. 14. II.
20 To fetch about this form of speech = To bring about this turn of affairs.

21-33 (*D*, p. 426). **DAVID'S RECALL OF ABSALOM.**
(*Repeated Alternation and Introversion.*)

D | G[1] | 21. David's decision to receive Absalom.
  H | j | 22. Joab's thanks.
    k | 23. Absalom in Jerusalem.
  G[2] | 24-27. David's direction and Absalom's person.
  H | *k* | 28. Absalom in Jerusalem.
    j | 29-33-. Joab's appeal.
  G[3] | -33. David's reception of Absalom.

21 Behold. Fig. *Asterismos.* Ap. 6.
I. Some codices read "thou".
22 thanked = blessed.
26 for. Note the Fig. *Parenthesis.* Ap. 6.
king's weight: to distinguish it from the sacred shekel. See Ap. 51. II.
27 three sons. Did not survive him. Cp. 18. 18.

935 **33** So Joab came to the king, and told him:
and when he had called for Absalom, he came
to the king, and bowed himself on his face to
the ground before the king:
G³ (p. 427) and the king kissed Absalom.

Y² J l n (p. 428) 934 **15** And °it came to pass after this, that
Absalom prepared him chariots and
°horses, and fifty °men to °run before him.
2 And Absalom °rose up early, and stood beside the way of the gate: and it was *so*, that
when any ¹man that had a controversy came
to the king for judgment, then Absalom called
unto him, and said, "Of what city *art* thou?"
And he said, "Thy servant *is* of one of the
tribes of Israel."
3 And Absalom said unto him, "See, thy °mat-
ters *are* good and right; but *there is* °no man
deputed of the king to hear thee."
4 Absalom said moreover, "Oh that I were
made judge in the land, that every ¹man which
hath any suit or cause might come unto me,
and I would do him justice!"
5 And it was *so*, that when any ¹man came
nigh *to him* to do him obeisance, he put forth
his hand, and took him, and kissed him.
6 And on this manner did Absalom to all
Israel that came to the king for judgment:
o so Absalom stole the °hearts of the °men of
Israel.
m **7** And it came to pass after °forty years, that
Absalom said unto the king, "I pray thee, let
me go and pay °my vow, which I have vowed
unto °the LORD, in °Hebron.
8 For thy servant °vowed a vow while I abode
at Geshur in Syria, saying, 'If ⁷the LORD shall
bring me again indeed to Jerusalem, then I will
serve ⁷the LORD.'"
m **9** And the king said unto him, "Go in peace."
So he arose, and went to Hebron.
n **10** But Absalom sent spies throughout all the
tribes of Israel, saying, "As soon as ye hear the
sound of the trumpet, then ye shall say, 'Absalom reigneth in Hebron.'"
11 And with Absalom went two hundred ¹men
out of Jerusalem, *that were* called; and they
went in their simplicity, and they knew not
any thing.
12 And Absalom °sent for °Ahithophel the
Gilonite, David's counsellor, from °his city,
even from Giloh, while he °offered sacrifices.
And the conspiracy was strong; for the People
°increased continually with Absalom.
o **13** And there came a messenger to David,
saying, "The hearts of the ¹men of Israel are
after Absalom."
L p¹ **14** And David said unto all his servants that
were with him at Jerusalem, "Arise, and let
us flee; for we shall not *else* escape from Absalom: make speed to depart, lest he overtake us
suddenly, and bring °evil upon us, and smite
the °city with the edge of the sword."
15 And the king's servants said unto the king,
°"Behold, thy servants *are ready to do* whatsoever my lord the king shall °appoint."
16 And the king went forth, and all his household after him. And the king left ten women,
which were concubines, to keep the house.
17 And the king went forth, and all the People
after him, and tarried in °a place that was far
off.
18 And all his servants passed on beside him;
and all the Cherethites, and all the Pelethites,
and all the °Gittites, six hundred ¹men which

15. 1—19. 43 (Y², p. 424). ABSALOM'S REBELLION. (*Alternations, Simple and Extended*).

Y² | J | 15. 1-13. Rebellion made.
  K | L | 15. 14-37. David. Departure.
    M | 16. 1-14. Mephibosheth. Ziba. Shimei.
      N | 16. 15—17. 23. Jerusalem. Absalom's entry.
 J | 17. 24—19. 8. Rebellion quelled.
  K | *L* | 19. 9-15. David. Return.
    M | 19. 16-30. Mephibosheth. Shimei. Ziba.
      N | 19. 31-43. Jerusalem. David. Re-entry.

15. 1-13 (J, above). REBELLION MADE. (*Introversion and Alternation.*)

J | l | n | 1-6-. Machinations. } Treason (secret).
  o | -6. Their success. }
   m | 7, 8. Request. } Departure of Absalom.
   m | 9. Permission. }
 l | *n* | 10-12. Machinations. } Treason (open).
  o | 13. Their success. }

1 it came to pass. Cp. Ps. 3 and chs. 15—18. David was now fifty-six, Absalom twenty-four, Solomon six.
horses. A sign of his pride (Deut. 17. 16, 20).
men. Heb. *'īsh.* Ap. 14. II.
run before. To clear the way. Mark of royalty or dignity. (Still done in Cairo.) Cp. 1 Sam. 8. 11. 1 Kings 1. 5; 18. 46.
2 rose = used to rise, &c.
3 matters: i. e. plea, cause, or suit.
no man = no one.
6 hearts. Put by Fig. *Metonymy* (of Adjunct), Ap. 6, for affections and adhesion.
men. Heb. *'ěnōsh.* Ap. 14. III.
7 forty years: i. e. from David's anointing (1 Sam. 16. 13): i. e. 974–934.
my vow, which I have vowed. Fig. *Polyptōton* (Ap. 6) = my solemn vow.
the LORD. Heb. Jehovah. Ap. 4.
Hebron. Where he was born, and had friends.
8 vowed a vow = made a solemn vow. Fig. *Polyptōton.* Ap. 6.
12 sent for. Sept. reads "sent and called".
Ahithophel. David's counsellor. Cp. Ps. 41. 9; 55. 13. See note on "Uriah", 11. 3.
his city. Cp. Josh. 15. 51.
offered sacrifices. See Ap. 43. I. iv.
increased. Cp. Ps. 3. 1.

14-37 (L, above). DAVID'S DEPARTURE. (*Repeated Alternation.*)

L | p¹ | 14-22. Adherents. (Ittai.)
  q¹ | 23. Weeping of country.
 p² | 24-29. Adherents. (Zadok and sons.)
  q² | 30. Weeping of David.
 p³ | 31-. Defection. (Ahithophel.)
  q³ | -31. Prayer of David.
 p⁴ | 32-37. Adherents. (Hushai.)

14 evil. Heb. *rā'a'.* Ap. 44. viii.
city. Put by Fig. *Metonymy* (of Subject), for its inhabitants. Ap. 6.
15 Behold. Fig. *Asterismos.* Ap. 6.
appoint = choose.
17 a place that was far off. Heb. *Beth-hammerḥāh.* Probably a proper name.
18 Gittites. From Gath, the city of Goliath, now David's choicest followers.

934 came after him from Gath, passed on before the king.

19 Then said the king to Ittai the Gittite, "Wherefore goest thou also with us? return to thy place, and abide with the king: for thou *art* a °stranger, and also an exile.

20 Whereas thou camest *but* yesterday, should I this day make thee go up and down with us? seeing I go whither I may, return thou, and take back thy brethren: °mercy and °truth *be* with thee."

21 And Ittai answered the king, and said, "*As* [7]the LORD liveth, and *as* my lord the king liveth, surely in what place my lord the king shall be, whether in death or life, even there also will thy servant be."

22 And David said to Ittai, "Go and pass over." And Ittai the Gittite passed over, and all his [6]men, and all the little ones that *were* with him.

q[1] (p. 428) 23 And °all the °country wept with a loud voice, and all the People passed over: the king also himself passed over the brook Kidron, and all the People passed over, toward the way of the wilderness.

p[2] 24 And °lo Zadok also, and all the Levites *were* with him, bearing the ark of the covenant of °God: and they set down the ark of °God; and Abiathar went up, until all the people had done passing out of the city.

25 And the king said unto Zadok, "Carry back the ark of [24]God into the city: °if I shall find favour in the eyes of [7]the LORD, He will bring me again, and shew me *both* it, and His habitation:

26 But if He thus say, 'I have no delight in thee;' [15]behold, *here am* I, let Him do to me °as seemeth good unto Him."

27 The king said also unto Zadok the priest, "*Art not* thou a seer? return into the city in peace, and your two sons with you, Ahimaaz thy son, and Jonathan the son of Abiathar.

28 °See, I will tarry in the plain of the wilderness, until there come word from you to certify me."

29 Zadok therefore and Abiathar carried the ark of [25]God again to Jerusalem: and they tarried there.

q[2] 30 And David went up by the ascent of *mount* °Olivet, and °wept as he went up, and had his °head covered, and he went °barefoot: and all the People that *was* with him covered [1]every man his head, and they went up, weeping as they went up.

p[3] 31 And *one* °told David, saying, "Ahithophel *is* among the conspirators with Absalom."

q[3] And David said, "O [7]LORD, I pray thee, °turn the counsel of Ahithophel into foolishness."

p[4] 32 And it came to pass, that *when* David was come to °the top *of the mount*, where he worshipped °God, °behold, °Hushai the °Archite came to meet him with his °coat rent, and earth upon his head:

33 Unto whom David said, "If thou passest on with me, then thou shalt be a burden unto me:

34 But if thou return to the city, and say unto Absalom, 'I will be thy servant, O king; *as* I *have been* thy father's servant hitherto, so *will* I now also *be* thy servant:' then mayest thou for me defeat the counsel of Ahithophel.

35 And °*hast thou* not there with thee Zadok and Abiathar the priests? therefore it shall be, *that* what thing soever thou shalt hear out of the king's house, thou shalt tell *it* to Zadok and Abiathar the priests.

36 [32]Behold, *they have* there with them their two sons, Ahimaaz Zadok's *son*, and Jonathan Abiathar's *son*; and by them ye shall send unto me every thing that ye can hear."

37 So Hushai David's friend came into the city, and Absalom came into Jerusalem.

16 And when David was a little past the °top *of the hill*, °behold, Ziba the servant of °Mephibosheth met him, with a couple of asses saddled, and upon them two hundred *loaves* of bread, and an hundred bunches of M r (p. 429)

19 stranger = foreigner.

20 mercy = lovingkindness, or grace.

truth = faithfulness. Sept. and Syr. read "Jehovah will deal with thee in lovingkindness and faithfulness".

23 all: i. e. all the country round him. Fig. *Synecdoche* (of the Whole). Ap. 6.

country. Put by Fig. *Metonymy* (of Subject) for the people. Fig. *Prosopopœia*. Ap. 6.

24 lo. Fig. *Asterismos.* Ap. 6.

God = ha-Elohim (with art.) = the [triune] God. Ap. 4. I.

25 if I shall find favour, &c. God's grace is the basis of all blessing. Cp. Num. 14. 8. Deut. 10. 15. 2 Sam. 22. 20. 1 Kings 10. 9. 2 Chron. 9. 8. Ps. 18. 19; 41. 11; 86. 2 (marg). Acts 7. 46.

26 as = according as.

28 See. Fig. *Asterismos.* Ap. 6.

30 Olivet. Name due to the Vulg. *Oliveti* in Acts 1. 12.

wept. Cp. Luke 19. 41.

head covered. Symbol for self-condemnation.

barefoot. Symbol of mourning. Isa. 20. 2, 4. Ezek. 24. 17.

31 told David. The news came when the trial was greatest. Cp. Ps. 41. 9 and 55. 12-14.

turn, &c. Cp. Pss. 41; 55; 69; 109.

32 the top. Doubtless a high place where God was worshipped. Nob was near where the Tabernacle once stood.

God. Heb. Elohim. Ap. 4. I.

behold. Fig. *Asterismos.* Ap. 6.

Hushai. David's friend. Cp. *v.* 37; 16. 16. 1 Chron. 27. 33.

Archite. Probably = a native of Archi, on frontier of Benjamin and Ephraim.

coat = the long tunic with sleeves.

35 hast thou not . . .? Fig. *Erotēsis.* Ap. 6.

16. 1-14 (M, p. 428). MEPHIBOSHETH, ZIBA, &c. (*Introversion.*)

M | r | 1, 2. Refreshment brought.
  | s | 3, 4. Slander of Ziba.
  | *s* | 5-13. Imprecations of Shimei.
  | *r* | 14. Refreshment partaken of.

1 top. Cp. 15. 32.

behold. Fig. *Asterismos.* Ap. 6.

Mephibosheth. Now thirty-one. Born in 965. Cp. 4. 4.

934 raisins, and an hundred of summer fruits, and
a ° bottle of ° wine.
2 And the king said unto Ziba, "What meanest thou by these?" And Ziba said, "The asses *be* for the king's household to ride on; and the bread and summer fruit for the young men to eat; and the wine, that such as be faint in the wilderness may drink."

s 3 And the king said, "And where *is* thy mas-
(p. 429) ter's son?" And Ziba said unto the king, [1] "Be-
hold, he abideth at Jerusalem: for ° he said, 'To day shall the house of Israel restore me the kingdom of my father.'"
4 Then said the king to Ziba, [1] "Behold, thine *are* all that *pertained* unto Mephibosheth." And Ziba said, "I humbly beseech thee *that* I may find grace in thy sight, my lord, O king."

s t 5 And when king David came to ° Bahurim,
(p. 430) [1] behold, thence came out a ° man of the family
of the house of Saul, whose name *was* Shimei, the son of Gera: he came forth, and cursed still as he came.
6 And he cast stones at David, and at all the servants of king David: and all the People and all the mighty men *were* on his right hand and on his left.
7 And thus said Shimei when he cursed, "Come out, ° come out, thou ° bloody [5] man, and ° thou [5] man of Belial:
8 ° The LORD hath returned upon thee all the blood of the house of Saul, in whose stead thou hast reigned; and ° the LORD hath delivered the kingdom into the hand of Absalom thy son: and, [1] behold, thou *art taken* in thy mischief, because thou *art* a [7] bloody [5] man."

u 9 Then said Abishai the son of Zeruiah unto
the king, "Why should this ° dead dog curse my lord the king? ° let me go over, I pray thee, and take off his head."

u 10 And the king said, ° "What have I to do
with you, ye ° sons of Zeruiah? so ° let him curse, because [8] the LORD hath said unto him, 'Curse David.' ° Who shall then say, 'Wherefore hast thou done so?'"
11 And David said to Abishai, and to all his servants, ° "Behold, my son, which came forth of my bowels, seeketh my ° life: ° how much more now *may this* Benjamite *do it?* let him alone, and let him curse; for [8] the LORD hath bidden him.
12 It may be that [8] the LORD will ° look on mine affliction, and that [8] the LORD will ° requite me good for his cursing this day."

t 13 And as David and his ° men went by the
way, Shimei went along on the hill's side over against him, and cursed as he went, and threw stones at him, and ° cast dust.

r 14 And the king, and all the People that *were*
(p. 429) with him, came ° weary and refreshed themselves there.

N v 15 And Absalom, and all the People the [5] men
(p. 430) of Israel, came to Jerusalem, and Ahithophel
with him.
16 And it came to pass, when Hushai the Archite, David's friend, was come unto Absalom, that Hushai said unto Absalom, "God save the king, God save the king."

bottle = skin-bottle (Josh. 9. 4. Matt. 9. 17).
wine. Heb. *yayin*. See Ap. 27. I.
3 he said. This was slander. See 19. 24–30, and cp. the two Structures.

16. 5–13 (*s*, p. 429). IMPRECATION OF SHIMEI.
(*Introversion.*)

s | t | 5–8. Imprecations.
  u | 9. Resentment of Abishai.
  u | 10–12. Forbearance of David.
  t | 13. Imprecations.

5 Bahurim. On east side of Olivet; "in tribe of Benjamin".
man. Heb. *'ish*. Ap. 14. II.
7 come out. Fig. *Epizeuxis* (Ap. 6): i.e. out = Begone! or Get out!
bloody man = man of bloods (pl. denoting much blood).
thou man of Belial. Cp. 1 Sam. 1. 16; 10. 27.
8 the LORD. Heb. Jehovah. Ap. 4. II.
9 dead dog. Fig. *Antiprosopopœia*. Ap. 6. Cp. 1 Sam. 17. 43.
let me go. Cp. 1 Sam. 26. 8.
10 What have I to do . . . ? First occurrence of this idiom. Fig. *Erotēsis* (Ap. 6). Cp. 19. 22. 1 Kings 17. 18. 2 Kings 3. 13. Matt. 8. 29. Mark 1. 24. Luke 4. 34. John 2. 4.
sons of Zeruiah. Cp. 3. 39 and Luke 9. 55.
let him curse. Uriah's murder closed David's mouth (12. 9).
Who shall then . . . ? Fig. *Erotēsis*. Ap. 6.
11 Behold. Fig. *Asterismos*. Ap. 6.
life = soul. Heb. *nephesh*. Ap. 13.
how much . . . ? Fig. *Erotēsis*. Ap. 6.
12 look on mine affliction. This is one of the eighteen emendations of the *Sōpherīm* (Ap. 33). The primitive text reads "Jehovah will behold with His eye". This was thought to be too anthropomorphic, and so was altered, and the alteration recorded.
requite. Cp. Ps. 109. 26–28.
13 men. Heb. *'ĕnōsh*. Ap. 14. III.
cast dust. Heb. "dusted him with dust". Fig. *Polyptōton* (Ap. 6): i.e. cast much dust.
14 weary. Heb. *'Ăyiphīm*. Perhaps the name of a place, or of a caravansary with that name, "for the weary".

16. 15–17. 23 (N, p. 428). JERUSALEM. ABSALOM'S ENTRY. (*Introversion.*)

N | v | 16. 15–19. Hushai's mission. Ahithophel's defeat.
  w | 16. 20–17. 4. Ahithophel. Counsel given.
  x | 17. 5–13. Hushai. Counsel given.
  x | 17. 14. Hushai. Counsel taken.
  w | 17. 15–22. Ahithophel. Counsel reported.
  v | 17. 23. Hushai's success. Ahithophel's death.

18 choose = hath chosen.

17 And Absalom said to Hushai, "*Is* this thy kindness to thy friend? why wentest thou not with thy friend?"
18 And Hushai said unto Absalom, "Nay; but whom [8] the LORD, and this People, and all the [5] men of Israel, ° choose, his will I be, and with him will I abide.
19 And again, whom should I serve? *should I* not *serve* in the presence of his son? as I have served in thy father's presence, so will I be in thy presence."

20 Then said Absalom to Ahithophel, "Give w
counsel among you what we shall do."

934 21 And Ahithophel ° said unto Absalom, "Go
in unto thy father's concubines, which he hath
left to keep the house; and all Israel shall hear
that thou art abhorred of thy father: then
shall the hands of all that *are* with thee be
strong."
22 So they spread Absalom a tent upon ° the
top of the house; and Absalom went in unto
his father's concubines in the sight of all Israel.
23 And the counsel of Ahithophel, which he
counselled in those days, *was* ° as if a [5]man had
enquired at the ° oracle of [16]God: so *was* all
the counsel of Ahithophel both with David and
with Absalom.

17 Moreover Ahithophel said unto Absalom,
"Let me now ° choose out twelve thousand ° men, and ° I will arise and pursue after
David ° this night:
2 And [1]I will come upon him while he *is* weary
and weak handed, and will make him afraid:
and all the People that *are* with him shall flee;
and I will smite the king only:
3 And I will bring back all the People unto
thee: the [1]man whom thou seekest *is* as if all
returned: *so* all the People shall be in peace."
4 And the saying ° pleased Absalom well,
° and all the elders of Israel.

x (p. 430) 5 Then said Absalom, ° "Call now Hushai the
Archite also, and let us hear likewise what he
saith."
6 And when Hushai was come to Absalom,
Absalom spake unto him, saying, "Ahithophel
hath spoken after this manner: shall we do
after his saying? if not; speak thou."
7 And Hushai said unto Absalom, "The ° counsel that Ahithophel hath ° given *is* not good at
this time.
8 For," said Hushai, "thou knowest thy father
and his ° men, that they *be* ° mighty men, and
they *be* ° chafed in their ° minds, as a bear
robbed of her whelps in the field: and thy
father *is* a [1]man of war, and will not lodge
with the People.
9 ° Behold, he is hid now in some pit, or in
some *other* place: and it will come to pass,
when some of them be overthrown at the first,
that whosoever heareth it will say, 'There is
a slaughter among the people that follow Absalom.'
10 And he also *that is* valiant, whose heart *is*
as the heart of a lion, shall utterly melt: for
all Israel knoweth that thy father *is* a [8]mighty
man, and *they* which *be* with him *are* ° valiant
men.
11 Therefore I counsel that all Israel be generally gathered unto thee, from Dan even to Beer-
sheba, ° as the sand that *is* by the sea for
multitude; and that ° thou go ° to battle ° in
thine own person.
12 So shall we come upon him in some place
where he shall be found, and we will light
upon him ° as the dew falleth on the ground:
and of him and of all the [8]men that *are* with
him there shall not be left so much as one.
13 Moreover, if he be gotten into a city, then
shall all Israel bring ropes to that city, and we
will draw it into the river, until there be not
one small stone found there."

x 14 And Absalom and all the [1]men of Israel
said, "The counsel of Hushai the Archite *is*
better than the counsel of Ahithophel." For
° the LORD had appointed to defeat the good
counsel of Ahithophel, to the intent that ° the
LORD might bring ° evil upon Absalom.

15 Then said Hushai unto Zadok and to *w*
Abiathar the priests, "Thus and thus did Ahithophel counsel Absalom and the elders of
Israel; and thus and thus have I counselled.
16 Now therefore send quickly, and tell David,
saying, 'Lodge not this night in the plains of
the wilderness, but speedily pass over; lest the
king be swallowed up, and all the People that
are with him.'"
17 Now Jonathan and Ahimaaz stayed by
° En-rogel; for they might not be seen to come
into the city: and ° a wench went and told
them; and they went and told king David.
18 Nevertheless a lad saw them, and told Absalom: but they went both of them away

21 said. Instigated by feelings of private revenge against David for his sin with Bath-sheba; she being the daughter of his son, Eliam. See 23. 34. Cp. 11. 3. Foretold by Nathan (12. 11, 12).
22 the top of the house. Cp. 11. 2.
23 as = according as.
oracle = word. The first occurrence of "oracle" as a rendering (fifteen times) of *dābār*, word. The holy of holies, because there the word of Jehovah was heard. Other occurrences: see 1 Kings 6. 5, 16, 19, 20, 22, 23, 31; 8. 6, 8. 2 Chron. 3. 16; 4. 20; 5. 7, 9. Ps. 28. 2 Cp. N.T. usage in plural: Acts 7. 38. Rom. 3. 2. Heb. 5. 12. 1 Pet. 4. 11.

17. 1 choose out. Sept. and Vulg. read "choose for myself". **men.** Heb. *'ish.* Ap. 14. II.
I will. Ahithophel manifests personal vengeance. See note on 16. 21 and 17. 11.
this night. Cp. Ps. 4. 8. Ps. 4 is concerning inheritances. David's was in jeopardy (*v.* 2), but his trust was in Jehovah's favour (15. 25; 22. 20. Ps. 18. 19).
4 pleased = was good in the eyes of.
and = and [in the eyes of] all.
5 Call now. Heb. = "Call thou" (cp. "thou", *v.* 6); but Sept. and Vulg. read "Call ye".
7 counsel . . . given. Heb. counsel . . . counselled. Fig. *Polyptōton* (Ap. 6) = the good counsel (but "not good" now).
8 men. Heb. *'ĕnōsh.* Ap. 14. III.
mighty men. Heb. *gibbōrim.* Ap. 14. IV.
chafed = bitter.
minds = souls. Heb. *nephesh.* Ap. 13.
9 Behold. Fig. *Asterismos.* Ap. 6.
10 valiant men = sons of valour.
11 as. Fig. *Parœmia.* Ap. 6.
thou = thou thyself. Heb. "thy face". Fig. *Synecdoche* (of Part), Ap. 6, put to emphasise the whole person.
to battle. Heb. *kārāb*, never used of battle (which is *milḥāmāh*). *Biḳkrab*, rendered "to battle", is an abbreviation for *b^ekirbah* = "in the midst of them", which is the reading of the Sept. and Vulg.
in thine own person. By all this emphasis Hushai represents Ahithophel's personal malice (which need not disturb Absalom) as being personal pride aimed against Absalom. See *vv.* 1–3, "I will arise"; "I will come"; "I will smite"; "I will bring back", &c.
12 as = according as.
14 the LORD. Heb. Jehovah. Ap. 4. II.
evil = the evil. Heb. *rā'a'.* Ap. 44. viii.
17 En-rogel. Now the Virgin's Fount, on east side of Ophel, or Jebus, from which the *Zinnor* runs up to the citadel. See note on 5. 8. Cp. Josh. 15. 7; 18. 16, and Ap 68, on "Zion".
a wench = a maidservant. Cp. Matt. 26. 69. Mark 14. 66. Luke 22. 56. John 18. 17.

934 quickly, and came to a [1]man's house in Bahurim, which had a well in his court; whither they °went down.

19 And the woman took and spread a covering over the well's mouth, and spread ground corn thereon; and the thing was not known.

20 And when Absalom's servants came to the woman to the house, they said, "Where *is* Ahimaaz and Jonathan?" And the woman °said unto them, "They be gone over the brook of water." And when they had sought and could not find *them*, they returned to Jerusalem.

21 And it came to pass, after they were departed, that they came up out of the well, and went and told king David, and said unto David, "Arise, and pass quickly over the water: for thus hath Ahithophel counselled against you."

22 Then David arose, and all the People that *were* with him, and they passed over °Jordan: by the morning light there lacked not one of them that was not gone over Jordan.

v (p. 430) **23** And when Ahithophel saw that his counsel was not followed, he saddled *his* ass, and arose, and gat him home to his house, to his city, and °put his household in order, and °hanged himself, and died, and was buried in the sepulchre of his father.

J O¹ y (p. 432) **24** Then David came to Mahanaim.

z And Absalom passed over Jordan, he and °all the [1]men of Israel with him.

25 And Absalom °made Amasa °captain of the host instead of Joab: which Amasa *was* a [1]man's son, whose name *was* °Ithra an Israelite, that °went in to °Abigail the daughter of Nahash, °sister to Zeruiah Joab's mother.

26 So Israel and Absalom pitched in the land of Gilead.

y **27** And it came to pass, when David was come to Mahanaim, that Shobi the son of °Nahash of Rabbah of the children of Ammon, and °Machir the son of Ammiel of Lo-debar, and Barzillai the Gileadite of Rogelim,

28 Brought beds, °and basons, and earthen vessels, and wheat, and barley, and flour, and parched *corn*, and beans, and lentiles, and parched *pulse*,

29 And honey, and °butter, and sheep, and cheese of kine, for David, and for the People that *were* with him, to eat: for they said, "The People *is* hungry, and weary, and thirsty, in the wilderness."

z **18** And David °numbered the People that *were* with him, and set captains of thousands and captains of hundreds over them.

2 And David sent forth a third part of the People under the hand of Joab, and a third part under the hand of Abishai the son of Zeruiah, Joab's brother, and a third part under the hand of Ittai the Gittite. And the king said unto the People, "I will surely go forth with you myself also."

3 But the People answered, "Thou shalt not go forth: for if we flee away, they will not care for us; neither if half of us die, will they care for us: but now *thou art* worth ten thousand of us: therefore now *it is* better that thou °succour us out of the city."

4 And the king said unto them, "What seemeth you best I will do." And the king stood by the gate side, and all the People came out by hundreds and by thousands.

5 And the king commanded Joab and Abishai and Ittai, saying, "*Deal* gently for my sake with the young man, *even* with Absalom." And all the People °heard when the king gave all the captains charge concerning Absalom.

6 So the People went out into the field against Israel: and the battle was in the °wood of Ephraim; P a

7 Where the People of Israel were slain before the servants of David, and there was there a great slaughter that day of twenty thousand *men*.

---

18 went down. Wells mostly dry in summer.

20 said. Probably misdirecting them.

22 Jordan. Cp. Pss. 42. 6 and 43; both Pss. referring to this period.

23 put his household in order = gave charge unto his household.

hanged himself. Not so much because his counsel was not taken, but because his revenge was not taken on David (see note on 11. 3; 16. 21, and 17. 1), and that the conspiracy must fail. Same word in Matt. 27. 5 as in Sept. here (*apēgxatō*), as though to invite the comparison of Judas with Ahithophel.

17. 24—18. 5 (*J*, p. 428). REBELLION QUELLED. (*Introversion.*)

J | O¹ | 17. 24—18. 5. Mahanaim. David. Preparation.
  P | 18. 6-18. The battle.
  O² | 18. 19—19. 8. Mahanaim. David. Report to.

17. 24—18. 5 (O¹, above). MAHANAIM, &c. (*Alternation.*)

O¹ | y | 17. 24-. Mahanaim. Arrival.
  z | 17. -24-26. Camp of Absalom.
  y | 17. 27-29. Mahanaim. Refreshments.
  z | 18. 1-5. Camp of David.

24 all. Fig. *Synecdoche* (of Genus). Ap. 6. The whole put for the greater part

25 made = set, or appointed.

captain of = captain over.

Ithra an Israelite = Jether an Ishmeelite. See 1 Chron. 2. 17.

went in to. Probably meaning seduced. If so, it would be during David's stay in Moab (1 Sam. 22. 3, 4).

Abigail. David was probably half-brother to Abigail and Zeruiah, having the same mother; he having Jesse for his father, they having Nahash.

sister to Zeruiah. Implying that she was not sister to David.

27 Nahash. Cp. 10. 2.

Machir. He had brought up Mephibosheth. Cp. 9. 5.

28 and. Note the Fig. *Polysyndeton* (Ap. 6) in *vv.* 28 and 29, emphasising the items.

29 butter. Scarce in Lo-debar. Cp. 9. 4. The word means place of "no pasture".

18. 1 numbered = mustered, or inspected. David was now fifty-six.

3 succour us out of the city = come to us out of the city with succour by prayer and counsel.

5 heard. This explains *v.* 12.

6-18 (P, above). THE BATTLE. (*Alternation.*)

P | a | 6-8. The battle. Fought.
  b | 9-15. Absalom. Death.
  a | 16. The battle. Return from.
  b | 17, 18. Absalom. Burial.

6 wood of Ephraim. Cp. Josh. 17. 15-18.

933 **8 For the battle was there scattered over °the face of all the country: and the wood °devoured more people that day than the sword devoured.**

b (p. 432) **9 And Absalom met the servants of David. And Absalom rode upon a mule, and the mule went under the thick boughs of a great oak, and his head caught hold of the oak, and he was °taken up between the heaven and the earth; and the mule that *was* under him went away.**

10 And a certain °man saw *it*, and told Joab, and said, °"Behold, I saw Absalom hanged in an oak."

11 And Joab said unto the [10]man that told him, "And, [10]behold, thou sawest *him*, and why didst thou not smite him there to the ground? and I would have given thee ten *shekels* of silver, and a °girdle."

12 And the [10]man said unto Joab, "Though I should receive a thousand *shekels* of silver in mine hand, *yet* would I not put forth mine hand against the king's son: for in °our hearing the king charged thee and Abishai and Ittai, saying, °'Beware that none *touch* the young man Absalom.'

13 Otherwise I should have wrought falsehood against mine own °life: for there is no matter hid from the king, and thou thyself wouldest have set thyself against *me*."

14 Then said Joab, "I may not tarry thus with thee." And he took three °darts in his hand, and thrust them through the heart of Absalom, while he *was* yet alive in the midst of the oak.

15 And ten young men that bare Joab's °armour compassed about and smote Absalom,
933 **and °slew him.**

a **16 And Joab blew the trumpet, and the People returned from pursuing after Israel: for Joab held back the People.**

b **17 And they took Absalom, and cast him into a great pit in the wood, and laid a very great °heap of stones upon him: and all Israel fled every one to his tent.**

18 (Now Absalom in his lifetime had taken and reared up for himself a °pillar, which *is* in the king's dale: for he said, "I have °no son to keep my name in remembrance:" and he called the °pillar after his own name: and it is called unto this day, Absalom's °place.)

Q^1 R c (p. 433) **19 Then said Ahimaaz the son of Zadok, "Let me now run, and bear the king tidings, how that °the LORD hath avenged him of his enemies."**

d **20 And Joab said unto him, "Thou shalt not bear tidings this day, but thou shalt bear tidings another day: but this day thou shalt bear no tidings, because the king's son is dead."**

e **21 Then said Joab to Cushi, "Go tell the king what thou hast seen." And Cushi bowed himself unto Joab, and ran.**

c **22 Then said Ahimaaz the son of Zadok yet again to Joab, "But howsoever, let me, I pray thee, also run after Cushi."**

d **And Joab said, "Wherefore wilt thou run, my son, seeing that thou hast no tidings ready?"**

23 "But howsoever," *said he*, "let me run." And he said unto him, "Run." Then Ahimaaz ran by the way of the plain, and overran Cushi. e

24 And David sat °between the two gates: S

and the watchman went up to the roof over the gate unto the wall, and lifted up his eyes, and looked, and [10]behold a [10]man running alone. *R* f

25 And the watchman cried, and told the king. And the king said, °"If he *be* alone, *there is* tidings in his mouth." And he came apace, and drew near.

26 And the watchman saw another [10]man running: and the watchman called unto the g

---

8 the face. Fig. *Pleonasm*, with *Prosopopœia*. Ap. 6.
devoured. Heb. "multiplied to devour", to emphasise the great number. Fig. *Prosopopœia*. Ap. 6.
9 taken up. The tradition about his "hair" comes from Josephus (VII. 10. 2).
10 man. Heb. *'ish*. Ap. 14. II.
Behold. Fig. *Asterismos*. Ap. 6.
11 girdle. A common present, made of silk, linen, or leather, and worked sometimes in gold. Used for fastening up loose garments.
12 our hearing. See *v.* 5.
Beware that none touch = Watch any one who [would touch] the, &c. After "Watch", Sept., Aram., Syr., and Vulg. add "for my sake", as in *v.* 5.
13 life = soul. Heb. *nephesh*. Ap. 13.
14 darts = clubs. Heb. *shēbet*, a club with a long spike at the end. Still used in Palestine.
15 armour = weapons.
slew him. David being fifty-seven years old; Absalom, twenty-four; Solomon, seven.
17 heap of stones. Not a memorial to honour but to warn (Josh. 7. 26; 8. 29). See note on *v.* 18.
18 pillar. Marks ambition's aim, while the heap of stones (*v.* 17) marks ambition's end.
no son. Cp. 14. 27. Therefore built before the first-born; or after his sons (14. 27) were dead.
place = monument. About a quarter of a mile east of Jerusalem, in the Valley of Jehoshaphat.
19 the LORD. Heb. Jehovah. Ap. 4. II.

18. 19—19. 8 (O^2, p. 432). MAHANAIM. REPORT. (*Division.*)

O^2 | Q^1 | 18. 19-33. Sorrow indulged.
| Q^2 | 19. 1-8. Sorrow restrained.

19-33 (Q^1, above). SORROW INDULGED. (*Alternation.*)

Q^1 | R | 19-23. Tidings borne.
S | 24-. David's seat.
R | -24-32. Tidings delivered.
S | 33. David's lamentation.

24 between the two gates. The outer and inner gates of the city wall.

19-23 (R, above). TIDINGS BORNE (*Extended Alternation.*)

R | c | 19. Request (Cushi).
d | 20. Refusal.
e | 21. Permission.
c | 22-. Request (Ahimaaz).
d | -22. Reluctance.
e | 23. Permission.

-24-32 (*R*, above). TIDINGS DELIVERED. (*Alternation.*)

R | f | -24, 25. The first runner.
g | 26. The second runner.
f | 27-30. Name of first, Ahimaaz.
g | 31, 32. Name of second, Cushi.

25 If he be alone. Otherwise it would be flight.

933 °porter, and said, [24] "Behold *another* [10] man
running alone." And the king said, "He also
bringeth tidings."

f (p. 433) 27 And the watchman said, "Me thinketh
the running of the foremost is like the running
of Ahimaaz the son of Zadok." And the king
said, "He *is* a °good [10] man, and cometh with
°good tidings."

28 And Ahimaaz called, and said unto the
king, "All is well." And he fell down to the
earth upon his face before the king, and said,
°"Blessed *be* [19] the LORD thy °God, Which hath
delivered up the °men that lifted up their hand
against my lord the king."

29 And the king said, "*Is* the young man
Absalom safe?" And Ahimaaz answered,
"When Joab sent the king's servant, °and *me*
thy servant, I saw a great tumult, but I knew
not °what *it was*."

30 And the king said *unto him*, "Turn aside,
and stand here." And he turned aside, and
stood still.

g 31 And, [10] behold, Cushi came; and Cushi
said, "Tidings, my lord the king: for [19] the
LORD hath avenged thee this day of all them
that rose up against thee."

32 And the king said unto Cushi, "*Is* the
young man Absalom safe?" And Cushi answered,
"The enemies of my lord the king,
and all that rise against thee to do *thee* hurt,
°be as *that* young man *is*."

S 33 And the king was much moved, and went
up to the chamber over the gate, and wept:
and as he went, thus he said, "O °my son
Absalom, my son, °my son Absalom! would
[28] God I had died °for thee, O Absalom, °my
son, °my son!"

Q^2 h^1 (p. 434) **19** And it was told Joab, °"Behold, the
king weepeth and mourneth for Absalom."

i^1 2 And the victory that day was *turned* into
mourning unto all the People: for the People
heard say that day how the king was grieved
for his son.

3 And the People gat them by stealth that
day into the city, °as people being ashamed
steal away when they flee in battle.

h^2 4 But the king °covered his face, and the
king cried with a loud voice, "O °my son Absalom,
O Absalom, °my son, °my son!"

i^2 5 And Joab came into the house to the king,
and said, "Thou hast shamed this day the
faces of all thy servants, which this day have
saved thy °life, °and the °lives of thy sons and
of thy daughters, and the °lives of thy wives,
and the °lives of thy concubines;

6 In that thou lovest thine enemies, and
hatest thy friends. For thou hast °declared
this day, that thou regardest neither princes
nor servants: for this day I perceive, that if
Absalom had lived, and all we had died this
day, then it had pleased thee well.

7 °Now therefore arise, go forth, and speak
°comfortably unto thy servants: for I swear by
°the LORD, if thou go not forth, there will not
tarry one with thee this night: and that will
be worse unto thee than all the evil that befell
thee from thy youth until °now."

8 Then the king arose, and sat in the gate. h^3
And they told unto all the People, saying,
"Behold, the king doth sit in the gate." And
all the People came before the king: for °Israel
had fled every °man to his tent.

9 And all the People were at strife through- L
out all the tribes of Israel, saying, "The king
saved us out of the hand of our enemies, and
He delivered us out of the hand of the Philistines;
and now he is fled out of the land for
Absalom.

10 And Absalom, whom we anointed over us,
is dead in battle. Now therefore why speak
ye not a word of bringing °the king back?"

11 And king David sent to Zadok and to k
Abiathar the priests, saying, "Speak unto the
elders of Judah, saying, 'Why are ye the last
to bring the king back to his house? seeing

---

26 porter = gatekeeper. No gates without the "Bawab" or gatekeeper. Cp. 2 Kings 7. 17. 1 Chron. 9. 21.

27 good. Cp. 1 Kings 1. 42.

28 Blessed be the LORD thy God. Some codices, with three early printed editions, reverse the order, thus changing the emphasis, and read: "Jehovah thy God be blessed".

God. Heb. Elohim. Ap. 4. I.

men. Heb. *'ěnōsh.* Ap. 14. III.

29 and = even.

what it was = what [it meant].

32 be as that young man. Fig. *Euphemism.* Ap. 6.

33 my son . . . my son. Fig. *Epizeuxis.* Ap. 6.

for = instead of.

19. 1-8 (Q^2, p. 433). SORROW RESTRAINED.
(*Repeated Alternation.*)

Q^2 | h^1 | 1. Mourning of David.
  i^1 | 2, 3. People. Sympathy with the king.
 h^2 | 4. Mourning of David.
  i^2 | 5-7. Joab. Remonstrance with the king.
 h^3 | 8. Mourning of David and People.

1 Behold. Fig. *Asterismos.* Ap. 6.

3 as = according as.

4 covered his face. Symbol of mourning. Occurs only here.

my son . . . my son. Fig. *Epizeuxis.* Ap. 6. Cp. 18. 33.

5 life . . . lives = soul . . . souls. Heb. *nephesh.* Ap. 13.

and. Note the Fig. *Polysyndeton.* Ap. 6.

6 declared = made clear.

7 Now. Note the Fig. *Epanadiplosis* (Ap. 6), to emphasise the completeness of Joab's reasoning.

comfortably. Heb. *'al-lēb,* to the heart. Cp. Isa. 40. 2.

the LORD. Heb. Jehovah. Ap. 4. II.

8 Israel. Note this name for Absalom's forces (17. 24, 26; 18. 6, 7).

man. Heb. *'īsh.* Ap. 14. II.

9-15 (L, p. 428). DAVID. RETURN.
(*Introversion.*)

L | j | 9, 10. King's return. Desired.
  k | 11, 12. Message to Judah.
  k | 13. Message to Amasa.
 j | 14, 15. King's return. Accomplished.

10 the king. Note the Fig. *Anadiplosis* (Ap. 6), "bringing back the king. And the king".

933 the speech of all Israel is come to the king, *even* to his house.
12 Ye *are* my brethren, ye *are* my bones and my flesh: wherefore then are ye the last to bring back the king?'

k (p. 434) 13 And say ye to Amasa, °'*Art* thou not of
° my bone, and of my flesh? °God do so to me, and more also, if thou be not captain of the host before me continually in the room of Joab.'"

j 14 And he bowed the heart of all the [8]men of Judah, even as *the heart of* one [8]man; so that they sent *this word* unto the king, "Return thou, and all thy servants."
15 So the king returned, and came to Jordan. And Judah came to °Gilgal, °to go to meet the king, to conduct the king over Jordan.

M l (p. 435) 16 And °Shimei the son of Gera, °a Benjamite, which *was* of Bahurim, hasted and came down with the [8]men of Judah to meet king David.

m 17 And *there were* a thousand [8]men of Benjamin with him, and Ziba the servant of the house of Saul, and his fifteen sons and his twenty servants with him; and they went over Jordan before the king.
18 And there went over a ferry boat to carry over the king's household, and to do what he thought good.

l n And Shimei the son of Gera fell down before the king, as he was come over Jordan;
19 And said unto the king, "Let not my lord impute °iniquity unto me, neither do thou remember that which thy servant did perversely the day that my lord the king went out of Jerusalem, that the king should take it to his heart.
20 For thy servant doth know that I have sinned: therefore, [1]behold, I am come the first this day of all the house of °Joseph [15]to go down to meet my lord the king."

o 21 But °Abishai the son of Zeruiah answered and said, "Shall not Shimei be put to death for this, because he cursed [7]the LORD's anointed?"

o 22 And David said, °"What have I to do with you, ye sons of Zeruiah, that ye should this day be °adversaries unto me? °shall there any [8]man be put to death this day in Israel? °for do not I know that I *am* this day king over Israel?"

n 23 Therefore the king said unto Shimei, "Thou shalt not die." And the king sware unto him.

m p 24 And Mephibosheth the °son of Saul came down to meet the king, and had °neither dressed his feet, nor trimmed his beard, nor washed his clothes, from the day the king departed until the day he came *again* in peace.

q 25 And it came to pass, when he was come to Jerusalem to meet the king, that the king said unto him, "Wherefore wentest not thou with me, Mephibosheth?"

r 26 And he answered, "My lord, O king, my servant deceived me: for thy servant said, °'I will saddle me an ass, that I may ride thereon,

13 Art . . .? Fig. *Erotēsis*. Ap. 6.
my bone, &c.: i. e. my near relation = my nephew (17. 25). Son of David's sister Abigail (1 Chron. 2. 17.)
God. Heb. Elohim. Ap. 4. I.
15 Gilgal. Here Samuel renewed the kingdom. 1 Sam. 11. 14. Cp. Josh. 5. 9; 9. 6; 10. 6. 1 Sam. 7. 16; 15. 33.
to go. Some codices, with one early printed edition, read "to go down". Cp. *v.* 20.

19. 16-30 (*M*, p. 428). SHIMEI, ZIBA, AND MEPHIBOSHETH. (*Alternation.*)

M | l | 16. Shimei. Reception.
  m | 17, 18-. Ziba. Deception.
  l | -18-23. Shimei. Forgiveness.
  m | 24-30. Ziba. Discovery.

16 Shimei. Cp. 16. 5.
a = the. Evidently a prominent Benjamite.

-18-23 (*l*, above). SHIMEI. FORGIVEN. (*Introversion.*)

l | n | -18-20. Shimei. Confession.
  o | 21. Abishai. Resentment.
  o | 22. Abishai. Resented.
  n | 23. Shimei. Forgiveness.

19 iniquity. Heb. *'āvāh*. Ap. 44. iv.
20 Joseph. Put by Fig. *Metonymy* (of Adjunct) for the two tribes (Ephraim and Manasseh), or for the ten tribes, Israel (Amos 5. 6, 15; 6. 6. Obad. 18. Zech. 10. 6). Cp. *v.* 43. In Ps. 80. 1 and 81. 5, Joseph is put for the twelve tribes.
21 Abishai. Always impetuous. 1 Sam. 26. 8; 2 Sam. 16. 9.
22 What have I to do . . .? See note on 16. 10.
adversaries. Heb. Satan.
shall . . .? Fig. *Erotēsis*. Ap. 6.
for do not I . . .? Fig. *Erotēsis*. Ap. 6.

24-30 (*m*, above). ZIBA. DISCOVERY. (*Introversion.*)

m | p | 24. Mephibosheth. Mourning.
  q | 25. David. Reproach.
  r | 26. Ziba. Deception.
  r | 27, 28. Ziba. Slander.
  q | 29. David. Reparation.
  p | 30. Mephibosheth. Comfort.

24 son = grandson.
neither dressed, &c. A symbol and proof of great grief.
26 I will saddle. Sept. reads "Saddle for me the ass". A command which Ziba disobeyed, and went off himself instead. But was there only *one* ass in Jerusalem? See note on *v.* 29
to = with.
28 For all, &c. Some codices, with one early printed edition, read "When in all the house of my father were none other than dead men".
dead men. Heb. men of death: i. e. doomed men. Heb. *'ĕnōsh*. Ap. 14. III.
What right . . .? Fig. *Erotēsis* (Ap. 6), to emphasise the free grace of David.

and go °to the king;' because thy servant *is* lame.

27 And he hath slandered thy servant unto my lord the king; but my lord the king *is* as an angel of [13]God: do therefore *what is* good in thine eyes. *r*
28 °For all *of* my father's house were but °dead men before my lord the king: yet didst thou set thy servant among them that did eat at thine own table. °What right therefore have I yet to cry any more unto the king?"

q (p. 435) 933 29 And the king said unto him, °"Why speakest thou any more of thy matters? °I have said, °'Thou and Ziba divide °the land.'"

p 30 And Mephibosheth said unto the king, "Yea, let him take all, °forasmuch as my lord the king is come again in peace unto his own house."

N s (p. 436) 31 And Barzillai the Gileadite came down from Rogelim, and went over Jordan with the king, to conduct him over Jordan.

32 Now Barzillai was a very aged man, *even* fourscore years old: and he had provided the king of sustenance while he lay at Mahanaim; for he *was* a very great [8]man.

33 And the king said unto Barzillai, "Come thou over with me, and I will feed thee with me in Jerusalem."

34 And Barzillai said unto the king, °"How long have I to live, that I should go up with the king unto Jerusalem?

35 I *am* this day fourscore years old: *and* °can I discern between good and °evil? °can thy servant taste what I eat or what I drink? °can I hear any more the voice of singing men and singing women? wherefore then should thy servant be yet a burden unto my lord the king?

36 Thy servant will go a little way over Jordan with the king: and why should the king recompense it me with such a reward?

37 Let thy servant, I pray thee, turn back again, that I may die in mine own city, *and be buried* by the grave of my father and of my mother. But [1]behold thy servant Chimham; let him go over with my lord the king; and do to him what shall seem good unto thee."

38 And the king answered, "Chimham shall go over with me, and I will do to him that which shall seem good unto thee: and whatsoever thou shalt require of me, *that* will I do for thee."

t 39 And all the people went over Jordan.

s And when the king was come over, the king kissed Barzillai, and blessed him; and he returned unto his own place.

40 Then the king went on to Gilgal, and Chimham went on with him:

t u[1] and °all the People of Judah conducted the king, and also °half the People of Israel.

v[1] 41 And, [1]behold, all the [8]men of Israel came to the king, and said unto the king, °"Why have our brethren the [8]men of Judah stolen thee away, and have brought the king, and his household, and all David's [28]men with him, over Jordan?"

u[2] 42 And all the [8]men of Judah answered the men of Israel, "Because the king *is* near of kin to us: wherefore then be ye angry for this matter? have we eaten at all of the king's *cost?* or hath he given us any gift?"

v[2] 43 And the [8]men of Israel answered the [8]men of Judah, and said, "We have ten parts in the king, and we have also more *right* in David than ye: why then did ye despise us, that our advice should not be first had in bringing back our king?"

u[3] And the words of the [41]men of Judah were fiercer than the words of the [41]men of Israel.

29 Why speakest . . . ? Fig. *Erotēsis* (Ap. 6), to show dissatisfaction with Mephibosheth's defence. Hence his division of Saul's estate. See note on *v.* 26.

I have said. Cp. 9. 10. David revokes 16. 4, and falls back on 9. 10.

Thou and Ziba. Cp. 16. 4.

the land: i. e. Saul's estate.

30 forasmuch = now that.

19. 31-43 (*N*, p. 428). JERUSALEM. DAVID'S RE-ENTRY. (*Alternation.*)

N | s | 31–38. Barzillai.
 t | 39–. The People.
 s | –39, 40–. Barzillai.
 t | –40–43. The People.

34 How long . . . ? Fig. *Erotēsis.* Ap. 6.

35 can . . . ? . . . can . . . ? Fig. *Anaphora.* Ap. 6.

evil. Heb. *rā'a'.* Ap. 44. viii.

–40–43 (*t*, above). THE PEOPLE. (*Repeated Alternation.*)

t | u[1] | –40. Judah and Israel. Escort of king.
 v[1] | 41. Israel. Complaint.
 u[2] | 42. Judah. Answer.
 v[2] | 43–. Israel. Complaint.
 u[3] | –43. Judah and Israel. Prevalence.

40 all . . . half. A whole-hearted act on the part of Judah: and a half-hearted act on the part of Israel. This explains what follows.

41 Why . . . ? Fig. *Erotēsis.* Ap. 6.

20. 1-22 (Y[3], p. 424). SHEBA'S REVOLT. (*Introversion.*)

Y[3] | w | 1, 2–. Sheba. Revolt made.
 x | –2. Judah's loyalty.
 y | 3. David's concubines.
 x | 4–13. Judah's loyalty.
 w | 14–22. Sheba. Revolt quelled.

1 man. Heb. *'ish.* Ap. 14. II.

son of Bichri = a descendant of Becher (Gen. 46. 21).

tents. One of the emendations of the *Sōpherim* (Ap. 33), by which they transposed the middle two letters of the primitive text and made it read "tents" instead of "gods". The same was done in 1 Kings 12. 16, and 2 Chron. 10. 16. See notes there.

4-13 (*x*, above). JUDAH'S LOYALTY. (*Repeated Alternation.*)

x | z[1] | 4, 5. Amasa. Disloyalty.
 a[1] | 6, 7. Joab and Abishai. Pursuit.
 z[2] | 8–10–. Amasa. Murder.
 a[2] | –10, 11. Joab and Abishai. Proclamation.
 z[3] | 12, 13–. Amasa. Dead.
 a[3] | –13. Joab. Pursuit.

20 And there happened to be there a °man of Belial, whose name *was* Sheba, the °son of Bichri, a Benjamite: and he blew a trumpet, and said, "We have no part in David, neither have we inheritance in the son of Jesse: every °man to his °tents, O Israel." Y[3] w

2 So every [1]man of Israel went up from after David, *and* followed Sheba the son of Bichri:

but the [1]men of Judah clave unto their king, from Jordan even to Jerusalem. x

3 And David came to his house at Jerusalem; and the king took the ten women *his* concubines, whom he had left to keep the house, and put them in ward, and fed them, but went not in unto them. So they were shut up unto the day of their death, living in widowhood. y

4 Then said the king to Amasa, "Assemble me the [1]men of Judah within three days, and be thou here present." *x* z[1]

933 5 So Amasa went to assemble *the men of* Judah: but he tarried longer than the set time which he had appointed him.

a[1] (p. 436) 6 And David said to Abishai, "Now shall Sheba the son of Bichri do us more harm than *did* Absalom: take °thou thy lord's servants, and pursue after him, lest he get him fenced cities, and escape us."

7 And there went out after him Joab's °men, and the Cherethites, and the Pelethites, and all the mighty men: and they went out of Jerusalem, to pursue after Sheba the son of Bichri.

z[2] 8 When they *were* at the great stone which *is* in Gibeon, Amasa went before them. And Joab's garment that he had put on was girded unto him, and upon it a girdle *with* a sword fastened upon his loins in the sheath thereof; and °as he went forth it fell out.

9 And Joab said to Amasa, °"*Art* thou in health, my brother?" And Joab took Amasa by the beard with the right hand to kiss him.

10 But Amasa took no heed to the sword that *was* in Joab's hand: so he smote him therewith in the fifth *rib*, and shed out his bowels to the ground, and struck him not again; and he died.

a[2] So Joab and Abishai his brother pursued after Sheba the son of Bichri.

11 And one of Joab's [1]men stood by him, and said, "He that favoureth Joab, and he that *is* for David, *let him go* after Joab."

z[3] 12 And Amasa wallowed in blood in the midst of the highway. And when the [1]man saw that all the People stood still, he removed Amasa out of the highway into the field, and cast a cloth upon him, when he saw that every one that came by him stood still.

13 When °he was removed out of the highway,

a[3] all the °People went on after Joab, to pursue after Sheba the son of Bichri.

w b (p. 437) 14 And °he went through all the tribes of Israel unto Abel, and to Beth-maachah, and all the °Berites: and they were gathered together, and went also after °him.

c 15 And they came and besieged him in Abel of Beth-maachah, and they cast up a °bank against the city, and it stood in the °trench: and all the People that *were* with Joab battered the wall, to throw it down.

b 16 Then cried a wise woman out of the city, "Hear, °hear; say, I pray you, unto Joab, 'Come near hither, that I may speak with thee.'"

17 And when he was come near unto her, the woman said, "*Art* thou Joab?" And he answered, "*I am he.*" Then she said unto him, "Hear the words of thine handmaid." And he answered, "I do hear."

18 Then she spake, saying, "They were wont to speak in old time, saying, °'They shall surely ask *counsel* at Abel:' and so they ended *the matter*.

19 *I am one of them that are* peaceable *and* faithful in Israel: thou seekest to destroy °a city and a mother in Israel: why wilt thou swallow up the inheritance of °the LORD?"

20 And Joab answered and said, "Far be it, °far be it from me, that I should swallow up or destroy.

21 The matter *is* not so: but a [1]man of °mount Ephraim, Sheba the son of Bichri by name, hath lifted up his hand against the king, *even* against David: deliver him only, and I will depart from the city." And the woman said unto Joab, °"Behold, his head shall be thrown to thee over the wall."

22 Then the woman went unto °all the people in °her wisdom. And they cut off the head of Sheba the son of Bichri, and cast *it* out to Joab.

And he blew a trumpet, and they retired from the city, every [1]man to his °tent. And Joab returned to Jerusalem unto the king. c

23 Now Joab *was* over all the host of Israel: and °Benaiah the son of Jehoiada *was* over the Cherethites and over the Pelethites: *K* d

24 And °Adoram *was* over the tribute: and Jehoshaphat the son of Ahilud *was* recorder: e

25 And Sheva *was* °scribe: and Zadok and Abiathar *were* the priests: *d*

26 And Ira also the Jairite was a °chief ruler about David. *e*

---

6 thou. Some codices, with two early printed editions, read "now", and others, with Sept., read "now therefore".

7 men. Heb. *'ĕnōsh.* Ap. 14. III.

8 as he went forth it fell out = and it (the sword) dropped out, and fell.

9 Art thou . . . ? Fig. *Erotēsis.* Ap. 6.

13 he was removed, or, thrust.

people. Heb. *'ish.* Ap. 14. II.

20. 14-22 (*w*, p. 436). SHEBA. REVOLT QUELLED. (*Alternation.*)

w | b | 14. Abel. Flight to.
  c | 15. Siege laid.
 b | 16-22-. Abel. Parley at.
  c | -22. Siege raised.

14 he = Joab.

Berites = Bichrites (*v.* 1).

him = Sheba.

15 bank = mound.

trench = rampart.

16 hear. Repeated by Fig. *Epizeuxis.* Ap. 6.

18 They shall, &c. Fig. *Parœmia.* Ap. 6.

19 a city and a mother = a city, a mother city, too. Fig. *Hendiadys* (Ap. 6): i. e. a metropolitan city.

the LORD. Heb. Jehovah. Ap. 4. II.

20 far be it. Repeated by Fig. *Epizeuxis.* Ap. 6.

21 mount = hill country.

Behold. Fig. *Asterismos.* Ap. 6.

22 all. Some codices, with three early printed editions, omit "all".

her wisdom. Cp. Ecc. 9. 14, 15.

tent. Cp. 19. 8.

23-26 (*K*, p. 414). DAVID'S OFFICERS. (*Alternation.*)

K | d | 23. Military.
  e | 24. Civil.
 d | 25. Ecclesiastical.
  e | 26. Civil.

23 Benaiah. Cp. 8. 18; 23. 20. 1 Kings 1. 8; 2. 34.

24 Adoram. Same name as Adoniram (1 Kings 4. 6).

25 scribe, or secretary. Cp. 8. 17.

26 chief ruler. Cp. 8. 18; 23. 38.

L f (p. 438) 932 to 930 **21** Then there was a °famine in the days of David three years, °year after year; and David enquired of °the LORD. And °the LORD answered, "*It is* for Saul, and for *his* bloody house, because he slew the Gibeonites."

g 2 And the king called the °Gibeonites, and said unto them; °(now the Gibeonites °*were* not of the °children of Israel, but of the remnant of the Amorites; and the °children of Israel had sworn unto them: and Saul sought to slay them in his zeal to the °children of Israel and Judah.)

3 Wherefore David said unto the Gibeonites, "What shall I do for you? and wherewith shall I make the atonement, that ye may bless the inheritance of [1]the LORD?"

4 And the Gibeonites said unto him, "We will have no silver nor gold of Saul, nor of his house; neither for us shalt thou kill °any man in Israel." And he said, "What ye shall say, *that* will I do for you."

5 And they answered the king, "The [4]man that consumed us, and that devised against us *that* we should be destroyed from remaining in any of the °coasts of Israel,

6 Let seven °men of his sons be delivered unto us, and we will hang them up unto [1]the LORD in Gibeah of Saul, *whom* [1]the LORD did choose." And the king said, "I will give *them*."

7 But the king spared Mephibosheth, the son of Jonathan the son of Saul, because of [1]the LORD'S oath that *was* between them, between David and Jonathan the son of Saul.

8 But the king took the two sons of Rizpah the daughter of Aiah, whom she bare unto Saul, Armoni and Mephibosheth; and the five sons of °Michal the daughter of Saul, whom she brought up for Adriel the son of Barzillai the Meholathite:

9 And he delivered them into the hands of the Gibeonites, and they hanged them in the hill before [1]the LORD: and they fell *all* seven together, and [2]were put to death in the days of harvest, in the first *days*, in the beginning of barley harvest.

h 10 And Rizpah the daughter of Aiah took sackcloth, and spread it for her upon the rock, from the beginning of harvest until water dropped upon them out of heaven, and suffered neither the birds of the air to rest on them by day, nor the beasts of the field by night.

11 And it was told David what Rizpah the daughter of Aiah, the concubine of Saul, had done.

g 12 And David went and took the bones of Saul and the bones of Jonathan his son from the °men of Jabesh-gilead, which had stolen them from the °street of Beth-shan, where the Philistines had hanged them, °when the Philistines had slain Saul in Gilboa:

13 And he brought up from thence the bones of Saul and the bones of Jonathan his son; and they gathered the bones of them that were hanged.

14 And the bones of Saul °and Jonathan his son buried they in the country of Benjamin in Zelah, in the sepulchre of Kish his father: and they performed °all that the king commanded.

And after that °God was intreated for the land. *f*

15 Moreover the Philistines had yet °war again with Israel; and David went down, and his servants with him, and fought against the Philistines: and David °waxed faint. M i[1] 930 to 923

16 And Ishbi-benob, which *was* of the sons of the °giant, the weight of whose spear *weighed* three hundred *shekels* of brass in weight, he being girded with a new *sword*, °thought to have slain David. k[1]

17 But Abishai the son of Zeruiah succoured him, and smote the Philistine, and killed him. Then the [6]men of David sware unto him, saying, "Thou shalt go no more out with us to battle, that thou quench not the °light of Israel."

18 And it came to pass after this, that there was again a battle with the Philistines at °Gob: i[2]

then Sibbechai the Hushathite slew Saph, which *was* of the sons of the [16]giant. k[2]

---

21. 1-14 (*L*, p. 414). DAVID'S ZEAL.
(*Introversion.*)

L | f | 1. The land. God's judgment on it.
  g | 2-9. Saul's sons. Reparation.
   h | 10, 11. Rizpah. Mourning.
  g | 12-14-. Saul's sons. Recovery of bones.
 f | -14. The land. God intreated for it.

1 famine. One of the thirteen mentioned. See note on Gen. 12. 10.

year after year=the year after that year: i. e. 932. David being now fifty-eight.

the LORD. Heb. Jehovah. Ap. 4. II.

2 Gibeonites. Cp. Josh. 9. 3, 16, 17.

now. Note the Fig. *Parenthesis.* Ap. 6.

were=they [were]. **children**=sons.

4 any man. Heb. *'ish.* Ap. 14. II.

5 coasts=borders.

6 men. Heb. *'ĕnōsh.* Ap. 14. III.

8 Michal. Some codices, cited in the *Massōrah*, with Sept. and Syr., read "Merab", as in 1 Sam. 18. 19.

12 men = lords, or masters (Heb. *baalīm*). Cp. 1 Sam. 31. 10, 13.

street. The open space by the gate (2 Chron. 32. 6. Neh. 8. 1, 3, 16). **when**=in the day.

14 and Jonathan. Some codices, with two early printed editions, and Sept., read "the bones of Jonathan".

all. Some codices, with one early printed edition, read "according to all".

God. Heb. Elohim. Ap. 4. I.

15-22 (*M*, p. 414). WARS AND EVENTS.
(*Repeated Alternation*).

M | i[1] | 15. War with Philistines.
  k[1] | 16, 17. Giant (Ishbi-benob). Slain by Abishai.
 i[2] | 18-. Battle at Gob.
  k[2] | -18. Giant (Saph). Slain by Sibbechai.
 i[3] | 19-. Battle at Gob.
  k[3] | -19. Giant (brother of Goliath). Slain by Elhanan.
 i[4] | 20-. Battle at Gath.
  k[4] | -20, 21. Giant. Slain by Jonathan.
 i[5] | 22. End of war.

15 war again. 930-923 B.C.

waxed faint. David was now sixty.

16 giant=Rapha. See Ap. 23 and 25.

thought to have slain, or, said he would slay.

17 light=lamp. Cp. Gen. 15. 17. 1 Kings 15. 4. Prov. 13. 9; 20. 20, though not the same word in Gen. 15. 17.

18 Gob. Some codices, with two early printed editions, read "Nob".

i3 19 And there was again a battle in [18]Gob with
(p. 438) the Philistines,
930-923
where Elhanan the son of Jaare-oregim, a
k3 Beth-lehemite, slew °*the brother of* °Goliath
the Gittite, the °staff of whose spear *was* like
a weaver's beam.

i4 20 And there was yet a battle in Gath,

k4 where was a [4]man of *great* stature, that had
on every hand six fingers, and on every foot
six toes, four and twenty in number; and he
also was born to the [16]giant.
21 And when he °defied Israel, Jonathan the
son of Shimeah the brother of David slew him.

i5 22 These four were born to the [16]giant in
Gath, and fell by the hand of David, and by
the hand of his servants.

H T1 **22** And °David spake unto °the LORD the
(p. 439) words of °this song in the day *that* °the
LORD had delivered him out of the hand of all
his enemies, and out of the hand of Saul:

U 2 And he said,
[1]"The LORD *is* my °rock, and my fortress,
and my deliverer;
3 °The °God of my °rock; in Him will I
trust:
He is my shield, and the horn of my salvation,
My high tower, and my refuge,
My saviour; Thou savest me from violence.

V l A 4 I will call on [1]the LORD, *Who is* worthy
to be praised:
So shall I be saved from mine enemies.

B 5 °When the waves of death compassed me,
The floods of °ungodly men made me
afraid;

B 6 The °sorrows of hell compassed me about;
The snares of death prevented me;

A 7 In my distress I called upon [1]the LORD,
And cried to my [3]God:
And He did hear my voice out of His
temple,
And my cry *did enter* into His ears.

m C 8 Then the earth shook and trembled;

D °The foundations of heaven moved
And shook, because He was wroth.
9 There went up a smoke out of His nostrils,
And fire out of His mouth devoured:
Coals were kindled by it.
10 He bowed the heavens also, and came
down;

E And darkness *was* under His feet.

F 11 And He rode upon a cherub, and did °fly:
And He °was seen upon the wings of the
°wind.

E 12 And He made darkness pavilions round
about Him,
°Dark waters, *and* thick clouds of the
skies.

D 13 Through the brightness before Him were
coals of fire kindled.

19 the brother of Goliath. Omit the italics, and understand another giant of the same name as the Goliath of 1 Sam. 17.
staff. Heb. "wood", put by Fig. *Metonymy* (of Cause) for what was made from it. Ap. 6.
21 defied = reproached.

22. 1—23. 7 (*H*, p. 414). WORSHIP. (*Division.*)

H | T1 | 22. 1-51. Song of David.
| T2 | 23. 1-7. Last words of David.

1-51 (T1, above). SONG OF DAVID. (*Introversion and Alternation.*)

T1 | U | 2, 3. Praise.
V | l | 4-7. Prayer made.
m | 8-16. Overthrow of enemies. Tempest.
V | *l* | 17-28. Prayer answered.
m | 29-49. Overthrow of enemies. Arms.
U | 50, 51. Praise.

1 David spake. At this point in his history (about 1018 B.C.). This song was written and edited by him later as Ps. 18, with the full liberty of all other editors of their own work.
the LORD. Heb. Jehovah. Ap. 4.
this song. Cp. Ex. 15. Deut. 32.
2 rock. Heb. *sel'a* = a shadow, or shelter. First occurrence.
3 The God of my rock. Sept. and Syr. read "My God was my rock" = immovable defence (Deut. 32. 4).
God. Heb. Elohim. Ap. 4. I.
rock. Heb. *zūr* = a cliff, *in situ*. See Ps. 18. 2; 31. 3; 42. 9; 71. 3.

4-7 (l, above). PRAYER MADE. (*Introversion.*)

l | A | 4. Call for deliverance.
B | 5. Compassed by pangs.
B | 6. Compassed by sorrows.
A | 7. Call for deliverance.

5 When, or, For. **ungodly men** = Belial.
6 sorrows of hell = meshes of Sheol. See Ap. 35.

8-16 (m, above). OVERTHROW OF ENEMIES. TEMPEST. (*Introversion.*)

m | C | 8-. On earth. Wonders.
D | -8-10-. In heaven. Fire.
E | -10. Darkness.
F | 11. Speedy succour.
E | 12. Darkness.
D | 13-15. In heaven. Fire.
C | 16. On earth. Wonders.

8 The. Some codices, with Sept. and Syr., read "and the".
11 fly. Fig. *Anthropopatheia.* Ap. 6.
was seen. Some codices, with two early printed editions, read "and darted".
wind. Heb. *rūach.* Ap. 9.
12 Dark = gathering of.
14 the MOST HIGH. Heb. *Elyōn.* Ap. 4. VI
16 channels. Heb. *'ăphīkim*, a watercourse, constrained by rocks or pipes or rocky channels. First occurrence. See Job 6. 15; 12. 21; 40. 18; 41. 15. Ps. 18. 15; 42. 1; 126. 4. Song 5. 12. Isa. 8. 7. Ezek. 6. 3; 31. 12; 32. 6; 34. 13; 35. 8; 36. 4, 6. Joel 1. 20; 3. 18. See notes on these eighteen passages for the various renderings.

14 [1]The LORD thundered from heaven,
And °the MOST HIGH uttered His voice.
15 And He sent out arrows, and scattered
them;
Lightning, and discomfited them.

16 And the °channels of the sea appeared, *C*

930 to 923 The foundations of the world were ° discovered,
At the rebuking of [1] the LORD,
At the ° blast of the ° breath of His nostrils.

l G (p. 440) 17 He sent from above, He took me;
He drew me out of many waters;
18 He delivered me from my strong enemy,
And ° from them that hated me:

H For they were too strong for me.

H 19 They ° prevented me in the day of my calamity:

G But [1] the LORD was my stay.
20 He brought me forth also into a large place:
He delivered me, because He delighted in me.
21 [1] The LORD rewarded me according to my righteousness:
According to the cleanness of my hands hath He recompensed me.
22 For I have kept the ways of [1] the LORD,
And have not wickedly departed from my [3] God.
23 For all His ° judgments *were* before me:
And *as for* His statutes, I did not depart from them.
24 I was also ° upright before Him,
And have kept myself from mine ° iniquity.
25 Therefore [1] the LORD hath recompensed me according to my righteousness;
According to my cleanness in His eye sight.
26 With the ° merciful Thou wilt shew Thyself ° merciful,
° *And* with the [24] upright ° man Thou wilt shew Thyself [24] upright.
27 With the pure Thou wilt shew Thyself pure;
And with the froward Thou wilt ° shew Thyself ° unsavoury.
28 And the afflicted people Thou wilt save:
But Thine eyes *are* upon the haughty,
That Thou mayest bring *them* down.

m J 29 For Thou *art* my ° lamp, [1] O LORD:
And [1] the LORD will lighten my darkness.

K 30 For by Thee I have run through a troop:
° By my [3] God have I leaped over a wall.
31 *As for* ° GOD, His way *is* perfect;
The ° word of [1] the LORD ° *is* tried:
He *is* a buckler to all them that trust in Him.
32 For ° who *is* [31] GOD, save [1] the LORD?
And ° who *is* a rock, save our [3] God?

L 33 [31] GOD *is* my ° strength *and* ° power:
And He ° maketh my way perfect.
34 He maketh my feet like hinds' *feet*:
And ° setteth me upon ° my high places.
35 He teacheth my hands to war;
So that a bow of steel is broken by mine arms.
36 Thou hast also given me the shield of Thy salvation:
And Thy gentleness hath made me great.
37 Thou hast enlarged my steps under me;
So that my feet did not slip.
38 I have pursued mine enemies, and destroyed them;
And turned not again until I had consumed them.

39 And I have consumed them, and wounded them, that they could not arise:
Yea, they are fallen under my feet.
40 For Thou hast girded me with strength to battle:
Them that rose up against me hast Thou subdued under me.

41 Thou hast also given me the necks of mine enemies, M
That I might destroy them that hate me.
42 They ° looked, but *there was* none to save;
Even unto [1] the LORD, but He answered them not.
43 Then did I beat them as small as the dust of the earth,
I did stamp them as the mire of the street,
And did spread them abroad.
44 Thou also hast delivered me from the ° strivings of my People,

---

discovered = laid bare.
blast = *neshāmāh*. Ap. 16.
breath. Heb. *rūach*. Ap. 9.

22. 17-28 (*l*, p. 439). **PRAYER ANSWERED.** (*Introversion.*)

l | G | 17, 18-. Deliverance.
  H | -18. Enemies.
  H | 19-. Enemies.
  G | -19-28. Deliverance.

18 from. Some codices, with Syr. and Vulg., read "and from". Cp. Ps. 18. 17.
19 prevented = got before.
23 judgments. Cp. Deut. 4. 1, note.
24 upright = blameless. Heb. *tāmīm*.
iniquity. Heb. *'āvāh*. Ap. 44. iv.
26 merciful = gracious.
And. Some codices, with two early printed editions, Sept., Syr., and Vulg., read this "And" in text.
man. Heb. *gibbōr*. Ap. 14. IV.
27 shew Thyself unsavoury = show Thyself ready to contend.
unsavoury = a wrestler. Cp. Ps. 18. 26.

29-49 (*m*, p. 439). **OVERTHROW OF ENEMIES. ARMS.** (*Extended Alternation.*)

m | J | 29. Jehovah my light.
  K | 30-32. God my avenger.
  L | 33-40. God my strength.
  M | 41-46. Deliverance.
  J | 47. Jehovah my life.
  K | 48. God my avenger.
  L | 49-. God my exalter.
  M | -49. Deliverance.

29 lamp = light.
30 By. Some codices, with two early printed editions, Sept., Aram., and Syr., read "And by".
31 GOD. Heb. *'El*. Ap. 4. IV.
word = statements. Heb. *'imrah*, what is said. See Ap. 73. v.
is tried = hath been proved.
32 who . . . ? Fig. *Erotēsis*. Ap. 6.
33 strength = fortress.
power = strength.
maketh my way perfect: or, showeth to the blameless His way. Some codices, with two early printed editions, read "my way", as in Ps. 18. 32.
34 setteth = maketh me to stand firm.
my high places. Contrast the "high places" so fatal to Jonathan and Saul (1. 25).
42 looked = looked about. But Aram., Sept., Syr., and Vulg. read "cried out". Cp. Ps. 18. 41.
44 strivings = contentions.

930 to 923 Thou hast kept me *to be* head of the °heathen:
A people *which* I knew not shall serve me.
45 °Strangers °shall submit themselves unto me:
As soon as they hear, they shall be obedient unto me.
46 [45] Strangers shall fade away,
And they °shall be afraid out of their close places.
J (p. 440) 47 [1] The LORD liveth; and blessed *be* my rock;
And exalted be the [3] God of the rock of my salvation.
K 48 It *is* [31] GOD That avengeth me,
And That bringeth down the °People under me,
L 49 And That bringeth me forth from mine enemies:
Thou also hast lifted me up on high above them that rose up against me:
M Thou hast delivered me from the °violent °man.
U 50 Therefore I will give thanks unto Thee, O [1] LORD, among the [44] heathen,
And I will sing praises unto Thy name.
51 *He is* the °tower of salvation for His king:
And sheweth mercy to His anointed,
Unto David, and to his seed for evermore."

T² W¹ X¹ (p. 441) **23** Now these *be* the °last °words of David.
David the son of Jesse °said,
And the °man *who was* raised up on high,
The anointed of the °God of Jacob,
And the sweet psalmist of Israel, °said,
X² 2 "The °Spirit of °the LORD °spake by me,
And His °word *was* in my tongue.
3 The [1] God of °Israel °said,
The Rock of °Israel °spake to me,
W² n 'He that ruleth over °men *must be* just,
o Ruling in the fear of [1] God.
o p 4 °And *he shall be* as the light of the morning, *when* the °sun riseth,
q *Even* a morning without clouds;
p *As* the tender grass *springing* out of the earth
q By clear shining after rain.'
n r¹ s 5 °Although my house *be* not so with °GOD;
t °Yet He hath made with me an everlasting covenant,
Ordered in all *things*, and sure:
t °For *this is* all my salvation, and all *my* desire,
s °Although He make °*it* not to grow.

heathen = Gentile nations.
45 Strangers = foreigners.
shall submit themselves, or give a feigned and unwilling obedience.
46 shall be afraid out of their close places = shall come forth trembling from their hiding-places.
48 People = Peoples.
49 violent man: i. e. Saul.
man. Heb. *'ish.* Ap. 14. II.
51 tower. Fig. *Prosopopœia.* Ap. 6.

23. 1-7 (T², p. 439). LAST WORDS OF DAVID. (*Division.*)

T² | W¹ | 1-3-. The speaker.
| W² | -3-7. His words.

1-3- (W¹, above). THE SPEAKER. (*Division.*)

W¹ | X¹ | 1. David's mouth.
| X² | 2, 3-. Not David's words.

Chapter 23 follows 24, but is placed here (by the Fig. *Hysterologia*) so as to include David's "last words" with his "song" under his "worship", and make the correspondence shown in the Structure. See p. 414.
1 last words. Hence their importance.
words = discourse, message, oracle, revelation. Heb. *dabar.* Ap. 73. x.
said. Heb. *nā'am* = to speak with assurance and authority. **man.** Heb. *geber.* Ap. 14. IV.
God. Heb. 'Elohim. Ap. 4. I.
God of Jacob: i. e. the God Who met Jacob when he had nothing and deserved nothing (but wrath), and promised him all = therefore "the God of all grace". Cp. Ps. 146. 5 and 1 Pet. 5. 10, referring to the grace which had called David.
2 Spirit = *rūach.* Ap. 9.
the LORD. Heb. Jehovah. Ap. 4. II.
spake: referring to the *substance* of the Divine revelation. Heb. *dabar* = to utter. See Ap. 73. x.
word. Heb. *millāh.* Used of a royal or divine decree (Ps. 19. 14. Dan. 3. 22, 28, &c.).
3 Israel. The higher title (not Jacob), because human instrumentality not in question here.
said. Here Heb. *'āmar*, referring to the *matter* of the Divine revelation. See Ap. 73. v.
spake. See note on "spake", *v.* 2.
men. Heb. *'ādām.* Ap. 14. I.

-3-7 (W², above). THE WORDS. (*Introversion.*)

W² | n | -3-. The ruler. Ideal. } The Ruler, and his rule.
| o | -3. The ideal rule.
| *o* | 4. The ideal rule.
| *n* | 5-7. The ruler. Actual.

4 (*o*, above). THE IDEAL RULE. (*Introversion.*)

o | p | 4-. The light. Effect in heavens. } This is the order in Heb.
| q | -4-. Its clearness.
| *q* | -4. Its clearness.
| *p* | -4-. The light. Effect on earth.

4 And he shall be. Translate in present tense, describing such an ideal rule.
sun. Cp. Ps. 72. 6, 7, 16. Jer. 23. 5, 6. Mal. 4. 2.

5-7 (*n*, above). THE RULER. ACTUAL. (*Division.*)

n | r¹ | 5. The ruler.
| r² | 6, 7. The ruled.

5 (r¹, above). THE RULER. (*Introversion.*)

r¹ | s | 5-. David's house.
| t | -5-. God's covenant with David.
| *t* | -5-. God's covenant with David.
| *s* | -5. David's house.

5 Although = For (Heb. *kī*). **GOD.** Heb. El. Ap. 4. IV. **Yet** = for (Heb. *kī*). **For** (Heb. *kī*). Punctuate and translate:

r¹ | s | For is not my house thus through God?
| t | For He hath made a covenant . . . sure (2 Sam. 7). } The Covenant.
| *t* | For this (Covenant) is all my . . . desire.
| *s* | For shall He not cause it to prosper?

it = i. e. my house.

r[2] u 6 But *the sons* of Belial *shall be* all of them
(p. 442) as thorns °thrust away,
930-923 Because they cannot be °taken with hands:
v
v 7 But the °man *that* shall touch them must
be °fenced with iron and the staff of
a spear;
u And they shall be utterly burned with fire
°in the *same* place."

J Y 8 These *be* the names of °the mighty men
whom David had:
Z A w[1] °The Tachmonite that sat in the seat, chief
among the captains; the same *was* Adino the
Eznite:
x[1] *he lift up his spear* against eight hundred,
whom he slew at one time.
w[2] 9 And after him *was* Eleazar the son of Dodo
the Ahohite, *one* of the three [8]mighty men with
David, when they defied the Philistines *that*
were there gathered together to battle, and
°the men of Israel were gone away:
x[2] 10 He arose, and smote the Philistines until
his hand was weary, and his hand clave unto
the sword: and °the LORD wrought a great
victory that day; and the people returned after
him only to spoil.
w[3] 11 And after him *was* °Shammah the son of
Agee the Hararite. And the Philistines were
gathered together °into a troop, where was a
piece of ground full of °lentiles: and the people
°fled from the Philistines.
x[3] 12 But he stood in the midst of the ground,
and defended it, and slew the Philistines: and
[10]the LORD wrought a great victory.
B 13 And °three of the °thirty chief went down,
and came to David in the harvest time unto
the cave of Adullam: and the troop of the
Philistines pitched in the valley of °Rephaim.
14 And David *was* then in °an hold, and the
garrison of the Philistines *was* then *in* Beth-
lehem.
15 And David longed, and said, "Oh that one
would give me drink of the water of the well
of Beth-lehem, which *is* by the gate!"
16 And °the three [8]mighty men brake through
the host of the Philistines, and drew water out
of the well of Beth-lehem, that *was* by the
gate, and took *it*, and brought *it* to David:
nevertheless he would not drink thereof, but
poured it out unto [2]the LORD.
17 And he said, "Be it far from me, O [2]LORD,
that I should do this: °*is not this* the blood
of the °men that went °in jeopardy of their
°lives?" therefore he would not drink it.
These things did these three mighty men.
A w[4] 18 And °Abishai, the brother of Joab, the son
of Zeruiah, °was chief °among [13]three.
x[4] And he lifted up his spear against three hundred, *and* slew *them*, and had the name
among [13]three.
19 °Was he not most honourable °of three?
therefore he was their captain: howbeit he
attained not unto the *first* [13]three.
w[5] 20 And Benaiah the son of Jehoiada, the son
of a valiant [7]man, of Kabzeel, who had done
many acts,
he slew two °lionlike men of Moab: he went x[5]

23. 6, 7 (r[2], p. 441). THE RULED. (*Introversion.*)

r[2] | u | 6-. The sons of Belial. Put to flight.
| v | -6. How they cannot be ruled.
| *v* | 7-. How they can be ruled.
| *u* | -7. The sons of Belial. Consumed.

6 thrust away = put to flight, chased away.
taken = handled.
7 man. Heb. *'ish.* Ap. 14. II. **fenced** = furnished.
in the same place = on the spot.

8-39 (*J*, p. 414). DAVID'S MIGHTY MEN. (*Introversion.*)

J | Y | 8-. Names.
| Z | -8-24-. Principal.
| *Z* | -24-39-. Subordinate.
| *Y* | -39. Number.

-8-24- (Z, above). THE PRINCIPAL. (*Introversion and Repeated Alternation.*)

Z | A | w[1] | -8-. Adino.
| x[1] | -8. His achievement.
| w[2] | 9. Eleazar.
| x[2] | 10. His achievement.
| w[3] | 11. Shammah.
| x[3] | 12. His achievement. } First three.
| B | 13-17. Three together.
| *A* | w[4] | 18-. Abishai.
| x[4] | -18, 19. Achievement and rank.
| w[5] | 20-. Benaiah.
| x[5] | -20-23. Achievement and rank.
| w[6] | 24-. Asahel. } Second three.

8 the mighty men. Heb. *gibbor.* Ap. 14. IV. This rehearsal comes at the end of David's reign, immediately before the setting up of the kingdom under Solomon. Even so will it be, at the time of the end, with the true David.

The Tachmonite that sat in the seat. A.V. marg. and R.V. text = "Josheb-bassebet the Tachmonite". Really = Ish-bosheth, put for Ish-baal = "man of Baal, son of a Hachmonite" (cp. 1 Chron. 11. 11), altered later to Adino. Cp. St. Peter's exploit (Acts 2), and Stephen's (Acts 6. 7).

9 the men of Israel were gone away. This is the time for true courage to be manifested. Cp. *v.* 11. 2 Tim. 1. 15; 4. 16, 17.

10 the LORD (Heb. Jehovah, Ap. 4. II) **wrought.** Cp. *v.* 12, and see Acts 14. 27; 15. 4, 12; 21. 19.

11 Shammah. Like Acts 14. 3.
into a troop. Probably = the place, Lehi.
lentiles. See note on 1 Chron. 11. 13.
fled. See note on *v.* 9, "gone away".
13 three . . . thirty. See note on 1 Chron. 27. 1.
Rephaim = Rapha. A noted descendant of the *Nephīlīm.* See Ap. 23 and 25.
14 an hold = a fort, or garrison.
16 the three. The three referred to in *v.* 13.
17 is not this . . . ? Supply instead "shall I drink?"
men. Heb. *'ěnōsh.* Ap. 14. III.
in jeopardy of their lives = with their lives [in their hands].
lives = souls. Heb. *nephesh.* Ap. 13. "Soul" put by Fig. *Metonymy* (of Adjunct), Ap. 6, for "blood", which is another name for it. Cp. Gen. 9. 4. Lev. 17. 11. Deut. 12. 23. Ap. 13.
18 Abishai. Mentioned in 10. 10, 14; 16. 9; 18. 2; 19. 21. 1 Sam. 26. 6-9.
was = he [was]. **among** = of.
19 Was he not . . . ? Fig. *Erotēsis.* Ap. 6.
of three = of [the second] three. See the Structure above, and note on *v.* 13.
20 lionlike men. Men of Ariel. Ariel, proper name, occurs only here and twice in Isa. 29. 1, 2.

930 to 923 down also and slew °a lion in the midst of °a pit in time of °snow:
21 And he slew an Egyptian, a °goodly [7]man: and the Egyptian had a spear in his hand; but he went down to him with a staff, and plucked the spear out of the Egyptian's hand, and slew him °with his own spear.
22 These *things* did Benaiah the son of Jehoiada, and had the name among three [8]mighty men.
23 He was more honourable than the thirty, but he attained not to the *first* [13]three. And David set him over his guard.

w6 (p. 442) 24 °Asahel the °brother of Joab *was* one of the [13]thirty;

Z Elhanan the son of Dodo of Beth-lehem,
25 Shammah the Harodite,
Elika the Harodite,
26 Helez the Paltite,
Ira the son of Ikkesh the Tekoite,
27 Abiezer the Anethothite,
Mebunnai the Hushathite,
28 Zalmon the Ahohite,
Maharai the Netophathite,
29 Heleb the son of Baanah, a Netophathite,
Ittai the son of Ribai out of Gibeah of the children of Benjamin,
30 Benaiah the Pirathonite,
Hiddai of the brooks of Gaash,
31 Abi-albon the Arbathite,
Azmaveth the Barhumite,
32 Eliahba the Shaalbonite,
Of the sons of Jashen, Jonathan,
33 Shammah the Hararite,
Ahiam the son of Sharar the Hararite,
34 Eliphelet the son of Ahasbai, °the son of the Maachathite,
Eliam the °son of Ahithophel the Gilonite,
35 Hezrai the Carmelite,
Paarai the Arbite,
36 Igal the son of Nathan of Zobah,
Bani the Gadite,
37 Zelek the Ammonite,
Nahari the Beerothite, °armourbearer to Joab the son of Zeruiah,
38 Ira an Ithrite,
Gareb an Ithrite,
39 °Uriah the Hittite:

Y °thirty and seven in all.

E A (p. 443) 24 °And again the anger of °the LORD was kindled against Israel,

B a and °He moved David against them to say, "Go, number Israel and Judah."
2 For the king said to Joab the captain of the host, which *was* with him, "Go now through all the tribes of Israel, from Dan even to Beer-sheba, and number ye the People, that I may know the number of the People."

b 3 And Joab said unto the king, "Now [1]the LORD thy °God add unto the People, how many soever they be, an hundredfold, and that the eyes of my lord the king may see *it*: but why doth my lord the king delight in this thing?"
4 Notwithstanding the king's word prevailed against Joab, and against the captains of the host. And Joab and the captains of the host went out from the presence of the king, to number the People of Israel.

b 5 And they passed over Jordan, and pitched in Aroer, on the °right side of the city that *lieth* in the midst of the °river of Gad, and toward Jazer:
6 Then they came to Gilead, and to the land of °Tahtim-hodshi; and they came to °Dan-jaan, and °about to Zidon,

---

a . . . a . . . snow. All these have the Art., as being a well-known exploit.

21 goodly of appearance. Heb. = a sight to see. 1 Chron. 11. 23 = stature.

with his own spear. Often done now spiritually by the servants of the true David.

24 Asahel. The third of the second three.

brother of Joab, but not Joab. His *name* here but not *himself*, because when the time of the end comes, with its "last words", *loyalty* will be the one test. Joab remained true in Absalom's rebellion, but fell away in Adonijah's. Hence in 1 Cor. 16. 22 "*love*" is the test, in the light of "Maran-atha", *not* the "strifes" of ch. 3, or the wrong judgments of ch. 4, or the uncleanness of ch. 5, or going to law of ch. 6; not the fornication of ch. 7, not a wrong conscience of chs. 9, 10, not ecclesiastical disorders of ch. 11, not the misuse of special gifts (chs. 12, 13, 14), not orthodoxy (ch. 15), but "love" and loyalty to the Person of Christ, the true David, David's son and David's Lord.

34 the. Probably "Hanan", the son, &c. (1 Chron. 11. 43), making three named in this verse.

son of Ahithophel. But not Ahithophel himself, on account of his disloyalty. See note on *v.* 24, above.

37 armourbearer. Joab's armourbearer named, but not Joab himself. See note on *v.* 24, above.

39 Uriah. Is doubly honoured, being named with his son; but Joab or Ahithophel are not named. Read Jer. 9. 23, 24.

thirty and seven in all: i. e. first three + second three + thirty-one of *vv.* 24–39.

24. 1–25 (*E*, p. 414). DAVID'S SIN IN NUMBERING. (*Alternation.*)

E | A | 1–. Jehovah. Anger.
  B | –1–10. Sin committed.
 A | 11–16–. Jehovah. Judgment.
  B | –16–25. Sin expiated.

–1–10 (B, above). SIN COMMITTED. (*Introversion.*)

B | a | –1, 2. David. Command.
  b | 3, 4. Joab's objection.
  b | 5–9. Joab's obedience.
 a | 10. David. Confession.

1 And again. The history in this chapter precedes ch. 23, by Fig. *Hysterologia* (Ap. 6). See note on 23. 1.

the LORD. Heb. Jehovah. Ap. 4. II.

He moved = He suffered him to be moved. By Hebrew idiom (and also by modern usage) a person is said to do that which he *permits* to be done. Here we have the historical fact. In 1 Chron. 21. 1 we have the real fact from the Divine standpoint. Here the *exoteric*, in 1 Chron. 21. 1 the *esoteric*. For examples, see Ex. 4. 21; 5. 22. Jer. 4. 10. Ezek. 14. 9; 20. 25. Matt. 11. 25; 13. 11. Rom. 9. 18; 11. 7, 8. 2 Thess. 2. 11. God's permission, but Satan's suggestion (Jas. 1. 13, 14); or, *yāṣath*, may be taken impersonally, "David was moved".

3 God. Heb. Elohim. Ap. 4. I.

5 right side: i. e. the south side, facing east.

river of Gad = the river valley belonging to Gad, which was the Jabbok.

6 Tahtim-hodshi. Site unknown. If translated = the lower parts of the country where the new moon was worshipped. Like Beth-shemesh = House of the Sun.

Dan-jaan = Dan in the wood, perhaps Laish-Dan (Josh. 19. 47. Judg. 18. 29). **about** = passed round.

930 7 And came to the °strong hold of Tyre, and
to to all the cities of the Hivites, and of the Ca-
923 naanites: and they °went out to the °south of
Judah, *even* to Beer-sheba.
8 So when they had gone through all the
land, they came to Jerusalem at the end of
°nine months and twenty days.
9 And Joab gave up the sum of the number
of the People unto the king: and there were in
°Israel eight hundred thousand valiant °men
that drew the sword; and the °men of °Judah
were five hundred thousand °men.

a 10 And David's heart smote him after that he
(p. 443) had numbered the People. And David said
unto [1]the LORD, °"I have °sinned greatly in
that I have done: and now, I beseech thee,
O [1]LORD, °take away the °iniquity of Thy
servant; for I have done very foolishly."

A c 11 °For when David °was up in the morning,
(p. 444) the word of [1]the LORD came unto the prophet
°Gad, David's seer, saying,
12 "Go and say unto David, 'Thus saith [1]the
LORD, °'I offer thee three *things;* choose thee
one of them, that I may *do it* unto thee.'"
13 So [11]Gad came to David, and told him, and
said unto him, "Shall °seven years of famine
come unto thee in thy land? or wilt thou flee
three months before thine enemies, while they
pursue thee? or that there be three days' pestilence in thy land? now °advise, and see what
answer I shall return to Him That sent me."

d 14 And David said unto [11]Gad, "I am in
a great strait: let us fall now into the hand
of the LORD; for His °mercies *are* °great:
and let me not fall into the hand of °man."

d 15 So [1]the LORD sent a pestilence upon Israel
from the morning even to the °time appointed:
and there died of the People from Dan even to
Beer-sheba seventy thousand [9]men.

c 16 And when the angel stretched out his
hand upon Jerusalem to destroy it, [1]the LORD
°repented Him of the °evil,

B e and said to the angel that destroyed the People, "It is enough: stay now thine hand."
And the angel of [1]the LORD was by the
threshingplace of °Araunah the Jebusite.
17 And David spake unto [1]the LORD when
he saw the angel that smote the People, and
said, °"Lo, I have sinned, and I have done
°wickedly: but these sheep, what have they
done? let Thine hand, I pray Thee, be against
me, and against my father's house."

f 18 And Gad came that day to David, and
said unto him, "Go up, rear an altar unto [1]the
LORD in the threshingfloor of [16]Araunah the
Jebusite."

g h[1] 19 And David, according to the saying of Gad,
went up °as [1]the LORD commanded.

i[1] 20 And [16]Araunah °looked, and saw the king
and his servants °coming on toward him: and
[16]Araunah went out, and bowed himself before
the king on his face upon the ground.
21 And Araunah said, "Wherefore is my
lord the king come to his servant?"
h[2] And David said, "To buy the threshingfloor of
thee, to build an altar unto [1]the LORD, that
the plague may be stayed from the people."

22 And [16]Araunah said unto David, "Let my i[2]
lord the king take and offer up what *seemeth*
good unto him: behold, *here be* oxen for
°burnt sacrifice, and threshing instruments
and *other* instruments of the oxen for wood."
23 All these *things* did [16]Araunah, *as* a king,
give unto the king. And Araunah said unto
the king, [1]"The LORD thy [3]God accept thee."

24 And the king said unto [16]Araunah, "Nay; h[3]
but I will surely buy *it* of thee at a price:

---

7 strong hold. Cp. Josh. 19. 29.
went out. Some codices read "came [in]".
south = the *Negeb*. Some codices read "land". See note on Gen. 13. 1.
8 nine months, &c. The long time implies a period of great peace.
9 Israel = 800,000 "valiant men". Heb. *'ish.* Ap. 14. II. **Judah** = 500,000 "men". Heb. *'ish.* Ap. 14. II. [Cp. 1 Chron. 21. 5, a different classification. Israel = 1,100,000, "all they of Israel that drew sword": i. e. all adults, not necessarily "valiant". Judah = 470,000 "men that drew sword"; not all the "men" by 30,000.]
10 I have sinned. Probably conviction of pride or other sinful motive. Heb. *ḥāṭāh.* Ap. 44. i.
take away = cause to pass over. See 12. 13.
iniquity. See Ap. 44. iv.

24. 11-16- (*A*, p. 443). JEHOVAH. JUDGMENT. (*Introversion.*)

A | c | 11-13. Divine offers.
  d | 14. David's decision made.
  d | 15. David's decision carried out.
  c | 16-. Divine forbearance.

11 For = And. **was** = rose.
Gad. Cp. 1 Sam. 9. 9. Gad last mentioned, 1 Sam. 22. 5. Probably inspired to write this history.
12 I offer thee = I impose on thee (Heb. *naṭal*). A choice out of God's four sore judgments (Ezek. 14. 21).
13 seven years. 1 Chron. 21. 12 = three years; also Sept. The Heb. numeral letters for three and seven were probably very much alike. Hence perhaps mistaken by an ancient scribe. Both may be right = "seven, or even three." **advise** = consider, or know.
14 mercies = compassions.
great = manifold. **man.** Heb. *'ādām.* Ap. 14. I.
15 time appointed. Sept. and Syr. say the plague lasted only till noon. So this "time" may mean for the evening sacrifice, 3 p.m. (cp. *v.* 18).
16 repented. Fig. *Anthropopatheia.* Ap. 6.
evil. Heb. *rā'a'.* Ap. 44. viii.

-16-25 (*B*, p. 443). EXPIATION OF THE SIN. (*Introversion and Repeated Alternation.*)

B | e | -16, 17. Entreaty for the Land. David's.
  f | 18. David. Command given to.
  g | h[1] | 19. David's obedience.
    i[1] | 20, 21-. Araunah's reception.
    h[2] | -21. David's request.
    i[2] | 22, 23. Araunah's offer.
    h[3] | 24. David's refusal.
  f | 25-. David. Obedience.
  e | -25. Entreaty for the Land. Jehovah.

Araunah the Jebusite. Perhaps spared in the taking of Jebus. See note on 5. 8.
17 Lo. Fig. *Asterismos.* Ap. 6.
wickedly. Heb. *'āvāh.* Ap. 44. iv.
19 as = according as.
20 looked = looked down.
coming on = crossing over.
22 burnt sacrifice. See Ap. 43. I. ii.

930 to 923 neither will I °offer [22]burnt offerings unto
[1]the LORD my [3]God of that which doth cost
me nothing." So David bought °the threshingfloor and the oxen for fifty °shekels of silver.

f (p. 444) 25 And David built °there an altar unto [1]the
LORD, and offered burnt offerings and peace
offerings.

e So [1]the LORD was intreated for the land, and
the plague was stayed from Israel.

24 offer. See Ap. 43. I. vi.

the threshingfloor and the oxen for fifty shekels of silver. Heb. *goren* (Ruth 3. 2), mentioned in *vv.* 16, 18, 21. Not the "place", Heb. *mākōm*, of 1 Chron. 21. 25 (Ruth 4. 10), which was afterward the Temple area, about eight acres, and for which David gave the much larger sum of 600 shekels of gold. Two separate purchases effected, the one here was hurried, as an earnest, and the other was made later.

shekels. See Ap. 51. II.

25 there. See note on 1 Chron. 22. 1.

1 AND 2 KINGS.

THE STRUCTURE OF THE TWO BOOKS * AS A WHOLE.

THE KINGDOM.

(*Division.*)

A¹ | 1 Kings **1. 1 — 12. 15.** THE KINGDOM. UNITED.

A² | 1 Kings **12. 16** — 2 Kings **25. 30.** THE KINGDOM. DIVIDED.

(Covering a period of 444 years : viz. 921-477).

---

1 Kings **1. 1 — 12. 15** (**A**¹, above). THE KINGDOM. UNITED.

(*Division.*)

A¹ | **B**¹ | 1 Kings 1. 1—2. 11. DAVID.

B² | 1 Kings 2. 12—11. 43. SOLOMON.

B³ | 1 Kings 12. 1-15. REHOBOAM.

---

1 Kings **12. 16** — 2 Kings **25. 30** (**A**², above). THE KINGDOM. DIVIDED.

(*Introversion and Repeated Alternation.*)

A² | **C**¹ | 1 Kings 12. 16-19. THE DIVISION OF THE KINGDOM.

D¹ | **E**¹ | 1 Kings 12. 20—14. 20. ISRAEL (JEROBOAM I).

F¹ | 1 Kings 14. 21—15. 24. JUDAH (REHOBOAM, 14. 21-31; ABIJAM, 15. 1-8; ASA, 15. 9-24).

E² | 1 Kings 15. 25—22. 40. ISRAEL (NADAB, 15. 25-31; BAASHA, 15. 32—16. 7; ELAH, 16. 8-14; ZIMRI, 16. 15-20; (INTERREGNUM, 16. 21, 22); OMRI, 16. 23-28; AHAB, 16. 29—22. 40.

F² | 1 Kings 22. 41-50. JUDAH (JEHOSHAPHAT).

E³ | 1 Kings 22. 51—2 Kings 8. 15. ISRAEL (AHAZIAH, 1 Kings 22. 51—2 Kings 1. 18; (ELIJAH'S Translation, 2 Kings 2. 1-25). JORAM, 2 Kings 3. 1—8. 15).

F³ | 2 Kings 8. 16—9. 29. JUDAH (JEHORAM, 8. 16-24; AHAZIAH, 8. 25—9. 29).

E⁴ | 2 Kings 9. 30—10. 36. ISRAEL (JEHU).

F⁴ | 2 Kings 11. 1—12. 21. JUDAH (ATHALIAH, 11. 1-16; JOASH, 11. 17—12. 21).

} DISRUPTION OF ISRAEL AND JUDAH. †

D² | **E**⁵ | 2 Kings 13. 1-25. ISRAEL (JEHOAHAZ, 13. 1-9; JEHOASH, 13. 10-25).

F⁵ | 2 Kings 14. 1-22. JUDAH (AMAZIAH, 14. 1-20; UZZIAH, 14. 21, 22).

E⁶ | 2 Kings 14. 23-29. ISRAEL (JEROBOAM II).

F⁶ | 2 Kings 15. 1-7. JUDAH (UZZIAH).

E⁷ | 2 Kings 15. 8-31. ISRAEL (ZACHARIAH, 15. 8-12; SHALLUM, 15. 13-16; MENAHEM, 15. 17-22; PEKAHIAH, 15. 23-26; PEKAH, 15. 27-31).

F⁷ | 2 Kings 15. 32—16. 20. JUDAH (JOTHAM, 15. 32-38; AHAZ, 16. 1-20).

E⁸ | 2 Kings 17. 1-41. ISRAEL (HOSHEA).

F⁸ | 2 Kings 18. 1—24. 20. JUDAH (HEZEKIAH, 18. 1—20. 21; MANASSEH, 21. 1-18; AMON, 21. 19-26; JOSIAH, 22. 1—23. 30; JEHOAHAZ, 23. 31-35; JEHOIAKIM, 23. 36—24. 7; JEHOIACHIN, 24. 8-16; ZEDEKIAH, 24. 17-20.

} DISPERSION OF ISRAEL AND CAPTIVITY OF JUDAH. †

C² | 2 Kings 25. 1-30. THE ENDING OF THE KINGDOM.

---

* For the cause of the division of the book of KINGS into two books, and for their relation to the two books of SAMUEL, see note on page 366.

† Note the division of the eight pairs into two groups, by the events which characterise the last pair of each group.

THE °FIRST BOOK OF THE °KINGS,

COMMONLY CALLED,

THE °THIRD BOOK OF THE KINGS.

B¹ G¹ J (p. 447) 921 **1** Now °king David was °old *and* stricken in years; and they covered him with clothes, but he °gat no heat.

K **2** Wherefore his °servants said unto him, "Let there be sought for my lord the king a young °virgin: and let her stand before the king, and let her cherish him, and let her lie in thy bosom, that my lord the king may get heat."

3 So they sought for a fair damsel throughout all the °coasts of Israel, and found Abishag a Shunammite, and brought her to the king.

4 And the damsel *was* very fair, and cherished the king, and ministered to him: but the king knew her not.

H L a **5** Then °Adonijah the son of Haggith exalted himself, saying, "I will be king:" and he prepared him chariots and horsemen, and fifty °men to run before him.

6 And his father had not displeased him at any time in saying, "Why hast thou done so?" and he also *was a* very goodly *man;* and °*his mother* bare him after Absalom.

7 And he conferred with °Joab the son of Zeruiah, and with Abiathar the priest: and they following Adonijah helped *him.*

b **8** But Zadok the priest, and Benaiah the son of Jehoiada, and Nathan the prophet, and Shimei, and Rei, and the °mighty men which *belonged* to David, were not with Adonijah.

a **9** And Adonijah slew sheep and oxen and fat cattle by the stone of Zoheleth, which *is* by °En-rogel, and called all his brethren the king's sons, and all the °men of Judah °the king's servants:

b **10** But Nathan the prophet, and Benaiah, and the [8] mighty men, and Solomon his brother, he called not.

TITLE, First . . . third. See note on p. 366. The wrong division into two books cuts up the histories of Ahaziah and Elijah.

THE STRUCTURE OF 1 AND 2 KINGS AS RELATED TO 1 AND 2 SAMUEL:

x | 2 Sam. 2. 1—4. 12. The Divided kingdom.
 y | 2 Sam. 5. 1—24. 25. The United kingdom.
 y | 1 Kings 1. 1—12. 15. The United kingdom.
x | 1 Kings 12. 16—2 Kings 25. 30. The Divided kingdom.

Kings. As compared with Chronicles, Kings and Samuel give the history from the human point of view, while Chronicles gives the same history from the Divine standpoint. The former, as man ruled the history; the latter, as God overruled it. Cp. Saul's death, 1 Sam. 31. 6, with 1 Chron. 10. 13, 14; and in Kings, three verses given to Hezekiah's reformation, and in Chronicles, three chapters.

For the parallel passages in the Book of Chronicles, see Ap. 56, and note on Title of 1 Samuel, p. 366.

1. 1—2. 11 (**B¹**, p. 446). DAVID.
(*Repeated Alternation with Introversions.*)

B¹ | G¹ | J | 1. 1. David. Length of years.
  K | 1. 2-4. Advice of servants to David.
   H | L | 1. 5-10. Solomon. Wrongful succession.
    M | N | 1. 11-14. Nathan. } Counter-
     O | 1. 15-. Bathsheba. } action.
 G² | -15. David. Very old.
   H | *M* | *O* | 1. 16-21. Bathsheba. } Counter-
     N | 1. 22-27. Nathan. } action.
    L | 1. 28-53. Solomon. Rightful succession.
 G³ | *K* | 2. 1-9. Advice of David to Solomon.
  J | 2. 10, 11. David. Length of reign.

1 king David: occurs in 2 Sam. 6. 12, 16; 7. 18; 8. 8, 11; 9. 5; 13. 21, 39; 16. 5, 6; 17. 17, 21; 19. 11, 16. Book begins with king David and ends with king of Babylon. Opens with Temple built, and closes with Temple burnt. Begins with David's first successor on the throne of his kingdom, and ends with David's last successor released from the house of his captivity. Characters of all are tested by the standard of David. **old:** about seventy. Cp. 2 Sam. 5. 4, 5. **gat no heat.** Cp. Ps. 32. 3, 4. **2 servants:** i. e. his advisers, probably medical. **virgin**=damsel. Heb. *bethûlâh.* **3 coasts**=borders.

5-10 (L, above). SOLOMON. WRONGFUL SUCCESSORS. (*Alternation.*)

L | a | 5-7. His adherents. Invited.
 b | 8. Non-adherents.
 a | 9. His adherents. Invited.
 b | 10. Non-invited.

5 Adonijah. Fourth son of David (2 Sam. 3. 4). Amnon dead (2 Sam. 13. 29), Absalom dead (2 Sam. 18. 14), and probably Chileab (2 Sam. 3. 3). **men.** Heb. *'ish.* Ap. 14. II. **6 his mother:** i. e. "Haggith". See *v.* 5. **7 Joab.** This is why his name is not in 2 Sam. 23. See note on 2 Sam. 23. 24. **8 mighty men.** See 2 Sam. 23. 8, 9, 16, 22. **9 En-rogel**=well or spring of Rogel. South side of Jerusalem, in the Kidron valley. **men.** Heb. *'ěnôsh.* Ap. 14. III. **the king's.** Some codices, with Syr., read "and the", &c.

M N c (p. 448) 921 11 Wherefore Nathan spake unto Bath-sheba the mother of Solomon, saying, "Hast thou not heard that Adonijah the son of Haggith doth reign, and David our lord knoweth *it* not?

d 12 Now therefore come, let me, I pray thee, give thee counsel, that thou mayest save thine own °life, and the °life of thy son Solomon.

d 13 Go and get thee in unto king David, and say unto him, °'Didst not thou, my lord, O king, swear unto thine handmaid, saying, 'Assuredly Solomon thy son shall reign after me, and he shall sit upon my throne?' °why then doth Adonijah reign?'

c 14 °Behold, while thou yet talkest there with the king, I also will come in after thee, and confirm thy words."

O 15 And Bath-sheba went in unto the king into the chamber:

G² and the king was very old; and Abishag the Shunammite ministered unto the king.

M O e 16 And Bath-sheba bowed, and did obeisance unto the king. And the king °said, "What wouldest thou?"

f 17 And she said unto him, °"My lord, thou swarest by °the LORD thy °God unto thine handmaid, *saying*, 'Assuredly Solomon thy son shall reign after me, and he shall sit upon my throne.'

g 18 And now, [14]behold, Adonijah reigneth; and °now, my lord the king, thou knowest *it* not:

h 19 And he hath slain oxen and fat cattle and sheep in abundance, and hath called all the sons of the king, and Abiathar the priest, and Joab the captain of the host: but Solomon thy servant hath he not called.

i 20 And °thou, my lord, O king, the eyes of all Israel *are* upon thee, that thou shouldest tell them who shall sit on the throne of my lord the king after him.

21 Otherwise it shall come to pass, when my lord the king shall °sleep with his fathers, that I and my son Solomon shall be counted °offenders."

N e 22 And, °lo, while she yet talked with the king, Nathan the prophet also came in.

23 And they told the king, saying, °"Behold Nathan the prophet." And when he was come in before the king, he bowed himself before the king with his face to the ground.

f 24 And Nathan said, "My lord, O king, hast thou said, Adonijah shall reign after me, and he shall sit upon my throne?

g 25 For he is gone down this day, and hath slain oxen and fat cattle and sheep in abundance, and hath called all the king's sons, and the captains of the host, and Abiathar the priest;

h and, [23]behold, they eat and drink before him, and say, [17]'God save king Adonijah.'

26 But me, *even* me thy servant, and Zadok the priest, and Benaiah the son of Jehoiada, and thy servant Solomon, hath he not called.

27 Is this thing done by my lord the king, and thou hast not shewed *it* unto thy servant, who should sit on the throne of my lord the king after him?" *i*

28 Then king David answered and said, "Call me Bath-sheba." And she came into the king's presence, and stood before the king. P¹ Q¹ j¹

29 And the king sware, and said, "*As* [17]the LORD liveth, That hath redeemed my °soul out of all distress, k¹

1. 11-14 (N, p. 447). NATHAN AND BATH-SHEBA. COUNTERACTION. (*Introversion.*)

N | c | 11. Bath-sheba. Danger.
  d | 12. Advice for David.
  d | 13. Advice for Bath-sheba.
  c | 14. Bath-sheba. Support.

12 life = soul. Heb. *nephesh*. Ap. 13.
13 Didst not thou . . . ? Fig. *Erotēsis*. Ap. 6.
why then . . . ? Fig. *Erotēsis*. Ap. 6.
14 Behold. Fig. *Asterismos*. Ap. 6. Some codices, with Aram., Sept., Syr., and Vulg., read "And behold".

16-27 (*M*, p. 447). NATHAN AND BATH-SHEBA. COUNTERACTION. (*Extended Alternation.*)

M | O | e | 16. Obeisance of Bath-sheba.
  f | 17. Rightful successor?
  g | 18. Adonijah.
  h | 19. Feast.
  i | 20, 21. Expectation.
} Nathan's advice followed.
N | *e* | 22, 23. Obeisance of Nathan.
  f | 24. Wrongful successor.
  g | 25-. Adonijah.
  h | -25, 26. Feast.
  i | 27. Inquiry.
} Nathan's promise fulfilled.

16 said. Some codices, with Syr. and Vulg., add "to her".
17 My lord. Some codices, with Sept. and Syr., add "O king".
the LORD. Heb. Jehovah. Ap. 4. II.
God. Heb. Elohim. Ap. 4. I.
18 now. A special reading (*Sevīr*, Ap. 34), with three early printed editions, Aram., Sept., Syr., and Vulg., read "thou". But the *Massōrah* (Ap. 30) says the scribes were misled in reading *'attāh* (thou) instead of *'attāh* (now).
20 thou = thou therefore. Some codices, with three early printed editions, and Aram., read "And now". See note on *v.* 18.
21 sleep with his fathers. See note on Deut. 31. 16.
offenders. See Ap. 44. i.
22 lo. Fig. *Asterismos*. Ap. 6.
23 Behold. Fig. *Asterismos*. Ap. 6.

28-53 (*L*, p. 447). SOLOMON. RIGHTFUL SUCCESSOR. (*Division.*)

L | P¹ | 28-40. Proclamation and anointing.
  P² | 41-53. Adonijah. Rebellion quelled.

28-40 (P¹, above). PROCLAMATION AND ANOINTING. (*Extended and Repeated Alternation.*)

P¹ | Q¹ | j¹ | 28. Call for Bath-sheba (David).
  k¹ | 29, 30. Command. Given.
  l¹ | 31. Acquiescence. Reverence.
Q² | j² | 32. Call for Zadok (David).
  k² | 33-35. Command. Given.
  l² | 36, 37. Acquiescence. Benediction.
Q³ | j³ | 38. Call for Solomon (Zadok).
  k³ | 39. Command. Obeyed.
  l³ | 40. Acquiescence. Rejoicing.

29 soul. Heb. *nephesh*. Ap. 13.

921 30 Even °as I swear unto thee by [17]the LORD [17]God of Israel, saying, 'Assuredly Solomon thy son shall reign after me, and he shall sit upon my throne in my stead;' even so will I certainly do this day."

l[1] (p. 448) 31 Then Bath-sheba bowed with *her* face to the earth, and did reverence to the king, and said, "Let my lord king David live for ever."

Q[2] j[2] 32 And king David said, "Call me Zadok the priest, and Nathan the prophet, and Benaiah the son of Jehoiada." And they came before the king.

k[2] 33 The king also said unto them, "Take with you the servants of your lord, and cause Solomon my son to ride upon °mine own mule, and bring him down to Gihon:

34 And let Zadok the priest and Nathan the prophet anoint him there king over Israel: and blow ye with the trumpet, and say, [17]'God save king Solomon.'

35 Then ye shall come up after him, that he may come and °sit upon my throne; for he shall be king in my stead: and I have appointed him to be ruler over Israel and over Judah."

l[2] 36 And Benaiah the son of Jehoiada answered the king, and said, "Amen: [17]the LORD [17]God of my lord the king say so *too*.

37 [30]As [17]the LORD hath been with my lord the king, even so be He with Solomon, and make his throne greater than the throne of my lord king David."

Q[3] j[3] 38 So Zadok the priest, and Nathan the prophet, and Benaiah the son of Jehoiada, and the Cherethites, and the Pelethites, went down, and caused Solomon to ride upon king David's mule, and brought him to Gihon.

k[3] 39 And Zadok the priest took an horn of oil out of the °tabernacle, and anointed Solomon. And they blew the trumpet; and all the People said, [17]"God save king Solomon."

l[3] 40 And all the People came up after him, and the People °piped with pipes, and °rejoiced with great joy, so that °the earth rent with the sound of them.

P[2] m (p. 449) 41 And Adonijah and all the guests that *were* with him heard *it* as they had made an end of eating. And when Joab heard the sound of the trumpet, he said, "Wherefore *is this* noise of the city being in an uproar?"

n 42 And while he yet spake, [23]behold, Jonathan the son of Abiathar the priest came: and Adonijah said unto him, "Come in; for thou *art* a valiant [5]man, and bringest good tidings."

43 °And °Jonathan answered and said to Adonijah, °"Verily our lord king David hath made Solomon king.

44 And the king hath sent with him Zadok the priest, and Nathan the prophet, and Benaiah the son of Jehoiada, and the °Cherethites, and the Pelethites, and they have caused him to ride upon the king's mule:

45 And Zadok the priest and Nathan the prophet have anointed him king in Gihon: and they are come up from thence rejoicing, so that the city rang again. This *is* the noise that ye have heard.

46 And also Solomon °sitteth on the throne of the kingdom.

47 And moreover the king's servants came to bless our lord king David, saying, °'God make the name of Solomon better than thy name, and make his throne greater than thy throne.' And the king °bowed himself upon the bed.

48 And also thus said the king, 'Blessed *be* [17]the LORD [17]God of Israel, Which hath given *one* to sit on my throne this day, mine eyes even seeing *it*.'"

49 And all the guests that *were* with Adonijah were afraid, and rose up, and went every [5]man his way. m

50 And Adonijah feared because of Solomon, and arose, and went, and caught hold on the horns of the altar.

51 And it was told Solomon, saying, [23]"Behold, Adonijah feareth king Solomon: for, °lo, he hath caught hold on the horns of the altar, saying, 'Let king Solomon swear unto me to day that he will not slay his servant with the sword.'" n

52 And Solomon said, "If he will °shew himself a °worthy man, there shall °not an hair of him fall to the earth: but if wickedness shall be found in him, he shall die."

53 So king Solomon sent, and they brought him down from the altar. And he came and bowed himself to king Solomon: and Solomon said unto him, "Go to thine house."

30 as = according as.
33 mine own mule. David had not disobeyed Deut. 17. 16, as Absalom had done (2 Sam. 15. 1) and Adonijah (1 Kings 1. 5).
35 sit, &c. As associate king, Solomon being nineteen years of age.
39 tabernacle = tent. Heb. *'ohel.* Not the Tabernacle at Gibeon, but David's tabernacle (2 Sam. 6. 17). See Ap. 40.
40 piped with pipes = playing loudly on pipes. Fig. *Polyptōton.* Ap. 6.
rejoiced with great joy = greatly rejoiced. Fig. *Polyptōton.* Ap. 6.
the earth rent. Fig. *Hyperbolē.* Ap. 6.

41-53 (P[2], p. 448). **ADONIJAH. REBELLION QUELLED.** (*Alternation.*)

P[2] | m | 41. Alarm.
n | 42-48. Tidings brought to Adonijah.
m | 49, 50. Fear and flight.
n | 51-53. Tidings brought to Solomon.

43 And = But.
Jonathan. David's faithful messenger of 2 Sam. 15. 36 and 17. 17.
Verily = of a truth; or, truth to tell.
44 Cherethites, &c. A bodyguard (1 Sam. 30. 14).
46 sitteth = hath taken [his] seat.
47 God. Heb. Elohim. Ap. 4. I. Some codices read, "thy God".
bowed = worshipped. Cp. Gen. 47. 31.
51 lo. Fig. *Asterismos.* Ap. 6.
52 shew himself. Some codices, with one early printed edition, add "toward me".
worthy man = a son of valour.
not an hair, &c. Fig. *Parœmia.* Ap. 6.

K o 2 Now the days of David drew nigh that he
(p. 450) should die;
p q and he °charged Solomon his son, saying,
921 2 "I go °the way of all the earth: be thou
to °strong therefore, and shew thyself a °man;
920 3 And keep the °charge of °the LORD thy
°God, to walk in His ways, °to keep His
statutes, and His commandments, and His
judgments, and His testimonies, °as it is
written in the law of Moses, that thou mayest
°prosper in all that thou doest, and whithersoever thou turnest thyself:
4 That [3]the LORD may °continue His word
which He spake concerning me, saying, 'If thy
°children take heed to their way, to walk before Me in truth with all their heart and with
all their °soul, there shall not °fail thee' (said
He) 'a [2]man on the throne of Israel.'
r 5 Moreover thou knowest also what °Joab the
son of Zeruiah °did to me, *and* what he did to
the two captains of the hosts of Israel, unto
°Abner the son of Ner, and unto °Amasa the
son of Jether, whom he slew, and shed the
blood of war in peace, and put the blood of
war upon his girdle that *was* about his loins,
and in his shoes that *were* on his feet.
6 Do therefore according to thy wisdom, and
let not his hoar head go down to °the grave in
peace.
p q 7 But shew kindness unto the sons of °Bar-
zillai the Gileadite, and let them be of those
that eat at thy table: for so they came to me
when I fled because of Absalom thy brother.
r 8 And, °behold, *thou hast* with thee °Shimei
the son of Gera, a Benjamite of Bahurim, which
cursed me with a grievous curse in the day
when I went to Mahanaim: but he came down
to meet me at Jordan, and °I sware to him by
[3]the LORD, saying, 'I will not put thee to death
with the sword.'
9 Now therefore hold him not guiltless: °(for
thou *art* a wise [2]man, and knowest what thou
oughtest to do unto him); °but his hoar head
bring thou down to [6]the grave with blood."
J o 10 So David °slept with his fathers, and was
buried in the city of David.
960 11 And the days that David reigned over Is-
to rael *were* forty years: seven years reigned he
920 in Hebron, and thirty and three years reigned
he in Jerusalem.
B^2 R 12 Then sat °Solomon upon the throne of
920 David his father;
S T V and his kingdom was established greatly.
W X^1 s 13 And Adonijah the son of Haggith came to
(p. 450) Bath-sheba the mother of Solomon. And she
said, "Comest thou peaceably?" And he said,
"Peaceably."
14 He said moreover, "I have somewhat to
say unto thee." And °she said, "Say on."
15 And he said, "Thou knowest that the kingdom was mine, and *that* all Israel set their
faces on me, that I should reign: howbeit the
kingdom is turned about, and is become my
brother's: for it was his from [3]the LORD.

2. 1-10 (*K*, p. 447). ADVICE OF DAVID TO SOLOMON. (*Introversion and Alternations.*)

K | o | 1-. David. End near.
  p | q | -1-4. For good. Solomon.
    r | 5, 6. For retribution. Joab.
  p | *q* | 7. For good. Barzillai.
    r | 8, 9. For retribution. Shimei.
o | 10. David. Death.

1 charged. Cp. Josh. 1. 6-9.
2 the way of all the earth. Cp. Josh. 23. 14.
strong = resolute. Necessary advice for Solomon = the peaceable. **man.** Heb. *'ish.* Ap. 14. II.
3 charge. Cp. Lev. 8. 35; 18. 30.
the LORD. Heb. Jehovah. Ap. 4. II.
God. Heb. Elohim. Ap. 4. I.
to keep. Some codices, with three early printed editions, read "and to keep", thus enlarging the Fig. *Polysyndeton* (Ap 6) in this verse.
as it is written. Cp. Deut. 17. 18, 19. Josh. 1. 6-8. Note the emphasis laid on God's Word written. See note on Ex. 17. 14, and Ap. 47.
prosper = do wisely. **4 continue** = establish.
children = sons. Cp. 2 Sam. 7. 8, 11-16.
soul. Heb. *nephesh.* Ap. 13. **fail** = be cut off from.
5 Joab . . . Zeruiah. David's own sister's son.
did to me. David does not mention the worst sin, the death of Absalom.
Abner. Cp. 2 Sam. 3. 27, 39.
Amasa. Cp. 2 Sam. 20. 9-11. 1 Chron. 2. 17.
6 the grave. Heb. *Sheōl.* Ap. 35. Note "the", not "a". Cp. *v.* 9.
7 Barzillai. Cp. 2 Sam. 17. 27, 29; 19. 31, 32.
8 behold. Fig. *Asterismos.* Ap. 6.
Shimei. Cp. 2 Sam. 16. 5-13; 19. 18-23.
I sware. Cp. 2 Sam. 19-23.
9 for. Note the parenthesis as indicated. Fig. *Epitrechon* (Ap. 6).
but = neither, as in Ps. 38. 1, the second negative being omitted, as is frequently the case. Lit. "and [not]". See Ps. 9. 18 (R. V. nor); 38. 1 (neither); 75. 5. Prov. 24. 12; 25. 27. Isa. 38. 18. The Ellipsis must be supplied here, as it is in the above passages. The Heb. *Vav* (ו) is *disjunctive* (as well as conjunctive), and is frequently translated "or" (see note on Judg. 11. 31), and with a negative "nor" and "neither", as it should be here (1 Kings 2. 9). Cp. Ex. 20. 17. Num. 16. 14 (R.V.); 22. 26. Deut. 7. 25. 2 Sam. 1. 21. Ps. 26. 9. Prov. 6. 4. Solomon obeyed David's former alternative and did not "hold him guiltless" (*v.* 36); but punished him for a fresh offence (*vv.* 42-46).
10 slept with his fathers. See note on Deut. 31. 16.

2. 12—11. 43 (**B^2**, p. 446). SOLOMON. (*Introversion.*)

B^2 | R | 2. 12-. Solomon. Accession.
  S | 2. -12—11. 40. Reign. Events.
  S | 11. 40-42. Reign. Record of events.
R | 11. 43-. Solomon. Death and burial.

12 Solomon. Born in 940. Now twenty years old.

2. -12—11. 40 (S, above). REIGN. EVENTS. (*Alternation.*)

S | T | 2. -12-46. Government.
  U | 3. 1. Marriage.
  T | 3. 2—10. 29. Government.
  U | 11. 1-40. Marriages, &c.

2. -12-46 (T, above). GOVERNMENT. (*Introversion and Repeated Alternation.*)

T | V | -12. Establishment of kingdom.
  W | X^1 | 13-25. Execution. Adonijah.
    Y^1 | 26, 27. Deposition. Abiathar.
   X^2 | 28-34. Execution. Joab.
    Y^2 | 35. Substitution. Benaiah and Zadok.
   X^3 | 36-46-. Execution. Shimei.
V | -46. Establishment of kingdom.

13-25 [For Structure see next page].

14 she said. Some codices, with two early printed editions, Sept., Syr., and Vulg., add "unto him".

920 16 And now I ask one petition of thee, °deny me not." And she said unto him, "Say on."

t 17 And he said, "Speak, I pray thee, unto Solomon the king, (for he will not °say thee nay,) that he give me Abishag the Shunammite to wife."

u 18 And Bath-sheba said, °"Well; I will speak for thee unto the king."

s 19 Bath-sheba therefore went unto king Solomon, to speak unto him for Adonijah. And the king rose up to meet her, and bowed himself unto her, and sat down on his throne, and caused a °seat to be set for the king's mother; and she sat on his right hand.

20 Then she said, "I desire one small petition of thee; *I pray thee,* [17]say me not nay." And the king said unto her, "Ask on, my mother: for I will not [17]say thee nay."

t 21 And she said, "Let Abishag the Shunammite °be given to Adonijah thy brother to wife."

u 22 And king Solomon answered and said unto his mother, "And why dost thou ask Abishag the Shunammite for Adonijah? ask for him the kingdom also; for he *is* mine elder brother; even for him, and for Abiathar the priest, and for Joab the son of Zeruiah."

23 Then king Solomon sware by [3]the LORD, saying, [3]"God do so to me, and more also, if Adonijah have not spoken this word against his own °life.

24 Now therefore, *as* [3]the LORD liveth, Which hath established me, and set me on the throne of David my father, and Who hath made me an house, °as He °promised, Adonijah shall be put to death this day."

25 And king Solomon sent by the hand of Benaiah the son of Jehoiada; and he fell upon him that he died.

W Y[1] (p. 450) 26 And unto Abiathar the priest said the king, "Get thee to °Anathoth, unto thine own °fields; for thou *art* °worthy of death: but I will not at this time put thee to death, because thou barest the ark of the °Lord GOD before David my father, and because thou hast been afflicted in all wherein my father was afflicted."

27 So Solomon thrust out Abiathar from being priest unto [3]the LORD; that he might °fulfil the word of [3]the LORD, which He spake concerning the house of Eli in °Shiloh.

X[2] 28 Then tidings came to Joab: for Joab had turned after Adonijah, though he turned not after °Absalom. And Joab fled unto the °tabernacle of [3]the LORD, and caught hold on the horns of the altar.

29 And it was told king Solomon that Joab was fled unto the [28]tabernacle of [3]the LORD; and, [8]behold, *he is* by the altar. Then Solomon sent Benaiah the son of Jehoiada, saying, "Go, fall upon him."

30 And Benaiah came to the tabernacle of [3]the LORD, and said unto him, "Thus saith the king, 'Come forth.'" And he said, °"Nay; but I will die here." And Benaiah brought the king word again, saying, "Thus said Joab, and thus he answered me."

2. 13-25 (X[1], p. 450). EXECUTION. ADONIJAH.
(*Extended Alternation.*)

X[1] | s | 13-16. Bath-sheba. Approached by Adonijah.
 t | 17. Adonijah's request.
 u | 18. Promise made.
 s | 19, 20. Bath-sheba. Approach to Solomon.
 t | 21. Adonijah's request.
 u | 22-25. Promise fulfilled. Result.

16 deny me not. Heb. idiom = "turn not away my face": face being put by Fig. *Synecdoche* (of Part) for the whole person. Ap. 6.

17 say thee nay = turn away thy face. See note above.

18 Well = good.

19 seat = throne.

21 be given. The verb is masc., as it usually is when a woman acts a man's part.

23 life = soul. Heb. *nephesh.* Ap. 13.

24 as = according as.

promised. Cp. 2 Sam. 7. 12, 13.

26 Anathoth. Cp. Josh. 21. 18.

fields. Some codices, with three early printed editions, Sept., Syr., and Vulg., read "estate".

worthy of death. Heb. idiom = "a man of death" = doomed to death. Heb. *'îsh.* Ap. 14. II.

Lord GOD = Adonai Jehovah. Ap. 4. II, and VIII (2).

27 fulfil. Cp. 1 Sam. 2. 31, 36. Already partly fulfilled (1 Sam. 4. 11; and now, wholly, in *v.* 35).

Shiloh. Cp. 1 Sam. 2. 35.

28 Absalom. Syr. and Vulg. read "Solomon".

tabernacle. Heb. *'ohel,* tent. See Ap. 40.

30 Nay; but . . . here. The famous *Mugah* codex quoted in the *Massōrah* adds "to him". Ap. 30.

32 men. Heb. *'ĕnōsh.* Ap. 14. III.

36 any whither. Fig. *Paronomasia.* Ap. 6. Heb. *'āneh vā'ānāh* = hither and thither.

37 on the day. Same as Gen. 2. 17. Here several days must have elapsed.

31 And the king said unto him, "Do [24]as he hath said, and fall upon him, and bury him; that thou mayest take away the innocent blood, which Joab shed, from me, and from the house of my father.

32 And [3]the LORD shall return his blood upon his own head, who fell upon two °men more righteous and better than he, and slew them with the sword, my father David not knowing *thereof, to wit,* Abner the son of Ner, captain of the host of Israel, and Amasa the son of Jether, captain of the host of Judah.

33 Their blood shall therefore return upon the head of Joab, and upon the head of his seed for ever: but upon David, and upon his seed, and upon his house, and upon his throne, shall there be peace for ever from [3]the LORD."

34 So Benaiah the son of Jehoiada went up, and fell upon him, and slew him: and he was buried in his own house in the wilderness.

35 And the king put Benaiah the son of Jehoiada in his room over the host: and Zadok the priest did the king put in the room of Abiathar. Y[2]

36 And the king sent and called for Shimei, and said unto him, "Build thee an house in Jerusalem, and dwell there, and go not forth thence °any whither. X[3]

37 For it shall be, *that* °on the day thou goest out, and passest over the brook Kidron, thou

920 shalt know for certain that thou °shalt surely die: thy blood shall be upon °thine own head."

38 And Shimei said unto the king, "The saying *is* good: [24]as my lord the king hath said, so will thy servant do." And Shimei dwelt in Jerusalem many days.

39 And it came to pass at the end of three years, that two of the servants of Shimei ran away unto Achish son of Maachah king of Gath. And they told Shimei, saying, [8]"Behold, thy servants *be* in °Gath."

40 And Shimei arose, and saddled his ass, and went to Gath to Achish to seek his servants: and Shimei went, and brought his servants from Gath.

41 And it was told Solomon that Shimei had gone from Jerusalem to Gath, and was come again.

42 And the king sent and called for Shimei, and said unto him, "Did I not make thee to swear by [3]the LORD, and protested unto thee, saying, 'Know for a certain, on the day thou goest out, and walkest abroad any whither, that thou shalt surely die?' and thou saidst unto me, 'The word *that* I have heard *is* good.'

43 Why then hast thou not kept the oath of [3]the LORD, and the commandment that I have charged thee with?"

44 The king said moreover to Shimei, "Thou knowest all the °wickedness which thine heart is privy to, that thou didst to David my father: therefore [3]the LORD shall return thy °wickedness upon thine own head;

45 And king Solomon *shall be* blessed, and the throne of David shall be established before [3]the LORD for ever."

46 So the king commanded Benaiah the son of Jehoiada; which went out, and fell upon him, that he died.

V (p. 450) And the kingdom was established in the hand of Solomon.

3 And Solomon made °affinity with Pharaoh king of Egypt, and took Pharaoh's daughter, and brought her into the city of David, until he had made an end of building his own house, and the house of °the LORD, and the wall of Jerusalem round about.

T A v (p. 452) 2 °Only the people sacrificed °in high places, because there was no house built unto the name of [1]the LORD, until those days.

3 And Solomon loved [1]the LORD, walking in the °statutes of David his father: [2]only he sacrificed and burnt incense in °high places.

4 And the king went to °Gibeon to sacrifice there; for that *was* the great high place: a thousand burnt offerings did Solomon °offer upon that altar.

w 5 In Gibeon [1]the LORD appeared to Solomon in a °dream by night:

x y and °God said, "Ask what I shall give thee."

z 6 And Solomon °said, "Thou hast shewed unto Thy servant David my father great °mercy, according as he walked before Thee in truth, and in righteousness, and in uprightness of heart with Thee; and Thou hast kept for him this great kindness, that Thou hast given him a son to sit on his throne, as *it is* this day.

7 And now, O [1]LORD my [5]God, Thou hast made Thy servant king instead of David my father: and I *am but* °a little child: °I know not *how* °to go out or come in.

---

shalt surely die. Fig. *Polyptōton*. Ap. 6. Heb. "a dying thou shalt die", as in Gen. 2. 17.

thine own head = thyself, "head" being put by Fig. *Synecdoche* (of the Part) for the whole person. Ap. 6. See note on 2. 9.

39 Gath. Sixty-four miles away. Therefore the expression "in the day" must refer to a longer period.

44 wickedness. Heb. *rā'a'*. Ap. 44. viii.

3. 1 affinity = relationship by marriage.

the LORD. Heb. Jehovah. Ap. 4.

3. 2—10. 29 (*T*, p. 450). GOVERNMENT.

(*Alternations, Simple and Extended, with Introversion.*)

T A | 3. 2–15. First appearance of Jehovah to Solomon.
  B | C | 3. 16—4. 34. Wisdom and riches. Two women.
    D | E | 5. 1–12. Contract with Hiram.
      F | 5. 13–18. Levy.
        G | 6. 1—8. 66. Temple (part).
A | 9. 1–9. Second appearance of Jehovah to Solomon.
  B | *D* | *E* | 9. 10–14. Contract with Hiram.
      F | 9. 15–24. Levy.
        G | 9. 25. Temple (general).
    C | 9. 26—10. 29. Riches and wisdom. One woman (Queen of Sheba).

2 Only. May imply regret rather than censure. Cp. 15. 14, &c.

in high places. Deut. 12. 11, 14, 26, 27, not obeyed since Jehovah had forsaken Shiloh. Cp. Ps. 78. 60, 67–69. Jer. 7. 12–14.

3. 2-15 (A, above). FIRST APPEARANCE OF JEHOVAH TO SOLOMON.

(*Introversion and Alternation.*)

A | v | 2–4. Solomon's worship at Gibeon.
  w | 5–. Dream.
    x | y | –5. Jehovah. Offer.
      z | 6–9. Solomon. Choice.
    x | *y* | 10. Jehovah. Approbation.
      z | 11–14. Solomon. Gifts.
  w | 15–. Dream.
v | –15. Solomon's worship at Jerusalem.

3 statutes of David. Contrast "the statutes of Omri" (Mic. 6. 16), and "statutes of the heathen" (2 Kings 17. 8).

high places. Not necessarily idolatrous (see note on *v.* 2, and cp. 1 Chron. 16. 39; 21. 29. 2 Chron. 1. 3, 13), though perhaps copied from Canaanites. Practice too deeply rooted for even Asa and Hezekiah to remove. Josiah it was who finally desecrated them. Anglo-Saxon = Hoes.

4 Gibeon = a high place, where the Tabernacle was. Cp. Josh. 9. 3. 2 Sam. 2. 12, 13.

offer = offer up. See Ap. 43. I. vi.

5 dream. One of the twenty in Scripture. See note on Gen. 20. 3.

God. Heb. Elohim. Ap. 4.

6 said: i.e. in his sleep. Cp. *v.* 15. See note on Ps. 127. 2.

mercy = grace, or lovingkindness.

7 a little child. In his father's eyes a "wise man" (2. 6, 9).

I know not = I shall not know. Some codices, with Sept., Syr., and Vulg., read "and know not", indicating the Fig. *Polysyndeton* here, and in the following verses. Ap. 6.

to go out or come in. Cp. Num. 27. 17. Fig. *Synecdoche* (of Part). Ap. 6. Put for whole manner of life.

920 **8 And Thy servant *is* in the midst of Thy People which Thou hast chosen, a great People, that cannot be numbered nor counted for multitude.**

9 °Give therefore Thy servant an °understanding heart to judge Thy People, that I may discern between good and bad: for who is able to judge this Thy so great a People?"

x y (p. 452) **10 And the speech pleased °the LORD*, that Solomon had asked this thing.**

z **11 And [5]God said unto him, "Because thou hast asked this thing, and hast not asked for thyself long life; neither hast asked riches for thyself, nor hast asked the °life of thine enemies; but hast asked for thyself understanding to discern judgment;**

12 °Behold, I have done according to thy words: °lo, I have given thee a wise and an understanding heart; so that there was none °like thee before thee, neither after thee shall any arise like unto thee.

13 And I have also given thee that which thou hast not asked, both riches, and honour: so that there shall not be °any among the kings [12]like unto thee all thy days.

14 And if thou wilt walk in My ways, to keep My statutes and My commandments, °as °thy father David did walk, then I will lengthen thy days."

w **15 And Solomon awoke; and, [12]behold, *it was* a dream.**

v **And he came to Jerusalem, and stood before the ark of the covenant of [10]the LORD*, and [4]offered up burnt offerings, and °offered peace offerings, and made a feast to all his servants.**

C H a (p. 453) **16 Then came there two women, *that were* harlots, unto the king, and stood before him.**

17 And the one woman said, "O my lord, I and this woman dwell in one house; and I was delivered of a child with her in the house.

18 And it came to pass the third day after that I was delivered, that this woman was delivered also: and we *were* together; °*there was* no stranger with us in the house, save we two in the house.

19 And this woman's °child died in the night; because she °overlaid it.

20 And she arose at midnight, and took my son from beside me, while thine handmaid slept, and laid it in her bosom, and laid her dead child in my bosom.

21 And when I rose in the morning to give my child suck, [12]behold, it was dead: but when I had considered it in the morning, behold, it was not my son, which I did bear."

22 And the other woman said, "Nay; but the living *is* my son, and the dead *is* thy son." And this said, "No; but the dead *is* thy son, and the living *is* my son." Thus they °spake before the king.

b **23 Then said the king, "The one saith, 'This *is* my son that liveth, and thy son *is* the dead:' and the other saith, 'Nay; but thy son *is* the dead, and my son *is* the living.'"**

24 And the king said, "Bring me a sword." And they brought a sword before the king.

25 And the king said, "Divide the living child in two, and give half to the one, and half to the other."

a **26 Then spake the woman whose the living child *was* unto the king, for her bowels yearned upon her son, and she said, "O my lord, give her the living child, and in no wise slay it." But the other °said, "Let it be neither mine nor thine, *but* divide *it*."**

b **27 Then the king answered and said, "Give her the living child, and in no wise slay it: she *is* the mother thereof."**

28 And all Israel heard of the judgment which the king had judged; and they feared the king: for they saw that the °wisdom of [5]God *was* in him, to do judgment.

J c[1] **4 So king Solomon was king over °all Israel.**

2 And these *were* the princes which he had; Azariah the son of Zadok the priest,

3 Elihoreph and Ahiah, the sons of Shisha,

9 Give. Cp. 2 Chron. 1. 10.
understanding = hearing. Solomon began by asking wisdom from God. Rehoboam (his son) began by asking counsel from man (12. 6, 8).
10 the LORD*. One of the 134 places where the *Sōpherim* put "Adonai" instead of "Jehovah". See Ap. 32, and cp. Ap. 30.
11 life = soul. Heb. *nephesh.* Ap. 13.
12 Behold . . . lo. Fig. *Asterismos.* Ap. 6.
like thee. Supply Fig. *Ellipsis* (Ap. 6), by adding "among the kings" from *v.* 13 and 10. 23.
13 any = a man. Heb. *'īsh.* Ap. 14. II.
14 as = according as. **thy father David.** Cp. 15. 5.
15 offered = prepared. See Ap. 43. I. iii. Showing that the Ceremonial Law was in writing before the days of Solomon, and not a later production, as asserted and assumed by some.

3. 16–4. 34 (C, p. 452). WISDOM AND RICHES. (*Introversion.*)

C | H | 3. 16–28. Wisdom.
  J | 4. 1–28. Dominion and riches.
  H | 4. 29–34. Wisdom.

3. 16–28 (H, above). WISDOM. (*Alternation.*)

H | a | 16–22. Case propounded.
  b | 23–25. Sentence pronounced.
  a | 26. Case withdrawn.
  b | 27, 28. Judgment executed.

18 there was no stranger. Some codices, with Sept., Syr., and Vulg., read "and there was no stranger".
19 child = son.
overlaid. One of the ten deaths occasioned by women. See note on Judg. 4. 21.
22 spake = talked [very much]. Fig. *Ellipsis* (Ap. 6) to be thus supplied.
26 said = kept on saying.
28 wisdom of God = Divine wisdom. Genitive of Character. See Ap. 17, and cp. note on *v.* 9 above.

4. 1–28 (J, above). DOMINION AND RICHES. (*Repeated Alternation.*)

J | c[1] | 1–19. Solomon. Riches (officers).
  d[1] | 20. People. Prosperity.
  c[2] | 21. Solomon. Dominion (foreign).
  d[2] | 22–23. People. Provision.
  c[3] | 24. Solomon. Dominion (foreign).
  d[3] | 25. People. Security.
  c[4] | 26–28. Solomon. Riches (officers).

1 all Israel. Expression not peculiar to any writer or period.

920 to 917 scribes; Jehoshaphat the son of Ahilud, the °recorder.

4 And Benaiah the son of Jehoiada *was* over the host: and Zadok and Abiathar *were* the priests:

5 And Azariah the son of °Nathan *was* over the officers: and Zabud the son of °Nathan *was* °principal officer, *and* °the king's friend:

6 And Ahishar *was* over the household: and Adoniram the son of Abda *was* over the tribute.

7 And Solomon had °twelve officers over all Israel, which provided victuals for the king and his household: each man his month in a year made provision.

8 And these *are* their names: The son of Hur, in °mount Ephraim:

9 The son of Dekar, in Makaz, and in Shaalbim, and Beth-shemesh, and °Elon-beth-hanan:

10 The son of Hesed, in Aruboth; to him *pertained* Sochoh, and all the land of Hepher:

11 The son of Abinadab, in all the region of °Dor; which had Taphath the daughter of Solomon to wife:

12 Baana the son of Ahilud; *to him pertained* Taanach and Megiddo, and all Beth-shean, which *is* by Zartanah beneath Jezreel, from Beth-shean to °Abel-meholah, *even* unto *the place that is* beyond Jokneam:

13 The son of Geber, in °Ramoth-gilead; to him *pertained* the towns of Jair the son of Manasseh, which *are* in Gilead; to him *also pertained* the °region of °Argob, which *is* in Bashan, threescore great cities with walls and brasen bars:

14 Ahinadab the son of Iddo *had* °Mahanaim:

15 Ahimaaz *was* in Naphtali; he also took Basmath the daughter of Solomon to wife:

16 Baanah the son of °Hushai *was* in Asher and in Aloth:

17 Jehoshaphat the son of Paruah, in Issachar:

18 Shimei the son of Elah, in Benjamin:

19 Geber the son of Uri *was* in the country of Gilead, *in* the country of Sihon king of the Amorites, and of Og king of Bashan; and °*he was* the only °officer which *was* °in the land.

d[1] (p. 453) 20 Judah and Israel *were* many, °as the sand which *is* by the °sea in multitude, eating and drinking, and making merry.

c[2] 21 And Solomon reigned over all kingdoms from °the river °unto the land of the Philistines, and unto the border of Egypt: they °brought presents, and served Solomon all the days of his life.

d[2] 22 And Solomon's °provision for one day was thirty °measures of fine flour, and threescore measures of meal,

23 Ten fat oxen, and twenty oxen out of the pastures, and an hundred sheep, beside harts, and roebucks, and fallowdeer, and fatted fowl.

c[3] 24 For he had dominion over all *the region* °on this side [21]the river, from Tiphsah even to Azzah, over all the kings on this side the river: and he had peace on all sides round about him.

d[3] 25 And Judah and Israel dwelt °safely, every °man under his vine and under his fig tree, from °Dan even to Beer-sheba, all the days of Solomon.

3 recorder = remembrancer. Cp. 1 Chron. 18. 15.
5 Nathan. Probably David's son. Cp. Luke 3. 31.
principal officer = priest. See Heb. (2 Sam. 8. 18).
the king's friend, as Hushai had been David's (2 Sam. 15. 37).
7 twelve officers. Cp. David's twelve captains (1 Chron. 27. 2–15).
8 mount = hill country.
9 Elon-beth-hanan. Some codices, with three early printed editions, read "Elon-ben-hanan". Other codices read "Elon and Beth-hanan". Sept. reads "Elon as far as Beth-hanan".
11 Dor. Cp. Josh. 11. 2; 12. 23; 17. 11.
12 Abel-meholah. The country of Elisha (19. 16, 21). Cp. Judg. 7. 22.
13 Ramoth-gilead. In the tribe of Gad. Famous for Ahab's last battle (22. 20). Cp. Josh. 20. 8. Judg. 11. 29.
region. A sharply defined border, defining the rocky rampart encircling the "Lejah" as it is called to-day.
Argob = Edrei, one of "the giant cities of Bashan". See Ap. 23 and 25.
14 Mahanaim. Cp. Gen. 32. 2. Josh. 13. 26.
16 Hushai. See note on *v.* 5.
19 he = Geber.
officer. Not the same word as in *v.* 7.
in the land = in the land [of Bashan].
20 as the sand. Fig. *Parœmia.* Ap. 6. Cp. Gen. 13. 16; 22. 17, &c.
sea. Some codices, with Syr., read "sea shore".
21 the river = the Euphrates. Cp. Gen. 15. 18. Josh. 1. 4.
unto = even unto. Cp. 2 Chron. 9. 26.
brought presents. Cp. Ps. 72. 10, 11.
22 provision. Heb. bread, put by Fig. *Synecdoche* (of the Species) for all kinds of food. Ap. 6.
measures. See Ap. 51. III. 3.
24 on this side, or beyond.
25 safely = confidently.
man. Heb. *'ish.* Ap. 14. II.
Dan even to Beer-sheba. The two extremities. Cp. Judg. 20. 1 and 1 Sam. 3. 20, &c.
26 forty thousand. In 2 Chron. 9. 25 it is 4,000, which is much more likely to be correct. The 12,000 are the same in both places. The ancient Hebrew characters were Phoenician, and may be seen on the Moabite Stone. These were in current use till about 140 B.C., and were gradually replaced by the modern Hebrew "square" characters. Mistakes in copying occurred through the similarity of certain letters. See notes on 2 Sam. 24. 10. Jer. 3. 8. Ezek. 6. 4; 22. 20.
horses. A breach of Deut. 17. 16. It began by breeding mules (1. 33, 38, 44), which was a breach of Lev. 19. 19.

4. 29–34 (*H*, p. 453). **WISDOM.**
(*Alternation.*)

H | e | 29. Extent.
  f | 30, 31. Others. Pre-eminence over.
  e | 32, 33. Extent.
  f | 34. Others. Resort by.

29 God. Heb. Elohim. Ap. 4. I.

26 And Solomon had °forty thousand stalls of °horses for his chariots, and twelve thousand horsemen. c[4]

27 And those officers provided victual for king Solomon, and for all that came unto king Solomon's table, every [25]man in his month: they lacked nothing.

28 Barley also and straw for the horses and dromedaries brought they unto the place where *the officers* were, every [25]man according to his charge.

29 And °God gave Solomon wisdom and *H* e (p. 454)

920 understanding °exceeding much, and largeness
to of heart, even [20]as the sand that *is* on the sea
917 shore.
f 30 And Solomon's wisdom excelled the wis-
(p. 454) dom of all the °children of the east country,
and all the wisdom of Egypt.
31 For he was wiser than °all °men; than
°Ethan the Ezrahite, and Heman, and Chalcol,
and Darda, the sons of Mahol: and his °fame
was in all nations round about.
e 32 And he spake three thousand °proverbs:
and his °songs were a thousand and five.
33 And he spake of trees, from the cedar tree
that *is* in Lebanon even unto the hyssop that
springeth out of the wall: he spake also of
beasts, and of fowl, and of creeping things, and
of fishes.
f 34 And there came of all °people to hear the
wisdom of Solomon, from all kings of the earth,
which had heard of his wisdom.

E h **5** And °Hiram king of Tyre sent his serv-
(p. 455) ants unto Solomon; for he had heard
that they had anointed him king in the room
of his father: for Hiram was ever a °lover of
David.
i k 2 And Solomon sent to Hiram, saying,
3 °"Thou knowest how that David my father
°could not build an house unto the name of
°the LORD his °God for the wars which were
about him on every side, until °the LORD put
them under the soles of his feet.
4 But now [3]the LORD my [3]God hath given
me rest on every side, *so that there is* neither
°adversary nor evil occurrent.
5 And, behold, I purpose to build an house
unto the name of [3]the LORD my [3]God, °as
[3]the LORD spake unto David my father, saying, 'Thy son, whom I will set upon thy
throne in thy room, he shall build an house
unto My name.'
6 Now therefore command thou that they
hew me cedar trees out of Lebanon; and my
servants shall be with thy servants:
l and unto thee will I give hire for thy servants
according to all that thou shalt appoint: for
thou knowest that *there is* not among us °any
that can skill to hew timber like unto the
Sidonians."
i k 7 And it came to pass, when Hiram heard
the words of Solomon, that he rejoiced greatly,
and said, "Blessed *be* [3]the LORD this day,
Which hath given unto David a wise son over
this great People."
8 And Hiram °sent to Solomon, saying, "I
have considered the things which thou sentest
to me for: *and* I will do all thy desire concerning timber of cedar, and concerning timber
of °fir.
9 My servants shall °bring *them* down from
Lebanon unto the sea: and I will convey them
by sea in floats unto the place that thou shalt
appoint me, and will cause them to be discharged there, and thou shalt receive *them*:
and thou shalt accomplish my desire, in giving
food for my household."
10 So Hiram °gave Solomon cedar trees and
[8]fir trees *according to* all his desire.

exceeding much = very great. Syr. reads this in connection with "largeness of heart", instead of with "understanding".

30 children = sons.

31 all men = any man.

men. Heb. *'ādām*, with Art. (Ap. 14. I) = any human being.

Ethan. The same four names occur among the sons of Zerah the son of Judah (1 Chron. 2. 6), except Dara for Darda; but cp. 1 Chron. 6. 44 and 33.

fame = name.

32 proverbs. Some included in the book of that name.

songs. Cp. Ps. 72 and 127.

34 people = peoples. Cp. ch. 10.

5. 1-12 (E, p. 452). CONTRACT WITH HIRAM.
(*Introversion and Alternation.*)

E | h | 1. Hiram and Solomon. Congratulations.
  i | k | 2-6-. Timber required.
     l | -6. Payment.
  i | *k* | 7-10. Timber required.
     l | 11. Payment.
  h | 12. Hiram and Solomon. Covenant.

1 Hiram. Born of a Jewish mother (7. 14. 2 Chron. 2. 14).

lover = ally. Hebrews always at amity with the Phoenicians. Never with Canaanites.

3 Thou knowest. Cp. 2 Sam. 5. 11. 1 Chron. 14. 1; 22. 4.

could not. There were three reasons altogether: (1) not the *time* (2 Sam. 7); (2) not the *opportunity* (1 Kings 5. 3); (3) not the *man* (1 Chron. 22. 8; 28. 3, &c.).

the LORD. Heb. Jehovah. Ap. 4. II.

God. Heb. Elohim. Ap. 4. I.

4 adversary. Heb. *sāṭān*.

5 as the LORD spake = according as Jehovah spake. Cp. 2 Sam. 7. 12, 13. 1 Chron. 17. 11, 12.

6 any = a man. Heb. *'īsh*. Ap. 14. II.

8 sent: i. e. wrote. Cp. 2 Chron. 2. 11. See note on Ex. 17. 14, and Ap. 47.

fir. Or, cypress.

9 bring them down. Note the illustration in the conversion of sinners. Cut down from nature's standing; down through the waters of death (Rom. 6. 11), before finding their place in the temple of God (Eph. 2. 20-22). Same with the stones. See note on *v.* 17.

10 gave = continued to give. Cp. Ps. 45. 12.

11 gave. Not the same as 2 Chron. 2. 10. That was for Hiram's *workmen* in Lebanon. This was for his royal household at Tyre.

measures. See Ap. 51. III. 3.

pure = bruised (as in a mortar), not crushed in a press.

12 as = according as. Cp. 3. 12.

league = a covenant. For breaking which Tyre was judged later. See Amos 1. 9.

13 levy = tribute of men for free labour, not the bond-service of 9. 21, 22. Cp. 4. 6. 2 Sam. 20. 24. Foretold in 1 Sam. 8. 16. David employed forced service of resident aliens (1 Chron. 22. 2; and notes on 2 Sam. 12. 31).

11 And Solomon °gave Hiram twenty thou- *l*
sand °measures of wheat *for* food to his
household, and twenty °measures of °pure
oil: thus gave Solomon to Hiram year by
year.
12 And [3]the LORD gave Solomon wisdom, *h*
°as He promised him: and there was peace
between Hiram and Solomon; and they two
made a °league together.
13 And king Solomon raised a °levy out of F
(p. 452)

920 to 917 all Israel; and the levy was thirty thousand °men.

14 And he sent them to Lebanon, ten thousand a month by courses: a month they were in Lebanon, *and* two months at home: and Adoniram *was* over the levy.

15 And Solomon had threescore and ten thousand that bare burdens, and fourscore thousand hewers in the mountains;

16 Beside the chief of Solomon's officers which *were* over the work, three thousand and three hundred, which ruled over the people that wrought in the work.

17 And the king commanded, and they °brought °great stones, costly stones, *and* hewed stones, to lay the foundation of the house.

18 And Solomon's builders and Hiram's builders did hew *them*, and the °stonesquarers: °so they prepared timber and stones to build the house.

G K M (p. 456) 917 **6** And it came to pass in the °four hundred and eightieth year after the °children of Israel were come out of the land of Egypt, in the fourth year of Solomon's reign over Israel, in the month Zif, which *is* the second month, that he began to build °the house of °the LORD.

N m 2 And the house which king Solomon built for [1]the LORD, the length thereof *was* threescore °cubits, and the breadth thereof twenty *cubits*, and the height thereof thirty cubits.

n 3 And the porch before the temple of the house, twenty [2]cubits *was* the length thereof, °according to the breadth of the house; *and* ten cubits *was* the breadth thereof before the house.

4 And for the house he made windows of narrow lights.

5 And against the wall of the house he built chambers round about, *against* the walls of the house round about, *both* of the temple and of the °oracle: and he made chambers round about:

6 The nethermost chamber *was* five [2]cubits broad, and the middle *was* six cubits broad, and the third *was* seven [2]cubits broad: for without *in the wall* of the house he made narrowed rests round about, that *the beams* should not be fastened in the walls of the house.

m 7 And the house, when it was in building, was built of stone °made ready °before it was brought thither: so that there was neither hammer nor axe *nor* any tool of iron °heard in the house, while it was in building.

n 8 The door for the middle chamber *was* in the right side of the house: and they went up with winding stairs into the middle *chamber*, and out of the middle into the third.

O 9 So he built the house, and finished it; and covered the house with beams and boards of cedar.

10 And *then* he built chambers against all the house, five cubits high: and they rested on the house with timber of cedar.

men. Heb. *'ish*. Ap. 14. II.

17 brought = quarried.

great stones. These stones illustrate the work of conversion in the sinner. Hewed out of nature's dark quarry (Isa. 51. 1, 2), cut and carved for a place in the temple of glory (Eph. 2. 20–22).

18 stonesquarers = men of Gebal, or Giblites, as Ezek. 27. 9, now Jubeil, forty miles north of Sidon. Cp. Ps. 83. 7. Phoenician masons' marks still visible on them.

so = and.

6. 1–8. 66 (G, p. 452). THE TEMPLE. (PARTICULAR.) (*Introversion.*)

G | K | 6. 1–38. The Temple.
  L | 7. 1–12. Other buildings.
  K | 7. 13–8. 66. The Temple.

6. 1–38 (K, above). THE TEMPLE. (*Introversion.*)

K | M | 1. Date of commencement.
  N | 2–8. Exterior of house.
    O | 9, 10. Completion.
      P | 11–13. Word of Jehovah.
    O | 14. Completion.
  N | 15–36. Interior of house.
  M | 37, 38. Date of completion.

1 four hundred and eightieth year. Note that the number is *Ordinal* (not Cardinal) = the 480th year of some longer and larger period, viz. the 490 years from the Exodus to the Dedication of the Temple; the difference of ten years being made up of seven years in building (*v.* 38) and three years in furnishing. Dedicated not in seventh year, for Completion took place in the eighth month of one year (*v.* 38), and the Dedication in the seventh month of another (8. 2). The *chronological* period was 40 years in wilderness + 450 years under judges + 40 years of Saul + 40 years of David + 3 years of Solomon (*v.* 1) = 573 (from 1490–917). The *mystical* period of 480 years is obtained by deducting the period of 93 years, when Israel's national position was in abeyance. Thus: 8 (Judg. 3. 8) + 18 (Judg. 3. 14) + 20 (Judg. 4. 3) + 7 (Judg. 6. 1) + 40 (Judg. 13. 1) = 93. (N.B. The eighteen years of Judg. 10. 7, 9, was local and beyond Jordan. It did not affect the national position). Hence 573 − 93 = 480 (from 873–93). See Ap., pp. 41, 56.

children = sons.

the house of the LORD = the Temple. Similar in plan to the Tabernacle, but double the size.

the LORD. Heb. Jehovah. Ap. 4.

6. 2–8 (N, above). EXTERIOR OF HOUSE. (*Alternation.*)

N | m | 2. House. Dimensions.
  n | 3–6. Accessories. Porch, &c.
  m | 7. House. Materials.
  n | 8. Accessories. Door, &c.

2 cubits. See Ap. 51. III. 2.

3 according to. Or, in the front of.

5 oracle. See note on 2 Sam. 16. 23.

7 made ready = made perfect.

before: i.e. in the quarries afar off, or beneath the city.

heard. So in the spiritual house. Eph. 2. 20–22.

12 which I spake unto David. Cp. 2 Sam. 7. 13, 1 Chron. 22. 10.

11 And the word of [1]the LORD came to Solomon, saying, P

12 "*Concerning* this house which thou art in building, if thou wilt walk in My statutes, and execute My judgments, and keep all My commandments to walk in them; then will I perform My word with thee, °which I spake unto David thy father:

917 13 And I will dwell °among the [1]children of
Israel, and will not forsake My people Israel."

O (p. 456) 14 So Solomon built the house, and finished it.

N o[1] (p. 457) 15 And he built the walls of the house within
with boards of cedar, both the floor of the
house, and the walls of the cieling: *and* he
°covered *them* on the inside with wood, and
covered the floor of the house with planks of fir.

p[1] 16 And he built twenty [2]cubits on the sides of
the house, both the floor and the walls with
boards of cedar: he even built *them* for it
within, *even* for the [5]oracle, *even* for the most
holy *place*.
17 And the house, that *is*, the temple before
it, was forty [2]cubits *long*.

o[2] 18 And the cedar of the house within *was*
carved with knops and open flowers: all *was*
cedar; there was °no stone seen.

p[2] 19 And the [5]oracle he prepared in the house
within, to set there the ark of the covenant of
[1]the LORD.
20 And the [5]oracle in the forepart *was* twenty
[2]cubits in length, and twenty [2]cubits in breadth,
and twenty [2]cubits in the height thereof: and
he °overlaid it with pure gold; and *so* [15]covered
the altar *which was of* cedar.

o[3] 21 So Solomon [20]overlaid the house within
with pure gold: and he made a partition by
the chains of gold before the oracle; and he
overlaid it with gold.
22 And the °whole house he [20]overlaid with
gold, until he had finished all the house: also
the whole altar that *was* by the [5]oracle he
overlaid with gold.

p[3] 23 And within the [5]oracle he made °two
cherubims *of* °olive tree, *each* ten [2]cubits high.
24 And five [2]cubits *was* the one wing of the
cherub, and five [2]cubits the other wing of the
cherub: from the uttermost part of the one
wing unto the uttermost part of the other *were*
ten [2]cubits.
25 And the other cherub *was* ten [2]cubits:
both the cherubims *were* of one measure and
one size.
26 The height of the one cherub *was* ten
[2]cubits, and so *was it* of the other cherub.
27 And he set the cherubims within the inner
house: and they stretched forth the wings of
the cherubims, so that the wing of the one
touched the *one* wall, and the wing of the
other cherub touched the other wall; and their
wings touched one another in the midst of the
house.
28 And he [20]overlaid the cherubims with
gold.
29 And he carved all the walls of the house
round about with carved figures of cherubims
and palm trees and open flowers, within and
without.

o[4] 30 And the floor of the house he [20]overlaid
with gold, within and without.

p[4] 31 And for the entering of the [5]oracle he
made doors *of* olive tree: the lintel *and* side
posts *were* a fifth part *of the wall*.
32 The °two doors also *were of* olive tree;
and he carved upon them carvings of cheru-

13 among = in the midst of.

6. 15-36 (*N*, p. 456). INTERIOR OF HOUSE.
(*Repeated Alternation.*)

N | o[1] | 15. Covering. Walls, within, covered, cedar.
p[1] | 16, 17. Oracle. Dimensions.
o[2] | 18. Covering. Walls, within, carved, cedar.
p[2] | 19, 20. Oracle. Ark, &c.
o[3] | 21, 22. Covering. Walls, within, gold.
p[3] | 23-29. Oracle. Cherubim.
o[4] | 30. Covering. Floor, covered, gold.
p[4] | 31-36. Oracle. Entrances.

15 covered. Note that all the stonework was covered with cedar wood; and the cedar wood covered with gold. Even so the saved sinner is covered with Christ's human and Divine righteousness imputed to him. Cp. Luke 15. 22. Phil. 3. 9.
18 no stone seen. Fig. *Pleonasm*. Ap. 6. Words not necessary for grammar, or sense; but used to emphasise the completeness of our covering by Christ's merits. Cp. Eph. 1. 6. Col. 1. 28; 2. 10; 4. 12.
20 overlaid. See note on covered, 15 and 18.
22 whole house. Fig. *Synecdoche* (of Whole). Ap. 6. Put for every part of it.
23 two cherubims. See Ap. 41.
olive tree = oil tree, as in Isa. 41. 19: rendered pine (Neh. 8. 15); but, *Oleaster* according to Tristram.
32 two doors = two-leaved (or double) doors.
33 door = entrance.
37 Zif. The second month.
38 eighth month. See note on *v.* 1, and cp. Dedication later, in "seventh month" (8. 2); so that more than one, and probably three, years in completing the appointments. parts = appointments.
seven years. See note on *v.* 1. Seven years for the building itself, and probably three years for the "appointments". Contrast these seven with the thirteen of 7. 1, and see Ap. 10.

7. 1-12 (L, p. 456). OTHER BUILDINGS.
(*Introversion.*)

L | q | 1. Solomon's own house. Time.
r | 2-8-. House of forest of Lebanon.
r | -8. House of the queen.
q | 9-12. Solomon's house. Materials.

1 thirteen. Cp. 6. 38, and see Ap. 10.

bims and palm trees and open flowers, and
overlaid *them* with gold, and spread gold upon
the cherubims, and upon the palm trees.
33 So also made he for the °door of the
temple posts *of* olive tree, a fourth part *of the
wall*.
34 And the two doors *were of* fir tree: the
two leaves of the one door *were* folding, and
the two leaves of the other door *were* folding.
35 And he carved *thereon* cherubims and
palm trees and open flowers: and covered *them*
with gold fitted upon the carved work.
36 And he built the inner court with three
rows of hewed stone, and a row of cedar beams.

37 In the fourth year was the foundation of M
the house of [1]the LORD laid, in the month °Zif: (p. 456)
38 And in the eleventh year, in the month 917
Bul, which *is* the °eighth month, was the house to
finished throughout all the °parts thereof, and 910
according to all the fashion of it. So was he
°seven years in building it.

7 But Solomon was building his own house L q
°thirteen years, and he finished all his (p. 457)
house. 910-897

r (p. 457) 910 to 897 2 He built also the house of the forest of Lebanon; the length thereof *was* an hundred °cubits, and the breadth thereof fifty °cubits, and the height thereof thirty °cubits, upon four rows of cedar pillars, with cedar beams upon the pillars.

3 And *it was* covered with cedar above upon the beams, that *lay* on forty five pillars, fifteen *in* a row.

4 And *there were* windows *in* three rows, and light *was* against light *in* three ranks.

5 And all the °doors and posts *were* square, with the windows: and light *was* against light *in* three ranks.

6 And he made a porch of pillars; the length thereof *was* fifty [2]cubits, and the breadth thereof thirty [2]cubits: and the porch *was* before them: and the *other* pillars and the thick beam *were* before them.

7 Then he made a porch for the throne where he might judge, *even* the porch of judgment: and *it was* covered with cedar from one side of the floor to the other.

8 And his house where he dwelt *had* another court within the porch, *which* was of the like work.

r Solomon made also an house for Pharaoh's daughter, whom he had taken *to wife*, like unto this porch.

q 9 All these *were of* costly stones, according to the measures of hewed stones, °sawed with saws, within and without, even from the foundation unto the coping, and *so* on the outside toward the great court.

10 And the foundation *was of* costly stones, even great stones, stones of ten [2]cubits, and stones of eight [2]cubits.

11 And above *were* costly stones, after the measures of hewed stones, and cedars.

12 And the great court round about *was* with three rows of hewed stones, and a row of cedar beams, both for the inner court of the house of °the LORD, and for the porch of the house.

K Q^1 R^1 (p. 458) 13 And king Solomon sent and fetched Hiram out of Tyre.

14 He *was* °a widow's son of the tribe of °Naphtali, and his father *was* a °man of Tyre, a worker in brass: and he was filled with wisdom, and understanding, and °cunning to work all °works in brass.

R^2 S s And he came to king Solomon, and wrought all his work.

t 15 For he °cast °two pillars of brass, of °eighteen [2]cubits high °apiece: and a line of twelve [2]cubits did compass either of them about.

16 And he made two °chapiters *of* molten brass, to set upon the tops of the pillars: the height of the one °chapiter *was* °five [2]cubits, and the height of the other °chapiter *was* five [2]cubits:

17 *And* °nets of checker work, and wreaths of chain work, for the [16]chapiters which *were* upon the top of the pillars; seven for the one [16]chapiter, and seven for the other [16]chapiter.

18 And he made the pillars, and two rows round about upon the one network, to cover the [16]chapiters that *were* upon the top, with pomegranates: and so did he for the other [16]chapiter.

19 And the [16]chapiters that *were* upon the top of the pillars *were* of lily work in the porch, four [2]cubits.

20 And the [16]chapiters upon the two pillars *had pomegranates* also above, over against the °belly which *was* by the network: and the

2 cubits. See Ap. 51. III. 2.

5 doors=entrances.

9 sawed with saws. Fig. *Polyptōton.* Ap. 6.

7. 13—8. 66 (*K*, p. 456). THE TEMPLE.
(*Division.*)

K | Q^1 | 7. 13-51. The work itself.
| Q^2 | 8. 1-66. The dedication of the work.

7. 13-51 (Q^1, above). THE WORK.
(*Division.*)

Q^1 | R^1 | 13, 14-. The worker.
| R^2 | -14-51. The works.

12 the LORD. Heb. Jehovah. Ap. 4. II.

14 a widow's. One of nine widows specially mentioned. See note on Gen. 38. 19.

Naphtali: by marriage. By birth, of Dan (2 Chron. 2. 14). Dan furnished Aholiab, one of the builders of the Tabernacle (Ex. 31. 6).

man. Heb. *'ish.* Ap. 14. II.

cunning = knowing, or skilful. Cp. 1 Sam. 16. 18. 1 Chron. 22. 15.

works in brass=castings in bronze. These were the subjects of later prophecy (Jer. 27. 19), fulfilled in 2 Kings 25. 13-17.

7. -14-51 (R^2, above). THE WORKS.
(*Alternation.*)

R^2 | S | -14-40-. Description.
| T | -40. Completion.
| *S* | 41-50. Enumeration.
| *T* | 51. Completion.

7. -14-40 (S T, above). DESCRIPTION.
(*Introversion.*)

S | s | -14. Hiram commences the work.
| t | 15-22. The position of pillars.
| u | 23-37. The sea. } Water.
| *u* | 38. The lavers. } Water.
| *t* | 39, 40-. The position of sea and lavers.
T | *s* | -40. Hiram completes the work.

15 cast. Heb. fashioned.

two pillars=the two pillars: i. e. the two notable pillars, for ornament, not for support, and hollow (Jer. 52. 21).

eighteen cubits high apiece. So 2 Kings 25. 17 and Jer. 52. 21. But 2 Chron. 3. 15 (marg.) says thirty-five cubits long: i. e. together, the top of "each" being reckoned separately. Therefore the height here was $17\frac{1}{2}+\frac{1}{2}$ cubit being taken up in the joining on of the capital.

apiece. This is the reckoning here. In 2 Chron. 3. 15 they are reckoned together. See margin.

16 chapiters. Old French *chapiteau*, from Lat. *capitulum*=capitals, or crowns.

five cubits. So 2 Chron. 3. 15. But 2 Kings 25. 17 says three cubits, not including the "wreathen" or lattice work, which is described separately, and must have been two cubits.

17 nets=frames, or net- or lattice-work. These are *included* in the five cubits here and in 2 Chron. 3. 15, but not in 2 Kings 25. 17.

20 belly=swell, or protuberance.

910 pomegranates *were* °two hundred in rows
to round about upon the other [16]chapiter.
897 21 And he set up the pillars °in the porch of the temple: and he set up the right pillar, and called the name thereof °Jachin: and he set up the left pillar, and called the name thereof °Boaz.

22 And upon the top of the pillars *was* lily work: so was the work of the pillars finished.

u (p. 458) 23 And he made a °molten sea, ten [2]cubits from the one brim to the other: *it was* round all about, and his height *was* five [2]cubits: and °a line of thirty [2]cubits did compass it round about.

24 And under the brim of it round about *there were* knops compassing it, ten in a [2]cubit, compassing the sea round about: the knops *were* cast in two rows, when it was cast.

25 It stood upon twelve oxen, three looking toward the north, and three looking toward the west, and three looking toward the south, and three looking toward the east: and the sea *was set* above upon them, and all their hinder parts *were* inward.

26 And it *was* an hand breadth thick, and the brim thereof was wrought like the brim of a cup, with flowers of lilies: it contained °two thousand °baths.

27 And he made ten bases of brass; four [2]cubits *was* the length of one base, and four [2]cubits the breadth thereof, and three [2]cubits the height of it.

28 And the work of the bases *was* on this *manner:* they had °borders, and the °borders *were* between the ledges:

29 And on the borders that *were* between the ledges *were* lions, oxen, and cherubims: and upon the ledges *there was* a base above: and beneath the lions and oxen *were* certain °additions made of thin work.

30 And every base had four brasen °wheels, and °plates of brass: and the four corners thereof had °undersetters: under the laver *were* °undersetters molten, °at the side of every [29]addition.

31 And the mouth of it within the [16]chapiter and above *was* a [2]cubit: but the mouth thereof *was* round *after* the work of the base, a [2]cubit and an half: and also upon the mouth of it *were* gravings with their °borders, foursquare, not round.

32 And under the [28]borders *were* four [30]wheels; and the axletrees of the wheels *were joined* to the base: and the height of a wheel *was* a [2]cubit and half a [2]cubit.

33 And the work of the wheels *was* like the work of a chariot wheel: their axletrees, and their °naves, and their °felloes, and their °spokes, *were* all molten.

34 And *there were* four [30]undersetters to the four corners of one base: *and* the [30]undersetters *were* of the very base itself.

35 And in the top of the base *was there* a round compass of half a [2]cubit high: and on the top of the base the ledges thereof and the borders thereof *were* of the same.

36 For on the plates of the ledges thereof, and on the borders thereof, he graved cherubims, lions, and palm trees, according to the °proportion of every one, and [29]additions round about.

37 After this *manner* he made the ten bases: all of them had one casting, one measure, *and* one size.

38 Then made he ten lavers of brass: one u
laver contained forty [26]baths: *and* every laver was four [2]cubits: *and* upon every one of the ten bases one laver.

39 And he put five bases on the right side of t
the house, and five on the left side of the house: and he set the sea on the right side of the house eastward over against the south.

40 And Hiram made the °lavers, and the shovels, and the basons.

So Hiram made an end of doing all the work T s
that he °made king Solomon for the house of [12]the LORD:

41 The two pillars, and the *two* bowls of the S
[16]chapiters that *were* on the top of the two pillars; and the two °networks, to cover the two bowls of the [16]chapiters which *were* upon the top of the pillars;

42 And four hundred pomegranates for the two networks, *even* two rows of pomegranates for one network, to cover the two bowls of the [16]chapiters that *were* °upon the pillars;

43 And the ten bases, and ten lavers on the bases;

---

two hundred. In *v.* 42 called four hundred, because two hundred reckoned to each, as in 2 Chron. 4. 13. In 2 Chron. 3. 16 they are called one hundred, because reckoned one hundred to each row. In Jer. 52. 23 they are ninety-six "on a side" (Heb. *rūachah* = to windward: i. e. exposed to the wind or open air. The others within, or sheltered).

21 in the porch = for the porch.
Jachin = He (God) will establish. } Referring to His
Boaz = In Him (God) is strength. } People Israel.

23 molten sea = brazen laver. "Sea" put by Fig. *Metonymy* (of Adjunct) for what contained it.
a line of thirty cubits. Here the proportion of the diameter to the circumference (1 : 3) was revealed, while human wisdom was still searching it out.

26 two thousand. 2 Chron. 4. 5 says three thousand. But 1 Kings 7. 26 speaks of what it *did* (usually) contain; while 2 Chron. 4. 5 speaks of what it *could* "receive and hold". No bath in use is filled to its full capacity. **baths.** See Ap. 51. III. 3.

28 borders = panels, or enclosures.

29 additions = connections. Probably wreaths. Occurs only here and *vv.* 29, 30, 36.

30 wheels: showing that these lavers were movable; and indicating that when "that which is perfect should come (viz. the washing with spirit, Acts 1. 5), the type (water) was to be wheeled away".
plates = axletrees.
undersetters = projections, or supports.
at the side of = opposite.

31 borders = panels. Removed by Ahaz (2 Kings 16. 17). Replaced by Hezekiah (2 Chron. 29. 19). Existed at taking of Temple (Jer. 52. 17, 20).

33 naves = felloes. **felloes** = spokes.
spokes = naves.

36 proportion: i.e. on a reduced scale, as the plates required.

40 lavers = cauldrons (for boiling the peace offerings). Some codices, with three early printed editions, Sept., and Vulg., read "pans". Cp. *v.* 45 and 2 Chron 4. 11.
made = made for.

41 networks = lattices.

42 upon = upon the face of. Fig. *Pleonasm.* Ap. 6.

910 to 897 **44** And one sea, and twelve oxen under the sea;

45 And the pots, and the shovels, and the basons: and all these vessels, which Hiram made to king Solomon for the house of [12]the LORD, *were of* bright brass.

46 In the plain of Jordan did the king cast them, in the clay ground between Succoth and Zarthan.

47 And Solomon left all the vessels *unweighed*, because they were °exceeding many: neither was the weight of the brass °found out.

48 And Solomon made all the °vessels that *pertained* unto the house of [12]the LORD: the °altar of gold, and the table of gold, whereupon the shewbread *was*,

49 And the °candlesticks of °pure gold, five on the right *side*, and five on the left, before the oracle, with the flowers, and the lamps, and the tongs *of* gold,

50 And the bowls, and the snuffers, and the basons, and the spoons, and the censers *of* pure gold; and the hinges *of* gold, *both* for the doors of the inner house, °the most holy *place*, *and* for the doors of the house, *to wit*, of the temple.

T (p. 458) **51** So was ended all the work that king Solomon made for the house of [12]the LORD. And Solomon brought in °the things which David his father had dedicated; *even* the silver, and the gold, and the vessels, did he put among the treasures of the house of [12]the LORD.

Q² U v (p. 460) **8** Then Solomon assembled °the elders of Israel, °and all the heads of the tribes, the chief of the °fathers of the °children of Israel, unto king Solomon in Jerusalem, that they might bring up the ark of the covenant of °the LORD °out of the city of David, which *is* Zion.

2 And all the °men of Israel assembled themselves unto king Solomon at the feast in the month °Ethanim, which *is* °the seventh month.

3 And all the elders of Israel came, and the priests °took up the ark.

4 And they brought up the ark of [1]the LORD, and °the tabernacle of the congregation, and all the holy vessels that *were* in °the tabernacle, even those did the °priests and the °Levites bring up.

w **5** And king Solomon, and all the congregation of Israel, that were assembled unto him, *were* with him before the ark, sacrificing sheep and oxen, that could not be told nor numbered for multitude.

v **6** And the priests brought in the ark of the covenant of [1]the LORD unto his place, into the °oracle of the house, to °the most holy *place*, *even* under the wings of the cherubims.

7 For the cherubims spread forth *their* two wings °over the place of the ark, and the cherubims covered the ark and the staves thereof above.

8 And they drew out the staves, that the ends of the staves were seen out in the holy *place* before the [6]oracle, and they were not seen °without: and there they are °unto this day.

9 *There was* nothing in the ark °save the two tables of stone, which Moses put there at Horeb, °when [1]the LORD made *a covenant* with the [1]children of Israel, when they came out of the land of Egypt.

10 And it came to pass, when the priests were come out of the holy *place*, that the cloud °filled the house of [1]the LORD, w

11 So that the priests could not stand to minister because of the cloud: for the glory of [1]the LORD had filled the house of [1]the LORD.

---

47 exceeding many. Heb. many many. Fig. *Epizeuxis* (Ap. 6) for emphasis: thus well rendered.

found out = sought out.

48 vessels = furniture.

altar: i. e. the altar of incense. Cp. 6. 22.

49 candlesticks. Cp. 2 Chron. 4. 20. Solomon exceeded the pattern in number but followed the design in shape. Size not stated.

pure gold. In Palestine, gold has the least possible alloy, and is exceedingly malleable.

50 the most holy place = the holy of holies.

51 the things which David his father had dedicated = the holy things of David. Heb. *ḳodesh.* See note on Ex. 3. 5.

8. 1-66 (Q², p. 458). THE DEDICATION. (*Introversion and Alternation.*)

Q² | U | 1-11. The Feast.
  V | W | Y | 12-21. Blessing.
      Z | 22. Station.
       X | 23-53. PRAYER.
  V | *W* | *Z* | 54, 55. Station.
       Y | 56-61. Blessing.
      X | 62-64. WORSHIP.
 U | 65, 66. The Feast.

1-11 (U, above). THE FEAST. (*Alternation.*)

U | v | 1-4. The Ark brought up.
  w | 5. "Could not be numbered." (Multitude.)
 v | 6-9. The Ark brought in.
  w | 10, 11. "Could not stand." (Cloud.)

1 the elders. Some codices, with Sept., Syr., and Vulg., read "all the elders".

and. Some codices, with three early printed editions, Aram., and Sept., omit "and".

fathers = fathers' houses = families.

children = sons.

the LORD. Heb. Jehovah. Ap. 4.

out of the city of David: i. e. up out of Zion (the former Jebus, 2 Sam. 5. 6-9) to Moriah, where the Temple had been built (1 Chron. 21. 28—22. 1). Cp. 2 Sam. 6. See Ap. 68.

2 men. Heb. *'ish.* Ap. 14. II.

Ethanim. Same as Tisri.

the seventh month. Cp. Lev. 23. 24. See note on 6. 38.

3 took up. As commanded in Num. 4. 5, 15, 19.

4 the tabernacle = the tent. Heb. *'ohel.* See Ap. 40. Brought from Gibeon (2 Chron. 1. 3, 4). Probably put among the treasures of 7. 51.

priests: the ministers of sacrifice.

Levites: the ministers of praise.

6 oracle = the most holy place. Cp. 2 Sam. 16. 23.

the most holy place = the holy of holies.

7 over. Heb. text reads "unto". A.V. "over" agrees with Aram., Sept., and Vulg. Cp. 2 Chron. 5. 8.

8 without = outside: i. e. outside the holy place.

unto this day: i. e. 1 Kings written while Temple was still standing; therefore before its destruction by Nebuchadnezzar, and before the Captivity. Cp. 2 Chron. 5. 9, and see 9. 21; 12. 19. 2 Kings 8. 22; 10. 27.

9 save, &c. Heb. 9. 4 speaks of the Ark as it was in the Tabernacle, not as in the Temple. Cp. Heb. 9. 2, 3, 4.

when . . . Israel. The Sept. reads "the Tables which Moses placed [there] in Horeb, which [Tables] the LORD covenanted with the sons of Israel".

10 filled. Cp. Ex. 40. 34.

Y x[1] (p. 461) 910 **12** Then spake Solomon, [1] "The LORD said that He would ° dwell in the thick darkness.

y[1] **13** I have surely built Thee an ° house to dwell in, a settled place for Thee to abide in for ever."

x[2] **14** And the king turned his face about, and blessed all the ° congregation of Israel: (and all the ° congregation of Israel stood;)

15 And he said, "Blessed *be* [1] the LORD ° God of Israel, Which spake with His mouth unto David my father, and hath with His hand fulfilled *it*, ° saying,

16 'Since the day that I brought forth My People Israel out of Egypt, I chose no city out of all the tribes of Israel to build an house, that My name might be ° therein; but I chose David to be over My People Israel.'

y[2] **17** And it was in the heart of David my father to build an house for the name of [1] the LORD [15] God of Israel.

x[3] **18** And [1] the LORD ° said unto David my father, 'Whereas it was in thine heart to build an house unto My name, thou didst well that it was in thine heart.

19 Nevertheless thou shalt not build the house; but thy son that shall come forth out of thy loins, he shall build the house unto My name.'

y[3] **20** And [1] the LORD hath performed His word that He spake, and I am risen up in the room of David my father, and sit on the throne of Israel, as [1] the LORD promised, and have built an house for the name of [1] the LORD [15] God of Israel.

21 And I have set there a place for the ark, wherein *is* ° the covenant of [1] the LORD, which He made with our fathers, when He brought them out of the land of Egypt."

Z (p. 460) **22** And Solomon ° stood before the altar of [1] the LORD in the presence of all the [14] congregation of Israel, and ° spread forth his hands toward heaven:

X A[1] a (p. 461) **23** And he said, [1] "LORD [15] God of Israel, *there is* no [15] God like Thee, in heaven above, or on earth beneath, Who keepest covenant and ° mercy with Thy servants that walk before Thee with all their heart:

24 Who hast kept with Thy servant David my father that Thou promisedst him: Thou spakest also with Thy mouth, and hast fulfilled *it* with Thine hand, as *it is* this day.

b **25** Therefore now, [1] LORD [15] God of Israel, keep with Thy servant David my father that Thou promisedst him, saying, 'There shall not fail thee a [2] man in My sight to sit on the throne of Israel; ° so that thy [1] children take heed to their way, that they walk before Me ° as thou hast walked before Me.'

26 And now, O ° God of Israel, let Thy ° word, I pray Thee, be verified, which Thou spakest unto Thy servant David my father.

a **27** But ° will [15] God ° indeed [12] dwell on the earth? ° behold, the ° heaven and heaven of heavens cannot contain Thee; ° how much less this house that I have builded?

8. 12-21 (Y, p. 460). THE BLESSING.
(*Repeated Alternation.*)

Y | x[1] | 12. Words of and to Jehovah.
  y[1] | 13. The house.
 x[2] | 14-16. Words of and to Jehovah.
  y[2] | 17. The house.
 x[3] | 18, 19. Words of and to Jehovah.
  y[3] | 20, 21. The house.

12 dwell. Fig. *Anthropopatheia*. Ap. 6.
13 house to dwell in. Heb. *beth zebūl* = Assyrian *bit-zabali* = high or lofty house. Cp. Zebulun (Gen. 30. 20).
14 congregation = assembly.
15 God. Heb. Elohim. Ap. 4.
saying. Cp. 2 Sam. 7. 6.
16 therein = there, with Sept. and 2 Chron. 6. 5. The Sept. adds after this word "and I have chosen Jerusalem that My Name might be there". This is preserved in 2 Chron. 6. 6. The scribe's eye, in copying, went back to the next word, "I have chosen David", and went on from there, omitting the sentence given above.
18 said. Cp. 2 Sam. 7. 12.
21 the covenant. Put by Fig. *Metonymy* (of Subject), Ap. 6, for the two tables of stone on which it was written. Cp. *v.* 9.
22 stood = took his position: position, not posture. See note on *v.* 54.
spread forth. He did this kneeling. See *v.* 54 and 2 Chron. 6. 13.
23 mercy = lovingkindness, or grace.

23-53 (X, p. 460). THE PRAYER.
(*Division.*)

X | A[1] | 23-30. General. Jehovah and himself.
 | A[2] | 31-53. Special. The people.

23-30 (A[1], above). GENERAL.
(*Alternation.*)

A[1] | a | 23, 24. Jehovah's faithfulness.
  b | 25, 26. Solomon's plea.
 a | 27. Jehovah's immensity.
  b | 28-30. Solomon's plea.

25 so that = provided that.
as = according as.
26 God = Elohim. Ap. 4. I. Some codices, with Sept., Syr., and Vulg., read "Jehovah Elohim". Ap. 4. I, II.
word. Heb. *dābār*. Put by Fig. *Metonymy* (of Subject), Ap. 6, for the promises made by it. See *v.* 56, and Ap. 73. x.
27 will . . . ? Fig. *Erotēsis*. Ap. 6. Cp. 2 Chron. 6. 18. Isa. 66. 1. Acts 7. 48, 49.
indeed = in truth.
behold. Fig. *Asterismos*. Ap. 6.
heaven, &c. Fig. *Polyptōton* (Ap. 6), for emphasis.
how much . . . ? Fig. *Erotēsis*. Ap. 6.
28 prayer. Includes every thought of the heart which is Godward.
supplication = entreaty (for favour).
cry = the vehement utterance of either.
29 toward. So written, but some codices read "upon".
make toward. Hence Daniel's act (Dan. 6. 10).

28 Yet have Thou respect unto the ° prayer of Thy servant, and to his ° supplication, O [1] LORD my [15] God, to hearken unto the ° cry and to the prayer, which Thy servant prayeth before Thee to day: *b*

29 That Thine eyes may be open toward this house night and day, *even* ° toward the place of which Thou hast said, 'My name shall be there:' that Thou mayest hearken unto the prayer which Thy servant shall ° make toward this place.

910 30 And hearken Thou to the supplication of Thy servant, and of Thy People Israel, when they shall pray [29] toward this place: and hear Thou in heaven Thy °dwelling place: and when Thou hearest, forgive.

A² B c¹ (p. 462) 31 °If any [2] man °trespass against his neighbour, and an oath be laid upon him to cause him to swear, °and the oath come before Thine altar in this house:

d¹ 32 Then hear Thou in heaven, and do, and judge Thy servants, condemning the wicked, to bring his way upon his head; and justifying the righteous, to give him according to his righteousness.

C c² 33 °When Thy People Israel be smitten down before the enemy, because they have °sinned against Thee, and shall turn again to Thee, and confess Thy name, and pray, and make supplication unto Thee in this house:

d² 34 Then hear Thou in heaven, and forgive the [33] sin of Thy People Israel, and °bring them again unto the land which Thou gavest unto their fathers.

c³ 35 °When heaven is shut up, and there is no rain, because they have [33] sinned against Thee; if they pray toward this place, and confess Thy name, and turn from their sin, when Thou afflictest them:

d³ 36 Then hear Thou in heaven, and forgive the [33] sin of Thy servants, and of Thy People Israel, °that Thou teach them the good way wherein they should walk, and give rain upon Thy land, which Thou hast given to Thy People for an inheritance.

c⁴ 37 If there be in the land famine, if there be °pestilence, °blasting, mildew, locust, *or* if there be caterpiller; if their enemy besiege them in the land of their °cities; whatsoever plague, whatsoever sickness *there be;*

38 What [28] prayer and [28] supplication soever be *made* by any °man, *or* by all Thy People Israel, which shall °know °every man the °plague of his own heart, and spread forth his hands toward this house:

d⁴ 39 Then hear Thou in heaven Thy [30] dwelling place, and forgive, and do, and give to [38] every man according to °his ways, whose heart Thou knowest; (°for Thou, *even* Thou only, knowest the hearts of all the [1] children of °men;)

40 That they may fear Thee all the days that they live in the land which Thou gavest unto our fathers.

B c⁵ 41 Moreover concerning a °stranger, that *is* not of Thy People Israel, but cometh out of a far country for Thy name's sake;

42 ([39] For °they shall hear of Thy great name, and of Thy strong hand, and of Thy stretched out arm;) when he shall come and pray toward this house;

d⁵ 43 Hear Thou in heaven Thy [30] dwelling place, and do according to all that the stranger calleth to Thee for: that all people of the earth may know Thy name, to fear Thee, as *do* Thy People Israel; and that they may know that this house, which I have builded, is called by Thy name.

44 If Thy people go out to battle against their °enemy, whithersoever Thou shalt send them, and shall pray unto [1] the LORD [29] toward the city which Thou hast chosen, and *toward* the house that I have built for Thy name: *C* c⁶

45 Then hear Thou in heaven their prayer and their supplication, and maintain their °cause. d⁶

46 If they [33] sin against Thee, ([39] for °*there is* no man that [33] sinneth not,) and Thou be angry with them, and deliver them to the enemy, so that they carry them away captives unto the land of the enemy, far or near; c⁷

31-53 (A², p. 461). SPECIAL. THE PEOPLE.
(*Introversion and Repeated Alternation.*)

A² | B | c¹ | 31. Subject.
| | d¹ | 32. "Hear Thou". } Individual.
| C | c² | 33. Subject.
| | d² | 34. "Hear Thou".
| | c³ | 35. Subject.
| | d³ | 36. "Hear Thou". } National.
| | c⁴ | 37, 38. Subject.
| | d⁴ | 39, 40. "Hear Thou".
| *B* | c⁵ | 41, 42. Subject.
| | d⁵ | 43. "Hear Thou". } Individual.
| *C* | c⁶ | 44. Subject.
| | d⁶ | 45. "Hear Thou".
| | c⁷ | 46-48. Subject.
| | d⁷ | 49-53. "Hear Thou". } National.

30 dwelling place. Fig. *Anthropopatheia*. Ap. 6.

31 If = When, or Whosoever shall.
trespass. See Ap. 44. i. This shows an acquaintance with the Pentateuch. See *v.* 33, and Ap. 47.
and the oath come. Omitted by Aram., Sept., Syr., and Vulg. versions.

33 When. Note how these petitions are based on the *Pentateuch*. Cp. Lev. 26. 17. Deut. 28. 25.
sinned. Heb. *chāṭā'*. Ap. 44. i.

34 bring them again. See Deut. 30. 1-8. Neh. 1. 8, 9.

35 When heaven is shut up. Cp. Lev. 26. 19. Deut. 11. 17. Cp. ch. 17. 1.

36 that Thou teach = because Thou wilt teach.

37 pestilence = death. Cp. Lev. 26. 26.
blasting = blight.
cities. Heb. gates. Put by Fig. *Metonymy* (of Adjunct) for cities.

38 man. Heb. *'ādām*. Ap. 14. I.
know = perceive in his own heart. Lat. *conscio*, or have conscience.
every man. Heb. *'ish*. Ap. 14. II.
plague = punishment. Put by Fig. *Metonymy* (of Cause), Ap. 6, for the sin which produces it.

39 his = all his, as in 2 Chron. 6. 30.
for Thou, &c. Fig. *Epitrechon*. Ap. 6.
men. Heb. *'ādām*. Ap. 14. I.

41 stranger = foreigner, or alien. Already contemplated in Num. 15. 14. Deut. 10. 19.

42 they shall hear. Cp. 10. 1, 6, 7.

44 enemy. Some codices, with Aram., Sept., Syr., and Vulg., read "enemies".

45 cause. Heb. judgment: i. e. execute judgment for them.

46 there is no man that sinneth not. Fig. *Parœmia*. Ap. 6. Cp. Prov. 20. 9. Ecc. 7. 20. Jas. 3. 2. 1 John 1. 8, 10.

910 47 *Yet* °if they shall °bethink themselves in the land whither they were carried captives, and repent, and make supplication unto Thee in the land of them that carried them captives, °saying, 'We have [33]sinned, and have done perversely, we have committed °wickedness;'
48 And *so* return unto Thee with all their heart, and with all their °soul, in the land of their enemies, which led them away captive, and pray unto Thee °toward their land, which Thou gavest unto their fathers, °the city which Thou hast chosen, and the house which °I have built for Thy name:

d7 (p. 462) 49 Then hear Thou their prayer and their supplication in heaven Thy [30]dwelling place, and maintain their [45]cause,
50 And °forgive Thy People that have [33]sinned against Thee, and all their °transgressions wherein they have °transgressed against Thee, and °give them compassion before them who carried them captive, that they may have compassion on them:
51 For they *be* Thy People, and Thine inheritance, which Thou broughtest forth out of Egypt, from the midst of the °furnace of iron:
52 That Thine eyes may be open unto the supplication of Thy servant, and unto the supplication of Thy People Israel, to hearken unto them in all that they call for unto Thee.
53 For Thou °didst separate them from among all the °people of the earth, *to be* Thine inheritance, [25]as Thou spakest °by the hand of °Moses Thy servant, when Thou broughtest our fathers out of Egypt, O °Lord °GOD."

Z (p. 460) 54 And it was *so*, that when Solomon had made an end of °praying all this °prayer and supplication unto [1]the LORD, he arose from before the altar of [1]the LORD, from °kneeling on his knees with his hands spread up to heaven.
55 And he stood, and blessed all the [14]congregation of Israel with a loud voice, saying,

Y e (p. 463) 56 "Blessed *be* [1]the LORD, That hath °given rest unto His People Israel, according to all that He promised:

f there hath °not failed one word of all His good promise, which He promised by the hand of °Moses His servant.

f 57 [1]The LORD our [15]God be with °us, [25]as He was with our fathers: °let Him not leave us, nor forsake us:
58 That He may °incline our hearts unto Him, to walk in all His ways, and to keep His commandments, and His statutes, and His judgments, which He commanded our fathers.
59 And let these my words, wherewith I have made supplication before [1]the LORD, be nigh unto [1]the LORD our [15]God day and night, that He maintain the [45]cause of His servant, and the [45]cause of His people Israel °at all times, as the matter shall require:
60 That all the [53]people of the earth °may know that [1]the LORD °*is* [15]God, *and that there is* none else.

e 61 Let your heart therefore be °perfect with [1]the LORD our [15]God, to walk in His statutes, and to keep His commandments, as at this day."

47 if, &c. Deuteronomy supplied the Lord with answers in His temptation; and supplied Solomon with petitions for his prayer. Cp. 30. 1-3, 4, 20; 9. 26, 29 (cp. *vv.* 51, 52 below); 7. 9 (cp. *v.* 23 above); and 10. 14 (cp. *v.* 27 above), &c.

bethink themselves = call themselves to their right mind. (The verb is in the Hiphil.)

saying, We have sinned. Cp. Neh. 1. 6, 7. Dan. 9. 8.

wickedness. Heb. *rāsha'*. Ap. 44. x.

48 soul. Heb. *nephesh*. Ap. 13.

toward their land. Cp. Dan. 6. 10; 9. 5-19. Ezra 9. 5-15; 10. 1. Neh. 9. 16-35. Ps. 106. 6.

the city. Some codices, with two early printed editions, and Vulg., read "and the city".

I have built. Heb. text written "Thou hast built", but some codices, with three early printed editions, Aram., Sept., and Vulg., read "I have built", as in A.V.

50 forgive Thy People. Cp. Lev. 26. 40, 42.

transgressions . . . transgressed. Heb. *pāsha'*. Ap. 44. ix.

give them. Cp. Ezra 1. 1, 3.

51 furnace = furnace for the smelting of iron; not made of iron. Cp. Gen. 15. 17.

53 didst separate. Cp. Lev. 20. 24, 26.

people = peoples.

by the hand. Fig. *Pleonasm*. Ap. 6.

Moses Thy servant. First of three occurrences. Cp. Neh. 1. 8; 9. 14.

Lord GOD = Adonai Jehovah. Ap. 4. II.

54 praying . . . prayer = making this solemn prayer. Fig. *Polyptōton*. Ap. 6.

kneeling. See note on *v.* 22, and cp. 19. 18. Isa. 45. 23. Ezra 9. 5. 2 Chron. 6. 13. Dan. 6. 10. Ps. 95. 6. Standing was the earlier practice (1 Sam. 1. 26).

8. 56-61 (*Y*, p. 460). **THE BLESSING.**
(*Introversion.*)

Y | e | 56-. The faithfulness of Jehovah. Celebrated.
| f | -56. Retrospective. Praise.
| *f* | 57-60. Prospective. Prayer.
| *e* | 61. The faithfulness of His People. Exhortation.

56 given rest. Cp. Ex. 33. 14.

not failed. Not fallen [to the ground]. Heb. *nāphal*, to fall. Solomon knows Josh. 23. 14. Cp. Josh. 21. 45.

Moses His servant. See note on Ex. 14. 31.

57 us. Note that Solomon includes himself.

let Him not leave us, &c. See note on Gen. 28. 15. Cp. Deut. 31. 6. Josh. 1. 5.

58 incline our hearts. Cp. Lev. 26. 3-13. Deut. 28. 1-14. Some codices, with three early printed editions, Sept., and Vulg., read "heart".

59 at all times. Heb. the matter of a day in its day: i. e. day by day.

60 may know. Cp. Deut. 4. 39.

is = He [is].

61 perfect with = loyal: i. e. not divided between Jehovah and other gods; hence wholly devoted to. Not heeded by Solomon himself. Cp. 9. 6; 11. 4. 1 Chron. 29. 19.

62 offered sacrifice. Heb. sacrificed a sacrifice. Fig. *Polyptōton* (Ap. 6) = offered a great or abundant sacrifice. See Ap. 43. I. iv. Jehovah accepted them by fire from heaven, as recorded in 2 Chron. 7. 1. See note on Gen. 4. 4.

62 And the king, and all Israel with him, °offered sacrifice before [1]the LORD. *X*
63 And Solomon [62]offered a sacrifice of peace offerings, which he [62]offered unto [1]the LORD, two and twenty thousand oxen, and an hundred and twenty thousand sheep. So the king and all the [1]children of Israel dedicated the house of [1]the LORD.
64 The same day did the king hallow the middle of the court that *was* before the house

910 of [1]the LORD: for there he °offered burnt offerings, and meat offerings, and the fat of the
peace offerings: because the brasen altar that
was before [1]the LORD *was* too little to receive
the burnt offerings, and meat offerings, and
the fat of the peace offerings.

65 And at that time Solomon held °a feast,
and all Israel with him, a great [14]congregation,
from the entering in of Hamath unto the river
of Egypt, before [1]the LORD our [15]God, °seven
days and seven days, *even* fourteen days.
66 On the eighth day he sent the People away:
and they blessed the king, and went unto their
tents joyful and glad of heart for all the goodness that [1]the LORD had done °for David His
servant, and for Israel His People.

A E[1] (p. 464) 897 9 And it came to pass, when Solomon had
finished the building of the house of °the
LORD, and the king's house, and all Solomon's
desire which he was pleased to do,
2 That [1]the LORD appeared to Solomon the
second time, °as He had appeared unto him at
Gibeon.

E[2] 3 And [1]the LORD said unto him, "I have heard
thy prayer and thy supplication, that thou hast
made before Me: I have hallowed this house,
which thou hast built, to put My name there
for ever; and °Mine eyes and °Mine heart shall
be there perpetually.

E[3] g 4 And if thou wilt walk before Me, as David
thy father walked, in integrity of heart, and
in uprightness, to do according to all that I
have commanded thee, °*and* wilt keep My
statutes and My judgments:

h 5 Then I will establish the throne of thy
kingdom upon Israel for ever, °as I promised
to David thy father, saying, 'There shall not
fail thee a °man upon the throne of Israel.'

g 6 *But* if ye shall at all turn from following
Me, ye or your °children, and will not keep My
commandments [4]*and* My statutes which I have
set before you, but go and serve other gods,
and worship them:

h 7 Then will I cut off Israel out of the land
which I have given them; and this house,
which I have hallowed for My name, will I
cast out of My sight; and Israel shall be a
proverb and a byword among all °people:
8 °And at this house, *which* is high, every
one that passeth by it shall be astonished, and
shall hiss; and they shall say, 'Why hath [1]the
LORD done thus unto this land, and to this
house?'
9 And they shall answer, 'Because they forsook [1]the LORD their °God, Who brought forth
their fathers out of the land of Egypt, and
have taken hold upon other gods, and have
worshipped them, and served them: therefore hath [1]the LORD brought upon them all
this °evil.'"

B D E (p. 452) 10 And it came to pass at the end of °twenty
917 years, when Solomon had built the two houses,
to the house of [1]the LORD, and the king's house,
897 11 (°*Now* Hiram the king of Tyre had furnished Solomon with cedar trees and °fir trees,
and with gold, according to all his desire,) that
then king Solomon gave Hiram twenty cities
in the land of Galilee.
12 And Hiram came out from Tyre to see the
cities which Solomon had given him; and they
pleased him not.
13 And he said, °"What cities *are* these
which thou hast given me, my brother?"
And he called them the land of °Cabul unto
this day.
14 And Hiram °sent to the king sixscore
°talents of gold.
15 And this *is* the °reason of the °levy which *F* i (p. 464)

---

64 offered = prepared. Ap. 43. I. iii.
65 a feast = the feast: viz. the Feast of Tabernacles. See note on *v.* 2.
seven days and seven days. Fig. *Epizeuxis.* Ap. 6. The first seven the Feast of Dedication; the second the Feast of Tabernacles.
66 for David: i. e. in the person of Solomon his son. Fig. *Synecdoche* (of Part). Cp. 10. 9 and 2 Chron. 7. 10.

9. 1-9 (*A*, p. 452). SECOND APPEARANCE OF JEHOVAH. (*Division.*)

A | E[1] | 1, 2. Appearance.
| E[2] | 3. Acceptance.
| E[3] | 4-9. Admonition.

1 the LORD. Heb. Jehovah. Ap. 4. II.
2 as He had appeared. See 3. 5.
3 Mine eyes . . . Mine heart. Fig. *Anthropopatheia.* Ap. 6.

4-9 (E[3], above). ADMONITION. (*Alternation.*)

E[3] | g | 4. Obedience.
| h | 5. Establishment.
| *g* | 6. Disobedience.
| *h* | 7-9. Rejection.

4 and. Sept., Syr., and Vulg. read this "and" in the text.
5 as = according as.
man. Heb. *'ish.* Ap. 14. II.
6 children = sons.
7 people = peoples.
8 And at this house, &c. Render thus: "And this house will become conspicuous; every passer by will be astonished, and hiss; and they will say", &c.
9 God. Heb. Elohim. Ap. 4. I.
evil. Heb. *rā'a'.* Ap. 44. viii.
10 twenty years. Cp. 7. 1.
11 Now Hiram. Fig. *Parenthesis.* Ap. 6.
fir, or cypress.
13 What cities . . . ? Fig. *Erotēsis.* Ap. 6.
Cabul. The point of the sarcasm is not apparent to us on account of our not knowing the meaning of the word. It has been variously suggested as meaning "worthless", "not to my taste" (Josephus). Galilee always despised. Sept. says "frontier"; others, "received as a pledge"; others, "good for nothing".
14 sent: referring to *v.* 11. Perhaps this was an advance for which the cities of *v.* 11 were the security.
talents. Ap. 51. II.

15-24 (*F*, p. 452). THE LEVY. (*Extended Alternation.*)

F | i | 15. Levy for buildings.
| k | 16. Pharaoh's daughter. City given.
| l | 17-19. Buildings. Gezer, &c.
| *i* | 20-23. Levy for builders.
| *k* | 24-. Pharaoh's daughter. House built.
| *l* | -24. Building. Millo.

15 reason = account, or schedule.
levy: i. e. tribute of men. Same word as 5. 13-18; not the same word as *v.* 21. See Structure, F and *F*, p. 452.

897 king Solomon raised; for to build the house of
to [1]the LORD, and his own house, and °Millo, and
880 °the wall of Jerusalem, and °Hazor, and °Megiddo, and °Gezer.

k 16 *For* Pharaoh king of Egypt had gone up,
(p. 464) and taken [15]Gezer, and burnt it with fire, and slain the Canaanites that dwelt in the city, and given it *for* a °present unto his daughter, Solomon's wife.

l 17 And Solomon °built Gezer, and Beth-horon the nether,
18 And Baalath, and °Tadmor in the wilderness, in the land,
19 And all the cities of store that Solomon had, and cities for his chariots, and cities for his horsemen, and that which Solomon desired to build in Jerusalem, and in Lebanon, and in all the land of his dominion.

i 20 *And* all the people *that were* left of the Amorites, Hittites, Perizzites, Hivites, and Jebusites, which *were* not of the [6]children of Israel,
21 Their [6]children that were left after them in the land, whom the [6]children of Israel also were not able utterly to destroy, upon those did Solomon levy a tribute of °bondservice unto this day.
22 But of the [6]children of Israel did Solomon °make no bondmen: but they *were* °men of war, °and his servants, and his princes, and his captains, and rulers of his chariots, and his horsemen.
23 These *were* the chief of the officers that *were* over Solomon's work, five hundred and fifty, which bare rule over the People that wrought in the work.

k 24 But Pharaoh's daughter came up out of the city of David unto her house which *Solomon* had built for her:

l then did he build Millo.

G 25 And °three times in a year did Solomon
(p. 452) °offer burnt offerings and peace offerings upon the altar which he built unto [1]the LORD, and he burnt incense upon the altar that *was* before [1]the LORD. So he finished the house.

C G[1] 26 And king Solomon made a navy of ships
(p. 465) in °Ezion-geber, which *is* beside Eloth, on the shore of the Red sea, in the land of Edom.
27 And Hiram sent in the navy his servants, shipmen that had knowledge of the sea, with the servants of Solomon.
28 And they came to °Ophir, and fetched from thence gold, four hundred and twenty talents, and brought *it* to king Solomon.

H[1] **10** And when the °queen of °Sheba °heard of the °fame of Solomon concerning the name of °the LORD, she came to prove him with °hard questions.
2 And °she came to Jerusalem with a very great train, with camels that bare spices, and very much gold, and precious stones: and when she was come to °Solomon, she communed with him of all that was in her heart.
3 And Solomon told her all her questions: there was not *any* thing hid from the king, which he told her not.

Millo = the Millo. Part of Jebusite city, or the filling up between Jebus and Moriah. Hezekiah strengthened it. Shechem had a "Millo" (Judg. 9. 6). Cp. *v.* 24; 11. 27. 2 Sam. 5. 9. 1 Chron. 11. 8. 2 Chron. 32. 54.

the wall. Begun by David (2 Sam. 5. 9. 1 Chron. 11. 8). Solomon closed the breaches (11. 27).

Hazor, an old Canaanitish town (Josh. 11. 1).

Megiddo, the same (Josh. 12. 21. Judg. 1. 27; 5. 19, and 1 Kings 4. 12).

Gezer. Gezer was formerly under the suzerainty of Egypt. Correspondence of the time of Amen-hotep III and IV, about 1450 B.C., has been found at Tel-el-Amarnah explorations, which mentions Yapakhi as "king" of Gezer. Letters from Abdkhiba, king of Jerusalem, complain of the Gezerites. First mentioned in Josh. 10. 33. Conquest only partial (Josh. 16. 10. Judg. 1. 29). Allotted to Levites (Josh. 21. 21). In excavation by Palestine Exploration Fund a contract was found, dated 649 B.C. (in Assyrian). Gezer then still under an Egyptian Governor. Another contract, dated 647 B.C., was found, showing an Assyrian occupation in the time of Manasseh. This may explain the "captains" of 2 Chron. 33. 11.

16 present = dowry.

17 built = rebuilt and fortified.

18 Tadmor. Called, later, Palmyra (from its palms).

21 bondservice. See note on *v.* 22.

22 make no bondmen. According to Lev. 25. 39. The levy, of 5. 13; 11. 28, was a levy for free service. This was for bondservice (*v.* 21).

men. Heb. *'ĕnōsh.* Ap. 14. III.

and. Note the Fig. *Polysyndeton* (Ap. 6) in this verse.

25 three times in a year. Cp. Ex. 23. 14-17. Deut. 16. 16. 2 Chron. 8. 13.

offer = offer up. See Ap. 43. I. vi.

9. 26—10. 29 (*C*, p. 452). **RICHES AND WISDOM.** (*Repeated Alternation.*)

C | G[1] | 9. 26-28. Riches. Navy.
  H[1] | 10. 1-10. Wisdom. Queen of Sheba.
 G[2] | 10. 11, 12. Riches. Navy.
  H[2] | 10. 13. Wisdom. Queen of Sheba.
 G[3] | 10. 14-29. Riches. Possessions.

26 Ezion-geber. Cp. Num. 33. 35. Deut. 2. 8. Position lost when Edom revolted (2 Kings 8. 20). Restored by Uzziah (2 Kings 14. 22). Finally lost by Ahaz (2 Kings 16. 6).

28 Ophir. See note on 2 Chron. 8. 18.

10. 1 queen of Sheba. Cp. 2 Chron. 9. 1.

Sheba, a grandson of Cush, settled in Ethiopia (Gen. 10. 7): i. e. Nubia and North Abyssinia, where female sovereigns were not unusual. Cp. Acts 8. 27.

heard = kept hearing. By the commercial intercourse of 9. 26-28. Cp. 2 Chron. 8. 17; 9. 1. Note her seven steps: heard (*v.* 1); came (*v.* 2); communed (*v.* 2); saw (*v.* 4); said (*v.* 6); gave (*v.* 10); returned (*v.* 13).

fame = report.

the LORD. Heb. Jehovah. Ap. 4. II.

hard = abstruse, or difficult.

2 she came. Note the use of this made by the Lord Jesus in Matt. 12. 42. Luke 11. 31.

Solomon. Some codices, with four early printed editions, Syr., and Vulg., read "King Solomon".

4 and. Note the Fig. *Polysyndeton* (Ap. 6), *vv.* 4, 5.

5 sitting = seated assembly.

attendance = standing.

4 And when the queen of Sheba had seen all Solomon's wisdom, °and the house that he had built,
5 And the meat of his table, and the °sitting of his servants, and the °attendance of his ministers, and their apparel, and his cupbearers,

897 and his °ascent by which he went up unto the
to house of [1] the LORD; there was no more °spirit
880 in her.
6 And she said to the king, "It was a true
report that I heard in mine own land of thy
°acts and of thy wisdom.
7 Howbeit I believed not the words, until I
came, and mine eyes had seen *it*: and, °behold,
the half was not told me: thy wisdom and
prosperity exceedeth the fame which I heard.
8 Happy *are* thy °men, happy *are* these thy
servants, which stand continually before thee,
and that hear thy wisdom.
9 Blessed be [1] the LORD thy °God, Which °de-
lighted in thee, to set thee on the throne of
Israel: because [1] the LORD loved Israel for ever,
therefore made He thee king, to do judgment
and °justice."
10 And she gave the king an hundred and
twenty °talents of gold, and of spices very
great store, and precious stones: there came
no more such abundance of spices as these which
the queen of Sheba gave to king Solomon.

G² 11 And the °navy also of Hiram, that brought
(p. 465) gold from °Ophir, brought in from Ophir great
plenty of °almug trees, and precious stones.
12 And the king made of the [11] almug trees
pillars for the house of [1] the LORD, and for
the king's house, harps also and psalteries for
singers: there came no such [11] almug trees, nor
were seen unto this day.

H² 13 And king Solomon gave unto the queen of
Sheba all her desire, whatsoever she asked,
beside *that* which Solomon gave her °of his
royal bounty. So she turned and went to her
own country, she and her servants.

G³ m p 14 Now the weight of gold that °came to
(p. 466) Solomon in one year was °six hundred threescore and six talents of gold,

q 15 Beside *that he had* of the merchantmen,
and of the traffick of the spice merchants, and
of all the kings of Arabia, and of the governors
of the country.

n r 16 And king Solomon made two hundred
targets *of* beaten gold: six hundred *shekels* of
gold went to one target.
17 And *he made* three hundred °shields *of*
beaten gold; three °pound of gold went to one
shield: and the king put them in the house of
the forest of Lebanon.
18 Moreover the king made a great throne of
ivory, and overlaid it with °the best gold.
19 The throne had six steps, and the °top of
the throne *was* round behind: and *there were*
°stays on either side on the place of the seat,
and two lions stood beside the stays.
20 And twelve lions stood there on the one
side and on the other upon the six steps: there
was not the like made in any kingdom.
21 And all king Solomon's drinking vessels
were of gold, and all the vessels of the house
of the forest of Lebanon *were of* pure gold;
none *were of* silver: it was nothing accounted
of in the days of Solomon.

s 22 For the king had at sea a °navy of Tharshish with the navy of Hiram: once in three
years came the navy of Tharshish, bringing
gold, and silver, °ivory, and °apes, and peacocks.

ascent. The covered stairway connecting Mount Zion (Jebus) with Mount Moriah. Cp. 2 Kings 16. 18. Ascent is the word for burnt or "ascending offering", by the merits of which we ascend now.
spirit. Heb. *rūach*. Ap. 9.
6 acts = words.
7 behold. Fig. *Asterismos*. Ap. 6.
8 men. Heb. pl. of *'īsh* or *'ĕnōsh*. Ap. 14.
9 God. Heb. Elohim. Ap. 4. I.
delighted. See note on Num. 14. 8. 2 Sam. 15. 26.
justice = righteousness.
10 talents. See Ap. 51. II.
11 navy also of Hiram. Joined with Solomon (*v.* 22; 9. 27, 28). **Ophir.** See note on 2 Chron. 8. 18.
almug. Not sandal wood, because found, too, in Lebanon (2 Chron. 2. 8). Cuneiform, GIZ-KU = precious wood; and Accadian, GIZ-DAN = strong wood.
13 of his royal bounty. Heb. according to the hand of king Solomon.

10. 14-29 (G³, p. 465). RICHES. POSSESSIONS.
(*Introversion and Alternation.*)

G³ | m | p | 14. Gold. Material.
q | 15. Means. Merchandise.
n | r | 16–21. Manufactures. Armour, &c.
s | 22. Means. Navy.
o | 23, 24. Pre-eminence.
n | s | 25. Means. Presents.
r | 26. Manufactures. Chariots, &c.
m | p | 27, 28-. Silver, cedars, &c. Material.
q | -28, 29. Means. Merchandise.

14 came. Probably in tariffs.
six hundred threescore and six = 666. Symbolical of the height or essence of man's desire, but all vanity (Ap. 10). Cp. Ecc. 2. 8, 11. 1 Tim. 6. 10.
17 shields. Taken away by Shishak in the reign of Rehoboam (14. 26).
pound. Heb. *maneh*. See Ap. 51. II. 4.
18 the best = pure.
19 top = canopy.
stays = supports. Lit. hands.
22 navy of Tharshish = Tharshish ships, a name for large ocean-going ships (like English "East-Indiamen"). When mentioned as a place it is identified by Oppert with Tartessis = the Andalusia of to-day, noted for silver (not gold), iron, tin, and lead (Jer. 10. 9. Ezek. 27. 12). They sailed from Tyre to the West Mediterranean, and from Ezion-geber to Ophir (Arabia, India, and East Africa), 9. 26–28 and 10. 11.
ivory = elephants' tusks.
apes, and peacocks. The Heb. for these are Indian words (Tamil).
25 brought = kept bringing.
every man. Heb. *'īsh*. Ap. 14. II.
27 as stones. Fig. *Hyperbolē*. Ap. 6.
sycomore. Not English, but Eastern; a kind of fig, or mulberry.

23 So king Solomon exceeded all the kings of o
the earth for riches and for wisdom.
24 And all the earth sought to Solomon, to hear
his wisdom, which [9] God had put in his heart.

25 And they °brought °every man his present, n s
vessels of silver, and vessels of gold, and garments, and armour, and spices, horses, and
mules, a rate year by year.

26 And Solomon gathered together chariots r
and horsemen: and he had a thousand and (p. 466)
four hundred chariots, and twelve thousand
horsemen, whom he bestowed in the cities for
chariots, and with the king at Jerusalem.

27 And the king made silver *to be* in Jeru- m p
salem °as stones, and cedars made he *to be* as
the °sycomore trees that *are* in the vale, for
abundance.

897-880 28 And Solomon had °horses brought out of Egypt, and °linen yarn:
q the king's merchants received °the linen yarn at a price.

29 And a chariot came up and went out of Egypt for six hundred *shekels* of silver, and an horse for an hundred and fifty: and so for all the °kings of the Hittites, and for the kings of Syria, did they bring *them* out °by their means.

U t (p. 467) **11** But king Solomon loved many °strange women, together with the daughter of Pharaoh, women of the Moabites, Ammonites, Edomites, Zidonians, *and* Hittites;

2 Of the nations *concerning* which °the LORD said unto the °children of Israel, "Ye shall not go in to them, neither shall they come in unto you: *for* surely they will turn away your heart after their gods:" Solomon clave unto these in love.

3 And he had seven hundred wives, princesses, and three hundred concubines: and his wives turned away his heart.

4 For it came to pass, when Solomon was old, *that* his wives turned away his heart after other gods: and his heart was °not perfect with [2]the LORD his °God, °as *was* the heart of David his father.

5 For Solomon went after °Ashtoreth the goddess of the Zidonians, and after °Milcom the °abomination of the Ammonites.

6 And Solomon did °evil in the sight of [2]the LORD, and went not fully after [2]the LORD, [4]as *did* David his father.

7 Then did Solomon build an high place for °Chemosh, the [5]abomination of Moab, in °the hill that *is* before Jerusalem, and for °Molech, the [5]abomination of the [2]children of Ammon.

8 And likewise did he for all his [1]strange wives, which burnt incense and sacrificed unto their gods.

u 9 And [2]the LORD was °angry with Solomon,
t because his heart was turned from [2]the LORD [4]God of Israel, Which had appeared unto him °twice,

10 And °had commanded him concerning this thing, that he should not go after other gods: but he kept not that which [2]the LORD °commanded.

u J¹ 11 Wherefore [2]the LORD said unto Solomon, "Forasmuch as this is done of thee, and thou hast not kept My covenant and My statutes, which I have commanded thee, °I will surely rend the kingdom from thee, and will give it to thy servant.

12 Notwithstanding in thy days I will not do it for David thy father's sake: *but* I will rend it out of the hand of thy son.

13 Howbeit I will not rend away all the kingdom; *but* will give °one tribe to thy son for David My servant's sake, and for Jerusalem's sake which I have chosen."

J² v x 14 And [2]the LORD stirred up °an adversary unto Solomon, Hadad the Edomite: he *was* of the king's seed in Edom.

---

28 horses. Cp. Isa. 31. 1; 36. 9. Also Ezek. 17. 15.

linen yarn. Probably = by strings, or droves (i. e. the horses).

29 kings of the Hittites. Cp. 1 Sam. 26. 6. 2 Kings 7. 6. These passages alleged to be unhistoric! but they are confirmed by the discoveries made in 1874 throughout Asia Minor and North Syria, which identify them with the "sons of Heth" (Gen. 23. 3, 5, 7; 25. 10; 27. 46; 49. 32), the *Khatta* of the Acadian and the *Kheta* of the Egyptian records. They contended on equal terms with Assyria and Egypt. Crushed by Sargon II, 717 B.C. Chief centres, Carchemish on the Euphrates and Kadesh on the Upper Orontes.

by their means. Heb. by their hand. Hand put by Fig. *Metonymy* (of Cause), Ap. 6, for what is done by it:—by means of Solomon's merchants.

11. 1-40 (*U*, p. 450). MARRIAGES.
(*Alternation.*)

U | t | 1-8. Sins. Committed.
  u | 9-. Jehovah's anger.
 t | -9, 10. Sins. Charged.
  u | 11-40. Jehovah's punishment.

1 strange = foreign. Note the frequent reference to these in the Book of Proverbs. Note the three steps in Solomon's fall: wealth, weapons, and women. Cp. Deut. 17. 16-17, where note the items in which Solomon failed.

2 the LORD (Heb. Jehovah) **said.** Ap. 4. II. See Ex. 34. 16. **children** = sons.

4 not perfect. See note on 8. 61.

God. Heb. Elohim. Ap. 4. I.

as = according to. David was faultless as to idolatry.

5 Ashtoreth. Cp. Judg. 2. 13. 1 Sam. 7. 3; 12. 10; 31. 10.

Milcom. Same as *Malcham*, the Aramaic pronunciation of Molech (*v.* 7). See Zeph. 1. 5. Translated "their king" (Jer. 49. 1. Amos 1. 15).

abomination. The word used for an idol by Fig. *Metonymy* (of Effect), because of Jehovah's hatred which it produced. Cp. 2 Kings 23. 13. Dan. 9. 27.

6 evil = the evil. Heb. *rā'a'*. Ap. 44. viii.

7 Chemosh. Cp. Num. 21. 29. Jer. 48. 7, 13, 46. 2 Kings 23. 13.

the hill, &c. = Mount of Olives! Hence called "the Mount of Corruption" (2 Kings 23. 13).

Molech. Generally has the article and denotes the king-idol (Lev. 18. 21; 20. 2, 3, 4, 5. 1 Kings 11. 7. 2 Kings 23. 10. Jer. 32. 35). Isa. 30. 33 and 57. 9 may be Molech, the idol, and not *Melek*, "king".

9 angry. Fig. *Prosopopœia.* Ap. 6. Heb. *'ānaph.* Used only of *Divine* anger. Occurs fourteen times: six in the *Hithpael* = to force one's self to be angry (as with one loved). See the six: Deut. 1. 37; 4. 21; 9. 8, 20. 1 Kings 11. 9. 2 Kings 17. 18.

twice. Cp. 3. 5; 9. 2.

10 had commanded him. Cp. 6. 12.

commanded. Some codices, with three early printed editions, Sept., Syr., and Vulg., add "him".

11-40 (*u*, above). JEHOVAH. PUNISHMENT.
(*Division.*)

u | J¹ | 11-13. Threatening (diminution).
  | J² | 14-40. Execution (adversaries).

11 I will surely rend = a rending I will rend. Fig. *Polyptōton.* Ap. 6. See note on Gen. 26. 28.

13 one tribe. Benjamin reckoned as part of Judah. Cp. *vv.* 30-32.

14-40 (J², above). EXECUTION (ADVERSARIES).
(*Introversion.*)

J² | v | x | 14. Hadad.
   | y | 15-22. Cause.
   | w | 23-25. Rezon.
  | *v* | *x* | 26. Jeroboam.
   | *y* | 27-40. Cause.

14 an adversary = a Satan.

y 15 For °it came to pass, when David was in
(p. 467) Edom, and °Joab the captain of the host was
897 gone up to bury the slain, after he had smitten
to °every male in Edom;
880 16 (For °six months did Joab remain there
with all Israel, until he had cut off every male
in Edom:)

17 That Hadad fled, he and certain Edomites of his father's servants with him, to go into Egypt; Hadad *being* yet a little child.

18 And they arose out of Midian, and came to Paran: and they took °men with them out of Paran, and they came to Egypt, unto Pharaoh king of Egypt; which gave him an house, and appointed him victuals, and gave him land.

19 And Hadad found great favour in the sight of Pharaoh, so that he gave him to wife the sister of his own wife, the sister of Tahpenes the queen.

20 And the sister of Tahpenes bare him Genubath his son, whom Tahpenes weaned in Pharaoh's house: and Genubath was in Pharaoh's household among the sons of Pharaoh.

21 And when Hadad heard in Egypt that David °slept with his fathers, and that Joab the captain of the host was dead, Hadad said to Pharaoh, "Let me depart, that I may go to mine own country."

22 Then Pharaoh said unto him, "But what hast thou lacked with me, that, °behold, thou seekest to go to thine own country?" And he answered, "Nothing: howbeit let me go in any wise."

w 23 And [4]God stirred him up *another* [14]adversary, Rezon the son of Eliadah, which fled from his lord Hadadezer king of Zobah:

24 And he gathered [18]men unto him, and became captain over a band, when David slew them *of Zobah:* and they went to Damascus, and dwelt therein, and reigned in Damascus.

25 And he was [14]an adversary to Israel all the days of Solomon, beside the mischief that Hadad *did:* and he abhorred Israel, and °reigned over Syria.

v x 26 And Jeroboam the son of Nebat, an °Ephrathite of Zereda, Solomon's servant, whose mother's name *was* Zeruah, °a widow woman, even he lifted up *his* hand against the king.

y 27 And this *was* the cause that he lifted up *his* hand against the king: Solomon built °Millo, *and* repaired the breaches of the city of David his father.

28 And the °man Jeroboam *was* a mighty man of valour: and Solomon seeing the young man that he was industrious, he °made him ruler over all the charge of the house of Joseph.

29 And it came to pass at that time when Jeroboam went out of Jerusalem, that the prophet °Ahijah the °Shilonite found him in the way; and he had clad himself with a new garment; and they two *were* alone in the field:

30 And Ahijah caught the new garment that *was* on him, and °rent it *in* twelve pieces:

31 And he said to Jeroboam, "Take thee ten pieces: for thus saith [2]the LORD, the [4]God of Israel, °'Behold, I will rend the kingdom out of the hand of Solomon, and will give °ten tribes to thee:

32 (°But he shall have °one tribe for My servant David's sake, and for Jerusalem's sake, the city which I have chosen out of all the tribes of Israel:)

33 Because that they have forsaken Me, and have worshipped °Ashtoreth the goddess of the Zidonians, °Chemosh the god of the Moabites, and °Milcom the god of the [2]children of Ammon, and have not walked in My ways, to do *that which is* right in Mine eyes, and *to keep* My statutes and My judgments, as *did* David his father.

34 Howbeit I will not take the whole kingdom out of his hand: but I will make him prince all the days of his life for David My servant's sake, whom I chose, because he kept My commandments and My statutes:

35 But °I will take the kingdom out of his son's hand, and will give it unto thee, *even* ten tribes.

36 And unto his son will I give one tribe, that David My servant may have a °light alway before Me in Jerusalem, the city which I have chosen Me to put My name there.

37 And I will take thee, and thou shalt reign according to all that thy °soul desireth, and shalt be king over Israel.

---

15 **it came to pass, &c.** Cp. 2 Sam. 8. 3-13.
Joab. Cp. Ps. 60, title, and see note on 2 Sam. 8. 13.
every male: i. e. who did not flee, as Hadad did. Supply Fig. *Ellipsis* (Ap. 6), "every male [whom he found] in Edom". See *v.* 17.
16 **six months.** See note on 2 Sam. 8. 13. Note also Fig. *Parenthesis* (Ap. 6), *v.* 16.
18 **men.** Heb. *'ĕnōsh.* Ap. 14. III.
21 **slept with his fathers.** See note on Deut. 31. 16.
22 **behold.** Fig. *Asterismos.* Ap. 6.
25 **reigned.** David had subdued Syria (2 Sam. 8. 3, 6; 10. 8, 18). Now Solomon, weakened by sin, loses Syria.
26 **Ephrathite** = Ephraimite, as in 1 Sam. 1. 1. Not a Bethlehemite, as in Ruth 1. 2. Zealous therefore for his tribe as against Judah.
a widow. One of the nine widows mentioned in Scripture. See note on Gen. 38. 19.
27 **Millo** = the Millo. See note on 9. 15.
28 **man.** Heb. *'ish.* Ap. 14. II.
made him ruler = gave him oversight, which gave him opportunity to oppress and create disaffection.
29 **Ahijah.** He afterwards rebuked Jeroboam (14. 6-16).
Shilonite = a native of Shiloh, where the Tabernacle and Ark had been placed (Josh. 18. 1). Cp. 1 Sam. 4. 3.
30 **rent it.** Symbolic act. Cp. 22. 11. Isa. 20. 2, &c. Jer. 19. 1-13. Ezek. 12. 1-20. Zech. 11. 7, 10, 14.
31 **Behold.** Fig. *Asterismos.* Ap. 6.
ten. Levi not reckoned.
32 **But he, &c.** Note the Fig. *Parenthesis* (Ap. 6) of this verse.
one tribe. Put for, and including, Simeon, Benjamin, and Levi, and others who joined later. Cp. 12. 23. 2 Chron. 11. 13; 15. 9. All included in 12. 20 by Fig. *Synecdoche* (of the Part), Ap. 6.
33 **Ashtoreth.** / **Chemosh.** / **Milcom.** } See notes on *vv.* 5 and 7.
35 **I will take.** Fulfilled in 12. 16-20.
36 **light** = lamp. Cp. the "furnace" of 8. 51, and see note on Gen. 15. 17. Cp. 2 Kings 8. 19. Ps. 18. 28. Jer. 25. 10: implying the continued existence of the Divine purpose.
37 **soul.** Heb. *nephesh.* Ap. 13.

897 38 And it shall be, °if thou wilt hearken unto
to all that I command thee, and wilt walk in My
880 ways, and do *that is* right in My sight, to keep
My statutes and My commandments, as David
My servant did; that I will be with thee, and
build thee °a sure house, as I built for David,
and will give Israel unto thee.
39 And I will for this afflict the seed of David,
but °not for ever.'"
40 Solomon sought therefore to kill Jeroboam.
And Jeroboam arose, and fled into °Egypt, unto
Shishak king of Egypt, and was in Egypt until
the death of Solomon.
41 And the rest of the acts of Solomon, and
all that he did, and his wisdom, *are* they not
°written in the book of the acts of Solomon?
42 And the time that Solomon reigned in Jeru-
920 salem over all Israel *was* °forty years.
to 43 And Solomon [21] slept with his fathers, and
880 was buried in the city of David his father: and
Rehoboam his son reigned in his stead.

B[3] z (p. 469) **12** And Rehoboam went to °Shechem: for
all Israel were come to Shechem to make
him king.
a c 2 And it came to pass, when Jeroboam the
son of Nebat, who was yet in Egypt, heard *of*
it, (°for he was fled from the presence of king
Solomon, and Jeroboam dwelt in Egypt;)
3 That they sent and called him. And Jeroboam and all the °congregation of Israel came,
and spake unto Rehoboam, saying,
4 "Thy father °made our yoke grievous: now
therefore make thou the grievous service of thy
father, and his heavy yoke which he put upon
us, lighter, and we will serve thee."
d 5 And he said unto them, "Depart yet *for*
three days, then come again to me." And the
People departed.
b 6 And king Rehoboam consulted with the
old men, that stood before Solomon his father
while he yet lived, and said, "How do ye
advise that I may answer this People?"
7 And they spake unto him, saying, "If thou
wilt be a servant unto this People this day,
and wilt serve them, and answer them, and
speak good words to them, then they will be
thy servants °for ever."
8 But he forsook the counsel of the old men,
which they had given him, and consulted with
the young men that were grown up with him,
and which stood before him:
9 And he said unto them, "What counsel
give ye that we may answer this People, who
have spoken to me, saying, 'Make the yoke
which thy father did put upon us lighter?'"
10 And the young men that were grown up
with him spake unto him, saying, "Thus shalt
thou speak unto this People that spake unto
thee, saying, 'Thy father made our yoke heavy,
but make thou *it* lighter unto us;' thus shalt
thou say unto them, °'My little *finger* shall be
thicker than my father's loins.
11 And now whereas my father did lade you
with a heavy yoke, I will add to your yoke:
my father hath chastised you with °whips, but
I will chastise you with °scorpions.'"
a d 12 So Jeroboam and all the People came to

38 if thou wilt hearken. Same conditions as in 9. 4.

a sure house: i.e. a long and unbroken line of descendants.

39 not for ever. Thus confirming the prophecy of Gen. 49. 10, which refers to the *tribal pre-eminence* of Judah (not national existence), which was preserved till fulfilled in Christ, when David's line ended in Him.

40 Egypt. This explains much. He must have thought of Joseph's exaltation, and the blessing pronounced on Ephraim (Gen. 48. 13-20; 49. 22-26); and by Moses (Deut. 33. 13-17). It explains also the origin of the "golden calves" (12. 28).

41 written in the book. See note on Ex. 17. 14, and Ap. 47.

42 forty years: 920-880 B.C.

12. 1-15 (B[3], p. 446). REHOBOAM.
(Introversions.)

B[3] | z | 1. Rehoboam. Accession to kingdom.
  a | c | 2-4. Petition of Jeroboam. Made.
    d | 5. Dismissal.
      b | 6-11. Answer considered.
  a | *d* | 12. Return.
    c | 13, 14. Petition of Jeroboam. Answered.
z | 15. Rehoboam. Rending of kingdom.

1 Shechem. A national sanctuary (Josh. 24. 1). Now *Nablous*, corruption of Neapolis, the (New town) of Vespasian. The site of Abraham's first altar. Jacob's first home. Here the tribes met. Here Joseph was buried. All this before Jebus became Jerusalem. Hence the envy of Ephraim for Judah (Isa. 11. 13). Degraded by new name, Sychar = drunkenness (Isa. 28. 1-7). Yet here alone in all the world is the Paschal lamb still slain.

2 for. Note the Fig. *Parenthesis*. Ap. 6.

3 congregation = assembly.

4 made our yoke grievous. Made by Jeroboam himself owing to the opportunity afforded by Solomon's action (11. 28).

7 for ever. Heb. all the days: i.e. always.

10 My little finger. Fig. *Paræmia*. Ap. 6.

11 whips. The badge of the taskmaster on the Egyptian monuments. Cp. Ex. 1. 10, 14; 5. 13, 14 ("beaten").

scorpions. A knotted whip, so called; as we call another kind of whip the "cat".

12 as = according as.

13 gave him = counselled him.

15 the cause = the turning (of events), or overruling.

the LORD. Heb. Jehovah. Ap. 4. II.

spake. Cp. 11. 31.

Rehoboam the third day, °as the king had appointed, saying, "Come to me again the third
day."
13 And the king answered the People roughly, *c*
and forsook the old men's counsel that they
°gave him;
14 And spake to them after the counsel of the
young men, saying, "My father made your yoke
heavy, and I will add to your yoke: my father
also chastised you with [11] whips, but I will chastise you with [11] scorpions."
15 Wherefore the king hearkened not unto *z*
the People; for °the cause was from °the LORD,
that He might perform His saying, which °the
LORD °spake by Ahijah the Shilonite unto
Jeroboam the son of Nebat.
16 So when all Israel saw that the king heark- C[1]
ened not unto them, the people answered the (p. 446)

880 king, saying, °"What portion have we in
David? neither *have we* inheritance in °the
son of Jesse: °to your tents, O Israel: now
see to thine own house, David." So Israel departed unto their tents.
17 But *as for* the °children of °Israel which
dwelt in the cities of Judah, Rehoboam reigned
over them.
18 Then king Rehoboam sent Adoram, who
was over the tribute; and all Israel °stoned
him with stones, that he died. Therefore king
Rehoboam °made speed to get him up to his
chariot, to flee °to Jerusalem.
19 So Israel rebelled against the house of David °unto this day.
E[1] K (p. 470) 20 And it came to pass, when all Israel heard
that Jeroboam was come again, that they sent
and called him unto the congregation, and made
him king over all Israel: there was none that
followed the house of David, but the tribe of
°Judah only.
L 21 And when Rehoboam was come to Jerusalem, he assembled all the house of Judah,
with the tribe of Benjamin, °an hundred and
fourscore thousand chosen men, which were
warriors, to fight against the house of Israel,
to bring the kingdom again to Rehoboam the
son of Solomon.
22 But the word of °God came unto °Shemaiah
°the °man of °God, saying,
23 "Speak unto Rehoboam, the son of Solomon, king of Judah, and unto all the house of
Judah and Benjamin, and to the remnant of
the People, saying,
24 'Thus saith [15]the LORD, "Ye shall not go
up, nor fight against your brethren the [17]chil-
dren of Israel: return °every man to his house;
for °this thing is from Me."'" They hearkened
therefore to the word of [15]the LORD, and returned to depart, according to the word of
[15]the LORD.
L M 25 Then Jeroboam °built Shechem in °mount
Ephraim, and dwelt therein; and went out
from thence, and built °Penuel.
N e O[1] 26 And Jeroboam said in his heart, "Now
shall the kingdom return to the house of
David:
27 °If this People go up to do sacrifice in the
house of [15]the LORD at Jerusalem, then shall
the heart of this People turn again unto their
lord, *even* unto Rehoboam king of Judah, and
they shall kill me, and go again to Rehoboam
king of Judah."
O[2] g[1] 28 Whereupon the king °took counsel, and
made two calves *of* gold, and said unto them,
"It is too much for you to go up to Jerusalem:
°behold thy gods, O Israel, which brought thee
up out of the land of Egypt."
29 And he set the °one in Beth-el, and the
other put he °in Dan.

16 What portion . . . ? Fig. *Erotēsis*. Ap. 6.
the son of Jesse. Used in contempt. Cp. 1 Sam. 16. 18; 20. 31; 22. 7, 8, 9; 25. 10. 2 Sam. 20. 1.
to your tents. One of the emendations of the *Sōpherīm*. Ap. 33. The primitive text was "to your gods", because the sin here was apostasy from Jehovah's worship in Jerusalem. Two letters transposed made it read "to your tents". See note on 2 Sam. 20. 1, and cp. 2 Chron. 10. 16.
17 children = sons.
Israel which dwelt in . . . Judah. Here was a nucleus of true worshippers constantly increased (1 Kings 12. 19. 1 Chron. 9. 3. 2 Chron. 10. 17; 11. 3, 16, 17; 15. 9; 16. 1; 19. 8; 23. 2; 30. 1, 5, 10, 11; 31. 6). In Ezra 1. 5; 2. 2, 59, 70; 7. 13; 9. 1; 10. 5, those returning of Judah's captivity are called "of Israel", and "all Israel", 2. 2, 70; 3. 1; 6. 21; 7. 10, 13; 8. 25; 9. 1; 10. 1, 2, 5, 10, 25. Neh. 2. 10; 7. 7, 61, 73; 8. 17; 10. 33; 11. 3; 12. 47. Judah was thus always representative of "all Israel". Hence Acts 4. 27, "the People of Israel", and Acts 2. 14, 22, 36, "of Judah". The two words are used interchangeably, except where otherwise stated. See note on "all the house of Israel", Ex. 16. 31. Also on 1 Chron. 22. 17; 23. 2. 2 Chron. 12. 6, "princes of Israel", used of Judah before the division. Also, on the cause of the increase of Judah, see note on 2 Chron. 13. 3.
18 stoned him. One of the nine stonings recorded. See note on Lev. 24. 14.
made speed. Heb. strengthened himself.
to Jerusalem: from Shechem.
19 unto this day. Cp. 8. 8. This was written certainly before the removal of Israel in 2 Kings 17.

12. 20—14. 20 (E[1], p. 446). ISRAEL.
JEROBOAM I. (*Introversion.*)

E[1] | K | 12. 20. Jeroboam. Accession.
  L | 12. 21-24. Reign. Assured.
  L | 12. 25—14. 18. Reign. Events.
 K | 14. 19, 20. Jeroboam. Record.

20 Judah only. See note on "one tribe" (11. 32).
21 an hundred, &c. 180,000. In David's time there were 470,000. See note on 2 Sam. 24. 9.
22 God. Heb. Elohim. Ap. 4.
Shemaiah. Cp. 2 Chron. 11. 2; 12. 5.
the man of God = prophet. See the first occurrence, Deut. 33. 1, and Ap. 49.
24 every man. Heb. *'īsh*. Ap. 14. II.
this thing: i. e. the division of the kingdom. Not the rebellion of Jeroboam. Cp. 2 Chron. 13. 4-12.

12. 25—14. 18 (*L*, above). REIGN. EVENTS.
(*Introversion and Alternation.*)

L | M | 12. 25. Reign. Beginning.
  N | e | 12. 26-33. Idolatry. Commenced.
   f | 13. 1-32. Warning. Prophet from Judah.
  N | *e* | 13. 33, 34. Idolatry. Persistence.
   f | 14. 1-17. Warning. Ahijah.
 M | 14. 18. Reign. End.

25 built = rebuilt, or repaired. This doubtless included increased fortification (2 Chron. 11. 11). Mesha uses the word (on Moabite stone) of cities he took. See Ap. 54.
mount = hill-country.
Penuel. On east of Jordan (Gen. 32. 30. Judg. 8. 8).

12. 26-33 (e, above). IDOLATRY. COMMENCED.
(*Division.*)

e | O[1] | 26, 27. Jeroboam. Fear.
 | O[2] | 28-33. Jeroboam. Expedients.

27 If this People. His apostasy was wilful, designed, and deliberate.

12. 28-33 (O[2], above). JEROBOAM. EXPEDIENTS. (*Division.*)

O[2] | g[1] | 28-30. Idolatry. The two calves.
 | g[2] | 31-33. Idolatry. The high places.

28 took counsel: "but not of Jehovah" (Isa. 30. 1). **behold.** Fig. *Asterismos*. Ap. 6. Cp. Ex. 32. 4. Hos. 8. 5, 6; 10. 5. **29 one in Beth-el:** was desecrated by Josiah (2 Kings 23. 15). **in Dan.** See note on Gen. 49. 17. Carried away by Tiglath-pileser (2 Kings 15. 29). The sons of Jonathan, the grandson of Moses (see note on Judg. 18. 30), were ready to act as priests.

880 30 And this thing °became a sin: for the
to People went *to worship* before the one, *even*
858 unto Dan.

g² 31 And he made an °house of high places,
(p. 470) and made priests of the lowest of the People,
which were not of the sons of Levi.

32 And Jeroboam ordained a feast in the eighth month, on the fifteenth day of the month, like unto the feast that *is* in Judah, and he °offered upon the altar. (°So did he in Beth-el,) sacrificing unto the calves that he had made: and he placed in Beth-el the priests of the high places which he had made.

33 So he [32]offered upon the altar which he had made in Beth-el the fifteenth day of the eighth month, *even* in the month which he had devised °of his own heart; and ordained a feast unto the [17]children of Israel: and he offered upon the altar, and burnt incense.

f h i¹ 13 And, °behold, there came °a °man of
(p. 471) °God out of Judah by the word of °the
LORD unto Beth-el: and Jeroboam stood by the altar to burn incense.

2 And he cried against the altar in the word of [1]the LORD, and said, °"O altar, altar, thus saith [1]the LORD; [1]'Behold, a °child shall be born unto the house of David, °Josiah by name; and upon thee shall he °offer the priests of the high places that burn incense upon thee, and °men's bones °shall be burnt upon thee.'"

j¹ 3 And he gave °a sign the same day, saying, "This *is* the sign which [1]the LORD hath spoken; [1]Behold, the altar [2]shall be rent, and the ashes that *are* upon it shall be poured out."

i² 4 And it came to pass, when king Jeroboam heard the saying of the [1]man of [1]God, which had cried against the altar in Beth-el, that he °put forth his hand from the altar, saying, "Lay hold on him." And his hand, which he put forth against him, dried up, so that he could not pull it in again to him.

j² 5 The altar also was rent, and the ashes poured out from the altar, according to the sign which the man of [1]God had given by the word of [1]the LORD.

i³ 6 And the king answered and said unto the [1]man of [1]God, "Intreat now the face of [1]the LORD °thy [1]God, and pray for me, that my hand may be restored me again." And the man of [1]God besought [1]the LORD, and the king's hand was restored him again, and became as *it was* before.

h k¹ 7 And the king said unto the [1]man of God, "Come home with me, and refresh thyself, and I will give thee a reward."

8 And the [1]man of [1]God said unto the king, "If thou wilt give me °half thine house, I will not go in with thee, neither will I eat bread nor drink water in this place:

9 For so was it charged me by the word of [1]the LORD, saying, 'Eat no bread, nor drink water, nor turn again by the same way that thou camest.'"

10 So he went another way, and returned not by the way that he came to Beth-el.

l¹ 11 Now there dwelt an old prophet °in Beth-el; °and his sons came and told him all the works that the [1]man of [1]God had done that day in Beth-el: °the words which he had spoken unto the king, them they told also to their father.

12 And their father said unto them, "What way went he?" For his sons had seen what way the [1]man of [1]God went, which came from Judah.

13 And he said unto his sons, "Saddle °me the ass." So they saddled °him the ass: and he rode thereon,

14 And went after the [1]man of [1]God, and found him sitting under °an oak: and he said unto him, "*Art* thou the [1]man of [1]God that camest from Judah?" And he said, "I *am*."

15 Then he said unto him, "Come home with me, and eat bread." k²

16 And he said, "I may not return with thee, nor go in with thee: neither will I eat bread nor drink water with thee in this place:

17 For it was °said to me by the word of [1]the

30 became a sin. See Ap. 44. i. Hence the repeated stigma who "made Israel to sin". Cp. 13. 34; 14. 16; 15. 26, 30, 34; 16. 2, 19, 26, &c.
31 house = a temple. Not merely "high places".
32 offered = offered up. Ap. 43. I. vi.
So did he, &c. Note the Fig. *Parenthesis.* Ap. 6.
33 of his own heart. Heb. text reads "by himself". Some codices, with three early printed editions, Aram., Sept., Syr., and Vulg., read as A.V. Man-made feasts go with man-made priests (*v.* 31).

13. 1-32 (f, p. 470). WARNING. BY MAN OF GOD. (*Repeated Alternation.*)

f | h | i¹ | 1, 2. Jeroboam. Warned.
j¹ | 3. Sign given.
i² | 4. Jeroboam. Smitten. } Arrival.
j² | 5. Sign fulfilled.
i³ | 6. Jeroboam. Healed.
h | k¹ | 7-10. Obedience.
l¹ | 11-14. Old prophet.
k² | 15-19. Disobedience. } Return.
l² | 20-32. Old prophet.

1 behold. Fig. *Asterismos.* Ap. 6.
a man of God. Cp. Deut. 33. 1, and see Ap. 49.
man. Heb. *'ish.* Ap. 14. II.
God. Heb. Elohim. Ap. 4. I.
the LORD. Heb. Jehovah. Ap. 4. II.
2 O altar, altar. Figs. *Apostrophe* and *Epizeuxis.* Ap. 6. **child** = son.
Josiah by name. Cyrus is the only other so foretold (177 years before). Josiah knew (2 Kings 23. 17, 18). Cyrus knew (2 Chron. 36. 22, 23. Isa. 44. 28).
offer (in sacrifice) = slay, or slaughter. Ap. 43. I. iv.
men's: human. Heb. *'ādām.* Ap. 14. I.
shall be. This was fulfilled in 2 Kings 23. 16 (360 years later).
3 a sign. We have similar signs in Ex. 3. 12. 2 Kings 19. 29; 20. 8. Isa. 7. 14; 8. 18.
4 put forth his hand. One of the eleven rulers who thus assaulted Jehovah's witnesses. See note on Ex. 10. 28.
6 thy God. He dare not say "my God".
8 half thine house. Remembering Num. 22. 18; 24. 13.
11 in Beth-el. A true prophet could not have remained there. Cp. 2 Chron. 11. 16, 17.
and his sons. Sept. reads "whose sons".
the words. Syr. and Vulg. read "and the words".
13 me = for me. **him** = for him.
14 an oak = the oak.
17 said. Cp. "charged": showing a weakening from *v.* 9.

880 to 858 LORD, ‘Thou shalt °eat no bread nor drink water there, nor turn again to go by the way that thou camest.’ ”

18 He said unto him, “I *am* a prophet also as thou *art;* and °an angel spake unto me by the word of [1]the LORD, saying, ‘Bring him back with thee into thine house, that he may eat bread and drink water.’ ” *But* he lied unto him.

19 So he went back with him, and did eat bread in his house, and drank water.

1[2] (p. 471) 20 And it came to pass, as they sat at the table, that the word of [1]the LORD came unto the prophet that brought him back:

21 And he cried unto the [1]man of [1]God that came from Judah, saying, “Thus saith [1]the LORD, ‘Forasmuch as thou hast °disobeyed the mouth of [1]the LORD, and hast not kept the commandment which [1]the LORD thy [1]God commanded thee,

22 But camest back, and hast eaten bread and drunk water in the place, of the which *the* LORD did say to thee, ‘Eat no bread, and drink no water;’ thy carcase shall not come unto the °sepulchre of thy fathers.’ ”

23 And it came to pass, after he had eaten bread, and after he had drunk, that he saddled for him the ass, °*to wit,* for the prophet whom he had brought back.

24 And when he was gone, °a lion met him by the way, and slew him: and his carcase was cast in the way, and the ass stood by it, the lion also stood by the carcase.

25 And, °behold, °men passed by, and saw the carcase cast in the way, and the lion standing by the carcase: and they came and told *it* in the city where the old prophet dwelt.

26 And when the prophet that brought him back from the way heard *thereof,* he said, “It *is* the [1]man of [1]God, who was °disobedient unto the word of [1]the LORD: therefore [1]the LORD hath delivered him unto the lion, which hath torn him, and slain him, according to the word of [1]the LORD, °which He spake unto him.”

27 And he spake to his sons, saying, “Saddle [13]me the ass.” And they saddled *him.*

28 And he went and found his carcase cast in the way, and the ass and the lion standing by the carcase: the lion had not eaten the carcase, nor torn the ass.

29 And the prophet took up the carcase of the [1]man of [1]God, and laid it upon the ass, and brought it back: and the old prophet came to the city, to mourn and to bury him.

30 And he laid his carcase in his own °grave; and they mourned over him, *saying,* “Alas, my brother!”

31 And it came to pass, after he had buried him, that he spake to his sons, saying, “When I am dead, then bury me in the sepulchre wherein the [1]man of [1]God *is* buried; °lay my bones beside his bones:

32 For the saying which °he cried by the word of [1]the LORD against the altar in Beth-el, and against all the houses of the high places which *are* in the cities of Samaria, shall surely come to pass.”

N e (p. 470) 33 After this thing Jeroboam returned not from his evil way, but made again of the lowest of the People priests of the high places: whosoever would, he consecrated him, and he °became *one* of the priests of the high places.

34 And this thing °became sin unto the house of Jeroboam, even to cut *it* off, and to destroy *it* from off °the face of the earth.

14 At that time Abijah the son of Jeroboam fell sick. f m[1] (p. 472) about 863

2 And Jeroboam said to his wife, “Arise, I pray thee, and disguise thyself, that thou be not known to be the wife of Jeroboam; and °get thee to Shiloh: °behold, there *is* Ahijah the prophet, which told me that *I should be* king over this People.

3 And take with thee ten loaves, and cracknels, and a °cruse of honey, and go to him: °he shall tell thee what shall become of the child.”

4 And Jeroboam's wife did so, and arose, and went to Shiloh, and came to the house of Ahijah. But Ahijah could not see; for his eyes °were set by reason of his age.

5 And °the LORD said unto Ahijah, [2]“Behold, the wife of Jeroboam cometh to ask a n[1]

---

eat no bread. To avoid what might have been offered to idols.

18 an angel spake. A solemn warning for all who listen to any revelation outside Scripture which purports to come from God, even though an “old prophet” asserts it. Cp. Gal. 1. 8, 9. Of all such it may be said “he lied unto him”.

21 disobeyed = rebelled against. The same expression used of Moses and Aaron at Meribah (Num. 20. 24; 27. 14). Safety found only in the path of obedience. Cp. *v.* 26.

22 sepulchre. Heb. *ḳeber,* a burying-place.

23 to wit = that is to say.

24 a lion. For lions in Palestine see Judg. 14. 5. 1 Sam. 17. 34. 2 Sam. 23. 20. 1 Kings 20. 36.

25 behold. Fig. *Asterismos.* Ap. 6.

men. Heb. *'ĕnōsh.* Ap. 14. III.

26 disobedient, by listening to the alleged word of an angel, instead of obeying the voice of Jehovah. See note on *v.* 18.

which He spake. Cp. *v.* 22.

30 grave = sepulchre. Heb. *ḳeber,* a burying-place, a pit. Cp. Ap. 35.

31 lay my bones: i. e. lay them not with the bones of those referred to in *v.* 2. Cp. 2 Kings 23. 18.

32 he cried. Cp. *v.* 2.

33 became one of the priests. Sept., Syr., and Vulg. reads “became priest”.

34 became sin = became the sin. See note on 12. 30.

the face of. Fig. *Pleonasm.* Ap. 6.

14. 1-17 (*f*, p. 470). **WARNING FROM AHIJAH.**
(*Repeated Alternation.*)

f | m[1] | 1-4. Message from Jeroboam by his wife.
  n[1] | 5, 6. Messenger revealed to Ahijah.
 m[2] | 7-11. Message from Jehovah to Jeroboam.
  n[2] | 12, 13. Messenger to return.
 m[3] | 14-16. Message from Jehovah.
  n[3] | 17. Messenger returns.

2 get thee to Shiloh. He had no confidence in his own gods. They were only political expedients. See the Structure of O[2], p. 470.

behold. Fig. *Asterismos.* Ap. 6.

3 cruse = flask, or bottle.

he. Some codices, with Sept., read “and he”.

4 were set. Cp. 1 Sam. 4. 15. One of the nine afflicted with blindness. See note on Gen. 19. 11.

5 the LORD. Heb. Jehovah. Ap. 4. II.

about 863 thing of thee for her son; for he *is* sick: thus
and thus shalt thou say unto her: for it shall
be, when she cometh in, that she shall feign
herself *to be* another *woman*."
6 And it was *so*, when Ahijah heard the sound
of her feet, as she came in at the °door, that
he said, "Come in, thou wife of Jeroboam;
why feignest thou thyself *to be* another? for
I *am* sent to thee *with* heavy *tidings*.

m[2] (p. 472) 7 Go, tell Jeroboam, 'Thus saith [5]the LORD
°God of Israel, "Forasmuch as I exalted thee
from among the People, and made thee prince
over My People Israel,
8 And rent the kingdom away from the house
of David, and gave it thee: and *yet* thou hast
not been as My servant David, who kept My
commandments, and who followed Me with all
his heart, to do *that* only *which was* right in
Mine eyes;
9 But hast done °evil above °all that were before thee: for thou hast gone and made thee
°other gods, and molten images, to provoke
Me to anger, and hast cast Me behind thy back:
10 Therefore, [1]behold, I will bring evil upon
the house of Jeroboam, and will cut off from
Jeroboam °him that pisseth against the wall,
and him that is °shut up and left in Israel,
and will take away the remnant of the house
of Jeroboam, °as a man taketh away dung, till
it be all gone.
11 Him that dieth of Jeroboam in the city
shall the dogs eat; and him that dieth in the
field shall the fowls of the air eat: for [5]the
LORD hath spoken *it*."'

n[2] 12 Arise thou therefore, get thee to thine own
house: *and* when thy feet enter into the city,
the child shall die.
13 And all Israel shall mourn for him, and
bury him: for he only of Jeroboam shall come
to the °grave, because in him there is found
some good thing toward [5]the LORD [7]God of
Israel in the house of Jeroboam.

m[3] 14 Moreover [5]the LORD shall raise Him up a
king over Israel, who shall cut off the house of
Jeroboam that day: °but what? °even now.
15 For [5]the LORD shall °smite Israel, as a
reed is shaken in the water, and He shall root
up Israel out of °this good land, which He gave
to their fathers, and shall scatter them beyond
°the river, because they have made their
°groves, provoking [5]the LORD to anger.
16 And He shall give Israel up because of the
°sins of Jeroboam, who did sin, and who °made
Israel to sin."

n[3] 17 And Jeroboam's wife arose, and departed,
and came to °Tirzah: *and* when she came to
the threshold of the [6]door, the child died;

M (p. 470) 18 And they buried him; and all Israel mourned
for him, according to the word of [5]the LORD,
which He spake °by the hand of His servant
Ahijah the prophet.

K 19 And °the rest of the acts of Jeroboam, how
he warred, and how he reigned, [2]behold, they
are written in the book of the chronicles of the
kings of Israel.
20 And the days which Jeroboam reigned
880-858 *were* °two and twenty years: and he °slept
with his fathers, and Nadab his son reigned in
his stead.

21 And Rehoboam the son of Solomon reigned F[1] P[1] O
in Judah. Rehoboam *was* forty and one years (p. 473)
old when he began to reign, and he reigned 880
seventeen years in Jerusalem, the city which to
[5]the LORD did choose out of all the tribes of 863

---

6 door = entrance.
7 God. Heb. Elohim. Ap. 4. I.
9 evil. Heb. *rā'a'*. Ap. 44. viii.
all. Not merely kings, but all other rulers. No anachronism.
other gods. Jehovah does not recognise the calves as being what Jeroboam intended, mere political expedients. See note on *v.* 2.
10 him that, &c. = every male.
shut up and left. The commentators speak of the text being obscure or corrupt. But *'āzab* is a *Homonym*, meaning: (1) *to leave* (as in Gen. 2. 24; 39. 6. Neh. 5. 10. Ps. 49. 10. Mal. 4. 1); and (2) *to restore, repair, fortify* (as in Neh. 3. 8. Ex. 23. 5 (see note there). Deut. 32. 36. 1 Kings 14. 10. 2 Kings 14. 26. Jer. 49. 25). Here it means "strengthened and fortified": i. e. they will not escape. Cp. 21. 21. 2 Kings 9. 8.
as = according as.
13 grave = a burying-place. Heb. *ķeber*, not *sh^eōl*. See Ap. 35.
14 but what? even now. Here again the text is supposed to be obscure. It is on account of the Figures of speech (Ap. 6) used: (1) Ellipsis = "But what [am I saying 'That day'?] Even now [hath He raised him up]". (2) Note the Fig. *Amphidiorthōsis*. Ap. 6.
15 smite Israel, [shaking him] as a reed is shaken, &c. The Fig. *Ellipsis* (Ap. 6) to be thus supplied.
this good land. Occurs only here and Josh. 23. 13, 15.
the river: i. e. the Euphrates. **groves** = *'Ashērīm*. See Ap. 42. **16 sins.** Heb. *chāṭā'*. Ap. 44. i.
made Israel to sin. The first of twenty-one occurrences in these two books: 14. 16; 15. 26, 30, 34; 16. 19, 26; 21. 22; 22. 52. 2 Kings 3. 3; 10. 29, 31; 13. 2, 6, 11; 14. 24; 15. 9, 18, 24, 28; 16. 13; 17. 21; 23. 15.
17 Tirzah. Afterward made the capital by Baasha (15. 21), till Samaria was built by Omri (15. 33; 16. 8, 15, 23, 24).
18 by the hand. Fig. *Pleonasm*. Ap. 6.
19 the rest. See 2 Chron. 13. 3-20.
20 two and twenty years. In 15. 25 Nadab reigned two years, and began in the second year of Asa, which was the twenty-first of Jeroboam, so that Nadab's two years fall within the time of his father's twenty-two. But from 2 Chron. 13. 20 we learn that Jeroboam was stricken with a languishing disease, in which time Nadab reigned with him, and died the same year as his father. The number "twenty-two" is associated with disorganisation and disintegration (= 2 × 11). It is associated with the worst two reigns: Jeroboam, here; and Ahab in 16. 29.
slept with his fathers = died. See notes on Deut. 31. 16. Said of the wicked Jeroboam and Ahab, as well as of good David and Jehoshaphat.

14. 21—15. 24 (F[1], p. 446). JUDAH.
(Division.)

F[1] | P[1] | 14. 21-31. Rehoboam.
| P[2] | 15. 1-8. Abijam.
| P[3] | 15. 9-24. Asa.

14. 21-31 (P[1], above). REHOBOAM.
(Introversion).

P[1] | O | 21. Introduction.
| P | 22-24. Sins. Committed.
| *P* | 25-28. Sins. Punished.
| *O* | 29-31. Conclusion.

880-863 Israel, to put His name there. And his
°mother's name *was* Naamah an °Ammonitess.
P 22 And Judah did [9]evil in the sight of [5]the
(p. 473) LORD, and they provoked Him to °jealousy
with their [16]sins which they had committed,
above all that their fathers had done.
23 For they also built them high places, and
images, and °groves, on every high hill, and
under every green tree.
24 And there were also °sodomites in the land:
and they did according to all the abominations
of the nations which [5]the LORD cast out before
the °children of Israel.
P 25 (And it came to pass in the fifth year of
875 king Rehoboam, *that* °Shishak king of Egypt
came up °against Jerusalem:
26 And he took away the treasures of the
house of [5]the LORD, and the treasures of the
king's house; he even took away °all: and he
took away °all the shields of gold which Solomon had made.
27 And king Rehoboam made in their stead
brasen shields, and committed *them* unto the
hands of the chief of the guard, which kept
the [6]door of the king's house.
28 And it was *so*, when the king went into
the house of [5]the LORD, that the guard bare
them, and brought them back into the guard
chamber.)
O 29 Now the rest of the acts of Rehoboam,
and all that he did, *are* they not written in the
book of the chronicles of the kings of Judah?
30 And there was war between °Rehoboam
and Jeroboam all *their* days.
31 And Rehoboam [20]slept with his fathers,
and was buried with his fathers in the city of
David. And his mother's name *was* Naamah
an [21]Ammonitess. And °Abijam his son reigned
in his stead.

P² q **15** Now in the eighteenth year of king Jero-
(p. 474) boam the son of Nebat reigned °Abijam
863 over Judah.
2 °Three years reigned he in Jerusalem. And
his °mother's name *was* °Maachah, the daughter of °Abishalom.
r 3 And he walked in all the °sins of his father,
which he had done before him: and his heart
was not perfect with °the LORD his °God, as
the heart of David his °father.
s 4 Nevertheless for David's sake did [3]the LORD
his [3]God give him a °lamp in Jerusalem, to
set up his son after him, and to establish Jerusalem:
5 Because David did *that which was* right in
the eyes of [3]the LORD, and turned not aside
from any *thing* that He commanded him all
the days of his life, save only in the matter of
Uriah the Hittite.
r 6 °And there was war between Rehoboam and
Jeroboam all the days of his life.
q 7 Now °the rest of the acts of Abijam, and
all that he did, °*are* they not written in the
book of the chronicles of the kings of Judah?
And there was war between Abijam and Jeroboam.
8 And Abijam °slept with his fathers; and
they buried him in the city of David: and Asa
his son reigned in his stead.
9 And in the twentieth year of Jeroboam king P³ t
of Israel reigned Asa over Judah. 860
10 And forty and one years reigned he in to
Jerusalem. And his [2]mother's name *was* [2]Maa- 819
chah, the daughter of [2]Abishalom.
11 And Asa did *that which was* °right in the u
eyes of [3]the LORD, as *did* David his [3]father.
12 And he took away the °sodomites out of
the land, and removed all the °idols that his
fathers had made.
13 And also [2]Maachah his mother, even her
he removed from *being* queen, because she had

21 mother's name. Mentioned here and in the case of each successive king (cp. 15. 10; 22. 42. 2 Kings 8. 26, &c.); because the king's character stands connected with the *mother*; and because of the position which the queen dowager occupied (cp. 2. 19; 15. 13. Jer. 13. 18).
Ammonitess. Twice mentioned, and in connection with Jerusalem. See *v.* 31.
22 jealousy. Fig. *Anthropopatheia.* Ap. 6.
23 groves. See note on Ex. 34. 13, and Ap. 42.
24 sodomites. Committers of the sin of Sodom (Gen. 19). Male prostitutes, dedicated to idolatry involving this sin. Connected with the *'Ashērah.* Ap. 42. Cp. Deut. 23. 17. 1 Kings 15. 12; 22. 46. 2 Kings 23. 7.
children = sons.
25 Shishak. Founder of the twenty-second dynasty. Campaign described on the wall of the temple in Karnak, near Thebes, with portrait of Rehoboam.
against. See note on Judg. 1. 8, and Ap. 53.
26 all = "all [he could find]".
all the shields. Some codices, with three early printed editions, and Vulg., omit "all".
30 Rehoboam. Being named first he was probably the aggressor, contrary to 12. 24.
31 Abijam = Abijah.

15. 1-8 (P², p. 473). ABIJAH. (*Introversion.*)

P² q | 1, 2. Introduction.
  r | 3. Sins. Committed.
    s | 4, 5. Divine forbearance.
  r | 6. Sins. Punished.
q | 7, 8. Conclusion.

1 Abijam = Abijah.
2 Three years. Not full years, for he died in the twentieth year of Jeroboam (*v.* 9).
mother's. Put by Fig. *Synecdoche* (of Genus) for ancestor. Here = grandmother.
Maachah, or Michaiah (2 Chron. 13. 2).
Abishalom = Absalom (2 Chron. 11. 21).
3 sins. Heb. *chāṭā'.* Ap. 44. i.
the LORD. Heb. Jehovah. Ap. 4. II.
God. Heb. Elohim. Ap. 4. I.
father. Put by Fig. *Synecdoche* (of Genus), Ap. 6, for ancestor.
4 lamp. See note on 11. 36. Peculiarly used of David.
6 And, &c. This is repeated (from 14. 30) to complete Structure above.
7 the rest. See 2 Chron. 13. 3, &c.
are they not . . . ? Fig. *Erotēsis.* Ap. 6.
8 slept with his fathers. See note on 14. 20.

15. 9-24 (P³, p. 473). ASA. (*Introversion.*)

P³ | t | 9, 10. Introduction.
  u | 11-15. Events. Religious.
  u | 16-22. Events. Military.
t | 23, 24. Conclusion.

11 right. Therefore his days "long in the land" (*v.* 23). Contemporary with seven Israelite kings.
12 sodomites. See note on 14. 24.
idols = filthy idols.

860 made an °idol in a grove; and Asa destroyed
to her idol, and burnt *it* by the brook Kidron.
819 **14** But the high places were °not removed:
nevertheless Asa's heart was perfect with [3]the
LORD all his days.
15 And he brought in the °things which his
father had °dedicated, and the things which
himself had dedicated, into the house of [3]the
LORD, silver, and gold, and vessels.

u v (p. 475) **16** And there was °war between Asa and
Baasha king of Israel all their days.

w **17** And Baasha king of Israel went up against
Judah, and built °Ramah, that he might not
suffer any to °go out or come in to Asa king of
Judah.

x **18** Then Asa took all the silver and the gold
that were left in the treasures of the house of
[3]the LORD, and °the treasures of the king's
house, and delivered them into the hand of
his servants: and king Asa sent them to Ben-
hadad, the son of Tabrimon, the son of Hezion,
king of Syria, that dwelt at Damascus, saying,

y **19** °"*There is* a °league between me and thee,
°*and* between my father and thy father: °be-
hold, I have sent unto thee a present of silver
and gold; come and break thy °league with
Baasha king of Israel, that he may depart
from me."

x **20** So Ben-hadad hearkened unto king Asa,
and sent the captains of the °hosts which he
had against the cities of Israel, and smote
°Ijon, and Dan, and Abel-beth-maachah, and
all Cinneroth, with all the land of Naphtali.

w **21** And it came to pass, when Baasha heard
thereof, that he left off building of Ramah,
and °dwelt in Tirzah.

v **22** Then king Asa made a proclamation
throughout all Judah; none *was* exempted:
and they took away the stones of Ramah, and
the timber thereof, wherewith Baasha had
builded; and king Asa built with them Geba
of Benjamin, and Mizpah.

t (p. 474) **23** °The rest of all the acts of Asa, and all his
might, and all that he did, and the cities which
he built, °*are* they not written in the book of
the chronicles of the kings of Judah? Nevertheless in the time of his old age he was diseased
in his feet.
24 And Asa [8]slept with his fathers, and was
buried with his fathers in the city of David his
°father: and Jehoshaphat his son reigned in
his stead.

E[2] Q[1] z (p. 475) 858-857 **25** And Nadab the son of Jeroboam began to
reign over Israel in the second year of Asa
king of Judah, and reigned over Israel two
years.

a **26** And he did °evil in the sight of [3]the LORD,
and walked in the way of his father, and in
his °sin wherewith he °made Israel to sin.

b **27** And Baasha the son of Ahijah, of the
house of Issachar, conspired against him; and
Baasha smote him at Gibbethon, which *belonged* to the Philistines; for Nadab and all
Israel laid siege to Gibbethon.
28 Even in the third year of Asa king of
Judah did Baasha slay him, and reigned in
his stead.
29 And it came to pass, when he reigned, *that*
he smote all the house of Jeroboam; he left
not to Jeroboam any °that breathed, until he
had destroyed him, according unto °the saying
of [3]the LORD, which He spake by His servant
Ahijah the Shilonite:

30 Because of the [26]sins of Jeroboam which *a*
he sinned, and which he [26]made Israel sin, by
his provocation wherewith he provoked [3]the
LORD [3]God of Israel to anger.

31 Now the rest of the acts of Nadab, and all *z*
that he did, [23]*are* they not written in the book
of the chronicles of the kings of Israel?

---

13 idol in a grove = a monstrous '*Ashērah.* See Ap. 42.
14 not removed: not till the reign of Hezekiah (22. 43. 2 Kings 12. 3; 18. 4).
15 things . . . dedicated = holy things of his father. See note on Ex. 3. 5.

15. 16-22 (*u*, p. 474). EVENTS. MILITARY.
(*Introversion.*)

u | v | 16. War with Baasha. Begun.
w | 17. Baasha's building of Ramah. Begun.
x | 18. Ben-hadad. Subsidy to.
y | 19. Former league appealed to.
x | 20. Ben-hadad. Help from.
w | 21. Baasha's building of Ramah. Left.
v | 22. War with Baasha. Ended.

16 war. Only border fighting. No campaign. Cp. *v.* 32.
17 Ramah = the modern *er Rām*, five miles north of Jerusalem, which it was intended to menace. See 2 Chron. 16. 1.
go out or come in. But in vain. See 12. 27; 15. 9, &c.
18 the. Some codices, with two early printed editions, read "among the".
19 There is. Supply Fig. *Ellipsis* (Ap. 6). [Let there be.] **league** = covenant.
and. Supply [as] instead of "and".
behold. Fig. *Asterismos.* Ap. 6.
20 hosts = forces.
Ijon, &c. All in the neighbourhood of Gennesaret.
21 dwelt in. Sept. and Vulg. read "returned to". See note on 14. 17.
23 The rest. Cp. 2 Chron. 14. 9—15. 10.
are they not . . .? Fig. *Erotēsis.* Ap. 6.
24 father = forefather. Fig. *Synecdoche* (of Species), Ap. 6.

15. 25—22. 40 (E[2], p. 446). ISRAEL.
(*Division.*)

E[2] | Q[1] | 15. 25-31. Nadab.
Q[2] | 15. 32—16. 7. Baasha.
Q[3] | 16. 8-14. Elah.
Q[4] | 16. 15-20. Zimri.
(¶ Interregnum, 16. 21, 22.)
Q[5] | 16. 23-28. Omri.
Q[6] | 16. 29—22. 40. Ahab.

25-31 (Q[1], above). NADAB. (*Introversion.*)

Q[1] | z | 25. Introduction.
a | 26. Evil-doing.
b | 27-29. Conspiracy of Baasha.
a | 30. Evil-doing.
z | 31. Conclusion.

26 evil. Heb. *rā'a'.* Ap. 44. viii.
sin. Same as "evil", above.
made Israel to sin. See note on 14. 16.
29 that breathed. Heb. *n^eshāmāh.* Ap. 16.
the saying. Cp. 14. 7-11.

Q² c (p. 476) 32 And there was °war between Asa and
Baasha king of Israel all their days.
857 33 In the third year of Asa king of Judah
to began Baasha the son of Ahijah to reign over
833 all Israel °in Tirzah, °twenty and four years.

d 34 And he did [26]evil in the sight of [3]the LORD,
and walked in the way of Jeroboam, and in
his [26]sin wherewith he [26]made Israel to sin.

d **16** Then the word of °the LORD came to
°Jehu the son of Hanani against Baasha, saying,
2 "Forasmuch as I exalted thee out of the
dust, and made thee °prince over My People
Israel; and thou hast walked in the way of
Jeroboam, and hast made My People Israel to
°sin, to provoke Me to anger with their °sins;
3 °Behold, I will take away the posterity of
Baasha, and the posterity of his house; and
will make thy house °like the house of Jeroboam the son of Nebat.
4 Him that dieth of Baasha in the city shall
the dogs eat; and him that dieth of his in the
fields shall the fowls of the air eat."

c 5 Now the rest of the acts of Baasha, and
what he did, and his might, *are* they not written in the book of the chronicles of the kings
of Israel?
6 So Baasha °slept with his fathers, and was
buried in Tirzah: and Elah his son reigned in
his stead.
7 And also by the hand of the prophet Jehu
the son of Hanani came the word of [1]the LORD
against Baasha, and against his house, even
for all the °evil that he did in the sight of [1]the
LORD, in provoking Him to anger with the
work of his hands, in being like the house of
Jeroboam; and because he killed him.

Q³ e 8 In the twenty and sixth year of Asa king of
834 Judah began Elah the son of Baasha to reign
over Israel in Tirzah, two years.

f g 9 And his servant Zimri, captain of half *his*
chariots, conspired against him, as he was in
Tirzah, °drinking himself drunk in the house
of Arza steward of *his* house in Tirzah.
10 And Zimri went in and smote him, and
killed him, in the twenty and seventh year of
Asa king of Judah, and reigned in his stead.

h 11 And it came to pass, when he began to
reign, as soon as he sat on his throne, *that* he
slew all the house of Baasha: he left him °not
one that pisseth against a wall, neither of
his °kinsfolks, nor of his friends.

f g 12 Thus did Zimri destroy all the house of
Baasha, according to the word of [1]the LORD,
which He spake °against Baasha by [1]Jehu the
prophet,

h 13 For all the [2]sins of Baasha, and the [2]sins
of Elah his son, by which they [2]sinned, and by
which they made Israel to [2]sin, in provoking
[1]the LORD °God of Israel to anger with their
°vanities.

e 14 Now the rest of the acts of Elah, and all
that he did, *are* they not written in the book of
the chronicles of the kings of Israel?

Q⁴ i 15 In the twenty and seventh year of Asa king
of Judah did Zimri reign seven days in Tirzah. 833

And the People *were* encamped against Gib- k
bethon, which *belonged* to the Philistines.
16 And the People *that were* encamped heard
say, "Zimri hath conspired, and hath also slain
the king:"

wherefore all Israel made Omri, the captain of l
the host, king over Israel that day in the camp.

17 And Omri went up from Gibbethon, and all *l*
Israel with him, and they besieged Tirzah.

18 And it came to pass, when Zimri saw that *k*
the city was taken, that he went into the palace
of the king's house, and burnt the king's house
over him with fire, and died,
19 For his °sins which he [2]sinned in doing
[7]evil in the sight of [1]the LORD, in walking in
the way of Jeroboam, and in his [2]sin which
he did, to °make Israel to [2]sin.

---

15. 32—16. 7 (Q², p. 475). BAASHA.
(*Introversion.*)

Q² | c | 15. 32, 33. Introduction.
  d | 15. 34. Evil-doing. Committed.
  d | 16. 1-4. Evil-doing. Punished.
| *c* | 16. 5-7. Conclusion.

32 war. Only border fighting (cp. *vv.* 16, 32. 2 Chron. 14. 1; 15. 19); no actual campaign, as in 2 Chron. 16. 1.
33 in Tirzah. See notes on 14. 17 and *v.* 21.
twenty and four years. Began in the third year of Asa. Therefore he died in the twenty-sixth year of Asa (16. 8). Yet in the thirty-sixth year Baasha came and made war against Judah (2 Chron. 16. 1). This would be nine or ten years after he was dead. But see note on 2 Chron. 16. 1, where the word "reign" should be rendered "kingdom": i. e. the thirty-sixth year from the kingdom of Israel. See Ap. 50. V, p. 57.

16. 1 the LORD. Heb. Jehovah. Ap. 4.
Jehu the son of Hanani. Cp. 2 Chron. 16. 7-10; 19. 2.
2 prince: or captain = one raised up. Heb. *nāgīd.*
sin. Heb. *chāṭā'.* Ap. 44. i.
3 Behold. Fig. *Asterismos.* Ap. 6.
like. Cp. 15. 29; 14. 11.
6 slept, &c. See note on Deut. 31. 16.
7 evil. Same as "sin", *v.* 2.

16. 8-14 (Q³, p. 475). ELAH. (*Introversion.*)

Q³ | e | 8. Introduction.
  f | g | 9, 10. Zimri. Conspiracy.
    h | 11. Elah. Cut off.
  f | *g* | 12. Zimri. Prophecy.
    h | 13. Elah cut off. Reason.
| *e* | 14. Conclusion.

9 drinking himself drunk. Fig. *Polyptōton* (Ap. 6) for emphasis.
11 not one, &c. = not one male.
kinsfolks = kinsmen-redeemers.
12 against. Some codices read "unto". Others read "concerning".
13 God. Heb. Elohim. Ap. 4. I.
vanities = idols. Cp. *v.* 26.

15-20 (Q⁴, p. 475). ZIMRI. (*Introversion.*)

Q⁴ | i | 15-. Introduction.
  k | -15, 16-. Zimri. Conspiracy.
    l | -16. Omri. Elected.
    l | 17. Omri. Siege of Tirzah.
  k | 18, 19. Zimri. Suicide.
| *i* | 20. Conclusion.

19 sins. Some codices read "sin", as in *v.* 26. Committed not merely during the seven days' reign, but during his whole life, of course.
make Israel to sin. See note on 14. 16.

i (p. 476) 833 20 Now the rest of the acts of Zimri, and his treason that he wrought, °*are* they not written in the book of the chronicles of the kings of Israel?

¶ m[1] (p. 477) 21 Then were the People of Israel divided into two parts: half of the People followed Tibni the son of Ginath, to make him king; and half followed Omri.

m[2] 22 But the People that followed °Omri prevailed against the People that followed Tibni the son of Ginath: so Tibni died, and Omri reigned.

Q[5] n 833-821 23 In the °thirty and first year of Asa king of Judah began °Omri to reign over Israel, twelve years: (°six years reigned he in Tirzah.)

o 24 And he bought the hill Samaria of Shemer for two °talents of silver, and built on the hill, and called the name of the city which he built, after the name of Shemer, °owner of the hill, °Samaria.

o 25 But Omri wrought [7]evil in the eyes of [1]the LORD, and did worse than all that *were* before him.

26 For he walked in all the way of Jeroboam the son of Nebat, and in his [19]sin wherewith he °made Israel to sin, to provoke [1]the LORD [13]God of Israel to anger with their [13]vanities.

n 27 Now the rest of the acts of Omri °which he did, and his might that he shewed, [20]*are* they not written in the book of the chronicles of the kings of Israel?

28 So Omri [6]slept with his fathers, and was buried in Samaria: and Ahab his son reigned in his stead.

Q[6] R 822-800 29 And in the thirty and eighth year of Asa king of Judah began Ahab the son of Omri to reign over Israel:

S T p and Ahab the son of Omri reigned over Israel in Samaria °twenty and two years.

q 30 And Ahab the son of Omri did [7]evil in the sight of [1]the LORD °above all that *were* before him.

31 And it came to pass, as if it had been a light thing for him to walk in the [2]sins of Jeroboam the son of Nebat, that he took to wife °Jezebel the daughter of Ethbaal king of the Zidonians, and went and served Baal, and worshipped him.

q 32 And he reared up an altar for Baal in the house of Baal, which he had built in Samaria.

33 And Ahab made a °grove;

p and Ahab did more to provoke [1]the LORD [13]God of Israel to anger than all the kings of Israel that were before him.

U V[1] 34 In his days did Hiel the Beth-elite °build Jericho: he laid the foundation thereof °in Abiram his firstborn, and set up the gates thereof °in his youngest *son* Segub, according to the word of [1]the LORD, °which He spake by Joshua the son of Nun.

[2] W Y r (p. 478) **17** And °Elijah the °Tishbite, *who was* of the °inhabitants of Gilead, said unto Ahab, "*As* °the LORD °God of Israel liveth, °before Whom I stand, there shall not be °dew

---

20 are they not written . . .? Fig. *Erotēsis.* Ap. 6.

16. 21, 22 (¶, p. 475). INTERREGNUM.
(*Division.*)

¶ | m[1] | 21. People. Division for Tibni.
  | m[2] | 22. People. Prevalence for Omri.

22 Omri. Note the Introversion of these names in this verse.

23-28 (Q[5], p. 475). OMRI. (*Introversion.*)

Q[5] | n | 23. Introduction.
  o | 24. Events. Building Samaria.
  o | 25, 26. Events. Evil-doing.
  n | 27, 28. Conclusion.

23 thirty and first year. He reigned twelve years (833-821), and yet in *v.* 29 Ahab began in the thirty-eighth year of Asa. Omri began to reign *de jure* when he slew Zimri, in the twenty-seventh year of Asa; but only *de facto* on the death of Tibni the usurper.
Omri. See Ap. 55.
six years. Beginning in Asa's thirty-first and ending in Asa's thirty-eighth (*v.* 29).

24 talents. See Ap. 51. II. owner = lord.
Samaria. This is the origin of the city.

26 made Israel to sin. See note on 14. 16.

27 which. Some codices, with four early printed editions, Sept., and Syr., read "and all that".

16. 29—22. 40 (Q[6], p. 475). AHAB.
(*Introversion and Alternation.*)

Q[6] | R | 16. 29-. Introduction.
  S | T | 16. -29-33. Personal evil. Idolatry.
    U | 16. 34—20. 43. Public events. War with Syria.
  S | *T* | 21. 1-29. Personal evil. Naboth.
    U | 22. 1-38. Public events. War with Syria.
  R | 22. 39, 40. Conclusion.

29 twenty and two years. For spiritual significance, see note on 14. 20, and Ap. 10.

-29-33 (T, above). PERSONAL EVIL.
(*Introversion.*)

T | p | -29. Ahab. Length of reign.
  q | 30, 31. Personal evil.
  q | 32, 33-. Public evil.
  p | -33. Ahab. Character of reign.

30 above all. The reign of Ahab opens a new era in Israel's history.

31 Jezebel, daughter of a regicide and fratricide (Josephus *c. Apion* 1. 18, *Ant.* viii. 3. 1), priest of the Phoenician goddess Astarte.

33 grove. See note on Ex. 34. 13, and Ap. 42.

16. 34—20. 43 (U, above). PUBLIC EVENTS.
(*Division.*)

U | V[1] | 16. 34. The rebuilding of Jericho.
  V[2] | 17. 1—19. 21. The drought.
  V[3] | 20. 1-43. War with Syria.

34 build = to fortify and complete. It had been partially restored (Judg. 3. 13. 2 Sam. 10. 5), but now became a fortified city of Israel.
in = at the cost of.
which He spake. Cp. Josh. 6. 26.

17. 1—19. 21 [For Structures see next page].

1 Elijah. First mention = GOD (*El*) is JAH (or Jehovah). See Ap. 4. II.
Tishbite = sojourner. Probably a priest.
inhabitants = sojourners.
the LORD. Heb. Jehovah. Ap. 4. II.
God. Heb. Elohim. Ap. 4. I.
before, &c. Probably a priest. See note above.
dew = night-mist. Cp. Deut. 32. 2. 2 Sam. 1. 21. Job 38. 28.

822 to 800 nor rain °these years, but according to my word."

2 And the word of [1]the LORD came unto him, saying,

3 "Get thee hence, and turn thee eastward, and hide thyself by the brook Cherith, that *is* °before Jordan.

4 And it shall be, *that* thou shalt drink of the brook; and °I have commanded the °ravens to feed thee °there."

s (p. 478) 5 So he went and did according unto the word of [1]the LORD: for he went and dwelt by the brook Cherith, that *is* before Jordan.

6 And the [4]ravens brought him bread and flesh in the morning, and bread and flesh in the evening; and he drank of the brook.

t 7 And it came to pass after a while, that the brook dried up, because there had been no rain in the land.

Y r 8 And the word of [1]the LORD came unto him, saying,

9 "Arise, get thee to °Zarephath, which *belongeth* to Zidon, and dwell there: °behold, [4]I have commanded °a widow woman there to sustain thee."

s 10 So he arose and went to Zarephath.

t Z^1 u^1 And when he came to the gate of the city, [9]behold, the widow woman *was* there gathering of sticks: and he called to her, and said, "Fetch me, I pray thee, a little water in a vessel, that I may drink."

11 And as she was going to fetch *it,* he called to her, and said, "Bring me, I pray thee, a morsel of bread in thine hand."

v^1 12 And she said, "*As* [1]the LORD thy [1]God liveth, I have not a cake, but an handful of meal in a barrel, and °a little oil in a °cruse: and, [9]behold, I *am* gathering two sticks, that I may go in and dress it for me and my son, that we may eat it, and die."

u^2 13 And Elijah said unto her, "Fear not; go *and* do as thou hast said: but make me thereof a little cake first, and bring *it* unto me, and after make for thee and for thy son.

14 For thus saith [1]the LORD [1]God of Israel, 'The °barrel of meal shall not waste, neither shall the [12]cruse of oil fail, until the day *that* [1]the LORD sendeth rain upon the earth.'"

v^2 15 And she went and did according to the saying of Elijah:

u^3 and She, and he, and her house, did eat *many* days.

16 *And* the barrel of meal wasted not, neither did the [12]cruse of oil fail, according to the word of [1]the LORD, which He spake by Elijah.

Z^2 w y 17 And it came to pass after these things, *that* the son of the woman, the mistress of the house, fell sick; and his sickness was so sore, that there was no °breath left in him.

z 18 And she said unto Elijah, °"What have I to do with thee, O thou °man of [1]God? art thou come unto me to call my °sin to remembrance, and to slay my son?"

x a 19 And he said unto her, "Give me thy son." And he took him out of her bosom, and carried him up into a loft, where he abode, and laid him upon his own bed.

20 And he cried unto [1]the LORD, and said, "O [1]LORD my [1]God, hast Thou also brought b

17. 1–19. 21 (V^2, p. 477). THE DROUGHT.
(*Alternation.*)

V^2 W | 17. 1-24. Elijah's retirement.
  X | 18. 1-46. Mission to Ahab.
 W | 19. 1-14. Elijah's flight.
  X | 19. 15-21. Mission to Hazael and others.

17. 1-24 (W, above). ELIJAH'S RETIREMENT.
(*Extended Alternation.*)

W | Y | r | 1-4. Command.
  s | 5, 6. Obedience.
  t | 7. Circumstance. The brook and ravens.
 Y | *r* | 8, 9. Command.
  s | 10-. Obedience.
  t | -10-24. Circumstance. The widow.

these years (not three years). No definite period stated. "Years" is pl., not dual. In Luke 4. 25 and Jas. 5. 17 = "three years and six months". These six months must be reckoned before the three years, not added at the end because of "the third year" (18. 1): i. e. the third full year.

3 before Jordan: i. e. on the east side.

4 I have commanded. Elijah miraculously fed *three* times: (1) by ravens (17. 6); (2) by a widow (17. 9); (3) by an angel (19. 5, 6).

ravens. Note "I have commanded". All things possible when He speaks. Almighty power is a better and easier explanation than all rationalistic inventions.

there. Nowhere else. Note the special lesson. Anywhere but in God's appointed place he would have perished.

9 Zarephath = the Sarepta of Luke 4. 26.

behold. Fig. *Asterismos.* Ap. 6.

a widow. One of nine widows mentioned. See note on *v.* 4 and Gen. 38. 19.

-10-24 (*t*, above). CIRCUMSTANCE. THE WIDOW.
(*Division.*)

t | Z^1 | -10-16. Maintenance.
 | Z^2 | 17-24. Bereavement.

-10-16 (Z^1, above). MAINTENANCE.
(*Repeated Alternation.*)

Z^1 | u^1 | -10, 11. Elijah. Request.
  v^1 | 12. The widow. Excuse.
 u^2 | 13, 14. Elijah. Promise.
  v^2 | 15-. The widow. Compliance.
 u^3 | -15, 16. Elijah. Promise fulfilled.

12 a little oil. From Josh. 19. 24-28 Zidon fell to Asher. From Deut. 33. 24 Asher had abundance of oil, though water was scarce. Cp. Gen. 49. 20.

cruse = flask. Cp. Matt. 25. 4.

14 barrel of meal. Fig. *Hypallage* (Ap. 6) = meal in the barrel.

17-24 (Z^2, above). BEREAVEMENT.
(*Introversion and Alternation.*)

Z^2 | w | y | 17. Son. Death.
  z | 18. Widow. Complaint.
 x | a | 19. Son taken.
  b | 20, 21. Prayer made.
 x | *b* | 22. Prayer answered.
  a | 23-. Son restored.
 w | *y* | -23. Son. Life.
  z | 24. Widow. Acknowledgment.

17 breath. Heb. *neshāmāh.* Ap. 16.

18 What have I . . .? See note on 2 Sam. 16. 10.

man of God. See note on Deut. 33. 1, and Ap. 49.

sin. Heb. *'āvōn.* Ap. 44. iii.

822 °evil upon the widow with whom I sojourn,
to by slaying her son?"
800 21 And he °stretched himself upon the child
three times, and cried unto [1]the LORD, and
said, "O [1]LORD my [1]God, I pray Thee, let this
child's °soul come into him again."

x b (p. 478) 22 And [1]the LORD heard the voice of Elijah;
and the [21]soul of the child came into him again,
and he revived.

a 23 And Elijah took the child, and brought him
down out of the chamber into the house, and
delivered him unto his mother:

w y and Elijah said, "See, thy son °liveth."

z 24 And the woman said to Elijah, "Now by
this I know that thou *art* a [18]man of [1]God, *and*
that the word of [1]the LORD in thy mouth *is*
truth."

X A (p. 479) **18** And it came to pass *after* many days,
that the word of °the LORD came to
Elijah in the °third year, saying, "Go, shew
thyself unto Ahab;

B and I will send rain upon the earth."

A C 2 And Elijah went to shew himself unto Ahab.
And *there was* a sore °famine in Samaria.
3 And Ahab called Obadiah, which *was* the
°governor of *his* house. (°Now Obadiah feared
[1]the LORD greatly:
4 For it was *so*, when °Jezebel cut off the prophets of [1]the LORD, that Obadiah took an hundred prophets, and hid them by °fifty in a cave,
and fed them with bread and water.)
5 And Ahab said unto Obadiah, °"Go into
the land, unto all fountains of water, and unto
all brooks: peradventure we may find grass
to save the horses and mules alive, that we
lose not all the beasts."
6 So they divided the land between them to
pass throughout it: Ahab went one way by
himself, and Obadiah went another way by
himself.

D 7 And as Obadiah was in the way, °behold,
Elijah met him: and he knew him, and fell
on his face, and said, "*Art* thou that my lord
Elijah?"
8 And he answered him, "I *am*:

E c go, tell thy lord, 'Behold, Elijah *is here*.'"

d e 9 And he said, °"What have I sinned, that
thou °wouldest deliver thy servant into the hand
of Ahab, to slay me?

f g 10 *As* [1]the LORD thy °God liveth, there is no
nation or kingdom, whither my lord hath not
sent to seek thee: and when they said, '*He is*
not *there*;' he took an oath of the kingdom
and nation, that they found thee not.

h 11 And now thou sayest, 'Go, tell thy lord, 'Behold, Elijah *is here*.''

f g 12 And it shall come to pass, *as soon as* I am
gone from thee, that the °Spirit of [1]the LORD
shall carry thee whither I know not; and *so*
when I come and tell Ahab, and he cannot find
thee, he shall slay me: but I thy servant fear
[1]the LORD from my youth.
13 Was it not told my lord what I did when

20 evil. Heb. *rā'a'*. Ap. 44. viii.
21 stretched = measured.
soul = life. Cp. *v.* 23, "liveth". Heb. *nephesh*. Ap. 13.
23 liveth. The result of life's being given, making the child "a living soul" (Gen. 2. 7).

18. 1-46 (X, p. 478). MISSION TO AHAB.
(*Alternation.*)

X | A | 1-. Command.
  B | -1. Promise of rain. Given.
A | 2-40. Obedience.
  B | 41-46. Promise of rain. Fulfilled.

1 the LORD. Heb. Jehovah. Ap. 4. II.
third year: i.e. the third or last full year toward the end of the three and a half years.

2-40 (*A*, above). OBEDIENCE.
(*Extended Alternation.*)

A | C | 2-6. Ahab and Obadiah.
  D | 7, 8-. Elijah.
   E | -8-16-. Ahab. Elijah's message.
C | -16, 17. Ahab and Elijah.
  D | 18. Elijah.
   E | 19-40. Ahab. Elijah's proposal.

2 famine. One of the thirteen famines mentioned in Scripture. See note on Gen. 12. 10.
3 governor of = governor over.
Now. Fig. *Parenthesis*. Ap. 6.
4 Jezebel. The first record of using the civil power against the true religion (and by a woman). See note on Judg. 4. 21.
fifty in a cave = fifty men. Heb. *'ish*. Ap. 14. II.
5 Go into = Sept. and Syr. read "Go and let us pass through".
7 behold. Fig. *Asterismos*. Ap. 6.

-8-16- (E, above). AHAB. ELIJAH'S MESSAGE.
(*Introversion.*)

E | c | -8. Command to Obadiah.
  d | 9-14. Expostulation of Obadiah.
  d | 15. Assurance of Elijah.
 c | 16-. Obedience of Obadiah.

9-14 (d, above). EXPOSTULATION OF OBADIAH.
(*Introversion and Alternation.*)

d | e | 9. Danger of Obadiah.
  f | g | 10. Ahab's search for Elijah (past).
    h | 11. Command. Of Elijah.
  f | *g* | 12, 13. Ahab's search for Elijah (future).
    h | 14-. Command. Of Elijah.
  e | -14. Danger of Obadiah.

9 What ...? Fig. *Erotēsis*. Ap. 6.
wouldest deliver = art giving.
10 God. Heb. Elohim. Ap. 4. I.
12 Spirit. Heb. *rūach*. Ap. 9.
13 men. Heb. *'ish*. Ap. 14. II.
15 before, &c. See note on 17. 1.

Jezebel slew the prophets of [1]the LORD, how
I hid an hundred °men of [1]the LORD'S prophets by [4]fifty in a cave, and fed them with
bread and water?

14 And now thou sayest, 'Go, tell thy lord, *h*
'Behold, Elijah *is here*:''

and he shall slay me." *e*

15 And Elijah said, "*As* [1]the LORD of hosts *d*
liveth, °before Whom I stand, I will surely
shew myself unto him to day."

16 So Obadiah went to meet Ahab, and told *c*
him:

and Ahab went to meet Elijah. *C*

822 to 800 17 And it came to pass, when Ahab saw Elijah, that Ahab said unto him, "*Art* thou he that °troubleth °Israel?"

D (p. 479) 18 And he answered, "I have not troubled [17]Israel; but thou, and thy father's house, in that ye have forsaken the commandments of [1]the LORD, and thou hast followed Baalim.

E i (p. 480) 19 Now therefore send, *and* gather to me all Israel unto mount °Carmel, and the prophets of Baal four hundred and fifty, and the prophets of the °groves four hundred, which eat at Jezebel's table."

20 So Ahab sent unto all the °children of Israel, and gathered the prophets together unto mount Carmel.

k F 21 And Elijah came unto all the people, and said, °"How long °halt ye between two opinions? if [1]the LORD *be* [10]God, follow Him: but if Baal, *then* follow him." And the People answered him not a word.

22 Then said Elijah unto °the People, °"I, *even* °I only, remain a prophet of [1]the LORD; but Baal's prophets *are* four hundred and fifty [13]men.

23 Let them therefore give us two bullocks; and let them choose one bullock for themselves, and cut it in pieces, and lay *it* on wood, and put no fire *under*: and I will dress the other bullock, and lay *it* on wood, and put no fire *under*:

24 And call ye on the name of your °gods, and I will call on the name of [1]the LORD: and the [10]God That answereth °by fire, let Him be [10]God." And all the people answered and said, "It is well spoken."

G l 25 And Elijah said unto the prophets of Baal, "Choose you one bullock for yourselves, and dress *it* first; for ye *are* many; and call on the name of your [24]gods, but put no fire *under*."

m 26 And they took the bullock which was given them, and they dressed *it*, and called on the name of Baal from morning even until noon, saying, "O Baal, hear us." But *there was* no voice, nor any that answered. And they °leaped upon the altar which °was made.

l 27 And it came to pass at noon, that Elijah mocked them, and said, °"Cry aloud: for he *is* a god; either he is talking, or he is °pursuing, or he is in a journey, *or* peradventure he sleepeth, and must be awaked."

m 28 And they cried aloud, and cut themselves after their manner with knives and °lancets, till the blood gushed out upon them.

29 And it came to pass, when midday was past, and they prophesied until the *time* of the offering of the °*evening* sacrifice, that *there was* neither voice, nor any to answer, nor any that regarded.

F 30 And Elijah said unto all the People, "Come near unto me." And all the People came near unto him.

G n¹ And he °repaired the altar of [1]the LORD *that was* °broken down.

31 And Elijah took twelve stones, according to the number of the tribes of the sons of °Jacob, unto whom the word of [1]the LORD came, saying, °"Israel shall be thy name:"

32 And with the stones he built an altar in the name of [1]the LORD:

o¹ and he made a trench about the altar, as great as would contain two °measures of seed.

n² 33 And he put the wood in order, and cut the bullock in pieces, and laid *him* on the wood,

o² and said, "Fill four barrels with °water, and pour *it* on the burnt sacrifice, and on °the wood."

34 And he said, "Do *it* the second time." And they did *it* the second time. And he said, "Do

---

17 troubleth. Cp. Josh. 7. 25 with 6. 18, and 1 Chron. 2. 7.
Israel. Put by Fig. *Metonymy* (of Cause), Ap. 6, for Israelitish people.

18. 19-40 (*E*, p. 479). AHAB. ELIJAH'S PROPOSAL. (*Introversion.*)

E | i | 19, 20. Baal's prophets. Assembled.
  k | 21-38. Conflict with prophets.
  k | 39. Confession of the People.
i | 40. Baal's prophets. Slain.

19 Carmel. Eighteen miles from Jezreel; sixteen miles from the sea. The Kishon below, but now dry. At the foot a perennial spring, with a roofed reservoir, eight feet deep. Carmel is still called "Mar-Elias".
groves = the *'Ashērah.* See note on Ex. 34. 13, and Ap. 42.
20 children = sons.

21-38 (k, above). CONFLICT WITH THE PROPHETS. (*Alternation.*)

k | F | 21-24. The People. Elijah's appeal.
  G | 25-29. Bullock of the prophets.
  F | 30-. The People. Elijah's call.
  G | -30-38. Bullock of Elijah.

21 How long . . .? Fig. *Erotēsis.* Ap. 6.
halt = leap. Cp. *v.* 26.
22 the People. Some codices read "all the people".
I . . . I. Fig. *Epizeuxis* (Ap. 6), for emphasis.
24 gods = god, as in *v.* 25. So R.V.
by fire. This was Jehovah's way of showing His acceptance of the offering. See note on Gen. 4. 4.

25-29 (G, above). BULLOCK OF THE PROPHETS. (*Alternation.*)

G | l | 25. Elijah.
  m | 26. The prophets of Baal.
  l | 27. Elijah.
  m | 28, 29. The prophets of Baal.

26 leaped upon = leaped over. Cp. *v.* 21.
was made = had been made.
27 Cry aloud, &c. Fig. *Eironeia.* Ap. 6.
pursuing. Occurs only here.
28 lancets = lances. Done by Dervishes to the present day.
29 evening sacrifice. The usual meal offering. There was also a morning meal offering as well (Num. 28. 8). Cp. 2 Kings 16. 15.

-30-38 (*G*, above). THE BULLOCK OF ELIJAH. (*Repeated Alternation.*)

G | n¹ | -30-32-. Altar. Its repairing.
  o¹ | -32. The trench.
  n² | 33-. Altar. Arrangement of wood.
  o² | -33-35. The water.
  n³ | 36, 37. Altar. Time for offering. Prayer.
  o³ | 38. The fire.

30 repaired. Carmel had been a *local* altar for *lay* (individual) offerings, but had been broken down. Cp. 19. 10. These *lay* altars had no horns.
broken down: i. e. purposely.
31 Jacob. Some codices, with one early printed edition, and Sept., read "Israel", in harmony with *v.* 36.
Israel. See note on Gen. 32. 28.
32 measures. See Ap. 51. III. 3.
33 water. See note on *v.* 19.
the wood. Sept. adds "and they did so".

822 *it* the third time." And they did *it* the third
to time.
800 35 And the water ran round about the altar;
and he filled the trench also with water.

n³ 36 And it came to pass at *the time of* the
(p. 480) offering of the *evening* sacrifice, that Elijah the
prophet came near, and said, [1]"LORD [10]God of
Abraham, Isaac, and of °Israel, let it be known
this day that Thou *art* [10]God in Israel, and *that*
I *am* Thy servant, and *that* I have done all
these things at Thy word.
37 Hear me, O [1]LORD, hear me, that this
People may know that Thou *art* [1]the LORD
[10]God, and *that* Thou hast turned their heart
back again."

o³ 38 °Then the fire of [1]the LORD fell, °and consumed the °burnt sacrifice, and the wood, and
the stones, and the dust, and licked up the
water that *was* in the trench.

k 39 And when all the People saw *it*, they fell
on their faces: and they said, °"The LORD, He
is the [10]God; [1]the LORD, He *is* the [10]God."

i 40 And Elijah said unto them, °"Take the
prophets of Baal; let not °one of them escape."
And they took them: and Elijah brought them
down to the brook °Kishon, and °slew them
there.

B H r 41 And Elijah said unto Ahab, "Get thee up,
(p. 481) eat and drink;

s for *there is* a sound of abundance of rain."

J K t 42 So Ahab went up to eat and to drink.

u And Elijah went up to the top of Carmel; and
he °cast himself down upon the earth, and put
his face between his knees,

L 43 And said to his °servant, "Go up now,
look toward the sea." And he went up, and
looked, and said, "*There is* nothing." And
he said, "Go again seven times."
44 And it came to pass at the seventh time,
that he said, [7]"Behold, there ariseth a little
cloud out of the sea, like a [13]man's hand."

H r And he said, "Go up, say unto Ahab, 'Prepare
thy chariot, and get thee down,

s that the rain stop thee not.'"

J L 45 And it came to pass in the mean while,
that the heaven was black with clouds and
°wind, and there was a great rain.

K t And Ahab rode, and went to Jezreel.

u 46 And the °hand of [1]the LORD was on Elijah; and he °girded up his loins, and °ran
before Ahab to the entrance of Jezreel.

W M¹ **19** And Ahab told Jezebel all that Elijah
had done, and withal °how he had slain
°all the prophets with the sword.
2 Then Jezebel sent a messenger unto Elijah,
saying, "So let the gods do °*to me*, and more
also, if I make not thy °life as the °life of one
of them by to morrow about this time."

N¹ v 3 And when he saw *that*, °he arose, and went
for his [2]life, and came to Beer-sheba, which
belongeth to Judah, and left his °servant
there.

36 Israel, not Jacob. See note on Gen. 32. 28.
38 Then the fire of the LORD fell. Aram. and Sept. read "Then fire from Jehovah fell". See note on Gen. 4. 4. "Fire of Jehovah" occurs only here and Num. 11. 1, 3.
and. Note the Fig. *Polysyndeton*. Ap. 6.
burnt sacrifice. See Ap. 43. II. ii.
39 The LORD, &c. Fig. *Epizeuxis*. Ap. 6. Heb. Jehovah. Ap. 4. II.
40 Take = seize, lay hold of.
one = a man. Heb. *'ish*. Ap. 14. II.
Kishon. Cp. Judg. 4. 13; 5. 21.
slew. Heb. idiom, caused them to be slain.

18. 41-46 (*B*, p. 479). PROMISE OF RAIN. FULFILLED. (*Alternation and Introversion*.)

B | H | r | 41-. Command. To Ahab.
s | -41. Reason.
J | K | t | 42-. Obedience of Ahab.
u | -42. Elijah. Ascent of Carmel.
L | 43,44-. Rain. Expectation of.
H | *r* | -44-. Command. To servant.
s | -44. Reason.
J | *L* | 45-. Rain. Fall of.
K | *t* | -45. Obedience of Ahab.
u | 46. Elijah. Run to Jezreel.

42 cast himself down. A rare word. Only here and 2 Kings 4. 34, 35. = Kneeling, and then placing forehead on the ground. **43** servant = young man.
45 wind. Heb. *rūach*. Ap. 9.
46 hand. Put by Fig. *Metonymy* (of Cause), Ap. 6, for power put forth.
girded. Girdles worn by all. Taken off when resting. Put on when preparing for work or journeying. See Ex. 12. 11. 2 Kings 4. 29; 9. 1. Luke 12. 37; 17. 8. Acts 12. 8.
ran. For over twenty miles Elijah acted as the royal "runner" across the great plain of Esdraelon. Possibly none at hand in the king's hasty departure.

19. 1-14 (*W*, p. 478). ELIJAH'S FLIGHT. (*Repeated Alternation*.)

W | M¹ | 1, 2. Jezebel's threat.
N¹ | v | 3, 4. Elijah. To the desert.
w | 5-7. Coming of angel.
v | 8, 9-. Elijah. To Horeb.
w | -9. Coming of word of Jehovah.
M² | 10. Jezebel's threat.
N² | x | 11-. Elijah. Command.
y | -11, 12. Jehovah. Manifestations.
x | 13-. Elijah. Awe.
y | -13. Jehovah. Inquiry.
M³ | 14. Jezebel's threat.

1 how he had slain: or, all about how he had slain.
all. Some codices, with Sept., omit this word "all".
2 to me. These words in italics are read in some codices, with Sept., Syr., and Vulg. Cp. 20. 10.
life = soul. Heb. *nephesh*. Ap. 13.
3 he arose. Some codices, with Aram. MS., Sept., Syr., and Vulg., read "And he feared and arose".
servant = young man.
4 himself = his soul. Heb. *nephesh*. Ap. 13.
LORD. Heb. Jehovah. Ap. 4. II.
5 behold. Fig. *Asterismos*. Ap. 6.
6 cake . . . cruse. Elijah miraculously fed three times. See notes on 17. 4, 6.

4 But he himself went a day's journey into
the wilderness, and came and sat down under
a juniper tree: and he requested for °himself
that he might die; and said, "It is enough;
now, O °LORD, take away my [2]life; for I *am*
not better than my fathers."

5 And as he lay and slept under a juniper w
tree, °behold, then an Angel touched him, and
said unto him, "Arise *and* eat."
6 And he looked, and, [5]behold, *there was*
a °cake baken on the coals, and a °cruse of

822 water at his °head. And he did eat and drink,
to and laid him down again.
800 7 And the Angel of [4]the LORD came again
the second time, and touched him, and said,
"Arise *and* eat; because the journey *is* too
great for thee."

v 8 And he arose, and did eat and drink, and
(p. 481) went in the strength of that meat °forty days
and °forty nights unto °Horeb the mount of
°God.
9 And he came thither unto a cave, and
°lodged there;

w and, [5]behold, the word of [4]the LORD *came* to
him, and He said unto him, °"What doest thou
here, Elijah?"

M[2] 10 And he said, "I have been very jealous
for °the LORD God of hosts: for the °children
of Israel have forsaken Thy covenant, °THROWN
DOWN THINE °ALTARS, AND SLAIN THY PROPHETS WITH THE
SWORD; AND °I, *even* I ONLY, AM LEFT; AND THEY SEEK MY
[2]LIFE, TO TAKE IT AWAY."

N[2] x 11 And He said, °"Go forth, and stand upon
the mount before [4]the LORD."

y And, [5]behold, [4]the LORD passed by, and a great
and strong °wind rent the mountains, and brake
in pieces the rocks before [4]the LORD; *but* [4]the
LORD *was* not in the °wind: and after the
°wind an earthquake; *but* [4]the LORD *was*
not in the earthquake:
12 And after the earthquake a fire; *but* [4]the
LORD *was* not in the fire: and after the fire °a
still small voice.

x 13 And it was *so*, when Elijah heard *it*, that
he °wrapped his face in his mantle, and went
out, and stood in the entering in of the cave.

y And, [5]behold, *there came* a voice unto him,
and °said, "What doest thou here, Elijah?"

M[3] 14 And he said, "I have been very jealous
for [4]the LORD [8]God of hosts: because the
[10]children of Israel have forsaken Thy covenant, thrown down Thine [10]altars, and slain
Thy prophets with the sword; and [10]I, *even*
I only, am left; and they seek my [2]life, to take
it away."

X O z 15 And [4]the LORD said unto him, "Go, re-
(p. 482) turn °on thy way to the wilderness of Damascus:

a and when thou comest, °anoint Hazael *to be*
king over Syria:
16 And Jehu the °son of Nimshi shalt thou
anoint *to be* king over Israel: and °Elisha the
son of Shaphat of Abel-meholah shalt thou
anoint *to be* prophet in thy room.

P b[1] 17 And it shall come to pass, *that* him that
escapeth °the sword of Hazael shall Jehu slay:
and him that escapeth from the sword of Jehu
shall °Elisha slay.

b[2] 18 Yet °I HAVE LEFT *me* SEVEN THOUSAND IN ISRAEL,
ALL THE KNEES WHICH HAVE NOT °BOWED UNTO BAAL,
and every mouth which hath not °kissed
him."

O z 19 So he departed thence,

a and found Elisha the son of Shaphat, who *was*
plowing *with* °twelve yoke *of oxen* before
him, and he with the twelfth: and Elijah
passed by him, and cast his °mantle upon
him.
20 And he left the oxen, and ran after Elijah,
and said, "Let me, I pray thee, kiss my father
and my mother, and *then* I will follow thee."
And he said unto him, "Go back again: for
°what have I done to thee?"
21 And he returned back from him, and took
a yoke of oxen, and slew them, and boiled
their flesh with the °instruments of the oxen,
and gave unto the people, and they did eat.
Then he arose, and went after Elijah, and
ministered unto him.

head = bolster, or pillow.
8 forty. The number of Probation. See Ap. 10.
Horeb. About 180 miles.
God. Heb. Elohim. Ap. 4. I.
9 lodged = passed the night.
What . . .? Fig. *Anthropopatheia* (Ap. 6), as though He did not know.
10 the LORD God of hosts. First occurrence of this title. See Ap. 4 = *Jehovah Elohim ẓebāōth*. It occurs in 2 Sam. 5. 10, but in narrative, not address. "The LORD (*Jehovah*) God (*Elohim*) of hosts" occurs only here in Kings and Chronicles. Often in Psalms (59. 5; 69. 6; 80. 4, 19; 84. 8; 89. 8). In Isa. 10. 23, 24; 22. 5, 12, 14, 15; 28. 22. Jer. 2. 19; 5. 14; 15. 16; 35. 17; 49. 5; 50. 25, 31. Hos. 12. 5. Amos 5. 15. After the return from captivity "LORD of hosts" occurs fourteen times in Haggai; about fifty in Zechariah; and twenty-five in Malachi. But "LORD God of hosts" is not found in those books.
children = sons. **thrown, &c.** Quoted in Rom. 11. 2, 3.
altars. There were *lay* altars (local) for customary individual offerings by laymen, as well as at Jerusalem. These had no horns.
I . . . I. Fig. *Epizeuxis*. Ap. 6.
11 Go forth. Sept. adds "to-morrow".
wind. Heb. *rūach*. Ap. 9.
12 a still small voice = the sound of stillness. Cp. Job 4. 16. Sept. = a gentle breeze, usually misquoted "the still", &c.
13 wrapped: as Moses at the bush (Ex. 3. 6).
said. Some codices, with Syr., add "unto him". Cp. *v.* 9.

19. 15-21 (*X*, p. 478). **MISSION TO HAZAEL AND OTHERS.** (*Introversion and Alternation.*)

X | O | z | 15-. Return of Elijah. Commanded.
  | | a | -15, 16. Anointings. Commanded.
  | P | b[1] | 17. Prophecy.
  | | b[2] | 18. History.
  | *O* | *z* | 19-. Return of Elijah. Effected.
  | | *a* | -19-21. Anointings. Effected.

15 on thy way = to thy way: i. e. out of which he had deviated.
anoint: i. e. cause to be anointed. Cp. 2 Kings 9. 1-7.
16 son of Nimshi. Son put by Fig. *Metonymy* (of Subject), Ap. 6, for grandson or descendant (2 Kings 9. 2).
Elisha = El = my GOD [is] salvation.
17 the sword. Put by Fig. *Metonymy* (of Cause), Ap. 6, for judgments inflicted by it. Cp. 2 Kings 9 and 10. The first prophecy given to Elijah.
Elisha slay: i. e. declare should be slain. Heb. idiom. See Jer. 1. 10. Hos. 6. 5.
18 I have left, &c. Rom. 11. 4.
bowed. } Put by Fig. *Metonymy* (of Adjunct), Ap. 6, for
kissed. } worshipping. Cp. Hos. 3. 12.
kissed him. Heb. kissed to him. Cp. Job 31. 26, 27.
19 twelve: seven separate ploughs following each other. Often seen to-day. **mantle.** Cp. Zech. 13. 4.
20 what have I done . . .? Fig. *Erotēsis* (Ap. 6), or "what is the meaning of what I did?"
21 instruments = implements. Cp. 2 Sam. 24. 22.

V^3 c^1 (p. 483) 822 to 800 **20** And °Ben-hadad the king of Syria gathered all his °host together: and *there were* °thirty and two kings with him, and horses, and chariots: and he went up and besieged Samaria, and warred against it.

d^1 e^1 2 And he sent messengers to Ahab king of Israel into the city, and °said unto him, "Thus saith Ben-hadad,

3 'Thy silver and thy gold *is* mine; thy wives also and thy °children, *even* the goodliest, *are* mine.'"

f^1 4 And the king of Israel answered and said, "My lord, O king, according to thy saying, I *am* thine, and all that I have."

e^2 5 And the messengers came again, and said, "Thus speaketh Ben-hadad, saying, 'Although I have sent unto thee, saying, 'Thou shalt deliver me thy silver, and thy gold, and thy wives, and thy [3]children;

6 Yet I will send my servants unto thee to morrow about this time, °and they shall °search thine house, and the houses of thy servants; and it shall be, *that* whatsoever is pleasant in thine eyes, they shall put *it* in their hand, and take *it* away.''"

f^2 7 Then the king of Israel called all the elders of the land, and said, "Mark, I pray you, and see how this *man* seeketh mischief: for he sent unto me for my wives, and for my [3]children, and for my silver, and for my gold; and I denied him not."

8 And all the elders and all the People said unto him, "Hearken not *unto him*, nor consent."

9 Wherefore he said unto the messengers of Ben-hadad, "Tell my lord the king, 'All that thou didst send for to thy servant at the first I will do: but this thing I may not do.'" And the messengers departed, and brought him word again.

e^3 10 And Ben-hadad sent unto him, and said, "The gods do so unto me, and more also, if the dust of Samaria shall suffice for handfuls for all the people that follow me."

f^3 11 And the king of Israel answered and said, "Tell *him*, °'Let not him that girdeth on *his harness* boast himself as he that putteth it off.'"

c^2 12 And it came to pass, when *Ben-hadad* heard this °message, as he *was* drinking, he and the kings in the °pavilions, that he said unto his servants, "Set *yourselves in array*." And they set *themselves in array* against the city.

d^2 13 And, °behold, there came a prophet unto Ahab king of Israel, saying, "Thus saith °the LORD, °'Hast thou seen all this great multitude? behold, I will deliver it into thine hand this day; and thou shalt know that I *am* °the LORD.'"

14 And Ahab said, "By whom?" And he said, "Thus saith [13]the LORD, '*Even* by the °young men of the princes of the provinces.'" Then he said, "Who shall order the battle?" And he answered, "Thou."

15 Then he numbered the young men of the princes of the provinces, and they were two hundred and thirty two: and after them he numbered all the People, *even* all the [3]children of Israel, *being* seven thousand.

16 And they went out at noon. But Ben-hadad *was* drinking himself drunk in the pavilions, he and the kings, the thirty and two kings that helped him.

17 And the young men of the princes of the provinces went out first; and Ben-hadad sent out, and they told him, saying, "There are °men come out of Samaria."

18 And he said, "Whether they be come out for peace, take them alive; or whether they be come out for war, take them alive."

19 So these young men of the princes of the provinces came out of the city, and the army which followed them.

20 And they slew every one his °man: and the Syrians fled; and Israel pursued them: and Ben-hadad the king of Syria escaped on an horse with the horsemen.

21 And the king of Israel went out, and smote the horses and chariots, and slew the Syrians with a great slaughter.

22 And the prophet came to the king of Israel, and said unto him, "Go, strengthen thyself, and mark, and see what thou doest: for at the °return of the year the king of Syria will come up against thee." c^3

20. 1-43 (V^3, p. 477). WAR WITH SYRIA.
(*Repeated Alternation.*)

V^3
- c^1 | 1. Syria. First invasion.
  - d^1 | 2-11. Israel. Negotiations.
- c^2 | 12. Syria. Siege of Samaria.
  - d^2 | 13-21. Israel. Sortie by Ahab.
- c^3 | 22-26. Syria. Second invasion.
  - d^3 | 27. Israel. Numbering of.
- c^4 | 28-30. Syria. Defeat.
  - d^4 | 31-33-. Israel. Ahab's forbearance
- c^5 | -33, 34. Syria. Covenant with Ahab.
  - d^5 | 35-43. Israel. God reproves Ahab.

1 Ben-hadad. Perhaps the son of the Ben-hadad of 15. 18.
host = force.
thirty and two. Probably vassal princes. Cp. *v.* 24.

2-11 (d^1, above). NEGOTIATIONS.
(*Repeated Alternation.*)

d^1
- e^1 | 2, 3. Ben-hadad. First demand.
  - f^1 | 4. Ahab. Compliance.
- e^2 | 5, 6. Ben-hadad. Second demand.
  - f^2 | 7-9. Ahab. Refusal.
- e^3 | 10. Ben-hadad. Threatening.
  - f^3 | 11. Ahab. Retort.

2 said. A special various reading (*Sevīr*, Ap. 34) reads "they said".
3 children = sons.
6 and. Note the Fig. *Polysyndeton.* Ap. 6.
search: as from the top: i. e. ransack.
11 Let not him. Fig. *Parœmia.* Ap. 6.
12 message = word. Put by Fig. *Metonymy* (of Adjunct), Ap. 6, for the message contained.
pavilions = tents.
13 behold. Fig. *Asterismos.* Ap. 6.
the LORD. Heb. Jehovah. Ap. 4. II.
Hast . . . ? Fig. *Erotēsis.* Ap. 6.
14 young men = the servants, or esquires.
17 men. Heb. *'ĕnōsh.* Ap. 14. III.
20 man. Heb. *'īsh.* Ap. 14. II.
22 return of the year: the spring. Cp. 2 Sam. 11. 1.

822 to 800 23 And the servants of the king of Syria said unto him, "Their gods *are* gods of the hills; therefore they were stronger than we; but let us fight against them in the plain, and surely we shall be stronger than they.

24 And do this thing, Take the kings away, every [20] man out of his place, and put °captains in their rooms:

25 And number thee an army, like the army that thou hast lost, horse for horse, and chariot for chariot: and we will fight against them in the plain, *and* surely we shall be stronger than they." And he hearkened unto their voice, and did so.

26 And it came to pass at the [22] return of the year, that Ben-hadad numbered the Syrians, and went up to °Aphek, to fight against Israel.

d³ (p. 483) 27 And the [3] children of Israel °were numbered, and were all present, and went against them: and the [3] children of Israel pitched before them like two little °flocks of kids; but the Syrians filled the country.

c⁴ 28 And there came a °man of °God, and spake unto the king of Israel, and said, "Thus saith [13] the LORD, 'Because the Syrians have said, [13] 'The LORD *is* °God of the hills, but He *is* not °God of the valleys,' therefore will I deliver all this great multitude into thine hand, and °ye shall know that I *am* [13] the LORD.' "

29 And they pitched one over against the other seven days. And *so* it was, that in the seventh day the battle was joined: and the [3] children of Israel slew of the Syrians an hundred thousand footmen in one day.

30 But the rest fled to Aphek, into the city; and *there* a wall fell upon twenty and seven thousand of the [20] men *that were* left. And Ben-hadad fled, and came into the city, into an inner chamber.

d⁴ 31 And his servants said unto him, °"Behold now, we have heard that the kings of the house of Israel *are* merciful kings: let us, I pray thee, put sackcloth on our loins, and ropes upon our heads, and go out to the king of Israel: peradventure he will save thy °life."

32 So they girded sackcloth on their loins, and *put* ropes on their heads, and came to the king of Israel, and said, "Thy servant Ben-hadad saith, 'I pray thee, let °me live.' " And he said, "*Is* he yet alive? he *is* my °brother."

33 Now the [17] men °did diligently observe whether °*any thing would come* from him, and did hastily catch *it:* and they said, "Thy brother Ben-hadad."

c⁵ Then he said, "Go ye, bring him." Then Ben-hadad came forth to him; and he caused him to come up into the chariot.

34 And *Ben-hadad* said unto him, "The cities, which my father took from thy father, I will restore; and thou shalt make °streets for thee in Damascus, °as my father made in Samaria." Then °*said Ahab,* "I will send thee away with this covenant." So he made a covenant with him, and sent him away.

d⁵ g (p. 484) 35 And a certain °man of the sons of the prophets said unto his neighbour in the word of [13] the LORD, "Smite me, I pray thee." And the [20] man refused to smite him.

36 Then said he unto him, "Because thou hast not obeyed the voice of [13] the LORD, [31] behold, as soon as thou art departed from me, a lion shall slay thee." And as soon as he was departed from him, a lion found him, and slew him.

37 Then he found another [20] man, and said, "Smite me, I pray thee." And the [20] man smote him, so that in smiting he wounded *him.*

38 So the prophet departed, and waited for the king by the way, and disguised himself with °ashes upon his face.

39 And as the king passed by, he cried unto the king: and he said, "Thy servant went out into the midst of the battle; and, [31] behold, a [20] man turned aside, and brought a [20] man unto me, and said, 'Keep this [20] man: if by any means he be missing, then shall thy [31] life be for his [31] life, or else thou shalt pay a °talent of silver.' h

40 And as thy servant was busy here and there, he was gone."

And the king of Israel said unto him, "So *shall* thy judgment *be;* thyself hast decided *it.*" i

41 And he hasted, and took the [38] ashes away from his face; and the king of Israel discerned him that he *was* of the prophets. *g*

42 And he said unto him, "Thus saith [13] the LORD, 'Because thou hast let go out of *thy* hand a [20] man whom I appointed to utter destruction, therefore thy [31] life shall go for his [31] life, and thy people for his people.' " *h*

43 And the king of Israel went to his house heavy and displeased, and came to Samaria. *i*

24 captains = governors, or pashas.
26 Aphek. Probably east of the Sea of Galilee.
27 were numbered = enrolled themselves.
flocks = newborn kids. Heb. *ḥāsaph.* Occurs only here.
28 man of God = a prophet. See Ap. 49.
God. Heb. Elohim. Ap. 4. I.
ye shall know. Sept. reads "so shalt thou know". Cp. *v.* 13 above.
31 Behold. Fig. *Asterismos.* Ap. 6.
life = soul. Heb. *nephesh.* Ap. 13.
32 me = my soul. Heb. *nephesh.* Ap. 13.
brother: i. e. a brother-king.
33 did diligently observe. Heb. divined and hasted. Fig. *Hendiadys* (Ap. 6) = quickly divined.
any thing would come. These italics are wrongly supplied, not knowing the two readings of E. and W. recensions, caused by a different division of words. The E. recension reads "and they pressed [to find out] whether it was from him and said". The W. recension reads "and they pressed it out from him, and they said": i. e. they wanted to know whether he confirmed the word of his own accord.
34 streets = broadways, or bazaars.
as = according as.
said. Fig. *Ellipsis* (Ap. 6) to be supplied by repetition from previous clause.

35-43 (d⁵, p. 483). ISRAEL. GOD REPROVES AHAB. (*Extended Alternation.*)

d⁵ | g | 35-38. Prophet disguised.
  h | 39, 40-. Symbol used.
   i | -40. Ahab's sentence.
 g | 41. Prophet discovered.
  h | 42. Symbol interpreted.
   i | 43. Ahab's heaviness.

35 man. Heb. *'ish.* Ap. 14. II. Josephus identifies him with Micaiah (22. 8).
38 ashes, &c. = bandage.
39 talent. See Ap. 51. II.

T Q¹ j (p. 485) 822 to 800 **21** And it came to pass after these things,
that Naboth the Jezreelite °had a vine-
yard, which *was* in °Jezreel, hard by the palace
of Ahab king of Samaria.
2 And Ahab spake unto Naboth, saying,
°"Give me thy vineyard, that I may have it
for a garden of herbs, because it *is* near unto
my house: and I will give thee for it a better
vineyard than it; *or*, if it seem good to thee,
I will give thee the worth of it in money."
3 And Naboth said to Ahab, °"The LORD
forbid it me, that I should give °the inheritance of my fathers unto thee."
k l 4 And Ahab came into his house heavy and
displeased because of the word which Naboth
the Jezreelite had spoken to him: for he had
said, "I will not give thee the inheritance of
my fathers." And he laid him down upon his
bed, and turned away his face, and would eat
no bread.
m 5 But Jezebel his wife came to him, and said
unto him, "Why is thy °spirit so sad, that thou
eatest no bread?"
j 6 And he said unto her, "Because I spake
unto Naboth the Jezreelite, and said unto him,
'Give me thy vineyard for money; or else, if it
please thee, I will give thee *another* vineyard
for it:' and he answered, 'I will not give thee
my vineyard.'"
k m 7 And Jezebel his wife said unto him, °"Dost
thou now govern the kingdom of Israel? arise,
and eat bread, and let thine heart be merry:
I will give thee the vineyard of Naboth the
Jezreelite."
8 So she wrote letters in Ahab's name, °and
°sealed *them* with his seal, and sent the letters
unto the elders and to the nobles that *were* in
his city, dwelling with Naboth.
9 And she wrote in the letters, saying, "Proclaim a fast, and set Naboth °on high among
the People:
10 And set °two °men, °sons of Belial, before
him, to bear witness against him, saying,
'Thou didst °blaspheme °God and the king.'
And *then* carry him out, and stone him, that
he may die."
11 And the [10]men of his city, *even* the elders
and the nobles who were the inhabitants in
his city, did °as Jezebel had sent unto them,
and as it *was* written in the letters which she
had sent unto them.
12 They proclaimed a fast, and set Naboth [9]on
high among the People.
13 And there came in two [10]men, [10]children of
Belial, and sat before him: and the [10]men of
Belial witnessed against him, *even* against
Naboth, in the presence of the People, saying,
"Naboth did [10]blaspheme [10]God and the king."
Then they carried him forth out of the city,
and °stoned him with stones, that he died.
14 Then they sent to Jezebel, saying, "Naboth
is stoned, and is dead."
15 And it came to pass, when Jezebel heard
that Naboth was stoned, and was dead, that
Jezebel said to Ahab, °"Arise, take possession
of the vineyard of Naboth the Jezreelite, which
he refused to give thee for money: for Naboth
is not alive, but dead."
l 16 And it came to pass, when Ahab heard
that Naboth was dead, that Ahab rose up to
go down to the vineyard of Naboth the Jezreelite, to take possession of it.
17 And the word of [3]the LORD came to Elijah Q² R n
the Tishbite, saying,
18 "Arise, go down to meet Ahab king of
Israel, which *is* in Samaria: °behold, *he is* in
the vineyard of Naboth, whither he is gone
down to possess it.
19 And thou shalt speak unto him, saying,
'Thus saith [3]the LORD, °'Hast thou °killed,
and also taken possession?'' And thou shalt
speak unto him, saying,

21. 1-29 (*T*, p. 477). PERSONAL EVIL. NABOTH. (*Division.*)

T | Q¹ | 1-16. Evil committed.
| Q² | 17-29. Evil to be judged.

1-16 (Q¹, above). EVIL COMMITTED. (*Alternation and Introversion.*)

Q¹ | j | 1-3. Ahab's covetousness. Fact.
k | l | 4. Ahab's heaviness.
m | 5. Jezebel's inquiry.
j | 6. Ahab's covetousness. Recital.
k | *m* | 7-15. Jezebel's promise.
l | 16. Ahab's gratification.

1 had a vineyard = a vineyard came to be his (by inheritance).
Jezreel. In the plain of Esdraelon.
2 Give me. Cp. 1 Sam. 8. 14, of which this is a fulfilment.
3 The LORD. Heb. Jehovah. Ap. 4. II.
the inheritance of my fathers. Naboth respected the Law of God (Lev. 25. 23. Num. 36. 7, 8).
5 spirit. Heb. *rūach.* See Ap. 9.
7 Dost . . . ? Fig. *Erotēsis.* Ap. 6.
8 and. Note the Fig. *Polysyndeton* (Ap. 6) in *vv.* 8-10.
sealed . . . with his seal. Fig. *Polyptōton.* Ap. 6. Sealing was done by rubbing ink on the seal, moistening the paper, and pressing the seal thereon.
9 on high: i. e. in a conspicuous place; or, perhaps, before the bar of justice.
10 two. Cp. Deut. 17. 6.
men. Heb. *'ěnōsh.* Ap. 14. III.
sons of Belial. Cp. Deut. 13. 13. 1 Sam. 1. 16; 2. 12, &c.
blaspheme. The current Heb. text reads "bless". In spite of this the A.V. and R.V. render it "blaspheme". It is one of the emendations of the *Sōpherim* (Ap. 18), and is correctly rendered "blaspheme", but should have had a marginal note of explanation.
God. Heb. Elohim. Ap. 4. I.
11 as = according as.
13 stoned him. One of the nine cases of stoning. See note on Lev. 24. 14.
15 Arise. This form of the imperative is only found in connection with Jehovah, and always with reference to the promised land. And the lengthened form is found only in Moses' mouth in Num. 10. 35.

17-29 (Q², above). EVIL TO BE JUDGED. (*Double Introversion and Alternation.*)

Q² | R | n | 17-19-. Call to Elijah to go to Ahab.
o | -19. Judgment pronounced.
S | p | 20. Altercation.
q | 21, 22. Judgment. Particular.
T | 23. Jezebel.
S | *q* | 24. Judgment. Particular.
p | 25, 26. Provocation.
R | *n* | 27-29-. Call to Elijah to see Ahab humbled.
o | -29. Judgment mitigated.

18 behold. Fig. *Asterismos.* Ap. 6.
19 Hast thou . . . ? Fig. *Erotēsis.* Ap. 6.
killed = murdered.

o
822-800
'Thus saith ³ the LORD, 'In the place where dogs licked the blood of Naboth shall dogs lick thy blood, even thine.'''

S p
(p. 485)
20 And Ahab said to Elijah, "Hast thou found me, O mine enemy?" And he answered, "I have found *thee:* because thou hast sold thyself to work °evil in the sight of ³ the LORD.

q
21 ¹⁸ Behold, I will bring ²⁰ evil upon thee, and will take away thy posterity, and will cut off from Ahab °him that pisseth against the wall, and him that is °shut up and left in Israel,
22 And will make thine house like the house of °Jeroboam the son of Nebat, and like the house of Baasha the son of Ahijah, for the provocation wherewith thou hast provoked *Me* to anger, and °made Israel to sin."

T
23 And of Jezebel also spake ³ the LORD, saying, "The dogs shall eat Jezebel ° by the wall of ° Jezreel.

S q
24 Him that dieth of Ahab in the city the dogs shall eat; and him that dieth in the field shall the fowls of the air eat."

p
25 But there was °none like unto °Ahab, which did sell himself to work °wickedness in the sight of ³ the LORD, whom Jezebel his wife stirred up.
26 And he did very abominably in following °idols, according to all *things* as did the Amorites, whom ³ the LORD cast out before the ¹³ children of Israel.

R n
27 And it came to pass, when Ahab heard those words, that he °rent his clothes, and put sackcloth upon his flesh, and fasted, and lay in sackcloth, and °went softly.
28 And the word of ³ the LORD came to Elijah the Tishbite, saying,
29 °"Seest thou how Ahab humbleth himself before Me?

o
because he humbleth himself before Me, I will °not bring the ²⁰ evil in his days: *but* in his son's days will I bring the ²⁰ evil upon his house."

U V¹
(p. 486)
22 And they continued °three years without war between Syria and Israel.
2 And it came to pass in the third year, that Jehoshaphat the king of Judah °came down to the king of Israel.

W¹ r¹
3 And the king of Israel said unto his servants, "Know ye that °Ramoth in Gilead *is* °ours, and we *be* still, *and* take it not out of the hand of the king of °Syria?"
4 And he said unto Jehoshaphat, "Wilt thou go with me to battle to Ramoth-gilead?" And Jehoshaphat said to the king of Israel, "I *am* as thou *art,* my People as thy People, my horses as thy horses."

s¹ X t¹
5 And Jehoshaphat said unto the king of Israel, "Enquire, I pray thee, at the word of °the LORD to day."

u¹
6 Then the king of Israel gathered the °prophets together, about four hundred °men, and said unto them, "Shall I go against Ramoth-gilead to battle, or shall I forbear?" And they

---

20 evil = the evil. Heb. *rā'a'.* Ap. 44. viii.
21 him that, &c. = every male. Cp. 14. 10.
shut up and left. See note on 14. 10.
22 Jeroboam. Cp. 16. 3.
made Israel to sin. See note on 12. 30.
23 by the wall. The word *b^eḥēl* is thought by Ginsburg to be an abbreviation for *b^eḥeleḳ* = "in the portion of", as in 2 Kings 9. 10, 36: i. e. within the rampart.
Jezreel. Not Samaria the capital, but Jezreel where Naboth had been murdered.
25 The Structure (p. 485) places the member ("*p*"), *vv.* 25, 26, as within a parenthesis.
none like unto Ahab. Out of twenty bad kings Ahab was the worst. Cp. 16. 30, 33.
wickedness. Same word as the "evil" (*v.* 20).
26 idols = filthy idols. Cp. Lev. 26. 30.
27 rent his clothes. His repentance was outward, not real.
went softly: i. e. humbly.
29 Seest thou . . .? Fig. *Erotēsis.* Ap. 6.
not bring. So the judgment on Solomon was postponed (11. 12) for his father's sake.

22. 1-38 (*U*, p. 477). PUBLIC EVENTS. WAR WITH SYRIA.
(*Repeated Alternation and Introversion.*)

U | V¹ | 1, 2. Ahab. Visited by Jehoshaphat.
  | W¹ | r¹ | 3, 4. Ramoth-gilead. Plan of Ahab.
  | | s¹ | 5-28. Jehoshaphat's uneasiness.
  | | r² | 29. Ramoth. Battle fought.
  | V² | 30. Ahab's expedient.
  | W² | r³ | 31. Ramoth-gilead. Plan of king of Syria.
  | | s² | 32. Jehoshaphat's danger.
  | | r⁴ | 33-36. Ramoth-gilead. Battle won.
  | V³ | 37, 38. Ahab's death.

1 three years. Probably reckoned from the peace of 20. 34. During this time Jehoshaphat "strengthened himself against Israel" (2 Chron. 17. 1): not mentioned here because *esoteric.* See note on title of 1 Kings.
2 came down. In every sense of the word; and this after 2 Chron. 17. 1. First was the *matrimonial* alliance (2 Chron. 18. 1), cp. 2 Kings 8. 18; and then the *military* alliance (*v.* 4 and 2 Chron. 18. 3). No mention here of the former, which was the secret cause that led up to it. Both fatal. Compare the *commercial* alliance of Jehoshaphat in 2 Chron. 20. 35-37, and the experience gained by Jehoshaphat in ch. 22. 48, 49.
3 And the king of Israel. Note the Fig. *Anadiplosis* (Ap. 6) with *v.* 2.
Ramoth. One of the Cities of Refuge.
ours. Given by Jehovah. Therefore presumably a "good work" to take it. But "good works" are "prepared works" (Eph. 2. 10), and this was not so prepared. See 2 Chron. 19. 1, 2.
Syria. Probably taken in former war (U, 16. 34—20. 43, p. 477) by Ben-hadad I from Omri, which his son Ben-hadad II agreed to restore.

5-28 (s¹, above). JEHOSHAPHAT'S UNEASINESS.
(*Introversion and Repeated Alternation.*)

s¹ | X¹ | t¹ | 5. Jehoshaphat.
   | | u¹ | 6. Ahab.
   | | t² | 7. Jehoshaphat.
   | | u² | 8, 9. Ahab.
   | | t³ | 10-. Jehoshaphat.
   | | u³ | -10-12. Ahab.
   | | Y | x¹ | 13. Micaiah. Messenger to.
   | | | x² | 14. Micaiah. To messenger.
   | X² | v¹ | 15. Micaiah.
   | | w¹ | 16. The king.
   | | v² | 17. Micaiah.
   | | w² | 18. The king.
   | | v³ | 19-25. Micaiah.
   | | w³ | 26, 27. The king.
   | | v⁴ | 28. Micaiah.

---

5 the LORD. Heb. Jehovah. Ap. 4. II.   **6** prophets: i. e. Ahab's false prophets. men. Heb. *'īsh.* Ap. 14. II.

822-800 said, "Go up; °for °the LORD * shall deliver *it*
into the hand of the king."
t[2] 7 And Jehoshaphat said, "*Is there* not here
(p. 486) a prophet of [5]the LORD °besides, that we
might enquire of him?"
u[2] 8 And the king of Israel said unto Jehoshaphat, "*There is* yet one [6]man, Micaiah the son
of Imlah, by whom we may enquire of [5]the
LORD: but I hate him; for he doth not prophesy good concerning me, but °evil." And
Jehoshaphat said, "Let not the king say so."
9 Then the king of Israel called an officer,
and said, "Hasten *hither* Micaiah the son of
Imlah."
t[3] 10 And the king of Israel and Jehoshaphat
the king of Judah sat each on his throne,
having put on their robes, in a °void place in
the entrance of the gate of Samaria;
u[3] and all the [6]prophets prophesied before them.
11 And Zedekiah the son of Chenaanah made
him horns of iron: and he said, "Thus saith
[5]the LORD, 'With these shalt thou push the
Syrians, until thou have consumed them.'"
12 And all the [6]prophets prophesied so, saying, "Go up to Ramoth-gilead, and prosper:
[6]for [5]the LORD shall deliver *it* into the king's
hand."
Y x[1] 13 And the messenger that was gone to call
Micaiah spake unto him, saying, °"Behold
now, the words of the prophets *declare* good
unto the king with one mouth: let thy °word,
I pray thee, be like the word of one of them,
and speak *that which is* good."
x[2] 14 And Micaiah said, "*As* [5]the LORD liveth,
what [5]the LORD saith unto me, that will I
speak."
X[2] v[1] 15 So he came to the king. And the king
said unto him, "Micaiah, shall we go against
Ramoth-gilead to battle, or shall we forbear?"
And he answered him, °"Go, and prosper:
[12]for [5]the LORD shall deliver *it* into the hand
of the king."
w[1] 16 And the king said unto him, "How many
times °shall I adjure thee that thou tell me
nothing but *that which is* true in the name of
[5]the LORD?"
v[2] 17 And he said, "I saw all Israel scattered
upon the hills, as sheep that have not a shepherd: and [5]the LORD said, 'These have no
master: let them return every [6]man to his
house in peace.'"
w[2] 18 And the king of Israel said unto Jehoshaphat, °"Did I not tell thee that he would prophesy no good concerning me, but [8]evil?"
v[3] 19 And he said, "Hear thou therefore the
word of [5]the LORD: I saw [5]the LORD sitting
on His throne, and all the host of °heaven
standing by Him on His right hand and on
His left.
20 And [5]the LORD said, 'Who shall °persuade
Ahab, that he may go up and fall at Ramoth-
gilead?' And one said on this manner, and
another said on that manner.
21 And there came forth °a spirit, and stood
before [5]the LORD, and said, 'I will [20]persuade
him.'
22 And [5]the LORD said unto him, 'Wherewith?' And he said, 'I will go forth, and I
will be a lying [21]spirit in the mouth of all his
prophets.' And He said, °'Thou shalt [20]per-
suade *him*, and prevail also: go forth, and
do so.'
23 Now therefore, [13]behold, [5]the LORD hath
put a lying [21]spirit in the mouth of all these
thy prophets, and [5]the LORD hath °spoken
[8]evil concerning thee."
24 But Zedekiah the son of Chenaanah went
near, and smote Micaiah on the cheek, and said,
°"Which way went the [21]Spirit of [5]the LORD
from me to speak unto thee?"
25 And Micaiah said, "Behold, thou shalt see
in that day, when thou shalt go into an inner
chamber to hide thyself."
26 And the king of Israel said, "Take Micaiah, w[3]
and carry him back unto Amon the governor of
the city, and to Joash the king's son;
27 And say, 'Thus saith the king, °"Put this
fellow in the prison, and feed him with bread
of affliction and with water of affliction, until I
come in peace."'"
28 And Micaiah said, "If thou return at all in v[4]
peace, [5]the LORD hath not spoken by me."
And he said, "Hearken, O °People, °every one
of you."
29 So the king of Israel and Jehoshaphat the r[2]
king of Judah went up to Ramoth-gilead.
30 And the king of Israel said unto Jehosha- V[2]
phat, °"I will disguise myself, and enter into
the battle; but put thou on thy robes." And
the king of Israel disguised himself, and went
into the battle.

for = and.
the LORD*. This is one of the 134 places where "Jehovah" was changed to "Adonai" by the *Sôpherim*. See Ap. 32.
7 besides. Jehoshaphat uneasy, well knowing that Ahab's prophets were not the prophets of Jehovah.
8 evil. Heb. *rā'a'*. Ap. 44. viii.
10 void place = level place, or threshing-floor.
13 Behold. Fig. *Asterismos*. Ap. 6.
word. So to be read; but written "words". In some codices, with three early printed editions, Syr., and Vulg., it is both written and read "word". Cp. 2 Chron. 18. 12.
15 Go, and prosper. Fig. *Eironeia*. Ap. 6. Doubtless repeating the words he had heard in *vv.* 6, 13.
16 shall: or must.
18 Did I not . . . ? Fig. *Erotēsis*. Ap. 6.
19 heaven = the heavens, as always.
20 persuade = entice.
21 a spirit = the spirit. Heb. *rūach*. Ap. 9.
22 Thou shalt, &c. Illustrating 2 Thess. 2. 9-12. Cp. Ezek. 14. 9: "I have deceived" = I have permitted it. This is quite in harmony with Prov. 12. 22. That refers to the sphere of God's *grace*; this to the sphere of His *judgment*. We are governed by His Word, not by His ways. Prov. 12. 22 refers to the world of *men*. This to the world of *spirits*.
23 spoken: in *v.* 17.
24 Which way . . . ? or, Which way then?
27 Put this fellow, &c. One of the eleven rulers offended with God's servants for speaking the truth. See note on Ex. 10. 28.
28 People = peoples.
every one = all.
30 I will. See note on *v.* 22. A feigned compliment, and piece of treachery.

W[2] r[3] 31 But the king of Syria commanded his
822 thirty and two captains that had rule over his
to chariots, saying, "Fight neither with small
800 nor great, save only with the king of Israel."
s[2] 32 And it came to pass, when the captains of
(p. 486) the chariots saw Jehoshaphat, that they said,
"Surely °it *is* the king of Israel." And they
turned aside to fight against him: and Jehoshaphat °cried out.

r[4] 33 And it came to pass, when the captains of
the chariots perceived that [32] it *was* not the king
of Israel, that they turned back from pursuing
him.

34 And a *certain* [6] man drew a bow °at a venture, and smote the king of Israel between the joints of the °harness: wherefore he said unto the driver of his chariot, °"Turn thine hand, and carry me out of the host; for I am wounded."

35 And the battle increased that day: and the king °was stayed up in his chariot against the Syrians, and died at even: and the blood ran out of the wound into the midst of the chariot.

36 And there went a proclamation throughout the host about the going down of the sun, saying, °"Every man to his city, and °every man to his own country."

V[3] 37 So the king died, and was brought to Samaria; and they buried the king in Samaria.

38 And *one* washed the chariot in the pool of Samaria; and the dogs licked up his blood; and they washed his armour; according unto the word of [5] the LORD which He spake.

R 39 Now the rest of the acts of Ahab, and all that he did, and the ivory house which he made, and all the cities that he built, *are* they not written in the book of the chronicles of the kings of Israel?

40 So Ahab °slept with his fathers; and Ahaziah his son reigned in his stead.

F[2] A[1] 41 And °Jehoshaphat the son of Asa began to
(p. 488) reign over Judah in the fourth year of Ahab
king of Israel.

42 Jehoshaphat *was* thirty and five years old when he began to reign; and he reigned twenty and five years in Jerusalem. And his mother's name *was* Azubah the daughter of Shilhi.

B[1] 43 °And he walked in all the ways of Asa his father; he turned not aside from it, doing *that which was* right in the eyes of [5] the LORD: nevertheless the high places were not taken away; *for* the People °offered and burnt incense yet in the high places.

44 And Jehoshaphat made peace with the king of Israel.

A[2] 45 Now the rest of the acts of Jehoshaphat, and his might that he shewed, and how he warred, [39] *are* they not written in the book of the chronicles of the kings of Judah?

B[2] 46 And the remnant of the °sodomites, which remained in the days of his father Asa, he took out of the land.

47 *There was* then °no king in Edom: a °deputy *was* king.

48 Jehoshaphat °made °ships of °Tharshish

32 it = he.
cried out. See note on 2 Chron. 18. 31.
34 at a venture = in his innocence, or to its full stretch.
harness = coat of mail.
Turn thine hand. This is Ahab's history; 2 Chron. 18 is Jehoshaphat's. Hence nothing about Jehovah's help.
35 was stayed up = stayed himself up, as in 2 Chron. 18. 34. Difference caused by pointing of the word *mā'ǎmād* (here), and *ma'amid* in Chronicles. The only occurrence of this participle, cp. 2 Chron. 18. 34.
36 Every man. Supply Fig. *Ellipsis* (Ap. 6), "Let every man go".
every man. Omitted in some codices, with two early printed editions, Sept., and Vulg.
40 slept with his fathers. See note on Deut. 31. 16.

41-50 (F[2], p. 446). JUDAH (JEHOSHAPHAT).
(Repeated Alternation.)

F[2] | A[1] | 41, 42. Jehoshaphat. Accession.
B[1] | 43, 44. Personal. Well- and wrong-doing.
A[2] | 45. Jehoshaphat. Political events. Record.
B[2] | 46-49. Personal. Well- and wrong-doing.
A[3] | 50. Jehoshaphat. Death and burial.

41 Jehoshaphat. Cp. 2 Chron. 17. 1.
43 And he walked. The 19th *Seder* begins here, and ends with 2 Kings 2. 14. See note on p. 366.
offered = sacrificed. See Ap. 43. I. iv.
46 sodomites. See note on 14. 23, 24.
47 no king. As later in 2 Kings 8. 20.
deputy. Appointed by the king of Judah.
48 made ships, &c. This was subsequent to 2 Chron. 20. 35-37. Here Jehoshaphat made "Tharshish ships" to go to Ophir, and, profiting by the experience and warning of 2 Chron. 20. 37, refused the request of Ahaziah, king of Israel. In 2 Chron. 20. 35 he had joined himself with Ahaziah to make (ordinary) ships to go to Tharshish, which was quite a different thing.
ships of Tharshish = Tharshish ships: i.e. large ocean-going ships.
Tharshish. See note on 10. 22.
50 buried: in further explanation of preceding clause.

1 Kings 22. 51—2 Kings 8. 15 (E[3], p. 446).
ISRAEL. *(Introversion.)*

E[3] | C[1] | 1 Kings 22. 51—2 Kings 1. 18. Ahaziah.
D | 2 Kings 2. 1-25. Elijah.
C[2] | 2 Kings 3. 1—8. 15. Joram.

This Structure exhibits the cause of the break between the two books mentioned in note on titles (pp. 366 and 446). If originally divided by design instead of from exigency, the break would not have occurred in the midst of the House of ISRAEL, and the reign of Ahaziah.

1 K. **22. 51**—2 K. **1. 18** [For Structure see next page].

to go to Ophir for gold: but they went not; for the ships were broken at Ezion-geber.

49 Then said Ahaziah the son of Ahab unto Jehoshaphat, "Let my servants go with thy servants in the ships." But Jehoshaphat would not.

50 And Jehoshaphat [40] slept with his fathers, A[3]
and was °buried with his fathers in the city of David his father: and Jehoram his son reigned in his stead.

51 Ahaziah the son of Ahab began to reign E[3] C[1] E
over Israel in Samaria the seventeenth year of (p. 488)
Jehoshaphat king of Judah, and reigned two years over Israel.

52 And he did [8] evil in the sight of [5] the LORD, F
and walked in the way of his father, and in

822 to 800 the way of his mother, and in the way of Jeroboam the son of Nebat, who °made Israel to sin:

53 For he served Baal, and worshipped him, and provoked to anger °the LORD God of Israel, according to all that his father had done.

1 Kings **22. 51**—2 Kings **1. 18** (C[1], p. 488).

AHAZIAH. (*Introversion.*)

C[1] | E | 1 Kings 22. 51. Introduction. Accession.
  F | 1 Kings 22. 52, 53. Personal. Evil-doing.
    G | 2 Kings 1. 1. Political. Rebellion of Moab.
  F | 2 Kings 1. 2-16. Personal. Evil-doing.
E | 2 Kings 1. 17, 18. Conclusion. Death and burial.

52 made Israel to sin. See first occurrence (14. 16).

53 the LORD God (Heb. Jehovah Elohim) **of Israel.** Cp. 1. 30, and see Ap. 4. II and I.

[THE SECOND BOOK OF THE KINGS,

COMMONLY CALLED,

THE FOURTH BOOK OF THE KINGS.]

G (p. 489) **1** Then °Moab rebelled against Israel °after the death of Ahab.

F H a 2 And Ahaziah fell down through a °lattice in his upper chamber that *was* in Samaria, and was sick: and he sent messengers, and said unto them, "Go, enquire of °Baal-zebub the god of °Ekron whether I shall recover of this disease."

b 3 But the °Angel of °the LORD said to °Elijah the Tishbite, "Arise, go up to meet the messengers of the king of Samaria, and say unto them, '*Is it* not because *there is* not a °God in Israel, *that* ye go to enquire of [2] Baal-zebub the god of Ekron?

c 4 Now therefore thus saith [3] the LORD, 'Thou shalt not come down from that bed on which thou art gone up, but °shalt surely die.' ' " And Elijah departed.

J 5 And when the messengers turned back unto him, he said unto them, "Why are ye now turned back?"

J 6 And they said unto him, "There came a °man up to meet us, and said unto us, 'Go, turn again unto the king that sent you, and say unto him, 'Thus saith [3] the LORD, '*Is it* not because *there is* not a [3] God in Israel, *that* thou sendest to enquire of Baal-zebub the god of Ekron? therefore thou shalt not come down from that bed on which thou art gone up, but [4] shalt surely die.' ' ' "

7 And he said unto them, "What manner of [6] man *was he* which came up to meet you, and told you these words?"

8 And they answered him, "*He was* an °hairy [6] man, and girt with a °girdle of leather about his loins." And he said, "It *is* Elijah the Tishbite."

H a 9 Then the king sent unto him a captain of fifty with his fifty. And he went up to him: and, °behold, he sat on the top of an hill. And he spake unto him, "Thou °man of [3] God, the king hath said, 'Come down.' "

10 And Elijah answered and said to the captain of fifty, "If I *be* a [9] man of [3] God, then °LET FIRE COME DOWN FROM HEAVEN, AND CONSUME thee AND THY FIFTY." And there came down fire from heaven, and consumed him and his fifty.

11 Again also he sent unto him another captain of fifty with his fifty. And he answered and said unto him, "O [9] man of [3] God, thus hath the king said, 'Come down quickly.' "

1. 1 Moab rebelled. Moab had been subdued by David (2 Sam. 8. 2; 23. 20); and when the kingdom was divided it passed to Israel. It was greatly oppressed by Omri and Ahab, and, on the death of the latter (cp. 3. 5), Mesha, king of Moab, rebelled. See the record of the event on "the Moabite stone". Ap. 54.

The verse is introduced here to complete the symmetry of the introversion. See "G" in the Structure above.

after. The inscription on the Moabite stone leaves the exact date indefinite. Line five, "Israel perished", may refer to the death of Ahab.

2-16 (*F*, above). AHAZIAH. PERSONAL. EVIL-DOING. (*Introversion and Extended Alternation.*)

F | H | a | 2. Mission to Baal-zebub.
    b | 3. Reproof of Elijah.
      c | 4. Assurance of death.
    J | 5. Messengers. Inquiry.
    J | 6-8. Messengers. Report.
  H | *a* | 9-15. Missions to Elijah.
    b | 16-. Reproof of Elijah.
      c | -16. Assurance of death.

2 lattice = network or balustrade, which protected the open window of the upper chamber. Cp. Judg. 3. 20; 5. 28. 1 Kings 17. 19. 2 Kings 4. 10.

Baal-zebub = Lord of flies. Later Jews polluted it by changing it to Beel-zebul (Lord of dung or dunghills). In Matt. 12. 24 it is in Greek Baal-zebul = lord of abominable idols; the prince of idols and idolatry; the worst and chief of all wickedness. Imagine the blasphemy.

Ekron. One of the five Philistine cities. Josh. 13. 3.

3 Angel of the LORD. See note on Ex. 3. 2. He who directed Moses directs Elijah.

the LORD. Heb. Jehovah. Ap. 4. II.

Elijah = my GOD is JAH. See Ap. 4. III.

God. Heb. Elohim. Ap. 4. I.

4 shalt surely die. Same as Gen. 2. 17.

6 man. Heb. *'ish.* Ap. 14. II.

8 hairy = clad in a garment consisting of a skin. Prophets wore coarse clothing (Zech. 13. 4. Matt. 3. 4).

girdle of leather. Worn by Palestine peasants to-day.

9 behold. Fig. *Asterismos.* Ap. 6.

man of God. The people's name for a prophet. See Ap. 49.

10 let fire come down. Quoted in Luke 9. 54.

12 unto them. Some codices, with Sept. and Syr., read "unto him".

fire of God. Occurs only here and Job 1. 16. Some codices, with Aram., Sept., and Vulg., omit "of God", as in *v.* 10.

12 And Elijah answered and said °unto them, "If I *be* a [9] man of [3] God, let fire come down from heaven, and consume thee and thy fifty." And the °fire of [3] God came down from heaven, and consumed him and his fifty.

802 13 And he sent again a captain of the third
to fifty with his fifty. And the third captain of
800 fifty went up, and came and fell on his knees
before Elijah, and besought him, and said unto him, "O [9]man of [3]God, I pray thee, let my °life, and the °life of these fifty thy servants, be precious in thy sight.

14 [9]Behold, there came fire down from heaven, and °burnt up the two captains of the former fifties with their fifties: therefore let [13]my life now be precious in thy sight."

15 And the Angel of [3]the LORD said unto Elijah, "Go down with Him: be not afraid of him." And he arose, and went down with Him unto the king.

b (p. 489) 16 And he said unto him, "Thus saith [3]the LORD, 'Forasmuch as thou hast sent messengers to enquire of [2]Baal-zebub the god of Ekron, °*is it* not because *there is* no [3]God in Israel to enquire of His word?

c therefore thou shalt not come down off that bed on which thou art gone up, but shalt surely die.'"

E 17 So he died according to the word of [3]the LORD which Elijah had spoken. And Jehoram reigned in his stead in the second year of Jehoram the son of Jehoshaphat king of Judah; because he had no son.

18 Now the rest of the acts of Ahaziah which he did, *are* they not written in the book of the chronicles of the kings of Israel?

D d (p. 490) **2** And it came to pass, when °the LORD would take up Elijah into °heaven by a whirlwind,

e that Elijah went with °Elisha °from Gilgal.

d f 2 And Elijah said unto Elisha, "Tarry here, I pray thee; for [1]the LORD hath sent me to Beth-el." And [1]Elisha said *unto him*, "*As* [1]the LORD liveth, and *as* °thy soul liveth, I will not leave thee." So they went °down to Beth-el.

3 And the sons of the prophets that *were* at Beth-el came forth to Elisha, and said unto him, "Knowest thou that [1]the LORD will take away thy master °from thy head to day?" And he said, "Yea, I know *it;* hold ye your peace."

g 4 And Elijah said unto him, "Elisha, tarry here, I pray thee; for [1]the LORD hath sent me to Jericho." And he said, "*As* [1]the LORD liveth, and *as* [2]thy soul liveth, I will not leave thee." So they came to Jericho.

5 And the sons of the prophets that *were* at Jericho came to Elisha, and said unto him, "Knowest thou that [1]the LORD will take away thy master [3]from thy head to day?" And he answered, "Yea, I know *it;* hold ye your peace."

h i 6 And Elijah said unto him, "Tarry, I pray thee, here; for [1]the LORD hath sent me to Jordan." And he said, "*As* [1]the LORD liveth, and *as* [2]thy soul liveth, I will not leave thee." And they two went on.

k 7 And fifty °men of the sons of the prophets went, and stood to view afar off: and they two stood by Jordan.

13 life = soul. Heb. *nephesh*. Ap. 13.
14 burnt up = consumed, as in *vv.* 10, 12.
16 is it not . . . ? Fig. *Erotēsis* (Ap. 6), or "was it because", &c.

2. 1-25 (D, p. 488). ELIJAH. TRANSLATION. (*Alternation.*)

D | d | 1-. Translation purposed.
  e | -1. Elisha accompanies Elijah from Gilgal.
  d | 2-24. Translation effected.
  e | 25. Elisha returns to Samaria.

1 the LORD. Heb. Jehovah. Ap. 4. II.
heaven = heavens, and elsewhere.
Elisha = my God [is] salvation. See his call (1 Kings 19. 16) ten years before.
from Gilgal. The reverse route taken by Israel on entering the Land.

2-24 (*d*, above). TRANSLATION EFFECTED. (*Introversion.*)

d | f | 2, 3. Beth-el. } Journey.
  g | 4, 5. Jericho. } Journey.
  h | 6-18. Jordan. Translation.
  g | 19-22. Jericho. } Return.
  f | 23, 24. Beth-el. } Return.

2 thy soul = thyself. Heb. *nephesh*. Ap. 13.
down. Therefore Gilgal in *v.* 1 cannot be the well-known Gilgal near Jericho, but another between Tibneh and Shiloh. See 4. 38. Gilgal = circle; and there may have been several such.
3 from thy head = from over thee: "head," put by Fig. *Synecdoche* (of Part), Ap. 6, for himself.

6-18 (h, above). JORDAN. TRANSLATION. (*Introversion.*)

h | i | 6. Their journey thither.
  k | 7. Sons of the prophets. Observation.
  l | 8. Passage of Jordan. From Jericho.
  m | 9, 10. Elisha. Request made.
  n | 11. Translation of Elijah.
  m | 12. Elisha. Request granted.
  l | 13, 14. Repassage of Jordan. To Jericho.
  k | 15. Sons of the prophets. Observation.
  i | 16-18. Their journey thither, and return.

7 men. Heb. *'īsh*. Ap. 14. II.
9 double portion. See note on *v.* 15.
spirit. Heb. *rūach*. Ap. 9. Put by Fig. *Metonymy* (of Cause) for the gifts and operations of the Spirit of God.
10 nevertheless. The verse needs no italics.
see = clearly see.
11 a whirlwind. Not a fiery chariot, according to a certain hymn. Cp. *v.* 1.

8 And Elijah took his mantle, and wrapped *it* together, and smote the waters, and they were divided hither and thither, so that they two went over on dry ground. l

9 And it came to pass, when they were gone over, that Elijah said unto Elisha, "Ask what I shall do for thee, before I be taken away from thee." And Elisha said, "I pray thee, let a °double portion of thy °spirit be upon me." m

10 And he said, "Thou hast asked a hard thing: °*nevertheless*, if thou °see me *when I am* taken from thee, it shall be so unto thee; but if not, it shall not be *so*."

11 And it came to pass, as they still went on, and talked, that, behold, *there appeared* a chariot of fire, and horses of fire, and parted them both asunder; and Elijah went up by °a whirlwind into [1]heaven. n

m (p. 490) 802 to 800 12 And Elisha [11]saw *it,* °and he cried, °"My father, my father, the chariot of Israel, and the horsemen thereof." And he [11]saw him no more: and he took hold of his own clothes, and rent them in two pieces.

l 13 He took up also the mantle of Elijah that fell from him, and went back, and stood by the bank of Jordan;

14 And he took the mantle of Elijah that fell from him, [12]and smote the waters, and said, °"Where *is* °the LORD God of Elijah?" and when he also had smitten the waters, °they parted hither and thither: and Elisha went °over.

k 15 And when the sons of the prophets which *were* to view at Jericho saw him, they said, "The [9]spirit of Elijah °doth rest on Elisha." And they came to meet him, and bowed themselves to the ground before him.

i 16 And they said unto him, "Behold now, there be with thy servants fifty strong °men; let them go, we pray thee, and seek thy master: lest peradventure the [9]Spirit of [1]the LORD hath taken him up, and cast him upon some mountain, or into some valley." And he said, "Ye shall not send."

17 And when they urged him till he was ashamed, he said, "Send." They sent therefore fifty [7]men; and they sought three days, but found him not.

18 And when they came again to him, (for he tarried at Jericho,) he said unto them, "Did I not say unto you, 'Go not'?"

g 19 And the [16]men of the city said unto Elisha, "Behold, I pray thee, the situation of this city *is* pleasant, as my lord seeth: but the water *is* naught, and the ground barren."

20 And he said, "Bring me a new °cruse, and put salt therein." And they brought *it* to him.

21 And he went forth unto the spring of the waters, and °cast the salt in there, and said, "Thus saith [1]the LORD, 'I have healed these waters; there shall not be from thence any more death or barren *land.*'"

22 So the waters were healed unto this day, according to the saying of Elisha which he spake.

f 23 And he went up from thence unto °Beth-el: and as he was going up by the way, there came forth °little children out of the city, and mocked him, and said unto him, °"Go up, thou °bald head; °go up, thou bald head."

24 And he turned back, and looked on them, and cursed them in the name of [1]the LORD. And there came forth two she °bears out of the wood, and tare forty and two °children of them.

e 25 And he went from thence to mount Carmel, and from thence he returned to Samaria.

12 and. Note the Fig. *Polysyndeton* (Ap. 6) in *v.* 12.
My father. Fig. *Epizeuxis.* Ap. 6. The repetition = my revered, or beloved father.
14 Where . . . ? Fig. *Erotēsis.* Ap. 6.
the LORD God = Jehovah Elohim; or, Where is Jehovah the God of Elijah? After this the Heb. text has *'aph hu'* = "even he". The Vulg. reads this as the end of the question. But the Massorites, by the accent (*athnach*), throw it on to the next sentence, "and when even he smote the waters", &c.
they parted. The first of sixteen miracles. See note on *v.* 15.
over. The 19th *Seder* ends here. See note on p. 366.
15 doth rest = hath rested. Cp. 1 Pet. 4. 14. Rest in "double portion" according to *v.* 9. Seen in the fact that Elijah wrought eight miracles and Elisha sixteen, and all were parables in action.

Elijah's eight Miracles (1 and 2 Kings).

1. Shutting heaven (17. 1).	5. Rain (18. 45).
2. Oil multiplied (17. 14).	6. Fire on 50 (2 Kings 1. 10).
3. Widow's son raised (17. 22, 23).	7. Fire on 50 (2 Kings 1. 12).
4. Fire from heaven (18. 38).	8. Jordan (2 Kings 2. 8).

Elisha's sixteen Miracles (2 Kings).

1. Jordan divided (2. 14).	9. Bread multiplied (4. 43).
2. Waters healed (2. 21).	10. Naaman healed (5. 10).
3. Bears from wood (2. 24).	11. Gehazi smitten (5. 27).
4. Water for kings (3. 20).	12. Iron to swim (6. 6).
5. Oil for widow (4. 1-6).	13. Sight to blind (6. 17).
6. Gift of son (4. 16, 17).	14. Smiting blindness (6. 18)
7. Raising from dead (4. 35).	15. Restoring sight (6. 20).
8. Healing of pottage (4. 41).	16. One after death (13. 21).

16 men. Heb. *'ĕnōsh.* Ap. 14. III.
20 cruse. Occurs only here.
21 cast the salt. Elisha's second miracle.
23 Beth-el. One of the seats of Israel's calf-worship (1 Kings 12. 26-30).
little children = young men. Heb. *na'ar.* Used of Isaac (twenty-eight years old); Joseph (thirty-nine); Rehoboam (forty).
Go up, &c. An open insult, avenged by Elisha's God in a way suited for that dispensation, though not for this. "Go up" may have referred to Elijah's translation; and thus, a blasphemous insult outraging Jehovah's own act.
bald head. Baldness premature. Elisha lived fifty years longer (13. 14).
go up, &c. Fig. *Epizeuxis.* Ap. 6.
24 bears. See 1 Sam. 17. 34-36.
children = progeny. Not the same word as *v.* 23.

3. 1–8. 15 (C², p. 488). **JORAM.**
(*Division.*)

C² | K¹ | 3. 1-3. Events. Personal.
   | K² | 3. 4–8. 15. Events. Political.

2 evil = the evil. Heb. *ra'a'.* Ap. 44. viii.
the LORD. Heb. Jehovah. Ap. 4. II.
his mother. Jezebel, who lived through the whole of his reign (9. 30).
image = pillar, or statue (which Ahab had made. Cp. 10. 18). 1 Kings 19. 18. Others remained (10. 26, 27).
3 sins. Heb. *chātā'.* Ap. 44. i.
made Israel to sin. See note on 1 Kings 14. 16.

3. 4–8. 15 [For Structure see next page].

4 Mesha. See Ap. 54 on "the Moabite stone".

C² K¹ (p. 491) **3** Now Jehoram the son of Ahab began to reign over Israel in Samaria the eighteenth year of Jehoshaphat king of Judah, and reigned twelve years.

2 And he wrought °evil in the sight of °the LORD; but not like his father, and like °his mother: for he put away the °image of Baal that his father had made.

3 Nevertheless he cleaved unto the °sins of Jeroboam the son of Nebat, which °made Israel to sin; he departed not therefrom.

4 And °Mesha king of Moab was a sheepmaster, and rendered unto the king of Israel an hundred thousand lambs, and an hundred thousand rams, with the wool. K² L O o (p. 492)

801 to 788 5 But it came to pass, when °Ahab was dead, that the king of Moab rebelled against the king of Israel.

p q (p. 492) 6 And king Jehoram went out of Samaria the same time, and numbered all Israel.
7 And he went and sent to Jehoshaphat the king of Judah, saying, "The king of Moab hath rebelled against me: wilt thou go with me against Moab to battle?" And he said, "I will go up: °I *am* as thou *art*, my People as thy People, *and* my horses as thy horses."
8 And °he said, °"Which way shall we go up?" And °he answered, "The way through the wilderness of Edom."
9 So the king of Israel went, and the king of Judah, and the king of Edom: and they °fetched a compass of seven days' journey:

r s and there was no water for the host, and for the cattle that followed them.

t u 10 And the king of Israel said, °"Alas! that [2]the LORD hath called these three kings together, to deliver them into the hand of Moab!"

v w 11 But Jehoshaphat said, °"*Is there* not here a prophet of [2]the LORD, that we may enquire of [2]the LORD by him?" And one of the king of Israel's servants answered and said, "Here *is* Elisha the son of Shaphat, which °poured water on the hands of Elijah."
12 And Jehoshaphat said, "The word of [2]the LORD is with him." So the king of Israel and °Jehoshaphat and the king of Edom went down to him.

x 13 And Elisha said unto the king of Israel, °"What have I to do with thee? get thee to the prophets of thy father, and to the prophets of thy mother."

u And the king of Israel said unto him, °"Nay: for [2]the LORD hath called these three kings together, to deliver them into the hand of Moab."

v x 14 And Elisha said, "*As* [2]the LORD of hosts liveth, °before Whom I stand, surely, were it not that I regard the presence of Jehoshaphat the king of Judah, I would °not look toward thee, nor see thee.

w S[1] 15 But now bring me a °minstrel." And it came to pass, when the minstrel played, that the °hand of [2]the LORD came upon him.
16 And he said, "Thus saith [2]the LORD, 'Make this °valley full of °ditches.'

S[2] T[1] y 17 For thus saith [2]the LORD, 'Ye shall not see °wind, neither shall ye see rain; yet that valley shall be filled with water, that ye may drink, both ye, and your cattle, and your beasts.'

z 18 And this is *but* a light thing in the sight of [2]the LORD: He will deliver the Moabites also into your hand.
19 And ye shall smite every fenced city, and every choice city, and shall fell every good tree, and stop all wells of water, and °mar every good piece of land with stones."

T[2] *y* 20 And it came to pass in the morning, when the °meat offering was °offered, that, behold,

3. 4—8. 15 (K[2], p. 491). EVENTS. POLITICAL.
(*Extended Alternation and Introversion.*)

K[2] | L | O | 3. 4-27. War with Moab. Mesha.
P | 4. 1-7. Elisha. Creditor and widow.
M | Q | 4. 8-37. Shunammite.
R | 4. 38-44. Famine. Miraculous supplies.
N | 5. 1-27. Mission to Elisha (Naaman).
L | *P* | 6. 1-7. Elisha. Residence and axe head.
O | 6. 8-23. War with Syria.
M | *R* | 6. 24—7. 20. Famine. Miraculous supplies.
Q | 8. 1-6. Shunammite.
N | 8. 7-15. Mission to Elisha (Ben-hadad).

4-27 (O, above). WAR WITH MOAB. MESHA.
(*Alternations and Introversion.*)

O | o | 4, 5. Mesha's rebellion.
p | q | 6-9-. Allies advance.
r | s | -9. Exigence.
t | 10-25. How met.
o | 26-. Mesha's defeat.
p | *r* | *s* | -26. Exigence.
t | 27-. How met.
q | -27. Allies retire.

5 Ahab was dead. Cp. 1. 1. He and his son Ahaziah both died in the same year (800 B.C.). See Ap. 50. V, p. 58.
7 I am, &c. Cp. 1 Kings 22. 4.
8 he said: i. e. Jehoram.
Which way . . . ? Either by crossing Jordan north of the Dead Sea and attacking Moab from the north; or by Edom, which was under Judah (1 Kings 22. 47).
he answered: i. e. Jehoshaphat answered.
9 fetched a compass = made a circuit. Cp. Acts 28. 13.

10-25 (t, above). EXIGENCY. HOW MET.
(*Alternation and Introversion.*)

t | u | 10. Trouble of the three kings.
v | w | 11, 12. Elisha. Help sought.
x | 13-. Reproof.
u | -13. Trouble of the three kings.
v | *x* | 14. Reproof.
w | 15-25. Elisha. Help given.

10 Alas! Fig. *Ecphōnēsis*. Ap. 6.
11 Is there not here . . . ? A similar question asked before by Jehoshaphat (1 Kings 22. 7).
poured water, &c. Put by Fig. *Metonymy* (of Adjunct), Ap. 6, for being an attendant.
12 Jehoshaphat. Some codices, with Sept., Syr., and Vulg., add "king of Judah".
13 What . . . ? See note on 2 Sam. 16. 10. Fig. *Erotēsis*. Ap. 6. **Nay** = Say not so.
14 before, &c. Implying Elisha's priesthood.
not look. Jehoram was wicked in himself (*v.* 2), as well as being the son of Ahab. Elisha less austere later (ch. 6).

15-25 (*w*, above). ELISHA. HELP GIVEN.
(*Division.*)

w | S[1] | 15, 16. Means.
S[2] | 17-25. Ends.

15 minstrel = harper. From Heb. *nāgan*, to harp.
hand. Fig. *Prosopopœia* (Ap. 6). But some codices, with Aram., read "the Spirit".
16 valley = a dry watercourse.
ditches = trenches. Heb. ditches ditches. Fig. *Epizeuxis* (Ap. 6) = full of.

17-25 (S[2], above). ENDS. (*Alternation.*)

S[2] | T[1] | y | 17. Water. } Prophecy.
z | 18, 19. Victory. }
T[2] | *y* | 20. Water. } Fulfilment.
z | 21-25. Victory. }

17 wind. Heb. *rūach*. Ap. 9.
19 mar = spoil. Fig. *Prosopopœia*. Ap. 6.
20 meat offering = meal offering. Heb. *minhah*. See Ap. 43. II. iii = gift offering.
offered = offered up. See Ap. 43. I. vi.

801–788 °there came water by the way of Edom, and
the country was filled with water.

z 21 And when all the Moabites heard that the
(p. 492) kings were come up to fight against them, they
gathered all that were able to °put on armour,
and upward, and stood in the border.
22 And they rose up early in the morning,
and the sun shone upon the water, and the
Moabites saw the water on the other side *as*
°red as blood:
23 And they said, "This *is* blood: the kings
are surely °slain, and they have smitten one
another: now therefore, Moab, to the spoil."
24 And when they came to the camp of Israel,
the Israelites rose up and smote the Moabites,
so that they fled before them: but they °went
forward smiting the Moabites, even in *their*
country.
25 And they beat down the cities, and on
every good piece of land cast °every man his
stone, and filled it; and they stopped all the
wells of water, and felled all the good trees:
only in °Kir-haraseth left they the °stones
thereof; °howbeit the slingers went about *it*,
and smote it.

o 26 And when the king of Moab saw that the
battle was too sore for him, he took with him
seven hundred [25]men that drew swords, to break
through *even* unto the king of Edom:

p r s but they could not.

t 27 Then he took his eldest son that should
have reigned in his stead, and °offered him
for °a burnt offering upon °the wall. And
there was great °indignation against Israel:

q and °they departed °from him, and returned
to °*their own* land.

P **4** Now there cried a certain woman of the
wives of the sons of the prophets unto
Elisha, saying, "Thy servant my °husband is
dead; and thou knowest that thy servant did
fear °the LORD: and the creditor is come to
take unto him my two sons to be °bondmen."
2 And Elisha said unto her, "What shall I
do for thee? tell me, what hast thou in the
house?" And she said, "Thine handmaid
hath not any thing in the house, save a pot
of oil."
3 Then he said, "Go, borrow thee vessels
abroad of all thy neighbours, *even* empty vessels; °borrow not a few.
4 And when thou art come in, thou shalt shut
the door upon thee and upon thy sons, and
shalt pour out into all those vessels, and thou
shalt set aside that which is full."
5 So she went from him, and shut the door
upon her and upon her sons, °who brought *the*
vessels to her; and °she poured out.
6 And it came to pass, when the vessels were
full, that she said unto her son, "Bring me yet
a vessel." And he said unto her, "*There is*
not a vessel more." And the oil stayed.
7 Then she came and told the °man of °God.
And he said, "Go, sell the oil, and pay thy
°debt, and live thou and thy °children of the
rest."

1 Q U a 8 And it fell on a day, that Elisha passed to
(p. 493)

there came water. Elisha's fourth miracle. See note on 2. 15.

21 put on armour. Heb. gird a girdle.

22 red as blood. Implied as owing to the action of the sun. Equally a miracle.

23 slain = destroyed.

24 went forward. Some codices, &c., add "still further", and connect this with entering. Other codices, with six early printed editions, Sept., Syr., and Vulg., connect these words with the *smiting*, and read "still further smote", or "went on smiting".

25 every man. Heb. *'ish*. Ap. 14. II.

Kir-haraseth = The city of the hill. The capital of Moab.

stones [in the wall] thereof. Supply Fig. *Ellipsis*. Ap. 6.

howbeit, &c. = and [till] the slingers should surround and smite it.

27 offered him = offered him up. Ap. 43. I. vi.

a burnt offering. Ap. 43. II. ii. Recording a fact on which Mesha is silent on the Moabite stone. Ap. 54.

the wall. i.e., the higher of the two. Heb. *hōmah* not *ḳir* as in *vv.* 4, 10.

indignation = wrath. This led probably to Moab's subsequent success.

they departed. This expresses the failure of Israel's expedition, while Mesha goes on to record his subsequent successes, which were great—all the cities taken by him (Ap. 54) being those belonging to Reuben and Gad.

from him: i.e. from the king of Moab.

their own. The Syr. and Vulg. have these words in the text.

4. 1 husband = man. Heb. *'ish*. Ap. 14. II.

the LORD. Heb. Jehovah. Ap. 4. II.

bondmen. Cp. Lev. 25. 39 and Neh. 5. 5.

3 borrow not a few = scant not.

5 who brought = they bringing.

she poured out. Elisha's fifth miracle. See note on 2. 15.

7 man. Heb. *'ish*. See Ap. 14. II.

God. Heb. Elohim. Ap. 4. I.

debt = creditor. children = sons.

4. 8-37 (Q, p. 492). THE SHUNAMMITE.
(*Introversion.*)

Q | U | 8–17. Son given.
  V | 18–20. Son's death.
    W | 21. Elisha's bed. Placed on.
      X | 22–24. Her Mission to Elisha.
        Y | 25–27. Her Arrival.
      X | 28–31. Her Converse with Elisha.
    W | 32, 33. Elisha's bed. Found on.
  V | 34, 35. Son raised.
U | 36, 37. Son restored.

8-17 (U, above). SON GIVEN.
(*Alternation.*)

U | a | 8. Resort of Elisha (general).
  b | 9, 10. Accommodation.
  a | 11. Resort of Elisha (particular).
  b | 12–17. Compensation.

8 Shunem. In the plain of Esdraelon. The native place of Abishag (1 Kings 1. 3).

great = wealthy, or a person of position (2 Sam. 19. 32).

9 holy. See note on Ex. 3. 5.

10 chamber = upper chamber, or wall-chamber.

°Shunem, where *was* a °great woman; and
she constrained him to eat bread. And *so* it
was, *that* as oft as he passed by, he turned in
thither to eat bread.

9 And she said unto her [1]husband, "Behold b
now, I perceive that this *is* an °holy [7]man of
[7]God, which passeth by us continually.
10 Let us make a little °chamber, I pray thee,

801 on the wall; and let us set for him there a bed,
to °and a table, and a stool, and a °candlestick:
788 and it shall be, when he cometh to us, that he
shall turn in thither."

a 11 And it fell on a day, that he came thither,
and he turned into the chamber, and lay there.

b 12 And he said to Gehazi his °servant, "Call
this Shunammite." And when he had called
her, she stood before him.
13 And he said unto him, "Say now unto her,
[9]'Behold, thou hast been °careful for us with
all this °care; what *is* to be done for thee?
wouldest thou be °spoken for to the king, or to
the captain of the host?'" And she answered,
"I dwell among mine own people."
14 And he said, "What then *is* to be done
for her?" And Gehazi answered, "Verily
she hath no [7]child, and her [1]husband is old."
15 And he said, "Call her." And when he
had called her, she stood in the °door.
16 And he said, "About this season, according to the time of life, thou shalt embrace a
son." And she said, "Nay, my lord, *thou* [7]man
of [7]God, do not lie unto thine handmaid."
17 And the woman conceived, and bare a son
at that season that Elisha had said unto her,
according to the time °of life.

V 18 And when the °child was grown, it fell on
a day, that he went out to his father to the
reapers.
19 And he said unto his father, "My head,
°my head." And he said to a lad, "Carry him
to his mother."
20 And when he had taken him, and brought
him to his mother, he sat on her knees till
noon, and *then* died.

W 21 And she went up, and laid him on the bed
of the [7]man of [7]God, and shut *the door* upon
him, and went out.

X 22 And she called unto her [1]husband, and said,
"Send me, I pray thee, one of the young men,
and one of the asses, that I may run to the
[7]man of [7]God, and come again."
23 And he said, "Wherefore wilt thou go to
him to day? *it is* neither new moon, nor sabbath." And she said, "*It shall be* well."
24 Then she saddled an ass, and said to her
servant, "Drive, and go forward; slack not
thy riding for me, except I bid thee."

Y 25 So she went and came unto the [7]man of
[7]God to mount Carmel. And it came to pass,
when the [7]man of [7]God saw her afar off, that he
said to Gehazi his [12]servant, [9]"Behold, *yonder*
is that Shunammite:
26 Run °now, I pray thee, to meet her, and say
unto her, '*Is it* well with thee? *is it* well with
thy [7]husband? *is it* well with the [18]child?'"
And she answered, "*It is* well."
27 And when she came to the [7]man of [7]God
to the hill, she caught him by the feet: but
Gehazi came near to thrust her away. And
the [7]man of [7]God said, "Let her alone; for
°her soul *is* °vexed within her: and [1]the LORD
hath hid *it* from me, and hath not told me."

X 28 Then she said, °"Did I desire a son of my
lord? °did I not say, 'Do not °deceive me?'"
29 Then he °said to Gehazi, "Gird up thy
loins, and take my staff in thine hand, and go
thy way: if thou meet any [7]man, °salute him
not; and if °any salute thee, answer him not
again: and lay my staff upon the face of the
°child."
30 And the mother of the [29]child said, "*As* [1]the
LORD liveth, and *as* °thy soul liveth, I will
not leave thee." And he arose, and followed her.
31 And Gehazi passed on before them, and
laid the staff upon the face of the [29]child; but
there was neither voice, nor hearing. Wherefore he went again to meet him, and told him,
saying, "The [29]child is not awaked."

32 And when Elisha was come into the house, W
[9]behold, the [29]child was dead, *and* laid upon
his bed.
33 He went in therefore, and shut the door
upon them twain, and prayed unto [1]the LORD.

34 And he went up, and lay upon the [18]child, V
and put his mouth upon his mouth, and his eyes
upon his eyes, and his hands upon his hands:
and he stretched himself upon the [18]child; and
the flesh of the [18]child waxed warm.
35 Then he returned, and walked in the house
to and fro; and went up, and stretched himself
upon him: and the [29]child sneezed seven times,
and the [29]child opened his eyes.

36 And he called Gehazi, and said, "Call this U
Shunammite." So he called her. And when
she was come in unto him, he said, °"Take
up thy son."
37 Then she went in, and fell at his feet, and
bowed herself to the ground, and took up her
son, and went out.

38 And Elisha came again to Gilgal: and R c
(p. 494)

---

and. Note the Fig. *Polysyndeton.* Ap. 6.
candlestick = lampstand. Very little furniture used in the East to-day.
12 servant = young man.
13 careful . . . care. Fig. *Polyptōton* (Ap. 6) = exceedingly careful.
spoken for to the king. This confidence in his influence with the king is accounted for by the miraculous aid recently given by Elisha in 3. 16-19.
15 door = entrance.
17 of life, or of spring. Read "that season about the time of spring of which Elisha had said unto her". The sixth miracle. Cp. 2. 15.
18 child = progeny.
19 my head. Fig. *Epizeuxis.* Ap. 6.
26 now. Some codices, with two early printed editions, read "now therefore".
27 her soul = herself. Heb. *nephesh.* Ap. 13.
vexed = bitter.
28 Did I . . . ? Fig. *Erotēsis.* Ap. 6.
deceive = cajole.
29 said. In what Elisha said the signs given are put by Fig. *Metonymy* (of Adjunct), Ap. 6, for the things symbolised by them.
salute him not. Idiom. The salutation being ceremonial and taking time.
any = a man. Heb. *'ish.* Ap. 14. II.
child. Heb. *na'ar* = youth.
30 thy soul = thou. Heb. *nephesh.* Ap. 13.
36 Take up thy son. The seventh miracle (2. 15).

4. 38-44 (R, p. 492). **FAMINE.**
(Alternation.)

R | c | 38-. Dearth.
  | d | -38-41. Supply. Eighth miracle.
  | c | 42. Firstfruits.
  | d | 43, 44. Supply. Ninth miracle.

801-788 *there was* °a dearth in the land; and the sons
of the prophets *were* sitting before him:
d and he said unto his servant, "Set on the great
(p. 494) pot, and °seethe pottage for the sons of the prophets."

39 And one went out into the field to gather
herbs, and found a °wild vine, and gathered
thereof wild gourds his lap full, and came and
shred *them* into the pot of pottage: for they
knew *them* not.

40 So they poured out for the °men to eat.
And it came to pass, as they were eating of
the pottage, that they cried out, and said, "O
thou [7]man of [7]God, *there is* °death in the
pot." And they could not eat *thereof*.

41 But he said, "Then bring meal." And he
cast *it* into the pot; and he said, "Pour out
for the people, that they may eat." And
there was °no harm in the pot.

c 42 And there came a [7]man from Baal-shalisha,
and brought the [7]man of God bread of the first-fruits,
twenty loaves of barley, and full ears of
corn in the husk thereof. And he said, "Give
unto the people, that they may eat."

d 43 And his °servitor said, "What, should I
set this before °an hundred [7]men?" He said
again, "Give the people, that they may eat:
for thus saith [1]the LORD, 'They shall eat, and
shall leave *thereof*.'"

44 So he set *it* before them, and they did eat,
and left *thereof*, according to the word of [1]the
LORD.

N e **5** Now °Naaman, captain of the host of the
(p. 495) king of Syria, °was a great °man with his
master, and honourable, because °by him °the
LORD had given °deliverance unto Syria: he
was also a mighty °man in valour, °*but he was*
°a leper.

f 2 And the Syrians had gone out by °companies,
and had brought away captive out
of the land of Israel a little maid; and she
waited on Naaman's wife.

3 And she said unto her mistress, °"Would
God my lord *were* with the prophet that *is*
°in Samaria! for he would recover him of his
leprosy."

4 And *one* went in, and told his lord, saying,
"Thus and thus said the maid that *is* of the
land of Israel."

5 And the king of Syria said, "Go to, go, and
I will send a letter unto the °king of Israel."
And he departed, and took with him ten
°talents of silver, and six thousand *pieces*
of gold, and ten °changes of raiment.

6 And he brought the letter to the [5]king of
Israel, saying, "Now when this letter is come
unto thee, behold, I have *therewith* sent Naaman
my servant to thee, that thou mayest
°recover him of his leprosy."

7 And it came to pass, when the king of Israel
had read the letter, that he rent his clothes,
and said, °"*Am I* °God, to kill and to make
alive, that this [1]man doth send unto me to
recover a [1]man of his leprosy? wherefore consider,
I pray you, and see how he seeketh a
quarrel against me."

8 And it was *so*, when Elisha the °man of
[7]God had heard that the king of Israel had
rent his clothes, that he sent to the king, saying,
"Wherefore hast thou rent thy clothes?
let him come now to me, and he shall know
that there is a prophet in Israel."

9 So Naaman came with his horses and with g
his chariot, and stood at the °door of the house
of Elisha.

10 And Elisha sent a messenger unto him, h
saying, °"Go and °wash in Jordan seven
times, and thy flesh shall come again to thee,
and thou shalt be clean."

---

38 a dearth = the dearth. One of thirteen famines. See note on Gen. 12. 10. **seethe** = boil.

39 wild vine: i. e. a plant with vine-like tendrils. Not the grape, but probably the colocynth.

40 men. Heb. *'ĕnôsh*. Ap. 14. III.

death. Put by Fig. *Metonymy* (of Effect), Ap. 6, for that which causes death.

41 no harm = no evil thing. Elisha's eighth miracle Cp. 2. 15.

43 servitor = attendant. Old English = one who serves.

an hundred men. Elisha's ninth miracle. See note on 2. 15. One of three (Ap. 10) miracles of feeding multitudes. Cp. Matt. 14. 20; 15. 34, 38.

5. 1-27 (N, p. 492). **MISSION TO ELISHA.** (*Introversion.*)

N | e | 1. Leprosy of Naaman. Providential.
f | 2-8. Negotiation. Naaman and king of Israel.
g | 9. Naaman's visit to Elisha.
h | 10. Elisha's direction. Given.
i | 11, 12. Naaman. Resentment.
i | 13. Naaman. Compliance.
h | 14. Elisha's direction. Taken.
g | 15-. Naaman's return to Elisha.
f | -15-26. Negotiations. Naaman with Elisha and [Gehazi.
e | 27. Leprosy of Gehazi. Judicial.

1 Naaman. Note the five servants in this chapter:—
1. The King's servant (Naaman), *v.* 1.
2. Naaman's wife's servant (the maid), *v.* 2.
3. Jehovah's servant (Elisha), *v.* 8.
4. Naaman's servants (*v.* 13).
5. The Prophet's servant (Gehazi), *v.* 20.

was = had come to be.

man. Heb. *'îsh*. Ap. 14. II.

by him. An unconscious instrument.

the LORD. Heb. Jehovah. Ap. 4. II.

deliverance. Probably from the Assyrians.

but, &c. Fig. *Anesis*. Ap. 6.

a leper. Cp. Lev. 13. Not regarded ceremonially by heathen. Not far gone (cp. *v.* 19). Probably only in initial stage. One of nine so afflicted. See note on Ex. 4. 6. The story of Naaman may be compared with the parallel in John 9.

2 companies = marauding bands. Cp. 6. 23.

3 Would God, &c. Fig. *Ejaculatio*. Ap. 6.

in Samaria. This is the girl's expression. Samaria was where she had heard of him.

5 king of Israel. Probably Jehoram.

talents. See Ap. 51. II.

changes of raiment. See Gen. 45. 22.

6 recover. A *Homonym*, with another meaning, to snatch away or destroy, as in Ps. 26. 9 and Jer. 16. 5. See notes there.

7 Am I God . . . ? Fig. *Erotēsis*. Ap. 6.

God. Heb. Elohim (the Creator). Ap. 4. I.

8 man of God. See Ap. 49.

9 door = entrance.

10 Go and wash. Cp. John 9. 7, and other commands: "Go, call" (John 4. 16); "Go, sell" (Matt. 19. 21).

wash = bathe (ceremonially). See note on Lev. 14. 9.

i 11 But Naaman was wroth, and went away,
(p. 495) and said, °"Behold, °I thought, he will surely
801 come out to me, and stand, and call on the
to name of [1] the LORD his [7] God, and °strike his
788 hand over the place, and recover the leper.

12 °*Are* not °Abana and Pharpar, °rivers of °Damascus, better than all the waters of Israel? may I not wash in them, and be clean?" So he turned and went away °in a rage.

i 13 And his °servants came near, and spake unto him, and said, °"My father, *if* the prophet had bid thee *do some* great thing, wouldest thou not have done *it?* how much rather then, when he saith to thee, 'Wash, and be clean?'"

h 14 Then went he down, and dipped himself seven times in Jordan, according to the saying of the [8] man of [8] God: and his flesh °came again like unto the flesh of a little °child, and he was clean.

g 15 And he °returned to the [8] man of [8] God, he and all his company, and came, and stood before him:

f and he said, [11] "Behold, °now I know that *there is* no [7] God in all the earth, but in Israel: now therefore, I pray thee, °take a °blessing of thy servant."

16 But he said, "*As* [1] the LORD liveth, °before Whom I stand, I will receive none." And he urged him to take *it;* but he refused.

17 And Naaman said, "Shall there not then, I pray thee, be given to thy servant two mules' burden of °earth? for thy servant will henceforth °offer neither burnt offering nor sacrifice unto other gods, but unto [1] the LORD.

18 In this thing [1] the LORD pardon thy servant, *that* when my master goeth into the house of °Rimmon to °worship there, and he °leaneth on my hand, and I bow myself in the house of °Rimmon: when I bow down myself in the house of Rimmon, °the LORD pardon thy servant in this thing."

19 And he said unto him, °"Go in peace." So he departed from him °a little way.

20 But Gehazi, the °servant of Elisha the [8] man of [8] God, said, [11] "Behold, my master hath spared Naaman this Syrian, in not receiving at his hands that which he brought: but, *as* [1] the LORD liveth, I will run after him, and take °somewhat of him."

21 So Gehazi followed after Naaman. And when Naaman saw *him* running after him, he lighted down from the chariot to meet him, and said, °"*Is* all well?"

22 And he said, "All *is* well. My master hath sent me, saying, [11] 'Behold, even now there be come to me from °mount Ephraim two young men of the sons of the prophets: give them, I pray thee, a °talent of silver, and two changes of garments.'"

23 And Naaman said, "Be content, °take two [22] talents." And he urged him, and bound two [22] talents of silver in two bags, with two changes of garments, and laid *them* upon two of his servants; and they bare *them* before him.

24 And when he came to the tower, he took *them* from their hand, and bestowed *them* in the house: and he let the °men go, and they departed.

11 Behold. Fig. *Asterismos.* Ap. 6.

I thought. Cp. *v.* 15, "Now I know". Human thought and Divine certitude.

strike = wave, move, or pass.

12 Are not . . . ? Fig. *Erotēsis.* Ap. 6.

Abana. Some codices, and three early printed editions, read "Amana".

rivers. Heb. *nāhār*, an ever-flowing stream. (Not *naḥal*, a summer stream.) Rising in Mount Hermon and losing themselves in a lake near Damascus.

Damascus. Used of the district, or of the city near which they flowed and were known.

in a rage. One of eleven rulers offended with God's servants for speaking the truth. See note on Ex. 10. 28.

13 servants. Again used by God. Cp. *vv.* 2-4.

My father. A title of honour and affection.

14 came again. The tenth miracle of Elisha. See note on 2. 15. **child** = boy.

15 returned. About thirty miles.

now I know. Cp. "Behold, I thought", *v.* 11.

take = accept.

blessing = a present. Cp. Gen. 33. 11. Judg. 1. 15.

16 before, &c. A phrase referring to priesthood, for the sacrifices Naaman speaks of (*v.* 17).

17 earth = soil. Naaman may have heard of Ex. 20. 24.

offer = prepare. See Ap. 43. I. iii.

18 Rimmon. The Assyrian storm-god Ramman.

worship = bow down himself.

leaneth. Cp. 7. 2, 17.

the LORD pardon = Jehovah pardon. Some codices add "I pray thee", but marked "to be cancelled".

19 Go in peace. God's servants are not "directors of conscience", but ministers of His Word. To have sanctioned it would have recognised idolatry. To have forbidden it would have put Naaman under a yoke to Elisha. It was for Naaman to decide whether he could do this thing, and be at "peace".

a little way. A phrase found only here and Gen. 35. 16 and 48. 7. = a stone's throw.

20 servant = young man.

somewhat = a trifle.

21 Is all well? Heb. Is it peace?

22 mount Ephraim. There were two schools of the prophets there: Beth-el and Gilgal. Cp. 2. 1, 3.

talent. See Ap. 51. II.

23 take = accept. Some codices, with one early printed edition, read "and accept".

24 men. Heb. *'ĕnōsh.* Ap. 14. III.

26 Went not . . . ? Fig. *Erotēsis.* Ap. 6. = Did not my heart beat?

Is it . . ? Fig. *Erotēsis.* Ap. 6. Cp. Hag. 1. 4.

and. Note the Fig. *Polysyndeton.* Ap. 6.

27 cleave. Elisha's eleventh miracle. See note on 2. 15.

a leper. One of the nine afflicted with leprosy. See note on Ex. 4. 6.

as snow. i.e. completely a leper; but not clean ceremonially. See note on Lev. 13. 13.

25 But he went in, and stood before his master. And Elisha said unto him, "Whence *comest thou,* Gehazi?" And he said, "Thy servant went no whither."

26 And he said unto him, °"Went not mine heart *with thee,* when the [1] man turned again from his chariot to meet thee? °*Is it* a time to receive money, °and to receive garments, and oliveyards, and vineyards, and sheep, and oxen, and menservants, and maidservants?

27 The leprosy therefore of Naaman shall °cleave unto thee, and unto thy seed for ever." *e*
And he went out from his presence °a leper *as white* °as snow.

P j (p. 497) 801 to 788 **6** And the sons of the prophets said unto Elisha, °"Behold now, the place where we dwell with thee is too °strait for us.
2 Let us go, we pray thee, unto Jordan, and take thence every °man a beam, and let us make us a place there, where we may dwell." And he answered, "Go ye."

k 3 And °one said, "Be content, I pray thee, and go with thy servants." And he answered, "I will go."
4 So he went with them. And when they came to Jordan, they °cut down °wood.

j 5 But as [3]one was felling a beam, the °axe head fell into the water: and he cried, and said, °"Alas, master! for it was borrowed."

k 6 And the °man of °God said, "Where fell it?" And he shewed him the place. And he °cut down °a stick, and cast *it* in thither; and the °iron did swim.
7 Therefore said he, "Take *it* up to thee." And he put out his hand, and took it.

O l 8 Then the °king of Syria warred against Israel, and took counsel with his servants, saying, "In such and such a place *shall be* my camp."
9 And the [6]man of [6]God sent unto the °king of Israel, saying, "Beware that thou pass not such a place; for thither the Syrians are come down."
10 And the king of Israel sent to the place which the [6]man of [6]God told him and warned him of, and saved himself there, not once nor twice.
11 Therefore the heart of the king of Syria was sore troubled for this thing; and he called his servants, and said unto them, "Will ye not shew me which of us *is* for the king of Israel?"
12 And one of his servants said, "None, my lord, O king: °but Elisha, the prophet that *is* in Israel, telleth the king of Israel the words that thou speakest in thy bedchamber."

m 13 And he said, "Go and spy where he *is*, that I may send and fetch him." And it was told him, saying, [1]"Behold, *he is* in Dothan."
14 Therefore sent he thither horses, and chariots, and a great host: and they came by night, and compassed the city about.

n 15 And when °the servant of the [6]man of [6]God was risen early, and gone forth, [1]behold, an host compassed the city both with horses and chariots. And °his servant said unto him, [5]"Alas, my master! how shall we do?"
16 And he answered, "Fear not: for they that *be* with us *are* more than they that *be* with them."
17 And Elisha prayed, and said, °"LORD, I pray thee, °open his eyes, that he may °see." And °the LORD opened the eyes of the young man; and he °saw: and, [1]behold, the mountain *was* full of horses and chariots of fire °round about Elisha.

n 18 And when they came down to him, Elisha prayed unto [17]the LORD, and said, "Smite this people, I pray Thee, with °blindness." And He smote them with blindness according to the word of Elisha.

m 19 And Elisha said unto them, "This *is* not the way, neither *is* this the city: follow me, and °I will bring you to the °man whom ye seek." °But °he led them to Samaria.

20 And it came to pass, when they were come into Samaria, that Elisha said, [17]"LORD, °open the eyes of these *men*, that they may [17]see." And [17]the LORD opened their eyes, and they [17]saw; and, [1]behold, *they were* in the midst of Samaria. *l*
21 And the king of Israel said unto Elisha, when he saw them, "My father, shall I smite *them?* shall I smite *them?*"
22 And he answered, "Thou shalt not smite *them:* °wouldest thou smite those whom thou hast taken captive with thy sword and with thy bow? set bread and water before them, that they may eat and drink, and go to their master."
23 And he prepared great provision for them: and when they had eaten and drunk, he sent them away, and they went to their master. So

---

6. 1-7 (*P*, p. 492). ELISHA. RESIDENCE, &c. (*Alternation.*)

P | j | 1, 2. Sons of the prophets. Proposal.
  k | 3, 4. Elisha. Consent.
  j | 5. Sons of prophets. Accident.
  k | 6, 7. Elisha. Miracle.

1 Behold. Fig. *Asterismos.* Ap. 6.
strait = narrow. **2 man.** Heb. *'ish.* Ap. 14. II.
3 one = the one: i. e. of *v.* 3.
4 cut down. Heb. *nāzar.* Cp. *v.* 6. **wood** = logs.
5 axe head. Heb. "iron", put by Fig. *Metonymy* (of Cause), Ap. 6, for the axe head made of iron. Cp. *v.* 6, where the Fig. is translated literally.
Alas. Fig. *Ecphōnēsis.* Ap. 6.
6 man of God. See Ap. 49.
cut down. Not same word as *v.* 3. Heb. *kāzab* = to cut evenly: i. e. shape or size evenly. Occurs only here and Song 4. 2 ("even shorn").
a stick = a helve.
iron did swim = made him see the iron: by causing it to rise to the surface. Elisha's twelfth miracle. See note on 2. 15. The spiritual application is thus put by John Newton:—

"Not one concern of ours is small
If we belong to Him;
To teach us this, the Lord of all
Once made the iron to swim".

8-23 (*O*, p. 492). WAR WITH SYRIA. (*Introversion.*)

O | l | 8-12. King of Syria. Hostility.
  m | 13, 14. Elisha. Baffling.
  n | 15-17. Eyes of servant opened.
  n | 18. Eyes of Syrians closed.
  m | 19. Elisha. Leading.
  l | 20-23. King of Israel. Benevolence.

8 king of Syria. Probably Ben-hadad of *v.* 24. 1 Kings 20. 1. **9 king of Israel.** Jehoram.
12 but = for: i. e. "[the fact is] that".
15 the servant = attendant. Heb. *m[e]shārēth.*
his servant = young man. Heb. *na'ar.*
17 the LORD. Heb. Jehovah. Ap. 4. II.
open his eyes. Elisha's thirteenth miracle. See note on 2. 15. **see . . . saw** = see . . . saw clearly.
round about. Cp. Ps. 34. 7; 91. 4.
18 blindness. Elisha's fourteenth miracle. See note on 2. 15. One of nine instances of persons so afflicted. See note on Gen. 19. 11.
19 I will bring. So he did.
man. Heb. *'ish.* Ap. 14. II.
But = And; or, So. Heb. *Vav* (ו).
he led them to Samaria: where they found the man they sought: i. e. Elisha himself.
20 open. Elisha's fifteenth miracle. See note on 2. 15.
22 wouldest . . . ? Fig. *Erotēsis.* Ap. 6.

801-788 the °bands of Syria came no more into the land of Israel.

R A o (p. 498) 24 And it came to pass after this, that Ben-hadad king of Syria °gathered all his host, and went up, and besieged Samaria.

25 And there was a great °famine in Samaria: and, [1]behold, they besieged it, until an °ass's head was *sold* for fourscore °*pieces* of silver, and the fourth part of a °cab of °dove's dung for five °*pieces* of silver.

p 26 And as the king of Israel was passing by upon the wall, there cried a woman unto him, saying, "Help, my lord, O king."

27 And he said, °"If [17]the LORD do not help thee, whence shall I help thee? out of the barnfloor, or out of the winepress?"

28 And the king said unto her, "What aileth thee?" And she answered, "This °woman said unto me, 'Give thy son, that we may eat him to day, and we will eat my son to morrow.'

29 So °we boiled my son, and did eat him: and I said unto her on the next day, 'Give thy son, that we may eat him:' and she hath hid her son."

q 30 And it came to pass, when the king heard the words of the woman, that he rent his clothes; and he passed by upon the wall, and the People looked, and, [1]behold, *he had* sackcloth within upon his flesh.

p 31 Then he said, [6]"God do so and more also to me, if the head of Elisha the son of Shaphat shall stand on him this day."

o 32 But Elisha sat in his house, and the elders sat with him; and *the king* sent a [19]man from before him: but ere the messenger came to him, he said to the elders, "See ye how this son of a murderer hath sent to take away mine head? look, when the messenger cometh, shut the door, and °hold him fast at the door: *is* not the sound of his master's feet behind him?"

33 And while he yet talked with them, [1]behold, the °messenger came down unto him: and he said, [1]"Behold, this °evil *is* of [17]the LORD; °what should I wait for [17]the LORD any longer?"

B **7** °Then Elisha said, "Hear ye the word of °the LORD; Thus saith °the LORD, 'To morrow about this time *shall* a °measure of fine flour *be sold* for a °shekel, and two °measures of barley for a °shekel, in the gate of Samaria.'"

2 Then a lord on whose hand the king °leaned answered the °man of °God, and said, °"Behold, *if* [1]the LORD would make windows in heaven, might this thing be?" And he said, °"Behold, °thou shalt see *it* with thine eyes, but shalt not eat thereof."

A r[1] s[1] t 3 And there were four °leprous °men at the entering in of the gate: and they said one to another, "Why sit we here until we die?

4 If we say, 'We will enter into the city,' then the °famine *is* in the city, and we shall die there: and if we sit still here, we die also. Now therefore come, and let us fall unto the °host of the Syrians: if they save us alive, we shall live; and if they kill us, we shall but die."

---

23 bands = marauding bands. Quite different from the organised host of *v.* 24.

6. 24—7. 20 (*R*, p. 492). FAMINE IN SAMARIA. (*Alternation.*)

R A | 6. 24–33. Famine. Suffered.
B | 7. 1, 2. Prediction of supply.
A | 7. 3–15. Famine. Relieved.
B | 7. 16–20. Prediction. Supplies received.

24–33 (A, above). FAMINE. SUFFERED. (*Introversion.*)

A | o | 24, 25. Origin. Second cause.
p | 26–29. Effects. Experienced
q | 30. King's mourning.
p | 31. Effects. Threatening.
o | 32, 33. Origin. First cause.

24 gathered. This was organised war, in contrast with the freebooting irregular bands of *v.* 23.

25 famine. One of the thirteen recorded in Scripture. See note on Gen. 12. 10.

ass's head. This was unclean food.

pieces. Supply Fig. *Ellipsis* (Ap. 6), "shekels" instead of "pieces".

cab. Only occurrence. See Ap. 51. III. 3.

dove's dung. A *Euphemism* (Ap. 6) is included in official Massoretic lists as being substituted for this indelicate expression, the word meaning "decayed leaves". Whichever is the meaning, it was always highly valuable as manure, especially to force growth during dearth.

27 If the LORD do not help thee. Heb. reads "Let not Jehovah help thee", as in A.V. marg. The R.V. "Nay, let Jehovah help thee", is contrary to the normal sense of this negative. Ginsburg suggests that *'al* (not) is an abbreviation for *'im l'o*, which is the exact equivalent for the A.V. text.

28 woman. One of the ten deaths occasioned by women. See note on Judg. 4. 21.

29 we boiled. Cp. Deut. 28. 53.

32 hold him fast at the door: or, hold the door fast against him. Ap. 6.

33 messenger. Heb. *hammāl'āk*, without the *'aleph* ('a), as in Sept. and Syr. In 1 Sam. 11. 4 the case is reversed. The *Massōrah* informs us that the *aleph* was wrongly inserted, making it read messengers instead of "kings". The king must have followed on his heels, for Elisha addresses him directly in 7. 1, 2. Cp. 7. 17.

evil. Heb. *ra'a'*. Ap. 44. viii.

what . . . ? = why? Fig. *Erotēsis*. Ap. 6. These are the words of the king.

7. 1 Then Elisha. The Structure shows that verses 1, 2 should be read with 6. 33.

the LORD. Heb. Jehovah. Ap. 4. II.

measure. See Ap. 51. III. 3.

shekel. Cp. 6. 25. See Ap. 51. II.

measures = seahs. See Ap. 51. III. 3.

2 leaned. Cp. 5. 18.

man of God. See Ap. 49.

Behold. Fig. *Asterismos*. Ap. 6.

thou shalt see it. Cp. *vv.* 19, 20.

7. 3–15 (*A*, above). FAMINE. RELIEVED. (*Division.*)

A | r[1] | 3–11. Discovery by lepers.
r[2] | 12–15. Confirmation by scouts.

3–11 (r[1], above). DISCOVERY BY LEPERS. (*Alternation.*)

r[1] | s[1] | t | 3, 4. Consultation.
u | 5–8. Discovery. Made.
s[2] | *t* | 9. Consultation.
u | 10, 11. Discovery. Reported.

3 leprous men. One of the nine cases of affliction with leprosy. See note on Ex. 4. 6.

men. Heb. *'ĕnōsh*. Ap. 14. III.

4 famine. Cp. 6. 25. **host** = camp.

u 5 And they rose up in the °twilight, to go
(p. 498) unto the camp of the Syrians: and when they
801 were come to the uttermost part of the camp
to of Syria, behold, *there was* no °man there.
788 6 For °the LORD* had made the host of the
Syrians to hear a noise of chariots, °and a
noise of horses, °*even* the noise of a great
host: and they said one to another, °"Lo, the
king of Israel hath hired against us the °kings
of the Hittites, and the °kings of the Egyptians,
to come upon us."
7 Wherefore they arose and fled in the [5]twilight, and left their tents, and their horses, and
their asses, even the camp as it *was*, and fled
for °their life.
8 And when these lepers came to the °uttermost part of the camp, they went into one
tent, and did eat and drink, and carried thence
silver, and gold, and raiment, and went and
hid *it;* and came again, and entered into
another tent, and carried thence *also*, and
went and hid *it*.
s[2] t 9 Then they said one to another, °"We do not
well: this day *is* a day of good tidings, and we
hold our peace: if we tarry till the morning
light, some °mischief will come upon us: now
therefore come, that we may go and tell the
king's household."
u 10 So they came and called unto the porter
of the city: and they told them, saying, "We
came to the camp of the Syrians, and, [2]behold,
there was no [5]man there, neither voice of °man,
but horses tied, and asses tied, and °the tents
°as they *were*."
11 And °he called the porters; and they told
it to the king's house within.
r[2] 12 And the king arose in the night, and said
unto his servants, "I will now shew you what
the Syrians have done to us. They know that
we *be* hungry; therefore are they gone out of
the camp to hide themselves in the field, saying, 'When they come out of the city, we shall
catch them alive, and get into the city.'"
13 And one of his servants answered and said,
"Let *some* take, I pray thee, five of the horses
that remain, which are left in the city, ([2]behold, they *are* as all the multitude of Israel
°that are left in it: [2]behold, *I say,* they *are*
even as all the multitude of the Israelites that
are consumed:) and let us send and see."
14 They took therefore two chariot horses;
and the king sent after the host of the Syrians,
saying, "Go and see."
15 And they went after them unto Jordan:
and, [6]lo, all the way *was* full of garments and
vessels, which the Syrians had cast away in
their haste. And the messengers returned,
and told the king.
B 16 And the People went out, and spoiled the
tents of the Syrians. So a [1]measure of fine
flour was *sold* for a °shekel, and two [1]measures
of barley for a °shekel, according to the word
of the LORD.
17 And the king appointed the lord on whose
hand he [2]leaned to have the charge of the
gate: and the People trode upon him in the
gate, and he died, as the [2]man of [2]God had
said, who spake when the °king came down
to him.

18 And it came to pass as the [2]man of [2]God
had spoken to the king, saying, "Two [1]measures of barley for a [16]shekel, and a [1]measure of
fine flour for a [16]shekel, shall be to morrow
about this time in the gate of Samaria:"
19 And that lord answered the [2]man of [2]God,
and said, "Now, [2]behold, *if* [1]the LORD should
make windows in heaven, °might such a thing
be?" And he said, "Behold, thou shalt see it
with thine eyes, but shalt not eat thereof."
20 And so it fell out unto him: for the people
trode upon him in the gate, and he died.

8 Then spake Elisha unto the woman, Q
°whose son he had restored to life, say- (p. 492)
ing, "Arise, and go thou and thine household,
and sojourn wheresoever thou canst sojourn:
for °the LORD hath called for a °famine; and
°it shall also come upon the land °seven years."
2 And the woman arose, and did after the
saying of the °man of °God: and she went with
her household, and sojourned in the land of
the Philistines seven years.
3 And it came to pass at the seven years' end,
that the woman returned out of the land of the

5 twilight = darkness. See note on the *Homonym*, 1 Sam. 30. 17. **man.** Heb. *'ish.* Ap. 14. II.

6 the LORD* = Jehovah. One of the 134 occurrences of Jehovah which the *Sōpherim* altered to Adonai. See Ap. 32.

and a noise. Note the Figs. *Polysyndeton* and *Repetitio* (Ap. 6) for great emphasis.

even = and. Some codices, with one early printed edition, Syr., and Vulg., read "and a noise", as in the two preceding clauses.

Lo. Fig. *Asterismos.* Ap. 6.

kings of the Hittites. The Hittites were divided into several tribes, each with its king or chief. Their empire extended from the Euphrates to Asia Minor. Cp. 1 Sam. 26. 6. The Assyrian monuments speak of a confederacy of twelve existing at this time.

kings of the Egyptians. The monuments of this date speak of a large number of names at this time.

7 their life = their soul. Heb. *nephesh.* Ap. 13.

8 uttermost = outermost.

9 We do not well. The application of this is full of instruction to others in like circumstances, for all time.

mischief = punishment.

10 man. Heb. *'ādām.* Ap. 14. I.

the tents = their tents. So Sept. **as** = just as.

11 he called the porters. The Sept., and a special reading called *Sevīr* (Ap. 34), read "the porters called".

13 that are left . . . Israelites. These words are repeated by *Homœoteleuton* (instead of omitted, as is usually the case with *Homœoteleuton*). They are not in many codices, or Sept., Syr., or Vulg. This accounts for the parenthesis in A.V.

16 shekel. See Ap. 51. II. 5.

17 king came down. See note on 6. 33.

19 might such a thing be? This is the reading of some codices, and four early printed editions, with Sept. and Syr. The current Heb. text reads "could it be according to this word?"

8. 1 whose son. Cp. 4. 35.

the LORD. Heb. Jehovah. Ap. 4. II.

famine = the famine, which had already begun. Probably the same as 4. 38. Occasion is not determined by the text, but *v.* 3 takes up the history at the end of the seven years.

it shall also come = it is come.

seven years: i. e. "[to last] seven years".

2 man of God. See Ap. 49.

801 to 788 Philistines: and she went forth to cry unto the
king °for her house and °for her °land.
4 And the king talked with Gehazi the servant of the [2]man of [2]God, saying, "Tell me, I pray thee, °all the great things that Elisha hath done."
5 And it came to pass, as he was telling the king how he had °restored a dead body to life, that, °behold, the woman, whose son he had restored to life, cried to the king °for her house and °for her land. And Gehazi said, "My lord, O king, this *is* the woman, and this *is* her son, whom Elisha restored to life."
6 And when the king asked the woman, she told him. So the king appointed unto her a certain officer, saying, "Restore all that *was* hers, and all the °fruits of the field since the day that she left the land, even until now."

N (p. 492)
7 And Elisha came to Damascus; and Ben-hadad the king of Syria was sick; and it was told him, saying, "The [2]man of [2]God is come hither."
8 And the king said unto °Hazael, "Take a °present in thine hand, and go, meet the [2]man of [2]God, and enquire of [1]the LORD by him, saying, 'Shall I recover of this disease?'"
9 So Hazael went to meet him, and took a [8]present with him, even of °every good thing of Damascus, forty camels' burden, and came and stood before him, and said, "Thy son Ben-hadad king of Syria hath sent me to thee, saying, 'Shall I recover of this disease?'"
10 And Elisha said unto him, "Go, say unto him, 'Thou °mayest certainly recover:' howbeit [1]the LORD hath shewed me that he shall °surely die."
11 And °he settled his countenance stedfastly, until °he was °ashamed: and the [2]man of [2]God wept.
12 And Hazael said, "Why weepeth my lord?" And he answered, "Because I know °the evil that thou wilt do unto the °children of Israel: their strong holds wilt thou set on fire, and their young men wilt thou slay with the sword, and wilt dash °their children, and rip up their women °with child."
13 And Hazael said, "But what, *is* thy servant °a dog, that he should do this great thing?" And Elisha answered, [1]"The LORD hath shewed me that thou *shalt be* king over Syria."
14 So he departed from Elisha, and came to his master; who said to him, "What said Elisha to thee?" And he answered, "He told me *that* thou shouldest °surely recover."
15 And °it came to pass on the morrow, that he took a thick cloth, and dipped *it* in water, and spread *it* on his face, so that he died: and Hazael reigned in his stead.

F[3] C[1] v (p. 500)
16 And in the fifth year of Joram the son of Ahab king of Israel, °Jehoshaphat *being* then king of Judah, Jehoram the son of Jehoshaphat king of Judah °began to reign.
17 Thirty and two years old was he when he [16]began to reign; and he reigned eight years in Jerusalem.

w
18 And he walked in the way of the kings of Israel, °as did the house of Ahab: for the °daughter of Ahab was his wife: and he °did [12]evil in the sight of [1]the LORD.

for . . . for. Heb. *'el* = "for [to recover]". Not same word as *v.* 5.
land = field: i.e. estate.
4 all the great things. See note on 2. 15.
5 restored a dead body. Cp. 4. 35.
behold. Fig. *Asterismos.* Ap. 6.
for . . . for. Heb. *'al* = for [to call attention to].
6 fruits = produce.
8 Hazael. One of Ben-hadad's servants.
present. It does not say that Elisha accepted it.
9 every good = every kind of. Fig. *Synecdoche* (of Genus). Ap. 6.
10 mayest certainly recover, &c. = "so far as recovering goes, thou wilt recover. And [yet] Jehovah hath made me plainly see that he will surely die."
surely die. Fig. *Polyptōton* (Ap. 6). See notes on Gen. 2. 17 and 26. 28.
11 he: i.e. Hazael.
ashamed. The thought of murder came into his mind.
12 the evil. Described in 10. 32; 12. 17; 13. 3, 22. Hos. 10. 14. Amos 1. 3, 4. Heb. *rā'a'.* Ap. 44. viii.
children = sons.
their children = little ones. Heb. *'ūl.*
with child. Heb. *hārāh.*
13 a dog. Cp. 1 Sam. 17. 43; 24. 14. 2 Sam. 9. 8.
14 surely recover. See note on *v.* 10. A false report.
15 it came to pass. The inscriptions of Shalmanezer II agree with this. The name of Jehu appears on them with Hazael's.

8. 16—9. 29 (F[3], p. 446). JUDAH.
(Division.)

F[3] | C[1] | 8. 16-24. Jehoram.
| C[2] | 8. 25—9. 24. Ahaziah.

16-24 (C[1], above). JEHORAM.
(Introversion.)

C[1] | v | 16, 17. Introduction.
| w | 18, 19. Evil-doing. Personal.
| *w* | 20-22. Evil events. Political.
| *v* | 23, 24. Conclusion.

16 Jehoshaphat being then king. Jehoram associated with him in Joram's fifth year, and reigned solely in Joram's sixth year. Cp. 9. 29. Joram (of Ahab) began in Jehoshaphat's eighteenth year (2 Kings 3. 1). His fifth year is therefore Jehoshaphat's twenty-third year, when Jehoram is associated with him as king, in the third year before his death. See Ap. 50. V, p. 58.
16 began to reign: i.e. in consort with his father.
18 as = according as.
daughter of Ahab. Cp. *v.* 26. See Ap. 55.
did evil. Cp. 2 Chron. 21. 2-4.
19 as He promised. Cp. 2 Sam. 7. 13.
light. Cp. 1 Kings 11. 36. See note on Gen. 15. 17. Heb. *nēr.* Found only four times, and always of David (2 Sam. 21. 17. 1 Kings 11. 36. 2 Kings 8. 19. 2 Chron. 21. 7).
and to his children. Many codices, and five early printed editions, read "for his children": i.e. sons.
20 Edom revolted. Cp. 2 Chron. 21. 8 with 1 Kings 22. 47, and see above (3. 9).

19 Yet [1]the LORD would not destroy Judah for David His servant's sake, °as He promised him to give him alway a °light, °*and* °to his °children.

20 In his days °Edom revolted from under the hand of Judah, and made a king over themselves. *w*
21 So Joram went over to Zair, and all the chariots with him: and he rose by night, and smote the Edomites which compassed him

about, and the captains of the chariots: and °the people fled into their tents.

22 °Yet Edom revolted from under the hand of Judah unto °this day. °Then Libnah revolted at the same time.

v (p. 500) 23 And °the rest of the acts of °Joram, and all that he did, °*are* they not written in the book of the chronicles of the kings of Judah?

24 And Joram °slept with his fathers, and was buried with his fathers in the city of David: and °Ahaziah his son reigned in his stead.

C² x (p. 501) 789 to 788 25 In the twelfth year of Joram the son of Ahab king of Israel did Ahaziah the son of Jehoram king of Judah begin to reign.

26 °Two and twenty years old *was* °Ahaziah when he began to reign; and he reigned one year in Jerusalem. And his mother's name *was* Athaliah, the °daughter of Omri king of Israel.

27 And he walked in the way of the house of Ahab, and did [12] evil in the sight of [1] the LORD, as *did* the house of Ahab: for he *was* the son in law of the house of Ahab.

y z 28 And °he went with Joram the son of Ahab to the war against Hazael king of Syria in °Ramoth-gilead; and the Syrians wounded Joram.

29 And king Joram went back to be healed in Jezreel of the wounds which the Syrians had given him at °Ramah, when he fought against Hazael king of Syria. And Ahaziah the son of Jehoram king of Judah went down to see Joram the son of Ahab in Jezreel, because he was sick.

a **9** And Elisha the prophet called one of the °children of the prophets, and said unto him, "Gird up thy loins, and take this °box of °oil in thine hand, and go to °Ramoth-gilead:

2 And when thou comest thither, look out there °Jehu the son of Jehoshaphat the son of Nimshi, and go in, and make him arise up from among his brethren, and carry him to an inner chamber;

3 Then take the [1] box of oil, and pour *it* on his head, and say, 'Thus saith °the LORD, "I have anointed thee °king °over Israel."' Then open the door, and flee, and tarry not."

4 So the young man, *even* the young man the prophet, went to Ramoth-gilead.

5 And when he came, °behold, the captains of the host *were* sitting; and he said, "I have an errand to thee, O captain." And Jehu said, "Unto which of all us?" And he said, "To thee, O captain."

6 And °he arose, and went into the house; and °he poured the oil on his head, and said unto him, "Thus saith [3] the LORD °God of Israel, 'I have anointed thee [3] king [3] over the People of [3] the LORD, *even* over Israel.

7 And thou shalt smite the house of Ahab thy master, that I may avenge the blood of My servants the prophets, and the blood of all the servants of [3] the LORD, at the hand of Jezebel.

8 For the whole house of Ahab shall perish: and I will cut off from Ahab °him that pisseth against the wall, and him that is shut up and left in Israel:

9 And I will make the house of Ahab °like the house of Jeroboam the son of Nebat, and like the house of Baasha the son of Ahijah:

10 And the dogs shall eat Jezebel in the portion of Jezreel, and *there shall be* none to bury *her*.'" And he opened the door, and fled.

11 Then Jehu came forth to the servants of his lord: and °*one* said unto him, °"*Is* all well? wherefore came this mad *fellow* to thee?" And he said unto them, °"Ye know the °man, and his communication."

21 the people: i. e. of Judah.

22 Yet Edom, &c. The success of Edom accounted for from the end of *v.* 21, and Gen. 27. 40.

this day. Written therefore before the captivity of Judah.

Then Libnah revolted. Cp. 2 Chron. 21. 10. Libnah was a city of the priests (Josh. 21. 13), and Jehoram with his wife and sons had "broken up" the Temple worship (2 Chron. 24. 7). The *priests* therefore, headed by Jehoiada (2 Chron. 23. 1), led this revolt, and were afterwards active in repairing the house of the Lord (2 Chron. 24. 1-14).

23 the rest. Cp. 2 Chron. 21.

Joram = Jehoram.

are they not . . . ? Fig. *Erotēsis*. Ap. 6.

24 slept with his fathers. See note on Deut. 31. 16.

Ahaziah his son: i. e. his youngest son; all the rest being slain. See 2 Chron. 21. 17; 22. 1; and Ap. 55.

8. 25—9. 29 (C², p. 500). AHAZIAH.

(*Introversion and Alternation.*)

C² | x | 8. 25-27. Introduction.
  y | z | 8. 28, 29. Joram, Ramoth-gilead, and Hazael.
    a | 9. 1-14-. Conspiracy of Jehu.
  y | *z* | 9. -14, 15-. Joram, Ramoth-gilead, and Hazael.
    a | 9. -15-26. Conspiracy of Jehu.
  x | 9. 27-29. Conclusion.

26 Two and twenty years. See note on 2 Chron. 22. 2.

Ahaziah. Note that Ahaziah, Joash, and Amaziah, omitted in Matt. 1. 8, all died violent deaths (9. 27; 12. 20; 14. 19).

daughter. Put by Fig. *Synecdoche* (of Genus), Ap. 6, for grand-daughter; and even for successors not in descent by blood.

28 he went with Joram. His uncle.

Ramoth-gilead. It was then in the hands of Israel, but threatened by Syria. Cp. 9. 14.

29 Ramah = Ramoth-gilead.

9. 1 children = sons.

box of oil = oil flask.

oil. For its use in consecration see 1 Sam. 10. 1; 16. 13.

Ramoth-gilead. Israelite army on guard here. Cp. *v.* 14.

2 Jehu the son of Jehoshaphat. In the Assyrian inscriptions he is called the son of Omri.

3 the LORD. Heb. Jehovah. Ap. 4. II.

king = to be king. **over**, or unto.

5 behold. Fig. *Asterismos*. Ap. 6.

6 he arose: i. e. Jehu arose.

he poured: i. e. the prophet poured.

God. Heb. Elohim. Ap. 4. I.

8 him that, &c. = every male.

9 like the house of Jeroboam, &c. Both these houses had been exterminated (1 Kings 15. 29; 16. 11).

11 one said. A special various reading called *Sevîr* (Ap. 34), some codices, with two early printed editions, Sept., Syr., and Vulg., read "they said".

Is all well? Heb. Is it peace?

Ye know, &c. = Why, ye are in the secret, or ye know all about the man.

man. Heb. *'ish*. Ap. 14. II.

789 to 788 12 And they said, "*It is* false; tell us now."
And he said, "Thus and thus spake he to me,
saying, 'Thus saith [3]the LORD, 'I have anointed
thee [3]king [3]over Israel.'"'"

13 Then they hasted, and took [11]every man
his garment, and put *it* under him on the top
of the °stairs, and blew with trumpets, saying,
"Jehu °is king."

14 So Jehu the son of Jehoshaphat the son of
Nimshi conspired against Joram.

y z (Now Joram °had kept Ramoth-gilead, he and
(p. 501) all Israel, because of Hazael king of Syria.

15 But king Joram °was returned to be healed
in Jezreel of the wounds which the Syrians had
given him, when he fought with Hazael king of
Syria.)

a And Jehu said, "If it be your °minds, *then* let
none go forth *nor* escape out of the city to go
to tell *it* in Jezreel."

16 So Jehu rode in a chariot, and went to
Jezreel; for Joram lay there. And Ahaziah
king of Judah was come down to see Joram.

17 And there stood a watchman on the tower
in Jezreel, and he spied the company of Jehu
as he came, and said, "I see a company."
And Joram said, "Take °an horseman, and
send to meet them, and let him say, '*Is it*
peace?'"

18 So there went one on horseback to meet
him, and said, "Thus saith the king, '*Is it*
peace?'" And Jehu said, °"What hast thou
to do with peace? turn thee behind me." And
the watchman told, saying, "The messenger
came to them, but he cometh not again."

19 Then he sent out a second on horseback,
which came to them, and said, "Thus saith
the king, '*Is it* peace?'" And Jehu answered,
[18]"What hast thou to do with peace? turn
thee behind me."

20 And the watchman told, saying, "He came
even unto them, and cometh not again: and
the driving *is* like the driving of Jehu the son
of Nimshi; for he driveth furiously."

21 And Joram said, "Make ready." And his
chariot was made ready. And Joram king of
Israel and Ahaziah king of Judah went out,
each in his chariot, and they went out against
Jehu, and met him in the portion of Naboth
the Jezreelite.

22 And it came to pass, when Joram saw
Jehu, that he said, "*Is it* peace, Jehu?" And
he answered, [18]"What peace, so long as the
°whoredoms of thy mother Jezebel and her
°witchcrafts *are so* many?"

23 And Joram °turned his hands, and fled,
and said to Ahaziah, "*There is* treachery, O
Ahaziah."

24 And Jehu drew a bow with his full strength,
and smote Jehoram °between his arms, and the
arrow went out at his heart, and he sunk down
in his chariot.

25 Then said *Jehu* to Bidkar his captain,
"Take up, *and* cast him in the portion of the
field of Naboth the Jezreelite: for remember
how that, when I and thou rode together after
Ahab his father, [3]the LORD °laid this °burden
upon him;

26 'Surely I have seen yesterday the blood of
Naboth, and °the blood of his sons,' °saith [3]the
LORD; 'and I will requite thee in this °plat,'
°saith [3]the LORD. Now therefore take *and* cast
him into the plat *of ground*, according to the
word of [3]the LORD."

27 But when Ahaziah the king of Judah saw x
this, he fled by the way of the garden house.
And Jehu followed after him, and said, "Smite
him also in the chariot." °*And they did so* at
the going up to Gur, which *is* by Ibleam. And
he fled to Megiddo, and died there.

28 And his servants carried him in a chariot
°to Jerusalem, and buried him in his sepulchre
with his fathers in the city of David.

29 And in the eleventh year of Joram the 789
son of Ahab began Ahaziah to reign over
Judah.

30 And when Jehu was come to Jezreel, E[4] D F[1]
Jezebel °heard *of it;* and she painted her °face, (p. 502)
and °tired her head, and looked out at °a
window.

---

13 stairs = steps. Acts 21. 35, 40.
is king = reigneth.
14 had kept = had been keeping.
15 was returned. Cp. 8. 29.
minds = souls. Heb. *nephesh.* Ap. 13. The parenthesis in *vv.* 14, 15 is so placed by the Structure. See above.
17 an horseman, or a charioteer.
18 What . . . ? Fig. *Anteisagogē* (Ap. 6).
22 whoredoms = idolatry. } Joined together. Cp.
witchcrafts = spiritism. } Num. 24. 1; 25. 1; 31. 16.
23 turned his hands: i. e. to wheel his chariot round.
24 between his arms: i. e. between his shoulders.
25 laid, &c. Cp. 1 Kings 21. 29.
burden = a prophetic pronouncement of doom. Cp. Isa. 13. 1; 15. 1; 17. 1. Nah. 1. 1. Hab. 1. 1.
26 the blood of his sons. Additional information here given to that in 1 Kings 21. 13.
saith the LORD = [is] Jehovah's oracle.
plat = portion. Cp. *v.* 21.
27 And they did so. Supply Fig. *Ellipsis* (Ap. 6) thus: "and they smote him".
28 to Jerusalem. Sept. reads "and brought him to Jerusalem".

9. 30—10. 36 (E[4], p. 446). JEHU.
(*Alternation.*)

E[4] | D | 9. 30—10. 28. Events. Public.
| E | 10. 29-31. Personal character.
| *D* | 10. 32, 33. Events. Political.
| *E* | 10. 34-36. Personal.

9. 30—10. 28 (D, above). EVENTS. PUBLIC.
(*Enumeration.*)

D | F[1] | 9. 30-37. End of Jezebel.
| F[2] | 10. 1-11. End of Ahab's house.
| F[3] | 10. 12-14. End of Ahaziah's brethren.
| F[4] | 10. 15-17. End of Ahab's seed in Samaria.
| F[5] | 10. 18-28. End of Baal-worship.

9. 30-37 (F[1], above). END OF JEZEBEL.
(*Introversion.*)

F[1] | b | 30-32. Exclamation of Jezebel.
| c | 33. Jezebel's death.
| *c* | 34, 35. Jezebel's carcase.
| *b* | 36, 37. Exclamation of Jehu.

30 heard of it: i.e. of the murder of her grandson.
face = eyebrows and eyelids.
tired = adorned.
a window = the lattice.

788 31 And as Jehu entered in at the gate, she said, °"*Had* Zimri peace, who slew his °master?"

32 And he lifted up his face to the window, and said, "Who *is* on my side? who?" And there looked out to him two *or* three eunuchs.

c (p. 502) 33 And he said, "Throw her down." So they threw her down: and *some* of her blood was sprinkled on the wall, and on the horses: and he trode her under foot.

c 34 And when he was come in, he did eat and drink, and said, "Go, see now this cursed *woman*, and bury her: for she *is* °a king's daughter."

35 And they went to bury her: but they found no more of her than the skull, and the feet, and the palms of *her* hands.

b 36 Wherefore they came again, and told him. And he said, "This *is* the word of [3]the LORD, which °He spake by His servant Elijah the Tishbite, saying, 'In the portion of Jezreel shall dogs eat the flesh of Jezebel:

37 And the carcase of Jezebel shall be as dung upon the face of the °field in the portion of Jezreel; °*so* that they shall not say, 'This *is* Jezebel.'"

F2 **10** And Ahab had seventy °sons in Samaria. And Jehu wrote letters, and sent to Samaria, °unto the °rulers °of Jezreel, to the elders, and to them that brought up Ahab's *children*, saying,

2 "Now as soon as this letter cometh to you, seeing your master's sons *are* with you, and *there are* with you chariots and horses, a fenced city also, and armour;

3 Look even out the best and meetest of your master's sons, and set *him* on his father's throne, and fight for your master's house."

4 But they were exceedingly afraid, and said, °"Behold, two kings stood not before him: how then shall we stand?"

5 And he that *was* over the house, and he that *was* over the city, the elders also, and the bringers up *of the children*, sent to Jehu, saying, "We *are* thy servants, and will do all that thou shalt bid us; we will not make any king: do thou *that which is* good in thine eyes."

6 Then he wrote a letter the second time to them, saying, "If ye *be* °mine, and *if* ye will hearken unto my voice, take ye the heads of °the men [2]your master's sons, and come to me to Jezreel by to morrow this time." Now the king's sons, *being* seventy °persons, *were* with the great °men of the city, which brought them up.

7 And it came to pass, when the letter came to them, that they took the king's sons, and slew seventy [6]persons, and put their heads in °baskets, and sent him *them* to Jezreel.

8 And there came a messenger, and told him, saying, "They have brought the heads of the king's sons." And he said, "Lay ye them in two heaps at the entering in of the gate until the morning."

9 And it came to pass in the morning, that he went out, and stood, and said to all the people, °"Ye *be* righteous: behold, I conspired against my master, and slew him: but who slew all these?

10 Know now that there shall fall unto the earth nothing of °the word of °the LORD, which °the LORD spake concerning the house of Ahab: for °the LORD hath done *that* which He spake °by His servant Elijah."

11 So Jehu slew all that remained of the house of Ahab in Jezreel, and all his great [6]men, and his °kinsfolks, and his priests, until he left him none remaining.

12 And he arose and departed, and came to Samaria. *And* as he *was* at the shearing house in the way, F3

13 Jehu met with the °brethren of Ahaziah king of Judah, and said, "Who *are* ye?" And they answered, "We *are* the brethren of Ahaziah; and we go down to salute the °children of °the king and the °children of °the queen."

14 And he said, "Take them alive." And they took them alive, and slew them at the pit of the shearing house, *even* two and forty [6]men; neither left he any of them.

15 And when he was departed thence, he lighted on °Jehonadab the son of Rechab *coming* to meet him: and he saluted him, and said to him, "Is thine heart right, °as my heart *is* with thy heart?" And Jehonadab answered, F4

---

31 Had Zimri peace . . . ? Fig. *Erotēsis*. Ap. 6. See 1 Kings 16. 9-20. Suggesting the wisdom of coming to terms with her. **master** = lord.

34 a king's daughter. A daughter of Eth-baal, king of Zidon (1 Kings 16. 31).

36 He spake. Cp. 1 Kings 21. 23.

37 field. Some codices, with Sept. and Vulg., read "ground".

so that, &c. = [something] of which they shall not say, &c.

10. 1 sons. Put by Fig. *Synecdoche* (of Part), Ap. 6, for grandsons and great-grandsons.

unto. Some codices, with Sept., Syr., and Vulg., read "and unto". **rulers** = elders.

of Jezreel. Doubtless they had fled to Samaria, being in great fear (*v.* 4) from what Jehu had done in Jezreel.

4 Behold. Fig. *Asterismos*. Ap. 6.

6 mine = for me.

the men. Heb. *'ĕnōsh*. Ap. 14. III.

persons. Heb. *'ish*. Ap. 14. II.

men. Heb. *'ish*. Ap. 14. II.

7 baskets = the baskets. Heb. *dūd*, for carrying fruit. Still used for this purpose. Not *ṣal* (bread-basket), which Gideon (Judg. 6. 19), and Pharaoh's baker (Gen. 40. 17) used.

9 Ye be righteous. Said by way of flattery and to allay disaffection.

10 the word of the LORD = the word of Jehovah. Cp. 1 Kings 21. 19-29.

the LORD. Heb. Jehovah. Ap. 4. II.

by = by the hand of.

11 kinsfolks = acquaintance.

13 brethren. Put by Fig. *Synecdoche* (of the Part) for near relatives. Cp. 2 Chron. 22. 8, where we have "sons of the brethren".

children = sons. **the king** = Joram.

the queen = Jezebel, the queen-mother.

15 Jehonadab. He was a Kenite (1 Chron. 2. 55), descendants of the father-in-law of Moses (Num. 10. 29. Judg. 1. 16; 4. 11. 1 Sam. 15. 6). See Jer. 35.

as = according as.

"It is." "If it be, °give *me* thine hand." And he gave *him* his hand; and he took him up to him into the chariot.

16 And he said, "Come with me, and °see my °zeal for [10]the LORD." So they made him ride in his chariot.

17 And when he came to Samaria, he slew all that remained unto Ahab in Samaria, till he had destroyed him, according to the saying of [10]the LORD, which He spake to Elijah.

F[5] d (p. 504) 18 And Jehu gathered all the People together, and said unto them, "Ahab served Baal a little; *but* Jehu shall serve him much.

19 Now therefore call unto me all the prophets of Baal, all his servants, and all his priests; let none be wanting: for I have a great sacrifice *to do* to Baal; whosoever shall be wanting, he shall not live." But Jehu did *it* in subtilty, to the intent that he might destroy the °worshippers of Baal.

e 20 And Jehu said, °"Proclaim a solemn assembly for Baal." And they proclaimed *it*.

21 And Jehu sent through all Israel: and all the [19]worshippers of Baal came, so that there was not a °man left that came not. And they came into the house of Baal; and the house of Baal was °full from one end to another.

f 22 And he said unto him that *was* over the vestry, "Bring forth vestments for all the [19]worshippers of Baal." And he brought them forth vestments.

g 23 And Jehu went, and Jehonadab the son of Rechab, into the house of Baal, and said unto the worshippers of Baal, "Search, and look that there be here with you none of the servants of [10]the LORD, but the worshippers of Baal only."

f 24 And when they went in to °offer sacrifices and burnt offerings, Jehu appointed fourscore [21]men without, and said, "*If* any of [6]the men whom I have brought into your hands escape, *he that letteth him go*, his °life *shall be* for the °life of him."

e 25 And it came to pass, as soon as he had made an end of [24]offering the burnt offering, that Jehu said to the guard and to the captains, "Go in, *and* slay them; let none come forth." And they smote them with the edge of the sword; and the guard and the captains cast *them* out, and went to °the city of the house of Baal.

d 26 And they brought forth the °images out of the house of Baal, and burned them.

27 And they brake down the image of Baal, and brake down the house of Baal, and made it a °draught house unto this day.

28 Thus Jehu destroyed Baal out of Israel.

E (p. 502) 29 Howbeit *from* the °sins of Jeroboam the son of Nebat, who °made Israel to sin, Jehu departed not from after them, °*to wit*, the golden calves that *were* in Beth-el, and that *were* °in Dan.

30 And [10]the LORD said unto Jehu, "Because thou hast done well in executing *that which is* right in Mine eyes, *and* hast done unto the house of Ahab according to all that *was* in Mine heart, thy [13]children of the °fourth *generation* shall sit on the throne of Israel."

31 But Jehu took no heed to walk in the law of [10]the LORD °God of Israel with all his heart: for he departed not from °the [29]sins of Jeroboam, which [29]made Israel to sin.

32 In those days [10]the LORD began °to cut Israel short: and Hazael smote them in all the °coasts of Israel; *D*

33 From Jordan °eastward, all the land of Gilead, the Gadites, and the Reubenites, and the Manassites, from Aroer, which *is* by the river Arnon, even Gilead and Bashan.

34 Now °the rest of the acts of Jehu, and all that he did, and all his might, °*are* they not written in the book of the chronicles of the kings of Israel? *E*

35 And Jehu °slept with his fathers: and they buried him in Samaria. And Jehoahaz his son reigned in his stead.

36 And the time that Jehu reigned over Israel in Samaria *was* twenty and eight years.

---

give me thine hand. Cp. the pledge (Ezra 10. 19. Ezek. 17. 18).

16 see = be eyewitnesses of.

zeal for the LORD. Not pure. See *vv.* 29-31.

10. 18-28 (F[5], p. 502). END OF BAAL-WORSHIP. (*Introversion.*)

F[5] | d | 18, 19. Jehu's purpose formed.
  e | 20, 21. Baal-worshippers. Assembled.
   f | 22. Vestments brought out.
    g | 23. Search made.
   f | 24. Offerings brought in.
  e | 25. Baal-worshippers. Slain.
 d | 26-28. Jehu's purpose effected.

19 worshippers = servants.

20 Proclaim = Sanctify, Hallow, or Solemnise.

21 man. Heb. *'īsh.* Ap. 14. II.

full, &c. = so full [that they stood] mouth to mouth. *Ellipsis* to be thus supplied, as in A.V. margin.

24 offer = prepare. See Ap. 43. I. iii.

life = soul. Heb. *nephesh.* Ap. 13.

25 the city = Heb. *'īr*, the innermost or most inaccessible part, whether of a city (= the citadel) or a house (as here).

26 images, or statues. **them** = each of them.

27 draught house = dunghill, middens, *latrinæ.*

29 sins. Heb. *chāṭā'.* Ap. 44. i.

made Israel to sin. See note on 1 Kings 14. 16.

to wit = namely.

in Dan. See 1 Kings 12. 29, 30, and cp. Gen. 49. 17.

30 fourth generation. See 15. 12. These were Jehoahaz, Joash, Jeroboam II, and Zachariah. Jehu's dynasty was the longest in all Israel.

31 God. Heb. Elohim. Ap. 4. I.

the sins. Heb. *chāṭā'.* Ap. 44. i. Some codices read "all the sins".

32 to cut Israel short: or, to cut off the outskirts, or make inroads into.

coasts = borders.

33 eastward = toward the sun-rising.

34 the rest. An Assyrian inscription (now in the British Museum) records that Jehu paid tribute to Shalmaneser II, who in 842 B.C. defeated Hazael, king of Syria. Jehu bought Shalmaneser II off by giving him, as tribute, bars of silver and gold; a golden ladle and golden goblets and pitchers were among his gifts.

are they not . . . ? Fig. *Erotēsis.* Ap. 6.

35 slept with his fathers. See note on Deut. 31. 16.

F[1] G[1] h (p. 505) 788 **11** And when °Athaliah the mother of Ahaziah saw that her son was dead, °she arose and °destroyed all the seed royal.

i 2 But °Jehosheba, the daughter of king Joram, sister of Ahaziah, took Joash the son of Ahaziah, and stole him °from among the king's sons *which were* slain; and they hid him, *even* him and his nurse, in the bedchamber from Athaliah, so that he was not slain.

788 3 And he was with her °hid in the house of °the LORD °six years.

k And Athaliah did reign over the land.

l 782 4 And the seventh year °Jehoiada sent and fetched the °rulers over hundreds, with the captains and the guard, and brought them to him into the house of [3]the LORD, and made a covenant with them, and took an oath of them in the house of [3]the LORD, and shewed them °the king's son.

5 And he commanded them, saying, "This *is* the thing that ye shall do; A third part of you °that enter in on the sabbath shall even be keepers of the watch of the king's house;

6 And a third part °*shall be* at the gate of Sur; and a third part at the gate behind the guard: so shall ye keep the watch of the house, that it be not broken down.

7 And two parts of all you that go forth on the sabbath, even they shall keep the watch of the house of [3]the LORD about the king.

8 And ye shall compass the king round about, every °man with his weapons in his hand: and he that cometh within the ranges, let him be slain: and be ye with the king as he goeth out and as he cometh in."

9 And the captains over the hundreds did according to all *things* that Jehoiada the priest commanded: and they took [8]every man his °men that were to come in on the sabbath, with them that should go out on the sabbath, and came to Jehoiada the priest.

10 And to the captains over hundreds did the priest give °king David's spears and shields, that *were* in the temple of [3]the LORD.

11 And the guard stood, [8]every man with his weapons in his hand, round about the king, from the right corner of the temple to the left corner of the temple, *along* by the altar and the temple.

12 And he brought forth the king's son, and put the crown upon him, and °*gave him* the °testimony; and they made him king, and anointed him; and they clapped their hands, and said, "God save the king."

11. 1–12. 21 (F[4], p. 446). JUDAH. (*Division.*)

F[4] | G[1] | 11. 1–16. Athaliah.
| G[2] | 11. 17—12. 21. Joash.

11. 1–16 (G[1], above). ATHALIAH. (*Introversion.*)

G[1] | h | 1. The slaying of the seed-royal.
| i | 2, 3–. Joash. Rescue of.
| k | –3. Athaliah. Reign.
| l | 4–12. Manifestation of Joash.
| *k* | 13, 14. Athaliah. Alarm.
| *i* | 15. Joash. Capture of the murderess.
| *h* | 16. The slaying of the usurper.

1 Athaliah. For genealogy see Ap. 55.
she arose, &c. Another of the ten occasions of deaths being caused by a woman. See note on Judg. 4. 21.
destroyed: or thought she did. They were left for dead.
2 Jehosheba. She was the wife of Jehoiada, the high priest (2 Chron. 22. 11); Jehoiada being brother-in-law to Ahaziah (2 Chron. 22. 11), and therefore uncle to Joash.
from among. Expressive words, pointing to our Joash, raised from the dead and now hidden in the house of God on high; and we with Him (Col. 3. 1-3).
3 hid in the house of the LORD. This was the safest possible place: for it had been broken up, and everything removed to the house of Baal (2 Chron. 24. 7) The Temple courts were deserted. Hence, Jehoiada and the priests were plotting for the restoration of the rightful heir. See note on Libnah, 8. 22.
the LORD. Heb. Jehovah. Ap. 4.
six years. The number of man's defiance and disorder. See Ap. 10.
4 Jehoiada. See note on Jehosheba, *v.* 2.
rulers. For their names see 2 Chron. 23. 1.
the king's son. Cp. 2 Chron. 23. 3.
5 that enter in = must come inside.
shall even be = and must be.
6 shall be = must be.
8 man. Heb. *'ish.* Ap. 14. II.
9 men. Heb. *'ĕnōsh.* Ap. 14. III.
10 king David's. All prepared by him against such a day as this (2 Sam. 8. 7).
12 gave him. The Fig. *Zeugma* (Ap. 6), by which the second verb has to be thus supplied.
testimony. See note on Ex. 17. 14, and Ap. 47.
14 behold. Fig. *Asterismos.* Ap. 6.
a pillar = the pillar.
Treason, Treason. Fig. *Epizeuxis* (Ap. 6), for great emphasis.
16 laid hands on her = made way for her.

11. 17—12. 21 (G[2], above). JOASH. (*Introversion.*)

G[2] | m | 11. 17–21. Conspiracy of Athaliah. Defeated.
| n | 12. 1. Joash. Accession.
| o | p[1] | 12. 2, 3. Personal. Well-doing.
| | p[2] | 12. 4–16. Ecclesiastical. Reform.
| | p[3] | 12. 17, 18. Political. Invasion.
| *n* | 12. 19. Joash. Record.
| *m* | 12. 20, 21. Conspiracy of servants. Successful.

k 13 And when Athaliah heard the noise of the guard *and* of the People, she came to the People into the temple of [3]the LORD.

14 And when she looked, °behold, the king stood by °a pillar, as the manner *was,* and the princes and the trumpeters by the king, and all the People of the land rejoiced, and blew with trumpets: and Athaliah rent her clothes, and cried, °"Treason, Treason."

i 15 But Jehoiada the priest commanded the captains of the hundreds, the officers of the host, and said unto them, "Have her forth without the ranges: and him that followeth her kill with the sword." For the priest had said, "Let her not be slain in the house of [3]the LORD."

16 And they °laid hands on her; and she went by the way by the which the horses came into the king's house: and there was she slain. *h*

17 And Jehoiada made a covenant between [3]the LORD and the king and the People, that they should be [3]the LORD'S People; between the king also and the People. G[2] m

18 And all the People of the land went into

782 the °house of Baal, and brake it down; his
altars and his images brake they in pieces
thoroughly, and slew Mattan the priest of
Baal before the altars. And the priest appointed officers over the house of [3]the LORD.
19 And he took the rulers over hundreds, and
the captains, and the guard, and all the People
of the land; and they brought down the king
from the house of [3]the LORD, and came by the
way of the gate of the guard to the king's
house. And he sat on the throne of the kings.
20 And all the People of the °land rejoiced,
and the °city was in quiet: and they slew
Athaliah with the sword °*beside* the king's
house.
21 Seven years old *was* Jehoash when he
began to reign.

n **12** In the seventh year of Jehu Jehoash be-
(p. 505) gan to reign; and forty years reigned
782–742 he in Jerusalem. And his mother's name *was*
Zibiah of Beer-sheba.
o p[1] 2 And Jehoash did *that which was* right in
the sight of °the LORD °all his days wherein
°Jehoiada the priest instructed him.
3 But the high places were not taken away:
the People still sacrificed and burnt incense in
°the high places.
p[2] 4 And Jehoash said to °the priests, "All the
(p. 506) money of the °dedicated things that is brought
into the house of [2]the LORD, *even* the money
of °every one that passeth °*the account*, the
money °that every man is set at, *and* all the
money that cometh into °any man's heart to
bring into the house of [2]the LORD,
5 Let [4]the priests take *it* to them, [4]every
man of his acquaintance: and let them repair
the breaches of the house, wheresoever any
breach shall be found."
r 6 But it was *so, that* in the three and twentieth year of king Jehoash the priests had not
repaired the breaches of the house.
q 7 Then king Jehoash called for Jehoiada the
priest, and the *other* priests, and said unto
them, "Why repair ye not the breaches of the
house? now therefore receive no *more* money
of your acquaintance, but deliver it for the
breaches of the house."
8 And [4]the priests °consented to receive no
more money of the people, neither to repair the
breaches of the house.
9 But Jehoiada the priest took a chest, and
°bored a hole in the lid of it, and set it beside
the altar, on the right side as [4]one cometh into
the house of [2]the LORD: and [4]the priests that
kept the door put therein all the money *that*
was brought into the house of [2]the LORD.
10 And it was *so*, when they saw that *there*
was much money in the chest, that the king's
scribe and the high priest came up, and they
put up in bags, and °told the money that was
found in the house of [2]the LORD.
r 11 And they gave the money, °being told, into the hands of them that did the work, that
had the oversight of the house of [2]the LORD:
and they laid it out to the carpenters and
builders, that wrought upon the house of [2]the
LORD,

18 house of Baal. Built by Jehoram and Athaliah (2 Chron. 24. 7).

20 land rejoiced. } When? When the usurper had
city was in quiet. } been cast out, and slain.
So shall it be when judgment shall be executed on the "prince" and "god" of this world (Rev. 19. 1, 2, 7).

beside the king's house = in the king's house.

12. 2 the LORD. Heb. Jehovah. Ap. 4.

all his days: i.e. all the days of Jehoiada. Cp. 2 Chron. 24. 14–18.

Jehoiada. His uncle. See note on Jehosheba, 11. 2.

3 the high places. They were first abolished by Hezekiah, and then (after their revival by Manasseh) by Josiah. Note the Fig. *Epanadiplosis*. Ap. 6.

12. 4–16 (p[2], p. 505). ECCLESIASTICAL REFORM. (*Alternation.*)

p[2] | q | 4, 5. Money. Command.
  r | 6. Neglect.
 q | 7–10. Money. Obedience.
  r | 11–16. Attention.

4 the priests. See note on Libnah, 8. 22.

dedicated = sacred. See note on Ex. 3. 5.

every one. Heb. *'îsh.* Ap. 14. II.

the account. These italics are not needed. Heb. *'ābar* = to pass over.

that every man, &c. Heb. "of the souls (= persons. Heb. *nephesh.* Ap. 13) of his [the priest's] valuation" (Lev. 27. 2–8). any man's. Heb. *'îsh.* Ap. 14.

8 consented = acquiesced. Heb. *'ôth*, a rare word, occurring only here and Gen. 34. 15, 22, 23.

9 bored a hole. There were two chests made on account of the slackness of the priests. The first by Jehoiada named here (in Kings), beside the altar of burnt-offering in the court. The other at the king's commandment without a hole bored (in 2 Chron. 24. 8, 14), outside "at the gate". In the former there was not room enough for the vessels of the house; in the latter there was abundance for all.

10 told = counted.

11 being told = being weighed or balanced.

15 men. Heb. *'ĕnōsh.* Ap. 14. III.

16 trespass. Heb. *'āshāh.* Ap. 44. ii.

sin. Heb. *chātā'.* Ap. 44. i.

17 Gath. One of the five Philistine cities, to reach which Hazael must have passed through Israel. Probably connected with his attacks on Jehu and Jehoahaz (10. 32; 13. 3, 4). to = against.

18 hallowed = set apart. Heb. *kodesh.* See note on Ex. 3. 5.

12 And to masons, and hewers of stone, and
to buy timber and hewed stone to repair the
breaches of the house of [2]the LORD, and for all
that was laid out for the house to repair *it*.
13 Howbeit there were not made for the house
of [2]the LORD bowls of silver, snuffers, basons,
trumpets, any vessels of gold, or vessels of silver, of the money *that was* brought into the
house of [2]the LORD:
14 But they gave that to the workmen, and
repaired therewith the house of [2]the LORD.
15 Moreover they reckoned not with the °men,
into whose hand they delivered the money to be
bestowed on workmen: for they dealt faithfully.
16 The °trespass money and °sin money was
not brought into the house of [2]the LORD: it
was the priests'.

17 Then Hazael king of Syria went up, and p[3]
fought against °Gath, and took it: and Hazael
set his face to go up °to Jerusalem.
18 And Jehoash king of Judah took all the
°hallowed things that Jehoshaphat, and Jeho-

782 ram, and Ahaziah, his fathers, kings of Judah,
had dedicated, and his own °hallowed things,
and all the gold *that was* found in the °treasures
of the house of [2]the LORD, and in the king's
house, and sent *it* to Hazael king of Syria:
and he went away from Jerusalem.

k (p. 505) 19 And °the rest of the acts of Joash, and all
that he did, °*are* they not written in the book of
the chronicles of the kings of Judah?

m 20 And his servants arose, and made a conspiracy, and °slew Joash in the house of °Millo,
which goeth down to Silla.
21 For Jozachar the son of Shimeath, and
Jehozabad the son of Shomer, his servants,
742 smote him, and he died; and they buried him
with his fathers in the city of David: and Amaziah his son reigned in his stead.

E[5] H[1] s (p. 506) 759-742 13 IN the °three and twentieth year of Jo-
ash the son of Ahaziah king of Judah
Jehoahaz the son of Jehu began to reign over
Israel in Samaria, *and reigned* seventeen years.

t 2 And he did *that which was* °evil in the sight
of °the LORD, and followed the °sins of Jeroboam the son of Nebat, which °made Israel to
sin; he departed not therefrom.

t 3 And the anger of [2]the LORD was kindled
against Israel, and He delivered them into the
hand of Hazael king of Syria, and into the
hand of Ben-hadad the son of Hazael, °all *their*
days.
4 And Jehoahaz besought [2]the LORD, and
[2]the LORD hearkened unto him: for He saw
the oppression of Israel, because the king of
Syria oppressed them.
5 (°And [2]the LORD gave Israel °a saviour,
so that they went out from under the hand of
the Syrians: and the °children of Israel dwelt
in their tents, as beforetime.
6 Nevertheless they departed not from the
[2]sins °of the house of Jeroboam, who [2]made
Israel [2]sin, *but* °walked °therein: and there
°remained °the grove also in Samaria.)
7 Neither did He leave of the People to Jehoahaz but fifty horsemen, and ten chariots, and
ten thousand footmen; for the king of Syria
had destroyed them, and had made them °like
the dust by threshing.

s 8 Now the rest of the acts of Jehoahaz, and
all that he did, and his might, °*are* they not
written in the book of the chronicles of the
kings of Israel?
9 And Jehoahaz °slept with his fathers; and
they buried him in Samaria: and °Joash his
son reigned °in his stead.

H[2] u 745 to 729 10 In the °thirty and seventh year of Joash
king of Judah began Jehoash the son of Jehoa-
haz to reign °over Israel in Samaria, *and
reigned* sixteen years.

v 11 And he did *that which was* [2]evil in the
sight of [2]the LORD; he departed not from all
the [2]sins of Jeroboam the son of Nebat, who
[2]made Israel sin: *but* he [6]walked [6]therein.

u 12 And the rest of the acts of Joash, and all
that he did, and his might wherewith he fought
against Amaziah king of Judah, [8]*are* they not
written in the book of the chronicles of the
kings of Israel?
13 And Joash [9]slept with his fathers; and
°Jeroboam sat upon his throne: and Joash was
buried in Samaria with the kings of Israel.

14 Now Elisha was fallen °sick of his sick- v w[1]
ness whereof he died. And Joash the king of

---

treasures = treasuries.

19 the rest of the acts of Joash. His punishment is recorded in Kings; the causes of it are found in Chronicles. See note on "Kings" (p. 446). See the *esoteric* causes in 2 Chron. 24. 25.

are they not . . . ? Fig. *Erotēsis.* Ap. 6.

20 slew Joash. See note on 8. 26.

Millo. See note on 1 Kings 9. 15. "The house" would be in connection with it.

13. 1-25 (E[5], p. 446). ISRAEL. (*Division.*)

E[5] | H[1] | 1-9. Jehoahaz.
  | H[2] | 10-25. Jehoash.

1-9 (H[1], above). JEHOAHAZ. (*Introversion.*)

H[1] | s | 1. Introduction.
  | t | 2. Events. Personal.
  | *t* | 3-7. Events. Political.
  | *s* | 8, 9. Conclusion.

1 three and twentieth year. See note on *v.* 10.

2 evil. Heb. *rā'a'.* Ap. 44. viii.

the LORD. Heb. Jehovah. Ap. 4. II.

sins. Heb. *chāṭā'.* Ap. 44. i.

made Israel to sin. See note on 1 Kings 14. 16.

3 all their days. Supply Fig. *Ellipsis* (Ap. 6), by reading "all [his] days". Cp. *vv.* 22-25.

5 And the LORD = And Jehovah. Note the parenthesis of *vv.* 5 and 6.

a saviour. Some think an angel; some, Elisha; some, a general of Jehoahaz. Cp. *v.* 25; 14. 27.

children = sons.

6 of the house of. Some codices, with Aram. and Syr., omit these words.

walked. Heb. "he [Israel] walked".

therein. Heb. in it: i. e. in Jeroboam's way; but some codices, with Aram., Sept., Syr., and Vulg., read "in them". **remained** = stood.

the grove = the *'Ashērah.* See Ap. 42.

like the dust, &c. A powerful emblem, true to Eastern life.

8 are they not . . . ? Fig. *Erotēsis.* Ap. 6.

9 slept with his fathers. See note on Deut. 31. 16.

Joash, or Jehoash. **in his stead:** i. e. alone.

10-25 (H[2], above). JEHOASH. (*Alternation.*)

H[2] | u | 10. Introduction.
  | v | 11. Events. Personal.
  | *u* | 12, 13. Conclusion.
  | *v* | 14-25. Events. Political.

10 thirty and seventh. Joash (of Israel) became king in the thirty-seventh year of Joash (of Judah). Amaziah, son of Joash (of Judah), became king in the second year of Joash (of Israel), 14. 1. Therefore Amaziah became associate king in the thirty-ninth year of Joash of Judah: i. e. one year before Joash died, for he "reigned forty years in Jerusalem" (2 Chron. 24. 1). The cause of Amaziah's kingship in Joash's lifetime is not named in Kings, but we see it in the "diseases" of 2 Chron. 24. 25.

over: i. e. in consort with his father. Cp. 14. 1.

13 Jeroboam. Usually known as Jeroboam II.

14-25 (*v*, above). EVENTS. POLITICAL. (*Division.*)

v | w[1] | 14-21. Domestic.
  | w[2] | 22-25. Foreign.

14 sick of his sickness. Fig. *Polyptōton.* Ap. 6. Elisha's long ministry of sixty-six years was now drawing to a close, after forty-five years' silence. We hear of no sickness of Elijah.

743 Israel came down unto him, and wept over his
face, and said, "O my father, °my father, °the
chariot of Israel, and the horsemen thereof."
15 And Elisha said unto him, "Take bow
and arrows." And he took unto him bow and
arrows.
16 And he said to the king of Israel, "Put
thine hand upon the bow." And he put his
hand *upon it:* and Elisha put his hands upon
the king's hands.
17 And he said, "Open the window eastward." And he opened *it.* Then Elisha said,
"Shoot." And he shot. And he said, °"The
arrow of ²the LORD'S deliverance, and the
arrow of deliverance from Syria: for thou
shalt smite the Syrians in Aphek, till thou
have consumed *them.*"
18 And he said, "Take the arrows." And
he took *them.* And he said unto the king of
Israel, "Smite upon the ground." And he
smote thrice, and stayed.
19 And the °man of °God was wroth with
him, and said, "Thou shouldest have smitten
five or six times; then hadst thou smitten
Syria till thou hadst consumed *it:* whereas
now thou shalt smite Syria *but* thrice."
20 And Elisha °died, and they buried him.
And the bands of the Moabites invaded the
land at the °coming in of the year.
21 And it came to pass, as °they were burying
a °man, that, °behold, they spied a band *of
men;* and they cast the °man into the sepulchre
of Elisha: and when the °man was let down,
and touched the bones of Elisha, °he revived,
and stood up on his feet.

w^2 (p. 507) 22 But Hazael king of Syria oppressed Israel
all the days of Jehoahaz.
23 °And ²the LORD was gracious unto them,
°and had compassion on them, °and had respect
unto them, because of His covenant with Abraham, Isaac, and Jacob, and would not destroy
them, neither cast He them from His presence
as yet.
24 So Hazael king of Syria died; and °Ben-
hadad his son reigned in his stead.
25 And Jehoash the son of Jehoahaz took
again out of the hand of Ben-hadad the son of
Hazael the cities, which he had taken out of
the hand of Jehoahaz his father °by war.
°Three times did Joash beat him, and recovered the cities of Israel.

F^5 J^1 K (p. 508) 743 to 714 **14** In the °second year of Joash son of
Jehoahaz king of Israel reigned Ama-
ziah the son of Joash king of Judah.
2 He was twenty and five years old when he
began to reign, and reigned twenty and nine
years in Jerusalem. And his mother's name
was Jehoaddan of Jerusalem.

L 3 And he did *that which was* right in the
sight of °the LORD, yet not like David his
father: he did according to all things °as Joash
his father did.
4 Howbeit °the high places were not taken
away: as yet the People did sacrifice and burnt
incense on the high places.

L M^1 5 And it came to pass, as soon as the kingdom
was confirmed in his hand, that he slew his
servants which had slain the king his father.

---

my father. Fig. *Epizeuxis.* Ap. 6.
the chariot of Israel. A memory of 2. 12, wondering whether his end would be like Elijah's.
17 The arrow of the LORD's deliverance. Fig. *Metonymy* (of Subject), Ap. 6. The arrow put for the deliverance Jehovah would give.
19 man of God. See Ap. 49.
God. Heb. Elohim with Art. Ap. 4. I.
20 died. He was called in the days of Ahab (1 Kings 19. 19), and ministered fifty years.
coming in of the year: i. e. the spring. Cp. 2 Sam. 11. 1.
21 they: prob. those who were evading the Moabite marauders.
man. Heb. *'ish.* Ap. 14.
behold. Fig. *Asterismos.* Ap. 6.
he revived = he lived. The sixteenth miracle. See note on 2. 15.
23 And = But.
and had. Note the Fig. *Polysyndeton.* Ap. 6.
24 Ben-hadad. Probably the third of that name. Cp. 1 Kings 15. 18; 20. 1.
25 by war = in the war.
Three times. According to *v.* 18.

14. 1-22 (F^5, p. 446). JUDAH. (*Division.*)

F^5 | J^1 | 1-20. Amaziah.
| J^2 | 21, 22. Uzziah, or Azariah.

1-20 (J^1, above). AMAZIAH. (*Introversion.*)

J^1 | K | 1, 2. Introduction.
| L | 3, 4. Events. Personal.
| *L* | 5-14. Events. Political.
| *K* | 15-20. Conclusion.

1 second year of Joash. According to 13. 10, Joash (king of Israel) began to reign in the thirty-seventh year of Joash (king of Judah). If Amaziah began in the second year of Joash (king of Israel), he would have reigned only thirty-nine years. But he reigned forty (12. 1). All depends on mode of reckoning from Nisan, and counting parts of years for complete years. This would at once explain the difference. See Ap. 50. V, p. 58. Our difficulty, as usual, arises from our ignorance.
3 the LORD. Heb. Jehovah. Ap. 4.
as Joash his father. He began well and ended badly.
4 the high places. See 1 Kings 15. 14.

5-14 (*L*, above). EVENTS. POLITICAL. (*Division.*)

L | M^1 | 5, 6. Domestic.
| M^2 | 7-14. Foreign.

6 children = sons.
written in the book of the law of Moses. See note on Ex. 17. 14, and Ap. 47.
every man. Heb. *'ish.* Ap. 14. II.
sin. Heb. *chāṭā'.* Ap. 44. I.

7-14 (M^2, above). FOREIGN. (*Introversion.*)

M^2 | w | 7. Victory over Edom.
| x | 8. Jehoash. Message to.
| *x* | 9, 10. Jehoash. Reply from.
| *w* | 11-14. Defeat by Israel.

7 He slew. The account in Chronicles supplies additional particulars. See 2 Chron. 25. 5-11.

---

6 But the °children of the murderers he slew
not: according unto that which is °written in the
book of the law of Moses, wherein ³the LORD
commanded, saying, "The fathers shall not be
put to death for the °children, nor the °chil-
dren be put to death for the fathers; but °every
man shall be put to death for his own °sin."
7 He slew of Edom in the valley of salt ten M^2 w
thousand, and took Selah by war, and called
the name of it Joktheel unto this day.

x 8 Then Amaziah sent messengers to Jehoash,
(p. 508) the son of Jehoahaz son of Jehu, king of Israel,
743-714 saying, "Come, let us °look one another in the
face."
x 9 And Jehoash the king of Israel sent to Amaziah king of Judah, saying, °"The thistle that
was in Lebanon °sent to the cedar that *was*
in Lebanon, saying, 'Give thy daughter to my
son to wife:' and there passed by a wild beast
that *was* in Lebanon, and trode down the
thistle.
10 Thou hast indeed smitten Edom, and thine
heart hath lifted thee up: glory *of this*, and
tarry at home: for why shouldest thou meddle
to *thy* hurt, that thou shouldest fall, *even* thou,
and Judah with thee?"
w 11 But Amaziah would not hear. Therefore
Jehoash king of Israel went up; and he and
Amaziah king of Judah [8]looked one another
in the face at °Beth-shemesh, which *belongeth*
to Judah.
12 And Judah was °put to the worse before
Israel; and they fled °every man to their tents.
13 And Jehoash king of Israel took Amaziah
king of Judah, the son of Jehoash the son of
Ahaziah, at Beth-shemesh, and came to Jerusalem, and brake down the wall of Jerusalem
from the gate of Ephraim unto the corner gate,
four hundred °cubits.
14 And he took all the gold and silver, °and
all the vessels that were found in the house of
[3]the LORD, and in the treasures of the king's
house, and °hostages, and returned to Samaria.
K 15 Now the rest of the acts of Jehoash °which
he did, and his might, and how he fought with
Amaziah king of Judah, °*are* they not written
in the book of the chronicles of the kings of
Israel?
16 And Jehoash slept with his fathers, and
was buried in Samaria with the kings of Israel;
and Jeroboam his son reigned in his stead.
17 And Amaziah the son of Joash king of
Judah lived after the death of Jehoash son of
729 Jehoahaz king of Israel °fifteen years.
to 18 And the rest of the acts of Amaziah, *are*
714 they not written in the book of the chronicles of
the kings of Judah?
19 Now they made a conspiracy against him
in Jerusalem: and he fled to °Lachish; but
they sent after him to Lachish, and °slew him
there.
20 And they brought him on horses: and he
was buried at Jerusalem with his fathers in
the city of David.

J^2 y 21 And all the people of Judah took °Aza-
(p. 509) riah, which *was* °sixteen years old, and made
him king instead of his father Amaziah.
z 22 He °built °Elath, and restored it to Judah,
y after that the king °slept with his fathers.
E^6 a 23 In the fifteenth year of Amaziah the son
728 of Joash king of Judah Jeroboam the son of
to Joash king °of Israel began to reign in Samaria,
687 *and reigned* °forty and one years.
b 24 And he did *that which was* evil in the
sight of [3]the LORD: he departed not from all
the [6]sins of Jeroboam the son of Nebat, who
°made Israel to [6]sin.

8 look one another, &c. Fig. *Tapeinosis* (Ap. 6), meaning very much more (*vv.* 11, 12).

9 The thistle, or briar or thorn. Heb. *choch*, rendered *thistle* here, and in 2 Chron. 25. 18. Job 31. 40; *thorn* in 2 Chron. 33. 11. Job 41. 2. Prov. 26. 9. Song 2. 2. Hos. 9. 6; and *bramble* in Isa. 34. 13.

sent. For a similar fable, see Judg. 9. 8. Fig. *Prosopopœia.* Ap. 6.

11 Beth-shemesh = house of the sun, on frontier of Judah and Dan, fifteen miles west of Jerusalem (Josh. 15. 10). Now *Aīn Shems.* A city of the priests (Josh. 21. 9, 13, 16). Afterward associated with idolatry, and now with defeat.

12 put to the worse = smitten.

every man. Heb. *'ish.* Ap. 14. II.

13 cubits. See Ap. 51. III. 2.

14 and. Note the Fig. *Polysyndeton.* Ap. 6.

hostages. Heb. sons of the securities. Occurs only here and in 2 Chron. 25. 24.

15 which he did. Some codices, with Syr., read "and all that he did".

are they not . . . ? Fig. *Erotēsis.* Ap. 6.

17 fifteen years: i.e. from 729–714. See Ap. 50. V, p. 58.

19 Lachish. On the Philistine border in Judah (Josh. 15. 39). Now *Tel-el-Hesy*, and recently excavated with important results.

slew him there. See note on 8. 26.

14. 21, 22 (J^2, p. 508). **UZZIAH, OR AZARIAH.**
(*Introversion.*)

J^2 | y | 21. Introduction. Accession.
  z | 22-. Events.
 y | -22. Conclusion. Father's death.

21 Azariah. Called also Uzziah (15. 13, 30, 32. 2 Chron. 26. 1. Isa. 1. 1; 6. 1. Hos. 1. 1. Amos 1. 1. Zech. 14. 5). In Chronicles called Azariah (1 Chron. 3. 12). These different names are common, having the same or similar meanings.

sixteen years: i.e. when "made" king. Only three years old at his father's death. See note on 15. 1.

22 built = rebuilt or fortified. This implies the subjugation of Edom.

Elath. On the Red Sea. Cp. 1 Kings 9. 26, and, for its eventual loss, 2 Kings 16. 6.

slept with his fathers. See note on Deut. 31. 16.

23-29 (E^6, p. 446). **ISRAEL. JEROBOAM II.**
(*Introversion.*)

E^6 | a | 23. Introduction. Accession.
  b | 24. Events. Personal.
  b | 25-27. Events. Political.
 a | 28, 29. Conclusion. Death.

23 of Israel. Some codices, with one early printed edition, and Sept., read "over Israel".

forty and one years. See note on 15. 8.

24 made Israel to sin. See note on 1 Kings 14. 16.

25 coast = border, or boundary.

entering of Hamath. The pass between Lebanon and Hermon. **the sea of the plain.** The Dead Sea.

God. Heb. Elohim. Ap. 4. I.

Jonah. Named by the Lord Jesus (Matt. 12. 39, 40).

26 not any shut up, nor any left = not any [place] strengthened or fortified. See note on Ex. 23. 5. Deut. 32. 36. 1 Kings 14. 10.

25 He restored the °coast of Israel from the b
°entering of Hamath unto °the sea of the
plain, according to the word of [3]the LORD °God
of Israel, which He spake by the hand of His
servant °Jonah, the son of Amittai, the prophet,
which *was* of Gath-hepher.
26 For [3]the LORD saw the affliction of
Israel, *that it was* very bitter: for *there*
was °not any shut up, nor any left, nor any
helper for Israel.
27 And [3]the LORD said not that He would

blot out the name of Israel from under heaven: but He saved them by the hand of Jeroboam the son of Joash.

a (p. 509) 28 Now the rest of the acts of Jeroboam, and all that he did, and his might, how he warred, and how he °recovered Damascus, and Hamath, *which belonged* to Judah, for Israel, [15] *are* they not written in the book of the chronicles of the kings of Israel?

687 29 And Jeroboam [22] slept with his fathers, *even* with the kings of Israel; and Zachariah his son °reigned in his stead.

F6 c (p. 510) **15** In the °twenty and seventh year of Jeroboam king of Israel began °Azariah son of Amaziah king of Judah to reign.

2 Sixteen years old was he when he began to reign, and he reigned two and fifty years in Jerusalem. And his mother's name *was* Jecholiah of Jerusalem.

d 3 And he did *that which was* right in the sight of °the LORD, °according to all that his father Amaziah had done;

4 °Save that the high places were not removed: the People sacrificed and burnt incense still on the high places.

d 649 5 And °the LORD smote the king, so that he was °a leper unto the day of his death, and dwelt in a °several house. And Jotham the king's son *was* °over the house, judging the People of the land.

c 6 And °the rest of the acts of Azariah, and all that he did, °*are* they not written in the book of the chronicles of the kings of Judah?

7 So °Azariah °slept with his fathers; and they buried him with his fathers in the city of David: and °Jotham his son reigned °in his stead.

E7 N1 e 663 8 In the °thirty and eighth year of Azariah king of Judah did Zachariah the son of Jeroboam reign over Israel in Samaria six months.

f 9 And he did *that which was* °evil in the sight of [3] the LORD, °as his fathers had done: he departed not from the °sins of Jeroboam the son of Nebat, who °made Israel to °sin.

f 10 And Shallum the son of Jabesh conspired against him, °and °smote him before the People, and slew him, and reigned in his stead.

e 11 And the rest of the acts of Zachariah, °behold, they *are* written in the book of the chronicles of the kings of Israel.

12 This *was* the word of [3] the LORD which °He spake unto Jehu, saying, "Thy sons shall sit on the throne of Israel unto the fourth *generation*." And so it came to pass.

28 recovered Damascus, and Hamath. Both were included in Solomon's kingdom (1 Kings 4. 21). Damascus lost to Rezin (1 Kings 11. 23-25). This recovery did not last long. See Amos 1. 3.

29 reigned. After an interregnum of eleven years. See 2 Kings 15. 8.

15. 1-7 (F6, p. 446). JUDAH. UZZIAH.
(*Introversion.*)

F6 | c | 1, 2. Introduction. Accession.
| d | 3, 4. Events. Personal.
| *d* | 5. Events. Political.
| *c* | 6, 7. Conclusion. Death.

1 twenty and seventh year. So in 2 Chron. 26. 1-3. Azariah being then sixteen (*v.* 2), and therefore only three on the death of his father Amaziah. Hence, there were thirteen years interregnum (16 − 3 = 13). Amaziah died in the fourteenth year of Jeroboam. Therefore Azariah began to reign in the twenty-seventh year of Jeroboam (13 + 14 = 27). This is the twenty-seventh year of Jeroboam's partnership with his father on his going to the Syrian wars.

Azariah = Uzziah. See note on 14. 21.

3 the LORD. Heb. Jehovah. Ap. 4. II.

according to all: i. e. he began well, but see 2 Chron. 26. 3-23.

4 Save that. Cp. 1 Kings 12. 31.

5 the LORD smote = Jehovah smote. Chronicles comes in here to explain why. See 2 Chron. 26. 16-21, and note on "Kings" in title of 1 Kings (p. 447).

a leper. One of nine afflicted with leprosy. See note on Ex. 4. 6. No reason is given here, but it is given in Chronicles according to the object of the latter book. See note above.

several house = a lazar house. See note on *v.* 7.

over the house, or palace: i. e. the king's house, as regent or co-regent.

6 the rest of the acts. For details see 2 Chron. 26. 1-15. The writings of HOSEA, JOEL, AMOS, and JONAH belong to this period: from the latter days of Joash (king of Judah) to the end of Uzziah. See the notes on the events in these reigns in their respective prophecies. They foretell the doom of Judah.

are they not . . . ? Fig. *Erotēsis.* Ap. 6.

7 Azariah. In the year of his death (649) Isaiah had his vision (Isa. 6. 1-9. John 12. 41), when the "voice" from the Temple prophesied the Dispersion (see the Structure of Isaiah). Uzziah had been driven from the Temple to a lazar house, when Isaiah saw the vision of the Temple in heaven.

slept with his fathers. See note on Deut. 31. 16.

Jotham. The first-named of the four kings in whose reigns Isaiah prophesied (Isa. 1. 1). Micah also began to prophesy and mourn over the coming dispersion of Israel.

in his stead. There had been an interregnum of eleven or twelve years.

8-31 (E7, p. 446). ISRAEL.
(*Division.*)

E7 | N1 | 8-12. Zachariah.
| N2 | 13-16. Shallum.
| N3 | 17-22. Menahem.
| N4 | 23-26. Pekahiah.
| N5 | 27-31. Pekah.

8-12 (N1, above). ZACHARIAH. (*Introversion.*)

N1 | e | 8. Introduction. Accession.
| f | 9. Events. Personal.
| *f* | 10. Events. Political.
| *e* | 11, 12. Conclusion. Record and death.

8 thirty and eighth year. Cp. with 14. 29. Jeroboam died in the fourteenth year of Azariah (or Uzziah). There must have been an interregnum of twenty-four years. See Ap. 50. V, p. 59, and note on 15. 1. **9 evil.** Heb. *rā'a'.* Ap. 44. viii. **as** = according as. **sins.** Heb. *chāṭā'.* Ap. 44. i. **made Israel to sin.** See note on 1 Kings 14. 16. **10 and.** Note the Fig. *Polysyndeton.* Ap. 6. **smote him:** as prophesied (Amos 7. 9). **11 behold.** Fig. *Asterismos.* Ap. 6. **12 He spake.** Cp. 10. 30 and Hos. 1. 4.

N² g **13 Shallum the son of Jabesh began to reign**
(p. 511) **in the nine and thirtieth year of °Uzziah king**
662 **of Judah; and he reigned a full month in Sa-**
maria.

h **14 For Menahem the son of Gadi went up**
from °Tirzah, and came to Samaria, and smote
Shallum the son of Jabesh in Samaria, and
slew him, and reigned in his stead.

g **15 And the rest of the acts of Shallum, and his**
conspiracy which he made, [11] behold, they *are*
written in the book of the chronicles of the
kings of Israel.

h **16 Then Menahem smote Tiphsah, and all**
that *were* therein, and the coasts thereof from
Tirzah: because they opened not *to him*, there-
fore he smote *it; and* all the women therein
that were with child he ripped up.

N³ i **17 In the nine and thirtieth year of °Azariah**
662 **king of Judah began °Menahem the son of**
to **Gadi to reign over Israel, *and reigned* ten**
652 **years in Samaria.**

k **18 And he did *that which was* [9] evil in the**
sight of [3] the LORD: he departed not all his
days from °the sins of Jeroboam the son of
Nebat, who [9] made Israel to sin.

k **19 *And* °Pul the king of Assyria °came**
against the land: and Menahem gave Pul a
thousand °talents of silver, that his hand
might be with him to confirm the kingdom in
his hand.

20 And Menahem °exacted the money of Is-
rael, *even* of all the mighty men of wealth, of
each °man fifty °shekels of silver, to give to
the king of Assyria. So the king of Assyria
turned back, and stayed not °there in the land.

i **21 And the rest of the acts of Menahem, and**
all that he did, [6] *are* they not written in the
book of the chronicles of the kings of Israel?

22 And Menahem [7] slept with his fathers;
and Pekahiah his son reigned in his stead.

N⁴ l **23 In the °fiftieth year of Azariah king of**
651 **Judah Pekahiah the son of Menahem began to**
to **reign over Israel in Samaria, *and reigned* two**
649 **years.**

m **24 And he did *that which was* [9] evil in the**
sight of [3] the LORD: he departed not from the
[9] sins of Jeroboam the son of Nebat, who [9] made
Israel to sin.

m **25 But °Pekah the son of Remaliah, a captain**
of his, conspired against him, and smote him
in Samaria, in the palace of the king's house,
with Argob and Arieh, and with him fifty
[20] men of the Gileadites: and he killed him, and
reigned in his room.

l **26 And the rest of the acts of Pekahiah, and**
all that he did, [11] behold, they *are* written in the
book of the chronicles of the kings of Israel.

N⁵ n **27 In the two and fiftieth year of Azariah**
649 **king of Judah Pekah the son of Remaliah began**
to **to reign over Israel in Samaria, *and reigned***
629 **°twenty years.**

o **28 And he did *that which was* [9] evil in the**
sight of [3] the LORD: he departed not from the
sins of Jeroboam the son of Nebat, who [18] made
Israel to sin.

15. 13-16 (N², p. 510). SHALLUM. (*Alternation.*)

N² | g | 13. Introduction. Accession.
  h | 14. Event. Personal.
 g | 15. Conclusion. Record.
  h | 16. Events. Political.

13 Uzziah. See note on 14. 21.

14 Tirzah. The capital before Samaria (1 Kings 14. 17; 15. 21; 16. 8). Now *Telluzah*, about nine miles north of Samaria.

17-22 (N³, p. 510). MENAHEM. (*Introversion.*)

N³ | i | 17. Introduction. Accession.
  k | 18. Events. Personal.
  k | 19, 20. Events. Political.
 i | 21, 22. Conclusion. Record. Death.

17 Azariah. See note on 14. 21.

Menahem. Their names are mentioned, together with Rezin (16. 9), in Tiglath-pileser's inscriptions.

18 the sins. Some codices, with Aram. and Sept., read "any of the sins". See note on 1 Kings 14. 16.

19 Pul. Thought to be the same as Tiglath-pileser (a throne name). But see 1 Chron. 5. 26.

came against. Probably at invitation of Menahem. Cp. Hos. 5. 13; 7. 11; 8. 9.

talents. See Ap. 51. II. 6.

20 exacted. Judah usually bought off foreign invaders (12. 18; 16. 8; 18. 15).

man. Heb. *'ish.* Ap. 14. II.

shekels. See Ap. 51. II. 5.

there=then. Heb. *shām.* Cp. Judg. 5. 11. Ps. 14. 5.

23-26 (N⁴, p. 510). PEKAHIAH. (*Introversion.*)

N⁴ | l | 23. Introduction. Accession.
  m | 24. Events.
  m | 25. Events.
 l | 26. Conclusion. Record.

23 fiftieth year. From *v.* 17 there appears to be an interregnum of some months.

25 Pekah. Cp. Isa. 7. 1.

27-31 (N⁵, p. 510). PEKAH. (*Introversion.*)

N⁵ | n | 27. Introduction. Accession.
  o | 28. Events. Personal.
  o | 29, 30. Events. Political.
 n | 31. Conclusion. Record.

27 twenty years. See Ap. 50. V, p. 59. The Assyrian inscription shows only four years. But why is writing on stone always assumed to be correct, and on parchment, always wrong? There were two chronological mistakes on the Duke of Cambridge's monument erected in Whitehall, London, which were the subject of a correspondence in the London newspapers of that date. (The Duke died in March, 1904.) On the coffin-plate of King Edward VII, his death is put as occurring in the "ninth" instead of in the "tenth" year of his reign. In the inscription of DARIUS HYSTASPIS on the *Behistūn* Rock (see Ap. 57), no less than *fourteen* "mistakes" made by the graver (one of them actually corrected by himself) are noted as such by the authors of the exhaustive work on that subject issued by the Trustees of the British Museum.

29 Tiglath pileser. See note on "Pul", *v.* 19.

Abel-beth-maachah . . . Gilead. These names are mentioned in Tiglath's own inscriptions.

carried them captive. This deportation took place in 734 B.C., and is referred to in Isa. 9. 1, 2.

29 In the days of Pekah king of Israel came o
°Tiglath-pileser king of Assyria, and took
Ijon, and °Abel-beth-maachah, and Janoah,
and Kedesh, and Hazor, and °Gilead, and
Galilee, all the land of Naphtali, and °carried
them captive to Assyria.

30 And Hoshea the son of Elah made a con-
spiracy against Pekah the son of Remaliah,
[10] and smote him, and slew him, (and reigned in

his stead,) in the °twentieth year of Jotham the son of Uzziah.

n (p. 511) **31** And the rest of the acts of Pekah, and all that he did, [11] behold, they *are* written in the book of the chronicles of the kings of Israel.

F[7] O[1] p (p. 512) **32** In the second year of Pekah the son of Remaliah king of Israel began [7] Jotham the son of Uzziah king of Judah to reign.

33 Five and twenty years old was he when he began to reign, and he reigned °sixteen years in Jerusalem. And his mother's name *was* Jerusha, the daughter of °Zadok.

q **34** And he did *that which was* right in the sight of [3] the LORD: he did according to °all that his father Uzziah had done.

r **35** Howbeit the high places were not removed: the People sacrificed and burned incense still in the high places. °He built the higher gate of the house of [3] the LORD.

r **36** Now °the rest of the acts of Jotham, and all that he did, °*are they* not written in the book of the chronicles of the kings of Judah?

q **37** In those days [3] the LORD began to send against Judah °Rezin the king of Syria, and Pekah the son of Remaliah.

p **38** And Jotham [7] slept with his fathers, and was buried with his fathers in the city of David his father: and Ahaz his son reigned in his stead.

O[2] s 632 to 616 **16** In the seventeenth year of Pekah the son of Remaliah °Ahaz the son of Jotham king of Judah began to reign.

2 °Twenty years old *was* Ahaz when he began to reign, and reigned °sixteen years in Jerusalem,

t and did not *that which was* right in the sight of °the LORD his °God, like David his father.

3 But °he walked in the way of the kings of Israel, yea, and made his °son °to pass through the fire, according to the abominations of the °heathen, whom [2] the LORD cast out from before the °children of Israel.

4 And he sacrificed and burnt incense in the high places, and on the hills, and under every green tree.

u **5** Then °Rezin king of Syria and Pekah son of Remaliah king of Israel °came up to Jerusalem to war: and they besieged Ahaz, but °could not overcome *him*.

6 At that time Rezin king of Syria recovered Elath to °Syria, and drave the Jews from °Elath: and the °Syrians came to Elath, and dwelt there unto this day.

7 So Ahaz °sent messengers to Tiglath-pileser king of Assyria, saying, I *am* thy servant and thy son: come up, and save me out of the hand of the king of Syria, and out of the hand of the king of Israel, which rise up against me.

8 And Ahaz took the silver and gold that was found in the °house of [2] the LORD, and in the treasures of the king's house, and sent *it for* °a present to the king of Assyria.

twentieth year, i.e. in 629. This was nine years before he succeeded in obtaining the throne, which was in the twelfth year of Ahaz (17. 1). In *v.* 33, sixteen years. So this twentieth year must be reckoned from his father's being struck with leprosy, as distinctly stated in *v.* 5.

15. 32—16. 20 (**F**[7], p. 446). JUDAH. (*Division.*)

F[7] | O[1] | 15. 32-38. Jotham.
  | O[2] | 16. 1-20. Ahaz.

32-38 (O[1], above). JOTHAM. (*Introversion.*)

O[1] p | 32, 33. Introduction.
  q | 34. Events. Personal.
   r | 35. Events. Public.
   r | 36. Events. Public.
  q | 37. Event. Personal.
 p | 38. Conclusion.

33 sixteen years: i.e. from his accession, on the death of Uzziah his father, for whom he reigned four years. See note on *v.* 30 above.

Zadok. The high priest (1 Chron. 6. 12). Perhaps this was why he invaded the priests' office.

34 all: i.e. all [the good].

35 He built. Cp. 2 Chron. 27. 3.

36 the rest. Cp. 2 Chron. 27. 2-8.

are they not . . .? Fig. *Erotēsis.* Ap. 6.

37 Rezin. The war which broke out in the reign of Ahaz was already threatening. Cp. Isa. 7. 1-16.

16. 1-20 (O[2], above). AHAZ. (*Introversion.*)

O[2] | s | 1, 2-. Introduction. Accession.
  t | -2-4. Personal. Apostasy.
   u | 5-9. Events. Political.
  t | 10-18. Personal. Apostasy.
 s | 19, 20. Conclusion. Record and death.

1 Ahaz. One of the four kings in whose reign Isaiah prophesied. Cp. 2 Chron. 28. 1. Isa. 1. 1.

2 Twenty years old . . . sixteen. There is no reason for concluding that "there must be an error in one of the passages" (viz. 16. 2 and 18. 2), for Ahaz begins in 622 and reigns till 616. As he was twenty when he began, he was born in 652, and died when thirty-six. Hezekiah begins in 617, and reigns twenty-nine years, till 588. As he was twenty-five when he began he was therefore born in 642, and died when he was fifty-four. From this it is clear that Ahaz was between ten and eleven when his son Hezekiah was born. This sounds improbable only to Western ears. But, to Eastern ears and physiological phenomena, there is nothing unusual, and nothing to justify a conclusion that the text is corrupt—the usual excuse for ignorance of the facts.

the LORD. Heb. Jehovah. Ap. 4. II.

God. Heb. Elohim. Ap. 4. I.

3 he walked. Cp. 2 Chron. 28. 2.

son. See note on 2 Chron. 28. 3.

to pass through the fire. The first king of Judah to do this. Followed in it by Manasseh (21. 6; 23. 10). Cp. Jer. 7. 31. Ezek. 20. 26, and Lev. 18. 21.

heathen = nations. **children** = sons.

5 Rezin. Cp. Isa. 7. He and Pekah are the two firebrands of Isa. 7. 4. The events in *vv.* 5-9 are said by some to contradict 2 Chron. 28. 5-20; but the event recorded in 2 Chron. happened the year before, directly after (2 Chron. 28. 5-20), in 631 (see Ap. 50. V, p. 59). Rezin and Pekah both attacked directly after his accession (successfully). But they confederated unsuccessfully.

came up. Pekah's design to persuade Ahaz failed; and he tried to supersede him himself ("Tabeal" being a cipher for Remaliah). Cp. Isa. 7. 6.

could not: because of the promise to David. Cp. Isa. 7. 7, 16.

6 Syria. Probably Edom (for *Aram*). See note below. **Elath.** It had belonged to Edom (14. 22).

7 sent messengers. This was opposed by Isaiah (7. 17). Cp. Hos. 5. 13; 7. 11, 12; 8. 9; 11. 5. Tiglath-pileser is the "razor" of Isa. 7. 20. **8 house.** Some codices, with two early printed editions, and Sept., read "treasures of the house". **a present.** Tiglath-pileser regarded it (in his inscriptions) as tribute.

632 to 616 9 And the king of Assyria hearkened unto
him: for the king of Assyria went up against
Damascus, and took it, and carried *the people*
of it captive to Kir, and slew Rezin.

t v (p. 513) 10 And king °Ahaz went to Damascus °to
meet Tiglath-pileser king of Assyria, and saw
an altar that *was* at Damascus: and king Ahaz
sent to Urijah the priest the °fashion of the
altar, and the °pattern of it, according to all
the workmanship thereof.
11 And °Urijah the priest built an altar according to all that king Ahaz had sent from
Damascus: so Urijah the priest made *it* against
king Ahaz came from Damascus.
12 And when the king was come from Damascus, the king saw the altar: °and the king
approached to the altar, and offered thereon.
13 [12]And he °burnt his burnt offering [12]and
his °meat offering, and poured his drink offering, and sprinkled the blood of his peace
offerings, upon the altar.

w 14 [12]And he brought also the °brasen altar,
which *was* before [2]the LORD, from the forefront of the house, from between °the altar and
the house of [2]the LORD, [12]and put it on the
north side of °the altar.

v 15 [12]And king Ahaz commanded [11]Urijah the
priest, saying, "Upon the °great altar burn
the morning burnt offering, [12]and the evening
meat offering, and the king's burnt sacrifice,
and his meat offering, with the burnt offering
of all the People of the land, and their meat
offering, and their drink offerings; and sprinkle
upon it all the blood of the burnt offering, and
all the blood of the sacrifice: and the brasen
altar shall be for me °to enquire *by*."
16 Thus °did Urijah the priest, according to
all that king Ahaz commanded.

w 17 And king Ahaz cut off the borders of the
bases, and removed °the laver from off them;
and took down °the sea from off the brasen
oxen that *were* under it, and put it upon a
pavement of stones.
18 And the °covert for the sabbath that they
had built in the house, and the king's entry
without, turned he from the house of [2]the LORD
°for the king of Assyria.

s (p. 512) 616 19 Now °the rest of the acts of Ahaz °which
he did, °*are they* not written in the book of the
chronicles of the kings of Judah?
20 And Ahaz °slept with his fathers, and was
°buried with his fathers °in the city of David:
and Hezekiah his son reigned in his stead.

E^8 P (p. 513) 620-611 **17** In the °twelfth year of Ahaz king of
Judah began Hoshea the son of Elah to
reign in Samaria over Israel °nine years.

Q 2 And he did *that which was* °evil in the sight
of °the LORD, but °not as the kings of Israel
that were before him.

Q 3 Against him came up Shalmaneser king of
Assyria; and Hoshea became his servant, and
gave him presents.
4 And the king of Assyria found conspiracy
in Hoshea: for he had sent messengers to °So
king of Egypt, and brought no present to the
king of Assyria, as *he had done* year by year:
therefore the king of Assyria shut him up, and
bound him in prison.
5 Then °the king of Assyria came up throughout all the land, and went up to Samaria, and
besieged it °three years.

16. 10-18 (*t*, p. 512). AHAZ. PERSONAL. APOSTASY. (*Alternation.*)

t | v | 10-13. The Altar.
  | w | 14. Removal.
  | *v* | 15, 16. The Altar.
  | *w* | 17, 18. Alterations.

10 Ahaz. Called Jehoahaz in Tiglath-pileser's great triumphal inscriptions. The first syllable of his name dropped in Scripture, as he was unworthy of it.

to meet: and do him honour. Hence the solemn warnings of Isa. 8. 13, 14, 19.

fashion = likeness, or sketch. **pattern,** or model.

11 Urijah. Perhaps the Uriah of Isa. 8. 2. His name does not occur in the list of high priests (1 Chron. 6. 3-15). Note the emphatic repetition of "Ahaz the king" and "Urijah the priest".

12 and. Note the Fig. *Polysyndeton* (Ap. 6) in *vv.* 12-15.

13 burnt = offered up. Ap. 43. I. vi.

burnt his burnt offering. Fig. *Polyptōton* (Ap. 6) for emphasis.

meat offering = meal offering. Ap. 43. II. iii.

14 brasen altar. Cp. 1 Kings 8. 64.

the altar: i. e. the new altar.

15 great altar: i. e. the new altar.

to enquire = to consider further [what shall be done with it]. Fig. *Ellipsis.* Ap. 6. Heb. *bāḳar.* Occurs seven times (16. 15. Lev. 13. 36; 27. 33. Ps. 27. 4. Prov. 20. 25. Ezek. 34. 11, 12).

16 did Urijah. Unlike Azariah in 2 Chron. 26. 17, 18.

17 the laver. Cp. 1 Kings 7. 23-39. 2 Chron. 28. 24, 25. **the sea.** Cp. 1 Kings 7. 23-26.

18 covert = the covered way. **for** = because of.

19 the rest. Cp. 2 Chron. 28. 24, 25. He shut up the house of the Lord altogether.

which. Some codices, with Aram. (MS.) and Syr., read "and all that".

are they not . . . ? Fig. *Erotēsis.* Ap. 6.

20 slept with his fathers. See note on Deut. 31. 16.

buried . . . in the city of David. But not in the tombs of the kings. Cp. 2 Chron. 28. 27, where observe the phrase "kings of Israel".

17. 1-41 (E^8, p. 446). ISRAEL. HOSHEA. (*Introversion.*)

E^8 | P | 1. Introduction.
  | Q | 2. Events. Personal. Evil-doing.
  | *Q* | 3-6. Event. Political. Captivity.
  | *P* | 7-41. Conclusion. Causes.

1 twelfth year. There was anarchy for nine years between Pekah and Hoshea. For, in 15. 30, Hoshea conspired against Pekah in the twentieth year of Jotham, which was the third year of Ahaz (20 − 12 = 8): for Ahaz began in Pekah's seventeenth year (16. 1), and Hoshea began in Ahaz's twelfth year. But Pekah's twenty years end in Ahaz's third year. (See Ap. 50. V, p. 59.)

nine years: reckoned from twelfth of Ahaz. Hoshea kept under by the Assyrians till then. Cp. Hos. 10. 14, where Shalman[eser] spoiled Beth-arbel in his first expedition, and would spoil Beth-el at his second.

2 evil. Heb. *rā'a'.* Ap. 44. viii.

the LORD. Heb. Jehovah. Ap. 4. II.

not as the kings of Israel . . . before him: thus, we do not read that he opposed Hezekiah's invitation (2 Chron. 30. 5-11).

4 So. The Heb. drops the embarrassing "k" of *Sabako,* his Ethiopian name. Afterward vanquished by Tirhakah. See note on 19. 9.

5 the king of Assyria. Shalmaneser (*v.* 3), who commenced the siege, but died before Sargon, his successor, captured Samaria in 611 B.C.

three years. From 613-611.

611 6 In the ninth year of Hoshea the °king of Assyria °took Samaria, and °carried Israel away into Assyria, and placed them in °Halah and in Habor *by* the river of Gozan, and in the cities of the Medes.

P x[1] (p. 514) 7 For *so* it was, that the °children of Israel had °sinned against [2]the LORD their °God, Which had brought them up out of the land of Egypt, from under the hand of Pharaoh king of Egypt, and had feared other gods,

8 And walked in the statutes of the °heathen, whom [2]the LORD cast out from before the [7]children of Israel, and of the kings of Israel, which they had made.

9 And the [7]children of Israel did secretly *those* things that *were* not right against [2]the LORD their [7]God, and they built them high places in all their cities, °from the tower of the watchmen to the fenced city.

10 And they set them up °images and °groves in every high hill, and under every green tree:

11 And there they burnt incense in all the high places, as *did* the heathen whom [2]the LORD carried away before them; and wrought wicked things to provoke [2]the LORD to anger:

12 For they served °idols, whereof [2]the LORD had said unto them, "Ye °shall not do this thing."

y[1] 13 Yet [2]the LORD testified against Israel, and against Judah, by all the prophets, *and by* °all the seers, saying, "Turn ye from your °evil ways, °and keep My commandments °*and* My statutes, according to all the law which I commanded your fathers, and which I sent to you °by My servants °the prophets."

x[2] 14 Notwithstanding they would not hear, but hardened their necks, °like to the neck of their fathers, that did not believe in [2]the LORD their [7]God.

15 And they rejected His statutes, °and His covenant that He made with their fathers, and His testimonies which He testified against them; and they followed °vanity, and became vain, and went after the heathen that *were* round about them, *concerning* whom [2]the LORD had charged them, that they should not do like them.

16 And they left all the commandments of [2]the LORD their [7]God, [15]and made them molten images, *even* two calves, and made a [10]grove, and worshipped all the host of heaven, and served Baal.

17 And they caused their sons [15]and their daughters to °pass through the fire, and used °divination and enchantments, and sold themselves to do [13]evil in the sight of [2]the LORD, to provoke Him to anger.

y[2] 18 Therefore [2]the LORD was very angry with Israel, and removed them out of his sight: there was none left but the tribe of °Judah only.

x[3] 19 Also Judah kept not the commandments of [2]the LORD their [7]God, °but walked in the statutes of Israel which they made.

y[3] 20 And [2]the LORD rejected °all the seed of Israel, and afflicted them, and delivered them into the hand of spoilers, until He had cast them out of His sight.

21 For He rent Israel from the house of David; and they made Jeroboam the son of Nebat king: and Jeroboam drave Israel from following [2]the LORD, and °made them °sin a great sin.

22 For the [7]children of Israel walked in all the [7]sins of Jeroboam which he did; they departed not from them; x[4]

6 king of Assyria = Shalmaneser. See *v.* 3.

took Samaria. Here, in the days of Hoshea (king of Israel); and in ch. 18 as connected with the days of Hezekiah (king of Judah). Cp. 18. 9.

carried Israel away. Sargon's own inscription says 27,290. Cp. 18. 9-12.

Halah. Some codices, with four early printed editions, read "Halath".

17. 7-41 (*P*, p. 513). CONCLUSION. CAPTIVITY. CAUSES. (*Repeated Alternation.*)

P | x[1] | 7-12. Provocation of Israel.
y[1] | 13. Remonstrance.
x[2] | 14-17. Obduracy of Israel.
y[2] | 18. Removal.
x[3] | 19. Disobedience of Judah.
y[3] | 20, 21. Rejection and rending.
x[4] | 22, 23-. Obduracy of Israel.
y[4] | -23-33. Removal.
x[5] | 34-40. Transplanting of Israel; and sequel.
y[5] | 41. Replaced people.

7 children = sons.

sinned. Heb. *chāṭa.* Ap. 44. i.

God. Heb. Elohim. Ap. 4. I.

8 heathen = nations.

9 from the tower . . . to the fenced city: from the remote watchtower in the country to the fortified city = the whole country.

10 images = statues.

groves = *'Ashērah.* See note on Ex. 34. 13, and Ap. 42.

12 idols = filthy, or manufactured idols.

shall not do this thing. Cp. Ex. 20. 3; 23. 13. Lev. 26. 1. Deut. 12. 31, &c.

13 all the seers = every one who had a vision.

evil. Heb. *rā'a'.* See Ap. 44. viii.

and. Note the Fig. *Polysyndeton.* Ap. 6.

and My statutes. Some codices, with two early printed editions, Aram., Sept., Syr., and Vulg., read "and My statutes" (the "and" being in the text).

by = by the hand of; and so generally. Cp. *v.* 23.

the prophets. Those in ISRAEL were Ahijah, Jehu (son of Hanani), Elijah, Elisha, Micaiah, Jonah, Oded, Amos, and Hosea. Those in JUDAH were Shemaiah, Iddo, Azariah, Hanani, Jehu, Zechariah (son of Jehoiada), Micah, and Isaiah.

14 like to. Supply Fig. *Ellipsis* (Ap. 6), "as their fathers' neck [was stiffened]".

15 and. Note the Fig. *Polysyndeton* (Ap. 6) in *vv.* 15-17. Sixteen "ands" emphasising each detail.

vanity. A term often applied to idols.

17 pass through the fire. Cp. Lev. 18. 21. Deut. 12. 31; 18. 10.

divination and enchantments: i. e. traffic with evil spirits and demons, and familiar spirits. Identical with modern spiritism. Cp. Deut. 18. 10, and see 1 Sam. 28. 8. Acts 16. 16. Rev. 9. 21.

18 Judah only. Fig. *Synecdoche* (of the Part), Ap. 6. Levites and Benjamin and additions from Israel are of course included.

19 but walked. Cp. Athaliah (8. 18, 27; 16. 3, &c.).

20 all the seed. A prophetic anticipation.

21 made. See note on 1 Kings 14. 16.

sin a great sin. Fig. *Polyptōton* (Ap. 6) for emphasis. Heb. *chāṭa'.* Ap. 44. i.

23 Until [2]the LORD removed Israel out of His sight, °as He had said [13]by all His servants the prophets.

y[4] z[1] (p. 515) 611 to 603 So was Israel carried away out of their own land to Assyria unto this day.

24 And the king of Assyria °brought *men* from Babylon, °and from °Cuthah, and from °Ava, and from °Hamath, and from °Sepharvaim, and placed *them* in the cities of Samaria instead of the [7]children of Israel: and they possessed Samaria, and dwelt in the cities thereof.

25 And *so* it was at the beginning of their dwelling there, *that* they feared not [2]the LORD:

a[1] therefore [2]the LORD sent °lions among them, which °slew *some* of them.

z[2] 26 Wherefore they spake to the king of Assyria, saying, "The nations which thou hast removed, and placed in the cities of Samaria, know not the manner of the [7]God of the land: therefore He hath sent lions among them, and, °behold, they slay them, because they know not the manner of the [7]God of the land."

a[2] 27 Then the king of Assyria commanded, saying, "Carry thither °one of the priests whom ye brought from thence; and let them go and dwell there, and let him teach them the manner of the [7]God of the land."

28 Then [27]one of the priests whom they had carried away from Samaria came and dwelt in Beth-el, and taught them how they should fear [2]the LORD.

z[3] 29 Howbeit every nation made gods of their own, and put *them* in the houses of the high places which the Samaritans had made, every nation in their cities wherein they dwelt.

30 °And the °men of Babylon made Succoth-benoth, °and the °men of Cuth made Nergal, and the °men of Hamath made Ashima,

31 [30]And the Avites made Nibhaz and Tartak, [30]and the Sepharvites °burnt their [7]children in fire to Adrammelech and Anammelech, the gods of Sepharvaim.

32 So they feared [2]the LORD, and made unto themselves of the °lowest of them priests of the high places, which sacrificed for them in the houses of the high places.

33 They °feared [2]the LORD, and served their own gods, after the manner of the nations °whom they carried away from thence.

x[5] (p. 514) 34 Unto this day °they do after the former manners: they fear not [2]the LORD, neither do they after their °statutes, or after their ordinances, or after the law and commandment which [2]the LORD commanded the [7]children of Jacob, °whom He named Israel;

35 With whom [2]the LORD had made a covenant, and charged them, saying, "Ye shall not fear other gods, nor bow yourselves to them, nor serve them, nor sacrifice to them:

36 But [2]the LORD, Who brought you up out of the land of Egypt with great power and a stretched out arm, Him shall ye fear, and Him shall ye worship, and to Him shall ye do sacrifice.

37 And the [34]statutes, and the ordinances, and the law, and the commandment, °which He wrote for you, ye shall observe to do for evermore; and ye shall not fear other gods.

38 And the covenant that I have made with you ye shall not forget; neither shall ye fear other gods.

39 But [2]the LORD your [7]God ye shall fear; and He shall deliver you out of the hand of all your enemies."

40 Howbeit they did not hearken, but they did after their former manner.

41 So these nations [33]feared [2]the LORD, and served their graven images, both their [7]children, and their [7]children's [7]children: °as did their fathers, so do they unto this day. y[5]

18 Now it came to pass in the °third year of Hoshea son of Elah king of Israel, *that* Hezekiah the son of Ahaz king of Judah began to reign. F[8] R[1] S (p. 516) 617

---

17. -23-33 (y[4], p. 514). REMOVAL.
(*Repeated Alternation.*)

y[4] | z[1] | -23-25-. Peoples exchanged. "No fear of God."
a[1] | -25. Punishment. Lions.
z[2] | 26. Peoples. Report. Ignorance.
a[2] | 27, 28. Remedy proposed: to fear Jehovah.
z[3] | 29-33. People. Corrupt fear of Jehovah.

23 as = according as.

24 brought men. These were the substituted people forming the nucleus of the later Samaritans; but subsequently intermixed with Israelites returning with Ezra and Nehemiah (Neh. 13. 3, 23-31). In N.T. called "foreigners" (Luke 17. 18). Cp. Matt. 10. 5, 6. Sargon refers to this in his inscriptions. Only one figure remains (7) of the number he gives.

and. Note the Fig. *Polysyndeton.* Ap. 6.

Cuthah. Ten miles north-east of Babylon. In the first year of Sargon there was war between Cuthah and Babylon, and the people of Cuthah were transported to Syria and Palestine.

Ava = either the Ivah of 18. 34, or the Ahava of Ezra 8. 15. **Hamath.** The one in Syria.

Sepharvaim (Dual). The two Sippars in Babylonia. *Sippar sa Samas* (the sun-god) and *Sippar sa Anuituv.*

25 lions. For lions in Palestine see note on 1 Kings 13. 24. **slew** = kept on slaying. Omit "some".

26 behold. Fig. *Asterismos.* Ap. 6.

27 one of the priests. An idolatrous Israelite priest from Samaria (*v.* 28).

30 men. Heb. *'ĕnōsh.* Ap. 14. III.

and. Note the Fig. *Polysyndeton* (Ap. 6) emphasising the five nations brought into Palestine. Cp. *v.* 24. Each brought its own gods. Thus (according to the language of the O.T.) Samaria committed adultery (idolatry) with five husbands (cp. Isa. 54. 5 with Isa. 23. 17. Jer. 22. 20. Hos. 2. 10-12). Repeated individually in John 4. 18. No wonder the woman worshipped she knew not what (John 4. 22).

31 burnt = burnt up. See Ap. 43. I. viii.

32 lowest. Cp. 1 Kings 12. 31. **33 feared.** Cp. *v.* 41.

whom they carried away from thence: or, whence they (the settlers) had carried them away.

34 they. These, according to the Structure, are the Israelites. The member (x[5], 34-40, p. 514) records their continued obduracy in their dispersion.

statutes. See note on Deut. 4. 1.

whom, &c. Render: "after the manner of the [several] nations; [gods] which had caused them [i. e. the Israelites] to go captive thence [i. e. out of the Land]. Gen. 32. 28. 1 Kings 18. 31.

37 which He wrote, &c. See note on Ex. 17. 14, and Ap. 47. **41 as** = according as.

18. 1—24. 20 [For the Structure see next page].

1 third year of Hoshea. Hoshea began in the twelfth year of Ahaz. Therefore Hezekiah began in the fifteenth year of Ahaz. Ahaz reigned sixteen years, but was deposed by Shalmaneser (17. 3, 4), who set up Hezekiah. Hezekiah rebelled (*v.* 7), which shows he was under Assyria till then. See Ap. 50. V, p. 59.

617 2 Twenty and five years old was he when he
to began to reign; and he reigned twenty and
588 nine years in Jerusalem. His mother's name
also *was* °Abi, the daughter of Zachariah.

T 3 And he did *that which was* right in the
(p. 516) sight of °the LORD, according to all that David
his father did.

4 He removed the high places, and brake the
images, and cut down the °groves, and brake
in pieces the °brasen serpent that Moses had
made: for unto those days the °children of
Israel did burn incense to it: and he called it
°Nehushtan.

5 He °trusted in [3]the LORD °God of Israel; so
that after him was °none like him among all
the kings of Judah, nor *any* that were before
him.

6 For he clave to [3]the LORD, °*and* departed
not from following Him, but kept His commandments, which [3]the LORD commanded
Moses.

7 And [3]the LORD was with him; *and* he
prospered whithersoever he went forth:
U V and he °rebelled against the king of Assyria,
and served him not.

W 8 He smote the °Philistines, *even* unto Gaza,
and the borders thereof, from the tower of the
watchmen to the fenced city.

V X[1] 9 And °it came to pass in the fourth year of
613 king Hezekiah, which *was* the seventh year of
Hoshea son of Elah king of Israel, *that* °Shal-
maneser king of Assyria came up against Samaria, and besieged it.

10 And at °the end of three years °they took
611 it: *even* in the sixth year of Hezekiah, that *is*
the ninth year of Hoshea king of Israel, Samaria was taken.

11 And the king of Assyria did carry away
Israel unto Assyria, and put them in °Halah
and in Habor *by* the river of Gozan, and in the
cities of the Medes:

12 Because they obeyed not the voice of [3]the
LORD their [5]God, but °transgressed His covenant, *and* all that °Moses the servant of [3]the
LORD commanded, and would not hear *them*,
nor do *them*.

X[2] Y[1] 13 Now in °the fourteenth year of king Heze-
603 kiah did Sennacherib king of Assyria come up
against °all the fenced cities of Judah, and took
them.

14 And Hezekiah king of Judah °sent to the
king of Assyria to Lachish, saying, °"I have
offended; return from me: that which thou
puttest on me will I bear." And the king of
Assyria appointed unto Hezekiah king of
Judah °three hundred °talents of silver and
thirty °talents of gold.

15 And Hezekiah gave *him* all the silver that
was found in the house of [3]the LORD, and in
the °treasures of the king's house.

16 At that time did Hezekiah cut off *the gold
from* the doors of the temple of [3]the LORD,

18. 1—24. 20 (F[8], p. 446). JUDAH.
(*Division.*)

F[8] | R[1] | 18. 1—20. 21. Hezekiah.
R[2] | 21. 1-18. Manasseh.
R[3] | 21. 19-26. Amon.
R[4] | 22. 1—23. 30. Josiah.
R[5] | 23. 31-35. Jehoahaz.
R[6] | 23. 36—24. 7. Jehoiakim.
R[7] | 24. 8-16. Jehoiachin.
R[8] | 24. 17-20. Zedekiah.

18. 1—20. 21 (R[1], above). HEZEKIAH.
(*Introversion.*)

R[1] | S | 18. 1, 2. Introduction. Accession.
T | 18. 3-7-. Personal. Well-doing.
U | 18. -7—19. 37. Events. Political.
T | 20. 1-19. Personal. Sickness.
S | 20. 20, 21. Conclusion. Record and death.

2 Abi. In 2 Chron. 29. 1 it is "Abijah", but "Abi" may be the abbreviation of "Abijah", the "i" or "j" standing for "jah".

3 the LORD. Heb. Jehovah. Ap. 4. II.

4 groves = *'Asherah*, sing. See note on Ex. 34. 13, and Ap. 42.

brasen serpent. Cp. Num. 21. 9. Now 835 years old. (From 1452 to 617 = 835). **children** = sons.

Nehushtan = a brass thing.

5 trusted = confided. Heb. *batah*. Ap. 69. i.

God. Heb. Elohim. Ap. 4. I.

none like him: i. e. for trust in Jehovah. Same praise given of Josiah (23. 25), but in a different respect.

6 and. This "and" is contained in some codices, two early printed editions, Syr., and Vulg. The Fig. *Polysyndeton* (Ap. 6) emphasising the Fig. *Synonymia*, by which the phrases are heaped up to express Hezekiah's goodness.

18. -7—19. 37 (U, above). EVENTS. POLITICAL.
(*Introversion.*)

U | V | 18. -7. Assyria. Hezekiah's rebellion.
W | 18. 8. Philistines. Smitten.
V | 18. 9—19. 37. Assyria. Shalmaneser's invasions.

7 rebelled. Hezekiah had hitherto been dependent on him. See note on *v.* 15.

8 Philistines. As prophesied by Isaiah (14. 28-32).

18. 9—19. 37 (*V*, above). ASSYRIA. INVASIONS.
(*Division.*)

V | X[1] | 18. 9-12. Invasions of Israel (Shalmaneser).
X[2] | 18. 13—19. 37. Invasions of Judah (Sennacherib).

9 it came to pass. Cp. 17. 3-6.

Shalmaneser. Commenced the siege; Sargon, his successor, completed it after three years. Cp. 17. 5, 6, where we have the same interval as here. In Sargon's own inscription he refers to the "tributes imposed upon them by the former king".

10 the end of three years. See note on 17. 5.

they. Sept. and Syr. read "he": i. e. Sargon. See note on 17. 5, 6. Sargon took it after Shalmaneser's death.

11 Halah. Some codices, with two early printed editions, read "Halath".

12 transgressed. Heb. *'abar*. Ap. 44. vii.

Moses the servant of the LORD. See note on Deut. 34. 5.

18. 13—19. 37 (X[2], above). INVASIONS OF JUDAH. (*Division.*)

X[2] | Y[1] | 18. 13-16. First invasion.
Y[2] | 18. 17—19. 37. Second invasion.

13 the fourteenth year. This was the first invasion of Judah which Sennacherib's inscription enlarges upon, but is only mentioned here. See note on *v.* 17. Cp. Isa. 36, 37, and 2 Chron. 32. **all the fenced cities.** Forty-six are mentioned in the inscriptions (see Ap. 67. xi). **14 sent.** Sennacherib had not approached Jerusalem yet. **I have offended.** See *v.* 7. **three hundred talents.** The Assyrian inscriptions say 800, the exact equivalent of 300 Hebrew (silver) talents. See note on "twenty" (15. 27). **talents.** See Ap. 51. II. **15 treasures** = treasuries. See note on Isa. 39. 2.

603 and *from* the °pillars which Hezekiah king of
Judah had overlaid, and gave °it to the king
of Assyria.

Y² A¹ 17 And the °king of Assyria °sent °Tartan
(p. 517) and °Rabsaris and °Rab-shakeh from °Lachish
to king Hezekiah with a °great host °against
Jerusalem. And they went up and came to
Jerusalem. And when they were come up,
they came and stood by the conduit of the
°upper pool, which *is* in the highway of the
fuller's field.

18 And when they had called to the king, there came out to them Eliakim the son of Hilkiah, which *was* over the °household, and Shebna the scribe, and Joah the son of Asaph the recorder.

19 And °Rab-shakeh said unto them, "Speak ye now to Hezekiah, 'Thus saith the great king, the king of Assyria, °'What confidence *is* this wherein thou [5]trustest?

20 Thou sayest, (but *they are but* °vain words,) *I have* counsel and strength for the war. Now [19]on whom dost thou [5]trust, that thou rebellest against me?

21 Now, °behold, thou °trustest upon the staff of this °bruised reed, *even* upon Egypt, on which if a °man lean, it will go into his hand, and pierce it: so *is* Pharaoh °king of Egypt unto all that [5]trust on him.

22 But °if ye say unto me, 'We [5]trust in [3]the LORD our [5]God:' [19]*is* not that He, Whose high places and whose altars Hezekiah hath taken away, and hath said to Judah and Jerusalem, 'Ye shall worship before this altar in Jerusalem?'''

23 Now therefore, I pray thee, give pledges to my lord the king of Assyria, and I will deliver thee two thousand horses, if thou be able on thy part to set riders upon them.

24 [19]How then wilt thou turn away the face of one captain of the least of my master's servants, and put thy [5]trust on Egypt for chariots and for horsemen?

25 Am I now come up °without [3]the LORD against this place to destroy it? [3]The LORD said to me, 'Go up against this land, and destroy it.'"

26 Then said Eliakim the son of Hilkiah, and Shebna, and Joah, unto Rab-shakeh, "Speak, I pray thee, to thy servants in the °Syrian language; for we understand *it:* and talk not with us in the Jews' language in the ears of the people that *are* on the wall."

27 But Rab-shakeh said unto them, "Hath my master sent me to thy master, and to thee, to speak these words? *hath he* not *sent me* to the °men which sit on the wall, that they may eat their own dung, and drink their own piss with you?"

28 Then Rab-shakeh stood and cried with a loud voice in the Jews' language, and spake, saying, "Hear the °word of the great king, the king of Assyria:

29 Thus saith the king, 'Let not Hezekiah °deceive you: for he shall not be able to deliver you out of °his hand:

30 Neither let Hezekiah make you [5]trust in [3]the LORD, saying, [3]'The LORD will surely deliver us, and this city shall not be delivered into the hand of the king of Assyria.'

31 Hearken not to Hezekiah:' for thus saith the king of Assyria, °'Make *an agreement* with me by a present, and °come out to me, and *then* eat ye °every man of his own vine, and every one of his fig tree, and drink ye every one the waters of his cistern:

32 Until I come and take you away to °a land

---

16 pillars, or supports.
it = them.

18. 17—19. 37 (Y², p. 516). SECOND INVASION.
(*Repeated and Extended Alternation.*)

Y² | A¹ | 18. 17-36. King of Assyria. Mission.
  B¹ | a | 18. 37. Report.
    b | 19. 1. Conduct.
      c | 19. 2-5. Message to Isaiah.
        d | 19. 6, 7. Answer of Isaiah. } Hezekiah.
A² | 19. 8-13. King of Assyria. Letter.
  B² | *a* | 19. 14-. Letter.
    b | 19. -14. Conduct.
      c | 19. 15-19. Prayer to Jehovah.
        d | 19. 20-34. Answer of Jehovah. } Hezekiah.
A³ | 19. 35-37. King of Assyria. Destruction.

17 king of Assyria. Some suppose Sargon, and treat Sennacherib as a mistake here. But probably Sennacherib was the co-regent in the field. Cp. Jerusalem's being taken by Nebuchadnezzar, while Nabopolassar was king in Babylon. So Belshazzar was co-regent with Nabonnedus at the taking of Babylon.

sent. The gift of *vv.* 14-16 did not prevent a further assault. Compromise seldom does.

Tartan. A title = commander-in-chief.

Rabsaris. A title = chief of the heads.

Rab-shakeh. A title = chief of the captains; possibly a political officer.

Lachish. Ten miles south-east of Jerusalem, on Sennacherib's way to Egypt. See note on 19. 8.

great host = heavy force.

against Jerusalem. See note on Judg. 1. 8.

upper pool. On east side of Jebus = Gihon.

18 household = palace.

19 Rab-shakeh said. See the references to this in Hezekiah's "Songs of the degrees". Pss. 120. 2, 3; 123. 3, 4, and cp. Isa. 37. 4. See Ap. 67. ii.

What confidence . . . ? Note the Fig. *Erotēsis* (Ap. 6), which the Rab-shakeh constantly uses. See *vv.* 20, 22, 24, 25, 27, 33, 34, 35. Figure used for emphasis.

20 vain words. Heb. word of lips = lip-words.

21 behold. Fig. *Asterismos.* Ap. 6.

trustest, &c. A policy opposed by Isaiah (Isa. 30. 2; 31. 4).

bruised reed. Cp. Ezek. 29. 6.

man. Heb. *'ish.* Ap. 14. II.

king of Egypt. Probably Shabako, the successor of So. See note on 19. 9, and cp. 17. 3, 4.

22 if ye say. Isa. 36. 7. If thou say. Spoken to one, but meant for all.

25 without the LORD. Either said in pretence, or from having heard Jehovah's prophecies (cp. 19. 25 with Isa. 10. 5).

26 Syrian = Aramaic.

27 men. Heb. *'ěnōsh.* Ap. 14. III.

28 word = message. Some codices, with two early printed editions, Sept., and Syr., read "words".

29 deceive = raise false hopes. Note the ל (*Lamed*) here, as in the first occurrence (Gen. 3. 13).

his hand = his [i. e. Asshur's king's] hand. Some codices, with one early printed edition, and Vulg., read "my hand".

31 Make [an agreement] = Get a blessing out of my coming. Lit. Make with me a blessing.

come out: i. e. capitulate.

every man. Heb. *'ish.* Ap. 14. II.

32 a land. Note the Fig. *Anaphora* (Ap. 6) for emphasis.

603 like your own land, a land of corn and °wine, a land of bread and vineyards, a land of oil olive and of honey, that ye may live, and not die: and hearken not unto Hezekiah, when he persuadeth you, saying, [3]'The LORD will °deliver us.'

33 Hath any of the gods of the nations [32]delivered at all his land out of the hand of the king of Assyria?

34 Where *are* the gods of °Hamath, and of °Arpad? where *are* the gods of °Sepharvaim, °Hena, and °Ivah? have they [32]delivered °Samaria out of mine hand?

35 Who *are* they among all the gods of the countries, that have [32]delivered their country out of mine hand, that [3]the LORD should deliver Jerusalem out of mine hand?'"

36 But the people held their peace, and answered Him not a word: for the king's commandment was, saying, "Answer him not."

B[1] a (p. 517) 37 Then came Eliakim the son of Hilkiah, which *was* over the household, and Shebna the scribe, and Joah the son of Asaph the recorder, to Hezekiah with *their* clothes rent, and told him the words of Rab-shakeh.

b **19** And °it came to pass, when king Hezekiah heard *it*, that he rent his clothes, and covered himself with sackcloth, and went into the house of °the LORD.

c 2 And he sent Eliakim, which *was* over the household, and Shebna the scribe, and the elders of the priests, covered with sackcloth, to °Isaiah the prophet the son of Amoz.

3 And they said unto him, "Thus saith Hezekiah, 'This day *is* a day of trouble, and of rebuke, and blasphemy: for the °children are come to the birth, and *there is* not strength to bring forth.

4 It may be [1]the LORD thy °God will hear °all the words of Rab-shakeh, whom the king of Assyria his master hath sent to °reproach the living °God; and will reprove the words which [1]the LORD thy °God hath heard: wherefore °lift up *thy* prayer for the remnant that are left.'"

5 So the servants of king Hezekiah came to Isaiah.

d 6 And °Isaiah said unto them, "Thus shall ye say to your master, 'Thus saith [1]the LORD, 'Be not afraid of the words which thou hast heard, with which the servants of the king of Assyria have °blasphemed Me.

7 °Behold, I will send °a blast upon him, and he shall °hear a rumour, and shall return to his own land; and I will cause him to fall by the sword in his own land.'''

A[2] 8 So Rab-shakeh returned, and found the king of Assyria warring against Libnah: for he had heard that he was °departed from Lachish.

9 And when he heard say of °Tirhakah king of Ethiopia, "Behold, he is come out to fight against thee:" he sent messengers again unto Hezekiah, saying,

10 "Thus shall ye speak to Hezekiah king of Judah, saying, 'Let not thy [4]God in Whom thou °trustest deceive thee, saying, 'Jerusalem shall not be delivered into the hand of the king of Assyria.'

11 Behold, thou hast heard what the kings of Assyria have done to all lands, by destroying them utterly: °and shalt thou be [32]delivered?

12 Have the gods of the nations [32]delivered them which my fathers have destroyed; *as* Gozan, and Haran, and Rezeph, and the [3]children of Eden which *were* in Thelasar?

13 Where *is* the king of °Hamath, and the king of Arpad, and the king of the city of Sepharvaim, of [34]Hena, and Ivah?'"

14 And Hezekiah received the letter of the hand of the messengers, and read it: B[2] *a*

and Hezekiah went up into °the house of [1]the LORD, and spread it before [1]the LORD. *b*

15 And Hezekiah °prayed before [1]the LORD, and said, "O [1]LORD [4]God of Israel, Which °dwellest *between* the cherubims, Thou °art the [4]God, *even* Thou alone, of all the king- *c*

wine. Heb. *tīrōsh*. See Ap. 27. II.
deliver = rescue.
34 Hamath. Cp. 17. 24.
Arpad. A city of Syria, north-west of Aleppo. Now identified with *Tell Erfūd*.
Sepharvaim. On the Euphrates, north of Babylon. See note on 17. 24.
Hena, and Ivah. Probably the names of gods or goddesses.
Samaria. See note on 17. 5, 24. Hamath, Arpad, and Samaria are all mentioned in the inscriptions at Khorsabad. See note on 17. 21.

19. 1 it came to pass. Cp. Isa. 37. 1.
the LORD. Heb. Jehovah. Ap. 4. II.
2 Isaiah. The first occurrence in the historical books. Hezekiah was one of the four kings in whose reign he prophesied (Isa. 1. 1). The chapters in Isaiah which refer to these events are 10. 5—12. 6; 14. 24-27; 17. 12-14; 22; 29—33; 36, and 37. **3 children** = sons.
4 God. Heb. Elohim. Ap. 4. I.
all. Some codices, with Syr., omit "all".
reproach = disparage, taunt, or flout.
lift up thy prayer. Hezekiah's "Songs of the degrees" witness to this prayer in his distress. See Pss. 120. 1; 130. 1, 2. Ap. 67. iv.
6 Isaiah. In Greek (N.T.) = Esaias.
blasphemed = reviled, or vilified.
7 Behold. Fig. *Asterismos*. Ap. 6.
a blast. Heb. *rūach*. Ap. 9.
hear a rumour. Fig. *Polyptōton* (Ap. 6), "hear a hearing" = hear a serious report. See note on Gen. 26. 28.
8 departed from Lachish. Sennacherib had laid siege against it (2 Chron. 32. 9), but had found it difficult, as Joshua had (Josh. 10. 31, 32, "the second day"); and "left" it untaken (Jer. 34. 7).
9 Tirhakah. An Ethiopian by birth; king of Egypt by conquest. Defeated later by Esarhaddon, son of Sennacherib, after fifteen days' battle. Esarhaddon is shown on a *stelē*, recently discovered, leading Tirhakah with cords.
10 trustest = confidest. Heb. *bataḥ*. Ap. 69. i.
11 and shalt thou be delivered? Note the Fig. *Erotēsis* here, and in *vv.* 12, 13, and 25.
13 Hamath, &c. See note on 18. 34.
14 the house of the LORD. Hezekiah's zeal for the house of Jehovah is seen in his "Songs of the degrees". Cp. Pss. 122. 1, 9; 134. 1, 2. See Ap. 67. xiii.
15 prayed. When assaulted by the king of terrors he "turned his face to the wall and prayed" (Isa. 38. 2). But when the king of Babylon came with a present he did not pray, and fell into the snare (Isa. 39. 1, 2). Note the Structure of Isaiah, chs. 36—39, and see Ap. 67. iv.
dwellest. Cp. his prayer in Ps. 123. 1. Ap. 67. iv.
art the God = art Thyself the God.

603 doms of the earth; °Thou hast made heaven and earth.

16 [1]LORD, bow down Thine ear, and hear: open, [1]LORD, Thine eyes, and see: and hear the words of Sennacherib, which hath sent him to [4]reproach the °living [4]God.

17 Of a truth, [1]LORD, the kings of Assyria have destroyed the nations and their lands,

18 And have cast their gods into the fire: for they *were* no gods, but the work of men's hands, wood and stone: therefore they have destroyed them.

19 Now therefore, O [1]LORD our [4]God, I beseech thee, save Thou us out of his hand, that all the kingdoms of the earth may know that Thou *art* [1]the LORD [4]God, *even* Thou only."

d e (p. 519) 20 Then Isaiah the son of Amoz sent to Hezekiah, saying, "Thus saith [1]the LORD [4]God of Israel, '*That* which thou hast prayed to Me against Sennacherib king of Assyria I have heard.'

f 21 This *is* the word that [1]the LORD hath spoken concerning him;

'The virgin the daughter of Zion hath despised thee, *and* laughed thee to scorn;
The daughter of Jerusalem hath shaken her head °at thee.

22 Whom hast thou [4]reproached and [6]blasphemed?
And against Whom hast thou exalted *thy* voice, and lifted up thine eyes on high?
Even against the Holy *One* of Israel.

23 By thy messengers thou hast reproached °the LORD*, and hast said,
'With the multitude of my chariots I am come up to the height of the mountains,
To the sides of Lebanon,
And °will cut down the tall cedar trees thereof,
And the choice fir trees thereof:
And I °will enter into the lodgings of his borders,
And into the forest of his Carmel.

24 I have digged and drunk strange waters,
And with the sole of my feet have I dried up all the rivers of besieged places.'

25 Hast thou not heard long ago *how* I have °done it,
And of ancient times that I have formed it?
Now have I brought it to pass,
That thou shouldest be to lay waste fenced cities *into* ruinous heaps.

26 Therefore their inhabitants were of small power,
They were dismayed and confounded;
They were °*as* the grass of the field,
And *as* the green herb, *as* the grass on the house tops,
And *as corn* °blasted before it be grown up.

27 But I know thy °abode,
And thy going out, and thy coming in,
And °thy rage against Me.

28 Because [27]thy rage against Me and thy °tumult is come up into Mine ears,
Therefore I will put My hook in thy nose,
And My bridle in thy lips,
And I will °turn thee back by the way by which thou camest.'

e 29 And this *shall be* a sign unto thee, Ye shall °eat this year such things as grow of themselves, and in the second year that which springeth of the same; and in the third year sow ye, and reap, and plant vineyards, and eat the fruits thereof.

30 And the remnant that is escaped of the house of Judah shall yet again take root downward, and bear fruit upward.

31 For °out of Jerusalem shall go forth a °remnant, and they that escape out of mount Zion: the zeal of °the LORD *of hosts* shall do this.

32 Therefore thus saith [1]the LORD concern- f
ing the king of Assyria, 'He shall not come into this city, nor shoot an arrow there, nor come before it with shield, nor °cast a bank against it.

33 By the way that he came, by the same shall he return, and shall not come into this city,' saith [1]the LORD.

34 'For I will °defend this city, to save it, °for Mine own sake, and for My servant David's sake.'"

35 And °it came to pass °that night, that A³ (p. 517)
°the Angel of [1]the LORD went out, and smote in the camp of the Assyrians an hundred fourscore and five thousand: and when °they arose

---

Thou hast made heaven and earth. Cp. Gen. 1. 1. Hezekiah, in his "Songs of the degrees", repeats this phrase as witnessing to the power of God, as Creator, to defeat the enemy. See Pss. 121. 1, 2; 123. 1; 124. 8; 134. 3. See Ap. 67. v.

16 living God. Always used in contrast with idols.

19. 20-37 (*d*, p. 517). ANSWER OF JEHOVAH.
(*Alternation.*)

d | e | 20. Jehovah. Prayer regarded.
  | f | 21-28. Defiance of the foe.
  | e | 29-31. Jehovah. Sign given.
  | f | 32-34. Defeat of the foe.

21 at thee = after thee: i. e. after she hath seen thy back turned.

23 the LORD*. This is one of the 134 places where the *Sōpherīm* altered "Jehovah" to "Adonai" (Ap. 32). will = have, as in *v.* 24.

25 done it = made it: i. e. the earth.

26 as the grass, &c. Note Hezekiah's reference to this in his "Song of the degrees" (Ps. 129. 5-7). See Ap. 67. ii. blasted = blighted.

27 abode, &c. = downsitting, and thy outgoing, and thy incoming.

thy rage = thy enraging thyself. Very emphatic. The Hithpael gerund occurs only here and Isa. 37. 28, 29.

28 tumult = arrogance.

turn thee back. See the reference to this in Hezekiah's "Song of the degrees" (Ps. 129. 4, 5). See Ap. 67. iii.

29 eat this year, &c. See the reference to Jehovah's sign in Hezekiah's "Songs of the degrees" (Pss. 126. 5, 6; 128. 2). See Ap. 67. ix.

31 out of Jerusalem . . . remnant: i. e. the country people who had retired into Jerusalem for safety. remnant. Cp. *v.* 4, and see Isa. 10. 20.

the LORD of hosts = Jehovah of hosts. Some codices, with three early printed editions, Aram., Sept., Syr., and Vulg., read "of hosts" in the text.

32 cast a bank: i. e. erect an earthwork.

34 defend = spread, or be a shield over.

for Mine own sake. Man's sins cannot foil God's purpose. He does not go outside of His own will to explain His actions in grace.

35 it came to pass. Cp. 37. 36.

that night: i. e. the night of the prophecy when the promise was fulfilled. Cp. "that day" (Luke 21. 34. 1 Thess. 5. 4).

the Angel of the LORD: i. e. the destroying Angel. Cp. 2 Sam. 24. 16. they: i. e. the king and his people.

603 early in the morning, [7]behold, they *were* all
°dead corpses.
36 So Sennacherib king of Assyria °departed,
°and went and returned, and dwelt at Nineveh.
37 And it came to pass, as he was worshipping
in the house of °Nisroch his god, that Adrammelech and Sharezer °his sons °smote him
with the sword: and they escaped into the
land of °Armenia. And °Esarhaddon his son
reigned in his stead.

T C[1] g (p. 520) **20** In °those days was Hezekiah sick unto
death. And the prophet Isaiah the son
of Amoz came to him, and said unto him, "Thus
saith °the LORD, °'Set thine house in order;
for thou shalt °die, and not live.' "
h 2 Then °he turned his face to the wall, and
°prayed unto [1]the LORD, saying,
3 "I beseech thee, O [1]LORD, remember now
how I have °walked before Thee in truth and
with °a perfect heart, and have done *that
which is* good in Thy sight." And Hezekiah
°wept sore.
g 4 And it came to pass, afore Isaiah was gone
out into the middle court, that the word of
[1]the LORD °came to him, saying,
5 "Turn again, and tell Hezekiah the captain
of My people, 'Thus saith [1]the LORD, the °God
of David thy father, 'I have heard thy prayer,
I have seen thy tears: °behold, I will heal
thee: on the third day thou shalt °go up unto
the house of [1]the LORD.
603 to 588 6 And I will add unto thy days °fifteen years;
and I will deliver thee and this city out of the
hand of the king of Assyria; and I will °defend
this city for Mine own sake, and for °My servant David's sake.' ' "
7 And Isaiah said, "Take a °lump of figs."
And they took and laid *it* on the boil, and he
recovered.
h 8 And Hezekiah said unto Isaiah, °"What
shall be the sign that [1]the LORD will heal me,
and that I shall °go up into the house of [1]the
LORD the third day?"
9 And Isaiah said, "This sign shalt thou have
of [1]the LORD, that [1]the LORD will do the thing
that He hath spoken: shall the shadow go forward ten °degrees, or go back ten °degrees?"
10 And Hezekiah answered, "It is a light
thing for the shadow to go °down ten [9]degrees:
nay, but let the shadow return backward ten
[9]degrees."
11 And Isaiah the prophet cried unto [1]the
LORD: and He brought the shadow ten [9]de-
grees backward, by which it had gone down
in the °dial of °Ahaz.
C[2] i[1] 12 At that time °Berodach-baladan, the son
of Baladan, °king of Babylon, °sent letters

dead corpses. Fig. *Pleonasm* (Ap. 6), for emphasis.

36 departed. There is no mention of the capture of Jerusalem in Sennacherib's inscription. This omission is more remarkable than what Sennacherib says. Had he taken Jerusalem, the omission would be unaccountable. Cp. 2 Chron. 32. 21 and Ps. 129. 4, 5.

and. Note the Fig. *Polysyndeton* (Ap. 6) to greatly emphasise the fact of his defeat.

37 Nisroch. Mentioned in the inscriptions.

his sons. A cylinder recently acquired (1910) by, and now in the British Museum, states: "On the twentieth day of the month Tebet (Dec.), Sennacherib, king of Assyria, his son slew him in a rebellion." The rebellion (it says) lasted till the twenty-eighth of Sivan (June) of next year, "when Esarhaddon his son sat on the throne of Assyria." The will, or rather deed of gift, of Sennacherib (2 inches by 1, containing eleven lines; in the Kouyoujik Gallery) gives all to Esarhaddon. This probably led to Esarhaddon having afterwards to fight his two brothers, Sennacherib's murderers.

smote him. Some years later; but mentioned here as the sequel to this history. **Armenia.** Heb. Ararat.

Esarhaddon. See note, above.

20. 1-19 (*T*, p. 516). PERSONAL. SICKNESS.
(*Division*.)

T | C[1] | 1-11. Hezekiah's miraculous healing.
  | C[2] | 12-19. Berodach's embassy.

1-11 (C[1], above). HEZEKIAH'S HEALING.
(*Alternation*.)

C[1] | g | 1. Isaiah's warning.
  | h | 2, 3. Hezekiah's prayer.
  | *g* | 4-7. Isaiah's promise.
  | *h* | 8-11. Hezekiah's sign.

1 those days. About the time of the second invasion (18. 13), but before the deliverance of 19. 35.

the LORD. Heb. Jehovah. Ap. 4. II.

Set thine house in order = Give charge concerning thine house. See the Structure of Isa. 36—39.

die, and not live. Fig. *Pleonasm* (Ap. 6), a double emphasis.

2 he. Some codices, with four early printed editions, Sept., and Syr., read "Hezekiah".

prayed. See note on *v.* 15. See his references to this in his "Songs of the degrees" (Pss. 120. 1; 123. 1-3; 130. 1, 2); and Ap. 67. iv.

3 walked = walked to and fro: i.e. habitually walked.

a perfect = whole, or undivided.

wept sore. Heb. "wept with a great weeping" = wept bitterly. Fig. *Polyptōton*. Ap. 6. See note on Gen. 26. 28.

4 came. The only occurrence of this in the case of Isaiah. Cp. Gen. 15. 1.

5 God of David (Heb. Elohim). This tells us the nature of Hezekiah's prayer. He had no heir to the throne, but remembered Jehovah's word to David in 2 Sam. 7. 12-16. Hence his anxiety, as manifested in his "Songs of the degrees". Cp. Pss. 127. 3-5; 128; and 132. See Ap. 67. xiv. (Manasseh not born till three years later, 600 B.C.)

behold. Fig. *Asterismos*. Ap. 6. Introducing the fivefold (Ap. 10) promise and answer to his prayer in *vv.* 5 and 6.

go up, &c. This also must have been a subject of prayer.

6 fifteen years. 603-588 B.C.

defend = be a shield to. Cp. 19. 34.

My servant David's sake. See note on *v.* 5 and Ps. 132. **7 lump** = cake, or plaister. **8 What shall be the sign . . .?** Contrast Ahaz (Isa. 7. 11, 12). **go up into the house of the LORD.** See note on 19. 14, and Ap. 67. xiii. **9 degrees.** It is to these degrees that Hezekiah's fifteen Songs refer (Pss. 120—134). The word "degrees" is repeated here six times (in the history), but five times in Isaiah's gracious words (38. 8). **10 down** = forward (*v.* 9). **11 dial** = degrees. **Ahaz.** See note on *v.* 8.

20. 12-19 [For the Structure see next page].

12 Berodach. Some codices, with Sept. and Syr., read "Merodach". Cp. Isa. 39. 1. **king of Babylon.** First occurrence of this title. Babylon and Nineveh the two great cities competing henceforward for supremacy in Assyria. Finally settled by Nabopolassar and his son Nebuchadnezzar, "the head of gold" (Dan. 2. 37, 38). **sent letters and a present.** These did what the king of Assyria and the king of terrors could not do. See the Structure "*C*" of Isa. 36—39.

603-588 and a °present unto Hezekiah: for he had heard
that Hezekiah had been sick.

j[1] (p. 521) 13 And Hezekiah °hearkened unto them, and
shewed them °all the house of °his precious
things, the silver, °and the gold, and the spices,
and the precious ointment, and °*all* the house
of his armour, and all that was found in his
°treasures: there was nothing in his house, nor
in all his dominion, that Hezekiah shewed
them not.

i[2] 14 °Then came Isaiah the prophet unto king
Hezekiah, and said unto him, °"What said
these °men? and from whence came they unto
thee?" And Hezekiah said, "They are come
from °a far country, *even* from Babylon."

j[2] 15 And he said, [14]"What have they seen in
thine house?" And Hezekiah answered, "All
the things that *are* in mine house have they
seen: there is nothing among my [13]treasures
that I have not shewed them."

i[3] 16 And Isaiah said unto Hezekiah, "Hear the
word of [1]the LORD.

17 °'Behold, the days come, that all that *is* in
thine house, and that which thy fathers have
laid up in store unto this day, shall be carried
°into Babylon: nothing shall be left,' saith [1]the
LORD.

18 'And of thy sons that shall issue from thee,
which thou shalt beget, shall °they take away;
and they shall be °eunuchs in the palace of the
king of Babylon.'"

j[3] 19 Then said Hezekiah unto Isaiah, °"Good
is the word of [1]the LORD which thou hast
spoken." And he said, °"*Is it* not *good*, if
peace and truth be in my days?"

S (p. 516) 20 And the rest of the acts of Hezekiah, and
all his might, and how he made °a pool, and °a
conduit, and °brought water into the city, *are*
they not written in the book of the chronicles of
the kings of Judah?

21 And Hezekiah °slept with his fathers: and
Manasseh his son reigned in his stead.

R[2] k (p. 521) 588-583 **21** °Manasseh *was* °twelve years old when
he began to reign, and reigned fifty and
five years in Jerusalem. And his mother's
name *was* °Hephzi-bah.

l 2 And he °did *that which was* °evil in the
sight of °the LORD, after the abominations of
the °heathen, whom °the LORD cast out before
the °children of Israel.

3 For he built up again °the high places
which Hezekiah his father had destroyed;
and he reared up altars for Baal, and made
°a grove, °as °did Ahab king of Israel; and
worshipped all °the host of heaven, and served
them.

4 And he built altars in the house of [2]the
LORD, of which [2]the LORD said, "In Jerusalem
will I put My name."

---

20. 12-19 (C[2], p. 520). BERODACH'S EMBASSY.
(*Repeated Alternation.*)

C[2] | i[1] | 12. Messengers from Babylon.
| j[1] | 13. Hezekiah. Ostentation.
| i[2] | 14. Messengers from Babylon.
| j[2] | 15. Hezekiah. Ostentation.
| i[3] | 16-18. Messenger from Jehovah.
| j[3] | 19. Hezekiah. Submission.

present. Cp. 2 Chron. 32. 22, 23. These presents account for the treasures exhibited to the Babylonian ambassadors, and explain Hezekiah's wealth (2 Chron. 32. 27, 28) so soon after the depletion of his treasures in 18. 15, 16.

13 hearkened. He did not pray as in *v.* 2, or as in 19. 15. See the notes and Isa. 39. 2, "was glad".

all. Some codices, with Syr. and Vulg., omit this "all". It was omitted also in A.V. edition, 1611.

his. The depletion of 18. 15, 16 was not of "his" house, but of the house of Jehovah as well as "the king's house".

and. Note the Fig. *Polysyndeton* (Ap. 6) emphasising each item.

all the house of his armour = all his armoury.

treasures = treasuries.

14 Then came Isaiah. He was to Hezekiah what Nathan was to David (2 Sam. 12. 1).

What said . . . ? Fig. *Anthropopatheia.* Ap. 6: for God knew who the men were, and what they had said.

men. Heb. *'ĕnōsh.* Ap. 14. III.

a far country. Some codices, with three early printed editions, Aram., Sept., Syr., and Vulg., add "unto me".

17 Behold. Fig. *Asterismos.* Ap. 6.

into Babylon. Cp. 2 Chron. 33. 11, and see note on *v.* 12. A remarkable prophecy, as Babylon was of little account as yet (cp. Isa. 39. 6). The return from Babylon was also foretold (Isa. 48, 49).

18 they. Heb. text reads "he". But some codices, with 3 early printed editions, read "they". Cp. Isa. 39. 7.

eunuchs: i. e. courtiers, chamberlains, &c. Cp. Gen. 37. 36 and Dan. 1. 3, 4.

19 Good. Hezekiah's submission was like Eli's. Cp. 1 Sam. 3. 18.

Is it not good, if: or, Is it not that, &c. Fig. *Erotēsis.* Ap. 6. Sept. reads "Let there be good".

20 a pool = the pool. Cp. 18. 17. The pool of Siloam fed by the conduit mentioned below.

a conduit = the conduit. A long underground channel discovered by Sir Charles Warren (in 1867) running from Gihon (now the Virgin's Fount) down to Siloam. An inscription found in it describes the making of it. Cp. 2 Chron. 32. 30.

brought water = brought the water. This is referred to by Hezekiah in Psalm 46. 4, where it is contrasted with the raging waters of *v.* 3. Cp. this with Isa. 8. 6-8.

21 slept with his fathers. See note on Deut. 31. 16.

21. 1-18 (R[2], p. 516). MANASSEH. (*Introversion.*)

R[2] | k | 1. Introduction. Accession.
| l | 2-9. Events. Personal. Evil-doing.
| m | 10-15. Threatening of Jehovah.
| *l* | 16. Events. Personal. Evil-doing.
| *k* | 17, 18. Conclusion. Record and death.

1 Manasseh = forgetting. So named because God had made Hezekiah forget his troubles (cp. Joseph, Gen. 41. 51). A sad name for him who became the worst of Judah's kings. His name appears second in a list of kings who brought gifts to Esar-haddon.

twelve years. Therefore not born till the third of Hezekiah's fifteen added years. See note on 20. 18.

Hephzi-bah = my delight is in her. Cp. reference to the marriage in Isa. 62. 4. A prophecy, given at the time of Hezekiah, foretelling a happier time; even the "good" of 20. 19, and note.

2 did . . . evil = did the evil. Heb. *rā'a'.* Ap. 44. viii. Generally associated with idolatry. **the LORD.** Heb. Jehovah. Ap. 4. II. **heathen** = nations. **children** = sons. **3 the high places.** Restoring what his father had destroyed (18. 4, 22). **a grove** = an *'Ashērah.* See note on Ex. 34. 13. Ap. 42. **as** = according as. **did Ahab.** See 11. 18, and cp. 1 Kings 16. 31, 32. **the host of heaven.** Never before done in Judah. Cp. Deut. 4. 19; 17. 3.

588 5 And he built altars for all the host of heaven
to in the °two courts of the house of [2]the LORD.
533 6 And he made °his son °pass through the
fire, and °observed times, and °used enchantments, and dealt with °familiar spirits and
°wizards: he wrought much °wickedness in
the sight of [2]the LORD, to provoke °*Him* to
anger.
7 And he set °a graven image of °the grove
that he had made in the house, of which [2]the
LORD said to David, and to Solomon his son,
"In this house, and in Jerusalem, which I have
chosen out of all tribes of Israel, will I put My
name for ever:
8 Neither will I make °the feet of Israel °move
any more out of the land which I gave their
fathers; only if they will observe to do according to all that I have commanded them, and
according to all the law that °My servant
Moses commanded them."
9 But they hearkened not: and Manasseh
°seduced them to °do more evil than did the
nations whom [2]the LORD destroyed before the
[2]children of Israel.
m 10 And [2]the LORD spake °by His servants
(p. 521) the prophets, saying,
11 "Because Manasseh king of Judah hath
°done these abominations, *and* hath done
wickedly above all that the °Amorites did,
which *were* before him, and hath made Judah
also to °sin with his °idols:
12 Therefore thus saith [2]the LORD °God of
Israel, °'Behold, I *am* bringing *such* [2]evil upon
Jerusalem and Judah, that whosoever heareth
of it, °both his ears shall tingle.
13 And I will stretch over Jerusalem °the line
of Samaria, and °the plummet of the house of
Ahab: and I will °wipe Jerusalem [3]as *a man*
°wipeth a dish, °wiping *it*, and turning *it* upside
down.
14 And I will forsake the °remnant of Mine
inheritance, and deliver them into the hand of
their enemies; and they shall become a prey
and a spoil to all their enemies;
15 Because they have done *that which was*
evil in My sight, and have provoked Me to
anger, since the day their fathers came forth
out of Egypt, even unto this day.'"
l 16 Moreover Manasseh shed °innocent blood
very much, till he had filled Jerusalem from
one end to another; beside his sin wherewith
he made Judah to sin, in doing *that which was*
evil in the sight of [2]the LORD.
k 17 Now °the rest of the acts of Manasseh, and
all that he did, and his °sin that he [2]sinned,
°*are* they not written in the book of the chronicles of the kings of Judah?
18 And Manasseh °slept with his fathers, and
was buried °in the garden of his own house,
in the garden of Uzza: and Amon his son
reigned in his stead.
R³ n 19 Amon *was* twenty and two years old
(p. 522) when he began to reign, and he reigned two
533 years in Jerusalem. And his mother's name
to *was* Meshullemeth, the daughter of Haruz of
531 °Jotbah.
o 20 And he did *that which was* [2]evil in the
sight of [2]the LORD, [3]as his father Manasseh
did.

21 And he walked in all the way that his
father walked in, and served the [11]idols that
his father served, and worshipped them:
22 And he forsook [2]the LORD [12]God of his
fathers, and walked not in the way of [2]the
LORD.

23 And the servants of Amon conspired a- *o*
gainst him, and slew the king in his own
house.

24 And the People of the land slew all them
that had conspired against king Amon; and
the People of the land made Josiah his son
king in his stead.

---

5 two courts. See note on 1 Kings 7. 12.
6 his son. Son put by Fig. *Synecdoche* (of Part), Ap. 6, for his sons. Cp. 2 Chron. 33. 6.
pass through the fire. As Ahaz had done (16. 3; cp. 23. 10. Deut. 18. 10). The name of Moloch was common at this time (Zeph. 1. 5).
observed times. Cp. Deut. 18. 10.
used enchantments. The same as modern spiritism. Cp. Lev. 19. 31. Deut. 18. 11.
familiar spirits. Heb. a familiar spirit. See note on Lev. 19. 31.
wizards = mediums.
wickedness. Heb. *rā'a'.* Ap. 44. viii. Same word as 'evil', *v.* 2.
Him. Some codices, with four early printed editions, Aram., Sept., Syr., and Vulg., read "Him" in text.
7 a graven image of the grove = a carved *'Ashērah* (*v.* 3). Removed by Josiah (23. 6). See Ap. 42.
8 the feet. Fig. *Pleonasm.* Ap. 6.
move = wander.
My servant Moses. See note on Num. 12. 7.
9 seduced. Not said of any previous king. Cp. Jer. 15. 4.
do more evil = do the evil more.
10 by = through. Heb. by the hand of. Fig. *Metonymy* (of Cause). Ap. 6.
11 done = made.
Amorites. One of the seven nations of Canaan, descendants of the *Nephīlīm.* Ap. 23 and 25.
sin. Heb. *chātā'.* Ap. 44. i.
idols = filthy, or manufactured idols.
12 God. Heb. Elohim. Ap. 4. I.
Behold. Fig. *Asterismos.* Ap. 6.
both his ears, &c. Cp. 1 Sam. 3. 11.
13 the line . . . the plummet. Put by Fig. *Metonymy* (of the Cause), Ap. 6, for what is measured by them.
wipe . . . wipeth . . . wiping. Fig. *Polyptōton* (Ap. 6), emphasising the completeness of the work.
14 remnant. Cp. 19. 30. Jerusalem survived the calamities of 18. 13, but would not survive those that were coming.
16 innocent blood. Tradition says that Isaiah was one who suffered martyrdom (Jos. *Ant.* x. 3. 1).
17 the rest. Cp. 2 Chron. 33. 12-19. His captivity in Babylon, &c.
sin that he sinned = his great sin. Fig. *Polyptōton.* Ap. 6.
are they not written . . . ? Fig. *Erotēsis.* Ap. 6.
18 slept with his fathers. His father was the best of Judah's kings, and he was the worst. See note on Deut. 31. 16.
in the garden. Not in the sepulchres of the kings.

21. 19-26 (R³, p. 516). **AMON.**
(*Introversion.*)

R³ | n | 19. Introduction. Accession.
  o | 20-22. Events. Personal. Evil-doing.
  o | 23, 24. Events. Political. Retribution.
  n | 25, 26. Conclusion. Burial.

19 Jotbah. Cp. Num. 33. 33. Deut. 10. 7.

n 25 Now the rest of the acts of Amon °which
(p. 522) he did, [17] *are* they not written in the book of the
533 chronicles of the kings of Judah?
to 26 And °he was buried in his °sepulchre [18] in
531 the garden of Uzza: and Josiah his son reigned
in his stead.

R[4] D **22** Josiah *was* °eight years old when he
(p. 523) began to reign, and he reigned thirty
531 and one years in Jerusalem. And his mother's
to name *was* Jedidah, the daughter of Adaiah of
500 °Boscath.
E p 2 And he did *that which was* right in the
sight of °the LORD, and walked in all the °way
of David his father, and °turned not aside to
the right hand or to the left.

q F r[1] 3 And it came to pass in °the eighteenth year
of king Josiah, *that* the king sent °Shaphan
the son of Azaliah, the son of Meshullam, the
scribe, to the house of [2] the LORD, saying,
4 "Go up to °Hilkiah the high priest, that he
may °sum the silver which is brought into the
house of [2] the LORD, which the keepers of the
door have gathered of the People:
5 And let them deliver it into the hand °of
the doers of the work, that have the oversight
of the house of [2] the LORD: and let them give
it °to the doers of the work which *is* in the
house of [2] the LORD, to repair the breaches of
the house,
6 Unto carpenters, and builders, and masons,
and to buy timber and hewn stone to repair
°the house."
7 Howbeit there was no reckoning made with
them of the money that was delivered into
their hand, because they dealt faithfully.
s[1] 8 And Hilkiah the high priest said unto Shaphan the scribe, "I have found °the book of
the law in the house of [2] the LORD." And
Hilkiah gave the book to Shaphan, and he
read it.
r[2] 9 And Shaphan the scribe came to the king,
and brought the king word again, and said,
"Thy servants have gathered the money that
was found in the house, and have delivered it
into the hand of them that do the work, that
have the oversight of the house of [2] the LORD."
s[2] 10 And Shaphan the scribe shewed the king,
saying, "Hilkiah the priest hath delivered me
a book." And Shaphan °read it before the
king.
11 And it came to pass, when the king had
heard the words of the book of the law, that
°he rent his clothes.
G t[1] 12 And the king commanded Hilkiah the
priest, and °Ahikam the son of Shaphan, and
°Achbor the son of Michaiah, and Shaphan
the scribe, and Asahiah a servant of the king's,
saying,
13 "Go ye, enquire of [2] the LORD for me, and
for the people, °and for all Judah, concerning
the words of this book that is found: for great

25 which he did. Some codices, with Aram. and Syr., read "and all that which he did".

26 he was buried = one buried him. But some codices, with three early printed editions, Aram., Sept., Syr., and Vulg., read "and they buried him".

sepulchre. Heb. *ķeber*, a (not "the") grave, or tomb. Cp. 22. 20.

22. 1—23. 30 (R[4], p. 516). JOSIAH.
(*Introversion and Alternations.*)

R[4] | D | 22. 1. Introduction. Accession.
E | p | 22. 2. Event. Personal well-doing.
q | 22. 3—23. 24. Josiah's reformation.
E | *p* | 23. 25. Event. Personal well-doing.
q | 23. 26, 27. Manasseh's provocation.
D | 23. 28-30. Conclusion.

1 eight years. Manasseh began at twelve, bred under godly Hezekiah. Josiah began at eight, bred by ungodly Amon. Contrast the two characters.

Boscath. In Judah. Cp. Josh. 15. 39.

2 the LORD. Heb. Jehovah. Ap. 4. II.

way. Edition of 1611 had "ways".

turned not aside. Josiah is the only king of whom this is said.

22. 3—23. 24 (q, above). JOSIAH'S REFORMATION. (*Alternations.*)

q | F | r[1] | 22. 3-7. Repairs of Temple.
s[1] | 22. 8. Book found.
r[2] | 22. 9. Repairs of Temple.
s[2] | 22. 10, 11. Book found.
G | t[1] | 22. 12, 13. Command. } Inquiry.
u[1] | 22. 14. Obedience. }
t[2] | 22. 15-17. Threatening. Judah. } Answer.
u[2] | 22. 18-20. Consolation. Josiah. }
F | r[3] | 23. 1, 2-. Assemblage of people.
s[3] | 23. -2. Book read.
G | t[3] | 23. 3. Josiah's well-doing. Covenant made.
u[3] | 23. 4-20. Evil removed.
t[4] | 23. 21-23. Josiah's well-doing. Passover.
u[4] | 23. 24. Evil removed.

3 the eighteenth year. Marks the completion of the work (23. 23). Begun in the twelfth year (2 Chron. 34. 3, 8). Jeremiah was called in Josiah's thirteenth year (Jer. 1. 2; 25. 3), and was to Josiah what Isaiah had been to Hezekiah.

Shaphan. Eight relatives mentioned in 2 Kings and 2 Chronicles: (1) His grandfather, Meshullam (2 Kings 22. 3); (2) his father, Azaliah (*v.* 3); (3) his son, Ahikam (*v.* 12); (4) his son, Gemariah (Jer. 36. 10); (5) his son, Elasah (Jer. 29. 3); (6) his son, Jaazaniah (Ezek. 8. 11); (7) his grandson, Michaiah (Jer. 36. 11, 13); (8) his grandson, Gedaliah (Jer. 39—43).

4 Hilkiah. The son of Shallum and father of Azariah (1 Chron. 6. 13).

sum = pour out, or pay away.

5 of the doers. These were the overseers.

to the doers. These were the labourers.

6 the house. Some codices, with two early printed editions, and Sept., read "the breaches of the house", as in *v.* 5.

8 the book of the law: i. e. the original copy of the Pentateuch, laid up by the side of the Ark (Deut. 31. 24-26). Probably secreted during the reigns of Manasseh (21. 16) and Amon (21. 21). See Ap. 47.

10 read it. Especially those parts applicable to the then circumstances, such as Lev. 26. Deut. 28, &c.

11 he rent his clothes. Not necessarily on account of his surprise, but on account of the solemnity of the words. **12 Ahikam.** The friend of Jeremiah (Jer. 26. 24) and father of Gedaliah (cp. 25. 22. Jer. 39. 14; 40. 5). See note on "Shaphan" (*v.* 3). **Achbor.** Not the same person as Abdon, in 2 Chron. 34. 20. The two books are independent. **13 and for all Judah.** Some codices, with two early printed editions, read "and for the remnant in Israel and in Judah". Cp. 2 Chron. 34. 21.

513 *is* the wrath of [2]the LORD that is kindled against us, because our fathers have not hearkened unto the words of this book, to do according unto all that which is written concerning us."

u[1] (p. 523) 14 So Hilkiah the priest, and Ahikam, and Achbor, and Shaphan, and Asahiah, went unto Huldah °the prophetess, °the wife of Shallum the son of Tikvah, the son of Harhas, keeper of the °wardrobe; (°now she dwelt in Jerusalem °in the college;) and they communed with her.

t[2] 15 And she said unto them, "Thus saith [2]the LORD [12]God of Israel, 'Tell the °man that sent you to me,

16 'Thus saith [2]the LORD, °'Behold, I will bring °evil upon this place, and upon the inhabitants thereof, *even* all the words of the book which the king of Judah hath read:

17 Because they have °forsaken Me, and have burned incense unto other gods, that they might provoke Me to anger with all the works of their hands; therefore My wrath shall be kindled against this place, and shall not be quenched.''

u[2] 18 But to the king of Judah which sent you to enquire of [2]the LORD, thus shall ye say to him, 'Thus saith [2]the LORD °God of Israel, °'*As touching* the words which thou hast °heard;

19 °Because thine heart was tender, and thou hast humbled thyself before [2]the LORD, when thou heardest what I spake against this place, and against the inhabitants thereof, that they should become °a desolation and a curse, and hast rent thy clothes, and wept before Me; I also have heard *thee*,' saith [2]the LORD.

20 [16]'Behold therefore, I will gather thee unto thy fathers, and thou shalt be °gathered into °thy grave °in peace; and thine eyes shall not see all the evil which I will bring upon this place.''"" And they brought the king word again.

F r[3] 23 And the king sent, and they gathered unto him all the elders of Judah and of Jerusalem.

2 And the king went up into the house of °the LORD, and all the °men of Judah and all the inhabitants of Jerusalem with him, and the priests, and the °prophets, and all the People, both small and great:

s[3] and he °read °in their ears all the words of the book of the covenant which was found in the house of °the LORD.

G t[3] 3 And the king stood °by a pillar, and made a covenant before [2]the LORD, to walk after [2]the LORD, and to keep His commandments and His testimonies and His statutes with all *their* heart and all *their* °soul, to perform the words of this covenant that were °written in this book. And all the People °stood to the covenant.

u[3] 4 And the king commanded Hilkiah the high priest, and the °priests of the second order, and the keepers of the door, to bring forth out of the temple of [2]the LORD all the vessels that were made for Baal, and for °the grove, and for all the °host of heaven: and he °burned them without Jerusalem in the fields of Kidron, and carried the ashes of them °unto Beth-el.

5 And he put down the °idolatrous priests, whom the kings of Judah had ordained to burn incense in the high places in the cities of Judah, and in the places round about Jerusalem; them also that burned incense unto Baal, to the sun, and to the moon, and to the °planets, and to all the host of heaven.

6 And he brought out [4]the grove from the house of [2]the LORD, without Jerusalem, unto

14 the prophetess. Others mentioned are: Miriam (Ex. 15. 20. Mic. 6. 4); Deborah (Judg. 4. 4); Noadiah (Neh. 6. 14); Isaiah's wife (Isa. 8. 3); Anna (Luke 2. 36); and Philip's daughters (Acts 21. 9).

the wife. Cp. the usage (Judg. 4. 4). The employment of a woman as prophet shows the degeneracy of the times, deplored by Isaiah (9. 15), denounced by Jeremiah (5. 7, 8; 14. 14; 23. 14–30; 37. 19. Lam. 2. 14), and by Ezekiel (13. 2–23). Inferred also from Huldah's words (*vv.* 15–18), and Jer. 5. 31.

wardrobe: i. e. vestry, or vestments.

now. Note the Fig. *Parenthesis.* Ap. 6.

in the college. Heb. in the second. Some supply "part", or "city". Probably = "second gate [of the city]". Cp. 2 Chron. 34. 22 and Zeph. 1. 10.

15 man. Heb. *'īsh.* Ap. 14. II.

16 Behold. Fig. *Asterismos.* Ap. 6.

evil. Heb. *rā'a'.* Ap. 44. viii.

17 forsaken Me. Huldah adopts the words of Deut. 29. 25–27.

18 God. Heb. Elohim. Ap. 4. I.

As touching. No Ellipsis here, but at end of verse. See below.

heard, or hearkened to. Supply Fig. *Ellipsis* (Ap. 6) thus: "Thus saith Jehovah Elohim: the words which thou hast hearkened to [shall surely come to pass]. In that thine heart was tender . . . I also have heard thee".

19 Because = In that.

a desolation and a curse. These words are from Deut. 11. 26; 28. 15–19; 29. 19; 30. 1. Cp. Jer. 44. 22.

20 gathered. See note on Gen. 49. 33.

thy grave. Heb. *keber* (not Sheol). In 21. 26 rendered sepulchre.

in peace. Josiah died in war (23. 29); but why not "in peace" of mind and heart as well? Cp. Isa. 57. 2.

23. 2 the LORD. Heb. Jehovah. Ap. 4. II.

men. Heb. *'īsh.* Ap. 14. II.

prophets. Some codices read "Levites", as in 2 Chron. 34. 30.

read. Either himself; or, by Heb. idiom, "caused to be read".

in their ears. Cp. Neh. 8. 1–4, &c. The king did not keep it to himself. God's word is for all.

3 by a pillar: or, on the pillar, or, platform. Cp. 11. 14.

soul. Heb. *nephesh.* Ap. 13.

written. See Ap. 47.

stood. But not for long. See Jer. 11. 2–20.

4 priests of the second order (or degree), i. e. ordinary priests.

the grove = the *'Ashērah.* See Ap. 42.

host of heaven. Cp. 21. 3.

burned them. As prescribed in Deut. 7. 25.

unto Beth-el. To defile the altar there, according to the prophecy in 1 Kings 13. 2.

5 idolatrous priests = black-robed; not *kohēn*, as appointed by God, but *kemārīm*, as appointed by man. Cp. Hos. 10. 5; Zeph. 1. 4.

planets = stations: i. e. the twelve signs of the Zodiac. Heb. *mazzālōth.* Spelt *Mazzārōth* in Job 38. 32 = *stations.* The Babylonian name for the *divisions* of the zodiac. Called in the Assyrian inscriptions "Mauzalti". (See *Western Asiatic Inscriptions.*)

513 the brook Kidron, and burned it at the brook Kidron, and stamped *it* small to powder, and cast the powder thereof upon the °graves °of the °children of the people.

7 And he brake down the houses of the °sodomites, that *were* by the house of [2]the LORD, where the women wove °hangings for the [4]grove.

8 And he brought all the priests out of the cities of Judah, and defiled °the high places where the priests had burned incense, from °Geba to °Beer-sheba, and brake down the high places of the gates that *were* in the entering in of the gate of Joshua the governor of the city, which *were* on a °man's left hand at the gate of the city.

9 Nevertheless the °priests of the high places came not up to the altar of [2]the LORD in Jerusalem, but they did eat of the unleavened bread among their brethren.

10 And he defiled °Topheth, which *is* in the °valley of the [6]children of Hinnom, that no [8]man might make his son or his daughter to pass through the fire to °Molech.

11 And he took away the horses that the °kings of Judah had given to the sun, at the entering in °of the house of [2]the LORD, °by the chamber of Nathan-melech the °chamberlain, which *was* in the °suburbs, and burned the chariots of the sun with fire.

12 And the altars that *were* on the °top of the upper chamber of Ahaz, which the kings of Judah had made, and the altars which Manasseh had made in the two courts of the house of [2]the LORD, did the king beat down, and °brake *them* down from thence, and cast the dust of them into the brook Kidron.

13 And the high places that *were* °before Jerusalem, °which *were* on the right hand of the °mount of corruption, which Solomon the king of Israel had builded for Ashtoreth the abomination of the Zidonians, and for °Chemosh the abomination of the Moabites, and for Milcom the abomination of the [6]children of Ammon, did the king defile.

14 And he brake in pieces the °images, and cut down the [4]groves, and filled their places with the bones of °men.

15 Moreover °the altar that *was* at Beth-el, *and* the high place which Jeroboam the son of Nebat, who °made Israel to sin, had made, both that altar and the high place he brake down, and burned the high place, *and* stamped *it* small to powder, and burned the [4]grove.

16 And as Josiah turned himself, he spied the °sepulchres that *were* there in the mount, and sent, and took the bones out of the °sepulchres, and burned *them* upon the altar, and polluted it, according to °the word of [2]the LORD which °the man of °God °proclaimed, who proclaimed these words.

17 Then he said, "What °title *is* that that I see?" And the °men of the city told him, "*It is* the [16]sepulchre of [16]the man of [16]God, which came from Judah, and proclaimed these things that thou hast done against the altar of Beth-el."

18 And he said, "Let him alone; let no man move his bones." So they let his bones alone, with the bones of the prophet that came out of Samaria.

19 And all the houses also of the high places that *were* in the cities of [18]Samaria, which the kings of Israel had made to provoke °*the LORD* to anger, Josiah took away, and did to them according to all the acts that he had done in Beth-el.

20 And he °slew all the priests of the high places that *were* there upon the altars, and burned [2]men's bones upon them, and returned to Jerusalem.

21 And the king commanded all the people, saying, °"Keep the passover unto [2]the LORD t[4] (p. 523)

6 graves. Heb. *ḳeber.* See note on 21. 26.
of the children of the people = of the common people in Jer. 26. 23. In 2 Chron. 35. 5 it = the laity as distinguished from Levites.
children = sons.
7 sodomites = male prostitutes. Suppression directed in Deut. 23. 17, 18. See note on 1 Kings 14. 23, 24.
hangings. Heb. houses. Probably veils to cover the *'Ashērah*, as it is covered in Romish processions to-day.
8 the high places. Seemingly (from *v.* 9) some were used for the worship of Jehovah. See notes on 1 K. 18. 29; 19. 10, 14.
Geba. Now *Jeba* (Josh. 18. 24).
Beer-sheba. Southern boundary (Gen. 21. 31. Judg. 20. 1). Cp. Amos 5. 5; 8. 14.
man's. Heb. *'ish.* Ap. 14. II.
9 priests of the high places. Not idolatrous priests. See note on *v.* 8.
10 Topheth = the Topheth. First occurrence. Put by Fig. *Metonymy* (of Adjunct), Ap. 6, put for anything abhorrent.
valley, &c. The junction of the three valleys uniting south of Jerusalem. The continual fires burning there gave the Greek name *Gehenna* (from the Heb. *Gē Hinnom* = valley of Hinnom).
Molech. Cp. Jer. 7. 31, 32; 19. 2–6. Prohibited Deut. 18. 10. Cp. 1 Kings 11. 7.
11 kings of Judah. Presumably Manasseh and Amon. See 21. 3–5.
of = from.
by = to.
chamberlain = eunuch, or officer.
suburbs, or outskirts.
12 top = roof, "[the roof] of", &c.
brake them down. The marg. of A.V. seems preferable here: "hurried away [with them] from thence".
13 before Jerusalem: i. e. the east side. See Zech. 16. 4.
which, &c. Fig. *Polyonymia.* Ap. 6.
mount of corruption: i. e. the Mount of Olives. Thus called on account of the idolatries connected with it.
Chemosh. Cp. 1 Kings 11. 5, 7.
14 images = pillars, or statues.
men. Heb. *'ādām.* Used collectively. Ap. 14. I.
15 the altar. Cp. 1 Kings 12. 32, 33.
made Israel to sin. See note on 1 Kings 14. 16.
16 sepulchres. Heb. pl. of *ḳeber.* See note on 21. 26.
the word. See 1 Kings 13. 2.
the man of God. See note on Deut. 33. 1. Ap. 49.
God. Heb. Elohim. Ap. 4. I.
proclaimed. Supply Fig. *Ellipsis* (Ap. 6) thus: "proclaimed [when Jeroboam stood by the altar at the feast], who proclaimed these words" 369 years before. See 1 Kings 13. 1, 2.
17 title = monument.
men. Heb. *'ĕnōsh.* Ap. 14. III.
19 the LORD. Sept., Syr., and Vulg. read "Jehovah" in the text.
20 slew = sacrificed. See Ap. 43. I. iv.
21 Keep the passover. See note on Ex. 12. 28.

513 your [16]God, as *it is* written in °the book of
this covenant."
22 Surely there was °not holden such a passover from the days of the °judges that judged
Israel, nor in all the days of the kings of Israel,
nor of the kings of Judah;
23 But in the eighteenth year of king Josiah,
wherein this passover was holden to [2]the LORD
in Jerusalem.
u[4] 24 Moreover the *workers with* °familiar
(p. 523) spirits, and the wizards, and the °images,
and the °idols, and all the abominations that
were spied in the land of Judah and in Jerusalem, did Josiah °put away, that he might
perform the words of the law which were
written in the book that °Hilkiah the priest
found in the house of [2]the LORD.
Ep 25 And °like unto him was there no king
before him, that turned to [2]the LORD with all
his heart, and with all his °soul, and with all
his might, according to all the law of Moses;
neither after him arose there *any* °like him.
q 26 Notwithstanding [2]the LORD turned not
from the fierceness of His great wrath, wherewith His anger was kindled against Judah,
because of all the provocations that Manasseh
had provoked Him withal.
27 And [2]the LORD said, "I will remove Judah
also out of My sight, °as I have removed Israel,
and will cast off this city Jerusalem which °I
have chosen, and the house of which I said,
'My Name shall be there.'"
D 28 Now the rest of the acts of Josiah, and all
that he did, °*are* they not written in the book
of the chronicles of the kings of Judah?
29 In his days °Pharaoh-nechoh king of
Egypt went up against °the king of Assyria
to the river Euphrates: and king Josiah °went
500 against him; and °he slew °him at °Megiddo,
when he had °seen him.
30 And his servants carried him in a chariot
dead from Megiddo, and brought him to Jerusalem, and °buried him in his own [16]sepulchre.
And the People of the land took Jehoahaz the
son of Josiah, and anointed him, and made him
king in his father's stead.
R[5] H 31 °Jehoahaz *was* twenty and three years old
(p. 526) when he began to reign; and he reigned three
500 months in Jerusalem. And his mother's name
was Hamutal, the daughter of Jeremiah of
Libnah.
I 32 And he did *that which was* °evil in the
sight of [2]the LORD, according to all that his
fathers had done.
H 33 And Pharaoh-nechoh put him in bands
°at Riblah in the land of Hamath, °that he
might not reign in Jerusalem; and put the land
to a tribute of an hundred °talents of silver,
and a °talent of gold.
500 34 And Pharaoh-nechoh made °Eliakim the
son of Josiah king °in the room of Josiah his
father, and turned his name to Jehoiakim, and
took Jehoahaz away: and he came to Egypt,
and °died there.
35 And Jehoiakim gave the silver and the
gold to Pharaoh; but he °taxed the land to
give the money according to the commandment of Pharaoh: he exacted the silver and
the gold of the People of the land, of every
one according to his taxation, to give *it* unto
Pharaoh-nechoh.
36 Jehoiakim *was* twenty and five years old R[6] v

the book of this covenant = this covenant-book. A.V., 1611, reads "this book of the covenant".

22 not holden such. Cp. Hezekiah's passover, of which the same is said (2 Chron. 30. 26). Both statements true. Hezekiah's greater than any before it. Josiah's greater than Hezekiah's. See the details (2 Chron. 35. 1-19). There were larger numbers, and the law was more exactly followed. Hezekiah's passover kept just before the dispersion of Israel. Josiah's passover kept just before the captivity of Judah.

judges that judged. Fig. *Polyptōton.* Ap. 6.

24 familiar spirits. See note on Lev. 19. 31.

images = teraphim = household gods.

idols = manufactured gods. **put** = clear.

Hilkiah the priest found. See 22. 8, &c.

25 like unto. Note the Fig. *Epanadiplōsis* (Ap. 6), by which (for emphasis) the statement begins and ends with the same words.

soul. Heb. *nephesh.* Ap. 13.

27 as = according as.

I have chosen = I once, or erewhile, chose.

28 are they not . . . ? Fig. *Erotēsis.* Ap. 6.

29 Pharaoh-nechoh: i. e. Nechoh II, the sixth king of the twenty-sixth dynasty. His father was a tributary to Assyria, but had secured independence for Egypt.

the king of Assyria: i. e. the king of Babylon, who had just conquered Nineveh, the rival capital.

went against him. His motive not known.

he = the king of Egypt. **him** = Josiah.

Megiddo. Southern margin of the plain of Esdraelon, celebrated for Syria's defeat by Barak (Judg. 5. 19).

seen. Fig. *Tapeinosis* (Ap. 6), to emphasise the fact that he did much more than "see" him. Cp. 14. 8 and 2 Chron. 35. 21, 22.

30 buried him. For the sorrow attending this, see 2 Chron. 35. 25.

23. 31-35 (R[5], p. 516). JEHOAHAZ.
(*Division.*)

R[5] | H | 31. Appointment by People (*v.* 30).
  I | 32. Personal character.
 H | 33-35. Appointment by Pharaoh-nechoh.

31 Jehoahaz. Also called Johanan (Jer. 22. 11. 1 Chron. 3. 15). He was the younger brother of Jehoiakim (*v.* 36).

32 evil. Heb. *rā'a'.* Ap. 44. viii.

33 at Riblah. After his defeat by Nebuchadrezzar at Carchemish. Riblah was a centre from whence roads branched to the Euphrates and Nineveh, or by Palmyra to Babylon. The southern roads led to Palestine, Lebanon, and Egypt. Riblah still bears this name, and is about twenty-five miles south-south-west of Emesa.

that he might not reign. Heb. text reads "when he reigned". A.V. follows some codices, with Aram., Sept., and Vulg.

talents. See Ap. 51. II.

34 Eliakim. Name changed, to assert Pharaoh-nechoh's authority.

in the room. Refusing to recognise the People's appointment of *v.* 30.

died there. As Jeremiah (22. 11, 12) foretold.

35 taxed = assessed.

23. 36—24. 7 (R[6], p. 516). JEHOIAKIM.
(*Alternation.*)

R[6] | v | 23. 36. Introduction.
  w | x[1] | 23. 37. Events. Personal.
    | x[2] | 24. 1-4. Events. Political.
 v | 24. 5, 6. Conclusion.
  w | x[3] | 24. 7-. Event. Non-invasion from Egypt.
    | x[4] | 24. -7. Event. Reason.

500 when he began to reign; and he reigned eleven
to years in Jerusalem. And his mother's name
489 *was* Zebudah, the daughter of Pedaiah of
Rumah.

w x[1] 37 And he °did *that which was* [32]evil in the
(p. 526) sight of [2]the LORD, according to all that his
fathers had done.

x[2] **24** In his days °Nebuchadnezzar king of
496 Babylon °came up, and Jehoiakim became his servant three years: then he turned
and rebelled against him.
2 And °the LORD sent against him °bands of
the Chaldees, and bands of the Syrians, and
bands of the Moabites, and bands of the °chil-
dren of Ammon, and sent them against Judah
to destroy it, according to the word of °the
LORD, which He spake °by His servants the
prophets.
3 Surely at the °commandment of [2]the LORD
came *this* upon Judah, to remove *them* out of
His sight, for the sins of Manasseh, °according
to all that he did;
4 And also for the innocent °blood that he
shed: for he filled Jerusalem with innocent
blood; which [2]the LORD would not pardon.

v 5 Now °the rest of the acts of Jehoiakim, and
all that he did, °*are* they not written in the
book of the chronicles of the kings of Judah?
6 So Jehoiakim °slept with his fathers: and
Jehoiachin his son reigned in his stead.

x[3] 7 And the king of Egypt came not again any
more out of his land:

x[4] for the king of Babylon had taken from the
river of Egypt unto the river Euphrates all
that pertained to the king of Egypt.

R[7] J 8 °Jehoiachin *was* °eighteen years old when
(p. 527) he began to reign, and he reigned in Jeru-
489 salem °three months. And his mother's name
was Nehushta, the daughter of Elnathan of
Jerusalem.

K 9 And he did *that which was* °evil in the sight
of [2]the LORD, according to all that his father
had done.

J y 10 At that time °the servants of Nebuchadnezzar king of Babylon came up against Jerusalem, and the city was besieged.
11 And Nebuchadnezzar king of Babylon
came against the city, °and his servants °did
besiege it.

z 12 And Jehoiachin the king of Judah went
out to the king of Babylon, he, and his mother,
and his servants, and his princes, and his
°officers:

z and the king of Babylon took him in °the
489 eighth year of his reign.
13 And he carried out thence all the treasures
of the house of [2]the LORD, and the treasures
of the king's house, and cut in pieces all the
vessels of gold which Solomon king of Israel
had made in the temple of [2]the LORD, °as [2]the
LORD °had said.
14 And he °carried away all Jerusalem, [11]and
all the princes, and all the mighty men of
valour, *even* ten thousand captives, and all the
°craftsmen and smiths: none remained, save
the poorest sort of °the People of the land.
15 And he carried away °Jehoiachin to Babylon, [11]and the king's mother, and the king's

37 did that which was evil. See 2 Chron. 36. 5-8. Jer. 22. 17; 24. 8; 26. 22, 23. N.B. Jer. 13—20, and probably 22; 26; 35; 36; belong to this period.

24. 1 Nebuchadnezzar. Or Nebuchadrezzar (Jer. 21. 2, 7; 22. 25), or Nebuchadonosor in Josephus and Berosus, Sept., and Vulg. This is the first occurrence of his name in Scripture.

came up. In the fourth year of Jehoiakim (Jer. 25. 1; 46. 2). Daniel says in third year (1. 1); but he writes from Babylon, whence Nebuchadnezzar set out, and here (cp. Jer. 46. 2), it refers to the actual coming. The Babylonian Servitude begins here (496 to 426 B.C.).

2 the LORD. Heb. Jehovah. Ap. 4. II.

bands = marauding bands. **children** = sons.

by = through. Heb. by the hand of. "Hand" put by Fig. *Metonymy* (of Cause), Ap. 6, for what is effected by it.

3 commandment. Heb. mouth. Put by Fig. *Metonymy* (of Cause), Ap. 6, for what is spoken by it.

according to all. A special reading called *Sevir* (Ap. 34) reads "in all". So some codices.

4 blood. Put by Fig. *Synecdoche* (of Species), Ap. 6, for murder, and the guilt of it.

5 the rest. See 2 Chron. 36. 6-8.

are they not . . . ? Fig. *Erotēsis.* Ap. 6.

6 slept with his fathers. Only the fact referred to here. Not the *manner* of his death and burial, for which see Jer. 22. 18, 19; 36. 29, 30. It was as foretold. The expression "slept with his fathers" is used even of Ahab; and every king of Judah whose *death* is recorded is said also to have been *buried*, except Jehoiakim. See note on Deut. 31. 16.

24. 8-17 (R[7], p. 516). **JEHOIACHIN.**
(*Introversion.*)

R[7] | J | 8. Event. Internal. Accession.
  K | 9. Personal character.
 J | 10-17. Events. External. Supercession.

8 Jehoiachin. Called also Coniah and Jeconiah (Jer. 22. 24; 24. 1).

eighteen. This was his age. In 2 Chron. 36. 9 he is said to be eight. See note there.

three months. Is put by Fig. *Synecdoche* (of the Part), Ap. 6, for three months and ten days. Cp. 2 Chron. 36. 9.

9 evil. Heb. *rā'a'.* Ap. 44. viii.

10-17 (*J*, above). **EVENTS. EXTERNAL.**
(*Alternation.*)

J | y | 10, 11. Nebuchadnezzar besieges Jerusalem.
  z | 12-. Jehoiachin surrenders.
  z | -12-16. Jehoiachin made captive.
 y | 17. Nebuchadnezzar makes Mattaniah king.

10 the servants of. Some codices, with two early printed editions, Sept. and Syr., omit these words, and read "came up".

11 and. Note the Fig. *Polysyndeton* (Ap. 6) in *vv.* 11-16 to emphasise every detail.

did besiege = were besieging.

12 officers: i.e. eunuchs or chamberlains.

the eighth year. Computed from the time that his father entrusted him with regal authority. This was the 4th year of Jehoiakim (Jer. 25. 1, cp. 32. 1).

13 as = according as.

had said. Cp. 20. 17.

14 carried away. This deportation was eleven years before that of Zedekiah (25. 18). Mordecai was in this deportation. See note on 2 Chron. 36. 6. The Captivity begun in 489. **craftsmen** = artificers.

the People of the land. Cp. 23. 6.

15 Jehoiachin to Babylon. Where he was captive for thirty-seven years.

489 wives, and his [12]officers, and °the mighty of
the land, *those* carried he into captivity from
Jerusalem to Babylon.
16 And all the °men of might, *even* seven
thousand, and [14]craftsmen and °smiths a thousand, all *that were* strong *and* apt for war,
even them the king of Babylon brought captive to Babylon.

y (p. 527) 17 And the king of Babylon made Mattaniah
his father's brother king in his stead, and
°changed his name to Zedekiah.

R[8] a (p. 528) 488 to 477 18 Zedekiah *was* twenty and one years old
when he began to reign, and he reigned eleven
years in Jerusalem. And his mother's name
was °Hamutal, the daughter of Jeremiah of
Libnah.

b 19 And he °did *that which was* [9]evil in the
sight of [2]the LORD, according to all that Jehoiakim had done.

a 20 For through the anger of [2]the LORD it
came to pass in Jerusalem and Judah, until He
had cast them out from His presence, that Zedekiah °rebelled against the king of Babylon.

C[2] L N 479 **25** °And °it came to pass in the °ninth year
of his reign, in the tenth month, in the
tenth *day* of the month,

O c *that* Nebuchadnezzar king of Babylon came,
he, and all his host, against Jerusalem, and
pitched against it; and they built forts against
it round about.
477 2 And the city was besieged unto the eleventh
year of king Zedekiah.

d 3 And on the ninth *day* of the °*fourth* month
°the famine prevailed in the city, and there
was no bread for the People of the land.

c 4 And the city was °broken up,

d and all the °men of war °*fled* by night by the
way of the gate between °two walls, which *is*
by the king's garden: °(now the Chaldees *were*
against the city round about:) and *the king*
went the way toward the plain.

P 5 And the army of the Chaldees pursued after
the king, and overtook him in the plains of
Jericho: and all his army were scattered from
him.
6 So they took the king, and brought him up
to the king of Babylon to °Riblah; and °they
°gave judgment upon him.
7 And they slew the sons of Zedekiah before
his eyes, and °put out the eyes of Zedekiah,
and bound him with fetters of brass,

Q and carried him to Babylon.

N 477 8 And in the fifth month, on the °seventh *day*
of the month, which *is* the nineteenth year of
king Nebuchadnezzar king of Babylon, came
Nebuzaradan, °captain of the guard, a servant
of the king of Babylon, unto Jerusalem:

O e 9 And he burnt the house of °the LORD, and
the king's house, and all the houses of Jerusalem, and every °great *man's* house burnt he
with fire.

f 10 And all the army of the Chaldees, that

---

the mighty of the land. Princes and potentates, priests and prophets (Jer. 29. 1). Among them Ezekiel (1. 12), Daniel, and Nehemiah.

16 men. Heb. *'ĕnôsh.* Ap. 14. III.

smiths = armourers.

17 changed his name. See note on 23. 34.

24. 18-20 (R[8], p. 516). ZEDEKIAH.
(*Introversion.*)

R[8] | a | 18. Accession.
  b | 19. Personal. Evil-doing.
 a | 20. Rebellion.

18 Hamutal. Therefore only half-brother to Jehoiakim, but full brother to Jehoahaz.

19 did that which was evil. See 2 Chron. 36. 12-16. Jer. 24. 8; 37. 2; 38. 2, 5.

20 rebelled. Though bound by oath (2 Chron. 36. 13. Ezek. 17. 13).

25. 1-30 (C[2], p. 446). THE KINGDOM ENDED.
(*Introversion.*)

C[2] | L | 1-21. Nebuchadnezzar and Zedekiah.
  M | 22-25. Remnant. In the land.
  M | 26. Remnant. Migration to Egypt.
 L | 27-30. Evil-Merodach and Jehoiachin.

25. 1-21 (L, above). NEBUCHADNEZZAR AND ZEDEKIAH. (*Extended Alternation.*)

L | N | 1-. Date. Ninth of Zedekiah (Jer. 39. 1).
  O | c | -1, 2. City besieged.
   d | 3. Famine.
   c | 4-. City broken up.
   d | -4. Flight.
    P | 5-7-. Executions at Riblah.
     Q | -7. Carrying away of Zedekiah.
 N | 8. Date. Nineteenth of Nebuchadnezzar.
  O | e | 9. Temple burned.
   f | 10. City wall broken down.
   f | 11, 12. City. Inhabitants. Flight.
   e | 13-17. Temple spoiled.
    P | 18-21-. Executions at Riblah.
     Q | -21. Carrying away of Judah.

1 And. Note the Fig. *Polysyndeton* (Ap. 6) in *vv.* 1-7, to emphasise every detail.

it came to pass. Cp. 2 Chron. 36. 11-13 and Jer. 52. The prophecy of Jer. 39—44 is the Divine comment on the history.

ninth year, &c. The day revealed to Ezekiel in exile (Ezek. 24. 1). Cp. Jer. 39. 1.

3 fourth. This numeral is supplied from Jer. 52. 6.

the famine. The ninth recorded in Scripture. See note on Gen. 12. 10. Fulfilling Lev. 26. 29. Deut. 28. 53-57. Jer. 15. 2; 27. 13. Lam. 2. 20-22. Ezek. 4. 16. Sufferings described in Jer. 21. 7-9. Lam. 4. 9, 10; 5. 10, &c.

4 broken up = breached. Before this an Egyptian force approached and the Babylonians retired (Jer. 37. 5-11). The relief was only temporary, as predicted.

men. Heb. *'ĕnôsh.* Ap. 14. III.

fled. Some codices, with Syr., read "the men of war fled, and went forth by night". Cp. Jer. 39. 4; 52. 7.

two = the two.

now. Note Fig. *Parenthesis.* Ap. 6.

6 Riblah. See note on 23. 33.

they. Some codices, with Sept., Syr., and Vulg., read "he".

gave judgment = passed sentence. Cp. 24. 20.

7 put out the eyes. So that he did not "see" Babylon, though he was to die there (Ezek. 12. 13). But he did "see" the king of Babylon, according to Jer. 32. 4; 34. 3. See note on Gen. 19. 11.

8 seventh day. Jer. 52. 12 says tenth day. He may have set fire to it on the seventh day, and it burnt until the tenth.

captain of the guard = chief of the royal executioners.

9 the LORD. Heb. Jehovah. Ap. 4. II.

great man's house. See note on Prov. 17. 19.

477 *were with* the [8]captain of the guard, brake
down the walls of Jerusalem round about.

f (p. 528) 11 Now the rest of the People *that were* left
in the city, and the fugitives that fell away to
the king of Babylon, with the remnant of the
multitude, did Nebuzar-adan the [8]captain of
the guard carry away.
12 But the [8]captain of the guard left of the
poor of the land *to be* vinedressers and °hus-
bandmen.

e 13 And the pillars of brass that *were* in the
house of [9]the LORD, and the bases, and the
brasen sea that *was* in the house of [9]the LORD,
did the Chaldees break in pieces, and carried
the brass of them to Babylon.
14 And the pots, and the shovels, and the
snuffers, and the spoons, and all the vessels
of brass wherewith they ministered, took they
away.
15 And the firepans, and the bowls, *and* such
things as *were* of gold, *in* gold, and of silver,
in silver, the [8]captain of the guard took away.
16 The two pillars, one sea, and the bases
which Solomon had made for the house of [9]the
LORD; the brass of all these vessels was without weight.
17 °The height of the one pillar *was* eighteen
°cubits, and the chapiter upon it *was* brass:
and the height of the chapiter three °cubits;
and the °wreathen work, and pomegranates
upon the chapiter round about, all of brass:
and like unto these had the second pillar with
°wreathen work.

P 18 And the [8]captain of the guard took °Seraiah
the °chief priest, and Zephaniah the °second
priest, and the three keepers of the °door:
19 And out of the city he took an officer that
was set over the men of war, and five [4]men of
them that °were in the king's presence, which
were found in the city, and the °principal scribe
of the host, which mustered the People of the
land, and threescore [4]men of the People of the
land *that were* found in the city:
20 And Nebuzar-adan [8]captain of the guard
took these, and brought them to the king of
Babylon to Riblah:
21 And the king of Babylon smote them, and
slew them at Riblah in the land of Hamath.

Q °So Judah was carried away out of °their land.

M g 22 And *as for* the people that remained in
the land of Judah, whom Nebuchadnezzar king
of Babylon had left, even over them he made
Gedaliah the son of °Ahikam, the son of Shaphan, ruler.

h 23 And °when all the captains of the armies,
they and their [4]men, heard that the king of
Babylon had made Gedaliah governor, there
came to Gedaliah to Mizpah, even °Ishmael
the son of Nethaniah, and °Johanan the son of
Careah, and Seraiah the son of Tanhumeth
the Netophathite, and Jaazaniah the son of
a Maachathite, they and their [4]men.

g 24 And Gedaliah sware to them, and to their
[4]men, and said unto them, "Fear not to be the
servants of the Chaldees: dwell in the land,
and serve the king of Babylon; and °it shall
be well with you."

25 But it came to pass in the °seventh month, h
that Ishmael the son of Nethaniah, the son of
Elishama, of the seed royal, came, and ten [4]men
with him, and °smote Gedaliah, that he died,
and the Jews and the Chaldees that were with
him at Mizpah.

26 And all the People, both small and great, M (p. 528)
and the captains of the armies, arose, and 489-452
°came to Egypt: for they were afraid of the
Chaldees.

27 And it came to pass in the seven and L
thirtieth year of the captivity of Jehoiachin
king of Judah, in the twelfth month, on the
seven and twentieth *day* of the month, *that*
°Evil-merodach king of Babylon in the year
that he began to reign did °lift up the head of
Jehoiachin king of Judah °out of prison;
28 And he spake °kindly to him, and set his
°throne above the °throne of the kings that
were with him in Babylon;

12 husbandmen. Cp. Jer. 52. 16.
17 The height of the one pillar. See note on 1 Kings 7. 15.
cubits. See Ap. 51. III. 2.
wreathen work=network.
18 Seraiah. The grandfather or great-grandfather of Ezra (1 Chron. 6. 14. Ezra 7. 1).
chief priest. See note on Lev. 4. 3.
second priest. See note on 23. 4. Probably a deputy high priest. No provision for such in the Law.
door=threshold.
19 were in the king's presence. Heb. saw the king's face.
principal scribe=scribe of the captain of the host.
21 So Judah was carried away. Thus ended the kingdom of Judah, as Jeremiah had predicted (Jer. 20. 4).
their=his.

25. 22-26 (M, p. 528). THE REMNANT. MIGRATION TO EGYPT. (*Alternation.*)

M | g | 22. Governor. Gedaliah.
  h | 23. Ishmael. Visit of.
g | 24. Governor's reception.
  h | 25. Ishmael. Murders by.

22 Ahikam. He had befriended Jeremiah (Jer. 26. 24)
23 when all the captains, &c. For fuller account see Jer. 40. 7—43. 13.
Ishmael. He was of the seed royal (*v.* 25), and laid claim to the throne. Cp. Jer. 40. 8; 41. 1-18. Josephus, *Ant.* X. 9. 2.
Johanan. Who, with others, warned Gedaliah of Ishmael's treachery (Jer. 40. 13; 41. 16).
24 it shall be well with you. So God designed it (Jer. 27. 5, 6, 11).
25 seventh month. Afterward observed as a fast. Cp. Zech. 7. 5.
smote Gedaliah. Instigated by Baalis, king of Ammon (Jer. 40. 7—43. 13).
26 came to Egypt. In defiance of the counsel of Jeremiah (whom they took with them). See Jer. 42 and 43. 8-13, who foretold that Egypt also would be given to the king of Babylon (Jer. 44. 29, 30).
27 Evil-merodach. The son and successor of Nebuchadnezzar.
lift up the head. Heb. idiom=show favour to.
out of prison. Some codices, with Sept. and Syr., read "and brought him forth out of his prison". Cp. Jer. 52. 31.
28 kindly=good words.
throne=seat (Prov. 9. 14). Cp. Lam. 1. 1.

29 And changed his prison garments: and he °did eat bread continually before him all the days of his life.

30 And his allowance *was* a continual allowance given him of the king, a daily rate for every day, all the days of his life.

29 did eat bread. He was a guest at the royal table. Cp. 2 Sam. 19. 33. 1 Kings 2. 7.

This chapter, compared with the last chapter of Jeremiah, points to his authorship. The (one) book of Kings brings the history of Israel and Judah down to the Captivity, and ends there. See the Structure, p. 413. The (one) book of Chronicles begins from Adam, and leads on from the Captivity to the book of Ezra-Nehemiah.

1 AND 2 CHRONICLES.

THE STRUCTURE OF THE TWO BOOKS* AS A WHOLE.

(*Alternation.*)

A | 1 Chron. 1. 1—9. 1. UP TO THE CAPTIVITY. } GENEALOGY.
B | 1 Chron. 9. 2-44. AFTER THE RETURN. } GENEALOGY.

A | 1 Chron. 10. 1—2 Chron. 36. 21. UP TO THE CAPTIVITY. } HISTORY.
B | 2 Chron. 36. 22, 23. AFTER THE RETURN. } HISTORY.

* For the division of Chronicles into two books, see note on the Structure of the two Books of Samuel as a whole (p. 366).

THE °FIRST BOOK OF THE

°CHRONICLES.

A A[1] B[1] 1 °ADAM, °Sheth, Enosh,
(p. 531) 2 °Kenan, Mahalaleel, Jered,
.004-2948 3 Henoch, Methuselah, Lamech,
4 Noah, °Shem, Ham, and Japheth.
C a[1] 5 The sons of °Japheth; Gomer, and Magog,
and Madai, and Javan, and Tubal, and Meshech, and Tiras.
6 And the sons of Gomer; Ashchenaz, and
°Riphath, and Togarmah.
7 And the sons of Javan; Elishah, and Tarshish, Kittim, and °Dodanim.
a[2] 8 The sons of Ham; °Cush, and Mizraim, Put,
and Canaan.
9 And the sons of Cush; Seba, and Havilah,
and Sabta, and Raamah, and Sabtecha. And
the sons of Raamah; Sheba, and Dedan.
10 And Cush begat °Nimrod: he began to be
mighty upon the earth.
11 And Mizraim begat Ludim, and Anamim,
and Lehabim, and Naphtuhim,
12 And Pathrusim, and Casluhim, (of whom
came the Philistines,) and Caphthorim.
13 And Canaan begat Zidon his firstborn, and
Heth,
14 The Jebusite also, and the Amorite, and
the Girgashite,
15 And the Hivite, and the Arkite, and the
Sinite,
16 And the Arvadite, and the Zemarite, and
the Hamathite.
a[3] 17 The sons of Shem; Elam, and Asshur, and
Arphaxad, and Lud, and Aram, and °Uz, and
Hul, and Gether, and °Meshech.
18 And Arphaxad begat Shelah, and Shelah
begat Eber.
19 And unto Eber were born two sons: the
name of the one *was* °Peleg; because in his
days the earth was divided: and his brother's
name *was* Joktan.
20 And °Joktan begat Almodad, and Sheleph,
and Hazarmaveth, and Jerah,
21 Hadoram also, and Uzal, and Diklah,
22 And Ebal, and Abimael, and Sheba,
23 And Ophir, and Havilah, and Jobab. All
these *were* the sons of Joktan.
B[2] 2446 24 °Shem, Arphaxad, Shelah,

TITLE, First. See note on p. 530.

Chronicles. Heb. name, *Dibrêi hayyāmīm* = words of the days. Greek name, *Paraleipomena* = things omitted. Latin name, *Chronicon*, from whence comes English title, Chronicles. These books belong to quite another part of the O.T., and do not follow in sequence on the books of Kings. See Ap. 1. They are, according to the Heb. Canon, the conclusion of the O.T.; and the genealogies here lead up to that of Matt. 1. 1, and the commencement of the N.T. They end with the ending of the kingdom; and the question of Cyrus, "Who is there?" (2 Chron. 36. 23) is followed by the answer, "Where is He?" (Matt. 2. 2), and the proclamation of the kingdom by the rightful King and His forerunner. It begins with the first Adam and leads on to the "last Adam".

For the relation of Chronicles to Kings see notes on title "Kings" (p. 447); and for the parallel passages in Samuel and Kings see Ap. 56.

It deals with the kingdom of Judah, because Christ was proclaimed as the successor of David.

It refers to other books:—*Kings* (2 Chron. 16. 11; 27. 7; 33. 18); *Prophets* (1 Chron. 29. 29. 2 Chron. 9. 29; 12. 15; 13. 22; 20. 34; 26. 22; 32. 32). It gives the histories from the Divine standpoint, pointing the moral, and giving the *reason* of both the judgments and the mercies (cp. 1 Chron. 10. 13. 2 Chron. 12. 12; 25. 20; 27. 6, &c.).

1. 1—9. 1 (**A**, p. 530). UP TO THE CAPTIVITY (GENEALOGY). (*Division.*)

A | A[1] | 1. 1—8. 40. In detail.
  | A[2] | 9. 1. In sum.

1. 1—8. 40 (A[1], above). IN DETAIL. (*Repeated Alternation.*)

A[1] | B[1] | 1. 1-4. Direct. Adam to Noah (4004-2948).
  | C[1] | 1. 5-23. Collateral. Japhet (5-7), Ham (8-16).
  | B[2] | 1. 24-28. Direct. Shem to Abraham (2446-1996).
  | C[2] | 1. 29-33. Collateral. Ishmael.
  | B[3] | 1. 34. Direct. Abraham to Israel (1996-1836).
  | C[3] | 1. 35-54. Collateral. Esau and Edom.
  | B[4] | 2. 1-12. Direct. Israel to Jesse (1836-1050?).
  | C[4] | 2. 13-55. Collateral. Jesse and Caleb.
  | B[5] | 3. 1-24. Direct. David to Zedekiah (990-509).
  | C[5] | 4. 1—8. 40. Collateral. Other tribes.

1 Adam. Cp. Gen. 1. 26; 2. 7.
Sheth. Cp. Gen. 4. 25; 5. 3.
2 Kenan = Cainan (Gen. 5. 9).

1. 5-23 (C[1], above). COLLATERAL. (*Division.*)

C[1] | a[1] | 5-7. The sons of Japheth.
  | a[2] | 8-16. The sons of Ham.
  | a[3] | 17-23. The other sons of Shem.

4 Shem. Cp. Gen. 5. 32; 10. 21. In cases where there are several sons of one father, the collateral are dealt with first, and the main line taken up later. Hence Shem's main line is not dealt with till *v.* 24, after the sons of Japheth and Ham have been given. **5 Japheth.** Cp. Gen. 10. 2, &c. **6 Riphath.** Some codices, with four early printed editions, Syr. and Vulg., read "Riphath", others "Diphath", owing to Heb. ד ("D") and ר ("R"). **7 Dodanim, or Rodanim.** See above note. **8 Cush.** Recent discoveries at Pterium, in Cappadocia, show that the Babylonians called Cappadocia *Kus.* The great king of the Hittites had his palace there, and was called "king of *Kus*". The river Gihon (classic, Pijramus) flows into the Mediterranean. Cp. Gen. 10. 6, 7. Isa. 11. 11. **10 Nimrod.** Cp. Gen. 10. 8. **17 Uz . . . Meshech** were sons of Aram (Shem's youngest son). No error, for grandsons are often reckoned, by descent, as sons. See Laban (Gen. 29. 5), Mephibosheth (2 Sam. 19. 24). Of the "sons of Judah" (4. 1-4) only the first-named was his son. It is assumed that we are acquainted with Genesis, and shall supply the links dealt with here with such brevity. **19 Peleg** = disruption. See note on Gen. 10. 25. **20 Joktan.** Cp. Gen. 10. 26. **24 Shem.** Direct descent taken up here, from *v.* 4. See Structure, B[2].

25 Eber, Peleg, Reu,

26 Serug, Nahor, Terah,

1996 27 Abram; the same *is* Abraham.

28 The sons of Abraham; Isaac, and Ishmael.

C^2 b^1 (p. 532) 29 These *are* their generations: The firstborn of Ishmael, Nebaioth; then Kedar, and Adbeel, and Mibsam,

30 Mishma, and Dumah, Massa, Hadad, and Tema,

31 Jetur, Naphish, and Kedemah. These are the sons of Ishmael.

b^2 32 Now the sons of Keturah, Abraham's concubine: she bare Zimran, and Jokshan, and Medan, and Midian, and Ishbak, and Shuah. And the sons of Jokshan; Sheba, and Dedan.

33 And the sons of Midian; Ephah, and Epher, and Henoch, and Abida, and Eldaah. All these *are* the sons of Keturah.

B^3 34 And Abraham begat Isaac. The sons of

1896–1836 Isaac; Esau and Israel.

C^3 c^1 35 The sons of °Esau; Eliphaz, Reuel, and Jeush, and Jaalam, and Korah.

36 The sons of Eliphaz; Teman, and Omar, °Zephi, and Gatam, Kenaz, and °Timna, and Amalek.

37 The sons of Reuel; Nahath, Zerah, Shammah, and Mizzah.

38 And the °sons of Seir; Lotan, and Shobal, and Zibeon, and Anah, and Dishon, and Ezar, and Dishan.

39 And the sons of Lotan; Hori, and Homam: and Timna *was* Lotan's sister.

40 The sons of Shobal; °Alian, and Manahath, and Ebal, Shephi, and Onam. And the sons of Zibeon; Aiah, and Anah.

41 The °sons of Anah; Dishon. And the sons of Dishon; °Amram, and Eshban, and Ithran, and Cheran.

42 The sons of Ezer; Bilhan, and Zavan, *and* °Jakan. The sons of Dishan; Uz, and Aran.

c^2 43 Now these *are* the kings that reigned in the land of Edom °before *any* king reigned over the °children of Israel; Bela the son of Beor: and the name of his city *was* Dinhabah.

44 And when Bela was dead, Jobab the son of Zerah of Bozrah reigned in his stead.

45 And when Jobab was dead, Husham of the land of the Temanites reigned in his stead.

46 And when Husham was dead, Hadad the son of Bedad, which smote Midian in the field of Moab, reigned in his stead: and the name of his city *was* °Avith.

47 And when Hadad was dead, Samlah of Masrekah reigned in his stead.

48 And when Samlah was dead, Shaul of Rehoboth by the river reigned in his stead.

49 And when Shaul was dead, Baal-hanan the son of Achbor reigned in his stead.

50 And when °Baal-hanan was dead, °Hadad reigned in his stead: and the name of his city *was* °Pai; and his wife's name *was* Mehetabel, the daughter of Matred, the daughter of Mezahab.

51 [50] Hadad died also.

c^3 And the °dukes of Edom were; duke Timnah, duke °Aliah, duke Jetheth,

1. 29-33 (C^2, p. 531). COLLATERAL. (*Division*).

C^2	b^1	29–31. The sons of Ishmael.
	b^2	32, 33. The sons of Keturah.

35-54 (C^3, p. 531). COLLATERAL. (*Division*.)

C^3	c^1	35–42. The sons of Esau.
	c^2	43–51–. The kings of Edom.
	c^3	–51–54. The dukes of Edom.

35 Esau. Cp. Gen. 36. 9, 10.

36 Zephi. Some codices, with one early printed edition, read "Zepho" (cp. Gen. 36. 11), owing to the slight difference between the Heb. ו ("O") and י ("I").

Timna. There was a Timna a daughter of Seir. The Timna here is a son of Eliphaz.

38 sons of Seir. Horites dwelling in Seir before the descendants of Esau (Gen. 36. 20).

40 Alian. Some codices, with two early printed editions, read "Alvan" (Gen. 36. 23).

41 sons. A special various reading called *Sevir* reads "son". See Ap. 34. Gen. 36. 25 tells of a daughter. This shows that *bānim* may include daughters.

Amram. Some codices read "Hemdan" (cp. Gen. 36. 26). These names are more alike in Hebrew than in English.

42 Jakan. Some codices, with Sept., read "and Akan", with the "and" in the text.

43 before any king. See note on Gen. 36. 31, which must have been before the writer's eyes.

children = sons.

46 Avith. Heb. text reads "Ayūth". But some codices, with two early printed editions, read "Avith", which A.V. follows.

50 Baal-hanan. Some codices, with one early printed edition, add "son of Achbor". Cp. Gen. 36. 39.

Hadad. Some codices, with four early printed editions, read "Hadar". See note on Amram, *v.* 41, and cp. Gen. 36. 39.

Pai. Some codices read "Pau". See note on Zephi, *v.* 36, and cp. Gen. 36. 39.

51 dukes of Edom were. Read, "there arose chiefs to Edom", viz. These seem to have superseded the kings.

Aliah. Some codices, with two early printed editions, read "Alvah". See note on Zephi, *v.* 36, and cp. Gen. 36. 40.

2. 1-12 (B^4, p. 531). DIRECT DESCENT. (*Division*.)

B^4	d^1	1, 2. Israel (Jacob) to Judah.
	d^2	3–12. Judah to Jesse.

1 Israel. See notes on Gen. 32. 28; 43. 8; 45. 26, 28.

Reuben. For the order of these names see Ap. 45

3 Judah. Put first because of his being chief. Cp. Gen. 38. 1–11.

evil. Heb. *rā'a'*. Ap. 44. viii. Cp. Gen. 38. 1–11.

the LORD. Heb. Jehovah. Ap. 4. II.

52 Duke Aholibamah, duke Elah, duke Pinon,

53 Duke Kenaz, duke Teman, duke Mibzar,

54 Duke Magdiel, duke Iram. These *are* the dukes of Edom.

2

These *are* the sons of °Israel; °Reuben, Simeon, Levi, and Judah, Issachar, and Zebulun, B^4 d^1 1836 to 1050?

2 Dan, Joseph, and Benjamin, Naphtali, Gad, and Asher.

3 The sons of °Judah; Er, and Onan, and Shelah: *which* three were born unto him of the daughter of Shua the Canaanitess. And Er, the firstborn of Judah, was °evil in the sight of °the LORD; and He slew him. d^2

1836 to 1050? 4 And °Tamar his daughter in law bare him Pharez and Zerah. All the sons of Judah *were* five.
5 The sons of °Pharez; Hezron, and Hamul.
6 And the sons of Zerah; Zimri, and Ethan, and Heman, and Calcol, and Dara: five of them in all.
7 And the °sons of Carmi; °Achar, the troubler of Israel, who °transgressed in the thing accursed.
8 And the [7]sons of °Ethan; Azariah.
9 The sons also of Hezron, that were born unto him; Jerahmeel, and °Ram, and °Chelubai.
10 And Ram begat Amminadab; and Amminadab begat °Nahshon, prince of the °children of Judah;
11 And Nahshon begat °Salma, and Salma begat Boaz,
12 And Boaz begat Obed, and Obed begat
1050 Jesse,

C[4] e[1] (p. 533) 13 And Jesse begat his firstborn Eliab, and Abinadab the second, and Shimma the third,
14 Nethaneel the fourth, Raddai the fifth,
990 15 Ozem the sixth, °David °the seventh:
16 Whose sisters *were* °Zeruiah, and Abigail. And the sons of Zeruiah; Abishai, and Joab, and Asahel, three.
17 And Abigail bare Amasa: and the father of Amasa *was* °Jether the Ishmeelite.

e[2] 18 And °Caleb the son of Hezron begat *children* of Azubah *his* wife, and of Jerioth: her sons *are* these; Jesher, and Shobab, and Ardon.
19 And when Azubah was dead, Caleb took unto him °Ephrath, which bare him Hur.
20 And Hur begat Uri, and Uri begat °Bezaleel.

e[3] 21 And afterward Hezron went in to the daughter of °Machir the father of Gilead, whom he married when he *was* threescore years old; and she bare him Segub.
22 And Segub begat Jair, who had °three and twenty cities in the land of Gilead.
23 And he took °Geshur, and Aram, with the towns of Jair, from °them, with Kenath, and the towns thereof, *even* °threescore cities. All these °*belonged to* the sons of Machir the father of Gilead.
24 And after that Hezron was °dead in Caleb-ephratah, then Abiah Hezron's wife bare him Ashur the father of Tekoa.

e[4] 25 And the sons of °Jerahmeel the firstborn of Hezron were, Ram the firstborn, and Bunah, and Oren, and Ozem, °*and* Ahijah.
26 Jerahmeel had also another wife, whose name *was* Atarah; she *was* the mother of Onam.
27 And the sons of Ram the firstborn of Jerahmeel were, Maaz, and Jamin, and Eker.
28 And the sons of Onam were, Shammai, and Jada. And the sons of Shammai; Nadab, and Abishur.
29 And the name of the wife of Abishur *was* Abihail, and she bare him Ahban, and Molid.
30 And the sons of Nadab; Seled, and Appaim: but Seled died without [10]children.
31 And the [7]sons of Appaim; Ishi. And the [7]sons of Ishi; Sheshan. And the [10]children of Sheshan; Ahlai.
32 And the sons of Jada the brother of Shammai; Jether, and Jonathan: and Jether died without [10]children.

4 Tamar. Cp. Gen. 38. 18, 29, 30; and Matt. 1. 3.
5 Pharez. Ruth 4. 18.
7 sons. Put for "son" by Fig. *Synecdoche* (of Genus), Ap. 6.
Achar = Achan. Cp. Josh. 7. 25.
transgressed. Heb. *mā'al.* Ap. 44. xi.
8 Ethan. Not the same person as "Ethan the Ezrahite" (1 Kings 4. 31), who was probably a Levite (see 1 Chron. 6. 27–29; 15. 17–19), and not of Judah, as the Heman and Ethan here.
9 Ram. Christ's genealogy traced through Jerahmeel. Called Aram in Matt. 1. 3, 4.
Chelubai = Caleb. Cp. *vv.* 18, 42.
10 Nahshon. He led the van of Israel at the Exodus. Cp. Num. 2. 3, 9.
children = sons.
11 Salma = Salmon, who married Rahab (Ruth 4. 21). He led on entry into Canaan. Cp. *vv.* 50, 51.

2. 13–55 (C[4], p. 531). COLLATERAL. (*Division.*)

C[4]	e[1]	13–17.	Jesse's posterity.
	e[2]	18–20.	Caleb, the son of Hezron.
	e[3]	21–24.	Hezron by daughter of Machir.
	e[4]	25–33.	Jerahmeel's posterity.
	e[5]	34–41.	Sheshan's posterity.
	e[6]	42–49.	Caleb's posterity.
	e[7]	50–55.	Caleb, the son of Hur.

15 David. The different spelling of many of these names in the Heb. is due to certain vowels being written out in full ("*plene*"). Where not written they are called "defective". The fact of this difference in Chronicles shows an independent origin.
the seventh. Jesse begat eight sons (1 Sam. 16. 5–11 and 17. 12–14). Here seven are numbered and named, and David is the seventh and the youngest; the eighth may have died young and left no issue. While it was proper to mention the eight in the *history*, it is unnecessary to do so in the *genealogy*.
16 Zeruiah. Sister of David. Nahash (2 Sam. 17. 25) may have been the father of Jesse's wife. Otherwise, she and Abigail were half-sisters.
17 Jether. Cp. 2 Sam. 17. 25 (marg.). Another name was Ithra.
18 Caleb the son of Hezron. The ancestor of "Caleb the son of Jephunneh" (Num. 13. 6, 30; 14. 6, 24; 32. 12; 34. 19. Josh. 14. 6, 14), who is distinguished from this Caleb in 4. 15. This shows the present genealogy to be independent.
19 Ephrath. Called Ephratah, *v.* 50. Cp. 4. 4.
20 Bezaleel. Gifted for the construction of the Tabernacle (Ex. 31. 2; 35. 30; 36. 1, 2; 37. 1). This proves those to be wrong who assume that the Caleb of *v.* 18 is the same as Caleb the son of Jephunneh (Bezaleel's great-grandfather), thus creating their own difficulty.
21 Machir. Cp. Num. 32. 40. Deut. 3. 15.
22 three and twenty. Increased afterward to thirty (Judg. 10. 4).
23 Geshur. North-east of Bashan (Deut. 3. 14. Josh. 12. 5. 2 Sam. 15. 8).
them: the Manassites. Cp. Num. 32. 41. Deut. 3. 14.
threescore cities. Cp. Num. 32. 33. Deut. 3. 4.
belonged to. Supply the Fig. *Ellipsis* (Ap. 6) by inserting "took" instead of "belonged to".
24 dead in Caleb-ephratah. Some wrongly affirm that this grandson of Judah must have died in Egypt. True, Hezron *lived* in Egypt, but did no one ever leave Egypt? Had he not heard of Abraham's sepulchre and Jacob's funeral? Had he no faith and no thoughts of God's promises? The difficulty is created gratuitously. His death there gave the name to the place, afterward called Beth-lehem.
25 Jerahmeel. See 1 Sam. 27. 10; 30. 29.
and: or, supply "of".

33 And the sons of Jonathan; Peleth, and
Zaza. These were the sons of Jerahmeel.
e5 34 Now Sheshan had no sons, but daughters.
(p. 533) And Sheshan had a servant, an Egyptian,
whose name *was* Jarha.
35 And Sheshan gave his daughter °to Jarha
his servant to wife; and she bare him Attai.
36 And Attai begat Nathan, and Nathan begat Zabad,
37 And Zabad begat Ephlal, and Ephlal begat
Obed,
38 And Obed begat Jehu, and Jehu begat
Azariah,
39 And Azariah begat Helez, and Helez begat
Eleasah,
40 And Eleasah begat Sisamai, and Sisamai
begat Shallum,
41 And Shallum begat Jekamiah, and Jekamiah begat Elishama.

e6 42 Now the sons of °Caleb the brother of
Jerahmeel *were*, Mesha his firstborn, which
was the °father of Ziph; and the sons of
°Mareshah the °father of °Hebron.
43 And the sons of Hebron; Korah, and
°Tappuah, and °Rekem, and Shema.
44 And Shema begat Raham, the father of
Jorkoam: and Rekem begat Shammai.
45 And the son of Shammai *was* °Maon: and
Maon *was* the [42]father of Beth-zur.
46 And Ephah, Caleb's concubine, bare Haran,
and Moza, and Gazez: and Haran begat Gazez.
47 And the sons of Jahdai; Regem, and Jotham, and Gesham, and Pelet, and Ephah, and
Shaaph.
48 Maachah, Caleb's concubine, bare Sheber,
and Tirhanah.
49 She bare also Shaaph the father of Madmannah, Sheva the father of Machbenah, and
the father of Gibea: and °the daughter of
Caleb *was* Achsa.

e7 50 These were the [7]sons of °Caleb the son of
Hur, the firstborn of Ephratah; Shobal the
[42]father of °Kirjath-jearim,
51 °Salma the father of Beth-lehem, Hareph
the [42]father of °Beth-gader.
52 And Shobal the [42]father of [50]Kirjath-jearim
had sons; Haroeh, *and* °half of the Manahethites.
53 And the families of [50]Kirjath-jearim; the
Ithrites, and the Puhites, and the Shumathites,
and the Mishraites; of them came the °Zareath-
ites, and the °Eshtaulites.
54 The sons of Salma; Beth-lehem, and the
Netophathites, Ataroth, the house of Joab, and
half of the Manahethites, the Zorites.
55 And the families of the scribes which dwelt
at °Jabez; the Tirathites, the Shimeathites,
and Suchathites. These *are* the °Kenites
that came of Hemath, the father of the house
990-509 of °Rechab.

B5 f1 **3** Now these were the sons of David, which
(p. 534) were °born unto him °in Hebron; the first-
960 born Amnon, of Ahinoam the Jezreelitess; the
to second °Daniel, of Abigail the Carmelitess:
953 2 The third, Absalom the son of Maachah the
daughter of Talmai king of Geshur: the fourth,
Adonijah the son of Haggith:

35 to Jarha. So to make him his heir. The laws of Khammurabi included this, § 191. See Ap. 15.
42 **Caleb the brother of Jerahmeel** and son of Hezron (*v.* 18).
father. Here used in the sense of ruler. Cp. *v.* 54; 4. 4.
Mareshah. The name of a city, also in Judah (Josh. 15. 44. 2 Chron. 11. 8).
Hebron. The name of a city, also in Judah. (Gen. 13. 18; 23. 2, 19). See note on Num. 13. 22. Given to Caleb by Joshua (14. 13).
43 **Tappuah.** Also the name of a city (Josh. 15. 34).
Rekem. Also a city, of Benjamin (Josh. 18. 27).
45 **Maon.** Also the name of a city (Josh. 15. 55). Mentioned in connection with David (1 Sam. 23. 24).
49 **the daughter of Caleb was Achsa.** "Caleb the son of Jephunneh" had a daughter named Achsah, who married Othniel (Josh. 15. 16, 17). Judg. 1. 12, 13). Hence the "discrepancy" assumed by some. See note on *v.* 18.
50 **Caleb the son of Hur.** The son of the Caleb in *v.* 19, Hur giving him the name of his own father. It is possible that this Caleb (*v.* 50) may have been the son of Jephunneh (Num. 13. 6), Jephunneh being the surname of the Hur of Ex. 17. 10; 24. 14; 31. 2; 35. 30.
Kirjath-jearim. An old Gibeonite city (Josh. 9. 17; 15. 60), where the Ark tarried long, and whence it was brought to Zion by David (1 Sam. 6. 21; 7. 2. 2 Sam. 6. 2. 1 Chron. 13. 5, 6).
51 **Salma.** A family name, repeated in Ruth 4. 20 and *v.* 11 above.
Beth-gader. Probably the same as Geder in 12. 4; 27. 28. Cp. Josh. 12. 13.
52 **half.** For the other half see *v.* 54.
53 **Zareathites . . . Eshtaulites** = of Zerah . . . of Eshtaol, two cities of Judah (Josh. 15. 33. Judg. 13. 25; 16. 31).
55 **Jabez.** Supposed to have been founded by Jabez. See below on 4. 9.
Kenites. These were the posterity of Jethro and Hobab. See Judg. 1. 16; and cp. 1 Sam. 15. 6; 27. 10. They became an ascetic people, and, by being mentioned here in connection with "scribes," may have been teachers. This perhaps accounts for Jehu's action in 2 Kings 10. 15, 16. **Rechab.** Cp. Jer. 35.

3. 1-24 (B5, p. 531). DIRECT DESCENT. DAVID TO ZEDEKIAH. (*Division.*)

B5	f1	1-9.	The sons of David.
	f2	10-16.	David's line to Zedekiah.
	f3	17-24.	The descendants of Jeconiah.

1 **born . . . in Hebron.** Cp. 2 Sam. 3. 2-5.
Daniel. Another name of Chileab (2 Sam. 3. 3).
3 **Eglah his wife.** The only woman in this list called David's "wife". Perhaps his original wife.
5 **born . . . Jerusalem.** Cp. 2 Sam. 5. 13-16.
Nathan. The son through whom the genealogy of Joseph is traced in Luke 3; and in Matt. 1, after Solomon's line failed in Jeconiah. See note on *v.* 17.
Solomon. Through whom the line is traced in Matt. 1.
Bath-shua. Another name for Bath-sheba. Cp. 2 Sam. 11. 3.
Ammiel, or Eliam. Cp. 2 Sam. 11. 3.

3 The fifth, Shephatiah of Abital: the sixth,
Ithream by °Eglah his wife.
4 *These* six were [1]born unto him in Hebron;
and there he reigned seven years and six
months: and in Jerusalem he reigned thirty 953
and three years. to
5 And these were °born unto him in °Jeru- 920
salem; Shimea, and Shobab, and °Nathan,
and °Solomon, four, of °Bath-shua the daughter of °Ammiel:
6 Ibhar also, and Elishama, and Eliphelet,
7 And Nogah, and Nepheg, and Japhia,

8 And Elishama, and Eliada, and Eliphelet, °nine.
9 *These were* all the sons of David, beside the sons of the concubines, and °Tamar their sister.

f^2 10 And Solomon's son *was* Rehoboam, Abia
(p. 534) his son, Asa his son, Jehoshaphat his son,
880 11 Joram his son, Ahaziah his son, Joash his son,
12 Amaziah his son, Azariah his son, Jotham his son,
13 Ahaz his son, Hezekiah his son, Manasseh his son,
14 Amon his son, Josiah his son.
15 And the sons of Josiah *were*, the firstborn °Johanan, the second °Jehoiakim, the third °Zedekiah, the fourth °Shallum.
499-488 16 And the sons of Jehoiakim: °Jeconiah his son, Zedekiah his son.

f^3 17 And the °sons of Jeconiah; °Assir, Salathiel his son,
18 Malchiram also, and Pedaiah, and Shenazar, Jecamiah, Hoshama, and Nedabiah.
19 And the [17]sons of Pedaiah *were*, °Zerubbabel, and Shimei: and the [17]sons of Zerubbabel; Meshullam, and Hananiah, and Shelomith their sister:
20 And Hashubah, and Ohel, and Berechiah, and Hasadiah, Jushab-hesed, five.
21 And the [17]sons of Hananiah; Pelatiah, and Jesaiah: the sons of Rephaiah, the sons of Arnan, the sons of Obadiah, the sons of Shechaniah.
22 And the [17]sons of Shechaniah; Shemaiah: and the sons of Shemaiah; Hattush, and Igeal, and Bariah, and Neariah, and Shaphat, °six.
23 And the [17]sons of Neariah; Elioenai, and Hezekiah, and Azrikam, three.
24 And the sons of Elioenai *were*, Hodaiah, and Eliashib, and Pelaiah, and Akkub, and Johanan, and Dalaiah, and Anani, seven.

C^5 g^1 **4** The °sons of Judah; Pharez, Hezron, and
(p. 535) Carmi, and °Hur, and Shobal.
1748 2 And Reaiah the son of Shobal begat Jahath; and Jahath begat Ahumai, and Lahad. These *are* the families of the °Zorathites.
3 And °these *were of* the father of Etam; Jezreel, and Ishma, and Idbash: and the name of their sister *was* Hazelelponi:
4 And Penuel the °father of Gedor, and Ezer the father of Hushah. These *are* the sons of Hur, the firstborn of Ephratah, the father of Beth-lehem.

g^2 5 And °Ashur the father of Tekoa had two wives, Helah and Naarah.
6 And Naarah bare him Ahuzam, and Hepher, and Temeni, and Haahashtari. These *were* the sons of Naarah.
7 And the sons of Helah *were*, Zereth, and Jezoar, and °Ethnan.
8 And Coz begat Anub, and Zobebah, and the families of Aharhel the son of Harum.

g^3 9 And Jabez was °more honourable than his brethren: and his mother called his name °Jabez, saying, "Because I bare him °with sorrow."
10 And Jabez called on °the God of °Israel, saying, "Oh that Thou wouldest bless me indeed, and enlarge my °coast, and that Thine hand might be with me, and that Thou wouldest keep *me* from °evil, that it may not °grieve me!" And °God granted him that which he requested.

8 nine. Eleven are mentioned in 2 Sam. 5. 14-16; but probably two died young, and their names were not needed in the genealogy. Cp. 2 Sam. 5. 15.
9 Tamar. Cp. 2 Sam. 13.
15 Johanan. Or Jehoahaz. 2 Kings 23. 30.
Jehoiakim. Called Eliakim by his father, but Jehoiakim by Pharaoh-nechoh, king of Egypt (2 Kings 23. 34).
Zedekiah. The same as Mattaniah. Cp. 2 Kings 24. 17, 18. He was the last king of Judah.
Shallum. The same as Jehoahaz, the successor of Josiah (Jer. 22. 11. 2 Kings 23. 31, 34).
16 Jeconiah. Called also Jehoiachin (2 Kings 24. 6), and Coniah (Jer. 22. 24, 28). Cp. 2 Chron. 36. 9. 2 Kings 24. 8.
17 sons. Cp. Jer. 22. 28-30.
Assir = the captive, perhaps referring to Zedekiah, and not a proper name.
19 Zerubbabel. According to Matt. 1. 12 and Ezra 3. 2; 5. 2, the son of Shealtiel.
22 six. Heb. *Shishshah*, which may be a proper name and not the numeral.

4. 1—8. 40 (C^5, p. 531). COLLATERAL. (*Division.*)

C^5	g^1	4. 1-4. Judah's posterity.
	g^2	4. 5-8. Ashur.
	g^3	4. 9, 10. Jabez.
	g^4	4. 11-20. Caleb the son of Hur.
	g^5	4. 21-23. The sons of Shelah.
	g^6	4. 24-43. The sons of Simeon.
	g^7	5. 1-10. The sons of Reuben (to the Captivity).
	g^8	5. 11-17. The sons of Gad.
	g^9	5. 18-26. Reuben, Gad, and half Manasseh.
	g^{10}	6. 1-3. The sons of Levi.
	g^{11}	6. 4-15. The Priests (to the Captivity).
	g^{12}	6. 16-48. Gershom, Kohath, and Merari.
	g^{13}	6. 49-53. The sons of Aaron.
	g^{14}	6. 54-81. The cities of Priests and Levites.
	g^{15}	7. 1-5. The sons of Issachar.
	g^{16}	7. 6-12. The sons of Benjamin.
	g^{17}	7. 13. The sons of Naphtali.
	g^{18}	7. 14-19. The sons of Manasseh.
	g^{19}	7. 20-29. The sons of Ephraim.
	g^{20}	7. 30-40. The sons of Asher.
	g^{21}	8. 1-32. The sons of Benjamin.
	g^{22}	8. 33-40. The stock of Saul and Jonathan.

1 sons = descendants.
Hur, and Shobal. These were sons of Caleb, the son of Hezron (2. 18, 20, 50, 52).
2 Zorathites. See 2. 53.
3 these were of. Some codices, with Sept., read "these were the sons of".
4 father: or lord, or prince. See note on 2. 42.
5 Ashur. A son of Hezron. Cp. 2. 24.
7 Ethnan. Supply Fig. *Ellipsis* (Ap. 6) thus: "Ethnan, and Coz, [and Coz] begat Anub". Cp. *v.* 13.
9 more honourable. Perhaps his going up with Caleb and Othniel against the Canaanites is referred to. See Judg. 1. 2, 4, 9-15. Josh. 15. 13-19.
Jabez. The transposition of letters in Heb. may intimate a change of experiences, and mean "may he have pain or grief reversed."
with sorrow. Cp. Gen. 3. 16 (same word).
10 the God of Israel (Heb. Elohim, Ap. 4). A suitable title and prayer before going on the expedition.
Israel. The nation as descended from him for whom God orders all. See notes on Gen. 32. 28; 43. 6; 45. 26, 28.
coast = border or boundary.
evil. Heb. *rā'ā'*. Ap. 44. viii.
grieve = pain. Note Fig. *Aposiopēsis.* Ap. 6. No conclusion to his prayer.

g4 (p. 535) **11** And Chelub the brother of Shuah begat Mehir, which *was* the father of Eshton.
12 And Eshton begat Beth-rapha, and Paseah, and Tehinnah the father of Ir-nahash. These *are* the °men of Rechah.
13 And the sons of Kenaz; Othniel, and Seraiah: and the sons of Othniel; °Hathath.
14 And Meonothai begat Ophrah: and Seraiah begat Joab, the [4]father of the °valley of Charashim; for they were craftsmen.
15 And the sons of °Caleb the son of Jephunneh; Iru, Elah, and Naam: and the [13]sons of Elah, even Kenaz.
16 And the sons of Jehaleleel; Ziph, and Ziphah, Tiria, and Asareel.
17 And the sons of Ezra *were*, Jether, and Mered, and Epher, and Jalon: and she bare Miriam, and Shammai, and Ishbah the father of Eshtemoa.
18 And his wife °Jehudijah bare Jered the father of Gedor, and Heber the father of Socho, and Jekuthiel the father of Zanoah. And these *are* the sons of °Bithiah the daughter of Pharaoh, which Mered took.
19 And the sons of *his* wife °Hodiah the sister of Naham, the father of Keilah the Garmite, and Eshtemoa the Maachathite.
20 And the sons of Shimon *were*, Amnon, and Rinnah, Ben-hanan, and Tilon. And the sons of Ishi *were*, Zoheth, and Ben-zoheth.

g5 **21** The sons of Shelah the son of Judah *were*, Er the father of Lecah, and Laadah the father of Mareshah, and the families of the house of them that wrought °fine linen, of the house of Ashbea,
22 And Jokim, and the [12]men of Chozeba, and Joash, and Saraph, who °had the dominion in Moab, and °Jashubi-lehem. And *these are* ancient °things.
23 These *were* the potters, and °those that dwelt among plants and hedges: there they dwelt with the king for his work.

g6 1750 **24** The sons of Simeon *were*, Nemuel, and Jamin, Jarib, Zerah, *and* Shaul:
25 Shallum his son, Mibsam his son, Mishma his son.
26 And the sons of Mishma; Hamuel his son, Zacchur his son, Shimei his son.
27 And Shimei had sixteen sons and six daughters; but his brethren had not many °children, neither did all their family multiply, like to the °children of Judah.
28 And they dwelt at °Beer-sheba, and Moladah, and Hazar-shual,
29 And at Bilhah, and at Ezem, and at Tolad,
30 And at Bethuel, and at Hormah, and at °Ziklag,
31 And at Beth-marcaboth, and Hazar-susim, and at Beth-birei, and at Shaaraim. These *were* their cities °unto the reign of David.
32 And their villages *were*, Etam, and Ain, Rimmon, and Tochen, and Ashan, five cities:
33 And all their villages that *were* round about the same cities, unto °Baal. These *were* their habitations, and °their genealogy.
34 And Meshobab, and Jamlech, and Joshah the son of Amaziah,
35 And Joel, and Jehu the son of Josibiah, the son of Seraiah, the son of Asiel,
36 And Elioenai, and Jaakobah, and Jeshohaiah, and Asaiah, and Adiel, and Jesimiel, and Benaiah,
37 And Ziza the son of Shiphi, the son of Allon, the son of Jedaiah, the son of Shimri, the son of Shemaiah;
38 These mentioned by *their* names *were* princes in their families: and the house of their fathers increased greatly.
39 And they went to the entrance of °Gedor, *even* unto the east side of the valley, to seek pasture for their flocks.
40 And they found fat pasture and good, and the land *was* wide, and quiet, and peaceable; for *they* of Ham had dwelt there of old.
41 And these °written by name came in the days of Hezekiah king of Judah, and smote their tents, and °the habitations that were found there, and destroyed them utterly unto this day, and dwelt in their rooms: because *there was* pasture there for their flocks.
42 And *some* of them, *even* of the sons of Simeon, °five hundred [12]men, went to mount Seir, having for their captains Pelatiah, and Neariah, and Rephaiah, and Uzziel, the sons of Ishi.
43 And they smote °the rest of the Amalekites that were escaped, and dwelt there °unto this day.

12 men. Heb. *'ĕnōsh.* Ap. 14. III.
13 Hathath. Supply Fig. *Ellipsis* (Ap. 6) thus: "Hathath and Meonothai [and Meonothai] begat Ophrah".
14 valley of Charashim = Ge-harashim, the name of the place.
15 Caleb the son of Jephunneh. Not the son of Hezron (2. 18).
18 Jehudijah = the Jewess.
Bithiah, the daughter of Pharaoh. Is Bithiah the same as Jehudijah, and did she turn a Jewess? Mered was evidently a man of position.
19 Hodiah. The Jehudijah of *v.* 18.
21 fine linen: or *byssus*, a fine white Egyptian linen.
22 had the dominion: or became lords to Moab.
Jashubi-lehem. The Vulg. renders it "and returned to Beth-lehem", like Naomi and Ruth (1. 1-4, 19).
things: or records.
23 those that dwelt, &c. The inhabitants of Netaim and Gedera.
27 children = sons.
28 Beer-sheba. Cp. Josh. 19. 2-5.
30 Ziklag. Given later to David by the Philistines (1 Sam. 27. 6).
31 unto the reign of David. The Codex *Hilleli*, with one early printed edition, Sept., Syr., and Vulg. read "unto king David".
33 Baal. Another name for Baalath-beer in Josh. 19. 8.
their genealogy: or, "and they had their own genealogical register."
39 Gedor. Probably south of Simeon, toward Mount Seir.
41 written by name: i. e. in the foregoing list.
the habitations = Maonites, or Mehumims (2 Chron. 26. 7). Cp. 20. 1 and Judg. 10. 12.
42 five hundred. If these could accomplish such things, what could not the whole of Israel have done? Cp. *v.* 10 and 5. 20.
43 the rest of the Amalekites. Not all destroyed in 1 Sam. 15. 8. A number survived. Cp. 1 Sam. 27. 8; 30. 1. 2 Sam. 8. 12. Est. 3. 1. See note on Ex. 17. 16.
unto this day. Evidently not disturbed by the king of Babylon in the deportation of Israel.

g7 (p. 535) 1751 **5** Now the sons of Reuben the firstborn of Israel, °(for he *was* the firstborn; but, °forasmuch as he defiled his father's bed, his birthright was given unto the sons of Joseph the son of Israel: and the genealogy is °not to be reckoned after the °birthright.

2 For °Judah prevailed above his brethren, and of him °*came* the °chief ruler; but the [1]birthright *was* Joseph's:)

3 The sons, *I say*, of Reuben the firstborn of Israel *were*, Hanoch, and Pallu, Hezron, and Carmi.

4 The sons of Joel; Shemaiah his son, Gog his son, Shimei his son,

5 Micah his son, Reaia his son, Baal his son.

6 Beerah his son, whom Tilgath-pilneser king of Assyria °carried away *captive:* he *was* prince of the Reubenites.

7 And his brethren by their families, when the genealogy of their generations was reckoned, *were* the chief, Jeiel, and Zechariah,

8 And Bela the son of °Azaz, the son of Shema, the son of Joel, who dwelt in °Aroer, even unto °Nebo and °Baal-meon:

9 And eastward he inhabited unto the entering in of the wilderness from the river Euphrates: because their cattle were multiplied in the land of Gilead.

10 And in the days of Saul they made war with the °Hagarites, who fell by their hand: and they dwelt in their tents throughout all the east *land* of Gilead.

g8 11 And the °children of Gad dwelt over against them, in the land of Bashan unto Salcah:

12 Joel the chief, and Shapham the next, and Jaanai, and Shaphat in Bashan.

13 And their brethren of the house of their fathers *were*, Michael, and Meshullam, and Sheba, and Jorai, and Jachan, and Zia, and °Heber, seven.

14 These *are* the children of Abihail the son of Huri, the son of Jaroah, the son of Gilead, the son of Michael, the son of Jeshishai, the son of Jahdo, the son of Buz;

15 Ahi the son of Abdiel, the son of Guni, chief of the house of their fathers.

16 And they dwelt °in Gilead in Bashan, and in her towns, and in all the suburbs of Sharon, upon their borders.

17 All these were reckoned by genealogies in the days of °Jotham king of Judah, and in the days of °Jeroboam king of Israel.

g9 18 The sons of Reuben, and the Gadites, and half the tribe of Manasseh, of °valiant men, °men able to bear buckler and sword, and to shoot with bow, and skilful in war, *were* four and forty thousand seven hundred and threescore, that went out to the war.

19 And they made war with the Hagarites, with Jetur, and Nephish, and Nodab.

20 And they were °helped against them, and the Hagarites were delivered into their hand, and all that *were* with them: for they cried to °God in the battle, and He was intreated of them; because they put their °trust in Him.

21 And they took away their cattle; of their camels fifty thousand, and of sheep two hundred and fifty thousand, and of asses two thousand, and of °men an hundred thousand.

22 For there fell down many slain, because the war *was* of [20]God. And they dwelt in their steads °until the captivity.

23 And the [11]children of the °half tribe of Manasseh dwelt in the land: they increased from Bashan unto Baal-hermon and Senir, and unto mount Hermon.

24 And these *were* the heads of the house of their fathers, °even Epher, and Ishi, and Eliel, and Azriel, and Jeremiah, and Hodaviah, and Jahdiel, °mighty men of valour, famous [18]men, *and* heads of the house of their fathers.

25 And they °transgressed against the [20]God of their fathers, and went a whoring after the gods of the °people of the land, whom [20]God destroyed before them.

5. 1 for. Note the Fig. *Parenthesis*. Ap. 6.
forasmuch. Cp. Gen. 35. 22; 49. 4.
not to be reckoned, &c. = not to be enrolled in the place of the firstborn.
birthright. See note on Gen. 25. 31.
2 Judah prevailed. Cp. Gen. 49. 8, referring to intertribal precedence.
came. Supply Fig. *Ellipsis* (Ap. 6) with "is".
chief ruler. Referring to the regal line, and the coming of the Messiah. A.V., 1611, had "rulers".
6 carried away. This was the *first* carrying away, and took place in 654. Cp. *v.* 26. The *second* was by Tiglath-Pileser (= Pul) in the reign of Pekah (649-629). This was the Galilee-Naphtali carrying away (2 Kings 15. 29. Isa. 9. 1) referred to in Matt. 4. 15. The *third* was the Samaria deportation in the ninth year of Hoshea and sixth of Hezekiah (611 B.C.), and ended the kingdom of Israel (2 Kings 17. 3-23; 18. 9-12). It was begun by Shalmaneser and ended by Sargon (613-611).
8 Azaz. Some codices, with four early printed editions, read "Azan", or "Azzan".
Aroer . . . Nebo . . . Baal-meon. All east of Dead Sea. See Num. 32. 34, 38. Deut. 2. 36.
10 Hagarites. Tracing their descent from Hagar through Ishmael. Cp. *v.* 19 with 1. 31, and Ps. 83. 6.
11 children = sons.
13 Heber. Some codices, with two early printed editions and Sept., read "Hebed", mistaking *Resh*, ר ("r") for *Daleth*, ד ("d").
16 in Gilead: i. e. in part of it, other parts having been allotted to the half-tribes of Reubenites and Manassites (Num. 32. 39-40. Deut. 3. 13. Josh. 13. 31).
17 Jotham . . . Jeroboam. Jotham (647-631) and Jeroboam II (728-687). See Ap. 50. V, p. 59. Consequently, the statement here refers to consensusses at different times.
18 valiant men = sons of valour.
men. Heb. *'ĕnōsh.* Ap. 14. III. These two and a half tribes, east of Jordan, chose their own portions, but were nearest to the enemy, and were the first to be carried away. Cp. Lot, Gen. 13. 10, 11, with 14. 11, 12. Better to have our "lot" chosen for us by Jehovah (Gen. 13. 14, 15).
20 helped: i. e. by God (2 Chron. 26. 17. Ps. 28. 7). This victory should have shown them that there could have been no captivity had they obeyed God (see note on 4. 43).
God. Heb. Elohim. Ap. 4. I.
trust. Heb. *baṭaḥ.* Ap. 69. i.
21 men. Heb. "souls (*nephesh*) of men (*'ādām*)". Ap. 13 and 14. I. Cp. Num. 31. 35.
22 until the captivity. Cp. 2 Kings 15. 29; 17. 6; 18. 9-12: i. e. that of Tiglath-pileser.
23 half: i. e. the half beyond Jordan.
24 even. Sept. and Vulg. omit this word "even".
mighty men. Heb. *gibbōr.* Ap. 14. IV.
25 transgressed = acted faithlessly. Ap. 44. xi.
people = peoples.

26 And the °God of Israel stirred up the
°spirit of °Pul king of Assyria, and the °spirit
of [6]Tilgath-pilneser king of Assyria, and he
about carried them away, even the Reubenites, and
654 the Gadites, and the half tribe of Manasseh,
and brought them unto °Halah, °and Habor,
and Hara, and to the river °Gozan, °unto this
day.

g[10] **6** The sons of °Levi; °Gershon, °Kohath,
(p. 535) and Merari.
1749 2 And the sons of Kohath; Amram, Izhar,
and Hebron, and Uzziel.
3 And the °children of Amram; °Aaron, and
Moses, and Miriam. The sons also of Aaron;
°Nadab, and Abihu, °Eleazar, and Ithamar.

g[11] 4 Eleazar begat Phinehas, °Phinehas begat
Abishua,
5 And Abishua begat Bukki, and Bukki begat Uzzi,
6 And Uzzi begat Zerahiah, and Zerahiah
begat Meraioth,
7 Meraioth begat Amariah, and Amariah
begat Ahitub,
8 And Ahitub begat Zadok, and °Zadok begat
°Ahimaaz,
9 And Ahimaaz begat Azariah, and Azariah
begat Johanan,
10 And Johanan begat Azariah, (°he *it is*
that executed the priest's office in the °temple
that Solomon built in Jerusalem:)
11 And Azariah begat Amariah, and Amariah
begat Ahitub,
12 And Ahitub begat Zadok, and Zadok begat
Shallum,
13 And °Shallum begat °Hilkiah, and Hilkiah
begat Azariah,
14 And Azariah begat °Seraiah, and Seraiah
begat Jehozadak,
15 And °Jehozadak went *into captivity*, when
°the LORD carried away Judah and Jerusalem
by the hand of Nebuchadnezzar.

g[12] 16 The °sons of [1]Levi; [1]Gershom, Kohath,
and Merari.
17 And these *be* the names of the sons of
Gershom; Libni, and Shimei.
18 And the sons of Kohath *were*, Amram, and
Izhar, and Hebron, and Uzziel.
19 The sons of Merari; Mahli, and Mushi.
And these *are* the families of the Levites
according to their fathers.
20 Of [1]Gershom; Libni his son, Jahath his
son, Zimmah his son,
21 Joah his son, Iddo his son, Zerah his son,
Jeaterai his son,
22 The sons of Kohath; °Amminadab his son,
Korah his son, Assir his son,
23 °Elkanah his son, and Ebiasaph his son,
and °Assir his son,
24 Tahath his son, Uriel his son, Uzziah his
son, and Shaul his son.
25 And the sons of [23]Elkanah; Amasai, and
Ahimoth.
26 *As for* Elkanah: °the sons of Elkanah;
Zophai his son, and Nahath his son,
27 Eliab his son, Jeroham his son, Elkanah
his son.
1060 28 And the sons of Samuel; °the firstborn
Vashni, and Abiah.

29 The sons of Merari; Mahli, Libni his son,
Shimei his son, Uzza his son,
30 Shimea his son, Haggiah his son, Asaiah
his son.
31 And these *are they* whom David set over 951
the °service of song in the house of [15]the LORD, to
after that the °ark had rest. 948
32 And they ministered before the °dwelling
place of the °tabernacle of the congregation

26 God of Israel. Note Elohim: not Jehovah, as dealing with Gentiles; but Israel, as not forgetting His covenant-relation though stirring up enemies.

spirit. Heb. *rūach*. Ap. 9.

Pul . . . and . . . Tilgath-pilneser. Two names of one person: Pul, the original and official name in Babylon of this usurper; Tilgath, his official name in Assyria, which he assumed from an earlier king. Cp. 2 Kings 15. 19.

Halah . . . Gozan. Whither the Israelites west of Jordan were deported by Sargon (2 Kings 15. 29; 17. 6; 18. 11).

and. Note the Fig. *Polysyndeton*. Ap. 6.

unto this day. See note on 4. 43.

6. 1 Levi. This care to give these genealogies after the captivities was to show that God's promises to preserve the nation would be faithfully kept. Cp. Jer. 23. 5, 6.

Gershon. Cp. Ex. 6. 16. The Western Massorite spelling; the eastern spelling being "Gershom".

Kohath. The second son placed first because Aaron descended from him. **3 children** = sons.

Aaron, and Moses. One of the six passages where Aaron precedes Moses (23. 13. Ex. 6. 20, 26. Num. 3. 1; 26. 59).

Nadab, and Abihu. Perished at Sinai for offering "strange fire". See note on Lev. 10. 1. Cp. Num. 3. 4. 1 Chron. 24. 2.

Eleazar. His line given without a break up to the Captivity. Cp. *v.* 15. In Ezra 7. 1-5 an abbreviated genealogy is given. Moses not enumerated here, though a priest (Ps. 99. 6), because separated for civil government before the appointment of the Levitic priesthood.

4 Phinehas. Cp. Ex. 6. 25. Ps. 106. 30. Num. 25. 11.

8 Zadok. Cp. 2 Sam. 8. 17; 15. 27. 1 Chron. 24. 3, 6, 31.

Ahimaaz. Cp. *v.* 53. 2 Sam. 15. 27, 36; 18. 19, 22, 27.

10 he. Note the Fig. *Parenthesis*. Ap. 6. See 2 Chron. 26. 17. **temple** = house.

13 Shallum. In Neh. 11. 11 called Meshullam.

Hilkiah. The high priest in reign of Josiah (2 Kings 22. 4. 2 Chron. 34. 9).

14 Seraiah. Carried away by Nebuchadnezzar, and put to death at Riblah (2 Kings 25. 18, 21).

15 Jehozadak. The Jozadak was the father of Joshua the high priest, who returned from the Captivity (Ezra 3. 2; 5. 2. Neh. 12. 26. Hag. 1. 1, 12. Zech. 6. 11).

the LORD. Heb. Jehovah. Ap. 4. II.

16 sons of Levi. These were not high priests.

22 Amminadab. His other name was Izhar, *vv.* 2 and 38.

23 Elkanah. A common Levitical name. Cp. *vv.* 25, 27, and see 1 Sam. 1. 1. **Assir.** Cp. Ex. 6. 24.

26 the sons of Elkanah. Some codices, with Sept. and one early printed edition, omit this second "Elkanah"; the Heb. reads "his son".

28 the firstborn Vashni. Cp. 1 Sam. 8. 2, where the firstborn's name "came to be" Joel. From 1 Chron. 6. 28 it seems to have been originally Vashni. From *v.* 33 he seems to have had two names.

31 service = the hands: hands being put by Fig. *Metonymy* (of Cause), Ap. 6, for the work done by them.

ark had rest. See 16. 1, notes on 13. 3, and Ex. 25. 22.

32 dwelling place = tabernacle. Heb. *mishkan*. Ap. 40.

tabernacle = tent of meeting. Heb. *'ohel-mōēd*. Ap. 40.

with singing, until Solomon had built the house of [15]the LORD in Jerusalem: and *then* they waited on their office according to their order.
33 And these *are* they that °waited with their °children. Of the sons of the Kohathites: °Heman a singer, °(the son of °Joel, the son of °Shemuel,
34 The son of Elkanah, the son of Jeroham, the son of Eliel, the son of Toah,
35 The son of Zuph, the son of Elkanah, the son of Mahath, the son of Amasai,
36 The son of Elkanah, the son of Joel, the son of Azariah, the son of Zephaniah,
37 The son of Tahath, the son of Assir, the son of Ebiasaph, the son of Korah,
38 The son of Izhar, the son of Kohath, the son of Levi, the son of °Israel).
39 And °his brother Asaph, who stood on his right hand, (*even* Asaph the son of Berachiah, the son of Shimea,
40 The son of Michael, the son of °Baaseiah, the son of Malchiah,
41 The son of Ethni, the son of Zerah, the son of Adaiah,
42 The son of °Ethan, the son of Zimmah, the son of Shimei,
43 The son of Jahath, the son of Gershom, the son of Levi.)
44 And °their brethren the sons of °Merari *stood* on the left hand: Ethan (the son of Kishi, the son of Abdi, the son of Malluch,
45 The son of Hashabiah, the son of Amaziah, the son of Hilkiah,
46 The son of Amzi, the son of Bani, the son of Shamer,
47 The son of Mahli, the son of Mushi, the son of Merari, the son of Levi.)
48 Their brethren also the Levites *were* appointed unto °all manner of service of the [32]tabernacle of the house of °God.
g[13] (p. 535) 49 But °Aaron and his sons °offered upon the altar of the burnt offering, and on the °altar of incense, *and were appointed* for all the work of the *place* °most holy, and to make an atonement for Israel, according to all that °Moses the servant of °God had commanded.
50 And °these *are* the sons of Aaron; Eleazar his son, Phinehas his son, Abishua his son,
51 Bukki his son, Uzzi his son, Zerahiah his son,
52 Meraioth his son, Amariah his son, Ahitub his son,
53 Zadok his son, Ahimaaz his son.
g[14] 54 Now these *are* °their dwelling places throughout their °castles in their °coasts, of the sons of Aaron, of the families of the Kohathites: for theirs °was the lot.
55 And they gave them Hebron in the land of Judah, and the °suburbs thereof round about it.
56 But the fields of the city, and the villages thereof, they gave to Caleb the son of Jephunneh.
57 And to the sons of Aaron they gave the cities of Judah, *namely*, Hebron, *the city* of refuge, and Libnah with her [55]suburbs, and Jattir, and Eshtemoa, with their [55]suburbs,
58 And °Hilen with her [55]suburbs, Debir with her [55]suburbs,

33 waited = stood. **children** = sons.
Heman, &c. = Heman the singer, Samuel's grandson. See 15. 17–19; 25. 1–6. Cp. 1 Kings 4. 31, and see his name in the Psalm titles (Ap. 63. viii).
the son. Note the parenthesis, *vv.* 33–38.
Joel. See note on *v.* 28 above.
Shemuel = Samuel. Twenty-one generations given.
38 Israel. Traced back to fountain head.
39 his brother Asaph: i. e. his brother in service. Fifteen generations.
40 Baaseiah. Some codices, with three early printed editions, Sept., and Syr., read "Maaseiah".
42 Ethan. The same as Jeduthun (9. 16; 16. 41; 25. 1. 2 Chron. 35. 15). Fourteen generations.
44 their brethren. Heman, from Kohath (Levi's second son); Asaph, from Gershom (Levi's eldest son); Ethan, from Merari (Levi's youngest son).
Merari. The youngest son of Levi (Ex. 6. 16).
48 all manner of service. Cp. ch. 23 below.
God. Heb. *ha-'Elohim* (Ap. 4), the [Triune] God.
49 Aaron and his sons. Cp. Num. 18. 1–7. Lev. 8. 2. This refutes the assertions of some that the kings of Judah were allowed to offer sacrifices or burn incense. Cp. 1 Kings 8. 64.
offered = burnt incense. Heb. *ḳaṭar.* Ap. 43. I. vii. Cp. Lev. 1. 9.
altar of incense. Cp. Ex. 30. 7.
most holy = holy of holies. See note on Ex. 3. 5.
Moses the servant of God. This expression occurs only four times: here, 2 Chron. 24. 9. Neh. 10. 29, and Dan. 9. 11. For other titles descriptive of Moses, as a servant, see notes on Ex. 14. 31. Num. 12. 7. Deut. 34. 5. 1 Kings 8. 53.
God. Heb. Elohim. Ap. 4. I.
50 these. Restating by way of summary.
54 their dwelling places. Cp. Josh. 21. 4–42. This was the basis of their claim for reinstatement after their return from Babylon. Probably many of these places had changed their names in spelling or otherwise since those days. This accounts for all the variations.
castles = districts.
coasts = borders.
was the lot. Supply Fig. *Ellipsis* (Ap. 6): "was the [first] lot".
55 suburbs = pasture land (as distinguished from "field" or arable land). So throughout the rest of this chapter. See *v.* 56.
58 Hilen = Holon of Josh. 21. 15. Some codices, with one early printed edition, read "Helez".

59 And Ashan with her [55]suburbs, and Beth-shemesh with her [55]suburbs:
60 And out of the tribe of Benjamin; Geba with her [55]suburbs, and Alemeth with her [55]suburbs, and Anathoth with her [55]suburbs. All their cities throughout their families *were* thirteen cities.
61 And unto the sons of Kohath, *which were* left of the family of that tribe, *were cities given* out of the half tribe, *namely, out of* the half *tribe* of Manasseh, by lot, ten cities.
62 And to the sons of Gershom throughout their families out of the tribe of Issachar, and out of the tribe of Asher, and out of the tribe of Naphtali, and out of the tribe of Manasseh in Bashan, thirteen cities.
63 Unto the sons of Merari *were given* by lot, throughout their families, out of the tribe of Reuben, and out of the tribe of Gad, and out of the tribe of Zebulun, twelve cities.
64 And the [33]children of Israel gave to the Levites *these* cities with their [55]suburbs.
65 And they gave by lot out of the tribe of the [33]children of Judah, and out of the tribe of

the [33]children of Simeon, and out of the tribe of the [33]children of Benjamin, these cities, °which are called by *their* names.

66 °And *the residue* of the families of the sons of Kohath had °cities of their coasts out of the tribe of Ephraim.

67 And they gave unto them, *of* the cities of refuge, °Shechem in °mount Ephraim with her [55]suburbs; *they gave* also °Gezer with her [55]suburbs,

68 And Jokmeam with her [55]suburbs, and Beth-horon with her [55]suburbs,

69 And Aijalon with her [55]suburbs, and Gath-rimmon with her [55]suburbs:

70 And out of the half tribe of Manasseh; Aner with her [55]suburbs, and Bileam with her [55]suburbs, for the family of the remnant of the sons of Kohath.

71 Unto the sons of Gershom *were given* out of the family of the half tribe of Manasseh, Golan in Bashan with her [55]suburbs, and Ashtaroth with her [55]suburbs:

72 And out of the tribe of Issachar; Kedesh with her [55]suburbs, Daberath with her [55]suburbs,

73 And Ramoth with her [55]suburbs, and Anem with her [55]suburbs:

74 And out of the tribe of Asher; Mashal with her [55]suburbs, and Abdon with her [55]suburbs,

75 And Hukok with her [55]suburbs, and Rehob with her [55]suburbs:

76 And out of the tribe of Naphtali; Kedesh in Galilee with her [55]suburbs, and Hammon with her [55]suburbs, and Kirjathaim with her [55]suburbs.

77 Unto °the rest of the [33]children of Merari *were given* out of the tribe of Zebulun, Rimmon with her [55]suburbs, Tabor with her [55]suburbs:

78 And on the other side Jordan by Jericho, on the east side of Jordan, *were given them* out of the tribe of Reuben, Bezer in the wilderness with her [55]suburbs, and Jahzah with her [55]suburbs,

79 Kedemoth also with her [55]suburbs, and Mephaath with her [55]suburbs:

80 And out of the tribe of Gad; Ramoth in Gilead with her [55]suburbs, and Mahanaim with her [55]suburbs,

81 And Heshbon with her [55]suburbs, and Jazer with her [55]suburbs.

g[15] 7 °Now the sons of Issachar *were,* Tola, and
(p. 535) Puah, Jashub, and Shimrom, four.
1746 2 And °the sons of Tola; Uzzi, and Rephaiah, and Jeriel, and Jahmai, and Jibsam, and Shemuel, heads of their father's house, *to wit,* of Tola: *they were* °valiant men of might in their generations; whose number *was* °in the days of David two and twenty thousand and six hundred.

3 And the °sons of Uzzi; Izrahiah: and the sons of Izrahiah; Michael, and Obadiah, and Joel, Ishiah, five: all of them chief men.

4 And with them, by their generations, after the house of their fathers, *were* bands of soldiers for war, six and thirty thousand *men:* for they had many wives and sons.

5 And their brethren among all the families of Issachar *were* °valiant men of might, reckoned in all by their genealogies fourscore and seven thousand.

65 which are called by their names: or, which are mentioned by name.

66 And the residue. Supply Fig. *Ellipsis* (Ap. 6) thus: "[as for some] of the families", &c.

cities of their coasts = the cities of their lot. Cp. Josh. 21. 20.

67 Shechem. Only Shechem in this list is a city of refuge. No list of the six is intended to be given, although all are named. See *vv.* 57, 67, 71, 76, 78, 80.

mount = hill country of.

Gezer. See note on 1 Kings 9. 15–17.

77 the rest of = those remaining from.

7. 1 Now the sons of Issachar were = And to the sons of Issachar belonged. Issachar born 1746 B.C.

2 the sons of Tola. Descendants of younger sons are contrasted with his firstborn Uzzi (*vv.* 3, 4). These names occur nowhere else, and prove Chronicles to be entirely independent.

valiant men. Heb. *gibbōr.* Ap. 14. IV.

in the days of David. When he numbered the people (2 Sam. 24).

3 sons. A special various reading called *Sevīr* (Ap. 34) reads "son".

5 valiant. A.V., 1611, omits this word.

6 three. In Gen. 46. 21 there were ten. When Chronicles was written the others probably had become extinct. Even in Num. 26. 38 only five are mentioned. In 8. 1, 2 only five are given.

mighty men. Heb. *gibbōr.* Ap. 14. IV.

11 their fathers. Fig. *Ellipsis* (Ap. 6), "their fathers [houses]".

12 children = sons.

Hushim, the sons of Aher = Hushim the son of another, that other being Dan (Gen. 46. 23). Not named here. For reason, see note below, and on Gen. 49. 17.

sons. Put by Fig. *Synecdoche* (of the Whole), Ap. 6, for "son".

Aher. Heb. *'āḥēr* = another.

14 she = his wife.

Aramitess = Aramæan, or woman of Syria.

6 *The sons* of Benjamin; Bela, and Becher, g[16]
and Jediael, °three. 1728

7 And the sons of Bela; Ezbon, and Uzzi, and Uzziel, and Jerimoth, and Iri, five; heads of the house of *their* fathers, °mighty men of valour; and were reckoned by their genealogies twenty and two thousand and thirty and four.

8 And the sons of Becher; Zemira, and Joash, and Eliezer, and Elioenai, and Omri, and Jerimoth, and Abiah, and Anathoth, and Alameth. All these *are* the sons of Becher.

9 And the number of them, after their genealogy by their generations, heads of the house of their fathers, [7]mighty men of valour, *was* twenty thousand and two hundred.

10 The [3]sons also of Jediael; Bilhan: and the sons of Bilhan; Jeush, and Benjamin, and Ehud, and Chenaanah, and Zethan, and Tharshish, and Ahishahar.

11 All these the sons of Jediael, by the heads of °their fathers, [7]mighty men of valour, *were* seventeen thousand and two hundred *soldiers,* fit to go out for war *and* battle.

12 Shuppim also, and Huppim, the °children of Ir, *and* °Hushim, the °sons of °Aher.

13 The sons of Naphtali; Jahziel, and Guni, g[17]
and Jezer, and Shallum, the sons of Bilhah. 1748

14 The sons of Manasseh; Ashriel, whom g[18]
°she bare: (*but* his concubine the °Aramitess bare Machir the father of Gilead:

15 And Machir took to wife *the sister* of

Huppim and Shuppim, whose sister's name *was*
Maachah;) and the name of the °second *was*
Zelophehad: and Zelophehad had °daughters.
16 And Maachah the wife of Machir bare
a son, and she called his name Peresh; and
the name of his brother *was* Sheresh; and his
sons *were* Ulam and Rakem.
17 And the [3]sons of Ulam; °Bedan. These
were the sons of Gilead, the son of Machir, the
son of Manasseh.
18 And °his sister Hammoleketh bare Ishod,
and Abiezer, and °Mahalah.
19 And the sons of °Shemidah were, Ahian,
and Shechem, and Likhi, and Aniam.
g[19] (p. 535) 1712 20 And the sons of Ephraim; Shuthelah, and
Bered his son, and Tahath his son, and Eladah
his son, and Tahath his son,
21 And Zabad his son, and Shuthelah his son,
and Ezer, and Elead, whom the men of Gath
that were born in *that* land slew, because
°they came down to take away their cattle.
22 And Ephraim their father mourned many
days, and his brethren came to comfort him.
23 And when °he went in to his wife, she
conceived, and bare a son, and he called his
name °Beriah, because it went evil with his
house.
24 °(And his daughter *was* Sherah, who built
Beth-horon the nether, and the upper, and
Uzzen-sherah.)
25 And Rephah *was* his son, also Resheph,
and Telah his son, and Tahan his son,
26 Laadan his son, Ammihud his son, Elishama his son,
27 °Non his son, Jehoshuah his son.
28 And their possessions and habitations
were, Beth-el and the towns thereof, and eastward Naaran, and westward °Gezer, with the
°towns thereof; Shechem also and the towns
thereof, unto °Gaza and the °towns thereof:
29 And by the borders of the [12]children of
Manasseh, Beth-shean and her towns, Taanach
and her towns, Megiddo and her [28]towns, Dor
and her [28]towns. In these dwelt the [12]children
of Joseph the son of Israel.
g[20] 1746 30 The sons of Asher; Imnah, and Isuah, and
Ishuai, and [23]Beriah, and Serah their sister.
31 And the sons of [23]Beriah; Heber, and Malchiel, who *is* the father of Birzavith.
32 And Heber begat Japhlet, and Shomer,
and Hotham, and Shua their sister.
33 And the sons of Japhlet; Pasach, and
Bimhal, and Ashvath. These *are* the [12]chil-
dren of Japhlet.
34 And the sons of °Shamer; Ahi, and
Rohgah, Jehubbah, and Aram.
35 And the °sons of his brother Helem; Zophah, and Imna, and Shelesh, and Amal.
36 The sons of Zophah; Suah, and Harnepher,
and Shual, and Beri, and Imrah,
37 Bezer, and Hod, and Shamma, and Shil-
shah, and Ithran, and Beera.
38 And the sons of Jether; Jephunneh, and
Pispah, and Ara.
39 And the sons of Ulla; Arah, and Haniel,
and Rezia.
40 All these *were* the [12]children of Asher,
heads of *their* father's house, choice *and*
[7]mighty men of valour, chief of the princes.
And the number throughout the genealogy
of them that were apt to the war *and* to battle
was twenty and six thousand [21]men.

8 Now °Benjamin °begat Bela his firstborn, g[21] 1728
Ashbel the second, and Aharah the third,
2 °Nohah the fourth, and °Rapha the fifth.
3 And the sons of Bela were, °Addar, and
°Gera, and Abihud,
4 And Abishua, and Naaman, and Ahoah,
5 And °Gera, and Shephuphan, and Huram.
6 And these *are* the sons of Ehud: °these
are the heads of the fathers of the inhabitants
of °Geba, °and °they removed them to Manahath:

15 second: i. e. second son of Manasseh, Machir being the first. **daughters.** Not sons (Num. 27. 1).
17 Bedan. The name of a judge (1 Sam. 12. 11).
18 his sister: i. e. Gilead's sister.
Mahalah. Supply Fig. *Ellipsis* (Ap. 6), "Mahalah [and Shemidah] and the sons". The name of one of the daughters of Zelophehad (Num. 26. 33).
19 Shemidah. Occurs only here, Num. 26. 32, and Josh. 17. 2.
21 they: i. e. the sons of Ephraim. A pre-Exodus raid, presuming perhaps on their descent from Joseph (Gen. 46. 20), the governor of Egypt.
23 he = Ephraim. Born 1712. Cp. Gen. 41. 50.
Beriah. An ancestor of Joshua. Not to be confounded with Beriah of Benjamin (8. 13), who made a reprisal on Gath; or with Beriah of Asher (*v.* 30).
24 And. Note the Fig. *Parenthesis.* Ap. 6.
27 Non = Nun, of Num. 13. 8.
28 Gezer. See note on 1 Kings 9. 15–17.
towns. Heb. daughters. Put by Fig. *Catachrēsis* (Ap. 6) for villages.
Gaza. Not the Gaza in Philistia assigned to Judah (Josh. 15. 47). **34 Shamer**: or Shomer, *v.* 32.
35 sons. Heb. "son". A special various reading called *Sevīr* (Ap. 34), and some codices, with one early printed edition, read "sons". This reading was followed by first edition of A.V., 1611.

8. 1 Benjamin. This tribe is now dealt with, and brought down to Saul and Jonathan.
The date of writing is Post-Exilic. See *v.* 28; 9. 3, 27, and compare with Ezra 2 and Neh. 10, which show that Benjamin was brought back to the Land after being nearly extinguished in Judg. 20. Loyalty to Judah and the house of God had been rewarded. Note the passages which connect Benjamin with Judah and with the blessings of the return from Babylon: Ezra 1. 5; 2; 4. 1. Neh. 7; 11. 4, 7, 31; 12. 34. The genealogy of Saul leads up to the subject of the book.
begat. The former genealogy (7. 6–12) is not full, but specifies only the families to be dealt with later.
2 Nohah . . . Rapha. Nowhere else mentioned in O.T. Cp. Gen. 46. 21. Perhaps grandsons. But these names show independence of Chronicles.
3 Addar. Called Ard in Gen. 46. 21. Num. 26. 40.
Gera. Name derived from a son of Benjamin (Gen. 46. 21). Repeated in *v.* 5.
5 Gera. Another Gera. Cp. *v.* 7.
6 these are the: or, "and these are they—the".
Geba. Near Gibeah of Saul (Josh. 18. 24. 1 Sam. 10. 26; 13. 3). Cp. Judg. 19. 12.
and. Read: "but they were carried away to Manahath".
they (the Gebaites) **removed** = were carried away, (same word as in 5. 26). The occasion is not known, but probably *after* they returned from captivity, as Geba is mentioned in Ezra 2. 26. Lod and Ono in *v.* 12 are named in Ezra 2. 33, and "the sons of Gibeon" in Neh. 7. 25. Cp. Ezra 2. 20.
Other names found here are mentioned in Neh. 10. 14, 20, 22, 24, 26, 27: e. g. Meshullam (*v.* 17), Hanan (*v.* 23), Elam and Hananiah (*v.* 24).

7 And Naaman, and Ahiah, and °Gera, he [6]removed them, and begat Uzza, and °Ahihud.

8 And Shaharaim begat *children* in the country °of Moab, after he had sent °them away; Hushim and Baara *were* his wives.

9 And he begat of °Hodesh his wife, Jobab, and Zibia, and Mesha, and Malcham,

10 And Jeuz, and Shachia, and Mirma. These *were* his sons, heads of the fathers.

11 And of Hushim he begat Abitub, and Elpaal.

12 The sons of Elpaal; Eber, and Misham, and °Shamed, who built °Ono, and Lod, with the towns thereof:

13 °Beriah also, and Shema, who *were* heads of the fathers of the inhabitants of °Aijalon, who °drove away the inhabitants of Gath:

14 And Ahio, Shashak, and Jeremoth,

15 And Zebadiah, and Arad, and Ader,

16 And Michael, and Ispah, and Joha, the sons of Beriah;

17 And Zebadiah, and [6]Meshullam, and Hezeki, and Heber,

18 °Ishmerai also, and Jezliah, and Jobab, the sons of Elpaal;

19 And Jakim, and Zichri, and Zabdi,

20 And Elienai, and Zilthai, and Eliel,

21 And Adaiah, and Beraiah, and Shimrath, the sons of Shimhi;

22 And Ishpan, and °Heber, and Eliel,

23 And Abdon, and Zichri, and [6]Hanan,

24 And [6]Hananiah, and [6]Elam, and Antothijah,

25 And Iphedeiah, and Penuel, the sons of Shashak;

26 And Shamsherai, and Shehariah, and Athaliah,

27 And Jaresiah, and Eliah, and Zichri, the sons of Jeroham.

28 These *were* heads of the fathers, by their generations, chief *men*. °These dwelt in Jerusalem.

29 And °at Gibeon dwelt the °father of Gibeon; whose wife's name *was* Maachah:

30 And his firstborn son Abdon, and Zur, and Kish, and Baal, and Nadab,

31 And Gedor, and Ahio, and °Zacher.

32 And Mikloth begat Shimeah. And [28]these also dwelt with their brethren in Jerusalem, over against them.

g[22] (p. 535) 1030 33 And °Ner begat Kish, and Kish begat Saul, and Saul begat Jonathan, and Malchishua, and Abinadab, and °Esh-baal.

34 And the son of Jonathan *was* °Merib-baal; and Merib-baal begat Micah.

35 And the sons of Micah *were*, Pithon, and Melech, and Tarea, and Ahaz.

36 And Ahaz begat Jehoadah; and Jehoadah begat Alemeth, and Azmaveth, and Zimri; and Zimri begat Moza,

37 And Moza begat Binea: Rapha *was* his son, Eleasah his son, Azel his son:

38 And Azel had six sons, whose names *are* these, Azrikam, °Bocheru, and Ishmael, and Sheariah, and Obadiah, and [6]Hanan. All these *were* the sons of Azel.

39 And the sons of Eshek his brother *were*, Ulam his firstborn, Jehush the second, and Eliphelet the third.

40 And the sons of Ulam °were °mighty men of valour, °archers, and had many sons, and sons' sons, an hundred and fifty. All these *are* of the sons of Benjamin.

9 So all Israel were reckoned by genealogies; and, °behold, they *were* written °in the book of the kings of °Israel and Judah, *who* A[2]

Gera. A third Gera. Cp. *vv.* 3, 6.

Ahihud. Supply Fig. *Ellipsis* (Ap. 6): "and Ahihud [and Shaharaim]. And Shaharaim begat", &c.

8 of Moab. As Boaz did. **them**: i.e. his wives.

9 Hodesh: i.e. his Moabitish wife.

12 Shamed. Some codices, with Sept. and Syr., read "Shemer". Cp. 7. 34.

Ono . . . Lod. Mentioned only after the exile (Ezra 2. 33. Neh. 7. 37). See note on *v.* 6.

13 Beriah. See notes on 7. 23, 30.

Aijalon. In Josh. 19. 42, it was in Dan. In Josh. 21. 24 it was a Levitical city. In 2 Chron. 28. 18 it was occupied by Philistines, under Ahaz. But here occupied by Benjamites, because (1) of Dan's idolatry (see note on Gen. 49. 17), and (2) of different distribution after the exile.

drove away. A reprisal later than 7. 21. See notes on 7. 23, 30.

18 Ishmerai = Ishmar-yah. The *Yod* (י) = *y*, being the abbreviation for *Yah* = Jehovah.

22 Heber. Most codices, and nine early printed editions, read "Heber". Some MSS. read "Hebed".

28 These dwelt. Cp. *v.* 32; 9. 34. Neh. 11. 1-4. Another token of God's faithfulness to Benjamin (cp. Deut. 33. 12), for adhering to Judah and the worship of the true God.

29 at Gibeon. Repeated in 9. 35-44.

father = lord, chief, or ruler. Cp. 9. 35. Called Jehiel there.

31 Zacher. Supply Ellipsis thus: "and Zacher [and Mikloth]. And Mikloth", &c.

33 Ner begat Kish. There are three genealogies of the house of Saul. We place the *facts*, (1) that persons often had two names (*v.* 34. Judg. 6. 32, &c.), and (2) that the same name recurs in the same family, against the *assumption* that the opposite is the case. It is this assumption which creates the difficulties in "reconciling" 1 Sam. 9. 1; 14. 51; and 1 Chron. 9. 38.

The following makes all the lists agree:

Jehiel (or Zeror, 1 Sam. 9. 1).

Abdon Zur Kish Baal Ner (or Abiel, 1 Sam. 9. 1; 14. 51).

(1 Sam. 14. 51) Abner Kish (1 Sam. 14. 51).

Saul (born 1030).

Esh-baal. Another name for Ish-bosheth (2 Sam. 2. 8).

34 Merib-baal. Another name by which Mephibosheth was known. Cp. 2 Sam. 2. 8; 4. 4. See note on *v.* 33 above.

The addition "bosheth" (= shame) came to be substituted for "Baal" as the latter word became associated with idolatry. Cp. Judg. 6. 32 with 2 Sam. 11. 21.

38 Bocheru. Some codices, with Sept. and Syr., read "his firstborn" (*b^ekhorō*).

40 were = became.

mighty men. Heb. *gibbōr*. Ap. 14. IV.

archers. Cp. 2 Chron. 14. 8.

9. 1 behold. Fig. *Asterismos.* Ap. 6.

in the book of the kings of Israel and Judah. Not the existing books of Samuel and Kings, but another book, being a collection of matters from them. Referred to in 2 Chron. 16. 11; 25. 26; 27. 7; 28. 26; 32. 32; 35. 27; 36. 8.

Israel. Punctuate and read "Israel: and Judah was carried away", &c.

were carried away to Babylon for their °transgression.

B D (p. 543) 454-400 2 Now °the first inhabitants that *dwelt* in their possessions in their cities *were*, °the Israelites, the priests, °Levites, and °the Nethinims.

E h[1] 3 And in °Jerusalem dwelt of the °children of Judah, and of the °children of Benjamin, and of the °children of °Ephraim, and Manasseh;

4 Uthai the son of Ammihud, the son of Omri, the son of Imri, the son of Bani, of the [3] children of Pharez the son of Judah.

5 And of the °Shilonites; Asaiah the firstborn, and his sons.

6 And of the sons of Zerah; Jeuel, and °their brethren, °six hundred and ninety.

7 And of the sons of Benjamin; °Sallu the son of Meshullam, the son of Hodaviah, the son of °Hasenuah,

8 And Ibneiah the son of Jeroham, and Elah the son of Uzzi, the son of Michri, and Meshullam the son of Shephathiah, the son of Reuel, the son of Ibnijah;

9 And their brethren, according to their generations, °nine hundred and fifty and six. All these °men *were* chief of the fathers in the house of their fathers.

h[2] 10 And of the priests; °Jedaiah, and Jehoiarib, and Jachin,

11 And °Azariah the son of Hilkiah, the son of Meshullam, the son of Zadok, the son of Meraioth, the son of Ahitub, °the ruler of the house of °God;

12 And °Adaiah the son of Jeroham, the son of Pashur, the son of Malchijah, and °Maasiai the son of Adiel, the son of Jahzerah, the son of Meshullam, the son of Meshillemith, the son of Immer;

13 And their brethren, heads of the house of their fathers, °a thousand and seven hundred and threescore; °very able °men for the work of the service of the house of [11] God.

h[3] 14 And of the Levites; °Shemaiah the son of Hasshub, the son of Azrikam, the son of Hashabiah, of the sons of Merari;

15 And Bakbakkar, Heresh, and Galal, and Mattaniah the son of Micah, the son of Zichri, the son of Asaph;

16 And Obadiah the son of Shemaiah, the son of Galal, the son of Jeduthun, and Berechiah the son of °Asa, the son of Elkanah, that °dwelt in the villages of the °Netophathites.

17 And the °porters *were*, Shallum, and Akkub, and Talmon, and Ahiman, and their brethren: Shallum *was* the chief;

18 Who °hitherto *waited* in °the king's gate eastward: they *were* porters in the companies of the [3] children of Levi.

19 And Shallum the son of Kore, the son of Ebiasaph, the son of Korah, and his brethren, of the house of his father, the °Korahites, *were* over the work of the service, keepers of the °gates of the °tabernacle: and their fathers, *being* over the host of °the LORD, *were* keepers of the entry.

20 And °Phinehas the son of Eleazar was the ruler over them °in time past, *and* [19] the LORD *was* with him.

transgression = defection. Heb. *mā'al*. Ap. 44. xi.

9. 2-44 (**B**, p. 530). AFTER THE RETURN (GENEALOGY). (*Introversion.*)

B | D | 2. In the cities.
  E | 3-34. In Jerusalem.
 D | 35-44. In Gibeon.

2 the first inhabitants: i. e. after the reoccupation on the return from Babylon, under Zerubbabel, Joshua, Nehemiah, and Ezra, 454-400 B. C. See Ap. 50. V, VI, p. 60 and VII (5), p. 67.

the Israelites. Heb. "Israel": i. e. the "Israel of God". Cp. Neh. 11. 3. See note on "Israel" (Gen. 32. 28; 43. 6; 45. 26, 28). Called "Israel", although only the return of Judah and Benjamin. See note on 1 Kings 12. 17. **Levites** = the Levites.

the Nethinims. Taken from the people in proportion of one in fifty to assist the Levites (Num. 31. 47. Ezra 8. 20).

9. 3-34 (E, above). IN JERUSALEM. (*Division.*)

E | h[1] | 3-9. Judah.
 | h[2] | 10-13. The Priests.
 | h[3] | 14-34. The Levites.

3 Jerusalem. As distinct from the Land (*v.* 2). Cp. Neh. 11. 1. **children** = sons.

Ephraim, and Manasseh. So that others beside Judah and Benjamin were included in the People now known as "Jews". Cp. Ezra 6. 21. Neh. 10. 28, 29. See note on 1 Kings 12. 17.

5 Shilonites = Shelonites. Not from the place Shiloh, but from Shelah the son of Judah. Cp. 2. 3. Num. 26. 28. Neh. 9. 5. So that some from each of the three lines of Judah were included, viz. Pharez, Shelah, Judah.

6 their: i. e. Uthai (*v.* 4) and Asaiah (*v.* 5). (Jewish.)

six hundred and ninety. These were the sons of Zerah. The 468 in Neh. 11. 6 were sons of Perez (i. e. Pharez).

7 Sallu. At the head of the Benjamites (Neh. 11. 7).

Hasenuah. In Neh. 11. 9 called Senuah.

9 nine hundred and fifty and six. In Neh. 11. 8 we have 928. The dates of the enumeration are independent and not identical.

men. Heb. *'ĕnōsh*. Ap. 14. III.

10 Jedaiah, &c. Cp. Neh. 11. 10 and 12. 6.

11 Azariah. In Neh. 11. 11 the same enumeration, but Seraiah. This is explained in 6. 12-14 above.

the ruler of the house of God. Applied to the high priest: at this time Ahitub (6. 11). Later it was Joshua the high priest (Ezra 3. 2. Zech. 3. 1-8; 6. 11-13). Cp. 2 Chron. 31. 13; 35. 8.

God. Heb. Elohim (with Art.) = the (true) God. Ap. 4. I.

12 Adaiah. Cp. Neh. 11. 12.

Maasiai. Cp. 24. 14 and Neh. 11. 13.

13 a thousand and seven hundred and threescore. In Neh. 11. 12-14, 1,192, which must have been before the priests had settled in the priestly cities.

very able men = mighty men of valour. Heb. *gibbōr*. Ap. 14. IV.

14 Shemaiah. Cp. Neh. 11. 15.

16 Asa. Some codices, with two early printed editions (one marg.), and Syr., read "Asaph".

dwelt in the villages. Till the priestly cities were rebuilt.

Netophathites. Cp. Neh. 12. 28.

17 porters = gatekeepers. Cp. Neh. 12. 25.

18 hitherto. Referring to the ancient practice.

the king's gate. Leading from the royal palace to the Temple.

19 Korahites. The descendants of Korah. Cp. Num. 16; 26. 9-11; and see Pss. 42; 44—49; 84; 85; 87; 88.

gates = thresholds.

tabernacle = tent. Heb. *'ohel*. See Ap. 40. III.

the LORD. Heb. Jehovah. Ap. 4. II.

20 Phinehas. Cp. Ex. 6. 23.

in time past: i. e. previous to the writing of this history. 1434-1383?

454 to 400 21 *And* Zechariah the son of Meshelemiah *was* porter of the °door of the [19]tabernacle of the congregation.

22 All these *which were* chosen to be [17]porters in the [19]gates *were* °two hundred and twelve. These were reckoned by °their genealogy in their [16]villages, whom David and °Samuel the seer °did ordain in their set office.

23 So they and their [3]children *had* the oversight of the gates of the house of the [19]LORD, *namely*, the house of the [19]tabernacle, by °wards.

24 In four °quarters were the [17]porters, toward the east, west, north, and south.

25 And their brethren, *which were* in their [16]villages, *were* to come after seven days from time to time with them.

26 For these Levites, the four °chief [17]porters, were in *their* °set office, and were over the °chambers and treasuries of the house of [11]God.

27 And they lodged round about the house of [11]God, because the charge *was* upon them, and the °opening thereof every morning *pertained* to them.

28 And *certain* of them had the charge of the °ministering vessels, that they should bring them in and out °by tale.

29 *Some* of them also *were* appointed to oversee the vessels, °and all the instruments of the sanctuary, °and the fine flour, and the wine, and the oil, and the frankincense, and the °spices.

30 And *some* of the sons of the priests °made the ointment of the spices.

31 And Mattithiah, *one* of the Levites, who *was* the firstborn of Shallum the Korahite, had the [26]set office over the things that were made °in the pans.

32 And *other* of their brethren, of the sons of the Kohathites, *were* over the shewbread, to prepare *it* °every sabbath.

33 And °these *are* the singers, chief of the fathers of the Levites, *who remaining* in the chambers *were* °free: for they were employed in *that* work day and night.

34 These chief fathers of the Levites *were* chief throughout their generations; these dwelt at Jerusalem.

D (p. 543) 35 And °in Gibeon dwelt the °father of Gibeon, °Jehiel, whose wife's name *was* Maachah:

36 And his firstborn son Abdon, then Zur, and Kish, and Baal, and Ner, and Nadab,

37 And Gedor, and Ahio, and Zechariah, and Mikloth.

38 And Mikloth begat Shimeam. And they also dwelt with their brethren at Jerusalem, over against their brethren.

39 And °Ner begat Kish; and Kish begat Saul; and Saul begat Jonathan, and Malchi-shua, and Abinadab, and Esh-baal.

40 And the son of Jonathan *was* Merib-baal: and Merib-baal begat Micah.

41 And the sons of Micah *were*, Pithon, and Melech, and Tahrea, °*and Ahaz*.

42 And Ahaz begat Jarah; and Jarah begat Alemeth, and Azmaveth, and Zimri; and Zimri begat Moza;

43 And Moza begat Binea; and Rephaiah his son, Eleasah his son, Azel his son.

44 And Azel had six sons, whose names *are* these, °Azrikam, Bocheru, and Ishmael, and Sheariah, and Obadiah, and Hanan: these *were* the sons of Azel.

10 Now °the Philistines fought against Israel; and the °men of Israel fled from before the Philistines, and fell down slain in mount Gilboa. A F[1] i (p. 544) 960

2 And the Philistines followed hard after Saul, and after his sons; and the Philistines slew Jonathan, and °Abinadab, and Malchi-shua, the sons of Saul. k

3 And the battle went sore against Saul, and

---

21 door = entrance.

22 two hundred and twelve. These were for the Tabernacle (*v.* 21). In Neh. 11. 19, 172, excluding those in the villages. Not the 4,000 of 23. 5, or their ninety-three heads (ch. 26), which were for the future Temple.

their genealogy = [Was registered] in their villages. There is no record of this. But Samuel stood at the head.

did ordain = founded. Cp. 23. 1-6. Cp. Acts 3. 24.

23 wards = watches, twenty-four quarters. Heb. *rūach* = winds.

26 chief. Heb. *gibbōr.* Ap. 14. IV. Some codices, with one early printed edition, Sept. and Syr., read "mighty men of the gates".

set office = trust. **chambers** = storehouses.

27 opening thereof, &c. = were over the key. Cp. Judg. 3. 25. Isa. 22. 22.

28 ministering vessels = vessels of service.

by tale = by number.

29 and. Note the Fig. *Polysyndeton* (Ap. 6), to emphasise all the details.

and the fine flour = and over the fine flour.

spices. Cp. Ex. 30. 22-38.

30 made = compounded.

31 in the pans = on the flat plates.

32 every sabbath. Cp. Ex. 25. 30. Lev. 24. 5-8.

33 these are the singers. Referring to *vv.* 14-16, and Neh. 11. 22. 2 Chron. 34. 12.

free = exempt from duty.

35 in Gibeon dwelt. Verses 35-44 are an abridgment of 8. 29-38. Could not suitably be introduced there. Reserved to be inserted here, to lead up to Saul's death in ch. 10.

the father of Gibeon = parent-family of Gibeon: Jehiel, &c.

Jehiel. Had another name, "Zoror", in 1 Sam. 9. 1. See note on 8. 33.

39 Ner begat Kish. See note on 8. 33.

41 and Ahaz. Supplied from 8. 35.

44 Azrikam, Bocheru. Some codices, with one early printed edition, Sept. and Syr., read "Azrikam his firstborn".

10. 1—2 Chron. 36. 21 (*A*, p. 530). HISTORY. (UP TO THE CAPTIVITY.) (*Division*.)

A | F[1] | 1 Chron. 10. 1-14. The house of Saul overthrown.
| F[2] | 1 Chron. 11. 1—2 Chron. 36 21. The house of David established.

10. 1-14 (F[1], above). THE HOUSE OF SAUL OVERTHROWN. (*Extended Alternation*.)

F[1] | i | 1. Flight of Israel.
| k | 2, 3. Philistines' pursuit of Saul.
| l | 4-6. "So Saul died, and". (Event.)
| *i* | 7. Flight of Israel.
| *k* | 8-12. Philistines' indignities to Saul.
| *l* | 13, 14. "So Saul died, for". (Reason.)

1 the Philistines fought. Cp. 1 Sam. 31. 1-6 and 2 Sam. 1. 9, 10.

men. Heb. *'ish.* Ap. 14. II.

2 Abinadab. Another name was Ishui (1 Sam. 14. 49).

960 the archers hit him, and he was wounded of
the archers.
l 4 Then said Saul to his armourbearer, "Draw
(p. 544) thy sword, and thrust me through therewith;
lest these uncircumcised come and °abuse me."
But his armourbearer would not; for he was
sore afraid. So Saul took a sword, and fell
upon it.
5 And when his armourbearer saw that Saul
was dead, he fell likewise on the sword, and
died.
6 °So Saul died, and °his three sons, and °all
his °house died together.
i 7 And when all the [1]men of Israel that *were*
in the valley saw that they fled, and that Saul
and his sons were dead, then they forsook
their cities, and fled: and the Philistines came
and dwelt in them.
k 8 And it came to pass on the morrow, when
the Philistines came to strip the slain, that
they found Saul and his sons fallen in mount
Gilboa.
9 And when they had stripped him, they
°took his head, and his armour, and sent into
the land of the Philistines round about, to
carry tidings unto their idols, and to the
people.
10 And they put his armour in the house of
their °gods, and fastened °his head in the
temple of Dagon.
11 And when all Jabesh-gilead heard all that
the Philistines had done to Saul,
12 They arose, all the valiant [1]men, and took
away the body of Saul, and the bodies of his
sons, and brought them to Jabesh, and °buried
their bones under °the oak in Jabesh, and
fasted seven days.
l 13 So Saul died °for his °transgression which
he committed against °the LORD, *even* against
the word of °the LORD, which he kept not,
and also for asking *counsel* of *one that had* a
°familiar spirit, °to enquire *of it;*
14 And [13]enquired not of [13]the LORD: therefore °He slew him, and turned the kingdom
unto David the son of Jesse.

F² J L **11** °Then all Israel gathered themselves to
(p. 545) David unto Hebron, saying, "Behold,
953 we *are* thy bone and thy flesh.
2 And moreover in time past, even when
Saul was king, thou *wast* he that leddest out
and broughtest in Israel: and °the LORD thy
°God said unto thee, 'Thou shalt feed My People Israel, and thou shalt be ruler over My
People Israel.'"
3 Therefore came all the elders of Israel to
the king to Hebron; and David made a covenant with them in Hebron before [2]the LORD;
and they anointed David king over Israel,
according to the word of [2]the LORD °by
Samuel.
M N 4 And David and all Israel °went to Jerusa-

4 abuse = insult, or mock.

6 So Saul died. Here, the event. In *v.* 13, the reason. See the Structure above.

his three sons = three of his sons.

all. Fig. *Synecdoche* (of the Whole), Ap. 6, put for greater part. See 2 Sam. 2. 8; 21. 8.

house. Put by Fig. *Metonymy* (of Subject), Ap. 6, for family or household.

9 took his head. Fig. *Ellipsis* (Ap. 6), "head [which they had cut off] and his armour".

10 gods. Ashtaroth. Cp. 1 Sam. 31. 10.

his head. This is additional to 1 Sam. 31. 10. "His body", there, is additional to this passage. The two books thus independent and complementary.

12 buried their bones. After they had burnt them (1 Sam. 31. 12).

the oak. Cp. 1 Sam. 31. 13.

13 for. In this book the reason; in 1 Sam. only the event. See Ap. 56.

transgression = disobedience, shown in his faithlessness or defection. Heb. *mā'al.* Ap. 44. xi. Cp. 1 Sam. 13. 13, 14; 15. 1-9; 28. 7.

the LORD. Heb. Jehovah. Ap. 4. II. Note it is not Elohim (God).

familiar spirit. See note on Lev. 19. 31.

to enquire = to seek and consult. Heb. *dārash,* to seek earnestly. Saul sought thus with the medium, but not with Jehovah. See note on 1 Sam. 28. 6, 7.

14 He: i. e. Jehovah. 1 Chron. gives the esoteric cause. 1 Sam. gives the exoteric event, which men could see. See Ap. 56.

11. 1—2 Chron. 36. 21 (F², p. 544). THE HOUSE OF DAVID ESTABLISHED. (*Division.*)

F²	G¹	1 Chron. 11. 1—29. 30. David.	21 Kings of the House of David (3 × 7)
	G²	2 Chron. 1. 1—9. 31. Solomon.	
	G³	2 Chron. 10. 1—12. 16. Rehoboam.	
	G⁴	2 Chron. 13. 1—14. 1-. Abijah.	
	G⁵	2 Chron. 14. -1—16. 14. Asa.	
	G⁶	2 Chron. 17. 1—21. 1-. Jehoshaphat.	
	G⁷	2 Chron. 21. 1-, -20. Jehoram.	
	G⁸	2 Chron. 22. 1-9. Ahaziah.	
	(G⁹)	(2 Chron. 22. 10—23. 21. Athaliah.)	
	G¹⁰	2 Chron. 24. 1-27. Joash.	
	G¹¹	2 Chron. 25. 1-28. Amaziah.	
	G¹²	2 Chron. 26. 1-23. Uzziah.	
	G¹³	2 Chron. 27. 1-9. Jotham.	
	G¹⁴	2 Chron. 28. 1-27. Ahaz.	
	G¹⁵	2 Chron. 29. 1—32. 33. Hezekiah.	
	G¹⁶	2 Chron. 33. 1-20. Manasseh.	
	G¹⁷	2 Chron. 33. 21-25. Amon.	
	G¹⁸	2 Chron. 34. 1—35. 27. Josiah.	
	G¹⁹	2 Chron. 36. 1-4. Jehoahaz.	
	G²⁰	2 Chron. 36. 5-8. Jehoiakim.	
	G²¹	2 Chron. 36. 9, 10. Jehoiachin.	
	G²²	2 Chron. 36. 11-21. Zedekiah.	

11. 1—29. 30 (G¹, above). DAVID. (*Division.*)

G¹	H¹	11. 1—29. 25. Events in detail.
	H²	29. 26-30. Events in sum.

11. 1—29. 25 (H¹, above). EVENTS IN DETAIL. (*Introversion.*)

H¹	J	11. 1—12. 40. David. Accession.
	K	13. 1—16. 43. The Tent. David's bringing up the Ark for it.
	K	17. 1—22. 19. The Temple. David's preparation for it.
	J	23. 1—29. 25. David. Resignation.

11. 1—12. 40 (J, above). [For Structure see next page.]

1 Then all Israel. Cp. 2 Sam. 5. 2. Omitting all events in Hebron (2 Sam. 2. 1-4). See Ap. 56. In this chapter we have 1-3 David's Coronation; 4-9, David's Capital; 10-47, David's Captains. **2 the LORD.** Heb. Jehovah. Ap. 4. II. **God.** Heb. Elohim. Ap. 4. I. **3 by Samuel.** Heb. by the hand of Samuel: "hand" being put by Fig. *Metonymy* (of Cause), Ap. 6, for what is done or written by it. **4 went to Jerusalem.** This is the first event recorded in Chronicles. See note on 2 Sam. 5. 6-10.

953 lem, which *is* Jebus; where the Jebusites *were*,
to the °inhabitants of the land.
952 5 And the inhabitants of Jebus °said to
David, "Thou shalt not come hither." Nevertheless David took the castle of °Zion, which
is the city of David.

O 6 And David said, "Whosoever smiteth the
(p. 546) Jebusites first shall be chief and captain." So
Joab the son of Zeruiah went first up, and was
chief.

M N 7 And David dwelt in the castle; therefore
they called it the city of David.
8 And he built the city round about, even
from °Millo round about: and Joab °repaired
the rest of the city.
9 So David waxed greater and greater: for
[2]the LORD of hosts *was* with him.

O P^1 m 10 These also *are* the chief of °the mighty
953 men whom David had, who strengthened
to themselves with him in his kingdom, *and*
920 with all Israel, to make him king, according
to the word of [2]the LORD concerning Israel.
11 And this *is* the number of [11]the mighty men
whom David had;

n °Jashobeam, an Hachmonite, the chief of the
°captains: he lifted up his spear against three
hundred slain *by him* at one time.
12 And after him *was* Eleazar the son of
°Dodo, the Ahohite, who *was one* of [11]the °three
mighties.
13 °He was with David at °Pas-dammim, and
there the Philistines were gathered together
to battle, where was a parcel of ground full of
°barley; and the People fled from before the
Philistines.
14 And °they set themselves in the midst of
that parcel, and delivered it, and slew the
Philistines; and [2]the LORD °saved *them* by
a great deliverance.

o 15 Now three of the °thirty captains went
down to the rock to David, into the cave of
Adullam; and the host of the Philistines encamped in the valley of °Rephaim.
16 And David *was* then in the hold, and the
Philistines' garrison *was* then at Beth-lehem.
17 And David longed, and said, °"Oh that
one would give me drink of the water of the
well of Beth-lehem, that *is* at the gate!"
18 And the three brake through the host of
the Philistines, and drew water out of the well
of Beth-lehem, that *was* by the gate, and took
it, and brought *it* to David: but David would
not drink *of* it, but poured it out to [2]the LORD,
19 And said, "My [2]God forbid it me, that I
should do this thing: shall I drink the blood
of these °men °that have put their °lives in
jeopardy? for with *the jeopardy of* their
°lives they brought it." Therefore he would
not drink it. These things did these three
[11]mightiest.

n 20 And Abishai the brother of Joab, he °was
chief of °the three: for lifting up his spear
against three hundred, he slew *them*, and °had
a name among the three.

11. 1—12. 40 (J, p. 545). DAVID. ACCESSION.
(*Introversion and Alternation.*)

J | L | 11. 1-3. Accession over all Israel.
  M | N | 11. 4, 5. The taking of Jebus.
    O | 11. 6. Forces. (Chief, Joab.)
  M | *N* | 11. 7-9. The taking of Jebus.
    O | 11. 10—12. 37. Forces. Chiefs, mighty men.
L | 12. 38-40. Accession over all Israel.

inhabitants. The descendants of the *Nephīlim.* Ap. 23 and 25.
5 said. 2 Sam. 5. 6-8 is supplementary to this.
Zion, which is the city of David. See notes on 2 Sam. 5.
8 Millo = the filling up: i. e. of the valley north of Jebus and south of Moriah. Cp. 2 Sam. 5. 9.
repaired = rebuilt.

11. 10—12. 37 (*O*, above). THE FORCES.
(*Division.*)

O | P^1 | 11. 10-47. David's mighty men.
  | P^2 | 12. 1-37. Their auxiliaries.

11. 10-47 (P^1, above). DAVID'S MIGHTY MEN.
(*Introversion.*)

P^1 | m | 10, 11-. The mighty men. The chiefs.
  n | -11-14. Severally.
    o | 15-19. Collectively.
  n | 20-25. Severally.
m | 26-47. The valiant men of the armies.

10 the mighty men. Heb. *gibbōr.* Ap. 14. IV. Introduced here, at *beginning* of reign, instead of *end* of it (2 Sam. 23. 8-39). Both positions full of instruction: Samuel, *chronological*; Chronicles, *moral* (according to the word of the LORD). See Ap. 56.
11 Jashobeam. See note on "Tachmonite" (2 Sam. 23. 8).
captains, or thirty.
12 Dodo. Sept. reads "Dodai". Cp. 27. 4.
three. See note on 1 Chron. 27. 1.
13 He was with David. Eleazar. In 2 Sam. 23. 11, 12, Shammah also was *with him.* Note the *plural* verbs in next verse, "they set . . . and [they] delivered it and [they] slew". This account is supplementary, not contradictory.
Pas-dammim. Probably Ephes-dammim, between Shocoh and Azekah (1 Sam. 17. 1).
barley. In 2 Sam. 23. 11, "lentiles". Therefore the field contained both: and the accounts are complementary, not contradictory.
14 they: i. e. David and Eleazar. See note on *v.* 13.
saved them by a great deliverance. Sept. and Syr. read "wrought a great victory". Cp. 2 Sam. 23. 10, 12.
15 thirty. See note on 27. 1.
Rephaim. Heb. *Rapha.* One of the great among the *Nephīlim*, like Anak; giving his name to this valley. Cp. Josh. 15. 8. 2 Sam. 5. 18, 22; 23. 13. Isa. 17. 5. See note on Num. 13. 22, 28. Deut. 1. 28, and Ap. 23, 25.
17 Oh that one, &c. Fig. *Ecphonēsis.* Ap. 6.
19 men. Heb. *'ĕnōsh.* Ap. 14. III.
that have put their lives in jeopardy? Heb. "with their lives". Cp. Judg. 12. 3. 1 Sam. 19. 5; 28. 21. Job 13. 14.
lives = souls. Heb. *nephesh.* Ap. 13.
20 was = came to be (as in Gen. 1. 2).
the three: i. e. who performed the foregoing act.
had. Some codices, with five early printed editions, Sept., Syr., and Vulg., read "he had".
22 a lion. See note on 1 Kings 13. 24.

21 Of the three, he was more honourable than
the two; for he was their captain: howbeit he
attained not to the *first* [12]three.
22 Benaiah the son of Jehoiada, the son of
a valiant [1]man of Kabzeel, who had done many
acts; he slew two lionlike men of Moab: also
he went down and slew °a lion in a pit in a
snowy day.

953 to 920 23 And he slew an Egyptian, a [1]man of *great* stature, five °cubits high; and in the Egyptian's hand *was* a spear like a weaver's beam; and he went down to him with a staff, and plucked the spear out of the Egyptian's hand, and slew him with his own spear.

24 These *things* did Benaiah the son of Jehoiada, and had the name among the [12]three mighties.

25 °Behold, he was honourable among the [15]thirty, but attained not to the *first* [12]three: and David set him over his °guard.

m (p. 546) 26 Also the °valiant men of the armies *were*, Asahel the brother of Joab, Elhanan the son of Dodo of Beth-lehem,

27 Shammoth the Harorite, Helez the °Pelonite,

28 Ira the son of Ikkesh the Tekoite, Abi-ezer the Antothite,

29 Sibbecai the Hushathite, Ilai the Ahohite,

30 Maharai the Netophathite, Heled the son of Baanah the Netophathite,

31 Ithai the son of Ribai of Gibeah, *that pertained* to the °children of Benjamin, Benaiah the Pirathonite,

32 Hurai of the brooks of Gaash, Abiel the Arbathite,

33 Azmaveth the Baharumite, Eliahba the Shaalbonite,

34 The sons of Hashem the Gizonite, Jonathan the son of Shage the Hararite,

35 Ahiam the son of Sacar the Hararite, Eliphal the son of Ur,

36 Hepher the Mecherathite, Ahijah the Pelonite,

37 Hezro the Carmelite, Naarai the son of Ezbai,

38 °Joel the brother of Nathan, Mibhar the son of Haggeri,

39 Zelek the Ammonite, Naharai the Berothite, the armourbearer of Joab the son of Zeruiah,

40 Ira the Ithrite, Gareb the Ithrite,

41 Uriah the Hittite, Zabad the son of Ahlai,

42 Adina the son of Shiza the Reubenite, a captain of the Reubenites, and thirty with him,

43 Hanan the son of Maachah, and Joshaphat the Mithnite,

44 Uzzia the Ashterathite, Shama and Jehiel the sons of Hothan the Aroerite,

45 Jediael the son of Shimri, and Joha his brother, the Tizite,

46 Eliel the Mahavite, and Jeribai, and Joshaviah, the sons of Elnaam, and Ithmah the Moabite,

47 Eliel, and Obed, and Jasiel °the Mesobaite.

P² R (p. 547) 962 to 960 **12** Now °these *are* they that came to David to Ziklag, while he yet kept himself close because of °Saul the son of Kish: and they *were* among the °mighty men, helpers of the war.

S p 2 *They were* armed with bows, and °could use both the right hand and the left in *hurling* stones and *shooting* arrows out of a bow, *even* of °Saul's brethren of Benjamin.

3 The chief *was* Ahiezer, then Joash, the sons of Shemaah the Gibeathite; and Jeziel, and Pelet, the sons of Azmaveth; and Berachah, and Jehu the Antothite,

4 And Ismaiah the Gibeonite, a [1]mighty man °among the thirty, and over the thirty; and Jeremiah, and Jahaziel, and Johanan, and Josabad the Gederathite,

5 Eluzai, and Jerimoth, and Bealiah, and Shemariah, and Shephatiah the Haruphite,

6 Elkanah, and Jesiah, and Azareel, and Joezer, and Jashobeam, the Korhites,

7 And Joelah, and Zebadiah, the sons of Jeroham of Gedor.

8 And of the Gadites there °separated themselves unto David into the hold to the wilderness °men of might, *and* °men of war *fit* for the battle, that could handle shield and °buckler, whose faces *were like* the faces of lions, and *were* as swift as the roes upon the mountains; q

9 Ezer the first, Obadiah the second, Eliab the third,

10 Mishmannah the fourth, Jeremiah the fifth,

11 Attai the sixth, Eliel the seventh,

12 Johanan the eighth, Elzabad the ninth,

13 Jeremiah the tenth, Machbanai the eleventh.

14 These *were* of the sons of Gad, captains of the host: one of the least *was* over an hundred, and the greatest over a thousand.

---

23 cubit = about 18 inches. See Ap. 51. III. 2.
25 Behold. Fig. *Asterismos*. Ap. 6.
guard = audience chamber.
26 valiant men. Heb. *gibbōr*. Ap. 14. IV. The list contains several non-Israelites. Cp. Ps. 18. 43, 44.
27 Pelonite. Syr. reads "Paltite". Cp. 2 Sam. 23. 26.
31 children = sons.
38 Joel the brother of Nathan. Not to be confused with Igal the son of Nathan. The lists are supplementary and independent, Chronicles being of later date, and adding several names after Uriah (*v.* 41).
47 the Mesobaite. Sept. and Vulg. read "of (or from) Zobah".

12. 1-37 (P², p. 546). THEIR AUXILIARIES. (*Alternation.*)

P² | Q | R | 1. General. } At Ziklag.
| | S | 2-22. Particular.
| *Q* | *R* | 23. General. } At Hebron.
| | *S* | 24-37. Particular.

1 these are they. These not included elsewhere: showing the independence of Chronicles.
Saul the son of Kish. See note on 8. 33.
mighty men. Heb. *gibbōr*. Ap. 14. IV.

2-22 (S, above). AUXILIARIES. AT ZIKLAG (PARTICULAR). (*Alternation.*)

S | p | 2-7. Benjamites.
| q | 8-15. Others, from Israel (Gadites).
| *p* | 16-18. Benjamin and Judah.
| *q* | 19-22. Others, from Israel (Manasseh).

2 could use, &c. Cp. Judg. 3. 15; 20. 15, 16.
Saul's brethren: i. e. his fellow-tribesmen. Cp. *v.* 29.
4 among the thirty. Probably another "thirty" at a later period. Ismaiah not in the list. 2 Sam. 23. 24, &c.
8 separated themselves. Another example of how Judah came to be *representative* of the whole of Israel. See note on 1 Kings 12. 17.
men of might. Heb. *gibbōr*. Ap. 14. IV.
men. Heb. *'ĕnōsh*. Ap. 14. III.
buckler. Heb. = spear. But some codices, with one early printed edition and Syr., read "buckler". Cp. Jer. 46. 3.

962 15 These *are* they that went over Jordan in
to °the first month, when it had °overflown all
960 his banks; and they put to flight all *them* of
the valleys, *both* toward the east, and toward
the west.

p 16 And there came of the °children of Benja-
(p. 547) min and Judah to the hold unto David.
17 And David went out to meet them, and
answered and said unto them, °"If ye be come
peaceably unto me to help me, mine heart
shall be °knit unto you: but if *ye be come* to
betray me to mine enemies, seeing *there is* no
°wrong in mine hands, the °God of our fathers
look *thereon*, and rebuke *it*."
18 Then °the Spirit °came upon °Amasai,
who was chief of the captains, *and he said*,
"Thine *are we*, David, and on thy side, thou
son of Jesse: °peace, peace *be* unto thee, and
peace *be* to thine helpers; for thy [17] God helpeth
thee." Then David received them, and made
them captains of the band.

q 19 And °there fell *some* of Manasseh to
David; when he came with the Philistines
against Saul to battle: but °they helped °them
not: for the °lords of the Philistines °upon
advisement sent him away, saying, "He will
fall to his master Saul °to *the jeopardy of* our
heads."
20 As he went to Ziklag, [19] there fell to him
of Manasseh, Adnah, and Jozabad, and Jediael,
and Michael, and Jozabad, and Elihu, and
Zilthai, captains of the thousands that *were*
of Manasseh.
21 And they °helped David against °the band
of the rovers: for they *were* all [1] mighty men
of valour, and were captains in the host.
22 For at *that* time day by day there came
to David to help him, until *it was* °a great host,
like the host of [17] God.

R 23 And these *are* the numbers of the bands
that were ready armed to the war, *and* came
to David to Hebron, to turn the kingdom of
Saul to him, according to the °word of °the
LORD.

S T^1 24 The [16] children of Judah that bare shield
(p. 548) and spear *were* six thousand and eight hun-
953 dred, ready armed to the war.
T^2 25 Of the [16] children of Simeon, [1] mighty men
of valour for the war, seven thousand and one
hundred.

T^3 26 Of the [16] children of Levi four thousand
and six hundred.
27 And °Jehoiada *was* the leader of the
Aaronites, and with him *were* three thousand
and seven hundred;
28 And °Zadok, a young man [1] mighty of
valour, and of his father's house twenty and
two captains.

T^4 29 And of the [16] children of Benjamin, the
°kindred of Saul, three thousand: for hitherto
the greatest part of them had °kept the ward
of the house of Saul.

T^5 30 And of the [16] children of Ephraim twenty
thousand and eight hundred, [1] mighty men of
valour, °famous throughout the house of their
fathers.

T^6 31 And of the half tribe of Manasseh eighteen
thousand, which were expressed by name, to come and make David king. 953

T^7 32 And of the [16] children of Issachar, *which*
were men that °had understanding of °the
times, to know what Israel ought to do; the
heads of them *were* two hundred; and all
their brethren *were* at their °commandment.

T^8 33 Of Zebulun, such as went forth to battle,
expert in war, with all instruments of war,

15 the first month. Nisan, or Abib.
overflown. Cp. Josh. 3. 15.
16 children = sons.
17 If ye be come, &c. A second band made David suspicious.
knit unto = one with.
wrong = act of violence. Heb. *ḥamas*, not same word as 16. 21.
God. Heb. Elohim. Ap. 4. I.
18 the Spirit. Heb. *rūach*. Ap. 9.
came upon = clothed: i. e. clothed him with wisdom and power: *i.e.*, employed him as His mouthpiece.
Amasai. Probably the same as Amasa, David's nephew (2. 17). Cp. 2 Sam. 19. 13.
peace, peace. Fig. *Epizeuxis*. Ap. 6.
19 there fell some of Manasseh, beside the Gadites (see the Structure above). See note on 1 Kings 12. 17 for the strengthening of Judah and making it representative of the whole nation.
they: David and his men. See 1 Sam. 28. 1, 2; 29.
them: the Philistines.
lords, or princes.
upon advisement = advisedly, or by counsel. Cp. 21. 12.
to the jeopardy of our heads. Heb. with our heads; or, at the cost of our heads.
21 helped David = helped with David.
the band: i. e. the Amalekites, who had burned Ziklag during his absence. See 1 Sam. 30. 1-20. It is assumed that we know of this.
22 a great host. About 300,000 men.
23 word = mouth. Put by Fig. *Metonymy* (of Cause), Ap. 6, for what was spoken by it.
the LORD. Heb. Jehovah. Ap. 4. II.

12. 24-37 (*S*, p. 547). AUXILIARIES AT HEBRON. (PARTICULAR). (*Division*.)

S	T^1	24. Judah.
	T^2	25. Simeon.
	T^3	26-28. Levi.
	T^4	29. Benjamin.
	T^5	30. Ephraim.
	T^6	31. Half Manasseh.
	T^7	32. Issachar.
	T^8	33. Zebulon.
	T^9	34. Naphtali.
	T^{10}	35. Dan.
	T^{11}	36. Asher.
	T^{12}	37. Those beyond Jordan.

27 Jehoiada. Not the high priest; for Abiathar held that office (1 Sam. 23. 9; 30. 7).
28 Zadok. Probably the same as Solomon's high priest (2 Sam. 8. 17; 15. 29, 35; 20. 25. 1 Kings 1. 8, 26; 2. 35).
29 kindred. Heb. brethren. Fig. *Synecdoche* (of Species), Ap. 6, "brethren" put for other relatives.
kept the ward = kept the charge. Fig. *Metonymy* (of Effect), Ap. 6, charge put for keeping what was commanded.
30 famous. Heb. men of names.
32 had understanding. Understood statesmanship.
the times. Fig. *Metonymy* (of Adjunct), Ap. 6, put for what is (or ought to be) done in them.
commandment. Heb. mouth. Put by Fig. *Metonymy* (of Cause), Ap. 6, for what is commanded by it.

953 °fifty thousand, which could keep rank: *they*
were not of °double heart.

T[9] 34 And of Naphtali a thousand captains, and
(p. 548) with them with shield and spear thirty and
seven thousand.

T[10] 35 And of the °Danites expert in war twenty
and eight thousand and six hundred.

T[11] 36 And of Asher, such as went forth to battle,
expert in war, forty thousand.

T[12] 37 And °on the other side of Jordan, of the
Reubenites, and the Gadites, and of the half
tribe of Manasseh, with all manner of instruments of war for the battle, an hundred and
twenty thousand.

L r 38 All these [8]men of war, that could keep
(p. 549) rank, came with °a perfect heart to Hebron,
to make David king over all Israel:

s and all the rest also of Israel *were* of °one
heart to make David king.

s 39 And there they were with David three
days, °eating and drinking: for their brethren
had prepared for them.

r 40 Moreover they that were nigh them, *even*
unto Issachar and Zebulun and Naphtali,
brought bread on asses, °and on camels, and
on mules, and on oxen, *and* meat, meal, cakes
of figs, and bunches of raisins, and wine, and
oil, and oxen, and sheep abundantly: for *there*
was joy in Israel.

K U t
952 **13** And David consulted with the captains
of thousands and hundreds, *and* with
every leader.
2 And David said unto all the °congregation
of Israel, "If *it seem* good unto you, and °*that*
it be of °the LORD our °God, let us send
abroad unto our °brethren every where, *that*
are left in all the land of Israel, and with them
also to the °priests and Levites *which are* in
their cities *and* suburbs, that they may gather
themselves unto us;
3 And let us °bring again °the ark of our
[2]God to us: for we °enquired not at it in the
days of Saul."
4 And all the [2]congregation said that they
would do so: for the thing was right in the
eyes of all the People.
5 So David gathered all Israel together, from
°Shihor of Egypt even unto the °entering of
Hemath, to bring [3]the ark of [2]God from
Kirjath-jearim.
6 And David went up, and all Israel, to
Baalah, *that is*, to °Kirjath-jearim, which
belonged to Judah, to bring up thence [3]the
ark of °God [2]the LORD, that dwelleth *between*
the cherubims, °Whose name is called *on it*.

u 7 And they carried [3]the ark of [2]God in °a new
cart out of the house of Abinadab: and Uzza
and Ahio °drave the cart.

33 fifty thousand. Zebulun the greatest number of any tribe.

double heart. Heb. a heart and a heart. Contrast with a perfect heart, and one heart, *v.* 38.

35 Danites. So far from none being in Palestine after 1285 B.C., the tribe could send more to help David than Ephraim or Manasseh, and more than Judah, Simeon, Levi, and Benjamin put together.

37 on = from.

38-40 (*L*, p. 546). ACCESSION OVER ALL ISRAEL. (*Introversion.*)

L | r | 38-. Assemblage. Men.
  s | -38. Unanimity. One heart.
  s | 39. Festivity. Three days.
 r | 40. Assemblage. Supplies.

38 a perfect heart. In contrast with a double heart. Cp. *v.* 33. Heart being put by Fig. *Metonymy* (of Subject), Ap. 6, for its desires.

one heart. See note on Ps. 133. 1, and its references to 2 Sam. 19. 9. 2 Chron. 30. 12. See Ap. 67 (xv).

39 eating and drinking. A covenant generally followed by festivities (Gen. 31. 44, 46). Cp. 1 Kings 1. 9.

40 and on camels. Note the Fig. *Polysyndeton* (Ap. 6), emphasising the fact that there were *no horses.*

13. 1—16. 43 (K, p. 545). THE TENT. DAVID'S BRINGING UP THE ARK FOR IT. (*Introversion.*)

K | U | 13. 1-14. Removal of Ark from Kirjath-jearim.
  V | 14. 1. House for David.
   W | 14. 2. Kingdom. Its establishment.
    X | 14. 3-7. David's family.
   W | 14. 8-17. Kingdom. Its defence.
  V | 15. 1-. House for David.
 U | 15. -1—16. 43. Removal of Ark from house of Obed-edom.

13. 1-14 (U and *U*, above). REMOVAL FROM KIRJATH-JEARIM. (*Extended Alternation.*)

15. 1—16. 43 (U and *U*, above). REMOVAL FROM OBED-EDOM. (*Extended Alternation.*)

U | t | 13. 1-6. Preparation. Of People.
  u | 13. 7. Conveyance. New cart.
   v | 13. 8. Music.
    w | 13 9-11. Offence of Uzzah.
     x | 13. 12-14-. Ark carried aside.
      y | 13. -14. Blessing *from* Jehovah.
 } Removal from Kirjath-jearim.

U | *t* | 15. 1. Preparation. Of House.
  u | 15. 2-15. Conveyance. Levites.
   v | 15. 16-28. Music.
    w | 15. 29. Offence of Michal.
     x | 16. 1. Ark set in its place.
      y | 16. 2-43. Blessing *of* Jehovah.
 } Removal from house of Obed-edom.

2 congregation = military assembly, or muster.

that it be. Supply Fig. *Ellipsis* (Ap. 6), "if it be".

the LORD. Heb. Jehovah. Ap. 4. II.

God. Heb. Elohim. Ap. 4. I.

brethren. So the true David calls them (Heb. 2. 11).

priests and Levites. Not mentioned in 2 Sam. 6. 1-19.

3 bring again. Compare the Structure above.

the ark of our God. Note its titles in these two books of Chronicles: the Ark, fifteen times; the Ark of God, twelve times; the Ark of the LORD, four times; the Ark of the Covenant of the LORD, eleven times; the Ark of the Covenant of God, once; the Ark of Thy strength, once; the holy Ark, once; the Ark of our God, once. Forty-six in all. See note on Ex. 25. 22.

enquired not at it. Heb. *dārash*, to seek diligently. See note on 10. 13. **5 Shihor.** Not the Nile, but the brook (or Wady) of Egypt (Num. 34. 5. Josh. 15. 4, 47) = El Arish. **entering of Hemath** = the pass of Hamath, on the extreme north (Num. 34. 8). **6 Kirjath-jearim.** Cp. 2 Sam. 6. 2, where it is Baale of Judah. **God.** Elohim (with Art.) = the [true] God. Ap. 4. I. **Whose name is called on it** = where His Name is invoked. **7 a new cart.** See note on 1 Sam. 6. 7. 2 Sam. 6. 3. **drave** = were leading beside: or, escorting.

v (p. 549) 952 8 And David and all Israel played before [5]God °with all *their* might, °and with singing, and with harps, and with psalteries, and with °timbrels, and with °cymbals, and with trumpets.

w 9 And when they came unto the threshing-floor of °Chidon, Uzza put forth his hand to hold [3]the ark; for the oxen stumbled.

10 And the anger of [2]the LORD was kindled against °Uzza, and He smote him, because he put his hand to [3]the ark: and there he °died before [2]God.

11 And David was °displeased, because [2]the LORD had made a breach upon Uzza: wherefore that place is called Perez-uzza to this day.

x 12 And David was afraid of [5]God that day, saying, °"How shall I bring [3]the ark of [5]God *home* to me?"

13 So David °brought not [3]the ark *home* to himself to the city of David, but carried it aside into the house of Obed-edom the Gittite.

14 And [3]the ark of [5]God remained with the family of Obed-edom in his house three months.

y And [2]the LORD blessed the house of Obed-edom, and all that he had.

V **14** Now °Hiram king of Tyre sent messengers to David, and timber of cedars, with masons and carpenters, to build him an house.

W 2 And David perceived that °the LORD had confirmed him king over Israel, for his kingdom was lifted up on high, because of His People Israel.

X 3 And David took °more wives at Jerusalem: and David begat more sons and daughters.

4 Now these *are* the names of *his* °children which he had in Jerusalem; Shammua, and Shobab, Nathan, and Solomon,

5 And Ibhar, and Elishua, and Elpalet,

6 And Nogah, and Nepheg, and Japhia,

7 And Elishama, and °Beeliada, and Eliphalet.

W a (p. 550) 8 And when the Philistines heard that David was anointed king over all Israel, all the Philistines went up to °seek David. And David heard *of it*, and °went out against them.

b c 9 And the Philistines came and spread themselves in the valley of °Rephaim.

d 10 And David enquired of °God, saying, "Shall I go up against the Philistines? and wilt Thou deliver them into mine hand?" And [2]the LORD said unto him, "Go up; for I will deliver them into thine hand."

e 11 So they came up to Baal-perazim; and David smote them there. Then David said, [10]"God hath broken in upon mine enemies by mine hand like the breaking forth of waters:" therefore they called the name of that place Baal-perazim.

12 And when they had °left their gods there, David gave a commandment, and °they were burned with fire.

8 with all their might. Cp. 2 Sam. 6. 5. No need to arbitrarily make this correspond. They are two independent books, complementary in their information.

and. Note the Fig. *Polysyndeton* (Ap. 6) in this verse, emphasising each item.

timbrels. See note on Ex. 15. 20.

cymbals. Heb. *meziltayim*: two metal discs, making a clashing sound. Always so rendered. Not to be confounded (as in A.V. and R.V.) with *zilzelim* = timbrels, which make a rustling sound, but rendered "cymbals" in 2 Sam. 6. 5. Ps. 150. 5.

9 Chidon. See 2 Sam. 6. 6; where he has another name, Nachon.

10 Uzza. See 2 Sam. 6. 6, 7.

died before God. Showing the sin of disobeying the Divine commands.

11 displeased = grieved, sad.

12 How shall I . . . ? Fig. *Erotēsis.* Ap. 6.

13 brought not the ark home. See 2 Sam. 6. 10, 11.

14. 1 Hiram. See note on 2 Sam. 5. 11.

2 the LORD. Heb. Jehovah. Ap. 4. II.

3 more wives. Cp. 3. 9. 2 Sam. 5. 13–16.

4 children: of both sexes.

7 Beeliada. In 2 Sam. 5. 16 called Eliada, which was a later name, perhaps changed from Beeliada because of the name "Baal", or lord, which, at first innocent, came to be associated with idolatry. See note on 8. 34.

14. 8–17 (*W*, p. 549). THE KINGDOM. ITS DEFENCE. (*Introversion, and Extended Alternation.*)

W | a | 8. Fame heard by Philistines.
b | c | 9. Philistines' array.
d | 10. Inquiry, and promise.
e | 11, 12. Defeat of Philistines.
b | *c* | 13. Philistines' array.
d | 14, 15. Inquiry and direction.
e | 16. Defeat of Philistines.
a | 17. Fame heard in all lands.

8 seek = search for. Heb. *bāķķesh*, especially to seek for blood or life. Cp. 2 Sam. 4. 11, "require".

went out against them. 2 Sam. 5. 17 says "went down to the hold". But this was earlier; for the later command was "thou shalt bestir thyself", which corresponds with the command "Go up" (*v.* 10) here, as well as with "thou shalt bestir thyself" of 2 Sam. 5. 24.

9 Rephaim = Rapha. See note on 11. 15.

10 God. Heb. Elohim. Ap. 4. I. In 2 Sam. 5. 19 it is Jehovah. Here, it is God's power as Creator. In 2 Sam. 5. 19 it is Jehovah's faithfulness to David. Both pleas were in David's mind, and the accounts are complementary. Cp. them in this narrative. Here, Elohim six times; Jehovah once. In 2 Sam., Jehovah six times; Elohim not once.

12 left their gods. Cp. 1 Sam. 4. 7.

they were burned with fire. This is supplementary information. In 2 Sam. 5. 21 David "took them away": i. e. to burn them, as recorded here.

16 Gibeon. In 2 Sam. 5. 25, Geba. But both places were close together, and the accounts are independent.

Gazer = Gezer. See note on 1 Kings 9. 15–17.

13 And the Philistines yet again spread themselves abroad in the valley. *b c*

14 Therefore David enquired again of [10]God; and [10]God said unto him, "Go not up after them; turn away from them, and come upon them over against the mulberry trees. *d*

15 And it shall be, when thou shalt hear a sound of going in the tops of the mulberry trees, *that* then thou shalt go out to battle: for [10]God is gone forth before thee to smite the host of the Philistines."

16 David therefore did as [10]God commanded him: and they smote the host of the Philistines from °Gibeon even to °Gazer. *e*

a (p. 550) 17 And the fame of David went out into all
lands; and [2]the LORD brought the fear of him
upon °all nations.

V (p. 549) 951-950 **15** And *David* made him houses in the city
of David,
U t and prepared a place for °the ark of °God, and
°pitched for it a tent.
u 2 Then David said, °"None ought to carry
[1]the ark of °God but the Levites: for them
hath °the LORD chosen to carry [1]the ark of
[1]God, and to minister unto Him °for ever."
3 And David gathered all Israel together to
Jerusalem, to bring up [1]the ark of [2]the LORD
unto his place, which he had prepared for it.
4 And David assembled the °children of
Aaron, and the Levites:
5 Of the °sons of Kohath; Uriel the chief,
and his brethren an hundred and twenty:
6 Of the sons of Merari; Asaiah the chief,
and his brethren two hundred and twenty:
7 Of the sons of Gershom; Joel the chief, and
his brethren an hundred and thirty:
8 Of the sons of Elizaphan; Shemaiah the
chief, and his brethren two hundred:
9 Of the sons of Hebron; Eliel the chief, and
his brethren fourscore:
10 Of the sons of Uzziel; Amminadab the
chief, and his brethren an hundred and twelve.
11 And David called for °Zadok and Abiathar
the priests, and for the Levites, for Uriel,
Asaiah, and Joel, Shemaiah, and Eliel, and
Amminadab,
12 And said unto them, "Ye *are* the chief of
the fathers of the Levites: sanctify yourselves,
both ye and your brethren, that ye may bring
up [1]the ark of [2]the LORD [1]God of Israel unto
the place that I have prepared for it.
13 For because ye *did it* not at the first, [2]the
LORD our [1]God made a breach upon us, for
that we sought Him not after °the due order."
14 So the priests and the Levites sanctified
themselves to bring up [1]the ark of [2]the LORD
[1]God of Israel.
15 And the [4]children of the Levites bare [1]the
ark of [1]God upon their shoulders with the
staves thereon, °as Moses commanded according to the word of [2]the LORD.
v 16 And David spake to the chief of the
Levites to appoint their °brethren *to be* the
singers with instruments of musick, psalteries
and harps and cymbals, sounding, by lifting
up the voice with joy.
17 So the Levites appointed °Heman the son
of Joel; and of his [16]brethren, °Asaph the son
of Berechiah; and of the sons of Merari their
[16]brethren, °Ethan the son of Kushaiah;
18 And with them their [16]brethren of the
second *degree*, Zechariah, Ben, and Jaaziel,
and Shemiramoth, and Jehiel, and Unni,
Eliab, and Benaiah, and Maaseiah, and Mattithiah, and Elipheleh, and Mikneiah, and
Obed-edom, and Jeiel, the porters.
19 So the singers, [17]Heman, Asaph, and
Ethan, *were appointed* to sound with cymbals
of brass;
20 And Zechariah, and °Aziel, and Shemiramoth, and Jehiel, and Unni, and Eliab, and
Maaseiah, and Benaiah, with psalteries °on
°Alamoth;
21 And Mattithiah, and Elipheleh, and Mikneiah, and Obed-edom, and Jeiel, and Azaziah,
with harps [20]on the °Sheminith °to excel.
22 And Chenaniah, °chief of the Levites, °*was*
for song: he instructed °about the song, because he *was* skilful.
23 And Berechiah and Elkanah *were* door-
keepers for [1]the ark.
24 And Shebaniah, and Jehoshaphat, and
Nethaneel, and Amasai, and Zechariah, and
Benaiah, and Eliezer, the priests, did blow
with the trumpets before [1]the ark of [1]God:
and Obed-edom and Jehiah *were* doorkeepers
for [1]the ark.
25 So David, and °the elders of Israel, and
the captains over thousands, went to bring up

17 all nations. Fig. *Synecdoche* (of Genus), Ap. 6, put for nations in all parts of the world.

15. -1—16. 43 (*U*, p. 549). REMOVAL OF ARK FROM HOUSE OF OBED-EDOM.

1 the ark. See notes on 13. 3 and Ex. 25. 22.

God. Heb. Elohim. Ap. 4. I.

pitched for it a tent. Had the Tabernacle of Moses been brought to Jerusalem, difficulties would have arisen in building the Temple. David's Tabernacle was merely provisional. The provision will yet be repeated, before the erection of the future Temple. See Acts 15. 16.

2 None ought to carry. David's mistake in the matter of the "new cart" was not to be repeated. Cp. 13. 7.

God. In most codices = Jehovah. But Cod. Hillel, and one early printed edition, read "God". See note on *v.* 1.

the LORD. Heb. Jehovah. Ap. 4. II.

for ever. Fig. *Synecdoche* (of the Whole), Ap. 6, put for a long time.

4 children = sons.

5 sons of Kohath. Of the six Ark-carriers, four were chosen from Kohath, one from Merari, and one from Gershom.

11 Zadok is put first, of the line of Phinehas. Abiathar was afterward disloyal (cp. 1 Kings 2. 26, 35). See note on 2 Sam. 8. 17.

13 the due order = according to the rule.

15 as = according as.

16 brethren: i. e. fellow-tribesmen. See note on the names in *v.* 17 below.

17 Heman. Samuel's grandson (a Kohathite). 1 Chron. 2. 6.

Asaph. A Gershonite. Cp. 6. 39, and 1 Kings 4. 31.

Ethan, or Jeduthun, a Merarite. See the three Psalms connected with him (Pss. 38, 61, 76).

20 Aziel. Another name, Jaaziel, in *v.* 18.

on. Heb. *'al*, relating to.

Alamoth. The maidens' choir (see Ap. 65. ii). One of three special choirs, the other two being *Sheminith* (a men's choir, see Ap. 65. xix); and Jeduthun's choir. "Alamoth" found only once as the subscript of Ps. 45. See note there. This choir was processional, not ecclesiastical. Cp. Ps. 68. 11, 25, which refers to this event, not to the Exodus.

21 Sheminith = *the* eighth. (See Ap. 65. xix.)

to excel = to lead.

22 chief = prince. Not by birth, but by merit. Probably "the chief musician".

was for song, or, was for service: especially the service of carrying up the Ark.

about the song. Three Psalms appointed: 1 Chron. 16. 7-36. Pss. 5 and 11; which, being suitable for general use, were afterwards handed over to "the chief musician". See note on the subscript at end of Ps. 3.

25 the elders. As representing "all Israel" (2 Sam. 6. 15).

[1]the ark of the covenant of [2]the LORD out of the house of Obed-edom with joy.

26 And it came to pass, when [1]God °helped the Levites that bare [1]the ark of the covenant of [2]the LORD, that °they offered seven bullocks and seven rams.

27 And David *was* clothed with a robe of fine linen, and all the Levites that bare [1]the ark, and the singers, and Chenaniah the master of the song with the singers: David also *had* upon him °an ephod of linen.

28 Thus all Israel brought up [1]the ark of the covenant of [2]the LORD with shouting, and with sound of the cornet, and with trumpets, and with cymbals, making a noise with psalteries and harps.

w (p. 549) 29 And it came to pass, *as* [1]the ark of the covenant of [2]the LORD came to the city of David, that Michal the daughter of Saul looking out at a window saw king David dancing and playing: and she °despised him in her heart.

x **16** So they °brought °the ark of °God, and set it in the midst of °the tent that David had pitched for it: and they °offered burnt sacrifices and peace offerings before °God.

y Y (p. 552) 951 to 950 2 And when °David had made an end of °offering the burnt offerings °and the peace offerings, he blessed the People in the name of °the LORD.

3 And he dealt to °every one of Israel, both °man and woman, to °every one a loaf of bread, and a good piece of flesh, and a flagon *of wine*.

Z 4 And he appointed *certain* of the Levites to minister before the [1]ark of [2]the LORD, and °to record, and to thank and praise [2]the LORD [1]God of Israel:

5 Asaph the chief, and next to him Zechariah, Jeiel, and Shemiramoth, and Jehiel, and Mattithiah, and Eliab, and Benaiah, and Obed-edom: and Jeiel with psalteries and with harps; but Asaph made a sound with cymbals;

6 Benaiah also and Jahaziel the priests with trumpets °continually before [1]the ark of the covenant of [1]God.

A 7 Then on that day David delivered first °*this psalm* to thank [2]the LORD into the hand of Asaph and his brethren.

B z[1] 8 Give thanks unto [2]the LORD,
Call upon His name,
Make known His deeds among the °people.
9 Sing unto Him,
Sing psalms unto Him,
°Talk ye of all His wondrous works.
10 Glory ye in His holy name:
Let the heart of them rejoice that seek [2]the LORD.
11 Seek [2]the LORD and °His strength,
Seek His face continually.
12 Remember His marvellous works that He hath done,
His wonders, and the °judgments of His mouth;
13 O ye seed of °Israel His servant,
Ye °children of °Jacob, His chosen ones.
14 He *is* [2]the LORD our [1]God;
His [12]judgments *are* in all the earth.
15 °Be ye mindful always of His covenant;
The word *which* He commanded to a thousand generations;
16 *Even of the covenant* which He made °with Abraham,
And of His oath unto °Isaac;
17 And hath confirmed the same to °Jacob for a law,
And to [13]Israel *for* an everlasting covenant,

---

26 helped. With His favour; there being no miscarriage now, as there had been in ch. 13.
they offered = sacrificed. Heb. *zābach*. Ap. 43. I. iv. 2 Sam. 6. 13 is complementary, not contradictory.
27 an ephod. Cp. 2 Sam. 6. 14.
29 despised him. Implying treatment with contempt.

16. 1 brought the ark. See note on 15. 3. This was in 951–950 B.C. A Sabbatic year.
the ark. See notes on 13. 3, and Ex. 25. 22.
God. Heb. Elohim. Ap. 4. I. See note on 14. 10–16.
the tent. See note on 15. 1.
offered = brought near. Heb. *ḳārab*. Ap. 43. I. i.

16. 2–43 (*y*, p. 549). THE BLESSING OF JEHOVAH. (*Introversion.*)

y | Y | 2, 3. The People blessed.
  Z | 4–6. Ministrations. Persons.
    A | 7. Delivery of Psalm to leaders.
      B | 8–36–. The Psalm of Praise.
    A | –36. Response by People.
  Z | 37–42. Ministrations. Persons.
Y | 43. The People dismissed.

2 David. Not with his own hand, but by the priests'.
offering = offering up. Heb. *'ālah*. Ap. 43. I. vi.
and. Note the Fig. *Polysyndeton* (Ap. 6) in *vv.* 2–4.
the LORD. Heb. Jehovah. Ap. 4. II. See note on 14. 10–16.
3 every one = every one, to a man. Heb. *'īsh*. Ap. 14. II.
man. Heb. *'īsh*. Ap. 14. II.
4 to record. Cp. titles of Pss. 38 and 70.
6 continually: i.e. morning and evening, as prescribed.
7 this psalm. Supply the Ellipsis thus: "Delivered first [the following words] to thank", &c. Other Psalms were probably 5, 11, and 68. Originally provided for this event, Ps. 68 was afterward divided up and incorporated in Pss. 105. 1–15; 96. 1–13; 106. 1, 47, 48. Exactly the same has been done since then by many human authors. It is those who say they "treat the Bible like any other book" who deny to the Divine Author this right to do as He will with His own.

8–36– (B, above). THE PSALM OF PRAISE. (*Repeated Alternation.*)

B | z[1] | 8–22. The peoples. (Ps. 105. 1–18).
  a[1] | 23–27. The earth.
  z[2] | 28, 29. The peoples. } (Ps. 96. 1–13.)
  a[2] | 30–33. The earth.
  z[3] | 34–36–. The People. (Ps. 106. 47, 48.)

8 people = Peoples.
9 Talk ye = meditate.
11 His strength. Fig. *Metonymy* (of Subject), Ap. 6. "Strength" put for the Ark, which was the sign of the presence of Jehovah, and the symbol of His strength. Cp. Ps. 105. 4 and 132. 8, and see note on 13. 3 and Ex. 25. 22.
12 judgments = righteous rules.
13 Israel. When adapted for more general worship, in Ps. 105, this was changed to the more general term "Abraham" (*v.* 6).
children = sons.
Jacob. See notes on Gen. 32. 28; 43. 6; 45. 26, 28.
15 Be ye mindful. This was specially for this occasion. In Ps. 105. 8, where it is for more general use, David (in editing) changed it to "He hath remembered". See note on *v.* 7.
16 with Abraham . . . Isaac. See note on Gen. 50. 24, and cp. Gen. 17. 2; 26. 3; 28. 13.
17 Jacob. See note on Gen. 50. 24 and *v.* 13 above.

951 18 Saying, "Unto thee will I give the land of
to Canaan,
950 The °lot of your inheritance;"
19 When °ye were but few,
Even a few, and strangers in it.
20 And *when* they went from nation to nation,
And from *one* kingdom to another people;
21 He suffered no [3]man to °do them wrong:
Yea, He °reproved kings for their sakes,
22 *Saying,* "Touch not °Mine anointed,
And do My prophets no harm."

a[1] 23 Sing unto [2]the LORD, all the earth;
(p. 552) Shew forth from day to day His salvation.
24 Declare His glory among the °heathen;
His marvellous works among all °nations.
25 For great *is* [2]the LORD, and greatly to be praised:
He also *is* to be feared above all gods.
26 For all the gods of the °people *are* °idols:
But [2]the LORD made the heavens.
27 Glory and honour *are* in His presence;
Strength and gladness *are* °in His place.

z[2] 28 °Give unto [2]the LORD, ye °kindreds of the [26]people,
Give unto [2]the LORD glory and strength.
29 [28]Give unto [2]the LORD the glory *due* unto His name:
Bring an °offering, and °come before Him:
Worship [2]the LORD in °the beauty of holiness.

a[2] 30 Fear before Him, all the earth:
The world also shall be stable,
That it °be not moved.
31 Let the heavens be glad,
And let the earth rejoice:
And let *men* say among the nations, [2]"The LORD reigneth."
32 Let the sea roar, and the fulness thereof:
Let the fields rejoice, and all that *is* therein.
33 Then shall the °trees of the wood sing out at the presence of [2]the LORD,
Because He cometh to judge the earth.

z[3] 34 O give thanks unto [2]the LORD; for *He is* good;
For His mercy °*endureth* for ever.
35 °And say ye, "Save us, O [1]God of our salvation,
And °gather us together,
And °deliver us from the [24]heathen,
That we may give thanks to Thy °holy Name,
And glory in Thy praise."
36 Blessed *be* [2]the LORD [1]God of Israel for ever and ever.

A And all the People said, "Amen," and praised [2]the LORD.

Z 37 So he left there °before [1]the ark of the
covenant of [2]the LORD °Asaph and his brethren, to minister before [1]the ark continually,
as every day's work required:
38 And Obed-edom with their brethren,
threescore and eight; Obed-edom also the son
of Jeduthun and Hosah *to be* porters:
39 And Zadok the priest, and his brethren
the priests, before °the tabernacle of [2]the LORD
in the high place that *was* at Gibeon,
40 To °offer burnt offerings unto [2]the LORD
upon the altar of the burnt offering continually
morning and evening, and *to do* according to
all that is written in the law of [2]the LORD,
which He commanded Israel;
41 And with them Heman and °Jeduthun,
and the rest that were chosen, who were expressed by name, to give thanks to [2]the LORD,
because His °mercy *endureth* for ever;
42 And with them Heman and Jeduthun with
trumpets and cymbals for those that should
make a sound, and with musical instruments
of [1]God. And the sons of Jeduthun °*were*
porters.
43 And all the People departed [3]every man Y
to his house: and David returned °to bless his
house.

18 lot=measuring line. Put by Fig. *Metonymy* (of Cause), Ap. 6, for the boundaries marked out by it.

19 ye. In Ps. 105. 12 it is "they". See notes on *vv.* 13 and 15 above.

21 do them wrong=oppress them. Heb. *'āshaḳ.* **reproved kings.** Cp. Gen. 12. 17; 20. 3.

22 Mine anointed. Israel was regarded as a kingdom of anointed kings and priests (Ex. 19. 6).

24 heathen=nations. **nations**=peoples.

26 people=peoples. Not same word as 12. 17. **idols**=things of naught, or nothings.

27 in His place=in His dwelling-place: i. e. the place of the Ark of the Covenant. In Ps. 96. 6, which is more general, it is "in His sanctuary". Cp. *vv.* 7 and 15.

28 Give=ascribe, as in Ps. 96. 7, 8. **kindreds**=families.

29 offering=gift offering. See Ap. 43. II. iii. **come before Him.** In Ps. 96. 8, which is more general, it is "come into His courts". **the beauty of holiness.** Cp. 2 Chron. 20. 21 and Ps. 96. 9, from which the meaning seems to be "in His glorious sanctuary".

30 be not moved. The Creator knows how to speak of the work of His hands.

33 trees of the wood. Referring specially to the wood at Kirjath-jearim (the city of woods). Cp. Ps. 132. 6.

34 endureth for ever=is age-abiding.

35 And say ye. A liturgical direction suited to this *special* occasion. Not needed for subsequent *general* use in Ps. 106. 47. See notes. Cp. *vv.* 7 and 15. **gather us . . . deliver us.** David knew from Deut. 4. 27; 28. 64; and 32, that the scattering of Israel had been foretold; and this prayer was based upon that revelation. So with Solomon. 1 Kings 8. 46–50. **holy.** See note on Ex. 3. 5.

37 before the ark. This was now in Zion (2 Sam. 6. 12–17). But the altars and vessels were in the Tabernacle at Gibeon (2 Chron. 1. 3–6). **Asaph and his brethren.** These were left in Zion "before the Ark", while the priests ministered "before the Tabernacle" (see *v.* 39 below), until Divine worship should be reconstructed in the Temple.

39 the tabernacle. Heb. *mishkān*=dwelling-place. Ap. 40.

40 offer=offer up. Heb. *'ālāh.* Ap. 43. I. vi.

41 Jeduthun. One of the three directors of the Temple-worship. Cp. 25. 1–6. 2 Chron. 5. 12. A descendant of Merari (cp. 16. 38 with 26. 10). Called also "Ethan" (15. 17, 19, and cp. 25. 1, 3, 6. 2 Chron. 35. 15). Jeduthun=to confess, give thanks. Pss. 38; 61; and 76, as printed in this edition of the Bible. (In Heb., A.V., and R.V., these Psalms are 39; 62; 77.) See Ap. 65. **mercy**=lovingkindness, or, grace.

42 were porters=were for the gate.

43 to bless his house. This was when Michal met him (15. 29). Cp. 2 Sam. 6. 20.

K C F
(p. 554)
950-948

17 Now it came to pass, °as David sat in his house, that David said to Nathan the prophet, °"Lo, 𝔍 dwell in an house of cedars, but °the ark of the covenant of °the LORD °*remaineth* under curtains."

G 2 Then Nathan said unto David, "Do all that *is* in thine heart; for °God *is* with thee."

G b 3 And it came to pass the same night, that the word of [2]God came to °Nathan, saying,
4 "Go and tell David My servant, 'Thus saith [1]the LORD,

c °'𝔗𝔥𝔬𝔲 shalt not build Me an house to dwell in:

d 5 For I have not dwelt in °an house since the day that I brought up °Israel unto this day; but have gone from tent to tent, and from *one* tabernacle *to another*.
6 Wheresoever I have °walked with all Israel, spake I a word to any of the °judges of Israel, whom I commanded to feed °My People, saying, 'Why have ye not built Me an house of cedars?'"

e 7 Now therefore thus shalt thou say unto My servant David, 'Thus saith [1]the LORD of hosts, '𝔍 took thee from the sheepcote, *even* from following the sheep, that thou shouldest be ruler over My People Israel:

e 8 And I have been with thee whithersoever thou hast walked, and have cut off all thine enemies from before thee, and have made thee °a name like the name of the great men that *are* in the earth.

d 9 Also I will ordain a place for My People Israel, and will plant them, and they shall dwell in their place, and shall be moved no more; neither shall the °children of °wickedness °waste them any more, as at the beginning,
10 And since the time that I commanded judges *to be* over My People Israel. Moreover I will subdue all thine enemies. Furthermore I tell thee that [1]the LORD will build thee an house.

c 11 And it shall come to pass, when thy days be expired that thou must °go *to be* with thy fathers, that I will raise up thy seed after thee, which shall be of thy sons; and I will establish his kingdom.
12 𝔋𝔢 shall build Me an house, and I will stablish his throne for ever.
13 𝔍 will be his father, and 𝔥𝔢 shall be My son: and I will not take My °mercy away from him, as I took *it* from *him* that was before thee:
14 But I will settle him in °Mine house and in °My kingdom for ever: and his throne shall be established for evermore.'"'

b 15 According to all these words, and according to all this vision, so did Nathan speak unto David.

F H f 16 And David the king came and sat before [1]the LORD, and said, °"Who *am* 𝔍, O [1]LORD [2]God, and what *is* mine house, that Thou hast brought me °hitherto?

g 17 And *yet* this was a small thing in Thine eyes, O [2]God; for Thou hast *also* spoken of

17. 1–22. 19 (*K*, p. 545). THE TEMPLE. DAVID'S PREPARATION FOR IT. (*Introversion.*)

K | C | 17. 1–27. Purpose declared.
  D | 18. 1–13. Conquests.
    E | 18. 14–17. Household.
  D | 19. 1—20. 8. Conquests.
C | 21. 1—22. 19. Place predicated.

17. 1-27 (C, above). PURPOSE DECLARED. (*Introversion.*)

C | F | 1. David sitting in his own house. (Who 𝔍 am.)
  G | 2. Nathan's reply from himself.
  G | 3–15. Nathan's reply from Jehovah.
F | 16–27. David sitting before Jehovah. (Who am 𝔍?)

17. 3–15 (*G*, above). NATHAN'S REPLY FROM JEHOVAH. (*Introversion.*)

G | b | 3, 4–. Message sent.
  c | –4. Jehovah's House. "Thou shalt not build".
    d | 5, 6. Jehovah's condescension.
      e | 7. Jehovah's election.
      e | 8. Jehovah's protection.
    d | 9, 10. Jehovah's promise.
  c | 11–14. Jehovah's House. "He shall build".
b | 15. Message delivered.

1 as David = according as David. Cp. 2 Sam. 7. 1-3 with the royal title "king". Here the personal name, "David". The two accounts are complementary.
Lo. Fig. *Asterismos.* Ap. 6.
the ark. See notes on 13. 3, and Ex. 25. 22.
the LORD. Heb. Jehovah. Ap. 4. II.
remaineth. Better supply *Ellipsis* with "dwelleth".
2 God. Heb. Elohim (with Art.). Ap. 4. I.
3 Nathan. Some codices, with Syr., add "the prophet".
4 Thou shalt not build, or, "Thou art not he who shall build." **an** = the.
5 Israel. Some codices, with six early printed editions, read "the sons of Israel".
6 walked = walked to and fro.
judges. 2 Sam. 7. 7 = "tribes". These could "feed" only by judges, so both agree.
My People. Western MSS. read *'Ammī* = My People. The Eastern MSS. read *'Ammō* = His People.
8 a name. Some codices, with Syr., read "a great name", as in 2 Sam. 7. 9.
9 children = sons.
wickedness. Heb. *'āval.* Ap. 44. vi.
waste them = wear them out. Some codices, with three early printed editions, read "cause them to languish".
11 go to be. Sept. reads "sleep" (2 Sam. 7. 12).
13 mercy = lovingkindness, or, grace.
14 Mine . . . My. 2 Sam. 7. 16 = Thine . . . Thy. Both alike, for the kingdom was David's because it was God's gift to him.

17. 16–27 (*F*, above). DAVID SITTING BEFORE JEHOVAH. (*Introversions.*)

F | H | f | 16. Self: abased.
    g | 17. Revelation.
      h | 18. Plea.
    g | 19. Promise.
  f | 20. God: exalted.
} David's person.
  J | 21. Israel pre-eminent.
  J | 22. Israel pre-eminent.
H | i | 23, 24. Establishment.
    k | 25–. Revelation.
      l | –25. Plea.
    k | 26. Promise.
  i | 27. Continuance.
} David's House.

16 Who am I? Fig. *Erotēsis.* Ap. 6. See notes on 2 Sam. 7. 18. **hitherto** = to this point.

950 Thy servant's house for a great while to come,
to and hast °regarded me according to the °estate
948 of °a man of high degree, O [1] LORD [2] God.
h 18 °What can David *speak* more to Thee for
(p. 554) the honour of Thy servant? for Thou knowest
Thy servant.

g 19 O [1] LORD, for Thy servant's sake, and
according to Thine own heart, hast Thou done
all this greatness, in making known all *these*
great things.

f 20 O [1] LORD, *there is* °none like Thee,
neither *is there any* [2] God beside Thee, according
to all that we have heard with our ears.

J 21 And [18] what one nation in the earth *is* like
Thy People Israel, whom °God went to °redeem
to be His own People, to make °Thee a name
of greatness and terribleness, by driving out
nations from before Thy People, whom Thou
hast °redeemed out of Egypt?

J 22 For Thy People Israel didst Thou make
Thine own People for ever; and Thou, [1] LORD,
becamest their [2] God.

H i 23 Therefore now, [1] LORD, let the thing that
Thou hast spoken concerning Thy servant and
concerning his house be established for ever,
and do °as Thou hast said.
24 Let it even be established, that Thy name
may be magnified for ever, saying, [1] 'The LORD
of hosts *is* the [2] God of Israel, *even* a [2] God to
Israel:' and *let* the house of David Thy servant
be established before Thee.

25 For Thou, O my [2] God, °hast told Thy
servant that Thou wilt build him an house:
l therefore Thy servant hath found *in his heart*
to pray before Thee.

k 26 And now, [1] LORD, Thou art [2] God, and hast
promised this goodness unto Thy servant:

i 27 Now therefore let it please Thee to °bless
the house of Thy servant, that it may be before
Thee for ever: for Thou °blessest, O [1] LORD,
and *it shall be* °blessed for ever."

D m **18** Now after this °it came to pass, that
(p. 555) David smote the Philistines, and sub-
948 dued them, and took °Gath and °her towns
out of the hand of the Philistines.
2 And he °smote Moab; and the Moabites
became David's servants, *and* brought gifts.
3 And David smote °Hadarezer king of
°Zobah unto Hamath, as he went °to stablish
his dominion by the river Euphrates.
4 And David took from him a thousand
chariots, and °seven thousand horsemen, and
twenty thousand footmen: David also houghed
all the chariot *horses*, but reserved of them
°an hundred chariots.
5 And when the Syrians of Damascus came
to help [3] Hadarezer king of [3] Zobah, David slew
of the Syrians two and twenty thousand
°men.

n 6 Then David put °*garrisons* in Syria-damascus;

o and the Syrians became David's servants,
and brought gifts.

17 regarded. Cp. "art mindful" of Ps. 8. 4.
estate. Heb. *tōr*, abbreviation of *tōrah* = law. See note on 2 Sam. 7. 19.
a man. Heb. *hā-'ādām* = the Man, of Ps. 8. 5, 6, Who is to have dominion over all the earth.
18 What can . . . ? Fig. *Erotēsis.* Ap. 6.
20 none like Thee. This is ever the worship rendered by all true worshippers. See note on 1 Sam. 2. 2.
21 God. Heb. *hā-'Elohim*, the [great] God. Ap. 4. I.
redeem . . . redeemed. See notes on Ex. 6. 6; 13. 13.
Thee = for Thyself.
23 as = according as.
25 hast told = revealed to the ear.
27 bless . . . blessest . . . blessed. Fig. *Polyptōton.* Ap. 6.

18. 1-13 (D, p. 554). CONQUESTS.
(*Extended Alternation.*)

D | m | 1-5. Conquests.
  n | 6-. Garrisons in Syria.
   o | -6-. Subjection.
    p | -6. Preservation.
 m | 7-12. Conquests.
  n | 13-. Garrisons in Edom.
   o | -13-. Subjection.
    p | -13. Preservation.

1 it came to pass. Cp. the parallel (2 Sam. 8. 1-8); and note that the two accounts are supplementary and complementary, not contradictory.
Gath. See note on "Metheg-ammah" (2 Sam. 8. 1). In the time of Solomon (1 Kings 2. 39) Gath was tributary.
her towns. Heb. her daughters. Fig. *Prosopopœia.* Ap. 6.
2 smote Moab. Thus fulfilling Num. 24. 17.
3 Hadarezer. Some codices, with two early printed editions, read "Hadadezer" as in 2 Sam. 8. 5.
Zobah. Cp. Ps. 60, title, and 1 Sam. 14. 47. It was in the neighbourhood of Damascus. In 19. 6 we have the provocation which led to this war. Cp. 2 Sam. 10. 16.
to stablish his dominion. It had been impaired. Cp. 2 Sam. 8. 3.
4 seven thousand. See note on 2 Sam. 8. 4
an = for an.
5 men. Heb. *'ish.* Ap. 14. II.
6 garrisons. Some codices, with Aram., Sept., and Syr., read this word in the text, as in 2 Sam. 8. 6.
the LORD. Heb. Jehovah. Ap. 4.
8 Tibhath. Called also Beta and Berothai (2 Sam. 8. 8): unless the four names represent four cities.
the pillars: i. e. the two pillars afterward made by Solomon (1 Kings 7. 15, 21. 2 Chron. 3. 15-17).
9 Tou. Called also Toi (2 Sam. 8. 9).
10 Hadoram. Called also Joram in 2 Sam. 8. 10.
had war = was a man (Heb. *'ish.* Ap. 14. II) of war.

Thus °the LORD preserved David whitherso- p
ever he went.

7 And David took the shields of gold that *m*
were on the servants of Hadarezer, and brought
them to Jerusalem.
8 Likewise from °Tibhath, and from Chun,
cities of [3] Hadarezer, brought David very much
brass, wherewith Solomon made the brasen
sea, and °the pillars, and the vessels of brass.
9 Now when °Tou king of Hamath heard
how David had smitten all the host of Hadarezer
king of Zobah;
10 He sent °Hadoram his son to king David,
to enquire of his welfare, and to congratulate
him, because he had fought against [5] Hadarezer,
and smitten him; (for [3] Hadarezer °had
war with Tou;) and *with him* all manner of
vessels of gold and silver and brass.

948 to 942 11 Them also king David dedicated unto [6]the LORD, with the silver and the gold that he brought from all *these* nations; °from Edom, and from Moab, and from the °children of Ammon, and from the Philistines, and from Amalek.

12 Moreover Abishai the son of Zeruiah slew of the Edomites in the valley of salt °eighteen thousand.

n (p. 555) 13 And he put garrisons in Edom;

o and all the Edomites became David's servants.

p Thus [6]the LORD preserved David whithersoever he went.

E q (p. 556) 14 So David reigned over all Israel, and executed judgment and justice among all his People.

r 15 And Joab the son of Zeruiah *was* over the host;

s and Jehoshaphat the son of Ahilud, °recorder.

t 16 And °Zadok the son of Ahitub, and °Abimelech the son of Abiathar, *were* the priests;

s and °Shavsha was scribe;

r 17 And Benaiah the son of Jehoiada *was* over the Cherethites, and °the Pelethites;

q and the sons of David *were* °chief °about the king.

D K[1] u **19** Now °it came to pass after this, that Nahash the king of the °children of Ammon died, °and his son reigned in his stead.

2 And David said, "I will shew kindness unto Hanun the son of Nahash, because his father shewed kindness to me."

v And David sent °messengers to comfort him concerning his father. So the servants of David came into the land of the [1]children of Ammon to Hanun, to comfort him.

w 3 But the princes of the [1]children of Ammon said to Hanun, °"Thinkest thou that David doth honour thy father, that he hath sent comforters unto thee? are not his servants come unto thee for to search, and to overthrow, and to spy out the land?"

v 4 Wherefore Hanun took David's servants, and shaved them, and cut off their garments in the midst hard by their buttocks, and sent them away.

u 5 Then there went *certain*, and told David how the °men were served. And he sent to meet them: for the °men were greatly ashamed. And the king said, "Tarry at Jericho until your beards be grown, and *then* return."

K[2] L[1] x 6 And when the [1]children of Ammon saw that they had made themselves odious to David, Hanun and the [1]children of Ammon sent a thousand talents of silver to hire them chariots and horsemen out of °Mesopotamia, and out of Syria-maachah, and out of Zobah.

7 So they hired thirty and two thousand °chariots, and the king of Maachah and his people; who came and pitched before Medeba. And the [1]children of Ammon gathered themselves together from their cities, and came to battle.

11 from Edom. In 2 Sam. 8. 14 we have another exploit included in this summary. See note on *v.* 12.

children = sons.

12 eighteen thousand. This was Abishai's command. In 2 Sam. 8. 13 we have David's command; while in Ps. 60 (title) we have Joab's share in the campaign (1 Kings 11. 16). There is no contradiction, but independent and separate exploits. Abishai's number was 18,000. We do not know how long Abishai's took him. Joab's (which took him six months longer) was 10,000.

18. 14-17 (E, p. 554). HOUSEHOLD. (*Introversion.*)

E | q | 14. David himself.
  r | 15-. Chief captain.
   s | -15. Recorder.
    t | 16-. Priests.
   s | -16. Scribe.
  r | 17-. Captain.
 q | -17. David's sons.

15 recorder: or remembrancer.

16 Zadok. Cp. 6. 8. 2 Sam. 8. 17; 15. 29.

Abimelech. Some codices, with Aram., Sept., Syr., and Vulg., read "Ahimelech". Cp. 2 Sam. 8. 17.

Shavsha. Called also Seraiah (2 Sam. 8. 17).

17 the. Some codices, with Sept., and two early printed editions, read "over the".

chief = heads, because David's sons were not priests.

about = at the hand of.

19. 1—20. 8 (*D*, p. 554). CONQUESTS. (*Division.*)

D | K[1] | 19. 1-5. The provocation.
 | K[2] | 19. 6—20. 8. The wars.

19. 1-5 (K[1], above). THE PROVOCATION. (*Introversion.*)

D | u | 1, 2-. David hears of Hanun's bereavement.
  v | -2. Condolence sent to Hanun.
   w | 3. Suspicion.
  v | 4. Condolence requited with indignity.
 u | 5. David hears of Hanun's action.

1 it came to pass. See 2 Sam. 10. 1-19.

children = sons.

and his son. Sept. reads "and Hanun his son", as in 2 Sam. 10. 1.

2 messengers to comfort = consolers.

3 Thinkest thou . . .? Fig. *Erotēsis.* Ap. 6.

5 men. Heb. pl. of *'ish* or *'ĕnōsh.* Ap. 14.

19. 6—20. 8 (K[2], above). THE WARS. (*Division.*)

K[2] | L[1] | 19. 6-19. Wars with Ammon and Syrians.
 | L[2] | 20. 1-3. Siege of Rabbah.
 | L[3] | 20. 4-8. Wars with Philistines.

6-19 (L[1], above). WARS WITH AMMON AND SYRIANS. (*Extended Alternation.*)

L[1] | x | 6-13. Assemblage of armies.
  y | 14-. Engagement with Syrians.
   z | -14. Flight of Syrians.
    a | 15. Flight of Ammonites.
 x | 16, 17-. Assemblage.
  y | -17. Engagement with Syrians.
   z | 18. Flight of Syrians.
    a | 19. Submission of Syrians.

6 Mesopotamia. Heb. *'Aram-nahăraim* = Syria of the two rivers.

7 chariots = cavalry. Used of men as well as horses, see *v.* 18. Cp. 2 Sam. 10. 6.

8 mighty men. Heb. *gibbōr.* Ap. 14. IV.

9 gate = entrance.

8 And when David heard *of it*, he sent Joab, and all the host of the °mighty men.

9 And the [1]children of Ammon came out, and put the battle in array before the °gate of the

948 to 942 city: and the kings that were come *were* by themselves in the field.

10 Now when Joab saw that the battle ° was set against him before and behind, he chose out of all the choice of Israel, and put *them* in array against the Syrians.

11 And the rest of the People he delivered unto the hand of Abishai his brother, and they set *themselves* in array against the [1] children of Ammon.

12 And he said, "If the Syrians be too strong for me, then thou shalt help me: but if the ° children of Ammon be too strong for thee, then I will help thee.

13 Be of good courage, and let us behave ourselves valiantly for our People, and for the cities of our ° God: and let ° the LORD do *that which is* good in His sight."

y (p. 556) 14 So Joab and the People that *were* with him drew nigh before the Syrians unto the battle;

z and they fled before him.

a 15 And when the [12] children of Ammon saw that the Syrians were fled, they likewise fled before Abishai his brother, and entered into the city. Then Joab came to Jerusalem.

x 16 And when the Syrians saw that they were put to the worse before Israel, they sent messengers, and drew forth the Syrians that *were* beyond the ° river: and Shophach the captain of the host of ° Hadarezer *went* before them.

17 And it was told David; and he gathered all Israel, and passed over Jordan, and came upon them, and set *the battle* in array against them.

y So when David had put the battle in array against the Syrians, they fought with him.

z 18 But the Syrians fled before Israel; and David slew of the Syrians seven thousand *men which fought in* ° chariots, and forty thousand footmen, and killed Shophach the captain of the host.

a 19 And when the servants of [16] Hadarezer saw that they were put to the worse before Israel, they made peace with David, and became his servants: neither would the Syrians help the [12] children of Ammon any more.

L[2] **20** And ° it came to pass, that after the year was expired, at the time that kings go out *to battle*, Joab led forth the power of the army, and wasted the country of the ° children of Ammon, and came and besieged Rabbah. But ° David tarried at Jerusa-
942 lem. And Joab smote Rabbah, and destroyed it.

2 And ° David took the crown of ° their king from off his head, and found it to weigh a talent of gold, and *there were* precious stones in it; and it was set upon David's head: and he brought also exceeding much spoil out of the city.

3 And he brought out the people that *were* in it, and ° cut *them* with saws, and with harrows of iron, and with axes. Even so dealt David with all the cities of the [1] children of Ammon. And David and all the People returned to Jerusalem.

10 was set against him = confronted him.
12 children = sons.
13 God. Heb. Elohim. Ap. 4. I.
the LORD. Heb. Jehovah. Ap. 4. II.
16 river = Euphrates.
Hadarezer. Some codices, with two early printed editions, read "Hadadezer". Cp. 18. 3.
18 chariots. See note on *v.* 7, and cp. 2 Sam. 10. 18.

20. 1 it came to pass. Cp. 2 Sam. 11. 1; 12. 26-31; 21. 18-22. children = sons.
David tarried at Jerusalem. No reference is made here to the result of this tarrying, which is recorded in 2 Sam. 11. 1—12. 25.
2 David took. No discrepancy here, for Joab had summoned David for the purpose (2 Sam. 12. 27).
their king. Probably Milcom, their king-idol.
3 cut. Heb. *sūr.* Occurs only here; the meaning "cut" is arbitrary. It must be explained by 2 Sam. 12. 31, where it is *sūm*, and is rendered "put" = "appointed them [to work] with". See notes there. *Sūr* is probably from *yashar* = to regulate, or rule.
4 Gezer. See note on 1 Kings 9. 15-17.
children = those born.
the giant. Heb. *rāphāh*, a descendant of one *Rapha*, who came of the *Nephīlīm*. See 2 Sam. 21. 18-22, and Ap. 23, 25. 6 man. Heb. *'īsh.* Ap. 14. II.

21. 1—22. 1 (*C*, p. 554). SITE OF TEMPLE PREDICATED. (*Alternation.*)

C | M | 21. 1. Incitement.
  N | 21. 2-8. The sin.
 M | 21. 9-15-. Punishment.
  N | 21.-15—22. 1. Expiation.

1 Satan. See note on 2 Sam. 24. 1.

2-8 (N, above). THE SIN. (*Alternation.*)

N | b | 2. Command of David.
  c | 3, 4. Objection.
 b | 5, 6. Obedience to command.
  c | 7, 8. Result.

3 The LORD. Heb. Jehovah. Ap. 4. II.

4 (And it came to pass after this, that there L[3] 930 to 923
arose war at ° Gezer with the Philistines; at which time Sibbechai the Hushathite slew Sippai, *that was* of the ° children of ° the giant: and they were subdued.

5 And there was war again with the Philistines; and Elhanan the son of Jair slew Lahmi the brother of Goliath the Gittite, whose spear staff *was* like a weaver's beam.

6 And yet again there was war at Gath, where was a ° man of *great* stature, whose fingers and toes *were* four and twenty, six *on each hand*, and six *on each foot:* and he also was the son of [4] the giant.

7 But when he defied Israel, Jonathan the son of Shimea David's brother slew him.

8 These were born unto [4] the giant in Gath; and they fell by the hand of David, and by the hand of his servants).

21 And ° Satan stood up against Israel, and provoked David to number Israel. C M (p. 557) 923

2 And David said to Joab and to the rulers of the People, "Go, number Israel from Beer-sheba even to Dan; and bring the number of them to me, that I may know *it.*" N b

3 And Joab answered, ° "The LORD make His People an hundred times so many more as c

923 they be: but, my lord the king, °are they not
all my lord's servants? °why then doth my
lord require this thing? °why will he be a
cause of °trespass to Israel?"
4 Nevertheless the king's word prevailed
against Joab. Wherefore Joab departed, and
went throughout all Israel, and came to Jerusalem.

b 5 And Joab gave °the sum of the number of
922 the People unto David. And all *they of* Israel
were a thousand thousand and an hundred
thousand °men that drew sword: and Judah
was four hundred threescore and ten thousand
°men that drew sword.
6 But Levi and Benjamin counted he not
among them: for the king's word was abominable to Joab.

c 7 And °God was displeased with this thing;
therefore He smote Israel.
8 And David said unto [7]God, "I have °sinned
greatly, because I have done this thing: but
now, I beseech Thee, do away the °iniquity of
Thy servant; for I have done very foolishly."

M d 9 And [3]the LORD spake unto Gad, David's
(p. 558) seer, saying,
10 "Go and tell David, saying, 'Thus saith
[3]the LORD, 'I offer thee three *things:* choose
thee one of them, that I may do *it* unto
thee.'''
11 So Gad came to David, and said unto him,
"Thus saith [3]the LORD, 'Choose thee
12 Either °three years' famine; or three
months to °be destroyed before thy foes, while
that the sword of thine enemies overtaketh
thee; or else three days the sword of [3]the
LORD, even the pestilence, in the land, and the
angel of [3]the LORD destroying throughout all
the °coasts of Israel.' Now therefore advise
thyself what word I shall bring again to Him
That sent me."

e 13 And David said unto Gad, "I am in a great
strait: let me fall now into the hand of [3]the
LORD; for very °great *are* His mercies: but
let me not fall into the hand of °man."

e 14 So [3]the LORD sent pestilence upon Israel: and there fell of Israel seventy thousand
[5]men.

d 15 And [7]God sent an angel unto Jerusalem
to destroy it: and as he was destroying, [3]the
LORD beheld, and °He repented Him of the
evil, and said to the angel that destroyed,
"It is enough, stay now thine hand."

N O And the angel of [3]the LORD stood by the
threshingfloor of °Ornan the Jebusite.

P 16 And David lifted up his eyes, and saw the
Angel of [3]the LORD stand between the earth
and the heaven, having a drawn sword in his
hand stretched out over Jerusalem.

P Then David and the elders *of Israel, who
were* clothed in sackcloth, fell upon their
faces.
17 And David said unto [7]God, °"*Is it* not I
that commanded the People to be numbered?
even I it is that have [8]sinned and done °evil
indeed; but *as for* these sheep, what have
they done? let Thine hand, I pray Thee, O
[3]LORD my [7]God, be on me, and on my father's
house; but not on Thy People, that they should
be plagued."

18 Then the angel of [3]the LORD commanded O Q
Gad to say to David, that David should go up,
and set up an altar unto [3]the LORD in the
threshingfloor of [15]Ornan the Jebusite.

19 And David went up °at the saying of Gad, R f
which he spake in the name of [3]the LORD.

20 And [15]Ornan turned back, and saw the g
angel; and his four sons with him °hid themselves. Now [15]Ornan °was threshing wheat.
21 And as David came to [15]Ornan, [15]Ornan
looked and saw David, and went out of the
threshingfloor, and bowed himself to David
with *his* face to the ground.
22 Then David said to [15]Ornan, "Grant me *g*

---

are . . . why . . . why . . . ? Fig. *Erotēsis.* Ap. 6.
trespass = guilt. Heb. *'ashām.* Ap. 44. ii. See Ex. 30. 11-16. The Tabernacle was erected with the *ransom* paid for 600,000. The site of the Temple obtained at the cost of 70,000 souls.
5 the sum. See note on 2 Sam. 24. 9.
men. Heb. *'īsh.* Ap. 14. II.
7 God. Heb. Elohim (with Art.) = the [true] God. Ap. 4. I.
8 sinned. Heb. *chāṭa'.* Ap. 44. i. David's repentance and confession preceded Gad's visit to him.
iniquity = perverseness. Cp. *v.* 4. Heb. *'āvāh.* Ap. 44. iv.

21. 9-15- (*M*, p. 557). PUNISHMENT.
(*Introversion.*)

M | d | 9-12. Divine offers.
  e | 13. Choice made.
  e | 14. Choice carried out.
 d | 15-. Divine forbearance.

12 three years. See note on 2 Sam. 24. 13.
be destroyed. Sept. and Vulg. read "flee", as in 2 Sam. 24. 13.
coasts = borders.
13 great = many.
man. Heb. *'ādām.* Ap. 14. I.
15 He repented. Fig. *Anthropopatheia.* Ap. 6.
Ornan: or Araunah in 2 Sam. 24.

21. -15—22. 1 (*N*, p. 557). EXPIATION.
(*Introversion.*)

N | O | -15. Angel. Station.
  P | 16-. David. Seeing.
  P | -16, 17. David. Humiliation.
 O | 18—22. 1. Angel. Message.

17 Is it not I . . . ? Fig. *Erotēsis.* Ap. 6.
evil. Heb. *rā'a'.* Ap. 44. viii.

21. 18—22. 1 (*O*, above). ANGEL. MESSAGE.
(*Alternation.*)

O | Q | 21. 18. Angel's command to David.
  R | 21. 19-26. David. Site of Altar.
 Q | 21. 27. Jehovah's command to Angel.
  R | 21. 28—22. 1. David. Site of Temple.

21. 19-26 (R, above). DAVID. SITE OF ALTAR.
(*Introversion.*)

R | f | 19. Obedience. Visit commenced.
  g | 20, 21. Reception.
  g | 22-25. Negotiation.
 f | 26. Obedience. Object effected.

19 at = according to.
20 hid = were hiding themselves.
was = had been.

922 °the place of *this* threshingfloor, that I may
build an altar therein unto [3]the LORD: thou
shalt grant it me for the full price: that the
plague may be stayed from the People."
23 And [15]Ornan said unto David, "Take *it* to
thee, and let my lord the king do *that which*
is good in his eyes: lo, I give *thee* the oxen
also for burnt offerings, and the °threshing
instruments for wood, and the wheat for the
°meat offering; I give it all."
24 And king David said to [15]Ornan, "Nay; but
I will verily buy it for the full price: for I will
not take *that* which *is* thine for the LORD, nor
°offer burnt offerings without cost."
25 So David gave to [15]Ornan for [22]the place
six hundred shekels of gold by weight.

f (p. 558) 26 And David built there an altar unto [3]the
LORD, and [24]offered burnt offerings and peace
offerings, and called upon [3]the LORD; and He
answered him °from heaven by fire upon the
altar of burnt offering.

Q 27 And [3]the LORD commanded the Angel;
and he put up his sword again into the °sheath
thereof.

R h (p. 559) 28 At that time when David saw that the
LORD had answered him in the threshing-
floor of [15]Ornan the Jebusite, then °he sacrificed
there.

i 29 (For the °tabernacle of [3]the LORD, which
Moses made in the wilderness, and the altar
of the burnt offering, *were* at that season in
the high place at °Gibeon.

h 30 But David could not go before it to enquire
of [7]God: for he was °afraid because of the
sword of the Angel of [3]the LORD.)

i 22 Then David said, °"This *is* the house of
°the LORD °God, and this *is* the altar
of the burnt offering for Israel."

J S U j 2 And David commanded to gather together
the °strangers that *were* in the land of Israel;
k and he set °masons to hew wrought stones to
build the house of God.

l n 3 And David prepared °iron in abundance for
the nails for the doors of the gates, and for
the joinings; and brass in abundance without
weight;
4 Also cedar trees in abundance: for °the
Zidonians and they of Tyre brought much
cedar wood to David.

o 5 And David said, "Solomon my son *is* °young
and tender,
m and the house *that is* to be builded for [1]the
LORD *must be* exceeding magnifical, °of fame
and of glory °throughout all countries: I will
therefore now make preparation for it." So
David prepared abundantly before his death.

l o 6 Then he called for Solomon his son, and
charged him to build an house for [1]the LORD
[1]God of Israel.
7 And David said to Solomon, "My son, as
for me, it was in my mind to build an house
unto the name of [1]the LORD my [1]God:
8 But the word of [1]the LORD came to me, °say-
ing, 'Thou hast shed blood abundantly, and
hast made great wars: thou shalt not build
an house unto My name, because thou hast
shed much blood upon the earth in My sight.
9 Behold, a son shall be born to thee, who

22 the place. Heb. *mākōm*, as in Ruth 4. 10. Referring to the whole place, afterward the Temple area. Not Heb. *goren*, as in 2 Sam. 24. 24, which was merely the threshingfloor, as in Ruth 3. 2. Hence 600 shekels of gold for the former, but only 50 shekels of silver for the latter. Two distinct transactions.

23 threshing instruments = threshing sledges composed of balks of timber, with sharp stones or iron spikes beneath. Cp. Isa. 41. 15. 2 Sam. 24. 22. Heb. *mōrag*. Called to-day in Palestine *moarej*.

meat offering = meal offering. Heb. *minchah*, gift offering. Ap. 43. II. iii.

24 offer = offer up. Heb. *'ālāh*. Ap. 43. vi.

26 from heaven by fire. All sacrifices accepted by God were consumed by fire from heaven, not kindled on earth. See note on Gen. 4. 4.

27 sheath. Occurs only here.

21. 28—22. 1 (*R*, p. 558). DAVID. SITE OF TEMPLE. (*Alternation.*)

R | h | 21. 28. David's sacrifice.
  i | 21. 29. Station of Tabernacle.
 h | 21. 30. David's fear.
  i | 22. 1. Site of Temple.

28 he sacrificed there; i. e. by the priests.

29 tabernacle = dwelling-place. Heb. *mishkān*.

Gibeon. Cp. 16. 39. 2 Chron. 1. 3. 1 Kings 3. 4.

30 afraid: i. e. afraid [to delay] because, &c. Otherwise Gibeon was only about eight miles away.

22. 1 This is the house of the LORD God. The place where grace had been manifested was the place where alone true worship could be offered. This it is that makes "the house of God".

the LORD. Heb. Jehovah. Ap. 4.

God. Heb. Elohim. Ap. 4.

22. 2—29. 25 (*J*, p. 545). THE RESIGNATION OF DAVID. (*Introversion and Alternation.*)

J | S | U | 22. 2-19. Intention to build the Temple.
   V | 23. 1. Solomon. First investiture.
  T | 23. 2. Princes, Priests, &c. Assemblage.
  T | 23. 3—27. 34. Princes and Priests. Appointments.
 S | *U* | 28. 1—29. 22-. Intention to build Temple.
   V | 29. -22-25. Solomon. Second investiture.

22. 2-19 (U, above). INTENTION TO BUILD THE TEMPLE. (*Introversions.*)

U | j | 2-. David's command about strangers.
 k | -2. Workmen.
  l | n | 3, 4. Preparation.
   o | 5-. Solomon. Youth.
    m | -5. The glory of the house.
  l | *o* | 6-13. Solomon. Charge.
   n | 14. Preparation.
 k | 15, 16. Workmen.
 j | 17-19. David's command to princes.

2 strangers = foreigners. Cp. 20. 3. 2 Chron. 2. 17. These were the forced labourers David had prepared in 2 Sam. 12. 31. Cp. 1 Sam. 8. 2. 1 Kings 5. 13; 9. 15, 22; and see Deut. 29. 11. Josh. 9. 27. The word "tribute" (Judg. 1. 28) means forced labour. Cp. 2 Sam. 20. 24. 1 Kings 9. 21. **masons.** See above note.

3 iron. None in Tabernacle.

4 the Zidonians, &c. See note on 2 Sam. 5. 11. Cp. 1 Kings 5. 1-15.

5 young and tender. Cp. 29. 1.

of fame and of glory. Fig. *Hendiadys* (Ap. 6) = of glorious fame.

throughout: or for. Cp. Isa. 56. 7.

8 saying. See ch. 17; 28. 3. 2 Sam. 7. 13.

922 shall be a °man of rest; and I will give him
rest from all his enemies round about: for his
name shall be °Solomon, and I will give °peace
and quietness unto Israel in his days.
10 He shall build an house for My name; and
he shall be My son, and I *will be* his father;
and I will establish the throne of his kingdom
over Israel for ever.'
11 Now, my son, [1]the LORD be with thee;
and prosper thou, and build the house of [1]the
LORD thy [1]God, °as He hath said of thee.
12 Only [1]the LORD °give thee wisdom and
understanding, and give thee charge concerning Israel, that thou mayest keep °the law of
[1]the LORD thy [1]God.
13 Then shalt thou prosper, if thou takest
heed to fulfil °the statutes and °judgments
which [1]the LORD charged Moses with concerning Israel: °be strong, and of good courage;
dread not, nor be dismayed.

n (p. 560) 14 Now, behold, °in my trouble I have °prepared for the house of [1]the LORD an hundred
thousand °talents of gold, and a thousand thousand °talents of silver; and of brass and iron
without weight; for it is in abundance: timber
also and stone have I prepared; and thou
mayest add thereto.
k 15 Moreover *there are* °workmen with thee in
abundance, hewers and workers of stone and
timber, and all manner of °cunning men for
every manner of work.
16 Of the gold, the silver, and the brass, and
the iron, *there is* no number. Arise *therefore*,
and be doing, and [1]the LORD be with thee."
j 17 David also commanded all the princes of
Israel to help Solomon his son, *saying*,
18 "*Is* not [1]the LORD your [1]God with you?
and hath He *not* given you rest on every side?
for He hath given the inhabitants of the land
into mine hand; and the land is subdued before
[1]the LORD, and before His People.
19 Now set your heart and °your soul to seek
[1]the LORD your [1]God; arise therefore, and
build ye the sanctuary of [1]the LORD °God, to
bring °the ark of the covenant of [1]the LORD,
and the °holy vessels of °God, into the house
that °is to be built to the name of [1]the LORD."

J V (p. 559) 921 **23** So when David was °old and °full of
days, he °made Solomon his son king
over Israel.
T 2 And he gathered together all the princes of
Israel, with the priests and the Levites.
T W[1] X (p. 560) 3 Now the Levites were numbered from the
age of °thirty years and upward: and their
number by their polls, °man by °man, was
thirty and eight thousand.
4 Of which, twenty and four thousand *were*
to °set forward the work of the house of °the
LORD; and six thousand *were* officers and
judges:
5 Moreover °four thousand *were* porters; and
four thousand praised [4]the LORD with the instruments "which I made," *said David*, "to
praise *therewith*."
Y 6 And David divided them into °courses
among the sons of Levi, *namely*, Gershon,
Kohath, and Merari.

man. Heb. *'ish*. Ap. 14. II.
Solomon . . . peace. Fig. *Paronomasia*. Ap. 6. Heb. *Shᵉlomoh . . . shālōm*. **11 as** = according as.
12 give thee wisdom. This was Solomon's prayer in 1 Kings 3. 5-15.
the law. }
13 the statutes and judgments. } The whole Levitical code. Ex. 21. 1. Deut. 4. 1.
be strong, and of good courage. See note on Deut. 31. 7.
14 in my trouble: i. e. in the unsettled years of his warlike reign; and of the trouble brought on by his sin with Bath-sheba, and by Absalom's rebellion. The Sept. reads "according to my poverty".
prepared for the house. The Tabernacle was built with the spoils of Egypt: the Temple from spoils of David's wars (2 Sam. 8. 7-12. 1 Chron. 18. 7-11).
talents. See Ap. 51. II. 6.
15 workmen. See note on "strangers", *v.* 2 above.
cunning = skilful. Cp. Ex. 26. 1. One of the words which have been degraded in meaning, through the fall of man. Cunning = knowing; but those who *know*, generally know too much.
19 your soul = you (emph.). Heb. *nephesh*. Ap. 13.
God. Heb. Elohim (with Art.) = the [true] God. Ap. 4. I.
the ark. See note on 13. 3.
holy. See note on Ex. 3. 5.
is to be built. And thus supersede the Tabernacle.

23. 1 old and full of days. Cp. Abraham (Gen. 25. 8), and Isaac (Gen. 35. 29). David born in 990. Now in his seventieth year. full of = satisfied with.
made Solomon his son king. During his lifetime. This was a common practice in those days; and these co-regnant kings explain many chronological problems.

23. 3—27. 34 (*T*, p. 559). PRINCES AND PRIESTS. APPOINTMENTS. (*Division.*)

T | W[1] | 23. 3—26. 28. Sacred.
| W[2] | 26. 29—27. 34. Civil.

23. 3—26. 28 (W[1], above). SACRED APPOINTMENTS. (*Introversion.*)

W[1] | X | 23. 3-5. The dedicated tribe.
Y | 23. 6. Division. Courses of the priests.
Z | p[1] | 23. 7-11. Gershonites.
| p[2] | 23. 12-20. Kohathites.
| p[3] | 23. 21-23. Merarites.
A | 23. 24-32. The service of the house.
Z | p[4] | 24. 1-19. Sons of Aaron.
| p[5] | 24. 20-31. Sons of Levi.
| p[6] | 25. 1-31. Sons of Asaph.
Y | 26. 1-25. Division. Porters and treasurers.
X | 26. 26-28. The dedicated things.

3 thirty years. According to Num. 4. 3, 23, 35, 47. Changed to twenty-five years by Jehovah (Num. 8. 24); and, by David's "last words", to twenty years (*v.* 27). Cp. Ezra 3. 8.
man = strong man. Heb. *geber*. Ap. 14. IV.
4 set forward = oversee.
the LORD. Heb. Jehovah. Ap. 4. II.
5 four thousand . . . porters. In ch. 26 we have the ninety-three chiefs. The 212 in 9. 22 pertained to the Tabernacle, not to the Temple (9. 21).
6 courses: or classes. See note on 24. 1, &c.

7 Of the Gershonites *were*, Laadan, and Z p[1]
Shimei.
8 The sons of Laadan; the chief *was* Jehiel,
and Zetham, and Joel, three.
9 The sons of Shimei; Shelomith, and Haziel,
and Haran, three. These *were* the chief of the
fathers of Laadan.
10 And the sons of Shimei *were*, Jahath, Zina,
and Jeush, and Beriah. These four *were* the
sons of Shimei.
11 And Jahath was the chief, and Zizah the
second: but Jeush and Beriah had not many

921 sons; therefore they were in one reckoning,
according to *their* father's house.
p² 12 The sons of Kohath; Amram, Izhar,
(p. 560) Hebron, and Uzziel, four.
13 The sons of °Amram; °Aaron and Moses:
and Aaron was separated, that he should
sanctify the most °holy things, he and his sons
for ever, to burn incense before [4] the LORD, to
minister unto Him, and to bless in His name
for ever.
14 Now *concerning* Moses °the °man of °God,
his sons were named of the tribe of Levi.
15 The sons of Moses *were,* Gershom, and
Eliezer.
16 Of the sons of Gershom, °Shebuel *was* the
°chief.
17 And the sons of Eliezer *were,* Rehabiah
the [16] chief. And Eliezer had none other sons;
but the sons of Rehabiah were very many.
18 Of the sons of Izhar; Shelomith the [16] chief.
19 Of the sons of Hebron; Jeriah the °first,
Amariah the second, Jahaziel the third, and
Jekameam the fourth.
20 Of the sons of Uzziel; Micah the [19] first,
and Jesiah the second.

p³ 21 The sons of Merari; Mahli, and Mushi.
The sons of Mahli; Eleazar, and Kish.
22 And Eleazar died, and had no sons, but
daughters: and their °brethren the sons of
Kish °took them.
23 The sons of Mushi; Mahli, and Eder, and
Jeremoth, three.

A 24 These *were* the sons of Levi after the
house of their fathers; *even* the [16] chief of the
fathers, as they were counted by number of
names by their polls, that did the work for
the service of the house of [4] the LORD, from
the age of °twenty years and upward.
25 For David said, [4] "The LORD [14] God of
Israel hath given rest unto His People, that
they may dwell in Jerusalem for ever:
26 And also unto the Levites; they shall no
more carry the tabernacle, nor any vessels of
it for the service thereof."
27 For by °the last words of David the
Levites *were* numbered from [24] twenty years
old and above:
28 Because their °office *was* to wait on the
sons of Aaron for the service of the house of
[4] the LORD, in the courts, °and °in the chambers,
and in the purifying of all [13] holy things, and
the work of the service of the house of [14] God;
29 °Both for the shewbread, and for the fine
flour for °meat offering, and for the unleavened
cakes, and for *that which is baked in* the pan,
and for that which is fried, and for all manner
of °measure and size;
30 °And to stand every morning to thank
and praise [4] the LORD, and likewise at even;
31 And to °offer all burnt sacrifices unto [4] the
LORD in the sabbaths, in the new moons, and
on the °set feasts, by number, according to the
order commanded unto them, continually before [4] the LORD:
32 And that they should °keep the charge of
the °tabernacle of the congregation, and the
charge of the [13] holy *place,* and the charge of
the sons of Aaron their brethren, in the service of the house of [4] the LORD.

13 Amram. Cp. Ex. 6. 20.
Aaron and Moses. See note on Ex. 6. 20.
holy. See note on Ex. 3. 5.
14 the man of God. See Ps. 90, title. Ap. 49.
man. Heb. *'ish.* Ap. 14. II.
God. Heb. Elohim (with Art.) = the [true] God. Ap. 4. I.
16 Shebuel. See note on Judg. 18. 30. The Chald. paraphrase asserts that this name "Shebuel" (which means "he returned to *'El,* the true God") was given to Jonathan after he had returned to the fear of the Lord. **chief** = head. **19 first** = head.
22 brethren: or kinsmen. **took**: i. e. by lot.
24 twenty. See note on *v.* 3 above. According to David's "last words", *v.* 3. **27 the** = these.
28 office = station.
and. Note the Fig. *Polysyndeton* (Ap. 6) in *vv.* 28-32.
in = over. **29 Both** = And. See note above.
meat offering = meal offering. Heb. *minḥa.* Ap. 43. II. iii.
measure and size. The standards were committed to the Levites. Honesty in dealing is part of true religion. Cp. Lev. 19. 36. Deut. 25. 15. Prov. 11. 1; 16. 11; 20. 23. Mic. 6. 11. If this be so in the secular sphere, how much more in sacred things.
30 And. See note on *v.* 28.
31 offer = offer up. Heb. *'ālāh.* Ap. 43. I. vi.
set feasts. Cp. Num. 28 and 29.
32 keep the charge. This is the idiom of the Pentateuch. Cp. Gen. 26. 5. Num. 18. 3-5.
tabernacle = tent. Heb. *'ohel.* Ap. 40. III.

24. 1 divisions . . . Aaron. Ch. 24 is concerning the courses of the priests, as ch. 23 is of the Levites. Cp. 23. 6. **2 children** = sons.
3 distributed = divided into courses, as in 23. 6.
4 chief men = strong men. Heb. *geber.* Ap. 14. IV. Here denoting the heads of houses, or families.
5 divided by lot. See note on the Urim and Thummim (Ex. 28. 30. Num. 26. 55).
God. Heb. Elohim (with Art.) = the [true] God. Ap. 4. I.
and of. Some codices, with four early printed editions, Aram., Syr., and Vulg., read "and from among".
6 the scribe = the secretary. Cp. 27. 32. See note on 2 Sam. 8. 17.
Ahimelech. So that Abiathar had a son named Ahimelech, who assisted him, as Hophni and Phinehas assisted Eli.

24 Now *these are* the °divisions of the Z p⁴
sons of Aaron. The sons of Aaron;
Nadab, and Abihu, Eleazar, and Ithamar.
2 But Nadab and Abihu died before their
father, and had no °children: therefore Eleazar and Ithamar executed the priest's office.
3 And David °distributed them, both Zadok
of the sons of Eleazar, and Ahimelech of the
sons of Ithamar, according to their offices in
their service.
4 And there were more °chief men found of
the sons of Eleazar than of the sons of Ithamar; and *thus* were they divided. Among
the sons of Eleazar *there were* sixteen °chief
men of the house of *their* fathers, and eight
among the sons of Ithamar according to the
house of their fathers.
5 Thus were they °divided by lot, one sort
with another; for the governors of the sanctuary, and governors *of the house* of °God,
were of the sons of Eleazar, °and of the sons
of Ithamar.
6 And Shemaiah the son of Nethaneel °the
scribe, *one* of the Levites, wrote them before
the king, and the princes, and Zadok the
priest, and °Ahimelech the son of Abiathar,

921 and *before* the chief of the fathers of the priests and Levites: °one principal household being taken for Eleazar, and *one* °taken for Ithamar.

7 Now the first °lot came forth to °Jehoiarib, the second to Jedaiah,

8 The third to Harim, the fourth to Seorim,

9 The fifth to Malchijah, the sixth to Mijamin,

10 The seventh to Hakkoz, the eighth to Abijah,

11 The ninth to Jeshuah, the tenth to Shecaniah,

12 The eleventh to Eliashib, the twelfth to Jakim,

13 The thirteenth to Huppah, the fourteenth to Jeshebeab,

14 The fifteenth to Bilgah, the sixteenth to Immer,

15 The seventeenth to Hezir, the eighteenth to Aphses,

16 The nineteenth to Pethahiah, the twentieth to Jehezekel,

17 The one and twentieth to Jachin, the two and twentieth to Gamul,

18 The three and twentieth to Delaiah, the four and twentieth to Maaziah.

19 These *were* °the orderings of them in their service to come into the house of °the LORD, according to their manner, under Aaron their father, °as °the LORD [5]God of Israel had commanded him.

p[5] 20 And °the rest of the sons of Levi *were*
(p. 560) *these:* Of the sons of Amram; °Shubael: of the sons of Shubael; Jehdeiah.

21 Concerning Rehabiah: of the sons of Rehabiah, the first *was* Isshiah.

22 Of the Izharites; Shelomoth: of the sons of Shelomoth; Jahath.

23 And the sons *of Hebron;* °Jeriah *the first,* Amariah the second, Jahaziel the third, Jekameam the fourth.

24 *Of* the sons of Uzziel; Michah: of the sons of Michah; Shamir.

25 The brother of Michah *was* Isshiah: of the sons of Isshiah; Zechariah.

26 The sons of Merari *were* Mahli and Mushi: the sons of Jaaziah; °Beno.

27 The sons of Merari by Jaaziah; Beno, and Shoham, and Zaccur, and Ibri.

28 Of Mahli *came* Eleazar, who had no sons.

29 Concerning Kish: the son of Kish *was* Jerahmeel.

30 The sons also of Mushi; Mahli, and Eder, and Jerimoth. These *were* the sons of the Levites after the house of their fathers.

31 These likewise °cast lots °over against their brethren the sons of Aaron in the presence of David the king, and Zadok, and Ahimelech, and the chief of the fathers of the priests and Levites, even the principal fathers over against their younger brethren.

p[6] **25** Moreover David and the °captains of the host separated to the service of the sons of Asaph, and of Heman, and of °Jeduthun, who should °prophesy with harps, with psalteries, and with cymbals: and the number of the workmen according to their service was:

2 Of the sons of Asaph; Zaccur, and Joseph, and Nethaniah, and Asarelah, the sons of Asaph under the hands of Asaph, which prophesied according to the order of the king.

3 Of [1]Jeduthun: the sons of [1]Jeduthun; Gedaliah, and Zeri, and Jeshaiah, Hashabiah, and Mattithiah, °six, under the hands of their father Jeduthun, who prophesied with a harp, to give thanks and to praise °the LORD.

4 Of Heman: the sons of Heman; Bukkiah, Mattaniah, Uzziel, Shebuel, and Jerimoth, Hananiah, Hanani, Eliathah, °Giddalti, and Romamti-ezer, Joshbekashah, Mallothi, Hothir, *and* Mahazioth:

5 All these *were* the sons of Heman the king's seer in °the words of °God, to lift up the horn. And °God gave to Heman fourteen sons and three daughters.

6 All these *were* under the hands of their father for song *in* the house of [3]the LORD, with cymbals, psalteries, and harps, for the service of the house of [5]God, according to

---

one principal household . . . Ithamar. Some codices, with Sept. and Syr., read "an ancestral house, one by one for Eleazar, and one by one for Ithamar".

taken: i.e. by lot. Heb. *'āḥar.*

7 lot came forth. See notes on Ex. 28. 30.

Jehoiarib. The twenty-four courses took, and kept, the names of these first heads (*vv.* 7-18). Each officiated a week (Sabbath to Sabbath), and Zacharias belonged to the eighth (Luke 1. 5). Cp. Neh. 12.

Solomon appointed the same courses, which were continued by Hezekiah and Josiah. Only four returned from the Captivity (Ezra 2. 36-39. Neh. 7. 39-42; 12. 1-21). Luke 1. 5 shows that they must have been made complete.

19 the orderings = the appointments: i.e. the order in which they fulfilled their service was all of Jehovah.

the LORD. Heb. Jehovah. Ap. 4. II.

as = according as.

20 the rest of the sons of Levi. Verses 20-30 give the names of the heads of the twenty-four courses of Levites enumerated in 23. 6-23.

Shubael. Cp. 23. 16.

23 Jeriah. Some codices, with eight early printed editions, Sept., and Syr., read "and the sons of Jeriah", but the Ellipses are rightly supplied from ch. 23. 19.

26 Beno = his son; Jaaziah being a third son of Merari. "Ben" (15. 18) prob. an abbreviation.

31 cast lots. See notes on the Urim and Thummim (Ex. 28. 30. Num. 26. 55). Cp. *vv.* 6, 7.

over against = equally with.

25. 1 captains of the host = the heads of the Temple service. This word "host" applied to Levites in Num. 4. 3. Rendered "service" (marg. *warfare*) in Num. 4. 23, 30, 35, 39, 43; 8. 24.

Jeduthun. Probably another name for Ethan. See note on 16. 41.

prophesy with harps. Not "perform", or "render". The music therefore eminently spiritual. See note on *v.* 5.

3 six. Only five named. The sixth is Shimei (*v.* 17).

the LORD. Heb. Jehovah. Ap. 4. II.

4 Giddalti. The fact that the meanings of these six names form a complete sentence in Hebrew is no more proof that this is a mistaken "obscure and ancient prayer", than that the chronicler has strung together a list of six names in order to form a sentence. What it shows is that Heman, in naming his sons, did so with this set purpose, as parents have often done since his day. The supposed prayer would read:

"I have magnified, and I have raised up help;
Sitting in trouble, I have spoken many oracles."

5 the words of God. Not the words of man. None but Divine words used in Divine worship.

God. Heb. Elohim (with Art.) = the [true] God. Ap. 4. I.

921 the king's order to Asaph, Jeduthun, and Heman.

7 So the number of them, with their brethren that were instructed in the °songs of [3]the LORD, *even* all that were °cunning, was °two hundred fourscore and eight.

8 And they °cast lots, °ward against *ward*, as well the small as the great, the teacher as the scholar.

9 Now the first lot °came forth for Asaph °to Joseph: the second to Gedaliah, who with °his brethren and sons *were* twelve:

10 The third to °Zaccur, *he*, his sons, and his brethren, *were* twelve:

11 The fourth to °Izri, *he*, his sons, and his brethren, *were* twelve:

12 The fifth to Nethaniah, *he*, his sons, and his brethren, *were* twelve:

13 The sixth to Bukkiah, *he*, his sons, and his brethren, *were* twelve:

14 The seventh to °Jesharelah, *he*, his sons, and his brethren, *were* twelve:

15 The eighth to Jeshaiah, *he*, his sons, and his brethren, *were* twelve:

16 The ninth to Mattaniah, *he*, his sons, and his brethren, *were* twelve:

17 The tenth to Shimei, *he*, his sons, and his brethren, *were* twelve:

18 The eleventh to °Azareel, *he*, his sons, and his brethren, *were* twelve:

19 The twelfth to Hashabiah, *he*, his sons, and his brethren, *were* twelve:

20 The thirteenth to Shubael, *he*, his sons, and his brethren, *were* twelve:

21 The fourteenth to Mattithiah, *he*, his sons, and his brethren, *were* twelve:

22 The fifteenth to Jeremoth, *he*, his sons, and his brethren, *were* twelve:

23 The sixteenth to Hananiah, *he*, his sons, and his brethren, *were* twelve:

24 The seventeenth to Joshbekashah, *he*, his sons, and his brethren, *were* twelve:

25 The eighteenth to Hanani, *he*, his sons, and his brethren, *were* twelve:

26 The nineteenth to Mallothi, *he*, his sons, and his brethren, *were* twelve:

27 The twentieth to Eliathah, *he*, his sons, and his brethren, *were* twelve:

28 The one and twentieth to Hothir, *he*, his sons, and his brethren, *were* twelve:

29 The two and twentieth to Giddalti, *he*, his sons, and his brethren, *were* twelve:

30 The three and twentieth to Mahazioth, *he*, his sons, and his brethren, *were* twelve:

31 The four and twentieth to Romamti-ezer, *he*, his sons, and his brethren, *were* twelve.

Y (p. 560) **26** Concerning the °divisions of the °porters: Of the °Korhites *was* Meshelemiah the son of Kore, of the sons of °Asaph.

2 And the sons of Meshelemiah *were*, Zechariah the firstborn, Jediael the second, Zebadiah the third, Jathniel the fourth,

3 Elam the fifth, Jehohanan the sixth, Elioenai the seventh.

4 Moreover the sons of Obed-edom *were*, Shemaiah the firstborn, Jehozabad the second, Joah the third, and Sacar the fourth, and Nethaneel the fifth,

5 Ammiel the sixth, Issachar the seventh, Peulthai the eighth: for °God blessed °him.

7 songs of the LORD. Not of man.
cunning=skilful. See note on 22. 15. Cp. Ex. 26. 1.
two hundred fourscore and eight. (288=24×12.) Twelve (the number of Governmental perfection) is a factor in all that pertains to government. Cp. 27. 1. See Ap. 10.
8 cast lots. See notes on the Urim and Thummim (Ex. 28. 30. Num. 26. 55).
ward=charge. A word belonging to usage of Pentateuch. Cp. 23. 32.
9 came forth: i. e. out of the ephod, the bag behind the high priest's breastplate; the lap, or bag of Prov. 16. 33. Cp. Josh. 21. 4, and see note on Ex. 28. 30. Num. 26. 55.
to Joseph. Not the eldest son. Cp. *v.* 2.
his brethren. Fig. *Synecdoche* (of Genus), Ap. 6, for relatives. **10 Zaccur,** the son of Asaph (*v.* 2).
11 Izri. Another spelling of Zeri (*v.* 3). Just as we spell the same name differently: e g. Esther and Hester, Elisabeth and Elizabeth, Ellen and Helen, Catharine and Katharine, Norah and Nora.
14 Jesharelah=Asarelah of *v.* 2.
18 Azareel=Uzziel of *v.* 4.
26. 1 divisions=courses. The names of the chiefs are given, as of the courses of priests and Levites. Ninety-three chiefs here; 4,000 under them (23. 5). The 212 of ch. 9. 22 were connected with the Tabernacle (9. 21), not the Temple.
porters = gatekeepers. See 9. 17, 18-26; 15. 18; 16. 38, 42. They were drawn from three families, viz. Meshelemiah (the Shallum of 9. 19 and Shelemiah of *v.* 14), Obed-edom (*v.* 4), and Hosah (*v.* 10).
Korhites. Cp. 9. 19, 31.
Asaph=Ebiasaph of 6. 37; 9. 19.
5 God. Heb. Elohim. Ap. 4. I.
him: i. e. Obed-edom (*v.* 4). Cp. 13. 14.
6 mighty men. Heb. *gibbōr.* Ap. 14. IV.
7 strong men. Heb. sons of valour.
8 men. Heb. *'ish.* Ap. 14. II. In sing. to show that each one was equally qualified.
10 children=sons. **chief**=head.
12 chief men. Heb. pl. of *geber.* Ap. 14. IV.
the LORD. Heb. Jehovah. Ap. 4. II.
13 cast lots. See note on 25. 8, 9.
for every gate. This ordering of David was according to the plan of the Temple, given by God "in writing" to David. See 28. 11-13, 19. So was the Tabernacle plan shown to Moses in the mount (Ex. 25. 40. Heb. 9. 5).

6 Also unto Shemaiah his son were sons born, that ruled throughout the house of their father: for they *were* °mighty men of valour.

7 The sons of Shemaiah; Othni, and Rephael, and Obed, Elzabad, whose brethren *were* °strong men, Elihu, and Semachiah.

8 All these of the sons of Obed-edom: they and their sons and their brethren, able °men for strength for the service, *were* threescore and two of Obed-edom.

9 And Meshelemiah had sons and brethren, [7]strong men, eighteen.

10 Also Hosah, of the °children of Merari, had sons; Simri the °chief, (for *though* he was not the firstborn, yet his father made him the °chief;)

11 Hilkiah the second, Tebaliah the third, Zechariah the fourth: all the sons and brethren of Hosah *were* thirteen.

12 Among these *were* the [1]divisions of the [1]porters, *even* among the [10]chief °men, *having* wards one against another, to minister in the house of °the LORD.

13 And they °cast lots, as well the small as the great, according to the house of their fathers, °for every gate.

921 14 And the lot eastward fell to °Shelemiah. Then for Zechariah his son, a wise counsellor, they cast lots; and his lot came out northward.

15 To Obed-edom southward; and to his sons the °house of Asuppim.

16 To °Shuppim and Hosah *the lot came forth* westward, with the gate °Shallecheth, by °the causeway of the going up, ward against ward.

17 Eastward *were* six Levites, northward four a day, southward four a day, and toward [15]Asuppim two *and* two.

18 At °Parbar westward, four at the causeway, *and* two at Parbar.

19 These *are* the divisions of the porters among the sons of Kore, and among the sons of Merari.

20 And °of the Levites, Ahijah *was* over the °treasures of the house of [5]God, and over the °treasures of the °dedicated things.

21 *As concerning* the sons of Laadan; the sons of the Gershonite Laadan, °chief fathers, *even* of Laadan the Gershonite, *were* Jehieli.

22 The sons of Jehieli; Zetham, and Joel his brother, *which were* over the [20]treasures of the house of [12]the LORD.

23 Of the Amramites, *and* the Izharites, the Hebronites, *and* the Uzzielites:

24 And °Shebuel the son of Gershom, the son of Moses, *was* ruler of the [20]treasures.

25 And his brethren by Eliezer; Rehabiah his son, and Jeshaiah his son, and Joram his son, and Zichri his son, and Shelomith his son.

X (p. 560) 26 Which Shelomith and his brethren *were* over all the [20]treasures of the [20]dedicated things, which David the king, and the [21]chief fathers, the captains over thousands and hundreds, and the captains of the host, had dedicated.

27 Out of the spoils won in battles did they °dedicate to maintain the house of [12]the LORD.

28 And all that Samuel the seer, and Saul the son of Kish, and Abner the son of Ner, and Joab the son of Zeruiah, had dedicated; *and* whosoever °had dedicated *any thing, it was* under the hand of Shelomith, and of his brethren.

W² B (p. 564) 29 Of the Izharites, Chenaniah and his sons *were* for the °outward business over Israel, for °officers and judges.

30 *And* of the Hebronites, Hashabiah and his brethren, °men of valour, a thousand and seven hundred, *were* officers among them of Israel on this side Jordan westward in all the business of [12]the LORD, and in the service of the king.

31 Among the Hebronites *was* Jerijah the [10]chief, *even* among the Hebronites, according to the generations of his fathers. In the fortieth year of the reign of David they were sought for, and there were found among them [6]mighty men of valour at Jazer of Gilead.

32 And his brethren, [7]men of valour, *were* two thousand and seven hundred [21]chief fathers, whom king David made rulers over the Reubenites, the Gadites, and the half tribe of Manasseh, for every matter pertaining to [5]God, and affairs of the king.

14 Shelemiah. The Meshelemiah of *v.* 1. See note on 25. 11.

15 house of Asuppim = the treasuries (from Heb. *'āsaph*, to gather). Cp. 2 Chron. 25. 24, where Joash took what was in Obed-edom's charge. So named because of the two gates called Asuppim.

16 Shuppim. Not an "accidental repetition" or "unintelligible intrusion", but a proper name.

Shallecheth = a casting up. Occurs only here, and Isa. 6. 13. Another gate made by Solomon (1 Kings 10. 5. 2 Chron. 9. 4).

the causeway of the going up. Made by Solomon (1 Kings 10. 5. 2 Chron. 9. 4). Connected with "Millo", between Zion (Jebus) and Moriah.

18 Parbar. Another gate connected with this causeway. Cp. 2 Kings 23. 11, rendered "suburbs". Cp. 2 Kings 11. 16.

20 of the Levites, Ahijah was. The Sept. reads "the Levites their brethren were" (reading *Aḥikem* instead of Ahijah).

treasures = treasuries. There were several in divers places, with various names.

dedicated = holy. See note on Ex. 3. 5.

21 chief fathers = heads of the fathers.

24 Shebuel. See note on 23. 16.

27 dedicate = set apart.

28 had dedicated. A practice dating from the time of Moses (Num. 31. 28-47), and Joshua (6. 24).

26. 29—27. 34 (W², p. 560). APPOINTMENTS. CIVIL. (*Introversion.*)

W² | B | 26. 29-32. Magistrates.
  C | 27. 1-15. Overseers.
    D | 27. 16-22. Tribes.
      E | 27. 23, 24. Exceptions.
    D | 27. 25. Treasurers.
  C | 27. 26-31. Overseers.
B | 27. 32-34. Counsellors.

29 outward business: outside the Temple (Neh. 10. 32-39; 11. 16), as distinguished from the worship within (which was the "business of the house of God". Neh. 11. 22).

officers and judges. See Deut. 16. 18 (same Heb.), 6,000 appointed. Provision made for them in Ex. 18. 13-26.

30 men of valour = sons of valour. Cp. *v.* 7.

27. 1 children = sons.

chief fathers = heads of the fathers.

captains of thousands. The host comprised all males over twenty. From this were organised twelve divisions of 24,000 men, commanded by twelve of the thirty. David's 600 (1 Sam. 23. 13, &c.) divided into three of 200 each (consisting of ten subdivisions of twenty each, commanded by the "thirty"), commanded by the "three". The commander of the "thirty" was not one of the "three", but next below them. See notes on ch. 11 and 2 Sam. 23.

2 Jashobeam. Cp. 11. 11.

3 Perez = Pharez, son of Judah. See note on 25. 11.

chief = head.

27 Now the °children of Israel after their number, *to wit*, the °chief fathers and °captains of thousands and hundreds, and their officers that served the king in any matter of the courses, which came in and went out month by month throughout all the months of the year, of every course *were* twenty and four thousand. C

2 Over the first course for the first month *was* °Jashobeam the son of Zabdiel: and in his course *were* twenty and four thousand.

3 Of the [1]children of °Perez *was* the °chief of all the captains of the host for the first month.

4 And over the course of the second month

921 *was* °Dodai an Ahohite, and of his course *was*
Mikloth also the °ruler: in his course likewise
were twenty and four thousand.
5 The third captain of the host for the third
month *was* °Benaiah the son of Jehoiada, a
°chief priest: and in his course *were* twenty
and four thousand.
6 This *is that* Benaiah, *who was* °mighty
°*among* the thirty, and above the thirty: and
in his course *was* Ammizabad his son.
7 The fourth *captain* for the fourth month
was Asahel the brother of Joab, and Zebadiah
his son after him: and in his course *were*
twenty and four thousand.
8 The fifth captain for the fifth month *was*
°Shamhuth the °Izrahite: and in his course
were twenty and four thousand.
9 The sixth *captain* for the sixth month *was*
°Ira the son of Ikkesh the Tekoite: and in his
course *were* twenty and four thousand.
10 The seventh *captain* for the seventh month
was °Helez the Pelonite, of the [1] children of
Ephraim: and in his course *were* twenty and
four thousand.
11 The eighth *captain* for the eighth month
was °Sibbecai the Hushathite, of the Zarhites:
and in his course *were* twenty and four thousand.
12 The ninth *captain* for the ninth month
was °Abiezer the Anetothite, of the Benjamites: and in his course *were* twenty and four
thousand.
13 The tenth *captain* for the tenth month
was °Maharai the Netophathite, of the Zarhites:
and in his course *were* twenty and four thousand.
14 The eleventh *captain* for the eleventh
month *was* °Benaiah the Pirathonite, of the
[1] children of Ephraim: and in his course *were*
twenty and four thousand.
15 The twelfth *captain* for the twelfth month
was °Heldai the Netophathite, of Othniel: and
in his course *were* twenty and four thousand.

D 16 Furthermore over °the tribes of Israel: the
(p. 564) ruler of the Reubenites *was* Eliezer the son of
Zichri: of the Simeonites, Shephatiah the son
of Maachah:
17 Of the Levites, Hashabiah the son of Kemuel:
Of the Aaronites, Zadok:
18 Of Judah, °Elihu, *one* of the brethren of
David:
Of Issachar, Omri the son of Michael:
19 Of Zebulun, Ishmaiah the son of Obadiah:
Of Naphtali, Jerimoth the son of Azriel:
20 Of the [1] children of Ephraim, Hoshea the
son of Azaziah:
Of the half tribe of Manasseh, Joel the son
of Pedaiah:
21 Of the half *tribe* of Manasseh in Gilead,
Iddo the son of Zechariah:
Of Benjamin, Jaasiel the son of Abner:
22 Of Dan, Azareel the son of Jeroham.
These *were* the princes of the tribes of Israel.

E 23 But David took °not the number of them
from twenty years old and under: because
°the LORD had said He would increase Israel
like to °the stars of the heavens.
24 Joab the son of Zeruiah began to number,
but he finished not, because °there fell wrath
for it against Israel; neither was the number
put in the account of the chronicles of king
David.

25 And °over the king's °treasures *was* Azma- D
veth the son of Adiel: and over the storehouses in the fields, in the cities, and in the
villages, and in the °castles, *was* Jehonathan
the son of Uzziah:

26 And over them that did the work of the C
field for tillage of the ground *was* Ezri the son
of Chelub:
27 And over the vineyards *was* Shimei the
Ramathite: over the increase of the vineyards
for the wine cellars *was* Zabdi the Shiph-
mite:
28 And over the olive trees and the sycomore
trees that *were* in the low plains *was* Baal-
hanan the Gederite: and over the cellars of
oil *was* Joash:
29 And over the herds that fed in Sharon
was Shitrai the Sharonite: and over the herds
that were in the valleys *was* Shaphat the son
of Adlai:
30 Over the camels also *was* Obil the °Ish-
maelite: and over the asses *was* Jehdeiah the
Meronothite:
31 And over the flocks *was* Jaziz the Hagerite.
All these *were* the rulers of the substance which
was king David's.

---

4 Dodai = Dodo (2 Sam. 23. 9). See note on 25. 11.
ruler = divisional officer.
5 Benaiah. Cp. 11. 22–25. 2 Sam. 23. 20–23.
chief priest. Read "Jehoiada the priest"—a head (1 Kings 4. 4).
6 mighty. Heb. *gibbōr.* Ap. 14. IV.
among = "a hero [of] thirty".
8 Shamhuth = Shammah (2 Sam. 23. 11), and Shammoth (11. 27), and see note on 25. 11.
Izrahite. Cp. 25. 11.
9 Ira. One of the thirty (see 11. 28 and 2 Sam. 23. 26).
10 Helez. Cp. 2 Sam. 23. 26.
11 Sibbecai. Cp. 11. 29 and 2 Sam. 21. 18.
12 Abiezer. Cp. 11. 28. 2 Sam. 23. 27.
13 Maharai. Cp. 11. 30. 2 Sam. 23. 28.
14 Benaiah. Cp. 11. 31. 2 Sam. 23. 30.
15 Heldai. Cp. 11. 30. Heled, 2 Sam. 23. 29 (Hildai, see note on 25. 11).
16 the tribes of Israel. Each tribe had a ruler, called (*v.* 22) "the princes of the tribes":
1. The first four sons of Leah, in order of their birth.
2. Issachar and Zebulun, fifth and sixth (Gen. 30. 18, 20).

Thus the first six are Leah's sons.
Her maid Zilpah's (Gad and Asher) not mentioned.
Then Naphtali (Bilhah, Rachel's maid).
Then Ephraim and Manasseh (Rachel's, through Joseph).
Then Benjamin (Rachel's other son).
Dan comes last! See note on Gen. 49. 17.

18 Elihu. Probably Eliab (2. 13), Jesse's eldest son (1 Sam. 16. 6).
23 not the number. Only the fighting men. See 21. 5 and 2 Sam. 24. 9.
the LORD. Heb. Jehovah. Ap. 4. II.
the stars of the heavens. Fig. *Parœmia.* Ap. 6. See note on Gen. 15. 5.
24 there fell wrath. Cp. 21. 6, 7.
25 over the king's treasures. There were twelve of these stewards. See Ap. 10.
treasures = treasuries. castles = fortresses.
30 Ishmaelite. Camels appropriately committed to him.

B (p. 564) 921 32 Also Jonathan °David's uncle was a counsellor, °a wise °man, and a scribe: and Jehiel the son of Hachmoni *was* with the king's sons:

33 And Ahithophel *was* the king's counsellor: and Hushai the Archite *was* the king's companion:

34 And after Ahithophel *was* Jehoiada the son of Benaiah, and Abiathar: and the °general of the king's °army *was* Joab.

U F H (p. 566) **28** And David °assembled all the °princes of Israel, the princes of the tribes, and the °captains of the companies that ministered to the king by course, and the °captains over the thousands, and °captains over the hundreds, and the °stewards over all the substance and possession of the king, and of his sons, with the officers, and with °the mighty men, and with all the valiant men, unto Jerusalem.

J q 2 Then David the king °stood up upon his feet, and said, "Hear me, my brethren, and my people: *As for me,* I *had* in mine heart to build an house of rest for °the ark of the covenant of °the LORD, °and for °the footstool of our °God, and had made ready for the building:

3 But [2]God said unto me, 'Thou shalt not build an house for My name, because thou *hast been* a °man of war, and hast shed blood.'

4 Howbeit [2]the LORD [2]God of Israel °chose me before all the house of my father to be king over Israel for ever: for He hath °chosen Judah *to be* the ruler; and of the house of Judah, the house of my father; and among the sons of my father He liked me to make *me* king over all Israel:

5 And of all my sons, (for [2]the LORD hath given me many sons,) He hath °chosen Solomon my son to sit upon the throne of the kingdom of [2]the LORD over Israel.

6 And °He said unto me, 'Solomon thy son, he shall build My house and My courts: for I have chosen him *to be* My son, and I will be his father.

7 Moreover I will establish his kingdom for ever, if he be constant to do My commandments and My judgments, as at this day.'

8 Now therefore in the sight of all Israel the °congregation of [2]the LORD, and in the audience of our °God, keep and °seek for all the commandments of [2]the LORD your [2]God: that ye may possess this good land, and leave *it* for an inheritance for your °children after you for ever.

r 9 And thou, Solomon my son, know thou the [2]God of thy father, and serve Him with a perfect heart and with a willing °mind: for [2]the LORD searcheth all hearts, and understandeth all the imaginations of the thoughts: if thou seek Him, He will be found of thee; but if thou forsake Him, He will cast thee off for ever.

10 °Take heed now; for [2]the LORD hath [5]chosen thee to build an house for the sanctuary: be strong, and do *it*."

K s 11 Then David gave to Solomon his son °the pattern of the porch,

t °and of the houses °thereof, and of the treasuries thereof, and of the upper chambers thereof, and of the inner parlours thereof; and of the place of the °mercy seat,

12 And [11]the pattern of all that he had °by the Spirit, of the courts of the house of [2]the LORD, and of all the °chambers round about,

32 David's uncle. In 20. 7 and 2 Sam. 21. 21 Jonathan is the son of Shimea, David's brother. The Heb. *dād* may thus be used of a brother's son as well as a father's brother's son.

a wise man = a man of understanding ("man". Heb. *'ish.* Ap. 14. II.).

34 general = prince. **army** = host.

28. 1—29. 22- (*U*, p. 559). INTENTION TO BUILD THE TEMPLE. (*Alternation.*)

U | F | 28. 1—29. 8. Preparation. Persons.
  G | 29. 9. Joy.
 F | 29. 10-20. Preparation. Devotions.
  G | 29. 21, 22-. Feasting.

28. 1—29. 8 (F, above). PREPARATIONS. PERSONS. (*Introversions.*)

F | H | 28. 1. Princes. Gifts.
  J | q | 28. 2-8. People addressed.
   r | 29. 9, 10. Solomon charged.
    K | 28. 11-19. The pattern delivered.
   J | *r* | 28. 20, 21. Solomon charged.
    q | 29. 1-5. People addressed.
 H | 29. 6-8. Princes. Gifts.

1 assembled = convoked, or mustered.

princes of Israel. Cp. 27. 16-22.

captains = princes (throughout the chapter). See note on 27. 1.

stewards. Cp. 27. 25-31. Each body consisted of twelve persons. See Ap. 10.

the mighty men. Heb. *gibbōr.* Ap. 14 IV.

2 stood up upon his feet. Note David's three attitudes: lying on the earth as a *penitent* (2 Sam. 12. 16. Cp. Ps. 51); sitting before Jehovah as a *worshipper* (2 Sam. 7. 18. 1 Chron. 17. 16); and standing on his feet as a *servant* (28. 2).

the ark. See note on 13. 3 and Ex. 25. 22.

the LORD. Heb. Jehovah. Ap. 4. II.

and = even.

the footstool of our God = the Ark. Fig. *Anthropopatheia.* Ap. 6. **God.** Heb. Elohim. Ap. 4. I.

3 man. Heb. *'ish.* Ap. 14. II.

4 chose me. Cp. 1 Sam. 16. 12.

chosen Judah. Cp. Gen. 49. 10.

5 chosen Solomon. Cp. 22. 9. 2 Sam. 12. 25.

6 He said unto me. Cp. 22. 9. 2 Sam. 7. 13, 14.

8 congregation = assembly as in *v.* 1.

seek. Heb. *dārash.* See notes on 10. 13, 14. 1 Sam. 28. 6, 7. **children** = sons.

9 mind = soul. Heb. *nephesh.* Ap. 13.

10 Take heed, &c. The 11th *Seder* begins here, and ends with 2 Chron. 2. 2. See note on p. 366.

28. 11-19 (K, above). THE PATTERN DELIVERED. (*Introversion.*)

K | s | 11-. The pattern given *by* David.
  t | -11, 12. The house and its parts.
   u | 13. The service of the house.
  t | 14-18. The house and its furniture.
 s | 19. The pattern given *to* David.

11 the pattern. Same word as of Tabernacle to Moses (Ex. 25. 9, 40: See Heb. 9. 5).

and. Note the Fig. *Polysyndeton* (Ap. 6) in *vv.* 11-13, for emphasis. **thereof:** i.e. of the sanctuary.

mercy seat = the propitiatory. See note on Ex. 25. 17.

12 by the Spirit. Heb. "by the Spirit (*rūach.* Ap. 9) with (or in) me". The pattern without, and the worship within, all of God. Nothing can be offered in worship but what comes from God (John 4. 24). Therefore said to be built by David in *intention*, and by Solomon in *fact.*

chambers = attached chambers.

921 of the treasuries of the house of [2]God, and of the treasuries of the °dedicated things:

u (p. 566) 13 Also for the courses of the priests and the Levites, and for all the work of the service of the house of [2]the LORD, and for all the vessels of service in the house of [2]the LORD.

t 14 *He gave* of gold by weight for *things* of gold, for all instruments of all manner of service; *silver also* for all instruments of silver by weight, for all instruments of every kind of service:
15 Even the weight for the °candlesticks of gold, and for their lamps of gold, by weight for every °candlestick, and for the lamps thereof: and for the °candlesticks of silver by weight, *both* for the °candlestick, and *also* for the lamps thereof, according to the use of every °candlestick.
16 And by weight *he gave* gold for the tables of shewbread, for every table; and *likewise* silver for the tables of silver:
17 Also pure gold for the fleshhooks, and the bowls, and the cups: and for the golden °basons *he gave gold* by weight for every °bason; and *likewise silver* by weight for every °bason of silver:
18 And for the altar of incense refined gold by weight; and gold for the pattern of the chariot °of the cherubims, that spread out *their wings*, and covered [2]the ark of the covenant of [2]the LORD.

s 19 "All *this*," *said David*, [2]"the LORD made me understand in writing by *His* hand upon me, *even* all the works of this pattern."

J r 20 And David said to Solomon his son, °"Be strong and of good courage, and do *it*: fear not, nor be dismayed: for [2]the LORD [2]God, *even* my [2]God, *will be* with thee; °He will not fail thee, nor forsake thee, until thou hast finished all the work for the service of the house of [2]the LORD.
21 And, °behold, the courses of the priests and the Levites, *even they shall be with thee* for all the service of the house of [2]God: and *there shall be* with thee for all manner of workmanship every willing skilful man, for any manner of service: also the princes and all the People *will be* wholly at thy commandment."

q **29** Furthermore David the king said unto all the °congregation, "Solomon my son, °whom alone °God °hath chosen, *is yet* °young and tender, and the work *is* great: for °the palace *is* not for man, but for °the LORD °God.
2 Now I have prepared with all my might for the house of my [1]God the °gold for *things to be made* of gold, °and the °silver for *things* of silver, and the °brass for *things* of brass, the °iron for *things* of iron, and wood for *things* of wood; °onyx stones, and *stones* to be set, glistering stones, and of divers colours, and all manner of precious stones, and marble stones in abundance.
3 Moreover, because I have set my affection to the house of my [1]God, °I have of °mine own proper good, of gold and silver, *which* I have given to the house of my [1]God, °over and above all that I have prepared for the °holy house,
4 *Even* three thousand talents of gold, of the gold of Ophir, and seven thousand talents of refined silver, to overlay the walls of the °houses *withal*:
5 The gold for *things* of [2]gold, and the [2]silver for *things* of silver, and for all manner of work *to be made* by the hands of artificers. And who *then* is willing °to consecrate his service this day unto [1]the LORD?"

6 Then the [1]chief of the fathers and princes of the tribes of Israel, and the captains of thousands and of hundreds, with the rulers of the king's work, offered willingly, H
7 And gave for the service of the house of [1]God of gold five thousand talents and ten thousand °drams, and of silver ten thousand talents, and of brass eighteen thousand talents, and one hundred thousand talents of iron.
8 And they with whom *precious* stones were found gave *them* to the treasure of the house of [1]the LORD, °by the hand of Jehiel the Gershonite.

9 Then the People rejoiced, for that they offered willingly, because with perfect heart G

---

dedicated = holy. See note on Ex. 3. 5.
15 candlesticks = lampstands.
17 basons = covered bowls.
18 of = even. Genitive of Apposition. See Ap. 17.
20 Be strong, and of a good courage. See note on Deut. 31. 7.
He will not fail thee. See notes on Deut. 4. 31; 31. 6.
21 behold. Fig. *Asterismos.* Ap. 6.

29. 1 congregation. Same word as in 28. 8.
whom = the one whom.
God. Heb. Elohim. Ap. 4. I.
hath chosen. Cp. 22. 9. 2 Sam. 12. 25.
young and tender. Cp. 22. 5.
the palace. Heb. *bîrāh.* Used only here and *v.* 19. Est. 1. 2, 5; 2. 3, 5, 8, 15; 8. 14; 9. 6, 11, 12. Neh. 1. 1; 2. 8; 7. 2. Dan. 8. 2. The name for a Persian royal palace, which shows the date of these books. (See note on "drams", *v.* 7), and why it is found among the *Kethubim*, or later books (and not with the historical books); and why Daniel is there too (and not among the prophets).
the LORD. Heb. Jehovah. Ap. 4. II.
2 gold . . . silver . . . brass . . . iron. Put by Fig. *Metonymy* (of Cause), Ap. 6, for what is made from them. The Fig. is completed by the words in italics.
and. Note the Fig. *Polysyndeton* (Ap. 6), to emphasise the fifteen gifts of grace (3 × 5, see Ap. 10). A.V., 1611, omits this first "and".
onyx. Cp. Gen. 2. 12. Ex. 25. 7; 28. 9.
3 I have of mine own proper good = Seeing I have a treasure of mine own. Omit the word "which".
mine own proper good. Heb. only one word, *segullāh* = personal treasure. Occurs only in Ex. 19. 5. Deut. 7. 6; 14. 2; 26. 18. 1 Chron. 29. 3. Ps. 135. 4. Ecc. 2. 8. Mal. 3. 17 (see margin). See note on Ex. 19. 5.
over and above. Cp. 22. 14.
holy. See note on Ex. 3. 5.
4 houses. Cp. 28. 11.
5 to consecrate. See notes on Ex. 28. 41. Lev. 9. 17.
6 chief = prince. See note on 27. 16.
7 drams. Heb. *'adarkonîm, darics.* Only here, and Ezra 27. A Persian coin Probably so called from the appellative "Darius" = the king's coin (like English "sovereign"). Indicates date of book. See note on "the palace", *v.* 1, and consult Ap. 51. I. 1, p. 73.
8 by the hand = unto the hand: i. e. under the direction of. Lit. "[laying them] upon the hand".

921 they offered willingly to [1]the LORD: and
David the king also °rejoiced with great joy.

F L (p. 568) 10 Wherefore David blessed [1]the LORD before all the [1]congregation: and °David said,
"Blessed *be* Thou, [1]LORD [1]God of Israel our
father, for ever and ever.
11 Thine, O [1]LORD, *is* the °greatness, °and
the °power, and the °glory, and the °victory,
and the °majesty: for all *that is* in the heaven
and in the earth *is Thine;* Thine *is* the kingdom, O [1]LORD, and Thou art exalted as head
above all.

M N 12 Both riches and honour *come* °of Thee,
and Thou reignest over all; and in Thine hand
is power and might; and in Thine hand *it is*
to make great, and to give strength unto all.

O v 13 Now therefore, our [1]God, we thank Thee,
and praise Thy glorious name.

w 14 But °who *am* I, and what *is* my People,
that we should be able to offer so willingly
after this sort? for all things *come* of Thee,
and of Thine own have we given Thee.
15 For °we *are* strangers before Thee, and
sojourners, as *were* all our fathers: our days
on the earth *are* as a shadow, and *there is*
°none abiding.

M N 16 O [1]LORD our [1]God, all this store that we
have prepared to build Thee an house for
Thine [3]holy name *cometh* of Thine hand, and
is all Thine own.

O w 17 I know also, my [1]God, that Thou °triest the
heart, and hast pleasure in uprightness. As
for me, in the uprightness of mine heart I have
willingly offered all these things: and now
have I seen with joy Thy People, which are
°present here, to offer willingly unto Thee.

v 18 O [1]LORD [1]God of °Abraham, Isaac, and of
Israel, our fathers, keep this for ever in the
imagination of the thoughts of the heart of
Thy People, and prepare their heart unto Thee:
19 And give unto Solomon my son a perfect
heart, to keep Thy commandments, Thy testimonies, and Thy statutes, and to do all *these*
things, and to build [1]the palace, *for* the which
I have made provision."

L 20 And David said to all the °congregation,
"Now bless [1]the LORD your [1]God." And all
the °congregation blessed [1]the LORD [1]God of
their fathers, and bowed down their heads,
and °worshipped [1]the LORD, and the king.

G (p. 566) 21 And they °sacrificed sacrifices unto [1]the
LORD, and °offered burnt offerings unto the
LORD, on the morrow after that day, *even* a
thousand bullocks, a thousand rams, *and* a
thousand lambs, with their drink offerings, and
sacrifices in abundance for all Israel:
22 And °did eat and drink before [1]the LORD
on that day with great gladness.

V x (p. 568) And they made Solomon the son of David king
°the second time, and anointed *him* unto [1]the
LORD *to be* the chief governor, and °Zadok *to*
be priest.

y 23 Then Solomon sat on the throne of [1]the
LORD as king instead of David his father, and
prospered; and all Israel obeyed him.

y 24 And all the princes, and °the mighty men,
and all the sons likewise of king David, °sub-
mitted themselves unto Solomon the king.

25 And [1]the LORD magnified Solomon ex- *x*
ceedingly in the sight of all Israel, and °be-
stowed upon him *such* royal majesty as had
not been on any king before him in Israel.

26 Thus David the son of Jesse reigned over H² z
all Israel. 960
27 And the time that he reigned over Israel to
was forty years; seven years reigned he in 920
Hebron, and thirty and three *years* reigned he
in Jerusalem.

---

9 rejoiced with great joy = rejoiced exceedingly. Fig. *Polyptōton* (Ap. 6), for emphasis.

29. 10-20 (*F*, p. 566). PREPARATION. DEVOTIONS. (*Introversions and Alternations.*)

F | L | 10, 11. Blessing.
  M | N | 12. Acknowledgment.
    O | v | 13. Praise.
      w | 14, 15. Personal. Self-abasement.
  M | *N* | 16. Acknowledgment.
    O | *w* | 17. Personal. Integrity.
      v | 18, 19. Prayer.
  L | 20. Blessing.

10 David said. A wonderful ascription of praise follows, tracing all good to Jehovah's sovereign grace.

11 greatness. Cp. Ps. 145. 3.

and. Note the Fig. *Polysyndeton* in *vv.* 11-13, fourteen "ands", (including "Both" (*v.* 12) and "Now" (*v.* 12) placing great emphasis on the fifteen separate clauses of praise and prayer.

power. Cp. *v.* 12 and Ps. 21. 13.

glory. Cp. *v.* 13. Ps. 96. 6 ("beauty").

victory. Cp. 1 Sam. 15. 29 ("Strength").

majesty. Cp. Ps. 21. 5 ("honour").

12 of Thee. Heb. from thy face. Fig. *Anthropopatheia*. Ap. 6.

14 who am I . . . ? See note on 2 Sam. 7. 18.

15 we are strangers. Cp. Pss. 39. 12; 119. 19.

none abiding = no hope of continuance.

17 triest the heart. Cp. 28. 9. 1 Sam. 16. 7.

present = found.

18 Abraham, Isaac, and of Israel. See note on Ex. 32. 13.

20 congregation = assembly.

worshipped = did homage to. Heb. *shaḥah*. First occurrence in Gen. 18. 2.

21 sacrificed sacrifices. Ap. 43. I. iv, and 43. II. xii.

offered = offered up. Ap. 43. I. vi, and 43. II. ii.

22- did eat = they did eat.

-22-25 (*V*, p. 559). SOLOMON. SECOND INVESTITURE. (*Introversion.*)

V | x | -22. Solomon. Aggrandisement by man.
  y | 23. Accession.
  y | 24. Submission.
x | 25. Solomon. Aggrandisement by Jehovah.

-22 the second time. The first is recorded in 23. 1 and 1 Kings 1. 39.

Zadok. Solomon completed this act of David by removing Abiathar after David's death (1 Kings 2. 27).

24 the mighty men. Heb. *gibbōr*. Ap. 14. IV.

submitted. Heb. gave the hand unto: "hand" being put by Fig. *Metonymy* (of Adjunct), Ap. 6, for the submission implied by it. Cp. 2 Chron. 30. 8.

25 bestowed. Cp. 1 Kings 3. 13. 2 Chron. 1. 12. Ecc. 2. 9.

in = over.

26-30 (H², p. 545). EVENTS. IN SUM (DAVID). (*Introversion.*)

z | 26, 27. Reign over all Israel. Particulars.
  a | 28-. David's death.
  a | -28. David's successor.
z | 29, 30. Reign over all Israel. Record.

a (p. 568) 920 28 And he died in a good old age, °full of days, riches, and honour:
a and Solomon his son reigned in his stead.

z 29 Now the acts of David the king, first and last, °behold, they *are* written in the book of Samuel °the seer, and in the book of Nathan °the prophet, and in the book of °Gad the seer,
30 With all his reign and his °might, and °the times that went over him, and over Israel, and over all the kingdoms of the countries.

28 full of = satisfied with.
29 behold. Fig. *Asterismos.* Ap. 6.
the seer. Heb. *ro-'eh,* a seer of visions. Samuel was known as a *ro'eh,* but the *ro'eh* afterwards became known as a *nābī*. See note on 1 Sam. 9. 9.
the prophet. Heb. *nābī',* a spokesman, one who spoke for another. Cp. Ex. 7. 1 with Ex. 4. 16; and see notes there, and on Deut. 33. 1, and Ap. 49. First occurrence Gen. 20. 7.
Gad the seer. Heb. *ḥozeh,* a seer. *Ro'eh* = one who sees *more* clearly than the *ḥozeh.* First occ. 2 Sam. 24. 11.
30 might: or royal estate.
the times. Fig. *Metonymy* (of Adjunct), Ap. 6, put for all the events that happened in those times.

THE °SECOND BOOK OF THE °CHRONICLES.

G² A (p. 569) 920 BCE **1** AND Solomon the son of David °was strengthened in his kingdom,
and °the LORD his °God *was* with him, and magnified him exceedingly.
F 2 Then °Solomon spake unto all Israel, to the °captains of thousands and of hundreds, and to the judges, and to every governor in all Israel, the °chief of the fathers.
3 So Solomon, and all the °congregation with him, °went to the high place that *was* at °Gibeon; for there was the °tabernacle of the °congregation of God, which °Moses the servant of the LORD had made in the wilderness.
4 °But °the ark of [1] God had David °brought up from Kirjath-jearim to *the place which* David had prepared for it: for he had pitched a tent for it at Jerusalem.
5 Moreover °the brasen altar, that Bezaleel the son of Uri, the son of Hur, had made, °he put before °the [3] tabernacle of the LORD: and Solomon and the congregation sought unto it.
6 And Solomon went up thither to the brasen altar °before [1] the LORD, which *was* at the [3] tabernacle of the °congregation, and °offered a thousand burnt offerings upon it.
G a 7 °In that night did [1] God appear unto Solomon, and said unto him, "Ask what I shall give thee."
b 8 And Solomon said unto [1] God, "Thou hast shewed great °mercy unto David my father, and hast made me to reign in his stead.
9 Now, O [1] LORD [1] God, let Thy promise °unto David my father be established: for Thou hast made me king over a People °like the dust of the earth in multitude.
b 10 Give me now wisdom and °knowledge, that

TITLE, Second. See notes on p. 366.
Chronicles. See note on title of first book; and, for the parallel passages in the book of Kings, see Ap. 56. The Structure of the two books is given as a whole on p. 530.

2 Chron. **1. 1—9. 31** (G², p. 545). SOLOMON.
(Introversion and Alternation.)

G² | A | 1. 1-. Introduction.
  | B | C | 1. -1-17. Appearance of Jehovah. Personal details.
  | | D | 2. 1—7. 11. Building of Temple. Sacred.
  | *B* | *C* | 7. 12-22. Appearance of Jehovah. National details.
  | | *D* | 8. 1—9. 28. Building of cities. Secular.
  | *A* | 9. 29-31. Conclusion.

(B–*D*: Events.)

-1-17 (C, above). APPEARANCE OF JEHOVAH.
(Introversion.)

C | E | -1. Magnificence of Solomon's kingdom.
  | F | 2-6. Journey to Gibeon.
  | G | 7-12. Appearance of God.
  | *F* | 13. Return to Jerusalem.
  | *E* | 14-17. Magnificence of Solomon's kingdom.

1 was strengthened: i. e. after the events recorded in 1 Chron. 28 and 29. 1 Kings 1 and 2.
the LORD. Heb. Jehovah. Ap. 4. II.
God. Heb. Elohim. Ap. 4. I.
2 Solomon spake. Thus beginning his reign as David had ended his (1 Chron. 28. 1) by a solemn assembly.
captains = princes. **chief** = heads.
3 congregation = convocation, or muster.
went. For the reason, see 1 Kings 3. 4.
Gibeon = a high place.
tabernacle = tent. Heb. *'ohel.* Ap. 40. 3.
congregation = assembly.
Moses the servant of the LORD. See note on Deut. 34. 5. **4 But** = But indeed.
the ark. See note on 1 Chron. 13. 3. Ex. 25. 22.
brought up. Cp. 2 Sam. 6. 2, 17. 1 Chron. 15. 1.

5 the brasen altar. This is additional and supplementary to the account in 1 Kings 3. **he put.** So some codices, with two early printed editions; but many codices, with four early printed editions, Sept., and Vulg., read "was there". **the.** Sept., Syr., and Vulg. read "all the". **6 before.** A special various reading called *Sevīr* (Ap. 34) reads "which [was] before". **congregation** = assembly. **offered** = offered up. Heb. *'ālāh.* Ap. 43. I. vi.

1. 7-12 (G, above). APPEARANCE OF GOD. *(Introversion.)*

G | a | 7. God. Appearance and offer.
  | b | 8, 9. Solomon. Acknowledgment.
  | *b* | 10. Solomon. Choice.
  | *a* | 11, 12. God. Reason and gift.

7 In that night. Cp. 1 Kings 3. 5-15. **8 mercy** = lovingkindness, or grace. **9 unto** = with. **like the dust.** Figs. *Parœmia* and *Hyperbolē.* Ap. 6. **10 knowledge.** Heb. *maddā'.* A rare word = inner consciousness. Occurs only here, *vv.* 11, 12. Ecc. 10. 20 ("thought"). Dan. 1. 4 ("science"), 17 = knowledge (gained by experience, Gen. 2. 9); while "wisdom" = knowledge (gained by study).

920 I may °go out and °come in before this People:
for °who can judge this Thy °People, *that is* so
great?"

a (p. 569) 11 And [1] God said to Solomon, "Because °this
was in thine heart, and thou hast not asked
riches, wealth, or honour, nor °the life of thine
enemies, neither yet hast asked °long life; but
hast asked wisdom and [10] knowledge for thyself, that thou mayest judge My People, over
whom I have made thee king:

12 Wisdom and [10] knowledge *is* granted unto
thee; and I will give thee riches, and wealth,
and honour, such as none of the kings have
had that *have been* before thee, neither shall
there any after thee have the like."

F 13 Then Solomon °came *from his journey* to
the high place that *was* at Gibeon to Jerusalem, from before the [3] tabernacle of the [3] congregation, and reigned over Israel.

E 14 And Solomon gathered chariots and horsemen: and he had a thousand and four hundred
chariots, and twelve thousand horsemen, which
he placed in the chariot cities, and with the
king at Jerusalem.

15 And the king made silver and gold at
Jerusalem *as plenteous* °as stones, and cedar
trees made he °as the sycomore trees that *are*
in the vale for abundance.

16 And Solomon had °horses brought out of
Egypt, and °linen yarn: the king's merchants
received the linen yarn at a °price.

17 And they fetched up, and brought forth out
of Egypt a chariot for six hundred *shekels* of
silver, and an horse for an hundred and fifty:
and so brought they out *horses* for all the
kings of the Hittites, and for the kings of
Syria, °by their means.

D H (p. 570) 920-917 **2** And Solomon determined to build an
house for °the name of °the LORD, and
°an house for his kingdom.

J d 2 °And Solomon told out threescore and ten
thousand °men to bear burdens, and fourscore
thousand to hew in the mountain, and °three
thousand and six hundred to oversee them.

e 3 And Solomon sent to Huram the king of
Tyre, saying, °"As thou didst deal with David
my father, and didst send him cedars to build
him an house to dwell therein, °*even so deal
with me.*

4 °Behold, I build an house to the name of
[1] the LORD my °God, to dedicate *it* to Him,
and to burn before Him °sweet incense, and
for °the continual shewbread, and for the burnt
offerings morning and evening, on the sabbaths,
and on the new moons, and on the solemn feasts
of the [1] LORD our °God. This *is an ordinance*
for ever to Israel.

5 And the house which I build *is* °great: for
great *is* our [4] God above all gods.

6 But °who is able to build Him an house,
seeing the °heaven and heaven of °heavens
cannot contain Him? who *am* I then, that I
should build Him an house, save only to burn
sacrifice before Him?

7 Send me now therefore a [2] man °cunning to
work in gold, °and in silver, and in brass, and
in iron, and in purple, and crimson, and blue,
and that °can skill to grave with the °cunning
men that *are* with me in Judah and in Jerusalem, whom David my father did provide.

8 Send me also cedar trees, °fir trees, and
°algum trees, out of Lebanon: for I know
that thy servants [7] can skill to cut timber in
Lebanon; and, [4] behold, my servants *shall be*
with thy servants,

9 Even to prepare me timber in abundance:
for the house which I am about to build *shall
be* °wonderful great.

10 And, [4] behold, °I will give to thy servants,
the hewers that cut timber, twenty thousand

---

go out . . . come in. Fig. *Synecdoche* (of Species), Ap. 6, put for manner of life in general.
who can judge . . . ? Fig. *Erotēsis*. Ap. 6.
People, that is so great? or, this Thy great People?
11 this was in thine heart. Supplementary to the account in Kings.
the life = the soul. Heb. *nephesh*. Ap. 13.
long life = many days.
13 came from his journey to. Sept. and Vulg. read "came from".
15 as stones . . . as the sycomore trees. Fig. *Hyperbolē*. Ap. 6.
16 horses. Cp. Deut. 17. 16.
linen yarn = in droves. See note on 1 Kings 10. 28, 29.
price = tariff.
17 by their means. Cp. 1 Kings 10. 26–29.

2. 1—7. 11 (D, p. 569). BUILDING OF TEMPLE (EVENTS: SACRED). (*Introversion.*)

D | H | 2. 1. Determination to build.
  J | 2. 2–18. Preparation.
    K | 3. 1—5. 1. Execution.
  J | 5. 2—7. 10. Dedication.
H | 7. 11. Completion of building.

1 the name of. Fig. *Pleonasm*. Ap. 6. See note on Ps. 20. 1. **the LORD.** Heb. Jehovah. Ap. 4. II.
an house for his kingdom. This is described in 1 Kings 7, which is complementary to 2 Chron. 8. 1.

2–18 (J, above). PREPARATION. (*Introversion.*)

J | d | 2. Labourers.
  e | 3–10. Embassy to Hiram. Request.
  e | 11–16. Embassy to Hiram. Agreement.
d | 17, 18. Labourers.

2 And Solomon, &c. The 11th *Seder* ends here. See note on p. 366.
men. Heb. *'īsh*. Ap. 14. II.
three thousand and six hundred. Cp. 1 Kings 5. 16.
3 As = according as.
even so deal with me. Fig. *Ellipsis* (absolute). Ap. 6.
4 Behold. Fig. *Asterismos*. Ap. 6.
God. Heb. Elohim. Ap. 4. I.
sweet incense = incense of spices.
the continual shewbread. See note on Ex. 25. 30; 40. 4.
5 great. In magnificence, not in size. Not for People; but, for Jehovah's presence with them.
6 who is able . . . ? Fig. *Erotēsis*. Ap. 6.
heaven and heaven of heavens. Fig. *Polyptōton*. Ap 6.
7 cunning = clever, or skilful. See note on 1 Chron. 22. 15; 25. 7, and Ex. 26. 1.
and. Note the Fig. *Polysyndeton*. Ap. 6.
can skill = know how.
8 fir = cypress.
algum. See note on 1 Kings 10. 11.
9 wonderful great. Heb. "great and wonderful". Fig. *Hendiadys* (Ap. 6) = great, yea, wonderfully great.
10 I will give to thy servants. No discrepancy here with 1 Kings 5. 11. There the allowance was for Hiram's household at Tyre; here for Hiram's labourers in Lebanon.

920 °measures of °beaten wheat, and twenty thou-
to sand measures of barley, and twenty thousand
917 °baths of wine, and twenty thousand baths of
oil."

e 11 Then Huram the king of Tyre answered in
(p. 570) writing, which he sent to Solomon, "Because
[1]the LORD hath loved His People, He hath
made thee king over them."

12 Huram said moreover, "Blessed *be* [1]the LORD [4]God of Israel, That made °heaven and earth, Who hath given to David the king a wise son, endued with prudence and understanding, that might build an house for [1]the LORD, and an house for his kingdom.

13 And now I have sent a [7]cunning [2]man, endued with understanding, of Huram my father's,

14 The son of °a woman of the daughters of Dan, and his father *was* a [2]man of Tyre, skilful to work in gold, and in silver, in brass, in iron, in stone, and in timber, in purple, in blue, and in fine linen, and in crimson; also to grave any manner of graving, and to find out every device which shall be put to him, with thy [7]cunning men, and with the [7]cunning men of my lord David thy father.

15 Now therefore the wheat, and the barley, the oil, and the wine, which my lord hath spoken of, let him send unto his servants:

16 And **we** will cut wood out of Lebanon, as much as thou shalt need: and we will bring it to thee in °floats by sea to Joppa; and **thou** shalt carry it up to Jerusalem."

d 17 And Solomon numbered all °the strangers that *were* in the land of Israel, after the numbering wherewith David his father had numbered them; and they were found an hundred and fifty thousand and three thousand and six hundred.

18 And he set threescore and ten thousand of them *to be* bearers of burdens, and fourscore thousand *to be* hewers in the mountain, and three thousand and six hundred overseers to °set the people a work.

K L **3** Then Solomon began to build the house
(p. 571) of °the LORD at Jerusalem in °mount
917 °Moriah, °where *the LORD* appeared unto
David his father, in the place that David °had
prepared in the threshingfloor of Ornan the
Jebusite.

2 And he began to build in the second *day* of the second month, in the fourth year of his reign.

M N f 3 Now these *are the things wherein* Solomon was instructed for the building of the house of °God. The length by °cubits after the first measure *was* threescore cubits, and the breadth twenty cubits.

g 4 And the porch that *was* in the front *of the house,* the length *of it was* °according to the breadth of the house, twenty cubits, and the height *was* °an hundred and twenty: and he overlaid it within with pure gold.

f 5 And °the greater house he °cieled with °fir tree, which he overlaid with °fine gold, and set thereon °palm trees and °chains.

6 And he garnished the house with precious stones for beauty: and the gold *was* gold of Parvaim.

7 He overlaid also the house, the beams, the °posts, and the walls thereof, and the doors thereof, with gold; and graved cherubims on the walls.

8 And he made °the most holy house, the length whereof *was* according to the breadth of the house, twenty cubits, and the breadth thereof twenty cubits: and he overlaid it with fine gold, *amounting* to six hundred °talents.

9 And the °weight of the nails *was* fifty shekels of gold. And he overlaid the upper chambers with gold.

10 And in [8]the most holy °house he made two cherubims of °image work, and overlaid **them** with gold.

---

measures = *kor.* See Ap. 51. III. 3.
beaten wheat: i. e. wheat prepared for food.
baths. See Ap. 51. III. 3.
12 heaven and earth. See note on Deut. 4. 26.
14 a woman . . . of Dan. By birth. In 1 Kings 7. 14, a widow . . . of Naphtali. By marriage. No discrepancy, as alleged.
16 floats = rafts.
17 the strangers. See note on 2 Sam. 12. 31, and cp. 1 Chron. 22. 2.
18 set . . . a work = keep the people at work.

3. 1—5. 1 (K, p. 570). EXECUTION.
(*Introversion and Alternation.*)

K | L | 3. 1, 2. Commencement.
  M | N | 3. 3-17. The house.
      O | 4. 1-8. Its furniture.
  M | *N* | 4. 9. The courts.
      O | 4. 10, 11-. Their furniture.
  L | 4. -11—5. 1. Completion.

1 the LORD. Heb. Jehovah. Ap. 4. II.
mount Moriah. Not mentioned since Gen. 22. 2, nor ever again.
Moriah. Vision of Jah. Refers here to "where Jehovah appeared".
where. See note on 1 Chron. 22. 1.
had prepared. Cp. 1 Chron. 22. 14; 2 Chron. 2. 7.

3. 3-17 (N, above). THE HOUSE.
(*Alternation.*)

N | f | 3. The house.
  g | 4. Its porch.
  f | 5-14. The house.
  g | 15-17. Its pillars.

3 God. Heb. *hā-'ĕlohīm*, the [true or triune] God.
cubits. See Ap. 51. III. 2.
4 according to = in the front of.
an hundred and twenty. Read "twenty" by a transposition of letters.
5 the greater house: i. e. the holy of holies.
cieled = covered. Walls as well as roof.
fir = cypress. **fine** = pure.
palm trees: i. e. artificial.
chains = wreathen work. Only found in connection with Tabernacle and Temple.
7 posts = thresholds.
8 the most holy = the holy of holies. See note on Ex. 3. 5.
talents. See Ap. 51. II. 6.
9 weight of the nails. These small and simple things not excluded. They held all together; and, though out of sight, are remembered and named by God.
10 house. In A.V., 1611 = place.
image work = carved work. This was no breach of the second commandment, for it was by the Divine Lawgiver's own direction.

917 11 And the wings of the cherubims *were*
to twenty cubits long: one wing *of the one*
910 *cherub was* five cubits, reaching to the wall
of the house: and the other wing *was likewise*
five cubits, reaching to the wing of the other
cherub.
12 And *one* wing of the other cherub *was*
five cubits, reaching to the wall of the house:
and the other wing *was* five cubits *also*, joining to the wing of the other cherub.
13 The wings of these cherubims spread
themselves forth twenty cubits: and they stood
on their feet, and their faces *were* ° inward.
14 And he made ° the vail *of* blue, and purple,
and crimson, and fine linen, and wrought
cherubims thereon.

g 15 Also he made before the house two pillars
(p. 571) of ° thirty and five cubits high, and the chapiter
that *was* on the top of each of them *was* five
cubits.
16 And he made ° chains, *as* in ° the oracle,
and put *them* on the heads of the pillars; and
made an hundred pomegranates, and put *them*
on the chains.
17 And he reared up the pillars before the
temple, one on the right hand, and the other
on the left; and called the name of that on the
right hand ° Jachin, and the name of that on
the left ° Boaz.

13 inward = toward the Ark.
14 the vail. Not mentioned in 1 Kings 6.
15 thirty and five cubits. In 1 Kings 7. 15 = eighteen cubits. But there it is "apiece"; here they are reckoned together. See note on 1 Kings 7. 15.
16 chains = wreathen work.
the oracle. See note on 2 Sam. 16. 23.
17 Jachin . . . Boaz. See notes on 1 Kings 7. 21.

4. 1 cubits. See Ap. 51. III. 2.
3 in a cubit: or, to the height of a cubit (i.e. one-fifth of the brazen sea).
5 received and held three thousand baths. 1 Kings 7. 26 says 2,000; and it is alleged that "there must be a mistake in the figures". But no: 1 Kings 7. 26 speaks of what it usually "contained", while here it speaks of what it could actually "receive and hold".
6 offered = offered up. Heb. *'ālāh*. Ap. 43. I. vi.
7 candlesticks = lampstands.
8 basons = bowls for sprinkling.
9 court of the priests. None in Tabernacle.
11 God. Heb. Elohim. Ap. 4. I.
12 pommels = bowls.
wreaths = network.
13 upon = upon the face of.
16 the LORD. Heb. Jehovah. Ap. 4.
18 found out = searched out.
20 after the manner: i.e. the prescribed order. Cp. *v.* 7 and Ex. 27. 20, 21.
the oracle. See note on 2 Sam. 16. 23.
21 perfect = of purest. Heb. the perfections of.

O **4** Moreover he made an altar of brass,
twenty ° cubits the length thereof, and
twenty ° cubits the breadth thereof, and ten
cubits the height thereof.
2 Also he made a molten sea of ten [1] cubits
from brim to brim, round in compass, and five
[1] cubits the height thereof; and a line of thirty
[1] cubits did compass it round about.
3 And under it *was* the similitude of oxen,
which did compass it round about: ten ° in a
[1] cubit, compassing the sea round about. Two
rows of oxen *were* cast, when it was cast.
4 It stood upon twelve oxen, three looking
toward the north, and three looking toward
the west, and three looking toward the south,
and three looking toward the east: and the
sea *was set* above upon them, and all their
hinder parts *were* inward.
5 And the thickness of it *was* an handbreadth,
and the brim of it like the work of the brim
of a cup, with flowers of lilies; *and* it ° received and held three thousand baths.
6 He made also ten lavers, and put five on
the right hand, and five on the left, to wash
in them: such things as they ° offered for the
burnt offering they washed in them; but the
sea *was* for the priests to wash in.
7 And he made ten ° candlesticks of gold
according to their form, and set *them* in the
temple, five on the right hand, and five on
the left.
8 He made also ten tables, and placed *them*
in the temple, five on the right side, and five
on the left. And he made an hundred ° basons
of gold.

M N 9 Furthermore he made the ° court of the
priests, and the great court, and doors for the
court, and overlaid the doors of them with
brass.

10 And he set the sea on the right side of O
the east end, over against the south.
11 And Huram made the pots, and the
shovels, and the basons.

And Huram finished the work that he was L
to make for king Solomon for the house of
° God;
12 *To wit*, the two pillars, and the ° pommels,
and the chapiters *which were* on the top of the
two pillars, and the two ° wreaths to cover
the two ° pommels of the chapiters which
were on the top of the pillars;
13 And four hundred pomegranates on the
two [12] wreaths; two rows of pomegranates on
each wreath, to cover the two [12] pommels of
the chapiters which *were* ° upon the pillars.
14 He made also bases, and lavers made he
upon the bases;
15 One sea, and twelve oxen under it.
16 The pots also, and the shovels, and the
fleshhooks, and all their instruments, did
Huram his father make to king Solomon for
the house of ° the LORD of bright brass.
17 In the plain of Jordan did the king cast
them, in the clay ground between Succoth and
Zeredathah.
18 Thus Solomon made all these vessels in
great abundance: for the weight of the brass
could not be ° found out.
19 And Solomon made all the vessels that
were for the house of [11] God, the golden altar
also, and the tables whereon the shewbread
was set;
20 Moreover the candlesticks with their
lamps, that they should burn ° after the
manner before ° the oracle, of pure gold;
21 And the flowers, and the lamps, and the
tongs, *made he of* gold, *and* that ° perfect
gold;

917 22 And the snuffers, and the basons, and the
to spoons, and the censers, *of* °pure gold: and
910 the entry of the house, the inner doors thereof
for the most °holy *place*, and the doors of the
house of the temple, *were of* gold.

910 **5** Thus all the work that °Solomon made
for the house of °the LORD was finished:
and Solomon brought in *all* the °things that
David his father had °dedicated; °and the
silver, and the gold, and °all the instruments,
put he °among the treasures of the house of
°God.

J P j (p. 573) 2 °Then Solomon assembled the elders of
Israel, and all the heads of the tribes, the
chief of the fathers of the °children of Israel,
unto Jerusalem, to bring up °the ark of the
covenant of [1]the LORD out of the city of
David, which *is* Zion.
3 Wherefore all the °men of Israel assembled
themselves unto the king in °the feast which
was in the seventh month.
4 And all the elders of Israel came; and °the
Levites took up [2]the ark.
5 And they brought up [2]the ark, and the
°tabernacle of the congregation, and all the
°holy vessels that *were* in the tabernacle, these
did °the priests *and* the Levites bring up.

k 6 Also king Solomon, and all the °congrega-
tion of Israel that were assembled unto him
before [2]the ark, sacrificed sheep and oxen,
which could not be told nor numbered for
multitude.

j 7 And °the priests brought in [2]the ark of the
covenant of [1]the LORD unto his place, to °the
oracle of the house, into °the most holy *place*,
even under the wings of the cherubims:
8 For the cherubims spread forth *their* wings
over the place of the ark, and the cherubims
covered [2]the ark and the staves thereof above.
9 And they °drew out the staves *of the ark*,
that the ends of the staves were seen from [2]the
ark before [7]the oracle; but they were not seen
without. And there it is °unto this day.
10 *There was* °nothing in [2]the ark save the
two tables which Moses put *therein* at Horeb,
when [1]the LORD made *a covenant* with the
[2]children of Israel, when they came out of
Egypt.

k 11 And it came to pass, when the priests
were come out of the [5]holy *place*: (for °all the
priests *that were* present °were sanctified, *and*
did not *then* wait by course:
12 Also the Levites *which were* the singers,
all of them of Asaph, of Heman, of °Jeduthun,
with their sons and their brethren, *being*
arrayed in white linen, having cymbals and
psalteries and harps, stood °at the east end
of the altar, and with them an hundred and
twenty priests sounding with trumpets:)
13 It came even to pass, as the trumpeters
and singers *were* as one, to make one sound
to be heard in praising and thanking [1]the
LORD; and when they lifted up *their* voice
with the trumpets and cymbals and instruments of musick, and praised [1]the LORD, *saying*, °"For *He is* good; for His °mercy *endureth* for ever:"

22 **pure** = purified. **holy.** See note on Ex. 3. 5.

5. 1 Solomon. Some codices, with one early printed edition, read "the King Solomon".
the LORD. Heb. Jehovah. Ap. 4. II.
things . . . dedicated = holy things. See note on Ex. 3. 5. **and.** Sept., Syr., and Vulg. omit this "and".
all. Some codices, with Sept. and Syr., omit "all".
among the treasures = in the treasuries.
God. Heb. Elohim (with Art.) = the [true] God. Ap. 4. I.

5. 2—7. 10 (*J*, p. 570). DEDICATION OF HOUSE.
(*Introversion and Alternation.*)

J | P | 5. 2-13-. The feast.
  Q | h | 5. -13. The cloud.
    i | 5. 14. Inability to minister.
      R | 6. 1-11. Solomon's blessing.
        S | 6. 12, 13. His station.
      R | 6. 14-42. Solomon's prayer.
  Q | *h* | 7. 1. The fire.
    i | 7. 2, 3. Inability to minister.
  P | 7. 4-10. The feast.

5. 2-13- (P, above). THE FEAST. (*Alternation.*)

P | j | 2-5. The Ark brought up.
  k | 6. Sacrifices.
  j | 7-10. The Ark brought in.
  k | 11-13-. Worship.

2 Then Solomon. Cp. 1 Kings 8. 1-11.
children = sons.
the ark. See notes on 1 Chron. 13. 3 and Ex. 25. 22.
3 men. Heb. *'ish*. Ap. 14. II.
the feast: i. e. the Feast of Tabernacles (Lev. 23. 33, &c.).
4 the Levites took up. These were the *bearers*, but the priests (being Levites also) brought it into the house (as stated in *v.* 7 and 1 Kings 8. 3). Hence, in *v.* 5 they are called "the priests and the Levites". See note on Deut. 17. 9.
5 tabernacle = tent. Heb. *'ohel*. Ap. 40. III.
holy vessels = sanctuary vessels. See note on Ex. 3. 5.
the priests and the Levites. See note on Deut. 17. 9. **6 congregation** = convocation, or muster.
7 the priests. See note on *v.* 4.
the oracle. See note on 2 Sam. 16. 23.
the most holy place = the Holy of Holies.
9 drew out. Cp. 1 Kings 8. 8.
unto this day. This is a copy of 1 Kings 8. 6-8, or an addendum by Ezra; because it is not applicable to "the day" of the writer, as may be seen from 36. 22, 23. But may this possibly have a mysterious reference to Rev. 11 19?
10 nothing in the ark save. See note on 1 Kings 8. 9.
11 all. On this occasion all served; not "by course". Note the parenthesis in *vv.* 11, 12.
were sanctified = had sanctified themselves.
12 Jeduthun. See note on 1 Chron. 16. 41.
at the east end: i. e. facing west.
13 For He is good, &c. Cp. Ezra 3. 11.
mercy = lovingkindness, or grace.
cloud, even the house of. Sept. reads "cloud of the glory of".

6. 1-11 [For Structure see next page].

1 said. The first thirty-nine verses repeat 1 Kings 8. 12-50, with one or two complementary items, 1 Kings 8. 51-61 being omitted, and three verses added.
The LORD. Heb. Jehovah. Ap. 4. II.

that *then* the house was filled with a °cloud, Q h
even the house of [1]the LORD;

14 So that the priests could not stand to i
minister by reason of the cloud: for the glory
of [1]the LORD had filled the house of [1]God.

6 Then °said Solomon, °"The LORD hath R T l[1] (p. 574)
said that He would dwell in the thick
darkness.

m[1] 2 But I have built an house of habitation for
910 Thee, and a place for Thy dwelling for ever."

U 3 And the king turned his face, and blessed the whole °congregation of Israel: and all the °congregation of Israel stood.

U 4 And he said, "Blessed *be* [1]the LORD °God of Israel, Who hath with His °hands fulfilled *that* which He spake with His mouth to my father David, saying,

T l[2] 5 'Since the day that I brought forth My People out of the land of Egypt I chose no city among all the tribes of Israel to build an house in, that My name might be there; °neither chose I any °man to be a ruler over My People Israel:

6 But I have chosen Jerusalem, that My name might be there; and have chosen David to be over My People Israel.'

m[2] 7 Now °it was in the heart of David my father to build an house for the name of [1]the LORD [4]God of Israel.

l[3] 8 But [1]the LORD said to David my father, 'Forasmuch as it was in thine heart to build an house for My name, thou didst well in that it was in thine heart:

9 Notwithstanding thou shalt not build the house; but thy son which shall come forth out of thy loins, he shall build the house for My name.'

m[3] 10 [1]The LORD therefore hath performed His word that He hath spoken: for I am risen up in the room of David my father, and am set on the throne of Israel, °as [1]the LORD promised, and have built the house for the name of [1]the LORD [4]God of Israel.

11 And in it have I put [2]the ark, wherein *is* the covenant of [1]the LORD, that He made with the °children of Israel."

S (p. 573) 12 And he °stood before the altar of [1]the LORD in the presence of all the [3]congregation of Israel, and spread forth his hands:

13 For Solomon °had made a brasen °scaffold, of five °cubits long, and five °cubits broad, and three °cubits high, and had set it in the midst of the court: and upon it he [12]stood, and kneeled down upon his knees before all the [3]congregation of Israel, and spread forth his hands toward heaven,

R n q (p. 574) 14 And said, "O [1]LORD [4]God of Israel, *there is* no [4]God like Thee in the heaven, nor in the earth; Which keepest covenant, and *shewest* °mercy unto Thy servants, that walk before Thee with all their hearts:

15 Thou Which hast kept with Thy servant David my father that which Thou hast promised him; and spakest with Thy mouth, and hast fulfilled *it* with Thine hand, as *it is* this day.

r 16 Now therefore, O [1]LORD [4]God of Israel, keep with Thy servant David my father that which Thou hast promised him, saying, 'There shall not fail thee a [5]man in My sight °to sit upon the throne of Israel; °yet so that thy [11]children take heed to their way to walk in My law, °as thou hast walked before Me.'

17 Now then, O [1]LORD [4]God of Israel, let Thy word be °verified, which Thou hast spoken unto Thy servant David.

18 But will [4]God in very deed dwell with °men on the earth? °behold, °heaven and the heaven of heavens cannot contain Thee; °how much less this house which I have built! *q*

19 Have respect therefore to the prayer of Thy servant, and to his supplication, O [1]LORD my [4]God, to hearken unto the cry and the prayer which Thy servant prayeth before Thee: *r*

20 That Thine eyes may be open °upon this house day and night, upon the place whereof Thou hast said that Thou wouldest put Thy

---

6. 1-11 (R, p. 573). SOLOMON'S BLESSING.
(*Introversion and Repeated Alternation.*)

R | T | l[1] | 1. Words of Jehovah. Recited.
m[1] | 2. The house. Built.
U | 3. Blessing. The People.
U | 4. Blessing. Jehovah.
T | l[2] | 5, 6. Words of Jehovah. To David. Rehearsed.
m[2] | 7. The house. David's purpose.
l[3] | 8, 9. Words of Jehovah. Rehearsed.
m[3] | 10, 11. The house. Built.

3 congregation = assembly, muster, or convocation.
4 God. Heb. Elohim. Ap. 4. I.
hands. Some codices *write* "hand", but *read* "hands" (pl.).
5 neither chose I. This true of Saul. God did not choose him as He chose David; though He overruled the choice of the People. Cp. 1 Sam. 8. 5.
man. Heb. *'ish.* Ap. 14. II.
7 it was in the heart. Cp. 2 Sam. 7. 2, 3. 1 Chron. 28. 2.
10 as = according as. **11 children** = sons.
12 stood. And then knelt down. See *v.* 13. No discrepancy, as alleged.
13 had made. This also is complementary to 1 Kings 8.
scaffold: or platform (round, and bowl-like, like a pulpit). Heb. same word as rendered laver.
cubits. See Ap. 51. III. 2.

14-42 (*R*, p. 573). SOLOMON'S PRAYER.
(*Introversion.*)

R | n | 14-20. For himself.
o | 21-39. For others. The People.
p | 40, 41-. The house.
o | -41. For others. The priests.
n | 42. For himself.

14-20 (n, above). FOR HIMSELF.
(*Alternation.*)

n | q | 14, 15. Plea. Jehovah's faithfulness.
r | 16, 17. Prayer.
q | 18. Plea. Jehovah's condescension.
r | 19, 20. Prayer.

14 mercy = lovingkindness, or grace.
16 to sit = sitting.
yet so = if only. Same condition as 2 Sam. 7. 14. Conditional to Solomon, but unconditional to David, as the Land was to Abraham (Gen. 15). Therefore the throne must, and will yet be, filled by David's son and David's Lord. **as** = according as.
17 verified. Some codices, with one early printed edition, Sept., and Syr., read "I beseech Thee".
18 men. Heb. *'ādām* (with Art. = mankind). Ap. 14. I.
behold. Fig. *Asterismos.* Ap. 6.
heaven . . . heaven . . . heavens. Fig. *Polyptōton* (Ap. 6), for emphasis.
how much less. Cp. Acts 7. 48-50.
20 upon = toward.

910 name there; to hearken unto the prayer which Thy servant prayeth toward this place.

o s u^1 (p. 575) 21 Hearken therefore unto the supplications of Thy servant, and of Thy People Israel, which they shall make toward this place:

v^1 hear Thou from Thy dwelling place, *even* from heaven; and when Thou hearest, forgive.

u^2 22 If a [5]man °sin against his neighbour, °and an oath be laid upon him to make him swear, and the oath come before Thine altar in this house;

v^2 23 Then hear Thou from heaven, and do, and judge Thy servants, by requiting the °wicked, by recompensing his way upon his own head; and by °justifying the righteous, by giving him according to his righteousness.

u^3 24 And if Thy People Israel be put to the worse before the enemy, because they have [22]sinned against Thee; and shall return and confess Thy name, and pray and make supplication before Thee in this house;

v^3 25 Then hear Thou from the heavens, and forgive the [22]sin of Thy People Israel, and bring them again unto the land which Thou gavest to them and to their fathers.

u^4 26 When the heaven is shut up, and there is no rain, because they have [22]sinned against Thee; *yet* if they pray toward this place, and confess Thy name, and turn from their [22]sin, when Thou dost afflict them;

v^4 27 Then hear Thou from heaven, and forgive the sin of Thy servants, and of Thy People Israel, when Thou hast taught them the °good way, wherein they should walk; and send rain upon Thy land, which Thou hast given unto Thy People for an inheritance.

u^5 28 If there be dearth in the land, if there be pestilence, if there be blasting, or mildew, locusts, or caterpillers; if their °enemies besiege them in the cities of their land; whatsoever sore or whatsoever sickness *there be:*

v^5 29 *Then* what prayer *or* what supplication soever shall be made of any [18]man, or of all Thy People Israel, when every one shall know his own sore and his own grief, and shall spread forth his hands in this house:

30 Then hear Thou from heaven Thy dwelling place, and forgive, and render unto [5]every man according unto all his ways, whose heart Thou knowest; (for Thou only knowest the hearts of the °children of [18]men:)

31 That they may fear Thee, to walk in Thy ways, so long as they live °in the land which Thou gavest unto our fathers.

t 32 Moreover concerning the stranger, which is not of Thy people Israel, but is come from a far country for Thy great name's sake, and Thy mighty hand, and Thy stretched out arm; if they come and pray °in this house;

t 33 Then hear Thou from the heavens, *even* from Thy dwelling place, and do according to all that the stranger calleth to Thee for; that all °people of the earth may know Thy name, and fear Thee, as *doth* Thy people Israel, and may know that this house which I have built is °called by Thy name.

s w 34 If Thy People go out to war against their enemies by the way that Thou shalt send them, and they pray unto Thee toward this city which Thou hast chosen, and the house which I have built for Thy name;

x 35 Then hear Thou from the heavens their prayer and their supplication, and °maintain their cause.

w 36 If they [22]sin against Thee, (°for *there is* no [18]man which [22]sinneth not,) and Thou be angry with them, and deliver them over before *their* enemies, and they carry them away captives unto a land far off or near;

37 Yet *if* they bethink themselves in the land whither they are carried captive, and turn and pray unto Thee in the land of their captivity, saying, 'We have [22]sinned, we have done amiss, and have dealt °wickedly;'

38 If they return to Thee with all their heart and with all their °soul in the land of their captivity, whither they have carried them captives, and pray toward their land, which Thou gavest unto their fathers, and *toward* the city which Thou hast chosen, and toward the house which I have built for Thy name:

x 39 Then hear Thou from the heavens, *even* from Thy dwelling place, their prayer and their supplications, and maintain their cause,

6. 21-39 (o, p. 574). PRAYER. FOR THE PEOPLE. (*Introversion.*)

o | s | 21-31. Israel.
  t | 32. Stranger.
  t | 33. Stranger.
s | 34-39. Israel.

21-31 (s, above). ISRAEL. (*Extended Alternation.*)

s | u^1 | 21-. Worship.
  v^1 | -21. Regard.
u^2 | 22. Trouble. Sin.
  v^2 | 23. Regard.
u^3 | 24. Trouble. Defeat.
  v^3 | 25. Regard.
u^4 | 26. Trouble. Drought.
  v^4 | 27. Regard.
u^5 | 28. Trouble. Pestilence, &c.
  v^5 | 29-31. Regard.

22 sin. Heb. *chāṭā'*. Ap. 44. I.
and an oath be laid upon = and he [his neighbour] lay an oath upon (Ex. 22. 7-11. Lev. 5. 1. Prov. 29. 4. Heb. 6. 16).

23 wicked = lawless. Heb. *rāsha'*. Ap. 44. x.
justifying = acquitting.

27 good: i. e. hast directed them into the good way (cp. Gen. 46. 28).

28 enemies. Sept. reads "enemy", as in 1 Kings 8. 37.

30 children = sons.

31 in the land. Heb. "upon the face of the land". Figs. *Pleonasm* and *Prosopopœia*. Ap. 6.

32 in = toward, as in *v.* 20.

33 people = Peoples. called by: or invoked upon.

34-39 (*s*, above). ISRAEL. (*Alternation.*)

s | w | 34. Trouble. Battle.
  x | 35. Regard.
w | 36-38. Trouble. Captivity.
  x | 39. Regard.

35 maintain: or vindicate.

36 for there is, &c. Fig. *Parœmia* (by way of *Parenthesis*). Ap. 6.

37 wickedly = lawlessly. Heb. *rāsha'*. Ap. 44. x.

38 soul. Heb. *nephesh*. Ap. 13.

910 and forgive Thy People which have [22] sinned against Thee.

p (p. 574) 40 Now, my [4] God, let, I beseech Thee, Thine eyes be open,
And *let* Thine ears *be* attent unto the prayer *that is made* in this place.

41 Now therefore °arise, O [1] LORD [4] God, into Thy resting place,
Thou, and [2] the ark of Thy strength:

o Let Thy priests, O [1] LORD [4] God, be clothed with salvation,
And let Thy °saints rejoice in °goodness.

n 42 O [1] LORD [4] God, turn not away the face of °Thine Anointed:
Remember °the mercies of David Thy servant."

Q h (p. 573) **7** Now when Solomon had made an end of praying, °the fire came down from heaven, and consumed the burnt offering and the °sacrifices; and the glory of °the LORD filled the house.

i 2 And the priests could not enter into the house of [1] the LORD, because the glory of [1] the LORD had filled [1] the LORD'S house.

3 And when all the °children of Israel saw how [1] the fire came down, and the glory of [1] the LORD upon the house, they bowed themselves with their faces to the ground upon the pavement, and worshipped, and praised [1] the LORD, *saying*, "For *He is* good; for His °mercy *endureth* for ever."

P V[1] y (p. 576) 4 Then the king and all the People °offered sacrifices before [1] the LORD.

5 And king Solomon offered a sacrifice of twenty and two thousand oxen, and an hundred and twenty thousand sheep: so the king and all the People dedicated the house of °God.

z 6 And the priests waited on their offices:

z the Levites also with instruments of musick of [1] the LORD, which David the king had made to praise [1] the LORD, because His mercy *endureth* for ever, when David praised by their ministry; and the priests sounded trumpets before them, and all Israel stood.

y 7 Moreover Solomon °hallowed the middle of the court that *was* before the house of [1] the LORD: for there he °offered burnt offerings, and the fat of the peace offerings, because the brasen altar which Solomon had made was not able to receive the burnt offerings, and the meat offerings, and the fat.

V[2] a 8 Also at the same time Solomon kept °the feast seven days, and all Israel with him, a very great °congregation, from the entering in of Hamath unto °the river of Egypt.

b 9 And in the eighth day they made a solemn assembly:

b for they kept the dedication of the altar seven

a days, and the feast seven days.

10 And on the three and twentieth day of the seventh month he sent the People away into their tents, glad and merry in heart for the goodness that [1] the LORD had shewed unto David, and to Solomon, and to Israel His People.

11 Thus Solomon finished the house of [1] the LORD, and the king's house: and all that came into Solomon's heart to make in the house of [1] the LORD, and in his own house, he prosperously effected. H (p. 570)

12 And [1] the LORD °appeared to Solomon by night, and said unto him, "I have heard thy prayer, C W c (p. 576) 897

and have chosen this place to Myself for an house of sacrifice. d

13 If I shut up heaven that there be no rain, or if I command the locusts to devour the land, or if I send pestilence among My People; X e

14 If My People, °which are called by My name, shall humble themselves, f

41 arise. The following words are found in Pss. 68. 1; 132. 8, 9, by which Solomon connects his own work with David's.

saints = gracious ones. Heb. "men of grace": i.e. those who are the subjects of Jehovah's saving grace.

goodness = prosperity, well-being, blessedness.

42 Thine Anointed. Heb. Messiah.

the mercies of David. Genitive of Relation (Ap. 17) = the mercies, or lovingkindnesses, shown and assured to David (Ps. 89. 49).

7. 1 the fire came down: i.e. to consume the sacrifices. See note on Gen. 4. 4. This is complementary to 1 Kings 8. 63, 64.

sacrifices = victims. Heb. *zebah*. Ap. 43. II. xii.

the LORD. Heb. Jehovah. Ap. 4. II.

3 children = sons. **mercy** = grace.

7. 4-10 (*P*, p. 573). THE FEAST. (*Double Introversion.*)

P | V[1] | y | 4, 5. Sacrifices.
z | 6-. The priests.
z | -6. The Levites.
y | 7. Sacrifices.
V[2] | a | 8. The feast.
b | 9-. Convocation.
b | -9-. Dedication.
a | -9, 10. The feast.

4 offered = sacrificed. Heb. *zebach*. Ap. 43. I. iv.

5 God. Heb. *ha-'Elohim* = the [true] God. Ap. 4. I.

7 hallowed. See note on "holy" (Ex. 3. 5).

offered = prepared. Heb. *'āsāh*. Ap. 43. I. iii.

8 the feast: i.e. of Tabernacles.

congregation = assembly, or muster.

the river = torrent, or Wady. Heb. *nahal*.

12-22 (*C*, p. 569). APPEARANCE OF JEHOVAH (SECOND). (*Alternations and Introversion.*)

C | W | c | 12-. Prayer accepted.
d | -12. House accepted.
X | e | 13. Jehovah. Displeasure.
f | 14-. People. Humiliation.
f | -14-. People. Prayer.
e | -14. Jehovah. Regard.
W | *c* | 15. Prayer accepted.
d | 16. House accepted.
X | g | 17. Solomon. Obedience.
h | 18. Jehovah. Establishment.
g | 19. Solomon. Disobedience.
h | 20-22. Jehovah. Rejection.

12 appeared to Solomon. This was thirteen years after the dedication. Cp. 7. 1 and 8. 1. 1 Kings 6. 37; 9. 1. The fire from heaven was the immediate answer to Solomon's prayer. This later answer shows that the prayers of God's people are ever fresh before Him.

14 which are called by My name = upon whom My name is called.

f and pray, and seek My face, and turn from
(p. 576) their °wicked ways;
910 then will I °hear from heaven, and will for-
e give their °sin, and will heal their land.
W c 15 Now Mine eyes shall be open, and Mine
ears attent unto the prayer *that is made* in
this place.
d 16 For now have I chosen and sanctified this
house, that My name may be there for ever:
and Mine eyes and Mine heart shall be there
perpetually.
X g 17 And as for thee, if thou wilt walk before
Me, °as David thy father walked, and do
according to all that I have commanded thee,
and shalt observe My statutes and My judgments;
h 18 Then will I stablish the throne of thy
kingdom, according as I have °covenanted
with David thy father, saying, 'There shall
not °fail thee a °man *to be* ruler in Israel.'
g 19 But if ye turn away, and forsake My
statutes and My commandments, which I
have set before you, and shall go and serve
other gods, and worship them;
h 20 Then will I pluck them up by the roots
out of My land which I have given them; and
this house, which I have sanctified for My
name, will I cast out of My sight, and will
make it *to be* a proverb and a byword among
all °nations.
21 And this house, which is high, shall be
°an astonishment to every one that passeth
by it; so that he shall say, 'Why hath [1]the
LORD done thus unto this land, and unto this
house?'
22 And it shall be answered, 'Because they
forsook [1]the LORD °God of their fathers, Which
brought them forth out of the land of Egypt,
and laid hold on other gods, and worshipped
them, and served them: therefore hath He
brought all this °evil upon them.'"

D Y¹ i **8** And it came to pass at the end of °twenty
(p. 577) years, wherein Solomon had built the
897 house of °the LORD, and his own house,
2 That the cities which Huram had °restored
to Solomon, Solomon built them, and caused
the °children of Israel to dwell there.
3 And Solomon went to °Hamath-zobah, and
prevailed against it.
4 And he built °Tadmor in the wilderness,
and all the store cities, which he built in
Hamath.
5 Also he °built Beth-horon the upper, and
Beth-horon the nether, fenced cities, with
walls, °gates, and bars;
6 And Baalath, and all the store cities that
Solomon had, and all the chariot cities, and
the cities of the horsemen, and all that
Solomon desired to build in Jerusalem, and
in Lebanon, and throughout all the land of
his dominion.
k 7 *As for* all the people *that were* left of the
Hittites, and the Amorites, and the Perizzites,
and the Hivites, and the Jebusites, which
were not of Israel,
8 *But* of their [2]children, who were left after
them in the land, whom the [2]children of Israel °consumed not, them did Solomon °make
to pay tribute until this day.
9 But of the [2]children of Israel did Solomon
make no servants for his work; but they *were*
°men of war, and chief of his captains, and
captains of his chariots and horsemen.
10 And these *were* the chief of king Solomon's
officers, *even* two hundred and fifty, that bare
rule over the people.
11 And Solomon brought up °the daughter l
of Pharaoh out of the city of David unto the
house that he had built for her: °for he said,
"My wife shall not dwell in the house of
David king of Israel, because *the places are*
°holy, whereunto °the ark of [1]the LORD hath
come."
12 Then Solomon °offered burnt offerings k
unto [1]the LORD on the altar of [1]the LORD,
which he had built before the porch,
13 Even after a certain rate every day,
[12]offering according to the commandment of
Moses, on the sabbaths, and on the new
moons, and on the solemn feasts, °three times

---

wicked. Heb. *rūʻaʻ*. Ap. 44. viii.
hear. Fig. *Anthropopatheia*. Ap. 6.
sin. Heb. *chāṭāʼ*. Ap. 44. i.
17 as = according as.
18 covenanted = confirmed by covenant.
fail thee = be cut off from thee.
man. Heb. *ʼīsh*. Ap. 14. II.
20 nations = the peoples.
21 an astonishment. Fig. *Metonymy* (of Cause), Ap. 6 = a cause of astonishment to others.
22 God. Heb. Elohim. Ap. 4. I.
evil. Same as "wicked", *v.* 14.

8. 1—9. 28 (*D*, p. 569). EVENTS. BUILDING OF CITIES, &c. (*Repeated Alternations.*)

D | Y¹ | 8. 1-18. Acquired. Riches.
  Z¹ | 9. 1-12. Admired. Riches and wisdom.
 Y² | 9. 13-22. Acquired. Riches.
  Z² | 9. 23, 24. Admired. Riches and wisdom.
 Y³ | 9. 25-28. Acquired. Riches.

8. 1-18 (X¹, above). ACQUIRED. RICHES. (*Introversion.*)

Y¹ | i | 1-6. Hiram. Cities given and rebuilt.
  k | 7-10. Service. Civil.
   l | 11. House for Pharaoh's daughter.
  k | 12-16. Service. Sacred.
 i | 17, 18. Hiram. Navy built.

1 twenty. The number of Expectancy and Waiting, 21 – 1. Divine completeness (21) minus one (1). (Ap. 10). Cp. Gen. 31. 38, 41. Judg. 4. 3; 15. 20; 16. 31. 1 Sam. 7. 2.
the LORD. Heb. Jehovah. Ap. 4. II.
2 restored = given. Evidently these had been previously given by Solomon as pledges or "security" (1 Kings 9. 10-14). children = sons.
3 Hamath-zobah. Not identified. Perhaps = *Hama*, in the valley of Orontes N. of Damascus.
4 Tadmor = Palmyra, 150 miles north-east of Damascus.
5 built = rebuilt. Cp. Josh. 16. 3, 5. 1 Chron. 7. 22-24.
gates = double doors.
8 consumed not = destroyed not.
make to pay tribute = raise a levy of bondmen.
9 men. Heb. pl. of *ʼĕnōsh*. Ap. 14. III.
11 the daughter of Pharaoh. Taking it for granted that we know she was Solomon's wife.
for he said. The reason is complementary to 1 Kings 9. 24. holy. See note on Ex. 3. 5.
the ark. See note on 1 Chron. 13. 3. Ex. 25. 22.
12 offered = offered up. Heb. *ʻālāh*. Ap. 43. I. vi.
13 three times. Cp. Ex. 23. 14. Deut. 16. 16.

897 in the year, *even* in the feast of unleavened
to bread, and in the feast of weeks, and in the
880 feast of tabernacles.
14 And he appointed, according to the order
of David his father, the °courses of the priests
to their service, and the Levites to their charges,
to praise and minister before the priests, as
the duty of every day required: the °porters
also by their courses at every gate: for so had
David °the man of °God commanded.
15 And they departed not from the °com-
mandment of the king unto the priests and
Levites concerning any matter, or concerning
the °treasures.
16 Now all the work of Solomon was prepared °unto [1]the day of the foundation of the
house of the LORD, and until it was finished.
So the house of [1]the LORD was perfected.
i 17 Then went Solomon to Ezion-geber, and
(p. 577) to Eloth, at the sea side in the land of Edom.
18 And Huram sent him °by the hands of
his servants °ships, and servants °that had
knowledge of the sea; and they went with
the servants of Solomon to °Ophir, and took
thence four hundred and fifty °talents of gold,
and brought *them* to king Solomon.

Z[1] m 9 And °when the queen of Sheba heard of
(p. 578) the fame of Solomon, she came to prove
894? Solomon with hard questions at Jerusalem,
with a very great company,
n and camels that bare spices, and gold in
abundance, and precious stones: and when
she was come to Solomon, she communed with
him of all that was in her heart.
o 2 And Solomon told her all her °questions:
and there was nothing hid from Solomon
which he told her not.
p 3 And when the queen of Sheba had seen the
°wisdom of Solomon, °and the house that he
had built,
4 [3]And the meat of his table, and the sitting
of his servants, and the attendance of his
ministers, and their apparel; his cupbearers
also, and their apparel; and his °ascent by
which he went up into the house of °the LORD;
there was no more °spirit in her.
o 5 And she said to the king, °"*It was* a true
report which I heard in mine own land of
thine acts, and of thy wisdom:
6 Howbeit I believed not their words, until
I came, and mine eyes had seen *it*: and, °be-
hold, the one half of the greatness of thy
wisdom was not told me: *for* thou exceedest
the fame that I heard.
7 Happy *are* thy °men, and happy *are* these
thy servants, which stand continually before
thee, and hear thy wisdom.
8 Blessed be [4]the LORD thy °God, Which
delighted in thee to set thee on His throne,
to be king for [4]the LORD thy °God: because
thy °God loved Israel, to establish them for
ever, therefore made He thee king over them,
to do judgment and °justice."
n 9 And she gave the king an hundred and
twenty °talents of gold, and of spices great
abundance, and precious stones: neither was
there any such spice as the queen of Sheba
gave king Solomon.

14 courses. Cp. 1 Chron. 24. 1.
porters = gatekeepers. Cp. 1 Chron. 9. 17.
man. Heb. *'ish.* Ap. 14. II.
the man of God. See Ap. 49.
God. Heb Elohim. Ap. 4. I.
15 commandment: or commandments.
treasures = treasuries.
16 unto. Sept., Syr., and Vulg. read "from".
18 by the hands of. Fig. *Pleonasm.* Ap. 6.
ships. From Tyre, in the Mediterranean, to the Red Sea. To show that this was not insuperable (as some have imagined) the next clause is added.
that had knowledge of the sea. This is the explanation of the possibility of such voyages being possible. And why not?
Ophir. First occurrence Gen. 10. 29, where Ophir, the son of Joktan, was the ancestor of several Arabian tribes. Rhodesia is probably the land indicated. About five hundred ruins are scattered over a large area. There are evidences of gold-smelting in the great Zimbawe buildings, where the ancient ruins resemble the ruins in Syria, temple and fortress being combined. The name Africa may have come from א (A or O), פ (ph), ר (r), with the Latin termination "ica". *Afur*, on the Zambesi, may also be connected with the ancient name. Tharshish ships for Ezion-geber sailed thither to East Africa, as well as to Arabia and India. The Queen of Sheba being mentioned in close connection with Ophir (*v.* 10), as hearing about Solomon, furnishes further evidence. Cp. 1 Kings 9. 28.
talents. See Ap. 51. II. 6.

9. 1-12 (Z[1], p. 577). ADMIRED. RICHES AND WISDOM. (*Introversion.*)

Z[1] | m | 1-. Queen of Sheba. Journey.
  n | -1. Presents brought.
   o | 2. What she heard.
    p | 3, 4. What she saw.
   o | 5-8. What she said.
  n | 9-11. Presents exchanged.
 m | 12. Queen of Sheba. Return.

1 when the queen of Sheba heard. For further notes, see the parallel passages in 1 Kings 10. Ap. 56.
2 questions = words, or matters.
3 wisdom. Put by Fig. *Metonymy* (of Cause) for the effects produced by it.
and. Note the Fig. *Polysyndeton* (Ap. 6) in *vv.* 3 and 4.
4 ascent: i. e. the causeway of 1 Chron. 26. 16, 18.
the LORD. Heb. Jehovah. Ap. 4. II.
spirit. Heb. *rūach.* Ap. 9.
5 It was a true report. Heb. The word was truth.
6 behold. Fig. *Asterismos.* Ap. 6.
7 men. Heb. pl. *'ěnōsh.* Ap. 14. III.
8 God. Heb. Elohim. Ap. 4. I.
justice = righteousness.
9 talents. See Ap. 51. II. 6.
10 algum trees. See note on 1 Kings 10. 11.
11 terraces = stairs, or balustrades. Cp. 1 Kings 10. 12.
12 she had brought. This, like other differences, is complementary.

10 And the servants also of Huram, and the
servants of Solomon, which brought gold from
Ophir, brought °algum trees and precious
stones.
11 And the king made *of* the algum trees
°terraces to the house of [4]the LORD, and to
the king's palace, and harps and psalteries for
singers: and there were none such seen before
in the land of Judah.
12 And king Solomon gave to the queen of *m*
Sheba all her desire, whatsoever she asked,
beside *that* which °she had brought unto the
king. So she turned, and went away to her
own land, she and her servants.

Y² q (p. 579) 897 to 880 13 Now the weight of gold that came to Solomon in one year was °six hundred and threescore and six [9]talents of gold;
14 Beside *that which* °chapmen and merchants brought. And all the kings of Arabia and governors of the country brought gold and silver to Solomon.

r 15 And king Solomon made two hundred °targets *of* beaten gold: six hundred *shekels* of beaten gold went to one °target.
16 And three hundred °shields *made he of* beaten gold: three hundred *shekels* of gold went to one °shield. And the king put them in the °house of the forest of Lebanon.
17 Moreover the king made a great throne of ivory, and overlaid it with pure gold.
18 And *there were* °six steps to the throne, with a footstool of gold, *which were* fastened to the throne, and °stays on each side of the sitting place, and two lions standing by the stays:
19 And twelve lions stood there on the one side and on the other upon the [18]six steps. There was not the like made in any kingdom.
20 And all the drinking vessels of king Solomon *were of* gold, and all the vessels of the [16]house of the forest of Lebanon *were of* °pure gold: none *were of* silver; it was *not* any thing accounted of in the days of Solomon.

q 21 For the king's ships went to Tarshish with the servants of Huram: every three years once came °the ships of Tarshish bringing gold, and silver, ivory, and apes, and peacocks.

r 22 And king Solomon passed all the kings of the earth in riches and wisdom.

Z² (p. 577) 23 And all the kings of the earth sought the presence of Solomon, to hear his wisdom, that [8]God had put in his heart.
24 And they brought °every man his present, vessels of silver, and vessels of gold, and raiment, °harness, and spices, horses, and mules, a rate year by year.

Y³ 25 And Solomon had °four thousand stalls for horses and chariots, and twelve thousand horsemen; whom he bestowed in the chariot cities, and with the king at Jerusalem.
26 And he °reigned over all the kings from the °river even unto the land of the Philistines, and to the °border of Egypt.
27 And the king made silver in Jerusalem as stones, and cedar trees made he as the sycomore trees that *are* in the low plains in abundance.
28 And they brought unto Solomon °horses out of Egypt, and out of all lands.

A (p. 569) 29 Now the rest of the acts of Solomon, first and last, *are* they not written in the book of Nathan the °prophet, and in the prophecy of Ahijah the Shilonite, and in the visions of Iddo the °seer °against Jeroboam the son of Nebat?
30 And Solomon reigned in Jerusalem over all Israel forty years.
31 And Solomon °slept with his fathers, and he was buried in the city of David his father: and Rehoboam his son reigned in his stead.

9. 13-22 (Y², p. 577). ACQUIRED. RICHES.
(*Alternation.*)

Y² | q | 13, 14. Importation.
   r | 15-20. Manufacture.
   q | 21. Importation.
   r | 22. Possession.

13 six hundred and threescore and six. Ap. 10.
14 chapmen. Heb. *tūr*, travellers, or merchants. Eng. = cheapmen, or traffickers.
15 targets = pointed or bossed shields. Heb. *ẓinnah.*
16 shields = covering or protecting shields. Heb. *māginnīm.*
house of the forest of Lebanon. This is the palace of cedar in Jerusalem (1 Kings 7. 2).
18 six. See Ap. 10.
stays = supports. Heb. = hands.
20 pure = purified.
21 the. No article in the Heb. here.
24 every man. Heb. *'ish.* Ap. 14. II.
harness = armour.
25 four thousand. See note on 1 Kings 4. 26.
26 reigned = was suzerain.
river: i. e. Euphrates.
border. Not river. Gen. 15. 18 yet waits fulfilment.
28 horses. Yet horses out of Egypt had a leading part in destroying Judah. Cp. 12. 3, 4, 9. Ps. 33. 17.
29 prophet . . . seer. Heb. *nabī . . . chōzeh.* See note on 1 Chron. 29. 29.
against Jeroboam. So that he had warning from God.
31 slept with his fathers. See note on Deut. 31. 16. Solomon died at the age of sixty.

10. 1—12. 16 (G³, p. 545). REHOBOAM.
(*Repeated Alternation*).

G³ | A¹ | 10. 1. Personal events. Accession.
   B¹ | 10. 2—11. 4. Public events. Revolt of Jeroboam.
   A² | 11. 5—12. 1. Personal events.
   B² | 12. 2-12. Public events. Invasion of Shishak.
   A³ | 12. 13-16. Personal. Records and death.

1 Rehoboam went. Cp. 1 Kings 12. 1-19.
all. "All" put by Fig. *Synecdoche* (of the Whole) for the greater part or representatives.

10. 2—11. 4 (B¹, above). REVOLT OF JEROBOAM. (*Introversion.*)

B¹ | C | 2, 3-. Jeroboam and Rehoboam.
   D | -3-5. First application.
   D | 6-19. Second application.
   C | 11. 1-4. Jeroboam and Rehoboam.

2 Jeroboam the son of Nebat. Our acquaintance with him is assumed (1 Kings 11. 26-40).

10. 3-19 (D and *D*, above). APPLICATIONS.

D	s¹	-3, 4. Petition made.	The first.
	t¹	5. Dismissal.	
D	s²	6-12. Petition. Considered.	The second.
	t²	12-14. Answer. Returned.	
	s³	15. Petition. Repeated.	
	t³	16-19. Answer. Consequences.	

G³ A¹ (p. 579) **10** And °Rehoboam went to Shechem: for to Shechem were °all Israel come to make him king.
B¹ C 2 And it came to pass, when °Jeroboam the son of Nebat, who *was* in Egypt, whither he had fled from the presence of Solomon the king, heard *it*, that Jeroboam returned out of Egypt.
3 And they sent and called him.
D s¹ So Jeroboam and all Israel came and spake to Rehoboam, saying,
880 4 "Thy father made our yoke grievous: now therefore ease thou somewhat the grievous

servitude of thy father, and his heavy yoke that he put upon us, and we will serve thee."

t[1] (p. 579) 5 And he said unto them, "Come again unto me °after three days." And the People departed.

s[2] 6 And king Rehoboam took counsel with the old men that had stood before Solomon his father while he yet lived, saying, "What counsel give ye *me* to return answer to this People?"

7 And they spake unto him, saying, "If thou be kind to this People, and please them, and speak good words to them, they will be thy servants for ever."

8 But he forsook the counsel which the old men gave him, and took counsel with the young men that were brought up with him, that stood before him.

9 And he said unto them, "What °advice give ye that we may return answer to this People, which have spoken to me, saying, 'Ease somewhat the yoke that thy father did put upon us?'"

10 And the young men that were brought up with him spake unto him, saying, "Thus shalt thou answer the People that spake unto thee, saying, 'Thy father made our yoke heavy, but make thou *it* somewhat lighter for us;' thus shalt thou say unto them, 'My little *finger* shall be thicker than my father's loins.

11 For whereas my father put a heavy yoke upon you, I will put more to your yoke: my father chastised you with whips, but I *will chastise you* with scorpions.'"

t[2] 12 So Jeroboam and all the People came to Rehoboam on the third day, °as the king bade, saying, "Come again to me on the third day."

13 And the king answered them roughly; and king Rehoboam forsook the counsel of the old men,

14 And answered them after the [9]advice of the young men, saying, "My father °made your yoke heavy, but I will add thereto: my father chastised you with whips, but I *will chastise you* with scorpions."

s[3] 15 So the king hearkened not unto the People: for the cause was of °God, that °the LORD might perform His °word, which He spake by the hand of Ahijah the Shilonite to Jeroboam the son of Nebat.

t[3] 16 And when [1]all Israel °*saw* that the king would not hearken unto them, the People answered the king, saying, "What portion have we in David? and *we have* none inheritance in the son of Jesse: °every man to °your °tents, O Israel: *and* now, David, see to thine own house." So all Israel went to their tents.

17 But *as for* the °children of Israel that °dwelt in the cities of Judah, Rehoboam reigned over them.

18 Then king Rehoboam sent Hadoram that *was* over the tribute; and the [17]children of Israel °stoned him with stones, that he died. But king Rehoboam made speed to get him up to *his* chariot, to flee to Jerusalem.

19 And Israel rebelled against the house of David unto this day.

C **11** And when Rehoboam was come to Jerusalem, he gathered of the house of Judah and °Benjamin an hundred and fourscore thousand chosen *men*, which were warriors, to fight against Israel, that he might bring the kingdom again to Rehoboam.

2 But the word of °the LORD came to °Shemaiah °the man of °God, saying,

3 "Speak unto Rehoboam the son of Solomon, king of Judah, and to all Israel in Judah and Benjamin, saying,

4 'Thus saith [2]the LORD, 'Ye shall not go up, nor fight against your brethren: return °every man to his house: for °this thing is done of Me.'''" And they obeyed the words of [2]the LORD, and returned from going against Jeroboam.

5 And Rehoboam dwelt in Jerusalem, and °built cities °for defence in Judah. A[2] E (p. 580)

6 He built even Beth-lehem, and Etam, and Tekoa,

7 And Beth-zur, and Shoco, and Adullam,

8 And Gath, and Mareshah, and Ziph,

9 And Adoraim, and Lachish, and Azekah,

10 And Zorah, and Aijalon, and Hebron, which *are* in Judah and in Benjamin fenced cities.

11 And he fortified the strong holds, and put captains in them, and store of victual, and of oil and wine.

12 And in every several city *he put* shields and spears, and made them exceeding strong, having Judah and Benjamin on his side.

---

5 after three days: i. e. the third day (cp. *v.* 12).

9 advice = counsel. **12 as** = according as.

14 made. So some codices, with six early printed editions, Sept., Syr., and Vulg. (as 1 Kings 12. 14); but the current Heb. text reads "I will make".

15 God. Heb. Elohim. Ap. 4. I.

the LORD. Heb. Jehovah. Ap. 4. II.

word, which He spake. Our acquaintance with 1 Kings 11. 29–39 is taken for granted.

16 saw. Some codices, with seven early printed editions, read this word "saw", in the text.

every man. Heb. *'ish.* Ap. 14. II.

your tents. Primitive text reads "your gods". One of the emendations of the *Sōpherim.* See Ap. 33, and cp. 2 Sam. 20. 1.

tents = homes. Cp. 2 Sam. 18. 17; 19. 8; 20. 1.

17 children = sons.

dwelt in the cities of Judah. See note on 1 Kings 12. 17.

18 stoned him with stones. Fig. *Polyptōton.* Ap. 6. See note on Lev. 24. 14.

11. 1 Benjamin. See 1 Kings 11. 36.

2 the LORD. Heb. Jehovah. Ap. 4. II.

Shemaiah. Cp. 12. 5 and 1 Kings 12. 22. See note on Ps. 90, title. **the man of God.** See Ap. 49.

God. Heb. Elohim. Ap. 4. I.

4 every man. Heb. *'ish.* Ap. 14. II.

this thing is done of Me. As a chastisement for the apostasy of Solomon, and the arrogance of Rehoboam.

11. 5–12. 1 (A[2], p. 579). PERSONAL EVENTS. (*Alternation.*)

A[2] | E | 11. 5–12. Residence.
F | 11. 13–17. Faithfulness.
E | 11. 18–23. Marriage.
F | 12. 1. Apostasy.

5–12 These particulars are complementary. Ap. 56.

5 built = rebuilt.

for defence. Evidently these fifteen cities were for defence against Egypt, because of Jeroboam's influence there (10. 2). His fears were well grounded (12. 2, 4 and 1 Kings 14. 25).

F (p. 580) 13 And the priests and the Levites that *were*
in °all Israel resorted to him out of all their
°coasts.
14 For the Levites left their suburbs and
their possession, and came to Judah and Jerusalem: for Jeroboam and his sons had cast
them off from executing the priest's office unto
[2]the LORD:
15 And he ordained him priests for the high
places, and for the °devils, and for the calves
which °he had made.
16 And °after them °out of all the tribes of
Israel such as °set their hearts to seek [2]the
LORD [2]God of Israel came to Jerusalem, to
sacrifice unto [2]the LORD [2]God of their fathers.
17 So they strengthened the kingdom of
880 Judah, and made Rehoboam the son of Solo-
to mon strong, °three years: for three years they
877 walked in the way of David and Solomon.

E 18 And Rehoboam °took him Mahalath the
daughter of Jerimoth the son of David to wife,
and Abihail the daughter of Eliab the son of
Jesse;
19 °Which bare him °children; Jeush, and
Shamariah, and Zaham.
20 And after her he took °Maachah the
daughter of °Absalom; which bare him Abijah, and Attai, and Ziza, and Shelomith.
21 And Rehoboam loved [20]Maachah the
daughter of [20]Absalom above all his wives
and his concubines: (°for he took eighteen wives,
and threescore concubines; and begat twenty
and eight sons, and threescore daughters.)
22 And Rehoboam made Abijah the son of
Maachah the °chief, *to be* ruler among his
brethren: for *he thought* to make him king.
23 And he dealt wisely, and dispersed of all
his [19]children throughout all the countries of
Judah and Benjamin, unto every fenced city:
and he gave °them victual in abundance. And
he desired many °wives.

F **12** And it came to pass, when Rehoboam
had established the kingdom, and had
strengthened himself, °he forsook the law of
°the LORD, and °all Israel with him.

B² u (p. 581) 875 2 And it came to pass, *that* in the °fifth year of
king Rehoboam °Shishak king of Egypt came
up °against Jerusalem, because they had °trans-
gressed against [1]the LORD,
3 With twelve hundred chariots, and threescore thousand horsemen: and the people *were*
without number that came with him out of
Egypt; the °Lubims, the °Sukkiims, and the
Ethiopians.
4 And he took the fenced cities which *pertained* to Judah, and came to Jerusalem.

v 5 Then came °Shemaiah the prophet to Rehoboam, and *to* the princes of Judah, that were
gathered together to Jerusalem because of
Shishak, and said unto them, "Thus saith
[1]the LORD, 'Ye have forsaken Me, and therefore have I also left you in the hand of
Shishak.'"

w 6 Whereupon the °princes of °Israel and the
king humbled themselves; and they said,
[1]"The LORD *is* righteous."

x 7 And when [1]the LORD saw that they
humbled themselves, the word of [1]the LORD
came to Shemaiah, saying, "They have
humbled themselves; *therefore* I will not
destroy them, but I will grant them °some
deliverance; and My wrath shall not be
poured out upon Jerusalem by the hand of
Shishak.
8 Nevertheless they shall be his servants;
that they may know °My service, and the
service of the kingdoms of the countries."

9 So Shishak king of Egypt came up °against u
Jerusalem, and took away the treasures of
the house of [1]the LORD, and the treasures
of the king's house; he took all: he carried
away also the shields of gold which Solomon
°had made.
10 Instead of which king Rehoboam made v

---

13 all Israel resorted to him. Thus the mingling of Israel with Judah was continued. See note on 1 Kings 12. 17. **coasts** = borders.
15 devils = hairy ones, or goats representing demons. **he** = Jeroboam.
16 after them = following them.
out of all the tribes. See notes on *vv.* 13, 14 above, and 1 Kings 12. 17. **set** = gave.
17 three years. See note on 12. 2.
18 took him Mahalath . . . and Abihail. Render "took him with Malahath . . . Abihail".
19 Which, i.e. Which [latter]. **children** = sons.
20 Maachah. Her other name was Michaiah (13. 2). **Absalom.** Same as Abishalom (1 Kings 15. 2).
21 for. Note the Fig. *Parenthesis.* Ap. 6.
22 chief = head. **23 them:** i.e. the sons. **wives** = wives [for them].

12. 1 he forsook. It is taken for granted that we know the details of 1 Kings 14. 22-24.
the LORD. Heb. Jehovah. Ap. 4. II.
all. Fig. *Synecdoche* (of Whole), Ap. 6, put for the part (viz. the ten tribes).

12. 2-12 (B², p. 579). PUBLIC EVENTS. INVASION BY SHISHAK. (*Extended Alternation.*)

B² | u | 2-4. Invasion.
 v | 5. Threatening of Jehovah.
 w | 6. Humiliation.
 x | 7, 8. Mitigation.
 u | 9. Invasion.
 v | 10, 11. Preparation of Rehoboam.
 w | 12-. Humiliation.
 x | -12. Mitigation.

2 fifth year. If the 390 years of Ezek. 4. 5 date back from the 5th year of Jehoiakin's captivity, they end 874, the close of Shishak's invasion.
Shishak. There is an inscription by Shishak on the outside of the south wall of the temple of Ammon at Karnac, in which he names the "king of Judah", and gives a list of 120 fortified cities he took.
against Jerusalem. See Ap. 53.
transgressed. Heb. *mā'al.* Ap. 44. xi.
3 Lubims = Libyans, west of Egypt.
Sukkiims, on east coast of Africa.
5 Shemaiah. Cp. 11. 2 and 1 Kings 12. 22.
6 princes of Israel. See note on 1 Kings 12. 17.
Israel. A special various reading called *Sevir* (Ap. 34) reads "Judah", as well as in 1 Chron. 22. 17; 23. 2. Otherwise "Israel" is put for "Judah".
7 some = for a little while. See note on Prov. 5. 14.
8 My service. In contrast with the service of their enemies. The difference between God's service and men's servitude. A few codices, and six early printed editions, read "his service".
9 against Jerusalem. See note on Judg. 1. 8, and Ap. 53. **had made.** Cp. 10. 17.

874 shields of brass, and committed *them* to the
hands of the °chief of the °guard, that kept
the entrance of the king's house.
11 And when the king entered into the house
of [1]the LORD, the [10]guard came and fetched
them, and brought them again into the [10]guard
chamber.

w (p. 581) 12 And when he humbled himself,
x the wrath of [1]the LORD turned from him, that
He would not destroy *him* altogether: and
also in Judah °things went well.

A[3] (p. 579) 880 to 863 13 So king Rehoboam strengthened himself
in Jerusalem, and reigned: for Rehoboam *was*
one and forty years old when he began to
reign, and he reigned seventeen years in Jerusalem, the city which [1]the LORD °had chosen
out of all the tribes of Israel, to put His name
there. And his mother's name *was* Naamah
°an Ammonitess.
14 And °he did °evil, because he °prepared
not his heart to seek [1]the LORD.
15 Now the acts of Rehoboam, first and last,
°*are* they not written in the °book of Shemaiah
the prophet, and of °Iddo the °seer concerning
genealogies? And *there were* °wars between
Rehoboam and Jeroboam continually.
16 And Rehoboam °slept with his fathers,
and was buried in the city of David: and
°Abijah his son reigned in his stead.

G[4] A (p. 582) 863 to 860 **13** Now in the °eighteenth year of king
Jeroboam began Abijah to reign over
Judah.
2 He reigned three years in Jerusalem.
His mother's name also *was* °Michaiah the
daughter of °Uriel of Gibeah. And there was
war between Abijah and Jeroboam.

B 3 And Abijah set the battle in array with
an army of valiant °men of war, *even* °four
hundred thousand chosen °men: Jeroboam
also set the battle in array against him with
°eight hundred thousand chosen °men, *being*
°mighty men of valour.

C a 4 And Abijah stood up upon mount Zemaraim,
which *is* in °mount Ephraim, and said, "Hear
me, thou Jeroboam, and all Israel;
5 °Ought ye not to know that °the LORD
°God of Israel gave the kingdom over Israel
to David for ever, °*even* to him and to his sons
by °a covenant of salt?

b 6 Yet Jeroboam the son of Nebat, the servant
of Solomon the son of David, is risen up, and
hath °rebelled against his °lord.

c 7 And there are gathered unto him vain
°men, the °children of Belial, and have
strengthened themselves against Rehoboam
the son of Solomon, when Rehoboam °was
°young and tenderhearted, and could not
withstand them.

a 8 And now ye think to withstand °the kingdom of [5]the LORD in the hand of the sons
of David;

b and ye *be* a great multitude, and *there are*
with you golden calves, which Jeroboam
°made you for gods.
9 °Have ye not cast out the priests of [5]the
LORD, the sons of Aaron, and the Levites,
and have made you priests after the manner

---

10 chief = princes. **guard** = runners.
12 things went well. Heb. "there were good words [spoken]": i. e. there were congratulations.
13 had chosen. Cp. 6. 6 and 1 Kings 12. 25-33.
an = the.
14 he did evil. Cp. 1 Kings 14. 22-24.
evil. Heb *ra'a'*. Ap. 44. viii.
prepared, or fixed. Cp. Ps. 57. 7; 108. 1; and 112. 7.
15 are they not . . . ? Fig. *Erotēsis*. Ap. 6.
book = words. **Iddo.** Cp. 9. 29; 13. 22.
seer. Heb. *ḥōzeh*. See note on 1 Chron. 29. 29.
wars. Cp. 1 Kings 14. 30.
16 slept with his fathers. See note on Deut. 31. 16.
Abijah. Called Abijam (1 Kings 14. 31). See note on 1 Chron. 25. 11.

13. 1—14. 1- (G[4], p. 545). ABIJAH.
(*Introversion.*)

G[4] | A | 13. 1, 2. Introduction.
B | 13. 3. War declared.
C | 13. 4-12. Address to Jeroboam.
B | 13. 13-21. War made.
A | 13. 21—14. 1-. Conclusion.

1 eighteenth year. Cp. 1 Kings 15. 1.
2 Michaiah. Called also Maachah in 11. 20; 1 Kings 15. 2. See note on 1 Chron. 25. 11. Michaiah = Who is like Jehovah? This name used of her as the queen-mother; but she is called Maachah = oppression, when speaking of her idolatry (15. 16).
Uriel of Gibeah. Josephus (*Ant.* VIII. 10. 1) says he was the husband of Tamar the daughter of Absalom, and the mother of Michaiah. See above, 11. 20. 1 Kings 15. 2.
3 men of. Heb. *gibbōr*. Ap. 14. IV.
four hundred . . . eight hundred. Note the steady increase of Judah and the decrease of Israel: Rehoboam could assemble 180,000; Abijah (eighteen years later), 400,000; Asa (six years later), 580,000; Jehoshaphat (thirty-two years later), 1,160,000. On the other hand, with Israel, Jeroboam could assemble 800,000, while Ahab's army was compared to "two little flocks of kids" (1 Kings 20. 27), which could not stand against the Syrians. This increase of Judah was caused by the constant emigration of Israelites from the ten tribes. See note on 1 Kings 12. 17.
men. Heb. *'ish*. Ap. 14. II.
mighty men. Heb. *gibbōr*. Ap. 14. IV.

13. 4-12 (C, above). ADDRESS TO JEROBOAM.
(*Extended Alternation.*)

C | a | 4, 5. Kingdom given.
b | 6. Rebellion against Rehoboam.
c | 7. Dependence of Jeroboam on man.
a | 8-. Kingdom withstood.
b | -8-11. Rebellion against Jehovah.
c | 12. Dependence of Abijah on God.

4 mount = hill country: i. e. of Ephraim.
5 Ought ye not . . . ? Fig. *Erotēsis*. Ap. 6.
the LORD. Heb. Jehovah. Ap. 4. II.
God. Heb. Elohim. Ap. 4. I.
even to him. Israel's king must be of David's line.
a covenant of salt. See notes on Lev. 2. 13 and Num. 18. 19. This is the third of the three occurrences.
6 rebelled. Cp. 1 Kings 11. 26.
lord. A.V., 1611, had "LORD". Heb. *'Adonai*. Ap. 4. VIII. 1. Heb. pl. = his overlord.
7 men. Heb. pl. *'ěnōsh*. Ap. 14. III.
children = sons.
was. Heb. *hāyāh* = became, or showed himself [to be young and weak]. **young.** Cp. 10. 8; 12. 13.
8 the kingdom of the LORD. Once pertaining to the whole nation (1 Chron. 28. 5. 2 Chron. 9. 8), now confined to Judah. **made you.** Cp. 1 Kings 12. 28.
9 Have ye not . . . ? Cp. 11. 14. Fig. *Erotēsis*. Ap. 6.

863 of the °nations of *other* lands? so that who-
to soever cometh to °consecrate himself with
860 a young bullock and °seven rams, *the same*
may be a priest of *them that are* no gods.
10 But as for **us**, [5]the LORD *is* our [5]God, and
we have not forsaken Him; and the priests,
which minister unto [5]the LORD, *are* the sons
of Aaron, and the Levites *wait* upon *their*
business:
11 And they °burn unto [5]the LORD every
morning and every evening burnt sacrifices
and sweet incense: the shewbread also *set
they in order* upon the pure table; and the
°candlestick of gold with the lamps thereof,
to burn every evening: for **we** keep the charge
of [5]the LORD our [5]God; but **ye** have forsaken
Him.

c 12 And, °behold, [5]God Himself *is* with us
(p. 582) for *our* captain, and His priests with °sound-
ing trumpets to cry alarm against you. O
[7]children of Israel, fight ye not against [5]the
LORD [5]God of your fathers; for ye shall not
prosper."

B d 13 But Jeroboam caused an ambushment to
(p. 583) come about behind them: so they were before
Judah, and the ambushment *was* behind them.

e 14 And when Judah looked back, °behold, the
battle *was* before and behind: and they cried
unto [5]the LORD, and the priests sounded with
the trumpets.
15 Then the [3]men of Judah gave a shout:
and as the [3]men of Judah shouted, it came to
pass, that [5]God smote Jeroboam and all Israel
before Abijah and Judah.

d 16 And the [7]children of Israel fled before
Judah: and [5]God delivered them into their
hand.
17 And Abijah and his People slew them
with a great slaughter: so there fell down
slain of Israel five hundred thousand chosen
[3]men.
18 Thus the [7]children of Israel were brought
under at that time, and the [7]children of Judah
prevailed, because they relied upon [5]the LORD
[5]God of their fathers.

e 19 And Abijah pursued after Jeroboam, and
took cities from him, Beth-el with the towns
thereof, and °Jeshanah with the towns thereof,
and °Ephrain with the towns thereof.
20 Neither did Jeroboam recover strength
again in the days of Abijah: and [5]the LORD
struck him, and °he died.

A 21 But Abijah waxed mighty, and married
fourteen wives, and begat twenty and two
sons, and sixteen daughters.
22 And the rest of the acts of Abijah, and
his ways, and his sayings, *are* written in the
°story of the prophet °Iddo.

14 So Abijah °slept with his fathers, and
they buried **him** in the city of David:
G^5 D and Asa his son reigned in his stead. In his
860 days the land was °quiet ten years.
to 2 And Asa did *that which was* good and
850 right in the eyes of °the LORD his °God:

E F^1 f 3 For he °took away the altars of the strange
gods, and °the high places, and brake down
the °images, and cut down the °groves:

nations = Peoples.
consecrate. See note on Ex. 28. 41. Lev. 9. 17.
seven rams. In Ex. 29. 1 and Lev. 8. 2 only "two rams" appointed. But religion and ritual, being for the flesh, always add outward things while they diminish the spiritual.
11 burn = "burn [as incense]". Heb. *kāṭar*. Ap. 43. I. vii. **candlestick** = lampstand.
12 behold. Fig. *Asterismos*. Ap. 6.
sounding trumpets. Cp. Num. 10. 9; 31. 6.

13. 13-20 (*B*, p. 582). WAR MADE.
(*Alternation*.)

B | d | 13. Jeroboam. Assault.
  e | 14, 15. Abijah. Cry to Jehovah.
 d | 16-18. Jeroboam. Defeat.
  e | 19, 20. Abijah. Victory through Jehovah.

14 behold. Fig. *Asterismos*.
19 Jeshanah. Now, probably *'Ain Sīnia*, in Valley north of Bethel.
Ephrain. Identified as "Ephraim" (John 11. 54).
20 he died. Fig. *Hysterologia*. Ap. 6. Jeroboam outlived Abijah. See note on 1 Kings 14. 20.
22 story. Heb. *midrash* = a historical commentary, having in view the moral instruction rather than the historic facts. Occurs only here and 24. 27.
Iddo. Cp. 9. 29; 12. 15.

14. -1—16. 14 (G^5, p. 545). ASA
(*Introversion*.)

G^5 | D | 14. -1, 2. Introduction.
  E | 14. 3-8. Events. Personal. Well-doing.
  E | 14. 9—16. 10. Events. Public. War.
 D | 16. 11-14. Conclusion.

1 slept, &c. See note on Deut. 31. 16.
quiet ten years. There was only border fighting (1 Kings 15. 19, 32), but no actual campaign. See note on 15. 19.
2 the LORD. Heb. Jehovah. Ap. 4. II.
God. Heb. Elohim. Ap. 4. I.

14. 3-8 (E, above). EVENTS. PERSONAL.
(*Introversions*.)

E | F^1 | f | 3. Removal of idolatry.
  g | 4-. Exhortation to Judah. Faith.
  g | -4. Exhortation to Judah. Works.
  f | 5. Removal of idolatry.
 F^2 | h | 6. Defence. Cities.
  i | 7-. Exhortation to Judah. Works.
  i | -7. Exhortation to Judah. Faith.
  h | 8. Defence. Armies.

3 took away . . . the high places. No "discrepancy" between this and 15. 17; for the high places referred to there belonged to "Israel", not Judah. Asa could do nothing in Israel.
images = sun images.
groves. Heb. *'Asherim*. See note on Ex. 34. 13, and Ap. 42. See note on Isa. 17. 8.
7 gates = double doors.

4 And commanded Judah to seek [2]the LORD g
[2]God of their fathers,
and to do the law and the commandment. *g*

5 Also he took away out of all the cities of *f*
Judah the high places and the images: and
the kingdom was quiet before him.

6 And he built fenced cities in Judah: for the F^2 h
land had rest, and he had no war in those
years; because [2]the LORD had given him rest.

7 Therefore he said unto Judah, "Let us i
build these cities, and make about *them* walls,
and towers, °gates, and bars, *while* the land
is yet before us;

i because we have sought [2]the LORD our [2]God,
(p. 583) we have sought *Him*, and He hath given us
860-819 rest on every side." So they built and
prospered.

h 8 And Asa had °an army *of men* that bare
targets and spears, out of Judah °three hundred
thousand; and out of Benjamin, that bare
shields and drew bows, °two hundred and
fourscore thousand: all these *were* °mighty
men of valour.

E G 9 And there came out against them °Zerah
(p. 584) the Ethiopian with an host of a thousand
847 thousand, and three hundred chariots; and
or came unto °Mareshah.
846 10 Then Asa went out against him, and they
set the battle in array in the valley of °Zephathah at [9]Mareshah.
11 And Asa cried unto [2]the LORD his [2]God,
and said, [2]"LORD, *it is* nothing with Thee to
help, whether with many, or with them that
have no power: help us, O [2]LORD our [2]God;
for we rest on Thee, and in Thy name we go
against this multitude. O [2]LORD, Thou *art*
our [2]God; let not °man prevail against Thee."
12 So [2]the LORD smote the Ethiopians before
Asa, and before Judah; and the Ethiopians fled.
13 And Asa and the People that *were* with
him pursued them unto °Gerar: and the
Ethiopians were overthrown, that they could
not recover themselves; for they were °destroyed before [2]the LORD, and before °His
host; and they carried away very much spoil.
14 And they smote all the cities round about
Gerar; for °the fear of [2]the LORD came upon
them: and they spoiled all the cities; for
there was exceeding much spoil in them.
15 They smote also the tents of cattle, and
carried away sheep and camels in abundance,
and returned to Jerusalem.

H j **15** °And °the Spirit of °God came upon
°Azariah the son of °Oded:
2 And he went out to meet Asa, and said
unto him, "Hear ye me, Asa, and all Judah
and Benjamin; °The LORD *is* with you, while
ye be with Him; and if ye seek Him, He will
be found of you; but if ye forsake Him, He
will forsake you.

k 3 Now for a long season Israel °*hath been*
°without the true [1]God, °and without °a
teaching priest, and without law.

l 4 But when they in their trouble did turn
unto [2]the LORD [1]God of Israel, and sought
Him, He was found of them.

k 5 And in those times *there was* °no peace to
him that went out, nor to him that came in,
but great °vexations *were* upon all the inhabitants of °the countries.
6 And nation was destroyed of nation, and
city of city: for [1]God did vex them with all
°adversity.

j 7 Be ye strong therefore, and let not your hands
be weak: for your work shall be rewarded."

J K 8 And when Asa heard these words, °and the
prophecy of Oded the prophet, he took
courage, and put away the °abominable idols
out of all the land of Judah and Benjamin, and
out of °the cities which he had taken from
°mount Ephraim, and renewed the altar of

8 an army = a force.
three hundred . . . two hundred (580,000). An increase of 180,000 on his father's. See note on 13. 3.
mighty men. Heb. *gibbōr*. Ap. 14. IV.

14. 9—16. 10 (*E*, p. 583). EVENTS. PUBLIC.
(*Extended Alternation.*)

E | G | 14. 9-15. Invasion by Zerah.
  H | 15. 1-7. Word of Jehovah by Azariah.
    J | 15. 8-19. Obedience.
  G | 16. 1-6. Invasion by Baasha.
    H | 16. 7-9. Word of the Lord by Hanani.
      J | 16. 10. Disobedience.

9 Zerah. Cp. 12. 2-9.
Mareshah. Now *Khan Mer'ask*. In the plain belonging to Judah (11. 8; 14. 9; 10; 20. 37. Josh. 15. 44). Mic. 1. 15.
10 Zephathah at. Sept. reads "Zaphonah, northward to".
11 man = mortal man. Heb. *'ĕnōsh*. Ap. 14. III.
13 Gerar. Now *Khan Umm Jerrar*. Six miles south of Gaza, twenty-five from Beer-sheba, thirty miles south-west of Mareshah (*v.* 10).
destroyed = broken.
His host = His People's battles are His own (1 Sam. 18. 17; 25. 28).
14 the fear of the LORD came. Cp. 17. 10; 20. 29.

15. 1-7 (H, above). THE WORD OF JEHOVAH BY AZARIAH. (*Introversion.*)

H | j | 1, 2. Threatening.
  k | 3. Trouble. The cause.
    l | 4. Humiliation.
  k | 5, 6. Trouble. The consequence.
j | 7. Encouragement.

1 And. This chapter supplementary to 1 Kings 15.
the Spirit. Heb. *rūach*. Ap. 9. Put by Fig. *Metonymy* (of Cause), for His gift of prophecy. One of the eight occurrences outside the book of Samuel.
God. Heb. Elohim. Ap. 4. I.
Azariah. Not mentioned elsewhere.
Oded. See 28. 9. Heb. *'ōdēd*.
2 The LORD. Heb. Jehovah. Ap. 4.
3 hath = had.
without. Figs. *Anaphora* and *Polysyndeton*. Ap. 6.
and. Fig. *Polysyndeton*. Ap. 6.
a teaching priest. Teaching was the great priestly function. But, as generally with priests, teaching was neglected for ritual. See note on Deut. 17. 11; 33. 10. Mal. 2. 7.
5 no peace. As in the days of Deborah and Gideon (Judg. 5. 6; 6. 6).
vexations = consternations. Cp. Deut. 7. 23. 1 Sam. 5. 9. Amos 3. 9. Zech. 14. 13. Heb. *mᵉhūmāh* = specially trouble from God.
the countries: i. e. the different tribal divisions.
6 adversity. By civil wars.

15. 8-19 (J, above). OBEDIENCE.
(*Repeated Alternation and Introversion.*)

J | K | 8. Removal of idols.
  L | m | 9-12. Covenant.
    n | 13-15-. Exception, then. The queen mother's idol. (Destroyed later, *v.* 16).
      M | -15. Rest.
  K | 16. Removal of idol.
    L | *n* | 17. Exception. Israel's high places.
      m | 18. Dedicated things.
        M | 19. Rest.

8 and the prophecy, &c. Render: "and the prophecy (Oded was the prophet) he took", &c.
abominable idols = abominations. Referring specially to the *'Asherim*. Ap. 42.
the cities . . . taken. Probably by Abijah (13. 19).
mount = the hill country.

60 to 819 [2] the LORD, that *was* before the porch of [2] the
LORD.
L m (9 And he gathered all Judah and Benjamin,
(p. 584) and the ° strangers with them out of ° Ephraim
and Manasseh, and out of ° Simeon: for they
° fell to him out of Israel in abundance, when
they saw that [2] the LORD his [1] God *was* with
him.
10 So they gathered themselves together at
Jerusalem in the ° third month, in the ° fifteenth
845 year of the reign of Asa.
11 And they ° offered unto [2] the LORD the
same time, of ° the spoil *which* they had
brought, seven hundred oxen and seven
thousand sheep.
12 And they entered into a covenant to seek
[2] the LORD [1] God of their fathers with all their
heart and with all their ° soul;
n 13 That whosoever would not seek [2] the
LORD [1] God of Israel ° should be put to death,
whether small or great, whether ° man or
woman.
14 And they sware unto [2] the LORD with
a loud voice, and with shouting, and with
trumpets, and with cornets.
15 And all Judah rejoiced at the oath: for
they had sworn with all their heart, and
sought Him with their whole desire; and He
was found of them:
M and [2] the LORD gave them rest round about.
K 16 And also *concerning* ° Maachah the
° mother of Asa the king, he removed her from
being queen, because she had made an ° idol
in a grove: and Asa cut down her ° idol, and
° stamped *it*, and burnt *it* at the brook Kidron.
L n 17 But the high places were ° not taken away
out of Israel: nevertheless the heart of Asa
was ° perfect all his days.
m 18 And he brought into the house of [1] God the
° things that his father had ° dedicated, and
that he himself had ° dedicated, silver, and
gold, and vessels.)
M 19 And there was ° no *more* war unto the five
845 and thirtieth year of the ° reign of Asa.

G 16 ° In the ° six and thirtieth year of the
844 ° reign of Asa Baasha king of Israel
° came up against Judah, and built Ramah, to
the intent that he might ° let none go out or
come in to Asa king of Judah.
2 Then Asa brought out silver and gold out
of the ° treasures of the house of ° the LORD and
of the king's house, and sent to Ben-hadad
king of Syria, that dwelt at Damascus, saying,
3 ° "*There is* a league between me and thee,
as *there was* between my father and thy
father: ° behold, I have sent thee silver and
gold; go, break thy league with Baasha king
of Israel, that he may depart from me."
4 And Ben-hadad hearkened unto king Asa,
and sent the captains of his armies against
the cities of Israel; and they smote Ijon, and
Dan, and Abel-maim, and all the ° store cities
of Naphtali.
5 And it came to pass, when Baasha heard *it*,
that he left off building of Ramah, and let his
work cease.
6 Then Asa the king took all Judah; and
they carried away the stones of Ramah, and
the timber thereof, wherewith Baasha was
building; and he built therewith Geba and
Mizpah.
7 And at that time ° Hanani the ° seer came *H*
to Asa king of Judah, and said unto him,
° "Because thou hast relied on the king of
Syria, and not relied on [2] the LORD thy ° God,
therefore is the host of the king of Syria escaped out of thine hand.
8 ° Were not the Ethiopians and the Lubims
a huge host, with very many chariots and
horsemen? yet, because thou didst rely on [2] the
LORD, He delivered them into thine hand.
9 For ° the eyes of [2] the LORD run to and fro
throughout the whole earth, to shew Himself
strong in the behalf of *them* whose heart *is*

9 strangers = sojourners: i. e. those not of Judah. Heb. *gūr*. See note on Prov. 5. 3.
Ephraim. Jeroboam's own tribe.
Simeon. Always more or less reckoned with Judah.
fell to him out of Israel. See note on 1 Kings 12. 17.
10 third month. The feast of Pentecost.
fifteenth year. The dates of *vv.* 9-19 refer to the parenthesis which concern 14. 9-15.
11 offered = sacrificed. Heb. *zābăch*. Ap. 43. I. iv.
the spoil. Taken from the Ethiopians, &c. (14. 13-15).
12 soul. Heb. *nephesh*. Ap. 13.
13 should be put to death. Cp. Deut. 17. 2-6.
man or woman. Heb. *'īsh* or *'ishshāh*.
16 Maachah. See note on 13. 2.
mother = the queen-mother. Put by Fig. *Synecdoche* (of Genus) for grandmother (1 Kings 15. 2). Ap. 6.
idol in a grove = a monstrous *'Ashērah* for a grove. Cp. 1 Kings 15. 13. See Ap. 42.
stamped it = beat it small.
17 not taken away. Not from "Israel" (15. 17), but from Judah (14. 3). Fig. *Palinodia*. Ap. 6.
perfect: i. e. so far as idolatry was concerned.
18 things . . . dedicated = holy things. See note on Ex. 3. 5.
19 no more war = no actual campaign (as in 16. 1). There was quiet between the two kings (14. 1), but there was border fighting (as in 1 Kings 15. 16, 32). See note on 14. 1.
reign = kingdom. Cp. Num. 24. 7. 1 Sam. 20. 31. 1 Kings 2. 12. 1 Chron. 11. 10; 14. 2; 17. 14; 22. 10; 28. 5.
16. 1 In the, &c. This chapter is complementary to 1 Kings 15. 17-24.
six and thirtieth. The thirty-sixth year of the kingdom: i. e. from the disruption of the kingdom of Judah. This agrees with all the other dates and lengths of reigns. See Ap. 50. V, and note on p. 57.
reign. See note on 15. 19.
came up against. There had been quiet between the two kingdoms as such (14. 1; 15. 19), though there had been border fighting (1 Kings 15. 16, 32).
let none go out. This shows that there was a tide of population streaming into Judah from Israel. See note on 1 Kings 12. 17. **2 treasures** = treasuries.
the LORD. Heb. Jehovah. Ap. 4. II.
3 There is. Supply *Ellipsis* (Ap. 6) by "Let there be".
behold. Fig. *Asterismos*. Ap. 6.
4 store cities = the storehouses of the cities. Sept. reads "the surrounding cities".
7 Hanani. Cp. 1 Kings 16. 1, 7; 19. 2; 20. 34.
seer. Heb. *rā'āh*. See note on 1 Chron. 29. 29.
Because. Cp. similar protests against resting on foreign alliances (Isa. 30. 1; 31. 1).
God. Heb. Elohim. Ap. 4. I.
8 Were not . . . ? Fig. *Erotēsis*. Ap. 6.
9 the eyes of the LORD. Fig. *Anthropopatheia*. Ap. 6. Cp. Prov. 15. 3. Job 34. 21. Ps. 139. 2. Jer. 16. 17. Zech. 4. 10.

°perfect toward Him. Herein thou hast done
foolishly: therefore from henceforth thou shalt
have wars."
J 10 Then Asa was °wroth with the [7]seer, and
(p. 584) put him in a prison house; for *he was* in a rage
with him because of this *thing*. And Asa
oppressed *some* of the People the same time.
D 11 And, °behold, the acts of Asa, first and last,
(p. 583) °lo, they *are* written in the book of the kings
of Judah and Israel.
12 And Asa in the thirty and ninth year of
his reign was diseased in his feet, until his
disease *was* exceeding *great*: yet in his disease
he °sought not to [2]the LORD, but to the °physicians.
13 And Asa °slept with his fathers, and died
in the one and fortieth year of his reign.
14 And they buried him in his own °sepulchres,
which he had °made for himself in the city of
David, and laid him in the bed which was filled
with °sweet odours and divers kinds *of spices*
prepared by the apothecaries' art: and they
made a °very great burning for him.

G[6] N Q **17** °And Jehoshaphat his son reigned in
(p. 586) his stead, and °strengthened himself
against Israel.
2 And he placed forces in all the °fenced cities
of Judah, and set garrisons in the land of Judah,
and in the cities of Ephraim, which °Asa his
father had taken.
R S o 3 And °the LORD °was with Jehoshaphat, because he walked in °the first ways of his father
David, and sought not unto Baalim;
4 But sought to the *LORD* °God of his father,
and walked in His commandments, and not
after the doings of °Israel.
5 Therefore [3]the LORD stablished the kingdom in his hand;
p and all Judah °brought to Jehoshaphat presents; and he had riches and honour in abundance.
q 6 And his heart was °lifted up in the ways of
[3]the LORD: moreover °he took away the high
places and °groves out of Judah.
7 Also in the third year of his reign he sent
to his °princes, *even* to Ben-hail, and to Obadiah, and to Zechariah, and to Nethaneel, and
to Michaiah, °to teach in the cities of Judah.
8 And with them *he sent* Levites, *even* Shemaiah, and Nethaniah, and Zebadiah, and
Asahel, and Shemiramoth, and Jehonathan,
and Adonijah, and Tobijah, and Tob-adonijah,
Levites; and with them Elishama and Jehoram, priests.
9 And they taught in Judah, and *had* °the
book of the law of [3]the LORD with them, and
°went about throughout all the cities of Judah,
and taught the People.
T o 10 And the °fear of [3]the LORD °fell upon all
the kingdoms of the lands that *were* round
about Judah, so that they made no war against
Jehoshaphat.
p 11 Also *some* of the Philistines [5]brought
Jehoshaphat presents, and tribute silver; and
the Arabians [5]brought him flocks, seven thousand and seven hundred rams, and seven
thousand and seven hundred he goats.
q 12 And Jehoshaphat waxed great exceed-

perfect = whole, as in Deut. 27. 6.

10 wroth with the seer. One of the eleven rulers offended with God's servants. See note on Ex. 10. 28.

11 behold . . . lo. Fig. *Asterismos.* Ap. 6.

12 sought not. Contrast Hezekiah (2 Kings 20. 2. Isa. 38. 2, 3.)

physicians = healers. First occurrence of mention of them among the Hebrews. These belonged to the priestly tribe, with traditional knowledge, more or less superstitious. Cp. Job 13. 4. In N.T. we have Luke (Col. 4. 14).

13 slept with his fathers. See note on Deut. 31. 16.

14 sepulchres = a great sepulchre. Pl. of majesty.

made for himself. Not infrequently done. Cp. Matt. 27. 60. John 19. 38–42.

sweet odours and divers kinds. Fig. *Hendiadys* (Ap. 6), emphasising the many kinds of odours. Omit "of spices".

very great burning: i. e. of the odours previously mentioned, but not of incense, or of the sin offering. Cp. 21. 19. Heb. *sāraph.* Ap. 43. I. viii.

17. 1–21. 1- (G[6], p. 545). JEHOSHAPHAT.
(*Extended and Simple Alternations, with Introversion.*)

G[6] | N | Q | 17. 1, 2. Introduction. Accession.
  R | S | 17. 3–9. Personal. Reformation.
    T | 17. 10–19. The kingdom. Established.
  O | U | 18. 1–34. Alliance with Ahab.
    V | 19. 1–3. Remonstrance. Jehu.
  P | 19. 4. Jerusalem. Dwelling.
N | *R* | *S* | 19. 5–11. Personal. Reformation.
    T | 20. 1–30. The kingdom. Invaded.
  Q | 20. 31–34. Conclusion. Reign.
  O | *U* | 20. 35, 36. Alliance with Ahaziah.
    V | 20. 37. Remonstrance. Eliezer.
  P | 21. 1. Jerusalem. Death.

1 And. This chapter is supplementary to 1 Kings 22. 41–43.

strengthened himself. Without this we could not understand his subsequent alliances with the worst of Israel's kings (18. 1, 2; 20. 35, 36).

2 fenced = fortified.

Asa . . . had taken (15. 8).

3–19 (R, above; S, *vv.* 3–9; T, *vv.* 10–19). PERSONAL. REFORMATION. (*Extended Alternation.*)

S | o | 3–5-. Divine presence.
  p | -5. Presents from Judah.
  q | 6–9. Goodness.
T | *o* | 10. Divine protection.
  p | 11. Presents from Philistines.
  q | 12–19. Greatness.

3 the LORD. Heb. Jehovah. Ap. 4. II.

was with. Thus approving his strengthening himself against idolaters and idolatry.

the first ways: i. e. David's earlier ways were of faith.

4 God. Heb. Elohim. Ap. 4. II.

Israel. The worship of the calves, and Baal.

5 brought . . . presents. In token of subjection and loyalty at beginning of reign (1 Sam. 10. 27. 1 Kings 10. 25).

6 lifted up = encouraged.

he took away. But "the people" failed in their part (20. 33. 1 Kings 22. 43). Jehoshaphat did his by *commanding* that they should be taken away; not, of course, doing this with his own hands. Cp. 19. 3.

groves. Heb. the *'Asherim.* See notes on Ex. 34. 13, and Ap. 42.

7 princes. These organized the Levites and priests (*v.* 8) into a teaching mission. The first so recorded.

to teach. This was the special function of the priests. See notes on Deut. 17. 9–12; 33. 10.

9 the book of the law. See note on Ex. 17. 14, and Ap. 47.

went about (2 Kings 23. 2. Neh. 8. 3–18).

10 fear = dread. **fell** = came, or was.

ingly; and he built in Judah castles, and cities of store.
13 And he °had much business in the cities of Judah: °and the °men of war, °mighty men of valour, *were* in Jerusalem.
14 And these *are* the numbers of them according to the house of their fathers: Of Judah, the captains of thousands; Adnah the chief, and with him [13]mighty men of valour °three hundred thousand.
15 And °next to him *was* Jehohanan the captain, and with him two hundred and fourscore thousand.
16 And next him *was* Amasiah the son of Zichri, who willingly offered himself unto [3]the LORD; and with him two hundred thousand [13]mighty men of valour.
17 And of Benjamin; Eliada a [13]mighty man of valour, and with him armed men °with bow and shield two hundred thousand.
18 And next him *was* Jehozabad, and with him an hundred and fourscore thousand ready prepared for the war.
19 These waited on the king, beside *those* whom the king put in the fenced cities °throughout all Judah.

U W r (p. 587) **18 °Now Jehoshaphat had °riches and honour in abundance, and °joined affinity with Ahab.**
s **2 °And °after *certain* years he went down to Ahab to Samaria. °And Ahab killed sheep and oxen for him in abundance, and for the People that *he had* with him, and °persuaded him to go up *with him* to °Ramoth-gilead.**
r **3 And Ahab king of Israel said unto Jehoshaphat king of Judah, "Wilt thou go with me to [2]Ramoth-gilead?" And he answered him, "I *am* as thou *art*, and my People as thy People; and °*we will be* with thee in the war."**
s Y v **4 And Jehoshaphat said unto the king of Israel, °"Enquire, I pray thee, at the word of °the LORD to day."**
w **5 Therefore the king of Israel gathered together of °prophets four hundred °men, and said unto them, "Shall we go to Ramoth-gilead to battle, or shall I forbear?" And they said, "Go up; for °God will deliver *it* into the king's hand."**

13 had much business = was busily engaged.
and the men of. Heb. pl. *'ĕnōsh.* Ap. 14. III.
mighty men. Heb. *gibbōr.* Ap. 14. IV.
14 three hundred thousand. So far from these numbers being exaggerated, they are a token of Jehovah's prospering grace. Jehoshaphat could muster 1,600,000; David, 1,300,000.
15 next to him = under his direction. Heb. "at his hand" (1 Chron. 25. 2).
17 with bow and shield. Fig. *Zeugma* (Ap. 6), by which the second verb is omitted. If we supply the first, the second follows: "[armed] with bow and [using] shield". **19 throughout all Judah.** Cp. *v.* 2.

18. 1-34 (U, p. 586). ALLIANCES WITH AHAB. (*Alternation and Introversion.*)

U | W | r | 1. Alliance. Matrimonial.
s | 2. Jehoshaphat's consent.
r | 3. Alliance. Military.
s | 4-27. Jehoshaphat's anxiety.
X | 28. The expedition.
W | t | 29-. Ahab's device.
u | -29. Jehoshaphat's consent.
u | 30, 31. Jehoshaphat's concern.
t | 32-34. Ahab's death.

1 Now, &c. This chapter is complementary to 1 Kings 22.
riches and honour in abundance. This is repeated from 17. 5, to show that there was no need for any alliance of any kind.
joined affinity. By marrying his son Jehoram to Athaliah the daughter of Ahab (21. 6. 2 Kings 8. 18). Contrast 17. 1, where he began by strengthening himself against Ahab, and now "joined affinity" with him. See Ap. 55. Cp. Asa's alliance with Syria (1 Kings 15. 17-19).
Note the three alliances or unequal yokes: (1) Marriage (18. 1; 21. 6); (2) War (18. 2-34); (3) Commerce (20. 35, 36). The consequence of this alliance was that Jerusalem ran with blood. The same was seen when James I of England married his son Charles I to Henrietta of France. England ran with blood, Charles lost his head, and his son James II lost his throne.
2 And. Note the Fig. *Polysyndeton* (Ap. 6), emphasising the consequent details.
after certain years. The third year of the peace between Ahab and Syria (1 Kings 22. 1, 2).
And Ahab killed, &c. Ahab's "sheep and oxen" did what all his men of war could never have done (17. 2, 10-19).
persuaded = seduced. Heb. *sūth,* to incite; our "sooth"; hence to deceive (Deut. 13. 6. 1 Sam. 26. 19. 1 Kings 21. 25. Jer. 38. 22).
Ramoth-gilead. Now, probably *Reimūn,* in Gilead. One of the cities of refuge (Deut. 4. 43). God's gift to Israel.
3 we will be with thee. Jehoshaphat was deceived by its seeming to be a "good work". But "good" works are only "prepared" works (Eph. 2. 10). It could not be "good" if done "with thee" (cp. 19. 2). "Better is he that ruleth his spirit than he that taketh a city" (Prov. 16. 32). But Jehoshaphat did not "take it".

18. 4-27 (*s,* above). JEHOSHAPHAT'S ANXIETY. (*Introversions and Alternations.*)

s | Y | v | 4. Jehoshaphat. Inquiry.
w | 5. Ahab. Compliance.
v | 6. Jehoshaphat. Further inquiry.
w | 7. Ahab. Reply.
Z | 8. True prophet sent for. Micaiah.
A | 9, 10. False prophets. Zedekiah.
A | 11. False prophets. All.
Z | 12, 13. True prophet brought. Micaiah.
Y | x | 14-. Inquiry made. Ahab.
y | -14. Micaiah's answer. Ironical.
x | 15. Inquiry adjured. Ahab.
y | 16-27. Micaiah's answer. Serious.

4 Enquire, &c. This shows his consciousness that he was not doing right. **the LORD.** Heb. Jehovah. Ap. 4. II. **5 prophets**: i. e. the false prophets of Baal. **men.** Heb. *'īsh.* Ap. 14. II. **God.** Heb. Elohim. Ap. 4. I. They knew not experimental relationship with Jehovah.

v (p. 587) 6 But Jehoshaphat said, "*Is there* not here a
prophet of [4]the LORD °besides, that we might
enquire of him?"

w 7 And the king of Israel said unto Jehoshaphat, "*There is* yet one [5]man, by whom we
may enquire of [4]the LORD: but °I hate him;
for he never prophesied good unto me, but
always °evil: the same *is* °Micaiah the son of
Imla." And Jehoshaphat said, "Let not the
king say so."

Z 8 And the king of Israel called for one *of his*
officers, and said, "Fetch quickly Micaiah the
son of Imla."

A 9 And the king of Israel and Jehoshaphat
king of Judah sat either of them on his throne,
clothed in *their* robes, and they sat in a void
place at the entering in of the gate of Samaria;
and all the prophets °prophesied before them.
10 And Zedekiah the son of Chenaanah had
made him horns of iron, and said, "Thus saith
[4]the LORD, 'With these thou shalt push Syria
until °they be consumed.'"

A 11 And all the prophets prophesied so, saying,
"Go up to Ramoth-gilead, and prosper: for [4]the
LORD shall deliver *it* into the hand of the king."

Z 12 And the messenger that went to call Micaiah
spake to him, saying, °"Behold, the words of
the prophets *declare* good to the king with
one °assent; let thy word therefore, I pray
thee, be like one of theirs, and speak thou good."
13 And Micaiah said, "*As* [4]the LORD liveth,
even what my [5]God saith, that will I speak."

Y x 14 And when he was come to the king, the
king said unto him, "Micaiah, shall °we go to
Ramoth-gilead to battle, or shall °I forbear?"

y And he said, "Go °ye up, and prosper, and they
shall be delivered into your hand."

x 15 And the king said to him, "How many
times shall I adjure thee that thou say nothing
but the truth to me in the name of [4]the LORD?"

y B[1] a (p. 588) 16 Then he said, "I did see all Israel scattered
upon the mountains, as sheep that have no
shepherd: and [4]the LORD said, 'These have
no master; let them return *therefore* [5]every
man to his house in peace.'"

b 17 And the king of Israel said to Jehoshaphat,
"Did I not tell thee *that* he would not prophesy good unto me, but [7]evil?"

a 18 Again he said, "Therefore hear the word
of [4]the LORD; I saw [4]the LORD sitting upon
His throne, and all the host of heaven standing
on His right hand and *on* His left.
19 And [4]the LORD said, 'Who shall entice
Ahab king of Israel, that he may go up and
fall at Ramoth-gilead?' And one spake saying
after this manner, and another saying after
that manner.
20 Then there came out a °spirit, and stood
before [4]the LORD, and said, 'I will entice him.'
And [4]the LORD said unto him, 'Wherewith?'
21 And he said, 'I will go out, and be a lying
[20]spirit in the mouth of all his prophets.' And
the LORD said, 'Thou shalt entice *him*, and thou
shalt also prevail: go out, and do *even* so.'

b 22 Now therefore, [12]behold, [4]the LORD hath
put a lying [20]spirit in the mouth of °these thy
prophets, and [4]the LORD hath spoken [7]evil
against thee."

B[2] c 23 Then Zedekiah the son of Chenaanah
came near, and smote Micaiah upon the cheek,
and said, "Which way went the [20]Spirit of
[4]the LORD from me to speak unto thee?"

d 24 And Micaiah said, "Behold, °thou shalt
see on that day when thou shalt go into an
inner chamber to hide thyself."

c 25 Then the king of Israel said, "Take ye
Micaiah, and °carry him back to Amon the
governor of the city, and to Joash the king's
son;
26 And say, 'Thus saith the king, °'Put this
fellow in the prison, and feed him with °bread
of affliction and with water of affliction, until
I return in peace.'"

d 27 And Micaiah said, "If thou certainly return in peace, *then* hath not [4]the LORD spoken
by me." And he said, "Hearken, all ye °people."

X (p. 587) 28 So the king of Israel and Jehoshaphat the
king of Judah went up to Ramoth-gilead.

W t 29 And the king of Israel said unto Jehoshaphat, °"I will disguise myself, and will go to
the battle; but put thou on thy robes."

---

6 besides. He thus shows that he knew they were false prophets.

7 I hate him = I have always hated him. True prophets are always hated by the Lord's enemies.

evil. Heb. *ra'a'*. Ap. 44. viii.

Micaiah = Who is like Jehovah?

9 prophesied before them. Jehoshaphat well knowing that they were not the prophets of Jehovah.

10 they. Note the characteristic ambiguity of such communications.

12 Behold. Fig. *Asterismos*. Ap. 6.

assent = mouth. Put by Fig. *Metonymy* (of Cause) for what is spoken by it.

14 we . . . I . . . ye. Note the change in number.

18. 16-27 (*y*, p. 587). MICAIAH'S ANSWER.
(*Repeated Alternation.*)

y | B[1] | a | 16. Vision seen. | Communicated.
	b	17. Understood.
	a	18-21. Vision seen.
	b	22. Interpreted.
B[2]	c	23. Zedekiah.	Received.
	d	24. Micaiah.
	c	25, 26. Ahab.
	d	27. Micaiah.

20 spirit. Heb. *rūach*. Ap. 9.

22 these. Some codices, with Sept., Syr., and Vulg., read "all these".

24 thou shalt see = art going to see; or, art about to see; or, thou wilt soon see.

25 carry him back. Implying that Micaiah was already a prisoner.

26 Put this fellow. One of the eleven rulers offended with God's servants. See note on Ex. 10. 28, and Ap. 10.

bread of affliction. Genitive of relation. Bread accompanied by, or eaten in, affliction; also because of its quality, or scant allowance.

27 people = Peoples.

29 I will disguise myself, and will go. Heb. text reads "to disguise myself and to go". This is either Fig. *Heterōsis* (of Moods), Ap. 6, the Infinitive being put for the Indicative, thus beautifully rendered; or, Fig. *Ellipsis* (Ap. 6), which might be supplied thus: "I [am about] to disguise myself and go".

u (p. 587) So the king of Israel disguised himself; and
°they went to the battle.
800 30 °Now the king of Syria had commanded
u the captains of the chariots that *were* with
him, saying, "Fight ye not with small or
great, save only with the king of Israel."
31 And it came to pass, when the captains of
the chariots saw Jehoshaphat, that they said,
"It *is* the king of Israel." Therefore they
compassed about him to fight: but Jehoshaphat cried out, and °the LORD °helped him;
and °God moved them *to depart* from him.
t 32 For it came to pass, that, when the captains
of the chariots perceived that it was not the
king of Israel, they turned back again from
pursuing him.
33 And a *certain* °man drew a bow °at a venture, and smote the king of Israel between the
joints °of the harness: therefore he said to
his chariot man, "Turn thine hand, °that thou
mayest carry me out of the host; for I am
°wounded."
34 And the battle increased that day: howbeit the king of Israel stayed *himself* up in
his chariot against the Syrians until the even:
800 and about the time of the sun going down °he
died.

V (p. 586) **19** And Jehoshaphat the king of Judah
returned to his house °in peace to Jerusalem.
2 And °Jehu the son of Hanani the seer went
out to meet him, and said to king Jehoshaphat, °"Shouldest thou help the °ungodly, and
love them that hate °the LORD? therefore *is*
°wrath upon thee from before °the LORD.
3 °Nevertheless there are good things found
in thee, in that thou hast taken away °the
groves out of the land, and hast prepared
thine heart to seek °God."
P 4 And Jehoshaphat dwelt at Jerusalem: and
he went out again through the People °from
Beer-sheba to °mount Ephraim, and brought
them back unto [2]the LORD [3]God of their
fathers.
S C[1] e (p. 589) 5 And he set judges in the land throughout
all the fenced cities of Judah, city by city,
f 6 And said to the judges, "Take heed what
ye do: for ye judge not for °man, but for [2]the
LORD, Who *is* with you °in the judgment.
7 Wherefore now let the °fear of [2]the LORD
be upon you; take heed and do *it:* for *there is*
no iniquity with [2]the LORD our [3]God, nor °re-
spect of persons, nor taking of °gifts."
C[2] *e* 8 °Moreover in Jerusalem did Jehoshaphat
set of the Levites, and *of* the priests, and of
the °chief of the fathers of Israel, for the judgment of [2]the LORD, and for controversies, when
they returned to Jerusalem.
f 9 And he charged them, saying, "Thus shall
ye do in the °fear of [2]the LORD, faithfully, and
with a perfect heart.
10 And what cause soever shall come to you
of your brethren that dwell in their cities, between blood and blood, between law and commandment, statutes and judgments, ye shall
even °warn them that they °trespass not
against [2]the LORD, and *so* wrath come upon
you, and upon your brethren: this do, and ye
shall not °trespass.
11 And, °behold, °Amariah the chief priest *is*
over you in °all matters of [2]the LORD; and
Zebadiah the son of Ishmael, the ruler of the
house of Judah, for all the king's matters:
also the Levites *shall be* officers before you.
°Deal courageously, and [2]the LORD shall be
with the good."

---

they went = they entered. But some codices, with two early printed editions, Aram., Syr., and Vulg., read "he entered". Cp. 1 Kings 22. 30.

30 Now, &c. Having been taken into the camp of Israel and allowed to hear what Ahab said, we are now taken into the camp of Syria to overhear what the king of Syria said. This is to enable us to understand what follows.

31 the LORD. Heb. Jehovah. Ap. 4. II.

helped him: i. e. Jehoshaphat, for Jehovah was his Covenant God.

God moved them. Heb. Elohim. Ap. 4. I. He stood, to the Syrians, only in the relation of the Creator to His creatures.

33 man. Heb. *'ish.* Ap. 14. II.

at a venture = in his innocence, or ignorance.

of the harness = of the armour.

that thou mayest = and.

wounded = sore wounded.

34 he died. Not fell asleep! No details of his death, here, in Chronicles, which is concerned only with Judah. Details given in Kings (1 Kings 22. 35-38).

19. 1 in peace. In contrast with Ahab's return (18. 33, 34, 37).

2 Jehu the son of Hanani. He had reproved Baasha, king of Israel, at Tirzah (1 Kings 16. 1); and now rebukes Jehoshaphat, king of Judah, at Jerusalem.

Shouldest thou . . . ? Fig. *Erotēsis* (Ap. 6), for emphasis. Here we have Jehovah's opinion as to alliances with idolaters (Ahab, 18. 1, &c), and as to what constitutes a "good work". See note on *v.* 3.

ungodly = lawless one (sing.). Ap. 44. x.

the LORD. Heb. Jehovah. Ap. 4. II.

wrath. Manifested in the wars recorded in 20. 1-3.

3 Nevertheless. Fig. *Palinodia.* Ap. 6.

the groves = the *'Asherōth.* See Ap. 42.

God. Heb. Elohim (with Art.) = the [true] God. Ap. 4. I.

4 from Beer-sheba, &c. The two outermost bounds.

mount = hill country of.

19. 5-11 (*S*, p. 586). PERSONAL REFORMATION.
(*Alternation.*)

S | C[1] | e | 5. Judges. — In Judah.
| | f | 6, 7. Exhortation. — In Judah.
| C[2] | *e* | 8. Levites. — In Jerusalem.
| | *f* | 9-11. Exhortation. — In Jerusalem.

6 man. Heb. *'ādām.* Ap. 14. I.

in the judgment = in the word or matter of judgment.

7 fear = dread, as in 20. 29; not as in *v.* 9 below, which is "reverence".

respect of persons. Closely following Deut. 16. 18-20.

gifts = bribes.

8 Moreover, &c. Cp. Deut. 17. 8-13.

chief = head.

9 fear = reverence. See note on *v.* 7 above.

10 warn. Used of warning or enlightenment as to God's word (Ps. 19. 11). Out of twenty-two occurrences fifteen are in Ezekiel.

trespass. Heb. *'āsham.* Ap. 44. ii.

11 behold. Fig. *Asterismos.* Ap. 6.

Amariah. The fifth high priest from Zadok (1 Chron. 6. 11), Jehoshaphat being the fifth king from David.

all matters of the LORD. Probably refers to spiritual, or ecclesiastical matters.

Deal courageously = be strong, and act.

T g 20 It came to pass ° after this also, *that* the
(p. 590) ° children of Moab, and the ° children of
799 Ammon, and with them *other* beside the
Ammonites, came against Jehoshaphat to
battle.
2 Then there came some that told Jehoshaphat, saying, "There cometh a great multitude against thee from beyond the sea on this side Syria; and, ° behold, they *be* in Hazazon-tamar, which *is* En-gedi."

h 3 And Jehoshaphat feared, and set ° himself
to seek ° the LORD, and proclaimed a fast
throughout all Judah.

i 4 And Judah gathered themselves together,
° to ask *help* of [3] the LORD: even out of all the
cities of Judah they came to seek [3] the LORD.

k l 5 And Jehoshaphat ° stood in the ° congregation of Judah ° and Jerusalem, in the house of [3] the LORD, before ° the new court,
6 And said, [3] "O LORD ° God of our fathers, ° *art* not Thou ° God in heaven? and ° rulest *not* Thou over all the kingdoms of the ° heathen? and ° in Thine hand ° *is there not* power and might, ° so that none is able to withstand Thee?
7 *Art* not Thou our [6] God, *Who* didst drive out the inhabitants of this land before Thy People Israel, and gavest it to the seed of ° ABRAHAM THY FRIEND for ever?
8 And they dwelt therein, and have built Thee a sanctuary therein for Thy name, saying,
9 'If, *when* ° evil cometh upon us, *as* the ° sword, judgment, or pestilence, or famine, we stand before this house, and in Thy presence, (for ° Thy name *is* in this house,) and cry unto Thee in our ° affliction, then Thou wilt hear and help.'
10 And now, behold, the [1] children of Ammon and Moab and ° mount Seir, whom Thou ° wouldest not let Israel invade, when they came out of the land of Egypt, but they turned from them, and destroyed them not;
11 [2] Behold, *I say, how* they reward us, to come to cast us out of Thy possession, which Thou hast given us to inherit.
12 O our [6] God, ° wilt Thou not ° judge them? for we have no might against this great ° company that cometh against us; neither know we what to do: but our eyes *are* upon Thee."
13 And all Judah stood before [3] the LORD, with their little ones, their wives, and their [1] children.

m 14 Then upon ° Jahaziel the son of Zechariah,
the son of Benaiah, the son of Jeiel, the son of Mattaniah, a Levite of the sons of ° Asaph, came the ° Spirit ° of [3] the LORD in the midst of the [5] congregation;
15 And he said, "Hearken ye, all Judah, and ye inhabitants of Jerusalem, and thou king Jehoshaphat, Thus saith [3] the LORD unto you, ° 'Be not afraid nor dismayed by reason of this great multitude; for the battle *is* not yours, but [6] God's.
16 To morrow go ye down against them: behold, they come up by the ° cliff of Ziz; and ye shall find them at the end of the ° brook, before the wilderness of Jeruel.
17 Ye shall not *need* to fight in this *battle*: set yourselves, ° stand ye *still*, and see the salvation of [3] the LORD with you, O Judah and Jerusalem: fear not, nor be dismayed; to morrow go out against them: for [3] the LORD *will be* with you.'"

18 And Jehoshaphat bowed his head with *his* face to the ground: and all Judah and the inhabitants of Jerusalem fell before [3] the LORD, worshipping [3] the LORD. k l
19 And the Levites, of the [1] children of the Kohathites, and of the [1] children of the Korhites, stood up to praise [3] the LORD [6] God of Israel with a loud voice on high.

---

20. 1-30 (*T*, p. 586). THE KINGDOM. INVADED.
(*Introversion and Alternation.*)

T | g | 1, 2. Invasion. Made and reported.
  h | 3. Fear of Moab. Jehoshaphat.
   i | 4. Assemblage. To seek Jehovah.
    k | l | 5-13. Prayer.
      m | 14-17. Prophecy. Given.
    k | l | 18, 19. Praise.
      m | 20-25. Prophecy. Fulfilled.
   i | 26-28. Assemblage. To bless Jehovah.
  h | 29. Fear of God. The kingdoms.
 g | 30. Invasion. Repelled.

1 after this: i. e. after Ahab's death (2 Kings 3. 5).
children = sons.
2 behold. Fig. *Asterismos.* Ap. 6.
3 himself = his face.
the LORD. Heb. Jehovah. Ap. 4. II.
4 to ask = to seek. Supply "counsel" here.
5 stood. On the platform provided for such purposes as this (2 Kings 11. 14; 23. 3).
congregation = assembly. Heb. *ḳāhal.* See note on "multitude" (Gen. 28. 3).
and. Some codices, with one early printed edition, Sept., and Syr., read "in".
the new court. The court of the priests, built by Solomon (4. 9; 15. 8).
6 God. Heb. Elohim. Ap. 4. I.
art not . . . rulest not . . . is there not? Fig. *Erotēsis.* Ap. 6.
heathen = nations (Dan. 4. 34, 35).
in Thine hand. The words of David were accessible to Jehoshaphat (1 Chron. 29. 12). See Ap. 47.
so that none = and there is none.
7 Abraham Thy friend. Three times so called: here, Isa. 41. 8, quoted in Jas. 2. 23. Cp. Moses (Ex. 33. 11).
9 evil. Heb. *rā'a'.* Ap. 44. viii.
sword. Put by Fig. *Metonymy* (of Cause), Ap. 6, for the execution done by it. Cp. 1 Kings 8. 37. 2 Chron. 6. 28.
Thy name = Thy presence.
affliction = distress. Some codices, with two early printed editions, read "distresses".
10 mount Seir. The Edomite Mehunim. See *v.* 1.
wouldest not, &c. Cp. Deut. 2. 9.
12 wilt Thou not . . . ? Fig. *Erotēsis.* Ap. 6.
judge = bring judgments. Put by Fig. *Metonymy* (of Cause), Ap. 6, for the judgments themselves.
company = rout.
14 Jahaziel . . . Asaph. Probably Ps. 83 written at that time.
Spirit. Heb. *rūach.* Ap. 9.
of: or from. Genitive of Origin: i. e. spiritual power from Jehovah.
15 Be not afraid = "Be not [ye] afraid".
16 cliff = ascent.
brook = valley.
17 stand ye still. Cp. Ex. 14. 13.

m (p. 590) 799 20 And they rose early in the morning, and went forth into the wilderness of Tekoa: and as they went forth, Jehoshaphat stood and said, "Hear me, O Judah, and ye inhabitants of Jerusalem; Believe in [3]the LORD your [6]God, so shall ye be established; believe His prophets, so shall ye prosper."

21 And when he had consulted with the People, he appointed singers unto [3]the LORD, and that should praise °the beauty of holiness, as they went out before the army, and to say, °"Praise [3]the LORD; for His °mercy *endureth* for ever."

22 And when they began to sing and to praise, °the LORD set °ambushments against the [1]children of Ammon, Moab, and mount Seir, which were come against Judah; and they were smitten.

23 For the [1]children of Ammon and Moab stood up against the inhabitants of mount Seir, utterly to slay and destroy *them:* and when they had made an end of the inhabitants of Seir, every one helped to destroy another.

24 And when Judah came toward the watch tower in the wilderness, they looked unto the multitude, and, [2]behold, they *were* dead bodies fallen to the earth, and none escaped.

25 And when Jehoshaphat and his People came to take away the spoil of them, they found among them in abundance both riches with °the dead bodies, and precious jewels, which they °stripped off for themselves, more than they could carry away: and they were three days in gathering of the spoil, it was so much.

i 26 And on the fourth day they assembled themselves in the valley of °Berachah; for there they blessed [3]the LORD: therefore the name of the same place was called, The valley of Berachah, unto this day.

27 Then they returned, °every man of Judah and Jerusalem, and Jehoshaphat in the forefront of them, to go again to Jerusalem with joy; for [3]the LORD had made them to rejoice over their enemies.

28 And they came to Jerusalem with psalteries and harps and trumpets unto the house of [3]the LORD.

h 29 And the °fear of [6]God was on all the kingdoms of *those* countries, when they had heard that [3]the LORD fought against the enemies of Israel.

g 30 So the realm of Jehoshaphat was quiet: for his [6]God gave him rest round about.

Q 31 And Jehoshaphat reigned over Judah: *he*
(p. 586) *was* thirty and five years old when he began
819 to reign, and he reigned twenty and five years
to in Jerusalem. And his mother's name *was*
794 Azubah the daughter of Shilhi.

32 And he walked in the way of °Asa his father, and departed not from it, doing *that which was* right in the sight of [3]the LORD.

33 Howbeit the high places were °not taken away: for as yet the People had not prepared their hearts unto the [6]God of their fathers.

34 Now the rest of the acts of Jehoshaphat, first and last, [2]behold, they *are* written in the °book of °Jehu the son of Hanani, who *is* mentioned in the book of the kings of Israel.

35 And °after this did Jehoshaphat king of Judah °join himself with Ahaziah king of Israel, °who did very °wickedly: O U (p. 586)

36 And he [35]joined himself with him °to make ships to go to Tarshish: and they made the ships in Ezion-gaber.

37 Then °Eliezer the son of Dodavah of Mareshah prophesied against Jehoshaphat, saying, "Because thou hast [35]joined thyself with Ahaziah, [3]the LORD hath °broken thy works." And the ships were broken, that they were not able to go to Tarshish. V

21 Now Jehoshaphat °slept with his fathers, and was buried with his fathers in the city of David. P 794

And °Jehoram his son reigned in his stead. G[7] D (p. 591)

---

21 the beauty of holiness = in His glorious sanctuary. See note on 1 Chron. 16. 29.

Praise the LORD = Praise Jehovah. Ap. 4. II.

mercy = lovingkindness, or grace.

22 the LORD. Some think the "Yod" (= J) was an abbreviation for "Judah".

ambushments = liers in wait. The Targum interprets them of angelic powers.

25 the dead bodies. Some codices, with five early printed editions and Vulg., read "apparel".

stripped off = raked together.

26 Berachah = Blessing.

27 every man. Heb. *'ish.* Ap. 14. II.

29 fear = dread, as in 19. 7 (not as in 19. 9). Genitive of Character = a great dread.

32 Asa his father. Some codices, with six early printed editions, read "his father Asa".

33 not taken away. See note on 17. 6.

34 book = words. Jehu. Cp. 19. 2.

35 after this. In the twentieth or twenty-first year of his reign. Cp. 1 Kings 22. 51. See Ap. 50. V, and note. "After" this wonderful deliverance. "After" the solemn warning of 19. 2. "After" his experience in 18. 31.

join himself. This was the third alliance (Commercial). See note on 18. 1. Note the Fig. *Repetitio* (Ap. 6), by which great emphasis is laid on these words by their repetition in *vv.* 36 and 37.

who did very wickedly. This is added to show that the reason against such an alliance was just as strong with Ahaziah as with Ahab.

wickedly = lawlessly. Ap. 44. x.

36 to make ships to go to Tarshish. This was prior to the similar event recorded in 1 Kings 22. 48, 49, where he made (himself) "Tarshish ships to go to Ophir". Ahaziah again sought to implicate Jehoshaphat. But he failed in the attempt, for we there read "Jehoshaphat would not" (*v.* 49). And the ships "did not go", for they were "broken" (*v.* 48). The marginal note in A.V. is neither correct nor necessary.

37 Eliezer. Sent by Jehovah, just as Jehu had been sent (19. 2).

broken. A *Homonym.* Heb. *pāraz,* to break. Rightly so rendered here. Its other meaning, *to increase,* as rightly given in Gen. 30. 43. Ex. 1. 12.

21. 1- slept with his fathers. See note on Deut. 31. 16; and contrast his ally's end (18. 34).

21. -1-20 (G[7], p. 545). JEHORAM.

(Introversion.)

G[7] | D | -1-5. Introduction.
| E | 6, 7. Events. Personal.
| *E* | 8-19. Events. Public.
| *D* | 20. Conclusion.

-1 Jehoram. He was designated to be king in the seventeenth year of his father, but crowned in his father's twenty-third year. He reigned eight years in Jerusalem: two with his father, and six after his father's death (cp. 2 Kings 1. 17; 8. 16).

796 2 And he had brethren the sons of Jehosha-
to phat, Azariah, and Jehiel, and Zechariah, and
788 Azariah, and Michael, and Shephatiah: all
these *were* the sons of Jehoshaphat king of
°Israel.
3 And their father gave them great gifts of
silver, and of gold, and of precious things,
with fenced cities in Judah: but the kingdom
gave he to Jehoram; because he *was* the firstborn.
4 Now when Jehoram was risen up to the
kingdom of his father, he strengthened himself, and °slew all his brethren with the sword,
and *divers* also of the princes of Israel.
5 Jehoram *was* thirty and two years old when
he began to reign, and he reigned eight years
in Jerusalem.

E (p. 591) 6 And he walked in the way of the kings of
Israel, like as did the house of Ahab: for he
had °the daughter of Ahab to wife: and he
wrought *that which was* °evil in the eyes of
°the LORD.
7 Howbeit [6]the LORD would not destroy the
house of David, because of °the covenant that
He had made with David, and °as He promised to give °a light to him and to his sons
for ever.

E n (p. 592) 8 In his days °the Edomites revolted from
under the dominion of Judah, and made themselves a king.
9 Then Jehoram °went forth with his princes,
and all his chariots with him: and he rose up
by night, and smote the Edomites which compassed him in, and the captains of the chariots.
10 So [8]the Edomites revolted from under
the hand of Judah °unto this day. The same
time *also* °did Libnah revolt from under his
hand; because he had forsaken [6]the LORD
°God of his fathers.

o 11 Moreover he made high places in the °mount-
ains of Judah, and caused the inhabitants of
Jerusalem to commit °fornication, and °com-
pelled Judah *thereto*.
12 And °there came a writing to him from
°Elijah the prophet, saying, "Thus saith [6]the
LORD [10]God of David thy father, 'Because thou
hast not walked in the ways of Jehoshaphat
thy father, nor in the ways of Asa king of
Judah,
13 But hast walked in the way of the kings
of Israel, and hast made Judah and the inhabitants of Jerusalem to go a whoring, like to the
whoredoms of the house of Ahab, and also
hast slain thy brethren of thy father's house,
which were better than thyself:
14 °Behold, with a great plague will [6]the
LORD smite thy People, °and thy °children,
and thy wives, and all thy goods:
15 And thou *shalt have* great sickness by
disease of thy bowels, until thy bowels fall out
by reason of the sickness day by day.'"

n 16 Moreover [6]the LORD stirred up against
Jehoram the °spirit of °the Philistines, and of
the Arabians, that °*were* near the Ethiopians:
17 And they came up °into Judah, and brake
into it, and carried away all the substance
that was found in the king's house, and his
sons also, and °his wives; so that there was
°never a son left him, save °Jehoahaz, the
youngest of his sons.

2 Israel. This word was originally represented by the abbreviation ׳ (i or y), which was read for "Israel" as well as Judah. The reading in the Severus Codex (see Ap. 34) is "Judah", and this is supported by the first edition of the *Hagiogrăpha* (Naples, 1486-1487), the Complutensian Polyglot, Sept., Syr., and Vulg. This same note applies to 28. 19, where the same phenomena occur.

4 slew all his brethren. The mischief of his marriage (18. 1) was thus soon seen. The enemy's design in breaking into the royal line so as to destroy the promises of Gen. 3. 15 and 2 Sam. 7. 16 is seen. See Ap. 23, 25. Jehoshaphat made the beginning (18. 1); Jehoram follows it up (21. 4); the Arabians continue the assault (21. 17; 22. 1); Athaliah nearly succeeds in accomplishing the design of Satan (22. 10).

6 the daughter of Ahab: i. e. Athaliah. See Ap. 23 and 55.

evil. Heb. *rā'a'*. Ap. 44. viii.

the LORD. Heb. Jehovah. Ap. 4. II.

7 the covenant. Cp. 2 Sam. 7. 12-17.

as = according as.

a light = a lamp. Cp. 1 Kings 15. 4; 11. 36. The word always refers to this promise to David.

21. 8-19 (*E*, p. 591). EVENTS. PUBLIC.
(*Alternation.*)

E | n | 8-10. Revolts. Edom and Libnah.
  | o | 11-15. Judgments. Prophesied.
  | *n* | 16, 17. Invasions. Philistines and Arabians.
  | *o* | 18, 19. Judgments. Fulfilled.

8 the Edomites revolted. Thus fulfilling Gen. 27. 40. Cp. 2 Kings 8. 20.

9 went forth with his princes. Cp. 2 Kings 8. 21. They went to Zair.

10 unto this day. Cp. 2 Kings 8. 22.

did Libnah revolt. Libnah was a city of the priests (Josh. 21. 13). The Temple was broken up (24. 4, 7), and the priests combined to dethrone Athaliah, and to restore the worship of Jehovah (23. 14-17; 24. 4-11).

God. Heb. Elohim. Ap. 4. I.

11 mountains. A special various reading called *Sevīr* (Ap. 34), some codices, with one early printed edition, Sept., and Vulg., read "cities".

fornication. Literal as well as spiritual, connected with the worship of the *'Ashērah* (Ap. 42).

compelled. Cp. Deut. 4. 19.

12 there came = was brought. Why assume that Elijah then sent it? It might have "come" as Holy Scripture comes to us to-day, though written in the past. It does not say a "letter" (which would be *'iggereth*, or *sepher*, a book), but *mich^etāb*, any writing, written at any time; probably a prophetic writing to be delivered at this particular time.

Elijah. Long since raptured (2 Kings 2: cp. 3. 11). This is the only mention of Elijah in Chronicles.

14 Behold. Fig. *Asterismos*. Ap. 6.

and. Note the Fig. *Polysyndeton* (Ap. 6) in *vv.* 14, 15.

children = sons.

16 spirit. Heb. *rūach*. Ap. 9. Put by Fig. *Metonymy* (of Cause), Ap. 6, for life in its manifestations.

the Philistines. These were tributaries before this (17. 11).

were near: or were under the direction of.

17 into Judah. And as far as Jerusalem, which also they took.

his wives. Except Athaliah.

never a son left him. This shows how nearly the plot of the great enemy succeeded in breaking up the royal line. See Ap. 23, and cp. note on *v.* 4 above.

Jehoahaz, or Ahaziah (22. 1), **or Azariah** (22. 6). All the same meaning = Jehovah taketh hold. On the various spelling of proper names, see note on 1 Chron. 25. 11.

o (p. 592) 18 And after all this [6]the LORD smote him in
his bowels with an incurable disease.
796 19 And it came to pass, that in process of
time, after the end of two years, his bowels
fell out by reason of his sickness: so he died
of sore diseases. And his people made °no
burning for him, like the burning of his
fathers.

D (p. 591) 20 Thirty and two years old was he when
he began to reign, and he reigned in Jerusalem eight years, and departed °without
being desired. Howbeit they buried him in
the city of David, but not in the sepulchres
of the kings.

G[8] p (p. 593) **22** And the inhabitants of Jerusalem made
°Ahaziah his youngest son king in his
stead: for the band of men that came with the
Arabians to the camp had °slain all the eldest.
So Ahaziah the son of Jehoram king of Judah
reigned.
790 i. e. 789-788 2 °Forty and two years old *was* Ahaziah
when he began to reign, and he reigned one
year in Jerusalem. His mother's name also
was Athaliah the °daughter of Omri.

q 3 He also walked in the °ways of the house of
Ahab: for his mother was his counsellor to do
wickedly.
4 Wherefore he did °evil in the sight of °the
LORD like the house of Ahab: for they were his
counsellors after the death of his father to his
destruction.

q 5 He walked also after their counsel, and
went °with Jehoram the son of Ahab king of
Israel to war against Hazael king of Syria
at Ramoth-gilead: and the Syrians smote
°Joram.
6 And he returned to be healed in Jezreel
because of the wounds which were given him
at Ramah, when he fought with Hazael king
of Syria. And °Azariah the son of Jehoram
king of Judah went down to see Jehoram the
son of Ahab at Jezreel, because he was sick.
7 And the °destruction of Ahaziah was of
°God by coming to Joram: for when he was
come, he went out with Jehoram against Jehu
the son of Nimshi, °whom [4]the LORD had anointed to cut off the house of Ahab.
8 And it came to pass, that, when Jehu was
executing judgment upon the house of Ahab,
and found the princes of Judah, and the sons
of the brethren of Ahaziah, that ministered
to Ahaziah, he slew them.
9 And he sought Ahaziah: and they caught
him, (for he was °hid °in Samaria,) and °brought
him °to Jehu: and when they had slain him,
they buried him: "Because," said they, "he *is*
the son of Jehoshaphat, who sought [4]the LORD
with all his heart."

p So the house of Ahaziah had no power to keep
still the kingdom.

G[9] F[1] 788 10 But when Athaliah the mother of Ahaziah
saw that her son was dead, °she arose and
destroyed all the seed royal of the house of
Judah.

G[1] 11 But Jehoshabeath, the daughter of the king,
took Joash the son of Ahaziah, and stole him
°from among the king's sons that were slain,
and put him and his nurse in a °bedchamber.
So Jehoshabeath, °the daughter of king Jehoram, °the wife of Jehoiada the priest, (for
she was the sister of Ahaziah,) hid him from
Athaliah, so that she slew him not.
12 And he was with them [9]hid °in the house 788-782
of [7]God °six years:
and Athaliah reigned over the land. F[2]

---

19 no burning: i. e. of spices.
20 without being desired = unregretted.

22. 1-9 (G[8], p. 545). AHAZIAH. (*Introversion.*)

G[8] | p | 1, 2. Introduction.
  q | 3, 4. Events. Personal.
  q | 5-9-. Events. Public.
p | -9. Conclusion.

1 Ahaziah. See note on Jehoahaz (21. 17).
slain all the eldest. See note on 21. 17.
2 Forty and two years old = a son of forty-two years: i. e. of the house of Omri, on account of his connection with it through his mother (832-790 = 42). In 2 Kings 8. 26 Ahaziah's actual age (twenty-two years) is given when he began to reign (790) during the two years of his father's disease. His father, Jehoram, was thirty-two when he began to reign with Jehoshaphat, two years before the latter's death (2 Kings 8. 16). This was in 796. Jehoram therefore was born in 828. Ahaziah, his son, being twenty-two when he began his co-regency, was therefore born in 812; his father being sixteen years old. See Ap. 50. V, pp. 57, 58.
daughter of Omri. Daughter put by Fig. *Synecdoche* (of Genus) for granddaughter. See Ap. 55.
3 ways. Cp. 2 Kings 8. 27.
4 evil = the evils. Heb. *rā'a'*. Ap. 44. viii.
the LORD. Heb. Jehovah. Ap. 4. II.
5 with Jehoram. Cp. 2 Kings 8. 28, &c.
Joram. Another spelling of Jehoram. See note on 1 Chron. 25. 11.
6 Azariah. Same as Ahaziah. See note on *v.* 1 and 21. 17. **7 destruction.** Cp. 2 Kings 9. 21-27.
God. Heb. Elohim. Ap. 4. I.
whom the LORD had anointed. Cp. 2 Kings 9. 6, 7.
9 hid = hiding himself.
in Samaria. The province, not the city.
brought him. His wounds being partially healed.
to Jehu. Who must have been then at Megiddo (2 Kings 9. 27).

22. 10—23. 21 (G[9], p. 545). ATHALIAH. (USURPATION.) (*Repeated Alternation.*)

G[9] | F[1] | 22. 10. Athaliah. Murderess.
  G[1] | 22. 11, 12-. Joash. Rescue and concealment.
F[2] | 22. -12. Athaliah. Usurpation.
  G[2] | 23. 1-11. Joash. Investiture.
F[3] | 23. 12. Athaliah. Alarm.
  G[3] | 23. 13-. Joash. Station.
F[4] | 23. -13-15. Athaliah. Execution.
  G[4] | 23. 16-20. Joash. Exaltation.
F[5] | 23. 17. Athaliah. End.

10 she arose and destroyed. The enemy's third attempt, at this time, to destroy the royal succession: (1) 21. 4; (2) 21. 17; 22. 1; (3) 22. 10. This time he well-nigh succeeded. See Ap. 25.
11 from among . . . slain. As Christ, the Antitype, Who was raised from among the dead, and is now hidden on high (Acts 3. 21).
bedchamber. One formerly used by the priests.
the daughter of king Jehoram: i. e. of the former king of that name (2 Kings 11. 2).
the wife of Jehoiada the priest. Hence her action. See note on "Libnah" (21. 10).
12 in the house of God. The safest of all places at that time; for its courts were deserted (24. 7).
six. The number of man. See Ap. 10.

G² r (p. 594) 782 **23** °And in the °seventh year Jehoiada
°strengthened himself, and took the cap-
tains of hundreds, Azariah the son of Jeroham,
and Ishmael the son of Jehohanan, and Azariah
the son of Obed, and Maaseiah the son of
Adaiah, and Elishaphat the son of Zichri, into
covenant with him.
2 And they went about in Judah, and gathered
the Levites out of all the cities of Judah, and
the chief of the fathers of °Israel, and they
came to Jerusalem.
3 And all the °congregation made a covenant
with the king in the house of °God.
s And he said unto them, °"Behold, the king's
son shall reign, °as °the LORD °hath said of
the sons of David.
r 4 This *is* the thing that ye shall do; A third
part of you entering on the sabbath, of the
priests and of the Levites, *shall be* porters of
the °doors;
5 And a third part *shall be* at the king's house;
and a third part at the gate of the foundation:
and all the People *shall be* in the courts of the
house of [3]the LORD.
6 But let none come into the house of [3]the
LORD, save the priests, and they that minister
of the Levites; they shall go in, for they *are*
°holy: but all the People shall keep the watch
of [3]the LORD.
7 And the Levites shall compass the king
round about, °every man with his weapons in
his hand; and whosoever *else* cometh into the
house, he shall be put to death: but be ye with
the king when he cometh in, and when he
goeth out."
8 So the Levites and all Judah did according to all things that Jehoiada the priest had
commanded, and took [7]every man his °men
that were to come in on the sabbath, with
them that were to go *out* on the sabbath: for
Jehoiada the priest dismissed not the courses.
9 Moreover Jehoiada the priest delivered to
the captains of hundreds spears, and bucklers,
and shields, that *had been* king David's, which
were in the house of [3]God.
10 And he set all the People, every man having his weapon in his hand, from the right
side of the °temple to the left side of the temple, along by the altar and the °temple, by the
king round about.
s 11 Then they brought out the king's son, and
°put upon him the crown, and *gave him* the
testimony, and made him king. And Jehoiada
and his sons anointed him, and said, [3]"God
save the king."
F³ (p. 593) 12 Now when Athaliah heard the noise of
the People running and praising the king, she
came to the People into the house of [3]the
LORD:
G³ 13 And she looked, and, °behold, the king
°stood at his pillar at the entering in, and the
princes and the trumpets by the king: and all
the People of the land rejoiced, and sounded
with trumpets, also the singers with instruments of musick, and such as taught to sing
praise.
F⁴ Then Athaliah rent her clothes, and said,
°"Treason, Treason."
14 Then Jehoiada the priest °brought out the
captains of hundreds that were set over the
°host, and said unto them, "Have her forth
of the ranges: and whoso followeth her, let
him be slain with the sword." For the priest
said, "Slay her not in the house of [3]the LORD."
15 So they °laid hands on her; and when
she was come to the entering of the horse gate 782
by the king's house, they slew her there.
16 And Jehoiada made a covenant between G⁴
him, and between all the People, and between
the king, that they should be [3]the LORD'S
People.
17 Then all the People went to °the house of
Baal, and brake it down, and brake his altars
and his images in pieces, and °slew Mattan
the priest of Baal before the altars.
18 Also Jehoiada appointed the offices of the
house of [3]the LORD by the hand of the priests
°the Levites, whom David had distributed in
the house of [3]the LORD, to offer the burnt offerings °of [3]the LORD, as *it is* written in the law
of Moses, with rejoicing and with singing,
as it was ordained °by David.
19 And he set the porters at the gates of the
house of [3]the LORD, that none *which was* unclean in any thing should enter in.

23. 1-11 (G², p. 593). JOASH. INVESTITURE.
(*Alternation.*)

G² | r | 1-3-. Assemblage.
| s | -3. The king's son. Revealed.
| r | 4-10. Arrangements.
| s | 11. The king's son. Crowned.

1 And. This chapter is complementary to 2 Kings 11. 4-20. See Ap. 56.
seventh. The number of spiritual perfection. Ap. 10.
strengthened himself. Chronicles mentions the military (*v.* 1), but enlarges on the Levites (*vv.* 2, &c.). Kings recognises the Levites (2 Kings 11. 4-12), but enlarges on the military. See note on Title of 1 Chronicles, and Ap. 56.
2 Israel. Note this word here, and see note on 1 Kings 12. 17.
3 congregation = assembly, or muster.
God. Heb. Elohim (with Art.) = the [true] God. Ap. 4. I.
Behold. Fig. *Asterismos* (Ap. 6), to emphasise the text or sermon of Jehoiada, which was the faithfulness of Jehovah to His word.
as = according as.
the LORD. Heb. Jehovah. Ap. 4. II.
hath said. This is the great point. Cp. 6. 16; 7. 18. 2 Sam. 7. 12. 1 Kings 2. 4; 9. 5.
4 doors = thresholds. Especially that of Sur (2 Kings 11. 6).
6 holy. See note on Ex. 3. 5.
7 every man. Heb. *'ish.* Ap. 14. II.
8 men. Heb. *'ish.* Ap. 14. III.
10 temple = house, as in preceding context.
11 put upon him the crown, and the testimony. Fig. *Zeugma* (Ap. 6), by which there is an Ellipsis (Ap. 6) of the second verb, rightly supplied in A.V., "gave him".
testimony: i. e. the book of the Law.
13 behold. Fig. *Asterismos.* Ap. 6.
stood = standing.
Treason, Treason. Fig. *Epizeuxis.* Ap. 6.
14 brought out. Syr. reads "commanded". Cp. 2 Kings 11. 15.
host = force.
15 laid hands on her: or, made way for her.
17 the house of Baal. All the vessels of the Temple had been removed thither by Jehoram and Athaliah (24. 7).
slew Mattan. According to Deut. 13. 9.
18 the Levites. Sept., Syr., and Vulg. read "and the Levites".
of. Some codices, with six early printed editions, read "to".
by David. Heb. "upon (or by) the hands of David".

782 20 And he took the captains of hundreds, and the nobles, and the governors of the People, and all the People of the land, and brought down the king from the house of [3]the LORD: and they came through the high gate into the king's house, and set the king upon the throne of the kingdom.

F[5] (p. 593) 21 And all the People of the land °rejoiced: and the city was °quiet, after that they had slain Athaliah with the sword.

G[10] H (p. 595) 782 to 742 **24** °Joash *was* seven years old when he began to reign, and he reigned forty years in Jerusalem. His mother's name also *was* Zibiah of Beer-sheba.

2 And Joash did *that which was* right in the sight of °the LORD all the days of Jehoiada the priest.

3 And Jehoiada took °for him two wives; and he begat sons and daughters.

K M O 4 And °it came to pass after this, *that* Joash was minded °to repair the house of [2]the LORD.

P t 5 And he gathered together the priests and the Levites, and said to them, "Go out unto the cities of Judah, and gather °of all Israel °money to repair the house of your °God from year to year, and see that ye hasten the matter."

u Howbeit the Levites hastened *it* not.

v 6 And °the king called for Jehoiada the chief, and said unto him, "Why hast thou not required of the Levites to bring in out of Judah and out of Jerusalem the °collection, *according to the commandment* of °Moses the servant of [2]the LORD, and of the °congregation of Israel, for the °tabernacle of witness?"

7 For the °sons of Athaliah, °that wicked woman, had broken up the house of [5]God; and also all the °dedicated things of the house of [2]the LORD did they bestow upon Baalim.

t 8 And at the king's commandment they made a chest, and set it without at the gate of the house of [2]the LORD.

9 And they made a proclamation through Judah and Jerusalem, to bring in to [2]the LORD [6]the collection *that* °Moses the servant of [5]God *laid* upon Israel in the wilderness.

u 10 And all the princes and all the People rejoiced, and brought in, and cast into the chest, until they had made an end.

v 11 Now it came to pass, that at what time the chest was brought unto the king's office by the hand of the Levites, and when they saw that *there was* much money, the king's scribe and the high priest's officer came and emptied the chest, and took it, and carried it to his place again. Thus they did day by day, and gathered money in abundance.

O 12 And the king and Jehoiada gave it to °such as did the work of the service of the house of [2]the LORD, and hired masons and carpenters to repair the house of [2]the LORD, and also such as wrought iron and brass to mend the house of [2]the LORD.

21 rejoiced . . . quiet. "After" Athaliah was slain! So will it be when the great usurper shall be finally cast down.

24. 1-27 (G[10], p. 545). JOASH.
(*Introversion.*)

G[10] | H | 1-3. Introduction.
  J | 4-26. Events.
 H | 27. Conclusion.

1 Joash. Cp. 2 Kings 12. 1, 2.
2 the LORD. Heb. Jehovah. Ap. 4. II.
3 for him: i. e. Joash. Was this because the line was almost extinct, or from lack of faith?

4-26 (J, above). EVENTS.
(*Introversion.*)

J | K | 4-22. Administration of Jehoiada.
  L | 23, 24. Invasion by Syrians.
 K | 25, 26. Conspiracy of servants.

4-22 (K, above). ADMINISTRATION OF JEHOIADA. (*Alternation.*)

K | M | 4-14. House of God. Repaired.
  N | 15, 16. Jehoiada. Death.
 M | 17-20. House of God. Forsaken.
  N | 21, 22. Jehoiada's son. Death.

4-14 (M, above). HOUSE OF GOD. REPAIRED.
(*Alternation.*)

M | O | 4. Repairs. Purposed.
  P | 5-11. Collection. Made.
 O | 12, 13. Repairs. Effected.
  P | 14. Collection. Surplus.

4 it came to pass. Cp. 2 Kings 12. 4, 5.
to repair. See *v.* 7.

5-11 (P, above). COLLECTION. MADE.
(*Extended Alternation.*)

P | t | 5-. Command of Joash.
  u | -5. Delay of Levites.
   v | 6, 7. Need and expostulation.
 t | 8, 9. Command of Joash.
  u | 10. Alacrity of princes and people.
   v | 11. Need supplied. Abundance.

5 of all Israel. See note on 1 Kings 12. 17.
money = silver.
God. Heb. Elohim. Ap. 4. I.
6 the king called. In the twenty-third year (2 Kings 12. 6).
collection = the tribute of the half-shekel redemption money (Ex. 30. 13-16). See Ap. 51. I.
Moses the servant of the LORD. See note on Deut. 34. 5. **congregation** = assembly.
tabernacle. Heb. *'ohel.* Ap. 40.
7 sons of Athaliah. Ahaziah and his brethren before they were slain (21. 17), which may have been allowed in consequence of their sin. Cp. 21. 10-12.
that wicked woman. The term found only here.
dedicated = holy. See note on Ex. 3. 5.
9 Moses the servant of God. See note on 1 Chron. 6. 49.
12 such as did the work. Heb. text reads sing., "him who did". The A.V., following some codices, with Aram., Sept., Syr., and Vulg., reads pl.
13 by them: i. e. by their hand: i. e. by their direction.

13 So the workmen wrought, and the work was perfected °by them, and they set the house of [5]God in his state, and strengthened it.

14 And when they had finished *it*, they brought the rest of the money before the king and Jehoiada, whereof were made vessels for *P*

782 to 742 the house of [2]the LORD, *even* vessels to minister, °and to offer *withal*, and spoons, and vessels of gold and silver. And they offered burnt offerings in the house of [2]the LORD continually all the days of Jehoiada.

N (p. 595) 15 But Jehoiada waxed old, and was full of days when he died; °an hundred and thirty years old *was he* when he died.

16 And they buried him in the city of David °among the kings, because he had done good in Israel, both toward [5]God, and toward His house.

M 17 Now after the death of Jehoiada came the princes of Judah, and °made obeisance to the king. Then the king hearkened unto them.

18 And they left the house of [2]the LORD [5]God of their fathers, and served °groves and °idols: and °wrath came upon Judah and Jerusalem for this their °trespass.

19 Yet He sent prophets to them, to bring them again unto [2]the LORD; and °they testified against them: but they would not give ear.

20 And the °Spirit of [5]God °came upon °Zechariah the son of Jehoiada the priest, which stood above the People, and said unto them, "Thus °saith [5]God, 'Why transgress ye the commandments of [2]the LORD, that ye cannot prosper? because ye have forsaken [2]the LORD, He hath also forsaken you.'"

N 21 And they conspired against him, and °stoned him with stones °at the commandment of the king in the court of the house of [2]the LORD.

22 Thus Joash the king remembered not the kindness which Jehoiada his father had done to him, but slew his son. And when °he died, he said, [2]"The LORD look upon *it*, °and require *it*."

L 23 And it came to pass at the end of the year, *that* the °host of Syria came up against him: and they came to Judah and Jerusalem, and °destroyed all the princes of the People from among the People, and sent all the spoil of them unto the king of Damascus.

24 For the army of the Syrians came with a small company of °men, and [2]the LORD delivered a very great [23]host into their hand, because they had forsaken [2]the LORD [5]God of their fathers. So they executed judgment against Joash.

K 25 And when they were departed from him, (for they left him in great diseases,) his own servants conspired against him for the blood of the °sons of Jehoiada the priest, and slew him on his bed, and he died: and they buried him in the city of David, but they buried him °not in the sepulchres of the kings.

26 And these are they that conspired against him; °Zabad the son of Shimeath an Ammonitess, and °Jehozabad the son of °Shimrith a Moabitess.

H 27 Now *concerning* his sons, and the greatness of the °burdens *laid* upon him, and the °repairing of the house of [5]God, °behold, they *are* written in the °story of the book of the kings. And Amaziah °his son reigned in his stead.

14 and. Note the Fig. *Polysyndeton* (Ap. 6), emphasising the details.

15 an hundred and thirty years. Unprecedented since Joshua (24. 29). Born in Solomon's reign, he lived through six others.

16 among the kings. An honour refused to Joash. Cp. *v.* 25.

17 made obeisance. With the view of obtaining the king's consent to their renewal of idolatry.

18 groves. Heb. *'Ashērah.* See Ap. 42.

idols = grievous images.

wrath came. From Jehovah. Cp. *vv.* 23, 24.

trespass. Heb. *'āsham.* Ap. 44. ii.

19 they testified against them. The Vulg. reads *quos protestantes* = who in protesting against them. Thus, the first instance of the word "Protestant" is found in the Vulgate, and not in the history of the Reformation. *Pro* = for, and *testans* = witnessing, is positive, not negative. It denotes a witnessing *for* God and His truth, not merely against evil.

20 Spirit. Heb. *rūach.* Ap. 9.

came upon = clothed.

Zechariah the son of Jehoiada. In Zech. 1. 1 and Matt. 23. 35 a *second* name is given, "son of Barachias". On the use of two or more names see note on 1 Chron. 25. 11. It is quite needless to assume that there is any error, when so simple a solution lies on the surface.

saith = hath said. A rare form of the verb.

21 stoned him. One of nine persons stoned. See note on Lev. 24. 14.

at the commandment of the king. One of eleven rulers offended with God's servants. See note on Ex. 10. 28. **22 he**: i.e. Zechariah.

and require it. The very words twice used by the Lord Jesus in Luke 11. 50, 51. Cp. Matt. 23. 35.

23 host = force.

destroyed all the princes. Who had led the People astray. This is how the "wrath came" (*v.* 18).

24 men. Heb. *'ěnōsh.* Ap. 14. III.

25 sons. Put by Fig. *Synecdoche* (of Genus), Ap. 6, for Jehoiada's one son: thus emphasising the son who was slain (*vv.* 20, 21). The Sept. and Vulg. read it "son" (without the Fig.).

not in the sepulchres. As Ahaz (28. 27).

26 Zabad . . . Jehozabad. Slaves, but the executioners of God's judgment. Zabad had another name (Jozachar), used in 2 Kings 12. 21.

Shimrith. In 2 Kings 12. 21 he has another name, "Shomer", if not his father's name.

27 burdens laid upon him. By the king of Syria (2 Kings 12. 18). **repairing** (*vv.* 4–14).

behold. Fig. *Asterismos.* Ap. 6.

story = the commentary. See note on 13. 22, the only other place in which the word is found.

his son. Not so in Israel. There they set up whom they chose (1 Kings 15. 27; 16. 15, 22). Here is seen Jehovah's faithfulness, in "the sure mercies of David" (2 Sam. 7. 16. Ps. 89. 34–36).

25. 1–28 (G[11], p. 545). **AMAZIAH.**

(*Introversion and Alternation.*)

G[11] | Q | 1, 2. Introduction.
  R | S | 3, 4. Home events. Requital.
    T | 5–13. Foreign events. War.
  R | *S* | 14–16. Home events. Apostasy.
    T | 17–24. Foreign events. War.
Q | 25–28. Conclusion.

1 Amaziah. Cp. 2 Kings 14. 1–3. Complementary to Kings (see Ap. 56); *vv.* 5–10 and 13–16 are additional.

25 °Amaziah *was* twenty and five years old *when* he began to reign, and he reigned twenty and nine years in Jerusalem. And his mother's name *was* Jehoaddan of Jerusalem. G[11] Q (p. 596) 743 to 714

2 And he did *that which was* right in the

743-714 sight of °the LORD, °but not with a perfect heart.

R S (p. 596) **3** Now it came to pass, when the kingdom was °established to him, that he slew his servants that had °killed the king his father.

4 But he slew not their children, but *did* °as *it is* written °in the law in the book of Moses, where [2]the LORD commanded, saying, "The fathers shall not die for the °children, neither shall the °children die for the fathers, but °every man shall die for his own °sin."

T w (p. 597) **5** Moreover Amaziah gathered Judah together, and made them captains over thousands, and captains over hundreds, according to the houses of *their* fathers, throughout all Judah and Benjamin: and he numbered them from twenty years old and above, and found them three hundred thousand choice *men, able* to go forth to war, that could handle spear and shield.

x **6** He hired also an hundred thousand mighty men of valour out of Israel for an hundred °talents of silver.

7 But there came °a °man of °God to him, saying, "O king, °let not the °army of °Israel go with thee; for [2]the LORD *is* °not with Israel, *to wit, with* ° all the [4]children of °Ephraim.

8 But if thou wilt go, do *it*, °be strong for the battle: [7]God shall make thee fall before the enemy: for [7]God hath power to help, and to cast down."

9 And Amaziah said to the [4]man of [7]God, "But what shall we do for the hundred [6]talents which I have given to the °army of Israel?" And the [4]man of [7]God answered, [2]"The LORD is able to give thee much more than this."

10 Then Amaziah separated them, *to wit*, the [9]army that was come to him out of [7]Ephraim, to go home again: wherefore their anger was greatly kindled against Judah, and they returned home in great anger.

w **11** And Amaziah strengthened himself, and led forth his People, and went to the °valley of salt, and smote of °the [4]children of Seir ten thousand.

12 And *other* ten thousand *left* alive did the [4]children of Judah carry away captive, and brought them unto the top of the rock, and cast them down from the top of the rock, that they all were broken in pieces.

x **13** But the soldiers of the army which Amaziah sent back, that they should not go with him to battle, fell upon the cities of Judah, from Samaria even unto Beth-horon, and smote three thousand of °them, and took much spoil.

R S (p. 596) **14** Now it came to pass, after that Amaziah was come from the slaughter of the Edomites, that he brought the gods of the [4]children of Seir, and °set them up *to be* his gods, and bowed down himself before them, and burned incense unto them.

15 Wherefore the anger of [2]the LORD was kindled against Amaziah, and He °sent unto him a prophet, which said unto him, "Why hast thou sought after the gods of the people, which could not °deliver their own people out of thine hand?"

16 And it came to pass, as he talked with him, that *the king* said unto him, °"Art thou made °of the king's counsel? forbear; why shouldest thou be smitten?" Then the prophet forbare, and said, "I know that [7]God hath °determined to destroy thee, because thou hast done this, and hast not hearkened unto my counsel."

17 Then Amaziah king of Judah took °advice, and sent to Joash, the son of Jehoahaz, the son of Jehu, king of Israel, saying, "Come, let us °see one another in the face." T y (p. 597)

18 And Joash king of Israel sent to Amaziah king of Judah, saying, "The °thistle that *was* in Lebanon sent to the cedar that *was* in Lebanon, saying, 'Give thy daughter to my son to wife:' and there passed by a wild beast that *was* in Lebanon, and trode down the °thistle. z

19 Thou sayest, Lo, thou hast smitten the Edomites; and thine heart lifteth thee up to boast: abide now at home; why shouldest

---

2 the LORD. Heb. Jehovah. Ap. 4. II.
but not. Cp. *vv.* 6-9, 14, 17. Cp. 2 Kings 14. 4.
3 established = confirmed.
killed the king (24. 25, 26).
4 as it is written. Cp. Deut. 24. 16.
in the law in the book of Moses. See Ap. 47.
children = sons.
every man. Heb. *'ish.* Ap. 14. II.
sin. Heb. *chāṭā'.* Ap. 44. i.

25. 5-13 (T, p. 596). FOREIGN EVENTS. WAR WITH EPHRAIM. (*Alternation.*)

T | w | 5. Home levies. Raised.
  x | 6-10. Mercenaries. Prohibition.
  w | 11, 12. Home levies. Led.
  x | 13. Mercenaries. Sent back.

6 talents. See Ap. 51. I.
7 a man of God. See Ap. 49.
man. Heb. *'ish.* Ap. 14. II.
God. Heb. Elohim. Ap. 4.
let not. For similar protests cp. 19. 2; 20. 37.
army = host.
Israel. These were mercenaries gathered out of the ten tribes, to be used against Edom (*v.* 6).
not with. This is the measure by which our alliances of all kinds should be tried.
all the children of Ephraim = any of the sons of Ephraim. Of these were the kings of Israel.
Ephraim. Put here for the whole northern kingdom.
8 be strong. Fig. *Eironeia.* Ap. 6.
9 army = troop.
11 valley of salt. South of the Dead Sea.
the children of Seir: i. e. the Edomites.
13 them: i. e. men, not villages.
14 set them up. For a similar action see 28. 23.
15 sent unto him a prophet. When He might have sent a sore judgment.
deliver = rescue.
16 Art thou made of, &c. = Have we given thee to be of.
of the king's counsel = for counsellor to the king.
determined = counselled.

17-24 (*T*, p. 596). FOREIGN EVENTS. WAR. (*Introversion.*)

T | y | 17. Amaziah. Challenge.
  z | 18-20. Challenge given.
  z | 21. Challenge accepted.
  y | 22-24. Amaziah. Defeat.

17 advice = counsel, as in *v.* 16. He took man's counsel, but not God's.
see = look. Idiom for desire to fight.
18 thistle = thorn. Cp. 2 Kings 14. 9.

743 thou meddle to *thine* hurt, that thou shouldest
to fall, *even* thou, and Judah with thee?"
714 20 But Amaziah would not hear; for it *came*
of [7]God, that He might deliver them into the
hand *of their enemies,* because they sought
after the gods of Edom.
z 21 So Joash the king of Israel went up; and
(p. 597) they °saw one another in the face, *both* he and
Amaziah king of Judah, at Beth-shemesh,
which *belongeth* to Judah.
y 22 And Judah was put to the worse before
Israel, and they fled [4]every man to his tent.
23 And Joash the king of Israel took Amaziah king of Judah, the son of Joash, the son of
Jehoahaz, at Beth-shemesh, and brought him
to Jerusalem, and brake down the wall of Jerusalem from the gate of Ephraim to the corner
gate, four hundred °cubits.
24 And *he took* all the gold and the silver,
and all the vessels that were found in the house
of [7]God with °Obed-edom, and the treasures of
the king's house, the °hostages also, and returned to Samaria.
Q 25 And Amaziah the son of Joash king of
(p. 596) Judah lived after the death of Joash son of
729 Jehoahaz king of Israel fifteen years.
to 26 Now the rest of the acts of Amaziah, first
714 and last, behold, °*are* they not written in the
book of the kings of Judah and Israel?
27 Now after the time that Amaziah did turn
away from following [2]the LORD they °made a
conspiracy against him in Jerusalem; and he
fled to Lachish: but they sent to Lachish after
him, and slew him there.
28 And they brought him upon horses, and
buried him with his fathers in °the city of
Judah.

G[12] U **26** °Then all the People of Judah took
(p. 598) °Uzziah, who *was* sixteen years old,
and made him king in the room of his father
Amaziah.
2 He built Eloth, and restored it to Judah, after
that the °king °slept with his fathers.
3 Sixteen years old *was* Uzziah when he
701 °began to reign, and he reigned fifty and two
to years in Jerusalem. His mother's name also
649 *was* Jecoliah of Jerusalem.
V 4 And he did *that which was* °right in the
sight of °the LORD, according to all that his
father Amaziah did.
5 And he sought °God in the days of Zechariah, °who had understanding in the visions of
°God: °and as long as he sought [4]the LORD,
°God made him to prosper.
W X 6 And he went forth and warred against the
Philistines, and brake down the wall of Gath,
and the wall of °Jabneh, and the wall of Ashdod, and built °cities about Ashdod, and among
the Philistines.
7 And [5]God helped him against the Philistines, and against the Arabians that dwelt in
Gur-baal, and the °Mehunims.
Y 8 And the Ammonites gave gifts to Uzziah:
and his name °spread abroad *even* to the entering in of Egypt; for he strengthened *himself*
exceedingly.
W X a 9 Moreover Uzziah built towers in Jerusalem
at the corner gate, and at the valley gate, and
at the turning *of the wall,* and fortified them.

21 saw. See note on "see" (*v.* 17).
23 cubits. See Ap. 51. III. 2.
24 Obed-edom. He and his family were the Temple treasurers (1 Chron. 26. 15).
hostages. Heb. "sons of securities".
26 are they not . . . ? Fig. *Erotēsis.* Ap. 6.
27 made a conspiracy = conspired a great conspiracy. Fig. *Polyptōton* (Ap. 6).
28 the city of Judah = Jerusalem. The only occurrence of the expression. Some codices, with Sept. and Syr. and Vulg., read "the city of David".

26. 1-23 (G[12], p. 545). **UZZIAH.**
(*Introversion and Alternation.*)

G[12] | U | 1-3. Introduction.
  V | 4, 5. Personal. Well-doing.
    W | X | 6, 7. Events. Foreign wars.
      Y | 8. Renown.
    W | *X* | 9-15-. Events. Home affairs.
      Y | -15. Renown.
  V | 16-21. Personal. Evil-doing.
U | 22, 23. Conclusion.

1 Then. This chapter largely complementary to 2 Kings 15. 1-7. See Ap. 56.
Uzziah. Another spelling is Azariah. In Chronicles and the Prophets it is usually Uzziah, except in 1 Chron. 3. 12. **2 king:** i. e. Amaziah.
slept with his fathers. See note on Deut. 31. 16.
3 began to reign. 2 Kings 15. 1 says he began to reign in the 27th of Jeroboam. This leaves a gap of thirteen years (714-701). See Ap. 50. V, pp. 58, 59.
4 right. Cp. 25. 2 and 2 Kings 15. 3.
the LORD. Heb. Jehovah. Ap. 4. II.
5 God. Heb. Elohim, with Art. = the [true] God. Ap. 4. I.
who had understanding in the visions of God. This is the Fig. *Periphrasis* (Ap. 6) for a prophet.
and. Note: a more or less complete *Polysyndeton* (Ap. 6) runs through this account of Uzziah, to emphasise the details.
6 Jabneh, now "*Yebnah*". Between Joppa and Ashdod, on northern boundary of Judah.
cities = fortresses.
7 Mehunims. See note on 20. 1 and 1 Chron. 4. 41.
8 spread abroad. Cp. *v.* 15, and see Structure above.

9-15- (*X*, above). **EVENTS. HOME AFFAIRS.**
(*Introversion.*)

X | a | 9. Jerusalem. Fortifications.
  b | 10. Defences. Forts, &c.
    c | 11-13. Armies.
  b | 14. Defences. Armour.
a | 15-. Jerusalem. Fortifications.

11 host = force.
by bands = troops, or for foray.
by the hand = under the direction of.
12 chief = head.
the mighty men. Heb. *gibbōr.* Ap. 14. IV.

10 Also he built towers in the desert, and b
digged many wells: for he had much cattle,
both in the low country, and in the plains:
husbandmen *also,* and vine dressers in the
mountains, and in Carmel: for he loved husbandry.
11 Moreover Uzziah had an °host of fighting c
men, that went out to war °by bands, according to the number of their account °by the
hand of Jeiel the scribe and Maaseiah the
ruler, under the hand of Hananiah, *one* of
the king's captains.
12 The whole number of the °chief of the
fathers of °the mighty men of valour *were* two
thousand and six hundred.
13 And under their hand *was* an army,
three hundred thousand and seven thousand

701-649 and five hundred, that made war with mighty
power, to help the king against the enemy.

b (p. 598) 14 And Uzziah prepared for them throughout all the [11]host shields, °and spears, and helmets, and °habergeons, and bows, and slings *to cast* stones.

a 15 And he made in Jerusalem °engines, invented by °cunning men, to be on the towers and upon the bulwarks, to shoot arrows and great stones withal.

Y And his name spread far abroad; for he was °marvellously helped, °till he was strong.

V d (p. 599) 652? 16 But °when he was strong, his heart was lifted up to *his* destruction: for he °transgressed against [4]the LORD [5]his God, and went into the temple of [4]the LORD to burn incense upon the altar of incense.

e 17 And Azariah the priest went in after him, and with him fourscore priests of [4]the LORD, *that were* °valiant men:

18 And they withstood Uzziah the king, and said unto him, "*It appertaineth* not unto thee, Uzziah, to burn incense unto [4]the LORD, but to the priests the sons of Aaron, that are °consecrated to burn incense: go out of the sanctuary; for thou hast °trespassed; neither *shall it be* for thine honour from [4]the LORD [5]God."

d 19 Then Uzziah °was wroth,

e and *had* a censer in his hand to burn incense: and while he °was wroth with the priests, °the leprosy even rose up °in his forehead before the priests in the house of [4]the LORD, from beside the incense altar.

20 And Azariah °the chief priest, and all the priests, looked upon him, and, °behold, he *was* leprous in his forehead, and they thrust him out from thence; yea, °himself hasted also to go out, because [4]the LORD had smitten him.

21 And Uzziah the king was a leper unto the day of his death, and dwelt in a °several house, *being* a leper; for he was cut off from the house of [4]the LORD: and Jotham his son *was* over the king's house, judging the People of the land.

U (p. 598) 22 Now the rest of the acts of Uzziah, first and last, did °Isaiah the prophet, the son of Amoz, write.

23 So Uzziah °slept with his fathers, and they buried him with his fathers in °the field of the burial which *belonged* to the kings; for they said, "He *is* a leper:" and Jotham his son reigned in his stead.

G[13] A (p. 599) 647 to 631 **27** Jotham *was* °twenty and five years old when he began to reign, and he reigned sixteen years in Jerusalem. His mother's name also *was* Jerushah, the daughter of Zadok.

B 2 And he did *that which was* right in the sight of °the LORD, °according to all that his father Uzziah did: howbeit he °entered not into the temple of °the LORD. And the people did yet corruptly.

B 3 He built the °high gate of the house of [2]the LORD, and on the wall of °Ophel he built much.

4 Moreover he built cities in the mountains of Judah, and in the forests he built castles and towers.

5 He fought also with the king of the Ammonites, and prevailed against them. And the °children of Ammon gave him the same year an hundred °talents of silver, and ten thousand °measures of wheat, and ten thousand of barley. So much did the °children of Ammon pay unto him, both the second year, and the third.

6 So Jotham °became mighty, because he

---

14 and. Note the Fig. *Polysyndeton.* Ap. 6.
habergeons = bucklers, or coats of mail.
15 engines. The Roman balista, or catapults that would cast stones up to 300 lb. a quarter of a mile.
cunning. Old Eng. = knowing, or skilful.
marvellously helped: or, marvelled at for being helped.
till he was strong. This is the zone of real danger. When we are weak, then are we strong (2 Cor. 12. 9, 10; 13. 4).

26. 16-21 (*V*, p. 598). PERSONAL. EVIL-DOING. (*Alternation.*)

V | d | 16. Uzziah. Transgression.
 e | 17, 18. Jehovah. Opposition.
 d | 19-. Uzziah. Anger.
 e | -19-21. Jehovah. Judgment.

16 when he was strong. See note on *v.* 15.
transgressed. Heb. *mā'al.* Ap. 44. xi.
17 valiant men = sons of valour.
18 consecrated = sanctified, or set apart. See note on Ex. 28. 41.
trespassed. Same word as "transgressed" (*v.* 16).
19 was wroth. One of eleven rulers offended with God's faithful servants. See note on Ex. 10. 28.
the leprosy. One of nine so affected. See note on Ex. 4. 6. The death penalty of Num. 18. 7 was thus limited.
in his forehead. In contrast with the high priest's frontlet, "Holiness to Jehovah".
20 the chief priest. See note on Lev. 4. 3.
behold. Fig. *Asterismos.* Ap. 6.
himself hasted. As Haman (Est. 6. 12).
21 several house = the separate house, or lazar house.
22 Isaiah. Raised up to prophesy in his reign. Wrote parts of 2 Kings, and his prophecy, cp. 32. 32.
23 slept with his fathers. See note on Deut. 31. 16.
the field of the burial. Not in the royal sepulchres.

27. 1-9 (G[13], p. 545). JOTHAM. (*Introversion.*)

G[13] | A | 1. Introduction.
 B | 2. Events. Personal.
 B | 3-6. Events. Public.
 A | 7-9. Conclusion.

1 twenty and five years old: i.e. when he began to reign alone. He was twenty when his father was smitten, and when he became co-regent. At his father's death he was twenty-five, and Ahaz was five. See Ap. 50. V, p. 59.
2 the LORD. Heb. Jehovah. Ap. 4. II.
according to all: i.e. to all the good, not the evil. Hence the "howbeit", which follows.
entered not into. As his father had done (26. 16). Not like Ahaz (28. 24). **3 high** = upper.
Ophel = the Ophel; or, the lofty place or tower at the north end of the hill of Zion, between Zion and the Temple.
5 children = sons. **talents.** See Ap. 51. II.
measures. Heb. *kor.* Ap. 51. III. 3.
6 became mighty = strengthened himself.

°prepared his ways before [2]the LORD his °God.

A (p. 599) 7 Now the rest of the acts of Jotham, and all his wars, and his ways, °lo, they *are* written in the book of the kings of Israel and Judah.

647 to 631 8 He was °five and twenty years old when he began to reign, and reigned sixteen years in Jerusalem.

9 And Jotham °slept with his fathers, and they buried him in the city of David: and Ahaz his son reigned in his stead.

G[14] C (p. 600) 632 to 616

28

Ahaz *was* °twenty years old °when he began to reign, and he reigned sixteen years in Jerusalem: but he did °not *that which was* right in the sight of °the LORD, like David his father:

D 2 °For he walked in the ways of the kings of Israel, and made also molten images for Baalim.

3 Moreover he burnt incense in the valley of the son of Hinnom, and burnt his °children in the fire, after the abominations of the °heathen whom [1]the LORD had cast out before the °children of Israel.

4 He °sacrificed also and burnt incense in the high places, and on the hills, and under every green tree.

E F 5 Wherefore [1]the LORD °his °God delivered him into the hand of °the king of Syria; and °they smote him, and carried away a great multitude of them captives, and brought *them* to Damascus. And he was also delivered into the hand of the king of Israel, who smote him with a great slaughter.

6 For °Pekah the son of Remaliah slew in Judah an hundred and twenty thousand in one day, *which were* all °valiant men; because they had forsaken [1]the LORD [5]God of their fathers.

7 And Zichri, a °mighty man of Ephraim, slew Maaseiah the king's son, and Azrikam the governor of the house, and Elkanah *that was* next to the king.

8 And the [3]children of Israel carried away captive of their brethren two hundred thousand, °women, sons, and daughters, and °took also away much spoil from them, and brought the spoil to Samaria.

9 But a prophet of [1]the LORD was there, whose name *was* °Oded: and he °went out before the host that came to Samaria, and said unto them, "Behold, because [1]the LORD [5]God of your fathers was wroth with Judah, He hath delivered them into your hand, and ye have slain them in a rage *that* °reacheth up unto heaven.

10 And now ye purpose to keep under the [3]children of Judah and Jerusalem for bondmen and bondwomen unto you: *but* °*are there* not with you, even with you, °sins against [1]the LORD your [5]God?

11 Now hear me therefore, and deliver the captives again, which ye have taken captive of your brethren: for the fierce wrath of °the LORD *is* upon you."

12 Then °certain of the °heads of the [3]children of Ephraim, Azariah the son of °Johanan, Berechiah the son of Meshillemoth, and Jehizkiah the son of Shallum, and Amasa the son of Hadlai, stood up against them that came from the war,

13 And said unto them, "Ye shall not bring in the captives hither: for whereas we have °offended against [1]the LORD *already*, ye intend to add *more* to our °sins and to our °trespass: for our °trespass is great, and *there is* fierce wrath against Israel."

14 So the armed men left the captives and the spoil before the princes and all the °congregation.

---

6 prepared = fixed, or established.
God. Heb. Elohim. Ap. 4. I.
7 lo. Fig. *Asterismos*. Ap. 6.
8 five and twenty. Repeated here from *v.* 1, to show that he continued his well-doing.
9 slept, &c. See note on Deut. 31. 16.

28. 1-27 (G[14], p. 545). AHAZ.
(*Introversion and Alternation.*)

G[14] | C | 1. Introduction.
  D | 2-4. Personal. Evil-doing.
    E | F | 5-15. Defeat by Syria and Israel.
        G | 16. Embassy. Sent to Assyria.
    E | *F* | 17-19. Defeat by Edomites and Philistines.
        G | 20, 21. Embassy. Failure.
  D | 22-25. Personal. Evil-doing.
C | 26, 27. Conclusion.

This chapter is complementary to 2 Kings 16. See Ap. 56.
1 twenty years . . . sixteen years. Yet his son Hezekiah was twenty-five years old when he died (29. 1). See note on 2 Kings 16. 1.
when he: i. e. when he (Jotham). Cp. Jehoiakim and Jehoachin (36. 9. 2 Kings 24).
not . . . like. Nor like his own father Jotham, or his son Hezekiah.
the LORD. Heb. Jehovah. Ap. 4. II.
2 For. He outdid the kings of Israel: cp. 2 Kings 16. 3, 4, which brought forth the prophecies of Isaiah, Micah, Nahum, and others.
3 children = sons.
heathen = nations.
4 sacrificed. Cp. 2 Kings 16. 4.
5 his. Which should have been his.
God. Heb. Elohim. Ap. 4. I.
the king of Syria: i. e. Rezin, whom God raised up as a scourge.
they smote him: i. e. when they took Elath (2 Kings 16. 6).
6 Pekah the son of Remaliah. Cp. 2 Kings 15. 27 and Isa. 7. As Pekah ends three years before Ahaz begins, this must have taken place between 632 and 629 B. C.
valiant men = sons of valour.
7 mighty man. Heb. *gibbōr*. Ap. 14. IV.
8 women, &c. These also were guilty. Cp. Jer. 7. 18.
took also away: i. e. from Jerusalem. See Ap. 53.
9 Oded = establishing. His name is prophetic.
went out before the host. Showing his courage.
reacheth up unto heaven. Fig. *Hyperbolē* (Ap. 6), to express the greatness of the rage.
10 are there not . . . ? Fig. *Erotēsis*. Ap. 6.
sins = trespasses, or guilt. Heb. *'āshām*. Ap. 44. ii.
11 the LORD. A.V., 1611, had "God".
12 certain = men. Heb. *'ěnōsh*. Ap. 14. III.
heads. Not the king.
Johanan. Should be Jehohanan.
13 offended = trespassed. Heb. *'āshām*. Ap. 44. ii.
sins. Heb. *chātā'*. Ap. 44. i.
trespass. Heb. *'āshām*. Ap. 44. ii.
14 congregation = assembly.

632 to 616 15 And the °men which were expressed by
name rose up, and took the captives, and with
the spoil clothed all that were naked among
them, and arrayed them, and shod them, and
gave them to eat and to drink, and anointed
them, and carried all the °feeble of them upon
asses, and brought them to Jericho, °the city
of palm trees, to their brethren: °then they returned to Samaria.
G (p. 600) 16 At that time did king Ahaz send unto the
°kings of Assyria to help him.
E F 17 For again the Edomites had come and
smitten Judah, and carried away captives.
18 The °Philistines also had invaded the
cities of the low country, and of the south of
Judah, and had taken Beth-shemesh, and
Ajalon, and Gederoth, and Shocho with the
villages thereof, and Timnah with the villages
thereof, Gimzo also and the villages thereof:
and they dwelt there.
19 For [1]the LORD brought Judah low because
of Ahaz king of °Israel; for he made Judah
°naked, and °transgressed sore against [1]the
LORD.
G 20 And °Tilgath-pilneser king of Assyria
came unto him, and distressed him, but
strengthened him not.
21 For Ahaz took away a portion *out* of the
house of [1]the LORD, and *out* of the house of
the king, and of the princes, and gave *it* unto
the king of Assyria: but he helped him not.
D 22 And in the time of his distress did he
°trespass yet more against [1]the LORD: °this *is*
that king Ahaz.
23 For he sacrificed unto the gods of Damascus, °which smote him: and he said, "Because
the gods of the kings of Syria °help them,
therefore will I sacrifice to them, that they
may help me." But they were °the ruin of him,
and of all [19]Israel.
24 And Ahaz °gathered together the vessels
of the house of [5]God, and cut in pieces the
vessels of the house of [5]God, and °shut up
the doors of the house of [1]the LORD, and he
made him altars in every corner of Jerusalem.
25 And in every several city of Judah he
made high places to burn incense unto other
gods, and provoked to anger [1]the LORD [5]God
of his fathers.
C 26 Now the rest of his acts and of °all his
ways, first and last, °behold, they *are* written
in the book of the kings of Judah and Israel.
27 And Ahaz °slept with his fathers, and
they buried him °in the city, *even* in Jerusalem:
but they brought him not into the sepulchres
of the kings of [19]Israel: and Hezekiah his son
reigned in his stead.

G[15] H (p. 601) 617 to 588 **29** Hezekiah °began to reign *when he was*
five and twenty years old, and he
reigned nine and twenty years in Jerusalem.
And his mother's name *was* °Abijah, the daughter of Zechariah.
J K 2 And he did *that which was* right in the
sight of °the LORD, according to all that David
his father had done.
L M[1] 3 He in °the first year of his reign, in the first
month, °opened the doors of the house of [2]the
LORD, and repaired them.

15 men. Heb. pl. of *'ish* or *'enosh*. Ap. 14.
feeble = tottering.
the city of palm trees. Cp. Deut. 34. 3.
then they returned to Samaria. Cp. this account with Luke 10. 30-37.
16 kings = the great king. Pl. of majesty.
18 Philistines. These behind, and the Syrians before. Cp. Isa. 9. 12, 13.
19 Israel. See note on 21. 2.
naked: i. e. had stripped Judah of the worship and service of God.
transgressed = acted treacherously; i. e. been grievously unfaithful. Heb. *mā'al*. Ap. 44. xi.
20 Tilgath-pilneser. Cp. 2 Kings 16. 10. The accounts in Kings and Chronicles are complementary. See Ap. 56.
22 trespass. Heb. *mā'al*. Ap. 44. xi. See note on "transgressed", *v.* 19.
this is that king Ahaz. Cp. three specially branded transgressors: Cain (Gen. 4. 15); Dathan (Num. 26. 9); and Ahaz, here. Contrast Hezekiah (32. 12, 30).
23 which smote him: i. e. which [as he believed] smote him. **help them.** So he falsely reasoned.
the ruin of him. As the idolatry of the Edomites ruined Amaziah (25. 14, 15).
24 gathered together. Cp. 2 Kings 16. 8.
shut up the doors. His son Hezekiah's first act was to open them (29. 3). **26 all his ways.** Cp. 27. 7.
behold. Fig. *Asterismos*. Ap. 6.
27 slept with his fathers. See note on Deut. 31. 16.
in the city. Not in the sepulchres.

29. 1—32. 33 (G[15], p. 545). HEZEKIAH.
(*Introversions.*)

G[15] | H | 29. 1. Introduction. Accession.
  J | K | 29. 2. Personal. Well-doing.
    L | 29. 3—31. 21. Events. Reformation.
  J | *L* | 32. 1-23. Events. Invasion.
    K | 32. 24-31. Personal. Sickness.
  H | 32. 32, 33. Conclusion. Record and Death.

1 began to reign. In the third year of Hoshea, king of Israel. Therefore in the last year but one of his father's reign. Hezekiah began his reformation in 616, the first year of his sole reign. See Ap. 50. V, p. 59.
Abijah. In 2 Kings 18. 2 it is given as *'Ābi*, here it is *'Ābijah*. But the "i" in the former stands for the abbreviation of "jah" in the latter.
2 the LORD. Heb. Jehovah. Ap. 4. II.

29. 3—31. 21 (L, above). EVENTS. REFORMATION. (*Double Introversion.*)

L | M[1] | 29. 3. The house of Jehovah. Reformation.
  N[1] | 29. 4-36. Restoration of worship.
  N[2] | 30. 1-27. Restoration of the Passover.
 M[2] | 31. 1. Idolatry. Abolition.
  N[3] | 31. 2. Restoration of ministry.
  N[4] | 31. 3-10. Restoration of offerings.
 M[3] | 31. 11-21. The worship of Jehovah. Preparation.

3 the first year. Yea, on the first day (*v.* 17). Only three verses occupied with this in Kings, but three chapters in Chronicles. For the reason and object see Ap. 56.
opened the doors. Cp. 28. 24. Note his zeal for the house of the LORD in his "Songs of the degrees" (Pss. 122. 1, 9; 134. 1, 2). See Ap. 67. xiii.

29. 4-36 (N[1], above). RESTORATION OF WORSHIP. (*Extended Alternation.*)

N[1] | O | 4-. Assemblage of priests and Levites.
  P | -4. The place. The East street.
   Q | 5-11. The sanctification of the priests and Levites.
    R | 12-19. The cleansing of the house.
 O | 20-. Assemblage of the rulers of the city.
  P | -20. The place. The house of Jehovah.
   Q | 21-30. The offerings for their sanctification.
    R | 31-36. The offerings of the People.

4 And he brought in the priests and the N[1] O
Levites,

P (p. 601) and gathered them together into °the east street,
616 5 And said unto them, "Hear me, °ye Levites, sanctify now yourselves, and sanctify the
Q f (p. 602) house of [2]the LORD °God of your fathers, and carry forth the filthiness out of the °holy *place*.
g 6 For our fathers have °trespassed, °and done *that which was* °evil in the eyes of [2]the LORD our [5]God, and have forsaken Him, and have turned away their faces from the °habitation of [2]the LORD, and turned *their* backs.
7 °Also they have °shut up the doors of the porch, and put out the lamps, and have not burned incense nor °offered burnt offerings in the [5]holy *place* unto the [5]God of Israel.
8 Wherefore the wrath of [2]the LORD °was upon Judah and Jerusalem, and He hath delivered them to °trouble, to astonishment, and to hissing, °as ye see with your eyes.
9 For, °lo, our fathers have fallen by the sword, and our sons and our daughters and our wives *are* in captivity °for this.
g 10 Now *it is* °in mine heart to make a covenant with [2]the LORD [5]God of Israel, that His fierce wrath may turn away from us.
f 11 My sons, be not now negligent: for [2]the LORD hath chosen you to stand before Him, to serve Him, and that ye should minister unto Him, and burn incense."
R S1 12 °Then the Levites arose, Mahath the son of Amasai, and Joel the son of Azariah, of the sons of the Kohathites: and of the sons of Merari, Kish the son of Abdi, and Azariah the son of Jehalelel: and of the Gershonites; Joah the son of Zimmah, and Eden the son of Joah:
13 And of the sons of Elizaphan; Shimri, and Jeiel: and of the sons of Asaph; Zechariah, and Mattaniah:
14 And of the sons of Heman; Jehiel, and Shimei: and of the sons of Jeduthun; Shemaiah, and Uzziel.
15 And they gathered their brethren, and sanctified themselves, and came, according to the commandment of the king, °by the words of [2]the LORD, to cleanse the house of [2]the LORD.
S2 16 And the priests went into °the inner part of the house of [2]the LORD, to cleanse *it*, and brought out all the uncleanness that they found in the temple of [2]the LORD into the court of the house of [2]the LORD. And the Levites took *it*, to carry *it* out abroad into the brook Kidron.
st Nisan 616 17 Now they began on °the first *day* of the first month to sanctify, and on the eighth day of the month came they to the porch of [2]the LORD: so they sanctified the house of [2]the LORD in eight days; and in the sixteenth day of the first month they made an end.
18 Then they went °in to Hezekiah the king, and said, "We have cleansed all the house of [2]the LORD, and the altar of burnt offering, with all the vessels thereof, and the shewbread table, with all the vessels thereof.
19 Moreover all the vessels, which king °Ahaz in his reign did °cast away in his °transgression, have we prepared and sanctified, and, °behold, they *are* before the altar of [2]the LORD."

20 Then Hezekiah the king °rose early, and gathered the °rulers of the city, *O* (p. 601)
and °went up to the house of [2]the LORD. *R*

21 And they brought seven bullocks, and seven rams, and seven lambs, and seven he goats, for a sin offering for the kingdom, and for the sanctuary, and for Judah. And he *Q* h (p. 602)

---

4 the east street = the broad place at the east. Cp. Ezra 10. 9.

29. 5-11 (Q, p. 601). THE SANCTIFICATION OF THE PRIESTS AND LEVITES. (*Introversion.*)

Q | f | 5. Sanctification.
g | 6-9. Reasons.
g | 10. Object.
f | 11. Sanctification.

5 ye Levites. Reformation must begin with the ministry. All priests were Levites, but not all Levites were priests.
God. Heb. Elohim. Ap. 4. I.
holy. See note on Ex. 3. 5.
6 trespassed = acted unfaithfully. Heb. *mā'al*. Ap. 44. xi.
and. Note the Fig. *Polysyndeton* (Ap. 6) in *vv.* 6, 7.
evil = the evil. Heb. *rā'a'* (with Art.). Ap. 44. viii.
habitation = dwelling place. Heb. *mishkān*. Ap. 40.
7 Also = And, carrying the Fig. *Polysyndeton* into this verse.
shut up the doors. Cp. 28. 24.
offered = offered up. Heb. *'ālāh*. Ap. 43. I. vi.
8 was = came.
trouble = commotion.
as = according as.
9 lo. Fig. *Asterismos*. Ap. 6.
for this: for the sins rehearsed in *vv.* 6, 7.
10 in mine heart. Put there by God.

12-19 (R, p. 601). THE CLEANSING OF THE HOUSE. (*Division.*)

R | S1 | 12-15. The persons.
S2 | 16-19. The house.

12 Then the Levites arose. They were from each of the three leading families (Gershom, Kohath, and Merari); two from the family of Elizaphan (Kohath's grandson. Ex. 6. 18, 22. Num. 3. 30); two from the posterity of Asaph (of Gershom); two of Heman (of Kohath); two of Jeduthun (of Merari). Fourteen in all. See Ap. 10.
15 by the words: or in the business. Cp. *v.* 30.
16 the inner part. All true reformation begins there, and proceeds outward. Man makes clean the outside, and never gets any farther (Matt. 15. 11, 17-20; 23. 25, 26. Luke 11. 39).
17 the first day of the first month. Note the six events which took place on that day (Gen. 8. 13).
18 in = inside.
19 Ahaz . . . cast away. Cp. 2 Kings 16. 14, 17.
transgression = defection. Heb. *mā'al*. Ap. 44. xi.
behold. Fig. *Asterismos*. Ap. 6.
20 rose early . . . went up. Note the zeal of Hezekiah for the house of Jehovah in his Songs of the degrees. See Pss. 122. 1, 9; 134. 1, 2; and cp. Isa. 37. 1, 14; 38. 20. 2 Kings 20. 8, and Ap. 67. xiii.
rulers = princes.

21-30 (*Q*, p. 601). THE OFFERINGS FOR THEIR SANCTIFICATION. (*Alternation.*)

Q | h | 21-24. The sin offering.
i | 25, 26. Worship.
h | 27. The burnt offering.
i | 28-30. Worship.

616 commanded the priests the sons of Aaron to [7]offer *them* on the altar of [2]the LORD.

22 So they killed the bullocks, and the priests received the blood, and sprinkled *it* °on the altar: likewise, when they had killed the rams, they sprinkled the blood upon the altar: they killed also the lambs, and they °sprinkled the blood upon the altar.

23 And they brought °forth the he goats *for* the sin offering before the king and the °congregation; and °they °laid their hands upon them:

24 And the priests killed them, and they made °reconciliation with their blood upon the altar, to make an °atonement °for all Israel: for the king commanded *that* the burnt offering and the sin offering *should be made* °for all Israel.

i (p. 602) 25 And he set the Levites in the house of [2]the LORD with cymbals, with psalteries, and with harps, according to the commandment of °David, and of Gad the king's °seer, and Nathan the prophet: for *so was* the commandment °of [2]the LORD °by His prophets.

26 And the Levites stood with the instruments °of David, and the priests with the trumpets.

h 27 And Hezekiah commanded to offer the burnt offering upon the altar. And when the burnt offering began, the song of [2]the LORD began *also* with the trumpets, and with the instruments *ordained* by David king of Israel.

i 28 And all the [23]congregation worshipped, and the singers sang, and the trumpeters sounded: *and* all *this continued* until the burnt offering was finished.

29 And when they had made an end of offering, the king and all that were present with him bowed themselves, and worshipped.

30 Moreover Hezekiah the king and the princes commanded the Levites to sing praise unto [2]the LORD with the words of David, and of Asaph the seer. And they sang praises with gladness, and they bowed their heads and worshipped.

R k (p. 603) 31 Then Hezekiah answered and said, "Now ye have °consecrated yourselves unto [2]the LORD, come near and bring sacrifices and thank offerings into the house of [2]the LORD."

l And the [23]congregation brought in sacrifices and thank offerings; and as many as were of a free heart burnt offerings.

m 32 And the number of the burnt offerings, which the [23]congregation brought, was threescore and ten bullocks, an hundred rams, *and* two hundred lambs: all these *were* for a burnt offering to [2]the LORD.

33 And the °consecrated things *were* six hundred oxen and three thousand sheep.

l 34 But the priests were too few, so that they could not flay all the burnt offerings: wherefore their brethren the Levites did help them, till the work was ended, and until the *other* priests had sanctified themselves: for the Levites *were* more upright in heart to sanctify themselves than the priests.

35 And also the burnt offerings *were* in abundance, with the fat of the peace offerings, and the drink offerings for *every* burnt offering. So the service of the house of [2]the LORD was set in order.

36 And Hezekiah rejoiced, and all the People, that [5]God had prepared the People: for the thing was *done* suddenly. *k*

30 And Hezekiah °sent to °all Israel and Judah, and wrote letters °also to Ephraim and Manasseh, that they should come to the house of °the LORD at Jerusalem, to °keep the passover unto °the LORD °God of Israel. N² T n (p. 603)

2 For the king had taken counsel, and his princes, and all the °congregation in Jerusalem, to keep the passover in °the second month. o

3 For they could not keep it °at that time, because the priests had not sanctified themselves sufficiently, neither had the People gathered themselves together to Jerusalem.

---

22 on = toward.
sprinkled the blood. According to Lev. 4. 30-34; 8. 15.
23 forth = near. congregation = assembly.
they. The A.V. of 1611 omitted "they".
laid their hands. According to Lev. 4. 15; 8. 22; 16. 21.
24 reconciliation = cleansing.
atonement. See note on Ex. 29. 33.
for all Israel. Note the reference to this in Hezekiah's "Songs of the degrees" (Ps. 133, and cp. 30. 1-3, 5, 6, 11, 12, 14, 18, 25, 26). See note on 1 Kings 12. 17 and Ap. 67. xv.
25 David. Cp. 1 Chron. 15. 16; 23. 5; 25. 1.
seer. Heb. *chozeh*. See note on 1 Chron. 29. 29.
of = by the hand of. by = by the hand of.
26 of. Genitive of Relation = appointed by. Cp. *v.* 27.

29. 31-36 (*R*, p. 601). THE OFFERINGS OF THE PEOPLE. (*Introversion.*)

R | k | 31-. Hezekiah's command.
l | -31. Obedience of assembly.
m | 32, 33. The offerings.
l | 34, 35. Obedience of priests.
k | 36. Hezekiah's joy.

31 consecrated. See note on verb (Ex. 28. 41. Lev. 9. 17).
33 consecrated things = holy things. See note on Ex. 3. 5.

30. 1-27 (N², p. 601). RESTORATION OF THE PASSOVER. (*Introversion.*)

N² | T | 1-13. The feast. Preparation.
U | 14. Idolatrous altars in Jerusalem taken away.
T | 15-27. The feast. Observance.

1-13 (T, above). THE FEAST. PREPARATION. (*Alternation.*)

T | n | 1. The invitation. General.
o | 2-5. Time. The second month.
n | 6-12. The invitation. Particular.
o | 13. Time. The second month.

1 sent. This was before the Removal of Israel.
all Israel. See note on *v.* 24 and Ap. 67. xv.
also. He wrote letters, as well as sent messengers.
the LORD. Heb. Jehovah. Ap. 4. II.
keep the passover. One of the ten observances of this feast. See note on Ex. 12. 28.
God. Heb. Elohim. Ap. 4. I.
2 congregation = assembly. See note on Gen. 28. 3.
the second month. As provided by the law (Num. 9. 6-13).
3 at that time: i. e. the first month, while all the work was going on. Cp. Ex. 12. 18.

616 4 And the thing °pleased the king and all the [2] congregation.

5 So they established a decree to make proclamation °throughout [1] all Israel, from Beer-sheba even to Dan, that they should come to [1] keep the passover unto [1] the LORD [1] God of Israel at Jerusalem: for they °had not done *it* of a long *time in such sort* as it was written.

n (p. 603) 6 So the °posts went with the letters °from the king and his princes throughout all Israel and Judah, and according to the commandment of the king, saying, "Ye °children of Israel, turn again unto [1] the LORD [1] God of °Abraham, Isaac, and Israel, and He will return to the remnant of you, that are escaped out of the hand of °the kings of Assyria.

7 And be not ye like your fathers, and like your brethren, which °trespassed against [1] the LORD [1] God of their fathers, *Who* therefore gave them up to desolation, °as ye see.

8 Now be ye not °stiffnecked, as your fathers *were, but* °yield yourselves unto [1] the LORD, and enter into His sanctuary, which He hath sanctified for ever: and serve [1] the LORD your [1] God, that the fierceness of His wrath may turn away from you.

9 For if ye turn again unto [1] the LORD, your brethren and your [6] children *shall find* compassion before them that °lead them captive, so that they shall come again into this land: for [1] the LORD your [1] God *is* °gracious and merciful, and will not turn away *His* face from you, if ye return unto Him."

10 So the [6] posts passed from city to city through the country of Ephraim and Manasseh even unto Zebulun: but they laughed them to scorn, and mocked them.

11 Nevertheless °divers °of Asher and Manasseh and of Zebulun humbled themselves, and came to Jerusalem.

12 Also in Judah the hand of °God was to give them °one heart to do the commandment of the king and of the princes, °by the word of [1] the LORD.

o 13 And there assembled at Jerusalem much People to keep the feast of unleavened bread in [2] the second month, a very great [2] congregation.

U 14 And they arose and took away the °altars that *were* in Jerusalem, and all the altars for incense took they away, and cast *them* into the °brook Kidron.

T p (p. 604) 14th Zif 616 15 Then they killed the passover on the fourteenth *day* of [2] the second month: and the priests and the Levites were ashamed, and sanctified themselves, and brought in the burnt offerings into the house of [1] the LORD.

16 And they °stood in their place after their manner, according to °the law of Moses °the man of God: the priests sprinkled the blood, *which they received* of the hand of the Levites.

17 For *there were* many in the [2] congregation that were not sanctified: therefore the Levites had the charge of the killing of the °passovers for every one *that was* not clean, to sanctify *them* unto [1] the LORD.

18 For a multitude of the people, *even* many of Ephraim, and Manasseh, Issachar, and Zebulun, had not cleansed themselves, yet did they eat the passover °otherwise than it was written.

But Hezekiah prayed for them, saying, "The good [1] LORD pardon every one q

19 *That* prepareth his heart to seek [1] God, [1] the LORD [1] God of his fathers, though *he be* not *cleansed* according to the purification of the sanctuary."

20 And [1] the LORD hearkened to Hezekiah, and °healed the People. r

21 And the [6] children of Israel that were *p*

---

4 pleased=was right in the eyes of.

5 throughout all Israel. The king, Hoshea, not objecting. Cp. 2 Kings 17. 2.

had not done it. Not since the division of the kingdom.

6 posts=couriers. Cp. Est. 3. 13, 15; 8. 10, 14. Jer. 51. 31. Elsewhere rendered "footmen" (1 Sam. 22. 17), or "guard" (1 Kings 14. 27, 28. 2 Kings 10. 25. 2 Chron. 12. 10, 11).

from=from the hand of: i. e. by his direction.

children=sons.

Abraham, Isaac, and Israel. See note on 1 Kings 18. 36 for the 5 occurrences of this expression.

the kings of Assyria. Pul and Tilgath-pilneser (2 Kings 15. 19. 1 Chron. 5. 26). These escaped captives were from the large numbers which had already been removed. See note on *v.* 9 and Ap. 67. xii.

7 trespassed. Heb. *mā'al.* Ap. 44. xi.

as=according as.

8 stiffnecked. Fig. *Metonymy* (of Adjunct), Ap. 6, put for obstinacy.

yield yourselves=submit yourselves. Heb. "give the hand", "hand" being put by Fig. *Metonymy* (of Adjunct), Ap. 6, for submission. Cp. 1 Chron. 29. 24.

9 lead them captive. Though the ten tribes, as such, had not been deported, yet thousands had been led captive. Hezekiah's Song of the degrees (Ps. 126. 1) refers to this. Cp. *v.* 6, and see Ap. 67. xii.

gracious, &c. Cp. Ex. 34. 6.

11 divers=men. Heb. *'ĕnōsh.* Ap. 14. III.

of Asher. These must have remained with Judah. Cp. Luke 2. 36, showing that Judah was representative of the whole nation. See note on 1 Kings 12. 17.

12 God. Heb. *Elohim* (with Art.)=the [true] God. Ap. 4. I.

one heart. It is to this that Hezekiah refers in his Song of the degrees (Ps. 133. 1). It is a Psalm of David, selected by Hezekiah because David knew the blessedness of this "unity". See 2 Sam. 19. 9, 14 and Ap. 67. xv.

by. Some codices, with six early printed editions and Syr., read "according to".

14 altars. The brazen serpent also. See 2 Kings 18. 4. **brook**=ravine.

30. 15-27 (*T*, p. 603). **THE FEAST. OBSERVANCE.**
(*Extended Alternation.*)

T | p | 15-18-. Passover eaten.
q | -18, 19. Intercession of Hezekiah.
r | 20. Acceptance by Jehovah.
p | 21-26. Feast kept.
q | 27-. Blessing of the priests.
r | -27. Acceptance by Jehovah.

16 stood, &c. Heb. "stood in their standing"; i. e. stood in their appointed place. Fig. *Polyptōton* (Ap. 6).

the law of Moses. Cp. 29. 22.

the man of God. See note on Deut. 33. 1, and Ap. 49.

17 passovers. Put by Fig. *Metonymy* (of Adjunct), Ap. 6, for the "passover lambs".

18 otherwise. Hezekiah considered this to be the lesser of two evils.

20 healed. And did not visit according to Lev. 15. 31.

616 °present at Jerusalem kept the feast of unleavened bread seven days with great gladness: and the Levites and the priests praised [1]the LORD day by day, *singing* with loud instruments unto [1]the LORD.

22 And Hezekiah spake °comfortably unto all the Levites that taught the good knowledge of [1]the LORD: and they did eat throughout the feast seven days, °offering peace offerings, and making confession to [1]the LORD [1]God of their fathers.

23 And the whole assembly took counsel to keep °other seven days: and they kept *other* seven days with gladness.

24 For Hezekiah king of Judah did give to the [2]congregation a thousand bullocks and seven thousand sheep; and the princes gave to the [2]congregation a thousand bullocks and ten thousand sheep: and a great number of priests sanctified themselves.

25 And all the [2]congregation of Judah, with the priests and the Levites, and all the [2]congregation that came out of Israel, and the °strangers that came out of the land of Israel, and that dwelt in Judah, rejoiced.

26 So there was great joy in Jerusalem: for since the time of Solomon the son of David king of Israel *there was* °not the like in Jerusalem.

q 27 Then °the priests the Levites arose and
(p. 604) blessed the People:

r and their voice was heard, and their prayer came *up* to His °holy dwelling place, *even* unto heaven.

M[2] **31** Now °when all this was finished, °all
(p. 601) Israel that were °present went out to the °cities of Judah, and brake the images in pieces, and cut down the °groves, and threw down the high places and the altars out of all Judah and Benjamin, in Ephraim also and Manasseh, until they had utterly destroyed them all. Then all the °children of Israel returned, °every man to his possession, into their own cities.

N[3] 2 And Hezekiah appointed °the courses of the priests and the Levites after their courses, [1]every man according to his service, the priests and Levites for burnt offerings and for peace offerings, to minister, and to give thanks, and to praise in the gates of the tents of °the LORD.

N[4] s 3 *He appointed* also °the king's portion of
(p. 605) his substance for the burnt offerings, *to wit*, for the morning and evening burnt offerings, and the burnt offerings for the sabbaths, and for the new moons, and for the set feasts, as *it is* °written in the law of [2]the LORD.

4 Moreover he commanded the people that dwelt in Jerusalem to give the portion of the priests and the Levites, that they might be encouraged in the law of [2]the LORD.

t 5 And as soon as the commandment came abroad, the [1]children of Israel brought in abundance the firstfruits of corn, wine, and oil, and honey, and of all the increase of the field; and the tithe of all *things* brought they in abundantly.

6 And *concerning* the [1]children of Israel and Judah, that dwelt in the cities of Judah, they also brought in the °tithe of oxen and sheep, and the tithe of holy things which were consecrated unto [2]the LORD their °God, and laid *them* °by heaps.

7 In the °third month they began °to lay the foundation of the heaps, and finished *them* in the °seventh month.

8 And when Hezekiah and the princes came and saw the heaps, they blessed [2]the LORD, and His People Israel.

9 Then Hezekiah questioned with the priests and the Levites concerning the heaps. s

10 And Azariah the chief priest of the house of Zadok answered him, and said, "Since *the People* began to bring the offerings into the house of [2]the LORD, we have had enough to eat, and have left plenty: for [2]the LORD hath blessed His People; and that which is left *is* this great store." t

11 Then Hezekiah commanded to prepare °chambers in the house of [2]the LORD; M[3] u
and they prepared *them*, v

---

21 present = found.
22 comfortably. Cp. Isa. 40. 2.
offering. Heb. *zābach*. Ap. 43. I. iv.
23 other seven days. As at Solomon's Dedication.
25 strangers = sojourners. Ex. 12. 48, 49.
26 not the like. Referring to the extra days of *v.* 23. Perfectly true; for this was "*since* the time of Solomon". Josiah's passover (2 Kings 23. 22, 23) was *after* Hezekiah's.
27 the priests the Levites. Cp. Deut. 17. 9. But some codices, with Sept. and Vulg., read "and the".
holy. See note on Ex. 3. 5.

31. 1 when. After, not before. All true reformation begins within and works outward. Cp. Phil. 2. 12, 13.
all Israel. See note on 30. 1.
present = found.
cities. Jerusalem had been cleansed before the passover. Cp. 30. 14.
groves = the *'Asherim*. Ap. 42. **children** = sons.
every man. Heb. *'ish*. Ap. 14. II.
2 the courses of the priests. 1 Chron. 24—26.
the LORD. Heb. Jehovah. Ap. 4. II.
3 the king's portion. Cp. 32. 27-29 and Num. 18; 28; and 29.
written in the law. See Ap. 47.

31. 3-10 (N[4], p. 601). RESTORATION OF OFFERINGS. (*Alternation.*)

N[4] | s | 3, 4. Hezekiah. Command.
  t | 5-8. Obedience of the people.
 s | 9. Hezekiah. Question.
  t | 10. Answer of the chief priests.

6 tithe. A.V., 1611, read "tithes" (pl.).
God. Heb. Elohim. Ap. 4. I.
by heaps. Heb. "heaps, heaps" = great heaps. Fig. *Epizeuxis*. Ap. 6.
7 third . . . seventh: i. e. Sivan, Thammuz, Ab, Elul, Ethanim. See Ap. 51. 5, p. 74.
to lay the foundation: i. e. to begin to build up the heaps.

11-19 (M[3], p. 601). THE WORSHIP OF JEHOVAH. PREPARATION. (*Introversion.*)

M[3] | u | 11-. Hezekiah. Command.
  v | -11. Storehouses prepared.
  v | 12-. Storehouses filled.
 u | -12-21. Hezekiah. Overseers.

11 chambers = storehouses.

v (p. 605) 616 12 And brought in the °offerings and the
tithes and the °dedicated *things* faithfully:
over which Cononiah the Levite *was* ruler,
u and Shimei his brother *was* the next.
13 And Jehiel, and Azaziah, and Nahath,
and Asahel, and Jerimoth, and Jozabad, and
Eliel, and Ismachiah, and Mahath, and Benaiah, *were* overseers under the hand of
Cononiah and Shimei his brother, at the commandment of Hezekiah the king, and [10]Azariah
the ruler of the house of °God.
14 And Kore the son of Imnah the Levite,
the porter °toward the east, *was* over the freewill offerings of [13]God, to distribute the °obla-
tions of [2]the LORD, and °the most holy things.
15 And next him *were* °Eden, and Miniamin,
and Jeshua, and Shemaiah, Amariah, and
Shecaniah, in the cities of the priests, in *their*
°set office, to give to their brethren by
courses, as well to the great as to the small:
16 Beside their genealogy of males, from
three years old and upward, *even* unto every
one that entereth into the house of [3]the LORD,
his daily portion for their service in their
charges °according to their courses;
17 Both to the genealogy of the priests by
the house of their fathers, and the Levites
from twenty years old and upward, in their
charges °by their courses;
18 And to the genealogy of all their little
ones, their wives, and their sons, and their
daughters, through all the °congregation: for
in their [15]set office they °sanctified themselves
in holiness:
19 Also of the sons of Aaron the °priests,
which were in the fields of the suburbs of
their cities, in every several city, the °men
that were expressed by name, to give portions
to all the males among the priests, and to all
that °were reckoned by genealogies among
the Levites.
20 And thus did Hezekiah throughout all
Judah, and wrought *that which was* good and
right and truth before [2]the LORD his [6]God.
21 °And in every work that he began in the
service of the house of [6]God, and in the law,
and in the commandments, to seek his [6]God,
he did *it* with all his heart, and prospered.

J L V (p. 606) 603 32 °After these things, and the °establish-
ment thereof, Sennacherib king of As-
syria came, and entered into Judah, and encamped against the fenced cities, and thought
°to win them for himself.
W w 2 And when Hezekiah saw that Sennacherib
was come, and that he was purposed to fight
against Jerusalem,
3 He took counsel with his princes and his
°mighty men °to stop the waters of the fountains which *were* without the city: and they
did help him.
4 So there was gathered much people together, who stopped all the fountains, and
°the brook that ran through the midst of the
land, saying, "Why should the °kings of Assyria come, and find much water?"
5 Also he strengthened himself, and built up
all the wall that was broken, and raised *it* up
to the towers, and another wall without, and
°repaired Millo *in* the city of David, and made
darts and shields in abundance.

12 offerings = heave offerings. See note on Ex. 29. 27, and Ap. 43. II. viii.
dedicated = holy. See note on Ex. 3. 5.
13 God. Heb. Elohim (with Art.) = the [true] God. Ap. 4. I. **14 toward the east.** Cp. 1 Chron. 9. 18.
oblations = heave offerings, as in *v.* 12.
the most holy things. Cp. Lev. 2. 3; 6. 17, 25, 29.
15 Eden. Cp. 29. 12.
set office = office of trust.
16 according to. Some codices, with seven early printed editions, read "in".
17 by. Some codices, with one early printed edition, read "according to".
18 congregation = assembly. See note on Gen. 28. 3.
sanctified themselves in holiness: or, devoted themselves [as] a holy body. See note on Ex. 3. 5.
19 priests. Some codices, with Syr., read "priest".
men. Heb. *'ĕnōsh* (no Art.). Ap. 14. III.
were reckoned by genealogies: or, registered themselves.
21 And. A special various reading called *Sevīr* (Ap. 34) omits "And".

32. 1-23 (*L*, p. 601). THE INVASION OF SENNACHERIB. (*Introversion.*)

L | V | 1. Sennacherib. Invasion.
  | W | 2-8. Defence. Preparation.
  | X | 9-19. Sennacherib. Message and letters.
  | *W* | 20. Defence. Prayer.
  | *V* | 21-23. Sennacherib. Destruction.

1 After these things. Thirteen years after the events in chapter 31.
establishment = "[done in] faithfulness".
to win. Heb. to break them up. Supply Fig. *Ellipsis* (Ap. 6) thus: "to break them up [and annex them] for himself".

2-8 (W, above). DEFENCE. PREPARATION. (*Alternation.*)

W | w | 2-5. Hezekiah. His works.
  | x | 6-. The People. Captains over them.
  | *w* | -6-8-. Hezekiah. His encouragement.
  | *x* | -8. The People. Confidence.

3 mighty men. Heb. *gibbōr.* Ap. 14. IV.
to stop. By covering up the fountain En-rogel (now known as "The Virgin's Fount"), or Gihon (upper pool), on east side of Ophel. Discovered by Sir Charles Warren in 1867. This was brought down to the west side of the city by Hezekiah (*v.* 30. Cp. 2 Kings 20. 20). En-rogel was stopped on the east side, and a channel cut through to the lower pool of Gihon on the west, and south to Siloam, a shaft running down to the water beneath Zion: referred to in Ps. 46. 4. This is contrasted with the Assyrian host, which is compared in the previous verse to raging waters. Isaiah refers to these works (Isa. 22. 9-11).
4 the brook = the overflow: i. e. Gihon, which frequently did so.
kings = the [great] king. Pl. of majesty.
5 repaired Millo. See notes on 2 Sam. 5. 9. 1 Kings 11. 27. 1 Chron. 11. 8. **6 street** = broad space.
spake comfortably. Cp. Isa. 40. 2.
7 Be strong, &c. Heb. "be ye strong", &c. See note on Deut. 31. 6. Josh. 10. 25.
multitude. Compared to raging waters (Ps. 46. 2, 3).
with us. Note the *Introversion* in *vv.* 7, 8 called *Antimetabolē* (Ap. 6), with us, with him, with him, with us. Cp. 2 Kings 6. 16.

6 And he set captains of war over the People, x
and gathered them together to him in the
°street of the gate of the city,
and °spake comfortably to them, saying, w
7 °"Be strong and courageous, be not afraid
nor dismayed for the king of Assyria, nor for
all the °multitude that *is* with him: for *there*
be more °with us than with him:

603 8 With him *is* an arm of flesh; but with us
is °the LORD our °God to help us, and to fight
our battles."
x (p. 606) And the People rested themselves upon the
words of Hezekiah king of Judah.
X y (p. 607) 9 °After this did Sennacherib king of Assyria
°send his servants to Jerusalem, (but he
himself laid siege °against Lachish, and all
his °power with him,) unto Hezekiah king of
Judah, and unto all Judah that *were* at Jerusalem,
saying,
z a 10 "Thus saith Sennacherib king of Assyria,
°'Whereon do ye °trust, that ye abide in
the siege in Jerusalem?
11 Doth not Hezekiah persuade you to give
over yourselves to die by famine and by thirst,
saying, [8]'The LORD our [8]God shall °deliver us
out of the hand of the king of Assyria?'
12 Hath not °the same Hezekiah taken away
His high places and His altars, and commanded
Judah and Jerusalem, saying, 'Ye
shall worship before one altar, and burn incense
upon it?'
b 13 Know ye not what I and my fathers
have done unto all the °people of *other* lands?
were the gods of the nations of those lands
any ways able to [11]deliver their lands out of
mine hand?
14 °Who *was there* among all the gods of
those nations that my fathers utterly destroyed,
that could [11]deliver his people out of
mine hand, that your [8]God should be able to
deliver you out of mine hand?
15 Now therefore let not Hezekiah deceive
you, nor persuade you on this manner, neither
yet believe him: for no °god of any nation or
kingdom was able to [11]deliver his people out of
mine hand, and out of the hand of my fathers:
how much less shall your [8]God [11]deliver you out
of mine hand?'"
y 16 And his servants spake yet *more* against
[8]the LORD °God, and against His servant
Hezekiah.
z b 17 He wrote also letters °to rail on [8]the LORD
[8]God of Israel, and to speak against Him, saying,
"As the gods of the nations of *other* lands
have not [11]delivered their people out of mine
hand, so shall not the [8]God of Hezekiah [11]deliver
His people out of mine hand."
a 18 Then they cried with a loud voice in the
Jews' speech unto the people of Jerusalem
that *were* on the wall, to affright them, and
to trouble them; that they might take the city.
19 And they spake against the °God of Jerusalem,
as against the gods of the people of the
earth, *which were* the work of the hands of
°man.
W (p. 606) 20 And for this *cause* Hezekiah the king, and
the prophet Isaiah the son of Amoz, °prayed
and cried to °heaven.
V 21 And [8]the LORD sent an angel, which cut
off all [8]the mighty men of valour, and the
leaders and captains in the camp of the king
of Assyria. So he °returned with shame of
face to his own land. And when he was come
into the house of his god, °they that came forth
of his own bowels slew him there with the
sword.

8 the LORD. Heb. Jehovah. Ap. 4. II.
God. Heb. Elohim. Ap. 4. I.

32. 9-19 (X, p. 606). SENNACHERIB. MESSAGE AND LETTERS. (*Alternation and Introversion.*

X | y | 9. Sennacherib's servants.
  z | a | 10-12. Hezekiah's weakness. } Railing message.
     b | 13-15. Sennacherib's strength. }
  y | 16. Sennacherib's servants.
  z | *b* | 17. Sennacherib's strength. } Railing letters.
     a | 18, 19. Hezekiah's weakness. }

9 After this. Omitting the account of the surrender of 2 Kings 18. 14-16.
send his servants. Cp. 2 Kings 18. 17-37; 19. 1-35. Isa. 10. 8-11; 36; 37.
against Lachish. A difficult task, for Rab-shakeh found Sennacherib had abandoned the siege (2 Kings 19. 8). Joshua had found it the same (see note on "second day", Josh. 10. 31, 32). In Jer. 34. 7 it still belonged to Judah.
power=royal retinue.
10 Whereon . . . ? Note the Fig. *Erotēsis* (Ap. 6), used throughout Rab-shakeh's message, *vv.* 10-14.
trust=confide. Heb. *bataḥ*. Ap. 69. I. Note the reference to Hezekiah's "trust in Jehovah" in his Songs of the degrees (121. 3; 125. 1-3; 127. 1; 130. 5-8, and see Ap. 67. x.
11 deliver=rescue.
12 the same Hezekiah. Contrast Ahaz (28. 22). See Ap. 67. i.
13 people=peoples.
14 Who . . . ? Fig. *Erotēsis*. Ap. 6.
15 god. Heb. *'ĕlōah*. Ap. 4. V.
God. Heb. Elohim. Ap. 4. I. Pl., with verb "deliver" in sing.
16 God. Elohim (with Art.)=the [true] God.
17 to rail. It is this railing which is referred to in Hezekiah's "Songs of the degrees": e. g. Pss. 120. 2, 3; 123. 3, 4; 129. 5-7.
19 God of Jerusalem. A remarkable title used by heathen.
man. Heb. *'ādām* (with Art.). Ap. 14. I.
20 prayed and cried. This is what Hezekiah refers to in his "Songs of the degrees" (Pss. 120. 1; 123. 1-3; 130. 1, 2). Cp. Isa. 38. 10-20. 2 Kings 19. 15-19; 20. 2, 3. See Ap. 67. iv. One of the few O.T. instances of united prayer.
heaven. Put by Fig. *Metonymy* (of Subject), Ap. 6, for God Himself. "Heaven" used here because the prayer was made to God, as "the Maker of heaven and earth" (2 Kings 19. 15. Isa. 37. 16). This is referred to in Hezekiah's "Songs of the degrees" (Pss. 121. 1, 2; 123. 1; 124. 8). See Ap. 67. v.
21 returned with shame. This is referred to in Hezekiah's "Songs of the degrees" (Ps. 129. 4, 5). R.V. "be ashamed and turned backward". See Ap. 67. iii.
they that came forth of his own bowels. The phrase occurs only here. See notes on 2 Kings 19. 37.
23 brought gifts . . . presents. This explains *v.* 27, and tells us how he could show treasures to the ambassadors from Babylon (2 Kings 20. 13. Isa. 39. 1, 2), after he had stripped himself for Sennacherib in 2 Kings 18. 15.
nations=the nations.

24-31 [For Structure see next page].

24 In those days. While Sennacherib's host was still surrounding Jerusalem. This is a brief summary of what is described in 2 Kings 20 and Isaiah 38.

22 Thus [8]the LORD saved Hezekiah and the
inhabitants of Jerusalem from the hand of
Sennacherib the king of Assyria, and from
the hand of all *other*, and guided them on
every side.
23 And many °brought gifts unto [8]the LORD
to Jerusalem, and °presents to Hezekiah king
of Judah: so that he was magnified in the
sight of all nations from thenceforth.
24 °In those days Hezekiah was sick to the *K c* (p. 608)

603-588 **death, and prayed unto [8]the LORD: and He spake unto him, and He °gave him a sign.**

d (p. 608) **25 But Hezekiah rendered not again according to the benefit *done* unto him; for his heart was lifted up: therefore there was wrath upon him, and upon Judah and Jerusalem.**

26 Notwithstanding Hezekiah humbled himself for °the pride of his heart, *both* he and the inhabitants of Jerusalem, so that the wrath of [8]the LORD came not upon them in the days of Hezekiah.

c **27 And Hezekiah had exceeding much riches and honour: °and he made himself treasuries for silver, and for gold, and for precious stones, and for spices, and for shields, and for all manner of pleasant jewels;**

28 Storehouses also for the increase of corn, and °wine, and oil; and stalls for all manner of beasts, and °cotes for flocks.

29 Moreover he provided him cities, [27]and possessions of flocks and herds in abundance: for [8]God had given him substance very much.

30 [12]This same Hezekiah also °stopped the upper watercourse of Gihon, [27]and brought it straight down to the west side of the city of David. And Hezekiah prospered in all his works.

d **31 Howbeit in *the business of* the ambassadors of the princes of °Babylon, who sent unto him to enquire of °the wonder that was *done* in the land, [15]God left him, to try him, that he might know all *that was* in his heart.**

H (p. 608) **32 Now the rest of the acts of Hezekiah, and his °goodness, °behold, they *are* written in the vision of °Isaiah the prophet, the son of Amoz, °*and* in the book of the kings of Judah and Israel.**

33 And Hezekiah °slept with his fathers, and they buried him in the chiefest of the sepulchres of the sons of David: and all Judah and the inhabitants of Jerusalem did him honour at his death. And Manasseh his son reigned in his stead.

G[16] Y (p. 608) 588-533 **33 °Manasseh *was* twelve years old when he began to reign, and he reigned fifty and five years in Jerusalem:**

Z e i **2 But did *that which was* evil in the sight of °the LORD, like unto the abominations of the °heathen, whom °the LORD had cast out before the °children of Israel.**

k l **3 For he built again the high places which Hezekiah his father had broken down, and he reared up altars for Baalim, and made °groves, and worshipped all °the host of heaven, and served them.**

m **4 Also he built altars in the house of [2]the LORD, whereof [2]the LORD °had said, "In Jerusalem shall My °name be for ever."**

5 And he built altars for all [3]the host of heaven in the two courts of the house of [2]the LORD.

k l **6 And he caused his [2]children to °pass through the fire in the valley of the son of Hinnom: also he °observed °times, and used enchantments, and used witchcraft, and dealt with a °familiar spirit, and with wizards: he wrought much °evil in the sight of [2]the LORD, to provoke Him to anger.**

32. 24-31 (*K*, p. 601). PERSONAL. SICKNESS. (*Alternation.*)

K | c | 24. Sickness.
  d | 25, 26. Transgression. Ingratitude.
 c | 27-30. Prosperity.
  d | 31. Transgression. Pride.

gave him a sign. Recorded in 2 Kings 20. 1-11. The going back of the shadow on the sun-dial of Ahaz ten degrees, which caused him to give the title of the fifteen "Songs of the degrees" (Pss. 120—134). See Ap. 67.

26 the pride=the lifting up. Cp. *v.* 25.

27 and. Note the Fig. *Polysyndeton* (Ap. 6) in *vv.* 27-30.

28 wine=new wine. Heb. *tīrōsh.* Ap. 27. ii.

cotes. Anglo-Saxon for enclosures.

30 stopped. The latest discoveries prove that the upper pool (Gihon) is identical with En-rogel (=the Fuller's Spring), now "the Virgin's Fount". A rock-hewn channel was cut from this westward to "the lower pool of Gihon, and eastward to Siloam". On the water supply at that time, see Isa. 7. 3; 8. 6; 22. 9-11; 36. 2. Cp. *v.* 3, 4 and 2 Kings 20. 20.

31 Babylon. The first occurrence of the name in connection with Judah.

the wonder. Cp. *v.* 24. 2 Kings 20. 10, 11. Isa. 38. 7, 8.

32 goodness=kindnesses.

behold. Fig. *Asterismos.* Ap. 6.

Isaiah. See Isa. 36-39.

and in, or [following] upon.

33 slept with his fathers. See note on Deut. 31. 16.

33. 1-20 (G[16], p. 545). MANASSEH. (*Introversion.*)

G[16] | Y | 1. Introduction.
 Z | 2-13. Events. Personal. Apostasy.
  A | 14. Public events. Buildings.
 Z | 15-17. Events. Personal. Reformation.
Y | 18-20. Conclusion.

1 Manasseh. This chapter is complementary to 2 Kings 21; *vv.* 11-17, concerning his reformation, are supplementary. See Ap. 56.

2-13 (Z, above). EVENTS. PERSONAL. APOSTASY, AND REPENTANCE (*Introversion.*)

Z | e | 2-9. Manasseh. His apostasy from Jehovah.
 f | 10-. Jehovah's remonstrance.
  g | -10. Disregard.
   h | 11. Captivity.
   h | 12, 13-. Deliverance.
  g | -13-. Regard.
 f | -13-. Jehovah's restoration.
e | -13. Manasseh. His acknowledgment of Jehovah.

2-9 (e, above). HIS APOSTASY. (*Introversion.*)

e | i | 2. Evil-doing. General.
 k | l | 3. Heathen high places rebuilt.
   m | 4, 5. Temple profaned. } Particular.
 k | *l* | 6. Heathen practices resumed.
   m | 7, 8. Temple profaned.
i | 9. Evil-doing. General.

2 the LORD. Heb. Jehovah. Ap. 4. II.

heathen=nations. **children**=sons.

3 groves=*'Ashērōth.* See Ap. 42.

the host of heaven. Cp. Deut. 17. 3.

4 had said. In Deut. 12. 11. 1 Kings 8. 29; 9. 3. 2 Chron. 6. 6; 7. 16. **name.** See note on Ps. 20. 1.

6 pass through the fire. Cp. Lev. 18. 21. Deut. 18. 10. 2 Kings 23. 10. 2 Chron. 28. 3.

observed times. Consulted auguries.

times=clouds, which were watched for auguries.

familiar spirit. See note on Lev. 19. 31.

evil=the evil. Heb. *rā'a'* (with Art.). Ap. 44. viii.

m 7 And he set a carved image, the °idol which
(p. 608) he had made, in the house of °God, of which
588 °God had said to David °and to Solomon his
to son, "In this house, and in Jerusalem, which
533 I have chosen before all the tribes of Israel,
will I put My [4] name for ever:
8 Neither will I any more remove the foot of
Israel from out of the land which I have appointed for °your fathers; °so that they will
take heed to do all that I have commanded
them, according to the whole law and the
statutes and the ordinances by the hand of
Moses."

i 9 So Manasseh made Judah and the inhabitants of Jerusalem to err, *and* to do worse than
the [2] heathen, whom [2] the LORD had destroyed
before the [2] children of Israel.

f 10 And [2] the LORD spake to Manasseh, and
to his People:

g but they would not hearken.

h 11 Wherefore [2] the LORD brought upon them
the °captains of the host of °the king of Assyria,
which took Manasseh °among the thorns, and
bound him with fetters, and carried him to
Babylon.

h 12 And when he was in affliction, he besought
[2] the LORD his [7] God, and humbled himself
greatly before the [7] God of his fathers,
13 And prayed unto Him:

g and He was intreated of him,

f and heard his supplication, and brought him
again to Jerusalem into his kingdom. Then
e Manasseh knew that [2] the LORD He *was* [7] God.

A 14 Now after this he built a wall without the
city of David, on the west side of °Gihon, in
the valley, even to the entering in at the fish
gate, and compassed about °Ophel, and raised
it up a very great height, and put captains of
war in all the fenced cities of Judah.

Z 15 And he took away the strange gods, and
the [7] idol out of the house of [2] the LORD, and all
the altars that he had built in the mount of
the house of [2] the LORD, and in Jerusalem, and
cast *them* out of the city.
16 And he repaired the altar of [2] the LORD,
and sacrificed thereon peace offerings and
thank offerings, and commanded Judah to serve
[2] the LORD [7] God of Israel.
17 Nevertheless the People did sacrifice still
in the high places, *yet* unto [2] the LORD their
[7] God only.

Y 18 Now the rest of the acts of Manasseh, and
his prayer unto his [7] God, and the words of the
seers that spake to him in the name of [2] the
LORD [7] God of Israel, °behold, they *are written*
in the book of the kings of °Israel.
19 °His prayer also, and *how God* was intreated of him, and all his °sins, and his °trespass, and the places wherein he built high
places, and set up [3] groves and graven °images,
before he was humbled: behold, they *are*
written among the sayings of °the seers.
20 So Manasseh °slept with his fathers, and
they buried him °in his own house: and
Amon his son reigned in his stead.

21 °Amon *was* two and twenty years old G[17] n
when he began to reign, and reigned two (p. 609)
years in Jerusalem. 533-531

22 But he did *that which was* °evil in the o
sight of [2] the LORD, °as did Manasseh his
father: for Amon sacrificed unto all the
carved [19] images which Manasseh his father
had made, and served them;
23 And humbled not himself before [2] the
LORD, as Manasseh his father had humbled himself; °but Amon °trespassed more and more.

24 And his servants conspired against him, o
and slew him in his own house.

25 But °the People of the land slew all them n
that had conspired against king Amon; and
the People of the land made Josiah his son
king in his stead.

34 °Josiah *was* eight years old when he G[18] B
began to reign, and he reigned in Jeru- 531
salem one and thirty years. to
2 And he did *that which was* right in the 500

---

7 idol = similitude.
God. Heb. Elohim (with Art.) = the [true] God. Ap. 4. I.
and = even.
8 your. Sept., Syr., and Vulg. read "their". Cp. 2 Kings 21. 8.
so that = if only.
11 captains = princes. See note on "Gezer", 1 Kings 9. 15–17.
the king of Assyria. Esar-haddon.
among the thorns = with hooks, or rings. A monument has been found showing this king Esar-haddon leading two captives with hooks or rings through their lips. And in an inscription he says: "I transported (from Syria) into Assyria men and women innumerable . . . I counted among the vassals of my realm twelve kings of Syria, beyond the mountains, Balou king of Tyre, Manasseh king of Judah".
14 Gihon. See notes on 32. 3, 4, 30.
Ophel. Northern part of Zion, south of Temple.
18 behold. Fig. *Asterismos.* Ap. 6.
Israel. See note on 1 Kings 12. 17.
19 His prayer. Not recorded. That given in the Apocrypha not considered genuine.
sins. Heb. *chāṭā'.* Ap. 44. i. A.V., 1611, reads "sin".
trespass. Heb. *mā'al.* Ap. 44. xi.
images. Same word as *v.* 22 and Deut. 7. 5. Always pl. in O.T.
the seers = the *chozai.* See note on 1 Chron. 29. 29.
20 slept with his fathers. See note on Deut. 31. 16.
in his own house. The Sept. reads "in the garden of his own house". Cp. 2 Kings 21. 18.

33. 21-25 (G[17], p. 545). AMON. (*Introversion.*)

G[17] | n | 21. Introduction.
  o | 22, 23. Personal. Evil-doing. Committed.
  o | 24. Personal. Evil-doing. Punished.
 n | 25. Conclusion.

21 Amon. Cp. 2 Kings 21. 19–24.
22 evil. Heb. *rā'a'.* Ap. 44. viii.
as = according as.
23 but Amon = "but he Amon".
trespassed more and more = he multiplied trespass. Heb. *'āshām.* Ap. 44. ii.
25 the People of the land = the commonalty. Cp. 36. 1.

34. 1—35. 27 (G[18], p. 545). JOSIAH. (*Introversion.*)

G[18] | B | 34. 1, 2. Introduction.
  C | 34. 3—35. 19. Events. Ecclesiastical.
  C | 35. 20-25. Events. Military.
 B | 35. 26, 27. Conclusion.

1 Josiah. These two chapters are complementary to 2 Kings 22. 1—23. 30. See Ap. 56.

sight of °the LORD, and walked in the ways
of David his father, and °declined *neither* to
the right hand, nor to the left.

D¹ E G (p. 610) 523 to 519 3 For in the eighth year of his reign, while
he was yet young, °he began to seek after the
°God of David his father: and in the twelfth
year he began to purge Judah and Jerusalem
from the high places, and the °groves, and
the °carved images, and the molten images.
4 And they °brake down the altars of Baalim
in his presence; °and the images, that *were*
on high above them, he cut down; and the
[3]groves, and the [3]carved images, and the
molten images, he brake in pieces, and made
dust *of them*, and strowed *it* upon the °graves
of them that had sacrificed unto them.
5 And he °burnt the bones of the priests
upon their altars, and cleansed Judah and
Jerusalem.
6 And *so did he* in the cities of Manasseh,
and Ephraim, and Simeon, even unto Naphtali,
°with their mattocks round about.
7 And when he had broken down the altars
and the [3]groves, and had beaten the graven
images into powder, and cut down all the
idols throughout all the land of Israel, he
returned to Jerusalem.

H p¹ 513 8 Now in the eighteenth year of his reign,
when he had purged the land, and the house,
°he sent Shaphan the son of Azaliah, and
Maaseiah the governor of the city, and Joah
the son of Joahaz the recorder, °to repair the
house of [2]the LORD his [3]God.
9 And when they came to °Hilkiah the high
priest, they delivered the money that was
brought into the house of [3]God, which the
Levites that kept the doors had gathered of
the hand of Manasseh and Ephraim, and of
all the remnant of Israel, and of all Judah
and Benjamin; and they returned to Jerusalem.
10 And they put *it* in the hand of the workmen
that had the oversight of the house of
[2]the LORD, and they gave it to the workmen
that wrought in the house of [2]the LORD, to
repair and amend the house:
11 Even to the artificers and builders gave
they *it*, to buy hewn stone, and timber for
couplings, and to floor the houses which the
kings of Judah had destroyed.
12 And °the men did the work faithfully: and
the overseers of them *were* Jahath and Obadiah,
the Levites, of the sons of Merari; and
Zechariah and Meshullam, of the sons of the
Kohathites, to set *it* forward; and *other of*
the Levites, °all that could skill of instruments
of musick.
13 °Also *they were* over the bearers of burdens,
and *were* overseers of all that wrought
the work in any manner of service: and of
the Levites *there were* scribes, and officers,
and porters.

q¹ 14 And when they brought out the money
that was brought into the house of [2]the LORD,
Hilkiah the priest °found a book of the law of
[2]the LORD *given* °by Moses.
15 And Hilkiah answered and said to Shaphan
the scribe, "I have [14]found the book of
the law in [2]the house of [2]the LORD." And
Hilkiah delivered the [14]book to Shaphan.

16 And Shaphan carried the [14]book to the
king, and brought the king word back again,
saying, "All that was committed °to thy p²
servants, they do *it*.
17 And they have °gathered together the
money that was found in the house of [2]the
LORD, and have delivered it into the hand of
the overseers, and to the hand of the workmen."
18 Then Shaphan the scribe told the king, q²
saying, "Hilkiah the priest hath °given me
a [14]book." And Shaphan read it before the
king.

---

2 the LORD. Heb. Jehovah. Ap. 4. II.
declined = turned aside or swerved.

34. 3—35. 19 (C, p. 609). EVENTS. ECCLESIASTICAL. (*Division.*)

C | D¹ | 34. 3-33. Reformation made.
  | D² | 35. 1-19. Passover kept.

3-33 (D¹, above). REFORMATION. MADE.
(*Introversion. Compound Alternations.*)

D¹ | E | G | 3-7. Judah and Jerusalem. The purging.
   | | H | p¹ | 8-13. Temple. Repair.
   | | | q¹ | 14-16-. Book found and delivered.
   | | | p² | -16, 17. Temple. Repair.
   | | | q² | 18, 19. Book found and read.
   | F | r | 20, 21. Jehovah. Inquiry. (Consequences.)
   | | s | 22. Servant's obedience.
   | *F* | *r* | 23-28-. Jehovah. Answer.
   | | *s* | -28. Servant's return.
   | *E* | *G* | 29. Judah and Jerusalem. The assembling.
   | | *H* | p³ | 30-. Temple. Entry of Josiah.
   | | | q³ | -30. Book read.
   | | | p⁴ | 31-. Temple. Station of Josiah.
   | | | q⁴ | -31-33. Book obeyed.

3 he began. Doubtless Zephaniah and Jeremiah were used in influencing Josiah. Both prophesied during his reign. Zephaniah began in first year of Josiah; Jeremiah in his thirteenth year, i. e. in 510.
God. Heb. Elohim. Ap. 4. I.
groves = *'Ashērim*. See Ap. 42.
carved images. Same as Deut. 7. 5.
4 brake down. Note the Fig. *Synonymia* (Ap. 6), by which the words are heaped together to impress us with the thoroughness of the work: e.g. "brake down", "cut down", "brake in pieces", "made dust of them", "strowed it", and "burnt".
and. Note the Fig. *Polysyndeton* (Ap. 6), connecting these particulars in *vv.* 4, 5.
graves. Heb. *ḳeber* = a burial place, from *ḳābar*, to bury (Gen. 23. 4, 20, &c.). Primary idea is heaping up a tumulus. *Ḳeber* = *a* grave; *Sh^eōl* = *the* grave. See Ap. 35.
5 burnt the bones. Thus fulfilling 1 Kings 13. 2.
6 with their mattocks: or, in their ruins.
8 he sent. This is supplementary to 2 Kings 22. 3.
to repair. This had been done before by Joash (2 Kings 12. 4-15).
9 Hilkiah. Cp. 1 Chron. 6. 13.
12 the men. Heb. *'ĕnōsh*. Ap. 14. III.
all that could skill = all that had understanding, or ability.
13 Also. Some think this should be omitted with the italics "they were" and "were".
14 found a book of the law. Without doubt the book which Moses himself wrote, the original copy of the Pentateuch. Cp. 2 Kings 22. 8, and see Ap. 47.
by = by the hand of. **16 to** = to the hand of.
17 gathered together. Heb. poured out, or melted down. **18 given me** = given to me.

513 19 And it came to pass, when the king had heard the words of the law, that he rent his clothes.

F r (p. 610) 20 And the king commanded Hilkiah, and Ahikam the son of Shaphan, and °Abdon the son of Micah, and Shaphan the scribe, and Asaiah a servant of the king's, saying,

21 "Go, enquire of [2]the LORD for me, and for them that are left in Israel and in Judah, concerning the words of the [14]book that is found: for great *is* the wrath of [2]the LORD that is poured out upon us, because our fathers have not kept °the word of [2]the LORD, to do after all that is written in this [14]book."

s 22 And Hilkiah, and *they* that the king °*had appointed*, went to Huldah the prophetess, the wife of Shallum the son of Tikvath, the son of Hasrah, keeper of the wardrobe; (now she dwelt in Jerusalem in the °college:) and they spake to her to that *effect*.

F r 23 And she answered them, "Thus °saith [2]the LORD [3]God of Israel, 'Tell ye the °man that sent you to me,

24 'Thus saith [2]the LORD, °'Behold, I will bring evil upon this place, and upon the inhabitants thereof, *even* all the curses that are °written in the book which they have read before the king of Judah:

25 Because they have forsaken Me, and have burned incense unto other gods, that they might provoke Me to anger with all the °works of their hands; therefore °My wrath shall be poured out upon this place, and shall not be quenched.'''

26 And as for the king of Judah, who sent you to enquire of [2]the LORD, so shall ye say unto him, 'Thus [23]saith [2]the LORD [3]God of Israel *concerning* the words which thou hast heard;

27 'Because thine heart was tender, and thou didst humble thyself before [3]God, when thou heardest °His words against this place, and against the inhabitants thereof, and humbledst thyself before Me, and didst rend thy clothes, and weep before Me; I have even heard *thee* also,' [23]saith [2]the LORD.

28 "Behold, I will °gather thee to thy fathers, and thou shalt be °gathered to thy [4]grave in peace, neither shall thine eyes see all the °evil that I will bring upon this place, and upon the inhabitants of the same.'''

s So they brought the king word again.

E G 29 Then the king sent and gathered together all the elders of Judah and Jerusalem.

H p³ 30 And the king went up into the house of [2]the LORD, °and all the [23]men of Judah, and the inhabitants of Jerusalem, and the priests, and °the Levites, and all the People, great and small:

q³ and he read in their ears all the words of the [14]book of the covenant that was found in the house of [2]the LORD.

p⁴ 31 And the king °stood in his place,

q⁴ and made °a covenant before [2]the LORD, to walk after [2]the LORD, and to keep His commandments, and His testimonies, and His statutes, with all his heart, and with all his °soul, to perform the words of the covenant which are written in this book.

20 Abdon: or Achbor. Cp 2 Kings 22. 12. See note on 1 Chron. 25. 11.

21 the word. Some codices, with Sept., Syr., and Vulg., read "the words" (pl.).

22 had appointed. The Sept. reads "named"; the Syr. reads "sent".

college: or second quarter [of the city].

23 saith=hath said.

man. Heb. *'ish.* Ap. 14. II.

24 Behold. Fig. *Asterismos.* Ap. 6.

written in the book. See note on *v.* 14; 35. 12, and Ap. 47.

25 works. Some codices, with one early printed edition and Syr., read "workmanship". Cp. 2 Kings 22. 17.

My wrath shall be poured out. Heb. text reads "that My wrath might be poured out". Some codices, with nine early printed editions and Sept., read "My wrath hath been poured out".

27 His words. Some codices, with Sept., read "My words".

28 gather thee to thy fathers. This is explained by the next sentence. See note on 2 Sam. 12. 23.

gathered to thy grave. Fig. *Euphemismos* (Ap. 6), for dying. **evil.** Heb. *ra'a'.* Ap. 44. viii.

30 and. Note the Fig. *Polysyndeton* (Ap. 6) in *vv.* 30–33.

the Levites. And prophets (2 Kings 23. 2).

31 stood in his place: or stood on his stand. Fig. *Polyptōton* (Ap. 6). **a**=the.

soul. Heb. *nephesh.* Ap. 13.

32 present=found.

33 took away. Cp. 2 Kings 23. 4–8.

children=sons.

serve, even to serve. Fig. *Epizeuxis.* Ap. 6.

all his days. Significant words, showing that in their hearts the people were still inclined to worship other gods, as Jeremiah testifies (Jer. 25. 3). See also Jer. 11 and 13.

35. 1-19 (D², p. 610). **PASSOVER KEPT.**
(Introversion.)

D² t | 1-. Passover. Kept.
  u | -1. Time. Fourteen days.
    v | 2-6. Command.
      w | 7. Donation of the king.
      w | 8, 9. Donation of the princes and others.
    v | 10-16. Obedience.
  u | 17. Time. Seven days.
t | 18, 19. Passover. None like it.

1 Josiah. This passover kept in the eighteenth year of his reign (2 Kings 23. 21–23).

kept a passover. One of the ten observances recorded. See note on Ex. 12. 28.

the LORD. Heb. Jehovah. Ap. 4. II.

fourteenth day. In this respect it was unlike Hezekiah's. Cp. 30. 2, 3. 2 Kings 23. 22, 23.

2 he set the priests, &c. This passover is interesting from the succinct description of its observance.

32 And he caused all that were °present in Jerusalem and Benjamin to stand *to it*. And the inhabitants of Jerusalem did according to the covenant of [3]God, the [3]God of their fathers.

33 And Josiah °took away all the abominations out of all the countries that *pertained* to the °children of Israel, and made all that were present in Israel to °serve, *even* to serve [2]the LORD their [3]God. *And* °all his days they departed not from following [2]the LORD, the [3]God of their fathers.

35 Moreover °Josiah °kept a passover unto °the LORD in Jerusalem: D² t (p. 611)
and they killed the passover on the °fourteenth *day* of the first month. u

2 And °he set the priests in their charges, v

513 and encouraged them to the service of the house of [1]the LORD,

3 And said unto the Levites °that taught °all Israel, which were °holy unto [1]the LORD, °"Put °the °holy ark in the house which Solomon the son of David king of Israel did build; *it shall* not *be* a burden upon *your* shoulders: serve now [1]the LORD your °God, and His People Israel,

4 And prepare *yourselves* by the houses of your fathers, after your courses, according to °the writing of David king of Israel, and according to °the writing of Solomon his son.

5 And stand in the [3]holy *place* according to the °divisions of °the families of the fathers of your brethren °the People, and *after* the division of the families of the Levites.

6 So kill the passover, and sanctify yourselves, and prepare your brethren, that *they* may do according to the word of [1]the LORD °by the hand of Moses."

w 7 And Josiah gave to [5]the People, of the flock, lambs and kids, all for the passover offerings, for all that were present, to the number of thirty thousand, and three thousand bullocks: these *were* of the king's substance.

w 8 And his princes gave willingly unto the People, to the priests, and to the Levites: °Hilkiah and Zechariah and Jehiel, rulers of the house of °God, gave unto the priests for the passover offerings two thousand and six hundred *small cattle*, and three hundred oxen.

9 Conaniah also, and °Shemaiah and Nethaneel, his brethren, and Hashabiah and Jeiel and °Jozabad, chief of the Levites, gave unto the Levites for passover offerings five thousand *small cattle*, and five hundred oxen.

v 10 So the service was prepared, and the priests stood in their place, and the Levites in their courses, according to the king's commandment.

11 And °they killed the passover, and the priests sprinkled *the blood* from their hands, and the Levites flayed *them*.

12 And they removed the burnt offerings, that they might give according to the divisions of [5]the families of [5]the People, to °offer unto [1]the LORD, as *it is* written in °the book of Moses. And so *did they* with the oxen.

13 And they roasted the passover with fire according to the ordinance: but the *other* [3]holy *offerings* °sod they in pots, and in caldrons, and in pans, and divided *them* speedily among all [5]the People.

14 And °afterward they made ready for themselves, and for the priests: because the priests the sons of Aaron *were busied* in °offering of burnt offerings and the fat until night; therefore the Levites prepared for themselves, and for the priests the sons of Aaron.

15 And the singers the sons of Asaph *were* in their place, according to the commandment of °David, and Asaph, and Heman, and Jeduthun the king's °seer; and the porters *waited* at every gate; °they might not depart from their service; for their brethren the Levites prepared for them.

16 So all the service of [1]the LORD was prepared the same day, to keep the passover, and to offer burnt offerings upon the altar of [1]the LORD, according to the commandment of king Josiah.

17 And the °children of Israel that were present kept the passover at that time, and the feast of unleavened bread seven days. *u*

18 And there was °no passover like to that kept in Israel from the days of Samuel the prophet; neither did all the kings of Israel keep such a passover as Josiah kept, and the priests, and the Levites, and all Judah and Israel that were present, and the inhabitants of Jerusalem. *t*

19 In the eighteenth year of the reign of Josiah was this passover °kept.

---

3 that taught all Israel. This was the great and special duty of the priests and Levites. But they neglected it for their ritual, as too many priests have done from that day to this. See notes on Deut. 33. 10; 17. 11, &c. **all Israel.** Not Judah only.
holy. See note on Ex. 3. 5.
Put the holy ark. It had probably been removed during the reparation of the Temple.
the holy ark = the Sanctuary's Ark. See note on Ex. 25. 22 and 1 Chron. 13. 3.
God. Heb. Elohim. Ap. 4. I.
4 the writing of David. Cp. 1 Chron. 28. 19; 2 Chron 29. 25, 27, 30.
the writing of Solomon. Cp. 2 Chron. 8. 14.
5 divisions. The word occurs only here.
the families = the houses.
the People = the sons of the People: i. e. the common people.
6 by the hand of Moses. This is Divine testimony as to the authorship of the Pentateuch (Ex. 12).
8 Hilkiah. The high priest (34. 9).
God. Heb. Elohim (with Art.) = the [true] God. Ap. 4. I.
9 Shemaiah . . . Jozabad. Cp. 31. 12-15.
11 they: i. e. the Levites.
12 offer = bring near. Heb. *ḳārab*. Ap. 43. I. i.
the book of Moses: i. e. Exodus. See Ap. 47.
13 sod = boiled.
14 afterward. Contrast Ezek. 34.
offering = offering up. Heb. *'ālāh*. See Ap. 43. I. vi.
15 David, and Asaph. Cp. 1 Chron. 25. 1; 6. 33, 39, 44.
seer. See notes on Judg. 9. 9. 1 Chron. 29. 29.
they might not: or they need not.
17 children = sons.
18 no passover like to that. Cp. 2 Kings 23. 22. No discrepancy with Hezekiah's passover (30. 26); none like Hezekiah's till then. This, of Josiah's, was later, and exceeded it.
19 kept. The Septuagint Version adds here [with a colon after kept]: ": after all these things that Josiah did in the house, who also burnt those who had familiar spirits, and the wizards, and the images, and the idols, and the sodomites, which were in the land of Judah and in Jerusalem, that he might confirm the words of the law that were written in the book which Hilkiah the priest had found in the house of the LORD. There was no one like him before him, who turned to the LORD with all his heart, and all his soul, and all his strength, according to all the law of Moses, and after him there rose up none like him. Nevertheless the LORD turned not from the anger of His great wrath, wherewith the LORD was greatly angry against Judah, for all the provocations wherewith Manasseh provoked Him. And the LORD said: 'I shall even remove Judah also from My presence, as I have removed Israel; and I have rejected the city which I chose, even Jerusalem, and the house of which I said, 'My Name shall be there.'' "

C x^1 20 °After all this, when Josiah had prepared
(p. 613) the °temple, °Necho king of Egypt came up
500 to fight °against °Charchemish by Euphrates:
y^1 and Josiah went out against him.

x^2 21 But °he sent ambassadors to him, saying, "What have I to do with thee, thou king of Judah? *I come* not against thee this day, but against the house wherewith I have war: for [3]God commanded me to make haste: forbear thee from *meddling with* [3]God, Who *is* with me, that He destroy thee not."

y^2 22 Nevertheless Josiah would not turn his face from him, but °disguised himself, that he might fight with him, and hearkened not unto the words of [20]Necho from the mouth of [3]God, and came to fight in the valley of °Megiddo.

x^3 23 And the archers shot at king Josiah; and the king said to his servants, "Have me away; for I am sore wounded."

y^3 24 His servants therefore took him out of that chariot, and put him in the second chariot that he had; and they brought him to Jerusalem, and he died, and was buried in *one of* the °sepulchres of his fathers. And all Judah and Jerusalem mourned for Josiah.
25 And °Jeremiah lamented for Josiah: and all the singing men and the singing women spake of Josiah in their lamentations to this day, and made them an ordinance in Israel: and, °behold, they *are* written in the lamentations.

B 26 Now the rest of the acts of Josiah, and his
(p. 609) °goodness, according to *that which was* written in the law of [1]the LORD,
27 And his deeds, first and last, behold, they *are* written in the book of the kings of Israel and Judah.

G^{19} a **36** Then °the People of the land took Je-
(p. 613) hoahaz the son of Josiah, and made him king in his father's stead in Jerusalem.
2 Jehoahaz *was* twenty and three years old
500 when he began to reign, and he reigned three months in °Jerusalem.

b 3 And the king of Egypt put him down at Jerusalem, and condemned the land in an hundred °talents of silver and °a talent of gold.

b 4 And the king of Egypt made Eliakim his brother king over Judah and Jerusalem, and turned his name to Jehoiakim.

a And Necho took Jehoahaz his brother, and carried him to °Egypt.

G^{20} c 5 Jehoiakim *was* twenty and five years old
500 when he began to reign, and he reigned
to eleven years in Jerusalem: and he did *that*
489 *which was* °evil in the sight of °the LORD his °God.

d 6 Against him °came up °Nebuchadnezzar

35. 20-25 (*C*, p. 609). EVENTS. MILITARY. (*Repeated Alternation.*)

C | x^1 | 20-. Pharaoh-necho. Invasion.
y^1 | -20. Josiah. Advance.
x^2 | 21. Pharaoh-necho. Embassy.
y^2 | 22. Josiah. Persistence.
x^3 | 23. Pharaoh-necho. Victory.
y^3 | 24, 25. Josiah. Death. Lamentation.

20 After all this. Thirteen years after.
temple = house.
Necho. Called also Pharaoh-necho. Said to be the founder of the twenty-fifth dynasty, about the thirty-fifth year of Manasseh: i. e. in 553 B.C.
against = at.
Charchemish = the fortress of Chemosh. Pharaoh-necho's object was to share the spoils of the falling empire of Assyria. Nineveh was taken 607 B.C. Cp. Jer. 46. 2.
21 he. Pharaoh-necho.
22 disguised himself. As Ahab had done (18. 29. 1 Kings 22. 30).
Megiddo. Cp. 2 Kings 23. 29.
24 sepulchres = graves. Heb. *keber*, as in 34. 4.
25 Jeremiah lamented. This does not refer to the book of that name (Lamentations), though Josiah is referred to in it (Lam. 4. 20 and Jer. 22. 10-18). Cp. Zech. 12. 11. 2 Kings 23. 31.
behold. Fig. *Asterismos.* Ap. 6.
26 goodness = kindnesses. Fig. *Metonymy* (of Cause), Ap. 6, put for acts of kindness. See 32. 32.

36. 1-4 (G^{19}, p. 545). JEHOAHAZ. (*Introversion.*)

G^{19} | a | 1, 2. Jehoahaz. Accession.
b | 3. King of Egypt puts him down.
b | 4-. King of Egypt sets his brother up.
a | -4. Jehoahaz. Captivity.

1 the People of the land = the commonalty. Cp. 33. 35. Not lawfully, for Jehoahaz was not the eldest son.
2 Jerusalem. The Sept. adds here, probably owing to the *Homœoteleuton* in the word Jerusalem: "Jerusalem, and his mother's name was Amital, daughter of Jeremiah of Lobnah: and he did that which was evil in the sight of the LORD, according to all that his fathers had done: and Pharaoh-neckhao bound him in Deblatha, in the land of Aimath, that he might not reign in Jerusalem".
3 talents . . . a talent. See Ap. 51. II. 6.
4 Egypt. The Sept. adds: "Egypt, and he died there: and they had given the silver and the gold to Pharaoh: at that time the land began to be taxed to give the money at the command of Pharaoh; and every one, as he could, kept demanding the silver and the gold of the People of the land, to give it to Pharaoh-neckhao".

5-8 (G^{20}, p. 545). JEHOIAKIM. (*Introversion*).

G^{20} | c | 5. Introduction.
d | 6. Nebuchadnezzar. Jehoiakim taken.
d | 7. Nebuchadnezzar. Temple spoiled.
c | 8. Conclusion.

5 evil. Heb *ra'a'*. Ap. 44. viii.
the LORD. Heb. Jehovah. Ap. 4. II.
God. Heb. Elohim. Ap. 4. I. The Sept. adds here: "according to all that his fathers did. In his days came Nebuchadnezzar king of Babylon into the land, and he served him three years, and then revolted from him. And the LORD sent against them the Chaldeans, and bands of Syrians, and bands of Moabites, and the sons of Ammon and Samaria; but after this, they rebelled according to the word of the LORD, by the hand of his servants the prophets. However, the anger of the LORD was upon Judah, to remove him from His presence, because of the sins of Manasseh in all that he did, and for the innocent blood which Jehoiakim had shed; and he had filled Jerusalem with innocent blood; yet the LORD refused to utterly destroy them".
6 came up. See Ap. 53.
Nebuchadnezzar. The son of Nabopolassar.

500-489 king of Babylon, and bound him in °fetters, °to carry him to Babylon.

d (p. 613) 7 [6]Nebuchadnezzar also carried of the vessels of the house of [5]the LORD to Babylon, and put them in his temple at Babylon.

c 8 Now the rest of the acts of Jehoiakim, and his abominations which he did, and that which was °found in him, behold, they *are* written in the °book of the kings of Israel and Judah: and Jehoiachin his son reigned in his stead.

G[21] e (p. 614) 489-488 9 °Jehoiachin *was* °eight years old when he began to reign, and he reigned three months and ten days in Jerusalem: and he did *that which was* [5]evil in the sight of [5]the LORD.

f 10 And when the year was expired, king [6]Nebuchadnezzar °sent, and °brought him to Babylon,

f with the goodly vessels of the house of [5]the LORD,

e and made °Zedekiah °his brother king over Judah and Jerusalem.

G[22] g 488 to 477 11 Zedekiah *was* one and twenty years old when he began to reign, and reigned eleven years in Jerusalem.
12 And he did *that which was* [5]evil in the sight of [5]the LORD his [5]God, *and* °humbled not himself before Jeremiah the prophet *speaking* from the °mouth of [5]the LORD.

h 13 And he also rebelled against king [6]Nebuchadnezzar, who had °made him swear by [5]God:

i but he stiffened his neck, and hardened his heart from turning unto [5]the LORD [5]God of Israel.

k 14 Moreover all the chief of the priests, and the People, °transgressed very much after all the abominations of the °heathen; and polluted the house of [5]the LORD which He had °hallowed in Jerusalem.

i 15 And [5]the LORD [5]God of their fathers sent to them by His messengers, °rising up betimes, and sending; because He had compassion on his People, and on His dwelling place:
16 But °they mocked the messengers of °God, and despised His words, and misused His prophets, until the wrath of [5]the LORD arose against His People, till *there was* °no remedy.

h 17 Therefore °He brought upon them the king of the Chaldees, who slew their young men with the sword in the house of °their sanctuary, and had no compassion upon young man or maiden, old man, or him that stooped for age: He gave *them* °all into his hand.
18 And [17]all the vessels of the house of [16]God, great and small, and the treasures of the house of [5]the LORD, and the treasures of the king, and of his princes; all *these* he brought to Babylon.

477 19 And they burnt the house of [16]God, and brake down the wall of Jerusalem, and burnt all the palaces thereof with fire, and destroyed all the goodly vessels thereof.

g 20 And them that had escaped from the

---

fetters. Heb. brasses, or bronzes (Dual). Put by Fig. *Metonymy* (of Cause), Ap. 6, for the two chains or fetters made of brass.
to carry him to Babylon. There were four deportations: (1) Manasseh (33. 11), no date given, but apparently 580-570 B.C.; (2) Jehoiakim (36. 6, Daniel in this; Dan. 1. 1), 496 B.C; (3) Jehoiachin (*v.* 10. 2 Kings 24. 14, Mordecai in this. Est. 2. 5, 6), 489 B.C.; (4) Zedekiah (36. 20. 2 Kings 25, Nehemiah in this), 477 B.C. From this last are reckoned the seventy years of 36. 21. Jer. 25. 9, 11, 12.
8 found in him = found upon him. On this is grounded the belief that he was tattooed with idolatrous marks or signs forbidden by Lev. 19. 28. Cp. Rev. 13. 16, 17; 14. 9, 11; 16. 2; 19. 20; 20. 4.
book. See Ap. 47.

36. 9, 10 (G[21], p. 545). JEHOIACHIN.
(*Introversion.*)

G[21] e | 9. Accession.
f | 10-. King. Captive.
f | -10-. Temple. Spoiled.
e | -10. Supercession.

9 Jehoiachin. Called also Jeconiah (1 Chron. 3. 16) and Coniah (Jer. 22. 24, 28). Cp. 2 Kings 24. 8. The "Je" (= Jehovah) being cut off from his name.
eight years. Some codices, with Sept. and Syr., read "eight", but 2 Kings 24. 8 reads "eighteen". The "eighteen" must include his co-regency, the "eight" to his reigning alone. This practice was common in Israel and Judah as well as in ancient contemporary kingdoms.
10 sent. N.B., not "came".
brought him = had him brought.
Zedekiah. Originally Mattaniah. Cp. 2 Kings 24. 17, &c.
his brother: i.e. his next of kin. In this case his uncle (2 Kings 24. 17. 1 Chron. 3. 15).

11-21 (G[22], p. 545). ZEDEKIAH.
(*Introversion.*)

G[22] g | 11, 12. Evil-doing. Against Jehovah.
h | 13-. Nebuchadnezzar. Rebellion.
i | -13. Jehovah. Obduracy of Zedekiah.
k | 14. Priests and people. Evil-doing.
i | 15, 16. Jehovah. Remonstrance.
h | 17-19. Nebuchadnezzar. Revenge.
g | 20, 21. Evil-doing. Requited by Jehovah.

12 humbled not himself, &c. Cp. Jer. 34. 8; 37. 2; and 38. 17, &c.
mouth. Put by Fig. *Metonymy* (of Cause), Ap. 6, for what is spoken by it.
13 made him swear. Ezekiel refers to this (Ezek. 17. 11-20).
14 transgressed very much = abounded in treachery. Heb. "multiplied to transgress transgression". Fig. *Polyptōton* (Ap. 6), for emphasis. Heb. *mā'al.* Ap. 44. xi.
heathen = nations.
hallowed. See note on Ex. 3. 5.
15 rising up betimes. Fig. *Anthropopatheia.* Ap. 6.
16 they mocked = they kept mocking. Cp. Matt. 23. 37. Especially Urijah (Jer. 26. 20-23) and Jeremiah (chaps. 37 and 38).
God. Heb. Elohim (with Art.) = the [true] God. Ap. 4. I.
no remedy. These words, occurring as they do on the last page of the Hebrew Bible, led to the conversion of the late Joseph Rabinovitch, of Kischeneff.
17 He brought. To leave us in no doubt as to the real cause. Cp. Judg. 1. 8, and see Ap. 53.
their sanctuary. No longer Jehovah's. Compare and contrast "My Father's house" (John 2. 16) and "your house" (Matt. 23. 38). The former at the beginning of His ministry; the latter at the close.
all = the whole that came into her hand.

477 to 426 sword carried he away to Babylon; where
they were °servants to him and his sons until
the reign of °the kingdom of Persia:
21 To °fulfil the word of [5]the LORD by the
mouth of °Jeremiah, until the land had enjoyed her sabbaths: *for* °as long as she lay
desolate she kept sabbath, to °fulfil °threescore
and ten years.

B[3] (p. 530) 426 22 Now in °the first year of Cyrus king of
Persia, that the word of [5]the LORD *spoken*
by the mouth of [21]Jeremiah might be accomplished, [5]the LORD stirred up the °spirit of
Cyrus king of Persia, that he made a proclamation throughout all his kingdom, and *put it*
also in writing, saying,
23 "Thus saith Cyrus king of Persia, 'All the
kingdoms of the earth hath [5]the LORD °God
of heaven given me; and °He hath charged me
to build Him an house in Jerusalem, which *is*
in Judah. Who *is there* among you of all His
People? [5]The LORD his [5]God *be* with him,
and let him go up'".

20 servants. Cp. Jer. 27. 6, 7. Dan. 1. This was foretold in 2 Kings 20. 17, 18. Isa. 39. 7.
the kingdom of Persia. See the Chronological Structure of Ezra-Nehemiah (p. 618), and notes there.
21 fulfil . . . fulfil. At beginning and end of *v.* in Heb. Note the emphasis by the Fig. *Epanadiplōsis.* Ap. 6.
Jeremiah. Cp. Jer. 25. 9, 12; 29. 10.
as long as = all the days. Thus completing a period of seventy years. This was foretold also (Lev. 23. 32; 26. 34, 35).
threescore and ten years. See special note on 36. 21, below.
22 the first year of Cyrus. See note on Ezra 1. 1.
spirit. Heb. *rūach*.
23 God of heaven. First occurrence of this expression. Now used because His People was *Lo Ammi* (= "not My People"), and He (Jehovah) had withdrawn from their midst. It is the title peculiar to the times of the Gentiles, while God acts from heaven, and not from between the cherubim as Jehovah the God of Israel, or as "the Lord of all the earth" (His millennial title). See the other occurrences (twenty in all = 3 × 6, Ap. 10): Ezra 1, 2; 5. 11, 12; 6. 9, 10; 7. 12, 21, 23. Neh. 1. 4, 5; 2. 4, 20. Ps. 136. 26. Dan. 2. 18, 19, 37, 44. Jonah 1. 9. Rev. 11. 13; 16. 11.
He hath charged me. Cp. Isa. 44. 28; 45. 13.

SPECIAL NOTE ON 2 Chron. 36. 21.

THE "SERVITUDE", THE "CAPTIVITY", AND THE "DESOLATIONS".

Three Periods of *seventy years* are assigned to these three respectively, and it is necessary that they should be differentiated.

i. The "SERVITUDE" began in the fourth year of JEHOIAKIM, and the first of NEBUCHADNEZZAR, when the "KINGDOM" passed under CHALDEAN rule for seventy years (Jer. 25. 1). This period closed with the capture of BABYLON by DARIUS the MEDIAN (ASTYAGES), and the "Decree" of CYRUS to rebuild the Temple. It lasted from 496–426 B.C.

ii. The "CAPTIVITY" commenced, and is dated by EZEKIEL from the carrying away to BABYLON of JECHONIAH, in the eighth year of NEBUCHADNEZZAR (2 Kings 24. 8-16). This was in 489 B.C. Consequently, when the "Servitude" ended in 426 B.C., the "Captivity" had lasted for sixty-three (9 × 7) years.

Seven years later CYRUS died, in 419 B.C. That year (419) is further notable for:

1. The appointment of Nehemiah as Governor of Jerusalem by Cambysses (Neh. 5. 14).
2. The completion of "the wall" in fifty-two days (Neh. 6. 15); and
3. The fact it marks the end of the *fifth* of the "seven sevens" of Dan. 9. 25. (See Appendix 50. VI, p. 60; and 50. VII (5), p. 67. The "Captivity" lasting from 489 to 419 B.C.

iii. The "DESOLATIONS" commenced with the beginning of the *third* and last siege of JERUSALEM by NEBUCHADNEZZAR in 479 B.C., and cover a period of "seventy years", ending in the second year of DARIUS HYSTASPIS: i. e. in 409 B.C.

This "threescore and ten years" which is referred to here (2 Chron. 36. 21), is the fulfilment of Lev. 26. 32-35, and has reference to "the LAND".

It is this period of which DANIEL says he "understood by books", as being the number of the years that Jehovah "would accomplish in the Desolations of Jerusalem" (Dan. 9. 2).

The DARIUS here (Dan. 9. 1) is evidently CYRUS, the son of ASTYAGES (see notes on p. 618, and Ap. 57); and as the first year of his reign was 426 B.C., it follows that *seventeen* years had, then, yet to run before the "Desolations" of the LAND were ended, in 409 B.C.

Hence, DANIEL's prayer, that follows, resulted in the giving to him the famous prophecy of the "seventy sevens" of years contained in Dan. 9. 20-27.

EZRA-NEHEMIAH.

THE STRUCTURE OF THE TWO BOOKS AS A WHOLE*,

ACCORDING TO THEIR CANONICAL ORDER.

(*Division.*)

A[1] | EZRA. THE REBUILDING OF THE TEMPLE.

A[2] | NEHEMIAH. THE REBUILDING OF THE WALLS.

(A[1], above). EZRA. THE REBUILDING OF THE TEMPLE.

(*Introversion.*)

A[1] | B | 1. 1-4 (N†). THE PEOPLE. EMANCIPATION.
- C | 1. 5—2. 70 (P). THE RETURN UNDER ZERUBBABEL.
  - D | 3. 1-6 (Q). THE ALTAR. BUILDING AND FEAST.
  - *D* | 3. 7—6. 22 (*Q*). THE TEMPLE. BUILDING AND FEAST.
- *C* | 7. 1—8. 36 (*P*). THE RETURN UNDER EZRA.

B | 9. 1—10. 44 (*N*). THE PEOPLE. DEDICATION. REFORMATION.

(A[2], above). NEHEMIAH. THE REBUILDING OF THE WALLS.

(*Introversion and Alternation.*)

A[2] | E | 1. 1—6. 19 (K†). THE WALL. REBUILDING. DISORDERS OVERCOME.
- F | H | 7. 1-4 (N). JERUSALEM. CHARGE OVER.
  - J | 7. 5-73- (P). THE RETURN UNDER ZERUBBABEL.
    - G | 7. -73—8. 18 (Q). FEAST OF THE SEVENTH MONTH (426 B.C.).
    - *G* | 9. 1—10. 39 (*N*). FEAST OF THE SEVENTH MONTH (404 B.C.).
- *F* | *H* | 11. 1-36 (*N*). JERUSALEM. RESIDENTS IN.
  - *J* | 12. 1-26 (*N*). THE RETURN UNDER EZRA.

E | 12. 27—13. 31 (*K*). THE WALL. DEDICATION. DISORDERS OVERCOME.

* In Hebrew manuscripts of the Bible, and the early printed editions of the Hebrew text, these two books are always treated and reckoned as one book: the 685 verses being numbered from the first verse of Ezra to the last verse of Nehemiah; the middle verse of the one book being given by the Massorites as Neh. 3. 32; while of the ten Sedarim (or Cycles for public reading), the fourth begins at Ezra 8. 35 and ends with Neh. 2. 10. See note at foot of p. 632. Moreover, the notes which the Massorites place at the end of each book are placed at the end of Nehemiah, and not at the end of Ezra. Cp. note on the books of SAMUEL, KINGS, and CHRONICLES, p. 366.

The Structure of the one book is set forth as above, the two Divisions being given in their CANONICAL ORDER.

EZRA confines himself mainly to the events connected with the TEMPLE.

NEHEMIAH confines himself mainly to the events connected with the WALL and the CITY.

Ezra comes first in the Canonical Order, because the TEMPLE is more important than the WALL, morally and spiritually.

Nehemiah follows, because the WALL is of secondary importance.

When the whole of the events are looked at in their CHRONOLOGICAL and HISTORICAL order, a different Structure is necessarily observed: this Structure is determined by certain *fixed points*, common to both Orders. These fixed points determine the place of the remaining events recorded in the two parts respectively. See Table of Events and CHRONOLOGICAL Structure on p. 618, and the Harmony of Events in Ap. 58.

† The letters of this fount (in brackets) correspond with the same letters in the CHRONOLOGICAL Structure on page 617.

CERTAIN FIXED POINTS IN THE TWO DIVISIONS OF THE JOINT BOOKS

May be exhibited as follows, in brief: a complete list of all the events will be found in Appendix 58.

EZRA.		NEHEMIAH.	
		1. 1—6. 19.	The WALL. Rebuilding. External disorders overcome.
1. 1-4.	The People. Emancipation.		
		7. 1-4.	The condition of the city. (People few. Houses not built.)
1. 5—2. 70.	The Return under Zerubbabel. (The Temple still desolate: and for sixteen years later. Hag. 1. 1-4.)	7. 5—73-.	The Return under Zerubbabel.
	Feast of the Seventh Month (426 B.C.).	7. -73—8. 18.	Feast of the Seventh Month (426 B.C.).
3. 1-13.	Temple. Foundation laid.		
4. 1—6. 15.	The Temple: building.		
6. 16-22.	Dedication of the Temple.		
7. 1—8. 36.	The Return under Ezra.		
9. 1-4.	Feast, &c., of the Seventh Month (404 B.C.).	9. 1-37.	Feast, &c., of the Seventh Month (404 B.C.).
9. 5.	Separation of the People. Ezra's Prayer.	9. 38.	Separation of the People. Levites' Prayer.
10. 1-44.	Strange wives put away, and the Covenant made.	10. 1-39.	Strange wives put away, and the Covenant made.
		11. 1—12-26.	Residents in Jerusalem.
		12. 27-47.	Dedication of the wall.
		13. 1-31.	Reformation of the People.

We are now in a position to complete the CHRONOLOGICAL Structure of the joint books.

THE STRUCTURE OF EZRA–NEHEMIAH AS A WHOLE,

ACCORDING TO

THE HISTORICAL AND CHRONOLOGICAL ORDER OF EVENTS.*

(*Introversions and Alternation.*)

A[1] A[2] **K** | Neh. 1. 1—6. 19 (E †). THE WALL. REBUILDING. EXTERNAL DISORDERS OVERCOME.

  L **N** | Neh. 7. 1-4 (H). JERUSALEM. CHARGE OVER IT.

    O | Ezra 1. 1-4 (B). THE PEOPLE. EMANCIPATION.

      M **P** | Neh. 7. 5-73- (J). / Ezra 1. 5—2. 70 (C). } THE RETURN UNDER ZERUBBABEL.

        Q | Neh. 7. -73—8. 18 (G). / Ezra 3. 1-7 (D). } FEAST OF THE SEVENTH MONTH (426 B.C.).

          R | Ezra 3. 8-13 (*D*). THE TEMPLE. FOUNDATION.

          R | Ezra 4. 1—6. 22 (*D*). THE TEMPLE. BUILDING AND DEDICATION.

      M *P* | Ezra 7. 1—8. 36 (*C*). THE RETURN UNDER EZRA.

        Q | Neh. 9. 1-3 (*G*). / Ezra 9. 1-4 (*B*). } FEAST OF THE SEVENTH MONTH (404 B.C.).

  L *O* | Neh. 9. 4—10. 39 (*G*). / Ezra 9. 5—10. 44 (*B*). } THE PEOPLE. SEPARATION.

    N | Neh. 11. 1—12. 26 (*F*). JERUSALEM. RESIDENTS IN IT.

K | Neh. 12. 27—13. 31 (*E*). THE WALL. DEDICATION. INTERNAL DISORDERS OVERCOME.

* See notes on p. 618.

† The Index letters (in brackets) correspond with the same letters which indicate the same members in the CANONICAL Structure, on page 616.

NOTES TO THE CHRONOLOGICAL STRUCTURE (p. 617).

The Chronological Order of Events, and the Structure based thereon, revolutionises the traditional view, which treats this one book as two books; places Ezra historically as preceding Nehemiah; and inserts the book of Esther between Ezra, chapters 6 and 7, instead of before Ezra–Nehemiah. (See date, Est. 1. 3.)

Those who thus dislocate the two divisions of this book proceed to speak of certain portions as being "misplaced", and "not original", and as having "false connections". These so-called "discrepancies", after having thus been first made by the commentators, are charged home on the inspired writers themselves.

That the "difficulties" exist only in the minds of the critics will be seen if we note the following facts:—

1. The fixed points, common to the two parts of the book, determine for us the true position of all the other parts, and result in giving us the Chronological Structure of the whole on page 617.

2. The traditional view places the building of the temple by Ezra as coming many years before Nehemiah 1. But this is inconceivable in view of the report brought by Hanani to Nehemiah concerning the desolations (Neh. 1. 3) and repeated to the king (Neh. 2. 3).

3. Nehemiah would surely have inquired about the welfare of the 42,360 exiles who are supposed to have returned to Jerusalem, and not about "the Jews that had escaped, which were left of the captivity" (Neh. 1. 2).

4. When the wall was finished, "the houses were not yet builded" (Neh. 7. 1-4).

5. When the Feast of the seventh month was kept (Neh. 8), "the foundation of the temple of the Lord was not yet laid" (Ezra 3. 1-6).

6. When the people dwelt in their "cieled houses", the house of the Lord still lay waste (Hag. 1. 1-4). These facts are more certain than all chronology, and are more important and conclusive than all reasoning.

7. The names of some of the kings mentioned have been hitherto regarded as proper names; whereas, according to Sir Henry Rawlinson, Professor Sayce, *The Encyclopædia Britannica*, and *The Century Encyclopædia of Names*, three at least are appellatives (like Pharaoh, Abimelech, Czar, Shah, Sultan); viz. Ahasuerus, which means "The venerable king", Artaxerxes, which means "The great king", and Darius, which means "The maintainer". See the Genealogy of the Persian kings (Ap. 57). If these appellatives denote separate and different individual kings, no place can be found for them all on the page of history.

8. See the longer notes on special passages at the end of Nehemiah, page 653.

°EZRA.

A[1] B (p. 616) (N) (p. 617) 426

1 NOW in the first year of °Cyrus king of Persia, that the word of °the LORD by the °mouth of Jeremiah might be fulfilled, °the LORD stirred up the °spirit of °Cyrus king of Persia, that he made a proclamation throughout all his kingdom, and *put it* also in writing, saying,

2 "Thus saith Cyrus king of Persia, [1]'The LORD °God of heaven °hath given me all the kingdoms of the earth; and He hath °charged me to build Him °an house at Jerusalem, which *is* in Judah.

3 °Who *is there* among you of all His People? his [2]God be with him, and let him go up to Jerusalem, which *is* in Judah, and °build the house of [1]the LORD [2]God of Israel, (He *is* the [2]God,) which *is* in Jerusalem.

4 And °whosoever °remaineth in any place where he sojourneth, let °the °men of his place help him with silver, and with gold, °and with goods, and with beasts, beside the freewill offering for the [2]house of °God that *is* in Jerusalem.'"

C (P) A (p. 619)

5 Then rose up °the °chief of the fathers of °Judah and Benjamin, and the priests, and the Levites, with all *them* whose [1]spirit [2]God had raised,

B a

to go up to build the house of [1]the LORD which *is* in Jerusalem.

b

6 And all they that *were* about them strengthened °their hands with vessels of silver, with gold, with goods, and with beasts, and with precious things, beside all *that* was willingly offered.

7 Also Cyrus the king brought forth the vessels of the house of [1]the LORD, °which Nebuchadnezzar had brought forth out of Jerusalem, and had put them in the house of his gods;

8 Even those did Cyrus king of Persia bring forth by the hand of Mithredath the treasurer, and numbered them unto °Sheshbazzar, the prince of Judah.

9 And this *is* the number of them: thirty °chargers of gold, a thousand °chargers of silver, nine and twenty knives,

10 Thirty basons of gold, silver basons of a second *sort* four hundred and ten, *and* other vessels a thousand.

11 All the vessels of gold and of silver *were* five thousand and four hundred. All *these* did [8]Sheshbazzar bring up with *them of* the captivity that were brought up from Babylon unto Jerusalem.

TITLE, Ezra. For the Structure of the two books (Ezra–Nehemiah) as a whole, in their canonical order, see p. 616. For the Structure of the chronological order, see p. 617 and the reasons for it, on p. 618.

The book of Esther precedes (chronologically) the book of Ezra–Nehemiah.

1 Cyrus. The son of Astyages and Esther. See Ap. 57, 58, on the genealogy of the Persian kings. So named nearly 200 years before he was born (Isa. 44. 28).

The book of Esther precedes the book of Ezra–Nehemiah, and Neh. 1. 1—7. 4 precedes Ezra 1. 1–14. See note on Neh. 1. 2. Est. 3. 8; 10. 3, and Ap. 57, 58.

the LORD. Heb. Jehovah. Ap. 4. II.

mouth. Cp. 2 Chron. 36. 21–23. Jer. 29. 10–14.

spirit. Heb. *rūach*. Ap. 9.

2 God. Heb. Elohim. Ap. 4. I.

God of heaven. See note on 2 Chron. 36. 23. Appropriate in the mouth of Cyrus, and in contrast with all heathen inscriptions.

hath given me. The son of Astyages (the venerable king = Ahasuerus) and Esther. Trained by Mordecai and Nehemiah, he was brought up in the knowledge of God and His Word.

charged me to build. Cp. Isa. 44. 24–28; 45. 1–6, 13.

an house. This proclamation put first, as it is the great subject treated of by Ezra.

3 Who is there . . . ? Fig. *Erotēsis*. Ap. 6.

build = rebuild.

4 whosoever [of the captive people] **remaineth in any place, &c.** Note the Fig. *Ellipsis*. Ap. 6.

remaineth = is left.

the men of his place: i. e. his Persian neighbours.

men. Heb. *'īsh.* Ap. 14. II.

and. Note the Fig. *Polysyndeton*. Ap. 6.

God. Heb. Elohim (with Art.) = the [true] God. Ap. 4. I.

1. 5—2. 70 (**C**, p. 616; **P**, p. 617). THE RETURN UNDER ZERUBBABEL.

(*Alternation and Introversion.*)

C | A | 1. 5–. The chief of the fathers.
  B | a | 1. –5. Return to Jerusalem.
      b | 1. 6–11. Assistance (*v.* 6 by Persians, *vv.* 7–11 by the king).
  A | 2. 1–67. The sons of the Province.
  B | *b* | 2. 68, 69. Assistance (by Israelites).
      a | 2. 70. Residents in the cities.

5 the chief of the fathers: i. e. those named in the next chapter.

chief = heads.

Judah and Benjamin. But the other tribes found representatives. Cp. 2. 59, 70, where the terms "of Israel" and "all Israel" are used. In 1 Chron. 9. 3, Ephraim and Manasseh are mentioned by name. See note on 1 Kings 12. 17.

6 their hands = them. Put by Fig. *Synecdoche* (of Part), Ap. 6, for themselves.

7 which Nebuchadnezzar had brought. Cp. 2 Kings 24. 13; 25. 14. 2 Chron. 36. 7. Jer. 27. 18–22; 28. 6; 52. 18, 19. Dan. 1. 2; 5. 2.

8 Sheshbazzar = the Chaldean name of the prince of Judah. Not Zerubbabel, which means born at Babel. Probably = Nehemiah, for he was the son of Hachaliah and Zidkijah (Neh. 10. 1), and therefore a "prince of Judah". **9 chargers** = basons or bowls. Heb. *'ăgartāl.* In Numbers *ḳeʽārāh*, plate or dish. Eng. "charger", from French *charger*, to load. Hence used of both a dish and a horse.

A c (p. 620) 426 **2** Now °these *are* the °children of °the Province that went up out of the captivity, of those which had been carried away, whom Nebuchadnezzar the king of Babylon had carried away unto Babylon, and came again unto Jerusalem °and Judah, every °one unto his city;

2 Which °came with Zerubbabel: °Jeshua, °Nehemiah, °Seraiah, Reelaiah, °Mordecai, Bilshan, Mizpar, Bigvai, Rehum, Baanah. The number of the °men of °the People of Israel:

d **3** The [1]children of Parosh, two thousand an hundred seventy and two.

4 The [1]children of Shephatiah, three hundred seventy and two.

5 The [1]children of Arah, seven hundred seventy and five.

6 The [1]children of Pahath-moab, of the [1]children of Jeshua *and* Joab, two thousand eight hundred and twelve.

7 The [1]children of Elam, a thousand two hundred fifty and four.

8 The [1]children of Zattu, nine hundred forty and five.

9 The [1]children of Zaccai, seven hundred and threescore.

10 The [1]children of Bani, six hundred forty and two.

11 The [1]children of Bebai, six hundred twenty and three.

12 The [1]children of Azgad, a thousand two hundred twenty and two.

13 The [1]children of Adonikam, six hundred sixty and six.

14 The [1]children of Bigvai, two thousand fifty and six.

15 The [1]children of Adin, four hundred fifty and four.

16 The [1]children of Ater of Hezekiah, ninety and eight.

17 The [1]children of Bezai, three hundred twenty and three.

18 The [1]children of Jorah, an hundred and twelve.

19 The [1]children of Hashum, two hundred twenty and three.

20 The [1]children of Gibbar, ninety and five.

21 The [1]children of Beth-lehem, an hundred twenty and three.

22 The [2]men of Netophah, fifty and six.

23 The [2]men of Anathoth, an hundred twenty and eight.

24 The [1]children of Azmaveth, forty and two.

25 The [1]children of °Kirjath-arim, Chephirah, and Beeroth, seven hundred and forty and three.

26 The [1]children of Ramah and Gaba, six hundred twenty and one.

27 The [2]men of Michmas, an hundred twenty and two.

28 The [2]men of Beth-el and Ai, two hundred twenty and three.

29 The [1]children of Nebo, fifty and two.

30 The [1]children of Magbish, an hundred fifty and six.

31 The [1]children of the other Elam, a thousand two hundred fifty and four.

32 The [1]children of Harim, three hundred and twenty.

33 The [1]children of Lod, Hadid, and Ono, seven hundred twenty and five.

34 The [1]children of Jericho, three hundred forty and five.

35 The [1]children of Senaah, three thousand and six hundred and thirty.

36 The priests: the [1]children of °Jedaiah, of the house of Jeshua, nine hundred seventy and three.

37 The [1]children of °Immer, a thousand fifty and two.

38 The [1]children of °Pashur, a thousand two hundred forty and seven.

39 The [1]children of °Harim, a thousand and seventeen.

40 The Levites: the [1]children of Jeshua and Kadmiel, of the [1]children of Hodaviah, seventy and four.

41 The singers: the [1]children of Asaph, an hundred twenty and eight.

42 The [1]children of the porters: the [1]children of Shallum, the [1]children of Ater, the [1]children of Talmon, the [1]children of Akkub, the [1]children of Hatita, the [1]children of Shobai, *in* all an hundred thirty and nine.

43 The °Nethinims: the [1]children of Ziha, the [1]children of Hasupha, the [1]children of Tabbaoth,

44 The [1]children of Keros, the [1]children of Siaha, the [1]children of Padon,

---

2. 1-67 (*A*, p. 619). THE SONS OF THE PROVINCE. (*Introversion.*)

A | c | 1, 2. In sum. The number.
  d | 3–58. Names found.
  d | 59–63. Names not found.
  c | 64–67. In sum.

1 these are. This chapter is parallel with Neh. 7. 69. See the Structure, M P, p. 617, and Ap. 58.

children = sons.

the Province: i. e. the Persian province of Judah. Cp. Neh. 1. 3.

and Judah. Some codices read "and unto Judæa". Cp. Neh. 7. 6.

one. Heb. *'ish.* Ap. 14. II.

2 came with Zerubbabel. But not till *after* Neh. 1. 1—7. 4. See note on Neh. 1. 2, 3. In Neh. 7. 4 no houses built, but in Hag. 1. 4, houses built and yet Temple lying waste.

Jeshua. The great helper of Zerubbabel.

Nehemiah. Cp. Neh. 1. 1; 10. 1. See note on "Sheshbazzar", 1. 8.

Seraiah = Azariah (Neh. 7. 7). Not Seraiah the high priest, put to death with Zedekiah (2 Kings 25. 18–21).

Mordecai. He had been taken in Jehoiachin's deportation (Est. 2. 5, 6).

men. Heb. pl. of *'enōsh.* Ap. 14. III.

the People of Israel. See note on 1. 5. So 2. 59, 70; 3. 1; 7. 13; 9. 1; 10. 5. Cp. 1 Kings 12. 17.

25 Kirjath-arim. Now *Khan 'Erma.* Some codices, with Sept. and Vulg., read "Kirjath-jearim".

36 Jedaiah. The head of the ninth course (1 Chron. 24. 11).

37 Immer. The head of the sixteenth course (1 Chron. 24. 14).

38 Pashur. Cp. Jer. 20. 1; 21. 1 and 1 Chron. 9. 12. Probably belonging to the fifth course, as son of Malchijah. Cp. 1 Chron. 24. 9 with Neh. 11. 12.

39 Harim. The third course. These four were subdivided into six each, making the twenty-four.

43 Nethinims = men given to God or His service. Temple servants. Cp. *v.* 58; 7. 7, 24; 8. 17, 20. Neh. 3. 26; 10. 28; 11. 21. 1 Chron. 9. 2.

426 45 The [1] children of Lebanah, the [1] children of Hagabah, the [1] children of Akkub,
46 The [1] children of Hagab, the [1] children of °Shalmai, the [1] children of Hanan,
47 The [1] children of Giddel, the [1] children of Gahar, the [1] children of Reaiah,
48 The [1] children of Rezin, the [1] children of Nekoda, the [1] children of Gazzam,
49 The [1] children of Uzza, the [1] children of Paseah, the [1] children of Besai,
50 The [1] children of Asnah, the [1] children of Mehunim, the [1] children of Nephusim,
51 The [1] children of Bakbuk, the [1] children of Hakupha, the [1] children of Harhur,
52 The [1] children of Bazluth, the [1] children of Mehida, the [1] children of Harsha,
53 The [1] children of Barkos, the [1] children of Sisera, the [1] children of Thamah,
54 The [1] children of Neziah, the [1] children of Hatipha.
55 The [1] children of Solomon's servants: the [1] children of Sotai, the [1] children of Sophereth, the [1] children of Peruda,
56 The [1] children of Jaalah, the [1] children of Darkon, the [1] children of Giddel,
57 The [1] children of Shephatiah, the [1] children of Hattil, the [1] children of Pochereth of Zebaim, the [1] children of Ami.
58 All the [43] Nethinims, and the [1] children of Solomon's servants, *were* three hundred ninety and two.
59 And these *were* they which went up from Tel-melah, Tel-harsa, Cherub, Addan, *and* Immer: but they could not shew their father's house, and their seed, whether they *were* °of Israel:
60 The [1] children of Delaiah, the [1] children of Tobiah, the [1] children of Nekoda, six hundred fifty and two.

d (p. 620) 61 And of the [1] children of the priests: the [1] children of Habaiah, the [1] children of Koz, the [1] children of Barzillai; which took a wife of the daughters of Barzillai the Gileadite, and was called after their name:
62 These sought their register *among* those that were reckoned by genealogy, but they were not found: therefore were they, °as polluted, put from the priesthood.
63 And the °Tirshatha said unto them, that they should °not eat of the most °holy things, till there stood up a priest °with °Urim and °with Thummim.

c 64 The whole °congregation together *was* °forty and two thousand three hundred *and* threescore,
65 Beside their servants and their °maids, of whom *there were* seven thousand three hundred thirty and seven: and *there were* among them two hundred singing men and singing women.
66 Their horses *were* seven hundred thirty and six; their mules, two hundred forty and five;
67 Their camels, four hundred thirty and five; *their* asses, six thousand seven hundred and twenty.

B b (p. 619) 68 And °*some* of the °chief of the fathers, when they came to the house of °the LORD which *is* at Jerusalem, offered freely for the house of °God to set it up in his place:

46 Shalmai. Some codices, with one early printed edition, Sept. and Syr., read "Selami".
59 of Israel. See note on 2. 2, and cp. 1 Kings 12. 17.
62 as polluted, put. R.V. = deemed polluted and put. Heb. *gā'al*, to pollute; not *gā'al*, to redeem. Supply *Ellipsis* thus: "therefore were they [rejected] from the priesthood as polluted". So in Neh. 7. 64; 13. 29. Isa. 59. 3; 63. 3. Lam. 4. 14. Zeph. 3. 1. Mal. 1. 7.
63 Tirshatha = governor (Persian title). Here refers to Nehemiah, as in Neh. 8. 9; 10. 1; 12. 26. The Heb. title is *Peḥah* (Neh. 5. 14, 18; 12. 26). Whence the Turkish *Pashah*. See note on 5. 3.
not eat of the most holy things: i. e. the remains of the meal offering, sin offering, and right shoulder of the peace offerings. Cp. Lev. 2. 3; 10. 12-14, 16, 17. Num. 18. 9, 10.
holy. See note on Ex. 3. 5. **with** = for.
Urim and with Thummim. See note on Ex. 28. 30. Num. 26. 55.
64 congregation = assembly, or muster.
forty and two thousand three hundred and threescore. This number (42,360) agrees with Neh. 7. 66. The two lists of *names* are not alike; but there is no "discrepancy". The two lists, while they agree in the numbers, and vary in names, yet have the totals identical. This shows the independence of the two accounts.

Numbered in Ezra 2.		42,360
Named in Ezra	29,818	
" in Neh., not in Ezra ...	1,765	31,583
Difference between names and numbers		10,777
Numbered in Neh. 7.		42,360
Named in Nehemiah	31,089	
" in Neh., not in Ezra ...	494	31,583
Difference between names and numbers		10,777

65 maids = handmaids.
68 some = a portion. Ezra mentions what *one* portion gave. Nehemiah (7. 70) mentions what *he and two other* portions gave. Hence the numbers "perforce" cannot be the same, and there is no "discrepancy".
chief = heads.
the LORD. Heb. Jehovah. Ap. 4. II.
God. Heb. Elohim (with Art.) = the [true] God. Ap. 4. I.
69 treasure = treasury.
drams. See Ap. 51. I. 1 (2).
pound. See Ap. 51. II. 4 (1).
70 all Israel. See note on 2. 2, and 1 Kings 12. 17.

3. 1-13 (D, p. 616; Q, p. 617). THE TEMPLE. FOUNDATION AND FEAST. (*Division*).

D | C^1 | 1-6. The setting up of the altar.
  | C^2 | 7-13. The foundation of the house.

1-7 [For Structure of C^1 see next page].

1 seventh month. Tisri. See Ap. 51. III. 5.
children = sons.
of Israel. See note on 2. 2, and 1 Kings 12. 17.
the cities. Some codices, with Sept., Syr., and Vulg., read "their cities". **man.** Heb. *'ish*. Ap. 14. II.
to = in. Therefore this was *after* Neh. 7. 1-4.

69 They gave after their ability unto the °treasure of the work threescore and one thousand °drams of gold, and five thousand °pound of silver, and one hundred priests' garments.
70 So the priests, and the Levites, and *some* of the people, and the singers, and the porters, and the Nethinims, dwelt in their cities, and °all Israel in their cities. a

3 And when the °seventh month was come, and the °children °of Israel *were* in °the cities, the People gathered themselves together as one °man °to Jerusalem. D C^1 D (p. 622) 426

E e (p. 622) 426 2 Then stood up °Jeshua the son of °Jozadak, and his brethren the priests, and °Zerubbabel the son of Shealtiel, and his brethren, and builded the altar of the °God of Israel, to °offer burnt offerings thereon, as *it is* °written in the law of Moses °the [1] man of God.

3 And they set the altar upon his bases; for fear *was* upon them because of the °people of those countries: and they [2] offered burnt offerings thereon unto °the LORD, *even* burnt offerings morning and evening.

f Tisri 15–21 4 They °kept also the feast of tabernacles, °as *it is* written, and *offered* the daily burnt offerings by number, according to the custom, as the duty of every day required;

f 5 And afterward *offered* the continual burnt offering, both of the new moons, and of all the set feasts of [3] the LORD that were consecrated,
e and of every one that willingly offered a freewill offering unto [3] the LORD.

D 6 From the first day of the seventh month began they to offer burnt offerings unto [3] the LORD. But the foundation of the temple of [3] the LORD was not *yet* laid.

C² g¹ 425 7 They gave money also unto the masons, °and to the °carpenters; and meat, and drink, and oil, unto them of Zidon, and to them of Tyre, to °bring cedar trees from Lebanon to the sea of °Joppa, according to the °grant that they had °of Cyrus king of Persia.

8 Now in the second year of their coming unto the house of °God at Jerusalem, in the second month, began Zerubbabel the son of Shealtiel, and Jeshua the son of Jozadak, and the remnant of their brethren the priests and the Levites, and all they that were come out of the captivity unto Jerusalem; and appointed the Levites, from twenty years old and upward, to °set forward the work of the house of [3] the LORD.

h¹ 9 Then stood Jeshua *with* his sons and his brethren, Kadmiel and his sons, the sons of °Judah, together, to [8] set forward the workmen in the house of [8] God: the sons of Henadad, *with* their sons and their brethren the Levites.

g² 10 And when the builders laid the foundation of the temple of [3] the LORD,
h² °they set the priests in their apparel with trumpets, and the Levites the sons of Asaph with °cymbals, to praise [3] the LORD, after the ordinance of David king of Israel.

11 And they sang together by course in praising and giving thanks unto [3] the LORD; because *He is* good, for His °mercy *endureth* for ever toward Israel. And all the People °shouted with a great shout, when they praised [3] the LORD, because the foundation of the house of [3] the LORD was laid.

g³ 12 But many of the priests and Levites and °chief of the fathers, °*who were* ancient men, that had seen the first house, when the foundation of this house was laid before their eyes,
h³ wept with a loud voice; and many °shouted aloud for joy:

13 So that the People could not discern the noise of the shout of joy from the noise of the weeping of the People: for the People shouted with a loud shout, and the noise was heard afar off.

4

D G (p. 623) Now when the °adversaries of Judah and Benjamin heard that the °children of the captivity builded °the temple unto °the LORD °God of Israel;

---

3. 1-7 (C¹, p. 621). SETTING UP THE ALTAR. (*Alternations.*)

C¹ | D | 1. Time. Seventh month.
  E | e | 2, 3. Altar and offerings.
    f | 4. Feast of Tabernacles.
  E | *f* | 5-. Other Feasts.
    e | -5. Altar and offerings.
  D | 6-. Time. Seventh month.

2 Jeshua. The high priest. Spelt Joshua in Hag. 1. 1; 2. 2. Zech. 3. 1.

Jozadak. The son of Seraiah (1 Chron. 6. 14, 15). But Ezra was the son of Seraiah (Ezra 7. 1). Therefore Ezra was brother to Jozadak and uncle to Joshua the high priest.

Zerubbabel. Cp. Matt. 1. 12. Luke 3. 27, called Zorobabel.

God. Heb. Elohim (with Art.) = the [true] God. Ap. 4. I.

offer = offer up. Heb. *'ālāh.* Ap. 43. I. vi.

written in the law of Moses. See note on Ex. 17. 14, and Ap. 47.

the man of God (with Art.) = the [true] God. See note on Deut. 33. 1; and Ap. 49.

3 people = peoples.

the LORD. Heb. Jehovah. Ap. 4. II.

4 kept, &c. As recorded also in the parallel passage (Neh. 8. 1-18).

as it is written. See Lev. 23. 34-43. Deut. 16. 13-15, and cp. 1 Kings 8. 2, 65.

3. 7-13 (C², p. 621). THE FOUNDATION OF THE HOUSE. (*Repeated Alternation.*)

C² | g¹ | 7, 8. The work set forward.
  h¹ | 9. The priests. Stationed.
  g² | 10-. The work. Foundation laid.
  h² | -10, 11. The priests. Praise.
  g³ | 12-. The work. Contrasted.
  h³ | -12, 13. The priests. Emotion.

7 and. Note the Fig. *Polysyndeton* (Ap. 6), to emphasise each detail.

carpenters = artificers.

bring cedar trees. Cp. 1 Kings 5. 6. 2 Chron. 2. 8, 10.

Joppa. Cp. Josh. 19. 46. Acts 9. 35, 43. Jon. 1. 3.

grant. Occurs only here.

of = from. Genitive of Origin. See Ap. 17.

8 God. Heb. Elohim (with Art.) = the [true] God. Ap. 4. I.

set forward = oversee.

9 Judah: or Hodaviah, as in 2. 40.

10 they set the priests: or, the priests took their stand.

cymbals. Heb. *mᵉziltayim.* Dual form, meaning two metal discs struck together, making a clashing sound. Not *zilzilīm*, which = timbrels, but is translated cymbals in 2 Sam. 6. 5 and Ps. 150. 5, from the rustling sound. See note on 1 Chron. 13. 8.

11 mercy = lovingkindness, or grace.

shouted with a great shout. Fig. *Polyptōton.* Ap. 6.

12 chief = heads.

who were. Some codices, with one early printed edition and Vulg., read "and the".

shouted aloud for joy. Thus fulfilling Jer. 33. 10, 11.

4. 1—6. 22 [For Structures see next page].

1 adversaries. The Samaritans (*v.* 10). See note on 2 Kings 17. 24, 26.

children = sons.

the temple. The walls and gates already built by Nehemiah. See Structures (pp. 616, 617), and notes on Neh. 1. 2. The desolations did not end with Ezra 1, though the servitude did. Cp. Jer. 25. 11. 2 Chron. 36. 21. See special note at end of 2 Chronicles, p. 615.

the LORD. Heb. Jehovah. Ap. 4. II.

God. Heb. Elohim. Ap. 4. I.

425 2 Then they came to ° Zerubbabel, and to the
° chief of the fathers, and said unto them, "Let
us build with you: for ° we seek your [1] God, as
ye *do*; and ° we do sacrifice unto Him since the
days of ° Esar-haddon king of ° Assur, which
brought us up hither."

H (p. 623) 3 But [2] Zerubbabel, and ° Jeshua, and the rest
of the [2] chief of the fathers of Israel, said unto
them, "Ye have nothing to do with us to build
an house unto our [1] God; but we ourselves
together will build unto [1] the LORD [1] God of
° Israel, ° as king Cyrus the king of Persia hath
commanded us."

J N 4 Then the people of the land weakened the
hands of the People of Judah, and ° troubled
them in building,
5 And hired counsellors against them,

O from 425–410 to frustrate their purpose, all the days of
° Cyrus king of Persia, even until the reign of
° Darius king of Persia.

N (6 And in the reign of ° Ahasuerus, in the
beginning of his reign, wrote they *unto him*
an accusation against the inhabitants of Judah
and Jerusalem.)
(7 And in the days of ° Artaxerxes, wrote
Bishlam, Mithredath, Tabeel, and the rest of
their ° companions, unto Artaxerxes king of
Persia; and the writing of the letter *was*
written in ° the Syrian tongue, and interpreted
in the Syrian tongue.
8 ° Rehum ° the chancellor and Shimshai ° the
scribe wrote a letter against Jerusalem to
[7] Artaxerxes the king ° in this sort:
9 Then *wrote* [8] Rehum the chancellor, and
Shimshai [8] the scribe, and the rest of their
[7] companions; the ° Dinaites, the ° Apharsathchites, the ° Tarpelites, the ° Apharsites, the
° Archevites, the Babylonians, the ° Susanchites, the ° Dehavites, *and* the ° Elamites,
10 And the rest of the ° nations whom the
great and noble ° Asnapper brought over, and
set in the cities of Samaria, and the rest *that*
are ° on this side the river, and ° at such a time.
11 This *is* the copy of the letter that they
sent unto him, *even* unto [7] Artaxerxes the
king; "Thy servants the ° men [10] on this side
the river, and [10] at such a time.

O P i 12 Be it known unto the king, that the ° Jews
which came up from thee to us are come unto
Jerusalem, building the rebellious and the bad

4. 1—6. 22 (*D*, p. 616; *Q*, p. 617). THE TEMPLE. BUILDING AND DEDICATION. (*Division.*)

D | F[1] | 4. 1—6. 15. The building.
| F[2] | 6. 16–22. The dedication.

4. 1—6. 15 (F[1], above). THE BUILDING. (*Extended Alternation.*)

F[1] | G | 4. 1, 2. Adversaries. Temptation.
H | 4. 3. Obedience to God's word.
J | 4. 4–16. Opposition. Letter to Cyrus.
K | 4. 17–22. King's answer. Success of plot.
L | 4. 23, 24–. Work. Cessation.
M | –24. Duration of cessation.
G | 5. 1. Helpers. (Prophets.) Exhortation.
H | 5. 2. Obedience to God's word.
J | 5. 3–17. Opposition. Letter to Darius.
K | 6. 1–12. King's answer. Defeat of plot.
L | 6. 13, 14. Work. Recommencement.
M | 6. 15. Date of completion.

2 Zerubbabel. See note on 3. 2. **chief** = heads.

we seek your God. A priest had been sent to these Samaritans (2 Kings 17. 28–33).

we do sacrifice unto Him. Heb. text = "although we have not been sacrificing". Some codices, and two early printed editions, with Sept. and Syr., add "unto Him".

Esar-haddon. The son and successor of Sennacherib (see notes on 2 Kings 19. 37, and 2 Chron. 33. 11).

Assur = Assyria. **3 Jeshua.** See note on 3. 2.

Israel. See note on 2. 2 and 1 Kings 12. 17.

as = according as.

4. 4–16 (J, above). OPPOSITION. LETTER TO CYRUS. (*Alternation.*)

J | N | 4. 4, 5–. Opponents. Counsellors.
O | –5. Action. To frustrate.
N | 6–11. Opponents. Writers.
O | 12–16. Action. Writing.

4 troubled them in = terrified them from.

5 Cyrus. The son of Astyages and Esther. See Ap. 57, 58.

Darius: i. e. Darius Hystaspis (see Ap. 57, 58). "Darius" being only an appellative (= the maintainer), needs "Hystaspis" to be added, to identify him; as Astyages, when called Darius, needs the addition of "the Mede". See Ap. 58, and notes on p. 618.

6 Ahasuerus = the venerable king. See Ap. 57, 58, and p. 618. An appellative, used here of Cyrus (*v.* 5), or retrospectively of Astyages; or, this verse may be retrospective, and should be in parenthesis.

7 Artaxerxes = the great king. Used here of the Cyrus of *v.* 3. See Ap. 57, 58, and p. 618. Verses 7–23 may also be retrospective of Neh. 2. 20—6. 15.

companions = colleagues or associates.

the Syrian tongue: i. e. in Aramaic characters as well as in the Aramaic language. Cp. Est. 1. 22; 8. 9, where "writing" (Heb. *kāthab*, to grave) is the same word as in this book.

8 Rehum. From here to 6. 18 is in Syriac, which was like the French of to-day. Cp. 2 Kings 18. 26. From 6. 19—7. 11 is Hebrew; and Syriac again from 7. 12–27; then Hebrew. **the chancellor** = the master of judgments or decrees. **the scribe**: or secretary. **in this sort** = after this manner. **9 Dinaites.** Probably from a Persian city. **Apharsathchites.** A Medo-Persian tribe. **Tarpelites.** Probably from east of Elymais. **Apharsites.** Of Persian origin. **Archevites.** From Babylonia. Cp. Gen. 10. 10. **Susanchites.** From the Persian province or city of Shushan, the capital of Elam. **Dehavites** = the Dahae of Herodotus (i. 125). **Elamites.** From a province of Persia. **10 nations** = peoples. **Asnapper** = Assur-bani-pal, or Sardanapalus, the only Assyrian king who got into Elam, or held Shushan (now Susa) its capital. **on this side** = beyond, on the west side: regarded from the east side of the Euphrates. **at such a time.** This may refer to the date of the letter; or be rendered, as in R.V., "and so forth". **11 men.** Chald. *'ěnōsh.* See Ap. 14. iii.

4. 12–16 (*O*, above). ACTION. WRITING. (*Introversion and Alternation.*)

O | P | i | 12. Notification.
k | 13. Hypothesis. "If".
Q | 14. Concern. Maintenance.
Q | 15. Advice. Search.
P | *i* | 16–. Certification.
k | –16. Hypothesis. "If".

12 Jews. Nehemiah, Hanani, and friends. Occurs eight times in Ezra, viz. 4. 12, 23; 5. 1, 5; 6. 7, 7, 8, 14. The name by which they were known to Gentiles, because the majority belonged to Judah.

425 city, and have °set up the walls *thereof*, and
joined the foundations.

k 13 Be it known now unto the king, that, if
(p. 623) this city be builded, and the walls set up
again, *then* will they not pay toll, tribute, and
custom, and *so* thou shalt endamage the
revenue of the kings.

Q 14 Now because °we have maintenance from
the king's palace, and it was not meet for us to
see the king's dishonour, therefore have we
sent and certified the king;

Q 15 That search may be made in the book of
the records of thy fathers: so shalt thou find
in the book of the records, and know that this
city *is* a rebellious city, and hurtful unto kings
and provinces, and that they have moved
sedition within the same of old time: for
which cause was this city destroyed.

P i 16 We certify the king that,

k if this city be builded *again*, and the walls
thereof set up, by this means thou shalt have
no portion on this side the river."

K l 17 *Then* sent the king an °answer unto
(p. 624) [8]Rehum the chancellor, and *to* Shimshai the
scribe, and *to* the rest of their [7]companions
that dwell in Samaria, and *unto* the rest beyond
the river, "Peace, and at such a time.

m 18 The letter which ye sent unto us hath
been plainly read before me.

m 19 And °I commanded, and search hath been
made, and it is found that this city of old time
hath °made insurrection against kings, and
that rebellion and sedition have been made
therein.
20 There have been °mighty kings also over
Jerusalem, which have ruled over all *countries*
beyond the river; and toll, tribute, and custom,
was paid unto them.

l 21 Give ye now °commandment to cause
these °men to cease, and that this city be not
builded, until *another* °commandment shall
be given from me.
22 Take heed now that ye fail not to do this:
why should damage grow to the hurt of the
kings?")

L 23 Now when the copy of king [7]Artaxerxes'
(p. 623) letter *was* read before [8]Rehum, and Shimshai
the scribe, and their [7]companions, they went
up in haste to Jerusalem unto the [12]Jews, and
made them to cease °by force and power.)
24 Then ceased the work of the house of
°GOD which *is* at Jerusalem.

M So it ceased unto the second year of the reign
425-410 of [5]Darius king of Persia.

G **5** Then the prophets, °Haggai the prophet,
1st Elul and °Zechariah the son of Iddo, prophesied
410 unto the Jews that *were* in Judah and
Jerusalem in the name of the °GOD °of Israel,
°*even* unto them.

H 2 Then rose up Zerubbabel the son of Shealtiel,
and Jeshua the son of Jozadak, and began
to build the house of [1]GOD which *is* at Jerusalem:
and with them *were* the prophets of
°GOD helping them.

3 At the same time came to them Tatnai, *J* R
°governor on this side the river, and Shethar- (p. 624)
boznai, and their °companions, and said thus
unto them, "Who hath °commanded you to
build this house, and to °make up this wall?"
4 Then °said °we unto them °after this
manner, "What are the names of the °men
that °make this building?"

---

set up the walls. Quite true; for Nehemiah's work had long preceded this. See the Chronological Structure, p. 617, and notes on p. 618; also Ap. 58. And note that, when Nehemiah's work was done (7. 4) and the houses built, the house of God was still lying waste (Hag. 1. 1-4). The Temple not mentioned here.

14 we have maintenance = the salt of the palace is our salt. See note on Num. 18. 19.

4. 17-22 (K, p. 623). KING'S ANSWER. SUCCESS OF PLOT. (*Introversion*.)

K | l | 17. Mission.
  m | 18. Reception.
  m | 19, 20. Verification.
  l | 21, 22. Prohibition.

17 answer. Chald. *pithgām* = an order or decree. A Persian word. Occurs only here and 5. 5, 11; 6. 11. Dan. 3. 16; 4. 17. **19 I commanded** = I made a decree.
made insurrection. Chald. lifted itself up.
20 mighty kings. Such as David and Solomon.
21 commandment = decree.
men = strong men, *gubrayya'a*. Chald. form of Ap. 14. IV.
23 by force. Chald. by arm; "arm" being put by Fig. *Metonymy* (of Cause), Ap. 6, for the force put forth by it.
24 GOD. Chald. *'ělāhā'* (*ha*, emphatic), sing., same as Heb. Eloah. Ap. 4. V.

5. 1 Haggai. The prophet of that name. In the second year of Darius (Hag. 1. 1), "sixth month".
Zechariah. The prophet of that name. In the second year of Darius, "eighth month" (Zech. 1. 1).
GOD. Chald. *'ělah* (sing.). Same as Eloah. Ap. 4. V.
of Israel. Still "Israel", because representative of the whole nation. See note on 1 Kings 12. 17.
even unto them: or "[which was] over them".
2 GOD. Chald. *'ělāhā'*, as in 4. 24. Heb. Eloah (emph.). Ap. 4. V.

5. 3-17 (*J*, p. 623). OPPOSITION. LETTER TO DARIUS. (*Extended Alternation*.)

J | R | 3, 4. Governor. "Who commanded?" } Verbal.
  S | 5-. Non-cessation. Fact.
  T | -5. Appeal to Darius.
  R | 6-10. Governor. "Who commanded?" } Letter.
  S | 11-16. Non-cessation. Reason.
  T | 17. Appeal to Darius.

3 governor. Chald. *pechāh* (modern "Pasha"). Tatnai was governor in Syria, Zerubbabel was governor in Judah. Cp. *vv.* 6, 14; 6. 6, 7, 13; 8. 36. Dan. 3. 2, 3, 27; 6. 7; and Hag. 1. 1, 14; 2. 2, 21.
companions = colleagues or associates.
commanded you = made a decree to you; given a firman.
make up = build. So the wall had already been built by Nehemiah. See the Chronological Structure, p. 617, and notes on p. 618; and Ap. 58.
4 said = told. Chald. *'āmar*, which must be followed by the words spoken (which are given in next clause).
we. Note this pronoun (first person sing. and pl.). Here, and 7. 27—9. 15, and Neh. 1. 1—7. 73; 12. 27-43; 13. 4-31. Sept., Syr., and Arab. read "they".
after this manner. Verse 4 should be rendered "we told them what the names were, accordingly the names of the men", &c. It is not a question.
men. As in 4. 21.
make this building. Heb. "build this building". Fig. *Polyptōton* (Ap. 6), for emphasis.

S 5 But ° the eye of their [1] GOD was upon the
(p. 624) ° elders of the Jews, that they could not cause
410 them to cease,
T till the matter came to ° Darius: and then
they returned ° answer by letter concerning
this *matter*.
R 6 The copy of the letter that ° Tatnai, [3] governor on this side the river, and Shethar-
boznai, and his [3] companions the ° Apharsach-
ites, which *were* on this side the river, sent
unto [5] Darius the king:
7 They sent a letter unto him, wherein was
written thus; "Unto [5] Darius the king, all
peace.
8 Be it known unto the king, that we went
into the ° province of Judea, to the house of
the great [2] GOD, which is builded with ° great
stones, and timber is laid in the walls, and
this work goeth fast on, and prospereth in
their hands.
9 Then asked we those elders, *and* said unto
them thus, 'Who commanded you to build
this house, and to make up these walls?'
10 We asked their names also, to certify
thee, that we might write the names of the
[4] men that *were* the ° chief of them.
S U n 11 And thus they returned us answer, saying,
(p. 625) 'We are the servants of ° the [1] GOD of heaven
and earth,
o and build the house that was builded ° these
many years ago, which a great king of Israel
builded ° and set up.
V 12 But after that our fathers had provoked
the [11] GOD of heaven unto wrath,
V He ° gave them into the hand of Nebuchadnezzar the king of Babylon, the Chaldean, who
destroyed this house, and carried the People
away into Babylon.
U n 13 But in the first year of ° Cyrus the king
426 of ° Babylon *the same* king Cyrus made a decree to build this house of [2] GOD.
14 And ° the vessels also of gold and silver of
the house of [2] GOD, which Nebuchadnezzar
took out of the temple that *was* in Jerusalem,
and brought them into the temple of Babylon,
those did Cyrus the king take out of the temple
of Babylon, and they were delivered unto *one*,
whose name *was* ° Sheshbazzar, whom he
had made [3] governor;
15 And said unto him, 'Take these vessels,
go, ° carry them into the temple that ° *is* in Jerusalem, and let the house of [2] GOD be builded in
his place.'
o 16 Then came the same [14] Sheshbazzar, *and*
laid the foundation of the house of [2] GOD
which *is* in Jerusalem: and since that time
even until now hath it been in building, and
yet it is not finished.'
T 17 Now therefore, if *it seem* good to the king,
(p. 624) let there be search made in the king's treasure
house, which *is* there at [13] Babylon, whether it
be *so*, that a decree was made of Cyrus the
king to build this house of [2] GOD at Jerusalem,
and let the king send his pleasure to us concerning this matter."

5 the eye. Fig. *Anthropopatheia*. Ap. 6.
elders. Chald. *sîb* = grey, hoary. Used only of Ezra here and 6, 7, 8, 14.
Darius. See note on 4. 5.
answer. See note on 4. 17.
6 Tatnai. His name has been recently found in a contract. **Apharsachites.** See note on 4. 9.
8 province. Cp. Neh. 1. 3.
great = rolling: i. e. too heavy to be moved without rolling. **10 chief** = head.

5. 11-16 (*S*, p. 624). **CESSATION. REASON.**
(*Introversion and Alternation.*)

S | U | n | 11-. Answer of builders.
o | -11. The building.
V | 12-. People. Provocation.
V | -12. People. Captivity.
U | *n* | 13-15. Answer of Cyrus.
o | 16. The building.

11 the GOD of heaven. See note on 2 Chron. 36. 23.
GOD. Chald. *'ĕlah*. Same as Eloah. Ap. 4. V.
these many years ago. Nearly 500 years.
and set up. Cp. 1 Kings 6. 1.
12 gave them. Cp. 2 Kings 24. 2; 25. 8-11.
13 Cyrus. Cp. 1. 1.
Babylon. Included now with Persia. Cp. 6. 1. Neh. 13. 6.
14 the vessels. Cp. Ezra 1. 7, 8; 6. 5.
Sheshbazzar. See note on 1. 8. This was Nehemiah, who was present, though the stone was actually laid by Zerubbabel (Zech. 4. 9).
15 carry them into = set them down, or deposit them in. **is** = is to be.

6. 1-12 (*K*, p. 623). **KING'S ANSWER. DEFEAT OF PLOT.** (*Alternation.*)

K | p | 1. Darius. Search made.
q | 2-5. Decree found (Cyrus).
p | 6, 7. Darius. Forbearance ordered.
q | 8-12. Decree made (Darius).

1 Darius: i. e. Darius (Hystaspis). See Chronological Structure and notes (pp. 617, 618), and Ap. 57, 58.
Babylon. See note on 5. 13.
2 Achmetha = Ecbatana, the capital of ancient Media.
3 first year of Cyrus. Cp. 1. 1.
GOD. Chald. *'ĕlāhā* = Heb. Eloah (Ap. 4. V.); the final "ha" is for emphasis.
offered. Chald. *deba'ḥ*. Same as Heb. *zebach*. Ap. 43. I. iv. **cubits.** See Ap. 51. III. 2.
4 rows = layers or stories, as in 1 Kings 6. 36.
new timber. Should be "timber, one": i. e. one row. In changing the ancient characters into the modern square characters the *aleph* ('a) in *ḥad'a* ("one"), in the ancient character, was mistaken for א, Tau, the "th" in *ḥadath* ("new"), and so was transliterated. The Sept. has preserved the original reading, and the R.V. notes it in the margin. The two lines should read: "layers of great stones, three; and a layer of timber, one".
house = treasury: "house" being put by Fig. *Metonymy* (of Adjunct), Ap. 6, for the treasures in it.

6 Then ° Darius the king made a decree, and *K p*
search was made in the house of the rolls, (p. 625)
where the treasures were laid up in ° Babylon.
2 And there was found at ° Achmetha, in the q
palace that *is* in the province of the Medes,
a roll, and therein *was* a record thus written:
3 "In the ° first year of Cyrus the king *the same*
Cyrus the king made a decree *concerning* the
house of ° GOD at Jerusalem, Let the house be
builded, the place where they ° offered sacrifices,
and let the foundations thereof be strongly
laid; the height thereof threescore ° cubits, *and*
the breadth thereof threescore cubits;
4 *With* three ° rows of great stones, and a
row of ° new timber: and let the expences be
given out of the king's ° house:

410 **5 And also let the golden and silver °vessels of the house of [3]GOD, which Nebuchadnezzar took forth out of the temple which °*is* at Jerusalem, and brought unto Babylon, be restored, and brought again unto the temple which *is* at Jerusalem, *every one* to his place, and place *them* in the house of [3]GOD."**

p **6 "Now *therefore*, °Tatnai, governor beyond the river, Shethar-boznai, and your °companions the Apharsachites, which *are* beyond the river, be ye far from thence:**

7 Let the work of this house of [3]GOD alone; let the governor of the °Jews and the elders of the Jews build this house of [3]GOD in his place.

q **8 Moreover °I make a decree what ye shall do to the elders of these [7]Jews for the building of this house of [3]GOD: that of the king's goods, *even* of the tribute beyond the river, forthwith expences be given unto these °men, that they be not hindered.**

9 And that which they have need of, both young bullocks, and rams, and lambs, for the burnt offerings of the °GOD of heaven, wheat, salt, °wine, and oil, according to the appointment of the priests which *are* at Jerusalem, let it be given them day by day without fail:

10 That they may offer sacrifices of °sweet savours unto the [9]GOD of heaven, and pray for the life of the king, and of his sons.

11 Also I have made a decree, that whosoever shall °alter this word, let timber be pulled down from his house, and being set up, let him be hanged thereon; and let his house be made a dunghill for this.

12 And the [3]GOD That hath caused His name to dwell there destroy all kings and people, that shall put to their hand to °alter *and* to destroy this house of [3]God which *is* at Jerusalem. I Darius have made a decree; let it be done with speed."

L **13 Then [6]Tatnai, governor on this side the river, Shethar-boznai, and their companions, according to that which [1]Darius the king had sent, so they did speedily.**

14 And the elders of the [7]Jews builded, and they prospered through the prophesying of Haggai the prophet and Zechariah the son of Iddo. And they builded, and finished *it*, according to the °commandment of the [9]GOD of Israel, and according to the °commandment of °Cyrus, and °Darius, and °Artaxerxes king of Persia.

M 405 **15 And this house was finished on the third day of the month °Adar, which was in the sixth year of the reign of [1]Darius the king.**

F[2] r **16 And the °children of Israel, the priests, and the Levites, and the rest of the °children of the captivity, kept the dedication of this house of [3]GOD with joy,**

s **17 And °offered at the dedication of this house of [9]GOD an hundred bullocks, two hundred rams, four hundred lambs; and for a sin offering for °all Israel, twelve he goats, according to the number of the tribes of Israel.**

5 vessels. Cp. 1. 7. **is** = was.
6 Tatnai, governor = Tatnai, pasha. See notes on 5. 3, 6.
companions = fellow-labourers or colleagues.
7 Jews. See note on 4. 12.
8 I make a decree. This was a new decree of Darius Hystaspis.
men = strong men. Chald. *gubbrayya'*. Heb. *geber*. Ap. 14. IV.
9 GOD. Chald. *'elah*. (Sing.) Same as Heb. Eloah. Ap. 4.
GOD of heaven. See note on 2 Chron. 36. 23.
wine = strong red wine. Heb. *chemer*. See Ap. 27. iii.
10 sweet savours. See note on Lev. 1. 9.
11 alter. A similar strong threat in the inscription of Darius on the Behistūn rock (Ap. 57). Cp. Dan. 3. 29.
12 alter. Supply Fig. *Ellipsis* (Ap. 6): "alter [this decree]".
14 commandment = decree.
Cyrus, and Darius, and Artaxerxes. Note the Fig. *Polysyndeton*, to mark the important fact that *three* kings, at various times, were concerned in the rebuilding of Jerusalem. The last named was the first in order.
Darius was Darius Hystaspis, and Artaxerxes was Astyages (the father of Cyrus), the same as in Neh. 2. 1. See Ap. 57 and 58; and notes on p. 618.
15 Adar = the twelfth month. See Ap. 51. III. 4.

6. 16-22 (F[2], p. 623). THE DEDICATION.
(*Introversion.*)

F[2] r | 16. Feast of Dedication. "Kept with joy."
  s | 17. The People. Their offerings.
   t | 18. The priests. Set.
    u | 19. The passover kept.
   t | 20. The priests. Purified.
  s | 21. The People. Their purification.
 r | 22. Feast of passover. "Kept with joy."

16 children = sons.
17 offered = brought near. Ap. 43. I. i.
all Israel. See note on 1 Kings 12. 17. Note the number "twelve". Ap. 10.
18 as it is written = according to the writing.
the book of Moses: i. e. the Pentateuch. See Ap. 47.
19 And, &c. Here recommences the Hebrew language. See note on 4. 8.
kept the passover. One of the ten so recorded. See note on Ex. 12. 28. **21 heathen** = nations.
the LORD. Heb. Jehovah. Ap. 4. II.
God. Heb. Elohim. Ap. 4. I.

18 And they set the priests in their divisions, and the Levites in their courses, for the service of [9]GOD, which *is* at Jerusalem; °as it is written in °the book of Moses. t

19 °And the [16]children of the captivity °kept the passover upon the fourteenth *day* of the first month. u

20 For the priests and the Levites were purified together, all of them *were* pure, and killed the passover for all the [16]children of the captivity, and for their brethren the priests, and for themselves. *t*

21 And the [16]children of Israel, which were come again out of captivity, and all such as had separated themselves unto them from the filthiness of the °heathen of the land, to seek °the LORD °God of Israel, did eat, *s*

22 And kept the feast of unleavened bread seven days with joy: for [21]the LORD had made them joyful, and turned the heart of the king *r*

405 of Assyria unto them, to strengthen their hands in the work of the house of [21] God, the [21] God of Israel.

C (*P*) W^1 (p. 627) **7** Now after these things, in the reign of ° Artaxerxes king of Persia,

X^1 v^1 404 °Ezra the °son of °Seraiah, the son of Azariah, the son of Hilkiah,

2 The son of Shallum, the son of Zadok, the son of Ahitub,

3 The son of Amariah, the son of Azariah, the son of Meraioth,

4 The son of Zerahiah, the son of Uzzi, the son of Bukki,

5 The son of Abishua, the son of Phinehas, the son of Eleazar, the son of Aaron the chief priest:

6 This Ezra went up from Babylon; and he *was* a °ready scribe in the law of Moses, which °the LORD °God of Israel had given: and the king granted him all his request, according to the hand of °the LORD his °God upon him.

w^1 7 And there went up *some* of the °children of Israel, °and of the priests, and the Levites, and the singers, and the porters, and the °Nethinims, unto Jerusalem,

W^2 in the seventh year of Artaxerxes the king.

404 X^2 v^2 1st Nisan to 1st Ab 8 And he came to Jerusalem in the °fifth month, which *was* in the seventh year of the king.

9 For upon °the first *day* of the °first month began he to go up from Babylon, and on the first *day* of the fifth month came he to Jerusalem, according to the good [6]hand of his [6]God upon him.

w^2 10 For Ezra had prepared his heart to seek the law of [6]the LORD, and to do *it*, and °to teach in °Israel statutes and judgments.

W^3 Y 11 Now this *is* the copy of the letter that the king [1]Artaxerxes gave unto Ezra the priest, °the scribe, *even* a scribe of the words of the commandments of [6]the LORD, and of His statutes to [10]Israel.

12 [1]"Artaxerxes, king of kings, unto Ezra the priest, a scribe of the law of the °GOD of heaven, perfect *peace*, and at such a time.

Z x 13 I make a °decree, that all they of the People of [10]Israel, and *of* °his priests and Levites, in my realm, which are minded of their own freewill to go up to Jerusalem, go with thee.

y z 14 Forasmuch as thou art sent of the king, and of his °seven counsellors, to enquire concerning Judah and Jerusalem, according to the law of thy [12]GOD which *is* in thine hand;

15 And to carry the silver and gold, which the king and his counsellors have freely offered unto the [12]GOD of °Israel, Whose habitation *is* in Jerusalem,

16 And all the silver and gold that thou canst find in all the province of Babylon, with the freewill offering of the People, and of the priests, offering willingly for the house of their [12]GOD which *is* in Jerusalem:

a 17 That thou mayest buy speedily with this money bullocks, rams, lambs, with their °meat offerings and their drink offerings, and offer

7. 1—8. 36 (*C*, p. 616; *P*, p. 617). THE RETURN UNDER EZRA. (*Repeated Alternation.*)

C | W^1 | 7. 1-. Artaxerxes. Time.
  X^1 | v^1 | 7. -1-6. Ezra. Journey. Hand of God.
    w^1 | 7. 7-. His companions.
 W^2 | 7. -7. Artaxerxes. Date.
  X^2 | v^2 | 7. 8, 9. Ezra. Journey. Hand of God.
    w^2 | 7. 10. His purpose.
 W^3 | 7. 11-26. Artaxerxes. Decree.
  X^3 | v^3 | 7. 27, 28-. Ezra. Blessing.
    w^3 | 7.-28. His companions. "Chief men."
 W^4 | 8. 1. Artaxerxes. Time.
  X^4 | w^4 | 8. 2-14. Companions of Ezra.
    v^4 | 8. 15-36. Ezra. Journey. Hand of God.

1 Artaxerxes = the great king: i.e. Darius (Hystaspis). See notes on p. 618. Ap. 57 and 58.

Ezra. By this genealogy (*vv.* 1-5), compared with 1 Chron. 6. 15, Ezra was brother to Jehozadak and uncle to the high priest Joshua. Ezra was deported with Zedekiah.

son = descendant.

Seraiah. Slain at Riblah (2 Kings 25 18-21).

6 ready = skilful.

the LORD. Heb. Jehovah. Ap. 4. II.

God. Heb. Elohim. Ap. 4. I.

7 children = sons.

and. Note the Fig. *Polysyndeton* (Ap. 6) in this verse.

Nethinims. See note on 2. 43.

8 fifth month. Nisan (March–April). Ap. 51. III. 4.

9 the first day of the first month. See note on Gen. 8. 13.

first month. Ab (July–August). Ap. 51. III. 4.

10 to teach in Israel. This was the chief duty of priests. See note on Deut. 33. 10.

Israel. Judah contained representatives of the whole Nation. See note on 1 Kings 12. 17.

7. 11-26 (W^3, above). ARTAXERXES. DECREE. (*Introversion.*)

W^3 | Y | 11, 12. Introduction.
  Z | 13-25. The decree for Ezra.
 Y | 26. Conclusion.

11 the scribe . . . a scribe = a perfect scribe. Fig. *Epizeuxis* (Ap. 6).

12 GOD. Chald. *'ĕlāh.* Same as Heb. Eloah. Ap. 4. V.

GOD of heaven. See note on 2 Chron. 36. 23.

13 decree. This decree (*vv.* 12-26) is in Chaldee, not in Hebrew. An inscription found at Susa commences with the same words. Cp. Dan. 2. 37.

13-25 (Z, above). THE DECREE FOR EZRA. (*Alternation.*)

Z | x | 13. To companions.
  y | 14-20. To Ezra. Supplies.
 x | 21-24. To treasurers.
  y | 25. To Ezra. Magistracy.

13 his: i. e. Israel's priests.

14-20 (y, above). TO EZRA. SUPPLIES. (*Introversion.*)

y | z | 14-16. The king's money.
  a | 17, 18. For service. Offerings.
  a | 19. For service. Vessels.
 z | 20. The king's treasury.

14 seven counsellors. Cp. Est. 1. 10, 14.

15 Israel. See note on 1 Kings 12. 17.

17 meat offerings = meal offerings. Heb. gift offerings. Ap. 43. II. iii.

404 them upon the altar of the house of your [12] GOD
which *is* in Jerusalem.
18 And whatsoever shall seem good to thee,
and to thy brethren, to do with the rest of the
silver and the gold, that do after the will of
your [12] GOD.

a (p. 627) 19 The °vessels also that are given thee for
the service of the house of thy [12] GOD, *those*
deliver thou before the [12] GOD of Jerusalem.

z 20 And whatsoever more shall be needful for
the house of thy [12] GOD, which thou shalt have
occasion to °bestow, bestow *it* out of the king's
treasure house.

x 21 And °I, *even* I Artaxerxes the king, do
make a decree to all the treasurers which *are*
beyond the river, that whatsoever Ezra the
priest, the scribe of the law of the [12] GOD of
heaven, shall require of you, it be done
speedily,
22 Unto an hundred °talents of silver, and
to an hundred °measures of wheat, and to an
hundred °baths of °wine, and to an hundred
baths of oil, and salt °without prescribing *how
much.*
23 Whatsoever is commanded by the [12] GOD
of heaven, let it be °diligently done for the
house of the [12] GOD of heaven: for °why should
there be wrath against the realm of the king
and his sons?
24 Also we certify you, that touching any of
the priests and Levites, singers, porters, [7] Nethinims, or ministers of this house of °GOD, it
shall not be lawful to impose toll, tribute, or
custom, upon them.

y 25 And thou, Ezra, after the wisdom of thy
[12] GOD, that *is* in thine hand, set magistrates
and judges, which may judge all the People
that *are* beyond the river, all such as know the
laws of thy [12] GOD; and [10] teach ye them that
know *them* not.

Y 26 And whosoever will not do the law of thy
[12] GOD, and the law of the king, let judgment be
executed speedily upon him, whether *it be* unto
death, or °to banishment, or to confiscation of
goods, or to imprisonment."

X³ v⁸ 27 °Blessed *be* [6] the LORD [6] God of our fathers,
Which hath put *such a thing* as this in the
king's heart, to beautify the house of [6] the LORD
which *is* in Jerusalem:
28 And hath extended °mercy unto me before
the king, and his counsellors, and before all
the king's °mighty princes.

w³ And I was strengthened as the hand of [6] the
LORD my [6] God *was* upon me, and I gathered
together out of Israel °chief men to go up with
me.

W⁴ **8** These *are* now the °chief of their fathers,
and *this is* the genealogy of °them that
went up with me from Babylon, in the reign
of °Artaxerxes the king.

X⁴ w⁴ 2 Of the sons of Phinehas; Gershom: of the
sons of Ithamar; Daniel: of the sons of David;
Hattush.
3 Of the sons of Shechaniah, of the sons of
Pharosh; Zechariah: and with him were
reckoned °by genealogy of the males an hundred and fifty.

19 vessels. See note on 1. 1.
20 bestow, bestow. Fig. *Anadiplōsis* (Ap. 6), for emphasis.
21 I, even I. Fig. *Epizeuxis* (Ap. 6), for emphasis.
22 talents. See Ap. 51. II.
measures . . . baths. See Ap. 51. III. 3.
wine. Cp. 6. 9. Heb. *chemer.* Ap. 27. iii.
without prescribing how much = without measure.
23 diligently = quickly, exactly. A Persian word, *'adrazda'.* Occurs only here.
why . . . ? Fig. *Erotēsis.* Ap. 6.
24 GOD. Chald. *'ĕlahah* = Heb. Eloah (emph.). See Ap. 4. V.
26 to banishment: or exclusion from the assembly. Chald. = to rooting out. Occurs only here.
27 Blessed, &c. These two verses (27, 28) resume the Hebrew language.
28 mercy = lovingkindness, or grace.
mighty. Heb. *gibbōr.* Ap. 14. IV.
chief = heads.

8. 1 chief = heads: i. e. heads of houses.
them that went up. Most of these names appear in ch. 2 and Neh. 10. The number is 1,496. If there were no women with them, this might be the cause of the "strange" marriages in ch. 10 and Neh. 10.
Artaxerxes: i. e. Darius (Hystaspis). See Ap. 57 and 58.
3 by genealogy = a lineage.
4 Pahath-moab. Cp. 2. 6.
5 sons of Shechaniah. Sept. reads "sons of Zattu, Shechaniah".
9 Of. Some codices, with one early printed edition and Sept., read "And of".
10 sons of Shelomith. Sept. reads "sons of Bani, Shelomith".
12 ten. Some codices, with Syr., read "twenty".
13 last. In contrast with others.
these. The only case where there were three heads. In all other cases (except *v.* 14, where there are two) only one head is mentioned.
14 them. Heb. text reads "him"; but some codices, with one early printed edition, read "them", as in A.V.

4 Of the sons of °Pahath-moab; Elihoenai
the son of Zerahiah, and with him two hundred males.
5 Of the °sons of Shechaniah; the son of
Jahaziel, and with him three hundred males.
6 Of the sons also of Adin; Ebed the son of
Jonathan, and with him fifty males.
7 And of the sons of Elam; Jeshaiah the son
of Athaliah, and with him seventy males.
8 And of the sons of Shephatiah; Zebadiah
the son of Michael, and with him fourscore
males.
9 °Of the sons of Joab; Obadiah the son of
Jehiel, and with him two hundred and eighteen males.
10 And of the °sons of Shelomith; the son
of Josiphiah, and with him an hundred and
threescore males.
11 And of the sons of Bebai; Zechariah the
son of Bebai, and with him twenty and eight
males.
12 And of the sons of Azgad; Johanan the
son of Hakkatan, and with him an hundred
and °ten males.
13 And of the °last sons of Adonikam, whose
names *are* °these, Eliphelet, Jeiel, and Shemaiah, and with them threescore males.
14 Of the sons also of Bigvai; Uthai, and
Zabbud, and with °them seventy males.

v⁴ A (p. 629) 404 15 And I gathered them °together to the river that runneth to °Ahava; and there °abode we in tents three days: and I viewed the People, and the priests, and found there °none of the sons of Levi.

16 Then sent I °for Eliezer, for Ariel, for Shemaiah, and for Elnathan, and for Jarib, and for Elnathan, and for Nathan, and for Zechariah, and for Meshullam, °chief men; also for °Joiarib, and for Elnathan, °men of understanding.

17 And I sent them with commandment unto Iddo the chief at the place °Casiphia, and I told them what they should say unto Iddo, *and* to his brethren the °Nethinims, at the place °Casiphia, that they should bring unto us ministers for the house of our °God.

18 And by the good hand of our [17]God upon us they brought us °a man of understanding, of the sons of Mahli, the son of Levi, the son of Israel; and Sherebiah, with his sons and his brethren, eighteen;

19 And Hashabiah, and with him Jeshaiah of the sons of Merari, his brethren and their sons, twenty;

20 Also of the [17]Nethinims, whom David and the princes had appointed for the service of the Levites, two hundred and twenty [17]Nethinims: all of them were expressed by name.

B b 21 Then I proclaimed a fast there, at the river °of [15]Ahava, that we might afflict ourselves before our [17]God, to seek of Him a right way for us, and for our little ones, and for all our substance.

22 For I was ashamed to require of the king a band of soldiers and horsemen to help us against the enemy in the way: because we had spoken unto the king, saying, "The hand of our [17]God *is* upon all them for good that seek Him; but His power and His wrath *is* against all them that forsake Him."

23 So we fasted and besought our [17]God for this: and He was intreated of us.

c 24 Then I separated twelve of the °chief of the priests, Sherebiah, Hashabiah, and ten of their brethren with them,

25 And weighed unto them the silver, and the gold, and the vessels, *even* the °offering of the house of our [17]God, which the king, and his counsellors, and his lords, and °all Israel *there* present, had offered:

26 I even weighed unto their hand six hundred and fifty °talents of silver, and silver vessels an hundred °talents, *and* of gold an hundred °talents;

27 Also twenty °basons of gold, °of a thousand °drams; and two vessels of °fine copper, precious as gold.

28 And I said unto them, "Ye *are* °holy unto °the LORD; the vessels *are* °holy also; and the silver and the gold *are* a freewill offering unto °the LORD [17]God of your fathers.

29 Watch ye, and keep *them*, until ye weigh *them* before the [24]chief of the priests and the Levites, and chief of the fathers of [25]Israel, at Jerusalem, in the chambers of the house of [28]the LORD."

30 So took the priests and the Levites the weight of the silver, and the gold, and the vessels, to bring *them* to Jerusalem unto the house of our [17]God.

B b 31 Then we departed from the river of Ahava on the twelfth *day* of the first month, to go unto Jerusalem: and the hand of our [17]God was upon us, and He delivered us from the hand of the enemy, and of such as lay in wait by the way. 12th Nisan to 4th Ab

32 And we came to Jerusalem, and abode there three days.

33 Now on the fourth day was the silver and the gold and the vessels weighed in the house of our [17]God by the hand of Meremoth the son of Uriah the priest; and with him *was* Eleazar the son of Phinehas; and with them *was* Jozabad the son of Jeshua, and Noadiah the son of Binnui, Levites; c

34 °By number *and* by weight of every one: and all the weight was written at that time.

35 °*Also* the °children of those that had been carried away, which were come out of the captivity, offered burnt offerings unto the [17]God of Israel, twelve bullocks for all Israel, ninety and six rams, seventy and seven lambs, twelve he goats *for* a sin offering: all *this was* a burnt offering unto [28]the LORD.

36 And they delivered the king's °commissions unto the king's °lieutenants, and to the governors on this side the river: and they furthered the People, and the house of °God. *A*

---

8. 15-36 (v⁴, p. 627). EZRA. JOURNEY.
(*Introversion and Alternation.*)

v⁴ | A | 15-20. Mission. Commenced.
B | b | 21-23. Difficulty. Encountered.
c | 24-30. Charge.
B | *b* | 31, 32. Difficulty. Overcome.
c | 33-35. Charge.
A | 36. Mission. Completed.

15 together = out.

Ahava. Ahava. The name of the river, and of the city. Cp. *v.* 21. **abode** = encamped.

none of the sons of Levi. Only priests and laymen. The Levites were slack. Cp. 2. 40. Only a small number accompanied Zerubbabel (2. 36). Not so the priests (2. 36-39).

16 for. The Syr. and Vulg. omit the word "for" throughout this verse, and read "then sent I Eliezer", &c., as in *v.* 17. **chief men** = heads.

Joiarib. A.V., 1611, read "Jarib".

men of understanding. Fig. *Antimereia* (of Noun), Ap. 6 = wise and prudent men, especially for teaching.

17 Casiphia. Not identified. Probably near Babylon.

Nethinims. These were the ministers of the Levites. Originally Gibeonites. See note on 2. 43.

God. Heb. Elohim. Ap. 4. I.

18 a man. Heb. *'ish.* Ap. 14. II.

21 of. Omitted in A.V., 1611. **24 chief** = princes.

25 offering = heave offering. Ap. 43. II. viii.

all Israel. See note on 2. 2 and 1 Kings 12. 17.

26 talents. See Ap. 51. II. 6.

27 basons = bowls. **of** = valued at.

drams. Heb. *darics.* See Ap. 51. I, and cp. 2. 69 and 1 Chron. 29. 7.

fine copper, &c. = copper shining like gold.

28 holy = a holy body. See note on Ex. 3. 5.

the LORD. Heb. Jehovah. Ap. 4. II.

34 By number and by weight of every one: or, the whole by number and weight.

35 Also, &c. The fourth of the ten *Sedarim* (or cycles for public reading) begins here and goes on to Neh. 2. 10, where it ends; thus uniting the two books in one. See note, p. 632. **children** = sons.

36 commissions = Royal decrees. Heb. *dath.* See note on Est. 1. 8.

lieutenants. Heb. *satraps.* A Persian title.

God. Heb. Elohim (with Art.) = the [true] God. Ap. 4. I.

B C^1 D^1 (p. 630) 404

9 Now when these things were done, °the princes came to me, saying, "The °People of Israel, and the priests, and the Levites, have not separated themselves from the °people of the lands, *doing* according to their abominations, *even* of the °Canaanites, the Hittites, the Perizzites, the Jebusites, the Ammonites, the Moabites, the Egyptians, and the Amorites.

2 For they have taken of their daughters for themselves, and for their sons: so that the °holy seed have mingled themselves with the people of *those* lands: yea, the hand of the princes and rulers hath been chief in this °trespass."

E^1 d^1 3 And when I heard this thing, I °rent my garment and my mantle, and plucked off the hair of my head and of my beard, and sat down °astonied.

e^1 4 Then were assembled unto me every one that °trembled at the words of the °God of [1]Israel, because of the °transgression of those that had been carried away;

E^2 d^2 F and I sat [3]astonied until the evening °sacrifice.

5 And at the evening sacrifice I arose up from my heaviness; and °having rent my garment and my mantle, °I fell upon my knees, and spread out my hands unto °the LORD my [4]God,

G f^1 6 And said, "O my [4]God, I am ashamed and blush to lift up my face to Thee, my [4]God: for our °iniquities are increased over *our* head, and our °trespass is grown up unto the heavens.

7 Since the days of our fathers *have* we *been* in a great [6]trespass unto this day; and for our [6]iniquities have we, our kings, *and* our priests, °been delivered into the hand of the kings of the lands, to the sword, to captivity, and to a spoil, and to °confusion of face, as *it is* this day.

g^1 8 And now for °a little °space grace hath been *shewed* from [5]the LORD our [4]God, to leave us a °remnant to escape, and to give us °a nail in His °holy place, that our [4]God may lighten our eyes, and give us a little reviving in our bondage.

9 For °we *were* °bondmen; yet our [4]God hath not forsaken us in our bondage, but hath extended °mercy unto us in the sight of the °kings of Persia, to give us a reviving, to set up the house of our [4]God, and °to repair the desolations thereof, and to °give us a wall in Judah and in Jerusalem.

f^2 10 And now, O our [4]God, °what shall we say after this? for we have forsaken Thy commandments,

11 Which Thou hast commanded °by Thy servants the prophets, saying, 'The land, unto which ye go to possess it, is an unclean land with the °filthiness of the [1]people of the lands, with their abominations, which have filled it from one end to another with their uncleanness.

12 Now therefore give not your daughters unto their sons, neither take their daughters unto your sons, °nor seek their peace or their wealth for ever: that ye may be strong, and eat the good of the land, and leave *it* for an inheritance to your °children for ever.'

9. 1—10. 44 (*B*, p. 617). THE PEOPLE. DEDICATION. REFORMATION. (*Division.*)

B | C^1 | 9. 1—10. 17. The evil-doing. Confessed.
| C^2 | 10. 18-44. The evil-doers. Reformed.

9. 1—10. 17 (C^1, above). THE EVIL-DOING. (*Introversion and Alternation.*)

C^1 | D^1 | 9. 1, 2. The evil reported to Ezra.
E^1 | d^1 | 9. 3. Ezra. Grief.
e^1 | 9. 4-. Assembly. Trembling.
E^2 | d^2 | 9. -4—10. 1-. Ezra. Prayer.
e^2 | 10. -1-4. Assembly. Weeping.
E^3 | d^3 | 10. 5-8. Ezra. Grief.
e^3 | 10. 9. Assembly. Trembling.
E^4 | d^4 | 10. 10, 11. Ezra. Charge.
e^4 | 10. 12-14. Assembly. Obedience.
D^2 | 10. 15-17. The evil removed by Ezra.

1 the princes. Not all of them. Cp. *v.* 2.

People of Israel. See note on 2. 2 and 1 Kings 12. 17.

people = peoples, or nations.

Canaanites. Contrary to the law (Ex. 34. 12-16. Deut. 7. 1-3). See Ap. 23 and 25.

2 holy seed, or the sanctuary's seed. See note on Ex. 3. 5 and cp. Dan. 2. 43. Ex. 19. 6; 22. 31. Deut. 7. 6; 14. 2.

trespass = defection. Heb. *mā'al.* Ap. 44. xi. Not the same word as in *v.* 6.

3 rent my garment, &c. These were signs of inward mourning. See *v.* 5. Josh. 7. 6. 1 Sam. 4. 12. 2 Sam. 1. 2; 13. 31. 2 Kings 18. 37. Job 1. 20. Matt. 26. 65.

astonied: i. e. causing astonishment in such as saw me.

4 trembled at the words, &c. Cp. Isa. 66. 2.

God. Heb. Elohim. Ap. 4. I.

transgression = defection. Heb. *mā'al.* Ap. 44. xi.

9. -4—10. 1- (d^2, above). EZRA. PRAYER. (*Introversion and Alternation.*)

d^2 | F | 9. -4, 5. Prostration and astonishment (Acts).
G | f^1 | 9. 6, 7. Confession.
g^1 | 9. 8, 9. Divine mercy.
f^2 | 9. 10-12. Confession.
g^2 | 9. 13, 14. Divine wrath.
f^3 | 9. 15. Confession.
} (Words).
F | 10. 1-. Prostration and weeping (Acts).

sacrifice = meal offering. Heb. *minchah.* Ap. 43. II. iii.

5 having rent = having already rent.

I fell upon my knees. Cp. 10. 1. 2 Chron. 6. 13. Dan. 6. 10. Luke 22. 41. Acts 7. 60; 9. 40; 20. 36; 21. 5.

the LORD. Heb. Jehovah. Ap. 4. II.

6 iniquities. Heb. *'āvāh.* Ap. 44. iv.

trespass. Heb. *'ashma* (fem.) = guilt incurred. The masc. = guilt imputed (as in Lev. 5. 7. Num. 5. 8. 2 Kings 12. 16. Ps. 68. 21). Ap. 44. ii. Not the same word as in *v.* 2. Cp. *vv.* 7, 13, 15.

7 been delivered. For these selfsame sins! as in *v.* 2.

confusion of face. Cp. Dan. 9. 5-7.

8 a little space = a little while. Heb. *kim'at.* See note on "almost" (Prov. 5. 14). Referring to the respite which had been begun by the kings of Assyria (6. 22. Neh. 9. 32) and continued by the kings of Persia.

remnant to escape. The same which Nehemiah had already inquired about (Neh. 1. 2, 3).

a nail = a peg surely driven in. Put by Fig. *Metonymy* (of Adjunct), Ap. 6, for the dwelling secured by it.

holy place = Jerusalem, or sanctuary. Cp. Ps. 24. 3. Isa. 56. 7; 57. 13.

9 we were. Or, supply the Ellipsis "we [are]".

bondmen. The subjects of the Persians (Neh. 9. 36).

mercy = lovingkindness, or grace.

kings of Persia. See Ap. 57.

to repair the desolations. Cp. Neh. 1. 2, 3.

give us a wall. This helps to prove that the task of Nehemiah had already been effected. See the Structure on p. 617, notes on p. 618, and Ap. 58.

10 what shall we say . . . ? Fig. *Erotēsis.* Ap. 6.

11 by = by the hand of.

filthiness. Showing Ezra's acquaintance with the Pentateuch. Cp. Gen. 15. 16. Deut. 9. 5. 1 Kings 21. 26.

12 nor seek their peace. Ref. to Pent.: the very words of Deut. 23. 6.

children = sons.

g[2] (p. 630) 404 13 And after all that is come upon us for our
°evil deeds, and for our great [6]trespass, seeing
that Thou our God hast punished us less than
our [6]iniquities *deserve*, and hast given us
°*such* deliverance as this;
14 °Should we again break Thy commandments, and join in affinity with the [1]people
of these abominations? wouldest not Thou be
angry with us till Thou hadst consumed *us*, so
that *there should be* no remnant nor escaping?

f[3] 15 O [5]LORD [4]God of Israel, Thou *art* righteous: for °we remain yet escaped, as *it is*
this day: °behold, we *are* before Thee in our
[6]trespasses: for we cannot stand before Thee
because of this."

F **10** Now °when Ezra had prayed, and
when he had confessed, weeping and
casting himself down before the house of °God,

e[2] there assembled unto him out of °Israel a very
great °congregation of °men and women and
12th Tisri °children: for the People °wept very sore.
2 And Shechaniah the son of Jehiel, *one* of
°the sons of Elam, °answered and said unto
Ezra, "We have °trespassed against our [1]God,
and have taken strange wives of the °people
of the land: yet now there is hope °in [1]Israel
concerning this thing.
3 Now therefore let us make a covenant with
our [1]God to put away all the wives, and °such
as are born of them, according to the °counsel
of °my LORD*, and of those that °tremble at
the commandment of our [1]God; and let it be
done °according to the law.
4 °Arise; for *this* matter *belongeth* unto
thee: we also *will be* with thee: be of good
courage, and do *it*."

E[3] d[3] 5 Then arose Ezra, and made °the chief
priests, °the Levites, and all [1]Israel, to swear
that they should do according to this word.
And they sware.
6 °Then Ezra rose up from before the house
of [1]God, and went into the chamber of °Johanan the son of Eliashib: and *when* he
°came thither, he did eat no bread, nor drink
water: for he °mourned because of the °transgression of them that had been carried away.
7 And they made proclamation throughout
Judah and Jerusalem unto all the °children
of the °captivity, that they should gather themselves together unto Jerusalem;
8 And that whosoever would not come within three days, according to the counsel of the
princes and the elders, all his substance should
be °forfeited, and himself separated from the
[1]congregation of those that had been °carried
away.

e[3] 9 Then all the [1]men of °Judah and Benjamin
gathered themselves together unto Jerusalem
29th Chisleu within three days. It *was* the °ninth month,
on the twentieth *day* of the month; and all
the people sat in the °street of the house of
[1]God, [3]trembling because of *this* matter, and
for the great rain.

E[4] d[4] 10 And Ezra the priest stood up, and said
unto them, "Ye have [6]transgressed, and have
taken strange wives, to increase the °trespass
of [1]Israel.
11 Now therefore make confession unto °the
LORD [1]God of your fathers, and do His pleasure: and separate yourselves from the [2]people
of the land, and from the strange wives."

12 Then all the [1]congregation answered and e[4]
said with a loud voice, °"As thou hast said,
so must we do.
13 But the People *are* many, and *it is* °a time
of much rain, and we are not able to stand
without, neither *is this* a work of one day or
two: for we are many that have °transgressed
in this thing.

13 evil. Heb. *rā'a'*. Ap. 44. viii.
such deliverance: or, such a reserved survival.
14 Should we . . . ? Fig. *Erotēsis.* Ap. 6.
15 we remain yet escaped: or, we are left but a remnant that is escaped. Cp. Neh. 1. 2, 3.
behold. Fig. *Asterismos.* Ap. 6.

10. 1 when Ezra had prayed. Note the change to the third person. This does not imply another authorship. Such changes are common. Cp. Isa. 6. 5-8; 7. 3; 37. 6 with other passages. Also Jer. 20. 1-6 with *v.* 7; and 21. 1 and 28. 1, 5.
God. Heb. Elohim (with Art.) = the [true] God. Ap. 4. I.
Israel. Cp. 1. 5; 2. 2, 59, 70; 6. 21; 7. 10, 13; 8. 25; 9. 1. See note on 1 Kings 12. 17.
congregation = assembly. Assembled 24th Tisri. Cp. Neh. 9. 3.
men. Heb. *'ĕnōsh.* Ap. 14. III.
children = little ones. Heb. *yeled.* Not the same word as in *v.* 7.
wept very sore. Heb. "wept a great weeping". Fig. *Polyptōton.* Ap. 6. See note on Gen. 26. 28.
2 the sons of Elam. Cp. *v.* 26.
answered and said. A Heb. idiom, by which the first verb "answered" must be rendered according to the context. Here = "confessed and said".
trespassed = acted treacherously. Heb. *mā'al.* Ap. 44. xi.
people = peoples. **in** = for.
3 such as are born. It does not appear that Shechaniah's proposal was carried out. Cp. *vv.* 11, 14.
counsel. See Ps. 33. 11; 73. 24; 106. 13. Prov. 8. 14; 19. 21. Isa. 46. 10, 11.
my LORD* = Jehovah. One of the 134 places where *Jehovah* was altered by the *Sōpherīm* to *Adonay.* See App. 32 and 4. viii. 2. **tremble.** Cp. 9. 4.
according to the law. See Deut. 24. 1, 2.
4 Arise. It would seem that Ezra continued kneeling.
5 the chief priests = the princes of the priests. Cp. 2 Chron. 36. 14.
the Levites. Some codices, with one early printed edition, read "and the Levites".
6 Then Ezra rose up. In response to Shechaniah.
Johanan. The son of Eliashib, the high priest who succeeded Joiakim, the successor of Jeshua (Neh. 12. 10, 23).
came thither. According to Syr. and Arabic = "lodged (or spent the night) there".
mourned. Cp. the first occ. of Heb. *'ābāl.* Gen. 37. 34.
transgression = unfaithfulness. Heb. *mā'al.* Ap. 44. xi. Cp. *v.* 2 and 10.
7 children = sons. Not the same word as in *v.* 1.
captivity = exile. As in *vv.* 6, 8, 16; 1. 11; 2. 1; 4. 1; 6. 19, 20, 21; 8. 35; 9. 4.
8 forfeited = devoted.
carried away = into captivity.
9 Judah and Benjamin. Yet spoken of as containing representatives of all Israel. See note on *v.* 1.
ninth month. That is Chisleu (= Nov.-Dec.), four months after Ezra's arrival (7. 8).
street = broad place.
10 trespass. Heb. *'āshah.* See note on 9. 6. Ap. 44. ii.
11 the LORD. Heb. Jehovah. Ap. 4. II.
12 As thou hast said = according to thy words. Heb. marg. reads "word".
13 a time of much rain = the rainy season.
transgressed = rebelled. Heb. *pāsha'.* Ap. 44. ix.

404 14 Let now our °rulers of all the [1]congregation
stand, and let all them which have taken
strange wives in our cities come at appointed
times, and with them the elders of every city,
and the judges thereof, until the fierce wrath
of our [1]God ° for this matter be turned from
us."

D² 15 ° Only Jonathan the son of Asahel and
(p. 630) Jahaziah the son of ° Tikvah ° were employed
about this *matter:* and Meshullam and Shabbethai the Levite helped them.
16 And the [7]children of the [7]captivity did so.
And Ezra the priest, *with* ° certain ° chief of the
fathers, after the house of their fathers, and
all of them by *their* names, were separated,
1st and sat down in the first day of the tenth
Tebeth month to examine the matter.
403 17 And they made an end with all the [1]men
1st that had taken strange wives by ° the first day
Nisan of the first month.

C² 18 And among the sons of the priests there
were found that had taken strange wives:
namely, of ° the sons of Jeshua the son of
Jozadak, and his brethren; Maaseiah, and
Eliezer, and Jarib, and Gedaliah.
19 And they ° gave their hands that they
would put away their wives; and ° *being*
guilty, *they offered* ° a ram of the flock for
their [10]trespass.
20 And of the sons of Immer; Hanani, and
Zebadiah.
21 And of the sons of Harim; Maaseiah, and
Elijah, and Shemaiah, and Jehiel, and Uzziah.
22 And of the sons of Pashur; Elioenai,
Maaseiah, Ishmael, ° Nethaneel, Jozabad, and
Elasah.
23 Also of the Levites; Jozabad, and Shimei, and Kelaiah, (the same *is* Kelita,) Pethahiah, Judah, and Eliezer.
24 Of the singers also; Eliashib: and of the
porters; Shallum, and Telem, and Uri.
25 Moreover of [1]Israel: of the sons of Parosh; Ramiah, and Jeziah, and Malchiah, and
Miamin, and Eleazar, and Malchijah, and
Benaiah.
26 And of the sons of Elam; Mattaniah,
Zechariah, and Jehiel, and Abdi, and Jeremoth, and Eliah.
27 And of the sons of Zattu; Elioenai, Eliashib, Mattaniah, and Jeremoth, and Zabad,
and Aziza.
28 Of the sons also of Bebai; Jehohanan,
Hananiah, Zabbai, *and* Athlai.
29 And of the sons of Bani; Meshullam,
Malluch, and Adaiah, Jashub, and Sheal,
° and Ramoth.
30 And of the sons of Pahath-moab; Adna,
and Chelal, Benaiah, Maaseiah, Mattaniah,
Bezaleel, and Binnui, and Manasseh.
31 And ° *of* the sons of Harim; Eliezer, Ishi-
jah, Malchiah, Shemaiah, Shimeon,
32 Benjamin, Malluch, *and* Shemariah.
33 Of the sons of Hashum; Mattenai, Mat-
tathah, Zabad, Eliphelet, Jeremai, Manasseh,
and Shimei.
34 Of the sons of Bani; Maadai, Amram,
and Uel,
35 Benaiah, Bedeiah, Chelluh,
36 Vaniah, Meremoth, Eliashib,
37 Mattaniah, Mattenai, and Jaasau,
38 And Bani, and Binnui, Shimei,
39 And Shelemiah, and Nathan, and Adaiah,
40 Machnadebai, Shashai, Sharai,
41 Azareel, and Shelemiah, Shemariah,
42 Shallum, Amariah, *and* Joseph.
43 Of the sons of Nebo; Jeiel, Mattithiah,
Zabad, Zebina, Jadau, and Joel, Benaiah.
44 All these had taken ° strange wives: and
some of them had wives by whom they had
[7]children.

14 rulers = princes.
for. Heb. *'ad* = "until", as in the previous clause. Translate and supply Fig. *Ellipsis* (Ap. 6) thus: "until the fierce wrath of our God be turned from us, until this matter [be carried out]".
15 Only = But, or, Nevertheless.
Tikvah. Cp. 2 Kings 22. 14 and 2 Chron. 34. 22.
were employed, &c. = superintended [the business].
16 certain = men. Heb. *'ĕnōsh.* Ap. 14. III.
chief = heads.
17 the first day of the first month. See note on Gen. 8. 13. Ezra's last date. The commission, therefore, sat for eighty-eight days.
18 the sons of Jeshua. Who had come up with Zerubbabel (2. 2). There were 973 priests of that house (2. 36). There were found guilty seventeen priests, ten Levites singers and porters, and eighty-six lay people, making 113 in all.
19 gave their hands. Heb. idiom for giving their word. Cp. 2 Kings 10. 15.
being guilty. Cp. Lev. 5. 1.
a ram. See Lev. 5. 14–19.
22 Nethaneel. Some codices, with five early printed editions, read "and Nethaneel".
29 and Ramoth. Heb. text reads "Jeremoth". Marg. reads "and Ramoth".
31 of. Some codices, with one early printed edition, Sept., Syr., and Vulg., have this word "of" in the text.
44 strange = foreign.
Thus ends the first part of this book "Ezra-Nehemiah"; not abruptly; as it is followed by the second part, which is concerned mainly with the rebuilding of the city and the walls, instead of with the Temple. The incidents recorded in Neh. 1. 1—7. 4 had taken place before the first return under Zerubbabel. See the Structures and notes on pp. 617, 618, and Ap. 58. Cp. also Neh. 7. 4 with Hag. 1. 1–4.

[N.B. This division of the book Ezra–Nehemiah, in the later printed Hebrew Bibles, is quite modern. It breaks up the *fourth* of the ten *Sedarim* (or cycles for public reading) which begins at Ezra 8. 35 and ends with Neh. 2. 10. See note on p. 617, and cp. note on p. 366.]

THE TEN *SEDARIM*

are as follows:

(1) Ezra 1. 1—3. 12.	(6) Neh. 3. 38—6. 14.
(2) ,, 3. 13—6. 17.	(7) ,, 6. 15—8. 9.
(3) ,, 6. 18—8. 34.	(8) ,, 8. 10—10. 1 (Heb. 9. 37).
(4) ,, 8. 35—Neh. 2. 10.	(9) ,, 10. 1 (Heb. 2)—12. 25.
(5) Neh. 2. 11—3. 37.	(10) ,, 12. 26—13. 31.

THE BOOK OF NEHEMIAH.

E H^1 J (p. 633) 455 **1** °THE words of °Nehemiah the son of Hachaliah. And it came to pass in the month °Chisleu, in the °twentieth year, as °I °was in °Shushan the palace,

K L 2 That °Hanani, one of my brethren, came, he and *certain* °men of Judah; and °I asked them concerning °the Jews that had °escaped, which were left of the captivity, and concerning Jerusalem.

3 And °they said unto me, °"The remnant that are °left of the captivity there in the °Province *are* in great affliction and reproach: the wall of Jerusalem also *is* °broken down, and the gates thereof are burned with fire."

M h k 4 And it came to pass, when I heard °these words, that I sat down and wept, and mourned *certain* days, and fasted, and °prayed before the °God of heaven,

5 And said, "I beseech thee, O °LORD [4] God of heaven, the great and terrible °GOD, That °keepeth covenant and mercy for them that love Him and °observe His commandments:

6 Let Thine °ear now be attentive, and Thine eyes open, that Thou mayest hear the prayer of Thy servant, which I pray before Thee now, day and night, for the °children of Israel Thy servants,

l and confess the °sins of the °children of Israel, which we have °sinned against Thee: both °I and my father's house have °sinned.

7 We have dealt very corruptly against Thee, and have not kept the commandments, nor the statutes, nor the judgments, which °Thou commandedst °Thy servant Moses.

m 8 Remember, I beseech Thee, the word that [7] Thou commandedst [7] Thy servant Moses, saying, °'*If* ye °transgress, I will scatter you abroad among the nations:

1. 1—6. 19 (**E**, p. 616; **K**, p. 617). THE WALL. BUILDING. EXTERNAL DISORDERS OVERCOME. (*Division.*)

E | H^1 | 1. 1—2. 20. Desolation.
| H^2 | 3. 1—6. 19. Reparation.

1. 1—2. 20 (H^1, above). DESOLATION. (*Alternation and Introversion.*)

H^1 | J | 1. 1. Date.
K | L | 1. 2, 3. The desolations. Reported.
M | h | 1. 4-11-. Prayer.
i | 1. -11. Office. King's cupbearer.
J | 2. 1-. Date.
K | *M* | *i* | 2.-1-4-. Office. King's cupbearer.
h | 2. -4. Prayer.
L | 2. 5-20. The desolations. Repeated.

1 The words. Divine revelation in writing must be made up of words (see Ap. 47). The "words" here were written, *chronologically*, long before the book of Ezra. See the Structures (pp. 616, 617, notes on p. 618; also Ap. 50, 57, and 58).

Nehemiah = comforter of (= appointed by) Jehovah. From 10. 1 he was one of the "princes" (9. 38) who signed the Solemn Covenant: a prince of Judah, for the "king's seed" and "princes" were taken to Babylon (Dan. 1. 3), according to the prophecy in 2 Kings 20. 17, 18. The next who signed was Zidkijah, a son of king Jehoiakim (1 Chron. 3. 16). Hanani (*v.* 2), his brother or near kinsman (a shortened form of Hananiah, cp. *v.* 2, and 7. 2), was another "prince", renamed Shadrach (Dan. 1. 3-6), Nehemiah was the Sheshbazzar of Ezra 1. 8. Five parties seen in action in this book: Nehemiah, Ezra, the People, their enemies, and the God of heaven.

Chisleu. The ninth month. See Ap. 51. III. 4.

twentieth year. See Ap. 50. VI and VII. 5. Cp. 2. 1. Forty-two years from the beginning of the Babylonian *Servitude*, thirty-five years from Jehoiachin's captivity, and twenty-three years from the destruction of Jerusalem, and the beginning of the *Desolations.* See special note on p. 615.

I was in Shushan. Like Joseph in Egypt, Obadiah in Samaria, Daniel in Babylon, and the saints in Cæsar's household (Phil. 4. 22). **was** = came to be.

Shushan. He had been there about sixteen years, and was removed thither from Babylon. Excavations in 1909 by M. de Morgan, at Susa, exposed the remains of three cities. Among them, four black stone pillars, with the Code of Khammurabi (see Ap. 15). Bricks of his palace or temple were also found. Occupied by Babylonians in 2800 B. C. **2 Hanani.** Shortened form of Hananiah. Cp. 7. 2. See note above, and cp. Dan. 1. 3, 6. **men.** Heb. *'ĕnōsh.* See Ap. 14. III. **I asked.** Not about Ezra, and the 42,360 who are supposed to have been already in the Province of Judah: this Nehemiah would surely have done if they had really been there. **the Jews.** Mentioned eleven times in this book (1. 2; 2. 16; 4. 1, 2, 12; 5. 1, 8, 17; 6. 6; 13. 23, 24). **escaped:** i. e. from the lands of their captivity. See Jer. 44. 13, 14. Why escape if already set free (Ezra 1. 3)? **3 they said:** that which could not have been said if Ezra and his thousands had been already there. **The remnant.** For the history of this "remnant" see Jer. 40—44. Only a few poor serfs there (Jer. 52. 15, 16). **left.** Not carried away or returned (Jer. 52. 15, 16). **Province** = Judah. See Ezra 5. 8. **broken down.** Just as left by Nebuchadnezzar (2 Kings 25. 9, 10. Jer. 52. 12-14). For the subsequent history see Jer. 40 to 44.

4-11- (h, above). PRAYER. (*Introversion.*)

h | k | 4-6-. Regard.
l | -6, 7. Confession. People's sins.
m | 8, 9. Remembrance.
l | 10. Confession. Jehovah's goodness.
k | 11-. Regard.

4 these words. Evidently the first authentic news he had heard. No wonder he was heartbroken. **prayed.** Nehemiah a man of prayer. Cp. 4. 4, 5; 5. 19; 6. 9, 14; 13. 14, 22, 29, 31. **God of heaven.** See note on 2 Chron. 36. 23. This title peculiar to the "times of the Gentiles", when God dwells no longer "between the Cherubim", but acts as from a distance. Heb. Elohim. Ap. 4. I, and cp. the title "Lord of all the earth" in Zech. 6. 5, when He again claims the land, as in Josh. 3. 11, 13. See note on 2 Chron. 36. 23. **5 LORD** = Jehovah. See Ap. 4. II. **GOD.** Heb. *'El* (with Art.). See Ap. 4. IV. **keepeth covenant.** Nehemiah goes back to the language of the Pentateuch (Deut. 7. 9). **observe** = keep. Cp. Ex. 20. 6; 34. 6, 7. **6 ear.** Fig. *Anthropopatheia.* Ap. 6. Nehemiah refers to Lev. 26. 40-45, and 1 Kings 8. 46-52. **children** = sons. **sins . . . sinned . . . sinned.** Heb. *chāṭā'.* Ap. 44. i. **I.** Like Daniel, he includes himself. Cp. Dan. 9. 3-19. **7 Thou commandedst.** Again a reference to the Pentateuch: as being well known. See Lev. 26. 33, 39-45. Deut. 4. 25-31; 28. 64; 30. 1-4. **Thy servant Moses.** See note on first occurrence, 1 Kings 8. 53. **8 If.** This word is clearly implied in Heb. Cp. Deut. 4. 25, &c. **transgress.** Heb. *mā'al.* Ap. 44. xi.

455 9 But [8]*if* ye °turn unto Me, and keep My
commandments, and do them; though there
were of you cast out unto the uttermost part
of the heaven, *yet* will I gather them from
thence, and will bring them unto the place that
I have chosen to set My name there.'

l 10 Now these *are* Thy servants and Thy Peo-
(p. 633) ple, whom Thou hast °redeemed by Thy great
power, and by Thy strong hand.

k 11 O °LORD*, I beseech Thee, let now Thine
ear be attentive to the prayer of Thy servant,
and to the prayer of Thy servants, who °desire
to fear Thy name: and prosper, I pray Thee,
Thy servant this day, and grant him °mercy
in the sight of this °man."

i For I was the king's cupbearer.

J **2** And it came to pass in the month °Nisan, in
454 °the twentieth year of °Artaxerxes the king,
K M i *that* °wine *was* before him: and I took up the
°wine, and gave *it* unto the king. Now I had
not been *beforetime* sad in his presence.
2 Wherefore the king said unto me, "Why
is thy countenance sad, seeing thou *art* not
sick? this *is* nothing *else* but °sorrow of
heart." Then I was very sore afraid,
3 And said unto the king, °"Let the king live
for ever: why should not my countenance be
sad, when the city, the place of my fathers'
sepulchres, °*lieth* waste, and the gates thereof
are consumed with fire?"
4 Then the king said unto me, "For what dost
thou make request?"
h So I prayed to the °God of heaven.
L N n 5 And I said unto the king, "If it please the
(p. 634) king, and if thy servant have found favour in
thy sight, that thou wouldest send me unto
Judah, unto the city of my fathers' sepulchres,
that I may build it."
6 And the king said unto me, (°the queen also
°sitting °by him,) "For how long shall thy journey be? and when wilt thou return?" So °it pleased the king to send me; and I set him a time.
o 7 Moreover I said unto the king, "If it please
the king, let letters be given me to the °gover-
nors beyond the river, that they may convey
me over till I come into Judah;
8 And a letter unto Asaph the keeper of the
king's °forest, that he may give me timber to
make beams for the gates of the palace which
appertained to the house, and for the °wall of
the city, and for the house °that I shall enter
into." And the king granted me, according to
the good °hand of my °God upon me.
p 9 Then I came to the governors beyond the
river, and gave them the king's letters. Now
the king had sent °captains of the °army and
horsemen with me.
q 10 When °Sanballat the °Horonite, and
(p. 634)

9 turn unto Me. National repentance was ever the one great condition of Israel's national blessing (Deut. 30. 2, &c.); and is still the condition. Cp. Acts 3. 19-21, which, with Acts 28. 17, 23-29, was the last national call.

10 redeemed. Heb. *pādāh.* See note on Ex. 6. 6; 13. 13.

11 LORD*. Heb. Adonai. See Ap. 4. VIII. 2. But it is one of the 134 alterations of the *Sōpherīm.* See Ap. 34.

desire to fear = delight in revering.

mercy = tender mercies.

man. Heb. *'ish.* Ap. 14. II.

2. 1 Nisan. The first month (Abib, Ex. 12. 2, &c.), called Nisan after the Captivity. This was four months after receiving the news (see Ap. 51. III. 5).

the twentieth year. See longer notes on p. 653.

Artaxerxes = the great king. An appellative (like Pharaoh, Czar, &c.) used of several kings of Persia. Synonymous with Artachshast (Arta = great, and Kshatza = king, preserved in the modern "Shah"). See Ap. 57 and 58. This Artaxerxes was the great king ASTYAGES (of Herodotus), and ARSAMES (of Darius Hystaspis' Inscription), the husband of Esther, and father of Cyrus. He was also the Ahasuerus of Est. 1. 1, which means "the venerable king"; and he was also the "Darius the Mede" of Ezra 6. 14 and Dan. 5. 31. See Ap. 57 and 58.

wine. Heb. *yayin.* See Ap. 27. I.

2 sorrow of heart. See Prov. 15. 13.

3 Let the king live. The usual Oriental salutation.

lieth waste. Cp. 1. 3. Impossible if Ezra with his 42,360 returned exiles were already there, and had rebuilt the temple! See notes on 1. 2; 5. 5, and on the Chronological Structure (p. 617, with the notes on p. 618). See also note on Ezra 4. 12, p. 624.

God of heaven. See note on 1. 5.

2. 5-20 (*L*, p. 633). THE DESOLATIONS. (REPEATED.) (*Alternations.*)

L | N | n | 5, 6. Desolations. Repeated to king and queen.
o | 7, 8. Letters requested.
p | 9. The governors beyond the river.
q | 10. Opposition.
O | 11-15. Nehemiah. Inspection.
N | *n* | 16, 17. Desolations. Repeated to rulers.
o | 18-. Letters, and king's words reported.
p | -18. Rulers in Jerusalem.
q | 19. Opposition.
O | 20. Nehemiah. Encouragement.

6 the queen. Heb. *ha-shēgāl* = wife. Occurs only here and in Ps. 45. 9. Dan. 5. 2, 3, 23. Not a Heb. word, but borrowed from the Akkadian *sha* = a bride, and *gal* = great. Used of a foreign queen. Here it would exactly suit "the great bride" or "foreign (Jewish) queen", Esther. (See notes on the Chronological Structure of Ezra-Nehemiah, p. 618.) Esther is introduced here (parenthetically) because of her sympathy and interest, which Nehemiah so greatly needed at this juncture, as Mordecai had needed it before (Est. 4. 14).

sitting. Not reclining. **by** = close to.

it pleased the king. The fruit of Nehemiah's prayer (*v.* 4). **7 governors** = pashas.

8 forest = park. Heb. *pārdēṣ.* A Persian word which occurs only here, Ecc. 2. 5, and Song 4. 13, where it is rendered "orchards". Sept. renders it "paradise", which occurs twenty-eight times: (nine times = Eden, nineteen times = garden, Heb. *gan.*)

wall. Some codices, with one early printed edition, Syr., and Vulg., read "walls" (pl.). These walls are the main subject of Nehemiah's section of the joint book. **that I shall enter into**: or, whereunto I shall come. **hand.** Fig. *Anthropopatheia.* Ap. 6. Also put by Fig. *Metonymy* (Ap. 6) for God's purpose (Acts 4. 28, 30); power (1 Chron. 29. 16); sovereignty (Ps. 31. 15); providence (1 Chron. 29. 16); supply (Ps. 104. 28); prosperity (Neh. 2. 8); security (John 10. 28, 29). **God.** Heb. Elohim. Ap. 4. I. **9 captains** = princes. **army** = force. **10 Sanballat.** An Aramaic papyrus, recently (1909) discovered at Elephantine (in Egypt), was written by two Jews (Delaya and Shelemya) to the sons of this Sanballat, who is called the "governor of Samaria". It is dated the seventeenth year of Darius Nothos (son of Darius Hystaspis). See Ap. 57 (Nothos = Greek "bastard"). Here ends the fourth of the ten *Sedarim* (or, Cycles for public reading) which commenced with Ezra 8. 35; thus showing that the two books were and are to be regarded as one. See note on p. 632; and cp. notes on p. 366. **Horonite.** Not of Beth-horon (Josh. 10. 10), but an alien (ch. 13. 27, 28) of Horonaim, a Moabite. Cp. Isa. 15. 5. Jer. 48. 3, 5, 34. See also the Moabite Stone. Ap. 54.

°Tobiah the servant, the Ammonite, °heard
of it, °it grieved them exceedingly that there
was come a °man to seek the welfare of the
°children of °Israel.
O 454 11 So I came to Jerusalem, and was there three
days.
12 And I arose in the night, I and some few
°men with me; neither told I *any* [10]man what
my [8]God had put in my heart to do °at Jerusalem: neither *was there any* beast with me,
save the beast that I rode upon.
13 And I went out °by night by °the gate of
the valley, even before the dragon well, and
to the dung °port, and °viewed the walls of
Jerusalem, °which were broken down, and the
gates thereof were consumed with fire.
14 Then I went on to [13]the gate of the fountain, and to the king's pool: but *there was* no
place for the beast *that was* under me to pass.
15 Then went I up in the night by °the brook,
and viewed the wall, and turned back, and entered by the gate of the valley, and *so* returned.
n 16 And the °rulers knew not whither I went,
or what I °did; neither had I as yet told *it* to
the Jews, °nor to the priests, °nor to the nobles,
°nor to the rulers, °nor to °the rest that did the
work.
17 Then said I unto them, "Ye see °the distress that we *are* in, how Jerusalem [3]*lieth*
waste, and the gates thereof are burned with
fire: come, and let us build up the wall of Jerusalem, that we be no more a reproach."
o 18 Then I told them of the [8]hand of my [8]God
which was good upon me; as also the king's
words that he had spoken unto me.
p And they said, "Let us rise up and build." So
they strengthened their hands for *this* °good
work.
q 19 But when Sanballat the [10]Horonite, and
[10]Tobiah the servant, the Ammonite, and
°Geshem the °Arabian, heard *it*, °they laughed
us to scorn, and despised us, and said, "What
is this thing that ye do? will ye rebel against
the king?"
O 20 Then answered I them, and said unto them,
"The [4]God of heaven, He will prosper us; therefore we His servants will arise and build: but
ye have no portion, nor right, nor memorial, in
Jerusalem."

H^2 P R (p. 635) **3** Then °Eliashib the high priest rose up
with his brethren the priests, and they
builded °the sheep gate; they sanctified it, and
set up the °doors of it; even unto the tower of
Meah, they sanctified it, unto the tower of
°Hananeel.
2 And °next unto him builded °the men of
Jericho. And next to them builded Zaccur the
son of Imri.
r^1 (p. 635) 3 But the °fish gate did the sons of Has-
senaah build, who *also* laid the beams thereof,
and set up the [1]doors thereof, the locks thereof,
and the bars thereof.
4 And [2]next unto them repaired Meremoth
the son of Urijah, the son of Koz. And next

Tobiah the servant. Probably a freed slave. Still called so by Fig. *Ampliatio*. Ap. 6. Also an alien, an Ammonite.

heard. Nehemiah had come through Samaria. Cp. 4. 1-13.

it grieved them. This is the first of six (see Ap. 10) forms which the opposition took. Note them, and observe how Nehemiah met each respectively: (1) Grief (2. 10); (2) laughter (2. 19); (3) wrath and indignation (4. 1-3); (4) fighting (4. 7, 8); (5) subtilty (6. 1, 2); (6) compromise (6. 5-7).

man. Heb. *'ādām*. Ap. 14. I = any human being.

children = sons.

Israel. Again used of Judah. See note on Ezra 2. 2, and 1 Kings 12. 17.

12 men. Heb. *'ĕnōsh*. Ap. 14. III.

at Jerusalem: or, for Jerusalem.

13 by night. Could Nehemiah have gone thus secretly if Ezra had 42,360 Jews there? And what need for it? Nehemiah had only a few men, and was in the midst of enemies.

the gate. Note the twelve gates (corresponding with the twelve gates of Rev. 21. 21). See Ap. 59.

port = gate. **viewed** = kept peering into.

which were, &c. Heb. text so written; but to be read, with some codices and three early printed editions, "how they were broken down".

15 the brook. Heb. *naḥal*, a torrent, mostly fed by rains. Not *nāhār*, a constant river.

16 rulers. Heb. *s^egānīm*, used of the Babylonian magistrates or prefects; occurs only in Ezra and Nehemiah. **did** = was doing.

nor. Note the Fig. *Paradiastolē*. Ap. 6.

the rest: i. e. of those who had accompanied Nehemiah.

17 the distress. How so, if the Temple was already built?

18 good work. This work was "good" because it was "prepared" by God. See Eph. 2. 10.

19 Geshem. Called Gashmu (6. 6), an Arab Sheik. Like the other two, an alien. In Ps. 83. 6, all three nationalities associated as the enemies of Israel.

Arabian. Descendants of Hagar. Hence Hagarenes.

they laughed, &c. The second form of opposition. See note on "grieved", *v.* 10.

3. 1–6. 19 (H^2, p. 633). **REPARATION.**
(Alternation.)

H^2 | P | 3. 1-32. Commencement of work.
  Q | 4. 1—6. 14. Opposition. Wrath. Mockery (III).
 P | 6. 15. Completion of work.
  Q | 6. 16-19. Opposition. Wrath. Hostility (IV).

3. 1-32 (P, above). **COMMENCEMENT OF WORK.**
(Introversion.)

P R | 1, 2. From the sheep gate.
 r^1 3-5. The fish gate.
 r^2 6-12. The old gate.
 r^3 13. The valley gate.
 r^4 14. The dung gate.
 r^5 15-24. The fountain gate. } The other gates.
 r^6 25. The prison gate.
 r^7 26, 27. The water gate.
 r^8 28, 29-. The horse gate.
 r^9 -29, 30. The east gate.
 r^{10} 31. The Miphkad gate.
R | 32. To the sheep gate.

1 Eliashib = God restores. The son of Joiakim, the son of Jeshua (cp. 12. 10). He was earnest in material work, but negligent of what was spiritual (see 13. 4, 7).

the sheep gate. Near the present St. Stephen's gate, at north-east corner of Temple area. So called because the sheep for sacrifice were brought in here. Cp. John 5. 2. This was the point of beginning and ending. See Ap. 59.

doors. Heb. *dal* = a door or gate hanging on hinges; not the same word as *v.* 20.

Hananeel. Cp. 12. 39. The partial fulfilment of Jer. 31. 38, which stretches on to what is still future. Cp. Zech. 14. 10. The two towers were on either side of the sheep gate. **2 next unto him** = at his hand. **the men of Jericho.** Cp. Ezra 2. 34. The gate opposite to their city. Heb. *'ĕnōsh*. Ap. 14. III. **3 fish gate.** See note on 2. 13, and Ap. 59.

454 unto them repaired Meshullam the son of
Berechiah, the son of Meshezabeel. And
next unto them repaired Zadok the son of
Baana.
5 And [4]next unto them the Tekoites repaired;
but their nobles put not their necks to the
work of their °LORD.

r[2] 6 Moreover the °old gate repaired Jehoiada
the son of Paseah, and Meshullam the son of
Besodeiah; they laid the beams thereof, and
set up the [1]doors thereof, and the locks thereof,
and the bars thereof.
7 And [4]next unto them repaired Melatiah
the Gibeonite, and Jadon the Meronothite,
the [2]men of °Gibeon, and of Mizpah, unto
the throne of the °governor on this side °the
river.
8 °Next unto him repaired Uzziel the son of
Harhaiah, of the °goldsmiths. Next unto him
also repaired Hananiah the son of *one of* the
°apothecaries, and they °fortified Jerusalem
unto the broad wall.
9 And [4]next unto them repaired Rephaiah
the son of Hur, the °ruler of the half °part of
Jerusalem.
10 And [4]next unto them repaired Jedaiah
the son of Harumaph, °even °over against his
°house. And [4]next unto him repaired Hattush
the son of Hashabniah.
11 Malchijah the son of Harim, and Hashub
the son of Pahath-moab, repaired the °other
piece, and the °tower of the °furnaces.
12 And [4]next unto him repaired Shallum the
son of Halohesh, the [9]ruler of the half part of
Jerusalem, he and °his daughters.

r[3] 13 The valley gate repaired Hanun, and the
inhabitants of °Zanoah; they built it, and set
up the [1]doors thereof, the locks thereof, and the
bars thereof, and a thousand °cubits on the
wall unto the dung gate.

r[4] 14 But the dung gate repaired Malchiah the
son of Rechab, the [9]ruler of [9]part of °Beth-
haccerem; he built it, and set up the [1]doors
thereof, the locks thereof, and the bars
thereof.

r[5] 15 But the °gate of the fountain repaired
Shallun the son of Col-hozeh, the ruler of
[9]part of Mizpah; he built it, and covered it,
and set up the [1]doors thereof, the locks thereof, and the bars thereof, and the wall of the
pool of °Siloah by the °king's garden, and
unto the °stairs that go down from the city
of David.
16 After him repaired Nehemiah the son of
Azbuk, the [9]ruler of the half [9]part of °Beth-zur,
unto *the place* over against °the sepulchres of
David, and to the °pool that was made, and
unto the [10]house of the °mighty.
17 After him repaired the Levites, Rehum the
son of Bani. [2]Next unto him repaired Hashabiah, the [9]ruler of the half [9]part of °Keilah, in
his part.
18 After him repaired their brethren, Bavai
the son of Henadad, the [9]ruler of the half [9]part
of [17]Keilah.
19 And [4]next to him repaired Ezer the son of
Jeshua, the [9]ruler of [7]Mizpah, another piece
over against the going up to the armoury at
the turning *of the wall*.
20 After him Baruch the son of Zabbai
°earnestly repaired the [11]other piece, from the
turning *of the wall* unto the °door of the [10]house
of Eliashib the high priest.
21 After him repaired Meremoth the son of
Urijah the son of Koz another piece, from
the [20]door of the [10]house of Eliashib even to
the end of the [10]house of Eliashib.
22 And after him repaired the priests, the
[2]men of the plain.
23 After him repaired Benjamin and Hashub
[10]over against their [10]house. After him repaired Azariah the son of Maaseiah the son of
Ananiah by his [10]house.
24 After him repaired Binnui the son of
Henadad another piece, from the °house of
Azariah unto the turning *of the wall*, even
unto the corner.

5 LORD. Heb. Adonim. Ap. 4. VII. 3. As in Ps. 8. 1, 9. The A.V., 1611, had "LORD".
6 old gate. See note on 2. 13, and Ap. 59.
7 Gibeon . . . Mizpah. Now *'el Jib. . . . Sûf*, about 4 and 5½ miles north-north-west of Jerusalem respectively.
governor. The Persian governor.
the river. The Euphrates.
8 Next = at his hand. Some codices, with five early printed editions, Sept., and Vulg., read "and at".
goldsmiths = refiners.
apothecaries = perfumers.
fortified. Heb. *Homonym*, *'āzab*. See note on Ex. 23. 5.
9 ruler = prince. Heb. *sar*. Not the same word as 2. 16.
part = circuit.
10 even. Some codices, with two early printed editions, omit this word.
over against his house. So *v.* 23. A true principle in all reformation work.
house = temporary erection, dwelling, home; not having doors with hinges as in *vv.* 1, 3, 6, 13, 14, 15, but only an "entrance" as in *v.* 20. See notes on *v.* 20, and 7. 4.
11 other = second. Cp. *vv.* 20, 21.
tower of the furnaces. At the north-west corner of the city. Cp. 12. 38.
furnaces: or ovens.
12 his daughters. Showing how women may contribute to the work of reformation.
13 Zanoah. Now *Zanu'a*, about 2½ miles south of Beth-Shemesh.
cubits. See Ap. 51. III. 2 (1).
14 Beth-haccerem = house of the vineyards (Jer. 6. 1): not identified yet. Perhaps *'Ain Karīm*.
15 gate. See Ap. 59.
Siloah = sent. See John 5. 1, 2. Cp. John 9. 7. At south-east corner of Ophel.
king's garden. See 2 Kings 25. 4.
stairs. On east side of the city. This fixes the site of Zion. See note on first occurrence (2 Sam. 5. 7). Cp. 12. 37. Discovered by Dr. Bliss, *Quarterly Statement*, Palestine Exploration Fund, Jan., 1897.
16 Beth-zur. Now *Beit Sūr*, about four miles north of Hebron.
the sepulchres of David. These therefore were in Zion, and include those of his descendants.
pool. See 2 Kings 20. 20.
mighty = mighty men. Heb. pl. of *gibbōr*. Ap. 14. IV.
17 Keilah. Now *Kīla*, about fifteen miles south-east of Jerusalem, in the Hebron mountains. See 1 Sam. 23. 1-13.
20 earnestly = zealously. This is said, to the everlasting memory, of Baruch. Prov. 10. 7.
door. Heb. *pethach* = entrance. Not same word as *vv.* 1, 3, 6, 13, 14, 15. See longer note on 7. 4.
24 house. See note on 7. 4.

r6 (p. 635) 454 25 Palal the son of Uzai, over against the
turning *of the wall*, and the tower which lieth
out from the king's °high [10]house, that *was* by
the °court of the prison. After him Pedaiah
the son of Parosh.

r7 26 °(Moreover the °Nethinims dwelt in °Ophel,
unto *the place* over against °the water gate toward the east, and the tower °that lieth out.)
27 After them the Tekoites repaired another
piece, over against the great tower [26]that lieth
out, even unto the wall of [26]Ophel.

r8 28 From above °the horse gate repaired the
priests, every °one [10]over against his [10]house.
29 After them repaired Zadok the son of
Immer [10]over against his [10]house.

r9 After him repaired also Shemaiah the son of
Shechaniah, the keeper of the east gate.
30 After him repaired Hananiah the son of
Shelemiah, and Hanun the sixth son of Zalaph,
another piece. After him repaired Meshullam
the son of Berechiah over against his chamber.

r10 31 After him repaired Malchiah °the goldsmith's son unto the place of the [26]Nethinims,
and of the merchants, over against the °gate
Miphkad, and to the going up of the corner.

R 32 °And between the going up of the corner
unto the °sheep gate repaired the goldsmiths
and the merchants.

Q S U1 (p. 637) **4** °But it came to pass, that when °Sanballat
heard that we °builded the wall, he was
°wroth, and took great indignation, and mocked
the Jews.
2 And he spake before his brethren and the
°army of Samaria, and said, °"What do these
feeble Jews? will they °fortify themselves?
°will they sacrifice? will they make an end in
a day? will they revive the stones out of the
heaps of the rubbish which are burned?"
3 Now °Tobiah the Ammonite *was* by him, and
he said, "Even that which they build, if a fox go
up, he shall even break down their stone wall."

V1 4 °Hear, O our °God; for we are °despised: and
turn their reproach upon their own head, and
give them for a prey in the land of °captivity:
5 And °cover not their °iniquity, and let not
their °sin be blotted out from before Thee: for
they have provoked *Thee* to anger before the
builders.

W1 6 So built we the wall; and all the wall was
joined together °unto the half thereof: for the
People had a °mind to work.

U2 7 °But it came to pass, *that* when Sanballat,
°and Tobiah, and the Arabians, and the Ammonites, and the Ashdodites, heard that the
walls of Jerusalem were made up, *and* that
the breaches began to be °stopped, then they
were very [1]wroth,
8 And conspired all of them together to come
and to fight against Jerusalem, and to °hinder it.

V2 9 Nevertheless we made our prayer unto our
[4]God, and °set a watch against them day and
night, because of them.

W2 10 And Judah said, "The strength of the
bearers of burdens is decayed, and *there is*
much rubbish; so that we °are not able to build
the wall."

25 high house: or upper, i. e. the site or ruin of it. Not yet rebuilt. Cp. 7. 4.

court of the prison. Where Jeremiah had been imprisoned more than once (Jer. 32. 2; 33. 1; 38. 7, 13).

26 Moreover. Note the Parenthesis of *v.* 26.

Nethinims. Their work was to carry wood and water for the Temple. Hence their dwelling. See note on Ezra 2. 43.

Ophel = the Ophel: the hill south of Moriah. Formerly Jebus, afterward Zion. See Ap. 68.

the water gate. By Gihon. Now 'Ain Umm ed Dĕraj, "the Virgin's Fount". On east side of Ophel, in Kedron valley. See Ap. 59 and 68.

that lieth out. Probably the "tower in Siloam", Luke 13. 4.

28 the horse gate. See Ap. 59.

one = man. Heb. *'ish.* Ap. 14. II.

31 the goldsmith's son: or, the son of Zorphi.

gate Miphkad: or, gate of review or registry. Probably north-east of Temple. See Ap. 59.

32 And. This is reckoned in the *Massōrah* as the middle verse of the 685 verses of the whole book "Ezra-Nehemiah", showing that the two books were one.

sheep gate. See Ap. 59. The work thus ended where it had been begun. Cp. *v.* 1.

4. 1—6. 14 (Q, p. 635). OPPOSITION.
(*Introversion.*)

Q | S | 4. 1-23. Opposition. Wrath (III). Fighting (IV).
  T | 5. 1-5. Grievance.
  T | 5. 6-19. Redress.
  S | 6. 1-14. Opposition. Compromise (V and VI).

4. 1-23 (S, above). OPPOSITION. THIRD AND FOURTH. (*Extended and Repeated Alternation.*)

S | U1 | 1-3. Opposition. Wrath and mockery (III).
  V1 | 4, 5. Prayer.
  W1 | 6. Perseverance.
  U2 | 7, 8. Opposition. Conspiracy to fight (IV).
  V2 | 9. Prayer.
  W2 | 10. Despondency.
  U3 | 11. Opposition. Hostility.
  V3 | 12. Warning.
  W3 | 13-23. Encouragement. Sword and trowel.

1 But = And.

Sanballat. See note on 2. 10.

builded = were building.

wroth. The third form of opposition. See note on 2. 10.

2 army = force.

What . . . ? Fig. *Erotēsis.* Ap. 6.

fortify. Heb. *Homonym,* *'āzab.* See note on Ex. 23. 5. Marg. note of A.V. and R.V. neither needed nor correct.

will they sacrifice? Showing that no altar was as yet built or sacrificial worship being carried on.

3 Tobiah. See note on 2. 10.

4 Hear . . . turn. Fig. *Apostrophe.* Ap. 6. Nehemiah's prayer an echo of Pss. 120; 121; 123. 3, 4; 124; 125; 127; 129. In accord with that dispensation.

God. Heb. Elohim. Ap. 4. I.

despised = become a taunt.

captivity. Some codices, with six early printed editions and Syr., read "their captivity".

5 cover not. Heb. *kāṣāh* = conceal not. Not *kāphar,* to cover by atonement.

iniquity. Heb. *'āvāh.* Ap. 44. iv.

sin. Heb. *chāṭā'.* Ap. 44. i.

6 unto the half. The circuit complete to *half the height.*

mind = heart.

7 But. In Heb. text ch. 4 begins here.

and. Note the Fig. *Polysyndeton* (Ap. 6), for emphasis.

stopped = repaired. So the only other occurrence of the Heb. (2 Chron. 24. 13).

8 hinder = cause a miscarriage.

9 set a watch. The result of the prayer.

10 are not = shall not.

U^3 (p. 637) 454 11 And our adversaries said, "They shall not know, neither see, till we come in the midst among them, and slay them, and °cause the work to cease."

V^3 12 And it came to pass, that when the Jews which dwelt °by them came, they said unto us °ten times, "From all places whence ye shall return unto us °*they will be upon you.*"

W^3 s (p. 638) 13 Therefore set I in °the lower places behind the wall, *and* on the higher places, I even set the people after their families with their swords, their spears, and their bows.

t 14 And I looked, and rose up, and said unto the nobles, and to the °rulers, and to the rest of the People, "Be not ye afraid of them: remember °the LORD*, *Which is* great and terrible, and fight for your brethren, your sons, and your daughters, your wives, and your houses."

15 And it came to pass, when our enemies heard that it was known unto us, and [4]God had °brought their counsel to nought, that we returned all of us to the wall, every °one unto his work.

u 16 And it came to pass from that time forth, *that* the half of my °servants wrought in the work, and the other half of them held both the spears, the shields, and the bows, and the °habergeons; and the °rulers *were* °behind all the house of Judah.

17 They which builded on the wall, and they that bare burdens, with those that laded, *every one* with one of his hands wrought in the work, and with the other *hand* held a weapon.

18 °For the builders, every [15]one had his sword girded by his side, and *so* builded.

s And he that sounded the trumpet *was* by me.

t 19 And I said unto the nobles, and to the [14]rulers, and to the rest of the people, "The work *is* great and large, and we are separated upon the wall, [15]one far from another.

20 In what place *therefore* ye hear the sound of the trumpet, resort ye thither unto us: our [4]God shall fight for us."

u 21 So we laboured in the work: and half of them held the spears from the rising of the morning till the stars appeared.

22 Likewise at the same time said I unto the people, "Let every [15]one with his [16]servant °lodge within Jerusalem, that in the night they may be a guard to us, and labour on the day."

23 So neither I, nor my brethren, nor my [16]servants, nor °the °men of the guard which followed me, °none of us put off our clothes, *saving that* every [15]one put them off for washing.

T v **5** And there was °a great cry of °the people and of their wives against their brethren the Jews.

w 2 For there were that said, "We, our sons, and our daughters, *are* many: therefore we take up corn *for them*, that we may eat, and live."

3 *Some* also there were that said, "We °have mortgaged our lands, vineyards, and houses, that we might buy corn, because of °the dearth."

4 There were also that said, "We have borrowed money for the king's tribute, *and that upon* our lands and vineyards.

v 5 Yet now our flesh *is* as the flesh of our brethren, our °children as their °children: and, °lo, we bring into bondage our sons and our daughters to be servants, and *some* of our daughters are brought unto bondage *already*: neither *is it* in our power *to redeem them;*

for other men have our lands and vineyards." *w*

6 And I was very angry when I heard their cry and these words. T x^1

---

11 cause, &c. = suspend the work.

12 by = close to. ten times. Cp. Gen. 31. 7.

they will be upon you. Fig. *Ellipsis* (Ap. 6). Render: "From all quarters to which ye will turn [they will be] upon us".

13 the lower places behind: or, the lowest parts of the space behind.

4. 13-23 (W^3, p. 637). ENCOURAGEMENT.
(*Extended Alternation.*)

W^3 | s | 13. Weapons.
  t | 14, 15. Encouragement to nobles, &c.
   u | 16-18-. Division of labour and defence.
 s | -18. Trumpets.
  t | 19, 20. Encouragement to nobles, &c.
   u | 21-23. Division of labour and guard.

14 rulers. See note on 2. 16.

the LORD* = Jehovah. One of the 134 places where the *Sōpherim* altered Jehovah to *Adonai*. See Ap. 32, and cp. Ap. 4. II, VIII (2).

15 brought, &c. Cp. Job 5. 12; Ps. 33. 10.

one = man. Heb. *'ish*. Ap. 14. II.

16 servants = young men.

habergeons = corselets or coats of mail.

rulers = princes. Heb. *sār*.

behind. To encourage, and help if needed.

18 For = And.

22 lodge = pass the night. Few, or no houses yet. See 7. 4; 13. 21. Cp. Heb. *lūn*. First occurrence Gen. 19. 2; 24. 23, 25, 54, &c. See longer note on p. 653.

23 the men of the guard. The Persian guard attached to Nehemiah.

men. Heb. *'ěnōsh*. Ap. 14. III.

none of us, &c. The Heb. is lit. "none of us put off our clothes; each man went with his weapon (or tool) [and his] water". A single and measured part of the ration "water" being put for the whole. Fig. *Synecdoche* (of the Part), Ap. 6; just as we use "salt" for "salary", because it was once the most important part of the salary. Or, the water may have been required for making the mortar. The Fig. is used to emphasise the exigency of the circumstances. The text is thus not "defective".

5. 1-5 (T, p. 637). GRIEVANCE. (*Alternation.*)

T | v | 1. Complaint.
  w | 2-4. Cause. Debt (Particular).
 v | 5-. Complaint.
  w | -5. Cause. Alienation (General).

1 a great cry. So there were troubles within as well as without. Cp. 2 Cor. 7. 5.

the people = the common people, in contrast with the nobles and rulers (*v.* 7), who had returned with Nehemiah.

3 have mortgaged = are mortgaging.

the dearth. One of the thirteen famines (Ap. 10) recorded in Scripture. See note on Gen. 12. 10.

5 children = sons. lo. Fig. *Asterismos*. Ap. 6.

6-19 (*T*, p. 637). REDRESS.
(*Repeated Alternation.*)

T | x^1 | 6-8-. Nehemiah. Anger and remonstrance.
  y^1 | -8. People. Silence.
 x^2 | 9-11. Nehemiah. Expostulation.
  y^2 | 12-. People. Promise.
 x^3 | -12, 13-. Nehemiah. Adjuration.
  y^3 | -13. People. Performance.
 x^4 | 14-19. Nehemiah. Example.

454 7 °Then I consulted with myself, and I rebuked the nobles, and the °rulers, and said
unto them, "Ye °exact usury, every °one of his
brother." And I °set a great °assembly °a-
gainst them.
8 And I said unto them, "We after our ability
have °redeemed our brethren the Jews, which
were sold unto the °heathen; and will ye even sell
your brethren? or shall they be sold unto us?"
y^1 (p. 638) Then held they their peace, and found nothing
to answer.
x^2 9 Also I said, "It *is* not good that ye °do:
°ought ye not to walk in the fear of our
°God because of the °reproach of the heathen
our enemies?
10 I likewise, *and* my brethren, and my °serv-
ants, might exact of them money and corn: I
pray you, let us °leave off this usury.
11 Restore, I pray you, to them, even this
day, their lands, their vineyards, their oliveyards, and their houses, also °the hundredth
part of the money, and of the corn, °the °wine,
and the oil, that ye exact of them."
y^2 12 Then said they, "We will restore *them,*
and will require nothing of them; so will we
do °as thou sayest."
x^3 Then I °called the priests, and took an oath
of them, that they should do according to this
promise.
13 Also I shook my lap, and said, "So [9]God
shake out every °man from his house, and from
his labour, that performeth not this promise,
even thus be he shaken out, and emptied."
y^3 And all the °congregation said, "Amen," and
praised °the LORD. And the people did according to this promise.
x^4 (14 °Moreover from the °time that I was appointed to be their °governor in the land of
Judah, °from the twentieth year even unto
the two and thirtieth year of °Artaxerxes the
king, *that is,* twelve years, I and my brethren have not eaten °the bread of the °governor.
15 But the former governors that *had been*
before me were chargeable unto the People,
and had taken of them bread and wine, °beside
forty °shekels of silver; yea, even their servants bare rule over the People: but so did not
I, because of the fear of [9]God.
16 Yea, also I continued in the work of this
wall, neither bought °we any land: and all my
[10]servants *were* gathered thither unto the work.
17 Moreover *there were* at my table an hundred and °fifty of the Jews and [7]rulers, beside
those that came unto us from among the °hea-
then that *are* about us.
18 Now *that* which was °prepared *for me*
daily *was* one ox *and* six choice sheep; also
fowls were prepared for me, and once in ten days
store of all sorts of °wine: yet for all this required not I the bread of the governor, because
the bondage was heavy upon this People.
19 °Think upon me, my [9]God, for good,
according to all that I have done for this
people.)

S X (p. 639) **6** Now it came to pass, when °Sanballat,
°and °Tobiah, and °Geshem the Arabian,
and the rest of our enemies, heard that I had
builded the wall, and *that* there was no breach
left therein; (though at that time I had not set
up the doors upon the gates;)
2 That [1]Sanballat and [1]Geshem sent unto Y a^1
me, saying, "Come, let us meet together in

7 Then = And. **rulers.** See note on 2. 16.
exact usury. It was twelve per cent. See *v.* 11.
one = man. Heb. *'ish.* Ap. 14. II.
set = appointed.
assembly = body [of witnesses.] Heb. *kehallah* (fem.). Occurs only here and Deut. 33. 4. **against** = over.
8 redeemed = re-purchased. Heb. *ḳānāh,* to acquire by purchase; not *gā'al,* to redeem by purchase; or *pādāh,* to deliver by power. See notes on Ex. 6. 6; 13. 13.
heathen = nations.
9 do = are doing.
ought ye . . . ? Fig. *Erotēsis.* Ap. 6.
God. Heb. Elohim. Ap. 4. I.
10 servants = young men.
leave off. Heb. *Homonym, 'āzab.* Here means to leave off. See note on 3. 8.
11 the hundredth part. Paid at one per cent. per month, as was the custom; it was twelve per cent. per annum.
the wine. Some codices, with two early printed editions and Syr., read "and the new wine".
wine. Heb. *tīrōsh.* Ap. 27. II.
12 as = according as.
called: i. e. as witnesses.
13 man. Heb. *'ish.* Ap. 14. II.
congregation = assembly or muster.
the LORD. Heb. Jehovah. Ap. 4. II.
14 Moreover. See special note on *vv.* 14-19, on p. 653, and longer notes on p. 653.
time = day. **governor** = Pasha.
from the twentieth year. See Ap. 50. VI and VII (5).
Artaxerxes = the great king, viz. Astyages. See notes on p. 618, and Ap. 57.
the bread of the governor. The supplies due to him from the people.
15 beside. Heb. *'aḥar* = after: i. e. after the rate of, as in Jer. 3. 17; 18. 12. Rendered "beside" only here, out of several hundred times.
shekels. See Ap. 51. II.
16 we. Some codices, with Sept., Syr., and Vulg., read "I".
17 fifty of = fifty men of (Heb. *'ish.* Ap. 14. II).
heathen = nations.
18 prepared. At Nehemiah's own cost.
wine. Heb. *yayin.* Ap. 27. I.
19 Think. Fig. *Apostrophe* (Ap. 6) and Fig. *Anthropopatheia* (Ap. 6).

6. 1-14 (*S,* p. 637). OPPOSITION. FIFTH AND SIXTH: (COMPROMISE). (*Extended Alternation.*)

S | X | 1. Occasion.
  Y | 2-8. First stratagem. (V) Compromise.
    Z | 9-. Fear.
      A | -9. Prayer.
X | 10-. Occasion.
  Y | -10-12. Second stratagem. (VI) Affrighting.
    Z | 13. Fear.
      A | 14. Prayer.

1 Sanballat . . . Tobiah. See notes on 2. 19; 4. 7.
and. Note the Fig. *Polysyndeton* (Ap. 6), for emphasis.
Geshem. Another spelling in Sanballat's letter (*v.* 6), *Gashmu.*

2-8 (Y, above). FIRST STRATAGEM. (V) COMPROMISE. (*Repeated Alternation.*)

Y | a^1 | 2. Application. Made.
  b^1 | 3. Nehemiah. Refusal.
a^2 | 4-. Application. Repeated. Four times.
  b^2 | -4. Nehemiah. Refusal repeated. Four times.
a^3 | 5-7. Accusation.
  b^3 | 8. Nehemiah. Denial.

454 °*some one of* the villages in the °plain of °Ono." But they thought to do me °mischief.

b¹ (p. 639) 3 And I sent messengers unto them, saying, "I *am* doing a great work, so that I cannot come down: °why should the work cease, whilst I leave it, and come down to you?"

a² 4 Yet they sent unto me °four times after this sort;

b² and I answered them °after the same manner.

a³ 5 Then sent Sanballat his °servant unto me in like manner the fifth time with an °open letter in his hand;

6 Wherein *was* written, "It is reported among the °heathen, and ¹Gashmu saith *it, that* thou and the Jews think to rebel: for which cause thou buildest the wall, that thou mayest be their king, according to these words.

7 And thou hast also appointed prophets to preach of thee at Jerusalem, saying, °'*There is* a king in Judah:' and now shall it be reported to the king according to these words. °Come now therefore, and let us take counsel together."

b³ 8 Then I sent unto him, saying, "There are no such things done as thou sayest, but thou °feignest them out of thine own heart."

Z 9 For they all °made us afraid, saying, "Their hands shall be weakened from the work, that it be not done."

A °Now therefore, *O God*, strengthen my °hands.

X 10 Afterward I came unto the house of °Shemaiah the son of Delaiah the son of Mehetabeel, who *was* °shut up;

Y c (p. 640) and he said, "Let us meet together in °the house of °God, within the temple, and let us °shut the doors of the temple:

d for they will come to slay thee; yea, in the night will they come to slay thee."

c 11 And I said, °"Should such a °man as I flee? and who *is there*, that, *being* as I *am*, would go into the temple to save his life? I will not go in."

d 12 And, °lo, I perceived that ¹⁰God had not sent him; but that he pronounced this prophecy against me: for ¹Tobiah and ¹Sanballat had hired him.

Z (p. 639) 13 °Therefore *was* he hired, that I should be afraid, and do so, and °sin, and *that* they might have *matter* for an evil report, that they might reproach me.

A 14 My ¹⁰God, °think thou upon ¹Tobiah and ¹Sanballat according to these their works, and on the prophetess Noadiah, and the rest of the prophets, that would have put me in fear.

P (p. 635) 15 So the wall was finished in the twenty and fifth *day of the month* Elul, in °fifty and two days.

Q 16 And it came to pass, that when all our enemies heard *thereof*, and all the °heathen that *were* about us saw *these things*, they were much cast down in their own eyes: for they perceived that this work was wrought of our ¹⁰God.

17 Moreover in those days °the nobles of Judah sent many letters unto Tobiah, and *the letters* of Tobiah came unto them.

18 For *there were* many in Judah sworn unto him, because he *was* the °son in law of Shechaniah the son of Arah; and his son Johanan had taken the daughter of °Meshullam the son of Berechiah.

19 Also they reported his good deeds before me, and uttered my words to him. *And* Tobiah sent letters to put me in fear.

7 Now it came to pass, when the wall was built, and I had set up the doors, and the porters and the singers and the Levites were appointed, H (O) (p. 616)

2 That I gave my brother °Hanani, °and Ha-

2 some one of the villages = in *Cephīrim* (7. 29. Ezra 2. 25); now *Kefr 'Ana*, twenty-five miles from Jerusalem; eight miles east of Jaffa; six miles north of Lydda.
plain = valley, or combe.
Ono. Now *Kefr 'Ana*, five miles north of Lydda (Ezra 2. 33). Cp. ch. 11. 31.
mischief: to kill or capture Nehemiah. Cp. Prov. 26. 24.
3 why . . . ? Fig. *Erotēsis*. Ap. 6.
4 four times. The enemy takes no denial.
after the same manner. The only sure and safe procedure. Cp. 1 Sam. 17. 30.
5 servant = young man.
open letter. That others might read it.
6 heathen = nations.
7 There is a king: or, he hath become king.
Come now, &c. The object still compromise.
8 feignest. Only here and 1 Kings 12. 33 (devise).
9 made us afraid. Sought to make them afraid, but Nehemiah had no fear. See *v.* 11.
Now. Some codices, with three (and one in marg.) early printed editions, read "Thou".
hands. Some codices, with six early printed editions, read "hand".
10 Shemaiah. A professed friend, but a false prophet. See *v.* 12.
shut up = confined, as in prison. Heb. *'āṣar*. See Jer. 33. 1; 36. 5; 39. 15.

6. -10-12 (*Y*, p. 639) **SECOND STRATAGEM. (VI) (AFFRIGHTING).** (*Alternation.*)

Y	c	-10-.	Stratagem. Made.
	d	-10.	Pretence. Feigned.
	c	11.	Stratagem. Failure.
	d	12.	Pretence. Discovered.

the house of God. This must have been a temporary structure. Nehemiah would not be without some place wherein to worship. The Altar not yet erected. The Temple not yet built. See notes on 7. 4, and p. 618; also Ap. 58.
God. Heb. Elohim (with Art.) = the [true] God. Ap. 4. I.
shut = close, so as to conceal.
11 Should. Fig. *Erotēsis*. Ap. 6. Heb. *ṣāgar*. Cp. 13. 19.
man. Heb. *'ish*. Ap. 14. II.
12 lo. Fig. *Asterismos*. Ap. 6.
13 Therefore = to this end.
sin. Heb. *chāṭā'*. Ap. 44. i.
14 think. Fig. *Anthropopatheia*. Ap. 6. Cp. 5. 19.
15 fifty and two days. If finished on twenty-fifth Elul, and work took fifty-two days, it must have been commenced on third of Ab (fifth month). Work rapid, because all materials there: and God's good hand was there upon them.
17 the nobles = certain nobles. Not necessarily all.
18 son in law. Connected also with a high priest Eliashib. Cp. 13. 4.
Meshullam. Cp. 3. 4, 30.

7. 2 Hanani. He must have returned to Jerusalem with Nehemiah. Cp. 1. 2.
and = even. Cp. 1. 2.

454 naniah the ruler of the °palace, charge over Jerusalem: for he °*was* a faithful °man, and °feared °God above many.

3 And I said unto them, "Let not the gates of Jerusalem be opened until the sun be hot; and while they °stand by, let them °shut the doors, and bar *them:* and appoint watches of the inhabitants of Jerusalem, every °one in his watch, and every °one *to be* over against his °house."

4 Now the city *was* °large and great: but the People *were* °few therein, and the °houses *were* not builded.

J (P) B (p. 641) 5 And my °God put into mine heart to gather together the nobles, and the rulers, and the People, that they might be reckoned by genealogy.

C (And I °found °a register of the genealogy of them which came up at the first, and found written therein,

6 "These *are* the °children of the province, that went up out of the captivity, of those that had been carried away, whom Nebuchadnezzar the king of Babylon had carried away, and came again to Jerusalem and to Judah, every one unto his city;

7 Who °came with Zerubbabel, Jeshua, Nehemiah, Azariah, Raamiah, Nahamani, Mordecai, Bilshan, Mispereth, Bigvai, Nehum, Baanah. The number, *I say,* of the °men of °the People of Israel *was this;*

C e[1] 8 The [6]children of Parosh, two thousand an hundred seventy and two.

9 The [6]children of Shephatiah, three hundred seventy and two.

10 The [6]children of Arah, six hundred fifty and two.

11 The [6]children of Pahath-moab, of the [6]children of Jeshua and Joab, two thousand and eight hundred *and* eighteen.

12 The [6]children of Elam, a thousand two hundred fifty and four.

13 The [6]children of Zattu, eight hundred forty and five.

14 The [6]children of Zaccai, seven hundred and threescore.

15 The [6]children of Binnui, six hundred forty and eight.

16 The [6]children of Bebai, six hundred twenty and eight.

17 The [6]children of Azgad, two thousand three hundred twenty and two.

18 The [6]children of Adonikam, six hundred threescore and seven.

19 The [6]children of Bigvai, two thousand threescore and seven.

20 The [6]children of Adin, six hundred fifty and five.

21 The [6]children of Ater of Hezekiah, ninety and eight.

22 The [6]children of Hashum, three hundred twenty and eight.

23 The [6]children of Bezai, three hundred twenty and four.

24 The [6]children of Hariph, an hundred and twelve.

25 The [6]children of Gibeon, ninety and five.

26 The [7]men of Beth-lehem and Netophah, an hundred fourscore and eight.

27 The [7]men of Anathoth, an hundred twenty and eight.

28 The [7]men of Beth-azmaveth, forty and two.

29 The [7]men of Kirjath-jearim, Chephirah, and Beeroth, seven hundred forty and three.

30 The [7]men of Ramah and Gaba, six hundred twenty and one.

31 The [7]men of Michmas, an hundred and twenty and two.

32 The [7]men of Beth-el and Ai, an hundred twenty and three.

33 The [7]men of °the other Nebo, fifty and two.

34 The [6]children of °the other Elam, a thousand two hundred fifty and four.

---

palace = stronghold. Cp. 2. 8. North of Temple area.
was a faithful man = was as [it were] truth's own man.
man. Heb. *'ish.* Ap. 14. II. Here, with *kaph veritatis* (*k^e'ish 'ĕmeth*), for emphasis. **feared** = revered.
God. Heb. *'eth-hā'ĕlohim* = the [true, or triune] God. See Ap. 4. I.
3 stand by: as on guard.
shut. Heb. *gūph,* to close, as a gate.
one. Heb. *'ish.* Ap. 14. II.
house = dwelling. See note on 7. 4.
4 large and great = wide, or open, and large.
few therein. This could not have been said if Zerubbabel had already returned with nearly 50,000 people (Ezra 2. 64-67).
houses were not builded. See longer notes on p. 653.

7. 5-73 (J, p. 616; P, p. 617). THE RETURN UNDER ZERUBBABEL. (*Introversion.*)

J | B | 5-. Assembly and genealogy.
  C | -5-7. Register. Found (General).
  C | 8-69. Register. Contents (Particular).
B | 70-73. Assembly. Contributors.

This portion corresponds with Ezra 1. 5—2. 70. Therefore all that precedes (1. 1—7. 4) must come, chronologically, before Ezra 1. 5. Nehemiah's record here interrupted, and resumed after some twelve years. See 5. 14. This portion was written after the Temple had been rebuilt (cp. 8. 5, 16), when Darius Hystaspis was reigning (see Ap. 57, 58, and 50. VII. 5).

5 God. Heb. Elohim. Ap. 4. I.
found. This account probably written long after this date (426): say, between 404 and 400 B.C. Heb. = I find that the list of names was, &c. See longer note on p. 653.
a register, which is here inserted. It consists of Judah and Benjamin. Levi was not here as a distinct community (cp. Deut. 10. 8, 9).
6 children = sons.
7 came with Zerubbabel. That was in 426 B.C. The covenant and separation did not take place till 404 B.C. twenty-two years later (ch. 10, where Zerubbabel is not mentioned, probably because then dead).
men. Heb. pl. *'ĕnōsh.* Ap. 14. III.
the People of Israel. Another proof that Israel is not exclusively used of the ten tribes. See *vv.* 61, 73; 12. 47; and note on 1 Kings 12. 17.
The names are repeated from Ezra 2. See note on *v.* 66, p. 642.

8-69 (*C*, above). **REGISTER. CONTENTS. (PARTICULAR.)** (*Repeated Alternation.*)

C | e[1] | 8-62. Names found. Detail.
  f[1] | 63-65. Not found. Priests.
  e[2] | 66. Names found. Sum.
  f[2] | 67. Not found. Servants and strangers.
  e[3] | 68, 69. Possessions. Animals.

33 the other. Some codices, with two early printed editions, read *'echad* = a certain, instead of *'achēr* = another, or the other (rival).
34 the other. Some codices, with one early printed edition, read "one", or "a certain", as above.

426 35 The [6]children of Harim, three hundred and twenty.

36 The [6]children of Jericho, three hundred forty and five.

37 The [6]children of Lod, Hadid, and Ono, seven hundred twenty and one.

38 The [6]children of Senaah, three thousand nine hundred and thirty.

39 The priests: the [6]children of Jedaiah, of the house of Jeshua, nine hundred seventy and three.

40 The [6]children of Immer, a thousand fifty and two.

41 The [6]children of Pashur, a thousand two hundred forty and seven.

42 The [6]children of Harim, a thousand and seventeen.

43 The Levites: the [6]children of Jeshua, of Kadmiel, *and* of the [6]children of Hodevah, seventy and four.

44 The singers: the [6]children of Asaph, an hundred forty and eight.

45 The porters: the [6]children of Shallum, the children of Ater, the [6]children of Talmon, the [6]children of Akkub, the [6]children of Hatita, the [6]children of Shobai, an hundred thirty and eight.

46 °The Nethinims: the [6]children of Ziha, the [6]children of Hashupha, the [6]children of Tabbaoth,

47 The [6]children of Keros, the [6]children of Sia, the [6]children of Padon,

48 The [6]children of Lebana, the [6]children of Hagaba, the [6]children of Shalmai,

49 The [6]children of Hanan, the [6]children of Giddel, the [6]children of Gahar,

50 The [6]children of Reaiah, the [6]children of Rezin, the [6]children of Nekoda,

51 The [6]children of Gazzam, the [6]children of Uzza, the [6]children of Phaseah,

52 The [6]children of Besai, the [6]children of Meunim, the [6]children of Nephishesim,

53 The [6]children of Bakbuk, the [6]children of Hakupha, the [6]children of Harhur,

54 The [6]children of Bazlith, the [6]children of °Mehida, the [6]children of Harsha,

55 The [6]children of Barkos, the [6]children of Sisera, the [6]children of Tamah,

56 The [6]children of Neziah, the [6]children of Hatipha.

57 The [6]children of Solomon's servants: the [6]children of Sotai, the [6]children of Sophereth, the [6]children of Perida,

58 The [6]children of Jaala, the [6]children of Darkon, the [6]children of Giddel,

59 The [6]children of Shephatiah, the [6]children of Hattil, the [6]children of Pochereth of Zebaim, the [6]children of Amon.

60 All [46]the Nethinims, and the [6]children of Solomon's servants, *were* three hundred ninety and two.

61 And these *were* they which went up *also* from Tel-melah, Tel-haresha, Cherub, Addon, and Immer: but they could not shew their father's house, nor their seed, whether they *were* of [7]Israel.

62 The [6]children of Delaiah, the [6]children of Tobiah, the [6]children of Nekoda, six hundred forty and two.

f[1] (p. 641) 63 And of the priests: the [6]children of Habaiah, the [6]children of Koz, the [6]children of Barzillai, which took *one* of the daughters of Barzillai the Gileadite to wife, and was called after their name.

64 These sought their register °*among* those that were reckoned by genealogy, but °it was not found: therefore were they, °as polluted, put from the priesthood.

65 And the °Tirshatha said unto them, that they should not eat of the most °holy things, till there stood *up* a priest with °Urim and Thummim.

66 The whole °congregation together *was* °forty and two thousand three hundred and threescore, e[2]

67 Beside their manservants and their maidservants, of whom *there were* seven thousand three hundred thirty and seven: and they had two hundred forty and five singing men and singing women. f[2]

68 °Their horses, seven hundred thirty and six: their °mules, two hundred forty and five: e[3]

69 *Their* camels, four hundred thirty and five: six thousand seven hundred and twenty asses.)

70 And °some of the °chief of the fathers gave unto the work. The [65]Tirshatha °gave to the treasure a thousand °drams of gold, fifty basons, five hundred and thirty priests' garments. B

71 And *some* of the [70]chief of the fathers gave to the treasure of the work twenty thousand

46 The Nethinims. Descendants of the Gibeonites and other foreigners. Only 612 returned from Babylon: 392 with Zerubbabel (Ezra 2. 58. Neh. 7. 60), and 220 with Ezra (Ezra 8. 20. Neh. 11. 21). See note on Ezra 2. 43.

54 Mehida. Some codices, with four early printed editions, read "Mehira" (with r, ר *Resh*) instead of Mehida (with d, ד *Daleth*).

64 among those, &c. = wherein they were registered. Cp. Ezra 2. 62.

it was. Some codices, with six early printed editions, read "they were".

as polluted, put. See note on Ezra 2. 62.

65 Tirshatha. See note on Ezra 2. 63.

holy. See note on Ex. 3. 5.

Urim and Thummim = the Urim and the Thummim. See notes on Ex. 28. 30. Num. 26. 55.

66 congregation = assembly, convocation, or muster. Cp. Ezra 2. 64. Heb. *ḳāhāl*.

forty and two thousand three hundred and threescore. This number (42,360) agrees with Ezra 2. 64. Though the two lists are not identical, there is no discrepancy, but the difference shows the independence of the two accounts:

Numbered in Neh. 7.		42,360
Named in Neh.	31,089	
,, not in Ezra	494	31,583
Difference between names and numbers		10,777

See note on Ezra 2. 64, which shows the same result.

68 Their horses . . . mules. This verse is found in some codices, with six early printed editions.

70 some = a portion.

chief = heads.

gave. Nehemiah mentions what he, the chiefs, and the rest of the people gave. Ezra (2. 68, 69) mentions what only *one* portion gave. Hence the numbers are necessarily different.

drams. Chald. *darkᵉmōnīm*. See Ap. 51. I. 1 (2).

426 [70]drams of gold, and two thousand and two hundred °pound of silver.

72 And *that* which the rest of the people gave *was* twenty thousand [70]drams of gold, and two thousand pound of silver, and threescore and seven priests' garments.

73 So the priests, and the Levites, and the porters, and the singers, and *some* of the People, and °the Nethinims, and all [7]Israel, dwelt in their cities;

G (Q) U (p. 643) and when °the seventh month came, the [6]children of Israel *were* in their cities.

Tisri 426 **8** °And all the People gathered themselves together as one °man into the °street that *was* before °the water gate;

V W¹ g and they spake unto Ezra the scribe to bring °the book of the law of Moses, which °the LORD had commanded to Israel.

2 And °Ezra the priest brought the law before the °congregation both of [1]men and women, and all that could hear with understanding, °upon the first day of the seventh month.

X h 3 And he read therein before the [1]street that *was* before [1]the water gate from the °morning until midday, before the °men and the women, and those that could understand; and the ears of all the People *were attentive* unto the book of the law.

i 4 And Ezra the scribe stood upon a °pulpit of wood, which they had made for the purpose; and °beside him stood Mattithiah, and Shema, and Anaiah, and Urijah, and Hilkiah, and Maaseiah, on his right hand; and on his left hand, Pedaiah, °and Mishael, and Malchiah, and Hashum, and Hashbadana, Zechariah, *and* Meshullam.

g 5 And Ezra °opened the book °in the sight of all the People;

X i (for he was above all the People;) and when he opened it, all the People °stood up:

6 And Ezra blessed [1]the LORD, the great °God. And all the people answered, °"Amen, Amen," with °lifting up their hands: and they bowed their heads, and worshipped [1]the LORD with *their* faces to the ground.

7 Also Jeshua, and Bani, and Sherebiah, Jamin, Akkub, Shabbethai, Hodijah, Maaseiah, Kelita, Azariah, Jozabad, Hanan, Pelaiah, and the Levites, caused the People to understand the law: and the People *stood* in their place.

h 8 So they °read in [1]the book in the law of [6]God °distinctly, °and °gave the sense, °and °caused *them* to understand the reading.

W² j 9 And °Nehemiah, which *is* the Tirshatha, and Ezra the priest the scribe, and the Levites that taught the People, said unto all the People, "This day *is* °holy unto [1]the LORD your [6]God; mourn not, nor weep." For all the People wept, when they heard the words of the law.

k 10 Then he said unto them, "Go your way, eat the fat, and drink the sweet, and send portions unto them for whom nothing is prepared:

71 pound. Heb. *māneh.* Ap. 51. II. 4 (1).

73 the Nethinims. See note on Ezra 2. 43.

7. -73—8. 18 (G, p. 616; Q, p. 617). THE FEAST OF THE SEVENTH MONTH (426 B.C.). (*Introversion.*)

G | U | 7. -73—8. 1-. The solemn assembly.
  V | 8. -1-12. The first day.
  V | 8. 13-18-. The second and following days.
U | 8. -18. The solemn assembly.

the seventh month. This was in 426 B.C., not in 404 B.C., which is referred to in 9. 1-3 and Ezra 9. 1-4. See Ap. 58.

8. -1-12 (V, above). THE FIRST DAY. (*Division.*)

V | W¹ | 8. -1-8. The book. Opened and read.
  | W² | 8. 9-12. The book. Effect of reading.

8. -1-8 (W¹, above). THE BOOK. OPENED AND READ. (*Alternation and Introversion.*)

W¹ | g | -1, 2. The book brought forth.
  X | h | 3. The reading.
    i | 4. Station of Ezra and others.
  g | 5-. The book opened.
  X | *i* | -5-7. Station of Ezra and others.
    h | 8. The reading.

1 And = Then. **man.** Heb. *'īsh.* Ap. 14. II.

street = broad or open space. See *vv.* 3, 16; 3. 26; 12. 36, 37, 40.

the water gate. See notes on 3. 26 and 5. 9.

the book = scroll. The well-known book (Deut. 31. 10, 11). See Ap. 47.

the LORD. Heb. Jehovah (with *'eth*). Ap. 4. II.

2 Ezra the priest. It was the priest's duty at this and at all times to teach the people the Word of God. See note on Deut. 17. 11; 33. 10; and cp. Mal. 2. 7.

congregation = assembly or muster.

upon the first day, &c. This was according to the requirement of Deut. 31. 9-12, every seventh year. Cp. Lev. 23. 23-25.

3 morning = daylight. **men.** Heb. pl. *'ĕnōsh.* Ap. 14. III.

4 pulpit = high platform. Eng. "pulpit" from Lat. *pulpitum*, a stage of a theatre.

beside him. Thirteen priests with him: fourteen in all. Ap. 10.

and. Some codices, with five early printed editions, omit this "and".

5 opened the book = unrolled the scroll.

in the sight = before the eyes.

stood up. In token of reverence (Judg. 3. 20. Job 29. 8; 37. 14).

6 God. Heb. Elohim (with Art.) = the [true] God. Ap. 4. I.

Amen, Amen. Fig. *Epizeuxis* (Ap. 6), emphasising the great solemnity.

lifting up. Heb. *mo'āl.* Occurs only here. Cp. 1 Tim. 2. 8.

8 read in the book: i. e. the Heb. text of the Pentateuch. See Ap. 47.

distinctly = a distinct [reading], i. e. (according to the Talmud) translating and interpreting it in the Chaldee paraphrase.

and. Note the Fig. *Polysyndeton* (Ap. 6), to emphasise each clause.

gave the sense: i. e. divided the sentences, &c., according to sense.

caused them to understand the reading: i. e. gave the traditional pronunciation of the words (which were then without the vowel points).

8. 9-12 (W², above). THE BOOK. EFFECT OF READING. (*Extended Alternation.*)

W² | j | 9. Prohibition. No weeping.
  k | 10-. Dismissal.
    l | -10. Joy.
j | 11. Prohibition. No grieving.
  k | 12-. Departure.
    l | -12. Joy.

9 Nehemiah. He now uses the third person. This is not necessarily a sign of change of authorship.

holy. See note on Ex. 3. 5.

Tisri 426 for *this* day °*is* [9]holy unto our °LORD: neither be ye sorry;

l (p. 643) for the °joy of °the LORD °is your °strength."

j 11 So the Levites stilled all the People, saying, "Hold your peace, for the day *is* [9]holy; neither be ye grieved."

k 12 And all the people went their way

l to eat, and to drink, and to send portions, and to make great mirth, because they had understood the words that were declared unto them.

V m (p. 644) 13 And on the second day were gathered together the °chief of the fathers of all the People, the priests, and the Levites, unto Ezra the scribe, even to understand the words of the law.

n o 14 And they °found °written in the law which [1]the LORD had commanded by Moses, that the °children of Israel should dwell in °booths in the feast of the seventh month:

p 15 And that they should publish and proclaim in all their cities, and in Jerusalem, saying, "Go forth unto the °mount, and fetch olive branches, and pine branches, and myrtle branches, and palm branches, and branches of thick trees, to make booths, °as *it is* written."

p 16 So the People went forth, °and brought *them*, and made themselves booths, every °one upon the roof of his house, and in their courts, and in the courts of the house of [6]God, and in the [1]street of [1]the water gate, and in the [1]street of the gate of Ephraim.

o 17 And all the [2]congregation of them that were come again out of the captivity made booths, and sat under the booths: for since the days of °Jeshua the son of Nun unto that day had °not the [14]children of °Israel °done so. And there was very great gladness.

m 18 Also day by day, from the first day unto the last day, °he read in [1]the book of the law of [6]God.

n And they kept the feast seven days;

U and on the eighth day *was* a solemn °assembly, according unto the °manner.

G (*N*) Y^1 Tisri 404 **9** Now in the twenty and fourth day of °this month the °children of Israel were assembled with fasting, and with sackclothes, and earth upon them.

2 And the seed of Israel separated themselves from all °strangers, and stood and confessed their °sins, and the °iniquities of their fathers.

3 And they stood up in their place, and read in °the book of the law of °the LORD their °God *one* fourth part of the day; and *another* fourth part they confessed, and worshipped °the LORD their °God.

Z^1 q^1 4 Then stood up upon the °stairs, of the Levites, Jeshua, and Bani, Kadmiel, Shebaniah, Bunni, Sherebiah, °Bani, *and* °Chenani,

r^1 and cried with a loud voice unto [3]the LORD their [3]God.

q^2 5 Then the °Levites, Jeshua, and Kadmiel, Bani, Hashabniah, Sherebiah, Hodijah, Shebaniah, *and* Pethahiah, said,

---

10 is = it [is].
LORD. Heb. Adonim. Ap. 4. VIII (3).
joy. Chald. *ḥedvāh*. Occurs only here, 1 Chron. 16. 27, and Ezra 6. 16.
the LORD. Heb. Jehovah. Ap. 4. II.
is = that [is],
strength = defence, or refuge.

8. 13-18 (*V*, p. 643). THE SECOND AND FOLLOWING DAYS. (*Alternation.*)

V | m | 13. Second day. Reading.
n | 14-17. Feast. Tabernacles (manner).
m | 18-. Every day. Reading.
n | -18-. Feast. Tabernacles (continuance).

14-17 (n, above). FEAST. TABERNACLES (MANNER). (*Introversion.*)

n | o | 14. Command. To dwell in booths.
p | 15. To go forth, &c.
p | 16. The going forth, &c.
o | 17. Obedience. Dwelling in booths.

13 chief = heads.
14 found: i. e. they came to the place where direction was given.
written. See note on Ex. 17. 14, and Ap. 47.
children = sons.
booths. Cp. Lev. 23. 39-43. Deut. 16. 13-15.
15 mount = hill country.
as it is written. See Lev. 23. 42.
16 and. Note the Fig. *Polysyndeton* (Ap. 6), to mark the minuteness of the obedience.
one = man. Heb. *'ish*. Ap. 14. II.
17 Jeshua. Another spelling of Joshua.
not . . . done so. 2 Chron. 8. 13 speaks only of the offerings required by the Law, which Solomon offered. Nothing is said *there* of what the People did; so that there is no "discrepancy", as is alleged.
Israel. See note on 1 Kings 12. 17.
18 he. Some codices, with Syr., read "they".
assembly = restraint: i. e. restraint from work.
manner = regulation, or ordinance.

9. 1—10. 39 (*G*, p. 616; (*N*), p. 617). THE SEPARATION OF THE PEOPLE. (*Repeated Alternations.*)

G | Y^1 | 9. 1-3. The People. Separation and worship.
Z^1 | q^1 | 9. 4-. The Levites. Cry to Jehovah.
r^1 | 9. -4. Prayer.
q^2 | 9. 5-. The Levites. Blessing Jehovah.
r^2 | 9. -5-38. Praise.
Y^2 | 10. 1-27. The People. Covenant made.
Z^2 | q^3 | 10. 28-. The Levites. Themselves.
r^3 | 10. -28-. Separation from foreigners.
q^4 | 10. -28. The Levites. Their families.
r^4 | 10. 29-. Cleaving to their brethren.
Y^3 | 10. -29-39. The People. Ordinances.

Neh. 9. 1—10. 39 is parallel with Ezra 9. 1—10. 44. Ezra 4. 1—8. 36 comes between Neh. 8. 18 and 9. 1. See the Table and Structure on p. 617, notes on p. 618, and Ap. 58.
1 this month. In 404 B.C., not in 426 B.C. (7. 73). Same as Ezra 9. 1-4. See Ap. 58.
children = sons.
2 strangers = sons of the foreigner.
sins. Heb. *chāṭā'*. Ap. 44. i.
iniquities. Heb. *'āvāh*. Ap. 44. iv.
3 the book of the law. See Ap. 47.
the LORD. Heb. Jehovah. Ap. 4. II.
God. Heb. Elohim. Ap. 4. I.
4 stairs = platform. Omit the comma.
Bani, and Chenani. Some codices, with Sept., read "sons of Chenani".
5 Levites. For these names, cp. 3. 17; 7. 43; 10. 10; 12. 8, 24. Ezra 2. 40; 3. 9.

r² A¹ (p. 645) Tisri 404 °"Stand up *and* bless [3]the LORD your [3]God for ever and ever: and °blessed be Thy glorious name, which is exalted above all blessing and praise.

6 °Thou, *even* °Thou, °*art* [3]LORD alone; °Thou hast made °heaven, the °heaven of heavens, with all their host, the earth, °and all *things* that *are* therein, the seas, and all that *is* therein, and °Thou preservest them all; and the host of heaven worshippeth Thee.

B¹ s 7 Thou [6]*art* [3]the LORD the [3]God, Who didst °choose Abram, [6]and broughtest him forth out of Ur of the Chaldees, and gavest him the name of °Abraham;

8 And foundest his heart °faithful before Thee, [6]and madest a °covenant with him to give the land of the Canaanites, the Hittites, the Amorites, and the Perizzites, and the Jebusites, and the Girgashites, to give *it, I say,* to his seed, and hast performed Thy words; for Thou *art* righteous:

9 [6]And didst see the °affliction of our fathers in Egypt, and heardest their cry by the Red sea;

10 [6]And °shewedst signs and wonders upon Pharaoh, and on all his servants, and on all the people of his land: for thou knewest that they dealt proudly against them. So didst Thou get Thee a name, as *it is* this day.

11 [6]And Thou didst divide the sea before them, so that they went through the midst of the sea on the dry land; and their °persecutors Thou threwest into the deeps, as a stone into the °mighty waters.

12 Moreover Thou °leddest them in the day by a °cloudy pillar; [6]and in the night by a pillar of fire, to give them light in the way wherein they should go.

13 °Thou camest down also upon mount Sinai, [6]and spakest with them from heaven, and gavest them right judgments, and °true laws, °good statutes and commandments:

14 [6]And °madest known unto them Thy °holy °sabbath, and commandedst them precepts, statutes, and laws, by the hand of Moses Thy servant:

15 [6]And °gavest them bread from heaven for their hunger, and broughtest forth °water for them out of the rock for their thirst, and °promisedst them that they should go in to possess the land which Thou hadst °sworn to give them.

t¹ 16 But they and our fathers °dealt proudly, [6]and hardened their necks, and hearkened not to Thy commandments,

17 [6]And refused to obey, neither were mindful of Thy wonders that Thou didst °among them; but hardened their necks, and in their rebellion °appointed a captain to return °to their bondage:

s² but Thou *art* °a °GOD °ready to pardon, gracious and merciful, slow to anger, and °of great kindness, and forsookest them not.

t² 18 Yea, when they had made them °a molten calf, [6]and said, °'This *is* thy [3]God That brought thee up out of °Egypt,' and had wrought great provocations;

---

9. -5-38 (r², p. 644). PRAISE. CONFESSION. PRAYER. (*Repeated Alternation.*)

r² | A¹ | -5, 6. Praise of Jehovah.
B¹ | 7-31. Confession.
A² | 32. Prayer to Jehovah.
B² | 33-37. Confession.
A³ | 38. Covenant with Jehovah.

5 Stand up, &c. One of the most glorious of all Doxologies. **blessed be** = let them bless.

6 Thou . . . Thou . . . Thou. Fig. *Epizeuxis* (Ap. 6), for emphasis.

art LORD = [art] He, Jehovah. **heaven** = the heavens.

heaven of heavens. Fig. *Polyptōton* (Ap. 6), for emphasis.

and. Note the Fig. *Polysyndeton* (Ap. 6), throughout this confession.

7-31 (B¹, above). CONFESSION. (*Repeated Alternation.*)

B¹ | s¹ | 7-15. Jehovah. Grace.
t¹ | 16, 17-. Israel. Ingratitude. Pride.
s² | -17. Jehovah. Pardon.
t² | 18. Israel. Ingratitude. Provocation.
s³ | 19-25. Jehovah. Manifold mercies.
t³ | 26. Israel. Rebellion.
s⁴ | 27-. Jehovah. Punishment.
t⁴ | -27-. Israel. Humiliation. Cry.
s⁵ | -27. Jehovah. Manifold mercies.
t⁵ | 28. Israel. Evil-doing repeated.
s⁶ | -28-. Jehovah. Punishment.
t⁶ | -28-. Israel. Humiliation. Cry.
s⁷ | -28, 29-. Jehovah. Mercies.
t⁷ | -29. Israel. Ingratitude. Pride.
s⁸ | 30-. Jehovah. Forbearance.
t⁸ | -30-. Israel. Obstinacy.
s⁹ | -30, 31. Jehovah. Judgment. Forbearance.

7 choose Abram. Cp. Gen. 11. 31; 12. 1; 17. 5. Josh. 24. 1-3.

Abraham. See note on Gen. 17. 5, and Ap. 50. III. The letter ה (*Hē*) = five. This is the number of *grace* (Ap. 10), put into the middle of the names (Abram and Sarai), as a symbol of the grace that called him. See Ap. 50. III for the repetition of five in its multiples all through his life.

8 faithful. Because He had made it so. Cp. Jas. 3. 6.

covenant. Cp. Gen. 15. 1, 18; 17. 7, 8.

9 affliction = humiliation. Cp. Ex. 2. 23-25.

10 shewedst signs, &c. See Ex. 7. 7, 8-10; 12 and 14. Pss. 105. 27; 106. 7; 135. 9.

11 persecutors = pursuers.

mighty waters. Cp. Ex. 15. 5.

12 leddest them = leddest them gently.

cloudy pillar. Cp. Ex. 13. 21.

13 Thou camest down. Cp. Ex. 19. 20; 20. 1.

true laws. Heb. laws of truth. See note on John 1. 17.

good statutes. See note on Gen. 26. 5. Deut. 4. 7.

14 madest known . . . Thy, &c. Jehovah's Sabbath was in Gen. 2. 1-3. Made known to Israel (Ex. 20. 9-11). Established as a sign (Ex. 31. 13-17).

holy. See note on Ex. 3. 5.

sabbath = cessation (from work), rest. This rest was made for man (Mark 2. 27).

15 gavest them bread. Ex. 16. 14, 15. Cp. John 6. 57, 58. **water.** Ex. 17. 6. Num. 20. 9-11.

promisedst. Deut. 1. 8.

16 dealt proudly = fostered pride.

17 among = with.

appointed a captain. See Num. 14. 4.

to their bondage. Some codices, with one early printed edition, read *bᵉmizrāīm* = to Egypt, instead of *bᵉmiryām* = in their rebellion.

a. The A.V. of 1611 had "the".

GOD. Heb. *Eloah.* See Ap. 4. V.

ready to pardon = of forgivenesses.

of great kindness = abounding in lovingkindness.

18 a molten calf. Ex. 32. 4.

This. Singular number: i. e. "This [calf]".

Egypt. Some codices, with six early printed editions and Syr., read "the land of Egypt". Cp. Ex. 32. 4.

s3 (p. 645) Tisri 404 **19** Yet Thou in Thy °manifold mercies forsookest them not in the wilderness: the pillar of the cloud °departed not from them by day, to [12]lead them in the way; neither the pillar of fire by night, to shew them light, and the way wherein they should go.

20 Thou gavest also Thy good °spirit to instruct them, [6]and withheldest not Thy °manna from their mouth, and gavest them [15]water for their thirst.

21 Yea, forty years didst Thou sustain them in the wilderness, *so that* they lacked nothing; their °clothes waxed not old, and their feet swelled not.

22 Moreover Thou gavest them kingdoms and °nations, and didst °divide them into corners: so they possessed the land of °Sihon, and the land of the king of Heshbon, and the land of °Og king of Bashan.

23 Their [1]children also multipliedst Thou as the stars of heaven, and broughtest them into the land, concerning which Thou hadst promised to their fathers, that they should go in to possess *it*.

24 So the [1]children went in and possessed the land, and Thou subduedst before them the inhabitants of the land, the Canaanites, and gavest them into their hands, with their kings, and the °people of the land, that they might do with them as they would.

25 And they took strong cities, and a °fat land, and possessed houses full of all goods, °wells digged, vineyards, and oliveyards, and fruit trees in abundance: so they did eat, and were filled, and became fat, and °delighted themselves in Thy great goodness.

t3 **26** Nevertheless they were disobedient, and rebelled against Thee, and cast Thy law behind their backs, and °slew Thy prophets which °testified against them to turn them to Thee, and they wrought great provocations.

s4 **27** Therefore Thou deliveredst them into the hand of their °enemies, who vexed them:

t4 and in the time of their trouble, when they cried unto Thee,

s5 Thou heardest *them* from heaven; and °according to Thy [18]manifold mercies Thou °gavest them saviours, who saved them out of the hand of their °enemies.

t5 **28** But after they had rest, they did °evil again before Thee:

s6 therefore leftest Thou them in the hand of their °enemies, so that they had the dominion over them:

t6 yet when they returned, and cried unto Thee, Thou heardest *them* from heaven;

s7 and many times didst Thou deliver them °according to Thy mercies;

29 And [26]testifiedst against them, that Thou mightest bring them again unto Thy law:

t7 yet they [16]dealt proudly, and hearkened not unto Thy commandments, but °sinned against Thy judgments, (which if °a man do, °he shall live in them;) and withdrew the shoulder, and hardened their neck, and would not hear.

s8 **30** Yet many years didst Thou forbear them, and [26]testifiedst against them by Thy spirit °in Thy prophets:

yet would they not give ear: t8

therefore gavest Thou them into the hand of the [24]people of the lands. s9

31 Nevertheless for Thy great mercies' sake Thou didst not utterly consume them, nor forsake them; for Thou *art* a gracious and merciful °GOD.

32 Now therefore, our [3]God, the great, the mighty, and the terrible [31]GOD, Who keepest covenant and °mercy, let not all the trouble seem little before Thee, that hath come upon us, on our kings, on our princes, °and on our priests, and on our prophets, and on our fathers, and on all Thy People, since the time of the kings of Assyria unto this day. A2

33 Howbeit Thou *art* just in all that is brought upon us; for Thou hast done right, but °we °have done wickedly: B2

34 Neither have our kings, our princes, our priests, nor our fathers, kept Thy law, nor hearkened unto Thy commandments and Thy testimonies, wherewith Thou didst [26]testify against them.

35 For they have not served Thee in their kingdom, and in Thy great goodness that Thou gavest them, and in the large and fat land which Thou gavest before them, neither turned they from their °wicked works.

19 manifold mercies. Cp. *v.* 27 and Ps. 106. 45.
departed not. Cp. Ex. 13. 21, 22.
20 spirit. Heb. *rūach*. Ap. 9. Cp. Num. 11. 16, 17. Deut. 34. 9. Ps. 143. 10, and *v.* 30 below.
manna. Cp. Ex. 16. 15. Josh. 5. 12.
21 clothes. Cp. Deut. 8. 4; 29. 5.
22 nations = peoples.
divide them into corners = apportion them their lot. Heb. *pē'āh* = quarter, region. See Lev. 19. 9; 23. 22. Cp. Jer. 9. 26; 49. 32. The word occurs in the allotment of the Land, in Josh. 15. 5; 18. 12, 14, 15, 20.
Sihon . . . Og. Cp. Num. 21. 21, &c.
24 people = peoples. **25 fat land** = rich soil.
wells digged. Heb. *bōr*, cisterns hewed. See note on Gen. 21. 19.
delighted themselves = made their Eden. Heb. *'ānag*. Hithp. pret. only here.
26 slew Thy prophets. See 1 Kings 19. 10. Cp. Matt. 23. 37. Acts 7. 52.
testified against = solemnly admonished.
27 enemies = adversaries.
according to. Some codices, with seven early printed editions and Sept., read "in".
gavest them saviours. See Judg. 3. 9.
28 evil. Heb. *rā'a'*. Ap. 44. viii.
enemies = oppressors.
according to. Some codices, with two early printed editions, Sept., and Vulg., read "in".
29 sinned. Heb. *chāṭā'*. Ap. 44. i.
a man. Heb. *'ādām*. Ap. 14. I.
he shall live, &c. See note on Lev. 18. 2.
30 in = by the hand of; "hand" put by Fig. *Metonymy* (of Cause), Ap. 6, for the ministry or agency of the prophets. **31 GOD.** Heb. *El*. Ap. 4. IV.
32 mercy = lovingkindness, or grace.
and. Some codices, with six early printed editions, omit this "and".
33 we. Note how Nehemiah (here), Ezra (9. 6-11), and Daniel (9. 5-19) associate themselves with the people in their confessions.
have done wickedly. Heb. *rāshā'*. Ap. 44. x.
35 wicked. Heb. *rā'a'*. Ap. 44. viii.

Tisri 404 36 °Behold, we *are* servants this day, and
°*for* the land that Thou gavest unto our fathers
to eat the fruit thereof and the good thereof,
behold, we *are* servants in it:
37 And it yieldeth much increase unto the
kings whom Thou hast set over us because of
our °sins: also they have dominion over our
bodies, and over our cattle, at their pleasure,
and we *are* in great distress.

A^3 (p. 645) 38 °And because of all this we make a sure
covenant, and write *it;* and our °princes,
Levites, *and* priests, seal *unto it.*"

Y^2 u **10** Now °those that sealed *were*, Nehemiah,
the °Tirshatha, the son of Hachaliah,
v and Zidkijah,
2 Seraiah, Azariah, Jeremiah,
3 Pashur, Amariah, Malchijah,
4 Hattush, Shebaniah, Malluch,
5 Harim, Meremoth, Obadiah,
6 Daniel, Ginnethon, Baruch,
7 Meshullam, Abijah, Mijamin,
8 Maaziah, Bilgai, Shemaiah: these *were* the
priests.

v 9 And the Levites: both Jeshua the son of
Azaniah, Binnui of the sons of Henadad, Kadmiel;
10 And their brethren, Shebaniah, Hodijah,
Kelita, Pelaiah, Hanan,
11 Micha, Rehob, Hashabiah,
12 Zaccur, Sherebiah, Shebaniah,
13 Hodijah, Bani, Beninu.

u 14 The °chief of the people; Parosh, Pahath-
moab, Elam, Zatthu, Bani,
15 Bunni, Azgad, Bebai,
16 Adonijah, Bigvai, Adin,
17 Ater, Hizkijah, Azzur,
18 Hodijah, Hashum, Bezai,
19 Hariph, Anathoth, Nebai,
20 Magpiash, Meshullam, Hezir,
21 Meshezabeel, Zadok, Jaddua,
22 Pelatiah, Hanan, Anaiah,
23 Hoshea, Hananiah, Hashub,
24 Hallohesh, Pileha, Shobek,
25 Rehum, Hashabnah, Maaseiah,
26 And Ahijah, Hanan, Anan,
27 Malluch, Harim, Baanah.

q^3 (p. 644) 28 And the rest of the People, the priests, the
Levites, the porters, the singers, the °Nethinims,
r^3 and all they that had separated themselves from
the °people of the lands unto °the law of °God,
q^4 their wives, their sons, and their daughters,
every one having knowledge, and having
understanding;
r^4 29 They clave to their brethren, their nobles,
Y^3 w (p. 647) and entered into a curse, and into an oath, to
walk in [28] God's law, which was °given by °Moses
the servant of [28] God, and to observe and
do all the commandments of °the LORD °our
Lord, and His judgments and His °statutes;
30 And that we would not give our daughters
unto the [28] people of the land, nor take their
daughters for our sons:

x 31 And *if* the [28] people of the land bring °ware
or any victuals °on the sabbath day to sell,
that we would not buy it of them on the sabbath,
or on the °holy day: and *that* we would
°leave °the seventh year, and °the exaction of
every debt.

32 Also we made ordinances for us, to charge x C^1

---

36 Behold. Fig. *Asterismos.* Ap. 6. **for**=as to.

37 sins. Heb. *chātā'.* Ap. 44. i.

38 And because, &c. Ch. 10 in Heb. text begins with this verse.

princes. Nehemiah and Hananiah, if not others, were members of the royal family of Judah. See 1. 1.

10. 1-27 (Y^2, p. 644). THE PEOPLE. COVENANT MADE. (*Introversion.*)

Y^2 | u | 1-. The chief. Nehemiah the Governor.
  v | -1-8. The priests.
  v | 9-13. The Levites.
 u | 14-27. The chiefs of the people.

This chapter is parallel with the last chapter of Ezra (10. 1-44). Consequently all beyond it is supplementary (chronologically). See note on 9. 1, the Structure on p. 617, notes on p. 618, and Ap. 58.

1 those that sealed. These are stated by the Talmudical writings, and the unanimous voice of tradition, to have formed "The Great Synagogue". It consisted at first of 120 members, but was afterward reduced to seventy. It represented the five divisions of the nation: (1) the chiefs of the priests; (2) the chief Levites; (3) the chiefs of the people; (4) the representatives of the cities; (5) the doctors of the law. Its work was (by solemn oath): (1) not to intermarry with the heathen; (2) to keep the sabbath; (3) to keep the sabbatical year; (4) to pay annually ⅓ of a shekel to the temple; (5) to supply wood for the altar; (6) to pay the priestly dues; (7) to collect and preserve the canonical scriptures. The Great Synagogue lasted 110 years: from Nehemiah to Simon the Just, when, having completed its work, it became known as the *Sanhedrim* of the N.T., the supreme council of the Jewish nation; which rejected the kingdom, and crucified the King (Messiah).

Tirshatha. See note on Ezra 2. 63.

14 chief=heads.

28 Nethinims. See note on Ezra 2. 43.

people=peoples.

the law of God. See Ex. 17. 14 and Ap. 47.

God. Heb. Elohim (with Art.)=the [true] God. Ap. 4. I.

-29-39 (Y^3, p. 644). THE PEOPLE. ORDINANCES. (*Introversion.*)

Y^3 | w | -29, 30. The People. Marriages.
  x | 31. The sabbath.
  x | 32-37. The Temple.
 w | 38, 39. The Priests, &c. Service.

29 given. See Ap. 47.

Moses the servant of God. The first of four occurrences of this expression in the Hebrew Bible. See Dan. 9. 11. 1 Chron. 6. 49; 2 Chron. 24. 9.

the LORD. Heb. Jehovah. Ap. 4. II.

our Lord. Heb. our Adonai. Ap. 4. VIII (3) = our sovereign Lord. Cp. Ps. 8. 1, 9.

statutes. See note on Deut. 4. 1.

31 ware=wares. Heb. pl. only here.

on the sabbath. Cp. 9. 14; 13. 15, 16, 18, 19, 21. This observation of the sabbath ensured the reading of God's Word, and the multiplication of copies.

holy. See note on Ex. 3. 5.

leave, &c.: i. e. forego the produce of the seventh year.

the seventh year. See Ex. 23. 10, 11. Lev. 25. 2, 7.

the exaction of every debt. Heb. = the burden of every bond. Cp. 5. 10, 11, and Deut. 15. 2; especially in the year of release.

32-37 (*x*, above). THE TEMPLE. (*Division.*)

x | C^1 | 32. Money.
  C^2 | 33, 34. Provisions.
  C^3 | 35-39. Firstfruits and tithes.

Tisri 404 ourselves yearly with the third part of a °shekel for the service of the house of our [28]God;

C² (p. 647) 33 For the shewbread, and for the continual °meat offering, and for the continual °burnt offering, of the sabbaths, of the new moons, for the set feasts, and for the °holy *things*, and for the sin offerings to make an atonement for °Israel, and *for* all the work of the house of our [28]God.

34 And we cast the lots among the priests, the Levites, and the people, for °the wood offering, to bring *it* into the house of our [28]God, after the houses of our fathers, at times appointed year by year, to °burn upon the altar of [29]the LORD our [28]God, as *it is* °written in the law:

C³ 35 And to bring the firstfruits of our ground, and the firstfruits of all fruit of all trees, year by year, unto the house of [29]the LORD:

36 Also the firstborn of our sons, and of our cattle, as *it is* [34]written in the law, and the firstlings of our herds and of our flocks, to bring to the house of our [28]God, unto the priests that minister in the house of our [28]God:

37 And *that* we should bring the firstfruits of our dough, and our °offerings, and the fruit of all manner of trees, of °wine and of oil, unto the priests, to the chambers of the house of our [28]God; and the tithes of our ground unto the Levites, that the same Levites might have the tithes in all the cities of our tillage.

w 38 And the priest the son of Aaron shall be with the Levites, when the Levites take tithes: and the Levites shall bring up the tithe of the tithes unto the house of our [28]God, to the chambers, °into the treasure house.

39 For the °children of Israel and the °children of Levi shall bring the offering of the corn, of the new wine, and the oil, unto the chambers, where *are* the vessels of the sanctuary, and the priests that minister, and the porters, and the singers: and we will °not forsake the house of our [28]God.

H (N) D (p. 648) 404-403 **11** And the °rulers of the People °dwelt at Jerusalem:

E the rest of the People also cast lots, to bring one of ten to dwell in Jerusalem the °holy city, and nine parts *to dwell* in *other* cities.

A D 2 And the People blessed all the °men, that willingly offered themselves to dwell at Jerusalem.

E F¹ 3 Now these *are* the °chief of the province that dwelt in Jerusalem:

G¹ °but in the cities of Judah dwelt every °one in his possession in their cities, *to wit*, °Israel, the priests, and the Levites, and °the Nethinims, and the °children of Solomon's servants.

F² H¹ t 4 And at Jerusalem dwelt *certain* of the [3]children of Judah,

u and of the [3]children of Benjamin.

t Of the [3]children of Judah; Athaiah the son of Uzziah, the son of Zechariah, the son of Amariah, the son of Shephatiah, the son of Mahalaleel, of the [3]children of Perez;

5 And Maaseiah the son of Baruch, the son of Col-hozeh, the son of Hazaiah, the son of Adaiah, the son of Joiarib, the son of Zechariah, the son of °Shiloni.

6 All the sons of Perez that dwelt at Jerusalem *were* four hundred threescore and eight valiant [2]men.

7 And these *are* the sons of Benjamin; Sallu the son of Meshullam, the son of Joed, the son of Pedaiah, the son of Kolaiah, the son of Maaseiah, the son of Ithiel, the son of Jesaiah. u

---

32 shekel. See Ap. 51. II. 5.
33 meat offering = gift, or meal offering. Heb. *minchah.* See Ap. 43. II. iii.
burnt offering. Ap. 43. II. ii.
holy. See note on Ex. 3. 5.
Israel. See note on 1 Kings 12. 17.
34 the wood offering. Heb. the offering of wood. Fig. *Hypallage.* Ap. 6. Not prescribed by the law. Josephus calls it *Xylophory*, or wood-bearing. A feast kept on the 22nd of Ab, and at other times.
burn. Heb. *bā'ar*, to consume. Not *yāzath* (as in 1. 3; 2. 17); or *sāraph* (as in 4. 2. Ap. 43. I. viii.).
written in the law. See note on Ex. 17. 14, and Ap. 47.
37 offerings = heave offerings. See Ap. 43. II. viii.
wine = new wine. Heb. *tīrōsh.* Ap. 27. ii.
38 into = attached to.
39 children = sons.
not forsake: not fail to provide for. Sept. has same word as Heb. 10. 25, *egkataleipontes.*

11. 1-36 (*H*, p. 616; (*N*), p. 617). **JERUSALEM. RESIDENCES IN.** (*Alternation.*)

H | D | 1-. Dwelling. Proportion.
  E | -1. The dwellers. Distribution.
  D | 2. Dwelling. Blessing.
  E | 3-36. The dwellers. Distribution.

1 rulers = princes.
dwelt. At this time more thickly peopled than 7. 4.
holy. See note on Ex. 3. 5.
2 men. Heb. pl. of *'ĕnōsh.* Ap. 14. III.

3-36 (*E*, above). **THE DWELLERS.** (*Repeated Alternation.*)

E | F¹ | 3-. In Jerusalem.
  G¹ | -3. In the cities.
  F² | 4-19. In Jerusalem.
  G² | 20. In the cities.
  F³ | 21-24. In Jerusalem.
  G³ | 25-36. In the villages.

3 chief = heads. **but** = and.
one. Heb. *'īsh.* Ap. 14. II.
Israel. See note on 1 Kings 12. 17. The common name of the nation, not of the ten tribes merely.
the Nethinims. See note on Ezra 2. 43.
children = sons. Cp. 7. 57, 60. Ezra 2. 55, 58.

4-19 (F², above). **IN JERUSALEM.** (*Division.*)

F² | H¹ | 4-9. Civil.
  H² | 10-19. Sacred.

4-9 (H¹, above). **CIVIL.** (*Alternation.*)

H¹ | t | 4-. Judah.
  u | -4-. Benjamin.
  t | -4-6. Judah.
  u | 7-9. Benjamin.

5 Shiloni = the Shilonite.

404 8 And after him Gabbai, Sallai, nine hundred
to twenty and eight.
403 9 And Joel the son of Zichri *was* their overseer: and Judah the son of Senuah *was* second over the city.

H² J¹ 10 Of the priests: Jedaiah the son of Joiarib,
(p. 649) Jachin.

11 Seraiah the son of Hilkiah, the son of Meshullam, the son of Zadok, the son of Meraioth, the son of Ahitub, *was* the ruler of the house of °God.

12 And their brethren that did the work of the house *were* eight hundred twenty and two: and Adaiah the son of Jeroham, the son of Pelaliah, the son of Amzi, the son of Zechariah, the son of Pashur, the son of Malchiah,

13 And his brethren, °chief of the fathers, two hundred forty and two: and Amashai the son of Azareel, the son of Ahasai, the son of Meshillemoth, the son of Immer,

14 And their brethren, °mighty men of valour, an hundred twenty and eight: and their overseer *was* Zabdiel, the son of *one of* the great men.

J² 15 Also of the Levites: Shemaiah the son of Hashub, the son of Azrikam, the son of Hashabiah, the son of Bunni;

16 And Shabbethai and Jozabad, of the[13] chief of the Levites, *had* the oversight of the outward business of the house of °God.

17 And Mattaniah the son of Micha, the son of Zabdi, the son of Asaph, *was* °the principal to begin the thanksgiving in prayer: and Bakbukiah the second among his brethren, and °Abda the son of Shammua, the son of Galal, the son of Jeduthun.

18 All the Levites in the °holy city *were* two hundred fourscore and four.

J³ 19 Moreover the porters, Akkub, Talmon, and their brethren that kept the gates, *were* an hundred seventy and two.

G² 20 And the residue of Israel, of the priests,
(p. 648) *and* the Levites, *were* in all the cities of Judah, every °one in his inheritance.

F³ 21 But °the Nethinims dwelt in Ophel: and Ziha and Gispa *were* over °the Nethinims.

22 The overseer also of the Levites at Jerusalem *was* Uzzi the son of Bani, the son of Hashabiah, the son of Mattaniah, the son of Micha. Of the sons of Asaph, the singers *were* over the business of the house of[11] God.

23 For *it was* °the king's commandment concerning them, that a certain portion should be for the singers, due for every day.

24 And Pethahiah the son of Meshezabeel, of the[3] children of Zerah the son of Judah, *was* at the king's hand in all matters concerning the people.

G³ K¹ 25 And for the °villages, °with their fields,
(p. 649) *some* of the[3] children of Judah dwelt at Kirjath-arba, and *in* the °villages thereof, and at Dibon, and *in* the °villages thereof, and at Jekabzeel, and *in* the °villages thereof,

26 And at Jeshua, and at Moladah, and at Beth-phelet,

27 And at Hazar-shual, and at Beer-sheba, and *in* the[25] villages thereof,

28 And at Ziklag, and at Mekonah, and in the[25] villages thereof,

29 And at °En-rimmon, and at Zareah, and at Jarmuth,

30 °Zanoah, Adullam, and *in* their[25] villages, at Lachish, and the fields thereof, at Azekah, and *in* the[25] villages thereof. And they °dwelt from Beer-sheba unto the valley of Hinnom.

31 The[3] children also of Benjamin from Geba *dwelt* at Michmash, and Aija, and Beth- K²
el, and *in* their[25] villages,

32 *And* at Anathoth, Nob, Ananiah,

33 Hazor, Ramah, Gittaim,

34 Hadid, Zeboim, Neballat,

35 Lod, and Ono, °the valley of °craftsmen.

36 And of the Levites °*were* divisions *in* K³
Judah, *and* in Benjamin.

12 Now °these *are* the priests and the J v
Levites that went up with Zerubbabel the son of Shealtiel, and Jeshua: Seraiah, Jeremiah, °Ezra,

---

11. 10-19 (H², p. 648). SACRED.
(*Division.*)

H² | J¹ | 10-14. The priests.
| J² | 15-18. The Levites.
| J³ | 19. The porters.

11 God. Heb. Elohim. Ap. 4. I.

13 chief=heads.

14 mighty men. Heb. *Gibbōr.* Ap. 14. IV.

16 God. Heb. Elohim (with Art.)=the [true] God. Ap. 4. I.

17 the principal to begin the thanksgiving. Or, [was] head: "the starting point [was], he was to praise at the time of prayer."

Abda the son of Shammua. Probably=Obadiah the son of Shemaiah, as in 1 Chron. 9. 16.

18 holy. See note on Ex. 3. 5, or, = the Sanctuary's city.

20 one=man. Heb. *'ish.* Ap. 14. II.

21 the Nethinims . . . the Nethinims. Fig. *Epanadiplōsis.* Ap. 6. The clause beginning and ending with the same word. See note on Ezra 2. 43.

23 the king's: i. e. Darius Hystaspis. Cp. Ezra 7. 24. See Ap. 57 and 58.

25-36 (G³, p. 648). IN THE VILLAGES.
(*Division.*)

G³ | K¹ | 25-30. Judah. } Civil.
| K² | 31-35. Benjamin. }
| K³ | 36. Levites. Sacred.

25 villages. Heb. daughters, i. e. of the mother city.

with their fields=in their fields: i. e. unwalled (Lev. 25. 31). Cp., for the names that follow, Josh. 15. 13, &c.

29 En-rimmon. Now *Khan Umm er Rŭmāmīm.* (Cp. Josh. 15. 32; 19. 7; 1 Chron. 4. 32.)

30 Zanoah. Now *Khan Zanūta.*

dwelt=encamped.

35 the valley of craftsmen. Cp. 6. 2 and 1 Chron. 4. 14.

craftsmen=artificers.

36 were divisions, &c.: or, "Judah's divisions [were assigned] to Benjamin".

12. 1-26 (*J*, p. 616; (*N*), p. 617). THE RETURN UNDER EZRA. (*Alternation.*)

J | v | 1-7. Priests. }
| w | 8, 9. Levites. } Names.
| *v* | 10-21. Priests. }
| *w* | 22-26. Levites. }

1 these. Nehemiah had given the heads of families (7. 6-73) and the numbers of the four classes of priests (7. 39-42). Cp. Ezra 2. 36-39. Here he inserts twenty-two names, the heads of priests' classes, or courses formed out of these four, "in the days of Jeshua" (*v.* 7). See Ezra 6. 18.

Ezra. Not *the* Ezra of the book of Ezra.

408 2 Amariah, Malluch, Hattush,
3 Shechaniah, Rehum, Meremoth,
4 Iddo, Ginnetho, Abijah,
5 Miamin, Maadiah, Bilgah,
6 Shemaiah, and Joiarib, Jedaiah,
7 Sallu, Amok, Hilkiah, Jedaiah. These *were* the °chief of the priests and of their brethren in the days of Jeshua.

w (p. 649) 8 Moreover °the Levites: Jeshua, Binnui, Kadmiel, Sherebiah, Judah, *and* Mattaniah, *which was* over the thanksgiving, he and his brethren.
9 Also Bakbukiah and Unni, their brethren, *were* °over against them °in the watches.

v 10 And Jeshua begat Joiakim, Joiakim also begat Eliashib, and Eliashib begat Joiada,
11 And Joiada begat Jonathan, and Jonathan begat Jaddua.
12 And in the days of Joiakim were priests, the [7] chief of the fathers: of Seraiah, Meraiah; of Jeremiah, Hananiah;
13 Of Ezra, Meshullam; of Amariah, Jehohanan;
14 Of Melicu, Jonathan; of °Shebaniah, Joseph;
15 Of Harim, Adna; of Meraioth, °Helkai;
16 Of Iddo, Zechariah; of Ginnethon, Meshullam;
17 Of Abijah, Zichri; of Miniamin, of Moadiah, Piltai;
18 Of Bilgah, Shammua; of Shemaiah, Jehonathan;
19 And of Joiarib, Mattenai; of Jedaiah, Uzzi;
20 Of Sallai, Kallai; of Amok, Eber;
21 Of Hilkiah, Hashabiah; of Jedaiah, Nethaneel.

w 22 The Levites in the days of Eliashib, Joiada, and Johanan, and Jaddua, *were* recorded [7] chief of the fathers: also the priests, to the reign of °Darius the Persian.
23 The sons of Levi, the [7] chief of the fathers, *were* written in °the book of the chronicles, even until the days of Johanan the son of Eliashib.
24 And the [7] chief of the Levites: Hashabiah, Sherebiah, and Jeshua the son of Kadmiel, with their brethren over against them, to praise *and* to give thanks, according to the commandment of David °the °man of °God, ward over against ward.
25 Mattaniah, and Bakbukiah, Obadiah, Meshullam, Talmon, Akkub, *were* porters keeping the °ward at the °thresholds of the gates.
26 These *were* in the days of Joiakim the son of Jeshua, the son of Jozadak, and in the days of Nehemiah the °governor, and of Ezra the priest, the scribe.

E L^1O^1 (p. 650) 27 And at the dedication of the wall of Jerusalem they sought the Levites out of all their places, to bring them to Jerusalem, to keep the dedication with gladness, both °with thanksgivings, and with singing, *with* cymbals, psalteries, and with harps.

P^1 28 And the sons of °the singers gathered themselves together, both out of the °plain country round about Jerusalem, and from the villages of Netophathi;

7 chief = heads.
8 the Levites. Cp. Ezra 2. 40 and 7. 43, above.
9 over against = corresponding to those in *v.* 8.
in the watches: i. e. the courses, or waitings.
14 Shebaniah. Some codices, with two early printed editions, Sept., and Syr., read "Shechaniah".
15 Helkai. Some codices, with six early printed editions, read "Hilkai".
22 Darius = Darius Hystaspis. See Ap. 57 and 58.
23 the book of the chronicles: i. e. the public records or registers.
24 the man of God. See Ap. 49.
man. Heb. *'ish*. Ap. 14. II.
God. Heb. Elohim (with Art.) = the [true] God. Ap. 4. I.
25 ward = charge.
thresholds = gatherings or storehouses.
26 governor = Pasha. Chald. *pechah*.

12. 27—13. 31 (*E*, p. 616; (*K*), p. 617). THE WALL. DEDICATION. INTERNAL DISORDERS OVERCOME. (*Division.*)

E | L^1 | 12. 27-47. Dedication of the wall.
| L^2 | 13. 1-31. Internal disorders overcome.

12. 27-47 (L^1, above). DEDICATION OF THE WALL. (*Introversion.*)

L^1 | M | O^1 | 27. Assemblage. Levites.
P^1 | 28, 29. Singers.
P^2 | 30. Priests and Levites.
O^2 | 31-. Assemblage. Princes of Judah.
N | Q^1 | -31-. The two companies.
R^1 | -31-37. Right hand. Thanksgiving.
N | R^2 | 38, 39. Left hand. Thanksgiving.
Q^2 | 40-. The two companies.
M | O^3 | -40-42. Assemblage. In detail.
P^3 | 43. Offerings. Rejoicing.
P^4 | 44. Offerings. Rejoicing.
O^4 | 45-47. Assemblage. In sum.

27 with thanksgivings. Ps. 147 would have been a suitable psalm for the occasion, and Ps. 122.
28 the singers. Mentioned in *v.* 24.
plain country = surrounding country.
29 the house of Gilgal. Heb. Beth-Gilgal.
31 companies of them that gave thanks. Heb. celebrations; "celebrations", or thanksgivings, put for the choirs who rendered them, by Fig. *Metonymy* (of Effect), Ap. 6.
32 Hoshaiah. Cp. Jer. 42. 1; 43. 2.
33 Ezra. Not Ezra the scribe.

29 Also from °the house of Gilgal, and out of the fields of Geba and Azmaveth: for the singers had builded them villages round about Jerusalem.

30 And the priests and the Levites purified themselves, and purified the People, and the gates, and the wall. P^2

31 Then I brought up the princes of Judah upon the wall, O^2

and appointed two great °*companies of them that gave* thanks, N Q^1

whereof one went on the right hand upon the wall toward the dung gate: R^1
32 And after them went °Hoshaiah, and half of the princes of Judah,
33 And Azariah, °Ezra, and Meshullam,
34 Judah, and Benjamin, and Shemaiah, and Jeremiah,
35 And *certain* of the priests' sons with

403 trumpets; *namely*, Zechariah the son of Jonathan, the son of Shemaiah, the son of Mattaniah, the son of Michaiah, the son of Zaccur, the son of Asaph:
36 And his brethren, Shemaiah, and Azarael, Milalai, Gilalai, Maai, Nethaneel, and Judah, Hanani, with the musical instruments °of David [24] the man of [24] God, and Ezra the scribe before them.
37 And at the fountain gate, which was over against them, they went up by °the stairs of the city of David, at the going up of the wall, above the house of David, even unto the water gate eastward.
N R² (p. 650) 38 And the other [31] *company of them that gave* thanks went over against *them*, and I after them, and the half of the people upon the wall, from beyond the tower of the furnaces even unto the broad wall;
39 And from above the gate of Ephraim, and above the old gate, and above the fish gate, and the tower of Hananeel, and the tower of Meah, even unto the sheep gate: and they stood still in the prison gate.
Q² 40 So stood the two [31] *companies of them that gave* thanks °in the house of [24] God,
M O³ and I, and the half of the rulers with me:
41 And the priests; Eliakim, Maaseiah, Miniamin, Michaiah, Elioenai, Zechariah, *and* Hananiah, with trumpets;
42 And Maaseiah, and Shemaiah, and Eleazar, and Uzzi, and Jehohanan, and Malchijah, and Elam, and Ezer. And the singers sang loud, with Jezrahiah *their* overseer.
P³ 43 Also that day they °offered great sacrifices, and rejoiced: for [24] God had made them rejoice with great joy: the wives also and the °children rejoiced: so that the joy of Jerusalem was heard even afar off.
P⁴ 44 And at that time were °some appointed over the chambers for the treasures, for the °offerings, for the firstfruits, and for the tithes, to gather °into them out of the fields of the cities the portions °of the law for the priests and Levites: for Judah rejoiced for the priests and for the Levites that waited.
O⁴ 45 And both the singers and the porters kept the °ward of their °God, and the ward of the purification, according to the commandment of David, *and* of Solomon his son.
46 For in the days of David and Asaph of old *there were* chief of the singers, and songs of praise and thanksgiving unto [45] God.
47 And °all Israel in the days of Zerubbabel, and in the days of Nehemiah, gave the portions of the singers and the porters, every day his portion: and they sanctified *holy things* unto the Levites; and the Levites sanctified *them* unto the °children of Aaron.

L² S x (p. 651) **13** °On that day they read in °the book of Moses in the audience of the People; and therein °was found written, that the Ammonite and the °Moabite should not come into the °congregation of °God for ever;
2 °Because they met not the °children of Israel with bread and with water, but °hired Balaam against °them, that he should °curse
them: howbeit our °God turned the curse into a blessing.
y 3 Now it came to pass, when they had heard the law, that they separated from Israel all the °mixed multitude.
x 4 °And before this, Eliashib the priest, having the oversight of the chamber of the house of our [2] God, *was* allied unto Tobiah:
5 And he had prepared for him a great chamber, where aforetime they laid the °meat offerings, the frankincense, and the vessels, and the tithes of the corn, the °new wine, and the oil, which was commanded *to be given* to the Levites, and the singers, and the porters; and the °offerings of the priests.
6 But in all this *time* was °not I at Jerusalem: for in °the two and thirtieth year of

36 of David: i. e. dating from, or invented by him.
37 the stairs. See 3. 15.
40 in = at.
43 offered. Heb. *zābăch*. Ap. 43. I. iv.
children = offspring.
44 some = men. Heb. *'enōsh*. Ap. 14. III.
offerings = heave offerings. Heb. *t^erūmāh*. Ap. 43. II. viii.
into them = by them: i. e. these officers; not into the chambers, for "chambers" is fem. and "them" is masc.
of the law. So in Cod. Hillel; but some codices, with one early printed edition, read "portions for thanksgiving".
45 ward = charge.
God. Heb. Elohim. Ap. 4. I.
47 all Israel. Used of Judah, Benjamin, and those who returned with them. See note on 1 Kings 12. 17.
children = sons.

13. 1-31 (L², p. 650). INTERNAL DISORDERS OVERCOME. (*Introversion.*)

L² | S | 1-9. Strangers.
  T | 10-14. Sin. Cheating.
  T | 15-22. Sin. Sabbath-breaking.
S | 23-31. Strangers.

1-9 (S, above). STRANGERS. (*Alternation.*)

S | x | 1, 2. Lawful exclusion.
  y | 3. Separation.
  x | 4-7. Unlawful inclusion.
  y | 8, 9. Separation.

1 On that day: i. e. of which he is about to write.
the book of Moses. See Ap. 47.
was found written = they came to the place or passage (viz. Deut. 23. 3-6). Not a discovery, but in the course of the public reading (as in Luke 4. 17). Cp. 8. 14.
Moabite (masc.). This did not therefore exclude Ruth, a female, though married to Mahlon before Boaz.
congregation = assembly, or muster.
God. Heb. Elohim (with Art.) = the [true] God. Ap. 4. I.
2 Because they (pl.). Num. 22. 56. Deut. 23. 3, 4.
children = sons.
hired Balaam. Num. 22. 5, 6. Josh. 24. 9, 10.
them (sing.), i. e. Israel.
curse. Heb. *ķālal* = reproach, imprecate.
God. Heb. Elohim. Ap. 4. I.
3 mixed multitude. Always a snare. Cp. Num. 11. 4.
4 And before this. See longer note on 13. 4-9, p. 653.
5 meat offerings = gift offerings. Heb. *minchah*. Ap. 43. II. iii.
new wine. Heb. *tīrōsh*. Ap. 27. ii.
offerings = heave offerings. Ap. 43. II. viii.
6 not I at Jerusalem. Nehemiah did not return with Haggai and Zachariah at the beginning of this reign. See longer note on p. 653.
the two and thirtieth year. See longer note on p. 653.

403 ° Artaxerxes king of Babylon came I unto the
king, and after certain days ° obtained I leave
of the king:

7 And I came to Jerusalem, and understood
of the ° evil that Eliashib did for Tobiah, in
preparing him a chamber in the courts of the
house of [1] God.

y (p. 651) 8 And it grieved me sore: therefore ° I cast
forth all the household stuff of Tobiah out of
the chamber.

9 Then I commanded, and they cleansed the
chambers: and thither brought I again the
vessels of the house of [1] God, with the [5] meat
offering and the frankincense.

T z (p. 652) 10 And I perceived that the portions of the
Levites had not been given *them:* for the
Levites and the singers, that did the work,
were fled every ° one to his field.

a 11 Then contended I with the rulers, and
said, "Why is the house of [1] God forsaken?"
And I gathered them together, and set them
in their place.

12 Then brought all Judah the tithe of the
corn and the new [5] wine and the oil unto the
treasuries.

13 And ° I made treasurers over the treasuries,
Shelemiah the priest, and Zadok the scribe, and
of the Levites, Pedaiah: and ° next to them
was Hanan the son of Zaccur, the son of ° Mattaniah:
for they were counted faithful, and
their office *was* to distribute unto their brethren.

b 14 Remember me, O my [1] God, concerning
this, and wipe not out my ° good deeds that
I have done for the house of my [1] God, and for
the ° offices thereof.

T z 15 In those days saw I in Judah *some* treading
° wine presses on the sabbath, and bringing
in sheaves, and lading asses; as also wine,
grapes, and figs, and all *manner of* burdens,
which they brought into Jerusalem on the
sabbath day: and I testified *against them* in
the day wherein they sold victuals.

16 There dwelt men of Tyre also therein,
which brought fish, and all manner of ware,
and sold on the sabbath unto the [2] children of
Judah, ° and in Jerusalem.

a 17 Then I contended with the nobles of Judah,
and said unto them, "What [7] evil thing *is*
this that ye do, and profane the sabbath day?

18 Did not your fathers thus, and did not our
[1] God bring all this [7] evil upon us, and upon this
city? yet ye bring more wrath upon Israel by
° profaning the ° sabbath."

19 And it came to pass, that when the gates
of Jerusalem began to be dark before the sabbath,
I commanded that the gates should be
shut, and charged that they should not be
opened till after the sabbath: and *some* of my
servants set I at the gates, *that* there should
no burden be brought in on the sabbath day.

20 So the merchants and sellers of all kind of
ware lodged without Jerusalem once or twice.

21 Then I testified against them, and said
unto them, "Why ° lodge ye about the wall?
if ye do *so* again, I will lay hands on you."
From that time forth came they no *more* on
the sabbath.

22 And I commanded the Levites that they
should cleanse themselves, and *that* they
should come *and* keep the gates, to sanctify
the sabbath day.

Remember me, O my [1] God, *concerning* this b
also, and spare me according to the ° greatness
of Thy ° mercy.

23 In those days also saw I Jews *that* ° had S U
married wives of ° Ashdod, of Ammon, *and* of
Moab:

24 And their [2] children spake half in the speech
of Ashdod, and could not speak in the Jews'
language, but ° according to the language of
each people.

25 And I contended with them, and ° cursed V c
them, and ° smote ° certain of them, and plucked
off their hair,

Artaxerxes = Darius Hystaspis. See longer note on p. 653.

obtained I leave = I earnestly requested. Heb. *shā'al*. See note on "enquire", 1 Sam. 28. 6, 7.

7 evil. Heb. *rā'a'*. Ap. 44. VIII.

8 I cast forth. His authority was not disputed. Malachi (2-4) also rebukes the People.

13. 10-22 (T and *T*, p. 651). NON-PAYMENT. (*Extended Alternation.*)

T | z | 10. Neglect. Tithes.
  a | 11-13. Reformation.
    b | 14. Prayer.
T | *z* | 15, 16. Neglect. Sabbath.
  a | 17-22-. Reformation.
    b | -22. Prayer.

10 one = man. Heb. *'ish*. Ap. 14. II.

13 I made treasurers: or, I set in charge.

next to them: or, to help them.

Mattaniah. Cp. 11. 17.

14 good deeds = kindnesses.

offices = charges.

15 wine presses. Heb. *gath*, a wine press; not *yekeb*, a wine vat.

16 and. Some codices, with six early printed editions, Syr., and Vulg., omit this "and".

18 profaning. Notwithstanding the covenant made in 10. 31.

sabbath. A special various reading called *Sevîr* (Ap. 34), one early printed edition, and Syr., add the word "day", as in *v.* 17.

21 lodge. See note on 4. 22.

22 greatness = abundance.

mercy = lovingkindness, or, grace.

23-31 (*S*, p. 651). STRANGERS. (*Alternations.*)

S | U | 23, 24. Unlawful marriages. (General.)
  V | c | 25-. Action.
    d | -25. Adjuration.
    c | 26. Words.
    d | 27. Adjuration.
U | 28-. Unlawful marriage. (Particular.)
  V | e | -28. Action. Expulsion.
    f | 29. Prayer.
    e | 30, 31-. Action. Cleansing.
    f | -31. Prayer.

23 had married. Notwithstanding the covenant of 10. 30 and Ezra 10. 12, 14.

Ashdod. Now, *Esdûd*. Josh. 15. 46. 1 Sam. 5 and 6. The Azotus of Acts 8. 40.

24 according to the language. Some codices, with four early printed editions, read "but with the tongue"

25 cursed: i. e. caused them to be cursed. Heb. idiom. Heb. *kālal*, as in *v.* 2.

smote. Heb. idiom = caused them to be smitten (as in Matt. 27. 26. Mark 15. 15. John 19. 1).

certain = men. Heb. *'ĕnōsh*. Ap. 14. III.

d (p. 652) 403 and made them swear by [1]God, *saying*, "Ye shall not give your daughters unto their sons, nor take their daughters unto your sons, or for yourselves.

c 26 °Did not Solomon king of Israel °sin by these things? yet among °many nations was there no king like him, who was beloved of his [1]God, and [1]God made him king over all Israel: nevertheless even him did °outlandish women cause to °sin.

d 27 °Shall we then hearken unto you to do all this great °evil, to °transgress against our [1]God in marrying °strange wives?"

U 28 And °*one* of the sons of Joiada, the son of Eliashib the high priest, *was* son in law to Sanballat the Horonite:

V e therefore I chased him from me.

f 29 Remember them, O my [1]God, because °they have defiled the priesthood, and the °covenant of the priesthood, and of the Levites.

e 30 Thus cleansed I them from all [27]strangers, and appointed the °wards of the priests and the Levites, every [10]one in his business;

31 And for °the wood offering, at times appointed, and for the firstfruits.

°Remember me, O my [1]God, for good. f

26 Did not Solomon . . . ? Fig. *Erotēsis*. Ap. 6. Cp. 1 Kings 11. 2 Sam. 12. 24, 25.
sin. Heb. *chāṭā'*. Ap. 44. i.
many = the many.
outlandish = the foreign. Heb. *nakrī*.
27 Shall we . . . ? Fig. *Erotēsis*. Ap. 6.
evil. Heb. *rā'a'*. Ap. 44. viii.
transgress. Heb. *mā'al*. Ap. 44. xi.
strange = foreign. Heb. *nakar*, as in *v.* 30.
28 one of the sons, &c. Joiada the son of Eliashbi was led astray by the degeneracy of his father (*v.* 4), and married the daughter of Sanballat (2. 10). Joiada's son was Manasseh, who, according to Josephus (*Ant.* xi. 8. 3), fled to Samaria, where Sanballat built the Samaritan temple at Gerizim, and made Manasseh the high priest of it.
29 they have defiled. Cp. Mal. 2. 1-8. Heb. *gā'al*, a *Homonym*. See note on Ezra 2. 62.
covenant. Cp. 9. 38.
30 wards of = charges for. N.B. no Art. here.
31 the wood offering. See note on 10. 34, 35.
Remember me. Thus ends the latest sacred history of the O.T.; chronological, not canonical. In 2 Macc. 2. 13 it is recorded of Nehemiah "how he, founding a library, gathered together the books about the kings and prophets, and the books of David, and letters of kings about sacred gifts".

LONGER NOTES ON SPECIAL PASSAGES IN NEHEMIAH.

2. 1 the twentieth year. The "seventy sevens" of Dan. 9. 24-27 begin here (454 B.C.).

The "seven sevens" (Dan. 9. 25), or forty-nine years begin here, and end in 405 B.C.; marked by the completion and dedication of the second Temple.

The "threescore and two sevens" (Dan. 9. 26), or 434 years begin (or rather, follow on) in 405 B.C., and end in A.D. 29, the year of the Cross.

The last "seven" is therefore, still future.

The first four of the "seven sevens" ended in 426 B.C., marked by the Decree of Cyrus, which ended the Babylonian Servitude of seventy years. See Ap. 50, 57, and 58.

5. 14-19 Moreover from the time that I was appointed, &c. Verses 14-19 are put within brackets for the following reasons:

As Nehemiah's record must have been written many years later, after the dedication both of the Temple (405 B.C.) and the Wall (403 B.C.), the reference to his policy during the twelve years of his governorship, from the twentieth to the thirty-second year of ARTAXERXES (DARIUS HYSTASPIS, 419-407 B.C.), is introduced here, in order to emphasise the contrast between the rapacity of "the nobles and rulers" (5. 7), and his own conduct. For he says that, not only at that time (454 B.C.) did he not exploit the people for his own advantage, but that during his governorship (which ended in 407 B.C., some four or five years at least before the time of his writing the final record, more than forty years later than 454), when, according to Eastern views, he would have been justified in getting as much as he could out of his office, he not only lived entirely at his own charges but supported others also. See note below on 13. 4-9.

7. 4 the houses were not builded = no sign of houses being built. This statement refers to the permanent stable habitations of the city proper which Haggai speaks of as being in existence forty-four years later (Hag. 1. 4, 9). The word *bayith*, house, means a dwelling, and in 2. 3 and 3. 31 is rendered "place", which clearly indicates its meaning in these passages. Among the ruined houses left by Nebuchadnezzar many might easily have been made habitable sufficiently to fulfil the conditions of 8. 16.

7. 5 I found a register of the genealogy of them which came up at the first. It must be borne in mind that Nehemiah wrote long after this date (426 B.C.); probably between 403 and 400 B.C. It is quite natural therefore that he should write of finding such a book as this. When he says, "I found a book", &c., it does not mean that Nehemiah found or discovered the register *at that time*; but, writing long after, he says, "I find that the list of names was, so and so", &c.

13. 4-9 And before this . . . the two and thirtieth year of Artaxerxes king of Babylon (13. 6). The ARTAXERXES (= great king) here is DARIUS HYSTASPIS. The record here *must* have been written *after* the dedication of both Temple (405 B.C.) and Wall (403 B.C.). The thirty-second year is that of the king's age, not of his reign, for he only succeeded CAMBYSES in 411 B.C. His twentieth year (5. 14) was 419 B.C., when, on the death of Cyrus, NEHEMIAH was "appointed" to be "governor in the land of Judah".

Consequently Nehemiah's twelve years of governorship end in 407 B.C., two years before the completion and dedication of the Temple, and when DARIUS HYSTASPIS had been reigning three years.

In that year (407) NEHEMIAH evidently receives a report from his deputy (probably HANANI still) as to the Temple progress, and doubtless of the ELIASHIB-TOBIAH scandal. He determines to go himself, obtains leave of absence (with difficulty, apparently, 13. 6), and comes to Jerusalem. Arriving there, he "understands" the evil concerning Eliashib, casts forth TOBIAH and his "stuff", and hurries on the Temple work towards completion.

ESTHER.

THE STRUCTURE OF THE BOOK AS A WHOLE.

(Introversions and Alternations.)

A[1] | 1. 1. AHASUERUS. REIGN. EXTENT OF KINGDOM.

B[1] | D[1] | 1. 2—2. 20. AHASUERUS. ON HIS THRONE.

E[1] | F | 2. 21-23. MORDECAI. DISCOVERY OF PLOT (BIGTHAN AND TERESH).

G | 3. 1-15. HAMAN. HIS PLOT.

F | 4. 1-3. MORDECAI. DISCOVERY OF HAMAN'S PLOT.

C[1] | 4. 4—5. 14. ESTHER. HER INTERCESSION.

B[2] | D[2] | 6. 1. AHASUERUS. ON HIS BED.

E[2] | H | 6. 2, 3. MORDECAI. KING'S INQUIRY.

J | 6. 4-9. HAMAN. KING'S INQUIRY.

H | 6. 10-14. MORDECAI. KING'S COMMAND.

C[2] | 7. 1. ESTHER. HER BANQUET.

B[3] | D[3] | 7. 2-. AHASUERUS. AT ESTHER'S TABLE.

E[3] | K | 7. -2. KING. INQUIRY AND PROMISE.

L | 7. 3, 4. ESTHER. PLEA FOR LIFE.

K | 7. 5-10. KING. INQUIRY AND WRATH.

C[3] | 8. 1-. ESTHER. HER ROYAL GIFT.

B[4] | D[4] | 8. -1, 2. AHASUERUS. ON HIS THRONE.

E | M | 8. 3-6. ESTHER. PLEA FOR HER PEOPLE.

N | 8. 7-17. KING. DECREE.

M | 9. 1-28. ESTHER. PLEA FOR HER PEOPLE.

C[4] | 9. 29-32. ESTHER. HER ROYAL AUTHORITY.

A[2] | 10. 1-3. AHASUERUS. REIGN. EXTENT OF KINGDOM.

THE °BOOK OF ESTHER.

A[1] 472–422 (Regnal)
1 °Now it came to pass in the days of °Ahasuerus, (°this *is* Ahasuerus which reigned, °from India even unto Ethiopia, *over* °an hundred and seven and twenty provinces:)

D[1] A[1] a (p. 655)
2 *That* °in those days, when the king [1]Ahasuerus °sat on the throne of his kingdom, which *was* in °Shushan the °palace,
3 In °the third year of his reign, he made °a feast unto all his princes and his servants; the °power of °Persia and Media, the nobles and princes of the provinces, *being* before him:

b
4 When he shewed the riches of his glorious kingdom and the honour of his excellent majesty many days, *even* °an hundred and fourscore days.

a
5 And when these days were expired, the king made [3]a feast unto all the people that were present in Shushan the [2]palace, both unto great and small, seven days, in the court of the garden of the king's °palace;
6 *Where were* white, green, and blue, *hangings*, fastened with cords of fine linen and purple to silver rings and pillars of marble: the °beds *were of* gold and silver, upon a pavement of red, and blue, and white, and black, marble.
7 And they gave *them* drink in vessels of gold, (°the vessels being diverse one from another,) and royal °wine in abundance, according to the state of the king.
8 And the drinking *was* according to the °law; none did compel: for so the king had appointed to all the officers of his house, that they should do according to every °man's pleasure.
9 Also °Vashti the queen made a feast for the women *in* the royal house which *belonged* to king Ahasuerus.

b
10 On the seventh day, when the heart of the king was merry with wine, he °commanded Mehuman, Biztha, Harbona, Bigtha, and Abagtha, Zethar, and Carcas, the °seven chamberlains that served in the presence of [1]Ahasuerus the king,
11 To bring [9]Vashti the queen before the king with the crown royal, to shew the °people and the princes her beauty: for she *was* fair to look on.
12 But the queen [9]Vashti °refused to come at

TITLE, Book of Esther. One of the five *Megilloth*. For its place in the Hebrew Canon see Ap. 1. Read at the Feast of Purim. Comes *chronologically* thus: (1) Daniel; (2) Esther; (3) Nehemiah; (4) Ezra. The Divine name does not occur, except five times in the form of an *Acrostic* (Ap. 6). See Ap. 60, and notes on Est. 1. 20; 5. 4, 13; 7. 5, 7.

1 Now it came to pass in the days of. See important note of Rabbinical commentators on Gen. 14. 1.

Ahasuerus = the venerable king. An appellative, like Pharaoh, Czar, Shah, &c. See notes on p. 618 and Ap. 57 and 58.

this. Implying that others were so called, from whom he is to be distinguished. This Ahasuerus was Astyages (Gr.), Arsames (Persian). See Ap. 57 and 58. "This Ahasuerus" emphasises the one who was specially renowned. Fig. *Parenthesis*. Ap. 6.

from India even unto Ethiopia: i. e. the two extreme boundaries of the known world.

an hundred and seven and twenty provinces. Dan. 6. 1 says 120 princes. The number continually altered to suit the requirements of government. Only in Dan. 6. 1 do we find 120. Plato says that "when Darius (i. e. 'the Maintainer' = Astyages) came to the throne, being one of the seven, he divided the country into seven portions" (*De Legibus* iii). These are the seven named in *vv.* 13, 14. When Babylon afterward fell into his hands, he divided his newly acquired kingdom into 120 parts (Dan. 9. 1. Cp. 6. 1). Why should he not have added these to the seven he already possessed, and thus have made the 127 of Est. 1. 1; 9. 30? In the later days of Darius (Hystaspis) these had reduced to twenty-three, as stated and named on the *Behistūn* inscription.

1. 2—2. 20 (D[1], p. 654). AHASUERUS. ON HIS THRONE. (*Division.*)

D[1]	A[1]	1. 2-12. Queen Vashti. Offence.
	A[2]	1. 13—2. 1. Queen Vashti. Degradation.
	A[3]	2. 2-20. Queen Esther. Substituted.

1. 2-12 (A[1], above). QUEEN VASHTI. OFFENCE. (*Alternation.*)

A[1]	a	2, 3. Feast: king's to nobles.
	b	4. Display of riches.
	a	5-9. Feasts: king's to people; queen's to women.
	b	10-12. Display of Vashti.

2 in those days: i. e. the days when these events took place. At other times he dwelt at Ecbatana, or elsewhere. Verse 1 mentions the ruler; *v.* 2, the place; *v.* 3, the time. **sat** = took his seat, or came to.

Shushan. Now, the ruins of *Susa*, on the river Shapur, east of Persian Gulf.

palace = castle, or fortress. Cp. Neh. 1. 1.

3 the third year: i. e. in 471; six years after the destruction of Jerusalem. Astyages now seventeen or eighteen years. See Ap. 50. VII (5). In this year Xerxes (who is supposed to be this king), according to *Herod.* vii. 8, and *Diod. Sic.* xi. 2, was preparing his expedition against Greece; whereas this chapter presupposes a season of peace and quiet. **a feast.** For its own sake. No reason is given. **power.** Put by Fig. *Metonymy* (of Effect), Ap. 6, for those who exercised it: viz. the people of power. **Persia and Media.** In this book this is always the order, except 10. 2. In Daniel it is the reverse. **4 an hundred and fourscore days.** This was to allow all peoples to be feasted in turn. Not all at the same time; or one feast of that duration. **5 palace** = house, or, large house. **6 beds** = couches. **7 the vessels.** Note the frequent *Parentheses* (Ap. 6) in *vv.* 1, 7, 13, 14, 20. **wine.** Heb. *yayin*. Ap. 27. I. **8 law.** Heb. *dath* = royal decree, or special mandate, as in *vv.* 13, 15, 19; 3. 8; 4. 11, 16. **man's.** Heb. *'ish*. Ap. 14. II. **9 Vashti.** The daughter of Alyattes (king of Lydia), married by Cyaxares to his son Astyages after the battle of Halys. See Ap. 57. **10 commanded.** Heb. *'āmar*. So rendered in *vv.* 15, 17; 2. 20; 4. 13; 6. 1; 9. 14, 25. Note the different words rendered "command" and "decree" in this book. **seven chamberlains** = seven eunuchs. This shows the minuteness of the writer's knowledge. **11 people** = peoples. **12 refused.** Probably because sent for by servants; not by the nobles (*v.* 3), and before the "peoples" (*v.* 5).

471 the king's °commandment by *his* chamberlains: therefore was the king very wroth, and his anger burned in him.

A[2] c (p. 656) 13 Then the king said to the wise men, which knew the times, °(for so *was* the king's manner toward all that knew [8]law and judgment:

14 And the next unto him *was* Carshena, Shethar, Admatha, Tarshish, Meres, Marsena, *and* Memucan, the [10]seven princes of [3]Persia and Media, which saw the king's face, *and* which sat the first in the kingdom;)

15 "What shall we do unto the queen Vashti according to [8]law, because she hath not performed the [10]commandment of the king [1]Ahasuerus [12]by the chamberlains?"

d 16 And Memucan answered before the king and the princes, [9]"Vashti the queen hath not done wrong to the king only, but also to all the princes, and to all the [11]people that *are* in all the provinces of the king [1]Ahasuerus.

17 For *this* deed of the queen shall come abroad unto all women, so that they shall despise their husbands in their eyes, when it shall be reported, 'The king [1]Ahasuerus [10]commanded [9]Vashti the queen to be brought in before him, but she came not.'

18 *Likewise* shall the °ladies of [3]Persia and Media say this day unto all the king's princes, which have heard of the deed of the queen. Thus *shall there arise* too much contempt and wrath.

19 If it please the king, let there go a royal [12]commandment from him, and let it be written among the [8]laws of the [3]Persians and the Medes, that it be °not altered, That [9]Vashti come no more before king [1]Ahasuerus; and let the king give her royal estate unto another that is better than she.

20 And when the king's °decree which he shall make shall be published throughout all his empire, [7](for °it is great,) °ALL THE WIVES SHALL GIVE to their husbands honour, both to great and small."

c 21 And the saying pleased the king and the princes; and the king did according to the word of Memucan:

d 22 For he sent letters into all the king's provinces, into every province according to the writing thereof, and to every people after their language, that every [8]man should bear rule in his own house, and that *it* should be published according to the language of every people.

A[3] B[1] **2** °After these things, when the wrath of king °Ahasuerus was appeased, he remembered °Vashti, and what she had done, and what was decreed against her.

2 Then said the king's servants that ministered unto him, "Let there be fair young °virgins sought for the king:

3 And let the king appoint officers in all the provinces of his kingdom, that they may gather together all the fair young [2]virgins unto Shushan the palace, to the house of the women, unto the °custody of Hege the king's °chamberlain, keeper of the women; and let their things for purification be given *them*:

4 And let the °maiden which pleaseth the king be queen instead of [1]Vashti." And the thing pleased the king; and he did so.

commandment. Heb. *dābar* = word, precept. Occurs *v.* 19; 2. 8; 3. 15; 8. 14, 17. See note on *v.* 10.

13 for. See note on the parentheses, *v.* 7.

1. 13-22 (A[2], p. 655). QUEEN VASHTI. DEGRADATION. (*Alternation.*)

A[2] | c | 13-15. King's inquiry of wise men.
d | 16-20. Advice. Given.
c | 21. King's agreement with wise men.
d | 22. Advice. Acted on.

18 ladies = princesses.

19 not altered. Cp. Dan. 6. 8.

20 decree = rescript. Only here and Ecc. 8. 11.

it is great: i. e. the decree is important.

ALL THE WIVES SHALL GIVE. This is the first of the five *Acrostics* (Ap. 6), exhibiting in the initials the Divine name. See Ap. 60.

2. 1-20 (A[3], p. 655). QUEEN ESTHER. SUBSTITUTED. (*Repeated Alternation and Introversions.*)

A[3] | B[1] | 1-4. Maidens. Sought.
C[1] | e[1] | 5, 6. Mordecai. Position.
f[1] | 7. Esther. Relation.
B[2] | 8-. Maidens. Gathered.
C[2] | f[2] | -8, 9. Esther. Included.
e[2] | 10, 11. Mordecai. Solicitude.
B[3] | 12-14. Maidens. Rotation.
C[3] | f[3] | 15-18. Esther. Selection.
e[3] | 19, 20. Mordecai. Station.

1 After these things: i. e. in 467. Astyages was now twenty-one. In the seventh year (*v.* 16); one of these spent in preparations (*v.* 12).

Ahasuerus. See note on 1. 1.

Vashti. See note on 1. 9.

2 virgins. Heb. *bethūlah.* See note on Gen. 24. 43.

3 custody = hand. **chamberlain** = eunuch.

4 maiden = a young person. Heb. *na'ar.*

5 a certain Jew = a man (Heb. *'ish.* Ap. 14. II), a Jew. The contrast between Judah and Israel was lost in a strange land; and, as Nebuchadnezzar's campaign was against Judah, so "Jew" became the name used by Gentiles.

Mordecai. Daniel and Ezekiel taken to Babylon (2 Kings 24. 14, 15); Nehemiah and Mordecai to Shushan; and Mordecai dwelt in the royal palace, as did Daniel and others (Dan. 1. 4. 2 Kings 20. 16-18).

a Benjamite. Thus Mordecai, a Benjamite, ends Jehovah's war against Amalek. Ex. 17. 16. Cp. 3. 1 with 7. 10; 9. 10. A work entrusted to Saul (a Benjamite). 1 Sam. 15. 2-33.

6 Jeconiah = Jehoiachin (2 Kings 24. 6).

carried away. Cp. 2 Kings 24. 14, 15. Jer. 52. 24-34. 133 years before the generally received date (i. e. 598-465 = 133), which, therefore, cannot be correct. From the carrying away of Jeconiah to the marriage of Esther to Astyages in his seventh year was only twenty-two years (489-467). See Ap. 50. VII (5).

7 Hadassah = myrtle. Not living with Mordecai (who was in the palace, *v.* 5), but brought up by him.

Esther = star. But Rabbi Yehudah derives it from *sathar*, to hide, because she was hidden in her guardian's house; and her nationality also was concealed (*v.* 10).

father. Abihail: now dead. See *v.* 15; 9. 29.

5 *Now* in Shushan the palace there was °a certain Jew, whose name *was* °Mordecai, the son of Jair, the son of Shimei, the son of Kish, °a Benjamite; C[1] e[1]

6 Who had been carried away from Jerusalem with the captivity which had been carried away with °Jeconiah king of Judah, whom Nebuchadnezzar the king of Babylon had °carried away.

7 And he brought up °Hadassah, that *is*, °Esther, his uncle's daughter: for she had neither °father nor mother, and the [4]maid *was* fair and beautiful; whom Mordecai, when her f[1]

467 father and mother were dead, took for his own daughter.

B[2] (p. 656) 8 So it came to pass, when the king's °commandment and his °decree was heard, and when many [4]maidens were gathered together unto Shushan the palace, to the [3]custody of Hegai,

C[2] f[2] that [7]Esther was brought also unto the king's house, to the custody of Hegai, keeper of the women.

9 And the [4]maiden pleased him, and she °obtained kindness of him; and he speedily gave her her things for purification, with such things as belonged to her, and seven [4]maidens, *which were* meet to be given her, out of the king's house: and he °preferred her and her [4]maids unto the best *place* of the house of the women.

e[2] 10 Esther had °not shewed her People nor her kindred: for [5]Mordecai had charged her that she should not shew *it*.

11 And [5]Mordecai walked every day before the court of the women's house, °to know how [7]Esther did, and what should become of her.

B[3] 12 Now when every [4]maid's turn was come to go in to king [1]Ahasuerus, after that she had been twelve months, according to the manner of the women, °(for so were the days of their purifications accomplished, *to wit*, six months with oil of myrrh, and six months with sweet odours, and with *other* things for the purifying of the women;)

13 Then thus came *every* [4]maiden unto the king; whatsoever she desired was given her to go with her out of the house of the women unto the king's house.

14 In the evening she went, and on the morrow she returned into the second house of the women, to the [3]custody of Shaashgaz, the king's [3]chamberlain, which kept the concubines: she came in unto the king no more, except the king delighted in her, and that she were called by name.

C[3] f[3] 15 Now when the turn of [7]Esther, the daughter of Abihail the uncle of Mordecai, who had taken her for his daughter, was come to go in unto the king, she required nothing but what Hegai the king's [3]chamberlain, the keeper of the women, appointed. And [7]Esther [9]obtained favour in the sight of all them that looked upon her.

16 So [7]Esther was taken unto king Ahasuerus into his house royal in the tenth month, which *is* the month °Tebeth, in the °seventh year of his reign.

17 And the king loved [7]Esther above all the women, and she [9]obtained grace and favour in his sight more than all the [1]virgins; so that he set the royal crown upon her head, and made her queen instead of [1]Vashti.

18 Then the king made a great feast unto all his princes and his servants, *even* [7]Esther's feast; and he made a °release to the provinces, and gave gifts, according to the state of the king.

e[3] 19 And °when the [1]virgins were gathered together the second time, then [5]Mordecai °sat in the king's gate.

20 Esther had [10]not *yet* shewed her kindred nor her People; °as [5]Mordecai had charged her: °for Esther did the °commandment of [5]Mordecai, like as when she was brought up with him.

21 In those days, while [5]Mordecai [19]sat in the king's °gate, F g (p. 657)

two of the king's chamberlains, Bigthan and Teresh, of those which kept the °door, were wroth, and sought to lay hand on the king Ahasuerus. h

22 And the thing °was known to [5]Mordecai, who told *it* unto [7]Esther the queen; and Esther certified the king *thereof* in [5]Mordecai's name. *g*

23 And when inquisition was made of the matter, it was found out;

therefore they were both hanged on a tree: and it was °written in the book of the chronicles before the king. *h*

3 °After these things did king °Ahasuerus promote Haman the son of Hammedatha the °Agagite, and advanced him, and set his seat above all the princes that *were* with him. G D i (p. 658)

---

8 commandment = word. Heb. *dābar*. See note on 1. 12.
decree = Imperial decree. Heb. *dāth*, as in 3. 15; 4. 3, 8; 8. 14, 17; 9. 1, 13, 14.
9 obtained = won.
preferred = promoted. Probably influenced by Mordecai.
10 not shewed. Not till 7. 3-5. This was Mordecai's wisdom. Cp. *v.* 20.
11 to know. This was Mordecai's solicitude. All this proves that these events must have taken place before the emancipation made by Cyrus (the son of this Astyages, Ap. 57), recorded in Ezra 1. No such secrecy would have been necessary, and no thought of allowing the People, whom he had just emancipated, to be exterminated, as is described in the book of Esther: But Cyrus, being her son, would be carefully prepared by her and Mordecai to begin his reign by such emancipation from Babylon (note, not from Shushan: cp. Ezra 1. 1 with Jer. 25. 11, 12), thus fulfilling Isa. 44. 28 and 45. 1-4.
12 for. Another *Parenthesis*. Ap. 6. See note on 1. 7.
16 Tebeth. See Ap. 51. VII. 5.
seventh year. The first feast was in the third year. The search probably took one year; the preparation another; oblations another. Other seasons are unnamed.
18 release = a holiday. Heb. *hănāhah*.
19 when, &c. = while they were collecting, &c.
sat in the king's gate. Mordecai was of the king's household. See *v.* 5. This guarded Esther's interests, and enabled him to obtain all information. (N.B. Haman lived in his own house with his family in the city.)
20 as = according as.
for, &c. Thus revealing a new characteristic of Esther. This secrecy was hardly needed if the emancipation of Ezra 1. 1 had already taken place.
commandment. Heb. *'āmar*, as in 1. 10, 15, 17.

2. 21-23 (**F**, p. 654). MORDECAI. DISCOVERY OF PLOT. (*Alternation.*)

F | g | 21-. Mordecai. Station.
  | h | -21. Conspiracy. Made.
  | *g* | 22, 23-. Mordecai. Discovery.
  | *h* | -23. Conspiracy. Punished.

21 gate. Heb. *sha'ar* = the lofty gate of a palace, not the same word as "door", *v.* 21; 6. 2.
door = threshold. Heb. *saph*.
22 was known. Mordecai sat in the king's gate: the very place to hear all news.
23 written. See note on 6. 1.

3. 1-15 [For Structure see next page].

1 After these things. Haman was not made Grand Vizier till five years later. See *v.* 7.
Ahasuerus. See note on 1. 1.
Agagite. A descendant of Amalekite kings (Num. 24. 7. 1 Sam. 15. 8, 32). Called an Amalekite by Josephus (*Ant.* xi. 6. 5).

467 2 And all the king's servants, that *were* in the
king's °gate, °bowed, and reverenced Haman:
for the king had so °commanded concerning him.
k (p. 658) But °Mordecai °bowed not, nor did *him*
reverence.
3 Then the king's servants, which *were* in
the king's gate, said unto [2] Mordecai, "Why
°transgressest thou the king's commandment?"
4 Now it came to pass, when they spake daily
unto him, and he hearkened not unto them,
that they told Haman, to see whether [2] Mordecai's matters would stand: for he had told
them that he *was* a Jew.

E l 5 And when Haman saw that [2] Mordecai
bowed not, nor did him reverence, then was
Haman full of wrath.
6 And he thought scorn to lay hands on
[2] Mordecai alone; for they had shewed him
the People of Mordecai: wherefore °Haman
sought to destroy all the Jews that *were*
throughout the whole kingdom of [1] Ahasuerus,
even the People of [2] Mordecai.

m 1st Nisan 462 7 In the first month, (that *is*, the month Nisan,) in the twelfth year of king Ahasuerus,
°they cast °Pur, that *is*, the lot, before Haman
from day to day, and from month to month,
to the twelfth *month*, that *is*, the month Adar.

D i 8 And °Haman said unto king [1] Ahasuerus,
°"There is a certain People °scattered abroad
and dispersed among the people in all the
provinces of thy kingdom; and their °laws
are diverse from all people; neither keep they
the king's °laws: therefore it *is* not for the
king's profit to suffer them.
9 If it please the king, let it be written that
they may be destroyed: and I will pay ten
thousand °talents of silver to the hands of
those that have the charge of the business, to
bring *it* into the king's treasuries."

k 10 And the king took his ring from his hand,
and gave it unto Haman the son of Hammedatha the Agagite, °the Jews' enemy.
11 And the king said unto Haman, "The
silver *is* given to thee, °the People also, to do
with them as it seemeth good to thee."

E m 12 Then were the king's scribes called on
°the thirteenth day of the first month,

l and there was written according to all that
Haman had [2] commanded unto the king's lieutenants, and to the governors that *were* over
every province, and to the rulers of every
people of every province according to the
writing thereof, and *to* every people after their
language; in the name of king [1] Ahasuerus
was it written, and sealed with the king's ring.
13 And the letters were sent by °posts into all
the king's provinces, to °destroy, to °kill, and
to °cause to °perish, all Jews, both young and
old, little children and women, in one day,
13th Adar 461 *even* upon [12] the thirteenth *day* of the twelfth
month, which *is* the month Adar, and *to*
°*take* the spoil of them for a prey.
14 The copy of the writing for a °commandment to be given in every province was
published unto all °people, that they should be
ready against that day.
15 The [13] posts went out, being hastened by
the king's °commandment, and the °decree was
given in Shushan the palace. And the king
and Haman °sat down to drink; but °the
city Shushan was °perplexed.

4 When Mordecai perceived all that was *F* n¹
°done, Mordecai rent his clothes, and put

3. 1-15 (**G**, p. 654). HAMAN. PLOT.
(*Alternations and Introversion.*)

G | D | i | 1, 2-. Haman. Advancement.
k | -2-4. The king. Command *re* Haman.
E | l | 5, 6. The plot. Devised.
m | 7. Pur. The month by lot. Twelfth month.
D | *i* | 8, 9. Haman. Plot purposed.
k | 10, 11. The king. Compliance with Haman.
E | *m* | 12-. Pur. The day by lot. Thirteenth day.
l | -12-15. The plot. Succeeds.

2 gate = lofty porch. Heb. *sha'ar*. See note on 2. 21.
bowed. Heb. *kāra'*. *Kāra'*, used of idols (1 Kings 19. 18. 2 Chron. 29. 29). *Shaḥah* is the word used of bowing to kings and others.
commanded = appointed or charged. Heb. *ẓavah*.
Mordecai. See note on 2. 5.
bowed not. He could not bow to an Amalekite, against whom Jehovah had declared perpetual war. See note on Ex. 17. 16.
3 transgressest. Heb. *'ābar*. Ap. 44. VII.
6 Haman sought. Another assault of Satan against the nation through whom the Seed of the woman was to come. See Ap. 23, p. 27.
7 they cast. From 1st Nisan 462 to 13th Adar 462.
Pur. Persian for "lot". The reference is to "the monthly prognosticators" of Isa. 47. 13. This was to fix on a fortunate time. Cp. 9. 24.
8 Haman said. Having got the month and the day (the thirteenth, see *v.* 13, cp. Ap. 10), he could go to the king.
There is a certain People. Would it have been necessary for Haman thus to have explained and described the Jews, if they had already received their emancipation? Impossible! We are asked to believe this according to the traditional teaching. But see note on 10. 3, and Ap. 57 and 58.
scattered abroad, &c. Cp. 2 Chron. 36. 23. Ezra 1. 1-4. There is no reference to any emancipation here.
laws. See note on 1. 8. **9 talents.** See Ap. 51. II.
10 the Jews' enemy. Haman so called four times: 3. 10; 8. 1; 9. 10, 24. No one else so called in Scripture.
11 the People also. This was the aim of the great enemy, who was using Haman as he had tried to use Pharaoh in Egypt. See Ap. 23.
12 the thirteenth day. Ominous number. See Ap. 10. Note the three thirteens: 3. 12, 13; 8. 12.
13 posts = the hand of the runners. Cp. 8. 10.
destroy . . . kill . . . cause to perish. Note the Fig. *Synonymia* (Ap. 6), to emphasise the utter destruction contemplated.
perish. Heb. *'ābad*. Here and 4. 16; 7. 4; 8. 11: not 9. 28. **take the spoil.** See note on 9. 10.
14 commandment = Imperial decree. Heb. *dath*. See note on 2. 8. **people** = peoples.
15 commandment = word. Heb. *dābar*. See note on 1. 12. **decree.** Heb. *dath*. See notes on 1. 8; 2. 8.
sat down to drink. So Joseph's brethren (Gen. 37. 25), and Herod (Matt. 14. 6. Mark 6. 21). So will it be (Rev. 11. 7-10).
the city. Put by Fig. *Metonymy* (of Adjunct), Ap. 6, for the inhabitants.
perplexed. A rare word. Ex. 14. 3, "entangled". Joel 1. 18. This verse speaks of the effect on the Persians. Ch. 4 speaks of the effect on the Jews. Contrast 8. 15.

4. 1-3 (*F*, p. 654). MORDECAI. DISCOVERY OF (HAMAN'S) PLOT. (*Division.*)

F | n¹ | 1, 2. Bitter cry. Mordecai. Shushan.
n² | 3. Bitter cry. Jews. Provinces.

1 done = being done.

462 on sackcloth with ashes, and went out into the midst of the city, and cried with a loud and a °bitter cry;

2 And came °even before the king's gate: for none *might* enter into the king's gate clothed with sackcloth.

n² (p. 658) 3 And in every province, whithersoever the king's °commandment and his °decree came, *there was* great mourning among the Jews, °and °fasting, °and weeping, °and wailing; °and many lay in sackcloth and ashes.

C¹ G¹ H (p. 659) 4 So Esther's °maids and her °chamberlains came and told *it* her. Then was the queen exceedingly grieved; and she sent raiment to clothe Mordecai, and to take away °his sackcloth from him: but he received *it* not.

J o 5 Then called Esther for Hatach, *one* of the king's [4] chamberlains, whom he had appointed to attend upon her, and gave him a °commandment to Mordecai, to know what it *was*, and why it *was*.

6 So Hatach went forth to Mordecai unto the street of the city, which *was* before the king's gate.

p 7 And Mordecai told him of all that had happened unto him, and of °the sum of the money that Haman had promised to pay to the king's treasuries for the Jews, to destroy them.

8 Also he gave him the copy of the writing of the [3] decree that was given at Shushan to destroy them, to shew *it* unto Esther, and to declare *it* unto her, and to charge her that she should go in unto the king, to make supplication unto him, and to make request before him for her People.

9 And Hatach came and told Esther the words of Mordecai.

J o 10 Again Esther spake unto Hatach, and gave him [5] commandment unto Mordecai;

11 "All the king's servants, and the people of the king's provinces, do know, that whosoever, whether °man or woman, shall come unto the king into the inner court, who is not called, *there is* one °law of his to put *him* to death, except such to whom the king shall hold out the golden sceptre, that he may live: but I have not been called to come in unto the king these thirty days."

p 12 And they told to Mordecai Esther's words.

13 Then Mordecai °commanded to answer Esther, "Think not with °thyself that thou shalt escape in the king's house, more than all the Jews.

14 For if thou altogether holdest thy peace at this time, *then* shall there °enlargement and deliverance arise to the Jews from another place; but thou and thy father's house shall be destroyed: and °who knoweth whether thou art come to the kingdom for *such* a time as this?"

H 15 Then Esther bade *them* return Mordecai *this answer*,

16 "Go, gather together all the Jews that are present in Shushan, and fast ye for me, and neither eat nor drink °three days, night or day: I also and my [4] maidens will fast likewise; and so will I go in unto the king, which *is* not according to the [11] law: and if °I perish, I perish."

bitter cry. Not (we may be sure) without confession and prayer, as with Nehemiah (ch. 1), and Daniel (ch. 9).

2 even = as far as.

3 commandment = word. See note on 1. 12.

decree = Imperial decree. Heb. *dāth*. See notes on 1. 8; 2. 8.

and. Note the Fig. *Polysyndeton* (Ap. 6), to emphasise the greatness and universality of the mourning.

fasting, &c. These were the accompaniments of true repentance.

4. 4—5. 14 (**C¹**, p. 654). ESTHER. INTERCESSION. (*Division.*)

C¹ | G¹ | 4. 4-17. Esther and Mordecai.
  | G² | 5. 1-14. Esther and the king.

4. 4-17 (G¹, above). ESTHER AND MORDECAI. (*Introversion and Alternation.*)

G¹ | H | 4. Esther. Information.
  J | o | 5, 6. Esther. Inquiry of Mordecai.
    p | 7-9. Mordecai. Reply and request.
  J | *o* | 10, 11. Esther. Message to Mordecai.
    p | 12-14. Mordecai. Reply and expostulation.
  H | 15-17. Esther. Decision.

4 maids. See note on 2. 4.

chamberlains = eunuchs.

his. Edition of A.V., 1611, reads "the".

5 commandment = charge. Heb. *ẓavāh*. See 3. 2.

7 the sum of the money = the exact sum of the money. Mordecai knew of this, but how we cannot tell. He evidently did not know that the king had made Haman a present of it (3. 11).

11 man. Heb. *'ish*. Ap. 14. II.

law = Imperial decree. Heb. *dāth*. See note on 1. 8.

13 commanded. Heb. *'āmar*. See note on 1. 10.

thyself = thy soul. Heb. *nephesh*. Ap. 13.

14 enlargement = respite.

who knoweth . . . ? Note the Fig. *Erotēsis* (Ap. 6), for emphasis. Used here of hope and trust in God and His overruling grace.

16 three days, night or day. The Jerusalem Talmud says "a day and night together make up a *nukthēmeron*, and that any part of such period is counted as a whole". Cp. 1 Sam. 30. 12, 13. Jonah 1. 17. Matt. 12. 40.

I perish. See note on 3. 13.

17 went his way = passed over: i.e. over the river Ulai, on which Shushan is built, to the Jewish quarter, to accomplish his part of the compact.

5. 1-14 (G², above). ESTHER AND THE KING. (*Alternations.*)

G² | K | 1, 2. King on royal throne.
  L | q | 3. King. Inquiry.
    r | 4. Esther. Invitation given.
    q | 5-. King. Compliance.
    r | -5. Esther. Invitation accepted.
  K | 6-. King at Esther's banquet.
  L | s | -6. King. Promise.
    t | 7, 8. Esther. Second invitation.
    s | 9-. Haman's joy.
    t | -9-14. Esther. Second invitation.

1 the third day. The beginning of a new life for Israel. See Ap. 10.

inner court. All houses had courts; a palace had several. **over against** = right opposite.

upon his royal throne. To transact business.

gate = porch, or entrance. Heb. *pethaḥ*.

17 So Mordecai °went his way, and did according to all that Esther had [5] commanded him.

5 Now it came to pass on °the third day, that Esther put on *her* royal *apparel*, and stood in the °inner court of the king's house, °over against the king's house: and the king sat °upon his royal throne in the royal house, °over against the °gate of the house. G² K 3rd Nisan 462

462 2 And it was so, when the king saw Esther the queen standing in the court, *that* she °obtained favour in his sight: and the king held out to Esther the golden sceptre that *was* in his hand. So Esther drew near, and touched the top of the sceptre.

L q (p. 659) 3 Then said the king unto her, "What wilt thou, queen Esther? and what *is* thy request? it shall be even given thee to the half of the °kingdom."

r 4 And Esther answered, "If *it seem* good unto the king, °LET THE KING AND HAMAN COME THIS DAY unto the banquet that I have prepared for him."

q 5 Then the king said, "Cause Haman to make haste, that he may do as Esther hath said."

r So the king and Haman came to the banquet that Esther had prepared.

K 6 And the king said unto Esther at the banquet of wine, °"What *is* thy °petition? and it shall be granted thee: and what *is* thy °request?

L s even to the half of the [3]kingdom it shall be performed."

t (p. 659) 7 Then answered Esther, and said, "My petition and my request *is;*

8 If I have found favour in the sight of the king, and if it please the king to grant my petition, and to perform my request, let the king and Haman come to the banquet that I shall prepare for them, and I will °do to morrow as the king hath said."

s 9 Then went Haman forth that day joyful and with a glad heart:

t u but when Haman saw Mordecai in the king's gate, that he °stood not up, nor °moved for him, he was full of indignation against Mordecai.

v 10 Nevertheless Haman refrained himself: and when he came home, he sent and called for his friends, and °Zeresh his wife.

11 And Haman °told them of the glory of his riches, and the multitude of his °children, and all *the things* wherein the king had promoted him, and how he had advanced him above the princes and servants of the king.

v 12 Haman said moreover, "Yea, Esther the queen did let no man come in with the king unto the banquet that she had prepared but myself; and to morrow am I invited unto her also with the king.

u 13 Yet all °THIS AVAILETH ME NOTHING, so long as I see °Mordecai the Jew sitting at the king's gate."

14 Then said [10]Zeresh his wife and all his friends unto him, "Let a °gallows be made of fifty °cubits high, and °to morrow speak thou unto the king that Mordecai may be hanged thereon: then go thou in merrily with the king unto the banquet." And the thing pleased Haman; and he caused the °gallows to be made.

D^3 (p. 654) **6** °On that night °could not the king sleep, and he °commanded to bring the book of records of the chronicles; and °they were read before the king.

---

2 obtained = won. Cp. 4. 11.

3 kingdom. Put by Fig. *Metonomy* (of Adjunct), Ap. 6, for a year's revenue. Cp. Mark 6. 23.

4 LET THE KING AND HAMAN COME THIS DAY. This is the second of the five *Acrostics* (Ap. 6) of the Divine name (Ap. 4. II) in this book. See Ap. 60. The second pivot on which the history turns.

6 What is thy petition? He must have seen that there was something behind the mere banquet.

petition = question. request = wish.

8 do to morrow. She still keeps back her petition, showing the king that he had rightly divined that there was something important behind it.

5. -9-14 (*t*, p. 659). ESTHER. SECOND INVITATION. (*Introversion.*)

t | u | -9. Mordecai. Haman's indignation.
 v | 10, 11. Haman. Ostentation.
 v | 12. Haman. Pride.
 u | 13, 14. Mordecai. Haman's gallows.

9 stood not up. Notwithstanding the crisis reached; and well knowing the cause of it.

moved = stirred. Only here, and Ecc. 12. 3.

Zeresh his wife. By *Gematria* = 507 ($13^3 \times 3$). See note on 9. 10, also Ap. 10.

11 told = recounted.

children = sons. He had ten sons. See 9. 10.

13 THIS AVAILETH ME NOTHING. This is the third of the five Acrostics of this book, exhibiting the Divine names (Ap. 4. II) to the eye. See Ap. 60.

Mordecai. The enmity was not merely personal, but religious; which is the worst form enmity can take.

14 gallows = tree: i. e. a stake to which a criminal was fastened till he died. The same word for cross. Cp. 2. 23; 7. 9; and see Acts 5. 30; 10. 39; 13. 29. 1 Pet. 2. 24.

cubits. See Ap. 51. III (2).

to morrow. There was no delay; but, quick as the action was, it was none too soon for its real usefulness.

6. 1 On that night. The time for Divine action had come. See Ap. 23, p. 27.

could not the king sleep. God uses small things to accomplish His purposes. See note on Judg. 3. 21. We know not what He used here. But the time had come for Him to work.

commanded. Heb. *'āmar.* See note on 1. 10.

they . . . read. The very portion which God ruled for the working out of His plan.

2 Mordecai had told. See 2. 21, 22.

door = threshold. Heb. *saph.* Cp. 2. 21.

4 Now Haman was come. This was the next step. The Fig. *Parenthesis* (Ap. 6) is used to emphasise the importance of it. gallows = tree. See note on 5. 14.

5 Behold. Fig. *Asterismos.* Ap. 6.

standeth in the court. As explained in the *Parenthesis, v.* 4.

come in. Note the Fig. *Anaaıplosis* (Ap. 6); *v.* 5 ending with the same verb which begins the next sentence.

---

2 And it was found written, that °Mordecai had told of Bigthana and Teresh, two of the king's chamberlains, the keepers of the °door, who sought to lay hand on the king Ahasuerus. E^2 H

3 And the king said, "What honour and dignity hath been done to Mordecai for this?" Then said the king's servants that ministered unto him, "There is nothing done for him."

4 And the king said, "Who *is* in the court?" J
°(Now Haman was come into the outward court of the king's house, to speak unto the king to hang Mordecai on the °gallows that he had prepared for him.)

5 And the king's servants said unto him, °"Behold, Haman °standeth in the court." And the king said, "Let him °come in."

462 6 So Haman °came in. And the king said
unto him, "What shall be done unto the °man
whom the king delighteth to honour?" Now
Haman °thought in his heart, "To whom
would the king delight to do honour more
than to myself?"
7 And Haman answered the king, "For the
[6]man whom the king delighteth to honour,
8 Let the royal apparel be brought which the
king *useth* to wear, °and the horse that the
king rideth upon, °and the crown royal which
is set upon his head:
9 [8]And let this apparel [8]and horse be delivered
to the hand of °one of the king's most noble
princes, that they may array the man *withal*
whom the king delighteth to honour, [8]and
bring him on horseback through the street of
the city, [8]and proclaim before him, 'Thus shall
it be done to the [6]man whom the king delighteth to honour.'"

H (p. 654) 10 Then the king said to Haman, °"Make
haste, *and* take the apparel and the horse,
°as thou hast said, and do even so to Mordecai
the Jew, that sitteth at the king's gate: let
nothing fail of all that thou hast spoken."
11 Then took Haman the apparel and the
horse, and arrayed Mordecai, and brought him
on horseback through the street of the city,
and proclaimed before him, "Thus shall it be
done unto the [6]man whom the king delighteth
to honour."
12 And Mordecai came again to the king's
gate. But Haman °hasted to his house mourning, °and having his head covered.
13 [12]And Haman told °Zeresh his wife [12]and all
his friends every *thing* that had befallen him.
Then said his wise men and °Zeresh his wife
unto him, "If Mordecai *be* of the seed of the
Jews, before whom thou hast begun to fall,
thou shalt not prevail against him, but shalt
surely fall before him."
14 And °while they *were* yet talking with
him, came the king's chamberlains, and [12]hasted
to bring Haman unto the banquet that Esther
had prepared.

C[2] **7** So the king and Haman came to banquet
with Esther the queen.
B[3] D[3] 2 And the king said again unto Esther on the
second day at the banquet of wine,
E[3] K "What *is* thy °petition, queen Esther? and
it shall be granted thee: and what *is* thy
°request? and it shall be performed, *even* to
the half of the °kingdom."
L 3 Then Esther the queen answered and said,
"If I have found favour in thy sight, O king,
and if it please the king, let °my life be given
me at my petition, and my People at my request:
4 For we °are °sold, I and my People, to be
°destroyed, to be °slain, and to °perish. But
if we had been sold for bondmen and bondwomen, I had held my tongue, although the
enemy could not °countervail the king's
damage."
K 5 Then the king Ahasuerus °answered and
said unto Esther the queen, °"WHO IS °HE, AND
WHERE IS HE, that durst presume in his heart
to do so?"

6 And Esther said, "The adversary and
enemy *is* this wicked Haman." Then Haman
was afraid before the king and the queen.
7 And the king arising from the banquet
of wine in his wrath *went* into the palace
garden: and Haman stood up to make request
for his °life to Esther the queen; for he saw
°THAT THERE WAS °EVIL DETERMINED AGAINST HIM by °the king.
8 Then the king returned out of the [7]palace
garden into the place of the banquet of wine;
and Haman was fallen upon the °bed whereon Esther *was*. Then said the king, °"Will
he force the queen also before me in the
house?" As the word went out of the king's
mouth, they covered Haman's face.
9 And Harbonah, one of the chamberlains,
said before the king, °"Behold also, the °gallows
fifty °cubits high, which Haman had made for
Mordecai, who had spoken good for the king,
standeth in the house of Haman." Then the
king said, "Hang him thereon."
10 So °they hanged Haman on the [9]gallows
that he had prepared for Mordecai. Then
was the king's wrath pacified.

6 came in. See note on *v.* 5.
man. Heb. *'ish.* Ap. 14. II. **thought** = said.
8 and. Note the Fig. *Polysyndeton* (Ap. 6) in *vv.* 8, 9, to emphasise the eagerness with which Haman enumerated the honours his heart desired.
9 one = a man. Heb. *'ish.* Ap. 14. II.
10 Make haste = be expeditious. Heb. *māhar*, as in 5. 5; not *daḥaph* (to urge oneself), as in *v.* 12; 3. 15; or *bāhal* (to hurry away), as in *v.* 14; 8. 14.
as = according as.
12 hasted. Heb. *daḥaph.* See note on *v.* 10.
and. Note the Fig. *Polysyndeton* (Ap. 6) in *vv.* 12, 13, emphasising the excitement which had seized him.
13 Zeresh. See note on 5. 14.
14 while. Everything was hastening to the approaching crisis.

7. 2 petition . . . request. See note on 5. 6.
kingdom. See note on 5. 3.
3 my life = my soul. Heb. *nephesh.* Ap. 13. Life put before petition, and her People put before her request.
4 are = have been.
sold. Implying that a bargain had been made.
destroyed . . . slain . . . perish. Note the Fig. *Synonymia* (Ap. 6), to emphasise the urgency of her petition. Cp. 3. 13. **perish.** See note on 3. 13.
countervail = make good, or compensate.
5 answered and said. Note the idiom = threatened and said. See note on Deut. 1. 41.
WHO IS HE, AND WHERE IS HE . . . ? This is the fifth Acrostic, which gives (not Jehovah but) the Divine Name "I AM" of Ex. 3. 14. See Ap. 60.
HE. Note the emphatic repetition of this pronoun.
7 life = soul. Heb. *nephesh.* Ap. 13.
THAT THERE WAS EVIL DETERMINED AGAINST HIM. This is the fourth, and last, of the four acrostics exhibiting the name Jehovah in this book. See Ap. 60.
evil. Heb. *ra'a'.* Ap. 44. viii.
the king. Note the Fig. *Epanadiplōsis* (Ap. 6), the verse beginning and ending with the same word, marking and emphasising its importance.
8 bed = couch.
Will he force . . . ? Fig. *Erotēsis.* Ap. 6.
9 Behold. Fig. *Asterismos.* Ap. 6.
gallows. See note on 5. 14.
cubits. See Ap. 51. III. 2 (1).
10 they hanged Haman. See note on "Benjamite" (2. 5).

C³ (p. 654) 462 **8** °On that day did the king Ahasuerus give the house of Haman °the Jews' enemy unto Esther the queen.
D¹ And Mordecai came before the king; for Esther had told what he *was* unto her.
2 And the king took off his ring, which he had taken from Haman, and °gave it unto Mordecai. And Esther set Mordecai °over the house of Haman.

E¹ M 3 And Esther spake yet again before the king, and fell down at his feet, and besought him with tears to put away the °mischief of °Haman the Agagite, and his device that he had devised against the Jews.
4 Then the king held out the golden sceptre toward Esther. So Esther arose, and stood before the king,
5 And said, °"If it please the king, and if I have found favour in his sight, and the thing *seem* right before the king, and I *be* pleasing in his eyes, let it be written to reverse the letters devised by Haman the son of Hammedatha the Agagite, which he wrote to destroy °the Jews which *are* in all the king's provinces:
6 For how can I endure to see the °evil that shall come unto my People? or how can I endure to see the destruction of my kindred?"

N w (p. 662) 7 Then the king Ahasuerus said unto Esther the queen and to Mordecai the Jew,
x y °"Behold, I have given Esther the house of Haman, and him they have hanged upon the °gallows, because he laid his hand upon the Jews.
z a 8 Write ye also for the Jews, as it °liketh you, in the king's name, and seal *it* with the king's ring: for the writing which is written in the king's name, and sealed with the king's ring, °may no man reverse."
9 Then were the king's scribes called at that time in the third month, that *is*, the month
23rd Sivan 461 °Sivan, on the three and twentieth *day* thereof; and it was written according to all that Mordecai °commanded unto the Jews, and to the lieutenants, and the deputies and rulers of the provinces which *are* from India unto Ethiopia, an hundred twenty and seven provinces, unto every province according to the writing thereof, and unto every People after their language, and to the Jews according to their writing, and according to their language.
10 And he wrote in the king Ahasuerus' name, and sealed *it* with the king's ring, and sent letters by °posts on horseback, *and* riders on mules, camels, *and* young dromedaries:
x y 11 Wherein the king granted the Jews which *were* in every city to gather themselves together, and to stand for °their life, to °destroy, to °slay, and to cause to °perish, all the °power of the people and province that would assault them, *both* °little ones and women, and *to take* the spoil of them for a prey,
12 Upon one day in all the provinces of king
13th Adar 461 Ahasuerus, *namely*, upon the °thirteenth *day* of the twelfth month, which *is* the month Adar.
z b 13 The copy of the writing for °a commandment to be given in every province *was* published unto all °people, and that the Jews should be ready against that day to avenge themselves on their enemies.

14 *So* the [10]posts that rode upon mules *and* camels went out, being °hastened and pressed on by the king's °commandment. And the °decree was given at Shushan the palace. *a*

15 And Mordecai went out from the presence of the king in royal apparel of blue and white, and with a great crown of gold, and with a garment of fine linen and purple: and the city of Shushan rejoiced and was glad. *w*
16 The Jews had °light, °and gladness, °and joy, °and honour.

8. 1 On that day. Contrast "On that night", 6. 1.
the Jews' enemy. See note on 3. 10.
2 gave it unto Mordecai. Cp. 3. 10. Note how God honoured godly Jews in foreign courts: Joseph next to Pharaoh; Moses the heir to the throne of Egypt; Daniel next to Darius in Babylon; Mordecai next to Astyages in Shushan.
over the house of Haman. Wonderful retribution.
3 mischief. Heb. *rā'a'*. Ap. 44. viii. Same word as "evil", 7. 7.
Haman the Agagite. See notes on 2. 5 and 3. 1.
5 If it please the king. Note the *Alternation* in this verse:—

a | The king. "If it please the king."
  b | Esther. "And if I have found favour."
a | The king. "And . . . before the king."
  b | Esther. "And I be pleasing in his eyes."

the Jews. Some codices, with Aram. and Syr., read "all the Jews".
6 evil. Same word as "mischief", *v.* 3.

8. 7-17 (N, p. 654). KING. DECREE.
(*Introversions and Alternation.*)

N | w | 7-. The king.
  x | y | -7. Grant to Esther.
    z | a | 8. The writing. Commanded. } Decree.
      b | 9, 10. The writing. Written. }
  x | *y* | 11, 12. Grant to Esther's People.
    z | *b* | 13. The writing. Copied. } Decree.
      a | 14. The writing. Dispatched. }
w | 15-17. The king.

7 Behold. Fig. *Asterismos.* Ap. 6.
gallows. See note on 5. 14.
8 liketh = pleaseth. Cp. 3. 11.
may no man reverse. But cp. 3. 12, and see Ap. 23, p. 27. **9 Sivan.** See Ap. 51. III. 4.
commanded unto = charged. Heb. *zavah*. See note on "law", 3. 2.
10 posts on horseback = couriers on horseback. Haman's "posts" were runners on foot (3. 13, 15), but speed was now essential. See 9. 1.
11 their life = themselves. Heb. *nephesh*. Ap. 13.
destroy . . . slay . . . perish. Fig. *Synonymia* (Ap. 6), for emphasis. See note on 3. 13.
power = force. Heb. *ḥayil*, as in 1. 3. Not *shālaṭ* = mastery, as in 9. 1; or *toḳeph* = authority, as in 9. 29.
little ones. These were spared, notwithstanding. Cp. 9. 6. **12 thirteenth.** See note on 3. 12.
13 a commandment = an imperial decree. Heb. *dāth*. See note on 2. 8. **people** = the peoples.
14 hastened. Heb. *bāhal*. See note on 6. 10.
commandment = word. Heb. *dābar*. See note on 1. 12.
decree. Heb. *dāth*. See note on 2. 8.
16 light. Put by Fig. *Metonymy* (of Adjunct), Ap. 6, for joy.
and. Note the Fig. *Polysyndeton* (Ap. 6), to emphasise the greatness of the joy.

461 17 And in every province, and in every city, whithersoever the king's [14] commandment and his [14] decree came, the Jews had joy and gladness, a feast and a good day. And many of the people of the land ° became Jews; for the fear of the Jews fell upon them.

M N¹ c¹ (p. 663) 9 Now in the twelfth month, that *is*, the month Adar, on the °thirteenth day of the same, when the king's ° commandment and his ° decree drew near to be put in execution, in the day that the enemies of the Jews hoped to have ° power over them, °(though it was turned to the contrary, that ° the Jews had rule over them that hated them;)

2 The Jews gathered themselves together in their cities throughout all the provinces of the king Ahasuerus, to lay hand on such as sought their hurt: and no ° man could ° withstand them; for the fear of them fell upon all ° people.

3 And all the rulers of the provinces, and the lieutenants, and the deputies, and officers of the king, helped the Jews; because the fear of Mordecai fell upon them.

4 For ° Mordecai *was* great in the king's house, and his fame went out throughout all the provinces: for this [2] man Mordecai waxed greater and greater.

d¹ 5 Thus the Jews smote all their enemies with the stroke of the ° sword, ° and ° slaughter, ° and ° destruction, ° and did what they would unto those that hated them.

6 And in Shushan the palace the Jews slew and ° destroyed five hundred [2] men.

7 ° And Parshandatha, and Dalphon, and Aspatha,

8 And Poratha, and Adalia, and Aridatha,

9 And Parmashta, and Arisai, and Aridai, and Vajezatha,

10 ° The ten sons of Haman the son of Hammedatha, ° the enemy of the Jews, ° slew they;

e¹ but on the spoil ° laid they not their hand.

O i 11 On that day the number of those that were slain in Shushan the palace was brought before the king.

k 12 And the king said unto Esther the queen, "The Jews have slain and destroyed five hundred [2] men in Shushan the palace, and the ten sons of Haman; what have they done in the rest of the king's provinces? now what *is* thy petition? and it shall be granted thee: or what *is* thy request further? and it shall be done."

13 Then said Esther, "If it please the king, let it be granted to the Jews which *are* in Shushan to do to morrow also according unto this day's [1] decree, and ° let Haman's ten sons ° be hanged upon the gallows."

i 14 And the king ° commanded it so to be done: and the [1] decree was given at Shushan; and they hanged Haman's ten sons.

17 became Jews = made common cause with the Jews.

9. 1-28 (*M*, p. 654). ESTHER. PLEA FOR HER PEOPLE. (*Repeated Alternation and Introversion.*)

M | N¹ | c¹ | 1-4. Assemblage.
d¹ | 5-10-. Slaughter. Palace.
e¹ | -10. Abstention from plunder.
O | i | 11. King. Receives report.
k | 12, 13. Esther's request.
i | 14. King. Makes another decree.
N² | c² | 15-. Assemblage.
d² | -15-. Slaughter. Shushan. City.
e² | -15. Abstention from plunder.
c³ | 16-. Assemblage.
d³ | -16-. Slaughter. Provinces.
e³ | -16. Abstention from plunder.
O | l | 17. Feasting. Provinces. One day (13th).
m | 18. Feasting. Shushan. Three days (13th, 14th, and 15th).
l | 19. Feasting. Villages. One day (14th).
N³ | f | 20. Letters of Mordecai.
g | 21, 22. Days. Commemoration.
h | 23, 24. Observance.
f | 25. Letters of the king.
g | 26. Days. Names (Purim).
h | 27, 28. Observance.

1 thirteenth. See note on 3. 12.
commandment. Heb. *dābar*. See note on 1. 12.
decree. Heb. *dāth*. See note on 2. 8.
power = mastery. See note on 8. 11.
though, &c. Note the *Parenthesis*. Ap. 6.
the Jews = the Jews themselves.
2 man. Heb. *'ish*. Ap. 14. II.
withstand = stand before. **people** = the peoples.
4 Mordecai = the man (Heb. *'ish*. Ap. 14. II) Mordecai, greatly emphasising the person. Cp. Num. 12. 3. 1 Kings 11. 28. Dan. 9. 21.
5 sword . . . slaughter . . . destruction. Note the Fig. *Synonymia* (Ap. 6), for emphasis.
and. Note the Fig. *Polysyndeton*. Ap. 6.
6 destroyed, &c. Note that they took no advantage of the permission given in 8. 11.
7 And. Note the Fig. *Polysyndeton* (Ap. 6) in *vv.* 7-9, particularising each one of Haman's ten sons.
10 The ten sons. In all Heb. MSS. and printed editions these ten names are written with the word *v^eēth*, being the demonstrative pronoun = self, or this same, or himself, thus:

vᵉēth	Parshandatha,
vᵉēth	Dalphon,
vᵉēth	Aspatha,
vᵉēth	Poratha,
vᵉēth	Adalia,
vᵉēth	Aridatha,
vᵉēth	Parmashta,
vᵉēth	Arisai,
vᵉēth	Aridai,
vᵉēth	Vajezatha.

It has been suggested that it is because they were hanged one above another. But, as each Hebrew character is a *number* as well as a letter, the numerical value of these names (regarded as an addition sum) amounts to 10,244, or 13 × 788; while Haman the Agagite = 117 (13 × 9), and Zeresh = 507 (13 × 39), and the whole family = 10,868 (13 × 836). See Ap. 10 for the significance of this. On the other hand, *'Eth-Hadassah hi' Esther* (2. 7) adds up 1,152 = 8 × 12², and "Mordecai", son of Jair, son of Shimei, son of Kish, a Benjamite (2. 5), adds up 1,912 = (8 × 239). See Ap. 10. **the enemy of the Jews.** See note on 3. 10. **slew they.** See note on "Benjamite" (2. 5). **laid they not their hand.** Cp. note on "take the spoil" (3. 13). They probably remembered taking the spoil instead of obeying in 1 Sam. 15. Hence the emphasis on this in *vv.* 10, 15, 16. **13 let Haman's ten sons be hanged.** One of the ten deaths occasioned or obtained by women. See note on Judg. 4. 21. **be hanged.** Not alive, but hanged up after death. They were slain in conflict first. See *vv.* 6, 7. **14 commanded.** Heb. *'āmar*. See note on 1. 10.

N^2 c^2 (p. 663) 461 15 For the Jews that *were* in Shushan gathered themselves together on the fourteenth day also of the month Adar,

d^2 and slew three hundred [2] men at Shushan;

e^2 but on the prey they [10] laid not their hand.

c^3 16 But the other Jews that *were* in the king's provinces gathered themselves together,

d^3 and stood for °their lives, and °had rest from their enemies, and slew of their foes seventy and five thousand,

e^3 but they [10] laid not their hands on the prey,

O 1 17 On the [1] thirteenth day of the month Adar; and on the fourteenth day of the same rested they, and made it a day of feasting and gladness.

m 13–15 Adar 461 18 But the Jews that *were* at Shushan assembled together on the [1] thirteenth *day* thereof, and on the fourteenth thereof; and on the fifteenth *day* of the same they rested, and made it a day of feasting and gladness.

l 19 Therefore the Jews of the villages, that dwelt in the unwalled towns, made the fourteenth day of the month Adar *a day of* gladness and feasting, and a good day, and of sending portions one to another.

N^3 f 20 And Mordecai wrote these things, and sent letters unto all the Jews that *were* in all the provinces of the king Ahasuerus, *both* nigh and far,

g 21 To °stablish *this* among them, that they should keep the fourteenth day of the month Adar, and the fifteenth day of the same, yearly,

22 As the days wherein the Jews rested from their enemies, and the month which was turned unto them from sorrow to joy, and from mourning into a good day: that they should make them days of feasting and joy, and of sending portions one to another, and gifts to the poor.

h 23 And the Jews undertook to do as they had begun, and as Mordecai had written unto them;

24 Because Haman the son of Hammedatha, the Agagite, [10] the enemy of all the Jews, had devised against the Jews to destroy them, and had cast Pur, that *is*, the lot, to consume them, and to destroy them;

f 25 But when *Esther* came before the king, he [14] commanded by letters that his wicked °device, which he devised against the Jews, should return upon his own head, and that he and his sons should be hanged on the gallows.

g 26 Wherefore they called these days °Purim after the name of °Pur. Therefore for all the words of this letter, and *of that* which they had seen concerning this matter, and which had come unto them,

h 27 The Jews °ordained, and took upon them, and upon their seed, and upon all such as joined themselves unto them, so as it should not fail, that they would keep these two days according to their writing, and according to their *appointed* time every year;

28 And *that* these days *should be* remembered and kept throughout every generation, every family, every province, and every city; and *that* these days of [26] Purim °should not fail from among the Jews, nor the memorial of them °perish from their seed.

16 their lives = themselves Heb. *nephesh.* Ap. 13.
had rest from. Dr. Ginsburg thinks the Heb. should read "to avenge themselves upon". Cp. 8. 13.
21 stablish = ordain. Heb. *ḳūm*, as in *vv.* 29, 31.
25 device, which he devised = his great device. Fig. *Polyptōton.* Ap. 6.
26 Purim = lots. The name of the feast to this day.
Pur. See note on 3. 7.
27 ordained. Heb. *ḳūm*, as in *vv.* 21, 31.
28 should not fail. This sounds like a prophecy, and sets a seal on the inspiration of the book.
perish = come to an end. See note on 3. 13.

9. 29-32 (**C**[4], p. 654). ESTHER. ROYAL AUTHORITY. (*Alternation.*)

C[4] | n | 29–. Esther. Authority.
  o | –29–31–. Confirmation.
  n | –31. Esther. Authority.
  o | 32. Confirmation.

29 the daughter of Abihail. See 2. 15.
confirm. Heb. *ḳūm*, as in *vv.* 21, 31.
30 hundred, &c. See note on 1. 1.
31 enjoined = ordained. Heb. *ḳūm.*
as = according as.
decreed = ordained. Heb. *ḳūm*, as in *vv.* 27, 29, 31.
themselves = their souls. Heb. *nephesh.* Ap. 13.
32 decree = command. Heb. *ma'ămar.* Occurs only in Esther (1. 15; 2. 20).
10. 1 isles = coasts.
2 power. Heb. *toḳeph.* See note on 8. 11.
are they not . . . ? Fig. *Erotēsis.* Ap. 6.
3 next = the second = the Grand Vizier. Cp. 8. 2.
speaking peace = maintaining peace.
his seed: i. e. the People of Israel. N.B. in Persia, not Judæa.

Thus was prepared the way for the emancipation of the Jews, which, not long after, was proclaimed by Cyrus (Ezra 1. 1), the son of Astyages and Esther (see Ap. 57), and is further proof that this book comes, chronologically, before the book Ezra-Nehemiah. N.B. the year 461 is the midway year of the Babylonian Servitude (496–426). See special note on p. 615.

29 Then Esther the queen, °the daughter of Abihail, and Mordecai the Jew, wrote with all authority, **C**[4] n (p. 664)

to °confirm this second letter of [26] Purim. o

30 And he sent the letters unto all the Jews, to the °hundred twenty and seven provinces of the kingdom of Ahasuerus, *with* words of peace and truth,

31 To [29] confirm these days of [26] Purim in their times *appointed*,

according as Mordecai the Jew and Esther the queen had °enjoined them, and °as they had °decreed for °themselves and for their seed, the matters of the fastings and their cry. *n*

32 And the °decree of Esther confirmed these matters of [26] Purim; and it was written in the book. o

10 And the king Ahasuerus laid a tribute upon the land, and *upon* the °isles of the sea. A^2 (p. 654)

2 And all the acts of his °power and of his might, and the declaration of the greatness of Mordecai, whereunto the king advanced him, °*are* they not written in the book of the chronicles of the kings of Media and Persia?

3 For Mordecai the Jew *was* °next unto king Ahasuerus, and great among the Jews, and accepted of the multitude of his brethren, seeking the wealth of his People, and °speaking peace to all °his seed.

JOB.

THE STRUCTURE OF THE BOOK AS A WHOLE.

(*Introversion.*)

A | 1. 1-5. INTRODUCTION. HISTORICAL.

B | 1. 6—2. 10. SATAN'S ASSAULT. JOB STRIPPED OF ALL.

C | 2. 11-13. THE THREE FRIENDS. THEIR ARRIVAL

D | 3 1—31. 40. JOB AND HIS FRIENDS

E | 32. 1—37. 24. THE MINISTRY OF ELIHU: THE MEDIATOR*.

D | 38. 1—42. 6. JOB AND JEHOVAH.

C | 42. 7-9. THE THREE FRIENDS THEIR DEPARTURE

B | 42. 10-13 SATAN'S DEFEAT. JOB BLESSED WITH DOUBLE.

A | 42. 14-17. CONCLUSION. HISTORICAL

*** Note that by this grand *Introversion* the ministry of ELIHU, the Mediator, is placed in the middle, summing up the ministry of JOB's three friends, and introducing the ministry of JEHOVAH.**

NOTE ON THE DATE AND AUTHORSHIP OF THE BOOK OF JOB.

A lengthened account of the discussion of these questions would be without profit.

But, if JOB was the son of ISSACHAR (Gen. 46. 13), then we have a clue that may help us to a decision of both.

It is better to keep within the Bible itself for the settlement of its problems; and to treat the whole Book as the context of all its parts.

There is no reason why JOB should not be the son of ISSACHAR, and no better evidence is forthcoming for a different view.

The three friends of Job were descendants of ESAU; they would therefore be contemporaries.

ELIPHAZ, of TEMAN, in Idumea, was a son of ESAU, and had a son called TEMAN, from whom his country took its name (Gen. 36. 10, 11). It was noted for its "wise men" (Jer. 49. 7); and is mentioned with EDOM (Amos 1. 11, 12). Compare Jer. 25. 23, where both are connected with BUZ, the brother of Uz (Gen. 22. 21).

BILDAD the Shuhite. SHUAH was the sixth son of ABRAHAM by KETURAH (Gen. 25. 2); and is mentioned in connection with ESAU, EDOM, and TEMAN (Jer. 49. 8).

ZOPHAR the Naamathite. NAAMAH (now *Nā'aneh*, six miles south of Lod, in the lowlands of Judah).

If JOB was the son of ISSACHAR (Gen. 46. 13), he would have gone down to Egypt with his father.

ISSACHAR was forty at "the going down to Egypt". (See Ap. 50. III, p. 52.)

If JOB was the third son (Gen. 46. 13), he would have been about twenty at that time (1706 B. C.).

We are told that he lived 140 years after his "double" blessing (42. 10). If that "double" blessing included length of years, then his age would have been 70 + 140 = 210 (i. e. three seventies of years). His lifetime would be from 1726-1516 B. C.

According to this, he was born the year after JOSEPH was sold, and died 119 years after the death of JOSEPH (in 1635 B. C.). When JOSEPH died, JOB was ninety-one. If his "double" blessing did include length of years, then his affliction took place twenty-one years previously, when he was seventy. His removal from EGYPT to Uz must therefore have taken place earlier still.

When JOB died (1516 B. C.) MOSES was fifty-five, and had been in MIDIAN fifteen years (twenty-five years before the Exodus).

This would account for JOB being a worshipper of the God of ABRAHAM, and explains how Moses could have been the author of the book, and perhaps an eye- and ear-witness of the events it records in Midian. If so, the time has come (as Dr. Stier foretold and hoped[1]) when this book would be regarded as "the *Porch* of the Sanctuary"; and when this "fundamental wisdom of original revelation will cease to be ascribed, as it now is by some of the best, to a later poet in Israel".

---

[1] *The Words of the Lord Jesus.* Vol. iv, p. 406.

°THE
BOOK OF JOB.

A A (p. 667) 1726-1516 **1** °THERE °was a °man in the land of °Uz, whose name *was* °Job; and °that °man °was °perfect and upright, and one that feared °God, and eschewed °evil.

B **2 And there were born unto him seven sons and three daughters.**

C **3 His substance also was seven thousand sheep, °and three thousand camels, and five hundred yoke of oxen, and five hundred she asses, and a very great household;**

C **so that this [1]man was the greatest of all the °men of the east.**

B **4 And his sons went and feasted *in their* houses, every °one °his day; and sent and called for their three sisters to eat and to drink with them.**

A **5 And it was so, when the days of *their* feasting °were gone about, that Job sent and sanctified them, and rose up early in the morning, and °offered burnt offerings *according* to the number of them all: for Job said, "It may be that my sons have °sinned, and °cursed [1]God in their hearts." Thus did Job continually.**

B D a **6 Now there [1]was a day when the °sons of [1]God came to °present themselves before °the LORD, and °Satan came also among them.**

TITLE, The Book of Job has always formed an integral part of the Hebrew Canon; and some fifty-seven passages in it are quoted or referred to in the other books of the Bible. See Ap. 61.

The object of the book is to show "the end of the LORD" (Jas. 5. 11): the end to which Job was brought in 40. 4, 5; 42. 5, 6; viz. the confession of human *impotence* in attaining righteousness, and thankfully casting himself on Divine *omnipotence* for salvation. All tends to this "end". The three friends show the impotence of human experience (Eliphaz), human tradition (Bildad), and human merit (Zophar). Elihu points to God as the giver of a Divine righteousness for helpless guilty sinners. See note on p. 666.

1. 1-5 (**A**, p. 665). THE INTRODUCTION. HISTORICAL. (*Introversion.*)

A | A | 1. Job's character.
  B | 2. His sons and daughters. Their number.
    C | 3-. His possessions. Great.
    C | -3. His position. Great.
  B | 4. His sons and daughters. Their unanimity.
A | 5. Job's conduct.

1 There was a man = A man came to be. This settles the question as to the historical fact.

was = came to be. See note on p. 666.

man. Heb. *'ish*. Ap. 14. II.

Uz. In Gen. 22. 20, 21, immediately after the offering of Isaac, Abraham hears that his brother Nahor has eight sons, and among them two named *Uz* and *Buz*, and *Kemuel* the father of *Aram*. Uz gives his name to the land. Buz and Aram are connected with Elihu (32. 2). See Ap. 62.

The land of Uz is mentioned in Jer. 25. 20 and Lam. 4. 21. South of Edom, west of Arabia, extending to the borders of Chaldea. **Job.** In Heb. *'Iyyōb* = afflicted. **that** = this. **was** = came to be, as in Gen. 1. 2. **perfect** = inoffensive. None are "perfect" in the English sense of the word. Heb. *tām*. See Gen. 20. 5. **God.** Heb. Elohim. Ap. 4. I. **evil.** Heb. *rā'a'*. Ap. 44. viii. **3 and.** Note the Fig. *Polysyndeton*. Ap. 6. **men** = sons. **4 one** = man, as in *v.* 1. **his day.** Probably = birthday. Cp. *v.* 5; 3. 3. Gen. 40. 20. **5 were gone about** = came round. **offered** = offered up. Ap. 43. I. vi. Showing that, from Gen. 4 onward, the institution was observed. **sinned.** Heb. *chāṭā'*. Ap. 44. i. **cursed.** One of the eighteen emendations of the *Sōpherīm* (Ap. 33), by which the primitive Heb. text, *kālal* = to curse, was changed to *barak* = to bless, as in *v.* 11 and 2. 5, 9. Translated "cursed" in A.V., and "renounced" in R.V., in spite of *bārak* (blessed) standing in the printed text. See notes on 2 Sam. 12. 14 and Ps. 10. 3.

1. 6—2. 10 (**B**, p. 665). SATAN'S ASSAULT. (*Extended Alternation.*)

B | D | a | 1. 6. Presentation of the Adversary.
  b | 1. 7. Jehovah's question.
  c | 1. 8. His approbation of Job.
  d | 1. 9-11. Calumniation of the Adversary.
  e | 1. 12-. Limited permission given.
  f | 1. -12. Departure of the Adversary.
  g | 1. 13-19. Inflictions (Job's possessions).
  h | 1. 20, 21. Job's patience.
  i | 1. 22. Job not sinning.
D | *a* | 2. 1. Presentation of the Adversary.
  b | 2. 2. Jehovah's question.
  c | 2. 3. His approbation of Job.
  d | 2. 4, 5. Calumniation of the Adversary.
  e | 2. 6. Limited permission given.
  f | 2. 7-. Departure of the Adversary.
  g | 2. -7. Infliction (Job's person).
  h | 2. 8-10-. Job's patience.
  i | 2. -10. Job not sinning.

6 sons of God = the angels. Cp. 38. 7, and see Ap. 23. **present themselves** = take their stations. **the LORD.** Heb. Jehovah. Ap. 4. II. **Satan** = the Adversary.

b (p. 667) 7 And [6]the LORD said unto [6]Satan, "Whence comest thou?" Then [6]Satan answered [6]the LORD, and said, "From going to and fro in the earth, and from walking up and down in it."

c 8 And [6]the LORD said unto [6]Satan, "Hast thou considered My servant Job, that *there is* none like him in the earth, a [1]perfect and an upright [1]man, one that feareth [1]God, and escheweth °evil?"

d 9 Then [6]Satan answered [6]the LORD, and said, °"Doth Job fear [1]God for nought?

10 °Hast not Thou made an hedge about him, and about his house, and about all that he hath on every side? Thou hast blessed the work of his hands, and his substance is increased in the land.

11 But put forth Thine °hand now, and °touch all that he hath, and He will [5]curse Thee to Thy face."

e 12 And [6]the LORD said unto [6]Satan, °"Behold, all that he hath *is* in thy °power; only upon himself put not forth thine hand."

f So [6]Satan went forth from the presence of [6]the LORD.

g 13 And °there [1]was °a day when his sons and
1656 his daughters *were* eating and drinking °wine in their eldest brother's house:

14 And there came a messenger unto Job, °and said, "The oxen were plowing, and the asses feeding beside them:

15 And °the Sabeans fell *upon them*, and took them away; yea, they have slain the °servants with the edge of the sword; and I only am escaped alone to tell thee."

16 °While he *was* yet speaking, there came also another, and said, °"The fire of [1]God is fallen from heaven, [14]and hath burned up the sheep, and the servants, and consumed them; and I only am escaped alone to tell thee."

17 [16]While he *was* yet speaking, there came also another, and said, "The Chaldeans made out three bands, [14]and fell upon the camels, and have carried them away, yea, and slain the servants with the edge of the sword; and I only am escaped alone to tell thee."

18 [16]While he *was* yet speaking, there came also another, and said, "Thy sons and thy daughters *were* eating and drinking [13]wine in their eldest brother's house:

19 And, °behold, there came a great °wind from the wilderness, and smote the four corners of the house, and it fell upon the young men, and they are dead; and I only am escaped alone to tell thee."

h 20 Then Job arose, and rent his mantle, and °shaved his head, and fell down upon the ground, and worshipped,

21 And said, "Naked came I out of my mother's womb, and naked shall I return thither: [6]the LORD gave, and [6]the LORD hath taken away; blessed be the name of [6]the LORD."

i 22 In all °this Job °sinned not, nor charged [1]God °foolishly.

D a **2** Again there °was °a day when °the sons of °God came to present themselves before °the LORD, and °Satan came also among them to present himself before °the LORD.

---

8 evil. Heb. *rāʿaʿ*. Ap. 44. viii.
9 Doth Job . . . ? Fig. *Erotēsis*. Ap. 6.
10 Hast not Thou . . . ? Fig. *Erotēsis*. Ap. 6.
11 hand. Put by Fig. *Metonymy* (of Cause), Ap. 6, for power exercised by it.
touch = hurt. Fig. *Tapeinosis* (Ap. 6), meaning much more than "touch".
12 Behold. Fig. *Asterismos*. Ap. 6.
power. Heb. "hand". Put by Fig. *Metonymy* (of Cause), Ap. 6, for power exercised by it.
13 there was a day = the fit, or usual day. When Job was seventy. See notes on p. 666.
wine. Heb. *yayin*. Ap. 27. i.
14 and. Note the Fig. *Polysyndeton* (Ap. 6), to emphasise the details in all these reports of the calamities.
15 the Sabeans. Heb. Sheba. Put by Fig. *Metonymy* (of the Subject), Ap. 6, for the people of Sheba. Cp. 6. 19. Isa. 60. 6. servants = young men.
16 While he was yet speaking. Repeated three times to show the rapidity and vehemence of Satan's assault.
The fire of God = A fire of Elohim. Fig. *Enallage* (Ap. 6) = a great (or terrible) fire. Elohim used as an adj. Cp. Song 8. 6. Ps. 80. 10.
19 behold. Fig. *Asterismos*. Ap. 6.
wind. Heb. *rūach*. Ap. 9.
20 shaved his head. Symbolic of mourning (Lev. 21. 5. Jer. 7. 29; 16. 6. Mic. 1. 16).
22 this: i. e. these calamities.
sinned. Heb. *chāṭāʾ*. Ap. 44. i.
foolishly = with injustice.

2. 1 was = came to be. a day = the fit, or usual.
the sons of God. See note on 1. 6.
God. Heb. Elohim. Ap. 4. I.
the LORD. Heb. Jehovah. Ap. 4. II, and Ap. 23.
Satan = the Adversary.
3 perfect and an upright. See note on 1. 1.
man. Heb. *'īsh*. Ap. 14. II.
evil. Heb. *rāʿaʿ*. Ap. 44. viii.
4 Skin. Fig. *Synecdoche* (of Part), Ap. 6, one part of the body put for the whole. Also Fig. *Parœmia*. Ap. 6.
life = soul. Heb. *nephesh*. Ap. 13.
5 But = However.
put forth Thine hand. See note on 1. 11.
touch = touch bone to his.
curse. See note on 1. 5.
6 save his life = save his soul. Heb. *nephesh*. Ap. 13.

---

2 And [1]the LORD said unto [1]Satan, "From whence comest thou?" And [1]Satan answered [1]the LORD, and said, "From going to and fro in the earth, and from walking up and down in it." *b*

3 And [1]the LORD said unto [1]Satan, "Hast thou considered My servant Job, that *there is* none like him in the earth, a °perfect and an upright °man, one that feareth [1]God, and escheweth °evil? and still he holdeth fast his integrity, although thou movedst Me against him, to destroy him without cause." *c*

4 And [1]Satan answered [1]the LORD, and said, °"Skin for skin, yea, all that a [3]man hath will he give for his °life. *d*

5 °But °put forth Thine hand now, and °touch his bone and his flesh, and he will °curse Thee to Thy face."

6 And [1]the LORD said unto [1]Satan, "Behold, he *is* in thine hand; but °save his life." *e*

7 So went [1]Satan forth from the presence of [1]the LORD, *f*

and smote Job with sore boils from the sole of his foot unto his crown. *g*

h (p. 667) 1656 8 And he took him a potsherd to scrape himself withal; and he °sat down among the ashes.
9 Then said his wife unto him, °"Dost thou still °retain thine integrity? [5]curse [1]God, and die."
10 But he said unto her, "Thou speakest as one of the foolish women speaketh. °What? °shall we receive good at °the hand of °God, and shall we not receive [3]evil?"

i In all °this did not Job °sin with his lips.

C E j (p. 669) 11 Now when Job's three friends heard of all this [3]evil that was come upon him, they came °every one from his own place; °Eliphaz the Temanite, and °Bildad the Shuhite, and °Zophar the Naamathite:

k for they had made an appointment together to come to mourn with him and to comfort him.

F 12 And when they lifted up their eyes afar off, and knew him not, they lifted up their voice, and wept;

F and they rent [11]every one his mantle, and sprinkled dust upon their heads toward heaven.

E j 13 So they sat down with him upon the ground seven days and seven nights, and none spake a word unto him:

k for they saw that *his* grief was very great.

D G[1] L[1] 3 °After this opened Job his mouth, and °cursed °his day.
2 And Job °spake, and said,
3 "Let the day perish wherein I was born, °and the night *in which* it was said, 'There is a °man child conceived.'
4 Let that day be °darkness; let not °GOD regard it from above, neither let the light shine upon it.
5 Let [4]darkness and °the shadow of death °stain it; let a cloud dwell upon it; let the blackness of the day terrify it.
6 *As for* that night, let °darkness seize upon it; let it not be joined unto the days of the year, let it not come into the number of the months.

8 sat down = was sitting.
9 Dost thou . . . ? Fig. *Erotēsis*. Ap. 6.
retain = remain firm in.
10 What? shall we . . . ? Fig. *Erotēsis*. Ap. 6.
the hand = from. Fig. *Metonymy* (of Cause), Ap. 6.
God. Heb. Elohim (with Art.) = the [true] God. Ap. 4. I.
this = these calamities. **sin.** Heb. *chāṭā'*. Ap. 44. i.

2. 11-13 (C, p. 665). THE THREE FRIENDS. THEIR ARRIVAL.
(*Introversion and Alternation.*)

C | E | j | 11-. Their visit. *Hearing* of Job's calamities.
  | | k | -11. The reason.
  | F | 12-. Their sorrow. (Real.)
  | *F* | -12. Their sorrow. (Symbolical.)
  | *E* | *j* | 13-. Their visit. *Seeing* Job's calamities.
  | | *k* | -13. The reason.

11 every one. Heb. *'ish*. Ap. 14. II.
Eliphaz. From Teman, which is connected with Esau and Edom (Gen. 36. 4, 11. 1 Chron. 1. 35, 36, 53, &c.). Temanites famed for wisdom. He argued from the standpoint of human *experience*.
Bildad. Probably descended from Shuah, youngest son of Keturah by Abraham (Gen. 25. 2). Settled east of Palestine (Gen. 25. 6). He argued from human *tradition*.
Zophar. Probably from Naamah, southern frontier of Judah. He argued from the ground of human *merit*.

3. 1—31. 4 (D, p. 665). JOB AND HIS FRIENDS.
(*Introversion and Repeated Alternation.*)

D | G[1] | 3. 1-26. Job's lamentation. Introduction.
H[1] | J[1] | 4. 1—5. 27. Eliphaz's first address.
  K[1] | 6. 1—7. 21. Job's reply to Eliphaz.
  J[2] | 8. 1-22. Bildad's first address.
  K[2] | 9. 1—10. 22. Job's reply to Bildad.
  J[3] | 11. 1-24. Zophar's first address.
  K[3] | 12. 1—14. 22. Job's reply to Zophar.
H[2] | J[4] | 15. 1-35. Eliphaz's second address.
  K[4] | 16. 1—17. 16. Job's reply to Eliphaz.
  J[5] | 18. 1-21. Bildad's second address.
  K[5] | 19. 1-29. Job's reply to Bildad.
  J[6] | 20. 1-29. Zophar's second address.
  K[6] | 21. 1-34. Job's reply to Zophar.
H[3] | J[7] | 22. 1-30. Eliphaz's third address.
  K[7] | 23. 1—24. 25. Job's reply to Eliphaz.
  J[8] | 25. 1-6. Bildad's third address.
  K[8] | 26. 1—27. 10. Job's reply to Bildad.
  J[9] | 27. 11—28. 28. Zophar's third address.[1]
G[2] | 29. 1—31. 40. Job's self-justification. Conclusion.

[1] For the reasons for this division, see note on 27. 11.

3. 1-26 (G[1], above). JOB'S LAMENTATION. (*Repeated Alternation.*)

G[1] | L[1] | 3. 1-9. Birth lamented.
  M[1] | 10. Reasons.
  L[2] | 11, 12. Infancy lamented.
  M[2] | 13-19. Reasons.
  L[3] | 20-23. Manhood lamented.
  M[3] | 24-26. Reasons.

1 After this: i. e. after this long restraint. **cursed.** Here we have the Heb. *ḳālal*, which was in the primitive text. See note on 1. 5. **his day:** i. e. his birthday. Cp. *v.* 3. **2 spake** = answered, i. e. began, or lamented. Heb. idiom. See note on Deut. 1. 41. **3 and** = or. He knew not which it was. Cp. Judg. 11. 31. **man.** Heb. *geber*. Ap. 14. IV. **4 darkness.** Heb. *ḥashak*. **GOD.** Heb. Eloah. See Ap. 4. V. **5 the shadow of death.** Heb. *zalmaveth* = the darkness of death. **stain it** = pollute it. Heb. *ga'al*, to pollute; not *gā'al*, to redeem. **6 darkness** = intense or thick darkness. Heb. *'ophel*. Not *ḥāshak* (*vv.* 4, 5, 9) which is less intense.

(A New Metrical Version.)

JOB'S LAMENTATION.

3. 3-26 (G[1], above).

L[1] (p. 669)
3 Perish the day when born I was to be,
Or night which said a man-child is brought forth.
4 That day! may it be darkness evermore;
Let not Eloah care for it above,
And let not light shed on it one clear ray.
5 Let darkness stain it and the shade of death.
Let densest clouds upon it settle down;
Let gathering darkness fill it with alarm.
6 That night! Let darkness take it for its own;
Be it not joyous, 'mid the other days,
Nor come into the number of the months.

1656 7 °Lo, let that night be solitary, let no joyful voice come therein.

8 Let them curse it that curse the day, who are ready to raise up °their mourning.

9 Let the stars of the twilight thereof be °dark; °let it look for light, but *have* none; neither let it see the dawning of the day:

M[1] (p. 669) 10 Because it shut not up the doors of my *mother's* womb, nor hid sorrow from mine eyes.

L[2] 11 °Why died I not °from the womb? *why* did I *not* °give up the ghost when I came out of the belly?

12 [11]Why did °the knees °prevent me? or why the breasts that I should suck?

M[2] 13 For now should I have lain still and been quiet, I should have slept: then had I been at rest,

14 With kings and counsellors of the earth, which built °desolate places for themselves;

15 Or with princes that had gold, who filled their houses with silver:

16 Or as an hidden untimely birth I had not been; as infants *which* never saw light.

17 There the °wicked cease *from* troubling; and there the °weary be at rest.

18 *There* the prisoners rest together; they hear not the voice of the °oppressor.

19 The small and great are there; and the servant *is* free from his °master.

L[3] 20 °Wherefore is light given to him that is in misery, and life unto the bitter *in* °soul;

21 Which °long for death, but it *cometh* not; and dig for it more than for hid treasures;

22 Which rejoice exceedingly, *and* are glad, when they can find the °grave?

23 °*Why is light given* to a [3]man whose way is hid, and whom °GOD hath hedged in?

M[3] 24 For my sighing cometh before °I eat, and my roarings are poured out like the waters.

25 For the thing which I greatly feared is come upon me, and that which I was afraid of is come unto me.

26 I was not in safety, neither had I rest, neither was I quiet; yet trouble came."

N 1 (p. 671) **4** Then Eliphaz the Temanite °answered and said,

2 "*If* we °assay °to commune with thee, wilt thou be grieved?

m but °who can withhold himself from °speaking?

7 Lo. Fig. *Asterismos.* Ap. 6.

8 their mourning = a dragon. Referring probably to what the constellation signified.

9 dark. Heb. *ḥāshak.* See *v.* 4.

let it look. Fig. *Prosopopœia.* Ap. 6.

11 Why . . . ? Fig. *Erotēsis.* Ap. 6.

from = in, or within.

give up the ghost = die. Heb. *gavā'*, to expire. Cp. 10. 18; 13. 19; 14. 10.

12 the knees [of the mother]. Fig. *Ellipsis.* Ap. 6.

prevent = come before, so as to meet.

14 desolate places = ruins: i. e. places (tombs or monuments) already going to ruins.

17 wicked = lawless agitators. Heb. *rāsha'.* Ap. 44. x.

weary = worn out [of strength].

18 oppressor = taskmaster.

19 master = masters. Heb. pl. for emphasis.

20 Wherefore . . . ? Fig. *Erotēsis.* Ap. 6.

soul. Heb. *nephesh.* Ap. 13.

21 long = wait, or look for.

22 grave = sepulchre. Heb. *ḳeber.* See Ap. 35.

23 Why . . . ? Fig. *Ellipsis.* Ap. 6. A.V. supplies the sentence from *v.* 20; but it may be repeated from *v.* 22, "the grave", regarding *vv.* 21, 22 as a parenthesis.

GOD. Heb. Eloah. Ap. 4. V.

24 I eat = my food.

4. 1—5. 27 [For Structure see next page].

1 answered and said = replied and said. The *idiom* (Ap. 6) requires that the first verb (where nothing has been as yet said) must be rendered according to the context: "spake", "prayed", "began", "concluded", &c. Here it = replied and said. See note on Deut. 1. 41.

2 assay = attempt, or try. **to commune** = a word.

who . . . ? Fig. *Erotēsis.* Ap. 6.

speaking. Heb. *millah* = words composing the matter of what is said.

---

7 Lo! let that night be cheerless evermore;
And let no joyful sound be heard therein.
8 Let those engaged in banning days curse this;
Those ready e'en to rouse Leviathan.
9 Let all the twilight stars thereof be dark:
Let it look forth for light, but look in vain;
Nor ever see the eyelids of the dawn.

M[1] 10 Because it shut not up my mother's womb,
And from mine eyes hid all this misery.

L[2] 11 Why should I not have died within the womb?
Or, when brought forth, why not have then expired?
12 Wherefore were [nursing] knees prepared for me?
Or why were breasts [prepared] that I should suck?

M[2] 13 For then, in silence had I been laid down;
I should have sunk to sleep and been at rest
14 With monarchs and with counsellors of Earth;
(The men who build their mouldering monuments),
15 With princes who [in life] possessed much gold,
(And who, with silver, had their houses filled).
16 Would I had been but an untimely birth,
Like stillborn babes which never see the light.
17 For there the wicked cause no more annoy.
And there the wearied ones [at last] find rest:
18 Together with them captives find repose,
And hear no more the harsh taskmasters' voice.
19 The small and great alike are gathered there;
The servant from his masters is set free.

L[3] 20 Wherefore unto the toilworn gives He light?
Or life [prolongs] to the embittered soul?
21 (To those who look for death that cometh not,
And seek for it as those who treasure seek,
22 Who would rejoice with exultation—yea!
Be glad indeed, if they could find the grave).
23 The grave—'Tis for the man whose way is hid,
For him whom GOD hath hedged round about.

M[3] 24 For sighing cometh in, in place of food,
My groanings are like water pourèd forth.
25 For, that which I so feared hath come on me,
And what I dreaded, that hath come to me.
26 I was not careless; nor did feel secure;
Nor rested without thought: yet, trouble came.

ELIPHAZ. FIRST ADDRESS.

4. 1—5. 27 (J[1], p. 669).

N 1 (p. 671) 2 If one replies to thee, wouldst thou be grieved?
m Yet, who from speaking can refrain himself?

O (p. 671) 1656
3 °Behold, thou hast instructed many, and thou hast strengthened the weak hands.
4 Thy °words have upholden him that was °falling, and thou hast strengthened the feeble knees.
5 But now it is come upon thee, and thou faintest; it toucheth thee, and thou art troubled.

P Q
6 °*Is* not *this* thy fear, thy confidence, thy hope, and the uprightness of thy ways?

R n
7 Remember, I pray thee, °who *ever* perished, being innocent? or where were the righteous cut off?

o
8 Even as I have seen, they that plow °iniquity, and sow °wickedness, reap the same.
9 By the °blast of °GOD they perish, and by the °breath of His °nostrils are they consumed.
10 The roaring of the lion, and the voice of the fierce lion, and the teeth of the young lions, are broken.
11 The old lion perisheth for lack of prey, and the stout lion's whelps are scattered abroad.

Q p[1]
12 Now a thing was secretly brought to me, and mine ear received °a little thereof.
13 In thoughts from the visions of the night, when deep sleep falleth on °men,
14 Fear came upon me, and trembling, which made °all my bones to shake.
15 Then °a spirit passed before my face; the hair of my flesh stood up:
16 It stood still, but I could not discern the form thereof: an image *was* before mine eyes, *there was* silence, and I heard a voice, *saying*,

p[2]
17 °"Shall °mortal man be more just than [9]GOD? shall a °man be more pure than his Maker?
18 [3]Behold, He °put no trust in His °servants; and His angels He °charged with folly:
19 How much less *in* them that dwell in °houses of clay, whose foundation *is* in the dust, *which* are crushed °before the moth?
20 They are destroyed from morning to evening: they perish for ever without any regarding *it*.

4. 1—5. 27 (J[1], p. 669). ELIPHAZ. FIRST ADDRESS. (*Introversion and Alternations.*)

J[1] | N | l | 4. 1, 2-. Apprehension.
| | m | 4. -2. Apology.
| O | 4. 3-5. Trouble. (Particular.)
| P | Q | 4. 6. Righteousness. (Particular.)
| | R | n | 4. 7. General proposition. } Appeal to experience.
| | | o | 4. 8-11. Proof. "I have seen." }
| *P* | *Q* | 4. 12—5. 1. Righteousness. (General.)
| | *R* | *n* | 5. 2. General proposition. } Appeal to experience.
| | | *o* | 5. 3-5. Proof. "I have seen." }
| *O* | 5. 6-26. Trouble. (General.)
| *N* | *l* | 5. 27-. Research.
| | *m* | 5. -27. Recommendation.

3 Behold. Fig. *Asterismos.* Ap. 6.
4 words = sayings. Heb. *millah.* See note on "speaking" (*v.* 2). **falling** = stumbling.
6 Is not . . . ? Fig. *Erotēsis.* Ap. 6. The A.V. of 1611 reads "confidence; the uprightness of thy ways and thy hope?" First altered in the Cambridge edition of 1638. Name of editor is unknown.
7 who . . . ? Fig. *Erotēsis.* Ap. 6.
8 iniquity. Heb. *'āven.* Ap. 44. iii.
wickedness. Heb. *'āmāl.* Ap. 44. v.
9 blast. Heb. *neshāmāh.* Ap. 16.
GOD. Heb. Eloah. Ap. 4. V.
breath = spirit. Heb. *rūach.* Ap. 9.
nostrils. Fig. *Anthropopatheia.* Ap. 6.

4. 12—5. 1 (*Q*, above). RIGHTEOUSNESS. (GENERAL.) (*Division.*)

Q | p[1] | 4. 12-16. Vision.
| p[2] | 4. 17—5. 1. Voice. (Angelic, *v.* 18. Human, *vv.* 19-21).

12 a little = a whispering.
13 men. Heb. pl. of *'ĕnōsh.* Ap. 14. III.
14 all = the multitude of.
15 a spirit. Heb. *rūach.* Ap. 9: i. e. a movement of air, caused by something unseen.
17 Shall . . . ? Fig. *Erotēsis.* Ap. 6.
mortal man. Heb. *'ĕnōsh.* Ap. 14. III.
man = strong man. Heb. *geber.* Ap. 14. IV.
18 put no trust = putteth no faith in. Heb. *'āman.* Ap. 69. III. Cp. 15. 15, 31.
servants = messengers (Ps. 104. 4).
charged = will charge.
19 houses of clay. Cp. 2 Cor. 5. 1.
before = sooner than.

O (p. 671)
3 Behold, how many others thou hast taught;
And hast been wont to nerve enfeebled hands.
4 The faltering step thy words have lifted up;
And thou hast strengthened oft the feeble knees.
5 But now, to thee [misfortune] comes, what grief!
Because it toucheth thee, thou art dismayed!

P Q
6 [Ought] not thy fear [of God to be] thy trust?
And the uprightness of thy ways thy hope?

R n
7 Reflect; when has the guiltless been destroyed?
Or when were any upright ones cut off?

o
8 Aye have I seen that they who evil plough
And mischief sow, do ever reap the same.
9 They perish, smitten by the blast of GOD,
And by His angry blast they are consumed.
10 [Hushed is] the lion's roar! the young lion's growl!
And broken are the strong young lion's teeth!
11 The fierce lion perisheth for lack of prey;
The lion's whelps are scattered far and wide.

12 Now, unto me a thing was brought by stealth; P p[1]
Mine ear did catch a whispering thereof.
13 When thoughts arise, in visions of the night,
When falls on mortals vision-seeing sleep.
14 Great fear did come on me, and trembling [dread];
It made my very bones to stand in awe!
15 And o'er my face there then did pass a breath,
Which made my very hair to stand on end.
16 It stopped: but nothing could I then discern;
I looked: and lo, an image without form.
Silence: and then I heard a voice—[which said]—

17 "CAN MORTAL MAN MORE RIGHTEOUS BE THAN GOD? p[2]
OR BOASTFUL MAN BEFORE HIS MAKER PURE?
18 IN HIS OWN SERVANTS HE WILL PUT NO TRUST,
HIS ANGELS HE WILL CHARGE WITH IGNORANCE.
19 How much more those who dwell in houses made
Of clay; with their foundation laid in dust:
[So frail], they will be crushed before a moth;
20 'Tween morn and eve destroyèd will they be:
Will perish utterly—with none to save.

1656 21 Doth not their excellency *which is* in them go away? they die, even without wisdom."

5 Call now, if there be any that will answer thee; and °to which of the °saints wilt thou turn?

R n (p. 671) 2 For wrath killeth the foolish man, and envy slayeth the °silly one.

o 3 I have seen the foolish taking root: but °suddenly I °cursed his habitation.

4 His °children are far from safety, and they are crushed in the gate, neither *is there* any to deliver *them*.

5 Whose harvest the hungry eateth up, and taketh it even out of the thorns, and the robber swalloweth up their substance.

O q (p. 672) 6 Although affliction cometh not forth of the dust, neither doth trouble spring out of the ground;

7 Yet °man is °born unto trouble, as the °sparks fly upward.

r s 8 °I would seek unto °GOD, and unto °God would I commit my cause:

t 9 Which doeth great things and unsearchable; °marvellous things without number:

10 Who giveth rain upon the earth, and sendeth waters upon the °fields:

11 To set up on high those that be low; that those which mourn may be exalted to safety.

12 He disappointeth the devices of the crafty, so that their hands cannot perform *their* °enterprise.

13 °HE TAKETH THE WISE IN THEIR OWN CRAFTINESS: and the counsel of the °froward is carried headlong.

14 They °meet with darkness in the daytime, and grope in the noonday as in the night.

15 But He saveth the °poor from the sword, °from their mouth, and from the hand of the mighty.

16 So the poor hath hope, and °iniquity stoppeth her mouth.

r s 17 °Behold, HAPPY *is* THE °MAN WHOM °GOD CORRECTETH: therefore despise not thou the chastening of °THE ALMIGHTY:

t 18 For He maketh sore, and °bindeth up: He woundeth, and °His hands make whole.

5. 1 to which . . . ? Fig. *Erotēsis*. Ap. 6. In the Vulgate versions this is changed to a command: and it is quoted in support of "the invocation of saints".

saints = holy ones: i. e. the angels. Cp. 15. 15. Deut. 33. 2. Jude 14. So Sept. See note on "holy". Ex. 3. 5.

2 silly. English = Anglo-Saxon *saelig* = inoffensive. Heb. *pāthāh* = credulous. Cp. Hos. 7. 11.

3 suddenly = at once.

cursed = noted, stigmatized, or pointed out. Heb. *nāḳab*: i. e. "declared [the fate of] his habitation." Supply Fig. *Ellipsis* (Ap. 6) by adding "saying", and mark *vv.* 4, 5 as being what he said. See translation, below.

4 children = sons.

5. 6-26 (*O*, p. 671). TROUBLE. (GENERAL.)
(*Introversion and Alternation.*)

O q	6, 7. Trouble. Inevitable.		
r s	8. Trust in God.	Third person.	
t	9-16. Reason. (God's greatness.)		
r s	17. Trust in God.	Second person.	
t	18. Reason. (God's goodness.)		
q	19-26. Trouble. Deliverance from it.		

7 man. Heb. *'ādām*. Ap. 14. I.

born unto trouble, &c. Fig. *Paræmia*. Ap. 6.

sparks. Heb. sons of flame.

8 I would seek. The pronoun "I" is emphatic, and stands in contrast with "thou" in *v.* 1.

GOD. Heb. El. Ap. 4. IV.

God. Heb. Elohim. Ap. 4. I.

9 marvellous. Some codices, with Sept., Syr., and Vulg., read "and marvellous".

10 fields = out-places.

12 enterprise = something stable. See note on "sound wisdom". Prov. 2. 7.

13 He taketh, &c. This is quoted in 1 Cor. 3. 19 direct.

froward = perverse. Heb. *pāthal*, to twist.

14 meet = meet repeatedly.

15 poor = needy.

from. Some codices, with Aram., Syr., and Vulg., read "of".

16 iniquity. Heb. *'āval*. Ap. 44. vi.

17 Behold. Fig. *Asterismos*. Ap. 6. Cp Ps. 94. 12. Prov. 3. 11, 12. Heb. 12. 5. Jas. 1. 12.

man. Heb. *'ĕnōsh*. Ap. 14. III.

GOD. Heb. El. Ap. 4. iv.

THE ALMIGHTY. Heb. Shaddai. See Ap. 4. VII.

18 bindeth up . . . His hands. Fig. *Anthropopatheia*. Ap. 6.

---

21 Is not their life within them soon removed?
They die before to wisdom they attain."
5 Call now! exists there one to answer thee?
To whom among the holy wilt thou turn?
R n (p. 671) 2 The foolish man is killed by his own wrath;
And jealousy will slay the simple one.
o 3 I, when I saw the foolish striking root,
Have forthwith shown what would take place [and said]:
4 "Afar from safety will his children be,
And crushed to death when passing in the gate,
With no one near at hand to rescue them.
5 His harvest will a hungry one eat up,
And snatch it even from [protecting] thorns.
His children's wealth a robber waits to seize."
O q (p. 672) 6 Be sure that evil comes not from the dust;
Nor trouble springeth not from out the ground.
7 Ah no! Man's trouble from his birth begins,
Thence rises it, as rise the sparks from fire.
r s 8 But I—'tis unto GOD that I would seek;
Yea, before God would I set forth my cause;

t 9 Who doeth great things and unsearchable,
And wondrous things till they are numberless:
10 Who giveth rain upon the thirsty earth,
And sendeth water on the open fields:
11 Who setteth up the lowly ones on high,
And mourning ones He doth in safety set:
12 And so frustrates the schemes of subtil men,
That nothing stable can they bring to pass.
13 Who takes the wise in their own subtilty,
So that their shifty plans are all forestalled.
14 [Such men] do meet with darkness in the day,
And at the noonday grope, as in the night.
15 But from the sword's devouring mouth He saves
A needy one, and plucks him from their hand.
16 Thus for the poor there comes a ground for hope;
[And so] iniquity doth shut her mouth.

r s 17 Lo! happy is the man whom GOD corrects:
O spurn not the ALMIGHTY's discipline.

t 18 For He it is Who wounds, yet bindeth up:
He smiteth; yet 'tis His own hands that heal.

q (p. 672) 19 He shall deliver thee in °six troubles: yea,
in seven there shall no °evil touch thee.
1656 20 In °famine He shall redeem thee from
death: and in war from the °power of the
sword.
21 Thou shalt be hid from the scourge of
the tongue: neither shalt thou be afraid of
destruction when it cometh.
22 At destruction and °famine thou shalt
°laugh: neither shalt thou be afraid of the
beasts of the earth.
23 For °thou shalt be in league with the
°stones of the field: and the beasts of the field
shall be at peace with thee.
24 And thou shalt know that thy °tabernacle
shall be in peace; and thou shalt visit thy
habitation, and °shalt not °sin.
25 Thou shalt know also that thy seed *shall
be* °great, and thine offspring as the grass of
the earth.
26 Thou shalt come to *thy* °grave in a full
age, like as a °shock of corn °cometh in in his
season.

N l 27 Lo this, we have searched it, so it *is*;
m hear it, and know thou *it* for °thy good."

K¹ S (p. 673) **6** But Job °answered and said,
2 °"Oh that °my grief were throughly
weighed, and my calamity laid in the balances
together!
3 For now it would be heavier than the sand of
the sea: therefore my words are swallowed up.
4 For the °arrows of °THE ALMIGHTY *are*
within me, the poison whereof °drinketh up
my °spirit: the °terrors of °GOD do set themselves in array against me.
5 °Doth the wild ass °bray when he hath
grass? or °loweth the ox over his fodder?
6 °Can that which is unsavoury be eaten
without salt? or is there *any* taste in the
°white of an egg?
7 The things *that* my °soul refused to touch
are as my sorrowful °meat.

T 8 ²Oh that I might have my request; and
that ⁴GOD would grant *me* °the thing that
I long for!
9 Even that it would please ⁴GOD to °destroy
me; that He would let loose His hand, and
cut me off!

19 six. Named in the following verses.
evil. Heb. *rā'a'*. Ap. 44. viii.
20 famine=famishing. Heb. *rā'gab*. Cp. *v.* 22.
power. Heb.=hands. Fig. *Metonymy* (of Adjunct), Ap. 6; hands put for the destructive power which is in them.
22 famine=pains of hunger. Heb. *kāphān*. Not the same word as *v.* 20.
laugh. Fig. *Metonymy* (of Adjunct), Ap. 6, put for the feeling of security expressed by it.
23 thou shalt be in league=thy covenant shall be.
stones. Fig. *Synecdoche* (of Species), Ap. 6, put for whatever is hurtful to the soil.
24 tabernacle=tent, or less settled house.
shalt not sin=shalt nothing miss. Heb. *chāṭā'*. Ap. 44. i. See below. **25 great**=many.
26 grave. Heb. *ķeber*. See Ap. 35.
shock=stack. Heb. *gadīsh*, a heap of sheaves of corn.
cometh in=mounteth up. **27 thy good**=thyself.

6. 1—7. 21 (K¹, p. 669). **JOB'S REPLY TO ELIPHAZ'S FIRST ADDRESS.** (*Introversion.*)

K¹ | S | 6. 1-7. Job's excessive grief.
T | 6. 8-13. Death to be desired.
U | 6. 14-21. Remonstrance. (Their feelings.)
U | 6. 22-30. Remonstrance. (Their words.)
T | 7. 1-10. Death to be desired.
S | 7. 11-21. Job's excessive grief.

1 answered=spake, but Heb. idiom=replied. See note on 4. 1 and Deut. 1. 41.
2 Oh. Fig. *Ecphōnēsis*. Ap. 6.
my grief: i.e. the cause of my grief.
4 arrows. Fig. *Anthropopatheia*. Ap. 6. Cp. Deut. 32. 23, 42. Ps. 38. 2. Ezek. 5. 16. Zech. 9. 14.
THE ALMIGHTY. Heb. Shaddai. Ap. 4. VII.
drinketh=draineth.
spirit. Heb. *rūach*. Ap. 9. Perhaps in the sense of taking away his courage.
terrors. Only here and Ps. 88. 16.
GOD. Heb. Eloah. Ap. 4. V.
5 Doth . . . loweth . . . ? Fig. *Erotēsis*. Ap. 6. Only here and 1 Sam. 6. 12.
bray. Only here and 30. 7. **when he hath**=over.
6 Can . . . ? Fig. *Erotēsis*. Ap. 6.
white of an egg. "Egg" occurs only here. "White" (Heb. *rīr*) is found elsewhere only in 1 Sam. 21. 13, where it is rendered "spittle".
7 soul. Heb. *nephesh*. Ap. 13.
meat=bread. Fig. *Synecdoche* (of Species), Ap. 6, put for all kinds of food.
8 the thing that I long for=my expectation. Fig. *Metonymy* (of Adjunct), Ap. 6, put for the thing desired.
9 destroy=crush.

---

q (p. 672) 19 In troubles six He will deliver thee;
Yea! e'en in seven shall no misfortune harm.
20 In famine He will ransom thee from death;
In battle from the power of the sword;
21 In slander thou shalt be in safety hid;
And when destruction comes thou shalt not fear:
22 At dearth and devastation thou wilt laugh;
And of the beasts thou shalt not be afraid.
23 For with the field stones thou wilt be in league;
And e'en wild beasts shall be at peace with thee.
24 Yea, thou shalt know that peace is in thy tent;
And, looking through thy home, wilt nothing miss.
25 And thou shalt know thy offspring numerous;
Thy progeny as herbage of the field:
26 And thou, in ripe old age unto thy grave
Shalt come; like sheaves in harvest gathered in.

N l 27- Lo! this we well have pondered; so it is:
m -27 Hear it, and treasure it for thine own good.

JOB'S REPLY TO ELIPHAZ'S FIRST ADDRESS.
6. 1—7. 21 (K¹, p. 669).

2 Oh, that my woe could be exactly weighed, K¹ S (p. 673)
And my bemoaning set in scale therewith!
3 The woe more heavy than the sand would weigh:
'Tis this that makes my utterances wild.
4 For Shaddai's arrows now [stick fast] in me,
The heat whereof my spirit drinketh up:
GOD'S terrors now against me are arrayed.
5 Will the wild ass o'er tender herbage bray?
Or lows the ox while fodder he doth eat?
6 Can tasteless food be eaten without salt?
Or is there any taste in white of egg?
7 The very things my soul refus'd to touch
Are, as it were, my uninviting food.

8 Oh, that my prayer might come [before my God]: T
That Eloah would grant my heart's desire:
9 That it would Eloah please to crush me quite;
That He would loose His hand, and cut me off.

1656 10 Then should I yet have comfort; yea,
°I would harden myself in sorrow: let Him
not spare; for I have not concealed the words
of the Holy One.
11 °What *is* my strength, that I should hope?
and °what *is* mine end, that I should prolong
my °life?
12 *Is* my strength the strength of stones? or
is my flesh of brass?
13 *Is* not my help in me? and is °wisdom
driven quite from me?

U (p. 673) 14 To him that is afflicted pity *should be*
shewed from his friend; but he forsaketh the
fear of ⁴THE ALMIGHTY.
15 My brethren have dealt deceitfully as
a brook, *and* as °the stream of brooks they
pass away;
16 Which are blackish by reason of the ice,
and wherein the snow is hid:
17 What time they wax warm, they vanish:
when it is hot, they are consumed out of their
place.
18 The paths of their way are turned aside;
they go °to nothing, and perish.
19 The °troops of Tema looked, the °com-
panies of Sheba waited for them.
20 They were confounded because they had
hoped; they came thither, and were ashamed.
21 For now ye are nothing; ye see *my* casting down, and are afraid.

U 22 °Did I say, 'Bring unto me?' or, 'Give
a reward for me of your °substance?'
23 Or, 'Deliver me from the enemy's hand?'
or, 'Redeem me from the hand of the °mighty?'
24 Teach me, and I will hold my tongue:
and cause me to understand wherein I have
erred.
25 How forcible are right °words! but what
doth your arguing °reprove?
26 Do ye imagine to reprove words, and the
speeches of one that is desperate, *which are* as
°wind?
27 Yea, ye overwhelm the fatherless, and ye
dig *a pit* for your friend.

10 I would harden, &c. Occurs only here. = Let me even exult in my anguish (should He not spare) that I have not concealed, &c.
11 What . . . ? Fig. *Erotēsis*. Ap. 6. Continued in *vv.* 12, 13. **life** = soul. Heb. *nephesh*. Ap. 13.
13 wisdom = stability. See note on Prov. 2. 7.
15 the stream of brooks. Heb. *'ăphīķ* = a torrent restrained in a narrow channel, natural or artificial, open as in a gorge, or covered as in an aqueduct, passing away, inaccessible, and out of sight. See note on first occurrence, 2 Sam. 22. 16.
18 to nothing = into a waste. Heb. *tohū*, as in Gen. 1. 2.
19 troops = caravans.
companies = travellers.
22 Did I say . . . ? Fig. *Erotēsis*. Ap. 6. Continued in *v.* 23.
substance. Heb. strength; put by Fig. *Metonymy* (of Adjunct), Ap. 6, for what is produced by it.
23 mighty = adversary. Cp. chs. 1 and 2.
25 words = sayings.
reprove = convince, or confute: i. e. what can a reproof from you reprove? See translation, below.
26 wind. Heb. *rūach*. Ap. 9.
30 Is there . . . ? cannot . . . ? Fig. *Erotēsis*. Ap. 6.

7. 1 Is there not . . . ? Fig. *Erotēsis*. Ap. 6.
an appointed time = a warfare. Cp. 14. 14.
man = mortal man. Heb. *'ěnōsh*. Ap. 14. III.
are not . . . ? Fig. *Erotēsis*. Ap. 6.
2 the shadow = the shade: i. e. daytime.
work. Put by Fig. *Metonymy* (of Effect), Ap. 6, for the wages or reward gained by work: i. e. evening.

28 Now therefore be content, look upon me;
for *it is* evident unto you if I lie.
29 Return, I pray you, let it not be iniquity;
yea, return again, my righteousness *is* in it.
30 °Is there iniquity in my tongue? °cannot
my taste discern perverse things?

7 °*Is there* not °an appointed time to °man *T*
upon earth? °*are not* his days also like
the days of an hireling?
2 As a servant earnestly desireth °the
shadow, and as an hireling looketh for *the*
reward of his °work:

---

10 I then should comfort find; yea, e'en in this,—
(Though HE spare not, that I could yet endure),—
The Holy One whom I have not yet denied.
11 But what then is my strength, that I should hope?
Or what mine end, though I be patient still?
12 My strength; has it become the strength of stones?
Or has my flesh become like flesh of brass?
13 [Alas!] if my help lie not in myself,
All that is stable hath been driv'n from me.

U (p. 673) 14 E'en to th' afflicted, love is due from friends;
E'en though the fear of Shaddai he forsake.
15 But MY friends prove illusive, like a brook;
Like streams whose flowing waters disappear,
16 And are not seen by reason of the ice,
[Or of the] snow, which, falling, covers them.
17 What time it waxeth warm, the streams dry up;
When it is hot they vanish from their place:
18 They turn aside from out their usual course;
Are lost; and gone up into empty air.
19 The caravans of Tema look about;
The travellers of Sheba long for them.
20 They feel ashamed that they had trusted them.
They reach the spot; they stand; and are amazed.

21 [And thus it is with you]. Ye come to me;
Ye see a fearful sight; and are dismayed.
22 Came ye because I said, "Give aught to me?" *U*
Or, "Of your substance bring to me a gift?"
23 Or, "Snatch me from the adversary's power?"
Or, "Ransom me from the oppressor's hand?"
24 Teach me, I pray; and I will hold my peace!
And make me understand where I have erred.
25 How forcible are words of uprightness!
But wherein doth your arguing convince?
26 Do YE reprove by fast'ning on MY words,
When one in sheer despair [at random] speaks
27 Like to the wind? Orphans ye might as well
Assail; and on your friend's disasters feast.
28 Be satisfied then. Do but look on me.
And 'twill be plain to you if I speak false.
29 Return, I pray you; let not wrong prevail;
Yea, turn again; my cause is truly just.
30 Is there, I ask, perverseness in my tongue?
And can I not discern iniquity?
7 Is not a mortal's life a warfare here *T*
On earth? and as a hireling's day, his days?
2 As [weary] labourer panteth for the shade,
And as the hireling longeth for his wage,

1656 **3** So am I made to possess months of vanity, and wearisome nights are appointed to me.

4 When I lie down, I say, 'When shall I arise, and the night be gone?' and I am full of tossings to and fro unto the °dawning of the day.

5 My flesh is clothed with worms and clods of dust; my skin is broken, and become loathsome.

6 My days are swifter than a weaver's shuttle, and are spent without hope.

7 O remember that my life *is* °wind: mine eye shall no more see good.

8 The eye of him that hath seen me shall see me no *more:* Thine eyes *are* upon me, and I *am* not.

9 *As* the cloud is consumed and vanisheth away: so he that goeth down to °the grave shall come up no *more.*

10 He shall return no more to his house, neither shall his place °know him any more.

S (p. 673) **11** Therefore I will not refrain my mouth; I will speak in the anguish of my °spirit; I will complain in the bitterness of my °soul.

12 °*Am* I a sea, or a °whale, that Thou settest a °watch °over me?

13 When I say, 'My bed shall comfort me, my couch shall ease my °complaint;'

14 Then Thou scarest me with dreams, and terrifiest me through visions:

15 So that my [11]soul chooseth strangling, *and* death °rather than my °life.

(**16** I °loathe *it;* I would not live alway): let me alone; for my days *are* vanity.

17 °What *is* [1]man, that Thou shouldest magnify him? and that Thou shouldest set Thine heart upon him?

18 And *that* Thou shouldest visit him °every morning, *and* try him every moment?

19 How long wilt Thou not depart from me, nor let me alone till I swallow down my spittle?

20 I have sinned; what shall I do unto Thee, O Thou Preserver of °men? why hast Thou set me as a mark against Thee, so that I am a burden °to myself?

21 And why dost Thou not pardon my °transgression, and take away mine °iniquity? for now shall I sleep in the dust; and Thou shalt seek me in the morning, but I *shall* not *be.*"

8 Then answered Bildad the Shuhite, and said, J^2 V (p. 675)

2 °"How long wilt thou speak these *things?* and *how long shall* the °words of thy mouth *be like* a strong °wind?

4 dawning. Heb. *nesheph.* A Homonym, having two meanings: (1) as here, daylight; (2) darkness. See notes on 1 Sam. 30. 17. 2 Kings 7. 5, 7.
7 wind. Heb. *rūach.* Ap. 9.
9 the grave. Heb. *Sheōl.* See Ap. 35.
10 know=recognise.
11 spirit. Heb. *rūach.* Ap. 9.
soul. Heb. *nephesh.* Ap. 13.
12 Am I . . . ? Fig. *Erotēsis.* Ap. 6.
whale=a sea-monster.
watch=a bound. Cp. Jer. 5. 22.
over=about, as in 13. 27. Prov. 8. 29.
13 complaint=complainings.
15 rather than my life=by mine [own] hands.
life=bones, or limbs: i. e. hands.
16 loathe [it]=loathe [life], *v.* 16 is parenthetical, being the thought of suicide, which intrudes itself upon him.
17 What is man . . . ? Fig. *Erotēsis.* Ap. 6.
18 every morning. Fig. *Synecdoche* (of Part), Ap. 6, put for all time: i. e. continuously.
20 men. Heb. *'ādām.* Ap. 14. I.
to myself. One of the emendations of the *Sōpherīm* (Ap. 33), by which the primitive text "unto Thee" was altered to the current text (by the omission of the last letter) to "unto myself".
21 transgression. Heb. *pāsha'.* Ap. 44. ix.
iniquity. Heb. *'āvāh.* Ap. 44. iv.

8. 1-22 (J^2, p. 669). BILDAD'S FIRST ADDRESS.
(Introversion and Alternation.)

J^2 | V | 8. 1, 2. Reproof of Job.
  W | X | 3. Appeal to Reason.
    Y | 4-7. Application to Job.
  W | *X* | 8-19. Appeal to tradition.
    Y | 20. Application to Job.
V | 21, 22. Comfort for Job.

2 How long . . . ? Fig. *Erotēsis.* Ap. 6.
words=sayings. wind. Heb. *rūach.* Ap. 9.

3 So I inherit months of vanity;
And nights of weariness have been my lot.
4 As soon as I lie down to sleep, I say:
'How long till I arise, and night be gone?'
And I am full of tossings till the dawn.
5 My flesh is clothed with worms, and clods of earth;
My broken skin heals up; then runs afresh.
6 Swifter than weaver's shuttle are my days,
And they are spent without a gleam of hope.
7 Remember that my life is but a breath,
Mine eye shall not again enjoyment see.
8 The eyes that see me now, will see no more,
But Thine will see me, though I shall not be.
9 As wasted cloud that vanishes away,
So he that goes to Sheōl comes not back;
10 No more doth he return unto his house.
The place that knew him knoweth him no more.
S (p. 673) 11 [And hence my grief]. I cannot check my words;
In anguish of my spirit I must speak,
And utt'rance find for bitterness of soul.
12 Am I a [restless] sea? or monster of
The deep, that Thou about me sett'st a bound?
13 Should I have said, "My bed shall comfort me;
My couch shall yield a respite from my moans."
14 Anon Thou terrifiest me with dreams,
And with alarming visions fillest me,
15 So that my soul e'en strangling would prefer—
Death [self-inflicted, wrought]—by mine own hands.
16 I loathe my life: I would not thus live on.
Let me alone; my days are vanity.
17 What is frail man that Thou shouldst lift him up?
Or that Thou shouldest set Thy heart on him?
18 That every morning Thou shouldst visit him,
And ev'ry moment put him to the test?
19 How long e'er Thou wilt turn away from me?
Wilt Thou not for one instant let me be?
20 Watcher of men, what shall I do to Thee,
If I have sinned? why set me as Thy butt,
As if I were a burden unto Thee?
21 Why, rather, dost Thou not forgive my sin,
And take all mine iniquity away?
For in the dust I soon shall lay me down;
And thou shalt seek me, but I shall not be.

BILDAD'S FIRST ADDRESS.
8. 1-29 (J^2, p. 669).

2 How long wilt thou pour forth such talk as this? J^2 V (p. 675)
And thy mouth's words be like the blustering wind?

W X (p. 675) 1656 3 °Doth °GOD pervert judgment? or °doth °THE ALMIGHTY pervert justice?

Y 4 If thy °children have sinned against Him, and He have cast them away °for their °transgression;

5 If thou wouldest seek unto [3]GOD betimes, and make thy supplication to [3]THE ALMIGHTY;

6 If thou *wert* pure and upright; surely now He would °awake for thee, and make the °habitation of thy righteousness prosperous.

7 Though thy beginning was small, yet thy latter end should greatly increase.

W X 8 For enquire, I pray thee, of the former age, and prepare thyself to the search of their fathers:

9 (For we *are but of* yesterday, and know nothing, because our days upon earth *are* a shadow:)

10 °Shall not they teach thee, °*and* tell thee, and utter words out of their °heart?

11 °Can the rush grow up without mire? can the flag grow without water?

12 Whilst it *is* yet in his greenness, *and* not cut down, it withereth before any *other* herb.

13 °So *are* °the paths of all that forget [3]GOD; and the hypocrite's hope shall perish:

14 Whose °hope shall be cut off, and whose trust *shall be* a spider's web.

15 He shall lean upon his house, but it shall not stand: he shall hold it fast, but it shall not endure.

16 °He *is* green before the sun, and his branch shooteth forth in his garden.

17 His roots are wrapped about °the heap, *and* °seeth the °place of stones.

18 If he destroy °him from his place, then °*it* shall deny him, *saying*, I have not seen thee.

19 °Behold, this °*is* the joy of his way, and out of the earth shall others grow.

Y 20 [19]Behold, [3]GOD will not cast away a perfect *man*, neither will He °help the evil doers:

21 Till He fill thy mouth with laughing, and thy lips with °rejoicing. *V*

22 They that hate thee shall be °clothed with shame; and the °dwelling place of the °wicked shall come to nought."

3 Doth . . . ? Fig. *Erotēsis*. Ap. 6.
GOD. Heb. *El.* Ap. 4. IV.
THE ALMIGHTY. Heb. *Shaddai.* Ap. 4. VII.
4 children=sons.
for=by the hand of; by their own act.
transgression=rebellion. Heb. *pāsh'a.* Ap. 44. ix.
6 awake for thee: i. e. hear thy prayer. Cp. Sept. and Pss. 7. 6; 35. 23; 44. 23.
habitation of thy righteousness=thy righteous home. Fig. *Antimereia* (of Noun). Ap. 6.
10 Shall . . . ? Fig. *Erotēsis.* Ap. 6.
and. Some codices, with Aram., Sept., and Syr., read this "and" in the text.
heart. Supply *Ellipsis* (Ap. 6), by adding the words "such as these": referring to what follows in *vv.* 11–19 (see below).
11 Can . . . ? Fig. *Erotēsis.* Ap. 6. This is the first simile. See the second, *vv.* 16–19.
13 So are, &c. The application of the first simile.
the paths. The Sept. reads "the latter end".
14 hope=confidence.
16 He. Supply *Ellipsis* (Ap. 6), "He [like a tree]". This is the second simile, and the application is in *v.* 20. The first simile is in *v.* 11, with its application in *vv.* 13–15.
17 the heap=a spring, or fountain, as in Song 4. 12. Heb. *gal.* Pl. in Josh. 15. 19, &c.
seeth=overlooks: i. e. overtops.
place=house.
18 him . . . it. See translation, below: "him" and "it" refer to the tree.
19 Behold. Fig. *Asterismos.* Ap. 6.
is. Supply "ends" instead of "is".
20 help=take by the hand.
21 rejoicing=shouting for joy.
22 clothed with shame. Cp. Pss. 35. 26; 109. 29; 132. 18.
dwelling place=tent.
wicked=lawless. Heb. *rāshā'.* Ap. 44. x.

W X (p. 675)
3 The [righteous] GOD: Will He in judgment err?
Or, Shaddai: Will He e'er pervert the right?

Y
4 It may be that thy SONS 'gainst Him have sinned;
And He, through THEIR rebellion, cut them off.
5 If thou wouldst now seek unto GOD thyself,
And supplication unto Shaddai make;
6 If thou thyself wert only right and pure;
Then surely He would hear thine earnest prayer,
And prosperous make thy righteous dwelling place.
7 However small thy first estate might seem,
Thy latter end should be exceeding great.

W X
8 Enquire, I pray thee, of the former age;
And of their fathers set thyself to learn;
9 (For we're of yesterday, and nothing know;
Yea, as a shadow are our days on earth).
10 Shall THEY not speak to thee, and wise things tell
To thee from their experience: [such as these]?
11 "The reed: can it grow high without the mire?
And can the flag thrive where no water is?
12 While yet 'tis green, and while it stands uncut,
Sooner than any grass it withers up.
13 So is the end of all who GOD forget;
So perisheth the hypocrite's vain hope.
14 His confidence shall worthless prove to him;
And that on which he trusts, a spider's house.
15 He leans upon it, and it giveth way,
He clings to it; but it will not endure.
16 [Or like the tree] so green before the sun,
Whose boughs spread forth o'er all his garden-bed;
17 Beside the fountain are its roots entwined;
It overtops the [lofty] house of stone;
18 If one uproot it from its place, at once
It doth disown him, with 'I know thee not.'
19 Behold [thus ends] the joy of its brief life,
While, where it grew shall other trees spring up."

20 But upright men GOD never casts away; *Y*
Nor takes He evil doers by the hand.

21 [Then wait]; and one day He will fill thy mouth *V*
With laughter, and thy lips with shouts of joy.
22 [While] they who hate thee shall be clothed with shame,
And tents of wicked men exist no more.

K² Z¹ A¹ (p. 677) 1656 **9** Then Job °answered and said,
2 "I know *it is* so of a truth: but °how should °man be just with °GOD?
3 If he °will contend with Him, he cannot answer Him one of a thousand.
4 *He is* wise in heart, and mighty in strength: °who hath hardened *himself* against Him, and hath prospered?

B u 5 Which removeth the mountains, and °they know not: Which overturneth them in His anger.
6 Which shaketh the earth out of her place, and the pillars thereof tremble.
7 Which commandeth the sun, and it riseth not; and sealeth up the stars.
8 Which alone spreadeth out the heavens, and treadeth upon the °waves of the sea.
9 Which maketh °Arcturus, °Orion, and °Pleiades, and the °chambers of the south.
10 Which doeth great things past finding out; yea, and wonders without number.

v 11 °Lo, He goeth by me, and I see *Him* not: He passeth on also, but I perceive Him not.
12 °Behold, He taketh away, ⁴who can hinder Him? ⁴who will say unto Him, 'What doest Thou?'

A² 13 *If* °GOD will not °withdraw His anger, the proud °helpers do stoop under Him.
14 How much less shall I answer Him, *and* choose out my words *to reason* with Him?
15 Whom, though I were righteous, *yet* would I °not answer, *but* I would make supplication to my Judge.
16 If I had called, and He had answered me; *yet* would I not believe that He had hearkened unto my voice.
17 For He breaketh me with a tempest, and multiplieth my wounds without cause.
18 He will not suffer me to take my °breath, but filleth me with bitterness.

B u 19 If *I speak* of strength, lo, *He is* strong: and if of judgment, ⁴who shall set me a time *to plead?*
20 If I justify myself, mine own mouth shall condemn me: *if I say, 'I am* perfect,' it shall also prove me perverse.

9. 1—10. 22 (K², p. 669). JOB'S REPLY TO BILDAD'S FIRST ADDRESS. (*Division.*)

K² | Z¹ | 9. 1-35. Job's answer to Bildad.
| Z² | 10. 1-22. Job's expostulation with God.

9. 1-35 (Z¹, above). JOB'S ANSWER TO BILDAD. (*Alternations.*)

Z¹ | A¹ | 1-4. Job unable to answer.
| B | u | 5-10. God's power. Works unsearchable. } General.
| | v | 11, 12. God's dealings. Ways inscrutable. }
| A² | 13-18. Job unable to answer.
| *B* | *u* | 19-24. God's exercise of power. Unequal. } Personal.
| | *v* | 25-31. God's dealings. Unequal. }
| A³ | 32-35. Job unable to answer.

1 answered = responded. See note on 4. 1.
2 how . . . ? Fig. *Erotēsis.* Ap. 6. This is the one great question of the book.
man = mortal man. Heb. *'ĕnōsh.* Ap. 14. III.
GOD. Heb. El. Ap. 4. IV.
3 will = desire to.
4 who . . . ? Fig. *Erotēsis.* Ap. 6. Cp. 2 Chron. 36. 13. Isa. 48. 4.
5 they know. Fig. *Prosopopœia.* Ap. 6.
8 waves of the sea. The celebrated Mugah Codex (the earliest quoted in the *Massōrah* itself), Ap. 30, reads "cloud": i. e. thick cloud.
9 Arcturus. Heb. *'āsh.* A name still connected with "the Great Bear" (the more ancient name being "the greater sheepfold": Arab. *al naish*, the assembled (as in a fold). See 38. 31, 32, and Ap. 12, p. 18.
Orion. Heb. *kᵉsîl.* Cp. 38. 31. Amos 5. 8. A strong one, or the coming prince. See Ap. 12, p. 17.
Pleiades. Heb. *kīmāh* = the congregation of the judge. See 38. 31, 32. Amos 5. 8, and Ap. 12, p. 17. A constellation in the neck of Taurus.
chambers of the south: i. e. the [hidden] recesses, or the invisible spaces; on the latitude of Job's residence.
11 Lo. 12 Behold. } Fig. *Asterismos.* Ap. 6.
13 GOD. Heb. Eloah. Ap. 4. V.
withdraw = avert.
helpers = confederates.
15 not answer = not [dare to] answer.
18 breath. Heb. *rūach.* Ap. 9.

JOB'S REPLY TO BILDAD'S FIRST ADDRESS.
9. 2—10. 22 (K², p. 669).

Z¹ A¹ (p. 677) **9** 2 Most surely do I know that this is so;
But how can mortal man be just with GOD?
3 If man contend in argument with HIM,
Of thousand things he could not answer one.
4 However wise of heart, and stout of limb,
Who ever bravèd HIM, and prosperèd?

B u 5 Who moveth mountains, and they know it not;
Who overturneth them in His fierce wrath;
6 Who maketh Earth to tremble from her place,
So that its pillars rock themselves in fear.
7 Who bids the sun, and it withholds its light,
And round about the stars he sets a seal.
8 Who arch'd the heavens by Himself alone,
And marcheth on upon the cloudy heights.
9 Who made the Fold, Orion, Pleiades,
Yea, [stars in] the recesses of the South.
10 Who doeth mighty works, past finding out,
And wondrous things, in number infinite.

v 11 Behold! He passeth, but I see Him not;
He sweepeth by, but is invisible.
12 Lo, He doth seize; who then can hold Him back?
Or, who shall say to Him "What dost Thou?"

13 Should GOD, at length, His anger not avert, A²
Helpers of pride must stoop beneath His hand.
14 How then can I [address or] answer Him?
Or choose my words [for argument] with Him?
15 I could not be induced to make reply,
Though just: but I would supplicate my Judge.
16 If I had called, and He had answered me,
Yet could I not feel sure that He had heard—
17 He Who o'erwhelms me with [destructive] storm,
And multiplies my wounds without a cause:
18 Who hardly suffers me to take my breath,
But fills me with excess of bitterness.

19 If I appeal to strength; Lo! He is strong. *B u*
And if to justice; who could summon Him?
20 Should I attempt to justify myself,
My mouth would instantly the act condemn:
And, if I say that I am free from blame,
Then it would only my perverseness prove.

1656 21 *Though* 𝔍 *were* perfect, *yet* would I not
know °my soul: I would despise my °life.
22 𝔗𝔥𝔦𝔰 *is* one *thing*, therefore I said *it*, '𝔋𝔢
destroyeth the perfect and °the wicked.
23 If the scourge slay suddenly, He will laugh
at the trial of the innocent.
24 The earth is given into the hand of [22]the
wicked: He °covereth the faces of the judges
thereof;' if not, where, *and* who *is* 𝔋𝔢?

v (p. 677) 25 Now my days are swifter than a °post:
they flee away, they see no good.
26 They are passed away as the °swift
ships: as the eagle *that* hasteth to the prey.
27 If I say, 'I will forget my °complaint,
I will leave off my heaviness, and comfort
myself:'
28 I am afraid of all my sorrows, I know
that Thou wilt not hold me innocent.
29 *If* 𝔍 be °wicked, °why then labour I in
vain?
30 If I wash myself with snow water, and
make my hands °never so clean;
31 Yet shalt Thou plunge me in the ditch,
and mine own clothes shall °abhor me.
A³ 32 For *He is* not a °man, as I *am*, *that*
I should answer Him, *and* we should come
together in judgment.
33 °Neither is there °any Daysman betwixt
us, *that* might lay His hand upon us both.
34 Let Him take His rod away from me,
and let not °His fear °terrify me:
35 °*Then* would I speak, and not fear Him;
but *it is* not so with 𝔪𝔢.

Z² C (p. 678) **10** My °soul is weary of my °life; I will
°leave my °complaint °upon myself;
I will speak in the bitterness of my °soul.
2 I will say unto °𝔊𝔒𝔇, 'Do not condemn
me; shew me wherefore Thou contendest
with me.
D w 3 *Is it* good unto Thee that Thou shouldest
oppress, that Thou shouldest despise the work
of Thine °hands, and shine upon the counsel
of the °wicked?

21 my soul=myself. Heb. *nephesh*. Ap. 13.
life. Heb. *chāyai*.
22 the wicked=a lawless one. Heb. *rāshā'*. Ap. 44. x.
24 covereth: i. e. so that they cannot discern between right and wrong.
25 post=runner, or courier. Cp. Est. 3. 13, 15.
26 swift ships=ships of *ēbeh*. Hence vessels of bulrush (*ēb*); vessels of desire (*'ābeh*), i. e. desiring to reach their haven; vessels of enmity (*'ēybāh*), i. e. pirate vessels; or vessels of the Nile (*'ābai*, Abyssinian for Nile). Others, vessels of Joppa. Perhaps the last is best.
27 complaint=complaining.
29 wicked. Heb. *rāshā'*. Ap. 44. x.
why...? Fig. *Erotēsis*. Ap. 6.
30 never so clean=clean with soap.
31 abhor. Fig. *Prosopopœia*.
32 man. Heb. *'īsh*. Ap. 14. II.
33 Neither is there. Some codices, with Sept. and Syr., read "Oh that there were".
any Daysman=any umpire, arbiter, or mediator. In Job's case He was found in Elihu; in ours, in Christ.
34 His fear=the fear that He causes.
terrify=startle, or scare. Cp. 13. 21; 33. 7.
35 Then would I=Fain would I.

10. 1-22 (Z², p. 677). **JOB'S EXPOSTULATION WITH GOD.** (*Introversion and Alternation.*)

Z² | C | 1, 2. Petition.
  D | w | 3-7. Expostulation. God's power.
     x | 8-13. His creature.
  D | *w* | 14-17. Expostulation. God's ways.
     x | 18, 19. His creature.
C | 20-22. Petition.

1 soul. Heb. *nephesh*. Ap. 13. life. Heb. *chāyai*.
leave=let go, let loose: i. e. tell forth, give vent to.
complaint=complaining. upon=about.
2 𝔊𝔒𝔇. Heb. Eloah. Ap. 4. V.
3 hands. Fig. *Anthropopatheia*. Ap. 6. Cp. Pss. 119. 73; 138. 8; and 139. 5, 10.
wicked=lawless. Heb. *rāshā'*. Ap. 44. x.
4 Hast...? seest...? Fig. *Erotēsis*. Ap. 6.
man=mortal man. Heb. *'ĕnōsh*. Ap. 14. III.
5 man's=a strong man's. Heb. *geber*. Ap. 14. IV.

4 °Hast Thou eyes of flesh? or °seest Thou
as °man seeth?
5 *Are* Thy days as the days of [4]man? *are*
Thy years as °man's days,
6 That thou enquirest after mine iniquity,
and searchest after my sin?

---

21 Though I could say, "My heart and life are pure,"
I should [indeed] despise [and loathe] myself.
22 'Tis all the same: therefore I say it out:
The good and wicked He [alike] destroys.
23 If pestilential scourge slay suddenly,
He mocketh at the trouble of the good!
24 The earth is given over to a lawless one;
The faces of its judges He doth veil;
If not; then who is he [that doth all this]?

v (p. 677) 25 My days have gone more swiftly than a post,
They fled apace; as if no good they saw.
26 They passèd by like swift papyrus boat,
Or as the vulture pounceth on its food.
27 If I should say
"I will forget my grief,
Cast off my heaviness and comfort take;"
28 Then, with a shudder, I recall my woe.
I know Thou wilt not hold me innocent;
29 [Thou wilt] account me guilty. [Be it so];
Then wherefore should I labour thus in vain?
30 E'en though I bathe in water pure as snow,
And wash my hands [and make them] clean with soap;
31 E'en then Thou wouldest plunge me in the ditch;
And make me an abhorrence to my clothes.

32 For He is not a man such as myself, A³
Whom I might answer—"Meet me: let us plead!"
33 Oh! that there were with us an Arbiter,
One Who could put His hand upon us both!
34 Oh! that He would remove from me His rod,
So that His terror might not make me fear.
35 Fain would I speak, and boldly plead my cause:
But now, [alas], it is not so with me.

10 My soul hath grown a-weary of my life; Z² C (p. 678)
I yield myself unto my inward grief;
Let me tell out my bitterness of soul:
2 To 𝔊𝔒𝔇 then will I say, "Condemn me not;
But make it known why Thou dost strive with me.

3 Is it a pleasure that Thou should'st oppress? D w
And thus despise the work of Thine own hands,
And shine upon the schemes of wicked men?
4 Hast Thou then eyes of flesh [like mortal man]?
Dost Thou behold indeed as he beholds?
5 Are Thy days like the days of mortal man?
Or, like the days of mighty man, Thy years?
6 That Thou should'st seek for mine iniquity,
And for my sin should'st [diligently] search?

1656 7 Thou knowest that I am not °wicked; and *there is* none that can deliver out of Thine hand.

x (p. 678) 8 Thine [3]hands have made me and fashioned me together round about; yet Thou dost destroy me.

9 Remember, I beseech Thee, that Thou hast made me as the clay; and wilt Thou bring me into dust again?

10 [4]Hast Thou not poured me out as milk, and curdled me like cheese?

11 Thou hast clothed me with skin and flesh, and hast °fenced me with bones and sinews.

12 Thou hast granted me life and favour, and Thy visitation hath preserved my °spirit.

13 And these *things* hast Thou hid in Thine heart: I know that this *is* with Thee.

D w 14 If I sin, then Thou markest me, and Thou wilt not acquit me from mine °iniquity.

15 If I be [7]wicked, woe unto me; and *if* I be righteous, *yet* will I not lift up my head. *I am* full of °confusion; therefore see Thou mine affliction;

16 For it increaseth. Thou huntest me as a fierce lion: and again Thou shewest thyself marvellous upon me.

17 Thou renewest Thy witnesses against me, and increasest Thine indignation upon me; °changes and war *are* against me.

x 18 °Wherefore then hast Thou brought me forth out of the womb? °Oh that I had °given up the ghost, and no eye had seen me!

19 I should have been as though I had not been; I should have been carried from the womb to the grave.

C 20 °*Are* not my days few? cease *then, and* let me alone, that I may take comfort a little,

21 Before I go *whence* I shall not return, *even* to the land °of °darkness and the shadow of death;

22 A land of °darkness, as °darkness *itself; and* of the shadow of death, without any order, and *where* the light *is* °as darkness.' "

7 wicked. Heb. *rāshā'.* Ap. 44. x.
11 fenced me = knit me together.
12 spirit = breath. Heb. *rūach.* Ap. 9.
14 iniquity. Heb. *'āvāh.* Ap. 44. iv.
15 confusion. Heb. *ḳālōn* = shame. First occurrence.
17 changes and war = successions, yea hostile successions. Fig. *Hendiadys* (Ap. 6) = one thing: i. e. a constant succession.
18 Wherefore . . . ? Fig. *Erotēsis.* Ap. 6.
Oh . . . ! Fig. *Ecphonēsis.* Ap. 6.
given up the ghost = died. Heb. *gāva'.* Cp. 3. 11; 13. 19; 14. 10. Not 11. 20.
20 Are not . . . ? Fig. *Erotēsis.* Ap. 6.
21 of darkness and the shadow = deep darkness. Fig. *Hendiadys.* Ap. 6. Not two things, but one.
darkness. Heb. *ḥāshak.* See note on 3. 6.
22 darkness. Heb. *'ēyphāh.* See note on 3. 6.
darkness itself. Heb. *'ophel.* See note on 3. 6.
as darkness. Heb. *'ophel.* See above.

11. 1-20 (J[3], p. 669). ZOPHAR'S FIRST ADDRESS.
(Introversion and Alternations.)

J[3] | E | 1-6. Rebuke. God's judgments (particular) on Job.
 | F | y | 7, 8. Human ignorance.
 | | z | 9-12. Divine knowledge.
 | *F* | *y* | 13, 14. Human merit.
 | | *z* | 15-19. Divine reward.
 | *E* | 20. Rebuke. God's judgments (general) on the wicked.

1 answered = spake. See note on 4. 1.
Zophar. See note on 2. 11.
2 Should . . . ? Fig. *Erotēsis.* Ap. 6.
man. Heb. *'ish.* Ap. 14. II.
3 lies = babblings.
men. Heb. *m^ethīm.* Ap. 14. V.
no man = none.

11 Then °answered °Zophar the Naamathite, and said, J[3] E (p. 679)

2 °"Should not the multitude of words be answered? and °should a °man full of talk be justified?

3 Should thy °lies make °men hold their peace? and when thou mockest, shall °no man make thee ashamed?

---

7 Thou know'st that guilty I shall not be proved,
But from Thy hand can none deliver me.

x (p. 678) 8 Thy hands took pains with me and fashioned me.
At once, all round Thou hast engulphed me!
9 Remember, that as clay Thou mouldedst me;
And wilt Thou turn me back again to dust?
10 Didst Thou not erstwhile pour me forth like milk?
And make me to coagulate like cheese?
11 With skin and flesh hast Thou not clothèd me?
With bones and sinews fortified my frame?
12 Both life and favour Thou hast given me;
Thy watchful providence preserved my breath.
13 Yet these things Thou wast planning in Thy heart:
I know that this was in Thy mind long since.

D w 14 If I had sinned, then Thou wouldst it have marked,
And wouldst not have acquitted me from guilt.
15 Had I been wicked, woe is unto me!
And were I just, I would not lift my head,
So full of shame am I. Behold my woe.
16 And should I [dare to] lift it, then wouldst Thou,
Like howling lion, still pursue my soul,
And yet against me show Thy wondrous power.
17 Against me wouldst Thou bring new witnesses,
Thine indignation toward me would increase,
Troop after troop against me they would come.

x 18 Then wherefore didst Thou bring me from the womb?
I might have died, and no eye looked on me.
19 I should have been as if I had not been;
And from the womb been carried to the grave."

C 20 How few my days! Oh! let Him then desist,
And leave me, that I may some comfort take,
21 Before I go whence I shall not return,
Into the darkness and the shades of death,
22 A land of darkness, dark as darkest night.
The land of death-shade, where no order reigns,
And where the day is like the midnight—dark.

ZOPHAR'S FIRST ADDRESS.
11. 1-20 (J[3], p. 669).

J[3] E (p. 679) 2 Will not a mass of words admit reply?
And must a man, verbose, perforce be right?
3 Thy talk may put to silence mortal men:
Thou may'st mock THEM, none putting thee to shame.

1656 4 For thou hast said, 'My doctrine *is* pure, and I am clean in Thine eyes.'
5 But oh that °GOD would speak, and open His °lips against thee;
6 And that He would shew thee the secrets of wisdom, that *they are* °double to °that which is! Know therefore that [5]GOD °exacteth of thee *less* than thine °iniquity *deserveth.*

F y (p. 679) 7 °Canst thou by searching find out [5]GOD? canst thou find out °THE ALMIGHTY unto perfection?
8 *It is* as high as heaven; °what canst thou do? deeper than °hell; °what canst thou know?

z 9 The measure thereof *is* longer than the earth, and broader than the sea.
10 If He °cut off, and shut up, or gather together, then °who can hinder Him?
11 For He knoweth vain [3]men: He seeth °wickedness also; °will He not then consider *it?*
12 For °vain [2]man would be wise, though °man be born *like* a wild ass's colt.

F y 13 °If thou prepare thine heart, and stretch out thine hands toward Him;
14 If °iniquity *be* in thine hand, put it far away, and let not [11]wickedness dwell in thy °tabernacles.

z 15 For then shalt thou lift up thy face without spot; yea, thou shalt be stedfast, and shalt not fear:
16 °Because thou shalt forget *thy* misery, *and* remember *it* as waters *that* pass away:
17 And *thine* °age shall be clearer than the noonday; thou shalt °shine forth, thou shalt be as the morning.
18 And thou shalt °be secure, because there is hope; yea, thou shalt °dig *about thee, and* thou shalt take thy rest in safety.
19 Also thou shalt lie down, and none shall make *thee* afraid; yea, many shall °make suit unto thee.

E 20 But the eyes of the °wicked shall fail, and they shall not escape, and their hope *shall be as* the giving up of the °ghost."

5 GOD. Heb. Eloah. Ap. 4. V.
lips. Fig. *Anthropopatheia.* Ap. 6.
6 double: i. e. manifold.
that which is. Cp. note on Prov. 2. 7.
exacteth. Theology. Zophar's mistake. God is no exactor. **iniquity.** Heb. *'āvāh.* Ap. 44. iv.
7 Canst . . . ? Fig. *Erotēsis.* Ap. 6.
THE ALMIGHTY. Heb. El Shaddai. Ap. 4. VII.
8 what . . . ? Fig. *Erotēsis.* Ap. 6.
hell. Heb. *Sheōl.* Ap. 35. **10 cut off**=pass by.
who . . . ? Fig. *Erotēsis.* Ap. 6.
11 wickedness=iniquity. Heb. *'āven.* See Ap. 44. iii.
will He not then, &c.=although He seemeth not to perceive it.
12 vain man would be wise. Fig. *Paronomasia.* Ap. 6. "A man", *nābub yillābēb*="a man senseless [would become] sensible" if God did always punish immediately. **man.** Heb. *'ādām.* Ap. 14. I.
13 If thou prepare. This was Zophar's false theology.
14 iniquity. Heb. *'āven.* Ap. 44. iii.
tabernacles=tents. Some codices, with one early printed edition, Aram., Sept., Syr., and Vulg., read "tent" (sing.). Ap. 40.
16 Because. Syr. reads "For now".
17 age. Put by Fig. *Metonymy* (of Adjunct), Ap. 6, for the things done in it. See below. Heb. *heled,* like Greek *aiōn.*
shine forth=soar or shoot upward like the rays of the rising sun.
18 be secure. On this verse see translation below.
dig=look about, as in Josh. 2. 2. Cp. ch. 39. 29: i. e. before lying down (*v.* 19).
19 make suit, &c. Heb. intreat thy face: i. e. seek thy favour.
20 wicked=lawless. Heb. *rāshā'.* Ap. 44. x.
ghost=breath. Heb. *nephesh.* Ap. 13.

12. 1—14. 22 (K[3], p. 669). **JOB'S REPLY TO ZOPHAR'S FIRST ADDRESS.** (*Repeated Alternation.*)

K[3] | G | 12. 1-4. Non-inferiority of Job to his friends.
  H | 12. 5-12. Job's appeal to his friends.
   J | 12. 13-25. God. Job declares Him.
 G | 13. 1-5. Non-inferiority of Job to his friends.
  H | 13. 6-18. Job's appeal to his friends.
   J | 13. 19—14. 22. God. Job appeals to Him.

1 answered. See note on 4. 1.
2 No doubt, &c. Fig. *Eironeia.* Ap. 6.

K[3] G (p. 680) **12** And Job °answered and said,
2 °"No doubt but ye *are* the people, and wisdom shall die with you.

---

4 Thou mayest say indeed [to one of THEM],
"Pure is my doctrine: I have shown myself
5 Pure in His eyes." Would but Eloah speak,
And ope' His lips with thee, and show thee some
6 Of wisdom's secrets: how they far surpass
All that is seen. Know, then, that GOD exacts
Not more than thine iniquity deserves.

F y (p. 679) 7 Eloah's wisdom deep canst thou search out!
Or, Shaddai's perfect way canst thou attain?
8 It is as high as heaven: What canst thou do?
Deeper than Sheol's depths: What canst thou know?

z 9 Its measurement is longer than the earth;
[Its breadth is] broader than the ocean wide.
10 If He pass by, and make arrest, or should
To judgment call; who then shall Him resist?
11 For well HE knows the vanity of men:
And marks their sin, though seeming not to heed.
12 But man, vain man, doth understanding lack:
Yea, man is born like a wild ass's colt.

F y 13 [But as for thee]: Hadst thou prepared thy heart,
And stretched forth thy hands to Him in prayer:
14 If sin were in thy hand, put it far off;
Nor dwell there, in thy tent, iniquity,

z 15 Thou wouldst thy face uplift without a stain;
Yea, firm thou wouldest stand, and need not fear:
16 For all thy misery thou wouldst then forget;
Or, think of it as waters passed away.
17 A time would come far brighter than the noon:
And thou soar upward like the rays of morn.
18 Thou wouldst have confidence; for there is hope;
And, having look'd around, mightst rest secure,
19 And lay thee down, with none to make afraid;
Nay, many will be paying court to thee.

E 20 But as for wicked men, their eyes will fail,
And every refuge to them useless prove;
Their hope will vanish like a puff of breath.

JOB'S REPLY TO ZOPHAR'S FIRST ADDRESS.
12. 2—14. 22 (K[3], p. 669).

K[3] G (p. 680) **12** 2 Ye are the people: not a doubt of that:
And, as for wisdom, it will die with you:

1656 3 But I have understanding as well as you; I *am* not inferior to you: yea, ° who knoweth not such things as these?
4 I am *as* one mocked of his neighbour, who calleth upon ° GOD, and He answereth him: the just upright *man is* laughed to scorn.

H (p. 680) 5 He that is ready to slip with *his* feet *is as* a lamp despised in the thought of him that is at ease.
6 The tabernacles of robbers prosper, and they that provoke ° GOD are secure; into whose hand [4] GOD bringeth *abundantly*.
7 But ask now the beasts, and ° they shall teach thee; and the fowls of the air, and ° they shall tell thee:
8 Or speak to the earth, and it [7] shall teach thee: and the fishes of the sea [7] shall declare unto thee.
9 [3] Who knoweth not in all these that ° the hand of ° the LORD hath wrought this?
10 In Whose hand *is* the ° soul of every living thing, and the ° breath of all ° mankind.
11 Doth not the ear try words? and the mouth taste his meat?
12 With the ° ancient *is* wisdom; and in length of days understanding.

J 13 With ° Him *is* wisdom and strength, He hath counsel and understanding.
14 ° Behold, He breaketh down, and it cannot be built again: He ° shutteth up a ° man, and there can be no ° opening.
15 [14] Behold, He withholdeth the waters, and they dry up: also He sendeth them out, and they overturn the earth.
16 With Him *is* strength and ° wisdom: the deceived and the deceiver *are* His.
17 He leadeth counsellors away spoiled, and maketh the judges fools.
18 He looseth the bond of kings, and girdeth their loins with a girdle.
19 He leadeth princes away spoiled, and overthroweth the mighty.
20 He removeth away ° the speech of the ° trusty, and taketh away the understanding of the aged.
21 He poureth contempt upon princes, and ° weakeneth the ° strength of the mighty.
22 He ° discovereth deep things out of darkness, and bringeth out to light the shadow of death.
23 He ° increaseth the nations, and destroyeth them: He enlargeth the nations, and straiteneth them *again*.
24 He taketh away the ° heart of the chief of the people of the earth, and causeth them to wander in a ° wilderness *where there is* no way.
25 They grope in the dark without light, and He maketh them to stagger like *a* drunken *man*.

3 who knoweth not . . . ? Fig. *Erotēsis*. Ap. 6.
4 GOD. Heb. Eloah. Ap. 4. V.
6 GOD. Heb. El. Ap. 4. IV.
7 they shall, &c. Fig. *Prosopopœia*. Ap. 6.
9 the hand. Fig. *Anthropopatheia*. Ap. 6.
the LORD. Heb. Jehovah. Ap. 4. II.
10 soul=life. Heb. *nephesh*. Ap. 13.
breath=spirit. Heb. *rūach*. Ap. 9.
mankind=flesh of man. Heb. *'īsh*. Ap. 14. II.
12 ancient=aged. Heb. word found only here and 15. 10; 29. 8; and 32. 6.
13 Him: i. e. Jehovah (*v.* 9).
14 Behold. Fig. *Asterismos*. Ap. 6.
shutteth . . . opening. Heb. idiom for exercising authority. Cp. Rev. 3. 7. Fig. *Parœmia*. Ap. 6.
man. Heb. *'īsh*. Ap. 14. II.
16 wisdom=stability. See note on Prov. 2. 7.
20 the speech=the lip. Put by Fig. *Metonymy* (of Cause), Ap. 6, for what is spoken by it.
trusty=faithful. Heb. *'āman*. See Ap. 69. III. Rendered by "trust" three times in Job (4. 18; 15. 15, 31).
21 weakeneth=looseneth.
strength=girdle. Occurs only here and Ps. 109. 19 and Isa. 23. 10.
22 discovereth=uncovereth.
23 increaseth=maketh them great. Occurs only here and 36. 24.
24 heart. Put by Fig. *Metonymy* (of Cause), Ap. 6, for the courage given by it.
wilderness=a pathless *tohū*. Cp. note on Gen. 1. 2.

3 But I have intellect as well as you;
And I am not inferior to you:
Who hath not knowledge of such things as these?
4 My neighbours come and mock me; and they say
"Aha! he calls on GOD, that He should answer him!"
And I, an upright man, am made their sport.

H (p. 680) 5 A lamp is scorned by one who feeleth safe;
But 'tis prepared for them of tottering feet.
6 Prosp'rous and peaceful are the spoilers' tents.
Security is theirs who GOD provoke:
Abundance doth Eloah give to them.
7 Ask now the beasts: each will thy teacher be;
The birds of heav'n shall learning to thee bring.
8 Hold converse with the Earth, and it will speak;
Yea, fishes of the sea will tell their tale.
9 Who knoweth not, by every one of these,
That 'tis Jehovah's hand that doeth this?
10 In Whose hand lieth every living soul,
The spirit of all flesh,—of every man.
11 Doth not the ear discern the sense of words,
Just as the palate doth distinguish food?
12 So with the aged wisdom should be found,
And length of days should understanding give.

J 13 With HIM, then, there must wisdom be, and might;
Counsel [to plan] and wisdom [to adapt].
14 Lo! He casts down, and no one can raise up.
He shutteth up, and no man openeth.
15 The waters He withholds; the streams run dry:
He sends them forth; they devastate the earth.
16 To Him [belong] both strength and wisdom's might,
To Him [are known] deceivers and deceived;
17 'tis He Who leadeth counsellors, from whom
He wisdom strips; and maketh judges fools.
18 'tis He Who breaks [confed'rate] bonds of kings,
And girds their loins with cords [as prisoners led];
19 He leadeth priests [of their pretensions] stripped,
And overthrows the long-established [thrones].
20 The trusted [speaker] He deprives of speech;
And takes away discernment from the old.
21 'tis He Who doth on princes pour contempt;
And strippeth of their strength [the stout] and strong.
22 Deep things from out of darkness He reveals;
Yea, bringeth things to light from out death's shade.
23 He maketh nations great; and then destroys:
Increaseth them; and then, doth captive lead.
24 Princes of Earth of reason He deprives,
And makes them wander in a pathless waste.
25 They grope in darkness, as in densest night:
He makes them stagger like a drunken man.

G (p. 680) 1656 **13** °Lo, mine eye hath seen °all *this,* mine ear hath heard and understood it.
2 What ye know, *the same* do I know also: I *am* not inferior unto you.
3 Surely I would speak to °THE ALMIGHTY, and I desire to reason with °GOD.
4 But ye *are* °forgers of lies, ye *are* all physicians of no value.
5 °O that ye would altogether hold your peace! and it should be your wisdom.

H 6 Hear now my reasoning, and hearken to the pleadings of my lips.
7 °Will ye speak wickedly for [3]GOD? and talk deceitfully for Him?
8 [7]Will ye accept His person? [7]will ye contend for [3]GOD?
9 °Is it good that He should search you out? or as one man °mocketh °another, do ye *so* mock Him?
10 He will surely reprove you, if ye do secretly accept persons.
11 Shall not His excellency make you afraid? and His dread fall upon you?
12 Your °remembrances *are* °like unto ashes, your °bodies to °bodies of clay.
13 Hold your peace, let me alone, that I may speak, and let come on me what *will.*
14 °Wherefore do I °take my flesh in my teeth, and put my °life in mine °hand?
15 Though He slay me, yet will I °trust in Him: but I will maintain mine own ways before Him.
16 He also *shall be* my salvation: for an hypocrite shall not come before Him.
17 °Hear diligently my speech, and my °declaration with your ears.
18 °Behold now, I have °ordered *my* cause; I know that I shall be justified.

J 19 °Who *is* he *that* will plead with me? for now, if I hold my tongue, I shall °give up the ghost.
20 Only do not two *things* unto me: then will I not hide myself from Thee.
21 Withdraw Thine hand far from me: and let not Thy dread make me afraid.
22 Then call Thou, and I will answer: or let me speak, and answer Thou me.
23 °How many *are* mine °iniquities and °sins? make me to know my °transgression and my °sin.
24 [14]Wherefore hidest Thou Thy face, and holdest me for Thine enemy?
25 [7]Wilt Thou break a leaf driven to and fro? and [7]wilt Thou pursue the dry stubble?

13. 1 Lo. Fig. *Asterismos.* Ap. 6.
all this. Some codices, with Syr. and Vulg., read "all these things". Cp. 33. 29.
3 THE ALMIGHTY. Heb. *Shaddai.* Ap. 4. VII.
GOD. Heb. El. Ap. 4. IV.
4 forgers of = besmearers with. Occurs only here, 14. 7 and Ps. 119. 69.
5 O. Fig. *Ecphōnēsis.* Ap. 6.
7 Will ye . . . ? / **9 Is it . . ?** } Fig. *Erotēsis.* Ap. 6.
mocketh = befooleth.
another. Heb. *'ěnōsh.* Ap. 14. III.
12 remembrances = memorable or weighty sayings.
like unto ashes = similitudes of ashes: i. e. light.
bodies = defences. Heb. *gab* = mounds. Add "[like to] clay defences": i. e. weak.
14 Wherefore . . . ? Fig. *Erotēsis.* Ap. 6.
take my flesh in my teeth. Fig. *Parœmia.* Ap. 6. Still preserved in Arabic for rushing into danger. Like the next clause, which is a proverb preserved in English. **life** = soul. Heb. *nephesh.* Ap. 13.
hand. Some codices, with Sept., Syr., and Vulg., read "hands" (pl.).
15 trust in Him = wait for Him. Heb. *yāḥal.* See Ap. 69. VI.
17 Hear diligently. Fig. *Polyptōton.* Ap. 6. "Hear ye, hearing": i. e. Listen attentively; or, give diligent heed. Cp. Isa. 6. 9. See note on Gen. 26. 28.
declaration = opinion. Occurs only here.
18 Behold. Fig. *Asterismos.* Ap. 6.
ordered = set in order.
19 Who . . . ? Fig. *Erotēsis.* Ap. 6.
give up the ghost = to expire. See note on 3. 11.
23 How many . . . ? Fig. *Erotēsis.* Ap. 6.
iniquities. Heb. *'āvāh.* Ap. 44. iv.
sins. Heb. *chāṭā'.* Ap. 44. viii.
transgression. Heb. *pāsha'.* Ap. 44. ix.

G (p. 680) **13** Behold, mine own eye hath seen all these things,
Mine ear hath heard; and understood them all.
2 What ye know, I know also, even I:
In no one thing do I fall short of you.
3 It is to Shaddai that I fain would speak;
With GOD to reason, that is my desire.
4 But as for YOU, smirchers with lies are YE;
Physicians of no value are ye all.
5 Would ye but altogether hold your peace;
That, of itself, would show that ye were wise.

H 6 But hear, I pray, the reasoning of my mouth,
And to the pleadings of my lips attend.
7 Is it for GOD ye utter what is wrong?
Is it on His behalf ye speak deceit?
8 Dare ye show partiality to Him?
Is it, indeed, for GOD that ye contend?
9 Would it be well that He should search YOU out
Or can ye mock at Him, as at frail man?
10 YOU He will openly convict, be sure,
If you in partiality acquit.
11 Will not His majesty make you afraid?
And will not dread of Him upon YOU fall?
12 Your weightiest words are as the ashes—light;
Your arguments, like clay defences—weak.
13 Hold ye your peace; let me alone, that I
May speak,—and then, let come on me what will.
14 Aye, come what may, I willingly the risk
Will take; and put my life into my hand.
15 Though He may slay me, I will wait for Him;
And, before Him, my doings would defend.
16 Yes, even He shall my salvation be,
For ne'er will hypocrite before Him stand.
17 Hear now [my friends], give heed unto my word,
And keep my declaration in your ears.
18 Behold now, I have orderèd my cause;
I know that I shall be declarèd just.

19 Who then is he that will contend with me? J
For now, if I keep silence, I should die.
20 Only, [O God] do not two things to me;
And then I will not hide me from Thy face:
21 Thy hand—from off me—take Thou far away,
Nor let Thy terror fill me with alarm.
22 Then call Thou [me, and] I will answer [Thee];
Or, I will speak, and do Thou answer me.
23 How many are my sins,—iniquities,—
Transgressions?—These, oh! make Thou me to know.
24 Why hidest Thou from me Thy countenance?
Why shouldst Thou count me as Thine enemy?
25 Wilt Thou pursue me as a driven leaf?
And chase me as the stubble [light and] dry?

1656 26 For Thou writest bitter things against me, and makest me to possess the °iniquities of my youth.

27 Thou puttest my feet also in the stocks, and lookest narrowly unto all my paths; Thou °settest a print upon the heels of my feet.

28 And °he, as a rotten thing, consumeth, as a garment that is moth eaten.

14 °Man *that is* born of a woman *is* of few days, and full of trouble.

2 He cometh forth like a flower, and is cut down: he fleeth also as a shadow, and continueth not.

3 And °dost Thou open Thine eyes upon such an one, and bringest °me into judgment with Thee?

4 °Who can bring a clean *thing* out of an unclean? not one.

5 Seeing his days *are* determined, the number of his months *are* with Thee, Thou hast appointed his °bounds that he cannot pass;

6 Turn from him, that he may rest, till he shall accomplish, as an hireling, his day.

7 °For there is hope of a tree, if it be cut down, that it will sprout again, and that the tender branch thereof will not cease.

8 Though the root thereof wax old in the earth, and the stock thereof die in the ground;

9 *Yet* through the scent of water it will bud, and bring forth boughs like a °plant.

10 But °man dieth, and °wasteth away: yea, [1]man °giveth up the ghost, and °where *is* he?

11 *As* the waters fail from the sea, and the flood decayeth and drieth up:

12 So °man lieth down, and riseth not: till the heavens *be* no more, they shall not awake, nor be raised out of their sleep.

13 °O that Thou wouldest hide me in °the grave, that Thou wouldest keep me secret, until Thy wrath be past, that Thou wouldest appoint me a set time, and remember me!

14 If a [10]man die, °shall he °live *again?* all the days of my °appointed time will I wait, till my °change come.

15 Thou shalt call, and I will answer Thee: Thou wilt have a °desire to the work of Thine hands.

16 For now Thou numberest my steps: [3]dost Thou not °watch over my °sin?

26 iniquities. Heb. *'āvāh.* Ap. 44. iv.
27 settest a print = they make a print on my feet.
28 He, &c. = they (my feet) waste away.

14. 1 Man. Heb. *'ādām.* Ap. 14. I. "Man" is to *v.* 1 what *v.* 1 is to the whole paragraph. The Heb. accent (*Dᵉḥī*) emphasises the word "man", and divides the verse into two members; viz. (1) man and (2) his characteristics which are three: (1) his origin (born in sin), (2) his brevity of life, and (3) his fulness of sorrow.
3 dost . . . ? Fig. *Erotēsis.* Ap. 6.
me. Sept., Syr., and Vulg. read "him".
4 Who . . . ? Fig. *Erotēsis.* Ap. 6. Fig. *Parœmia.* Ap. 6.
5 bounds. Four early printed editions read "fixed times".
7 For there is hope of a tree. This is a positive independent statement, about which there is no doubt. There should be a full stop here. Then the Heb. accents mark off two hypotheses: (1) if it is cut down (*v.* 7) the Spring will wake its sap; (2) if waxing old (*v.* 8) it may still send forth a new growth. But there is no hope of man's living again like a tree. If he is to "live again" he must be raised from the dead.
9 plant = a new plant.
10 man = strong man. Heb. *geber.* Ap. 14. IV.
wasteth away = will decompose.
giveth up, &c. See note on 3. 11.
where . . . ? Fig. *Erotēsis.* Ap. 6.
12 man. Heb. *'ish.* Ap. 14. II.
13 O. Fig. *Ecphonēsis.* Ap. 6.
the grave = Sheōl. Ap. 35.
14 shall . . . ? Fig. *Erotēsis.* Ap. 6.
live again: i. e. in resurrection. Cp. John 11. 25, 26.
appointed time = service, or warfare.
change = improvement. Heb. *ḥalaph* = a change for the better. See note on Lev. 27. 10.
15 desire = a longing.
16 sin. Heb. *chāṭā'.* Ap. 44. i.

---

26 For bitter things, against me, Thou dost write,
And dost entail on me my sins of youth.
27 My feet Thou settest fast within the stocks,
And lookest closely into all my ways,
Branding Thy mark upon my very feet.
28 While these, thus marked, in rottenness wear out,
As garment when the moth hath eaten it.

* * * * * * *

14 [Frail son of] man that is of woman born,
How few his days; and these, of trouble full!
2 He springeth like a flow'r, and is cut down:
He fleeth as a shadow; makes no stay.
3 Yet, op'nest Thou Thine eyes on such an one?
And bring'st him into judgment with Thyself?
4 Oh that a clean thing could come forth from out
A thing unclean! But there is no such one.
5 If now his days are all [by Thee] decreed,
And fixed the number of his months with Thee,
If Thou hast made him bounds he may not pass,
6 Then look away from him, that he may rest,
And, like a hireling, may fulfil his day.
7 For of a tree, indeed, there still is hope
That, if it be cut down, 'twill sprout again;
And that its suckers will not cease [to grow].
8 Though, in the earth, the root thereof wax old,
Though in the dust [of earth] its stump should die;
9 [Yet] will the scent of water make it bud,
And put forth shoots like newly-planted tree.
10 But man—he dies; and, fallèn, he departs:
Yea, man—when he expireth—Where [is he]?
11 As waters fail, and vanish from the sea,
And as a river wasteth and dries up;
12 So man lies down and rises not again:
Until the heavens are no more, they ne'er
Awake; nor are arousèd from their sleep.

* * * * * * *

13 Oh! that in Sheol Thou wouldst cover me;
Conceal me, till Thine anger turn away;
Fix me a time; and then remember me.

* * * * * * *

14 If a man dieth, will he live again?
Then—all my days of service I will wait,
Until the time of my reviving come;
15 Then shalt Thou call, and I will answer Thee;
For Thou wilt yearn toward Thy handiwork.

* * * * * * *

16 But now—Thou numberest my ev'ry step:
And Thou wilt not pass over [all] my sin.

1656 17 My °transgression *is* sealed up in a bag,
and Thou sewest up mine °iniquity.
18 And surely the mountain falling cometh to
nought, and the rock is removed out of his
place.
19 °The waters wear the stones: Thou
washest away the things which grow *out* of
the dust of the earth; and Thou destroyest
the hope of °man.
20 Thou prevailest for ever against him, and
he passeth: Thou changest his countenance,
and sendest him away.
21 His sons come to honour, and he knoweth
it not; and they are brought low, but he perceiveth *it* not of them.
22 °But his flesh upon him shall have pain,
and °his soul °within him shall °mourn."

J^4 K^1 a (p. 684) **15** Then °answered °Eliphaz the Temanite,
and said,
2 °"Should a wise man utter °vain knowledge, and fill his belly with the east °wind?
3 ²Should he reason with unprofitable talk?
or with speeches wherewith he can do no
good?

b 4 Yea, thou castest off °fear, and restrainest
prayer before °GOD.
5 For thy mouth uttereth thine °iniquity, and
thou choosest the tongue of the crafty.
6 Thine own mouth condemneth thee, and
not I: yea, thine own lips testify against
thee.

a 7 °*Art* thou the first °man *that* was born? or
wast thou °made before the hills?
8 °Hast thou °heard the °secret of °GOD?
and dost thou restrain wisdom to thyself?
9 °What knowest thou, that we know not?
what understandest thou, which *is* not in us?
10 With us *are* both the grayheaded and very
aged men, much elder than thy father.
11 °*Are* the consolations of ⁴GOD small with
thee? is there any °secret thing with thee?
12 °Why doth thine heart carry thee away?
and what do thy eyes wink at,
13 That thou turnest thy °spirit against
⁴GOD, and lettest *such* words go out of thy
mouth?

17 transgression. Heb. *pāsha'*. Ap. 44. ix.
iniquity. Heb. *'āvāh*. Ap. 44. iv.
19 The waters, &c. Fig. *Parœmia*. Ap. 6.
man = a mortal. Heb. *'ĕnōsh*. Ap. 14. III.
22 But. This verse describes what happens while he is alive. See below.
his soul = he himself. Heb. *nephesh*. Ap. 13.
within = over.
mourn: i. e. mourn "over himself". Heb. *'ālāiv*, as in Hos. 10. 5.

15. 1-35 (J^4, p. 669). ELIPHAZ. SECOND ADDRESS. (*Division.*)

J^4 | K^1 | 15. 1-16. On Job's reasonings.
| K^2 | 15. 17-35. On God's dealings.

1-16 (K^1, above). ON JOB'S REASONINGS. (*Alternations.*)

K^1 | a | 1-3. Questions concerning Job's words.
| b | 4-6. Proofs in answer.
| *a* | 7-14. Questions concerning Job's character.
| *b* | 15, 16. Proofs in answer.

1 answered = replied. See note on 4. 1.
Eliphaz. See note on 2. 11. This is the second of his three addresses.
2 Should . . . ? Fig. *Erotēsis*. Ap. 6.
vain = empty. i.e. windy science.
wind. Heb. *rūach*. Ap. 9.
4 fear = reverence.
GOD. Heb. El. Ap. 4. IV.
5 iniquity. Heb. *'āvāh*. Ap. 44. iv.
7 Art . . . ? Fig. *Erotēsis*. Ap. 6.
man. Heb. *'ādām*. Ap. 14. I.
made = brought forth.
8 Hast . . . ? Fig. *Erotēsis*. Ap. 6.
heard = overheard.
secret. Heb. *sōd* = secret counsellings, used of two or more in council. **GOD.** Heb. Eloah. Ap. 4. V.
9 What . . . ? / **11 Are . . . ?** } Fig. *Erotēsis*. Ap. 6.
secret = concealed. Heb. *lā'at*. Rendered by Theodotion (R. Sept.), *mustērion* (= secret); Aquila (R. Sept.), *aporrhētā* (= forbidden); Symmachus (R. Sept.), *homilia* (= intercourse).
12 Why . . . ? Fig. *Erotēsis*. Ap. 6.
13 spirit. Heb. *rūach*. Ap. 9.

---

17 For, sealed is my guilt, as in a bag,
And mine iniquity Thou fast'nest up.

* * * * * *

18 Yes!—e'en a mountain falling, wastes away;
The rock may be removed from its place;
19 The [flowing] waters wear away the stones;
The floods thereof may wash away the soil:
E'en so the frail man's hope Thou dost destroy;
20 Thou overpow'rest him, and he is gone;
His face doth fade; Thou sendest him away.
21 His sons are honoured, but he knows it not;
They are brought low, but he perceives it not.
22 Only [till then] he feels pain over it,
Only [till then] he over it doth mourn.

ELIPHAZ. SECOND ADDRESS.

(J^4, 15. 2-35).

K^1 a (p. 684) 2 A wise man, should he give vain knowledge forth,
Or fill himself with words like blustering wind?
3 Should he contend with words of no avail,
Or speeches wherewith he can do no good?

4 But thou—thou wouldst make void the fear of GOD, b
And weaken [all] devotion [due] to Him.
5 Thy mouth declares thine own iniquity;
And thou thyself dost choose the crafty tongue.
6 Thine own mouth and not I doth thee condemn;
Yea, thine own lips against thee testify.

7 Art thou the first man who was [ever] born? *a*
Wast thou brought forth before the hills [were made]?
8 Eloah's secret counsel didst thou hear?
And to [His] wisdom canst thou e'er attain?
9 What knowest thou, that is not known to us?
What understandest thou, that we do not?
10 (The grey-haired and the agèd is with us,
More full of days than thine own father was).
11 GOD'S comfortings, are they too small for thee?
Or is there any secret [sin] with thee?
12 Why let thy feelings carry thee away?
What meaneth, then, this quiv'ring of thine eyes?
13 That thou shouldst turn thy rage against [thy] GOD,
And cause such words to issue from thy mouth.

1656 14 °What *is* °man, that he should be °clean? and *he which is* born of a woman, that he should be righteous?

b (p. 684) 15 °Behold, He putteth no °trust in His °saints; yea, the heavens are not clean in His °sight.
16 How much more abominable and filthy *is* °man, which drinketh °iniquity like water?

K² c 17 I will shew thee, hear me; and that *which* I have seen I will declare;
18 Which wise men have told from their fathers, and have not hid *it*:
19 Unto whom alone the earth was given, and no stranger passed among them.
20 The °wicked man °travaileth with pain all *his* days, and the number of years is hidden to the oppressor.
21 A dreadful sound *is* in his ears: in prosperity the destroyer shall come upon him.
22 He believeth not that he shall return out of darkness, and he is °waited for of the sword.
23 He wandereth abroad for bread, *saying*, 'Where *is it*?' he knoweth that the day of darkness is ready at his hand.
24 Trouble and anguish shall make him afraid; they shall prevail against him, as a king ready to the battle.

d 25 For he stretcheth out his hand against ⁴GOD, and strengtheneth himself against °THE ALMIGHTY.
26 He runneth upon Him, *even* on *his* neck, upon the thick bosses of his bucklers:
27 Because he covereth his face with his fatness, and maketh °collops of fat on *his* flanks.

c 28 And he dwelleth in desolate cities, *and* in houses which no man inhabiteth, which are ready to become heaps.
29 He shall not be rich, neither shall his substance continue, neither °shall he prolong the perfection thereof upon the earth.
30 He shall not depart out of darkness; the flame shall dry up his branches, and by the °breath of His mouth shall he go away.
31 Let not him that is deceived trust in vanity: for vanity shall be his recompence.
32 It shall be accomplished before his time, and his branch shall not be green.
33 He shall shake off his unripe grape as the vine, and shall cast off his flower as the olive.
34 For the °congregation of hypocrites *shall be* desolate, and fire shall consume the °tabernacles of bribery.

14 man = a mortal. Heb. *'ĕnōsh*. Ap. 14. III. See note on 14. 1.
clean = pure.
15 Behold. Fig. *Asterismos*. Ap. 6.
trust = faith. Heb. *'āman*. Cp. *v.* 31. Ap. 69. III.
saints = holy ones. Here = angels. Cp. 4. 18.
sight = eyes.
16 man. Heb. *'īsh*. Ap. 14. II.
iniquity. Heb. *'āval*. Ap. 44. vi.

15. 17-35 (K², p. 669). ON GOD'S DEALINGS.
(Alternation.)

K²
c | 15. 17-24. God's judgments.
d | 25-27. Reasons. The procuring cause.
c | 28-34. God's judgments.
d | 35. Reasons. The procuring cause.

20 wicked man = lawless one. Heb. *rāshā'*. Ap. 44. x. From *v.* 20 to *v.* 35 Eliphaz repeats what he had heard from tradition.
travaileth = "he travaileth".
22 waited for of the sword = destined to the power of the sword.
25 THE ALMIGHTY. Heb. 'El Shaddai. Ap. 4. VII.
27 collops = lumps, or slices.
29 shall he prolong the perfection thereof. The Sept. reads "shall their shadow stretch along upon the ground".
30 breath. Heb. *rūach*. Ap. 9.
34 congregation = assembly.
tabernacles = tents.

---

14 What is a mortal, that he should be pure?
Or he of woman born, that he be just?

b (p. 684) 15 Lo! in His holy ones He puts no faith;
(The very heavn's in His sight are not pure.)
16 How much less [man], corrupt, defiled! Yea, man,
Who drinks, like water [his] iniquity.

K² c 17 Give heed to me; and I will thee instruct;
And that which I have seen I will declare:
18 (Which wise men plainly have made known to us,
And have not hid them—truths their fathers taught;
19 The men to whom alone the land was given,
And among whom no alien passed): [They said]:
20 "The wicked sorely labours all his days,
His years reserved for the oppressor's greed.
21 A voice of terror ever fills his ears;
And when he prospers, then the spoiler comes.
22 He has no hope from darkness to return;
[And thinks] that he is destined for the sword;
23 He wanders forth and asks :—'O, where is bread'
Well knowing that a dark day draweth nigh.
24 Distress and anguish fill him with alarm;
They overpow'r him like a warrior's charge.

25 Because he stretchèd out his hand 'gainst GOD d
And haughtily El Shaddai did defy,
26 [Because] he used to run with stiffened neck
Against Him, with the bosses of his shield;
27 Because his face he clothed with his own fat,
And gathered rolls of fat upon his loins.

28 Therefore he dwelleth in a ruined place; c
In houses where none other deigns to live;
In places destined to be ruined heaps.
29 He will not long be rich, nor will his wealth
Endure, nor will his shadow lengthen out.
30 From darkness he will nevermore escape;
His tender branch the flame shall wither up;
In God's hot anger he will pass away.
31 Let no one put his faith in vain deceit:
For vanity will be his recompense;
32 [And] he will be cut off before his time,
So that his palm will not be always green.
33 As shaketh off the vine its unripe fruit,
Or as the olive casts away its flower,
34 So will the household of the vile be naught;
And fire consume the tents of the corrupt

d (p. 685) 1656 35 They conceive °mischief, and bring forth vanity, and their °belly prepareth deceit."

K^4 L^1 (p. 686) **16** Then Job °answered and said,
2 "I have heard many such things: °miserable comforters *are* ye all.
3 °Shall °vain words have an end? or °what emboldeneth thee that thou answerest?
4 I also could speak as ye *do*: if °your soul were in °my soul's stead, I could heap up words against you, and shake mine head at you.
5 *But* I would strengthen you with my mouth, and the moving of my lips should asswage *your grief*.
6 Though I speak, my grief is not asswaged: and *though* I forbear, what am I eased?
M^1 7 But now He hath made me weary: Thou hast made desolate all my company.
8 And Thou hast filled me with wrinkles, *which* °is a witness *against me*: and my °leanness rising up in me beareth witness to my face.
9 He teareth *me* in His wrath, Who hateth me: He gnasheth upon me with His teeth; mine enemy sharpeneth His eyes upon me.
10 They have gaped upon me with their mouth; they have smitten me upon the cheek reproachfully; they have gathered themselves together against me.
11 °GOD hath delivered me to °the ungodly, and turned me over into the hands of °the wicked.
12 I was at ease, but He hath broken me asunder: He hath also taken *me* by my neck, and shaken me to pieces, and set me up for His mark.
13 His archers compass me round about, He cleaveth my reins asunder, and doth not spare; He poureth out my gall upon the ground.
14 He breaketh me with breach upon breach, He runneth upon me like a °giant.
15 I have °sewed sackcloth upon my skin, and defiled my horn in the dust.

35 mischief. Heb. *'āmāl.* Ap. 44. v.
belly. Put by Fig. *Metonymy* (of Subject), Ap. 6, for the thoughts produced by emotion.

16. 1—17. 16 (K^4, p. 669). JOB'S REPLY TO ELIPHAZ'S SECOND ADDRESS.
(*Repeated Alternation.*)

K^4 | L^1 | 16. 1-6. Reproof.
M^1 | 16. 7-16. Despondency.
L^2 | 16. 17-21. Reply.
M^2 | 16. 22—17. 1. Despondency.
L^3 | 17. 2-10. Challenge.
M^3 | 17. 11-16. Despondency.

1 answered = replied. See note on 4. 1.
2 miserable = wearisome.
3 Shall . . . ? Fig. *Erotēsis.* Ap. 6.
vain words = empty words. Heb. words of wind.
what . . . ? Fig. *Erotēsis.* Ap. 6.
4 your soul = you (emph.). Heb. *nephesh.* Ap. 13.
my soul = me (emph.). Heb. *nephesh.* Ap. 13.
8 is = is become.
leanness. Fig. *Prosopopœia.* Ap. 6.
11 GOD. Heb. El. Ap. 4. IV.
the ungodly = an evil one. Heb. *'āvāl.* Ap. 44. vi.
the wicked = the lawless ones. Heb. *rāshā'.* Ap. 44. x.
14 giant = mighty man. Heb. *gibbōr.* Ap. 14. IV.
15 sewed sackcloth, &c. Put by Fig. *Metonymy* (of Adjunct), Ap. 6, for the sorrow which accompanied it.
16 shadow of death. Not a mere shade or shadow, but the deep darkness of the grave. Cp. 3. 5; 10. 21; 12. 22; 24. 17; 28. 3; 34. 22, &c.
17 injustice = violence. Only occurrence of English word in O.T.
18 O. Fig. *Ecphōnēsis.* Ap. 6.
cover not . . . my blood. The reference is to the practice which remains to this day, based on Num. 35. 33. Lev. 17. 13. Job's desire is that the evidence of his sufferings may not be hidden.
19 behold. Fig. *Asterismos.* Ap. 6.

16 My face is foul with weeping, and on my eyelids *is* the °shadow of death;
17 Not for *any* °injustice in mine hands: also my prayer *is* pure. L^2
18 °O earth, °cover not thou my blood, and let my cry have no place.
19 Also now, °behold, my Witness *is* in heaven, and my record *is* on high.

---

d (p. 685) 35 For evil they conceive, and mischief bear;
Their heart doth travail with iniquity."

JOB'S REPLY TO ELIPHAZ'S SECOND ADDRESS.
16. 1—17. 16 (K^4, p. 669).

K^4 L^1 (p. 686) **16** 2 Of such like things I have abundance heard;
[Yea] ministers of trouble are ye all.
3 Shall such vain words come never to an end?
Or what emboldens thee to answer still?
4 For I could also speak as well as ye.
If YE were in distress instead of ME,
Against you I could heap together words;
Against you I could shake my head in scorn;
5 I with MY mouth could [also] harden you;
And with my lip I, too, could you restrain.
6 Though, if I speak, my grief is not assuaged;
If I forbear, how much of it departs?

M^1 7 Ah! God hath verily exhausted me!
Yea all my family Thou hast destroyed;
8 And shrivelled up my skin. Look! what a sight!
My leanness, like a witness, riseth up
And testifies my ruin to my face.
* * * * * * *
9 His anger rends, and maketh war on me,
And He hath gnashed upon me with His teeth.
He is mine enemy; His eyes are swords:
10 [And vile] men gape upon me with their mouths;
And, with contempt, they smite me on my cheeks,
And band themselves against me all at once.
11 GOD to the evil one delivers me,
And headlong casts me into hands malign.
12 At ease I was, when He did shatter me:
He seized my neck, and dashed me to the ground:
Then picked me up, and set me for His mark.
13 His archers did encompass me around.
One cleaves my reins asunder—spares me not;
Another pours my gall upon the earth;
14 Another breaketh me with breach on breach.
He runneth at me like a man of war.
15 I have sewn sackcloth round about myself:
My glory is defilèd in the dust:
16 My face with weeping has become inflamed:
And o'er mine eyelids comes the shade of death.

17 [All this] was not for wrong that I had done; L^2
My prayer was pure [made in sincerity].
18 (O Earth! do thou not cover up my blood;
And let my cry [for vengeance] have no rest.)
19 E'en now, lo! in the heav'ns my Witness is;
And He Who voucheth for me is on high.

1656 20 My °friends scorn me: *but* mine eye poureth
out *tears* unto °GOD.
21 O that one might plead for a °man with
[20] God, as a °man *pleadeth* for his neighbour!
M[2] (p. 686) 22 When a few years are come, then I shall
go °the way *whence* I shall not return.
17 My °breath °is °corrupt, my days are
°extinct, °the graves *are ready* for me.
L[3] 2 *Are there* not mockers with me? and doth
not mine eye °continue in their provocation?
3 °Lay down now, °put me in a surety with
Thee; °who *is* He *that* will °strike hands
with me?
4 For Thou hast hid their heart from understanding: therefore shalt Thou not exalt *them.*
5 °"He that speaketh flattery to *his* friends,
even the eyes of his °children shall
°fail."
6 He hath made me also a byword of the
people; and °aforetime I was as a °tabret.
7 Mine eye also is dim by reason of sorrow,
and all my °members *are* as a shadow.
8 Upright *men* shall be astonied at this, and
the innocent shall stir up himself against the
hypocrite.
9 The righteous also shall hold on his way,
and he that hath clean hands shall be stronger
and stronger.
10 But as for °you all, do ye return, and
come now: for I cannot find *one* wise *man*
among you.
M[3] 11 My days are past, my purposes are broken
off, *even* the thoughts of my heart.
12 They change the night into day: the
light *is* short because of °darkness.
13 If I wait, °the grave *is* mine house: I
have made my bed in the darkness.
14 I have said to corruption, 'Thou *art* my
father:' to the worm, '*Thou art* my mother,
and my sister.'
15 And where *is* now my hope? as for my
hope, who shall see it?
16 They shall go down to the bars of °the
pit, when *our* rest together *is* in the dust."

18 Then °answered °Bildad the Shuhite, N[1] (p. 687)
and said,
2 °"How long *will it be ere* ye make °an end
of words? mark, and afterwards we will
speak.

20 friends = neighbours.
GOD. Heb. Eloah. Ap. 4. V.
21 man = strong man. Heb. *geber*. Ap. 14. IV.
man = son of man. Heb. *ben-'ādām*. Ap. 14. I.
22 the way, &c. Fig. *Euphemism* (Ap. 6), for death.
17. 1 breath = spirit. Heb. *rūach*. Ap. 9.
is = has become.
corrupt = consumed.
extinct. Heb. *zā'ak*. Occurs only here.
the graves. The Sept. reads as in translation below.
2 continue in = constantly dwell on.
3 Lay down now = Appoint it so, I pray.
put me, &c. = be thou my bond. Cp. Isa. 38. 14 ("undertake").
who is he . . . ? Fig. *Erotēsis*. Ap. 6. The answer is given in *v.* 4 by Fig. *Ellipsis* (Ap. 6), "[not they]".
strike hands. The idiom for making a compact. Cp. Prov. 6. 1; 11. 15; 17. 18; 22. 26, &c.
5 He that, &c. Supply Ellipsis, as in translation below; and treat *v.* 5 as a quotation.
children = sons.
fail = look in vain.
6 aforetime = in former times. Cp. Ruth 4. 7.
tabret = a drum. Heb. *topheth*. To the sound and warning of which people gave heed. See note on 1 Sam. 10. 5. After this verse imagine a pause.
7 members = limbs.
10 you. So some codices, with Syr. and Vulg., which A.V. and R.V. followed. Other codices read "them".
12 darkness. Heb. *ḥāshak*. See note on 3. 6.
13 the grave. Heb. *Sheōl*. Ap. 35. Cp. *v.* 16.
16 the pit. Heb. *Sheōl*. Ap. 35. Cp. *v.* 13.

18. 1-21 (J[5], p. 669). BILDAD'S SECOND ADDRESS. (*Division.*)

J[5] | N[1] | 1-4. Reproof of Job.
| N[2] | 5-21. Doom of the wicked.

1 answered. See note on 4. 1.
Bildad. See note on 2. 11.
2 How long . . . ? Fig. *Erotēsis*. Ap. 6.
an end: or, a perversion.

20 My friends are they who scorn me, [mock my grief]:
But to Eloah I pour out my tears,
21 That He may justify me with Himself,
E'en as a son of man pleads for his friend.

M[2] (p. 686) 22 For yet a few more years will come and go,
And I shall go the way whence none return.
17 My spirit's gone; extinguished are my days:
A grave I seek, and [yet I shall] not find.

L[3] 2 Surely do those who mock beset me round;
Mine eye doth on their provocation rest.
3 Arrange a pledge, I pray; be Thou my bond;
Who is there [else] will pledge himself for me?
4 [Not they]. Their heart from wisdom Thou hast hid:
Thou wilt not, then, let them prevail. ['Tis said]
5 "When one for profit doth betray his friends;
His very children look to him in vain."
6 But me the people's byword He hath made:
Whereas, aforetime, I was as a drum,
[And all did heed the warning that I gave].
7 Therefore mine eye becometh dim from grief;
And all my limbs are to a shadow shrunk.
8 The upright will astounded be at this,
The pure be stirr'd by [treatment so] unjust.
9 But still the righteous on his way will hold;
The innocent will go from strength to strength.
10 [Despite] them all, come now, I beg of you;
Shall I not find among you one wise man?

11 My days are passed; [and all] my purposes M[3]
Are broken off;—my heart's most cherished plans.
12 Night is appointed me instead of day:
[My] light is drawing near to darkness [deep].
13 If I should hope, lo, Sheōl is my home;
Yea, in the darkness I should make my bed;
14 "My father thou"—I say now to the grave;
"My mother" and "my sister"—to the worm.
15 ["If I should hope," I said;] "where then is hope?
And who [alas!] should see my blessedness?
16 With me to Sheōl would they both go down,
And rest together, with me, in the dust."

BILDAD'S SECOND ADDRESS.
18. 2-21 (J[5], p. 669).

18 2 How long will you thus hunt about for words? N[1] (p. 687)
Pray understand, and after, let us speak.

1656 **3 ° Wherefore are we counted as beasts, *and* reputed ° vile in ° your sight?**
4 He teareth ° himself in his anger: ° shall the earth be forsaken for thee? and shall the rock be removed out of his place?

N² O¹ e (p. 688) **5 Yea, the ° light of the ° wicked shall be put out, and the spark of his fire shall not shine.**
6 The [5]light shall be ° dark in his ° tabernacle, and his ° candle shall be put out ° with him.

f **7 The ° steps of his strength shall be straitened, and his own counsel shall cast him down.**
8 For he is cast into a net by his own feet, and he ° walketh upon a snare.
9 ° The ° gin shall take *him* by the heel, *and* ° the ° robber shall prevail against him.
10 The snare *is* ° laid for him in the ground, and a trap for him in the way.
11 Terrors shall make him afraid on every side, and shall ° drive him to his feet.
12 His ° strength shall be hungerbitten, and destruction *shall be* ready at his side.
13 It shall devour the ° strength of his ° skin: *even* the ° firstborn of death shall devour his ° strength.
14 His confidence shall be rooted out of his [6]tabernacle, and it shall bring him to the ° king of terrors.
15 ° It shall dwell in his [6]tabernacle, because *it is* ° none of his: brimstone shall be scattered upon his habitation.
16 His roots shall be dried up beneath, and above shall his branch be cut off.

e **17 His remembrance shall perish from the earth, and he shall have no name in the street.**
18 He shall be driven from light into darkness, and chased out of the world.
19 He shall neither have son nor ° nephew among his people, nor any remaining in his dwellings.

f **20 They that come after *him* shall be astonied at his ° day, as they that went before were affrighted.**

O² **21 Surely such *are* the dwellings of the ° wicked, and this *is* the place *of him that* knoweth not ° GOD."**

3 Wherefore . . . ? Fig. *Erotēsis.* Ap. 6.
vile: or, stupid.
your sight. Sept. and Syr. read "thine eyes".
4 himself = his soul. Heb. *nephesh.* Ap. 13.
shall . . . ? Fig. *Erotēsis.* Ap. 6.

18. 5-21 (N², p. 687). DOOM OF THE WICKED. (*Division.*)

N² | O¹ | 5-20. Particular.
| O² | 21. General.

5-20 (O¹, above). DOOM. (PARTICULAR.) (*Alternation.*)

O¹ e | 5, 6. Extinction.
f | 7-16. Result. { *vv.* 7, 8. Evils from himself. / *vv.* 9-16. Evils from others.
e | 17-19. Extinction.
f | 20. Result. Astonishment of others.

5 light. The reference is to the universal practice of burning a light during the night.
wicked = lawless. Heb. *rāshā'.* Ap. 44. x.
6 dark. Heb. *ḥashak*: see note on 3. 6; showing that the man is dead, and not alive to keep the light burning.
tabernacle = tent. **candle** = lamp.
with him = over him: see note on "dark", above.
7 steps of his strength = his firm step. Gen. of character. Ap. 17. 1.
8 walketh = walketh habitually.
9 the gin = a gin. A.V., 1611, reads "grin" = a snare. Same meaning, but now obsolete. **the** = a.
robber = noose.
10 laid = hidden.
11 drive him to his feet = follow at his feet. Cp. 1 Sam. 25. 42.
12 strength, &c. i.e. shall be weakened by hunger. Same word as *v.* 7, not same as *v.* 13.
13 strength = parts or members of his body.
skin. Put by Fig. *Synecdoche* (of the Part), Ap. 6, for the whole body. Cp. Ex. 22. 26.
firstborn of death: i.e. the chief, or worst, or cruellest death. Fig. *Euphemismos.* Ap. 6.
14 king of terrors. Euphemy, for death.
15 It: i.e. every one of the terrors.
none of his = not, indeed, his own.
19 nephew = grandson (Judg. 12. 14).
20 day. Put by Fig. *Metonymy* (of Adjunct), Ap. 6, for the thing done in the day: i.e. his fall.
21 wicked. Heb. *'āval.* Ap. 44. vi. Occurs elsewhere only in 27. 7; 29. 17; 31. 3, and Zeph. 3. 5.
GOD. Heb. El. Ap. 4. IV.

---

3 Wherefore are we accounted like the beasts,
[And wherefore] held as stupid in thine eyes?
4 Lo! in his anger 'tis himself he rends!
For thee, shall Earth be rendered desolate?
Or shall the rock be movèd from its place?

N² O¹ e (p. 688) 5 Yes! True! the sinner's light shall be put out;
And from his fire shall no bright flame ascend.
6 Daylight shall darkness in his tent become;
The lamp which hangs above him shall go out.

f 7 His once firm step shall [halt, and] weakened be,
And his own counsel cast him headlong down.
8 By his own feet he's urged into a net,
For in his chosen way there lies a snare.
9 The [hidden] snare shall seize him by the heel;
The noose shall [catch him and shall] hold him fast.—
10 The snare lies hidden for him in the ground;
The trap in ambush waits beside his path.
11 Terrors shall startle him on every side;
[At every step] they make his feet to start.
12 Through pangs of hunger shall his strength decline:
A dire disease stands ready at his side
13 The members of his body to consume;
Yea, Death's Firstborn his members shall devour,
14 Uproot him from his tent (in which he trusts),
And to the King of Terrors hurry him.
15 These terrors in his tent shall dwell,—yet not
His own. Brimstone upon it shall descend;
16 [While] from beneath his roots shall be dried up,
And from above his branch shall be cut off.

17 His memory has perish'd from the Earth, e
No name is left to him in all the land.
18 From light to darkness do they thrust him forth,
And from the world they drive him far away:
19 Childless among his people he is left:
In all his habitation none survives.

20 They who come after wonder at his doom, *f*
As they who went before were seized with fear.

21 Such are the dwellings of [all] wicked men; O²
Yea, such the place of him who knows not GOD.

K⁵ P (p. 689) 1656

19 Then Job °answered and said,
2 "How long will ye vex °my soul,
and break me in pieces with words?
3 These ten times have ye reproached me:
ye are not ashamed *that* ye °make yourselves
strange to me.
4 And be it indeed *that* I have °erred, mine
°error °remaineth with myself.
5 If indeed ye will magnify *yourselves* against
me, and plead against me my reproach.

Q
6 Know now that °GOD hath overthrown
me, and hath compassed me with His net.
7 °Behold, I cry out of wrong, but I am not
heard: I cry aloud, but *there is* no judgment.
8 He hath fenced up my way that I cannot
pass, and He hath set darkness in my paths.
9 He hath stripped me of my glory, and
taken the crown *from* my head.
10 He hath °destroyed me on every side, and
I am gone: and mine hope hath He °removed
like a tree.
11 He hath also kindled His wrath against
me, and He counteth me unto Him as *one of*
His enemies.
12 His troops come together, and raise up
their way against me, and encamp round
about my °tabernacle.
13 He hath put my brethren far from me,
and mine acquaintance are verily estranged
from me.
14 My kinsfolk have failed, and my familiar
friends have forgotten me.
15 They that dwell in mine house, and my
maids, count me for a stranger: I am an alien
in their sight.
16 I called my servant, and he gave *me* no
answer; I intreated him with my mouth.
17 My °breath is °strange to my wife, °though
I intreated for the °children's *sake* of mine
own body.
18 Yea, °young children despised me; I
°arose, and they spake against me.
19 All my °inward friends abhorred me: and
they whom I loved are turned against me.
20 My bone cleaveth to my skin and to my
flesh, and I am escaped with °the skin of my
teeth.
21 °Have pity upon me, have pity upon me, Q
O ye my friends; for °the hand of ⁶GOD hath
°touched me.
22 Why do ye persecute me as °GOD, and
are not satisfied with my flesh?

19. 1-29 (K⁵, p. 669). JOB'S REPLY TO BILDAD'S SECOND ADDRESS. (*Introversion.*)

K⁵ P | 1-5. Censure of his friends for their reproaches.
Q | 6-20. Complaints of God's dealings as his enemy.
Q | 21-27. Appeal to his hope in God as his Redeemer.
P | 28, 29. Warning to his friends to cease their reproaches.

1 answered = replied. See note on 4. 1.
my soul = me. Heb. *nephesh*. Ap. 13.
3 make yourselves strange to me: or, are insolent to me.
4 erred . . . error. Heb. *shāgā*. Ap. 44. xii.
remaineth with myself: i. e. is mine own affair.
6 GOD. Heb. Eloah. Ap. 4. V.
7 Behold. Fig. *Asterismos*. Ap. 6. See translation below.
10 destroyed = crushed.
removed = uprooted.
12 tabernacle = tent.
13, 14. Note the Alternation in these two verses.
17 breath. Heb. *rūach*. Ap. 9.
strange = offensive.
though I, &c. See rendering below.
children's = sons': i. e. had his sons not died.
18 young children = the very boys; or, young miscreants.
arose = would fain rise.
19 inward = intimate. Heb. men of my counsel = my confidential friends.
20 the skin of my teeth = the gums. See rendering below.
21 Have pity, &c. Fig. *Ecphōnēsis*. Ap. 6.
the hand. Fig. *Anthropopatheia*. Ap. 6.
touched = stricken. Fig. *Tapeinōsis*. Ap. 6.
22 GOD. Heb. El. Ap. 4. IV.

JOB'S REPLY TO BILDAD'S SECOND ADDRESS.
19. 2-29 (K⁵, p. 669).

K⁵ P (p. 689)
2 How long will ye [thus grieve and] vex my soul,
And break me all to pieces with your words?
3 Already ten times have ye taunted me;
And still are not ashamed to wrong me thus.
4 Be it that I have sinnèd, [as ye say],
My sense of sin abideth with myself.
5 If 'gainst me still ye magnify yourselves,
And plead against me that I [must have] sinned:

Q
6 Then know ye that Eloah hath o'erthrown
My cause; and made His net to close me round.
7 Behold, I cry out [" Wrong!"] but am not heard:
I cry out "Help!" but there is no redress:
8 My path He hedgeth up; I cannot pass;
And on my way He maketh darkness rest:
9 From me my glory He hath strippèd off,
And from my head hath He removed the crown.
10 On all sides I am crush'd, where'er I go:
He hath my hope uprooted like a tree:
11 Against me He hath made His anger burn,
And counts me toward Him as His enemy.
12 Together ['gainst me] do His troops come on;
Against me they their earthworks have cast up,
And round about my tent have they encamped.
13 My brethren hath He put far off from me,
And mine acquaintance from me are estranged.
14 My near-of-kin have ceased [and failèd] me,
And my familiar friends forgotten me.
15 The dwellers in my house, the very maids,
Account [and treat] me as a stranger now:
I am become an alien in their eyes.
16 I called my servant,—but he answered not,
[Though] I entreated him with mine own mouth.
17 My breath is grown offensive to my wife,
So would my fondling to my sons appear.
18 Yea—e'en the very boys despise me now;
They jeer at me when I attempt to rise.
19 My confidential friends from me recoil:
And those I loved turn right away from me.
20 My bone cleaves fast unto my skin and flesh,
All shrunk away the cov'ring of my teeth.
21 Have pity; oh, have pity, ye, my friends; Q
Eloah's hand [alas!] hath stricken me.
22 Wherefore pursue me as if ye were GOD?
Will not my body's [ills] suffice for you?
* * * * * *

1656 23 °Oh that my words were now written!
oh that they were printed in a book!
24 That they were °graven with an iron pen
and lead in the rock for ever!
25 For I °know *that* my °Redeemer liveth,
and *that* He shall stand at the latter *day* upon
the °earth:
26 And *though* after my °skin *worms* destroy this *body*, yet in my flesh shall I see
[6]GOD:
27 Whom I shall see for myself, and mine
eyes shall behold, and not °another; *though*
my reins be consumed within me.
P (p. 689) 28 °But ye should say, 'Why persecute we
him, °seeing the root of the matter is found in
°me?
29 Be ye afraid of the sword: for wrath
bringeth the °punishments of the sword, that
ye may know °*there is* a judgment."

J[6] R (p. 690) **20** Then °answered °Zophar the Naamathite, and said,
2 "Therefore do my thoughts cause me to
answer, and for *this* I make haste.
3 I have heard the °check °of my reproach,
and the °spirit of my understanding causeth
me to answer.
4 °Knowest thou *not* this °of old, since °man
was placed upon earth,
5 That the triumphing of the °wicked *is*
short, and the joy of the hypocrite *but* for
a moment?
S 6 Though his excellency mount up to the
heavens, and his head reach unto the clouds;
7 *Yet* he shall perish for ever like his own
°dung: they which have seen him shall say,
'Where *is* he?'
8 He shall fly away as a dream, and shall not
be found: yea, he shall be chased away as a
vision of the night.
9 The eye also *which* saw him shall *see him*
no more; neither shall his place any more behold him.
10 His °children shall °seek to please the
°poor, and his hands shall restore their goods.
11 His bones are full *of the sin* of his youth,
which shall lie down with him in the dust.
12 Though °wickedness be sweet in his mouth,
though he hide it under his tongue;

23 Oh! Fig. *Ecphōnēsis*. Ap. 6.
24 graven = engraven. See translation below.
25 know. Put by Fig. *Metonymy* (of Cause), Ap. 6, to include all the effects of knowing.
Redeemer = next of kin. Heb. *gō'ēl*. See notes on Ex. 6. 6, and cp. Ruth 2. 20; 4. 1, 3, 6. Isa. 59. 20.
earth = dust of [the earth].
26 skin. Put by Fig. *Synecdoche* (of Part), Ap. 6, for the whole body.
27 another = a stranger. A pause must be made between *vv.* 27 and 28.
28 But ye: or, Ye shall [then] say.
seeing. Fig. *Ellipsis* (Ap. 6). Supply by repeating the question, "Why see a root of blame in him?"
me. Some codices, with Aram., Sept., and Vulg., read "him".
29 punishments = sins; "sins" put by Fig. *Metonymy* (of Cause), Ap. 6, for the punishments called for by them.
there is a judgment = that judgment will be executed.

20. 1-29 (J[6], p. 669). ZOPHAR'S SECOND ADDRESS. (*Introversion.*)

J[6] | R | 1-5. His theme stated.
  S | 6-28. Expansion of the theme.
 R | 29. The theme restated.

1 answered = spake again. See note on 4. 1.
Zophar. See note on 2. 11.
3 check = correction.
of = for: i. e. meant to confound me, referring to chap. 19.
spirit of = spirit from. Heb. *rūach*. Ap. 9.
4 Knowest thou not this? This was Zophar's reply to Job in 19. 25, implying that Job had no such hope.
of old = from of old.
man. Heb. *'ādām*. Ap. 14. I.
5 wicked = lawless. Heb. *rāshā'*. Ap. 44. x.
7 dung. See note on Isa. 25. 10.
10 children = sons.
seek to please = pay court to.
poor = impoverished. Heb. *dūl*. See note on Prov. 6. 11.
12 wickedness. Heb. *rā'a'*. Ap. 44. viii.

---

23 Oh that my words could now be written down!
Oh that a record could be graved with pen
24 Of iron, cut in rock [and filled] with lead,
A witness evermore. [The words are these].
25 I KNOW THAT MY REDEEMER [EVER] LIVES,
AND AT THE LATTER DAY ON EARTH SHALL STAND;
26 AND AFTER [WORMS] THIS BODY HAVE CONSUMED,
YET IN MY FLESH I SHALL ELOAH SEE:
27 WHOM I, E'EN I, SHALL SEE UPON MY SIDE.
MINE EYES SHALL SEE HIM—STRANGER, NOW, NO MORE:
[FOR THIS] MY INMOST SOUL WITH LONGING WAITS.
* * * * * * *
P (p. 689) 28 Ye shall [then] say,
"Why did we him pursue?
Why seek to find in him a root of blame?"
29 Beware! and of the sword be ye afraid:
For wrathful are the sword's dread punishments;
And ye shall know indeed its judgment [sure].

ZOPHAR'S SECOND ADDRESS.
20. 2-29 (J[6], p. 669).

J[6] R **20** 2 Not so: my thoughts impel me to respond,
And therefore is my haste within me [roused].
3 Correction meant for my reproof, I hear,
But zeal, with knowledge, gives me a reply.
4 Know'st thou [not] this?—a truth of olden time,
Since Adam first was placed upon the earth:
5 That brief the triumph of the wicked is,
And momentary is the sinner's joy?
6 His joy may mount up to the [very] skies, S
His head reach up unto the [highest] clouds:
7 Like his own stubble he is swept away;
And they who see shall say, "Where has he gone?"
8 He fleeth as a dream, and is not found:
Is chased away, like visions of the night.
9 The eye which saw him sees him not again;
His dwelling-place descrieth him no more.
10 His children shall pay court unto the poor;
And his own hands give back again his wealth.
11 His bones are filled with sins in secret done,
And with him in the dust they shall lie down.
12 Though wickedness, while in his mouth, be sweet,
Though underneath his tongue he keep it hid,—

1656 13 *Though* he spare it, and forsake it not;
but keep it still within his °mouth:
14 *Yet* his °meat in his bowels is turned, *it is*
the gall of asps within him.
15 He hath swallowed down riches, and he
shall vomit them up again: °GOD shall cast
them out of his belly.
16 He shall suck the poison of asps: the
viper's tongue shall slay him.
17 He shall not see the °rivers, the °floods,
the °brooks of honey and butter.
18 That which he laboured for shall he
restore, and shall not swallow *it* down: according to *his* substance *shall* the restitution
be, and he shall not rejoice *therein*.
19 Because he hath oppressed *and* hath
forsaken the [10]poor; *because* he hath violently taken away an house which he builded
not;
20 Surely he shall not °feel quietness in his
belly, he shall not save of that which he
desired.
21 There shall none of his [14]meat be left;
therefore shall no man look for his goods.
22 In the fulness of his sufficiency he shall
be in straits: °every °hand of the °wicked
shall come upon him.
23 *When* he is about to fill his belly, *God*
shall cast the fury of His wrath upon him,
and shall rain *it* upon him while he is
eating.
24 He shall flee from the iron weapon, *and*
the bow of steel shall strike him through.
25 It is drawn, and cometh out of the body;
yea, the glittering sword cometh out of his gall:
terrors *are* upon him.
26 All darkness *shall be* hid in his secret
places: a fire °not blown shall consume him;
it shall go ill with him that is left in his
°tabernacle.
27 The heaven shall reveal his °iniquity;
and the earth shall rise up against him.
28 The increase of his house shall depart,
and his goods shall °flow away in the day of
His wrath.
R (p. 690) 29 This *is* the portion of a [5]wicked °man
from °God, and the heritage appointed unto
him by [15]GOD."

21 But Job °answered and said, K6 T1 (p. 691)
2 °"Hear diligently my speech, and let
this be your consolations.
3 Suffer me that I may speak; and after that
I have spoken, °mock on.
4 As for me, *is* my complaint to °man? and
if *it were so*, °why should not °my spirit be
troubled?

13 mouth=palate.
14 meat=bread; "bread" put by Fig. *Synecdoche* (of Species) Ap. 6, for all kinds of food.
15 GOD. Heb. El. Ap. 4. IV.
17 rivers=divisions of water for irrigation, as in a garden. Heb. *palgey mayim*. See notes on Prov. 21. 1, and Ps. 1. 3.
floods=rivers. Heb. *nāhār*, everflowing.
brooks=wadys. Heb. *nāḥal*, summer streams.
20 feel=know, or experience.
22 every hand of the wicked=all power of trouble.
hand. Put by Fig. *Metonymy* (of Cause), Ap. 6, for the power exercised by it.
wicked. Heb. *'āmāl*. Ap. 44. v.
26 not blown. Not blown up, or produced by man.
tabernacle=tent.
27 iniquity. Heb. *'āvāh*. Ap. 44. iv.
28 flow away=melt away, disappear.
29 man. Heb. *'ādām*. Ap. 14. I.
God. Heb. Elohim. Ap. 4. I.

21. 1-34 (K^6, p. 669). **JOB'S REPLY TO ZOPHAR'S SECOND ADDRESS.** (*Repeated Alternation.*)

K^6 | T^1 | 1-6. Appeal to his friends.
  U^1 | 7-26. Contrasted cases. The wicked (*vv.* 7-21). The good (*vv.* 22-26).
 T^2 | 27-29. Appeal to his friends.
  U^2 | 30-33. Contrasted cases. The wicked: in life (*vv.* 30, 31); in death (*vv.* 32, 33).
 T^3 | 34. Appeal to his friends.

1 answered=replied. See note on 4. 1.
2 Hear diligently. See note on 13. 17.
3 mock on=mock [thou] on, as if pointing to him.
4 man. Heb. *'ādām*. Ap. 14. I.
why . . . ? Fig. *Erotēsis*. Ap. 6.
my spirit=myself. Heb. *rūach* (Ap. 9). Put by Fig. *Synecdoche* (of the Part), Ap. 6, for the whole person, for emphasis.

---

13 Keeping it long, and loth to let it go,
Retaining it within his palate's taste;
14 Yet in his bowels is his food all changed;
Within him it becomes the gall of asps.
15 He swallowed wealth, but vomiteth it up:
Yea, from his belly GOD will drive it forth.
16 The venom of the adder shall he suck;
The poison of the viper slayeth him.
17 He shall not look upon the [flowing] streams,
Or floods, or brooks of honey and of milk.
18 In vain he toiled, he shall not swallow [it];
Like wealth giv'n back, in it he has no joy.
19 Because he crush'd, and helpless left, the poor;
[And] seized upon a house he did not build:
20 Because content within he never knew,
Nor let escape him ought that he desired,
21 (No, not a shred that he devourèd not):
Therefore it is, his wealth shall not endure.
22 When it is at its height, his straits begin;
The power of distress shall come on him.
23 For, when he is about to eat his food,
Then [God] shall send on him His burning wrath,
And rain it on him for his punishment.
24 [Though] he may flee away from lance of steel,
The [shaft from] bow of brass shall pierce him through:
25 [And if] one draws it forth from out his flesh,
The gleaming arrow-head from out his gall,
[Then other] terrors shall upon him come.
26 For his hid treasures every trouble waits;
A fire not blown [by man] devours them all;
It shall consume what in his tent is left.
27 The heav'ns shall his iniquity reveal:
Against him riseth up the [very] earth:
28 The increase of his house to exile goes,
Like flowing waters, in God's day of wrath.
29 Such is the sinner's portion sent from God; R (p. 690)
And such the doom GOD hath appointed him.

JOB'S REPLY TO ZOPHAR'S SECOND ADDRESS.
21. 1-34 (K^6, p. 669).

2 Oh, do but list with patience to my words K6 T1 (p. 691)
And so let this your consolation be.
3 Oh, bear with me, I pray, and let me speak;
And after I have done, thou canst mock on.
4 Is it to man that my appeal I make?
Might I not in that case impatient be?

1656 **5 Mark me, and be astonished, and °lay *your***
hand upon *your* mouth.
6 Even when I remember I am afraid, and
trembling taketh hold on my flesh.

U^1 g^1 (p. 692) **7 Wherefore do the ° wicked live, become old,**
yea, are mighty in power?
8 Their seed is established in their sight with
them, and their offspring before their eyes.
9 Their houses ° *are* safe from fear, neither *is*
the rod of ° GOD upon them.
10 °Their bull gendereth, and faileth not;
° their cow calveth, and casteth not her calf.
11 They send forth their little ones like a flock,
and their ° children dance.
12 They take the timbrel and harp, and re-
joice at the sound of the ° organ.
13 They spend their days in wealth, and in a
moment ° go down to ° the grave.
14 Therefore they say unto ° GOD, 'Depart
from us; for we desire not the knowledge of
Thy ways.
15 ° What *is* ° THE ALMIGHTY, that we should
serve Him? and ° what profit should we have,
if we pray unto Him?'
16 ° Lo, their good *is* not in their hand: the
counsel of the [7] wicked is far from me.

h^1 **17 °How oft is the °candle of the °wicked**
put out! and *how oft* cometh their destruction
upon them! ° *God* distributeth sorrows in His
anger.
18 °They are as °stubble before the °wind, and
as chaff that the storm carrieth away.
19 ° GOD layeth up ° his ° iniquity for his
° children: He rewardeth him, and he shall
know *it*.
20 His eyes shall see his destruction, and he
shall drink of the wrath of [15] THE ALMIGHTY.
21 For what pleasure *hath* he in his house
after him, when the number of his months
is cut off in the midst?

g^2 **22 Shall *any* teach [14] GOD knowledge? see-**
ing He judgeth those that are high.

5 lay your hand, &c. A token of having no answer.

7-26 (U^1, p. 691). **30-33** (U^2, p. 691). **CONTRASTED CASES.** (*Repeated Alternation.*)

U^1	g^1	7-16. Prosperity.	The wicked.
	h^1	17-21. Adversity.	
	g^2	22-24. Prosperity.	The good.
	h^2	25, 26. Adversity.	
U^2	g^3	30, 31. Prosperity in life.	The wicked.
	h^3	32, 33. Prosperity in death.	

7 wicked = lawless. Heb. *rāshā'*. Ap. 44. x.
9 are safe = are in peace.
GOD. Heb. Eloah. Ap. 4. V.
10 their = each.
11 children = lads.
12 organ. Heb. *'ūgab* = a wind instrument. Cp. Gen. 4. 21. Job 30. 31. Ps. 150. 4.
13 go down = get dashed.
the grave. Heb. *Sheōl.* Ap. 35.
14 GOD. Heb. El. Ap. 4. IV.
15 What . . . ? Fig. *Erotēsis.* Ap. 6.
THE ALMIGHTY. Heb. Shaddai. Ap. 4. VII.
16 Lo. Fig. *Asterismos.* Ap. 6.
17 How oft . . . ? Fig. *Erotēsis.* Ap. 6. These words must be repeated to supply the *Ellipsis* (Ap. 6) at the beginning of *vv.* 18 and 19, as in middle of *v.* 17.
candle = lamp.
wicked = lawless. Heb. *rāshā'*. Ap. 44. x.
God. Supply "How oft He", &c., instead of "*God*".
18 They: i.e. [How oft] they.
stubble = crushed straw. Heb. *teben* (not *ḳash* = straw. **wind.** Heb. *rūach.* Ap. 9.
19 GOD = [How oft] Eloah. Ap. 4. V.
his: i.e. the lawless man's children.
iniquity. Heb. *'āven.* Ap. 44. iii. Put by Fig. *Metonymy* (of Cause) Ap. 6, for punishment brought on by it.
children = sons.
24 breasts = skin bottles.
25 soul. Heb. *nephesh.* Ap. 13.

23 One dieth in his full strength, being wholly
at ease and quiet.
24 His ° breasts are full of milk, and his bones
are moistened with marrow.

25 And another dieth in the bitterness of his h^2
° soul, and never eateth with pleasure.
26 They shall lie down alike in the dust, and
the worms shall cover them.

---

5 Turn now, and look on me, and stand amazed,
And lay ye now your hand upon your mouth.
6 For, when I think of it, I am dismayed,
And trembling taketh hold upon my flesh.

U^1 g^1 (p. 692) 7 Why [suffers God] ungodly men to live,
And to grow old; yea, to wax strong in power?
8 With them their seed is 'stablished; yea, with them
Their offspring [live and] grow before their eyes.
9 Their houses are in peace; they know no fear;
No scourge descends upon them from GOD'S hand.
10 Their bull engendereth, and doth not fail;
Their cow doth calve, and casteth not her calf.
11 Their little children skip about like lambs;
Their elder children mingle in the dance.
12 With timbrel and with harp they lift their voice;
And merry make with cheerful sound of pipe.
13 They in prosperity complete their days,
And in a moment to the grave go down.
14 Yet, unto GOD they say:
"Depart from us;
No knowledge of THY ways do we desire.
15 [Pray] Who is Shaddai that we Him should serve?
And what the profit if to Him we pray?"
* * * * * * *

16 But lo! their good comes not from their own hand.
Far be the way of wicked men from me.
17 [But yet, YE say] h^1
"How oft goes out the lamp of evil men!
[How oft] calamity doth on them come!
[How oft] are pangs apportioned them in wrath!
18 [How oft] are they as straw before the blast,
Like chaff the storm and tempest drive away!"
19 [Ye say]; "Eloah lays up for the sons
The father's evil life, in recompense,
20 That his own eyes may [all] the trouble see.
When from the wrath of Shaddai he shall drink.
21 What pleasure hath he in prosperity,
When cut off is the number of his months?"
22 Is it to GOD that one can knowledge teach? g^2
Seeing 'tis He Who judgeth things on high!
23 [For, lo]: one dieth in the very height
Of his prosperity, calm, and at ease:
24 His breasts are full of nourishment; his bones
With marrow are well moistened [and fresh].
25 Another dies in bitterness of soul, h^2
And never has he tasted any good.
26 Together in the dust they both lie down:
Alike, o'er both, the worm its covering spreads.

T² (p. 691) 1656
27 °Behold, I know your thoughts, and the devices *which* ye wrongfully imagine against me.
28 For ye say, °'Where *is* the house of the °prince? and °where *are* the dwelling places of the ⁷wicked?'
29 °Have ye not asked them that go by the way? and do ye not know their tokens,

U² g³ (p. 692)
30 °That the ⁷wicked is reserved to the day of destruction? they shall be brought forth to the day of wrath.
31 °Who shall declare his way to his face? and °who shall repay him *what* he hath done?

h³
32 Yet shall he be brought to °the grave, and shall remain in the °tomb.
33 The °clods of the valley shall be sweet unto him, and every °man shall draw after him, as *there are* innumerable before him.

T³ (p. 691)
34 How then comfort ye me in vain, seeing in your answers there remaineth °falsehood?"

J⁷ V¹ (p. 693)
22 Then °Eliphaz the Temanite °answered and said,
2 °"Can a °man be profitable unto °GOD, °as he that is wise may be profitable unto himself?
3 °*Is it* any pleasure to °THE ALMIGHTY, that thou art righteous? or *is it* gain *to Him*, that thou makest thy ways perfect?
4 °Will He reprove thee for fear of thee? °will He enter with thee into judgment?

W X
5 °*Is* not thy °wickedness great? and thine °iniquities °infinite?
6 For thou hast taken a pledge from thy brother for nought, and °stripped °the naked of their clothing.
7 Thou hast not given water to the weary to drink, and thou hast withholden bread from the hungry.
8 But *as for* the mighty °man, he had the earth; and the honourable man dwelt in it.
9 Thou hast sent widows away empty, and the arms of the fatherless have been broken.

10 Therefore snares *are* round about thee, and sudden fear troubleth thee; Y
11 Or darkness, *that* thou canst not see; and abundance of waters cover thee.

27 Behold. Fig. *Asterismos*. Ap. 6.
28 Where . . . ? Fig. *Erotēsis*. Ap. 6.
prince = noble.
29 Have ye not . . . ? Fig. *Erotēsis*. Ap. 6.
30 That. Supply *Ellipsis* (Ap. 6) before "That" = "[They say] that". See translation below.
31 Who . . . ? Fig. *Erotēsis*. Ap. 6.
32 the grave = sepulchre. Heb. *ḳeber*. Ap. 35.
tomb = tumulus, or sepulchral mound.
33 clods. Heb. *degeb* = soft, or moist clods. Occurs only here and 38. 38. **man.** Heb. *'ādām*. Ap. 14. I.
34 falsehood = perverseness. Heb. *mā'al*. Ap. 44. xi.

22. 1-30 (J⁷, p. 669). ELIPHAZ. THIRD ADDRESS. (*Alternations*.)

J⁷ | V¹ | 1-4. Argument. (General.) Concerning God.
  W | X | 5-9. Accusation. (Particular.)
    Y | 10, 11. Punishment. (Particular.)
  V² | 12. Argument. (General.) Concerning God.
  W | X | 13, 14. Accusation. (Particular.)
    Y | 15-20. Punishment. (General.)
  V³ | 21-30. Argument. (Particular.) Concerning God, and Job.

1 Eliphaz. See note on 2. 11.
answered = spake. See note on 4. 1.
2 Can . . . ? Fig. *Erotēsis*. Ap. 6.
man = a strong man. Heb. *geber*. Ap. 14. IV.
GOD. Heb. El. Ap. 4. IV.
as = nay. The Heb. accent (*Tᵉbir*) on *kī*, "as", is disjunctive, and means "nay". See note on Isa. 28. 28.
3 Is it . . . ? Fig. *Erotēsis*. Ap. 6.
THE ALMIGHTY. Heb. Shaddai. Ap. 4. VII.
4 Will He . . . ? } Fig. *Erotēsis*. Ap. 6.
5 Is not . . . ? }
wickedness. Heb. *'āval*. Ap. 44. vi.
iniquities. Heb. *rāshā'*. Ap. 44. x.
infinite = without end.
6 stripped the naked. Fig. *Oxymoron*. Ap. 6.
the naked = the poorly clad, or threadbare.
8 man. Heb. *'īsh*. Ap. 14. II. See translation below.

T² (p. 691)
27 Behold, [my friends], I know your thoughts, which ye
Against me do so wrongfully maintain.
28 Ye say
"Where is the dwelling of the Prince?
And where the tent wherein the wicked dwell?"
29 Have ye not asked of travellers? Do not
Ignore what they have noted down. [They say]:—
U² g³ (p. 692)
30 "The wicked, in the day of wrath, is spared;
Yea, in the day of wrath he doth escape."
31 Who, to his face, will dare denounce his way?
Who shall requite him that which he hath done?
h³
32 He too will be escorted to the tomb;
And o'er his monument one keepeth watch.
33 The valley's clods do gently cover him:
Behind, [the mourners] come in lengthened train;
Before, they all in countless numbers walk.
T³ (p. 691)
34 How then console ye me with worthless [words],
Seeing your answers only failure prove?

ELIPHAZ'S THIRD [AND LAST] ADDRESS.
22. 1-30 (J⁷, p. 669).

J⁷ V¹ (p. 693)
22 2 Will mighty man advantage bring to GOD?
Nay, he, though wise, can profit but himself.
3 To Shaddai is it gain if thou be just?
Or any profit if thy ways be pure?
4 From awe of thee will He debate with thee?
Or into judgment with thee will He come?

5 It may be that thy wickedness is great, W X
And without number thine iniquities:
6 That thou didst take thy brother's pledge for naught;
Or didst strip off the garments of the poor;
7 Or, that thou didst not give the weary drink,
Or from the hungry thou withheldest bread.
8 [Thou may'st have said]—
"The land is for the strong";
And, "favoured men [alone] should dwell therein:"
9 Widows [thou may'st] have sent away unhelped,
And robbed the fatherless of their support.

10 This may be why the snares are round thee spread, Y
And terror cometh on thee suddenly:
11 [And why] the darkness thou canst not explain;
[And why] the waterfloods o'erwhelm thy soul.

V² (p. 693) 1656 **12** °*Is* not °GOD in the height of heaven? and °behold the height of the stars, how high they are!

W X **13** °And thou sayest, °'How doth ³GOD know? can He judge through the °dark cloud?

14 Thick clouds *are* a covering to Him, that He seeth not; and He °walketh in the °circuit of heaven.'

Y **15** Hast thou marked the old way which °wicked °men have trodden?

16 Which were cut down out of time, whose foundation was overflown with a flood:

17 Which said unto ²GOD, 'Depart from us:' and what can ³THE ALMIGHTY do for them?

18 Yet He filled their houses with good *things*: but the counsel of the °wicked is far from me.

19 The righteous see *it*, and are glad: and the innocent laugh them to scorn.

20 °Whereas our substance is not cut down, but the remnant of them the fire consumeth.

V³ **21** °Acquaint now thyself with Him, and be at peace: thereby °good shall come °unto thee.

22 Receive, I pray thee, the law from His mouth, and lay up His words in thine heart.

23 If thou °return to ³THE ALMIGHTY, thou shalt be built up, thou shalt put away °iniquity far from thy °tabernacles.

24 Then shalt thou lay up gold as dust, and the *gold* of Ophir as the stones of the brooks.

25 Yea, ³THE ALMIGHTY shall be thy defence, and thou shalt have plenty of silver.

26 For then shalt thou have thy delight in ³THE ALMIGHTY, and shalt lift up thy face unto ¹²GOD.

27 Thou shalt make thy prayer unto Him, and He shall hear thee, and thou shalt pay thy vows.

28 Thou shalt also decree a thing, and it shall be established unto thee: and the light shall shine upon thy ways.

29 When *men* are cast down, then thou shalt say, '*There is* lifting up; and He shall save °the humble person.

12 Is not . . . ? Fig. *Erotēsis*. Ap. 6.
GOD. Heb. Eloah. Ap. 4. V.
behold. Fig. *Asterismos*. Ap. 6.
13 And, &c. = "and [yet may be] thou sayest".
How . . . ? Fig. *Erotēsis*. Ap. 6.
dark cloud. Heb. *'ărāphel*. See note on 3. 6.
14 walketh = walketh habitually.
circuit = vault. Heb. *ḥûg*.
15 wicked. Heb. *'āven*. Ap. 44. iii.
men. Heb. *m^ethîm*. Ap. 14. V.
18 wicked = lawless. Heb. *rāshā'*. Ap. 44. x.
20 Whereas. Supply Ellipsis (Ap. 6), "[and say] Surely", &c. See translation below.
21 Acquaint. This is the false theology of Eliphaz. Cp. 42. 8.
good = blessing. **unto** = upon. } Most codices, with Aram., Sept., Syr., and Vulg., read "thy gain shall be blessing".
23 return. Sept. adds "and submit thyself".
iniquity. Heb. *'āvah*. Ap. 44. iv.
tabernacles = tents. Some codices, with four early printed editions, Sept., Syr., and Vulg., read "tent"; others, with six early printed editions (and one in margin), read "tents" (pl.).
29 the humble. Heb. the man of downcast eyes. Cp. Luke 18. 13.
30 the island of. Island put by Fig. *Metonymy* (of Subject), Ap. 6, for coasts, or borders; but the words are omitted by the Sept.
it. The Aram., Sept., Syr., and Vulg. read "thou".

23. 1—24. 25 [For Structure see next page].

1 answered = replied [a third time]. See note on 4. 1.
2 complaint = complaining.
my. Sept. and Syr. read "His".
stroke = hand. Put by Fig. *Metonymy* (of Cause), Ap. 6, for the calamity occasioned by it. Cp. 13. 21; 19. 21.

30 He shall deliver °the island of the innocent: and °it is delivered by the pureness of thine hands.' "

23 Then Job °answered and said, K⁷ A j (p. 695)
2 "Even to day *is* my °complaint bitter: °my °stroke is heavier than my groaning.

V² (p. 693) 12 [Is not] Eloah high in Heav'n sublime?
Behold the highest of the stars, how high!

W X 13 [And yet, may be] thou say'st
"How doth GOD know?
And through the thickest darkness can He judge?
14 Thick clouds enrobe Him, that He cannot see;
Alone He walketh in the vault of heaven."

Y 15 Oh that thou wouldst consider well the way
Which wicked men of old have ever trod.
16 They who were snatched away before their time,
Their strong foundation swept, as with a flood.
17 Who unto GOD did say "Depart from us!"
[And ask'd] "what good could Shaddai do to them!"
18 Yet, He it was Who filled their homes with good.

* * * * * *

The way of wicked men is far from me.
19 The righteous see that THEY may well rejoice;
The innocent will laugh at them, [and say],
20 "Surely our substance hath not been destroyed;
While their abundance is consumed with fire."

V³ 21 Acquaintance make with Him, and be at peace;
For thereby blessing shall upon thee come.

22 Receive, I pray, instruction from His mouth,
And lay up [all] His words within thy heart.
23 To Shaddai come thou back: submit thyself:
[And], from thy tent put far away thy sin:
24 Then shalt thou lay up treasure as the dust,
And [gold] of Ophir as the pebble-stones.
25 Yea, Shaddai, He shall be thy precious ore,
And [His] great strength as silver unto thee.
26 For then in Shaddai thou shalt take delight,
And to Eloah thou wilt lift thy face.
27 Then shalt thou pray to Him, and He will hear,
And unto Him thou wilt perform thy vows.
28 The thing thou purposest shall come to pass:
And over all thy ways the light shall shine.
29 When others are depressed, then thou shalt say
'Look up! For, humble men HE will exalt;
30 Yea, HE doth let the innocent escape.'

* * * * * *

So too shalt THOU, through innocence of hands.

JOB'S REPLY TO ELIPHAZ'S THIRD ADDRESS.

23. 1—24. 25 (K⁷, p. 669).

23 2 To-day again my plaint is bitter, still: K⁷ A j (p. 695)
His hand is heavier than all my groans.

1656 3 °Oh that I knew where I might find Him! *that* I might come *even* to His seat!
4 I would order *my* cause before Him, and fill my mouth with arguments.
5 I would know the words *which* He would answer me, and understand what He would say unto me.

k (p. 695) 6 Will He plead against me with *His* great power? No; but He would put *strength* in me.
7 There the righteous might dispute with Him; so should I be delivered for ever from my Judge.

j 8 Behold, I go forward, but He *is* not *there;* and backward, but I cannot perceive Him:
9 On the left hand, where He doth work, but I cannot behold *Him:* He hideth Himself on the right hand, that I cannot see *Him:*

k 10 But He knoweth the way that I °take: °*when* He hath tried me, I °shall come forth as gold.

B 11 My foot hath held His steps, His way have I kept, and not declined.
12 Neither have I gone back from the commandment of His lips; I have esteemed the words of His mouth more than °my necessary *food.*

A 13 But He *is* in one *mind,* and who can turn Him? and *what* °His soul desireth, even *that* He doeth.
14 For He performeth *the thing that is* appointed for me: and many such *things are* with Him.
15 Therefore am I troubled at His presence: when I consider, I am °afraid of Him.
16 For °GOD maketh my heart °soft, and °THE ALMIGHTY troubleth me:
17 °Because I was not cut off before the °darkness, *neither* hath He covered the °darkness from my face.

24 °Why, seeing °times are not hidden from °THE ALMIGHTY, do they that know Him not °see His °days?

B l 2 °*Some* remove the °landmarks; they violently take away flocks, and feed *thereof.*
3 They drive away the ass of the fatherless, they °take the widow's ox for a pledge.

23. 1—24. 25 (K⁷, p. 669). JOB'S REPLY TO ELIPHAZ'S THIRD ADDRESS. (*Alternation.*)

K⁷ | A | 23. 1-10. God's inscrutability.
B | 23. 11, 12. Job's integrity.
A | 23. 13—24. 1. God's inscrutability.
B | 24. 2-25. Man's iniquity.

23. 1-10 (A, above). GOD'S INSCRUTABILITY. (*Alternation.*)

A | j | 1-5. Job's wish for trial.
k | 6, 7. His confidence of the issue.
j | 8, 9. Job's search for trial.
k | 10. His confidence of the issue.

3 Oh. Fig. *Ecphōnēsis.* Ap. 6.
10 take: or choose.
when he hath: or, if He would.
shall=should.
12 my necessary food. Heb. my own law=my appointed portion: i. e. my ordinary allowance; "law" being put by Fig. *Synecdoche* (of the Genus), Ap. 6, for what is allowed by it. Cp. Gen. 47. 22. Prov. 30. 8.
13 His soul=Himself. Heb. *nephesh.* Ap. 13. Fig. *Anthropopatheia.* Ap. 6.
15 afraid. See note on Deut. 28. 66.
16 GOD. Heb. El. Ap. 4. IV.
soft=faint, or unnerved. Cp. Deut. 20. 3. Isa. 7. 4.
THE ALMIGHTY. Heb. Shaddai. Ap. 4. VII.
17 Because, &c. See translation below.
darkness. Heb. *ḥashak.* See note on 3. 6.
darkness. Heb. *'ophel.* See note on 3. 6.

24. 1 Why . . . ? Fig. *Erotēsis.* Ap. 6.
times. Put by Fig. *Metonymy* (of Adjunct) for the events which take place in them.
THE ALMIGHTY. Heb. Shaddai. Ap. 4. VII.
see=perceive, or understand.
days. Put by Fig. *Metonymy* (of Adjunct), Ap. 6, for His doings in them: e. g. visitation, or judgment, &c. Cp. 18. 20. Pss. 37. 13; 137. 7. Ezek. 21. 29. Obad. 12. Luke 19. 42. 1 Cor. 4. 3.

24. 2-25 (*B*, above). MAN'S INIQUITY. (*Alternation.*)

B | l | 2-17. Crimes of lawless men.
m | 18-20. What the issue ought to be.
l | 21, 22. Crimes of lawless men.
m | 23-25. What the issue commonly is.

2 Some: i. e. the lawless men, whose various crimes are detailed in the following verses.
landmarks. Cp. Deut. 19. 14.
3 take . . . for a pledge. Cp. *v.* 9 and Deut. 24. 6, 17. Amos 2. 8.

---

3 Oh, that I knew where I might find Him: knew
How I might come unto His [judgment] seat!
4 I would set out my cause before His face;
And I would fill my mouth with arguments.
5 And well I know how He would answer me,
And understand what He to me would say.

k (p. 695) 6 Would He with His great pow'r contend with me?
Nay, He would surely set on me His heart.
7 There I, an upright man, would plead with Him,
And [so] for ever from my Judge go free.

j 8 Lo, to the East I go: He is not there;
And to the West, but I perceive Him not:
9 Or North, where He doth work, I look in vain;
Or in the South, He hides where none can see.

k 10 But mine habitual way He knoweth well;
If tried, I know I should come forth as gold.

B 11 My foot unto His steps hath firmly held;
His way I have observed, nor gone aside:
12 From His commands I have not turnèd back;
His words I prized more than my daily food.

13 But He is [God] alone: Who turneth Him? *A*
What He desireth, even that He doth.
14 What is decreed for me He will perform:
And many such [decrees] He hath in store.
15 [Shut] from His presence out, I am in fear;
I think of Him and I am sore afraid.
16 For GOD [it is] Who maketh faint my heart;
Yea, Shaddai is the One Who troubleth me.
17 Not from the darkness am I thus dismayed;
Nor yet because thick darkness veils my face.
24 Since, then, events from Shaddai are not hid,
Why do not they who love Him know His ways?

2 [The lawless men, their neighbours'] landmarks move; *B* l
They seize on flocks, and feed them [as their own].
3 [Some] from the fatherless drive off their ass,
And take the widow's ox from her in pledge;

1656 4 ° They turn the needy out of the way: the ° poor of the earth hide themselves together.

5 ° Behold, *as* wild asses in the desert, go they forth to their work; rising betimes for a prey: the wilderness *yieldeth* food for them *and* for *their* ° children.

6 They reap ° *every one* ° his corn in the field: and they gather the vintage of ° the wicked.

7 They cause the ° naked to lodge without clothing, that *they have* no covering in the cold.

8 They are wet with the showers of the mountains, and embrace the rock for want of a shelter.

9 They pluck the fatherless from the breast, and take a pledge of the poor.

10 They cause *him* to go [7] naked without clothing, and they take away the sheaf *from* the hungry;

11 *Which* make oil within their walls, *and* tread *their* winepresses, and suffer thirst.

12 ° Men groan from out of the ° city, and the ° soul of the wounded crieth out: yet ° GOD layeth not folly *to them*.

13 ° They are of those that rebel against the light; they know not the ways thereof, nor abide in the paths thereof.

14 The murderer rising with the light killeth the poor and needy, ° and in the night is as a thief.

15 The eye also of the adulterer waiteth for the ° twilight, saying, 'No eye shall see me:' and disguiseth *his* face.

16 In the dark ° they dig through houses, *which* they had marked for themselves in the daytime: they know not the light.

17 For the morning *is* to them even as the shadow of death: ° if *one* know *them, they are in* the terrors of the shadow of death.

m (p, 695) 18 He *is* swift as the waters; their portion is cursed in the earth: ° he ° beholdeth not ° the way of the vineyards.

19 Drought and heat consume the snow waters: *so doth* ° the grave *those which* have ° sinned.

20 The womb shall forget him; the worm shall feed sweetly on him; he shall be no more remembered; and ° wickedness shall be broken as a tree.

21 ° He evil entreateth the barren *that* beareth not: and doeth not good to the widow. l

22 He draweth also the mighty with his power: he riseth up, and no *man* is sure of life.

23 *Though* it be given him *to be* in safety, whereon he resteth; yet His eyes *are* upon their ways. m

---

4 They: [while others]. See translation below.
poor = wretched.
5 Behold. Fig. *Asterismos.* Ap. 6.
children = offspring.
6 every one. Fig. *Ellipsis.* Ap. 6.
his corn. Heb. *bᵉlīlō.* But if divided thus, *bᵉlī lō,* it means "not his own". The word "corn" must be supplied as an *Ellipsis* of the Acc. See translation below.
the wicked = a lawless one. Heb. *rāshā'.* Ap. 44 x.
7 naked. Put by Fig. *Synecdoche* (of the Whole), Ap. 6, for scantily clad, or threadbare.
12 Men. Heb. *mᵉthīm.* Ap. 14. V.
city. The Sept. adds "and houses".
soul. Heb. *nephesh.* Ap. 13.
GOD. Heb. Eloah. Ap. 4. V.
13 They. There is a pause between *vv.* 12 and 13. "They" is emphatic = These. Note the three stages of the lawless: (1) avoiding the light (*v.* 16. John 3. 20); (2) consequent ignorance; (3) final result.
14 and = and [then again].
15 twilight = darkness. A Homonym. See notes on 1 Sam. 30. 17. 2 Kings 7. 5. **16 they**: i. e. burglars.
17 if one know them. See translation below.
18 he. Some codices, with Sept. and Vulg., read "and he".
beholdeth = returneth. **the** = to the.
19 the grave. Heb. Sheōl. Ap. 35.
sinned. Heb. *chāṭā'.* Ap. 44. i.
20 wickedness. Heb. *'āval.* Ap. 44. vi. Put by Fig. *Metonymy* (of Subject), Ap. 6, for the wicked man.
21 He evil entreateth. See translation below.

---

4 [While others] turn the needy from their way;
And all the poor [and wretched] hide themselves.
5 Behold them! As wild-asses they go forth,
And, on the plains, they early seek their prey;
The barren steppe doth yield their children food.
6 They reap [down corn] in fields which are not theirs;
The vineyard of the wicked they do dress.
7 Ill-clad, they lodge without a covering,
And without shelter are they from the cold.
8 With sweeping-rain from mountain-storm they're wet;
For want of refuge they embrace the rock.
9 These [tyrants] tear the orphan from the breast;
That which is on the poor they take to pledge.
10 Stripped of their [scanty] clothing they go forth,
And, hungry, carry [their task-masters'] sheaves:
11 Within their walls these poor press out their oil;
Their wine-presses they tread, yet suffer thirst.
12 From city and from houses groans ascend;
With shrieks those being murdered cry for help;
Yet GOD regards not this enormity!

* * * * * *

13 [Others again] rebel against the light;
They have no knowledge of its [blessèd] ways,
Neither abide they in the paths thereof.
14 The murderer at day-break riseth up,
That he may slay the poor and destitute;
And [then again] at night he plays the thief.
15 Th' adulterer for [midnight's] darkness waits,
"No eye [saith he] shall see the path I take;"
And so he puts a covering on his face.
16 [Burglars] break into houses in the dark,
Which they had set a mark on in the day;
For such as these the daylight do not love.
17 To such, the light is as the shade of death;
For [in the light] death's terrors they discern.
18 Swift as the [rushing] waters' face, [so will] m (p. 695)
His cursèd portion vanish from the earth:
Nor will he to his vineyard e'er return.
19 As drought and heat to water turn the snows,
[E'en so] will Sheōl deal with those who sin.
20 The womb which bore him doth forget him there;
The worm doth [feed on him and] find him sweet:
He will not be remembered any more:
The wicked man lies, shivered, like a tree.
21 [Again, the wicked] wrongs the barren [wife]; l
And to the widow no compassion shows.
22 And by his might he drags the strong away:
He riseth up, no one is sure of life.
23 [God] lets them rest secure, and confident: m
Though still His eyes are ever on their ways.

1656 24 They are exalted for a little while, but are gone and brought low; they are taken out of the way as all *other*, and cut off as the tops of the ears of corn.

25 And if *it be* not *so* now, who will make me a liar, and make my speech nothing worth?"

J8 C1 (p. 697) **25** Then °answered °Bildad the Shuhite, and said,

2 "Dominion and fear *are* with Him, He maketh peace in His high places.

3 °Is there any number of His armies? and upon whom doth not His light arise?

C2 4 °How then can °man be justified with °GOD? or how can he be °clean *that is* born of a woman?

5 °Behold even to the moon, and it shineth not; yea, the stars are not pure in His sight.

6 °How much less [4]man, *that is* a °worm? and the son of °man, *which is* a °worm?

K8 D **26** But Job °answered and said,

2 °"How hast thou helped *him that is* without power? °*how* savest thou the arm *that hath* no strength?

3 [2]How hast thou counselled *him that hath* no wisdom? and [2]*how* hast thou plentifully declared the thing °as it is?

4 To whom hast thou uttered words? and whose °spirit came from thee?

E 5 °Dead *things* °are formed from under the waters, and the inhabitants thereof.

6 °Hell *is* naked before Him, and °destruction hath no covering.

7 He stretcheth out the °north over the empty place, *and* hangeth the earth °upon nothing.

8 He bindeth up the waters in His thick clouds; and the cloud is not rent under them.

9 He holdeth back the face of His throne, *and* spreadeth His cloud upon it.

10 He hath compassed the waters with bounds, until the day and night come to an end.

11 The pillars of heaven °tremble and are °astonished at His reproof.

12 He divideth the sea with His power, and by His understanding He smiteth through the proud.

25. 1-6 (J8, p. 669). BILDAD'S THIRD ADDRESS. (*Division.*)

J8 | C1 | 1-3. God. His omnipotence.
| C2 | 4-6. Man. His impotence.

1 answered = concluded. See note on 4. 1.
Bildad. See note on 2. 11.
3 Is there . . . ?
4 How . . . ? } Fig. *Erotēsis*. Ap. 6.
man = mortal man. Heb. *'ĕnōsh*. Ap. 14. III.
GOD. Heb. El. Ap. 4. iv.
clean = pure. **5 Behold.** Fig. *Asterismos*. Ap. 6.
6 How much less . . . ? Fig. *Erotēsis*. Ap. 6.
worm. Heb. *rimmah*, put by Fig. *Metonymy* (of Adjunct), Ap. 6, for that which is corruptible.
man. Heb. *'ādām*. Ap. 14. I.
worm = maggot. Heb. *tōlā'*, put by Fig. *Metonymy* (of Adjunct), Ap. 6, for that which is weak.

26. 1—27. 10 (K8, p. 669). JOB'S REPLY TO BILDAD'S THIRD ADDRESS. (*Alternation.*)

K8 | D | 26. 1-4. Appeal to his friend.
| E | 26. 6-14. God's ways: His power incomparable.
| *D* | 27. 1-5. Appeal to his friends.
| *E* | 27. 6-10. Job's ways: his righteousness unblameable.

1 answered = replied [to Bildad]. See note on 4. 1.
2 How . . . ? Figs. *Exouthenismos*, *Erotēsis*, and *Eironeia*. Ap. 6.
3 as it is = the thing that is. See note on "sound wisdom". Prov. 2. 7.
4 spirit. Heb. *neshāmāh*. Ap. 16.
5 Dead things are formed from under the waters. The Ellipsis must be supplied thus: "[The place where] the Rephaim stay [which is] beneath the waters, and the things that are therein." This place thus answers to the other place, Sheōl, the grave, in the next verse.
Dead things. Heb. "The Rephaim", the offspring of the fallen angels, akin to the *Nephīlīm* (Gen. 6. 4. See Ap. 23 and 25 and note on Isa. 26. 14, 19).
are formed = remain. Heb. *ḥul*, a Homonym with three meanings: (1) *to stay, remain*, as here; Gen. 8. 10. Judg. 3. 25. 2 Sam. 3. 29. Lam. 4. 6. Hos. 11. 6: even *to wait*, hence *to trust*, Job 35. 14. Cp. Ps. 37. 7. Lam. 3. 26; (2) *to be in pain*, and hence *to bring forth*, Deut. 2. 25. Isa. 23. 4; 26. 18; 54. 1; 66. 8. Ps. 29. 9, &c.; (3) *to be formed* as made or brought forth, 26. 13. Pss. 51. 5; 90. 2. Deut. 32. 18. Prov. 8. 24, 25; 26. 10. Job 15. 7.
6 Hell. Heb. *Sheōl*. Ap. 35.
destruction. Heb. *Abaddōn*.
7 north. See note on Ps. 75. 6. Isa. 14. 13, 14.
upon nothing = not on any thing.
11 tremble . . . astonished. Fig. *Prosopopœia*. Ap. 6.

---

24 They tower a little while, and then are gone;
Brought low, they are, like others, gathered in;
Or cut off even as the ears of corn.
25 If this be not so who can prove me wrong?
Or make my words to be of no account?

BILDAD'S THIRD ADDRESS.
25. 1-6 (J8, p. 669).

J8 C1 (p. 697) With HIM dominion is and reverence;
2 'tis He Who maketh harmony on high;
3 The number of His armies who can count?
Yea, upon whom ariseth not His light?
C2 4 How then can mortal man be just with GOD?
Or he be pure who is of woman born?
5 Behold the moon: to Him it shineth not;
The very stars in His sight are not pure.
6 How much less mortal man—[the food of] worms—
Or any son of man—himself a worm!

JOB'S REPLY TO BILDAD'S THIRD ADDRESS.
26. 1—27. 10 (K8, p. 669).

K8 D 2 How hast thou helpèd him who hath no pow'r?
Or succour brought to him who hath no strength?
3 How hast thou counselled him who is unlearned?
Or hast made fully known the thing that is?
4 By whom hast thou [been taught] to speak these words?
Whose inspiration hath come forth to thee?

5 Where stay the [mighty] Rephaim [of old]? E
Beneath the sea, and things that are therein!—
6 [Open] before Him, Sheōl naked lies,
And deep Abaddon hath no covering.
7 The North He stretches o'er the empty space,
And hangeth not the Earth on anything.
8 He bindeth up the waters in thick clouds,
And [yet] the cloud beneath them is not rent.
9 He closeth fast the entrance to His throne,
And over it He spreadeth His dark cloud.
10 The round horizon bounds the waters' face,
And there the fading light with darkness blends.
11 The pillars of the heav'ns He makes to rock;
And they are terrified at His rebuke.
12 By His great pow'r He calms the [raging] sea;
And by His wisdom He subdues the proud.

1656 13 By His °spirit He hath °garnished the heavens; His hand °hath formed the °crooked °serpent.
14 Lo, these *are* parts of His ways: °but how little a portion is heard of Him? but the thunder of His power who can understand?"

D (p. 697) **27** Moreover Job continued his parable, and said,
2 "*As* °GOD liveth, *Who* hath taken away my judgment; and °THE ALMIGHTY, *Who* hath vexed °my soul;
3 All the while my °breath *is* in me, and the °spirit of °GOD *is* in my nostrils;
4 My lips shall not speak °wickedness, nor my tongue utter deceit.
5 °God forbid that I should justify you: till I °die I will not remove mine integrity from me.
E 6 My righteousness I hold fast, and will not let it go: my heart shall not reproach *me* so long as I live.
7 Let mine enemy be as the °wicked, and he that riseth up against me as the °unrighteous.
8 For °what *is* the hope of the hypocrite, though he hath gained, when [3]GOD °taketh away °his soul?
9 °Will [2]GOD hear his cry when trouble cometh upon him?
10 [9]Will he delight himself in [2]THE ALMIGHTY? [9]will he °always call upon [3]GOD?
J^9 F (p. 698) 11 °I will teach you by the hand of [2]GOD: *that* which *is* with [2]THE ALMIGHTY will I not conceal.
12 °Behold, all ye yourselves have seen *it*; why then are ye thus altogether vain?
13 °This *is* the portion of a [7]wicked °man with [2]GOD, and the heritage of oppressors, *which* they shall receive of [2]THE ALMIGHTY.
14 If his °children be multiplied, *it is* for the sword: and his offspring shall not be satisfied with bread.
15 Those that remain of him shall be °buried in death: and °his widows shall not weep.

13 spirit. Heb. *ruach*. Ap. 9.
garnished = beautified.
hath formed = doth stay. See note on *v.* 5.
crooked = fleeing. Heb. *bariḥ*. The word occurs only here; Isa. 27. 1; 43. 14, referring to the constellation "Serpens".
serpent = *naḥash*, the shining one. Hence a serpent; here, the constellation so called.
14 but how little a portion = 'tis but a whisper.

27. 2 GOD. Heb. El. Ap. 4. IV.
THE ALMIGHTY. Heb. Shaddai. Ap. 4. vii.
my soul = me. Heb. *nephesh*. Ap. 13.
3 breath. Heb. *neshāmāh*. Ap. 16.
spirit = breath. Heb. *rūach*. Ap. 9.
GOD. Heb. Eloah. Ap. 4. V.
4 wickedness. Heb. *'āvāl*. Ap. 44. vi.
5 God forbid = Far be it from me. Fig. *Deisis*. Ap. 6. die = expire.
7 wicked = lawless. Heb. *rāshā'*. Ap. 44. x.
unrighteous. Heb. *'āvvāl*. Ap. 44. vi. See note on "wicked", 18. 21.
8 what . . .? Fig. *Erotēsis*. Ap. 6.
taketh away his soul. By a different division of the letters it means "when he lifteth up his soul to God", or "when God demandeth his soul".
his soul = himself; or, his life. Heb. *nephesh*. Ap. 13.
9 Will . . .? Fig. *Erotēsis*. Ap. 6.
10 always = continually.

27. 11—28. 28 (J^9, p. 669). ZOPHAR'S THIRD ADDRESS. (*Introversion and Alternations.*)

J^9 | F | 27. 11-23. Unwisdom.
  G | n | 28. 1-6. What man knows.
    o | 28. 7, 8. What man does NOT know.
  G | n | 28. 9-11. What man can do.
    o | 12-19. What man can NOT do.
F | 28. 20-28. Wisdom.

11 I will teach you. This is Zophar's third and last address. (1) It is required by the Structure on p. 669 to complete the symmetry of the book. (2) The sentiments of 27. 11—28. 28 demand it, for they are the very opposite of Job's and the same as Zophar's in 27. 13; 20. 29. (3) If these are Job's words, then his friends had convinced him, which Elihu declares they had not done (32. 12). (4) The Heb. of 29. 1 does not mean "continued", but "*added* to take up his discourse", which may mean conclusion as well as continuance. (5) It marks off and separates 29. 1—31. 40 from Job's ordinary replies. Instead of replying to Zophar, Job utters his "self-justification" (in 29. 1—31. 40), which corresponds with his lamentation in 3. 1-26, and forms the conclusion (G^2) as that had been the introduction (G^1), and prepares us for "the words of Job are ended" in 31. 40. (6) Kennicott, Bernard, and Wolfsson assign a third address to Zophar. **12 Behold.** Fig. *Asterismos*. Ap. 6. **13 This is the portion, &c.** Zophar thus takes up the words with which he had concluded his second address (20. 29). **man.** Heb. *'ādām*. Ap. 4. 1. **14 children** = sons. **15 buried in death** = buried through pestilence. **his widows.** The widow of each one of them.

13 The heav'ns so fair His Spirit beautifies,
The Serpent [constellation] He hath formed.
14 Lo, these are but the outlines of His ways;
A whisper only, that we hear of Him;
His wondrous pow'r, who then, can comprehend?

* * * * * *

D (p. 697) **27** Moreover Job did add these words, and say:
2 As GOD doth live Who takes away my right,
E'en Shaddai, Who hath so embittered me;
3 So long as breath remaineth in [my mouth],
And in my nostrils is Eloah's breath,
4 These lips of mine shall not perverseness speak,—
My tongue shall never utter what is false.
5 No; never will I grant that you are right,
Nor, while I live, my innocence let go;
E 6 My right I hold; I will not give it up!
My heart shall not reproach me all my days,
7 E'en were the Evil One mine enemy,
And he—th' Unjust—should my accuser be.

8 What hope is left the godless man, what gain,
When once Eloah doth his life demand?
9 Will GOD [indeed] give ear unto his cry
When [trouble or] distress on him shall come?
10 He is not one who doth in Shaddai joy!
Or on Eloah calls, at any time!

ZOPHAR'S THIRD ADDRESS
27. 11—28. 28 (J^9, p. 669).

11 I now would speak about the ways of GOD, J^9 F (p. 698)
And Shaddai's dealings [with you] not conceal.
12 Ye, surely, must have seen them for yourselves;
Or are ye, then, so altogether vain?
13 This is the lot of wicked men from GOD;
Th' oppressor's heritage from Shaddai's hand:
14 If sons do multiply, 'tis for the sword:
Of bread his offspring will not have enough:
15 Their issue buried, killed by pestilence,
Their widows will not lamentation make.

1656 16 Though he heap up silver as the dust, and
prepare raiment as the clay;
17 He may prepare *it*, but the just shall
put *it* on, and the innocent shall divide the
silver.
18 He buildeth his house as a moth, and as a
°booth *that* the °keeper maketh.
19 The rich man shall lie down, but °he
shall not be °gathered: he openeth his eyes,
and °he *is* not.
20 Terrors take hold on him as waters, a
tempest stealeth him away in the night.
21 The east wind carrieth him away, and he
departeth: and as a storm hurleth him out of
his place.
22 For °*God* shall cast upon him, and not
spare: he °would fain flee out of his hand.
23 *Men* shall clap their hands at him, and
shall hiss him out of his place.

G n (p. 698) **28** °Surely there °is a °vein for the silver,
and a place for gold *where* they fine
it.
2 Iron is taken out of the °earth, and brass *is*
molten *out of* the stone.
3 °He setteth an end to darkness, and searcheth out all perfection: the stones of darkness,
and the shadow of death.
4 The flood breaketh out from the inhabitant; *even the waters* forgotten of the foot:
they are dried up, they are gone away from
°men.
5 *As for* the earth, out of it cometh bread:
and under it is turned up as it were fire.
6 The stones of it *are* the place of sapphires:
and it hath dust of gold.
o 7 *There is* a path which no fowl knoweth,
and which the vulture's eye hath not seen:
8 The °lion's whelps have not trodden it,
°nor the fierce lion passed by it.
G n 9 He putteth forth his hand upon the °rock;
he overturneth the mountains by the roots.

18 booth. Generally made of branches of trees. Cp. Isa. 1. 8. Jonah 4. 5. Lev. 23. 40-42.
keeper = watcher: i. e. vineyard watcher.
19 he = it: i. e. his wealth which is out at interest.
gathered = gathered in, or collected.
he = it: i. e. his wealth is gone. Not he, the rich man, for if he opens his eyes, he "is", not "is not".
22 God is wrongly supplied. It means "he who was wont in times past to flee from the rich man will now come down on him".
would fain flee. Heb. a fleeing would flee. Fig. *Polyptōton* (Ap. 6) = would hastily flee.

28. 1 Surely. This is the continuation of Zophar's last address. Not Job's words. Cp. 35. 16; 38. 2. They are opposed to his own words, and confirm those of his friends. Cp. his second address, 20. 1-29.
is = doth exist.
vein = outlet: i. e. mine, or shaft.
2 earth = dust.
3 He = man: i. e. the miner.
4 men = mortal men. Heb. *'ĕnōsh*. Ap. 14. III.
8 lion's whelps = sons of pride: i. e. ravenous beasts.
nor = and . . . not.
9 rock = flint.

10 He cutteth out rivers among the rocks;
and his eye seeth every precious thing.
11 He bindeth the floods from overflowing;
and *the thing that is* hid bringeth he forth to
light.

12 But where shall wisdom be found? and o
where *is* the place of understanding?
13 ¹Man knoweth not the price thereof;
neither is it found in the land of the living.
14 The depth saith, 'It *is* not in me:' and
the sea saith, '*It is* not with me.'
15 It cannot be gotten for gold, neither shall
silver be weighed *for* the price thereof.
16 It cannot be valued with the gold of Ophir,
with the precious onyx, or the sapphire.
17 The gold and the crystal cannot equal it:
and the exchange of it *shall not be for* jewels
of fine gold.

16 Though silver, like the dust, he heapeth up,
And garments, made in number like the sand,
17 Though he prepare, the just will put them on;
His silver will the innocent divide.
18 The house he builds, 'tis frail as is the moth's,
Or as the booth which vineyard watcher makes.
19 He lies down rich, [his wealth] not gathered in:
He openeth his eyes, and it is gone!
20 Terrors will overtake him as a flood:
A whirlwind in the night will sweep him off.
21 The east wind catcheth him, and he is gone;
Yea, as a storm, it hurls him from his place.
22 He who, before, was wont to flee from him,
Will now come down on him, and will not spare.
23 In triumph he will clap his hands at him;
And hiss him forth from out his dwelling-place.

* * * * * *

G n (p. 698) 28 Yes, for the silver there exists a vein;
A place withal for gold which they refine.
2 From out the earth iron may be brought up;
And copper may be smelted from the ore.
3 To darkness ['neath the earth] man sets a bound;
In all directions he explores [beneath];
Yea, e'en the ores of earth in darkness [hid].
4 A shaft he sinks, 'neath where the settler dwells:
And there, forgotten by the well-worn way,
The miners bore, and pass away [from sight].

5 As for the earth, bread cometh forth from it:
Yet underneath it fire is stirrèd up.
6 Among its stones are glowing sapphires found;
And in its dust are nuggets of pure gold.
7 There is a path no bird of prey hath known; o
Nor hath the eagle's eye discovered it.
8 [A path] which no proud beast hath ever trod:
Not e'en the lion ever passed that way.
9 Man lays his hand upon the flinty rock; *G n*
The hills he overturneth by their roots.
10 He cutteth water-channels in the rocks:
His eye detecteth every precious thing.
11 The overflowing floods he doth restrain:
The hidden things he bringeth forth to light.
12 But wisdom—whence can wisdom be obtained? o
And understanding: where is found its place?
13 No mortal man doth know the way thereto;
Among the living it can not be found.
14 Th' abyss exclaims "[Wisdom] is not in me."
And ocean roars—"Nor dwelleth it with me."
15 Fine gold cannot be given in its stead,
Neither can silver for its price be weighed.
16 With Ophir's gold it never can be bought;
Nor with the onyx, or the sapphire gem.
17 Crystal and gold cannot compare with it;
Nor vessels of pure gold be its exchange.

1656 18 No mention shall be made of coral, or of
pearls: for the price of wisdom *is* above
rubies.
19 The topaz of Ethiopia shall not equal it,
neither shall it be valued with pure gold.
F (p. 698) 20 °Whence then cometh wisdom? and
°where *is* the place of understanding?
21 Seeing it is hid from the eyes of all living,
and kept close from the fowls of the air.
22 °Destruction and death °say, 'We have
°heard the fame thereof with our ears.'
23 °God understandeth the way thereof, and
He knoweth the place thereof.
24 For He looketh to the ends of the earth,
and seeth under the whole heaven;
25 To make the weight for the °winds; and
He weigheth the waters by measure.
26 When He made a decree for the rain, and
a way for the lightning of the thunder:
27 Then did He see it, and declare it; He
prepared it, yea, and searched it out.
28 And unto °man He said, °'Behold, °the
fear of °the LORD*, °that *is* wisdom; and to
depart from evil *is* understanding.'"

H^1 J p (p. 700) 29 °Moreover Job °continued his parable,
and said,
2 °"Oh that °I were as *in* months past, as
in the days *when* °GOD preserved me;
3 When His °candle shined upon my head,
and when by His light I walked *through*
darkness;
4 As I was in the days of my °youth, when
the °secret of ²GOD *was* upon my °taber-
nacle;
5 When °THE ALMIGHTY *was* yet with me,
when my °children *were* about me;
6 When I washed my steps with butter, and
the rock poured me out °rivers of oil;
q 7 When I went out to the gate through the
city, *when* I prepared my seat in the °street!

20 Whence ... where ...? Fig. *Erotēsis*. Ap. 6.
22 Destruction. Heb. *Abaddōn*.
say ... heard. Fig. *Prosopopœia*. Ap. 6.
23 God. Heb. *Elohim*. Ap. 4. I.
25 winds. Heb. *rūach*. Ap. 9.
28 man. Heb. *'ādām*. Ap. 14. I.
Behold. Fig. *Asterismos*. Ap. 6.
the fear = the reverence.
the LORD*. One of the 134 alterations of the *Sōpherīm* (Ap. 32), by which the name "Jehovah" in the primitive text, was changed to Adonai.
that is wisdom. This was a libel on Job, for Job had this "fear" or reverence; yet he was suffering. That was the very point in question, and leads up to the answer. This was Zophar's philosophy. The fear of the LORD is not true wisdom; it is only "the *beginning* of wisdom" (Ps. 111. 10. Prov. 1. 7; 9. 10). True wisdom is to take the place of the sinner before God, and Job takes this place (42. 5, 6). This is "the end of the LORD" (Jas. 5. 11), and it is "the end" of this book. This wisdom "justifies God" (Ps. 51. 3, 4, 6. Matt. 11. 19. Luke 7. 35). True wisdom is "given", and we have to be "made" to know it (Prov. 30. 24. 2 Tim. 3. 15. Job 38. 36). Cp. 33. 27, 28; 34. 31; 35. 11; 39. 17. Zophar's was *human* wisdom founded on human merit. To depart from evil is what every prudent man would do from good policy.

29. 1—31. 40 (G^2, p. 669). **JOB'S SELF-JUSTIFICATION.** (*Division.*)

G^2	H^1	29. Saddened retrospect of past prosperity.
	H^2	30. Sorrowful description of present misery.
	H^3	31. Solemn asseveration of innocence.

29. 1-25 (H^1, above). **SADDENED RETROSPECT OF PAST PROSPERITY.** (*Introversion.*)

H^1	J	p	1-6. Job's prosperity.	(What he was.)
		q	7-11. His honour.	(What he had.)
	K	r	12. Redress of wrong.	(What Job did.)
		s	13. Beneficence	
		t	14-. Righteousness.	
	K	*t*	-14. Justice.	
		s	15, 16. Beneficence.	
		r	17. Redress of wrong.	
	J	*p*	18-20. Job's prosperity.	(What he thought.)
		q	21-25. His honour.	(What he had.)

1 Moreover = And.
continued his parable: i.e. again took up his impressive discourse. This is Job's last address (G^2), corresponding with his first (G^1). See the Structure on p. 669. **2 Oh.** Fig. *Ecphōnēsis*. Ap. 6. **I.** Note the frequency of "I" (self-occupation). In ch. 29, the "I" of prosperity; in ch. 30, the "I" of adversity; in ch. 31, the "I" of self-righteousness. Contrast the "I" of 42. 2-6, the "end". **GOD.** Heb. Eloah. Ap. 4. V. **3 candle** = lamp. **4 youth** = autumn's prime, or maturity. **secret** = counsel. **tabernacle** = tent. **5 THE ALMIGHTY.** Heb. Shaddai. Ap. 4. VII. **children** = youths. **6 rivers** = divisions. Hence the little channels made in garden irrigation. See note on Ps. 1. 3, and Prov. 21. 1. **7 street** = broad or open place.

18 Corals and pearls can not with it be named;
The worth of rubies wisdom far excels.
19 The topaz gem of Cush vies not therewith;
And purest gold with it can not be weighed.
F (p. 698) 20 Whence, then, this wisdom? [Whence, then, doth it come]?
And understanding, where is found its place?
21 So hidden from the eyes of all who live;
And from the birds of heav'n so close concealed.
22 Death and Destruction [both alike] declare:—
"The rumour of it, it hath reached our ears."
23 Eloah, though, hath understood the way;
And He discerns the [secret] place thereof.
24 For HE can look to Earth's remotest bounds,
And all beneath the heavens He beholds.
25 So that He gives the air its density;
And waters meteth out by measurement.
26 When for the rain He issued a decree,
A way appointed for the thunder-flash;
27 Then did He see it; then declared it [good];
Yea, He established it and showed it forth:
28 And to the sons of Adam thus He saith:—
"Lo! Wisdom is to reverence the Lord;
And understanding is to flee from sin."

JOB'S SELF-JUSTIFICATION. CONCLUSION.
29. 1—31. 40 (G^2, p. 669).

2 Oh that I were as in the olden times; H^1 J p (p. 700)
As in the days when GOD watched over me.
3 When shone His lamp so brightly o'er my head,
And, by His light, I could in darkness walk.
4 As fared I in the spring-time of my life,
With GOD'S own secret presence in my tent.
5 When Shaddai yet was with me as my stay,
And round me were my children in their youth.
6 When with abundant milk my feet I bathed,
And oil from out the rock flowed forth for me.
7 When to the city's gate I made my way, q
And in the open place prepared my seat;

1656 8 The young men saw me, and hid themselves: and the aged arose, *and* stood up.
9 The princes refrained talking, and °laid *their* hand on their mouth.
10 The nobles held their peace, and their tongue cleaved to the roof of their mouth.
11 When the ear heard *me*, then °it blessed me; and when the eye saw *me*, it °gave witness to me:
K r (p. 700) 12 Because I delivered the °poor that cried, and the fatherless, and *him that had* none to help him.
s 13 The blessing of him that was ready to perish came upon me: and I caused the widow's heart to sing for joy.
t 14 I put on righteousness, and it clothed me:
K t my judgment *was* as a robe and a diadem.
s 15 I was eyes to the blind, and feet *was* I to the lame.
16 I *was* a father to the °poor: and the cause *which* I knew not I searched out.
r 17 And I brake the jaws of the °wicked, and plucked the spoil out of his teeth.
J p 18 Then I said, 'I shall °die in my nest, and I shall multiply *my* days °as the sand.'
19 My root *was* spread out by the waters, and the dew lay all night upon my branch.
20 My glory *was* fresh in me, and my bow was renewed in my hand.
q 21 Unto me *men* gave ear, and waited, and kept silence at my counsel.
22 After my words they spake not again; and my speech dropped upon them.
23 And they waited for me °as for the rain; and they opened their mouth wide *as* for the latter rain.
24 *If* I laughed on them, they believed *it* not; and the light of my countenance they cast not down.
25 I chose out their way, and sat chief, and dwelt as a king in the army, as one *that* comforteth the mourners.

9 **laid their hand, &c.** In token of silence and submission.
11 **it blessed . . . gave witness.** Fig. *Prosopopœia*. Ap. 6.
12 **poor** = wretched. Heb. *'ānah*. See note on Prov. 6. 11.
16 **poor** = helpless. Heb. *'ebyōn*. See note on Prov. 6. 11.
17 **wicked.** Heb. *'avvīl*. Ap. 44. vi. See note on 18. 21.
18 **die in my nest.** The Sept. reads "grow old as a palm trunk".
as the sand. A note in Cod. (No. 1 in King's Lib., Brit. Mus.) states that the Western School points this to mean "as a phœnix". The Vulg. reads "as a palm".
23 **as for the rain**: i. e. the early rain, which is sometimes so late as to cause anxiety.

30. 1-31 (H², p. 700). SORROWFUL DESCRIPTION OF PRESENT MISERY. (*Alternation.*)

H² | L | 1-14. From others. (*vv.* 1-8, their character. *vv.* 9-14, their conduct.)
  M | 15-18. In himself. (*vv.* 15, 16, mental. *vv.* 17, 18, bodily.)
  L | 19-24. From God. (*vv.* 19, 20, silence. *vv.* 21-24, action.)
  M | 25-31. In himself.

1 **I.** Note the "I" of adversity in ch. 30. See note on 29. 2.

30 But now *they that are* younger than °I have me in derision, whose fathers I would have disdained to have set with the dogs of my flock. H² L (p. 701)
2 Yea, whereto *might* the strength of their hands *profit* me, in whom old age was perished?
3 For want and famine *they were* solitary; fleeing into the wilderness in former time desolate and waste.
4 Who cut up mallows by the bushes, and juniper roots *for* their meat.
5 They were driven forth from among *men*, (they cried after them as *after* a thief;)

---

8 The young men saw me, and withdrew themselves;
Yea, all the elders would rise up, and stand.
9 The rulers, too, from talking would refrain,
And lay their hand, for silence, on their mouth.
10 The nobles' voice was hush'd; they held their peace;
Their tongue, in silence, to their palate clave:
11 The ear that heard me blessed me as it heard;
The eye that saw me witness bore to me,
K r (p. 700) 12 That I did save the poor when he cried out:
The fatherless, and him who had no help.
s 13 The perishing to me his blessing gave;
I caused the widow's heart to sing for joy.
t 14 My righteousness I put on as my robe:
K t My justice, as my cloak and diadem.
s 15 I was instead of eyes unto the blind,
And to the lame I was instead of feet.
16 A father was I to the needy ones;
The cause I did not know I searchèd out.
r 17 I loved to break the jaws of evil men,
And pluck the prey, still living, from their teeth.
J p 18 I said, "I shall grow old as doth the palm;
Yea, multiplied like sand my days shall be:
19 My root unto the waters shall spread out,
And all night long the dew be on my branch,
20 My glory shall remain with me still fresh;
My bow, within my hand, renew its strength."
21 To me men hearkened, waited, and gave ear, *q*
And at my counsel silence they did keep.
22 When I had spoken, none replied again,
So that on them my wisdom still might fall.
23 Yea, they would wait, as men for showers wait,
And open wide their mouths as for the rain.
24 That I should mock them they would ne'er believe,
Nor would they cause a shadow on my face;
25 'Twas mine to choose their way, and sit as chief;
As king among his subjects so I dwelt;
And among mourners as a comforter.

30 But, now, my juniors hold me up to scorn, H² L (p. 701)
Whose fathers I would have disdained to put
On level with the dogs that watched my flock.
2 What profit would their strength have been to me
When they had lost their ripened manhood's powers?
3 Through hunger they were like the barren rock,
These vagrants, driven from the land of drought,
For ages past a desolation wild;
4 Who pluck among the bushes bitter herbs,
And make the roots of juniper their food.
5 From human intercourse are they chased forth,
[And] men cry after them, as after thieves:

1656 6 To dwell in the °cliffs of the valleys, *in* caves of the earth, and *in* the rocks.

7 Among the bushes they brayed; under the nettles they were gathered together.

8 *They were* °children of fools, yea, °children of base men: they were °viler than the earth.

9 And now am I their song, yea, I am their byword.

10 They abhor me, they flee far from me, and spare not to spit in my °face.

11 Because He hath loosed my cord, and afflicted me, they have also let loose the bridle before me.

12 Upon *my* right *hand* rise the youth; they push away my feet, and they raise up against me the ways of their destruction.

13 They mar my path, they set forward my calamity, °they have no helper.

14 They came *upon me* as a wide breaking in *of waters:* in the desolation they rolled themselves *upon me.*

M (p. 701) 15 Terrors are turned upon me: they pursue °my soul as the °wind: and my welfare passeth away as a cloud.

16 And now my °soul is poured out upon me; the days of affliction have taken hold upon me.

17 My bones are pierced in me in the night season: and my sinews take no rest.

18 By the great force *of my disease* is my garment changed: it bindeth me about as the °collar of my coat.

L 19 He hath cast me into the mire, and I am become like dust and ashes.

20 I cry unto Thee, and Thou dost not °hear me: I stand up, and Thou regardest me *not.*

21 Thou art become cruel to me: with Thy strong hand Thou opposest thyself against me.

22 Thou liftest me up to the [15] wind; Thou causest me to ride *upon it,* and dissolvest °my substance.

23 For I know *that* Thou wilt bring me *to* death, and *to* the house appointed for all living.

24 Howbeit He will not stretch out *His* hand to the °grave, though they cry in °his destruction.

25 °Did not I weep for him that was in trouble? was *not* my [16] soul grieved for the °poor? *M*

26 When I looked for good, then evil came *unto me:* and when I waited for light, there came °darkness.

27 My bowels boiled, and rested not: the days of affliction °prevented me.

28 I went mourning without the sun: I stood up, *and* I cried in the °congregation.

29 I am a brother to dragons, and a companion to owls.

6 cliffs = ravines; or, most dreadful ravines.
8 children = sons.
viler than the earth = smitten or scourged out of the land. **10 face** = presence.
13 they have no helper = they derive no help or benefit from it.
15 my soul = what is noble or excellent in me. Not *nephesh* (Ap. 13) here, as in *vv.* 16 and 25.
wind. Heb. *rūach.* Ap. 9.
16 soul. Heb. *nephesh.* Ap. 13.
18 collar: the opening in the tunic for the neck.
20 hear = answer.
22 my substance. See note on "sound wisdom". Prov. 2. 7.
24 grave. Heb. *bī'ī,* a mound or tumulus. But others point it *be'ī* = a prayer.
his destruction = their calamity.
25 Did not I . . . ? Fig. *Erotēsis.* Ap. 6.
poor = helpless. Heb. *'ebyōn.* See note on Prov. 6. 11.
26 darkness. Heb. *'ophel.* See note on 3. 6.
27 prevented = came on.
28 congregation = assembly.

---

6 In dark ravines they make their dwellingplace,
In holes of earth, and caverns of the rocks;
7 Among the desert scrub they raise their shouts,
[And] under bramble bushes herd [like beasts].
8 Children of fools, yea, sons without a name,
As outcasts they are driven from the land.
9 But, now, I have become their mocking-song;
I have become a by-word unto them.
10 They [all] abhor and stand aloof from me;
And spare not now to spit before my face.
11 Since He hath loosed my bow, and humbled me,
They too, before me, cast off all restraint.
12 At my right hand this rabble rises up;
They thrust aside my feet; [leave me no room];
Against me they oppose their hostile ways:
13 They mar my path; [my movements they impede];
They seek my hurt, although it helps them not,
14 As [waters] through a breach, they come [on me];
And like a tempest they rush in on me.

M (p. 701) 15 All now is overthrown: and, like the wind,
Terrors my dignity have scattered far;
And gone, like clouds, is my prosperity.
16 And now my soul within me is poured out;
The days of my affliction hold me fast.
17 By night my bones are pierced [with pains] without;
My throbbing nerves [within me] never rest.
18 By great exertion is my garment changed;
It girds me as my tunic girds my neck.

19 Into the mire His hand hath cast me down; *L*
To dust and ashes I may be compared.
20 I cry aloud to Thee, Thou answ'rest not;
I stand [in prayer], but Thou dost not regard.
21 Thou art become relentless [to my prayer];
And dost assail me with Thy mighty hand.
22 Thou used'st to uplift me on the wind;
[Yea] Thou didst cause me [thereupon] to ride:
[But now] my substance Thou dost bring to naught.
23 I know that Thou wilt turn me o'er to death,—
E'en to the place ordained for all who live.
24 Ah! prayer [for these] is vain. He will not help,
Though when in trouble they may cry [to Him].

25 Did not I weep for him whose lot was hard? *M*
Was I not for the helpless sorely grieved?
26 Yet, when I looked for good, then evil came;
And darkness [deep], when I expected light.
27 My bowels boil, and they are never still;
So suddenly has trouble come on me.
28 Shrouded in gloom I go, without the sun.
I rose in the assembly, and cried "Help!"
29 Brother am I become to howling brutes,
And a companion to the screeching birds.

1656 30 My skin is black upon me, and my bones are burned with heat.

31 My harp also is *turned* to mourning, and my °organ into the voice of them that weep.

H^3 N^1 u^1 (p. 703) **31** °I made a covenant with mine eyes; °why then should I think upon a maid?

v^1 2 For what portion of °GOD *is there* from above? and *what* inheritance of °THE ALMIGHTY from on high?

3 °*Is* not destruction to the °wicked? and a strange *punishment* to the workers of °iniquity?

4 °Doth not He see my ways, and count all my steps?

N^2 u^2 5 If I have walked with vanity, or if my foot hath hasted to deceit;

v^2 6 Let me be weighed in an even balance, that ²GOD may know mine integrity.

N^3 u^3 7 If my step hath turned out of the way, and mine heart °walked after mine eyes, and if any blot hath cleaved to mine hands;

v^3 8 *Then* let me sow, and let another eat; yea, let my offspring be rooted out.

N^4 u^4 9 If mine heart have been deceived by a woman, or *if* I have laid wait at my neighbour's door;

v^4 10 *Then* let my wife grind unto another, and let others bow down upon her.

11 For this *is* an heinous °crime; yea, it *is* an °iniquity *to be punished by* the judges.

12 For it *is* a fire *that* consumeth to destruction, and would root out all mine increase.

N^5 u^5 13 If I did despise the cause of my manservant or of my maidservant, when they contended with me;

v^5 14 What then shall I do when °GOD riseth up? and when He visiteth, what shall I answer Him?

15 Did not He That made me in the womb make him? and did not One fashion us in the womb?

N^6 u^6 16 If I have withheld the °poor from *their* desire, or have caused the eyes of the widow to fail;

17 Or have eaten my morsel myself alone, and the fatherless hath not eaten thereof;

18 (For from my youth he was brought up with me, as *with* a father, and I have guided her from my mother's womb;)

31 organ = lute.

31. 1-40 (H^3, p. 700). SOLEMN ASSEVERATION OF HIS INNOCENCE. (*Repeated Alternation.*)

H^3 | N^1 | u^1 | 1. Sin. (Unchastity.)
v^1 | 2-4. Consequence.
N^2 | u^2 | 5. Sin. (Deceit.)
v^2 | 6. Consequence. (Trial desired.)
N^3 | u^3 | 7. Sin. (Dishonesty.)
v^3 | 8. Consequence. (Imprecation.)
N^4 | u^4 | 9. Sin. (Adultery.)
v^4 | 10-12. Consequence. (Imprecation.)
N^5 | u^5 | 13. Sin. (Injustice.)
v^5 | 14, 15. Consequence. (Penalty.)
N^6 | u^6 | 16-21. Sin. (Inhumanity.)
v^6 | 22, 23. Consequence. (Imprecation.)
N^7 | u^7 | 24-27. Sins of heart. (Covetousness, 24, 25. Idolatry, 26, 27.)
v^7 | 28. Consequence. (Penalty.)
N^8 | u^8 | 29-34. Sins of heart. (Malignity, 29-31. Inhospitality, 32. Hypocrisy, 33, 34.)
v^8 | 35-37. Consequence. (Trial desired.)
N^9 | u^9 | 38, 39. Sin. (Fraud.)
v^9 | 40. Consequence.

1 I. Note the "I" of self-justification; and see note on 29. 2.

why . . . ? Fig. *Erotēsis*. Ap. 6.

2 GOD. Heb. Eloah. Ap. 4. V.

THE ALMIGHTY. Heb. Shaddai. Ap. 4. VII.

3 Is not . . . ? Fig. *Erotēsis*. Ap. 6.

wicked. Heb. *'āvvīl*. Ap. 44. vi. See note on 18. 21.

iniquity. Heb. *'āven*. Ap. 44. iii.

4 Doth not He . . . ? Fig. *Erotēsis*. Ap. 6.

7 walked. Fig. *Prosopopœia*. Ap. 6.

11 crime. Heb. *zimmah*. Ap. 44. xiii.

iniquity. Heb. *'āvāh*. Ap. 44. iv.

iniquity to be punished by the judges = a judicial iniquity; or, an iniquity in the eye of the law.

14 GOD. Heb. El. Ap. 4. iv.

16 poor. Heb. *dal* = impoverished or reduced in means. See note on Prov. 6. 11.

---

30 Without: my skin is all burnt up, and black;
Within: my bones are all consumed with heat.
31 Therefore my harp to mourning has been turned;
My lyre is like the voice of them that weep.

H^3 N^1 u^1 (p. 703) **31** A covenant mine eyes had made [with God];
How then could I upon a virgin gaze?
v^1 2 What would my judgment be from GOD above?
Or what my lot from Shaddai in the height?
3 Is not calamity for evil men?
To those who sin is not disaster due?
4 Would not Eloah see my [evil] way?
[Would He not] take account of all my steps?
N^2 u^2 5 If I have walked in ways of falsity,
Or if my foot hath hasted to deceit;
v^2 6 Then let Him weigh me in just balances,
And let Eloah know my blamelessness.
N^3 u^3 7 If from THE way, my step aside hath swerved,
And I have coveted what I had seen,
Or any stain has cleaved unto my hands:
v^3 8 Then let me sow and let another reap,
And let my plantings all be rooted up.

9 By woman if my heart have been enticed, N^4 u^4
And at my neighbour's door I have laid wait:
10 Then let my wife grind for another man, v^4
Let others humble her [as if their slave].
11 For such a deed would be a heinous sin,
A sin that must be brought before the judge;
12 A fire 'twould be that to Abaddon burns,
Destroying all my increase at the root.

13 If I had spurned my servants' righteous cause, N^5 u^5
When they had brought before me their complaint:
14 What then could I have done when GOD rose up? v^5
When He required, could I have answered Him?
15 Who in the womb made ME, made He not him?
And from one source gave being to us both?

16 If from the poor man's prayer I turned away, N^6 u^6
[Or if] I caused the widow's eyes to fail;
17 Or if I ate my morsel all alone,
So that the fatherless ate none thereof:—
18 [But no]! As with a father he grew up
With me: and from my birth I guided her.

1656 19 If I have seen any perish for want of
clothing, or any °poor without covering;
20 If his °loins have not blessed me, and *if*
he were *not* warmed with the fleece of my
sheep;
21 If I have lifted up my hand against the
fatherless, when I saw my °help in the gate:

v[6] (p. 703) 22 *Then* let mine arm fall from my shoulder
blade, and mine arm be broken from °the
bone.
23 For destruction *from* [14] GOD *was* a terror
to me, and by reason of His °highness I could
not °endure.

N[7] u[7] 24 If I have made gold my hope, or have
said to the fine gold, '*Thou art* my confidence;'
25 If I rejoiced because my wealth *was* great,
and because mine hand had gotten much;
26 If I beheld °the sun when it shined, or the
moon walking *in* brightness;
27 And my heart hath been secretly enticed,
or °my mouth hath kissed my hand:

v[7] 28 This also *were* an [11] iniquity *to be punished by* the judge: for I should have denied
the [14] GOD *That is* above.

N[8] u[8] 29 If I rejoiced at the destruction of him that
hated me, or lifted up myself when °evil °found
him:
30 (Neither have I suffered my mouth to °sin
by wishing a curse to °his °soul.)
31 If the °men of my °tabernacle said not,
'Oh that we had of his flesh! we cannot be
satisfied.'
32 The stranger did not lodge in the street:
but I opened my doors to the traveller.
33 If I covered my °transgressions °as Adam,
by hiding mine °iniquity in my bosom:
34 Did I fear a great multitude, or did the
contempt of families terrify me, that I kept
silence, *and* went not out of the door?

19 poor = helpless. Heb. *'ebyōn.* See note on Prov. 6. 11.
20 loins have not blessed. Fig. *Prosopopœia,* Ap. 6: i. e. the loins so covered.
21 help. Put by Fig. *Metonymy* (of Adjunct), Ap. 6, for those who would be on his side.
22 the bone. A.V. marg., "the chanel bone". Obsolete Eng. for channel = what is channelled or scooped out: i. e. the socket. **23 highness** = majesty. endure = escape. **26 the sun** = the light.
27 my mouth hath kissed my hand: i. e. the outward sign of homage [to, or in worship, of the sun].
29 evil. Heb. *rā'a'.* Ap. 44. viii. found. Fig. *Prosopopœia.* Ap. 6.
30 sin. Heb. *chāṭā'.* Ap. 44. i. his. A special various reading called *Sevīr* (Ap. 34) reads "their". soul. Heb. *nephesh.* Ap. 13.
31 men. Heb. *m^ethīm.* Ap. 14. V. tabernacle = tent.
33 transgressions. Heb. *pāsha'.* Ap. 44. ix. Some codices, with two early printed editions, Sept., and Vulg., read "transgression" (sing.). as Adam. Cp. Gen. 3. 10. iniquity. Heb. *'āvah.* Ap. 44. iv.
35 Oh! Fig. *Ecphōnēsis.* Ap. 6. behold. Fig. *Asterismos.* Ap. 6. adversary = man (Heb. *'īsh.* Ap. 14. II) of my quarrel.
38 land cry . . . complain. Fig. *Prosopopœia.* Ap. 6.
39 have caused, &c. = made the souls of the owners groan. life = soul. Heb. *nephesh.* Ap. 13.

35 °Oh that one would hear me! °behold, v[8]
my desire *is, that* [2] THE ALMIGHTY would answer me, and *that* mine °adversary had written a book.
36 Surely I would take it upon my shoulder,
and bind it *as* a crown to me.
37 I would declare unto Him the number of
my steps; as a prince would I go near unto
Him.

38 If my °land cry against me, or that the N[9] u[9]
furrows likewise thereof °complain;
39 If I have eaten the fruits thereof without
money, or °have caused the owners thereof to
lose their °life:

19 If e'er I saw one perishing [with cold],
Or any needy without covering:
20 Have not his [very] loins blessed me indeed,
When he has felt the warmth of my lambs' fleece?
21 If 'gainst the orphan I have raised my hand,
Because I saw the judge would take my part:

v[6] (p. 703) 22 [Then] let my shoulder from its socket fall,
And [let] my arm be broken from its blade.
23 No! GOD'S destruction ever was my dread,
Before His majesty I could not stand.

N[7] u[7] 24 If I have put my confidence in gold,
Or to the fine gold said ["Thou art] my trust":
25 If I rejoiced because my wealth was great,
Because my hand had vast abundance gained:
26 If on the sun I looked as it shone forth,
Or on the moon, so bright, as it marched on,
27 And secretly my heart hath been enticed,
So that my hand [in worship] touched my mouth:

v[7] 28 This, too, had been a sin before the law;
For then I had denied the GOD above.

N[8] u[8] 29 Over my foe's misfortune had I joyed?
Or e'er exulted when ill came on him?
30 (Nay, not my mouth would I permit to sin,
By asking for a curse upon his soul.)
31 Though have not those of mine own household said,
"Oh! that we had [our foeman's] flesh [to eat],
That we might satiate ourselves [therewith]."
32 The stranger never lodged outside [my tent];
My doors I opened to the traveller.
33 If I, like Adam, my transgression hid,
And in my breast concealed my secret sin:
34 Then let me tremble at the rabble crowd,
Yea, let the scorn of men of rank affright,
And let me silence keep, and not go forth.

35 (Oh! that I had but one to hear what I v[8]
Have noted down! Let Shaddai answer me!
Or, let mine adversary write HIS charge!
36 Would I not on my shoulder lift it up,
Or bind it as a crown upon [my head]?
37 The number of my steps I would declare;
Yea, as a prince I would draw near to him.)

38 If all my land against me had cried out, N[9] u[9]
And [if] its furrows all together wept;
39 If without having paid, I ate its fruits,
And made the souls of those who owned it groan:

v9 (p. 703) 1656 40 °Let thistles grow instead of wheat, and cockle instead of barley." The words of Job are °ended.

O1 (p. 705) **32** So these three °men ceased to answer Job, because he *was* righteous in his own eyes.
2 Then was kindled the wrath of °Elihu the son of °Barachel the °Buzite, of the kindred of °Ram: against Job was his wrath kindled, because he justified °himself rather than °God.
3 Also against his three friends was his wrath kindled, because they had found no answer, and *yet* had °condemned Job.
4 Now Elihu had waited till Job had spoken, because they *were* elder than he.
5 When Elihu saw that *there was* no answer in the mouth of *these* three [1]men, then his wrath was kindled.

O2 P1 y 6 And Elihu the son of Barachel the Buzite answered and said, "I *am* young, and ye *are* very old;
z wherefore I was afraid, and durst not shew you mine opinion.
7 I said, °'Days should speak, and multitude of °years should teach wisdom.'
y 8 But *there is* a °spirit in [1]man: and the °inspiration of °THE ALMIGHTY giveth them understanding.
9 Great [1]men are not *always* wise: neither do the aged understand judgment.
z 10 Therefore I said, 'Hearken to me; I also will shew mine opinion.'
11 °Behold, I waited for your words; I gave ear to your reasons, whilst ye searched out what to say.
12 Yea, I attended unto you, and, [11]behold, *there was* none of you that °convinced Job, *or* that answered his °words:
13 Lest ye should say, 'We have found out wisdom:' °GOD thrusteth him down, not °man.
14 Now he hath not directed *his* words against me: neither will I answer him with your speeches."
15 (They were amazed, they answered no more: they left off speaking.

40 Let thistles grow. This is not an imprecation, but an argument in favour of his integrity: i.e. Had he been as his friends alleged, would he not have had bad instead of bountiful harvests? See translation below.

ended: so far as his friends were concerned. He had words for God (ch. 42. 1-6).

32. 1—37. 24 (E, p. 665). THE MINISTRY OF ELIHU: THE MEDIATOR. (*Division.*)

E | O1 | 32. 1-5. The connecting narrative.
  | O2 | 32. 6—37. 24. The ministry proper.

32. 1-5 (O1, above). THE CONNECTING NARRATIVE. (*Alternation.*)

O1 | w | 1. The three men. Job's friends.
   | x | 2, 3. Anger of Elihu.
   | *w* | 4. The one man. Job.
   | *x* | 5. Anger of Elihu.

1 men. Heb. pl. of *'ĕnōsh.* Ap. 14. III.

2 Elihu=God is Jehovah; or, my God is He. Not named before. His addresses occupy six chapters. His two counts of indictment (*vv.* 2, 3) are based upon what precedes, and lead up to "the end of the Lord" in what follows from *v.* 13.

Barachel=whom God hath blessed.

Buzite. Descended from Buz, the second son of Nahor, the brother of Abraham (Gen. 22. 20, 21). See notes on p. 666.

Ram=Aram, related to Buz (Gen. 22. 21).

himself=his soul. Heb. *nephesh.* Ap. 13.

God. Heb. *Elohim.* Ap. 4. I.

3 condemned Job. The primitive text reads "condemned God", but was altered from motives of false reverence by the *Sōpherīm* to "Job". See Ap. 33.

32. 6—37. 24 (O2, above). ELIHU'S MINISTRY. (*Repeated Alternation.*)

O2 | P1 | 32. 6-22. Elihu. Introduction.
   | Q1 | 33. 1-33. His first address to Job.
   | P2 | 34. 1. Elihu. Continuation.
   | Q2 | 34. 2-37. His words to Job's friends.
   | P3 | 35. 1. Elihu. Continuation.
   | Q3 | 35. 2-16. His second address to Job.
   | P4 | 36. 1. Elihu. Conclusion.
   | Q4 | 36. 2—37. 24. His words on God's behalf.

32. 6-22 (P1, above). ELIHU. INTRODUCTION. (*Alternation.*)

P1 | y | 6-. Personal. Seniority.
   | z | -6, 7. Reason for not speaking before.
   | *y* | 8, 9. Personal. Qualification.
   | *z* | 10-22. Reason for speaking now.

7 Days . . . years. Put by Fig. *Metonymy* (of Adjunct), Ap. 6, for men of years: aged men.

8 spirit. Heb. *rūach.* Ap. 9.

inspiration. Heb. *neshāmāh.* Ap. 16. **THE ALMIGHTY.** Heb. Shaddai. Ap. 4. VII. **11 Behold.** Fig. *Asterismos.* Ap. 6. **12 convinced**=convicted. Man condemns without convicting; but God convicts first, that the man may condemn himself. **words**=arguments. **13 GOD.** Heb. El. Ap. 4. IV. **man.** Heb. *'ish.* Ap. 14. II.

v9 (p. 703) 40 [Then] thorns had thrived instead of wheat I'd sowed,
And noxious weeds, instead of barley, grown.
Job's words are ended: [he will say no more].

ELIHU'S ADDRESSES.

32. 6—37. 24 (E, p. 665).

INTRODUCTION, 32. 6-22.

O2 P1 y (p. 705) **32** 6 I am but young in years, and ye are old:
z Therefore it was that I held back in fear,
And durst not show what my opinion was.
7 For those of many days should speak, I thought;
A multitude of years should wisdom teach.
y 8 Howe'er, a spirit dwells in mortal man,
And Shaddai's breath makes them to understand:
9 The greatest men are not at all times wise;
Nor do the aged [always] rightly judge.

10 Therefore I said, "O hearken unto me; z
I too will show my knowledge, even I."
11 Lo! I have listened unto your discourse;
To all your reas'nings I have given ear,
Waiting till ye have searched out what to say.
12 But, though to you I carefully gave heed,
There was not one of you convicted Job;
Not one who really answered what he said.
13 I pray you, say not "We have wisdom found;
'tis GOD alone Who thrusts him down, not man."
14 Since not 'gainst ME hath he arrayed his words,
I will not with YOUR words reply to him.
15 (All broken down, they answer him no more:
They have not any more a word to say.

1656 16 When I had waited, (for they spake not,
but stood still, *and* answered no more;)
17 *I said,* '𝔍 will answer also my part, 𝔍 also
will shew mine opinion.
18 For I am full of °matter, the [8] spirit within me constraineth me.
19 [11] Behold, my belly *is* as °wine *which*
hath no vent; it is ready to burst like new
°bottles.
20 I will speak, that I may be refreshed: I
will open my lips and answer.
21 Let me not, I pray you, accept any
[13] man's person, neither let me give flattering
titles unto °man.
22 For I know not to give flattering titles;
in so doing my Maker would °soon take me
away.'

Q[1] R[1] a[1] (p. 706) **33** Wherefore, Job, I pray thee, hear my
speeches, and hearken to all my words.
2 °Behold, now I have opened my mouth, my
tongue hath spoken in my mouth.
b[1] 3 °My words *shall be of* the uprightness of
my heart: and my lips shall utter knowledge
clearly.
4 The °Spirit of °GOD hath made me, and
the °breath of °THE ALMIGHTY hath given me
life.
a[2] 5 If thou canst answer me, set *thy words* in
order before me, stand up.
b[2] 6 [2] Behold, 𝔍 *am* according to °thy wish in
[4] GOD'S stead: 𝔍 also am formed out of the
clay.
7 [2] Behold, my terror shall not make thee
afraid, neither shall my hand be heavy upon
thee.
S c 8 Surely thou hast spoken in mine hearing,
and I have heard the voice of °*thy* words,
saying,
9 '𝔍 am clean without °transgression, 𝔍 *am*
innocent; neither *is there* °iniquity in me.
10 [2] Behold, He °findeth occasions against
me, °He counteth me for His enemy,
11 He putteth my feet in the stocks, He
marketh all my paths.'
12 [2] Behold, *in* this thou art not just: I will
answer thee, that °𝔊𝔒𝔇 is °greater than
°man. d

18 matter. Heb. *millah* = the matter of what is said.
19 wine. Heb. *yayin.* Ap. 27. i.
bottles = skin bottles; which, if fermentation is not completed, sometimes burst.
21 man. Heb. *'ādām.* Ap. 14. I.
22 soon. See note on Prov. 5. 14.

33. 1-33 (Q[1], p. 705). ELIHU'S WORDS TO JOB.
(*Alternations.*)

Q[1] | R[1] | a[1] | 1, 2. Call for attention.
b[1] | 3, 4. His fitness. { g | 3. Internal. h | 4. External.
a[2] | 5. Call for answer.
b[2] | 6, 7. His fitness. { *h* | 6. External. *g* | 7. Internal.
S | c | 8-11. Job's error. Justification of himself.
d | 12. Answer. God's greatness (in Creation).
S | *c* | 13. Job's error. Charge against God.
d | 14-30. Answer. God's goodness (in Revelation).
R[2] | a[3] | 31-. Call for silence.
b[3] | -31. His fitness. "I will speak."
a[4] | 32. Call for answer.
b[4] | 33. His fitness. "I will teach."

2 Behold. Fig. *Asterismos.* Ap. 6.
3 My words. In this chapter are to be found most of the fundamental doctrines of the N.T.
4 Spirit. Heb. *rūach.* Ap. 9.
GOD. Heb. El. Ap. 4. IV.
breath. Heb. *n^eshāmāh.* See Ap. 16.
THE ALMIGHTY. Heb. Shaddai. Ap. 4. VII.
6 thy wish. Cp. 13. 3, 18-24; 16. 21; 23. 3-9; 30. 20; 31. 35.
8 thy words. Cp. 9. 17; 10. 7; 11. 4; 16. 17; 23. 10, 11; 27. 5; 29. 14; 31. 1.
9 transgression. Heb. *pāsha'.* Ap. 44. ix.
iniquity. Heb. *'āvah.* Ap. 44. iv.
10 findeth = seeketh. Cp. Num. 14. 35; 32. 7.
He counteth. Some codices, with one early printed edition, Sept., Syr., and Vulg., read "that He may count".
12 𝔊𝔒𝔇. Heb. Eloah. Ap. 4. V.
greater than man. This is the theme of Elihu's addresses.
man = mortal man. Heb. *'ĕnōsh.* Ap. 14. III.

---

16 And still I waited, though they could not speak,
But silent stood and offered no reply.)
17 I will reply—e'en I:—on mine own part;
I too will show my knowledge, even I.
18 For I am fillèd full with [wisdom's] words;
The spirit in my breast constraineth me.
19 It is as wine secured, without a vent,
Like wine-skins new, which are at point to burst.
20 So, I will speak, that I may find relief;
Open my lips, and take up my discourse.
21 I will not now regard the face of man,
And to no man will flattering titles give.
22 I know not how to flatter. Otherwise
My Maker soon would summon me away.

ELIHU. FIRST ADDRESS TO JOB. 33. 1-33.

Q[1] R[1] a[1] (p. 706) **33** And now, O Job, I pray thee hear me speak,
And be attentive to my every word.
2 Behold now that I have begun to speak;
My tongue shall utt'rance give, distinct and clear:
b[1] 3 For all that I shall say comes from my heart,
My lips shall speak what is sincere and true.
4 GOD'S Spirit made me [at the first], and [still]
'tis the Almighty's breath must quicken me.

5 If thou be able, answer me, I pray: a
Array thy words in order; take thy stand.

6 Lo, I am here—thou wishedst—in GOD'S stead. b[2]
And of the clay I have been formed, [like thee].
7 Behold, my terror will not make thee fear;
Nor heavy will my hand upon thee press.

8 But, surely, thou hast spoken in mine ears, S c
And I have heard a voice of words like these:
9 "A man without transgression, pure, am I:
Yea, I am clean; without iniquity.
10 He is against me; seeking grounds of strife,
That He may count me as His enemy;
11 My feet He setteth fast within the stocks,
And taketh observation of my ways."

12 Behold, thou art not just: I answer thee: d
HOW GREAT IS 𝔊𝔒𝔇 COMPARED WITH
MORTAL MAN?

S c (p. 706) 1656 **13 Why dost thou strive against Him? for He giveth not account of any of His matters.**

d e¹ (p. 707) **14 For** [4] **GOD speaketh once, yea twice,** ***yet man*** **perceiveth it not.**
15 In a dream, in a vision of the night, when deep sleep falleth upon [12] **men, in slumberings upon the bed;**

f¹ **16 Then He openeth the ears of** [12] **men, and sealeth their instruction,**
17 That He may withdraw °man ***from his*** **purpose, and hide pride °from man.**
18 He keepeth back his °soul from the °pit, and his life from perishing by the sword.

e² **19 He is chastened also with pain upon his bed, and the multitude of his bones with strong** ***pain:***
20 So that his life abhorreth bread, and his [18] **soul dainty meat.**
21 His flesh is consumed away, that it cannot be seen; and his bones ***that*** **were not seen stick out.**
22 °Yea, his [18] **soul draweth near unto the °grave, and his life to the destroyers.**

f² **23 °If there be a messenger with Him, an °interpreter, one among a thousand, to shew unto** [17] **man °His uprightness:**
24 Then He is gracious unto him, and saith, 'Deliver him from going down to the [18] **pit: I have found °a Ransom.'**
25 His flesh shall be fresher than a child's: he shall return to the days of his youth:
26 He shall pray unto [12] **GOD, and He will be favourable unto him: and he shall see His face with °joy: for He will render unto** [12] **man** [23] **His righteousness.**
27 He looketh upon [12] **men, and** ***if any*** **say, °'I have °sinned, and perverted** ***that which was*** **right, and it profited me not;'**
28 He will deliver his [18] **soul from going into the** [18] **pit, and his life shall see the light.**

33. 14-30 (*d*, p. 706). **GOD'S GOODNESS: IN REVELATION.** (*Repeated Alternation.*)

d
- e¹ | 14, 15. Means. (Dreams and visions.) — In detail.
- f¹ | 16-18. Ends. (Negative.)
- e² | 19-22. Means. (Afflictions.)
- f² | 23-28. Ends. (Positive.)
- e³ | 29. Means. (All these means.) — In sum.
- f³ | 30. Ends. (Neg. 30-. Pos. -30.)

17 man. Heb. *'ādām.* Ap. 14. I.
from man. Heb. from *geber.* Ap. 4. III.
18 soul. Heb. *nephesh.* Ap. 13.
pit. Heb. *shachath* = the grave, as dug out of the earth.
22 Yea. This "Yea" was not in the A.V. of 1611, nor in editions of 1646 and 1648.
grave. Heb. *shachath,* as in *v.* 18.
23 If there be. This is another way by which God speaks.
interpreter. To reveal God and His truth. Cp. John 1. 18.
His: i. e. God's righteousness.
24 a Ransom = an Atonement. Heb. *kopher,* a covering by shedding of blood, or the price of expiation, or atonement.
26 joy = shouts of joy.
27 I have sinned. This is true wisdom. See note on 28. 28. This is "the end of the Lord" (Jas. 5. 11), to which all was leading, and which is reached at length in 42. 2-5.
sinned. Heb. *chata'.* Ap. 44. i.
29 Lo. Fig. *Asterismos.* Ap. 6.
33 hearken = hearken thou.

29 °Lo, all these ***things*** **worketh** [4] **GOD oftentimes with** [17] **man,** e³
30 To bring back his [18] **soul from the** [18] **pit, to be enlightened with the light of the living.** f³

31 Mark well, O Job, hearken unto me: R² a³ (p. 706)
hold thy peace, and I will speak. b³
32 If thou hast anything to say, answer me: speak, for I desire to justify thee. a⁴
33 If not, °hearken unto me: hold thy peace, and I shall teach thee wisdom." b⁴

S c (p. 706) 13 Why, then, 'gainst Him didst thou dare make complaint,
That by no word of His He answ'reth thee?

d e¹ (p. 707) 14 For GOD DOTH speak. He speaks in sundry ways:
Again, again, though man regard it not.
15 He speaks in dreams, and visions of the night,
When, deep in slumber, lying on their bed,
There falls on men an overwhelming sleep.

f¹ 16 Then opens He their ear, that they may hear,
Pressing, as with a seal, the warning given,
17 To make a man withdraw himself from sin,
Or keep him from the [dangerous] way of pride.
18 Back from the pit 'tis thus He keeps a man,
And saves his life from falling by the sword.

e² 19 He speaks again, when, chastened, on his bed
Another lies, his bones all rack'd with pain;
20 So that his daily food he doth abhor,
And turns against his choicest dainty meat.
21 His flesh, it wastes away and is not seen:
His bones, before concealed, show through his skin.
22 Unto destruction he is drawing nigh,
And death's dark angel waits to end his life.

f² 23 Then, then, He speaks with him by Messenger
Who can interpret;—One, 'mong thousands chief,
Who will reveal to man HIS righteousness.

24 Then He doth show him grace [Divine, and saith]:—
"Deliver him from going down to death;
A Ransom I have found—Redemption's price."
25 Young as a child's becomes his flesh again,
And to his youthful days he doth return.
26 He, supplication to Eloah makes,
Who grace and kindly favour showeth him,
So that he looketh up to God with joy.
Thus, doth [He] give to man HIS righteousness.
27 This, then, becomes the burden of his song:—
"I sinned! and I perverted what was right!
Although no profit from it came to me."
28 His soul HE hath redeemed from the pit:
His life will yet again behold the light.

29 Thus doth GOD speak, in all these sundry ways: e³
Time after time; and yet again He speaks:

30 That from destruction He may save a soul, f³
And make him joy in light—the light of life.

31 Mark this, O Job, and hearken unto me. R² a³ (p. 706)

I will now speak: and, as for thee, hold thou b³
Thy peace, while I with words of wisdom teach.

32 If there be any answer, answer me. a⁴
Speak: for I long to see thee justified.

33 If not; do thou then hearken unto me: b⁴
Hold thou thy peace, while wisdom I impart.

P²
(p. 705)
1656
Q¹ T g
(p. 708)

34 Furthermore Elihu °answered and said,
2 "Hear my °words, O ye wise *men;* and give ear unto me, ye that have knowledge.
3 For the ear trieth words, as the °mouth tasteth meat.
4 Let us choose to us judgment: let us know among ourselves what *is* good.
h 5 For Job hath said, °"I am righteous: and °GOD hath taken away my judgment.
6 Should I lie against my right? my wound *is* incurable without °transgression."
i 7 What °man *is* like Job, *who* drinketh up scorning like water?
8 Which goeth in company with the workers of °iniquity, and walketh with °wicked °men.
9 For he hath said, 'It profiteth a [7]man nothing that he should delight himself with °God.'
U j 10 Therefore hearken unto me, ye [8]men of understanding:
k far be it from [5]GOD, *that He should do* [8]wickedness; and *from* °THE ALMIGHTY, *that He should commit* [8]iniquity.
11 For the work of a °man shall He render unto him, and cause °every man to find according to *his* ways.
12 Yea, surely [5]GOD will not do [8]wickedly, neither will [10]THE ALMIGHTY pervert judgment.
13 °Who hath given Him a charge over the earth? or °who hath disposed the whole world?
14 If He set His heart upon °man, *if* He gather unto Himself his °spirit °and his °breath;
15 All flesh shall °perish together, and [11]man shall °turn again unto dust.
U j 16 If now *thou hast* understanding, hear this: hearken to the voice of my words.
k 17 °Shall even he that hateth right govern? and wilt thou condemn Him that is most just?
18 °*Is it fit* to say to a king, '*Thou art* °wicked?' *and* to °princes, '*Ye are* °ungodly?'

34. 1 answered = addressed. See note on 4. 1.

34. 2-37 (Q², p. 705). ELIHU'S WORDS TO JOB'S FRIENDS. (*Introversion and Alternations.*)

Q⁴ | T | g | 2-4. Appeal to his hearers.
h | 5, 6. Job's error. (5, Himself. 5, 6, God.)
i | 7-9. His reproof.
U | j | 10-. Call for attention.
k | -10-15. Vindication of God.
U | *j* | 16. Call for attention.
k | 17-33-. Vindication of God.
T | *g* | -33, 34. Appeal to his hearers.
h | 35. Job's error.
i | 36, 37. His reproof.

2 words = speech.
3 mouth = palate.
5 I am righteous. Cp. 9. 21-24; 10. 15; 27. 6; 13. 15, 18, 23; 16. 17; 19. 7; 23. 7, 10-12; 27. 5, &c.
GOD. Heb. El. Ap. 4. IV.
6 transgression. Heb. *pāsha'.* Ap. 44. ix.
7 man = strong man. Heb. *geber.* Ap. 14. IV.
8 iniquity. Heb. *'āven.* Ap. 44. iii.
wicked. Heb. *rāshā'.* Ap. 44. x.
men. Heb. pl. of *'ěnōsh.* Ap. 14. III.
9 God. Heb. Elohim. Ap. 4. I.
10 THE ALMIGHTY. Heb. Shaddai. Ap. 4. VII.
11 man. Heb. *'ādām.* Ap. 14. I.
every man. Heb. *'ish.* Ap. 14. II.
13 Who ...? Fig. *Erotēsis.* Ap. 6.
14 man = him.
spirit. Heb. *rūach.* Ap. 9.
and = even; or, Fig. *Hendiadys* (Ap. 6), one thing meant by the two words.
breath. Heb. *neshāmāh.* Ap. 16. Cp. Gen. 2. 7.
15 perish = expire.
turn again. Cp. Gen. 3. 19. Ecc. 12. 7.
17 Shall ...? / **18 Is it ...?** } Fig. *Erotēsis.* Ap. 6.
wicked = Belial.
princes = nobles.
ungodly. Heb. *rāshā'.* Ap. 44. x. Cp. *v.* 8.

ELIHU. ADDRESS TO JOB'S FRIENDS.
34. 1-37 (Q², p. 705).

P²
(p. 705)
Q² T g
(p. 708)

34 Elihu then addressed [Job's friends] and said:
2 Hear now my words, ye wise [and clever] men;
And ye who knowledge have, give ear to me.
3 For 'tis the ear that [proves and] trieth speech,
E'en as the palate shows what food is good.
4 Then, let us, what is right, choose for ourselves:
Let us decide among us, what is good.

h 5 Now Job hath said—
"I am and have been just:
But GOD my righteous cause hath turned away.
6 Shall I against my right speak what is false?
Sore is my wound; though through no sin of mine."

i 7 Where is the worthy man [who] like to Job,
Drinks up as water all your scornful words?
8 And keepeth company with those who sin,
And doth associate with wicked men?
9 For he hath said—
"It profiteth not man
That he should take delight in Elohim."
10 To this, ye wise men, list to my reply: U j
Far be such evil from the mighty GOD, k
And far from Shaddai such iniquity.
11 For, sure, man's work He will repay to him,
And will requite according to his ways.
12 Nay, surely, GOD will not do wickedly,
And Shaddai never will pervert the right.
13 Who e'er to Him did delegate the charge
Of earth? or trusted Him with all the world?
14 Should He think only of Himself, [and all]
His breath, the breath of life withdraw; [what then?]
15 All flesh together would [at once] expire,
And man would straight to dust return again.

16 Now, if thou understanding hast, hear this; *U j*
Give heed unto the teaching of my words.

17 Can one who hateth justice rule [the world]? *k*
Wilt thou condemn the Just, the Mighty One?
18 Shall one say to a King—"Thou worthless man"?
Or, unto nobles, "Ye ungodly men"?

1656 19 °*How much less to Him* That °accepteth not the persons of [18]princes, nor °regardeth the rich more than the °poor? for they all *are* °the work of His hands.

20 In a moment shall they die, and the people shall be troubled at midnight, and pass away: and the mighty shall be taken away °without hand.

21 For His eyes *are* upon the ways of °man, and He seeth all his goings.

22 *There is* no °darkness, nor shadow of death, where the workers of [8]iniquity may hide themselves.

23 For He will not lay upon [21]man more *than right;* that he should enter into judgment with [5]GOD.

24 He shall break in pieces mighty men without number, and set others in their stead.

25 Therefore He knoweth their works, and He overturneth *them* in the night, so that they are °destroyed.

26 He striketh them as [8]wicked men in the open sight of others;

27 Because they turned back °from Him, and would not consider any of His ways:

28 So that they cause the cry of the [19]poor to come unto Him, and He heareth the cry of the afflicted.

29 °When He giveth quietness, who then can make trouble? and °when He hideth *His* face, who then can behold Him? whether *it be done* against a nation, or against a [11]man only:

30 That the hypocrite reign not, lest the people be ensnared.

31 Surely it is meet to be said unto [5]GOD, 'I have borne *chastisement,* I will not offend *any more:*

32 *That which* I see not teach Thou me: if I have done [8]iniquity, I will do no more.'

33 °*Should it be* according to thy mind? He will recompense it, whether thou refuse, or whether thou choose; and not I:

T g (p. 708) therefore speak what thou knowest.

19 How . . . ? Fig. *Erotēsis.* Ap. 6.
accepteth not, &c. Cp. Deut. 10. 17. 2 Chron. 19. 7. Luke 20. 21. Acts 10. 34.
regardeth. A Homonym (Heb. *nākar*), with three meanings: (1) here, to regard; (2) to mistake, Deut. 32. 27; (3) to deliver, 1 Sam. 23. 7.
poor: i. e. reduced in circumstances. Heb. *dal.* See note on Prov. 6. 11.
the work, &c. Cp. 10. 3; 14. 15; 31. 15; 37. 7, &c.
20 without hand. Cp. Dan. 2. 34, 45; 8. 25; and see 1 Sam. 26. 11. 2 Sam. 24. 16.
21 man. Heb. *'īsh.* Ap. 14. II.
22 darkness. Heb. *ḥāshak.* See note on 3. 6.
25 destroyed=crushed. **27 from**=from after.
29 When . . . ? Fig. *Erotēsis.* Ap. 6.
30 hypocrite=profane man (Heb. *'ādām.* Ap. 14. I).
33 Should it be. See rendering below.
35 without wisdom. See note on 33. 27.
36 wicked. Heb. *'āven.* Ap. 44. iii.
37 rebellion. Heb. *pāsha'.* Ap. 44. ix.
sin. Heb. *chāṭā'.* Ap. 44. i.

35. 2-16 (Q^3, p. 705). ELIHU'S WORDS TO JOB.
(*Repeated Alternation.*)

Q^3 | V^1 | l^1 | 2, 3. Error. Job's. } Personal.
m^1 | 4-8. Answer.
V^2 | l^2 | 9. Error. Man's. } General.
m^2 | 10-13. Answer.
V^3 | l^3 | 14-. Error. Job's. } Personal.
m^3 | -14-16. Answer.

2 GOD'S. Heb. El. Ap. 4. IV.

34 Let [8]men of understanding tell me, and let a wise [7]man hearken unto me.

35 Job hath spoken without knowledge, and his words *were* °without wisdom. h

36 My desire *is that* Job may be tried unto the end because of *his* answers for °wicked [8]men. i

37 For he addeth °rebellion unto his °sin, he clappeth *his hands* among us, and multiplieth his words against [5]GOD."

35 Elihu spake moreover, and said, P3 (p. 705)

2 "Thinkest thou this to be right, *that* thou saidst, 'My righteousness *is* more than °GOD'S?' Q^3 V^1 l^1 (p. 709)

19 How much less wilt thou say it then to Him?
Who [neither] doth accept the face of kings,
Nor doth regard the rich above the poor,
For they are all the work of His own hands.
20 They in a moment die, e'en in a night;
The people tremble when they pass away:
The mighty fall, but by no [human] hand.
21 For on the ways of men His eyes are set,
And all their footsteps He doth see [and note].
22 There is no darkness, and no shade of death,
Where workers of iniquity may hide.
23 Man doth not need repeated scrutiny,
When he to GOD for [final] judgment comes.
24 He breaks the strong in ways we cannot trace;
And others, in their stead, He setteth up.
25 To this end takes He knowledge of their works;
And, in a night He overthroweth them,
[In such a way] that they are [all] destroyed.
26 [Sometimes] He smites the wicked where they stand,
In open sight of all men who behold;
27 Because they turnèd back from after Him,
Nor any of His ways would they regard;
28 But, [by oppression,] brought the poor man's cry
To Him Who hears the plaint of the oppressed.
29 When He gives quiet, who can e'er disturb?
Or who can see Him when He hides His face?
(Whether it be a nation or a man,
30 Whether because the godless may not reign,
Or those who of the people make a prey.)
31 If Job had [spoken] unto GOD, [and] said:
"I have borne chastisement: and never more
32 Will I transgress; that which I do not see
Teach me Thyself: if in the past I wrought
Iniquity, I will not work it more:"
33 Should He requite on thine own terms, [and say]:
"As thou wilt choose [so be it], not as I?"
Say therefore, now, O Job, if thou dost know. T g (p. 708)
34 For ME would men of understanding speak;
Yea, every wise man listening now [will say]:
35 "Job, without knowledge, spoke in ignorance; h
And void of understanding were his words."
36 Oh would that Job were proved unto the end, i
For his replies are those of evil men.
37 Rebellion he doth add unto his sin:
Defiant in our midst he claps his hands;
And, against GOD he multiplies his words.

ELIHU. SECOND ADDRESS TO JOB.
35. 1-16 (Q^3, p. 705).

1 Elihu further spake to Job and said:— P3 (p. 705)
2 Dost thou count this sound judgment? Thou didst say, Q^3 V^1 l^1 (p. 709)
"My righteousness surpasseth that of GOD:"

1656 3 For thou saidst, °'What advantage will it
be unto thee?' *and*, °'What profit shall I
have, *if I be cleansed* from my °sin?'

m[1] 4 I will answer thee, and thy companions
(p. 709) with thee.

5 °Look unto the heavens, and see; and behold the clouds *which* are higher than thou.

6 If thou [3]sinnest, what doest thou against Him? or *if* thy °transgressions be multiplied, what doest thou unto Him?

7 If thou be righteous, what givest thou Him? or what receiveth He of thine hand?

8 Thy °wickedness *may hurt* °a man as thou *art*; and thy righteousness *may profit* the son °of man.

V[2] l[2] 9 By reason of the multitude of oppressions they make *the oppressed* to cry: they cry out by reason of the arm of the mighty.

m[2] 10 But none saith, 'Where *is* °GOD my Maker, Who giveth songs in the night;

11 Who teacheth us more than the beasts of the earth, and maketh us wiser than the fowls of heaven?'

12 There they cry, but none giveth answer, because of the pride of °evil men.

13 Surely [2]GOD will not hear vanity, neither will °THE ALMIGHTY regard it.

V[3] l[3] 14 Although thou sayest thou shalt not see Him,

m[3] *yet* judgment *is* before Him; therefore °trust thou in Him.

15 But now, because *it is* not *so*, °He hath visited in His anger; yet He knoweth *it* not in great extremity:

16 Therefore doth Job open his mouth in vain; he multiplieth words without knowledge."

P[1] (p. 705) **36** Elihu also proceeded, and said,

Q[4] W (p. 710) 2 "Suffer me a little, and I will shew thee that *I have* yet to speak on °GOD'S behalf.

3 I will fetch my knowledge from afar, and will ascribe righteousness to my Maker.

4 For truly my words *shall* not *be* false: He That is perfect in knowledge *is* with thee.

5 °Behold, °GOD °*is* mighty, and despiseth not *any: He is* mighty in strength *and* wisdom. X n

6 He preserveth not the life of the °wicked: but giveth right to the °poor. o

7 He withdraweth not His eyes from the righteous: but with kings *are they* on the throne; yea, He doth establish them for ever, and they are exalted.

3 What . . . ? Fig. *Erotēsis*. Ap. 6.
sin. Heb. *chāṭā'*. Ap. 44. i.
5 Look = Look attentively.
6 transgressions. Heb. *pāsha'*. Ap. 44. ix.
8 wickedness. Heb. *rāsha'*. Ap. 44. x.
a man. Heb. *'ish*. Ap. 14. II.
of man. Heb. *'ādām*. Ap. 14. I.
10 GOD. Heb. Eloah. Ap. 4. V.
12 evil. Heb. *rā'a'*. Ap. 44. viii.
13 THE ALMIGHTY. Heb. El Shaddai = GOD ALMIGHTY. Ap. 4. VII.
14 trust thou in = stay thyself upon. Heb. *ḥūl*. See Ap. 69. IV.
15 He. Supply Ellipsis: "[thou sayest] He".

36. 2—37. 24 (Q[4], p. 705). **ELIHU'S WORDS ON GOD'S BEHALF.** (*Introversion and Alternations.*)

Q[4] | W | 36. 2-4. Introduction. "On God's behalf."
X | n | 36. 5. His attribute. "God is great."
o | 36. 6-15. Manifested in Providence.
p | 36. 16-25. Application and exhortation to fear His wondrous wrath.
X | *n* | 36. 26. His attribute. "God is great."
o | 36. 27—37. 13. Manifested in Creation.
p | 37. 14-22-. Application and exhortation to consider His "wondrous works."
W | 37. -22, 24. Conclusion. "On God's behalf."

2 GOD'S. Heb. Eloah. Ap. 4. V.
5 Behold. Fig. *Asterismos*. Ap. 6.
GOD. Heb. El. Ap. 4. IV.
is mighty. This is the text of Elihu's discourses, leading up to God's own addresses to Job. Cp. *v.* 26; and 33. 12. **6 wicked** = lawless. Heb. *rāshā'*. Ap. 44. x.
poor = wretched. Heb. *'anī*. See note on Prov. 6. 11.

3 Yea—thou dost ask "What is the gain to thee?"
And, "Shall I profit more than by my sin?"
m[1] (p. 709) 4 I—even I, will make reply to thee,
And, with thee, to these friends of thine as well.
5 Look up unto the heav'ns; consider them;
Survey the skies, so high above thy head.
6 If thou hast sinned, what doest thou to Him?
Be thy sins many, what dost thou to Him?
7 If thou art just, what dost thou give to Him?
Or from thy hand what [gift] will He receive?
8 Thy sin may hurt a mortal like thyself;
Thy righteousness may profit one like thee.
V[2] l[2] 9 Men make an outcry when they are oppressed:
They cry for help when 'neath the tyrant's pow'r.
m[2] 10 But no one saith, "Where is my Maker, GOD,
Who giveth songs to us in sorrow's night;
11 And teacheth us beyond the beasts of earth,
And makes us wiser than the fowl of heav'n?"
12 But the true reason why He answereth not,
Although they cry, is—evil doers' pride,
13 For vanity GOD will in no wise hear,
Nor will th' Almighty hold it in regard.
V[3] l[3] 14 How much less, then, when thou dost say to Him—
"I see Him not: [He doth not hear my cry]."
Yet judgment is before Him: therefore wait.
15 But now, because He hath not punished thee,
[Thou say'st]:— "His anger doth not visit sin;
Nor strictly mark wide-spread iniquity."
16 Thus Job doth fill his mouth with vanity;
And, without knowledge, multiplieth words.

ELIHU. WORDS ON GOD'S BEHALF. P[1] (p. 705)
36. 2—37. 24 (Q[4], p. 705).

Q[4] W (p. 710) 2 Bear with me, while I, briefly, make thee see
There yet are words to say on GOD'S behalf.
3 My knowledge I shall gather from afar;
And to my Maker righteousness ascribe.
4 For truly, nothing false is in my words:
Th' Omniscient One it is Who deals with thee.
5 Lo! GOD IS GREAT,—but naught doth He despise: X n
In power great, in wisdom great, is He.
6 He will not let the wicked ever live: o
But He will right the cause of the oppressed,
7 And not take from a righteous man His eyes.
He seateth them with kings upon the throne;
He makes them sit in glory; raised on high.

1656 8 And if *they be* bound in fetters, *and* be
holden in cords of affliction;
9 Then He sheweth them their work, and
their °transgressions that they have exceeded.
10 He openeth also their ear to discipline,
and commandeth that they return from °iniquity.
11 If they obey and serve *Him*, they shall
spend their days in prosperity, and their years
in pleasures.
12 But if they obey not, they shall perish by
the sword, and they shall die without knowledge.
13 But the hypocrites in heart heap up
wrath: they cry not when He bindeth them.
14 °They die in youth, and their life *is*
among the °unclean.
15 He delivereth the [6]poor in his affliction,
and openeth their ears in oppression.

p (p. 710) 16 Even so would He have removed thee out
of the strait *into* a broad place, where *there is*
no straitness; and that which should be set
on thy table *should be* full of fatness.
17 But thou hast fulfilled the judgment of the
[6]wicked: judgment and justice take hold *on*
thee.
18 Because *there is* wrath, *beware* lest He
take thee away with *His* stroke: then a great
ransom cannot deliver thee.
19 °Will He esteem thy riches? *no*, not gold,
nor all the forces of strength.
20 Desire not the night, when people are cut
off in their place.
21 Take heed, regard not [10]iniquity: for this
hast thou chosen rather than affliction.
22 [5]Behold, [5]GOD exalteth by His power:
°who teacheth like Him?
23 [22]Who hath enjoined Him His way? or
[22]who can say, 'Thou hast wrought °iniquity?'
24 Remember that thou magnify His work,
which °men behold.

9 transgressions. Heb. *pāsha'*. Ap. 44. ix.
10 iniquity. Heb. *'āven*. Ap. 44. iii. Not the same word as *v.* 23.
14 They die = their souls die. Heb. *nephesh*. Ap. 13.
unclean = sodomites. See note on Deut. 23. 17.
19 Will He . . . ?
22 who . . . ? } Fig. *Erotēsis*. Ap. 6.
iniquity. Heb. *'āval*. Ap. 44. vi. Not the same word as *vv.* 10, 21.
24 men. Heb. pl. of *'ĕnōsh*. Ap. 14. III.
25 Every man. Heb. every *'ādām*. Ap. 14. I.
man may behold = all mankind have gazed.
26 is great. See note on *v.* 5.
His years. Fig. *Anthropopatheia*. Ap. 6.
29 can any . . . ? Fig. *Erotēsis*. Ap. 6.
spreadings = suspensions, or floatings.
tabernacle = booth. Heb. *ṣukkāh*.
30 bottom = roots or offspring, i. e. clouds.
31 people = peoples.
33 sheweth = announceth.

25 °Every man may see it; °man may [24]behold *it* afar off.

26 Behold, [5]GOD °*is* great, and we know X n
Him not, neither can the number of °His
years be searched out.
27 For He maketh small the drops of water: o
they pour down rain according to the vapour
thereof:
28 Which the clouds do drop *and* distil upon
[25]man abundantly.
29 Also °can *any* understand the °spreadings of the clouds, *or* the noise of His °tabernacle?
30 [5]Behold, He spreadeth His light upon it,
and covereth the °bottom of the sea.
31 For by them judgeth He the °people; He
giveth meat in abundance.
32 With clouds He covereth the light; and
commandeth it *not to shine* by *the cloud* that
cometh betwixt.
33 The noise thereof °sheweth concerning it,
the cattle also concerning the vapour.

8 And, if they be in [iron] fetters bound,
Or, [if] they be held fast in sorrow's bonds,
9 [It is] that He may show to them their deeds
And their transgressions which have sprung from pride.
10 Thus openeth He their ear, and doth instruct
And warn them from iniquity to turn.
11 Then, if they hearken and obey [His voice],
They in prosperity shall spend their days,
[And end] their years in peace and pleasantness.
12 Should they not heed, they perish by the sword;
And die, not knowing [how it is, or why].
13 But hypocrites in heart will heap up wrath,
[Because] they cry not when He bindeth them.
14 [Wherefore] they die while they are yet in youth,
Their life is spent among polluted ones.
15 Yet He doth save the poor in all his woes,
And openeth their ear in their distress.
p (p. 710) 16 Thus, in like manner, He would THEE allure,
And from the mouth of trouble draw thee out
Into a pleasant place:—no trouble there;
Thy table well prepared with richest food.
17 But [if] with sinners' pleadings thou be filled,
Judgment and justice will lay hold on thee.
18 For, there is wrath; [beware, then,] of its stroke;
For, then, a ransom great will not suffice,
19 Nor treasure turn the threatened stroke aside,
Nor precious ore avail, nor all thy strength.
20 Oh, long not for the night [of death], in which
[Whole] nations get upheaved from out their place!
21 Take heed! regard not thou iniquity;
For this thou didst prefer to all thy woes.
22 Lo, GOD will be exalted in His pow'r:
Who can convey instruction like to Him?
23 Who is it that assigns to Him His way?
Or who can say to Him—"Thou hast done wrong"?
24 Remember that thou should'st extol His work,
Which men have contemplated, [and have sung]:
25 Yea, all have gazed in wonder thereupon;
And mortal man beholds it from afar.

26 Lo! GOD IS GREAT,—[greater] than we can know; X n
The number of His years past finding out.
27 'Tis He Who draweth up the vapour-clouds; o
And they distil [from heaven] in rain and mist:
28 E'en that which from the [low'ring] skies doth fall,
And poureth down on man abundantly.
29 Can any man explain the rain-clouds' balancings,
The rumbling thunders of His canopy?
30 Behold, He spreadeth out His light thereon,
While making dark the bottom of the sea.
31 (Yet He His judgment executes by these:
By these He giveth food abundantly.)
32 He [graspeth] in His hand the lightning flash,
And giveth it commandment where to strike.
33 Of this the noise thereof quick notice gives,
The [frightened] cattle warn of coming storm.

1656 **37** At this also my heart trembleth, and is moved out of his place.

2 Hear attentively the noise of °His voice, and the sound *that* goeth out of °His mouth.

3 He directeth it under the whole heaven, and His lightning unto the ends of the earth.

4 After it a voice roareth: He thundereth with the voice of His excellency; and He will not stay them when His voice is heard.

5 °GOD thundereth marvellously with His voice; great things doeth He, which we cannot comprehend.

6 For He saith to the snow, 'Be thou *on* the earth;' likewise to the small rain, and to the great rain of His strength.

7 He sealeth up the hand of every °man; that all °men may know His work.

8 Then the beasts go into dens, and remain in their °places.

9 Out of the south cometh the whirlwind: and cold out of the north.

10 By the °breath of [5]GOD frost is given: and the breadth of the waters is straitened.

11 Also by watering He wearieth the thick cloud: He scattereth His bright cloud:

12 And it is turned round about by His counsels: that they may do whatsoever He commandeth them upon the face of the °world in the earth.

13 He causeth it to come, whether for correction, or for His land, or for mercy.

p (p. 710) 14 Hearken unto this, O Job: stand still, and consider the wondrous works of [5]GOD.

15 °Dost thou know when °GOD disposed them, and caused the light of His cloud to shine?

16 [15]Dost thou know the balancings of the °clouds, the wondrous works of Him Which is perfect in knowledge?

17 How thy garments *are* warm, when He quieteth the earth by the south *wind*?

37. 2 His voice . . . His mouth. Fig. *Anthropopatheia.* Ap. 6.
5 GOD. Heb. El. Ap. 4. IV.
7 man. Heb. *'ādām.* Ap. 14. I.
men. Heb. pl. of *'ĕnōsh.* Ap. 14. III.
8 places=lurking-places, or lairs.
10 breath. Heb. *neshāmah.* Ap. 16.
12 world=vast expanse, or the habitable world. Heb. *tēbēl.*
15 Dost . . . ? Fig. *Erotēsis.* Ap. 6.
GOD. Heb. Eloah. Ap. 4. V.
16 clouds=thick clouds.
18 sky=skies.
looking glass=mirror.
20 man. Heb. *'īsh.* Ap. 14. II.
21 wind. Heb. *rūach.* Ap. 9.
23 THE ALMIGHTY. Heb. Shaddai. Ap. 4. VII.
power. The Heb. accents mark off three distinct attributes: (1) power supreme; (2) righteousness abundant; (3) the consequent reverence from men, *v.* 24.

18 Hast thou with Him spread out the °sky, *which is* strong, *and* as a molten °looking glass?

19 Teach us what we shall say unto Him; *for* we cannot order *our speech* by reason of darkness.

20 Shall it be told Him that I speak? if a °man speak, surely he shall be swallowed up.

21 And now *men* see not the bright light which *is* in the clouds: but the °wind passeth, and cleanseth them.

22 Fair weather cometh out of the north: with [15]GOD *is* terrible majesty. W

23 *Touching* °THE ALMIGHTY, we cannot find Him out: *He is* excellent in °power, and in judgment, and in plenty of justice: He will not afflict.

24 [7]Men do therefore fear Him: He respecteth not any *that are* wise of heart."

37 [The rumbling thunder] makes my heart to quake,
And [startled] it leaps up from out its place.
2 Hear ye, O hear, the roaring of His voice,
The loud reverberations from His mouth,
3 As under heaven's expanse the sound goes forth,
His lightning to the Earth's extremities
4 [He sends], and after it the thunder roars:
He thund'reth with His voice of majesty:
One cannot trace Him, though His voice be heard.
5 GOD'S voice is wondrous when He thundereth.
Great things He doth: we comprehend them not.
6 For to the snow He saith—"Fall thou on Earth:"
And to the show'r, yea, to the flooding rains
7 Which stop the work of man and make it cease,
That all men of His doing may take note;
8 Then must the beasts each to his covert go,
And in their lairs must they [perforce] remain.
9 Out from the south proceedeth the hot blast;
And from Mezarim comes the biting cold.
10 The wind of GOD produces the hoar-frost;
The waters wide are all congealed by it.
11 With rain He ladeneth the thick dark cloud,
And dissipates the filmy cumulus:
12 It turneth round about as He doth guide,
That His commandment it may execute
Upon the [vast] expanse of all the earth,
13 Whether in chastisement, or for His land,
Or else in mercy cause He it to come.

14 O Job! [I pray thee] hearken unto this: p
Stand still and contemplate GOD'S wondrous works. (p. 710)
15 Know'st THOU how Eloah gives charge to them,
And how He makes His light on them to shine?
16 Or dost thou know the thick-clouds' balancings,
His wondrous works, Whose knowledge hath no bound?
17 How [is it that] thy garments [feel so] warm,
When He makes still the Earth with southern heat?
18 Wast thou with Him [when] He spread out the sky;
And made it like a molten mirror [firm]?
19 Oh, tell me that which we should say to Him:
We know not what to say; so dark we are!
20 Must He be told that I would speak to Him!
And if I speak, can man see Him and live.
21 But now, [though] men see not the light [of God],
Yet He is bright [in splendour] in the skies:
But when the wind has passed and cleared the clouds,
22 Then from the north there comes a golden light.

Ah! but with GOD there is a majesty W
23 Divine. And Shaddai's paths we cannot find;
So great, so great is He in pow'r; so full
Of righteousness and truth: He will not crush.
24 Therefore can men but stand in awe of Him:
For none can know Him, be they e'er so wise.

Y A¹ (p. 713) 1656 **38** Then °the LORD °answered Job out of the whirlwind, and said,
2 °"Who *is* this that °darkeneth counsel by words without knowledge?
3 Gird up now thy loins like a °man; for I will demand of thee, and °answer thou Me.
B¹ C 4 °Where wast thou when I laid the foundations of the earth? declare, if thou °hast understanding.
5 Who hath laid the measures thereof, if thou knowest? or who hath stretched the line upon it?
6 Whereupon are the °foundations thereof °fastened? or who laid the corner stone thereof;
7 When the morning °stars sang together, and all the °sons of °God shouted for joy?
D q¹ 8 Or *who* shut up the sea with doors, when it brake forth, *as if* it had issued out of the womb?
9 When I made the cloud the garment thereof, and °thick darkness a swaddlingband for it,
10 And °brake up for it My decreed *place*, and set bars and doors,
11 And said, 'Hitherto shalt thou come, but no further: and here shall thy proud waves be stayed'?
r¹ 12 Hast thou commanded °the morning since thy days; *and* caused the dayspring to know his place;
13 That it might take hold of the ends of the earth, that °the wicked might be shaken out of it?
14 It is turned as clay *to* the seal; and they stand as a garment.
15 And from ¹³the wicked their light is withholden, and the high arm shall be broken.
q² 16 Hast thou entered into the springs of the sea? or hast thou walked in the °search of the depth?

38. 1—42. 6 (*D*, p. 665). JOB AND JEHOVAH. (*Alternation.*)

D | Y | 38. 1—40. 2. Jehovah's first address.
  Z | 40. 3-5. Job's first answer.
  Y | 40. 6—41. 34. Jehovah's second address.
  Z | 42. 1-6. Job's second answer.

38. 1—40. 2 (Y, above). JEHOVAH'S FIRST ADDRESS. (*Repeated Alternation.*)

Y | A¹ | 38. 1-3. Jehovah's *first* appeal to Job.
  B¹ | 38. 4-35. The inanimate creation. Wisdom exhibited in outward activities.
  A² | 38. 36-38. Jehovah's *second* appeal to Job.
  B² | 38. 39—39. 30. The animate creation. Wisdom manifested "in the inward parts."
  A³ | 40. 1, 2. Jehovah's *third* appeal to Job.

1 the LORD. Heb. Jehovah. Ap. 4. II.
answered. See note on 4. 1. We now have Jehovah's own ministry, and the theme is Himself. Elihu's ministry furnishes the text: "God is greater than man" (33. 12). This leads up to "the end of the Lord" (Jas. 5. 11). "How should mortal man be just with God?" See 4. 17; 9. 2; 15. 14; 33. 9; 34. 5. How different from the ministry of the three friends, which, like most ministries of to-day, consists in the effort to make men "good" by persuasion.
2 Who is this . . . ? Fig. *Erotēsis.* Ap. 6.
darkeneth. Heb. *ḥashak.* See note on 3. 6.
3 man. Heb. *geber.* Ap. 14. IV.
answer thou Me=cause Me to know.

38. 4-35 (B¹, above). THE INANIMATE CREATION. WISDOM EXHIBITED IN OUTWARD ACTIVITIES. (*Introversions.*)

B¹ | C | 4-7. The earth.
  D | q¹ | 8-11. The sea.
    r¹ | 12-15. The morn, and dawn.
    q² | 16-18. The springs of the sea. } Things pertaining to the earth.
  E | 19-. Light.
  E | -19-21. Darkness. } Things pertaining to both the earth and the heavens.
  D | q³ | 22, 23. Snow and hail.
    r² | 24-27. Lightning.
    q⁴ | 28-30. Rain, dew, and frost. } Things pertaining to the heavens.
  C | 31-35. The heavens.

4 Where wast thou . . . ? Figs. *Erotēsis* and *Irony.* Ap. 6. **hast understanding**=knowest. **6 foundations**=sockets. **fastened**=sunk. **7 stars sang.** Fig. *Prosopopœia.* Ap. 6. See Ap. 12. **sons of God**=angels. See note on Gen. 6. 2: and the eight occurrences of the expression in O.T. See also Ap. 23 and 25. **God.** Heb. Elohim. Ap. 4. I. **9 thick darkness.** Heb. *'ărāphel.* See note on 3. 6. **10 brake up**=assigned. **12 the morning.** See the Alternation below, *vv.* 12-14. **13 the wicked**=lawless. Heb. *rāshā'.* Ap. 44. x. Here and *v.* 15 the letter Ayin (ע) is suspended (see note on Judg. 18. 30). Without it the word means "heads", with it "the lawless". All the ancient versions and early printed editions read "the lawless". **16 search**=secret.

JEHOVAH'S TWO ADDRESSES TO JOB.
38. 1—42. 6 (*D*, p. 665).
JEHOVAH'S FIRST ADDRESS.
38. 1—40. 2 (Y, above).

Y A¹ (p. 713) **38** Then from the storm Jehovah spake to Job,
2 Pray, who is it that maketh counsel dark
By words devoid of knowledge, [and of truth]?
3 Gird up thy loins, now, like a man; for I
Will ask of thee, and do thou answer Me.
B¹ C 4 Where wast thou when I earth's foundations laid?
Say, if thou know'st, and hast intelligence.
5 Who fix'd its measurements? (for thou wilt know),
Or who upon it stretched the measuring line?
6 On what were its foundations made to rest?
Or who its corner-stone [so truly] laid,
7 (When all the morning stars together sang,
And all the sons of God did shout for joy)?
8 Or, who fenced in with doors the [roaring] sea, D q¹
When bursting forth from [Nature's] womb it came?
9 What time I made the clouds its covering-robe,
And darkness deep the swaddling-band thereof;
10 When I decreed for it My boundary,
And set its bars and doors, and to it said,
11 "Thus far—no farther, Ocean, shalt thou come:
Here shalt thou stay the swelling of thy waves"?
12 Hast thou called Morning forth since thou wast born? r¹
Or taught the early Dawn to know its place?
13 [Bid Morn] lay hold on outskirts of the earth;
[Taught Dawn] to rout the lawless from their place?
14 [Bid Morn] change earth as clay beneath the seal;
[Bid Dawn] enrobe the beauteous world with light?
15 Thus Morning robs the wicked of their prey,
And stays, arrested, the uplifted arm.
16 The fountains of the sea hast thou explored? q²
Or, hast thou searched the secrets of the deep?

1656 17 Have the gates of death been opened unto thee? or hast thou seen the °doors of the shadow of death?

18 Hast thou perceived the breadth of the earth? declare if thou knowest it all.

E (p. 713) 19 Where *is* the °way *where* light dwelleth?
E and *as for* darkness, where *is* the place thereof,

20 That thou shouldest take it to the bound thereof, and that thou shouldest know the paths *to* the house thereof?

21 Knowest thou *it*, because thou wast then born? or *because* the number of thy days *is* great?

D q^3 22 Hast thou entered into the °treasures of the snow? or hast thou seen the °treasures of the hail,

23 Which I have reserved against the time of trouble, against the day of battle and war?

r^2 24 By what way is the light °parted, *which* scattereth the east wind upon the earth?

25 Who hath divided a watercourse for the overflowing of waters, or a way for the lightning of thunder;

26 To cause it to rain on the earth, *where* no °man *is; on* the wilderness, wherein *there is* no °man;

27 To satisfy the desolate and waste *ground;* and to cause the bud of the tender herb to spring forth?

q^4 28 Hath the rain a father? or who hath begotten the drops of °dew?

29 Out of whose womb came the ice? and the hoary frost of heaven, who hath gendered it?

30 The waters are hid as *with* a stone, and the face of the deep is frozen.

C 31 Canst thou bind the sweet influences of °Pleiades, or loose the bands of °Orion?

32 Canst thou bring forth °Mazzaroth in his season? or canst thou guide °Arcturus with his sons?

33 Knowest thou the °ordinances of heaven? canst thou set °the dominion thereof in the earth?

17 doors = gates.
19 way. Supply Ellipsis: "Where is the way [to the place where] light", &c.
22 treasures = treasuries.
23 against the day, &c.: e.g. as in Josh. 10. 11.
24 part = divide up into parts: as the rays of light in a prism. **26** man. Heb. *'ish*. Ap. 14. II. man. Heb. *'ādām*. Ap. 14. I.
28 dew = night mist. See note on Ps. 133. 3.
31 Pleiades. Heb. *kīmah*. See Ap. 12. Orion. Heb. *k^esīl*. Ap. 12.
32 Mazzaroth = the twelve signs of the Zodiac marking the path of the sun in the heavens. Ap. 12. Arcturus. Heb. *'āyish* = the greater sheepfold: known to day as "the great bear". See Ap. 12.
33 ordinances = statutes. the = his.
36 in the inward parts. Heb. *ṭuchōth*: occ. only here and Ps. 51. 6. See note on 28. 28 and Prov. 1. 7.

38. 39—39. 30 (B^2, p. 713). THE ANIMATE CREATION. WISDOM MANIFESTED "IN THE INWARD PARTS". (*Introversion and Alternation.*)

B^2 | F | 38. 39-41. Sustenance. (The lion, *vv.* 39, 40. The raven, *v.* 41.)
  G | H | 39. 1-4. Young. (The wild goats, *v.* 1-. The hinds, *vv.* -1-4.)
    J | 39. 5-12. Attribute. Freedom. (The wild ass, *vv.* 5-8. The wild bull, *vv.* 9-12.)
  G | *H* | 39. 13-18. Young. (The ostrich.)
    J | 39. 19-25. Attribute. Courage. (The war-horse.)
F | 39. 26-30. Sustenance. (The hawk, *v.* 26. The eagle, *vv.* 27-30.)

34 Canst thou lift up thy voice to the clouds, that abundance of waters may cover thee?

35 Canst thou send lightnings, that they may go, and say unto thee, 'Here we *are*'?

36 Who hath put wisdom °in the inward parts? or who hath given understanding to the heart? A^2

37 Who can number the clouds in wisdom? or who can stay the bottles of heaven,

38 When the dust groweth into hardness, and the clods cleave fast together?

39 Wilt thou hunt the prey for the lion? or fill the appetite of the young lions, B^2 F (p. 714)

17 The gates of Death: have they been shown to thee?
Or hast thou seen the portals of its shade?
18 The utmost breadths of earth hast thou surveyed?
Reply, if thou hast knowledge of it all.
E (p. 713) 19 Where lies the way that leads to Light's abode?
E And, as for Darkness, where is found its place;
20 That thou shouldst bring each to its proper bound,
And know the paths that lead unto its house?
21 THOU know'st [of course]: THOU must have then been born,
And great must be the number of thy days!
D q^3 22 The treasuries of Snow hast thou approach'd?
Or, Hast thou seen the storehouse of the hail,
23 Which 'gainst a time of trouble I have kept,
Against the day of battle and of war?
r^2 24 The Light: by what way do its rays break up?
How drives the east wind o'er the earth its course?
25 Who cleft a channel for the floods of rain?
Or passage for the sudden thunder-flash?
26 So that it rains on lands where no one dwells,
On wilderness where no man hath his home,
27 To saturate the wild and thirsty waste,
And cause the meadow's tender herb to shoot?
q^4 28 The Rain, hath it a father [beside Me]?
The drops of Dew: who hath begotten them?
29 Whose is the womb whence cometh forth the Ice?
And heaven's hoar-frost: who gave it its birth?
30 As, turned to stone, the waters hide themselves;
The surface of the deep, congeal'd, coheres.
31 Canst thou bind fast the cluster Pleiades? C
Or, canst thou loosen [great] Orion's bands?
32 Canst thou lead forth the Zodiac's monthly Signs?
Or, canst thou guide Arcturus and his sons?
33 The statutes of the heavens: know'st thou these?
Didst thou set their dominion o'er the earth?
34 The clouds: canst thou to them lift up thy voice,
That plenteousness of rain may cover thee?
35 Canst thou send lightnings forth, that they may go,
And say to thee "Behold us! Here are we?"
36 Who hath put wisdom in the inward parts? A^2
Or understanding given to the heart?
37 Who by his wisdom piles the clouds in tiers?
Or, who inclines the rain-clouds of the skies,
38 When dust, like metal fused, becometh hard,
And clods cleave fast together solidly?
39 The Lion: wilt thou hunt for him his prey? B^2 F (p. 714)
Or satisfy the hunger of his young,

1656 40 When they couch in *their* dens, *and* abide in the covert to lie in wait?
41 Who provideth for the raven his food? when his young ones cry unto °GOD, they wander for lack of meat.

G H (p. 714) **39** °Knowest thou the time when the wild goats of the rock bring forth? *or* canst thou mark when the hinds do calve?
2 Canst thou number the months *that* they fulfil? or knowest thou the time when they bring forth?
3 They bow themselves, they bring forth their young ones, they cast out their sorrows.
4 Their young ones are in good liking, they grow up °with corn; they go forth, and return not unto them.

J 5 Who hath sent out the wild °ass free? or who hath loosed the bands of the wild °ass?
6 Whose house I have made the wilderness, and the barren land his dwellings.
7 He scorneth the multitude of the city, neither regardeth he the crying of the driver.
8 The range of the mountains *is* his pasture, and he searcheth after every green thing.
9 Will the unicorn be willing to serve thee, or abide by thy crib?
10 Canst thou bind °the unicorn with his band in the furrow? or will he harrow the valleys after thee?
11 Wilt thou °trust him, because his strength *is* great? or wilt thou leave thy labour to him?
12 Wilt thou believe him, that he will bring home thy seed, and gather *it into* thy barn?

G II 13 °*Gavest thou* the goodly wings unto the peacocks? or wings and feathers unto the ostrich?
14 Which leaveth her eggs in the earth, and warmeth them in dust,
15 And forgetteth that the foot may crush them, or that the wild beast may break them.
16 She is hardened against her young ones, as though *they were* not hers: her labour is in vain without fear;
17 Because °𝔊𝔒𝔇 hath deprived her of wisdom, neither hath He imparted to her understanding.
18 What time she lifteth up herself on high, she scorneth the horse and his rider.

19 Hast thou given the horse strength? hast thou clothed his neck with °thunder? J
20 Canst thou make him °afraid as a °grasshopper? the glory of his °nostrils *is* terrible.
21 He paweth in the valley, and rejoiceth in *his* strength: he goeth on to meet the armed men.
22 He mocketh at fear, and is not affrighted; neither turneth he back from the sword.
23 The quiver rattleth against him, the glittering spear and the shield.

---

41 GOD. Heb. El. Ap. 4. IV.

39. 1 Knowest thou . . . ? Note the Fig. *Erotēsis* (Ap. 6), used by Jehovah throughout this chapter for emphasis.

4 with corn = in the open field. Heb. *bar.* A *Homonym* with three meanings: (1) *pure, clear, clean* (11. 4. Song 6. 9, 10. Pss. 19. 8; 24. 4; 73. 1, &c.); hence corn winnowed and cleansed (Gen. 41. 35, 49. Ps. 65. 13. Prov. 11. 26. Joel 2. 24, &c.); (2) *the ground,* or *open field* (Job 39. 4), because bare and clean. Cp. Prov. 14. 4; (3) *son*: see note on Ps. 2. 12.

5 ass. Probably = mule.

10 the unicorn = the wild bull.

11 trust = confide in. Heb. *bāṭaḥ.* Ap. 69. I.

13 Gavest thou. The Ellipsis (Ap. 6) is correctly supplied.

17 𝔊𝔒𝔇. Heb. Eloah. Ap. 4. V.

19 thunder = rustling mane.

20 afraid = leap.
grasshopper = locust.
nostrils = snorting.

---

40 What time within their dens they lay them down,
Or in their jungle lairs they lie in wait?
41 Who is it that provides the Raven meat;
When unto GOD his young ones lift their cry,
And wander forth abroad from lack of food?

G H (p. 714) **39** Know'st thou the time the Rock-Goat gendereth?
Observest thou the calving of the Hinds?
2 The months they fill, didst thou their number set,
And know the time when they to birth should bring?
3 They bow themselves: they bring their offspring forth;
And to the winds cast all their pangs away.
4 Strong grow their young; they fatten on the plains;
And to their parents never more return.

J 5 Who is it that sent forth the Wild Ass free?
Or who hath loosened the swift runner's bands?
6 Whose dwelling I have made the wilderness;
His haunts the salt and arid desert waste.
7 The city's busy tumult he doth scorn;
The driver's shouts and cries he doth not hear.
8 The mountains are his ample pasture ground;
There roameth he in quest of all things green.
9 The Wild Bull: will he be thy willing slave,
Or pass the night, contented, by thy crib?
10 Canst thou in harness lead him forth to plough?
To harrow, will he follow after thee?
11 Wilt thou, for all his strength, confide in him?
Or leave to him the tillage of thy ground?
12 Canst thou be sure he will bring home thy seed,
Or gather corn to fill thy threshing-floor?
13 The Ostrich wing, admirèd tho' it be;
Is it the pinion of the kindly Stork?
14 Nay! she it is that leaves to earth her eggs,
And in the dust she letteth them be warmed;
15 Unmindful that the passing foot might crush,
Or that the roaming beast might trample them.
16 She dealeth sternly with her young, as if
Not hers: and fears not that her toil be vain.
17 For God created her devoid of sense;
Nor gave her in intelligence a share.
18 Yet, when she lifteth up herself for flight,
The horse and rider both alike she scorns.
19 The War-horse: didst thou give to him his strength? J
Or clothe his arching neck with rustling mane?
20 Make him leap lightly, as the locust does?
The glory of his snorting fills with dread:
21 He paws the plain, rejoicing in his strength;
He rusheth on to meet the armèd host:
22 He mocks at fear, and cannot be dismayed;
Nor from the sword will he turn back or flee,
23 Though 'gainst him rain the arrows of the foe,
The glitter of the lance, and flash of spear.

1656 24 He swalloweth the ground with fierceness
and rage: neither believeth he that *it is* the
sound of the trumpet.
25 He saith among the trumpets, 'Ha, ha;'
and he smelleth the battle afar off, the thunder of the captains, and the shouting.

F (p. 714) 26 Doth the hawk fly by thy wisdom, *and*
stretch °her wings toward the south?
27 Doth the eagle mount up at thy command,
and make [26]her nest on high?
28 °She dwelleth and abideth on the rock,
upon the crag of the rock, and the strong
place.
29 From thence [28]she seeketh the prey, *and*
her eyes behold afar off.
30 [26]Her young ones also suck up blood:
and °where the slain *are,* there *is* °she."

A³ (p. 713) **40** Moreover °the LORD answered Job,
and said,
2 °"Shall °he that contendeth with °THE
ALMIGHTY instruct *Him?* °he that reproveth
°GOD, let him answer it."

Z 3 Then Job answered [1]the LORD, and said,
4 °"Behold, °I am vile; °what shall I answer Thee? I will °lay mine hand upon my
mouth.
5 °Once have I spoken; but I will not
answer: yea, °twice; °but I will proceed no
further."

Y K¹ (p. 716) 6 Then answered [1]the LORD unto Job out of
the whirlwind, and said,
7 "Gird up thy loins now like a °man: I will
demand of thee, and declare thou unto Me.
8 Wilt thou also disannul My judgment?
wilt thou condemn Me, that thou mayest be
righteous?
9 Hast thou °an arm like °GOD? or canst
thou thunder with a voice like Him?
10 Deck thyself now *with* majesty and excellency; and array thyself with glory and
beauty.
11 Cast abroad the °rage of thy wrath: and
behold every one *that is* proud, and abase
him.
12 Look on every one *that is* proud, *and*
bring him low; and tread down the °wicked
in their place.
13 Hide them in the dust together; *and* bind
their faces in secret.
14 Then will I also confess unto thee that L¹
thine own right hand can save thee.

26 her. Heb. = his. **28** She = He.
30 where the slain are, &c.: i. e. on a field of battle. Cp. Matt. 24. 28. Luke 17. 37.
she. A.V., 1611, reads "he".
40. 1 the LORD. Heb. Jehovah. Ap. 4. II.
2 Shall . . . ? Fig. *Erotēsis.* Ap. 6.
he that contendeth = the caviller, or reprover.
THE ALMIGHTY. Heb. Shaddai. Ap. 4. VII.
he that reproveth = contender with, or disputer.
GOD. Heb. Eloah. Ap. 4. V.
4 Behold. Fig. *Asterismos.* Ap. 6.
I am vile. This is true wisdom. This is "the end of the Lord" (Jas. 5. 11), and the "end" of this whole book.
what . . . ? Fig. *Erotēsis.* Ap. 6.
lay mine hand, &c. Symbolic of silence and submission.
5 Once . . . twice. Heb. idiom (Ap. 6) for doing a thing repeatedly. Cp. Ps. 62. 11.
but. Some codices, with Sept. and Syr., omit "but".

40. 6—41. 34 (*Y*, p. 713). JEHOVAH'S SECOND ADDRESS. (*Repeated Alternation.*)

Y | K¹ | 40. 6-13. Jehovah's *first* appeal to Divine power. (General.)
  L¹ | 40. 14. Consequent admission.
K² | 40. 15—41. 10-. Jehovah's *second* appeal to Divine power. (Special.) Behemoth (40. 15-24). Leviathan (41. 1-10-).
  L² | 41. -10, 11. Consequent inference.
K³ | 41. 12-34. Jehovah's *third* appeal to Divine power. (Special.) Leviathan, continued.

7 man. Heb. *geber.* Ap. 14. IV.
9 an arm. Fig. *Anthropopatheia.* Ap. 6.
GOD. Heb. El. Ap. 4. IV.
11 rage = overflowings.
12 wicked = lawless. Heb. *rāshā'.* Ap. 44. x.

---

24 With noise and fury stampeth he the earth:
Nor standeth steady when the trumpet sounds.
25 And when it sounds amain he saith, "Aha!"
And from afar the coming battle scents,
The captain's thunder, and the shout of war.

F (p. 714) 26 Is it by thine instruction that the Hawk
Soars high, and spreads his pinions to the south?
27 Is it at thy command the Eagle mounts,
And builds his eyrie in the lofty heights?
28 The rock he makes his home; and there he dwells
On crag's sharp tooth, and [lonely] fastnesses:
29 And thence he keenly spieth out the prey:
His piercing eye beholds it from afar.
30 His young ones learn full soon to suck up blood;
And where the slain are lying, there is he.

A³ (p. 716) **40** Thus spake Jehovah from the storm to Job,
2 "Shall caviller to Shaddai knowledge give?
Reprover of Eloah; answer Me!"

JOB'S FIRST REPLY TO JEHOVAH.

40. 3-5 (Z, p. 713).

Z 3 Then Job confess'd, and made reply; and said,
4 "Lo! I am vile! What shall I answer Thee?
Rather, I lay my hand upon my mouth.
5 Already have I spoken far too much;
I cannot answer. I will add no more."

JEHOVAH'S SECOND ADDRESS.

40. 6—41. 34 (*Y*, p. 713).

JEHOVAH'S FIRST APPEAL TO JOB.

40. 6-13 (K¹, above).

6 Again Jehovah said, from out the storm:— *Y* K¹
7 Now like a strong man, gird thou up thy loins:
'tis I Who ask thee: make thou Me to know.
8 Wilt thou indeed My judgment disannul?
And Me condemn, that thou mayst righteous seem?
9 Hast thou an arm, then, like the mighty GOD?
Or, canst thou thunder with a voice like His?
10 Deck thyself now with glory and with might:
Array thyself with majesty and power:
11 Send far and wide thy overflowing wrath:
And on each proud one look, and bring him low:
12 Each proud one single out, and humble him;
Yea, crush the evil-doers where they stand:
13 Hide them away together in the dust;
And in the deepest dungeon have them bound.
14 THEN, ALSO, I MYSELF WILL OWN TO THEE L¹
THAT THY RIGHT HAND TO SAVE THEE
WILL SUFFICE.

K² 15 [4] Behold now ° behemoth, which I made
(p. 716) with thee; he eateth grass as an ox.
1656 16 ° Lo now, his strength *is* in his loins, and
his force *is* in the ° navel of his belly.
17 He moveth his tail like a cedar: the sinews of his stones are wrapped together.
18 His bones *are as* strong pieces of brass; his bones *are* like bars of iron.
19 He *is* the chief of the ways of [9] GOD: He That made him can make His sword to approach *unto him.*
20 Surely the mountains bring him forth food, where all the beasts of the field play.
21 He lieth under the shady trees, in the covert of the reed, and fens.
22 The shady trees cover him *with* their shadow; the willows of the brook compass him about.
23 [4] Behold, he drinketh up a river, *and* hasteth not: he ° trusteth that he can draw up Jordan into his mouth.
24 He taketh it with his eyes: *his* nose pierceth through snares.

41 ° Canst thou draw out ° leviathan with an hook? or his tongue with a cord *which* thou lettest down?
2 Canst thou put an ° hook into his nose? or bore his jaw through with a thorn?
3 Will he make many supplications unto thee? will he speak soft *words* unto thee?
4 Will he make a covenant with thee? wilt thou take him for a servant for ever?
5 Wilt thou play with him as *with* a bird? or wilt thou bind him for thy maidens?
6 Shall the companions make a banquet of him? shall they part him among the merchants?
7 Canst thou fill his skin with barbed irons? or his head with fish spears?

behemoth: probably the hippopotamus (Greek for river-horse).
16 Lo. Fig. *Asterismos.* Ap. 6.
navel = muscles.
23 trusteth = believeth. Heb. *baṭah.* Ap. 69. I.
41. 1 Canst thou . . . ? Note the Fig. *Erotēsis* (Ap. 6) throughout this chapter.
leviathan: probably the crocodile.
2 hook = reed.
9 Behold. Fig. *Asterismos.* Ap. 6.
11 prevented = anticipated.
is = that is.
13 discover = uncover.
with = within.
double bridle = double row of teeth.
16 air. Heb. *rūach.* Ap. 9.

8 Lay thine hand upon him, remember the battle, do no more.
9 ° Behold, the hope of him is in vain: shall not *one* be cast down even at the sight of him?
10 None *is so* fierce that dare stir him up:
who then is able to stand before Me? L²
11 Who hath ° prevented Me, that I should repay *him? whatsoever is* under the whole heaven ° is Mine.
12 I will not conceal his parts, nor his power, K³
nor his comely proportion.
13 Who can ° discover the face of his garment? *or* who can come *to him* ° with his ° double bridle?
14 Who can open the doors of his face? his teeth *are* terrible round about.
15 *His* scales *are his* pride, shut up together *as with* a close seal.
16 One is so near to another, that no ° air can come between them.
17 They are joined one to another, they stick together, that they cannot be sundered.

JEHOVAH'S SECOND APPEAL TO JOB.

40. 15—41. 10- (K², p. 716).

K² 15 Behold Behėmoth now, which I have made
(p. 716) As well as thee. Grass like the ox he eats.
16 Behold, his massive strength is in his loins:
His force doth in his belly's muscles lie;
17 Shakes he his tail? 'tis like a cedar tree.
The sinews of his thighs are firm entwined.
18 His bones are strong, like unto tubes of brass;
His ribs with bars of iron may compare.
19 A masterpiece of all GOD'S ways is he:
Only his Maker can bring nigh His sword.
20 The mountains will bring produce forth for him,
While all the beasts do, fearless, round him play.
21 Beneath the shady trees he lieth down,
And rests in covert of the reed and fen:
22 The shady trees weave o'er him each its shade;
While willows of the brook encompass him.
23 Suppose the stream should swell; he will not blench:
For he believes that Jordan he can drink.
24 Shall any take him while he lies on watch?
Or with a hook shall any pierce his nose?
41 Canst thou draw up Leviathan with hook?
Or catch, as with [an angler's] line, his tongue?
2 Canst thou insert into his nose a reed?
Or canst thou pierce his jaw through with a thorn?
3 Will he make many humble pray'rs to thee?
Or will he ever say soft things to thee?
4 Will he engage in covenant with thee,
That thou shouldst take him for thy lifelong slave?
5 Wilt thou, as with some linnet, play with him?
Or wilt thou cage him for thy maidens' sport?
6 Will trading dealers haggle o'er his price?
And rétail him among the merchantmen?
7 Wilt thou with darts essay to fill his skin?
Or [pierce] his head with spears for catching fish?
8 Lay thou thy hand upon him, though but once:
Think only of the contest: do no more.
9 Behold, all hope of taking him is vain:
E'en at the sight of him one is cast down:
10- None so foolhardy as to stir him up:
-10 BEFORE ME, THEN, [HIS MAKER], WHO CAN STAND? L²
11 WHO E'ER FIRST GAVE TO ME, THAT I SHOULD HIM
REPAY? SINCE ALL BENEATH THE HEAV'NS IS MINE?

JEHOVAH'S THIRD APPEAL TO JOB.

41. 12-36 (K³, p. 716).

12 Silence I shall not keep about his parts: K³
His wondrous strength: his well-proportioned frame;
13 His coat of mail: who hath e'er stripped this off?
His double row of teeth: who enters there?
14 The doors which close his mouth: who opens them?
His teeth's surroundings are a scare to see.
15 The scales which form his armour are his pride:
Each one shut up and closed as with a seal.
16 So near one to another do they lie
That air between them cannot find a way:
17 So close unto each other do they cleave,
And cling so fast, that none can sunder them.

1656 **18 By his °neesings a light doth shine, and**
his eyes *are* like the eyelids of the morning.
19 Out of his mouth go burning lamps, *and*
sparks of fire leap out.
20 Out of his nostrils goeth smoke, as *out* of
a seething pot or caldron.
21 His °breath kindleth coals, and a flame
goeth out of his mouth.
22 In his neck remaineth strength, and sor-
row is turned into joy before him.
23 The flakes of his flesh are joined together:
they are firm in themselves; they cannot be
moved.
24 His heart is as firm as a stone; yea, as
hard as a piece of the nether *millstone.*
25 When he raiseth up himself, the mighty
are afraid: by reason of °breakings they
°purify themselves.
26 The sword of him that layeth at him can-
not hold: the spear, the °dart, nor the °haber-
geon.
27 He esteemeth iron as straw, *and* brass as
rotten wood.
28 The arrow cannot make him flee: sling-
stones are turned with him into stubble.
29 °Darts are counted as stubble: he °laugh-
eth at the shaking of a spear.
30 Sharp stones *are* under him: he spread-
eth sharp pointed things upon the mire.
31 He maketh the deep to boil like a pot: he
maketh the sea like a pot of ointment.
32 He maketh a path to shine after him; *one*
would think the deep *to be* hoary.
33 Upon earth there is not his like, who is
made without fear.
34 He beholdeth all high *things:* he *is* a king
over all the °children of pride."

Z (p. 713) **42 Then Job answered °the LORD, and**
said,
2 "I know that Thou canst do every *thing,*
and *that* no thought can be withholden from
Thee.
3 °Who *is* he that hideth counsel without
knowledge? therefore have I uttered that I
understood not; things too wonderful for me,
which I knew not.
4 °Hear, I beseech Thee, and I will speak:
°I will demand of thee, and declare thou unto
me.
5 I have heard of Thee by the hearing of the
ear: but now mine eye seeth Thee.
6 Wherefore °I abhor *myself,* and repent in
dust and ashes."

7 And it was *so,* that after [1]the LORD had M (p. 718)
spoken °these words unto Job,
[1]the LORD said to Eliphaz the Temanite, N

18 neesings. Obsolete for sneezings. From A.S. *fneósan.* Chaucer spells it *fnesen.*
21 breath=soul. Heb. *nephesh.* Ap. 13.
25 breakings=terrors.
purify themselves=mistake their way; are bewildered; or, beside themselves.
26 dart=missile. Not same word as in *v.* 29. (Heb. *massā'*). **habergeon**=coat of mail.
29 darts=clubs. Not same word as in *v.* 26. (Heb. *tōthāk*).
laugheth. Fig. *Prosopopœia.* Ap. 6.
34 children of pride=sons of pride, or proud beasts.
42. 1 the LORD. Heb. Jehovah. Ap. 4. II.
3 Who is he . . . ? Supply the obvious *Ellipsis* (Ap. 6) thus: "[Thou askedst] 'Who is this?'" &c.; which Jehovah did ask in 38. 1-3. **4 Hear**=Hear, now.
I will demand of thee. Supply the *Ellipsis* (Ap. 6): "[Thou saidst]: 'Let him answer Me'" (see 40. 2).
6 I abhor myself, and repent. "The end of the Lord" (i. e. what Jehovah designed as the great lesson of this book) is at length reached. Cp. Jas. 5. 11.

42. 7-9 (*C*, p. 665). **THE THREE FRIENDS.**
(*Introversion and Alternation.*)

C | M | 7-. Jehovah ceases to speak to Job.
  N | -7-. Job's friends spoken to by Jehovah.
    O | s | -7-. What He said.
      t | -7. The reason. "Because."
    O | *s* | 8-. What He said.
      t | -8. The reason. "Because."
  N | 9-. Job's friends obey Jehovah.
M | -9. Jehovah accepts Job.

7 these words: i. e. ch. 38. 1—41. 34.

18 His sneezings are a flashing forth of light.
His eyes are like the eyelids of the Dawn.
19 Out of his mouth vapours like torches go,
And sparks like fire therefrom make their escape.
20 Out of his nostrils goeth forth a smoke,
As from a boiling pot on reed-fire set.
21 His breath,—as if it would set coals aflame;
And from his mouth a flame seems issuing forth:
22 His strength abideth ever in his neck;
Before his face grim terror dancing goes.
23 His softer folds of flesh, though hanging, cleave
So close on him that moved they cannot be.
24 His heart is hard, hard as a stone is hard;
Yea, like a nether millstone, firm and hard.
25 Whene'er he riseth up, the mighty cow'r;
And, at the waves he makes, their fright is great.
26 Let one encounter him—no sword will stand:
No spear, nor dart, nor iron coat of mail.
27 Iron he counts no better than a straw,
And brass no better is than rotten wood.
28 The arrow will not make him flee away:
Slingstones to him are stubble, and no more;
29 Like harmless chaff he counts the pond'rous club,
And at the whizzing of a spear will laugh.
30 His under-parts are sharply pointed spikes:
He spreads like threshing-drag upon the mire.
31 Like boiling pot he makes the deep to foam;
And, like a well-stirr'd ointment pot, the Nile.
32 His wake he makes a sparkling, shiny path,
So that the deep will look like hoary hair.
33 His equal is not found on all the earth:
He hath been made insensible of fear:
34 On all things high he looketh [dauntlessly];
And over all proud beasts he is a king.

JOB'S SECOND REPLY TO JEHOVAH.
42. 1-6 (*Z*, p. 713).

1 Then answered Job, and to Jehovah said:— Z (p. 713)
2 "I know, I know, that THOU canst all things do:
No purposes of THINE can be withstood.
3 [Thou askedst (38. 3; 40. 2)]—
'Who is this that counsel hides,
And darkens all, because of knowledge void?'
'tis I! I uttered things I could not know;
Things far too wonderful, beyond my ken.
4 Hear now, I pray thee: let me speak this once.
[Thou saidst (40. 2)]:—
''tis I who ask thee: Answer Me.'
5 I heard of Thee by hearing of the ear,
But now mine eye hath seen Thee, I abhor
6 [Myself]. In dust and ashes I repent."

O s (p. 718) "My wrath is kindled against thee, and against thy two friends:
1656 t for ye have °not spoken of Me *the thing that is* right, °as My servant Job *hath.*

O s 8 Therefore take unto you now °seven bullocks and seven rams, and go to My servant Job, and offer up for yourselves a °burnt offering; and My servant Job shall pray for you:

t for °him will I accept: lest I deal with you *after your* folly, in that ye have not spoken of Me *the thing which is* right, like My servant Job."

N 9 So Eliphaz the Temanite and Bildad the Shuhite *and* Zophar the Naamathite went, and did according as [1]the LORD commanded them:

M [1]the LORD also accepted °Job.

B P (p. 719) 10 And [1]the LORD °turned the captivity of Job, when he prayed for his friends: also [1]the LORD gave Job °twice as much as he had before.

Q 11 Then came there unto him all his brethren, and all his sisters, and all they that had been of his acquaintance before, and did eat bread with him in his house: and they bemoaned him, and comforted him over all the °evil that [1]the LORD had brought upon him: °every man also gave him a °piece of money, and °every one an earring of gold.

P 12 So [1]the LORD blessed the latter end of Job more than his beginning: for he had fourteen thousand sheep, °and six thousand camels, and a thousand yoke of oxen, and a thousand she asses.

Q 13 He had also [8]seven sons and three daughters.

A R 14 And he called the name of the first, °Jemima; and the name of the second, °Kezia; and the name of the third, °Keren-happuch.
15 And in all the land were no women found *so* fair as the daughters of Job: and their father gave them inheritance among their brethren.

S 1656-1516 16 After this lived °Job an hundred and forty years,

and saw his sons, and his sons' sons, *even* four generations. R

17 So Job died, *being* old and °full of days. S

---

not spoken of Me the thing that is right. We have, therefore, an inspired record of what they said; but all they said was not inspired, and cannot be quoted as the Word of Jehovah.

as My servant Job hath: i.e. in 42. 1-6.

8 seven. See Ap. 10.

burnt offering. Heb. *'ōlah.* Ap. 43. II. ii. See Ap. 15.

him = his face: face being put by Fig. *Synecdoche* (of the Part), Ap. 6, for the whole person.

9 Job. Heb. the face of Job, as in *v.* 8.

10-13 (*B*, p. 665). SATAN'S DEFEAT. (JOB BLESSED WITH DOUBLE.) (*Alternation.*)

B | P | 10. Job's blessing.
Q | 11. His family.
P | 12. Job's blessing.
Q | 13. His family.

10 turned the captivity. Fig. *Paronomasia* (Ap. 6), *shāb eth sh būth*, emphasising recovery or deliverance from any trouble, as in Ps. 126. 1, 4, &c.

twice as much. This blessing was included in "the end of the Lord" (Jas. 5. 11). See note on p. 666.

11 evil = calamity. Heb. *rā'a'.* Ap. 44. viii. Cp. Isa. 45. 7.

every man. Heb. *'īsh.* Ap. 14. II.

piece = weight, as in Gen. 33. 19. The Sept. reads "a lamb, and four drachms weight of gold, even of unstamped [gold]"; or, "a piece of gold stamped with a lamb."

every one. Heb. *'īsh.* Ap. 14. II.

12 and. Note the Fig. *Polysyndeton* (Ap. 6), in *vv.* 12-15, to emphasise each particular thing.

14-16 (*A*, p. 665). CONCLUSION. (*Alternation.*)

A | R | 14, 15. Job's children.
S | 16-. His life.
R | -16-. Job's descendants.
S | -16. His death.

14 Jemima = beautiful as the day (Sept. and Vulg.) or as a dove.

Kezia = fragrant as cassia (i. e. cinnamon).

Keren-happuch = horn of beauty or plenty. Cp. *v.* 15.

16 an hundred and forty years: i.e. from 1656 to 1516. See note on p. 666.

17 full of days = satisfied with days.

The Sept. has a long sub-scription, for which see Ap. 62. The Arabic has a similar sub-scription, which professes to have been taken from the Syriac, but it is not in the Syriac version as given in Walton's *Polyglot.*

THE PSALMS.

THE STRUCTURE OF THE BOOK AS A WHOLE*.

1—150. THE FIVE BOOKS†.

A[1] | 1—41. THE GENESIS BOOK‡: CONCERNING MAN. The counsels of God‖ concerning him. All blessing bound up in obedience (cp. 1. 1 with Gen. 1. 28). Obedience is man's "tree of life" (cp. 1. 3 with Gen. 2. 16). Disobedience brought ruin (cp. Ps. 2 with Gen. 3). The ruin repaired only by the SON OF MAN in His atoning work as the seed of the woman (cp. Ps. 8 with Gen. 3. 15). The book concludes with a Benediction and double Amen.

B[1] | 42—72. THE EXODUS BOOK‡: CONCERNING ISRAEL AS A NATION. The counsels of God‖ concerning ISRAEL'S RUIN, ISRAEL'S REDEEMER, and ISRAEL'S REDEMPTION (Ex. 15. 13). Cp. Ps. 68. 4 with Ex. 15. 3, "JAH". It begins with Israel's cry for deliverance, and ends with Israel's king reigning over the redeemed nation. The book concludes with a Benediction and a double Amen.

C[1] | 73—89. THE LEVITICUS BOOK‡: CONCERNING THE SANCTUARY. The counsels of God‖ concerning the Sanctuary in its relation to man, and the Sanctuary in relation to Jehovah. The Sanctuary, Congregation, Assembly, or Zion, &c., referred to in nearly every Psalm. The book concludes with a Benediction and a double Amen.

B[2] | 90-106. THE NUMBERS BOOK‡: CONCERNING ISRAEL AND THE NATIONS OF THE EARTH. The counsels of God‖ concerning the EARTH, showing that there is no hope or rest for the Earth apart from Jehovah. Its figures and similes are from this world as a wilderness (cp. the references to mountains, hills, floods, grass, trees, pestilence, &c.). It begins with the prayer of Moses (the Man of the Wilderness), Ps. 90, and closes with a rehearsal of ISRAEL'S rebellions in the wilderness (Ps. 106). Note "the New Song" for "all the earth" in Ps. 96. 11, where the theme is contained in one sentence which gives an Acrostic, spelling the word "Jehovah": "Let the heavens rejoice, and let the earth be glad" (see note on 96. 11). The book concludes with a Benediction and Amen, Hallelujah.

A[2] | 107—150. THE DEUTERONOMY BOOK‡: CONCERNING GOD AND HIS WORD. The counsels of God‖ concerning His Word, showing that all blessings for MAN (Book I), all blessings for ISRAEL (Book II), all blessings for the EARTH and the NATIONS (Book IV), are bound up with living on the words of God (Deut. 8. 3). Disobedience to Jehovah's words was the source of MAN'S sorrows, ISRAEL'S dispersion, the SANCTUARY'S ruin, and EARTH'S miseries. Blessing is to come from that Word written on the heart (cp. Jer. 31. 33, 34. Heb. 8. 10-12; 10. 16, 17). Ps. 119 is in this book. The Living Word (John 1. 1) began His ministry by quoting Deut. 6. 13, 16; 8. 3; 10. 20 in Matt. 4. 4, 7, 10. The book begins with Ps. 107, and in *v.* 20 we read, "He sent HIS WORD and healed them", and it concludes with five Psalms (one for each of the five books), each Psalm beginning and ending with "Hallelujah".

---

* Manuscript and Massoretic authorities, the Talmud (*Kiddushin* 33a) as well as the ancient versions, divide the Psalms into five books. The *Midrash* on Ps. 1. 1 says, "Moses gave to the Israelites the five books of the Law; and corresponding with these David gave them the five books of the Psalms."

The Structure of each Psalm being perfect in itself, we may well expect to find the same perfection in the arrangement of the five books respectively as well as of the one hundred and fifty Psalms as a whole.

Many attempts have been made from ancient times to discover the reason for the classification of the Psalms under these five books; but none of them is so satisfactory as to preclude this further attempt.

It is certain that the present order in which we have the Psalms is the same as it was when they were in the hands of our Lord, and were quoted repeatedly by Him, and by the Holy Spirit through the Evangelists and Apostles. Indeed, in Acts 13. 33, the Holy Spirit by Paul expressly mentions "the *second* Psalm". This puts us upon sure ground.

There must be a reason therefore why "the *second* Psalm" is not (for example) the *seventy-second*; and why the *ninetieth* (which is the most ancient of all the Psalms, being a prayer of Moses) is not the *first*.

The similar endings to each book are noted above. There are in all seven "Amens", and twenty-four Hallelujahs. All the latter (except the four in Book IV) are in Book V.

† For the relation of the five books of the Pentateuch to each other see Ap. 1.

‡ For the relation of the five books of the Psalms to the Pentateuch, see above, and the Structures prefixed to each book.

‖ For the Divine Names and Titles occurring in the Psalms see Ap. 63. V.

1—41 (𝔄¹, p. 720). THE FIRST OR GENESIS BOOK*. MAN.

(*Division.*)

𝔄¹ | A¹ | 1—8. "MAN", AND "THE SON OF MAN" (8. 4).
| A² | 9—15. "THE MAN OF THE EARTH" (ANTICHRIST, 10. 18).
| A³ | 16—41. "THE MAN CHRIST JESUS."

1—8 (A¹, above). "MAN", AND "THE SON OF MAN."

(*Introversion and Alternations.*)

A¹ | B | D | 1†. MAN BLESSED. THE LAW OF JEHOVAH HIS DELIGHT (REFERS TO PARADISE).
E | 2†. REBELLIOUS MAN. VAINLY MEDITATING AGAINST THE SON OF GOD, THROUGH WHOM ALONE UNIVERSAL DOMINION CAN BE RESTORED (*v.* 12 and Heb. 1. 5).
C | F | 3. PRAYER IN VIEW OF THIS REBELLION (MORNING). "JEHOVAH MY SHIELD" (*v.* 3). } ENEMIES WITHOUT.
G | 4. PRAYER IN VIEW OF THIS REBELLION (NIGHT). "HOW LONG?" (*v.* 2).
C | *F* | 5. PRAYER IN VIEW OF THIS REBELLION (MORNING). "JEHOVAH MY KING" (*v.* 2). } SORROWS WITHIN.
G | 6. PRAYER IN VIEW OF THIS REBELLION (NIGHT). "HOW LONG?" (*v.* 3).
B | *D* | 7. MAN BLESSED. TRUST IN JEHOVAH HIS DEFENCE.
E | 8. REBELLIOUS SUBDUED. THE SON OF MAN EXALTED WITH DOMINION IN THE EARTH.

9—15 (A², above). "THE MAN OF THE EARTH."

(*Introversion.*)

A² | H | 9 (H¹), 10 (H²)‡. "THE MAN OF THE EARTH." THE ANTICHRIST. HIS DAYS, CHARACTER, AND END. "THE TIMES OF TROUBLE" (9. 9; 10. 1). THE GREAT TRIBULATION. THE TWO PSALMS LINKED TOGETHER BY AN ACROSTIC ALPHABET, BROKEN, LIKE THOSE "TIMES".
J | K | 11. PRAYER IN VIEW OF (9 and 10) THOSE "TIMES OF TROUBLE".
L | 12. THE VANITY OF MAN.
J | *K* | 13. PRAYER IN VIEW OF (9 and 10) THOSE "TIMES OF TROUBLE".
L | 14. THE DEPRAVITY OF MAN.
H | 15. THE PERFECT MAN. HIS CHARACTER AND ETERNAL ABIDING. LEADING UP TO A³.

16—41 (A³, above). "THE MAN CHRIST JESUS."

(*Extended Alternations.*)

A³ | M | P | 16‖. TAKING HIS PLACE OF SUFFERING. JEHOVAH APPORTIONING HIS LOT.
Q | 17. PRAYER AND APPEAL IN VIEW OF PS. 16 (P).
R | 18. ANSWER TO THE PRAYER OF PS. 17, AND PROMISE OF DELIVERANCE AND TRIUMPH.
N | S | 19. HIS PEOPLE ACKNOWLEDGING GOD'S GLORY IN CREATION AND REVELATION.
T | 20. THEIR PRAYER AS THEY SEE IN MESSIAH THEIR OWN SALVATION.
U | 21. THEIR EXULTATION IN MESSIAH'S EXALTATION.
O | V | 22. THE GOOD SHEPHERD IN DEATH (John 10. 11). ATONEMENT THE BASIS OF *ALL* BLESSING.
W | 23. THE GREAT SHEPHERD IN RESURRECTION (Heb. 13. 20). RESURRECTION THE BASIS OF *PRESENT* BLESSING.
X | 24. THE CHIEF SHEPHERD IN GLORY (1 Pet. 5. 4). ADVENT THE BASIS OF ALL *FUTURE* BLESSING.
M | *P* | 25. PRAYER WITH REFERENCE TO PS. 16 (P). THE "PATH" AND THE "WAY" (cp. *vv.* 4, 8-10, 12 with 16. 11).
Q | 26. PRAYER WITH REFERENCE TO PS. 17 (Q). APPEAL TO INTEGRITY (cp. 17. 1, 3, 4).
R | 27 (*R*¹), 28 (*R*²). PRAYERS WITH REFERENCE TO PS. 18 (R). ANSWER FROM JEHOVAH, AS HIS "ROCK" AND "DELIVERER".
N | *S* | 29. HIS PEOPLE'S PRAISE FOR GOD'S GLORY IN CREATION. Cp. 19 (S).
T | 30 (*T*¹), 31 (*T*²), §32 (*T*³), 34 (*T*⁴). THEIR PRAISE AS THEY SEE THE ANSWER TO PS. 20 (PS. 33 BEING THE FIRST "NEW SONG" IN THE PSALTER).
U | 34. THEIR EXULTATION IN MESSIAH'S EXALTATION. As in "U", Ps. 21.
O | *V* | 35 (*V*¹), 36 (*V*²). PRAYER AND PRAISE WITH REFERENCE TO ATONEMENT AS BEING THE BASIS OF *ALL* BLESSING. Cp. 22 (V).
W | 37. INSTRUCTION AS TO *PRESENT* BLESSING, IN VIEW OF PS. 23 (W).
X | 38 (*X*¹), 39 (*X*²), 40 (*X*³), 41 (*X*⁴). PRAYER AND PRAISE WITH REFERENCE TO *FUTURE* BLESSING. Cp. 41. 12, THE DIVINE ANSWER TO 24. 3 (X).

---

* For notes, see p. 722.

NOTES ON THE STRUCTURE, PAGE 721.

* In the first Book of the Psalms the leading thought *corresponds* with that of the first Book of the Pentateuch. The counsels of God are shown from the beginning to the end in relation to MAN.

As Genesis begins with the Divine *blessing* on *Man* (1. 28), so Psalm 1 opens with "*Blessed is the man*". All blessedness for man is shown to consist in subjection to, and occupation with, God's Law. It is the Tree of Life to him; and, meditating on this, he becomes like a well-watered tree in the Paradise of God.

But, in Gen. 3, Man rebelled against that Law: and Ps. 2 describes the consequences of that rebellion; while Ps. 3 takes its title from one who rebelled against God's King. The ruin can be repaired only by "THE MAN Christ Jesus" (the Seed of the woman, Gen. 3. 15): and in the Psalms of this first Book (the *third* section) we see Him in His atoning work, which alone sets man again in the blessedness which he had lost.

The first Book consists of *forty-one* Psalms. The central Psalm is 21, which sets forth the eternal life and blessedness of God's King. All that have titles (37) are David's—the man of God's choice.

Of the Divine Titles, Jehovah occurs 279 times, and Elohim only 48 times, 9 of which are joined with Jehovah. (See Ap. 4.) Note also the references to the events, &c., of Genesis in this first Book. (See Ap. 63. V.)

† Pss. 1 and 2 are linked together by having no Titles; and by Ps. 1 opening, and Ps. 2 closing with "Blessed".

The first or GENESIS book is divided into three sections, which (on p. 721) are stated thus:—

1. The *First* (Pss. 1-8) concerning "MAN".
2. The *Second* (Pss. 9-15) concerning "THE MAN OF THE EARTH" (the Antichrist).
3. The *Third* (Pss. 16-41) concerning "THE MAN CHRIST JESUS" (the Messiah).

‡ Pss. 9 and 10 are linked together by having an irregular alphabet running acrostically through the two. The alphabet is broken and irregular, like the "times of trouble", "the great tribulation", of which they speak.

‖ Ps. 16 is the first *Michtam* Psalm. The others are Pss. 56-60. See Ap. 65. xii.

§ Ps. 32 is the first *Maschil* Psalm, denoting *instruction*.

THE °PSALMS.

BOOK I.

A C (p. 723) **1** °BLESSED *is* the °man that °walketh not in the counsel of the °ungodly,
Nor standeth in the way of °sinners,
Nor sitteth in the seat of the °scornful.

D a 2 But his delight *is* in °the law of °the LORD;
And in His °law doth he °meditate day and night.

b 3 And he shall °be °like a tree °planted by the °rivers of water,
That bringeth forth his fruit in his season;
His leaf also shall not wither;
And whatsoever he doeth shall °prosper.

B *D a* 4 The [1]ungodly °*are* not so:

b But *are* °like the chaff which the °wind driveth away.

C 5 Therefore the [2]ungodly shall not °stand in the judgment,
Nor [1]sinners in the °congregation of the °righteous.

A 6 °For [2]the LORD °knoweth the way of the [5]righteous:

B But the way of the ungodly shall °perish.

E E (p. 723) **2** °**Why do the °heathen °rage,**
And the °people °imagine a vain thing?
2 The kings of the earth °set themselves,
And the rulers °take counsel together,
Against °the LORD, and against His °Anointed, °*saying*,
3 "Let us break °their bands asunder,
And cast away their cords from us."

F 4 He That sitteth in the heavens shall °laugh:
°The LORD* shall have them in derision.

TITLE, Psalms. See Ap. 63, and the Structures, pp. 720, 721. Cp. Luke 20. 42; 24. 44. Acts 1. 20.

1–8. MAN, AND THE SON OF MAN (**A**[1], p. 721).

1 (**D**, p. 721). MAN BLESSED. LAW OF JEHOVAH. (*Alternation.*)

D | A | 1–3. The godly.
B | 4, 5. The ungodly.
A | 6–. The godly.
B | –6. The ungodly.

1–5 (A, 1–3; B, 4, 5). (*Introversion and Alternation.*)

A | C | 1. Godly. Not standing with ungodly. Now.
D | a | 2. Their character. } Their way. } The godly.
b | 3. Comparison.
B | *D* | *a* | 4–. Their character. } Their way. } The ungodly.
b | –4. Comparison.
C | 5. Ungodly. Not standing with godly. Then.

1 BLESSED = How happy. The first Psalm begins thus, and Ps. 2 ends thus. So does the last Psalm of Book I (Ps. 41. 1, 13). Fig. *Antiptōsis* (Ap. 6). Cp. Jer. 17. 7, 8. See Ap. 63. vi for the Beatitudes in the Psalms.
man. Heb. *'ish.* Ap. 14. II. Put by Fig. *Synecdochē* (of Species), Ap. 6, for all of both sexes.
walketh, &c.: i. e. who never did walk . . . stand . . . sit. Fig. *Anabasis* (Ap. 6), three triplets:

walketh	counsel	ungodly	= continue in.
standeth	way	sinners	= carry out.
sitteth	seat	scornful	= settle down.

ungodly = lawless. Heb. *rāshā'.* Ap. 44. x.
sinners. Heb. *chāṭā'.* Ap. 44. i.
scornful = scoffers. Heb. *lūẓ.*
2 the law = instruction: i. e. the whole Pentateuch which contains it.
the LORD. Heb. Jehovah. Ap. 4. II.
meditate: i. e. continually and habitually.
3 be = become, or prove. Fig. *Simile.* Ap. 6.
like a tree. The first of two comparisons. See *v.* 4.
planted: i. e. in a garden. Not a "tree of the field".
rivers = divisions irrigating a garden. Heb. *palgēymāyim.* See note on Prov. 21. 1.

3 prosper. Cp. Gen. 39. 3, 23. **4 are not so,** &c. = not so the ungodly. **like the chaff.** The other comparison. See *v.* 3. Cp. 35. 5. **wind.** Heb. *rūach.* Ap. 9. **5 stand** = rise. No part in first resurrection. Rev. 20. 5, 6. Cp. Ps. 49. 14. **congregation** = assembly. **righteous** = justified. **6 For.** *Effect* latent in first clause: *cause* latent in second clause. **knoweth** = approveth, or acknowledgeth. Fig. *Metonymy* (of Cause), Ap. 6. Cp. Nah. 1. 7. 2 Tim. 2. 19. **perish** = come to naught.

2 (**E**, p. 721). REBELLIOUS MAN. (*Repeated Alternation.*)

E | E | 1–3. Mankind. Speaking.
F | 4, 5. Jehovah. Fig. *Chleuasmos.* Ap. 6.
G | 6–9. The Son. His rule.
E | 10. Mankind. Spoken to.
F | 11. Jehovah. Fig *Apostrophe.* Ap. 6.
G | 12. The Son. His judgment.

The second Psalm of each book has to do with the enemy. See Ap. 10.

1 Why . . .? Fig. *Erotēsis.* Ap. 6. Repeat at beginning of *v.* 2. Cp. Acts 4. 25, 26. **heathen** = nations. Note the quadruple *Anabasis* (Ap. 6): nations, peoples, kings, rulers. Cp. 1. 1. **rage** = tumultuously assemble. **people** = peoples. **imagine.** Same as meditate in 1. 2. **2 set themselves** = take their stand. **take counsel together** = have gathered by appointment. So the Sept. and Aram. Cp. 48. 4. **the LORD.** Heb. Jehovah. Ap. 4. II. **Anointed** = Messiah. So Pss. 18. 50; 20. 6; 28. 8; 84. 9; 89. 38, 51; 132. 10, 17. In Dan. 9. 25, 26, rendered Messiah. **saying.** The Fig. *Ellipsis* (Ap. 6) correctly supplied. **3 their:** i. e. Jehovah's, and Messiah's. **4 laugh.** Fig. *Anthropopatheia.* Ap. 6. **The LORD*.** Primitive text was Jehovah. Altered by the *Sōpherim* to Adonai. See Ap. 32.

5 Then shall He speak unto them in His wrath,
And vex them in His sore displeasure.

G (p. 723) 6 Yet have I °set My king
Upon °My °holy hill of °Zion.
7 I will declare °the decree:
[2]The LORD hath said unto Me, °"**Thou art My Son;**
This day have I °begotten Thee.
8 °**Ask of me, and I shall give *Thee* the [1]heathen *for* Thine inheritance.**
And the uttermost parts of the earth *for* Thy possession.
9 **Thou shalt °break them with a °rod of °iron;**
Thou shalt dash them in pieces like a potter's vessel."'

E 10 °Be wise now therefore, O ye kings:
Be instructed, ye judges of the earth.
F 11 Serve °the LORD with fear,
And rejoice with trembling.
G 12 °Kiss the °Son, lest °He be angry, and ye perish °*from* the way,
°When His wath is kindled but °a little.
°Blessed *are* all they that °put their trust in Him.

934 B. C. **3** °A Psalm of David, °when he fled from Absalom his son.

H c (p. 724) 1 °LORD, °how are they °increased that trouble me!
°Many *are* they that rise up against me.
d 2 °Many *there be* which say of °my soul,
"*There is* no °help for him in °God."
°Selah.
e 3 But Thou, O [1]LORD, °*art* a shield °for me;
My glory, and the lifter up of °mine head.
I 4 I °cried unto [1]the LORD with my voice,
And He °heard me out of His °holy hill.
°Selah.
I 5 I laid me down and °slept;
I awaked; for [1]the LORD °sustained me.
c 6 I will not be afraid of ten thousands of people,
That have set *themselves* against me round about.
d 7 Arise, O [1]LORD; save me, O my [2]God:
e For Thou hast smitten all mine enemies *upon* the cheek bone;
Thou hast broken the teeth of the °ungodly.

6 set=founded. Not the same word as *v.* 2.
My holy hill. Fig. *Antimereia* (Ap. 6). Heb. = "mount of my Sanctuary".
holy. See note on Ex. 3. 5.
Zion. The mount immediately south of Moriah. See note on 2 Sam. 5. 7. Occurs thirty-eight times in Psalms. "Jerusalem" occurs seventeen times. See Ap. 68. **7 the**=for a.
Thou art my Son. Quoted in Acts 13. 33. Heb. 1. 5; 5. 5. This is the Divine formula for anointing. Cp. Matt. 3. 17, for Prophet; Matt. 17. 5, for Priest; and Heb. 1. 5, 6, for King.
begotten Thee. Fig *Anthropopatheia* (Ap. 6). It refers to resurrection (Acts 13. 33. Rom. 1. 3, 4. Col. 1. 18. Rev. 1. 5).
8 Ask of me. Referring not to this present dispensation of grace, but to coming dispensation of judgment.
I shall give, &c. Quoted in Rev. 2. 27; 12. 5; 19. 15.
9 break them=rule, or govern them. So Sept., Syr., and Vulg. **rod**=sceptre.
iron. Put by Fig. *Metonymy* (of Adjunct), Ap. 6, for unbending authority.
10 Be wise. Fig. *Apostrophe.* Ap. 6.
11 the LORD. Heb. *'eth* Jehovah. Ap. 4. II (objective).
12 Kiss=submit to, or be ruled by. Heb. *nashak.* Occurs thirty-two times (first in Gen. 27. 26, 27). Always so rendered except 1 Chron. 12. 2. 2 Chron. 17. 17. Ps. 78. 9 (where it is Poel Part.) "armed"; Ezek. 3. 13 "touched" (marg. "kissed"); and Gen. 41. 40, "be ruled" (marg. "be armed", or "kiss").
Son. Aram. *bar,* a *Homonym* with two meanings: (1) *son* (Dan. 3. 25. Ezra 5. 1, 2, 2; 6. 14. Dan. 3. 25; 5. 22; 7. 13, and Prov. 31. 2, 2, 2 (king Lemuel); (2) *ground,* Dan. 2. 38; 4. 12, 15, 21, 23, 23, 25, 32. See note on Job 39. 4. So here in Ps. 2. 12 = kiss the ground, Fig. *Metonymy* (of Adjunct), Ap. 6, for prostrate yourselves in submission. The usual Heb. for "son" is *bēn,* and is translated "son" or "sons" 2,890 times, and "child" or "children" (where it ought always to be "son" or "sons"), 1,549 times: making 4,439 in all. The Aram. *ben* is also used for "son".
He: i. e. Jehovah, *v.* 11.
from the way. No Fig. *Ellipsis* (Ap. 6) here, "from" not needed = "perish, way [and all]". Ending like Ps. 1. 6. Cp. 146. 9. So 2 Kings 3. 4 = wool [and all].
When His wrath is kindled: or, His wrath will soon be kindled (R.V.).
a little=quickly. See note on "almost", Prov. 5. 14.
Blessed=How happy. Fig. *Beatitudo.* See note on 1. 1.
put their trust=flee for refuge to. Heb. *ḥasah.* See Ap. 69. ii.

3 [For Structure see below].

Title. A Psalm. See Ap. 65. XVII.
when. The first psalm with an historical title. See Ap. 63. viii and 64. Cp. 2 Sam. chs. 15-18.
1 LORD. Heb. Jehovah. Ap. 4. II.
how . . . ! Fig. *Exclamatio* (Ap. 6), for emphasis.
increased=multiplied. **Many**=what multitudes.
2 Many. Fig. *Anaphora.* Ap. 6.
my soul=me, or myself. Heb. *nephesh.* Ap. 13. **help**=salvation, or deliverance. **God.** Heb. Elohim. Ap. 4. I. **Selah.** Connecting the contrast between "man" (as a creature) who knows God (Elohim) only as Creator, with the speaker (David), who knew *Jehovah* as his Covenant God. See Ap. 4. I, II, and 66. ii. **3 art a shield.** Fig. *Metaphor* (Ap. 6); "shield" put by Fig. *Metonymy* (of Adjunct), Ap. 6, for defence. **for me**=about me. **mine head.** Fig. *Synecdoche* (of Part), Ap. 6, put for whole person. **4 cried**=shall cry. **heard**=will answer. **holy hill.** See note on 2. 6. **Selah.** Connecting the peace which comes from prayer, as in Phil. 4. 6. See Ap. 66. II. **5 slept**=have slept. At Mahanaim (2 Sam. 17. 27-29). **sustained**=was sustaining. **7 ungodly**=lawless. Heb. *rāshā'.* Ap. 44. x.

3 (**F**, p. 721). PRAYER IN VIEW OF PSALM **2** (MORNING). (*Introversion and Repeated Alternation.*)

F | H | c | 1. Numbers of enemies against me.
  d | 2. No salvation (they say).
  e | 3. Thou my help. (Experience. 2nd person.)
 I | 4. Prayer answered. } (Experience. 3rd person.)
 I | 5. Confidence justified. }
 H | *c* | 6. Numbers of enemies against me.
  d | 7-. Save me (I say).
  e | -7, 8. Thou my help. (Experience. 2nd person.)

8 °Salvation *belongeth* unto [1]the LORD:
°Thy blessing *is* upon Thy People. °Selah.

°To the chief Musician on °Neginoth.

4

°A Psalm of David.

G J (p. 725) 1 °Hear me when I call, O °God of my righteousness:
Thou hast enlarged me *when I was* in distress;
°Have mercy upon me, and hear my prayer.

K f 2 O ye sons of °men, °how long *will ye turn* my glory into shame?

g *How long* will ye love vanity, *and* seek after °leasing? °Selah.

K f 3 But know that °the LORD hath °set apart °him that is godly for Himself:
°The LORD will [1]hear when I call unto Him.

g 4 °Stand in awe, and °sin not:
Commune with your own heart upon your bed, and be °still. °Selah.
5 °Offer the °sacrifices of righteousness,
And put your °trust in [3]the LORD.

J 6 *There be* many °that say, "Who will shew us *any* °good?"
[3]LORD, °lift Thou up the light of Thy °countenance upon us.
7 Thou hast put °gladness in my heart,
More than in the time *that* °their corn and their °wine increased.
8 I will both lay me down in peace, °and sleep:
For Thou, [3]LORD, only °makest me dwell in °safety.

°To the chief Musician °upon Nehiloth.

5

°A Psalm of David.

F L (p. 725) 1 °Give ear to my words, O °LORD,
°Consider my °meditation.
2 °Hearken unto the °voice of °my cry, my King, and my °God:
For unto Thee will I pray.
3 My voice shalt Thou hear in the morning, O [1]LORD;
In the morning will I °direct *my prayer* unto Thee, and will °look up.

8 Salvation=deliverance, same word as "help", *v.* 2.
Thy blessing is=Thy blessing hast been, and wilt be: i.e. whatever may happen to me. In this spirit he sends back the Ark (2 Sam. 15. 25).
Selah. Connecting Ps. 3 with Ps. 4, which has the same subject. See Ap. 66. II.
To the chief Musician. See Ap. 64.
Neginoth=smitings; from *nāgan*, to strike, as on strings. See Ap. 65. xv. Here the reference is to the smitings with words in Ps. 3, as in Lam. 3. 63 (cp. Job 30. 9. Lam. 3. 14). Cp. the other *Neginoth* Psalms: 3. 2; 5. 6; 53. 1; 54. 3; 60. 1, 11, 12; 66. 10-12; 75. 4-6 (cp. 77. 7, Isa. 38. 20, and Hab. 3. 19).

4 (**G**, p. 721). PRAYER IN VIEW OF PSALM **2** (EVENING). (*Introversion and Alternation.*)

G | J | 1. Prayer to Jehovah.
  K | f | 2-. The sons of men. (David.)
    g | -2. The sons of men. (Themselves.)
  K | *f* | 3. The sons of men. (David.)
    g | 4, 5. The sons of men. (Themselves.)
J | 6-8. Prayer to Jehovah.

Title. A Psalm. See Ap. 65. xvii.
1 Hear=Answer.
God. Heb. Elohim. Ap. 4. I.
God of my righteousness = My righteous God. Genitive of relation or object.
Have mercy=be gracious, or show favour to.
2 men. Heb. *'ish.* Ap. 14. II.
how long=until when. Ellipsis correctly supplied.
leasing = falsehood. Anglo-Saxon = *leasung*; Mid. Eng. = *lesing.*
Selah. Connecting and contrasting his enemies' acts with his own sure defence. See Ap. 66. ii.
3 the LORD. Heb. Jehovah. Ap. 4. II.
set apart. All depended on Jehovah's favour (Num. 14. 8). Some codices, with Sept. and Vulg., read "hath given distinction to".
him that is godly: i.e. a subject of grace.
4 Stand in awe, &c.=Stand in awe and [so] sin not.
sin. Heb. *chāṭā'.* Ap. 44. i. **still**=silent.
Selah. Connecting their sin with its being put away. See Ap. 66. ii.
5 Offer the sacrifices. No Art. Heb. *zabaḥ.* Ap. 43. I. iv.
sacrifices of righteousness = righteous sacrifices. Genitive of Character. How could they offer these while in rebellion against the Lord's Anointed?
trust=confide. Heb. *bataḥ.* See Ap. 69. i.
6 that say . . . good. See note on 144. 12-15.
lift Thou up. No priest with David to give the blessing of Num. 6. 24-26. See 2 Sam. 15. 32-37.
countenance. Fig. *Anthropopatheia.* Ap. 6.
7 gladness. This was true "good".
their corn. See note on Ps. 144. 15.
wine=new wine. Heb. *tīrōsh.* Ap. 27. II.
8 and sleep=sleep at once. This reference is to 2 Sam. 17. 2. See note there.
makest=wilt make. **safety**=confidence.

To the chief Musician. See Ap. 64. **upon Nehiloth**; better, *nᵉḥālōth* = concerning inheritances. Referring to Jehovah's favour as being the true inheritance of godly Israelites, as shown in *vv.* 3, 6, 7. Cp. Ps. 144. 12-15, the other *Nᵉḥālōth* Psalm. See Ap. 65. xvi.

5 (*F*, p. 721). PRAYER IN VIEW OF PSALM **2** (MORNING). (*Repeated Alternation.*)

F | L | 1-3. Prayer to Jehovah.
  M | 4. "For": Reason. Character of Jehovah.
    N | 5, 6. The lawless and their wickedness.
      O | 7. "But": The true worshippers. (*Shemīnīth.*)
L | 8. Prayer to Jehovah.
  M | 9. "For": Reason. Character of the wicked.
    N | 10. The wicked and their judgment.
      O | 11, 12. "But": The true worshippers. (*Shemīnīth.*)

Title. A Psalm. See Ap. 65. XVII. **1 Give ear . . . Consider . . . 2 Hearken.** Fig. *Synonymia.* Ap. 6. **LORD.** Heb. Jehovah. Ap. 4. II. **meditation.** Connecting this Psalm with 1. 2; 2. 1. **2 voice.** The voice marks the tone of any cry. First occurrence here. **my cry.** Connecting this Psalm with 3. 4. **God.** Heb. Elohim. Ap. 4. I. **3 direct**=set in order (as the wood on the altar). Cp. Gen. 22. 9. Ex. 40. 4, 23. **look up**=look out, or watch for [an answer].

M (p. 725) 4 For Thou *art* not a °GOD That hath pleasure in °wickedness:
Neither shall °evil dwell with Thee.

N 5 The °foolish shall not stand in Thy sight:
Thou hatest all workers of °iniquity.
6 Thou shalt destroy them that speak °leasing:
[1]The LORD will abhor the bloody and deceitful °man.

O 7 But °as for me, I will come *into* Thy house in the °multitude of Thy °mercy:
And in Thy fear will I worship toward Thy °holy °temple.

L 8 Lead me, O [1]LORD, in Thy righteousness because of mine enemies;
Make °Thy way straight before my face.

M 9 For *there is* no °faithfulness in °their mouth;
°Their inward part *is* very wickedness;
°Their throat *is* an open sepulchre;
°They flatter with their °tongue.

N 10 °Destroy Thou them, O [2]God;
Let them fall °by their own counsels;
Cast them out in the multitude of their °transgressions;
For they have rebelled against Thee.

O 11 But let all those that °put their trust in Thee rejoice:
Let them ever shout for joy, because Thou °defendest them:
Let them also that love °Thy name be joyful in Thee.
12 For Thou, [1]LORD, wilt °bless the righteous;
With °favour wilt Thou compass him °as *with* °a shield.

°To the chief Musician °on Neginoth °upon Shemînîth.

6

°A Psalm of David.

G P (p. 721) 1 O °LORD, rebuke me not in Thine anger,
Neither chasten me in Thy hot displeasure.
2 °Have mercy upon me, O [1]LORD; for I *am* weak:
O [1]LORD, heal me; for my bones are vexed.
3 °My soul is also °sore vexed:
But Thou, O [1]LORD, °how long?
4 Return, O [1]LORD, deliver [3]my soul:
Oh save me for Thy °mercies' sake.
5 For in death *there is* °no remembrance of Thee:
In °the grave who shall give Thee thanks?

Q 6 I am weary with my groaning;
R All the night make I my bed to swim;
R I water my couch with my tears.

Q 7 Mine eye is °consumed because of grief;
It waxeth old because of all mine °enemies.

P 8 °Depart from me, all ye workers of °iniquity;
For [1]the LORD hath °heard the voice of my weeping.
9 [1]The LORD hath °heard my supplication;
[1]The LORD will °receive my prayer.
10 Let all mine enemies be ashamed and sore vexed:
Let them return *and* be ashamed suddenly.

---

4 GOD. Heb. El. Ap. 4. IV. First occ. in Psalms.
wickedness=lawlessness. Heb. *rāshā'*. Ap. 44. x.
evil. Heb. *ra'a'*. Ap. 44. viii.
5 foolish=boasters.
iniquity. Heb. *'āven*. Ap. 44. iii.
6 leasing=falsehood. See note on 4. 2.
man. Heb. *'ish*. Ap. 14. II.
7 as for me. Cp. 17. 15; 26. 11; 35. 13; 41. 12; 55. 16; 69. 13; 73. 2.
multitude=abundance.
mercy=lovingkindness, or grace.
holy. See note on Ex. 3. 5.
temple. Heb. *hēykāl* = palace: i. e. heaven itself, which was the pattern for the earthly "house" or tent, as being the dwelling-place of Jehovah. Hence it is used of the Tabernacle (1 Sam. 1. 9; 3. 3). Cp. Pss. 11. 4; 18. 6.
8 Thy way: not mine.
9 faithfulness=steadfastness, or stability.
their=his. Referring to the man of *v.* 6.
Their. Three times repeated; refers to the "foolish" and "workers" of *v.* 5.
tongue. Put by Fig. *Metonymy* (of Cause), Ap. 6, for what is spoken by it.
10 Destroy Thou them=Deal with them as guilty.
by their own counsels. Answered in Ahithophel (2 Sam. 15. 31; 17. 14, 23). A prayer suited for the dispensation in which David lived. See Ap. 63. IX.
transgressions. Heb. *pāsha'*. Ap. 44. ix.
11 put their trust=flee for refuge to. Heb. *ḥāsāh*. See Ap. 69. ii.
defendest=coverest.
Thy name=Thee Thyself. "Name" put by Fig. *Metonymy* (of Adjunct), Ap. 6, for the person and character: i. e. all that the name implies and includes.
12 bless the righteous=bless the justified one. Cp. Pss. 1. 1; 2. 12; 3. 8.
favour. This is the "shield". In His favour is "life" (30. 5); "preservation" (86. 2, marg.); "security" (41. 11); "mercy" (Isa. 60. 10). Hence the prayer of 106. 4.
as. Fig. *Simile*. Ap. 6.
a shield. Heb. *zinnah*, a shield of the largest size. See 1 Sam. 17. 7, 41. Only here, 35. 2 (buckler), and 91. 4 in the Psalms. In other Psalms it is *māgēn*, smaller both in size and weight (cp. 1 Kings 10. 17. 2 Chron. 9. 16). The shield is the "favour" of Jehovah mentioned above.
To the chief Musician. See Ap. 64.
on Neginoth. See sub-scription to Ps. 3 above, and Ap. 65. xv.
upon Shemînîth=relating to the class so called: viz. true worshippers (*v.* 7), circumcised on the eighth day="the righteous" of *v.* 12. Cp. the other Shemînîth Psalm (Ps. 11). See Ap. 65. xix.

6 (*G*, p. 721). PRAYER IN VIEW OF PSALM 2 (NIGHT). (*Introversion.*)

G | P | 1-5. Prayer offered.
  Q | 6-. Exhaustion.
    R | -6-. Tears.
    R | -6. Tears.
  Q | 7. Exhaustion.
P | 8-10. Prayer answered.

Title. A Psalm. See Ap. 65. XVII.
1 LORD. Heb. Jehovah. Ap. 4. II.
2 Have mercy=Be gracious, or show favour to.
3 My soul=I. Heb. *nephesh*. Ap. 13.
sore vexed=troubled. Same as John 12. 27. Cp. 42. 5, 6.
how long?=until when? Fig. *Erotēsis*; and, before and after these words, the Fig. *Aposiopēsis*. Ap. 6.
4 mercies'=mercy's. Heb. lovingkindness.
5 no remembrance. See 30. 9; 88. 10-12; 115. 17; 118. 17. Isa. 38. 18, 19. Ecc. 9. 10.
the grave. Heb. Sheōl. Ap. 35.
7 consumed=wasted.
enemies=adversaries.
8 Depart, &c. Fig. *Apostrophe*. Ap. 6.
iniquity. Heb. *'āven*. Ap. 44. iii.
heard . . . 9 receive. Fig. *Synonymia*. Ap. 6.

964 B. C.

7 °Shiggaion of David, which he sang unto the LORD, concerning the °words of °Cush °the °Benjamite.

D S (p. 727) 1 O °LORD my °God, in Thee °do I °put my trust:

T Save me from all them that °persecute me, and deliver me:

U 2 Lest °he °tear °my soul like a lion, Rending *it* in pieces, °while *there is* none to deliver.

V 3 O [1]LORD my [1]God, if I have done this; If there be °iniquity °in my hands;
4 If I have rewarded °evil unto him that was at peace with me;

V (Yea, I have °delivered him that without cause is mine °enemy:)

U 5 Let the °enemy °persecute [2]my soul, and °take °*it;* Yea, let him °tread down my life upon the earth, And lay mine honour in the dust. °Selah.

T 6 Arise, O [1]LORD, in Thine anger, Lift up Thyself because of the rage of mine [4]enemies: And awake for me *to* the judgment *that* Thou hast commanded.
7 So shall the congregation of the °people °compass Thee about: For their sakes therefore return Thou on high.
8 [1]The LORD shall judge the [7]people: Judge me, O [1]LORD, according to my righteousness, and according to mine integrity *that is* in me.
9 Oh let the °wickedness of the °wicked come to an end; but establish the just: For the righteous [1]God trieth the hearts and reins.

S 10 My °defence *is* of [1]God, Which saveth the °upright in heart.
11 [1]God judgeth the °righteous, And °GOD is angry *with the wicked* every day.
12 If he turn not, °He will whet °His sword; He hath bent His °bow, and made it ready.
13 He hath also prepared for him the instruments of death; He °ordaineth His arrows against the persecutors.
14 °Behold, he °travaileth with °iniquity, And hath °conceived °mischief, and °brought forth falsehood.
15 He made a pit, and digged it, And is fallen into the ditch *which* he made.
16 His [14]mischief shall return upon his own head, And his violent dealing shall come down upon his own °pate.
17 I will praise [1]the LORD according to His righteousness: And will sing praise to the name of [1]the LORD °MOST HIGH.

To the chief Musician °upon Gittith.

8 A Psalm of David.

E W (p. 728) 1 O °LORD our °LORD, How excellent *is* °Thy name in all °the earth!

7 (*D*, p. 721). MAN BLESSED. TRUST IN JEHOVAH. (*Introversion.*)

D S | 1-. Trust in Jehovah for defence.
T | -1. Prayer for deliverance.
U | 2. The evil to be delivered from.
V | 3, 4-. Demerit.
V | -4. Merit.
U | 5. The evil to be delivered from.
T | 6-9. Prayer for deliverance.
S | 10-17. Trust in Jehovah for defence.

Title. Shiggaion = a loud cry in danger or joy, from *shā'ag*, always rendered "roar". Occurs twenty-one times. Both meanings are seen in this Psalm, and Hab. 3. 1 (pl. "set to" = concerning), the only two occurrences. See Ap. 65. XX.
words = matters, or business.
Cush. Who it was is not known: an evidence of genuineness. **the** = a.
Benjamite. Hence probably an adherent or servant of Saul, and therefore long before Shimei and Absalom.
1 LORD. Heb. Jehovah. Ap. 4. II.
God. Heb. Elohim. Ap. 4. I. **do I** = have I.
put my trust = flee for refuge. Heb. *ḥāṣāh*. See Ap. 69. ii.
persecute = pursue me. Refers probably to Saul.
2 he: i. e. Cush.
tear. Heb. *ṭaraph.* Refers to *living* prey.
my soul = me. Heb. *nephesh.* Ap. 13.
while there is none to deliver. Sept., Syr., and Vulg. read "and there be no deliverer to rescue". Better, no sign of a rescuer. Cp. Lam. 5. 8.
3 iniquity. Heb. *'āval.* Ap. 44. vi, not the same as *v.* 14.
in my hands. Hands put by Fig. *Metonymy* (of Cause), Ap. 6, for what is done by them.
4 evil. Heb. *rā'a'.* Ap. 44. viii.
delivered = rescued. Aram. and Syr. read "oppressed".
enemy = adversary. Heb. *ẓārar.*
5 enemy = foe. Heb. *'oyeb.*
persecute . . . take . . . tread. Fig. *Anabasis.* Ap. 6.
it = me.
Selah. Connecting the treading down of *v.* 5 with the rising up of Jehovah. See Ap. 66. II.
7 people = peoples.
compass Thee about = gather round Thee: i. e. to hear Thy judgment.
9 wickedness . . . wicked = lawlessness . . . lawless. Heb. *rāshā'.* Ap. 44. x.
10 defence = shield. See note on "shield", 6. 12.
upright. Plural. **11 righteous.** Plural.
GOD. Heb. El. Ap. 4. IV. **12 He**: i. e. God.
His sword . . . bow. Fig. *Anthropopatheia.* Ap. 6.
13 ordaineth = will ordain.
14 Behold. Fig. *Asterismos.* Ap. 6.
travaileth . . . conceived . . . brought forth. Fig. *Anabasis.* Ap. 6. **travaileth** = will travail.
iniquity. Heb. *'āven.* Ap. 44. iii, not same word as *v.* 3.
mischief. Heb. *'āmal.* Ap. 44. v.
16 pate = head; especially the smooth skull. Put by Fig. *Synecdoche* (of Part), Ap. 6, for the whole person, for emphasis. From "plate" = the smooth top of the head (Skeat).
17 MOST HIGH. Heb. *Elyōn.* See Ap. 4. VI. First occurrence in Psalms. The first of thirty-six occurrences in O.T. is Gen. 14. 18.
To the chief Musician. See Ap. 64.
upon Gittith = relating to the Feast of Tabernacles (for which it was suited), because it commemorated safe dwelling after deliverance. See Ap. 65.

8 (*E*, p. 721). [For Structure see next page].

Title. A Psalm. See Ap. 65. xvii.
1 LORD. Heb. Jehovah. Ap. 4. II.
LORD. Heb. *Adonim.* Ap. 4. VIII (3).
Thy name: i. e. Jehovah Himself; "name" being put by Fig. *Metonymy* (of Adjunct), Ap. 6, for His character, person, and attributes. See 20. 1. Cp. 5. 11.
the earth: i. e. the great subject of this Psalm. See note on *vv.* 4, 6.

X h (p. 728) Who hast set Thy °glory above the heavens.

j **2 °Out of the mouth of °babes and sucklings hast Thou °ordained °strength**
Because of Thine °enemies,
That Thou mightest still the °enemy and the °avenger.

X h 3 When I consider Thy heavens, the °work of Thy °fingers,
The moon and the stars, which Thou hast [2]ordained;

j **4 °What is °man, that Thou art °mindful of him?**
And °the son of °man, that Thou °visitest him?
5 For Thou hast made him a little lower than °the angels,
And hast °crowned him with glory and honour.
6 Thou madest °him to have °dominion over the °works of Thy °hands;
Thou °hast put °all *things* under his feet:
7 All sheep and oxen,
Yea, and the beasts of the field;
8 The fowl of the air, and the fish of the sea,
And whatsoever passeth through the paths of the seas.

W 9 O [1]LORD our [1]LORD,
How excellent *is* Thy name in all [1]the earth!

°To the chief Musician °upon Muth-labben.

9

°A Psalm of David.

A² H¹ Y (p. 728) 1 (א) °I will praise *Thee*, O °LORD, with my whole heart;
I will shew forth all Thy marvellous works.
2 (א) I will be glad and rejoice in Thee:
I will sing praise to Thy name, O Thou °MOST HIGH.

Z A 3 (ב) When mine enemies are turned back,
They shall fall and perish °at Thy presence.

8 (*E*, p. 721). REBELLIOUS MAN. SUBDUED.

E | W | 1-. Greatness of Jehovah in the earth.
X | h | -1. Glory of Jehovah in the heavens.
j | 2. His condescension to man.
X | *h* | 3. Glory of Jehovah in the heavens.
j | 4-8. His condescension to man.
W | 9. Greatness of Jehovah in the earth.

glory = majesty, or excellence.

2 Out of, &c. Quoted in Matt. 21. 16.

babes. Referring to his own youth. A still more definite reference to 1 Sam. 17. 14, 33, 42, 55, 56.

ordained = appointed. Heb. *yāṣad.*

strength. Put by Fig. *Metonymy* (of Subject) for the praise due for what is put forth by it.

enemies = adversaries. enemy = foe.

avenger = the revenger.

3 work. The Western *Massorites* (Ap. 30), with Sept. and Vulg., read "works" (pl.).

fingers. Fig. *Anthropopatheia.* Ap. 6.

ordained = established. Heb. *kūn.*

4 What . . . ? Fig. *Erotēsis.* Ap. 6. Quoted in Heb. 2. 5-8. Cp. 1 Cor. 15. 27 and Eph. 1. 22.

man = mortal man. Heb. *'ěnōsh.* Ap. 14. III.

mindful . . . visitest. Fig. *Anabasis.* Ap. 6.

the son of man. No Art. Occurs 3 times before this (Num. 23. 19. Job 25. 6; 35. 8). In sing. 111 times in O.T. and 39 times in pl. (the other occurrences in the Pss. (49. 2; 144. 3) is a different word). Here (8. 4) the title *relates* to *dominion in the earth.* Cp. *vv.* 1, 6-9, and see notes on Ezek. 2. 1, Mat. 8. 20, and Rev. 14. 4.

man. Heb. *'ādām.* Ap. 14. I.

5 the angels. Heb. Elohim. See Ap. 4. I. Rendered "angels" in Heb. 2. 7; also here, in Sept., Vulg., Syr., and Arab. See also Ps. 97. 7. Heb. 1. 6.

crowned, &c. This refers to "the second man". See notes on Heb. 2. 8, and 2 Pet. 1. 17.

6 him: i. e. the "first man", Adam (Gen. 1. 26).

dominion, &c. This he lost in the Fall.

works. Some codices, with three early printed editions and Syr., read "work" (sing.).

hands. Fig. *Anthropopatheia.* Ap. 6.

hast = didst. See Gen. 1. 26.

all things. Six are enumerated in *vv.* 7 and 8. (The number of man. See Ap. 10.)

To the chief Musician. See Ap. 64.

upon Muth-labben = relating to the death of the champion (Goliath). Cp. 1 Sam. 17. 4, 46, &c., and 144, which has, in the Sept., the title "A Psalm of David concerning Goliath".

9—15 (**A²**, p. 721). "THE MAN OF THE EARTH". (*Division.*)

A² | H¹ | 9. The Lawless one. (General.)
H² | 10. The Lawless one. (Particular.)

9 (**H¹**, above). THE LAWLESS ONE. (GENERAL.)

H¹ | Y | 1, 2. Thanksgiving.
Z | 3-10. Excision of the wicked.
Y | 11. Thanksgiving.
Z | 12-20. Excision of the wicked.

Psalms 9 and 10 are linked together by an irregular Acrostic (see notes on pp. 721, 722, and Ap. 63. VII), beginning at 9. 1 and ending with 10. 18. Seven letters are omitted. The Acrostic is irregular, corresponding with the "times of trouble". The notes will show how one subject pervades them (see **H**, p. 721). Cp. "the lawless one" (9. 5, 16 and 10. 2, 4, 13, 15); "times of trouble" (9. 9 and 10. 1); "the oppressed" (Heb. *dāk*, crushed, 9. 9 and 10. 18; occurs only here and 74. 21); "mortal men" (9. 19, 20 and 10. 18); "forget" (9. 12, 17, 18 and 10. 11, 12); "humble" (9. 12, 18, and 10. 12, 17); "not alway" (9. 18, and "never", 10. 11); "for ever and ever" (9. 5 and 10. 16); "arise, Jehovah" (9. 19 and 10. 12).

Title. A Psalm. See Ap. 65. XVII. **1** I will = Let me. LORD. Heb. Jehovah. Ap. 4. II.

2 MOST HIGH. Heb. *Elyōn.* Ap. 4. VI.

9. 3-10 (Z, above). EXCISION OF THE WICKED. (*Alternations and Introversion.*)

Z | A | 3. The wicked. Excision.
B | k | 4-. Deliverance.
l | -4, 5. Judgment.
A | 6. The wicked. Apostrophe.
B | *l* | 7, 8. Judgment.
k | 9, 10. Deliverance.

3 at Thy presence = from before Thee.

B k (p. 728) 4 For Thou hast maintained my right and my cause;
l Thou °satest in the throne judging °right.
5 (ג) Thou hast rebuked the °heathen, Thou hast destroyed °the wicked,
Thou hast °put out their name °for ever and ever.
A 6 (ה) O °thou enemy, °destructions are come to °a perpetual end:
And thou hast destroyed cities;
Their memorial is perished with them.
l 7 (ו) But [1]the LORD shall °endure for ever:
He hath prepared His throne for judgment.
8 (ו) And °He **shall judge °the world in righteousness,**
He shall minister judgment to the °people in uprightness.
k 9 (ו) [1]The LORD also will be a refuge for °the oppressed,
A [1]refuge in °times of trouble.
10 (ו) And they that know °Thy name will °put their trust in Thee:
For Thou, [1]LORD, hast not forsaken them that seek Thee.
Y 11 (ז) Sing praises to [1]the LORD, Which dwelleth in °Zion:
Declare among the [8]people His doings.
Z C m (p. 729) 12 When He °maketh inquisition for blood,
He remembereth °them:
He °forgetteth not the °cry of the °humble.
n 13 (ח) °Have mercy upon me, O [1]LORD;
Consider my trouble *which I suffer* of them that hate me,
Thou That liftest me up from the gates of death:
o 14 That I may shew forth all Thy °praise
In the gates of the daughter of [11]Zion:
°I will rejoice in Thy salvation.
D 15 (ט) The [5]heathen are sunk down in the pit *that* they made:
In the net which they hid is their own foot taken.
E 16 [1]The LORD is known *by* the judgment *which* He executeth:
[5]The wicked is snared in the work of his own hands. °Higgaion. °Selah.
E 17 (י) The °wicked shall be °turned into °hell,
D *And* all the nations that [12]forget °God.
C m 18 (כ) For °the needy shall not alway be [12]forgotten:
The expectation of the °poor shall °*not* perish for ever.
n 19 Arise, O [1]LORD; let not °man prevail:
Let the heathen be judged °in Thy sight.
20 °Put them in fear, O [1]LORD:
o *That* the °nations may know themselves *to be but* [19]men. °Selah.

H[2] F (p. 729) 10 (ל) °Why standest Thou afar off, O °LORD?
°*Why* hidest Thou *Thyself* in °times of trouble?
G I 2 °The wicked in *his* pride doth °persecute °the poor:
Let them be taken in the devices that they have imagined.

4 satest = hast sat. **right** = righteously.
5 heathen = nations.
the wicked = a lawless one: i. e. the Antichrist. Cp. 10. 3, 13, 14, 15. Heb. *rāshā'*. Ap. 44. x.
put out = blotted out. **for ever, &c.** Cp. 10. 16.
6 thou enemy. Same as the lawless one of *v.* 5.
destructions are come = complete is the destruction.
a perpetual end = for evermore. Some codices, with two early printed editions, Sept., Syr., and Vulg., read "swords are abandoned".
7 endure = sit as king.
8 He, &c. Quoted in Acts 17. 31.
the world = the habitable world. Heb. *tēbēl*. First occurrence in Psalms; never found with the Art.
people = peoples.
9 the oppressed = the crushed one. Cp. 10. 18.
times of trouble = the great time of trouble: i. e. the tribulation of Matt. 24, Jer. 30, &c. Cp. 10. 1.
10 Thy name. See note on 5. 11.
put their trust = confide. Heb. *bāṭaḥ*. See Ap. 69. I.
11 Zion. See Ap. 68.

12-20 (*Z*, p. 728). EXCISION OF THE LAWLESS.
(*Introversion and Extended Alternations.*)

Z | C | m | 12. Remembrance of oppressed.
  n | 13. Prayer.
  o | 14. Effect of the prayer.
 D | 15. The nations.
  E | 16. The wicked.
  E | 17-. The wicked.
 D | -17. The nations.
C | *m* | 18. Remembrance of oppressed.
  n | 19, 20-. Prayer.
  o | -20. Effect of the prayer.

12 maketh inquisition for = inquireth concerning.
them: i. e. those named in *v.* 10.
forgetteth not. Cp. *vv.* 17, 18 and 10. 11, 12.
cry = outcry.
humble = oppressed. Cp. *v.* 18 and 10. 12, 17.
13 Have mercy = Be gracious, or favourable to.
14 praise. So some codices, with four early printed editions (one in margin). Other codices read "praises".
I will = that I may.
16 Higgaion = soliloquy, or meditation. See Ap. 66. I.
Selah. Connecting the wicked one (sing.) of *v.* 16 with the wicked ones (pl.) of *v.* 17. See Ap. 66. II.
17 wicked = wicked ones (pl.). Heb. *rāshā'*. Ap. 44. x.
turned = returned. Cp. Job 21. 26; 34. 15. Ps. 104. 29. Ecc. 3. 20; 12. 7.
hell = the grave. Heb. Sheol. Ap. 35.
God. Heb. Elohim. Ap. 4. I.
18 the needy = a needy one.
poor = oppressed. Cp. *v.* 12.
not. Ellipsis of second negative. See note on Gen. 2. 6.
19 man. Heb. *'ĕnōsh*. Ap. 14. III.
in Thy sight = before Thee: i. e. at Thy coming.
20 Put them in fear = Appoint them some terror.
nations. As in *v.* 5, "heathen".
Selah. Connecting Ps. 9, concerning "men" generally, with Ps. 10, "the man of the earth". See **H**, p. 728, and Ap. 66. II.

10 (**H**[2], p. 728). THE MAN OF THE EARTH. (PARTICULAR.) (*Introversion and Alternations.*)

H[2] | F | 1. Appeal to Jehovah.
 G | I | 2-5. The lawless one. His acts.
  J | 6. His thoughts (concerning himself.)
 G | *I* | 7-10. The lawless one. His acts.
  J | 11. His thoughts (concerning God.)
F | 12-18. Appeal to Jehovah.

1 Why . . . ? Fig. *Erotēsis*. Ap. 6.
LORD. Heb. Jehovah. Ap. 4. II.
times of trouble = the great time of tribulation. Cp. 9. 9.
2 The wicked = a lawless one. Heb. *rāshā'*. Ap. 44. x. Cp. *vv.* 4, 13, 15, and 9. 5, 16.
persecute = hotly pursue.
the poor = an oppressed one. Cp. *v.* 18, and 9. 9. Heb. *'ānī*. See note on Prov. 6. 11.

3 For [2]the wicked boasteth of his °heart's desire,
And °blesseth the covetous, *whom* [1]the LORD abhorreth.
4 The [2]wicked, through the pride of his countenance, will not seek *after God:*
°God *is* not in all his thoughts.
5 His ways are always grievous;
Thy judgments *are* far above out of his °sight:
As for all his °enemies, he °puffeth at them.
J (p. 729) 6 He hath °said in his heart, "I shall not be moved:
For *I shall* never *be* in adversity."
G I p (p. 730) 7 °**His mouth is full of cursing and deceit and fraud:**
Under his tongue *is* mischief and vanity.
q 8 He sitteth in the lurking places of the villages:
In the secret places doth he murder the innocent:
p His eyes are privily set against °the poor.
q 9 He lieth in wait secretly as a lion in his den:
He lieth in wait to catch [2]the poor:
He doth catch [2]the poor, when he draweth him into his net.
10 He croucheth, *and* humbleth himself,
That [8]the poor may fall by his strong ones.
J 11 He hath [6]said in his heart, °"GOD hath °forgotten:
(p. 729) He hideth his face; He will °never see *it.*"
F 12 (ק) °Arise, O [1]LORD; O [11]GOD, lift up Thine hand:
Forget not °the humble.
13 °Wherefore doth [2]the wicked contemn [4]God?
He hath said in his heart, "Thou wilt not °require *it.*"
14 (ר) °Thou hast seen *it;* for Thou beholdest mischief and spite, to requite *it* with Thy hand:
[8]The poor committeth himself unto Thee;
Thou art the helper of the fatherless.
15 (ש) Break Thou the arm of [2]the wicked and [2]the evil *man:*
Seek out his [2]wickedness *till* Thou find none.
16 °**The [1]LORD is King °for ever and ever:**
The °heathen are perished out of His land.
17 (ת) [1]LORD, Thou hast °heard the desire of the [12]humble:
Thou wilt °prepare their heart, Thou wilt °cause Thine °ear to hear:
18 To judge the fatherless and the °oppressed,
That °the man of the earth may no more oppress.

°To the chief Musician.

11

°*A Psalm* of David.

K L (p. 730) 1 In °the LORD °put I my trust:
How say ye to °my soul,
"Flee °*as* a bird to your mountain?"
M 2 For, lo, °the wicked bend *their* bow,
They make ready their arrow upon the string,
That they may °privily shoot at °the upright in heart.
N 3 If °the foundations be destroyed,
What can °the righteous °do?
O 4 [1]The LORD *is* in His holy temple,
[1]The LORD'S throne *is* in heaven:
O His °eyes behold, His °eyelids try, the °children of °men.

---

3 heart's = soul's. Heb. *nephesh.* Ap. 13.
blesseth, &c. One of the emendations of the *Sopherim* (see Ap. 33). The primitive text of this line read, "the covetous man (or robber) blasphemeth, yea, abhorreth Jehovah". Cp. 1 Kings 21. 10, 13. Job 1. 5, 11; 2. 5, 9.
4 God. Heb. Elohim. Ap. 4. I: i.e. "no sign of God in all his thoughts".
5 sight = ken. **enemies** = adversaries.
puffeth at = despiseth.
6 said in his heart. Cp. *v.* 11.

10. 7-10 (*I*, p. 729). THE LAWLESS ONE. ACTS. (*Alternation.*)

I | p | 7. His mouth and tongue.
  q | 8-. Comparison to beast of prey.
 p | -8. His eyes.
  q | 9, 10. Comparison to beast of prey.

7 His mouth, &c. Quoted in Rom. 3. 14.
8 the poor = a weak one. Heb. *hēlkāh.*
11 GOD. Heb. El. Ap. 4. IV.
forgotten. Cp. *v.* 12, and 9. 12, 17, 18.
never see it. Cp. *v.* 14 and 9. 18.
12 Arise. Cp. 9. 19.
the humble = the humble ones. Cp. *v.* 17, and 9. 12, 18.
13 Wherefore . . . ? Fig. *Erotēsis.* Ap. 6.
require it = investigate.
14 Thou hast seen. Cp. *v.* 11.
15 the evil = an evil one. Heb. *rā'a'.* Ap. 44. viii.
16 The LORD, &c. Quoted in Rev. 11. 15.
for ever and ever. Cp. 9. 5.
heathen = nations. Cp. 9. 5, 15.
17 heard . . prepare . . cause. Fig. *Anabasis.* Ap. 6.
prepare = establish.
ear. Fig. *Anthropopatheia.* Ap. 6.
18 oppressed. Cp. 9. 9.
the man. Heb. *'ĕnōsh.* Ap. 14. III.
the man of the earth. Spoken of above as the "lawless one". **To the chief Musician.** See Ap. 64.

11 (**K**, p. 721). PRAYER IN VIEW OF PSALMS **9** and **10**. (*Introversion.*)

K | L | 1. Trust in Jehovah. Defender of the righteous.
 M | 2. The lawless. Violence manifested.
  N | 3. The righteous. Tried.
   O | 4-. Jehovah's temple and throne in heaven.
   O | -4. Jehovah's eyes and eyelids on earth.
  N | 5-. The righteous. Tried.
 M | -5, 6. The lawless. Violence revenged.
 L | 7. Trust in Jehovah. Lover of the righteous.

Title. A Psalm. See Ap. 65. XVII.
1 the LORD. Heb. Jehovah. Ap. 4. II.
put I my trust = I have fled for refuge. Heb. *ḥaṣah.* See Ap. 69. II.
my soul = me (for emphasis). Heb. *nephesh.* Ap. 13.
as. The Aram., Sept., Syr., and Vulg. read this "as" (or "like") in the text.
2 the wicked = the lawless ones. Heb. *rāshā'.* Ap. 44. x. **privily** = in the darkness.
the upright = upright ones.
3 the foundations: *hashshāthōth* = settled order of truth or institutions; not the roof or walls. **the** = a.
do. Not say or think, but lawfully and effectually "do".
4 eyes . . . eyelids. Fig. *Anthropopatheia.* Ap. 6.
children = sons.
men. Heb. *'ādām.* Ap. 14. I.

N (p. 730) 5 [1]The LORD trieth °the righteous:
M But the [2]wicked and him that loveth violence °His soul hateth.
6 Upon the [2]wicked He shall rain snares,
Fire and brimstone, and an horrible °tempest: *this shall be* the portion of their cup.
L 7 For the righteous [1]LORD loveth righteousness;
°His countenance °doth behold °the upright.

°To the chief Musician °upon Sheminith.

12

°A Psalm of David.

L P (p. 731) 1 °Help, °LORD; for the °godly man °ceaseth;
For the °faithful fail from among the °children of men.
Q r 2 °They speak vanity every one with his neighbour:
With flattering lips *and* with a °double heart do they speak.
s 3 [1]The LORD shall cut off all flattering lips, *and*
°The tongue that speaketh proud things:
4 Who have said, °"With our tongue will we prevail;
Our lips *are* our own: who *is* lord over us?"
R 5 "For the oppression of the °poor, for the sighing of the needy,
Now will I arise," °saith [1]the LORD;
R "I will set *him* in safety °*from him that* puffeth at °him."
Q r 6 The °words of [1]the LORD *are* pure °words:
As °silver tried in a °furnace °of °earth,
°Purified seven times.
s 7 Thou shalt keep °them, O [1]LORD,
Thou shalt preserve °them from this generation for ever.
P 8 The °wicked walk on every side,
When the vilest °men are exalted.

°To the chief Musician.

13

°A Psalm of David.

K S[1] t (p. 731) 1 °How long wilt Thou °forget me, O °LORD? for ever?
How long wilt Thou hide Thy °face from me?
2 How long shall I take counsel in °my soul,
Having sorrow in my heart daily?
u How long shall mine enemy be exalted over me?
t 3 Consider *and* °hear me, O [1]LORD my °God:
°Lighten mine eyes, lest I °sleep the *sleep of* death;
u 4 Lest mine enemy say, "I have prevailed against him;"
And those that trouble me rejoice when I am moved.

5 the righteous = a righteous one.
His soul = He (emphatic). Heb. *nephesh.* Ap. 13. Fig. *Anthropopatheia.* Ap. 6.
6 tempest = blast. Heb. *rūach.* Ap. 9.
7 His countenance doth behold the upright = An upright one shall gaze upon His face. One of the emendations of the *Sōpherim.* See Ap. 33, and note on Ex. 34. 20. **To the chief Musician.** See Ap. 64.
upon Sheminith = the *Sheminīth.* See Ap. 65. XIX.

12 (L, p. 721). THE VANITY OF MAN.
(Introversion and Alternation.)

L | P | 1. Decrease of the godly and faithful.
  Q | r | 2. Man's words.
      s | 3, 4. The speakers. "Cut off."
    R | 5-. The oppression of the humble.
    R | -5. Deliverance from the oppression.
  Q | *r* | 6. Jehovah's words.
      s | 7. The hearers. "Preserved."
P | 8. Increase of the lawless and vile.

Title. A Psalm. See Ap. 65. XVII.
1 Help = Save. **LORD.** Heb. Jehovah. Ap. 4. II.
godly man = "gracious [man]".
ceaseth = is no more. Cp. Isa. 57. 1. Mic. 7. 2.
faithful. Fig. *Metonymy* (of Adjunct), Ap. 6, put for faithful men.
children of men = sons of men. (Heb. *'ādām.* Ap. 14. I.)
2 They speak. Man's words contrasted with Jehovah's words. Cp. *v.* 6, and see Structure above.
double = deceitful. Heb. "a heart and a heart". Cp. 1 Chron. 12. 33.
3 The tongue, &c. Quoted in Jas. 3. 5.
4 With our tongue will we prevail = Thanks to our tongue, we will prevail.
5 poor = wretched. Heb. *'ānī.* See note on Prov. 6. 11.
saith the LORD = let Jehovah say.
from him that puffeth at him = let him [the oppressed] despise it [the oppression].
him = it: i.e. the oppression.
6 words = the spoken words, sayings, or utterances. Cp. 119. 38. **silver tried**: i.e. pure silver.
furnace = crucible. Put a full stop after this word.
of = to, or pertaining to (referring to the "words"). The letter lamed (ל = L) is the sign of the Dative case, not the Genitive.
earth. Heb. *'erez* (the earth), not *'ădāmāh* (the ground): i.e. "words for, or pertaining to the earth", but purified seven times: i.e. with spiritual perfection (see Ap. 10). Some are used with a higher meaning; some in a different sense. Verse 6 is an alternation.
Purified. The verb is sing., agreeing with silver. Cp. "u", and "*u*".

r | t | The words of Jehovah are pure words.
  u | As silver tried in a furnace:
t | [Words] pertaining to the earth:
  u | Purified seven times.

7 them: i.e. the godly. Pl. ref. to "the faithful" of *v.* 1.
them = **him**: refers to the man of grace (*v.* 1).
8 wicked = lawless. Heb. *rāshā'.* Ap. 44. x.
men: i.e. the sons of Adam, as in *v.* 1, "P".
To the chief Musician. See Ap. 64.

13 (*K*, p. 721). PRAYER IN VIEW OF PSALMS 9, 10. *(Division.)*

K | S[1] | 1-4. Prayer.
  S[2] | 5, 6. Praise.

1-4 (S[1], above). PRAYER.

S[1] | t | 1, 2-. For himself.
  u | -2. Against the enemy.
t | 3. For himself.
  u | 4. Against the enemy.

Title. A Psalm. See Ap. 65. XVII.

1 How long . . . ? = Until when? Fig. *Erotēsis.* Ap. 6. Four times repeated is the Fig. *Anaphora.* Ap. 6. **forget . . . face.** Fig. *Anthropopatheia.* Ap. 6. See 9. 12, 17, 18, and 10. 11, 12. **LORD.** Heb. Jehovah. Ap. 4. II. **2 my soul** = myself (emph.). Heb. *nephesh.* Ap. 13. **3 hear** = answer. **God.** Heb. Elohim. Ap. 4. I. **Lighten mine eyes** = Revive me. **sleep the sleep of death** = sleep my last sleep. Heb. Fig. *Polyptōton.* Ap. 6.

S² v (p. 732) **5** But I have °trusted in Thy °mercy;
My heart shall rejoice in Thy salvation.
w **6** I will sing unto [1]the LORD,
w Because He hath °dealt bountifully with me.
v °To the chief Musician.

14

A Psalm of David.

L x¹ (p. 732) **1** °The fool hath said in his heart, "*There is* °no °GOD*."
They are corrupt, they have done abominable works,
°*There is* none that °doeth good.

y¹ **2** °The LORD °looked down from heaven upon the °children of °men,
°To see if there were any that did understand,
And seek [1]GOD*.

x² **3** They are °all gone aside, they are *all* together become °filthy:
There is none that doeth good, no, not one.

y² **4** Have all the workers of °iniquity no knowledge?
Who °eat up My People *as* they eat bread,
And call not upon [2]the LORD.

x³ **5** There °were they in great fear:
For [1]GOD* *is* in the °generation of the °righteous.
6 Ye have shamed the counsel of the °poor,
Because [2]the LORD *is* his refuge.

y³ **7** °Oh that the salvation of [7]Israel *were come* out of °Zion!
When [2]the LORD °bringeth back the captivity of His people,
°Jacob shall rejoice, *and* °Israel shall be glad.

15

°A Psalm of David.

H T (p. 732) **1** °LORD, who shall abide in Thy °tabernacle?
Who shall °dwell in Thy °holy hill?

U a **2** He that °walketh °uprightly, and °worketh righteousness,
And °speaketh the °truth in his heart.

b **3** °*He that* backbiteth not with his tongue,
Nor doeth °evil to his °neighbour,
Nor °taketh up a reproach against his neighbour.

U a **4** In whose eyes a vile person is contemned;
But he honoureth them that fear [1]the LORD.

b *He that* sweareth °to *his own* hurt, and changeth not.
5 *He that* putteth not out his money to °usury,
Nor taketh °reward against the innocent.

T He that doeth these *things* shall °never be moved.

---

13. 5, 6 (S², p. 731). PRAISE. (*Introversion.*)

S² | v | 5-. Past.
  w | -5. Future.
  w | 6-. Future.
v | -6. Past.

5 trusted = confided. Heb. *baṭāḥ*. Ap. 69. I.
mercy = lovingkindness, or grace.
6 dealt bountifully with = compensated.
To the chief Musician. See Ap. 64.

14 (*L*, p. 721). THE DEPRAVITY OF MAN. (*Repeated Alternation.*)

L | x¹ | 1. The lawless. Their words.
  y¹ | 2. Jehovah. His inspection.
x² | 3. The lawless. Their deeds.
  y² | 4. Jehovah. His expostulation.
x³ | 5, 6. The lawless. Their feelings.
  y³ | 7. Jehovah. His interposition.

1 The fool: i.e. the impious man. Cp. 10. 4; 53. 1.
no = no sign of a.
GOD*. The primitive text was "Jehovah" (Ap. 4. II), but the *Sōpherīm* say that they altered it to El (Ap. 4. IV). So *vv.* 2 and 5. See Ap. 32.
There is, &c. Quoted in Rom. 3. 10-12 with other scriptures.
doeth good. The Sept. adds "no not one". This completes the Fig. *Epanadiplosis* with *v.* 3 (Ap. 6).
2 The LORD. Heb. Jehovah. Ap. 4. II. Fig. *Epanadiplosis* (Ap. 6). The verse beginning and ending with "Jehovah" (see note on "GOD", *v.* 1). Psalm not for public use: but for David's private use.
looked . . . To see. Fig. *Anthropopatheia*. Ap. 6.
children = sons. **men.** Heb. *'ādām*. Ap. 14. I.
3 all = the whole mass. Cp. "No, not one", Rom. 3. 10-12. **filthy** = corrupt.
4 iniquity. Heb. *'āven*. Ap. 44. iii.
eat up My People. Cp. Jer. 10. 25. Amos 8. 4. Mic. 3. 3.
Between *vv.* 3 and 4 the Sept., Syr., and Vulg. insert four verses; three are retained in P.B.V. Probably an ancient marginal note which found its way into a MS.
5 were they in great fear. Fig. *Polyptōton*. Ap. 6. Heb. they feared a fear.
generation = circle. Heb. *dōr*, company, or class.
righteous = righteous man.
6 poor = an oppressed one. Cp. Pss. 9 and 10.
7 Oh . . .! Fig. *Epiphonēma*. Ap. 6. **Zion.** See Ap. 68.
bringeth back the captivity. Fig. *Paronomasia* (Ap. 6). See note on Deut. 30. 3.
Jacob . . . Israel. On these names, see notes on Gen. 32. 28; 43. 6; 45. 26, 28.

15 (*H*, p. 721). THE PERFECT MAN. (*Introversion and Alternation.*)

H | T | 1. His eternal abiding. Question.
  U | a | 2. Positive. } Answers.
    b | 3. Negative }
  U | *a* | 4-. Positive. }
    b | -4, 5-. Negative. }
T | -5. His eternal abiding. Question.

The Structure is due to the Fig. *Synezeugmenon* (see *Zeugma*, Ap. 6), by which all the statements are yoked on together to one verb at the end instead of each having its own verb. For scope of Ps. 15 see the Structure of **A**², p. 721. Note contrasts with Ps. 12.

This Psalm forms the text of the Sermon on the Mount (Matt. 5—7). See Ap. 70. The theology pertains to the Kingdom, not to the Church of God. Not true of this present Dispensation. See Ap. 63. IX.

Title. A Psalm. See Ap. 65. XVII. **1 LORD.** Heb. Jehovah. Ap. 4. II. **tabernacle** = tent: i.e. dwelling, or home. Some codices, with one early printed edition, read "tents"; pl. of majesty = Thy heavenly home. See Ap. 40. 3. **dwell** = abide continually. Fig. *Anabasis*. Ap. 6. **holy hill** = holy mountain: i.e. Mount Zion; the type of the heavenly kingdom. **2 walketh** = walketh habitually. **walketh . . . worketh . . . speaketh.** Note Fig. *Anabasis*. Ap. 6. **uprightly** = without blame. **truth.** First occ. in the Psalms. **3 He that** = that never hath. So in the following two lines. **evil.** Heb. *rā'a'*. Ap. 44. viii. **neighbour** = friend. **taketh up** = receiveth. **4 to his own hurt.** Sept., Syr., and Vulg., read "to his neighbour". **5 usury.** Cp. Ex. 22. 25. Lev. 25. 36, 37. Deut. 23. 19, 20. **reward** = bribery. Cp. Ex. 23. 8. Deut. 27. 25. **never be moved.** See *v.* 1. Contrast 9. 15, 17, and cp. Matt. 7. 24-27. Pss. 16. 8; 125. 1.

16

°Michtam °of °David.

P V¹ c (p. 733) 1 °Preserve me, O °GOD: for in Thee do I °put my trust.

d 2 O *my soul,* °thou hast said unto °the LORD, "Thou *art* my °LORD*:

e °My goodness *extendeth* not to Thee;
3 °*But* to the °saints that *are* °in the earth,
And °*to* the excellent, °in whom *is* all °my delight."

e 4 Their sorrows shall be multiplied *that* hasten *after* another *god:*
Their drink offerings of blood will I not offer,
Nor take up °their names into my lips.

d 5 ²The LORD *is* the °portion of mine inheritance and of my cup:
Thou °maintainest my °lot.
6 The °lines are fallen unto me in pleasant *places;*
Yea, I have a goodly heritage.

c 7 I will bless ²the LORD, Who hath given me counsel:
My °reins also °instruct me in the night seasons.

V² f **8 °I have set ²the LORD always before me:**
Because *He is* at my right hand, I shall °not be moved.

g **9 Therefore °my heart is glad, and my °glory rejoiceth:**
°My flesh also shall rest in hope.

g **10 For °Thou wilt not leave °my soul in °hell;**
Neither wilt Thou °suffer Thine °Holy One to °see °corruption.

f **11 Thou wilt shew me °the path of life:**
In Thy presence *is* fulness of joy;
At °Thy right hand *there are* pleasures for evermore.

17

A °Prayer of David.

Q W m (p. 734) 1 °Hear the °right, O °LORD, °attend unto my cry,
°Give °ear unto my prayer, *that goeth* not out of °feigned lips.
2 °Let my sentence come forth from Thy presence;
Let Thine eyes behold the things that are equal.

n 3 Thou hast proved mine heart; Thou hast visited *me* in the night;
Thou hast tried me, *and* shalt °find nothing;
I am purposed *that* my mouth shall not °transgress.

16–41 (**A**³, p. 721). "THE MAN CHRIST JESUS".

16 (**P**, p. 721). TAKING HIS PLACE OF SUFFERING. (*Division.*)

P | V¹ | 1-7. David speaketh to Jehovah and to the saints.
| V² | 8-11. "David speaketh concerning" Messiah (Acts 2. 25-28).

1-7 (V¹, above). HIMSELF. HIS TRUST. (*Introversion.*)

V¹ | c | 1. Prayer. For preservation. } David to Jehovah.
| d | 2-. My Adonai. My good.
| e | -2, 3. The saints.
| *e* | 4. The apostates. } David to saints.
| *d* | 5, 6. My portion. My heritage.
| *c* | 7. Praise. For counsel.

Title. Michtam. See Ap. 65. XII.
of=relating to.
David. And therefore refers to David's Son, and David's Lord, as do all the Davidic Psalms.
1 Preserve. Cp. Heb. 5. 7-9.
GOD. Heb. El. Ap. 4. IV.
put my trust=flee for refuge. Heb. *ḥāṣāh.* Ap. 69. II.
2 thou hast said. Some codices, with two early printed editions, Sept., Syr., and Vulg., read "I said", in which case there is no Ellipsis, and "O my soul" should be omitted.
the LORD. Heb. Jehovah. Ap. 4. II.
LORD*. One of the 134 places where the *Sōpherim* changed Jehovah (of the primitive text) to Adonai (Ap. 32).
My goodness, &c.=I have no good beyond Thee.
3 But to=As for.
saints=holy (or separated) ones. See note on Ex. 3. 5.
in the earth=in His own Land.
to. Omit "to". **in whom**=in them.
my: or, His: i. e. Jehovah's. So the Sept.
4 their names: i. e. the names of their gods.
5 portion. Note the four things: portion (*v.* 5); path, presence, pleasures (*v.* 11).
maintainest=wilt maintain.
lot. } Put by Fig. *Metonomy* (of Cause), Ap. 6, for
6 lines. } the land thus allotted by it.
7 reins. Put by Fig. *Metonymy* (of Subject), Ap. 6, for thoughts.
instruct=will instruct.

16. 8-11 (V², above). HIS MISSION AND WORK. (*Introversion.*)

V² | f | 8. Jehovah at My right hand. (Life.)
| g | 9. Rest in hope. Positive. (Death.)
| *g* | 10. Not left in Sheōl. Negative. (Resurrection.)
| *f* | 11. I at His right hand. (Ascension.)

8 I have set, &c. Quoted in Acts 2. 25-28; 13. 35.
not be moved. Cp. 15. 5.
9 my heart=I myself, like "my soul". Fig. *Synecdoche* (of Part). Ap. 6.
glory. Put by Fig. *Metonymy* (of Effect), Ap. 6, for the powers of the mind which give the glory.
My flesh also shall rest. Refers to Messiah's *death.*
10 Thou wilt not leave, &c. Refers to the *Resurrection.*
my soul=me. Heb. *nephesh.* Ap. 13.
hell=the grave. Heb. Sheōl. Ap. 35.
suffer=give, or allow.
Holy One, or Thy beloved: i. e. Christ the Messiah (Acts 2. 27). See note on 52. 9.

see=experience, or know. **corruption.** Showing that it is the body that is referred to. **11 the path of life.** Refers to *Ascension.* **Thy right hand.** Cp. *v.* 8, and see Structure above ("f" and "*f*").

17 [For Structure see next page].

Title. Prayer. Heb. *Tᵉphillah.* One of five Psalms so called (17; 86; 90; 102; 142). See Ap. 63. It is a prayer of Messiah, the true David; in view of Ps. 16. 6-11, cp. 17. 15. **1 Hear . . . attend . . . Give ear.** Fig. *Anabasis.* Ap. 6. **right**=righteousness. Cp. *v.* 15, and Structure. **LORD.** Heb. Jehovah. Ap. 4. II. **ear.** Fig. *Anthropopatheia.* Ap. 6. Cp. *vv.* 2, eyes; 7, hand; 8, wings; 15, face. **feigned**=guileless. **2 Let my sentence, &c.**=From thy presence my judgment will come: Thine eyes will discern upright ones. **3 find nothing.** None but Christ could say this. See John 14. 30. **transgress.** Heb. *'ābar.* Ap. 44. vii.

4 Concerning the works of °men, by the word of Thy lips
I have °kept *me from* the paths of °the destroyer.
n 5 Hold up my goings in Thy °paths,
(p. 734) *That* my footsteps slip not.
m 6 I have called upon Thee, for Thou wilt °hear me, O °GOD:
Incline Thine [1]ear unto me, *and hear* my speech.
X i 7 Shew Thy marvellous lovingkindness, O Thou That savest by Thy right hand them which °put their trust *in Thee*
From those that rise up *against them.*
8 Keep me °as the °apple of the °eye,
°Hide me under the shadow of Thy °wings,
k 9 From °the wicked that oppress me,
From °my deadly enemies, *who* compass me about.
l 10 They are inclosed in their own fat:
With their mouth they speak proudly.
11 They have now compassed us in our °steps:
They have set their eyes bowing down to the earth;
Y 12 Like as a lion *that* is greedy of his prey,
Y And as it were a young lion lurking in secret places.
X i 13 Arise, O [1]LORD,
°Disappoint him, cast him down:
k Deliver °my soul from °the wicked, *which is* Thy °sword:
14 From °men *which are* Thy °hand, O [1]LORD,
l From °men of the °world, *which have* their portion in *this* life,
And whose belly Thou fillest with Thy °hid *treasure:*
°They are °full of °children,
And leave the rest of their *substance* to their babes.
W 15 As for me, °I will behold Thy °face in righteousness:
I shall be °satisfied, °when I awake, with °Thy likeness.

°To the chief Musician.

990-923 B.C. **18** *A Psalm* of °David °the servant of °the LORD, who spake unto °the LORD the words of this °song °in the day *that* °the LORD °**delivered him from the °hand of all his enemies,** and from the hand of Saul: And he said,

R A D 1 °I will love Thee, O °LORD, my °strength.
E 2 [1]The LORD *is* my °rock, and my °fortress, and my deliverer;

17 (Q, p. 721). PRAYER IN VIEW OF PSALM **16**.
(*Introversion and Repeated Alternation.*)

Q W | 1–6. I (*'ănī*) = As for me. The righteous sufferer.
X | i | 7, 8. Prayer for deliverance.
k | 9. From enemies.
l | 10, 11. Description of them.
Y | 12–. Comparison. Lion.
Y | –12. Comparison. Young lion.
X | *i* | 13–. Prayer for deliverance.
k | –13, 14–. From enemies.
l | –14. Description of them.
W | 15. I (*'ănī* = As for me). The righteous sufferer.

1–6 (W, above). THE RIGHTEOUS SUFFERER.
(*Introversion.*)

W | m | 1, 2. Prayer. "Hear me". ("Thine eyes".)
n | 3, 4. Purpose. Mouth not transgress.
n | 5. Purpose. Footsteps not slip.
m | 6. Prayer. "Hear me". ("Thine ear".)

4 men. Heb. *'ādām.* Ap. 14. I.
kept me from = I have marked.
the destroyer = the oppressor, or violent one. Only here in the Psalms. **5 paths** = tracks, or ruts.
6 hear = answer. See Structure, above.
GOD. Heb. El. Ap. 4. IV.
7 put their trust = flee for refuge. Heb. *ḥāṣah.* Ap. 69. II. **8 as.** Fig. *Simile.* Ap. 6.
apple ... eye ... wings. Fig. *Anthropopatheia.* Ap. 6.
Hide = Thou wilt hide.
9 the wicked = the lawless ones.
my deadly enemies = the foes of my soul. Heb. *nephesh.* Ap. 13.
11 steps = ways, or goings, as in *v.* 5.
13 Disappoint = anticipate.
my soul = me myself. Heb. *nephesh.* Ap. 13.
the wicked = a lawless one. Heb. *rāshā'.* Ap. 44. x.
sword. Fig. *Anthropopatheia.* Ap. 6.
14 men. Heb. *m^ethim.* Ap. 14. V.
hand. Fig. *Anthropopatheia.* Ap. 6. See note on "ear", *v.* 1.
world. Heb. *ḥeled.* The world as being transitory. See longer note on 49. 1.
hid. Fig. *Antimereia* (Ap. 6). Act. Part. put for Noun. Heb. thy hid = thy hidden, or secret thing.
They are = Let them be.
full = satisfied with. Cp. *v.* 15. **children** = sons.
15 I will behold Thy face. See note on Ex. 23. 15; 34. 20.
face. Fig. *Anthropopatheia.* Ap. 6. Cp. *v.* 1, and see note on Ex. 23. 15; 34. 20.
satisfied = full, as in *v.* 14.
when I awake = when I awake from the sleep of death in resurrection. This prayer is in view of 16. 9–11. Resurrection of the body is the true inheritance.
Thy likeness = Thine appearing, or a vision of Thee. Cp. 1 John 3. 2.
To the chief Musician. See Ap. 64.

18 [For Structure see next page].
Title. David. Like all Psalms of David, it finds its fulfilment in the true David. See the Structure of this book (A[3], p. 721). Cp. 18. 4, 5 with 17. 9. It is placed, as first written, in 2 Sam. 22; but it is edited and placed here to find its true relation to other Psalms. Why should not David have the right claimed by all other writers? to say nothing of the Holy Spirit's right to do as He pleases and wills. It was edited for its place here, when it was handed over "to the chief Musician". See the sub-scription, and Ap. 64.
the servant. Cp. Isa. 42. 1; 49. 6; 52. 13.

the LORD. Heb. Jehovah. Ap. 4. II. **song.** Heb. *shīrāh.* See Ap. 65. xxiv. **in the day.** Cp. 2 Sam. 22, and Ap. 18. **delivered, &c.** Cp. Luke 1. 74. **hand** = paw. **1 I will love Thee** = Fervently do I love Thee. Heb. *raḥam,* to yearn over. This verse was added by David when the Psalm was handed over to the chief Musician (sub-scription, and Ap. 64) for use in public worship. **LORD.** Heb. Jehovah. Ap. 4. II. **strength.** Put by Fig. *Metonymy* (of Effect), Ap. 6, for the source of all strength. Heb. *ḥazak,* strength (for holding fast); not the same word as *vv.* 2, 17, 17, 32, 39. **2 rock** = fortress. Heb. *ṣela'.* See notes on Deut. 32. 13, and Ex. 17. 6. Note the Figs. *Anthropopatheia* and *Exergasia.* Ap. 6. **fortress** = mountain stronghold. Heb. *m^eẓad.*

°My GOD, my °strength, in Whom I will °trust;
My °buckler, and °**the horn of my salvation,** *and* my high tower.

B F[1] m (p. 735) 3 I will call upon [1]the LORD, *Who is* °*worthy* to be praised:
So shall I be °saved from mine enemies.

n 4 The °sorrows of death compassed me,
And the floods of °ungodly men made me afraid.

n 5 The [4]sorrows of °hell compassed me about:
The °snares of death °prevented me.

m 6 In my distress I called upon [1]the LORD,
And °cried unto my °God:
He heard my voice out of His °temple,
And my cry came before Him, *even* into His °ears.

F[2] o 7 Then the earth °shook and °trembled;
The foundations also of the °hills moved
And were °shaken, because He was wroth.

p 8 There went up a smoke °out of His °nostrils,
And fire out of His °mouth devoured:
Coals were kindled by it.

q 9 He bowed the heavens also, and came down:
And °darkness *was* under His °feet.

r 10 And He °rode upon a °cherub, and did °fly:
r Yea, He did °fly upon the wings of the °wind.

q 11 He made °darkness His secret place; His pavilion round about Him
Were °dark waters *and* thick clouds of the skies.

p 12 At the brightness *that was* before Him His thick clouds passed,
Hail *stones* and coals of fire.
13 [1]The LORD also thundered °in the heavens,
And the °HIGHEST gave His voice;
Hail *stones* and coals of fire.
14 Yea, He sent out His arrows, and scattered them;
And He shot out lightnings, and discomfited them.

o 15 Then the °channels of waters were seen,
And the foundations of the °world were discovered
At Thy rebuke, O [1]LORD,
At the °blast of the °breath of Thy °nostrils.

F[3] s 16 He sent from above, He took me,
He drew me out of °many waters.

---

18 (**R**, p. 721). ANSWER TO PRAYER. (*Introversion.*)

R | A | D | 1. Jehovah spoken TO. Love.
  E | 2. Jehovah spoken OF. Deliverer.
   B | 3-19. Enemies. Deliverance from.
    C | 20-24. Equity of Jehovah's dealings. Me.
    C | 25-27. Equity of Jehovah's dealings. Others.
   B | 28-48. Enemies. Victory over.
 A | *D* | 49. Jehovah spoken TO. Praise.
  E | 50. Jehovah spoken OF. Deliverer.

2 My GOD. Heb. El. Ap. 4. IV.
strength = rock (in original situation): hence, refuge. Heb. *ẓūr*. See Deut. 32. 13; not same as *vv.* 17, 32, 39.
trust = flee for refuge. See Ap. 69. II.
buckler = shield. Heb. *māgēn*, as in *v.* 30 and Ps. 5. 12.
the horn, &c. Quoted in Luke 1. 69.

3-19 (B, above). ENEMIES. DELIVERANCE FROM. (*Division.*)

B | F[1] | 3-6. David's call for deliverance.
 F[2] | 7-15. Deliverance effected.
 F[3] | 16-19. Jehovah the deliverer.

3-6 (F[1], above). DAVID'S CALL FOR DELIVERANCE. (*Introversion.*)

F[1] | m | 3. David's call and confidence.
 n | 4. Compassed by enemies. } Cp. t and *t*, *v.* 18.
 n | 5. Compassed by danger. }
 m | 6. David's call and answer.

3 worthy to be praised. Fig. *Antimereia*. Ap. 6, Pass. Part. put for Adj. Heb. the praised One.
So shall I, &c. Quoted in Luke 1. 71.
saved = delivered (in the widest sense). Heb. *yasha'*.
4 sorrows = meshes, or snares (Heb. *ḥēbel*). Not bodily pains. **ungodly men** = Belial.
5 hell = the grave. Heb. Sheōl. Ap. 35.
snares. Heb. *yāḳash* = noose, or snare.
prevented = were beforehand with, or confronted.
6 God. Heb. Elohim. Ap. 4. I.
temple = palace. Put for heaven itself.
cried . . . ears. See note on *v.* 41.

7-15 (F[2], above). DELIVERANCE EFFECTED. (*Introversion.*)

F[2] | o | 7. Wonders on earth.
 p | 8. Fire from heaven.
  q | 9. Darkness in the heavens.
   r | 10-. Jehovah's speedy succour.
   r | -10. Jehovah's speedy succour.
  q | 11. Darkness in the heavens.
 p | 12-14. Fire from heaven.
 o | 15. Wonders on earth.

7 shook . . . trembled . . . shaken. Fig. *Paronomasia*. Ap. 6. Heb. *vattig'ash, vattir'ash*. Eng. = "shaked . . . quaked and shaked", or "rocked and reeled". **hills** = mountains.
8 out of = into.
nostrils . . . mouth. Fig. *Anthropopatheia*. Ap. 6.
9 darkness. Heb. *'ărāphel*. See note on Job 3. 6.
feet. } Fig. *Anthropopatheia*. Ap. 6.
10 rode . . . fly. }
cherub. See Ap. 41.
wind. Heb. *rūacḥ*. Ap. 9.

11 darkness . . . dark. Heb. *ḥāshak*. See notes on Job 3. 6. **13 in.** Some codices, with Aram., Sept., and Vulg., read "from" (2 Sam. 22. 14). **HIGHEST.** Heb. *Elyōn*. Ap. 4. VI. **15 channels.** Heb. *'ăphīḳīm*. See note on 2 Sam. 22. 16. **world.** Heb. *tēbēl* = the habitable world. Gr. *oikoumenē*. **blast.** Heb. *n*e*shamah*. Ap. 16. **breath.** Heb. *rūacḥ*. Ap. 9.

16-19 (F[3], above). JEHOVAH THE DELIVERER. (*Introversion.*)

F[3] | s | 16, 17-. Jehovah's deliverance.
 t | -17. Compassed by enemies. } Cp. n and *n*, *vv.* 4, 5.
 t | 18-. Compassed by enemies. }
 s | -18, 19. Jehovah's deliverance.

16 many waters. Put by Fig. *Metonymy* (of Adjunct), Ap. 6, for troubles.

17 He delivered me from my °strong enemy,
And from them which hated me:
t For they were too °strong for me.
t 18 They [5]prevented me in the day of my calamity:
(p. 735)
s But [1]the LORD was my stay.
19 He brought me forth also into a large place;
He delivered me, °because He delighted in me.
C 20 [1]The LORD rewarded me according to my righteousness;
According to the cleanness of my hands hath He recompensed me.
21 For I have kept the ways of [1]the LORD,
And have not wickedly departed from my [6]God.
22 For all His judgments *were* before me,
And I did not put away His statutes from me.
23 I was also upright °before Him,
And I kept myself from °mine iniquity.
24 Therefore hath [1]the LORD recompensed me according to my righteousness,
According to the cleanness of my hands in His eyesight.
C 25 With the °merciful Thou wilt shew Thyself merciful;
With an upright °man Thou wilt shew Thyself upright;
26 With the pure Thou wilt shew Thyself pure;
[25]And with °the froward Thou wilt shew Thyself °froward.
27 For Thou wilt [3]save the afflicted people;
But wilt bring down high looks.
B u 28 For Thou wilt light my °candle:
(p. 736) [1]The LORD my [6]God will enlighten my [9]darkness.
29 For by Thee I have °run through a troop;
And by my [6]God have I leaped over a wall.
30 *As for* °GOD, His way *is* perfect:
The °word of [1]the LORD is °tried:
He *is* a [2]buckler to all those that °trust in Him.
31 For who *is* °GOD save [1]the LORD?
Or who *is* a °rock °save our [6]God?
v 32 *It is* [30]GOD That girdeth me with °strength,
And maketh my way perfect.
33 He maketh my feet like hinds' *feet,*
And setteth me upon °my high places.
34 He teacheth my hands to war,
So that a bow of steel is °broken by mine arms.
35 Thou hast also given me the °shield of Thy salvation:
And Thy right hand hath holden me up,
And Thy °gentleness hath made me great.
36 Thou hast enlarged my steps under me,
That my feet did not slip.
37 I have °pursued mine enemies, and °overtaken them:
Neither did I turn again till they were °consumed.
38 I have °wounded them that they were not able to rise:
They are °fallen under my feet.
39 For Thou hast girded me with [32]strength unto the battle:

17 strong = strong (for might). Heb. *ʿāzaz.* Not same word as *vv.* 1, 2, 32, 39.
strong = strong (for activity). Heb. *'āmaz.* Not same word as *vv.* 1, 2, 32, 39.
19 because, &c. This is the one ground of blessing. See note on Num. 14. 8, and 2 Sam. 15. 25, 26.
23 before = with.
mine iniquity. Some codices read "the wicked". Heb. *ʿāvāh.* Ap. 44. iv. **25** merciful = gracious.
With. Some codices, with two early printed editions, Sept., Syr., and Vulg., read "And with".
man = strong man. Heb. *geber.* Ap. 14. IV.
26 the froward = the perverse. Heb. *ʿiḳēsh.*
froward = a wrestler, or contender.

18. 28-48 (*B*, p. 735). ENEMIES. VICTORY OVER. (*Extended Alternation.*)

B | u | 28-31. Help. General.
v | 32-39-. Vengeance on enemies.
w | -39-42. Subjugation of enemies.
x | 43-45. Deliverance.
u | 46. Help. General.
v | 47-. Vengeance on enemies.
w | -47. Subjugation of enemies.
x | 48. Deliverance.

28 candle = lamp. Used to-day, in the East, more for comfort than light. **29** run = broken through.
30 GOD. Heb. = the El. Ap. 4. IV.
word = sayings, as in Pss. 12. 6 (fem. pl.); 19. 14 (masc. pl.) (not *v.* 4); 119. 11 (see note there), &c.
tried = refined. Cp. Ps. 12. 6.
trust in = flee for refuge to. Heb. *ḥaṣah.* Ap. 69. II.
31 GOD. Heb. Eloah. Ap. 4. V.
rock. Heb. *ẓur.* See notes on Ex. 17. 6; 32. 13.
save = except.
32 strength = might (for valour). Heb. *ḥīl.* Not the same as *vv.* 1, 2, 17, 17.
33 my. Ginsburg thinks this should be omitted.
34 broken = bent.
35 shield. Heb. *māgēn,* rendered "buckler", *v.* 2. See note on Ps. 5. 12. gentleness = condescension.
37, 38 pursued . . . overtaken . . . consumed . . . wounded . . . fallen. Fig. *Anabasis.* Ap. 6. The tenses may be future, and prophetic.
41 cried . . . save. Fig. *Paronomasia.* Ap. 6. Heb. *y^{e}shavv^{e}ʿū . . . mōshīaʿ.* May be represented in Eng. "they cried with fear, but none gave ear."
42 wind. Heb. *rūach.* Ap. 9.
cast them out: or scatter them. Some codices, with Aram., Sept., Syr., and Vulg., read "crush". Cp. 2 Sam. 22. 43. **43** heathen = nations, or Gentile peoples.
44 strangers = sons of the foreigner.
submit = come cringing.

Thou hast subdued under me those that rose up against me. w
40 Thou hast also given me the necks of mine enemies;
That I might destroy them that hate me.
41 They °cried, but *there was* none to °save *them:*
Even unto [1]the LORD, but He answered them not.
42 Then did I beat them small as the dust before the °wind:
I did °cast them out as the dirt in the streets.
43 Thou hast delivered me from the strivings of the People; x
And Thou hast made me the head of the °heathen:
A People *whom* I have not known shall serve me.
44 As soon as they hear of me, they shall obey me:
The °strangers shall °submit themselves unto me.

45 The [44]strangers shall fade away,
And ° be afraid out of their close places.

u (p. 736) 46 [1]The LORD liveth; and blessed *be* my rock;
And let the [6]God of my salvation be exalted.

v 47 *It is* [30]GOD That avengeth me,

w And subdueth the People under me.

x 48 He delivereth me from mine enemies:
Yea, Thou liftest me up above those that rise up against me:
Thou hast delivered me from the violent °man.

A D (p. 735) 49 **°Therefore will I give thanks unto Thee, O [1]LORD, among the [43]heathen,**
And sing praises unto Thy name.

E 50 Great deliverance giveth He to His king;
And sheweth mercy to His ° ANOINTED,
To David, and to his seed for evermore.

°To the chief Musician.

19

° A Psalm of David.

S G H a (p. 737) 1 The heavens ° declare the glory of ° GOD;
And the ° firmament ° sheweth His handywork.

b 2 ° Day unto day ° uttereth ° speech,
And night ° unto night sheweth ° knowledge.

c 3 *There is* no [2]speech nor ° language,
° *Where* their ° voice is not heard.

b 4 **°Their °line is gone out through all the °earth, and their °words to the end of the °world.**

J a In them hath He set a ° tabernacle for the sun,
5 °Which *is* as a bridegroom coming out of his ° chamber,
° *And* rejoiceth as a ° strong man to run a race.
6 His going forth *is* from the end of the heaven,
And his circuit unto the ends of it:
And there is nothing hid from the heat thereof.

G H 7 The ° law of ° the LORD *is* ° perfect, ° converting ° the soul:
The ° testimony of ° the LORD *is* ° sure, making wise the simple.
8 The ° statutes of [7]the LORD *are* ° right, rejoicing the heart:
The commandment of [7]the LORD *is* pure, ° enlightening the eyes.

45 be afraid = come trembling.
48 man. Heb. *'ish.* Ap. 14. II.
49 Therefore, &c. Quoted in Rom. 15. 9.
50 Anointed = Messiah. Looking beyond David, to David's Son and David's Lord.
To the chief Musician. See Ap. 64. The changes from 2 Sam. 22 were made when David handed the Psalm over for general use in public worship.

19 (**S**, p. 721). ACKNOWLEDGMENT OF CHRIST'S GLORY IN CREATION, AND REVELATION.

S | G | H | 1-4-. The heavens. The word written there: (eight lines).
| | J | -4-6. In them (*bāhem*) the sun (six lines).
| *G* | *H* | 7-10. The Scriptures. The word written therein (eight lines).
| | *J* | 11-14. In them (*bāhem*) Thy servant (six lines).

The position of this Psalm in the Structure (p. 721) shows that it corresponds with "*S*", Ps. 29, with its two answering parts, the "Glory" and the "Voice" of Jehovah.

The verbs in the *first* part (1-6) are *literary*, and in the *second* part *astronomical*, thus interlacing and uniting the two parts in one whole.

Title. A Psalm of David. One Psalm: one whole, not two odd scraps strung together by some late "redactor". See Ap. 65. XVII.

1-6 (G, above). THE HEAVENS.
(*Introversion.*)

G | a | 1. The heavens.
| b | 2. Their testimony. Incessant. (Pos.)
| c | 3. Their words. Inaudible. (Neg.)
| *b* | 4-. Their testimony. Universal. (Pos.)
| *a* | -4-6. The heavens.

1 declare = rehearse (the Piel part. implying repetition. Cp. 71. 15. Gen. 24. 66. Fig. *Prosopopœia.* Ap. 6.
GOD. Heb. El. Ap. 4. IV.
firmament = expanse.
sheweth = is setting forth. Cp. first occurrence (Gen. 3. 11. Pss. 97. 6; 111. 6).
2 Day unto day = Day after day.
uttereth = constantly poureth forth. Heb. *nāba'*, to tell forth, or prophesy.
speech = speaking. See note on 18. 30.
unto = after.
knowledge = intelligence, information.
3 language = words.
Where. Omit this word. There is no *Ellipsis* (Ap. 6).
voice = sound: i. e. "their voice is not heard"
4 Their, &c. Quoted in Rom. 10. 18.
line = inheritance. Heb. measuring, or allotting line. Put by Fig. *Metonymy* (of Cause), Ap. 6, for inheritance. Sept., Syr., and Vulg., read "voice". So Rom. 10. 18, thus connecting the written word. See note on *v.* 7.
earth. Heb. *'ereẓ* = the earth (as created).
words = sayings, or teachings. See note on 18. 30.
world. Heb. *tēbēl* = the world (as inhabited). Gr. *oikoumenē.*
tabernacle = tent, or house. Hence the signs of the Zodiac are called the "houses" of the sun, because in them he moves and dwells, and completes his circuit. This corresponds with God's servants dwelling and moving in the written "Word" (*v.* 11). **5 Which** is = And he. **chamber** = bridal canopy. Heb. *chuppāh.* First occurrence; elsewhere, only in Isa. 4. 5 ("defence"). Joel 2. 16 ("closet"). **And.** Omit this "And". **strong man.** Heb. *gibbōr.* Ap. 14. IV. **7 law.** Note the synthetic parallelism of the second half of this Psalm, which compares the written words in the Scripture with the words written in the heavens, and preserved in the names of the signs of the Zodiac and the constellations. See Ap. 12. Note in *vv.* 7-9 the six *titles* of the Word, its six *attributes*, and its six *effects* (see Ap. 10). **the LORD.** Heb. Jehovah. Ap. 4. II. The Covenant God, in contrast with El (*v.* 1) the Creator. Occurs seven times in this latter half of the Psalm. **perfect:** like *all* His other works. Note the six words in *vv.* 7-9. **converting** = returning. As the sun returns in the heavens, so here the same word is used of the sinner's conversion (or returning). Note that all the verbs in this second half are *astronomical*, as those in the first half are *literary*. See note above. **the soul.** Heb. *nephesh.* Ap. 13. **testimony** = witness. Cp. 89. 37. **sure** = faithful and enduring; as the sun is "the faithful witness in the heavens" (89. 37). **8 statutes** = precepts. Heb. *pikkūdim.* Found only in the Psalms, and in the Pl. **right** = righteous: i. e. equitable and just. **enlightening** = giving light, as the sun (Gen. 1. 15, 17, 18. Isa. 60. 19).

9 The °fear of [7]the LORD *is* °clean, enduring for ever:
The °judgments of [7]the LORD *are* °true *and* righteous altogether.
10 More to be desired *are they* than gold, yea, than much fine gold:
Sweeter also than honey and the honeycomb.

J (p. 737) 11 Moreover °by them is Thy servant °warned:
And in °keeping of them °*there is* great reward.
12 Who can °understand °*his* °errors?
°Cleanse Thou me from °secret *faults*.
13 °Keep back Thy servant also °from presumptuous *sins;*
Let them not °have dominion over me: then shall I be upright,
And I shall be innocent from °the great °transgression.
14 Let the words of my mouth, and the °meditation of my heart, °be acceptable °in Thy sight,
O [7]LORD, my °strength, and my °redeemer.

°To the chief Musician.

20

A Psalm of David.

T K (p. 738) 1 °The LORD °hear thee in the day of trouble;
The °name of the °God of Jacob °defend thee;
2 Send °thee help from the sanctuary,
And °strengthen thee out of °Zion;
3 Remember °all thy °offerings,
And °accept thy burnt sacrifice; °Selah.
4 Grant thee according to thine own heart,
And fulfil all thy counsel.

L 5 We will rejoice in Thy salvation,
And in the [1]name of our [1]God we will set up *our* banners:

M [1]The LORD °fulfil all thy petitions.

M 6 Now know I that [1]the LORD saveth °His Anointed;
He °will hear him from His °holy heaven
°With the saving °strength of His °right hand.

L 7 °Some *trust* in chariots, and some °in horses:
But °**we** will remember the [1]name of [1]the LORD our [1]God.
8 **They** are brought down and fallen:
But **we** are risen, and °stand upright.

K 9 °Save, [1]LORD:
Let the king [1]hear us °when we call.

°To the chief Musician.

9 fear = reverence.
clean = cleansing (especially Levitically). Cp. Lev. 16. 30. Num. 8. 7, 21. Ezek. 36. 33, &c. Heb. *tahēr.*
judgments = judicial requirements.
true = faithful (in perpetuity).
11 by them = in them. Heb. *bāhem*, as in *v.* 4, going about the Scriptures, moving and dwelling in the written Word, as the sun does in the heavens. (Cp. 1 Tim. 4. 15; 3. 14.)
warned = enlightened; hence, taught or admonished.
keeping = observing, or watching; as observers watch the heavenly bodies. Cp. 130. 6. Isa. 21. 11.
there is great reward = great [is] the reward.
12 understand = discern.
his. Not in Hebrew text.
errors = wanderings. Like those of the "planets" (= wanderers).
Cleanse = clear, or acquit. Heb. *nāḳāh.*
secret = hidden things; things that are not discerned.
13 Keep back = restrain or hold back; as the motions of the heavenly bodies are controlled. First occurrence Gen. 20. 6; 22. 12, 16; 39. 9. Cp. 1 Sam. 25. 39, &c.
from presumptuous sins. Fig. *Hypallage.* Ap. 6. Heb. keep back presumptuous [men] from me.
have dominion over = rule, as the sun and moon rule the day and night (Gen. 1. 18. Ps. 136. 8, 9).
the great = much.
transgression. Heb. *pāsha'.* Ap. 44. ix.
14 meditation. Heb. *higgaion.* See Ap. 66. I.
be acceptable = come with acceptance.
in Thy sight = before Thee.
strength = rock. Heb. *ẓur.* See notes on 18. 1, 2.
redeemer. Heb. *gā'al.* See note on Ex. 6. 6. The Psalm begins with the *Creator* and ends with the *Redeemer.* Cp. the heavenly worship, where we have the same two in the same order (Rev. 4. 11 with 5. 9).
To the chief Musician. See Ap. 64.

20 (**T**, p. 721). HIS PEOPLE'S PRAYER IN VIEW OF **A**[3], p. 721). (*Introversion.*)

T | K | 1-4. Prayer.
  L | 5-. We. His People's trust.
    M | -5. Jehovah's Messiah.
    M | 6. Jehovah's Messiah.
  L | 7, 8. We. His People's trust.
K | 9. Prayer.

1 The LORD. Heb. Jehovah. Ap. 4. II.
hear = answer.
name. Put by Fig. *Metonymy* (of Adjunct), Ap. 6, for the person himself. Occurs three times in this Psalm: *v.* 1, the Defending Name; *v.* 5, the Displayed Name; *v.* 7, the Delivering Name.
God. Heb. Elohim. Ap. 4. I.
God of Jacob = Jacob's God: i. e. the God Who met Jacob when he had nothing and deserved nothing (but wrath), and gave him everything. The N.T. "God of all grace". See note on Gen. 32. 28; 43. 6; 45. 26, 28; this Divine title occurs in Pss. 46. 7, 11; 75. 9; 76. 6; 81. 1, 4; 84. 8; 94. 7; 114. 7; 146. 5. Cp. also Isa. 2. 3. Mic. 4. 2.
defend = shall defend. To this day the calling out the name of a person of rank or power will bring protection to one in danger from the violence of an enemy. In Psalms always used of God. Fut. as in *vv.* 2, 3, 4.
2 thee = thy.
strengthen = sustain, or support. Heb. *ṣa'ad.* Cp. *v.* 6 and 21. 1. **Zion.** See Ap. 68.
3 all thy offerings. Some codices, with eight early printed editions, read "every present of thine".
offerings = gift offerings, or presents. Heb. *minchāh.* Ap. 43 II. iii. **accept.** Heb. turn to ashes. This was the only way by which Jehovah accepted what was offered. See note on Gen. 4. 4. **Selah.** Here, connecting the prayer of *v.* 4 with the atonement or accepted sacrifice of *v.* 3; the only ground on which prayer can be answered. See Ap. 66. ii.
5 fulfil = will fulfil. **6 His Anointed** = His Messiah. **will hear** = answereth (continually). **holy.** See note on Ex. 3. 5. **With the saving strength** = by the mighty saving deeds. **strength** = might (inherent). Heb. *gābar.* Cp. Ap. 14. IV and *v.* 2 above. **right hand.** Fig. *Anthropopatheia.* Ap. 6. **7 Some trust in** = Some by, &c. **in** = by. **we will remember, &c.** = we by, &c. **8 stand upright** = are established. **9 Save, LORD,** or, O LORD, save. Or, with Sept., "Jehovah save the king". Cp. *v.* 6. **when** = in the day when. See Ap. 18. **To the chief Musician.** See Ap. 64.

21

°A Psalm °of David.

U N (p. 739) 953 1 The king shall joy in Thy °strength, O °LORD;
And in Thy salvation how greatly shall he rejoice!

O P 2 Thou hast given him his °heart's desire,
And hast not withholden the request of his lips. °Selah.
3 For Thou °preventest him with the blessings of goodness:
Thou settest a °crown of pure gold on his head.
4 He asked °life of Thee, *and* Thou gavest *it* him,
Even length of days for ever and ever.
5 His glory *is* great in Thy salvation:
°Honour and majesty hast Thou laid upon him.

Q d 6 For Thou hast made him most °blessed for ever:
Thou hast made him exceeding glad with Thy countenance.

e 7 For the king °trusteth in [1] the LORD,
And through the °mercy of the °MOST HIGH he shall not be moved.

O P 8 Thine hand shall find out all Thine enemies:
Thy right hand shall find out those that hate Thee.
9 Thou shalt °make them as a fiery oven in the time of Thine °anger:
[1] The LORD shall swallow them up in His wrath,
And the fire shall devour them.
10 Their fruit shalt Thou destroy from the earth,
And their seed from among the °children of °men.

Q e 11 For they intended °evil against Thee:
They imagined a mischievous device, *which* they °are not able *to perform.*

d 12 Therefore shalt Thou make them turn their back,
When Thou shalt make ready *Thine arrows* upon Thy °strings against the face of them.

N 13 Be Thou exalted, [1] LORD, in Thine own [1] strength:
So will we sing and praise Thy power.

°To the chief Musician, °upon °Aijeleth Shahar.

22

°A Psalm °of David.

R¹ S¹ T pp. 739 and 740) 1 °**My GOD, my GOD, why hast thou forsaken me?**
Why art Thou so far from helping me, *and from* the words of my °roaring?

21 (**U**, p. 721). HIS PEOPLE'S JOY IN VIEW OF **A**³: THE CORONATION OF THEIR KING.
(*Introversions and Alternations.*)

U | N | 1. Messiah. Strong in Jehovah's strength.
O | P | 2-5. Jehovah's dealings with the king.
Q | d | 6. His reward. } Reasons. } Jehovah addressed.
e | 7. His merit.
O | *P* | 8-10. The king's dealings with his enemies.
Q | *e* | 11. Their guilt. } Reasons. } The king addressed.
d | 12. Their defeat.
N | 13. Messiah. Strong in His own strength.

Title. A Psalm. See Ap. 65. XVII.
of=pertaining or relating to.
1 strength=prevailing strength. Heb. *'āraz*, as in *v.* 13. Cp. notes on 20. 2, 6.
LORD. Heb. Jehovah. Ap. 4. II.
2 heart's desire. Cp. 20. 4; 37. 4.
Selah. See Ap. 66. II. Here connecting the reason (*v.* 3) of the answer (*v.* 2) with the prayer of 20. 4; which, by the Selah of 20. 3, had been connected with the reason given there: i. e. atonement.
3 preventest=comest to meet. Cp. "settest" in *v.* 3.
crown. See Rev. 14. 14, and cp. Matt. 8. 20.
4 life: i. e. resurrection life. Cp. Isa. 53. 10. Heb. 2. 10-18; 5. 7.
5 Honour, &c. Cp. Rev. 5. 13.
6 blessed. Cp. Rev. 5. 13.
7 trusteth=confideth. Heb. *bāṭah*. Ap. 69. I.
mercy=lovingkindness, or grace.
MOST HIGH. Heb. *Elyōn.* Ap. 4. VI.
9 make them=place them as [in] a furnace of fire.
anger. Heb. face is put by Fig. *Metonymy* (of Subject), Ap. 6, for the anger manifested by it.
10 children=sons. **men.** Heb. *'ādām.* Ap. 14. I.
11 evil. Heb. *rā'a'.* Ap. 44. viii.
are not able to perform=could not accomplish.
12 strings=bow-strings.
13 To the chief Musician. See Ap. 64.
upon=relating to.
Aijeleth Shahar=the Day-dawn: David's Coronation, 953 B.C. Looking forward to the Day-dawn of Messiah's Coronation, which is the subject of the twenty-first Psalm, not of Ps. 22. Cp. 2 Sam. 23. 4; see note on 2 Pet. 1. 19, and Ap. 65. I. Cp. 139. 9.

22 (**V**, p. 721). MESSIAH. THE GOOD SHEPHERD, IN DEATH. (*Division.*)

V | R¹ | 1-21. Messiah. His "sufferings." } See Ap. 71.
R² | 22-31. Messiah. His "glory."

1-21 (R¹, above). MESSIAH. HIS "SUFFERINGS". (*Division.*)

R¹ | S¹ | 1-6. The "Sufferings." Messiah's prayer. Desertion.
S² | 7-21. The "Sufferings." Messiah's plea. Enemies.

1-6 [For Structure of S¹, see next page].

Title. A Psalm. See Ap. 65. XVII.
of David=relating to or concerning David's Son and David's Lord (Matt. 22. 41-45). "The root and the offspring of David" (Rev. 22. 16). David "being a prophet and knowing . . . spake of". These three Psalms (22, 23, 24) relate to the sufferings and the glory of "the Man Christ Jesus." 22=The Good Shepherd on Earth, in Death (John 10. 11). 23=The Great Shepherd, in Heaven, by Resurrection (Heb. 13. 20). 24=The Chief Shepherd, coming in His Glory to earth and Zion, again (1 Pet. 5. 4. Rev. 19). See the Structure of **O** (p. 721). Ps. 22 is Christ as the sin offering; Ps. 40, as the burnt offering; Ps. 69, as the trespass offering. **1 My GOD, my GOD.** Heb. my El (Ap. 4. IV). God as Almighty in relation to the *creature*; not Jehovah (Ap. 4. II), in covenant relation with His servant. Quoted in Matt. 27. 46. Mark 15. 34. The Psalm is Christ's prayer and plea on the Cross. It begins with "My God, my God" (Matt. 27. 46. Mark 15. 34), and it ends with "It is finished". See note on *v.* 31, and cp. John 19. 30. If the Lord uttered the whole of this Psalm on the cross, the dying malefactor must have "heard", and believed (Rom. 10. 17). Cp. Luke 23. 32, 40-42. The "kingdom" had been referred to by Christ in Ps. 22. 22-30. See note on "roaring", below. The Fig. *Epizeuxis* (Ap. 6) is used for solemn emphasis. **roaring**=lamentation. Heb. *shā'ag*=spoken of a lion, and of thunder.

2 O my °God, I cry in the daytime, but Thou °hearest not;
And in the night season, and am not silent.
U (p. 740) 3 °But Thou *art* °holy,
O Thou That °inhabitest the praises of Israel.
U 4 Our fathers °trusted in Thee:
They °trusted, and Thou didst deliver them.
5 They cried unto Thee, and were delivered:
They [4]trusted in Thee, and were not confounded.
T 6 But I *am* a °worm, and no °man;
A reproach of °men, and °despised of the People.
S² V X 7 °All they that see me laugh me to scorn:
They °shoot out the lip, they shake the head, *saying,*
8 °**"He °trusted on °the LORD *that* He would deliver him:**
Let Him deliver him, seeing He delighted in him."
g 9 [3]But Thou *art* he That took me out of the womb:
Thou didst °make me °hope *when I was* upon my mother's breasts.
10 I was cast upon Thee from the womb:
Thou *art* my [1]GOD from my mother's belly.
11 Be not far from me; for trouble *is* near;
For *there is* °none to help.
W h 12 Many bulls have compassed me:
Strong *bulls* of Bashan have beset me round.
13 They gaped upon me *with* their mouths,
As a ravening and a roaring lion.
i 14 I am poured out like water,
And all my bones are out of joint:
My heart is like wax;
It is melted °in the midst of my bowels.
15 My strength is °dried up like a potsherd;
And my tongue cleaveth to my jaws;
And Thou hast brought me into the dust of death.
W h 16 For °dogs have compassed me:
The °assembly of the °wicked have inclosed me:
°They pierced my hands and my feet.
i 17 I may °tell all my bones:
V f They °look *and* stare upon me.
18 **They °part my garments among them,**
And cast lots upon my vesture.
g 19 [3]But be not Thou far from me, O °LORD*:
O my strength, haste thee to help me.
20 Deliver my °soul from the sword;
My °darling from the °power of the [16]dog.
21 Save me from the °lion's mouth:
°For Thou hast °heard me °from the horns of the °unicorns.

22. 1-6 (S¹, p. 739). MESSIAH'S PRAYER. DESERTION. (*Introversion.*)

S¹ | T | 1, 2. His desertion. Mourned.
U | 3. Jehovah's holiness. Declared.
U | 4, 5. Jehovah's goodness. Experienced.
T | 6. His desertion. Experienced.

2 God. Heb. Elohim. Ap. 4. I.
hearest not=answerest not.
3 But Thou. And yet Thou. Cp. *vv.* 9 and 19. Note the emphasis.
holy. See note on Ex. 3. 5. Here=the Divine attribute.
inhabitest the praises. "Praises" put by Fig. *Metonymy* (of Adjunct), Ap. 6, for the Sanctuary, where the praises were offered. The various readings and renderings arise from trying to make sense, not seeing this Figure of speech. Cp. 80. 1; 99. 1.
4 trusted=confided. Heb. *bāṭaḥ.* See Ap. 69. i.
6 worm. Heb. *tōlā'*, not the ordinary word for "worm", but the crimson *coccus* from which the scarlet dye was obtained. Hence rendered "scarlet" in Ex. 25. 4; 26. 1, &c. See note on Josh. 2. 18, and Ex. 12. 13. Jacob, so called Isa. 41. 14. Christ thus took the lowest place of His People. **man.** Heb. *'ish.* Ap. 14. II.
men. Heb. *'ādām.* Ap. 14. I.
despised. Cp. Isa. 53. 3.

22. 7-21 (S², p. 739). MESSIAH'S PLEA. ENEMIES. (*Introversion and Alternations.*)

S² | V | f | 7, 8. Enemies.
g | 9-11. "But Thou".
W | h | 12, 13. "Bulls" (pl.). "Lion" (sing.).
i | 14, 15. "I".
W | *h* | 16. "Dogs" (pl.). "Lion" (sing.).
i | 17-. "I".
V | *f* | -17, 18. Enemies.
g | 19-21. "But Thou".

7 All. Fig. *Synecdoche* (of Genus), Ap. 6, put for most or greater part. (Some believed.) **shoot out**=open.
8 He, &c. Fig. *Eironeia* (Irony). Ap. 6. Quoted in Matt. 27. 43. Mark 15. 29. Luke 23. 35.
trusted, &c.=devolved all on Jehovah. Heb. *gālal.* See Ap. 69. V.
the LORD. Heb. Jehovah. Ap. 4. II.
9 make=cause.
hope=trust, or confide. Heb. *bāṭaḥ.* Ap. 69. I
11 none to help. Cp. 69. 20. He was alone in this wondrous work.
14 in the midst of my bowels=within me.
15 dried up. Cp. John 19. 28.
16 dogs. Fig. *Hypocatastasis.* Ap. 6. "Enemies" being implied (not expressed).
assembly=congregation: in civic aspect.
wicked=breakers up. Heb. *rā'a'.* Ap. 44. viii.
They pierced, &c.="As a lion [they break up] my hands and my feet". The Heb. text reads *kā'ări*=as a lion (the "k"=as). The A.V. and R.V., with Sept., Syr., and Vulg., take the "k" as part of the verb *k'āru*, and alter the vowel points, making it read "they pierced". It is better to translate the Heb. text literally, and supply the *Ellipsis* of the verb from Isa. 38. 13, "they break up". The meaning is exactly the same, and agrees with John 19. 37.
17 tell=count. The whole description applies to death by crucifixion only.
look and stare=look for and see. In this idiom the former verb includes the *feeling* implied by the context. Cp. 1 Sam. 17. 42.
18 part, &c. Quoted in Matt. 27. 35. Mark 15. 24. Luke 23. 34. John 19. 24. **19 LORD*.** One of the 134 emendations of the *Sōpherīm* (Ap. 32) by which "Jehovah" of the primitive text was changed to "Adonai". **20 soul.** Heb. *nephesh.* Ap. 13. **darling**=only one. Heb. *yāḥīd.* See note on Deut. 6. 4.=my one own priceless possession; put by Fig. *Metonymy* (of Subject), Ap. 6, for "my life", answering to "my soul" in the preceding line. Cp. *psuchē* (John 12. 27). **power.** Heb. hand, or paw. Put by Fig. *Metonymy* (of Cause), Ap. 6, for the power exercised by it. **21 lion's.** See note on "They pierced" (*v.* 16). **For**=Yea. **heard me**=answered me. Cp. *v.* 2. Supply Ellipsis, "[and delivered me]". **from the horns, &c.** This clause may be joined on to the end of the preceding line. "Thou hast heard me" may be read on to *v.* 22: "I will declare". **unicorns**=the bulls of *v.* 12.

R² X (p. 741) 22 °I will declare °Thy Name unto my °brethren:
In the midst of the °congregation will I praise Thee.

Y 23 °Ye °that fear 8 the LORD, praise Him;
Z j¹ All ye the seed of °Jacob, glorify Him;
And °fear Him, all ye the seed of °Israel.

k¹ 24 For He hath not 6 despised nor abhorred °the affliction of °the afflicted;
Neither hath He hid His face from him;
But when he cried unto Him, He 21 heard.

X 25 My praise *shall be* of Thee in the great 22 congregation:
I will pay my vows before them 23 that fear Him.

Y 26 The °meek shall eat and be satisfied:
They shall praise 8 the LORD that seek Him:
Your heart shall live for ever.

Z j² 27 All °the ends of the °world shall remember and turn unto 8 the LORD:
And all the kindreds of the nations shall worship before Thee.

k² 28 °For the kingdom *is* 8 the LORD'S:
And He *is* the Governor among the nations.

j³ 29 °All *they that be* fat upon earth shall eat and worship:
All they that go down to the dust °shall bow before Him:
°And none can keep alive his own 20 soul.
30 °A seed shall serve Him;
It shall be °accounted to 19 the LORD* °for a generation.
31 They shall come, and °shall declare His righteousness unto a People °that shall be born,

k³ °That °He hath done *this*.

23

°A Psalm °of David.

W A (p. 741) 1 °The LORD *is* °my shepherd; I shall °*not* want.
2 He °maketh me to °lie down in °green pastures:
He °leadeth me beside the °still waters.
3 He °restoreth my °soul:
He °leadeth me in the °paths of righteousness for His °name's sake.

B 4 °Yea, though I walk °through the °valley of the shadow of death,
I will fear no °evil: for °Thou *art* with me;
Thy °rod and Thy °staff they °comfort me.

22. 22-31 (R², p. 739). MESSIAH'S GLORY (Ap. 71).
(*Extended Alternations.*)

R² X | 22. "I". Messiah's praise. Promised.
Y | 23-. Praise to Jehovah.
Z | j¹ | -23. Israel to praise.
k¹ | 24. The reason. "For".
X | 25. "I". Messiah's praise. Awarded.
Y | 26. Praise to Jehovah.
Z | j² | 27. The nations to praise.
k² | 28. The reason. "For".
j³ | 29-31-. All to praise.
k³ | -31. The reason. "For".

Note here the Parenthesis of the present Dispensation: for which see Ap. 72. [rection. See Heb. 2. 12.

22 I will declare. These words are Christ's in resur-
Thy Name=Thee (emphatic). Put by Fig. *Metonymy* (of Adjunct), Ap. 6, for the Person and all His attributes. See note on Ps. 20. 1. **brethren.** Cp. John 20. 17.
congregation=assembly: in its military aspect.

23 Ye: i. e. the Gentiles of 18. 49; 117. 1. Deut. 32. 43. Isa. 11. 1, 10. [word as in third line.
that fear=that stand in awe. Heb. *gūr*. Not the same
Jacob . . . Israel. See notes on Gen. 32. 28; 43. 6; 45. 26, 28.
fear=revere. Referring to Israel. Heb. *yārē'*. Not the same word as in first line and *v.* 25.

24 the affliction=the humiliation.
the afflicted=the patient One.

26 meek=the patient or wronged ones.

27 the ends, &c. Put by Fig. *Metonymy* (of Subject), Ap. 6, for the people dwelling in the farthest regions.
world=earth. Heb. *'ĕrez*.

28 For, &c. Cp. Matt. 6. 13.

29 All they that be fat=All the great ones.
shall bow. Cp. Phil. 2. 9-11, and refs. there.
And none can=Even He cannot: ref. to Matt. 27. 42. Cp. Acts 1. 8. **soul.** Heb. *nephesh*. Ap. 13.

30 A seed. Sept. and Vulg. read "My seed". Cp. Isa. 53. 10. **accounted to**=recounted of.
for a generation=unto a generation that shall come (reading the first part of *v.* 31 with the end of *v.* 30).

31 shall declare His righteousness=His righteousness shall be declared.
that shall be born. Referring to the new birth as declared by Christ to Nicodemus (John 3. 3-7). Cp. Ezek. 36. 25-27. [not *v.* 21.
That=For. Corresponding with "for", *vv.* 24 and 28,
He hath done this=It is finished. Cp. John 19. 30. Thus concluding the Psalm. Cp. the beginning. Heb. *'āsāh*, to accomplish or finish, as in 2 Chron. 4. 11.
Not given to the chief Musician; the Psalm being for private study, and not public worship.

23 (**W**, p. 721). MESSIAH. THE GREAT SHEPHERD, IN RESURRECTION. (*Introversion.*)

W A | 1-3. Jehovah. Supply. "Pastures and waters". Spoken of. "He".
B | 4. Danger. "Death". "Rod and staff". Spoken to. "Thou".
B | 5. Danger. "Enemies". "Table and Cup". Spoken to. "Thou".
A | 6. Jehovah. Supply. "Goodness and Mercy". Spoken of. "His".

Title. A Psalm. See Ap. 65. XVII. **of.** See note on title of Ps. 22. **1 The LORD.** Heb. Jehovah. **The LORD . . . my shepherd.** One of the Jehovah Titles. See Ap. 4. II, "JEHOVAH-RO'I". Figs. *Metaphor* and *Anthropopatheia*. Ap. 6. **not want.** Because "Jehovah will provide", JEHOVAH-JIREH. See Ap. 4. II. **2 maketh me**=causeth me (implying continuance). **lie down.** We need *making* so as to feed, and not trample the pastures down. **green pastures**=choice pastures. Heb. "pastures of tender grass". **leadeth me**=causeth me to rest. Heb. *nāhal*, to lead flocks. **still waters.** Heb. "waters of rests", JEHOVAH-SHĀLŌM. Ap. 4. II. **3 restoreth**=bringeth back, as in Ps. 19. 8, JEHOVAH-ROPHEKA. Ap. 4. II. **soul.** Heb. *nephesh*. Ap. 13. **leadeth.** Heb. *naḥah*, to guide, conduct. **paths of righteousness**=righteous paths. JEHOVAH-ZIDKĒNŪ. Ap. 4. II. **name's**=own. See note on 20. 1. **4 Yea**=Moreover. **through.** Not into; but "through", and out of it, into resurrection life. **valley, &c.**=a valley of deep shade: may include (but not necessarily) death's dark valley. **evil.** Heb. *ra'a'*. Ap. 44. viii. **Thou art with me.** JEHOVAH-SHAMMAH. Ap. 4. II. **rod and . . . staff**=club and . . . crook. The only two things carried by the shepherd; the former for defence, the latter for help. The club for the sheep's enemies, the crook for the sheep's defence. A lesson for pastors to-day. **comfort**=gently lead. Same word as "leadeth" in *v.* 2.

B (p. 741) **5 Thou °preparest a °table before me in the presence of mine °enemies:**
Thou °anointest my head with oil; my °cup °runneth over.

A **6 Surely goodness and °mercy shall °follow me all the days of my life:**
And I will dwell in the house of [1]the LORD °for ever.

24

°A Psalm °of David.

X C^1 (p. 742) 953 **1 °The earth is °the LORD'S, and °the fulness thereof;**
The °world, and they that dwell therein.
2 For He hath °founded it upon the seas,
And established it upon the floods.

D^1 **3 Who shall ascend into °the hill of [1]the LORD?**
°Or who shall °stand in His °holy place?

E^1 **4 He that hath °clean hands, and a pure heart;**
Who hath not lifted up his °soul unto vanity,
Nor sworn deceitfully.
5 He shall receive the blessing from [1]the LORD,
°And °righteousness from the °God of his salvation.
6 °This *is* the °generation of them that seek Him,
That seek Thy face, °O °Jacob. °Selah.

C^2 **7 Lift up your heads, O ye gates;**
And be ye lift up, ye °everlasting doors;
And the °King of glory shall come in.

D^2 **8 Who *is* [7]this King of glory?**

E^2 **[1]The LORD strong and mighty,**
[1]The LORD mighty in battle.

C^3 **9 [7]Lift up your heads, O ye gates;**
Even [7]lift *them* up, ye [7]everlasting doors;
And [7]the King of glory shall come in.

D^3 **10 °Who is [7]this King of glory?**

E^3 **°The LORD of hosts,**
He *is* [7]the King of glory. °Selah.

25

A Psalm °of David.

M P F^1 (p. 743) 953 **(א) 1 Unto Thee, (ב) O °LORD, do I °lift up my °soul.**

---

5 preparest=settest in order.
table. Put by Fig. *Metonymy* (of Subject), Ap. 6, for what is on it. So that I may feast while He fights. JEHOVAH-NISSI. Ap. 4. II. The figure of the sheep is continued: for the "table" of *v.* 5 answers to the "pastures" of *v.* 2.
enemies=adversaries.
anointest. JEHOVAH-M^EKADDĪSHKEM. Ap. 4. II. Still referring to the sheep and the Shepherd's care: for the figure of the "sheep" is carried right through the Psalm.
cup: i. e. the Shepherd's cup of water for the sheep.
runneth over. See note on 73. 10.
6 mercy=lovingkindness, or grace.
follow=follow after, or closely. In Heb. present put [for future.
for ever=evermore. Heb. "to length of days".

24 (**X**, p. 721). MESSIAH. THE CHIEF SHEPHERD IN GLORY. (*Repeated Alternation.*)

X | C^1 | 1, 2. Right to the earth.
  D^1 | 3. Question. Who . . . ?
    E^1 | 4–6. Answer. Selah.
  C^2 | 7. His Own right.
    D^2 | 8–. Question. Who . . . ?
      E^2 | –8. Answer.
  C^3 | 9. His right with His People.
    D^3 | 10–. Question. Who . . . ?
      E^3 | –10. Answer.

(C2–D3: Right to millennial kingdom.)

Title. A Psalm. See Ap. 65. XVII.
of David=concerning David and the true David. Relates to the entrance of the Ark into Zion (see Ap. 68), typifying the coming glory of Heb. 1. 6. Cp. 2 Sam. 6. 2. 1 Chron. 15. 25. Ps. 68 relates to the setting out of the procession. Ps. 24 to the entrance up to Zion. Ps. 87 to the joy of the entrance with dancings and shoutings. Ps. 105, for subsequent celebrations of the event.
1 The earth. Heb. *'érez*, the earth (as created).
the LORD'S. Heb. Jehovah's. Ap. 4. II. The emphasis is on Jehovah="JEHOVAH'S is the earth".
the fulness=all that fills it. Quoted in 1 Cor. 10. 26.
world. Heb. *tēbēl*, the world (as inhabited).
2 founded, &c. Cp. 2 Pet. 3. 5. Ps. 136. 6. Gen. 1. 1.
3 the hill=the mountain (of Zion, south of Moriah). Seven times so called: here, and Gen. 22. 14. Num. 10. 33. Isa. 2. 3; 30. 29. Mic. 4. 2. Zech. 8. 3. See Ap. 68.
Or. The A.V., 1611, read "And". Changed in 1769 to "Or".
stand=rise up. Cp. 1. 5. **holy.** See note on Ex. 3. 5.
4 clean. Cp. Ps. 15 and Ex. 20. 13–16.
soul. Heb. *nephesh.* Ap. 13. **5 And**=Even.
righteousness. The gift received from Jehovah.
God. Heb. Elohim. Ap. 4. I.
6 This=Such: i. e. not a "new cart" (2 Sam. 6. 3), but the Kohathites. See Num. 7. 9; 4. 2, 15. Deut. 10. 8; 31. 9, &c; and cp. 2 Sam. 6. 13. 1 Chron. 15. 2.
generation=class or circle. Here, the Kohathites. Cp. 22. 30. **O Jacob.** Sept. and Syr. read "O God of Jacob". **Jacob.** See notes on Gen. 32. 28; 43. 6; 45. 26, 28. **Selah.** Connecting the first triad with the Ark of Jehovah: transferring our thoughts from the general claim to the particular making of the claim by this event. See note on *v.* 10, and Ap. 66. II.
7 everlasting doors=age-abiding entrances. The tabernacle (or tent) of David, on Mount Zion, was not ancient. This looks forward to the fulfilment of prophecy in times yet to come. **King of glory**=Glorious king. The repeated question points us both to 22. 6 ("a worm, and no man") and to 23. 1 (The Shepherd). **10 Who**=Who then, is He, this glorious King? **The LORD of hosts.** See note on first occurrence (1 Sam. 1. 3), and Structure above. **Selah.** Connecting Ps. 25 with Ps. 24. Ps. 24 referring to Zion, the new *place* of worship, and Ps. 25 referring to the worship itself, which was to be and could henceforward be offered there. Ps. 24 corresponds with 1 Chron. 15, and Ps. 25 with 1 Chron. 16, which together give a full description of the worship. Ps. 25 is further emphasised by being an Acrostic Psalm, in which the worthiness of Jehovah and the unworthiness of His worshippers stand out in vivid contrast.

25 (*P*, p. 721). [For Structure see next page.]

The second Acrostic Psalm (see Ap. 63. vii). The omission of ק (*Kōph*) makes twenty-one letters (7×3) instead of twenty-two, and marks off one verse (*v.* 11) as central, which is the first confession of sin in the Psalms; thus linking on *Repentance* to *Suffering* and Resurrection (Pss. 16, 22), as in Luke 24. 44–47. The double א (A=*Aleph*) in *vv.* 1, 2 connects the looking up of the worshipper with the double ר (R=*Resh*) of *vv.* 18, 19, which speaks of the looking down of Jehovah. These two are linked on to Ps. 25 by the Selah of 24. 10 and 24. 4. See note on Selah (24. 10). **Title. of David**=by David, or pertaining to the true David. **1 LORD.** Heb. Jehovah. Ap. 4. II. **lift up.** Verses 1 and 2 are connected with *vv.* 18, 19: the double *Aleph* (א), with the double *Resh* (ר), connecting David's looking up with Jehovah's looking down. **soul.** Heb. *nephesh.* Ap. 13.

2 (א) O my °God,
(ב) °I trust in Thee:
Let me °not be °ashamed,
Let °not mine °enemies triumph over me.
3 (ג) Yea, °let none that wait on Thee be [2]ashamed:
Let them be [2]ashamed which °transgress without cause.
4 (ד) Shew me Thy ways, O [1]LORD;
Teach me Thy paths.
5 (ה) Lead me in Thy truth, and teach me:
For Thou *art* the [2]God of my salvation;
(ו) °On Thee do I wait all the day.
6 (ז) °Remember, O [1]LORD, Thy tender °mercies and Thy lovingkindnesses;
For they *have been* ever of old.
7 (ח) [6]Remember not the °sins of my youth, nor my °transgressions:
According to Thy °mercy [6]remember Thou me
For Thy goodness' sake, O [1]LORD.
G¹ (p. 743) 8 (ט) Good and upright *is* [1]the LORD:
Therefore will He °teach [7]sinners in the way.
9 (י) The °meek will He guide °in judgment:
And the °meek will He teach His way
10 (כ) All the paths of [1]the LORD *are* [7]mercy and truth
Unto °such as keep His °covenant and His testimonies.
F² 11 (ל) For Thy °name's sake, O [1]LORD,
°Pardon mine °iniquity; for it *is* great.
G² 12 (מ) °What °man *is* he that °feareth [1]the LORD?
Him shall He [8]teach in the way *that* He shall choose.
13 (נ) °His soul shall dwell at ease;
And his seed shall inherit the °earth.
14 (ס) The °secret of [1]the LORD *is* with them that [12]fear Him;
And He will °shew them His covenant.
F³ 15 (ע) Mine eyes *are* °ever toward [1]the LORD;
For He shall pluck my feet out of the net.
16 (פ) Turn thee unto me, and °have mercy upon me;
For I *am* °desolate and afflicted.
17 (צ) The troubles of my heart are °enlarged:
°*O* bring thou me out of my distresses.
18 (ר) °Look upon mine °affliction and my pain;
And °forgive all my °sins.
19 (ר) °Consider mine °enemies; for they are many;
And they hate me with °cruel hatred.
20 (ש) O keep my [1]soul, and °deliver me:
Let me not be [2]ashamed; for I °put my trust in Thee.
21 (ת) Let integrity and uprightness preserve me;
For I wait on Thee.
22 Redeem Israel, O [2]God,
Out of all his troubles.

26

A Psalm °of David.

Q H¹ (p. 743) 1 °Judge me, O °LORD;
For I have walked in mine integrity:
J¹ I have °trusted also in the °LORD; *therefore* I shall not slide.
H² (p. 744) 2 Examine me, O [1]LORD, and prove me;
Try my °reins and my °heart.

25 (*P*, p. 721). PRAYER IN VIEW OF **P** (Ps. **16**).
(*Repeated Alternation.*)

P | F¹ | 1-7. Prayer and worship.
G¹ | 8-10. Teaching. Worshippers.
F² | 11. Prayer and worship.
G² | 12-14. Teaching. Worshippers.
F³ | 15-22. Prayer and worship.

2 God. Heb. Elohim. Ap. 4. I.
I trust = have confided. Heb. *baṭaḥ.* See Ap. 69. I. Not the same word as in *v.* 20.
not. Heb. *'al* (= Gr. *mē*), subjective. Cp. "none", *v.* 3.
ashamed = put to shame. Fig. *Metonymy* (of Cause) as a verb. So *v.* 20; 31. 1; 119. 116, &c.
enemies = foes.
3 let none. Heb. "none with (*l'o*; Gr. *ou*, objective) them". Cp. "not", *v.* 2.
transgress = act treacherously. Heb. *bāgad.*
5 On = For. Heb. *kī.* Some codices, with Sept., Syr., and Vulg., read *v^ekī*, "and for", thus restoring the Vav (ו), which otherwise is wanting.
6 Remember. Note the threefold object of this remembrance in *vv.* 6, 7.
mercies = compassions. Heb. *rāham.* Not the same word as in *vv.* 7, 16. **7 sins.** Heb. *chāṭā'.* Ap. 44. i.
transgressions. Heb. *pāsha'.* Ap. 44. ix.
mercy = grace. Heb. *ḥāsad.* Not the same word as in *vv.* 6, 16.
8 teach = direct. The subject of this member (G¹).
9 meek = patient, or good.
in judgment = to be vindicated.
10 such. The redeemed (*v.* 22) and righteous worshippers are the subject of this Psalm. See note above.
covenant. The first occurrence in the Psalms.
11 name's. See note on 20. 1.
Pardon. This is the first such plea in the Psalms. See note on "Selah" (24. 10). The central verse of this Psalm. Cp. *v.* 18.
iniquity. Heb. *'āvāh.* Ap. 44. iv.
12 What . . . ? Fig. *Erotēsis* (Ap. 6), to emphasise the worshippers. **man.** Heb. *'īsh.* Ap. 14. II.
feareth = revereth.
13 His soul = He. Heb. *nephesh.* Ap. 13.
earth = land. Cp. Matt. 5. 5.
14 secret = secret counsel.
shew them = cause them to know.
15 ever toward. Supply Fig. *Ellipsis* (Ap. 6), "ever [looking] toward". It is *salutary suspense* which keeps us thus looking.
16 have mercy upon = show kindness to. Heb. *ḥānan.* Not the same word as in *vv.* 6, 7.
desolate = [Thine] only One. Heb. *yāchīd.* See note on Deut. 6. 4. Sept. = *monogenēs*, only begotten.
17 enlarged, &c.: or, troubles have enlarged my heart: i. e. made it more sympathetic.
O bring: or Thou hast brought.
18 Look upon. See note on "lift up", *v.* 1.
affliction = humiliation.
forgive = bear away. First occurrence in the Psalms.
sins. Heb. *chāṭā'.* Ap. 44. i.
19 Consider. Same Heb. as "look upon", *v.* 18.
enemies = foes.
cruel hatred. Heb. "hatred of violence" = "violent hatred". Ginsburg thinks "hatred without a cause".
20 deliver = rescue.
put my trust = flee for refuge. Heb. *ḥasah.* See Ap. 69. II. Not the same word as in *v.* 1.
22 Redeem = Deliver: i. e. redeem *by putting forth power.* Heb. *pādāh.* See notes on Ex. 13. 13.

26 [For Structure see next page].

Title. of David = by David, or concerning the true David.
1 Judge me = Vindicate me, or Do me justice.
LORD. Heb. Jehovah. Ap. 4. II.
trusted = confided. Heb. *bāṭaḥ.* Ap. 69. I.
2 reins = kidneys.
reins . . . heart. Put by Fig. *Metonymy* (of Subject), Ap. 6, for thoughts and feelings.

J² (p. 744) 3 For Thy lovingkindness *is* before mine eyes:
And I have °walked in Thy truth.
4 I have not sat with vain persons,
Neither will I go in with dissemblers.
5 I have hated the °congregation of °evil doers;
And will not sit with the °wicked.
6 I will wash mine hands in innocency:
So will I compass Thine °altar, O ¹LORD:
7 That I may publish with the voice of thanksgiving,
And °tell of all Thy wondrous works.
8 ¹LORD, I have loved the °habitation of Thy °house,
And °the place where Thine honour °dwelleth.

H³ 9 °Gather not °my soul with °sinners,
Nor my life with bloody °men:
10 In whose hands *is* °mischief,
And their right hand is full of bribes.

J³ 11 But as for me, I will walk in mine integrity:
H⁴ °Redeem me, and °be merciful unto me.
J⁴ 12 My foot standeth in an even place:
In the °congregations will I bless ¹the LORD.

27

°*A Psalm* °of David.

*R*¹ K¹ (p. 744) 1 °The LORD *is* my °light and my salvation; whom shall I fear?
°The LORD *is* the °strength of my life; °of whom shall I be afraid?
2 When the °wicked, *even* mine °enemies and my foes, came upon me to eat up my flesh,
They stumbled and fell.
3 Though an host should encamp against me,
My heart shall not fear:
Though war should rise against me,
°In this *will I be* confident.

K² L l 4 One *thing* have I desired of ¹the LORD, that will I seek after;
That I may °dwell in the house of ¹the LORD all the days of my life,
To behold the °beauty of ¹the LORD, and to °enquire in His °temple.
m 5 For in the °time of trouble He shall °hide me in His °pavilion:
In the °secret of His °tabernacle shall He hide me;
He shall set me up upon a °rock.
n 6 And now shall mine head be lifted up above mine enemies round about me:
o Therefore will I °offer in His ⁵tabernacle °sacrifices of joy;
I will sing, yea, I will sing praises unto ¹the LORD.

L l 7 Hear, O ¹LORD, *when* I cry with my voice:
°Have mercy also upon me, and answer me.
8 °*When Thou saidst,* "Seek ye My face;" my heart said unto Thee,
"Thy face, ¹LORD, will I seek."
m 9 ⁵Hide not Thy ⁸face *far* from me;
Put not Thy servant away in anger:
Thou hast been my help;
Leave me not, neither forsake me, O °God °of my salvation.

26 (*Q*, p. 721). PRAYER WITH REFERENCE TO PSALM **17.** (*Repeated Alternation.*)

Q | H¹ | 1-. Prayer.
  J¹ | -1. Plea. "For".
 H² | 2. Prayer.
  J² | 3-8. Plea. "For".
 H³ | 9, 10. Prayer.
  J³ | 11-. Plea. Profession.
 H⁴ | -11. Prayer.
  J⁴ | 12. Plea. Profession.

3 walked = walked habitually.
5 congregation = assembly: in its military aspect.
evil. Heb. *rā'a'.* Ap. 44. viii.
wicked = lawless. Heb. *rāshā'.* Ap. 44. x.
6 altar. No need to suppose this to refer to the Temple or later period than David. The altars of burnt offering and incense were in use from the time of the Exodus. **7 tell of** = recount.
8 habitation = dwelling: implying safety.
house. Referring not to the Temple, but to David's Tabernacle on Zion. Cp. 5. 7, and see below.
the place, &c. = the place of Thy glorious Tabernacle.
dwelleth. Heb. *shākan.* See note on "placed" (Gen. 3. 24).
9 Gather not = Destroy not. Heb. *'āṣaph.* A Homonym. See note on "receive" (Num. 12. 14, 15).
my soul = me (emphatic). Heb. *nephesh.* Ap. 13.
sinners. Heb. *chāṭā'.* Ap. 44. i.
men. Heb. pl. of *'ěnōsh.* Ap. 14. III.
10 mischief = lewdness. [note on 25. 22.
11 Redeem = deliver (by power). Heb. *pādāh.* See
be merciful = show me favour, or be gracious.
12 congregations = assemblies; or pl. of majesty = the great assembly. Occurs only here, and 68. 26.

27 (*R*¹, p. 721). PRAYER IN VIEW OF PSALM **18.** (*Division.*)

*R*¹ | K¹ | 1-3. Confidence. The basis of the prayer.
 | K² | 4-14. Prayer. Resulting from the confidence.

Title. A Psalm. See Ap. 65. XVII.
of David = by David, or relating to the true David.
1 The LORD. Heb. Jehovah. Ap. 4. II.
light. Fig. *Metonymy* (of Effect), Ap. 6, not Fig. *Metaphor*; "light" put for Jehovah as the Author of joy.
strength = strength (for protection). Heb. *'āzaz.*
of whom, &c. Cp. Rom. 8. 31.
2 wicked. Heb. *rā'a'.* Ap. 44. viii.
enemies = adversaries. **3 In this** = in spite of this. In *v.* 1 we have the foundation of his confidence; in *v.* 2, the need of it; and in *v.* 3, the exercise of it.

4-14 (K², above). PRAYER. RESULTING FROM THE CONFIDENCE. (*Extended Alternation.*)

K² | L | l | 4. Seeking.
   m | 5. Hiding.
    n | 6-. Enemies.
     o | -6. Joy.
 } Prayer meditated.
 L | *l* | 7, 8. Seeking.
   m | 9, 10. Hiding.
    n | 11, 12. Enemies.
     o | 13, 14. Hope.
 } Prayer offered.

4 dwell, &c. Cp. Ps. 23. 6.
beauty = pleasantness, delightfulness.
enquire = contemplate with admiration.
temple = palace. Used generally of heaven, but also of the holy place (Gr. *naos*). **5 time** = day.
hide. Fig. *Metonymy* (of Adjunct), Ap. 6; hiding put for protection afforded by it. **pavilion** = dwelling.
secret = secret place, where no stranger was admitted.
tabernacle = tent, or habitation. Heb. *'ohel.* Ap. 40 (3).
rock. Heb. *ẓūr.* See note on 18. 1, 2.
6 offer = sacrifice. Heb. *zābach.* Ap. 43. I. iv.
sacrifices of joy = joyful sacrifices. Genitive of character. See Ap. 17. i: i. e. with shoutings of joy. **7 Have mercy** = Show favour, or Be gracious.
8 When, &c.: or, "To thee, my heart, He hath said, 'Seek thou My face'; Thy face, O Jehovah, will I seek". **9 God.** Heb. Elohim. Ap. 4. I. **of.** Genitive of Origin. Ap. 17 (2).

10 When my father and my mother forsake me,
Then [1] the LORD will ° take me up.

n (p. 744) 11 ° Teach me Thy way, O [1] LORD,
And lead me in a plain path,
Because of mine ° enemies.
12 Deliver me not over unto the ° will of mine ° enemies:
For false witnesses are risen up against me, and such as breathe out cruelty.

o 13 °*I had fainted*, unless I had believed to see the goodness of [1] the LORD
° In the land of the living.
14 ° Wait on [1] the LORD:
Be of good courage, and He shall strengthen thine heart:
° Wait, I say, on [1] the LORD.

28

°*A Psalm* ° of David.

R² M p (p. 745) 1 Unto thee will I cry, O ° LORD my ° rock;
be ° not silent to me:
Lest, *if* Thou ° be silent to me,
I become like them that go down into ° the pit.
2 Hear the voice of my supplications, when I cry unto Thee,
When I ° lift up my hands toward Thy ° holy ° oracle.

q 3 Draw me not away with the ° wicked,
And with the workers of ° iniquity,
Which speak peace to their neighbours,
But ° mischief *is* in their hearts.

N 4 Give ° them according to their ° deeds, and according to the [3] wickedness of their ° endeavours:
Give ° them after the ° work of their hands;
Render to ° them their desert.
5 Because they regard not the ° works of [1] the LORD,
Nor the ° operation of His hands,
He shall destroy them, and not build them up.

M p 6 Blessed *be* [1] the LORD,
Because He hath heard the voice of my supplications.

q 7 [1] The LORD *is* my strength and my ° shield;
My heart ° trusted in Him, and I am ° helped:
Therefore my heart greatly rejoiceth;
And with my song will I ° praise Him.
8 [1] The LORD *is* ° their strength,
And He *is* the ° saving strength ° of ° His anointed.

N 9 Save Thy People, and bless Thine inheritance:
° Feed them also, and lift them up for ever.

29

°A Psalm ° of David.

S O¹ (p. 745) 1 ° Give unto ° the LORD, O ye ° mighty,
° Give unto ° the LORD glory and strength.
2 [1] Give unto [1] the LORD [1] the glory due unto ° His name;
° Worship [1] the LORD in ° the beauty of holiness.

10 take me up = receive and protect me with His saints.
11 Teach = Point out, or Direct.
enemies = those that observe me.
12 will = soul. Heb. *nephesh*. Ap. 13.
enemies = adversaries.
13 I had fainted, unless. The Hebrew word has the extraordinary points (see Ap. 31) in the MSS. to show that the Massorites regarded it as not having been in the primitive text. Its presence accounts for the insertion (in italics) in the A.V. and R.V. They are not found in some codices, the Sept., Syr., or Vulg. The verse should read: "I have believed that I shall see the goodness", &c.
In the land of the living. See note on Isa. 38. 11.
14 Wait. Fig. *Apostrophe*. Ap. 6.

28 (*R²*, p. 721). PRAYER IN VIEW OF PSALM **18**.
(*Alternations*.)

R² | M | p | 1, 2. For audience. } Prayer.
| | q | 3. For discrimination. }
| N | 4, 5. Enemies. Imprecation.
| *M* | *p* | 6. For audience. } Praise.
| | *q* | 7, 8. For help. }
| *N* | 9. Enemies. Imprecation.

Title. A Psalm. Ap. 65. XVII.
of David = by David, or relating to the true David. The Psalm is a continuation of Ps. 27, and stands in relation to Ps. 18.
1 LORD. Heb. Jehovah. Ap. 4. II. In Pss. 28 and 29 there are twenty verses, and Jehovah occurs twenty times.
rock. Heb. *zūr*. See note on 18. 1, 2; and cp. 27. 5. The reference is to Ps. 18.
not silent = not deaf, and so dumb. Heb. *hārash*.
be silent = be quiet, or silent. Heb. *ḥashah*.
the pit. Heb. *bōr*, a sepulchre, as hewn (Gen. 21. 19).
2 lift up my hands. Put by Fig. *Metonymy* (of Adjunct), Ap. 6, for praying. **holy.** See note on Ex. 3. 5.
oracle = speaking place. Occurs only here in Psalms. See note on 2 Sam. 16. 23.
3 wicked = lawless. Heb. *rāshā'*. Ap. 44. x.
iniquity. Heb. *'āven*. Ap. 44. iii.
mischief. Heb. *rā'a'*. Ap. 44. viii.
4 them. Note the Fig. *Repetitio* (Ap. 6), for emphasis.
deeds = deed, or work. **endeavours** = practices.
work. Some codices, with Aram., Sept., and Vulg., read "works" (pl.). **5 works** = deeds.
operation = actual execution. Some codices pl., as in note above.
7 shield. Here is the link with Ps. 18. Cp. "strength", *v.* 8, below.
trusted = confided. Heb. *bataḥ*. Ap. 69. I.
trusted . . . helped . . . praise. Note the reference to past, present, and future.
8 their = [strength] to His People. The letter Aleph (א = ') being interchangeable with Ayin (ע = '). This orthography is attested by some codices, and by Sept. and Syr. Thus agreeing with 29. 11.
saving strength = great saving strength. Heb. "strength of salvations". Pl. of majesty.
of = to. **His anointed** = His Messiah, as in 2. 2.
9 Feed = tend as a shepherd. Cp. Ps. 23.

29 (*S*, p. 721). HIS PEOPLE'S PRAISE OF GOD'S GLORY IN CREATION. IN VIEW OF PSALM **19**.
(*Division*.)

S | O¹ | 1, 2. Praise promised.
| O² | 3–11. Praise rendered.

Title. A Psalm. See Ap. 65. XVII.
of David = by David, or relating to the true David. The sequel to Ps. 28, and the fulfilment of the promise in 28. 7. It is "the voice of Jehovah" in response to David's voice in 28. 6. It ends in the same manner.
1 Give = Ascribe, or Bring as due.
the LORD. Heb. Jehovah. Ap. 4. II. Occurs four times in O¹ and fourteen times in O². See note on 28. 1. **mighty.** The Targum reads "angels".
2 His name = Himself. See note on 20. 1. **Worship** = Bow down. **the beauty of holiness** = His glorious Sanctuary. Cp. 2 Chron. 20. 21. Ps. 96. 9. Ex. 28. 2.

O² P R (p. 746) 3 The °voice of [1]the LORD *is* upon the waters:
The °GOD of glory thundereth:
[1]The LORD *is* upon °many waters.
4 The [3]voice of [1]the LORD *is* °powerful;
The [3]voice of [1]the LORD *is* °full of majesty.

S r 5 The [3]voice of [1]the LORD breaketh the cedars;
Yea, [1]the LORD breaketh the cedars of Lebanon.

s 6 He maketh them also to skip like a calf;
Lebanon and °Sirion like a young °unicorn.

R 7 The [3]voice of [1]the LORD °divideth the flames of fire.

S s 8 The [3]voice of [1]the LORD shaketh the wilderness;
[1]The LORD shaketh the wilderness of °Kadesh.

r 9 The [3]voice of [1]the LORD maketh the hinds °to calve,
And °discovereth the forests:

Q And in His °temple °doth every one speak of *His* glory.

P 10 [1]The LORD °sitteth upon the flood;
Yea, [1]the LORD sitteth King for ever.

Q 11 [1]The LORD will give °strength unto His People;
[1]The LORD will bless His People with °peace.

951 B.C. **30** °A Psalm *and* °Song *at* the °dedication °of the house of David.

*T*¹ T (p. 746) 1 I will extol Thee, O °LORD; for Thou hast °lifted me up,
And hast not made my foes to rejoice over me.

U t 2 O [1]LORD my °God,
I cried unto Thee,

u And Thou hast healed me.
3 O [1]LORD, Thou hast brought up my °soul from °the grave:
Thou hast kept me alive, °that I should not go down to °the pit.

v 4 °Sing unto [1]the LORD, O ye °saints of His,
And give thanks at the remembrance of His holiness.

V 5 For His anger °*endureth but* a moment;
In His favour *is* life:
Weeping may °endure for a night,
But joy *cometh* in the morning.

V 6 And in my prosperity I said,
°"I shall never be moved."
7 [1]LORD, by Thy favour Thou hast made °my mountain to stand strong:
Thou didst °hide Thy °face, *and* I was troubled.

---

29. 3-11 (O², p. 745). PRAISE RENDERED. (*Alternation.*)

O² | P | 3-9-. Nature.
  Q | -9. Grace.
  P | 10. Nature.
  Q | 11. Grace.

3-9- (P, above). NATURE. (*Alternation and Introversion.*)

P | R | 3, 4. Waters.
  S | r | 5. Cedars.
    s | 6. Mountains.
  R | 7. Waters.
  S | *s* | 8. Wilderness.
    r | 9-. Forests.

3 voice=thunder. Fig. *Epibolē* or *Anaphora.* Ap. 6. Seven times: *vv.* 3, 4, 4, 5, 7, 8, 9.
GOD. Heb. El. Ap. 4. IV=the mighty Creator, the glorious God. **many**=mighty.
4 powerful=with power. **full of**=with.
6 Sirion=Hermon. Cp. Deut. 3. 9.
unicorn=the bull-calf of wild oxen. Cp. 22. 21. Job 39. 9.
7 divideth the flames: or, "cleaveth [with] flames of fire": i. e. lightning.
8 Kadesh: i. e. Kadesh-Naphtali, near Lebanon (*v.* 6); not Kadesh-barnea.
9 to calve. Through fright.
discovereth=strippeth bare; or, layeth open to view.
temple=palace: i. e. heaven itself.
doth every one speak of=doth every being there ascribe. See *v.* 1. Cp. Rev. 4. 8.
10 sitteth upon the flood. Corresponding with *v.* 3 ="sat enthroned at the flood", referring to Genesis. Heb. *mabbūl*, from *yābal*, to flow. Occurs only here and Gen. 6. 17; 7. 6, 7, 10, 17; 9. 11, 15, 28; 10. 1, 32; 11. 10.
11 strength. See note on 28. 8. He who has it (*v.* 1) will give it (*v.* 11).
peace=the (i. e. His) peace. Cp. Phil. 4. 7.

30 (*T*¹, p. 721). HIS PEOPLE'S PRAISE IN VIEW OF PSALM **20.** (*Introversion and Extended Alternation.*)

*T*¹ | T | 1. Thanksgiving promised.
  U | t | 2-. David's cry to Jehovah.
    u | -2, 3. The relief obtained.
    v | 4. Songs of praise.
  V | 5. Joy succeeds weeping.
  V | 6, 7. Prosperity precedes trouble.
  U | *t* | 8-10. David's cry to Jehovah.
    u | 11. The relief obtained.
    v | 12-. Songs of praise.
  T | -12. Thanksgiving promised.

Title. A Psalm. Heb. *mizmōr.* See Ap. 65. XVII.
Song. Heb. *Shīr.* The only *Shīr* in the first book. See Ap. 65. XXIII.
dedication. Heb. *ḥanak.* Used of houses in Deut. 20. 5.
of the house of David. Cp. 2 Sam. 7. 1, 2. Not the temple.
1 LORD. Heb. Jehovah. Ap. 4. II.
lifted me up=as out of a pit.
2 God. Heb. Elohim. Ap. 4. I.
3 soul. Heb. *nephesh.* Ap. 13.
the grave. Heb. Sheōl. See Ap. 35.
that I should not go down. So in some codices and one early printed edition; but other codices read "from among" [those who were going down], with Sept., Syr., and Vulg.
the pit=a sepulchre. Heb. *bōr.* See note on "well" (Gen. 21. 19).
4 Sing=Sing praises.
saints=favoured ones: lit. men endued with grace. The natural man cannot do this (1 Cor. 2. 14).

5 endureth, &c. Render "For a moment [is] His anger; for a lifetime [is] His favour". **endure**=lodge.
6 I shall, &c. Cp. 62. 6. **7 my mountain**: i. e. Zion, which David had but recently taken (2 Sam. 5. 7-10).
hide Thy face. Probably refers to a sickness which followed. **face.** Fig. *Anthropopatheia.* Ap. 6.

U t (p. 746) 8 I cried to Thee, O [1]LORD;
And unto °the LORD* I made supplication.
9 °What profit °*is there* in my °blood, when I go down to °the pit?
°Shall the dust praise Thee? °shall it declare Thy truth?
10 Hear, O [1]LORD, and have mercy upon me:
[1]LORD, be Thou my helper.

u 11 Thou hast °turned for me my mourning into dancing:
Thou hast °put off my °sackcloth, and °girded me with gladness;

v 12 To the end that °*my* glory may sing praise to Thee, and not be silent.

T O [1]LORD my [2]God, I will give thanks unto Thee for ever.

°To the chief Musician.

31

°A Psalm °of David.

T² W Y (p. 747) 1 In Thee, O °LORD, °do I put my trust; let me never be ashamed:
Deliver me in Thy righteousness.
2 Bow down Thine °ear to me; °deliver me speedily:
Be Thou my strong °rock, for an house of defence to save me.

Z A 3 For Thou *art* my °rock and my fortress;
Therefore for °Thy name's sake °lead me, and °guide me.
4 Pull me out of the net that they have laid privily for me:
For Thou *art* my strength.

B w 5 °**Into Thine °hand I °commit my °spirit:**
Thou hast °redeemed me, O [1]LORD °GOD of truth.

x 6 °I have hated them that regard °lying vanities:
But I °trust in [1]the LORD.

X 7 I will be glad and rejoice in Thy °mercy:
For Thou hast °considered my trouble;
Thou hast known °my soul in adversities;
8 And hast not shut me up into the hand of the enemy:
Thou hast set my feet in a large room.

W Z A 9 °Have mercy upon me, O [1]LORD, for I am in trouble:
Mine eye is consumed with grief, *yea*, [7]my soul and my °belly.
10 For my life is spent with grief, and my years with sighing:
My strength faileth
Because of mine °iniquity, and my bones are consumed.
11 I was a °reproach among all mine enemies,
But especially among °my neighbours, and a fear to mine acquaintance:
They that did see me without fled from me.
12 I am forgotten as a dead man out of mind:
I °am like a °broken vessel.
13 For I have heard the slander of many:
Fear *was* on every side:
While they took counsel together against me,
They devised to take away my °life.

B x 14 But I [6]trusted in Thee, O [1]LORD:
I said, "Thou *art* my °God."

---

8 the LORD*. One of the 134 places where "Jehovah" (in the primitive text) was altered to "Adonai". See Ap. 32. Some codices, with one early printed edition, read "Jehovah". Ap. 4. II.
9 What profit . . . ? Fig. *Erotēsis.* Ap. 6.
is there. Supply "[will there be]".
blood = soul. Cp. Lev. 17. 11.
the pit. Heb. *Shāchath* = destruction (55. 23; 103. 4), or corruption (16. 10; 49. 9. Jer. 2. 6).
Shall . . . ? Fig. *Erotēsis.* Ap. 6. Cp. 6. 5; 88. 11; 115. 17; 118. 17. Isa. 38. 18.
11 turned: denoting the act. See "girded", below.
put off = torn open, or off.
sackcloth. Put by Fig. *Metonymy* (of Adjunct), Ap. 6, for the sadness of which it was the sign.
girded: denoting the fact. See "turned", above.
12 my glory. Put by Fig. *Metonymy* (of Effect), Ap. 6, for "myself", referring either to the *tongue* (108. 1), or powers of mind which give the praise.
To the chief Musician. See Ap. 64. Though written for a special occasion, Ps. 30 was handed over to the chief Musician for public use, and in connection with any other dedication.

31 (*T*², p. 721). HIS PEOPLE'S PRAYER AND PRAISE IN VIEW OF PSALM **20.** (*Alternations and Introversions.*)

*T*²
 W | Y | 1, 2. Let me not be ashamed. "Thine ear". } Prayer.
   Z | A | 3, 4. Reason. "For". [Thrice.]
     B | w | 5. "Into Thine hand".
       x | 6. "I trust".
 X | 7, 8. Praise for benefits received.
 W | Z | *A* | 9-13. Reason. "For". [Thrice.] } Prayer.
     B | *x* | 14. "I trusted".
       w | 15. "In Thy hand".
   Y | 16-18. Let me not be ashamed. "Thy face".
 X | 19-24. Praise for benefits received.

Title. A Psalm. See Ap. 65. XVII.
of David = by David, or relating to the true David.
1 LORD. Heb. Jehovah. Ap. 4. II.
do I put my trust = have I fled for refuge to. See Ap. 69. II.
2 ear. Fig. *Anthropopatheia.* Ap. 6.
deliver = rescue.
rock. Heb. *zur.* } See note on 18. 1, 2.
3 rock. Heb. *sela'.* } See note on 18. 1, 2.
Thy name's sake. See note on 20. 1.
lead = Thou wilt gently lead.
guide = gently guide. **Pull** = Thou wilt pull.
5 Into, &c. Quoted in Luke 23. 46.
hand. Fig. *Anthropopatheia.* Ap. 6.
commit = I will commit.
spirit. Heb. *rūach.* Ap. 9.
redeemed = delivered by power. Heb. *pādah.* See note on Ex. 13. 13. Cp. Ex. 6. 6.
GOD. Heb. El. Ap. 4. IV.
6 I have hated. Some codices, with Aram., Sept., Syr., and Vulg., read "Thou hatest".
lying vanities = idols. See Jer. 8. 19; 10. 8. Cp. 2 Sam. 5. 21. Jonah 2. 8.
trust in = have fixed my hope on, or confidence in. Heb. *batah.* Ap. 69. I.
7 mercy = lovingkindness, or grace.
considered = looked upon.
my soul = me myself. Heb. *nephesh.* Ap. 13.
9 Have mercy upon = Show favour or grace to.
belly. Put by Fig. *Synecdoche* (of Part), Ap. 6, for "body".
10 iniquity. Heb. *'āvāh.* Ap. 44. iv. But Sept. and Syr. read "humiliation". **11 reproach** = derision.
my neighbours. Cp. 2 Sam. 6. 16, 20.
12 am = became. **broken:** or missing.
13 life = soul. Heb. *nephesh.* Ap. 13.
14 God. Heb. Elohim. Ap. 4. I.

w (p. 747) 15 My °times *are* in Thy hand:
[2]Deliver me from the hand of mine enemies, and from them that persecute me.

Y 16 Make Thy °face to shine upon Thy servant:
Save me °for Thy mercies' sake.
17 Let me not be ashamed, O [1]LORD; for I have called upon Thee:
Let the °wicked be ashamed, *and* let them be silent in °the grave.
18 Let the lying lips be put to silence;
Which speak °grievous things proudly and contemptuously against °the righteous.

X 19 *Oh* how great *is* Thy goodness, which Thou hast laid up for them that fear Thee;
Which Thou hast wrought for them that °trust in Thee before the sons of °men!
20 Thou shalt hide them in the secret of Thy presence from the °pride of °man:
Thou shalt keep them secretly in a °pavilion from the strife of tongues.
21 Blessed *be* the [1]LORD:
For He hath shewed me His marvellous °kindness in a °strong city.
22 For I said in my haste, "I am cut off from before Thine °eyes:"
Nevertheless Thou heardest the voice of my supplications when I cried unto Thee.
23 O love °the LORD, all ye His °saints:
For [1]the LORD preserveth the faithful,
And plentifully rewardeth the proud doer.
24 Be of good courage, and He shall strengthen your heart,
All ye that °hope in [1]the LORD.

32

A Psalm °of David, °Maschil.

T^3 C y (p. 748) 941 B.C. 1 °**Blessed *is* °*he whose* °transgression *is* °forgiven, *whose* °sin *is* °covered.**
2 [1]**Blessed *is* the °man unto whom °the LORD °imputeth not °iniquity,**
z And in whose °spirit *there is* no guile.
D a 3 When I °kept silence, my bones waxed old
Through my °roaring all the day long.
4 For day and night Thy °hand was heavy upon me:
My moisture °is turned °into the drought of summer. °Selah.
b 5 °I acknowledged my [1]sin unto thee, and mine [1]iniquity °have I not hid.
I said, "I will confess my °transgressions unto [2]the LORD;"
And °Thou forgavest the [2]iniquity of my [1]sin. °Selah.
6 For this °shall every one that is °godly pray unto Thee °in a time when Thou mayest be found:

15 times. Put by Fig. *Metonymy* (of Adjunct), Ap. 6, for what is done in them = all my affairs.
16 face. Fig. *Anthropopatheia.* Ap. 6.
for Thy mercies' sake = in Thy lovingkindness.
17 wicked = lawless. Heb. *rāshā'.* Ap. 44. x.
the grave. Heb. Sheōl. Ap. 35.
18 grievous = hard, or arrogant.
the righteous = a righteous one.
19 trust = put their trust. Same word as *v.* 1.
men. Heb. *'ādām.* Ap. 14. I.
20 pride = conspiracy.
man. Heb. *'īsh.* Ap. 14. II.
pavilion = booth, or tent.
21 kindness = lovingkindness, or grace.
strong = fortified: which Zion was.
22 eyes. Fig. *Anthropopatheia.* Ap. 6.
23 the LORD. Heb. 'eth Jehovah. Ap. 4. II. (Objective.)
saints = favoured, or graced ones.
24 hope in = wait for.

32 (*T^3*, p. 721). HIS PEOPLE'S PRAYER AND PRAISE IN VIEW OF PSALM **20**. (*Introversions and Alternations.*)

T^3
C | y | 1, 2-. The justified.
  z | -2. The sanctified. } David speaks.
D | a | 3, 4. Trouble.
  b | 5-7. Deliverance.
E | 8. Promise.
E | 9. Injunction. } God speaks.
D | *a* | 10-. Trouble.
  b | -10. Deliverance.
C | *y* | 11-. The justified.
  z | -11. The sanctified. } David speaks.

Title. of David = by David, or relating to the true David.
Maschil = giving instruction. This is the first of thirteen "Maschil" Psalms. These are 32, 42, 44, 45, 52, 53, 54, 55, 74, 78, 88, 89, 142; some in each Book, except Book IV. See Ap. 65. XI.
1 Blessed = How happy. See Ap. 63. VI. Quoted in Rom. 4. 7, 8.
he. Left to be supplied by *any* one who has this experience.
transgression = breaking away, rebellion. Heb. *pāsha',* referring to *thought.* Ap. 44. ix.
forgiven = taken up and carried away.
sin = erring, transgression. Heb. *chāṭā'.* Ap. 44. i.
covered = atoned (by the death and merit of a substituted sacrifice).
2 man. Heb. *'ādām.* Ap. 14. I.
the LORD. Heb. Jehovah. Ap. 4. II.
imputeth not. Forensic or legal righteousness. The N.T. righteousness is not *negative,* but *positive,* for the righteousness of One (Christ) is imputed or accounted to another, as it was to Abraham (Gen. 15. 6. Rom. 4. 13).
iniquity = sin in the nature, rather than breaches of the law in act = perverseness (never eradicated). Heb. *'āvōn.* Ap. 44. iii. **spirit.** Heb. *rūach.* Ap. 9.
3 kept silence: from confession. Probably during the year referred to in 2 Sam. 12. 1-5.
roaring = irrepressible anguish. Not yet articulate confession.
4 hand. Fig. *Anthropopatheia.* Ap. 6.
is = was.
into. Some codices, with Aram., read "like".
Selah. Connecting the *trouble* of conviction with the *confession* to which it led. See Ap. 66. II.
5 I acknowledged = I [made up my mind that I would] acknowledge.
have I not hid = did I not hide.

transgressions. Refers to 2 Sam. 12. 13 (941 B.C.). Some codices, with Sept. and Vulg., read it in sing., **Thou forgavest.** Divine forgiveness follows immediately on true confession to Him. Cp. 2 Sam. 12. 13. Gen. 44. 16, 17. Job 42. 5, 6. Isa. 6. 5-7. Dan. 10. 10-12. Luke 5. 8-10. **Selah.** Connecting this Divine forgiveness with prayer and worship, which can be accepted only from those who have this experience. Cp. *vv.* 4 and 7; and see Ap. 66. II. **6 shall** = let. **godly** = man of lovingkindness, who has experienced this Divine grace or favour. **in a time,** &c. = in a time of finding [his need].

Surely in the °floods of great waters they shall not come nigh unto him.
7 Thou *art* my °hiding place; Thou shalt preserve me from trouble;
Thou shalt compass me about with °songs of deliverance. °Selah.

E (p. 748) 8 °I will °instruct thee and teach thee in the way which thou °shalt go:
°I will guide thee with Mine eye.

E 9 Be ye not as the °horse, *or* as the °mule, *which* have no understanding:
Whose mouth must be held in with °bit and °bridle,
°Lest they °come near unto thee.

D a 10 Many sorrows *shall be* to °the wicked:
b But he that °trusteth in [2]the LORD, °mercy shall compass him about.

C y 11 Be glad in [2]the LORD, and rejoice, ye righteous:
z And shout for joy, all *ye that are* upright in heart.

T[4] F[1] G (p. 749) 33 °Rejoice in °the LORD, O ye righteous:
For praise is comely for the upright.
2 Praise [1]the LORD with harp:
Sing unto Him with the psaltery *and* an instrument of ten strings.
3 Sing unto Him °a new song;
Play skilfully with a loud noise.

H 4 For the Word of [1]the LORD *is* right;
And all His works *are done* in truth.
5 He loveth righteousness and judgment:
The earth is full of the °goodness of [1]the LORD.
6 °By the word of [1]the LORD were the heavens made;
And all the host of them by the °breath of His mouth.
7 He gathereth the waters of the sea together °as an heap:
He layeth up the °depth in storehouses.

G 8 Let all the earth fear [1]the LORD:
Let all the inhabitants of the °world stand in awe of Him.

H 9 For He °spake, and it °was *done;*
He °commanded, and it °stood fast.

F[2] J 10 [1]The LORD bringeth the counsel of the °heathen to nought:
He maketh the devices of the people of none effect.
11 The counsel of [1]the LORD standeth for ever,
The thoughts of His heart to all generations.

K 12 °Blessed *is* the nation whose °God *is* [1]the LORD;
And the People *whom* He hath chosen for His own inheritance.

J 13 [1]The LORD looketh from heaven;
He beholdeth all °the sons of men.
14 From the place of His habitation He looketh
Upon all the inhabitants of the earth.
15 He fashioneth their hearts alike;
He considereth all their works.

16 There is no king saved by the multitude of an host:
A mighty man is not delivered by much strength.

---

floods, &c. Fig. *Hypocatastasis.* Ap. 6. Put for the time of need in preceding line.

7 hiding place. Note Jehovah my *righteousness* (*v.* 5), my *hiding place* (*v.* 7), and my *guide* (*v.* 8). Cp. 9. 9; 27. 5; 31. 20; 119. 114.

songs = shoutings.

Selah. Connecting this worship and praise with the further instruction and guidance which such receive.

8 I will instruct. Jehovah now speaks. See the Structure on p. 748.

instruct. Hence the title "Maschil". See Ap. 65. XI. Note the Fig. *Anabasis* (Ap. 6): instruct, teach, guide.

shalt go = goest.

I will guide, &c. = Let me cause mine eye to take counsel concerning thee. Used of Jethro (Ex. 18. 19, &c.), Nathan (1 Kings 1. 12, &c.), Jeremiah (Jer. 38. 15).

9 horse . . . mule. Cp. Prov. 26. 3.

bit . . . bridle. See note on "eye", *v.* 8.

Lest = Otherwise they will not.

come near = draw near: i. e. for help and instruction, so as to understand what they are to do: (1) *to help*, Heb. *ḳārab*, Ap. 43. I. i (Deut. 4. 7. Pss. 34. 18; 119. 151; 145. 18. Neh. 13. 4); or (2) *in worship* (Lev. 16. 1. 1 Sam. 14. 36. Ezek. 40. 46; 44. 15).

10 the wicked = the lawless one. Heb. *rāshā'*. Ap. 44. x.

trusteth = confideth. Heb. *baṭaḥ*. Ap. 69. I.

mercy = lovingkindness, or grace.

33 (*T*[4], p. 721). HIS PEOPLE'S NEW SONG IN VIEW OF PSALM **20.** (*Division.*)

T[4] | F[1] | 1-9. Exhortation to praise Jehovah.
| F[2] | 10-22. Declarations concerning Jehovah.

1-9 (F[1], above). EXHORTATION TO PRAISE JEHOVAH. (*Alternation.*)

F[1] | G | 1-3. Exhortation for righteous to praise Jehovah.
| H | 4-7. Reason. "For". (The word and works of Jehovah.)
| *G* | 8. Exhortation to all to fear Jehovah.
| *H* | 9. Reason. "For". (The word and works of Jehovah.)

1 Rejoice = Shout for joy. Ps. 33 (without a title) is thus linked on to Ps. 32. 11. Other links may be noted: cp. 32. 8 with 33. 17; and 32. 8 with 33. 18, &c.

the LORD. Heb. Jehovah. Ap. 4. II.

3 a new song. First occurrence of seven new songs in the O.T. (six in the Psalms: 33. 3; 40. 3; 96. 1; 98. 1; 144. 9; 149. 1; and one in Isa. 42. 10). Heb. *ḥādāsh* = new, unheard of before.

5 goodness = lovingkindness.

6 By the word, &c. Quoted in 2 Pet. 3. 5.

breath = spirit. Heb. *rūach*. Ap. 9.

7 as an heap. Aram., Sept., and Syr. read "as a skin-bottle", taking the pointing as in Ps. 119. 83. The Massoretic pointing refers it to Ex. 15. 8.

depth = depths, or abysses.

8 world = world (as inhabited). Heb. *tēbēl*.

9 spake. Referring to the one act.

was done = it became. Refers to the permanent fact.

commanded. Refers to the one act.

stood fast. Refers to the abiding fact.

10-22 (F[2], above). DECLARATIONS CONCERNING JEHOVAH. (*Alternation.*)

F[2] | J | 10, 11. Mankind's relation to Jehovah.
| K | 12. Relation of Jehovah to His People.
| *J* | 13-17. Results of J.
| *K* | 18-22. Results of K.

10 heathen = nations, or peoples.

12 Blessed = How happy. See Ap. 63. VI. Cp. 144. 15.

God. Heb. Elohim. Ap. 4. I.

13 the sons of men = humanity. Heb. *'ādām* (with Art.). Ap. 14. I.

17 An horse *is* a vain thing for safety:
Neither shall he deliver *any* by his great strength.

K (p. 749) 18 °Behold, the °eye of [1]the LORD *is* upon them that fear Him,
Upon them that °hope in His °mercy;
19 To °deliver °their soul from death,
And to keep them alive in famine.
20 °Our soul waiteth for [1]the LORD:
He *is* our help and our °shield.
21 For our heart shall rejoice in Him,
Because we have °trusted in His °holy °name.
22 Let thy [18]mercy, O [1]LORD, be upon us,
According as we [18]hope in Thee.

969 B.C. **34** °*A Psalm* °of David, °when he changed his behaviour before °Abimelech; who drove him away, and he departed.

U L^1 M c 1 (א) I will bless °the LORD at all times:
His praise *shall* continually *be* in my mouth.
2 (ב) °My soul shall make her boast in °the LORD:
The °humble shall hear *thereof*, and be glad.

d 3 (ג) O magnify [2]the LORD with me,
And let us exalt His name together.

N 4 (ד) I sought [2]the LORD, and He °heard me,
And °delivered me from all my fears.

M c 5 (ה) °They °looked °unto Him,
(ו) And were lightened:
And their faces were not ashamed.
6 (ז) This poor man cried, and [2]the LORD [4]heard *him*,
And saved him out of all his °troubles.
7 (ח) °The angel of [2]the LORD °encampeth round about them that °fear Him,
And delivereth them.

d 8 (ט) **O °taste and see that [2]the LORD *is* good:**
°Blessed *is* the °man *that* °trusteth in Him.
9 (י) O [7]fear [2]the LORD, ye his °saints:
For *there is* no want to them that [7]fear Him.
10 (כ) The young lions do lack, and suffer hunger:
But they that seek [2]the LORD shall not want any good *thing*.

L^2 e^1 11 (ל) Come, ye °children, hearken unto me:
I will teach you the fear of [2]the LORD.
12 (מ) **°What °man *is he that* desireth °life,**
***And* loveth *many* days, that he may see good?**
13 (נ) **°Keep thy tongue from °evil,**
And thy lips from speaking guile.
14 (ס) **Depart from [13]evil, and do good;**
Seek peace, and pursue it.
15 (ע) **The eyes of [2]the LORD *are* upon the righteous,**
And His °ears *are open* unto their cry.

f^1 16 (פ) **The °face of [2]the LORD *is* against them that do [13]evil,**
To cut off the remembrance of them from the earth.

e^2 17 (צ) *The righteous* °cry, and [2]the LORD °heareth,
And [4]delivereth them out of all their [6]troubles.

---

18 Behold. Fig. *Asterismos.* Ap. 6.
eye. Fig. *Anthropopatheia.* Ap. 6. Some codices, with Sept., Syr., and Vulg., read "eyes" (pl.).
hope in = wait for.
mercy = lovingkindness, or grace.
19 deliver = rescue.
their soul = them themselves. } Heb. *nephesh* (Ap. 13),
20 Our soul = we ourselves. } for emphasis.
shield. Heb. *māgēn.* See note on 5. 12.
21 trusted = confided. Heb. *baṭaḥ.* Ap. 69. I.
holy. See note on Ex. 3. 5. name. See note on 20. 1.

34 (*U*, p. 721). HIS PEOPLE'S EXULTATION IN HIS EXALTATION: IN VIEW OF PSALM **21.**
(*Division.*)

U | L^1 | 1-10. Praise. (א—ל.)
| L^2 | 11-22. Instruction. (מ—ת.)

Title. A Psalm. Ap. 65. XVII.
of David = by, or relating to David.
when. Cp. 1 Sam. 21. 10—22. 1.
Abimelech. An appellative for the kings of Gath. This Abimelech was named Achish.
This is an Acrostic Psalm (see Ap. 63. VII). It is divided into two parts, eleven letters to the first and eleven to the second.

1-10 (L^1, above). PRAISE. (א—ל.)
(*Introversion and Alternation.*)

L^1 | M | c | 1, 2. The oppressed. "I" and "they".
| | d | 3. Invitation. "O magnify". "Ye".
| N | 4. Acknowledgment. "I".
| *M* | c | 5-7. The oppressed. "I" and "they".
| | *d* | 8-10. Invitation. ("O taste . . . see . . . fear"). "Ye".

1 the LORD. Heb. *'eth Jehovah.* Ap. 4. II (Objective).
2 My soul = I myself. Heb. *nephesh.* Ap. 13.
the LORD. Heb. Jehovah. Ap. 4. II.
humble = patient, oppressed.
4 heard = answered. **delivered** = rescued.
5 They looked. Some codices, with Sept., Syr., and Vulg., read Imperative, "Look . . !"
looked = looked expectantly. To this end Jehovah keeps us in salutary suspense.
unto Him. That is why they were radiant. To look within is to be miserable (see notes on 77). To look around is to be distracted (see notes on 73).
6 troubles = distresses.
7 The angel of the LORD. Occurs in Psalms only here and 35. 5. Here, in mercy; there, in judgment. Cp. Acts 12: delivering Peter (*vv.* 7-11), and smiting Herod (*v.* 23).
encampeth. Heb. *ḥānāh.* Hence the name "Mahanaim" = two camps in Jacob's vision, afterward to be noted in David's history (2 Sam. 17. 24, 27; 19. 32).
fear = revere.
8 taste, &c. Referred to in 1 Pet. 2. 3.
Blessed = How happy. See Ap. 63. VI.
man = strong man. Heb. *geber.* Ap. 14. IV. Trusting not in his own strength, but in Jehovah.
trusteth in = fleeth for refuge to. Heb. *ḥasah.* Ap. 69. II.
9 saints = separated ones. See note on Ex. 3. 5.

11-22 (L^2, above). INSTRUCTION. (מ—ת.)
(*Repeated Alternation.*)

L^2 | e^1 | 11-15. The righteous.
| f^1 | 16. The evil-doers.
| e^2 | 17-20. The righteous.
| f^2 | 21. The evil-doers.
| e^3 | 22. The righteous.

11 children = sons.
12 What . . . ? Referred to in 1 Pet. 3. 10-12.
man. Heb. *'ish.* Ap. 14. II.
life. Fig. *Metonymy* (of Adjunct), Ap. 6, put for all that makes life worth living.
13 Keep, &c. Fig. *Apostrophe.* Ap. 6.
evil. Heb. *rā'a'.* Ap. 44. viii.
15 ears. } Fig. *Anthropopatheia.* Ap. 6.
16 face. }
17 cry = have cried. **heareth** = hath heard.
delivereth = hath rescued.

18 (ק) [2] The LORD *is* nigh unto them that are of a broken heart;
And saveth such as be of a contrite °spirit.
19 (ר) Many *are* the afflictions of °the righteous:
But [2] the LORD delivereth him out of them all.
20 (ש) He keepeth all his °bones:
Not one of them is broken.
f² (p. 750) 21 (ת) [13] Evil shall slay °the wicked:
And they that hate [18] the righteous shall be °desolate.
e³ 22 (פ) [2] The LORD °redeemeth the °soul of His servants:
And none of them that [8] trust in Him shall be [21] desolate.

35

A Psalm °of David.

V¹ O g k¹ 1 °Plead *my cause*, O °LORD, with °them that strive with me:
l¹ °Fight against them that °fight against me.
k² 2 Take hold of °shield and buckler,
And stand up for mine help.
l² 3 Draw out also the spear, and °stop *the way* against them that °persecute me:
k³ Say unto °my soul, "I *am* thy salvation."
h 4 Let them be confounded and put to shame that seek after [3] my soul:
Let them be turned back and brought to confusion that devise my hurt.
5 Let them be as chaff before the °wind:
And let °the angel of [1] the LORD chase *them*.
6 Let their way be dark and slippery:
And let [5] the angel of [1] the LORD [3] persecute them.
7 For °without cause have they hid for me their °net *in* a pit,
Which °without cause they have digged for [3] my soul.
8 Let destruction come upon him at unawares;
And let his net that he hath hid catch himself:
Into that very destruction let him fall.
i 9 And [3] my soul shall be joyful in [1] the LORD:
It shall rejoice in His salvation.
10 °All my bones shall °say, [1] "LORD, °who *is* like unto Thee,
Which °deliverest the °poor from him that is °too strong for him,
Yea, the °poor and the needy from him that spoileth him?"
P 11 °False witnesses did rise up;
They laid to my charge *things* that I knew not.
Q 12 They rewarded me °evil for good
To the °spoiling of [3] my soul.
R 13 But as for me, when they were sick, my °clothing *was* sackcloth:
I humbled [3] my soul °with fasting;
And my prayer returned into mine own bosom.
14 I behaved myself as though *he had been* my friend *or* brother:

18 spirit. Heb. *rūach*. Ap. 9.
19 the righteous = a righteous one. Cp. "him", next clause.
20 bones. True (by *application*) of the members of Christ's body. See note on 35. 10. Eph. 5. 30. Hence John 19. 31-33. Ex. 12. 46. Heartbroken (69. 20), but not "bones".
21 the wicked = a lawless one. Heb. *rāshā'*. Ap. 44. x.
desolate = held guilty.
22 redeemeth = delivereth (by power). Heb. *pādāh.* See note on Ex. 13. 13; and cp. Ex. 6. 6.
soul. Heb. *nephesh.* Ap. 13.

35 (*V*¹, p. 721). MESSIAH'S PRAYER AND PRAISE IN VIEW OF PSALM **22.**
(*Introversion and Extended Alternation.*)

*V*¹ O | g | 1-3. Appeal for help.
h | 4-8. Imprecation.
i | 9, 10. Praise.
P | 11. Evildoers. Words.
Q | 12. Their evil for good. (Deeds.)
R | 13. His good for evil. (Deeds.)
R | 14. His good for evil. (Deeds.)
Q | 15. Their evil for good. (Deeds.)
P | 16. Evildoers. Words.
O | *g* | 17, 18. Appeal for help.
h | 19-26. Deprecation.
i | 27, 28. Praise.

Title. of David = by David, or relating to the true David.

1-3 (g, above). APPEAL FOR HELP.
(*Repeated Alternation.*)

g | k¹ | 1-. Defensive.
l¹ | -1. Offensive.
k² | 2. Defensive.
l² | 3-. Offensive.
k³ | -3. Defensive.

1 Plead = Contend, or strive. Note the Fig. *Exergasia* (Ap. 6) in the words "plead", "fight", "take hold", "stand up", "draw out", "stop", "say", &c.; continued in *vv.* 4, 5. Psalm probably written during and concerning the times of 1 Sam. 21—24, 26, and 27, but it relates also to David's Son and David's Lord, the Messiah, in view of Ps. 22. See the Structure on p. 721. Cp. especially *vv.* 15-21 with Matt. 26. 67. Mark 14. 65. Luke 22. 63. **LORD.** Heb. Jehovah. Ap. 4. II.
them that strive = my contenders.
Fight = make war.
2 shield, &c. Fig. *Anthropopatheia.* Ap. 6.
3 stop = close up. Some render "battle axe" or "barricade". persecute = pursue.
my soul = me (emph.). Heb. *nephesh.* Ap. 13.
5 wind. Heb. *rūach*. Ap. 9.
the angel of the LORD. See note on 34. 7.
7 without cause. See note on *v.* 19.
net in a pit: i.e. a pit covered with a net.
10 All my bones = all the members of my body. *Interpretation* belongs to the speaker. The *Application* belongs (1) to the O.T. saints (139. 13-16), and (2) to the later members referred to in Eph. 1. 22, 23; 2. 21; 4. 4-16. Note their experiences: 6. 2 (vexed); 22. 14 (out of joint); but "not broken" (34. 20 John 19. 36. Ex. 12. 46); His heart broken (69. 20); so our hearts (34. 18); but not ourselves (John 10. 27-29).
say. They speak: and always of HIM. Fig. *Prosopopœia* (Ap. 6), for emphasis. They all and always confess Christ as LORD (1 Cor. 12. 3. 1 Pet. 3. 15).
who is like . . ? Fig. *Erotēsis* (Ap. 6), for greater emphasis. Cp. their words (71. 19; 73. 25; 89. 6. 1 Sam. 2. 2. Deut. 33. 26, 27).
deliverest = rescuest. Cp. 2 Tim. 4. 18. 2 Pet. 2. 9. 1 Cor. 15. 54-57. 2 Cor. 1. 10. Hos. 13. 14.
poor = oppressed. Cp. 34. 6.
too strong. Law too strong (Gal. 3. 10, 13); sin too strong (Rom. 5. 21); the world too strong (John 16. 33); self too strong (Rom. 7. 24); death too strong (2 Tim. 1. 10).
11 False witnesses. "Many of them". Cp. Matt. 26. 60, 61; 27. 40. Mark 14. 55-59. **12 evil.** Heb. *ra'a'.* Ap. 44. viii. spoiling = bereaving. **13 clothing, &c.** Fig. *Metonymy* (of Adjunct), Ap. 6, put, by Symbol, for feelings of sorrow. with fasting = in the Fast: i.e. on the great Day of Atonement (Lev. 16).

I bowed down heavily, as one that mourneth *for his* mother.

Q (p. 751[1]) 15 But in mine °adversity they rejoiced, and gathered themselves together:
Yea, the °abjects gathered themselves together against me, and I knew °*it* not;
They did °tear *me*, and ceased not:

P 16 With °hypocritical mockers in feasts,
They gnashed upon me with their teeth.

O g 17 °LORD*, how long wilt Thou look on?
Rescue [3] my soul from their destructions,
°My darling °from the lions.

18 I will give Thee thanks in the great °congregation:
I will praise Thee among °much People.

h 19 Let not them that are mine enemies wrongfully rejoice over me:
Neither let them wink with the eye °**that hate me** °**without a cause.**

20 For they speak not peace:
But they devise °deceitful matters against *them that are* quiet in the land.

21 Yea, they °opened their mouth wide against me,
And said, °"Aha, aha, our eye °hath seen *it*."

22 *This* °Thou hast seen, O [1] LORD: keep not silence:
O [17] LORD*, be not far from me.

23 Stir up Thyself, and awake to my °judgment,
Even unto my cause, °my °God and my °Lord.

24 °Judge me, O [1] LORD my [23] God, according to Thy righteousness;
And let them not rejoice over me.

25 Let them not say in their hearts, "Ah, so would °we have it:"
Let them not say, "We have swallowed him up."

26 Let them be ashamed and brought to confusion together that rejoice at mine hurt:
Let them be °clothed with shame and dishonour that magnify *themselves* against me.

i 27 Let them shout for joy, and be glad, that favour °my righteous cause:
Yea, let them say continually, "Let [1] the LORD be magnified,
Which hath pleasure in the prosperity of His servant."

28 And my tongue shall speak of Thy righteousness
And of Thy praise all the day long.

°To the chief Musician.

36

A Psalm °of David °the servant of [5] the LORD.

V S (p. 752[2]) 1 The °transgression of °the wicked °saith °within my heart,
That °**there is no fear of** °**God before** °**his eyes.**

2 For he flattereth himself in his own eyes,
Until his °iniquity be found to be hateful.

3 The words of his mouth *are* °iniquity and deceit:
He hath left off to be wise, *and* to do good.

4 He deviseth °mischief upon his bed;
He °setteth himself in a way *that is* not good;
He abhorreth not °evil.

15 adversity = halting or falling. Cp. 38. 17. Jer. 20. 10.
abjects = outcasts.
it. Supply *Ellipsis* (Ap. 6), by reading "[them]".
tear me. Heb. *ḳār'ū* (with Ayin = '). Spelt with Aleph (*ḳar'ū*); it means "cry out". See note on Isa. 11. 4.
16 hypocritical mockers in feasts. Fig. *Ellipsis* (of Repetition) = "hypocrites [at feasts] mocking at the feast". Ap. 6. III. 1.
17 LORD*. The primitive text was Jehovah. Ap. 4. II. Altered to "Adonai" by the *Sōpherīm*. See Ap. 32.
My darling = My only one. See note on 22. 20.
from the lions. Cp. Ps. 22. 13, 16.
18 congregation = assembly, or convocation.
much = mighty.
19 that hate me. Quoted in John 15. 25.
without a cause. Note the same Greek word there (*dōrean*) as in Rom. 3. 24, rendered "freely", but meaning "without a cause". Cp. *v.* 7, and 69. 4; 109. 3.
20 deceitful matters. Heb. "words of frauds".
21 opened their mouth. Implying contempt.
Aha, aha. Fig. *Epizeuxis* (Ap. 6), for emphasis. See 40. 15; 70. 3. Cp. Mark 15. 29.
hath seen. Implying delight in so doing.
22 Thou hast seen. Another eye has seen.
23 judgment = vindication.
my God and my Lord. Cp. John 20. 28.
God. Heb. Elohim. Ap. 4. I.
Lord. Heb. Adonai. Ap. 4. VIII (2).
24 Judge = Vindicate.
25 we = our soul. Heb. *nephesh.* Ap. 13: i. e. we have our great desire at last.
26 clothed with shame. Cp. 109. 29; 132. 18.
27 my righteous cause = my justification.
28 To the chief Musician. See Ap. 64.

36 (*V*[2], p. 721). MESSIAH'S PRAYER AND PRAISE IN VIEW OF PSALM **22.** (*Introversion.*)

V[2] S | 1-4. The wicked. Their misdeeds.
  T | 5-9. The lovingkindness of Jehovah. Declaration.
  T | 10. The lovingkindness of Jehovah. Prayer.
S | 11, 12. The wicked. Their end.

Title. of David = by David.
the servant of the LORD. In the Heb. text these two words are reversed, and the title stands thus: "Relating to Jehovah's servant, by David". This is exactly what it is. His prayer and praise in view of Ps. 22 (see p. 721, and Isa. 42. 1, &c.), in death and resurrection. Ps. 18 is the only other Psalm so entitled.
1 transgression = rebellion. Heb. *pāsha'.* Ap. 44. ix.
the wicked = a lawless one. Heb. *rāshā'.* Ap. 44. x.
saith: declareth, as an oracle. Heb. *nā'am.* Cp. Jer. 23. 31 = declareth. Fig. *Prosopopœia.* Ap. 6.
within my heart = within me; "my heart" being put by Fig. *Synecdochē* (of the Part), Ap. 6, for the whole person: i. e. assureth or convinceth me that, &c. Not seeing the Fig., or the force of the Heb. *nā'am*, many follow the hypothesis of the Sept., Syr., and Vulg., and read "his heart".
there is, &c. Quoted in Rom. 3. 18.
God. Heb. Elohim. Ap. 4. I. His relation, as Creator, to His creatures. This lawless one knows not Jehovah; and fears not Elohim.
his eyes. Answering to "his heart" in preceding clause. **2 iniquity.** Heb. *'āvāh.* Ap. 44. iv.
3 iniquity. Heb. *'āven.* Ap. 44. iii.
4 mischief. Heb. *'āven*, as in *v.* 3, "iniquity".
setteth himself = taketh his stand.
evil. Heb. *rā'a'.* Ap. 44. viii.
5-9 [For Structure see next page].
5 mercy = lovingkindness, or grace (as in *v.* 7).
LORD. Heb. Jehovah. Ap. 4. II.

5 Thy °mercy, O °LORD, *is* in the heavens; T m[1]
And Thy faithfulness *reacheth* unto the clouds.

6 Thy righteousness *is* like °the great mountains;
°Thy judgments *are* a great deep:
n¹ O °LORD, Thou preservest °man and beast.
(p. 753) m² 7 How excellent *is* Thy °lovingkindness, O °God!
n² Therefore the °children of [6]men °put their trust under the shadow of Thy °wings.
8 They shall be abundantly satisfied with the fatness of Thy house;
And Thou shalt make them drink of the °river of Thy pleasures.
m³ 9 For with Thee *is* the fountain of life:
n³ In Thy light shall we see light.
T 10 O °continue Thy lovingkindness unto them that know Thee;
And Thy righteousness to the upright in heart.
S 11 Let not the foot of pride come against me,
(p. 752) And let not the hand of the [1]wicked remove me.
12 There are the workers of [3]iniquity fallen:
They are cast down, and shall not be able to rise.

37

A Psalm °of David.

W U¹ o 1 (א) °Fret not thyself because of °evildoers,
(p. 753) Neither be thou envious against the workers of °iniquity.
p 2 For they shall soon be cut down like the grass,
And wither as the green herb.
o 3 (ב) °Trust in °the LORD, and do good;
So shalt thou dwell in the land, and verily thou shalt be fed.
4 Delight thyself also in [3]the LORD;
And He shall give thee the desires of thine heart.
5 (ג) °Commit thy way unto [3]the LORD;
[3]Trust also in Him; and He shall bring *it* to pass.
6 And He shall bring forth thy righteousness as the light,
And thy °judgment as the noonday.
7 (ד) °Rest in [3]the LORD, and wait patiently for Him:
[1]Fret not thyself because of him who prospereth in his way,
Because of the °man who bringeth °wicked devices to pass.
8 (ה) Cease from anger, and forsake wrath:
[1]Fret not thyself in any wise to do °evil.
p 9 For [1]evildoers shall °be cut off:
But those that wait upon [3]the LORD, they shall inherit °the earth.
10 (ו) For yet a little while, and the °wicked *shall* not *be:*
Yea, thou shalt diligently consider his place, and it *shall* not *be.*
11 °**But the °meek shall inherit [9]the earth;**
And shall delight themselves in the abundance of peace.
V¹ q 12 (ז) The [10]wicked plotteth against the just,
And gnasheth upon him with his teeth.

36. 5-9 (T, p. 752). THE LOVINGKINDNESS OF JEHOVAH DECLARED. (*Repeated Alternation.*)

T | m¹ | 5, 6-. His attributes.
n¹ | -6. Their effects.
m² | 7-. His attributes.
n² | -7, 8. Their effects.
m³ | 9-. His attributes.
n³ | -9. Their effects.

6 the great mountains. Heb. mountains of El (Ap. 4. IV) = GOD'S mountains: i. e. great and mighty.
Thy judgments = And Thy just decrees. The "And" was cancelled by the Massorites (see the Bab. Talmud *Nedarim*, 37b-38a). Ginsburg *Int.* (pp. 307-8).
LORD = Jehovah, because of *preservation*, which is more than creation. See Ap. 4. II.
man. Heb. *'ādām.* Ap. 14. I.
7 lovingkindness. Cp. "mercy", *v.* 5 (m¹).
God. Heb. Elohim (Ap. 4. I), because of His creatures, the sons of men. **children** = sons.
put their trust under = flee for refuge to. Heb. *hāṣah.* Ap. 69. II. **wings.** Fig. *Anthropopatheia.* Ap. 6.
8 river = full stream. Heb. *naḥal.* Refers to Paradise.
10 continue = prolong.

37 (*W*, p. 721). INSTRUCTION AS TO PRESENT BLESSING IN VIEW OF PSALM **23.** (*Repeated Alternations.*)

W | U¹ | 1-11. Admonitions and reasons.
V¹ | 12-26. Contrasts. Lawless and righteous.
U² | 27-29. Admonition and reason.
V² | 30-33. Contrasts. Righteous and lawless.
U³ | 34. Admonition and reason.
V³ | 35-40. Contrasts. Lawless and righteous.

Ps. 37 is an Acrostic Psalm (see Ap. 63. VII), having four lines (a quatrain) assigned to each successive letter of the alphabet, except the fourth (ד, *v.* 7), the eleventh (כ, *v.* 20), the nineteenth (ק, *v.* 34), which each have three lines (a triplet) assigned to them. These three triplet verses occur in perfect order. The seventh verse is the seventh letter from the beginning; the thirty-fourth verse is the seventh letter from the end; while the middle verse (*v.* 20) marks the end of the first half with the first of the two middle letters (כ).
Title. of David = by David, and relating to the true David.
The Psalm is Messiah's admonition as to present blessing, arising from the fact that Jehovah is His Shepherd.

1-11 (U¹, above). ADMONITIONS AND REASONS. (*Alternation.*)

U¹ | o | 1. Trust. Fret not.
p | 2. Reason. "For".
o | 3-8. Trust. Delight. Commit.
p | 9-11. Reason. "For".

1 Fret not = Heat not thyself with vexation.
evildoers. Cp. Ps. 36. 11, 12. Heb. *rā'a'.* Ap. 44. viii.
iniquity. Heb. *'āval.* Ap. 44. vi.
3 Trust = Confide in. Heb. *batah.* Ap. 69. I.
the LORD. Heb. Jehovah. Ap. 4. II.
5 Commit = Roll upon, or Repose on. Cp. 55. 22. Heb. *gālal.* Ap. 69. V.
6 judgment = vindication. Some codices, with six early printed editions and Syr., read pl., "vindications" = pl. of majesty = thy complete vindication.
7 Rest. Heb. be silent for: i. e. wait for, or stand still. Cp. 62. 5. Ex. 14. 13. **man.** Heb. *'ish.* Ap. 14. II.
wicked. Heb. *'āshah.* Ap. 44. i.
8 evil. Heb. *rā'a'.* Ap. 44. viii.
9 be cut off: i. e. die. Used of Messiah (Dan. 9. 26), whose resurrection was sure. (Ps. 16, &c.).
the earth = the land, as in *vv.* 3, 29, 34.
10 wicked = lawless (pl.). Heb. *rāshā'.* Ap. 44. x.
11 But the meek = patient oppressed ones. Quoted in Matt. 5. 5.

12-26 (V¹, above). CONTRASTS. LAWLESS AND RIGHTEOUS. (*Alternation.*)

V¹ | q | 12-15. The lawless.
r | 16-19. The righteous.
q | 20-22. The lawless.
r | 23-26. The righteous.

13 °The LORD* shall °laugh at him:
For He seeth that his °day °is coming.
14 (ח) The [10]wicked have drawn out the sword, and have bent their bow,
To cast down °the poor and needy,
And to slay such as be °of upright conversation.
15 Their sword shall enter into their own heart,
And their bows shall be broken.
r (p. 753) 16 (ט) A little that a righteous man hath *is* better
Than the riches of many [10]wicked.
17 For the arms of the [10]wicked shall be broken:
But [3]the LORD upholdeth °the righteous.
18 ( ) The LORD °knoweth the days of the upright:
And their inheritance shall be for ever.
19 They shall not be ashamed in the [8]evil time:
And in the days of famine they shall be satisfied.
q 20 (כ) But the [10]wicked shall perish,
And the enemies of [3]the LORD *shall be* as the fat of lambs:
They shall consume; °into smoke shall they consume away.
21 (ל) The [10]wicked borroweth, and payeth not again:
But the righteous °sheweth mercy, and giveth.
22 For *such as be* blessed °of Him shall inherit [9]the earth;
And *they that be* cursed °of Him shall be [9]cut off.
r 23 (מ) The steps of a °*good* man are °ordered by [3]the LORD:
And He delighteth in his way.
24 Though he fall, he shall not be utterly cast down:
For [3]the LORD upholdeth *him with* His °hand.
25 (נ) I have been young, and *now* am old;
Yet have I not seen the righteous forsaken,
Nor his seed begging bread.
26 *He is* °ever °merciful, and lendeth;
And his seed *is* blessed.
U[2] 27 (ס) Depart from [8]evil, and do good;
And °dwell for evermore.
28 For [3]the LORD loveth judgment,
And forsaketh not His °saints;
(ע) °They are preserved for ever:
But the seed of the [10]wicked shall be cut off.
29 The righteous shall inherit °the land,
And dwell therein for ever.
V[2] 30 (פ) The mouth of °the righteous speaketh wisdom,
And his tongue talketh of °judgment.
31 The law of his °God *is* in his heart;
None of his steps shall slide.
32 (צ) The [10]wicked watcheth [30]the righteous,
And seeketh to slay him.
33 [3]The LORD will not leave him in his hand,
Nor condemn him when he is judged.
U[3] 34 (ק) Wait on [3]the LORD, and keep His way,
And He shall exalt thee to inherit [29]the land:

13 The LORD*. Heb. Jehovah. Altered by the *Sōpherīm* to Adonai. Ap. 32.
laugh. Fig. *Anthropopatheia.* Ap. 6.
day=judgment. "Day" put by Fig. *Metonymy* (of Adjunct), Ap. 6, for the judgment then to be executed.
is coming. So some codices, with Aram. and Syr. Heb. text=will come.
14 the poor and needy=a poor and needy one.
of upright conversation=upright in the (or their) way: i. e. in life. Some codices, with Sept. and Vulg., read "upright in heart".
17 the righteous. (Plural.)
18 knoweth. Put by Fig. *Metonymy* (of Cause), Ap. 6, for regarding with affection or favour. Cp. 1. 6; 31. 7.
20 into. Some codices, with Sept., Syr., and Vulg., read "like".
21 sheweth mercy=is gracious.
22 of. Genitive of Cause=by: i. e. His blessed ones.
23 good man. Heb. *geber.* Ap. 14. IV
ordered=prepared, or made firm.
24 hand. Fig. *Anthropopatheia.* Ap. 6.
26 ever=all the day, or all day long.
merciful=gracious.
27 dwell. Fig. *Heterōsis* (of Mood), Ap. 6, imp. for ind.=thou shalt dwell.
28 saints=favoured, or gracious ones.
They, &c. The letter *Ayin* (ע) is hidden behind the Prep. *Lamed* (ל), in the first word "for ever" (Heb. *leʿōlām*, לע). Dr. John Lightfoot says it is cut off like the "seed" of the "wicked" in same clause, both these words ending with *Ayin* (ע). He sees in this the seed of Joram being cut off (i.e. Ahaziah, Joash, and Amaziah. Matt. 1. 8). Cp. with 1 Chron. 3. 11, 12.
29 the land. See note on "the earth", *v.* 9.
30 the righteous=a righteous one.
judgment=justice.
31 God. Heb. Elohim. Ap. 4. I.

37. 35-40 (V[3], p. 753). CONTRASTS. THE LAWLESS AND THE RIGHTEOUS. (*Alternation.*)

V[3] | s | 35, 36. The lawless.
| t | 37. The righteous.
| s | 38. The lawless.
| t | 39, 40. The righteous.

35 the wicked=a lawless man.
in great power=ruthless.
a green bay tree=a green tree in its native soil. Sept. and Syr. read "cedars in Lebanon". Cp. Hos. 14. 6.
36 he. Aram., Sept., and Vulg. read "I".
37 the end=the hereafter, or future.
peace: or wellbeing.
38 transgressors. Heb. *pāshaʿ.* Ap. 44. ix.
39 But. Some codices, with Syr. and Vulg., omit "But", thus making the *Tau* (ת) the first letter instead of the second (ות).

When the [10]wicked are [9]cut off, thou shalt see *it*.
35 (ר) I have seen °the [10]wicked °in great power, V[3] s (p. 754)
And spreading himself like °a green bay tree.
36 Yet °he passed away, and, lo, he *was* not:
Yea, I sought him, but he could not be found.
37 (ש) Mark the perfect *man*, and behold the upright: t
For °the end of *that* [7]man *is* °peace.
38 But the °transgressors shall be destroyed together: s
The end of the [10]wicked shall be [9]cut off.
39 (ת) °But the salvation of the righteous *is* of [3]the LORD: t
He is their strength in the time of trouble.

40 And [3]the LORD shall help them, and deliver them:
He shall °deliver them from the [10]wicked, and save them,
Because they °trust in Him.

38 °A Psalm °of David, °to bring to remembrance.

X^1 W (p. 755) 1 O °LORD, rebuke me not in Thy wrath:
Neither chasten me in Thy hot displeasure.

X u 2 For Thine °arrows stick fast in me,
And Thy °hand presseth me sore.
3 *There is* no soundness in my flesh because of Thine anger;
Neither *is there any* rest in my bones because of my °sin.
4 For mine °iniquities are gone °over mine head:
As an heavy burden they are too heavy for me.
5 My wounds stink *and* are corrupt
Because of my foolishness.
6 I am troubled; I am bowed down greatly;
I go mourning all the day long.
7 For my loins are filled with a °loathsome *disease:*
And *there is* no soundness in my flesh.
8 I am feeble and sore broken:
I have roared °by reason of the disquietness of my heart.
9 °LORD*, all my desire *is* before Thee;
And my groaning is not hid from Thee.
10 My heart panteth, my °strength faileth me:
As for the light of mine eyes, it also is gone from me.

v 11 My lovers and my friends stand aloof from my °sore;
And my °kinsmen stand afar off.
12 They also that seek after my °life °lay snares *for me:*
And they that seek my hurt speak mischievous things,
And imagine deceits all the day long.
13 But I, as a deaf *man*, heard not;
And *I was* as a dumb man *that* openeth not his mouth.
14 Thus I was as a °man that heareth not,
And in whose mouth *are* no reproofs.
15 For in Thee, O [1]LORD, do I hope:
Thou wilt °hear, O [9]LORD* my °God.
16 For I said, "*Hear me*, lest *otherwise* they should rejoice over me:"
When my foot slippeth, they magnify *themselves* against me.

X u 17 For I *am* ready to °halt,
And my sorrow *is* continually before me.
18 For I will declare mine [4]iniquity;
I will be sorry for my °sin.

v 19 But mine enemies *are* lively, *and* they are strong:
And they that hate me wrongfully are multiplied.
20 They also that render °evil for good
Are mine adversaries; because I follow *the thing that* good *is*.

W 21 Forsake me not, O [1]LORD:
O my [15]God, be not far from me.
22 Make haste to help me,
O [9]LORD* my salvation.

°To the chief Musician, °*even* to Jeduthun.

39 °A Psalm °of David.

X^2 Y (p. 755) 1 °I said, "I will °take heed to my ways,
That I °sin not with my tongue:
I will °keep my mouth with °a bridle,
While °the wicked is before me."

---

40 deliver = have made them escape.
trust in = fled for refuge to. Heb. *ḥasah.* Ap. 69. II.

38 (X^1, p. 721). PRAYER AND PRAISE IN VIEW OF FUTURE BLESSING (Ps. **24**). (*Introversion and Alternation.*)

X^1 W | 1. Prayer. "Not rebuke".
X | u | 2-10. Sin and suffering. "For".
v | 11-16. Treatment from friends.
X | *u* | 17, 18. Sin and suffering. "For".
v | 19, 20. Treatment from enemies.
W | 21, 22. Prayer. "Not forsake".

Title. A Psalm = Mizmōr. See Ap. 65. XVII.
of David = by David.
to bring to remembrance. Used on the Day of Atonement.
This group of four Psalms closes the first book, and is similar in character to the four that end the second book.
Cp. 38 Title with 70 Title.
" 38. 4, 11, 22, with 69. 1, 2, 8, 13.
" 40. 2, 3, 6, 13-17, with 69. 14, 30, 31.
" 41. 1 with 72. 13.
" 41. 2, 3, 7, 8, with 71. 10, 13, 18.
" 41. 7, 8, with 71. 10, 11.
" 41. 13, with 72. 18, 19.

1 LORD. Heb. Jehovah. Ap. 4. II.
2 arrows . . . hand. Fig. *Anthropopatheia.* Ap. 6.
3 sin. Heb. *chāṭā'.* Ap. 44. i.
4 iniquities. Heb. *'āven.* Ap. 44. iii.
over mine head. The reference is to the burdens of porters and carriers, which often mount up and project over the head.
7 loathsome = burning.
8 by reason of the disquietness of my heart. Ginsburg suggests *lāvi'* instead of *lāvi* = "beyond the roaring of a lion".
9 LORD*. Primitive text was Jehovah. One of the 134 emendations of the *Sōpherīm.* Ap. 32.
10 strength. Strength to endure = vital strength. Heb. *koḥ.*
11 sore = stroke. Used of a leprous stroke.
kinsmen = neighbours.
12 life = soul. Heb. *nephesh.* Ap. 9.
lay snares. Some commentators make two lines in this verse; but the Heb. accents make three: the first = the *act*, the second = the *speech*, the third = the *motive.*
14 man. Heb. *'īsh.* Ap. 14. II.
15 hear = answer.
God. Heb. Elohim. Ap. 4. I.
17 halt. Cp. 35. 15 and Gen. 32. 31.
18 sin. Heb. *chāṭā'.* Ap. 44. i.
20 evil. Heb. *rā'a'.* Ap. 44. viii.
To the chief Musician. See Ap. 64.
even to Jeduthun. See Ap. 65. VI.

39 (X^2, p. 721). [For Structure see next page.]

Title. A Psalm = Mizmōr. See Ap. 65. XVII.
of David = by David, and relating to the true David.
The Psalm is a continuation of the subject of this last group of four Psalms. Verses 2 and 9 link it on to 38. 13; and *v.* 1 to 38. 17. See note on Title of 38, above.
1 I said = I formed this resolution (38. 7).
take heed = observe, keep, or guard.
sin. Heb. *chāṭā'.* Ap. 44. i.
keep: same as "take heed to", above. Sept. and Vulg. read "I did put".
a bridle = a muzzle.
the wicked = a lawless one. Heb. *rāshā'.* Ap. 44. x.

2 I was °dumb with silence, I held my peace,
even from °good;
And my sorrow was stirred.
3 My heart was hot within me,
While I was musing the fire burned:
Then spake I with my tongue,

Z (p. 756) 4 °LORD, make me to know mine end,
And the measure of my days, what it *is;*
That I may know how °frail I *am.*

A 5 °Behold, Thou hast made my days *as* an handbreadth;
And mine °age *is* as nothing before Thee:
B Verily every °man °at his best state *is* °altogether vanity. °Selah.
6 Surely °every man °walketh °in a vain shew:
Surely they are disquieted in vain:
He heapeth up *riches*, and knoweth not who shall gather them.

C D w 7 And now, °LORD*, what wait I for?
x My hope °*is* in Thee.
E y 8 Deliver me from all my °transgressions:
z Make me not the reproach of °the foolish.
Y 9 I was dumb, I opened not my mouth;
Because Thou didst *it.*
Z 10 Remove Thy stroke away from me
A I am consumed by the °blow of Thine °hand.
B 11 When Thou with rebukes dost correct °man for °iniquity,
Thou makest his beauty to consume away like a °moth:
Surely every [5]man *is* vanity. °Selah.
C E y 12 Hear my prayer, O [4]LORD, and give ear unto my cry;
z Hold not Thy peace at my tears:
D x For I *am* a stranger with Thee,
And a sojourner, as all my fathers *were.*
w 13 O spare me, that I may °recover strength,
Before I go hence, and be no more.

°To the chief Musician.

40

°A Psalm °of David.

X[3] F[1] G (p. 756) 1 °I waited patiently for °the LORD;
And He °inclined unto me, and °heard my cry.
2 He °brought me up also out of an horrible pit, out of the miry clay,
And set my feet upon a °rock, *and* established my goings.
3 And He hath put °a new song in my mouth,
even praise unto our °God:
Many shall °see *it*, °and fear,
H And shall °trust in [1]the LORD.

39 (*X*[2], p. 721). PRAYER AND PRAISE IN VIEW OF FUTURE BLESSING (Ps. **24**).
(*Extended Alternation and Introversion.*)

X[2] | Y | 1-3. Silent meditation.
Z | 4. Speech. Prayer.
A | 5-. The fading of life. "I".
B | -5, 6. Vanity of man. Selah.
C | D | w | 7-. Departure.
x | -7. Hope in Thee.
E | y | 8-. Supplication. } Prayer.
z | -8. Deprecation. } Prayer.
Y | 9. Silent meditation.
Z | 10-. Speech. Prayer.
A | -10. The fading of beauty. "I".
B | 11. Vanity of man. Selah.
C | *E* | *y* | 12-. Supplication. } Prayer.
z | -12-. Deprecation. } Prayer.
D | *x* | -12. Hope in Thee.
w | 13. Departure.

2 dumb: as if tongue-tied.
good. Perhaps the *Ellipsis* (Ap. 6) may be supplied "from good [words]". See P.B.V.
4 LORD. Heb. Jehovah. Ap. 4. II.
frail = shortlived.
5 Behold. Fig. *Asterismos.* Ap. 6.
age = lifetime. Heb. *ḥeled.* See note on "world" (49. 1). **man.** Heb. *'ādām.* Ap. 14. I.
at his best state = though standing fast, or firmly established.
altogether vanity = only all vanity. Some codices, with Syr., omit "all".
Selah. Connecting the vanity of *v.* 5 with the expansion and explanation of it in *v.* 6. See Ap. 66. II.
6 every man. Heb. *'ish.* Ap. 14. II.
walketh: i. e. walketh to and fro, or habitually.
in a vain shew = only in a mere form. Heb. *ẓelem.* Occurs thirty-three times. Always rendered image, except here and Dan. 3. 19 ("form").
7 LORD*. The primitive text read "Jehovah". This is one of the 134 places where the *Sōpherīm* altered Jehovah to "Adonai". See Ap. 32. **is** = "it [is]"
8 transgressions. Heb. *pāsha'.* Ap. 44. ix.
the foolish = a foolish one. **10 blow** = pressure.
hand. Fig. *Anthropopatheia.* Ap. 6.
11 man. Heb. *'ish.* Ap. 14. II. See note on "moth", below. **iniquity.** Heb. *'āvōn.* Ap. 44. iii.
moth. Heb. *'āsh.* Forming the Fig. *Paronomasia* (Ap. 6), connecting man (*'ish*) with a moth (*'āsh*).
Selah. Connecting human vanity with an abiding reality and a divinely provided resource—prayer, and hope in Jehovah. See Ap. 66. II.
13 recover strength = be comforted. Heb. "brighten up". **To the chief Musician.** See Ap. 64.

40 (*X*[3], p. 721). MESSIAH'S PRAYER AND PRAISE IN VIEW OF FUTURE BLESSING. (Ps. **24**).

X[3] | F[1] | 1-5. Deliverance by Jehovah.
F[2] | 6-10. Address to Jehovah.
F[3] | 11-17. Prayer to Jehovah.

Title. A Psalm. Heb. *Mizmōr.* Ap. 65. XVII.
of David = by David, and relating to the true David.

1-5 (F[1], above). DELIVERANCE BY JEHOVAH.
(*Introversion.*)

F[1] | G | 1-3-. Deliverance.
H | -3. Trust.
H | 4. Trust.
G | 5. Deliverance.

1 I waited patiently. Heb. in waiting I waited. Fig. *Polyptōton.* Ap. 6. **the LORD.** Heb. Jehovah. Ap. 4. II. **inclined** = hath inclined. **heard** = hath heard. **2 brought** = hath brought. **rock.** Heb. *sela'.* See notes on 18. 1, 2. **3 a new song.** See note on 33. 3. **God.** Heb. Elohim. Ap. 4. I **see . . . and fear.** Fig. *Paronomasia.* Ap. 6. Heb. *yir'ū . . . v'yira'ū* = peer and fear. **trust** = confide Heb. *bāṭaḥ.* Ap. 69. i.

H (p. 756) 4 °Blessed *is* that °man that maketh [1]the LORD his [3]trust,
And respecteth not the proud, nor such as turn aside to lies.

G 5 Many, O LORD my [3]God, *are* Thy wonderful works *which* Thou °hast done,
And Thy °thoughts *which are* to us-ward:
They cannot be reckoned up in order unto Thee:
°*If* I would declare and speak *of them*,
They are more than can be °numbered.

F[2] J (p. 757) 6 °**Sacrifice and °offering Thou didst not desire;**
Mine ears hast Thou °opened:
Burnt offering and sin offering °hast Thou not required

K w 7 °**Then said I, "Lo, I come:**
x **In the °volume of the book °*it is* written °of me,**

K w 8 **I °delight to do Thy °will, O my [3]God:**
x Yea, Thy law *is* °within my °heart.
9 I have °preached righteousness in the great °congregation:
J Lo, I have not refrained my lips,
O [1]LORD, Thou knowest.
10 I °have not hid Thy righteousness [8]within my heart;
I have declared Thy faithfulness and Thy °salvation:
I °have not concealed Thy lovingkindness and Thy truth °from the great [9]congregation.

F[3] L N a 11 °Withhold not Thou Thy tender mercies from me, O [1]LORD:
Let Thy lovingkindness and Thy truth continually preserve me.

b 12 For innumerable °evils have compassed me about:
Mine °iniquities have taken hold upon me, so that I °am not able to look up;
They °are more than the hairs of mine head: therefore my °heart °faileth me.

O 13 Be pleased, O [1]LORD, to deliver me:
O [1]LORD, make haste to help me.

P 14 Let them be ashamed and confounded together
That seek after my °soul to destroy it;
Let them be driven backward and put to shame
That wish me [12]evil.

4 Blessed = Happy. See Ap. 63. VI.
man = strong man. Heb. *geber*. Ap. 14. IV.
5 hast done = didst.
thoughts. Fig. *Anthropopatheia*. Ap. 6.
If I would = Fain would I.
numbered: or rehearsed.

40. 6-10 (F[2], p. 756). ADDRESS TO JEHOVAH. (*Introversion and Alternation.*)

F[2] J | 6. What Jehovah had done, and not done.
  K | w | 7-. Messiah's delighted obedience.
      x | -7. Reason. Written in the Book.
  K | *w* | 8-. Messiah's delighted obedience.
      x | -8. Reason. Written in His heart.
J | 9, 10. What Messiah had done, and not done.

6 Sacrifice. Heb. *zābāch*. Ap. 43. I. iv. Quoted in Heb. 10. 5-9.
offering. Heb. *minchah*. Ap. 43. II. iii. Cp. Heb. 10. 5-7. Note the four great offerings here, and separately: Ps. 40. 6- = any sacrifice; -6-, the meal offering; -6-, burnt offering; -6, sin offering (cp. Ps. 22); and in Ps. 69 = the trespass offering.
opened = digged. Kal Pret. of *kārāh* = opening by digging, or boring. Note the occurrences: Gen. 50. 5. Num. 24. 18. 2 Chron. 16. 14 (marg.). Pss. 7. 15 (marg.); 40. 6; 57. 6; 119. 85. Jer. 18. 22, 22, referring to the opening of the ear to hear; for which, in Isa. 50. 5 (cp. Isa. 48. 8), another word (*pāthāh*) is used with the meaning of opening (as of a door).
Note the *obedience*, which is the point emphasised by the alternation in *v.* 6.

J | y | Sacrifice and offering. Not desired.
  z | Mine ears hast Thou digged. (Pos.).
  y | Burnt-offering and sin-offering. Not required.
  z | Lo, I come to do. (Pos.).

Obedience is the great truth here conveyed; and, on the same grounds as in 1 Sam. 15. 22. Jer 7. 22, 23. Heb. 10. 5, is not a *quotation* of this verse: it is what Messiah "said" when He came into the world to *perform* what Ps. 40. 6 *prophesied*, when He had become Incarnate, and could say "I am come". He must change the word "ears" for the "body", in which that *obedience* was to be accomplished, and He had a right to change the words, and thus *adapt* them. It is not a question of *quotation*, or of the Sept. versus the Heb. text. Note the heaping up of these expressions to emphasise the obedience, and observe the alternation of pos. and neg. in *vv.* 9, 10.
hast = didst.
7 Then said I: i. e. at Incarnation, when He "came into the world" (Heb. 10. 5).
volume of the book = scroll, that is to say, the book. Genitive of Apposition, and Fig. *Pleonasm* (Ap. 6) = the book of the law (Ap. 47).
it is written = it is prescribed. Cp. 2 Kings 22. 13.
of me = for me. Joseph and Mary should have remembered what was "written" (Luke 2. 49).
8 delight. Note the double delight (Isa. 42. 1. Matt. 3. 17).
will = good pleasure.
within = in the midst.
heart = bowels: i. e. my inward parts.
9 preached = declared as glad tidings = *euaggelizō* in N.T.
congregation = assembly, or convocation.
10 have not hid = did not hide.
salvation = or deliverance.
have not concealed = did not conceal.
from = in.

11-17 (F[3], p. 756). PRAYER TO JEHOVAH. (*Introversions and Alternation.*)

F[3] | L | N | a | 11. Jehovah's care for Messiah.
          b | 12. Messiah's distress.
        O | 13. His prayer. "Make haste".
      P | 14, 15. Against enemies.
      P | 16. For friends.
  L | *N* | *b* | 17- Messiah's distress.
          a | -17-. Jehovah's care for Messiah.
        O | -17. His prayer. "Make no tarrying".

11 Withhold not Thou = Thou wilt not withhold.
12 evils = calamities. Heb. *rā'a'*. Ap. 44. viii.
iniquities. Put by Fig. *Metonymy* (of Cause), Ap. 6, for their punishment. Heb. *'āven*. Ap. 44. iii. Laid on Him as the substituted sacrifice.
am not able = was not able.
are more = were more.
heart. Put by Fig. *Metonymy* (of Adjunct), Ap. 6, for courage.
faileth me = failed me.
14 soul. Heb. *nephesh*. Ap. 13.

15 Let them be desolate for a reward of their shame
That say unto me, °'Aha, aha.'

P (p. 757) 16 Let all those that seek Thee rejoice and be glad in Thee:
°Let such as love Thy [10]salvation say continually,
[1]'The LORD be magnified.'

L N b 17 But I *am* °poor and needy;
Yet °the LORD* °thinketh upon me:

a Thou *art* my help and my deliverer;

O Make no tarrying, O my [3]God."

°To the chief Musician.

41

°A Psalm °of David.

X[4] Q (p. 758) 1 °Blessed *is* he that considereth °the poor:
°The LORD °will deliver him °in time of trouble.
2 [1]The LORD will preserve him, and °keep him alive; *and* he shall be [1]blessed upon the earth:
And Thou wilt not deliver him unto the °will of his enemies.
3 [1]The LORD will strengthen him upon °the bed of languishing:
Thou wilt make all his bed in his sickness.

R 4 I said, [1]"LORD, °be merciful unto me:
Heal °my soul; for °I have °sinned against Thee."

S c 5 Mine enemies speak °evil of me,

d "When shall he die, and his name perish?"

e 6 And if °he come to see *me*, he °speaketh vanity:
His heart gathereth iniquity to itself;
When he goeth abroad, he telleth *it*.

S c 7 All that hate me whisper together against me:
Against me do they devise my hurt.

d 8 °"An evil disease," *say they*, "cleaveth fast unto him:
And *now* that he lieth he shall rise up no more."

e 9 Yea, °mine own familiar friend, in °whom I °trusted, °**which did eat of my °bread, Hath lifted up *his* heel against me.**

R 10 But Thou, O [1]LORD, [4]be merciful unto me, and raise me up,
That I may °requite them.

Q 11 By this I know that Thou °favourest me,
Because mine enemy doth not °triumph over me.
12 And as for me, Thou upholdest me in mine integrity,
And settest me before °Thy face for ever.

Doxology to the Genesis book. 13 °Blessed *be* [1]the LORD °God of Israel
From everlasting, and °to everlasting.
°Amen, and Amen.

°To the chief Musician.

---

15 Aha, aha. Fig. *Epizeuxis*. Ap. 6. Cp. 35. 21; 70. 3.
16 Let. Some codices, with seven early printed editions, Aram., Sept., Syr., and Vulg., read "And let". Cp. 35. 27; 70. 4. **17 poor** = afflicted. Heb. *'ānāh*.
the LORD*. The primitive text read "Jehovah", but altered by the *Sōpherīm* to "Adonai". See Ap. 32. Some codices, with seven early printed editions, read "may Jehovah".
thinketh = will think. Put by Fig. *Metonymy* (of Cause), Ap. 6, for all that the thoughts can devise, plan, or order.
To the chief Musician. See Ap. 64.

41 (*X*[4], p. 721). MESSIAH'S PRAYER AND PRAISE IN VIEW OF FUTURE BLESSING (Ps. **24**).
(*Introversion and Extended Alternation.*)

X[4] | Q | 1–3. Jehovah's favour to Messiah.
  R | 4. Prayer.
   S | c | 5–. Enemies. What they do.
    d | –5. Enemies. What they say.
     e | 6. The Traitor.
   S | *c* | 7. Enemies. What they do.
    d | 8. Enemies. What they say.
     e | 9. The Traitor.
  R | 10. Prayer.
 Q | 11, 12. Jehovah's favour to Messiah.

v. 13. The concluding Doxology to the First Book.

Title. A Psalm = Mizmōr. See Ap. 65. XVII.
of David = by David, and relating to the true David.
1 Blessed. See Ap. 63. VI.
the poor = weak, or feeble. Heb. *dal.* Not the same as 40. 17. **The LORD.** Heb. Jehovah. Ap. 4. II.
will deliver = may the LORD deliver . . . preserve.
in time of trouble = in the evil day.
2 keep him alive = revive, so as to live again; hence, to give life to: here, in resurrection. Heb. *Piel* conjugation, to give life, quicken. Cp. Ps. 119. 25, 37, &c. Deut. 32. 39. Job 33. 4. Ecc. 7. 12. 1 Sam. 2. 6. Hence, *to preserve seed* (Gen. 19. 32, 34); *to repair*, in the sense of restoring what was lost (1 Chron. 11. 8. Neh. 4. 2. Hos. 6. 2; 14. 7. Ps. 85. 6).
will = soul. Heb. *nephesh.* Ap. 13.
3 the bed = the couch.
4 be merciful = be gracious, or show favour.
my soul = me. Heb. *nephesh.* Ap. 13.
I have sinned. Christ could say this of those whose sins He was bearing, which were laid upon Him.
sinned. Heb. *chāṭā'.* Ap. 44. i.
5 evil. Heb. *rā'a'.* Ap. 44. viii.
6 he come: i. e. the traitor; then Ahithophel, afterward Judas (see *v.* 9).
speaketh. Note the lying lips, the evil heart, the wicked slander.
8 An evil disease = a thing of Belial. Cp. 101. 3. Deut. 13. 13; 15. 9. Judg. 19. 22. 1 Sam. 2. 12. See 2 Sam. 16. 7.
9 mine own familiar friend: i. e. the one whom I was in the habit of saluting as my friend.
whom I trusted. These words not quoted by Christ (John 13. 18), for He knew what was in man (John 2. 24, 25).
trusted = confided. Heb. *baṭaḥ.* Ap. 69. I.
which did eat, &c. Quoted in John 13. 18.
bread. Put by Fig. *Synecdoche* (of Species), Ap. 6, for all kinds of food. [63. IX.
10 requite. Suited for that Dispensation. See Ap.
11 favourest = delightest, or hast pleasure in. Cp. Matt. 3. 17; 12. 18; 17. 5. Isa. 42. 1.
triumph = shout with triumph.
12 Thy face. See note on Ex. 34. 20.
13 Blessed, &c. Heb. *bārak*, not *'ashrei*, as in *v.* 1 and the Beatitudes (Ap. 63. VI). This Doxology concludes the first book of Psalms, also the second book (72. 18–20). They were the words of David when he brought up the Ark (1 Chron. 16. 36), also in 1 Kings 1. 47, 48, when this group (37—41) was written; also in 1 Chron. 29. 10. They are taken up again in Luke 1. 68–70. **God.** Heb. Elohim. Ap. 4. I. **to everlasting:** i. e. to the age to come. **Amen** = Truth. Fig. *Epizeuxis* (Ap. 6), for solemn emphasis. **To the chief Musician.** See Ap. 64.

42—72 (B[1], p. 720). THE SECOND, OR EXODUS BOOK *. ISRAEL.

(Division.)

B[1] | A[1] | **42—49.** CONCERNING ISRAEL'S RUIN.
  A[2] | **50—60.** CONCERNING ISRAEL'S REDEEMER.
  A[3] | **61—72.** CONCERNING ISRAEL'S REDEMPTION.

42—49 (A[1], above). ISRAEL'S RUIN.

(Introversion and Alternation.)

A1 | B | **42 (B[1]), 43 (B[2])** †. THE RUIN AND OPPRESSION REALISED (42. 9; 43. 2). NO HELP FROM MAN. IT OPENS WITH CRYING AND TEARS AS EXODUS DOES. (Cp. Ex. 2. 23; 3. 7-9; 6. 9.)
  C | D | **44.** THE CRY FOR HELP TO THE DELIVERER AND REDEEMER (*vv.* 23-26).
    E | **45.** THE DELIVERER PRAISED. ANSWER TO THE CRY.
  C | *D* | **46.** THE HELP OF THE DELIVERER. (Cp. 48. 8.)
    E | **47 (*E*[1]), 48 (*E*[2]).** THE DELIVERER PRAISED. (Cp. 48. 8 with 44. 1.)
 B | **49.** THE RUIN, AND NEED OF REDEMPTION REALISED. NO HELP FROM MAN (*v.* 7), ONLY FROM GOD (*v.* 15).

50—60 (A[2], above). ISRAEL'S REDEEMER.

(Introversion.)

A2 | F | **50.** GOD SPEAKS TO HIS PEOPLE. HE BREAKS THE SILENCE AS IN EXODUS 3. 4 Cp. Heb. 12. 25, 26.
  G | **51.** TRANSGRESSION. CONFESSED AND FORGIVEN.
  G | **52 (*G*[1]), 53 (*G*[2]), 54 (*G*[3]), 55 (*G*[4]).** TRANSGRESSORS. UNCONFESSED AND DESTROYED.
 F | **56 (*F*[1]), 57 (*F*[2]), 58 (*F*[3]), 59 (*F*[4]), 60 (*F*[5]).** GOD'S PEOPLE SPEAK TO HIM OF ISRAEL'S REDEEMER AND HIS WORK: TELLING OF DEATH AND RESURRECTION (MICHTAM. Ap. 65. XII).

61—72 (A[3], above). ISRAEL'S REDEMPTION.

(Alternations.)

A3 | H | K | **61 (K[1]), 62 (K[2]), 63 (K[3]), 64 (K[4]).** ISRAEL WAITS FOR DELIVERANCE "FROM THE ENDS OF THE EARTH", WHICH IS THE WORK OF GOD ALONE (64. 9).
    L | **65.** ZION WAITS FOR HER BLESSING.
      M | **66 (M[1]), 67 (M[2]).** PRAISE PROMISED. THE TROUBLE REMEMBERED (66. 10-12).
        J | **68** THE ANSWER TO 61—67. GOD ARISES. "BLESSED BE GOD" (*v.* 35).
 H | *K* | **69.** THE KING WAITS FOR DELIVERANCE (*v.* 14) FROM SUFFERINGS, SHAME, AND SORROW. (THE TRESPASS OFFERING) ‡.
    L | **70.** THE KING WAITS FOR HIS DELIVERANCE. "MAKE HASTE".
      M | **71.** PRAISE PROMISED (*vv.* 22-24). THE TROUBLE REMEMBERED (*v.* 20).
        J | **72.** THE ANSWER. THE KING REIGNS. "BLESSED BE THE LORD GOD" (*v.* 18). THIS WAS ALL HIS DESIRE (2 Sam. 23. 5). THE REDEEMED NATION BLESSED, AND A BLESSING TO ALL NATIONS.

---

* For notes, see p. 760.

NOTES ON THE STRUCTURE, PAGE 759.

* Exodus is the Greek ἔξοδος, and is the name given to the book by the Septuagint Translators as descriptive of its chief event—*the going out* of Israel from Egypt. But the Hebrew title for it is וְאֵלֶּה שְׁמוֹת (*v^{e}'ēlleh sh^{e}mōth*), "And these are the names." The Book is thus called because it begins with the *names* of those who came into the place whence they were *redeemed* and delivered from their ruin and oppression.

It is indeed the book of "the Names"; for not only does the Lord speak so pointedly of knowing Moses "by name" (33. 12, 17), but Moses asks by what Name he is to speak of the God of their fathers to the Israelites (3. 13), and the Lord reveals His Name (3. 14, 15); while in 6. 3; 33. 19; and 34. 5–7, He further proclaims it. So, again, of the "Angel" that was sent before the People (23. 20), Jehovah said, "My Name is in Him" (23. 21). Moses speaks to Pharaoh in the Name of Jehovah (5. 23); and Pharaoh is raised up "that My Name may be declared throughout all the earth" (9. 16). It is in this book that we first have the third Commandment concerning the Name of the Lord (20. 7). Bezaleel is said to have been "called" by name (31. 2), whereas a different phrase is used of Aholiab (31. 6) both here and in 35. 30 and 34. It is in Exodus also that we have the particular instructions as to the engraving of the names on the shoulder-stones of the ephod (28. 9–12), and on the breastplate stones (15–21), which were strictly carried out (39. 6, 7 and 8–14). Thus "the names of the sons of Israel" were borne before the Lord with the Redeeming Blood in the Holy of Holies. Moreover, these *names* appear at the *beginning* of Exodus, in connection with the Ruin; and at the *end* in connection with the Redemption "before God in the Sanctuary"; while we have the Name of the Redeemer proclaimed and celebrated throughout, "The Lord *is* His name" (Ex. 15. 3).

Exodus is therefore the Book of Redemption: and Redemption is individual and by name. It is the book in which the Redemption of the People is first mentioned: "Thou in Thy mercy hast led forth the People *which* Thou hast Redeemed: Thou hast guided them in Thy strength unto Thy holy habitation." (Exod. 15. 13).

The Title "Exodus" also occurs in Luke 9. 31 (rendered "decease" in A.V. and R.V.), where it is the subject of which Messiah spake with Moses and Elijah on "the holy mount". This subject was His Redemption work, viz. the "*exodus* which He should accomplish at Jerusalem", which was the great Antitype of that accomplished by Moses.

The types of Exodus are also types of Redemption. The Divine title Jah (יָהּ, see Ap. 4. III), the concentrated form of Jehovah, occurs for the first time in the Book of Exodus (15. 3); and it occurs also for the first time in the Psalms in this second or Exodus Book (Ps. 68. 4).

In this *second* Book of the Psalms we find the subject-matter corresponding with that of Exodus. Like the other books, its teaching is dispensational. In the Genesis Book, *Man* is the central thought; in this Exodus Book, it is the *Nation of Israel* around which the counsels and purposes of God are centred. It opens with the "cry" from the depth of the Ruin and Oppression, as Exodus does; and it ends with the King reigning over the redeemed Nation (Ps. 72), brought "again the second time" from the four corners of the earth (Isa. 11. 11); as it was brought the first time from Egypt; and, at length, made a blessing to all the families of the earth.

Of the Divine names and titles: Elohim occurs 262 times (two of them with Jehovah), El 14 times, and Jehovah only 37 times. Note the references to Sinai, Miriam, and other events in Exodus, in this second Book.

---

† Psalms 42 and 43 are linked together by a recurring question and answer. See the Structure (p. 759).

‡ As Ps. 32 is the Sin Offering and Ps. 40 the Burnt Offering, so Ps. 69 is the Trespass Offering.

BOOK II.

42 °Maschil, °for °the °sons of Korah.

B A¹ (p. 761) 1 As the hart °panteth °after the water °brooks,
So panteth °my soul °after Thee, O °God.
2 ¹My soul thirsteth for ¹God, for the living °GOD:
°When shall I come and °appear before ¹God?
3 My tears have been my meat day and night,
While they °continually say unto me, "Where *is* thy ¹God?"

B¹ 4 When I remember these *things*, I pour out ¹my soul in me:
For I °had gone with the multitude, I °went with them to the house of ¹God,
With the voice of joy and praise, with a multitude that kept °holyday.

C¹ 5 °Why art thou cast down, O ¹my soul?
°And *why* art thou disquieted in me?
Hope thou in ¹God: for I shall yet praise Him
For the °help of °His °countenance.

A² 6 °O my ¹God, ¹my soul is cast down within me:
Therefore will I remember Thee from the land of °Jordan,
And of °the Hermonites, from the °hill Mizar.
7 Deep calleth unto deep at the noise of Thy waterspouts:
All Thy waves and Thy billows are gone over me.

B² 8 °*Yet* °the LORD will command °His lovingkindness in the daytime,
And in the night °His song *shall be* with me,
And my prayer unto the °GOD of my life.
9 I will say unto °GOD my °rock, "Why hast Thou °forgotten me?
Why go I mourning because of the oppression of the enemy?"
10 °*As* with a sword in my bones, mine °enemies reproach me;
While they say daily unto me, "Where *is* thy ¹God?"

C² 11 ⁵Why art thou cast down, O my soul?
⁵And why art thou disquieted within me?
Hope thou in ¹God: for I shall yet praise Him,
Who is the °health of my ⁵countenance, and my ¹God.

42–72 (𝔅¹). THE EXODUS BOOK.

For the Structure, see p. 759. It has to do with ISRAEL; as the first book (1—41) had to do with MAN.

42–49 (A¹, p 759). ISRAEL'S RUIN.

42, 43 (B¹, B², p. 759). THE RUIN REALISED.
(Repeated Alternation.)

B | A¹ | 42. 1-3. Cry from afar.
  B¹ | 42. 4. Hope. "I remember".
    C¹ | 42. 5. Appeal. "Why cast down?" Praise.
A² | 42. 6, 7. Cry from afar.
  B² | 42. 8-10. Hope. "Jehovah will command", &c.
    C² | 42. 11. Appeal. "Why cast down?" Praise.
A³ | 43. 1, 2. Cry from afar.
  B³ | 43. 3, 4. Hope. "I will go".
    C³ | 43. 5. Appeal. "Why cast down?" Praise.

Pss. 42 and 43 are linked together, because (1) Ps. 43 has no title; (2) the Structure shows the correspondence of the repeated appeal.

Title. Maschil = Instruction. The second of thirteen so named. See note on Ps. 32, Title, and Ap. 65. XI.

for = by.

the sons of Korah. The first of the eleven Psalms so distinguished (42, 44, 45, 46, 47, 48, 49, 84, 85, 87, 88). Korah died by Divine judgment (Num. 16. 31-35), but his sons were spared in grace (Num. 26. 11). The men of Num. 16. 32 did not include the "sons". See notes, and Ap. 63. VIII. **sons** = descendants.

1 panteth = crieth, or longeth. Cp. Joel 1. 20. The cry of Israel in Egypt. **after** = for.

brooks = channels: water in gorges or pipes, difficult of approach. Heb. *'aphīkīm*. See note on 2 Sam. 22. 16.

my soul = I myself. Heb. *nephesh*. Ap. 13.

after = upon.

God. Heb. Elohim. Ap. 4. I. The Creator, not yet revealed as Jehovah to Israel in the Egyptian oppression.

2 GOD. Heb. El. Ap. 4. IV. Because "the living", in contrast with idols.

When shall I come, &c. Figs. *Interjectio*, *Erotēsis*, and *Apostrophe*. Ap. 6.

appear before God = see the face of God. So it is in some codices, with one early printed edition, Aram., and Syr. See notes on Ex. 23. 15; 34. 20.

3 continually = all the day.

4 had gone = shall go. **went** = shall go.

holyday = feast day.

5 Why . . . ? Fig. *Cycloides*. Ap. 6. The question repeated in *v.* 11 and 43. 5. See the Structure, above.

And why . . . ? This second "why" is in the text of some codices, with Sept., Syr., and Vulg., as in *v.* 11 and 43. 5.

help. Heb. pl. salvations. Pl. of majesty = great help, or great salvation.

His. Heb. text reads "my", so that, where I go I am delivered.

countenance. Fig. *Synecdoche* (of Part), Ap. 6, put for the whole person.

6 O my God. In some codices this is joined on to the end of *v.* 5 = "the great deliverance of me, and [praise] my God". Cp. *v.* 11 and 43. 5. **Jordan.** The reference is to 2 Sam. 17. 22. **the Hermonites** = the Hermons. Refers to the two peaks. **hill** = mountain. **8 Yet.** Omit this. **the LORD.** Heb. Jehovah. Ap. 4. II. **His lovingkindness . . . His song.** Fig. *Ellipsis* (Complex), Ap. 6, by which each is to be repeated in the other = "His lovingkindness [and His song] in the daytime; and in the night His song [and His lovingkindness] shall be with me". **GOD of my life.** Some codices, with Syr., read "the living GOD" (Ap. 4. IV). **9 GOD.** Heb. El. Ap. 4. IV. In edition of 1611 this was printed "My God". **rock** = mountain crag, or fortress. Heb. *sela'*. See note on Deut. 32. 13. Ps. 18. 1, 2. **forgotten.** Fig. *Anthropopatheia*. Ap. 6. **10 As with.** Some codices read "Like". **enemies** = adversaries. The second Psalm of each book has for its subject the enemy. See Ap. 10. **11 health** = salvation.

A³ (p. 761) **43** °Judge me, O °God, and plead my cause against an °ungodly nation:
O deliver me from the deceitful and unjust °man.
2 For Thou *art* the ¹God of °my strength: why °dost Thou °cast me off?
Why go I mourning because of the oppression of °the enemy?

B³ 3 O send out Thy °light and Thy truth: let them °lead me;
Let them °bring me unto °Thy °holy hill,
And to Thy °tabernacles.
4 Then will I go unto the altar of ¹God,
Unto °GOD my exceeding joy:
Yea, upon the harp will I praise Thee, O ¹God my ¹God.

C³ 5 °Why art thou cast down, O my soul?
And why art thou disquieted within me?
Hope in ¹God: for I shall yet praise Him,
Who is the °health of my countenance, and my ¹God.

°To the chief Musician.

603
D D a (p. 762) **44** °For the sons of Korah, °Maschil.

1 °We have heard with our ears, O °God, our fathers have °told us,
What work Thou didst in their days, in the times of old.
2 *How* Thou didst drive out the °heathen with Thy hand, and plantedst °them;
How Thou didst afflict the °people, and °cast them out.

b 3 For they got not the land in possession by their own sword,
Neither did their own arm save them:

c °But Thy right hand, and Thine arm, and the light of Thy countenance,
Because Thou hadst °a favour unto them.

d 4 °Thou °art my King, O ¹God:
Command °deliverances for Jacob.

a 5 Through Thee will we push down our °enemies:
Through °Thy name will we tread them under that rise up against us.

b 6 For I will not °trust in my °bow,
Neither shall my °sword save me.

c 7 °But Thou °hast saved us from our enemies,
And °hast put them to shame that hated us.

d 8 In ¹God we °boast all the day long,
And praise Thy name for ever. °Selah.

E F e (p. 763) 9 °But Thou hast °cast off, and put us to shame;
And goest not forth with our armies.

43. 1 Judge = Vindicate.
God. Heb. Elohim. Ap. 4. I.
ungodly = graceless. Fig. *Tapeinōsis*. Ap. 6.
man. Heb. *'ish.* Ap. 14. II.
2 my strength = my refuge, or my defending God.
dost = didst. **cast . . . off.** See 44. 8.
the enemy = an enemy.
3 light . . . truth. Probably an allusion to the Urim and Thummim (see notes on Ex. 28. 30), from which the Psalmist was now absent, in flight from Absalom.
lead = gently lead, or comfort.
bring: i. e. by their guiding counsel.
Thy holy hill: i. e. Zion. Therefore refers to times of David. **holy.** See note on Ex. 3. 5.
tabernacles = habitations. Pl. of majesty = thy great habitation. Heb. pl. of *mishkān.* Ap. 40.
4 GOD. Heb. El. Ap. 4. IV.
5 Why . . . ? See notes on 42. 5 for the whole of this verse. **health** = salvation. See note on 42. 5.
To the chief Musician. See Ap. 64.

44 (**D**, p. 759). THE CRY FOR A DELIVERER.
(*Introversions.*)

D | D | 1-8. God our help.
  E | F | 9-14. Us.
      G | 15. Me. Thy reproach. } Trouble.
  E | *G* | 16. Me. The reason. }
      F | 17-22. Us.
  D | 23-26. Jehovah our help.

Title. For the sons of Korah. The second of eleven so ascribed. See note on Title, Ps. 42, Ap. 63. VIII, and note on sub-scription below.
Maschil = Instruction. The third of thirteen Psalms so named. See note on Ps. 32, Title, and Ap. 65. XI. See note on Ps. 42, Title.

1-8 (D, above). GOD OUR HELP
(*Extended Alternation.*)

D | a | 1, 2. By Thee our fathers cast out.
  b | 3-. Not their own sword. } Reason.
  c | -3. But Thy right hand. }
  d | 4. Thou our confidence.
  a | 5. By Thee will we put down.
  b | 6. Not my own sword. } Reason.
  c | 7. But Thou. }
  d | 8. Thou our confidence.

1 We have heard. Refers to the exodus. See note on sub-scription. No time in reigns of David or Solomon to suit this Psalm. Temple-worship carried on. People in the land. Israel gone astray. Judah had turned away, but had returned (*vv.* 17, 18). The Psalm suits Hezekiah only. Sennacherib and Rab-shakeh referred to in *v.* 16. See the cylinder of Sennacherib (Ap. 67. xi, p. 98).
God. Heb. Elohim. Ap. 4. I.
told us = rehearsed. Cp. Ex. 12. 26; 13. 14. Josh. 4. 6, 7.
2 heathen = nations: i. e. the Canaanites.
them: thy People Israel.
people = peoples: i. e. the Canaanites.
cast them out = spread them about (as a vine, Isa. 5); "them" referring to Israel in both clauses.
3 But = For; giving the reason. See Structure above. Heb. *kī*, "for". **a favour.** Cp. Deut. 4. 37; 7 7, 8.
4 Thou = Thou Thyself.
art my King = art He my King.
deliverances. Pl. of majesty = a great deliverance.
5 enemies = adversaries.
Thy name. See note on 20. 1.
6 trust = confide. Heb. *batah.* Ap. 69. i.
bow . . . sword. Put by Fig. *Metonymy* (of Adjunct), Ap. 6, for military science. Cp. 2 Kings 19. 32.
7 But = For, as in *v.* 3. **hast saved** = didst save. Referring to *vv.* 1-4. **hast put** = didst put. Referring to *vv.* 1-4. **8 boast** = have boasted. **Selah.** Connecting the wondrous past with the distressing present, introducing the reason which called forth the Psalm itself, and marking the important break determining the Structure. See Ap. 66. II.

9-14 (F, above). [For Structure see next page.]

9 But = But now. Heb. *'aph* (not *kī*, as in *vv.* 3 and 7). Very emphatic, marking great contrast, as in 68. 16 ("Yea"). Some codices, with Aram., read "Howbeit". **cast off** (as with contempt). Cp. 43. 2. Some codices, with Syr., read "cast us off".

f (p. 763) 10 Thou makest us to turn back from the [5]enemy:
And they which hate us °spoil for themselves.
11 Thou hast given us like °sheep *appointed* for meat;
And hast °scattered us among the [2]heathen.
e 12 Thou sellest Thy people for nought,
And dost not increase *Thy wealth* by their price.
f 13 Thou makest us °a reproach to our neighbours,
A scorn and a derision to them that are round about us.
14 Thou makest us a byword among the heathen,
A shaking of the head among the people.
G 15 My confusion *is* continually before me,
And the shame of my face hath covered me,
E G (p. 762) 16 For the voice of him that reproacheth and blasphemeth;
By reason of the enemy and °avenger.
F g (p. 763) 17 All this is come upon us; yet have we not forgotten Thee,
Neither have we dealt falsely in Thy covenant.
18 Our heart is not turned back,
Neither have our °steps declined from Thy way;
h 19 Though Thou hast sore broken us in the °place of dragons,
And covered us with the shadow of death.
g 20 If we have forgotten the °name of our [1]God,
Or stretched out our hands to a strange °GOD;
21 Shall not [1]God search this out?
For He knoweth the secrets of the heart.
h 22 °**Yea, for Thy sake are we killed all the day long;**
We are counted as [11]sheep for the slaughter.
D i 23 °Awake, why °sleepest Thou, O °LORD*?
Arise, cast *us* not off for ever.
24 Wherefore hidest Thou Thy face,
And forgettest our affliction and our oppression?
k 25 For °our soul is bowed down to the dust:
k Our belly cleaveth unto the earth.
i 26 °Arise for our help,
And °redeem us for Thy °mercies' sake.
°To the chief Musician °upon °Shoshannim.

601 **45** °For the sons of Korah, °Maschil,
°A Song of °loves.

E H (p. 763) 1 My heart is °inditing a good °matter:
I speak of the things which I have made touching the king:
My tongue °*is* the pen of a °ready writer.

---

44. 9-14 (F, p. 762). US. TROUBLE.
(*Alternation.*)

F | e | 9. Thou hast cast us off. (Pos. and Neg.)
  | f | 10, 11. Enemies' acts.
  | *e* | 12. Thou hast cast us off. (Pos. and Neg.)
  | *f* | 13, 14. Enemies' words.

10 spoil for themselves = have plundered at their will; first occurrence Judg. 2. 14. See Sennacherib's boast on his cylinder. Ap. 67. xi, p. 98. Some codices, with Aram. and Syr., read "plundered us", &c.
11 sheep appointed for meat. Heb. sheep of devouring. Genitive of Relation (Ap. 17). Cp. Rom. 8. 36.
scattered us. Israel had already been removed. Sennacherib says he had taken away 200,150 (Ap. 67, p. 98).
13 a reproach. Cp. Rab-shakeh's harangue (2 Kings 18. 27-35) with *vv.* 13, 14. See Ap. 67. i.
16 avenger = him that taketh vengeance. Cp. 8. 2. Here = Sennacherib.

17-22 (*F*, p. 762). US. TROUBLE.
(*Alternation.*)

F | g | 17, 18. Righteousness.
  | h | 19. Calamities.
  | *g* | 20, 21. Righteousness.
  | *h* | 22. Calamities.

18 steps = goings. Pl. in many codices, with one early printed edition, Aram., Sept., Syr., and Vulg.; but some codices, with nine early printed editions, read singular.
19 place of dragons = place of jackals. Put by Fig. *Metonymy* (of Adjunct), Ap. 6, for a desert place.
20 name. See note on 20. 1.
GOD. Heb. El. Quoted in Ap. 4. IV.
22 Yea = Surely. Quoted in Rom. 8. 36.

23-26 (*D*, p. 762). JEHOVAH OUR HELP.
(*Introversion.*)

D | i | 23, 24. Prayer. "Awake".
  | k | 25-. Affliction.
  | *k* | -25. Affliction.
  | *i* | 26. Prayer. "Arise".

23 Awake . . . sleepest. Fig. *Anthropopatheia.* Ap. 6.
LORD*. Primitive text read "Jehovah". Altered by the *Sōpherīm* to "Adonai". See Ap. 32. Some codices, with two early printed editions, read "Jehovah".
25 our soul is = we ourselves are. Heb. *nephesh.* Ap. 13.
26 Arise. Fig. *Anthropopatheia.* Ap. 6.
redeem = deliver. Heb. *pādāh.* See notes on Ex. 6. 6; 13. 13.
mercies' = mercy's, or lovingkindness'.
To the chief Musician. See Ap. 64. Written by Hezekiah for his special circumstances; but on account of *vv.* 1-8 was handed over for general use at the Feast of the Passover. See note below.
upon = relating to, or concerning.
Shoshannim = Lilies. Put by Fig. *Metalepsis* for "Spring", and "Spring" put for the great spring festival, the Passover. See Ap. 65. XXI.

45 (**E**, p. 759). THE DELIVERER. PRAISED.
(*Introversion.*)

E | H | 1. The Psalmist.
  | J | 2-8. The king.
  | *J* | 9-16. The queen.
  | *H* | 17. The Psalmist.

Title. For the sons of Korah = By, &c. The third of nine so ascribed. See Title, Ps. 42, and Ap. 63. VIII.
Maschil = giving instruction. The fourth of thirteen so named. See Title, Ps. 32, and Ap. 65. XI.
A Song. Heb. *shīr*, as in Ps. 18. See Ap. 65. XXIII.

loves. Probably pl. of majesty = significant love. If in connection with the marriage of Hezekiah (2 Kings 21. 1 and Isa. 62. 4), its place here is accounted for between Pss. 44—48. Significant, because of its fulfilment in Messiah (Rev. 19. 7. Cp. Isa. 54. 5-8). Hephzi-bah (Isa. 62. 4) was the wife of Hezekiah. **1 inditing** = bubbling up: i. e. running over, or overflowing with. **matter** = theme. **is.** Supply Ellipsis: "tongue [is like] the pen". **ready:** i. e. with readiness of mind in respect of the subject treated of.

J K l (p. 764) 2 Thou art °fairer than the °children of °men:
Grace is poured into thy lips:

m Therefore °God hath blessed thee for ever.

L 3 Gird thy sword upon *thy* thigh, O °*most* mighty,
° With thy glory and thy majesty.
4 And in thy majesty ride prosperously
°Because of truth and meekness *and* righteousness;
And thy right hand shall teach thee terrible things.

L 5 Thine arrows *are* sharp in the °heart of the king's enemies;
Whereby the °people fall under thee.

K l **6 °Thy throne, O ²God, *is* for ever and ever:**
The sceptre of Thy °kingdom *is* a right sceptre.
7 Thou lovest righteousness, and hatest °wickedness:

m **Therefore ²God, Thy ²God, hath °anointed Thee**
With the oil of gladness above Thy °fellows.
8 °All thy garments *smell* of °myrrh, and aloes, *and* cassia,
Out of the ivory palaces, whereby they have made thee glad.

J M O n 9 Kings' daughters *were* among thy °honourable women:

o Upon thy right hand °did stand °the queen in gold of Ophir.

P 10 Hearken, O daughter, and °consider, and incline thine ear;
°Forget also thine own people, and thy father's house;
11 So shall the king greatly desire thy beauty:
For He *is* thy °LORD; and worship thou him.

N 12 And the °daughter of Tyre °*shall be there* with a gift;

N *Even* the rich among the people shall intreat thy favour.

M O o 13 The king's daughter °*is* °all glorious °within:
Her clothing *is* of wrought gold.
14 She shall be brought unto the king in °raiment of needlework:

n The virgins her companions that follow her
Shall be brought unto thee.
15 With °gladness and rejoicing shall they be brought:
They shall enter into the king's palace.

P 16 Instead of °thy fathers shall be °thy children,
Whom thou mayest make princes in all the earth.

H (p. 763) 17 I will make thy name to be remembered in all generations:
Therefore shall the °people praise thee for ever and ever.

°To the chief Musician °for the sons of Korah, °upon Alamoth.

45. 2-8 (*J*, p. 763). THE KING.
(*Introversion and Alternation.*)

J | K | l | 2-. The king's merits.
m | -2. His reward. "Therefore" (*'al kēn*).
L | 3, 4. His weapon, and its effects.
L | 5. His weapons, and their effects.
K | *l* | 6, 7-. The king's merits.
m | -7, 8. His reward. "Therefore" (*'al kēn*).

2 fairer: i. e. in His glory which follows the suffering described in Isa. 52. 14; 53. 2.
children = sons.
men. Heb. *'ādām.* Ap. 14. I.
God. Heb. Elohim. Ap. 4. I.
3 most mighty = mighty One. Heb. *gibbōr.* Ap. 14. IV.
With thy glory. Supply *Ellipsis* (Ap. 6), by repeating "[Gird thee] with Thy glory".
4 Because = On behalf.
5 heart. Put by Fig. *Metonymy* (of Adjunct), Ap. 6, for "in the midst".
people = peoples.
6 Thy throne, O God. Quoted in Heb. 1. 8, 9. Several attempts are made by certain commentators to get rid of this reference to Christ's Godhead; but not only would Heb. 1. 8, 9 have to go, but Isa. 9. 6, and Jer. 23. 6; 33. 16 as well.
kingdom. Cp. Pss. 20, 21, 24. Luke 1. 31-33, &c.
7 wickedness = lawlessness. Heb. *rāshā'.* Ap. 44. x.
anointed. Hence His name Messiah (Gr. Christ) = the anointed one.
fellows = companions.
8 All. Supply *Ellipsis* (Ap. 6): "[So that] all".
myrrh, and aloes. Cp. Ex. 30. 23, 24. John 12. 3; 19. 39.

45. 9-16 (*J*, p. 763). THE QUEEN.
(*Introversions and Alternation.*)

J | M | O | n | 9-. Maids of honour.
o | -9. The queen's apparel.
P | 10, 11. The queen addressed.
N | 12-. Suppliant.
N | -12. Suppliants.
M | *O* | *o* | 13, 14-. The queen's apparel.
n | -14, 15. Maids of honour.
P | 16. The queen addressed.

9 honourable women. Court ladies. English = maids of honour.
did = doth.
the queen. Type, Past, Hephzi-bah (2 Kings 21. 1. Isa. 62. 4); antitype, future, Israel, the bride of Messiah (Isa. 54. 5-8; 62. 45). Cp. Rev. 19. 7.
10 consider = see plainly, or observe.
Forget also thine own people. As did Rebekah (Gen. 24. 58), and Rachel (Gen. 31. 14), and Asenath (Gen. 41. 45), and Ruth (1. 16).
11 LORD. Heb. *Adonim.* Ap. 4. VIII. 3.
12 daughter of Tyre. Either the queen of Tyre, or the people of Tyre personified.
shall be there. Fig. *Ellipsis* (Complex), Ap. 6. III. 2, p. 10. Supply both clauses, repeating the verbs thus: "the daughter of Tyre [shall entreat thy favour] with a gift; even the rich among the people shall [come] and entreat thy favour". See note on 2 Chron. 32. 23.
13 is. The *Ellipsis* better supplied thus: "all glorious [sitteth enthroned] within". These Ellipses are caused by the bubbling over of the inditing heart, which is too quick for the pen.
all glorious = nothing but glory. Cp. Isa. 4. 5.
within: i. e. in the inner palace; not internally.
14 raiment of needlework = embroidered robes.

15 gladness. Heb. pl. of majesty = with great gladness. **16 thy . . . thy.** Heb. text, these pronouns are masc.; but the Syr. reads them fem. In this case they agree with and perfect the Structure above. **17 people** = peoples, or nations. **To the chief Musician.** See Ap. 64. Having been written for the marriage of Hezekiah, the Psalm was handed over for public use, as the glorious antitype of the marriage of Messiah in a yet future day (Rev. 19. 7-9). **for the sons, &c.** See note on Title, above. This and Ps. 87 are the only two Psalms where the Title is given at the beginning as well as the end. These two Psalms are for a good reason thus discriminated. **upon**: i.e. relating to. **Alamoth.** See Ap. 65. II.

603 **46** °A Song.

D Q[1] (p. 765) 1 °God *is* °our °refuge and strength,
A °very present help in trouble.

R p 2 Therefore will not we fear, though the earth °be removed,
And though the mountains be °carried into the °midst of the sea;

q 3 *Though* the °waters thereof °roar *and* be troubled,
Though the mountains shake with the swelling thereof. °Selah.

S 4 *There is* a °river, the °streams whereof shall make glad the city of [1]God,
°The holy *place* of the °tabernacles of the °MOST HIGH.

S 5 [1]God *is* °in the midst of her; she shall not be °moved:
[1]God shall help her, °*and that* right early.

R q 6 The °heathen °raged, the kingdoms °were moved:

p He uttered His voice, the earth melted.

Q[2] 7 °The LORD of hosts *is* with us;
The [1]God of Jacob *is* our °refuge. °Selah.

T r 8 Come, °behold the works of °the LORD,

s What desolations He hath made in the earth.

U 9 He maketh wars to cease unto the end of the earth;

U He breaketh the °bow, and cutteth the °spear in sunder;
He burneth the °chariot in the fire.

T r 10 °Be still, and know that I *am* [1]God:
I will be °exalted among the [6]heathen,

s I will be °exalted in the earth.

Q[3] 11 [7]The LORD of hosts *is* with us;
°The [1]God of Jacob *is* [7]our refuge. °Selah.

°To the chief Musician.

602 **47** °A Psalm °for the sons of Korah.

E[1] V t (p. 766) 1 O clap your hands, all ye °people;
Shout unto °God with the voice of triumph.

u 2 For °the LORD °MOST HIGH *is* °terrible;
He is °a great King over all the earth.

46 (*D*, p. 759). THE HELP OF THE DELIVERER.
(*Introversions and Alternations.*)

D | Q[1] | 1. God our refuge.
  R | p | 2. The earth moved. } Danger defied.
    q | 3. The waters roar. }
      S | 4. The holy city. } Zion defended.
      S | 5. The holy city. }
  R | *q* | 6-. The heathen rage. } Danger defied.
    p | -6. The earth melted. }
Q[2] | 7. God our refuge. Selah.
  T | r | 8-. Behold God, in His works. } Works seen.
    s | -8. The earth. His desolations. }
      U | 9-. The world. War. } Wars ended.
      U | -9. The world. Weapons. }
  T | *r* | 10-. Know God in Himself. } Himself known.
    s | -10. The earth. God's exaltation. }
Q[3] | 11. God our refuge. Selah.

Title. A Song. Heb. *shīr*. One of the "Songs" referred to in Isa. 38. 20 (though not the same word). See Ap. 65. XXIII. Doubtless Hezekiah's during Sennacherib's siege. No other period of Israel's history suits it. Not celebrating a victorious campaign, but a successful defence. See notes below. Pss. 46, 47, 48 a Trilogy referring to the same event. See note on "Selah", *v.* 11.

1 God. Heb. Elohim. Ap. 4. I.

our refuge. Fig. *Cycloides* (Ap. 6), because repeated in *vv.* 7 and 11. See Structure above.

refuge: to which one flees. Heb. *ḥāṣāh*. Ap. 69. V. Not the same word as *vv.* 7, 11.

very present=found (near); masc. refers to God (help is fem.).

2 be removed=quake. Same as "moved", *v.* 6.

carried=moved.

midst=Heb. heart. Fig. *Metonymy* (of Adjunct). Ap. 6.

3 waters thereof roar. Fig. *Hypocatastasis* (Ap. 6), implying the raging of the Assyrian host without.

roar. Same word as "raged" (*v.* 6).

Selah. Connecting the roaring of the waters without with the silent flowing river in the rock-cut channel beneath Zion, and contrasting the boastings of the enemy with the secret purposes of God. No refrain "dropped out" here, as some suggest. See the Structure above, and Ap. 68.

4 river. Heb. *nahar*, a constantly flowing river (not *naḥal*, a summer *wady*). It flows beneath Zion, filling *En Rogel* and supplying Siloam. See Ap. 68.

streams=channels. Heb. *pālag*. See note on Gen. 10. 25. Ps. 1. 3: i. e. the rock-cut channels beneath Zion. See Ap. 68. All other water-supplies cut off. Cp. 2 Chron. 32. 30. 2 Kings 20. 20. See Ap. 68, and Ecclesiasticus 48. 17.

The holy place of the tabernacles of the MOST HIGH. Sept. and Vulg. render this "The Most High hath hallowed His habitation". See note on Ex. 3. 5.

tabernacles=the great habitation. Pl. of majesty, implying greatness of glory, not of size. Heb. *mishkān*. Ap. 40. ii. **MOST HIGH.** Heb. *Elyōn*. Ap. 4. VI.

5 in the midst=in the middle, not the same as *v.* 2. **moved.** Same word as "carried", in *v.* 2. **and that right early.** Heb. at the turning of the morning: i. e. when the morning dawns. See 2 Kings 19. 31-35. Isa. 37. 35, 36. Cp. Ex. 14. 27. **6 heathen**=nations. **raged.** Same word as "roar", *v.* 3. **were moved**=moved. Same word as in *v.* 5. **7 The LORD of hosts.** See note on 1 Sam. 1. 3. **refuge**=an impregnable place. Heb. *miṣgāb*. Not the same word as in *v.* 1. **Selah.** Connecting this assured confidence in God's promise with its fulfilment in the deliverance of Zion from Sennacherib (Ap. 66. II). **8 behold**=gaze on. **the LORD.** Heb. Jehovah. Ap. 4. II. But some codices, with first printed edition and Syr., read "Elohim", God. Cp. 66. 5. **9 bow . . . spear . . . chariot.** The weapons of war, corresponding with the preceding line—war. See the Structure above. **10 Be still**=Desist; cease your efforts. Heb. *rāpha*. **exalted.** Heb. *rūm*, so most frequently rendered. **11 The God of Jacob.** See notes on 146. 5; and cp. Gen. 32. 28; 43. 6; 45. 26. **Selah.** Connecting Ps. 46 with Pss. 47 and 48, all three referring to the same events. See Ap. 66. II. **To the chief Musician.** See Ap. 64.

47 (*E*[1], p. 759) [For Structure see next page].

Title. A Psalm. Heb. *mizmōr*. See Ap. 65. XVII. Referring to the time of Hezekiah. One of three Psalms (46, 47, 48) in praise of Zion, delivered from Sennacherib's siege. **for the sons of Korah.** The fourth of nine so ascribed. See note on 42, and Ap. 65. VIII. **1 people**=peoples. **God.** Heb. Elohim. Ap. 4. I. **2 the LORD.** Heb. Jehovah. Ap. 4. II. **MOST HIGH.** Heb. *Elyōn*. Ap. 4. VI. **terrible**=to be reverenced. **a great King.** This in special contrast with Sennacherib (Isa. 36. 4).

W (p. 766) 3 °He shall subdue the [1] people under us,
And the °nations under our feet.
4 He °shall choose our inheritance for us,
The excellency of Jacob whom He loved.
°Selah.

X 5 [1] God is °gone up with a shout,
[2] The LORD with the sound of a trumpet.

V t 6 °Sing °praises °to [1] God, sing °praises:
Sing °praises unto our King, °sing °praises.

u 7 For [1] God *is* the King °of all the earth:
Sing ye praises °with understanding.
8 [1] God °reigneth over the °heathen:
[1] God sitteth upon the °throne of His holiness.

W 9 The princes of the [1] people are gathered together,
°*Even* the People of the [1] God of Abraham:

X For the °shields of the earth *belong* unto [1] God:
He is greatly °exalted.

602 **48** °A Song *and* °Psalm °for the sons of Korah.

E[2] Y (p. 766) 1 Great *is* °the LORD, and greatly to be praised
In °the city of our °God, *in* °the mountain of His holiness.

Z 2 Beautiful for °situation, the joy of the whole °earth,
Is °mount Zion, *on* °the sides of the north,
°The city of the great King.
3 [1] God °is known in her palaces for a refuge.

A 4 For, °lo, °the kings were assembled,
They passed by together.
5 They saw *it, and* so they marvelled;
They were troubled, *and* hasted away.
6 Fear took hold upon them there,
And pain, as of a woman in travail.
7 Thou breakest the ships of Tarshish
With an east °wind.
8 °As we have heard, so have we seen
In [1] the city of °the LORD of hosts, in [1] the city of our [1] God:
[1] God will establish it for ever. °Selah.

Y 9 We have °thought of Thy lovingkindness, O [1] God,
In the °midst of Thy temple.
10 According to Thy °name, O [1] God,
So *is* Thy praise unto the ends of the earth:
Thy right hand is full of righteousness.

Z 11 Let [2] mount Zion rejoice,
Let the °daughters of Judah be glad,
Because of Thy °judgments.

47 (*E*[1], p. 759). PRAISE TO THE DELIVERER.
(*Extended Alternations.*)

E[1]
V | t | 1. A call to praise.
u | 2. The reasons.
W | 3, 4. The nations, and Israel.
X | 5. God exalted.
V | *t* | 6. A call to praise.
u | 7, 8. The reason.
W | 9-. The nations, and Israel.
X | -9. God exalted.

3 He shall subdue = may He subdue.
nations = tribes of men.
4 shall choose = chooseth: referring to Israel's inheritance. Repeat this verb at the beginning of the next line.
Selah. Connecting the consideration of what God had done for Hezekiah and Zion and the exaltation claimed in 46. 10 with the exaltation given in 47. 5, 9 (Ap. 66. II).
5 gone up = exalted, as in *v.* 9 (same word).
6 Sing praises. Fig. *Epanadiplōsis* (Ap. 6), the verse beginning and ending with the same word.
praises. Pl. of majesty = great praise. Note the Fig. *Repetitio* (Ap. 6), for emphasis.
to God. Some codices, with Sept. and Vulg., read "to our God".
7 of. Some codices, with two early printed editions, read "over", as in *v.* 8.
with understanding. Cp. 49. 3 and 1 Cor. 14. 15, 16.
8 reigneth = hath become king.
heathen = nations.
throne of His holiness = His holy Throne. Genitive of Character.
9 Even. Perhaps better to supply Ellipsis (Ap. 6): "[unto] the People", or "[to be] a People". See the Structure, and cp. *v.* 4.
shields. Put by Fig. *Metonymy* (of Effect), Ap. 6, for princes (in preceding line), or, for defences in general Cp. 89. 18 (marg.) and Hos. 4. 18 (marg.).
exalted. Cp. *v.* 5. This is the object of the Psalm connected with 46 by the Selah in 46. 13.

48 (*E*[2], p. 759). PRAISE TO THE DELIVERER.
(*Repeated Alternation.*)

E[2]
Y | 1-. Praise.
Z | -1-3. Zion a joy. In her palaces, God known.
A | 4-8. The reason. "For". God's *power* shown in her establishment "for ever". Selah.
Y | 9, 10. Praise.
Z | 11-13. Zion to rejoice. In her towers, strength surveyed.
A | 14. The reason. "For". God's *favour* shown in guidance "for evermore".

Title. A Song. Heb. *Shīr.* See Ap. 65. XXIII.
Psalm. Heb. *mizmōr.* See Ap. 65. XVII.
for the sons of Korah. See Ap. 63. VIII. The fifth of nine so ascribed; and the last of the four Psalms celebrating the deliverance of Zion and Hezekiah (44, 46-48).
1 the LORD. Heb. Jehovah. Ap. 4. II.
the city: i. e. Zion, recently delivered from Sennacherib.
God. Heb. Elohim. Ap. 4. I.
the mountain of His holiness, or of His Sanctuary. Genitive of Character. **2 situation** = elevation. **earth**: or land. **mount Zion.** Immediately south of Moriah. See Ap. 68. **the sides of the north**: i. e. with Moriah and the Temple immediately on the north side. **The city of the great King** = [is] Jerusalem as a whole. Note the three points of view: (1) the elevated mount; (2) the south side of Moriah; (3) Jerusalem proper. Cp. Matt. 5. 35. **3 is known** = hath made Himself known. **4 lo.** Fig. *Asterismos.* Ap. 6. **the kings**: i. e. the vassal kings of Sennacherib. **7 wind.** Heb. *rūach.* Ap. 9. **8 As we have heard.** Thus linking on Ps. 44. 1. **the LORD of hosts.** Cp. 46. 7, 11. **Selah.** Connecting the demand of Ps. 46. 10, to "be still" and exalt Jehovah, with the "rest" in the thought of His lovingkindness. Connecting also the end of members A and *A* (*v.* 14). See Ap. 66. II. **9 thought** = been silent (Heb. *dāmah*), or stood still (46. 10) and rested in thought. **midst.** Same word as in 46. 5. **10 name.** See note on 20. 1. **11 daughters** = cities. Put by Fig. *Metonymy* (of Subject) Ap. 6, for cities (cp. Num. 21. 25. Josh. 17. 11, 16). These cities of Judah had cause for rejoicing, for they were now free from Sennacherib, who had captured them (Isa. 36. 1). See Sennacherib's cylinder. Ap. 67. xi, p. 98. **judgments**: on the Assyrian host.

12 °Walk about [2]Zion, and go round about her:
Tell the °towers thereof.
13 Mark ye well her °bulwarks,
°Consider her palaces;
That ye may tell *it* to the generation following.
A (p. 766) 14 For °this [1]God *is* our [1]God for ever and ever:
He will be our guide °*even* unto death.

°To the chief Musician.

12 **Walk about.** They were now free to do this.
towers. Many discovered on the east side of Ophel in recent excavations.
13 **bulwarks**=outer walls or ramparts.
Consider=single out. Occurs only here.
14 **this God**: or, such a God.
even unto death=for evermore, according to some codices, five early printed editions, Aram., Sept., and Vulg. The Massorites divided the one word (*'almūth*) into two (*'al mōth*), making it="over death". But the correspondence is with the preceding line, and with *v.* 8, as shown in the Structure, A and *A*.
To the chief Musician. Though written (probably by Hezekiah, Isa. 38. 20) for this special occasion, it was handed over for public use in the Temple worship.

B Int. (p. 767) **49** °A Psalm for the sons of °Korah.

1 Hear this, all *ye* °people;
Give ear, all *ye* inhabitants of the °world:
2 Both °low and °high,
Rich and °poor, °together.
3 My mouth shall speak of wisdom;
And the meditation of my heart *shall be* of understanding.
4 I will incline mine ear to a parable:
I will open my °dark saying upon the harp.

B v 5 Wherefore should I fear in the °days of °evil,
When the °iniquity °of my heels shall compass me about?

w 6 They that °trust in their wealth,
And boast themselves in the multitude of their riches;
7 °None *of them* can °by any means °redeem °his brother,
Nor give to °God °a ransom for °him:
8 (For the °redemption of °their soul *is* °precious,
And °it ceaseth for ever:)
9 °That he should °still live for ever,
And not see °corruption.

x 10 For °he seeth *that* wise men die,
Likewise the fool and the brutish person perish,
y °And leave their wealth to others.
11 Their inward thought *is, that* their houses *shall continue* for ever,
And their dwelling places to all generations;
They call *their* lands after their own names.

C 12 Nevertheless °man *being* in honour abideth not:
He is like the beasts *that* perish.

49 (*B*, p. 759). NEED OF REDEMPTION REALIZED. (*Alternations and Introversion.*)

INTRODUCTION.

Theme { I. 1, 2. All to hear.
II. 3, 4. I will speak.

The Theme announces an Enigma, and the solution is the Incarnation and work of the Redeemer.

I. *vv.* 1, 2.		II. *vv.* 3, 4.	
Hear.	Low.	Mouth.	Ear.
Peoples.	High.	Wisdom.	Parable.
Give ear.	Rich.	Heart.	Dark saying.
Inhabitants	Poor.	Understanding.	Harp.

B | B | v | 5. Why fear? (two lines).
w | 6-9. No redemption from man (four lines. Alt.).
x | 10-. Death (two lines).
y | -10, 11. Worldly wisdom (four lines. Int.)
C | 12. Man like the beasts (two lines).
B | *y* | 13. Worldly wisdom (two lines). Selah.
x | 14. Death (two lines. Int.).
w | 15. Redemption for me (two lines). Selah.
v | 16-19. Fear not! (four lines. Alt.).
C | 20. Man like the beasts (two lines).

NOTE.—In the first and third members the Introversion is alternated, the couplets in one being answered by quatrains in the other. If written by Hezekiah after his recovery the date would be about 602 B.C.

Title. A Psalm. The sixth of nine so ascribed. Heb. *mizmōr.* See Ap. 65. XVII.
Korah. See Ap. 63. VIII.
1 **people**=peoples.
world=age=transitoriness. Heb. *ḥeled*=the world as transitory, as in 17. 14. Cp. 39. 5, "age"; 89. 47, "time". Job 11. 17. These are all the occurrences.
2 **low**=sons of *'ādām.* Ap. 14. I.
high=sons of *'ish.* Ap. 14. II.
poor=helpless. Heb. *'ebyōn.* See note on Prov. 6. 11.
together=alike. 4 **dark**=deep.
5 **days of evil.** His were in Matt. 26. 38. Luke 22. 44, 53. John 12. 27. Heb. 5. 7.
evil. Heb. *rā'a'.* Ap. 44. viii.
iniquity=perverseness. Heb. *'āvāh.* Ap. 44. iv.
of my heels: or, my footsteps. Put by Fig. *Synecdoche* (of Part), Ap. 6, for the whole person, in order to call attention to, and thus emphasise, the reference to Gen. 3. 15. When our iniquities were laid upon Christ, then He was vulnerable and was wounded for our transgressions. 6 **trust.** Heb. *baṭaḥ.* See Ap. 69. I.
7 **None**=no man. Heb. *'ish.* Ap. 14. II. **by any means redeem.** Heb. Fig. *Polyptōton* (Ap. 6)="redeeming will redeem". **redeem**=deliver by power. Heb. *padāh.* See notes on Ex. 6. 6 and 13. 13.
his brother. Some codices read "surely" instead of "a brother". In this case the two lines read, "Surely no man (Heb. *'ish.* Ap. 14. II) can redeem, nor give to God atonement for himself". **God.** Heb. Elohim. Ap. 4. I. **a ransom**=atonement. Heb. *kāpher.* See Gen. 6. 14 ("pitch"). Ex. 29. 33. **him**=himself.
8 **redemption**=Heb. *padāh,* as "redeem", in *v.* 7. **their soul**=them. Heb. *nephesh.* Ap. 13. **precious** =costly, or, so costly is it that, &c. **it**=the redemption of themselves. 9 **That,** &c. Connect this with the end of *v.* 7. **still live for ever**=live on continually. **corruption.** Heb. *shāḥath*= destruction (with Art.): i.e. in the grave. 10 **he seeth**=it must be seen. **And leave**=They leave. *Homonym*: *'āzab.* See note on Ex. 23. 5; or, fortify, or strengthen by increasing or laying them up.
12 **man.** Heb. *'ādām.* Ap. 14. I. This corresponds with *v.* 20. See the Structure, above.

B y (p. 767) 13 This their way *is* their folly:
Yet their posterity approve their sayings. °Selah.

x 14 Like sheep they are laid in °the grave;
Death shall °feed on them;
And the upright shall have dominion over them in °the morning;
And their beauty shall consume in °the grave °from their dwelling.

u 15 But [7]God will [7]redeem °my soul from °the power of [14]the grave:
For He shall °receive me. °Selah.

v 16 °Be not thou afraid when °one is made rich,
When the glory of his house is increased;
17 For when he dieth he shall °carry nothing away:
His glory shall not descend after him.
18 °Though while he lived he blessed °his soul:
°And *men* will praise thee, when thou doest well to thyself.
19 °He shall go to the generation of °his fathers;
°They shall never see light.

C 20 [12]Man *that is* in honour, and understandeth not,
Is like the beasts *that* perish.

50

A Psalm °of Asaph.

F D (p. 768) 1 °The mighty God, *even* the LORD, hath spoken,
And called the earth from the rising of the sun unto the going down thereof.
2 Out of °Zion, the perfection of beauty,
°God hath shined.
3 Our [2]God °shall come, and shall °not keep silence:
A fire shall devour before Him,
And it shall be very tempestuous round about Him.
4 He shall call to the heavens from above,
And to the earth, that He may judge His People.
5 °Gather My °saints together unto Me;
Those that have made a covenant with Me °by sacrifice.
6 And the heavens shall declare his righteousness:
For [2]God *is* judge Himself. °Selah.

E F 7 Hear, O My People, and I will speak;
O Israel, and I will testify against thee:
I am [2]God, *even* thy [2]God.
8 I will not reprove thee for thy sacrifices
Or thy burnt offerings, *to have been* continually before Me.
9 I will take no bullock out of thy house,
Nor he goats out of thy folds.
10 For every beast of the forest *is* Mine,
And the cattle upon a thousand hills.
11 I know all the fowls of the mountains:
And the wild beasts of the field *are* Mine.
12 If I were hungry, I would not tell thee:
For the °world *is* Mine, and the fulness thereof.
13 Will I eat the flesh of bulls,
Or drink the blood of goats?

G 14 °Offer unto [2]God thanksgiving;
And pay thy vows unto the °MOST HIGH:

13 Selah. Connecting the *fact* of *v.* 14 with their *thought* of *vv.* 11, 12, and explaining the *folly* of *v.* 13. See Ap. 66. II.

14 the grave. Heb. *Shᵉōl.* Ap. 35. Occurs three times in this Psalm, *vv.* 14, 15.

feed on them = shepherd them. Fig. *Prosopopœia.* Ap. 6.

the morning: i.e. the resurrection morning = the "first" resurrection of Rev. 20. 6; resurrection of "life" (John 5. 29); "the just" (Acts 24. 15). Luke 14. 14. Dan. 12. 2, &c.

from their dwelling: i.e. [far] from their [former] lofty house. Heb. *zābal*, from similar Assyrian root = lofty [house], in contrast with "the grave". See note on 1 Kings 8. 13.

15 my soul = me, myself. Heb. *nephesh.* Ap. 13.

the power of the grave = the hand of *Shᵉōl*; "hand" being put by Fig. *Metonymy* (of Cause), Ap. 6.

receive me = take me out of [Sheol]; same word as "carry away" in *v.* 17. Cp. 50. 9; 73. 24; 78. 70.

Selah. Connecting the *fear* and the *folly* of the hopeless man with the true *hope* and *wisdom* which takes away fear. See Ap. 66. II.

16 Be not thou afraid. This, with *v.* 5, gives the scope of the Psalm. See the Structure (p. 767).

one = a man. Heb. *'īsh.* Ap. 14. II.

17 carry . . . away. See note on "receive", *v.* 15.

18 Though = For.

his soul = himself. Heb. *nephesh.* Ap. 13.

And men will praise = And [though] men praise thee when, &c.

19 He shall = [Yet] he shall, &c., continuing from *v.* 18.

his: i.e. the man's. **They**: i.e. those fathers.

50–60 (A[2], p. 759). ISRAEL'S REDEEMER.

50 (F, p. 759). HE BREAKS SILENCE.
(*Alternations.*)

F | D | 1–6. The Psalmist.
  E | F | 7–13. Reproof. Neg. Owns them. } His people addressed.
    G | 14, 15–. Duty. Praise and prayer.
    H | –15. Promise. I will deliver.
  D | 16–. The Psalmist.
  E | *F* | –16–22. Reproof. Pos. Disowns them. } The wicked addressed.
    G | 23–. Duty. Praise.
    H | –23. Promise. I will show.

Title. of Asaph = of, or for Asaph. The only Psalm of Asaph in Book II, the others being in Book III.

1 The mighty God, even the LORD. Heb. "El, Elohim, Jehovah" = The God of Gods, even Jehovah. Occurs only here and Josh. 22. 22 (twice). See Ap. 4. I, II, IV.

2 Zion. See Ap. 68.

God. Heb. Elohim. Ap. 4. I.

3 shall come. The promise of Ex. 3. 7, 8 turned into a prayer. Cp. Isa. 11. 11.

not keep silence. Now He is keeping silence. But He will speak again, and here we are told what He will say.

5 Gather = Gather in.

saints = those who have found favour with God. Cp. Matt. 24. 29–31.

by sacrifice. Cp. Ex. 24. 8.

6 Selah. Connecting the "call" to "hear" what *true worship* is (*vv.* 7–15), and to "consider" what *true service* is (*vv.* 16–22) when these things come into judgment (*v.* 6). Both are summed up in *v.* 23. (Ap. 66. II.)

12 world. Heb. *tēbēl* = the habitable world (Gr. *oikoumenē*).

14 Offer. Heb. *zabach.* Ap. 43. I. iv. Here is *true* worship. See *v.* 23; 40. 6; 51. 17. Heb. 13. 15. Cp. Isa. 1. 11–14. Jer. 7. 22, 23. Hos. 6. 6. Amos 5. 21. This is the opposite of "unthankful" (2 Tim. 3. 2).

MOST HIGH. Heb. Elyōn. Ap. 4. VI.

15 And call upon Me in the day of trouble:
H (p. 768) I will deliver thee, and thou shalt glorify Me.
D 16 But unto the °wicked [2]God °saith,
E F °"What hast thou to do to declare My statutes,
Or *that* thou shouldest take My covenant in thy mouth?
17 Seeing thou hatest instruction,
And castest My words behind thee.
18 When thou sawest a thief, then thou °consentedst with him,
And hast been partaker with adulterers.
19 Thou givest thy mouth to °evil,
And thy tongue °frameth deceit.
20 Thou sittest *and* speakest against thy brother;
Thou slanderest °thine own mother's son.
21 These *things* hast thou done, and °I kept silence;
Thou thoughtest that I was altogether *such an one* as thyself:
But I will reprove thee, and set *them* in order before thine eyes.
22 Now consider this, ye that forget °GOD,
Lest I tear *you* in pieces, and *there be* none to °deliver."

G 23 Whoso [14]offereth praise glorifieth Me:
H And to him that ordereth *his* °conversation *aright*
Will I shew the salvation of [2]God.

°To the chief Musician.

941 **51** °A Psalm of David, °when Nathan the prophet came unto him, after he had gone in to Bath-sheba.

G J (p. 769) 1 °Have mercy upon me, O °God, according to Thy °lovingkindness:
According unto the multitude of Thy tender mercies °blot out my °transgressions.
2 °Wash me throughly from mine °iniquity,
And °cleanse me from my °sin.
K 3 For I °acknowledge my [1]transgressions:
And my [2]sin *is* ever before me.
4 Against Thee, Thee °only, have I [2]sinned,
And done *this* °evil in Thy sight:
°That Thou mightest be justified °when Thou speakest,
***And* be °clear when Thou judgest.**
5 °Behold, I was shapen in [2]iniquity;
And in [2]sin did my mother conceive me.
L a 6 [5]Behold, Thou desirest truth °in the inward parts:
And in the hidden *part* Thou shalt °make me to know wisdom.
b 7 °Purge me with °hyssop, and I shall be clean:
[2]Wash me, and I shall be whiter than snow.
8 °Make me to hear joy and gladness;
That the bones *which* Thou hast broken may rejoice.
J 9 Hide Thy face from my [2]sins,
And [1]blot out all mine [2]iniquities.
10 °Create in me a clean heart, O [1]God;
And renew a °right °spirit within me.

16 wicked. Heb. *rāshā'*. Ap. 44. x.
saith = hath said.
What . . . ? Figs. *Erotēsis* and *Apodioxis*. Ap. 6. See Rom. 2. 21, 22.
18 consentedst with = foundest pleasure with. Aram., Sept., Syr., and Vulg. read "rannest".
19 evil. Heb. *rā'a'*. Ap. 44. viii.
frameth = weaveth.
20 thine own mother's son. Fig. *Periphrasis* (Ap. 6), for emphasis.
21 I kept silence; Thou thoughtest. Cp. Ecc. 8. 11-13. Isa. 3. 11; 26. 10.
22 GOD. Heb. Eloah. Ap. 4. V.
deliver = rescue.
23 conversation = way. Some codices, with five early printed editions, Sept., Syr., and Vulg., read "And there [will be] a way by which I will show to him", &c.
To the chief Musician. See Ap. 64.

51 (**G**, p. 759). THE RESPONSE OF HIS PEOPLE. (*Division.*)

G J | 1, 2. Prayer.
K | 3-5. Transgression. Confession.
L | a | 6. What God desires.
b | 7, 8. Prayer and resulting praise.
J | 9-12. Prayer.
K | 13. Transgressors. Instruction.
L | b | 14, 15. What God desires.
a | 16-19. Prayer and resulting praise.

Title. A Psalm. Heb. *mizmōr*. See Ap. 65. XVII.
when Nathan, &c. See 2 Sam. 11. 2; 12. 1. David's utterance when he lay all night upon the earth as a *penitent* (2 Sam. 12. 16). Cp. his utterance when he "sat before the LORD" as a *worshipper* (2 Sam. 7. 18-29), and when he "stood upon his feet" as a *servant* (1 Chron. 28. 2-10).
1 Have mercy upon me = Be gracious or favourable unto me. **God.** Heb. Elohim. Ap. 4. I.
lovingkindness: or, grace.
blot out = erase, as a debt from a book (Ex. 32. 32, 33. Num. 5. 23. Ps. 69. 28), or wipe out so as to remove (2 Kings 21. 13. Isa. 44. 22).
transgressions. Heb. *pāsha'*. Ap. 44. ix.
2 Wash: as a garment. Heb. *kabas*. Heb form = multiply to wash = wash thoroughly.
iniquity. Heb. *'āvah*. Ap. 44. iv.
cleanse: i. e. pronounce ceremonially clean.
sin. Heb. *chāṭā'*. Ap. 44. i.
3 acknowledge. Confession is ever the condition of forgiveness. See notes on 32. 5.
4 only = alone. This is primary, and contains the secondary. **evil.** Heb. *rā'a'*. Ap. 44. viii.
That, &c. Quoted in Rom. 3. 4.
when Thou speakest: i.e. in Thy word. Some codices, with three early printed editions, Sept., and Vulg., read "in Thy words" (pl.). Cp. Rom. 3. 4.
clear = pure; such moral purity as belongs not to man, only to God (Job 15. 14; 25. 4. Prov. 20. 9). Heb. *zakak*.
5 Behold. Fig. *Asterismos*. Ap. 6.
6 in the inward parts. More than the external acts. Heb. *ṭuchoth*. Only here and Job 38. 36.
make me, &c. See note on Job 28. 28. We need this *making*, for this wisdom is from above. Cp. 2 Tim. 3. 15.
7 Purge me = Thou wilt sin-cleanse me, or un-sin me: i. e. expiate by the blood of a sin offering.
hyssop. Put by Fig. *Metonymy* (of Cause), Ap. 6, for the atoning blood sprinkled by it. Cp. Num. 14. 18; 19. 6, 18. **8 Make me** = Thou wilt make me.
10 Create. Heb. *bārā'*, as in Gen. 1. 1. The new heart is not the old one changed, but newly created: i.e. "begotten" by God, as in John 3. 6-8.
right = steadfast. Cp. 78. 37; 112. 7.
spirit. Heb. *rūach*. Ap. 9. Put by Fig. *Synecdoche* (of Part), Ap. 6, for whole character.

11 Cast me not away from Thy presence;
And °take not Thy °Holy Spirit from me.
12 Restore unto me the joy of Thy salvation;
And uphold me °*with Thy* free °spirit.

K (p. 769) 13 *Then* will I teach [1]transgressors Thy ways;
And [2]sinners shall be converted unto Thee.

L b 14 °Deliver me from °bloodguiltiness, O [1]God,
Thou [1]God of my salvation:
And my tongue shall sing aloud of Thy righteousness.
15 O °LORD*, open Thou my lips;
And my mouth shall shew forth Thy praise.

a 16 For Thou °desirest not sacrifice; else would I give *it:*
Thou delightest not in burnt offering.
17 The °sacrifices of [1]God *are* a broken [12]spirit:
A broken and a contrite heart, O [1]God, Thou wilt °not despise.
18 Do good in Thy good pleasure unto °Zion:
Build Thou the walls of Jerusalem.
19 Then shalt Thou be pleased with the sacrifices of righteousness, with burnt offering and whole burnt offering:
Then shall they offer bullocks upon Thine altar.

°To the chief Musician.

968 **52** °Maschil, *A Psalm* of David, °when Doeg the Edomite came and told Saul, and said unto him, David is come to the house of Ahimelech.

G[1] M (p. 770) 1 °Why boastest thou thyself in mischief, O °mighty man?
The °goodness of °GOD *endureth* °continually.
2 Thy tongue deviseth °mischiefs;
Like a sharp rasor, working deceitfully.
3 Thou lovest °evil more than good;
And lying rather than to speak righteousness. °Selah.
4 Thou lovest all °devouring words,
O *thou* deceitful tongue.
5 [1]GOD shall likewise °destroy thee for ever,
He shall °take thee away, and °pluck thee out of *thy* dwelling place,
And °root thee out of the land of the living. °Selah.

N 6 The °righteous also shall see, and fear,
And shall laugh at him:

M 7 Lo, *this is* °the man *that* made not °God his strength;
But °trusted in the abundance of his riches,
And strengthened himself in his °wickedness.

N 8 But I *am* like a green olive tree in the house of [7]God:
I [7]trust in the °mercy of [7]God for ever and ever.
9 I will praise Thee for ever, because °Thou hast done *it:*
And I will wait on °Thy name; for *it is* good before °Thy saints.

°To the chief Musician °upon °Mahalath.

11 take not. Not a proper prayer for those now "in Christ": for, see John 14. 16.
Holy Spirit. See the only other O.T. occurrences of the expression (Isa. 63. 10, 11). Heb. *rūach*. Ap. 9.
12 with Thy free spirit: i. e. with a spirit of willing and unforced obedience. Heb. *rūach*. Ap. 9. Cp. Ex. 35. 5, 22.
14 Deliver = Rescue.
bloodguiltiness = bloods, pl. of majesty; put by Fig. *Synecdoche* (of Species), Ap. 6, for the great murder of Uriah (2 Sam. 11. 14-21). Cp. Gen. 4. 10.
15 LORD* = Jehovah. Ap. 4. II. One of the 134 alterations of the *Sōpherīm*. Ap. 32.
16 desirest not. Because death was the penalty. Was the child's life the substitute?
17 sacrifices. Pl. of majesty = the great sacrifice. Cp. Isa. 57. 15; 66. 2.
not despise. Fig. *Tapeinōsis* (Ap. 6), meaning that God will do infinitely more than words can express.
18 Zion. See Ap. 68.
If *vv.* 18, 19 are a later addition, then they were probably the work of Hezekiah in his editing the Psalms as well as the Proverbs, when the Psalm was handed over for public use. See Ap. 67. But David was "a prophet" (Acts 2. 30, 31).
To the chief Musician. See Ap. 64. The use in public worship makes it set forth the condition of national blessing. See its place in the Structure of Book II. Verses 18, 19 make the member "*a*" (above) agree with the member "a".

52 (G[1], p. 759). INSTRUCTION AS TO THE DEFEAT OF ENEMIES. (*Alternation.*)

G[1] | M | 1-5. The enemies apostrophised. (Doeg.)
N | 6. The righteous ones. (Pl. = Israel.)
M | 7. The enemies apostrophised. (Doeg.)
N | 8, 9. The righteous one. (Sing. = David.)

Title. Maschil = Instruction. The fifth of thirteen so named. See note on Title, Ps. 32, and Ap. 65. XI.
when Doeg, &c. See notes on 1 Sam. 21. 7; 22. 18. See note on *Mahălath*, in sub-scription at end of *v.* 9.
1 Why boastest . . . ? Relating to Doeg's treachery.
mighty man. Heb. *gibbōr*. Ap. 14. IV. P.B.V. = tyrant; Sept. = mighty lawless one. It is prophetic, and a type of Antichrist.
goodness = lovingkindness, or grace.
GOD. Heb. El. Ap. 4. IV.
continually = all the day.
2 mischiefs = malignity. Pl. for sing. = a great malignity.
3 evil. Heb. *rā'a'*. Ap. 44. viii.
Selah. Connecting the deceitful tongue of Doeg (*v.* 4) with the imprecation on it. See Ap. 66. II.
4 devouring words. Heb. words of swallowing up. Cp. 1 Sam. 22. 18.
5 destroy . . . take away . . . pluck out . . . root out. Note the Fig. *Anabasis*. Ap. 6.
Selah. Connecting God's judgment with the righteous onlookers. See Ap. 66. II.
6 righteous = righteous ones (pl.).
7 the man = the strong man (Heb. *geber*. Ap. 14. IV) **that made not God his strength.** The Gematria of this sentence = 2,197 (= 13^3). See Ap. 10.
God. Heb. Elohim. Ap. 4. I.
trusted = confided. Heb. *bāṭah*. Ap. 69. I.
wickedness. Aram. and Syr. read "wealth". Cp. 112. 3.
8 mercy = lovingkindness, or grace.
9 Thou hast done it. David ascribes all the glory to his God.
Thy name = Thyself. See note on 20. 1.
Thy saints. Some codices read sing. = Thy beloved (One).
To the chief Musician. See Ap. 64.
upon = relating to.
Mahalath, for *Maḥălōth* = the great dancings. See Ap. 65. IX.

53 ° Maschil, *A Psalm* of David.

G² O **1 The ° fool hath said in his heart, "*There is* no ° God."**

P a **Corrupt are they, and have done abominable ° iniquity:**
° *There is* none that doeth good.

b **2 ° God looked down from heaven upon the ° children of men,**
To see if there were *any* ° that did understand,
That did seek ° God.

P a **3 Every one of them is gone back: they are altogether become filthy;**
***There is* none that doeth good, no, not one.**

b **4 Have ° the workers of ° iniquity no knowledge?**
Who eat up my People *as* they eat bread:
They have not called upon ¹ God.

O **5 There were they in great fear, *where* no fear was:**
° For ¹ God hath scattered the bones of him that encampeth *against* thee:
Thou hast put *them* to shame, because ¹ God hath ° despised them.
6 ° Oh that the ° salvation of Israel *were come* out of ° Zion!
When ° God bringeth back the captivity of His People,
° Jacob shall rejoice, *and* ° Israel shall be glad.

° To the chief Musician ° on ° Neginoth.

about 965 **54** ° Maschil, *A Psalm* of David, ° when the Ziphims came and said to Saul, Doth not David hide himself with us?

G³ Q c (p. 771) **1 Save me, O ° God, by ° Thy name,**
And ° judge me by Thy strength.
2 Hear my prayer, O ¹ God;
Give ear to the words of my mouth.

d **3 For ° strangers are risen up against me,**
And oppressors seek after ° my soul:
They have not set ¹ God before them. ° Selah.

R **4 Behold, ¹ God *is* mine helper:**
The ° LORD* *is* with them that uphold ³ my soul.

R **5 He shall reward ° evil unto mine enemies:**
Cut them off in Thy truth.

Q c **6 I will ° freely sacrifice unto Thee:**
I will praise ¹ Thy name, O ° LORD; for *it is* good.

d **7 For He hath ° delivered me out of all trouble:**
And mine eye hath ° seen *his desire* upon mine enemies.

° To the chief Musician ° on ° Neginoth.

53 (*G*², p. 759). INSTRUCTION AS TO DEFEAT OF ENEMIES. (*Introversion and Alternation.*)

*G*² | O | 1-. The fool. God no-where.
| P | a | -1. Man. Depravity.
| | b | 2. God. Inspection.
| *P* | *a* | 3. Man. Depravity.
| | *b* | 4. God. Expostulation.
| *O* | 5, 6. The righteous. God now-here.

Title. Maschil = Instruction (the sixth of thirteen Psalms so named. See note on Title, Ps. 32, and Ap. 65. XI), as to the faction of the Tyrant of Ps. 52. This Psalm for public use. See note at end. Hence Elohim (Ap. 4. I), the Creator in relation to His creatures. A partial repetition of Ps. 14, which was not for public use (as Ps. 53 was); therefore Jehovah (David's God) there, and Elohim (the creature's Creator) here.

1 fool. May not this refer to Nabal?

God. Heb. Elohim. Ap. 4. I. Seven times in this Psalm. In Ps. 14 three times Elohim, and four times Jehovah. Elohim more characteristic of the second (or Exodus) book.

iniquity. In Ps. 14, Heb. *'ălīlāh* = doing; here, *'āval* = deceit. See Ap. 44. vi.

There is none, &c. Quoted in Rom. 3. 1-12.

2 God. Heb. *'eth 'Elohim* (Objective). Ap. 4. I. Note the Fig. *Epanadiplōsis* (Ap. 6), by which this verse is marked off as containing universal instruction, beginning and ending with the same word "God".

children of men = sons of Adam. Ap. 14. I.

that did understand. Heb. *Maschil.* See note on Title.

4 the workers. Some codices, with two early printed editions, Aram., Sept., Syr., and Vulg., read "all the workers".

iniquity. Heb. *'āvāh.* Ap. 44. iii.

5 For God hath scattered. This is an addition to Ps. 14.

despised them. Here, the wicked are in question. In Ps. 14. 5, the righteous.

6 Oh. Fig. *Ecphōnēsis.* Ap. 6.

salvation = great salvation, pl. of majesty. But some codices, with Sept. and Syr., read sing.

Zion. See Ap. 68.

God. Some codices, with Aram., Sept., and Syr., read "Jehovah".

Jacob . . . Israel: i. e. both natural and spiritual seed. See notes on Gen. 32. 28; 43. 6; 45. 26, 28.

To the chief Musician. This Psalm was edited for public use; hence the title Elohim. See notes above.

on = relating to.

Neginoth = smitings: referring to God's smitings with words and acts. See *v.* 5, which differs from 14. 5, 6. See Ap. 65. XV.

54 (*G*³, p. 759). INSTRUCTION AS TO THE DEFEAT OF ENEMIES. (*Introversion and Alternation.*)

*G*³ | Q | c | 1, 2. Prayer.
| | d | 3. Reason. Enemies assemble.
| R | 4. Jehovah my helper.
| *R* | 5. Jehovah my helper.
| *Q* | *c* | 6. Praise.
| | *d* | 7. Reason. Enemies scattered.

Title. Maschil = Instruction. The seventh of thirteen Psalms so named. See note on Title, Ps. 32, and Ap. 65. XI. **when, &c.** Cp. 1 Sam. 23. 19; 26. 1.

1 God. Heb. Elohim. Ap. 4. I.

Thy name = Thine own self. See note on Ps. 20. 1.

judge = vindicate.

3 strangers = aliens: the Ziphites, or the men of Keilah (1 Sam. 23. 12). Some codices, with two early printed editions and Aram., read "insolent men". Cp. 86. 14. **my soul** = me, or my life. Heb. *nephesh.* Ap. 13. **Selah.** Connecting David's danger with David's true and only source of help (Ap. 66. II). **4 LORD*.** One of the 134 alterations of Jehovah to Adonai by the *Sōpherim.* Ap. 32. **5 evil** = the evil. Heb. *rā'a'* (with Art.). Ap. 44. viii. **6 freely sacrifice:** Heb. with a freewill offering will I sacrifice. Cp. Num. 15. 3. **LORD.** Heb. Jehovah. Ap. 4. II. **7 delivered** = rescued. **seen his desire:** or, looked upon, and thus seen Jehovah's deliverance. **To the chief Musician.** See Ap. 64. **on** = relating to. **Neginoth** = smitings: i. e. the great smitings of my enemies by Jehovah. See Ap. 65. XV.

55 °Maschil, *A Psalm* of David.

G^4 S^1 e (p. 772) 934 1 Give ear to my prayer, O °God;
And hide not Thyself from my supplication.
2 Attend unto me, and °hear me:
I mourn in my complaint, and °make a noise;
f 3 Because of the voice of the enemy,
Because of the °oppression of the wicked:
For they cast °iniquity upon me,
And in wrath they hate me.
4 My heart is °sore pained within me:
And the terrors of death are fallen upon me.
5 Fearfulness and trembling are come upon me,
And horror hath overwhelmed me.
e 6 And I said, "Oh that I had wings like a dove!
For then would I fly away, and be at rest.
7 Lo, *then* would I wander far off,
And °remain in the °wilderness. °Selah.
8 I would °hasten my escape
From the °windy storm *and* tempest."
9 Destroy, O °LORD, *and* °divide their °tongues:
f For I have seen violence and strife in the city.
10 Day and night they go about it upon the walls thereof:
°Mischief also and sorrow *are* in the midst of it.
11 °Wickedness *is* in the midst thereof:
°Deceit and guile depart not from her streets.
T^1 12 For *it was* not an enemy *that* reproached me;
Then I could have borne *it*:
Neither *was it* he that hated me *that* did magnify *himself* against me;
Then I would have hid myself from him:
13 But *it was* thou, °a man °mine equal,
°My guide, and mine acquaintance.
14 We took sweet counsel together,
And walked unto the house of [1]God °in company.
S^2 g 15 Let death seize upon them,
And let them go down °quick into °hell:
h For °wickedness *is* in their dwellings, *and* among them.
g 16 As for me, I will call upon [1]God;
And °the LORD shall save me.
17 Evening, and morning, and at noon, will I °pray, and °cry aloud:
And He shall hear my voice.
18 He hath °delivered °my soul °in peace from the battle *that was* against me:
h For there were °many with me.
19 °GOD shall °hear, and afflict them,
(°Even He That abideth of old). °Selah.
°Because they have °no changes,
Therefore they fear not [1]God.

---

55 (G^4, p. 759). INSTRUCTION AS TO DEFEAT OF ENEMIES. (*Repeated Alternation.*)

G^4 | S^1 | e | 1–2. Prayer. Despondency.
f | 3–5. Reason. "For".
e | 6–9–. Prayer. Encouragement.
f | –9–11. Reason. "For".
T^1 | 12–14. Treachery of Ahithophel.
S^2 | g | 15–. Prayer. Imprecatory.
h | –15. Reason. "For".
g | 16–18–. Prayer. Encouragement.
h | –18, 19. Reason. "For".
T^2 | 20, 21. Treachery of Ahithophel.
S^3 | i | 22–. Prayer. Encouragement.
k | –22. Reason. Assurance.
i | 23–. Prayer. Imprecatory.
k | –23. Reason. Assurance.

Title. Maschil = Instruction. The eighth of thirteen so named. See note on Title, Ps. 32, and Ap. 65. XI. The occasion of this Psalm is seen in 2 Sam. 15. Hence 934 B.C. **1 God.** Heb. Elohim. Ap. 4. I.
2 hear = answer. **make a noise** = moan.
3 oppression: or outcry. The Heb. word *'āḳah* occurs only here.
iniquity = iniquitous words or devices. Heb. *'āven.* Ap. 44. iii. Fig. *Metonymy* (of Adjunct), Ap. 6.
4 sore pained . . . unto death. Cp. the words of the true David (John 13. 21) in reference to the Antitype (*v.* 18. Matt. 26. 38).
7 remain = lodge. The Sept. renders it by *aulizomai,* the word used in Matt. 21. 17. Cp. Luke 21. 37. See also Jer. 9. 2. **wilderness.** Cp. 2 Sam. 15. 28; 17. 16.
Selah. Connecting his despondency with his escape from the cause of it. It was not merely comfort he desired, but deliverance. See Ap. 66. II.
8 hasten my escape. Cp. 2 Sam. 15. 14.
windy storm = wind (Heb. *rūach.* Ap. 9) of storm.
9 LORD*. One of the 134 alterations of Jehovah to Adonai by the *Sōpherīm.* Ap. 32.
divide their tongues = cleave (as in Gen. 10. 25; 11. 1–9) their counsels; "tongues" being put by Fig. *Metonymy* (of Cause), Ap. 6, for counsels given by them. This prayer was literally answered (2 Sam. 17. 1–14).
tongues. Heb. sing.
10 Mischief. Heb. *'āven.* Ap. 44. iii.
11 Wickedness = pravities (pl.). Heb. *havāh* = cupidity. **Deceit** = Oppression, or violence.
13 a man = a mortal. Heb. *'ĕnōsh.* Ap. 14. III.
mine equal = as mine equal: i. e. esteemed by David as such; refers to Ahithophel.
My guide: or counsellor. Cp. 2 Sam. 16. 23 and Acts 1. 17.
14 in company = with the multitude. Heb. *regesh.* Occurs only here.
15 quick = alive. Cp. Num. 16. 30–33.
hell. Heb. *Sh^eōl.* Ap. 35.
wickedness. Heb. *rā'a'* (pl.). Ap. 44. viii.
16 the LORD. Heb. Jehovah. Ap. 4. II.
17 pray = meditate.
cry aloud. Heb. *hāmāh* = to make a noise. Onomatopoetic, like bees, or the cooing of a dove in Ezek. 7. 16. See note on sub-scription.
18 delivered = plucked (with power). Heb. *pādah.* See notes on Ex. 6. 6; 13. 13.
my soul = me (emphatic). Heb. *nephesh.* Ap. 13.
in peace. Note Ellipsis: "[and set it] in peace".
many with me = many [in conflict] with me. Fig. *Ellipsis.* Ap. 6.
19 GOD. Heb. El. Ap. 4. IV. The mighty Creator, because in conflict with His creatures.
hear = hear me. **afflict them** = answer them.
Even, &c. Fig. *Parenthesis.* Ap. 6.
Selah. Connecting the *true confidence* of David with the *false confidence* of the ungodly. David's true confidence was based on the fact that His GOD was the mighty One enduring for ever. "El" here is emphasised by the double accent *Pasek,* or "note line" each side of it. (Ap. 66. II.) **Because . . . no changes** = With whom are no changes (for the better): i. e. no improvement. See note on "alter" (Lev. 27. 10). Heb. *halaph.* Cp. Gen. 35. 2.

T² (p. 772²) 20 °He hath put forth his hands against such as be at peace with him:
He hath °broken his covenant.
21 *The words* of his mouth were smoother than butter,
But °war *was* in his heart:
His words were softer than oil,
Yet *were* they drawn swords.

S³ i 22 °**Cast thy °burden upon [16] the LORD, and He shall °sustain thee:**
k He shall never suffer °the righteous to be moved.
i 23 But Thou, O [1] God, shalt bring them down into the pit of destruction:
°Bloody and deceitful men shall not live out °half their days;
k But I will °trust in Thee.

°To the chief Musician °upon °Jonath-elem-rechokim.

962 **56** °Michtam of David, °when the Philistines took him in Gath.

F¹ U (p. 773) 1 °Be merciful unto me, O °God: for °man °would swallow me up;
He fighting °daily oppresseth me.
2 Mine °enemies would daily [1] swallow *me* up:
For *they be* many that fight against me, °O Thou Most High.
V 3 What time I am afraid,
I will °trust in Thee.
W 4 °In [1] God I will praise His word,
In [1] God I have put my [3] trust;
I will not fear what °flesh can do unto me.
U 5 °Every day they wrest my words:
All their thoughts *are* against me for °evil.
6 They gather themselves together, they hide themselves,
They mark my steps,
When they wait for °my soul.
7 Shall they escape by °iniquity?
In *Thine* anger cast down the °people, O [1] God.
8 Thou °tellest my °wanderings:
Put Thou my tears into °Thy bottle:
Are they not in °Thy book?
V 9 °When I cry *unto Thee,* then shall mine enemies turn back:
This I know; °for [1] God *is* °for me.
W 10 °In [1] God will I praise *His* word:
In °the LORD will I praise *His* word.
11 In [1] God have I °put my trust: I will not be afraid
What °man can do unto me.
12 Thy vows *are* upon me, O [1] God:
I will render praises unto Thee.
13 For Thou hast °delivered [6] my soul from death:
°*Wilt* not *Thou deliver* my feet from falling,
That I may walk before [1] God
°In the light of the living?

°To the chief Musician, °Al-taschith.

20 He: i. e. Ahithophel.
broken his covenant: by his disloyalty.
21 war was in his heart. Cp. 2 Sam. 14. 33 with 15. 5, 6. Referring to *v.* 19.
22 Cast, &c. = Commit unto. Quoted in 1 Pet. 5. 7.
burden = gift, or lot. Here = those very words of *v.* 21.
sustain thee = hold thee up.
the righteous = the righteous one (sing.).
23 Bloody and deceitful men = men of bloods and deceit. Genitive of Character. Heb. bloods = great bloodshed.
half their days. Referring to Absalom's untimely death.
trust = confide. Heb. *bāṭaḥ.* Ap. 69. I.
To the chief Musician. See Ap. 64.
upon = relating to.
Jonath-elem-rechokim = The dove of the distant Terebinths. Ap. 65. VII. A pictorial description of David in the wilderness, fleeing from Absalom. Cp. *vv.* 6–8; and the word *hāmāh* = to coo (as a dove). See note on "cry aloud" in *v.* 17.

56 (*F*¹, p. 759). ISRAEL'S REDEEMER, AND HIS WORK. (*Extended Alternation.*)

*F*¹ U | 1, 2. Complaint.
V | 3. Trust.
W | 4. Praise.
U | 5–8. Complaint.
V | 9. Trust.
W | 10–13. Praise.

Title. Michtam: i. e. Resurgam. See *v.* 13. One of six Psalms so called. The first is Ps. 16. See Ap. 65. XII. and sub-scription, *v.* 13.
when, &c. See 1 Sam. 21. 10; 27. 4; 29. 2–11.
1 Be merciful = Be gracious, or favourable.
God. Heb. Elohim. Ap. 4. I.
man. Heb. *'ěnōsh.* Ap. 14. III.
would swallow me up = thirst for my blood. Heb. *shā'aph*, used of wild beasts.
daily = all the day. See *v.* 5.
2 enemies = watchers, or observers.
O Thou Most High. Heb. *mārōm*, lofty, or exalted (not *Elyōn*).
3 trust = confide. Heb. *bāṭaḥ.* Ap. 69. I.
4 In God. Fig. *Cycloides.* Ap. 6. Cp. *v.* 10.
flesh. Put by Fig. *Synecdoche* (of Part), Ap. 6, for man.
5 Every day = all the day. See *v.* 5.
evil. Ap. 44. viii.
6 my soul = me. Heb. *nephesh.* Ap. 13.
7 iniquity. Heb. *'āven.* Ap. 44. iii.
people = peoples. (No Art.)
8 tellest = recordest.
wanderings . . . bottle Fig. *Paronomasia.* Ap. 6. Heb. *nodī . . . bᵉnʿodeka.*
Thy bottle. Fig. *Anthropopatheia.* Ap. 6. Tears of mourners were thus collected and buried with the dead. Hence often found in ancient tombs.
Thy book. Fig. *Anthropopatheia.* Ap. 6.
9 When I cry unto Thee = In the day of my cry.
for = that.
for me = mine.
10 In God, &c. Fig. *Cycloides.* Ap. 6. See *v.* 4.
the LORD. Heb. Jehovah. Ap. 4. II.
11 put my trust = confided. Cp. *v.* 3.
man = a man. (No Art.). Heb. *'ādām.* Ap. 14. I.
13 delivered = plucked.
Wilt not thou . . . ? Fig. *Erotēsis.* Ap. 6.
In the light of the living = in resurrection life. Hence the title "Michtam". Cp. Ps. 16, and other Michtam Psalms. See also Job 33. 30; and Ps. 116. 8, 9; where it is "land of the living".
To the chief Musician. See Ap. 64.
Al-taschith = Destroy not. See Ap. 65. III. The words of David in 1 Sam. 26. 9. 2 Sam. 24. 16, 17. Same word as in 2 Sam. 1. 14. Isa. 65. 8. Cp. 1 Chron. 21. 12, 15.

964 **57** °Michtam of David, °when he fled from Saul in °the cave.

F² X Z l (p. 774) **1** °Be merciful unto me, O °God, °be merciful unto me:
For my °soul °trusteth in Thee:
Yea, in the shadow of °Thy wings will I make my refuge,
°Until *these* calamities be overpast.

m **2** I will cry unto [1]God °MOST HIGH;
Unto °GOD That °performeth °*all things* °for me.

3 He shall send from heaven, and save me
From the reproach of him that would °swallow me up. °Selah.
n [1]God shall send forth His °mercy and His truth.

A **4** My [1]soul *is* among lions:
And I lie *even among* them that are set on fire,
Even the sons of °men, whose teeth *are* spears and arrows,
And their tongue a sharp sword.

Y **5** °Be Thou exalted, O [1]God, above the heavens;
Let Thy glory *be* above all the earth.

X A **6** They have prepared a net for my steps;
My [1]soul is bowed down:
°They have digged a pit before me,
Into the midst whereof they are fallen *themselves*. °Selah.

Z l **7** °My heart is °fixed, O [1]God, °my heart is fixed:
m I will sing and give praise.
8 °Awake up, my °glory; awake, psaltery and harp:
I *myself* °will awake early.
9 I will praise Thee, O °LORD*, among the °people:
I will °sing unto Thee among the nations.

n **10** For Thy °mercy *is* great unto the heavens,
And Thy °truth unto the °clouds.

Y **11** [5]Be Thou exalted, O [1]God, above the heavens:
Let Thy glory *be* above all the earth.

°To the chief Musician, °Al-taschith.

58 °Michtam of David.

F³ B (p. 774) **1** °Do ye indeed speak righteousness, °O congregation?
Do ye judge uprightly, O ye sons of °men?

---

57 (*F*², p. 759). ISRAEL'S REDEEMER, AND HIS WORK. (*Alternations and Introversions.*)

F² | X | Z | l | 1. Repetition. Prayer.
  m | 2, 3-. Resolve. "I will cry".
  n | -3. Mercy and truth. Sent.
 A | 4. Enemies.
  Y | 5. "Be Thou exalted".
X | *A* | 6. Enemies.
 Z | *l* | 7-. Repetition. Praise.
  m | -7-9. Resolve. "I will sing".
  n | 10. "Mercy and truth". Great.
  Y | 11. "Be Thou exalted".

Title. Michtam = Resurgam. One of the six Psalms so called. See Ap. 65. XII, and sub-scription.
when, &c. Cp. 1 Sam. 22. 1.
the cave. Probably at En-gedi (1 Sam. 24. 7, 8), where David probably used the words "Al-taschith". See the sub-scription.
1 Be merciful = Be gracious, or favourable. Cp. 56. 1.
God. Heb. Elohim. Ap. 4. I.
be merciful. Fig. *Epizeuxis* (Ap. 6), for emphasis.
soul. Heb. *nephesh*. Ap. 13.
trusteth in = hath fled for refuge to. Heb. *ḥasah*. Ap. 69. II. Same word as "make my refuge" in next line.
Thy wings. Fig. *Anthropopatheia*. Ap. 6.
Until, &c.: or, Until one shall have overpast these calamities. **2 MOST HIGH.** See note on 56. 2.
GOD. Heb. El. Ap. 4. IV.
performeth = bringeth to pass, and perfecteth, or completeth.
all things. Fig. *Ellipsis* (Absolute). Nothing particularised, that we may supply everything. To name one thing might seem to exclude all others. Cp. 138. 8.
for me = on my behalf.
3 swallow me up. See note on 56. 1.
Selah. Connecting and emphasising by repetition David's confidence (that God would assuredly send deliverance), with and because of His lovingkindness and truth. See Ap. 66. II.
mercy = lovingkindness, or grace. Note the Structure "n" and "*n*", above.
4 men. Heb. *'ādām*. Ap. 14. I.
5 Be Thou exalted. See the Structure. Fig. *Cycloides*. Ap. 6. See *v.* 11. Cp. similar *Cycloides* in 56. 4, 11.
6 They have digged, &c. Cp. 7. 15.
Selah. Connecting the bitterness of his enemies with his assured confidence in God. (Ap. 66. II.)
7 My heart . . . my heart. Fig. *Epizeuxis* (Ap. 6), as in *v.* 1. (See the Structure, above; also the Fig. *Ecphonēsis*. Ap. 6.) **fixed** = steadfast. Contrast 78. 37.
8 Awake. Fig. *Pœanismos*. Ap. 6.
glory. Fig. *Metonymy* (of Effect), Ap. 6, put for the tongue or the heart which gives the glory.
will awake early = will awake the dawn.
9 LORD*. One of the 134 places where the *Sōpherīm* altered Jehovah, of the primitive text, to Adonai. See Ap. 32.
people = peoples. **sing** = sing praise.
10 mercy . . . truth. See note on *v.* 3.
clouds = skies.
11 To the chief Musician. See Ap. 64.
Al-taschith = Destroy not. See notes on Title, and 56. 13; also Ap. 65. III.

---

58 (*F*³, p. 759). ISRAEL'S REDEEMER, AND HIS WORK. (*Introversion.*)

F³ | B | 1, 2. Man's judgment. Unrighteous.
 C | 3-5. The wicked. Their character.
  D | 6-9. Imprecation.
 C | 10. The righteous. Their rejoicing.
B | 11. God's judgment. Righteous.

Title. Michtam. See Ap. 65. XII. **1 Do ye indeed . . . ?** Fig. *Erotēsis*. Ap. 6. Render:
"Are ye indeed silent [when] ye should speak righteousness?
When ye should judge with equity, O ye sons of men?"
O congregation: or, O faction. Heb. *'ēlem*. Occurs only here and in the sub-scription of Ps. 55 = silent. So human judges are dumb when they ought to speak, and deaf when they ought to hear (*v.* 4). **men.** Heb. *'ādām*. Ap. 14. I.

2 Yea, in heart ye work ° wickedness;
° Ye weigh the violence of your hands in the earth.

C (p. 774) 3 The ° wicked are estranged from the womb:
They go astray as soon as they be born, speaking lies.
4 Their poison *is* like the poison of a serpent:
They are like the deaf adder *that* stoppeth her ear;
5 Which will not hearken to the voice of charmers,
Charming never so wisely.

D 6 Break their teeth, O ° God, in their mouth:
Break out the great teeth of the young lions, O ° LORD.
7 Let them melt away as waters *which* run continually:
When he bendeth *his bow to shoot* his arrows, let them be as ° cut in pieces.
8 As a snail *which* melteth, let *every one of them* pass away:
Like the untimely birth of a woman, *that* they may not see the sun.
9 Before your pots can feel ° the thorns,
He shall take them away as with a whirlwind, both living, and in *his* wrath.

C 10 The righteous shall rejoice when he seeth the vengeance:
He shall wash his feet in the blood of the [3]wicked.

B 11 So that a [1]man shall say, "Verily *there is* a reward for ° the righteous:
Verily ° He is a God That judgeth in the earth."

° To the chief Musician, ° Al-taschith.

970 **59** ° Michtam of David; ° when Saul sent, and they watched the house to kill him.

F[4] E (p. 775) 1 Deliver me from mine enemies, O my ° God:
° Defend me from them that rise up against me.
2 Deliver me from the workers of ° iniquity,
And save me from bloody ° men.
3 For, lo, they lie in wait for my ° soul:
The mighty are gathered against me;
Not *for* my ° transgression, nor *for* my ° sin, O ° LORD.
4 They run and prepare themselves without *my* fault:
Awake to help me, and behold.
5 Thou therefore, O ° LORD God of hosts, the [1]God of Israel,
Awake to visit all the ° heathen:
Be not merciful to any ° wicked ° transgressors. ° Selah.

F 6 They return at evening: they make a noise like a dog,
And go round about the city.

G 7 Behold, they belch out with their mouth:
Swords *are* in their lips:
For "who", *say they,* "doth hear"?

H 8 But Thou, O [3]LORD, shalt ° laugh at them;
Thou shalt have all the [5]heathen in derision.

2 wickedness. Heb. *'avvāl.* Cp. Ap 44. vi.
Ye weigh = Ye weigh out, or, dispense.
3 wicked = lawless. Heb. *rāshā'.* Ap. 44. x.
6 God. Heb. Elohim. Ap. 4. I.
LORD. Heb. Jehovah. Ap. 4. II.
7 cut in pieces = cut down [like grass].
9 the thorns. Put by Fig. *Metonymy* (of Cause), Ap. 6, for the fire caused by them (Ecc. 7. 6).
11 the righteous = the righteous one.
He is a God: or, There is a God, judges in the earth [will say]. Note the Introversion in this verse.
To the chief Musician. See Ap. 64.
Al-taschith = Destroy not. See Ap. 65. III.

59 (*F*[4], p. 759). ISRAEL'S REDEEMER, AND HIS WORK. (*Extended Alternation.*)

F[4]
- E | 1–5. Prayer. Enemies in the land. Selah.
  - F | 6. Comparison to a dog.
    - G | 7. Doggish characteristic. Barking.
      - H | 8, 9–. Psalmist's trust in God.
        - J | –9, 10. Reason. "God my defence".
- *E* | 11–13. Prayer. Enemies with them in the land. Selah.
  - *F* | 14. Comparison to a dog.
    - *G* | 15. Doggish characteristic. Greediness.
      - *H* | 16–. Psalmist's trust in God.
        - *J* | –16, 17. Reason. "God my defence".

Title. Michtam. See Ap. 65. XII.
when, &c. Cp. 1 Sam. 19. 11.
1 God. Heb. Elohim. Ap. 4. I.
Defend me = set me on high.
2 iniquity. Heb. *'āven.* Ap. 44. iii.
men. Heb. pl. of *'ĕnōsh.* Ap. 14. III.
3 soul. Heb. *nephesh.* Ap. 13.
transgression = rebellion. Heb. *pāsha'.* Ap. 44. ix.
sin. Heb. *chāṭā'.* Ap. 44. i.
LORD. Heb. Jehovah. Ap. 4. II.
5 LORD God of hosts = Jehovah Elohim Sabaoth. See note on 1 Sam. 1. 3.
heathen = nations.
wicked. Heb. *'āven.* Ap. 44. iii.
transgressors = hypocrites. Heb. *bāgad.*
Selah. Connecting the wicked transgressors with their true character as dogs of the Gentiles; and marking off and connecting the two prayers in *vv.* 1–5 (E), and *vv.* 11–13 (*E*). See Ap. 66. II.
8 laugh. Cp. Ps. 2. 4.
9 Because of his strength: or, O my strength, as in *v.* 17.
10 mercy = lovingkindness, or grace.
prevent = anticipate.
11 LORD*. One of the 134 places where the *Sōpherīm* altered "Jehovah" to "Adonai". Ap. 32.
12 sin. Heb. *chāṭā'.* Ap. 44. i.

9 ° *Because of* his strength will I wait upon Thee:
For [1]God *is* my defence. J
10 The [1]God of my ° mercy shall ° prevent me:
[1]God shall let me see *my desire* upon mine enemies.

11 Slay them not, lest my People forget: *E*
Scatter them by Thy power; and bring them down,
O ° LORD * our shield.
12 *For* the ° sin of their mouth *and* the words of their lips
Let them even be taken in their pride:
And for cursing and lying *which* they speak.

13 **Consume *them* in wrath, consume *them*,**
that they *may* not *be*:
And let them know that [1]God ruleth in
Jacob
Unto the ends of the earth. °Selah.

F 14 **And at evening let them return; *and* let**
(p. 775) **them make a noise like a dog,**
And go round about the city.

G 15 **Let them °wander up and down for meat,**
And °grudge if they be not satisfied.

H 16 **But I will sing of Thy °power;**
Yea, I will sing aloud of Thy [10]mercy in
the morning:

J **For Thou hast °been my °defence**
And refuge in the day of my trouble.
17 **Unto Thee, O my strength, will I °sing:**
For [1]God *is* my [16]defence, *and* the [1]God of
my [10]mercy.

°To the chief Musician °upon °Shushan-eduth.

about 895 **60** °Michtam of David, to teach; °when he strove with °Aram-naharaim and with Aram-zobah, when Joab returned, and smote of Edom in the valley of salt °twelve thousand.

F[5] K 1 **O °God, Thou hast cast us off, Thou hast**
(p. 776) **scattered us,**
Thou hast been displeased; O turn Thy-
self to us again.
2 **Thou hast made the earth to tremble;**
Thou hast °broken it:
Heal the breaches thereof; for it shaketh.
3 **Thou hast °shewed Thy people hard**
things:
Thou hast made us to drink the wine of
°astonishment.
4 **Thou hast given a banner to them that fear**
Thee,
That it may be displayed because of °the
truth. °Selah.
5 **That Thy beloved may be delivered;**
Save *with* Thy right hand, and °hear °me.

L o 6 **[1]God °hath spoken in His holiness; I will**
rejoice,
I will divide °Shechem, and mete out the
valley of °Succoth.
7 **°Gilead *is* mine, and °Manasseh *is* mine;**
°Ephraim also *is* the strength of mine
head;
°Judah *is* my °lawgiver;

p 8 **°Moab *is* my °washpot;**
Over °Edom will I °cast out my shoe:
°Philistia, triumph thou because of me.
9 **Who will bring me *into* °the strong city?**
Who will lead me into [8]Edom?

K 10 ***Wilt* not Thou, O [1]God, *Which* hadst cast**
us off?
And *Thou*, °O [1]God, *Which* didst not go
out with our armies?
11 **Give us °help from trouble:**
For vain *is* the °help of °man.

L o 12 **Through [1]God we shall do valiantly:**
p **For He *it is That* shall tread down our**
enemies.

°To the chief Musician °upon °Neginah.

---

13 Selah. See note on *v.* 5.
15 wander = prowl about.
grudge: or, stay all night.
16 power = strength, as in *v.* 9. **been** = proved.
defence = high tower. **17 sing** = sing praise.
To the chief Musician. See Ap. 64.
upon = relating to.
Shushan-eduth. It is "testimony" relating to the second Passover provided for in Num. 9. 5–14, and acted on in 2 Chron. ch. 30. See Ap. 65. XXII. The other of the two Psalms thus used is Ps. 79.

60 (*F*[5], p. 759). ISRAEL'S REDEEMER, AND HIS WORK. (*Alternations.*)

F[5] | K | 1–5. Prayer. (God, the object.)
  L | o | 6, 7. Israel. } (God, the subject.)
    p | 8, 9. Heathen. }
 K | 10, 11. Prayer. (God, the object.)
  L | *o* | 12–. Israel. } (God, the subject.)
    p | –12. Heathen. }

Title. Michtam. See Ap. 65. XII.
when, &c. See 2 Sam. 8. 13, 14.
Aram-naharaim, &c. = Mesopotamia or Syria. See 1 Chron. 18. 5, and note below on "twelve thousand".
twelve thousand. In 2 Sam. 8. 13, and 1 Chron. 18. 12, it is David's and Abishai's exploit, which was 18,000. Here, it is Joab's exploit, and his share was 12,000, but he took six months longer in finishing up his task (1 Kings 11. 15, 16). David's 22,000 in 1 Chron. 18. 5 were in a Syrian campaign. See notes on 2 Sam. 8. 12, 13.
1 God. Heb. Elohim. Ap. 4. I.
2 broken = made fissures. Occurs only here.
3 shewed = suffered . . . to see.
astonishment: or confusion, or trembling.
4 the truth: or [Thy] faithfulness. Heb. *ḳosheṭ*. Occurs only here in Psalms. Cp. Prov. 22. 21 = certainty, or exact, precise truth. (No Art.)
Selah. Connecting the gift, with the great and important object of it. (Ap. 66. II.) **5 hear** = answer.
me. Heb. text reads "us"; but some codices, with four early printed editions, Aram., Sept., Syr., and Vulg., read "me".
6 hath spoken. Verses 6–9 refer to the promise of the possession of the *whole* of Canaan, confirmed in 2 Sam. 7. 10. David here encourages himself by it.
Shechem . . . Succoth. West and east of Jordan.
7 Gilead . . . Manasseh. Eastern side.
Ephraim . . . Judah. Western side.
lawgiver. Cp. Gen. 49. 10. Num. 21. 18. Deut. 33. 21.
8 Moab . . . Edom. Spoken of as the chattels of a conqueror (2 Sam. 8. 12–14).
washpot = footbath: i. e. an ignominious vessel.
cast out my shoe. Idiom for taking possession.
Philistia. Syr. reads "over Philistia".
9 the strong city. Probably Sela or Petra, corresponding with Edom (cp. 2 Kings 14. 7). David claims the promise of Num. 24. 18.
10 O God. Some codices omit "O God".
11 help from trouble = succour out of trouble.
help of man = salvation or deliverance of man. Cp. "save", *v.* 5. **man.** Heb. *'ādām*. Ap. 14. I.
12 To the chief Musician. See Ap. 64.
upon = relating to.
Neginah = smitings. Ap. 65. XIV.

61 [For Structure see next page].

Title. of David: i. e. relating to David and to the true David. **1 God.** Heb. Elohim. Ap. 4. I.
2 the earth: or, the land.
that is higher than I = which will prove higher.

---

61 *A Psalm* °of David.

1 **Hear my cry, O °God;** **K**[1] M
Attend unto my prayer. (p. 776)
2 **From the end of °the earth will I cry unto**
Thee, when my heart is overwhelmed:
Lead me to the rock °*that* is higher than I.

N (p. 777) **3** For Thou hast been a °shelter for me,
And a strong tower from the enemy.
4 I will abide in Thy °tabernacle for ever:
I will °trust in the °covert of Thy °wings.
°Selah.

O **5** For Thou, O [1]God, hast heard my vows:
Thou hast given *me* the heritage of those
that °fear °Thy name.

N **6** Thou wilt prolong the king's life:
And his years as °many generations.
7 He shall °abide before [1]God for ever:
O °prepare °mercy and truth, *which* may
preserve him.

M **8** So will I sing praise unto [5]Thy name for
ever,
That I may daily perform my vows.

°To the chief Musician, °to °Jeduthun.

62

°A Psalm of David.

K[2] P[1] (p. 777) **1** °Truly °my soul °waiteth upon °God:
°From Him *cometh* my salvation.
2 He °only *is* my rock and my °salvation;
He is my °defence; I shall not be greatly
moved.

Q[1] **3** How long will ye °imagine mischief
against a °man?
Ye shall be slain all of you:
As a bowing wall *shall ye be, and as* a
tottering fence.
4 They [2]only consult to cast *him* down
°from his excellency:
They delight in lies:
They bless with their mouth, but they
curse inwardly. °Selah.

P[2] **5** [1]My soul, [1]wait thou [2]only upon [1]God;
For my expectation *is* from Him.
6 He [2]only *is* my rock and my [2]salvation:
He is my [2]defence; I shall not be moved.
7 °In [1]God *is* my [2]salvation and my glory:
The rock of my strength, *and* my refuge,
is in [1]God.

Q[2] **8** °Trust in Him °at all times; ye People,
Pour out your heart before Him:
[1]God *is* a refuge for us. °Selah.
9 °Surely °men of low degree *are* °vanity,
and °men of high degree *are* a lie:
To be laid in the balance,
They *are* °altogether *lighter* than °vanity.
10 [8]Trust not in oppression,
°And become not vain in robbery:
If riches increase, set not your °heart
upon them.

P[3] **11** [1]God hath spoken °once;
Twice have I heard this;
That °power *belongeth* unto [1]God.
12 Also unto Thee, O °LORD*, *belongeth*
°mercy:
For °Thou **renderest to °every man according to his work.**

61–72 (**A**[3], p. 759). ISRAEL'S REDEMPTION.

61 (**K**[1], p. 759). WAITED FOR BY ISRAEL.
(*Introversion.*)

K[1] M | 1, 2. Prayer.
N | 3, 4. Confidence.
O | 5. Reason.
N | 6, 7. Confidence.
M | 8. Praise.

3 shelter = refuge.
4 tabernacle. Heb. *'ohel*, tent (Ap. 40. 3), i. e. David's tent on Mount Zion. The Psalm probably refers to Absalom's rebellion.
trust = flee for refuge. Heb. *ḥaṣah.* Ap. 69. II.
covert = secret place.
wings. Fig. *Anthropopatheia.* Ap. 6.
Selah. Connecting the confidence with the only true ground of it. This is the central member of the Psalm. See the Structure above. (Ap. 66. II.)
5 fear = revere.
Thy name = Thee. See note on 20. 1.
6 many generations = from generation to generation.
7 abide = remain [enthroned].
prepare = number, or appoint, as in Jonah 1. 17.
mercy = lovingkindness, or grace.
8 To the chief Musician. See Ap. 64.
to = for.
Jeduthun. A precentor appointed by David, by name Ethan (see Ap. 65), afterward called Jeduthun = confession (1 Chron. 15. 17-19; 16. 41; 25. 1-6). Other Jeduthun Psalms are 38 and 76; in all three "vows" find a place.

62 (**K**[2], p. 759). ISRAEL'S REDEMPTION WAITED FOR. (*Repeated Alternation.*)

K[2] P[1] | 1, 2. Trust in God.
Q[1] | 3, 4. Enmity of foes.
P[2] | 5-7. Trust in God.
Q[2] | 8-10. Enmity of foes.
P[3] | 11, 12. Trust in God.

Title. A Psalm. Heb. *mizmōr.* See Ap. 65. XVII. A sequel to Ps. 61.
1 Truly = Only, or surely. Occurs six times in this Psalm: "truly" in *v.* 1; "only" in *vv.* 2, 4, 5, 6; "surely" in *v.* 9. Occurs four times in Ps. 38, another Jeduthun Psalm.
my soul = I myself (emph.). Heb. *nephesh.* Ap. 13.
waiteth = [waiteth in] silence; or, is become silent. See 37. 7.
God. Heb. Elohim. Ap. 4. I.
From. Some codices, with Sept., Syr., and Vulg., read "For from".
2 only = same word as "truly", *v.* 1.
salvation. Repeated for emphasis.
defence = high tower.
3 imagine mischief. Occurs only here. Probably = assault, or rise against.
man. Heb. *'ish.* Ap. 14. II.
4 from his excellency = from his dignity or high rank. Royal rank is implied.
Selah. Connecting the enmity of his foes with his trust in God. See Ap. 66. II.
7 In God is = Upon God [depends] my salvation.
8 Trust = Confide. Heb. *baṭaḥ.* Ap. 69. I.
at all times. Sept. and Vulg. read "all ye assembly of the People".
Selah. Connecting his trust in God with the nothingness of man. See Ap. 66. II.

9 Surely. Same word as "truly", *v.* 1. **men of low degree** = sons of *'ādām.* Ap. 14. I. **vanity** = a breath. **men of high degree** = sons of *'īsh.* Ap. 14. II. **altogether** = together. **10 And.** Ed. 1611 omits "And"; added in 1629. **heart.** Put by Fig. *Metonymy* (of Subject). Ap. 6, for the affections connected with it. **11 once; Twice.** Cp. Job 33. 14; 40. 5. Put for many times. **power** = strength. **12 LORD*.** One of the 134 alterations of Jehovah to Adonai by the *Sōpherīm.* Ap. 32. **mercy** = grace. **Thou renderest, &c.** Quoted in Matt. 16. 27. Rom. 2. 6. 1 Cor. 3. 8. 2 Tim. 4. 14. Rev. 2. 23; 20. 12, 13; 22. 12. **every man.** Heb. *'īsh.* Ap. 14. II.

about 964 **63** °A Psalm of David, °when he was in the wilderness of Judah.

K3 R1 (p. 778) 1 O °God, Thou *art* my °GOD; early will I seek Thee:
°My soul thirsteth for Thee, my flesh °longeth for Thee
°In a dry and °thirsty land, where no water is;
2 To see Thy power and Thy glory,
So *as* I have seen Thee in the sanctuary.

S1 3 Because Thy °lovingkindness *is* better than life,
My lips shall °praise Thee.

R2 4 Thus will I bless Thee while I live:
I will lift up my hands in Thy name.
5 [1]My soul shall be satisfied as *with* marrow and fatness;
And my mouth shall praise *Thee* with joyful lips:
6 When I remember Thee upon my bed,
°*And* meditate on Thee in the *night* watches.

S2 7 Because Thou hast been my help,
Therefore in the shadow of Thy °wings will I °rejoice.

R3 8 [1]My soul °followeth °hard after Thee:
Thy right °hand upholdeth me.
9 But those *that* seek [1]my soul, °to destroy *it*,
Shall go into °the lower parts of the earth.
10 They shall fall by the sword:
They shall be a portion for °foxes.

S3 11 But the king shall rejoice in [1]God;
Every one that sweareth by Him shall glory:

R4 But the mouth of them that speak lies shall be stopped.

°To the chief Musician.

64 °A Psalm °of David.

K4 T1 U q (p. 778) 1 Hear my voice, O °God, in my °prayer:
Preserve my life from fear of the enemy.

r 2 °Hide me from the °secret counsel of the °wicked;
From the °insurrection of the workers of °iniquity:

V 3 Who whet their tongue like a sword,
And bend *their bows to shoot* their arrows, *even* bitter words:
4 That they may shoot in secret at the perfect:
Suddenly do they °shoot at him, and °fear not.

U r 5 They encourage themselves *in* an °evil matter:
They commune of laying snares privily;
They say, "Who shall see them?"
6 They search out °iniquities; they accomplish a diligent search:

q Both the inward *thought* of every one *of them*, and the heart, *is* deep.

V 7 But [1]God shall °shoot at them
With an arrow; suddenly shall they be wounded.
8 So they shall make their own tongue to fall upon themselves:
All that see them shall flee away.

T2 9 And all °men °shall fear,
And shall declare the work of [1]God;
For they shall wisely consider of His doing.

T3 10 °The righteous shall be glad in °the LORD, and shall °trust in Him;
And all the upright in heart shall glory.

°To the chief Musician.

---

63 (K3, p. 759). ISRAEL'S REDEMPTION WAITED FOR. (*Repeated Alternation.*)

K3
- R1 | 1, 2. Assurance.
  - S1 | 3. Reason for praise.
- R2 | 4-6. Assurance.
  - S2 | 7. Reason for praise.
- R3 | 8-10. Assurance. (Enemies.)
  - S3 | 11-. Reason for praise.
- R4 | -11. Assurance. (Enemies.)

Title. A Psalm. Heb. *mizmōr.* Ap. 65. XVII.
when, &c. See 1 Sam. 22. 5; 23. 14-16.
1 God. Heb. Elohim. Ap. 4. I.
GOD. Heb. El. Ap. 4. IV.
My soul=I myself. Heb. *nephesh.* Ap. 13.
longeth=fainteth. Occurs nowhere else.
In. Some codices, with Syr., read "like".
thirsty=weary. **3 lovingkindness**=grace.
praise=commend, or extol. Heb. *shabaḥ*; used only by David and Solomon.
6 And. Supply Ellipsis (Ap. 6) by reading "[I will] meditate".
7 wings. Fig *Anthropopatheia.* Ap. 6.
rejoice: or, rest.
8 followeth. Supply Ellipsis by reading "[cleaveth to and] followeth". **hard**=close.
hand. Fig. *Anthropopatheia.* Ap. 6.
9 to destroy it. As Ahithophel did (2 Sam. 17. 1-3).
the lower parts: i. e. to Sheōl.
10 foxes=jackals.
11 To the chief Musician. See Ap. 64.

64 (K4, p. 759). ISRAEL'S REDEMPTION WAITED FOR. (*Division.*)

K4
- T1 | 1-8. Enemies.
- T2 | 9. Mankind in general.
- T3 | 10. The righteous in particular.

Title. A Psalm. Heb. *mizmōr.* Ap. 65. XVII.
of David=relating to David and the true David.

1-8 (T1, above). ENEMIES. (*Alternation and Introversion.*)

T1
- U | q | 1. The enemies. (Sing.)
  - r | 2. Enemies. (Pl.)
    - V | 3, 4. Their attempt to wound.
- *U* | *r* | 5, 6-. Enemies. (Pl.)
  - *q* | -6. The enemy. (Sing.)
    - *V* | 7, 8. Their wounding.

1 God. Heb. Elohim. Ap. 4. I. **prayer**=musing.
2 Hide. Put by Fig. *Metonymy* (of Adjunct), Ap. 6, for protect.
secret counsel=conspiracy (2 Sam. 16. 20-22; 17. 1-4).
wicked. Heb. *rā'a'.* Ap. 44. viii.
insurrection. The former, secret; this, open.
iniquity. Heb. *'āvāh.* Ap. 44. iv.
4 shoot ... fear. Fig. *Paronomasia.* Ap. 6. Heb. *yoruhū ... yīrā'ū.* **5 evil.** Heb. *rā'a'.* Ap. 44. viii.
6 iniquities. Heb. *'āval.* Ap. 44. vi.
7 shoot. Fig. *Anthropopatheia.* Ap. 6.
9 men. Heb. *'ādām.* Ap. 14. I.
shall fear. Some codices, with six early printed editions, read "will see".
10 The righteous=A righteous one.
the LORD. Heb. Jehovah. Ap. 4. II.
trust=make his refuge. Heb. *ḥasah.* Ap. 69. II.
To the chief Musician. See Ap. 64.

65

°A Psalm *and* °Song °of David.

L W (p. 779) 1 Praise °waiteth for Thee, O °God, in °Sion:
And unto Thee shall the vow be performed.

X 2 O Thou That hearest prayer,
Unto Thee shall all °flesh come.

W s 3 °Iniquities prevail against me:
t *As for* our °transgressions, Thou shalt °purge them away.

s 4 °Blessed *is the man whom* °Thou choosest, and causest to approach *unto Thee,*
That he may dwell in Thy °courts:
We shall be satisfied with the goodness of Thy house,
Even of Thy °holy °temple.

t 5 *By* terrible things in righteousness wilt Thou answer us,
O [1] God of our salvation;

X Y *Who art* the °confidence of all the ends of the earth,
And of them that are afar off *upon* the sea:

Z 6 °Which by His strength setteth fast the mountains;
Being girded with power:
7 Which stilleth the noise of the seas, the noise of their waves,
And the tumult of °the people.

Y 8 They also that dwell in the uttermost parts are afraid at Thy tokens:

Z u Thou makest the outgoings of the morning °and evening °to rejoice.

v 9 Thou visitest the earth, and waterest it:
Thou greatly enrichest it
With the °river of [1] God, *which* is full of water:
Thou preparest them corn, when Thou hast so provided for it.
10 Thou waterest the ridges thereof abundantly:
Thou settlest the furrows thereof:
Thou °makest it soft with showers:
Thou blessest the springing thereof.

u 11 Thou crownest the year with Thy goodness;
And Thy paths drop fatness.

v 12 They drop *upon* the pastures of the wilderness:
And the little hills rejoice on every side.
13 The pastures are clothed with flocks;
The valleys also are covered over with corn;
They shout for joy, they also sing.

°To the chief Musician.

66

A °Song *or* °Psalm.

M[1] A (p. 779) 1 Make a joyful noise unto °God, all °ye lands:
2 Sing forth the honour of His name:
°Make His praise glorious.

---

65 (**L**, p. 759). ISRAEL'S REDEMPTION. ZION WAITS. (*Alternation.*)

L | W | 1. Israel. Zion.
X | 2. Mankind.
W | 3-5-. Israel. Zion.
X | -5-13. Mankind.

Title. A Psalm. Heb. *mizmōr.* Ap. 65. XVII.
Song. Heb. *shīr.* Ap. 65. XXIII.
of David = by, or relating to David and the true David.
1 waiteth. As in 62. 1. Israel's silent waiting is now passed on to Zion. All is silent there as yet.
God. Heb. Elohim. Ap. 4. I.
Sion. See Ap. 68. David's tabernacle was there. This spelling with "S" comes through the Sept. and Vulg. Heb. is always "Z".
2 flesh. Put by Fig. *Synecdoche* (of Part), Ap. 6, for all mankind: i. e. the people.

3-5- (*W*, above). ISRAEL. ZION. (*Alternation.*)

W | s | 3-. Singular. "Me".
t | -3. Plural. "Our".
s | 4. Singular. "He".
t | 5-. Plural. "We".

3 Iniquities = iniquitous words. Heb. *'āvāh.* Ap. 44. iv.
transgressions. Heb. *pāsha'.* Ap. 44. ix.
purge them away = cover them by atonement.
4 Blessed = Happy. Fig. *Beatitudo.* Ap. 63. VI.
Thou choosest. Only those whom He calls can truly worship. See Lev. 1. 1, 2.
courts. Not the temple courts, but David's tabernacle on Zion. **holy.** See note on Ex. 3. 5.
temple. Heb. *heykal* = palace.

-5-13 (*X*, above). MANKIND. (*Alternation.*)

X | Y | -5. God the confidence of all afar off. } God spoken of.
Z | 6, 7. The power of God. }
Y | 8-. God the fear of all afar off. } God spoken to.
Z | -8-13. The goodness of God. }

5 confidence. Heb. *baṭaḥ.* See Ap. 69. I.
6 Which = Who. **7 the people** = peoples.

-8-13 (*Z*, above). THE GOODNESS OF GOD. (*Alternation.*)

Z | u | -8. Times. Morning and evening.
v | 9, 10. Places. Earth and water.
u | 11. Time. The year.
v | 12, 13. Places. Hills and valleys.

8 and evening. Supply Ellipsis (Ap. 6) from preceding clause: "and [the incomings of the] evening".
to rejoice = to shout for joy.
9 river. Heb. *peleg.* Always pl., except here; and always connected with a garden. See notes on 1. 3 and Prov. 21. 1. Cp. Rev. 22. 1, 2.
10 makest it soft = dissolvest it. Until the early rains fall, the ground is as hard as a rock.
13 To the chief Musician. See Ap. 64.

66 (**M**[1], p. 759). PRAISE PROMISED. TROUBLE REMEMBERED. (*Repeated Alternation.*)

M[1] | A | 1, 2. Exhortation to praise.
B | 3. Address. God's works in the world.
C | 4. Address. Promise for the world. Selah.
D | 5-7. Invitation. "Come and see," &c. Selah.
A | 8, 9. Exhortation to praise.
B | 10-12. Address. God's dealings with His People.
C | 13-15. Address. Promise for Psalmist. Selah.
D | 16-20. Invitation. "Come and hear," &c.

Title. Song. Heb. *shīr.* See Ap. 65. XXIII. **Psalm.** Heb. *mizmōr.* See Ap. 65. XVII. **1 God.** Heb. Elohim. Ap. 4. I. **ye lands** = the earth; earth being put by Fig. *Metonymy* (of Subject), Ap. 6, for its inhabitants. **2 Make His praise glorious.** Aram. and Syr. read "Celebrate the glory of His praise".

B (p. 779) 3 Say unto [1] God, "How terrible *art Thou in* Thy works!
Through the greatness of Thy power shall Thine enemies submit themselves unto Thee.

C 4 All ° the earth shall worship Thee,
And shall sing unto Thee;
They shall ° sing *to* Thy name." ° Selah.

D 5 ° Come and see the works of [1] God:
He is terrible *in His* doing toward the ° children of ° men.
6 He turned ° the sea into dry *land:*
They went through ° the flood on foot:
There did we rejoice in Him.
7 He ruleth by His power for ever;
His eyes behold the nations:
Let not the rebellious exalt themselves. ° Selah.

A 8 O bless ° our [1] God, ye ° people,
And make the voice of His praise to be heard:
9 Which holdeth ° our soul in life,
And suffereth not our ° feet to be moved.

B 10 For Thou, O [1] God, hast proved us:
Thou hast tried us, as silver is tried.
11 Thou broughtest us into the net;
Thou laidst ° affliction upon our loins.
12 Thou ° hast caused ° men to ride over ° our ° heads;
We went through fire and through water:
But Thou broughtest us out into a ° wealthy *place.*

C w (p. 780) 13 I will go into Thy house with burnt offerings:
x I will pay Thee my vows,
x 14 ° Which my lips have ° uttered,
And my mouth hath spoken, when I was in trouble.
w 15 I will ° offer unto Thee burnt sacrifices of fatlings,
With the incense of rams;
I will ° offer bullocks with goats. ° Selah.

D y 16 [5] Come *and* hear, all ye that fear [1] God,
And I will declare what He hath done for ° my soul.
z 17 I cried unto Him with my mouth,
And He was extolled with my tongue.
z 18 If I regard ° iniquity in my heart,
° The LORD* will not ° hear *me:*
y 19 *But* verily [1] God hath heard *me;*
He hath attended to the voice of my prayer.
20 Blessed *be* [1] God,
Which hath not ° turned away my prayer, nor His ° mercy from me.

° To the chief Musician ° on ° Neginoth.

67

A ° Psalm *or* ° Song.

M[2] E a (p. 781) 1 ° God be ° merciful unto us, and bless us;
And cause His face to shine upon us; ° Selah.
b 2 That Thy ° way may be known upon earth,
Thy ° saving health among all nations.

---

4 the earth. See note on "ye lands", *v.* 1.
sing=sing psalms.
Selah. Marking the Structure by showing that the member D (*vv.* 5–7) corresponds with the member *D* (*v.* 16); and connecting the exhortation of *vv.* 1–4 with the reason for it in *v.* 5. See Ap. 66. II.
5 Come and see. Note the correspondence of *v.* 16, "Come and hear".
children=sons.
men. Heb. *'ādām.* Ap. 14. I.
6 the sea: i. e. the Red Sea.
the flood: i. e. the river Jordan.
7 Selah. Repeating the exhortation to praise, and connecting the two halves of the Psalm. (Ap. 66. II.)
8 our God. Some codices, with one early printed edition, Aram., and Syr., omit "our".
people=peoples.
9 our soul. Heb. *nephesh.* Ap. 13. Some codices, with seven early printed editions, read pl.
feet. So some codices, with three early printed editions; others read "foot".
11 affliction=a heavy burden: i. e. in Egypt. Heb. *mū'āḳah.* Occurs only here.
12 hast caused=didst cause.
men. Heb. *'ěnōsh.* Ap. 14. III.
our heads=us. Fig. *Synecdoche* (of Part), Ap. 6.
heads. So some codices, with three early printed editions, Sept., and Vulg.; other codices read "head".
wealthy place. Aram., Sept., Syr., and Vulg. read "freedom". Cp. Ps. 18. 19.

66. 13–15 (*C*, p. 779). ADDRESS. PROMISE OF PSALMIST. (*Introversion.*)

C | w | 13-. Offerings.
  x | -13. Vows.
  x | 14. Vows.
  w | 15. Offerings.

14 Which. Fig. *Ellipsis* (Ap. 6)="which [vows]".
uttered=opened. Fig. *Ellipsis* (Ap. 6)="opened [and vowed]".
15 offer=prepare. Heb. *'āsāh.* Ap. 43. I. iii.
Selah. Connecting the members D and *D.* See note on *v.* 4, and Ap. 66. II.

16–20 (*D*, p. 779). INVITATION: "COME AND HEAR." (*Introversion*).

D | y | 16. God.
  z | 17. I.
  z | 18. I.
  y | 19, 20. God.

16 my soul=me (emph.). Heb. *nephesh.* Ap. 13.
18 iniquity. Heb. *'āven.* Ap. 44. iii.
The LORD*. One of the 134 places where the *Sōpherīm* say they altered Jehovah to Adonai. Ap. 32.
hear=answer.
20 turned away=turned away [from Himself]. Fig. *Ellipsis.* Ap. 6.
mercy=lovingkindness, or grace.
To the chief Musician. See Ap. 64.
on=relating to.
Neginoth=smitings: i. e. the smitings of Israel's enemies by God. See Ap. 65. XV.

67 [For Structure see next page].

Title. Psalm. Heb. *mizmōr.* Ap. 65. XVII.
Song. Heb. *shīr.* Ap. 65. XXIII. Some codices, with Sept. and Vulg., add "of David".
1 God. Heb. Elohim. Ap. 4. I.
merciful=favourable, or gracious.
Selah. Connecting the prayer (*v.* 1) with the object of it (*v.* 2). See Ap. 66. II.
2 way=dealings. See note on 103. 7.
saving health=salvation, or saving help.

F c (p. 781) 3 Let ° the people praise Thee, O [1] God;
Let all ° the people praise Thee.

d 4 O let ° the nations be glad and sing for joy:

G For Thou shalt judge [3] the people righteously,

G And ° govern ° the nations upon earth. ° Selah.

F c 5 Let [3] the people praise Thee, O [1] God;
Let all [3] the people praise Thee.

d 6 *Then* shall the earth yield her increase;

E a *And* ° God, *even* our own ° God, shall bless us.

b 7 ° God shall bless us;
And all the ends of ° the earth shall fear Him.

° To the chief Musician.

951 **68** A ° Psalm *or* ° Song of David.

J H[1] J[1] (p. 781) 1 ° Let ° God arise, ° let His enemies be scattered:
° Let them also that hate Him flee before Him.
2 As smoke is ° driven away, *so* drive *them* ° away:
As wax melteth before the fire,
So let the ° wicked perish at the presence of [1] God.

J[2] 3 But let the righteous be glad; ° let them rejoice before [1] God:
Yea, let them exceedingly rejoice.

H[2] K 4 Sing unto [1] God,
Sing praises to His name:
Extol Him That rideth upon the heavens
By His name ° JAH, and rejoice before Him.

L N 5 A father of the fatherless, and a judge of the widows,
Is [1] God in His ° holy habitation.
6 [1] God ° setteth the solitary in families:
He bringeth out those which are bound with chains:

O But ° the rebellious ° dwell in a dry *land.*

67 (M[2], p. 759). PRAISE PROMISED. TROUBLE REMEMBERED. (*Introversion and Alternations.*)

M[2] | E | a | 1. Prayer. "God be merciful".
b | 2. Object. Way known on earth.
F | c | 3. Injunction. "Let the people praise".
d | 4-. Effect. Peoples glad.
G | -4-. Address. People judged.
G | -4. Address. Nations governed.
F | *c* | 5. Injunction. "Let the people praise".
d | 6-. Effect. Earth fruitful.
E | *a* | -6. Prayer. "God be merciful".
b | 7. Object. God feared on earth.

3 the people = peoples. (No Art.)
4 the nations. (No Art.)
govern = gently lead.
Selah. Connecting the righteous rule of God of *v.* 4 (*d*) with renewed praise for it in *v.* 5 (*d*). See Ap. 66. II.

6, 7 (*d, E,* above). PRAYER. EFFECT AND OBJECT. According to the Hebrew. (*Introversion.*)

d | x | The earth shall yield.
E | y | God will bless us.
z | Our own God (Jehovah).
y | God will bless us.
x | All the ends of the earth shall fear.

6 God . . . God. } Fig. *Epizeuxis.* Ap. 6. Heb.
7 God shall bless us. } Elohim. Ap. 4. I.
the earth. Put by Fig. *Metonymy* (of Adjunct), Ap. 6, for its inhabitants. (No Art.)
To the chief Musician. See Ap. 64.

68 (J, p. 759). ISRAEL'S REDEMPTION. THE ANSWER TO PSALMS **61—67.** (*Division.*)

J | H[1] | 1-3. Introduction to psalm.
H[2] | 4-35. The psalm itself.

1-3 (H[1], above). THE INTRODUCTION. (*Division.*)

H[1] | J[1] | 1, 2. The wicked scattered.
J[2] | 3. The righteous made glad.

Title. Psalm. Heb. *mizmōr.* Ap. 65. XVII.
Song. Heb. *shīr.* Ap. 65. XXIII. It was written originally for use at the going up of the Ark to Zion 951, B.C., a Sabbatical year (2 Sam. 6 and 1 Chron. 15; see note on Title of Ps. 24); but, as it celebrates, among other things, the deliverance from Egypt, it was afterward appointed for public use at the Feast of the Passover. See notes on the sub-scription, and cp. *vv.* 1 and 4.

1 Let God arise. The Divine formula at the setting forth of the Ark. In the prayer (Num. 10. 35), "Rise up Jehovah" (Ap. 4. II); but here, God (Elohim. Ap. 4. I), because in connection with enemies. **Let.** Some codices, with one early printed edition, Sept., Syr., and Vulg., read "And let". **2 driven away** = driven about. **wicked** = lawless. Heb. *rāshā'.* Ap. 44. x. **3 let.** Some codices, with five early printed editions, Aram., Syr., and Vulg., read "and let".

4-35 (H[2], above). THE PSALM ITSELF. (*Introversion and Extended Alternation.*)

H[2] | K | 4. Exhortation to praise (four lines).
L | N | 5, 6-. Mercies to His People.
O | -6. Enemies judged.
P | 7-10. Goings in the wilderness (nine lines).
Q | 11-14. Jehovah's word. History (four verses).
M | 15, 16. Zion. Jehovah's chosen dwelling-place.
M | 17, 18. Zion. Jehovah's chosen dwelling-place.
L | *N* | 19, 20. Mercies to His People.
O | 21-23. Enemies judged.
P | 24-27. Goings in the sanctuary (nine lines).
Q | 28-31. God's command. Prophecy (four verses).
K | 32-35. Exhortation to praise (four verses).

4 JAH. See Ap. 4. III. Cp. Ex. 15. 2. The Divine Titles enrich this Psalm: Elohim occurs twenty-six times, because the Psalm has to do with the scattering of His enemies. The first occurrence of JAH is in Ex. 15. 2, and in the Psalms this first occurrence is in the second, or Exodus book. **5 holy habitation:** i. e. which David had prepared for the Ark on Zion. **6 setteth the solitary in families** = bringeth absent ones home. **the rebellious** = rebellious ones. **dwell** = have [ever] dwelt.

P e (p. 782) 7 O [1]God, °when Thou wentest forth before Thy People,
When Thou didst march through the wilderness; °Selah:

f 8 The earth shook,
The heavens also °dropped at the presence of [1]God:
Even Sinai itself *was moved* at the presence of [1]God, the [1]God of Israel.

g 9 Thou, O [1]God, didst send a plentiful rain, whereby
Thou didst confirm Thine inheritance, when it was weary.

h 10 °Thy congregation hath dwelt therein:
Thou, O [1]God, hast prepared of Thy goodness for °the poor.

Q (p. 781) 11 °The LORD* gave the word:
Great *was* the °company of °those that °published *it*.
12 °Kings of armies °did flee apace:
And she that °tarried at home divided the spoil.
13 Though ye have lien among the °pots, °*yet shall ye be*
As the wings of a dove covered with silver,
And her feathers with yellow gold.
14 When °the ALMIGHTY scattered kings °in it,
It °was *white* as snow in °Salmon.

M 15 The °hill of [1]God *is as* the °hill of Bashan;
An high °hill *as* the °hill of Bashan.
16 °Why °leap ye, ye high hills?
°*This is* the [15]hill *which* [1]God °desireth to dwell in;
Yea, °the LORD will dwell *in it* for ever.

M 17 The °chariots of [1]God *are* °twenty thousand, °*even* thousands of angels:
[11]The LORD* °*is* among them, *as in* Sinai, in the °holy *place*.
18 °**Thou hast °ascended on high, Thou hast °led °captivity captive:**
Thou hast °received gifts for °men;
°Yea, °*for* the rebellious also, that °THE LORD [1]God might °dwell *among them*.

L N 19 Blessed *be* the [11]LORD*, *Who* daily loadeth us *with benefits*,
Even °THE GOD °of our °salvation. °Selah.

---

68. 7-10 (P, p. 781); **24-27** (*P*, p. 781). GOINGS.
(*Extended Alternation.*)

P | e | 7. Goings in the wilderness.		
f | 8. Accompaniments.		In the wilderness.
g | 9. Address.		
h | 10. Thy congregation.		
P | *e* | 24. Goings in the sanctuary.		
f | 25. Accompaniments.		Into the sanctuary.
g | 26. Address.		
h | 27. The congregation.		

7 when Thou wentest forth: i. e. from Egypt. The whole deliverance of Israel is here rehearsed. See the sub-scription. For use at the Passover.

Selah. Connecting the first going up of the Ark in the wilderness with its accompaniments. See Ap. 66. II.

8 dropped: i. e. dropped [moisture].

10 Thy congregation=Thy living ones, or living host.

the poor=the humbled or oppressed one.

11 The LORD*. One of the 134 places where Jehovah was changed by the *Sōpherīm* to Adonai. See Ap. 32; also *vv.* 17, 19, 22, 26, 32.

company=host, or army.

those=the women. See note on *v.* 25. This is the women's part. Cp. 1 Sam. 18. 6, 7. Cp. Deborah.

published it. Always used of good news.

12 Kings, &c. Verses 12, 13, are the words of the women.

did flee apace. The rendering of the Fig. *Epizeuxis.* Ap. 6. Heb. "did flee, did flee". Cp. Judg. 5. 19; 7. 25.

tarried at home. Cp. 1 Sam. 30. 21-25.

13 pots. Heb. Dual, the two [or between the] brick-kilns: i. e. in Egypt. Not dirty vessels according to the Rabbinical commentators, but dirty places.

yet shall ye be. Referring to the deliverance and subsequent glory.

14 the ALMIGHTY. Heb. Shaddai. Ap. 4. VII.

in it: i. e. in His inheritance.

was white, &c. Supply Fig. *Ellipsis* (Ap. 6) thus, "was as [when He scatters] snow in Salmon": i. e. scatters by dispersing, as snow is melted away.

Salmon. Occurs only here and Judg. 9. 48.

15 hill=mountain. See note on Ezek. 28. 16.

16 Why . . . ? Fig. *Erotēsis.* Ap. 6.

leap=look askance at, or envy. Heb. *rāzad.* Occurs only here. By the Fig. *Prosopopœia* (Ap. 6), the other mountains are spoken of as envying Zion.

This is. Omit these italics, and punctuate thus: "Why will ye envy, O ye high hills, the hill Jehovah desired for His abode".

desireth. Cp. 78. 67, 68; 132. 13; and 1 Kings 11. 32. Neh. 1. 9.

the LORD. Heb. Jehovah. Ap. 4. II.

17 chariots. Fig. *Anthropopatheia.* Ap. 6.

twenty thousand. Heb. twice ten thousand thousands.

even thousands. Heb. thousands repeated: i. e. upon thousands.

is among them, &c. This line, according to the primitive orthography in the division of the word, reads; "Jehovah hath come from Sinai into the Sanctuary". See Ginsburg, *Int.*, pp. 161, 162. Or the printed text may stand with the *Ellipsis* (Ap. 6) supplied thus: "Jehovah among them (i. e. the angels and chariots) [hath come from] Sinai into the Sanctuary". **17 holy.** See note on Ex. 3. 5. **18 Thou.** Is this the poor one of *v.* 10? **ascended on high**=gone up to the high [mountain: i. e. Zion]; referring to the Ark; but a type of Christ's ascension, as is clear from Eph. 4. 8. **led**=led in procession. **captivity.** Put by Fig. *Metonymy* (of Adjunct), Ap. 6, for captives. **received gifts for men.** The Heb. *laḳaḥ* has a twofold meaning, i. e. *receiving* and *giving.* Here the *Ellipsis* must be supplied by the second, "received [and given] gifts among (or for) men". In Eph. 4. 8 the *Ellipsis* must be supplied by the former, "Thou hast [received] and given gifts among (or for) men". "Among" is one of the recognised renderings of *Beth* (ב=B) with a plural noun. (See 99. 6. 2 Sam. 15. 31. Lam. 1. 3. Cp. R.V.). **men.** Heb. *'ādām.* Ap. 14. I. **Yea.** Fig. *Epitrechon.* Ap. 6. **for the rebellious also.** This is a foreshadowing of true grace. **THE LORD.** Heb. Jah, as in *v.* 4. **dwell.** Heb. *shākan.* See note on "placed" (Gen. 3. 24)=dwell as in a tabernacle, the Ark being the symbol of His presence. Cp. Ex. 25. 8; 29. 45, 46. Josh. 18. 1; 22. 19. 1 Kings 6. 13; 8. 12, 13. 2 Chron. 6. 1, 2. It is from this verb that we have *Shekinah.* **19 THE GOD.** Heb. El (with Art.). Ap. 4. IV. **of our**="[Who is] our". **salvation.** Some codices, with one early printed edition, Sept., and Vulg., read "salvations" (pl.)=our great salvation. **Selah.** Connecting the exhortation to bless Jehovah (*v.* 19) with the reason for it (*v.* 20). See Ap. 66. II.

20 °*He That is* our [19] GOD *is* the [19] GOD of salvation;
And unto °GOD the Lord *belong* °the issues from °death.

O (p. 781) 21 But [1] God shall wound the head of His enemies,
And the hairy scalp of such an one as goeth on still in his °trespasses.
22 [11] The LORD * said, °"I will bring again from Bashan,
°I will bring °*My people* again from the depths of the sea:
23 That thy foot may be °dipped in the blood of *thine* enemies,
And the tongue of thy °dogs in the same."

P e (p. 782) 24 They have seen Thy °goings, O [1] God;
Even the °goings of my [19] GOD, my King, °in the sanctuary.

f 25 The singers °went before, the players on instruments °*followed* after;
°Among *them were* the °damsels playing with °timbrels.

g 26 Bless ye [1] God in the °congregations,
Even [11] the LORD *, °from the °fountain of Israel.

h 27 There *is* little °Benjamin *with* their ruler,
The princes of Judah °*and* their council,
The princes of °Zebulun, *and* the princes of Naphtali.

Q (p. 781) 28 °Thy [1] God hath commanded thy °strength:
°Strengthen, O [1] God, that which Thou hast wrought for us.
29 °Because of Thy temple °at Jerusalem
Shall kings bring presents unto Thee.
30 Rebuke °the company of spearmen,
°The multitude of the bulls, with the calves of the °people,
Till every one submit himself with °pieces of silver:
°Scatter Thou the °people *that* delight in war.
31 Princes shall come out of Egypt;
°Ethiopia shall soon °stretch out her hands unto [1] God.

K 32 Sing unto [1] God, ye kingdoms of the earth;
O sing praises unto [11] the LORD *; °Selah:
33 To Him That °rideth upon the heavens of heavens, *which were* °of old;
Lo, He doth send out °His voice, *and that* a mighty voice.
34 Ascribe ye strength unto [1] God:
His excellency *is* over Israel,
And His strength *is* in the clouds.
35 O [1] God, °*Thou art* terrible out of °Thy holy places:
The °GOD of Israel *is* He That giveth strength and °power unto *His* people.
Blessed *be* [1] God.

°To the chief Musician °upon °Shoshannim.

20 He That is. These italics may be omitted, or otherwise supplied. "The El [we have] is the El", &c.

GOD the Lord. Heb. Jehovah Adonai. Ap. 4. II. viii. 2.

the issues from = means of escape from. (No Art.)

death. With the Art., as in 116. 15. The ref. is to Ex. 12. 12, 13, 29.

21 trespasses. Heb. *'āshām.* Ap. 44. ii.

22 I will bring. Fig. *Epizeuxis* (Ap. 6), for emphasis = I will surely bring.

My people. Supply the *Ellipsis* (Ap. 6) from the context: "I will surely bring [mine enemies] from" wherever they may have fled, bring them again for judgment; the object being stated in the next verse. See the Structure, and cp. "O" and "*O*".

23 dipped. Aram., Sept., Syr., and Vulg. read "bathed". Cp. Isa. 63. 3, 4. Rev. 19. 13.

dogs in the same. Supply the *Ellipsis* (Ap. 6) from the context: "dogs [may lick] the same".

24 goings = progression, or procession. Cp. 2 Sam. 6. 1 Chron. 15. 16-21, where the order is given as in *vv.* 24, 25 here.

goings. Fig. *Epizeuxis.* Ap. 6. **in** = into.

25 went before. Cp. 1 Chron. 15. 16-21.

followed after = behind. **Among** = between.

damsels. Heb. *'ălāmōth*: i.e. the females of *v.* 11. See Ap. 65. II.

timbrels = drums. Heb. *toph.* See note on Ex. 15. 20. **26 congregations** = assemblies.

from. Supply the *Ellipsis* (Ap. 6), "[Ye that are] from, or of, the fountain of Israel".

fountain: i.e. the patriarch Abraham, or, Israel. Ginsburg suggests "the called of Israel".

27 Benjamin. The least of the tribes, and last on the jasper stone of Aaron's breastplate. Cp. Ex. 28. 20. Jasper is the first stone in the foundations of Rev. 21. 19. **and their council** = their company.

Zebulun. Four tribes named: two in the extreme south, and two in the extreme north.

28 Thy God hath commanded. Some codices, with Aram., Sept., Syr., and Vulg., read "Command, O God".

strength = strength (for defence). Heb. *'azaz.*

Strengthen, &c. "Strengthen, O God, the strength which Thou hast wrought for us from Thy temple". Connecting with this line the first words of *v.* 29.

29 Because of Thy temple. See note above.

at Jerusalem = unto Jerusalem (commencing a new line) shall kings bring presents, &c.

30 the company of spearmen = the wild beasts of the reeds.

The multitude of the bulls = the herd of mighty oxen. Cp. Jer. 46. 20, 21. **people** = peoples.

pieces of silver: i.e. tribute money.

Scatter Thou. So it should read with Sept., Syr., and Vulg., but Heb. text reads "He hath scattered".

31 Ethiopia. Put by Fig. *Metonymy* (of Subject), Ap. 6, for Ethiopians.

stretch out her hands. Put by Fig. *Metonymy* (of Adjunct), Ap. 6, either for bringing presents, as in *v.* 29, or for prayer, or for pledging loyalty with an oath.

32 Selah. Connecting the exhortation to praise with Him Who is to be praised, *vv.* 33-35. See Ap. 66. II.

33 rideth. Fig. *Anthropopatheia.* Ap. 6.

of old. Cp. 2 Pet. 3. 5, 6: referring to "the world that then was".

His voice. Omit the italics, and then we have the Fig. *Epizeuxis* (Ap. 6), "His voice a voice of strength".

35 Thou art terrible. Supply *Ellipsis* (Ap. 6) thus: "[To be feared] is God from His Sanctuary".

Thy holy places. Sept. and Vulg. read the sing. It is the pl. of majesty. **holy.** See note on Ex. 3. 5.

GOD. Heb. El. Ap. 4. IV.

power. Heb. pl. = mighty, or abundant power.

To the chief Musician. See Ap. 64. Originally written for the going up of the Ark to Zion; it was handed over to the chief Musician for public use. **upon** = relating to. **Shoshannim** = lilies. A poetic name for spring. Hence used at the Passover, the spring festival. See Ap. 65. XXI.

69

°A Psalm °of David.

K R[1] S (p. 784) 1 Save me, O °God;
T i For the °waters are °come in unto °*my* soul.
2 I °sink in deep °mire, where *there is* no standing:
I am come into deep [1]waters, where the floods overflow me.
k 3 I am weary of my crying: my throat is dried:
Mine eyes fail while I wait for my [1]God.
l 4 **They that °hate me without a cause are more than the hairs of mine head:**
They that would destroy me, *being* mine enemies wrongfully, are °mighty:
°Then I restored *that* which I took not away.
U 5 O [1]God, Thou knowest my foolishness;
And my °sins are not hid from Thee.
6 Let not them that wait on Thee, O °Lord GOD of hosts, be ashamed for my sake:
Let not those that seek Thee be confounded for my sake, O °God of Israel.
V m 7 Because for Thy sake I have borne reproach;
Shame hath covered my face.
n 8 I am become °a stranger unto my brethren,
And an alien unto my mother's °children.
9 For °**the zeal of Thine house hath eaten me up;**
And °**the reproaches of them that reproached Thee are fallen upon me.**
10 When °I wept, *and chastened* [1]my soul with fasting,
That was to my reproach.
o 11 I made °sackcloth also my garment;
And I became a °proverb to them.
p 12 They that sit in the gate speak against me;
And I *was* °the song of the drunkards.
S 13 But as for me, my prayer *is* unto Thee, O °LORD, °*in* an acceptable time:
O [1]God, in the °multitude of Thy °mercy
°Hear me, in the truth of Thy salvation.
T i 14 Deliver me out of the [2]mire, and let me not sink:
Let me be delivered from them that hate me, and out of the deep [1]waters.
15 Let not the waterflood overflow me,
Neither let the deep swallow me up,
And let not the pit shut her mouth upon me.
k 16 [13]Hear me, O [13]LORD; for Thy °lovingkindness *is* good:
Turn unto me according to the [13]multitude of Thy tender mercies.
17 And hide not Thy face from Thy servant;
For I am in trouble: [13]hear me speedily.
18 Draw nigh unto [1]my soul, *and* °redeem it:
l Deliver me because of mine enemies.
U 19 Thou hast known my reproach, and my shame, and my dishonour:
Mine adversaries *are* all before Thee.

---

69 (*K*, p. 759). ISRAEL'S REDEMPTION. THEIR REDEEMER WAITS FOR HIS DELIVERANCE.
(*Division.*)

K | R[1] | 1–21. Prayer.
| R[2] | 22–29. Imprecation.
| R[3] | 30–36. Praise.

1–21 (R[1], above). PRAYER.
(*Extended Alternation.*)

R[1] | S | 1–. Salvation.
T | –1–4. Trouble.
U | 5, 6. Appeal.
V | 7–12. Reproach. Treatment received.
S | 13. Salvation.
T | 14–18. Trouble.
U | 19. Appeal.
V | 20, 21. Reproach. Treatment received.

–1–4 (T, above); **14–18** (*T*, above). TROUBLE.
(*Alternation.*)

T | i | –1, 2. Mire and waters.
k | 3. Desire after God.
l | 4. Enemies.
T | *i* | 14, 15. Mire and waters.
k | 16–18–. Desire after God.
l | –18. Enemies.

Title. A Psalm. No Heb. for this.
of David. Relating to the true David, Israel's Redeemer. Ps. 22 is Christ as the sin offering; Ps. 40 as the whole burnt offering; and this, Ps. 69 as the trespass offering. Verse 9 refers to John 15. 25; *vv.* 14–20 refer to Gethsemane (Matt. 26. 36–45); *v.* 21 to the Cross (Matt. 27. 34, 48. John 19. 29); *vv.* 22–28 to Rom. 11. 9, 10; *v.* 25 to Judas (Acts 1. 20).
1 God. Heb. Elohim. Ap. 4. I.
waters. Put by Fig. *Hypocatastasis* (Ap. 6) for great troubles.
come in unto my soul: i. e. threaten my life.
my soul = me (emphatic). Heb. *nephesh.* Ap. 13.
2 sink = have sunk.
mire. See note on waters, *v.* 1.
4 hate me without a cause. Cp. 35. 19. Quoted in John 15. 25.
mighty. The Syr., by supplying the letter Ayin (ע), reads "stronger than my bones", thus completing the alternation of this verse.
Then. Ginsburg suggests "I" (emphatic) instead of "Then". **5** sins. Heb. *'āsham.* Ap. 44. ii.
6 Lord GOD. Heb. Adonai Jehovah. Ap. 4. VIII. 2 and II.
God of Israel. See note on Isa. 29. 23.

7–12 (V, above); **20, 21** (*V*, above). REPROACHES.
(*Extended Alternation.*)

V | m | 7. I. Reproached.
n | 8–10. Desolation.
o | 11, 12–. "I gave", &c.
p | –12. Drunkards.
V | *m* | 20–. I. Reproached.
n | –20. Desolation.
o | 21– "They gave", &c.
p | –21. Drink.

8 a stranger. Cp. John 1. 11. children = sons.
9 the zeal, &c. Quoted as fulfilled in John 2. 17.
the reproaches. Quoted in Rom. 15. 3.
10 I wept, and chastened my soul. The Sept. reads "I humbled my soul".
11 sackcloth. Put by Fig. *Metonymy* (of Adjunct), Ap. 6, for mourning attire.
proverb. Cp. John 8. 48. Matt. 27. 63.
12 the song = the mocking song.
13 LORD. Heb. Jehovah. Ap. 4. II.
in an acceptable time: i. e. at the time Thou pleasest.
multitude = abundance, or plenitude.
mercy = lovingkindness, or grace.
Hear = answer. lovingkindness = grace.
18 redeem. Heb. *gā'al.* See Ex. note on 6. 6.

V m (p. 784) 20 Reproach hath broken my heart; and I am full of heaviness:
n And I looked *for* °*some* to take pity, but *there was* none;
And for comforters, but I found none.
o 21 °They °gave me also °gall °for my °meat;
p And in my thirst they gave me vinegar to drink.
R² q (p. 785) **22 °Let their table become a snare before them:**
And *that which should have been* for their welfare, *let it become* a trap.
23 Let their eyes be darkened, that they see not;
And make their loins continually to shake.
24 Pour out Thine indignation upon them,
And let Thy wrathful anger take hold of them.
25 °Let their °habitation be desolate;
***And* let none dwell in their tents.**
r 26 For they persecute *him* whom Thou hast smitten;
And they talk to the grief of °those whom Thou hast wounded.
q 27 °Add °iniquity unto their °iniquity:
And let them not come into Thy righteousness.
28 Let them be blotted out of the book of °the living,
And not be written with the righteous.
r 29 But I *am* °poor and sorrowful:
°Let Thy salvation, O [1]God, set me up on high.
R³ W 30 I will °praise the °name °of [1]God °with a song,
And will magnify Him with thanksgiving.
31 *This* also shall please [13]the LORD °better than °an ox
Or bullock that hath °horns °and °hoofs.
X s 32 The humble shall see *this*, °*and* be glad:
And your °heart °shall live that seek °God.
t 33 For [13]the LORD heareth the °poor,
And despiseth not His prisoners.
W 34 Let the °heaven and earth praise Him,
The seas, and every thing that moveth therein.
X t 35 For [1]God will save °Zion, and °will build the cities of Judah:
That they may °dwell there, and °have it in possession.
s 36 The seed also of His servants shall inherit it:
And they that love His [30]name shall dwell therein.

°To the chief Musician.

70 *A Psalm* °of David, °to bring to remembrance.

L Y (p. 786) 1 °*Make haste*, O °God, to deliver me;
Make haste to help me, O °LORD.

20 some. Aram., Sept., Syr., and Vulg. read "one".
21 They gave. Fulfilled in Matt. 27. 34, 48. Mark 15. 23, 36. Luke 23. 36. John 19. 28–30.
gave=put. See note on Matt. 27. 34.
gall.=something bitter, probably the poppy. Heb. *r'osh*. In Deut. 29. 18; 32. 33, it is rendered "venom"; in Job 20. 16, "poison"; in Hos. 10. 4, "hemlock".
for=into.
meat=choice food. Occurs only here. A kindred form in 2 Sam. 13. 5, 7, 10.

69. 22–29 (R², p. 784). IMPRECATION.
(*Alternation.*)

R² | q | 22–25. Imprecation. "They".
  r | 26. Reason. They hurt Thine afflicted.
 | *q* | 27, 28. Imprecation.
  r | 29. Contrast. Thou savest Thine oppressed.

22 Let, &c. Imprecation. Suitable for a dispensation of Law and Judgment; not for this Day of Grace. See Rom. 11. 9, 10.
25 Let, &c. Quoted in Acts 1. 20.
habitation=palace: a place surrounded by a wall. Occurs only here in Psalms.
26 those whom Thou hast wounded=Thy wounded ones.
27 Add. Referring to the reading in *v.* 26.
iniquity. Heb. *'avah*. Ap. 44. iv. Put here by Fig. *Metonymy* (of Effect), Ap. 6, for the punishment deserved by it.
28 the living= life. See note on Lev. 18. 5.
29 poor=afflicted. Heb. *'ani*. See note on Prov. 6. 11. Not the same word as in *v.* 33. Constantly used of Christ in the Psalms. Cp. 22. 24 (afflicted); 34. 6; 35. 10; 40. 17; 70. 5; 109. 16, 22. **Let.** Omit.

30–36 (R³, above). PRAISE.
(*Alternation and Introversion.*)

R³ | W | 30, 31. "I will praise".
  X | s | 32. Promise to God's servants.
    t | 33. Reason. Jehovah's dealings.
 | *W* | 34. Let creation praise.
  X | *t* | 35. Reason. God's dealings.
    s | 36. Promise to God's servants.

30 praise. The sufferings never mentioned without praise. Cp. Ps. 22. Isa. 53, &c.
name: i. e. God Himself. Cp. Ps. 20. 1.
of. Genitive of Apposition. Ap. 17. 4.
with a song. Heb. *beshir*. Fig. *Paronomasia* (Ap. 6) with *mishshōr*, an ox, in *v.* 31.
31 better. Praise is the truest sacrifice.
an ox. See note on "song" (*v.* 30).
horns. Showing full age; not under three years (Gen. 15. 9).
and. So some codices, with two early printed editions, Sept., Syr., and Vulg.; but not in current printed Heb. text.
hoofs=divided hoof, showing it to be ceremonially clean (Lev. 11. 3). **32 and be glad**=they rejoice.
heart. Put by Fig. *Synecdoche* (of the Part), Ap. 6, for the whole being.
shall live: i. e. live again in resurrection. See note on Lev. 18. 5.
God. In A.V., 1611, this was printed "good". First printed "God" in ed. 1617.
33 poor=helpless. Heb. *'ebyōn*. See note on Prov. 6. 11.
34 heaven and earth. See note on Gen. 14. 19.
35 Zion. See Ap. 68.
will build. This is prophecy; for David was "a prophet" (Acts 2. 30).
dwell, &c. Not merely dwell and possess, but inherit and hand down.
have it in possession=inherit it. Note the *Introversion*.
36 To the chief Musician. See Ap. 64.

70 [For Structure see next page].
Title. of David=relating to David. **to bring to remembrance**: what is written in Ps. 40. 13–17. Repeated here to complete the Structure of this second book (see p. 759). **1 Make haste.** Supply *Ellipsis* (Ap. 6) from Ps. 40. 13: "Be pleased". **God.** Heb. Elohim. Ap. 4. I. **LORD.** Heb. Jehovah. Ap. 4. II.

Z (p. 786) 2 °Let them be ashamed and confounded
That seek after °my soul:
Let them be turned backward, and put to confusion,
That desire my hurt.
3 Let them be turned back for a reward of their shame
°That say, °"Aha, aha."

Z 4 Let all those that seek Thee °rejoice and be glad in Thee:
And let such as love Thy salvation say continually,
"Let °God be magnified."

Y 5 But I *am* °poor and needy:
Make haste unto me, O [1] God:
Thou *art* my help and my deliverer;
°O [1] LORD, make no tarrying.

M A C (p. 786) 71 In Thee, O °LORD, °do I put my trust:
Let me never be put to °confusion.
2 Deliver me in Thy righteousness, and cause me to escape:
Incline Thine °ear unto me, and save me.
3 Be Thou my °strong habitation, °whereunto I may continually resort:
Thou hast given commandment to save me;
For Thou *art* my °rock and my fortress.
4 °Deliver me, O my °God, out of the hand of the wicked,
Out of the hand of the unrighteous and cruel man.
5 For Thou *art* my °hope, O °Lord GOD:

D u *Thou art* my °trust from my youth.
6 By Thee have I been holden up °from the womb:
Thou art He That took me out of my mother's bowels:

v My praise *shall be* continually of Thee.
7 °I am as a wonder unto many;
But Thou °*art* my strong refuge.
8 Let my mouth be filled *with* Thy praise
And with Thy honour all the day.

w 9 Cast me not off in the time of old age;
Forsake me not when my strength faileth.
10 For mine enemies speak against me;
And they that lay wait for °my soul take counsel together,
11 Saying, [4] "God hath forsaken him:
Persecute and take him; for *there is* none to deliver *him*."
12 O [4] God, be not far from me:
O my [4] God, make haste for my help.

B x 13 Let them be confounded *and* consumed that are adversaries to [10] my soul;
Let them be covered *with* reproach and dishonour that seek my hurt.

y 14 But I will hope continually,
And will yet praise Thee more and more.
15 My mouth shall shew forth Thy righteousness
And Thy salvation all the day;
For I know not °the numbers *thereof*.
16 I will go in the °strength of the [5] Lord GOD:
I will make mention of Thy righteousness, *even* of Thine only.

A D u 17 O [4] God, Thou hast taught me from my youth:

v And hitherto have I declared Thy wondrous works.

---

70 (*L*, p. 759). ISRAEL'S REDEMPTION. THEIR REDEEMER WAITS FOR HIS DELIVERANCE. (*Introversion.*)

L | Y | 1. David.
  | Z | 2, 3. Imprecation.
  | *Z* | 4. Intercession.
  | *Y* | 5. David.

2 Let them. Note the repeated alternation here.
my soul = me (emphatic). Heb. *nephesh.* Ap. 13.
3 That say. Some codices, with Aram., Sept., Syr., and Vulg., read "Who are saying to me". Cp. 40. 15.
Aha, aha. Fig. *Epizeuxis.* Ap. 6.
4 rejoice. Put by Fig. *Metonymy* (of the Subject), Ap. 6, for "have cause to rejoice", &c.
God. Heb. Elohim. Ap. 4. I. Some codices, with Aram. and Vulg., read "Jehovah".
5 poor = wretched, or oppressed. Heb. *'ānāh.* See note on Prov. 6. 11.
O LORD. Some codices, with six early printed editions and Syr., read "O my God". Cp. 40. 17.

71 (*M*, p. 759). ISRAEL'S REDEEMER. PRAISE PROMISED. (*Alternations and Introversion.*)

M | A | C | 1–5–. Declaration of trust.
  | D | u | –5, 6–. Youth. Care. (Past.)
  | v | –6–8. Promise of praise. (Present.)
  | w | 9–12. Prayer for old age. (Future.)
  | B | x | 13. Confusion of enemies.
  | y | 14–16. Return for mercies.
  | *A* | *D* | *u* | 17–. Youth. Teaching. (Past.)
  | *v* | –17. Promise of praise. (Present.)
  | *w* | 18. Prayer for old age. (Future.)
  | *C* | 19–21. Declaration of trust.
  | *B* | *y* | 22–24–. Return for mercies.
  | *x* | –24. Confusion of enemies.

1 LORD. Heb. Jehovah. Ap. 4. II.
do I put my trust = have I fled for refuge. Heb. *ḥāsāh.* Ap. 69. II.
confusion = shame.
2 ear. Fig. *Anthropopatheia.* Ap. 6.
3 strong habitation = rock of habitation. Heb. *ẓūr,* a fortified place. Some codices, with six early printed editions, Aram., Sept., and Vulg., read "a rock of refuge".
whereunto I may continually resort, &c. Sept. reads "a place of security to save me".
rock. Heb. *ṣela'.* See note on 18. 1, 2. Ex. 17. 6. Deut. 32. 13.
4 Deliver = Cause me to escape.
the wicked = lawless one. Heb. *rāsha'.* Ap. 44. x.
God. Heb. Elohim. Ap. 4. I.
5 hope. Put by Fig. *Metonymy* (of Adjunct), Ap. 6, for the object of hope.
Lord GOD. Heb. Adonai Jehovah. Ap. 4. VIII. 2, and II.
trust = confidence. Heb. *baṭaḥ.* Ap. 69. I.
6 from the womb. Cp. Jer. 1. 5. Some have supposed that this Psalm was written by Jeremiah. See note on *v.* 22. But even then it points to Christ.
7 I am = I have become.
art. Supply the *Ellipsis* (Ap. 6), "hast been".
10 my soul = me (emphatic). Heb. *nephesh.* Ap. 13.
15 the numbers. Cp. 40. 5.
16 strength = strengths. Pl. of majesty = great strength.

w (p. 786) 18 °Now also °when I am old and grayheaded, O [4]God, forsake me not;
Until I have shewed °Thy strength unto *this* generation,
And Thy power to °every one *that* is to come.

C 19 Thy righteousness also, O [4]God, *is* very high,
Who hast done great things:
O [4]God, °who *is* like unto Thee!
20 *Thou*, Which hast shewed me great and sore troubles,
Shalt °quicken me again,
And shalt °bring me up again from the depths of the earth.
21 Thou shalt increase my greatness,
And comfort me on every side.

B y 22 I will also praise Thee °with the psaltery,
Even Thy truth, O my [4]God:
Unto Thee will I °sing with the harp,
O Thou °Holy One of Israel.
23 My lips shall greatly rejoice when I [22]sing unto Thee;
And [10]my soul, which Thou hast °redeemed.
24 My tongue also shall talk of Thy righteousness all the day long:

x For they are confounded, for they are brought unto shame, that seek my hurt.

921 # 72 *A Psalm* °for Solomon.

J E (p. 787) 1 Give °the king thy °judgments, O °God,
And Thy °righteousness unto the °king's son.

F G 2 He shall °judge Thy People with [1]righteousness,
And Thy °poor with °judgment.
3 The mountains shall bring °peace to the people,
And the little hills, by righteousness.
4 He shall °judge the [2]poor of the People,
He shall save the °children of the needy,
And shall break in pieces the oppressor.

H a 5 They shall fear Thee as long as the sun and moon endure,
Throughout all generations.

b 6 He shall come down °like rain upon the mown grass:
As showers *that* water the earth.
7 In his days shall °the righteous flourish;
And abundance of peace so long as the moon endureth.

c 8 He shall have dominion also °from sea to sea,
And from °the river unto the ends of the earth.
9 They that dwell in the wilderness shall bow before him;
And his enemies shall °lick the dust.

d 10 The kings of °Tarshish and of the °isles shall bring presents:
The kings of °Sheba and Seba shall °offer gifts.

18 Now also=Yea also.
when I am old and grayheaded=to old age and gray hairs.
Thy strength=Thine arm; "arm" being put by Fig. *Metonymy* (of Cause), Ap. 6, for the wonders wrought by it.
every one that is to come. A special reading called *Sevīr* (Ap. 34) reads "all who are to come".
19 who is like unto Thee. This is the cry of all God's saints. See note on Ex. 15. 11.
20 quicken me again=make me alive again.
bring me up again: i. e. in resurrection.
22 with=with the aid of. **sing**=sing praise.
Holy One of Israel. Occurs only three times in the Psalms (here, 78. 41; 89. 18). In Isaiah we find it thirty times. In Jeremiah twice (50. 29; 51. 5). See note on 78. 41.
23 redeemed. Heb. *pādāh.* See note on Ex. 13. 13 and 6. 6.

72 (*J*, p. 759). ISRAEL'S REDEMPTION. THE ANSWER TO PSALMS **69—71.**

(*Introversion and Extended Alternation.*)

J | E | 1. Prayer and theme of Psalm.
  F | G | 2-4. Messiah's goodness to the poor.
    H | 5-10. Other attributes.
      I | 11. General adoration.
  F | *G* | 12-14. Messiah's goodness to the poor.
    H | -15-17-. Other attributes.
      I | -17. General adoration.
  E | 18-20. Praise and doxology to Book II.

Title. for Solomon. Not of, but concerning. See Epilogue by David for his son Solomon, and for his 'Greater Son", the Messiah. Written after Solomon's second investiture, 1 Chron. 29. 23 (921 B.C.). The year before David's death.
1 the king: i. e. David himself.
judgments=just decisions (of David regarding Solomon).
God. Heb. Elohim. Ap. 4. I.
righteousness: i. e. in all his (Solomon's) judgments, according to 1 Kings 3. 5-9. 1 Chron. 29. 19, and 28. 5, 7.
king's son=Solomon; but to be yet fulfilled in Christ.
2 judge, &c.=rule in righteousness.
poor=oppressed (pl.). See note on 70. 5.
judgment=justice.
3 peace=prosperity.
4 judge=vindicate. **children**=sons.

5-10 (H, above); **15-17-** (*H*, above). OTHER ATTRIBUTES. (*Introversion.*)

H | a | 5. Eternity.
  b | 6, 7. Agricultural prosperity. (Moon.)
    c | 8, 9. The world. Dominion.
      d | 10. Gifts.
H | d | -15-. Gifts.
    c | -15. His People. Worship.
  b | 16. Agricultural prosperity. (Sun.)
a | 17-. Eternity.

6 like rain. Cp. 2 Sam. 23. 4.
7 the righteous. Some codices, with Sept., Syr., and Vulg., read "righteousness".
8 from sea to sea. From the Mediterranean to the Persian Gulf.
the river: i. e. the Euphrates. Same Fig. as above.
9 lick the dust. Put by Fig. *Metonymy* (of the Adjunct), Ap. 6, for utter subjugation.
10 Tarshish. On the west. See note on 1 Kings 10. 22.
isles=coastlands, or maritime countries.
Sheba, &c. On the east and south.
offer gifts=bring near their presents. Ap. 43. II. iii.

11 Yea, all kings shall fall down before him: I
All nations shall serve him.

F G (p. 787) 12 For he shall deliver °the needy when he crieth;
The [2] poor also, and *him* that hath no helper.
13 He shall spare the °poor and [12] needy,
And shall save the °souls of [12] the needy.
14 He shall °redeem °their soul from deceit and violence:
And precious shall their blood be in his sight.

H d 15 And °he shall °live,
And to him shall be °given of the °gold of Sheba:
c Prayer also shall be made °for him continually;
And °daily shall he be praised.

b 16 There shall be an °handful of corn in the earth upon the top of the mountains;
The fruit thereof shall shake like Lebanon:
And *they* of the city shall flourish like grass of the earth.

a 17 His name shall endure for ever:
His name shall be continued as long as the sun:

I °And *men* shall be °blessed °in him:
All nations shall call him °blessed.

E 18 °Blessed *be* °the LORD °God, the [1] God of Israel,
Who only doeth wondrous things.
19 And [18] blessed *be* His glorious °name for ever:
And let the whole earth be °filled *with* His glory;
Amen, and Amen.

12 the needy = a helpless one. Heb. *'ebyōn*. See note on Prov. 6. 11.

13 poor = impoverished. Heb. *dal*. See note on Prov. 6. 11.

souls. Heb. *nephesh*. Ap. 13.

14 redeem. Heb. *gā'al*. See notes on Ex. 6. 6; 13. 13.

their soul = them, or their life. Heb. *nephesh*. Ap. 13.

15 he shall live. The accent (*r^ebia*) on "he" marks it as emphatic, and as to be distinguished from the plurals of the preceding verses, and rendered "they", as it is in R.V. See the Structure, and note the members "G" and "*G*", which treat of Messiah's goodness to the poor. It is in *v.* 10 ("H d") and in *v.* 15 ("*H d*") that we have them, and their gifts to Him. He, the Head, delivers and saves them; and they, in *v.* -15, bring to Him a liberal hand, a praying heart, and a praising tongue.

live = live for ever. See note on Lev. 18. 5.

given, &c. Solomon the type (1 Kings. 10. 2, 10; 2 Chron. 9. 1). Fulfilment in Christ the Antitype.

gold. Fig. *Synecdoche* (of Species), Ap. 6, "gold" being put for precious gifts. Cp. Isa. 60. 6.

for = to.

daily = all the day.

16 handful = abundance.

corn = fine corn.

17 And men shall be blessed in him: All nations shall call him blessed = Yea, all nations shall be blessed in him—shall call him happy. "Blessed" is not the same word as in the preceding line. Heb. *'āshar*, cognate with *'ashrey*. See Ap. 63. VI.

in him. Thus confirming the promise to Abraham. See Gen. 12. 3; 18. 18; 22. 18; 26. 4; 28. 14.

18 Blessed, &c. This doxology closes the second book of the Psalms. Heb. *bārak*, not *'āsher*.

the LORD. Heb. Jehovah. Ap. 4. II.

God. Some codices omit "Elohim" here, with Sept., Syr., and Vulg.

19 name = self. See note on 20. 1.

filled, &c. Cp. Num. 14. 21.

20 are ended = are accomplished. When this Psalm is realised, all prophecy concerning Israel will be fulfilled: according to Dan. 9. 24, and see 2 Sam. 23. 1, where cp. the title, "son of Jesse".

EPILOGUE.

20 The prayers of David the son of Jesse °are ended.

73—89 (ℭ, p. 720). THE THIRD OR LEVITICUS BOOK * THE SANCTUARY.

(Division.)

ℭ | A¹ | 73—83. THE SANCTUARY IN RELATION TO MAN.
  | A² | 84—89. THE SANCTUARY IN RELATION TO JEHOVAH.

73—83 † (**A¹**, above). THE SANCTUARY IN RELATION TO MAN.
(Extended Alternation.)

A¹ **B** | **73.** THE EFFECT OF BEING OUTSIDE THE SANCTUARY. OCCUPATION OF HEART WITH OTHERS, AND CONSEQUENT DISTRACTION.
C | **74.** THE ENEMY IN THE SANCTUARY.
D | **75.** GOD'S ANOINTED IN THE SANCTUARY.
E | **76.** DESTRUCTION OF THE ENEMIES OF THE SANCTUARY.
B | **77** (*B*¹), **78** (*B*²). THE EFFECT OF BEING OUTSIDE THE SANCTUARY. OCCUPATION OF HEART WITH SELF, AND CONSEQUENT MISERY. **78** IS INSTRUCTION (MASCHIL ‡) AS TO **73** AND **77**, SHOWING HOW JEHOVAH FORSOOK "SHILOH" (*v.* 60), AND CHOSE NOT JOSEPH (*v.* 67): BUT CHOSE ZION (*vv* 68, 69), AND CHOSE DAVID (*vv.* 70–72).
C | **79.** THE ENEMY IN THE SANCTUARY.
D | **80** (*D*¹), **81** (*D*²), **82** (*D*³). GOD IN THE SANCTUARY.
E | **83.** DESTRUCTION OF THE ENEMIES OF THE SANCTUARY.

84—89 § (**A²**, above). THE SANCTUARY IN RELATION TO JEHOVAH.
(Repeated Alternation.)

A² **F¹** | **84** (**F**¹₁), **85** (**F**¹₂). THE BLESSEDNESS OF APPROACHERS TO THE SANCTUARY.
G¹ | **86.** PRAYER BEFORE GOD (IN THE SANCTUARY). MESSIAH'S HUMILIATION THE SECRET AND SOURCE OF THE BLESSING.
F² | **87.** THE BLESSEDNESS OF DWELLERS IN ZION.
G² | **88.** PRAYER BEFORE GOD. INSTRUCTION (MASCHIL ‡) AS TO MESSIAH'S HUMILIATION, AS THE SECRET AND SOURCE OF THE BLESSING.
F³ | **89.** THE BLESSEDNESS OF THOSE WHO "KNOW THE JOYFUL SOUND" (*v.* 15). GOD IN THE ASSEMBLY OF HIS SAINTS (*v.* 7). INSTRUCTION ‡ AS TO GOD'S DEALINGS IN HIS SANCTUARY, AND AS TO THE WHOLE BOOK.

---

* LEVITICUS is the title which man has given to the third book of the Pentateuch, because of its subject-matter: viz. the ordinances, &c., pertaining to the Levites. The title in the Hebrew Canon is וַיִּקְרָא (*vayyiḳra'*), "AND HE CALLED." It is emphatically the Book of the SANCTUARY. It tells how God is to be approached; and teaches us that none can worship except such as are "called" (65. 4), and whom "the Father seeks to worship Him" (John 4. 23, 24). In Lev. 1. 1, 2, we see the exemplification of the words: "Blessed *is the man whom* Thou choosest, and causest to approach *unto Thee*, that he may dwell in Thy courts: we shall be satisfied with the goodness of Thy house, *even* of Thy holy temple" (65. 4). The types in Leviticus are types of the Sanctuary: i.e. of Access and Worship.

In this Leviticus-Book of the Psalms we find the corresponding thought. Its teaching is Dispensational, as in the other books; but, in this, the counsels of God are seen, not in relation to *Man* (as in Genesis), not in relation to the *Nation* (as in Exodus), but in relation to the SANCTUARY, which is mentioned or referred to in nearly every Psalm of this third book. The Sanctuary is seen from its *ruin*, to its establishment in the fullness of blessing.

In the first Division (73-83, **A¹**) Elohim (Ap. 4. I) occurs sixty-five times (twice with Jehovah); and Jehovah only fifteen times. In the second Division (84-89, **A²**) Jehovah occurs fifty times, and Elohim only twenty-eight times (four of which are with Jehovah). El (Ap. 4. IV) occurs five times.

† All the Psalms in the first Division (**A¹**) are Psalms of Asaph.

‡ Maschil. See Ap. 65. XI.

§ All the Psalms (except 86 and 89) in the second Division (**A²**) are Psalms of the sons of Korah.

BOOK III.

73

° A Psalm ° of Asaph.

B A (p. 790) 1 ° Truly ° God *is* ° good to ° Israel,
Even to such as are of a clean heart.

B 2 But as for ° me, my feet were ° almost ° gone;
My steps had well nigh slipped.

C 3 For I was envious at the ° foolish,
When I saw the prosperity of the ° wicked.

D F 4 For *there are* no ° bands ° in their death:
But their strength ° *is* firm.
5 They *are* not ° in trouble *as other* ° men;
Neither are they plagued ° like *other* ° men.

G a 6 Therefore pride compasseth them about as a ° chain;
Violence covereth them *as* a garment.
7 Their eyes ° stand out with fatness:
° They have more than heart ° could wish.

b 8 They are corrupt, and speak ° wickedly *concerning* oppression:
They speak loftily.
9 They set their mouth against ° the heavens,
And their ° tongue walketh through the ° earth.

G a 10 Therefore ° His People ° return ° hither:
And waters of a full *cup* ° are ° wrung out to them.

b 11 And they say, ° "How doth ° GOD know?
And ° is there knowledge in the ° MOST HIGH?"

F 12 ° Behold, these *are* the ° ungodly,
Who prosper in ° the world; they increase *in* riches.

E 13 ° Verily ° I have cleansed my heart *in* vain,
And washed my hands in innocency.
14 For all the day long have I been plagued,
And chastened ° every morning.
15 If I say, "I will speak thus;"
° Behold, I should ° offend *against* the generation of thy ° children.
16 When I ° thought to ° know this,
It *was* ° too painful for me;

E 17 Until I went into ° the sanctuary of [11] GOD;
° *Then* understood I their ° end.

73—89 (C, p. 789). THE LEVITICUS BOOK.

73—83 (A[1] p. 789). THE SANCTUARY IN RELATION TO MAN.

This Third Book has to do with the SANCTUARY; as the First Book (1—41) had to do with MAN; and the Second Book (42-72) had to do with ISRAEL.

73 (B, p. 789). OUTSIDE THE SANCTUARY. EFFECT. DISTRACTION. (*Introversion.*)

B | A | 1. Occupation with God. Peace.
  B | 2. Occupation with others. My error.
   C | 3. Result. My discontent.
    D | 4-12. The wicked. Their prosperity.
     E | 13-16. Result. Distraction.
     E | 17. Remedy. The Sanctuary.
    D | 18-20. The wicked. Their end.
   C | 21. Result. My discontent.
  B | 22. Occupation with others. My error.
 A | 23-28. Occupation with God. Peace.

Title. A Psalm. Heb. *mizmōr*. See Ap. 65. XVII. **of Asaph.** The second of Asaph's twelve Psalms, Ps. 50 being the first. See Ap. 63. VIII.

1 Truly, &c. = Nothing but good is God to Israel. Occurs three times in this Psalm: here, rendered "Truly"; *v.* 13, "Verily"; *v.* 18, "Surely". The uniform rendering would be "Only" or, "After all".

God. Heb. Elohim. Ap. 4. I.

good. The conclusion is stated before the distraction of mind caused by occupation of heart with others is described.

Israel. This links on Book III with Book II.

2 me. Note the emphasis on this (by repetition of the first Person), which is the key to the Psalm.

almost = quickly. See note on Prov. 5. 14.

gone = stumbled.

3 foolish = arrogant, or boasters.

wicked = lawless. Heb. *rāshā'*. Ap. 44. x.

4-12 (D, above). THE WICKED. THEIR PROSPERITY. (*Introversion.*)

D | F | 4, 5. Their prosperity. (Negative.)
  G | a | 6, 7. Their pride and fulness.
     b | 8, 9. Their speech.
  G | *a* | 10. Their pride and fulness.
     b | 11. Their speech.
 F | 12. Their prosperity. (Positive.)

4 bands: or pangs. The *Massōrah* calls attention to this *Homonym* (*ḥarzuboth*) as occurring not only twice, but in two different senses. The other case is Isa. 58. 6.

in = at.

is. Supply Ellipsis by "continues".

5 in trouble as other = in the trouble of. Used first of Joseph (Gen. 41. 51.

men. Heb. *'ĕnōsh*. Ap. 14. III.

like: or with. **men.** Heb. *'ādām*. Ap. 14. I. **6 chain** = necklace. **7 stand out** = protrude. **They have,** &c.: or The imaginations of their heart overflow. **could wish** = could picture, or imagine. Heb. *maskīth*. See note on Prov. 25. 11. **8 wickedly.** Heb. *ra'a'*. Ap. 44. viii. **9 the heavens.** Put by Fig. *Metonymy* (of Subject), Ap. 6, for God, Who dwells there. **tongue walketh.** Fig. *Prosopopœia*. Ap. 6. **earth.** Supply the Ellipsis (Ap. 6), by adding "[they say]". Let "His People return hither" as in *v.* 10. **10 His People** = God's people. **return** = turn: i. e. follow. **hither** = to us. (Spoken by the wicked.) **are** = shall be. **wrung out to** = drained by. **11 How . . . ?** **is there . . . ?** Fig. *Erotēsis*. Ap. 6. **GOD.** Heb. El. Ap. 4. IV. **MOST HIGH.** Heb. *Elyōn*. Ap. 4. VI. **12 Behold.** Fig. *Asterismos*. Ap. 6. **ungodly** = lawless. Heb. *rāshā'*. (No Art.) Ap. 44. x. **the world** = this age. **13 Verily.** See note on "Truly", *v.* 1. **I have cleansed.** This is the result of occupation with *others*. Distraction. Cp. Structure, above. **14 every morning.** Put by Fig. *Synecdoche* (of Part), Ap. 6, for "continually". **15 Behold.** Fig. *Asterismos*. Ap. 6. **offend** = deal treacherously. Heb. *bāgad*. **children** = sons. **16 thought** = pondered [it]. Cp. the same word in 77. 5. **know** = reconcile, or understand. **too painful for me** = vexation in mine eyes. **17 the sanctuary.** This is the book of the Sanctuary, and nearly every Psalm in it contains some reference to it, or to the congregation who worship in it. **Then.** Supply "Until" by the Fig. *Anaphora*. Ap. 6. **end** = latter end, or hereafter.

D (p. 790) **18** °Surely Thou °didst set them in slippery places:
Thou castedst them down into destruction.
19 °How are they *brought* into desolation, as in a moment!
°They are utterly consumed with terrors.
20 As a dream when *one* awaketh;
So, O °LORD*, when Thou °awakest, Thou shalt despise their °image.

C **21** °Thus my heart was grieved,
And I was pricked in my reins.

B **22** So °foolish *was* I, and ignorant:
I was *as* a beast before Thee.

A c (p. 791) **23** °Nevertheless I *am* continually with Thee:
Thou hast holden *me* by my right hand.
24 Thou shalt guide me with Thy counsel,
And afterward receive me *to* glory.
25 °Whom have I in heaven *but Thee?*
And *there is* none upon earth *that* I desire beside Thee.
26 My flesh and my heart faileth:
But [1]God *is* the °strength of my heart, and my portion for ever.

d **27** For, lo, they that are far from Thee shall perish:

d Thou hast destroyed all them that go a °whoring from Thee.

c **28** But °*it is* good for me to draw near to [1]God:
I have °put my trust in °the Lord GOD,
That I may declare all Thy works.

74

°Maschil °of Asaph.

C H K (p. 791) **1** O °God, °why hast Thou °cast *us* off for ever?
°*Why* doth Thine anger °smoke against the °sheep of Thy pasture?

L **2** Remember Thy °congregation, *which* Thou hast °purchased °of old;
The °rod of Thine inheritance, *which* Thou hast °redeemed;
°This °mount Zion, wherein Thou hast dwelt.

M **3** °Lift up Thy °feet unto the °perpetual desolations;
Even all *that* the enemy hath done wickedly in the sanctuary.

M **4** Thine °enemies roar in the midst of °Thy congregations;
They set up °their °ensigns *for* °signs.
5 *A man* °was famous according as he had lifted up
°Axes upon the thick trees.
6 But now they break down the carved work thereof at once with axes and hammers.

18 Surely. See note on "Truly", *v.* 1.
didst set = wilt set.
19 How are they = How [is it that] they are.
They are = [How is it that] they are.
20 LORD*. One of the 134 emendations of the *Sōpherim* by which they changed Jehovah, of the primitive text, to Adonai. Ap. 32.
awakest = ariseth. Fig. *Anthropopatheia.* Ap. 6.
image = image of which they dreamt.
21 Thus. Cp. the Structure "C" (*v.* 3) and "*C*" (*v.* 21).
22 foolish = brutish.

73. 23-28 (*A*, p. 790). OCCUPATION WITH GOD. (*Introversion.*)

A | c | 23-26. I (emphatic).
| d | 27-. They. Far from Thee.
| *d* | -27. They. Departing from Thee.
| *c* | 28. I (emphatic).

23 Nevertheless I. Note the emphasis on Pronoun, according to the Structure, "c" (*v.* 23) and "*c*" (*v.* 28), "As for me, I".
25 Whom have I . . . ? This is ever the cry of God's saints. Fig. *Erotēsis.* Ap. 6. See note on Ex. 15. 11.
26 strength. Heb. *zur* = rock, or refuge.
27 whoring from. Supply Ellipsis (Ap. 6) thus: whoring [in departing] from. Refers (spiritually) to idolatry, or anything that takes us from God.
28 it is good for me. The Heb. accent (*pasek*) emphasises the Pronoun "me". Others may go "far from Thee" (*v.* 27), but "as for me, I will draw near to Thee" (cp. *v.* 23). The "good" is seen in the twofold result: (1) I find a refuge in Him; (2) I tell forth His praises.
put my trust = flee for refuge. Heb. *ḥāṣah.* Ap. 69. II.
the Lord GOD = Adonai Jehovah. Ap. 4. VIII. 2, and II.

74 (C, p. 789). THE ENEMY IN THE SANCTUARY. (*Introversion.*)

C | H | 1-11. Prayer. The enemy in the Sanctuary.
| J | 12. Plea. Former merciful deliverances.
| *J* | 13-17. Plea. Former merciful deliverances.
| *H* | 18-23. Prayer. The enemy in the Sanctuary.

The second Psalm of each book has to do specially with the enemy. See Ap. 10.

1-11 (H, above). PRAYER. (*Introversion.*)

H | K | 1. Expostulation.
| L | 2. Prayer. Memory. "Of old".
| M | 3. Enemies.
| *M* | 4-8. Enemies.
| *L* | 9. Prayer. Inquiry. "How long?"
| *K* | 10, 11. Expostulation.

Title. Maschil = Instruction. The ninth of thirteen so named. See note on Title, Ps. 32, and Ap. 65. XI.
of Asaph. The third of the twelve Asaph Psalms. See Ap. 63. VIII. Not David's Asaph, but a successor bearing the same name.
1 God. Heb. Elohim. Ap. 4. I.
why . . . ? Fig. *Erotēsis.* Ap. 6.
cast us off. Cp. 43. 2; 44. 9.
smoke. Fig. *Anthropopatheia.* Ap. 6. Cp. 18. 8.
sheep of Thy pasture. Occurs frequently in the Asaph Psalms (79. 13); also in Jer. 23. 1. Ezek. 34. 31.
2 congregation = assembly. The subject of Book II.
purchased = acquired as a possession. Heb. *kanah.* Cp. 78. 54. Ex. 15. 16. Ruth 4. 10.
of old = aforetime. Refers to Ex. 15. 16.
rod = sceptre.
redeemed. Heb. *gā'al.* See note on Ex. 6. 6. Cp. 13. 1'.
This. Shows that the writer wrote while the scenes described were enacted. Cp. 79 and Lam. 2. 1-9.
mount Zion. See Ap. 68.

3 Lift up Thy feet unto = Hasten to [and see]. Cp. Idiom (Gen. 29. 1). **feet.** Fig. *Anthropopatheia.* Ap. 6. **perpetual.** Same word as "for ever", *v.* 1. **4 enemies** = adversaries. **Thy congregations** = Thine assembly. **their.** Cp. "our", *v.* 9. **ensigns for signs** = signs as signs [for us]. **signs.** Same word as "ensigns" and "standard" in Num. 2. **5 was** = used to be [considered]. The contrast is with "now" in the next line. **Axes.** Cp. Jer. 46. 22, 23.

7 They have °cast fire into Thy °sanctuary,
They have defiled *by casting down* the °dwelling place of Thy name to the ground.
8 They said in their hearts, "Let us destroy them °together:"
They have burned up all the °synagogues of °GOD in the land.

L (p. 791) 9 We see not our °signs:
There is no more any °prophet:
Neither *is there* among us any that knoweth how long.

K 10 O [1]God, °how long shall the adversary reproach?
Shall the enemy blaspheme Thy name for ever?
11 Why withdrawest Thou Thy hand, even Thy right hand?
Pluck *it* out of Thy °bosom.

J 12 For [1]God *is* my King [2]of old,
Working °salvation °in the midst of the earth.

J N c (p. 792) 13 Thou didst °divide the sea by Thy strength:
d Thou brakest the heads of the °dragons in the waters.
d 14 Thou brakest the heads of leviathan in pieces,
And gavest him *to be* meat to the °people inhabiting the wilderness.
c 15 Thou didst °cleave the °fountain and the °flood:
Thou driedst up mighty rivers.
N e 16 The day *is* Thine, the night also *is* Thine:
f Thou hast prepared the °light and the sun.
f 17 Thou hast set all the borders of the earth:
e Thou hast made summer and winter.

H O 18 Remember this, *that* the enemy hath reproached, O °LORD,
And *that* the foolish people have blasphemed °Thy name.

P g 19 O deliver not °the soul of Thy turtledove unto the °multitude *of the wicked:*
Forget not the congregation of Thy °poor for ever.
h 20 Have respect unto °the °covenant:
For the dark places of °the earth are full of the habitations of cruelty.
P g 21 O let not °the oppressed °return ashamed:
Let °the poor and needy praise [18]Thy name.
h 22 Arise, O [1]God, plead Thine own cause:
O Remember how the foolish man reproacheth Thee daily.
23 Forget not the voice of Thine [4]enemies:
The tumult of those that rise up against Thee increaseth continually.

°To the chief Musician, °Al-taschith.

---

7 cast fire into, &c. = cast Thy holy place into the fire.
sanctuary. Some codices, with three early printed editions, read "holy places" (pl.).
dwelling place. Heb. *mishkān.* Ap. 40 (2).
8 together: or, at once.
synagogues = meeting-places. See note on "congregations", *v.* 4. This rendering comes from the Sept.
GOD. Heb. El. Ap. 4. IV.
9 signs: i. e. the signs of God's presence and power, or miraculous signs. Cp. "their" of *v.* 4 with "our", *v.* 9.
prophet. Put by Fig. *Metonymy* (of Cause), Ap. 6, for prophetic utterances.
10 how long . . . ? Fig. *Erotēsis.* Ap. 6. Cp. *v.* 1. Fig. *Ellipsis* (Ap. 6), "how long [this shall last]".
11 bosom. Fig. *Anthropopatheia.* Ap. 6. Sept. adds here "Selah". If this was in the primitive text, it marks the division of the Structure; and connects the conclusion of the prayer with the wonderful ground of the plea based upon it; which, with "J" (*v.* 12) and "*J*" (*vv.* 13-17) constitute the central members and subjects of the Psalm.
12 salvation = deliverances. Pl. of majesty = great deliverance.
in the midst, &c. Cp. Ex. 8. 22. (Heb. *v.* 15).

74. 13-17 (*J*, p. 791). PLEA. FORMER MERCIFUL DELIVERANCES. (*Introversions.*)

J | N | c | 13-. Dividing the sea.
d | -13. The breaking of Egypt.
d | 14. The breaking of Egypt.
c | 15. Dividing the Jordan.
N | e | 16-. Day and night.
f | -16. Heavens.
f | 17-. Earth.
e | -17. Summer and winter.

13 divide = cleave. Cp. Ex. 14. 21, describing a sudden vehement act. Heb. *pārar.*
dragons = crocodiles. (No Art.). Symbolical of Egypt.
14 people inhabiting = inhabitants: i. e. the wild beasts.
15 cleave = sunder, open a passage. Heb. *baka'.*
fountain. Cp. Ex. 17. 6. Num. 20. 11. Put by Fig. *Metonymy* (of Effect), Ap. 6, for the rock from which the water flowed.
flood. Cp. Josh. 3. 13, &c.
16 light. Sept., Syr., and Vulg. read "moon".

18-23 (*H*, above). PRAYER. THE ENEMY IN THE SANCTUARY. (*Introversion and Alternation.*)

H | O | 18. Remember the enemies' reproach.
P | g | 19. Deprecation. The oppressed.
h | 20. Prayer. "Thy covenant".
P | *g* | 21. Deprecation. The oppressed.
h | 22, 23. Prayer. "Thy cause".
O | -22. Remember the enemies' reproach.

18 LORD. Heb. Jehovah. Ap. 4. II.
Thy name = Thee. See note on Ps. 20. 1.
19 the soul = the life. Heb. *nephesh.* Ap. 13.
multitude = company, or host; same word as "congregation" in next line.
poor = oppressed. Heb. *'ānāh.* See note on Pr. 6. 11.
20 the. Sept., Syr., and Vulg. read "Thy".
covenant. Cp. Gen. 15. 18; 17. 7, 8.
the earth: or the land.
21 the oppressed = an oppressed one. Same as *v.* 19.
return. Cp. 6. 10.
the poor and needy praise = a poor one, and a needy one will praise.
23 To the chief Musician. See Ap. 64.
Al-taschith = Destroy not. See Ap. 65. III

75

A °Psalm *or* °Song °of Asaph.

D Q (p. 793) 1 Unto Thee, O °God, do we give thanks,
Unto Thee do we give thanks: for *that* °Thy name is near
°Thy wondrous works declare.

R S 2 When °I shall receive the congregation
°I will judge uprightly.
3 The earth

T And all the inhabitants thereof are dissolved:

S I °bear up the pillars of it. °Selah.

T 4 I said unto the °fools, "Deal not foolishly:"
And to the °wicked, "Lift not up the °horn:
5 Lift not up your [4] horn on high:
°Speak °*not with* a stiff neck.
6 For promotion *cometh* neither from the east, nor from the west,
Nor from the °south.
7 °But [1] God *is* the judge:
He putteth down one, and setteth up another.
8 For in the °hand of °the LORD *there is* °a cup, and the wine is °red;
It is full of °mixture; and He poureth out of the same:
But the dregs thereof, all the [4] wicked of the earth shall wring *them* out, *and* drink *them*."

Q 9 But I will °declare for ever;
I will sing praises to the °God of Jacob.

R 10 All the [4] horns of the [4] wicked also will I cut off;
But the [4] horns of °the righteous shall be exalted.

°To the chief Musician on °Neginoth.

76

°A Psalm *or* °Song °of Asaph.

E U[1] (p. 794) 1 In °Judah *is* °God °known:
His name *is* great in °Israel.
2 In °Salem also °is His °tabernacle,
And His dwelling place in °Zion.
3 °There °brake He the arrows of the bow,
The shield, and the sword, and the °battle. °Selah.

V[1] 4 Thou *art* more glorious *and* excellent than the °mountains of prey.

U[2] 5 The stouthearted are spoiled, they have slept their sleep:
And °none of the °men of might have °found their hands.

75 (D, p. 789). GOD'S ANOINTED IN THE SANCTUARY. (*Alternation.*)

D | Q | 1. Praise. Offered.
  R | 2-8. Judgment. Upright.
  Q | 9. Praise. Promised.
  R | 10. Judgment. Upright.

Title. Psalm. Heb. *mizmōr*. See Ap. 65. XVII.
Song. Heb. *shīr*. See Ap. 65. XXIII.
of Asaph. The fourth of the twelve Asaph Psalms. See Ap. 63. VIII.
In this Psalm the enemies of the Sanctuary are warned, and God's People are encouraged.
1 God. Heb. Elohim. Ap. 4. I.
Thy name. See note on 20. 1. It denotes God's saving presence. Sept., Syr., and Vulg. read "and we shall call on Thy name".
Thy wondrous works declare = Men tell of Thy wondrous works.

2-8 (R, above). JUDGMENT. UPRIGHT. (*Alternation.*)

R | S | 2, 3-. The earth.
  T | -3-. Its inhabitants.
  S | -3. The earth.
  T | 4-8. Its inhabitants.

2 I shall receive the congregation = The set time has come, &c.
I = I, even I. Very emphatic.
3 bear up = have established.
Selah. Connecting the set time of judgment with the judgment itself as it will affect the wicked and the righteous.
4 fools = arrogant.
wicked. Heb. *rāsha'*. Ap. 44. x.
horn. Put by Fig. *Metonymy* (of Adjunct), Ap. 6, for pride connected with the wearing of it.
5 Speak not with a stiff neck. According to the primitive orthography = nor speak arrogantly of the Rock. **not.** See note on "no" (Gen. 2. 6).
6 south. Therefore it comes from the north. The immediate place of God's throne, to which Satan aspires. Cp. Isa. 14. 12-14. See Job 26. 7. This is where promotion comes from.
7 But = No.
8 hand. Fig. *Anthropopatheia*. Ap. 6.
the LORD. Heb. Jehovah. Ap. 4. II.
a cup. The symbol of God's judgment. Isa. 51. 17-23 (cp. 19. 14). Hab. 2. 15, 16. Ezek. 23. 31, 34, &c. Jer. 25. 27; 48. 26; 49. 12. **red** = foaming.
mixture = spice. Cp. Rev. 14. 10.
9 declare. Sept. reads "exult".
God of Jacob: i. e. the God of Grace, who met Jacob when he had nothing, and deserved nothing but wrath.
10 the righteous = a righteous one.
To the chief Musician. See Ap. 64. II.
Neginoth = smitings; refers to the smitings of the wicked in judgment. See Ap. 65. XV.

76 [For Structure see next page].

Title. A Psalm. Heb. *mizmōr*. Ap. 65. XVII.
Song. Heb. *shīr*. Ap. 65. XXIII.
of Asaph = by Asaph. The fifth of the twelve Asaph Psalms. Ap. 63. VIII.

The members U[1], U[2], U[3], U[4] are in the third person. The members V[1], V[2], V[3] are in the second person. The Structure is determined by the two Selahs; and points to the historic event, the taking of Jebus by David (2 Sam. 5. 4-9) 960 B.C. **1 Judah.** Great emphasis on the locality. Note the three terms, Judah, Salem, Zion, and "there" (*v.* 3). **God.** Heb. Elohim. Ap. 4. I. **known** = made known, or making Himself known. **Israel.** Named because the taking of Jebus was in connection with David's taking of the throne of Israel. **2 Salem.** The ancient Jebusite name for Jerusalem. Cp. Gen. 14. 18. Heb. 7. 1, 2. **is** = is come, or is set up. **tabernacle:** i. e. David's tabernacle on Zion. In 18. 11 = pavilion, or dwelling. Heb. *ṣukkāh*, not *'ōhel*. **Zion.** This is where David's tabernacle was set up after the taking of Jebus. Cp. 2 Sam. 5. 6-10; 6; 7. 1, 2, &c. See Ap. 68. Zion had no place in history till this event. **3 There.** Emphatic. Heb. *shām*. Cp. Gen. 2. 8. Ex. 40. 3 (therein). Deut. 1. 39 (thither). 2 Chron. 6. 11 (in it). **brake He** = hath He broken in pieces. **battle.** Put by Fig. *Metonymy* (of Adjunct), Ap. 6, for other weapons used in battle. **Selah.** Connecting the Jebusite defeat with God Who gave it; and passing on from the third person to the second. See Ap. 66. II. Note the emphasis on "Thou". **4 mountains of prey.** The great mountain (Zion) which had become a prey: i. e. a prey seized, as in next verse; the mighty men had become a spoil, or been plundered. **5 none . . . found their hands.** Idiom for helplessness. Like losing heart or finding heart (2 Sam. 7. 27). **men.** Heb. *'ĕnōsh*. Ap. 14. III.

6 At Thy rebuke, O °God of Jacob,
°Both the chariot and horse are °cast into a dead sleep.
V² (p. 794) **7** Thou, *even* Thou, *art* to be feared:
And who may stand in Thy sight when once Thou art angry?
U³ **8** Thou didst cause judgment to be heard from heaven;
The earth feared, and was still,
9 When [1] God arose to judgment,
To save all the °meek of the earth. °Selah.
V³ **10** Surely the wrath of °man shall praise Thee:
The remainder of wrath shalt Thou restrain.
U⁴ **11** Vow, and °pay unto °the LORD your [1] God:
Let all that be round about Him bring °presents unto Him That ought to be feared.
12 He shall cut off the °spirit of princes:
He is terrible to the kings of the earth.

°To the chief Musician, °to Jeduthun.

77

°A Psalm °of Asaph.

B¹ W (p. 794) **1** I cried unto °God with my voice,
Even unto °God with my voice; and °He gave ear unto me.
2 In the day of my trouble I sought °the LORD*:
°My sore ran in the night, and °ceased not:
°My soul refused to be comforted.
3 I remembered [1] God, and was troubled:
I °complained, and °my spirit was overwhelmed. °Selah.
4 Thou holdest mine °eyes waking:
I am so troubled that I cannot speak.
5 I have considered the days of old,
The years of ancient times.
6 I call to remembrance °my song in the night:
I commune with mine own heart:
And [3] my spirit made diligent search.
X **7** °Will [2] the LORD* cast off for ever?
And will He be favourable no more?
8 Is His °mercy clean gone for ever?
Doth *His* °promise fail for evermore?
9 Hath °GOD forgotten to be gracious?
Hath He in anger shut up His tender mercies? °Selah.
W **10** And I said, "This *is* my infirmity:
But I will remember the years of the °right hand of °the MOST HIGH.
11 I will remember °the works of °THE LORD:
Surely I will remember Thy °wonders of old.
12 I will meditate also of all Thy °work,
And talk of Thy doings."
X Y i (p. 795) **13** Thy way, O [1] God, *is* in °the sanctuary:
°Who *is so* great a [9] GOD as *our* [1] God?

76 (**E**, p. 789). DESTRUCTION OF THE ENEMIES OF THE SANCTUARY. (*Repeated Alternation.*)

E | U¹ | 1-3. The Jebusites' defeat. Selah.
V¹ | 4. God. Thou art *glorious.*
U² | 5, 6. The Jebusites' defeat.
V² | 7. God. Thou art to be *feared.*
U³ | 8, 9. The Jebusites' defeat. Selah.
V³ | 10. God. Thou art to be *praised.*
U⁴ | 11, 12. The Jebusites' defeat,

6 God of Jacob. See note on 75. 9.
Both the chariot and horse are cast into a dead sleep. Sept., Syr., and Vulg. read "the horsemen are stunned".
cast into a dead sleep. One word in Heb. = stunned.
9 meek = the patient oppressed ones.
Selah. Connecting God's judgment on Jebusites, and making it a ground of praise. See Ap. 66. II.
10 man. Heb. *'ādām.* Ap. 14. I.
11 pay unto. Fig. *Ellipsis* (Ap. 6) = "pay [thy vows] unto".
the LORD. Heb. Jehovah. Ap. 4. II.
presents. Pl. of majesty: i. e. a great or ceremonial present.
12 spirit. Heb. *rūach.* Ap. 9.
To the chief Musician. See Ap. 64.
to Jeduthun. See Ap. 65. VI.

77 (*B*¹, p. 789). OUTSIDE THE SANCTUARY. EFFECT. MISERY. (*Alternation.*)

*B*¹ | W | 1-6. Occupation with self.
X | 7-9. Its sure result. Misery.
W | 10-12. Occupation with God.
X | 13-20. Its sure result. Happiness.

Title. A Psalm. Heb. *mizmōr.* Ap. 65. XVII.
of Asaph = for Asaph. The sixth of the twelve Asaph Psalms. Ap. 63. VIII.
1 God. Heb. Elohim. Ap. 4. I.
He gave ear. Inf. = "to give ear". Therefore supply *Ellipsis* (Ap. 6): "He [condescended] to give ear".
2 the LORD*. One of the 134 places where the *Sopherim* altered Jehovah to Adonai. See Ap. 32.
My sore ran. Heb. hand was outstretched: i. e. in prayer.
ceased not: i. e. to be outstretched.
My soul = I (emphatic). Heb. *nephesh.* Ap. 13.
3 complained = communed [with myself].
my spirit = I (emphatic). Heb. *rūach.* Ap. 9.
Selah. Connecting this self-introspection with its sure result—misery. See Ap. 66. II.
4 eyes = eyelids; or, Thou keepest mine eyelids from closing.
6 my song. Note that the whole of this member "W" (*vv.* 1-6) is occupation with self.
7 Will . . . ? Fig. *Erotēsis* (Ap. 6), emphasising the consequence of this introspection. It is continued through the whole of this member "X" (*vv.* 7-9).
8 mercy = lovingkindness, or grace.
promise = word. Put by Fig. *Metonymy* (of Cause), Ap. 6, for the promise given by it.
9 GOD. Heb. El. Ap. 4. IV.
Selah. Connecting all this misery with the only sure remedy—occupation with God: and passing from "I" and "my" to "Thou" and "Thy". (Ap. 66. II.)
10 right hand. Fig. *Anthropopatheia.* Ap. 6.
the MOST HIGH. Heb. *Elyōn.* Ap. 4. VI.
11 the works = doings.
THE LORD. Heb. Jah. Ap. 4. III.
wonders. Heb. work. Some codices, with Aram., Sept., Syr., and Vulg., read "wonders": i. e. wonderful ways or works.
12 work. Some codices, with Aram., Sept., Syr., and Vulg., read "works" (pl.).

13-20 [For Structure see next page].

13 the sanctuary. Only here, in God's presence, is found peace and happiness. **Who . . . ?** Fig. *Erotēsis* (Ap. 6), for emphasis. This is the cry resulting from occupation with God. Even the cry of His saints. See note on Ex. 15. 11.

k (p. 795) 14 Thou art the [9]GOD That doest wonders:
Thou hast °declared Thy strength among the °people.
15 Thou hast with *Thine* arm redeemed Thy people,
The sons of Jacob and °Joseph. °Selah.

Z l 16 The waters saw Thee, O God,
°The waters saw Thee; they were afraid:
°The depths also were troubled.

m 17 The °clouds poured out water:
The skies sent out a sound:
Thine °arrows also went abroad.

Z m 18 The voice of Thy thunder °*was* in the heaven:
°The lightnings °lightened the world:

l The earth trembled and shook.

Y i 19 Thy way °*is* in °the sea,
And Thy °path in the great waters,
And Thy °footsteps are not known.

k 20 Thou leddest Thy People like a flock
By the hand of °Moses and Aaron.

78

°Maschil °of Asaph.

A N r (p. 796) 1 Give ear, O my People, *to* my law:
Incline your °ears to the words of my mouth.
2 °**I will open my mouth in a °parable:**
I will utter °dark sayings of old:

s 3 Which we have heard and °known,
And our fathers have told us.

t 4 We will not hide *them* from their °children,
°Shewing to the generation to come the praises of °the LORD,
And His strength, and His °wonderful works that He hath done.

N r 5 For He established a testimony in Jacob,
And appointed a law in Israel,

s Which He °commanded our fathers,
That they should make them known to their [4]children:

t 6 That the generation to come might know *them, even* the [4]children *which* should be born;
Who should arise and declare *them* to their [4]children:
7 That they might set their hope in °God,
And not forget the works of °GOD,
But keep His commandments:

B D 8 And might not be as their fathers,
A stubborn and °rebellious generation;
A generation *that* set not their heart aright,
And whose °spirit was not stedfast °with [7]GOD.

E 9 The [4]children of °Ephraim, *being* armed, *and* °carrying bows,
Turned back in the day of battle.

F 10 They °kept not the covenant of [7]God,
And refused to walk in His law;
11 And forgat His works,
And His [4]wonders that He had shewed them.

---

77. 13-20 (*X*, p. 794). THE SURE RESULT. HAPPINESS. (*Introversions and Alternation.*)

X | Y | i | 13. God's way in the Sanctuary.
| | k | 14, 15. His people. Redeemed. Jacob and Joseph.
| Z | l | 16. The waters beneath. (Fear and trouble.)
| | m | 17. The heavens. (Clouds and skies.)
| *Z* | *m.* | 18-. The heavens. (Thunder and lightning.)
| | *l* | -18. The earth beneath. (Trembling and shaking.)
| *Y* | *i* | 19. God's way in the sea.
| | *k* | 20. His People. Led by Moses and Aaron.

14 declared = made known. **people** = peoples.

15 Joseph. Because his sons were not the direct sons of Jacob.

Selah. Connecting the redemption from Egypt with the accomplishment of it as recorded in "the scriptures of truth". See Ap. 66. II.

16 The waters. Fig. *Epizeuxis* (Ap. 6), for emphasis: i.e. the waters of the Nile, and the Red Sea (Ex. 14. 21-31).

The depths. Not referring to the "abyss" of Babylonian mythology, which was a corruption of primitive truth (Gen. 1. 2), but the Red Sea emphasised in the preceding clause.

17 clouds = the thick or dark clouds.

arrows. Put by Fig. *Metonymy* (of Adjunct), Ap. 6, for lightnings, mentioned below.

18 was in the heaven. Heb. *galgal* = rolled along.

The. Sept., Syr., and Vulg. read "Thy".

lightened = illumined.

19 is = was.

the sea. Not the sea-monster, the Ti'amat of Babylonian mythology, but the Red Sea mentioned above. See note on "The depths", *v.* 16.

path. Heb. text = "paths"; but some codices, with five early printed editions, as in A.V.

footsteps = footprints: i.e. when the waters return to their place.

20 Moses and Aaron. Only here in this third book.

78 [For Structure see next page].

Title. Maschil = Instruction. The tenth of thirteen so named. See note on Title, Ps. 32, and Ap. 65. XI.

of Asaph = by, or for Asaph. Asaph was a "seer" or prophet (2 Chron. 29. 30). This Psalm is concerning the choosing a site for the Sanctuary. The seventh of the twelve Asaph Psalms. Ap. 63. VIII.

1 ears. Heb. text = ear. Some codices, with Aram. and Syr., read "ears".

2 I will open, &c. Quoted in Matt. 13. 35.

parable . . . dark sayings. Cp. 49. 5. Same words. The Psalm has a moral: showing that Divine history contains more than appears on the surface.

3 known = come to know.

4 children = sons.

Shewing = Recounting.

the LORD. Heb. Jehovah. Ap. 4. II.

wonderful works = wonders. Cp. 77. 11, 14.

5 commanded our fathers. Cp. Ex. 10. 2; 12. 26, 27; 13. 8-10, 14, 15. Deut. 4. 9; 6. 7, 20, &c.

7 God. Heb. Elohim. Ap. 4. I.

GOD. Heb. El. Ap. 4. IV.

8 rebellious. Cp. Deut. 9. 24; 31. 27.

spirit. Heb. *rūach*. Ap. 9.

with. Some codices, with six early printed editions, read "toward".

9 Ephraim. The mention of Ephraim is not "perplexing". See explanation in next verse, and in the events of Judges 12. 1-6; 17, and 18: viz. the introduction of idolatry. It is sin which is spoken of. See *v.* 57, "deceitful bow". Cp. Hos. 7. 16; 10. 6-8.

carrying bows: i.e. though equipped as bowmen, yet were faithless. This is transferred to the moral application.

10 kept not. See note on *v.* 9.

G (p. 796) 12 Marvellous things did He in the sight of their fathers,
In the land of Egypt, *in* the field of ° Zoan.

H 13 He ° divided the sea, and caused them to pass through;
And He made the waters to stand ° as an heap.
14 In the daytime also He ° led them with a cloud,
And all the night with a light of fire.
15 He ° clave the ° rocks in the wilderness,
And gave *them* ° drink as *out of* the great depths.
16 He brought streams also out of the rock,
And caused waters to run down like rivers.

J 17 And they ° sinned yet more against Him
By provoking ° the MOST HIGH in the wilderness.
18 And they tempted [7] GOD in their heart
By asking meat for their ° lust.
19 Yea, they ° spake against [7] God;
They said, "Can [7] GOD furnish a table in the wilderness?
20 Behold, He smote the rock, that the waters gushed out,
And the streams overflowed;
Can He give bread also?
Can He provide flesh for His people?"

K 21 Therefore [4] the LORD heard *this*, and was wroth:
So a fire was kindled against Jacob,
And anger also came up against Israel;

C l¹ 22 Because they believed not in [7] God,
And ° trusted not in His salvation:

m¹ 23 Though He had commanded the ° clouds from above,
And ° opened the doors of heaven,
24 And had rained down ° manna upon them to eat,
And had given them of the corn ° of heaven.
25 ° Man did eat ° angels' food:
He sent them meat to the full.
26 He caused an east wind to blow in the heaven:
And by His power He brought in the south wind.
27 He ° rained flesh also upon them as dust,
And feathered fowls like ° as the sand of the sea:
28 And He let *it* fall in the midst of their camp,
Round about their habitations.

l² 29 So they did eat, and were well filled:
For He gave them their own desire;
30 They were ° not estranged from ° their lust.

m² But while their meat *was* yet in their mouths,
31 ° The wrath of [7] God came upon them,
And slew the fattest of them,
And smote down the chosen *men* of Israel.

l³ 32 ° For all this they [17] sinned still,
And believed not for His [4] wondrous works.

78 (*B*², p. 789). OUTSIDE THE SANCTUARY.
(*Introversion and Extended Alternation.*)

*B*² | A | 1-7. MOSAIC Institution. Giving of the Law.
B | D | 8. Provocation. General.
E | 9. Turning back.
F | 10, 11. Forgetfulness.
G | 12. Wonders in Egypt and Zoan.
H | 13-16. "Led" with mercies in wilderness.
J | 17-20. Provocation in wilderness.
K | 21. Wrath in wilderness.
C | 22-33. Unbelief in spite of wrath.
C | 34-39. Insincerity in spite of mercies.
B | *D* | 40. Provocation. General.
E | 41. Turning back.
F | 42. Forgetfulness.
G | 43-51. Wonders in Egypt and Zoan.
H | 52-55. "Led forth" from Egypt to wilderness.
J | 56-58. Provocation in the land.
K | 59-64. Wrath in the land.
A | 65-72. DAVIDIC Institution. Giving of Temple and monarchy.

1-7 (A, above). MOSAIC INSTITUTION.
(*Extended Alternation.*)

A | N | r | 1, 2. The Law.
s | 3. Taught us by our fathers.
t | 4. To be taught by us.
N | *r* | 5-. The Law.
s | -5. Taught us by our fathers.
t | 6, 7. To be taught by us.

12 Zoan. See note on Ex. 1. 10.
13 divided. Cp. Ex. 14. 21.
as an heap. Cp. Ex. 14. 22; 15. 8.
14 led them. Cp. Ex. 13. 21; 14. 24; and note the correspondence of H with *H*, in the Structure above.
15 clave. Heb. *bāḳa'* (in Piel), implying repeated cleaving.
rocks. Heb. *ẓūr.* Same word as in Ex. 17. The two events brought together here.
drink as out of. Some codices, with seven early printed editions, read "drink in the".
17 sinned. Heb. *chāṭā'*. Ap. 44. i.
the MOST HIGH. Heb. *Elyōn.* Ap. 4. VI. Cp. *v.* 35, and 77. 10.
18 lust=soul. Heb. *nephesh.* Ap. 13.
19 spake against. Cp. Num. 11. 4-6.

22-33 (C, above). UNBELIEF IN SPITE OF WRATH. (*Repeated Alternation.*)

C | l¹ | 22. Israel. Sin. Unbelief.
m¹ | 23-28. Jehovah. Mercies.
l² | 29, 30-. Israel. Sin. Lust.
m² | -30, 31. Jehovah. Wrath.
l³ | 32. Israel. Sin. Unbelief.
m³ | 33. Jehovah. Wrath.

22 trusted not=confided not. Heb. *baṭaḥ.* Ap. 69. I.
23 clouds=skies.
opened the doors. Fig. *Anthropopatheia.* Ap. 6. Cp. Gen. 7. 11.
24 manna. Bread; not "the drops of the tarfu or tamarisk tree", as alleged. See John 6. 31, 49-51.
of heaven: i.e. from heaven; not from trees.
25 Man. Heb. *'īsh.* Ap. 14. II.
angels' food=bread of the mighty ones. Sept., Syr., Arab., Ethiopic, with Targums, render it "bread of angels". The "of" may be Genitive of Agent. See Ap. 17.
27 rained. As in *v.* 24.
as the sand. Fig. *Parœmia.* Ap. 6.
30 not estranged=not turned away from.
their lust. What they had longed for.
31 The wrath, &c. Cp. John 3. 36. Eph. 5. 6. Col. 3. 6.
32 For all this=In, or amid all this.

m³ (p. 796) 33 Therefore their days did He consume °in vanity,
And their years in trouble.

C L n (p. 797) 34 When He slew them, then they sought Him:
And they returned and enquired early after ⁷GOD.

o 35 And they remembered that God *was* their rock,
And °THE HIGH ⁷GOD their °redeemer.

M p 36 Nevertheless they did flatter Him with their mouth,

q And they lied unto Him with their °tongues.

M p 37 For their heart was not right with Him,

q Neither were they stedfast in His °covenant.

L n 38 But He, *being* full of compassion, forgave *their* °iniquity, and °destroyed *them* not:
Yea, many a time turned He His anger away,
And did not stir up all His wrath.

o 39 For °He remembered that they *were but* °flesh;
°A wind that passeth away, and cometh not again.

B D (p. 796) 40 °How oft did they provoke Him in the wilderness,
And grieve Him in the desert!

E 41 Yea, they °turned back and tempted ⁷GOD,
And °limited °the Holy One of Israel.

F 42 °They remembered not His hand,
Nor the day when He °delivered them from the enemy.

G 43 How He had wrought His °signs in Egypt,
And His wonders in the field of ¹²Zoan:
44 And had °turned their rivers into blood;
And their floods, that they could not drink.
45 He sent divers sorts of °flies among them, which devoured them;
And °frogs, which ³⁸destroyed them.
46 He gave also their increase unto the °caterpiller,
And their °labour unto the locust.
47 He °destroyed their vines with °hail,
And their sycomore trees with °frost.
48 He gave up their cattle also to the ⁴⁷hail,
And their flocks to °hot thunderbolts.
49 He cast upon them the fierceness of His anger,
Wrath, and indignation, and trouble,
By °sending °evil angels *among them.*
50 He °made a way to His anger;
He spared not their °soul from death,
But gave their life over to the pestilence;
51 And smote all the firstborn in Egypt;
The chief of *their* °strength in the °tabernacles of °Ham:

H 52 But made His own People to go forth like sheep,
And guided them in the °wilderness like a flock.
53 And He °led them on safely so that they feared not:
But the sea °overwhelmed their enemies.
54 And He brought them to the border of °His sanctuary,
Even to °this mountain, *which* His right hand had purchased.

---

33 in vanity=in a breath i. e. the whole generation of men quickly died out. Cp. Num. 14. 29, 35; 26. 64, 65.

78. 34-39 (*C*, p. 796). INSINCERITY IN SPITE OF MERCIES. (*Introversion and Alternations.*)

C | L | n | 34. Repentance of Israel.
  o | 35. Remembrance of Israel.
   M | p | 36-. Mouth. } Positive.
    q | -36. Lied. }
   M | *p* | 37-. Heart. } Negative.
    q | -37. Unsteadfast. }
 L | *n* | 38. Repentance of Jehovah.
  o | 39. Remembrance of Jehovah.

35 THE HIGH GOD. Heb. *'El 'Elyōn*=EL MOST HIGH.
redeemer. Heb. *ga'al.* See note on Ex. 6. 6; 13. 13.
36 tongues. Heb.=tongue (sing.).
37 covenant. If that of Ex. 34. 5-10, then note the reference to it in *v.* 38, below.
38 iniquity. Heb. *'āvah.* Ap. 44. iv.
destroyed=laid waste.
39 He remembered. Fig. *Anthropopatheia.* Ap. 6. Cp. "They forgat", *v.* 11.
flesh. Cp. Gen. 6. 3; 8. 21. Ps. 103. 14-16.
A wind. Heb. *rūach.* Ap. 9.
40 How oft. Ten times at least in the first two years (Num. 14. 22).
41 turned back: i.e. again and again.
limited. Heb. *tāvāh*, to set a mark (Ezek. 9. 4), the only other occurrence of the *Hiphil*; hence, to set a limit.
the Holy One of Israel. This title occurs only three times in the Psalms: here (78. 41); in the last Davidic Psalm of the second book (71. 22); and in the last Psalm of this third book (89. 18).
42 They remembered not. Contrast *v.* 39, "He remembered".
delivered. Heb. *pādāh*, as in Ex. 13. 13.
43 signs in Egypt. The Psalm, *vv.* 44-51, does not profess to give a list of the "ten plagues"; so that there is no ground for the assumption as to only a "Jehovist" document being known to the writer. He selects according to his special purpose. He names the first and the last, and omits the third (lice), fifth (murrain), sixth (boils), and the ninth (darkness).
44 turned their rivers. The first plague (Ex. 7. 17, &c.).
45 flies. The fourth plague (Ex. 8. 21).
frogs. The second plague (Ex. 8. 5, 6).
46 caterpiller=corn locust. A more specific word than Ex. 10. 1-20. It occurs in Joel 1. 4; 2. 25.
labour. Put by Fig. *Metonymy* (of Cause), Ap. 6, for the fruit of labour. **47 destroyed**=killed.
hail. The seventh plague (Ex. 9. 18).
frost. Word occurs nowhere else. Prob.=hailstones.
48 hot thunderbolts: or lightnings (Ex. 9. 23).
49 sending=letting loose.
evil angels. In distinction from "demons". Cp. 1 Tim. 4. 1, where both are mentioned. Cp. Ex. 12. 23. 2 Sam. 24. 16.
50 made=pondered, or weighed. Cp. Prov. 4. 26; 5. 6, 21. Contrast Isa. 26. 7. **soul.** Heb. *nephesh.* Ap. 13.
51 strength=strengths (pl.). Manly vigour. Put by Fig. *Metonymy* (of Adjunct), Ap. 6, for the firstborn. Cp. Gen. 49. 3. Deut. 21. 17. Ps. 105. 36.
tabernacles=tents. Heb. *'ohel.* Ap. 40 (3).
Ham=Egypt. Cp. 105. 23, 27; 106. 22.
52 wilderness. Cp. Isa. 63. 11-14.
53 led=gently led. See the Structure (H and *H*), and cp. *vv.* 13-16. **overwhelmed.** Cp. Ex. 14. 27; 15. 10.
54 His sanctuary: i. e. Zion. See Ap. 68.
this mountain: viz. the one in the writer's view; not in "the memory of an exile in Babylon".

55 He cast out the °heathen also before them,
And divided them an inheritance °by line,
And made the tribes of Israel to dwell in their tents.

J (p. 796) 56 Yet they tempted and provoked °the MOST HIGH [7]God,
And kept not His testimonies:
57 But °turned back, and dealt unfaithfully like their fathers:
They were turned aside like °a deceitful bow.
58 For they provoked Him to anger with their high places,
And moved Him to jealousy with their °graven images.

K 59 °When [7]God °heard *this*, He was wroth,
And greatly abhorred Israel:
60 So that He forsook the °tabernacle of °Shiloh,
The tent *which* He placed among °men;
61 And delivered His °strength into captivity,
And His °glory into the enemy's hand.
62 He gave His People over also °unto the sword;
And was wroth with His inheritance.
63 The fire consumed their young men;
And their maidens °were not given to marriage.
64 Their °priests fell by the sword;
And their widows made no lamentation.

A 65 Then °the LORD* awaked °as one out of sleep,
And like a mighty man that shouteth by reason of wine.
66 And He smote His enemies in °the hinder parts:
He put them to a perpetual reproach.
67 Moreover He refused the [51]tabernacle of Joseph,
And °chose not the tribe of Ephraim:
68 But chose the tribe of Judah,
The mount Zion °which He loved.
69 And He built His [54]sanctuary like high *palaces*,
°Like the earth which He hath established for ever.
70 He °chose David also His servant,
And took him from the sheepfolds:
71 From following the ewes great with young He brought him
°To feed Jacob °His people, and °Israel His inheritance.
72 So he fed them according to the integrity of his heart;
And guided them by the °skilfulness of his hands.

79

°A Psalm °of Asaph.

C N (p. 798) 1 O °God, the °heathen are come into Thine inheritance;
Thy °holy °temple have they defiled;
They have laid Jerusalem °on heaps.
2 The dead bodies of Thy servants have they given *to be* meat unto the fowls of the heaven,
The flesh of Thy °saints unto the beasts of the earth.

55 heathen = nations.
by line. Sometimes this is put by Fig. *Metonymy* (of Cause), Ap. 6, for the inheritance itself which was measured off by it. Cp. Ps. 19. 4.
56 the MOST HIGH. Heb. *'eth 'Ĕlohīm 'Elyōn.* Ap. 4.
57 turned back. See the Structure (J and *J*).
a deceitful bow: disappointing the bowman. Cp. Hos. 7. 16.
graven images. Same word as Deut. 7. 5. Includes all images, whether carved, graven, or molten.
59 When God heard this, He. There is no "When" in the Heb. Render: "God heard this, and He was wroth".
heard. Fig. *Anthrōpopatheia.* Ap. 6.
60 tabernacle = habitation. Heb. *mishkān.* Ap. 40 (2).
Shiloh. Cp. Judg. 18. 1, 31. 1 Sam. 4. 3.
men. Heb. *'ādām.* Ap. 14. I.
61 strength. One of the names for the Ark of the Covenant (cp. 63. 2; 132. 8). See notes on Ex. 25. 22. 1 Chron. 13. 3.
glory. Another name for the Ark (1 Sam. 4. 22).
62 unto the sword. Cp. 1 Sam. 4. 10.
63 were not given to marriage = were not praised: i. e. had no marriage song.
64 priests. Cp. 1 Sam. 4. 11.
65 the LORD*. One of the 134 places where the *Sōpherīm* changed "Jehovah" to "Adonai". See Ap. 32.
as one out of sleep. Supply *Ellipsis* (Ap. 6) = "as one [awaketh] out of sleep".
66 the hinder parts = rear, or backward.
67 chose not. Ephraim did not lose inheritance, but lost precedence, which was transferred to Judah.
68 which He loved. The proof of which was the removal of the Ark to Zion.
69 Like the earth. Some codices, with two early printed editions, Sept., Syr., and Vulg., read ב (*Beth* = in) instead of כ (*Kaph* = like) = "In the land".
70 chose David. Cp. 1 Sam. 16. 11, 12. This is the climax of the Psalm.
71 To feed = To shepherd.
To feed Jacob. Cp. 2 Sam. 7. 7, 8.
His people. Some codices, with Sept. and Vulg., read "His servant".
Israel. Note the two names: Jacob, the natural seed; Israel, the spiritual seed. See notes on Gen. 32. 28; 43. 6; 45. 26, 28.
72 skilfulness = discernment, or understanding.

79 (*C*, p. 789). **THE ENEMY IN THE SANCTUARY** (cp. Ps. **74**). (*Introversion and Extended Alternation.*)

C | N | 1-3. Complaint.
O | 4. Our neighbours. Reproach.
P | r | 5. Question.
s | 6, 7. Prayer against nations.
t | 8, 9. Prayer for selves.
P | *r* | 10-. Question.
s | -10. Prayer against nations.
t | 11. Prayer for selves.
O | 12. Our neighbours. Reproach.
N | 13. Praise.

Title. A Psalm. Heb. *mizmōr.* See Ap. 65. XVII.
of Asaph. The eighth of the twelve Asaph Psalms. Cp. Ps. 74, the second of the third book. See Ap. 10. The Psalm is said to have "hardly any regular strophical divisions". But see the Structure above.
1 God. Heb. Elohim. Ap. 4. I.
heathen = nations.
holy. See note on Ex. 3. 5.
temple. See 1 Kings 14. 25, 26. 2 Chron. 12. 2-10. Pillaged, but not destroyed.
on heaps = in ruins. Cp. the prophecy in Mic. 3. 12.
2 saints = men of Thy lovingkindness, or gracious ones, or beloved.

3 Their blood have they °shed like water round about Jerusalem;
And *there was* none to bury *them*.

O (p. 798) 4 We are become a reproach to our neighbours,
A scorn and derision to them that are round about us.

P r 5 °How long, °LORD? wilt Thou be angry for ever?
Shall Thy jealousy burn like fire?

s 6 °Pour out Thy wrath upon the [1]heathen that have °not known Thee,
And upon the kingdoms that have not called upon Thy name.
7 For °they have devoured °Jacob,
And laid waste his °dwelling place.

t 8 O remember not against us former °iniquities:
Let Thy tender mercies speedily °prevent us:
For we are brought very low.
9 Help us, O [1]God of our salvation, for the glory of Thy name:
And deliver us, and °purge away our °sins, for °Thy name's sake.

P r 10 °Wherefore should the [1]heathen say, "Where *is* their [1]God?"

s Let Him be known among the [1]heathen in our sight
°*By* the revenging of the blood of Thy servants *which is* shed.

t 11 Let the sighing of the prisoner come before Thee;
According to the greatness of °Thy power °preserve Thou °those that are appointed to die;

O 12 And render unto our neighbours sevenfold into their bosom
Their reproach, wherewith they have reproached Thee, O °LORD*.

N 13 So we Thy people and sheep of Thy pasture
Will give Thee thanks for ever:
We will shew forth Thy praise to all generations.

°To the chief Musician °upon Shoshannim-Eduth.

80

°A Psalm °of Asaph.

D[1] Q[1] (p. 799) 1 Give ear, O °Shepherd of Israel,
Thou That leadest °Joseph like a flock;
Thou That dwellest °*between* the cherubims, shine forth.
2 °Before °Ephraim and Benjamin and Manasseh stir up Thy strength,
And come *and* save us.
3 °Turn us again, O °God,
And cause Thy face to shine; and we shall be saved.

R[1] 4 °O LORD God of hosts,
°How long wilt Thou be angry against the prayer of Thy people?

---

3 shed=poured out. Cp. same word in *v.* 6.
5 How long . . . ? Fig. *Erotēsis*. Ap. 6. Cp. P. r. (*v.* 5) with *P. r.* (*v.* 10). **LORD.** Heb. Jehovah. Ap. 4. II.
6 Pour out. Fig. *Anthropopatheia*. Ap. 6. See note on "shed", *v.* 3. **not known Thee.** Cp. Jer. 10. 25.
7 they have. So some codices, with Aram., Sept., Syr., and Vulg. Cp. Jer. 10. 25. But other codices read "he hath": i. e. the enemy.
Jacob. Put by Fig. *Metonymy* (of Subject), Ap. 6, for the riches of his descendants.
dwelling place=pasture.
8 iniquities. Heb. *'āvāh*. Ap. 44. iv.
prevent us=come to meet us. Eng. usage changed. Original sense obsolete.
9 purge away=cover, or atone for. Heb. *kāphar*. See note on Ex. 29. 33. **sins.** Heb. *chāṭā'*. Ap. 44. i.
Thy name's sake=Thine own sake. See 20. 1.
10 Wherefore . . . ? Fig. *Erotēsis*. Ap. 6. Cp. *v.* 5.
By. Supply Ellipsis from the preceding line: "[Let] the avenging . . . [be known]", &c.
11 Thy power. Heb. Thine arm. Put by Fig. *Metonymy* (of Effect), Ap. 6, for the power contained in and put forth by it. By Fig. *Anthrōpopatheia* (Ap. 6), an "arm" attributed to God. **preserve**=reserve.
those that are appointed to die=sons of death. Genitive of Relation. Cp. Rom. 8. 36.
12 LORD*. One of the 134 places where "Jehovah" was changed to "Adonai" by the *Sōpherīm*. See Ap. 32.
13 To the chief Musician. See Ap. 64.
upon Shoshannim-Eduth. The testimony relating to the Feast of the second Passover (Num. 9. 5-14. Cp. 2 Chron. 29. 25-35; 30. 23). The other of the two Psalms thus called is Ps. 59. See Ap. 65. XXII.

80 (*D*[1], p. 789). GOD IN THE SANCTUARY (cp. Ps. **75**). (*Repeated Alternation.*)

D[1] | Q[1] | 1-3. Prayer. Turn us. Shine.
R[1] | 4-6. Representation. The People.
Q[2] | 7. Prayer. Turn us. Shine.
R[2] | 8-13. Representation. The Vine.
Q[3] | 14, 15. Prayer. Turn Thou.
R[3] | 16. Representation. Vine and People.
Q[4] | 17-19. Prayer. Turn us. Shine.

Title. A Psalm. Heb. *mizmōr*. See Ap. 65. XVII.
of Asaph. The ninth of the twelve Asaph Psalms. See Ap. 63. VIII.
1 Shepherd of Israel. It is in the blessing of Joseph (Gen. 48. 15 and 49. 24) that God is spoken of as the Shepherd. And this is why Joseph is here mentioned.
Joseph is put by Fig. *Synecdoche* (of Part), Ap. 6, for all Israel. The kingdom was not yet divided. The Psalms are not arranged chronologically according to date, but logically according to subject, as required by the Structures of the various books (see p. 720, &c.). The subject of Ps. 80 corresponds with Ps. 79, and does not follow Ps. 79 chronologically.
between. Fig. *Ellipsis* (Ap. 6), "dwellest [enthroned above] the cherubim".
2 Before. A special various reading called *Sevīr* (Ap. 34) reads "For the sons of".
Ephraim and Benjamin and Manasseh. Note the Fig. *Polysyndeton* (Ap. 6), calling our attention to these three. They were descended from Rachel, and marched together in the rear (Num. 2. 18-22). As Judah, Issachar, and Zebulun marched in the van, the Ark (the symbol of God's presence) led them as a Shepherd (78. 13-16, 52-55. John 10. 4, 5).
3 Turn us again. Fig. *Cycloides* (Ap. 6) governing the Structure. Cp. *vv.* 7, 19. Not from captivity, but from idolatry to the true worship.
God. Heb. Elohim. Ap. 4. I. Note the significant order: *v.* 3, "O God"; *v.* 7, "O God of hosts"; *v.* 19, "O Jehovah, God of hosts". This Divine order rebukes our own loose use of the Divine titles; and shows us the importance of noting their Divine use, not heeding modern hypotheses.

4 O LORD God of hosts. Heb. Jehovah Elohim Zebaioth. See note on 1 Sam. 1. 3. Not common in the Psalms, but occurring in 59. 5 and 84. 8. **How long . . . ?** Fig. *Erotēsis*. Ap. 6.

5 Thou feedest them with the bread of tears;
And givest them tears to drink in great measure.
6 Thou makest us a strife unto our neighbours:
And our enemies °laugh among themselves.

Q² (p. 799) 7 [3] Turn us again, O [4] God of hosts,
And cause Thy face °to shine; and we shall be saved.

R² 8 Thou hast brought °a vine out of Egypt:
Thou hast cast out the °heathen, and planted it.
9 Thou preparedst *room* before it,
And didst cause it to take deep root, and it filled the land.
10 The hills were covered with the shadow of it,
And the boughs thereof *were like* °the goodly cedars.
11 She sent out her boughs unto °the sea,
And her °branches unto °the river.
12 °Why hast Thou *then* broken down her hedges,
So that all they which pass by the way do pluck her?
13 The boar out of °the wood doth waste it,
And the wild beast of the field doth devour it.

Q³ 14 °Return, we beseech Thee, O [4] God of hosts:
Look down from heaven, °and behold, and visit this vine;
15 °And the vineyard which Thy right hand hath planted,
And the °branch *that* Thou madest strong for Thyself.

R³ 16 *It is* burned with fire, *it is* cut down:
They perish at the rebuke of Thy countenance.

Q⁴ 17 Let Thy hand be °upon the °man of Thy [15] right hand,
°Upon the °son of man *whom* Thou madest strong for Thyself.
18 So will not we go back from Thee:
°Quicken us, and we will call upon Thy name.
19 [3] Turn us again, °O [4] LORD God of hosts,
Cause Thy face to shine; and we shall be saved.

°To the chief Musician °upon Gittith.

81

A Psalm °of Asaph.

D² S¹ T (p. 800) 1 Sing aloud unto °God our strength:
Make a joyful noise unto the °God of Jacob.
2 °Take a psalm, and bring hither the °timbrel,
The pleasant harp with the °psaltery.
3 Blow up the °trumpet in the new moon,
In the time appointed, on our solemn feast °day.

U 4 For this *was* a statute for Israel,
And a law of the [1] God of Jacob.
5 °This He ordained in Joseph *for* a testimony,
When °He went °out °through the land of Egypt:
Where °I heard a language *that* I understood not.

---

6 laugh among themselves. Some codices, with Sept., Syr., and Vulg., read "have mocked at us".

7 to shine. Cp. Num. 6. 25.

8 a vine. Cp. Isa. 5. 1-7; 27. 2-6. Jer. 2. 21; 12. 10. Verse 11 connects Joseph and Gen. 49. 22.

heathen=nations.

10 the goodly cedars=mighty cedars. Heb. "cedars of El". Ap. 4. IV.

11 the sea: i.e. the Mediterranean.

branches=roots, or suckers.

the river: i.e. the Euphrates.

12 Why . . . ? Fig. *Erotēsis* (Ap. 6), for emphasis.

13 the wood=forest. The Heb. word for forest here (*mīyyā'ar*), has the letter *Ayin* (ע) suspended (see note on Judg. 18. 30). This is the second of four such suspended letters (the other two being Job 38. 13, 15). Read *with* this letter, the word means "forest"; *without* it, and with an *Aleph* (א) instead, it is *mīyy'ar*, "river". The ancient Jewish interpreters took this suspended letter as denoting that, when innocent, Israel would be assailed only by a power weak as a river animal; but, when guilty, it would be destroyed by a power as strong as a land animal. Until the Roman power arose (whose military ensign was the "boar"), it was understood as "river" (meaning Egypt); but afterward the Sept., Chald., and Vulg. read "forest".

14 Return. Cp. *vv.* 3, 7, 19, and see the Structure above.

and. Note the Fig. *Polysyndeton* (Ap. 6) for emphasis. Almost an Ellipsis="[once more] look down, [once more] behold, [once more] visit".

15 And the. Supply the *Ellipsis* (Ap. 6), "And [protect] the".

branch=son. Some codices, with Sept., Syr., and Vulg., read "son of man", as in *v.* 17.

17 upon: or over. **man.** Heb. *'īsh.* Ap. 14. II.

son of man=son of Adam. Heb. *'ādām.* Ap. 14. I. See note on Ezek. 2. 1.

18 Quicken=make alive, restore, revive.

19 O LORD, &c. See note on *vv.* 3 and 7.

To the chief Musician. See Ap. 64.

upon Gittith=relating to the (Art.) wine-press, or the autumn Festival of Tabernacles; or to the vine and the vineyard, which are the subjects of the Psalm. See Ap. 65. IV.

81 (*D*², p. 789). GOD IN THE SANCTUARY. (*Division.*)

*D*² | S¹ | 1-10. Israel. God's call to praise and hearken.
| S² | 11-16. Israel. Refusal and consequence.

Title. of Asaph. The tenth of the twelve Asaph Psalms. Ap. 63. VIII. Relating to the worship of the Sanctuary.

1-10 (S¹, above). ISRAEL. GOD'S CALL TO PRAISE AND HEARKEN. (*Extended Alternation.*)

S¹ | T | 1-3. Call to praise. (Positive.)
  U | 4-6. Deliverance from Egypt. Reason.
    V | u | 7-. Israel. Prayer.
      v | -7. God's answer.
| *T* | 8, 9. Call to hear. (Negative.)
  U | 10-. Deliverance from Egypt. Reason.
    V | *u* | -10-. Israel. Command.
      v | -10. God's promise.

1 God. Heb. Elohim. Ap. 4. I. **Jacob.** See 75. 9.

2 Take a psalm=Raise a song.

timbrel. Heb. *toph.* See note on Ex. 15. 20.

psaltery=lute.

3 trumpet. Heb. *shophar.* See note on Num. 10. 2.

day. Some codices, with two early printed editions, Aram., and Syr., read "days" (pl.): i.e. festivals.

5 This. No Heb. for "This".

He: i.e. God. **out**=forth.

through=before: i.e. in the sight of. Cp. Num. 33. 3.

I=I [Israel].

6 °I removed his shoulder from the burden:
His hands were delivered from the ° pots.

V u (p. 800) 7 Thou calledst in trouble,
And I delivered thee;
v I answered thee ° in the secret place of thunder:
I ° proved thee at the waters of Meribah. ° Selah.

T 8 Hear, O My People, and I will testify unto thee:
O Israel, if thou wilt hearken unto Me;
9 There shall no ° strange ° god be in thee;
Neither shalt thou worship any ° strange ° god.

U 10 I *am* ° the LORD thy God,

V u Which brought thee out of the land of Egypt:

v Open thy mouth wide, and I will fill it.

S^2 W (p. 801) 11 But My People would not hearken to My voice;
And Israel ° would none of Me.

X 12 So I ° gave them up unto their own hearts' ° lust:
And they walked in their own counsels.

W 13 °Oh that My People had hearkened unto Me,
And Israel had ° walked in My ways!

X 14 I should ° soon have subdued their enemies,
And turned My hand against their adversaries.
15 The ° haters of ° the LORD should have submitted themselves unto Him:
But their time should have endured for ever.
16 He should have fed [12] them also with the finest of the wheat:
And with honey out of the rock ° should I have satisfied thee.

82

° A Psalm ° of Asaph.

D^3 Y (p. 801) 1 ° God ° standeth in ° the congregation of the mighty;
He judgeth among the ° gods.

Z 2 How long will ye judge unjustly,
And ° accept the persons of the ° wicked? ° Selah.
3 ° Defend ° the poor and fatherless:
Do justice to the afflicted and needy.
4 Deliver [3] the poor and needy:
Rid *them* out of the hand of the [2] wicked.

A 5 ° They know not, neither ° will they understand;

A They walk ° on in darkness:
All the foundations of the earth are out of course.

Z 6 ° **I have said, "Ye are [1] gods;**
And all of you *are* ° children of ° the MOST HIGH.
7 But ye shall die like ° men,
And fall like one of the ° princes."

Y 8 Arise, O [1] God, ° judge the earth:
For Thou shalt inherit all ° nations.

---

6 I = I [God].
pots = baskets. Depicted in Egyptian paintings as being used in brickmaking. Not same word as 68. 13, though the same things referred to. Cp. 2 Kings 10. 7.
7 in, or from.
proved. Cp. Ex. 17. 6. Num. 20. 1-13.
Selah. Connecting the merciful deliverance with the reason why Israel should hearken. See Ap. 66. II.
9 strange = foreign, or foreigner's.
strange god = god of the foreigner. Not the same as above. For the former, see 44. 20. Isa. 43. 12; for the latter, Deut. 32. 12.
god. Heb. *'el.* Ap. 4. IV.
10 the LORD thy God. Heb. Jehovah thy Elohim. Ap. 4. II. 1. The title of the Lawgiver.

81. 11-16 (S^2, p. 800). ISRAEL. REFUSAL, AND CONSEQUENCES. (*Alternation.*)

S^2 | W | 11. Refusal to hear.
  X | 12. Consequence. The worst possible.
 W | 13. If they had heard.
  X | 14-16. Consequence. The most blessed.

11 would none of Me = had no mind for Me.
12 gave them up = let him (Israel) go on. The greatest judgment God could have given them; or give us. **lust** = stubbornness.
13 Oh . . . ! Fig. *Œonismos.* Ap. 6.
walked. Plural.
14 soon. See note on "almost", Prov. 5. 14.
15 haters of the LORD: i. e. Israel's enemies.
the LORD. Heb. Jehovah. Ap. 4. II.
16 should I have satisfied thee. Some codices read "would I satisfy him". Sept., Syr., and Vulg., read "would He satisfy him".

82 (D^3, p. 789). GOD IN THE SANCTUARY. (*Introversion.*)

D^3 | Y | 1. God, the righteous Judge.
  Z | 2-4. Earthly judges indicted.
   A | 5-. Their wrong judgment. (Negative.)
   A | -5. Their wrong judgment. (Positive.)
  Z | 6, 7. Earthly judges condemned.
 Y | 8. God, the righteous Judge.

Title. A Psalm. Heb. *mizmōr.* Ap. 65. XVII.
of Asaph. The eleventh of the twelve Asaph Psalms.
1 God. Heb. Elohim. Ap. 4. I.
standeth: i. e. officially.
the congregation of the mighty = GOD'S (Heb. El. Ap. 4. IV) assembly (in its civil aspect).
gods. Elohim: used of earthly judges as representing Him. Cp. Ex. 21. 6; 22. 8, 9, 28 (quoted in Acts 23. 5). Hence, Moses is so spoken of (Ex. 7. 1). (It is used also of idols as representing even a false god.) See John 10. 34, 35.
2 accept the persons. Cp. Lev. 19. 15. Prov. 18. 5. 2 Chron. 19. 7.
wicked = lawless. Heb. *rāshā'.* Ap. 44. x.
Selah. Connecting the indictment with the command to judge righteously. See Ap. 66. II.
3 Defend = Vindicate. Cp. *vv.* 1, 2.
the poor = oppressed. Heb. *'ebyōn* = a helpless or expectant one. See note on Prov. 6. 11.
5 They = The oppressed.
will = can.
on = to and fro.
6 I have said. Cp. Ex. 22. 9, 28. John 10. 34, 35.
children = sons. Cp. Luke 6. 35.
the MOST HIGH. Heb. *Elyōn.* Ap. 4. VI.
7 men. Heb. *'ādām.* Ap. 14. I.
princes. Cp. Num. 16. 2, 35.
8 judge = judge Thou.
nations = the nations.

83

°A Song *or* °Psalm °of Asaph.

E B (p. 802) 1 °Keep not Thou silence, O °God:
°Hold not Thy peace, and be not still, O °GOD.

C y^1 2 For, lo, Thine enemies °make a tumult:
And they that hate Thee have °lifted up the head.
3 They have taken crafty counsel against Thy People,
And consulted against Thy hidden ones.

z^1 4 They have said, "Come, and let us cut them off °from *being* a nation;
That the name of Israel may be no more in remembrance."

y^2 5 For they have consulted together with one consent:
They °are confederate °against Thee:
6 The °tabernacles of °Edom, and the Ishmaelites;
Of Moab, and the Hagarenes;
7 Gebal, and Ammon, and Amalek;
The Philistines with the inhabitants of Tyre;
8 Assur also is joined with them:
They have holpen the °children of Lot. °Selah.

C y^3 9 Do unto them as *unto* the °Midianites;
As *to* °Sisera, as *to* °Jabin, at the brook of Kison:
10 *Which* perished at En-dor:
They became *as* dung for the °earth.
11 Make their nobles like °Oreb, and like °Zeeb:
Yea, all their princes as °Zebah, and as °Zalmunna:

z^2 12 Who said, "Let us take to ourselves
The °houses of [1]God in °possession."

y^4 13 O my [1]God, make them like a °wheel;
As the °stubble before the °wind.
14 As the fire burneth a wood,
And as the flame setteth the mountains on fire;
15 So °persecute them with Thy tempest,
And make them afraid with Thy storm.

B 16 Fill °their faces with shame;
That °they may seek Thy name, O °LORD.
17 Let °them be confounded and troubled for ever;
Yea, let °them be put to shame, and perish:
18 That °*men* may know that Thou, Whose name alone *is* °JEHOVAH,
Art the °MOST HIGH over all the earth.

°To the chief Musician °upon Gittith.

84

°A Psalm °for the sons of Korah.

F¹ F a (p. 803) 1 °How °amiable *are* Thy °tabernacles,
O °LORD of hosts!

83 (*E*, p. 789). DESTRUCTION OF THE ENEMIES OF THE SANCTUARY. (*Introversions.*)

E | B | 1. Appeal against enemies.
  C | y^1 | 2, 3. Their combination. "For".
    z^1 | 4. Their words.
   y^2 | 5-8. Their combination. "For".
  C | y^3 | 9-11. Enemies. Their punishment.
    z^2 | 12. Their words.
   y^4 | 13-15. Enemies. Their punishment.
 B | 16-18. Appeal against enemies.

Title. A Song. Heb. *shīr.* Ap. 65. XXIII.

Psalm. Heb. *mizmōr.* Ap. 65. XVII.

of Asaph. The last of the twelve Asaph Psalms. Probably Jahaziel's: cp. 2 Chron. 20. 14, 19-21, the Psalm being written on that occasion (about 804 B.C.), and 2 Chron. 20. 22-36 being the answer to this prayer. Cp. *v.* 12 with 2 Chron. 20. 11; and *vv.* 17, 18 with 2 Chron. 20. 29.

1 Keep not . . . Hold not. Fig. *Tapeinōsis.* Ap. 6.

God. Heb. Elohim. Ap. 4. I.

GOD. Heb. El. Ap. 4. IV.

2 make a tumult = roar like the waves of the sea, as in 46. 3.

lifted up the head. Put by Fig. *Metonymy* (of Adjunct), Ap. 6, for acting presumptuously. Cp. 3. 3; 27. 6. Judg. 8. 28.

4 from being a nation = that they be no more a nation. Cp. Jer. 48. 2. Isa. 7. 8.

5 are confederate = have solemnised a covenant.

against Thee. Not only against Thy People (*v.* 3).

6 tabernacles = tents. Heb. *'ohel.* See Ap. 40 (3).

Edom. Note the tenfold confederation of enemies in *vv.* 6-9, followed by the sevenfold destruction in *vv.* 10-12; the two making the number 17, the sum of the two numbers (10 ordinal perfection or completeness, and 7 spiritual perfection): 17 being the seventh prime number. Thus the three numbers correspond with the conspiracy of man, and judgment of God. See Ap. 10.

8 children = sons.

Selah. Connecting these two things together, the former being that which calls forth the prayer: and connecting the *past* confederacy with the future one of the "ten kingdoms" and the same Divine destruction.

9 Midianites. Cp. Judg. 7. 22. [Ap. 66. II.

Sisera. Cp. Judg. 4. 15. **Jabin.** Cp. Judg. 4. 23.

10 earth = ground, or soil. Heb. *'ădāmāh.* See note on Isa. 25. 10. **11 Oreb.** Cp. Judg. 7. 25.

Zeeb. Cp. Judg. 7. 25. **Zebah.** Cp. Judg. 8. 5, 21.

Zalmunna. Cp. Judg. 8. 5, 21.

12 houses = pleasant pastures. Heb. *ne'ōth* (pl.). Same word as in 23. 2; 65. 12.

possession = inheritance. Cp. 2 Chron. 20. 11.

13 wheel. Heb. *galgāl,* a rolling thing. Probably the wild artichoke, which throws out branches of equal length, and, when ripe and dry, breaks off at the root, and is carried by the wind, rolling like a wheel over the plains. Cp. Isa. 17. 13; where it is again used with "chaff", and rendered "a rolling thing" (marg. thistledown).

stubble = straw. Heb. *ḳash* = the dry haulm of grain, which is carried about by the wind like the *galgāl.*

wind. Heb. *rūach.* Ap. 9.

15 persecute = pursue.

16 their: i. e. the enemies.

they: i. e. Israel, or Thy People.

LORD. Heb. Jehovah. Ap. 4. II.

17 them: i. e. the enemies. **18 men**: Israel.

JEHOVAH. One of three places where, in A.V., this name is transliterated and printed in large capital letters (small in R.V.). See Ap. 48. Cp. Ex. 6. 3 and Isa. 26. 4.

MOST HIGH. Heb. *Elyōn.* Ap. 4. VI.

To the chief Musician. See Ap. 64. **upon Gittith** = relating to Gittith, a winepress—referring to the autumn Feast of Tabernacles. One of three winepress Psalms. See Ap. 65. IV. Cp. Pss. 7 and 80.

84 [For Structures see next page].

Title. A Psalm. Heb. *mizmōr.* See Ap. 65. XVII. **for the sons of Korah** = of, &c. The seventh of nine so ascribed. See note on Ps. 42, and Ap. 63. VIII. **1 How . . . !** Fig. *Ecphōnēsis.* Ap. 6. **amiable** = beloved. **tabernacles** = habitations. Heb. *mishkan* (Ap. 40. 2). Perhaps referring to the Mosaic (at Gibeon), and the Davidic (on Zion). **LORD of hosts.** Heb. Jehovah Sabaioth. Ap. 4. II. See note on 1 Sam. 1. 3.

b (p. 803) 2 °My soul longeth, yea, even fainteth for the °courts of °the LORD:
My heart and my flesh crieth out for the living °GOD.
c 3 °(Yea, the °sparrow hath found an house,
c And the swallow a °nest for herself, where she may lay her young,)
b °*Even* Thine °altars, O [1] LORD of Hosts, My King, and my °God.
a 4 °Blessed *are* they that dwell in Thy house: They will be °still praising Thee. °Selah.
G d 5 [4] Blessed *is* the °man whose strength *is* in Thee;
e In whose heart °*are* the ways *of them*.
f 6 *Who* passing through the valley °of Baca °make it °a well;
f The °rain also filleth the pools.
e 7 They go from strength to strength,
d °*Every one of them* °in Zion appeareth before [3] God.
E 8 O [1] LORD [3] God of Hosts, hear my prayer: Give ear, O °God of Jacob. °Selah.
E 9 Behold, O [3] God our °shield, And look upon the face of °Thine Anointed.
D F 10 For a day in Thy courts *is* better °than a thousand.
I had rather °be a doorkeeper in the house of my [3] God,
Than to dwell in the °tents of °wickedness.
G 11 For the [2] LORD [3] God °*is* a sun and [9] shield: The [2] LORD will give °grace and glory:
°No good *thing* will He withhold from them that walk uprightly.
12 O [1] LORD of hosts,
[4] Blessed *is* the [5] man that °trusteth in Thee.

°To the chief Musician.

84–89 (**A**[2], p. 789). THE SANCTUARY IN ITS RELATION TO JEHOVAH.

84 (**F**[1], p. 789). THE BLESSEDNESS OF ITS WORSHIPPERS. (*Introversion and Alternation.*)

F[1] | D | F | 1–4. Blessedness of dwellers.
  G | 5–7. Blessedness of approachers.
    E | 8. Prayer.
    E | 9. Prayer.
  D | *F* | 10. Blessedness of dwellers. "For". (Reason of F.)
    G | 11, 12. Blessedness of approachers. "For". (Reason of G.)

1–4 (F, above). BLESSEDNESS OF ITS DWELLERS. (*Introversion.*)

F | a | 1. "Thy tabernacles".
  b | 2. Desire for the courts of Jehovah.
    c | 3–. As the sparrow.
    c | –3–. As the swallow.
  b | –3. Desire for the altars of Jehovah.
a | 4. "Thy house".

2 My soul longeth=I, even I myself, long. Heb. *nephesh* (Ap. 13), for emphasis.
courts. Corresponding with "altars" (*v.* 3). See the Structure.
the LORD. Heb. Jehovah. Ap. 4. II.
GOD. Heb. El. Ap. 4. IV.
3 Yea, the sparrow, &c. These two lines are placed within a parenthesis. **sparrow**: or bird.
nest. Not in the altars. See note below.
Even Thine altars. Fig. *Ellipsis.* Ap. 6. Supply it by repeating the verb "found" from preceding clause ="[Even so have I found] Thine altars", &c. Nothing has "dropped out" from the text.
altars: i.e. the two altars; the brazen altar of burnt offering, and the golden altar of incense. Birds could not build their nests in these! These have no reference to the times of the Maccabees, but to Ex. 27. 1, and 30. 1. Cp. Num. 3. 31.
God. Heb. Elohim. Ap. 4. I.
4 Blessed. Cp. *vv.* 5, 12. See Ap. 63. VI. Fig. *Benedictio.* Ap. 6.
still praising. Cp. 1 Chron. 9. 33.
Selah. Connecting the dwellers in, and the approachers to, the House of Jehovah, with the common blessedness of all true worshippers. See Ap. 66. II.

5–7 (G, above). BLESSEDNESS OF APPROACHERS. (*Introversion.*)

G | d | 5–. Blessed is the man whose strength is in Thee. (Singular.)
  e | –5. [They] in whose heart are [Thy] ways. (Plural.)
    f | 6–. Those passing through the valley of the weeping, make it a place of springs. } The Valley.
    f | –6. The early rain filleth its pools. }
  e | 7–. They go from strength to strength. (Plural.)
d | –7. He (the "man" of *v.* 5, d) appeareth before God in Zion. (Singular.)

5 man: i.e. any one; not priest or Levite merely. Heb. *'ādām.* Ap. 14. I. **are the ways of them.** Supply Fig. *Ellipsis* (Ap. 6), "in whose heart are [Thy] highways" [leading thereunto]. **6 of Baca**=of weeping. All the ancient versions so render it. Cp. Judg. 2. 1, 5. **make it.** Sept. reads "He maketh it". **a well**=a place of springs. **rain**=the early rain. **7 Every one of them in Zion appeareth before God**=he appeareth before God in Zion. Note the sing., "he appeareth": i.e. "the man" of *v.* 5. See the Structure of *vv.* 5–7 (G), above. **in Zion.** See Ap. 68. The valley of *Baca* thus becomes the valley of *Berachah* (or blessing), 2 Chron. 20. 26. **8 God of Jacob.** Not Israel, but the God (Elohim, Ap. 4. I) Who met Jacob when he had nothing and deserved nothing (but wrath), and promised him everything: thus becoming "the God of all grace". **Selah.** Connecting the request for audience with the words of the prayer, and dividing the Psalm, structurally, into its two parts. **9 shield**: i.e. God's provision in Messiah. He is our Shield (Gen. 15. 1). Faith's shield (Eph. 6. 16). This shield includes: (1) Favour (5. 12); (2) Salvation (18. 35); (3) Truth (91. 4). And "Favour" includes Life (30. 5); Mercy (Isa. 60. 10); Preservation (86. 2); Security (41. 11); Remembrance and Salvation (106. 4). Cp. 115. 9–11. **Thine Anointed**=Thy Messiah. Not on us. **10 than a thousand.** Supply Ellipsis (Ap. 6) by adding "[elsewhere]". **be a doorkeeper**=to stand at the threshold. **tents**=habitations. **wickedness**=lawlessness. Heb. *rāshā'.* Ap. 44. x. **11 is a sun.** Fig. *Metaphor.* Ap. 6. The only occurrence, in the Psalms, of this metaphor. It is used of Messiah, Mal. 4. 2 (Heb. text, 3. 20). **grace and glory.** Not the former without the latter (Rom. 8. 29, 30). The former is the flower, the latter the fruit. **No good thing, &c.** Fig. *Tapeinōsis* (Ap. 6)=every good thing, beyond all mention, will He give. **12 trusteth**=places his confidence. Heb. *bāṭaḥ.* Ap. 69. I. **To the chief Musician.** Ap. 64.

85 °A Psalm °for the sons of Korah.

F² H (p. 804) 1 °LORD, Thou hast been favourable unto °Thy land:
Thou hast °brought back the captivity of °Jacob.
2 Thou hast forgiven the °iniquity of Thy People,
Thou hast °covered all their °sin. °Selah.
3 Thou hast taken away all Thy wrath:
Thou hast turned *thyself* from the fierceness of Thine anger.

J g 4 °Turn us, O °God of our salvation,
And cause Thine anger toward us to cease.

h 5 Wilt Thou be angry with us for ever?
Wilt Thou draw out Thine anger to all generations?
6 Wilt Thou not revive us again:
That Thy people may rejoice in Thee?

J g 7 Shew us Thy °mercy, O [1] LORD,
And grant us Thy salvation.

h 8 I will hear what °GOD [1] the LORD will speak:
For He will speak °peace unto His People, and to His °saints:
But let them °not turn again to folly.

H 9 Surely His salvation *is* nigh them that fear Him;
That °glory may dwell in our [1] land.
10 Mercy and truth are °met together;
Righteousness and peace have °kissed *each other*.
11 Truth shall spring out of the °earth;
And righteousness shall look down from heaven.
12 Yea, [1] the LORD shall give *that which is* good;
And °our land shall yield her increase.
13 Righteousness shall go before Him;
And shall set *us* in the way of His steps.

86 °A Prayer °of David.

G¹ K (p. 804) 1 Bow down Thine ear, O °LORD, °hear me:
For I *am* °poor and needy.
2 Preserve my °soul; for I *am* °holy:
O Thou my °God, save Thy servant that °trusteth in Thee.
3 °Be merciful unto me, O °LORD*:
For I cry unto Thee °daily.
4 Rejoice the [2] soul of Thy servant:
For unto Thee, O [3] LORD*, do I lift up [2] my soul.
5 For Thou, [3] LORD*, *art* good, and ready to forgive;
And °plenteous in °mercy unto all them that call upon Thee.
6 Give ear, O [1] LORD, unto my prayer;
And attend to the voice of my supplications.

L i 7 In the day of my trouble I will call upon Thee:

k For Thou wilt answer me.

M 8 Among the °gods *there is* none like unto Thee, O [3] LORD*;
Neither *are there any works* like unto Thy works. *M*

9 All nations whom Thou hast made shall come and worship before Thee, O [3] LORD*; *L i*
And °shall glorify Thy name.

---

85 (F², p. 789). PRAYER FOR THE LAND OF THE SANCTUARY. (*Introversion and Alternation.*)

F² | H | 1-3. Mercies to the Land.
  J | g | 4. Prayer.
    h | 5, 6. Questions.
  J | *g* | 7. Prayer.
    h | 8. Answer.
| *H* | 9-13. Mercies to the Land.

Title. A Psalm. Heb. *mizmōr*. Ap. 65. XVII.
for the sons of Korah. The eighth of eleven so ascribed. See note on Ps. 42, Title, and Ap. 63. VIII.
1 LORD. Heb. Jehovah. Ap. 4. II.
Thy land. Cp. connection with "People" (*v.* 2), as in Deut. 32. 43. Note "our" in *v.* 12.
brought back the captivity = restored the fortunes, as in 126. 1. Job 42. 10. No reference to the Babylonian captivity, but to the restoration of David's fortunes after Absalom's revolt.
Jacob. Refers to the natural seed, and to the earthly and material standpoint. See notes on Gen. 32. 28; 43. 6; 45. 26, 28.
2 iniquity = perverseness. Heb. *'āvāh*. Ap. 44. iv.
covered = concealed. Heb. *kāṣāh*; not *kāphar*, to atone. **sin.** Heb. *chāṭā'*. Ap. 44. i.
Selah. Connecting forgiveness with (as being the basis of) millennial blessing. See Ap. 66. II.
4 Turn us. Cp. "Thou hast turned" (*vv.* 2, 3).
God. Heb. Elohim. Ap. 4. I.
7 mercy = lovingkindness, or grace.
8 GOD. Heb. El. Ap. 4. IV.
peace. Referring to the war with Absalom.
saints = graced ones.
not turn again: i.e. rebel, as in Absalom's case.
9 glory may dwell: i.e. the glory of Jehovah's presence in the Shekinah, in the Tabernacle.
10 met . . . kissed. Fig. *Prosopopœia*. Ap. 6.
11 earth = land. Same word as *vv.* 1, 9, 12.
12 our land, &c. Note "Thy land" in *v.* 1. Cp. 67. 6.

86 (G¹, p. 789). PRAYER IN THE SANCTUARY. MESSIAH'S HUMILIATION. THE SECRET OF THE BLESSING. (*Introversion and Alternation.*)

G¹ | K | 1-6. Prayer.
  L | i | 7-. "I will call".
    k | -7. Reason. "For".
      M | 8-. Jehovah incomparable.
      M | -8. His works incomparable.
  L | *i* | 9. "All nations shall worship".
    k | 10. Reason. "For
| *K* | 11-17. Prayer.

Title. A Prayer = An Intercession, or Hymn. Cp. 72. 20, referring to the whole of Book II. Heb. *Tᵉphillāh*. See Ap. 63. I.
of David. The only Psalm in this third book ascribed to David. Refers to David's Son and Lord.
1 LORD. Heb. Jehovah. Ap. 4. II.
hear = answer.
poor = helpless. Heb. *'ebyōn*. See note on Prov. 6. 11.
2 soul. Heb. *nephesh*. Ap. 13.
holy = one whom Thou favourest.
God. Heb. Elohim. Ap. 4. I.
trusteth = confideth. Heb. *bāṭaḥ*. Ap. 69. I.
3 Be merciful = Show me favour, or Be gracious.
LORD*. One of the 134 places where the *Sōpherim* say they changed Jehovah to Adonai. See Ap. 32.
daily = all the day. **5 plenteous.** Cp. Ex. 34. 6.
mercy = lovingkindness, or grace.
8 gods. Heb. *'ĕlohim* = judges. See note on Ex. 21. 6; 22. 8, 9. **9 shall glorify.** Cp. Isa. 66. 23.

k (p. 804) 10 °For Thou *art* great, and °doest wondrous things:
Thou *art* ²God alone.

K l (p. 805) 11 Teach me Thy way, O ¹LORD; I will walk in Thy truth:
°Unite my heart to °fear Thy °name.
12 I will praise Thee, O ³LORD* my ²God, with all my heart:
And I will glorify Thy ¹¹name for evermore.

m 13 For great *is* Thy ⁵mercy toward me:
And Thou hast delivered ²my soul from °the lowest °hell.

n 14 O ²God, the proud are risen against me,
And the assemblies of violent *men* have sought after ²my soul;

n And have not set Thee before them.

m 15 But Thou, O ³LORD*, *art* a °GOD °full of compassion, and gracious,
Longsuffering, and plenteous in ⁵mercy and truth.

l 16 O turn unto me, and °have mercy upon me;
Give Thy strength unto Thy servant,
And save the son of Thine handmaid.
17 Shew me a token for good;
That they which hate me may see *it*, and be ashamed:
Because Thou, ¹LORD, hast holpen me, and comforted me.

87 °A Psalm *or* °Song °for the sons of Korah.

F² N¹ (p. 805) 1 °His foundation *is* in the °holy mountains.
2 °The LORD loveth the gates of °Zion
More than all the dwellings of °Jacob.

O¹ 3 Glorious things are spoken of thee,
O city of °God. °Selah.

N² 4 I will make mention of °Rahab and Babylon to them that know me:
Behold Philistia, and Tyre, with °Ethiopia;
This *man* was born there.

O² 5 And °of ²Zion it shall be said, "This and that °man was born in her:
And °the HIGHEST Himself shall establish her."

N³ 6 The ²LORD shall count, when He °writeth up the °people,
°*That* this *man* was born there. °Selah.

O³ 7 As well °the singers as °the players on instruments °*shall be there:*
All my °springs *are* in thee.

°A Song *or* Psalm for the sons of Korah, °to the chief Musician °upon Mahalath Leannoth.

10 For. Cp. *v.* 5 in the Structure. **doest** = a doer.

86. 11-17 (*K*, p. 804). PRAYER. (*Introversion.*)

K | l | 11, 12. Prayer, and consequence.
m | 13. Plea. Goodness of God.
n | 14-. Man's wickedness. Man-ward.
n | -14. Man's wickedness. God-ward.
m | 15. Pleas. Goodness of God.
l | 16, 17. Prayer, and object.

11 Unite my heart. Sept., Syr., and Vulg. read "Let my heart rejoice".
fear = revere. **name.** See note on 20. 1.
13 the lowest hell = *Sheōl* beneath.
hell. Heb. Sheōl. Ap. 35. Not the language of "Semitic heathenism", but the inspired revelation of *Divine eschatology.*
15 GOD. Heb. El. Ap. 4. IV.
full of compassion, &c. Cp. Ex. 34. 6.
16 have mercy upon = show favour, or be gracious to.

87 (F², p. 789). THE BLESSEDNESS OF THE DWELLERS IN ZION. (*Repeated Alternations.*)

F² | N¹ | 1, 2. Other dwellings spoken of.
O¹ | 3. Zion spoken to.
N² | 4. Other nations spoken of.
O² | 5. Zion spoken to.
N³ | 6. Other peoples spoken of.
O³ | 7. Zion spoken to.

Title. A Psalm. Heb. *mizmōr.* Ap. 65. XVII.
Song. Heb. *shīr.* Ap. 65. XXIII.
for the sons of Korah: i. e. of or by them. This title is repeated in the sub-scription after *v.* 7, to emphasise the occasion of its use in bringing up the Ark to Zion by David (951 B.C. a Sabbatic year). See note there, and on Title of Ps. 24.
1 His: i. e. Jehovah's (which He has laid in Zion).
holy. See note on Ex. 3. 5.
2 The LORD. Heb. Jehovah. Ap. 4. II.
Zion. See Ap. 68.
Jacob. Israel viewed in connection with the natural seed, and with material blessings. See notes on Gen. 32. 28; 43. 6; 45. 26, 28.
3 God. Heb. *hā-'Elohim* = the [true] God. Ap. 4. I.
Selah. Connecting the first alternation with the second, showing that it is to be a repeated alternation.
4 Rahab = pride, or haughtiness. Used as name for Egypt (by Fig. *Polyonymia*, Ap. 6), as in 89. 10; Isa. 51. 9. Cp. Job 9. 13 and 26. 12; not the same word as in Joshua 2.
Ethiopia. Supply Ellipsis of the verb "say": "Tyre with Ethiopia [say]" this, &c.
5 of = to. **man.** Heb. *'ish.* Ap. 14. II.
the HIGHEST = the MOST HIGH. Heb. *'Elyōn.* Ap. 4. VI.
6 writeth up = enrolleth.
people = peoples.
That. Instead of "*That*", supply "[and say] this one", &c.
Selah. Connecting the last repetition of the alternation, and completing the Structure. Thus, both the Selahs in this Psalm are structural. (Ap. 66. II).
7 the singers = they that shout.
the players on instruments = they that dance, as in bringing up the Ark. See note on the sub-scription.

shall be there. Supply *Ellipsis* (Ap. 6): "[shall say of Zion]". **springs** = fountains: i. e. fountains of delight. **A Song, &c.** Repeated from the title. Cp. 45 for a similar repetition. **to the chief Musician.** See Ap. 64. **upon Mahalath Leannoth** = relating to the shoutings with dancings in bringing up the Ark to Zion (2 Sam. 6. 12-15; and 1 Chron. 15. 25-29). As in Judg. 21. 21, 23 (cp. R.V.), and see Ap. 65. X.

88 °Maschil of °Heman the °Ezrahite.

G^2 P (p. 806) 1 O °LORD °God of my salvation,
I have cried day *and* night before Thee:
2 Let my prayer come before Thee:
Incline Thine ear unto my cry;
Q R 3 For my °soul is full of troubles:
And my life draweth nigh unto °the grave.
4 I °am counted with them that go down into the pit:
°I am as a °man *that hath* no strength:
5 °Free among the dead,
Like the slain that lie in °the grave,
Whom Thou rememberest no more:
And they are cut off from Thy hand.
6 Thou hast laid me in the lowest pit,
In darkness, in the deeps.
S 7 Thy wrath lieth hard °upon me,
And Thou hast afflicted *me* with all Thy waves. °Selah.
T 8 Thou hast put away mine acquaintance far from me;
Thou hast made me an abomination unto them:
I am shut up, and I cannot come forth.
9 Mine eye mourneth by reason of affliction:
P o [1] LORD, I have called daily upon Thee,
I have stretched out my hands unto Thee.
p 10 Wilt Thou shew wonders to the dead?
Shall the °dead arise *and* praise thee? °Selah.
11 Shall Thy lovingkindness be declared in [5] the grave?
Or Thy faithfulness in destruction?
12 Shall Thy wonders be known in the dark?
And Thy righteousness in the land of forgetfulness?
o 13 But unto Thee have I cried, O [1] LORD;
And in the morning shall my prayer °prevent Thee.
p 14 [1] LORD, why castest Thou off [3] my soul?
Why hidest Thou Thy °face from me?
Q R 15 I *am* afflicted and ready to die from *my* youth up:
While I suffer Thy terrors I am distracted.
S 16 Thy fierce wrath goeth °over me;
Thy terrors have cut me off.
17 They came round about me °daily like water;
They compassed me about together.
T 18 Lover and friend hast Thou °put far from me,
And mine acquaintance into darkness.

89 °Maschil of °Ethan the °Ezrahite.

F^3 U (p. 806) 1 I will sing of the °mercies of °the LORD for ever:
With my mouth will I make known Thy °faithfulness to all generations.

88 (G^2, p. 789). INSTRUCTION. MESSIAH'S HUMILIATION, THE SECRET SOURCE OF THE BLESSING. (*Alternation.*)

G^2 | P | 1, 2. Prayer.
  Q | R | 3–6. Dissolution near.
    S | 7. Wrath. Waves.
    T | 8, 9–. Desolation.
P | –9–14. Prayer.
  Q | R | 15. Dissolution near.
    S | 16, 17. Wrath. Waves.
    T | 18. Desolation.

Title. Maschil = Instruction. The eleventh of thirteen so named. See note on Title, Ps. 32, and Ap. 65. XI. The title, rearranged as above, removes the difficulty of this Psalm being ascribed to two different writers.

Heman. Celebrated for wisdom (with Ethan, 89), 1 Kings 4. 31. 1 Chron. 6. 33, 44; 25. 4. He was a Kohathite, while Ethan was a Merarite. See Ap. 63. VIII, and 64.

Ezrahite. Put for Zerahite. Probably the name of a district. Cp. the case of Elkanah (1 Sam. 1. 1).

The Psalm is prophetic of Messiah's humiliation, corresponding with Ps. 86. See the Structure, p. 789.

1 LORD. Heb. Jehovah. Ap. 4. II.

God. Heb. Elohim. Ap. 4. I.

3 soul. Heb. *nephesh* (Ap. 13), for emphasis.

the grave. Heb. *Sheōl.* Ap. 35

4 am = have been.

I am = I am become.

man. Heb. *geber.* Ap. 4. IV.

5 Free = Set free: i. e. by death, so as to be free from the Law (according to the Talmud, *Shabbath*, fol. 151. B).

the grave = sepulchre. Heb. *ķebēr.* See Ap. 35.

7 upon me. Same word as "over me", *v.* 16, with which the member corresponds.

Selah. Connecting *v.* 6 with its amplification in *vv.* 8, 9.

–9–14 (*P*, above). PRAYER. (*Alternation.*)

P | o | –9. Declaratory.
  p | 10–12. Interrogatory.
o | 13. Declaratory.
  p | 14. Interrogatory.

10 dead. Heb. *Rephaim*, who have no resurrection. See note on Isa. 26. 14, where it is rendered "deceased"; and 19, where it is rendered "the dead". Cp. Ap. 23 and 25.

Selah. Connecting *v.* 10 with its amplification in *vv.* 11–13. Cp. Selah, *v.* 7. See Ap. 66. II.

13 prevent = come before.

14 face. Fig. *Anthrōpopatheia.* Ap. 6.

16 over me. Same word as "upon me", *v.* 7.

17 daily = all the day.

18 put far from me. Cp. *v.* 8, the corresponding member.

89 (F^3, p. 789). INSTRUCTION AS TO BLESSING IN THE SANCTUARY. (*Introversion and Alternation.*)

F^3 | U | 1. Eternal praises.
  V | W | 2–4. Ethan reminds Jehovah of His covenant with David.
    X | 5–18. Ethan praises Jehovah's faithfulness.
  V | W | 19–37. Ethan reminds Jehovah of His covenant with David.
    X | 38–51. Ethan deplores Jehovah's visitation.
U | 52. Eternal praises.

Title. Maschil = Instruction. The twelfth of thirteen so named (the thirteenth being Ps. 142). See note on Ps. 32, and Ap. 65. XI.

Ethan. Mentioned with Heman (Ps. 88). A Merarite (1 Chron. 6. 44; 15. 17). He seems to have another name, "Jeduthun" (1 Chron. 25. 1, 3, 6; 16. 41, 42). The only Psalm ascribed to Ethan. See note on *v.* 30, and 88, Title.

Ezrahite. See note on 88, Title. Cp. the case of Elkanah (1 Sam. 1. 1). **1 mercies** = lovingkindnesses. Pl. of majesty = the great lovingkindness. **the LORD.** Heb. Jehovah. Ap. 4. II. **faithfulness** = truth. Heb. *'ĕmūnāh.* Seven times reiterated in this Psalm: *vv.* 1, 2, 5, 8, 24, 33, 49 ("in thy truth").

V W **2** For °I have said, °"Mercy shall be built up for ever:
Thy [1] faithfulness shalt Thou establish in the very heavens."
3 I have °made a °covenant with My chosen,
I have °sworn unto David My servant,
4 Thy seed will I establish for ever,
And build up thy throne to all generations. °Selah.

X q **5** And the heavens shall praise Thy wonders, O [1] LORD:
Thy [1] faithfulness also in the congregation of the °saints.

r **6** For °who in the °heaven can be compared unto [1] the LORD?
Who among the °sons of the mighty can be likened unto [1] the LORD?
7 °GOD is greatly to be feared in the °assembly of the [5] saints,
And to be had in reverence of all *them that are* about Him.

q **8** O [1] LORD °God of hosts,
[6] Who *is* a strong °LORD, like unto Thee?
Or to Thy [1] faithfulness round about Thee?
9 Thou rulest the raging of the sea:
When the waves thereof arise, Thou stillest them.
10 Thou hast broken °Rahab in pieces, as one that is slain;
Thou hast scattered Thine enemies with Thy strong °arm.
11 The heavens *are* Thine, the earth also *is* Thine:
As for °the world and the fulness thereof, Thou hast founded them.
12 The north and the south Thou hast created them:
°Tabor and Hermon shall rejoice in Thy name.
13 Thou hast a mighty [10] arm:
Strong is Thy °hand, *and* high is Thy right °hand.
14 °Justice and judgment *are* the °habitation of Thy throne:
[2] Mercy and truth shall go before Thy °face.
15 °Blessed *is* the People that know °the joyful sound:
They shall walk, O [1] LORD, in the light of Thy °countenance.
16 In °Thy name shall they rejoice all the day:
And in Thy righteousness shall they be exalted.
17 For Thou *art* the °glory of their strength:
And in Thy favour our °horn shall be exalted.

r **18** For [1] the LORD *is* our °defence;
And the Holy One of Israel *is* our king.

V W s **19** Then Thou spakest in vision to Thy Holy One,
And saidst, "I have laid help upon *one that is* mighty;
I have exalted *one* chosen out of the People.
20 °**I have found David My servant;**
With My holy oil have I anointed him:

2 I have said. Some codices, with Sept. and Vulg., read "Thou hast said". Cp. *v.* 19 (*W*, below). The words of Ethan, reminding Jehovah of His covenant with David.

Mercy=Lovingkindness, or grace. Note "Mercy" (*v.* 2); "covenant" (*v.* 3); "seed" (*v.* 4); repeated in *W*, below (*vv.* 19-32 and *vv.* 33-37). **3 made**=solemnised.

covenant. See 2 Sam. 7, where Jehovah, being the only party, the covenant is *unconditional*, and=a "promise" among "the sure mercies of David", &c. But it looks beyond David.

sworn. See 2 Sam. 7. 11, &c.; the word is not used there, but the terms of the oath are given.

Selah. Connecting the recital of Jehovah's covenant with the praise offered for it. See Ap. 66. II.

89 5-18 (X, p. 806). **PRAISE FOR JEHOVAH'S FAITHFULNESS.** (*Alternation.*)

X | q | 5. Jehovah addressed.
  r | 6, 7. Reason. "For".
  q | 8-17. Jehovah addressed.
  r | 18. Reason. "For".

5 saints=holy ones, or angels. See preceding line, &c.

6 who. Fig. *Erotēsis.* Ap. 6. This is the cry of all His saints. See note on Ex. 15. 11.

heaven=sky. Same word as *v.* 37.

sons of the mighty=sons of *Elīm*=the angels.

7 GOD. Heb. El. Ap. 4. IV.

assembly=secret conclave.

8 God. Heb. Elohim. Ap. 4. I.

LORD. Heb. Jah. Ap. 4. III.

10 Rahab=Egypt. See note on 87. 4.

arm. Fig. *Anthrōpopatheia.* Ap. 6.

11 the world. Heb. *tēbēl*=the world as inhabited.

12 Tabor and Hermon. West and east of the Holy Land; and, with north and south, completing the four points of the compass.

13 hand. Fig. *Anthrōpopatheia.* Ap. 6.

14 Justice=Righteousness.

habitation=foundation.

face. Fig. *Anthrōpopatheia.* Ap. 6.

15 Blessed = Happy. Fig. *Beatitudo.* Ap. 6. See Ap. 63. VI.

the joyful sound. Of the trumpet's assembling sound. Lev. 23.

countenance=face. See *v.* 14.

16 Thy name=Thyself. See note on 20. 1.

17 glory=beauty.

horn. Many codices, with four early printed editions, read "horns" (pl.); but seven early printed editions read sing.

18 defence=shield. Heb. *gānan*, to cover, or protect.

19-37 (*W*, p. 806). **ETHAN REMINDS JEHOVAH OF HIS COVENANT WITH DAVID.** (*Extended Alternation.*)

W | s | 19-27. David. "Faithfulness" (*v.* 2).
  t | 28. Covenant (*v.* 3).
  u | 29-32. Seed (*v.* 4).
  s | 33. David. "Faithfulness (*v.* 2).
  t | 34, 35. Covenant (*v.* 3).
  u | 36, 37. Seed (*v.* 4).

20 I have found, &c. Quoted in Acts 13. 22.

22 wickedness. Heb. *'avvāl.* Ap. 44. vi.

23 foes=adversaries.

21 With whom My hand shall be established:
Mine arm also shall strengthen him.
22 The enemy shall not exact upon him;
Nor the son of °wickedness afflict him.
23 And I will beat down his °foes before his face,
And plague them that hate him.
24 But My [1] faithfulness and My [2] mercy *shall be* with him:
And in [16] My name shall his horn be exalted.

25 I will set his hand also in the sea,
And his right hand in the rivers.
26 He shall cry unto Me, 'Thou *art* my father,
My [7]GOD, and the rock of my salvation.'
27 Also I will make him *My* firstborn,
°Higher than the kings of the earth.
t **28** My [2]mercy will I keep for him for evermore,
(p. 807) And My covenant shall stand fast with him.
u **29** His seed also will I make *to endure* for ever,
And his throne as the days of heaven.
30 °If his °children forsake My law,
°And walk not in My judgments;
31 If they °break My statutes,
°And keep not My commandments;
32 °Then will I visit their °transgression with the rod,
And their °iniquity with stripes.
s **33** °Nevertheless My °lovingkindness will I not utterly take from him,
Nor suffer My [1]faithfulness to fail.
t **34** My covenant will I not °break,
Nor °alter the thing that is gone out of My lips.
35 Once have I sworn by My holiness
That I will not lie unto David.
u **36** °**His seed shall endure for ever,**
And his throne as the sun before Me.
37 It shall be established for ever as the moon,
And *as* °a faithful witness in [6]heaven."
°Selah.
X Y[1] v **38** But Thou hast cast off and abhorred,
(p. 808) Thou hast been wroth with °Thine anointed.
w **39** Thou hast °made void the covenant of Thy servant:
Thou hast profaned his crown *by casting it* to the ground.
x **40** Thou hast broken down all his hedges;
Thou hast brought his strong holds to ruin.
y **41** All that pass by the way spoil him:
He is a reproach to his neighbours.
y **42** Thou hast set up the right hand of his adversaries;
Thou hast made all his enemies to rejoice.
x **43** Thou hast also turned the edge of his sword,
And hast not made him to stand in the battle.
w **44** Thou hast made his glory to cease,
And cast his throne down to the ground.
v **45** The days of his youth hast Thou shortened:
Thou hast covered him with shame. °Selah.
Y[2] z **46** How long, [1]LORD? wilt Thou hide thyself for ever?
°Shall Thy wrath burn like fire?
a **47** Remember how short my °time is:
Wherefore hast Thou made all °men in vain?

27 Higher = MOST HIGH. Heb. *'Elyōn*. Ap. 4. VI. This looks forward to Immanuel (Isa. 7. 13–15; 9. 6, 7. Mic. 5. 2).

30 If his children, &c. Ethan refers to the very words of warning given to Solomon (1 Kings 9. 6, 7; cp. 11. 11–13), which, with 2 Sam. 7, should be read with this Psalm. Ethan (we may suppose) outlived Solomon, and saw the break-up of the kingdom; and left this Psalm for Instruction (*Maschil*) for all future time.

children = sons.

And walk not. Fig. *Pleonasm* (Ap. 6), for emphasis.

31 break = profane.

And keep not. Fig. *Pleonasm* (Ap. 6), for emphasis.

32 Then will I. Cp. 2 Sam. 7. 14.

transgression = revolt. Heb. *pāsha'*. Ap. 44. ix.

iniquity. Heb. *'āvah*. Ap. 44. iv.

33 Nevertheless. Fig. *Palinodia*. Ap. 6. Cp. 2 Sam. 7. 15. **lovingkindness** = grace.

34 break = profane. **alter** = violate.

36 His seed, &c. Cp. John 12. 34.

37 a faithful witness: i. e. the sun (cp. *v.* 36). See note on "testimony" (Ps. 19. 7). Rev. 1. 5; 3. 14.

Selah. Connecting the above solemn warning with the fulfilment in the visitation of judgment in the next member. See Ap. 66. II.

89. 38–51 (*X*, p. 806). ETHAN DEPLORES THE DIVINE VISITATION. (*Division.*)

X | Y[1] | 38–45. Visitation.
| Y[2] | 46–51. Expostulation.

38–45 (Y[1], above). VISITATION. (*Introversion.*)

Y[1] | v | 38. Rejection.
w | 39. Degradation.
x | 40. Desolation.
y | 41. Enemies. Spoil.
y | 42. Enemies. Rejoice.
x | 43. Desolation.
w | 44. Degradation.
v | 45. Rejection.

38 Thine = Thine own.

39 made void = disowned only here and in Lam. 2. 7.

45 Selah. Connecting the visitation with the prayer for its removal. See Ap. 66. II.

46–51 (Y[2], above). EXPOSTULATION. (*Alternation.*)

Y[2] | z | 46. Complaint.
a | 47, 48. "Remember". Frailty.
z | 49. Complaint.
a | 50, 51. "Remember". Reproach.

46 Shall. Supply Ellipsis from preceding line: "[How long] shall", &c.

47 time = lifetime. **men** = sons of Adam. Ap. 14. I.

48 man = strong man. Heb. *geber*. Ap. 14. IV.

soul. Heb. *nephesh*. Ap. 13.

hand. Put by Fig. *Metonymy* (of Cause), Ap. 6, for the power exercised by it. **the grave.** Heb. *Sheōl*. Ap. 35.

Selah. Connecting the fact of man's frailty (even of the strongest) with the renewed and increased fervour of his complaint. See Ap. 66. II.

49 LORD*. One of the 134 places where the *Sōpherim* altered Jehovah to Adonai. See Ap. 32.

swarest. See 2 Sam. 7, and note on *v.* 3.

truth = faithfulness. Same word as rendered "faithfulness" in *v.* 1. Here, the last of the seven occurrences.

48 What °man *is he that* liveth, and shall not see death?
Shall he deliver his °soul from the °hand of °the grave? °Selah.
49 °LORD*, where *are* Thy former lovingkindnesses, *z*
Which Thou °swarest unto David in Thy °truth?

a (p. 808)

50 Remember, [49] LORD *, the reproach of Thy °servants;
How I do bear in my bosom *the* °*reproach of* all the °mighty °people;
51 Wherewith Thine enemies have reproached, O [1] LORD;
Wherewith they have reproached the footsteps of °Thine Anointed.

U (p. 806)

52 °Blessed *be* [1] the LORD for evermore.
°Amen, and Amen.

50 servants. Some codices, with Syr., read "servant" (sing.).
reproach. Aram. reads "insult". Cp. 69. 9. Ezek. 36. 15. Rom. 15. 3.
mighty people = many peoples: i.e. the enemies of Israel. **people** = peoples. No Art.
51 Thine Anointed = Thy Messiah.
52 Blessed. Fig. *Benedictio*, not *Beatitido*. Not the same word as in *v.* 15. Cp. Rom. 1. 25; 9. 5. 2 Cor. 11. 31.
Amen, and Amen. This closes the third (or Leviticus) book of the Psalms. Cp. the endings of the first book (Ps. 41), and the second book (Ps. 72).

NOTES ON THE STRUCTURE OF THE FOURTH BOOK (p. 810).

NUMBERS is the name that man has given to the fourth book of the Pentateuch, on account of the *numberings* recorded in chapters 1—3 and 26. The name is from the Latin Vulgate (*Numeri*), which is again a translation of the name given by the Septuagint Translators (*Arithmoi*). The title in the Hebrew Canon is *b^emidbar*, "IN THE WILDERNESS" (the fifth word in *v.* 1, Hebrew). This title covers *all* the events recorded in this book. "Numbers", therefore, is the Book of the WILDERNESS; and its types are wilderness types, or types of our pilgrimage.

In the Numbers-Book of the Psalms we find the corresponding subject. It opens with Psalm 90, "A prayer of Moses"—the man of the wilderness! Its teaching, like that of the other books, is Dispensational, with the EARTH as its central thought. God's counsels and purposes are celebrated with regard to the earth, and the nations of the earth, from the ruin to the glory; as we have seen them set forth in the other books with regard to (1) Man, (2) Israel, and (3) the Sanctuary.

Sin has come into the world, and ruined, not merely man, but the earth itself: "Cursed *is* the ground for thy sake." Sin has made the paradise of God a wilderness, and death has filled it with sorrow and sadness. There is no hope for the earth, no hope for the nations of the earth, and no hope for creation, apart from Jehovah. The first and second Psalms (90 and 91) set this forth, and give, as it were, the key-note and epitome of the whole book. Its figures are from this wilderness-world; as mountains, hills, floods, grass, pestilence, trees, &c., which the reader will notice for himself. Happiness for the world will be found only when He, "Whose right it is", shall come again to reign and "judge the world in righteousness". In Christ, the coming King, not only Israel, but all the nations of the earth, will be blessed. This is the theme of the book. (See note on Psalm 96. 11.)

It consists, like Book III, of *seventeen* Psalms, all of which are anonymous (though not all without titles) except 90 (and 91), Moses's, and 101, 103, which are David's.

Of the Divine Titles in this Fourth Book, Jehovah (Ap. 4. II) occurs 126 times, and Elohim (Ap. 4. I), 31 (10 of which are with Jehovah). El occurs 6 times.

Psalms 90 and 91[1] are evidently one Psalm in two parts, written by Moses at the beginning of the thirty-eight years of penal wanderings in the wilderness (in 1490 B.C.), which are the subject of this Fourth Book.

Psalm 90 is suggested by, and occupied with, the sorrows of the vast multitude (associated with the 603,550 "men of war") in the wilderness, *numbered*, and sentenced to death; all from 20 years old and upward (Num. 14. 29).

It is of these that verses 9 and 10 speak.

If a man was 20 when he was numbered (for the war) he died at or before 60
" 30 " " " " " " 70
" 40 " " " " " " 80

The average age would be 30, hence verse 10.

Psalm 91, on the other hand, presents the contrast of those under "the shadow of the Almighty". The deliverance of "the Church in the wilderness", from the causes and instrumentalities of death for the countless condemned thousands (in Psalm 90) whose carcases were to fall in the wilderness, is set forth at length.

If a man was 19 when the penal wanderings began, he would be 57 (19 + 38) at the close.

If a lad of 10, he would be 48; and so on.

This Psalm was therefore written for the comfort of "the Church in the wilderness" during the 40 years. Towards the close, myriads must have been cut off by the various agencies named:

The terror by night.
The arrow that flieth by day.
The pestilence in darkness.
The destruction (contagion) at noonday.
The lion and adder.

With regard to the latter, in the night journeyings (Num. 9. 21) they would be exposed to danger and death from the adders which infest the district, and from the attacks of wild beasts. From all of these the *trusters* would be delivered.

They would see with their eyes "the reward of the wicked"—thousands dying around, yet nothing permitted to assail them.

If *tents* is right in verse 10, this is confirmation that Moses wrote this Psalm, and at, or about, the time suggested—viz. 1490 B.C.

[1] If 91 be a Psalm of Moses (following Psalm 90), then *all* the Scriptures quoted in our Lord's temptation (even that which the evil one tried to quote) were from the writings of Moses!

90—106 (𝔅², p. 720). THE FOURTH, OR NUMBERS BOOK*. THE EARTH AND THE NATIONS.

(Division, with Prologue and Epilogue.)

PROLOGUE | **90.** THE REST. LOST, AND NEEDED.

𝔅² | A¹ | **91—94.** REST FOR THE EARTH DESIRED. NO HOPE FOR IT TILL "THE WICKED CEASE FROM TROUBLING".

A² | **95—100.** REST FOR THE EARTH ANTICIPATED. NOTE THE CENTRAL VERSE OF THE PSALTER (96. 11) AND THE REASON (96. 13).

A³ | **101—105.** REST FOR THE EARTH CELEBRATED. JEHOVAH'S THRONE IN THE HEAVENS, AND HIS KINGDOM OVER ALL (103. 19).

EPILOGUE | **106.** THE REST. HOW LOST, AND VALUED.

91–94 (A¹, above). REST FOR THE EARTH DESIRED.

(Alternation.)

A¹ | B | **91.** REST, ONLY IN JEHOVAH IN A PERISHING WORLD; AND, THE SECRET PLACE OF THE MOST HIGH THE ONLY PLACE OF SAFETY IN IT.

C | **92.** PRAYER FOR THAT "SABBATH-KEEPING" (YET TO COME, Heb. 4. 9) WHEN ALL "WORKERS OF INIQUITY" SHALL BE CUT OFF (*vv.* 7, 9), AND THE RIGHTEOUS SHALL FLOURISH (*v.* 12) IN JEHOVAH THEIR "ROCK" AND "DEFENCE" (*v.* 15).

B | **93.** REST, ONLY IN JEHOVAH. HIS THRONE WHEN ESTABLISHED WILL BE THE PLACE OF SAFETY. (See note on 93. 5.)

C | **94.** PRAYER FOR REST, TO JEHOVAH, "THE JUDGE OF THE EARTH", TO CUT OFF ALL "WORKERS OF INIQUITY" (*vv.* 4, 16, 23), AND TO GIVE THE RIGHTEOUS REST (*vv.* 13–15) IN JEHOVAH, THEIR "ROCK" AND "DEFENCE" (*v.* 22).

95–100 (A², above). REST FOR THE EARTH ANTICIPATED.

(Introversion and Alternation.)

A² | D | **95.** WORSHIP, IN VIEW OF REST ANTICIPATED. HIS "PEOPLE" AND "SHEEP" (*v.* 7) TO "COME BEFORE HIS PRESENCE WITH THANKSGIVING" (*v.* 2). REASON: "JEHOVAH IS GREAT" (*v.* 3).

E | F | **96.** A SUMMONS TO SING THE "NEW SONG". "FOR HE COMETH" (JUDGMENT).

G | **97.** THE NEW SONG. "JEHOVAH REIGNETH"

E | *F* | **98.** A SUMMONS TO SING THE "NEW SONG". "FOR HE COMETH" (JUDGMENT).

G | **99.** THE NEW SONG. "JEHOVAH REIGNETH".

D | **100.** WORSHIP, IN VIEW OF REST ANTICIPATED. HIS "PEOPLE" AND "SHEEP" (*v.* 3). TO "COME BEFORE HIS PRESENCE WITH SINGING" (*v.* 2). REASON: "JEHOVAH IS GOOD" (*v.* 5).

101–105 (A³, above). REST FOR THE EARTH CELEBRATED.

(Alternation.)

A³ | H¹ | **101.** THE COMING KINGDOM. ITS PRINCIPLES: "MERCY AND JUDGMENT" (*v.* 1). THE WICKED CUT OFF (*vv.* 5, 8).

J¹ | **102.** THE KING IN HIS HUMILIATION AND COMING GLORY AS THE ETERNAL CREATOR (*vv.* 12, 24–27). ALL ELSE PERISHING (*v.* 26).

H² | **103.** THE COMING KINGDOM. ITS MERCIES AND JUDGMENTS (*vv.* 4, 6, 17, 19).

J² | **104.** THE KING IN HIS COMING GLORY AS THE ETERNAL CREATOR (*v.* 31). ALL ELSE PERISHING (*vv.* 27–29).

H³ | **105.** THE COMING KINGDOM. BASED ON THE COVENANT (*vv.* 8–12; 42–45–) OF "MERCY AND JUDGMENT" (*vv.* 5–7).

* For notes, see p. 809.

BOOK IV.

90 °A Prayer of °Moses °the man of °God.

B A^1 a (p. 812) 1 °LORD*, Thou hast been our °dwelling place
In all generations.

b 2 Before the mountains were brought forth,
c °Or ever Thou hadst formed the earth and °the world,
c
b Even from everlasting to everlasting,
a Thou °*art* °GOD.

A^2 d^1 3 Thou turnest °man to destruction;
And sayest, °"Return, ye °children of men."

e^1 4 For °a thousand years in Thy sight
Are but as yesterday when it is past,
And *as* a watch in the night.

d^2 5 Thou carriest them away as with a flood; they are *as* a sleep:
In the morning *they are* like grass *which* groweth up.
6 In the morning it flourisheth, and groweth up;
In the evening it is cut down, and withereth.

e^2 7 For we are consumed by Thine anger,
And by Thy wrath are we troubled.

d^3 8 Thou hast set our °iniquities before Thee,
Our °secret *sins* in the light of Thy countenance.

e^3 9 For all our days °are passed away in Thy wrath:
We spend our years as °a tale *that is told.*

d^4 10 The days of °our years *are* °threescore years and ten;
And if by reason of °strength *they be* fourscore years,
Yet *is* °their strength labour and sorrow;

e^4 For it is soon cut off, °and we fly away.

d^5 11 °Who knoweth the °power of Thine anger?
Even according to Thy fear, *so is* Thy wrath.

A^3 f^1 (p. 813) 12 So teach *us* to °number [10] our days,
°That we may apply *our* hearts unto wisdom.

g^1 13 °Return, O °LORD, °how long?
And let it repent Thee concerning Thy servants.

90–106 (𝔅², p. 720). THE NUMBERS BOOK (**A**¹, p. 810). THE EARTH AND THE NATIONS.

For the Structure, see p. 810. The book has to do with the EARTH and the NATIONS, as the first book (1—41) had to do with MAN; the second book (42—72) with ISRAEL; and the third book (73—89) with the SANCTUARY.

90 (p. 810). PROLOGUE.
REST. LOST, AND NEEDED. (*Division.*)

B | A^1 | 1, 2. The eternity of Jehovah-El.
| A^2 | 3-11. The frailty of man.
| A^3 | 12-17. The application of both.

1, 2 (A^1, above). THE ETERNITY OF JEHOVAH-EL. (*Introversion.*)

A^1 | a | 1-. Jehovah our dwelling-place.
b | -1. In time.
c | 2-. Before the mountains.
c | -2-. Before the earth and the world.
b | -2-. In eternity.
a | -2. Thou art El.

Title. A Prayer. Heb. *Tᵉphillah.* See Ap. 63. I.
Moses: the man of the wilderness. Hence the wilderness, and works of creation, referred to.
the man of God. See Ap. 49. There are *seven* specially so called: Moses (Deut. 33. 1); Samuel (1 Sam. 9. 6-10; cp. *v.* 14); David (Neh. 12. 24); Elijah (1 Kings 17. 18); Elisha (2 Kings 4. 7); Shemaiah (2 Chron. 11. 2); Igdaliah (Jer. 35. 4); and four unnamed (1 Sam. 2. 27. 1 Kings 13. 1; 20. 28. 2 Chron. 25. 7).
God. Heb. Elohim (with Art.): i.e. the true God. Ap. 4. I.
1 Lord*. Heb. Adonai. Ap. 4. VIII (2) = The Lord specially in relation to the earth. This is why this fourth book commences with this title, denoting the Sovereign Lord.
dwelling place = habitation, or refuge.
2 Or = Ere. Positive, not comparative. Anglo-Saxon *aer*, from which we have our modern "ere"; found formerly as "er", "ear", and "yer". In A.V., 1611, Num. 11. 33 read "yer it was chewed".
the world = the habitable world. Heb. *tēbēl.*
art: or wast. **GOD.** Heb. El. Ap. 4. IV.

3-11 (A^2, above). THE FRAILTY OF MAN. (*Repeated Alternation.*)

A^2 | d^1 | 3. Declaration.
e^1 | 4. Reason. "For".
d^2 | 5, 6. Declaration.
e^2 | 7. Reason. "For".
d^3 | 8. Declaration.
e^3 | 9. Reason. "For".
d^4 | 10-. Declaration.
e^4 | -10. Reason. "For".
d^5 | 11. Declaration.

3 man = mortal man. Heb. *'ĕnōsh.* Ap. 14. III.
Return. Either to dust; or, in resurrection.
children of men = sons of Adam (sing.). See Ap. 14. I.
4 a thousand years. Cp. 2 Pet. 3. 8.
8 iniquities. Heb. *'āvah.* Ap. 44. iv.
secret. Heb. is sing.; hence we cannot supply "sins" but "[sin]". But some codices, with two early printed editions, read "secrets" (pl.). **9 are passed away** = have declined, or ended. **a tale that is told** = a thought, or a sigh. **10 our**: i. e. Moses, and those of whom he writes. **threescore years and ten.** This refers to the length of life in the wilderness in the time of Moses, which must have been shortened specially, so that the adults died off within the forty years. The "days" were, and could thus be, actually "numbered", as stated in *v.* 12; and in a way they could not have been since then. See notes on p. 809. **strength.** Heb. pl., meaning great strength (i. e. vigour, or strength for activity). Heb. *gābar.* Cp. Ap. 14. IV. **their strength** = their violence (i. e. strength for aggression). Heb. *rāhab.* See notes on p. 809. **and we fly away.** Fig. *Euphemy*, for dying. Ap. 6. **11 Who . . . ?** Fig. *Erotēsis.* Ap. 6. **power.** Heb. *'ōz.* Spelt with Ayin (ʽ) here, but *'ōz* (with Aleph) in Ps. 76. 7. See note on Isa. 11. 4.

12-17 [For Structure see next page].

12 number our days. See note on "threescore", *v.* 10, above. **That we may apply our hearts unto wisdom** = That we may bring home a heart of wisdom. **13 Return.** Same word as *v.* 3. **LORD.** Heb. Jehovah. Ap. 4. II. **how long.** Supply Ellipsis: "how long [shall we wait for Thy return]?"

f² (p. 813) 14 O satisfy us °early with Thy °mercy;
That we may rejoice and be glad all our days.
15 Make us glad °according to the days *wherein* Thou hast afflicted us,
And the °years *wherein* we have seen ³evil.

g² 16 Let Thy work appear unto Thy servants,
And Thy glory unto their °children.

f³ 17 And let the beauty of the ¹LORD* our °God be upon us:
And establish Thou the work of our hands upon us;
Yea, the work of our hands establish Thou it.

B¹ **91** He that dwelleth in the secret place of °the MOST HIGH
Shall abide under the shadow of °THE ALMIGHTY.

C¹ 2 °I will say of °the LORD, "*He is* my refuge and my fortress:
My °God; in Him will I °trust."

B² 3 Surely He shall deliver thee from the snare of the fowler,
And from the noisome pestilence.
4 He shall cover thee with His °feathers,
And under His °wings shalt thou °trust:
°His truth *shall be thy* shield and °buckler.
5 Thou shalt not be afraid for the terror by night;
Nor for the arrow *that* flieth by day;
6 *Nor* for the pestilence *that* walketh in darkness;
Nor for the destruction *that* wasteth at noonday.
7 A thousand shall fall at thy side,
And ten thousand at thy right hand;
But it shall not come nigh thee.
8 Only with thine eyes shalt thou behold
And see the reward of the °wicked.

C² 9 °Because thou hast made ²the LORD,
°*Which is* my refuge,

B³ °*Even* ¹the MOST HIGH, thy habitation;
10 There shall no °evil befall thee,
Neither shall any plague come nigh thy °dwelling.
11 For °**He shall give His angels charge over thee,**
To keep thee °in all thy ways.
12 **They shall °bear thee up °in *their* hands,**
Lest thou dash thy foot against a stone.
13 Thou shalt tread upon the lion and °adder:
The young lion and the dragon shalt thou trample under feet.

C³ 14 Because he hath set his love upon Me, therefore will I deliver him:
I will set him on high, because he hath known °My name.
15 He shall call upon Me, and I will answer him:
I *will be* with him in trouble;
I will deliver him, and °honour him.
16 With °long life will I satisfy him,
And shew him My salvation.

12-17 (A³, p. 811). THE APPLICATION.
(*Repeated Alternation.*)

A³ | f¹ | 12. Us. Our days. Numeration.
g¹ | 13. Thy servants. Favour.
f² | 14, 15. Us. Our days. Exhilaration.
g² | 16. Thy servants. Favour.
f³ | 17. Us. Our works. Establishment.

14 early = in the morning.
mercy = lovingkindness, or grace.
15 according to the days . . . years: i. e. the forty years in the wilderness.
evil. Heb. *rā'a'.* Ap. 44. viii.
17 God. Heb. Elohim. Ap. 4. I.

91 (**B**, p. 810). REST PROVIDED IN, AND FOR MESSIAH.
(*Alternations.*)

B² | B¹ | 1. Address *re* the dweller. "He" (the Spirit speaks).
C¹ | 2. His response. "My" (Messiah speaks).
B² | 3-8. Address to dweller. "Thee" (the Spirit speaks).
C² | 9-. His response. "My" (Messiah speaks).
B³ | -9-13. Address to dweller. "Thee" (the Spirit speaks).
C³ | 14-16. Jehovah's response. "I".

Without a Title, as are all the Psalms in Book IV, except 90, 101, 103. See notes on p. 809. If by Moses, then the "I" of the members C¹ (*v.* 2), and C² (*v.* 9-), may be Joshua, a type of Messiah. Cp. Deut. 1. 38; 3. 28; 31. 7, 23. If Moses were the author (this Psalm following his), then *all* the Scriptures quoted in Matt. 4 were from his writings. Note the refs. to Deut. 32. 1-14. It is not David's, for we have no more right to insert the name of "David" where it is not written, than to take it out where it is.

1 the MOST HIGH. Heb. *'Elyōn.* Ap. 4. VI.
THE ALMIGHTY. Heb. Shaddai. Ap. 4. VII.
2 I will say. Messiah speaks. See C¹, above.
the LORD. Heb. Jehovah. Ap. 4. II.
God. Heb. Elohim. Ap. 4. I.
trust = confide. Heb. *bāṭaḥ.* Ap. 69. I.
4 feathers . . . wings. Note the Fig. *Anthrōpopatheia* (Ap. 6) throughout the Psalm.
trust = flee for refuge. Heb. *ḥāṣāh.* Ap. 69. II. Not the same word as in *v.* 2.
His truth. See note on "shield" (84. 9).
buckler = coat of mail. Occurs only here.
8 wicked = lawless. Heb. *rāshā'.* Ap. 44. x.
9 Because thou, &c. Heb. reads "For thou, O LORD, [art] my refuge." The change of person marks the Structure, and is not due to "textual corruption".
Which is. Omit these italics.
Even, &c. Heb. reads "The MOST HIGH [thou hast made] thy habitation", supplying the Ellipsis from the preceding line.
10 evil. Heb. *rā'a'.* Ap. 44. viii.
dwelling = tent. Some codices, with one early printed edition and Aram., read "tents" (pl.). See notes on p. 809.
11 He shall give. See Matt. 4. 6. Luke 4. 10.
in all thy ways. These words were omitted by Satan, the Scripture being misquoted and misapplied. The words "at any time" are added in Matt. 4. 6. Verse 13 is also omitted, because it refers to Satan's own head being crushed (Gen. 3. 15).
12 bear thee up. Cp. 94. 18. **in** = on.
13 adder: or asp.
14 hath set His love. Heb. *ḥāshaḳ.* Indicates the deepest affection. Cp. Deut. 7. 7; 10. 15; Isa. 38. 17. Only here in the Psalms.
My name. See note on 20. 1.
15 honour = glorify.
16 long life = length of days.

92 °A Psalm *or* °Song for °the sabbath day.

C D j (p. 813) 1 *It is a* good *thing* to give thanks unto °the LORD,
And to sing praises unto Thy °name, O °MOST HIGH:
2 To shew forth Thy lovingkindness in the morning,
And Thy faithfulness °every night,
3 Upon an instrument of ten strings, and upon the psaltery;
Upon the harp with °a solemn sound.
k 4 For Thou, [1]LORD, hast made me glad through Thy °work:
I will triumph in the °works of Thy hands.
l 5 O [1]LORD, how great are Thy works!
And Thy thoughts are °very deep.
E m 6 A brutish °man knoweth not;
Neither doth a fool understand this.
n 7 When the °wicked spring as the grass,
And when all the workers of °iniquity do flourish;
It is that they shall be destroyed for ever:
8 But Thou, [1]LORD, °*art most* high for evermore.
F o 9 For, lo, Thine enemies, O [1]LORD,
For, lo, Thine enemies shall perish;
p All the workers of [7]iniquity shall be scattered.
G 10 But my horn shalt Thou exalt like °*the horn of* an °unicorn:
G I shall be anointed with fresh oil.
F o 11 Mine eye also shall °see *my desire* on mine enemies,
p *And* mine ears shall °hear *my desire* of the °wicked that rise up against me.
E m 12 °The righteous shall flourish like the °palm tree:
He shall grow like a °cedar in Lebanon.
n 13 Those that be planted in the house of [1]the LORD
Shall flourish in the courts of our °God.
14 They shall still bring forth °fruit in old age;
They shall be fat and flourishing;
D j 15 To shew that [1]the LORD *is* upright:
k *He is* my rock,
l And *there is* no unrighteousness in Him.

B H (p. 813) **93** °The LORD reigneth, He is °clothed with majesty;
°The LORD is °clothed with strength, *wherewith* He hath °girded Himself:
°The world also is °stablished, that it cannot be moved.
2 Thy throne *is* established of old:
Thou *art* from everlasting.
J 3 °The floods have lifted up, O [1]LORD,
°The floods have lifted up their voice;
°The floods lift up their waves.
J 4 [1]The LORD on high *is* mightier
Than the °noise of many waters,
Yea, than the mighty °waves of the sea.

---

92 (**C**, p. 810). PRAYER AND PRAISE FOR SABBATH REST. (*Introversion and Alternations.*)

C | D | j | 1-3. The praise of Jehovah.
k | 4. What He is to me.
l | 5. His attributes. Greatness.
E | m | 6. A wicked individual. (Sing.)
n | 7, 8. The wicked. (Plural.)
F | o | 9-. Thine enemies.
p | -9. Workers of iniquity.
G | 10-. Favour to me. (Future.)
G | -10. Favour to me. (Past.)
F | *o* | 11-. Mine enemies.
p | -11. Doers of evil.
E | *m* | 12. A righteous individual. (Sing.)
n | 13, 14. The righteous. (Plural.)
D | *j* | 15-. The praise of Jehovah.
k | 15-. What He is to me.
l | -15. His attributes. Righteousness.

Title. A Psalm. Heb. *mizmōr.* Ap. 65. XVII.
Song. Heb. *shīr.* Ap. 65. XXIII.
1 the sabbath day. Looking forward to the Day and Rest of Messiah's reign. May it not also have reference to the wilderness time, the cause being recorded in Num. 15. 32-41?
the LORD. Heb. Jehovah. Ap. 4. II.
name. See note on 20. 1.
MOST HIGH. Heb. 'Elyōn. Ap. 4. IV. Showing that it relates to His doings in the earth. See notes on p. 809.
2 every = in the.
3 a solemn sound. Heb. *higgiyōn* = soliloquy, or meditation. Occurs in three Psalms: 9. 16; 19. 14 ("meditation"); 92. 3 ("solemn sound"). See Ap. 66. I.
4 work = act. Heb. *pā'al.* Some codices, with two early printed editions and Syr., read "acts" (pl.).
works = labours. Heb. *'āsāh.*
5 very deep. Cp. 36. 6; 40. 5; 139. 17. Rom. 11. 33.
6 man. Heb. *'īsh.* Ap. 14. II.
7 wicked = lawless. Heb. *rāshā'.* Ap. 44. x.
iniquity. Heb. *'āven.* Ap. 44. iii. See note on *v.* 14.
8 art most high = [art enthroned] on high. Not as *v.* 1.
10 the horn of. Supply Ellipsis (Ap. 6), by "those of".
unicorn = buffalo, or wild ox.
11 see, &c. = look on. Omit my desire.
hear = hear of [the destruction of] the wicked.
wicked. Heb. *rā'a'.* Ap. 44. viii.
12 The righteous = A righteous one (sing.).
palm. In barren soil, watered deep at the roots. An *Endogen.*
cedar. In mountain snows and storms, the roots embedded in the rocks. An *Exogen.*
13 God. Heb. Elōhim. Ap. 4. I.
14 fruit. The righteous for fruit, the wicked for fuel.

93 (*B*, p. 810). THE REST DESIRED. (*Introversion.*)

B | H | 1, 2. Attributes of Jehovah.
J | 3. The floods. High.
J | 4. Jehovah. Higher.
H | 5. Attributes of Jehovah.

1 The LORD. Heb. Jehovah. Ap. 4. II.
The LORD reigneth. Three Psalms commence thus (93, 97, 99); they each end with the thought of "holiness" (the last has the word "holy" three times), indicating that, when He reigns, "all will be holy" (Isa. 23. 18. Zech. 14. 20, 21). This explains the cry of the *Zōa* (Rev. 4. 8), because His judgments will prepare the way for His reign.
clothed . . . girded. Fig. *Anthrōpopatheia.* Ap. 6.
The world. Heb. *tēbēl* = The habitable world. Cp. 1 Sam. 2. 8.
stablished. Aram., Sept., Syr., and Vulg. render "firmly fixed".
3 The floods. Note the Fig. *Anaphora* (Ap. 6), for emphasis. Generally applied to rivers.
4 noise of many waters. Cp. Rev. 1. 15; 14. 2; 19. 6.
waves = breakers.

H (p. 813) 5 Thy °testimonies are very sure:
°Holiness becometh Thine house,
O [1]LORD, for ever.

C K[1] (p. 814) **94** O °LORD °GOD, to Whom vengeance belongeth;
O °GOD, to Whom vengeance belongeth, °shew Thyself.
2 Lift up Thyself, Thou °judge of the earth:
Render a reward to the proud.
3 [1]LORD, °how long shall the °wicked,
How long shall the °wicked triumph?
4 *How long* shall they utter *and* speak hard things?
And all the workers of °iniquity boast themselves?
5 They break in pieces Thy People, O [1]LORD,
And afflict Thine heritage.
6 They slay the widow and the stranger,
And murder the fatherless.
7 Yet they say, °"THE LORD shall not see,
Neither shall the °God of Jacob regard *it*."

L[1] 8 Understand, ye brutish among the People:
And *ye* fools, when will ye be wise?
9 He that °planted the ear, shall He not hear?
He that formed the eye, shall He not see?
10 He that chastiseth the °heathen, shall not He correct?
He that teacheth °man knowledge, *shall not He know?*
11 **[1]The LORD °knoweth the thoughts of [10]man, That they *are* vanity.**

K[2] 12 °Blessed *is* the °man whom Thou chastenest, O [7]LORD,
And teachest him out of Thy law;
13 That Thou mayest give him rest from the days of adversity,
Until the pit be digged for °the wicked.

L[2] 14 °**For [1]the LORD will not cast off His People,**
Neither will He forsake His inheritance.
15 But judgment shall return unto righteousness:
And all the upright in heart shall follow it.
16 °Who will rise up for me against the °evildoers?
Or who will stand up for me against the workers of [4]iniquity?
17 Unless [1]the LORD *had been* my help,
My °soul had °almost °dwelt in silence.

K[3] 18 When I said, "my foot slippeth;"
Thy °mercy, O [1]LORD, °held me up.
19 In the multitude of my °thoughts within me
Thy °comforts delight my [17]soul.
20 Shall °the throne of °iniquity have fellowship with Thee,
Which frameth °mischief by a law?
21 They gather themselves together against the [17]soul of °the righteous,
And condemn the innocent °blood.

L[3] 22 But [1]the LORD is my defence;
And my [7]God *is* the rock of my refuge.
23 And He shall bring upon them their own [4]iniquity,
And shall cut them off in their own [3]wickedness;
Yea, [1]the LORD our [7]God shall cut them off.

5 testimonies. Cp. Ps. 19. 7.
Holiness. Cp. 97. 12; 99. 9; and see note on *v.* 1, above.

94 (*C*, p. 810). PRAYER FOR REST FOR THE EARTH. (*Repeated Alternation.*)

C | K[1] | 1-7. Address to Jehovah.
  L[1] | 8-11. Declaration concerning Him.
 K[2] | 12, 13. Address to Jehovah.
  L[2] | 14-17. Declaration concerning Him.
 K[3] | 18-21. Address to Jehovah.
  L[3] | 22, 23. Declaration concerning Him.

1 LORD. Heb. Jehovah. Ap. 4. II.
GOD. Heb. El. Ap. 4. IV. Note the Fig. *Anaphora* (Ap. 6) in this verse. **shew Thyself**=shine forth.
2 judge of the earth. This is in keeping with the subject of Book IV. See notes on p. 809.
3 how long. Note the Fig. *Anaphora.* Ap. 6.
wicked=lawless ones. Heb. *rāshā'.* Ap. 44. x. Not the same word as in *v.* 23.
4 iniquity. Heb. *'āven.* Ap. 44. iii. Same word as in *vv.* 16, 23; not *v.* 20.
7 THE LORD. Heb. Jah. Ap. 4. III.
God. Heb. Elohim. Ap. 4. I. See note on 20. 1.
9 planted the ear. Consult works on physiology for the wonders of this expression.
10 heathen=nations.
man. Heb. *'ādām.* Ap. 14. I.
11 knoweth, &c. See 1 Cor. 3. 20.
12 Blessed=Happy. See Ap. 63. VI.
man. Heb. *geber.* Ap. 14. IV.
13 the wicked=a wicked one. Same word as *v.* 3.
14 For the LORD. See Rom. 11. 1, 2.
16 Who . . . ? Fig. *Erotēsis.* Ap. 6.
evildoers. Heb. *rā'a'.* Ap. 44. viii.
17 soul. Heb. *nephesh.* Ap. 13.
almost=quickly. See note on Prov. 5. 14.
dwelt in silence. Fig. *Euphemy* (Ap. 6), for dying.
18 mercy=lovingkindness, or grace.
held me up. Cp. 91. 12.
19 thoughts=perplexities.
comforts. Occurs only here, Isa. 66. 11, and Jer. 16. 7, where it is rendered "consolations".
20 the throne of iniquity: i. e. the throne which administers injustice.
iniquity. Heb. *havvāh*=cupidity. Put by Fig. *Metonymy* (of Cause), Ap. 6, for the injustice produced by desire for gain.
mischief. Heb. *'āmāl.* Ap. 44. v.
21 the righteous=a righteous one (sing. no Art.).
blood. Put by Fig. *Synecdoche* (of Part), Ap. 6, for man.

95–100 (**A**[2], p. 810). REST FOR THE EARTH ANTICIPATED.

95 (**D**, p. 810). WORSHIP IN VIEW OF REST ANTICIPATED. (*Introversion and Alternation.*)

D | M[1] | 1-7-. Rest to be found in true worship. People speak.
 M[2] | -7-11. Rest lost through unbelief. God speaks.

1-7- (M[1], above). REST TO BE FOUND IN TRUE WORSHIP. (*Introversion and Alternation.*)

M[1] | N | q | 1, 2. Exhortation to praise.
   r | 3. Reason. "For".
  O | 4. The earth is His.
   P | 5-. The sea is His.
   P | -5-. He made the sea.
  O | -5. He formed the earth.
 N | *q* | 6. Exhortation to praise.
   r | 7-. Reason. "For".

The Psalm has two distinct parts, see Structure, above; not two independent Psalms strung together. The latter part is the complement of the former.
1 the LORD. Heb. Jehovah. Ap. 4. II.

95 O come, let us sing unto °the LORD: D M[1] N (p. 814)
Let us make a joyful noise to the rock of our salvation.

2 Let us come before His °presence with thanksgiving,
And make a joyful noise unto Him with psalms.
r 3 For [1]the LORD *is* a great °GOD,
(p. 814) And a great King above all °gods.
O 4 In His hand *are* the deep places of the earth:
The strength of the hills *is* His also.
P 5 The sea *is* His,
P And He made it:
O And His °hands formed the dry *land*.
N q 6 O come, let us worship and bow down:
Let us kneel before [1]the LORD our maker.
r 7 For He *is* our °God;
And we *are* the People of His pasture, and the sheep of His hand.
M² Q °**To day if ye will hear His voice,**
(p. 815) 8 **Harden not your heart, as °in the provocation,**
And **as** ***in*** **the day of °temptation in the wilderness:**
R 9 °**When your fathers °tempted Me,**
Proved Me, °and saw My work.
Q 10 **Forty years long was I grieved with °*this* generation,**
And said, "It *is* a People that do err in their heart,
And they have not known My ways:"
R 11 °**Unto whom I sware in My wrath**
That they should not enter into My °rest.

F S **96** O sing unto °the LORD °a new song:
(p. 815) Sing unto °the LORD, all °the earth.
2 Sing unto [1]the LORD, bless °His name;
Shew forth His salvation from day to day.
3 Declare His glory among the °heathen,
His wonders among all °people.
T 4 For [1]the LORD *is* great, and greatly to be praised:
He *is* to be feared above all °gods.
5 For °all the gods of the °nations *are* °idols:
But [1]the LORD made the heavens.
6 Honour and majesty *are* before Him:
Strength and °beauty *are* in His °sanctuary.
S 7 Give unto [1]the LORD, O ye kindreds of the [3]people,
Give unto [1]the LORD glory and strength.
8 Give unto [1]the LORD the glory *due unto* [2]His name:
Bring an °offering, and °come into His courts.
9 O worship [1]the LORD in °the beauty of holiness:
°Fear before Him, all [1]the earth.
10 Say among the [3]heathen *that* [1]the LORD reigneth:
The world also °shall be established that it shall not be moved:
He shall judge the [3]people righteously.
11 °Let the heavens rejoice, and let the earth be glad;
Let the sea roar, and the fulness thereof.
12 Let the field be joyful, and all that *is* therein:
°Then shall all the trees of the wood rejoice

---

2 presence. Heb. = face. See note on Ex. 23. 15; 34. 20. Hence the word "before" (*v.* 6; 96. 6, 9, 13; 92. 3, 5; 98. 6, 9; 100. 2; 102. 2, 10, 28, &c. This is the essence of all true worship.

3 GOD. Heb. El. Ap. 4. IV.

gods = rulers, or judges. Heb. *ĕlohīm.* Ap. 4. I. See note on Ex. 22. 9.

5 hands. Fig. *Anthrōpòpatheia.* Ap. 6.

7 God. Heb. Elohim. Ap. 4. I.

To day, &c. Cp. Heb. 3. 7-11; 4. 1.

-7-11 (M², p. 814). REST LOST THROUGH UNBELIEF. (*Alternation.*)

M² | Q | -7, 8. Time. "To-day".
  R | 9. Sin. Committal. Place (*'ăsher* = where).
 Q | 10. Time. "Forty years".
  R | 11. Sin. Punishment. Place (*'ăsher* = where.)

8 in the provocation = at Meribah (Num. 20. 13).

temptation = Massah (Ex. 17. 7).

9 When. Heb. *'ăsher* = where.

tempted. Fig. *Anthrōpopatheia.* Ap. 6.

and = yea.

10 this. Supply the Ellipsis by substituting "that".

11 Unto whom = Where: as in *v.* 9 (see note on "When", *v.* 9). Heb. *'ăsher.*

rest. The rest, thus lost, is to be yet found in the future (according to Heb. 3. 7-11, 15; 4. 3, 7).

96 (**F**, p. 810). SUMMONS TO SING THE NEW SONG. (*Alternation.*)

F | S | 1-3. Exhortation to sing the New Song.
 T | 4-6. Reasons. "For".
 S | 7-13-. Exhortation to sing the New Song.
 T | -13. Reasons. "For".

1 the LORD. Heb. Jehovah. Ap. 4. II.

a new song. Ps. 96 is the call; Ps. 97 is the answer. Cp. 98 and 99. The subject is the coming rest for the earth, to which creation looks forward (Rom. 8. 18-23).

the earth. This is the subject of Book IV. See notes on p. 809. **2 His name.** See note on 20. 1.

3 heathen = nations. people = peoples.

4 gods = rulers. Heb. *'ĕlohīm.* Ap. 4. I. See note on Ex. 22. 9.

5 all the gods . . . idols. Fig. *Paronomasia.* Ap. 6 Heb. *kāl-'ĕlohey . . . 'ĕlīlim.* nations = peoples.

idols = nothings. Cp. 1 Cor. 8. 4.

6 beauty. Some codices read "joy". Cp. 1 Chron. 16. 27.

sanctuary. Some codices read "dwelling-place". as in 1 Chron. 16. 27.

8 offering = presence offerings. Heb. *minchah.* Ap. 43. II. iii.

come into His courts. Some codices read "enter before Him". Cp. 1 Chron. 16. 29.

9 the beauty of holiness. See note on 1 Chron. 16. 29. Fear = Tremble.

10 shall be established. Sept., Syr., and Vulg. read "He hath fixed".

11 Let the heavens rejoice, and let the earth be glad. The initials of the four Hebrew words making this sentence form an acrostic (Ap. 6, 60, and 63. VII), giving the four letters of the word JEHOVAH (Y, H, V, H) thus:

Yismᵉhū Hashshāmayim Vᵉthāgēl Hā'ārez.

The *Massōrah* (Ap. 30) has a special rubric calling attention to this acrostic.

12 Then shall. Ginsburg thinks this should be "Yea, let".

13 °Before [1]the LORD:
T (p. 815) For °He cometh, for °He cometh to judge [1]the earth:
He shall °judge °the world with righteousness,
And the [3]people with His truth.

G U s (p. 816) **97** °The LORD °reigneth;
Let °the earth rejoice;
t Let the multitude of °isles be glad *thereof*.
V u 2 Clouds and darkness *are* round about Him:
v Righteousness
w And judgment
Are the °habitation of His throne.
V u 3 A fire goeth °before Him,
And burneth up His °enemies round about.
4 His lightnings enlightened °the world:
[1]The earth saw, and trembled.
5 The hills melted like wax at the °presence of [1]the LORD,
At the °presence of °THE Lord of the whole [1]earth.
v 6 °The heavens declare His righteousness,
And all the °people see His glory.
7 Confounded be all they that serve °graven images,
That boast themselves of °idols:
Worship Him, all *ye* °gods.
w 8 °Zion heard, and was glad;
And the °daughters of Judah rejoiced
Because of Thy judgments, O [1]LORD.
U s 9 For Thou, [1]LORD, *art* °HIGH above all [1]the earth:
Thou art exalted far above all [7]gods.
10 Ye that love [1]the LORD, hate °evil:
He preserveth the °souls of His °saints;
He delivereth them out of the hand of the °wicked.
t 11 Light is sown for the °righteous,
And gladness for the °upright in heart.
12 Rejoice in [1]the LORD, ye righteous;
And give thanks at the °remembrance of His °holiness.

98 °A Psalm.
F W (p. 816) 1 °O sing unto °the LORD a new song;
For He hath done marvellous things:
X His °right hand, and His holy °arm, hath gotten Him the victory.
2 [1]The LORD hath made known His salvation:
His righteousness hath He openly shewed in the sight of the °heathen.
3 He hath remembered His °mercy and His truth toward the house of Israel:
All the ends of the earth have seen the salvation of our °God.
W 4 Make a joyful noise unto [1]the LORD, all the earth:
Make a loud noise, and rejoice, and °sing praise.
5 Sing unto [1]the LORD with the harp;
With the harp, and the voice of °a psalm.
6 With trumpets and sound of cornet
Make a joyful noise °before [1]the LORD, the King.

---

13 Before. See note on "presence" (95. 2).
He cometh . . . He cometh. Fig *Epizeuxis* (Ap. 6), for emphasis.
the world = the habitable world. Heb. *tēbēl.* No rest or righteous rule for the world and its inhabitants until He comes. The next Psalm is "the New Song", celebrating this by anticipation.

97 (**G**, p. 810). THE NEW SONG.
(*Introversion and Alternations.*)

G | U | s | 1-. Jehovah reigneth.
    t | -1. Joy and gladness.
  V | u | 2-. Clouds, &c.
    v | -2-. Righteousness.
    w | -2. Judgment.
  V | *u* | 3-5. Lightnings, &c.
    v | 6, 7. Righteousness.
    w | 8. Judgment.
U | *s* | 9, 10. Jehovah reigneth.
  t | 11, 12. Joy and gladness.

Psalm 97 is the answer to the call of 96.
1 The LORD. Heb. Jehovah. Ap. 4. II.
The LORD reigneth. See note on 93. 1.
reigneth = hath taken a kingdom.
the earth. Note that this Book (IV) and its Psalms have relation to the earth or land. See notes on p. 809.
isles = coasts or coastlands beyond Palestine. Put for the Gentile world. **2 habitation** = foundation.
3 before. See note on "presence" (95. 2).
enemies = adversaries.
4 the world = the habitable world. Heb. *tēbēl.*
5 presence. See note on 95. 2.
THE Lord. Heb. Adon. Ap. 4. viii (1). Specially connected with His rule in the earth. Occurs in Josh. 3. 11, 13; 5. 14, and Zech. 6. 5.
6 The heavens. Put by Fig. *Metonymy* (of Adjunct), Ap. 6, for Him who dwells there. **people** = peoples.
7 graven images = an image, whether graven or molten (sing.).
idols = nothings. Cp. 96. 5 and 1 Cor. 8. 4.
gods = judges, or rulers. See note on Ex. 22. 9.
8 Zion. See Ap. 68.
daughters = daughter cities.
9 HIGH = MOST HIGH. Heb. *'Elyōn.* Ap. 4. VI.
10 evil. Heb. *rā'a'.* Ap. 44. viii.
souls. Heb. *nephesh.* Ap. 13.
saints = gracious (i. e. graced) ones.
wicked = lawless (pl.). Heb. *rāshā'.* Ap. 44. x.
11 righteous = a righteous one (sing.). **upright** (pl.).
12 remembrance = mention, or memorial.
holiness. See notes on 93. 1, 5.

98 (*F*, p. 810). SUMMONS TO SING THE NEW SONG. (*Alternation.*)

F | W | 1-. Exhortation to praise.
  X | -1-3. Reason. "For".
  W | 4-9-. Exhortation to praise.
  X | -9. Reasons. "For".

Title. A Psalm. Heb. *mizmōr.* Ap. 65. XVII.
1 O sing. Another summons to sing the New Song; but this time it is for what Jehovah has done for Israel.
the LORD. Heb. Jehovah. Ap. 4. II.
right hand . . . arm. Fig. *Anthrōpopatheia.* Ap. 6.
2 heathen = nations. **holy.** See note on Ex. 3. 5.
3 mercy = lovingkindness, or grace.
God. Heb. Elohim. Ap. 4. I.
4 sing praise. Fig. *Anadiplosis* (Ap. 6), for emphasis. See note on "psalm", *v.* 5.
5 a psalm = sing praise (Heb. *zimrāh*), at end of *vv.* 4 and 5, by Fig. *Anadiplōsis.* Ap. 6.
6 before. See note on "presence" (95. 2).

7 Let the sea roar, and the fulness thereof;
°The world, and they that dwell therein.
8 Let the °floods °clap *their* hands:
Let the hills be joyful together
9 [6]Before [1]the LORD;

X (p. 816) For He cometh to judge the earth:
With righteousness shall He judge the world,
And the °people with equity.

G Y x (p. 817) **99** °The LORD °reigneth; let the °people tremble:
He sitteth *between* the °cherubims; let °the earth be moved.
2 [1]The LORD *is* great in °Zion;
And He *is* high above all °the people.
3 Let them praise Thy great and terrible name;
For it *is* °holy.
4 The king's strength also loveth judgment;

y Thou dost establish equity,
Thou executest °judgment and righteousness in Jacob.

Z 5 Exalt ye [1]the LORD our °God,
And worship at His footstool;
For °He *is* [3]holy.

Y x 6 °Moses and Aaron among His priests,
And °Samuel among them that call upon His name;
°They called upon the LORD, and He answered them.
7 He spake °unto them in the cloudy pillar:
They kept His testimonies, and the ordinance *that* He gave them.

y 8 Thou answeredst °them, O [1]LORD our [5]God:
Thou wast a °GOD That forgavest °them,
Though Thou °tookest vengeance of °their inventions.

Z 9 Exalt [1]the LORD our [5]God,
And worship at His [3]holy hill;
For [1]the LORD our [5]God *is* [3]holy.

100 °A Psalm of °praise.

D A a (p. 817) 1 Make a joyful noise unto °the LORD, all °ye lands.
2 Serve °the LORD with gladness:

b Come before His °presence with singing.

B 3 Know ye that [1]the LORD He *is* °God:
It is He *That* hath made us, °and not we ourselves;
We are His °People, and the °sheep of His pasture.

A b 4 Enter into His gates with thanksgiving,
And into His courts with praise:

a Be thankful unto Him, *and* bless °His name.

B 5 For [1]the LORD *is* °good; His °mercy *is* everlasting;
And His truth *endureth* to all generations.

7 The world: i.e. as inhabited. Heb. *tēbēl*.
8 floods = rivers.
clap. Fig. *Prosopopœia*. Ap. 6.
9 people = peoples.

99 (*G*, p. 810). THE NEW SONG.
(*Alternations.*)

G | Y | x | 1-4-. Of Jehovah. } Motives.
| | y | -4. To Jehovah. }
| Z | 5. Exalt ye, &c.
| Y | x | 6, 7. Of Jehovah. } Examples.
| | y | 8. To Jehovah. }
| Z | 9. Exalt ye, &c.

1 The LORD. Heb. Jehovah. Ap. 4. II.
reigneth = hath taken a kingdom. See note on 93. 1.
people = peoples.
cherubims. See Ap. 41. The Psalm was therefore written while the Ark was in existence.
the earth. The subject of Book IV. See notes on p. 809.
2 Zion. See Ap. 68.
the people = the peoples. A.V., 1611, omitted "the".
3 holy. See notes on 93. 1, 5 and Ex. 3. 5.
4 judgment and righteousness. See 2 Sam. 8. 15 and 1 Chron. 18. 14. Cp. with 1 Kings 10. 9.
5 God. Heb. Elohim. Ap. 4. I.
He. Cp. *vv.* 3 and 9, and see note on 93. 1, 5.
6 Moses. He was the grandson of Levi, and exercised priestly functions before Aaron (Ex. 24. 6-8); even consecrating him (Ex. 28). He and Aaron are both included "among His priests".
Samuel. Cp. 1 Sam. 7. 9, 10; 12. 18.
They called. Omit "They", which obscures the sense, by leaving Moses and Aaron without a predicate. Cp. Ex. 15. 25; 32. 11-14; 33. 12-14. Num. 11. 2; 21. 7. Deut. 9. 20, 26. Ps. 106. 23.
7 unto them: i. e. to Moses and Aaron.
8 them = Moses and Aaron.
GOD. Heb. El. Ap. 4. IV
them . . . their = the People.
tookest vengeance. Cp. Num. 20. 12. Deut. 3. 26. Ps. 106. 32, 33.

100 (*D*, p. 810). WORSHIP, IN VIEW OF REST ANTICIPATED. (*Alternation and Introversion.*)

D | A | a | 1, 2-. Exhortation to worship.
| | b | -2. Entrance into His presence.
| B | 3. What Jehovah is. (Three declarations.)
| A | b | 4-. Entrance into His presence.
| | a | -4. Exhortation to worship.
| B | 5. What Jehovah is. (Three declarations.)

Title. A Psalm. Heb. *mizmōr*. Ap. 65. XVII.
praise = thanksgiving.
1 the LORD. Heb. Jehovah. Ap. 4. II.
ye lands. Heb. the land; Israel in the land.
2 the LORD = Jehovah's self. Heb. Jehovah with *'eth*.
presence. See note on 95. 2.
3 God. Heb. Elohim. Ap. 4. I. The Heb. accent places the chief pause on "God"; the minor pauses on "know" and "made": i. e. the knowledge of Jehovah as our God reveals to His People that He made them such, and that they are His "sheep" and His care.
and not we ourselves. Some codices, with six early printed editions, read *l'o* ("not"); but other codices, with one early printed edition, Aram., read *lō* (for Him or His), "and His we are", as in A.V. marg. The difference arises from spelling Heb. *lō* with an *Aleph* (א = 'o) or with a *Vau* (ו = ō). The *Massōrah* notes several such passages where the same variation occurs (Ex. 21. 8. Lev. 11. 21; 25. 30. 1 Sam. 2. 3. 2 Sam. 16. 18; 19. 7. Isa. 9. 2; 49. 5; 63. 9. Job 6. 21; 13. 15. Ps. 100. 3. Prov. 19. 7; 26. 2).
People . . . sheep. Note the correspondence between Pss. 100 and 95 (p. 810).
4 His name. See note on Ps. 20. 1.
5 good. Cp. Ps. 95. 3, "great" (p. 810).
mercy = lovingkindness, or grace.

101 °A Psalm °of David.

H¹ C (p. 818) 1 I will sing of °mercy and judgment:
Unto Thee, O °LORD, will I sing.
2 I will behave myself wisely in a °perfect way.
O °when wilt Thou come unto me?
I will walk within my house with a perfect heart.

D 3 I will set no °wicked thing before mine eyes:
I °hate °the work of them that turn aside;
It shall not cleave to me.
4 A °froward heart shall depart from me:
I will not know a °wicked *person*.
5 Whoso privily slandereth his neighbour,
Him will I °cut off:
Him that hath an high look and a °proud heart will not I suffer.

C 6 Mine eyes *shall be* upon the faithful of °the land, that they may dwell with me:
He that walketh in a [2]perfect way, He shall serve me.

D 7 He that worketh deceit shall not dwell within my house:
He that telleth lies shall not tarry in my sight.
8 I will °early destroy all the °wicked of [6]the land;
That I may [5]cut off all °wicked doers from °the city of [1]the LORD.

102 °A Prayer of the afflicted, when he is overwhelmed, and poureth out his complaint °before the LORD.

J¹ E c (p. 818) 1 Hear my prayer, O °LORD,
And let my cry come unto Thee.
2 Hide not Thy °face from me in the day *when* I am in trouble;
Incline Thine ear unto me:
In the day *when* I call answer me speedily.

d 3 For my days are consumed °like smoke,
And my bones are burned as °an hearth.
4 My heart is smitten, and withered like grass;
So that I forget to eat my °bread.
5 By reason of the voice of my groaning
My bones cleave to my °skin.
6 I am like °a pelican of the wilderness:
I am like an °owl of the desert.
7 I watch, and am
As a sparrow °alone upon the house top.
8 Mine enemies reproach me all the day;
And they that are mad against me °are sworn against me.
9 For I have eaten ashes like [4]bread,
And mingled my drink with weeping,
10 °Because of Thine indignation and Thy wrath:
For Thou hast lifted me up, and cast me down.
11 My days *are* like a shadow that declineth;
And I am withered like grass.

12 °But Thou, O [1]LORD, °shalt endure for ever; F
And °Thy remembrance unto all generations.

101-105 (**A**³, p. 810). REST FOR THE EARTH CELEBRATED.

101 (**H**¹, p. 810). THE COMING KING AND HIS RULE. (*Alternation.*)

H¹ | C | 1, 2. I. My. "The perfect way". "Mercy".
D | 3-5. Them that "turn aside" "cut off". "Judgment".
C | 6. I. Me, mine. "Perfect way". "Mercy".
D | 7, 8. He that "worketh deceit" "cut off". "Judgment".

Title. A Psalm. Heb. *mizmōr*. Ap. 65. XVII.
of David. Relating to the true David, and His coming rule to give "rest" to the earth. The king's vow to rule in righteousness. Cp. 2 Sam. 23. 3-5.
1 mercy = lovingkindness, or grace.
mercy and judgment. Note these two as the alternate subjects of the Structure above.
LORD. Heb. Jehovah. Ap. 4. II.
2 perfect = blameless.
when, &c.: i.e. as king shalt Thou come.
3 wicked thing = thing of Belial.
hate = have always hated.
the work: i.e. the doings, or business.
4 froward = perverse (from what is right).
wicked. Heb. *rāʿaʿ*. Ap. 44. viii.
5 cut off = destroy. See *v.* 8.
proud heart = broad of heart: i.e. large and blatant. Cp. Prov. 21. 4; 28. 25.
6 the land: i.e. Palestine, as in 100. 1.
8 early = morning by morning: i.e. the judgments of a day dealt with within the day. No prisons needed. Land kept clean.
wicked. Heb. *rāshāʿ*. Ap. 44. x.
wicked doers = workers of iniquity. Heb. *'āven*. Ap. 44. iii.
the city of the LORD: i.e. Zion. See Ap. 68.

102 (**J**¹, p. 810). THE KING, IN HIS HUMILIATION. (*Extended Alternation and Introversion.*)

J¹ | E | c | 1, 2. Prayer.
d | 3-11. Humiliation. "Days cut short".
F | 12. Jehovah everlasting.
G | 13-22. Favour to His People.
E | *d* | 23. Humiliation. "Days cut short".
c | 24-. Prayer.
F | -24-27. Jehovah everlasting.
G | 28. Favour to His People.

Title. A Prayer, &c. This refers to Messiah's humiliation.
before. See note on "presence" (95. 2).
1 LORD. Heb. Jehovah. Ap. 4. II.
face. See note on "presence" (95. 2).
3 like smoke. So some codices, with Aram., Sept., and Vulg.; other codices read "in smoke".
an hearth = charred wood.
4 bread. Put by Fig. *Synecdoche* (of Part), Ap. 6, for food in general.
5 skin = flesh.
6 a pelican . . . owl: both unclean birds.
alone. Some codices, with one early printed edition, read "flitting to and fro".
8 are sworn against me = are sworn [together] against me; as in Acts 23. 12-21.
10 Because of = from the face of. See note on 95. 2.
12 But Thou. Emphasising the great consolation.
shalt endure. Sittest, or wilt sit [enthroned].
Thy remembrance. Some codices read "Thy throne".

G H e (p. 819) 13 Thou shalt arise, *and* have °mercy upon °Zion:
For the time to favour her, yea, °the set time, is come.
14 For Thy servants take pleasure in her °stones,
And favour the dust thereof.
f 15 So the °heathen shall fear the °name of [1]the LORD,
And all the kings of the earth Thy °glory.
J g 16 When [1]the LORD shall build up [13]Zion,
He shall °appear in His [15]glory.
h 17 He will regard the prayer of the destitute,
And not despise their prayer.
K 18 This shall be written for °the generation to come:
K And °the people which shall be °created shall praise °THE LORD.
J g 19 For He hath looked down from °the height of His sanctuary;
From heaven did [1]the LORD behold the earth;
h 20 To hear the groaning of the prisoner;
To loose °those that are °appointed to death;
H e 21 To declare the [15]name of [1]the LORD in [13]Zion,
And His praise in Jerusalem;
f 22 °When [18]the people are gathered together,
And the kingdoms, to serve [1]the LORD.
E d (p. 818) 23 °He weakened my strength °in the way;
He shortened my days.
c 24 I said, "O °my GOD, take me not away in the midst of my days:"
F Thy years *are* throughout all generations.
25 °**Of old hast Thou laid the foundation of the earth:**
And the heavens *are* the work of Thy hands.
26 **They shall perish, but Thou shalt endure:**
Yea, all of them shall wax old like a garment;
As a vesture shalt Thou change them, and they shall be changed:
27 **But Thou *art* °the same,**
And Thy years shall have no end.
G 28 The °children of Thy servants °shall continue,
And their seed shall be established [1]before Thee.

H[2] L (p. 819) **103** *A Psalm* °of David.

1 °Bless °the LORD, O °my soul:
And all that is within me, *bless* His °holy °name.
2 Bless [1]the LORD, O [1]my soul,
And forget not °all His °benefits:
3 Who °forgiveth all thine °iniquities;
Who healeth all thy diseases;
4 Who °redeemeth thy life from destruction;
Who crowneth thee with lovingkindness and °tender mercies;
5 Who satisfieth thy mouth with good *things;*
So that thy youth is renewed like the eagle's.

102. 13-22 (G, p. 818). **FAVOUR TO HIS PEOPLE.** (*Introversion and Alternations.*)

G | H | e | 13, 14. Favour to Zion.
f | 15. Favour to the nations.
J | g | 16. Jehovah's glory in Zion.
h | 17. Jehovah's grace to the needy.
K | 18-. For a future People.
K | -18. For a future People.
J | *g* | 19. Jehovah's glory in Zion.
h | 20. Jehovah's grace to the needy.
H | *e* | 21. Favour to Zion.
f | 22. Favour to the peoples.

13 mercy=compassion. **Zion.** See Ap. 68.
the set time. First, the end of the seventy years (Dan. 9. 2. Neh. 2. 17-20; 3. 1-32); and second, the still future set time in God's counsels. All this is prophecy. No need to think it was written after Jerusalem's desolation. David was a prophet (Acts 2. 30, 31). Cp. Isa. 40. 2; 61. 2.
14 stones. Put by Fig. *Synecdoche* (of Part), Ap. 6, for the restored buildings.
15 heathen=nations. **name.** See note on 20. 1.
glory. Always mentioned in connection with Messiah's sufferings. Cp. *vv.* 1-12. See Ap. 71.
16 appear in His glory. This shows that all is prophetic. Cp. Isa. 60. 1-3.
18 the generation to come=a generation to come. Showing that all here is future. **the**=a.
created: i. e. the new Israel (Ps. 22. 31. Isa. 43. 1-7, 18-21; 66. 8). This is the new nation referred to in Matt. 21. 43.
THE LORD. Heb. Jah. Ap. 4. III.
19 the height of His sanctuary=His holy height.
20 those . . . appointed to death=the sons of death. Genitive of Relation. The Heb. word for "death" occurs only here and 79. 11. It is *fem.*, as though the mother. Cp. Rom. 8. 36, and see Ap. 17 (5).
22 When, &c. Cp. Pss. 22. 27; 68. 32. Isa. 45. 14. Fulfilling Gen. 49. 10.
23 He weakened. A return to the subject corresponding with "d" (*vv.* 3-11), above.
in the way: i. e. of His humiliation.
24 my GOD. Heb. *Eli*=my El. Ap. 4. IV.
25 Of old, &c. Quoted in Heb. 1. 10-12, which shows this Psalm is all prophetic of Messiah.
27 the same: or He. Cp. Isa. 41. 4; 43. 10.
28 children=sons.
shall continue=shall dwell [in the Land].

103 (H[2], p. 810). **THE COMING KINGDOM.** (*Introversion.*)

H[2] | L | 1-5. Exhortation to bless.
M | 6, 7. Jehovah's kingdom. Israel.
N | 8. Merciful goodness.
O | 9. Sparing goodness. Time.
P | 10. Pardoning goodness.
P | 11-13. Pardoning goodness.
O | 14-16. Sparing goodness. Time.
N | 17, 18. Merciful goodness.
M | 19. Jehovah's kingdom. Universal.
L | 20-22. Exhortation to bless.

Title. of David: i. e. relating to the true David.
1 Bless. Fig. *Apostrophe.* Ap. 6.
the LORD. Heb. Jehovah, with *'eth*=Jehovah Himself. Ap. 4. II.
my soul=me myself. Heb. *nephesh.* Ap. 13.
holy. See note on Ex. 3. 5. **name.** See note on 20. 1.
2 all=any of. **benefits**=dealings.
3 forgiveth=passeth over. This verb, with its adj. and subs., is never used but of God. Lit. That is the Forgiver. Cp. *v.* 14 and note there.
iniquities. Heb. *'āvāh.* Ap. 44. iv. So some codices, with one early printed edition, Sept., and Vulg. (pl.); other codices read singular.
4 redeemeth: i. e. as a kinsman. Heb. *gā'al.* See note on Ex. 6. 6; 13. 13.
tender mercies=compassions.

M (p. 819) 6 °The LORD executeth righteousness
And judgment for all that are oppressed.
7 He made known His °ways unto Moses,
His °acts unto the °children of Israel.

N 8 [6]The LORD *is* °merciful and gracious,
°Slow to anger, and plenteous in °mercy.

O 9 He will not always chide:
Neither will He keep °*His anger* for ever.

P 10 He hath not dealt with us after our °sins;
Nor rewarded us according to our [3]iniquities.

P 11 For as the heaven is high above the earth,
So °great is His [8]mercy °toward them that °fear Him.
12 As far as the east is from the west,
So far hath He removed our °transgressions from us.
13 Like as a father pitieth *his* [7]children,
So [6]the LORD pitieth them that [11]fear Him.

O 14 For He knoweth our °frame;
°He remembereth that we *are* °dust.
15 *As for* °man, his days *are* as grass:
As a flower of the field, so he flourisheth.
16 For the °wind passeth over it, and °it is gone;
And °the place thereof shall °know it no more.

N 17 °But the [8]mercy of [6]the LORD *is* from everlasting to everlasting upon them that [11]fear Him,
And His righteousness unto [7]children's [7]children;
18 To such as keep His covenant,
And to those that remember His commandments to do them.

M 19 [6]The LORD hath °prepared His throne in the heavens;
And His kingdom ruleth over all.

L 20 Bless [6]the LORD, °ye His angels,
°That excel in strength, that do His °commandments,
Hearkening unto the voice of His word.
21 Bless ye [6]the LORD, all *ye* His hosts;
Ye °ministers of His, that do His pleasure.
22 Bless [6]the LORD, all His works
In all places of His °dominion:
Bless the LORD, O [1]my soul.

J² Q (p. 820) **104** °Bless °the LORD, O °my soul.

R S¹ O °LORD my °God, Thou art °very great;
Thou art °clothed with honour and majesty.
2 Who coverest *Thyself* with light as *with* a garment:
Who stretchest out the heavens like a °curtain:

T¹ 3 Who layeth the beams of His chambers in the waters:
Who maketh °the clouds His °chariot:
Who walketh upon the wings of the °wind:
4 °**Who maketh His angels °spirits;**
His °ministers a flaming fire:
5 *Who* laid the °foundations of the °earth,
That it should not °be removed °for ever.

6 The LORD. Heb. Jehovah. Ap. 4. II.
7 ways: i. e. the *reasons* of His acts (esoteric) to Moses.
acts: i. e. the *acts* (exoteric) visible to the People.
children = sons.
8 merciful = compassionate, or pitiful. Cp. *v.* 13.
Slow to anger = long-suffering.
mercy = lovingkindness, or grace. Cp. Ex. 34. 6, 7.
9 His anger. The *Ellipsis* (Ap. 6) is correctly supplied from the preceding line.
10 sins. Heb. *chāṭā'*. Ap. 44. i.
11 great = mighty, or hath prevailed.
toward = upon. fear = revere.
12 transgressions. Heb. *pāsha'*. Ap. 44. ix.
14 frame = formation.
He remembereth. Cp. Isa. 29. 16; 45. 9, 10: i. e. God *remembers* what man forgets (i. e. our infirmities); and He *forgets* what man remembers (i. e. our sins). See Isa. 43. 25; 44. 22. Jer. 31. 34. Cp. Isa. 55. 8.
dust. See Gen. 2. 7; 3. 19. Ecc. 12. 7.
15 man. Heb. *'ĕnōsh*. Ap. 14. III.
16 wind. Heb. *rūach*. Ap. 9.
it is gone = there is no sign of it.
the place . . . know it. Fig. *Prosōpopœia*. Ap. 6.
know = recognise.
17 But. Blessed contrast. Note the Structure, "*N*", p. 819. **19** prepared = established.
20 ye. Some codices, with Sept. and Vulg., read "all ye". That excel = That are mighty.
commandments = commandment (sing.).
21 ministers: i. e. the angels. Cp. 104. 4. Heb. 1. 14.
22 dominion = sovereignty.

104 (J², p. 810). THE KING IN HIS COMING POWER AND GLORY.

(*Introversion and Repeated Alternation.*)

J² | Q | 1-. Jehovah to be praised.
  R | S¹ | -1, 2. Thou.
    T¹ | 3-5. He. Who. Day I. Earth.
   S² | 6-9. Thou. Day II. Waters.
    T² | 10-19. He. Who. } Day III, IV.
   S³ | 20-. Thou. } Earth. Light.
    T³ | -20-23. They.
   S⁴ | 24-30. Thou. Day V, VI. Water. Sun.
    T⁴ | 31, 32. He.
 Q | 33-35. Jehovah to be praised.

1 Bless. Fig. *Apostrophe*. Ap. 6.
the LORD. Heb. Jehovah, with *'eth* = Jehovah Himself. Ap. 4. II.
my soul = I myself. Heb. *nephesh*. Ap. 13.
LORD. Heb. Jehovah. Ap. 4. II.
God. Heb. Elohim. Ap. 4. I.
very great. The conception of Deity is grand; and the cosmogony is neither Hebrew nor Babylonian, but Divine.
clothed. Fig. *Anthrōpopatheia*. Ap. 6. So throughout the Psalm.
2 curtain. Of the fifty-three occurrences of this word, only one (here) in the Psalms. No less than forty-seven of them have to do with the Tabernacle; forty-three of them being in Ex. 26 and 36.
3 the clouds = the thick clouds.
chariot. Fig. *Anthrōpopatheia*. Ap. 6.
wind. Heb. *rūach*. Ap. 9.
4 Who, &c. Quoted in Heb. 1. 7.
spirits. Angels are spirits (Heb. *rūach*. Ap. 9), and are called so in Heb. 1. 7, 14. 1 Pet. 3. 19 (cp. 1 Pet. 3. 22).
ministers = servants. Cp. 103. 21.
5 foundations. Cp. Job 38. 4-6. Prov. 8. 29.
earth. Heb. *'ĕreẓ*. As in *vv.* 9, 13, 14, 24; not the same word as in *v.* 20. be removed = move.
for ever = for ever and aye.
6 The waters stood. Cp. 2 Pet. 3. 5, 6 with Gen. 1. 2-.

6 Thou coveredst it with the deep as *with* a garment: S²
°The waters stood above the mountains.

7 At Thy rebuke they fled;
At the voice of Thy thunder they hasted away.
8 They go up by the mountains; they go down by the valleys
Unto the place which Thou °hast founded for them.
9 Thou hast set a bound that they may not pass over;
That they turn not again to cover [5]the earth.

T² (p. 820) 10 He sendeth the springs into the valleys,
Which run among the hills.
11 They give drink to every beast of the field:
°The wild asses quench their thirst.
12 By them shall the fowls of the heaven have their habitation,
Which sing among the branches.
13 He watereth the hills from His chambers:
[5]The earth is satisfied with the fruit of Thy works.
14 He causeth the grass to grow for the cattle,
And herb for the service of °man:
That He may bring forth °food out of [5]the earth;
15 And °wine *that* maketh glad the heart of °man,
And oil to make *his* face to shine,
And bread *which* strengtheneth °man's heart.
16 The trees of °the LORD are full *of sap;*
The cedars of Lebanon, which He hath planted;
17 Where the birds make their nests:
As for the stork, the fir trees *are* her house.
18 The high hills *are* a refuge for the wild goats;
And the rocks for the °conies.
19 He appointed the moon for seasons:
The sun °knoweth his going down.

S³ 20 Thou makest darkness, and it is night:
T³ Wherein all the beasts of the forest do creep *forth:*
21 The young lions roar after their prey,
And seek their meat from °GOD:
22 The sun ariseth, they gather themselves together,
And lay them down in their dens:
23 Man goeth forth unto his work
And to his labour until the evening.

S⁴ 24 O [16]LORD, °how manifold are Thy works!
In wisdom hast Thou made them all:
[5]The earth is full of Thy riches.
25 *So is* this great and wide sea,
Wherein *are* things creeping innumerable,
Both small and great beasts.
26 There go the °ships:
There is that °leviathan, *whom* Thou hast °made to °play therein.
27 These wait all upon Thee;
That Thou mayest give *them* their meat in due season.
28 *That* Thou givest them they gather:
Thou openest Thine °hand, they are filled with good.
29 Thou hidest Thy face, they are °troubled:
Thou takest away their °breath, they die,
And °return to their dust.

8 hast founded = didst prepare.
11 The wild asses: are provided with water. Cp. *v.* 15.
14 man. Heb. *'ādām*, with Art. = humanity. Ap. 14. I.
food. Heb. bread. Put by Fig. *Synecdoche* (of Part), Ap. 6, for all food. Note the three, "grass", "herb", "food".
15 wine: is provided for man. Cp. *v.* 11. Heb. *yayin.* Ap. 27. I.
man = weak, mortal man. Heb. *'ĕnōsh.* Ap. 14. III.
16 the LORD. Heb. Jehovah. Ap. 4. II.
18 conies. Heb. *shaphan.* Not rabbits, which can burrow; but about their size, having smooth feet; therefore dwelling among the rocks, and not in the ground.
19 knoweth. Fig. *Prosopopœia.* Ap. 6.
21 GOD. Heb. El. Ap. 4. IV.
24 how manifold. Fig. *Apostrophe.* Ap. 6.
26 ships: or nautilus, the "small" of *v.* 25.
leviathan = sea monster, or the "great" of *v.* 25.
made = formed. play = sport.
28 hand. Fig. *Anthrōpopatheia.* Ap. 6.
29 troubled = dismayed.
breath = spirit. Heb. *rūach.* Ap. 9.
return. Cp. Gen. 3. 19. Ecc. 12. 7.
30 spirit. Heb. *rūach.* Ap. 9.
earth = ground. Heb. *'ădāmah.*
31 His works. His own works.
35 sinners. Heb. *chāṭā'.* Ap. 44. i.
the wicked = lawless ones. Heb. *rāsha'.* Ap. 44. x.
be no more = be there no sign of them. Cp. 103. 16.
Praise ye THE LORD (Heb. Jah. Ap. 4. III). Heb. *Halĕlu-jah.* This is the first "Hallelujah" in the O.T. The Talmud and the Midrash call attention to the fact that it is connected with the overthrow of the wicked. We may note that it is the same with the first Hallelujah in the N.T. (Rev. 19. 1, 2).

105 [For Structure see next page.]
For circumstances see note on 1 Chron. 16. 7.
1 the LORD. Heb. Jehovah. Ap. 4. II.
name. See note on 20. 1. people = peoples.
3 holy. See note on Ex. 3. 5.
4 face. Fig. *Anthrōpopatheia.* Ap. 6.
evermore = at all times, or continually.

30 Thou sendest forth Thy °spirit, they are created:
And Thou renewest the face of the °earth.
31 The glory of [16]the LORD shall endure for ever: T⁴
[16]The LORD shall rejoice in °His works.
32 He looketh on the °earth, and it trembleth:
He toucheth the hills, and they smoke.
33 I will sing unto [1]the LORD as long as I live: Q
I will sing praise to [1]my God while I have my being.
34 My meditation of Him shall be sweet:
I will be glad in [16]the LORD.
35 Let the °sinners be consumed out of the [32]earth,
And let °the wicked °be no more.
Bless thou [1]the LORD, O [1]my soul.
°Praise ye °THE LORD.

105 O give thanks unto °the LORD; call upon His °name: H³ U (p. 822)
Make known His deeds among the °people.
2 Sing unto Him, sing psalms unto Him:
Talk ye of all His wondrous works.
3 Glory ye in His °holy [1]name:
Let the heart of them rejoice that seek [1]the LORD.
4 Seek [1]the LORD, and His strength:
Seek His °face °evermore.

5 Remember His marvellous works °that He hath done;
His °wonders, and the °judgments of His mouth;
6 O ye seed of °Abraham His °servant,
Ye °children of Jacob His chosen.
7 He *is* [1] the LORD our °God:
His judgments *are* in all the earth.
V n (p. 822) 8 He hath remembered His covenant for ever,
The °word *which* He commanded to a thousand generations.
9 (Which *covenant* He °made with °Abraham,
And His oath unto °Isaac;)
10 And °confirmed the same unto °Jacob for a law,
And to °Israel *for* an °everlasting covenant:
o 11 Saying, "Unto thee will I give the land of Canaan,
°The lot of your inheritance:"
p 12 When °they were *but* a °few men in number;
Yea, very few, and strangers in it.
W i 13 °When they went from one nation to another,
From *one* kingdom to another people;
k 14 He suffered no °man to do them wrong:
Yea, He reproved kings for their sakes;
15 *Saying*, "Touch not Mine anointed,
And do My °prophets no harm."
l 16 Moreover He called for a famine upon the land:
He brake the whole staff of bread.
m q 17 He °sent a °man before °them,
°*Even* Joseph, *who* was sold for a servant:
r 18 °Whose feet they hurt with fetters:
°He was laid in °iron:
19 Until the time that °his word °came:
The °word of [1] the LORD °tried him.
s 20 °The king sent and loosed him;
Even the ruler of °the people, and let him go free.
21 He made him lord of his house,
And ruler of all his substance:
22 To bind his princes °at his pleasure;
And teach his °senators wisdom.

105 (**H**³, p. 810). THE COMING KINGDOM. AS BASED ON THE PAST. (*Introversion and Alternations.*)

H³ | U | 1–7. Exhortation to praise (2nd person pl.).
V | 8–2. Basis of praise. The Covenant in promise.
W | i | 13. Journeyings.
k | 14, 15. Favour.
l | 16. Affliction.
m | 17–22. Mission of deliverance. Joseph.
} History of Patriarchs.
W | *i* | 23. Journeyings.
k | 24. Favour.
l | 25. Affliction.
m | 26–41. Mission of deliverance. Moses and Aaron.
} History of Nation.
V | 42–45–. Basis of the praise. The Covenant in performance.
U | –45. Exhortation to praise (2nd person pl.).

5 that=which.
wonders: i. e. the miracles in Egypt.
judgments=just decisions (given at Sinai).
6 Abraham. Some codices read Israel. Cp. 1 Chron. 16. 13. **servant.** Sept. and Syr. read pl., "servants". **children**=sons.
7 God. Heb. Elohim. Ap. 4. I.

8–12 (V, above). COVENANT IN PROMISE.

42–45– (*V*, above). COVENANT IN PERFORMANCE. (*Extended Alternation.*)

V | n | 8–10. The Covenant remembered.
o | 11. The Land given.
p | 12. The People described.
V | *n* | 42, 43. The Covenant remembered.
o | 44. The Land possessed.
p | 45–. The People described.

8 word=promise, as in *v.* 42.
9 made=solemnised.
Abraham. Cp. Gen. 12. 7; 15. 18; 13. 14–17.
Isaac. Cp. Gen. 26. 3, 4.
10 confirmed=[He] established.
Jacob. Cp. Gen. 28. 13; 35. 12; 48. 1–4. See note on Gen. 50. 24; cp. Mic. 7. 20, and Heb. 11. 13.
Israel: i. e. the spiritual seed; in contrast with Jacob, the natural seed. See notes on Gen. 32. 28; 43. 6; 45. 26, 28.
everlasting covenant. See notes on Gen. 9. 15, and Isa. 44. 7.
11 The lot=measuring line. Put by Fig. *Metonymy* (of Cause), Ap. 6, for the inheritance measured off by it.
12 they. Some codices, with Aram. and Syr., read "ye": i. e. not the three Patriarchs, but the descendants of each one respectively.
few men in number=men (Heb. *m*ᵉ*thim.* Ap. 14. V) of number: i. e. soon numbered (see note on "almost", Prov. 5. 14). Cp. Gen. 34. 30. Deut. 4. 27; 26. 5. Jer. 44. 28. (The opposite is "without number", Ps. 40. 12.) This could not be said of the Patriarchs. **13 When they went.** Cp. *v.* 23. **14 man.** Heb. *'ādām.* Ap. 14. I.
15 prophets: i. e. those who were men of God, and His spokesmen. Abraham so called (Gen. 20. 7). See Ap. 49.

17–22 (m, above). THE MISSION OF JOSEPH.

26–41 (*m*, above). THE MISSION OF MOSES AND AARON. (*Extended Alternation.*)

m | q | 17. The sending of the Deliverer.
r | 18, 19. Trial by the Word (Joseph).
s | 20–22. The deliverance.
m | *q* | 26. The sending of the Deliverers.
r | 27–36. Trial by the Word (Egypt's).
s | 37–41. The deliverance.

17 sent=had sent. **man.** Heb. *'ish.* Ap. 14. II. **them**=their face. **Even Joseph.** Cp. Gen. 37. 28. **18 Whose feet.** Fig. *Hysteresis.* Ap. 6. Further particulars Divinely revealed. **He**=His soul. Heb. *nephesh.* Ap. 13. **iron.** Put by Fig. *Metonomy* (of Cause), Ap. 6, for manacles made from it. **19 his word**: i. e. Joseph's word: i. e. his interpretation of the dreams. **came**: came to pass. Cp. Judg. 7. 13, 21. 1 Sam. 9. 6. **word**=utterance, as in Ps. 119. 38=what is said; here, the prophetic promise. **tried**=proved: i. e. proved his faith in the Divine promise (Gen. 37. 5–11). **20 The king sent.** Cp. Gen. 41. 14, 39, 40, 44. **the people**=peoples. **22 at his pleasure**=according to his soul (i. e. his will). Heb. *nephesh.* Ap. 13. **senators**=elders.

W i (p. 822) 23 °Israel also came into Egypt;
And Jacob sojourned in the land of Ham.
k 24 And He increased His People greatly;
And made them stronger than their °enemies.
l 25 °He turned their heart to hate His People,
To deal subtilly with His servants.
m q 26 He sent °Moses His servant;
And Aaron whom He had chosen.
r 27 °They shewed °His signs among them,
And wonders in the °land of Ham.
28 He sent °darkness, and made it dark;
And °they rebelled not against His word.
29 He turned their waters into blood,
And slew their fish.
30 Their land °brought forth frogs in abundance,
°In the chambers of their kings.
31 He spake, and there came divers sorts of flies,
°*And* lice in all their °coasts.
32 He gave them hail for rain,
And flaming fire in their land.
33 He smote their vines also and their fig trees;
And brake the °trees of their [31] coasts.
34 He spake, and the locusts came,
And caterpillers, and that without number,
35 And did eat up all the herbs in their land,
And devoured the fruit of their ground.
36 He smote also all the firstborn in their land,
The °chief of all their °strength.
s 37 He brought them forth also with silver and gold:
And *there was* not one feeble *person* among °their tribes.
38 °Egypt was glad when they departed:
For the fear of them fell upon them.
39 He spread a cloud for a covering;
And fire to give light in the night.
40 *The People* asked, and He brought quails,
And satisfied them with the bread of heaven.
41 He opened the rock, and the waters gushed out;
They ran in the dry places *like* a river.
V n 42 For He remembered His [3] holy °promise,
And Abraham His servant.
43 And He brought forth His People with joy,
°*And* His chosen with gladness:
o 44 And °gave them the lands of °the heathen:
And they inherited the °labour of the °people;
p 45 That they might observe His statutes,
And keep His laws.
U °Praise ye °THE LORD.

X A (p. 823) **106** °Praise ye °THE LORD.
B O give thanks unto °the LORD; for *He is* good:
For His °mercy *endureth* for ever.

23 Israel also came = So Israel came. Cp. *v.* 13 and Gen. 46. 1.
24 enemies = adversaries.
25 He turned. Cp. Ex. 1. 10; 4. 21.
26 Moses. Cp. *v.* 17 above, and the Structure. See Ex. 3. 10.
27 They. Sept., Syr., and Vulg. read "He". Cp. 78. 43.
His signs = The words of His signs.
land of Ham: i.e. Egypt. Cp. 78. 51; 106. 22.
28 darkness. This was the ninth plague (Ex. 10. 21). All are not mentioned, not being needed. This is put first for the purpose implied in the next line.
they rebelled not: i.e. Israel did not rebel against the command for circumcision. According to Ex. 12. 48, no uncircumcised person could eat the Passover. This is implied in Josh. 5. 2 by the expression, the "second time".
30 brought forth = swarmed with.
In. Fig. *Ellipsis* (Ap. 6) = "[and they entered] into".
31 And = [And there came].
coasts = borders, or boundaries.
33 trees of their coasts = boundary trees.
36 chief = firstlings.
strength. Put by Fig. *Metonymy* (of Effect), Ap. 6, for those produced by their strength or manly vigour.
37 their = his: i.e. Israel's (or Jehovah's).
38 Egypt. Put by Fig. *Metonymy* (of Adjunct), Ap. 6, for Egyptians; the People (*masc.*), not "Land" (*fem.*).
42 promise. Same word as in *v.* 8, "word".
43 And His chosen. Pl. = Even His chosen [People].
44 gave. Cp. *v.* 11, "will I give", and see Structure.
the heathen = nations.
labour. Put by Fig. *Metonymy* (of Cause), Ap. 6, for that which is produced by it.
people = peoples.
45 Praise ye THE LORD. Heb. Hallelujah = Praise ye Jah. Ap. 4. III.

106 (*X*, p. 810). EPILOGUE. REST. HOW LOST, AND VALUED.
(*Introversion and Alternation.*)

X | A | 1-. Hallelujah.
B | -1-3. Exhortation to praise.
C | 4, 5. Prayer.
D | t[1] | 6, 7. Sin.
u[1] | 8-12. NEVERTHELESS.
E[1] | v[1] | 13-16. Sin.
w[1] | 17, 18. Punishment.
v[2] | 19-22. Sin.
w[2] | 23-. Punishment.
F[1] | -23. DELIVERANCE. Moses.
E[2] | v[3] | 24, 25. Sin.
w[3] | 26, 27. Punishment.
v[4] | 28, 29-. Sin.
w[4] | -29. Punishment.
F[2] | 30, 31. DELIVERANCE. Phinehas.
E[3] | v[5] | 32-. Sin.
w[5] | -32, 33. Punishment.
v[6] | 34-39. Sin.
w[6] | 40-42. Punishment.
F[3] | 43-. DELIVERANCE. "He".
D | *t* | -43. Sin.
u | 44-46. NEVERTHELESS.
C | 47. Prayer.
B | 48-. Exhortation to praise.
A | -48. Hallelujah.

1 Praise ye THE LORD. Heb. = Hallelu-jah.
THE LORD. Heb. Jah. Ap. 4. III.
the LORD. Heb. Jehovah. Ap. 4. II.
mercy = lovingkindness, or grace.

2 Who can utter the mighty acts of [1]the LORD?
Who can shew forth all His praise?
3 °Blessed *are* they that keep judgment,
And °he that doeth righteousness at all times.
C (p. 823) 4 Remember °me, O [1]LORD, with the favour *that Thou bearest unto* Thy People:
O visit °me with Thy salvation;
5 That I may see the good of Thy °chosen,
That I may rejoice in the gladness of Thy °nation,
That I may glory with Thine °inheritance.
D t[1] 6 We have °sinned with our fathers,
We have committed °iniquity, °we have done °wickedly.
7 Our fathers understood not Thy wonders in °Egypt;
They remembered not the multitude of Thy [1]mercies;
But °provoked *Him* at the sea, *even* at the Red sea.
u[1] 8 °Nevertheless He saved them for His name's sake,
That He might make His mighty power to be known.
9 He rebuked the Red sea also, and it was dried up:
So He led them through the depths, as through the wilderness.
10 And He saved them from the hand of him that hated *them*,
And °redeemed them from the hand of the enemy.
11 And the waters covered their °enemies:
There was not one of them left.
12 Then believed they His words;
They sang His praise.
E[1] v[1] 13 They °soon forgat His works;
They waited not for His counsel:
14 But lusted exceedingly in the wilderness,
And tempted °GOD in the desert.
15 And He gave them their request;
But sent leanness into their °soul.
16 They envied Moses also in the camp,
And Aaron the °saint of [1]the LORD.
w[1] 17 The earth opened and swallowed up °Dathan,
And °covered the company of °Abiram.
18 And a fire was kindled in their company;
The flame burned up the [6]wicked.
v[2] 19 They made a calf in °Horeb,
And worshipped the molten image.
20 Thus they changed °their °glory
Into the similitude of an ox that eateth grass.
21 They forgat [14]GOD their saviour,
Which had done great things in Egypt;
22 Wondrous works in the °land of Ham,
And terrible things by the Red sea.
w[2] 23 Therefore He said that He would destroy them,
F[1] Had not °Moses °His chosen stood before Him in the breach,
To turn away His wrath, lest He should destroy *them*.

3 Blessed = Oh how happy! Fig. *Beatitudo*. Ap. 63. VI.
he that doeth. Some codices, with two early printed editions, Aram., Sept., Syr., and Vulg., read "they that do".
4 me. Some codices, with Sept., Syr., and Vulg., read "us".
5 chosen . . . nation . . . inheritance. Note the three names of Jehovah's People.
6 sinned. Heb. *chāṭā'*. Ap. 44. i. } Note the three
iniquity. Heb. *'āvāh*. Ap. 44. iv. } classes of ill-doing.
we have. Some codices, with one early printed edition, read "and have".
wickedly = lawlessly. Heb. *rāshā'*. Ap. 44. x.
7 Egypt. It took forty hours to take Israel out of Egypt, but forty years to take Egypt out of Israel.
provoked Him = rebelled. Heb. *mārāh*. Same word as in *vv.* 33, 43; not the same as in *v.* 29.
8 Nevertheless. Cp. Structure, *v.* 44. Fig. *Palinodia*. Ap. 6.
10 redeemed, as a kinsman. Heb. *gā'al*. See notes on Ex. 6. 6; 13. 13.
11 enemies = adversaries.
13 soon forgat. Characteristic of human nature.
14 GOD. Heb. El. Ap. 4. IV.
15 soul. Heb. *nephesh*. Ap. 13.
16 saint = separated one. See note on Ex. 3. 5.
17 Dathan . . . Abiram. Korah not mentioned: not because of being an "older tradition" (as alleged), but because the "sons of Korah" were spared. See Ps. 42, Title, and cp. Num. 16. 1-35 and 26. 11.
covered = overwhelmed.
19 Horeb. So called here; not because the word of a later writer, but because "Horeb" was the higher name ("the mount of God", Ex. 3. 1. 1 Kings 19. 8), in order to show the heinousness of the sin.
20 their glory. The primitive text was "My glory", but this was changed by the *Sōpherīm* to "their" out of a mistaken reverence. See Ap. 33.
glory. Put by Fig. *Metonymy* (of Adjunct), Ap. 6, for God Himself, Who was and should have been He Whom they gloried in.
22 land of Ham. Cp. 78. 51; 105. 27.
23 Moses. Cp. Ex. 32. 10-14.
His chosen. Not theirs.
25 murmured. Occurs only here, Deut. 1. 27, and Isa. 29. 24.
And. Some codices, with two early printed editions, read this word in the text; others read "they".
27 overthrow. Sept. reads "disperse".
28 Baal-peor. Cp. Num. 25. 2, 3.
the dead. This pertains to necromancy. Cp. Deut. 18. 11. Isa. 8. 19.
29 provoked = grieved, or irritated. Heb. *kā'as*. Not the same word as in *vv.* 7, 33, 43.
Him. This word is read in text in some codices, with Sept., Syr., and Vulg.
inventions = doings. See *v.* 39 also.

24 Yea, they despised the pleasant land, E[2] v[3]
They believed not His word:
25 But °murmured in their tents,
°*And* hearkened not unto the voice of [1]the LORD.
26 Therefore He lifted up His hand against them, w[3]
To overthrow them in the wilderness:
27 To °overthrow their seed also among the nations,
And to scatter them in the lands.
28 They joined themselves also unto °Baal-peor, v[4]
And ate the sacrifices of °the dead.
29 Thus they °provoked °*Him* to anger with their °inventions:
And the plague brake in upon them. w[4]

F[2] (p. 823) 30 Then stood up °Phinehas, and executed judgment:
And *so* the plague was stayed.
31 And that was °counted unto him for righteousness
Unto all generations for evermore.

E[3] v[5] 32 They °angered *Him* also at the waters of °strife,

w[5] So that it °went ill with Moses for their sakes:
33 Because they [7] provoked °his °spirit,
So that he °spake unadvisedly with his lips.

v[6] 34 They °did not destroy the °nations,
Concerning whom [1] the LORD °commanded them:
35 But were mingled among the °heathen,
And learned their works.
36 And they served their idols:
°Which were a snare unto them.
37 Yea, they sacrificed their sons and their daughters unto °devils,
38 And shed innocent blood, *even* the blood of their sons and of their daughters,
Whom they sacrificed unto the idols of Canaan:
And the land was °polluted with blood.
39 Thus were they defiled with their own works,
And went a whoring with their own [29] inventions.

w[6] 40 Therefore was the wrath of [1] the LORD kindled against His People,
Insomuch that He abhorred His own inheritance.
41 And He gave them into the hand of the [35] heathen;
And they that hated them ruled over them.
42 Their enemies also oppressed them,
And they were brought into subjection under their hand.

F[3] 43 °Many times did He °deliver them;

D t But they [7] provoked *Him* with their counsel,
And were brought low for their °iniquity.

u 44 [8] Nevertheless He regarded their affliction,
When He heard their cry:
45 And He °remembered for them His covenant,
And °repented according to the multitude of His [1] mercies.
46 He made them also to be °pitied
°Of all those that carried them captives.

47 Save us, O [1] LORD our °God, *C*
And °gather us from among the heathen,
To give thanks unto Thy °holy °name,
And to triumph in Thy praise.

48 °Blessed *be* [1] the LORD [47] God of Israel *B*
From everlasting to everlasting:
And let all the People say, "Amen."

[1] Praise ye °THE LORD. *A*

---

30 Phinehas. Cp. Num. 25. 7, 8.
31 counted. Cp. Num. 25. 12, 13.
32 angered = caused indignation. Occurs only here in the Psalms.
strife. Heb. *Meribah.* Num. 20. 2–13.
went ill = fared ill.
33 his: i. e. Moses.
spirit. Heb. *rūach.* Ap. 9.
spake unadvisedly. A very rare Hebrew word. Occurs only here in the Psalms.
34 did not destroy. Cp. Judg. 1. 21–29, &c.
nations = peoples: i.e. the Canaanite nations. See Ap. 23 and 25.
commanded. Cp. Ex. 23. 32, 33: and often repeated. For the reason, see Ap. 23 and 25.
35 heathen = nations: i. e. the nations of Canaan. Cp. *v.* 38. See Ap. 23 and 25.
36 Which were = And they became. Some codices, with Sept. and Vulg., read "And it became".
37 devils = demons. Cp. Deut. 32. 17.
38 polluted. The strongest word that could be used. Cp. Num. 35. 33. Isa. 24. 5.
43 Many times. Cp. Judg. 2. 16. Neh. 9. 27, &c.
deliver = rescue.
iniquity. Heb. *'āvōn.* Ap. 44. iii.
45 remembered ... repented. Fig. *Anthrōpopatheia.* Ap. 6.
46 pitied. Cp. 2 Kings 25. 27–30. Daniel, Nehemiah, Esther, Ezra; showing that the prayer of Solomon was answered (1 Kings 8. 50).
Of = Before: i. e. By.
47 God. Heb. Elohim. Ap. 4. I.
gather us. Not necessary to suppose a late date for the Psalm. The Spirit of God spake by the prophets. David was a prophet (Acts 2. 30, 31). Moreover, the Dispersion was well known, being foretold in Deut. 28. 64. We might as well reason away 1 Kings 8. 46–50, for Solomon himself prays this prayer.
holy. See note on Ex. 3. 5.
name. See note on Ps. 20. 1.
48 Blessed. Fig. *Benedictio.* This Doxology closes this fourth book. Cp. the closing Psalms of the other books.
THE LORD. Heb. Jah. See Ap. 4. III.

107—150 (𝔄², p. 720). THE FIFTH, OR DEUTERONOMY BOOK*.

GOD'S WORD THE ONLY GOOD.

"He sent His Word, and healed them,
And delivered them from all their destructions." †
(107. 20 ; 147. 15, 18.)

(*Alternations and Introversion.*)

𝔄² | **A¹** | **107.** DELIVERANCE BY THE HEALING WORD.

B¹ | **C** | **E** | **108** (**E¹**), **109** (**E²**), **110** (**E³**). THE TRUE DAVID'S HUMILIATION, DELIVERANCE, AND EXALTATION (108. 6).

F | **111** (**F¹**), **112** (**F²**), **113** (**F³**). PRAISE. THREE HALLELUJAH PSALMS. THE FIRST TWO BEGINNING, AND THE THIRD, BOTH BEGINNING AND ENDING, WITH "HALLELUJAH". (Ps. 111 BEING PRAISE FOR JEHOVAH'S WORKS; 112, FOR HIS WAYS; AND 113, FOR HIMSELF.)

D | **G¹** | **114** (G^1_1), **115** (G^1_2). DELIVERANCE FROM EGYPT, AND EGYPT'S IDOLS.

H¹ | **116** (H^1_1), **117** (H^1_2), **118** (H^1_3). PRAISE. THREE PSALMS. THE FIRST TWO ENDING WITH "HALLELUJAH", AND THE THIRD BEGINNING AND ENDING WITH "O GIVE THANKS".

A² | **119** ‡. QUICKENING AND SUSTAINING ‖ BY THE REVEALING WORD.

B² | *D* | **G²** | **120** (G^2_1)—**134** (G^2_{15}) §. DELIVERANCE FROM SENNACHERIB TYPICAL OF ISRAEL'S FUTURE DELIVERANCE. FIFTEEN PSALMS ARRANGED IN FIVE TRIADS. (See Ap. 67.)

H² | **135** (H^2_1), **136** (H^2_2). PRAISE. TWO PSALMS LINKED TOGETHER BY ONE COMBINED STRUCTURE.

G³ | **137.** DELIVERANCE OF CAPTIVES. SENNACHERIB'S CAPTIVES (See notes)

H³ | **138.** PRAISE.

G⁴ | **139.** DELIVERANCE FROM AN EVIL HEART. (COMPARE Ezek 36. 26. Jer. 31. 33.)

H⁴ | **140** (H^4_1)—**144** (H^4_5). PRAYER AND PRAISE.

C | *E* | **145.** THE TRUE DAVID LEADING THE PRAISES OF HIS PEOPLE (144. 9).

F | **146** (F^1)—**150** (F^5). PRAISE. FIVE ¶ HALLELUJAH PSALMS, EACH BEGINNING AND ENDING WITH "HALLELUJAH".

---

* For notes, see p. 827.

NOTES ON THE STRUCTURE, PAGE 826.

* DEUTERONOMY is man's name for this book. It comes from the Greek Septuagint, and means "the second Law". It was given because Deuteronomy was a repetition of the Law, with variations, to suit the needs of the new generation in the Land. The title in the Hebrew Canon is אֵלֶּה הַדְּבָרִים, *'elleh hadd*^{e}*bārīm*, "THESE ARE THE WORDS". It is the book which contains the words of God; and consists almost wholly of the testimonies, statutes, judgments, &c., of Jehovah. It was from this book that the Saviour made His three quotations, when He met the tempter with the threefold "It is written". It follows the Book of the Wilderness; and gives the reason for all the trials of the pilgrimage: "The LORD thy God led thee these forty years . . . that He might make thee know that man doth not live by bread only, but by every *word* that proceedeth out of the mouth of the LORD doth man live" (Deut. 8. 2, 3). The natural life, the giving of which is recorded in Genesis, is nothing worth if man be not begotten by the Word, and if the new nature thus given be not nourished by the Word. For only thus can man be truly said to "live".

Hence, in this Deuteronomy-Book of the Psalms we have the same leading subject. Its teaching, like that of the other books, is Dispensational; and it is grouped around the WORD. All blessing for *Man* (Book I), all blessing for *Israel* (Book II), all blessing for *Zion* (Book III), all blessing for the *Earth and its Nations* (Book IV), is bound up in the Word and Law of God. The breaking of that Law had been the source of *Man's* sorrow, *Israel's* dispersion, the *Temple's* ruin, and the *Earth's* misery. It will yet be seen that all blessing for *Man*, the gathering of *Israel*, the building of *Zion*, and restoration for the *earth*, is bound up with the Word of God, and with His Law written by His Spirit on the fleshy tables of the heart (Jer. 31. 31-34. Ezek. 36. 24-38).

What a wonderful thing for one to be brought to say "O how I love Thy Law!" (Psalm 119. 97), when the breaking of that Law had brought in all the suffering! But it will be noted that this is said only after (in Psalm 118) the Resurrection of the Righteous Magnifier of that Law has been celebrated.

This is the theme of the Deuteronomy-Book of the Psalms. It consists of *forty-four* Psalms, in which the title Jehovah occurs 293 times; and Jah, 13; while Elohim occurs only 41 times (4 of which are with Jehovah); El, 10 times; Eloha, twice.

While the structure of the other books consists of two or three sections, this book is, like the Law of God itself, a perfect whole. It is the only book which has an even number of Psalms. Its first Psalm (107), as is the case with the first Psalms of the other books, is at once its key-note and epitome.

† Heb. *Sh*^{e}*ḥīth* = graves, or pits (from *Shāḥath* = to destroy), occurs only here and in Lam. 4. 20. The two passages, taken together, tell us that it is not merely the *written* Word which delivers from deep afflictions, but that the *Living* and Divine WORD, Who was "taken in their pits", is the alone Deliverer of His People from their graves.

‡ It will be noted that Ps. 119 is characteristic of the DEUTERONOMY Book of the Psalms; while Ps. 84 is characteristic of the LEVITICUS Book, and Ps. 90 of the NUMBERS Book. We cannot imagine these as being appropriate to any other Books.

‖ The Quickening and Sustaining Word. This is characteristic of Ps. 119. Cp. *vv.* 25, 37, 40, 50, 88, 93, 107, 149, 154, 156, 159 (eleven occurrences). Moreover, the verb *ḥāyāh* (= *to breathe, to live, to continue to live*) is used sixteen times in this Psalm, always in the sense of *keeping alive*, or *continuing in life*. See KAL (Future), *vv.* 17, 77, 116, 144, 175. PIEL (Pret.), *vv.* 50, 93. PIEL (Imperative), *vv.* 25, 37, 40, 88, 107, 149, 154, 156, 159.

In this connection, how suitable to Hezekiah. See Ap. 67, and note the *Distress*, which is the subject of the first Psalm of each of the five groups of "the songs of the Degrees"; and Hezekiah's earnest prayer. Ap. 67 (iv and xiv).

§ The Songs of THE Degrees are 15 in number (120—134, G^2, above). They correspond in number with the 15 years added to Hezekiah's life. Ten are by Hezekiah (corresponding with the number of "the Degrees" by which the shadow of the sun went backward on the sun-dial of Ahaz, 2 Kings 20. 8-11). Five are by others (4 by David and 1 by Solomon). Solomon's Psalm occupies the centre (127); and, of the 7 on either side, 2 in each 7 are by David; and 10 (5 in each 7) by Hezekiah.

In each 7 the name of JEHOVAH occurs 24 times, and JAH once in the third Psalm of each 7. In the central Psalm Jehovah occurs 3 times.

The fifteen Psalms are arranged in five groups of 3 each. In each group, the subject of the first is *Distress*; the second is *Trust in Jehovah*; while the third speaks of *Blessing and Peace in Zion*.

They are here in fulfilment of Hezekiah's promise recorded in Isa. 38. 20. (For further information see Ap. 73, and Dr. J. W. Thirtle's *Old Testament Problems*. London, Henry Frowde.)

¶ The last five Hallelujah Psalms (146—150, ***F***, p. 826) are an echo and reminiscence of the whole of the five books of the Psalter:—

F | J | 146. GENESIS. Compare *v.* 4 with Gen. 2. 7; *v.* 5 with Gen. 28; *v.* 6 with Gen 1.

K | 147. EXODUS. Compare *v.* 4 ("names") with Ex. 1. 1; *vv.* 2, 20 with the building up of the nation (Ex. 1. 7-20); and *vv.* 15, 19 with Ex. 20.

L | 148. LEVITICUS. Compare *v.* 14 ("a People near unto Him") with Lev. 10. 3.

K | 149. NUMBERS. Compare *vv.* 5-9 with Num. 14. 21; 24. 17-24. The nations ruled and blessed by the Saints.

J | 150. DEUTERONOMY. Compare *v.* 2 with Deut. 3. 24.

BOOK V.

A A (p. 828) **107** O give thanks unto °the LORD, for *He* *is* good:
For His °mercy *endureth* for ever.
2 Let the °redeemed of [1]the LORD say *so*,
Whom He hath °redeemed from the °hand of the °enemy;
3 And °gathered them out of °the lands,
From the east, and from the west,
From the north, and from the °south.

B C[1] a[1] 4 They wandered in the wilderness in °a solitary way;
They found no °city to dwell in.
5 Hungry and thirsty,
Their °soul fainted in them.
b[1] 6 Then they cried unto [1]the LORD in their °trouble,
c[1] *And* He delivered them out of their distresses.
7 And °He led them forth by °the right way,
That they might go to a [4]city of habitation.
d[1] 8 Oh that *men* would praise [1]the LORD *for* His °goodness,
And *for* His wonderful works to the °children of °men!
9 For He satisfieth the longing [5]soul,
And °**filleth the hungry [5]soul with goodness.**

C[2] a[2] 10 Such as sit in darkness and in the shadow of death,
Being bound in °affliction and iron;
11 Because they °rebelled against the °words of °GOD,
And °contemned the counsel of °the MOST HIGH:
12 Therefore He brought down their heart with labour;
They fell down, and *there was* °none to help.
b[2] 13 Then they cried unto [1]the LORD in their [6]trouble,
c[2] *And* He saved them out of their distresses.
14 He brought them out of darkness and the shadow of death,
And brake their bands in sunder.
d[2] 15 Oh that *men* would praise [1]the LORD *for* His [8]goodness,
And *for* His wonderful works to the [8]children of [8]men!
16 For He hath broken the gates of brass,
And cut the bars of iron in sunder.

C[3] a[3] 17 °Fools because of their °transgression,
And because of their °iniquities, °are afflicted.
18 Their [5]soul abhorreth all manner of meat;
And they draw near unto the gates of death.

107–150 (𝔄[2], p. 720). THE DEUTERONOMY BOOK.

GOD'S WORD: THE ONLY GOOD.

107 (**A**[1], p. 826). THE DELIVERING AND HEALING, OR LIVING WORD. (*Introversion.*)

A[1] | A | 1–3. Praise for Jehovah's lovingkindness.
B | 4–32. Distress and Deliverance.
B | 33–41. Judgment and Blessing.
A | 42, 43. Praise for Jehovah's lovingkindness.

The first Psalm of Book V. This book contains fifteen by David, one by Solomon (127), and the rest anonymous (probably by Hezekiah, see Ap. 67), certainly not later than his day. See notes on passages supposed to prove a later date.

1 the LORD. Heb. Jehovah. Ap. 4. II.
mercy = lovingkindness, or grace; as in *v.* 43.
2 redeemed. Heb. *gā'al*, to redeem by purchase. See notes on Ex. 6. 6, and cp. Ex. 13. 13.
hand. Put by Fig. *Metonymy* (of Cause), Ap. 6, for the power exercised by it.
enemy = adversary, or straitnesses.
3 gathered. This is the subject of this last book. Gathered by His Word; and according to His Word. See the Structure, p. 826, and note, p. 827.
the lands, &c. Fig. *Topographia* (Ap. 6), for emphasis. The Psalm looks forward to the final ingathering of Israel.
south = sea: i. e. the Red Sea.

4–32 (B, above). DISTRESS AND DELIVERANCE. (*Repeated and Extended Alternation.*)

B | C[1] | a[1] | 4, 5. Trouble. Wanderers. (Wilderness.)
b[1] | 6–. Cry.
c[1] | –6, 7. Deliverance.
d[1] | 8, 9. Praise, and Reason.
C[2] | a[2] | 10–12. Trouble. Rebels.
b[2] | 13–. Cry.
c[2] | –13, 14. Deliverance.
d[2] | 15, 16. Praise, and Reason.
C[3] | a[3] | 17, 18. Trouble. Fools.
b[3] | 19–. Cry.
c[3] | –19, 20. Deliverance.
d[3] | 21, 22. Praise, and Injunction.
C[4] | a[4] | 23–27. Trouble. Wanderers on Deep.
b[4] | 28–. Cry.
c[4] | –28–30. Deliverance.
d[4] | 31, 32. Praise, and Injunction.

4 a solitary way = a trackless waste.
city to dwell in = city of habitation, as in *v.* 7.
5 soul. Heb. *nephesh.* Ap. 13.
trouble = strait.
7 He led them forth. When this is the case, the way is always "right".
the right way. Because it is His way: not the shortest, or most direct, or most pleasant; but it is the way of Grace and Favour. It is the way of Trial (Deut. 8. 2–4); the way of Safety; the way of Divine Provision and Miraculous Supplies; and it ends "right".
8 goodness = lovingkindness, or grace; same word as "mercy" in *v.* 1.
children = sons.
men. Heb. *'ādām.* Ap. 14. I.
9 filleth the hungry soul. Quoted in Luke 1. 53.
10 affliction = oppression.
11 rebelled. This marks the subject of C[1].
words = sayings, utterances.
GOD. Heb. El. Ap. 4. IV.

---

contemned = despised. **the MOST HIGH.** Heb. *'Elyōn.* Ap. 4. VI. **12 none to help** = no sign of a helper. **17 Fools** = the Perverse, depending on their own wisdom, which is foolishness with God (1 Cor. 1. 20–25). Cp. Prov. 1. 7; 12. 15; 14. 3, 9; 15. 5; 27. 22. **transgression.** Heb. *pāsha'.* Ap. 44. ix. **iniquities.** Heb. *'āvah.* Ap. 44. iv. Not the same word as in *v.* 42. **are afflicted** = bring affliction on themselves.

b^3 (p. 828) 19 Then they cry unto [1]the LORD in their trouble,
c^3 *And* He saveth them out of their distresses.
20 °He °sent His Word, and °healed them,
And °delivered *them* from their °destructions.

d^3 21 Oh that *men* would praise [1]the LORD *for* His [8]goodness,
And *for* His wonderful works to the [8]children of [8]men!
22 And let them sacrifice the sacrifices of thanksgiving,
And declare His works with rejoicing.

C^4 a^4 23 °They that go down to the sea in ships,
That do business in great waters;
24 These see the °works of [1]the LORD,
And His wonders in the deep.
25 For He commandeth, and raiseth the stormy °wind,
Which lifteth up the waves thereof.
26 They mount up to the heaven, they go down again to the depths:
Their [5]soul is melted because of trouble.
27 They reel to and fro, and stagger like a drunken °man,
And °are at their wit's end.

b^4 28 Then they cry unto [1]the LORD in their trouble,
c^4 And He bringeth them out of their distresses.
29 He maketh the storm a calm,
So that the waves thereof are still.
30 Then are they glad because they be quiet;
So He °bringeth them unto their desired haven.

d^4 31 Oh that *men* would praise [1]the LORD *for* His [8]goodness,
And *for* His wonderful works to [8]the children of [8]men!
32 Let them exalt Him also in the °congregation of the people,
And praise Him in the °assembly of the elders.

B e (p. 829) 33 He turneth rivers into a wilderness,
And the watersprings into dry ground;
34 A fruitful land into barrenness,
For the °wickedness of them that dwell therein.

f 35 He turneth the wilderness into a standing water,
°And dry ground into watersprings.
36 And there He maketh the hungry to dwell,
That they may prepare a city for habitation;
37 And sow the fields, and plant vineyards,
Which may yield fruits of increase.
38 He blesseth them also, so that they are multiplied greatly;
And °suffereth not their cattle to decrease.

e 39 °Again, they are minished and brought low
Through oppression, affliction, and sorrow.

20 He sent His Word=He sendeth. This is the key-note to the whole book. All blessing is bound up in this. Note the prophetic reference to Christ, the *Living* Word (John 1. 1, 2, 14), and contrast with the *written* Word (Ps. 119). See the Structure, p. 826.
sent=sendeth. **healed**=healeth.
delivered=delivereth.
destructions=graves. Heb. *shāḥath.* Occurs only here and Lam. 4. 20. The Divine Deliverer was "taken in their pits", and He alone can deliver from the grave.

23 They that go down, &c. In the Heb. text, *vv.* 23–28 are marked by "inverted *Nūns*" (i.e. the letter *Nūn* (*N*), inverted ׆). There are nine altogether (see Ginsburg's *Massōrah*, Letter נ, § 15, Vol. II, p. 259). There are two in Num. 10. 35, 36 (see note there), and seven in this Psalm. Verses 23–28 each have one; also *v.* 40. These inverted letters are used as our "brackets" are, to indicate that, in the opinion of the *Sōpherīm*, the verses so marked should be transposed. But this is only an opinion, arrived at from not seeing the Structure of the Psalm, which, when examined, leaves nothing "inexplicable", as the transition from *v.* 38 to *v.* 39 is said to be.

24 works. Some codices, with two early printed editions, read "work" (sing.).
25 wind. Heb. *rūach.* Ap. 9.
27 man. Heb. *'īsh.* Ap. 14. II.
are at their wit's end. Heb. all their wisdom swallows itself.
30 bringeth=guideth: or, will gently guide.
32 congregation=assembly, or convocation.
assembly=session, or seated company.

107. 33–41 (*B*, p. 828). **JUDGMENT AND BLESSING.** (*Alternation.*)

B | e | 33, 34. Judgment.
  f | 35–38. Lovingkindness.
  e | 39, 40. Judgment.
  f | 41. Lovingkindness.

34 wickedness. Heb. *rā'a'.* Ap. 44. viii.
35 And. Note the Fig. *Polysyndeton* (Ap. 6) in *vv.* 35–38, emphasising each item which goes to make up the fulness of blessing.
38 suffereth not, &c. Fig. *Tapeinosis* (Ap. 6)=will abundantly multiply.
39 Again, &c. So far from the transition from *v.* 38 to 39 being "inexplicable", or *v.* 40 being an "interpolation", the perfection of the repetition of the subject ("judgment") is shown by the Structure above.
40 in the wilderness, where there is no way=a pathless waste.
wilderness. Heb. *tohū.* Rendered "without form" in Gen. 1. 2, describing what "the world that then was" had become by the disruption.
41 the poor=a needy one. Heb. *'ebyōn.* See note on Prov. 6. 11. **from**=after.
42 iniquity. Heb. *'āval.* Ap. 44. vi. Not the same word as in *v.* 17.
43 these. The edition of A.V., 1611, reads "those".
lovingkindness=lovingkindnesses (pl.). Same word as "mercy", in *v.* 1. A, thus corresponding with *A*, in Heb., though not in A.V.

40 He poureth contempt upon princes,
And causeth them to wander °in the °wilderness, *where there is* no way.
41 Yet setteth He °the poor on high °from affliction, *f*
And maketh *him* families like a flock.
42 The righteous shall see *it*, and rejoice: *A* (p. 828)
And all °iniquity shall stop her mouth.
43 Whoso *is* wise, and will observe °these *things*,
Even they shall understand the °lovingkindness of [1]the LORD.

108

°A Song *or* °Psalm °of David.

E[1] D (p. 830) 1 O °God, my heart is °fixed;
I will sing and give praise, even with °my glory.
2 Awake, psaltery and harp:
I *myself* will °awake early.
3 I will praise Thee, O °LORD, among the °people:
And I will sing praises unto Thee among the nations.
4 For Thy °mercy *is* great above the heavens:
And Thy truth *reacheth* unto the °clouds.
5 Be Thou exalted, O [1]God, above the heavens:
And Thy glory above all the earth;
6 That Thy °beloved may be delivered:
Save *with* Thy right hand, and answer me.

E g 7 [1]God hath °spoken in His holiness; I will rejoice,
I will divide Shechem, and mete out the valley of Succoth.
8 Gilead *is* mine; °Manasseh *is* mine;
Ephraim also *is* the strength of mine head;
Judah *is* my lawgiver;

h 9 Moab *is* my washpot;
Over Edom will I cast out my °shoe;
Over Philistia will I triumph.
10 Who will bring me into the strong city?
Who will lead me into Edom?

D 11 *Wilt* not °Thou, O [1]God, *Who* hast cast us off?
And wilt not Thou, O [1]God, go forth with our hosts?
12 Give us help from trouble:
For vain *is* the help of °man.

E g 13 Through [1]God we shall do valiantly:
h For He *it is That* shall tread down our enemies.

°To the chief Musician.

109

°A Psalm °of David.

E[2] F (p. 830) 1 Hold not Thy peace, O °God °of my praise;
2 For the mouth of °the wicked and the mouth of the deceitful are opened against me:
°They have spoken against me with a lying tongue.
3 They compassed me about also with °words of hatred;
And fought against me °without a cause.
4 For my love they are my adversaries:
But °I *give myself unto* prayer.
5 And they have °rewarded me °evil for good,
And hatred °for my love.

G 6 "(°Set Thou a [2]wicked man over him:
°And let °Satan stand at his right hand.
7 When he shall be judged, let him be condemned:
[6]And let his prayer become °sin.
8 Let his days be few;
And °let another take his °office.

108—110 (B[1], p. 827). THE TRUE DAVID'S HUMILIATION, DELIVERANCE, AND TRIUMPH.

108 (E[1], p. 826). THE TRUE DAVID'S DELIVERANCE. (*Alternations.*)

E[1] | D | 1-6. God spoken to. Prayer.
  E | g | 7, 8. Israel. } God spoken of.
    h | 9, 10. Enemies. }
  D | 11, 12. God spoken to. Prayer.
  E | *g* | 13-. Israel. } God spoken of.
    h | -13. Enemies. }

Title. A Song. Heb. *shîr.* Ap. 65. XXIII.
Psalm. Heb. *mizmōr.* Ap. 65. XVII.
of David. Pss. 108—110 relate to the true David, and His humiliation, deliverance, and triumph. The first of fifteen Davidic Psalms in this fifth book. This subject appears in each book as the root and source of all blessing. Instead of a new Psalm being written for this subject here, a composite Psalm is formed by a combination of parts of Pss. 57. 7-11 and 60. 5-12. See the notes there.
1 God. Heb. Elohim. Ap. 4. I. **fixed** = steadfast.
my glory. Put by Fig. *Metonymy* (of Effect), Ap. 6, for the heart or tongue which gives the glory. Cp. 7. 5; 16. 9; 30. 12; 57. 8. Lit. "Aye, fain would I glory", &c.
2 awake early = awake the dawn.
3 LORD. Heb. Jehovah. Ap. 4. II.
people = peoples.
4 mercy = lovingkindness, or grace.
clouds = skies. **6 beloved** = beloved ones (pl.).
7 spoken in: or sworn by.
8 Manasseh. Some codices, with one early printed edition, read "And Manasseh".
9 shoe. See note on 60. 8.
11 Thou. Some codices, with Sept., Syr., and Vulg., read "Thou" (emphatic) in the text.
12 man. Heb. *'ādām.* Ap. 14. I.
13 To the chief Musician. Ap. 64.

109 (E[2], p. 826). THE TRUE DAVID'S HUMILIATION AND DELIVERANCE. (*Extended Alternation.*)

E[2] | F | 1-5. Prayer for himself.
  G | 6-15. Enemies. Their cursing.
    H | 16-20. Reward of those who curse his soul.
  F | 21-27. Prayer for himself.
  G | 28, 29. Enemies. Their cursing.
    H | 30, 31. Deliverance from those who condemn his soul.

Title. A Psalm. Heb. *mizmōr.* Ap. 65. XVII.
of David. See note on Ps. 108 (Title).
1 God. Heb. Elohim. Ap. 4. I.
of. Genitive of Relation: i.e. Whom I praise. Cp. Deut. 10. 21.
2 the wicked = a lawless one. Heb. *rāshā'.* Ap. 44. x.
They have spoken against me. See *vv.* 6-19 for what they spoke. Cp. 38. 11, 12; 71. 10, 11.
3 words of hatred. Written down in *vv.* 6-15. Cp. 2 Sam. 16. 5-13 for the type.
without a cause. Cp. John 15. 25.
4 I give myself unto prayer = I [am all] prayer. Cp. 120. 7 "I [am all] peace". As here in *vv.* 1-5 (F) and *vv.* 21-27 (*F*).
5 rewarded me = set or put against me. Syr. reads "returned me". Not the same word as in *v.* 20, though the same thing is referred to.
evil. Heb. *rā'a'.* Ap. 44. viii.
for my love. Note here the *Ellipsis* of the verb "saying", emphasising what is said rather than the saying of it. This verb has often to be thus supplied. See Gen. 26. 7. 1 Kings 20. 34. Ps. 2. 2; 144. 12. Prov. 1. 21. Isa. 5. 9; 14. 8; 18. 2; 22. 13; 24. 14, 15; 28. 9. Jer. 9. 19; 11. 19; 50. 5. Lam. 3. 41. Hos. 14. 8. Acts 9. 6; 10. 15; 14. 22, &c. See note on Ps. 144. 12.
6 Set Thou = "[saying] Set Thou", &c. See note above. Note the *Parenthesis* (Ap. 6), *vv.* 6-15.
And let Satan = And then Satan will.
Satan = an adversary. **7 sin.** Heb. *chāṭā'.* Ap. 44. i.
8 let another, &c. Quoted, but not *fulfilled* in Acts 1. 20. **office** = overseership.

9 Let his °children be fatherless,
And his wife a widow.
10 Let his [9]children be continually °vagabonds, and beg:
Let them °seek *their bread* also out of their desolate places.
11 Let the extortioner °catch all that he hath;
And let the strangers spoil his labour.
12 Let there be none to extend °mercy unto him:
Neither let there be any to favour his fatherless [9]children.
13 Let his posterity be cut off;
And in the generation following let °their name be blotted out.
14 Let the °iniquity of his fathers be remembered with °the LORD;
And let not the [7]sin of his mother be blotted out.
15 °Let them be before [14]the LORD continually,
That He may cut off the memory of them from the earth)."

H (p. 830) 16 Because that he remembered not to shew [12]mercy,
But persecuted °the poor and needy °man,
That he might even slay °the broken in heart.
17 As he loved cursing, so let it come unto him:
As he delighted not in blessing, so let it be far from him.
18 As he clothed himself with cursing like as with his garment,
So let it come into his bowels like water,
And like oil into his bones.
19 Let it be unto him as the garment *which* covereth him,
And for a girdle wherewith he is girded continually.
20 °*Let* this *be* the °reward of mine adversaries °from [14]the LORD,
And of them that °speak [5]evil against my °soul.

F i (p. 831) 21 But do 𝔗𝔥𝔬𝔲 for me, O °GOD °the Lord, for Thy °name's sake:

k Because Thy [12]mercy *is* good, deliver Thou me.

l 22 For 𝔍 *am* °poor and needy,

m And my °heart is wounded within me.

n 23 I am gone like the shadow when it declineth:

n I am tossed up and down as the locust.

m 24 My knees are weak through fasting;
And my flesh faileth of fatness.

l 25 𝔍 became also a reproach unto them:
When they looked upon me they shaked their heads.

k 26 Help me, O [14]LORD my [1]God:
O save me according to Thy [12]mercy:

i 27 That they may know that °this *is* Thy hand;
That °𝔗𝔥𝔬𝔲, [14]LORD, hast done it.

G (p. 830) 28 °Let 𝔱𝔥𝔢𝔪 curse, but bless 𝔗𝔥𝔬𝔲:
When they arise, let them be ashamed;
but °let Thy servant rejoice.
29 °Let mine adversaries be clothed with shame,
And let them cover themselves with their own confusion, as with a mantle.

H 30 I will greatly praise [14]the LORD with my mouth;
Yea, I will praise Him among the multitude.
31 For °He shall stand at the right hand of the °poor,
To save *him* from those that °condemn his [20]soul.

---

9 children = sons.
10 vagabonds = wanderers.
seek their bread also out. Sept. and Vulg. read "driven out".
11 catch = lay a snare for. Cp. 1 Sam. 28. 9.
12 mercy = kindness, or grace.
13 their name. Some codices, with Sept. and Vulg., read "His name".
14 iniquity. Heb. *'āvāh.* Ap. 44. iv.
the LORD. Heb. Jehovah. Ap. 4. II.
15 Let them be, &c. This verse is the end of the Parenthesis, which begins with *v.* 6.
16 the poor = an oppressed one (*v.* 22).
man. Heb. *'ish.* Ap. 14. II.
the broken in heart = one broken in heart. Cp. *v.* 22; 69. 20.
20 Let this be = This is. Verse 16 is a return to the subject of *vv.* 1–5, and by the same speaker of *vv.* 1–5.
reward = work. Not the same word as in *v.* 5.
from the LORD = from Jehovah. It was He Who permitted it. Cp. *v.* 27, "This is Thy hand; Thou, LORD, hast done it". See 22. 15; 38. 2, 3; 39. 9, 10. Cp. 2 Sam. 16. 11, "the LORD hath bidden him".
speak evil. See *vv.* 6–19 for the evil spoken.
soul. Heb. *nephesh.* Ap. 13.

109. 21–27 (*F*, p. 830). **PRAYER FOR HIMSELF.** (*Introversion.*)

F i | 21–. "Thou".
k | –21. "Thy mercy".
l | 22–. My humiliation.
m | –22. My heart wounded.
n | 23–. Comparison to a shadow.
n | –23. Comparison to a locust.
m | 24. My body weakened.
l | 25. My emaciation.
k | 26. "Thy mercy".
i | 27. "Thou".

21 GOD. Heb. Jehovah. Ap. 4. II.
the Lord. Heb. Adonai. Ap. 4. VIII (2).
name's. See note on 20. 1.
22 poor = oppressed. Refers to Messiah. Cp. *v.* 16. See 40. 17; 69. 29; 70. 5; 86. 1.
heart. Cp. *v.* 16.
27 this is Thy hand. See note on "from the LORD", *v.* 20. Put by Fig. *Metonymy* (of Cause), Ap. 6, for what is done by the hand.
Thou, LORD, hast done it. See note on *v.* 20. The same is said of Messiah's exaltation. See 118. 23.
28 Let them curse. As in *vv.* 6–15.
let Thy servant rejoice = Thy servant shall rejoice.
29 Let mine, &c. Contrast this with the malignity of *vv.* 6–15 and characterised in *vv.* 16–19.
31 He shall stand, &c. Contrast this with *v.* 6.
poor = needy. Not the same word as in *v.* 16.
condemn his soul. Cp. the Structure, *v.* 20 (H), with *v.* 31 (*H*).

110 °A Psalm °of David.

E³ J (p. 832) **1 °The LORD °said unto °my Lord, °"Sit Thou at My right hand,**
°Until I °make Thine enemies Thy footstool."

K **2 ¹The LORD shall send the rod of Thy strength out of °Zion:**

L **Rule Thou in the midst of Thine °enemies.**

M **3 Thy People °*shall be* °willing in the day of Thy power,**
In °the beauties of holiness °from the womb of the morning:
Thou hast the dew of Thy °youth.

J **4 ¹The LORD hath °sworn, and will not repent,**
°Thou *art* a priest for ever
°After the order of °Melchizedek.

K **5 °The LORD* at Thy right hand**
Shall strike through kings in the day of His wrath.

L **6 He shall judge among the °heathen,**
°He shall fill *the places* with the dead bodies;
He shall wound the °heads over °many countries.

M **7 He shall drink °of the brook in the way:**
Therefore shall He lift up °the head.

F¹ N (p. 832) **111** °Praise ye THE LORD.
(א) I will praise °the LORD with *my* whole heart,
(ב) In the °assembly of the upright, and *in* the congregation.

O P **2 (ג) The °works of ¹the LORD *are* great,**
(ד) Sought out of all them that have pleasure therein.
3 (ה) His work *is* honourable and °glorious:
(ו) And His righteousness endureth for ever.

110 (**E³**, p. 826). THE TRUE DAVID'S EXALTATION. (*Extended Alternation.*)

E³ J | 1. What Jehovah has uttered.
  K | 2-. What He will do.
    L | -2. Messiah's enemies.
      M | 3. Refreshment. Dew.
J | 4. What Jehovah has uttered.
  K | 5. What He will do.
    L | 6. Messiah's enemies.
      M | 7. Refreshment. Brook.

Title. **A Psalm.** Heb. *mizmōr.* Ap. 65. XVII.
of David. Relating to the true David, and interpreted of Him and by Him. See note below.

1 The LORD. Heb. Jehovah. Ap. 4. II. Quoted in Matt. 22. 41-46. Acts 2. 34, 35. Heb. 1. 13.

said. Heb. *ne'um* Jehovah = "the Oracle (or oracular utterance) of Jehovah". It is almost always used of the immediate direct utterance of Jehovah Himself; seldom of that of the prophet; (Num. 24. 3, 15); David (2 Sam. 23. 1).

my Lord = Adonai, Ap. 4. VIII (2): i.e. David's Lord: i.e. the Messiah. Cp. Matt. 22. 41-46.

Sit Thou, &c. Fig. *Anthrōpopatheia.* Ap. 6.

Until I make, &c. Quoted or referred to seven times in N.T. (Matt. 22. 44. Mark 12. 36. Luke 20. 42. Acts 2. 34. Heb. 1. 13; 10. 13. 1 Cor. 15. 25).

make Thine enemies Thy footstool = set Thine enemies [as] a footstool for Thy feet. In N.T. Gr. = *tithēmi* (2 aor. subj.) = "shall have placed". 1 Cor. 15. 25 is the exception, where it is not "set as a footstool", but put "under", because Christ's session on His own throne (Matt. 25. 31. Rev. 3. 21) is there referred to, instead of His session on His Father's throne, as in all the other quotations.

2 the rod of Thy strength = Thy strong staff. Gen. of Character, Ap. 17. The reference is to the ancestral staff, marking the priest as well as the prince, and handed down here to Messiah, David's son.

Zion. See Ap. 68. Cp. Rom. 11. 25-27.

enemies = foes.

3 shall be. Supply *Ellipsis* (Ap. 6) thus: "[shall offer] themselves for voluntary offerings, in the day that Thou warrest".

willing = freewill offerings, as in Ex. 35. 29; 36. 3. 1 Chron. 29. 9, 14, 17. Ezra 3. 5; 8. 28.

the beauties of holiness. Some codices, with two early printed editions, read "in (or on) the holy mountains".

from the womb, &c. Supply *Ellipsis* (Ap. 6): "[as the dew] from the womb before the morning I have begotten thee [a son]". Cp. 2. 7. There should be no stop after the word "morning". **youth** = a son.

4 sworn. Corresponding with "said" (*v.* 1). **Thou**: i.e. Messiah (David's son and Lord), not David himself, who was not of the tribe of Levi. **Thou art, &c.** Quoted in Heb. 5. 6; 7. 17. **After the order.** Cp. Gen. 14. 18. Heb. 5. 6, 10; 6. 20; 7. 1-28. **Melchizedek.** His priesthood was unique, and did not pass to another, as did Aaron's. Hence, Christ's priesthood, being in Resurrection life and Ascension glory, will continue for ever, and He will be a priest upon His throne (Zech. 6. 13), and a priest for ever.

5 The LORD*. One of the 134 places where the *Sōpherim* changed Jehovah to Adonai. See Ap. 32.

6 heathen = nations. Cp. Joel 3. 9-17. Zech. 14. 1-4. **He shall fill, &c.** = "Let Him judge among the peoples [a region] full of corpses. **heads** = head (Rev. 19. 11-21): i.e. the Antichrist. **many countries** = a great land. **7 of** = from. The verse begins with this word (Heb. מ = M = from), and thus corresponds with the "from" of *v.* 3 (member M, above). **the head** = [his] head.

111 (**F¹**, p. 826). PRAISE FOR JEHOVAH'S WORKS. (*Introversion and Alternation.*)

F¹ N | 1. Praise to Jehovah.
  O | P | 2-4. For His works.
    Q | 5, 6. His bounty, and objects of it.
  O | *P* | 7, 8. For His works.
    Q | 9, 10-. His bounty, and objects of it.
N | -10. Praise to Jehovah.

The first of three Hallelujah Psalms; the first two being a pair of Acrostic Psalms, linked together by a corresponding arrangement.

111 | | 1-8. Eight couplets. א-ע.
  | 9, 10. Two triplets. פ-ת.
112 | | 1-8. Eight couplets. א-ע.
  | 9, 10. Two triplets. פ-ת.

1 Praise ye THE LORD. Heb. Hallelu-*Jah.* Ap. 4. III. **the LORD.** Heb. Jehovah. Ap. 4. II. **assembly** = conclave, or secret assembly. **2 works.** The great subject of this Psalm, as His *ways* are of the next. Cp. Rev. 15. 3. **3 glorious** = majestic.

4 (ז) He hath made His wonderful works to be remembered:
(ח) [2] The LORD *is* °gracious and full of compassion.

Q (p. 832) 5 (ט) He hath given °meat unto them that °fear Him:
(י) He will ever be mindful of His covenant.
6 (כ) He hath shewed His People the power of His works,
(ל) That He may give them the °heritage of the °heathen.

O P 7 (מ) The °works of His hands *are* verity and judgment;
(נ) All His commandments *are* sure.
8 (ס) They stand fast for ever and ever,
(ע) *And are* done in truth and uprightness.

Q 9 (פ) **°He sent °redemption unto His people:**
(צ) He hath commanded His covenant for ever:
(ק) °Holy and °reverend *is* His name.
10 (ר) The °fear of [2] the LORD *is* the °beginning of wisdom:
(ש) A good understanding have all they that do *His commandments:*

N (ת) His praise endureth for ever.

F² R o (p. 833) **112** Praise ye °THE LORD.
(א) °Blessed *is* the °man *that* feareth °the LORD,
(ב) *That* delighteth greatly in His commandments.
2 (ג) His seed shall be mighty upon earth:
(ד) The generation of the upright shall be blessed.
3 (ה) Wealth and riches *shall be* in his house:

p (ו) And his righteousness endureth for ever.
4 (ז) Unto °the upright there ariseth light in the darkness:

q (ח) *He is* gracious, and full of compassion, and righteous.
5 (ט) °A good [1] man sheweth favour, and °lendeth:
(י) He will guide his affairs with discretion.

S 6 (כ) Surely he shall not be moved for ever:
(ל) °The righteous shall be in everlasting remembrance.
7 (מ) He shall not be afraid of °evil tidings:
(נ) His heart is fixed, °trusting in °the LORD.
8 (ס) His heart *is* established, he shall not be afraid,
(ע) Until he see *his desire* upon his enemies.

R q 9 (פ) **°He hath dispersed, he hath given to the °poor;**

p (צ) **His righteousness endureth for ever;**

o (ק) His horn shall be exalted with honour.

S 10 (ר) °The wicked shall see *it*, and be grieved;
(ש) He shall gnash with his teeth, and melt away:
(ת) The °desire of °the wicked shall perish.

F³ T **113** °Praise ye °THE LORD.

U Praise, O ye servants of °the LORD,

V Praise the °name of °the LORD.

V 2 °Blessed be the [1] name of °the LORD
From this time forth and for evermore.

---

4 gracious, &c. See Ex. 34. 6, 7.
5 meat. Heb. "prey". Put by Fig. *Synecdochē* (of Species), Ap. 6, for food of all kinds.
fear = revere.
6 heritage = inheritance. **heathen** = nations.
7 works . . . are. Some codices read "work . . . is" (sing.).
9 He sent, &c. Quoted in Luke 1. 68.
redemption. Involves three things: (1) His People; (2) His covenant; (3) His name.
Holy. See note on Ex. 3. 5.
reverend = to be feared. Heb. *nōrā'*, from *yārē'*, to be afraid. The Niphal Part. (as here) rendered "dreadful" (5); "to be feared" (3); "fearful" (2); "fearfully" (1); "to be had in reverence" (1); "reverend" (1); "terrible" (24); "terrible acts" (1); "terrible things" (5); "terribleness" (1). Cp. 45. 4; 47. 2; 65. 5; 66. 3, 5; 68. 35; 76. 12; 99. 3; 106. 22, &c.
10 fear = reverence.
beginning. Not wisdom itself, or its *end*, but only the *beginning* of it. See notes on Job 28. 28. Prov. 1. 7.

112 (F², p. 826). PRAISE FOR JEHOVAH'S WAYS. (*Alternation and Introversion.*)

F² | 1-. HALLELUJAH.
R | o | -1-3-. Happiness.
  p | -3, 4-. Righteousness.
   q | -4, 5. Goodness.
    S | 6-8. Shall stand.
R | *q* | 9-. Goodness.
  p | -9-. Righteousness.
   o | -9. Happiness.
    S | 10. Shall fall.

The second of three Hallelujah Psalms, and of the pair (111, 112). See note above. Also an Acrostic Psalm. See Ap. 63. VII.
1 THE LORD. Heb. Jah. Ap. 4. III.
Blessed = Happy. See Ap. 63. VI.
man. Heb. *'ish.* Ap. 14. II.
the LORD. Heb. eth Jehovah: i. e. Jehovah Himself. Ap. 4. II.
4 the upright = upright ones (pl.).
5 A good man, &c. Or, Good [is] the man that, &c.
lendeth. Put by Fig. *Synecdoche* (of Species), Ap. 6, for all kinds of merciful acts.
6 The righteous = A righteous one.
7 evil tidings. Heb. "evil hearing"; put by Fig. *Metonymy* (of Adjunct), Ap. 6, for whatever bad news may be heard.
trusting = confiding. Heb. *baṭah.* See Ap. 69. I.
the LORD. Heb. Jehovah. Ap. 4. II.
9 He hath dispersed. Quoted in 2 Cor. 9. 9.
poor = helpless ones. Heb. *'ebyōn* (pl.). See note on Prov. 6. 11.
10 The wicked = A lawless one. Heb. *rāshā'*. Ap. 44. x.
desire. Probably = hope, as in 9. 18; Prov. 10. 28.
the wicked = lawless ones (pl.). Ap. 44. x.

113 (F³, p. 826). PRAISE TO JEHOVAH HIMSELF. (*Introversion.*)

F³ | T | 1-. HALLELUJAH.
 U | -1-. Praise Jehovah. } Command given.
  V | -1. Praise His Name. } Command given.
  V | 2, 3. Bless His Name. } Command obeyed.
 U | 4-9-. Praise Jehovah. } Command obeyed.
T | -9. HALLELUJAH.

The third of these three Hallelujah Psalms (111—113). The Psalms of this group are called the Hallel Psalms (113—118). Psalms 113, 114 were sung before the Paschal meal (but after the second of the four cups of wine); 115—118 after it. The last probably sung by the Lord Jesus (Matt. 26. 30).
1 Praise ye THE LORD. Heb. Hallelu-Jah.
THE LORD. Heb. Jah. Ap. 4. III.
the LORD. Heb. Jehovah. Ap. 4. II.
name. See note on 20. 1.
2 Blessed. Fig. *Benedictio*, not *Beatitudo.* Ap. 6.
the LORD. Heb. Jehovah. Ap. 4. II.

3 From the rising of the sun unto the going down of the same
[2]The LORD'S [1]name *is* to be praised.

U (p. 833) 4 [2]The LORD *is* high above all nations,
And His glory above the heavens.
5 °Who *is* like unto [2]the LORD our °God,
Who dwelleth on high,
6 Who humbleth *Himself* to behold
The things that are in °heaven, and in the earth!
7 He raiseth up °the poor out of the dust,
And lifteth °the needy out of the dunghill;
8 That He may set *him* °with princes,
Even °with the princes of His People.
9 He maketh the barren woman to keep house,
And to be a joyful mother of °children.
T [1]Praise ye [1]THE LORD.

G½ W (p. 834) **114** °When Israel went out of °Egypt,
The house of °Jacob from a people of strange language;
2 Judah °was His sanctuary,
And Israel His dominion.

X r 3 °The sea saw *it*, and fled:
°Jordan was driven back.
s 4 The mountains skipped like rams,
And the little hills like lambs.

X r 5 °What *ailed* thee, O thou [3]sea, that thou fleddest?
Thou [3]Jordan, *that* thou wast driven back?
s 6 Ye mountains, *that* ye skipped like rams;
And ye little hills, like lambs?

W 7 Tremble, thou earth, at the presence of °the Lord,
At the presence of the °GOD of [1]Jacob;
8 Which °turned the rock *into* a °standing water,
The flint into a fountain of waters.

G½ Y t (p. 834) **115** °Not unto us, O °LORD, °not unto us,
u But unto Thy °name give glory,
For Thy °mercy, °*and* for Thy truth's sake.

Z v 2 Wherefore should the °heathen say,
"Where *is* now their °God?"
w 3 But our [2]God *is* in the heavens:
He hath done whatsoever He hath pleased.

Z v x 4 Their idols *are* °silver and gold,
y The °work of °men's hands.
z 5 They have °mouths, but they speak not:
a Eyes have they, but they see not:
b 6 They have ears, but they hear not:
c °Noses have they, but they smell not:
b 7 They have hands, but they handle not:
a Feet have they, but they walk not:
z Neither °speak they through their throat.
y 8 They that make them are like unto them;
x °*So is* every one that °trusteth in them.

w 9 O °Israel, [8]trust thou in [1]the LORD:
°*He is* their help and their °shield.

---

5 Who is like . . . ? This is ever the outburst of the saints' praise. See note on Ex. 15. 11.
God. Heb. Elohim. Ap. 4. I.
6 heaven = the heavens.
7 the poor = an impoverished one.
the needy = a needy one. Cp. 1 Sam. 2. 8.
8 with princes . . . with the princes. Fig. *Anadiplōsis* (Ap. 6), for emphasis. **9 children** = sons.

114 (G½, p. 826). ISRAEL'S DELIVERANCE FROM EGYPT. (*Introversion and Alternation.*)

G½ | W | 1, 2. God's mercies to Jacob.
X | r | 3. By water. } Statements.
s | 4. On land.
X | *r* | 5. Water. } Questions.
s | 6. Land.
W | 7, 8. God's mercies to Jacob.

See note on Psalm 113, above.
1 When Israel. Cp. Ex. 13. 3.
Egypt. Not Babylon. The Psalm not post-exilic.
Jacob. See notes on Gen. 32. 28; 43. 6; 46. 27, 28.
2 was = became. See note on Gen. 1. 2.
3 The sea. Cp. Ex. 14. 21.
Jordan. Cp. Josh. 3. 13.
5 What . . . ? Fig. *Erotēsis.* Ap. 6.
7 the Lord. Heb. Adōn. Ap. 4. VIII (1).
GOD. Heb. Eloah. Ap. 4. V.
8 turned = changed. **standing** = pool.

115 (G½, p. 826). ISRAEL'S DELIVERANCE FROM EGYPT'S IDOLATRY. (*Introversion and Alternations.*)

G½ | Y | t | 1–. Negative. } The praise given.
u | –1. Positive.
Z | v | 2. Heathen theology.
w | 3. Israelitish.
Z | *v* | 4–8. Heathen theology.
w | 9–16. Israelitish.
Y | *t* | 17. Negative. } The praise-givers.
u | 18. Positive.

1 Not. Heb. *l'o* (not *'al*). Supply *Ellipsis* thus: "Not to us LORD, not to us [belongeth glory] but to Thy name give the glory". **LORD.** Heb. Jehovah. Ap. 4. II.
name. See note on 20. 1.
mercy = lovingkindness, or grace.
and. Some codices, with one early printed edition, Aram., Sept., Syr., and Vulg., read this "and" in the text.
2 heathen = nations.
God. Heb. Elohim. Ap. 4. I.

4-8 (*v*, above). HEATHEN THEOLOGY. (*Introversion.*)

v | x | 4–. The idols.
y | –4. Their fabrication.
z | 5–. Mouth without speech. (Sing.)
a | –5. Eyes without sight. (Pl.)
b | 6–. Ears without hearing. (Pl.)
c | –6. Nose without smell. (Sing.)
b | 7–. Hands without handling. (Pl.)
a | –7–. Feet without walking. (Pl.)
z | –7. Throat without voice. (Sing.)
y | 8–. The fabricators.
x | –8. The idolaters.

4 silver and gold. Put by Fig. *Metonymy* (of Cause), Ap. 6, for what is made from them. Cp. 135. 15-19.
work. Some codices, with Sept. and Vulg., read pl., "works". **men's.** Heb. *'ādām.* Ap. 14. I.
5 mouths = a mouth (sing.).
6 Noses = a nose (sing.).
7 speak = make a sound.
8 So is. Some codices, with Sept., Syr., and Vulg., read "And [so is]".
trusteth = confideth. Heb. *baṭaḥ.* Ap. 69. I.
9 Israel. Some codices, with Sept., Syr., and Vulg., read "house of Israel". See notes on Gen. 32. 28; 43. 6; 46. 27, 28.
He is their help, &c. Fig. *Epistrophe* (Ap. 6), in *vv.* 9, 11.
shield. See note on Ps. 84. 9.

10 O house of Aaron, [8]trust in [1]the LORD:
[9]He *is* their help and their shield.
11 Ye that fear [1]the LORD, [8]trust in [1]the LORD:
[9]He *is* their help and their shield.
12 [1]The LORD hath been mindful of us: °He will bless *us;*
°He will bless °the house of Israel;
He will bless the house of Aaron.
13 °He will bless them that °fear [1]the LORD,
Both °small °and great.
14 [1]The LORD shall increase you more and more,
You and your °children.
15 Ye *are* blessed of [1]the LORD
Which made heaven and earth.
16 The heaven, *even* the heavens, *are* [1]the LORD'S:
But the earth hath He given to the [14]children of [4]men.

Y t (p. 834) 17 The dead praise not °THE LORD,
Neither any that go down into silence.
u 18 But we will bless [17]THE LORD
From this time forth and for evermore.
°Praise [17]THE LORD.

H$_1^1$ A^1 (p. 835) **116** I love °the LORD, because He hath heard
°My voice *and* my supplications.
2 Because He hath inclined His ear unto me,
Therefore will I call upon *Him* as long as I live.
B 3 The °sorrows of death compassed me,
And the pains of °hell °gat hold upon me:
I found trouble and sorrow.
C E 4 °Then called I upon the name of [1]the LORD;
F d O [1]LORD, I beseech Thee, deliver °my soul.
e 5 °Gracious *is* [1]the LORD, and righteous;
Yea, our °God *is* °merciful.
6 [1]The LORD preserveth the °simple:
D I was brought low, and He helped me.
A^2 7 Return unto thy °rest, O [4]my soul;
°For [1]the LORD hath dealt bountifully with thee.
8 For Thou hast delivered [4]my soul from death,
Mine eyes from tears,
And my feet from falling.
9 I will walk before [1]the LORD
In the land of the living.
B 10 °**I believed, therefore have I spoken:**
I was greatly afflicted:
11 I said in my °haste,
°"All men *are* °liars."
C E 12 °What shall I render unto [1]the LORD
For all His benefits toward me?
13 °I will take the cup of salvation,
°And call upon the name of [1]the LORD.
14 I will pay my vows unto [1]the LORD
Now in the presence of all His people.
F e 15 °Precious in the sight of [1]the LORD
Is the death of His °saints.

12 He will bless us; He will bless. Fig. *Anadiplosis* (Ap. 6), for emphasis.
the house of Israel. Cp. 135. 19. See note on Ex. 16. 31.
13 He will bless. Fig. *Anaphora* (Ap. 6), taken with the last line of *v.* 12. **fear**=revere.
small and great. Both pl. Fig. *Syntheton.* Ap. 6.
and=with.
14 children=sons.
17 THE LORD. Heb. Jah. Ap. 4. III.
18 Praise THE LORD. Heb. Hallelu-Jah.

116 (**H**[1], p. 826). PRAISE FOR DELIVERANCE.
(*Extended Alternation.*)

H$_1^1$ | A^1 | 1, 2. Resolve to praise.
  B | 3. Afflictions.
    C | E | 4–. Promise.
      F | d | –4. Prayer.
        e | 5, 6–. The Lord's goodness to others.
          D | –6. His goodness to me.
A^2 | 7–9. Resolve to praise.
  B | 10, 11. Afflictions.
    C | *E* | 12–14. Promise.
      F | *e* | 15. The Lord's goodness to others.
        d | 16–. Prayer.
          D | –16. His goodness to me.
A^3 | 17–19. Resolve to praise.

1 the LORD. Heb. Jehovah. Ap. 4. II.
My voice and my supplications=My supplicating voice. Fig. *Hendiadys.* Ap. 6. So some codices, with Sept., Syr., and Vulg., read "the voice of my supplication".
3 sorrows=cords. Put by Fig. *Metonymy* (of Cause), Ap. 6, for the pains produced by them.
hell=Sheōl. See Ap. 35.
gat hold. Fig. *Prosopopœia.* Ap. 6.
4 Then called I=I will call, as in *v.* 13. See the Structure.
my soul=me (emphatic). Heb. *nephesh.* Ap. 13.
5 Gracious. Cp. Ex. 34. 6, 7.
God. Heb. Elohim. Ap. 4. I.
merciful=full of compassion.
6 simple=sincere or guileless ones; not "foolish" in the modern usage.
7 rest. Pl. for emphasis. **For**=Because.
10 I believed=I believed [Him]. Quoted in 2 Cor. 4. 13.
11 haste=hasting.
All men. Heb. *'ādām* (with Art.) = all humanity. Ap. 14. I.
liars: or false.
12 What shall I render . . . ? Note the answer in next verse.
13 I will take. The way to render thanks is to receive yet more grace.
And call=And [I will] call. Cp. Structure, E and *E.*
15 Precious. See note on 1 Sam. 3. 1.
saints=separated ones.
17 offer=sacrifice. Heb. *zābach.* Ap. 43. I. iv.
19 Praise ye THE LORD = Hallelu-Jah. See Ap. 4. III.

16 O [1]LORD, truly I *am* Thy servant; *d*
I *am* Thy servant, *and* the son of Thine handmaid:
Thou hast loosed my bonds. *D*
17 I will °offer to Thee the sacrifice of thanksgiving, A^3
And will call upon the name of [1]the LORD.
18 I will pay my vows unto [1]the LORD
Now in the presence of all His people,
19 In the courts of [1]the LORD'S house,
In the midst of thee, O Jerusalem.
°Praise ye THE LORD.

H½ G (p. 836) **117** °**O praise** °**the LORD, all ye nations:**
°**Praise Him, all ye** °**people.**
H **2** For His °merciful kindness °is great toward us:
H And the truth of [1]the LORD *endureth* for ever.
G °Praise ye °THE LORD.

H⅓ J (p. 836) **118** O give thanks unto °the LORD; for *He is* good:
Because His °mercy *endureth* for ever.
2 Let Israel now say,
That His [1]mercy *endureth* for ever.
3 Let the house of Aaron now say,
That His [1]mercy *endureth* for ever.
4 Let them now that fear [1]the LORD say,
That His [1]mercy *endureth* for ever.
K[1] L[1] **5** I called upon °THE LORD in distress:
°THE LORD answered me, °*and set me* in a large place.
M[1] e **6** °**The LORD *is* on my side; I will not fear:**
What can °**man do unto me?**
7 [1]The LORD taketh my part with them that help me:
Therefore shall I see *my desire* upon them that hate me.
f **8** °*It is* °better to °trust in [1]the LORD
°Than to °put confidence in °man.
9 [8]*It is* [8]better to [8]trust in [1]the LORD
[8]Than to [8]put confidence in princes.
f **10** °All nations compassed me about:
°But in the name of [1]the LORD will I destroy them.
11 °They compassed me about; yea, °they compassed me about:
[10]But in the name of [1]the LORD I will destroy them.
12 °They compassed me about like bees; they °are quenched as the fire of thorns:
For in °the name of [1]the LORD I will destroy them.
e **13** °Thou hast thrust sore at me that I might fall:
But [1]the LORD helped me.
K[2] L[2] **14** [5]THE LORD *is* my strength and °song,
And is become my °salvation.
M[2] g **15** The voice of rejoicing and salvation *is* in the °tabernacles of the righteous:
h °The right hand of [1]the LORD °doeth valiantly.
16 [15]The right hand of [1]the LORD is exalted:
[15]The right hand of [1]the LORD [15]doeth valiantly.
h **17** I shall not die, but live,
And declare the °works of [5]THE LORD.
18 [5]THE LORD hath °chastened me sore:
But He hath not given me over unto death.

117 (H½, p. 826). PRAISE.
(*Introversion.*)

H½ | G | 1. Praise.
  H | 2-. His lovingkindness. } Motives.
  H | -2. His truth. }
  G | -2. Praise.

1 praise, &c. Quoted in Rom. 15. 11.
the LORD. Heb. Jehovah with *'eth* = Jehovah Himself. Ap. 4. II.
Praise = Laud. See note on 63. 3.
people = peoples.
2 merciful kindness = lovingkindness, or grace.
is great toward = overcame, or prevailed over. Cp. 103. 11.
Praise ye THE LORD. Heb. Hallelu-Jah. Ap. 4. III.

118 (H⅓, p. 826). PRAISE).
(*Introversions and Alternations.*)

H⅓ | J | 1-4. O give thanks.
  K[1] | L[1] | 5. Acknowledgment. My deliverer.
    M[1] | e | 6, 7. Help.
      f | 8, 9. Trust. } Trust.
      f | 10-12. Trust. }
      e | 13. Help.
  K[2] | L[2] | 14. Acknowledgment. My strength.
    M[2] | g | 15-. Tents of the righteous. } Help.
      h | -15, 16. Cause. Hand.
      h | 17, 18. Effect. Life.
      g | 19, 20. Gates of righteousness.
  K[3] | L[3] | 21. Acknowledgment. My salvation.
    M[3] | i | 22-24. Messiah. Matt. 21. 42. } Triumph.
      k | 25-. Prayer.
      k | -25. Prayer.
      i | 26-28. Messiah. Matt. 21. 9.
  J | 29. "O give thanks".

1 the LORD. Heb. Jehovah. Ap. 4. II.
mercy = lovingkindness, or grace.
5 THE LORD. Heb. Jah. Ap. 4. III.
and set me in a large place. The current Heb. text = with the deliverance of JAH, *bammerḥab yāh* (two words). The Massoretic text reads it as one word, *bammerḥabyāh* = with deliverance. The A.V. and R.V. transfer the *yāh* to the beginning of the clause, and are then compelled to make out the sense by supplying "and set me". They do not even notice the Massoretic reading. The printed text reads:
"I called upon Jah in distress,
He answered me with the deliverance of *Yāh*."
The Massoretic text reads:
"I called upon Yah in distress,
He answered me with deliverance."
6 The LORD, &c. Heb. Jehovah. Ap. 4. II. Quoted in Heb. 13. 6.
man = a man. Heb. *'ādām*. Ap. 14. I.
8 It is better . . . Than. Fig. *Cœnotes* (Ap. 6), repeated in *v.* 9.
better = good. By Fig. *Heterōsis* (Ap. 6), the Positive is put for the Comparative, and is so rendered.
trust = flee for refuge. Heb. *ḥāṣāh*. Ap. 69. II.
put confidence. Heb. *bāṭaḥ*. Ap. 69. I.
man. Heb. *'ādām*. Ap. 14. I.
10 All. Put by Fig. *Synecdochē* (of Genus), Ap. 6, for a large number, or many.
But, &c. Fig. *Epistrophe* (Ap. 6), repeated in *v.* 11.
11 They compassed . . . they compassed. Fig. *Epizeuxis* (Ap. 6), for emphasis.
12 They compassed. Fig. *Anaphora* (Ap. 6), repeated from *v.* 11.

are quenched. Sept. reads "blazed up". **the name.** See note on 20. 1. **13 Thou.** Does this refer to the "man" of *v.* 6? **14 song.** Put by Fig. *Metonymy* (of Adjunct), Ap. 6, for the theme of the song. **salvation.** Cp. *v.* 21. Ex. 15. 2. Isa. 12. 2. Put by Fig. *Metonymy* (of Cause), Ap. 6, for Him Who saves = my Saviour. **15 tabernacles** = tents, or dwellings. Heb. *'ohel*. Ap. 40 (3). **The right hand.** Fig. *Anthrōpopatheia*. Ap. 6. **doeth valiantly.** Fig. *Cœnotes* (Ap. 6), repeated in *v.* 16. **17 works.** Some codices, with one early printed edition, read "work" (sing.). **18 chastened me sore.** The Fig. *Polyptōton* (Ap. 6), thus well rendered. Heb. = "chastening He chastened me".

g (p. 836) 19 Open to me the gates of righteousness:
I will go into them, *and* I will praise [5]THE LORD:
20 This gate of [1]the LORD,
Into which the righteous shall enter.

K[3] L[3] 21 I will praise Thee: for Thou hast heard me,
And art become my [14]salvation.

M[3] i 22 °**The stone *which* the builders °refused**
Is become the head *stone* of the corner.
23 °**This is [1]the LORD'S doing;**
It *is* marvellous in our eyes.
24 This *is* the day *which* [1]the LORD hath made;
We will rejoice and be glad in it.

k 25 °Save now, I beseech Thee, O [1]LORD:
k O [1]LORD, I beseech Thee, send now prosperity.

i 26 °**Blessed *be* he that cometh in the name of [1]the LORD:**
We have blessed °you out of the house of [1]the LORD.
27 °GOD *is* [1]the LORD, Which hath shewed us light:
°Bind the °sacrifice with °cords, °*even* unto the horns of the altar.
28 Thou *art* my [27]GOD, and I will °praise Thee:
Thou art my °God, I will exalt Thee.

J 29 O give thanks unto [1]the LORD; for *He is* good:
For His [1]mercy *endureth* for ever.

119

ℵ ALEPH.

A[2] N (p. 837) 1 (ℵ) °Blessed *are* the undefiled in the °way,
Who walk in the °law of °the LORD.

O 2 (ℵ) °Blessed *are* they that °keep His °testimonies,
And that seek Him with the whole heart.

P 3 (ℵ) They also do no °iniquity:
They walk in His [1]ways.

Q 4 (ℵ) Thou hast commanded *us*
To keep Thy °precepts diligently.

N 5 (ℵ) O that my [1]ways were directed
To keep Thy °statutes!

O 6 (ℵ) Then shall I not be °ashamed,
When I have respect unto all Thy °commandments.

P 7 (ℵ) I will °praise Thee with uprightness of heart,
When I shall have learned Thy °righteous °judgments.

Q 8 (ℵ) I will keep Thy [5]statutes:
O forsake me °not utterly.

---

22 The stone: i. e. the Messiah. See Gen. 49. 24. A stone of stumbling, Isa. 8. 14 (cp. Rom. 9. 33. 1 Pet. 2. 8); a "tried stone", "precious", "sure", Isa. 28. 16; the rejected stone (cp. Matt. 21. 42. Mark 12. 10, 11. Luke 20. 17. Acts 4. 11. 1 Pet. 2. 4). The true foundation, Isa. 28. 16 (cp. Matt. 16. 18. 1 Cor. 3. 11. Eph. 2. 20).

refused. See note above, and cp. Structure, "i" with "*i*", above. Here the present Dispensation comes in. See Ap. 72.

23 This is the LORD'S doing. Messiah's exaltation is thus like the humiliation (109. 27).

25 Save now, &c. Heb. "Hosanna" = Save, I pray. Not a Particle of *time*, but of *entreaty* (as in Ecc. 12. 1). Repeated four times for emphasis. Lit. "I pray Thee, Jehovah; Save; I pray Thee; I pray Thee, O Jehovah".

26 Blessed, &c. See Matt. 21. 9; 23. 39. Mark 11. 9. Luke 13. 35; 19. 38. John 12. 13.

you. Plural.

27 GOD. Heb. El. Ap. 4. IV.

Bind. Heb. *'āsar*, to bind, or join. Here, in its idiomatic usage, to join, so as to make ready (Gen. 46. 29. Ex. 14. 6. 1 Kings 18. 44. 2 Kings 9. 21), or begin (1 Kings 20. 14. 2 Chron. 13. 3).

sacrifice. Heb. *ḥāg* = a feast, or festal [sacrifice]. See note on Ex. 23. 18, and cp. Ex. 5. 1; 12. 14; 23. 14. Lev. 23. 39, 41. Num. 29. 12. Deut. 16. 15. Zech. 14. 16, 18, 19.

cords = wreaths, or garlands, as in Ex. 28. 14, 22, 24, 25; 39. 15, 17, 18.

even unto. Heb. *'ad* = up to or during: i. e. even until [it is consummated at] the horns of the altar. *'Ad* denotes progression in time. Translate: "Make ready the festal sacrifice with garlands until [it is consummated at] the horns of the altar." Cp. Acts 14. 13. There is nothing about "to the altar" here.

28 praise = give thanks.

God. Heb. Elohim. Ap. 4. I.

119. 1-8 (A[2], p. 826). QUICKENING BY THE WRITTEN WORD. (ℵ. ALEPH, *Extended Alternation.*)

ℵ | N | 1. The way.
O | 2. Condition. Happy.
P | 3. They, upright.
Q | 4. Command.
} Third Person. (General.)

N | 5. My ways.
O | 6. Condition. Not ashamed.
P | 7. I, upright.
Q | 8. Promise.
} First Person. (Individual.)

Probably by Hezekiah. See Ap. 67, Ps. 123. 3, and notes below.

An Acrostic Psalm (Ap. 63. VII), in which each verse in each of the twenty-two sections commences with the twenty-two successive letters of the Hebrew alphabet: i. e. the first eight begin with *Aleph* (= A), the second eight with *Beth* (= B), &c.: making 176 verses in all (i. e. 8 × 22).

For the ten words (corresponding with the Ten Commandments) which are characteristic of this Psalm, see Ap. 73.

1 Blessed = How happy (see Ap. 63. VI). Here pl. = O the great happiness.

way. The first of the ten words. See Ap. 73. The thirteen occurrences of this word in this Psalm are all noted below, as are those of the other nine.

law. The sixth in order of the ten words. See Ap. 73.

the LORD. Heb. Jehovah. Ap. 4. II.

2 Blessed. This Psalm begins with a double Beatitude. See Ap. 63. VI. **keep** = guard.

testimonies. The second in order of the ten words. See Ap. 73.

3 iniquity = perversity. Heb. *'āval.* Ap. 44. vi.

4 precepts. The third in order of the ten words. See Ap. 73. **5 statutes.** The ninth in order of the ten words. See Ap. 73. **6 ashamed** = put to shame; not shame of conscience. **commandments.** The tenth in order of the ten words. See Ap. 73. **7 praise** = give thanks, as in 92 1, &c. **righteous** = righteousness: i. e. judgments of Thy righteousness. The eighth in order of the ten words. See Ap. 73. **judgments.** The seventh in order of the ten words. See Ap. 73. **8 not utterly** = not in any wise. Cp. *v.* 43

ב BETH.

R (p. 838) 9 (ב) Wherewithal shall °a young man cleanse his °way?
°By taking heed *thereto* according to Thy °word.

S l[1] 10 (ב) With my whole heart have I sought Thee:
m[1] O let me not wander from Thy [6]commandments.

l[2] 11 (ב) Thy °word have I °hid in mine heart,
That I might not °sin against Thee.

m[2] 12 (ב) Blessed *art* Thou, O [1]LORD:
Teach me Thy [5]statutes.

l[3] 13 (ב) With my °lips have I °declared
All the [7]judgments of Thy mouth.
14 (ב) I have rejoiced in the [1]way of Thy [2]testimonies,
As *much as* in all riches.

R 15 (ב) I will meditate in Thy [4]precepts,
And have respect unto Thy ways.
16 (ב) I will delight myself in Thy statutes:
I will not forget Thy °word.

ג GIMEL.

T (p. 838) 17 (ג) Deal bountifully with Thy servant,
That I may live, and keep Thy [9]word.
18 (ג) °Open Thou mine eyes, that I may °behold
Wondrous things out of Thy [1]law.
19 (ג) I *am* a °stranger in the earth:
Hide not Thy [6]commandments from me.

U 20 (ג) My °soul °breaketh for the °longing
That it hath unto Thy [7]judgments at all times.
21 (ג) Thou hast rebuked the proud *that are* cursed,
Which do °err from Thy [6]commandments.

T 22 (ג) Remove from me °reproach and °contempt;
For I have kept Thy [2]testimonies.

U 23 (ג) Princes also did sit *and* speak against me:
But Thy servant did meditate in Thy [5]statutes.
24 (ג) Thy [2]testimonies °also *are* my delight
And °my counsellers.

ד DALETH.

V n (p. 838) 25 (ד) [20]My soul cleaveth unto the °dust:
o °Quicken Thou me according to Thy °word.

W p 26 (ד) I have declared my [1]ways, and Thou heardest me:
q Teach me Thy [5]statutes.
q 27 (ד) Make me to understand the [1]way of Thy [4]precepts:
p So shall I °talk of Thy wondrous works.

V n 28 (ד) [20]My soul °melteth for heaviness:
o Strengthen Thou me according unto Thy °word.

W r 29 (ד) Remove from me the [1]way of lying:
And grant me Thy [1]law graciously.

9-16 (ב BETH). CLEANSING OF THE WAY.
(*Introversion and Repeated Alternation.*)

ב | R | 9. The way to be cleansed. (Future.)
  S | l[1] | 10-. What I have done. My heart.
    m[1] | -10. Prayer. (Negative.)
    l[2] | 11. What I have done. My heart.
    m[2] | 12. Prayer. (Positive.)
    l[3] | 13, 14. What I have done. My lips.
  R | 15, 16. The way to be cleansed. (Future.)

9 a young man. The writer not necessarily a youth.
way=path. Not the same word as in *v.* 1.
By taking=So as to take. Put interrogation at end of the second line instead of the first.
word=the articulate subject-matter of what is said. The tenth in order of the ten words of this Psalm. See note on 18. 30. Ap. 73. Not the same word as in *v.* 11. Some codices, with Aram., Sept., Syr., and Vulg., read "words" (pl.).
11 word=the mode, or purport of what is said. The fifth in order of the ten words of this Psalm. See Ap. 73. Some codices, with one early printed edition, Aram., Sept., Syr., and Vulg., read "words" (pl.).
hid=treasured up. **sin.** Heb. *chāṭā'*. Ap. 44. i.
13 lips . . . declared. Fig. *Paronomasia*. Ap. 6: *bispātay sippartī*.
16 word. Same word as in *v.* 9 (not *v.* 11): but some codices, with two early printed editions, Aram., Sept., Syr., and Vulg., read "words" (pl.).

17-24 (ג GIMEL). PRAYER FOR STRENGTHENING.
(*Alternation.*)

ג | T | 17-19. Prayer and Reasons.
  U | 20, 21. Twofold statement. Himself and wicked.
  T | 22. Prayer and Reasons.
  U | 23, 24. Twofold statement. Himself and wicked.

18 Open=Unveil.
behold=discern, or see clearly.
19 stranger=foreigner sojourning.
20 soul. Heb. *nephesh*. Ap. 13.
breaketh for=hath broken owing to. Occurring again only in Lam. 3. 16.
longing=fervent desire; same word as *vv.* 40, 174, but not *v.* 131.
21 err=go far astray (through wine or passion). Same word as "wander" (*v.* 10), and "err" (*v.* 118). Heb. *shāgah*. Ap. 44. xii.
22 reproach and contempt. Cp. 123. 3, 4, confirming Hezekiah's suggested authorship.
24 also=nevertheless. See 129. 2.
my counsellors=men (Heb. *'īsh*. Ap. 14. II) of my counsel.

25-32 (ד DALETH). PRAYER. PRESERVATION.
(*Alternations and Introversion.*)

ד | V | n | 25-. Depression.
    o | -25. "Quicken me".
  W | p | 26-. Profession. (Past.)
      q | -26. Prayer. "Teach me".
      q | 27-. Prayer. (Future.)
      p | -27. Profession. "I will talk".
  V | *n* | 28-. Depression.
    o | -28. "Strengthen me".
  W | r | 29. Prayer. "Remove".
      s | 30, 31-. Profession. (Past.)
      r | -31. Prayer. "Put not to shame".
      s | 32. Profession. (Future.)

25 dust. Put by Fig. *Metonymy* (of Adjunct), Ap. 6, for the dead, as in Ps. 30. 9. Ecc. 12. 7.
Quicken . . . me=Give me life, or keep me alive. The first of nine prayers for quickening (Imperative), *vv.* 25, 37, 40, 88, 107, 149, 154, 156, 159. Twice as a statement of fact, *vv.* 50, 93.
word. As in *v.* 9; but some codices read "words" (pl.).
27 talk=meditate.
28 melteth=weepeth. Occurs only here. Job 16. 20. Ecc. 10. 18.
word. As in *v.* 9. Some codices read pl.; but other codices, with Sept. and Vulg., read "by (or in) thy words" (pl.).

s 30 (ד) I have chosen the [1] way of truth:
Thy [7] judgments have I °laid *before me*.
31 (ד) I have °stuck unto Thy [2] testimonies:
r (p. 838) O [1] LORD, put me not to shame.
s 32 (ד) I will run the [1] way of Thy [6] commandments,
When Thou shalt °enlarge my heart.

ה HE.

X t (p. 839) 33 (ה) °Teach me, O [1] LORD, the way of Thy [5] statutes;
And I shall keep it *unto* the end.
u 34 (ה) Give me understanding, and I shall keep Thy [1] law;
Y Yea, I shall observe it with *my* whole heart.
Z 35 (ה) Make me to go in the path of Thy [6] commandments;
For therein do I delight.
Y 36 (ה) Incline my heart unto Thy [2] testimonies,
And not to covetousness.
X t 37 (ה) Turn away mine eyes from beholding vanity;
And [25] quicken Thou me in Thy °way.
38 (ה) Stablish Thy [11] word unto Thy servant,
°Who *is devoted* to Thy fear.
39 (ה) Turn away my reproach which I °fear:
For Thy [7] judgments *are* good.
u 40 (ה) Behold, I have [20] longed after Thy [4] precepts:
[25] Quicken me °in Thy °righteousness.

ו VAU.

A (p. 839) 41 (ו) Let Thy °mercies come also unto me, O [1] LORD,
Even Thy salvation, according to Thy [11] word.
42 (ו) So shall I have °wherewith to answer him that °reproacheth me:
B For I °trust in Thy °word.
A 43 (ו) And take not the [9] word of truth utterly out of my mouth;
B For I have hoped in Thy [7] judgments.
44 (ו) So shall I keep Thy [1] law continually
°For ever and ever.
45 (ו) And I will walk °at liberty:
For I seek Thy [4] precepts.
46 (ו) I will speak of Thy [2] testimonies also before °kings,
And will not be ashamed.
47 (ו) And I will delight myself in Thy [6] commandments,
Which I °have loved.
48 (ו) °My hands also will I lift up unto Thy [6] commandments, which I have loved;
And I will meditate in Thy [5] statutes.

ז ZAIN.

C1 (p. 839) 49 (ז) Remember the [9] word unto Thy servant,
°Upon which Thou hast °caused me to hope.
D1 50 (ז) This *is* my °comfort in my affliction:
For Thy [11] word hath °quickened me.

30 laid = set.
31 stuck = cleaved, or adhered.
32 enlarge my heart = set my heart at liberty, as in Isa. 60. 5. 2 Cor. 6. 11, 13.

33-40 (ה HE). PRAYER. TEACHING.
(*Introversion and Alternation.*)

ה | X | t | 33. Eyes. Make me to see.
u | 34-. Mind. Its comprehension.
Y | -34. Heart.
Z | 35. Feet. Practical walking.
Y | 36. Heart.
X | *t* | 37-39. Eyes. Turn them away.
u | 40. Mind. Its desires.

33 Teach me = Show, or make me to see.
37 way. Some codices, with three early printed editions, Aram., and Syr., read "ways" (pl.).
38 Who is devoted to Thy fear. Supply Ellipsis thus: "Which [leadeth to] reverence of Thee"; or, "Which [pertaineth to]", &c. **39** fear = dread.
40 in: or by.
righteousness. Heb. *ẓedāḳāh*. See Ap. 73. viii.

41-48 (ו VAU). PRAYER. STRENGTHENING.
(*Alternation.*)

ו | A | 41, 42-. Prayer. (Positive.)
B | -42. Reason and Plea.
A | 43-. Prayer. (Negative.)
B | -43-48. Reasons and Pleas.

41 mercies = lovingkindnesses.
42 wherewith = a word. Heb. *dābār* as in *v.* 9. See Ap. 73. x.
reproacheth. See note on "contempt", 123. 3.
trust in = confide in. Heb. *baṭaḥ*. Ap. 69. I.
word. Some codices, with one early printed edition, Aram., Sept., and Syr., read "words" (pl.).
44 For ever and ever. Put by Fig. *Synecdoche* (of Whole), Ap. 6, for a part: i. e. the rest of his life.
45 at liberty = at large. Cp. 118. 5.
46 kings. So Hezekiah testified, doubtless, when kings sent presents and embassies to him (2 Chron. 32. 22, 23). No occasion to suggest a later date for this Psalm.
47 have loved = love. Sept. adds "much".

49-56 (ז ZAIN). PRAYER. COMFORT AND REMEMBRANCE. (*Repeated Alternation.*)

ז | C1 | 49. "Remember . . . Thou".
D1 | 50, 51. Statement as to consequences.
C2 | 52. "I remembered".
D2 | 53, 54. Statement as to consequences.
C3 | 55. "I have remembered".
D3 | 56. Statement as to consequences.

48 My hands, &c. Heb. idiom = to swear by, as in Gen. 14. 22. Ex. 6. 8 (marg.). Deut. 32. 40. Ezek. 20. 5, 6; 36. 7. See note on Ex. 17. 16.
49 Upon which. This is supported by the Sept. and Vulg. In Deut. 29. 25 it is rendered "Because".
caused me to hope. Our hope is based on believing what we have "heard" from God. Cp. Heb. 11. 1 with Rom. 10. 17.
50 comfort. The word occurs (as a noun) elsewhere only in Job 6. 10.
quickened me = kept me alive. See note on *v.* 25.
proud = insolent (like Rabshakeh).
53 Horror = Indignation.
wicked = lawless. Heb. *rāshā'*. Ap. 44. x.

51 (ז) The °proud have had me greatly in derision:
Yet have I not declined from Thy [1] law.
52 (ז) I remembered Thy [7] judgments of old, O [1] LORD; C2
And have comforted myself.
53 (ז) °Horror hath taken hold upon me D2
Because of the °wicked that forsake Thy [1] law.

54 (ז) Thy [5]statutes have been my °songs
In the house of my pilgrimage.

C³ (p. 839) 55 (ז) I have remembered Thy °name, O [1]LORD, in the night,
And have kept Thy [1]law.

D³ 56 (ז) °This I had,
Because I kept Thy [4]precepts.

ח CHETH.

E (p. 840) 57 (ח) *Thou art* my portion, O [1]LORD:
I have said that I would keep Thy [9]words.

58 (ח) I intreated Thy °favour with *my* whole heart:
Be °merciful unto me according to Thy [11]word.

59 (ח) I thought on my [1]ways,
And turned my feet unto Thy [2]testimonies.

60 (ח) I made haste, and delayed not
To keep Thy [6]commandments.

F 61 (ח) The bands of the [53]wicked have °robbed me:
But I have not forgotten Thy [1]law.

E 62 (ח) At midnight I will rise to give thanks unto Thee
Because of Thy [7]righteous [7]judgments.

63 (ח) I *am* a °companion of all *them* that °fear Thee,
And of them that keep Thy [4]precepts.

F 64 (ח) The earth, O [1]LORD, is full of Thy °mercy:
Teach me Thy [5]statutes.

ט TETH.

G (p. 840) 65 (ט) Thou hast dealt well with Thy servant,
O [1]LORD, according unto Thy [9]word.

H t 66 (ט) Teach me good judgment and knowledge:
For I have believed Thy [6]commandments.

u 67 (ט) °Before I was °afflicted I went astray:
°But now have I kept Thy [11]word.

H t 68 (ט) Thou *art* °good, and °doest good;
Teach me Thy [5]statutes.

u 69 (ט) The proud have forged a lie against me:
But I will keep Thy [4]precepts with *my* whole heart.

70 (ט) Their heart is as fat as grease;
But I delight in Thy [1]law.

71 (ט) °*It is* °good for me that I have been [67]afflicted;
That I might learn Thy [5]statutes.

G 72 (ט) The [1]law of Thy mouth *is* better unto me
Than thousands of °gold and silver.

י °JOD.

J (p. 840) 73 (י) Thy hands have made me and °fashioned me:
Give me understanding, that I may learn Thy [6]commandments.

54 songs. Put by Fig. *Metonymy* (of Subject), Ap. 6, for the theme of my songs.
55 name. See note on 20. 1.
56 This. Supply Ellipsis (Ap. 6) thus: "This [comfort] I had".

57-64 (ח CHETH). PRAYER AND PROFESSION. (*Alternation.*)

ח | E | 57-60. Jehovah my portion.
  F | 61. Statement *re* the work of the lawless.
 E | 62, 63. Jehovah my praise.
  F | 64. Statement *re* the favour of Jehovah.

57 The division is better made thus, dispensing with the supposed Ellipsis:
I have said "Jehovah is my portion,
That I might keep Thy word."
58 favour. Heb. face; put by Fig. *Metonymy* (of Adjunct), Ap. 6, for what is indicated by it.
merciful=gracious.
61 robbed=surrounded. Cp. Sennacherib's investment of Hezekiah. See Ap. 67.
63 companion=fellow of the same party.
fear=revere.
64 mercy=lovingkindness, or grace.

65-72 (ט TETH). PRAYER. JEHOVAH'S DEALINGS. (*Introversion and Alternation.*)

ט | G | 65. Thy dealings good.
  H | t | 66. Thy judgments good. Teach me.
    u | 67. Affliction good. Result.
  H | *t* | 68. Thou art good. Teach me.
    u | 69-71. Affliction good. Result.
 G | 72. Thy law good.

67 Before. If we begin this verse with the word "Till", and *v.* 71 with "'Tis", then each verse in this section will commence with "T", as it does in the Hebrew.
afflicted=oppressed.
But now. Cp. Heb. 12. 6-11, and references there.
68 good=kind. **doest good**=actest kindly.
71 It is. See note on *v.* 67.
good=right, or fitting.
72 gold and silver. Put by Fig. *Metonymy* (of Cause), Ap. 6, for coins made from these metals.

73-80 (י JOD). PRAYER. INSTRUCTION AND DELIVERANCE. (*Introversion.*)

י | J | 73. Prayer. "I".
  K | 74. "They that revere Thee".
   L | 75. Affliction. "I".
    M | 76. Lovingkindness.
    M | 77. Tender mercies.
   L | 78. Affliction. "I".
  K | 79. "They that fear Thee".
 J | 80. Prayer. "I".

Jod. This is the small letter referred to in Matt. 5. 18.
73 fashioned=formed. Cp. Job 31. 15; also Deut. 32. 18.
74 fear=revere.
75 right=righteousness, as in *v.* 7.
afflicted=humbled.
76 merciful kindness=lovingkindness, or grace.

74 (י) They that °fear Thee will be glad when they see me; K
Because I have hoped in Thy [9]word.

75 (י) I know, O [1]LORD, that Thy [7]judgments *are* °right, L
And *that* Thou in faithfulness hast °afflicted me.

76 (י) Let, I pray Thee, Thy °merciful kindness be for my comfort, M
According to Thy [11]word unto Thy servant.

.M (p. 840) 77 (י) Let Thy °tender mercies come unto me, that I may live:
°For Thy [1]law *is* my °delight.

L 78 Let the °proud be ashamed; for they dealt °perversely with me °without a cause:
But I will meditate in Thy [4]precepts.

K 79 (י) Let those that [74]fear Thee turn unto me,
And °those that have known Thy [2]testimonies.

J 80 (י) Let my heart be °sound in Thy [5]statutes;
That I be not ashamed.

כ CAPH.

N[1] O (p. 841) 81 (כ) [20]My soul fainteth for Thy salvation:
But I hope in Thy [9]word.
82 (כ) Mine eyes °fail for Thy [11]word,
P Saying, "When wilt Thou comfort me?"
O 83 (כ) For I am become like a °bottle in the smoke;
Yet do I not forget Thy [5]statutes.
84 (כ) How °many *are* the days of Thy servant?
P When wilt Thou °execute [7]judgment on them that persecute me?

N[2] Q[1] 85 (כ) The [78]proud have digged pits for me,
°Which *are* not °after Thy [1]law.
R[1] 86 (כ) All Thy [6]commandments *are* °faithful:
Q[2] They persecute me °wrongfully;
R[2] Help Thou me.
Q[3] 87 (כ) They had °almost °consumed me upon earth;
R[3] But I forsook not Thy [4]precepts.
88 (כ) [25]Quicken me after Thy lovingkindness;
So shall I keep the [2]testimony of Thy mouth.

ל LAMED.

S v (p. 841) 89 (ל) °For ever, O [1]LORD,
w Thy [9]word is °settled in heaven.
v 90 (ל) Thy faithfulness *is* unto all generations:
w Thou hast established the earth, and it °abideth.
91 (ל) °They °continue °this day according to Thine °ordinances:
For °all *are* Thy servants.
T 92 (ל) Unless Thy [1]law *had been* my [77]delights,
I should then have perished in mine affliction.
U 93 (ל) I will never forget Thy [4]precepts:
For with them Thou hast [25]quickened me.
U 94 (ל) I *am* Thine, save me;
For I have °sought Thy [4]precepts.
T 95 (ל) The [53]wicked have waited for me to destroy me:
But I will consider Thy [2]testimonies.
S 96 (ל) I have seen an end of °all perfection:
But °Thy [6]commandment *is* exceeding broad.

77 tender mercies = compassions.
For, &c. This is the ground of his prayer.
delight. Pl. as in *v.* 92 = great delight.
78 proud = insolent, or arrogant.
perversely = with falsehood.
without a cause. Cp. John 15. 25 with Rom. 3. 24 ("freely").
79 those that have known. Some codices read "and they shall know". **80 sound** = thorough.

81-88 (כ CAPH). PRAYER. IN DISTRESS. (*Division.*)

כ | N[1] | 81-84. Distress. Complaints and Pleas.
| N[2] | 85-88. Distress. Causes, Contrasts, and Prayers.

81-84 (N[1], above). COMPLAINTS AND PLEAS. (*Alternation.*)

N[1] | O | 81, 82-. Two complaints, with plea between.
P | -82. Question. When comfort?
O | 83, 84-. Two complaints, with plea between.
P | -84. Question. When vindicate?

82 fail. Same word as "fainteth", in *v.* 81.
83 bottle = wine-skin: i. e. black and shrivelled. Cp. Job 30. 30.
84 many: i. e. few at the most. Cp. 89. 47. 2 Sam. 19. 34.
execute judgment = vindicate.

85-88 (N[2], above). CAUSES, CONTRASTS, AND PRAYERS. (*Repeated Alternation.*)

N[2] | Q[1] | 85. Enemies. "They . . . me".
R[1] | 86-. Statement. "Thy".
Q[2] | -86-. Enemies. "They . . . me".
R[2] | -86. Statement. "Thou".
Q[3] | 87-. Enemies. "They . . . me".
R[3] | -87, 88. Statement. "Thy".

85 Which, &c. = "[Men] who are not", &c.
after = according to.
86 faithful = faithfulness.
wrongfully. See note on "perversely", *v.* 78.
87 almost = soon. See note on "almost" (Prov. 5. 14).
consumed = made an end of.

89-96 (ל LAMED). JEHOVAH AND HIS WORD. (*Introversion.*)

ל | S | 89-91. Jehovah's Word settled and eternal.
T | 92. Affliction cannot destroy my delight in it.
U | 93. Statement and reason. "For".
U | 94. Statement and reason. "For".
T | 95. The wicked cannot destroy my meditation in it.
S | 96. Jehovah's Word perfect and eternal.

89-91 (S, above). JEHOVAH'S WORD. (*Alternation.*)

S | v | 89-. Jehovah eternal. } The heavens
w | -89. His Word established. } (89. 37).
v | 90-. Jehovah's faithfulness eternal. } The earth
w | -90, 91. The earth established. } (89. 4).

89 For ever, O LORD. Supply *Ellipsis* (Ap. 6), "For ever [art Thou], O Jehovah [For ever] Thy Word", &c.
settled = standeth fast, as the earth: i.e. endureth for ever (102. 12, 26. Isa. 40. 8. Luke 16. 17. 1 Pet. 1. 25). So Christ, the Living Word (John 12. 34).
90 abideth = standeth, as in *v.* 91.
91 They: i. e. heaven and earth.
continue = stand, as in *v.* 90.
this day = [to] this day, or to-day.
ordinances = regulations. Heb. *mishpāt.* The seventh of the ten words. Ap. 73. Cp. *v.* 132.
all. With Art. = the whole [universe].
94 sought = inquired into, or studied. Cp. 105. 4.
96 all perfection = an end, or limit to all things. Cp. Job 26. 10; 28. 3.
Thy commandment, &c. = spacious exceedingly [are] Thy commandments: i. e. including all (as opposed to "end").

מ MEM.

V X (p. 842) **97** (מ) O how love I Thy [1]law!
𝔍t *is* my meditation all the day.

Y x¹ **98** (מ) Thou °through Thy [6]commandments hast made me wiser than mine enemies:
y¹ For °𝔱𝔥𝔢𝔶 *are* ever with me.

x² **99** (מ) I have more understanding °than all my teachers:
y² For Thy [2]testimonies *are* my meditation.

x³ **100** (מ) I understand more than the °ancients,
y³ Because I keep Thy [4]precepts.

W **101** (מ) I have refrained my feet from every °evil °way,
That I °might keep Thy °word.

W **102** (מ) I have not °departed from Thy [7]judgments:
For 𝔗𝔥𝔬𝔲 hast °taught me.

V X **103** (מ) How °sweet are Thy [11]words unto my taste!
Yea, sweeter than honey to my mouth!

Y **104** (מ) Through Thy [4]precepts I get understanding:
Therefore I hate every false [101]way.

נ NUN.

A a (p. 842) **105** (נ) Thy [9]word *is* a °lamp unto my feet,
And a light unto my path.

b **106** (נ) I have sworn, and °I will perform *it*,
That I will keep Thy [7]righteous [7]judgments.

B **107** (נ) I am afflicted very much:
[25]Quicken me, O [1]LORD, according unto Thy [9]word.

108 (נ) Accept, I beseech Thee, the freewill offerings of my mouth, O [1]LORD,
And teach me Thy [7]judgments.

B **109** (נ) [20]My soul *is* continually °in my hand:
Yet do I not forget Thy [1]law.

110 (נ) The [53]wicked have laid a snare for me:
Yet I °erred not from Thy [4]precepts.

A a **111** (נ) Thy [2]testimonies have I taken as an heritage for ever:
For 𝔱𝔥𝔢𝔶 *are* the rejoicing of my heart.

b **112** (נ) I have inclined mine heart to perform Thy [5]statutes alway,
Even unto the end.

ס SAMECH.

C (p. 842) **113** (ס) I hate *vain* °thoughts:
But Thy [1]law do I love.

114 (ס) 𝔗𝔥𝔬𝔲 *art* my °hiding place and my °shield:
I hope in Thy [9]word.

D **115** (ס) Depart from me, ye [101]evildoers:
For I will keep the [6]commandments of my °God.

E **116** (ס) Uphold me according unto Thy [11]word, that I may °live:
And let me not be ashamed of my hope.

E **117** (ס) Hold Thou me up, °and I shall be safe:
And I will °have respect unto Thy [5]statutes continually.

D **118** (ס) Thou hast °trodden down all them that [21]err from Thy [5]statutes:
For their deceit *is* falsehood.

97-104 (מ MEM). JEHOVAH'S WORD THE SOURCE OF WISDOM. (*Introversion and Alternations.*)

מ | V | X | 97. The Word of Jehovah. Precious.
  Y | 98-100. The source of Understanding and Reason.
   W | 101. The Psalmist's practice (Pos.) and motive.
   W | 102. The Psalmist's practice (Neg.) and Reason.
 V | *X* | 103. The Word of Jehovah. Precious.
  Y | 104. The source of Understanding and Consequences.

98-100 (Y, above). THE SOURCE OF UNDERSTANDING (Pos.). (*Repeated Alternation.*)

Y | x¹ | 98-. Wiser than mine enemies.
 y¹ | -98. Reason.
 x² | 99-. Wiser than my teachers.
 y² | -99. Reason.
 x³ | 100-. Wiser than the aged.
 y³ | -100. Reason.

98 through: or, as to.
𝔱𝔥𝔢𝔶 are = it [is]: i. e. the Law containing the commandments.
99 than all my teachers. Because Divinely taught Divine wisdom.
100 ancients = elders, or the aged ones.
101 evil. Heb. *rā'a'.* Ap. 44. viii.
way. Including religious way, in the sense of Acts 9. 2; 19. 9, 23; 24. 14. Cp. Acts 16. 17; 18. 26; especially in *v.* 104.
might. A.V., 1611, reads "may".
word. Same word as in *v.* 9. Some codices, with one early printed edition, with Aram., Sept., Syr., and Vulg., read "words" (pl.).
102 departed = swerved. **taught** = directed.
103 sweet = smooth, or agreeable. Not the same word as in 19. 10.

105-112 (נ NUN). JEHOVAH'S WORD THE SOURCE OF LIGHT AND JOY. (*Introversion and Alternation.*)

נ | A | a | 105. The Word my Light.
  b | 106. Purpose to keep it.
   B | 107, 108. Affliction and Prayer.
   B | 109, 110. Danger and Protestations.
 A | *a* | 111. The Word my Heritage and Joy.
  b | 112. Purpose to keep it.

105 lamp: or lantern, for light on the path for the feet; not merely a light for the eyes (19. 8).
106 I will perform it. Some cod., with seven early printed editions, Aram., Sept., Syr., and Vulg., read "I have performed it"; but some cod., with four early printed editions (1 in marg.), read "and will perform it".
109 in my hand. An idiom for great danger. Cp. Judg. 12. 3. 1 Sam. 19. 5; 28. 21. Job 13. 14.
110 erred = to err from the paths of virtue and piety. Heb. *tā'āh*; not the same word as in *vv.* 21, 118.

113-120 (ס SAMECH). JEHOVAH'S LAW. THE SECURITY GIVEN BY IT. (*Introversion.*)

ס | C | 113, 114. Protestations. "I".
  D | 115. Evildoers. Addressed concerning God.
   E | 116. Uphold me. From above and without.
   E | 117. Uphold me. From beneath and within.
  D | 118, 119. Evildoers. God addressed concerning them.
 C | 120. Protestations. "I".

113 thoughts = divided or doubting thoughts. Same root as 1 Kings 18. 21 (cp. Jas. 1. 8); or, them that are of double mind.
114 hiding place. Cp. 32. 7; 91. 1.
shield. Cp. 84. 9, and note. Fig. *Anthrōpopatheia.* Ap. 6.
115 God. Heb. Elohim. Ap. 4. I. But "my God" implies Jehovah.
116 live. See note ‖ on p. 827.
117 and I shall be safe = so shall I be saved.
have respect unto. Aram. and Syr. read "find dear delight in". Sept. reads "shall meditate".
118 trodden down: or set at naught.

119 (ס) °Thou puttest away all the [53] wicked of the earth *like* dross:
Therefore I love Thy [2] testimonies.

C (p. 842) 120 (ס) °My flesh trembleth for fear of Thee;
And I am afraid of Thy [7] judgments.

ע AIN.

F (p. 843) 121 (ע) I have done [7] judgment and °justice:
Leave me not to mine oppressors.

122 (ע) Be surety for Thy servant for good:
Let not the °proud oppress me.

G 123 (ע) Mine eyes fail for Thy salvation,
And for the [11] word of Thy righteousness.

H 124 (ע) Deal with Thy servant according unto Thy °mercy,
And teach me Thy [5] statutes.

125 (ע) I *am* Thy servant; give me understanding,
That I may know Thy [2] testimonies.

F 126 (ע) *It is* time for *Thee*, [1] LORD, °to work:
For they have made void Thy [1] law.

G 127 (ע) Therefore I love Thy [6] commandments
Above gold; yea, above fine gold.

128 (ע) Therefore I esteem all *Thy* [4] precepts *concerning* all *things to be* right;
H *And* I hate every false [101] way.

פ PE.

J (p. 843) 129 (פ) Thy [2] testimonies *are* °wonderful:
Therefore doth [20] my soul °keep them.

130 (פ) The °entrance of Thy [9] words giveth light;
It giveth understanding unto the °simple.

131 (פ) I opened my mouth, and panted:
For °I longed for Thy [6] commandments.

K 132 (פ) Look Thou upon me, and be °merciful unto me,
°As Thou usest to do unto those that love Thy °name.

K 133 (פ) °Order my steps °in Thy [11] word:
And let not any °iniquity have dominion over me.

134 (פ) °Deliver me from the oppression of °man:
So will I keep Thy [4] precepts.

135 (פ) Make Thy face to shine upon Thy servant;
And teach me Thy [5] statutes.

J 136 (פ) °Rivers of waters run down mine eyes,
Because they keep not Thy [1] law.

צ TZADDI.

L[1] (p. 843) 137 (צ) °Righteous *art* Thou, O [1] LORD,
And upright *are* Thy [7] judgments.

138 (צ) Thy [2] testimonies *that* Thou hast commanded *are* °righteous
And very faithful.

M[1] 139 (צ) My zeal hath consumed me,
Because mine enemies have forgotten Thy [9] words.

L[2] 140 (צ) Thy [11] word *is* °very pure:
Therefore Thy servant loveth it.

141 (צ) I *am* °small and despised: M[2]
Yet do not I forget Thy [4] precepts.

142 (צ) Thy [7] righteousness *is* an everlasting [7] righteousness, L[3]
And Thy [1] law °*is* the truth.

119 Thou puttest away. Sept. and Vulg. read "I have accounted".

120 My flesh trembleth: or, My flesh creeps (as we say). Cp. Job 4. 15: i.e. at the judgment executed on the wicked.

121-128 (ע AIN). JEHOVAH'S SERVANT'S CONFIDENCE. (*Extended Alternation.*)

ע | F | 121, 122. What I have done, and Prayer (Neg.).
  G | 123. The Word. Desire for it.
   H | 124, 125. Thy servant's prayer.
 F | 126. What Jehovah should do, and Plea (Pos.).
  G | 127, 128-. The Word. Love for it.
   H | -128. Thy servant's resolve.

121 justice = righteousness. Same word as in *v.* 7.

122 proud = arrogant. This is the only verse in this Psalm which has not one of the "ten words", unless we may include the Living Word Himself, Who is the "surety" for His people. See note on Prov. 11. 15, and cp. Heb. 7. 22. See Ap. 73.

124 mercy = lovingkindness, or grace.

126 to work: i. e. to intervene.

129-136 (פ PE). GUIDANCE BY THE WORD. (*Introversion.*)

פ | J | 129-131. Statements concerning the Word.
  K | 132. Prayer concerning the Righteous.
  K | 133-135. Prayer concerning the Wicked.
 J | 136. Statement concerning the Word.

129 wonderful. Same root as in *vv.* 18, 27.
keep = keep safely.

130 entrance = doorway; which was always an open way for the light, in the absence of windows.
simple = sincere, as opposed to crafty.

131 I longed. An Aramaic word (*yā'ab*). Occurs only here. Weaker than in *vv.* 20, 40, 174.

132 merciful = gracious.
As Thou usest to do = According to Thy ordinance. Heb. *mishpāt.* The seventh in order of the "ten words" (Ap. 73). So rendered in *v.* 91.
name. See note on 20. 1.

133 Order = Direct, or guide.
in = by. Some codices, with one early printed edition, Sept., and Vulg., read "according to".
iniquity. Heb. *'āven.* Ap. 44. iii.

134 Deliver: i. e. by power. Heb. *pādāh.* See notes on Ex. 6. 6 and 13. 13. Not the same word as *vv.* 153, 154, 170.
man. Heb. *'ādām.* Ap. 14. I.

136 Rivers of waters. Heb. *palgēy-mayim.* See note on Prov. 21. 1. Eng. idiom = Floods of tears.

137-144 (צ TZADDI). JEHOVAH'S WORD AND THE PSALMIST. (*Repeated Alternation.*)

צ | L[1] | 137, 138. Thy Word. Righteous.
  M[1] | 139. I. Consumed.
 L[2] | 140. Thy Word. Pure.
  M[2] | 141. I. Despised.
 L[3] | 142. Thy Word. Truth.
  M[3] | 143. I. Consumed.
 L[4] | 144. Thy Word. Righteous.

137 Righteous, &c. See *v.* 7. See also Rev. 16. 5, 7.

138 righteous and very faithful = righteousness and faithfulness.

140 very pure = refined.

141 small = insignificant. Cp. Judg. 6. 15.

142 is the truth = is truth (no Art.). Cp. John 17. 17.

M[3] (p. 843) 143 (צ) Trouble and anguish have °taken hold on me:
Yet Thy [6]commandments *are* my [77]delights.

L[4] 144 (צ) The righteousness of Thy [2]testimonies *is* everlasting:
Give me understanding, and I shall live.

ק KOPH.

N (p. 844) 145 (ק) I °cried with *my* whole heart; °hear me, O [1]LORD:
I will keep Thy [5]statutes.
146 (ק) I °cried unto Thee; save me,
And I shall keep Thy [2]testimonies.
147 (ק) I °prevented the °dawning of the morning, and cried:
I hoped in Thy °word.
148 (ק) Mine eyes °prevent the *night* °watches,
That I might meditate in Thy [11]word.
149 (ק) °Hear my voice according unto Thy lovingkindness:
O [1]LORD, [25]quicken me according to Thy [7]judgment.

O 150 (ק) They draw nigh that follow °after mischief:
They are far from Thy [1]law.
151 (ק) Thou *art* near, O [1]LORD;
And all Thy [6]commandments *are* truth.

P 152 (ק) Concerning Thy [2]testimonies, I have known of old
That Thou hast founded them for ever.

ר RESH.

N (p. 844) 153 (ר) Consider mine affliction, and °deliver me:
For I do not forget Thy [1]law.
154 (ר) Plead my cause, and °deliver me:
[25]Quicken me according to Thy [11]word.

O 155 (ר) Salvation *is* far from the [53]wicked:
For they seek not Thy [5]statutes.
156 (ר) Great *are* Thy °tender mercies, O [1]LORD:
[25]Quicken me according to Thy [7]judgments.
157 (ר) Many *are* my persecutors and mine °enemies;
Yet do I not decline from Thy [2]testimonies.
158 (ר) I beheld the °transgressors, and °was grieved;
Because they kept not Thy [11]word.
159 (ר) Consider how I love Thy [4]precepts:
[25]Quicken me, O [1]LORD, according to Thy lovingkindness.

P 160 (ר) Thy [9]word *is* true *from* the °beginning:
And every one of Thy [7]righteous [7]judgments *endureth* for ever.

ש SCHIN.

Q[1] (p. 844) 161 (ש) °Princes have persecuted me without a cause:
But my heart standeth in awe of Thy °word.

R[1] 162 (ש) I rejoice at Thy °word,
As one that findeth great spoil.

143 taken hold. Fig. *Prosopopœia.* Ap. 6.

145-152 (ק KOPH.) } PRAYER FOR FAITHFULNESS
153-160 (ר RESH.) } IN DISTRESS.
(*Extended Alternation.*)

ק | N | 145–149. The Psalmist's cry.
O | 150, 151. Jehovah near Psalmist. Foes nigh.
P | 152. The Word established for ever.

ר | *N* | 153, 154. The Psalmist's cry.
O | 155–159. Jehovah far from wicked. Foes many.
P | 160. The Word established for ever.

145 cried = called [unto Thee], as in *v.* 146.
hear = answer.
146 cried = called. Fig. *Anaphora.* Ap. 6.
147 prevented = anticipated, or forestalled.
dawning. A *Homonym.* Heb. *nesheph.* See note on 1 Sam. 30. 17. A.V. and R.V. correctly render it here, and in Job 7. 4; though not in 1 Sam. 30. 17. Job 24. 15.
word. Same as in *v.* 11; but some codices, with Sept. and Vulg., read "words" (pl.).
148 prevent = anticipate, or forestall.
watches. See Ap. 51. III. 4 (18), p. 74.
149 Hear. Emphatic = O do hear.
150 after mischief. Some codices, with Sept., Syr., and Vulg., read "after me maliciously".
153 deliver. Twenty-five Heb. words so rendered. Here, *ḥālaz* = rescue (with a gentle hand); not the same word as in *vv.* 134, 154, 170.
154 deliver. Heb. *gā'al* = redeem. See notes on Ex. 6. 6 and 13. 13. Not the same word as in *vv.* 134, 153, 170.
156 tender mercies = compassions.
157 enemies = adversaries: i.e. those who hem me in.
158 transgressors. Heb. *bāgad* = traitors, or treacherous men.
was grieved = loathed myself: i.e. seeing the same tendencies in myself. Cp. Job 42. 6.
160 beginning. Heb. *r'osh* = head. Put by Fig. *Synecdochē* (of Part), Ap. 6, for the whole (including the beginning, and "every one", as in next line) = sum and substance, word and words (Jer. 15. 16. John 17. 8, 14); rendered "sum" in 139. 17.

161-168 (ש SCHIN). JEHOVAH'S WORD GIVES PEACE AND COMFORT. (*Repeated Alternation.*)

ש | Q[1] | 161. Contrastive Statement.
R[1] | 162. Praise. "Thy".
Q[2] | 163. Contrastive Statement.
R[2] | 164. Praise. "Thy".
Q[3] | 165. Contrastive Statement.
R[3] | 166–168. Prayer. "Thy".

161 Princes = Rulers.
word. Same word as in *v.* 9. Some codices, with Sept. and Vulg., read "words" (pl.).
162 word. Same word as in *v.* 11. Some codices with Sept. and Vulg., read "words" (pl.).
163 lying = falsehood = what is false; especially false religion and idolatry.
164 Seven times. Not a "round" number, but the number of spiritual perfection. See Ap. 10.
165 peace. Put by Fig. *Synecdochē* (of Part), Ap. 6, for every blessing connected with peace.
offend them = make them stumble.

163 (ש) I hate and abhor °lying: Q[2]
But Thy [1]law do I love.
164 (ש) °Seven times a day do I praise Thee R[2]
Because of Thy [7]righteous [7]judgments.
165 (ש) Great °peace have they which love Thy [1]law: Q[3]
And nothing shall °offend them.
166 (ש) [1]LORD, I have hoped for Thy salvation, R[3]
And done Thy [6]commandments.

167 (ש) [20]My soul hath kept Thy [2]testimonies;
And I love them exceedingly.
168 (ש) I have kept Thy [4]precepts and Thy [2]testimonies:
For all my [1]ways *are* before Thee.

ת TAU.

S¹ (p. 845) 169 (ת) Let my cry come near before Thee, O [1]LORD:
Give me understanding according to Thy [9]word.
170 (ת) Let my supplication come before Thee:
°Deliver me according to Thy [11]word.
T¹ 171 (ת) My lips shall °utter praise,
When Thou hast taught me Thy [5]statutes.
172 (ת) My tongue shall °speak of Thy [11]word:
For all Thy [6]commandments *are* [7]righteousness.
S² 173 (ת) Let Thine °hand help me;
For I have chosen Thy [4]precepts.
T² 174 (ת) I have [20]longed for Thy salvation, O [1]LORD;
And Thy [1]law *is* my delight.
S³ 175 (ת) Let [20]my soul live, and it shall praise Thee;
And let Thy [7]judgments °help me.
T³ 176 (ת) I have gone astray like a °lost sheep; seek Thy servant;
S⁴ For I do not forget Thy [6]commandments.

120

°A Song of °degrees.

G¹₂ A (p. 845) 1 In my °distress I °cried unto °the LORD,
And He °heard me.
B 2 °Deliver °my soul, O [1]LORD, from lying °lips,
And from a deceitful °tongue.
B 3 What shall be given unto thee? or what shall be °done unto thee,
Thou false tongue?
4 Sharp arrows of the °mighty,
With coals of juniper.
A 5 Woe is me, that I sojourn in °Mesech,
That I dwell in the tents of °Kedar!
6 [2]My soul hath long dwelt
With °him that hateth peace.
7 °I *am for* peace:
But when I °speak, °they *are* for war.

121

°A Song of °degrees.

G²₂ C¹ a 1 I will lift up mine eyes unto the °hills,
b °From whence °cometh my help.

169-176 (ת TAU). PETITIONS AND STATEMENTS. (*Repeated Alternation.*)

ת S¹ | 169, 170. Prayer ("Let") and Plea.
T¹ | 171, 172. Statements. "I". Praise.
S² | 173. Prayer ("Let") and Plea ("For").
T² | 174. Statements. "I".
S³ | 175. Prayers ("Let").
T³ | 176–. Statement. "I". Confession.
S⁴ | –176. Prayer and Plea ("For").

170 Deliver=Rescue. Heb. *nāẓal*, to pluck out of the hands of an enemy; recover. Not the same word as in *vv.* 134, 153, 154.

171 utter = pour forth or bubble over with. Cp. Prov. 15. 2; 18. 4.

172 speak of. Heb. respond with. Put by Fig. *Synecdochē* (of Species), Ap. 6, for all kinds of speaking or singing; hence=praise.

173 hand. Fig. *Anthrōpopatheia* (Ap. 6); "hand" put by Fig. *Metonymy* (of Cause), Ap. 6, for power exercised by it.

175 it shall praise Thee. Refers to Isa. 38. 20.
help me. Refers to Isa. 37. 33–36.

176 lost=perishing. Cp. Matt. 18. 11; Luke 19. 10.

120 (G¹₂, p. 826). GROUP I. PSALM (FIRST). DISTRESS. (*Introversion.*)

G¹₂ A | 1. Hezekiah and Jehovah.
B | 2. His prayer to Jehovah.
B | 3, 4. His apostrophe to Rab-shakeh.
A | 5–7. Hezekiah and Jehovah.

Title. A Song. Heb. *shīr.* See Ap. 65. XXIII: viz. one of the Songs promised by Hezekiah in Isa. 38. 20.
degrees=the degrees, or steps. Heb. *hamma'ălōth* (with Art.): i.e. the "degrees" mentioned six times in 2 Kings 20. 8–11, and five times in Isa. 38. 8 (Heb.). No other "degrees" known to Scripture which are connected with the shadow of the sun.
For the origin, authorship, examination, and Structure, see Ap. 67, and note § on p. 827.

1 distress. The first Psalm of each of the five groups speaks of DISTRESS; the second of TRUST; the third of BLESSING AND PEACE IN ZION. The distress, here, refers to Sennacherib's siege of Jerusalem (2 Kings 19. 3. Isa. 37. 3)
cried. See 2 Kings 19. 3, 4, 14–19. 2 Chron. 32. 20. Isa. 37. 15–20; 38. 2, 3. See Ap. 67. iv.
the LORD. Heb. Jehovah. Ap. 4. II.
heard=answered.

2 Deliver=Pluck me. Heb. *nāẓal.* Same word as in 119. 170. The reference is to 2 Kings 18. 30, 32.
my soul=me. Heb. *nephesh.* Ap. 13.
lips. Heb.=lip: i.e. Rab-shakeh's. The reference is to 2 Kings 18. 19–35; 19. 8–13. 2 Chron. 32. 10–19. Isa. 36. 4–20; 37. 8–13. See Ap. 67. i.
tongue. Fig. *Epistrophe* (Ap. 6), with "tongue", *v.* 3.

3 done=heaped upon: i.e. added to. Cp. 1 Sam. 3. 17; 20. 13, &c.

4 mighty=Mighty [One].

5 Mesech . . . Kedar. Used typically of cruel and merciless peoples; as we use the terms Vandals, Goths, Philistines.

6 him. Some codices, with Sept., Syr., and Vulg., read "them".

7 I=I [even I]; or, I [am all] peace (emphatic).
speak=speak [of peace]. See note on 109. 4.
they are for war. The reference is to 2 Kings 18. 19. 2 Chron. 32. 2. Isa. 36. 5.

---

121 (G²₂, p. 826). GROUP I. PSALM (SECOND). TRUST. (*Division.*)

G²₂ | C¹ | 1, 2. Jehovah's help proclaimed.
| C² | 3–8. Jehovah's help promised.

Title. A Song. Heb. *shīr.* See Ap. 65. XXIII. **of degrees**=for, or relating to the degrees. Only here thus. Heb. *lamma'ălōth.* See note on Title of 120.

1, 2 (C¹, above). JEHOVAH'S HELP PROCLAIMED. (*Introversion.*)

C¹ | a | 1–. Contemplation of Creation.
b | –1. Whence can help come? Question.
b | 2–. Whence help cometh. Answer.
a | –2. Contemplation of the Creator.

1 hills=mountains. Add a full stop. **From whence, &c.?** Punctuate this line as a question. Cp. Jer. 3. 23. **cometh**=is to come.

b (p. 845) 2 °My help *cometh* [1] from °the LORD,
a °Which made heaven and earth.
C² c (p. 846) 3 He will °not suffer thy foot to be moved:
He That °keepeth thee will not slumber.
4 Behold, He That °keepeth Israel
Shall °neither slumber nor sleep.
d 5 [2] The LORD *is* thy °keeper:
[2] The LORD *is* thy shade upon thy right hand.
c 6 The sun shall not smite thee by day,
Nor the moon by night.
d 7 [2] The LORD °shall preserve thee from all °evil:
He °shall preserve thy °soul.
8 [2] The LORD [7] shall preserve °thy going out and thy coming in
From this time forth, and even for evermore.

122 °A Song °of degrees °of David.

G²₃ D 1 I was glad when they said unto me,
"Let us go into °the house of °the LORD."
E 2 Our feet °shall stand
Within thy gates, O °Jerusalem.
F 3 [2] Jerusalem is builded
As a city that is °compact together:
G 4 Whither the tribes °go up, the tribes of °THE LORD,
Unto the °testimony of Israel,
To give thanks unto the °name of [1] the LORD.
G 5 For there are set °thrones of judgment,
The °thrones of the house of David.
F 6 °Pray for the peace of Jerusalem:
E They shall prosper that love thee.
7 °Peace be within thy walls,
And prosperity within thy palaces.
8 For my brethren and companions' sakes,
I will now °say, [7] "Peace *be* within thee."
D 9 Because of [1] the house of [1] the LORD our °God
I will seek thy good.

123 °A Song of degrees.

G²₄ H 1 Unto Thee lift I up mine eyes,
O Thou That °dwellest in the heavens.

---

2 My help. Fig. *Anadiplosis*, repeated from end of *v.* 1.
the LORD=Jehovah (Ap. 4. II), not the hills.
Which made heaven and earth. The reference is to the burden of Hezekiah's prayer (2 Kings 19. 15. Isa. 37 16). Idols were only the work of men's hands (2 Kings 19. 18. 2 Chron. 32. 19. Isa. 37. 19). Rab-shakeh had reproached "the living God". See further references to this in 124. 8; 134. 3; and Ap. 67. v.

3-8 (C², p. 845). JEHOVAH'S HELP. PROMISED. (*Alternation.*)

C² | c | 3, 4. What Jehovah *will not* suffer. (Neg.)
   d | 5. What He *will* do as the Keeper. (Pos.)
   c | 6. What Jehovah *will not* do. (Neg.)
   d | 7, 8. What He *will* do as the Keeper. (Pos.)

3 not=May He not. Heb. *'al* (like Gr. *mē*). (Subjective, and conditional).
3 keepeth . . . 4 keepeth . . . 5 keeper. Note the Fig. *Polyptōton* (Ap. 6). Heb. *shomreka . . . shomēr . . . shomreka.* Repeated in *vv.* 7, 8.
4 neither. Heb. *l'o* (like Gr. *ou*). He will not. Absolute.
7 shall preserve thee. The repeated promise of Jehovah by Isaiah (2 Kings 19. 20-34. Isa. 37. 6, 7, 22-35.
7 shall preserve . . . shall preserve . . . 8 shall preserve. Note the Fig. *Polyptōton* (Ap. 6). Heb. *yishmarka . . . yishmor . . . yishmar.*
evil=calamity. Heb. *rā'a'.* Ap. 44. viii.
soul. Heb. *nephesh.* Ap. 13. See Isa. 38.
8 thy going out, &c. Idiom for life in general. The promise was fulfilled in 2 Chron. 32. 22.

122 (G²₃, p. 826). GROUP I. PSALM (THIRD). DELIVERANCE, BLESSING, AND PEACE IN ZION. (*Introversion.*)

G²₃ | D | 1. The house of Jehovah.
   E | 2. Jerusalem spoken to.
   F | 3. Jerusalem spoken of.
   G | 4. Description.
   G | 5. Description.
   F | 6-. Jerusalem spoken of.
   E | -6-8. Jerusalem spoken to.
   D | 9. The house of Jehovah.

Title. A Song. Heb. *shīr.* See note on Title of Ps. 120, and Ap. 65. XXIII.
of degrees=of the degrees (with Art.), as in Title of 120. See Ap. 67, and note on p. 827.
of David=by David. A Psalm which Hezekiah found ready to his hand. Some codices, with Aram. and Syr., omit "of David".
1 the house of the LORD. Heb. the house of Jehovah (Ap. 4. II). This was Hezekiah's constant care, desire, and thought. It filled his heart. He began his reign by "opening its doors" and cleansing it. See 2 Chron. 29—31, where it is mentioned seventeen times. He spread Sennacherib's letter before Jehovah there (Isa. 37. 14). In his mortal sickness his prayer and its answer related to it (2 Kings 20. 5). The "sign" he asked related to it (2 Kings 20. 8. Isa. 38. 22). His songs were to be sung there (Isa. 38. 20). See Ap. 67. xiii.
the LORD. Heb. Jehovah. Ap. 4. II.

2 shall stand=have stood [and shall still stand.] The reference is to the Passover, which had been kept for "all Israel". See Ap. 67. xv. **Jerusalem.** Note the Fig. *Anadiplosis* (Ap. 6), the word being repeated at the beginning of the next verse. **compact**=coupled together (as by a bridge), as Moriah was joined with Zion by the Millo. See note on 1 Kings 9. 15; 2 Kings 12. 20, and Ap. 68. **4 go up.** See Ap. 68. "ZION". **THE LORD.** Heb. Jah. Ap. 4. III. **testimony**: the Ark of Jehovah. **name.** See note on 20. 1. **5 thrones.** Pl. of Majesty=the great Throne. **6 Pray for the peace of Jerusalem.** Fig. *Paronomasia* (Ap. 6), *sha'ălū shelōm yerūshālām yishlāyū.* See Ap. 67. vi. **7 Peace be within.** Fig. *Epanadiplōsis* (Ap. 6), uniting *vv.* 7 and 8 by beginning and ending with the same words. **8 say**=speak [saying]. **9 God.** Heb. Elohim. Ap. 4. I.

123 (G²₄, p. 826). GROUP II. PSALM (FIRST). DISTRESS. (*Introversion.*)

G²₄ | H | 1. Prayer to Jehovah.
   J | 2-. As the eyes . . . look. } Comparison.
   J | -2. So our eyes look. }
   H | 3, 4. Prayer to Jehovah.

Title. A Song, &c. Same as Ps. 120. **1 dwellest in the heavens.** The reference is to 2 Kings 19. 15 and Isa. 37. 16.

J (p. 846) 2 °Behold, °as the eyes of servants *look* unto the hand of their masters,
And as the eyes of a maiden unto the hand of her mistress;

J So our eyes *wait* upon °the LORD our °God,
Until that He °have mercy upon us.

H 3 [2]Have mercy upon us, O [2]LORD, [2]have mercy upon us:
For we are exceedingly filled with °contempt.
4 °Our soul is exceedingly filled
With the °scorning of those that are °at ease,
And with the [3]contempt of the °proud.

124

°A Song of degrees of David.

G K (p. 847) 1 "If *it had not been* °the LORD Who was on our side,"
°Now may Israel say;
2 "If *it had not been* [1]the LORD Who was on our side,
When °men rose up against us:

L e 3 Then °they had swallowed us up °quick,
When their wrath was kindled against us:

f 4 Then the waters had overwhelmed us,
The °stream had gone over °our soul:
5 Then the proud waters had gone over [4]our soul.

M 6 Blessed *be* [1]the LORD,

L e Who hath not given us *as* a prey to their teeth.

f 7 [4]Our soul is escaped °as a bird out of the snare of the fowlers:
The snare is broken, and we are escaped.

K 8 Our help *is* in the °name of [1]the LORD,
°Who made heaven and earth."

125

°A Song of degrees.

G N (p. 847) 1 They that °trust in °the LORD
°*Shall be* as mount Zion, *which* cannot be removed, *but* abideth °for ever.
2 *As* the mountains *are* round about Jerusalem,
So [1]the LORD *is* round about His People
From henceforth even [1]for ever.
3 °For the °rod of °the wicked shall not °rest upon the °lot of the °righteous;
Lest the °righteous put forth their hands unto °iniquity.

O 4 Do good, O [1]LORD, unto *those that be* good,

P And to *them that are* upright in their hearts.

P 5 As for such as turn aside unto their crooked ways,

O [1]The LORD shall lead them forth with the workers of °iniquity:

N *But* peace *shall be* upon Israel.

---

2 Behold. Fig. *Asterismos.* Ap. 6.
as. Fig. *Simile.* Ap. 6.
the LORD. Heb. Jehovah. Ap. 4. II.
God. Heb. Elohim. Ap. 4. I.
2 have mercy=Be gracious. Fig. *Anaphora.* Ap. 6.
3 contempt=the mockery. Cp. 119. 22, referring to Rab-shakeh.
4 Our soul=we. Heb. *nephesh* (Ap. 13).
scorning=the scoffing. The reference is to the scoffing of Sennacherib and Rab-shakeh (2 Kings 18. 19-35; 19. 8-13. 2 Chron. 32. 10-19. Isa. 36. 4-21; 37. 8-13). Ap. 67. i.
at ease. Same Heb. as "tumult" in 2 Kings 19. 28, and Isa. 37. 29.
proud=proud oppressors.

124 (G, p. 826). GROUP II. PSALM (SECOND). TRUST. (*Introversion and Alternation.*)

G | K | 1, 2. Jehovah our help.
  L | e | 3. Voracity of enemies.
    f | 4, 5. Comparison. Waters.
      M | 6-. Blessed be Jehovah.
  L | *e* | -6. Voracity of enemies.
    f | 7. Comparison. Fowlers.
K | 8. Jehovah our help.

Title. See note on Title of Ps. 120.
1 the LORD. Heb. Jehovah. Ap. 4. II.
Now. Refers to Hezekiah's deliverance. See Ap. 67. x.
2 men. Heb. *'ādām.* Ap. 14. I. (Sing. refers to Sennacherib).
they. The pl., referring to Sennacherib's hosts; likened to a stream and waters in *vv.* 4, 5. See note on Ps. 46. 3.
3 quick=alive.
4 stream=torrent, or flood. Heb. *naḥal.* See Ap. 67.
our soul=us. Heb. *nephesh.* Ap. 13. Note the Fig. *Epistrophe* (Ap. 6) in the repetition at end of *v.* 5.
7 as a bird. The reference is to the words of Sennacherib on his cylinder, where he mentions Hezekiah by name, whom he had got "as a bird in a cage". See Ap. 67. xi.
8 name. See note on 20. 1.
Who made heaven and earth. See Ap. 67. v, and note on 121. 2 and 134. 3.

125 (G, p. 826). GROUP II. PSALM (THIRD). BLESSING AND PEACE IN ZION. (*Introversion.*)

G | N | 1-3. Israel's security.
  O | 4-. Jehovah's goodness.
    P | -4. The upright.
    P | 5-. The evildoers.
  O | -5-. Jehovah's judgment.
N | -5. Israel's security.

Title. Same as Ps. 120. See Ap. 67.
1 trust=confide. Heb. *bāṭaḥ.* Ap. 69. I.
the LORD. Heb. Jehovah. Ap. 4. II.
Shall be as mount Zion. Some codices, with one early printed edition and Syr., read "are in Mount Zion". Ap. 68.
for ever. Note the Fig. *Epistrophe* (Ap. 6), the words being repeated at the end of the next line.
3 For=Surely.
rod, or cudgel.
the wicked=the wicked (or lawless) one. Heb. *rāshā'.* Ap. 44. x. Here the reference is to Sennacherib (Isa. 30. 31), but it looks forward to 2 Thess. 2. 3, 4.
rest upon=continue over.
lot=heritage (as allotted).
righteous. Pl.: i. e. Hezekiah and the godly in Israel.
iniquity. Heb. *'āval.* Ap. 44. vi.
5 iniquity. Heb. *'āven.* Ap. 44. iii.

126

°A Song of degrees.

G 7/7 Q (p. 848) 1 When °the LORD °turned again the captivity of °Zion,
R We were °like them that dream.
S 2 Then was our mouth filled with laughter,
And our tongue with °singing:
Then °said they among the °heathen,
"°The LORD hath done great things for them."
3 [2]The LORD hath done great things for us;
Whereof we are glad.
Q 4 [1]Turn again our captivity, O [1]LORD,
R As the °streams °in the °south.
S 5 They that °sow in tears shall reap in joy.
6 He that goeth forth and weepeth, bearing precious seed,
Shall doubtless come again with rejoicing, bringing his sheaves *with him*.

127

A Song of degrees °for Solomon.

G 8/8 T g 1 Except °the LORD build °the house,
They labour in vain that build it:
h Except °the LORD keep °the city,
°The watchman waketh *but* in vain.
U 2 *It is* vain for you to rise up early, to sit up late,
To eat the bread of sorrows:
U °*For* so He giveth His °beloved °sleep.
T g 3 °Lo, °children *are* an heritage °of [1]the LORD:
And the fruit of the womb *is His* reward.
h 4 As arrows *are* in the hand of a mighty man;
So *are* [3]children of the youth.
5 °Happy *is* the °man that hath his quiver full of them:
°They shall °not be ashamed,
But they shall °speak with the enemies in the gate.

128

°A Song of degrees.

G 9/9 V 1 °Blessed *is* every one that °feareth °the LORD;
That walketh in His ways.

126 (G 7/7, p. 826). GROUP III. PSALM (FIRST). DISTRESS. (*Extended Alternation.*)

G 7/7 | Q | 1–. Distress.
R | –1. Its ending. As dreams.
S | 2, 3. Joy.
Q | 4–. Distress.
R | –4. Its ending. As streams.
S | 5, 6. Joy.

Title. Same as Ps. 120.

1 the LORD. Heb. Jehovah. Ap. 4. II.

turned . . . the captivity=turned the fortunes. This does not refer to a captivity or captives, but to a restoration to blessing. See Job 42. 10 and Ezek. 16. 53 and 55, where it is three times explained as "return to your former estate". See Ap. 67. xii. **Zion.** See Ap. 68.

like them that dream. The reference is to the waking in 2 Kings 19. 35. Isa. 37. 36. The illustration is in Luke 24. 41. Acts 12. 9 (603 B.C.).

2 singing: i. e. the songs of Isa. 38. 20.

said they=was it said.

heathen=nations. The reference is to 2 Chron. 32. 22, 23.

The LORD hath done great things. Fig. *Anadiplosis* (Ap. 6), because the phrase is repeated at the beginning of the next verse.

4 streams=torrents. Heb. *'ăphîḳîm.* See 2 Sam. 22. 16. Supply the *Ellipsis*, "as the streams [are turned] in the Negeb".

in the south=in the Negeb, where, in the hill-country of Judæa the *'ăphîḳîm* are turned about in their beds between the rocks and in the gorges.

south. Heb. Negeb; the hill-country of Judæa. See note on Gen. 13. 1, and Deut. 1. 7.

5 sow in tears. The reference is to the "sign" given in Isa. 37. 30. See Ap. 67. ix.

127 (G 8/8, p. 826). GROUP III. PSALM (SECOND). TRUST. (*Alternation.*)

G 8/8 | T | g | 1–. Human builders. Vain.
h | –1. Human defenders of city. Vain.
U | 2–. Human labours. Vain.
U | –2. Divine gifts.
T | *g* | 3. Divine provision of builders. Sons.
h | 4, 5. Divine provision of defenders.

Title. A Song of degrees. Same as 120 ("the degrees"). Ap. 67. The Structure, and the references to Hezekiah being childless (Ap. 67. xiv), show that this is not a Psalm "made up of two smaller Psalms, having no connection with each other".

for Solomon=of or by Solomon. The central Psalm of the fifteen. Selected by Hezekiah to complete and perfect the arrangement.

1 the LORD. Heb. Jehovah. Ap. 4. II. **the**=a.

2 For so=Thus.

beloved=beloved one (sing.). Heb. *yedīd.* This was Solomon's name (Jedidiah) given by Jehovah (2 Sam. 12. 25). Solomon was given because David was beloved of Jehovah. Some codices, with Sept., Syr., and Vulg., read pl. **sleep**=in sleep: i. e. while they sleep: i. e. without their labour. So He gave to Solomon (1 Kings 3. 5–15); to Adam (Gen. 2. 21, 22); Abraham (Gen. 15. 12, 13); Jacob (Gen. 28. 10–15); Samuel (1 Sam. 3. 3, 4), &c. **3 Lo.** Fig. *Asterismos.* Ap. 6. **children**=sons. The reference to the fact that Hezekiah was rejoicing in Isaiah's message that he should have a son, made it a suitable Psalm for Hezekiah to select (2 Kings 20. 12, 18. Isa. 39. 7). Cp. Ps. 128. See Ap. 67. xiv. When his trouble came, he was childless. Hence he remembered Jehovah's promise to David (132. 11). **of**=from. Hence he sings Jehovah's praise. **5 Happy is the man.** Hezekiah was that man. See the Beatitudes. Ap. 63. VI. **man.** Heb. *geber.* Ap. 14. IV. **They**: i. e. the sons. **not be ashamed.** Fig. *Tapeinosis* (Ap. 6): quite the opposite. **speak**=meet, whether for negotiation or for fighting.

128 (G 9/9, p. 826). GROUP III. PSALM (THIRD). DELIVERANCE, BLESSING, AND PEACE. (*Alternations.*)

G 9/9 | V | 1. Blessedness of those who revere Jehovah. (Third Person.)
W | i | 2. Thou. } Second Person.
k | 3–. Thy house and thy wife.
l | –3. Thy sons. Peace.
V | 4. Blessedness of those who revere Jehovah. (Third Person.)
W | *i* | –5. Thou. } Second Person.
k | –5. Thy city and thy life.
l | 6. Thy sons. Peace.

Title. A Song of degrees. Same as 120. See Ap. 67. **1 Blessed is**=O the happinesses of. See the Beatitudes. Ap. 63. VI. **feareth**=revereth. **the LORD.** Heb. Jehovah. Ap. 4. II.

W i (p. 848) 2 For thou shalt eat the °labour of °thine hands:
Happy *shalt* thou *be,* and *it shall be* well with thee.
k 3 Thy °wife *shall be* as a °fruitful vine by the sides of thine house:
l Thy °children like olive plants round about thy table.
V 4 °Behold, that thus shall the °man be °blessed
That [1]feareth [1]the LORD.
W i 5 [1]The LORD shall bless thee out of Zion:
k °And thou shalt see the good of Jerusalem all the days of thy life.
l 6 Yea, °thou shalt see thy [3]children's [3]children,
And °peace upon Israel.

129 °A Song of degrees.

G^{2}_{10} X (p. 849) 1 "Many a time have they afflicted me from my youth,"
May Israel now say:
2 °"Many a time have they afflicted me from my youth:
Y °Yet they have not prevailed against me.
X 3 °The plowers plowed upon my back:
They made long their furrows."
Y 4 °The LORD *is* °righteous:
He hath cut asunder the °cords of °the wicked.
5 Let them all be confounded and turned back
That hate °Zion.
6 Let them be °as the grass *upon* the housetops,
Which withereth afore it °groweth up:
7 Wherewith the mower filleth not his hand;
Nor he that bindeth sheaves his bosom.
8 Neither do they which go by say,
"The blessing of [4]the LORD *be* upon you:
We bless you in the °name of [4]the LORD."

130 °A Song of degrees.

G^{2}_{11} A (p. 849) 1 Out of the °depths have I cried unto Thee, O °LORD.
2 °LORD*, hear my voice:
Let Thine °ears be attentive
To the voice of my supplications.
3 If Thou, °LORD, shouldest mark iniquities,
O [2]LORD* who shall stand?
B 4 °But *there is* °forgiveness with Thee,
That Thou mayest be feared.
A 5 I wait for [1]the LORD, my °soul doth wait,
And in °His word do I hope.
6 My [5]soul *waiteth* for the [2]LORD*
More than they that °watch for the morning:
I say, more than they that watch for the morning.
7 Let Israel hope in [1]the LORD:
B For with the [1]LORD *there is* °mercy,
And with Him *is* °plenteous °redemption.
8 And He shall °redeem Israel
From all his °iniquities.

---

2 labour. Put by Fig. *Metonymy* (of Cause), Ap. 6, for that which is produced by labour.
thine hands: i.e. thine own hands, in contrast with the opposite (Lev. 26. 16. Deut. 28. 30–33, 39, 40). See also Amos 5. 11. Mic. 6. 15.
3 wife . . . fruitful. The reference is, as in Ps. 127, to the fact that Hezekiah was childless at this time and longed for an heir. See Ap. 67. xiv.
children = sons.
4 Behold. Fig. *Asterismos.* Ap. 6.
man = a strong man (pl.). Heb. *geber.* Ap. 14. IV.
blessed. Not the same word as in *v.* 1. That is happy (*Beatitudo*); this is blessed (*Benedictio*).
5 And thou shalt see: or, That thou mayest see.
6 thou shalt see. Hezekiah *did* see.
peace. Because this Psalm concludes a group.

129 (G^{2}_{10}, p. 826). GROUP IV. PSALM (FIRST). DISTRESS. (*Alternation.*)

G^{2}_{10} | X | 1, 2–. Distress. Caused by enemies.
Y | –2. Failure of enemies. Stated.
X | 3. Distress. Caused by enemies.
Y | 4–8. Failure of enemies. Prayed for.

Title. A Song of degrees. Same as 120. See Ap. 67.
2 Many a time. Fig. *Anaphora* (Ap. 6), being repeated from *v.* 1.
Yet = Nevertheless. Heb. *gam,* as in 119. 24 ("also"); Ezek. 16. 28. Ecc. 6. 7. Not "reduplicated by mistake, and then spelt differently to make sense", as is alleged by modern criticism.
3 The plowers. No Art.
4 The LORD. Heb. Jehovah. Ap. 4. II.
righteous = just: i.e. in His judgments.
cords: i.e. of bondage. Cp. 2. 3.
the wicked = lawless ones. Heb. *rāshā'.* Ap. 44. x.
5 Zion. See Ap. 68.
6 as the grass = as grass. The reference in *vv.* 6, 7 is not to "Egyptian monuments", but to the reply of Jehovah concerning Sennacherib, which Hezekiah quotes here. Cp. 2 Kings 19. 25, 26. Isa. 37. 27.
groweth up. Either unsheatheth itself into flower, or is plucked up (as Sept. and Vulg.).
8 name. See note on 20. 1.

130 (G^{2}_{11}, p. 826). GROUP IV. PSALM (SECOND). TRUST. (*Alternation.*)

G^{2}_{11} | A | 1–3. Waiting on Jehovah.
B | 4. Reason. "For".
A | 5–7–. Waiting for Jehovah.
B | –7, 8. Reason. "For".

Title. A Song of degrees. Same as 120. See Ap. 67.
1 depths. Symbolical of distress. Cp. 42. 7; 66. 12; 69. 2. **LORD.** Heb. Jehovah. Ap. 4. II.
2 LORD*. One of the 134 places where the *Sōpherīm* altered Jehovah to Adonai. See Ap. 32. So also *vv.* 3, and 6. **ears.** Fig. *Anthropopatheia.* Ap. 6.
3 LORD. Heb. Jah. Ap. 4. III.
4 But = For; or Because; corresponding with *v.* 7.
forgiveness = the forgiveness: viz. that which Hezekiah gave thanks for in Isa. 38. 17.
5 soul. Heb. *nephesh.* Ap. 13.
His word: as sent to Hezekiah by Jehovah through Isaiah.
6 watch. Heb. *shāmar* = to keep = observe. An astronomical word, as in 19. 11. Cp. 105. 45; 107. 43; 119. 34. Omit the italics, note the Fig. *Epizeuxis.* Ap. 6, and render: "More than watchers for the morning [while] watching for the morning."
7 mercy = lovingkindness, or grace.
plenteous redemption. Not only from the king of Assyria (Isa. 37), but from "the king of terrors".
redemption. Heb. *pādāh.* See notes on Ex. 13. 13.
8 redeem. Same as *v.* 7.
iniquities. Heb. *'āvāh.* Ap. 44. iv. (Isa. 38.)

131 °A Song of degrees °of David.

G^{2}_{12} C (p. 850) 1 °LORD, my heart is not haughty, nor mine eyes lofty:
Neither do I exercise myself in great matters,
Or in things too °high for me.

D 2 °Surely I have behaved and °quieted °myself,
As a child that is weaned of his mother:
D °My soul *is* even as a weaned child.

C 3 Let °Israel hope in [1]the LORD
From henceforth and for ever.

132 °A Song of degrees.

G^{2}_{13} (THEME) (p. 850) 1 °LORD, °remember °David,
And °all his afflictions:

F 2 How he sware unto the [1] LORD,
And vowed unto °the mighty *God* of Jacob;

G 3 Surely °I will not come into the °tabernacle °of my house,
Nor go up into my °bed;
4 I will not give sleep to mine eyes,
Or slumber to mine eyelids,
5 Until I find out a place for [1]the LORD,
°An habitation for [2]the mighty *God* of Jacob.

H 6 Lo, we °heard of °it at Ephratah:
We found °it °in the fields of the wood.
7 We will go into His °tabernacles:
We will worship at His °footstool.

J 8 °"Arise, O [1]LORD, into Thy rest;
Thou, and °the ark of Thy strength.

K 9 Let Thy priests be clothed with righteousness;

L And let Thy °saints °shout for joy.

M 10 For Thy servant David's sake
Turn not away the face of °Thine anointed."

F 11 The [1] LORD °hath sworn °*in* truth unto David;
He will not turn from it;

G °"**Of the fruit of thy body will I set upon thy throne.**

12 If thy °children will keep My covenant

---

131 (G^{2}_{12}, p. 826). GROUP IV. PSALM (THIRD) DELIVERANCE, BLESSING, AND PEACE. (*Introversion.*)

G^{2}_{12}
- C | 1. Jehovah. My comfort and peace.
  - D | 2-. I have comforted myself in Thee.
  - *D* | -2. I have comforted myself in Thee.
- *C* | 3. Jehovah. Israel's comfort and peace.

Title. A Song of degrees. Same as 120. Ap. 67.
of David = by David. For its place here see Ap. 67.
1 LORD. Heb. Jehovah. Ap. 4. II.
high = wonderful.
2 Surely = [See] whether I have not, &c.
quieted = silenced. Some codices, with Sept. and Vulg., read "soothed and uplifted": i.e. comforted.
myself = my soul. Heb. *nephesh.* Ap. 13.
My soul = Myself. Heb. *nephesh.* Ap. 13.
3 Israel. Not "a liturgical addition", but used to link the three Psalms of this group together (129. 1; 130. 7, 8; 131. 3). For Israel is to find rest and peace where their kings (David, and Hezekiah) found it.

132 (G^{2}_{13}, p. 826). GROUP V. PSALM (FIRST). DISTRESS. BLESSING FOR THE HOUSE OF JEHOVAH. (*Extended Alternation.*)

THE THEME. David's Distress.

G^{2}_{13}
- F | 2. David sware unto Jehovah.
  - G | 3-5. What David sware.
    - H | 6, 7. Dwelling-place for the Ark. Search.
      - J | 8. Prayer for the Ark's rest.
        - K | 9-. Prayer for the Priests.
          - L | -9. Prayer for the Saints.
            - M | 10. Prayer for Messiah.
- *F* | 11-. Jehovah sware unto David.
  - *G* | -11, 12. What Jehovah sware.
    - *H* | 13. Dwelling-place for the Ark. Designation.
      - *J* | 14, 15. Answer to Prayer (*v.* 8, J).
        - *K* | 16-. Answer to Prayer for Priests (*v.* 9, K).
          - *L* | -16. Answer to Prayer for Saints (*v.* 9, L).
            - *M* | 17, 18. Answer to Prayer for Messiah (*v.* 10, M).

Title. A Song of degrees. Same as 120. Ap. 67.
1 LORD. Heb. Jehovah. Ap. 4. II.
remember David = remember for David: i.e. remember to fulfil the promises made to him.
David. Hezekiah remembers David, and puts Jehovah in remembrance of him.
all his afflictions = all his being afflicted: all his anxious cares as to his work. The Temple was Hezekiah's care, as it had been David's. Not "post-exilic". We see these anxieties from the beginning of his reign (2 Sam. 7. 1 Chron. 13. 3; 21. 18—22. 1). The subjects of these last three Psalms are merged in blessing.
2 the mighty [God] of Jacob. The mighty One to Whom Jacob vowed his vow. Title occurs outside the Pentateuch, only here, and Gen. 49. 24; Isa. 1. 24 (Israel); 49. 26; 60. 16. Note the Fig. *Epistrophe* (Ap. 6) for emphasis in *v.* 5.

3 I will not come. Note the Fig. *Periphrases* (Ap. 6) in *vv.* 4, 5. **tabernacle** = tent. Heb. *'ohel.* Ap. 40. 3. Cp. Acts 7. 46. **of.** Gen. of Apposition = "the Tent: i.e. my house". The emphasis = my own house. **bed** = couch. **5 An habitation.** Pl. of Majesty. Heb. *mishkān* (Ap. 40. ii). **6 heard:** i.e. while he was at Ephratah. David's father was an Ephrathite (of Bethlehem-Ephratah. Cp. Gen. 35. 19. David had "heard" of it as being in Shiloh. **it:** i.e. the Ark. **in the fields of the wood** = at Jaar's fields: i.e. Kirjath-jearim (1 Chron. 13. 5.). **7 tabernacles** = the plural of Majesty. His great habitation. Heb. *Mishkān.* Ap. 40. 2. **footstool.** Fig. *Anthrōpopatheia.* Ap. 6. **8 Arise.** Fig. *Ellipsis* (Ap. 6) = [and will say] "Arise, O LORD", &c. This is what Solomon did say in 2 Chron. 6. 41: see Ps. 68. 1 (and note there), according to Num. 10. 35. Verses 8-10 record what David said. **the ark of Thy strength.** Occurs only here and 2 Chron. 6. 41. See notes on Ex. 25. 22 and 1 Chron. 13. 3. **9 saints** = favoured ones. **shout for joy.** That is exactly what they did. See the *sub*-scription of Ps. 87 and note there on "Mahalath-Leannoth". **10 Thine anointed** = i.e. David. Not "Zerubbabel", no such oath made to him. **11 hath sworn.** See 2 Sam. 7. 8-17. **in truth** = a truth. **Of the fruit of thy body.** This was what Hezekiah was concerned about; for he as yet had no son, and was in danger of death. Hence this pleading of Jehovah's oath to David. Quoted in Acts 2. 30. **12 children** = sons.

And °My testimony that I shall teach them,
Their °children shall also sit upon thy throne for evermore."

H (p. 850) 13 For [1] the LORD hath chosen °Zion;
He hath desired *it* for °His habitation.

J 14 This *is* My rest for ever:
Here will I dwell; for I have desired it.
15 I will abundantly bless °her provision:
I will satisfy her °poor with bread.

K 16 I will also clothe her priests with salvation:
L And her [9] saints shall shout aloud for joy.
M 17 There will I make °the horn of David °to bud:
I have ordained a °lamp for Mine [10] anointed.
18 His enemies will I clothe with shame:
But upon himself shall °his crown flourish.

133

°A Song of degrees °of David.

G^2_{14} N (p. 851) 1 °Behold, °how good and how pleasant *it is*
For brethren to dwell together in °unity!

O m 2 *It is* like the precious °ointment upon the head,
n That °ran down upon the beard,
Even Aaron's beard:
That °went down °to the skirts of his garments;

O m 3 °As the dew of Hermon,
n °*And as the dew* that °descended upon the mountains of °Zion:

N For °there °the LORD commanded the blessing,
Even life for evermore.

134

°A Song of degrees.

G^2_{15} P (p. 851) 1 °Behold, bless ye °the LORD, all *ye* °servants of °the LORD,
Q Which by night °stand in °the house of °the LORD.

Q 2 Lift up your hands *in* the sanctuary,
And bless [1] the LORD.

P 3 [1] The LORD That made °heaven and earth
°Bless thee °out of Zion.

My testimony. Heb. = "this My testimony". Some codices, with Aram., Sept., and Vulg., read "[these] my testimonies" (pl.). **children** = sons.

13 Zion. See Ap. 68.

His habitation = His dwelling. Fig. *Anthropopatheia* (Ap. 6).

15 her: i.e. Zion's. **poor** = needy ones.

17 the horn of David = a horn for David.

to bud: i.e. to bring forth: viz. a son and heir. See Ap. 67. xiv.

lamp. According to Gen. 15. 17; and note there.

18 his crown: i.e. his royal crown.

133 (G^2_{14}, p. 826). GROUP V. PSALM (SECOND). TRUST. BLESSING IN THE HOUSE OF JEHOVAH.

(*Introversion and Alternation.*)

G^2_{14}
N | 1. The blessing enjoyed. Unity.
O | m | 2-. Comparison to the anointing oil.
n | -2. Descent of the oil.
O | *m* | 3-. Comparison to Hermon's dew.
n | -3-. Descent of the dew.
N | -3. The blessing enjoyed. Life.

Title. A Song of degrees. Same as 120. The three subjects of the three Psalms of this last group are merged in blessing.

of David = by David. Hezekiah found this Psalm exactly suited for his purpose. David wrote it on the experience of a similar blessing of "unity," when "all Israel" were united "as the heart of ONE MAN" (2 Sam. 19. 9, 14). It was the same with Hezekiah. Read 2 Chron. 30. 5, 6, 11, 18, and note the "ONE HEART" (*v.* 12). See Ap. 67. xv.

1 Behold. The word of the Holy Spirit; as "yea" is of the Father; and "verily" of the Son. Note the Fig. *Asterismos.* Ap. 6.

how good. This was manifested in 2 Chron. 30. 25, 26.

unity = one. The reference is to the "one man" of 2 Sam. 19. 14 (David), and the "one heart" of 2 Chron. 30. 12 (Hezekiah). Heb. *yāhad* (not *'eḥad*. See note on Deut. 6. 4. Cp. Josephus (*Ant.* ix. 13. 2).

2 ointment = oil (Ex. 30. 23-25).

ran down = descended. Ex. 29. 7. Lev. 8. 12; 21. 10.

went down = descended, as in *v.* 3.

to the skirts, &c. = to the opening of his robes (see Ex. 28. 32). Heb. = mouth (or opening).

3 As = [It is] like, as in *v.* 2.

And as the dew. Omit these italics.

descended. Cp. *v.* 2.

Zion. The dew (or copious summer night mist) was *one.* The same dew descended on Zion in the south as on Hermon in the north. Zion's dew represents the tribe of Judah. Hermon's dew represents Asher, Ephraim, Manasseh, Zebulon, Issachar (2 Chron. 30. 11, 18, 25, 26). The idea is not in the *motion* of this dew, from Hermon to Zion, but in its uniting both in its copious descent.

there. Cp. Deut. 12. 5, 11, 14, 18, 21. Pss. 128. 5; 134. 3. Ps. 133 is blessing IN Zion; Ps. 132 is blessing FOR Zion; Ps. 134 is blessing FROM Zion.

the LORD. Heb. Jehovah. Ap. 4. II.

134 (G^2_{15}, p. 826). GROUP V. PSALM (THIRD). BLESSING FROM THE HOUSE OF JEHOVAH.

(*Introversion.*)

G^2_{15}
P | 1-. Blessing given TO Jehovah.
Q | -1. The Servants. Their Watch.
Q | 2. The Servants. Their Service.
P | 3. Blessing given BY Jehovah.

Title. A Song of degrees. Same as 120. See Ap. 67. **1 Behold.** See note on 133. 1. **the LORD.** Heb. Jehovah. Ap. 4. II. **servants.** Limited and defined in next clause, as in 135. 2. **stand.** The night-watchmen. The reference is to 2 Chron. 29. 11; 30. 16; 31. 2. There were no *seats* in the Tabernacle or Temple. Cp. Heb. 10. 11. **the house of the LORD.** The reference is to Hezekiah's interest in the Temple. See Ap. 67. xiii. **3 heaven and earth.** The reference is to 2 Chron. 32. 19. 2 Kings 19. 15. Isa. 37. 16. See Ap. 67. v. **Bless thee.** The reference may be to 2 Chron. 30. 27; 31. 10. This is the last of the fifteen Songs of THE Degrees, which are referred to in Isa. 38. 20. See Ap. 67. **out of Zion.** See note on "there", 133. 3.

$\mathbf{H}^2_1$ R (p. 852) **135** °Praise ye °THE LORD.

Praise ye the °name of °the LORD;

S Praise *Him,* O ye servants of °the LORD.

2 Ye that stand in the house of [1] the LORD,

In °the courts of the house of our °God,

3 Praise [1] THE LORD; for [1] the LORD *is* good:

Sing praises unto His [1] name; for °*it is* pleasant.

T V 4 For [1] THE LORD hath chosen °Jacob unto Himself,

And °Israel for His °peculiar treasure.

W 5 For I know that [1] the LORD *is* great,

And *that* °our LORD *is* above all °gods.

6 Whatsoever [1] the LORD pleased, *that* did He

In °heaven, and in earth, in the seas, and all deep places.

7 He causeth the vapours to ascend from the ends of the earth;

He maketh lightnings for the rain;

He bringeth the °wind out of His °treasuries.

8 Who °smote the firstborn of Egypt,

Both of °man and beast.

9 *Who* sent tokens and °wonders into the midst of thee, O Egypt,

Upon Pharaoh, and upon all his servants.

10 Who °smote great nations,

And slew mighty kings;

11 °Sihon king of the Amorites,

And °Og king of Bashan,

And °all the kingdoms of Canaan:

12 And °gave their land *for* an heritage,

°An heritage unto Israel His People.

U 13 °Thy [1] name, O [1] LORD, *endureth* for ever;

U *And* Thy memorial, O [1] LORD, throughout all generations.

T V 14 °For [1] the LORD will °judge His People,

And He will °repent Himself concerning His servants.

W o 15 °The idols of the °heathen *are* silver and gold,

p The work of [8] men's hands.

q 16 They have mouths, but they speak not;

r Eyes have they, but they see not;

r 17 They have ears, but they hear not;

q Neither is there *any* °breath in their mouths.

p 18 They that make them °are like unto them:

o *So is* every one that °trusteth in them.

S 19 Bless [1] the LORD, O °house of Israel:

Bless [1] the LORD, O house of Aaron:

20 Bless [1] the LORD, O house of °Levi:

Ye that fear [1] the LORD, bless [1] the LORD.

21 Blessed be [1] the LORD °out of Zion,

Which °dwelleth at Jerusalem.

R [1] Praise ye [1] THE LORD.

---

135 ($\mathbf{H}^2_1$, p. 826). PRAISE.

(*Introversion and Alternation.*)

$\mathbf{H}^2_1$ R | 1–. Hallelujah.

S | –1–3. Exhortation to praise. Servants.

T | V | 4. Jehovah's choice of Israel.

W | 5–12. Superiority over idols.

U | 13–. Jehovah addressed. Name.

U | –13. Jehovah addressed. Memorial.

T | *V* | 14. Jehovah's vindication of Israel.

W | 15–18. Superiority over idols.

S | 19–21–. Exhortation to praise. Israel.

R | –21. Hallelujah.

This Psalm is probably by Hezekiah, continuing the Songs of the Degrees. Corresponds with 114 and 115 ($\mathbf{H}^1$). See Structure (p. 826).

1 Praise ye THE LORD = Hallelu-jah. Ap. 4. III.

name. See note on 20. 1.

the LORD. Heb. Jehovah (Ap. 4. II). Note the three Jehovahs between Jah in *v.* 1 and Elohim in *v.* 2. Corresponding with the threefold blessing of Num. 6. 22–27.

2 the courts. This includes the People as well as the priests and Levites. **3 it:** i.e. His name.

God. Heb. Elohim. Ap. 4. I.

4 Jacob. Cp. Mal. 1. 2. Rom. 9. 13. Put also by Fig. *Metonymy* (of Cause) for his posterity (Ap. 6).

Israel. See notes on Gen. 32. 28; 43. 6; 45. 26, 28.

peculiar treasure = own possession. Heb. *segullāh.* See note on Ex. 19. 5.

5 our LORD = Adonim. Ap. 4. VIII (3).

gods. Heb. *'elohim.* Ap. 4. I. Used here of earthly rulers (82. 6), as representing God. See note on Ex. 22. 9, and cp. Rom. 13. 1–7.

6 heaven, and in earth. Hezekiah's expression. See Ap. 67. v.

7 wind. Heb. *rūach.* Ap. 9. Cp. *v.* 7 with Jer. 10. 13; 51. 16.

treasuries. Heb. = treasures, put by Fig. *Metonymy* (of Adjunct) for treasuries (Ap. 6), and rightly so rendered. Cp. Job 38. 22.

8 smote, &c. Cp. Ex. 12. 29.

man. Heb. *'ādām.* Ap. 14. I.

9 wonders. Cp. Ex. 7—14, and Ps. 136. 15.

10 smote, &c. Cp. Num. 21—26, 34, and 35.

11 Sihon. Cp. Num. 21. 21–34. Deut. 1. 4.

Og. Cp. Deut. 31. 4. Josh. 13. 31.

all. Cp. Josh. 12. 7.

12 gave their land. Cp. Josh. 12. 7.

An heritage. Repeated by Fig. *Anadiplosis.* Ap. 6.

13 Thy name. Cp. *v.* 13 with Ex. 3. 15.

14 For, &c. Cp. Deut. 32. 36.

judge = vindicate.

repent Himself = have compassion.

15–18 (*W,* above). SUPERIORITY OVER IDOLS.

(*Introversion.*)

W | o | 15–. The idols.

p | –15. Their fabrication.

q | 16–. Mouth without speech. (Sing.)

r | –16. Eyes without sight. (Pl.).

r | 17–. Ears without hearing. (Pl.)

q | –17. Mouth without breath. (Sing.)

p | 18–. Their fabricators.

o | –18. The idolaters.

15 The idols, &c., *vv.* 15–18. Not "borrowed" from Ps. 115, but repeated, and varied, because the object here is quite different. Ps. 115 = heathen theology; 135 = Divine theology. **heathen** = nations.

17 breath. Heb. *rūach.* Ap. 9.

18 are = will become.

trusteth = confideth. Heb. *baṭaḥ.* Ap. 69. I.

19 house of Israel. Includes all Israel. Cp. 115. 12. See note on Ex. 16. 31.

20 Levi. Not included in 115.

21 out of Zion. Shows that this Psalm is an expansion of Ps. 134.

dwelleth. Fig. *Anthropopatheia.* Ap. 6.

H $^2_2$ A E (p. 853) **136** O give thanks unto °the LORD; for *He* is good:
°For His °mercy *endureth* for ever.
2 °O give thanks unto the °God of °gods:
For His [1] mercy *endureth* for ever.
3 O give thanks to the °LORD of lords:
For His [1] mercy *endureth* for ever.

B F 4 To Him Who alone doeth great wonders:
For His [1] mercy *endureth* for ever.
5 To Him That by wisdom °made the heavens:
For His [1] mercy *endureth* for ever.
6 To Him That stretched out the earth °above the waters:
For His [1] mercy *endureth* for ever.
7 To Him That made °great lights:
For His [1] mercy *endureth* for ever:
8 The sun °to rule by day:
For His [1] mercy *endureth* for ever:
9 The moon and stars [8] to rule by night:
For His [1] mercy *endureth* for ever.

C s G 10 To Him That °smote Egypt in their firstborn:
For His [1] mercy *endureth* for ever:

t 11 And °brought out Israel from among them:
For His [1] mercy *endureth* for ever:

J 12 With a strong °hand, and with a stretched out °arm:
For His [1] mercy *endureth* for ever.

u 13 To Him Which divided the Red sea into parts:
For His [1] mercy *endureth* for ever:

K 14 And made Israel to pass through the midst of it:
For His [1] mercy *endureth* for ever:

D 15 But °overthrew Pharaoh and his host in the Red sea:
For His [1] mercy *endureth* for ever.

D 16 To Him Which led His People through the wilderness:
For His [1] mercy *endureth* for ever.

C s 17 To Him Which smote great kings:
For His [1] mercy *endureth* for ever:
18 And slew famous kings:
For His [1] mercy *endureth* for ever:
19 °Sihon king of the Amorites:
For His [1] mercy *endureth* for ever:
20 And Og the king of Bashan:
For His [1] mercy *endureth* for ever:

t J 21 And gave °their land for an heritage:
For His [1] mercy *endureth* for ever:
22 *Even* an heritage unto Israel His servant:
For His [1] mercy *endureth* for ever.

u K 23 Who remembered us in our low estate:
For His [1] mercy *endureth* for ever:
24 And hath °redeemed us from our °enemies:
For His [1] mercy *endureth* for ever.

B L 25 Who giveth °food to all °flesh:
For His [1] mercy *endureth* for ever.

A M 26 [1] O give thanks unto the °GOD of heaven:
For His [1] mercy *endureth* for ever.

136 (H $^2_2$, p. 826). PRAISE.
(*Introversion and Extended Alternation.*)

H $^2_2$
A | 1-3. Exhortation to praise.
  B | 4-9. General dealings. Creation.
    C | s | 10. Smote Egyptians.
          t | 11, 12. Brought Israel out of Egypt.
            u | 13, 14. Israel's rescue.
      D | 15. Overthrow of Enemies. Sea.
      D | 16. Guidance of His People. Desert.
    C | *s* | 17-20. Smote kings.
          t | 21, 22. Brought Israel into Canaan.
            u | 23, 24. Israel's rescue.
  B | 25. General dealings. Grace.
A | 26. Exhortation to praise.

Psalms 135 and 136 are a pair; and have a corresponding Structure when viewed together. This does not interfere with their own independent Structures. In Ps. 135, verses 19-22 are not "an addition" or "interpolation" from 135. 10, in order to make twenty-two verses (the number of letters in the Hebrew alphabet). Without these verses (*vv.* 19-22) the Structure below would fail.

PSALMS **135** AND **136** COMPARED.
(*Extended Alternation.*)

135 E | 1-5. Exhortation to praise.
  F | 6, 7. Creative wonders.
    G | 8, 9. Deliverance from Egypt.
      H | 10, 11. Deliverance on Journey.
        J | 12, 13. Gift of the Land.
          K | 14. Goodness to His People.
            L | 15-18. False gods.
              M | 19-21. Praise.
136 *E* | 1-3. Exhortation to praise.
  F | 4-9. Creative wonders.
    G | 10-15. Deliverance from Egypt.
      H | 16-20. Deliverance on Journey.
        J | 21, 22. Gift of the Land.
          K | 23, 24. Goodness to His People.
            L | 25. The True God.
              M | 26. Praise.

the LORD. Heb. Jehovah. Ap. 4. II.
For, &c. Figs. *Amœbaeon* and *Epistrophe*. Ap. 6.
mercy = lovingkindness, or grace.
2 O give thanks. Note the Figs. *Cœnotes* and *Anaphora* (Ap. 6) in *vv.* 1, 2, 3.
God of gods. Heb. Elohim of the elohim. Ap. 4. I.
gods. Heb. *'ĕlohim.* See note on 135. 5 and Ex. 22. 9.
3 LORD of lords. Heb. Adonīm of the adonim. Ap. 4. VIII. Cp. Deut. 10. 17.
5 made the heavens. Cp. Gen. 1. 1.
6 above. i.e. in Gen. 1. 1, and 2 Pet. 3. 5. By the overthrow of Gen. 1. 2 the earth became a ruin, being "overflowed" (2 Pet. 3. 6), and covered with "the deep" (Gen. 1. 2).
7 great lights. Gen. 1. 14, "lightholders".
8 to rule = to have dominion. Gen. 1. 16-18.
10 smote Egypt. Cp. Ex. 12. 29.
11 brought out Israel. Cp. Ex. 13. 17.
12 hand . . arm. Fig. *Anthrōpopatheia* (Ap. 6).
15 overthrew = shook off.
19 Sihon, &c. These two verses (*vv.* 19, 20) not an "interpolation". See note above.
21 their: i.e. Sihon's and Og's. Not a verse "clearly dropped out", which contained the noun for this pronoun. The kings named show "whose" land is referred to. An "interpolation" from which a verse has "dropped out" is a new idea in the field of imaginative criticism; and, if true, would be quite unworthy of a "commentator's" time and trouble.
24 redeemed = rescued. Heb. *pāraḳ* = to break. Thus to rescue, by breaking the bonds. Rendered "redeem" only here (and Dan. 4. 27 in the Vulgate versions: A.V. "break off"). **enemies** = adversaries.
25 food. Heb. = bread. Put by Fig. *Synecdoche* (of Species) for all kinds of food. Ap. 6. **flesh.** Put by Fig. *Synecdoche* (of Part) for all living beings. Ap. 6. **26 GOD.** Heb. El. Ap. 4. IV. **GOD of heaven.** See note on 2 Chron. 36. 23.

G³ N¹ (p. 854)
137 By the rivers of °Babylon,
There we sat down,
O¹ Yea, we wept,
When we remembered Zion.

N² 2 We hanged our harps
Upon the willows in the midst thereof.
3 For there °they that carried us away captive required of us a song;
And they that wasted us *required of us* mirth, *saying*,
"Sing us *one* of the songs of Zion."
4 How shall we sing °the LORD'S song
In a °strange land?

O² 5 °If I forget thee, O Jerusalem,
°Let my right hand forget *her cunning*.
6 If I do not remember thee,
Let my tongue cleave to the roof of my mouth;
If I prefer not Jerusalem
Above my chief joy.

N³ 7 Remember, O ⁴LORD, the °children of °Edom
O³ In the °day of Jerusalem;
°Who said, °"Rase *it*, rase *it*,
Even to the foundation thereof."

N⁴ 8 O daughter of Babylon, who art °to be destroyed;
°Happy *shall he be*, that °rewardeth thee
As thou hast served us.
9 ⁸Happy *shall he be*, that taketh and dasheth thy °little ones
Against the stones.

138 *A Psalm* °of David.

H³ P¹ (p. 854)
1 I will °praise Thee with my whole °heart:
Before the °gods will I sing praise unto Thee.
2 I will worship toward Thy °holy °temple,
And praise Thy °name for Thy lovingkindness and for Thy truth:
For Thou hast °magnified Thy °word above all Thy °name.
3 In the day when I cried Thou answeredst me,
And °strengthenedst me *with* strength in °my soul.
4 All the kings of the earth shall praise Thee, O °LORD,
When °they hear the ²words of Thy mouth.

137 (G³, p. 826). ISRAEL. DELIVERANCE FROM BABYLON. (*Repeated Alternation.*)

G³
- N¹ | 1–. Babylon. Weeping.
  - O¹ | –1. Zion. Remembrance.
- N² | 2–4. Babylon. Weeping.
  - O² | 5, 6. Jerusalem. Remembrance. "I".
- N³ | 7–. Edom. Remembrance.
  - O³ | –7. Jerusalem. Destruction.
- N⁴ | 8. Babylon. Destruction.

1 Babylon. The Psalm is anonymous, and probably by Hezekiah. No need to refer it to post-exilic times. The Psalm reads as though it were a reminiscence of past experience in Babylon, and a contrast with previous joys in Zion; not, as during or after the seventy years, or an experience of a then present exile in Babylon. The writer is in Jerusalem after an absence not of long duration; and is full of joy. The post-exilic captives were full of sorrow on their return (Ezra 3. 12. Hag. 2. 3). These exiles had obeyed Isaiah's call (Isa. 48. 20. Cp. 43. 14–21).

3 they that carried us away: i.e. the captives of Judah, as those of Israel had been by Shalmaneser and Sargon. The latter took away only 27,280 from Samaria. See note on 1 Chron. 5. 6; and Ap. 67. xi.

4 the LORD'S. Heb. Jehovah's. Ap. 4. II.

strange=foreigner's.

5 If I forget . . . do not remember. The writer's then present personal declaration.

Let my right hand forget. Supply "me" for the Ellipsis. Some codices, with Sept. and Vulg., read "let my right hand be forgotten".

7 children=sons.

Edom. Gen. 27. 39, 40 was not fulfilled until the reign of Joram (2 Kings 8. 20–23. 2 Chron. 21. 8–10 (cp. 1 Kings 22. 47). From that time they were implacable enemies.

day. Put by Fig. *Metonymy* (of Adjunct) for what happened at the time (Ap. 6). Cp. Job 18. 20. Hos. 1. 11. Joel 1. 15. Luke 17. 22, 26; 19. 42. 1 Cor. 4. 3.

Who said. The reference is to what they *said*, not to what they *did*; to the encouragement given to Sennacherib, not to the help given to Nebuchadnezzar. That is what Obadiah, a later prophet, refers to. Isaiah (Hezekiah's contemporary) refers to the earlier words. See Isa. 34. 6. Here Edom does not go beyond words.

Rase it, rase it. Fig. *Epizeuxis* (Ap. 6) for emphasis. This was *said*, not *done*, at that time.

8 to be destroyed. Hezekiah must have been familiar with Isaiah's prophecies, who employs the very words of *vv.* 8, 9. (Isa. 13. 6, 16–18; 21. 9; 47. 14, 15. Cp. Nahum 3. 10.)

Happy. See Ap. 63. VI. for the Beatitudes of the Psalms.

rewardeth. See notes above, which show that the "post-exilic" assumption involves insuperable difficulties if this Psalm is sundered from the contemporary prophecies of Isaiah (especially 13. 1–14; and 27), and from a Babylon under Assyrian rule.

9 little ones. The reference is to Isa. 13. 16–18, which belongs to a Dispensation of Law and Judgment, and is not to be interpreted of the present Dispensation of Grace.

138 (H³, p. 826). PRAISE. (*Repeated Alternation.*)

H³
- P¹ | 1–4. To Jehovah. Praise. (Second Person.)
  - Q¹ | 5, 6. Of Jehovah. (Third Person.)
- P² | 7. To Jehovah. (Second Person.)
  - Q² | 8–. Of Jehovah. (Third Person.)
- P³ | –8. To Jehovah. (Second Person.)

Title. of David=by David. Placed here by Hezekiah, to correspond with H¹, H² and H⁴. See p. 826. **1 praise Thee.** Some codices, with Aram., Sept., Syr., and Vulg., add "O Jehovah". **heart.** Sept. adds "for Thou hast heard the words of my mouth", probably from *v.* 4. **gods.** Heb. *'ĕlohīm.* Ap. 4. I. See note on Ex. 22. 8. **2 holy.** See note on Ex. 3. 5. **temple**=house or palace. Heb. *hēykāl.* **name.** See note on 20. 1. **magnified:** i.e. by fulfilling it beyond all expectation. **word**=sayings. Heb. *'imrah.* See Ap. 73. v. **name.** See note on 20. 1. **3 strengthenedst**=encouraged, or emboldened. **my soul**=myself (emphatic). Heb. *nephesh.* Ap. 13. **4 LORD.** Heb. Jehovah. Ap. 4. II. **they hear**=they have heard.

Q¹
(p. 854)

5 Yea, they shall sing °in the ways of ⁴the
   LORD:
  For great *is* the glory of ⁴the LORD.
6 Though ⁴the LORD *be* high, yet hath He
   °respect unto the lowly:
  But the proud He knoweth afar off.

P²

7 Though I walk in the midst of trouble,
   Thou wilt °revive me:
  Thou shalt stretch forth Thine °hand
   °against the wrath of mine enemies,
  And Thy right °hand shall save me.

Q²

8 ⁴The LORD will perfect *that which* concerneth me:

P³

Thy °mercy, O ⁴LORD, *endureth* for ever:
  Forsake not the °works of Thine own
  hands.
   °To the chief Musician.

139
   °A Psalm °of David.

G⁴ R
(p. 855)
S¹ T¹

1 O °LORD, Thou hast °searched me, and
   °known *me*.

2 𝔗𝔥𝔬𝔲 ¹knowest my °downsitting and mine
   °uprising,
  Thou understandest my °thought afar off.
3 Thou °compassest my path and my °lying
   down,
  And °art acquainted *with* all my ways.
4 For *there is* not a word in my tongue,
  But, lo, O ¹LORD, Thou ¹knowest it °al-
   together.
5 Thou hast beset me °behind and before,
  And laid Thine hand upon me.

U¹

6 *Such* knowledge *is* too wonderful for me;
  It is high, I cannot *attain* unto it.

S² T²

7 Whither shall I go from Thy °spirit?
  Or whither shall I flee from Thy °presence?
8 If I ascend up into heaven, 𝔗𝔥𝔬𝔲 *art* there:
  If I make my bed in °hell, °behold, Thou
   art there.
9 *If* I take the °wings of the morning,
  And dwell in the uttermost parts of the sea;
10 Even there shall Thy hand lead me,
   And Thy °right hand shall hold me.
11 If I say, "Surely the darkness shall cover
   me;"
  Even the night shall be light about me.
12 Yea, the darkness °hideth not from Thee;
  But the night shineth as the day:
  The darkness and the light *are* both alike
   to Thee.
13 For 𝔗𝔥𝔬𝔲 hast possessed my reins:
  𝔗𝔥𝔬𝔲 hast °covered me in my mother's
   womb.
14 I will praise Thee; for I am °fearfully
   and wonderfully made:
  Marvellous *are* Thy works;
  And *that* ° my soul ¹knoweth right well.
15 My °substance was not hid from Thee,
   When I was made in secret,
  And °curiously wrought in the lowest
   parts of the earth.
16 Thine eyes did see my °substance, yet
   being °unperfect;
  And in Thy book all *my members* were
   written,
  ° *Which* in continuance were fashioned,
  When *as yet there was* none of them.

---

5 in: or, of.
6 respect = regard.
7 revive = make alive, or sustain in life. See note 11
on p. 827.
hand. Some codices, with two early printed editions
and Sept., read "hands" (pl.). Fig. *Anthropopatheia*
(Ap. 6).
against. Some codices, with two early printed
editions, read "Yea, because of".
mercy = lovingkindness, or grace.
works. Some codices, with Syr., read "work" (sing.).
To the chief Musician. See Ap. 64.

139 (G⁴, p. 826). DELIVERANCE FROM SELF.
            (*Alternation*.)

G⁴ | R | 1. Divine searching
    | S¹ | T¹ | 2–5. Omniscience.
    | | U¹ | 6. Admiration.
    | S² | T² | 7–16. Omnipresence.
    | | U² | 17, 18. Admiration.
    | S³ | T³ | 19–. Omnipotence.
    | | U³ | –19–22. Detestation.
  | R | 23, 24. Divine searching.

Title. A Psalm. Heb. *mizmōr*. Ap. 65. XVII.
of David = by David. The words alleged to be
Chaldaisms in *vv.* 3, 4, 8, 20, are found in the earlier
books such as Lev. 1 and 2 Sam. There is no internal
evidence of non-Davidic authorship.
1 LORD. Heb. Jehovah. Ap. 4. II.
searched = search out as for treasures or secrets.
known = seen, so as to understand.
2 downsitting . . . uprising. Fig. *Synecdochē* (of
Species), Ap. 6, put for all movements.
thought = inward thought. Occurs only here and
in *v.* 17.
3 compassest = scrutinisest.
lying down = bed.
art acquainted with = well knowest, or hast inspected.
4 altogether = on every side, or, the whole of it.
5 behind and before. Fig. *Synecdoche* (of Species),
Ap. 6, put for every direction.
7 spirit. Heb. *rūach*. Ap. 9.
presence. Heb. = face. Fig. *Anthrōpopatheia*. Ap. 6.
8 hell = Sheol. See Ap. 35.
behold. Fig. *Asterismos*. Ap. 6.
9 wings of the morning. See note on *sub*-scription
of Ps. 21.
10 right hand. Fig. *Anthrōpopatheia*. Ap. 6.
12 hideth not from = cannot be too dark for.
13 covered = woven me together. Cp. Job 10. 8, 11.
14 fearfully and wonderfully. Heb. = fears and
wonders. Put by Fig. *Metonymy* (of Cause), Ap. 6, for
the feelings produced by the works.
my soul = myself. Heb. *nephesh*. Ap. 13.
15 substance = frame. Heb. = bone, as in Gen. 2.
21, 22.
curiously = skilfully. Heb. = embroidered. Cp. Ex.
26. 1; 35. 35.
16 substance . . . unperfect = unfinished substance.
Not the same word as in *v.* 15. One word in Hebrew.
unperfect. Not imperfect.
Which in continuance = the days which were
ordered, or in which they should be fashioned.
17 How precious. Fig. *Ecphonēsis*. Ap. 6. See
note on 1 Sam. 3. 1.
thoughts = desires. See *v.* 2.
GOD. Heb. El. Ap. 4. IV.
sum. Heb. pl. of majesty, denoting the fullness or
vastness of them.
18 more in number . . . sand. Fig. *Parœmia*. Ap. 6.

---

17 °How precious also are Thy °thoughts
   unto me, O °GOD!
  How great is the °sum of them!
18 *If* I should count them, they are °more in
   number than the sand:
  When I awake, I am still with Thee.

U²

T3 (p. 855) **19** °Surely °Thou wilt slay °the wicked, O °GOD:

U3 Depart from me therefore, ye °bloody °men.

20 For they speak against Thee °wickedly,
And Thine enemies take *Thy name* in vain.

21 Do not I hate them, O [1]LORD, that hate Thee?
And °am not I grieved with those that rise up against Thee?

22 I hate them with perfect hatred:
I count them mine enemies.

R **23** Search me, O [17]GOD, and [1]know my heart:
Try me, and [1]know my °thoughts:

24 And see if *there be any* °wicked °way in me,
And lead me in the °way everlasting.

°To the chief Musician.

140

°A Psalm °of David.

H† V1 (p. 856) **1** Deliver me, O °LORD, from °the evil °man:
Preserve me from the violent °man;

W1 **2** °Which imagine °mischiefs in *their* heart;
Continually are they gathered together *for* war.

3 They have sharpened their °tongues like a serpent;
Adders' poison *is* under their lips. °Selah.

V2 **4** Keep me, O [1]LORD, from the hands of the °wicked;
Preserve me from the violent [1]man;

W2 Who have purposed to overthrow my goings.

5 The proud have hid a snare for me, and cords;
They have spread a net °by the wayside;
They have set gins for me. [3]Selah.

V3 **6** I said unto the [1]LORD, "Thou *art* my °GOD:"
Hear the voice of my supplications, O [1]LORD.

7 O °GOD the Lord, the strength °of my salvation,
Thou hast °covered my head in the day of battle.

W3 **8** Grant not, O [1]LORD, the desires of the °wicked:
Further not his °wicked device; *lest* they exalt themselves. [3]Selah.

V4 **9** *As for* the head of °those that compass me about,
Let the °mischief of their own lips °cover them.

10 Let °burning coals fall upon them:
Let them be cast into the fire;
Into deep pits, °that they rise not up again.

11 Let not an °evil speaker be established in the earth:
°Evil shall hunt the violent [1]man to overthrow *him*.

19 Surely, &c. These six verses (19–24) are not an "interpolation". They are required to complete the Structure. See above.

Thou wilt slay, &c. This is Omnipotent work. Cp. Job 40. 9–14.

the wicked = a lawless one. Heb. *rāshā'*. Ap. 44. x.

GOD. Heb. Eloah. Ap. 4. V.

bloody = bloodthirsty.

men. Heb. *'ĕnōsh*. Ap. 14. III.

20 wickedly = rebelliously (pre-meditated).

21 am not I grieved with = do I not loathe.

23 thoughts = distractions or cares. Not the same word as in *vv.* 2, 17.

24 wicked = painful or grievous.

way. Put by Fig. *Metonymy* (of Cause), Ap. 6, for the grief produced by it.

way everlasting. Put by Fig. *Metonymy* (of Effect), Ap. 6, for the happiness which is the effect and end of everlasting life.

To the chief Musician. See Ap. 64.

140 (H‡, p. 826). PRAYER AND PRAISE.
(*Repeated Alternation.*)

H‡
V1 | 1. Prayer. Preservation from enemies.
W1 | 2, 3. The evil man. Purposes. (Selah.)
V2 | 4-. Prayer. Preservation from enemies.
W2 | -4, 5. The evil man. Purposes. (Selah.)
V3 | 6, 7. Prayer. Preservation from enemies.
W3 | 8. The evil man. Desires. (Selah.)
V4 | 9–11. Prayer. Destruction of enemies.

EPILOGUE (12, 13). Trust and Praise.

Title. A Psalm. Heb. *mizmōr*. See Ap. 65. XVII.

of David = by David.

1 LORD. Heb. Jehovah. Ap. 4. II.

the evil = an evil man. Heb. *rā'a'*. Ap. 44. viii.

man. Heb. *'ādām*. Ap. 14. I.

man. Heb. *'ish*. Ap. 14. II.

2 Which = Who.

mischiefs. Not the same word as in *v.* 9, but the same word as "evil" in *v.* 1.

3 tongues. Sing. See note on *v.* 11. Quoted in Rom. 3. 13.

Selah. Connecting the evil with the prayer to be delivered; thus marking the Structure (Ap. 66. II.)

4 wicked = lawless. Heb. *rāshā'*. Ap. 44. x.

5 by the wayside. See Job 18. 10.

6 GOD. Heb. El. Ap. 4. IV.

7 GOD the Lord. Heb. Jehovah Adonai. Ap. 4. II and VIII (2).

of. Genitive of character = my saving strength.

covered = screened or protected. Not the same word as in *v.* 9.

8 wicked. Heb. *rāshā'*. Sing. Ap. 44. x. The same word as in *v.* 4.

wicked device = devices or plots. Occurs only here.

9 those that compass me about = one word in Hebrew.

mischief = labour, toil. Heb. *'āmal*. Ap. 44. v.

cover = overwhelm. Not the same word as in *v.* 7.

10 burning coals. Put by Fig. *Metonymy* (of Adjunct), Ap. 6, for cruel words and hard speeches which wound the heart as fire wounds the body. Cp. Prov. 16. 27; 26. 23.

that they, &c. = let them not, &c.

11 evil speaker. Heb. a man of tongue; not "a man of lips" (= talkative. Job 11. 2), but with an evil motive = a slanderer. Cp. *v.* 3.

Evil shall hunt = Let evil hunt.

12 the afflicted = a poor one.

the poor = helpless ones.

13 name. See note on 20. 1.

dwell in Thy presence. Cp. 11. 7; 16. 11.

12 I know that [1]the LORD will maintain the cause of °the afflicted, EPILOGUE
And the right of °the poor.

13 Surely the righteous shall give thanks unto Thy °name:
The upright shall °dwell in Thy presence.

141

°A Psalm of David.

H^{4}_{2} X Z (p. 857) 1 °LORD, I cry unto Thee: make haste unto me;
Give ear unto my voice, when I cry unto Thee.
2 Let my prayer be set forth before Thee *as* °incense;
And the lifting up of my hands *as* the evening °sacrifice.

A 3 °Set a watch, O [1]LORD, before my mouth;
°Keep the door of my lips.
4 Incline not my heart to *any* °evil thing,
To practise °wicked works
With °men that work °iniquity:
And let me not °eat of their °dainties.
5 Let °the righteous smite me; *it shall be* a kindness:
And let him reprove me; *it shall be* °an excellent oil,
Which shall not break my head:

B s For °yet my prayer also *shall be* in their calamities.

t 6 °When their °judges are overthrown °in stony places,
°They shall hear my °words; for they are °sweet.

Y 7 °Our bones are scattered at °the grave's mouth,

Y As when one °cutteth and °cleaveth *wood* upon the earth.

X Z 8 But mine eyes *are* unto Thee, O °GOD the [1]Lord:
In Thee °is my trust; leave not °my soul destitute.

A 9 °Keep me from the °snares *which* they have laid for me,
And the °gins of the workers of [4]iniquity.

B t 10 Let °the wicked fall into their own nets,

s Whilst that I °withal °escape.

142

°Maschil °of David; A Prayer °when he was in the °cave.

H^{4}_{3} C (p. 857) 1 I cried unto °the LORD with my voice;
With my voice unto °the LORD did I make my supplication.
2 I poured out my complaint before Him;
I shewed before Him my trouble.

D 3 When my °spirit °was overwhelmed within me, °then Thou knewest my path.

141 (H^{4}_{2}, p. 826). PRAYER AND PRAISE.
(*Introversion and Extended Alternation.*)

H^{4}_{2} | X | Z | 1, 2. I cry to Thee. Help me.
  A | 3–5–. Prayer for preventing grace (*Shamar*).
   B | s | –5. Yet, I.
    t | 6. Punishment of wicked.
     Y | 7–. Bones scattered.
     Y | –7. Wood cleaved.
X | *Z* | 8. I look to Thee. Help me.
  A | 9. Prayer for preventing grace (*Shamar*).
   B | *t* | 10–. Punishment of wicked.
    s | –10. Yet, I.

Title. A Psalm of David. See Title of 140.
1 LORD. Heb. Jehovah. Ap. 4. II.
2 incense. Cp. Ex. 30. 7. Rev. 8. 3, 4.
sacrifice = gift offering. Ap. 43. II. iii.
3 Set a watch = Set a guard. Heb. *shāmrāh*. Same word as "keep", *v.* 9 (*A*). Occurs only here.
Keep = keep in safety. Not the same word as in *v.* 9.
4 evil. Heb. *rā'a'*. Ap. 44. viii.
wicked. Heb. *rāsha'*. Ap. 44. x.
men. Heb. *'ish*. Ap. 14. II.
iniquity. Heb. *'āven*. Ap. 44. iii.
eat: i.e. partake of, or have fellowship with.
dainties = pleasant things. Cp. *v.* 6.
5 the righteous = a righteous one.
an excellent oil = oil for the head. This verse is said to be "extremely obscure" and "corrupt to a degree". The Fig. *Metalepsis* (Ap. 6) makes all clear; "head", being first used for *hair*, and then for the *whole person* by Fig. *Synecdoche* (of the Part). Heb. = "as oil on the hair, I will not refuse it". Note the alternation of lines in this verse.
5 yet. Same root as "withal" in *v.* 10 (*B*).
6 When. Not in Hebrew text.
judges = rulers. Cp. 2 Kings 9. 33.
in stony places = as by a rock; or, over a rock. Heb. by the hands of a rock. **They**: i.e. the people.
words = sayings. Heb. *'imrah*. Ap. 73. v.
sweet. Cognate with "dainties", *v.* 4.
7 Our bones. Sept. (Vatican B, and Alex. A by second hand), Syr., Arab., and Ethiop. read "their bones"
the grave's. Heb. Sheol's. Ap. 35. Note the word "bones" in this connection.
cutteth = sliceth, as in 1 Sam. 30. 12. Song 4. 3; 6. 7 (elsewhere rendered "piece" or "pieces"). Never means "ploweth", as in R.V.
cleaveth. As in Ecc. 10. 9. Zech. 14. 4 (cp. Gen. 22. 3. 1 Sam. 6. 14).
8 GOD the Lord. Heb. Jehovah Adonai. Ap. 4. II. VIII (2).
is my trust = have I sought refuge. Heb. *ḥasah*. Ap. 69. II.
my soul = me (emphatic). Heb. *nephesh*. Ap. 13.
9 Keep. Same root as "watch" in *v.* 3. (Heb. *shāmrēnī*.)
snares. A.V., 1611, read "snares" (sing.). Since 1769, "snares" (pl.). Heb. text is sing.
gins = traps. Short for "engine" = an ingenious contrivance.
10 the wicked = lawless ones. Heb. *rāsha'*. Ap. 44. x.
withal = Same as "yet", *v.* 5 (B). **escape** = pass on [in safety].

142 (H^{4}_{3}, p. 826). PRAYER AND PRAISE. (*Extended Alternation.*)

H^{4}_{3} | C | 1, 2. I cried unto Jehovah.
  D | 3–. Trouble. Comfort in. } Statements.
   E | –3. Enemies. } Statements.
    F | 4. Friends. Desertion of.
C | 5. I cried unto Jehovah.
  D | 6–. Trouble. Deliverance from. } Pleas.
   E | –6. Enemies. } Pleas.
    F | 7. Friends. Surrounded by.

Title. **Maschil** = Instruction. See Ap. 65. XI. **of David** = by David. **when . . . cave.** Adullam (1 Sam. 22. 1) or En-gedi (1 Sam. 24. 3). The last of eight Psalms referring to this subject. **1 the LORD.** Heb. Jehovah. Ap. 4. II. **3 spirit.** Heb. *rūach*. Ap. 9. **was overwhelmed** = fainted. Heb. = was darkened. Cp. 77. 3; 107. 5; 143. 4. Elsewhere only Jonah 2. 8, and Lam. 2. 12. **then** = then [I remembered] Thou knewest, &c.

E (p. 857) In the way wherein I walked have they privily laid a snare for me.

F 4 I looked on *my* right hand, and °beheld, but *there was* no man that would °know me:
Refuge failed me; no man cared for °my soul.

C 5 I cried unto Thee, O [1] LORD:
I said, "Thou *art* my refuge
And my portion in °the land of the living."

D 6 Attend unto my cry; for I am brought very low:

E Deliver me from my °persecutors; for they are stronger than I.

F 7 Bring [4] my soul out of prison, that I may praise Thy name:
The righteous shall compass me about;
For Thou shalt deal bountifully with me.

143

°A Psalm of David.

H¾ G J (p. 858) 1 Hear my prayer, O °LORD, give ear to my supplications:
In Thy faithfulness answer me, *and* in Thy righteousness.
2 And °enter not into judgment with Thy servant:
For °in Thy sight shall °no man living °be justified.

K 3 For the enemy hath °persecuted °my soul;
He hath smitten my life down to the ground;
He hath made me to dwell in darkness, as those that have been long dead.
4 Therefore is °my spirit °overwhelmed within me;
My heart within me is desolate.

H 5 I °remember the days of old;
I meditate on all Thy works;
I °muse on °the work of Thy hands.

H 6 I stretch forth my hands unto Thee:
[3] My soul *thirsteth* after Thee, °as a thirsty land. °Selah.

G J 7 Hear me speedily, O [1] LORD: [4] my spirit faileth:
Hide not Thy face from me,
Lest I be like unto them that go down into °the pit.
8 Cause me to hear Thy °lovingkindness in the morning;
For in Thee do I °trust:
Cause me to know the way wherein I should walk;
For I lift up [3] my soul unto Thee.
9 °Deliver me, O [1] LORD, from mine enemies:
I °flee °unto Thee to hide me.
10 Teach me to do Thy °will; for Thou *art* my °God:
Thy °Spirit *is* good; °lead me into the °land of uprightness.
11 °Quicken me, O [1] LORD, for Thy °name's sake:
For Thy righteousness' sake bring [3] my soul out of trouble.
12 And of Thy °mercy cut off mine °enemies, K
And destroy all them that afflict [3] my soul:
For I *am* Thy servant.

4 beheld. Supply Ellipsis: "beheld [on my left hand], but", &c.
know = regard, or recognise.
my soul = me (emphatic). Heb. *nephesh*. Ap. 13.
5 the land of the living. See note on Ezek. 26. 20.
6 persecutors = pursuers.

143 (H¾, p. 826). PRAYER.
(*Introversion and Alternation.*)

H¾ | G | J | 1, 2. Prayer.
| | K | 3, 4. Enemy. Action.
| H | 5. Conduct. Past. Remembrance.
| *H* | 6. Conduct. Present. Desire.
| *G* | *J* | 7–11. Prayer.
| | *K* | 12. Enemies. Excision.

Title. A Psalm of David. Same as 140.
1 LORD. Heb. Jehovah. Ap. 4. II.
2 enter not. As in Job 9. 32; 22. 4.
in Thy sight. Cp. 1 Sam. 16. 7. Isa. 55. 8. Job 14. 3.
no man = no one. Cp. Job 15. 14, 15.
be justified = stand or appear [before Thee] just. The verb is Active. Sept., A.V., and R.V. render it passive. Cp. Rom. 3. 20. Gal. 2. 16.
3 persecuted = pursued.
my soul = me (emphatic). Heb. *nephesh*. Ap. 13.
4 my spirit = me. Heb. *rūach*. Ap. 9. Fig. *Synecdoche* (of Part), Ap. 6, put for the whole person, for emphasis.
overwhelmed. Same word as 77. 3; 107. 5; 142. 3.
5 remember. Cp. 77. 5, 10, 11.
muse = talk with myself.
the work of Thy hands. Some codices, with three early printed editions, Aram., Sept., and Vulg., read "works" (pl.).
6 as. Some codices, with seven early printed editions, read "in".
Selah. Connecting and returning to prayer (7–11) as the consequence of the reflection (5, 6). This is the last Selah (of seventy-one) in the Psalms. For three others, see Hab. 3. 3, 9, 13. See Ap. 66. II.
7 the pit = a grave. Heb. *bōr*. A sepulchre, as hewn out of the rock. Hence rendered cistern, or dry pit. Cp. Gen. 37. 20. See note on Gen. 21. 19.
8 lovingkindness: or grace.
trust = confide. Heb. *bāṭah*. Ap. 69. I.
9 Deliver me = pluck me [out of the hands of].
flee. A.V., 1611, reads "fly". Since 1629 the reading is "flee".
unto. Some codices, with one early printed edition and Sept., read "in". Cp. *v.* 8.
10 will = good pleasure.
God. Heb. Elohim. Ap. 4. I.
Spirit. Heb. *rūach*. Ap. 9.
lead, &c. = It will lead.
land. Some codices, with one early printed edition, read "way"; others, with Syr., read "path". Cp. 27. 11.
11 Quicken me = Give, or preserve me in life. See note ‖ on p. 827.
name's. See note on Ps. 20. 1.
12 mercy = lovingkindness, or grace.
enemies. Cp. Structure, *v.* 3 (K).

144

A Psalm °of David.

H$\frac{4}{5}$ L[1] (p. 859)

1 °Blessed *be* °the LORD my °strength,
Which teacheth my hands °to war,
And my fingers °to fight:
2 My °goodness, and my fortress;
My high tower, and my °deliverer;
My shield, and *He* in Whom I °trust;
Who subdueth °my People °under me.
3 [1] LORD, °what *is* °man, that Thou takest knowledge of him!
°*Or* the son of °man, that Thou makest account of him!
4 °Man is like to vanity:
His days *are* as a shadow that passeth away.
5 Bow Thy heavens, O [1] LORD, and come down:
Touch the mountains, and they shall smoke.
6 °Cast forth lightning, and scatter them:
Shoot out Thine °arrows, and destroy them.
7 °Send Thine °hand from above;
°Rid me, and °deliver me out of great waters,
From the hand of °strange children;

M[1]
8 Whose mouth °speaketh vanity,
And their right hand *is* a right hand of falsehood.

L[2]
9 I will sing a new song unto Thee, O °God:
Upon a psaltery *and* an instrument of ten strings will I sing praises unto Thee.
10 *It is He* That giveth salvation unto kings:
Who °delivereth °David His servant from the hurtful °sword.
11 [7] Rid me, and [7] deliver me from the hand of [7] strange children,
Whose mouth [8] speaketh vanity,
And their right hand *is* a right hand of falsehood:

M[2]
12 °That our sons °*may be* as plants grown up in their youth;
That our daughters °*may be* as corner stones, polished *after* the similitude of a palace:
13 *That* our garners [12] *may be* full, affording all manner of store:
That our °sheep may bring forth thousands and ten thousands in our °streets:
14 *That* our oxen [12] *may be* °strong to labour;
That there be °no breaking in, °nor going out;
That *there be* no complaining in our [13] streets.
15 °Happy *is that* people, that is °in such a case:

L[3]
°*Yea*, happy *is that* People, whose [9] God *is* [1] the LORD.

144 (**H**$\frac{4}{5}$, p. 826). PRAYER AND THANKSGIVING.
(*Repeated Alternation.*)

H$\frac{4}{5}$
| L[1] | 1–7. David's words. Praise and Prayer.
| M[1] | 8. Words of foreigners. Vain and false.
| L[2] | 9–11. David's words. Praise and Prayer.
| M[2] | 12–15–. Words of foreigners. Vain and false.
| L[3] | –15. David's words. Right and true.

Title. of David = by David. The Sept. adds "concerning Goliath." This may be because Ps. 8, which relates to David and Goliath (see its *sub*-scription), has the same words in *v.* 4 as in 144. 3. In any case, Ps. 144 is peculiarly appropriate to David's victory (1 Sam. 17). Not a "compilation" of "fragments" of some "lost Psalms", but a perfect whole with a perfect design, as shown by the Structure above.

1 Blessed. Fig. *Benedictio* (Ap. 6). Not *Beatitudo* as in *v.* 15.

the LORD. Heb. Jehovah. Ap. 4. II.

strength = rock, or fortress. Cp. Deut. 32. 4. 1 Sam. 2. 2; 2 Sam. 22. 47. Pss. 18. 2, 31, 46; 19. 14; 28. 1; 62. 2, 6.

to war . . . to fight. Not merely generally, but specially in the case of Goliath (1 Sam. 17). See Title.

2 goodness = lovingkindness. The Syr. reads "refuge".

deliverer = liberator. Heb. *pālaṭ*. Not the same word as in *vv.* 7, 10, 11. See notes below.

trust = flee for refuge. Heb. *ḥasah*. Ap. 69. II.

my People: A special reading called *Sevīr* (see Ap. 34), and some other codices, with Aram. and Syr., read "peoples". Cp. 18. 47.

under me. In some codices there is a marginal note: "under Him"; and this is read the text, in some codices.

3 what . . . ? Fig. *Erotēsis*. Ap. 6. Cp. 8. 4.

man. Heb. *'ādām*. Ap. 14. I.

Or. This word is read in some codices, with one early printed edition. **man.** Heb. *'ĕnōsh*. Ap. 14. III.

4 Man. Heb. *'ādām*. Ap. 14. I.

6 Cast forth = Flash. Heb. lighten lightnings. Fig. *Polyptōton* (Ap. 6). See note on Gen. 26. 28.

arrows. Fig. *Anthrōpopatheia*. Ap. 6.

7 Send = Put forth.

hand. Heb. text reads "hands" (pl.); but some codices, with one early printed edition, Aram., Sept., Syr., and Vulg., read "hand" (sing.), which A.V. and R.V. followed.

Rid = snatch. Heb. *pāẓah*; same word as in *v.* 11, and "delivereth", *v.* 10.

deliver = pluck, or rescue. Heb. *nāẓal*; same word as in *v.* 11, not the same as in *vv.* 2, 10.

strange. Always means foreign, in Hebrew, as in early English.

strange children = aliens. Heb. = 'sons of the foreigner.

8 speaketh. Cp. *v.* 11; and note the words they speak in *vv.* 12–15.

9 God. Heb. Elohim. Ap. 4. I.

10 delivereth = snatcheth; same word as "rid", *vv.* 7, 11.

David . . . sword; with special reference to Goliath's sword in 1 Sam. 17. 50, 51.

12 That = Who. Heb. *'āsher*. Supply the Ellipsis thus: "Who [say] our sons are, &c." All the words in italic type in *vv.* 12–15– may be omitted, or the Present Tense may be supplied throughout. The verb "say" or "saying" is very frequently to be thus understood. See note on 109. 5.

may be. Supply "Are" and omit "That".

13 sheep = flocks.

streets = open fields. Heb. that which is outside the house. **14 strong to labour** = well laden. **no breaking in** = no invasion. **nor going out** = no captivity. **15 Happy.** See Ap. 63. VI. **in such a case**: i.e. holding the false view that happiness consists in outward prosperity. Cp. 4. 6, 7, and 146. 3 and 5. **Yea.** Supply the Ellipsis (Ap. 6), not as in A.V. and R.V., but [Yea, rather], or [Nay]. The last member (L[3]) being David's own words; denying the vain and false words of the aliens (*vv.* 8 and 12–15), and declaring the truth as to that in which real happiness consists. See note on 4. 6, 7.

145 °David's *Psalm* of praise.

E N¹ u (p. 860) 1 (א) I will extol Thee, my °God, O king;
v And I will bless Thy °name for ever and ever.
u 2 (ב) Every day will I bless Thee;
v And I will praise Thy [1]name for ever and ever.
O¹ 3 (ג) Great *is* °the LORD, and greatly to be praised;
And His greatness *is* unsearchable.
N² w¹ 4 (ד) One generation shall praise Thy works to another,
And shall declare Thy mighty acts.
x¹ 5 (ה) I will speak of the °glorious honour of Thy majesty,
And of Thy °wondrous works.
w² 6 (ו) °And *men* shall speak of the might of Thy °terrible acts:
x² And I will declare Thy greatness.
w³ 7 (ז) They shall °abundantly utter the memory of Thy great goodness,
And shall sing of Thy righteousness.
O² 8 (ח) [3]The LORD *is* °gracious, and full of compassion;
Slow to anger, and °of great mercy.
9 (ט) [3]The LORD *is* good °to all:
And His °tender mercies *are* over all His works.
N³ y 10 (י) All Thy works shall praise Thee, O [3]LORD;
And Thy °saints shall bless Thee.
11 (כ) They shall speak of the glory of Thy kingdom,
z And talk of Thy °power;
z 12 (ל) To make known to the sons of °men His mighty acts,
y And the glorious majesty of His kingdom.
O³ a 13 (מ) Thy kingdom *is* °an everlasting kingdom,
And Thy dominion *endureth* throughout all °generations.
b 14 (ס) [3]The LORD upholdeth all that °fall,
And °raiseth up all *those that be* bowed down.
a 15 (ע) The °eyes of all wait upon Thee;
And Thou givest them their meat in due season.
16 (פ) °Thou openest Thine °hand,
And satisfiest the desire of every living thing.

145 (*E*, p. 826). DAVID'S [PSALM] OF PRAISE. (*Repeated Introversion.*)

E | N¹ | 1, 2. Praise promised. For Jehovah. (David.)
O¹ | 3. Praise offered.
N² | 4-7. Praise promised. For His work. (David and others.)
O² | 8, 9. Praise offered.
N³ | 10-12. Praise promised. For His kingdom. (The works.)
O³ | 13-20. Praise offered.
N⁴ | 21. Praise promised. David and all others.

Title. David's [Psalm] of praise. No other Psalm so entitled. An acrostic Psalm. See Ap. 63. VII.

1, 2 (N¹, above). DAVID ALONE. (*Alternation.*)

N¹ | u | 1-. Thee.
v | -1. Thy name.
u | 2-. Thee.
v | -2. Thy name.

1 God. Heb. Elohim. Ap. 4. I.
name. See note on 20. 1.
3 the LORD. Heb. Jehovah. Ap. 4. II.

4, 7 (N², above). DAVID AND OTHERS. PRAISE. (*Alternation.*)

N² | w¹ | 4. They shall.
x¹ | 5. I will.
w² | 6-. They shall.
x² | -6. I will.
w³ | 7. They shall.

5 glorious, &c. Heb. = the majesty of the glory of Thine honour.
wondrous works = instances or examples of Thy wonders. Heb. = words of Thy wonders.
6 And men = And they. See Structure (N², above).
terrible. See note on 111. 9.
7 abundantly utter = pour forth.
8 gracious, &c. Cp. Ex. 34. 6, 7.
of great mercy = great in lovingkindness, or grace.
9 to all. Sept. reads "to them that wait on Him".
tender mercies = compassions.

10-12 (N³, above). THE WORKS PRAISE. (*Introversion.*)

N³ | y | 10, 11-. Glory. } "Thy".
z | -11. Might. }
z | 12-. Might. } "His".
y | -12. Glory. }

10 saints = favoured or beloved ones. Cp. 16. 10.
11 power. Sing. of the Heb. word "mighty acts" (*v.* 4).
12 men. Heb. *'ādām* (with Art.) = mankind. Ap. 14. I.

13-20 (O³, above). PRAISE OFFERED. (*Alternation.*)

O³ | a | 13. Thou.
[b | נ, 14. He.]
a | 15, 16. Thou.
b | 17-20. He.

13 an everlasting kingdom = a kingdom for all ages. Looking backward (eternal, 77. 5) as well as forward (everlasting, 77. 7). These words, "Thy kingdom [O Christ] is an everlasting kingdom", were (up to 1893) to be seen on the wall of one of the largest Mosques in Damascus. Formerly it was a Temple of Rimmon. It was turned into the (Christian) Church of St. John the Baptist by Arcadius, later it was made into a Mosque by Caliph Walid I (705-717). It was destroyed by fire on Oct. 14, 1893, and subsequently rebuilt. (*Enc. Brit.* vol. 7, p. 785, Camb. (11th) edition.) **generations.** Following this verse (13) the Primitive Text read:

"Faithful is Jehovah in all His words
And holy in all His works",

the verse beginning with the missing letter נ (Nun) = *Neᵉmān* (= faithful). It is found in some codices, with Sept., Syr., Vulg., Arabic, and Ethiopic Versions. The Structure (O³, above) thus confirms the Ancient Versions. **14 fall** = are ready to fall. **raiseth up.** Occurs only here and 146. 8. **15 eyes of all wait.** Fig. *Prosopopœia.* Ap. 6. **16 Thou.** This is emphatic in Sept., Syr., and Vulg. Cp. 104. 26. **hand.** Fig. *Anthropopatheia.* Ap. 6.

b (p. 860) 17 (צ) [3] The LORD *is* [7] righteous in all His ways,
And ° holy in all His works.
18 (ק) [3] The LORD *is* ° nigh ° unto all them that call upon Him,
To all that call upon Him in truth.
19 (ר) He will fulfil the desire of them that fear Him:
He also will hear ° their cry, and will save them.
20 (ש) [3] The LORD preserveth all them that love Him:
But all the ° wicked will He destroy.

N^4 21 (ת) My mouth shall speak the praise of [3] the LORD:
And ° let ° all flesh bless His ° holy [2] name for ° ever and ever.

F^1 J P (p. 861) **146** ° Praise ye THE LORD.
° Praise ° the LORD, ° O my soul.
2 While I live will I praise [1] the LORD:
I will sing praises unto my ° God while I have any being.

Q c 3 Put not your ° trust in princes,
Nor in the son of ° man,
d In whom *there is* ° no help.
e 4 ° His ° breath goeth forth, he ° returneth to his ° earth;
In that very day his ° thoughts perish.

Q c 5 ° Happy *is he* that *hath* the ° GOD ° of Jacob for his help,
° Whose ° hope *is* in [1] the LORD his [2] God:
d 6 Which ° made heaven, and earth,
The sea, and all that therein *is*:
Which keepeth truth for ever:
7 Which executeth judgment for the oppressed:
Which giveth ° food to the hungry.
[1] The LORD looseth ° the prisoners:
8 [1] The LORD openeth *the eyes of* [7] the blind:
[1] The LORD raiseth them that are bowed down:
[1] The LORD loveth [7] the righteous:
9 [1] The LORD preserveth [7] the ° strangers;
He ° relieveth [7] the fatherless and widow:
But the way of the ° wicked He turneth upside down.

e 10 [1] **The LORD ° shall reign ° for ever,**
Even thy [2] God, O ° Zion, unto all generations.

P [1] Praise ye THE LORD.

F^2 K R S^1 f^1 (p. 862) **147** ° Praise ye THE LORD:
° For *it is* good to sing praises unto our ° God;
For *it is* pleasant; *and* praise is comely.

---

17 holy=gracious.

18 nigh: i.e. nigh to help. Cp. 34. 18; 119. 151. Deut. 4. 7.

unto all. Note the Fig. *Anadiplosis* (Ap. 6) in the repetition, "to all that call" (for emphasis).

19 their cry: i.e. for help in distress.

20 wicked=lawless. Heb. *rāshā'*. Ap. 44. x.

21 let all flesh=all flesh shall, as in *v.* 10; thus completing and perfecting the Structure above.

all flesh. Fig. *Synecdoche* (of the Part), Ap. 6, put for all men. **holy.** See note on Ex. 3. 5.

ever and ever. Many codices, with one early printed edition, here add:—

"And we will bless Jah:
From henceforth even for ever,
Praise ye Jah." Cp. Ps. 115. 18.

146 (J, p. 827). FIRST HALLELUJAH PSALM. (GENESIS.) *(Introversion and Extended Alternation.)*

J | P | 1, 2. Hallelujah.
  Q | c | 3-. Wrong trust. }
    d | -3. Powerless. } Man.
    e | 4. Mortal. }
  Q | *c* | 5. Right trust. }
    d | 6-9. Powerful. } Jehovah.
    e | 10-. Eternal. }
  P | -10. Hallelujah.

The first of the five "Hallelujah" Psalms concluding the whole book; each beginning and ending with this word. The first has GENESIS for its subject; the second, EXODUS; the third, LEVITICUS; the fourth, NUMBERS, and the fifth, DEUTERONOMY. See the Structure, p. 827, and notes below.

1 Praise ye THE LORD=Hallelu-JAH. Ap. 4. III.

Praise. Fig. *Apostrophe.* Ap. 6.

the LORD. Heb. Jehovah. Ap. 4. II.

O my soul=O I myself (emphatic). Heb. *nephesh*. Ap. 13. **2 God.** Heb. Elohim. Ap. 4. I.

3 trust=confidence. Heb. *bāṭaḥ*. Ap. 69. I.

man. Heb. *'ādām*. Ap. 14. I.

no help=no salvation, or saving help. Cp. 33. 16; 60. 11.

4 His breath, &c. This verse occurs in the Apocrypha (1 Macc. 2. 63); but why is it *assumed* that this verse is taken from the Book of Maccabees, instead of this verse in Maccabees being taken from this Psalm?

breath=spirit. Heb. *rūach*. Ap. 9. Not the same word as in 150. 6.

returneth. See Gen. 2. 7; 3. 19, and cp. Ecc. 12. 7. Ps. 104. 29.

earth=ground, or dust. Heb. *'ădāmāh*. Not *'erez*=the Earth. **thoughts**=purposes, or plans.

5 Happy. The last of the twenty-seven Beatitudes in the Book of Psalms. See Ap. 63. VI.

GOD. Heb. El. Ap. 4. IV.

of Jacob: i.e. the God who met Jacob (Gen. 28. 13) when he had nothing (Gen. 32. 10), and deserved nothing (but wrath, Gen. 27), and promised him everything. This title answers to the N.T. title "the God of all grace" (1 Pet. 5. 10). Happy indeed are all they who have this God for their God.

Whose. Supply the Ellipsis by repeating [Happy he] whose, &c. **hope**=expectation.

6 made heaven, and earth. Another reference to Genesis (ch. 1). Cp. *v.* 4 (above). See notes on Gen. 14. 19 and Deut. 4. 26.

7 food. Heb. bread. Put by Fig. *Synecdochē* (of Species), Ap. 6, for food in general.

the. No Art. in Heb. **9 strangers**=aliens.

relieveth. Plenty of saving "help" here. Cp. the contrast with "man", (d, *v.* 3), "no help". **wicked**=lawless. Heb. *rāsha'*. Ap. 44. x. **10 for ever.** Contrast *v.* 4. Cp. Rev. 11. 15. **Zion.** See Ap. 68.

147 [For Structure see next page].

The second of these five Hallelujah Psalms, the EXODUS Psalm. **1 Praise ye THE LORD.** Heb. Hallelu-JAH. Ap. 4. III. Not "inserted by mistake in verse 1 instead of in the title", but required here by the Structure. See the Structure. **For.** Not "come into the first line from the second by dittography", but an essential part of the second line, which is repeated by the Fig. *Anadiplosis* (Ap. 6) in the third line. The first verse thus *does* contain two lines (beside the "Hallelujah") like all the other verses. **God.** Heb. Elohim. Ap. 4. I.

2 °The LORD °doth build up Jerusalem:
He °gathereth together the °outcasts of Israel.
3 He healeth the broken in heart,
And bindeth up their wounds.

g[1] (p. 862) 4 He telleth the number of the °stars;
He calleth them all by *their* °names.
5 Great *is* °our LORD, and °of great power:
His understanding *is* infinite.

h[1] 6 [2] The LORD lifteth up °the meek:
He casteth the °wicked down to the ground.

S[2] f[2] 7 Sing unto [2] the LORD with thanksgiving;
Sing praise upon the harp unto our [1] God:

g[2] 8 Who covereth the heaven with clouds,
Who prepareth rain for the earth,
Who maketh grass to grow upon the °mountains.
9 He giveth to the beast his food,
And to the young ravens which cry.

h[2] 10 He delighteth not in the strength of the horse:
°He taketh not pleasure in the legs of a °man.
11 [2] The LORD taketh pleasure in them that fear Him,
In those that °hope in His mercy.

S[3] f[3] 12 °Praise [2] the LORD, O Jerusalem;
Praise thy [1] God, O °Zion.
13 For He hath strengthened the bars of thy gates;
He hath blessed thy °children within thee.
14 He maketh °peace *in* thy borders,
And filleth thee with the finest of the wheat.

g[3] 15 He sendeth forth His °commandment *upon* earth:
His word runneth very swiftly.
16 He giveth snow like wool:
He scattereth the hoarfrost like ashes.
17 He casteth forth his ice like morsels:
Who can stand before His cold?
18 He sendeth out His °word, and melteth them:
He causeth His °wind to blow, *and* the waters flow.

h[3] 19 He sheweth His °word unto °Jacob,
His statutes and His judgments unto °Israel.
20 He hath °not dealt so with any nation:
And *as for His* judgments, °they have not known them.

R [1] Praise ye THE LORD.

F[3] L T (p. 862) U i **148** °Praise ye THE LORD.
Praise ye °the LORD from the heavens:
Praise Him in the °heights.

k 2 Praise ye Him, all His angels:
Praise ye Him, all His hosts.
3 Praise ye Him, sun and moon:
Praise Him, all ye °stars of light.

147 (K, p. 827). THE SECOND HALLELUJAH PSALM. (EXODUS.)
(*Introversion and Extended Alternation.*)

K | R | 1–. Hallelujah.
S[1] | f[1] | –1–3. Praise. Kindness to Israel.
g[1] | 4, 5. General operations. Nature.
h[1] | 6. Contrast. What Jehovah does.
S[2] | f[2] | 7. Praise. Kindness to Israel.
g[2] | 8, 9. General operations. Nature.
h[2] | 10, 11. Contrast. What Jehovah delights in.
S[3] | f[3] | 12–14. Praise. Kindness to Israel.
g[3] | 15–18. General operations. Nature.
h[3] | 19, 20–. Contrast. What Jehovah has shown.
R | –20. Hallelujah.

2 The LORD. Heb. Jehovah. Ap. 4. II.
doth build up Jerusalem = is Jerusalem's builder (participle). No reference to post-exilic building. Cp. 122. 3. **gathereth** = will gather.
outcasts = the driven away.
4 stars . . . names. See Ap. 12. Cp. Isa. 40. 26.
names. The reference is to the knowledge of the "names" in building up the nation of Israel. Cp. *vv.* 2 and 20 with Ex. 1. 7–20; and *vv.* 15, 19 with Ex. 20.
5 our LORD. Heb. *'Adonim.* Ap. 4. VIII (3). Cp. 135. 5.
of great power = abounding in power. Cp. Isa. 40. 26.
6 the meek = meek or humble ones. Num. 12. 3.
wicked = lawless. Heb. *rāshā'.* Ap. 44. x.
8 mountains. The Sept. adds "and herb for the service of men". From thence it found its way into the Prayer Book Version. Cp. 104. 14. Here, the addition is out of place, as "man" is not introduced till *v.* 10.
10 He taketh not. Some codices, with Sept., Syr., and Vulg., read "Nor taketh delight".
man. Heb. *'ish.* Ap. 4. II.
11 hope in His mercy = wait for His lovingkindness.
12 Praise the LORD. Not the same word as in *v.* 1. Used only by David and Solomon.
Zion. See Ap. 68. Zion then still standing.
13 children = sons.
14 peace in thy borders = thy borders peace.
15 commandment = sayings, or utterances. Heb. *'imrah.* See Ap. 73. v. Cp. 33. 9; 107. 20.
18 word. Heb. *dābār* = the subject-matter of the articulate utterance (*v.* 15). See Ap. 73. x.
wind. Heb. *rūach.* Ap. 9.
19 word. Some codices, with Sept., Syr., and Vulg., read "word". Others read plural.
Jacob . . . Israel. See notes on Gen. 32. 28; cp. 43. 6; 45. 26, 28.
20 not dealt so, &c. The reference is to Exod. 20. Cp. Deut. 4. 7, 8; and see Ap. 15.
they have not known them. Sept. and Vulg. read "He maketh not known to them".

148 (L, p. 827). THE THIRD HALLELUJAH PSALM. (LEVITICUS.)
(*Introversion and Extended Alternation.*)

L | T | 1–. Hallelujah.
U | i | –1. Praise from the heavens. (2nd Person.)
k | 2–4. Things in the heavens.
l | 5–. Injunction. "Let them praise".
m | –5, 6. Reasons. "For".
U | *i* | 7–. Praise from the earth. (2nd Person.)
k | –7–12. Things in the earth.
l | 13–. Injunction. "Let them praise".
m | –13–14–. Reasons. "For".
T | –14. Hallelujah.

The third of the last five Hallelujah Psalms. The LEVITICUS Psalm. Cp. *v.* 14 with Lev. 10. 3.
1 Praise ye THE LORD. Hallelu-JAH. Ap. 4. III.
the LORD. Heb. Jehovah with *'eth* = Jehovah Himself. Ap. 4. II. **heights.** As in Job 16. 19; 25. 2.
3 stars of light. Gen. of Origin (Ap. 17. 2) = stars that give light = light-bearers, as in Gen. 1. 14–16.

4 Praise Him, ye heavens of heavens,
And ye waters that *be* above the heavens.

l (p. 862) 5 Let them praise the name of [1] the LORD:
For He commanded, and they were created.
m 6 He hath also stablished them for ever and ever:
He hath made a decree °which shall not pass.

U i 7 Praise [1] the LORD from °the earth,
k Ye °dragons, and all deeps:
8 Fire, and hail; snow, and vapours;
Stormy °wind fulfilling his word:
9 Mountains, and all hills;
Fruitful trees, and all cedars:
10 Beasts, and all cattle;
Creeping things, and flying fowl:
11 Kings of [7] the earth, and all °people;
Princes, and all judges of the earth:
12 Both young men, and maidens;
Old men, and children:

l 13 Let them praise the °name of [1] the LORD:
m For His °name alone is excellent;
His glory *is* above the °earth and heaven.
14 He also exalteth the horn of His People,
The praise of all His °saints;
Even of the °children of Israel, a People °near unto Him.

T [1] Praise ye THE LORD.

F[4] *K* V (p. 863) **149** °Praise ye THE LORD.
Sing unto °the LORD a new song,
W *And* His praise in the °congregation of °saints.
X 2 Let °Israel rejoice in Him That made him:
Let the °children of °Zion be joyful in their King.
Y n 3 Let them praise His °name
o In the dance:
Y n Let them sing praises unto Him
o With the °timbrel and harp.
X 4 For [1] the LORD °taketh pleasure in His People:
He will beautify the meek with salvation.
W 5 Let the [1] saints be joyful °in glory:
Let them sing aloud upon their °beds.
6 *Let* the °high *praises* of °GOD *be* in their mouth,
And a twoedged sword in their hand;
7 To execute vengeance upon the °heathen,
And punishments upon the °people;
8 To bind their kings with chains,
And their nobles with fetters of iron;
9 To execute upon them °the judgment written:
This honour have all His [1] saints.
V [1] Praise ye the LORD.

F[5] *J* A (p. 863) **150** °Praise ye THE LORD.
B Praise °GOD in His °sanctuary:
C Praise Him in the °firmament of His power.

---

6 which shall not pass: or, which [they] shall not pass.
7 the earth. Note the change and see Structure above.
dragons = sea monsters.
8 wind. Heb. *rūach.* Ap. 9.
11 people = peoples.
13 name. See note on 20. 1.
earth and heaven: i.e. combining the two subjects of *vv.* 1 and 7. This order of these two words occurs only here and Gen. 2. 4. Cp. note on Deut. 4. 26.
14 saints = favoured ones, or beloved.
children = sons.
near unto Him. The reference is to Leviticus and its leading thought. See Lev. 10. 3; 21. 21; and cp. 65. 4.

149 (*K*, p. 827). THE FOURTH HALLELUJAH PSALM. (NUMBERS.)
(*Introversion and Alternation.*)

K | V | 1–. Hallelujah.
W | –1. Saints to praise.
X | 2. Israel to rejoice in Jehovah.
Y | n | 3–. Praise. } In A.V.
o | –3–. How. } For Heb.
Y | *n* | –3–. Praise. } see note
o | –3. How. } below.
X | 4. Jehovah taketh pleasure in Israel.
W | 5–9–. Saints to praise.
V | –9. Hallelujah.

The fourth of the concluding five Hallelujah Psalms, answering to NUMBERS. Cp. *vv.* 5–9 with Num. 24. 17–24.
1 Praise ye THE LORD. Heb. Hallelu-JAH. Ap. 4. III.
the LORD. Heb. Jehovah. Ap. 4. II.
congregation = assembly (in its military aspect).
saints = favoured ones, or beloved, *v.* 5 (*W*).
2 Israel. Cp. the Structure.
children = sons.
Zion. See Ap. 68.
3 In the Hebrew this verse is an *Introversion*:—

Y | 3–. Let them praise His name.
Z | –3–. With the dance.
Z | –3–. With the timbrel and harp.
Y | –3–. Let them sing praises unto Him.

name. See note on 20. 1.
timbrel = drum. See note on Ex. 15. 20.
4 taketh pleasure. Cp. Isa. 54. 7, 8.
5 in glory = "with [ascriptions of] glory".
beds = couches.
6 high praises = extollings.
GOD. Heb. El. Ap. 4. IV.
7 heathen = nations.
people = peoples.
9 the judgment written. See Deut. 32. 40–43. Cp. Isa. 45. 14. Ezek. 25. 14; chs. 38 and 39. Zech. 14. The special reference is to NUMBERS 24. 17–24.

150 (*J*, p. 827). THE FIFTH HALLELUJAH PSALM. (DEUTERONOMY.) (*Introversion.*)

J | A | 1–. Hallelujah.
B | –1–. The Sanctuary.
C | –1. Praise of Jehovah's power.
C | 2. Praise of Jehovah's might.
B | 3–6–. Instruments of the Sanctuary.
A | –6. Hallelujah.

The fifth of the last five Hallelujah Psalms, answering to the great thought of DEUTERONOMY. Cp. *v.* 2 with Deut. 3. 24, and 32. 43.
1 Praise ye THE LORD. Heb. Hallelu-JAH. Ap. 4. III.
GOD. Heb. El. Ap. 4. IV.
sanctuary. The earthly sanctuary and the heavenly: the lower being formed on the pattern of the higher. See Heb. 8. 5; 9. 23; and cp. 1 Chron. 28. 11–13, 19.
firmament: Heb. = expanse (Gen. 1. 6).

C (p. 863) 2 Praise Him °for His °mighty acts:
Praise Him according to His °excellent greatness.

B 3 Praise Him with °the sound of the trumpet:
Praise Him with °the psaltery and harp.
4 Praise Him with [3]the °timbrel and dance:
Praise Him with stringed instruments and °organs.
5 Praise Him upon [3]the loud cymbals:
Praise Him upon the high sounding cymbals.
6 Let every thing that hath °breath °praise THE LORD.

A °Praise ye THE LORD.

2 for = in [the recital of] His mighty acts.
mighty acts. Some codices, with Aram. and Syr., read "His might".
excellent = the abundance of His greatness or grandeur.
3 the. No Art. in Heb. text.
4 timbrel = drum. See note on Ex. 15. 20.
organs = pipe, or reed (sing., never pl.).
6 breath. Heb. *n*[e]*shāmāh* (see Ap. 16): i.e. in contrast with material instruments.
praise THE LORD. Heb. *t*[e]*hallēl jah.*
Praise ye THE LORD. Heb. *Hal*[e]*lūjah*, thus fitly closing the Book of Psalms. Cp. the endings of the other four books; and see notes on p. 720.

THE PROVERBS[1].

THE STRUCTURE OF THE BOOK AS A WHOLE.

(*Introversion and Alternation.*)

INTRODUCTION. 1. 1–6–.

A | 1. –6—9. 18. "THE WORDS OF THE WISE". FOR SOLOMON. FOR A PRINCE AND A KING. SECOND PERSON ("MY SON", "THY", "THEE", "THOU", "THINE"). THE "MOTHER".

B | C | 10. 1—19. 19. PROVERBS BY SOLOMON. FOR ALL. THIRD PERSON ("HE", "HIS", "HIM", "THEY", "THEM").

D | 19. 20—24. 34. PROVERBS FOR SOLOMON. FOR A PRINCE AND A KING. SECOND PERSON ("MY SON", "THOU", "THY").

B | *C* | 25. 1—26. 28. PROVERBS BY SOLOMON. FOR ALL. "COPIED BY THE MEN OF HEZEKIAH". THIRD PERSON ("HE", "HIM", "HIS").

D | 27. 1—29. 27. PROVERBS FOR SOLOMON. FOR A PRINCE AND A KING. SECOND PERSON ("MY SON", "THEE", "THY").

A | 30. 1—31. 31. "THE WORDS OF AGUR" AND "THE WORDS OF LEMUEL". FOR SOLOMON. FOR A PRINCE AND A KING ("MY SON", "THY"). THE "MOTHER".

[1] For Introduction and Analysis explanatory of the above Structure, see Appendix 74.

°THE PROVERBS.

INT. (p. 864) **1** THE proverbs °of Solomon the son of David, king of Israel;
2 °To know °wisdom and °instruction;
°To perceive the °words of °understanding;
3 [2]To receive the [2]instruction of °wisdom,
Justice, and judgment, and equity:
4 [2]To give °subtilty to the °simple,
To the young man knowledge and discretion.
5 A wise *man* °will hear, and will increase learning;
And a man of [2]understanding shall attain unto wise counsels:
6 [2]To understand a proverb, and °the interpretation:
A A[1] (p. 865) The °words of the wise, and their dark sayings.
7 The °fear of °the LORD *is* °the beginning of knowledge:
But °fools °despise [2]wisdom and [2]instruction.

TITLE. The Proverbs. Heb. *Mishlai*; Greek, *Paroimiai* = any dark sententious saying; Vulg. *Proverbia*. Whence the English name. Heb. *Mishlai* is from *Māshāl* = to rule (Gen. 1. 18; 3. 16. Ex. 21. 8, &c.). Hence applied to words which are to *rule* and *govern* the life. Not a collection of human wisdom, but of Divine rules from heaven for earth.

The book is quoted in the N.T.:—

1. 16	in Rom. 3. 15.
3. 11, 12	in Heb. 12. 5, 6. Rev. 3. 19.
3. 34	in Jas. 4. 6. 1 Pet. 5. 5.
11. 31	in 1 Pet. 4. 18.
25. 21, 22	in Rom. 12. 20.
26. 11	in 2 Pet. 2. 22.

And also allusions, as in Rom. 12. 16, &c.

The Structure (p. 864) distinguishes the main divisions of the book, marked by such expressions as "My son"; "The words of the wise"; and the pronouns "thy", "thee", &c.; and the Proverbs "for"; and Proverbs "by" Solomon. Some proverbs are for a ruler, others are general, and for all men.

Māshāl is used of an Allegory (Ezek. 17. 2); a discourse (Num. 23. 7, 8); a taunt (Isa. 14. 4); an argument (Job 29. 1); a byword (Jer. 24. 9); a lament (Mic. 2. 4): all Proverbs are distinguished by parallelism of lines, synonymous, or gradational, or synthetic (i.e. constructive), or antithetic (i.e. contrastive). These again are arranged (as to order) either in alternate or introverted lines.

1 of. Genitive of Relation (Ap. 17), being the title or heading of the whole book, some being "for" him; others "by" him. If not, why the words of 10. 1? Chapters 10—19. 19 are not to "my son", but are in the third person, "he" and "him". See Ap. 74, and note also other sub-headings, 25. 1; 30. 1; 31. 1. All these are covered by the Genitive of Relation (Ap. 17). **2 To know** = For discerning. So in *vv.* 3, 4, 6. **wisdom.** Heb. *chokmah.* There are six words rendered "wisdom" in this book. (1) *chokmah*, rendered "wisdom" except in the passages below. It occurs thirty-nine times in sing., and three times in pl. (1. 20; 9. 1; 24. 7 = true wisdom); forty-two times altogether (6×7. See Ap. 10). (2) *bīnāh* = discernment or discrimination. Once rendered "wisdom" (23. 4). Elsewhere, in twelve passages rendered "understanding"; once "knowledge" (2. 3). (3) *lēb* = heart; rendered "wisdom" four times (10. 21; 11. 12; 15. 21; 19. 8). (4) *'ārmāh* = shrewdness; rendered "wisdom" only in 8. 5; elsewhere only in 1. 4 rendered "subtilty"; 1. 12 rendered "prudence". (5) *sākal* = prudence, or good sense, rendered "wisdom" once (1. 3); and (6) *sekel* = insight, rendered "wisdom" (12. 8; 23. 9); elsewhere rendered "understanding" (3. 4; 13. 15; 16. 22), and "prudence" (19. 11). For "sound wisdom", see note on 2. 7. **instruction** = admonition or discipline. Sometimes rendered "chastening". **words** = sayings. Heb. *'imrah.* See Ap. 73. No. V. **understanding.** Heb. *bīnāh.* See note on "wisdom", *v.* 2. **3 wisdom.** Heb. *sākāl.* See note on *v.* 2 (No. 5), above. **4 subtilty** = prudence. Same root as Gen. 3. 1. Cp. Matt. 10. 16. 1 Sam. 23. 22. Not the same word as Gen. 27. 35. **simple** = artless, guileless, unsuspecting. Cp. *vv.* 22, 32; 7. 7; 8. 5; 9. 4, 16; 14. 15, 18; 19. 25; 21. 11; 22. 3; 27. 12. **5 will hear.** Illustrations: Eunuch (Acts 8. 27, 39); Sergius Paulus (Acts 13. 7); the Bereans (Acts 17. 11, 12); Apollos (Acts 18. 24-28). **6 the interpretation** = satire, or the point of what is said. Occurs only here and Hab. 2. 6.

1. -6—9. 18 (**A**, p. 864). "THE WORDS OF THE WISE". FOR SOLOMON (FOR A PRINCE AND A KING). SECOND PERSON ("MY SON", "THY", "THEE", "THOU", "THINE"). THE "MOTHER".

(*Repeated Alternation.*)

A | A[1] | 1. -6—2. 15. Wisdom's Call.
 B[1] | 2. 16-22. The Foreign Woman.
A[2] | 3. 1—4. 27. Wisdom's Call.
 B[2] | 5. 1-23. The Foreign Woman.
A[3] | 6. 1-23. Wisdom's Call.
 B[3] | 6. 24-35. The Foreign Woman.
A[4] | 7. 1-4. Wisdom's Call.
 B[4] | 7. 5-27. The Foreign Woman.
A[5] | 8. 1—9. 12. Wisdom's Call.
 B[5] | 9. 13-18. The Foolish Woman.

words. Heb. *dabar.* Ap. 73. x. **7 fear** = reverence. This expression occurs fourteen times in Proverbs (1. 7, 29; 2. 5; 8. 13; 9. 10; 10. 27; 14. 26, 27; 15. 16, 33; 16. 6; 19. 23; 22. 4; 23. 17). See Ap. 75. **the LORD.** Heb. Jehovah. Ap. 4. II. **the beginning.** And only the "beginning", not the end. It is not "wisdom" itself. True wisdom is to justify God and condemn oneself. See note on Job 28. 28, and cp. 9. 10. Ps. 111. 10. **fools.** Heb. *'ĕvīl.* In this book three Heb. words are rendered "fools": (1) *'ĕvīl* = lax or careless habit of mind and body. Occurs nineteen times in Proverbs, viz. here, 7. 22; 10. 8, 10, 14, 21; 11. 29; 12. 15, 16; 14. 3, 9; 15. 5; 16. 22; 17. 28; 20. 3; 24. 7; 27. 3, 22; 29. 9. (2) *k^esīl* = fat, and then *dense*, or *stupid*, which comes of it, showing itself in impiety. Occurs forty-nine times in Proverbs, viz. *vv.* 22, 32; 3. 35; 8. 5; 10. 1, 18, 23; 12. 23; 13. 16, 19, 20; 14. 7, 8, 16, 24, 33; 15. 2, 7, 14, 20; 17. 10, 12, 16, 21, 24, 25; 18. 2, 6, 7; 19. 1, 10, 13, 29; 21. 20; 23. 9; 26. 1, 3, 4, 5, 6, 7, 8, 9, 10, 11, 12; 28. 26; 29. 11, 20; and eighteen times in Ecclesiastes. (3) *nābāl* = a vulgar churl. Occurs only three times in Proverbs: viz. 17. 7, 21; 30. 22; not in Ecclesiastes. **despise** = have always despised, &c. Illustrations: Cain (Gen. 4. 6-8); Hophni and Phinehas (1 Sam. 2. 12, 25); Nabal (1 Sam. 25. 25); Rehoboam (1 Kings 12. 13); Athenians (Acts 17. 18, 32); Jews and Greeks (1 Cor. 1. 18, 23, 24).

A[1] (*cont.*)
8 °My son, °hear the [2]instruction of °thy father,
And forsake not the law of °thy mother:
9 For °they *shall be* an °ornament of grace unto thy head,
And chains about thy °neck.
10 [8]My son, if °sinners entice thee,
°Consent thou not.
11 If they say, "Come with us,
Let us lay wait for °blood,
Let us lurk privily for °the innocent °without cause:
12 Let us swallow them up alive as °the grave;
And whole, as those that go down into the °pit:
13 We shall find all precious substance,
We shall fill our houses with spoil:
14 Cast in thy lot among us;
Let us all have one purse:"
15 My son, walk not thou in the way with them;
Refrain thy foot from their °path:
16 **For °their feet run to °evil,**
And make haste to shed blood.
17 Surely °in vain the net is spread
In the sight of any bird.
18 And they lay wait for their *own* blood;
They lurk privily for their *own* °lives.
19 So *are* the ways of every one that is greedy of gain;
Which taketh away the °life of the °owners thereof.

a (p. 866)
20 °Wisdom crieth °without;
She uttereth her voice in the °streets:
21 She crieth in the chief place of concourse,
In the openings of the gates:
In the city she uttereth her [2]words, °*saying,*

b
22 "How long, ye [4]simple ones, will ye °love simplicity?
And the scorners delight in their scorning,
And [7]fools hate knowledge?

c
23 °Turn you at my reproof:
°Behold, I will pour out my °spirit unto you,
I will make known my words unto you."

a
24 Because I have called, and ye °refused;
I have stretched out my hand, and no man regarded;
25 But ye have set at nought all my counsel,
And would none of my reproof:

b
26 °I also will laugh at your calamity;
I will mock when your °fear cometh;
27 When your fear cometh as °desolation,
And your °destruction cometh as a whirlwind;
When distress and anguish cometh upon you.
28 °Then shall they call upon me, but I will not answer;
They shall seek me early, but they shall not find me:
29 °For that they hated knowledge,
And did not choose the fear of [7]the LORD:

8 My son. See the Structure (p. 864) for the portions so addressed (1. -6—9. 18; 19. 20-34; 27. 1—29. 27; 30. 1—31. 31). Occurs fifteen times in this member (**A**), and only in the other corresponding members (**D**, *D*, *A*).

hear, &c. Illustrations: Isaac (Gen. 48. 15); Moses (Heb. 11. 23); Samuel (1 Sam. 1. 28; 2. 18; 3. 19-21); Timothy (2 Tim. 1. 5; 3. 15. Acts 16. 1, 2).

thy father. The address is educational, this being the duty of the father, corresponding with *A*, 31. 1-9, as contrasted with "the words of the wise", also addressed to "my son" (19. 20—24. 34; 27. 1—29. 27).

thy mother. Cp. 31. 1-9.

9 they: i. e. instruction and law.

ornament = garland.

neck. Showing cheerful and willing obedience, in contrast with stiffneckedness (Ex. 32. 9) and pride (Isa. 3. 16). See also Gen. 41. 42.

10 sinners. Heb. *chāṭā'*. Ap. 44. i.

Consent thou not: Illustrations: Joseph (Gen. 39. 9, 10); prophet (1 Kings 13. 8, 9); Jehoshaphat (1 Kings 22. 49, contrast 2 Chron. 18. 2; 20. 35-37); Joash (2 Chron. 24. 17, 18).

11 blood. Fig. *Metalepsis* (Ap. 6), "blood" put for bloodshedding, and then bloodshedding put for the one whose blood was shed. See Isa. 33. 15.

the innocent = an innocent one (sing.).

without cause. Cp. John 15. 25.

12 the grave. Heb. *sheʼōl.* Ap. 35.

pit. Heb. *bōr*, a hole bored or dug. Hence a dry pit or grave. Cp. Gen. 37. 20.

15 path. Some codices, with Aram., Sept., Syr., and Vulg., read "paths" (pl.).

16 their feet = they. Put by Fig. *Synecdochē* (of the Part), Ap. 6, for the persons who run. Quoted in Rom. 3. 15.

evil = mischief. Heb. *rā'a'.* Ap. 44. viii.

17 in vain, &c. = it avails not. Fig. *Parœmia.* Ap. 6. The sight of the net does not deter the birds. They (emphatic) still go on to their capture and death. The next verse requires this sense. So men go on in their evil ways, though they know it is to their own ruin (*v.* 18).

18 lives = souls. Heb. *nephesh.* Ap. 13.

19 life = soul. Heb. *nephesh.* Ap. 13.

owners. Heb. *ba'al*, as in *v.* 17. The "owners" of a soul are like the "owners" of wings, and are caught in their own trap with their eyes open.

20-33 (Note the *Extended Alternation* in these verses).

a | 20, 21. The Call made.
 b | 22. Expostulation of Wisdom with the simple.
  c | 23. Promise to hearers.
a | 24, 25. The Call made.
 b | 26-32. Expostulation of Wisdom with refusers.
  c | 33. Promise to hearers.

20 Wisdom. Heb. *chokmah.* See note on 1. 2.

without. The emphasis is on the publicity of her call.

streets = open or broad places, especially about the city gates (Deut. 13. 16), or open squares. Gen. 19. 2. Judg. 19. 15, 20. 2 Chron. 29. 4. Ezra 10. 9. Est. 6. 9, 11. Job 29. 7. Ps. 144. 14, &c. Isa. 59. 14, &c. Ezek. 16. 31.

21 saying. The Ellipsis of this verb has frequently to be supplied. See note on Ps. 109. 5.

22 love. The second feature. The first was ignorance in *v.* 7.

23 Turn, &c. = Turn [and listen to] my reproof.

Behold. Fig. *Asterismos* (Ap. 6), to emphasise the conditional promise.

spirit. Heb. *rūach.* Ap. 9. Put by Fig. *Metonymy* (of Subject) for all spiritual blessings.

24 refused: i. e. refused [to hear], *vv.* 24-33.

26 I: i. e. I, Wisdom.

fear = what you fear. "Fear" put by Fig. *Metonymy* (of Cause) Ap. 6, for the calamity which produced the fear. Note the Introversion in Heb. of "fear", "desolation", "destruction", "anguish", in *vv.* 26, 27.

27 desolation = tempest.

destruction = calamity. **28 Then, &c.** Illustration: Israel (Deut. 1. 45, 46). See also Isa. 1. 15. Jer. 11. 11. Ezek. 8. 18. Hos. 5. 6. **29 For that** = Forasmuch as.

b (cont.) 30 They would none of my counsel:
They despised all my reproof.
31 °Therefore shall they eat of the fruit of their own way,
And be filled with their own devices.
32 For the turning away of the [4]simple °shall slay them,
And the prosperity of [7]fools shall destroy them.
c (p. 866) 33 But whoso hearkeneth unto me °shall dwell safely,
And shall be quiet from fear of °evil."

2 °My son, if thou wilt receive my °words,
And °hide my commandments with thee;
2 So that thou °incline thine ear unto °wisdom,
°*And* apply thine heart to °understanding;
3 °Yea, if thou criest after knowledge,
And liftest up thy voice for [2]understanding;
4 If thou seekest her °as silver,
And searchest for her as *for* hid treasures;
5 °Then shalt thou [2]understand °the fear of °the LORD,
And °find the knowledge of °God.
6 For [5]the LORD °giveth wisdom:
°Out of His mouth °*cometh* knowledge and [2]understanding.
7 °He layeth up °sound wisdom for the righteous:
He is a °buckler to them that walk °uprightly.
8 °He keepeth °the paths of judgment,
And °preserveth the way of His °saints.
9 °Then shalt thou [2]understand righteousness, and judgment,
And equity; *yea*, every good path.
10 °When [2]wisdom entereth into thine heart,
And knowledge is pleasant unto °thy soul;
11 Discretion shall preserve thee,
[2]Understanding shall keep thee:
12 To °deliver thee from the way of the °evil *man*,
From the °man that speaketh °froward things;
13 Who leave [8]the paths of uprightness,
To walk in the ways of °darkness;
14 Who rejoice to do [12]evil,
And delight in the [12]frowardness of the °wicked;
15 Whose ways *are* crooked,
And *they* [12]froward in their paths:
B[1] (p. 865) 16 To [12]deliver thee from the °strange woman,
Even from the °stranger *which* flattereth with her [1]words;
17 Which forsaketh the guide of her youth,
And forgetteth the covenant of her [5]God.

31 Therefore, &c. Illustrations: Israel (Num. 11. 4-6. Ps. 106. 13, 14. Cp. Num. 11. 20-23 and Ps. 106. 15. See also Num. 14. 44, 45). Under Samuel (1 Sam. 8. 7, 19. Cp. 13. 6-23; 31. 1-10). Neglect of Sabbatical year (Ex. 21. 2. Lev. 25. 1-7. Deut. 15. 1, 2. Cp. 2 Chron. 36. 3-21. Jer. 34. 10-22). Saul (1 Sam. 28. 3. Cp. *vv.* 7, 15-20, and note 1 Chron. 10. 13).

32 shall slay them. Illustrations: Israel (Deut. 32. 15-25. Hos. 13. 6-8); Babylon (Isa. 47. 7-9); Moab (Jer. 48. 11-15); Sodom (Ezek. 16. 49); Tyre (Ezek. 28. 2, 7).

33 shall dwell safely. Illustrations: Noah (Gen. 6. 22; 7. 23. Heb. 11. 7); Shadrach, &c. (Dan. 3. 25. Ps. 138. 7); Daniel (Dan. 6. 10, 22. Ps. 119. 10); Christ's sheep (John 10. 28).

evil. Heb. *rā'a'.* Ap. 44. viii.

2. My son. Note this guide to the Structure on p. 864.

words=sayings. Heb. *'imrah.* Ap. 73. v.

hide=lay up. More than listening=hide as in a treasury. Illustrations: Deut. 6. 6. Ps. 119. 9, 11. Matt. 13. 44. Luke 2. 19, 51; 9. 44.

2 incline thine ear=hearken. Heb. prick up or point thine ear. Not the same word as in *v.* 18.

wisdom. Heb. *chokma.* See note on 1. 2.

And apply=[then] thou shalt incline or bend thy heart, &c. This is the first step, as *v.* 5 is the result.

understanding=discernment. Heb. *bīnāh.* Note on "wisdom" (1. 2), No. 2.

3 Yea=For if. (Heb. *kī 'im*). If thou goest further and criest and seekest, &c. Then the result is shown in *v.* 5.

4 as silver: or money. Probably the reference is to Job 28.

5 Then. In that case. See notes above.

the fear, &c. That is only "the beginning of wisdom", not the end. See note on 1. 7.

the LORD. Heb. Jehovah. Ap. 4. II.

find. What He has hidden (*v.* 7).

God. Heb. Elohim. Ap. 4. I.

6 giveth. The cry of *v.* 3 implies a Giver. Illustrations: Joseph (Gen. 41. 38, 39); Moses (Ex. 4. 12); Solomon (1 Kings 3. 12; 4. 29); Daniel (1. 17; 2. 23); Stephen (Acts 6. 5, 10); Lydia (Acts 16. 14); Paul's prayer (Eph. 1. 17. Col. 1. 9); John (1 John 5. 20).

Out of His mouth. A phrase common in the prophets, but only here in Proverbs.

cometh. Supply Ellipsis from preceding clause "He giveth".

7 He layeth up. Same word as "hide" in *v.* 1. The wicked cannot find. The righteous must dig. It is in safety from the enemy.

sound wisdom=something stable. Heb. *tushiyah*=that which is, or stability. May be so rendered in all its twelve occurrences. Cp. Job 5. 12 (enterprise=anything stable); 6. 13 (wisdom=stability); 11. 6; 12. 16 (wisdom = stability); 26. 3; 30. 22 (substance). Prov. 2. 7; 3. 21; 8. 14 (sound wisdom); 18. 1 (wisdom = all that is). Isa. 28. 29 (working=everything that is). Mic. 6. 9 (the man of wisdom = every one who is or exists). See Ap. 74.

buckler. Cp. Pss. 3. 3; 7. 10; 18. 2, 30, 35; 28. 7; 33. 20. Applied to God, as here. **uprightly**=blamelessly.

8 He keepeth=for preserving. See note on 4. 23.

the paths of judgment=righteous paths.

preserveth, &c. Illustrations: David (1 Sam. 25. 32-34; 27. 1. Cp. 2 Sam. 22. 1); Paul (2 Cor. 12. 7-9).

saints=favoured ones. Heb. *chasīdīm.* The first occurrence in Proverbs of this word which marks a later Jewish sect called *chasīdīm* or holy ones. **9 Then, &c.** Another conclusion, as in *vv.* 2 and 5.

10 When, &c.: or because. Commencing the particular instructions as to the practical power of wisdom, to keep from evil men (*vv.* 10-15) and the foreign woman (*vv.* 16-19); and in the way of good men (*vv.* 20-22). See Ap. 74. **thy soul**=thee. Heb. *nephesh.* Ap. 13. **12 deliver**=pluck, or rescue. **evil**=evil [man]. Heb. *rā'a'.* Ap. 44. viii. **man.** Heb. *'ish.* Ap. 14. II. **froward**=perverse. Heb. occurs nine times in Proverbs (*vv.* 12, 14; 6. 14; 8. 13; 10. 31, 32; 16. 28, 30; 21. 8); elsewhere only in Deut. 32. 20.

13 darkness. Put by Fig. *Metonymy* (of Effect), Ap. 6, for the evil which leads thither. Cp. Rom. 13. 12. Eph. 5. 11. **14 wicked.** Same word as "evil", *v.* 12.

2. 16-22 (B[2], p. 865). THE FOREIGN WOMAN.

16 strange woman. Heb. *zūr*=apostate to a false religion, of which prostitution formed part. **stranger**=foreigner. Heb. *nākar*=foreign woman. Not of Abraham's seed (Gen. 17. 12): ever a snare to Israel.

18 For her °house inclineth unto death,
And her paths unto °the dead.
19 None that go unto her °return again,
Neither °take they hold of the paths of life.
20 That thou mayest walk in the way of good *men*,
And keep the paths of the righteous.
21 For the upright shall °dwell in the land,
And the °perfect shall remain in it.
22 But the °wicked shall be cut off from the earth,
And the °transgressors shall be rooted out of it.

A[2] (p. 865) 3 °My son, forget not my law;
But let thine heart °keep my commandments:
2 For length of days, and long life,
And peace, shall °they °add to thee.
3 Let not °mercy and truth forsake thee:
°Bind them about thy neck;
Write them upon the table of thine heart:
4 So shalt thou find favour and good °understanding
In the sight of °God and °man.
5 °Trust in °the LORD °with all thine heart;
And lean not unto thine own °understanding.
6 In all thy ways °acknowledge Him,
And He shall °direct thy paths.
7 °**Be not wise in thine own eyes:**
°Fear °the LORD, and °depart from °evil.
8 It shall be °health to thy °navel,
And °marrow to thy bones.
9 °Honour [5]the LORD with thy °substance,
And with the firstfruits of all thine increase:
10 So shall thy barns be filled with plenty,
And thy °presses shall °burst out with °new wine.
11 [1]**My son, °despise not the chastening of [5]the LORD;**
Neither be weary of His correction:
12 **For °whom [5]the LORD loveth He correcteth;**
Even as a father the son *in whom* he delighteth.
13 °Happy *is* the [4]man *that* findeth °wisdom,
°And the [4]man *that* getteth [5]understanding.

18 house. Put by Fig. *Metonymy* (of Adjunct), Ap. 6, for household.
the dead. Heb. *R^ephaim*, who have no resurrection. Cp. Isa. 26. 14 ("deceased"), 19 ("the dead"); and see Ap. 25. This shows that a Canaanite woman is referred to here.
19 return again. Cp. "rooted out", *v.* 22, with Isa. 26. 19.
take . . . hold = attain to.
21 dwell in the land. Not be "cast out", as in *v.* 22.
perfect: or blameless.
22 wicked = lawless. Not the same word as in *v.* 14. Heb. *rāshā'*. Ap. 44. x.
transgressors = traitors, treacherous or faithless ones. Heb. *bāgad*.

3. 1—4. 27 (A[2], p. 865). WISDOM'S CALL.

1 My son. See note on 2. 1.
keep = watch, guard. See note on 4. 23.
2 they. Not the "law" and "commandments" of *v.* 1, for they are feminine, but the "days" of *v.* 2 (which are masculine, agreeing with the verb "add", which is masculine also). See Ap. 74.
add to thee. This, in the Hiphil = make increase for thee, or cause thee to increase or grow [in wisdom]: i. e. as the days and years lengthen and increase they will add to thy wisdom if thou forget not, &c. So in other passages where wisdom is supposed to promise long life, which it does not. See notes on *v.* 16; 4. 10; 9. 11; 10. 27.
3 mercy = lovingkindness, or grace.
Bind. Like the phylacteries. Cp. 6. 21; 7. 3; and see Ex. 13. 16.
4 understanding = insight. Heb. *sēkel*. See note on "wisdom" (1. 2), No. 6. Not the same word as in *v.* 5.
God. Heb. Elohim. Ap. 4. I.
man. Heb. *'ādām*. Ap. 14. I.
5 Trust = Confide. Heb. *bāṭah*. Ap. 69. I.
the LORD. Heb. Jehovah. Ap. 4. II.
with all thine heart. Illustrations: Abraham (Gen. 24. 1-8; cp. Prov. 19. 14); Eleazar (Gen. 24. 12-27); Jephthah (Judg. 11. 11); David (1 Sam. 30. 6-8); Asa (2 Chron. 14. 9-15); Hezekiah (2 Kings 18. 4-7; 19. 14-37); Nehemiah (1. 4-11; 2. 4-8).
understanding = discernment. Heb. *bīnāh*. See note on "wisdom" (1. 2), No. 2.
6 acknowledge = recognise, or own.
direct = rightly divide: i.e. dividing and thus showing what is right or pleasing to God. Heb. *yāshar*. Num. 23. 27. Cp. Judges 14. 3, 7. 1 Sam. 18. 20, 26. Rendered by Sept. *orthotomeō*, the same word as in 2 Tim. 2. 15.
7 Be not wise, &c. Illustrations: Ahab (1 Kings 22. 30, 34, 35); Jeroboam (1 Kings 12. 26-33; 13. 33, 34; Asa (1 Kings 15. 19); Ben-hadad (1 Kings 20. 10, 11); quoted Rom. 11. 25; 12. 16.
Fear = revere. See note on 1. 7.
the LORD. Jehovah (with *'eth*) = Jehovah Himself. Ap. 4. II.
depart from = shun, or avoid.
evil. Heb. *rā'a'*. Ap. 44. viii.
8 health = healing. Occurs only here.
navel. Put by Fig. *Synecdoche* (of Part) for the whole body (Ap. 6). But Sept. and Syr., following a different spelling, read "body".

marrow = moistening. **9 Honour . . . substance.** This proverb has led to a universal custom. Cp. 1 Tim. 5. 3, 17. Acts 5. 2 ("price" = honour); 19. 19. Illustrations: Abraham (Gen. 14. 20. Heb. 7. 2); Jacob (Gen. 28. 22); David (1 Chron. 29. 1-5, 28); Widow (Mark 12. 41-44); Woman (Mark 14. 3-9); Cornelius (Acts 10. 2, 4); Philippians (4. 15-19). **10 presses** = wine-vats. Heb. *yeḳeb*. Not *gath*; a wine-press. **burst out** = overflow. **new wine.** Heb. *tīrōsh*. Ap. 27. ii. **11 despise not** = shrink not from. Quoted from Job 1. 20-22, and in Heb. 12. 5, 6. Jas. 5. 17. Cp. Job. 34. 31, 32. One of the passages quoted in the N.T. from Proverbs, viz. 3. 11, 12 (in Heb. 12. 5, 6. Cp. Rev. 3. 19); 3. 34 (Jas. 4. 6); 11. 31 (in 1 Pet. 4. 18); 25. 21, 22 (in Rom. 12 20); 26. 11 (in 2 Pet. 2. 22). Illustrations: David (2 Sam. 15. 25, 26; 16. 10-12; 23. 5); Hezekiah (Isa. 39. 5-8, contrast Ahaz, 2 Chron. 28. 22, and Jehoram, 2 Kings 6. 31-33); Jerusalem (Zeph. 3. 2. Cp. Isa. 1. 5). **12 whom, &c.** Joseph (Gen. 37. 23-36; 39. 20; 40. 23. Cp. Ps. 105. 18); Israel (Deut. 8. 3-5, 15, 16); Jehoshaphat (2 Chron. 20. 35-37); Paul (2 Cor. 12. 7). **13 Happy** = Oh, the blessedness, as in Ps. 1. 1. Note the eight occurrences of this Beatitude in Proverbs: 3. 13; 8. 32, 34 (blessed); 14. 21; 16. 20; 20. 7 (blessed); 28. 14; 29. 18. **wisdom.** Heb. *chokmāh*. See note on 1. 2. **And** = yea, or even.

A[2] (cont.)

14 For °the merchandise of it *is* better than
the merchandise of silver,
And the gain thereof than fine gold.
15 ° She *is* more precious than ° rubies:
And all the things thou canst desire are
not to be compared unto her.
16 Length of days *is* ° in her right hand;
And in her left hand ° riches and
honour.
17 ° Her ways *are* ways of pleasantness,
And all her paths *are* ° peace.
18 [15] She *is* ° a tree of life to them that lay
hold upon her:
And happy *is every one* that retaineth her.
19 [5] The LORD by [13] wisdom hath founded the
earth;
By [5] understanding hath He established the
heavens.
20 By His knowledge the depths are broken
up,
And the ° clouds drop down the ° dew.
21 [1] My son, let not ° them depart from thine
eyes:
[1] Keep ° sound wisdom and discretion:
22 So shall they be life unto thy ° soul,
And grace to thy ° neck.
23 Then shalt thou walk in thy way
safely,
And thy foot shall not stumble.
24 When thou ° liest down, thou shalt not be
afraid:
Yea, thou shalt lie down, and thy sleep
shall be sweet.
25 ° Be not afraid of sudden fear,
Neither of the desolation of ° the wicked,
when it cometh.
26 For [5] the LORD shall be ° thy confidence,
And shall ° keep thy foot from being
taken.
27 ° Withhold not good from ° them to whom
it is due,
When it is in the power of thine ° hand to
do *it*.
28 Say not unto thy neighbour, "Go, and
come again,
And to morrow I will give;"
When thou hast it by thee.
29 Devise not ° evil against thy neighbour,
Seeing he dwelleth ° securely by thee.
30 Strive not with a [4] man without cause,
° If he have done thee no harm.
31 ° Envy thou not ° the oppressor,
And choose none of his ways.
32 For the ° froward *is* ° abomination to [5] the
LORD:
But His ° secret *is* with the righteous.
33 ° The curse of [5] the LORD *is* in the house
of ° the [25] wicked:
But ° He blesseth the habitation of ° the
just.
34 Surely ° **He scorneth the scorners:**
But he giveth grace unto the lowly.
35 The wise ° shall inherit glory:
But ° shame shall be the promotion of
° fools.

4 Hear, ye ° children, the ° instruction of a
father,
And attend to ° know understanding.
2 For I give you good doctrine,
Forsake ye not my law.

14 the merchandise of it: i. e. lit., her merchandise.
15 She. Emphatic = She, in herself.
rubies = corals, or pearls.
16 in her right hand = in her power; "hand" put by Fig. *Metonymy* (of Cause), Ap. 6, for use as a grand agency for good of all kinds. Not necessarily a long life conferred. See note on *v.* 2 and Ap. 75.
riches, &c. = to be used aright. See Ap. 75.
17 Her ways, &c. Illustration: Hezekiah (2 Chron. 29. 36; 30. 26. Contrast 2 Chron. 28). Cp. Acts 2. 46; 8. 6; 13. 52. 2 Cor. 8. 2.
peace = well-being, or prosperity.
18 a tree of life. See Gen. 2. 9; 3. 22, 24, and cp. Prov. 11. 30; 13. 12; 15. 4. Rev. 2. 7; 22. 2. 14.
20 clouds, &c. = skies.
dew = night mist. See note on Ps. 133. 3. "Dew" falls only when there are no clouds.
21 them. Is masculine, and so perhaps refers to the "mercy and truth" of 3. 3.
sound wisdom = what is stable. See note on 2. 7.
22 soul. Heb. *nephesh.* Ap. 13.
neck. Sept. adds, "Yea, it shall be healing to thy flesh; and refreshing to thy bones".
24 liest down. Sept. reads "sittest".
25 Be not afraid, &c. Illustrations: Moses (Ex. 14. 13, 14); Rahab (Josh. 6. 24, 25. Heb. 11. 31); Elisha (2 Kings 6. 16, 17); Ebed-melech (Jer. 39. 15–18).
the wicked = lawless ones. Heb. *rāsha'.* Ap. 44. x.
26 thy confidence. Sept. reads "in all thy ways".
keep = keep safe. Not the same word as in *vv.* 1, 21.
27 Withhold not. Illustrations: Ammonites, &c. (Deut. 23. 3, 4); Nabal (1 Sam. 25. 10, 11; cp. *v.* 15); Widow (1 Kings 17. 12. 2 Kings 4. 7); Parable (Luke 10. 30–35); Corinthians (2 Cor. 8. 1–11; 9. 1–7).
them to whom it is due = the owners thereof.
hand. Heb. text reads "hands", but some codices, with two early printed editions and Sept., read "hand" (sing.).
29 evil. Heb. *ra'a'.* Ap. 44. viii.
securely = confidently, or without suspicion.
30 If he, &c. (Heb. *'im l'o* = verily). Render: "he hath already done thee enough harm".
31 Envy thou not, &c. = Do not become excited against, &c. Illustrations: Moses (Heb. 11. 25, 26); Jezebel (1 Kings 21. 7–13. Cp. 2 Kings 9. 30–37). Ps. 34. 21.
the oppressor = the man (Heb. *'ish*) of violence. Ap. 14. II.
32 froward = those who turn aside. The same word as in 2. 15; not as elsewhere in Proverbs.
abomination to the LORD. Note all the things thus declared: 3. 32 (11. 20); 6. 16; 8. 7; 11. 1; 12. 22; 15. 8 (21. 27), 9, 16, 26; 16. 5; 17. 15, 15; 20. 10 (23); 28. 9.
secret = secret counsel. What is sealed up from all save those to whom He reveals it.
33 The curse, &c. Illustrations: Baasha (1 Kings 16. 1–4, 12, 13); Jehoiakim (Jer. 22. 13–19); Coniah (Jer. 22. 24–28); Jehu (2 Kings 19. 8–12. Hos. 1. 4); Hazael (Amos 1. 4); Jeroboam II (Amos 7. 9); Esau (Obad. 18).
the wicked = a lawless one (sing.).
He blesseth, &c. Illustrations: Abraham (Heb. 11. 12. Contrast Ahab, 2 Kings 10. 1–11); Jacob (Gen. 30. 27); Joseph (Gen. 39. 2, 21); Obed-edom (2 Sam. 6. 11); the widow (2 Kings 4. 2–7).
the just = just ones (pl.).
34 He scorneth, &c. Quoted in Jas. 4. 6. 1 Pet. 5. 5.
35 shall inherit, &c. Render: "the wise shall inherit glory, but a fool is piling up disgrace". Illustrations: Asaph (Ps. 73. 24); Paul (2 Tim. 4. 8); others (Jas. 1. 12. Dan. 12. 3. John 12. 26).
shame, &c. Illustrations: Jeroboam (1 Kings 21. 22. 2 Kings 13. 2, 11; 14. 24; 15. 9, 18, 24, 28). Cp. Prov. 24. 8.
fools. Heb. *k^esil.* See note on 1. 7.

4. 1 children = sons.
instruction = correction, or admonition.
know understanding = learn discernment.

A[2] (cont.) 3 For I was my father's °son,
Tender and °only *beloved* °in the sight of my mother.
4 He taught me also, and said unto me,
"Let thine heart retain my words:
°Keep my commandments, and °live.
5 °Get wisdom, get understanding:
Forget °*it* not; neither decline from the °words of my mouth.
6 Forsake °her not, and she shall °preserve thee:
Love her, and she shall °keep thee.
7 °Wisdom *is* the principal thing; *therefore* get wisdom:
And with all thy getting get understanding.
8 Exalt her, and she shall promote thee:
She shall bring thee to honour, °when thou dost embrace her.
9 She shall give to thine head an ornament of grace:
°A crown of °glory shall she °deliver to thee.
10 Hear, O °my son, and receive my °sayings;
And °the years of thy life shall be many.
11 I have °taught thee in the way of wisdom;
I have led thee in right paths.
12 °When thou goest, thy steps shall not be straitened;
And °when thou runnest, thou shalt not stumble.
13 °Take fast hold of instruction; °let *her* not go:
[6]Keep her; for °she *is* thy life.
14 °Enter not into the path of the °wicked,
And go not in the way of °evil *men*.
15 °Avoid it, pass not by it,
Turn from it, and pass °away.
16 °For they sleep not, except they have done mischief;
And their sleep is taken away, unless they cause *some* to fall.
17 For they eat the °bread °of °wickedness,
And drink the °wine °of violence.
18 °But the path of the just *is* as °the shining light,
That shineth more and more unto the °perfect day.
19 The °way of the [14]wicked *is* °as darkness:
They know not at what they stumble.
20 [10]My son, attend to my °words;
Incline thine ear unto my [10]sayings.
21 Let them not °depart from thine eyes;
[4]Keep them in the midst of thine heart.
22 For they *are* life unto those that find them,
And °health to all their flesh.

d (p. 871) 23 °Keep thy heart °with all diligence;
For out of it *are* the issues of life.

3 son. The Heb. accent (*Dechi*) emphasises this word to show (1) his own early training (*v.* 3); (2) those whom he would instruct (*vv.* 1, 2); (3) his instruction (*vv.* 5-9).

only beloved=unique.

in the sight of my mother. A special various reading, called *Sevir* (Ap. 34), reads "of my mother's sons". So in some codices, with several early printed editions.

4 Keep=Take heed to.

live: i.e. live again, in resurrection life. See note on Lev. 18. 5. Earthly life could be enjoyed without keeping commandments.

5 Get wisdom: *v.* 6 tells how to do it.

it=her.

words=sayings. Heb. *'imrah.* See Ap. 73. v.

6 her: i.e. wisdom.

preserve=guard.

keep=protect, as one protects the apple of one's eye. See note on *v.* 23.

7 Wisdom . . . wisdom. Heb. in four words, "Beginning—wisdom—get—wisdom" = as the principal thing, get wisdom.

8 when=because. Heb. *kī.*

9 A crown=A diadem.

glory=beauty: i.e. a beautiful diadem.

deliver=deliver fully and freely. Heb. *māgan* (a rare word). Occurs only in Gen. 14. 20, here, and Hos. 11. 8.

10 my son. See note on 1. 8.

sayings. Heb. *'imrah.* See Ap. 73. v.

the years of thy life shall be many=[my sayings] shall grow greater [through] the years of thy life. The verb denotes increase of size, not merely numbers. See notes on 3. 2, 16; 10. 27. The verb here is masculine, but "years of life" is feminine. The verb therefore refers to "sayings".

11 taught=directed.

12 When thou goest: or, as thou walkest; i.e. however hedged in our path seems, it opens out as we go forward.

when thou runnest=if thou runnest. To walk is obligatory; to run is optional.

13 Take fast hold. The Hiphils of this clause are emphatic.

let her not go=do not let her go.

she=she herself. Emphatic.

14 Enter not. Note the Fig. *Synonymia* (Ap. 6) in the verbs of *vv.* 14, 15. Illustrations: Lot (Gen. 13. 10-13); Solomon (2 Kings 23. 13. Cp. with 1 Kings 11. 5); Jehoshaphat (2 Chron. 18. 1; 21. 6. Cp. with 2 Chron. 19. 2; 22. 2, 3, 10, and Prov. 6. 27, 28).

wicked=lawless. Heb. *rāshā'.* Ap. 44. x.

evil. Heb. *rā'a'.* Ap. 44. viii.

15 Avoid=let that go; referring to *v.* 14. Note the Fig. *Synonymia.* Ap. 6. **away**=on.

16 For. Heb. *'im l'o*=because; i.e. the reason why they sleep not is because they mean mischief, and because they intend an occasion of stumbling.

17 bread. Put by Fig. *Synecdoche* (of Part) for food in general.

of=obtained. Gen. of Origin. Ap. 17 (2).

wickedness=lawlessness. Heb. *rāshā'.* Ap. 44. x.

wine. Heb. *yayin.* Ap. 27. i.

of violence=obtained by violence. Gen. of Origin. Ap. 17 (2).

18 But. Marking the contrast between the growth of wickedness (*vv.* 16, 17), and the growth of wisdom leading in right paths (*vv.* 11, 12).

the shining light=the dawning of day: advancing and brightening till noon.

perfect=stable part, when the sun seems stationary on the meridian. Illustrations: Jacob (Gen. 49. 10, 18. Heb. 11. 21); Nathanael (John 1. 46-51); Eunuch (Acts 8. 27-39); Cornelius (Acts 10. Cp. Prov. 15. 9). **19 way of the wicked.** Illustrations: Korah (Num. 16. 16-19); Ahab (1 Kings 16. 31); Babylon (Isa. 47. 11); Jews (Jer. 5. 19, 25; 44. 15-23. Ezek. 18. 29. Acts 28. 25, 26). **as.** Some codices, with one early printed edition, read "in". **20 words.** Heb. *dābar.* Ap. 73. x. **21 depart**=get away from. **22 health**=healing. **23 Keep . . . with all diligence.** Above all that must be guarded. The prep. M (מ) marks the place or person that keeps: the meaning being, guard the heart as the great citadel, for out of it are the source and outgoings of life. Same word as in *vv.* 6, 13. Not the same word as in *vv.* 4, 21.

A² (cont.) e 24 Put away from thee a °froward mouth,
And perverse lips put far from thee.
(p. 871) d 25 Let thine eyes look right on,
And let thine eyelids look straight before thee.
e 26 °Ponder the path of thy feet,
And let all thy ways be established.
27 Turn not to the right hand nor to the left:
Remove thy foot from [14]evil.

B² (p. 865) 5 °My son, attend unto my wisdom,
And bow thine ear to my °understanding:
2 That thou mayest °regard discretion,
And *that* thy lips may keep knowledge.
3 For the lips of °a strange woman °drop *as* an honeycomb,
And her mouth *is* smoother than oil:
4 But her end is bitter as wormwood,
Sharp as a twoedged sword.
5 Her feet go down to death;
Her steps take hold on °hell.
6 °Lest thou shouldest ponder the path of life,
Her ways are moveable, *that* thou canst not know *them.*
7 Hear me now therefore, O ye °children,
And depart not from the °words of my mouth.
8 Remove thy way far from her,
And come not nigh the °door of her house:
9 Lest thou give thine honour unto others,
And thy °years unto the cruel:
10 Lest [2]strangers be filled with thy °wealth;
And thy °labours *be* in the house of °a stranger;
11 And thou mourn at the last,
When thy flesh and thy body are consumed,
12 And say, 'How have I hated instruction,
And my heart despised reproof;
13 And have not °obeyed the voice of my teachers,
Nor inclined mine ear to them that instructed me!
14 °I was °almost in all °evil
In the midst of the congregation and assembly.'
15 Drink waters out of thine own cistern,
And running waters out of thine own well.
16 °Let thy °fountains be dispersed abroad,
°*And* °rivers of waters in the °streets.
17 Let them be only thine own,
And not [3]strangers' with thee.
18 Let °thy fountain be blessed:
And °rejoice with the wife of thy youth.
19 *Let her be as* the loving hind and pleasant roe;
Let her breasts satisfy thee at all times;
And be thou ravished always with her love.
20 And why wilt thou, my son, be ravished with a °strange woman,
And embrace the bosom of a °stranger?

froward. See notes on 2. 12 and 6. 12, the only other examples of frowardness of mouth.

4. 23-27. Note the *Alternation* in these verses.

d | 23. Positive. Heart.
e | 24. Negative. Mouth.
d | 25. Positive. Eyes.
e | 26, 27. Negative. Feet.

26 Ponder the path, &c. Illustrations: Abraham (Gen. 24. 1-9. See note on 3. 5, 6); Eleazar (Gen. 24. 5); Joshua (24. 15); Ruth (1. 16-18); David (Ps. 39. 1); Hezekiah (Ps. 119. 60); The good wife (Prov. 31. 27); Daniel (1. 8; 6. 3, 4); contrast Asa (2 Chron. 16. 1-9).

5. 1-23 (B², p. 865). THE FOREIGN WOMAN.

1 My son. See note on 1. 8.
understanding = discernment.
2 regard discretion, &c. Heb. infinitive = to guard deep counsels and knowledge. Let them mount guard over thy lips. Cp. Jas. 3. 8: "the tongue can no man tame".
3 a strange woman. Two words are used for "strange" and "stranger": one, Heb. *zūr*, an apostate Israelite woman gone over to the idolatrous impurities of heathen religion; the other *nākar*, a purely foreign woman of a similar character. The danger is religious rather than moral. Hence here it is *zūr*. See note on 2.16.
drop as an honeycomb = distil honey. The invitations of religious idolatry suit the tastes of the natural man.
5 hell = the grave. Heb. *sheōl.* Ap. 35.
6 Lest thou shouldest ponder. Render: So that she findeth not the level path of life; her ways are unstable and she knoweth it not.
7 children = sons.
words = sayings. Heb. *'imrah.* Ap 73. v.
8 door = entrance.
9 years. Put by Fig. *Metonymy* (of Adjunct), Ap. 6, for what happens in them.
10 wealth. Heb. strength: put by Fig. *Metonymy* (of Cause), Ap. 6, for what is produced by it.
labours. Put by Fig. *Metonymy* (of Cause), Ap. 6, for what is produced by it.
a stranger = a foreigner. Heb. *nākar.* Not the same word as in *vv.* 3, 17. See note above and on 2. 16.
13 obeyed = hearkened to.
14 I was almost in all evil. The *Beth Essentiae* denotes "in", in the sense of "as" = I soon became as an evil man, &c. See Ap. 75.
almost = in a little while. Heb. *kim'at.* Occurs eighteen times (Gen. 26. 10. 2 Sam. 19. 36. 1 Chron. 16. 19. 2 Chron. 12. 7. Ezra 9. 8. Job 32. 22. Ps. 2. 12; 73. 2; 81. 14; 94. 17; 105. 12; 119. 87. Prov. 5. 14; 10. 20. Song 3. 4. Isa. 1. 9; 26. 20. Ezek. 16. 47). It is rendered "almost" only in Ps. 73. 2, 119. 87, and here, where it may as well be rendered "soon" or "quickly" as in Job 32. 22. Ps. 81. 14; 94. 17 (marg.). It denotes in a little time, as in Ps. 2. 12; 105. 12 (= soon numbered). 2 Chron. 12. 7 (= a little while). Song 3. 4 (= a little while; i.e. scarcely). Isa. 26. 20.
evil. Heb. *rā'a'.* Ap. 44. viii.
16 Let thy fountains. Sept. reads "Let not thy fountain", &c. This must be the sense from the context. The R.V. obtains it by a question, "Should thy fountain . . . ?".
fountains. Plural of emphasis: i.e. thine own wife. Cp. Song 4. 12. **And** = As or nor [thy].
rivers of waters = divisions of waters. Heb. *palgēy māyim*: i.e. thy garden irrigation channels in the streets. See note on 21. 1.
streets = open places.
18 thy fountain: i.e. thine own wife. Cp. *v.* 16.
rejoice with = get thy joy with. Some codices, with Sept., Syr., and Vulg., read "in" instead of "with".
20 strange = apostate. Heb. *zūr.* See note on *v.* 3.
stranger = alien or foreigner. Heb. *nākar.* See note on *vv.* 3, 10.

B[2] (cont.)

21 For the ways of ° man *are* before the eyes of ° the LORD,
And He pondereth all his goings.
22 His own ° iniquities shall ° take the ° wicked himself,
And ° he shall be holden with the cords of his ° sins.
23 He shall ° die without instruction;
And in the greatness of his folly he shall go astray.

A[3] (p. 865)

6 ° My son, ° if thou be surety for thy ° friend,
If thou hast ° stricken thy hand with a ° stranger,
2 Thou art snared with the ° words of thy mouth,
Thou art taken with the ° words of thy mouth.
3 Do this now, my son, and ° deliver thyself,
When thou art come into the hand of thy friend;
Go, humble thyself, and make sure thy [1] friend.
4 Give not sleep to thine eyes,
Nor slumber to thine eyelids.
5 [3] Deliver thyself as a roe from the hand *of the hunter,*
And as a bird from the ° hand of the fowler."
6 Go to the ant, thou sluggard;
Consider her ways, and be wise:
7 Which having no guide,
Overseer, or ruler,
8 Provideth her meat ° in the summer,
And gathereth her food in the harvest.
9 How long wilt thou sleep, O sluggard?
When wilt thou arise out of thy sleep?
10 *Yet* a little sleep, a little slumber,
A little folding of the hands to sleep:
11 So shall thy ° poverty come ° as one that travelleth,
And thy want ° as an armed ° man.
12 A ° naughty person, a ° wicked [11] man,
Walketh with a ° froward mouth.
13 He winketh with his eyes, he speaketh with his feet,
He teacheth with his fingers;
14 ° Frowardness *is* in his heart, he deviseth mischief continually;
He ° soweth discord.
15 Therefore shall his calamity come suddenly;
Suddenly shall he be broken without remedy.
16 These ° six *things* doth ° the LORD hate:
° Yea, seven *are* an ° abomination ° unto Him:
17 ° A proud look, a lying tongue,
And hands that shed innocent blood,
18 An heart that deviseth [12] wicked imaginations,
Feet that be swift in running to mischief,
19 A false witness *that* speaketh lies,
And he that soweth discord among brethren.
20 [1] My son, keep thy father's commandment,
And forsake not the law of thy mother:
21 Bind ° them continually upon thine heart,
And tie them about thy neck.
22 When thou goest, ° it shall lead thee;
When thou ° sleepest, ° it shall keep thee;
And *when* thou awakest, ° it shall ° talk with thee.

21 man = a man. Heb. *'īsh.* Ap. 14. II. Illustrations: Cain (Gen. 4. 5, 6); Babel's builders (Gen. 11. 4–7); Sodom (Gen. 18. 21, &c.); Uzzah (2 Sam. 6. 6, 7; 1 Chron. 15. 13. Num. 4. 15); David (2 Sam. 12. 9); Baasha (1 Kings 15. 29. Cp. 16. 7); Ahab (1 Kings 21. 19); Belshazzar (Dan. 5. 22–28); Nathanael (John 1. 48); The Seven Assemblies (Rev. 2. 2, 9, 13, 19; 3. 1, 8, 15). Cp. 1 Sam. 16. 7.

the LORD. Heb. Jehovah. Ap. 4. II.

22 iniquities. Heb. *'āvāh.* Ap. 44. iv.

take = trap or entrap him.

wicked = a lawless man. Heb. *rāsha'.* Ap. 44. x.

he shall be holden. Illustrations: Saul (1 Sam. 18. 8, 9. Cp. 24. 16, 17; 26. 21; 28. 5–20); Jerusalem (Jer. 2. 16–19. Ezek. 22. 31); Ahithophel (2 Sam. 17. 23); Judas (John 12. 6. Matt. 26. 47–49). Cp. Prov. 23. 29, 35.

sins. Heb. *chāṭā'.* Ap. 44. i.

23 die without instruction. Illustration: Saul (1 Chron. 10. 13, 14).

6. 1–23 (A[3], p. 865). **WISDOM'S CALL.**

1 My son. See note on 1. 8.

if. This word should be supplied at the beginning of each line in *v.* 2, as well as in *v.* 1.

friend = neighbour.

stricken thy hand. Idiom for making a contract. Cp. Job 17. 3.

stranger = an apostate. Heb. *zūr.* See note on 5. 3.

2 words = sayings. Heb. *'imrah.* Ap. 73. v.

3 deliver = rescue.

5 hand. Aram., Sept., and Syr. read "snare".

8 in the summer. True of Eastern ants.

11 poverty = need. There are six words rendered poor or poverty in Proverbs: (1) *rūsh* = in want of necessaries of life (6. 11; 10. 4, 15; 13. 7, 8, 18, 23; 14. 20; 17. 5; 18. 23; 19. 1, 7, 22; 22. 2, 7; 24. 34; 28. 3, 6, 19, 27; 29. 13; 30. 8; 31. 7). (2) *dal* = impoverished, reduced (10. 15; 14. 31; 19. 4, 17; 22. 9, 16, 22, 22; 28. 3, 8, 11, 15; 29. 7, 14). (3) *ḥeṣer* = in want (11. 24; 21. 17; 28. 22). (4) *'ānāh* = wretched (14. 21). (5) *'ebyōn* = destitute, helpless; deficient in will and wealth (14. 31). (6) *yārash* = dispossessed (20. 13; 23. 21; 30. 9).

as one that travelleth = as a highwayman.

as an armed man = as a man with a shield. Cp. 24. 33, 34.

man. Heb. *'īsh.* Ap. 14. II.

12 naughty person. Heb. a man of Belial = a worthless person. Like Anglo-Saxon *nā* (= no, or not) and *wiht* (= a thing) = a thing of naught: i.e. worthless.

wicked. Heb. *'āven.* Ap. 44. iii.

froward = perverse. Same word as in 4. 24; 11. 20; 17. 20; 22. 5. Not the same as elsewhere in Proverbs.

14 Frowardness = Deceitfulness. See note on 2. 12. The same word as in 2. 12, 14; 8. 13; 10. 31, 32; 16. 28, 30. Not the same as elsewhere in Proverbs.

soweth = casteth forth [as seed].

16 six things. Epitomising *vv.* 12–14 (Ap. 10).

the LORD. Heb. Jehovah. Ap. 4. II.

Yea, seven. Fig. *Epanorthōsis.* Ap. 6. To imply that the list is not exhausted.

abomination. See note on 3. 32.

unto Him = unto His soul. Heb. *nephesh.* Ap. 13.

17 A proud look = eyes lifted up. Fig. *Synecdoche* (of Part), Ap. 6, put for pride, which is indicated by this act. This is the first, and the others proceed downward; "eyes", "tongue", "hands", "heart", "feet", and then the whole man.

21 them. This is masc., and cannot refer to the two, above. Does it refer to the "words" and "sayings" of 4. 20?

22 it = she: referring to the "commandment" or "law" of *v.* 20, which are fem. **sleepest** = liest down.

talk = commune. Three, the number of Divine completeness (Ap. 10). Not four (as some suppose) and one "dropped out"!

23 For the commandment *is* a lamp; and the °law *is* light;
And °reproofs of instruction *are* the °way of life:

B³ (p. 865) 24 To keep thee from the °evil woman,
From the flattery of the tongue of a °strange woman.
25 Lust not after her beauty in thine heart;
Neither let her take thee with her eyelids.
26 For by means of a whorish woman *a man is brought* to a piece of bread:
And the adulteress will hunt for °the precious °life.
27 °Can a [11] man °take fire in his bosom,
And his clothes not be burned?
28 Can one go upon hot coals,
And his feet not be burned?
29 So he that goeth in to his neighbour's wife;
Whosoever toucheth her shall not be innocent.
30 *Men* do not °despise a thief, if he steal
To satisfy his °soul when he is hungry;
31 But *if* he be found, he shall restore sevenfold;
He shall give all the substance of his house.
32 °*But* whoso committeth adultery with a woman lacketh °understanding:
He *that* doeth it destroyeth his own [30] soul.
33 A wound and dishonour shall he get;
And his reproach shall not be wiped away.
34 For jealousy *is* the rage of °a man:
Therefore he will not spare in the day of vengeance.
35 He will not regard any ransom;
Neither will he rest content, though thou givest many gifts.

A⁴ (p. 865) **7** °My son, °keep my °words,
And lay up my commandments with thee.
2 Keep my commandments, and °live;
And my law as the apple of thine eye.
3 °Bind them upon thy fingers,
Write them upon the °table of thine heart.
4 Say unto wisdom, "Thou *art* my °sister;"
And call understanding *thy* °kinswoman:

B⁴ f (p. 873) 5 That they may [1] keep thee from the °strange woman,
From the °stranger *which* °flattereth with her [1] words.

g 6 For at the window of my house
I looked through my casement,
7 And beheld among the °simple ones,
I discerned among the °youths,
A young man void of °understanding,
8 Passing through the °street near her corner;
And he °went the way to her house,
9 In the °twilight, in the °evening,
In the black and dark night:

f 10 And, behold, there met him a woman
With the attire of an harlot, and °subtil of heart.
11 (She *is* loud and stubborn;
Her feet abide not in her house:
12 Now *is she* without, now in the streets,
And lieth in wait at every corner.)
13 So she caught him, and kissed him,
And with an °impudent face said unto him,
14 "*I have* peace offerings with me;
This day have I payed my vows.
15 Therefore came I forth to meet thee,
Diligently to seek thy face, and I have found thee.
16 I have °decked my bed with coverings of tapestry,
With carved *works*, with fine linen of Egypt.
17 I have perfumed my bed
With myrrh, aloes, and cinnamon.
18 Come, let us °take our fill of love until the morning:
Let us solace ourselves with °loves.

---

23 law is light. Fig. *Paronomasia* (Ap. 6), *v tôrāh 'ôr*. In Latin it would be similar: *Lex est lux.*
reproofs of instruction = what is directed. Cp. *v.* 20.
way of life = way to life: i.e. life eternal. See note on Lev. 18. 5.

6. 24-35 (B³, p. 865). THE FOREIGN WOMAN.

24 evil. Heb. *rā'a'*. Ap. 44. viii.
strange woman = alien, or foreign woman. Heb. *nākar*. See note on 5. 3.
26 the . . . life = the soul. Heb. *nephesh*. Ap. 13.
27 Can a man . . . ? Fig. *Parœmia*. Ap. 6.
take = shovel up.
30 despise. Heb. *būz* (from *bāzah*), is here followed by ל (= L) = for. Render it therefore: "Men will not think it a trifle (or a light matter) for a thief that he should steal: [even] to satisfy", &c. . . . So if he be found, &c.
soul. Heb. *nephesh*. Ap. 13.
32 But whoso = How much more he who.
understanding. Heb. = heart: put by Fig. *Metonymy* (of Subject), Ap. 6, for understanding.
34 a man = a strong man. Heb. *geber*. Ap. 14. IV. Here, it is used of the jealous husband.

7. 1-4 (A⁴, p. 865). WISDOM'S CALL.

1 My son. See note on 1. 8. **keep** = watch.
words = sayings. Heb. *'imrah*. Ap. 73. v.
2 live: i.e. live for ever, in resurrection and eternal life. See note on Lev. 18. 5. Illustrations: Adam (Gen. 3. 22, 23); Lot's wife (Gen. 19. 26); Saul (1 Chron. 10. 13); Prophet (1 Kings 13).
3 Bind them. Cp. 3. 3. Deut. 6. 8; 11. 18.
table = tablet. **4 sister.** Cp. Matt. 12. 50.
kinswoman = close friend (masc.). Only other occ. Ruth 2. 1, of Boaz.

7. 5-23 (B⁴, p. 865). THE FOREIGN WOMAN.
(*Alternation.*)

B⁴ | f | 5. The woman.
| g | 6-9. The young man.
| *f* | 10-21. The woman.
| *g* | 22-27. The young man.

5 strange = apostate. Heb. *zūr*. See note on 5. 3.
stranger = alien, or foreigner. See note on 5. 3.
flattereth = maketh smooth.
7 simple. See note on 1. 4. **youths** = sons.
understanding. Heb. heart. Put by Fig. *Metonymy* (of Subject), Ap. 6, for understanding. Cp. 6. 32.
8 street = back street. **went** = sauntered.
9 twilight = darkness. A *Homonym*. See note on 1 Sam. 30. 17.
evening = evening of the day.
10 subtil = hidden. Heb. *nāzar*. Not the same word as in Gen. 3. 1. Same as in Isa. 48. 6.
13 impudent. Heb. hardened. Put by Fig. *Metonymy* (of Adjunct), Ap. 6, for boldness.
16 decked, &c. These words in *vv.* 16, 17 are rare words appropriately put into the lips of a foreigner.
18 take our fill = drink deep.
loves. Pl. = much love.

19 For the °goodman *is* not at home,
He is gone a long journey:
20 He hath taken a bag of money with him,
And will come home at °the day appointed."
21 With °her much fair speech she caused him to yield,
With the flattering of her lips she forced him.

g (p. 873) 22 He goeth after her °straightway,
As an ox goeth to the slaughter,
Or as a °fool to the correction of the stocks;
23 Till a dart strike through his liver;
As a bird hasteth to the snare,
And knoweth not that it *is* for his °life.
24 Hearken unto me now therefore, O ye °children,
And attend to the [1] words of my mouth.
25 Let not thine heart decline to her ways,
Go not astray in her paths.
26 For °she hath cast down many wounded:
Yea, many strong *men* have been slain by her.
27 Her house *is* the way to °hell,
Going down to the °chambers of death.

A⁵ C (p. 874) **8** Doth not °wisdom cry?
And understanding put forth her voice?

D E 2 She standeth in the top of °high places,
By the way °in the places of the paths.
3 She crieth at the gates, at the entry of the city,
At the coming in at the °doors.

F 4 Unto you, O °men, I call;
And my voice *is* to the sons of °man.
5 O ye °simple, understand °wisdom:
And, ye °fools, be ye of an understanding heart.
6 Hear; for I will speak of °excellent °things;
And the opening of my lips *shall be* right things.

G 7 For my mouth shall speak truth;
And °wickedness *is* an abomination to my lips.
8 All the °words of my mouth *are* in righteousness;
There is nothing °froward or perverse in them.
9 They *are* all plain to him that understandeth,
And right to them that find knowledge.

H J 10 Receive my instruction, and not silver;
And knowledge rather than choice gold.
11 For wisdom *is* °better than rubies;
And all the things that may be desired are not to be compared to it.

K L 12 °I [1] wisdom dwell with prudence,
And find out knowledge of °witty inventions.
13 °The fear of °the LORD *is* to °hate °evil:
Pride, and arrogancy, and the evil way,
And the °froward °mouth, do I hate.

---

19 goodman = master of the house. Cp. Matt. 24. 43. Luke 12. 39.
20 the day appointed = the new moon.
21 her. The A.V. of 1611 omitted "her".
22 straightway = suddenly.
fool. Heb. *'ĕvil.* See note on 1. 7.
23 life = soul. Heb. *nephesh.* Ap. 13.
24 children = sons. See the Structure, p. 864.
26 she hath cast down. Illustrations: Samson (Judg. 16. 4–21); David (2 Sam. 11); Solomon (1 Kings 11. Neh. 13. 26).
27 hell = the grave. Heb. *shᵉōl.* Ap. 35.
chambers = inner chambers. An explanation of Sheol.

8. 1—9. 12 (A⁵, p. 865). **WISDOM'S CALL.**
(*Simple and Extended Alternation.*)

A⁵ | C | 8. 1. Wisdom's call.
 D | E | 8. 2, 3. From high places.
  F | 8. 4–6. To the simple.
   G | 8. 7–9. Reasons.
    H | 8. 10–31. Wisdom self-commended.
 C | 8. 32–36. Wisdom's call.
 D | *E* | 9. 1–3. From high places.
  F | 9. 4–6. To the simple.
   G | 9. 7–9. Reasons.
    H | 9. 10–12. Wisdom self-commended.

1 wisdom. Heb. *chokmah* = wisdom personified. Cp. *v.* 12. See note on 1. 2.
2 high places = places of vantage.
in the places of the paths = in the places where the paths meet. **3 doors** = entrances.
4 men. Heb. *'ishim.* Ap. 14. II. } All classes.
man. Heb. *'ādām.* Ap. 14. I. }
5 simple. See note on 1. 4.
wisdom. Heb. *'ārmāh.* Not the same word as in *v.* 1 = shrewdness. See note on 1. 2.
fools. Heb. *k sil.* See note on 1. 7.
6 excellent. Heb. *nāgīd* = a prince, or representative.
things. Heb. *dābār* = words (see Ap. 73. x.). Hence = representative truths.
7 wickedness = lawlessness. Heb. *rāsha'.* Ap. 44. x.
8 words = sayings. Heb. *'imrah.* Ap. 73. v.
froward = twisted, or crafty.

10-31 (H, above). **WISDOM SELF-COMMENDED.**
(*Introversion and Extended Alternation.*)

H | J | 10, 11. Wisdom personified.
 K | L | 12–14. Prudence.
  M | 15, 16. Rule.
   N | 17. Recompense.
 K | *L* | 18, 19. Riches, &c.
  M | 20. Righteousness.
   N | 21. Recompense.
J | 22–31. Wisdom personified.

11 better. Note the seventeen occurrences of this rendering of Heb. *tōb* in Proverbs: 3. 14; 8. 11, 19; 12. 9; 15. 16, 17; 16. 32; 17. 1; 19. 1, 22; 21. 9, 19; 25. 7, 24; 27. 5, 10; 28. 6.
12 I wisdom dwell. Wisdom personified. Fig. *Prosōpopœia.* Ap. 6.
witty = sagacious. Anglo-Saxon *witan*, to know; like Greek *oida* = to know intuitively: not by effort, which is *ginōskō* = to get to know.
13 The fear, &c. See note on 1. 7.
the LORD. Heb. Jehovah. Ap. 4. II.
hate. This is far beyond Zophar's mistaken definition of it in Job 28. 28. A man may "depart" from evil from *policy*, while he loves it in his heart. But to "hate" it comes only from Divine wisdom. By nature men love evil (Jer. 17. 9. Matt. 7. 17; 15. 19. John 3. 19. Rom. 3. 10–18; 8. 7, 8. 1 Cor. 2. 14. Gal. 5. 17. Eph. 2. 2, 3, 12; 4. 17–22. Col. 1. 21. Tit. 3. 3. 1 John 5. 19).
evil. Heb. *rā'a'.* Ap. 44. viii.
froward = perverse.
mouth. Put by Fig. *Synecdochē* (of Part), Ap. 6, for the whole man.

14 Counsel *is* mine, and °sound wisdom:
𝔍 *am* °understanding; I have strength.
M (p. 874) 15 °By me kings reign,
And princes decree justice.
16 By me princes rule,
And nobles, *even* all the °judges of the earth.

N 17 𝔍 love them °that love me;
And those that seek me early shall find me.

K L 18 Riches and honour *are* with me;
Yea, durable riches and righteousness.
19 My fruit *is* [11] better than gold, yea, than fine gold;
And my revenue than choice silver.

M 20 I lead in the way of righteousness,
In the midst of the paths of judgment:
N 21 That I may cause those that love me to inherit substance;
And I will fill their °treasures.

J O (p. 875) 22 [13] The LORD °possessed me in the °beginning of °His way,
°Before His works of old.

P j[1] k 23 I was °set up °from everlasting, from the beginning,
Or ever the earth was.
l 24 When *there were* no depths, I was °brought forth;
When *there were* no fountains abounding with water.
j[2] 25 Before the mountains were °settled,
Before the hills was I [24] brought forth:
26 While as yet He had not made the °earth, nor the fields,
Nor °the highest part of the dust of the °world.
j[3] 27 When He prepared the heavens, 𝔍 *was* there:
When He set a °compass upon the face of the depth:
k 28 When He established the °clouds above:
When He strengthened the fountains of the °deep:
29 When He gave to the sea His decree,
That the waters should not pass His commandment:
j[4] When He °appointed the foundations of the earth:

O 30 Then °I was °by Him, °*as* one brought up *with Him:*
And I was daily *His* delight,
°Rejoicing always before Him;

14 sound wisdom. See note on 2. 7.
understanding = discernment. See note on 1. 2.
15 By me kings reign. See Ps. 75. 6, 7. Dan. 2. 21, 47. Rom. 13. 1-7.
16 judges of the earth. Some codices, with two early printed editions, Aram., Syr., read "righteous judges"; reading *zedek*, "righteousness", instead of *'ĕrez*, "earth". R.V. follows this.
17 that love me. Illustrations: Joseph (Gen. 37. 2, 13, 16, 17; 39. 3, 9; 41. 38); Samuel (1 Sam. 2. 26; 7. 3-17; cp. Jer. 15. 1); David (1 Sam. 17. 37, 45, 46); Abijah (1 Kings 14. 13); Obadiah (1 Kings 18. 4; cp. *vv.* 3, 12); Josiah (2 Chron. 34. 1-3, 27, 28); Daniel (1. 6, 8; cp. 9. 23; 10. 11-19).
21 treasures = treasuries.

8. 22-31 (*J*, p. 874). WISDOM PERSONIFIED.
(*Alternation.*)

J | O | 22. In eternity past. With Jehovah.
P | 23-29. Before the creation of man.
O | 30. In eternity past. With Jehovah.
P | 31. After the creation of man.

22 possessed = acquired, implying a definite act, as "constituted". Sept. and Syr. render it "created" (*ektise*). Cp. the use of the verb in this book (1. 5; 4. 5, 7; 16. 16; 17. 16; 18. 15; 19. 8; 20. 14; 22. 23). Heb. *ḳānāh*. Occurs eighty-six times in O.T.; rendered "possess" only four times. Cp. "wisdom" (Luke 11. 49).
beginning . . . Before. See Col. 1. 15-17; 2. 9. Rev. 3. 14. John 1. 1; 17. 5: "begotten before the world . . . born in the world". Elohim taking *creature* form in order to create; as He, later, took *human* form (flesh) to redeem. Hence "creation" and "redemption" combined in Christ (Rev. 4. 11; 5. 9). Man created in His likeness: that in which He appeared to the patriarchs and to Joshua (5. 13) was not temporary, or assumed for the moment, but was permanent.
His way. As distinct from His "works" (Ps. 103. 7).
Before. To this must be referred Eph. 1. 4, and Col. 1. 17. Three times we have "*before* the foundation (or disruption, Gen. 1. 2. See note on Matt. 13. 35) of the world" (John 17. 24. Eph. 1. 4, and 1 Pet. 1. 20). Cp. the expression "*from* (or, *since*) the foundation of the world", seven times (Matt. 13. 35; 25. 34. Luke 11. 50. Heb. 4. 3; 9. 26. Rev. 13. 8; 17. 8). See note on Matt. 13. 35. The former has to do with the "Church", the latter with the "Kingdom"; the former with God's "purpose", the latter with His "counsels".

23-29 (P, above). BEFORE CREATION.
(*Repeated Alternation and Introversion.*)

P | j[1] | k | 23. Before the earth.
l | 24. Before the seas.
j[2] | 25, 26. Before the earth.
j[3] | 27. When the heavens.
k | 28, 29-. When the seas.
j[4] | -29. When the earth.

23 set up = founded. Heb. *naṣak*, as in Ps. 2. 6, "set".
from everlasting = from the outset of the ages. Cp. Heb. 11. 3.
24 brought forth. Same root as Job 15. 7; 39. 1. Ps. 29. 9; 51. 5. Isa. 45. 10; 51. 2; 66. 8. Heb. *ḥûl*. Not the same word as in *v.* 30.

25 settled. Cp. Ps. 104. 8. **26 earth.** Heb. *'eretz*. **the highest part**: or, the first atoms or particles. **world** = the habitable world. Heb. *tēbēl* (not *'ĕretz* = earth). The Talmud (*Taanith* fol. 10A) distinguishes *'ĕretz* as meaning the land of Israel, from the world as meaning *the outside lands*. Cp. Matt. 2. 20. **27 compass** = a circle, or vault. **28 clouds** = skies, or finer clouds. **deep** = abyss. **29 appointed** = fixed by statute, or marked out. **30 I was by** = I became beside Him. John 1. 1. See note on "was", Gen. 1. 2. **by** = close by. **as one brought up with Him** = as one constantly with Him, or under His constant care. Heb. *'āmōn*, from root *'āman* = to be constant or steady, and denoting: (1) The making constant or steady (Ex. 17. 12). (2) The being constant, as a river (Isa. 33. 16. Jer. 15. 18); as a house (2 Sam. 7. 16. Isa. 7. 9); of words (Gen. 42. 20); of a prophet (1 Sam. 3. 20); an allowance (Neh. 11. 23). (3) The stability or faithfulness (Deut. 32. 20. Isa. 65. 16. Jer. 51. 15); hence "Amen", affirming and confirming assent. (4) Of the constant and steady care of a nurse, &c. (Est. 2. 7, 20. 2 Kings 10. 1, 5. Isa. 60. 4; 66. 12. Lam. 4. 5). (5) Of the constant and steady resting of the mind as trusting, relying, or depending upon (Gen. 15. 6; 45. 26. Ex. 4. 5. Deut. 28. 66. Judg. 11. 20). (6) Of the constant, steady hand required in a cunning workman (Song 7. 1 = hands of steadiness, meaning work not hastily done. The R.V. rendering of 8. 30, "a master workman", is made on insufficient ground). **Rejoicing.** Cp. *v.* 31.

P (p. 875) 31 [30] Rejoicing in °the habitable part of His earth;
And my delights *were* with the sons of °men.

C (p. 874) 32 Now therefore hearken unto me, O ye °children:
For °blessed *are they that* keep my ways.
33 Hear instruction, and be wise,
And refuse it not.
34 [32] Blessed *is* the [31] man that heareth me,
Watching daily at my gates,
Waiting at the posts of my doors.
35 For whoso findeth me °findeth life,
And shall obtain °favour of [13] the LORD.
36 But he that °sinneth against me wrongeth his own °soul:
All they that hate me °love death.

D E **9** °Wisdom hath builded her house,
She hath hewn out her seven pillars:
2 She hath killed her beasts; she hath °mingled her °wine;
She hath also furnished her table.
3 She hath °sent forth her °maidens: °she crieth
Upon the °highest places of the city,

F 4 Whoso *is* °simple, let him turn in hither:
As for him that wanteth °understanding, she saith to him,
5 Come, eat of my °bread,
And drink of the [3] wine *which* I have [2] mingled.
6 °Forsake the °foolish, and °live;
And go in the way of understanding.

G 7 °He that reproveth a scorner getteth to himself shame:
And he that rebuketh a °wicked *man* *getteth* himself a blot.
8 °Reprove not a scorner, lest he °hate thee:
Rebuke a wise man, and °he will love thee.
9 Give °*instruction* to a wise *man*, and he will be yet wiser:
Teach a just *man*, and he will increase in learning.

H 10 The fear of °the LORD *is* °the beginning of °wisdom:
And °the knowledge of °the holy *is* °understanding.
11 For by me thy days shall °be multiplied,
And the years of thy life °shall be increased.
12 If thou be wise, thou shalt be wise for thyself:
But *if* thou scornest, thou alone shalt bear *it*.

B[5] Q (p. 876) 13 °A foolish woman *is* clamorous:
She is [4] simple, and knoweth °nothing.

R S 14 For she sitteth at the °door of her house,
On a seat in the [3] high places of the city,

T 15 To call passengers
°Who go right on their ways:

Q 16 Whoso *is* [4] simple, let him turn in hither:
And *as for* him that wanteth [4] understanding, she saith to him,

R T 17 "Stolen waters are sweet,
And bread *eaten* in secret is pleasant."

S 18 But he knoweth not that °the dead *are* there;
And that her guests *are* in the depths of °hell.

---

31 the habitable part of His earth. Heb. *tēbēl 'areẓ*. See note on "world", *v.* 26.
men. Heb. *'ādām*. Ap. 14. I. Cp. Gen. 2. 19; 3. 8, 21. Made in His image. Gen. 1. 26, 27.
32 children = sons.
blessed = happy. See note on 3. 13.
35 findeth life: i.e. resurrection life, and life eternal. Cp. John 3. 36. 1 John 5. 12. See note on Lev. 18. 5.
favour = as shown in Rom. 6. 23.
36 sinneth. Heb. *chāṭā'*. Ap. 44. i.
soul. Heb. *nephesh*. Ap. 13.
love death = live and act so as to lose life. Fig. *Metonymy* (of Cause), Ap. 6.

9. 1 Wisdom. Pl. as in 1. 20; 9. 1; and 14. 1.
2 mingled. Cp. Isa. 5. 22. Not with water but with spices. **wine.** Heb. *yayin*. Ap. 27. I.
3 sent forth her maidens. An Eastern custom. In N.T. the invitation was carried by menservants (Matt. 22. 3. Luke 14. 17).
maidens = or young persons (masc. or fem.) Heb. *na'ar*. **she crieth:** or, each to cry.
highest places. Cp. 1 Sam. 10. 5, 10, &c.
4 simple. See note on 1. 4.
understanding. Heb. "heart". Put by Fig. *Metonymy* (of Subject), Ap. 6, for understanding.
5 bread. Put by Fig. *Synecdoche* (of Part), Ap. 6, for all kinds of food.
6 Forsake, &c. Illustrations: Moses (Heb. 11. 24-27); Caleb and Joshua (Num. 13. 30-33; 14. 6-9, 38); Rahab (Josh. 2. 9-13; 6. 25. Heb. 11. 31); Ruth (1. 16; 2. 11, 12); Dionysius and Damaris (Acts 17. 34); Ephesians (Acts 19. 19. Eph. 2. 13); members of Nero's household (Phil. 1. 13; 4. 22).
foolish = heartless. Heb. *pᵉthī* (masc. pl.). Not either of the three words in *v.* 13 or 1. 7, but the same word as in *v.* 4.
live: i.e. live for ever. See note on Lev. 18. 5.
7 He that reproveth, &c.: *vv.* 7-12 not "out of their proper context". See the Structure on p. 874.
wicked = lawless. Heb. *rāshā'*. Ap. 44. x.
8 Reprove not a scorner, &c. Illustrations: Joseph (Gen. 37. 2); the Prophet (2 Chron. 25. 16); Jews (Isa. 36. 21); the Baptist (Matt. 14. 1-10).
hate thee. We *condemn* one who has wronged us, and he condemns us. God's plan is to *convict* and make the sinner condemn himself.
he will love thee. Illustrations: Nathan (2 Sam. 12. Cp. 1 Chron. 3. 5 and 1 Kings 1. 32-34); the two disciples (Luke 24. 25, 29); Peter (John 21. 17); Peter (Gal. 2. 11-14. Cp. 2 Pet. 3. 15).
9 instruction, or supply "a hint".
10 the LORD. Heb. Jehovah. Ap. 4. II.
the beginning: not the end. See note on 1. 7.
wisdom. See note on 1. 2.
the knowledge, &c. Not departing from evil from policy, but hating it (8. 13).
the holy = the Holy One. (Pl. of majesty.)
understanding = discernment. See note on 1. 2.
11 be multiplied = become great [in importance or usefulness]. Not necessarily "many" in number.
shall be increased: i.e. in importance. Not necessarily in number. See note on 3. 16.

9. 13-18 (B[5], p. 865). THE FOOLISH WOMAN.
(*Alternation and Introversion.*)

B[5] | Q | 13. Her call.
  R | S | 14. From high places.
    T | 15. From the right way.
Q | 16. Her call.
  R | T | 17. To the wrong way.
    S | 18. To the lowest place.

13 A foolish woman. The contrast is with *v.* 1. Heb. *kᵉsīl*. See note on 1. 7. **nothing** = nothing whatever.
14 door = entrance.
15 Who go right, &c. = passing on their way, or [To call them] that go straightforward, &c.
18 the dead = Rephaim. (No Art.) See Ap. 25.
hell = Sheol. Ap. 35.

C U^1 W^1 (p. 877)

10 °The proverbs of Solomon.
°A wise son maketh a glad father:
But °a foolish son *is* the heaviness of his mother.
2 Treasures of °wickedness °profit nothing:
But °righteousness delivereth from °death.
3 °The LORD °will not suffer the °soul of °the righteous to famish:
But He °casteth away the substance of °the wicked.
4 He becometh °poor that dealeth *with* a °slack hand:
But the hand of the diligent maketh rich.
5 He that °gathereth in summer *is* a wise son:
But he that °sleepeth in harvest *is* a son that causeth shame.
6 °Blessings *are* upon the °head of °the just:
But °violence covereth the mouth of [3]the wicked.
7 °The memory of [6]the just *is* blessed:
But °the name of [3]the wicked shall rot.
8 The wise in heart °will receive commandments:
But °a prating fool shall fall.
9 He that walketh °uprightly walketh surely:
But he that perverteth his ways shall be known.
10 He that winketh with the eye causeth sorrow:
But a [8]prating fool shall fall.
11 The °mouth of a righteous *man is* a well of life:
But [6]violence covereth the mouth of the [3]wicked.
12 °Hatred stirreth up strifes:
But °love covereth all °sins.
13 In the °lips of him that hath understanding wisdom is found:
But a rod *is* for the back of him that is void of °understanding.
14 Wise *men* lay up knowledge:
But the [11]mouth of the °foolish *is* near destruction.
15 The rich man's wealth *is* °his strong city:
The °destruction of the °poor *is* their °poverty.
16 The labour of [3]the righteous *tendeth* to life:
The °fruit of °the [3]wicked to °sin.

10. 1—19. 19 (**C**, p. 864). PROVERBS BY SOLOMON. FOR ALL. Third Person ("HE", "HIM", "THEY"). (*Division.*)

C	U^1	10. 1—15. 33. The Pious and the Ungodly. With reference to others. Their lots in life. (Chiefly Antithetic.)
	U^2	16. 1—19. 19. The Pious and the Ungodly. With reference to God. Their life and character. (Chiefly Synthetic.)

10. 1—15. 33 (U^1, above). THE PIOUS AND THE UNGODLY. WITH REFERENCE TO OTHERS. (*Division.*)

U^1	W^1	10. 1-32. Their Life and Conduct. (General.)
	W^2	11. 1—15. 33. Their advantages and disadvantages. (Particular.)

For all men; not for any special person, such as "MY SON". See the Structure, p. 864.

1 The proverbs of Solomon. This is the heading of a distinct class of Proverbs marked off by different authorship. All are in two lines, except 19. 7, which has three lines. They are miscellaneous, having self-developing connections, finding their reasons in what follows.

A wise son. Illustration: Joseph (Gen. 47. 12. Cp. 48. 2).

a foolish son. Heb. *k^{e}sîl.* See note on 1. 7. Illustration: Esau (Gen. 26. 34, 35; 27. 45, 46).

2 wickedness = lawlessness. Heb. *rāsha'.* Ap. 44. x.

profit nothing. Illustrations: Rehoboam (2 Chron. 12. 1-4, 9); Gehazi (2 Kings 5. 20-27. Prov. 21. 6); Nebuchadnezzar (Dan. 4. 31, 33); Belshazzar (Dan. 5); the Rich Fool (Luke 12. 20, 21. Cp. 16. 23, 24). Cp. Prov. 11. 28.

righteousness delivereth, &c. Illustrations: Daniel (6. 22-30; 6. 22. Cp. Prov. 13. 6); Noah (Gen. 7. 1. Heb. 11. 7).

death. Put by Fig. *Metonymy* (of Effect), Ap. 6, for the things which lead to death.

3 The LORD. Heb. Jehovah. Ap. 4. II.

will not suffer, &c. Illustrations: Elijah (1 Kings 17); David (2 Sam. 17. 27-29).

soul. Heb. *nephesh.* Ap. 13.

the righteous = a righteous one.

casteth away = repel, &c. Illustrations: Israel (Judg. 6. 1-4); Samaria (1 Kings 18. 2. 2 Kings 6. 5); Jerusalem (Lam. 5. 10. Zeph. 1. 18); the Chaldeans (Hab. 2. 8).

the wicked = lawless ones. Heb. *rāshā'.* Ap. 44. x.

4 poor = needy. Heb. *rūsh.* See note on 6. 11.

slack = deceitful. As in 12. 24. Ps. 52. 2; 120. 2. Hos. 7. 16. Mic. 6. 12. **5 gathereth in summer,** &c. Illustrations: Isaac (Gen. 18. 19); Joseph (Gen. 47. 12); Timothy (2 Tim. 3. 15. Acts 16. 1, 2). **sleepeth in harvest.** Cp. 24. 30-34. **6 Blessings:** not simply good things, but good things bestowed by another. **head.** Put by Fig. *Synecdochē* (of Part), Ap. 6, for the whole person. **the just** = a just one. **violence,** &c.: or, the mouth of lawless ones conceal violence. **7 The memory** = What is remembered of him; not what he remembers; see Ps. 146. 4. Illustrations: Elisha (2 Kings 13. 21); Jehoiada (2 Chron. 24. 15, 16); the woman (Mark 14. 9); Mary (Luke 1. 28, 48); Dorcas (Acts 9. 36, 39. Cp. Prov. 22. 1); Antipas (Rev. 2. 13). **the name,** &c. Illustrations: Balaam (2 Pet. 2. 15. Jude 11. Rev. 2. 14); Ahaz (2 Chron. 28. 22); Athaliah (2 Chron. 24. 7); Herod (Acts 12. 22, 23. Cp. Ps. 9. 16). **8 will receive,** &c. Illustrations: Abraham (Gen. 22. Heb. 11. 8, 17); David (2 Sam. 7); widow (1 Kings 17. 10-16); Rechabites (Jer. 35. 6-10. Cp. Prov. 23. 22). **a prating fool** = a fool (Heb. *'ĕvīl.* See note on 1. 7) of lips: lips put by Fig. *Metonymy* (of Cause), Ap. 6, for what is spoken by them. Illustrations: Korah, &c. (Num. 16); Diotrephes (3 John 9, 10). Cp. 2 Pet. 2. 10. Jude 10, 13. **9 uprightly** = in integrity. **11 mouth.** Put by Fig. *Metonymy* (of Cause), Ap. 6, for what is spoken by it. **12 Hatred stirreth up strifes.** Illustrations: Ishmael (Gen. 21. 9-14. Gal. 4. 29); Jews (Acts 13. 50; 14. 2-4; 17. 5, 13). **love covereth.** The opposite action. Cp. 1 Cor. 13. 4. Illustrations: Joseph (Gen. 40. 15. Cp. 45. 5-8. Prov. 17. 9; 19. 11); David (2 Sam. 1); Paul (Philemon); Christ (Matt. 26. 41. Mark 16. 7. John 20. 25-27; 21. 15-19, &c.). **sins.** Heb. *pāsha'.* Ap. 44. ix. **13 lips.** Put by Fig. *Metonymy* (of Cause), Ap. 6, for what is spoken by them. **understanding.** Heb. "heart", put by Fig. *Metonymy* (of Subject), Ap. 6, for understanding. **foolish.** Same word as in *v.* 8. **15 his strong city.** Heb. city of his strength. Fig. *Antimereia.* Ap. 6. **destruction** = that which destroys them. Fig. *Metonymy* (of Effect), Ap. 6. **poor** = weak. Heb. *dal.* See note on 6. 11. **poverty** = *rūsh.* See note on 6. 11. **16 fruit** = produce. **the wicked** = a lawless one. **sin.** Heb. *chāṭā'.* Ap. 44. i.

W1 (cont.)

17 He *is in* the way of life that keepeth instruction:
But he that °refuseth reproof °erreth.
18 He that hideth hatred *with* lying lips,
And he that uttereth a slander, *is* a [1] fool.
19 In the multitude of words there °wanteth not [12]sin:
But he that °refraineth his lips *is* wise.
20 The °tongue of [6]the just *is as* choice silver:
The heart of [3]the wicked *is* little worth.
21 The [13]lips of [3]the righteous °feed many:
But [8]fools die °for want of °wisdom.
22 The blessing of [3]the LORD, °it maketh rich,
And He addeth no sorrow with it.
23 *It is* °as sport to a [1]fool to do mischief:
°But a °man of °understanding hath °wisdom.
24 The fear of [3]the wicked, it shall come upon him:
But the desire of °the righteous °shall be granted.
25 °As the whirlwind passeth, so *is* [3]the wicked no *more:*
But [3]the righteous *is* °an everlasting foundation.
26 As vinegar to the teeth, and as °smoke to the eyes,
So *is* the sluggard to them that send him.
27 °The fear of [3]the LORD °prolongeth days:
But the years of [3]the wicked shall be °shortened.
28 °The °hope of [24]the righteous *shall be* gladness:
But the °expectation of [3]the wicked shall perish.
29 The way of [3]the LORD *is* strength to °the upright:
But °destruction *shall be* to the workers of °iniquity.
30 [3]The righteous shall never be °removed:
But [3]the wicked shall not inhabit the °earth.
31 The mouth of [6]the °just °bringeth forth [23]wisdom:
But the °froward tongue shall be °cut out.
32 The [13]lips of [3]the righteous know what is acceptable:
But the mouth of [3]the wicked *speaketh* °frowardness.

W2 X1 (p. 878)

11 °A false balance *is* °abomination to °the LORD:
But a just °weight *is* His delight.
2 °*When* pride cometh, then cometh shame:
°But with the lowly *is* °wisdom.
3 The °integrity of °the upright shall guide them:
But the °perverseness of °transgressors shall destroy them.

17 refuseth. Some codices read "hateth". **erreth** = leadeth astray.

19 wanteth not sin = lacketh not sin. Illustrations: Job (32. 2; 34. 5, 12; 35. 16; 42. 3); Job's friends (32. 3; 42. 7, 8); the widows (1 Tim. 5. 13). Of the "Twelve", the one who spake most (Peter) erred most (Matt. 16. 22; 26. 74).

refraineth = restraineth. Illustrations: Eleazar (Gen. 24. 21. Cp. Prov. 4. 26; 15. 28); Aaron (Lev. 10. 3); Saul (1 Sam. 10. 27. Cp. Prov. 11. 12).

20 tongue. Put by Fig. *Metonymy* (of Cause), Ap. 6, for what is spoken by it.

21 feed = shepherd: i.e. instruct. Illustrations: Job (4. 3, 4; 29. 21, 22); David (Ps. 78. 70–72); Peter (Acts 4. 1–4); Philip (Acts 8. 5–8); Paul and Barnabas (Acts 11. 26; 14. 22–28); Judas and Silas (Acts 15. 32, 33).

for = through.

wisdom: Heb. "heart", put by Fig. *Metonymy* (of Subject), Ap. 6, for understanding.

22 it = itself: i.e. the uttered blessing, like the "words of the wise".

23 as sport. A.V. of 1611 read "as a sport".

But. Supply Fig. *Ellipsis* (Ap. 6), "But [to exercise] wisdom [is as sport] to a man of understanding".

man. Heb. *'ish.* Ap. 14. II.

understanding . . . wisdom. See note on 1. 2.

24 the righteous = righteous ones.

shall be granted. Illustrations: Hannah (1 Sam. 1. 20); Esther (4. 16; 8. 15–17); Daniel (2. 16–23); Simeon (Luke 2. 25–30).

25 As the whirlwind passeth, &c. Illustrations: Gen. 7. 21–23 (cp. Matt. 24. 37–39. Luke 17. 26, 27); Elah (1 Kings 16. 7–10); Sennacherib (2 Kings 19. 35–37).

an everlasting foundation. Cp. Matt. 7. 24–27.

26 smoke. In Eastern tents and houses, wood or charcoal fires, and no chimneys.

27 The fear of the LORD. See note on 1. 7.

prolongeth days = increaseth days; not necessarily in number, but in greater value and importance.

shortened = cut down, or made little, as in Isa. 50. 2; 59. 1. Mic. 2. 7. Num. 11. 23; 21. 4 (discouraged). Judg. 10. 16 (grieved); 16. 16 (vexed). Job 21. 4 (troubled). Zech. 11. 8 (loathed). Ps. 102. 23, where it refers to affliction, not to continued living.

28 The hope of the righteous, &c. Illustrations: Abraham (Rom. 4. 18–20); Joseph (Ps. 105. 17–21); Hezekiah (Ps. 126); Daniel (6. 10).

hope. Heb. *yāḥal* = an unlikely hope.

expectation = confidence. Heb. *tikvah* = a likely hope. Illustrations: Goliath (1 Sam. 17. 44, 51); Athaliah (2 Kings 11. 1–16); Sennacherib (2 Kings 19. 23, 37. 2 Chron. 32. 21); Herod (Matt. 2. 16).

29 the upright = an upright one.

destruction = ruin. Illustrations: Saul (1 Chron. 10. 13, 14. Prov. 11. 3); Jeroboam (1 Kings 14. 7–11. Isa. 50. 11). **iniquity.** Heb. *'āven.* Ap. 44. iii.

30 removed = moved, or shaken.

earth: or land [of promise].

31 just = righteous, as in *vv.* 30, 32.

bringeth forth: i.e. as a plant.

froward. See note on 2. 12.

cut out = cut off as unproductive.

32 frowardness. See note on 2. 12. Here pl. = great [perverseness.

11. 1–15. 33 [For Structure see next page].

11. 1-31 (X1, p. 879). WITH REFERENCE TO ONE'S NEIGHBOURS.

1 A false balance = False balances. **abomination.** See note on 3. 32. **the LORD.** Heb. Jehovah. Ap. 4. II. **weight** = stone. Put by Fig. *Metonymy* (of Cause), Ap. 6, for the weight it represents. This proverb is repeated three times (16. 11; 20. 10, 23). Cp. Lev. 19. 36. Deut. 25. 13–15, and Mic. 6. 11. There was a royal standard (2 Sam. 14. 26). **2 When pride cometh, then, &c.** Illustrations: Miriam (Num. 12. 10); Uzziah (2 Chron. 26. 16–21); Nebuchadnezzar (Dan. 4. 30); Moab (Zeph. 2. 8, 10); Nineveh (Zeph. 2. 15). **But with the lowly, &c.** Illustrations: Joseph (Gen. 41. 16, 38, 39); Daniel (Dan. 2. 20, 21. Cp. Prov. 2. 6). **wisdom.** See note on 1. 2. **3 integrity, &c.** Illustrations: Joseph (Gen. 39. 4, 22, 23; 50. 25. Heb. 11. 22). **the upright** = upright ones. **perverseness, &c.** = slipperiness. Illustrations: Israel (Deut. 1. 43, 44); Balaam (Num. 22. 32; 31. 8); Hophni and Phinehas (1 Sam. 2. 25; 4. 11); Saul (1 Sam. 15. 23); Absalom (2 Sam. 15. 3–6; 18); Ahithophel (2 Sam. 17. 1–3, 23); Ahab (1 Kings 21. 25, 26; 22. 34, 37); Jews (Jer. 34. 8–22); Jerusalem (Ezek. 9. 9, 10). **trangsressors** = traitors. Heb. *bāgad* = faithless to covenant. Not the same word as in 16. 10; 26. 10; 28. 21; but the same as in all other passages in this book.

X[1] (*cont.*)

4 Riches profit not in °the day of wrath:
But righteousness °delivereth from death.
5 The righteousness of the °perfect shall direct his way:
But °the °wicked shall fall by his own °wickedness.
6 The righteousness of [3]the upright shall [4]deliver them:
But [3]transgressors shall be taken in *their own* °naughtiness.
7 When a [5]wicked °man dieth, *his* °expectation shall perish:
And the hope of unjust *men* perisheth.
8 °The righteous is °delivered out of trouble,
And [5]the wicked cometh in his stead.
9 An hypocrite with *his* °mouth destroyeth his neighbour:
But through knowledge shall °the just be [8]delivered.
10 °When it goeth well with the righteous, the city rejoiceth:
And °when °the wicked perish, *there is* shouting.
11 By the blessing of the upright the city is exalted:
But it is °overthrown by the [9]mouth of [10]the [5]wicked.
12 He that is void of °wisdom °despiseth his neighbour:
But a °man of understanding holdeth his peace.
13 °A talebearer revealeth °secrets:
But he that is of a faithful °spirit concealeth the matter.
14 Where no °counsel *is*, the people fall:
But in the °multitude of counsellers *there is* °safety.
15 He that is surety °for a stranger shall °smart *for it:*
And he that hateth suretiship °is sure.
16 A °gracious woman retaineth honour:
°And strong *men* retain riches.
17 The °merciful [12]man doeth good to °his own soul:
But *he that is* cruel °troubleth his own flesh.
18 [5]The wicked °worketh a °deceitful work:
But °to him that soweth righteousness *shall be* a sure reward.
19 °As righteousness *tendeth* to life:
So he that pursueth °evil *pursueth it* to his own death.
20 They that are of a froward heart *are* °abomination to [1]the LORD:
But *such as are* upright in *their* way *are* His delight.

11. 1–15. 33 (W[2], p. 877). THE PIOUS AND UNGODLY. THEIR ADVANTAGES AND DISADVANTAGES. (*Division.*)

W[2]	X[1]	11. 1-31. With reference to one's Neighbours.
	X[2]	12. 1-28. With reference to Domestic and Public vocations.
	X[3]	13. 1-25. With reference to Temporal and Eternal good.
	X[4]	14. 1-35. With reference to Wise and Foolish; Rich and Poor; Masters and Servants.
	X[5]	15. 1-33. With reference to other relations in the religious sphere.

4 the day, &c. The day of [God's] wrath.
delivereth = rescueth. Heb. *nāẓal* here and in *v.* 9, but not in *vv.* 8, 9, or 21.
5 perfect = without blemish or blame. Heb. *tāmīm*: used of sacrifices.
the wicked . . . wickedness = a lawless one . . . lawlessness. Heb. *rāshā'*. Ap. 44. x. Not the same word as in *v.* 21.
6 naughtiness. See note on 6. 12.
7 man. Heb. *'ādām.* Ap. 14. I.
expectation shall perish. Illustrations: Balaam's (Num. 23. 10; 31. 8); Absalom's (2 Sam. 18. Cp. Prov. 20. 20). Cp. also Job 21. 7-13 and Ps. 73. 19. Luke 12. 16-20.
expectation. Heb. *ḳāvah.* See note on 10. 28.
8 The righteous = A righteous one.
delivered = drawn out, liberated with gentle effort. Heb. *chālaz*. The same word as in *v.* 9, but not the same as in *vv.* 4, 6, and 21. Illustrations: Mordecai and Haman (Est. 7. 9, 10); Daniel and his accusers (Dan. 6. 23, 24); Israel and Egyptians (Ex. 14, and Isa. 43. 3, 4).
9 mouth. Put by Fig. *Metonymy* (of Cause), Ap. 6, for what is said by it.
the just = righteous ones.
10 When it goeth well, &c. Illustrations: Hezekiah (2 Chron. 29. 3-36; 30. 26); Nehemiah (Neh. 2; 6. 15; 8. 17); Mordecai (Est. 8. 15, 16).
when the wicked perish, &c. Illustrations: Pharaoh (Ex. 15); Sisera (Judg. 5); Athaliah (2 Kings 11. 20).
the wicked = wicked ones.
11 overthrown; or ruined.
12 wisdom. Heb. "heart", put by Fig. *Metonymy* (of Subject), Ap. 6, for sense.
despiseth = reproacheth: in contrast with the next line.
man. Heb. *'īsh.* Ap. 14. II.
13 A talebearer = He that goes about talebearing: or, a pedlar in scandal. Cp. Lev. 19. 16. Jas. 1. 26. Illustrations: Doeg (1 Sam. 21. 7; 22. 9, 10. Ps. 52. 2. Cp. Prov. 24. 28); the nobles of Judah (Neh. 6. 17-19).
secrets = a secret.
spirit. Heb. *rūach.* Ap. 9.
14 counsel: or helmsman.
multitude of counsellers. Provided they are really "counsellers". **safety** = salvation.
15 for a stranger, &c. Christ became surety for His People, and they were "strangers" (Eph. 2. 12); and He smarted for it, blessed be His Name! Heb. *ẓūr*, an apostate. See note on 5. 3.

smart for it = be sore broken. See Ps. 38. 8; 69. 20. **is sure** = is secure. Heb. *baṭaḥ.* Ap. 69. i. **16 gracious woman.** Cp. the woman of Folly (9. 13). **And strong men, &c.** Sept. and Syr. read, "but the diligent". **17 merciful man** = man of lovingkindness, or grace. **his own soul** = his own self. Heb. *nephesh.* Ap. 13. Illustrations: the Kenites (1 Sam. 15. 6. Ecc. 11. 1); David (1 Sam. 30. 11-20); Jonathan (2 Sam. 9. 7; 21. 7); Job (Job 42. 10. Cp. Prov. 13. 2); the Centurion (Luke 7. 2-10); Cornelius (Acts 10. 4. Cp. Prov. 12. 14); the Maltese (Acts 28. 1-10). **troubleth, &c.** Illustrations: Cain (Gen. 4. 10-12); Joseph's brethren (Gen. 37; 42. 21); Adoni-bezek (Judg. 1. 6, 7); Agag (1 Sam. 15. 33); Haman (Est. 9. 25); Jonah (Jonah 4. 1-3); the miser (Ecc. 4. 8). **18 worketh, &c.** Pharaoh (Ex. 1. 20. Acts 7. 19). Caiaphas (John 11. 49, 50). Cp. Acts 8. 1, 4. **deceitful** = lie. Heb. *sheḳer.* The verb, adjective, and noun are the renderings of eight words in Proverbs: (1) *sheḳer* = a lie (11. 18; 20. 17; 31. 30); (2) *rāmāh* = cheating (12. 5, 17, 20; 14. 8, 25; 26. 19, 24); (3) *shāgāh* = wander, go astray (20. 1); (4) *kāzab* = fraud (23. 3); (5) *pāthāh* = delude (24. 28); (6) *nāshāh* (26. 26); (7) *'āthar.* See note on 27. 6; (8) *tok.* See note on 29. 13. **to him . . . a sure reward.** Illustrations: Noah (Gen. 6. 22; 7. Heb. 11. 7); Abraham (Heb. 6. 15); Joseph (Gen. 37—41. Cp. Ps. 37. 4-6); Simeon (Luke 2. 25-32. Lam. 3. 25, 26); Paul (2 Cor. 1. 12. 2 Tim. 4. 7, 8). **19 As righteousness** = Thus righteousness. Heb. *kēn.* Sept. and Syr. read Heb. *ben*, A righteous son. **evil.** Heb. *rā'a'.* Ap. 44. viii. **20 abomination.** See note on 3. 32.

X[1] (*cont.*)

21 *Though* °hand *join* in hand, [5]the °wicked shall not be unpunished:
But the seed of °the righteous shall °be delivered.
22 *As* a °jewel of gold in a swine's snout,
So is a °fair woman which is without discretion.
23 The desire of [21]the righteous *is* only good:
But the [7]expectation of [10]the [5]wicked *is* wrath.
24 There is that scattereth, and yet increaseth;
And *there is* that withholdeth more than is meet, but *it tendeth* to °poverty.
25 The liberal °soul shall be °made fat:
And he that watereth shall be watered also himself.
26 He that °withholdeth corn, the people shall curse him:
But blessing *shall be* upon the head of him that selleth *it*.
27 He that diligently seeketh good procureth favour:
But he that seeketh °mischief, it shall come unto him.
28 He that °trusteth in his riches shall fall
But [21]the righteous shall flourish as a branch.
29 He that troubleth his own house shall inherit °the wind:
And the °fool *shall be* servant to the wise of heart.
30 The fruit of [8]the righteous *is* a tree of life;
And he that °winneth [25]souls *is* wise.
31 Behold, [8]the righteous °shall be recompensed in the earth:
Much more [5]the wicked and °the sinner.

X[2] (p. 878)

12 Whoso loveth °instruction loveth knowledge:
But he that hateth reproof *is* brutish.
2 A good *man* obtaineth favour of °the LORD:
But a °man of °wicked devices °will He condemn.
3 A °man shall not be established by °wickedness:
But the root of °the righteous shall not be moved.
4 A °virtuous woman *is* a °crown to her husband:
But she that maketh ashamed *is* as rottenness in his bones.
5 The °thoughts of the righteous *are* °right:
But the °counsels of °the [2]wicked *are* °deceit.
6 The °words of [5]the [2]wicked *are* to lie in wait for blood:
But the mouth of °the upright shall deliver them.
7 [2]The [5]wicked are °overthrown, °and *are* not:
But the house of [3]the righteous shall stand.
8 A [2]man °shall be commended according to his °wisdom:
But he that is of a perverse heart °shall be despised.
9 °*He that is* despised, and hath a servant, *is* °better
Than he that honoureth himself, and lacketh bread.
10 A righteous *man* °regardeth the °life of his beast:
But the tender mercies of [5]the wicked *are* °cruel.

---

21 hand join in hand. Illustrations: the Babel builders (Gen. 11. 1–9); Korah (Num. 16); the Canaanite kings (Josh. 9. 1, 2); Adoni-zedek (Josh. 10); the Confederacy (Isa. 7. 1–16); the Ten Kingdoms (Rev. 19).
wicked. Not the same word as in *vv.* 5, 23, 31. Heb. *rā'a'*. Ap. 44. viii.
the righteous = righteous ones.
be delivered = escape. Not the same word as in *vv.* 4, 6, 8, 9. Heb. *mālat* = to slip away.
22 jewel = a nose-jewel, worn by women. See Gen. 24. 47. Isa. 3. 21. **fair** = beautiful.
23 Illustrated in *vv.* 24–31.
24 poverty = want. Heb. *ḥeser*. See note on 6. 11.
25 soul. Heb. *nephesh*. Ap. 13.
made fat = enriched. Illustrations: widow (1 Kings 17. 10, &c.); Shunammite (2 Kings 4. 8, 37); Publius (Acts 28. 7, 8). Cp. Phil. 4. 15.
26 withholdeth. Different from hoarding it in store as in Egypt (Gen. 41. 34–36; 53–57).
27 mischief. Heb. *rā'a'*. Ap. 44. viii.
28 trusteth = confideth. Heb. *bāṭaḥ*. Ap. 69. i.
29 the wind. Heb. *rūach*. Ap. 9.
fool. Heb. *'ĕvīl*. See note on 1. 7.
30 winneth = taketh, or catcheth.
31 shall be recompensed in the earth. This was the promise for that Dispensation (Ps. 37), not for this. See 1 Pet. 4. 18 and Ap. 63. ix. Rightly divide the Dispensations, and all difficulties are removed.
the sinner = a sinner. Heb. *chāṭā'*. Ap. 44. i.

12. 1–28 (X[2], p. 878). WITH REFERENCE TO DOMESTIC AND OTHER VOCATIONS.

1 instruction = discipline, or correction.
2 the LORD. Heb. Jehovah. Ap. 4. II.
man. Heb. *'ish*. Ap. 14. II.
wicked = lawless. Heb. *rāshā'*. Ap. 44. x.
will He condemn: or will pronounce him guilty, as Job 40. 8. **3 man.** Heb. *ādām*. Ap. 14. I.
wickedness = lawlessness. Heb. *rāshā'*. Ap. 44. x.
the righteous = righteous ones.
4 virtuous = worthy. See 31. 10 and Ruth 31. 11.
crown. Always used of a bridal or royal crown.
5 thoughts = plans.
right = just (as to their character). Illustrations: David (1 Sam. 23. 9; 26. 8–11); Daniel (Dan. 1. 8; 6. 4); Nathanael (John 1. 47).
counsels = steerings, or directions. Illustrations: Korah (Num. 16); Jeroboam (1 Kings 12. 28. Cp. *v.* 26); the prophet of Beth-el (1 Kings 13. 18. Cp. Prov. 11. 9); Sanballat (Neh. 6. 2); Haman (Est. 3. 5, 6, 8); Ishmael (Jer. 40. 14); Herod (Matt. 2. 8, 16); Pharisees (Matt. 22. 15, 16); Judas (John 12. 4–6).
the wicked = lawless ones.
deceit = deception. Heb. *rāmah*. See note on 11. 18.
6 words. Heb. *dābar*. Ap. 73. x.
the upright = upright ones.
7 overthrown. Cp. Gen. 19. 21, 25, 29. 2 Sam. 10. 3. 1 Chron. 19. 3, &c.
and are not = there is nothing of them left.
8 shall be commended. Illustration: Joseph (Gen. 41. 39). **wisdom.** Heb. *sākal*. See note on 1. 2.
shall be despised. Illustrations: Hophni and Phinehas (1 Sam. 1. 3; 2. 17, 30); Nabal (1 Sam. 25. 2, 17. Cp. Prov. 28. 6); Judah (Jer. 4. 22, 30. Lam. 1. 8); lost son (Luke 15. 15, 16).
9 He that is despised, and hath = Better to be little noticed and have, &c. **better.** See note on 8. 11.
10 regardeth, &c. = knoweth. Illustrations: Jacob (Gen. 33. 13, 14); David (1 Sam. 17. 34, 35).
life = soul. Heb. *nephesh*. Ap. 13.
cruel. Illustrations: Nahash (1 Sam. 11. 1, 2); Pilate (Luke 23. 16).

X[2] (*cont.*)

11 He that tilleth his land °shall be satisfied with bread:
But °he that followeth vain *persons is* void of °understanding.

12 °The [2]wicked desireth °the net °of °evil *men*:
But the root of [3]the righteous °yieldeth *fruit*.

13 °The wicked is snared by the °transgression of *his* °lips:
But °the just °shall come out of trouble.

14 A [2]man shall be satisfied with good by the fruit of *his* mouth:
And the recompence of a [3]man's hands shall be rendered unto him.

15 The way of a °fool *is* right in his own eyes:
But he that hearkeneth unto counsel *is* wise.

16 A [15]fool's wrath °is °presently known:
But a prudent *man* °covereth °shame.

17 *He that* speaketh truth sheweth forth righteousness:
But a false witness [5]deceit.

18 There is that speaketh °like the °piercings of a sword:
But the °tongue of the wise °*is* health.

19 The °lip of truth shall be established for ever:
But a lying tongue *is* °but for a moment.

20 [5]Deceit *is* in the heart of them that imagine [12]evil:
But to the counsellers of peace *is* joy.

21 There shall °no evil happen to [13]the just:
But [5]the wicked shall be filled with °mischief.

22 Lying [19]lips *are* °abomination to [2]the LORD:
But °they that deal truly *are* His delight.

23 A prudent [3]man °concealeth knowledge:
But the heart of °fools proclaimeth [15]foolishness.

24 The hand of the diligent °shall bear rule:
But the slothful shall be under tribute.

25 °Heaviness in the heart of man maketh it °stoop:
But a good word °maketh it glad.

26 °The righteous °*is* more excellent than his neighbour:
But the way of [5]the wicked °seduceth them.

27 The slothful *man* °roasteth not that which he took in hunting:
But the °substance of a diligent [3]man *is* precious.

28 In the way of righteousness *is* °life;
And *in* the pathway *thereof there is* °no death.

11 shall be satisfied. Illustrations: Isaac (Gen. 26. 12); Jacob (Gen. 31. 40; 32. 10).
he that followeth, &c. Illustrations: Abimelech's followers (Judg. 9. Cp. Prov. 24. 21); Theudas (Acts 5. 36, 37).
understanding. Heb. "heart", put by Fig. *Metonymy* (of Subject), Ap. 6, for sense. Sept. adds: "He that delighteth himself in the drinking of wine shall leave his own stronghold a disgrace."
12 The wicked = a lawless one.
the net. Put by Fig. *Metonymy* (of Cause), Ap. 6, for what is caught in it.
of evil men: i. e. which evil men use.
evil. Heb. *rā'a'*. Ap. 44. viii: not the same word as in *vv.* 13, 21.
yieldeth = giveth [to others]: i. e. instead of taking them as prey.
13 The wicked = an evil man. Heb. *rā'a'*. Same word as "evil" in *v.* 12.
transgression. Heb. *pāsha'*. Ap. 44. ix.
lips. Put by Fig. *Metonymy* (of Cause), Ap. 6, for what is spoken by them. Illustrations: Korah (Num. 16. 1-3, 31-35. Ps. 64. 8); the Amalekite (2 Sam. 1. 2-16); Adonijah (1 Kings 2. 23); Daniel's accusers (Dan. 6. 24); Jews (Matt. 27. 25).
the just = a righteous one.
shall come out, &c. Illustrations: Joshua and Caleb (Num. 14. 10, 24, 30); Esther and her People (Est. 7. 3; 8. 3-17; 9. 25); Peter (Acts 11. 2-18; 12. 3-18).
15 fool. Heb. *'ĕvil*. See note on 1. 7.
16 is = letteth itself be.
presently = immediately, at once, the same day. Illustrations: Jehoram (2 Kings 6. 31); Jezebel (1 Kings 19. 1, 2); Nebuchadnezzar (Dan. 3. 19); synagogue at Nazareth (Luke 4. 28).
covereth = concealeth.
shame = public ignominy. Fig. *Metonymy* (of Effect), Ap. 6, put for the affront which causes it. Illustrations: Gideon (Judg. 8. 2, 3. Cp. 8. 1); Hezekiah (Isa. 36. 21. Cp. Prov. 26. 4); David (1 Sam. 17. 29, 30. Cp. *v.* 28); Saul (1 Sam. 10. 27. Cp. 20. 30-33).
18 like the piercings, &c. Illustrations: Saul (1 Sam. 20. 30; and 18. 21. Cp. Ps. 57. 4, and Prov. 16. 27); Doeg (1 Sam. 22. 9-19); Jews (John 8. 48); Jeremiah (Lam. 3. 14. Heb. 11. 36).
piercings = stabs. Occurs only here.
tongue. Put by Fig. *Metonymy* (of Cause), Ap. 6, for what is spoken by it.
is health. Illustrations: Jethro (Ex. 18. 17-26); Abigail (1 Sam. 25. 24-33); the woman (2 Sam. 20. 16); Stephen (Acts 7. 59. Cp. 22. 20).
19 lip. Put by Fig. *Metonymy* (of Cause), Ap. 6, for what is spoken. Illustration: Caleb and Joshua (Num. 14. 30, 38).
but for a moment. Illustrations: Ahab (1 Kings 22. 30, 37; Hananiah (Jer. 28. 2, 11. Cp. *vv.* 15-17); Gehazi (2 Kings 5. 22, 25, 27. Prov. 10. 9); Ananias (Acts 5. 5, 10. Prov. 21. 6).
21 no evil = nothing in vain. Heb. *'āven*. Ap. 44. iii.
mischief. Heb. *rā'a'*. Same word as "evil" in *vv.* 12, 20.
22 abomination, &c. See note on 3. 32.
they that deal truly are, &c. Some codices, with Sept., read "is" (sing.) = he that dealeth, &c.
23 concealeth knowledge. Illustrations: Samuel (1 Sam. 9. 27. Cp. 10. 16); Nehemiah (Neh. 6. 2, 3).
fools. Heb. *kesil*. See note on 1. 7. Not the same word as in *vv.* 15, 16. **24 shall bear rule.** Illustrations: Eleazar (Gen. 24. 2, 10); Joseph (Gen. 39. 4, 22); Jeroboam (1 Kings 11. 28). **25 Heaviness** = Anxiety (fem.). **stoop** = bowed down. Illustrations: Ezra (Ezra 9. 3—10. 6); Nehemiah (Neh. 1. 4); David (Ps. 40. 12); Jeremiah (Jer. 8. 18). **maketh, &c.** = maketh [the man] glad [by driving it (fem.), the anxiety (fem.), away]. **26 the righteous** = a righteous one. **is more excellent than his neighbour** = guideth his neighbour. **seduceth them** = leadeth them astray. The clauses are not "unrelated", nor is the text "corrupt beyond restoration", when properly translated. **27 roasteth not, &c.** = starteth not his game (see the Oxford Gesenius). **substance**: i. e. that which the diligent man "starts" and obtains is substantial. The proverb is not "humorous". **28 life**: i. e. life eternal. See note on Lev. 18. 5. **no death** = immortality. Or take *nethībāh* (as in Judg. 5. 6. Isa. 59. 8) as denoting, with *derek*, no devious winding by-path. In this case we must read *'el*, "to", instead of *'al*, "no". This avoids the necessity of the italics.

X[3] (p. 878)

13 A wise son *heareth* his father's °instruction:
But a scorner heareth not rebuke.
2 A °man shall °eat good by the fruit of *his* mouth:
But the °soul of the °transgressors *shall eat* violence.
3 He that keepeth his mouth keepeth his °life:
But he that openeth wide his lips shall have destruction.
4 The [2]soul of the sluggard desireth, and *hath* nothing:
But the [2]soul of °the diligent shall be made fat.
5 A righteous *man* °hateth lying:
But a °wicked *man* is loathsome, and °cometh to shame.
6 Righteousness keepeth *him that is* upright in the way:
But °wickedness °overthroweth °the sinner.
7 There is that °maketh himself rich, yet *hath* nothing:
There is that °maketh himself °poor, yet *hath* great riches.
8 The °ransom of a [2]man's [3]life *are* his riches:
But °the [7]poor heareth not rebuke.
9 The light of °the righteous °rejoiceth:
But the °lamp of °the [5]wicked shall be °put out.
10 Only °by pride cometh contention:
But with the °well advised *is* wisdom.
11 Wealth *gotten* by vanity shall be diminished:
But he that gathereth °by labour shall increase.
12 Hope °deferred °maketh the heart °sick:
But *when* the desire cometh, *it is* °a tree of life.
13 Whoso despiseth °the word °shall be destroyed:
But he that feareth the commandment °shall be rewarded.
14 The law of °the wise *is* a fountain of life,
To depart from the snares of death.
15 Good understanding °giveth favour:
But the way of [2]transgressors *is* °hard.
16 Every prudent *man* dealeth with knowledge:
But a °fool layeth open *his* °folly.
17 A [5]wicked messenger falleth into °mischief:
But a faithful ambassador *is* °health.
18 °Poverty and shame *shall be to* him that refuseth instruction:
But he that regardeth reproof shall be honoured.
19 The desire accomplished is sweet to the [2]soul:
But *it is* abomination to °fools to depart from °evil.
20 He that walketh with wise *men* °shall be wise:
But °a companion of [16]fools °shall be destroyed.

13. 1-25 (X[3], p. 878). WITH REFERENCE TO TEMPORAL AND ETERNAL GOOD.

1 instruction=correction, or discipline.

2 man. Heb. *'ish.* Ap. 14. ii.

eat = get his food: "eat" being put by Fig. *Metonymy* (of Effect), Ap. 6, for what is gained by effort.

soul. Heb. *nephesh.* Ap. 13.

transgressors=traitors, faithless ones. Heb. *bāgad*, as in *v.* 15; 2. 22; 11. 3, 6; 16. 10; 21. 18, &c.

3 life=soul. Heb. *nephesh.* Ap. 13.

4 the diligent=diligent ones.

5 hateth lying. Illustrations: Joseph (Gen. 46. 31-34); Samuel (1 Sam. 3. 18); Micaiah (1 Kings 22. 13, 14; Prov. 14. 5); Elihu (Job 32. 22); Hezekiah (Ps. 119. 29, 163); David (Ps. 101. 7); Agur (Prov. 30. 8); Jeremiah (Jer. 26. 1-15); John Baptist (Matt. 14. 4).

wicked=lawless one. Heb. *rāshā'.* Ap. 44. x.

cometh to shame. Illustrations: Jehoram (2 Chron. 21. 18, 19); Gehazi (2 Kings 5. 27. Prov. 20. 17); Jezebel (2 Kings 9. 35); Manasseh (2 Kings 21. 7-13. Prov. 17. 15); Herod (Acts 12. 21-23).

6 wickedness=lawlessness. Heb. *rāshā'.* Ap. 44. x.

overthroweth=subverteth.

the sinner=the sin offering. Heb. *chāṭā'* = sin. Always so rendered in Leviticus. Ap. 43. II. v.

7 maketh himself rich: i.e. or pretendeth to be rich. Heb. *'āshar.* The Hithpael occurs only here.

poor=needy. Heb. *rūsh.* See note on 6. 11.

8 ransom=covering. Heb. *kopher.*

the poor, &c.: i.e. poor [becometh he that] heeded not rebuke.

9 the righteous=righteous ones.

lamp . . . put out. May mean that his family or line will become extinct. **the wicked**=lawless ones.

10 by pride cometh contention=by pride only cometh, &c. Illustrations: Korah (Num. 16); men of Ephraim (Judg. 12. 1-6); Rehoboam (1 Kings 12); the Apostles (Luke 22. 24). **well advised:** or modest.

11 by labour=by the hand: "hand" being put by Fig. *Metonymy* (of Cause), Ap. 6, for the labour effected by it.

12 deferred=protracted.

maketh . . . sick=enfeebleth. Illustrations: Abraham (Gen. 15. 2, 3); David (Ps. 42. 1-3); the Jews (Lam. 4. 17); the two disciples (Luke 24. 17, 21).

a tree of life. See Gen. 2. 9.

13 the word. Heb. *dābar* (no Art.). Ap. 73. x.

shall be destroyed. Illustrations: the world (Gen. 6. 1 Pet. 3. 20. 2 Pet. 2. 6); Israel (Deut. 28. 15-68); the lord (2 Kings 7. 2, 17-20); Joash (2 Chron. 24. 17-25); Amaziah (2 Chron. 25. 16-27. Prov. 15. 32); the priests and others (2 Chron. 36. 16); Jehoiakim (Jer. 26. 20-24); the Jews (Jer. 44. 17, 27).

shall be rewarded. Illustrations: Pharaoh's servants (Ex. 9. 20, 25); Amaziah (2 Chron. 25. 6-11); Ebed-melech (Jer. 39. 15-18). Contrast Josiah (2 Chron. 34. 27, 30) with Jehoiakim his son (Jer. 36. 23-30; 22. 18, 19).

14 the wise=a wise one.

15 giveth favour. Illustrations: Abraham (Gen. 23. 10, 11); Joseph (Gen. 39. 2); Joshua (Josh. 6. 27); David (1 Sam. 18. 14); Abigail (1 Sam. 25. 3, 18-34); Daniel (Dan. 1. 8, 9; 6. 3); Samuel (1 Sam. 2. 26. Prov. 22. 1).

hard=rough. This meaning may be substituted for its usual rendering "strong". See Gen. 49. 24. Ex. 14. 27. Num. 24. 21. Jer. 5. 15. Amos 5. 24. Mic. 6. 2, &c. Heb. *'ēythān.*

16 fool. Heb. *k^eṣīl.* See note on 1. 7.

folly. Heb. *'ĕvīl.* See note on 1. 7. Illustrations: Balaam (Num. 22. 29, 30); Ahasuerus (Est. 3. 10-15); Herod (Matt. 14. 7. Mark 6. 23).

17 mischief. Heb. *rā'a'.* Same word as "evil" in *v.* 19. Ap. 44. viii.

health=healing. Cp. 12. 18. **18 Poverty.** See note on "poor", *v.* 7. **19 fools.** Heb. *k^eṣīl.* See note on 1. 7. But some codices, with Sept. and Syr., read "lawless". **evil.** Heb. *rā'a'.* Ap. 44. viii. **20 shall be wise.** Illustrations: Uzziah (2 Chron. 26. 5); Joash (2 Chron. 24. 2); Ruth (1. 16); Elisha (2 Kings 2. 9); Andrew (John 1. 40, 41); Nathanael (John 1. 45-51). **a companion, &c.:** or he that feedeth (or entertaineth) fools shall be bankrupt. **shall be destroyed**=shall be broken.

X[3] (cont.)
21 [19]Evil pursueth [6]sinners:
But to [9]the righteous good shall be repayed.
22 A °good *man* leaveth °an inheritance to his °children's children:
And the wealth of the [6]sinner *is* laid up for the just.
23 Much food *is* °*in* the tillage of the [7]poor:
But there is *that is* destroyed for want of judgment.
24 He that °spareth his rod hateth his son:
But he that loveth him °chasteneth him betimes.
25 °The righteous eateth to the satisfying of his [2]soul:
But the belly of [9]the [5]wicked shall want.

X[4] (p. 878)
14 Every °wise woman °buildeth her house:
But °the foolish °plucketh it down with her hands.
2 He that walketh in his uprightness feareth °the LORD:
But *he that is* perverse in °his ways despiseth Him.
3 In the °mouth of [1]the foolish *is* a rod °of pride:
But the °lips of the wise shall °preserve them.
4 Where no °oxen *are*, the crib *is* clean:
But much increase *is* by the strength of the ox.
5 °A faithful witness will not lie:
But a false witness will utter lies.
6 A scorner °seeketh wisdom, °and *findeth it* not:
But knowledge *is* easy unto him that °understandeth.
7 Go from the presence of a °foolish °man,
°When thou perceivest not *in him* the lips of knowledge.
8 The °wisdom of °the prudent °*is* to understand his way:
But the [1]folly of [7]fools *is* °deceit.
9 [1]Fools °make a mock at °sin:
But among °the righteous *there is* °favour.
10 The heart knoweth °his own bitterness;
And °a stranger doth not intermeddle with his joy.
11 The house of °the wicked shall be overthrown:
But the °tabernacle of °the upright shall flourish.
12 There is a way which °seemeth right unto a [7]man,
But the end thereof °*are* the ways of death.
13 Even in laughter the heart °is sorrowful;
And the end of that mirth *is* heaviness.

22 good. Fig. *Anadiplōsis* (Ap. 6). Heb. text *v.* 21 ends with "good", which is repeated at the beginning of *v.* 22.
an inheritance. Not necessarily wealth; but a good name, &c.
children's=sons'. Illustrations: Jacob (Gen. 48. 15, 16, 20); Caleb (Num. 14. 24. Josh. 14. 14).
23 in the tillage of, &c.: i. e. with Jehovah's blessing.
24 spareth=withholdeth. Illustrations: Eli (1 Sam. 3. 13; 4. 11); David (2 Sam. 13. 39; 14. 25. 1 Kings 1. 6).
chasteneth him betimes=carefully seeketh correction (or discipline) for him: or, seeketh early, &c.

14. 1-35 (X[4], p. 878). WITH REFERENCE TO WISE AND FOOLISH, RICH AND POOR, &c.

1 wise. Heb. *chokmoth* (see note on 1. 2), wisdoms, pl. (with verb in sing.) for emphasis. Fig. *Hypallage* (Ap. 6)=the true wisdom of women, which is put for the *wise* woman. The word is pointed as an Adjective by mistake. See notes on 1. 20; 9. 1; 14. 1.
buildeth=has built. Preterite tense, implying the outcome of past wisdom.
the foolish=a foolish woman. Heb. *'ĕvil.* Same word as in *vv.* 3, 8, 9, 17, 18, 24, 29. Not the same word as in *vv.* 7, 8, 16, 24.
plucketh it down=will tear it down: future, because folly's present course is continuous to the end.
2 the LORD. Heb. Jehovah. Ap. 4. II.
his ways. It may mean Jehovah's ways: i. e. he who turns out of His ways becomes an apostate, like the "strange" woman.
3 mouth. Put by Fig. *Metonymy* (of Cause), Ap. 6, for what is spoken by it.
of pride. Gen. of Possession, "pride's sceptre". See Ap. 17 (3). On the one side, we have "pride", prating, and punishment; on the other side, prudence, piety, and preservation.
lips. Put by Fig. *Metonymy* (of Cause), Ap. 6, for what is spoken by them.
preserve=guard.
4 oxen. While these were multiplied, horses were prohibited.
5 A faithful witness, &c. See Matt. 26. 60, 61; Rev. 1. 5.
6 seeketh=every scorner hath sought repeatedly. Note the past tense.
and findeth it not. Illustrations: the Pharisees (John 9. 29. Cp. 7. 52, and 1 Cor. 2. 14); Jews (Acts 13. 41, 45); Athenians (1 Cor. 1. 23; 2. 8).
understandeth=is discerning. Illustration: Ethiopian (Acts 8. 27-39).
7 foolish. Heb. *k[e]sil.* See note on 1. 7. Same word as in *vv.* 16, 33; not the same word as in *vv.* 1, 3, 9, 17, 18, 29.
man. Heb. *'ish.* Ap. 14. II.
When thou perceivest not="And acknowledge not". Heb. *yāda'*, to know, as in *vv.* 10, 33, &c.
8 wisdom. Heb. *chokma.* See note on 1. 2.
the prudent=a prudent one. See note on "subtil", Gen. 3. 1.
is to understand. Not to vainly speculate about it, or to pry into the ways of others. **deceit**=lying. Heb. *rāmah.* See note on 11. 18. **9 make a mock.** The verb is singular, and probably the pl. "fools" means "A great fool makes a mock", &c. **sin**=guilt. The proper name for the trespass offering. Heb. *'āshām* (Ap. 44. ii.). Illustrations: the antediluvians (Luke 17. 26, 27. 1 Pet. 3. 20); Abner (2 Sam. 2. 14-17); Haman (Est. 3. 13-15. Prov. 29. 2); the Jews (Isa. 22. 13). **the righteous**=upright ones. **favour.** Those who offer the trespass offering, experience the Divine favour. **10 his own bitterness**=the bitterness of his soul (Heb. *nephesh.* Ap. 13). Illustrations: Hannah (1 Sam. 1. 8-13); Joab (2 Sam. 19. 5-7); the Shunammite (2 Kings 4. 27); Haman (Est. 5. 13); Job (Job 3); Herod (Mark 6. 16). **a stranger**=an apostate. Heb. *zūr.* See note on 2. 16; 5. 3. **11 the wicked**=lawless ones. Heb. *rāshā'.* Ap. 44. x. See notes on *v.* 32. **tabernacle**=tent, or dwelling. Heb. *'ohel.* Ap. 40. Put by Fig. *Metonymy* (of Adjunct), Ap. 6, for the dwellers therein. **the upright**=upright ones (as in *v.* 9). **12 seemeth right**=is pleasing. It only "seems" right. Illustrations: Jeroboam (1 Kings 12. 27-33; 14. 7-11. Cp. Prov. 3. 7); Josiah (2 Chron. 35. 20-24); Jews (Acts 13. 50; John 16. 2. Cp. Paul, Phil. 3. 4-7, and 1 Tim. 1. 13). **are**=is. **13 is:** i. e. may be. Illustrations: Nabal (1 Sam. 25. 36, 37); Solomon (Ecc. 2. 2); Belshazzar (Dan. 5. 1-6, 30); Israelites (Amos 6. 3-7); Babylon (Rev. 18. 7, 8).

X[4] (*cont.*)

14 The backslider in heart shall be °filled with his own ways:
And a good [7] man *shall be satisfied* °from himself.
15 The simple believeth every °word:
But [8] the prudent *man* looketh well to his going.
16 A wise *man* feareth, and departeth from °evil:
But the [7] fool °rageth, and is °confident.
17 *He that is* soon angry dealeth [1] foolishly:
And a [7] man of °wicked devices is hated.
18 The simple inherit [1] folly:
But °the [8] prudent are crowned with knowledge.
19 °The evil bow before the good;
And [11] the wicked at the gates of °the righteous.
20 °The poor is hated even of his own neighbour:
But °the rich *hath* many friends.
21 He that despiseth his neighbour °sinneth:
But he that °hath mercy on °the poor, °happy *is* he.
22 Do they not err that devise [16] evil?
But °mercy and truth *shall be* to them that devise good.
23 In all labour there is profit:
But the talk of the lips *tendeth* only to penury.
24 The crown of the wise *is* their riches:
But the [1] foolishness of [7] fools *is* [1] folly.
25 A true witness delivereth °souls:
But a [8] deceitful *witness* speaketh lies.
26 In °the fear of [2] the LORD *is* °strong confidence:
And His °children shall have a place of refuge.
27 [26] The fear of [2] the LORD *is* a fountain of life,
To °depart from the snares of death.
28 In the multitude of people *is* the king's honour:
But in the want of people *is* the destruction of the prince.
29 *He that is* slow to wrath *is* of great °understanding:
But *he that is* °hasty of °spirit exalteth [1] folly.
30 A sound heart *is* the life of the flesh:
But envy the rottenness of the bones.
31 He that oppresseth °the poor reproacheth °his Maker:
But he that honoureth Him [21] hath mercy on °the poor.
32 °The wicked is °driven away in his °wickedness:
But [19] the righteous °hath hope in his death.
33 [8] Wisdom resteth in the heart of him that hath understanding:
°But *that which is* in the midst of [7] fools is made known.
34 Righteousness °exalteth a nation:
°But [21] sin *is* a reproach to any °people.
35 The king's favour *is* toward a wise servant:
But his wrath is *against* him that causeth shame.

X[5] (p. 878)

15 A soft answer °turneth away wrath:
But °grievous words stir up anger.
2 The tongue of °the wise useth knowledge aright:

14 filled = satisfied.
from himself. Ginsburg thinks, "from his own doings." Cp. Jer. 17. 10.
15 word: or thing. **16 evil.** Heb. *rā'a'*. See Ap. 44. viii. **rageth** = rusheth on.
confident. Heb. *baṭaḥ*. Ap. 69. i.
17 wicked devices = deep schemes or intrigues.
18 the prudent = prudent ones.
19 The evil = evil ones. Heb. *rā'a'*. Ap. 44. viii.
the righteous = a righteous one.
20 The poor = A needy one. Heb. *rūsh*. See note on 6. 11. **the rich** = a rich man.
21 sinneth. Heb. *chāṭa'*.
hath mercy on = is gracious to.
the poor = an afflicted one. Heb. *'ānāh*. See note on 6. 11. **happy.** See note on 3. 13.
22 mercy = lovingkindness, or grace.
25 souls. Heb. *nephesh*. Ap. 13.
26 the fear of the LORD. See note on 1. 7.
strong confidence. Illustrations: Abraham (Gen. 22. 3–10. Heb. 11. 19); David (1 Sam. 30. 6); Hezekiah (2 Chron. 32. 7, 8, 22); Shadrach and others (Dan. 3. 17, 25, 27. Isa. 43. 2); Habakkuk (Hab. 3. 17–19); Peter (Acts 12. 6. Prov. 3. 24); Paul (2 Tim. 4. 6–8).
children = sons. **27 depart from** = avoid.
29 understanding = discernment. Heb. *t^ebūnāh*. See note on 1. 2.
hasty of spirit. Illustrations: Rehoboam (1 Kings 12. Cp. *v.* 16, above); Jehoram (2 Kings 5. 7); Jonah (Jonah 4. 8, 9); Martha (Luke 10. 40).
spirit. Heb. *rūach*. Ap. 9.
31 the poor = a weak one. Heb. *dal*. See note on 6. 11.
his Maker. An ancient title found in the book of Job (Job 35. 10), also in Prov. 17. 5; just as we speak of the "Creator". Used here because He is the Maker of the weak as well as the strong. We meet with it again in Isa. 17. 7; 51. 13; 54. 5. Not "confined to the later literature of Judaism".
the poor = a humble one. Heb. *'ebyōn*. See note on 6. 11.
32 The wicked = A lawless one. Heb. *rāshā'*. Ap. 44. x.
driven away in his wickedness = thrust down in his evil-doing. Illustrations: Dathan (Num. 16. 33); Israel (Ex. 32. 28. 1 Cor. 10. 7); Balaam (Num. 31. 8, 10. Rev. 2. 14). Canaanites (Josh. 2. 9; 5. 1; 10. Deut. 9. 5); Hophni and Phinehas (1 Sam. 4. 11); Baal's prophets (1 Kings 18. 40); Belshazzar (Dan. 5. 2–6, 30).
wickedness = lawlessness, as above.
hath hope in his death. Illustrations: Jacob (Gen. 49. 18); Joseph (Gen. 50. 24, 25. Heb. 11. 22); David (2 Sam. 23. 5. Ps. 17. 15); Stephen (Acts 7. 55, 60); Paul (2 Tim. 4. 6–8); Peter (2 Pet. 1. 14, 16; 3. 13).
33. But, &c. The verb being fem. may refer to "wisdom". If so we may render "and [even] in the midst of fools will make itself known".
34 exalteth ... But, &c. Illustrations: Deut. 4. 6; 28; 1 Kings 9. 7–9; 2 Chron. 15. 3, 5, 6; cp. Josh. 1. 8; 10. 42; 23. 14 with Judg. 1; 2, &c.; cp. 2 Chron. 17. 2–5, 10, 11, and 2 Kings 18. 7 with 2 Kings 16. Cp. the Canaanites (Lev. 18. 24–30); Egypt (Ex. 12. 12. Ezek. 29. 1–15); Amalekites (Ex. 17. 16. 1 Sam. 15); Babylon (Isa. 14. 4–23. Isa. 47. 6–15); Moab (Isa. 16. 6, 7); Tyre (Ezek. 28. 2–8. Isa. 23. 1–9): Nineveh (Zeph. 2. 13–15).
people = peoples.

15. 1–32 (X[5], p. 878). WITH REFERENCE TO OTHER RELATIONS IN THE RELIGIOUS SPHERE.

1 turneth away wrath. Illustrations: Aaron (Lev. 10. 16–20); Reubenites (Josh. 22. 15–34); Gideon (Judg. 8. 1–3. Prov. 15. 18); Hannah (1 Sam. 1. 15, 17); Abigail (1 Sam. 25. 23, &c.).
grievous = bitter, cutting, violent, &c. Illustrations: the Ephraimites (Judg. 12. 1–4); men of Israel and Judah (2 Sam. 19. 41–43. Prov. 30. 33); Saul and Jonathan (1 Sam. 20. 30–34); Rehoboam (2 Chron. 10. 13–16. Prov. 26. 21); Eliphaz (Job 22. 5, &c.); Paul and Barnabas (Acts 15. 39).
2 the wise, &c. = wise ones will use.

X5 (cont.) But the mouth of °fools poureth out °foolishness.
3 The eyes of °the LORD *are* °in every place, °Beholding °the evil and °the good.
4 °A wholesome tongue *is* a °tree of life: But perverseness therein *is* a breach in the °spirit.
5 °A fool despiseth his father's instruction: But he that regardeth reproof is °prudent.
6 In the house of °the righteous *is* much °treasure: But in the revenues of [1]the wicked is trouble.
7 The lips of the wise disperse knowledge: But the heart of the °foolish *doeth* not so.
8 The sacrifice of °the wicked °*is* an abomination to [3]the LORD: But the prayer of °the upright *is* His delight.
9 The way of [8]the wicked [8]*is* an abomination unto [3]the LORD: But He loveth him that followeth after righteousness.
10 Correction °*is* grievous unto him that forsaketh the way: *And* he that hateth reproof shall die.
11 °Hell and destruction *are* before [3]the LORD: How much more then the hearts of the °children of °men?
12 A scorner °loveth not one that reproveth him: Neither will he go unto the wise.
13 A °merry heart maketh a cheerful countenance: But by sorrow of the heart the [4]spirit is broken.
14 The heart of him that hath °understanding °seeketh knowledge: But the mouth of [2]fools feedeth on [2]foolishness.
15 All the days of the °afflicted *are* °evil: But he that is of a °merry heart *hath* a continual feast.
16 °Better *is* little with °the fear of [3]the LORD Than great treasure and trouble therewith.
17 [16]Better *is* a dinner of herbs where love is, Than a stalled ox and hatred therewith.
18 A wrathful °man stirreth up °strife: But *he that is* slow to anger appeaseth strife.
19 The way of the slothful *man is* as an hedge of thorns: But the way of °the righteous *is* °made plain.
20 A wise son maketh a glad father: But a foolish [11]man despiseth his mother.
21 [5]Folly *is* joy to *him that is* destitute of °wisdom: But a [18]man of [14]understanding walketh uprightly.
22 Without counsel purposes are disappointed: But in the multitude of °counsellers °they are established.
23 A [18]man hath joy by the answer of his mouth: And a word *spoken* °in due season, how good *is it!*
24 The way of life *is* °above to °the wise, That he may depart from [11]hell beneath.
25 [3]The LORD will destroy the house of the proud: But He will establish the °border of the widow.

fools. Heb. *k^{e}sīl*. See note on 1. 7.
foolishness. Heb. *'ĕvīl*. See note on 1. 7.
3 the LORD. Heb. Jehovah. Ap. 4. II.
in every place. Note the different places in the illustrations following:
Beholding=taking note, or observing. Illustrations: Adam (Gen. 3. 8, 9); Hagar (Gen. 16. 7, 13); Ethiopian (Acts 8. 29); Abraham (Gen. 22. 11, 15-18); Jacob (Gen. 28. 11-16; 46. 1-4); Joseph (Gen. 39. 21); Achan (Josh. 7. 10-18); Solomon (2 Chron. 7. 1-3, 12-16); David (Ps. 139. 7-13); Asa (2 Chron. 14. 11, 12); Jehoshaphat (2 Chron. 18. 31); Ahab (1 Kings 22. 34, 35); Hezekiah (2 Kings 20. 5, 13-18); Manasseh (2 Chron. 33. 12, 13); Ezekiel (Ezek. 3. 22); Nebuchadnezzar (Dan. 4. 29, 32); Belshazzar (Dan. 5. 5); Jonah (Jonah 2. 10); Nathanael (John 1. 48); Stephen (Acts 7. 55); Peter (Acts 10. 9-16); Herod (Acts 12. 23); Lydia (Acts 16. 13, 14); Paul (Acts 27. 23, 24. 2 Tim. 4. 17); the wedding guests (Matt. 22. 11-13. 1 Cor. 11. 28).
the evil=evil ones. Heb. *rā'a'*. Ap. 44. viii.
the good=good ones.
4 A wholesome tongue=Gentleness of tongue.
tree of life. See Gen. 2. 9; 3. 22, 24. Cp. Prov. 3. 18. Ezek. 27. 12. Rev. 22. 2, and notes there.
spirit. Heb. *rūach*. Ap. 9.
5 A fool. Heb. *'ĕvīl*. See note on 1. 7.
prudent. Sept. adds: "In abounding righteousness is great strength, but the ungodly will perish root and branch."
6 the righteous=a righteous one.
treasure. Heb. "strength", put by Fig. *Metonymy* (of Cause), Ap. 6, for the treasures procured by it.
the wicked=a lawless one. Heb. *rāshā'*. Ap. 44. x. In *v.* 8 it is plural. Not the same word as in *v.* 26.
7 foolish. Heb. *k^{e}sīl*. See note on 1. 7.
8 the wicked=lawless ones.
is an abomination, &c. See note on 3. 32. Illustrations: Cain (Gen. 4. 5. Heb. 11. 4); Saul (1 Sam. 15. 22, 23); Jews (Isa. 1. 11-15; 66. 3).
the upright=upright ones.
10 is grievous, &c. Illustrations: Asa (2 Chron. 16. 10); Jews (John 7. 7; 8. 23, 40).
11 Hell=the grave. Heb. *Sh^{e}ōl*. Ap. 35.
children=sons. **men.** Heb. *'ādām*. Ap. 14. I.
12 loveth not, &c. Illustrations: Ahab (2 Chron. 18. 7. Prov. 17. 4); the Jews (Amos 5. 10); Pharisees (Luke 7. 30); cp. Matt. 3. 7. Prov. 12. 1).
13 merry=joyful, or glad.
14 understanding. Heb. *bīnāh* (1. 2). Same word as in *v.* 21, but not in *v.* 32.
seeketh knowledge. Illustrations: Solomon (1 Kings 3. 5-10. Prov. 19. 8); Queen of Sheba (1 Kings 10. Matt. 12. 42); Mary (Luke 10. 39); Nicodemus (John 3. 1, 2); the Ethiopian (Acts 8. 28); the Bereans (Acts 17. 11).
15 afflicted. Heb. *'ānāh*. See note on "poverty", 6. 11.
evil=sad. Same word as in *v.* 3. **merry**=good.
16 Better. See note on 8. 11. Illustrations: the shepherds (Luke 2. 20. Cp. Matt. 2. 3); Paul in prison (Phil. 4. 11, 13, 18. 1 Tim. 6. 6). Contrast Ahab in palace (1 Kings 21. 4). Jehovah is a substitute for every good thing, but nothing is a substitute for Him.
the fear of the LORD. See note on 1. 7.
18 man. Heb. *'īsh*. Ap. 14. II.
strife=contention, or discord.
19 the righteous=upright ones.
made plain=a raised road. Illustration: Eleazar (Gen. 24. 12, 26, 27, 52. Ps. 37. 23).
21 wisdom. Heb. *lēb*="heart", put by Fig. *Metonymy* (of Adjunct), Ap. 6, for the knowledge it should possess. See note on 1. 2.
22 counsellers. But they must *be* "counsellers".
they are. Aram., Sept., and Syr. read "counsel is".
23 in due season=in its season.
24 above=upward.
the wise=a skilful one. Heb. *sākal*. See note on 1. 2.
25 border=landmark. Note the contrast with "house".

X[5] (cont.)

26 The thoughts of °the wicked *are* an [8]abomination to [3]the LORD:
But *the words* of the pure *are* pleasant words.
27 He that is greedy of gain troubleth his own house;
But he that hateth °gifts shall live.
28 The heart of [6]the righteous studieth to answer:
But the mouth of [8]the wicked poureth out °evil things.
29 [3]The LORD *is* far from [8]the wicked:
But He heareth the prayer of °the righteous.
30 The light of the eyes rejoiceth the heart:
And a good report maketh the bones fat.
31 The ear that heareth the reproof °of life
Abideth among the wise.
32 He that refuseth °instruction despiseth his own °soul:
But he that heareth reproof °getteth understanding.
33 [16]The fear of [3]the LORD *is* the [32]instruction of °wisdom;
And °before honour *is* humility.

U[2] Y[1] (p. 886)

16 The °preparations of the heart in °man,
And the °answer of the °tongue, *is* from °the LORD.
2 All the ways of a °man *are* °clean in his °own eyes;
But [1]the LORD °weigheth °the spirits.
3 Commit thy works unto [1]the LORD,
And thy °thoughts °shall be established.
4 [1]The LORD hath made all *things* for °Himself:
Yea, even °the wicked for the day of °evil.
5 Every one *that is* proud in heart *is* an °abomination to [1]the LORD:
Though °hand *join* in °hand, he shall not be °unpunished.
6 By °mercy and truth °iniquity is °purged:
And by °the fear of [1]the LORD *men* depart from [4]evil.
7 When a [2]man's ways please [1]the LORD,
He maketh even his enemies to be at peace with him.
8 °Better *is* a little with righteousness
Than great revenues without right.
9 A [1]man's heart °deviseth his way:
But [1]the LORD °directeth his steps.
10 °A divine sentence *is* in the °lips of the king:
His mouth °transgresseth not in judgment.
11 A just weight and balance *are* [1]the LORD'S:
All the weights of the bag *are* His °work.
12 *It is* an abomination to kings to commit °wickedness:
For the throne is established by righteousness.

26 the wicked = an evil-doer. Heb. *rāʿaʿ*, same word as "evil" in *v.* 3. Ap. 44. viii.
27 gifts = bribes. Cp. 18. 1; 20. 21.
28 evil. Heb. *rāʿaʿ*. Ap. 44. viii.
29 the righteous = righteous ones.
31 of = tending or leading to. Gen. of Relation. See Ap. 17 (5).
32 instruction = correction, or discipline. See note on 1. 7.
soul. Heb. *nephesh*. Ap. 13. Illustrations: Dathan (Num. 16. 12–14, 31–33); Zedekiah (2 Chron. 36. 12; Jer. 39. 1–7); Nebuchadnezzar (Dan. 4. 27–33); Belshazzar (Dan. 5. 22–30); Jews (Matt. 23. 34–38); Gadarenes (Luke 8. 37).
getteth understanding = possesseth a heart. "Heart" put by Fig. *Metonymy* (of Subject), Ap. 6, for "sense". Illustrations: Job's friends (Job 42. 7–9); the woman (John 4. 17, &c.); two disciples (Luke 24. 25–32); Paul (Acts 9. 6–22).
33 wisdom. Heb. *chākmāh*. See note on 1. 2.
before honour, &c. Illustrations: Joseph (Gen. 41. 16, 39, 40. Prov. 22. 4); Gideon (Judg. 6. 15); Hananiah (Neh. 7. 2); Daniel (Dan. 2. 30–48); Centurion (Matt. 8. 8, 10); Ephraim (Hos. 13. 1); John Baptist (John 1. 15, 30; 3. 30).

16. 1—19. 19 (U[2], p. 877). THE PIOUS AND UNGODLY WITH REFERENCE TO GOD. THEIR LIFE AND ACTION. (*Division.*)

U[2]	Y[1]	16. 1–33. Personal confidence in God.
	Y[2]	17. 1–28. Personal contentment and peace.
	Y[3]	18. 1–24. Personal virtues in social life.
	Y[4]	19. 1–19. Personal character. Humility, meekness, and gentleness.

1 preparations = arrangements or plans. The Ellipsis (Ap. 6) of the verb in the first clause must be supplied (as it is in the second clause): "To [ל] man [pertain] the plans of his heart; but from [מִן] Jehovah [comes] the final decree." Cp. *v.* 9. May be well rendered "the last word" (cp. *v.* 4). See Ap. 74. Illustrations: Balaam (Num. 23. 11, 12; 24. 10–13. Josh. 24. 9, 10. Neh. 13. 2). Cp. Jer. 10. 23.
man = man. Heb. *'ādām*. Ap. 14. I.
answer. Heb. *maʿăneh*, from *ʿānāh*, which is a word of wide meaning. The noun occurs only eight times (Job 32. 3, 5. Prov. 15. 1, 23; 16. 1, 4; 20. 19. Mic. 3. 7).
tongue. Put by Fig. *Metonymy* (of Cause), Ap. 6, for what is said by it. The silent and secret plans of man's heart are contrasted with the disclosures of the tongue, which come from Jehovah. See note on "Himself", *v.* 4.
tongue. Put by Fig. *Metonymy* (of Cause), Ap. 6, for what is said by it. **the LORD.** Heb. Jehovah. Ap. 4. II.
2 man. Heb. *'ish*. Ap. 14. II. **clean** = pure.
own eyes. Cp. 12. 15; 14. 12; 16. 25; 21. 2. Conscience is no safe guide, for it depends on what a man *believes*. Illustrations: Hazael (2 Kings 8. 13); Jehu (2 Kings 10. 16, 31); the Pharisee (Luke 18. 11–14); Paul (Acts 26. 9; cp. 9. 4. 1 Tim. 1. 13 and Rom. 7. 9).
weigheth. With moral and spiritual weights.
the spirits = spirits (no Art.). Heb. *rūach*. Ap. 9.
3 thoughts = plans. Cp. *v.* 1.
shall be established. Illustrations: Jacob (Gen. 32. 24–30; 46. 1–4); Ruth (Ruth 2. 12); David (1 Sam. 17. 45; 30. 8–19. 2 Sam. 5. 19–25); Ezra (Ezra 8. 21–23, 31, 32). Esther (Est. 4. 14–17; 8. 15–17); Daniel (Dan. 6. 10. Ps. 37. 4–6). **4 Himself.** Same word as "answer" (*v.* 1) = His decree, or His own end. See note on *v.* 1. **the wicked** = a lawless one. Heb. *rāshāʿ*. Ap. 44. x. **evil.** Heb. *rāʿaʿ*. Ap. 44. viii. **5 abomination, &c.** See note on 3. 32. **hand . . . hand.** Easterns walk thus: Westerns walk arm in arm. **unpunished** = acquitted, or held innocent. **6 mercy** = lovingkindness, or grace. **iniquity.** Heb. *ʿāvāh*. Ap. 44. iv. **purged** = covered: i. e. by a propitiatory covering. **the fear of the LORD.** See note on 1. 7. **8 Better.** See note on 8. 11. **9 deviseth his way.** See notes on *v.* 1. **directeth his steps.** Illustrations: Joseph's brethren (Gen. 37. 18–28, and 45. 5); Pharaoh's daughter (Ex. 2. 5); Saul (1 Sam. 9. 3, 15, 16; 23. 26–28); Jesse (1 Sam. 16. 8–11; 17. 23, 53); Syrians (2 Kings 5. 2); Zacchæus (Luke 19. 4, 5, 9); woman (John 4. 7); Saul (Acts 9. 1, &c.); Philemon. **10 A divine sentence** = an oracle. **lips.** Put by Fig. *Metonymy* (of Cause), Ap. 6, for what is uttered by them. **transgresseth not**: or, will not be unfaithful. **11 work** = something made: i. e. His ordinance. Lev. 19. 36. Cp. Prov. 11. 1. The shekel was the shekel "of the sanctuary". **12 wickedness** = lawlessness. Heb. *rāshāʿ*. Ap. 44. x.

Y[1] (cont.)
13 Righteous lips *are* the delight of °kings;
And °they love him that speaketh right.
14 The wrath of a king *is as* °messengers of death:
But a wise [2]man will °pacify it.
15 In the light of the king's countenance *is* life;
And his favour *is* as a °cloud of the latter rain.
16 How much [8]better *is it* to get °wisdom than gold!
And to get °understanding rather to be chosen than silver!
17 The highway of °the upright *is* to depart from [4]evil:
He that °keepeth his way preserveth his °soul.
18 °Pride *goeth* before destruction,
And an haughty [2]spirit before a fall.
19 [8]Better *it is to be* of an humble [2]spirit with the °lowly,
Than to divide the spoil with the proud.
20 He that handleth a matter wisely shall find good:
And whoso °trusteth in [1]the LORD, °happy *is* he.
21 The wise in °heart shall be called prudent:
And the sweetness of the [10]lips increaseth learning.
22 °Understanding *is* a wellspring of life unto him that hath it:
But the instruction of °fools *is* °folly.
23 The [21]heart of the wise °teacheth his mouth,
And addeth learning to his [10]lips.
24 Pleasant °words *are as* an honeycomb,
Sweet to the [17]soul, and °health to the °bones.
25 There is a way that seemeth right unto a [2]man,
But the end thereof *are* the ways of death.
26 °He that laboureth laboureth for himself;
For his °mouth °craveth it of him.
27 °An ungodly [2]man diggeth up [4]evil:
And in his lips *there is* as a burning fire.
28 A froward [2]man °soweth strife:
And a whisperer separateth chief friends.
29 A violent [2]man enticeth his neighbour,
And leadeth him into the way *that is* not good.
30 He shutteth his eyes to devise froward things:
Moving his lips he bringeth [4]evil to pass.
31 The °hoary head *is* a crown of glory,
If it be found in the way of righteousness.
32 *He that is* slow to anger *is* [8]better than °the mighty;
And he that ruleth his [18]spirit °than he that taketh a city.
33 The °lot is cast into the °lap;
But °the whole °disposing thereof *is* of [1]the LORD.

Y[2] (p. 887)
17 °Better *is* a dry morsel, and quietness therewith,
Than an house full of °sacrifices *with* strife.
2 A wise servant shall have rule over a son that causeth shame,
And shall have part of the inheritance among the brethren.
3 The fining pot *is* for silver, and the furnace for gold:
But °the LORD °trieth the hearts.
4 A °wicked doer giveth heed to false lips;
And a °liar giveth ear to a naughty tongue.

13 kings. Some codices, with Sept., Aram., and Syr., read "a king".
they love, &c., or, kings love the words of uprightness.
14 messengers, &c. Illustrations: Benaiah (1 Kings 2. 25); Haman (Est. 7. 8-10). **pacify it** = get it covered.
15 cloud = heavy cloud, &c. Specially valuable, falling just before harvest.
16 wisdom. Heb. *chākmāh.* See note on 1. 2.
understanding. Heb. *bīnāh.* See note on 1. 2.
17 the upright = upright ones.
keepeth = guardeth.
soul. Heb. *nephesh.* Ap. 13.
18 Pride goeth, &c. Illustrations: Asahel (2 Sam. 2. 18-23); Ben-hadad (1 Kings 20. 3, 11, 32); Babylon (Isa. 47. 10, 11); Azariah (Jer. 43. 2-11); Nebuchadnezzar (Dan. 4. 30, 31. Ps. 49. 11, 12); Edom (Obad. 3, 4); Herod Agrippa (Acts 12. 21-23).
19 lowly = wretched. Heb. *'ānāh.* See note on 6. 11.
20 trusteth = confideth. Heb. *baṭah.* Ap. 69. I.
happy. See note on 3. 13.
21 heart. Put by Fig. *Metonymy* (of Subject), Ap. 6, for understanding or discernment.
22 Understanding. Heb. *sēkel* See note on 1. 2.
fools . . . folly. Heb. *'ĕvīl.* See note on 1. 7.
23 teacheth = maketh wise. Illustrations: Eleazar (Gen. 24. 34-49); Jacob (47. 9); Peter (Acts 3. 12, &c.; 4. 19, &c.); Paul (Acts 13. 16-41; 14. 17; 17. 28; 17; 24. 25; 26. 2-27. Philem. 1 Tim. 1. 12-16).
24 words = sayings. Heb. *'imrah.* Ap. 73. v.
health = healing. Cp. 6. 8.
bones. Put by Fig. *Synecdoche* (of Part), Ap. 6, for whole body.
26 He that laboureth = the soul of him who laboureth. Heb. *nephesh.* Ap. 13. **mouth** = appetite.
craveth it of him = urgeth him on.
27 An ungodly man = A man of Belial.
28 soweth = sendeth forth. Illustrations: Princes of Ammon (2 Sam. 10. 3); Ziba (2 Sam. 16. 3); Chaldeans (Dan. 3. 8-13); Herodias (Mark 6. 19, 20).
31 hoary head, &c. Illustrations: Jacob (Gen. 47. 9; 48. 1, &c.); Samuel (1 Sam. 12. 2-4; 25. 1); Barzillai (2 Sam. 19. 32, 37); Elisha (2 Kings 13. 14); Jehoiada (2 Chron. 24. 15, 16).
32 the mighty = a mighty one.
than he that taketh a city. Illustration: Jehoshaphat (1 Kings 22. 3, 4. Even if the city had been taken, which it was not).
33 lot = stone. See next note.
lap = bosom (17. 23; 21. 14). The reference is to the bag of the ephod, in which were the two stones by which Jehovah gave true judgment or decision. See notes on Ex. 28. 30. Num. 26. 55. Illustrations: Haman (Est. 3. 7); Jonah (Jonah 1. 7); apostles (Acts 1. 15-26).
the whole disposing = its every decision.
disposing = judgment. Heb. *mishpāt,* as in Num. 27. 21.

17. 1-28 (Y[2], p. 886). PERSONAL CONTENTMENT AND PEACE.

1 Better. See note on 8. 11.
sacrifices = slain beasts. Heb. *zebach.* Ap. 43. II. xii.
3 the LORD. Heb. Jehovah. Ap. 4. II.
trieth the hearts. Illustrations: Abraham (Gen. 22. 1); Israel (Deut. 8. 2); Hezekiah (2 Chron. 32. 31); Martha and Mary (John 11. 5, 6); young man (Matt. 19. 16-22); woman (Matt. 15. 23-28).
4 wicked = mischief maker. Heb. *rā'a'.* Ap. 44. viii.
liar. Heb. "lie". Text not "corrupt"; but "lie" is put by Fig. *Metonymy* (of Effect), Ap. 6, for the man who habitually lies: i.e. a liar is always ready to believe a lie. Illustrations: Ahab (1 Kings 22. 6); Jews (Isa. 30. 9-11. Jer. 5. 30, 31. Mic. 2. 11).

Y[2] (*cont.*)

5 Whoso °mocketh °the poor reproacheth
his °Maker:
And he that is glad at calamities shall not
be °unpunished.
6 °Children's °children *are* the crown of old
men;
And the glory of °children *are* their fathers.
7 Excellent °speech becometh not a °fool:
Much less do [4]lying °lips a prince.
8 A gift *is as* a precious stone in the eyes of
°him that hath it:
Whithersoever it turneth, it °prospereth.
9 He that covereth a °transgression seeketh
love;
But he that repeateth a matter separateth
°*very* friends.
10 A reproof entereth more into a °wise man,
Than an hundred stripes into a °fool.
11 An °evil *man* seeketh only rebellion:
Therefore a cruel messenger shall be sent
against him.
12 Let °a bear robbed of °her whelps meet a
°man,
Rather than a [10]fool in his °folly.
13 Whoso rewardeth [11]evil for good,
[11]Evil shall not depart from his house.
14 The °beginning of strife *is as* °when one
letteth out water:
Therefore leave off contention, before it
°be meddled with.
15 He that °justifieth °the wicked, and he
that condemneth °the just,
Even they both *are* °abomination to [3]the
LORD.
16 °Wherefore *is there* a price in the hand of
a [10]fool to get °wisdom,
Seeing *he hath* no °heart *to it?*
17 A friend °loveth at all times,
And a brother is born for adversity.
18 A °man void of °understanding striketh hands,
And becometh surety in the presence of
his friend.
19 He loveth [9]transgression that loveth strife:
And °he that exalteth his gate seeketh
destruction.
20 He that hath a froward heart findeth no good:
And he that hath a perverse tongue falleth
into mischief.
21 He that begetteth a °fool *doeth it* to his
sorrow:
And the father of a °fool hath no joy.
22 A merry heart doeth good *like* a medicine:
But a broken °spirit drieth the bones.
23 A [15]wicked *man* taketh a °gift out of the
°bosom
To pervert the ways of judgment.
24 [16]Wisdom *is* °before him that hath understanding;
But the eyes of a [10]fool *are* in the ends of
the earth.
25 A [10]foolish son *is* a grief to his father,
And bitterness to her that bare him.
26 Also to punish the just *is* not good,
Nor to strike princes for equity.
27 He that hath knowledge °spareth his words:
And a [12]man of °understanding is of an
°excellent [22]spirit.
28 Even a °fool, when he holdeth his peace,
is counted [10]wise:
And he that shutteth his lips *is esteemed*
a [12]man of °understanding.

5 mocketh. Illustrations: princes of Judah (Isa. 3. 14, 15; 10. 1, 2. Jer. 34. 10, 11); rich (Jas. 5. 4).
the poor = a needy one. Heb. *rūsh*. See note on 6. 11.
Maker. See note on 14. 31.
unpunished = held guiltless. Illustrations: Tyrians (Ezek. 26. 2-6); Edom (Obad. 10-15).
6 Children's = Sons'.
7 speech. Heb. "lip", put by Fig. *Metonymy* (of Cause), Ap. 6, for what is spoken by it.
fool. Heb. *nabal*. See note on 1. 7. Not the same word as in *vv.* 10, 12, 16, 24, 25. **lips.** See above note.
8 him that hath it = its owner (the bribed, not the briber).
prospereth = it sparkles. And he loves to look at it and keep it. Cp. "gift", *v.* 23.
9 transgression. Heb. *pāsha'*. Ap. 44. ix.
very friends = true friends.
10 wise man. Heb. *bīnāh*. See note on 1. 2.
fool. Heb. *k^esīl*. See note on 1. 7.
11 evil = evil worker. Same word as "wicked", *v.* 4.
12 a bear = a he-bear (masc. because it is always construed with a masc. verb).
her whelps = his mate. **man.** Heb. *'ish*. Ap. 14. II.
folly. Heb. *'ĕvīl*. See note on 1. 7.
14 beginning of strife. Illustrations: Ephraimites (Judg. 12. 1-6); Abner (2 Sam. 2. 14-17); Rehoboam (2 Chron. 10. 1-16); Jeroboam (2 Chron. 13. 17); the Twelve (Matt. 20. 24).
when one letteth out = the letting loose (as by making a breach in a dam).
be meddled with = gathereth volume.
15 justifieth the wicked, &c. Illustrations: the counsellors (Ezra 4. 1-16); Tertullus (Acts 24. 1-9); Ahab and Jezebel (1 Kings 21. 5-24). Note the Fig. *Paronomasia* (Ap. 6). *Mazdīk rāshā' umarshīa' ẓadīk*, which may be Englished, "he who wrongs the right and rights the wrong".
the wicked = a lawless one. Heb. *rāshā'*. Ap. 44. x.
the just = a just one.
abomination, &c. See note on 3. 32.
16 Wherefore is there a price, &c. = Why is this ready money in the hand of a fool to get wisdom when he has no sense? Illustrations: Israel (2 Chron. 30. 10); the Jews (Luke 4. 28); Herod Antipas (Luke 23. 11); Jews (John 5. 40; 8. 45); Athenians (Acts 17. 32, 33); Felix (Acts 24. 25-27); Agrippa (Acts 26. 28).
wisdom. Heb. *chākmāh*. See note on 1. 2.
heart. Put by Fig. *Metonymy* (of Subject), Ap. 6, for the sense in it.
17 loveth at all times. Illustrations: Abraham (Gen. 14. 14. Cp. 13. 11); Joseph (Gen. 45. 5; 50. 21); Moses (Ex. 32. 11-13. Deut. 9. 18, 25-29. Cp. Acts 7. 40); Jonathan (1 Sam. 20. 33); Barzillai (2 Sam. 19. 32); Ahikam (Jer. 26. 24); Ebed-melech (Jer. 38. 7); Paul (Philem. 12, 20); Barnabas (Acts 9. 27); Aristarchus (Acts 19. 29; 20. 4; 27. 2. Philem. 24. Col. 4. 10); Luke (2 Tim. 4. 11); Epaphroditus (Phil. 2. 26).
18 man. Heb. *'ādām*. Ap. 14. I.
understanding. Heb. "heart", put by Fig. *Metonymy* (of Cause), Ap. 6, for the understanding in it. See note on 1. 2.
19 he that exalteth his gate, &c.: i.e. a rich man, who thus proclaimed his wealth (Eastern doors being generally low-pitched and uninviting), courted destruction. This explains 2 Kings 25. 9, where "every great man's house he (Nebuchadnezzar) burnt with fire".
21 fool. Heb. *nabal*, as in *v.* 7.
22 spirit. Heb. *rūach*. Ap. 9.
23 gift = bribe. Cp. *v.* 8. This is the act of the briber, not the bribed. **bosom** = lap. See note on 16. 33.
24 before = is the goal of.
27 spareth his words. Illustrations: Aaron (Lev. 10. 3); Moses (Num. 16. 4; 20. 6); Samuel (1 Sam. 8. 6-8); Christ (1 Pet. 2. 23).
understanding = discerning. Heb. *bīnāh*. See note on 1. 2. **excellent** = quiet.
28 fool. Heb. *'ĕvīl*, as in *vv.* 16, 22. See note on 1. 7.
understanding = wisdom (i. e. a wise man).

Y[3] (p. 886)

18 °Through desire a man, having separated himself, seeketh
And °intermeddleth with °all wisdom.
2 A °fool hath no delight in understanding,
But that his heart may °discover itself.
3 When °the wicked cometh, *then* cometh also contempt,
And with °ignominy °reproach.
4 The °words of a °man's mouth *are as* deep waters,
And the wellspring of °wisdom *as* a °flowing brook.
5 *It is* °not good °to accept the person of [3]the wicked,
°To °overthrow °the righteous in judgment.
6 A [2]fool's °lips enter into contention,
And his °mouth calleth for strokes.
7 A [2]fool's mouth *is* his destruction,
And his [6]lips *are* the snare of his °soul.
8 The words of a °talebearer °*are* as wounds,
And they go down into the innermost parts of the belly.
9 He also that is slothful in his work
Is brother to him that is °a great waster.
10 The °name of °the LORD *is* a strong tower:
[5]The righteous runneth into it, and is °safe.
11 The rich man's wealth *is* his strong city,
And °as an high wall in his own °conceit.
12 Before destruction the heart of [4]man °is haughty,
And before honour *is* °humility.
13 He that answereth a matter °before he heareth *it*,
It *is* [2]folly and shame unto him.
14 The °spirit of a [4]man will °sustain his infirmity;
But a wounded °spirit °who can bear?
15 The heart of °the prudent getteth knowledge;
And the ear of °the wise seeketh knowledge.
16 A °man's gift maketh room for him,
And bringeth him before great men.
17 *He that is* °first in his own cause *seemeth* just;
But his neighbour cometh and searcheth him.
18 The lot causeth contentions to cease,
And parteth between the mighty.
19 A brother °offended *is harder to be won* than a strong city:
And *their* contentions *are* like the bars of a castle.
20 A [4]man's belly shall be satisfied with the fruit of his mouth;
And with the increase of his lips shall he be filled.
21 Death and life *are* in the °power of °the tongue:
And they that love it shall eat the fruit thereof.
22 *Whoso* findeth °a wife findeth a good *thing*,
And obtaineth favour of [10]the LORD.
23 °The poor useth intreaties;
But the rich answereth roughly.
24 °A [4]man *that hath* °friends °must shew himself friendly:
And °there is °a friend *that* sticketh closer than a brother.

18. 1-24 (Y[3], p. 886). PERSONAL VIRTUES IN SOCIAL LIFE.

1 Through desire, &c. = Seeking his own pleasure, the recluse (or separatist) breaketh forth (or quarreleth) with everything that is stable.

intermeddleth = breaketh forth. Heb. *gāla'*. See note on "meddle", 17. 14.

all wisdom = everything that is stable. See note on 2 7.

2 fool. Heb. *k^e^sīl*. See note on 1. 7. Same word as in *vv.* 6, 7; not the same as in *v.* 13. **discover** = vent.

3 the wicked = a lawless one. Heb. *rāshā'*. Ap. 44. x.

ignominy = disgrace, or shame (i. e. outward).

reproach = reproachfulness.

4 words. Heb. *dābar*. Ap. 73. x.

man's. Heb. *'īsh*. Ap. 14. II.

wisdom. Heb. *chākmāh*. See note on 1. 2.

flowing brook = a gushing torrent. Heb. *naḥal*.

5 not good. Fig. *Tapeinōsis* (Ap. 6), meaning it is very bad. **to accept the person** = to show partiality.

To. Repeat the Ellipsis: "[It is not good] to".

overthrow = turn aside: i. e. pervert.

the righteous = a righteous one.

6 lips. Put by Fig. *Metonymy* (of Cause), Ap. 6, for what is spoken by them.

mouth. See above note. Illustrations: Judg. 8. 4-17; 2 Kings 2. 23, 24; Luke 19. 22.

7 soul = own self. Heb. *nephesh*. Ap. 13.

8 talebearer = whisperer, or tattler.

are as wounds = are as dainty morsels: i.e. are greedily swallowed.

9 a great waster = a master of destruction: i. e. an absolute destroyer.

10 name = person. See note on Ps. 20. 1.

the LORD. Heb. Jehovah. Ap. 4. II.

safe = set on high. Illustrations: Job (Job 19. 25, 26); Habakkuk (Hab. 3. 17, 19); Asa (2 Chron. 14. 11); Hezekiah (2 Kings 19. 14-20, 32-35. Isa. 38. 1-8); Apostles (Acts 4. 24-33). **11 as** = [it is] as.

conceit = imagination. See note on 25. 11.

12 is haughty. Illustration: Jezebel (2 Kings 9. 30-33).

humility. Cp. 15. 33. Illustration: contrast Goliath (1 Sam. 17. 8-10, 43, 44) with 1 Sam. 17. 45, 47.

13 before he heareth it. Illustrations: David (2 Sam. 16. 4; 19. 24-30); Ahasuerus (Est. 3. 10. Cp. 8. 5, &c.); Darius (Dan. 6. 9. Cp. 6. 14, 18); magistrates (Acts 16. 37-39).

14 spirit. Heb. *rūach*. Ap. 9.

sustain, &c. Illustrations: Job (Job 1. 20, 21; 2. 8, 9, 10); Paul (2 Cor. 12. 9. Acts 22. 24. Rom. 5. 3-5); Paul and Silas (Acts 16. 23-25, 37).

who can bear? Illustrations: Cain (Gen. 4. 13, 14); Eli's daughter-in-law (1 Sam. 4. 19-22. Cp. Prov. 15. 13); Saul (1 Sam. 28. 20; 2 Sam. 1. 9); Ahithophel (2 Sam. 17. 23); Zimri (1 Kings 16. 18); Pashur (Jer. 20. 4); Judas (Matt. 27. 5). **15 the prudent** = a prudent one.

the wise = wise ones.

16 man's. Heb. *'ādām*. Ap. 14. I.

17 first in his own cause. Illustrations: Saul (1 Sam. 15. 13. Cp. *v.* 26); Ziba (2 Sam. 16. 1-3. Cp. 19. 26); Tertullus (Acts 24. 5, 16. Cp. *v.* 13).

19 offended = dealt falsely with.

21 power. Heb. "hand", put by Fig. *Metonymy* (of Cause), Ap. 6, for the power put forth by it.

the tongue. Illustrations: the ten spies (Num. 14. 36, 37); Doeg (1 Sam. 22. 9, 10); Sennacherib (2 Kings 18. 28, 35; 19. 22-35. 2 Chron. 32. 21); Ammonites (Ezek. 25. 3-7); Sapphira (Acts 5. 5-10); Esther (Est. 7 and 8); Paul (Acts 16. 28-34); the Gospel (Rom. 1. 16. 2 Cor. 2. 16).

22 a wife. Some codices, Aram., Sept., Syr., and Vulg., read, "a good wife". Cp. 19. 14.

23 The poor = a needy one. Heb. *rūsh*. See note on 6. 11.

24 A man. A special various reading called *sevīr* reads *yēsh*, instead of *'īsh*, which means "there is", or "there are" instead of "a man". It occurs three times: here, 2 Sam. 14. 19, and Mic. 6. 10. **friends.** Heb. *rē'īm* = feeders, from *rā'āh* to feed (Ps. 23. 1, shepherd). **must shew himself friendly** = who break in pieces. Heb. *Hithpolel* of *rā'ā'* (Ap. 44. viii.) **there is.** Heb. *yēsh*, as in preceding line. **a friend** = a lover (who loves "without cause"). Note the Fig. *Paronomasia* (Ap. 6) in these words, which may be thus represented in English:—

"There are *friends* who *rend* us,
But there is a *lover* who is closer than a *brother*."

Y[4] (p. 886)

19 °Better *is* °the poor that walketh in his integrity,
Than °*he that is* perverse in his °lips, and is a °fool.
2 Also, *that* the °soul *be* without knowledge, *it is* °not good;
And he that °hasteth with *his* feet, °sinneth.
3 The °foolishness of °man °perverteth his way:
And his heart °fretteth against °the LORD.
4 Wealth maketh many friends;
But °the poor is separated from his neighbour.
5 A false witness shall not be °unpunished,
And *he that* °speaketh lies shall not escape.
6 Many will intreat the favour of the prince:
And every man *is* a friend to °him that giveth gifts.
7 All the brethren of [1]the poor do hate him:
How much more do his friends °go far from him?
He °pursueth *them with* words, *yet* they *are* wanting *to him*.
8 He that getteth °wisdom loveth his own [2]soul:
He that keepeth °understanding shall find good.
9 °A false witness shall not be [5]unpunished,
And *he that* [5]speaketh lies shall perish.
10 °Delight is not seemly for a [1]fool;
Much less for a servant to have rule over princes.
11 The discretion of a [3]man °deferreth his anger;
And *it is* his glory to pass over a transgression.
12 The king's wrath *is* as the roaring of a lion;
But his favour *is* as °dew upon the grass.
13 A [1]foolish son °*is* the calamity of his father:
And the contentions of a wife *are* a continual dropping.
14 House and riches *are* the inheritance of fathers:
And °a prudent wife *is* from [3]the LORD.
15 Slothfulness casteth into a deep sleep;
And an idle [2]soul shall suffer hunger.
16 He that °keepeth the commandment °keepeth his own [2]soul;
But he that despiseth his ways shall °die.
17 He that hath pity upon [4]the poor lendeth unto [3]the LORD;
And that which he hath given will He pay him again.
18 °Chasten thy son while there is hope,
And °let not thy [2]soul spare for his crying.
19 °A man of great wrath °shall °suffer punishment:
For if °thou deliver *him*, yet thou must do it again.

D A[1] (p. 891)

20 Hear counsel, and receive °instruction,
That thou mayest be wise in thy latter end.
21 *There are* °many devices in a °man's heart;
°Nevertheless the counsel of [3]the LORD, that shall stand.
22 The desire of a °man °*is* his kindness:
And a [1]poor [21]man *is* °better than °a liar.

19. 1-19 (Y[4], p. 886). PERSONAL CHARACTER, HUMILITY, &c.

1 Better. See note on 8. 11.

the poor = a needy one. Heb. *rūsh.* See note on 6. 11. Same as in *vv.* 7, 22; not the same as in *vv.* 4, 17.

he that is. Fig. *Ellipsis* (Ap. 6), better supplied thus: "Than [the rich that is] perverse", &c.

lips. Put by Fig. *Metonymy* (of Cause), Ap. 6, for what is spoken by them.

fool. Heb. *kᵉsīl.* See note on 1. 7. Same word as in *vv.* 10, 13, 29; not the same as in *v.* 3.

2 soul. Heb. *nephesh.* Ap. 13.

not good. Illustrations: Syrians (1 Kings 20. 28); Jews (Isa. 5. 12, 13); Saul (1 Tim. 1. 13. Acts 26. 11); People and Priests (Hos. 4. 6); Pharisees (Matt. 12. 7); Judah (Hos. 6. 6); Peter (Matt. 16. 22); the rulers (Acts 13. 27. 1 Cor. 2. 8); Job (Job 33. 8, 9; 34. 5, 9, 35; 35. 16; 42. 3, 5, 6); Hezekiah (2 Chron. 32. 31); Peter (Luke 22. 33, 34).

hasteth, &c. Illustrations: Joshua (Josh. 9. 15); Saul (1 Sam. 13. 9, 10, 13, 14; 14. 24-45); David (2 Sam. 16. 4); the Prophet (1 Kings 13. 18, 19); Peter (John 18. 10).

sinneth. Heb. *chāṭā'.* Ap. 44. i.

3 foolishness. Heb. *'ěvīl.* See note on 1. 7. Not the same word as in *vv.* 1, 10, 13, 29.

man. Heb. *'ādām.* Ap. 14. I.

perverteth: or subverteth.

fretteth against = is angry with. Illustrations: Adam (Gen. 3. 12); Cain (Gen. 4. 13, 14); Jehoram (2 Kings 3. 10, 13; 6. 33); Jonah (Jonah 4. 1, 4, 9); Israel (Num. 14. 2, 3; 20. 2-5; 21. 4-6. Deut. 9. 23, 24).

the LORD. Heb. Jehovah. Ap. 4. II.

4 the poor = a weak one. Heb. *dal.* See note on 6. 11. Same word as in *v.* 17; not the same word as in *vv.* 1, 7, 22.

5 unpunished = acquitted, or held innocent.

speaketh = breatheth forth.

6 him that giveth gifts. Heb. a man (*'īsh*, Ap. 14. II) of gifts = a generous man.

7 go far = withdraw.

pursueth, &c.: or, seeketh words [of friendship], but there are none.

8 wisdom. Heb. "heart", put by Fig. *Metonymy* (of Adjunct), Ap. 6, for the understanding. See note on 1. 2.

understanding. Heb. *bīnah.* See note on 1. 2.

9 A false witness, &c. The repetition of *v.* 5 is needed, and punishment is defined. **10 Delight** = Luxury.

11 deferreth his anger. Illustrations: Joseph (Gen. 40. 15); Moses (Num. 12); David (1 Sam. 24; 26. 5, &c.); the Prophet (1 Kings 13. 6, &c.).

12 dew = night mist.

13 is the calamity = is a great trouble to. Heb. "troubles" (pl.) for great trouble. Fig. *Metonymy* (of Effect), Ap. 6, put for action of the foolish son which brings it on. **14 a prudent wife.** See 18. 22.

16 keepeth = guardeth. **die** = die prematurely.

18 Chasten = Correct, or discipline.

let not, &c. This is not a caution against excess of severity, but against a cruel kindness which ends in death, by withholding seasonable correction.

19 A man of great wrath = one in a rage (cp. Dan. 11. 44. Cp. 2 Kings 22. 13). **shall suffer** = suffereth.

suffer punishment = incurreth a penalty. Heb. *'onesh* = a fine, or indemnity. (Oxford Gesenius).

thou deliver = thou rescue him [by paying the penalty] thou must do it continually.

19. 20—24. 34 [For Structure see next page].

20-27 (A[1], p. 891). CALL TO HEAR.

20 instruction = correction, or discipline.

21 many devices = many schemes.

man's. Heb. *'īsh.* Ap. 14. II.

Nevertheless, &c. Illustrations: Joseph's brethren (Gen. 37. 19, &c. Cp. Ps. 76. 10); Pharaoh (Ex. 1. 10. Cp. Ex. 15); the rulers (Matt. 27. 63-66); Saul (Acts 9. 1, 2. Cp. *vv.* 3-9, &c.); Herod (Acts 12. 1-3. Cp. *vv.* 5-19); the forty Jews (Acts 23. 12-15). **22 man.** Heb. *'ādām.* Ap. 14. I. This word stands in relation to *'īsh* in *v.* 21, and to a poor man in next clause = here, the commonest sort of man, or ordinary man. **is, &c.** = is [measured by] his kindness. **better.** See note on 8. 11. **a liar.** Heb. an *'īsh* [a man of the better sort who is] a liar. This proverb does not "remain a riddle".

A[1] (*cont.*) 23 °The fear of [3]the LORD *tendeth* to °life:
And *he that hath it* shall abide satisfied;
He shall not be visited with °evil.
24 A slothful *man* hideth his hand in *his* °bosom,
And will not so much as bring it to his mouth again.
25 Smite a °scorner, and the simple °will beware:
And °reprove one that hath understanding, °*and* he will understand knowledge.
26 He that °wasteth *his* father, *and* chaseth away *his* mother,
Is a son that causeth shame, and bringeth reproach.
27 Cease, °my son, to hear the instruction
That causeth to err from the °words of knowledge.
B[1] (p. 891) 28 °An ungodly witness scorneth judgment:
And the °mouth of °the wicked devoureth °iniquity.
29 Judgments are prepared for scorners,
And stripes for the back of [1]fools.

20 °Wine *is* a °mocker, °strong drink *is* °raging:
And whosoever °is deceived thereby °is not wise.
2 The fear of a king *is* as the roaring of a lion:
Whoso provoketh him to anger °sinneth *against* his own °soul.
3 *It is* an honour for a °man °to cease from strife:
But every °fool will be °meddling.
4 The sluggard will not °plow by reason of the °cold;
°*Therefore* shall he beg in harvest, and *have* nothing.
5 Counsel in the heart of [3]man *is like* deep water;
But a [3]man of understanding will draw it out.
6 Most °men will proclaim °every one °his own goodness:
But a faithful [3]man who can find?
7 The just *man* walketh in his integrity:
His °children *are* °blessed after him.
8 A king that sitteth in the throne of judgment
Scattereth away all °evil with his eyes.
9 Who °can say, "I have made my heart clean,
°I am pure from my [2]sin?"
10 Divers °weights, *and* divers °measures,
Both of them *are* alike °abomination to °the LORD.

19. 20—24. 34 (**D**, p. 864). PROVERBS **FOR** SOLOMON (22. 17; 24. 23); **FOR A PRINCE AND A** KING (20. 2, 8, 26; 21. 1). SECOND PERSON. (See below.) (*Repeated and Extended Alternation.*)

D | A[1] | 19. 20-27. Call to hear.
B[1] | 19. 28—21. 1. Personal conduct.
C[1] | 21. 2—22. 16. Personal character.
A[2] | 22. 17-21. Call to hear.
B[2] | 22. 22-29. Personal conduct.
C[2] | 23. 1-21. Personal character.
A[3] | 23. 22-25. Call to hear.
B[3] | 23. 26-35. Personal conduct.
C[3] | 24. 1-20. Personal character.
A[4] | 24. 21, 22. Call to hear.
B[4] | 24. 23-29. Personal conduct.
C[4] | 24. 30-34. Personal character.

D is addressed to "MY SON" (19. 27; 23. 15, 19, 26; 24. 13, 21); and is all in the Second Person: "THOU" (19. 20; 22. 24, 25, 26, 27; 23. 1, 5, 6, 13, 14, 19, 31, 34; 24. 1, 10, 11, 12); "THEE" (22. 19, 20, 21, 27; 23. 7); "THY" (22. 18; 23. 16, 22, 25; 24. 10, 27, 34); "THINE" (23. 12, 15, 17, 18, 19, 33); "THYSELF" (24. 27).

23 The fear of the LORD. See note on 1. 7.
life. Heb. pl. implying resurrection and eternal life.
evil. Heb. *rāʻaʻ*. Ap. 44. viii.
24 bosom = bowl or wide dish. 2 Kings 21. 13. 2 Chron. 35. 13. Cp. Matt. 26. 23.
25 scorner = scoffer.
will beware = will be made wise (note the force of the *Hiphil*). Illustrations: Israel (Ex. 14. 31); the stubborn (Deut. 21. 21); Gibeonites (Josh. 9. 3); Sergius Paulus (Acts 13. 6-12). **reprove** = set right.
and he will understand knowledge = will cause teaching to be discerned. Cp. 22. 17.
26 wasteth = preyeth upon.
27 my son. The presence of this word here and in 23. 15, 19, 26; 24. 13, 21, together with the employment of the second person, shows that these are proverbs *for* Solomon. See note under Structure above.
words = sayings. Heb. *'imrah*. Ap. 73. v.

19. 28—21. 1 (B[1], above). PERSONAL CONDUCT.
28 An ungodly witness. Heb. "A witness of Belial": i.e. a false witness.
mouth. Put by Fig. *Metonymy* (of Cause), Ap. 6, for the witness given by it.
the wicked = lawless ones. Heb. *rāshāʻ*. Ap. 44. x.
iniquity. Heb. *'āven*. Ap. 44. iii.

20. 1 Wine. Heb. *yayin*. See Ap. 27. I.
is. Fig. *Metaphor*. Ap. 6. **mocker** = scoffer.
strong drink. Heb. *shēkār*. Ap. 27. IV
raging = a brawler.
is deceived = erreth. Heb. *shāgah* = to go astray. See note on 11. 18. Not the same word as in *v.* 17.
is not wise. Illustrations: Noah (Gen. 7. 1. Cp. 9. 20, 21); Nabal (1 Sam. 25. 36); Elah (1 Kings 16. 8-10); Ben-hadad (1 Kings 20. 16-21); Ephraim (Isa. 28. 7); Belshazzar, &c. (Dan. 5. Jer. 51. 39, 57); Nineveh (Nah. 1. 10); and probably Nadab and Abihu (Lev. 10. 8, 9).
2 sinneth = erreth. Heb. *chāṭā'*. Ap. 44. i.

soul. Heb. *nephesh*. Ap. 13. **3 man.** Heb. *'īsh*. Ap. 14. II. **to cease from strife.** Illustrations: Abraham (Gen. 13. 7-9. Cp. Prov. 17. 14); David (1 Sam. 25. 32-34). **fool.** Heb. *'ěvīl*. See note on 1. 7. **meddling** = breaking out. See notes on 17. 14; 18. 1. The only other occurrences of *gālaʻ*. Not the same word as in *v.* 19. **4 plow.** Plowing always done during the early rains. **cold** = autumn. Put by Fig. *Metalepsis*, Ap. 6, "cold" put for Autumn, and "Autumn" put for abundance of fruits possessed at that time. **Therefore.** This word is read in the text in some codices, with five early printed editions. **6 men.** Heb. *'ādām*. Ap. 14. I. **every one.** Heb. *'īsh 'īsh*. Ap. 14. II. **his own goodness.** Illustrations: Absalom (2 Sam. 15. 4); Jehu (2 Kings 10. 16, 31); Scribes, &c. (Matt. 6. 2; 23. 5); the rich young man (Matt. 19. 20, 22). **7 children** = sons. **blessed** = happy. See note on 3. 13. **8 evil.** Heb. *rāʻaʻ*. Ap. 44. viii. **9 can** = is able to. **I am pure, &c.** Illustrations: Job before he learned his lesson (Job 9. 17; 10. 7; 11. 4; 16. 17; 23. 10, 11; 27. 5; 29. 14; 31. 1; cp. 33. 9. But not after, see 42. 5, 6). None of God's own people say this. Not David (2 Sam. 12. 13. Cp. Ps. 51. 1-7); not Psalmist (119. 176); not Ezra (Ezra 9. 6); not Nehemiah (Neh. 9. 33, 34); not Isaiah (Isa. 6. 5, 6); not Daniel (Dan. 9. 8); not Peter (Luke 5. 8); not John (1 John 1. 8); not James (Jas. 3. 2); not Paul (Rom. 7. 18. 1 Tim. 1. 15). **10 weights . . . measures.** Heb. "a stone and a stone, an ephah and an ephah". Ephah put by Fig. *Synecdoche* (of Species), Ap. 6, for all kinds of weights and measures. There is no word for "divers" = diverse. **abomination, &c.** Cp. *v.* 23, and 11. 1; 16. 11, &c. See note on 3. 32, and cp. Deut. 25. 13, &c. **the LORD.** Heb. Jehovah. Ap. 4. II.

B[1] (*cont.*)

11 Even a child is known by his doings,
Whether his work *be* °pure, and whether *it be* °right.
12 The °hearing ear, and the seeing eye,
[10] The LORD hath made even both of them.
13 Love not sleep, lest thou °come to poverty;
Open thine eyes, *and* thou shalt be satisfied with bread.
14 "*It is* °naught, *it is* °naught," saith the buyer:
But when he is gone his way, then he boasteth.
15 There is gold, and a multitude of rubies:
But the lips of knowledge *are* a precious jewel.
16 Take his garment that is surety *for* a °stranger:
And take a °pledge of him for a °strange woman.
17 °Bread of °deceit *is* sweet to a [3] man;
But afterwards his mouth shall be °filled with gravel.
18 *Every* purpose is established by counsel:
And with good advice make war.
19 He that goeth about *as* a talebearer revealeth secrets:
Therefore °meddle not with him that flattereth with his °lips.
20 Whoso °curseth his father or his mother,
His °lamp shall be put out in obscure darkness.
21 An inheritance *may be* gotten hastily at the beginning;
But the end thereof shall not be °blessed.
22 Say not thou, "I will recompense [8] evil;"
But wait °on [10] the LORD, and He shall save thee.
23 Divers [10] weights *are* an °abomination unto [10] the LORD;
And a false balance *is* not good.
24 °Man's goings *are* of [10] the LORD;
How can a °man then understand his own way?
25 *It is* a snare to the [24] man *who* °devoureth *that which is* °holy,
And after vows to make enquiry.
26 A wise king °scattereth the °wicked,
And bringeth °the wheel over them.
27 The °spirit of [24] man *is* the °candle of [10] the LORD,
Searching all the inward parts of °the belly.
28 °Mercy and truth preserve the king:
And his throne is upholden by °mercy.
29 The glory of young men *is* their strength:
And the beauty of old men *is* the gray head.
30 The blueness of a wound °cleanseth away °evil:
So *do* stripes the inward parts of the °belly.

21 The king's heart *is* in the hand of °the LORD, *as* °the rivers of water:
°He turneth it whithersoever He will.

C[1] (p. 891)

2 Every way of a °man *is* right in his own eyes:
But [1] the LORD °pondereth the hearts.

11 pure = accurate. **right** = correct.

12 hearing ear, &c. Illustrations: Moses (Ex. 4. 11); Hagar (Gen. 21. 19); Elisha's servant (2 Kings 6. 17); Lydia (Acts 16. 14).

13 come to poverty = become dispossessed. Heb. *yārash*. See note on 6. 11.

14 naught . . . naught = very bad. Fig. *Epizeuxis* (Ap. 6), for emphasis.

16 stranger = apostate. Heb. *zūr*. See notes on 2. 16; 5. 3.

pledge of him. Supply Fig. *Ellipsis* (Ap. 6), "[Who has become security for] a foreign woman."

strange woman = foreign woman. Heb. *nākar*. See notes on 2. 16; 5. 3.

17 Bread of deceit = Bread gained by deceit. Genitive of Origin. See Ap. 17 (2).

Bread. Put by Fig. *Synecdoche* (of Part), Ap. 6, for all kinds of food.

deceit = lying. Heb. *sheḳer*. See note on 11. 18.

filled with gravel: or grit. See note on Gen. 3. 14, implying utmost disappointment. See Ap. 19.

19 meddle = mingle, mix thyself up. Not the same word as in *v.* 3.

lips. Put by Fig. *Metonymy* (of Cause) for the flattery spoken by them (Ap. 6).

20 curseth = revileth.

lamp shall be put out. A Fig. *Hypocatastasis* (Ap. 6), denoting that he shall die childless.

21 blessed = happy. See note on 3. 13.

22 on = for.

23 abomination, &c. See note on 3. 32.

24 Man's = A strong man's. Heb. *geber*. Ap. 14. IV.

man = an ordinary man. Heb. *'ādām*. Ap. 14. I.

25 devoureth = rashly promises.

holy. See note on Ex. 3. 5.

26 scattereth = winnoweth out.

wicked = lawless. Heb. *rāshā'*. Ap. 44. x.

the wheel: i.e. of the threshing instrument. Cp. Isa. 28. 27.

27 spirit = breath. Heb. *n^eshāmāh*. See Ap. 16.

candle = lamp or light. Same word as in *v.* 20.

the belly. Put by Fig. *Metalepsis* (Ap. 6) for the heart, and the heart for its thoughts.

28 Mercy = lovingkindness, grace, or favour.

30 cleanseth away = is cleansing. Supply the Ellipsis (Ap. 6), "[though it be] an evil".

evil. Heb. *rā'a'*. Ap. 44. viii.

belly. Supply the Ellipsis from preceding clause, "[though they be an evil]"

21. 1 the LORD. Heb. Jehovah. Ap. 4. II.

the rivers of water. Heb. *palgēy mayīm* = the divisions of water [in a garden], from *palag*, to divide (Gen. 10. 25). The name given to the small channels which divide up an Eastern (walled) garden for purposes of irrigation. See note on "rivers", Ps. 1. 3. There is an Ellipsis in the second clause, and the verb must be supplied thus:

The king's heart [is] in the hand of Jehovah,
As the *palgēy mayīm* [are in the hand of the gardener].

See Ap. 74.

He turneth, &c. i. e. Jehovah directeth [the king's heart] whithersoever He will [as the gardener directeth the water with his foot] (Deut. 11. 10), not needing or deigning to use a tool; so easily is it done. Illustrations: Ahab (1 Kings 18. 10. Cp. *v.* 40); Ahasuerus (Est. 6. 1); Sennacherib (2 Kings 19. 27, 28, and Isa. 10. 5–7); Nebuchadnezzar (Ezek. 29. 16. Jer. 43. 10–12); the Jews (Jer. 32. 28. 2 Kings 24. 3); Cyrus (Ezra 1. 1. Isa. 45. 1); Darius (Ezra 6. 22); Augustus (Luke 2. 1–7. Cp. Mic. 5. 2).

21. 2—22. 16 (C[1], p. 891). PERSONAL CHARACTER.

2 man. Heb. *'īsh*. Ap. 14. II.

pondereth = weigheth, and thus testeth. See all the occurrences of *tākan*, to poise. 1 Sam. 2. 3. 2 Kings 12. 11 ("told"). Job 28. 25. Ps. 75. 3 (bear up). Prov. 16. 2; 21. 2 (pondereth); 24. 12 (pondereth). Isa. 40. 12 (meted), 13 (directed). In Ezekiel the *Niphal* is rendered "equal": 18. 25, 29; 33. 17, 20.

C[1] (cont.)

3 To do °justice and judgment
Is °more acceptable to [1]the LORD than sacrifice.
4 An high look, and a proud heart,
°*And* the °plowing of °the wicked, *is* °sin.
5 The °thoughts of °the diligent *tend* only to plenteousness;
But of every one *that is* hasty only to want.
6 The getting of treasures by a lying tongue
Is a vanity tossed to and fro of them that seek death.
7 The °robbery of [4]the wicked shall destroy them;
Because they refuse to do judgment.
8 °The way of [2]man *is* froward and strange:
But *as for* the °pure, his work *is* right.
9 *It is* °better to dwell in a corner of the housetop,
Than with a brawling woman in a wide house.
10 The °soul of °the [4]wicked desireth °evil:
His neighbour findeth no favour in his eyes.
11 When the °scorner is punished, the simple is made wise:
And when the wise is °instructed, he receiveth knowledge.
12 The righteous *man* wisely considereth the house of [10]the [4]wicked:
But God overthroweth [4]the wicked for *their* °wickedness.
13 Whoso stoppeth his ears at the cry of the °poor,
He also shall cry himself, but shall not be °heard.
14 A gift in secret pacifieth anger:
And a reward in the bosom strong wrath.
15 *It is* joy to °the just to do judgment:
But destruction *shall be* to the workers of °iniquity.
16 The °man that wandereth out of the way of understanding
Shall remain in the °congregation of the °dead.
17 He that loveth pleasure *shall be* a °poor [2]man:
He that loveth °wine and oil shall not be rich.
18 [10]The [4]wicked *shall be* a ransom for °the righteous,
And the °transgressor for the upright.
19 *It is* [9]better to dwell in the wilderness,
°Than with a contentious and an angry woman.
20 *There is* treasure to be desired and oil in the dwelling of the wise;
But a °foolish [16]man °spendeth it up.
21 He that followeth after righteousness and °mercy
Findeth life, righteousness, and honour.
22 A wise *man* scaleth the city of the mighty,
And °casteth down the strength of the confidence thereof.
23 Whoso °keepeth his °mouth and his °tongue
Keepeth his [10]soul from °troubles.
24 Proud *and* haughty [11]scorner *is* his name,
Who dealeth in proud wrath.
25 The desire of the slothful killeth him;
For his hands refuse to labour.
26 He °coveteth greedily all the day long:
But the righteous giveth and spareth not.
27 The sacrifice of [4]the wicked *is* abomination:
How much more, *when* he bringeth it with a wicked °mind?
28 A false witness °shall perish:
But the [2]man that heareth °speaketh constantly.
29 A [4]wicked [2]man hardeneth his face:
But *as for* the upright, he °directeth his way.
30 *There is* °no wisdom nor understanding
Nor counsel against [1]the LORD.
31 The horse *is* prepared against the day of battle:
But °safety *is* of [1]the LORD.

3 justice=righteousness.
more acceptable, &c. Illustrations: Saul (1 Sam. 13. 10-13; 15. 22); Israel (Jer. 7. 22, 23. Amos 5. 21-24); Judah (Isa. 1. 11-17); Pharisees (Matt. 9. 13). Note the contrast, *v.* 4. **4 And.** Omit this "And".
plowing: or tillage. See Ap. 74.
the wicked=lawless ones. Heb. *rāshā'*. Ap. 44. x.
sin. Heb. *chāṭā'*. Ap. 44. i. The special word for the sin offering. Render the verse "A lofty look and a proud heart, [which is] the tillage of the lawless, [is more acceptable to them than] the sin offering." This supply of the Ellipsis (Ap. 6. III) from the preceding verse completes the sense, and shows that the two are strictly related.
5 thoughts=reckonings, or calculatings.
the diligent=a diligent one.
7 robbery=rapacity. Illustrations: the princes of Judah (Isa. 1. 23, 24); the Jews (Jer. 7. 9-11, 15; 34. 10-22. Mic. 3. 9-12).
8 The way, &c. Render, "The way of a man laden with guilt is unsteady". Some codices, with Aram. and Syr., read "of a man who is an alien".
pure=upright. **9 better.** See note on 8. 11.
10 soul. Heb. *nephesh*. Ap. 13.
the wicked=a lawless one.
evil. Heb. *ra'a'*. Ap. 44. viii.
11 scorner=scoffer. **instructed**=corrected.
12 wickedness. Heb. *ra'a'*. Ap. 44. viii, same as "evil" in *v.* 10.
13 poor=weak. Heb. *dal*. See note on 6. 11.
heard=answered. Illustrations: the Jews (Zech. 7. 9-14. Jer. 34. 10-22); Parable (Matt. 18. 30-34).
15 the just=a just one.
iniquity. Heb. *'āven*. Ap. 44. iii.
16 man. Heb. *'ādām*. Ap. 14. I.
congregation=assembly.
dead=the Rephaim, who have no resurrection. See note on "deceased" and "dead" in Isa. 26. 14, 19, and Ap. 25.
17 poor=destitute. Heb *ḥeser*. See note on 6. 11.
wine. Heb. *yayin*. Ap. 27. I.
18 the righteous=a righteous one.
transgressor=traitor.
19 Than, &c. Supply the Ellipsis thus: Than [in a house, or palace].
20 foolish. Heb. *k^esîl*. See note on 1. 7.
spendeth it up=swalloweth it up.
21 mercy=lovingkindness, or grace.
22 casteth down. Illustrations: Joshua (Josh. 6. 3-21; 8. 4-8); wise woman (2 Sam. 20. 16-22. Cp. Ecc. 9. 13-15).
23 keepeth=guardeth.
mouth . . . tongue. Put by Fig. *Metonymy* (of Cause), Ap. 6, for what is uttered by them.
troubles. Some codices, with five early printed editions, Aram., Sept., and Syr., read "trouble" (sing.).
26 coveteth greedily=craving he craveth. Fig. *Polyptōton* (Ap. 6), for emphasis. **27 mind**=purpose.
28 shall perish. Illustrations: Pashur (Jer. 20. 4-6); Hananiah (Jer. 28. 1-4, 10-17); the false prophets (Jer. 29. 21); Shemaiah (Jer. 29. 31, 32); Amaziah (Amos 7. 10-17).
speaketh. Supply the Ellipsis (Ap. 6), "speaketh [the truth] evermore."
30 no wisdom . . . against the LORD. Illustrations: Pharaoh (Ex. 1. 10. See Ap. 23); Balak (Num. 24. 10); Ahaziah (2 Kings 1. 9-17); Sennacherib (2 Chron. 32. 21; Isa. 30. 31); Haman (Est. 5. 11-13; 7. 10).
31 safety, &c.=to Jehovah [belongeth] the salvation.

22 A good °name *is* rather to be chosen than great riches,
And loving favour rather than silver and gold.
2 The rich and ° poor meet together:
°The LORD *is* the Maker of them all.
3 A prudent *man* foreseeth the °evil, and hideth himself:
But the °simple pass on, and °are punished.
4 °By humility *and* °the fear of [2]the LORD
Are riches, and honour, and °life.
5 Thorns °*and* snares *are* in the way of the °froward:
He that doth keep his °soul shall be far from them.
6 °Train up a child °in the way he should go:
And when he is old, he will not depart from it.
7 °The rich ruleth over °the [2]poor,
And the borrower °*is* servant to the lender.
8 He that soweth °iniquity shall reap vanity:
And the rod of his anger °shall fail.
9 He that hath a bountiful eye shall be blessed;
For he giveth of his bread to °the poor.
10 Cast out the °scorner, and contention °shall go out;
Yea, strife and reproach shall cease.
11 °He that loveth °pureness of heart,
For the grace of his lips the king *shall be* his friend.
12 The eyes of [2]the LORD °preserve knowledge,
And He overthroweth the °words of the °transgressor.
13 The slothful *man* saith, *"There is* a lion without,
I shall be slain in the °streets."
14 The mouth of °strange women *is* a deep pit:
He that is abhorred of [2]the LORD shall fall therein.
15 °Foolishness *is* bound in the heart of a child;
But the rod of correction shall drive it far from him.
16 He that oppresseth [9]the poor to increase his *riches,*
And he that giveth to [7]the rich, *shall* surely *come* to want.

A[2] (p. 891) 17 Bow down thine ear, and hear the °words of the wise,
And apply °thine °heart unto °my °knowledge.
18 For *it is* a pleasant thing if thou keep them within thee;
They shall withal be fitted in thy lips.
19 That thy °trust may °be in [2]the LORD,
I have made known to °thee this day, even to °thee.
20 Have not I written °to thee °excellent things
°In counsels and knowledge,
21 That I might make thee know the certainty of the °words of truth;
That thou mightest answer the °words of truth to them that °send unto thee?

B[2] 22 Rob not [9]the poor, because he *is* poor:
Neither oppress °the afflicted in the gate:
23 For [2]the LORD will plead their cause,
And spoil the [5]soul of those that spoiled them.
24 Make no friendship with °an angry man;
And with a furious °man thou shalt not go:

22. 1 name. Note the Ellipsis (Ap. 6), and supply "good" from Ecc. 7. 1.

2 poor = needy. Heb. *rūsh.* See note on 6. 11. Same word as in *v.* 7. Not the same word as in *vv.* 9, 16, 22.

The LORD. Heb. Jehovah. Ap. 4. II.

3 evil = mischief. Heb. *rā'a'.* Ap. 44. viii.

simple. See note on 1. 4.

are punished = suffer for it, or pay the penalty.

4 By humility, &c. = The reward of humility [that is] the fear of the Jehovah, will be, &c.

the fear of the LORD. See note on 1. 7.

life: i.e. resurrection and eternal life. See note on Lev. 18. 5; not necessarily long life on earth.

5 and. Sept., Syr., and Vulg. read this "and" in the text.

froward = perverse. See note on 2. 12, 15; 3. 32. Illustrations: Israel (Judg. 2. 2, 3. Josh. 23. 12, 13; contrast with Josh. 21. 43-45; 24. 31); Ahab (1 Kings 17. 1; 18. 5; 21. 4, 20; 22. 6, 37). **soul.** Heb. *nephesh.* Ap. 13.

6 Train up = Hedge in: i.e. straiten him in, as cattle are guided.

in the way he should go = concerning his way. Heb. at the mouth of his way: "mouth" being put by Fig. *Metonymy* (of Adjunct), Ap. 6, for the opening or beginning of his way. C. H. Spurgeon applied it to "the way you wish you had gone yourself"!

7 The rich = a rich one. **the poor** = poor ones.

is servant, &c. Illustrations: the widow (2 Kings 4. 1); the Jews (Neh. 5. 3, 5).

8 iniquity = trickery. Heb. *'āval.* Ap. 44. vi. Illustration: Rebekah (Gen. 27. 6-17, 41-46).

shall fail. Illustrations: Balak (Num. 24. 10); Solomon (1 Kings 11. 14, 23, and 1 Kings 11. 31, 40); Ahaziah (2 Kings 1. 9-17); Sennacherib (2 Chron. 32. 21. Isa. 30. 31); Haman (Est. 5. 11-13; 7. 10). See note on 21. 30.

9 the poor = a weak one. Heb. *dal.* Same word as in *vv.* 16, 22. Not the same word as in *vv.* 2, 7. See note on 6. 11. **10 scorner** = scoffer.

shall go out. Illustration: Ishmael (Gen. 21. 9-12. Cp. Gal. 4. 29).

11 He that, &c. Aram., Sept., and Syr., read "Jehovah". **pureness of heart** = one pure of heart.

12 preserve = guard.

words: or affairs. Heb. *dābar.* Ap. 73. x.

transgressor = traitor. Heb. *bāgad.* Illustrations: Ahithophel (2 Sam. 17. 14); Noadiah (Neh. 6. 14-16); Ezra's opponents (Ezra 3. 3, 13. Cp. ch. 5 and 6); the Sanhedrin (Acts 5. 34). **13 streets** = open places.

14 strange = apostate. Heb. *zūr.* See notes on 2. 16 and 5. 3.

15 Foolishness. Heb. *'ĕvil.* See note on 1. 7.

17-21 (A[2], p. 891). CALL TO HEAR.

17 words of the wise. See the Structure of the whole book (p. 864). Referring to the wise men by whom Solomon was surrounded, such as Ethan, Heman, Chalcol, and Darda, the sons of Mahol (1 Kings 4. 31).

thine. Note the continuation of the second person, "the words of the wise" being addressed to Solomon.

heart. Put by Fig. *Metonymy* (of Subject), Ap. 6, for thoughts and powers.

my. Note the writer's personality as being other than Solomon. **knowledge** = teaching.

19 trust = confidence. Heb. *baṭaḥ.* See Ap. 69. i.

be = come to be.

thee. Note the emphasis on the second person.

20 to thee = for thee. See the Structure (p. 891).

excellent things. Heb. marg. reads "formerly", or "before". **In** = With.

21 words = sayings, or utterances. Heb. *'imrah.* See Ap. 73. v.

send unto = inquire of. Illustration: the queen of Sheba (1 Kings 10).

22-29 (B[2], p. 891). PERSONAL CONDUCT.

22 the afflicted = a wretched one. Heb. *'anī.* See note on 6. 11.

24 an angry man = a lord, or master, of anger.

man. Heb. *'īsh.* Ap. 14. II.

25 Lest thou learn his ways,
And get a snare to thy [5] soul.
26 Be not thou *one* of them that strike hands,
Or of them that are sureties for debts.
27 If thou hast nothing to pay,
Why should °he take away thy bed from under thee?
28 Remove not the °ancient °landmark,
Which thy fathers have set.
29 °Seest thou a °man diligent in his business? he shall stand before kings;
He shall not stand before °mean *men*.

C² (p. 891)
23 °When °thou sittest to eat with a ruler,
°Consider diligently °what *is* before thee:
2 °And put a knife to thy throat,
If thou *be* °a man given to °appetite.
3 Be not desirous of his °dainties:
For they *are* °deceitful meat.
4 °Labour not to be rich:
Cease from thine own °wisdom.
5 Wilt thou set thine eyes upon that which is not?
°For *riches* certainly make themselves wings;
They fly away as an eagle toward heaven.
6 Eat thou not the bread of *him that hath* an °evil eye,
Neither desire thou his [3] dainty meats:
7 For as he °thinketh in his °heart, so *is* he:
"Eat and drink," saith he to thee;
But his heart *is* not with thee.
8 The morsel *which* thou hast eaten shalt thou vomit up,
And lose thy sweet words.
9 Speak not in the ears of a °fool:
For °he will despise the °wisdom of thy °words.
10 Remove not the °old landmark;
And enter not into the °fields of the °fatherless:
11 For their °Redeemer *is* mighty;
He shall plead their cause with thee.
12 Apply thine heart unto instruction,
And thine ears to the words of knowledge.
13 Withhold not correction from the °child:
For *if* thou beatest him with the rod, he shall not die.
14 Thou shalt beat him with the rod,
And shalt °deliver his °soul from °hell.
15 My son, if thine heart be wise,
My heart shall rejoice, even mine.
16 Yea, my °reins shall rejoice,
When thy lips speak right things.
17 Let not thine heart envy °sinners:
But *be thou* in °the fear of °the LORD all the day long.
18 For surely there is °an end;
And thine °expectation shall not be cut off.
19 Hear thou, °my son, and be wise,
And guide thine heart in the way.
20 Be not among °winebibbers;
Among riotous °eaters of flesh:
21 For the drunkard and the glutton shall come to °poverty:
And drowsiness shall clothe *a man* with rags.

A³
22 °Hearken unto °thy father that begat thee,
And despise not thy mother when she is old.
23 Buy the truth, and sell *it* not;
Also °wisdom, and instruction, and understanding.
24 The father of °the righteous shall greatly rejoice:
And he that begetteth a wise *child* shall have joy of him.
25 [22] Thy father and thy mother shall be glad,
And she that bare thee shall rejoice.
26 [19] My son, give me thine °heart, B³
And let thine eyes °observe my ways.

---

27 he: i. e. the usurer. **28 ancient** = age-long.
landmark = boundary stone.
29 Seest thou . . . ? Fig. *Erotēsis*. Ap. 6.
man. Heb. *'īsh*. Ap. 14. II.
mean = mean ones: i. e. men who are obscure.

23. 1-21 (C², p. 891). PERSONAL CHARACTER.

1 When = Forasmuch as. Taking the act for granted.
thou. The second person is continued down to *v.* 24.
Consider = Discern. **what**: or, who.
2 And put = Then thou wilt put.
a man given, &c. Illustrations: Esau (Gen. 25. 30); Isaac (Gen. 25. 28; 27. 4); those referred to in Phil. 3. 18, 19.
appetite = soul. Heb. *nephesh*. Ap. 13.
3 dainties = dainty meals.
deceitful meat = meat that deceives. Heb. *kazah*. See note on 11. 18.
4 Labour not, &c. Illustrations: Lot (Gen. 13. 10, 13); the rich fool (Luke 12. 16-20. Cp. Prov. 10. 16). See Jeremiah's advice (Jer. 45. 5).
wisdom. Heb. *bīnāh*. See note on 1. 2. Not the same word as in *vv.* 9, 23.
5 For. This is the reason why "it is gone".
6 evil. Heb. *rā'a'*. Ap. 44. viii.
7 thinketh, &c. = estimates himself.
heart = soul. Heb. *nephesh*. Ap. 13.
9 fool. Heb. *kᵉsīl*. See note on 1. 7.
he will despise. Illustration: Amaziah (2 Chron. 25. 16).
wisdom = intelligence. Heb. *sekel*. See note on 1. 2. Not the same word as in *vv.* 4, 23.
words = sayings. Heb. *millāh* = discourse.
10 old landmark = ancient boundary. Cp. 22. 28.
fields. Some codices, with Aram., Sept., Syr., and Vulg., read "field" (sing.).
fatherless. Put by Fig. *Synecdoche* (of Species), Ap. 6 for all bereaved ones.
11 Redeemer = kinsman-redeemer. Heb. *gā'al*. See note on Ex. 6. 6; 13. 13. **13 child** = youth.
14 deliver = rescue. **soul.** Heb. *nephesh*. Ap. 13.
hell = hades. See Ap. 35.
16 reins = kidneys. Put by Fig. *Metonymy* (of Adjunct), Ap. 6, for affections and impulses.
17 sinners. Heb. *chāṭā'*. Ap. 44. i.
the fear of the LORD. See note on 1. 7.
the LORD. Heb. Jehovah. Ap. 4. II.
18 an end = a hereafter, or latter end.
expectation. Heb. *tiḳvah*. See note on 10. 28.
19 my son. Note the characteristic of this member **D** (p. 891).
20 winebibbers. Heb. *yayin* (Ap. 27. i) and *ṣābā'* = drinkers to excess. **eaters of flesh** = selfish eaters.
21 poverty = dispossession. Heb. *yārash*. See note on 6. 11.

22-25 (A³, p. 891). CALL TO HEAR.

22 Hearken. This determines the Structure (p. 891).
thy father. Note this mark of "Proverbs FOR Solomon". See the Structure of **D** (p. 891).
23 wisdom. Heb. *chākmāh*. See note on 1. 2. Not the same word as in *vv.* 4, 8.
24 the righteous = a just one.

26-33 (B³, p. 891). PERSONAL CONDUCT.

26 heart. Put by Fig. *Metonymy* (of Adjunct), Ap. 6, for attention. **observe** = delight in.

27 For a whore *is* a deep ditch;
And a °strange woman *is* a narrow pit.
28 She also lieth in wait as *for* a prey,
And increaseth the °transgressors among °men.
29 Who hath woe? who hath sorrow? who hath contentions?
Who hath babbling? who hath wounds without cause?
Who hath redness of eyes?
30 They that tarry long at the °wine;
They that go to seek °mixed wine.
31 Look not thou upon the [30]wine when it is red,
When it giveth °his colour in the cup,
When it moveth itself aright.
32 At the last it biteth like a serpent,
And stingeth like an adder.
33 Thine eyes shall behold °strange women,
And thine heart shall utter perverse things.
34 Yea, thou shalt be as he that lieth down in the °midst of the sea,
Or as he that lieth upon the °top of a mast.
35 "They have stricken me," *shalt thou say,* "*and* I was not sick;
They have beaten me, *and* I °felt *it* not:
When shall I awake? I will seek it yet again."

C^3 (p. 891)

24 °Be not thou envious against °evil °men,
Neither desire to be with them.
2 For their heart studieth destruction,
And their lips talk of °mischief.
3 Through °wisdom is an house builded;
And by understanding it is established:
4 And by knowledge shall the °chambers be filled
With all precious and pleasant riches.
5 °A wise °man *is* strong;
Yea, °a man of knowledge °increaseth strength.
6 For by wise counsel thou shalt make thy war:
And in °multitude of counsellers *there is* safety.
7 °Wisdom °*is* too high for a °fool:
He °openeth not his mouth in the gate.
8 He that deviseth to do [1]evil
Shall be called a °mischievous person.
9 The °thought of °foolishness *is* °sin:
And the °scorner *is* an abomination to °men.
10 °*If* thou faint in the day of adversity,
Thy strength *is* small.
11 °If thou forbear to °deliver *them that are* °drawn unto death,
And *those that are* ready to be slain;
12 If thou sayest, "Behold, we °knew it not;"
Doth not He that pondereth the heart consider *it?*
And He that keepeth thy °soul, doth *not* He know *it?*
And shall *not* He render to *every* [9]man according to his works?
13 °My son, eat thou honey, because *it is* good;
And the honeycomb, *which is* sweet to thy taste:
14 So *shall* the knowledge of [3]wisdom *be* unto thy [12]soul:
When thou hast found *it,* then there shall be a reward,
And thy expectation shall not be °cut off.
15 Lay not wait, O °wicked *man,* against the dwelling of °the righteous;
Spoil not his resting place:
16 For a °just *man* falleth seven times, and riseth up again:
But °the [15]wicked shall fall into °mischief.
17 °Rejoice not when thine enemy falleth,
And let not thine heart be glad when he stumbleth:
18 Lest °the LORD see *it,* and it displease Him,
And He turn away His wrath °from him.

---

27 strange = foreign. Heb. *nākar.* See note on 2. 16; 5. 3. Not the same word as in *v.* 33.
28 transgressors = traitors.
men. Heb. *'ādām.* Ap. 14. I.
30 wine. Heb. *yayin.* Ap. 27. I.
mixed wine. Heb. *mimṣāk.* See Ap. 27. VII.
31 his colour = its sparkle.
33 strange = apostate. Heb. *zūr.* See note on 2. 16; 5. 3. Not the same word as in *v.* 27.
34 midst. Heb. "heart".
top = basket: i.e. the look-out basket or cradle on the [mast.
35 felt = knew.

24. 1-20 (C^3, p. 891). PERSONAL CHARACTER.
1 Be not thou envious = Do not get excited. Cp. 23. 17. evil. Heb. *rā'a'.* Ap. 44. viii.
men. Heb. *'ĕnōsh.* Ap. 14. III.
2 mischief. Heb. *'āmal.* Ap. 44. v. Not the same word as in *vv.* 8 and 16.
3 wisdom. Heb. *chākmāh.* See note on 1. 2.
4 chambers = inner chambers.
5 A wise man, &c. = A strong man [if wise] is strong indeed. Aram., Syr., and Sept. read "[Better] a wise man than a mighty". man. Heb. *geber.* Ap. 14. IV.
a man. Heb. *'ish.* Ap. 14. II.
increaseth strength. Aram. and Syr. read "than one who is strong".
6 multitude, &c. But they must all be "counsellors". Cp. 11. 15 and 15. 22.
7 Wisdom. Heb. pl. = true wisdom. See notes on 1. 20; 9. 1; and cp. 14. 1.
is too high = seems to be, or is regarded as coral: i.e. as an ornament costly, and, to him, unattainable. Occurs three times (here, Job 28. 18, and Ezek. 27. 16).
fool. Heb. *'ĕvīl.* See note on 1. 7.
openeth not his mouth in the gate: i.e. where the judges sit. A fool is not appointed as a judge.
8 mischievous person = a genius at plots. Heb. *zimmāh* = plots. Not the same word as in *vv.* 2 and 16.
9 thought, &c. Cp. 4. 23. Job 1. 5. Jer. 4. 14. Matt. 9. 3, 4; 15. 19, 20.
foolishness = the foolish. Heb. *'ĕvīl* (*v.* 7).
sin. Heb. *chāṭā'.* Ap. 44. i. scorner = scoffer.
men. Heb. *'ādām.* Ap. 14. I. Same word as in *vv.* 12, 30.
10 If thou faint, &c. Adversity is sent to try our strength; and, if we fail, it is proved to be weakness. Illustrations: Jacob (Gen. 42. 36); David (1 Sam. 27. 1); Elijah (1 Kings 19. 3, 4); Jonah (Jonah 4. 8).
11 If thou forbear. This is counsel for a ruler or judge, and is FOR Solomon. See the Structure (p. 891). Illustrations: Doeg (1 Sam. 22. 18); Pilate (Luke 23. 22-24).
deliver = snatch, or rescue.
drawn, &c. = being taken to execution.
12 knew it not = we knew not of it.
soul. Heb. *nephesh.* Ap. 13.
13 My son. Confirming the Structure **D** (p. 891).
14 cut off. Cp. *v.* 20 and 23. 18.
15 wicked = lawless. Heb. *rāshā'.* Ap. 44. x. (sing.), *v.* 16 (pl.). the righteous = a just one.
16 just = righteous. the wicked = lawless ones.
mischief = calamity. Heb. *rā'a'.* Ap. 44. viii. Not the same word as in *vv.* 2 and 8.
17 Rejoice not. Illustrations: Tyre (Ezek. 26. 2-6); Ammon (Ezek. 25. 6); David (2 Sam. 1. 11, 12). Cp. Ps. 35. 13, 14); Jeremiah (Jer. 9. 1); Edom (Obad. 11-14).
18 the LORD. Heb. Jehovah. Ap. 4. II.
from him. Supply Ellipsis, "from him [to thee]".

19 °Fret not thyself because of °evil *men*,
Neither [1]be thou °envious at °the [15]wicked;
20 For there shall be no °reward to the [8]evil *man;*
The °candle of [19]the wicked shall be put out.

A⁴ (p. 891)
21 [13]My son, fear thou [18]the LORD and the king:
And °meddle not with °them that are given to change:

B⁴
22 For °their °calamity shall rise suddenly;
And who knoweth the °ruin of them °both?
23 These *things* also °*belong* to the wise.
It is not good to have respect of persons in judgment.
24 He that saith unto °the °wicked, "Thou *art* righteous;"
Him shall the °people curse, nations shall abhor him:
25 But to them that °rebuke *him* shall be delight,
And a good blessing shall come upon them.
26 *Every man* shall °kiss *his* lips
That giveth a °right answer.
27 Prepare thy work without,
And make it fit for thyself in the field;
And afterwards build thine house.
28 Be not a witness against thy neighbour without cause;
And °deceive *not* with thy lips.
29 Say not, "I will do so to him °as he hath done to me:
I will render to the [5]man according to his work."

C⁴
30 I went by the field of the slothful,
And by the vineyard of the [9]man void of °understanding;
31 And, °lo, it was all grown over with thorns,
And nettles had covered the face thereof,
And the stone wall thereof was broken down.
32 Then I °saw, *and* °considered *it* well:
I looked upon *it, and* received instruction.
33 *Yet* a little sleep, a little slumber,
A little folding of the hands to sleep:
34 So shall thy °poverty come *as* one that travelleth;
And thy want as °an armed [5]man.

C D¹ (p. 897)
25 These *are* also proverbs °of Solomon, which °the °men of Hezekiah king of Judah copied out.
2 *It is* the glory of °God to conceal a thing:
But the °honour of kings *is* to search out a matter.
3 The heaven for height, and the earth for depth,
And the heart of kings *is* unsearchable.
4 Take away the dross from the silver,
And there shall come forth a vessel for the °finer.
5 °Take away °the °wicked *from* before the king,
And his throne shall be established in righteousness.
6 Put not forth thyself in the presence of the king,
And stand not in the place of great *men:*
7 For °better *it is* that it be said unto thee, "Come up hither;"
Than that thou shouldest be put lower in the presence of the prince
Whom thine eyes have seen.

19 Fret not = Chafe not thyself. Cp. Ps. 37. 1, 7, 8.
evil men = evil-doers. Cp. Ps. 37. 1, 7, 8. Same word as in *v.* 8.
envious = excited. **the wicked** = lawless ones.
20 reward = posterity, or future.
candle = lamp. The idiom is used for having no posterity.

21 (A⁴, p. 891). CALL TO HEAR.

21 meddle not = mingle not, i.e. have nothing to do with.
them that are given to change = with them that make a difference [between a wicked king and a wicked common man].

22-29 (B⁴, p. 891). PERSONAL CONDUCT.

22 their: i.e. the king and a common man.
calamity = overthrow. **ruin** = catastrophe.
both: i.e. the two who are the subjects of this counsel.
23 belong to = are [the words of] the wise (pl.). R.V. = are [sayings] of the wise. See the Structure, p. 891, and note on 22. 17.
24 the wicked. Unto a wicked [king]: i.e. as well as to an ordinary man.
wicked = lawless. Heb. *rāshā'.* Ap. 44. x.
people = peoples.
25 rebuke him: i.e. rebuke a wicked king.
26 kiss his lips = do homage with his lips to him.
right = straightforward.
28 deceive. Heb. *pāthāh.* See note on 11. 18.
29 as = according as.

30-34 (C⁴, p. 891). PERSONAL CHARACTER.

understanding. Heb. "heart": put by Fig. *Metonymy* (of Adjunct), Ap. 6, for the discernment coming from it. See note on 1. 2.
31 lo. Fig. *Asterismos.* Ap. 6.
32 saw = gazed.
considered it well = set my heart upon it.
34 poverty = need. Heb. *rūsh.* See note on 6. 11.
an armed man = a man with a shield.

25. 1–26. 28 (*C*, p. 864). PROVERBS BY SOLOMON. THIRD PERSON ("HE", "HIM", "HIS"). (*Division.*)

C | D¹ | 25. 1-28. Admonition to the Fear of God.
  | D² | 26. 1-28. Warning against the Sins of Men.

25. 1-28 (D¹, above). ADMONITION TO THE FEAR OF GOD. (*Division.*)

1 of Solomon = by Solomon, as author: i.e. written by him. Characterising this section of the book.
the men of Hezekiah. Evidently a special guild of scribes employed in the work of editing and putting together the O.T. books. At the end of each book are three Majuscular letters, *Cheth* (ח = Ḥ), *Zayin* (ז = Z), and *Koph* (ק = Ḳ), which are the initials of Hezekiah, and his sign-manual, confirming the work done. This *tri-grammaton* is found in all MSS. and printed editions up to the end of 2 Kings. After the death of Hezekiah it obtains varied forms and additions; subsequent writers and editors having lost the origin and meaning of these three letters, and taken it as a word which means "Be strong", put there for their encouragement. See Ap. 67.
men. Heb. *'ĕnōsh.* Ap. 14. III.
2 God. Heb. Elohim. Ap. 4. I. Cp. Job 37. 14-24; and 38-41.
honour = glory, as in preceding line.
4 finer = refiner.
5 Take away, &c. Illustrations: David (1 Kings 2. 5, 6. Cp. *v.* 46); Asa (1 Kings 15. 13).
the wicked = a lawless one. Heb. *rāshā'.* Ap. 44. x.
7 better. See note on 8. 11.

D^1 (*cont.*) 8 °Go not forth hastily to strive,
Lest *thou know not* what to do in the end thereof,
When thy neighbour hath put thee to shame.
9 Debate thy cause °with thy neighbour *himself;*
And discover not a secret to another:
10 Lest he that heareth *it* put thee to °shame,
And thine infamy turn not away.
11 A word °fitly spoken
Is like °apples of gold in °pictures of silver.
12 *As* an earring of gold, and an ornament of fine gold,
So is a wise reprover upon an °obedient ear.
13 As the cold of snow °in the time of harvest,
So is a faithful messenger to them that send him:
For he refresheth the °soul of his masters.
14 Whoso boasteth himself of a °false gift
Is like clouds and °wind without rain.
15 By long forbearing is a °prince °persuaded,
And a soft °tongue °breaketh the bone.
16 Hast thou found honey? eat so much as is sufficient for thee,
Lest thou be filled therewith, and vomit it.
17 Withdraw thy foot from thy neighbour's house;
Lest he be °weary of thee, and *so* hate thee.
18 °A man that beareth false witness against his neighbour
Is a °maul, and a sword, and a sharp arrow.
19 Confidence in an °unfaithful man in time of trouble
Is like a broken tooth, and a °foot out of joint.
20 *As* he that °taketh away a garment in cold weather, *and as* vinegar upon °nitre,
°So *is* he that singeth songs to an heavy heart.
21 °**If thine enemy be hungry, give him bread to eat;**
And if he be thirsty, give him water to drink:
22 **For thou shalt °heap coals of fire upon his head,**
And °the LORD shall reward thee.
23 The north [14] wind °driveth away rain:
So *doth* °an angry countenance a backbiting tongue.
24 *It is* [7] better to dwell in the corner of the housetop,
Than with a °brawling woman and in a wide house.
25 *As* cold waters to a thirsty [13] soul,
So *is* °good news from a far country.
26 A righteous man falling down before the [5] wicked
Is as a °troubled fountain, and a corrupt spring.
27 *It is* not good to eat much honey:
So *for men* to search their own glory *is not* glory.
28 He that *hath* no rule over his own °spirit
Is like a city *that is* broken down, *and* without walls.

D^2 (p. 897) **26** As °snow in summer, and as °rain in harvest,
So honour is not seemly for °a fool.
2 As the bird °by wandering, as the swallow °by flying,
°So the curse causeless shall not come.

8 Go not forth, &c. Illustrations: Gaal (Judg. 9. 26-40); the ten tribes (Josh. 22. 12-34); Abner (2 Sam. 2. 14, 17); Asahel (2 Sam. 2. 18-23); Amaziah (2 Kings 14. 8-14); Josiah (2 Chron. 35. 20-24).

9 with thy neighbour. Illustrations: Abraham (Gen. 13. 8; 21. 25-32); Jephthah (Judg. 11. 12-27).

10 shame. A *Homonym.* Heb. *cheṣed,* meaning (1) mercy, or lovingkindness, but also (2) a disgraceful thing. Lev. 20. 14, 17. Job 37. 13. See notes there.

11 fitly = timely. As we say "on the spur of the moment".

apples of gold. The difficulty is not in this expression, for jewellery is evidently intended from the first clause of the next verse.

pictures = carved or sculptured work, put by Fig. *Metonymy* (of Effect), Ap. 6, for imaginative work made from it: i.e. baskets, or dishes. Golden fruit (the Rev. James Niel suggests oranges) in silver salvers would be the height of rarity, which it is the intention of the words to convey. Heb. *maskīth* occurs six times, 18. 11 ("conceit"); Lev. 26. 1. Num. 33. 52. Ps. 73. 7 ("could wish"); Ezek. 8. 12 ("imagery").

12 obedient = attentive.

13 in the time of harvest: i.e. most unusual. Cp. 26. 1. The emphasis is on "cold" as being refreshing.

soul. Heb. *nephesh.* Ap. 13.

14 false = pretended. Illustrations: Zedekiah (1 Kings 22. 11); Hananiah (Jer. 28. 1-4); Shemaiah (Jer. 29. 24-31); false apostles (2 Cor. 11. 13-15. Jude 12).

wind. Heb. *rūacḥ.* Ap. 9.

15 prince: or judge. **persuaded.** Cp. Gen. 26. 13-31.

tongue. Put by Fig. *Metonymy* (of Cause), Ap. 6, for what is spoken by it.

breaketh the bone: i.e. overcometh obstinacy.

17 weary = full of.

18 A man. Heb. *'īsh.* Ap. 14. II.

maul = a mallet, or large wooden hammer, or club. From the Latin *malleus.*

19 unfaithful = treacherous. Heb. *bāgad.* See note on "transgressors" (11. 3).

foot out of joint = a tottering foot. Illustrations: Micah (Judg. 18. 20); Ben-hadad (2 Kings 8. 8-15. 2 Chron. 28. 20, 21); Israelites (Isa. 30. 1-5); Zedekiah (Jer. 37. 5-7); cp. Ezek. 17. 15; 29. 7; and Prov. 19. 22.

20 taketh away, &c. = decketh himself out in. Heb. *'ādāh.* See Job 40. 10. Isa. 61. 10. Jer. 4. 30; 31. 4. Ezek. 16. 11, 13; 23. 40. Hos. 2. 13: i.e. he that thinks more of his appearance than his comfort and health.

nitre = *natron.* Now called soda. With any acid it causes strong effervescence.

So is he. The point is in the incongruity of the three things named.

21 If thine enemy be hungry, &c. Quoted in Rom. 12. 20; cp. 1 Sam. 24. 6; 26. 9. Illustrations: Azariah, Berachiah, &c. (2 Chron. 28. 12-15); Elisha (2 Kings 6. 19-23). By the Fig. *Synecdoche* (of Species), Ap. 6, these examples are put for all similar kinds.

22 heap, &c. = receive from thine enemy [and place] upon his head. Fig. *Ellipsis* (Relative), Ap. 6. As *ḥāthā* = receive, the Ellipsis must be thus supplied: i.e. If thou doest good to one whose burning words (16. 27; 26. 23) thou hast received, they will burn him in another sense. Illustration: David (1 Sam. 24. 16-22).

the LORD. Heb. Jehovah. Ap. 4. II.

23 driveth away = bringeth forth. Heb. *ḥūl.*

an angry countenance. Supply the Ellipsis thus: by adding "[produceth]".

24 brawling = wrangling.

25 good news, &c. Illustrations: Jacob (Gen. 45. 25-28); Paul (Col. 1. 3, 4. Eph. 1. 15, 16. Phil. 1. 3-6).

26 troubled = trampled, or fouled.

28 spirit. Heb. *rūacḥ.* Ap. 9.

26. 1-28 (D^2, p. 897). WARNING AGAINST THE SINS OF MEN.

1 snow in summer . . . rain. These are as rare and as exceptional as honour is to a fool.

a fool. Heb. k^e*sīl.* See note on 1. 7.

2 by . . . by = for . . . for: or [has cause] for.

So the curse, &c. Illustrations: Baalam's (Neh. 13. 2); Goliath's (1 Sam. 17. 43); Shimei's (2 Sam. 16. 5, 12).

3 A whip for the horse, a bridle for the ass,
And a rod for °the °fool's back.
4 °Answer not a [1]fool according to his °folly,
Lest thou also be like unto him.
5 [4]Answer a [1]fool according to his [4]folly,
Lest he be wise in his own °conceit.
6 He that °sendeth a message by the hand of a [1]fool
°Cutteth off the feet, *and* drinketh damage.
7 The °legs of the lame °are not equal:
So *is* a parable in the mouth of [1]fools.
8 As he that °bindeth a stone in a sling,
So *is* he that giveth honour to a [1]fool.
9 *As* a thorn goeth up into the hand of °a drunkard,
So *is* a parable in the mouth of [1]fools.
10 °The great *God* that formed all *things*
Both °rewardeth the [1]fool, and rewardeth transgressors.
11 °**As a dog returneth to his vomit,**
So a [1]fool °returneth to his [4]folly.
12 Seest thou a °man wise in his own [5]conceit?
There is more hope of a [1]fool than of him.
13 The slothful *man* saith, "*There is* °a lion in the way;
A lion *is* in the streets."
14 *As* the door turneth upon his hinges,
So *doth* the slothful upon his bed.
15 The slothful °hideth his hand in *his* °bosom;
°It grieveth him to bring it again to his mouth.
16 The sluggard *is* wiser in his own conceit
Than seven °men that can render a reason.
17 He that passeth by, *and* °meddleth with strife *belonging* not to him,
Is like one that taketh a dog by the ears.
18 As a mad *man* who casteth firebrands,
Arrows, and death,
19 So *is* the [12]man *that* °deceiveth his neighbour,
And saith, "Am not I in sport?"
20 Where no wood is, *there* the fire goeth out:
So where *there is* no talebearer, the strife ceaseth.
21 *As* coals *are* to burning coals, and wood to fire;
So *is* a contentious [16]man to kindle strife.
22 The words of a talebearer *are* as °wounds,
And they go down into the innermost parts of the belly.
23 °Burning lips and a °wicked heart
Are like a potsherd covered with °silver dross.
24 He that hateth dissembleth with his lips,
And layeth up [19]deceit within him;
25 When he °speaketh fair, believe him not:
For *there are* seven abominations in his heart.
26 *Whose* hatred is covered by °deceit,
His [23]wickedness shall be shewed before the *whole* °congregation.
27 Whoso diggeth a pit °shall fall therein:
And he that rolleth a stone, it will return upon him.
28 A lying tongue °hateth *those that are* afflicted by it;
And a flattering mouth worketh ruin.

D² E¹ (p. 899)
27 Boast not °thyself of to morrow;
For °thou knowest not what a day may bring forth.
2 °Let another man praise °thee, and not °thine own mouth;
A °stranger, and not thine own lips.
3 A stone *is* heavy, and the sand weighty;

3 the fool's back = the back of fools.
4 Answer not. The point of *v.* 3 is that you cannot reason with a fool: *v.* 4 gives the reason. If you answer not according to his folly, he will think he is wise like yourself. If you do answer him according to his folly, he will think you are a fool like he is: i. e. according to *v.* 3 you cannot *reason* with him. These are finely stated facts, not commands.
folly. Heb. *'ĕvīl.* See note on 1. 7. **5 conceit** = eyes.
6 sendeth a message: or, transacteth business.
Cutteth off the feet: i. e. his own feet = renders himself helpless.
7 legs = clothes; "legs" put by Fig. *Metonymy* (of Subject), Ap. 6, for the clothes on them.
are not equal = are lifted up: i. e. the clothes being lifted up expose the lame legs. So a fool exposes his folly in expounding a parable.
8 bindeth = bindeth tight: a foolish thing to do.
9 a drunkard: i. e. insensible to a thorn.
10 The great God, &c. Render: "A master [workman] formeth all himself aright: but he that hireth a fool, hireth a transgressor [who will spoil the work]."
rewardeth. Heb. *sākar*, to hire.
11 As a dog, &c. Quoted in 2 Pet. 2. 22.
returneth = repeateth. Illustrations: Pharaoh (Ex. 9. 27–34); Ahab (1 Kings 21. 27; 22. 6–8); Herod (Mark 6. 20–27). **12 man.** Heb. *'īsh.* Ap. 14. II.
13 a lion = a black lion. **15 hideth** = burieth.
bosom = dish, as in 2 Kings 21. 13. Prov. 19. 24.
It grieveth him = It is hard for him, or he is too lazy.
16 men. No Heb. for this word here.
17 meddleth = vexeth himself.
19 deceiveth. Heb. *rāmāh.* See note on 11. 18. Not the same word as in *v.* 26.
22 wounds = self-inflicted wounds. Cp. 18. 8.
23 Burning lips: i. e. warm professions.
wicked. Heb. *rā'a'.* Ap. 44. viii.
silver dross. Fig. *Hypallage* (Ap. 6). Heb. = silver of dross.
25 speaketh fair = maketh his voice gracious.
26 deceit. Heb. *nāshā'.* See note on 11. 18. Not the same word as in *vv.* 19, 24.
congregation = assembly.
27 shall fall therein. Illustrations: Jacob, who deceived with a kid (Gen. 27. 14), was deceived by a kid (Gen. 37. 31, 32); David and the sword (2 Sam. 11. 14, 15, and 2 Sam. 12. 10); Haman and the gallows (Est. 7. 10; see Ps. 9. 15); Daniel and his accusers (Dan. 6. 4–9, 13, and 24).
28 hateth, &c.: i. e.:—
"Forgiveness to the injured doth belong;
They ne'er pardon who have done the wrong."

27. 1–29. 27 (*D*, p. 864). "WORDS OF THE WISE". FOR SOLOMON (A KING AND PRINCE, 28. 16; 29. 4, 14). SECOND PERSON. "MY SON" (27. 11). "THYSELF" (27. 1). "THOU" (27. 1, 22, 23). "THY" (27. 10, 23, 26, 27).

D	E¹	27. 1–27. Against self-praise and arrogance.
	E²	28. 1–28. Against unscrupulous dealing.
	E³	29. 1–27. Against stubbornness and insubordination.

1 Boast not, &c. Cp. Jas. 4. 13–16.
thyself ... thou. Second person, marking the Structure.
thou knowest not. Illustrations: Jonathan (1 Sam. 23. 17. Cp. 31. 2); Abner (2 Sam. 3. 9, 10. Cp. 3. 27); Benhadad (1 Kings 20. 3–31. Cp. *v.* 11); Ahab (1 Kings 22. 26, 27, 34–37); Haman (Est. 5. 12; 7. 1, 10); Nebuchadnezzar (Dan. 4. 30, 31–33); the rich fool (Luke 12. 20).
2 Let another man praise thee. Illustrations: Centurion (Matt. 8. 10); John (Matt. 11. 11. John 5. 35); Luke (Col. 4. 14. 2 Tim. 4. 11); Epaphroditus (Phil. 2. 25). No Heb. for "man", here.
thee ... thine. Second person, marking the Structure.
stranger = one unknown. Heb. *nākar.* See note on 2. 16; 5. 10.

E[1] (cont.)
But a °fool's wrath *is* heavier than °them both.
4 Wrath *is* cruel, and anger *is* outrageous;
But who *is* able to stand before °envy?
5 Open rebuke *is* better
Than secret love.
6 °Faithful *are* the wounds of a friend;
But the kisses of an enemy *are* °deceitful.
7 The full °soul loatheth an honeycomb;
But to the hungry °soul every bitter thing
is sweet.
8 As a bird that wandereth from her nest,
So *is* a °man that wandereth from his place.
9 Ointment and perfume rejoice the heart:
So *doth* the sweetness of a [2]man's friend
by °hearty counsel.
10 Thine own friend, and °thy father's friend,
forsake not;
Neither go into thy brother's house in the
day of thy calamity;
For °better *is* a neighbour *that is* near
than a brother far off.
11 °My son, be wise, and make my heart glad,
That I may answer him that reproacheth me.
12 A prudent *man* foreseeth the °evil, *and*
hideth himself;
But the simple pass on, *and* °are punished.
13 Take his garment that is surety for a
°stranger,
And take a pledge of him for a °strange
woman.
14 He that blesseth his friend with a loud
voice, rising early in the morning,
It shall be counted a curse to him.
15 A continual dropping in a very rainy day
And a °contentious woman are alike.
16 Whosoever hideth her hideth the °wind,
°And the ointment of his right hand, *which*
bewrayeth *itself*.
17 Iron sharpeneth iron;
So a [8]man sharpeneth the countenance of
his friend.
18 Whoso keepeth the fig tree shall eat the
fruit thereof:
So he °that waiteth on his master shall be
°honoured.
19 As in water face *answereth* to face,
So the heart of °man to °man.
20 °Hell and destruction are never full;
So the eyes of [19]man are never satisfied.
21 *As* the fining pot °for silver, and the furnace
°for gold;
°So *is* a [8]man to his praise.
22 Though thou shouldest °bray a [3]fool in a
mortar among wheat with a pestle,
Yet will not his[3] foolishness depart from him.
23 Be thou diligent to know the state of thy flocks,
And look well to thy herds.
24 For °riches *are* not for ever:
And doth the crown *endure* to every
generation?
25 The hay appeareth, and the tender grass
sheweth itself,
And herbs of the mountains are gathered.
26 The lambs *are* for thy clothing,
And the °goats *are* the price of the field.
27 And *thou shalt have* goats' milk enough for
thy food, for the food of thy household,
And *for* the °maintenance for thy maidens.

E[2] (p. 899)
28 °The °wicked flee when no man pursueth:
But °the righteous °are °bold as a lion.

3 fool's. Heb. *'ĕvil.* See note on 1. 7.
them. Should be "they".
4 envy = jealousy.
6 Faithful, &c. Illustrations: Nehemiah (Neh. 5. 7–13. Cp. Neh. 6. 2); Jehu (2 Chron. 19. 2–11).
deceitful. Heb. *'āthar* = effusive (i. e. abundant) and empty (as vapour). See note on 11. 18. Cp. Matt. 26. 49.
7 soul. Heb. *nephesh.* Ap. 13.
8 man. Heb. *'īsh.* Ap. 14. II.
9 hearty counsel = counsel of the soul. Heb. *nephesh.* Ap. 13.
10 thy father's friend. Illustrations: Hiram (1 Kings 5. 1. Cp. *v.* 12); Mephibosheth (2 Sam. 9. 6, 7. Cp. 21. 7); Rehoboam (1 Kings 12. 6–8); Joash (2 Chron. 24. 17, 18; cp. *v.* 22).
better. See note on 8. 11.
11 My son. Marking the Structure (p. 899), as being the Words of the Wise, *for* Solomon.
12 evil. Heb. *rā'a'.* Ap. 44. viii.
are punished = pay the penalty.
13 stranger = an apostate. Heb. *zūr.* See note on 2. 16; 5. 3.
strange = foreign. See note above.
15 contentious = wrangling.
16 wind. Heb. *rūach.* Ap. 9.
And. Supply the Ellipsis, "And [hideth]", &c.
18 that waiteth . . . honoured. Illustrations: Deborah (Gen. 35. 8); Joseph (Gen. 39. 2–6, 22, 23); Elisha (2 Kings 3. 11); Centurion's servant (Luke 7. 8); disciples (Luke 12. 37); soldier (Acts 10. 7).
19 man . . . man. Heb. *'ādām.* Ap. 14. I.
20 Hell = Sheōl. Ap. 35.
21 for . . . for = trieth . . . trieth.
So is, &c. = So doth a man put his praise to the test.
22 bray = pound, pulverize.
24 riches. Consisted mainly in flocks and herds.
26 goats = he goats.
27 maintenance = life.

28. 1–28 (E[2], p. 899). **AGAINST UNSCRUPULOUS DEALING.**

1 The wicked flee, &c. = A lawless one flees. Illustrations: Adam (Gen. 3. 8); Joseph's brethren (Gen. 50. 15); the Jews (Lev. 26. 36); Ahab (1 Kings 21. 20); Herod Antipas (Matt. 14. 2. Cp. Prov. 20. 27); Felix (Acts 24. 25). Cp. Eph. 2. 13.
the wicked = a lawless one. Heb. *rāshā'.* Ap. 44. x.
the righteous = righteous ones.
are bold as a lion. Illustrations: Moses (Ex. 32. 20); the prophet (1 Kings 13. 1–10); Elijah (1 Kings 18. 15, 18. 2 Kings 1. 15); Azariah (2 Chron. 26. 17, 18); Nehemiah (Neh. 6. 11); Shadrach, &c. (Dan. 3); Peter and John (Acts 4. 18, 20; 5. 41, 42); Stephen (Acts 7. 51–60); Paul (Acts 20. 22–24).
bold = confident. Heb. *baṭaḥ.* Ap. 69. i.
2 transgression. Heb. *pāsha'.* Ap. 44. ix.
many: i. e. changes of dynasty in quick succession.
a man of understanding, &c., or a man knowing a discerning [man] when he sees him, &c. Cp. Pharaoh and Joseph; or Nebuchadnezzar and Daniel.
man. Heb. *'ādām.* Ap. 14. I.
3 poor = needy. Same root as in *vv.* 6, 19, 27. Not the same word as in *vv.* 3, 8, 11, 15, 22. Heb. *rūsh.* See note on 6. 11.
man = strong man. Heb. *geber.* Ap. 14. IV.
the poor = weak ones. Heb. *dal.* See note on "poverty" in 6. 11. Same word as in *vv.* 8, 11, 15.
4 praise the wicked = praise a lawless one. Illustrations: Saul (1 Sam. 23. 21); Absalom (2 Sam. 15. 6); Judah's nobles (Neh. 6. 19); false prophets (Jer. 5. 30, 31); Jews (Acts 12. 21–23).
contend with them. Illustrations: Nehemiah (Neh. 5. 7–11; 13. 11); John (Matt. 14. 4).

2 For the °transgression of a land °many
are the princes thereof:
But by °a °man of understanding *and* knowledge the state *thereof* shall be prolonged.
3 A °poor °man that oppresseth °the poor
Is like a sweeping rain which leaveth no food.
4 They that forsake the law °praise [1]the
[1]wicked:
But such as keep the law °contend with them.

E^2 *(cont.)*

5 °Evil °men °understand not judgment:
But they that seek °the LORD [2]understand all *things*.
6 °Better *is* °the [3]poor that walketh in his °uprightness,
°Than *he that is* perverse *in his* °ways, though he *be* rich.
7 Whoso keepeth the law *is* a °wise son:
But he that is a companion of riotous *men* °shameth his father.
8 He that by usury and unjust gain increaseth his substance,
He shall gather it for him that will pity [3]the poor.
9 He that turneth away his ear from hearing °the law,
Even his prayer *shall be* abomination.
10 Whoso causeth °the righteous to go astray in an °evil way,
He shall fall himself into his own °pit:
But the upright shall have good *things* in possession.
11 The rich °man *is* wise in his own °conceit;
But °the [3]poor that hath [2]understanding searcheth him out.
12 When °righteous *men* do rejoice, *there is* great glory:
But when °the [1]wicked rise, a [2]man is hidden.
13 °He that covereth his °sins shall not prosper:
But whoso °confesseth and forsaketh *them* shall have mercy.
14 °Happy *is* the [2]man °that feareth alway:
But °he that hardeneth his heart shall fall into mischief.
15 *As* a °roaring lion, and a ranging bear;
So is a [1]wicked ruler over [3]the poor people.
16 The prince that wanteth [2]understanding *is* also a great °oppressor:
But he that hateth covetousness shall prolong *his* days.
17 A [2]man that doeth violence to °the blood of *any* °person
Shall flee to the °pit; let °no man stay him.
18 Whoso walketh [6]uprightly shall be saved:
But *he that is* °perverse *in his* ways shall °fall at once.
19 He that tilleth his land shall have plenty of bread:
But he that followeth after °vain *persons* shall have °poverty enough.
20 A faithful [11]man shall abound with blessings:
But he that maketh haste to be rich shall °not be innocent.
21 To have respect of °persons *is* not good:
For for a piece of bread °*that* [3]man will °transgress.
22 He that hasteth to be rich *hath* an [5]evil eye,
And considereth not that °poverty shall come upon him.
23 He that rebuketh a [2]man afterwards shall find more favour
Than he that flattereth with the °tongue.
24 Whoso robbeth his father or his mother, and saith, "*It is* no [21]transgression;"
The same *is* the companion of a °destroyer.
25 He that is of a proud °heart stirreth up strife:
But he that putteth his °trust in [5]the LORD shall be made fat.
26 He that [25]trusteth in °his own heart is a °fool:
But whoso walketh wisely, he shall be delivered.
27 He that giveth unto [11]the [3]poor shall not lack:
But he that hideth his eyes shall have many a curse.
28 When [12]the [1]wicked rise, [2]men hide themselves:
But when they perish, [12]the righteous increase.

5 Evil. Heb. *rā'a'.* Ap. 44. viii.
men. Heb. *'ĕnōsh.* Ap. 14. III.
understand not, &c. Illustrations: Israel (Num. 16. 41); Ahab (1 Kings 18. 17); the Lord's enemies (Mark 4. 11, 12. John 5. 44); Pharisees (Luke 11. 42; 18. 9-14; 16. 14). Heb. *bīnāh.* See note on 1. 2.
the LORD. Heb. Jehovah. Ap. 4. II.
6 Better. See note on 8. 11.
the poor = a poor one. **uprightness** = integrity.
Than he . . . ways = Than [he that walketh] in double ways. Heb. *'āḳash.* See *v.* 18. Cp. Jas. 1. 8.
ways = double ways. As in *v.* 18.
7 wise = intelligent. Heb. *bīnāh.* See note on 1. 2.
shameth. Cp. 29. 15. **9 the law** = instruction.
10 the righteous = upright ones.
evil. Heb. *rā'a'.* Ap. 44. viii.
pit = a slough or clay pit. Heb. *sheḥūth.*
11 man. Heb. *'īsh.* Ap. 14. II. **conceit** = eyes.
the poor = a poor one. Heb. *dāl.* See note on 6. 11.
12 righteous = upright ones (pl.).
the wicked = lawless ones.
13 He that covereth, &c. Illustrations: Adam (Gen. 3. 12. See Job 31. 33); Cain (Gen. 4. 9); Saul (1 Sam. 15. 19-21).
sins = transgressions. Heb. *pāsha'.* Ap. 44. ix.
confesseth, &c. Illustrations: David (2 Sam. 12. 13. Ps. 51. 3); Manasseh (2 Chron. 33. 12, 13); Nineveh (Jer. 18. 7, 8. Jonah 3. 5-10. Matt. 12. 41); the lost son (Luke 15. 18-24). **14 Happy.** See note on 3. 13.
that feareth alway, &c. Illustrations: Joseph (Gen. 39. 9; 42. 18); Nehemiah (Neh. 5. 15); Job (Job 1. 5).
he that hardeneth, &c. Illustrations: Jews (Jer. 8. 12); Gentiles (Rom. 2. 3-5); Herod (Matt. 14. 1-10).
15 roaring = growling while *devouring* his prey, not roaring (as he *springs* upon it).
16 oppressor, &c. Supply the Relative *Ellipsis* (Ap. 6), "oppressor [and shall cut short his days]: but", &c., or, it may be the Fig. *Aposiopesis* (Ap. 6); and = [what of him].
17 the blood of any person = the blood of a soul.
person. Heb. *nephesh.* Ap. 13.
pit = the grave. Heb. *bōr.*
no man = none: i. e. A man oppressed with the guilt of murder (cp. Gen. 9. 4, 5) will flee to the pit [of destruction]: let none lay hold on him; there is no occasion for it; he is his own tormentor, and will probably be his own executioner, or will deliver himself up to justice.
18 perverse. Fig. *Ellipsis* (Ap. 6) = "perverse [and walketh in double] ways, shall fall in one". See *v.* 6.
fall at once: or fall in one of the two.
19 vain: or vanities.
poverty. Not the same word as *v.* 22. Heb. *rūsh,* as in *v.* 3. **20 not be innocent** = not go unpunished.
21 persons. Heb. "faces", put by Fig. *Synecdoche* (of Part), Ap. 6, for persons.
that man = [even] a strong man.
transgress. Heb. *pāsha'.* Ap. 44. ix.
22 poverty. Not the same word as in *v.* 19. Heb. *ḥeser* = want.
23 tongue. Put by Fig. *Metonymy* (of Cause), Ap. 6, for what is spoken by it.
24 destroyer = a destroying man. Heb. *'īsh.* Ap. 14. II.
25 heart = soul. Heb. *nephesh.* Ap. 13.
trust = confidence. Heb. *baṭah.* Ap. 69. i.
26 his . . . heart, &c. Put by Fig. *Synecdoche* (of Part), Ap. 6, for himself. Illustrations: Hazael (2 Kings 8. 13); Johanan (Jer. 42. 7-22; 43. 1-7); Peter (Matt. 26. 33, 74); David (2 Sam. 24. 2: cp. *v.* 10); Absalom (2 Sam. 15. 4). Contrast Solomon (1 Kings 3. 7-9).
fool. Heb. *kesīl.* See note on 1. 7. Cp. Jer. 17. 9.

E³ (p. 899)

29 He, that being °often reproved hardeneth *his* neck,
Shall suddenly be destroyed, and that without remedy.
2 When °the righteous are °in authority, the people rejoice:
But when °the wicked °beareth rule, the people mourn.
3 Whoso loveth °wisdom rejoiceth his father:
But he that keepeth company with harlots spendeth *his* substance.
4 The king by judgment establisheth the land:
But °he that °receiveth gifts overthroweth it.
5 A °man that flattereth his neighbour
°Spreadeth a net for his °feet.
6 In the transgression of an °evil °man *there is* a snare:
But °the righteous doth sing and rejoice.
7 ⁶The righteous °considereth the cause of °the poor:
But ²the wicked °regardeth not to know *it*.
8 °Scornful °men °bring a city into a snare:
But wise *men* °turn away wrath.
9 *If* a wise ⁶man contendeth with a °foolish ⁶man,
Whether he rage or laugh, *there is* no rest.
10 °The bloodthirsty °hate °the upright:
But °the just °seek his °soul.
11 A °fool uttereth all his °mind:
But a wise *man* °keepeth it in till afterwards.
12 If a ruler hearken to lies,
All his servants *are* ²wicked.
13 °The °poor and °the deceitful ⁶man °meet together:
°The LORD lighteneth both their eyes.
14 The king that faithfully judgeth °the ⁷poor,
His throne shall be established for ever.
15 The rod and reproof give ³wisdom:
But a child left *to himself* bringeth his mother to shame.
16 When °the ²wicked are °multiplied, °transgression increaseth:
But ²the righteous shall °see their fall.
17 Correct thy son, and he shall give thee rest;
Yea, he shall give delight unto thy ¹⁰soul.
18 Where *there is* °no vision, °the people perish:
But he that keepeth the law, °happy *is* he.
19 A servant will not be corrected by words:
For though he understand he will not answer.
20 °Seest thou a °man *that is* hasty in his words?
There is more hope of a ¹¹fool than of him.
21 He that delicately bringeth up his servant from a °child
Shall have him °become *his* °son at the length.
22 An angry ²⁰man stirreth up strife,
And a °furious man aboundeth in ¹⁶transgression.
23 A °man's pride °shall bring him low:

29. 1-27 (E³, p. 899). AGAINST STUBBORNNESS AND INSUBORDINATION.

1 often reproved, &c. Illustrations: Antediluvians (Gen. 6. 1 Pet. 3. 20. 2 Pet. 2. 5. Luke 17. 26, 27); Pharaoh (Ex. 7. 13, 14; 8. 15; 10. 1, 20, 27); Ahab (1 Kings 17. 1; 18. 18; 20. 42; 21. 20; 22).

2 the righteous = righteous ones.

in authority = increase, not necessarily in numbers, but in greatness. Cp. *v.* 16, and see note on 4. 10, and the next clause.

the wicked = a lawless one. Heb. *rāsha'*. Ap. 44. x.

beareth rule. Some codices, with Aram., Sept., Syr., and Vulg., read the plural here: "bear rule".

3 wisdom. Heb. *chākmah*. See note on 1. 2.

4 he = a man. Heb. *'īsh*. Ap. 14. II.

receiveth gifts = is open to bribes.

5 man. Heb. *geber*. Ap. 14. IV.

Spreadeth a net, &c. Illustrations: woman of Tekoah (2 Sam. 14. 3, 19, 20, 28, 29); spies (Luke 20. 21).

feet = footsteps. **6 evil.** Heb. *rā'a'*. Ap. 44. viii.

man. Heb. *'īsh*. Ap. 14. II.

the righteous = a righteous one.

7 considereth. Heb. "knoweth", put by Fig. *Metonymy* (of Cause), Ap. 6, for the result of knowing. Illustrations: Job (Job 29. 13-16. Cp. Ps. 37. 26; 112. 5. Prov. 31. 20); Josiah (Jer. 22. 16).

the poor = weak ones. Heb. *dal*. See note on "poverty", 6. 11.

regardeth not to know it: i.e. makes no attempt to know it; or, knowing it, does not consider it. Illustrations: Jews (Jer. 5. 28. Cp. Luke 10. 31, 32).

8 Scornful men = Scoffers. Heb. "men of scorning".

men. Heb. *'ĕnōsh*. Ap. 14. III.

bring a city, &c. Illustrations: Judah (2 Chron. 36. 16-21); rulers (Isa. 28. 14-22; and Matt. 27. 39-43).

turn away wrath. Illustrations: Moses (Ex. 32. 10-14) and Aaron (Num. 16. 48); Elijah (Jas. 5. 18). Contrast Sodom (Gen. 18. 32); and Jer. 5. 1. Ezek. 22. 30.

9 foolish. Heb. *'ĕvīl*. See note on 1. 7. Not the same word as in *vv.* 11, 20.

10 The bloodthirsty = men of bloods. Heb. *'ĕnōsh*. Ap. 14. III.

hate the upright. Illustrations: Ahab (2 Chron. 18. 7); Jezebel (1 Kings 18. 4; 19. 2); Jews (Acts 23. 12); Cain (Gen. 4. 8. Cp. 1 John 3. 12).

the upright = upright ones.

the just = an honest one.

seek his soul: i.e. to preserve it. Illustrations: Jonathan (1 Sam. 19. 2); Obadiah (1 Kings 18. 4); believers (Acts 12. 5); Priscilla and Aquila (Rom. 16. 4).

soul = life. Heb. *nephesh*. Ap. 13.

11 fool. Heb. *kesīl*. See note on 1. 7.

mind = spirit. Heb. *rūach*. Put by Fig. *Metonymy* (of Cause), Ap. 6, for the feeling manifested by it.

keepeth it. Illustrations: Abraham (Gen. 22); Joseph (Gen. 42. 7; 44. 18-34); Moses (Ex. 3. 10. Cp. 4. 18); Nathan (2 Sam. 12. 1-6, 7-13).

13 The poor = a needy man. Heb. *rūsh*. See note on 6. 11.

the deceitful = a crafty, or an oppressive man, especially a creditor or usurer. Occurs in plural only here, for emphasis. Cp. Ps. 10. 7 ("fraud"); 55. 11, and 72. 14 ("deceit"). Heb. *tōk*. See note on 11. 18.

meet together: i.e. unexpectedly; first occurrence Gen. 32. 17. Cp. 33. 8.

The LORD. Heb. Jehovah. Ap. 4. II.

14 the poor = weak ones.

16 the wicked = wicked ones.

multiplied = increased in authority or position. Not necessarily in number. Cp. *v.* 2, and see note on 4. 10.

transgression. Heb. *pāsha'*. Ap. 44. ix.

see their fall = see into (the symptoms and causes of) their fall: i.e. fall caused by external circumstances. **18 no vision, &c.** Illustration: Israel (1 Sam. 3. 1. 1 Kings 12. 28-32; 14. 14-16). **the** = a. **happy, &c.** See note on 3. 13. Illustrations: Hezekiah (2 Chron. 29); Josiah (2 Chron. 34. 33; 35. 18. Jer. 22. 16). **20 Seest thou, &c.?** Note Fig. *Erotēsis* (Ap. 6), for emphasis. **man.** Heb. *'īsh*. Ap. 14. II. **21 child** = youth. **become.** Some render "aspire to be"; others = become [insolent] like a son. **son** = offspring. **22 furious man** = a master or lord of wrath. Heb. *bā'al* = lord. **23 man's.** Heb. *'ādām*. Ap. 14. I. **shall bring him low.** Adam and Eve (Gen. 3. 5, 6); Hezekiah (2 Kings 20. 16-18); angels (2 Pet. 2. 4. Jude 6, 7).

But honour shall °uphold °the humble in °spirit.
24 Whoso is partner with a thief hateth his own [10]soul:
He heareth cursing, and bewrayeth *it* not.
25 °The fear of [23]man bringeth °a snare:
But whoso °putteth his trust in [13]the LORD shall be °safe.
26 Many seek the ruler's favour;
But *every* [6]man's judgment *cometh* from [13]the LORD.
27 An unjust [6]man *is* an abomination to °the just:
And *he that is* upright in the way *is* abomination to °the [2]wicked.

A F[1] G (p. 903) **30** The words of °Agur the son of °Jakeh, *even* the °prophecy:
The °man spake unto °Ithiel, even unto Ithiel and °Ucal,
2 °Surely I *am* more brutish than *any* °man,
And have not the °understanding of °a man.
3 I neither °learned °wisdom,
°Nor have the knowledge of °the holy.
H J[1] 4 °Who hath ascended up into heaven, or descended?
Who hath gathered °the wind in his fists?
Who hath bound the waters in a garment?
Who hath established all the ends of the earth?
What *is* his name, and what *is* his son's name, if thou canst tell?
K[1] 5 Every °word of °GOD *is* °pure:
He *is* a shield °unto them that °put their trust in Him.
J[2] 6 °Add thou not unto His words,
Lest He °reprove thee, and thou be found a liar.
G 7 Two *things* have I required of thee;
°Deny me *them* not before I die:
8 Remove far from me vanity and °lies:
Give me neither °poverty nor riches;
°Feed me with °food convenient for me:
9 Lest I be full, and deny *thee*, and say, "Who *is* °the LORD?"
Or lest I be °poor, and steal,
And °take the name of my °God *in vain*.
H J[3] 10 °Accuse not a servant unto his master,
Lest he curse thee, and thou be found guilty.
K[2] L 11 *There is* a generation *that* curseth their father,
And doth not bless their mother.
M N[1] 12 *There is* a generation *that are* pure in their own eyes,
And *yet* is not washed from their filthiness.
N[2] 13 *There is* a generation, O how lofty are their eyes!
And their eyelids are lifted up.
N[3] 14 *There is* a generation, whose teeth *are as* swords, and their jaw teeth *as* knives,
To devour the °poor from off the earth, and the needy from *among* °men.

uphold the humble. Illustrations: Solomon (1 Kings 3. 7, 9, 11–14); John (John 1. 26, 27; 3. 29, 31); Mary (Luke 1. 38); angels (Isa. 6. 2).
the humble = a humble one.
spirit. Heb. *rūach*. Ap. 9.
25 The fear of man. Refers to the inward feeling of timidity. See note on "fear", 2 Tim. 1. 7.
The fear . . . a snare. One of the two great snares. The other is "the praise of man": (John 12. 43. Cp. Rom. 2. 29. John 5. 44). Illustrations: parents (John 9. 22); rulers (John 12. 42); Nicodemus (John 3. 2; 7. 50. Contrast 19. 39); Joseph (John 19. 38); David (1 Sam. 16. 12, 13; 27. 1); Elijah (1 Kings 19. 3, &c.); Peter (Matt. 26. 69–74).
putteth his trust = confideth. Heb. *baṭah*. Ap. 69. i.
safe = set on high.
27 the just = just ones. **the wicked** = a lawless one.

30. 1—31. 31 (*A*, p. 864). THE WORDS OF AGUR AND LEMUEL, FOR SOLOMON: FOR A PRINCE AND RULER. (*Division.*)

F[1] | 30. 1–33. The words of AGUR.
F[2] | 31. 1–31. The words of king LEMUEL.

30. 1–33 (F[1], above). THE WORDS OF AGUR. (*Alternation and Introversions.*)

Title, *v.* 1-.

F[1] | G | -1–3. Confession. Himself.
  H | J[1] | 4. Address. } God.
    K[1] | 5. Declaration. } God.
    J[2] | 6. Address. } God.
  G | 7–9. Prayer. Himself.
  H | J[3] | 10. Address. } Man.
    K[2] | 11–31. Declaration. } Man.
    J[4] | 32, 33. Address. } Man.

1 Agur = I shall fear. Probably a master of assemblies, as in Ecc. 12. 11. Nothing is known of him, but we accept all that was in the Scriptures which the Lord Jesus referred to. We know as little of some of the Minor Prophets. **prophecy** = oracle, or burden.
man. Heb. *geber*. Ap. 14. IV.
Ithiel = El [is] with me. Ap. 4. IV.
Ucal = I shall be able.
2 Surely = [True it is] that.
man = an educated man, or peer. Heb. *'īsh*. Ap. 14. II.
understanding. Heb. *bīnāh*. See note on 1. 2.
a man. Heb. *'ādām*: a commoner. Ap. 14. I.
3 learned = have been taught; with emphasis on taught. **wisdom.** Heb. *chākmah*. See note on 1. 2.
Nor have = Nor yet have I.
the holy = holy ones: or, the Most Holy One.
4 Who . . . ? Can it mean that the speaker here is the speaker of ch. 8? viz. the "son" of the last clause of this verse? **the wind.** Heb. *rūach*. Ap. 9.
5 word = saying or utterance. Heb. *'imrah*. Ap. 73. v. The only occurrence of this word in Proverbs.
GOD. Heb. Eloah. Ap. 4. V. The only occurrence of this title in Proverbs. Occurs forty-one times in Job, four times in Psalms, twelve times in the other books.
pure = tried [in a furnace]. Cp. Ps. 12. 6.
unto them. Some codices read "unto all them".
put their trust = flee for refuge. Heb. *ḥaṣah*. Ap. 69. ii.
6 Add thou not, &c. A solemn warning based on Deut. 4. 2; 12. 32. Cp. Gal. 1. 8, 9. Rev. 22. 18, 19.
reprove thee. Emphatic = send a special reproof unto thee. **7 Deny** = Withhold.
8 lies = word of falsehood.
poverty = need. Heb. *rūsh*. See note on 6. 11.
Feed me = Cause me to be fed.
food convenient = allowance of food. Cp. Job 23. 12.
9 the LORD. Heb. Jehovah. Ap. 4. II.
poor: i. e. from being dispossessed. Heb. *yārash*. See note on "poverty", 6. 11.
take the name, &c. = assaileth Jehovah. Not a reference to the second Commandment. **God.** Heb. Elohim. Ap. 4. I. **10 Accuse not a servant** = Get not a servant accused. Note the Hiphil here; as in Ps. 101. 5.
11-31 [For Structure see next page].
14 poor = needy. Heb. *'ānī*. See note on 6. 11. Not the same word as in *vv.* 8, 9. **men.** Heb. *'ādām*. Ap. 14. I.

N[1] **15** **The °horseleach hath two daughters, *crying*, "Give, give."**
There are three *things that* are never satisfied,
***Yea*, four *things* say not, *It is* enough:**
16 °The grave; and the barren womb;
The earth *that* is not filled with water;
And the fire *that* saith not, "*It is* enough."

L **17** **The eye *that* mocketh at *his* father,**
And °despiseth to obey *his* mother,
°The ravens of the valley shall pick it out,
And the young eagles shall eat it.

M N[5] (p. 904) **18** **There be three *things which* are too wonderful for me,**
Yea, four which I know not:
19 The way of an eagle in the air;
The way of a serpent upon a rock;
The way of a ship in the midst of the sea;
And the way of a [1]man with a °maid.
20 Such *is* the °way of an adulterous woman;
She eateth, and wipeth her mouth,
And saith, "I have done °no wickedness."

N[6] **21** **For three *things* the earth is disquieted,**
And for four *which* it cannot bear:
22 For a servant when he reigneth;
And a °fool when he is filled with meat;
23 For an odious *woman* when she is married;
And an handmaid that °is heir to her mistress.

N[7] **24** **There be four *things which are* °little upon the earth,**
But they *are* °exceeding wise:
25 The ants *are* °a people °not strong,
Yet they °prepare their meat in the summer;
26 The °conies *are but* a feeble folk,
Yet make they their °houses in the °rocks;
27 The locusts have °no king,
Yet go they forth all of them °by bands;
28 The spider taketh hold °with her hands,
And is in °kings' palaces.

N[8] **29** **There be three *things* which go well,**
Yea, four are comely in going:
30 A lion *which is* strongest among beasts,
And turneth not away for any;
31 A greyhound; an he goat also;
And a king, against whom *there is* no rising up.

J[1] **32** **If thou hast done °foolishly in lifting up thyself,**
Or if thou hast °thought evil,
***Lay* thine hand upon thy mouth.**
33 Surely the churning of milk bringeth forth butter,
And the wringing of the nose bringeth forth blood:
So the forcing of wrath bringeth forth strife.

F[2] O[1] P (p. 904) **31** **°The words of °king Lemuel, the °prophecy that °his mother taught him.**
2 What, °my son? and what, the son of my womb?
And what, the son of my vows?

11-31 (K[2], p. 903). DECLARATION.
(*Alternation and Divisions.*)

K[2] | L | 11. Parents. Cursing of.
M | N[1] | 12. Impurity.
N[2] | 13. Pride.
N[3] | 14. Violence.
N[4] | 15, 16. Insatiableness.
} Four-fold enumeration.
L | 17. Parents. Mocking of.
M | N[5] | 18–20. Four things inscrutable (*m*).
N[6] | 21–23. Four things disquieting (*f*).
N[7] | 24–28. Four things little and wise (*m*).
N[8] | 29–31. Four things graceful (*m*).
} Four-fold enumeration.

15 horseleach. Occurs only here. It is like the "flesh" in man. In the natural and spiritual spheres "the dose has to be increased".

16 The grave = Sheōl. Ap. 35.

17 despiseth to obey = despiseth obedience to.

The ravens, &c. These birds of prey always begin with the eyes of a carcase.

19 maid. Heb. *'almah.* See note on Gen. 24. 43. Refers here probably to seduction.

20 way = manner, or conduct. Cp. Ps. 119. 9.

no wickedness = nothing: or, as we say, "no harm". Heb. *'āven.* Ap. 44. III.

22 fool. Heb. *nābal.* See note on 1. 7.

23 is heir to = has dispossessed, or become heiress to.

24 little upon the earth = earth's little ones.

exceeding wise. Heb. "wise, made wise". Fig. *Polyptōton.* Ap. 6. The Sept. and Vulg. render "wiser than the wise".

25 a people. So are those "made wise" (2 Tim. 3. 15) who are God's People (Ps. 100. 3).

not strong = very weak. Fig. *Tapeinosis.* So Rom. 5. 6 (cp. Isa. 40. 29; 45. 24. Job 12. 13).

prepare = will prepare. Hence 10. 5.

26 conies. About the size of a rabbit. Inhabit clefts in the rocks; because, having soft feet, they cannot burrow as a rabbit can. So God's people abide in Christ, their Rock.

houses . . . rocks = house . . . rock. Heb. singular.

27 no king. So we have no visible king, yet when "made wise" we see Him Who is invisible (John 14. 19. Cp. 1 Pet. 1. 8).

by bands = gathered together. So will God's People. Sept. renders it by *keleusmatos* = at one word of command. Same word as the assembling shout in 1 Thess. 4. 16. Cp. 1 Cor. 15. 23, "in his own order" or rank.

28 with her hands. So we, by the hand of faith, shall be found in the palace of the King of kings.

kings' palaces = king's palace.

32 foolishly = stupidly. Heb. *nābal.* See note on 1. 7. Same word as in *v.* 22.

thought evil = meditated [with evil intent].

31. 1-31 (F[2], p. 903). THE WORDS OF KING LEMUEL, FOR SOLOMON: A PRINCE AND KING.
(*Division.*)

F[2] | O[1] | 1–9. Warnings. Women and wine.
O[2] | 10–31. Example. The model woman.

31. 1-9 (O[1], above). WARNINGS. "MY SON" (*v.* 2). SECOND PERSON. "THY" (*vv.* 3, 8, 9).
(*Introversion.*)

O[1] | P | 1, 2. Call to attention.
Q | 3. Women.
Q | 4–7. Wine.
} Warning.
P | 8, 9. Call to advocacy.

1 The words, &c. The Heb. *dibrēy* has no governing noun; so one must be understood thus: "[An unnamed one's] words [addressed] to king Lemuel: a burden which his mother [repeatedly] taught him".

king Lemuel = to El and for El, a king. Cp. Jedidiah = beloved of Jah (2 Sam. 12. 25). Solomon was the royal seed in the line of Him Who is King of kings and Lord of lords. The Talmud says (*Avoth d'Rab. Nathan*, c. 39): "Solomon was called by six names: Solomon, Jedidiah, Koheleth, Son of Jakeh, Agur, and Lemuel".

prophecy = oracle, oracular utterance, or burden.

his mother. Cp. the Structure, **A** (p. 864).

2 my son? Cp. the Structure, **A** (p. 864).

Q 3 Give not thy strength unto women,
Nor thy ways to that which destroyeth kings.

Q 4 *It is* not for kings, O Lemuel, *it is* not for kings to drink °wine;
Nor for princes °strong drink:
5 Lest they drink, and forget the law,
And pervert the judgment of any of the afflicted.
6 Give ⁴strong drink unto him that is ready to perish,
And ⁴wine unto those that be °of heavy hearts.
7 Let him drink, and forget his °poverty,
And remember his misery no more.

P 8 Open thy mouth for the dumb
In the cause of all °such as are appointed to destruction.
9 Open thy mouth, judge righteously,
And plead the cause of °the poor and °needy.

O² R S 10 (א) °Who can find a °virtuous woman?
For her price *is* far above rubies.
11 (ב) The heart of her husband °doth safely trust in her,
So that he shall have °no need of °spoil.
12 (ג) She will do him good and not °evil
All the days of her life.

T 13 (ד) She seeketh wool, and flax,
And worketh °willingly with her hands.
14 (ה) She is like the merchants' ships;
She bringeth her food from afar.
15 (ו) She riseth also while it is yet night,
And giveth °meat to her household,
And a portion to her maidens.
16 (ז) She considereth a field, and buyeth it:
With the fruit of her hands she planteth a vineyard.
17 (ח) She girdeth her loins with strength,
And strengtheneth her arms.
18 (ט) She perceiveth that her merchandise *is* good:
Her °candle goeth not out by night.
19 (י) She layeth her hands to the spindle,
And her hands hold the distaff.

U 20 (כ) She stretcheth out her hand to °the poor;
Yea, she reacheth forth her hands to the needy.

V 21 (ל) She °is not afraid of the snow for her household:
For all her household *are* clothed with °scarlet.

W 22 (מ) She maketh herself coverings of tapestry;
Her clothing *is* silk and purple.

R S 23 (נ) Her husband is °known in the gates,
When he sitteth among the elders of the land.

T 24 (ס) She maketh fine linen, and selleth *it;*
And delivereth girdles unto the merchant.
25 (ע) Strength and honour *are* her clothing;
And °she shall rejoice in time to come.

U 26 (פ) She openeth her mouth with °wisdom;
And in her tongue *is* the law of kindness.

V 27 (צ) She looketh well to the ways of her household,
And eateth not the bread of idleness.
28 (ק) Her °children arise up, and call her blessed;
Her husband *also,* and he praiseth her.

29 (ר) Many daughters have done virtuously, *W*
But thou excellest them all.
30 (ש) Favour *is* °deceitful, and beauty *is* vain:
But a woman *that* feareth °the LORD, she shall be praised.
31 (ת) Give her of the fruit of her hands;
And let her own works praise her in the gates.

---

4 wine. Heb. *yayin.* Ap. 27. i.
strong drink. Heb. *shēkār.* Ap. 27. iv.
6 of heavy hearts = bitter of soul. Heb. *nephesh.* Ap. 13.
7 poverty. Heb. *rūsh.* See note on 6. 11.
8 such as are appointed to destruction. Heb. = sons of destruction. Genitive of Relation, as in Rom. 8. 36. Ap. 17 (5).
9 the poor = a poor one. Heb. *'ānī.* See note on Prov. 6. 11.
needy = a needy one. Heb. *'ebyōn.* See note on Prov. 6. 11.

31. 10-31 (O², p. 904). THE MODEL WOMAN.
(Extended Alternation.)

O² | R | S | 10-12. Her husband (א—ג).
T | 13-19. Her occupation (ד—י).
U | 20. Her character. Bounty (כ).
V | 21. Her household (ל).
W | 22. Herself. Without (מ).
R | *S* | 23. Her husband (נ).
T | 24, 25. Her occupation (ס and ע).
U | 26. Her character. Wisdom (פ).
V | 27, 28. Her household (צ and ק).
W | 29-31. Herself. Within (ר—ת).

10 Who can find . . . ? This heading is the Fig. *Erotēsis.* Ap. 6. The twenty-two verses which follow, each begin with the twenty-two successive letters of the Hebrew alphabet. The acrostic cannot be reproduced in English, because the letters of the two alphabets vary in their number, order, and equivalents. This is to emphasise the great lesson King Solomon was to learn. Note the warnings against foreign women (**A**, p. 865), which, alas! Solomon failed to heed. This is why the book closes with the eulogy of the model Israelitish matron. See the evidence in Ap. 74.
virtuous. The English use of this word limits it to one kind of excellence. The meaning of the Hebrew is wider: *ḥayil* = strong in all moral qualities. Ruth is the only one so called in the O.T. May it not be that we have here Bathsheba's or Solomon's (and David's) commendation of Ruth?
11 doth . . . trust in = hath confided in. Heb. *baṭaḥ.* Ap. 69. I.
no need = no lack. **spoil** = gain.
12 evil = mischief. Heb. *rā'a'.* Ap. 44. viii.
13 willingly with her hands = with her hands' good will.
15 meat = [live] prey. Put by Fig. *Synecdoche* (of Species), Ap. 6, for all kinds of food.
18 candle = lamp.
20 the poor = a poor one. Heb. *'ānī.* See note on "poverty", 6. 11.
21 is not = will not.
scarlet = double change of garments.
23 known. Fig. *Metonymy* (of Cause), Ap. 6, for the result of that knowledge; viz. respect from all at the city gate, which includes high and low, rich and poor, peasants, labourers and judges.
25 she shall rejoice, &c. = she laugheth at the future.
26 wisdom. Heb. *chākmah.* See note on 1. 2.
28 children = sons.
30 deceitful = Heb. *sheker.* See note on 11. 18.
the LORD. Heb. Jehovah. Ap. 4. II.

[1]ECCLESIASTES;
OR,
THE PREACHER.

THE STRUCTURE OF THE BOOK AS A WHOLE.

(*Introversion.*)

A | 1. 1. INTRODUCTION.

B | 1. 2—6. 9. THE CHIEF GOOD. WHAT IT IS NOT.

B | 6. 10—12. 12. THE CHIEF GOOD. WHAT IT IS.

A | 12. 13, 14. CONCLUSION.

[1] The name of this book comes direct from the Latin Vulgate through the Sept. version. The Hebrew name is KOHELETH = Assembler or Convener (an appellative, not a proper name). It is feminine, to agree with the word "Wisdom", which is feminine, and is therefore Wisdom personified (as in Prov. 1. 20; 8. 1, and always with masculine verbs. Cp. Matt. 11. 19. Luke 7. 35; 11. 49, 50). ḲOHELETH is from *ḳahal* = to call, assemble, or gather together. This is what Solomon did (1 Kings 8. 1, 2, 5). It occurs with a feminine verb in 7. 27. The word *Ḳoheleth* occurs *seven* times in the book (Ap. 10): *three* times at the beginning (1. 1, 2, 12); *three* times at the end (12. 8, 9, 10); and *once* in the middle (7. 27).

This book formed part of the Hebrew Bible long before the time of Christ, and is therefore included in His word, "the Scriptures" (Matt. 22. 29: 2 Tim. 3. 16, &c.). It is given in the list of canonical books by Josephus (A.D. 37), and is included in all the Ancient Versions made before Christ. It has been rejected by some, or put to a late date, on account of its alleged Theology. Theology is man's reasoning about the *Word* of God, as Science (so called) is man's reasoning about the *Works* of God. Because Genesis does not agree with *Science* that book is rejected by Rationalists. Because Ecclesiastes does not agree with *Theology*, this book is rejected, as uninspired, even by some Evangelical theologians.

True, the Bible contains an inspired record of what people said and did; and it does not follow that all that they said or did was inspired. Nevertheless, it is inconceivable that this can apply to a *whole book*, without a word of warning. Those who can imagine such a thing refuse the evidence that Christ in Luke 16. 19-30 is using the language of His enemies, and in *v.* 31 giving His own Divine pronouncement. They strain out the gnat and swallow the camel. They do not see that, if any one *whole book* is not a part of "THE ORACLES OF GOD", every Christian doctrine loses its foundation. There could have been in that case no Divine selection or preservation of books, and no Divine CANON OF SCRIPTURE. If ONE book is thus ruled out, then another may be. Doubt is thus cast upon the whole Bible, and we have no "Word of God" at all! If this book be not part of the Word and words of God, then we have no reply to those who reject Genesis, Daniel, Jonah, or the Apocalypse, who do so on the same ground of human reasoning. If the inner consciousness of each individual is to decide what is and what is not "Scripture", there is an end of Divine Revelation altogether.

In any case Solomon's "wisdom" was given him by God (1 Kings 3. 5-12; 4. 29-34), and this "wisdom" was therefore "from above" (Jas. 3. 17), as Luke's was (see note on Luke 1. 3). Moreover, Solomon did not lose it, for it "remained with" him (Ecc. 2. 9).

ECCLESIASTES;

OR, THE PREACHER.

A (p. 906) **1** °The words of °the Preacher, the son of David, king in Jerusalem.

A^1 B^1 D (p. 907) 2 °"Vanity of vanities," saith the [1] Preacher, "vanity of vanities; °all *is* °vanity.
3 What profit hath a °man of all his °labour which he taketh °under the sun?
4 *One* generation passeth away, and *another* generation cometh: but the earth °abideth °for ever.
5 The sun also ariseth, and the sun goeth down, and hasteth to his place where he arose.
6 The °wind goeth toward the south, and turneth about unto the north; °it whirleth about continually, and the °wind returneth again according to his circuits.
7 All the rivers run into the sea; yet the sea *is* not full; unto the place from whence the rivers come, thither °they return again.

E 8 All things *are* full of °labour; °man cannot utter *it:* °the eye is not satisfied with seeing, nor the ear filled with hearing.

D 9 The thing that hath been, it *is that* which shall be; and that which is done *is* that which shall be done: and *there is* no new *thing* [3] under the sun.
10 Is there *any* thing whereof it may be said, 'See, this *is* new?' it hath been already of old time, which was before us.

E 11 *There is* no °remembrance °of former *things;* neither shall there be *any* °remembrance of *things* that are to come with *those* that shall come °after.

C^1 F^1 a^1 (p. 908) 12 °I [1] the Preacher °was king °over Israel in Jerusalem.
13 And I gave my heart to seek and search out by °wisdom concerning all *things* that are

1 The words. Rashi says that, when this expression occurs at the beginning of a book, it shows that the book is meant for *reproof*, and he gives evidence from Deut. 1. 1 (cp. 32. 15). Amos 1. 1 (cp. 4. 1). Jer. 1. 1 (cp. 30. 6). David, 2 Sam. 23. 1 (cp. *v.* 6).

the Preacher. This comes from Luther's version "Prediger"; but "Koheleth" does not include the idea of preaching. Some of its teaching is individual (3. 17); and succeeding appeals are in the second person.

1. 2—6. 9 (B, p. 906). THE CHIEF GOOD. WHAT IT IS NOT.

(*Division and Repeated Introversion.*)

B | A^1 | B^1 | 1. 2–11. Man. His labour. Vanity.
      C^1 | 1. 12—2. 26. Personal search.
  A^2 | B^2 | 3. 1–9. Man. Times for his labour.
      C^2 | 3. 10—4. 16. Personal Observation.
  A^3 | B^3 | 5. 1–12. Man. His Works.
      C^3 | 5. 13—6. 9. Personal Observation.

1. 2-11 (B^1, above). MAN. HIS LABOUR. VANITY. (*Alternation.*)

B^1 | D | 2–7. Transience. "Passeth away".
  E | 8. Dissatisfaction.
  D | 9, 10. Recurrence.
  E | 11. Oblivion.

2 Vanity of vanities. Fig. *Polyptōton.* Ap. 6. Note also the Fig. *Epanadiplōsis* (Ap. 6), by which *v.* 2 begins and ends with the same word. These Figures are used for the greatest emphasis, and denote utter vanity.

all = the whole, or "the sum total". Not everything in the universe, but all the human labours of *vv.* 3, 8.

vanity. Heb. *hābal*, used of that which soon vanishes.

3 man. Heb. *'ādām* = the natural man. Ap. 14. I.

labour = toil.

under the sun. This expression is peculiar to this book, and occurs twenty-nine times: (1. 3, 9, 14; 2. 11, 17, 18, 19, 20, 22; 3. 16; 4. 1, 3, 7, 15; 5. 13, 18; 6. 1, 12; 8. 9, 15, 15, 17; 9. 3, 6, 9, 9, 11, 13; 10. 5). It is equivalent to "upon the earth" (5. 2; 8. 14, 16; 10. 7; 11. 2, 3). It refers to all that is connected with earthly things as such, and with man apart from God, but what is stated is inspired truth. If what is stated here seems to be a "discrepancy" when compared with other scriptures, then these latter must be dealt with and reconciled and harmonised as other supposed "discrepancies" usually are; not cast aside as uninspired. It may be that it is man's theology which has yet to be conformed to these inspired statements.

4 abideth = standeth still, as in first occurrence (Gen. 18. 8, 22; 19. 27. Josh. 18. 5. Ps. 119. 90).

for ever. Heb. *'ōlām* = for ages; *'ōlām* occurs in Ecc. seven times: 1. 4, 10; 2. 16; 3. 11, 14; 9. 6; 12. 5. See the notes thereon. It = the world in relation to time past and future: as we use it when we speak of the ancient world, the old world, the modern world, the world to come, the Roman world.

5 The Heb. pauses in this verse are remarkable, and need a semicolon between each clause.

6 wind. Heb. *rūach.* Ap. 9. The first part of *v.* 6 continues the motion of the sun, going to the south (in winter) and turning about to the north (in summer).

it whirleth: i. e. the wind whirleth. This is the subject of *v.* 6.

7 they return again. This is the point of the illustration. Cp. Job 36. 27.

8 labour = weariness.

man. Heb. *'īsh.* Ap. 14. II.

the eye. Some codices, with Aram., Sept., and Syr., read "and the eye".

11 remembrance = memorial.

of former things. Supply the Ellipsis (Ap. 6) with the word "men", to complete the argument from *vv.* 2–4–. The Chaldee for the former [men] version supplies the word "generation".

after = "after [them]", or at the last.

1. 12—2. 26 [For Structure see next page].

12 I. Solomon knew that the kingdom was to be rent (1 Kings 11. 11, 12) and the People scattered; therefore he sought to kill Jeroboam (1 Kings 11. 39–40). The Chald. Targum says, on *v.* 1: "These are the words of the *prophecy* which Koheleth delivered when Solomon foresaw, by the *Spirit of prophecy*, that the kingdom of Rehoboam his son would be divided by Jeroboam the son of Nebat".

was = came to be.

over Israel. Solomon was the only king of which this was wholly true.

13 wisdom. Heb. *chokmah.* See note on Prov. 1. 2.

done °under heaven: this sore travail hath
°God given to the sons of [3] man to be °exercised therewith.
14 I have seen all the works that are done
[3] under the sun; and, behold, all *is* °vanity and
°vexation of °spirit.
15 *That which is* crooked cannot be made
straight: and that which is wanting cannot
be numbered.

b¹ (p. 908) 16 I communed with mine own heart, saying, 'Lo, I am come to great estate, and have
gotten more [13] wisdom than all *they* that have
been before me in Jerusalem:' yea, °my
heart °had great experience of [13] wisdom and
knowledge.
17 And I gave my heart to know [13] wisdom,
and to know °madness and °folly: I perceived
that this also is °vexation of [14] spirit.
18 For in much [13] wisdom *is* much °grief: and
he that increaseth knowledge increaseth °sorrow.

c¹ **2** I said in mine heart, 'Go to now, I will
prove thee with mirth, therefore °enjoy
pleasure:' and, °behold, this also *is* vanity.
2 I said °of laughter, '°*It is* mad:' and °of
mirth, '°What doeth it?'
3 I sought °in mine heart °to give myself
unto °wine, yet acquainting mine heart with
°wisdom; and to lay hold on folly, till I might
see what *was* that good for the sons of °men,
which they should do °under the °heaven °all
the days of their life.

F² a² 4 I °made me great °works; I builded me
houses; I planted me vineyards:
5 I made me gardens and °orchards, and I
planted trees in them of all *kind of* fruits:
6 I made me pools of water, to water therewith the °wood that bringeth forth trees:
7 I °got *me* servants and maidens, and had
servants born in my house; also I had great
possessions of great and small cattle above all
that were in Jerusalem before me:
8 I °gathered me also silver and gold, and the
peculiar treasure of kings and of °the provinces: I gat me men singers and women
singers, and the delights of the sons of [3] men,
as musical instruments, and that of all sorts.

b² 9 So I was great, and increased more than all
that were before me in Jerusalem: also my
[3] wisdom °remained with me.

1. 12—2. 26 (C¹, p. 907). PERSONAL SEARCH.
(*Division and Extended and Repeated Alternation.*)

C¹ | F¹ | a¹ | 1. 12-15. Labour. Things done.
b¹ | 1. 16-18. Wisdom.
c¹ | 2. 1-3. Pleasure sought.
F² | a² | 2. 4-8. Labour. "Great works".
b² | 2. 9. Wisdom.
c² | 2. 10. Pleasure enjoyed.
F³ | a³ | 2. 11. Labour. "Great works".
b³ | 2. 12-16. Wisdom.
c³ | 2. 17-. Pleasure hated.
F⁴ | a⁴ | 2. -17-25. Labour. "All my labour".
b⁴ | 2. 26-. Wisdom.
c⁴ | 2. -26. Pleasure judged.

under heaven=under the heavens. Some codices, with one early printed edition, Aram., Syr., and Vulg., read "under the sun".
God. Heb. Elohim. Ap. 4. I. The title "Jehovah" is not used in Ecclesiastes, as this book refers to man in relation to his Creator only; not to man in covenant with Him as "Jehovah". Hence the frequent use of Heb. *'ādām* for "man" in this book.
exercised=humbled.
14 vanity. See note on 1. 2.
vexation of spirit=feeding on wind. The expression occurs nine times (1. 14, 17; 2. 11, 17, 26; 4. 4, 6, 16; 6. 9.).
spirit. Heb. *rūach.* Ap. 9.
16 my heart=I myself. **had**=saw.
17 madness=the opposite of wisdom, as displayed in the loss of self-control; raving with self-conceit. So elsewhere in this book.
folly=infatuation. Heb. *ṣākal.* See note on "wisdom", Prov. 1. 2.
vexation, &c. Not the same phrase in Heb. as in *v.* 14.
18 grief=mortification. **sorrow**=smarting.

2. 1 enjoy=look thou into.
behold. Fig. *Asterismos.* Ap. 6.
2 of laughter=to laughter.
It is mad. See note on "madness", 1. 17.
of mirth=to mirth.
What doeth it?=What doth she do?
3 in mine heart: i. e. resolved.
to give myself unto: or, how to enlist, by wine, my very flesh [in the work]: i. e. the work of proving the heart with mirth—"yet retaining wisdom".
wine. Heb. *yayin.* Ap. 27. I.
wisdom. See note on 1. 13.
men. Heb. *'ādām.* Ap. 14. I. Note the use of this word in Ecc. See note on 1. 13.
under the heaven. See note on 1. 3. Some codices, with Sept., Syr., and Vulg., read "sun", to which it is equivalent.
all the days=the numbered days.
4 made me great works=increased or multiplied my possessions.
works. Put by Fig. *Metonymy* (of Cause), Ap. 6, for the results and effects gained by work. Cp. Ex. 23. 12. 1 Sam. 25. 2. Isa. 26. 12.
5 orchards. Heb. *pardēṣīm* = paradises, parks, or pleasure grounds. Different from "gardens", which were cultivated (Deut. 11. 10. 1 Kings 21. 2). Paradises were formed by eastern monarchs. In the British Museum may be seen the inscriptions of Gudea, the greatest of the Sumerian rulers of Chaldea (2500 B.C.), and Tiglath-pileser I, king of Assyria (1120 B.C.), describing what could be only a botanical and zoological park. Assur-nazir-pal, king of Assyria (885 B.C.), founded such a public paradise, and describes how he stocked it; what he brought, and whence he brought the natural history collection. The British Museum contains a portion of a similar catalogue of Sennacherib. The Paradise in Rev. 2. 7; 22. 1, 2, refers to the future paradise, which will be as literal and real, not figurative. **6 wood**=forest. **7 got me servants**=bought me servants. Heb. bondage has nothing in common with Greek, Roman, or African slavery. There is no word for such slavery in Hebrew; *'ĕbĕd*=labourer, is the name of all Jehovah's servants. **8 gathered**=amassed. Heb. *kānaṣ*, said to be a later Hebrew word (see Ap. 76. i). **the provinces.** Heb. *m*[e]*dīnah*, from *dūn* = to rule, hence a country. There is no article before "kings", because they constantly change, whereas countries do not change. This is another word which is said to be of later date, but it is found in 1 Kings 20. 14, 15, 17, 19. Lam. 1. 1. Ezek. 19. 8. See Ap. 76. Cp. note on "event" in *v.* 14. **remained.** The Divine wisdom given by God (1 Kings 3. 5-15) had not been taken away. See note at foot of p. 906. This must be remembered in reading this book. Like Luke's "understanding" it came "from above". See note on "very first" (Luke 1. 3).

c2 (p. 908) 10 And whatsoever mine eyes desired I kept
not from them, I withheld not my heart from
any joy; for my heart rejoiced in all my
°labour: and this °was my °portion of all my
°labour.
F3 a3 11 °Then I °looked on all the works that my
hands had wrought, and on the [10]labour that I
had laboured to do: and, behold, all *was* °vanity
and °vexation of °spirit, and *there was* no
profit °under the sun.
b3 12 And I turned myself to °behold [3]wisdom,
and [2]madness, and folly: for what *can* the
[3]man *do* that cometh after the king? *even* that
which hath been already done.
13 Then I saw that [9]wisdom excelleth folly, as
far as light excelleth darkness.
14 The wise man's eyes *are* in his head; but
the °fool walketh in darkness: °and I myself
perceived also that one °event happeneth to
them all.
15 Then °said I in my heart, 'As it happeneth to the [14]fool, so it happeneth even
°to me; and why was I then more wise?'
Then °I said in my heart, that this also *is*
vanity.
16 For *there is* no °remembrance °of the wise
more than °of the [14]fool °for ever; °seeing
that which now *is* in the days to come shall
°all be forgotten. And how dieth the wise
man? °as the [14]fool.
c3 17 Therefore I hated °life;
F4 a4 Because the work that is wrought [11]under the
sun *is* grievous unto me: for all *is* [11]vanity and
[11]vexation of [11]spirit.
18 Yea, I hated all my °labour which I had
°taken [11]under the sun: because I should leave
it unto the [3]man that shall be after me.
19 And who knoweth whether he shall be a
wise *man* or a °fool? yet shall he °have rule
over all my [18]labour wherein I have laboured,
and wherein I have °shewed myself wise [11]un-
der the sun. This *is* also vanity.
20 Therefore I went about to cause my heart
to despair of all the [18]labour which I °took
[11]under the sun.
21 For °there is a [3]man whose labour *is* in
[3]wisdom, and in knowledge, and in equity; yet
to a [3]man that hath not laboured therein shall
he °leave it *for* his portion. This also *is*
vanity and a great °evil.
22 For what hath [3]man of all his [18]labour,
and of the °vexation of his heart, wherein he
hath [10]laboured [11]under the sun?
23 For all his days *are* sorrows, and his °tra-
vail grief; yea, his heart taketh not rest in the
night. This is also vanity.
24 *There is* °nothing °better for a [3]man, °*than*
that he should eat and drink, and *that* he
should make °his soul enjoy good in his
[10]labour. This also I saw, that °it *was* from
the hand of °God.
25 For who can eat, or °who else can hasten
hereunto, °more than I?
b4 26 For *God* giveth to a [3]man that *is* good in
His sight [3]wisdom, and knowledge, and joy:
but to the °sinner He giveth [23]travail, to °gather
and to heap up, that he may give to *him that is*
good before God.
c4 This also *is* [11]vanity and [11]vexation of [11]spirit.

10 labour=toil. **was**=came to be.
portion=share, as in 3. 22.
11 Then=But when.
looked=turned in order to look, as in *v.* 12.
vanity. See note on 1. 2.
vexation of spirit=feeding on wind. Cp. 1. 14.
spirit. Heb. *rūacḥ.* Ap. 9. **12 behold**=consider.
under the sun. See note on 1. 3.
14 fool. Heb. *k^e^ṣil*=fat, inert. Same word as in *vv.* 15, 16; not the same word as in *v.* 19.
and I myself perceived=and I too knew: i. e. as well as they.
event=a happening. Heb. *miḳreh.* Said to be a later word, but it occurs in 1 Sam. 6. 9; 20. 26. Ruth 2. 3. See note on *v.* 8.
15 said I in my heart=spake with myself.
to me. Heb. "to me, even to me" (emphatic).
16 remembrance=memorial, as in 1. 11, 11.
of=for. **for ever.** See note on 1. 4.
seeing that which now is=for, as in time past.
all. This "all" was not in the edition of A.V. 1611.
as the fool. Cp Ps. 49. 10. 2 Sam. 3. 33.
17 life. Put by Fig. *Metonymy* (of the Subject) for the pleasure enjoyed in it.
18 labour. Put by Fig. *Metonymy* (of Cause), Ap. 6, for all that is produced by toil. **taken**=toiled.
19 fool. Heb. *ṣakal*=stupid. Not the same word as in *vv.* 14, 15, 16.
have rule. Heb. *shalaṭ.* Supposed to be a later Hebrew word, but it occurs in Ps. 119. 133. Gen. 42. 6. See Ap. 75. **shewed myself wise**=acted wisely.
20 took=toiled. Some codices, with two early printed editions, add "and wherein I had acted wisely".
21 there=here. **leave it**="leave it [to another]".
evil=calamity. Heb. *rā'a'.* Ap. 44. viii.
22 vexation=feeding, or delight. Same word as in 1. 17; 4. 16. Not the same as in *vv.* 11, 17, 26.
23 travail=toil that brings about fatigue. The same word as in 1. 13; 2. 26; 3. 10; 4 8; 5. 14. Not the same word as in 4. 4, 6. Occurs only in Ecclesiastes.
24 nothing better=no goodness.
better. Occurs in Ecc. 2. 24; 3. 22; 4. 3, 6, 9, 13; 5. 5; 6. 3, 9; 7. 2, 3, 3, 5, 8, 8, 10; 8. 15; 9. 4, 16.
than. Ginsburg thinks this "than" should be in the text. **his soul**=himself. Heb. *nephesh.* Ap. 13.
it: i. e. true enjoyment. Omit the preceding italics.
God. Heb. *ha-'Elohim*=the [true] God (Ap. 4. I. with Art.). God (as Creator) is the subject which is continued through the next verse as the source and giver of all good. It is not therefore necessary to suppose that "another hand has been here at work".
25 who else can hasten hereunto=who can enjoy?
more than I. Some codices, with Sept., Syr., and Arab., read *mimmennū*, instead of *mimmennī*, "without Him" (i. e. without His favour).
26 sinner. Heb. *cḥāṭā'.* Ap. 44. i. Occurs again in Ecclesiastes six times. (5. 6; 7. 20, 26; 8. 12; 9. 2, 18).
gather=gather in. Not the same word as *v.* 8.

3. 1-9 (B2, p. 907). MAN. TIMES FOR HIS LABOUR. (*Introversion.*)

B2 | G | 1. Labour. Its appointment.
  H | 2-8. Seasons.
 G | 9. Labour. Its profit.

1 a season=an appointed time. Heb. *z^e^mān.* Cp. Ezra 10. 14. Neh. 2. 6. Est. 9. 27. A word is not necessarily a "later" word, because there has not been occasion for it to be used, or needed before. See Ap. 76.
a time=a season. Note the 28 "seasons" (=4×7. See Ap. 10.). In Heb. MSS. these are set out in 14 lines; 2 in a line, with a space between each pair.
purpose. Heb. *ḥēphez.* Alleged to be later Hebrew. See Ap. 76. v.
under the heaven. See note on 1. 3.

3 To every *thing there is* °a season, and °a B2 G (p. 909)
time to every °purpose °under the heaven:

H (p. 909) **2 A [1]time °to be born, and a [1]time °to die; a [1]time °to plant, and a [1]time °to pluck up *that which is* planted;**
3 A [1]time °to kill, and a [1]time °to heal; a [1]time °to break down, and a [1]time °to build up;
4 A [1]time °to weep, and a [1]time °to laugh; a [1]time °to mourn, and a [1]time °to dance;
5 A [1]time °to cast away stones, and a [1]time °to gather stones together; a [1]time °to embrace, and a [1]time °to refrain from embracing;
6 A [1]time °to get, and a [1]time °to lose; a [1]time °to keep, and a [1]time °to cast away;
7 A [1]time °to rend, and a [1]time °to sew; a [1]time °to keep silence, and a [1]time °to speak;
8 A [1]time °to love, and a [1]time °to hate; a [1]time °of war, and a [1]time °of peace.

G **9 What profit hath he that worketh in that wherein he °laboureth?**

C^2 J^1 d^1 (p. 910) **10 I have °seen the °travail, which °God hath given to the sons of °men to be exercised in it.**

e^1 **11 He hath made every *thing* beautiful in °his [1]time: also He hath °set °the world in °their heart, so that no [10]man can find out the work that °God °maketh from the °beginning to °the end.**

f^1 **12 I know that *there is* no good °in them, but for *a man* to rejoice, and to do good °in his life.**
13 And also that every [11]man should eat and drink, and enjoy the good of all his labour, it *is* the gift of [10]God.

J^3 d^2 **14 I know that, whatsoever [11]God doeth, it shall be °for ever: nothing can be put to it, nor any thing taken from it: and [11]God doeth *it*, that *men* should fear before Him.**
15 That which hath been is now; and that

2 to be born=to bear. Gen. 17. 17, 21; 18. 14; 21. 2.
to die. Ps. 31. 5, 15. Heb. 9. 27.
to plant (cp. 2. 5): it is beyond man's power to alter the seasons. Applied to a kingdom. Ps. 44. 2; 80. 8, 12, 13. Jer. 18. 9. Amos 9. 15. Matt. 15. 13.
to pluck up, &c. Jer. 18. 7, 9.
3 to kill: i. e. judicially. 1 Kings 2. 23, 24, 28, 29, 34; 36, 37, 46. Ps. 88. 31, 34. Jer. 12. 3. Out of its proper "time", "to kill" is to murder. There is no "time" for this.
to heal. Isa. 38. 5, 21; 57. 18. Ps. 107. 20; 147. 3.
to break down. Jer. 39. 2, 8. Ezek. 33. 21. Mal. 1. 4.
to build up (cp. 2. 4). Neh. 2. 17, 18, 20. Ps. 102. 13–16. Isa. 45. 13; 58. 12; 60. 10. Dan. 9. 25. Amos 9. 11.
4 to weep. Gen. 23. 2; 44. 30. 2 Sam. 12. 21. Joel 2. 17. Jer. 21. 9. Luke 6. 25.
to laugh (cp. 2. 1, 2). Gen. 21. 6. Ps. 2. 4; 37. 13. Matt. 5. 4; 9. 15. Luke 6. 21. Neh. 8. 9.
to mourn. Gen. 23. 2. 1 Sam. 16. 1. Prov. 29. 2. Isa. 38. 14; 61. 2. Joel 1. 9. Zech. 12. 10, 12.
to dance. 2 Sam. 6. 14. Ps. 149. 3; 150. 4. Jer. 31. 13.
5 to cast away stones: as out of a vineyard. Isa. 5. 2. Lev. 14. 40, 45. Judg. 20. 16. 1 Kings 15. 22. Lam. 4. 1.
to gather stones together (cp. 2. 4). Deut. 27. 4, 5. Josh. 4. 3, 8, 20. 1 Sam. 17. 40. 1 Kings 18. 31, 32. Ps. 102. 14. Isa. 54. 11.
to embrace (cp. 2. 3). Gen. 29. 13; 33. 4; 48. 10. 2 Kings 4. 16.
to refrain from embracing. Prov. 5. 20. Joel 2. 16. 1 Cor. 7. 5, 6.
6 to get=to buy, or acquire (cp. 2. 8). Gen. 42. 2, 7, 20. Ruth 4. 5. 2 Sam. 24. 21. Isa. 55. 1. Jer. 32. 7. Eph. 4. 28.
to lose. Gen. 31. 39. Matt. 10. 39; 16. 25. Isa. 47. 9.
to keep. 1 Sam. 16. 11. Prov. 7. 1. Luke 8. 15. 2 Tim. 1. 14. John 2. 10; 12. 7.
to cast away. Judg. 15. 17. 2 Kings 7. 15. Isa. 31. 7. Hos. 9. 17. Ecc. 11. 1.
7 to rend. 1 Sam. 15. 27, 28. 1 Kings 11. 11, 31; 12. 31; 14. 8. Joel 2. 13. John 19. 24.
to sew=to join together, adjust. Spoken of kingdom, as "rending" is: Ezek. 37. 15, 22, and refs. there. Cp. Ezra 4. 12, margin.
to keep silence. Lev. 10. 3. Ps. 32. 2. Amos 5. 13. 1 Tim. 2. 11, 12. 1 Pet. 2. 15. Cp. Deut. 3. 26. Luke 1. 22; 4. 41.
to speak. Ex. 7. 2. Num. 22. 8. 2 Sam. 7. 17. Ps. 2. 5; 145. 6, 11, 21. Ezek. 2. 7. Luke 1. 19, 20. John 16. 13. **8 to love.** Jer. 2. 2. Ezek. 16. 8. Dan. 1. 9. Gal. 5. 13. 2 Thess. 1. 3. **to hate.** 2 Sam. 13. 15. Ps. 105. 25. Prov. 25. 17. Luke 14. 26. Prov. 11. 15; 15. 27; 28. 16. John 12. 25. Jude 23. **of war.** Ex. 17. 16. Num. 1. 3, 20, 22; 26. 2. Deut. 3. 18. Judg. 3. 2. 2 Sam. 3. 1. Jer. 6. 4. Luke 14. 31. Rev. 12. 7; 19. 11, 19. **of peace.** Josh. 11. 23; 14. 15. Lev. 26. 6. Judg. 4. 17. 1 Sam. 7. 14. Ps. 72. 3; 85. 8. Prov. 16. 7. Isa. 9. 7. Zech. 9. 10. Rom. 5. 1. Eph. 4. 3. **9 laboureth**=toileth.

3. 10—4. 16 (C^2, p. 907). PERSONAL OBSERVATION.
(Repeated and Extended Alternation.)

C^2 | J^1 | d^1 | 3. 10. Labour. Sons of men.
  e^1 | 3. 11. Wisdom. Man ignorant of God's work.
  f^1 | 3. 12, 13. Pleasure, or enjoyment.
J^2 | d^2 | 3. 14, 15. Labour. God's work is for ever.
  e^2 | 3. 16–21. Wisdom. Man's ignorance like beasts'.
  f^2 | 3. 22. Pleasure, or enjoyment.
J^3 | d^3 | 4. 1–4. Labour. For others.
  e^3 | 4. 4, 5. Wisdom. The fool, none.
  f^3 | 4. 6. Pleasure, or enjoyment.
J^4 | d^4 | 4. 7–12. Labour. "For whom".
  e^4 | 4. 13, 14. Wisdom.
  f^4 | 4. 15, 16. Pleasure, or enjoyment. None.

10 seen the travail=considered the business. **travail.** See note on 2. 23. **God.** Heb. Elohim. Ap. 4. I. Occurs eight times in this chapter. See note on 1. 13. **men.** Heb. *'ādām.* Ap. 14. I. Observe the use of this word in Ecclesiastes. See note on 1. 10. **11 his time**=its proper season. **set**=put. **the world.** Heb. *'ōlām*=the ages; or the world (in relation to time). Here, put by Fig. *Metonymy* (of Subject) for that which is inscrutable by man, viz. obscurity as to the past and the future ages, resulting in man's incapacity for finding out, or comprehending the whole of what God doeth. This has resulted from the Fall. **their**: i. e. the sons of men (*v.* 10). **God.** Heb. Elohim (with Art.)=the true God, or the Deity. Ap. 4. I. **maketh**=hath made, or done. **beginning to the end.** The reason being given in *v.* 14. Man sees his own times of *vv.* 1–8; but what God doeth is from time past to time future (*v.* 14); so that man cannot find that out to the end from the beginning. **the end.** Heb. *sōph.* One of the words said to belong to later Hebrew, but it is found in 1 Chron. 20. 16 ("conclusion"), and Joel 2. 20 ("hinder part"). See also 7. 2; 12. 13, and Ap. 76. vi. **12 in them**: i. e. in God's works. **in**=during. **14 for ever.** Same word as "world" in *v.* 11. See note on 1. 4.

which is to be hath already been; and [10] God
requireth that which is past.
e2 (p. 910) 16 And moreover I saw ° under the sun the
place of judgment, *that* ° wickedness *was* there;
and the place of righteousness, *that* ° iniquity
was there.
17 I said in mine heart, [10] 'God shall judge
° the righteous and ° the wicked: for *there is*
a [1] time there for every [1] purpose and for every
work.'
18 I said in mine heart concerning the estate
of the sons of [10] men, that ° God might manifest
them, and that they might see that they
themselves are ° beasts.
19 For ° that which befalleth the sons of
[10] men befalleth [18] beasts; even ° one thing befalleth them: as the one dieth, so dieth the
other; yea, they have all ° one breath; so that
a [10] man hath ° no preeminence above a [18] beast:
for all *is* vanity.
20 All go unto ° one place; all are ° of the
dust, and all ° turn to dust again.
21 Who knoweth the ° spirit ° of [10] man ° that
goeth upward, and the ° spirit of the [18] beast
° that goeth downward to the earth?
f2 22 Wherefore I perceive that *there is* nothing
° better, than that a [11] man should rejoice in his
own works; for that *is* his ° portion: for who
shall bring him to see what shall be after
him?

J3 d3 **4** So I returned, and considered all the
oppressions that are done ° under the sun:
and behold the tears of *such as were* oppressed,
and they had no comforter; and on the ° side
of their oppressors *there was* power; but ° they
had no comforter.
2 Wherefore I ° praised the dead which are
already dead more than the living which are
yet alive.
3 Yea, ° better *is he* than both they, which
hath not yet been, who hath not seen the
° evil work that is done [1] under the sun.
e3 4 Again, I considered all ° travail, and ° every
right work, that for this a ° man is envied of
his neighbour. This *is* also vanity and ° vexation of ° spirit.
5 The ° fool foldeth his hands together, and
eateth his own flesh.
f3 6 [3] Better *is* an handful *with* quietness, than
both the hands full *with* [4] travail and [4] vexation
of [4] spirit.
J4 d4 7 Then I returned, and I saw vanity [1] under
the sun.
8 There is one *alone*, and *there is* not a
second; yea, he hath neither ° child nor brother: yet *is there* no end of all his labour;
neither is his eye satisfied with riches; neither
saith he, 'For whom do I ° labour, and bereave
° my soul of good?' This *is* also vanity, yea,
it *is* a sore ° travail.
9 Two *are* [3] better than one; because they
have a good reward for their labour.
10 For if they fall, the one will lift up his
fellow: but woe to him *that is* alone when he
falleth; for *he hath* not another to help him
up.
11 Again, if two lie together, then they have
heat: but how can one be warm *alone*?
12 And if one ° prevail against him, two shall
withstand him; and ° a threefold cord is not
quickly broken.
13 [3] Better *is* a ° poor and a wise child than e4
an old and foolish king, who will no more be
admonished.

16 under the sun. See note on 1. 3.
wickedness = lawlessness. Heb. *rāshā'*. Ap. 44. x.
iniquity. Same word as "wickedness" above. Fig. *Epizeuxis* (Ap. 6).
17 the righteous = a righteous one.
the wicked = a lawless one. Heb. *rāshā'*. Ap. 44. x.
18 God. Cp. *v.* 11, and note on 1. 11.
God might manifest them = God hath chosen them to show them that even they are beasts.
beasts = living creatures. As opposed to man = mammals: as opposed to creeping things = quadrupeds: as opposed to wild beasts = cattle.
19 that which befalleth. See note on "event", 2. 14; and Ap. 76. iii.
one thing: i.e. death.
one breath = one spirit. Heb. *rūach*. Ap. 9. Cp. Gen. 2. 7 with 1. 20, 21, 24, 30; and Ap. 13.
no preeminence, &c. Cp. Ps. 49. 12, 20; 146. 4.
20 one place: i.e. *Sheōl*, or the grave.
of the dust. See Gen. 1. 24; 2. 7, 19; 3. 19.
turn to dust again. See Gen. 3. 19. Ps. 22. 15; 104. 29; 146. 4. Job 10. 9; 34. 15. Cp. ch. 12. 7.
21 spirit. Heb. *rūach*. Ap. 9.
of man. Heb. "of the sons of Adam". See notes on *vv.* 10, 13; 1. 13.
that goeth, &c. This is mentioned as one of the emendations of the *Sōpherim*, though it is not included in the official lists (see Ap. 33). The primitive Text read the letter *He* (ה = H) as an interrogative, "whether it go" (cp. 2. 19; 6. 12). The Chald., Sept., Syr., Vulg., Luther, Geneva, and R.V. follow this reading. Another school took the *He* (ה = H) as the article pronoun and read "that goeth", &c., thus avoiding a supposed objection to its public reading. This was followed by Coverdale, the Bishops' Bible, and the A.V. It is therefore the Fig. *Erotēsis* (Ap. 6), leaving the question to be answered at the end of the book (12. 7).
22 better. See note on 2. 24. Cp. 11. 9.
portion = share, as in 2. 10: i.e. in the present life.

4. 1 under the sun. See note on 1. 3.
side. Heb. "hand": put by Fig. *Metonymy* (of Cause), Ap. 6, for the violence proceeding from it.
they: i.e. the oppressed. The phrase repeated for emphasis. Fig. *Epistrophe*. Ap. 6.
2 praised = commended, or pronounced happy. Heb. *shabach*, used only by David and Solomon.
3 better. See note on 2. 24.
evil. Heb. *ra'a'*. Ap. 44. viii.
4 travail = toil, as connected with trouble, sorrow. Not the same word as in 1. 13; 2. 23, 26; 3. 10; 4. 8; 5. 14.
every right work = all the dexterity in work.
man. Heb. *'ish*. Ap. 14. II.
vexation, &c. = feeding on wind. See note on 1. 14.
spirit. Heb. *rūach*. Ap. 9.
5 fool. Heb. *k^esil*, fat, inert. See note on Prov. 1. 7.
8 child = son.
labour = toil.
my soul = myself. Heb. *nephesh*. Ap. 13.
travail = fatigue from toil. See note on 2. 23, 26.
12 prevail against = overpower. Heb. *tākaph*, supposed to belong to later Hebrew, but it is found in Job 14. 20 and 15. 24 (the only three occurrences). See Ap. 76. vii.
a threefold cord. Cp. Num. 6. 24-26. Mic. 6. 8. Titus 2. 12, 13. 1 Thess. 1. 3 with 1. 9, 10.
13 poor = straitened in means, not able to profit others. Heb. *misken*. Not the same as in *v.* 14. Supposed to be a later Hebrew word, but a derivative of it is found in Deut. 8. 9. See Ap. 76. viii.

14 For °out of prison he cometh to reign; whereas also *he that is* °born in his kingdom becometh °poor.

f^4 (p. 910) 15 I considered all the living which walk [1]under the sun, with the second child that shall stand up in his stead.

16 *There is* no end of all the people, *even* of all that have been before them: they also that come after shall not rejoice in him. Surely this also *is* vanity and °vexation of [4]spirit.

B^3 K^1 (p. 912) **5** Keep thy foot when thou goest to the house of °God, and be more ready to °hear, than to give the sacrifice of °fools: for they consider not that they do °evil.

2 Be not rash with thy mouth, and let not thine heart be hasty to utter *any* °thing before [1]God: for [1]God *is* in heaven, and thou °upon earth: therefore let thy words be few.

L^1 3 For a dream cometh through the multitude of business; and a [1]fool's voice *is known* by multitude of words.

K^2 4 When thou °vowest a vow unto °God, defer not to pay it; for *He hath* no °pleasure in [1]fools: pay that which thou hast vowed.

5 °Better *is it* that thou shouldest not vow, than that thou shouldest vow and not pay.

6 Suffer not thy mouth °to cause thy flesh to °sin; neither say thou before the °angel, that it *was* an °error: °wherefore should [1]God be angry at thy °voice, and °destroy the °work of thine hands?

L^2 7 For in the multitude of dreams and many words *there are* also °*divers* vanities: but fear thou [1]God.

K^3 8 If thou seest the oppression of the °poor, and violent perverting of judgment and justice in a °province, marvel not at the °matter:

L^3 for °*He That is* higher than the highest regardeth; and *there be* higher than they.

K^4 9 Moreover the profit of the earth °is °for all: the king *himself* is served by the field.

10 He that loveth silver shall not be satisfied with silver; °nor he that loveth abundance with increase: this *is* also vanity.

11 When goods increase, they are increased that eat them: and what °good *is there* to the °owners thereof, saving the beholding *of them* with °their eyes?

12 The sleep of a labouring man *is* sweet, whether he eat little or much: but the abundance of the rich will not suffer him °to sleep.

C^3 M g^1 13 There is a sore [1]evil *which* I have seen °under the sun, *namely*, riches kept for the [11]owners thereof to [11]their hurt.

h^1 14 But those riches perish by [1]evil °travail: and he begetteth a son, and *there is* nothing in his °hand.

15 °As he came forth of his mother's womb, naked shall he return to go as he came, and shall take nothing of his labour, which he may carry away in his hand.

g^2 16 And this also *is* a sore [1]evil, *that* in all

---

14 out of prison, &c. Cp. Joseph (Gen. 41. 40); Daniel (Dan. 5. 29; 6. 1-3).

born, &c. Cp. Rehoboam, robbed by Shishak (1 Kings 14. 25-28).

poor=needy, in want. Heb. *rūsh.* See note on "poverty", Prov. 6. 11.

16 vexation. The same word as in 1. 17; 2. 22.

5. 1-12 (B^3, p. 907). **MAN. HIS WORKS.**
(Repeated Alternation.)

B^3 | K^1 | 1, 2. Works.
L^1 | 3. Reason.
K^2 | 4-6. Vows.
L^2 | 7. Reason.
K^3 | 8-. Perverting of judgment.
L^3 | -8. Reason.
K^4 | 9-12. Riches.

1 God. Heb. Elohim (with Art.)=the [true] God, or the Deity. Ap. 4. I. See note on 1. 13.

hear=obey.

fools=fat, inert. Heb. *kᵉṣīl.* See note on Prov. 1. 7.

evil. Heb. *rāʿaʿ.* Ap. 44. viii.

2 thing=word.

upon earth. Same idea as "under the sun". See note on 1. 3.

4 vowest a vow=makest a solemn vow. Fig. *Polyptōton* (Ap. 6). **God.** Heb. Elohim. Ap. 4. I.

pleasure. See note on "purpose", 3. 1, and Ap. 76. v.

5 Better. See note on 2. 24.

6 to cause, &c.: by vows made concerning the flesh, such as eating and drinking, marrying, &c.

sin. Heb. *chāṭāʾ.* Ap. 44. i.

angel=messenger. Cp. Mal. 2. 7.

error. Heb. *shāgag.* Ap. 44. xii.

wherefore . . . ? Fig. *Erotēsis.* Ap. 6.

voice. Put by Fig. *Metonymy* (of Cause), Ap. 6, for the vain words uttered by it; referring to *v.* 1.

destroy=confiscate.

work. Aram., Sept., and Vulg. read "works" (pl.).

7 divers vanities. Plural of emphasis = great vanity: i.e. in many dreams and many words, also [there is] great vanity: referring to *v.* 3 above.

8 poor=needy, in want. Heb. *rūsh,* as in 4. 14.

province. See note on 2. 8, and Ap. 76. ii.

matter. Heb. purpose or desire, put by Fig. *Metonymy* (of Cause), Ap. 6, for the effect of it. Heb. *ḥēphez,* one of the words supposed to be later Hebrew. See note on 3. 1, and Ap. 76. v.

He That is higher, &c.=the high One above the high one regardeth, even the Most High is over them.

9 is="it [is]."

for all=[consists] in the whole, i. e. not confined to one day.

10 nor he that loveth, &c.=And who is [ever] content with abundance without increase (capital without interest). No socialism or "corruption" of text here.

11 good=advantage.

owners. Plural of emphasis. **their**=his.

12 to sleep=to sleep soundly.

5. 13—6. 9 (C^3, p. 907). **PERSONAL OBSERVATION.** *(Alternations.)*

C^3 | M | g^1 | 5. 13. Self. Labour for.
h^1 | 5. 14, 15. Profitless.
g^2 | 5. 16. Self. Labour for.
h^2 | 5. 17. Profitless.
N | 5. 18-20. Long life.
M | g^3 | 6. 1, 2-. Self. Riches for.
h^3 | 6. -2. Profitless.
g^4 | 6. 3-. Self. Children.
h^4 | 6. -3. Profitless.
N | 6. 4-9. Long life.

13 under the sun. See note on 1. 3.

14 travail=fatigue from toil. See note on 2. 23, and 4. 4.

15 As=According as. Cp. Job 1. 21. Ps. 49. 17. 1 Tim. 6. 7.

points as he came, so shall he go: and what
°profit hath he that hath °laboured for the
°wind?
h² (p. 912) 17 All his days also he eateth in darkness,
and *he hath* much sorrow and wrath with his
sickness.
N 18 Behold *that* which I have seen: *it is* good
and °comely *for one* to eat and to drink, and
to enjoy the good of all his labour that he
taketh [13] under the sun all the days of his life,
which [1] God giveth him: for it *is* his portion.
19 Every °man also to whom [1] God hath given
riches and wealth, and hath given him power
to eat thereof, and to take his portion, and to
rejoice in his labour; this *is* °the gift of [4] God.
20 For he shall not much remember the days
of his life; because [1] God °answereth *him* in
the joy of his heart.

M g³ 6 There is an °evil which I have seen °under
the sun, and it *is* common among °men:
2 A °man to whom °God hath given riches,
°wealth, and honour, so that he wanteth nothing for °his soul of all that he desireth,
h³ yet °God giveth him not power to eat thereof, but
a stranger eateth it: this *is* °vanity, and it *is* an
[1] evil disease.
g⁴ 3 If a [2] man beget an hundred *children*, and
live many years, so that the days of his years
be many,
h⁴ and [2] his soul be not °filled with good, and also
that he have no burial; I say, *that* an untimely
birth *is* better than he.
4 For °he cometh in with [2] vanity, and departeth
in darkness, and his name shall be covered
with darkness.
5 Moreover he hath not seen the sun, nor
known *any thing:* this hath more rest than
the other.
N 6 Yea, though he live a thousand years twice
told, yet hath he seen no good: °do not all go
to °one place?
7 All the °labour of [1] man *is* for his mouth,
and yet °the appetite is not filled.
8 For °what hath °the wise more than °the
fool? °what hath °the poor, that knoweth
to walk before the living?
9 °Better *is* °the sight of the eyes than °the
wandering of °the desire: this *is* also vanity
and °vexation of °spirit.
B O¹ Q (p. 913) 10 °That which hath been is named already,
and it is known that it *is* [1] man: neither may
he contend with Him That is mightier than
he.
R 11 Seeing there be many things that increase
vanity, what *is* [1] man the better?
12 For who knoweth what *is* good for [1] man
in *this* life, °all the days of his vain life which
he spendeth as a shadow? °for who can tell a
[1] man what shall be after him [1] under the sun?

7 A °good °name *is* °better than °precious
°ointment; and the day of death than
the day of one's birth.
2 *It is* [1] better to go to the house of mourning,
than to go to the house of °feasting: for that
is °the end of all °men; and the living will lay
it to his heart.

16 profit = advantage. laboured = toiled.
wind. Heb. *rūach*. Ap. 9.
18 comely = well.
19 man. Heb. *'ādām.* Ap. 14. I. See note on 1. 13.
the gift = a gift.
20 answereth = causeth [things] to respond, as in Hos. 2. 21, 22. See note on 10. 19.

6. 1 evil. Heb. *rā'a'.* Ap. 44. viii.
under the sun. See note on 1. 3.
men. Heb. *'ādām* (with Art.) = humanity. Ap. 14. I. See note on 1. 13.
2 man. Heb. *'īsh.* Ap. 14. II.
God. Heb. Elohim (with Art.) = the [true] God, or the Deity. Ap. 4. I. See note on 1. 13.
wealth. See note on 5. 19.
his soul = himself. Heb. *nephesh.* Ap. 13.
vanity. See note on 1. 2.
3 filled = satisfied.
4 he cometh: i. e. in the untimely birth of *v.* 3.
6 do not all . . . ? Fig. *Erotēsis* (in Affirmation), Ap. 6. Cp. 3. 19-21. one place: i. e. Sheōl. Ap. 35.
7 labour = toil.
the appetite = the soul. Heb. *nephesh.* Ap. 13.
8 what = what [advantage].
the wise = a wise one, or sage.
the fool = a fool. Heb. *kesīl.* See note on Prov. 1. 7.
the poor = a wretched one. Heb *'ānāh.* See note on "poverty", Prov. 6. 11.
9 Better. See note on 2. 24.
the sight of = what is seen by.
the wandering of = what is pursued by.
the desire = soul. Heb. *nephesh.* Ap. 13. No Art.
vexation of spirit. See note on 1. 14.
spirit. Heb. *rūach.* Ap. 9.

6. 10—12. 12 (*B*, p. 906). THE CHIEF GOOD. WHAT IT IS. (*Repeated Alternation.*)

B | O¹ | 6. 10—7. 14. Man. In himself.
P¹ | 7. 15-29. Personal proving.
O² | 8. 1-8. Man. In his wisdom.
P² | 8. 9, 10. Personal observation.
O³ | 8. 11-13. Man. In his evil-doing.
P³ | 8. 14—9. 1. Personal observation.
O⁴ | 9. 2-10. Man. In his end.
P⁴ | 9. 11—10. 15. Personal inspection.
O⁵ | 10. 16—12. 8. Man. In his different portions.
P⁵ | 12. 9-12. Personal information.

6. 10—7. 14 (O¹, above). MAN. IN HIMSELF. (*Introversion.*)

O¹ | Q | 6. 10. Man and God.
R | 6. 11—7. 10. Good. Q. What is it?
R | 7. 11, 12. Good. Ans. What it is.
Q | 7. 13, 14. God and man.

10 That which hath been is named already, &c.: "What is he who hath been? (cp. 1. 9).
Long ago his name was given;
And it is understood what [that name was,]—
It was—Adam":
which means *vegetable mould*, made in the likeness of Elohim, Gen. 1. 27; 2. 7; 5. 1, 2. Made of "earth" he returns to earth (1 Cor. 15. 47): i.e. "vanity". This book is a comment on Pss. 144. 4. Cp. Pss. 39; 49; 62.
12 all the days of his vain life = the numbered days of his vain life. for = as to which.

7. 1 good. Note the Fig. *Epanadiplōsis* (Ap. 6), by which the sentence begins and ends with the same word "good" (rendered "precious").
name . . . ointment. Note the Fig. *Paronomasia* (Ap. 6), "*shēm mishshemen*".
better. See note on 2. 24.
precious = good. Same word as "good" at the beginning of the sentence.
2 the end. Heb. *sōph.* See note on 3. 11.
men. Heb. *'ādām* (with Art.) = mankind. Ap. 14. I. See note on 1. 13.

3 Sorrow *is* [1]better than laughter: for by the sadness of the countenance the heart is made [1]better.

4 The heart of the wise *is* in the house of mourning; but the heart of °fools *is* in the house of mirth.

5 *It is* [1]better to hear the rebuke of the wise, than for a °man to hear the song of [4]fools.

6 For as the °crackling of °thorns under a °pot, so *is* the laughter of the [4]fool: this also *is* °vanity.

7 Surely °oppression °maketh a wise man °mad; and °a gift destroyeth the heart.

8 [1]Better *is* the end of a thing than the beginning thereof: *and* the patient in °spirit *is* [1]better than the proud in °spirit.

9 Be not hasty in thy [8]spirit to be angry: for anger resteth in the bosom of [4]fools.

10 Say not thou, 'What is *the cause* that the former days were [1]better than these?' for thou dost not enquire wisely concerning this.

R (p. 913) 11 °Wisdom *is* good °with an inheritance: and *by it there is* profit to them that °see the sun.

12 For [11]wisdom *is* a defence, *and* money *is* a defence: but the excellency of knowledge *is*, *that* [11]wisdom giveth °life to them that have it.

Q 13 Consider the work of °God: for who can make *that* straight, which He hath made crooked?

14 In the day of prosperity be joyful, but in the day of adversity consider [13]God also hath set the one over against the other, to the end that [2]man should °find nothing after him.

P[1] S[1] l[1] (p. 914) 15 All *things* have I seen in the days of my vanity: there is a °just *man* that perisheth in his righteousness, and there is a °wicked *man* that prolongeth *his life* in his °wickedness.

16 Be not righteous °over much; neither make thyself °over wise:

m[1] why shouldest thou °destroy thyself?

S[2] l[2] (p. 914) 17 °Be not over much [15]wicked, neither be thou °foolish:

m[2] °why shouldest thou die before thy time?

18 *It is* good that thou shouldest take hold of this; yea, also from this withdraw not thine hand: for he that feareth [13]God shall °come forth of them all.

S[3] l[3] 19 [11]Wisdom strengtheneth °the wise more than ten mighty *men* which are in the city.

m[3] 20 For *there is* not a [15]just [2]man upon earth, that doeth good, and °sinneth not.

S[4] l[4] 21 Also take no heed unto all words that are spoken; lest thou hear thy servant °curse thee:

m[4] 22 For oftentimes also thine own heart knoweth that thou thyself likewise hast [21]cursed others.

S[5] l[5] 23 All this have I proved by [11]wisdom: I said, "I will be wise;" but it *was* far from me.

24 That which is far off, and °exceeding deep, who can find it out?

25 I applied mine heart to know, and to search, and to seek out [11]wisdom, and °the reason *of things*, and to know the °wickedness of [4]folly, even of [17]foolishness *and* [7]madness:

m[5] 26 And I find more bitter than death the woman, whose heart *is* snares and nets, *and* her hands *as* bands: whoso pleaseth [13]God shall escape from her; but the [20]sinner shall be taken by her.

S[6] l[6] 27 °Behold, this have I found," saith the preacher, °"*counting* one by one, to find out the °account:

---

4 fools=fat, inert. Heb. *kᵉsîl*. Same word as in *vv.* 5, 6, 9, 25 ("folly"). Not the same as "foolish" (*v.* 17), or "foolishness", *v.* 25. See note on "poverty", Prov. 1. 7.

5 man. Heb. *'îsh.* Ap. 14. II.

6 crackling. Same word as "voice" (Gen. 3. 8), used of any sound.

thorns . . . pot. Note Fig. *Paronomasia* (Ap. 6). Heb. *ḥaṣṣîrîm . . . ḥaṣṣîr.* May be Englished by "nettles . . . kettles".

vanity. See note on 1. 2.

7 oppression=oppressing: i. e. the act of oppressing.

maketh . . . mad. Referring to the madness of folly.

mad=beyond control. See note on 1. 17.

a gift=a bribe.

8 spirit. Heb. *rûach.* Ap. 9.

11 Wisdom. Heb. *chākmāh.* See note on Prov. 1. 2.

with, &c.=like, or as. See 2. 16; 8. 1. Gen. 18. 23, 25. Job 3. 14, 15; 9. 26; 21. 8; 40. 15. Pss. 73. 5, 25; 143. 7. Render: "Wisdom [is as] good as riches, and more advantageous to them that see the sun".

see the sun: i. e. the idiom for "are alive".

12 life=future life. See note on Lev. 18. 5.

13 God. Heb. Elohim (with Art.)=the [true] God: i. e. the Deity. Ap. 4. I.

14 find=discover.

7. 15-29 (P[1], p. 913). PERSONAL PROVING.
(Division and Repeated Alternation.)

P[1] | S[1] | l[1] | 15, 16-. Overmuch righteousness.
m[1] | -16. Reason.
S[2] | l[2] | 17-. Overmuch wickedness.
m[2] | -17, 18. Reason.
S[3] | l[3] | 19. Overmuch might.
m[3] | 20. Reason.
S[4] | l[4] | 21. Overmuch heed.
m[4] | 22. Reason.
S[5] | l[5] | 23-25. Overmuch wisdom.
m[5] | 26. Reason.
S[6] | l[6] | 27, 28-. Overmuch search.
m[6] | -28, 29. Reason.

15 just=righteous.

wicked . . . wickedness. Heb. *rāsha' . . . rā'a'.* Ap. 44. x, viii.

16 over much: i. e. depending on the merit of good works.

over wise: i. e. beyond what is necessary.

destroy thyself=make thyself lonely: i. e. forsaken. Cp. Job 16. 7.

17 Be not over much wicked=Be not very wicked: i. e. Be not wicked at all. For violation of nature's laws surely end in premature death.

foolish=stupid. Heb. *sākal*; not the same word as in *vv.* 4, 5, 6, 9, 25 ("folly"). See note on Prov. 1. 7.

why . . . ? Fig. *Erotēsis.* Ap. 6.

18 come forth of them all=make His way with both.

19 the wise=a wise man.

20 sinneth. Heb. *chāṭā'.* Ap. 44. I.

21 curse=revile.

24 exceeding deep. Heb. "deep, deep". Fig. *Epizeuxis.* Ap. 6.

25 the reason . . . madness=in order to know the reason (or cause) of folly's wickedness, and the madness of folly.

wickedness=lawlessness. Heb. *rāshā'.* Ap. 44. x.

27 Behold. Fig. *Asterismos.* Ap. 6.

counting, &c. Or, supply the Ellipsis thus: "[considering women] one by one", &c.

account=result.

28 Which yet °my soul °seeketh, but I find not: [11]one [2]man among a thousand have I found;
m[6] (p. 914) but a woman among all those have I not found.
29 °Lo, this only have I found, that [13]God hath made [2]man upright; but °they have sought out many °inventions.

O[2] T n (p. 915) **8** Who *is* °as the wise *man?* and °who knoweth the °interpretation of a thing?
o °a °man's °wisdom maketh his face to shine, and the °boldness of his face shall be changed.
U 2 °I *counsel thee* to keep the king's commandment, and *that* °in regard of the oath of °God.
3 Be not hasty to go out of his sight: °stand not in an °evil thing; for he doeth whatsoever pleaseth him.
U 4 Where the word of a king *is, there is* °power: and who may say unto him, 'What doest thou?'
T n 5 Whoso keepeth the commandment shall °feel no °evil thing: and a wise man's heart discerneth both °time and judgment.
o 6 Because to every °purpose °there is [5]time and judgment, °therefore the misery of [1]man *is* °great upon him.
7 For he knoweth not that which shall be: for who can tell him when it shall be?
8 *There is* no [1]man that hath [4]power over °the spirit to retain °the spirit; neither *hath he* [4]power in the day of death: and *there is* no °discharge in *that* war; neither shall °wickedness deliver °those that are given to it.
P[2] V 9 All this have I seen, and applied my heart unto every work that is done °under the sun:
W °*there is* a time wherein one [1]man ruleth over another to his own hurt.
V 10 And so °I saw °the wicked buried, who had °come and gone from the place of the holy,
W and they were forgotten in the city where they had so done: this *is* also vanity.
O[3] X 11 Because sentence against an [3]evil work is not executed speedily, therefore the heart of the sons of [1]men is fully set in them to do [3]evil.
Y 12 Though a °sinner do [3]evil an hundred times, and his °*days* be prolonged,
Z yet surely I know that it shall be well with them that fear °God, which fear before Him:
Z 13 But it shall not be well with °the [10]wicked,
Y neither shall he prolong *his* days, *which are* as a shadow;
X because he feareth not before [12]God.
P[3] A (p. 916) 14 There is a vanity which is done °upon the earth; that there be °just *men,* unto whom it happeneth according to the work of the [10]wicked; again, there be [10]wicked *men,* to

28 my soul = I myself. Heb. *nephesh.* Ap. 13.
seeketh = sought.
29 Lo. Fig. *Asterismos.* Ap. 6. Same as "Behold" in *v.* 27.
they = mankind: not merely the above classes. This verse is admittedly the inspired truth of God: so therefore are the other statements in this book. Moreover, "they" is emphatic. **inventions** = devices.

8. 1-8 (O[2], p. 913). MAN. IN HIS WISDOM.
(*Introversion and Alternation.*)

O[2] | T | n | 1-. Wisdom. Happiness of it.
o | -1. Reason.
U | 2, 3. King's commandment.
U | 4. King's word.
T | *n* | 5. Wisdom. Strength of it.
o | 6-8. Reason.

1 as = like.
who . . . ? Supply the Ellipsis (Ap. 6), from the preceding line: "Who [is like him that] knoweth?"
interpretation = understanding.
man's. Heb. *'ādām* (with Art.). Ap. 14. I. See note on 1. 13.
wisdom. Heb. *chākmāh.* See note on Prov. 1. 2.
boldness = sternness.
2 I counsel thee: or I say, then.
in regard of = on account of.
God. Heb. Elohim. Ap. 4. I. See note on 1. 13.
3 stand not = do not take thy stand. Some codices, with one early printed edition, Syr., and Vulg. read, "and stand not".
evil. Heb. *rā'a'.* Ap. 44. viii.
4 power = might, or control. Heb. *shilṭōn.* Occurs only here and in *v.* 8. **5 feel** = know.
evil = calamity. Heb. *rā'a'.* Ap. 44. viii.
time and judgment = a time, yea, a judgment time. Fig. *Hendiadys.* Ap. 6.
6 purpose. See note on 3. 1.
there is = there exists. Heb. *yēsh.*
therefore the misery = when the evil (Heb. *rā'a'.* Ap. 44. viii). **great** = heavy.
8 the spirit. Heb. *rūach.* Ap. 9. Some render "wind" and refer to 11. 5. Prov. 30. 4.
discharge in that war = no furlough in the battle [of life].
wickedness. Heb. *rā'a'.* Ap. 44. viii. Perhaps here = cunning: no cunning will save the wicked.
those that are given to it = its possessors.

8. 9, 10 (P[2], p. 913). PERSONAL OBSERVATION.
(*Alternation.*)

P[2] | V | 9-. Observation.
W | -9. Result.
V | 10-. Observation.
W | -10. Result.

9 under the sun. See note on 1. 3.
there is a time wherein = sometimes.
10 I saw = I have seen.
the wicked = lawless men (pl.). Heb. *rāshā'.* Ap. 44. x.
come and gone. Supply the complex Fig. *Ellipsis* (Ap. 6), "I have seen wicked men come [to the grave; and righteous men] depart [in death, Gen. 15. 2] from the place of the holy, and be forgotten", &c.

11-13 (O[3], p. 913). MAN IN HIS EVIL-DOING.
(*Introversion.*)

O[3] | X | 11. Consequence of God's suspended judgment.
Y | 12-. Evil-doing prolonged.
Z | -12. Evil-doers. Well with them.
Z | 13-. Evil-doers. Evil with them.
Y | -13-. Evil-doers' days not prolonged.
X | -13. Cause. No fear of God.

12 sinner. Heb. *chāṭā'.* Ap. 44. I. **days.** Supply the Ellipsis (Ap. 6) by "evil-doing". **God.** Heb. Elohim (with Art.) = the [true] God: the Deity. Ap. 4. I. See note on 1. 13. **13 the wicked** = a lawless one.

8. 14—9. 1 [For Structure see next page].

14 upon the earth. See note on 5. 2. **just** = righteous.

whom it happeneth according to the work of the righteous: I said that this also *is* vanity.

B[1] p[1] (p. 916) 15 Then I commended mirth, because a [1]man hath no °better thing [9]under the sun, than to eat, and to drink, and to be merry:

q[1] for that shall abide with him of his °labour the days of his life, which [12]God giveth him [9]under the sun.

B[2] p[2] 16 When I applied mine heart to know [1]wisdom, and to see the °business that is done [11]upon the earth:

q[2] (°for also *there is that* neither day nor night seeth sleep with his eyes:)

B[3] p[3] 17 Then I beheld all the work of [12]God, that a [1]man cannot find out the work that is done [9]under the sun:

q[3] because though a [1]man labour to seek *it* out, °yet he shall not find *it;* yea farther; though a wise *man* think to know *it*, yet shall he not be able to find *it*.

A **9** For all this °I considered in my heart °even to declare all this, that °the righteous, and the wise, and their works, *are* in the hand of °God: no °man knoweth either love or °hatred *by* all *that is* before °them.

O[4] C[1] 2 °All *things come* alike to all: *there is* °one event to the righteous, and to °the wicked; to the good and to the clean, and to the unclean; to him that sacrificeth, and to him that sacrificeth not: as *is* the good, so *is* the °sinner; *and* he that sweareth, as *he* that feareth an oath.

3 This *is* °an °evil among all *things* that are done °under the sun, that *there is* [2]one event unto all: yea, also the heart of the sons of [1]men is full of °evil, and °madness *is* in their heart while they live, and after that °*they go* to the dead.

D[1] 4 °For to him that is joined to all the living there is °hope: for °a °living dog °is °better than a dead °lion.

5 For the living know that they shall die:

C[2] but °the dead know not any thing, neither have they any more °a reward; for the °memory of °them °is forgotten.

6 Also their love, and their hatred, and their envy, is now °perished; neither have they any more a portion for ever in any *thing* that is done [3]under the sun.

D[2] 7 Go thy way, eat thy bread with joy, and drink thy °wine with a merry heart; for [1]God now accepteth thy works.

8 Let thy garments be always white; and let thy head lack no °ointment.

9 Live joyfully with the wife whom thou lovest all the days of the life of thy vanity, which He hath given thee [3]under the sun, all the days of thy vanity: for that *is* thy portion in *this* life, and in thy °labour which thou takest [3]under the sun.

8. 14—9. 1 (P[3], p. 913). PERSONAL OBSERVATION.
(*Introversion and Alternation.*)

P[3] | A | 8. 14. Contrariety. Man's happenings.
B[1] | p[1] | 8. 15-. Mirth commended.
q[1] | 8. -15. Reason.
B[2] | p[2] | 8. 16-. Wisdom. Man's work on earth.
q[2] | 8. -16. Reason.
B[3] | p[3] | 8. 17-. Wisdom. God's work on earth.
q[3] | 8. -17. Reason.
A | 9. 1. Contrariety. God's dealings.

15 better. See note on 2. 24. **labour**=toil.

16 business=travail.

for also there is, &c.=how that one doth not see sleep with his eyes by day or by night. Fig. *Catachresis* (Ap. 6).

17 yet he shall not find it. The A.V. of 1611 omitted these words. Inserted in a subsequent edition.

9. 1 I considered=I have taken to heart.

even to declare. Sept. and Syr. read, "and my heart proved".

the righteous=just ones.

God. Heb. Elohim (with Art.)=the [true] God: the Deity. Ap. 4. I.

man. Heb. *'ădām.* Ap. 14. I. See note on 1. 13.

hatred by all that is before them=hatred. All lies before them (i.e. in the future).

them: i.e. the righteous and the lawless.

9. 2-10 (O[4], p. 913). MAN. IN HIS END.
(*Repeated Alternation.*)

O[4] | C[1] | 2, 3. The dead.
D[1] | 4, 5-. The living.
C[2] | -5, 6. The dead.
D[2] | 7-10-. The living.
C[3] | -10. The dead.

2 All things come alike to all=Just as before all others. Reading on from *v.* 1.

one event: i.e. death. See note on 2. 14.

the wicked=a lawless one. Heb. *rāshā'.* Ap. 44. x.

sinner. Heb. *chāṭā'.* Ap. 44. i. All the nouns in this verse are sing.

3 an evil. The Preposition (ב=B) in *bbol*, gives the force of the superlative: i.e. the greatest or worst calamity of all, &c.

evil=calamity. Heb. *ra'a'.* Ap. 44. viii.

under the sun. See note on 1. 3.

madness. Pl. as elsewhere. See note on 1. 17.

they go. Omit these words and note the Fig. *Aposiopesis* (Ap. 6), "and after that—to the dead!" See the following note.

4 For to him that is joined. Connect this with the end of preceding verse and render "For who is excepted? To all the living", &c.

hope=confidence. Heb. *biṭṭāḥōn* (from *baṭah*). Ap. 69. i. Occurs only here, 2 Kings 18. 19, and Isa. 36. 4.

a living dog, &c. Fig. *Parœmia.* Ap. 6. Same proverb in Arabic.

living dog. Regarded by the Jews as the most unclean and despicable creature (1 Sam. 17. 43; 24. 14. 2 Sam. 9. 8; 16. 9. 2 Kings 8. 13. Matt. 7. 6; 15. 26. Rev. 22. 15). Hence Gentiles so called.

is=he [is]: i.e. even he.

better. See note on 2. 24.

lion. Regarded as the noblest of animals (Gen. 49. 10. Job 10. 16. Isa. 38. 13. Lam. 3. 10. Hos. 13. 7. Rev. 5. 5).

5 the dead know not any thing. See and cp. *v.* 10. Ps. 6. 5; 30. 9; 31. 17; 88. 11. Isa. 38. 18, 19.

a reward=any advantage [to them].

memory=the faculty of remembering. See note on "them", below.

them. The Heb. suffix "them" must be taken as the subject in all the four nouns alike. As in *v.* 6, the possessive pronoun "their" is, and must be, taken alike in each case. **is forgotten**=ceases to exist, as in Ps. 77. 9, where it is parallel with "clean gone for ever" and "evermore", and in the next verse here (*v.* 6), where it stands parallel with "perished" and "for ever". **6 perished.** Like the knowledge and memory of *v.* 5. **7 wine.** Heb. *yayin.* Ap. 27. I. **8 ointment**=perfume. **9 labour . . . takest**=toil . . . toilest.

10 Whatsoever °thy hand findeth to do, °do
it with thy might;
C3 (p. 916) for *there is* no work, nor device, °nor knowledge,
nor °wisdom, in °the grave, whither thou goest.
P4 E1 r1 (p. 917) 11 I returned, and saw [3]under the sun, that
the race *is* not to the swift, nor the battle to
the strong, neither yet bread to the wise, nor
yet riches to men of understanding, nor yet
favour to °men of skill; but time and °chance
°happeneth to them all.
12 °For °man also knoweth not his time:
s1 as the fishes that are taken in an [3]evil net, and
as the birds that are caught in the snare; so
are the sons of °men snared in an [3]evil time,
when it falleth suddenly upon them.
E2 r2 13 This [10]wisdom have I seen also [3]under the
sun, and it *seemed* great unto me:
14 *There was* °a little city, and few °men
within it; and there came a great king against
it, and besieged it, and built great bulwarks
against it:
15 Now °there was found in it a °poor wise
°man, and he by his [10]wisdom delivered the city;
s2 yet no [14]man remembered that same °poor
°man.
E3 r3 16 Then said I, [10]'Wisdom *is* [4]better than
strength:
s3 nevertheless the [15]poor man's [10]wisdom *is* despised, and his words are not heard.'
E4 r4 17 The words of wise *men are* heard in quiet
more than the cry of him that ruleth among
°fools.
18 [10]Wisdom *is* better than weapons of war:
s4 but one [2]sinner destroyeth much good.

E5 r5 **10** °Dead flies °cause the ointment of the
apothecary °to send forth a stinking
savour: *so doth* a little °folly °him that is in
reputation for °wisdom *and* honour.
s5 2 A wise man's heart *is* at his right hand;
but a °fool's heart at his left.
E6 r6 3 Yea also, when he that is a °fool walketh
by the way, his °wisdom faileth *him*,
s6 and he °saith to every one *that* °he *is* a °fool.
E7 r7 4 If the °spirit of the ruler rise up against
thee, leave not thy place; for °yielding pacifieth
great offences.
5 There is an °evil *which* I have seen °under
the sun, as an error *which* proceedeth from the
ruler:
s7 6 °Folly is set °in great dignity, and the rich
sit in low place.
7 I have seen servants upon °horses, and
princes walking as servants °upon the earth.
E8 r8 8 He that diggeth a pit shall fall into it; and
whoso breaketh an °hedge, a serpent shall
bite him.

10 thy hand findeth to do. Hand put by Fig. *Metonymy* (of Cause), Ap. 6, for the strength put forth by it (Lev. 12. 8; 25. 28).
do it with thy might = do it while thou art able, and have time to do it.
nor knowledge, &c. See note on *v.* 5, above.
wisdom. Heb. *chākmah.* See note on 1. 2.
the grave. Heb. Sheōl. Ap. 35. The only occurrence of the word in this book.

9. 11—10. 15 (P4, p. 913). PERSONAL INSPECTION. (*Division and Repeated Alternation.*)

P4 | E1 | r1 | 9. 11,12-. Wisdom. Unequally requited, &c.
s1 | 9. -12. Man snared by ignorance.
E2 | r2 | 9. 13-15-. Wisdom. Better than strength.
s2 | 9. -15. Man benefits by wisdom of poor.
E3 | r3 | 9. 16-. Wisdom. Better than strength.
s3 | 9. -16. Man despises wisdom of poor.
E4 | r4 | 9. 17-18-. Wisdom. Better than strength.
s4 | 9. -18. Man's folly destroys what is good.
E5 | r5 | 10. 1. Wisdom. Better than reputation.
s5 | 10. 2. Man's heart betrays his folly.
E6 | r6 | 10. 3-. Wisdom of the fool fails him.
s6 | 10. -3. Man's folly declares itself.
E7 | r7 | 10. 4, 5. Wisdom. Better than power.
s7 | 10. 6, 7. Man's folly often in high places.
E8 | r8 | 10. 8-10-. Wisdom. Better than labour.
s8 | 10. -10. Man's wisdom saves labour.
E9 | r9 | 10. 11, 12-. Wisdom's words are gracious.
s9 | 10. -12-15. Man's words destroy himself.

11 men. Heb. *gibbor.* Ap. 14. IV.
chance = occurrence. Heb. *phega'*: i.e. "time [of misfortune]". Occurs only here and 1 Kings 5. 4, where it is associated with "evil" (or calamity).
happeneth = meeteth, or befalleth.
12 For man, &c. Connect this sentence with *v.* 11.
man . . . men. Heb. *'ādām* (with Art.). Ap. 14. I.
14 a little city. For the application of *vv.* 14-16, note the following illustrations: poor (2 Cor. 8. 9. Phil. 2. 6-8); wise (1 Cor. 1. 24); delivered (1 Cor. 1. 18, 25); none remembered (Isa. 53. 3); despised (1 Cor. 1. 28); words heard in quiet (Job 6. 24. Ezek. 1. 24, 25. Luke 10. 39).
men. Heb. pl. of *'ĕnōsh.* Ap. 14. III.
15 there was found = [some one] was found.
poor = unfortunate. Heb. *misken.* See note on Prov. 6. 11.
poor wise. Some codices, with three early printed editions, Aram., Sept., and Vulg., read "poor but wise".
man. Heb. *'īsh.* Ap. 14. II.
17 fools = fat, inert. Heb. *kesil.* See note on Prov. 1. 7.

10. 1 Dead flies. Heb. flies of death: i.e. flies that bring or produce death. Supply the Fig. *Ellipsis*, "[as] dead". **cause** = [are that which will] cause, &c.
to send forth a stinking savour = to stink [and] ferment. Fig. *Hendiadys.* Ap. 6.
folly = stupidity. Heb. *sakal.* Same root as in *v.* 6. See note on Prov. 1. 7.
him. Note the Fig. *Ellipsis* (Ap. 6): "So doth stupidity [cause] him that is in reputation for wisdom and honour [to send forth an offensive savour]".
wisdom. Heb. *chākmah.* See note on 1. 2.
2 fool's = dullard's. Heb. *kesil* = fat, inert. Same word as in *v.* 12. See note on Prov. 1. 7.
3 fool. Heb. *sākal.* Same word as in *vv.* 6, 14, not *vv.* 2, 12, 15. **wisdom** = heart.
saith = tells. See note on Prov. 1. 7.
he = he himself (emph.).
4 spirit. Heb. *rūach.* Ap. 9.
yielding, &c. = gentleness preventeth greater outrages. **5 evil.** Heb. *rā'a'.* Ap. 44. viii. **under the sun.** See note on 1. 3. **6 Folly** = a great dullard. Heb. *sākal*, as in *vv.* 1, 3, 3, 14. **in great dignity** = in many high positions. **7 horses.** No evidence of a late origin of this book, for we read of them in 1 Kings 4. 26, 28; 10. 26, 28; 22. 4. 2 Kings 9. 33; 14. 20. If not in common use, it was because of the Law (Deut. 17. 16); and because of Solomon's disobedience (1 Kings 10. 28. 2 Chron. 1. 16, 17; 9. 28). **upon the earth.** See note on 5. 2. **8 hedge** = a wall built of loose stones without mortar. Heb. *gāder*, used especially of sheep-folds (Num. 32. 16, 24, 36. 1 Sam. 24. 3. Zeph. 2. 6); also for fencing pathways between the vineyards (Num. 22. 24. Ps. 62. 3; 80. 12). The crevices between the loose stones form hiding-places for lizards and other creeping things.

9 Whoso removeth stones shall be hurt therewith; *and* he that cleaveth wood shall be endangered thereby.

10 If the iron be blunt, and he do not whet the edge, then must he put to more strength:

s8 but [1] wisdom *is* profitable to direct.

E9 r9 (p. 917) 11 Surely the serpent will bite without enchantment; and a babbler is no better.

12 The words of a wise man's mouth *are* gracious;

s9 but the lips of a [2] fool will swallow up himself.

13 The beginning of the words of his mouth *is* °foolishness: and the end of his talk *is* mischievous °madness.

14 A [3] fool also is full of words: a °man cannot tell what shall be; and what shall be after him, who can tell him?

15 The °labour of the °foolish wearieth every one of them, because he knoweth not how to go to the city.

O5 F (p. 918) 16 Woe to thee, O land, when thy king *is* a child, and thy princes eat in the morning!

17 °Blessed *art* thou, O land, when thy king *is* the son of nobles, and thy princes eat in due season, for strength, and not for drunkenness!

G 18 By much slothfulness the °building decayeth; and through idleness of the hands the house °droppeth through.

H 19 A feast is made for laughter, and °wine °maketh merry: but money °answereth all *things*.

F 20 °Curse not the king, no not °in thy thought; and °curse not the rich in thy bedchamber: for a bird of the air shall carry the voice, and that which hath wings shall tell the matter.

G **11** Cast thy °bread °upon the waters: for thou shalt find °it after many days.

2 °Give °a portion to °seven, and also to °eight; for thou knowest not °what °evil shall be °upon the earth.

3 If the clouds be full of rain, they empty *themselves* [2] upon the earth: and if the tree fall toward the south, or toward the north, in the place where the tree falleth, there it shall be.

4 He that observeth the °wind °shall not sow; and he that regardeth the clouds °shall not reap.

5 °As thou knowest not what *is* the way of the °spirit, *nor* how the bones *do grow* in the womb of her that is with child: even so thou knowest not the works of °God Who maketh all.

6 In the morning sow thy seed, and in the evening withhold not thine hand: for thou knowest not whether shall °prosper, either this or that, or whether they both *shall be* alike good.

H J1 t1 7 Truly the light *is* sweet, and a pleasant *thing it is* for the eyes to behold the sun:

8 But if a °man live many years, °*and* rejoice in them all;

u1 yet let him remember the days of darkness; for they shall be many.

v1 All that cometh *is* vanity.

---

13 foolishness. Heb. *ṣākal*, as in *vv.* 3, 6, 14.
madness. See note on 1. 17.
14 man. Heb. *'ādām* (with Art.). Ap. 14. I. See note on 1. 13.
15 labour=toil.
foolish. Heb. *kesîl*, as in *vv.* 2 and 12; not *ṣākal*, as in *vv.* 3, 6, 13, 14.

10. 16—12. 8 (O5, p. 913). MAN IN HIS DIFFERENT PORTIONS. (*Extended Alternation.*)

O5 F | 10. 16, 17. Kings and the Land.
G | 10. 18. Builders.
H | 10. 19. Riches.
F | 10. 20. Kings and subjects.
G | 11. 1-6. Sowers.
H | 11. 7—12. 8. Youth.

17 Blessed=Happy. Heb. *'ashrēy*. The only occurrence in this book.
18 building decayeth=the roof falleth in.
droppeth through=leaketh.
19 wine. Heb. *yayin*. Ap. 27. i.
maketh merry=will gladden life. Cp. Ps. 104. 15.
answereth all things=maketh everything respond [to their requirements]: i.e. will procure both [feast and wine]. See note on 5. 19, the only two occurrences of *'ānāh* in this book.
20 Curse not the king=Revile not a king.
in thy thought=in thy secret thought: i.e. with all thy [acquired] knowledge. Heb. *maddā'*, a rare word. Occurs only six times. Rendered "thought", here; "knowledge" (2 Chron. 1. 10, 11, 12. Dan. 1. 17); "science" (Dan. 1. 4).

11. 1 bread. Put by Fig. *Metonymy* (of Effect), Ap. 6, for the seed from which it is produced.
upon=upon the surface of.
it=the profit or result of it.
2 Give: i.e. in charity.
a portion: i.e. a portion of the bread of *v.* 1.
seven . . . eight. An idiomatic phrase denoting several or many, like the idiom "once . . . twice"= several times (Job 33. 14. Ps. 62. 11); "twice . . . thrice"=often (Job 33. 29. Isa. 17. 6); "three and four"=frequently, or many (Ex. 20. 5; 34. 7. Prov. 30. 15, 18, 21. Amos 1. 3, 6, 9, 11, 13; 2. 1, 4, 6); "four and five" (Isa. 17. 6); "six and seven"=many (Job 5. 19); "seven and eight" (Mic. 5. 5).
what evil. As the verb is Masc. but "evil" is Fem., render "what will prove a misfortune".
evil=misfortune. Heb. *rā'a'*. Ap. 44. viii.
upon the earth. See note on 5. 2.
4 wind. Heb. *rūach*. Ap. 9.
shall not sow . . . shall not reap. The ploughing must be done when the early rains have come, even in the face of storm and tempest; otherwise there will be no reaping after the latter rains.
5 As=According as. See note on John 3. 8.
spirit. Heb. *rūach*. Ap. 9.
God. Heb. Elohim (with Art.)=the [true] God, or the Deity. Ap. 4. I. See note on 1. 13.
6 prosper. Heb. *kāshēr*: supposed to be a later Hebrew word, but a kindred form seems to be found in Ps. 68. 6, where "with chains" should be rendered "into prosperity". See Ap. 75. xi.

11. 7—12. 8 (*H*, above). YOUTH. (*Repeated Alternations.*)

H J1 t1 | 11. 7, 8-. Youth. Rejoice.
u1 | 11. -8-. Remembrance. Days of darkness.
v1 | 11. -8. Vanity.
J2 t2 | 11. 9-. Youth. Rejoice.
u2 | 11. -9. Knowledge. Day of judgment.
v2 | 11. 10. Vanity.
J3 t3 | 12. 1-. Youth. Remember.
u3 | 12. -1-7. Knowledge. Days of evil.
v3 | 12. 8. Vanity.

8 man. Heb. *'ādām* (with Art.). Ap. 14. I. See note on 1. 13.
and rejoice=let him rejoice.

J^2 t^2 (p. 918) 9 °Rejoice, O °young man, in thy °youth; and
let thy heart cheer thee in the days of °thy
youth, and walk in the ways of thine heart,
and in the sight of thine eyes:

u^2 but know thou, that for all these *things* [5] God
will bring thee into °judgment.

v^2 10 Therefore remove sorrow from thy heart,
and put away °evil from thy flesh: for childhood and °youth *are* vanity.

J^3 t^3 **12** Remember °now thy °Creator in the
days of thy youth,

u^3 w while the °evil days come not, nor the years
draw nigh, when thou shalt say, 'I have no
°pleasure in them;'

x y^1 2 While the sun, or the light, or the moon, or
the stars, be not darkened, nor the clouds return after the rain:
3 In the day when the °keepers of the °house
shall °tremble, and °the strong men shall bow
themselves, and °the grinders °cease because
they are few, and °those that look out of the
°windows be °darkened,
4 And °the doors shall be shut in the °streets,
when the °sound of the grinding is low, and
he shall °rise up at the voice of the bird, and
all °the daughters of musick shall be brought
low;

z^1 5 Also *when* they shall be °afraid of *that*
which is °high, and °fears *shall be* in the way,

y^2 and the °almond tree shall flourish, and the
°grasshopper °shall be a burden,

z^2 and °desire shall fail: (because °man goeth to
his long home, and the mourners go about the
°streets:)

y^3 6 °Or ever °the silver cord be loosed, or °the
golden bowl be broken, or the °pitcher be
broken at the fountain, or °the wheel broken
at the cistern.

w 7 Then shall the °dust return to the earth
°as it was: and the °spirit shall °return unto
°God Who gave it.

v^3 8 "Vanity of vanities," saith the preacher;
"all *is* vanity."

P^5 K a (p. 920) 9 And moreover, because the preacher was
wise, he still taught the People knowledge;
yea, he gave good heed, and sought out,

b *and* set in order many proverbs.
10 The preacher sought to find out acceptable
words:

L and *that which was* written *was* upright, *even*
words of truth.

9 Rejoice, &c. A positive command, not irony; qualified by the solemn fact: "but know thou", &c.
young man=a chosen youth, implying beauty and strength.
youth=childhood.
thy youth. Same word as "young man".
judgment=the judgment.
10 evil=sadness.
youth=dawn of life Heb. *shaharūth.* Occurs only here

12. 1 now=also.
Creator. Plural of Majesty=the [great] Creator, or a reference to the Trinity.

12. -1-7 (u^3, p. 918). KNOWLEDGE. DAYS OF EVIL. (*Introversion and Repeated Alternation.*)

u^3 | w | -1. Evil days. Approach. (Fig.).
x | y^1 | 2-4. Figures. Luminaries, &c. } External.
z^1 | 5-. Literal. Fear.
y^2 | -5-. Figures. Almond tree, &c.
z^2 | -5. Literal. Failure.
y^3 | 6. Figures. Silver cord, &c. } Internal.
w | 7. Evil days. (Literal.)

evil days=days of the misfortune: i.e. affliction and death. Heb. *rā'a'.* Ap. 44. viii: i.e. the days described in following verses.
pleasure. See note on 3. 1.
3 keepers of the house: i.e. the arms of the body.
house. The human body is often compared to a house (Isa. 38. 12. Job 4. 19. 2 Cor. 5. 1, 2. 2 Pet. 1. 13).
tremble. Occurs only here, Est. 5. 9 ("move"), and Hab. 2. 7 ("vex"). See Ap. 76. xii.
the strong men: i.e. the legs. Heb. *geber.* Ap. 14. iv.
the grinders: i.e. the teeth.
cease=fail, or become unfit for use. Heb. *baṭal*=a passage; prob.=the ear-passage. Occurs only in Solomon's writings. Here, *v.* 5, Prov. 7. 8, and Song 3. 2 (pl.).
those that look out of the windows: i.e. eyes ("those" is feminine, agreeing with Heb. "eyes").
windows=lattices=the eyelids.
darkened=dimmed.
4 the doors=the openings: i.e. the mouth and ears.
streets=street (sing.).
sound of the grinding is low: i.e. the mastication with gums instead of teeth is low.
rise up=start: referring to insomnia.
the daughters of musick: i.e. songs, &c., the product of music.
5 afraid: i.e. of ascending heights.
high=lofty, elevated.
fears shall be in the way: i.e. apprehensions of danger in journeying.
almond tree shall flourish: i.e. grey hairs shall grow scanty, or drop off, not "almond nuts be rejected"; for the teeth and eating have already been dealt with in *v.* 3.
grasshopper, or locust.
shall be a burden=shall become burdensome: i.e. as to weight.
desire shall fail. "Desire"=Heb.=the caperberry. Here the A.V. beautifully renders the figure of speech (as a *version* should do), while the R.V. renders it literally (as a *translation* too often does). The Fig. is *Metalepsis*: i.e. a double *Metonymy* (Ap. 6), by which (1) the "caperberry" is put for the *condiment* made from it, and then (2) the condiment is put for the *appetite* produced by it. And further, since, because of its shape, as well as from the notion that it was supposed to create sexual desire, all that is intended by the figure is included in the rendering "desire shall fail". **man.** Heb. *'ādām* (with Art). Ap. 14. I. See note on 1. 13. **6 Or,** &c. New figures now (in *v.* 6) introduced, referring to the *arrival* (y^3, above) of death itself. **the silver cord**: i.e. the spinal cord. **the golden bowl**: i.e. the head, or skull. **pitcher**: the failure of the heart. **the wheel.** On which the bucket is brought up by a rope from the cistern, or well. **7 dust.** Fig. *Metonymy* (of Cause), Ap. 6, put for the body which is made of dust (Gen. 2. 7; 3. 19. Ps. 104. 29. Job 34. 15, 16). **as it was.** Note the reference to Adam's creation. **spirit.** Heb. *rūach.* Ap. 9. Not *nephesh*, soul (Ap. 13). **return unto God.** Hence He is said to be the God of the spirits of all flesh (Num. 16. 22; 27. 16. Cp. Luke 23. 46. Acts 7. 59); "the Father of spirits" (Heb. 12. 9). **God.** Heb. Elohim (with Art.)=the (true or triune) God; the Deity. Ap. 4. I.

M c (p. 920) 11 ° The words of the wise
d *are* as goads,
d and as ° nails ° fastened
c ° *by* the masters of assemblies,
L *which* are given from ° one shepherd.
K a 12 ° And further,
b by these, my son, be admonished: of making many books *there is* no end; and much study *is* a weariness of the flesh.

A (p. 906) 13 Let us hear ° the conclusion of the whole matter: Fear ° God, and keep His commandments: for this *is* the whole *duty* of [5] man.
14 For [7] God shall bring every work into judgment, with every ° secret thing, whether *it be* good, or whether *it be* ° evil.

12. 9-12 (P[5], p. 913). PERSONAL INFORMATION AND COUNSEL. (*Alternation.*)

P[5] | K | a | 9-. And moreover (*yōthēr*).
b | -9, 10-. The efforts of *Koheleth*.
L | -10. What hath been written by one writer.
M | c | 11-. The words of the wise
d | -11-. like goads } well planted, } "The words of the wise".
d | -11-. like nails }
c | -11-. [are] rulers of assemblies.
L | -11. What hath been furnished by one Giver.
K | *a* | 12-. And further (*yōthēr*).
b | -12. The efforts of others.

11 The words of the wise. See notes on p. 864, and Ap. 7. 4.
nails. These were built into a wall, because Eastern walls were too hard or too soft for them to be hammered in. **fastened** = planted. Masc., while "nails" is Fem.: but the Accents unite the two words. The verb *nāṭaʿ* is found again only in 3. 2, where it is singular. **by the masters** = [are] the lords, or rulers. Heb. *baʿal.* **one shepherd.** The Inspirer. See Gen. 48. 15; 49. 24. Ps. 23. 1. **12 And further** = Beyond these. Note the Structure above. **13 the conclusion.** See note on "the end", 3. 11. **God.** Heb. *'eth ha-'Elohīm* = the [true and only] God; the great Creator, who throughout the book is put in contrast with man (Heb. *'ādām.* Ap. 14. I) the creature. Ap. 4. I. **14 secret** = hidden. **evil.** Heb. *rāʿaʿ.* Ap. 44. viii.

THE SONG OF SOLOMON*.

THE STRUCTURE OF THE BOOK AS A WHOLE†.

(*Introversion and Alternation.*)

A | 1. 1-11. THE INTRODUCTION. THE SHULAMITE SEPARATED. TAKEN BY SOLOMON FROM HER HOME AND HER BELOVED (SHEPHERD) INTO THE ROYAL TENTS, PITCHED NEAR THEM.

B | C | 1. 12—2. 7. THE SHULAMITE AND HER BELOVED TOGETHER.
D | 2. 8—3. 5. THE SHULAMITE AND HER BELOVED APART.

B | *C* | 3. 6—5. 1. THE SHULAMITE AND HER BELOVED TOGETHER.
D | 5. 2—8. 4. THE SHULAMITE AND HER BELOVED APART.

A | 8. 5-14. THE CONCLUSION. THE SHULAMITE RESTORED. RETURN FROM SOLOMON TO HER HOME WITH HER BELOVED (SHEPHERD).

* In the Hebrew, *lishᵉlomoh* is not the Genitive case, meaning "of Solomon", or "Solomon's" (*v.* 1). The Preposition ל (*Lamed* = l) means "to", or "for", as in the Psalm-Titles, and in the expression "*for* the chief Musician". It is therefore not necessarily limited to authorship, as may be further seen from the title of Ps. 72, where we have the same word (*lishᵉlomoh*) rendered "for Solomon". It may well mean *concerning* or *relating to* Solomon "the king's son". Moreover, the Relative Pronoun *'asher* (= which) takes it out of the category of ordinary authorship, and may rightly require the rendering "which [is] concerning Solomon". The Preposition has a wide range of meaning (divided into some twenty-two classes) according to the Verbs used; but, when used without a Verb (as it is here), it may refer to the *subject*, and be well rendered "concerning", as it is in Jer. 49. 1, 7, 23, 28, &c. The question of authorship therefore does not, of necessity, arise, and need not be discussed.

† For further notes on the book as a whole, see p. 921.

NOTE ON THE STRUCTURE OF THE SONG OF SOLOMON (PAGE 920).

The scope of the book is determined by the Structure of the book as a whole.

The story gradually develops itself; and, from the key which is found in the last chapter (8. 5-14), the whole may be pieced together in the words of Dr. C. D. Ginsburg (*Commentary*, London, 1857, pp. 4-6), to which the references have been added in order to connect the threads of the events.

"There was a family living at Shulem, consisting of a widowed mother, several sons, and one daughter, who maintained themselves by farming and pasturage. The brothers were particularly fond of their sister, and took her under their special care, promising that her prudence and virtue should be greatly rewarded by them (8. 8-14).

"In the course of time, while tending the flock, and, according to the custom of the shepherds, resorting at noon beneath a tree for shelter against the meridian sun, she met with a graceful shepherd youth to whom she afterward became espoused (1. 7; 2. 16; 6. 3).

"One morning, in the spring, this youth invited her to accompany him into the field; but the brothers, overhearing the invitation, and anxious for the reputation of their sister, sent her [in order to prevent their meeting] to take care of the vineyards (2. 15).

"The damsel, however, consoled her beloved and herself with the assurance that, though separated bodily, indissoluble ties subsisted between them, over which her brothers had no control (2. 16).

"She requested him to meet her in the evening (3. 1); and, as he did not come, she feared that some accident had befallen him on the way, and went in search of him (3. 2), and found him (3. 4).

"The evening now was the only time in which they could enjoy each other's company, as, during the day, the damsel was occupied in the vineyards.

"On one occasion, when entering a garden, she accidentally came into the presence of King Solomon (6. 11, 12), who happened to be on a summer visit to that neighbourhood (6. 6-11).

"Struck with the beauty of the damsel, the King conducted her into his royal tent (1. 2-4), and there, assisted by his court-ladies (1. 5-8), endeavoured with alluring flatteries and promises, to gain her affections, but without effect (1. 6-11).

"Released from the King's presence, the damsel soon sought an interview with her beloved shepherd (1. 12—2. 7).

"The King, however, took her with him to his capital in great pomp, in the hope of dazzling her with his splendour (3. 1-11); but neither did this prevail: for while even there, she told her beloved shepherd, who had followed her into the capital (4. 1-5), and obtained an interview with her, that she was anxious to quit the gaudy scene for her own home (4. 6).

"The shepherd, on hearing this, praised her constancy (4. 7-16); and such a manifestation of their mutual attachment took place, that several of the court-ladies were greatly affected by it (6. 1).

"The King, still determined if possible to win her affections, watched for another favourable opportunity; and with flatteries and allurements, surpassing all that he had used before, tried to obtain his purpose (6. 4—7. 9).

"He promised to elevate her to the highest rank, and to raise her above all his concubines and queens, if she would comply with his wishes; but, faithful to her espousals, she refused all his overtures, on the plea that her affections were pledged to another (7. 10—8. 4).

"The King, convinced at last that he could not possibly prevail, was obliged to dismiss her; and the shepherdess, in company with her beloved shepherd, returned to her native place (8. 5-14).

"On their way home (8. 5-7), they visited the tree under which they had first met, and there renewed their vows of fidelity to each other.

"On her arrival in safety at her home, her brothers, according to their promise, rewarded her greatly for her virtuous conduct" (8. 8, 9).

The above is an *Interpretation*. The *Application* is an incentive to loyalty and fidelity to the One "Who loved us and gave Himself for us"; and to stand fast, in our love and loyalty to Him, in the face of the fiercest temptations and severest trials.

To Israel this would be expressed: "Be thou faithful unto death" (Jas. 1. 3. 1 Pet. 1. 7. Heb. 10. 23); "To him that overcometh", &c. (Rev. 2. 7, 11, 17, 26; 3. 5, 12, 21); also Heb. 13. 9, 13. 1 Pet. 1. 4-7, &c.

To the Church of God this would be expressed in such passages as Gal. 5. 1. Eph. 4. 14; 6. 13, 18. Phil. 1. 6; 4. 1. Col. 1. 10, 22, 23; 2 7. 2 Tim. 3. 14. Tit. 1. 9.

THE SONG OF SOLOMON.

A A 1 THE ° song of songs, which *is* ° Solomon's.
B C 2 ° Let ° him kiss me with the kisses of his
(p. 922) mouth: for ° thy love *is* better than ° wine.
3 ° Because of the savour of thy good ointments ° thy name *is as* ointment poured forth,
therefore do the ° virgins love thee.
4 ° Draw me, we will ° run after thee: ° the
king hath brought me into his ° chambers: we
will be glad and rejoice in thee, we will ° remember [2] thy love more than [2] wine: ° the upright love thee.
D 5 I *am* ° black, but comely, O ye ° daughters
of Jerusalem, as the tents of ° Kedar, ° as the
curtains of Solomon.
6 ° Look not upon me, because I *am* black,
because ° the sun hath looked upon me: my
mother's ° children were angry with me; they
made me the keeper of the vineyards; *but*
mine own vineyard ° have I not kept.
B C 7 ° Tell me, O thou whom my ° soul loveth,
where thou ° feedest, where thou makest *thy*
flock to ° rest at noon: for why should I be
as one that ° turneth aside ° by the flocks of
thy companions?
D 8 ° If thou know not, O thou fairest among
women, go thy way forth by the footsteps of
the flock, and feed thy kids beside the shepherds' tents.
A 9 ° I have compared thee, O ° my love, to ° a
company of horses ° in Pharaoh's chariots.

1 song of songs, which is Solomon's. Heb. title *Shīr Hashshīrīm* = Song of Songs. In the Sept. it is *Asma Asmatōn*, Vulg. *Canticum Canticorum*, all with the same meaning. Fig. *Polyptōton* (Ap. 6), meaning the most beautiful or excellent song. It belongs to the third division of the O.T. Canon (see Ap. 1). The order of the five "Megilloth" (or Scrolls) is the order of the festivals on which they are read. The Song is read annually at the Feast of the Passover, as Ruth is read at Pentecost; Lamentations on 9th of Ab; Ecclesiastes at the Feast of Tabernacles; and Esther at the Feast of Purim.

From the most ancient times it has formed part of the Hebrew Canonical Scriptures. It is a poem based on the true facts of a story which unfolds itself as it proceeds. Various interpretations have been given of it: the *literal*, the *allegorical*, and the *typical*. The allegorical embrace Jehovah and Israel (which was the view of the Jewish commentators); the Roman Catholic views it of the Virgin Mary; the Protestant commentators view it of "Christ and the Church"; the typical view regards it as a type of Solomon's nuptials, or as that of Christ and the Gentiles. The allegorical view puts the coarse flatteries and language of a seducer into the lips of "Christ", which is inconsistent with His dignity and holiness (cp. 6. 4–10, 13; 7. 9). It is the language of seduction put into the mouth of Him "Who spake as never man spake".

The number of speakers forbids all the interpretations which depend on there being only *two*. There are *seven* in all, and they can be easily distinguished by the Structures: viz. (1) the Shulamite; (2) the daughters of Jerusalem; (3) Solomon: (4) the shepherd lover of the Shulamite; (5) the brothers of the Shulamite; (6) the companions of the shepherd; (7) the inhabitants of Jerusalem. **Solomon's.** See note on p. 920.

1. 1-11 (A, p. 920). THE INTRODUCTION.

Introducing most of the seven speakers of the book: the Shulamite's soliloquy of her beloved shepherd (*vv.* 2–4, 7); the king (*vv.* 4, 9–11); the court-ladies (*vv.* 5, 8); her brothers (*v.* 6).

(*Introversion and Alternation.*)

A | A | 1. SOLOMON'S Song about the Shulamite.
  B | C | 2–4. THE SHULAMITE soliloquizes about her beloved (shepherd).
    D | 5, 6. THE COURT-LADIES (who disdain her) answered by the Shulamite.
  B | *C* | 7. THE SHULAMITE soliloquizes about her beloved (shepherd).
    D | 8. THE COURT-LADIES (who tell her to return) answered by the Shulamite.
A | 9–11. SOLOMON'S admiration of the Shulamite.

The Shulamite speaks. She has been taken into Solomon's tents, and soliloquizes about her beloved (*vv.* 2, 3); she implores him to come and rescue her (*v.* 4); she repels the scorn of the court-ladies (*v.* 6); and implores her beloved to tell her where she may find him (*v.* 7); the court-ladies ironically reply (*v.* 8); meanwhile the king comes in and commences by expressing his admiration (*vv.* 9–11). **2 Let him kiss me** = Oh for a kiss. **him**: i.e. the Shulamite's beloved, the shepherd, from whom she has been taken by Solomon. **thy love is** = thy endearments [are]. Heb. *dodim.* Only here, *vv.* 4, 10, 10, and 7. 12. A man is addressed. **wine.** Heb. *yayin.* Ap. 27. I. **3 Because of the savour** = Sweet is the odour. **thy name** = thou (emph.). Name put for the person. See note on Ps. 20. 1. **virgins** = damsels. Heb. *'ălāmoth*, not *bethūloth* (virgins). **4 Draw me, &c.** = Draw me after thee, let us flee together! **run after** = run to any one for refuge. **the king.** This explains the circumstances described on p. 921. **chambers** = inner apartments. **remember** = praise. **the upright love thee** = upright ones have loved thee. **5 black** = swarthy (Fem.). **daughters of Jerusalem**: i.e. the ladies of Solomon's court. **Kedar** = dark. All Kedar's tents were black. **as.** Supply the Ellipsis (Ap. 6), "[but comely] as the curtains of Solomon". Required by the *Alternation*:—

a | swarthy. | *a* | as Kedar's tents.
b | comely. | *b* | as Solomon's curtains.

6 Look not upon me = Look not down on: i.e. regard me not. Cp. 1 Chron. 17. 17. Ps. 106. 44. **the sun hath looked.** Fig. *Prosopopœia* (Ap. 6), to emphasise the cause of her swarthiness. **children** = sons: i.e. her brothers are referred to as speaking as in 2. 15, and see note on p. 921 and cp. 8. 8. **have I not kept** = I never kept. She says this to show the harsh treatment of her brothers. **7 Tell me, &c.** Again soliloquizing. See Structure above. **soul.** Heb. *nephesh.* Ap. 13. **feedest** = shepherdest. This cannot refer to Solomon! **rest** = lie down. **turneth aside** = strayeth, or wandereth. **by** = to, or among. **8 If thou, &c.** Answer of the court-ladies: ironical. **9 I have, &c.** Solomon now speaks to her. **my love** = my friend, or one beloved. Heb. *ra'yāh.* Fem. here, *v.* 15; 2. 2, 10, 13; 4. 1, 7; 6. 4. **a company of horses** = my mare. **in Pharaoh's chariots** = in the chariot of Pharaoh.

10 Thy cheeks are comely with rows *of jewels,* thy neck with chains *of gold.*
11 We will make thee °borders of gold with studs of silver.
C E[1] (p. 923) 12 °While the king °*sitteth* at his table, °my spikenard °sendeth forth the smell thereof.
13 A °bundle of myrrh *is* °my wellbeloved unto me; °he shall lie all night betwixt my breasts.
14 °My beloved *is* unto me *as* a cluster of °camphire in the vineyards of En-gedi.
F[1] 15 Behold, thou *art* fair, °my love; behold, thou *art* fair; thou *hast* doves' eyes.
E[2] 16 Behold, thou *art* fair, °my beloved, yea, pleasant: also our °bed *is* °green.
17 The °beams of our house *are* °cedar, *and* our °rafters of °fir.

2 °I *am* the rose of Sharon, *and* °the lily of the valleys.
F[2] 2 °As the lily among °thorns, so *is* °my love among the °daughters.
E[3] 3 As °the apple tree among °the trees of the wood, so *is* °my beloved among the sons. I sat down under °his shadow with great delight, and °his fruit *was* sweet to my taste.
4 He brought me to the °banqueting house, and °his banner over me *was* °love.
5 °Stay me with °flagons, °comfort me with [3]apples: for I *am* sick °of [4]love.
6 His left hand *is* under my head, and his right hand °doth embrace me.
7 °I charge °you, O ye daughters of Jerusalem, by the °roes, and by the hinds of the field, that ye °stir not up, nor °awake °*my* love, °till he please.
D G[1] 8 The °voice of °my beloved! behold, °he °cometh leaping upon the mountains, °skipping upon the hills.

1. 12—2. 7 (**C**, p. 920). THE SHULAMITE AND HER BELOVED, TOGETHER.

In the royal tents, away from Jerusalem (3. 6-11); in the place where the court-ladies first saw her (6. 12); and "while the king is at his table".

(*Repeated Alternation.*)

C | E[1] | 1. 12-14. THE SHULAMITE to her shepherd lover. They meet and exchange their vows.
F[1] | 1. 15. THE BELOVED (shepherd) to the Shulamite. (It is thou who art beautiful; not I.)
E[2] | 1. 16—2. 1. THE SHULAMITE to her shepherd love. (No. It is thou who art comely; not I.)
F[2] | 2. 2. THE BELOVED (shepherd) to the Shulamite. (Thou art my loved one.)
E[3] | 2. 3-7. THE SHULAMITE to her shepherd lover: ending with an apostrophe to the court-ladies not to incite or excite her affection for another person till she herself desires it. See notes on "awake" (2. 7) and "love" (2. 7), and cp. 3. 5 and 8. 4.

11 borders = bead-rows.
12 While the king sitteth, &c. Solomon's advances fail; for, to his flattery she opposes her unabated love for her shepherd lover, with whom she has an interview in 1. 12—2. 7. **sitteth.** Supply "was".
my spikenard: i.e. her shepherd lover.
sendeth = sent. **13 bundle** = little bag.
my wellbeloved. Masculine, showing of, and to whom she is speaking.
he shall lie = it (i.e. the bag of myrrh) will lodge.
14 My beloved. Masculine. Same word as "wellbeloved" in *v.* 13.
camphire = henna, or cypress flowers.
15 my love. Here it is Feminine, showing that the shepherd lover is replying to his betrothed. See note on *v.* 9.
16 my beloved. Here it is Masculine. The Shulamite speaks again.
bed = couch. **green** = verdant.
17 beams of our house = our bower.
cedar = cedar arches. **rafters** = retreat.
fir = cypress roof.
2. 1 I am the rose of Sharon: i.e. I am a mere wild-flower of the plains: a flower found in great profusion: disclaiming her lover's compliment. **the** = a.
2 As the lily = As a lily: the shepherd, taking up her word in his reply. **thorns.** See note on 2 Kings 14. 9.
my love = my friend. Heb. *ra'yāh.* See note on 1. 9. Feminine again, showing that it is the shepherd who is speaking. **daughters** = damsels. Heb. *bānōth,* fem. pl. of *beyn,* a son. **3 the apple tree.** Occurs only six times in Scripture: four times in this book (2. 3, 5; 7. 8; 8. 5); once in Proverbs (25. 11); and once in Joel (1. 12); three times for the tree, and three times for the fruit. Probably the orange tree. **the trees of the wood**: i.e. the wild trees. **my beloved.** Masculine. Showing that it is the Shulamite speaking. **his** = its. **4 banqueting house** = vine-arbour or vineyard-bower. **his banner over me was love** = he overshaded me with love; *degel,* from *dāgal,* to shade; then an ensign because of the shade it gives and protection which it ensures. **love.** Heb. *'ahăbāh* (Fem.). See note on *v.* 7. **5 Stay** = Strengthen. **flagons** = grape-cakes. **comfort** = refresh. **of** = with. **6 doth embrace** = will embrace. **7 I charge** = I adjure. **you.** This and the verbs here are Masculine. It is not uncommon to find this: but when we do, we find true feminity has been lost. **roes** = gazelles. **stir not up** = excite not. Heb. *'ūr* (in the Hiphil). **awake** = incite. Heb. *'ūr* (in the Piel) = not to rouse from sleep, but to excite the passions. See Isa. 42. 13. Prov. 10. 12. **my love** = my feelings or affection (Fem.). **till he** = till she. It is Feminine, to agree with love, *'ahăbāh* = love never used in the abstract, as in 3. 10, and 8. 4 (a person). This is an appeal to the court-ladies not to try and incite her affection for Solomon.

2. 8—3. 5 (**D**, p. 920). THE SHULAMITE AND HER BELOVED, APART.

(She, still in the royal tents in the country, tells the court-ladies the story of her love.)

(*Repeated Alternation.*)

D | G[1] | 2. 8-14. THE SHULAMITE tells the court-ladies about her beloved: how he once came and invited her to go out with him.
H[1] | 2. 15. HINDERED by her brothers, she tells how they set her a task in the vineyards.
G[2] | 2. 16, 17. THE SHULAMITE tells the court-ladies how she waited for her beloved to come again in the evening.
H[2] | 3. 1-3. HINDERED by the watchmen, she tells how she went out and sought him.
G[3] | 3. 4. THE SHULAMITE tells the court-ladies how she found her beloved again.
H[3] | 3. 5. HINDERED by the court-ladies, she again adjures them not to hinder, as before, in 2. 7; in 3. 5, and again in 8. 4.

8 voice = sound: e.g. footsteps (Gen. 3. 8). **my beloved.** Masculine. Showing that the Shulamite is the speaker. **he**: emphatic = this (very one). **cometh** = came. **skipping** = bounding.

9 [8] My beloved is like a [7] roe or a young hart:
behold, he °standeth behind our wall, he °look-
eth forth at the windows, °shewing himself
through the lattice.
10 [8] My beloved spake, and said unto me,
"Rise up, [2] my love, my fair one, and come
away.
11 For, lo, the winter is past, °the rain is
over *and* gone;
12 The flowers appear °on the earth; the
time of the singing *of birds* is come, and
the °voice of the °turtle is heard in our land;
13 The fig tree °putteth forth her green figs,
and the vines °*with* the tender grape °give a
good smell. Arise, °my love, my fair one, and
come away.
14 O my dove, *that art* in the clefts of the
rock, in the °secret *places* of the stairs, let me
see thy countenance, let me hear thy voice;
for sweet *is* thy voice, and thy countenance *is*
comely."
H¹ (p. 923) 15 °"Take us °the foxes, °the little foxes, that
spoil the vines: for our °vines *have* tender
grapes."
G² 16 °My beloved *is* mine, and I *am* his: °he
feedeth among the lilies.
17 °Until the day break, and the shadows
flee away, °turn, [8] my beloved, and be thou
like a [7] roe or a young hart upon the mountains of °Bether.

H² 3 By night on my °bed I °sought him whom
°my soul loveth: I sought him, but I
found him not.
2 I will rise now, and go about the city in the
streets, and in the broad ways I will seek him
whom [1] my soul loveth: I sought him, but I
found him not.
3 The watchmen that go about the city found
me: *to whom I said,* "Saw ye him whom [1] my
soul loveth?"
G³ 4 °*It was* but °a little that I passed °from
them, °but I found him whom [1] my soul loveth:
I °held him, and would not let him go, until
I had brought him into my mother's house,
and into the °chamber of her that conceived me.
H³ 5 °I charge °you, O ye daughters of Jerusalem,
by the °roes, and by the hinds of the field,
that ye °stir not up, nor °awake *my* °love, till
°he please.
C J¹ (p. 924) 6 °Who *is* this that cometh °out of the wilderness like pillars of smoke, perfumed with
myrrh and frankincense, with all powders of
the merchant?
7 °Behold his °bed, which *is* Solomon's; threescore °valiant men *are* about it, of the valiant
of Israel.
8 They all hold swords, *being* expert in war:
°every man *hath* his sword upon his thigh because of fear in the °night.
9 °King Solomon made himself °a chariot of
the wood of Lebanon.
10 He made the pillars thereof *of* silver,
°the bottom thereof *of* gold, °the covering of

9 standeth = there he was standing.
looketh forth = looked through.
shewing himself = he glanced.
11 the rain. The first or early rains come about the end of October or beginning of November; and the wet season, i.e. the last or latter rains, in March or beginning of April. **12 on the earth** = in the fields.
voice: i.e. cooing.
turtle = turtle-dove. A migratory bird (Jer. 8. 7).
13 putteth forth = sweetens or ripens.
with the tender grape = blossoms.
give = they give.
my love = friend. Heb. *ra'yah*, as in *v.* 2. See note on 1. 9. Feminine. Showing that the shepherd is speaking to the Shulamite.
14 secret places of the stairs = the hiding places of the cliff.
15 Take us = Catch for us. The Shulamite here quotes the words of her brothers (H¹, p. 923). See note on "children" 1. 6.
the ... the. No Art. here in the Heb.
vines have tender grapes = vineyards are in bloom.
16 My beloved. Masculine. Showing the Shulamite as the speaker. he feedeth = he who feedeth.
17 Until the day break = When the day cools. This is clear from the words which follow.
turn = return. Bether = separation. See note on 8. 14.

3. bed = couch, not the same word as in 1. 16; 3. 7; 5. 13; 6. 2.
1 sought = still sought.
my soul = I myself. Heb. *nephesh*. Ap. 13.
4 It was but a little that = Scarcely.
a little = a little while. See note on "almost", Prov. 5. 14. from them = them.
but = when. held = seized.
chamber = inner chamber.
5 I charge you = I have adjured you.
you. See note on 2. 7.
roes = gazelles.
stir not up . . . awake. See note on 2. 7.
love. Heb. *'ahăbāh*. Fem. as in 2. 7; 8. 4. he = she.

3. 6–5. 1 (*C*, p. 920). THE SHULAMITE AND HER BELOVED, TOGETHER.

The procession of Solomon's court to Jerusalem.
(*Introversion and Repeated Alternation.*)

C | J¹ | 3. 6–11. The inhabitants of JERUSALEM see the procession approaching. Remark of one (*v.* 6); of another (*vv.* 7, 8); of a third (*vv.* 9, 10); of a fourth (*v.* 11).

K | L¹ | 4. 1–5. THE BELOVED (shepherd), who has followed the court, comes to Jerusalem to rescue the Shulamite. He obtains an interview, and again expresses his delight in her. [Contrast his modesty with Solomon's coarse flatteries in 6. 4–10, and 7. 1–9.]

M¹ | 4. 6. THE SHULAMITE proposes to return, referring to 2. 17.

L² | 4. 7–16–. THE BELOVED (shepherd) immediately proffers assistance, emboldened by her beauty (*vv.* 7–11) and by her faithfulness (*vv.* 12–16–).

M² | 4. –16. THE SHULAMITE declares that all she has is for his pleasure.

L³ | 5. 1–. THE BELOVED (shepherd) suitably responds: "I am coming".

J² | 5. –1. The daughters of JERUSALEM (some of the court-ladies) encourage them and urge them on.

6 Who is this? = What is that? A question asked by an inhabitant of Jerusalem.
out of the wilderness = up from the country.
7 Behold his bed = Lo! it is the litter or sedan. The answer by another inhabitant of Jerusalem. bed. Heb. *mittah*. Not the same as 1. 16; 3. 1; 5. 13; or 6. 2. valiant men. Heb. *gibbōr*. Ap. 14. IV. **8 every man.** Heb. *'īsh*. Ap. 14. II. night = nights (Pl.). **9 King Solomon made, &c.** The remark of a third inhabitant of Jerusalem. See the Structure (J¹, above). a chariot = a palanquin. **10 the bottom thereof** = its support. the covering of it = its seat.

it *of* purple, °the midst thereof °being paved
°*with* love, °for the daughters of Jerusalem.
11 °Go forth, O ye °daughters of Zion, and behold king Solomon with the crown wherewith
his mother crowned him in the day of his
°espousals, and in the day of the gladness of
his heart.

K L[1] (p. 924) **4** °Behold, thou *art* fair, °my love; °behold,
thou *art* fair; thou *hast* °doves' eyes °with-
in thy locks: thy hair *is* as a flock of goats,
°that appear from mount Gilead.
2 Thy teeth *are* like a flock *of sheep that*
are °*even* shorn, which came up from the
washing; °whereof every one bear twins, and
none *is* °barren among them.
3 Thy lips *are* like a °thread of scarlet, and
thy °speech *is* comely: thy °temples *are* like
a °piece of a pomegranate [1] within thy locks.
4 Thy neck *is* like the tower of David builded
for an armoury, whereon there hang a thousand bucklers, all shields of °mighty men.
5 Thy two breasts *are* like two young roes
that are twins, which feed among the lilies.
M[1] 6 °Until the day °break, and the shadows flee
away, I will get me to the °mountain of
myrrh, and to the hill of frankincense.
L[2] 7 °Thou *art* all fair, [1]my love; *there is* no
spot in thee.
8 °Come with me from °Lebanon, °*my*
spouse, with me from °Lebanon: look from the
top of °Amana, from the top of °Shenir and
°Hermon, from °the °lions' dens, from °the
mountains of the °leopards.
9 Thou hast °ravished my heart, my sister,
[8]*my* spouse; thou hast °ravished my heart with
°one of thine eyes, with one chain °of thy neck.
10 How °fair is thy °love, °my sister, [8]*my*
spouse! how much better is thy °love than
°wine! and the smell of thine ointments than
all spices!
11 Thy lips, O *my* [8]spouse, °drop *as* the
honeycomb: honey and milk *are* under thy
tongue; and the smell of thy garments *is* like
the smell of Lebanon.
12 °A garden °inclosed *is* my sister, *my*
[8]spouse; a spring °shut up, a fountain sealed.
13 Thy plants *are* °an orchard of pomegranates, with pleasant fruits; °camphire, with
spikenard,
14 Spikenard and saffron; calamus and cinnamon, with °all trees of frankincense; myrrh
and aloes, with all the chief °spices:
15 °A °fountain of gardens, a well of living
waters, and streams from Lebanon.
16 Awake, O north wind; and come, thou
south; blow upon my garden, *that* the spices
thereof may flow out.
M[2] °Let °my beloved come into his garden, and eat
°his pleasant fruits.

L[3] **5** °I am come into my garden, my sister, *my*
°spouse: °I have gathered my myrrh with
my spice; °I have eaten my honeycomb with my
honey; °I have drunk my °wine with my milk:
J[3] °eat, O friends; drink, yea, drink abundantly,
O beloved.

the midst thereof=its interior.
being paved=tesselated.
with love=most lovely. **for**=by.
11 Go forth. The remark of a fourth inhabitant of Jerusalem. See the Structure (J[1], p. 924).
daughters of Zion. Occurs only here, and Isa. 3. 16, 17; 4. 4; always by way of reproof. Can it be so here? Does it imply the envy or jealousy of 8. 6? (Cp. "haughty", Isa. 3. 16.) Note the difference between the sing. and pl. **espousals**=marriage.

4. 1 Behold. The words of the shepherd approaching the Shulamite.
my love=my friend. Heb. *ra'yāh*. See note on 1. 9. Feminine, showing the speaker and the one spoken to.
behold=gaze on.
doves' eyes. Referring to the large melting eye of the dove: a "clean" bird.
within thy locks=behind (or through) thy veil.
that appear=springing down. **2 even**=evenly.
whereof every one bear twins=all of which are paired. This is the force of the *Hiphil* of *tā'am*, to be double or pairs, like the *Poel* of *Kal* in Ex. 26. 24; 36. 29.
barren=bereaved, as in Jer. 18. 21.
3 thread=braid. **speech**=mouth.
temples=cheeks. **piece**=part.
4 mighty men. Heb. *gibbōr*. Ap. 14. IV.
6 Until=When. The Shulamite speaks in *v.* 6, referring to 2. 17, answering that that very evening she will quit Jerusalem and go to their delightful country.
break=cools. Cp. 2. 17.
mountain. The edition of A.V. 1611 had "mountains" (pl.).
7 Thou art all fair, my love. The shepherd speaks: "love" being here feminine again.
8 Come=Thou wilt come.
Lebanon . . . Amana . . . Shenir . . . Hermon . . . the lions' dens, . . . the mountains of the leopards. He gives these names to Jerusalem and the royal residence. **my spouse**=my betrothed.
lions . . . leopards: denote the king and his courtiers. Cp. Ezek. 19. 7; 22. 25. Nah. 2. 12.
9 ravished my heart=put heart into me.
one. It was customary to unveil one eye in conversation. **of:** or round.
10 fair=sweet.
love=endearments. Heb. *dodīm*, as in 1. 2, 4; and 7. 12.
my sister, my spouse=my sister—betrothed.
wine. Heb. *yayin*. Ap. 27. I.
11 drop as=drop [honey] as.
12 A garden. Note the *Alternation* in *vv.* 12-15:—
c | 12-. Garden.
d | -12. Spring.
c | 13, 14. Garden fruits.
d | 15. Fountain.
inclosed=closed: bolted and barred.
shut up. Same word as "inclosed" (above).
13 an orchard=a paradise. See note on Ecc. 2. 5.
camphire=henna, or cypress.
14 all trees of frankincense=all sorts of frankincense trees. **spices**=spice plants.
15 A fountain=[With] a fountain.
fountain of gardens=a garden-fountain, without which no garden was complete.
Let my beloved. The Shulamite speaks in response, with the eloquent brevity of her overwrought feelings.
my beloved. Here, masculine, which shows who the speaker of this sentence is. **his**=its.

5. 1 I am come=I am coming. This is the shepherd's suitable reply to her brief invitation.
spouse=betrothed, as in 4. 8, 9, 10, 12.
I have gathered=I am gathering.
I have eaten=I am eating.
I have drunk=I am drinking.
(The perfect tenses being used for the present. See Kautzsch's *Gesenius*, § 106.)

wine. Heb. *yayin*. Ap. 27. I. **eat, O friends.** The words of the court-ladies, encouraging the Shulamite and her beloved (masculine). See Structure (J[2], p. 924).

N¹ O¹ (p. 926) 2 °I sleep, but my heart °waketh: °*it is*
the voice of °my beloved °that knocketh, *say-*
ing, "Open to me, my sister, °my love, my
dove, my undefiled: for my head is filled with
dew, *and* my locks with the drops of the night.
3 °I have put off my coat; how shall I put it
on? I have washed my feet; how shall I °defile
them?"
4 ²My beloved °put in his hand by the hole *of*
the door, and °my bowels were moved °for him.
5 °I rose up to open to ²my beloved; and my
hands dropped *with* myrrh, and my fingers
with sweet smelling myrrh, upon the handles
of the lock.
6 I opened to ²my beloved; but ²my beloved
had withdrawn himself, *and* was gone: °my
soul failed when °he spake: I sought him, but
I could not find him; I called him, but he gave
me no answer.
7 The watchmen that °went about °the city
found me, they smote me, they wounded me;
the keepers of the walls °took away my veil
from me.
8 °I charge °you, O daughters of Jerusalem, if
ye find ²my beloved, that ye tell him, that I *am*
°sick °of °love.
P¹ 9 °What *is* thy beloved more than *another*
beloved, O thou fairest among women? what
is thy beloved more than *another* beloved,
that thou °dost so charge us?
O² 10 °My beloved *is* white and ruddy, °the
chiefest among ten thousand.
11 His head *is as* the most fine gold, his locks
are °bushy, *and* black as a raven.
12 His eyes *are* as *the eyes* of doves by the
°rivers of °waters, °washed with milk, *and*
°fitly set.
13 His cheeks *are* as °a bed of spices, *as*
sweet flowers: his lips *like* lilies, °dropping
°sweet smelling myrrh.
14 His hands *are* °as gold rings °set with the
beryl: his belly *is as* °bright ivory overlaid
with sapphires.
15 His legs *are as* pillars of °marble, set
upon °sockets of fine gold: his °countenance
is as Lebanon, °excellent as the cedars.
16 His °mouth *is* most sweet: yea, he *is*
°altogether lovely. °This *is* ²my beloved, and
°this *is* my friend, O daughters of Jerusalem.

P² **6** °Whither is °thy beloved gone, O thou fairest among women? whither is °thy beloved
turned aside? that we may seek him with thee.
O³ 2 °My beloved is gone down into his garden,
to the beds of spices, °to feed in the gardens,
and to gather lilies.
3 I *am* ²my beloved's, and ²my beloved *is*
mine: °he feedeth among the lilies.
N² Q¹ (p. 927) 4 °Thou *art* beautiful, O °my love, as °Tirzah,

5. 2—8. 4 (*D*, p. 920). THE SHULAMITE AND HER BELOVED, APART. (*Division.*)

D | N¹ | 5. 2—6. 3. Her colloquies with the court-ladies.
| N² | 6. 4—8. 4. Her colloquies with Solomon.

5. 2—6. 3 (N¹, above). HER COLLOQUIES WITH THE COURT-LADIES. (*Repeated Alternation.*)

N¹ | O¹ | 5. 2-8. THE SHULAMITE tells the court-ladies a dream she once had about her beloved (shepherd).
| P¹ | 5. 9. THE COURT-LADIES, astonished at her love, ask, "What is there in thy beloved more than any other?"
| O² | 5. 10-16. THE SHULAMITE describes him to them, and ends, "Such is my beloved".
| P² | 6. 1. THE COURT-LADIES wish to see such an one; and ask, "Where is he, that we may seek him?"
| O³ | 6. 2, 3. THE SHULAMITE evades their question, suspecting their motives.

2 I sleep=I was asleep, or sleepy.
waketh=kept awake. **it is.** Supply "it was".
my beloved. Heb. masculine.
that knocketh=he is knocking (masculine).
my love=my friend. Feminine. Heb. *ra'yāh*, as in 1. 9, 15; 2. 2, 10, 13; 4. 1, 7; 5. 2; 6. 4.
3 I have put off. She quotes (*v.* 3) the reply her shepherd lover gave in her dream. **defile**=soil.
4 put in his hand, &c.=withdrew his hand. Heb. "sent away his hand from the hole". So the Sept. and Rashbam.
my bowels were moved for him=my heart was disquieted within me.
for him. Many codices read "within me", and so A.V. margin. **5 I** (emph.): i.e. I immediately arose.
6 my soul=I (emph.). Heb. *nephesh.* Ap. 13.
he spake=when he was speaking of it.
7 went about: i.e. the patrol.
the city. She is still in Jerusalem and away from her country home. (See the notes, p. 920.)
took away my veil. This was gross insult to an Eastern woman.
8 I charge=I adjure. **you.** See note on 2. 7.
sick of love=love-sick. **of**=with.
love. Same word and sense as in 2. 7; 3. 5; and 8. 4.
9 What is . . . ? The speakers are the court-ladies, replying to the conclusion of her dream.
dost so charge us?=hast so adjured us?
10 My beloved. The Shulamite describes him further to them. See Structure (O², above).
the chiefest among ten thousand=distinguished or conspicuous above thousands. Heb. "signalized as by a banner".
11 bushy=flowing, waving, or curled.
12 rivers=channels, or gorges. Heb. *'aphīkim.* See note on 2 Sam. 22. 16.
waters. In A.V. 1611 this was "water" (sing.).
washed=bathed: i.e. the doves.
fitly set=set as gems in a ring.
13 a bed of spices=a raised bed of balsam. Some codices, with Sept., read "beds of balsam".
dropping=distilling. **sweet smelling**=liquid.
14 as gold rings=like golden cylinders.
set with the beryl=adorned with gems of Tarshish (alluding to the nails, of which great care was taken)
bright=polished. **15 marble**=white marble.
sockets=bases. **countenance**=aspect.
excellent=choice. **16 mouth**=voice, by Fig. *Metonymy* (of Cause), Ap. 6. **altogether lovely**=fervently cherished, or desired. Heb. *maḥmād.* Occurs only here in this book. **This**=Such.

6. 1 Whither, &c. Spoken by the court-ladies. See the Structure (P², above). **thy beloved.** Masc.
2 My beloved. The Shulamite speaks again in reply. See the Structure (O³, above). **to feed**=to feed [his flock]. **3 he feedeth**=he that feeds [his flock] as a shepherd.

6. 4—8. 4 [For Structure see next page].

4 Thou art beautiful. Solomon breaks in as soon as the Shulamite called for her beloved (shepherd), as he did in 1. 9. **my love**=my friend. Heb. *ra'yāh.* Feminine. See note on 1. 9. **Tirzah.** Became the royal residence of the kings of Israel after the division of the kingdom, until Omri built Samaria (1 Kings 14. 17; 15. 21, 33; 16. 8, 15, 17). Cp. 16. 24. Tirzah means "delightful". Hence the flattering comparison.

comely as Jerusalem, °terrible as °*an army*
with banners.
5 Turn away thine eyes from me, for they
have °overcome me: thy hair *is* °as a flock of
goats °that appear from Gilead.
6 °Thy teeth *are* as a flock of sheep which
go up from the washing, whereof every one
beareth twins, and *there is* not one barren
among them.
7 As a °piece of a pomegranate *are* thy temples °within thy locks.
8 °There are °threescore queens, and fourscore concubines, and °virgins without number.
9 °My dove, my undefiled is °*but* one; she *is*
the *only* one of her mother, she *is* the choice
one of her that bare her. The daughters saw
her, and blessed her; *yea*, the queens and the
concubines, and they °praised her.
10 "Who *is* she *that* looketh forth as the
morning, fair as the moon, clear as the sun,
and °terrible as ⁴*an army* with banners?"

R¹ (p. 927) 11 °I went down into the garden of nuts to
see the fruits of the valley, *and* to see whether
the vine flourished, *and* the pomegranates
budded.
12 °Or ever I was aware, °my soul °made me
like °the chariots of Ammi-nadib.

Q² 13 °Return, return, O °Shulamite; °return,
return, that we may °look upon thee.

R² °What will ye °see in the °Shulamite?

Q³ As it were °the company of two armies.
7 How beautiful are thy feet °with shoes, O
°prince's daughter! °the joints of thy
thighs *are* like jewels, the work of °the hands
of a cunning workman.
2 Thy navel *is like* a round goblet, *which*
wanteth not °liquor: thy °belly *is like* an
heap of wheat set about with lilies.
3 Thy two breasts *are* like two young °roes
that are twins.
4 Thy neck *is* as a tower of ivory; thine eyes

6. 4—8. 4 (N², p. 926). HER COLLOQUIES WITH SOLOMON. (*Repeated Alternation.*)

N² | Q¹ | 6. 4-10. SOLOMON comes forward with flatteries (*vv.* 4-9). What his court-ladies said was true (*v.* 10).
R¹ | 6. 11, 12. THE SHULAMITE explains that her meeting with him was "unwittingly" (see notes). She withdraws.
Q² | 6. 13-. SOLOMON: "Return, return".
R² | 6. -13- THE SHULAMITE: "What is there to look at in me?"
Q³ | 6. -13—7. 9. SOLOMON renews his flatteries.
R³ | 7. 10—8. 4. THE SHULAMITE rejects him: "I belong to my beloved; not to you". Calls on her beloved to fetch her away, and again adjures the court-ladies not to excite her feelings (as in 2. 7, and 3. 5).

terrible, &c. = majestic, or awe-inspiring, as bannered hosts.

an army with banners = the bannered [hosts]. Fem. pl., with no noun expressed. Perhaps a reference to the Hosts of Israel in their journeys in Num. 2.

5 overcome me = taken me by storm (as we say). This is the force of the *Hiphil*.

as = like. The A.V. edition of 1611 did not have "as".

that appear = springing down. Cp. 4. 1.

6 Thy teeth. See notes on 4. 2, where the same comparison is used by the shepherd, except that the latter uses *keẓûboth*, flocks, while the former uses *rāḥēl*, ewes.

7 piece = part.

within thy locks = behind thy veil. Cp. 4. 1, 3.

8 There are: i.e. I have.

threescore. The numbers are not the same as in 1 Kings 11. 3, because a different period is referred to.

virgins = damsels. See note on 1. 3.

9 My dove = But he is my dove.

but one = my only one. In contrast with the numbers of *v.* 8. Flattery enough to turn the heart of almost any woman.

praised her: supply the Ellipsis by adding [saying]. See note on Ps. 109. 5.

11 I went down. The Shulamite explains that she went down to the nut-garden quite innocently, and with no design on her part.

12 Or ever I was aware = Unwittingly, or I know not [how it was], &c.

my soul = I (emph.). Heb. *nephesh.* Ap. 13.

made me like = placed me at, or was brought. **the chariots of Ammi-nadib.** So various are the renderings that the text is said to be "hopelessly corrupt" by modern critics. The A.V. follows the Sept., Arab., Ethiopic, and Vulgate, by treating it as a proper name (with variations in the orthography). The Heb. is "the chariots of my People, the noble", or, of my noble People. From which, when we note the context, and who is speaking, and what fact she is referring to, the Shulamite plainly seems to be saying that she came unwittingly on the royal chariots and the retinue of nobles with Solomon when he first saw her (see p. 921). **13 Return, return.** This was the entreaty of Solomon, as she turned to go away, the moment her necessary explanation had been made. **Shulamite.** Shulem is thought to be the same as Shunem, now *Sōlam*, about three and a half miles from Zerin, north of Jezreel, mentioned in Josh. 19. 18. 1 Sam. 28. 4. 1 Kings 1. 3, 15; 2. 17, 21, 22. 2 Kings 4. 8, 12, 25, 36. Instead of this proper name causing "great difficulty", it is necessary, to enable us to fix the locality of the whole subject of the song. Abishag came from Shunem (1 Kings 1. 4); and is here used as being synonymous with "fairest among women" (1. 8; 5. 9; 6. 1). **look** = gaze on. **What will ye see . . . ?** This is her answer to Solomon's request as she was departing. **see** = gaze on. **the company of two armies.** Instead of "of two armies", the A.V. marg. and R.V. text reads "of Mahanaim", and the R.V. renders the phrase: "the dance (or steps) of Mahanaim". Modern critics say "This is another proper name which must in all probability vanish from the text". But the text needs this here, though it does not need "Ammi-nadib" in *v.* 12. *The Quarterly Statement* of the Palestine Exploration Fund (1891, pp. 244, 245) shows that in *kimḥolath hammaḥănāyim*, the root of the former word (*ḥūl*, to be round) is the common name for a circle (hence another suggested rendering is "like a dance to double choirs"; one even ventures on "a sword-dance"), or geographical "basin", and *meḥanāyim* as meaning a plain or camp on a plain. Remembering that a man was seen by David's watchman from "the wood Ephraim" (2 Sam. 18. 6. Cp. 17. 27) running on "a plain" (2 Sam. 18. 24-27. Cp. 2 Sam. 19. 32), and now putting the word "plain" by Fig. *Metonymy* (of Adjunct), Ap. 6, for the view obtained of it, we have the suitable rendering, "Like the view of Mahanaim", i.e. a view as beautiful as that, which would be the answer to her question, "What will ye behold in the Shulamite?" For "Mahanaim" see Gen. 32. 2.

7. 1 with shoes = with sandals. **prince's daughter** = noble maiden. **the joints of thy thighs** = thy rounded thighs. **the hands of a cunning workman** = hands of steadiness: i.e. work not hastily done. See note on "as one brought up", &c., Prov. 8. 30. **2 liquor** = spiced wine. **belly** = body. **3 roes** = fawns.

like the fishpools in Heshbon, by ° the gate of Bath-rabbim: thy nose *is* as the tower of Lebanon which looketh toward Damascus.

5 Thine head upon thee *is* like Carmel, and the hair of thine head like purple; the king *is* ° held in the galleries.

6 How fair and how ° pleasant art thou, O ° love, ° for delights!

7 This thy stature is like to a palm tree, and thy breasts to clusters *of grapes*.

8 I said, "I will go up to the palm tree, I will take hold of the boughs thereof:" now also thy breasts shall be as clusters of the vine, and the smell of thy nose like apples;

9 And ° the roof of thy mouth like the best ° wine for my beloved, that goeth *down* sweetly, causing ° the lips of those that are asleep to speak.

R³ (p. 927) 10 ° I *am* my beloved's, and his desire *is* toward me.

11 ° Come, my beloved, let us go forth into the field; let us lodge in the villages.

12 Let us get up early to the vineyards; let us see if the vine flourish, *whether* the tender grape appear, *and* the pomegranates bud forth: there will I give thee my ° loves.

13 The mandrakes ° give a smell, and at ° our gates *are* all manner of pleasant *fruits*, new and old, *which* I have ° laid up for thee, O my beloved.

8 O that thou *wert* as my brother, that sucked the breasts of my mother! *when* I should find thee without, I would kiss thee; yea, I should not be ° despised.

2 I ° would lead thee, *and* bring thee into my mother's house, ° *who* would instruct me: I would cause thee to drink of ° spiced wine of the juice of my pomegranate.

3 ° His left hand *should be* under my head, and his right hand should embrace me.

4 ° I charge ° you, O daughters of Jerusalem, that ye ° stir not up, nor ° awake *my* ° love, until ° he please.

A S¹ (p. 928) 5 ° Who *is* this that cometh up from ° the wilderness, leaning upon her beloved?

T¹ ° I raised thee up ° under the apple tree: ° there thy mother ° brought thee forth: there she ° brought thee forth *that* bare thee.

6 ° Set me as a ° seal upon thine heart, as a seal upon thine arm: for [4] love *is* strong as death; jealousy *is* ° cruel ° as the grave: ° the coals thereof *are* coals of fire, ° *which hath* a most vehement ° flame.

7 Many waters ° cannot quench [4] love, neither can the floods drown it: if ° a man would give all the substance of his house for [4] love, it would utterly be contemned.

---

4 the gate of Bath-rabbim = the populous gate.
5 held in the galleries = captivated by the ringlets.
Carmel = the [mount] Carmel.
6 pleasant = charming.
love. Heb. *'ahābāh* = love in the abstract. It is not the person who is here addressed. See note on 2. 7.
for delights = among delightsome things.
9 the roof of thy mouth = the palate. Put by Fig. *Metonymy* (of Adjunct), Ap. 6, for speech.
wine. Heb. *yayin.* Ap. 27. I.
the lips of those that are asleep = slumbering lips.
10 I am my beloved's = I belong to my beloved: referring to her beloved shepherd. The Shulamite speaks, and thus gently but firmly refuses the king's advances.
11 Come, my beloved. (Masc.). See note on 1. 2. Thus she apostrophises her beloved (shepherd).
12 loves = endearments. Heb. *dodīm,* as in 1. 2, 4; and 4. 10, 10.
13 give a smell = diffuse their fragrance.
our gates = our gateways. **laid up** = reserved.
8. 1 despised = reproached.
2 would lead thee = would fain lead thee thence [in triumph].
who would = thou wouldest, or she would.
spiced wine = the aromatic [wine]. Heb. *rekah.*
3 His left hand = [Let] his left hand [be].
4 I charge you = I have adjured you. In this last charge the addition is not "by the roes", &c. And we have *mah* instead of *'im* = Why incite, &c.
you. See note on 2. 7.
stir not up . . . awake. See note on 2. 7, and cp. 3. 5.
love. Heb. *'ahābāh* (Fem.). Used of love in the abstract. See notes on 2. 4, and 3. 5. **he** = she.

8. 5-14 (*A*, p. 920). THE CONCLUSION. THE SHULAMITE RESTORED.

The Shulamite returns home from Solomon, and is seen by her brothers and their companions, approaching; her beloved (shepherd) is with her.

(*Repeated Alternation.*)

A | S¹ | 5-. THE COMPANIONS of the shepherd see them approaching.
T¹ | -5-7. THE SHULAMITE and her beloved (shepherd) revisit the spot where they first plighted their troth; and renew their vows.
S² | 8, 9. THE BROTHERS confer as to their sister's dowry. "What shall we do for her?" "If she be a wall (i.e. virtuous) we will adorn her." "If she be a door (accessible to any) we will shut her up."
T² | 10-12. THE SHULAMITE: "I am a wall" (not a door). Solomon has many vineyards; I will keep my own.
S³ | 13. THE BELOVED (shepherd) asks her to tell them her story.
T³ | 14. THE SHULAMITE owns him her beloved. He is to hasten to her now and ever. No longer over the mountains which separated them (2. 8, 17), for these have given place to the mountains of delight.

5 Who is this? The companions of the shepherd are the speakers.
the wilderness = the plain of 3. 6. See note on "the company of two armies" above: i.e. the plain of Esdraelon, lying between Jezreel and Shunem.

I raised thee up: i.e. I awakened [love] in thy heart: i.e. I won thy heart. See note on "love", 2. 7. **under the apple tree** = under the orange tree. The place of the birth of their love. The orange-blossom is everywhere, now, the bridal flower. **there**: thither came she that bare thee. Confinements in the open air are of frequent occurrence. **brought thee forth** = to bring thee forth. **6 Set** = Oh place. **seal** = signet, regarded as good as a signature. Now that writing is more common it has become an ornament. It was worn round the neck (Gen. 38. 18, 25), or worn on the right hand (Jer. 22. 24). Cp. also Hag. 2. 23. **cruel** = inexorable, hard. **as the grave** = as Sheōl. See Ap. 35. **the coals thereof** = its flames. **which hath a most vehement flame.** Heb. "flames of Jah": *shalhebeth-yah.* Render this:

For love is strong as death, The flames thereof are flames of fire,
Jealously is inexorable as Sheol, The vehement flames of Jah.

flame. Same root as Gen. 3. 24. **7 cannot quench**: i.e. earthly things cannot destroy that which is divine. **a man.** Heb. *'ish.* Ap. 14. II.

S² (p. 928) **8 °We have a little sister, and °she hath no breasts: what shall we do for our sister in the day when she shall be °spoken for?**
9 °If she *be* a wall, we will build upon her a °palace of silver: and if she *be* °a door, we will inclose her with °boards of cedar.
T² **10 °I *am* a wall, and my breasts like towers: then was I in °his eyes as one that found favour.**
11 °Solomon had a vineyard at °Baal-hamon; he let out the vineyard unto °keepers; every one for the fruit thereof was to bring a thousand *pieces* of silver.
12 My vineyard, which *is* mine, °*is* before me: °thou, O Solomon, °*must have* a thousand, and °those that keep the fruit thereof two hundred.

S³ **13 °Thou that °dwellest in the gardens, °the companions °hearken to thy voice: cause °me to hear *it*.**

T³ **14 °Make haste, my beloved, and be thou like to a roe or to a young hart °upon the mountains of spices.**

8 We have. One of the brothers now speaks.
We have a little sister = Our sister is still young.
she hath no breasts. The idiom for not yet marriageable. This is what the brothers had once said in earlier days. The reference here is "not obscure" when we note who the speakers are, and when they said this.
spoken for. i. e. demanded [in marriage]. Cp. 1 Sam. 13. 9; 25. 39.
9 If she be a wall. Spoken by another brother: i.e. like a wall that keeps out all intruders.
palace = turret, or battlement.
a door: i.e. accessible to any one.
boards = planks, or panels.
10 I am a wall. The Shulamite thus replies: I stand firm against all the blandishments of Solomon. I am not a door admitting any one.
his eyes: i.e. her shepherd lover's, or the brother's who last spoke (not Solomon's. Solomon is mentioned in the next verse).
11 Solomon. The Shulamite, in demanding her reward, gives her reasons.
Baal-hamon. Not yet identified.
keepers = husbandmen: i.e. tenants.
12 is before me = is my own.
thou. Apostrophising the absent Solomon whom she had left.
must have. Instead of these words supply "[mayst keep his] thousand".
those that keep, &c. = the keepers [may keep] their two hundreds. **13 Thou that dwellest** = Oh thou that dwellest. Spoken by the shepherd. **dwellest in the gardens.** No longer in "the city" of 5. 7, but now abidest permanently. Heb. *yāshab.* **the companions** = my companions (who were the speakers of *v.* 5). **hearken** = are listening. **me, &c.:** or "me [and our companions] to hear". **14 Make haste, &c.** The Shulamite lets him hear it; and, before all, announces and avows him as her beloved, bidding him always to hasten to her like a gazelle. **upon** = [that turneth itself about] upon: or that boundeth over the mountains of spices (4. 6), "*Beṣāmīm*" (= spices); and no longer over the mountains of separation "*Bāther*" (2. 17).

THE BOOK OF THE PROPHET
ISAIAH.
THE STRUCTURE OF THE BOOK AS A WHOLE.

(*Introversion.*)

1. 1. THE TITLE.

A | 1. 2—5. 30. EXHORTATIONS : REPREHENSORY. PROPHETIC.

B | 6. 1-13. THE VOICE FROM THE TEMPLE. THE SCATTERING.

C | 7. 1—12. 6. HISTORIC. EVENTS AND PROPHECIES (AHAZ).

D | 13. 1—27. 13. BURDENS. ALTERNATED WITH ISRAEL'S BLESSINGS.

D | 28. 1—35. 10. WOES. ALTERNATED WITH JEHOVAH'S GLORIES.

C | 36. 1—39. 8. HISTORIC. EVENTS AND PROPHECIES (HEZEKIAH).

B | 40. 1-11. THE VOICE FROM THE WILDERNESS. THE GATHERING.

A | 40. 12—66. 24. EXHORTATIONS : PROMISSORY. PROPHETIC.

For the CANONICAL order and place of the Prophets, see Ap. 1 and notes on the Structure of the Minor Prophets as a whole (p. 1207).
For the CHRONOLOGICAL order of the Prophets, see Ap. 77.
For the Inter-relation of the Prophetic Books, see Ap. 78.
For the Prophets and their calling, see Ap. 49.
For the Formulæ of Prophetic Utterances, see Ap. 82.
For References to the Pentateuch in the Prophets, see Ap. 92.
For the Quotations and verbal allusions to ISAIAH in the New Testament, see Ap. 80.
For the Evidences of one Authorship, see Ap. 79.

The Structure, above, declares the unity of the book, and effectually disposes of the alleged dual authorship and the hypothetical division of the book by modern critics into two parts: the "former" part being chs. 1—39, the "latter" part chs. 40—66 The "Voice", in ch. 40. 1-11, is necessitated in order to complete the "Correspondence" with 6. 1-13; and, if an hypothesis is admitted on the one side, then it must be admitted on the other; and it is hypothetically incredible that this dual reference to the "voice" could have been the outcome of a dual authorship. For other evidences, see Ap. 79, 80, and 82.

The DATE of the book is given as "in the days of Uzziah, Jotham, Ahaz, and Hezekiah".

In ch. 6. 1, the prophecy there is given as being "in the year that king Uzziah died".

According to Ap. 50, p. 59 (cp. Ap. 77), Uzziah died in 649 B.C.

Historically, Isaiah disappears from view after delivering the great prophecy of the Babylonian Servitude (2 Kings 20. 16-18 and Isa. 39. 1-8). This was in the year 603 B.C., after Hezekiah's illness at the close of the siege of Jerusalem by Sennacherib in Hezekiah's fourteenth year (cp. Ap. 50, p. 60).

We have thus two fixed dates, and between them a period of forty-six years, during which, undoubtedly, "the Word of Jehovah came" through Isaiah, and "God spake" by him.

Though this period was covered and overlapped by the Prophet's life, it was not the whole of the period covered by the "vision", which goes far beyond the prediction of the Babylonish Captivity.

Hezekiah lived for fifteen years after his illness, dying therefore in 588 B.C. Manasseh, his son, born in the third of the fifteen added years, succeeded in the same year (588 B.C.).

How soon after his accession the Manassean persecution began we are not told; but it is highly improbable that a boy of *twelve* years would immediately commence the horrible things of which we are told in 2 Kings 21 and 2 Chron. 33.

The unutterable "religious" practices that lie behind the descriptive words in these chapters point clearly to some four or five years later, when Manasseh would be sixteen or seventeen.

According to Jewish tradition, Isaiah perished in the Manassean persecution; when, it is said, he took refuge inside a hollow mulberry tree, which Manasseh ordered to be sawn through. This may be referred to in Heb. 11. 37.

If we take the fifth year of Manasseh (584 B.C.) as the date of Isaiah's death (violent or natural, we have no means of determining), then, from "the year that king Uzziah died" (6. 1, which forcibly suggests the *terminus a quo* of the whole book) to this point, we have sixty-five years from the commencement of the "visions" till the supposed date of his death (649–584 B.C.=65). See Ap. 77.

If Isaiah was about the same age as Samuel, Jeremiah, and Daniel were, at the beginning of their ministries, viz. 16–18, then we may conclude that the length of his life was some 81–83 years.

There is no evidence that "the Word of the LORD came" to Isaiah after the reign of Hezekiah ended in 588 B.C., therefore the whole period covered by "the vision" of Isaiah is *sixty-one* years (649–588=61).

From that year onward till the *thirteenth* year of Josiah in 518 B.C., there were seventy years during which God did not speak "by the prophets" (588–518=70).

The chart of the Prophets (see Ap. 77) shows that

ISAIAH was contemporary with HOSEA from 649-611 B.C.=38 years;
with MICAH from 632-611 B.C.=21 ,, ;
and with NAHUM in the year 603 B.C.= 1 year.

THE °BOOK OF THE PROPHET
°ISAIAH.

649-588 **1** °THE vision of Isaiah the son of Amoz, which °he saw °concerning Judah and Jerusalem in the days of °Uzziah, °Jotham, °Ahaz, °*and* °Hezekiah, kings of Judah.

A E[1] F[1] (p. 931) **2** °Hear, O heavens, and give ear, O earth: °for °the LORD °hath °spoken,

G[1] I have nourished and °brought up °children, and they have °rebelled against Me.

3 The ox °knoweth his owner, and the ass his master's crib: *but* Israel doth °not know, °My People doth not consider.

H[1] **4** °Ah °sinful nation, a people °laden with °iniquity, a seed °of evildoers, [2]children that are °corrupters: they have °forsaken °the

TITLE. Book=Scroll. For its place in the Heb. Canon, see Ap. 1. For its relation to the other prophets, see Ap. 78.

Isaiah=the salvation of Jehovah. For the occurrences of his name in N.T., see Ap. 79. I. For quotations in the N.T., see Ap. 80. For the unity of the book as a whole, see the Structure on p. 930, and Ap. 79.

1 The vision of Isaiah. This is the title of the whole book.

he saw=he saw in vision. Heb. *chāzā*, to gaze on, as in 2. 1; 13. 1. Not the same word as in 6. 1, 6; 21. 6, 7; but Jehovah was the speaker. Isaiah's voice and pen, but Jehovah's words (*v.* 2).

concerning Judah and Jerusalem. This is the subject of the book. It is not concerning the "Church" or the "world": nor to other nations, except as they come in contact with "Judah and Jerusalem". Its theme is the salvation of the nation by Jehovah through judgment and grace, as being "life from the dead" (Rom. 11. 15). It is addressed to those who look for Messiah (8. 17; 45. 22) and those who "wait for Him" (8. 17; 25. 9; 26. 8; 33. 2). **Uzziah** (2 Chron. 26. 1-23. 649 B.C.). **Jotham** (2 Chron. 27. 1-9). **Ahaz** (2 Chron. 28. 1-27). **and.** The absence of conjunctions between these names, and the Hebrew accents attached to them, seem to indicate that some of them reigned for a time jointly. See Ap. 50, p. 59. **Hezekiah** (2 Chron. 29. 1—32. 33, and Isa. 36. 1—39. 8).

1. 2—5. 30 (**A**, p. 930). EXHORTATIONS: REPREHENSORY AND PROPHETIC. (*Introversion.*)

A | A | 1. 2-31. The Word of Jehovah. "Hear ye!" Zion the vineyard.
  B | 2. 1-5. Zion's future glory.
    C | 2. 6-22. The sin of Judah (men). Judgment pronounced.
      D | 3. 1-15. The political ruin of Judah.
    C | 3. 16—4. 1. The sin of Judah (women). Judgment pronounced.
  B | 4. 2-6. Zion's future glory.
A | 5. 1-30. The Song of Jehovah. "Judge ye!" Zion the vineyard.

1. 2-31 (A, above). THE WORD OF JEHOVAH. "HEAR YE!" ZION THE VINEYARD. (*Division, and Repeated and Extended Alternation.*)

A | E[1] | F[1] | 2-. Call to hear. Indictment.
    G[1] | -2, 3. Israel's sin. Cause: rebellion.
      H[1] | 4-9. Expostulation.
  E[2] | F[2] | 10. Call to hear. Instruction.
    G[2] | 11-15. Israel's sin. Aggravation: formality.
      H[2] | 16, 17. Exhortation.
  E[3] | F[3] | 18-. Call to hear. Rectification.
    G[3] | -18-20. Israel's sin. Remedy: Divine grace.
      H[3] | 21-31. Expostulation.

2 Hear, O heavens. Fig. *Apostrophe.* Ap. 6. Reference to Pentateuch (Ap. 92). It commences like the Song of Moses (Deut. 32. 1. See notes, p. 282), and is the commentary on it. Note the connection of the two books, Isaiah the necessary sequel to Deuteronomy. This verse was put on the title-page of early English Bibles, claiming the right of all to hear what Jehovah hath spoken. **for.** Note the reason given. **the LORD.** Heb. Jehovah. Ap. 4. II. **hath spoken**: i.e., articulately. Not Isaiah. All modern criticism is based on the assumption that it is a human book: and that prediction is a human impossibility (which we grant); and this ends in a denial of inspiration altogether. Against this God has placed 2 Pet. 1. 21. **spoken.** Jehovah is the Eternal One: "Who was, and is, and is to come". Hence, His words are, like Himself, eternal; and prophecy relates to the *then present* as well as to the *future*; and may have a *praeterist* and a *futurist* interpretation, as well as a now *present application* to ourselves. **brought up.** Cp. Ex. 4. 22; Deut. 14. 1; 32. 6, 18, 20. **children**=sons. **rebelled.** Heb. *pāsh'a.* Ap. 44. ix. **3 knoweth.** Put by Fig. *Metonymy* (of Cause), Ap. 6, for all that that knowledge implies. **not know.** Cp. Jer. 8. 7. All Israel's trouble came from the truth of this indictment. Cp. Luke 19. 42-44. The trouble will all be removed when 54. 13; 60. 16 are fulfilled. Jer. 31. 34. Isa. 11. 9. Cp. Jer. 9. 23, 24. **My People.** Some codices, with Sept., Syr., and Vulg., read "and My people". **4 Ah.** Fig. *Ecphōnēsis.* Ap. 6. Note the four exclamatory descriptions, and see note on "gone away", below. **sinful.** Heb. *chāṭā'.* Ap. 44. i. **sinful nation.** Note the Figs. *Apostrophe, Synonymia,* and *Anabasis* (Ap. 6) in *vv.* 4, 5. Contrast Ex. 19. 6. Deut. 7. 6; 14. 2, 21. **laden**=heavily burdened. **iniquity.** Heb. *'āvāh.* Ap. 44. iv. **of**=consisting of. Genitive of Apposition. Ap. 17. 4. **corrupters.** Ref. to Pent. (Deut. 32. 5). **forsaken.** Apostasy in disposition. Ref. to Pent. (Deut. 28. 20; 31. 16). Ap. 92. Occurs in the "former" portion here, *v.* 28; 6. 12; 7. 16; 10. 3 (leave), 14 (left); 17. 2, 9; 18. 6 (left); 27. 10; 32. 14: and in the "latter" portion, 41. 17; 49. 14; 54. 6; 55. 7; 58. 2; 60. 15; 62. 4, 12; 65. 11. Ap. 79. II. **the LORD.** Heb. Jehovah (with *'eth*)=Jehovah Himself (Ap. 4. II). Not the same as in *vv.* 2, 9, 10, 11, 20.

649-588 LORD, they have ° provoked ° the ° Holy One of
Israel unto anger, they are ° gone away backward.
5 ° Why should ye be stricken any more? ye
will revolt more and more: the whole head is
sick, and the whole heart faint.
6 From the sole of the foot even unto the
head *there is* no soundness in it; *but* ° wounds,
and bruises, and putrifying sores: they have
not been closed, neither bound up, neither
mollified with ° ointment.
7 Your country *is* ° desolate, ° your cities *are*
burned with fire: your ° land, ° strangers devour it in your presence, and *it is* ° desolate, as
overthrown by ° strangers.
8 And the daughter of Zion is left ° as a ° cottage in a vineyard, as ° a lodge in a garden of
cucumbers, as a besieged city.
9 ° Except ° the LORD of hosts had left unto us
a ° very small remnant, we should have been
° as Sodom, *and* we should have been like unto
Gomorrah.
E[2] F[2] 10 [2] Hear the word of [2] the LORD, ye ° rulers
(p. 931) of [9] Sodom; give ear unto ° the law of our
° God, ye ° people of Gomorrah.
G[2] 11 ° "To what purpose *is* the multitude of
your sacrifices unto Me?" ° saith [2] the LORD:
"I am full of the burnt offerings of rams, and
the fat of fed beasts; and I delight not in the
blood of bullocks, or of lambs, or of he goats.
12 When ye come ° to appear before Me, who
hath required this at your hand, to ° tread My
courts?
13 Bring no more vain ° oblations; incense
° is an abomination unto Me; the new moons
and sabbaths, the calling of ° assemblies, ° I cannot away with; *it is* ° iniquity, even the solemn
meeting.
14 Your new moons and your appointed feasts
° My soul hateth: they are a trouble unto Me;
I am weary to bear *them*.
15 ° And when ye ° spread forth your hands,
I will hide Mine eyes from you: yea, when ye
° make many prayers, I will not hear: your
hands are full of ° blood.
H[2] 16 Wash you, make you clean; put away the
° evil of your doings from before Mine eyes;
cease to do ° evil;
17 Learn to do well; seek judgment, relieve
the oppressed, judge the ° fatherless, plead for
the ° widow.
E[3] F[3] 18 Come now, and ° let us reason together,"
[11] saith [2] the LORD:
G[3] "though your ° sins be as scarlet, they shall
be as white as snow; ° though they be red like
crimson, they shall be as wool.

provoked = despised, blasphemed. Ref. to Pent. (Ap. 92). An old Mosaic word (Num. 14. 11, 23; 16. 30. Deut. 31. 20). Apostasy in words (see note above).

the Holy One of Israel. Occurs twenty-five times in Isaiah: twelve times in the "former" portion (1. 4; 5. 19, 24; 10. 20; 12. 6; 17. 7; 29. 19; 30. 11, 12, 15; 31. 1; 37. 23); and thirteen times in the "latter" portion (41. 14, 16, 20; 43. 3, 14; 45. 11; 47. 4; 48. 17; 49. 7; 54. 5; 55. 5; 60. 9, 14). Outside Isaiah it is used by Himself once (2 Kings 19. 22 first occurrence); three times in the Psalms (71. 22; 78. 41; 89. 18). Elsewhere found only three times (Jer. 50. 29; 51. 5; and Ezek. 39. 7 in Israel). **Holy.** See note on Ex. 3. 5.

gone away backward. Apostasy in act. See notes on *v.* 4, and notice the threefold apostasy in this verse. Compare also the fourfold exclamatory descriptions of which this apostasy is affirmed: making seven in all (see Ap. 10).

5 Why . . . ? Fig. *Erotēsis.* Ap. 6.

6 wounds. Note the Fig. *Synonymia* (Ap. 6). Heb. sing., as are the other two. **ointment** = oil.

7 desolate. Occurs in "former" portion here, 6. 11; 17. 9; 33. 8; and in the "latter" portion, 49. 8, 19; 54. 1, 3; 61. 4, 4; 62. 4.

your cities. Some codices, with Syr., read "and your cities". **land** = soil.

strangers = foreigners, or apostates. Heb. *zūr.* See note on Prov. 5. 3 (not the same word as in 2. 6).

8 as a cottage. Note the Fig. *Synonymia.* Ap. 6.

cottage = a booth, made of reeds. Cp. Job 27. 18.

a lodge. A platform on four poles, sheltered by leaves or sacking. Left to the weather at the close of harvest.

9 Except, &c. The first passage in Isaiah quoted in N.T. (Rom. 9. 29).

the LORD of hosts. See note on 1 Sam. 1. 3.

very small. Heb. *kimʿaṭ.* See note on Prov. 5. 14.

as Sodom. Ref. to Pent. (Gen. 19. 1-29. Deut. 29. 23.) (Ap. 92). Cp. 3. 9, for the reason.

10 rulers of: i.e. rulers who ruled as in Sodom.

the law. Ref. to whole Pentateuch. Twelve times in Isaiah (1. 10; 2. 3; 5. 24; 8. 16, 20; 24. 5; 30. 9; 42. 4, 21, 24; 51. 4, 7). See Ap. 92.

God. Heb. *Elohim.* Ap. 4. i.

people of: i.e. people who acted as the people in Gomorrah acted.

11 To what purpose, &c. Fig. *Synathrœsmos* (Ap. 6), in *vv.* 11-15. Also Fig. *Hypotyposis* (Ap. 6), for emphasis, in describing the hollowness of mere religious observances (as when Christ was on earth. Cp. John 2. 6, 7 with 14, 16). Matt. 15. 3-8.

saith the LORD. The Heb. fut. of *'āmar* (= *y'omar*), combined with a Divine title, is used thrice in the so-called "former" portion of Isaiah (1. 11, 18; 33. 10), and six times in the "latter" portion (40. 1, 25; 41. 21, 21; 66. 9). Elsewhere only in Ps. 12. 5, while the past tense is frequently used (see Ap. 92).

12 to appear, &c. Ref. to Pent. See note (Ex. 23. 15; 34. 20).

tread = trample, and thus profane. Heb. *rāmaṣ.* Ezek. 26. 11; 34. 18. Dan. 8. 7, 10.

13 oblations. Heb. *minchah* = gift-offering. Ap. 43. II. iii. **is** = itself [is].

assemblies = convocations. Heb. *miḳra'.* Ref. to Pent. (Ap. 92); out of twenty-three occurrences, twenty occur in Pent. Occurs only here, 4. 5, and Neh. 8. 8 (in a later sense "reading"), outside the Pentateuch. Not *ḳāhal.* See note on Gen. 28. 3; 49. 6; and Ap. 92.

I cannot away with. Heb. *yākol* = to be able. Here = "I am not able [to endure, or put up with]". The Fig. *Ellipsis* (Ap. 6) must be thus supplied. **iniquity** = vanity. (Not the same word as *v.* 4.) Heb. *'āven.* Ap. 44. iii. **iniquity, even the solemn meeting.** Heb. "iniquity and assembly". Fig. *Hendiadys* (Ap. 6) = your vain assembly. **14 My soul** = I (very emphatic). Heb. *nephesh.* Ap. 13. Fig. *Anthropopatheia.* Ap. 6. **15 And when** = Even when. **spread forth your hands.** Put by Fig. *Metonymy* (of Adjunct), Ap. 6, for "pray", in which the hands are spread forth. **make many prayers** = multiply your prayer. **blood.** Put by Fig. *Metonymy* (of Effect), Ap. 6, for the acts which shed the blood. **16 evil.** Heb. *rāʿaʿ.* Ap. 44. viii. **17 fatherless . . . widow.** Put by Fig. *Synecdoche* (of Species), Ap. 6, for all kinds of helpless and bereaved persons. **18 let us reason together** = let us put the matter right, or settle the matter. It means the putting an end to all reasoning, rather than an invitation to commence reasoning. **sins.** Heb. *chāṭā'.* Ap. 44. i. **though.** Some codices, with one early printed edition, Sept., Syr., and Vulg., read "yea, though".

649-588 19 If ye be willing and obedient, ye shall eat the good of the land:

20 But if ye refuse and rebel, ye shall be devoured with the sword: °for the mouth of [2]the LORD hath spoken *it*."

H³ J L (p. 933) 21 How °is the faithful city become an harlot! it was full of judgment; righteousness lodged in it; but now murderers.

M a 22 Thy silver is become dross, thy °wine mixed with water:

b 23 °Thy °princes *are* rebellious, and companions of thieves: every one loveth °gifts, and followeth after rewards: they judge not the [17]fatherless, neither doth the cause of the [17]widow come unto them.

K 24 Therefore saith °THE Lord, [9]the LORD of hosts, °the mighty One of Israel, "Ah, I will ease Me of Mine adversaries, and avenge Me of Mine enemies:

J M a 25 And I will °turn My hand upon °thee, and purely °purge away thy dross, and take away all thy °tin:

b 26 And I will restore thy °judges as at the first, and thy counsellors as at the beginning:

L afterward thou shalt be called, The city of righteousness, the °faithful city.

27 Zion shall be °redeemed with judgment, and °her converts with righteousness.

K 28 And the destruction of the °transgressors and of the [4]sinners *shall be* together, and they that [4]forsake [2]the LORD shall be consumed.

29 For they shall be ashamed of the °oaks which ye have desired, and ye shall be confounded for the gardens that ye have °chosen.

30 For ye shall °be as an oak whose °leaf fadeth, and as a garden that hath no water.

31 And °the strong shall be as tow, and °the maker of it as a spark, and they shall both burn together, and none shall quench *them*."

B (p. 931) **2** °The word that Isaiah the son of Amoz °saw °concerning Judah and Jerusalem.

2 And it shall come to pass °in the last days, *that* the °mountain of °the LORD'S house shall be established in the top of the mountains, and shall be exalted above the hills; and °all nations shall °flow unto it.

3 And many °people shall go and say, "Come ye, and let us °go up to the mountain of [2]the LORD, °to the house of the °God of Jacob; and He will teach us of His ways, and we will walk in His °paths:" for out of Zion shall go forth °the law, and the word of [2]the LORD from Jerusalem.

4 And He shall judge among the nations, and shall rebuke many [3]people: and they shall beat their °swords into plowshares, and their °spears into pruninghooks: °nation shall not lift up sword against nation, neither shall they learn war any more.

20 for the mouth of the LORD, &c. This sets the seal on this book as a whole, uniting all its parts. It occurs in the "former" portion (1. 20), and in the "latter" portion (40. 5, and 58. 14). Cp. 21. 17; 22. 25; 24. 3; 25. 8. See Ap. 79. II.
21 is=[is it that she].
22 wine=liquor, or drink. Heb. *ṣābā'*. Ap. 27. vi.

1. 21-31 (H³, p. 931). EXPOSTULATION.
(*Alternations and Introversion.*)

H³ | J | L | 21. The City.
  M | a | 22. Metals. (Fig.) } Inhabitants.
  b | 23. Officers. (Lit.) }
  K | 24. Judgment on enemies of Jehovah.
J | *M* | *a* | 25. Metals. (Fig.) } Inhabitants.
  b | 26-. Officers. (Lit.) }
  L | -26, 27. The City.
  K | 28-31. Judgment on the wicked among Jehovah's People.

23 Thy princes, &c. Fig. *Hermeneia* (Ap. 6). Interpreting the Figs. *Hypocatastasis* (Ap. 6) in *v.* 22.
princes are rebellious. *Sārīm sorᵉrīm*, not a "pun", but the Fig. *Paronomasia* (Ap. 6), for solemn emphasis. It may be Englished "thy rulers are unruly".
gifts=rewards, or bribes.
24 THE Lord. Heb. *Adōn*. Ap. 4. VIII (2).
the mighty One of Israel. Peculiar to Isaiah. Ref. to Pent. (Gen. 49. 24). Ap. 92. Cp. Isa. 49. 26; 60. 16.
25 turn My hand: i.e. repeat the judgment (*v.* 27).
thee: i.e. the city (*vv.* 21, 26, 27).
purge=refine. Cp. 1. 16; 6. 7. **tin**: i.e. alloy.
26 judges as at the first. Ref. to Pent. Ex. 18. 16-26. Num. 25. 5. Deut. 1. 16; 16. 18; 19. 17-19; 21. 2. Ap. 92. **faithful.** Cp. *v.* 21.
27 redeemed=delivered. Heb. *pādāh*. See notes on Ex. 6. 6 and 13. 13.
her converts=they that return of her.
28 transgressors=rebels. Ap. 44. ix.
29 oaks: the trees resorted to for idolatrous worship (57. 5; 65. 3; 66. 17. 2 Kings 16. 4; 17. 10. Ezek. 6. 13). Note the alternation of "oaks", "gardens", "oak", "garden" in *vv.* 29, 30.
chosen. Heb. *bachar*. Occurs four times in the "former" portion (here, 7. 15, 16; 14. 1), and sixteen times in the "latter" portion (40. 20; 41. 8, 9, 24; 43. 10; 44. 1, 2; 48. 10; 49. 7; 56. 4; 58. 5, 6; 65. 12; 66. 3, 4, 4). See Ap. 79. II. **30** be=become.
leaf. Some codices (one in marg.), with four early printed editions, Sept., Syr., and Vulg., read "leaves" (pl.).
31 the strong. Heb. *ḥāṣon*. Occurs only here, and Amos 2. 9.
the maker of it=his work (whatever it be): i.e. the idols (doubtless the *'asherāhs*. Ap. 42).
2. 1 The word that=That which. Cp. Mic. 4. 1-3, written seventeen years later.
saw=saw in vision. See note on 1. 1.
concerning Judah, &c. The repetition of 1. 1 shows that ch. 1 is to be regarded as a summary Introduction to the whole book.
2 in the last days: i.e. the days of Messiah.
mountain of the LORD'S house. Ps. 24. 3. Cp. Ps. 68. 15. See note on Ezek. 28. 16.
the LORD'S=Jehovah's. Ap. 4. II.
all nations. Fig. *Synecdoche* (of Genus)=many from all nations.
flow=stream. Same word as in Jer. 31. 12. Mic. 4. 1.
3 people=peoples.
go up. Note the Fig. *Zeugma* (Ap. 6). The second verb must be supplied (enter into).
to the house="[and enter] into the house", &c. The "and" is read in some codices, with two early printed editions, Sept., Syr., and Vulg. **God.** Heb. Elohim. Ap. 4. I. **paths.** Heb. *'orah*. Occurs in "former" portion here, 3. 12; 26. 7, 8; 30. 11; 33. 8 ("highways"); and in the "latter" portion, 40. 14; 41. 3. See Ap. 79. II. **the law**=law (no Art.). See note on 1. 10.
4 swords . . . spears. Put by Fig. *Synecdoche* (of the Part), Ap. 6, for all kinds of weapons; while plowshares and pruning-hooks put by the same Figure, for all implements of peace. The signs are Figures, but the things signified are literal. Cp. Ps. 72. 7. Jer. 23. 6. Zech. 9. 10. **nation.** Some codices, with four early printed editions, read "and nation".

649-588 5 O °house of Jacob, come ye, and let us walk in the light of [2] the LORD.

C N c (p. 934) 6 °Therefore Thou hast forsaken Thy people the [5] house of Jacob, because they be °replenished °from the east, and *are* °soothsayers like the Philistines, and they °please themselves in the °children of °strangers.

7 °Their land also is full of silver and gold, °neither *is there any* end of their treasures; °their land is also full of horses, °neither *is there any* end of their chariots:

8 Their land also is full of °idols; they worship the work of their own hands, that which their own fingers have made:

9 And the °mean man boweth down, and the °great man humbleth himself: therefore forgive them not.

d 10 Enter into the rock, and hide thee in the dust, for °fear of [2] the LORD, and for the glory of His majesty.

O e 11 The °lofty looks of °man shall be °humbled, °and the °haughtiness of °men shall be °bowed down,

f and [2] the LORD alone shall be °exalted in that day.

12 For °the day of °the LORD of hosts *shall be* upon every *one that is* °proud and °lofty, °and upon every *one that is* °lifted up; °and he shall be °brought low:

13 And upon all the cedars of Lebanon, *that are* °high and [12] lifted up, and upon all the oaks of Bashan,

14 And upon all the [13] high mountains, and upon all the hills *that are* [12] lifted up,

15 And upon every °high tower, and upon every fenced wall,

16 And upon all the °ships of °Tarshish, and upon all °pleasant pictures.

O e 17 And the °loftiness of [11] man shall be [11] bowed down, and the [11] haughtiness of [11] men shall be °made low:

f [2] and [2] the LORD alone shall be [11] exalted in that day.

N c 18 And the [8] idols He shall utterly abolish.

d 19 And they shall go into the holes of the rocks, and into the caves of the earth, for [10] fear of [2] the LORD, and for the glory of His majesty, when He ariseth to shake °terribly the earth.

20 In that day a [11] man shall cast his [8] idols of silver, and his [8] idols of gold, which they

5 house of Jacob. Generally has regard to the natural seed of Jacob, while Israel has regard to the spiritual. See notes on Gen. 32. 28; 43. 6; 45. 26, 28. The expression occurs nine times in Isaiah, six before ch. 40 (2. 5, 6; 8. 17; 10. 20; 14. 1; 29. 22), and three after ch. 40 (46. 3; 48. 1; 58. 1). See Ap. 79. II.

2. 6-22 (C, p. 931). THE SIN OF JUDAH: (MEN). JUDGMENT PRONOUNCED.
(*Introversion and Alternations.*)

C | N | c | 6-9. The sin of Judah. Idols made.
d | 10. Threatening.
O | e | 11-. Abasement of man } Day of the LORD.
f | -11-16. Exaltation of Jehovah.
O | *e* | 17-. Abasement of man. } Day of the LORD.
f | -17. Exaltation of Jehovah.
N | *c* | 18. The sin of Judah. Idols abolished.
d | 19-22. Threatening.

6 Therefore. Or, For.
replenished: or, full of divinations.
from the east. Especially diviners and mediums from an evil spirit (an *ob*). Cp. Lev. 19. 31; 20. 6. Deut. 18. 11. 1 Sam. 28. 3-7; and below, 8. 9; 19. 3; 29. 4, where *ob* occurs. See note on Lev. 19. 31.
soothsayers. Ref. to Pent. Lev. 19. 26 (observe times). Deut. 18. 10, 14 (observers of times). Same word in all four cases. Heb. *'ānan.* Occurs only here in the "former" portion, and only in 57. 3 (sorceress) in the "latter" portion. See Ap. 79. II.
please themselves = join hands with.
children = young children.
strangers. Heb. *nakar* = unknown persons; hence, foreigners.
7 Their land . . . neither (repeated). Note Fig. *Symploke* (Ap. 6).
8 idols = nothings. Ref. to Pent. (Lev. 26. 1. Deut. 17. 14-19). Ap. 92.
9 mean man. Heb. *'ādām.* Ap. 14. I. } Contrasting society's extremes.
great man. Heb. *'īsh.* Ap. 14. II.
10 fear = dread. Cp. 2 Thess. 1. 9, 10.
11 lofty = proud. Note the Fig. *Synonymia* (Ap. 6) to impress us with the far-reaching object and effect of Jehovah's dealings in "the day of the LORD", recorded in *vv.* 11-17. Heb. *gābah.* Same word as "high" (*v.* 15), and "loftiness" (*v.* 17). Not the same word as "lofty" (*v.* 12). **man.** Heb. *'ādām.* Ap. 14. I.
humbled = lowered. Note the Fig. *Synonymia* (Ap. 6), in *vv.* 11 and 17. Heb. *shāphal.* Same word as "brought low" (*v.* 12), "made low" (*v.* 17). Heb. = each shall be, &c.
and. Note the Fig. *Polysyndeton* (Ap. 6).
haughtiness. Heb. *rūm.* Same word as "lofty" (*v.* 12), "high" (*vv.* 13, 14).
men. Heb. pl. of *'ĕnōsh.* Ap. 14. III.
bowed down = brought low. Heb. *shāhah.* Same word as in *v.* 17.
exalted. Heb. *sāgab.* Same word as in *v.* 17.
12 the day of the LORD. This is the first of twenty occurrences. In sixteen it is simply "*yōm Jehovah*" (13. 6, 9. Ezek. 13. 5. Joel 1. 15; 2. 1, 11; 3. 14 (Heb. 4. 14). Amos 5. 18, 20. Obad. 15. Zeph. 1. 7, 14, 14. Mal. 4. 5). In four passages it is with *Lamed* (ל = L) prefixed = *for* or *to*: viz. 2. 12. Ezek. 30. 3. Zech. 14. 1 and 17 = a day *known* to Jehovah. In other places it is combined with other words, such as "wrath", "vengeance". In the N.T. it occurs four times: viz. 1 Thess. 5. 2. 2 Thess. 2. 2 (see note). 2 Pet. 3. 10. Rev. 1. 10 (see note). Thus the expression is stamped with the number "*four*" (see Ap. 10); for "the day of the LORD" is the day when everything done will be to abase man and exalt Jehovah. Now it is "man's day" (1 Cor. 4. 3, see note), when man exalts himself, and bows God out of the world He has created. **the LORD of hosts.** See note on 1 Sam 1. 3. **proud** = arrogant. Heb. *gā'āh.* Note the Fig. *Synonymia* (Ap. 6). **lofty** = haughty. Heb. (*rūm*). Same word as "haughtiness" (*vv.* 11, 17), "high" (*vv.* 13, 14). Note the Fig. *Synonymia* (Ap. 6). **and.** Note the Fig. *Polysyndeton* (Ap. 6), emphasising each of the details in *vv.* 11-18. **lifted up** = self-satisfied. Heb. *nās'a'.* Same as *vv.* 13, 14. **brought low.** Heb. *shāphal.* Same word as "humbled" (*v.* 11). Note the Fig. *Synonymia* (Ap. 6). **13 high.** Heb. *rūm.* Same word as "haughtiness" (*vv.* 11, 17); "lofty" (*v.* 12); "high" (*v.* 14). **15 high.** Heb. *gābah.* Same word as "lofty" (*v.* 11); "loftiness" (*v.* 17). **16 ships of Tarshish.** Occurs in the "former" portion only here and 23. 1, 14; and in the "latter" portion only in 60. 9. **Tarshish.** See note on 1 Kings 10. 22. **pleasant** = desirable. **17 loftiness.** Heb. *gābah.* Same word as "lofty" (*v.* 11). **made low.** Heb. *shāphal.* Same word as "humbled" (*v.* 11), "brought low" (*v.* 12). **19 terribly the earth.** Note the Fig. *Paronomasia* (Ap. 6). Heb. *le'ăroẓ hā'āreẓ.* Cp. *v.* 21.

649-588 made *each one* for himself to worship, to the moles and to the bats;

21 To go into the clefts of the rocks, and into the °tops of the ragged rocks, for fear of [2]the LORD, and for the glory of His majesty, when He ariseth to shake [19]terribly the earth.

22 °Cease ye from [11]man, whose °breath *is* in his nostrils: °for wherein is he to be °accounted of?

D P[1] g[1] (p. 935) **3** For, °behold, °the Lord, °the LORD of hosts, doth take away from Jerusalem and from Judah the °stay and the °staff, the whole stay of °bread, and the whole stay of °water,

2 °The °mighty man, and the °man of war, the judge, and the prophet, and the °prudent, and the °ancient,

3 The captain of fifty, and the °honourable man, and the counsellor, and the °cunning artificer, and the °eloquent orator.

h[1] 4 And I will give °children *to be* their princes, and °babes shall rule over them.

5 And the People shall be oppressed, every one by another, and every one by his neighbour: the °child shall behave himself proudly against the ancient, and the base against the honourable.

6 When a °man shall take hold of his brother of the house of his father, *saying,* "Thou hast °clothing, °be thou our ruler, and *let* this ruin *be* under thy hand:"

7 In that day shall he °swear, saying, "I will not be an healer; for in my house *is* neither bread nor clothing: make me not a ruler of the People."

Q[1] 8 For Jerusalem is °ruined, and Judah is fallen: because their tongue and their doings *are* against [1]the LORD, to provoke °the eyes of His glory.

9 The °shew of their countenance doth °witness against them; and they °declare their sin as °Sodom, they °hide *it* not. Woe unto °their soul! for they have rewarded °evil unto themselves.

P[2] g[2] 10 Say ye to °the righteous, that *it shall be* well *with him:* for they shall eat the fruit of their doings.

11 °Woe unto °the wicked! *it shall be* ill *with him:* for the reward of his °hands shall be °given him.

h[2] 12 *As for* My People, °children *are* their oppressors, and women rule over them.

Q[2] O My People, they which lead thee cause *thee* to err, and °destroy the way of thy °paths.

P[3] g[3] 13 [1]The LORD standeth up to plead, and standeth to judge the °people.

14 [1]The LORD will enter into judgment with the [2]ancients of His People, and the princes thereof: for ye have eaten up the vineyard; the spoil °of the °poor *is* in your houses.

h[3] 15 "What mean ye *that* ye °beat My People to pieces, and grind the faces of the [14]poor?" °saith °the Lord °GOD of hosts.

C R 16 Moreover [1]the LORD saith, "Because the °daughters of Zion are haughty, and walk with stretched forth necks and wanton eyes, walking and mincing *as* they go, and making a tinkling with °their feet:

---

21 tops = fissures or crevices. Cp. Rev. 6. 12-17.

22 Cease ye = Let go.

breath, &c. Heb. *n^eshāmāh* (Ap. 16). Occurs twice in the "former" portion (2. 22; 30. 33) and twice in the "latter" portion (42. 5; 57. 16, "soul"). Ap. 79: II. Ref. to Pent. (Gen. 2. 7). Ap. 92.

for wherein . . . ? Fig. *Erotēsis* (Ap. 6), for emphasis.

accounted of = reckoned on. Cp. Ps. 146. 3, 4. Jer. 17. 5

3. 1-15 (D, p. 931). THE POLITICAL RUIN OF JUDAH. (*Alternations.*)

D | P[1] | g[1] | 1-3. Judgment. Prophesied.
 h[1] | 4-7. Oppression.
 Q[1] | 8, 9. The ruin of Jerusalem and Judah.
 P[2] | g[2] | 10, 11. Judgment. Threatened.
 h[2] | 12-. Oppression.
 Q[2] | -12. The ruin of the People.
 P[3] | g[3] | 13, 14. Judgment. Assured.
 h[3] | 15. Oppression.

1 behold. Fig. *Asterismos* (Ap. 6), for emphasis.

the Lord. Heb. *hāh-'ādōn.* Ap. 4. VIII (1).

the LORD. Heb. Jehovah. Ap. 4. II.

the LORD of hosts. See note on 1 Sam. 1. 3.

stay . . . staff. Note the Fig. *Paronomasia* (Ap. 6). Heb. *mash'en* (masc.); *mish'an* (fem.).

bread . . . water. Put by Fig. *Synecdoche* (of Species), Ap. 6, for all kinds of food.

2 The. Note the absence of Articles in this verse.

mighty man. Heb. *gibbōr.* Ap. 14. IV.

man. Heb. *'ish.* Ap. 14. II.

prudent = diviner: i.e. the king. Cp. Prov. 16. 10.

ancient = elder.

3 honourable man = eminent or highly respected man. Cp. 2 Kings 5. 1.

cunning artificer = skilled in arts.

eloquent orator = skilled in magnetism.

4 children = youths, or boys. } Not the same word
babes = with caprice. } as in *v.* 12.
5 child = a youth, or a boy. }

6 man. Heb. *'ish.* Ap. 14. II.

clothing. Put by Fig. *Synecdoche* (of Species), Ap. 6, for all necessaries. **be** = become.

7 swear. Heb. "lift up [the hand]": i.e. swear. Ref. to Pent. (Gen. 14. 22. Ex. 6. 8. Num. 14. 30. Deut. 32. 40). Ap. 92. **8 ruined** = overthrown.

the eyes of His glory = His glorious presence, "eyes" being put by Fig. *Metonymy* (of Subject), Ap. 6, for the person as manifested.

9 shew = expression. **witness** = testify.

declare . . . hide it not = have declared . . . have not hidden. Fig. *Pleonasm* (Ap. 6), for emphasis.

Sodom. See 1. 9, 10.

their soul = them (emphatic). Heb. *nephesh.* Ap. 13.

evil. Heb. *rā'a'.* Ap. 44. viii.

10 the righteous = a righteous one.

11 Woe. Fig. *Maledictio.* Ap. 6.

the wicked, &c. = a lawless evil one (*rā'a'*, Ap. 44. viii), [it shall not be well]. Heb. *rāshā'.* Ap. 44. x.

hands. Put by Fig. *Metonymy* (of Cause), Ap. 6, for what is done with them. **given him** = done to him.

12 children = little ones.

destroy = have swallowed up.

paths. See note on 2. 3. **13 people** = peoples.

14 of. Genitive of Relation (Ap. 17. 5) = taken from.

poor = oppressed. Heb. *'ānī.* See note on "poverty" (Prov. 6. 11).

15 beat = crush. **saith** = is the oracle of.

the Lord. Heb. *'Ădonāi.* Ap. 4. VIII (2).

GOD. Heb. Jehovah. Ap. 4. II.

3. 16—4. 1 (*C*, p. 931). THE SIN OF JUDAH: (WOMEN). JUDGMENT PRONOUNCED. (*Introversion.*)

C | R | 3. 16. Pride. Manifested.
 S | 3. 17. Threatening. (General.)
 S | 3. 18-26. Threatening. (Particular.)
 R | 4. 1. Pride. Humbled.

16 daughters. Cp. the "kine of Bashan" (Amos 4. 1).

their. Heb. masc. Often used of women who act as men.

S 649-588 17 Therefore °the LORD* will smite with a
scab the crown of the head of the daughters
of Zion, °and [1]the LORD will discover their
°secret parts."

S (p. 935) 18 In that day [17]the Lord will take away the
°bravery of *their* tinkling °ornaments *about*
their feet, and *their* °cauls, and °*their* round
tires like the moon,
19 The °chains, [17]and the bracelets, and the
°mufflers,
20 The °bonnets, [17]and the °ornaments of
the legs, and the °headbands, and the °tablets,
and the °earrings,
21 The rings, and °nose jewels,
22 The °changeable suits of apparel, [17]and
the mantles, and the °wimples, and the °crisp-
ing pins,
23 The °glasses, [17]and the °fine linen, and
the °hoods, and the °vails.
24 [17]And it shall come to pass, *that* instead
of °sweet smell there shall be °stink; [17]and
instead of a girdle a °rent; and instead of °well
set hair baldness; and instead of a °stomacher
a °girding of sackcloth; *and* °burning instead
of beauty.
25 Thy °men shall fall by the sword, [17]and
thy °mighty in the war.
26 [17]And her °gates shall °lament and
°mourn; and she *being* desolate shall sit
upon the ground.

R **4** °And °in that day seven women shall take
hold of one °man, saying, "We will eat our
own bread, and wear our own apparel: only let
us be called by thy name, to take away our
reproach."

B T (p. 936) 2 °In that day shall °the Branch °of °the
LORD °be °beautiful and glorious, and the fruit
of °the earth *shall be* excellent and comely for
them that are °escaped of Israel.

U 3 And it shall come to pass, *that he that is*
left in Zion, and *he that* remaineth in Jerusalem,
shall be called °holy, *even* every one that is
written °among the living in Jerusalem:

U 4 When °the LORD* shall have washed away
the filth of the daughters of Zion, and shall
have °purged the °blood of Jerusalem from
the midst thereof by the °spirit of judgment,
and by the °spirit of burning.

T 5 And [2]the LORD will create upon °every
dwelling place of mount Zion, and upon her
°assemblies, a cloud and smoke by day, and
the shining of a flaming fire by night: for
°upon all the glory *shall be* °a defence.
6 And there shall be a °tabernacle for a
shadow in the daytime from the heat, and for
a place of refuge, and for a covert from storm
and from rain.

17 the LORD*. One of the 134 places where, in the primitive text, the *Sopherim* say they changed Jehovah to *Adonai*. See Ap. 32.
and. Note the Fig. *Polysyndeton* (Ap. 6) in *v.* 17—4. 1.
secret parts ; or, nakedness.
18 bravery = finery.
ornaments = metal crescent-shaped discs.
cauls = caps. Old French "*cale*".
their round tires like the moon = round crescent-shaped headbands.
19 chains = pendants. **mufflers** = light face-veils.
20 bonnets = headdress. Heb. p^{e}'er. Not therefore peculiar to the "latter" portion of Isaiah (61. 10) as alleged. See Ap. 79. II. **ornaments** = anklets.
headbands = girdles. Cp. 49. 18. Jer. 2. 32.
tablets = scent bottles. Heb. houses of the soul; *nephesh*, used in the sense of breath. See Ap. 13. VIII. 5.
earrings = amulets.
21 nose jewels. Worn in Palestine to-day.
22 changeable suits, &c. = robes: i.e. state or gala dresses. **wimples** = a neck binding (Old English).
crisping pins = reticules or purses.
23 glasses = mirrors (of polished metal).
fine linen = underclothing.
hoods = turbans. **vails** = long flowing vails.
24 sweet smell = perfume.
stink = rottenness, or stench. **rent** = a rope.
well set hair = richly plaited hair.
stomacher = sash or girdle, often worked in silk and gold. Still worn in Palestine.
girding of sackcloth = girding with a rope.
burning = branding.
25 men. Heb. m^{e}thîm. See Ap. 14. V.
mighty = might. Some codices, with Aram., Sept., Syr., and Vulg., read "mighty ones".
26 gates = entrances.
lament and mourn. Fig. *Prosopopœia.* Ap. 6.
mourn. Occ. in "former" portion here, 19. 8 (as adj.); 24. 4, 7; 33. 9; and in the "latter" portion, 57. 18 (as noun); 60. 20 (as noun); 61. 2, 3 (as adj.); 66. 10. Ap. 79. II.
4. 1 And. The Fig. *Polysyndeton* (Ap. 6) links this verse on to the preceding chapter. See the Structure, R, above.
in that day. Not emphatic, or at the beginning of the verse. **man.** Heb. *'îsh.* Ap. 14. II.

4. 2-6 (*B*, p. 931). ZION'S FUTURE GLORY.
(*Introversion.*)

B | T | 2. Glory. The Branch, Jehovah.
U | 3. Inhabitants of Jerusalem: holy.
U | 4. Inhabitants of Jerusalem: cleansed.
T | 5, 6. Glory. The marriage canopy.

2 In that day: i.e. after all the judgments.
the Branch: i.e. Messiah. So the Chaldee paraphrase has it. Heb. *ẓemach.* Not the same word as in 11. 1. See the Structure of "the Four Gospels" preceding the Structure of MATTHEW; and note the application of this expression to the Gospel of JOHN and the notes there. Used there to connect the four Titles of Messiah: MATTHEW: the *King* (Zech. 9. 9 with Jer. 23. 5, 6). MARK: the *Servant* (Isa. 42. 1 with Zech. 3. 8). LUKE: the MAN (Zech. 6. 12). JOHN: JEHOVAH (Isa. 40. 9, 10, with Isa. 4. 2).
of the LORD = Jehovah's Branch: i.e. Messiah. Heb. Jehovah. Ap. 4. II. **be** = become.
beautiful and glorious = for honour and for glory.
the earth = the land.
escaped of Israel: i.e. those who will have escaped destruction in the great tribulation. These could not be the "Church", for they are of "Israel"; and the blessings are the temporal blessings promised in 30. 23, &c. Ezek. 34. 29. Joel 2. 23-25. Amos 9. 11-15, &c.
3 holy. See note on Ex. 3. 5. **among the living** = written down or destined for life. Cp. Pss. 69. 28; 87. 5, 6. Mal. 3. 16. **4 the LORD*** = Jehovah. Ap. 4. II. One of the 134 places where Jehovah (in the primitive text) was changed to *Adonai.* See Ap. 32. **purged** = cast out. Heb. *duaḥ.* Cp. 1. 16; 6. 7.
blood. Put by Fig. *Metonymy* (of Effect), Ap. 6, for blood-guiltiness. **spirit** = blast, as in 11. 4. Cp. 2 Thess. 2. 8. Heb. *rûaḥ.* Ap. 9. **5 every dwelling place of mount Zion.** Not merely over the Tabernacle as in the old Dispensation. **assemblies** = convocation. Heb. *mikra'.* Ref. to Pent. See note on 1. 13. Some codices, with four early printed editions, read "assemblies" (pl.). **upon** = over.
a defence = a canopy. Heb. *chuppah*, the marriage canopy. Not translated "defence" elsewhere. Occurs only here, Ps. 19. 5, and Joel 2. 16. Cp. Isa. 62. 4. **6 tabernacle** = pavilion.

V¹ W¹ i (p. 937) 649–588. **5** Now will I sing to My wellbeloved °a song of My beloved touching his vineyard. My wellbeloved °hath a vineyard in °a very fruitful °hill:

2 And he fenced it, and gathered out the stones thereof, and planted it with the choicest °vine, and built a °tower in the midst of it, and also made a °winepress therein: and he looked that it should bring forth grapes, and it brought forth °wild grapes.

k 3 °And now, O inhabitants of Jerusalem, and °men of Judah, judge, I pray you, betwixt Me and My vineyard.

4 What could have been done more to My vineyard, that I have not done °in it? wherefore, when I looked that it should bring forth grapes, brought it forth [2]wild grapes?

X 5 [3]And now go to; I will tell you what I will do to My vineyard: I will take away the hedge thereof, and it shall be eaten up; *and* break down the wall thereof, and it shall be trodden down:

6 And I will lay it waste: it shall not be pruned, nor digged; but there shall come up briers and thorns: °I will also command the clouds that they rain no rain upon it.

W² *i* 7 For the vineyard of °the LORD of hosts *is* the °house of Israel, and the [3]men of Judah His pleasant plant:

k and He looked for °judgment, but behold °oppression; for °righteousness, but behold °a cry.

V² Y¹ 8 °Woe unto them that join house to house, *that* lay field to field, till *there be* °no place, that they may be placed alone in the midst of the earth!

Z¹ 9 "In Mine °ears" °*said* [7]the LORD of hosts, "Of a truth many houses shall be desolate, *even* great and fair, without inhabitant.

10 Yea, ten acres of vineyard shall yield one °bath, and the seed of an °homer shall yield an °ephah.

Y² 11 [8]Woe unto them that rise up early in the morning, *that* they may follow °strong drink; that continue until °night, *till* wine inflame them!

12 And the harp, and the viol, the °tabret, and °pipe, and °wine, are in their °feasts: but they regard not the work of °the LORD, neither consider the operation of His hands.

Z² l 13 Therefore My People are gone into captivity, because *they have* no knowledge: and their honourable °men *are* famished, and their multitude dried up with thirst.

m 14 Therefore °hell hath °enlarged °herself,

5. 1-30 (*A*, p. 931). THE SONG OF JEHOVAH. (*Division.*)

A | V¹ | 1-7. The Parable of the Vineyard.
  | V² | 8-30. The Parable interpreted.

5. 1-7 (V¹, above). THE PARABLE OF THE VINEYARD. (*Introversion and Alternation.*)

V¹ | W¹ | i | 1, 2. The Vineyard. Jehovah's care.
  k | 3, 4. Requital by Vineyard.
  X | 5. Jehovah's requital. Externals destroyed.
  X | 6. Jehovah's requital. Internals wasted.
 W² | *i* | 7-. The Vineyard. Jehovah's care.
  k | -7. Requital by Vineyard.

1 a song. Eight sentences describe the vineyard, of which seven give the characteristics, and one (*v.* 7) the result. This "song" sets forth the doom of the Vineyard: the Parable (Luke 20. 9-16), the doom of the husbandmen. **hath** = had.

a very fruitful = oil's son. Can it refer to David and his anointing? Cp. 1 Sam. 2. 10; 16. 13; Ps. 132. 7. Cp. *v.* 7-, below.

hill = horn. Heb. *ḳeren*, always "horn" (seventy-five times). Only "hill" here.

2 vine. For Israel as this vine, see 27. 2-6. Jer. 2. 21; 12. 10. Ps. 80. 8. Hos. 10. 1; 14. 5-7, &c. One of the three trees to which Israel is likened: the fig = *national* privilege; the olive = *religious* privilege; the vine = *spiritual* privilege. See note on Judg. 9. 8-13.

tower = a watchtower.

winepress = wine-vat. Heb. *yeḳeb*, not *gath*, a winepress. See note on Prov. 3. 10.

wild grapes = bad grapes. Heb. *beushim*, from *bashash*, to stink. The Heb. word occurs only in *vv.* 2, 4.

3 And now. Referring to time. Note the Fig. *Anacœnōsis* (Ap. 6). **men.** Heb. *'īsh.* Ap. 14. II.

4 in it. Some codices, with one early printed edition, Aram., Sept., Syr., and Vulg., read "to (or for) it".

6 I will, &c. Ref. to Pent. (Deut. 28. 23, 24. Lev. 26. 19).

7 the LORD of hosts. See note on 1. 9 and 1 Sam. 1. 3.

house of Israel. Occurs four times in Isaiah, twice before ch. 40 (5. 7; 14. 2), and twice after (46. 3; 63. 7). See Ap. 79. II. Note the *introversion*: "vineyard", "Israel", "Judah", "pleasant plant".

judgment . . . oppression. Note the Fig. *Paronomasia* (Ap. 6) for great and solemn emphasis, to attract our attention and impress our minds. Not a "pun" or a "play" on words. Heb. *mishpāt . . . mishpāch.*

righteousness . . . a cry. Fig. *Paronomasia* (Ap. 6). Heb. *ẓedāḳāh . . . ẓe'āḳāh.* See note above. These two lines may be Englished by "He looked for **equity**, but behold **iniquity**; for **right**, but behold **might**" (as used in oppression and producing a "cry").

8-30 (V², above). THE PARABLE INTERPRETED. (*Repeated Alternation.*)

V² | Y¹ | 8. Woe. Crimination. Covetousness.
  Z¹ | 9, 10. Threatening. Desolation.
 Y² | 11, 12. Woe. Crimination. Excess.
  Z² | 13-17. Threatening. Captivity.
 Y³ | 18-23. Woe. Crimination. Iniquity.
  Z³ | 24-30. Threatening. Destruction (24, 25). Invasion 26-30.

8 Woe. Fig. *Epibole.* Ap. 6. "Woe" repeated six times in succession (*vv.* 8, 11, 18, 20, 21, 22). Note the six subjects. **no.** Heb. *'ephes.* Occurs in "former" portion only here and in 34. 12; and in the "latter" portion in 40. 17; 41. 12, 29; 45. 6, 14; 46. 9; 47. 8, 10; 52. 4; 54. 15. Ap. 79. II. **9 ears.** Fig. *Anthrōpopatheia.* Ap. 6. **said.** Note *Ellipsis* of the verb "to say". See Ap. 6 and instructive examples in Pss. 109. 5; 144. 12. Isa. 28. 9. Jer. 9. 19, &c. **10 bath . . . homer . . . ephah.** See Ap. 51. III. 3. **11 strong drink.** Heb. *shēkār.* Ap. 27. IV. **night.** Heb. *nesheph.* A *Homonym.* Cp. 21. 4 and 59. 10. See notes on Job 24. 15, and 1 Sam. 30. 17. **12 tabret** = drum. Heb. *toph.* See note on 1 Sam. 10. 5. **pipe** = fife. **wine.** Heb. *yayin.* Ap. 27. I. **feasts** = banquets. **the LORD.** Heb. Jehovah. Ap. 4. II.

5. 13-17 (Z², above). THREATENING: CAPTIVITY. (*Introversion.*)

Z² | l | 13. Captivity.
 m | 14, 15. Judgment. Man abased.
 m | 16. Judgment. Jehovah exalted.
 l | 17. Restoration.

13 men. Heb. *methīm.* Ap. 14. v. **14 hell** = Sheōl. Ap. 35. **enlarged.** Fig. *Prosopopœia.* Ap. 6. **herself** = her soul. Heb. *nephesh.* Ap. 13.

649-588 and opened °her mouth without measure: and their glory, and their multitude, and their pomp, and he that rejoiceth, shall descend into it.

15 And °the mean man shall be brought down, and °the mighty man shall be humbled, and the eyes of the °lofty shall be humbled:

m (p. 937) 16 But [7]the LORD of hosts shall be exalted in judgment, and °GOD That is °holy shall be sanctified in righteousness.

l 17 Then shall the lambs feed after their manner, and the waste places of the fat ones shall °strangers eat.

Y3 18 [8]Woe unto them that draw °iniquity with °cords of vanity, and °sin as it were with a °cart rope:

19 °That say, 'Let Him make speed, *and* hasten His work, that we may see *it:* and let the counsel of °the Holy One of Israel draw nigh and come, that we may know *it!*'

20 [8]Woe unto them that °call °evil good, and good °evil; that °put darkness for light, and light for darkness; that °put bitter for sweet, and sweet for bitter!

21 [8]Woe unto *them that are* wise in their own eyes, and prudent in their own °sight!

22 [8]Woe unto *them that are* °mighty to drink [12]wine, and °men of strength to mingle [11]strong drink:

23 Which justify °the wicked for °reward, and take away the righteousness of °the righteous from °him!

Z3 24 Therefore as the fire devoureth the stubble, and the flame consumeth the chaff, *so* their root shall be as rottenness, and their blossom shall go up as dust: because they have cast away °the law of [7]the LORD of hosts, and despised °the word of [19]the Holy One of Israel.

25 Therefore is the anger of [12]the LORD kindled against His People, and He hath °stretched forth His hand against them, and hath smitten them: and the hills did tremble, and their carcases *were* °torn in the midst of the streets. °For all this His anger is not turned away, but His hand *is* °stretched out still.

26 And He will lift up an ensign to the nations from far, and will °hiss unto them from the end of the earth: and, behold, °they shall come with speed swiftly:

27 None shall be weary nor stumble among them; none shall slumber nor sleep; neither shall the girdle of their loins be loosed, nor the latchet of their shoes be broken:

28 Whose arrows *are* sharp, and all their bows bent, their horses' hoofs shall be counted like flint, and their wheels like a whirlwind:

29 Their roaring *shall be* like a lion, they shall roar like young lions: yea, they shall roar, and lay hold of the prey, and shall carry *it* away safe, and none shall deliver *it.*

30 And in that day they shall roar against them like the roaring of the sea: and if *one* look unto the land, behold darkness *and* sorrow, and the light is darkened in the °heavens thereof."

B A (p. 938) 649 **6** In °the year that °king Uzziah °died °I saw also °the LORD* sitting upon a throne, high and lifted up, and His train filled the temple.

2 Above °it stood the °seraphims: each one had six wings; with twain he covered his face, and with twain he covered his feet, and with twain he did fly. B n

14 her. All these feminine pronouns mean that the nouns belong to Sheōl.

15 the mean man=commoner. Heb. *'ādām.* Ap. 14. I.

the mighty man=peer. Heb. *'īsh.* Ap. 14. II. See notes on 2. 11, 17.

lofty=proud. Heb. *gābah.* See note on 2. 11.

16 GOD=the mighty God. Heb. 'El (with Art.). Ap. 4. iv. **holy.** See note on Ex. 3. 5.

17 strangers=foreigners.

18 iniquity. Heb. *'āvāh.* Ap. 44. iv.

cords, &c. Which draw on sin by the *load.*

sin. Heb. *chāṭā'.* Ap. 44. i.

cart rope. Implies sin by the cart-load.

19 That say, &c. Cp. Jer. 17. 15.

the Holy One of Israel. See notes on 1. 4 and Ps. 71. 22.

20 call=are calling.

evil. Heb. *rā'a'.* Ap. 44. viii.

evil good. Note the *Introversion* in each of the three clauses of this verse. **put**=give out.

21 sight. Heb. "face", put by Fig. *Metonymy* (of Subject), Ap. 6, for themselves, or their own view of matters.

22 mighty=strong men. Heb. *gibbōr.* Ap. 14. IV.

men. Heb. pl. of *'ěnōsh.* Ap. 14. III.

23 the wicked=a lawless one. Heb. *rāshā'.* Ap. 44. x.

reward=a bribe. **the righteous**=righteous ones.

him=them. **24 the law.** See note on 1. 10.

the word=saying, or spoken word. Heb. *'imrāh.* See Ap. 73. v.

25 stretched forth: in judgment.

torn in the midst of the streets=as the sweepings of the streets.

For all this, &c. Cp. the Ref. to Pent. in the fivefold consequence of Isa. 5. 25; 9. 12, 17, 21; 10. 4: with the fivefold cause in Lev. 26. 14, 18, 21, 24, 28.

stretched out still=remains stretched out. Same word as "stretched forth (above) in judgment". Ref. to Pent. (Ex. 6. 6. Deut. 4. 34; 5. 15; 7. 19; 9. 29; 11. 2; 26. 8).

26 hiss unto=hiss for (as men call bees). Fig. *Anthrōpopatheia.* Ap. 6.

they shall come. Note the Fig. *Hypotyposis* (Ap. 6) in *vv.* 26-30. **30 heavens**=skies.

6. 1-13 (B, 930). THE VOICE FROM THE TEMPLE. (*Alternations.*)

B | A | 1. The Vision. (General.)
  B | n | 2-4. The Seraphs.
    o | 5. The Prophet. (Defiled.)
    n | 6. A Seraph.
    o | 7. The Prophet. (Cleansed.)
  A | 8-. The Voice. (Particular.)
  B | p | -8. The Messenger. "Then said I."
    q | 9, 10. Answer and Message.
    p | 11-. The Messenger. "Then said I."
    q | -11-13. Answer and Promise.

1 king Uzziah. Contrast this leprous king with the glorious king of *v.* 5.

died. In a separate house. This completes the contrast. See 2 Chron. 26. 21.

I saw. Heb. *rā'āh*=to see clearly. As in *v.* 6; 21. 6, 7. Not the same word as in 1. 1; 13. 1.

the LORD*=Jehovah. One of the 134 places where, in the primitive text, Jehovah was changed to Adonai. See Ap. 32, and Ap. 4. VIII. 2. and II.

2 it: i. e. the throne.

seraphims=burning ones. No Art. Celestial beings, named but unexplained. Name used of the serpents (Num. 21. 6) because of the burning effect produced by them, just as *nāchāsh* was used of a snake because of its shining skin (Num. 21. 9), as well as of the shining one of Gen. 3. 1. See notes on Gen. 3. 1. Num. 21. 6, 9, and Ap. 19. Sept. reads "and seraphs stood round about Him".

649-588 3 And one cried unto another, and said,
°"Holy, holy, holy, *is* °the LORD of hosts:
the whole earth *is* full of His glory."
4 And the posts of the door moved at the
voice of him that cried, and the house was
filled with smoke.
o 5 Then said I, °"Woe *is* me! for I am °un-
(p. 938) done; because I *am* a °man of unclean lips,
and I dwell in the midst of a People of unclean
lips: for mine eyes have °seen the °King, [3]the
LORD of hosts."
n 6 Then °flew one of the [2]seraphims unto me,
having a live coal in his hand, *which* he had
taken with °the tongs from off the altar:
o 7 And he laid *it* upon my mouth, and said,
"Lo, this hath touched thy lips; and thine
°iniquity is taken away, and thy sin °purged."
A 8 Also I heard the °voice of [1]the LORD*,
saying, °"Whom shall I send, and who will
go for °Us?"
B p Then °said I, "Here *am* I; send me."
q 9 And He said, "**Go, and tell this People,**
°'**Hear ye indeed, but understand not; and**
°**see ye indeed, but perceive not.'**
10 °Make the °heart of this People fat, and
make their °ears heavy, and shut their °eyes;
lest they see with their °eyes, and hear with
their °ears, and understand with their °heart,
and °convert, and be healed."
p 11 Then said I, [1]"LORD*, °how long?"
q And He answered, "Until the cities be °wasted
°without inhabitant, and the houses without
°man, and the °land be utterly °desolate,
12 And °the LORD have removed [11]men far
away, and *there be* a great °forsaking in the
midst of the land.
13 °But yet in it *shall be* a tenth, and *it* shall
return, and °shall be eaten: as a °teil tree,
and as an oak, whose °substance °*is* in them,
when they °cast *their leaves: so* the °holy
seed *shall be* the substance thereof."

C C¹ **7** And °it came to pass in the days of °Ahaz
(p. 939) the son of Jotham, the son of Uzziah, king
631-630 of Judah, *that* °Rezin the king of Syria, and
°Pekah °the son of Remaliah, king of Israel,
went up toward Jerusalem to war against it,
but °could not prevail against it.

3 Holy, holy, holy. Fig. *Epizeuxis* (Ap. 6) for intense and solemn emphasis. Cp. the threefold blessing of Num. 6. 24-26 and Rev. 4. 8, a threefold unity.

the LORD of hosts. See note on 1. 9 and 1 Sam. 1. 3.

5 Woe. Fig. *Ecphonēsis*. Ap. 6.

undone=dumb, or lost. The essence of true conviction is a concern for what I *am*, not for what I have *done* or *not done*.

man. Heb. *'īsh*. Ap. 14. II. **seen.** Cp. Job 42. 5.

King. Contrast "king Uzziah", *v.* 1.

6 flew. Cp. "ran" (Luke 15. 20).

the tongs. Ref. to Pent. (Ex. 25. 38; 37. 23 ("snuffers"). Num. 4. 9). Ap. 92.

7 iniquity. Heb. *'āvāh*. Ap. 44. iv.

purged=covered. Heb. *kāphar*=to cover, and thus, here, atone. See note on Ex. 29. 33. Not the same word as in 1. 25; 4. 4.

8 voice. See the Structure (p. 930). This is the voice from the Temple concerning the "scattering", corresponding with 40. 3, 6, which is the voice from the wilderness concerning the "gathering".

Whom shall I send? This was not Isaiah's original commission to prophesy, but his special commission for *this* great dispensational prophecy. Chs. 1-5 form a general introduction to the whole book (see p. 930).

Us. Ref. to Pent. (Gen. 1. 26; 3. 22; 11. 7). Ap. 92.

said I. In edition 1611 this was "I said".

9 Hear ye indeed. Heb. "a hearing, hear ye". Fig. *Polyptōton* (Ap. 6) for emphasis. See note on Gen. 26. 28.

see ye indeed. Heb. "a seeing see ye". Fig. *Polyptoton*, as above.

10 Make, &c.=Declare or foretell that the heart of this People will be fat. Isaiah could do no more. A common Hebrew idiom.

This prophecy is of the deepest import in Israel's history. Written down seven times (Matt. 13. 14. Mark 4. 12. Luke 8. 10. John 12. 40. Acts 28. 26, 27. Rom. 11. 8). Solemnly quoted in three great dispensational crises:—

(1) By Christ (Matt. 13. 14), as coming from Jehovah on the day a council was held "to destroy Him".

(2) By Christ, as coming from Messiah in His glory (John 12. 40, 41) after counsel taken to "put Him to death" (John 11. 53, and cp. 12. 37).

(3) By Paul, as coming from the Holy Ghost when, after a whole day's conference, they "believed not" (Acts 28. 25-27).

heart. Note the Fig. *Epanodos* (Ap. 6), in verse 10:—

q | r | heart.
  s | ears.
    t | eyes.
    t | eyes.
  s | ears.
r | heart.

convert=turn or return.

11 how long? See the answer (Rom. 11. 25).

wasted=desolate.

without=for want of. **man.** Heb. *'ādām*. Ap. 14. I. **land**=ground, or soil. Heb. *'ădamah*. **desolate.** See note on 1. 7. **12 the LORD.** Heb. Jehovah. Ap. 4. II. **forsaking.** See note on 1. 4. **13 But yet in it shall be a tenth, &c.**=Still, there is in it (the land) a tenth part; and it (the tenth part) shall again be swept away; yet, as with terebinth and oak, whose life remains in them when felled, the holy seed will be the life thereof. This is no "interpolation"; it is necessary to complete the Structure (*q*, p. 938). **shall be.** Supply [there is]. **teil tree**=terebinth. **substance**=root-stock. **is in them:** or will be in them. A special reading called *Sevīr* (Ap. 34) reads "in it": i.e. in the land. **cast their leaves**=are felled. The *Ellipsis*, here, is wrongly supplied. **holy.** See note on Ex. 3. 5.

7. 1—12. 6 (C, p. 930). HISTORIC EVENTS AND PROPHECIES (AHAZ).
(Repeated Alternation.)

C | C¹ | 7. 1-9. Confederacy (Syria and Israel). (Particular.) "It shall not stand" (*v.* 7).
  D¹ | 7. 10—8. 8. Divine Interposition (7, 10). THE VIRGIN'S SON.
C² | 8. 9, 10. Confederacy. (General.) "It shall be brought to naught."
  D² | 8. 11—9. 7. Divine Interposition. IMMANUEL.
C³ | 9. 8—10. 32. Confederacy. (Jehovah's.) Particular. "I will punish".
  D³ | 10. 33—12. 6. Divine Interposition. THE SON OF DAVID.

7. 1 it came to pass in the days of. See note on Gen. 14. 1. **Ahaz.** For the history explaining this prophecy see 2 Kin. 15. 37—16. 5. **Rezin.** See 2 Kin. 16. 5-9. **Pekah.** His was the last prosperous reign in Israel. It began in the last year of Uzziah, king of Judah. **the son of Remaliah.** Repeated for emphasis in *vv.* 1, 4, 5, 9. A murderer (2 Kin. 15. 25). **could not prevail against it.** Cp. 2 Kin. 16. 5.

631-630 **2 And it was told ° the house of David, say-**
ing, "Syria is confederate with ° Ephraim."
And ° his heart was moved, and the heart of
his people, as the trees of the wood are moved
with the ° wind.
3 Then said ° the LORD unto Isaiah, "Go
forth now to meet Ahaz, thou, and ° Shear-
jashub thy son, at the end of the conduit of the
upper pool in the ° highway of the fuller's field;
4 And say unto him, 'Take heed, and be
quiet; fear not, neither be fainthearted ° for the
two tails of these smoking ° firebrands, ° for the
fierce anger of [1] Rezin with Syria, and of
[1] the son of Remaliah.
5 Because Syria, [2] Ephraim, and [1] the son of
Remaliah, have taken evil counsel against
thee, saying,
6 'Let us go up against Judah, and ° vex it,
and let us make a breach therein for us, and
set a king in the midst of it, *even* ° the son of
Tabeal:
7 Thus saith ° the Lord ° GOD, 'It shall not
stand, neither shall it come to pass.
8 For ° the head of Syria *is* ° Damascus, and
the head of Damascus *is* ° Rezin; ° and within
° threescore and five years shall [2] Ephraim be
broken, ° that it be not a people.
9 And the head of Ephraim *is* Samaria, and
the head of Samaria *is* Remaliah's son. ° If
° ye will not believe, ° surely ye shall not be
° established.'"
D[1] E G (p. 940) **10 ° Moreover [3] the LORD ° spake ° again unto**
Ahaz, saying,
11 "Ask thee a ° sign of [3] the LORD thy ° God;
ask it ° either in the depth, or in the height
above."
H **12 But Ahaz said, ° "I will not ask, neither**
will I tempt ° the LORD."
G **13 And ° he said, "Hear ye now, O [2] house of**
David; *Is it* a small thing for you to weary
° men, but will ye weary my [11] God also?
14 Therefore ° the LORD * Himself shall give
you a [11] sign; ° Behold, ° a ° virgin ° shall con-
ceive, and bear a son, and ° shall call his name
° Immanuel.

2 the house of David. Not to Ahaz only, but to the house which had received the promise of Jehovah's protection (2 Sam. 7).

Ephraim. The leading tribe, put by Fig. *Synecdoche* (of Part), Ap. 6, for the rest of the ten tribes. Sometimes called "Samaria" (1 Kin. 16. 24).

his, i.e. Ahaz.

wind. Heb. *rūach*. Ap. 9.

3 the LORD. Heb. Jehovah. Ap. 4. II.

Shear-jashub = the remnant shall return.

highway. Occurs in the "former" portion, here, 11. 16; 19. 23; 33. 8; 35. 8; 36. 2; and in the latter portion, 40. 3; 49. 11; 57. 14 (verb); 59. 7 (paths); 62. 10 (verb and noun). See Ap. 79. II.

4 for = because of.

firebrands. Cp. Amos 4. 11. Zech. 3. 2. Not like the stump of Judah (6. 13).

for = consisting of.

6 vex = terrify.

the son of Tabeal: i.e. Rezin, king of Syria.

7 the Lord. Heb. *Adonai*. Ap. 4. VIII (2).

GOD. Heb. Jehovah. Ap. 4. II and IX.

8 the = though the.

Damascus: which is soon to be spoiled.

Rezin: a firebrand soon to be quenched. He was the last independent king of Syria.

and = yet.

threescore and five years. To be made up thus: Ahaz 14 + Hezekiah 29 + Manasseh 22 = 65 (13 × 5). Fulfilled in 567–6 B.C.

that it be not a people = shall be no more a people. But Judah shall return (6. 13).

9 If ye will not believe, surely ye shall not be established. Note the Fig. *Paronomasia* (Ap. 6) for emphasis and to attract attention to the importance of the sentence. Heb. *'im l'o tha'ǎmīnū, kī l'o thē'āmēnū*, which may be Englished thus: "If ye will not trust, ye shall not be trusted". Or, have no *belief* . . . find no relief; or, will not *understand* . . . shall not *surely stand*; or, no *confiding* . . . no *abiding*. Verse 17 shows that Ahaz did not trust.

ye. But specially referring to Ahaz. See note on "shall call" (*v.* 14).

surely = [know] that.

7. 10—8. 8 (D[1], p. 939). **DIVINE INTERPOSITION. THE VIRGIN'S SON.** (*Alternation.*)

D[1] | E | 7. 10–17. The Son.
  F | 7. 18–25. Assyrian Invasion.
 E | 8. 1–4. The Son.
  F | 8. 5–8. Assyrian Invasion.

7. 10–17 (E, above). **THE SON.** (*Alternation.*)

E | G | 10, 11. The Sign offered.
  H | 12. Ahaz. Refusal of Sign.
 G | 13–16. The Sign given.
  H | 17. Ahaz. Prophecy concerning him.

10 Moreover. It seems as though Isaiah wanted to see what Ahaz would say to *v.* 9. **spake.** This identifies the words with Jehovah Himself, and not merely with Isaiah. It shows the vast importance of the coming prophecy. **again** = added. Lit. added to speak. Occurs in this connection only again in 8. 5 in this book. **11 sign.** Heb. *'ōth*, a present visible token or pledge, as in Gen. 1. 14. Ex. 4. 8, 9; 12. 13; and especially 8. 18. This word is used eight times in the "former" portion (here; *v.* 14; 8. 18; 19. 20; 20. 3; 37. 30; 38. 7, 22); and three times in the "latter" portion (44. 25; 55. 13; 66. 19). See Ap. 79. II, and cp. Hezekiah's sign (38. 7). **God.** Heb. Elohim. Ap. 4. I. **either.** Ahaz was not limited, and therefore without excuse. **12 I will not ask.** He had already made up his mind to appeal to Assyria, and had probably sent messengers to Tiglath-Pileser (2 Kings 16. 7. 2 Chron. 28. 16). His self-hardening is masked by his apparently pious words. **the LORD.** Heb. Jehovah (with *'ēth*) = Jehovah Himself. Ap. 4. II. **13 he:** i.e. Jehovah by the prophet; thus identifying Himself with this important prophecy. **men.** Heb. pl. of *'ĕnōsh*. Ap. 14. III. **14 the LORD*.** One of the 134 passages where Jehovah, in the primitive text, was altered by the Sopherīm to "Adonai". See Ap. 32. **Behold.** Fig. *Asterismos* (Ap. 6) for emphasis. **a virgin.** Heb. the virgin: i.e. some definite well-known damsel, whose identity was then unmistakable, though unknown to us. See Matt. 1. 21–23. Luke 1. 31. See Ap. 101. **virgin** = damsel. Heb. *ha-'almāh*. It occurs seven times (Gen. 24. 43. Ex. 2. 8. Ps. 68. 25. Prov. 21. 19. Song 1. 3; 6. 8, and Isa. 7. 14). The Heb. for virgin (in our technical sense) is *b^ethūlāh*, and occurs fifty times (2 × 5², see Ap. 10). Its first occurrence is Gen. 24. 16, where, compared with *v.* 43, it shows that while every *Bethulah* is indeed an *Almah*, yet not every *Almah* is a *Bethulah*. The prophecy does not lose its Messianic character, for Mary, in whom it was fulfilled, is designated by the same holy inspiring Spirit as "*parthenos*" (not *gunē*). As a sign to Ahaz this damsel was an *almah*. As a sign, when the prophecy was *fulfilled* (or filled full), it was Mary, the *parthenos* or virgin. **shall conceive, and bear** = is pregnant and beareth. Ref. to Pent. The two words occur together only here, Gen. 16. 11, and Judg. 13. 5, 7; and *v.* 12 shows that birth was imminent. Perhaps the *Almah* was "Abi" (2 Kings 18. 2. 2 Chron. 29. 1), but the son was not necessarily Hezekiah. See Ap. 101. **shall call.** Some codices, with three early printed editions, and Sept., read "thou (Ahaz) wilt call". **Immanuel** = "GOD (*'El*) with us". Most codices, and six early printed editions, give it as two words. Some, with two early printed editions, as one word.

631-630 15 °Butter and honey shall he eat, °that he may know to refuse the °evil, and °choose the good.
16 °For before the °child shall know to refuse the [15] evil, and [15] choose the good, °the land that thou °abhorrest °shall be forsaken °of °both her kings.

H (p. 940) 17 [3] The LORD shall bring upon thee, and upon thy people, and upon thy father's house, days that have not come, from the day that Ephraim departed from Judah; *even* °the king of Assyria.

F r[1] (p. 941) 18 And it shall come to pass in that day, *that* [3] the LORD shall hiss for the fly that *is* in the uttermost part of the °rivers of Egypt, and for the bee that *is* in the land of Assyria.

s[1] 19 And they shall come, and shall rest all of them in the desolate valleys, and in the holes of the rocks, and upon all °thorns, and upon all °bushes.

r[2] 20 In the same day shall [14] the LORD* shave with a rasor that is °hired, *namely*, by them beyond the river, by the king of Assyria, the

s[2] head, and the hair of the feet: and it shall also consume the beard.

r[3] 21 °And it shall come to pass in that day, *that* a °man °shall nourish a young cow, and two sheep;

s[3] 22 And it shall come to pass, for the °abundance of milk *that* they shall give he shall eat [15] butter: for °butter and honey shall every one eat that is left °in the land.

r[4] 23 And it shall come to pass in that day, *that* every place shall be, where there were a thousand vines at a thousand °silverlings, it shall *even* be for briers and thorns.
24 With arrows and with bows shall *men* come thither; because all the land shall become briers and thorns.

s[4] 25 And *on* all hills that °shall be digged with the mattock, there °shall not come thither °the fear of briers and thorns: but it shall be for the °sending forth of oxen, and for the °treading of lesser cattle."

E t **8** °Moreover °the LORD said unto me, "Take thee a great °roll, and write °in it with °a °man's pen °concerning °Maher-shalal-hash-baz."
2 And I took unto me faithful witnesses to record, °Uriah the priest, and °Zechariah the son of Jeberechiah.

u 3 And I went unto the prophetess; and she conceived, and bare a son.

u Then said [1] the LORD to me, "Call his name [1] Maher-shalal-hash-baz.

t 4 For °before the °child shall have knowledge to cry, 'My father, and my mother,' the riches of Damascus and the spoil of Samaria °shall be °taken away before the king of Assyria."

---

15 Butter = Curds. See Gen. 18. 8. Deut. 32. 14, &c.
that he may know = up to the time of his knowing: i.e. the prophecy shall come to pass while still a babe. See *v.* 16.
evil. Heb. *rā'a'.* Ap. 44. viii.
choose. See note on 1. 29.
16 For before. This was the sign to Ahaz and all present. Cp. the further sign, 8. 4, and see Ap. 101.
child = sucking child.
the land = the soil.
abhorrest: or vexest.
shall be forsaken. So it came to pass two years later. Cp. 2 Kings 15. 30; 16. 9. See note on 1. 4.
of = because of. Connect this with "abhorrest", not with "forsaken".
both her kings: i.e. Pekah and Rezin (*v.* 1).
17 the king of Assyria. This was fulfilled in 2 Kings 16. 7, and 2 Chron. 28. 19, 20.

7. 18-25 (F, p. 940). ASSYRIAN INVASION. (*Repeated Alternation.*)

F | r[1] | 18. Fly and Bee.
s[1] | 19. Destination.
r[2] | 20-. Rasor.
s[2] | -20. Destination.
r[3] | 21. Cow and Sheep.
s[3] | 22. Destination.
r[4] | 23, 24. Briers and thorns.
s[4] | 25. Destination.

18 rivers of Egypt. Ref. to Pent. Heb. *y^e'ōr.* Twenty-nine times in Genesis and Exodus (only twice in plural. Ex. 7. 19; 8. 5). Then, after, 2 Kings 19. 24; Job 28. 10; Ps. 78. 44; ten times in Isaiah. See Ap. 92.
19 thorns = the thorn bushes.
bushes = the pastures.
20 hired. By Ahaz himself.
21 And it shall come to pass. Note the Fig. *Anaphora* (Ap. 6), commencing *vv.* 21, 22, 23, emphasising the points of the prophecy.
man. Heb. *'ish.* Ap. 14. II.
shall nourish, &c.: i.e. no longer a land of olives and oil, but a poor pasturage. Cp. Jer. 39. 10.
22 abundance of milk. Not because of the number of the cattle, but on account of the fewness of the people.
butter and honey. Not corn and wine and oil.
in = in the midst of.
23 silverlings = shekels: i.e. as rent. Cp. Song 8. 11, and see Ap. 51. II (5).
25 shall be digged = should be digged (but were to go out of cultivation).
shall not come thither = thou wilt not come thither: i.e. venture to walk (without weapons, *v.* 24) where thou wast wont to plough in peace.
the fear of = for fear of.
sending forth = letting loose, or driving forth.
treading = trampling down.

8. 1-4 (*E*, p. 940). THE SON. (*Introversion.*)

E | t | 1, 2. The Prophecy
u | 3-. The Son. Birth.
u | -3. The Son. Name.
t | 4. The Prophecy.

8. 1 Moreover. There is no break in the prophecy.
the LORD. Heb. Jehovah. Ap. 4. II.
roll = tablet. Elsewhere only in 3. 23.
in it = on it.
a man's pen = the carving tool of the people. The writing was to be legible, in the language of the common people (not in the language of the priests or educated classes). Eastern languages have these two, down to the present day. Cp. Hab. 2. 2. "Pen" is put by Fig. *Metonymy* (of Cause), Ap. 6, for the writing written by it.
man's = a common man's. Heb. *'ĕnōsh.* Ap. 14. III.
concerning = "for Maher, &c." **Maher-shalal-hash-baz** = haste, spoil, speed, prey. (Note the *Alternation.*) These words are explained in *v.* 4, and may be connected thus: he hasteneth [to take the] spoil, he speeds [to seize] the prey. This child was a sign, as also the child in 7. 14.
2 Uriah = Urijah. See 2 Kings 16. 10.
Zechariah. Probably the father-in-law of Ahaz (2 Kings 18. 2).
4 before. The interval was twenty-one months from the prophecy, twelve from the birth.
child = sucking child: as in 7. 16. Not the same word as in *v.* 18.
shall be taken. So it was: in the third year of Ahaz, Damascus was sacked and Rezin was slain.
taken = carried away.

F v (p. 942) 631-630 5 [1]The LORD spake also unto me °again, saying,
6 "Forasmuch as this People refuseth the waters of °Shiloah that go softly, and °rejoice in Rezin and Remaliah's son;

w 7 Now therefore, behold, °the LORD* bringeth up upon them the waters of the river, strong and many, *even* the king of Assyria, and all his glory:

w and he shall come up over all his °channels, and go over all his banks:

v 8 And he shall pass through Judah; he shall overflow and go over, he shall reach *even* to the neck; and the stretching out of °his wings shall fill the breadth of thy land, O °Immanuel.

C[2] (p. 939) 9 °Associate yourselves, O ye °people, and ye shall be broken in pieces; and give ear, all ye of far countries: °gird yourselves, and ye shall be broken in pieces; °gird yourselves, and ye shall be broken in pieces.

10 Take counsel together, and it shall come to nought; speak the word, and it shall not stand: for °GOD *is* with us."

D[2] J x (p. 942) 11 For [1]the LORD spake thus to me with a strong hand, and instructed me that I should not walk in the way of this People, saying,

12 "Say ye not, 'A °confederacy,' °to all *them to* whom this People shall say, 'A °confederacy;' °**neither fear ye °their fear, nor be afraid.**

y 13 °**Sanctify °the LORD of hosts Himself**; and *let Him be* your fear, and *let Him* °*be* your dread.

14 And He shall be for a sanctuary; but °**for a stone of stumbling and for a rock of offence** to both the houses of Israel, for a °gin and for a snare to the inhabitants of Jerusalem.

15 And many among them shall °stumble, and fall, and be broken, and be snared, and be taken.

K 16 Bind up the °testimony, seal the °law among My °disciples."

17 And I will °wait upon [1]the LORD, That hideth His face from °the house of Jacob, °**and I will look for Him.**

L 18 **Behold, I and the °children whom [1]the LORD hath given me** *are* for °signs and for wonders in Israel from [13]the LORD of hosts, Which °dwelleth in mount Zion.

J x 19 "And °when they shall say unto you, 'Seek unto them that have °familiar spirits, and unto wizards that °peep, and that °mutter:'

y should not a people seek unto their °God? °for the living to the dead?

K 20 To the [16]law and to the [16]testimony: if they speak not according to this word, *it is* because °*there is* no light in them.

8. 5-8 (*F*, p. 940). THE ASSYRIAN INVASION. (*Introversion*.)

F | v | 5, 6. The Land. Its waters refused.
  w | 7-. Waters of Assyria. Approach.
  w | -7. Waters of Assyria. Arrival.
 v | 8. The Land. Assyrian waters overflow.

5 again. See note on 7. 10.

6 Shiloah: i.e. the waters beneath Zion running from Gihon to Siloam. See Ap. 68. II. (pp. 100, 101).

rejoice in Rezin. This is not "a wrong reading of the Hebrew text", but it refers to the trust reposed in the king of Syria instead of in Jehovah (7. 9). They despised God's covenant with Zion (symbolized by its secret stream), and preferred the help of the heathen; therefore the Assyrian floods should overwhelm them. (Cp. the same contrast in Ps. 46. 3, 4; and see notes there.) This applied specially to Israel: and the judgment overtook Israel first.

7 the LORD*. One of the 134 places where the *Sopherim* changed "Jehovah", of the primitive text, to *Adonai*. See Ap. 32.

channels. Heb. *'ăphīḳīm.* See note on 2 Sam. 22. 16.

8 his wings. Probably referring to the wings of his army.

Immanuel = GOD with us. This shows that the prophecy in 7. 14 was not to be exhausted with Ahaz and his times. See Ap. 101.

9 Associate yourselves = Make friendships.

people = nations.

gird yourselves. Note the Fig. *Repetitio* (Ap. 6) for emphasis. Occurs in "former" portion here only, and in the "latter" portion only in 45. 5 and 50. 11. Ap. 79. II.

10 GOD is with us = Heb. *Immanu-El.* See *v.* 8. Ap. 4. IV.

8. 11—9. 7 (D[2], p. 939). DIVINE INTERPOSITION. IMMANUEL. (*Extended Alternation.*)

D[2] | J | x | 8. 11, 12. False dependence. Confederacy.
  y | 8. 13-15. True dependence. Jehovah.
   K | 8. 16, 17. The Testimony and the Law.
    L | 8. 18. Messiah and His children.
 J | *x* | 8. 19-. False dependence: spirits.
  y | 8. -19. True dependence. God.
   K | 8. 20-22. The Law and the Testimony.
    L | 9. 1-7. Messiah. The Son.

12 confederacy. Heb. *ḳesher.* Never used in a good sense.

to all them to whom = whensoever, or whereof.

neither, &c. Quoted in 1 Pet. 3. 14, 15.

their fear = what they fear, or with their fear.

13 Sanctify = Hallow, regard as holy. Cp. 29. 23. See note on Ex. 3. 5. Ref. to Pent. (Num. 20. 12; 27. 14). Ap. 92.

the LORD of hosts. See note on 1. 9 and 1 Sam. 1. 9.

be your dread = inspire you with awe. Quoted in 1 Pet. 3. 13-15.

14 for a stone of stumbling. Cp. 1 Pet. 2. 7, 8. Luke 20. 17. Rom. 9. 32, 33; 11. 11. **gin** = a trap.

15 stumble . . . fall, &c. Note the Fig. *Synonymia.* Ap. 6.

16 testimony . . . law. No Art. either here or in *v.* 20. Note the Structure, above, and the *Introversion* of these two words in K and *K*. See note on 1. 10.

disciples = instructed ones. **17 wait.** Ref. to Pent. (Gen. 49. 18). See Ap. 92. **the house of Jacob.** See note on 2. 5. **and I will look, &c.** See Heb. 2. 13. **18 children** = young children. Not the same word as in *v.* 4. **signs.** See the Structure in Ap. 102. **signs and for wonders.** Cp. 20. 3. Ref. to Pent. Ex. 7. 3. Deut. 4. 34; 6. 22; 7. 19; 13. 1, 2; 26. 8; 28. 46; 29. 3; 34. 11. See note on 7. 11, and Ap. 92. **dwelleth** = is making His dwelling, or is about to dwell. **19 when** = should. **familiar spirits.** See note on Lev. 19. 31. **peep.** Heb. *ẓāphaph.* Occurs only in Isaiah; and this form, only in 10. 14: elsewhere, in 29. 4 (whisper); 38. 14 (chatter). It is used of an unearthly sound. **mutter**: i.e. with indistinct sounds. This refers to the low incantations which, in the Babylonian and Egyptian "mysteries", had to be recited in a whisper (like certain parts of the Roman Missal). A whole series is called "the ritual of the whispered charm". (See *The Religions of Ancient Egypt and Babylonia*, pp. 465, 466). **God.** Heb. Elohim. Ap. 4. I. **for the living to the dead.** Supply the Fig. *Ellipsis* from the preceding clause (Ap. 6), and render: "Should not any People seek unto its God? for [should] the living [seek unto] the dead?" This is a solemn warning against all ancient and modern Spiritists. **20 there is no light in them** = there shall be no morning for them. All are in darkness who do not speak by and appeal to the revealed Word of God.

631-630 21 And °they shall pass through °it, °hardly
bestead and hungry: and it shall come to pass,
that when they shall be hungry, they shall
°fret themselves, and curse their king and their
[19]God, and °look upward.
22 And they shall look unto °the earth;
and behold trouble and darkness, °dimness
of anguish; and *they shall be* °driven to
darkness.

L (p. 942) **9** °Nevertheless the °dimness *shall* not *be*
such as *was* in her °vexation, when °at
the first He lightly afflicted °**the land of Zebulun and the land of Naphtali**, and °afterward
did more grievously afflict *her by* **the way of the sea, beyond Jordan, in Galilee of the nations.**
2 The people °that walked in darkness °have seen a great light: °they that dwell in the land of the shadow of death, upon them hath the light shined."
3 °Thou °hast multiplied the nation, °*and* not
increased the joy: they joy before Thee according to the joy in harvest, *and* as *men* rejoice
when they divide the spoil.
4 For °Thou hast broken the yoke of his
burden, and the °staff of his shoulder, the °rod
of his oppressor, as in the °day of Midian.
5 For every battle of the warrior *is* with
confused noise, and garments rolled in blood;
but *this* shall be with burning *and* fuel of fire.
6 °**For unto us a Child °is born, unto us a Son °is °given**: and the °government shall be upon
His shoulder: and His °name shall be called
°Wonderful, Counseller, The mighty °GOD,
The everlasting Father, The Prince °of Peace.
7 Of the increase of *His* [6]government and
peace *there shall be* °no end, **upon the throne of David**, and upon His kingdom, to order °it,
and to establish °it with judgment and with
justice **from henceforth even for ever**. The
zeal of °the LORD of hosts will perform this.'

M[1] N[1] b[1] (p. 943) 8 °The LORD* °sent a word into °Jacob, and
it hath °lighted upon Israel.

21 they: i.e. they who live not in the light of God's Word.
it: i.e. Immanuel's land. The singular number and same verb, referring back to *v.* 8.
hardly bestead = in hard case.
fret themselves. Cp. Rev. 16. 11, 21.
look upward: [in vain].
22 the earth = the land.
dimness of anguish = the gloom of anguish.
driven to = thrust out into.
9. 1 Nevertheless = For. This member (*L*, 9. 1-7) relates to Messiah, the Son, referring back to 8. 9, 10; and carries 7. 14 on to its future fulfilment. See Ap. 102.
dimness . . . vexation. Almost the same two words as dimness . . . anguish (8. 22).
at the first. When Ben-hadad, in the reign of Baasha, "smote Ijon, and Dan, and Abel-beth-maachah, and all Cinneroth, with all the land of Naphtali" (1 Kings 15. 20). **the land, &c.** Quoted in Luke 1. 79.
afterward. Referring to the heavier scourge when Hazael "smote all the coasts of Israel from Jordan eastward, all the land of Gilead" (2 Kings 10. 32, 33). This land was the first to be afflicted by the armies of Assyria (2 Kings 15. 29), and was the first to see the promised light in the person of the Messiah.
2 that walked in darkness = the walkers in darkness.
have seen = saw. Quoted in Matt. 4. 14-16.
3 Thou: i.e. Jehovah.
hast. This is the Fig. *Prolepsis* (Ap. 6), by which the future is prophetically spoken of as present, or past.
and not increased the joy. The difficulty is not removed by reading *lō*, "to him", instead of *l'o*, "not" (which is the marginal reading of Heb. text, and is followed by the R.V. Dr. C. D. Ginsburg suggests that the word in question, *haggīl'o*, was wrongly divided into two words, and the last syllable (*l'o*) was treated as a separate word. Read as one word, the four lines form an *Introversion*, thus:—

z | Thou hast multiplied the exultation,
a | Thou hast increased the joy:
a | They joy before Thee according to the joy in harvest,
z | And as men exult when they divide the spoil.

4 Thou hast. Fig. *Prolepsis.* Ap. 6. See above (*v.* 3).
staff = rod: i.e. the rod that smites the shoulder.
rod = sceptre.
day of Midian. Refers to Judg. 7. 21, &c.
6 For unto us, &c. The prophecy of the "Divine Interposition" ends with Messiah, even as it began in 7. 14 (quoted in Luke 2. 11). See Ap. 102. **is.** Fig. *Prolepsis.* Ap. 6. **given.** The interval of this present dispensation comes between this word "given" and the next clause. **government.** The Heb. word *misrāh* occurs only in these verses (6, 7). Like *politeuma* (Phil. 3. 20). **name** = He Himself. See note on Ps. 20. 1. **Wonderful.** Cp. Judg. 13. 18. **GOD.** Heb. El. As in 10. 21. Ap. 4. IV. **of.** Genitive (of Origin), Ap. 17. 2; i.e. the Prince Who gives peace. Cp. Rom. 15. 16. **7 no end.** Cp. the angelic message (Luke 1 32, 33). **it.** Feminine, referring to the kingdom. **upon . . . henceforth.** Quoted in Luke 1. 32, 33. **the LORD of hosts.** See note on 1. 9, and 1 Sam. 1. 3.

9. 8—10. 32 (C[3], p. 939). **JEHOVAH'S CONFEDERACY.** (*Division.*)

C[3] | M[1] | 9. 8—10. 4. Made with Israel's enemies (in judgment).
| M[2] | 10. 5-32. Broken with enemies for Israel's deliverance (in grace).

9. 8—10. 4 (M[1], above). **JEHOVAH'S COVENANT MADE WITH ISRAEL'S ENEMIES.**
(*Repeated and Extended Alternation.*)

M[1] | N[1] | b[1] | 9. 8-10. Sin. Self-confidence.
c[1] | 9. 11, 12-. Threatening.
d[1] | 9. -12. Anger not turned away.
N[2] | b[2] | 9. 13. Sin. Impenitence.
c[2] | 9. 14-17-. Threatening.
d[2] | 9. -17. Anger not turned away.
N[3] | b[3] | 9. 18-. Sin. Lawlessness.
c[3] | 9. -18-21-. Threatening.
d[3] | 9. -21. Anger not turned away.
N[4] | b[4] | 10. 1, 2. Sin. Haughtiness.
c[4] | 10. 3, 4-. Threatening.
d[4] | 10. -4. Anger not turned away.

8 the LORD* = Jehovah. One of the 134 places where the *Sopherim* changed Jehovah (of the primitive text). to *Adonai.* See Ap. 32. **sent a word**: ch. 2. 5, 6, which had now been fulfilled. Cp. 5. 25. 2 Chron 28. 6-8. **Jacob.** See note on 2. 5. **lighted** = fallen.

631-630 9 And °all the People shall know, *even* E-
phraim and the inhabitant of Samaria, that
say in the pride and stoutness of heart,
10 "The bricks are °fallen down, but we will
build with hewn stones: the sycomores are
cut down, but we will change *them into* cedars."

c[1] (p. 943) 11 Therefore °the LORD shall set up the
°adversaries of Rezin against °him, and °join
his enemies together;
12 The Syrians before, and the Philistines
behind; and they shall devour Israel with
open mouth.

d[1] °For all this His anger is not turned away,
but His hand *is* °stretched out still.

N[2] b[2] 13 For the people °turneth not unto Him
That smiteth them, neither do they seek °the
LORD of hosts.

c[2] 14 Therefore [11] the LORD will cut off from Israel head and tail, branch and °rush, in one day.
15 The ancient and honourable, he *is* the °head;
and the prophet that teacheth lies, he *is* the °tail.
16 For °the leaders of this People cause *them*
to °err; and °*they that are* led of them *are*
°destroyed.
17 Therefore [8] the LORD* shall have no joy
in their young men, neither shall have mercy
on their fatherless and widows: for every one
is an hypocrite and an evildoer, and every
mouth speaketh folly.

d[2] [12]For all this His anger is not turned away,
but His hand *is* stretched out still.

N[3] b[3] 18 For °wickedness burneth as the fire: it

c[3] shall devour the briers and thorns, and shall
kindle in the thickets of the forest, and they
shall mount up *like* the lifting up of smoke.
19 Through the wrath of [7] the LORD of hosts
is the land darkened, and the People shall be
as the fuel °of the fire: no man shall spare his
brother.
20 And he shall snatch on the right hand,
and be hungry; and he shall °eat on the left
hand, and they shall °not be satisfied: they
shall eat °every man the flesh of his own arm:
21 Manasseh, Ephraim; and Ephraim, Manasseh: *and* they together *shall be* against Judah.

d[3] [12]For all this His anger is not turned away,
but His hand *is* stretched out still.

N[4] b[4] 10 Woe unto them that decree unrighteous
decrees, and that °write °grievousness
which they have °prescribed;
2 To turn aside the needy from judgment,
and to take away the right from the °poor of
My People, that widows may be their prey,
and *that* they may rob the fatherless!

c[4] 3 And what will ye do in the day of visitation, and in the °desolation *which* shall come
from far? to whom will ye flee for help? and
where will ye °leave your °glory?
4 Without Me they shall °bow down under the
prisoners, and they shall °fall under the slain.

d[4] °For all this His anger is not turned away,
but His hand *is* stretched out still.

M[2] O (p. 944) 5 °O, °Assyrian! the rod of Mine anger, and
the staff in their hand is Mine indignation.
6 I will send him against an °hypocritical nation, and against the People of My wrath will
I give him a charge, to take the spoil, and to
take the prey, and to tread them down like
the mire of the streets.

7 Howbeit °he meaneth not so, neither doth P e
his heart °think so; but *it is* in his heart to
destroy and cut off nations not a few.
8 For °he saith, "*Are* not my princes °alto-
gether kings?
9 *Is* not Calno as Carchemish? *is* not Hamath as Arpad? *is* not Samaria as Damascus?
10 °As my hand hath found the kingdoms of
the °idols, and whose graven images did excel
them of Jerusalem and of Samaria;

---

9 all the People, &c. "People" is singular, and "know" is plural = the People, all of them.
10 fallen down. Note the *Alternation* in this verse.
11 the LORD. Heb. Jehovah. Ap. 4. II.
adversaries. Some codices read "princes, or generals". **him**: i. e. Ephraim (not Rezin).
join, &c. = weave together, unite as allies.
12 For all this, &c. See note on 5. 25. Note the Fig. *Amœbœon* (Ap. 6), 5. 25; here, *vv.* 17, 21; 10. 4.
stretched out: in judgment. See note on 5. 25.
13 turneth not. Ref. to Pent. (Deut. 4. 29, 30). Ap. 92.
the LORD. Heb. Jehovah. with *'eth* = Jehovah Himself. Ap. 4. II. See note on 1 Sam. 1. 3.
14 rush. Heb. *'agmōn.* Occurs twice in "former" portion, here and 19. 15; and once in "latter" portion (58. 5, "bulrush"). Elsewhere only in Job 41. 2, 20. See Ap. 79. II.
15 head . . . tail. Ref. to Pent. Only here and Deut. 28. 13, 44. Ap. 92.
16 the leaders: or, flatterers. **err** = stray.
they that are led = they that are flattered.
destroyed = swallowed up.
18 wickedness = lawlessness. Heb. *rāshā'.* Ap. 44. x.
19 of = for. Genitive of Relation (Ap. 17. 5).
20 eat . . . not be satisfied. Ref. to Pent. (Lev. 26. 26). Ap. 92.
every man. Heb. *'ish.* Ap. 14. II.
10. 1 write = ordain, or register; legalize iniquities.
grievousness = oppression.
prescribed = written.
2 poor = Heb. *'anī.* See note on Prov. 6. 11.
3 desolation = storm.
leave = secure, or put in safe keeping. Heb. *'āzab,* a *Homonym* with two meanings. See note on Ex. 23. 5.
glory = honour.
4 bow down under the prisoners = captives will be enough to make you bow down.
fall under the slain = mortally wounded ones [will be enough] to make you fall.
For, &c. See note on 9. 12.

10. 5-32 (M[2], p. 943). JEHOVAH'S COVENANT. BROKEN FOR ISRAEL'S DELIVERANCE.
(*Introversion and Alternation.*)

M[2] O | 5, 6. Assyrian invasion. Mission.
  P | e | 7-11. Assyrian intention.
      f | 12-15. Jehovah's punishment of Assyria.
  P | *e* | 16-19. Assyrian work.
      f | 20-27. Jehovah's deliverance of Israel.
O | 28-32. Assyrian invasion. March.

5 O Assyrian. Not woe to the Assyrian. That woe comes later (cp. 17. 12, and 33. 1), after the latest woes on Ephraim and Judah. This is a Divine summons.
Assyrian. The monuments tell us that this was Sargon, the father of Sennacherib.
6 hypocritical = impious, profane, godless, or irreligious. Cp. 9. 17 and 33. 14, the only other occ. in Isaiah.
7 he meaneth not so = will not mean. The blindness of the instrument emphasises the truth of the prophecy.
think so = so intend.
8 he saith = he will say. **altogether** = all of them.
10 As = According as. **idols** = nothings.

631-630 11 Shall I not, [10]as I have done unto Samaria and her ° idols, so do to Jerusalem and her ° idols ?"

f
(p. 944) 12 °Wherefore it shall come to pass, *that* when ° the LORD* hath performed His whole work upon mount Zion and on Jerusalem, I will punish the fruit of the stout heart of the king of Assyria, and the glory of his high looks.

13 For he saith, "By the strength of my hand I have done *it*, and by my wisdom; for I am prudent: and I have removed the ° bounds of the ° people, and have robbed their treasures, and I have put down the inhabitants like a valiant *man*:

14 And my hand hath ° found as a nest the riches of the people: and as one gathereth eggs *that are* left, have I gathered all the earth; and there was none that moved the wing, or opened the mouth, or ° peeped."

15 ° Shall the axe ° boast itself against him that heweth therewith? *or* shall the ° saw magnify itself against him that shaketh it? as if the rod should ° shake *itself* against them that lift it up, *or* as if the staff should ° lift up *itself, as if it were* ° no wood.

Pe 16 Therefore shall ° THE Lord, ° the LORD of hosts, send among his fat ones leanness; and under his glory He shall ° kindle a ° burning like the burning of a fire.

17 And the light of Israel shall be for a fire, and his Holy One for a flame: and it shall burn and devour his thorns and his briers ° in one day;

18 And shall consume the glory of his forest, and of his fruitful field, both ° soul and ° body: and they shall be as when a standardbearer fainteth.

19 And the rest of the trees of his forest shall be few, that a ° child may ° write them.

f 20 And it shall come to pass in ° that day, *that* the remnant of Israel, and such as are escaped of ° the house of Jacob, shall no more again stay upon him that smote them; but shall stay upon ° the LORD, ° the Holy One of Israel, ° in truth.

21 ° The remnant shall return, *even* the remnant of Jacob, unto ° the mighty ° GOD.

22 For ° though Thy people Israel be ° as the sand of the sea, *yet* [21]a remnant of them shall return: the ° consumption decreed shall overflow ° with righteousness.

23 For ° the Lord ° GOD of hosts shall make a ° consumption, even ° determined, in ° the midst of ° all the land."

24 Therefore thus saith [23] the Lord [23] GOD of hosts, "O My people that dwellest in Zion, be not afraid of the Assyrian: he shall ° smite thee with a ° rod, and shall lift up his staff against thee, after the manner of Egypt.

25 For yet a very little while, and the indignation shall cease, and Mine ° anger in their destruction.

26 And [16] the LORD of hosts shall stir up a scourge for him ° according to the slaughter of ° Midian at the rock of Oreb: and *as* His rod *was* upon the sea, so shall He lift it up after the manner of Egypt.

27 And it shall come to pass in that day, *that* his burden shall be taken away from off thy shoulder, and his yoke from off thy neck, and the yoke ° shall be destroyed ° because of the anointing.

28 ° He is come to ° Aiath, he is passed to O

---

11 idols=effigies.
12 Wherefore=And.
the LORD*=Jehovah (Ap. 4. II). One of the 134 places where the *Sopherim* altered the primitive text from Jehovah to *Adonai*. See Ap. 32.
13 bounds of the people. Ref. to Pent. (Deut. 32. 8).
people=peoples.
14 found as a nest. Supply the Ellipsis (Ap. 6) thus: "found [means to reach] as a nest".
peeped. See note on 8. 19.
15 Shall . . . ? Note Fig. *Erotēsis* (Ap. 6) for emph.
boast itself. Heb. *pā'ar.* Not therefore peculiar to the "latter" portion of Isaiah (44. 23, &c.), as alleged. See Ap. 79. II. Ref. to Pent. (Ex. 8. 9).
saw. Heb. *massōr.* Occurs only here.
shake itself against=brandish.
lift up itself, as if it were no wood=raise him that lifteth it up.
no wood: i.e. the user of it (who is flesh and blood, not wood).
16 THE Lord. Heb. *'Adon* (with Article). See Ap. 4. VIII (1).
the LORD of hosts. See note on 1. 9 and 1 Sam. 1. 3.
kindle . . . burning=be like a burning. Note the Fig. *Paronomasia* (Ap. 6). Heb. *yēkad yekōd kīkōd*= kindle . . . kindling . . . kindling.
17 in one day. So it was (2 Kings 19. 35).
18 soul. Heb. *nephesh.* Ap. 13.
body=flesh. Put by Fig. *Synecdochē* (of Part), Ap. 6, for the whole body.
19 child=lad.
write=reckon.
20 that day. Passing on to the final fulfilment in the day of the LORD.
the house of Jacob. See note on 2. 5.
the LORD. Heb. Jehovah. Ap. 4. II.
the Holy One of Israel. See note on 1. 4.
in truth. Heb. *be'ĕmeth.* Occurs three times in the "former" portion (here; 16. 5; 38. 3); and twice in the "latter" portion (48. 1; 61. 8). See Ap. 79. II.
21 The remnant shall return. Heb. Shear-jashub. See 7. 3. So they did. Cp. 2 Chron. 30. 1–13, esp. *v.* 6.
the mighty GOD. Cp. 9. 6. Ref. to Pent. (Deut. 10. 17).
GOD. Heb. El. Ap. 4. IV.
22 though, &c. Quoted in Rom. 9. 27, 28.
as the sand, &c. Fig. *Parœmia* (Ap. 6). Ref. to Pent. (Gen. 22. 17; 32. 12, &c.).
consumption=full end, or finish. Heb. *killāyōn.* Ref. to Pent. Occurs only here, and Deut. 28. 65. Ap. 92.
with=in.
23 the Lord. Heb. *Adonai.* Ap. 4. VIII (2).
GOD. Heb. Jehovah. Ap. 4. II.
consumption=consummation. Heb. *kālāh.*
determined=decreed.
the midst of. Fig. *Pleonasm.* Ap. 6.
all. Some codices, with five early printed editions, omit "all".
24 smite thee with=smite thee [indeed] with, &c.
rod=club.
25 anger=anger [shall cease].
26 according to=like.
Midian. Cp. 9. 4, and Judg. 7. 25.
27 shall be destroyed=will rot.
because of the anointing=before the face (at the sight) of the oil: i.e. in Gideon's lamps; and of the anointed One (Messiah).
28 He is come. This is a prophetic description of Sennacherib's advance against Judah.
Aiath=Ai: now *et Tell*, or *Khan Haiyan.*

631-630 °Migron; at °Michmash he hath °laid up his °carriages:
29 They are gone over °the passage: they have taken up their lodging at °Geba; °Ramah is afraid; °Gibeah of Saul is fled.
30 Lift up thy voice, O daughter of °Gallim: cause it to be heard unto °Laish, O poor °Anathoth.
31 °Madmenah is removed; the inhabitants of °Gebim gather themselves to flee.
32 As yet shall he remain at °Nob that day: he shall shake his hand *against* the mount of the daughter of Zion, the hill of Jerusalem.

D³ Q (p. 946) 33 Behold, [16]THE Lord, [16]the LORD of hosts, shall lop the bough with terror: and the high ones of stature *shall be* hewn down, and the haughty shall be humbled.
34 And He shall cut down the thickets of the °forest with iron, and Lebanon shall fall by a mighty one.

R S **11** °And there shall come forth °a rod out of the °stem of Jesse, and a °Branch shall grow out of his roots:
2 And the °spirit of °the LORD shall °rest upon Him, the °spirit °of wisdom and °understanding, the °spirit of counsel and might, the °spirit of knowledge and of the fear of °the LORD;
3 And °shall make Him of quick understanding in the fear of [2]the LORD: °and He shall °not judge after the sight of His eyes, neither °reprove after the hearing of His ears:
4 But with righteousness shall He judge the °poor, and °reprove with equity for the meek of the earth: and He shall °smite °the earth with the rod of His mouth, and with the °breath of His lips shall He slay °the wicked.
5 And righteousness shall be the girdle of His loins, and faithfulness the girdle of His reins.

Migron. Not yet identified. Probably near Gibeah (1 Sam. 14. 2). Sennacherib mentions it as *Amgarron* (see Ap. 67. x. p. 98).

Michmash. Now *Mŭkmās*, seven miles north of Jerusalem (1 Sam. 13. 2–23; 14. 5, 31. Ezra 2. 27. Neh. 7. 31; 11. 31).

laid up. In anticipation of a speedy conquest of Jerusalem.

carriages = baggage (Old English). Put by Fig. *Metonymy* (of Adjunct), Ap. 6, for what is carried.

29 the passage = the ravine: i.e. Wady *Suweinit*. Cp. 1 Sam. 13. 23.

Geba. Now *Jeb'a*, near Michmash.

Ramah. Now *er Ram*, five miles north of Jerusalem.

Gibeah. Now *Tell el Ful*, between Jerusalem and Emmaus, two and a half miles north of Jerusalem.

30 Gallim. Not identified. Probably *Beitfāla'*, near Bethlehem.

Laish. Not Laish in the tribe of Dan.

Anathoth. Now *'Anāta*. Three miles north-east of Jerusalem.

31 Madmenah. Not identified. A town of Benjamin, near Jerusalem. See note on 25. 10.

Gebim. Not identified. North of Jerusalem.

32 Nob. A city of the priests, in sight of Jerusalem, from whence Sennacherib shook his hand against the city. Nob only a half day's journey from Jerusalem.

10. 33—12. 6 (D³, p. 939). DIVINE INTERPOSITION. (THE SON OF DAVID.)
(*Introversion and Alternation.*)

D³ | Q | 10. 33, 34. Prophecy of Jehovah's deliverance.
  R | S | 11. 1–5. The Deliverer. "The Offspring."
    T | 11. 6–9. His new Dispensation. (Moral.)
  R | *S* | 11. 10. The Deliverer. "The Root."
    T | 11. 11–16. His new Dispensation. (Political.)
  Q | 12. 1–6. Praise for Jehovah's deliverance.

34 forest. A.V., edition 1611, reads "forests" (pl.). These are Sennacherib's own figures of himself. See 2 Kings 19. 23. Cp. 29. 17. Ezek. 31. 3–8. Note the contrast in 11. 1.

11. 1 And = But. Note the same order of events in Rev. 19 and 20, as in Isa. 10 and 11. **a rod** = a sprout: occ. again only in Prov. 14. 3. Note the sublime contrast with 10. 33, 34. **stem** = stump. Appropriate for Jesse, not David. **Branch** = Shoot or Scion. Heb. *nezer*. Nothing to do with "Nazareth". See note on Matt. 2. 23. Not the same word as in 4. 2; see note there. **2 spirit.** Heb. *rūach*. Ap. 9. Same word as *v.* 4 "breath", and *v.* 15 "wind". **the LORD.** Heb. Jehovah. Ap. 4. II. **rest upon Him.** Cp. 61. 1. A prophecy which is appropriated by Christ (Luke 4. 16–21). **of.** Genitive of Origin and Efficient Cause. Ap. 17. 2. **understanding** = discernment. **3 shall make Him of quick understanding.** Or, His delight shall be; or, the reverence of Jehovah shall be fragrance to Him. Cp. Gen. 8. 21. Lev. 26. 31. **and.** Some codices, with two early printed editions, Aram., Sept., and Vulg., omit this "and". **not judge, &c.** Cp. 1 Sam. 16. 7. **reprove** = administer judgment. **4 poor** = impoverished, reduced. Heb. *dal*. See note on "poverty" (Prov. 6. 11). **reprove** = set right, or righten. **smite.** Same word as in *v.* 15. **the earth.** Some codices read *'āriz*, "the oppressor", for *erez*, "the earth". This reading is confirmed by the Structure of the clause (which is an Introversion):

g | He shall smite the *oppressor*
  h | with the rod of His *mouth*,
  h | and with the blast of His *lips*
g | shall He slay the *lawless one*.

This reading ("oppressor", for "the earth") depends on whether the first letter is *Aleph* (א = ') or *Ayin* (ע = '). If with א the word is *'erez*, earth; and if with ע it is *'ariz*, oppression. These two letters are often interchanged. See notes on Pss. 28. 8 (their); 35. 15 (tear me). Mic. 1. 10 (at all). Hos. 7. 6 (baker sleepeth). The word *gā'al* (to redeem) is spelt with Aleph ('), but it has been mistaken for *gā'al* (to pollute), and is actually so rendered in Ezra 2. 62. Neh. 7. 64. Isa. 59. 3; 63. 3. Lam. 4. 14. Dan. 1. 8. Zeph. 3. 1. Mal. 1. 7; while *ga'al* is properly so rendered in Lev. 26. 11, 15, 30, 43, 44. 2 Sam. 1. 21 (vilely = as polluted). Job 21. 10 (faileth), Jer. 14. 19 (lothed), Ezek. 16. 45. The word "power" is spelt *'ā* (with Aleph) in Ps. 76. 7, but *'oz* (with Ayin (')) in 90. 11. See further note on Hos. 7. 6 ("in their lying in wait"). The *Massōrah* contains several lists of words in which these letters are interchanged. See Ginsburg's *Massōrah* (Vol. I, p. 57, letter א, § 514 b, and Vol. II, p. 390, letter ע, §§ 352–360, &c.). **breath.** Heb. *rūach* = blast, as in Ex. 15. 8; 25. 4; 37. 7. 2 Kings 19. 7. **the wicked** = the lawless one. Heb. *rāshā'*. Ap. 44. x (sing. not pl.). Cp. 2 Thess. 2. 8.

T i (p. 947) 631-630 6 The °wolf also shall dwell with the lamb, and the leopard shall lie down with the kid; and the calf and the young lion and the fatling together;

k and a °little child shall lead them.

i 7 And the cow and the bear shall feed; their young ones shall lie down together: and the lion shall eat straw like the ox.

k 8 And the sucking child shall play on the hole of the asp, and the weaned child shall put his hand on the °cockatrice' den.

9 They shall not hurt nor destroy °in all My holy mountain: for the earth °shall be full of °the knowledge of [2]the LORD, as the waters cover the sea.

R S (p. 946) 10 And in that day **there °shall be a °Root of Jesse, which shall stand for an ensign of the °people; to It shall the °Gentiles seek:** and His rest shall be °glorious.

T l (p. 947) 11 And it shall come to pass in that day, *that* °the LORD* shall set His hand again °the second time to recover the remnant of His People, which shall be left, from Assyria, and from Egypt, and from °Pathros, and from Cush, and from Elam, and from Shinar, and from Hamath, and from the °islands of the sea.

12 And He shall set up an ensign for the nations, and shall °assemble the °outcasts of Israel, and °gather together the °dispersed of Judah from the four corners of the earth.

m 13 The envy also of °Ephraim shall depart, and the adversaries of Judah shall be cut off: Ephraim shall not envy Judah, and Judah shall not vex Ephraim.

m 14 But they shall °fly upon the shoulders of the Philistines toward the west; they shall spoil °them of the east together: they shall lay their hand upon Edom and °Moab; and the °children of Ammon shall obey them.

l 15 And [2]the LORD shall utterly destroy the °tongue of the Egyptian sea; and with °His mighty °wind shall He shake His hand over °the river, and shall [4]smite it in the seven streams, and make *men* go over °dryshod.

16 And there shall be an °highway for the remnant of His People, which shall be left, from Assyria; °like as it was to Israel °in the day that he came up out of the land of Egypt.

Q U n **12** And in that day thou shalt say, "O °LORD, I will praise Thee:

o though Thou wast angry with me, Thine anger is turned away, and Thou comfortedst me.

V 2 Behold, °GOD *is* my salvation; I will °trust, and not be afraid: for °THE LORD °JEHOVAH *is* °my strength and *my* song; he also is become my salvation.

3 Therefore with joy shall ye draw water out of the wells of °salvation."

U n 4 And in that day shall ye say,

o "Praise [1]the LORD, call upon His name, declare His doings among the °people, make mention that His name is °exalted.

11. 6-9 (T, p. 946). HIS NEW DISPENSATION. (MORAL.) (*Alternation.*)

T | i | 6-. Natural enemies, together.
  k | -6. A child not hurt by them.
  i | 7. Natural enemies, together.
  k | 8, 9. A child not hurt by them.

6 wolf. Fig. *Ampliatio.* Ap. 6.
little child=youth.
8 cockatrice'=viper's. Heb. *ẓepha'.* Occurs only here in "former" portion; and in 59. 5 in "latter". Ap. 79. II.
9 in all My holy mountain. This expression occurs in the "former" portion only here and 27. 13, and in the "latter" portion in 56. 7; 57. 13; 65. 25. It is to be distinguished from other expressions in which the word "mountain" occurs.
shall be=shall assuredly become.
the knowledge. This is the sign of the fulness of blessing. See note on 1. 3; cp. 6. 3. Ref. to Pent. (Num. 14. 21). Ap. 92.

11. 11-16 (*T*, p. 946). HIS NEW DISPENSATION. (POLITICAL.) (*Introversion.*)

T | l | 11, 12. Return of Remnant from Assyria.
  m | 13. Result. Adversaries cut off. Internal.
  m | 14. Result. Enemies' submission. External.
  l | 15, 16. Return of Remnant from Assyria.

10 shall be=shall come to be. Quoted in Rom. 15. 12.
Root=sapling. **people**=peoples.
Gentiles=nations. **glorious**=glory.
11 the LORD*=Jehovah. One of the 134 places (Ap. 32) where the *Sopherim* changed "Jehovah" (of the primitive text) to "Adonai".
the second time. Ref. to Pent. (the first time being Ex. 15. 16, 17). Ap. 92. **Pathros**=Upper Egypt.
islands=maritime countries. Heb. *'i.* Occurs in "former" portion, here; 20. 6; 23. 2, 6; 24. 15; and in the "latter" portion, in 40. 15; 41. 1, 5; 42. 4, 10, 12, 15; 49. 1; 51. 5; 59. 18; 60. 9; 66. 19.
12 assemble=gather in.
outcasts . . . dispersed. Note these two words as applied respectively to Israel and Judah: the former, masc.; the latter, fem.
gather together=gather out.
13 Ephraim. Put by Fig. *Synecdoche* (of Part), Ap. 6, for the whole of the ten tribes.
14 fly=flee. **them**=the sons of.
Moab. See note on 15. 1. **children**=sons.
15 tongue=gulf.
His mighty=the full force, spirit, or blast, as in *v.* 4 ("breath"). **wind**=Heb. *rūach.* Ap. 9.
the river: i. e. the Euphrates.
dryshod. Heb. in shoes.
16 highway. See note on 7. 3.
like as it was. Ref. to Pent. (Ex. 14. 22). Ap. 92.
in the day=when. See note on Gen. 2. 17, and Ap. 18.

12. 1-6 (Q, p. 946). PRAISE FOR JEHOVAH'S DELIVERANCE. (*Alternations.*)

Q | U | n | 1-. In that day. Praise.
  o | -1. Cause. Expressed in words.
  V | 2, 3. Jehovah . . . my song.
  U | *n* | 4-. In that day. Praise.
  o | -4. Cause. Expressed in words.
  V | 5, 6. Jehovah . . . my song.

1 LORD. Heb. Jehovah. Ap. 4. II.
2 GOD. Heb. El. Ap. 4. IV.
trust=confide in. Heb. *bāṭaḥ.* Ap. 69. i.
THE LORD. Heb. Jah. Ap. 4. III.
JEHOVAH. One of the four passages where Jehovah is transliterated instead of being translated (Ex. 6. 3. Ps. 83. 18, and Isa. 26. 4). Also one of several words where different type is used. See Ap. 48.
my strength and my song. Ref. to Pent. (Ex. 15. 2). Ap. 92.
3 salvation. Ref. to Pent. (Gen. 49. 18. Ex. 14. 13; 15. 2. Deut. 32. 15). Ap. 92.
4 people=peoples.
exalted. Cp. 2. 11, 17, "in that day".

V (p. 947) 631–630 5 °Sing unto ¹the LORD; for He hath done
excellent things: this *is* known in all the
earth.
6 Cry out and shout, thou °inhabitant of Zion:
for great *is* °the Holy One of Israel in the midst
of thee.'"

D W Y^1 B^1 (p. 948) 649–588 **13** The °burden of °Babylon, which °Isaiah
the son of Amoz did see.
2 Lift ye up a banner upon the high mountain,
exalt the voice unto them, shake the hand, that
they may go into the gates of the nobles.
3 I have commanded My °sanctified ones, I
have also called My °mighty ones for Mine
anger, *even* °them that rejoice in My highness.
4 The noise of a multitude in the mountains,
like as of a great people; a tumultuous noise
of the kingdoms of nations gathered together:
°the LORD of °hosts mustereth the °host of the
battle.
5 They come from a far country, from °the
end of heaven, *even* °the LORD, and the weapons
of His indignation, to destroy °the whole land.

C p 6 Howl ye; for °the °day of ⁵the LORD *is* at
hand; it shall come as a °destruction from °the
ALMIGHTY.

q 7 Therefore shall all hands be faint, and every
°man's heart shall melt:
8 And they shall be afraid: pangs and sorrows
shall take hold of them; they shall be in pain
as a woman that travaileth: they shall be
amazed one at another; their faces *shall be* °*as*
flames.

p 9 Behold, ⁶the day of ⁵the LORD cometh,
°cruel both with wrath and fierce anger, to lay
the land desolate: and He shall destroy the
sinners thereof out of it.
10 For the stars of heaven and the constellations
thereof °shall not give their light: the
sun shall be darkened in his going forth, and
the moon shall not cause her light to shine.
11 And I will punish °the world for *their*
°evil, and the °wicked for their °iniquity; and
I will cause the arrogancy of the proud to cease,
and will lay low the haughtiness of the terrible.
12 I will make a ⁷man more precious than
fine gold; even a °man than the golden wedge
of Ophir.

q 13 Therefore I will shake the heavens, and
the earth shall remove out of her place, in the
wrath of ⁴the LORD of hosts, and in the day of
His fierce anger.
14 And it shall be as the chased roe, and as a
sheep that no °man taketh up: they shall every
°man turn to his own people, and flee every one
into his own land.
15 Every one that is found shall be thrust

5 Sing = Sing praise. Ref. to Pent. (Ex. 15. 1, 21). Ap. 92.
6 inhabitant = inhabitress.
the Holy One of Israel. See note on 1. 4.

13. 1—27. 13 (**D**, p. 930). BURDENS, AND ISRAEL'S BLESSINGS.
(*Introversion and Alternations.*)

D | W | Y^1 | 13. 1–22. Burden of Babylon. (People, Land.)
Z^1 | 14. 1–3. Israel. Jehovah's mercy.
Y^2 | 14. 4–23. Burden of Babylon. (King.)
Z^2 | 14. 24–32. Israel. Jehovah's deliverance.
X | A^1 | 15. 1—16. 14. Burden. Moab.
A^2 | 17. 1–14. Burden. Damascus.
A^3 | 18. 1–7. Burden. Ethiopia.
A^4 | 19. 1—20. 6. Burden of Egypt.
A^5 | 21. 1–10. Burden. Desert of Sea.
A^6 | 21. 11, 12. Burden. Dumah.
A^7 | 21. 13–17. Burden. Arabia.
W | Y^3 | 22. 1–14. Burden of Valley of Vision.
Z^3 | 22. 15–25. Israel. Judgment and Mercy.
Y^4 | 23. 1–18. Burden of Tyre.
Z^4 | 24. 1—27. 13. Israel. Judgment and Mercy.

13. 1—14. 32 (W, above). BURDEN: BABYLON AND ISRAEL.
(*Repeated and Extended Alternations.*)

W | B^1 | 13. 1–5. Prophecy. Babylon's destruction.
C | p | 13. 6. The day of Jehovah.
q | 13. 7, 8. Consequences.
p | 13. 9–12. The day of Jehovah.
q | 13. 13–18. Consequences.
} The people.
D | 13. 19, 20. Depopulation.
E | 13. 21, 22. Devastation.
B^2 | 14. 1–3. Prophecy. Israel's restoration.
C | r | 14. 4–8. Oppressor ceased.
s | 14. 9–11. Taunt of dead. Fig.
r | 14. 12–15. Oppressor fallen.
s | 14. 16–20. Taunt of living.
} The King.
D | 14. 21, 22. Depopulation.
E | 14. 23. Devastation.
B^3 | 14. 24–32. Prophecy. Jehovah's purpose concerning both: Assyria, Philistia, and Israel.

1 burden = a prophetic oracle or warning. This begins the *fourth* great division of the book. See the Structure (p. 930), and above. Ref. to Pent. (Num. 24. 3). Ap. 92.

Babylon. This takes precedence, and stands for Chaldæa generally. It reached its height about 100 years later, under Nabopolassar and his son Nebuchadnezzar. A generation later it was captured by Cyrus and Darius the Mede (see Ap. 57). Babylon was of little importance at this time.

Isaiah. His name given in 1. 1; 2. 1; 7. 3; 13. 1; 20. 2, 3; 37. 2, 5, 6, 21; 38. 1, 4, 21; 39. 3, 5, 8.

3 sanctified ones = separated ones. Here = the armies of the Medes and Persians. Cp. 44. 28; 45. 1.

mighty ones = heroes. Heb. *gibbōr*. Ap. 14. IV.

them that rejoice in My highness = my proudly exulting ones.

4 the LORD of hosts. See note on 1. 9.

hosts . . . host. Note Fig. *Paronomasia* (Ap. 6). Heb. *ẓᵉba'ōth . . . ẓᵉbā'*.

5 the end of heaven: i.e. from afar.

the LORD. Heb. Jehovah. Ap. 4. II.

the whole land = all the land [of Chaldæa].

6 the day. Put by Fig. *Metonymy* (of Subject), Ap. 6, for the events (or judgments which shall take place in it. **day of the LORD.** See note on 2. 12. Occurs in fifteen other places in O.T.: (*v.* 9. Ezek. 13. 5. Joel 1. 15; 2. 1, 11, 31; 3. 14. Amos 5. 18, 18, 20. Obad. 15. Zeph. 1. 7, 14, 14. Mal. 4. 5 (total 4 × 4, Ap. 10). **destruction . . . ALMIGHTY.** Note Fig. *Paronomasia* (Ap. 6). Heb. *kᵉshod . . . mishshaddai.* **the ALMIGHTY** = the All-bountiful One. Heb. *Shaddai* (Ap. 4. VII). **7 man's** = mortal's. Heb. *'ĕnōsh.* Ap. 14. III. **8 as flames** = as [faces of] flames darkened. **9 cruel** = stern. **10 shall not give their light.** Quoted in Matt. 24. 29. Shall not celebrate [Thee]. Cp. Ps. 19. 1–3; 145. 10. Heb. *hālel.* Occurs twice in "former" portion (here and in 38. 18 "celebrate") and four times in "latter" portion (41. 16; 45. 25, "glory"; 62. 9; 64. 11, "praise"). See Ap. 79. II. **11 the world** = the habitable world. Heb. *tēbēl.* **evil.** Heb. *rā'a'.* Ap. 44. viii. **wicked** = lawless. Heb. *rāshā'.* Ap. 44. x. **iniquity.** Heb. *'āvāh.* Ap. 44. iv. **12 man.** Heb. *'ādām.* Ap. 14. I. **14 man.** Heb. *'īsh.* Ap. 14. II.

649-588 through; and every one that is joined *unto*
them shall fall by the sword.
16 Their °children also shall be dashed to
pieces before their eyes; their houses shall be
spoiled, and their wives ravished.
17 Behold, I will stir up the °Medes against
them, which shall not regard silver; and *as*
for gold, they shall not delight in it.
18 *Their* bows also shall dash the young men
to pieces; and they shall have no pity on the
fruit of the womb; °their °eye shall not spare
°children.
D 19 And Babylon, the glory of kingdoms, the
(p. 948) beauty of the Chaldees' excellency, shall be °as
when °God overthrew Sodom and Gomorrah.
20 It shall °never be inhabited, neither shall
it be dwelt in from generation to generation:
neither shall the Arabian pitch tent there;
neither shall the shepherds make their fold there.
E 21 But wild beasts of the desert shall lie there;
and their houses shall be full of °doleful creatures; and owls shall dwell there, and °satyrs
shall dance there.
22 And °the wild beasts of the islands shall
cry in their desolate houses, and °dragons in
their pleasant palaces: and her time *is* near to
come, and her days shall not be prolonged.

Z¹ B² **14** For °the LORD will °have mercy on
Jacob, and will yet °choose Israel, and
°set them in their own °land: and the °stran-
gers shall be joined with them, and they shall
cleave to °the house of Jacob.
2 And °the people shall take them, and bring
them to °their place: and °the house of Israel
shall °possess them in the land of [1]the LORD
for servants and handmaids: and they shall
take them captives, whose captives they were;
and they shall rule over their °oppressors.
3 And it shall come to pass in the day that
[1]the LORD shall give thee rest from thy sorrow,
and from thy fear, and from the hard bondage
wherein thou wast made to serve,
Y² C r 4 That thou shalt °take up this °proverb
against the °king of Babylon, and say, °"How
hath the oppressor ceased! the °golden city
ceased!
5 [1]The LORD hath broken the staff of the
°wicked, *and* the sceptre of the rulers.
6 He who smote [2]the people in wrath with a
°continual stroke, he that °ruled the nations
in anger, °is persecuted, *and* none hindereth.
7 The whole earth is at rest, *and* is quiet:
they °break forth into singing.
8 Yea, the °fir trees °rejoice at thee, *and* °the
cedars of Lebanon, *saying*, 'Since thou art °laid
down, no feller is come up against us.'
s 9 °Hell from beneath is moved for thee to
meet *thee* at thy coming: it stirreth up the
°dead for thee, *even* all the chief ones of the
earth; it hath raised up from their thrones all
the kings of the nations.
10 All they shall °speak and °say unto thee,
'Art thou also become weak as we? art thou
become like unto us?'
11 Thy pomp is brought down to °the grave,
and the noise of thy viols: the °worm is spread
under thee, and the worms °cover thee.
r 12 [4]How art thou fallen from heaven, O
°Lucifer, son of the morning! *how* art thou

16 children = babes.
17 Medes. Here only "Medes". In 21. 2, "Persians and Medes." In 45. 1 Cyrus named. The order is chronological.
18 their. Some codices, with two early printed editions, Sept., Syr., and Vulg., read "and their".
eye shall not spare. Fig. *Prosopopœia.* Ap. 6.
children = sons.
19 as when God, &c. Ref. to Pent. See note on 1. 9.
God. Heb. Elohim. Ap. 4. I.
20 never. See note on 25. 8.
never be inhabited. Cp. 14. 4–23; 15. 6, 7; 21. 9; 34. 11; 46. 1; 47. 1–11. Jer. 25. 12–14; 50. 1–46; 51. 1–64.
21 doleful creatures. Probably hyenas.
satyrs = goat-shaped demons worshipped by the Seirites (Edom). Cp. Lev. 17. 7. 2 Chron. 11. 15; 25. 14.
22 the wild beasts = jackals.
dragons, or wild dogs.

1 the LORD. Heb. Jehovah. Ap. 4. II.
have mercy. Note the Structure (B², p. 948).
choose. See note on 1. 29.
set them = make them rest. Cp. *v.* 3.
land = soil.
strangers = sojourners, foreign proselytes. Isaiah sees far beyond the Captivity. Heb. *gūr.* See note on 5. 17. Thus, the mention of strangers is not confined to latter part of Isaiah as alleged by some. See Ap. 79. II.
the house of Jacob. See note on 2. 5.
2 the people = peoples.
their place = their own place. See 49. 22; 60. 9; 66. 20.
the house of Israel. See note on 5. 7.
possess them. For servants and handmaids. This is to be fulfilled at a later day: still future (49. 23; 60. 9–14; 61. 5).
oppressors. Cp. 60. 14.
4 take up this proverb. Ref. to Pent. (Num. 23. 7, 24; 24. 3, 15, 20, 21, 23). Elsewhere only in Mic. 2. 4. Hab. 2. 6, and Job 27. 1; 29. 1.
proverb = triumph-song.
king of Babylon. Fig. *Polyonymia* (Ap. 6). One of the names for the Antichrist. See note on Dan. 7. 8.
How . . . ! Fig. *Chleuasmos.* Ap. 6.
golden city: or exactress of gold. Some, by reading ר (=R) for ד (=D) read "oppression".
5 wicked = lawless ones (pl.). Heb. *rāshā'.* Ap. 44. x.
6 continual = unremitting.
ruled the nations = trod down nations.
is persecuted, and none hindereth = with an unsparing persecution.
7 break forth into singing. This word (Heb. *pāẓah*) occurs once in the "former" portion (here), and five times in the "latter" portion (44. 23; 49. 13; 52. 9; 54. 1; 55. 12). See Ap. 92.
8 fir trees. Cp. 37. 24; 41. 19; 55. 13; 60. 13.
rejoice. Fig. *Prosopopœia.* Ap. 6.
the cedars of Lebanon, saying, &c. It refers to Nebuchadnezzar's and Esar-haddon's cutting down, as recorded in their *Inscriptions*, p. 58 (published by Oppert, Paris, 1865). They tell how they "brought the greatest trees from the summits of Lebanon to Babylon". Nebuchadnezzar moreover boasts that he will do it in his message to Hezekiah (37. 28. See Ap. 67, p. 98).
laid down = laid low.
9 Hell = the grave. Heb. Sheōl. Ap. 35.
dead = *Rephaim.* See Ap. 23 and 25. Cp. 26. 14, 19.
10 speak . . . say. Fig. *Prosopopœia* (Ap. 6), by which the dead are represented as speaking.
11 the grave. Heb. Sheōl. Ap. 35. Same word as "hell", *vv.* 9 and 15.
worm. This shows the meaning to be given to Heb. "Sheōl" in *vv.* 9, 15; as worms are *material*, not *spirit.* Cp. 66. 24. Mark 9. 44, 46, 48.
cover thee = are thy coverlet.
12 Lucifer = Morning-star. Worshipped by the Assyrians as male at sunrise, female at sunset. A name of Satan.

649-588 **cut down to the ground, which didst °weaken
the nations!**
**13 °For thou °hast said in thine heart, 'I will
°ascend into °heaven, I will exalt my throne
above the stars of °GOD: I will sit also upon
the °mount of the congregation, in the °sides
of °the north:**
**14 I will ascend above the heights °of the
clouds; I will be like °the MOST HIGH.'**
**15 Yet thou shalt be brought down to [9]hell,
to the [13]sides of the pit.**
s **16 They that see thee shall narrowly look**
(p. 948) **upon thee, *and* consider thee, *saying*, °'*Is* this
the °man that made the earth to °tremble, that
did shake kingdoms;**
**17 *That* made the °world as a wilderness, and
destroyed the cities thereof; *that* °opened not
the house of his prisoners?'**
**18 All the kings of the nations, *even* all of
them, °lie in °glory, every one in his own °house.**
**19 But thou art °cast out of thy °grave like an
°abominable branch, *and as* the raiment of
those that are slain, thrust through with a
sword, °that go down °to the °stones of the
°pit; as a carcase trodden under feet.**
**20 Thou shalt not be joined with them in
burial, because thou hast destroyed thy land,
and slain thy people: the seed of evildoers
shall never be renowned.**
D **21 Prepare °slaughter for his °children °for
the °iniquity of their fathers; that they do not
rise, nor possess the land, nor fill the °face of
the world with °cities."**
**22 "For I will rise up against them," saith
°the LORD of hosts, "and cut off from Babylon
the °name, and remnant, °and °son, and
°nephew," saith [1]the LORD.**
E **23 "I will also make it a possession for the
bittern, and pools of water: and I will sweep
it with the besom of destruction," saith [22]the
LORD of hosts.**
Z[2] B[3] **24 [22]The LORD of hosts °hath sworn, saying,
"Surely °as I have °thought, so shall it come
to pass; and as I have purposed, *so* shall it
stand:**
**25 That I will °break °the Assyrian in My
land, and upon My mountains tread him under
foot: then shall his °yoke depart from off them,
and his burden depart from off their shoulders.**
**26 This *is* the °purpose that is purposed upon
the whole earth: and this *is* the hand that is
°stretched out upon all the nations.**
**27 For [22]the LORD of hosts hath [26]purposed,
and who shall disannul *it?* and His hand *is*
[26]stretched out, and who shall turn it back?"**
616 **28 In the year that °king Ahaz died was this
°burden.**
**29 °Rejoice not thou, whole °Palestina, be-
cause the rod of °him that smote thee is broken:
°for out of the serpent's root shall come forth
a °cockatrice, and his fruit *shall be* a fiery
flying serpent.**
**30 And the °firstborn of the poor shall feed,
and the needy shall lie down in safety: and
I will kill thy root with famine, and he shall
slay thy remnant.**

weaken = subdue.
13 For = And. **hast said** = saidst.
ascend = mount up. **heaven** = the heavens.
GOD. Heb. El. Ap. 4. IV.
mount of the congregation. Not Zion, but the Divine assembly of judgment. Cp. Pss. 75. 2; 82. 1. Ezek. 28. 12-14.
sides = recesses. Same word as in *v.* 15; 37. 24, and 1 Sam. 24. 3. Ezek. 32. 23.
the north. This helps us to localize the dwelling place of God. No "Semitic conception", but Divine revelation of Him Who knows what Satan "said in his heart". Cp. Ps. 75. 6. Job 26. 7.
14 of = that is to say. Genitive of Apposition. **Ap. 17. 4.**
the MOST HIGH. Heb. *Elyōn.* Ap. 4. VI.
16 Is this the man . . . ? Fig. *Dialogismos.* Ap. 6.
man. Heb. *'īsh.* Ap. 14. II.
tremble = quake, forming the Fig. *Paronomasia* (Ap. 6), with "shake."
17 world = the habitable world. Heb. *tēbēl.*
opened not the house of = loosed not.
18 lie = sleep. Heb. *shākab.* So rendered twelve times in O.T. **glory** = state or honour.
house = burial-house, or mausoleum. 1 Kings 2. 10, 34. 1 Sam. 25. 1; 28. 3. Ecc. 12. 5.
19 cast out = flung out: out, or far away.
grave = sepulchre. Heb *ḳeber.* See Ap. 35.
abominable branch = a detested or despised scion.
that go down, &c. As those that go down . . . as, &c.
to. One school of Massorites reads "upon", another reads "up to".
stones. Cast upon those who were buried. No word has "evidently dropped out" of *v.* 20; for *v.* 19 *does* state that they were buried, but he was not.
pit = a rock-hewn buryingplace, as in Pss. 28. 1; 30. 3; 88. 5. Heb. *bōr.* See note on Gen. 21. 19, showing the sense in which we are to understand Sheōl in *vv.* 11, 15. Cp. English word "bore." Heb. *bōr* is rendered cistern, four times; dungeon, thirteen; fountain, one; well, nine; pit, thirty-nine times.
21 slaughter = a slaughter-house, or, instruments of slaughter. Heb. *maṭbēaḥ.* Occurs only here.
children = sons.
for the iniquity of their fathers. Ref. to Pent. (Ex. 20. 5). Ap. 92.
iniquity. Heb. *'āvāh.* Ap. 44. iv.
face = surface.
cities. The triumph-song which began in *v.* 4 ends here.
22 the LORD of hosts. See note on 1. 9. 1 Sam. 1. 3.
name and remnant. Note the Fig. *Homœopropheron* (Ap. 6) in this sentence and the next: "renown and remnant, scion and seed".
and. Some codices, with two early printed editions, omit this "and".
son, and nephew = scion and seed, or, son and son's son.
24 hath sworn. Fig. *Deasis.* Ap. 6. Ref. to Pent. (Deut. 1. 8; 2. 14; 4. 31, &c.). In Isaiah it occurs again: 45. 23; 54. 9; 62. 8. See Ap. 79. II.
as = according as. Cp. 46. 10, 11. Job 23. 13. Pss. 33. 9, 10; 92. 5. Prov. 19. 21; 21. 30. Lam. 3. 37. Matt. 11. 25. Acts 4. 28. Eph. 1. 9.
thought = intended.
25 break . . . yoke. Ref. to Pent. (Gen. 27. 40).
the Assyrian. Another name for the Antichrist. See note on Dan. 7. 8.
26 purpose . . . hand. Note the Alternation of these two words in *vv.* 26 and 27.
stretched out: i.e. in judgment.
28 king Ahaz died. Cp. 6. 1.
burden = rod: i.e. Babylon.
29 Rejoice not thou: i.e. at the death of Ahaz, and because the Davidic dominion was broken by the Syro-Ephraimitic war. **Palestina** = Philistia.
him = the Davidic power.
for out of the serpent's root, &c. That was how Philistia regarded Judah and Ahaz. **cockatrice** = viper (see note on 11. 8), which they would find in his son Hezekiah in the immediate future (2 Kings 18. 8). **30 firstborn of the poor** = the poorest of the poor. Heb. idiom. Heb. *dāl,* impoverished, reduced. See 11. 4. This looks forward to the fulfilment by Messiah (*v.* 32).

616 31 Howl, O °gate; cry, O °city; thou, whole
[29]Palestina, *art* dissolved: for there shall come
from the north a smoke, and °none *shall be*
alone °in his appointed times.
32 What shall °*one* then answer the messengers of °the nation? °That [1]the LORD hath
founded Zion, and °the poor of His People
shall °trust in it.

A^1 F (p. 951) 649-588 **15** The °burden of °Moab. °Because in the
night °Ar of Moab is °laid waste, *and*
°brought to silence; because in the night °Kir
of Moab is laid waste, *and* °brought to silence;

G^1 t^1 2 °He is gone up to °Bajith, and to °Dibon,
the high places, to weep: Moab shall howl
over °Nebo, and over °Medeba: on all their
heads *shall be* baldness, *and* every beard cut off.
3 In °their streets they shall gird themselves
with sackcloth: on the tops of °their houses,
and in °their °streets, every one shall howl,
°weeping abundantly.
4 And °Heshbon shall °cry, and °Elealeh:
their voice shall be heard *even* unto °Jahaz:
therefore the °armed soldiers of Moab shall
°cry out; his °life shall be °grievous unto him.
5 My heart shall [4]cry out for Moab; his fugitives *shall flee* unto °Zoar, °an heifer of three
years old: for by the °mounting up of °Luhith
with weeping shall they go it up; for in the
way of °Horonaim they shall raise up a [4]cry
of destruction.

u^1 6 For the waters of °Nimrim shall be °deso-
late: for the hay is withered away, the grass
faileth, there is no green thing.
7 Therefore the abundance they have gotten,
and that which they have laid up, shall they
carry away to the °brook of the willows.

t^2 8 For the cry is gone round about the borders
of Moab; the howling thereof unto °Eglaim,
and the howling thereof unto Beer-elim.

u^2 9 For the waters of °Dimon shall be full of
°blood: for I will bring °more upon °Dimon,
°lions upon him that escapeth of Moab, and
upon the remnant of the land.

G^2 t^3 **16** Send ye the °lamb °to the ruler of the
land from °Sela to the wilderness, unto
the mount of the daughter of Zion.

u^3 2 For it shall be, *that,* as a wandering bird
°cast out of the nest, *so* the daughters of Moab
shall °be at the fords of Arnon.

t^4 3 °Take counsel, °execute judgment; make
thy shadow as the night in the midst of the
noonday; hide the outcasts; bewray not him
that wandereth.

31 gate . . . city. Put by Fig. *Metonymy* (of Subject), Ap. 6, for the people in them.
none shall be alone = there shall be no stragglers.
in = at.
32 one then answer = what report shall the messengers or ambassadors of the nations take back?
the nation = a nation.
That, &c. This is the report.
the poor = oppressed ones. Heb. *'ānī.* See note on Prov. 6. 11.
trust in it = flee for refuge to it. Heb. *ḥasah.* Ap. 69. ii.

15. 1—16. 14 (A^1, p. 948). THE BURDEN OF MOAB. (*Introversion and Alternations.*)

A^1 | F | 15. 1. Past. Devastation of Moab.
  G^1 | t^1 | 15. 2-5. Moab. Cry.
    u^1 | 15. 6, 7. Reason.
    t^2 | 15. 8. Moab. Cry.
    u^2 | 15. 9. Reason.
  G^2 | t^3 | 16. 1. Moab. Advice.
    u^3 | 16. 2. Reason.
    t^4 | 16. 3, 4-. Moab. Advice.
    u^4 | 16. -4, 5. Reason.
  G^3 | t^5 | 16. 6. Moab. Pride.
    u^5 | 16. 7, 8. Result.
    u^6 | 16. 9-11. Result.
    t^6 | 16. 12. Moab. Pride.
 F | 16. 13, 14. Future. Enfeeblement of Moab.

1 burden. The first of the seven burdens (see **D**, p. 930). **Because** = Surely.
Moab. Had been subdued by Saul (1 Sam. 14. 47) and David (2 Sam. 8. 2); and paid tribute to Ahab (2 Kings 1. 1; 3. 4, 5); Jehoshaphat gained victories (2 Chron. 20. 1-30, and 2 Kings 3. 4-27). Tiglath-pileser carried away tribes east of Jordan, and received tribute from Moab as well as from Ahaz (2 Kings 16. 10).
Ar = Rabbah (Num. 21. 28; Deut. 2. 9, 18, 29).
laid waste . . . brought, &c. Note the Alternation in this verse.
brought to silence = cut off or destroyed. Cp. Hos. 4. 6; 10. 7, 15.
Kir. Now *Kirak,* east of south end of Dead Sea.
2 He: i.e. Moab. **Bajith.** Not identified.
Dibon. Now *Dhībān.* Num. 21. 30; 32. 3, 34; 33. 45, 46. Josh. 13. 9, 17. Jer. 48. 18, 22.
Nebo. Now *Jebel Neba* in Moab, overlooking the Jordan Valley.
Medeba. Same name to-day. Cp. Num. 21. 30. Josh. 13. 9, 16. 1 Chron. 19. 7.
3 their streets = his (i.e. Moab's) open streets.
weeping abundantly = coming down with weeping.
4 Heshbon. Now *Heshbān.* The capital of the Amorites. Rebuilt by Reuben (Num. 32. 37).
cry = cry in pain.
Elealeh. Now *el 'Al,* near Heshbon. Cp. 16. 9. Num. 32. 3, 37. Jer. 48. 34.
Jahaz. Not identified. Num. 21. 23. Deut. 2. 32. Judg. 11. 20.
armed soldiers = light-armed troopers.
cry out = shout for joy.
life = soul. Heb. *nephesh.* Ap. 13.
grievous unto him = vexed within him.
5 Zoar. Now (probably) *Tell esh Shaghūr.* Original name was Bela (Gen. 13. 10; 14. 2, 8; 19. 22, 23, 30. Deut. 34. 3. Jer. 48. 34. **an heifer** = [flee] like an heifer, &c. Cp. Jer. 48. 34. **mounting up** = ascent. **Luhith.** Now *Tel'at el Heith*; one mile west of Mount Nebo. Cp. Jer. 48. 5. **Horonaim.** Not identified; probably *Wady Ghūeir.* **6 Nimrim.** Probably *Wady Nimrim,* near south end of Dead Sea. **desolate** = desolations. **7 brook of the willows**: or valley of the Arabians. Probably the *Wady-el-Ahsy* separating Kerek from Djebal, or the brook Zered of Deut. 2. 13, 14. **8 Eglaim.** Not identified; probably the *En-eglaim* of Ezek. 47. 10. **9 Dimon.** Probably *Umm Deineh,* east of the Dead Sea. **Dimon . . . blood.** Note Fig. *Paronomasia* (Ap. 6). Heb. *Dīmon . . . dām.* **more** = more [howlings]. **lions** = a lion. Put by Fig. *Synecdoche* (of Species), Ap. 6, for all wild beasts.

16. 1 lamb = tribute lamb. **to the ruler** = of the ruler: i.e. Judah, as Mesha king of Moab had done (2 Kings 3. 4). **Sela.** Now *Petra* (so called by the Romans) in Mount Seir, near Mount Hor (2 Kings 14. 7). **2 cast out, &c.** = a forsaken nest. **be** = become. **3 Take counsel** = Bring advice. Some codices, with one early printed edition, Sept., Syr., and Vulg., read "Bring thou counsel". **execute judgment** = perform an arbitrator's duty. Heb. *pelīlah.* Occurs only here. Some codices, with seven early printed editions, Aram., Sept., Syr. and Vulg., read "execute thou".

649-588 4 °Let Mine outcasts °dwell with thee, Moab; be thou a covert to them from the face of °the spoiler:
u[4] (p. 951) for the °extortioner is at an end, the spoiler ceaseth, the °oppressors are consumed out of the land.
5 And °in °mercy shall the throne be established: and He shall sit upon it °in truth in the tabernacle of David, judging, and seeking judgment, and °hasting righteousness.

G[3] t[5] 6 °We have heard of the pride of Moab; *he is* very proud: *even* of his haughtiness, and his pride, and his wrath: *but* °his lies *shall* not *be* so.

u[5] 7 Therefore shall Moab howl for Moab, every one shall howl: for the foundations of °Kir-hareseth shall ye mourn; surely *they are* °stricken.
8 For °the fields of °Heshbon °languish, °*and* °the vine of °Sibmah: the °lords of the °heathen have broken down the principal plants thereof, they are come *even* unto °Jazer, they °wandered *through* the wilderness: her branches are stretched out, they are gone over the sea.

u[6] 9 Therefore I will bewail with the weeping of [8]Jazer the vine of [8]Sibmah: I will °water thee with My tears, O [8]Heshbon, and °Elealeh: for °the shouting for thy summer fruits and for thy harvest is fallen.
10 And gladness is taken away, and joy out of the °plentiful field; and in the vineyards there shall be no singing, neither shall there be shouting: the treaders shall tread out no °wine in *their* °presses; I have made *their vintage* shouting to cease.
11 Wherefore My bowels shall °sound like an harp for Moab, and Mine inward parts for °Kir-haresh.

t[6] 12 And it shall come to pass, when it is seen that Moab is weary °on the high place, that he shall come to his sanctuary to pray; but he shall not °prevail.

F 13 This *is* the word that °the LORD hath spoken concerning Moab since that time.
14 But now [13]the LORD hath spoken, saying, °"Within °three years, as the years of an hireling, and the glory of Moab shall be °contemned, with all that great multitude; and the remnant *shall be* very °small *and* °feeble."

A[2] H a (p. 952) **17** The °burden of °Damascus. "Behold, Damascus °is taken away from *being* a °city, and it shall be a ruinous °heap.
b 2 The °cities of °Aroer *are* °forsaken: they shall be for flocks, which shall lie down, and none shall make *them* afraid.
3 The fortress also shall cease from Ephraim, and the kingdom from Damascus, and the remnant of Syria: they shall be as the glory of the °children of Israel," saith °the LORD of hosts.

K c 4 "And in that day it shall come to pass, *that* the glory of Jacob shall °be made thin, and the fatness of his flesh shall wax lean.

4 Let Mine outcasts, &c. Some codices, with Aram., Sept., and Syr., read "Let the outcasts", &c.
dwell = sojourn. Cp. 1 Sam. 22. 3, 4.
the spoiler: i.e. Sennacherib.
extortioner. Heb. *mūẓ.* Occurs only here.
oppressors = treaders down. Heb. *rāmas.* Occurs only here.
5 in mercy. The burden goes beyond the immediate future to the ultimate future.
mercy = lovingkindness, or grace.
in truth. See note on 10. 20.
hasting righteousness = prompt in equity. Cp. 46. 13.
6 We. Cp. 6. 8. Gen. 1. 26.
his lies shall not be so = his resources do not correspond.
7 Kir-hareseth. Some codices read "Kir-harasheth". Cp. 15. 1.
stricken = worn away. Heb. *nākā'.* Occurs only here.
8 the fields = [as to] the fields. Cp. Deut. 32. 32. 2 Kings 23. 4. Jer. 31. 40 (feminine).
Heshbon. Cp. 15. 4.
languish = he [Moab] hath enfeebled.
and = supply [as to] and omit the colon.
the vine of Sibmah = Sibmah's vine.
Sibmah. Probably *Sūmia,* on the east of Jordan, two and a half miles west of Heshbon (Josh. 13. 19. Jer. 48. 32).
lords. Probably plural of Majesty for "great lord of the nations", a title claimed by the kings of Assyria.
heathen = nations.
Jazer. Probably *Beit Zer'ah,* on the east of Jordan (Num. 32. 1. Josh. 13. 25; 21. 39. 2 Sam. 24. 5. 1 Chron. 6. 81; 26. 31. Jer. 48. 32).
wandered through: or, strayed into.
9 water thee = make thee drunk.
Elealeh. See note on 15. 4.
the shouting for thy summer fruits and for thy harvest is fallen = on thy summer fruits and thy harvest a war-cry hath fallen.
10 plentiful = fruitful.
wine. Heb. *yayin.* Ap. 27. I.
presses = wine-vat. Heb. *yekeb,* not *gath.* See note on 5. 2.
11 sound = make a plaintive sound. Note the Fig. *Paronomasia* (Ap. 6). Heb. *vᵉkīrbī Ķīr.*
Kir-haresh. See note on 15. 1.
12 on. Some codices, with two early printed editions, read "unto": weary with climbing up to. Cp. 15. 2.
prevail = obtain anything.
13 the LORD. Heb. Jehovah. Ap. 4. II.
14 Within. Some codices, with two early printed editions, read "about".
three years. From the death of Ahaz.
contemned = brought low.
small = few. **feeble** = small.

17. 1-14 (A[2], p. 948). **BURDEN OF DAMASCUS.**
(*Introversion and Alternation.*)

A[2] H | a | 1. Ruin of Damascus.
  b | 2, 3. Other cities.
 J | K | c | 4, 5. Diminution.
   d | 6. The remnant.
  L | 7, 8. God. Looking unto Him.
 J | *K* | *d* | 9-. The remnant.
   c | -9. Desolation.
  L | 10. God. Not looking unto Him.
H | *a* | 11. Ruin of Damascus.
  b | 12-14. Other peoples.

1 burden. The second of the seven burdens (see **D**, p. 930). **Damascus.** The capital of Syria. **is taken away** = is swept away. This was by Tiglath-pileser, king of Assyria, and the slaughter of Rezin (632 B.C.). See 2 Kings 16. 9, and 7. 9, 16, above. **city . . . heap.** Note the Fig. *Paronomasia* (Ap. 6). Heb. *mē'īr . . . mᵉ'ī.* **2 cities of Aroer.** Note the Fig. *Paronomasia* (Ap. 6). Heb. *'ārey 'ărō'ēr.* **Aroer.** There were three other cities of that name (Deut. 2. 36. Num. 32. 34. 1 Sam. 30. 28), and this one, which is not identified. **forsaken.** See note on 1. 4. **3 children** = sons. **the LORD of hosts.** See note on 1. 9. **4 be** = become.

649-588 5 And °it shall [4]be as when the harvestman gathereth the corn, and reapeth the ears with his arm; and °it shall be as he that gathereth ears in the valley of °Rephaim.

d (p. 952) 6 Yet gleaning grapes shall be left in it, as the shaking of an olive tree, two *or* three berries in the top of the uppermost bough, four *or* five in the outmost fruitful branches thereof," saith °the LORD °God of Israel.

L 7 At that day shall °a man °look to his Maker, and his eyes shall °have respect to °the Holy One of Israel.

8 And he shall not look to the altars, the work of his hands, neither shall respect *that* which his fingers have made, either °the groves, or the °images.

J K d 9 In that day shall his strong cities [4]be as a [2]forsaken bough, and an uppermost branch, which they left because of the [3]children of Israel:

c and there shall be °desolation.

L 10 Because thou hast forgotten the [6]God of thy salvation, and hast not been mindful of the °Rock of thy strength, therefore shalt thou plant °pleasant plants, and shalt set it with °strange slips:

H a 11 °In the day shalt thou make thy plant to grow, and in the morning shalt thou make thy seed to flourish: *but* the harvest *shall be* a heap in the day of grief and of desperate sorrow.

b 12 Woe to the multitude of many °people, *which* make a noise like the °noise of the seas; and to the °rushing of nations, *that* make a °rushing like the °rushing of mighty waters!

13 The nations shall [12]rush like the [12]rushing of many waters: but °*God* shall rebuke them, and they shall flee far off, and shall be chased as the °chaff of the mountains before the °wind, and like °a rolling thing before the whirlwind.

14 And behold at eveningtide °trouble; *and* before the morning °he *is* not. This *is* the portion of them that spoil us, and the lot of them that rob us.

A³ M e (p. 953) **18** °Woe to the °land °shadowing with wings, which *is* °beyond the rivers of Ethiopia:

2 That sendeth ambassadors by °the sea, even in vessels of °bulrushes upon the waters, *saying*, "Go, ye swift messengers, to a nation °scattered and peeled, to a people °terrible from their beginning hitherto; a nation meted out and trodden down, °whose land the rivers have spoiled!"

f 3 All ye inhabitants of the world, and dwellers on the earth, see ye, when °He lifteth up an ensign on the mountains; and when °He bloweth a trumpet, hear ye.

N 4 For so °the LORD said unto me, "I will take My rest, and I will consider in My dwelling place like a clear heat upon herbs, *and* like a °cloud of dew in the heat of harvest."

5 it: i.e. Jacob's glory (*v.* 4).
it: i.e. Jacob's fatness (*v.* 4).
Rephaim. South-west of Jerusalem. So called after one "Rapha", a mighty one among the descendants of the *Nephilim*, as Anak was, who gave his name to another branch. See Ap. 23 and 25.
6 the LORD. Heb. Jehovah. Ap. 4. II.
the LORD God of Israel. Ref. to Pent. (Ex. 32. 27. Cp. Josh. 9. 18, 19; 10. 40, 42, &c.). See note on 29. 23 and Ap. 92. **God.** Heb. Elohim. Ap. 4. I.
God of Israel. Ref. to Pent. (Ex. 24. 10. Num. 16. 9). Occurs in latter part of Isaiah (41. 17; 45. 3; 48. 2). See Ap. 79. II and 92.
7 a man = Lit. the man. Heb. *'ādām*. Ap. 14. I.
look = have an eye unto.
have respect = have regard. Note the Alternation in *vv.* 7, 8: "look" and "have respect".
the Holy One of Israel. See note on 1. 4.
8 the groves = the *Ashêrahs*. See Ap. 42. Ref. to Pent. (Ex. 34. 13. Deut. 7. 5; 12. 3; 16. 21). Ap. 79. II.
images = sun images. Ref. to Pent. (Lev. 26. 30); both mentioned again (27. 9). Ap. 92.
9 desolation. See note on 1. 7.
10 Rock. Ref. to Pent. (Deut. 32. 13). Ap. 92.
pleasant plants. Probably = plantings of Adonis.
strange slips: or slips of a strange [God].
11 In the day = By day.
12 people = peoples. **noise** = booming, or roaring.
rushing. Note the Fig. *Repetitio* (Ap. 6), for emphasis.
13 God = One. **chaff** = dried grass.
wind. Heb. *rūach*. Ap. 9.
a rolling thing = a *galgal*. See note on Ps. 83. 13.
14 trouble = consternation.
he is not: or, he is no more. Some codices, with two early printed editions, Aram., Sept., Syr., and Vulg., read "and he is no more".

18. 1-7 (A³, p. 948). BURDEN OF ETHIOPIA.
(*Introversion and Alternation.*)

A³ | M | e | 1, 2. Israel. Spoiling.
    f | 3. Zion. Jehovah's ensign.
  N | 4. Jehovah's withdrawal. Cause of recall.
  N | 5, 6. Jehovah's act. Cause of spoiling.
M | *e* | 7-. Israel. Present to Jehovah.
    f | -7. Zion. Mount of Jehovah's name.

1 Woe = Ho! The third of the seven burdens (see **D**, p. 930).
land . . . beyond: i.e. land . . . beyond Abyssinia.
shadowing with wings = of the rustling *ẓalẓal* (from *ẓalal*, to tinkle, cp. Deut. 28. 42). Occurs only in Job 41. 7 (spears). 2 Sam. 6. 5 (cymbals). Ps. 150. 5 (cymbals). See note on 1 Chron. 13. 8.
2 the sea = the Nile. So called by the inhabitants of the Sudan to-day.
bulrushes = reeds. Not the papyrus, but its companion reed, the *ambach*, which reaches a height of fifteen feet and has yellow flowers. Ref. to Pent. Only here, 35. 7; Ex. 2. 3; and Job 8. 11. Ap. 79. II.
scattered and peeled = "tall and smooth-faced", as Professor Sayce describes them.
terrible. They formed the armies of "So" or Shabaka, and are the backbone of the Anglo-Egyptian army (see *Records of the Past*, vol. vii, part iv).
whose land the rivers have spoiled: i.e. the "sudd" or swamps (hence Sudan). The Dinka and Shilluk negroes live on the floating cakes of sudd.
3 He = Jehovah. See Structure, above.
4 the LORD. Heb. Jehovah. Ap. 4. II.
cloud of dew = summer night mist. Heb. *'āb*. Not a rain-cloud, which latter is never seen in harvest. Eight times rendered "thick clouds".
6 left. See note on "forsaken" (1. 4).
fowls . . . beasts. Note the Alternation.

N 5 For afore the harvest, when the bud is perfect, and the sour grape is ripening in the flower, he shall both cut off the sprigs with pruning hooks, and take away *and* cut down the branches.

6 They shall be °left together unto the °fowls

649-588 of the mountains, and to the °beasts of the
earth: and the fowls shall summer upon them,
and all the beasts of the earth shall winter
upon them.

M e (p. 953) 7 In that time shall the °present be brought
unto °the LORD of hosts of a people [2]scattered
and peeled, and from a people [2]terrible from
their beginning hitherto; a nation meted out
and trodden under foot, whose land the rivers
have spoiled,

f to the place of °the name of °the LORD of
hosts, the mount Zion."

A[4] O g (p. 954) **19** The °burden of Egypt. "Behold, °the
LORD °rideth upon a swift cloud, and
shall come into Egypt: and the idols of Egypt
shall be moved at His presence, and the heart
of Egypt shall melt in the midst of it.

h 2 And I will °set the Egyptians against the
Egyptians: and they shall fight °every one
against his brother, and every one against
his neighbour; city against city, *and* kingdom
against kingdom.

g 3 And the °spirit of Egypt shall fail in the
midst thereof; and I will destroy the counsel
thereof: and they shall seek to the °idols, and
to the °charmers, and to them that have °familiar spirits, and to the wizards.

h 4 And the Egyptians will I give over into the
hand of a °cruel lord; and a fierce king shall
rule over them," saith °THE Lord, °the LORD
of hosts.

P i 5 "And the waters shall °fail from the sea, and
°the river shall be wasted and dried up.
6 And °they shall turn the rivers far away;
and the °brooks of defence shall be °emptied
and dried up: the reeds and flags shall wither.

k 7 The °paper reeds by the [6]brooks, by the
mouth of the [6]brooks, and every thing sown
by the [6]brooks, shall °wither, be driven away,
°and be no *more*.

i 8 The fishers also shall °mourn, and all they
that cast angle into the [6]brooks shall lament,
and they that spread nets upon the waters
shall languish.

k 9 Moreover they that work in fine flax, and
they that °weave networks, shall be confounded.
10 And they shall be broken in the °purposes
thereof, all that °make sluices *and* ponds for
°fish.

Q l 11 Surely the princes of °Zoan *are* °fools, the
counsel of the wise counsellers of Pharaoh is
become brutish:

m how say ye unto Pharaoh, '𝔍 *am* the son of
the wise, the son of ancient kings?'
12 Where *are* they? where *are* thy wise *men*?
and let them tell thee now, and let them know
what [4]the LORD of hosts hath purposed upon
Egypt.

l 13 The princes of [11]Zoan are become fools, the
princes of Noph are deceived; they have also
seduced Egypt, *even they that are* the stay of
the tribes thereof.
14 [1]The LORD hath mingled a perverse [3]spirit
in the midst thereof: and they have caused
Egypt to err in every work thereof, as a drunken
man °staggereth in his vomit.

---

7 present. Heb. *shai*, because of being conveyed. Only here, and Ps. 68. 29; 76. 11.
the LORD of hosts. See note on 1. 9.
the name. See note on Ps. 20. 1.

19. 1—20. 6 (A[4], p. 948). BURDEN OF EGYPT. (*Introversion.*)

A[4] | O | 19. 1-4. Confusion. Assyria.
  P | 19. 5-10. Desolation.
   Q | 19. 11-17. The Lord of hosts. The cause.
  P | 19. 18-25. Healing.
 O | 20. 1-6. Captivity. Assyria.

19. 1-4 (O, above). CONFUSION. (*Alternation.*)

O | g | 1. Idols, &c.
  h | 2. War. Civil.
 g | 3. Idols, &c.
  h | 4. War. Foreign.

1 burden. The fourth of the seven burdens (see **D**, p. 930). **the LORD.** Heb. Jehovah. Ap. 4. II.
rideth. Fig. *Anthropopatheia*. Ap. 6.
2 set the Egyptians, &c. Referring to the anarchy consequent on the defeat of Egypt by Sargon (688 B.C.).
every one. Heb. *'ish.* Ap. 14. II.
3 spirit. Heb. *rūach.* Ap. 9.
idols. See note on 2. 8.
charmers. Heb. *'ittim* = mutterers. Occurs only here.
familiar spirits. See note on Lev. 19. 31. Ref. to Pent. (Lev. 20. 6, 27; Deut. 18. 11, &c.). Ap. 92.
4 cruel lord. Sing. adjective with pl. noun = the lord of the nations, as the kings of Assyria called themselves.
THE Lord = the *'Adōn*. Ap. 4. VIII (1).
the LORD of hosts. See note on 1. 9.

19. 5-10 (P, above). DESOLATION. (*Alternation.*)

P | i | 5, 6. Waters. } Things.
  k | 7. Vegetation. }
 i | 8. Waters. Fishers in them. } Persons.
  k | 9, 10. Vegetation. Workers therein. }

5 fail = be dried up. Heb. *nāshath.* Occurs only here in "former" portion, and only in 41. 17 in the "latter" portion. Elsewhere only in Jer. 51. 30. Ap. 79. II.
the river: i.e. the Nile.
6 they shall turn, &c. = the arms of the river shall stink.
brooks = canals of *Matzor*: i.e. Egypt. See note on 7. 18. **emptied** = shallow.
7 paper reeds = meadows. Occurs only here.
wither = be dried up.
and be no more: or, and disappear.
8 mourn. See note on 3. 26.
9 weave. Occurs in the "former" portion only here, and in 38. 12; and in the "latter" portion only in 59. 5. Ref. to Pent. (Ex. 28. 32; 35. 35; 39. 22). Ap. 92.
10 purposes: or, foundations. Cp. Ps. 11. 3.
make sluices . . . fish: or, work for wages shall be grieved in soul.
fish = souls. Heb. *nephesh.* Ap. 13. A.V. marg., "living things".

19. 11-17 (Q, above). THE CAUSE: THE LORD OF HOSTS. (*Alternation.*)

Q | l | 11-. Princes . . . fools.
  m | -11, 12. Cause. The LORD of hosts.
 l | 13-15. Princes . . . fools.
  m | 16, 17. Cause. The LORD of hosts.

11 Zoan. See note on 30. 4.
fools. Heb. *'aval.* See note on Prov. 1. 7.
14 staggereth = goeth astray, as in preceding clause.

649-588 15 Neither shall there be *any* work for Egypt,
which the head or tail, branch or °rush, may do.

m 16 °In that day shall Egypt be like unto
(p. 954) women: and it shall be afraid and fear because
of the shaking of °the hand of [4]the LORD of
hosts, which He shaketh over it.
17 And °the land of Judah shall be a terror
unto Egypt, every one that maketh mention
thereof shall be afraid in himself, because of the
counsel of [4]the LORD of hosts, which He hath
determined against it.

P n 18 [16]In that day shall °five cities in the land
(p. 955) of Egypt speak °the language of Canaan, and
swear to [4]the LORD of hosts; one shall be
called, The city of °destruction.

o 19 [16]In that day shall there be °an altar to
[1]the LORD in the midst of the land of Egypt,
and °a pillar °at the border thereof to [1]the
LORD.
20 And it shall be for a °sign and for a witness
unto [4]the LORD of hosts in the land of Egypt:
for they shall cry unto [1]the LORD because of the
oppressors, and He shall send them a Saviour,
and a great One, and He shall deliver them.
21 And [1]the LORD shall be known to Egypt,
and the Egyptians shall know [1]the LORD [16]in
that day, and shall °do sacrifice and oblation;
yea, they shall vow a vow unto [1]the LORD,
and perform *it.*
22 And [1]the LORD shall smite Egypt: He
shall smite and heal *it:* and they shall return
even to [1]the LORD, and He shall be intreated
of them, and shall heal them.

n 23 °In that day shall there be a °highway
out of Egypt to Assyria, and the Assyrian
shall come into Egypt, and the Egyptian into
Assyria, and the Egyptians shall serve with
the Assyrians.

o 24 [23]In that day shall Israel be the third with
Egypt and with Assyria, *even* a blessing in the
midst of the °land:
25 Whom [4]the LORD of hosts shall bless,
saying, 'Blessed *be* Egypt My people, and
Assyria the work of My hands, and Israel
Mine inheritance.'

O p **20** °In the year that °Tartan came unto
Ashdod, (when °Sargon the king of
Assyria °sent him,) and fought against Ashdod,
and took it;

q 2 At °the same time spake °the LORD °by
°Isaiah the son of Amoz, saying, "Go and loose
the sackcloth from off thy loins, and put off thy
shoe from thy foot." And he did so, walking
°naked and barefoot.

q 3 And [2]the LORD said, "Like as My servant
611-608 Isaiah hath walked [2]naked and barefoot three
years *for* a °sign and wonder upon Egypt and
upon Ethiopia;

p 4 So shall the king of Assyria lead away the
Egyptians prisoners, and the Ethiopians captives, young and old, [2]naked and barefoot,
even with *their* buttocks uncovered, to the
shame of Egypt.
5 And they shall be afraid and ashamed of
Ethiopia their °expectation, and of °Egypt
their glory.
6 And the inhabitant of this °isle shall say
in that day, 'Behold, such *is* our expectation,
whither we flee for help to be delivered from
the king of Assyria: and how shall we escape?' "

15 rush. See note on 9. 14.

16 In that day: i.e. the day when this burden should be fulfilled (not "the day of the Lord"). Note the six steps, *vv.* 16, 18, 19, 21, 23, 24.

the hand. Put for the judgments indicated by the act.

17 the land of Judah. The Assyrian armies came through Judah.

19. 18-25 (*P*, p. 954). HEALING.
(*Alternation.*)

P | n | 18. Cities.
o | 19-22. Healing.
n | 23. Highway.
o | 24, 25. Blessing.

18 five cities. These were probably Heliopolis, Leontopolis, Daphne, Migdol, and Memphis.

the language of Canaan: i.e. the Hebrew language, by the multitude of Jews that went thither.

destruction. The primitive reading was doubtless *ha-zedek* = "righteousness", which the Sept. simply transliterates, ἀσεδέκ. From a desire not to compete with "Jerusalem", which bore this name (Isa. 1. 26), it was altered to *cheres*, which in Chaldee = "the sun", or in Greek = "Heliopolis", which is the reading in many MSS., two early printed editions, and the margins of the A.V. and R.V. But when the temple at Jerusalem was cleansed and restored, the temple at Heliopolis was deemed schismatic; and, by altering one letter (ח = CH, for ה = H), *chereṣ* (the sun) was altered to *hereṣ* (destruction). Hence the present reading of the current Heb. text. See Ginsburg, *Introduction*, pp. 404-8, and Ap. 81.

19 an altar. See Ap. 81.

a pillar. Probably a boundary pillar. Heb. *nāẓab.* A pillar or monument. Not for worship.

at = close to. **20** sign. See note on 7. 11.

21 do sacrifice. "The third Ptolemy, when he had occupied all Syria by force, did not sacrifice thank-offerings to the gods in Egypt, but came to Jerusalem and made votive offerings" (Josephus, *c. Apion*, 11. 5).

23 In that day: i.e. the glorious future, the day of the LORD. Not the same as *v.* -11.

highway. See note on 7. 3. **24** land: or, earth.

20. 1-6 (*O*, p. 954). CAPTIVITY. ASSYRIA.
(*Introversion.*)

O | p | 1. Assyria.
q | 2. Isaiah. Symbol.
q | 3. Isaiah. Signification.
p | 4-6. Assyria.

1 In the year. Probably the year of Samaria's fall (611 B.C.).

Tartan. A title = commander-in-chief. Cp. 2 Kings 18. 17.

Sargon. Never once named by classic writers, and in Scripture only here. The monuments show that he was the son of Shalmaneser, and the father of Sennacherib.

sent him. This expedition is mentioned on the monument found at Khorsabad. A usurper, called "Javan", or "the Greek", had been put on the throne of Ashdod by Hezekiah in the place of "Akimit".

2 the same = that.

the LORD. Heb. Jehovah. Ap. 4. II.

by = by the hand of. Isaiah. See note on 13. 1.

naked. Put by Fig. *Synecdoche* (of the Whole), Ap. 6, for being scantily clad.

3 sign and wonder. Ref. to Pent. (see note on 7. 11 and 8. 18), and Ap. 92.

5 expectation. Put by Fig. *Metonymy* (of Adjunct), Ap. 6, for the help expected from Egypt.

Egypt their glory. Put by Fig. *Metonymy* (of Adjunct), Ap. 6, for the Egyptians, in whom they gloried.

6 isle = sea coast, or coast land. See note on 11. 11.

A5 r (p. 956) 649–588 **21** The °burden °of °the desert of °the sea.
As °whirlwinds in the south °pass
through; *so* it cometh from the desert, from
a terrible land.
2 A grievous vision is declared unto me; the
treacherous °dealer dealeth treacherously, and
the spoiler spoileth.
s °Go up, O Elam: besiege, O Media; all the
°sighing thereof have I made to cease.
3 Therefore are my loins filled with pain:
pangs have taken hold upon me, as the pangs
of a woman that travaileth: I was bowed down
at the hearing *of it;* I was dismayed at the
seeing *of it.*
4 My heart panted, fearfulness affrighted me:
the °night of my °pleasure hath he turned into
°fear unto me.
t 5 °Prepare the table, watch in the watchtower,
eat, drink: arise, ye princes, *and* anoint the
shield.
t 6 For thus hath °the LORD* said unto me,
"Go, set a watchman, let him declare what he
seeth."
7 And he saw °a chariot *with* a couple of
horsemen, °a chariot of asses, *and* a °chariot
of camels; and he hearkened diligently with
much heed:
8 And he cried, "°A lion: My [6]LORD*, I stand
continually upon the watchtower in the daytime, and I am set in my ward whole nights:
9 And, behold, here cometh a [7]chariot of °men,
with a couple of horsemen." And he answered
and said, °"Babylon is fallen, is fallen; and
all °the graven images of her gods he hath
broken unto the ground."
s 10 O my °threshing, and the °corn of my
floor:
r that which I have heard of °the LORD of hosts,
the °God of Israel, have I declared unto you."

A6 (p. 948) 11 The °burden of °Dumah. He calleth to me
out of °Seir, "Watchman, °what of the night?
Watchman, °what of the night?"
12 The watchman said, °"The morning
cometh, and also the night: °if ye will enquire,
enquire ye: return, come."

A7 u (p. 956) 13 The °burden °upon Arabia. In the forest
°in Arabia shall ye lodge, O ye °travelling
companies of °Dedanim.
14 The inhabitants of the land of °Tema
°brought water to him that was thirsty, they
°prevented with their bread him that fled.
v 15 For °they fled from the swords, from the
drawn sword, and from the bent bow, and from
the grievousness of war.
u 16 For thus hath [6]the LORD* said unto me,
°"Within a year, according to the years of an
hireling, and all the glory of °Kedar shall fail:

21. 1-10 (A5, p. 948). BURDEN OF THE DESERT OF THE SEA. (BABYLON). (*Introversion.*)

A5 | r | 1, 2-. Vision. Seen and declared.
 | s | -2-4. The besiegers (Media and Persia). Sent by God.
 | t | 5. The feasting of Babylon. } The besieged.
 | *t* | 6-9. The fall of Babylon. } The besieged.
 | *s* | 10-. The besiegers. Sent by God.
 | *r* | -10-12. Vision heard and declared.

1 burden. The fifth of the seven burdens (see **D**, p. 930).
of=relating to. Genitive of Relation. Ap. 17. 5.
the desert of the sea. A similar term used by Herodotus, "*pelagizein*" (i. 184).
the sea. The waters of the Euphrates in flood were so called, as the Nile was (19. 5). Cp. Rev. 17. 3, 15.
whirlwinds=storms. **pass**=sweep.
2 dealer=one.
Go up, O Elam. Note the Fig. *Paronomasia* (Ap. 6). Heb. *'ălī 'ēylām.*
sighing. Caused by the oppression of Babylon. Occurs in the "former" portion only here, and in 35. 10, and in the "latter" portion only in 51. 11. See Ap. 79. II.
4 night. A *Homonym.* Heb. *nĕsheph*=darkness, here, but daylight in Job 7. 4. 1 Sam. 30. 17. See notes there. The R.V., in doubt, renders it here "twilight".
pleasure=joy. **fear**=trembling.
5 Prepare, &c. Fig. *Irony.* Ap. 6.
6 the LORD*. One of the 134 instances where the *Sopherīm* say they changed the primitive text (Jehovah) to *Adonai.* Ap. 32.
7 a chariot=a troop.
a chariot with a couple of horsemen=a troop of horsemen in pairs.
8 A lion: My LORD*. Read: [as] a lion, "O LORD", &c. **9 men.** Heb. *'ish.* Ap. 14. II.
Babylon is fallen, &c. Note the Fig. *Epizeuxis* (Ap. 6), for emphasis.
the graven images of her gods. Ref. to Pent. Phrase peculiar to Deut. 7. 25; 12. 3. Ap. 92.
10 threshing. Put by Fig. *Metonymy* (of Cause) for the results of it. Here=my oppressed People. Cp. 41. 15. Mic. 4. 13. Jer. 51. 33.
corn of my floor. Lit. son of my threshingfloor.
the LORD of hosts. See note on 1. 9.
the God of Israel. See note on 29. 23.
God. Heb. Elohim. Ap. 4. I.
11 burden. The sixth of the seven burdens (see **D**, p. 930).
Dumah=Edom. An abbreviated form of fuller name "Idumea" (34. 5. Ezek. 35. 15; 36. 5. Mark 3. 8). Dumah=silence, prophetic of its end.
Seir. The inheritance of Esau (or Edom).
what of the night?=how far is it in the night? Note the Fig. *Epizeuxis* (Ap. 6). Repeated in an abbreviated form thus: Heb. *shomēr mah-millayᵉlah? shomēr ma-millēyl?*=how far gone is the night? how far gone the night? This is Edom's inquiry.
12 The morning cometh, &c. This may be the oracle of silence implied in the name "Dumah" (see above, and cp. Pss. 94. 17; 115. 17).
if ye will inquire. Isaiah had no answer. He is silent, but intimates that they may inquire again.

21. 13-17 (A7, p. 948). THE BURDEN OF ARABIA. (*Alternation.*)

A7 | u | 13, 14. Arabia.
 | v | 15. The flight.
 | *u* | 16. Arabia.
 | *v* | 17. The diminishing.

13 burden. The seventh and last of the seven burdens (see **D**, p. 930). **upon Arabia:** *ba'rāb*=in Arabia. **in Arabia:** or, in the evening, or, at sunset. The name is as significant as "Dumah" (*v.* 11). **travelling companies**=caravans. **Dedanim**=Dedanites. Descendants of Abraham by Keturah: Dedan, son of Midian (Gen. 25. 3. 1 Chron. 1. 32). **14 Tema.** Descendants of Abraham through Hagar and Ishmael (Gen. 25. 15. 1 Chron. 1. 30): both mentioned in Jer. 25. 23. Job 6. 19. See note on p. 666. **brought**=bring ye. **prevented**=meet ye. **15 they fled.** From the Assyrian invaders. **16 Within a year.** Later afflictions were foretold in Jer. 49. 28. **Kedar.** Another descendant of Abraham by Hagar through Ishmael (Gen. 25. 13).

v (p. 956) 649-588 17 And the residue of the number of archers, the °mighty men of the °children of Kedar, shall be diminished: for [1]the LORD [10]God of Israel hath spoken *it*."

Y[3] w (p. 957) **22** The °burden of the °valley of °vision. What aileth thee now, that thou art wholly °gone up to the housetops?
2 Thou that art full of °stirs, a tumultuous city, a joyous city: thy slain *men are* not slain with the sword, nor dead in battle.
3 All thy rulers are fled together, they are bound by the archers: all that are found in thee are bound together, *which* have fled °from far.

x 4 Therefore said I, "Look away from me; I will weep bitterly, labour not to comfort me, because of the spoiling of the daughter of my People."
5 For *it is* a day of trouble, and of treading down, and of perplexity by °the Lord °GOD of hosts in the [1]valley of vision, breaking down the walls, and of crying to the mountains.

y 6 And °Elam bare the °quiver with °chariots of °men °*and* horsemen, and Kir uncovered the shield.
7 And it shall come to pass, *that* thy choicest valleys shall be full of chariots, and the horsemen shall set themselves in array °at the gate.
8 And he °discovered the °covering of Judah, and thou didst look in that day to the armour of the house of the forest.
9 Ye °have seen also the breaches of the city of David, that they are many: and ye gathered together the waters of °the lower pool.
10 And ye have numbered the houses of Jerusalem, and the houses have ye broken down to fortify the wall.
11 Ye made also a °ditch between the two walls for the water of the old pool: but ye have not looked unto the maker thereof, neither had respect unto Him That fashioned it long ago.

x 12 And in that day did [5]the Lord [5]GOD of hosts call to weeping, and to mourning, and to baldness, and to girding with sackcloth:

w 13 And behold joy and gladness, slaying oxen, and killing sheep, eating flesh, and drinking wine: °"**let us eat and drink; for to morrow we shall die.**"
14 And it was revealed in mine ears by °the LORD of hosts, "Surely this °iniquity shall not be purged from you till ye die," saith [5]the Lord [5]GOD of hosts.

Z[3] R 15 Thus saith [5]the Lord [5]GOD of hosts,

S "Go, get thee unto this treasurer, *even* unto °Shebna, which *is* over the house, °*and say,*
16 'What hast thou here? and whom hast thou here, that thou hast hewed thee out a sepulchre here, °*as* he that heweth him out a sepulchre on high, *and* that graveth an habitation for himself in a rock?
17 °Behold, °the LORD °will carry thee away with a mighty captivity, and will surely cover thee.
18 He will °surely violently turn and toss thee *like* a ball into a large country: there shalt thou die, and there the chariots of thy glory *shall be* the shame of thy lord's house.
19 And I will °drive thee from thy °station, and from thy state shall He pull thee down.'

17 mighty men. Heb. *gibbōr*. Ap. 14. IV.
children = sons.

22. 1-14 (Y[3], p. 948). THE VALLEY OF VISION. PERSIAN INVASION. (*Introversion.*)

Y[3] | w | 1-3. The besieged. Impious joy.
  x | 4, 5. Day of trouble. Inflicted.
    y | 6-11. The invaders. Persians.
  x | 12. Day of mourning. Required.
w | 13, 14. The besieged. Impious joy.

1 burden = oracle.
valley of vision. The Sept. and Arabic versions render it Jerusalem, in relation to the high hills around. Similar names: "inhabitant of the valley," "rock of the plain" (Jer. 21. 13), "mountain in the fields" (Jer. 17. 3). The reference is to *v.* 5.
vision. Here the most solemn visions had been seen: Abraham (Gen. 22. 2, 14, cp. the name Jehovah-jireh); also David (1 Chron. 21. 16, 28), and the many visions of Isaiah (1. 1; 6. 1-4, &c.). The Sept. reads "Zion".
gone up, &c. Denoting a time of popular rejoicing. Refers to past time. Cp. Matt. 24. 16. Luke 21. 21.
2 stirs = outcries. Referring to the time of this prophecy.
3 from far = afar, or far away.
5 the Lord. Heb. *Adonai*. Ap. 4. VIII (2).
GOD. Heb. Jehovah. Ap. 4. II. See 1. 9.
6 Elam . . . Kir. The south and north limits of the Chaldæan forces.
quiver. Heb. *'ashpāh*. Occurs only here in "former" portion, and only in 49. 2 in the "latter" portion. Ap. 79. II.
chariots. See note on 21. 7.
men. Heb. *'ādām*. Ap. 14. I.
and. Some codices, with three early printed editions and Vulg., read this "and" in the text.
7 at = toward.
8 discovered = dismantled. covering = veil.
9 have seen = beheld.
the lower pool. The pool of Siloam. Cp. 7. 3; 2 Chron. 32. 30. The old pool. See notes on 2 Chron. 32. 3, 30, and Ap. 68. III, p. 101.
11 ditch = a gathering of waters.
13 let us, &c. Note Fig. *Ellipsis* (Ap. 6). Supply thus: "[saying,] 'Let us eat'," &c. Cp. 1 Cor. 15. 32.
14 the LORD of hosts. See note on 1. 9.
iniquity. Heb. *'āvāh*. Ap. 44. iv.
iniquity shall not be purged. Ref. to Pent. (Ex. 30. 10. Lev. 4. 20, &c.). Cp. 6. 7; 27. 9; and Ap. 92.

22. 15-25 (Z[3], p. 948). ISRAEL: JUDGMENT AND MERCY. (*Introversion.*)

Z[3] | R | 15-. Jehovah's word.
  S | -15-19. Shebna.
    T | 20-24. Eliakim.
  S | 25-. Shebna.
R | -25. Jehovah's word.

15 Shebna. See 2 Kings 18. 18, 26. Probably a foreigner, or heathenized Jew.
and say. Some codices, with Aram., Sept., Syr., and Vulg., read "and thou shalt say unto him".
16 as he . . . rock = (as . . . rock). Fig. *Parenthesis*. Ap. 6.
17 Behold. Fig. *Asterismos*. Ap. 6.
the LORD. Heb. Jehovah. Ap. 4. II.
will carry thee away with a mighty captivity, &c. = will hurl thee with the hurling of [a mighty] man.
18 surely violently turn and toss thee. Note the Fig. *Paronomasia* (Ap. 6). Heb. *ẓānōph, yiẓnāphka, ẓenēphāh*.
19 drive = thrust.
station = office, or administration.

T U (p. 958) 649-588 20 And it shall come to pass °in that day, that I will call My servant °Eliakim the son of Hilkiah:

V 21 And I will clothe him with thy robe, and strengthen him with thy °girdle, and I will commit thy °government into his hand: and he shall be a father to the inhabitants of Jerusalem, and to the house of Judah.

22 And the key of the house of David will I lay °upon his shoulder; °so he shall °open, and none shall shut; and he shall shut, and none shall open.

23 And I will fasten him *as* a nail in a sure place; and he shall be for a glorious throne to his father's house.

U 24 And they shall hang upon him all the glory of his father's house, °the offspring and the issue, all °vessels of small quantity, from the vessels of cups, even to all the vessels of flagons.'

S (p. 957) 25 °In that day," saith [14] the LORD of hosts, "shall °the nail that is fastened in the sure place be °removed, and be °cut down, and °fall; and the burden that *was* upon it shall be °cut off:

R for [17] the LORD hath spoken *it*."

Y[4] W[1] X (p. 958) **23** The °burden of °Tyre. Howl, ye °ships of °Tarshish;

Y a[1] for it is laid waste, so that there is no °house, no entering in: from the land of °Chittim °it is revealed to them.

2 Be still, ye inhabitants of the °isle; °thou whom the merchants of Zidon, that °pass over the sea, have replenished.

3 And by great waters the °seed of °Sihor, the °harvest of the °river, *is* her revenue; and °she is a °mart of nations.

4 Be thou ashamed, O °Zidon: for the sea hath spoken, *even* the strength of the sea, saying "°I travail not, nor bring forth °children, neither do I nourish up young men, *nor* bring up virgins."

b[1] 5 °As at the report concerning Egypt, *so* shall they be sorely pained at the report of Tyre.

22. 20-24 (T, p. 957). ELIAKIM.

T	U	20.	Eliakim. Called.
	V	21-23.	"I will". Jehovah's work.
	U	24.	Eliakim. Established.

20 in that day: i.e. in the day when this prophecy will be fulfilled. Cp. *v.* 25.

Eliakim = Whom God sets up. Hezekiah's minister. Probably superseded by Shebna in the evil days of Manasseh. See 36. 3, 22; 37. 2.

21 girdle. Ref. to Pent. Occurs here; and elsewhere only in Ex. 28. 4, 39, 40; 29. 9; 39. 29. Lev. 8. 7, 13; 16. 4. Ap. 92. A priestly vestment.

government = administration.

22 upon. Cp. 9. 6. **so** = and.

open and . . . shut. Put by Fig. *Metonymy* (of Adjunct), Ap. 6, for power of administration. Cp. Rev. 3. 7, which shows that the fulfilment culminates in Messiah.

24 the offspring and the issue: i.e. direct and collateral issue, and embraces his entire kindred.

the offspring. Heb. *hazze'ezā'īm.* Occurs only in Job and Isaiah (Job 5. 25; 21. 8; 27. 14; 31. 8, and Isa. 34. 1; 42. 5; 44. 3; 48. 19; 61. 9; 65. 23). See Ap. 79. II.

vessels. Put by Fig. *Metonymy* (of Subject), Ap. 6, for the kindred mentioned above.

25 In that day. Refers back to the day of *v.* 20: i.e. the day of Shebna's overthrow. This would be the day of Eliakim's exaltation.

the nail: which Shebna thought himself to be, but which Jehovah declared Eliakim to be.

removed . . . cut down . . . fall . . . cut off. Referring to *vv.* 17-19. Fig. *Synonymia* (Ap. 6), emphasising the completeness of Shebna's downfall. The *interpretation* belongs to the two men, but the *application* refers (1) to the two parties in Jerusalem, and (2) to the Messiah, in Whom the prophecy will be exhausted.

23. 1-18 (Y[4], p. 948). BURDEN OF TYRE.
(*Division.*)

Y[4]	W[1]	1-14.	The former time.
	W[2]	15-18.	The latter time.

1-14 (W[1], above). THE FORMER TIME.
(*Alternation.*)

W[1]	X	1-.	Howl.
	Y	-1-13.	Reason. Devastation.
	X	14-.	Howl.
	Y	-14.	Reason. Devastation.

1 burden = oracle.

Tyre. It had rejoiced in the misfortunes of Judah (Amos 1. 9); so it is punished by the same king of Babylon (*v.* 13). Ezek. 26. 2-21.

ships of Tarshish. See note on 2. 16 and 1 Kings 10. 22.

ships. Put by Fig. *Metonymy* (of Adjunct), Ap. 6, for the people in them. **house.** In this case "port".

-1-13 (Y, above). THE REASON. DEVASTATION.
(*Repeated Alternation.*)

Y	a[1]	-1-4.	Apostrophe to Tarshish and Zidon.
	b[1]	5.	Cause of sorrow. Report.
	a[2]	6-8.	Apostrophe to Tarshish.
	b[2]	9.	Cause. Jehovah.
	a[3]	10-12.	Apostrophe to Tarshish.
	b[3]	13.	Punishment. Chaldæans.

Chittim. Originally used of Cyprus, but extended to the islands and coast-lands of the Mediterranean. **it**: i.e. the fall of Tyre. **2 isle.** Here, Tyre itself. **thou whom** = which. **pass over** = cross, in trading. In *vv.* 6, 10, 12, imperative, implying flight. **3 seed**: or, grain. **Sihor** = the black river, the Nile (cp. Jer. 2. 18). **harvest.** Egypt was the field, the Phœnician coast its granary. **river.** Ref. to Pent. See note on 7. 18. "River" is here put by Fig. *Metonymy* (of Adjunct), Ap. 6, for the country (Egypt) through which it passes. **she is a mart of nations**: or, it became merchandise for the nations. **mart** = gain resulting from merchandise, as in *v.* 18 (45. 14. Prov. 3. 14; 31. 18). **4 Zidon.** Was a seaport, the mother city of Phœnicia, the granary of Egypt's harvests. The Zidonians had built Tyre on a rocky island, and connected it with the mainland. **I travail not** = I have not travailed. The verbs which follow in *v.* 4 are in the past tense. The sea speaks to the mother Zidon: thou seekest Tyre—thou findest only the sea. **children** = sons. **5 As at the report concerning, &c.**: or, When the report comes to Egypt they are forthwith in terror at the report concerning Tyre.

a[2] 6 [2] Pass ye over to [1] Tarshish; howl, ye in-
(p. 958) habitants of the [2] isle.
649–588 7 *Is* this your joyous *city*, whose ° antiquity *is*
of ancient days? her own ° feet shall carry her
afar off to sojourn.
8 Who hath taken this counsel against [1] Tyre,
the ° crowning *city*, whose merchants *are*
princes, whose traffickers *are* the honourable
of the earth?
b[2] 9 ° The LORD of hosts hath purposed it, to
° stain the pride of all glory, *and* to bring into
contempt all the honourable of the earth.
a[3] 10 [2] Pass through thy land as a [3] river, O
daughter of [1] Tarshish: *there is* no more
strength.
11 He stretched out his hand over the sea,
He shook the kingdoms: ° the LORD hath given
a commandment against ° the merchant *city*, to
destroy the strong holds ° thereof.
12 And He said, "Thou shalt no more rejoice,
O thou ° oppressed virgin, daughter of [4] Zidon:
arise, [2] pass over to [1] Chittim; there also shalt
thou have no rest."
b[3] 13 Behold the land of the Chaldeans; ° this
people was not, *till* the Assyrian founded it for
them that dwell in the wilderness: they set up
the towers thereof, they raised up the palaces
thereof; ° *and* ° He brought it to ruin.
X 14 Howl, ye [1] ships of Tarshish:
Y for your strength is laid waste.
W[2] c 15 And it shall come to pass in that day, that
(p. 959) Tyre shall be forgotten ° seventy years, according to the days of ° one king: after the end of
seventy years shall Tyre sing as an harlot.
d 16 ° Take an harp, go about the city, thou
harlot that hast been forgotten; make sweet
melody, sing many songs, that thou mayest be
remembered.
c 17 And it shall come to pass after the end of
seventy years, that [11] the LORD will visit Tyre,
d and she shall turn to her hire, and shall commit fornication with all the kingdoms of the
° world ° upon the face of the ° earth.
18 And her merchandise and her hire shall be
° holiness to [11] the LORD: it shall not be treasured nor laid up; for her merchandise shall
be for them that dwell before [11] the LORD, to eat
° sufficiently, and for durable clothing.

A[1] B e[1] **24** ° Behold, ° the LORD maketh the ° earth
° empty, and maketh it waste, and turn-
eth it upside down, and scattereth abroad the
inhabitants thereof.
f[1] 2 And it shall be, ° as with the people, so with
the priest; as with the servant, so with his
master; as with the maid, so with her mistress;
as with the buyer, so with the seller; as with
° the lender, so with ° the borrower; as with the
taker of usury, so with the giver of usury to
him.
e[2] 3 ° The land shall be ° utterly emptied, and
° utterly spoiled: for [1] the LORD hath spoken
this word.
4 [1] The earth ° mourneth *and* fadeth away,
° the world ° languisheth *and* fadeth away,
f[2] the haughty people of ° the earth do ° languish.

7 antiquity = origin.
feet. Put by Fig. *Metonymy* (of Subject), Ap. 6, for the vessels in which the Tyrians fled from Nebuchadnezzar.
8 crowning = crown-giver: i.e. conferring crowns on other Phœnician cities.
9 The LORD of hosts. See note on 1. 9.
stain = pollute.
11 the LORD. Heb. Jehovah. Ap. 4. II.
the merchant city = Tyre, or the Phœnician coast. Hos. 12. 7. **thereof**: or, which are upon it.
12 oppressed = humbled.
13 this people was not = a people that were no people (i.e. Assyria). Tyre boasted antiquity (*v.* 7). Assyria was their object-lesson and warning.
and: or, but. **He.** God.

23. 15–18 (W[2], p. 958). THE LATTER TIME (*Alternation.*)

W[2] | c | 15. Time. Seventy years.
d | 16. Rejoicing. Fig. *Irony.*
c | 17–. Time. Seventy years.
d | –17, 18. Restitution. Literal.

15 seventy years. See Jer. 25. 9–11; 27. 2–7. From the first year of Nebuchadnezzar (496 B.C.) to the conquest of Babylon by Cyrus (426 B.C.).
one. Heb. *'ehad*, a compound unity, hence "one" of a dynasty, here, the Babylonian dynasty. Not *yāhîd*, a single one. See note on Deut. 6. 4.
16 Take an harp, &c. Fig. *Apostrophe.* Ap. 6. Not a quotation.
17 world = the earth. Heb. *ha-'āreẓ*.
upon = which are upon.
earth = ground, or, soil. Heb. *ha-'ădāmāh.*
18 holiness = hallowed.
sufficiently = abundantly.

24. 1—27. 13 (Z[4], p. 948). ISRAEL. JUDGMENT AND MERCY. (*Division.*)

Z[4] | A[1] | 24. 1–23. Judgment.
A[2] | 25. 1—27. 13. Mercy.

24. 1–23 (A[1], above). ISRAEL. JUDGMENT. (*Alternations.*)

A[1] | B | e[1] | 1. Land.
f[1] | 2. People.
e[2] | 3, 4–. Land.
f[2] | –4–12. People.
C | 13–16–. Jehovah glorified from the ends of the earth.
B | e[3] | –16. Land.
f[3] | 17, 18. People.
e[4] | 19, 20. Land.
f4 | 21, 22. People.
C | 23. Jehovah glorified on Mount Zion.

1 Behold. Fig. *Asterismos* (Ap. 6). Note the Structure of Z[4] from p. 948, and that of Z[4] from **D** (p. 930).
the LORD. Heb. Jehovah. Ap. 4. II.
earth. Heb. *hā-'āreẓ.* Occurs sixteen times in this chapter. Rendered "land" in *vv.* 3, 11, 13.
empty. Note the Fig. *Synonymia*, "empty", "waste", "upside down", "scattered abroad". See Ap. 6.
2 as . . . so. Fig. *Simile.* Ap. 6.
the lender . . . the borrower. Ref. to Pent. (Ex. 22. 25, 27. Deut. 15. 2; 24. 10, 11). See Ap. 92
3 The land: Heb. *hā-'āreẓ*, as in *v.* 1.
utterly emptied. Note the Fig. *Paronomasia* (Ap. 6), for emphasis. Heb. *hibbōk tibbōk.*
utterly spoiled. Heb. *hibbōz tibbōz.*
4 mourneth. See note on 3. 26.
mourneth and fadeth away. Note Fig. *Paronomasia* (Ap. 6). Heb. *'āblāh nāblāh.*
the world = the habitable world. Heb. *tēbēl.*
the world languisheth and fadeth away . . . languish. Heb. *'umlelāh nāblāh tēbēl 'umlālū.*
the earth, &c. Fig. *Prosopopœia* (Ap. 6). This is one of the three places where (in the Heb.) one verse ends with "the earth" and the next verse begins with "the earth", being the Fig. *Anadiplosis* (Ap. 6). The other two passages are Gen. 1. 1, 2, and Hos. 2. 23, 24 (A.V. *vv.* 21, 22).

649–588 5 ° The earth also is defiled under the inhabitants thereof; because they have ° transgressed
° the laws, changed the ordinance, broken ° the
everlasting covenant.
6 ° Therefore hath the curse devoured the
° earth, and they that dwell therein are ° desolate: therefore the inhabitants of the ° earth are
burned, and few ° men left.
7 The ° new wine [4] mourneth, the vine languisheth, all the merryhearted do sigh.
8 The mirth of ° tabrets ceaseth, the noise of
them that rejoice endeth, the joy of the harp
ceaseth.
9 They shall not drink ° wine with a song;
° strong drink shall be bitter to them that
drink it.
10 The city of ° confusion is broken down:
every house is shut up, that ° no man may
come in.
11 *There is* a crying for [9] wine in the streets;
all joy is darkened, the mirth of [3] the land is
gone.
12 In the city is left ° desolation, and the gate
is smitten with destruction.

C 13 When thus it shall be in the midst of [3] the
(p. 959) land among the people, *there shall be* as the
shaking of an olive tree, *and* as the gleaning
grapes when the vintage is done.
14 They shall lift up their voice, they shall
sing for the majesty of [1] the LORD, they shall
cry aloud from the ° sea.
15 "Wherefore glorify ye [1] the LORD in the
° fires, *even* the name of [1] the LORD ° God of
Israel in the ° isles of the sea.
16 From the uttermost part of [1] the earth
have we heard songs, *even* glory to ° the
righteous."

B e[3] But ° I said, " ° My leanness, my leanness, woe
unto me! the ° treacherous dealers have dealt
treacherously; yea, the ° treacherous dealers
have dealt very treacherously."

f[3] 17 ° Fear, and the ° pit, and the ° snare, *are*
upon thee, O inhabitant of [1] the earth.
18 And it shall come to pass, *that* he who
fleeth from the noise of the ° fear shall fall
into the ° pit; and he that cometh up out of
the midst of the ° pit shall be taken in the
° snare: for ° the windows from on high
° are open, and the ° foundations of [6] the earth
do shake.

e[4] 19 [1] The earth is ° utterly broken down, the
[6] earth is ° clean dissolved, the [6] earth is ° moved
exceedingly.
20 The [6] earth shall ° reel to and fro like a
drunkard, and shall be ° removed like a cottage; and the ° transgression thereof shall be
heavy upon it; and it shall fall, and not rise
again.

f[4] 21 And it shall come to pass in that day, *that*
[1] the LORD shall punish the host of the high
ones ° *that are* on high, and the kings of the
° earth upon the ° earth.
22 And they shall be gathered together, *as*
prisoners are gathered in the ° pit, and shall be
shut up in the prison, ° and after many days
shall they be ° visited.

C 23 Then the moon shall be ° confounded, and
the sun ° ashamed, when ° the LORD of hosts
shall reign in mount Zion, and in Jerusalem,
and before His ° ancients ° gloriously.

5 The earth. See last note on p. 959.
transgressed. Heb. *'ābar.* Ap. 44. vii.
the laws . . . the everlasting covenant. Ref. to Pent. See note on Gen. 9. 16; and Ap. 92. The Pentateuch was as well known to Isaiah as to the kings in whose reigns he prophesied.
6 Therefore hath the curse devoured the earth. Some codices, with four early printed editions (one in margin), and Syr., read "Because of a curse the earth mourneth". **earth.** Heb. *'erez.*
desolate = laid waste. Heb. *'āsham.* Cp. *vv.* 10, 12, 23.
men. Heb. *'ĕnōsh.* Ap. 14. III.
7 new wine = must. Heb. *tīrōsh.* Ap. 27. II.
8 tabrets = drums. See note on drums, 1 Sam. 10. 5. Heb. *toph.* **9 wine.** Heb. *yayin.* Ap. 27. I.
strong drink. Heb. *shēkār.* Ap. 27. IV.
10 confusion = desolation. Heb. *tohū.* Same word as "without form". Ref. to Pent. (Gen. 1. 2). Occurs in "former" portion three times (here; 29. 21, "thing of naught;" 34. 11); and in the "latter" portion eight times (40. 17, 23; 41. 29; 44. 9, "vanity;" 45. 18, 19, "in vain;" 49. 4, "naught;" 59. 4, "vanity"). See Ap. 79. II.
no man = no one.
12 desolation = astonishment. Heb. *shamēm.* Cp. *vv.* 6, 10, 23.
14 sea. Note Fig. *Ellipsis* = sea [saying]. Ap. 6. See note on Ps. 109. 5. **15 fires.** Or, valleys.
God. Heb. *Elōhim.* Ap. 4. I.
God of Israel. Ref. to Pent. (Gen. 33. 20. Ex. 24. 10. Num. 16. 9). See note on 29. 23, and Ap. 92.
isles = maritime countries. See note on 11. 11.
16 the righteous = the righteous One (sing.): i.e. the One referred to in *v.* 15; or, the nation, as in 26. 2. Cp. Acts 3. 14; 7. 52; 22. 14.
I said = I had said: i.e the land. Fig. *Prosopopœia.* Ap. 6.
My leanness, my leanness. Fig. *Epizeuxis* (Ap. 6), for emphasis. This figure is used thrice in the "former" portion (here, and 26. 3; 29. 1); and twice in the "latter" portion (41. 27, and 65. 1). See Ap. 79. II.
treacherous dealers, &c. = traitors have betrayed. Note Fig. *Polyptōton* (Ap. 6), for emphasis.
17 Fear, and the pit, and the snare. Fig. *Synonymia* (Ap. 6), and Fig. *Paronomasia* (Ap. 6), not a "play on words", but for great and solemn emphasis. Heb. *paphad, vāpaḥath, happa vāppāph* (tr. Eng., scare, lair, snare).
18 fear . . . pit . . . snare. Fig. *Paronomasia* (Ap. 6) again. Heb. *happaḥad . . . happaḥath . . . happaḥath bappāḥ.* See Luke 21. 35, and cp. Jer. 48. 43, 44.
the windows from on high, &c. Ref. to Pent. (Gen. 7. 11). Ap 92. **are open** = have opened.
foundations of the earth. See 58. 12. Cp. 40. 21.
19 utterly broken down. Note Fig. *Polyptōton* (Ap. 6). Heb. breaking, breaks up. Same Fig. below.
clean dissolved. Heb. bursting, bursts up.
moved exceedingly. Heb. tottering, tottereth.
20 reel to and fro. Heb. staggering, staggereth.
removed. Heb. rocketh to and fro.
transgression = revolt. Heb. *pasha'.* Ap. 44. ix. Not the same word as in *v.* 5.
21 that are. Omit.
earth = the ground, or, soil. Heb. *hā-'ădāmāh.* Cp. 6. 12.
22 pit. Not the same word as in *vv.* 17, 18. Here, Heb. *bōr*, a dug-out pit, or dungeon. Occurs in Isa. 14. 15, 19; 36. 13; 38. 18; and in "latter" portion, 51. 1. Ap. 79. II.
and = even.
visited: i.e. with the judgments foretold in the preceding verses. Cp. 10. 3; 26. 14, 16; 29. 6.
23 confounded = blush (from shame).
ashamed = turn pale (from fear).
the LORD of hosts. See note on 1. 9.
ancients = elders. Cp. Rev. 4. 4.
gloriously = in glory, or "[shall be] a glory".

A² D G (p. 961) 649–588

25 O °LORD, Thou *art* my °God; °I will exalt Thee, °I will praise Thy name; for Thou hast done °wonderful *things; Thy* counsels of old *are* faithfulness *and* truth.

H g

2 For Thou hast made of a city an heap; *of* a defenced city a ruin: a palace of °strangers to be no city; it shall never be built.

3 Therefore shall the strong people glorify Thee, the city of the terrible nations shall fear Thee.

4 For Thou hast been a °strength to the °poor, a °strength to the needy in his distress, a refuge from the storm, a shadow from the heat, °when the °blast of the terrible ones *is* as a storm *against* the wall.

5 Thou shalt bring down the noise of ²strangers, as the heat in a dry place; *even* the heat with the shadow of a cloud: the °branch of the terrible ones shall °be brought low.

h

6 And in this mountain shall °the LORD of hosts make unto all °people °a feast °of fat things, °a feast of °wines on the lees, of fat things °full of marrow, °of wines on the lees well refined.

7 And He will °destroy in °this mountain the face of the covering °cast over all °people, and the vail that is spread over all nations.

8 **He will °swallow up death °in victory**; and °the Lord °GOD **will wipe away tears from off all faces**; and the °rebuke of His People shall He take away from off all the earth: for ¹the LORD hath spoken *it*.

G

9 And it shall be said in that day, "Lo, this *is* our ¹God; °we have waited for Him, and He will save us: this *is* ¹the LORD; °we have waited for Him, we will be glad and rejoice in His salvation."

H h

10 For in this mountain shall the hand of ¹the LORD rest,

g

and °Moab shall be °trodden down under Him, even °as °straw is °trodden down °for the dunghill.

11 And He shall °spread forth His hands in the midst of them, °as he that swimmeth °spreadeth forth *his hands* to swim: and He shall bring down their pride together with the °spoils of their hands.

12 And the fortress of the high fort of thy walls shall He °bring down, lay low, *and* bring to the ground, *even* to the dust.

E i¹ (p. 962)

26 °In that day shall this song be sung in the land of °Judah; We have a strong city; salvation will *God* appoint *for* walls and bulwarks.

---

25. 1—27. 13 (A², p. 959). MERCY.
(*Introversion.*)

A² | D | 25. 1-12. Praise.
  E | 26. 1-21. Song in Judah.
   F | 27. 1. The old serpent punished.
  E | 27. 2-6. Song of Israel.
 D | 27. 7-13. Acknowledgment.

25. 1-12 (D, above). PRAISE.
(*Alternation and Introversion.*)

D | G | 1. Praise.
  H | g | 2-5. Destruction of enemies.
    h | 6-8. Place. This mountain.
 G | 9. Praise.
  H | *h* | 10-. Place. This mountain.
    g | -10-12. Destruction of enemies.

1 LORD. Heb. Jehovah. Ap. 4. II.
God. Heb. Elohim. Ap. 4. I.
I will exalt Thee, I will praise Thy name. In Hebrew three words, two making the Fig. *Paronomasia* (Ap. 6); not for a "play on words", but for solemn emphasis, to attract our attention. Heb. *'ărōmimkā, 'ōdeh shimkā*. Ref. to Pent. (Ex. 15. 2). Ap. 92.
wonderful things = a wonderful deed.
2 strangers = foreigners. See note on 5. 17.
4 strength = stronghold.
poor. Heb. *dal* = impoverished, reduced. See note on "poverty", Prov. 6. 11.
when the blast of the terrible ones is = for the blast of the terrible ones [is], &c.
blast. Heb. *rūach* (Ap. 9), as in 37. 7. Ex. 15. 8. 2 Kings 19. 7. **5 branch** = triumphal song.
be brought low = become low.
6 the LORD of hosts. See note on 1 Sam. 1. 3.
people = the peoples.
a feast. Note the Fig. *Paronomasia* (Ap. 6) in this verse: **a feast** (Heb. *mishtēh*) **of fat things** (Heb. *shemānīm*), **a feast of** (Heb. *mishtēh*) **wines on the lees** (Heb. *shemārīm*); **of fat things** (Heb. *shemānīm*) **full of marrow** (Heb. *memuḥyim*), **of wines on the lees** (Heb. *shemārīm*). All these words are thus heaped together to impress us with the greatness of this feast.
wines on the lees. Heb. *shemārīm* (Ap. 27. VIII), see above = wines purified from the lees.
7 destroy = swallow up, as in *v.* 8.
this mountain: i.e. Zion (2. 1, 2; 24. 23).
cast = covered. **people** = the peoples.
8 swallow up. Same word as "destroy" (*v.* 7), so as to cause a thing to disappear and be no more. Cp. Num. 16. 30. Ps. 69. 15; 106. 17. Jonah 1. 17.
in victory. Heb. *nezaḥ* = for ever. Occurs in Isa. 13. 20; 28. 28; 33. 20; 34. 10; and in the "latter" portion, 57. 16; rendered "victory" in 1 Chron. 29. 11. 1 Sam. 15. 29. Quoted in 1 Cor. 15. 54: where we have the Holy Spirit's comment on the word, giving the additional thought of "victory". See Ap. 79. II.
the Lord = Adonai. Ap. 4. VIII (2).
GOD = Jehovah. Ap. 4. II. **rebuke** = reproach.
9 we have waited. Ref. to Pent. (Gen. 49. 18. See Ap. 36). Ap. 92.
we have waited. Fig. *Anaphora*. Ap. 6.
10 Moab . . . as straw . . . for the dunghill. Note the Fig. *Homœopropheron* (Ap. 6). Moab . . . *Māthbēn beMo Madmēnāh*.
straw. Instead of the usual word *teben*, the word *mathbēn*, which occurs only here, is used to complete the Fig. *Homœopropheron*. See above. **trodden down** = beaten to pieces by treading. **for the dunghill** = in Madmenah, as in 10. 31 and Jer. 48. 2 R.V. quite wrong, "in the water of the dunghill". Dung is never watered in the East, but dried, and used as fuel (Ezek. 4. 15), and is found only in the streets of towns and villages. In Ps. 83. 10 "earth" is *'ădāmāh* = ground. See note there. **11 spread forth His hands.** In the East all swimmers swim "hand over hand", and beat the water with a loud noise. Parallel with the beating of straw in *v.* 10. Cp. Isa. 63. . **as** = according as. **spoils** = devices, or artifices. **12 bring down, lay low, and bring to the ground.** Note the Fig. *Synonymia* (Ap. 6), to emphasise the certainty and reality of what had been expressed by the Fig. *Simile* in *vv.* 10, 11.

26. 1-21 [For Structure see next page].

1 In that day: i.e. in the yet future day, when these judgments shall have been accomplished. **Judah.** In ch. 26 we have the Song of Judah (*v.* 1); in ch. 27, the Song of Israel. Cp. *vv.* 6, 12.

649-588 2 Open ye the gates, that the righteous nation which °keepeth the truth may enter in.

3 Thou wilt keep *him* in °perfect peace, *whose* °mind *is* stayed *on Thee:* because he °trusteth in Thee.

4 [3]Trust ye in °the LORD for ever: for in °THE LORD °JEHOVAH *is* °everlasting strength:

k^1 q^1 (p. 962) 5 For He °bringeth down them that dwell on high; the lofty city, He layeth it low; He layeth it low, *even* to the °ground; He bringeth it *even* to the dust.

6 The foot shall tread it down, *even* the feet of the °poor, *and* the steps of the °needy.

i^2 7 The °way of °the just *is* °uprightness: Thou, most upright, dost °weigh the path of °the just.

8 Yea, in the [7]way of Thy judgments, O [4]LORD, have °we waited for Thee; the desire of *our* °soul *is* to Thy name, and to the °remembrance of Thee.

9 With my [8]soul have I desired Thee in the night; yea, with my °spirit within me will I seek Thee °early: for °when Thy judgments *are* in the earth, the inhabitants of the world will learn righteousness.

k^2 10 Let favour be shewed to °the wicked, *yet* will he not learn righteousness: in the land of uprightness will he deal unjustly, and will not behold the majesty of [4]the LORD.

11 [4]LORD, *when* Thy hand is lifted up, they will not see: *but* they shall see, and be ashamed for *their* envy at the people; yea, °the fire of Thine enemies shall devour them.

i^3 12 [4]LORD, Thou wilt °ordain peace for us: for Thou also hast wrought all our works °in us.

13 O [4]LORD our °God, *other* °lords beside Thee have °had dominion over us: *but* by Thee only will we °make mention of °Thy name.

k^3 14 °*They are* dead, they shall not live; *they are* °deceased, °they shall not rise: therefore hast Thou visited and destroyed them, and made all their memory to perish.

i^4 15 °Thou hast °increased °the nation, O [4]LORD, °Thou hast increased the nation: Thou art glorified: Thou °hadst removed *it* far *unto* all the ends of the earth.

16 [4]LORD, in trouble have they visited Thee, they poured out a prayer *when* Thy °chastening *was* upon them.

17 °Like as a woman with child, *that* draweth near the time of her delivery, is in pain, *and* crieth out in her pangs; so have we been in Thy sight, O [4]LORD.

18 We have been with child, we have been in pain, we have as it were brought forth °wind;

26. 1-21 (E, p. 961). SONG IN JUDAH. (*Repeated Alternation.*)

E | i^1 | 1-4. The righteous. Their salvation.
k^1 | 5, 6. The wicked. Brought down.
i^2 | 7-9. The righteous. Their way.
k^2 | 10, 11. The wicked. Devoured.
i^3 | 12, 13. The righteous. Their God.
k^3 | 14. The wicked (Rephaim). No resurrection.
i^4 | 15-19-. The righteous nation. Increased. Resurrection.
k^4 | -19. The wicked (Rephaim). No resurrection.
i^5 | 20. The righteous nation. Preserved.
k^5 | 21. The wicked. Destroyed.

2 keepeth the truth = maintaineth fidelity. No Article. Cp. Deut. 32. 20. Occurs only here, in Isaiah.

3 perfect peace. Heb. peace, peace. Fig. *Epizeuxis* (Ap. 6), for emphasis, beautifully expressed in the A.V. The same expression occurs in 57. 19, indicating the unity of the book. See note on 24. 16, and Ap. 79. II. Cp. 27. 5. **mind** = thought.

trusteth = confideth. Heb. *baṭaḥ*. See Ap. 69. I.

4 the LORD. Heb. Jehovah. Ap. 4. II.

THE LORD. Heb. Jah. Ap. 4. III. In Isaiah, only here and 12. 2; 38. 11, 11.

JEHOVAH. One of the four passages where the A.V. transliterates the word instead of translating it. See note on 12. 2, and Ap. 48.

everlasting strength = a rock of ages. Ref. to Pent. (Deut. 32. 4, 18, 30, same word as here). See Ap. 92. Found only in Deuteronomy and as applied to God (see Ap. 79. II); and here, and 30. 29, in the "former" portion; and 44. 8 in the "latter" portion. Cp. Hab. 1. 12. 1 Sam. 2. 2. 2 Sam. 23. 3, and Psalms.

5 bringeth down, &c. See note on 25. 12.

ground = earth. Heb. *'erez*.

6 poor = wretched, afflicted. Here singular. Heb. *'ānāh*. See note on Prov. 6. 11.

needy = lowly ones.

7 way. See note on "path", 2. 3.

the just = a just one.

uprightness = a perfect or level way.

weigh = ponder.

8 we waited. See note on 25. 9.

soul. Heb. *nephesh*. Ap. 13.

remembrance. Ref. to Pent. Same as "memorial" in Ex. 3. 15. The words are quoted again in Pss. 102. 12; 135. 13 and Hos. 12. 5, and nowhere else. Ap. 92.

9 spirit. Heb. *rūaḥ*. Ap. 9.

early = with the dawn.

when, &c. Hence the multitudes which come out of the great tribulation in Rev. 7. 14-17.

10 the wicked = a lawless one. Heb. *rāshā'*. Ap. 44. x.

11 the fire, &c. Or, fire shall devour Thine adversaries (R.V.). **12 ordain** = arrange.

in us = for us. Cp. Phil. 2. 13.

13 God. Heb. Elohim. Ap. 4. I.

lords = owners. Referring to the Canaanite oppressors of Israel and their false gods.

had dominion = domineered, or lorded it.

make mention = call upon.

Thy name = Thee. See note on Ps. 20. 1.

14 They are dead: i.e. the "other lords" of *v.* 13. Heb. *mēthīm*. Not dead men, as such, for "all" men shall rise again (Dan. 12. 2. John 5. 28, 29. Acts 23. 6, 8; 24. 15. 1 Cor. 15. 22. Rev. 20. 4-6, 13), but those referred to in *v.* 13.

deceased = the *Rephaim*. This is a proper name, and should not be translated. Where it is translated it is always rendered "giants" or "dead" (*v.* 19. Job 26. 5. Ps. 88. 10. Prov. 2. 18; 9. 18; 21. 16. Isa. 14. 9); why not so here? or transliterated, as it is in 17. 5. **they shall not rise.** These *Rephaim* will not rise. They were the progeny of the fallen angels: these latter are kept "in prison" (1 Pet. 3. 19), in "chains" (2 Pet. 2. 4. Jude 6), "reserved" unto judgment: but their progeny will "not rise" (*vv.* 14, 19) or be judged, for they have been "visited", "destroyed", and "perished". See Ap. 23 and 25. **15 Thou hast increased.** Fig. *Epizeuxis*. Ap. 6. **increased** = added to. **the nation:** i.e. Israel. The future nation of Matt. 21. 43. **hadst removed, &c.** = hast enlarged or extended all the boundaries of the land. Heb. *rachak*, as in Mic. 7. 11. **16 chastening** = discipline. **17 Like as a woman, &c.** Ref. to Pent. (Gen. 3. 16). Ap. 92. Cp. 13. 8; 37. 3; 42. 14; 66. 7, 9. These refer to the birth-pangs of the Great Tribulation, which issue in the new nation. **18 wind.** Heb. *rūaḥ*. Ap. 9.

649-588 **we have not wrought any deliverance in the**
earth; °neither have the inhabitants of the
°world fallen.
19 °Thy dead *men* shall live, *together with*
°my dead body °shall they arise. Awake and
sing, ye that °dwell in dust: for thy dew *is* °*as*
the dew of herbs,
k[4] **°and the earth shall °cast out °the dead.**
(p. 962) **20 °Come, My People, enter thou into thy**
i[5] **chambers, and shut thy doors about thee:**
hide thyself as it were for °a little moment,
until the indignation be overpast.
k[5] **21 For, behold, [4]the LORD [20]cometh out of His**
place to punish the inhabitants of the earth for
their °iniquity: the earth also shall °disclose
her blood, and shall no more cover her slain.

F **27 °In that day °the LORD with °His sore**
(p. 961) **and great and °strong sword shall**
punish °leviathan the °piercing serpent, even
leviathan that °crooked serpent; and He shall
slay the °dragon that *is* in the °sea.
E **2 [1]In that day °sing ye unto her, A vineyard**
of °red wine.
3 I [1]the LORD do keep it; I will water it
every moment: lest *any* hurt it, I will keep it
night and day.
4 °Fury *is* °not in Me: who would set the
°briers *and* thorns against Me in battle? I
would go through them, I would burn them
together.
5 °Or let him take hold of °My strength, *that*
he may make peace with Me; *and* he shall
make peace with Me.
6 °He shall cause them that come of Jacob
to take root: Israel shall blossom and bud,
and fill the face of °the world with fruit.
D l **7 Hath He smitten him, °as He smote those**
(p. 963) **that smote him? *or* is he slain according to**
the slaughter of them that are slain by him?
m **8 °In measure, °when it shooteth forth, °Thou**
wilt debate with it: He stayeth His °rough
°wind in the day of the °east °wind.
9 °By this therefore shall the °iniquity of
Jacob be °purged; and °this *is* all the fruit to
take away his °sin; when He maketh all the
stones of °the altar °as chalkstones that are
beaten °in sunder, °the groves and °images
shall °not stand up.

neither have the inhabitants of the world fallen = nor did the inhabitants of the world come to the light: i.e. by being born. The Heb. *nāphal*, to fall, is used of birth, as Heb. *nĕphel* occurs only in Job 3. 16. Ps. 58. 8. Ecc. 6. 3.

world = the inhabited world. Heb. *tēbēl*.

19 Thy dead men = Thy dead ones. Heb. *mēthīm*, as in *v.* 14. These are very different from the dead in *v.* 14. They are Jehovah's dead. These shall rise.

my dead body shall . . . arise = my corpse (a noun of multitude).

shall they arise (pl. verb): i.e. all the dead bodies of Jehovah's people. All these shall awake and sing (Ps. 17. 15).

dwell in dust = lie in the dust: i.e. buried in the dust of the earth.

as the dew of herbs = like the dew upon herbs: i.e. revivifying them. Cp. 66. 14.

and = but; introducing the important contrast already expressed in *v.* 14.

cast out: or, cast away. Not yield up in resurrection. Whom will the earth thus cast away? See the answer in the word which follows.

the dead = the *Rephaim*. See note on *v.* 14, and Ap. 23 and 25. These will "not rise".

20 Come = Go.

a little moment. See note on Prov. 5. 14.

21 iniquity. *'āvāh*. Ap. 44. iv.

disclose her blood. Ref. to Pent. (Gen. 4. 10, 11). Ap. 92.

27. 1 In that day: i.e. the period of judgment foretold in 26. 21.

the LORD. Heb. Jehovah. Ap. 4. II.

His . . . strong sword. Fig. *Anthropopatheia*. Ap. 6.

leviathan. Three great aquatic animals are here mentioned: probably referring to Israel's three great enemies: Assyria (with Nineveh, on the Tigris); Babylon (on the Euphrates); and Egypt (on the Nile); with Satan himself behind them all, as their great instigator.

piercing = fleeing, or fugitive (like the Tigris).

crooked—tortuous (like the winding Euphrates).

dragon = the crocodile of the Nile.

sea = the Nile, as in 19. 5. Nah. 3. 8.

2 sing: or, answer.

red wine. Heb. *chemer*. Ap. 27. III. Some codices, with one early printed edition, Aram., and Sept., read *chemed*, pleasant, or lovely.

4 Fury. Heb. *chēmah* = heat, wrath, displeasure.

not in Me: i.e. not now. There was in the other song (5. 5-7): but now, "in that day", all wrath will have gone.

briers and thorns: i.e. the *internal* enemies of the vineyard (as the wild beasts are the external enemies). These are now the objects of His wrath, not His vineyard.

5 Or: i.e. if such enemies wish to avert My wrath, then let them make peace with Me. **My strength** = Me, as a refuge or protection. **6 He shall cause,** &c. This verse is not an "addendum", or "irrelevant", or "an illegible gap". It is necessary in order to give us the subject of the song, which is reserved till this verse. The symbol is to tell us that Israel is the vineyard (cp. *v.* 12). See the Structure on p. 961; and note that in E (26. 1-21) we have the Song of Judah, while in *E* (27. 2-6) the Song concerning Israel. **the world** = the inhabited world. Heb. *tēbēl*.

27. 7-13 (*D*, p. 961). ACKNOWLEDGMENT. (*Alternation.*)

D | l | 7. Enemies.
| m | 8, 9. Israel.
| *l* | 10, 11. Enemies.
| *m* | 12, 13. Israel.

7 as, &c. = according to the stroke of those, &c. **8 In measure** = By measure. Referring to the smiting of Israel, as being in a limited measure. Heb. *ṣe'āh*. Ap. 51. III. 3. (11), (5). **when it shooteth forth** = when Thou didst send it forth (i.e. the stroke of *v.* 7). **Thou wilt debate with it** = Thou wilt curb it (i.e. the stroke of *v.* 7). Heb. *rīb* = plead, as in 1. 17; 3. 13; 51. 22. Jer. 2. 9, 29; 12. 1; 50. 34. Mic. 7. 9. **rough** = harsh, or severe. **wind.** Heb. *rūach*. Ap. 9. **east wind.** A violent, hot, scorching wind; pernicious to the fruit of a vineyard. **9 By this** = In this way. **iniquity.** Heb. *'āvāh*. Ap. 44. iv. **purged** = covered: i.e. atoned for. Heb. *kāphar*. See note on Ex. 29. 33. **this is all the fruit** = all this is the fruit or result. **sin.** Heb. *chāṭā'*. Ap. 44. i. **the altar** = [all] altars. **as** = no better than. **in sunder** = to pieces. **the groves** = the Asherahs. Ap. 42. **images** = images of Ashtoreth. See note on 17. 8. **not** = no more.

l (p. 963) 649-588 10 °Yet the defenced city *shall be* desolate, *and* the habitation °forsaken, and left like a wilderness: there shall the calf feed, and there shall he lie down, and °consume the branches thereof.
11 When °the boughs thereof are withered, °they shall be °broken off: the women come, *and* set them on fire: for it *is* a people of no understanding: therefore He That made them will not have mercy on them, and He That formed them will shew them no favour.

m 12 And it shall come to pass °in that day, *that* [1]the LORD shall °beat off from the °channel of the °river unto the stream of Egypt, and ye shall be gathered one by one, O ye °children of Israel.
13 And it shall come to pass [12]in that day, *that* the great trumpet shall be blown, and they shall come which were °ready to perish in the land of Assyria, and the outcasts in the land of Egypt, and shall worship [1]the LORD in the °holy °mount at Jerusalem.

D J¹K¹M n (p. 964) **28** °Woe to the °crown of pride, °to the drunkards of °Ephraim, whose glorious beauty *is* °a fading flower, which *are* on the head of the °fat valleys of them that are overcome with °wine!

o 2 °Behold, °the LORD* °hath a mighty and strong one, *which* as a tempest of hail *and* a destroying storm, as a flood of mighty waters overflowing, shall °cast down to the earth with the hand.
3 The [1]crown of pride, the drunkards of Ephraim, shall be trodden under feet:
4 And the glorious beauty, which *is* on the head of the [1]fat valley, shall °be [1]a fading flower, °*and* as the °hasty fruit before the summer; which *when* he that looketh upon it °seeth, while it is yet in his hand he °eateth it up.
5 In that day shall °the LORD of hosts be for a crown of glory, and for a diadem of beauty, unto the residue of His People,
6 And for a °spirit of judgment to him that sitteth in judgment, and for strength to them that °turn the battle to the gate.

n 7 But °they also have erred through [1]wine, and through °strong drink are out of the way; the priest and the prophet have erred through °strong drink, they are swallowed up of [1]wine, they are out of the way through °strong drink; they err in vision, they stumble *in* °judgment.
8 For all °tables are full of vomit *and* filthiness, *so that there is* no place *clean.*

N p 9 °Whom shall He teach knowledge? and whom shall He make to understand doctrine? *them that are* weaned from the °milk, *and* drawn from the °breasts.

q 10 °For precept °*must be* upon precept, pre-

10 Yet = For. **forsaken.** See note on 1. 4.
consume = devour.
11 the boughs, &c. = her harvest drieth up.
they. Fem., i. e. the "stones" of *v.* 9.
broken off = broken, or destroyed.
12 in that day: *vv.* 12, 13 refer to Israel, as *vv.* 7, 10, and 11 refer to Israel's enemies.
beat off: i.e. as olives from a tree = "beat off [his fruit]": i.e. gather the sons of Israel.
channel = flood.
river: i.e. the Euphrates. **children** = sons.
13 ready to perish. So the end will be like the beginning. See Deut. 26. 5.
holy. See note on Ex. 3. 5. **mount** = mountain.

28. 1—35. 10 (*D*, p. 930). WOES. ALTERNATED WITH JEHOVAH'S GLORIES.
(*Repeated Alternation.*)

D | J¹ | K¹ | 28. 1-22. Ephraim (Samaria and Israel).
  L¹ | 28. 23-29. Jehovah the Instructor.
J² | K² | 29. 1-21. Jerusalem and Lebanon.
  L² | 29. 22-24. Jehovah the Redeemer.
J³ | K³ | 30. 1-17. The Egyptian League.
  L³ | 30. 18-33. Jehovah the gracious One.
J⁴ | K⁴ | 31. 1-9. Apostates.
  L⁴ | 32. 1-20. Jehovah the righteous King.
J⁵ | K⁵ | 33. 1-12. The Assyrian spoiler.
  L⁵ | 33. 13-24. Jehovah the King in His beauty.
J⁶ | K⁶ | 34. 1-17. Gentile nations.
  L⁶ | 35. 1-10. Jehovah, the King in His glory.

28. 1-22 (K¹, above). EPHRAIM. (SAMARIA AND ISRAEL). (*Introversions and Alternation.*)

K¹ | M | n | 1. Ephraim. Pride.
  o | 2-6. Jehovah the Instructor.
  n | 7, 8. Judah. Drink.
N | p | 9. Whom shall He teach.
  q | 10, 11. Teaching. Mocking.
N | *p* | 12. Refusal to hear.
  q | 13. Teaching. Threatening.
M | r | 14, 15. Judah. Scorners.
  s | 16, 17. Jehovah's foundation.
  r | 18-22. Judah. Scorners.

1 Woe = Ho! We now come (in *D*, see above) to a cycle of woes corresponding with the "burdens" (in D, p. 930). In these "woes" Jehovah's purpose is alternately thrown into sharp contrast (see the Structure of *D*, above).
crown of pride = pride's crown, or proud crown (i.e. Samaria; cp. Amos 6. 1, 3). Fig. *Enallagē* (Ap. 6). Referring to the circle of towers which girdled Samaria.
to = of.
Ephraim = one tribe. Put by Fig. *Metonymy* (of Adjunct), Ap. 6, for all the tribes of Israel.
a fading flower. Cp. 1. 30; 40. 7.
fat = rich, or luxuriant.
wine. Heb. *yayin.* Ap. 27. I.
2 Behold. Fig. *Asterismos* (Ap. 6).
the LORD* = Jehovah (Ap. 4. II). One of 134 places where "Jehovah" of the primitive text was changed to "Adonai"; so some codices, with two early printed editions. See Ap. 32.
hath a mighty and strong one = hath a mighty one, immensely strong: i.e. Assyria (2 Kings 17. 5, 6; 18. 10).
cast down = cast [Ephraim] down.
4 be = become. **and.** Omit.

hasty fruit = early fig [becomes]. **seeth.** The A.V. of 1611 had "seeth it". **eateth it up** = swalloweth it. **5 the LORD of hosts.** See note on 1. 9. **6 spirit.** Heb. *rūach.* Ap. 9. **turn** = turn, or drive, back. **7 they.** Referring to Judah. **strong drink.** Heb. *shēkār.* Ap. 27. IV. **judgment** = pronouncing judgment. **8 tables.** Used at sacrificial feasts (Tabernacles, Harvest, &c.). 1 Sam. 20. 34. Ezek. 40. 39-43. Mal. 1. 7, 12. **9 Whom** = Whom [say they]. **milk . . . breasts?** (Two questions.) **10 For** = For [say they] mimicking the prophet as though he were teaching little children in a school. **must be:** or, [hath been]. The verse then reads:

"For it is *ẓav lāẓāv, ẓav lāẓāv*
ḳav lāḳāv, ḳav lāḳāv
zeʿēr shām, zeʿēr shām."

The Figs. *Epizeuxis* and *Paronomasia* (Ap. 6), for emphasis. It may be Englished by: "Law upon law, Saw upon saw".

649-588 cept upon precept; line upon line, line upon
line; here a little, *and* there a little:
11 °**For with °stammering lips and °another tongue will °He speak to this People.**

p (p. 964) 12 °To whom He said, "This *is* the rest *wherewith* ye may cause the weary to rest; and this *is* the refreshing:" yet they would not hear.

q 13 But the word of [5] the LORD °was unto them precept upon precept, precept upon precept; line upon line, line upon line; here a little, *and* there a little; that they °might go, and °fall backward, and be broken, and snared, and °taken.

M r 14 Wherefore hear the word of [5] the LORD, ye scornful °men, that rule this People which *is* in Jerusalem.
15 Because ye have said, "We have °made a covenant with death, and with °hell are we at agreement; when the overflowing scourge shall pass through, it shall not come unto us: for we have made lies our refuge, and under falsehood have we hid ourselves:"

s 16 Therefore thus saith °the Lord GOD, °"**Behold, °I lay °in Zion for a foundation °a stone, °a tried stone, a precious corner *stone*, °a sure foundation: he that believeth shall °not make haste.**
17 °Judgment also will I lay to the line, and righteousness to the plummet: and the hail shall sweep away the refuge of lies, and the waters shall overflow the hiding place.

r 18 And your [15] covenant with death shall be disannulled, and your agreement with [15] hell shall not stand; when the overflowing scourge shall pass through, then ye shall be trodden down by it.
19 From the time that it goeth forth it shall °take you: for morning by morning shall it pass over, by day and by night: and it shall be a °vexation only *to* understand the °report.
20 For °the bed is shorter than that *a man* can stretch himself *on it:* and the covering narrower than that he can wrap himself *in it.*
21 For [5] the LORD shall rise up as *in* mount °Perazim, He shall be wroth as *in* the valley of °Gibeon, that He may do His work, °His strange work; and bring to pass His act, °His strange act."
22 Now therefore be ye not mockers, lest your bands be made strong: for I have heard from [16] the Lord GOD of hosts a consumption, even determined, upon the whole °earth.

L[1] t (p. 965) 23 Give ye ear, and hear My voice; hearken, and hear My speech.
24 Doth the plowman °plow all day to sow? doth °he open and break the clods of his ground?
25 When he hath made plain the face thereof, doth he not cast abroad the fitches, and scatter

11 For = Yea, verily. Taking the words out of their own taunting lips, and turning them against themselves. Quoted in 1 Cor. 14. 21.
stammering = jabbering.
another = foreign. Referring to the Assyrian language they were (alas!) soon to hear (cp. 33. 19. Deut. 28. 49). **He speak**: i.e. by the Assyrians.
12 To whom He said: or, He (Jehovah) Who said to them: i.e. by His prophets (7. 4; 8. 6; 30. 15. Jer. 6. 16).
13 was = became. Giving back to the scoffers their own words (from *v.* 10) in the form of a threatening.
might = may.
fall backward, &c. Note the Fig. *Synonymia* (Ap. 6), by which the similar words are heaped together to impress on them the solemnity and certainty of the judgment. **taken** = caught.
14 men. Pl. of *'ĕnōsh.* Ap. 14. III.
15 made = cut, or solemnised.
made a covenant. It is alleged that the use of the word "covenant" is confined to Jehovah by the "second Isaiah" (i.e. after ch. 40): but it is so used before that (see 24. 5; 33. 8). But why should not a covenant be made with, and by, other parties as it is here in 28. 15, 18? See Ap. 79. II.
hell. Heb. Sheōl. Ap. 35.
16 the Lord GOD = Heb. Adonai Jehovah. See Ap. 4. VIII (2).
Behold. Fig. *Asterismos* (Ap. 6), emphasising the contrast between the false foundation of *v.* 15 with the true foundation. (This is quoted in Rom. 9. 33. 1 Pet. 2. 6.)
I lay = I have laid. So the Syr. and Sept. Laid, in the counsels of eternity: in Abraham's promise (Gen. 12); in David's covenant (2 Sam. 7).
in Zion. In Zion; not Zion itself.
a stone. This is a distinct reference to Gen. 49. 24. It is the Immanuel (of ch. 7), the promised Son (of ch. 9), the rod from Jesse's stem (of ch. 11).
a tried stone = a test stone: i.e. tested itself, and testing others. Cp. *v.* 17, and Zech. 3. 9.
a sure foundation. Fig. *Polyptōton* (Ap. 6), for emphasis. Heb. a foundation founded: i.e. a well-founded foundation, or a firm or sure foundation.
not make haste = be constant, steady, not fleeing away. See note on Prov. 8. 30. Note the Fig. *Metonymy* (of Subject), Ap. 6; by which the hastening, or flight, is put for the confusion and shame which is the cause of it. Sept. reads "ashamed". In Rom. 9. 33; 10. 11. 1 Pet. 2. 6, the Fig. is translated, and means therefore exactly the same thing: = shall have no need for hurried flight (cp. 49. 23).
17 Judgment also will I lay to the line, &c. = I will make judgment the line, and righteousness the plumb-line.
19 take you = take you away.
vexation = terror.
report = hearing. Put by Fig. *Metonymy* (of Adjunct), Ap. 6, for what is heard.
20 the bed, &c. This allegory is to show that their false security as to the approach of Sennacherib would afford them no real rest, it would soon be disturbed.
21 Perazim . . . Gibeon. This could not be known or understood without reference to 2 Sam. 5. 20, and Josh. 10. 10; and this reference must have been in writing: too long before (700 years) to be a matter of mere memory. See Ap. 92.
His strange work = strange His work [is]. Heb. *zūr* = foreign.
His strange act = unwonted [is] His act. Heb. *nākar.*
22 earth = land, or soil.

28. 23-29 (L[1], p. 964). JEHOVAH THE INSTRUCTOR. (*Alternation.*)

L[1] | t | 23-25. Ploughing and sowing.
  | u | 26. Divine instruction.
  | *t* | 27, 28. Threshing.
  | *u* | 29. Divine instruction.

24 plow all day: i.e. continually = ever keep ploughing? See the note on *v.* 28. **he open** = he [for ever] open.

649-588 the cummin, and cast in °the principal wheat and the appointed barley and the rie in their °place?

u (p. 965) 26 °For his °God doth instruct him to discretion, *and* doth teach him.

t 27 For the fitches are not threshed with a °threshing instrument, neither is a cart wheel turned about upon the cummin; but the fitches are beaten out with a staff, and the cummin with a rod.

28 °Bread *corn* is °bruised; °because he will not °ever be threshing it, nor break *it with* the wheel of his cart, nor °bruise it *with* his horsemen.

u 29 °This also cometh forth from [5] the LORD of hosts, *Which* is wonderful in counsel, *and* °excellent in °working.

J[2] K[2] v (p. 966) **29** °Woe °to °Ariel, to Ariel, °the city *where* David °dwelt! add ye °year to year; °let them kill sacrifices.

2 Yet I will distress [1] Ariel, and there shall be heaviness and sorrow: and it shall be unto Me °as Ariel.

3 And I will camp against thee round about, and will lay siege against thee with a mount, and I will raise forts against thee.

4 And thou shalt be brought down, *and* shalt speak out of the °ground, and thy speech shall be low out of the dust, and thy voice shall be, as of one that hath °a familiar spirit, out of the °ground, and thy speech shall °whisper out of the dust.

5 Moreover the multitude of thy °strangers shall be °like small dust, and the multitude of the °terrible ones *shall be* as chaff that passeth away: yea, it shall be at an instant suddenly.

6 Thou shalt be °visited of °the LORD of hosts with thunder, and with earthquake, and great noise, with storm and tempest, and the flame of devouring fire.

7 And the multitude of all the nations that fight against °Ariel, even all that fight against her and her munition, and that distress her, shall be as a dream of a night vision.

8 It shall even be °as when an hungry *man* dreameth, and, behold, he eateth; but he awaketh, and his °soul is empty: or as when a thirsty man dreameth, and, behold, he drinketh; but he awaketh, and, behold, *he is* faint, and his °soul hath appetite: so shall the multitude of all the nations be, that fight against mount Zion.

w 9 Stay yourselves, and wonder; cry ye out, and cry: they are drunken, but not with °wine; they stagger, but not with °strong drink.

10 For °**the LORD °hath poured out upon you the °spirit of deep sleep,** and hath closed your eyes: the prophets and your rulers, the seers hath He covered.

11 And the vision °of all is become unto you as the words of a °book that is sealed, which *men* deliver to one that is learned, saying, "Read this, I pray thee:" and he saith, "I cannot; for it *is* sealed:"

12 And the [11] book is delivered to him that is not learned, saying, "Read this, I pray thee:" and he saith, "I am not learned."

x 13 Wherefore °the LORD * °said, "Forasmuch as **this people draw near *Me* with their mouth, and with their lips do honour Me,** °but have

---

25 the principal wheat=wheat in rows. Only here.
place=due order. Connect "appointed" with "place", not with "barley".

26 For his God, &c. Render: "For One hath instructed him in the right course; his God doth teach him". **God.** Heb. Elohim. Ap. 4. I.

27 threshing instrument. Only here, and 41. 15.

28 Bread=Corn. Bread is put by Fig. *Metonymy* (of Effect), Ap. 6, for the corn of which it is made. Cp. Job 28. 5.

bruised=crushed: i.e. reduced to powder. Cp. Ex. 32. 20. 2 Kings 23. 6. Render, as a question: Is corn crushed?

because=nay. The Heb. accent *t^ebīr* is disjunctive and requires this rendering. Cp. R.V. marg., and Job 22. 2. **ever**=for ever.

29 This: i.e. this same design in His treatment of His people. His purpose is the same as that of the husbandman. Cp. Amos 9. 9.

excellent=lofty.

working=wisdom. The sort of wisdom which carries the purpose through to permanency. Heb. *tūshīyah.* See note on Prov. 2. 7.

29. 1-21 (K[2], p. 964). JERUSALEM AND LEBANON. (*Extended Alternation.*)

K[2] | v | 1-8. Woe. Jerusalem.
  w | 9-12. Stupefaction.
   x | 13, 14. Reason.
 v | 15-17. Woe. Lebanon.
  w | 18, 19. Illumination.
   x | 20, 21. Reason.

1 Woe. The second of the six woes, indicated in the Structure (*D*, p. 930).

to Ariel. Note the Fig. *Epizeuxis* (Ap. 6). See note on 24. 16.

Ariel=either a lion of GOD (El, Ap. 4. IV) (2 Sam. 23. 20); or the altar-hearth of GOD (Ezek. 43. 15, 16; and the Moabite Stone, line 12, Ap. 54). Jerusalem is called Har-el on old Egyptian monuments.

the city. Put by Fig. *Polyonymia* (Ap. 6) for Jerusalem. "City" is in the construct state:=city of [the spot] where David camped.

dwelt=encamped.

year. Put by Fig. *Metonymy* (of Adjunct), Ap. 6, for festival.

let them kill, &c.: or, let the feasts go round. Fig. *Eironeia.* Ap. 6.

2 as Ariel=as a veritable hearth of GOD.

4 ground=earth.

a familiar spirit=an *Ob.* See note on Lev. 19. 31.

whisper=peep, chirp, or mutter.

5 strangers: i.e. adversaries.

like, &c. . . . as, &c. Fig. *Hyperbole.* Ap. 6.

terrible ones=tyrants.

6 visited. These judgments (in *v.* 6) refer to the deliverance from Jerusalem's enemies.

the LORD of hosts. See note on 1 Sam. 1. 3.

7 Ariel. Here it is plainly Jerusalem.

8 as=according as.

soul. Heb. *nephesh.* Ap. 13.

9 wine. Heb. *yayin.* Ap. 27. I.

strong drink. Heb. *shēkār.* Ap. 27. IV.

10 the LORD. Heb. Jehovah. Ap. 4. II.

hath poured, &c. Quoted in Rom. 11. 8.

spirit. Heb. *rūach.* Ap. 9.

11 of all=of the whole, or altogether.

book=scroll, or document, in writing.

13 the LORD*. One of the 134 places where the *Sopherim* say they changed Jehovah of the primitive text to Adonai. See Ap. 32.

said. Quoted in Matt. 15. 7-9. Mark 7. 6.

but=though.

649-588 **removed their heart far from Me, and their fear toward Me is °taught by the precept of °men:**
14 Therefore, behold, I will proceed to do a marvellous work among this People, *even* a marvellous work and a wonder: °for **the °wisdom of their wise *men* shall perish, and the °understanding of their prudent *men* shall be hid."**

v 15 Woe unto them that seek deep to hide their counsel from [10]the LORD, and their works are in the dark, and they say, "Who seeth us? and who knoweth us?"
16 Surely your turning of things upside down shall be esteemed as the potter's clay: for shall the work °say of him that made it, "He made me not?" or shall the thing framed say of him that framed it, "He had no [14]understanding"?
17 *Is* it not yet a very little while, and Lebanon shall be turned into a fruitful field, and the fruitful field shall be esteemed as a forest?

w 18 And in that day shall the deaf hear the words of the °book, and the eyes of the blind shall see out of obscurity, and out of darkness.
19 The °meek also shall increase *their* joy in [10]the LORD, and the °poor among °men shall rejoice in °the Holy One of Israel.

x 20 For °the terrible one is brought to nought, and the scorner is consumed, and all that watch for °iniquity are cut off:
21 That °make a [19]man an offender for a word, and lay a snare for him that °reproveth in the gate, and turn aside the °just for °a thing of nought.

L² y (p. 967) 22 Therefore thus saith [10]the LORD, Who redeemed °Abraham, concerning °the house of Jacob, "Jacob shall not now be ashamed, neither shall °his face now wax pale.

z 23 But when he seeth his °children, the work of Mine hands, in the midst of him,

z they shall sanctify My °name, and sanctify [19]the Holy One of Jacob, and shall fear °the God of Israel.

y 24 They also that erred in [10]spirit °shall come to [14]understanding, and they that murmured shall °learn doctrine."

K³ O **30** °"Woe to the °rebellious °children," saith °the LORD, "that °take counsel, but not of Me; and that °cover with a covering, but not of °My Spirit, that they may add °sin to °sin:
2 That °walk to go down into Egypt, and have not asked at My mouth; to strengthen themselves in the °strength of Pharaoh, and to °trust in the shadow of Egypt!

P 3 Therefore shall the [2]strength of Pharaoh be your shame, and the [2]trust in the shadow of Egypt *your* confusion.
4 For °his princes were at °Zoan, and his ambassadors came to °Hanes.
5 They were all ashamed of a people *that* could not profit them, nor be an help nor profit, but a shame, and also a reproach."

---

taught by the precept of men = a commandment of men in which they have been schooled: i.e. taught by rote.
men = mortals. Heb. pl. of *'ĕnōsh.* Ap. 14. III.
14 for. Quoted in 1 Cor. 1. 19.
wisdom. Heb. *chākam.* } See notes on
understanding. Heb. *bīnāh.* } Prov. 1. 2.
16 say. Cp. 45. 9.
18 book = scroll. **19 meek** = oppressed.
poor = oppressed. Heb. *'ebyōn.* See note on Prov. 6. 11.
men. Heb. *'ādām.* Ap. 14. I.
the Holy One of Israel. See note on Isa. 1. 4.
20 the terrible one = the tyrant.
iniquity. Heb. *'āven.* Ap. 44. iii.
21 make a man an offender for a word = who bring a man into condemnation by a word (i.e. by false witness).
reproveth = decideth: i.e. in judgment.
just = righteous.
a thing of nought. See note on "confusion", 24. 10.

29. 22-24 (L², p. 964). **JEHOVAH THE REDEEMER.** (*Introversion.*)

L² | y | 22. The word of Jehovah. Spoken.
z | 23-. The work of Jehovah. Seen.
z | -23. The work of Jehovah. Effect.
y | 24. The word of Jehovah. Understood.

22 Abraham. Ref. to Pent. as well known. Ap. 92.
the house of Jacob. See note on 2. 5.
his face . . . wax pale. Put by Fig. *Metonymy* (of Adjunct), Ap. 6, for fear.
23 children = young children.
the God of Israel. This expression occurs seven times in Isaiah (here; 41. 17; 45. 3, 15; 48. 1, 2; 52. 12). Elsewhere twenty-nine times, without Jehovah preceding (Gen. 33. 20. Ex. 24. 10. Num. 16. 9. Josh. 22. 16. 1 Sam. 1. 17; 5. 7, 8, 8, 8, 10, 11; 6. 3, 5; 25. 32. 2 Sam. 23. 3. Ezra 3. 2; 8. 35; 9. 4. 1 Chron. 4. 10; 5. 26. 2 Chron. 29. 7. Ps. 69. 6. Ezek. 8. 4; 9. 3; 10. 19, 20; 11. 22; 43. 2).
24 shall come, &c. = shall know discernment.
learn doctrine = accept instruction.

30. 1-17 (K³, p. 964). **THE EGYPTIAN LEAGUE.** (*Extended Alternation and Introversion.*)

K³ | O | 1, 2. Rebellion against Jehovah.
P | 3-5. Egypt. Disappointment from.
Q | a | 6. Property. Removal.
b | 7. Reason. Egypt's help, vain.
O | 8-11. Rebellion against Jehovah.
P | 12-14. Egypt. Destruction of.
Q | *b* | 15. Egypt's help, vain.
a | 16, 17. Persons. Flight.

1 Woe. The third of the six woes (see *D*, p. 930).
rebellious = stubborn, or backsliding.
children = sons.
the LORD. Heb. Jehovah. Ap. 4. II.
take counsel = carry out a purpose.
cover with a covering: or, pour out a libation; and so, make an alliance.
My Spirit = Me. Heb. *rūach.* Ap. 9.
sin. Heb. *chata.* Ap. 44. i.
2 walk = are setting out. This prophecy had been given in the days of Hezekiah (617-588), and was then being fulfilled in Israel.
strength of Pharaoh. Cp. *v.* 7, where it is shown to be a vain help. In *vv.* 2, 3, "strength" is literal. In *v.* 7 it is a Figure.
trust = flee for refuge to. Heb. *hāṣah.* Ap. 69. II. Same word as in *v.* 3, but not the same as in *v.* 12.
4 his: i.e. Pharaoh's.
Zoan. Now *Ẓān.* In the time of Moses it was the capital or court of Pharaoh, and the scene of his miracles (Ps. 78. 12, 43), and the seat of wisdom (19. 11, 13). Occurs elsewhere Num. 13. 22. Ezek. 30. 14. At Zoan began the exodus. **Hanes.** Called Tahapanes (Jer. 2. 16). Now *Tell Defenneh,* about seventy miles from Cairo, the capital of a minor district. Succeeded Memphis as the capital before Abraham's time. Known to the Greeks as Hiracleopolis Magna. The name occurs only here in Scripture.

Q a (p. 967) 649–588 6 The °burden of the beasts of °the south: into the land of trouble and anguish, from whence *come* the young and old lion, °the viper and fiery flying serpent, they will carry their °riches upon the shoulders of young asses, and their treasures upon the bunches of camels, °to a people *that* shall not profit *them*.

b 7 For the Egyptians shall help in vain, and to no purpose: therefore °have I cried concerning this, °"Their strength *is* to sit still."

O 8 Now go, write it before them in °a table, and °note it in a book, that it may be for °the time to come for ever and ever:

9 That this *is* a rebellious People, lying °children, °children *that* will not hear the °law of [1]the LORD:

10 Which say to the seers, "See not;" and to the prophets, "Prophesy not unto us right things, speak unto us smooth things, prophesy deceits:

11 Get you out of the way, turn aside out of the °path, cause °the Holy One of Israel to cease from before us."

P 12 Wherefore thus saith [11]the Holy One of Israel, "Because ye despise this word, and °trust in oppression and perverseness, and stay thereon:

13 Therefore this °iniquity shall be to you as a breach ready to fall, swelling out in a high wall, whose breaking cometh suddenly at an instant.

14 And He shall break it °as the breaking of the potters' vessel that is broken in pieces; He shall not spare: so that there shall not be found in the bursting of it a sherd to take °fire from the hearth, or to take water *withal* out of the °pit."

Q b 15 For thus saith °the Lord GOD, [11]the Holy One of Israel; "In returning and rest shall ye be saved; in quietness and in °confidence shall be your °strength: and ye would not.

a 16 But ye said, 'No; for we will °flee upon °horses;' therefore °shall ye flee: and, 'We will ride upon the °swift;' therefore shall they that pursue you be °swift.

17 °One thousand °*shall flee* at the °rebuke of one; at the °rebuke of five shall °ye flee: till ye be left as °a beacon upon the top of a mountain, and as an °ensign on an hill."

L^3 c^1 (p. 968) 18 And therefore will [1]the LORD wait, that He may °be gracious unto you, and therefore will He be exalted, that He may °have mercy upon you: for [1]the LORD *is* a °God of judgment: °blessed *are* all they that °wait for Him.

19 For the people shall dwell in Zion at Jerusalem: thou shalt weep no more: He will be very gracious unto thee at the voice of thy cry; when He shall hear it, He will answer thee.

20 And °*though* the °LORD* give you the bread of adversity, and the water of afflic-

6 burden. Refers to the lading of the animals of the ambassadors who were going down to Egypt with rich gifts to secure an alliance, and thus reversing the steps of their national deliverance. It is not a fresh "burden", "the beginning of which has been lost".

the south = *the Negeb*, which must be passed through to get to Egypt. See notes on Gen. 13. 1, and Ps. 126. 4.

the viper, &c. Ref. to Pent. (Deut. 8. 15). Occurs in Isaiah only here, and in 59. 5. Ap. 92.

riches. Heb. *ḥāyil* = strength. Put by Fig. *Metonymy* (of Adjunct), Ap. 6, for the riches or treasures carried by it.

to = [relying] upon: i.e. the Egyptians, as stated in preceding clause.

7 have I cried concerning this = have I called (or named) her.

Their strength, &c. Heb. Egypt—sitting still (and thus not giving the help that was being sought). Rahab = pride, or strength, is put by Fig. *Metonymy* (of Adjunct), Ap. 6, for Egypt, the proud or strong one. Note the wrong but common use of this verse, through not heeding the context.

8 a table = a tablet.

note = inscribe. Ref. to Pent. (Ex. 17. 14; 24. 4; 34. 27, 28. Num. 33. 2. Deut. 31. 9, 24). Ap. 92.

the time to come = the latter day.

9 children = sons.

law: or, instruction contained in the law of Moses. See note on 1. 10.

11 path. See note on 2. 3.

the Holy One of Israel. See note on 1. 4. Ps. 71. 22.

12 trust = confide. Heb. *bāṭaḥ* (Ap. 69. i). Not the same word as in *vv.* 2, 3. Same as in *v.* 15.

13 iniquity. Heb. *'āvāh*. Ap. 44. iv.

14 as the breaking of the potters' vessel. The reference is to the manufacture of *ḥomrah*, by breaking up pottery to powder in order to make cement of it. Carried on in the valley of Hinnom. See note on Jer. 19. 1, 2.

fire from the hearth = that which is kindled.

pit = cistern.

15 the Lord GOD. Heb. Adonai Jehovah. Ap. 4. VIII.

confidence = trust: i.e. trust [in Jehovah]. Heb. *bāṭaḥ*, as in *v.* 12. Ap. 69. i.

strength = real power. Heb. *gᵉbūrah*. Not the same word as in *vv.* 2, 3: but the same as in 28. 6.

16 flee . . . horses . . . shall ye flee. Note the Fig. *Paronomasia* (Ap. 6). Heb. *nānūs . . . sūs . . . tᵉnūsūn*, for emphasis.

swift . . . shall they . . . be swift. Fig. *Paronomasia* (Ap. 6). Heb. *ḳal . . . yiḳḳallū*, for emphasis; not a mere "play on words".

17 One thousand shall flee. Ref. to Pent. (Lev. 26. 8. Deut. 28. 25; 32. 30). Ap. 92.

shall flee. The Fig. *Ellipsis* (Ap. 6) is correctly supplied from the next clause.

rebuke = threat.

ye flee = ye [all] flee.

a beacon = a pole, or mast. **ensign** = flagstaff.

30. 18–33 (L^3, p. 964). JEHOVAH THE GRACIOUS ONE. (*Repeated Alternation.*)

L^3 | c^1 | 18–21. Blessing for Israel. Spiritual.
d^1 | 22. Judgment on idols.
c^2 | 23–26. Blessing for Israel. Temporal.
d^2 | 27, 28. Judgment on nations.
c^3 | 29. Blessing for Israel. Spiritual.
d^3 | 30–33. Judgment on Assyria.

18 be gracious = show you favour, or grace.

have mercy upon you = show you compassion.

God. Heb. Elohim. Ap. 4. I.

blessed = O the happinesses [of all, &c.]. The first of three in Isaiah (32. 20; 56. 2).

wait = look for. **20 though.** Omit "though", and read it as a direct promise: "Jehovah will give you affliction [as] bread and adversity [as] water". **LORD*** = Jehovah (Ap. 4. II). One of the 134 places where the *Sopherim* changed Jehovah of the primitive text for Adonai (Ap. 32). Some codices, with three early printed editions, read "Jehovah" in the text.

649-588 tion, °yet shall not thy °teachers °be removed into a °corner any more, but thine eyes shall °see thy °teachers:

21 And thine ears shall hear a word behind thee, saying, "This *is* the way, walk ye in it," when ye turn to the right hand, and when ye turn to the left.

d[1] (p. 968) 22 Ye shall defile also the °covering of thy graven images of silver, and the °ornament of thy molten images of gold: thou shalt cast them away as a menstruous cloth; thou shalt say unto it, "Get thee hence."

c[2] 23 Then shall He give the rain of °thy seed, that thou shalt sow the ground withal; and bread of the increase of the °earth, and it shall be fat and plenteous: in that day shall thy cattle feed in large pastures.

24 The oxen likewise and the young asses that °ear the ground shall eat clean provender, which hath been winnowed with the shovel and with the fan.

25 And there shall be upon every high mountain, and upon every high hill, rivers *and* °streams of waters in the day of the great slaughter, when the towers fall.

26 Moreover the light of the moon shall be as the light of the sun, and the light of the sun shall be sevenfold, as the light of seven days, in the day that [1]the LORD bindeth up the breach of His People, and healeth the stroke of their wound.

d[2] 27 °Behold, °the name of [1]the LORD cometh from far, burning *with* His anger, and the burden *thereof is* heavy: His lips are full of indignation, and His tongue as a devouring fire:

28 And His °breath, as an overflowing stream, shall reach to the midst of the neck, to sift the nations with the sieve of vanity: and *there shall be* a bridle in the jaws of the °people, causing *them* to err.

c[3] 29 Ye shall have a song, as in the night °*when* a °holy solemnity is kept; and gladness of heart, as when one goeth with a pipe to come into °the mountain of [1]the LORD, to the °mighty One of Israel.

d[3] 30 And [1]the LORD shall cause His glorious voice to be heard, and shall shew the lighting down of His arm, with the indignation of *His* anger, and *with* the flame of a devouring fire, *with* scattering, and tempest, and hailstones.

31 For through the voice of [1]the LORD shall the Assyrian be beaten down, *which* smote with a rod.

32 And *in* °every place where the grounded staff shall pass, which [1]the LORD shall lay upon him, *it* shall be with °tabrets and harps: and in battles of °shaking will He fight with it.

33 For °Tophet *is* ordained of old; yea, for °the king it is prepared; He hath made *it* deep *and* large: the pile thereof *is* fire and much wood; the °breath of [1]the LORD, like a stream of brimstone, doth kindle it.

K[4] e[1] (p. 969) **31** °Woe to them that go °down to Egypt for help; and stay on horses, and °trust in chariots, because *they are* many; and in horsemen, because they are very strong;

but they look not unto °the Holy One of Israel, °neither seek °the LORD! f[1]

2 Yet He also *is* wise, and will bring °evil, and will not call back His words: but will arise against the house of the °evildoers, and against the help of them that work °iniquity.

---

yet shall not thy teachers = and thy teachers shall not.
corner. Heb. occurs only here.
teachers. Perhaps pl. of Majesty = thy great Teacher (i.e. Jehovah).
be removed into a corner = hide Himself.
see = be clearly seeing.
22 covering. Heb. *ẓāphā(ẓippōi)*. Ref. to Pent. Occurs only here, Ex. 38. 17, 19, and Num. 16. 38, 39. Ap. 92.
ornament. Heb. *'āphuddah* (rendered ephod). Ref. to Pent. Occurs only here, Ex. 28. 8, and 39. 5.
23 thy seed. Another reading (Ben Naphtali) is "thy land".
earth = ground, or soil.
24 ear. Old English = to plough: from Anglo-Saxon *erian*: and this from the Latin *arare*: the Aryan root AR entering into many words with a cognate reference. ARt (ploughing being the oldest art); oAR (with which the water is ploughed); ARtos (Greek for bread); eARth; ARatrum (Latin, a plough); ARare (to plough). The verb "ear" is found only here, Deut. 21. 4, and 1 Sam. 8. 12. The noun "earing" occurs in Gen. 45. 6, and Ex. 34. 21.
25 streams. Heb. *yiblēi* (from *yābal* = to bring, or conduct along). Occurs only here in the "former" portion, and only in 44. 4, in the "latter" portion of Isaiah, where it is rendered "watercourses". Ap. 79. II.
27 Behold. Fig. *Asterismos*. Ap. 6.
the name. See note on Ps. 20. 1.
28 breath = blast. Heb. *rūach*. Ap. 9. See note on 25. 4.
people = peoples.
29 when a holy solemnity is kept. Ref. to Pent. and the habitual keeping of the feasts there prescribed (Lev. 23. 2, &c.). See Ap. 92.
holy. See note on Ex. 3. 5.
the mountain of the LORD. See notes on 2. 3, and Ezek. 28. 16.
mighty One = Rock. Ref. to Pent. (Deut. 32. 4, 15, 18, 30, 31). Cp. Isa. 26. 4. Ap. 92.
32 every place where the grounded staff, &c. = every stroke of the staff of doom, which, &c.
tabrets = drums. See note on 1 Sam. 10. 5. Heb. *toph*, forming the Fig. *Paronomasia* with *Tophet* in next verse, for emphasis (Ap. 6).
shaking = tumult.
33 Tophet = the place of burning. In the valley of Hinnom, the place where continual fires consumed the refuse of Jerusalem. Cp. Rev. 19. 20; 20. 10.
the king = Moloch. See note on 1 Kings 11. 7.
breath. Heb. *nᵉshamah* (Ap. 16). See note on 2. 22.

31. 1-9 (K[4], p. 964). APOSTATES.
(*Repeated Alternation.*)

K[4] | e[1] | 1-. Trust in Egypt. Woe.
  f[1] | -1, 2. Jehovah. Rejection.
 e[2] | 3-. Trust in Egypt. Vain.
  f[2] | -3-6. Jehovah. Protection.
 e[3] | 7. Trust in Jehovah. Exhortation.
  f[3] | 8, 9. Jehovah. Deliverance.

1 Woe. The fourth of the six woes. See the Structure (*D*, p. 930).
down. It is always "down" to Egypt, geographically and morally.
trust = confide. Heb. *bāṭaḥ*. Ap. 69. i.
the Holy One of Israel. See note on 1. 4. Ps. 71. 22.
neither seek the LORD. Cp. 30. 2. Ref. to Pent. (Deut. 17. 16). Ap. 92.
the LORD. Heb. Jehovah (with *'eth*). Ap. 4. II.
2 evil . . . evildoers. Heb. *rā'a'*. Ap. 44. viii.
iniquity. Heb. *'āven*. Ap. 44. iii.

e^2 (p. 969) 3 Now the Egyptians *are* °men, and not °GOD;
and their horses °flesh, and not °spirit.
649-588 When [1] the LORD shall stretch out His hand,
f^2 both he that helpeth shall fall, and he that is
holpen shall fall down, and they all shall fail
together.
4 For thus hath [1] the LORD spoken unto me,
"Like as the lion and the young lion roaring
on his °prey, when a °multitude of shepherds is
called forth against him, *he* will not be afraid
of their voice, nor abase himself for the noise
of them: so shall °the LORD of hosts come
down to fight °for mount Zion, and °for the
hill thereof.
5 °As birds flying, so will [4] the LORD of hosts
°defend Jerusalem; °defending also He will deliver
it; and °passing over He will preserve *it.*"
6 °Turn ye unto *Him from* whom the °children
of Israel have deeply revolted.
e^3 7 "For in that day °every man shall cast away
his °idols of silver, and his °idols of gold, which
your own hands have made unto you *for* a °sin.
f^3 8 Then shall the Assyrian fall with the sword,
not of a °mighty man; and the sword, not of
a °mean man, shall devour him: but he shall
flee from the sword, and his young men shall
be °discomfited.
9 And he shall °pass over to his strong hold
for fear, and his princes shall be afraid of the
ensign," saith [1] the LORD, Whose fire *is* in
Zion, and His furnace in Jerusalem.

L^4 R (p. 970) **32** °Behold, °a king shall reign °in righteousness,
and princes shall rule °in
judgment.
S 2 °And a °man shall be as an hiding place
from the °wind, and a covert from the tempest;
as °rivers of water in a dry place, as the
shadow of a great rock in a °weary land.
T 3 [2] And the eyes of them that see shall not be dim,
and the ears of them that hear shall hearken.
4 °The heart also of the rash shall understand
knowledge, [2] and the tongue of the stammerers
shall be ready to speak plainly.
5 °The °vile person shall be no more called
°liberal, nor the °churl said *to be* bountiful.
6 For the °vile person will speak villany, and
his heart will work °iniquity, to practise hypocrisy,
and to utter error against °the LORD, to
make empty the °soul of the hungry, and he
will cause the drink of the thirsty to fail.
7 The °instruments also of the [5] churl *are*
°evil: **he** °deviseth °wicked °devices to destroy
the °poor with lying words, even when the
°needy speaketh right.
8 But the °liberal [7] deviseth °liberal things;
and by °liberal things shall **he** stand.
U i (pp. 970, 971) 9 Rise up, °ye women that are at ease; °hear
my voice, ye °careless daughters; give ear unto
my speech.

3 men, and not GOD. Fig. *Pleonasm* (Ap. 6). The statement put two ways for great emphasis (positive and negative). **men.** Heb. *'ādām.* Ap. 14. I.
GOD. Heb. 'El = the mighty God. Ap. 4. IV.
flesh, and not spirit. Fig. *Pleonasm* (Ap. 6). See above. **spirit.** Heb. *rūach.* Ap. 9.
4 prey = live prey. **multitude** = crowd.
the LORD of hosts. See note on 1. 9 and 1 Sam. 1. 3.
for : or, over.
5 As birds flying. As birds hovering [covering and protecting their nest with their wings], so will, &c. The Fig. *Ellipsis* is to be thus supplied. Ref. to Pent. (Deut. 32. 11). Ap. 92.
defend = shield. The verb is found only in Isaiah's utterances (2 Kings 19. 34, 20. 6. Isa. 31. 5; 37. 35; 38. 6; and Zech. 9. 15; 12. 8.
defending, &c. = shielding. Only used of God. Only here, 2 Kings 19. 34; 20. 6. Lit. "[then there will be] a shielding, and He will rescue; a passing over [as in Egypt at the Passover], and he will cause to escape."
passing over. Ref. to Pent. (Ex. 12. 13, 23, 27). Ap. 92. This word is nowhere else used in this sense.
6 Turn = Return. **children** = sons.
7 every man. Heb. *'īsh.* Ap. 14. II.
idols = nothings. **sin.** Heb. *chāṭā'.* Ap. 44. i.
8 mighty man. Heb. *'īsh.* Ap. 14. II.
mean man. Heb. *'ādām.* Ap. 14. I.
discomfited = become tributaries.
9 pass over. Not the same word as in *v.* 5 (which is *pāṣaḥ*). Here, Heb. *'ābar*, to cross over, or retreat.

32. 1-20 (L^4, p. 964). JEHOVAH'S RIGHTEOUS KING. (*Extended Alternation.*)

L^4 | R | 1. The king reigning in righteousness.
  S | 2. The Land. } Effect: Protection.
   T | 3-8. The People. }
    U | 9-14. Desolation.
 R | 15-. The Spirit poured out.
  S | -15-17. The Land. } Effect: Security.
   T | 18, 19. The People. }
    U | 20. Cultivation.

1 Behold. Fig. *Asterismos.* Ap. 6.
a king. Ref. to Pent. (Deut. 17. 14, 15). Ap. 92.
in = for, in the interest of.
2 And. Note the Fig. *Polysyndeton* (Ap. 6) in *vv.* 2-5, emphasising every detail.
man. Heb. *'īsh.* Ap. 14. II.
wind. Heb. *rūach.* Ap. 9.
rivers of water. Heb. *palgēi-māyim.* Channels for irrigation in a garden. See notes on Prov. 21. 1. Ps. 1. 3.
weary = thirsty.
4 The heart also = And the heart: preserving the Fig. *Polysyndeton* (*v.* 2). Ap. 6.
5 The vile person. Some codices, with two early printed editions, Sept., and Syr., read "And the", thus preserving the Fig. *Polysyndeton* (*v.* 1). Ap. 6.
vile person = fool. Heb. *nābal.* See note on Prov. 1. 7 and on 1 Sam. 25. 3. **liberal** = noble.
churl = miser, or covetous. Note the *Alternation* in *vv.* 5-7:—
g | 5-. vile.
 h | -5. churl.
g | 6. vile.
 h | 7. churl.
6 vile . . . villany. Note the Fig. *Paronomasia* (Ap. 6). Heb. *nābāl nebālāh.*
iniquity. Heb. *'āven.* Ap. 44. iii.
the LORD. Heb. Jehovah. Ap. 4. II.
soul. Heb. *nephesh.* Ap. 13.

7 instruments also of the churl. Note the Fig. *Paronomasia* (Ap. 6). Heb. *vekelay kēlayv.* Eng. chattels of the churl. **evil.** Heb. *rā'a'.* Ap. 44. viii. **deviseth** = counselleth. **wicked.** Heb. *rāshā'.* Ap. 44. x. **devices** = plans. **poor** = wretched. Heb. *'ānāh.* See note on Prov. 6. 11. **needy** = helpless, weak in will and wealth. Heb. *'ebyōn.* See note on Prov. 6. 11. **8 liberal** = noble: freehearted, freehanded.

32. 9-14 [For Structure see next page].

9 ye women. Fig. *Synecdoche* (of Species), "women" being put for the whole nation, now reduced by sin to utter weakness; or, a special message, as in 3. 16-26. **hear my voice.** Ref. to Pent. (Deut. 4. 33, 36), Ap. 92. **careless** = confident. Heb. *bāṭaḥ.* Ap. 69. i. Used here of self-confidence, in irony.

k (p. 971) 649–588 10 Many days and years shall ye be troubled, ye [9]careless women:
l for the vintage shall fail, the gathering shall not come.

i 11 Tremble, [9]ye women that are at ease; be troubled, ye [9]careless ones: strip you, and make you bare, and gird *sackcloth* upon *your* loins.

k 12 They shall lament for the teats, for the °pleasant fields, for the fruitful vine.
13 Upon the land of My people shall come up thorns *and* briers; yea, upon all the houses of joy *in* the joyous city:

l 14 Because the palaces shall be °forsaken; the multitude of the city shall be °left; the forts and towers shall be for dens °for ever, a joy of wild asses, a pasture of flocks;

R (p. 970) 15 Until the °spirit be °poured upon us from on high,
S and the wilderness be a fruitful field, and the fruitful field be counted for a forest.
16 Then judgment shall dwell in the wilderness, and righteousness remain in the fruitful field.
17 And the °work of righteousness shall be peace; and the effect of righteousness quietness and °assurance for ever.

T 18 And My People shall dwell in a peaceable habitation, and in sure dwellings, and in quiet resting places;
19 When it shall °hail, coming down on the forest; and the city shall be low in a low place.

U 20 °Blessed *are* ye that sow beside all waters, that send forth *thither* the feet of the ox and the ass.

K^5 m^1 (p. 971) 33 °Woe to thee °that spoilest, and thou *wast* not spoiled; and °dealest treacherously, and they dealt not treacherously with thee! when thou shalt cease to spoil, thou shalt be spoiled; *and* when thou shalt make an end to deal treacherously, they shall deal treacherously with thee.

n^1 2 O °LORD, be gracious unto us; we have waited for Thee: be Thou their °arm °every morning, our salvation also in the time of trouble.

m^2 3 At the noise of the tumult °the people fled; at the lifting up of Thyself °the nations were scattered.
4 And your spoil shall be gathered *like* the gathering of the °caterpiller: as the running to and fro of locusts shall He run upon them.

n^2 5 [2]The LORD is exalted; for He dwelleth on high: He hath filled Zion with judgment and righteousness.
6 And wisdom and knowledge shall be the stability of thy times, *and* strength of salvation: the fear of [2]the LORD °*is* his treasure.

m^3 7 °Behold, their valiant ones shall cry without: °the ambassadors of peace shall weep bitterly.
8 The °highways °lie waste, the °wayfaring man ceaseth: he hath broken the covenant, he hath despised the cities, he regardeth no °man.

9 The earth °mourneth *and* languisheth: Lebanon is ashamed *and* °hewn down: °Sharon is like a wilderness; and Bashan and Carmel °shake off *their fruits*.

10 "Now will I rise," °saith [2]the LORD; "now will I be exalted; now will I lift up Myself. n^3
11 Ye shall conceive chaff, ye shall bring forth stubble: your °breath, *as* fire, shall devour you.

---

32. 9–14 (U, p. 970). DESOLATION.
(*Extended Alternation.*)

U | i | 9. Women at ease. Call to hear.
  k | 10–. Trouble.
   l | –10. Reason.
 i | 11. Women at ease. Call to tremble.
  k | 12, 13. Trouble.
   l | 14. Reason.

12 pleasant fields = fields of desire. Fig. *Enallage.* Ap. 6.

14 forsaken = neglected.

left. See note on "forsake", 1. 4.

for ever. Fig. *Synecdoche* (of the Whole), Ap. 6. Put for a prolonged period. Note the limitation by the word "until" in the next verse.

15 spirit. Heb. *rūach.* Ap. 9. Cp. Joel 2. 28. Ezek. 36. 25–27.

poured. Heb. *'ārāh.* Occurs in Isa. 3. 17; 22. 6, and here in the "former" portion; and in 53. 12, the "latter" portion.

17 work = tillage.

assurance = confidence. Heb. *bāṭah* (Ap. 69. i). Same word as careless (*v.* 9), but not in irony.

19 hail, coming down. Note the Fig. *Paronomasia* (Ap. 6), for emphasis. Heb. *ūbārad beredeth*; Eng. *hail hailing.*

20 Blessed = O the happinesses of you, &c. The second of the three occurring in Isaiah. See note on 30. 18. Cp. 56. 2.

33. 1–12 (K^5, p. 964). THE ASSYRIAN SPOILER.
(*Repeated Alternation.*)

K^5 | m^1 | 1. The spoiler.
  n^1 | 2. Jehovah. Prayer to.
 m^2 | 3, 4. The spoiler.
  n^2 | 5, 6. Jehovah. Praise to.
 m^3 | 7–9. The spoiler.
  n^3 | 10–12. Jehovah. Answer of.

1 Woe. The fifth of the six Woes. See the Structure (*D*, p. 930). The Structure of K^5, above, will make this section quite clear, and show that the verses are not "out of place", or "disarranged".

that spoilest = thou plunderer.

dealest treacherously = thou traitor.

2 LORD. Heb. Jehovah. Ap. 4. II.

arm. Put by Fig. *Metonymy* (of Cause) for the strength and defence put forth by it. Ap. 6.

every morning: i. e. continually.

3 the people = peoples. the nations = nations.

4 caterpiller = locusts.

6 is = that [is].

7 Behold. Fig. *Asterismos.* Ap. 6.

the ambassadors. Note the Fig. *Asyndeton* (Ap. 6), in *vv.* 7–12.

8 highways. See note on 7. 3.

lie waste = are desolate. See note on 1. 7.

wayfaring man = he that walketh along the path. See note on "path", 2. 3.

man = mortal. Heb. *'ěnōsh.* Ap. 14. III.

9 mourneth. See note on 3. 26.

hewn down = withered.

Sharon. Occurs in the "former" portion, only here and 35. 2; and in the "latter" portion, only in 65. 10. Ap. 79. II.

shake off. Heb. *nā'ar.* A rare word. Occurs twice in the "former" portion (here, and *v.* 15), and once in the "latter" portion (52. 2). Ap. 79. II.

10 saith the LORD = may Jehovah say. See note on 1. 11.

11 breath, as fire = breath as a fire. Heb. *rūach.* Ap. 9.

649-588 12 And °the people shall be *as* the °burnings of lime: *as* °thorns cut up shall they be burned in the fire."

L^5 o^1 (p. 972) 13 Hear, °ye *that are* far off, °what I have done; and, ye *that are* near, acknowledge My might.

14 The sinners in Zion are afraid; °fearfulness hath °surprised the hypocrites. °Who °among us shall dwell with the devouring fire? °who among us shall dwell with everlasting burnings?

15 °He that walketh righteously, and speaketh uprightly; he that despiseth the gain of oppressions, that [9]shaketh his hands from holding of bribes, that stoppeth his ears from °hearing of °blood, and shutteth his eyes from seeing °evil;

16 °He shall dwell on high: his place of defence *shall be* the munitions of rocks: bread shall be given him; his waters *shall be* sure.

17 Thine eyes shall see °the king in his beauty: they shall behold the land that is very °far off.

p^1 18 Thine heart shall meditate terror. Where *is* the °scribe? where *is* the °receiver? where *is* °he that counted the towers?

19 Thou shalt not see a °fierce people, a people of a deeper speech than thou canst perceive; of a °stammering °tongue, *that thou canst* not understand.

o^2 20 °Look upon Zion, °the city of our °solemnities: thine eyes shall see Jerusalem a quiet habitation, a °tabernacle *that* shall not be taken down; not one of the stakes thereof shall ever be removed, neither shall any of the cords thereof be broken.

21 But there the glorious [2]LORD *will be* unto us a place of broad rivers *and* streams;

p^2 wherein shall go no galley with oars, neither shall °gallant ship pass thereby.

o^3 22 For [2]the LORD *is* our Judge, [2]the LORD *is* our Lawgiver, [2]the LORD *is* our King; He will save us.

p^3 23 Thy tacklings are loosed; they could not well strengthen their mast, they could not spread the sail: then is the prey of a great spoil divided; °the lame take the prey.

o^4 24 And the inhabitant shall not say, "I am sick:" the People that dwell therein *shall be* °forgiven *their* °iniquity.

K^6 V q **34** Come near, ye nations, to hear; and hearken, ye °people: let the earth hear, and all that is therein; the °world, and °all things that come forth of it.

2 For the indignation of °the LORD *is* upon all nations, and *His* fury upon all their armies: He hath °utterly destroyed them, He hath delivered them to the slaughter.

3 Their slain also shall be cast out, and their stink shall come up out of their carcases, and the °mountains shall be melted with their blood.

4 And all the host of heaven shall be dissolved, and the heavens shall be rolled together as a scroll: and all their host shall fall down, as the leaf falleth off from the vine, and as a falling fig from the fig tree.

r 5 For My sword shall be bathed in heaven:

12 the people = peoples.
burnings of lime: i.e. fuel for limekilns.
thorns cut up. These are the common fuel used in limekilns in Palestine.

33. 13-24 (L^5, p. 964). JEHOVAH. THE KING IN HIS BEAUTY. (*Repeated Alternation.*)

L^5 | o^1 | 13-17. The king. Seen in the Land.
| p^1 | 18, 19. Enemy not seen.
| o^2 | 20, 21-. The glorious Jehovah. Seen in Zion.
| p^2 | -21. Enemy not seen.
| o^3 | 22. Jehovah. Present to save.
| p^3 | 23. Enemy. Destroyed.
| o^4 | 24. Jehovah. His People forgiven.

13 ye: i.e. the heathen.
what I have done: i.e. in the destruction of Sennacherib's army.
14 fearfulness = trembling. Heb. *re'ādah.* Only here in Isaiah; and elsewhere, only in Job 4. 14. Pss. 2. 11; 48. 6. **surprised** = seized.
Who . . . ? who . . . ? Fig. *Erotēsis* (Ap. 6). The answer implied being the negative.
among = for.
15 He, &c. This is not the answer to *v.* 14, but the subject of the Promise in *v.* 16, "He . . shall dwell on high". Hence it is emphatic. Ref. to Pent. (Deut. 10. 17; 16. 19; 27. 25). Ap. 92. **hearing of** = listening to.
blood = murderers. Fig. *Metalepsis* (of Subject), Ap. 6; by which "blood" is first put for bloodshedding, and, secondly, bloodshedding put for those who shed it.
evil. Heb. *rā'a'.* Ap. 44. x.
17 the king. See *v.* 22. **far off** = far stretching.
18 scribe = the counter. **receiver** = the weigher.
he that counted, &c. Referring to Sennacherib's besieging army.
19 fierce, &c. Ref. to Pent. (Deut. 28. 49, 50). Ap. 92.
stammering = jabbering.
tongue. Put by Fig. *Metonymy* (of Cause), Ap. 6, for the language spoken by it.
20 Look = Gaze.
the city. Fig. *Polyonymia.* Ap. 6.
solemnities = festal-days. Ref. to Pent., where the word frequently occurs (cp. Lev. 23. Num. 15, &c.). Ap. 79. II.
tabernacle = tent. Heb. *'ohel.* Ap. 40. 3.
21 gallant = mighty, or noble.
23 the lame take the prey. Referring to the spoil taken from the dead of the Assyrian host. See 2 Kings 19. 35.
24 forgiven their iniquity. Ref. to Pent. (Ex. 23. 21; 32. 32. Num. 14. 19).
iniquity. Heb. *'āvāh.* Ap. 44. iv.

34. 1-17 (K^6, p. 964). GENTILE NATIONS. (*Extended Alternations.*)

K^6 | V | 1-8. Nations and armies.
| W | 9, 10. The land.
| X | 11-. Wild creatures.
| Y | -11. The line of confusion.
| *V* | 12. Nobles and Princes.
| *W* | 13-. The land.
| *X* | -13-16. Wild creatures.
| *Y* | 17. The line of confusion.

1-8 (V, above). NATIONS AND ARMIES. (*Introversion.*)

V | q | 1-4. Wrath.
| r | 5, 6-. Sword.
| *r* | -6, 7. Sacrifice.
| *q* | 8. Vengeance.

1 people = peoples.
world = the inhabited world. Heb. *tēbēl.*
all things, &c. = and all that is therein.
2 the LORD. Heb. Jehovah. Ap. 4. II.
utterly destroyed = devoted to destruction, or, placed under a Divine ban.
3 mountains shall be melted with their blood. Fig. *Hyperbole* (Ap. 6). So *vv.* 4 and 5.

649–588 behold, it shall come down upon Idumea, and
upon the people °of My curse, to judgment.
6 The sword of [2]the LORD is filled with blood,
it is made fat with fatness, *and* with the blood
of lambs and goats, with the fat of the kidneys
of rams:
r for [2]the LORD hath a sacrifice in Bozrah, and
(p. 972) a great slaughter in the land of Idumea.
7 And the °unicorns shall come down with
them, and the bullocks with the bulls; and
their land shall be °soaked with blood, and
their dust made fat with fatness.

q 8 For *it is* the day °of [2]the LORD'S vengeance,
and the year of recompences for the controversy
°of Zion.

W 9 And the streams thereof shall be turned into
pitch, and the dust thereof into brimstone, and
the land thereof shall become burning pitch.
10 It shall not be quenched night nor day;
the smoke thereof shall go up for ever: from
generation to generation it shall lie waste;
none shall pass through it for ever and ever.

X 11 But the cormorant and the bittern shall
possess it; the owl also and the raven shall
dwell in it:

Y and He shall stretch out upon it the line of
°confusion, and the °stones of °emptiness.

V 12 They shall call the nobles thereof to the
kingdom, but none *shall be* there, and all her
princes shall be nothing.

W 13 And thorns shall °come up in her palaces,
nettles and brambles in the fortresses thereof:

X and it shall be an habitation of dragons, *and*
a court for owls.
14 The wild beasts of the desert shall also
meet with the wild beasts of the island, and
the satyr shall cry to his fellow; the °screech
owl also shall rest there, and find for herself
°a place of rest.
15 There shall the great owl make her nest,
and lay, and hatch, and gather under her
shadow: there shall the vultures also be
gathered, every one with her mate.
16 °Seek ye out of °the book of [2]the LORD,
and read: no one of these shall °fail, none
shall want her mate: for My mouth it hath
commanded, and His °Spirit it hath gathered
them.

Y 17 And He hath cast the lot for them, and
His hand hath divided it unto them by line:
they shall possess it for ever, from generation
to generation shall they dwell therein.

5 of My curse: i.e. I have devoted.
7 unicorns: or, rhinocerots. Heb. *rᵉ'ēmīn*.
soaked = drunken. Fig. *Hyperbole*. Ap. 6.
8 of = for. **11 confusion.** See note on 24. 10.
confusion . . . emptiness. Heb. *tohū . . . bohū*. Ref. to Pent. (Gen. 1. 2), "without form and void" = waste and desolate. Only there, here, and Jer. 4. 23 beside. Ap. 92.
stones of emptiness. Fig. *Metonymy* (of Cause), Ap. 6, "stones" being put for what causes the land to lie empty or untilled. **13 come up in** = climb.
14 screech owl. Heb. *Lilith*. Used to-day of any being of the night, as the English "bogy" is used. Charms are used against it to-day in Palestine.
a place, &c. = a roost. **16 Seek** = Search.
the book of the LORD. This proves there was a book in existence, which could be searched. See Ap. 47.
fail = be missing. Heb. *'ādar*. Not the same word as in 19. 5 (see note there). Occurs here in "former" portion, and 40. 26 in "latter" portion. See Ap. 79. II.
Spirit. Heb. *rūach*. Ap. 9.

35. 1-10 (L[6], p. 964). JEHOVAH: THE KING IN HIS GLORY. (*Alternation*).

L[6] | s[1] | 1, 2. The Land.
  t[1] | 3-6-. The People.
 s[2] | -6-8-. The Land.
  t[2] | -8. The People.
 s[3] | 9-. The Land.
  t[3] | -9, 10. The People.

Ch. 35 is the sequel to this long series of Burdens (**D**) and Woes (*D*); it sets forth the future return of Israel.
1 The wilderness, &c.: i.e. the land of Edom referred to in 34. 9-16. While Edom becomes a waste, the Land becomes a paradise; and the way of the return thither a peaceful highway.
shall be glad for them = shall rejoice over them, as in the first occ. Deut. 28. 63; 30. 9, and Jer. 32. 41.
them: i.e. the noisome creatures of 34. 14-16, which were the evidences of the vengeance of 34. 8 and the glorious results as seen in 35. 4. The former portrays one aspect of it, and the latter the other. The wilderness is glad for the removal of the Edomites, of which removal the presence of the wild creatures (34. 13-17) was the token. See Ap. 82.
and = but; giving the contrast.
the desert shall rejoice, and blossom, &c. The description in this chapter leaves little to be interpreted. It requires only to be *believed*. No amount of spiritual blessing through the preaching of the Gospel can produce these physical miracles.
2 Sharon. See note on 33. 9.
the LORD. Heb. Jehovah. Ap. 4. II.
God. Heb. Elohim. Ap. 4. I.
3 Strengthen, &c. Quoted in Heb. 12. 11, 12.
5 Then the eyes, &c. When Messiah came, *these* miracles (not miracles *qua* miracles) were the evidence that He had indeed come to save His People (Matt. 11. 1-6), but they rejected Him. Hence, this with other similar prophecies are in abeyance. John had based his own claims on 40. 3, while the Lord based His claims on 35. 5, 6.

L[6] s[1] **35** °The wilderness and the solitary place
(p. 973) °shall be glad for °them; °and °the
desert shall rejoice, and blossom as the rose.
2 It shall blossom abundantly, and rejoice
even with joy and singing: the glory of Lebanon shall be given unto it, the excellency of
Carmel and °Sharon, they shall see the glory
of °the LORD, *and* the excellency of our °God.

t[1] 3 °**Strengthen ye the weak hands, and con-**
firm the feeble knees.
4 Say to them *that are* of a fearful heart, "Be
strong, fear not: behold, your [2]God will come
with vengeance, *even* [2]God *with* a recompence;
He will come and save you."
5 °Then the eyes of the blind shall be opened,
and the ears of the deaf shall be unstopped.
6 Then shall the lame *man* leap as an hart,
and the tongue of the dumb sing:

for in the wilderness shall waters break out, s[2]
and streams in the desert.
7 And the parched ground shall become a pool,
and the thirsty land springs of water: in the
habitation of dragons, where each lay, *shall be*
grass with reeds and rushes.

649-588 8 And an °highway shall be there, and a way,
and it shall be called °The way of holiness;
t² the unclean shall not pass over it; °but it *shall*
(p. 973) *be* for those: the wayfaring men, though fools,
shall not °err *therein.*
s³ 9 °No lion shall be there, nor *any* ravenous
beast shall go up thereon, it shall not be found
there;
t³ but the redeemed shall walk *there:*
10 And the ransomed of ²the LORD shall
return, and come to Zion with songs, and
everlasting joy upon °their heads: they shall
obtain joy and gladness, and sorrow and
°sighing shall flee away.

A¹ D u¹ **36** Now °it came to pass °in the fourteenth
(p. 974) year of king Hezekiah, *that* Senna-
603 cherib king of Assyria came up against all the
°defenced cities of Judah, °and took them.
2 And the king of Assyria sent °Rabshakeh
from °Lachish to Jerusalem unto king Hezekiah °with a great army. And °he stood by
the conduit of the upper pool in the °highway
of the fuller's field.
v¹ 3 Then came forth unto him °Eliakim, Hilkiah's son, which was over the °house, and
°Shebna the °scribe, and Joah, Asaph's son,
the recorder.
u² 4 And ²Rabshakeh said unto them, "Say ye
now to Hezekiah, 'Thus saith °the great king,
the king of Assyria, 'What confidence *is* this
wherein thou °trustest?
5 °I say, *sayest thou,* (but *they are but* °vain
words) '*I have* counsel and strength for war':
now on whom dost thou ⁴trust, that thou
rebellest against me?
6 Lo, thou ⁴trustest in the staff of this broken
reed, on Egypt; whereon if a °man lean, it will
go into his hand, and pierce it: so *is* Pharaoh
king of Egypt to all that ⁴trust in him.
7 But if °thou say to me, 'We ⁴trust in °the
LORD our °God': °*is it* not **He**, Whose high
places and Whose altars Hezekiah hath taken
away, and said to Judah and to Jerusalem, 'Ye
shall worship before this altar''?
8 Now therefore give pledges, I pray thee, to
my °master the king of Assyria, and I will
give thee two thousand horses, if thou be able
on thy part to set riders upon them.

8 highway. See note on 7. 3. Occurs only here.
The way, &c. = the holy road.
but, &c.: i.e. yet for those very persons it will exist.
err therein = go astray.
9 No lion shall be there, &c. Ref. to Pent. (Lev. 26. 6). Ap. 92.
10 their heads. Put by Fig. *Synecdoche* (of Part), Ap. 6, for themselves. **sighing.** See note on 21. 2.
Ch. 40 takes up this theme, after the historical episode of chs. 36-39, which is necessary for the understanding of the references to the Assyrian invasion.

36. 1—39. 8 (*C*, p. 930). HISTORIC EVENTS AND PROPHECIES. (HEZEKIAH.)
(*Extended and Repeated Alternation.*)

C | Z¹ | A¹ | 36. 1—37. 13. The King of Assyria. His summons to surrender Jerusalem.
B¹ | 37. 14-20. Hezekiah's fear and prayer.
C¹ | 37. 21-38. Isaiah. Answer to prayer, and promise of deliverance from Sennacherib.
Z² | A² | 38. 1. "The King of Terrors". His solemn summons to Hezekiah to surrender his life.
B² | 38. 2, 3. Hezekiah's fear and prayer.
C² | 38. 4-22. Isaiah. Answer to prayer and promise of deliverance from death.
Z³ | A³ | 39. 1. The King of Babylon. His letters and present.
B³ | 39. 2. Hezekiah. Fearless and prayerless.
C³ | 39. 3-8. Isaiah. His message of deliverance to Babylon.

36. 1—37. 13 (A¹, above). THE KING OF ASSYRIA. (*Introversion.*)

A¹ | D | 36. 1-21. Rabshakeh. First embassy.
E | 36. 22—37. 7. Hezekiah. Reception of message.
D | 37. 8-13. Rabshakeh. Second embassy.

36. 1-21 (D, above). RABSHAKEH. (FIRST EMBASSY.) (*Repeated Alternation.*)

D | u¹ | 1, 2. Rabshakeh. Mission.
v¹ | 3. Eliakim. Comes forth.
u² | 4-10. Rabshakeh. Message to Hezekiah.
v² | 11. Eliakim. Answer.
u³ | 12-20. Rabshakeh. Message to the People.
v³ | 21. Eliakim. Answer him not.

For the general notes on this chapter see notes on 2 Kings 18. 13—20. 19.

1 it came to pass. Note the insertion of these historical events in the midst of prophecy, corresponding with those concerning the reign of Ahaz (**C**, p. 930). Cp. 2 Kings 18. 13—20. 19, on which Isaiah is not dependent, and 2 Chron. 32. 1-33, which is not dependent on either (see Ap. 56). This history is a proof of Isaiah's prophetic mission and gifts. History and prophecy are thus combined: for the latter is history foretold, and the former is (in this and many cases) prophecy fulfilled: the two accounts being perfectly independent. **in the fourteenth year:** i.e. 628 B.C. See Ap. 50. V, pp. 59, 60. After Hezekiah's reformation (2 Chron. 29. 1—32. 1). Samaria had been taken by Shalmaneser in Hezekiah's sixth year (2 Kings 18. 10). The date (fourteenth year) no "error". **defenced cities** = fortified cities. **and took them.** See the list and number of them (forty-six) on Sennacherib's hexagonal cylinder in the British Museum. See Ap. 67 (xi), p. 98. **2 Rabshakeh:** or, "political officer". Probably a renegade Jew. **Lachish.** Now *Tell el Hesy*, or *Umm Lākis.* See the work on the excavations there, published by the "Palestine Exploration Fund". Cp. note on 2 Kings 18. 17; and 19. 8. **with a great army.** Foretold in 29. 1-6, as foretold in 22. 15-25. **he stood.** In the same spot where Isaiah stood with Ahaz twenty-eight years before. See 7. 3. **highway.** See note on 7. 3. **3 Eliakim.** See and cp. 22. 20-25. The promise of 22. 20, 21 was already fulfilled. **house.** Put by Fig. *Metonymy* (of Subject), Ap. 6, for household. Eliakim fulfils Shebna's office, as foretold in 22. 15-25. **Shebna.** See 22. 15. **scribe:** or, secretary. Title used of a state officer, first in 2 Sam. 8. 17. Connected with finance (2 Kings 22. 3). Jer. 52. 25. **4 the great king.** Contrast Ps. 47. 2. **trustest** = hast confided. Heb. *bāṭah.* Ap. 69. i. See Hezekiah's "Songs of the Degrees" (Pss. 121. 3; 125. 1, 2; 127. 1; 130. 5-8; and Ap. 67 (xi)). **5 I say, sayest thou.** Some codices read "Thou sayest", as in 2 Kings 18. 20. **vain words** = lip-talk. Heb. word of lips. **6 man.** Heb. *'ish.* Ap. 14. II. **7 thou.** Some codices read "ye", as in 2 Kings 18. 22. **the LORD.** Heb. Jehovah. Ap. 4. II. **God.** Heb. Elohim. Ap. 4. I. **is it not He . . .?** Manifesting Rabshakeh's ignorance. **8 master.** Heb. *'Adonai.* Ap. 4. VIII (2).

603 9 How then wilt thou turn away the face of one captain of the least of my master's servants, and put thy [4]trust on °Egypt for chariots and for horsemen?

10 And °am I now come up without [7]the LORD against this land to destroy it?' the LORD said unto me, 'Go up against this land, and destroy it.'"

v[2] (p. 974) 11 °Then said [3]Eliakim and [3]Shebna and Joah unto Rabshakeh, "Speak, I pray thee, unto thy servants in the Syrian language; for we understand *it*: and speak not to us in the °Jews' language, in the ears of the people that *are* on the wall."

u[3] 12 But [2]Rabshakeh said, "Hath my master sent me to thy master and to thee to °speak these words? *hath he* not *sent me* to the °men that °sit upon the wall, that they may eat their own dung, and drink their own piss with you?"

13 Then [2]Rabshakeh stood, and cried with a loud voice in the Jews' language, and said, "Hear ye the words of [4]the great king, the king of Assyria.

14 Thus saith the king, 'Let not Hezekiah deceive you: for he shall not be able to deliver you.

15 Neither let Hezekiah make you [4]trust in [7]the LORD, saying, [7]'The LORD will surely deliver us: °this city shall not be delivered into the hand of the king of Assyria.'

16 Hearken not to Hezekiah': for thus saith the king of Assyria, 'Make *an agreement* with me *by* a present, and come out to me: and eat ye °every one of his vine, and °every one of his fig tree, and drink ye °every one the waters of his own cistern;

17 Until I come and °take you away to a land like your own land, a land of corn and °wine, a land of °bread and vineyards.

18 *Beware* lest Hezekiah persuade you, saying, [7]'The LORD will deliver us.' °Hath any of the gods of the nations delivered his land out of the hand of the king of Assyria?

19 °Where *are* the gods of °Hamath and °Arphad? where *are* the gods of °Sepharvaim? and have they delivered Samaria out of my hand?

20 Who *are they* among all the gods of these lands, that have delivered their land out of my hand, that [7]the LORD should deliver Jerusalem out of my hand?'"

v[3] 21 But they held their peace, and answered him not a word: for the king's commandment was, saying, "Answer him not."

E w (p. 975) 22 Then came [3]Eliakim, the son of Hilkiah, that *was* over the household, and [3]Shebna the scribe, and Joah, the son of Asaph, the recorder, to Hezekiah with *their* clothes rent, and told him the words of [2]Rabshakeh.

x **37** And it came to pass, when king Hezekiah heard *it*, that he rent his clothes, and covered himself with sackcloth, and °went into the house of °the LORD.

w 2 And he sent °Eliakim, who *was* over the household, and °Shebna the scribe, and the °elders of the priests covered with sackcloth, unto Isaiah the prophet the son of Amoz.

3 And they said unto him, "Thus °saith Hezekiah, 'This day *is* a day of trouble, and of rebuke, and of °blasphemy: for the °children are come to the birth, and *there is* not strength to bring forth.

4 It may be [1]the LORD thy °God will hear the °words of °Rabshakeh, whom the king of Assyria his master hath sent to °reproach the living °God, and will reprove the °words which [1]the LORD thy °God hath heard: wherefore °lift up *thy* prayer for the remnant that is left.'"

5 So the servants of king Hezekiah came to Isaiah.

6 And °Isaiah said unto them, "Thus shall *x*
ye say unto your master, 'Thus saith [1]the LORD, 'Be not afraid of the [4]words that thou hast heard, wherewith the servants of the king of Assyria have [3]blasphemed Me.

7 Behold, I will send °a blast upon him, and

---

9 Egypt. Hezekiah at first looked for help there (see 20. 3-6; 30. 2-5; 2 Kings 18. 21).

10 am I now come up. As foretold twenty-eight years before (10. 6-8). If Rabshakeh knew of this, it shows the falsehood of "half the truth".

11 Then said, &c. This led only to grosser insults.

Jews'. The name by which the People were known of old, to foreigners. See note on *v.* 2. No proof of a later authorship. "Hebrew" is the later word for the *language* (cp. 19. 18).

12 speak these words. See Ap. 67 (i).

men. Heb. pl. of *'ĕnōsh.* Ap. 14. III.

sit upon the wall = maintain their posts: i.e. till reduced to these extremities.

15 this city. Some codices, with two early printed editions, Sept., and Syr., read "and this city": i.e. "therefore this city".

16 every one = man, as in *v.* 6.

17 take you away. As he did Israel (2 Kings 18. 11).

wine = new wine. Heb. *tīrōsh.* Ap. 27. II.

bread. Put by Fig. *Synecdoche* (of Part), Ap. 6, for all kinds of food.

18 Hath, &c.? = [Reflect]: Hath, &c.?

19 Where: or, Why, where. Some codices, with two early printed editions, read "Where then".

Hamath. Now *Hama,* north of Damascus (Amos 6. 14).

Arphad. Now *Tell Erfād,* 13 miles north of Aleppo.

Sepharvaim. Now *Sippara* on the Euphrates, above Babylon.

36. 22–37. 7 (E, p. 974). **HEZEKIAH. RECEPTION OF MESSAGE.** (*Alternation.*)

E | w | 36. 22. Hezekiah. Message received from Rabshakeh.
x | 37. 1. Jehovah. Answer sought from.
w | 37. 2-5. Hezekiah. Message sent to Isaiah.
x | 37. 6, 7. Jehovah. Answer sent from.

37. 1 went into the house of the LORD. See Hezekiah's reference to his love for, and use of, the Temple in his "Songs of the Degrees" (Pss. 122. 1, 9; 134. 1, 2; and Ap. 67 (xiii)).

the LORD. Heb. Jehovah. Ap. 4. II.

2 Eliakim . . Shebna. See note on 36. 3.

elders of the priests. These now added to the embassy. Joah absent.

3 saith = hath said.

blasphemy = reproach. Note the reference to this in Hezekiah's "Songs of the Degrees" in Pss. 120. 2, 3; 123. 3, 4; and Ap. 67 (i). **children** = sons.

4 God. Heb. Elohim. Ap. 4. I.

words. See note on "blasphemy" (*v.* 3).

Rabshakeh = the Rabshakeh. See note on 36. 2.

reproach = revile.

lift up thy prayer. Note the reference to Hezekiah's "Songs of the Degrees" in Pss. 120. 1; 123. 1-3; 130. 1, 2; and Ap. 67 (iv). Trust (36. 4, 7, 15) leads to prayer.

6 Isaiah said. The message in *vv.* 6, 7 is shorter and calmer than the second.

7 a blast. Heb. *rūacḥ.* Ap. 9. See 2 Kings 19. 35.

603 he shall hear °a rumour, and return to his own
land; and I will cause him to °fall by the sword
in his own land.'' "

D (p. 974) 8 So [4]Rabshakeh returned, and found the
king of Assyria warring against Libnah: for
he had heard that he °was departed from
Lachish.
9 And °he heard say concerning °Tirhakah
king of °Ethiopia, "He is come forth to make
war with thee." And when he heard *it*, he
sent messengers to Hezekiah, saying,
10 "Thus shall ye speak to Hezekiah king of
Judah, saying, 'Let not thy [4]God, in Whom
thou °trustest, deceive thee, saying, 'Jerusalem
shall not be given into the hand of the king of
Assyria.'
11 °Behold, thou hast heard what the kings
of Assyria have done to °all lands by destroying
them utterly; and shalt thou be delivered?
12 Have the gods of the nations delivered
them which my fathers have destroyed, *as*
°Gozan, and Haran, °and Rezeph, and the
°children of Eden which *were* in Telassar?
13 Where *is* the king of °Hamath, and the
king of °Arphad, and the king of the city of
°Sepharvaim, °Hena, and °Ivah?' "

B [1] 14 And Hezekiah received the letter from the
hand of the messengers, and read it: and
Hezekiah [1]went up unto the house of [1]the
LORD, and °spread it before [1]the LORD.
15 And Hezekiah prayed unto [1]the LORD,
saying,
16 "O °LORD of Hosts, °God of Israel, That
°dwellest *between* the cherubims, Thou *art*
°the °God, *even* Thou alone, of all the kingdoms
of the earth: Thou hast °made heaven
and earth.
17 Incline Thine °ear, O [1]LORD, and hear;
open Thine °eyes, O [1]LORD, and see: and
hear all the [4]words of Sennacherib, which
hath sent to [4]reproach the °living [4]God.
18 Of a truth, [1]LORD, the kings of Assyria
have laid waste all the °nations, and their
countries,
19 And have cast their gods into the fire: for
they *were* no gods, but the work of °men's
hands, wood and stone: therefore they have
destroyed them.
20 Now therefore, O [1]LORD our [4]God, °save
us from his hand, that all the kingdoms of
the earth may know that Thou *art* [1]the LORD,
even Thou only."

C[1] y (p. 976) 21 Then Isaiah the son of Amoz sent unto
Hezekiah, saying, "Thus [3]saith [1]the LORD
[16]God of Israel, 'Whereas °thou hast prayed
to me against Sennacherib king of Assyria:

z 22 This *is* the word which [1]the LORD hath
spoken concerning him; 'The virgin, the
daughter of Zion, hath °despised thee, *and*
°laughed thee to scorn; the daughter of Jerusalem
hath °shaken her head at thee.
23 Whom hast thou [4]reproached and [3]blasphemed?
and against whom hast thou exalted
thy voice, and lifted up thine eyes on high?
even against °the Holy One of Israel.
24 By thy servants hast thou [4]reproached
the °LORD*, and hast said, 'By the multitude
of my chariots °am I come up to the height
of the mountains, to the sides of °Lebanon;
and I will cut down the tall cedars thereof,
and the choice fir trees thereof: and I will
enter into the height of his border, *and* the
forest of his Carmel.
25 I have digged, and drunk water; and with
the sole of my feet have I dried up all the °rivers
of the °besieged places.'

---

a rumour. Not that of *vv.* 8, 9, but that of *v.* 36, on hearing which he returned to his own land (*v.* 37).

fall by the sword. See note on *v.* 37.

8 was departed from Lachish: having raised the siege. See note on 2 Kings 18. 17; 19. 8.

9 he heard. The "rumour" of *v.* 7.

Tirhakah. The Taracus of the inscriptions. The third and last of Manetho's twenty-sixth dynasty. This reference to the Ethiopian dynasty in Isaiah's time is an "undesigned coincidence".

Ethiopia. Judah's hope in Ethiopia was vain (see 20. 1-6).

10 trustest = confidest. Heb. *bāṭah.* Ap. 69. i. See note on 36. 4.

11 Behold. Fig. *Asterismos.* Ap. 6.

all lands = all the earths: i.e. all such countries specially connected with Israel.

12 Gozan, &c. These places are all in Mesopotamia.

and Rezeph. The Heb. pointing connects this with the next clause.

children = sons.

13 Hamath . . . Arphad . . . Sepharvaim. See notes on 36. 19.

Hena. Now (prob.) *'Anah*, on the Euphrates.

Ivah. Now (prob.) *Hīt*, on the Euphrates.

14 spread it, &c. See note on "lift up", &c. (*v.* 4).

16 LORD of Hosts. See note on 1. 9, and 1 Sam. 1. 3.

God of Israel. See note on 29. 23.

dwellest: or, sittest enthroned.

the. Heb. He, the [God]. Cp. 1 Kings 18. 39.

God. Heb. Elohim (with Art.) = the [true] God.

made heaven and earth. Note the reference to this in Hezekiah's "Songs of the Degrees" (Pss. 121. 1, 2; 123. 1; 124. 8; 134. 3; and Ap. 67 (v)).

17 ear . . . eyes. Fig. *Anthropopatheia.* Ap. 6.

eyes. Heb. text reads "eye". But A.V. reads "eyes", with some codices, five early printed editions, Sept., Syr., and Vulg.

living. In contrast with idols.

18 nations, and their countries. Heb. *hā-'ărāzōth . . . 'arzām*: as in *v.* 11. The latter word put by Fig. *Metonymy* (of Adjunct), Ap. 6, for the people inhabiting the lands. Note also the Fig. *Paronomasia* (Ap. 6). Some codices read "nations, and their land".

19 men's. Heb. *'ādām.* Ap. 14. I.

20 save us. Some codices add "I (or, we) pray Thee". Cp. 2 Kings 19. 19.

37. 21—38 (C[1], p. 974). **ISAIAH. ANSWER TO PRAYER.** (*Alternation.*)

C[1] | y | 21. Hezekiah. Prayer regarded.
| z | 22-29. King of Assyria. Apostrophe to.
| y | 30-32. Hezekiah. Sign given to.
| z | 33-38. King of Assyria. Destruction of.

21 thou hast prayed. See note on "lift up" (*v.* 4).

22 despised . . . laughed . . . shaken, &c. Fig. *Prosopopœia.* Ap. 6.

shaken = wagged. Denoting derision and scorn.

23 the Holy One of Israel. See note on 1. 4.

24 LORD*. One of the 134 places where the *Sōpherīm* changed "Jehovah" of the primitive text to "Adonai". See Ap. 32.

am I come up = have I scaled. Cp. 36. 10. These boasts probably refer to the future as well as the past.

Lebanon, &c. Cp. 2 Kings 19. 23. Fulfilling 14. 8 (see note there). As Hannibal later scaled the Alps.

25 rivers = arms, or canals. Cp. 19. 6, and Mic. 7. 12.

besieged places. Heb. *matzōr.* Put for Egypt.

603 26 Hast thou not heard long ago, *how* I have
done it; *and* of ancient times, that I have
°formed it? now have I brought it to pass,
that thou shouldest be to lay waste defenced
cities *into* ruinous heaps.
27 Therefore their inhabitants *were* of small
power, they were dismayed and confounded:
they were °*as* the grass of the field, and *as* the
green herb, *as* the grass on the housetops, and
as corn blasted before it be grown up.
28 But I know thy °abode, and thy °going out,
and thy coming in, and thy rage against Me.
29 Because thy rage against Me, and thy
°tumult, is come up into Mine ears, therefore
will I put °My hook in thy nose, and My bridle
in thy lips, and I will °turn thee back by the
way by which thou camest.'
y (p. 976) 30 And this *shall be* a °sign unto thee, °'Ye
shall eat *this* year such as °groweth of itself;
and the second year that which °springeth of the
same: and in the third year °sow ye, and reap,
and plant vineyards, and eat the fruit thereof.
31 And the remnant that is escaped of the
house of Judah °shall again take root downward, and bear fruit upward:
32 For out of Jerusalem [31] shall go forth a
remnant, and they that escape out of mount
Zion: the °zeal of [16] the LORD of hosts [31] shall
do this.'"
z 33 Therefore thus saith [1] the LORD concerning
the king of Assyria, "He [31] shall not come into
this city, nor shoot an arrow there, nor come
before it with shields, nor cast a bank against it.
34 By the way that he came, by the same
[31] shall he return, and shall not come into this
city," saith [1] the LORD.
35 "For I will °defend this city to save it for
Mine own sake, and for °My servant °David's
sake."
36 °Then the angel of [1] the LORD went forth,
and smote in the camp of the Assyrians a
hundred and fourscore and five thousand: and
when °they arose early in the morning, behold,
they *were* all dead corpses.
37 So Sennacherib king of Assyria departed,
°and went °and returned, °and dwelt at Nineveh.
38 [37] And it came to pass, as he was worshipping in the house of Nisroch his god, that
Adrammelech and Sharezer °his sons smote
him with the sword; and they escaped into the
land of Armenia: and °Esar-haddon his son
reigned in his stead.

Z^2 A^2 (p. 974) 603 **38** °In those days was Hezekiah °sick
unto death. And Isaiah the prophet
the son of Amoz came unto him, and said unto
him, "Thus saith °the LORD, °'Set thine house
in order: for thou shalt °die, and not live.'"
B^2 2 Then Hezekiah turned his face toward the
wall, and °prayed unto [1] the LORD,
3 And said, "Remember now, O [1] LORD, I
beseech Thee, how I have walked before Thee
°in truth and with a perfect heart, and have
done *that which is* good in Thy sight." And
Hezekiah °wept sore.
C^2 F (p. 977) 4 Then °came the word of [1] the LORD to
Isaiah, saying,
5 "Go, and say to Hezekiah, 'Thus saith
[1] the LORD, °the °God of David thy father, 'I

---

26 formed=purposed. Cp. 10. 5, 15; 30. 32.

27 as the grass. Note Hezekiah's reference to this in his "Songs of the Degrees" (Ps. 129. 5–7). See Ap. 67. ii.

28 abode=sitting down.

going out, and thy coming in. Put by Fig. *Synecdoche* (of Part), Ap. 6, for life in general.

29 tumult=arrogance.

My hook, &c. Assyrian sculptures represent captives thus led. Jehovah would treat them as they treated others.

turn thee back. See Hezekiah's reference to this (Ps. 129. 4, 5). Ap. 67. iii.

30 sign. See note on 7. 11.

Ye shall eat, &c. No seed would be sown on account of the (foretold) devastation wrought by the invasion. Hezekiah refers to this "sign" in his "Songs of the Degrees" (Pss. 126. 5, 6; 128. 2). See Ap. 67. ix.

groweth of itself. Ref. to Pent. (Lev. 25. 5, 11). Only here, 2 Kings 19. 29, and Job 14. 19.

springeth of the same=shooteth up of itself, or from the roots. Heb. *shaḥith*, occurs only here.

sow ye. See note above.

31 shall. Hezekiah refers to Jehovah's repeated promises on which he relies (cp. 2 Kings 19. 30–34). See Pss. 121. 2–8; 124. 1–3, 6; 125. 2; 126. 2, 3; 127. 1. See Ap. 67. vii.

32 zeal=jealousy. Ref. to Pent. Cp. 9. 7. See Ap. 92.

35 defend=shield. See note on Isa. 31. 5.

My servant. Three are so called in this book: David (here); Israel or Jacob (the nation) (41. 8; 42. 19; 43. 10; 44. 1; 45. 4; 48. 20; 49. 3 and whole chapter); and Messiah (42. 1; 65. 8).

David's sake. Note how Hezekiah refers to these words in his "Songs of the Degrees" (Ps. 132. 1, 10). See Ap. 67. viii.

36 Then, &c. Cp. 2 Kings 19. 35–37.

they: i.e. the Israelites.

37 and. Note the Fig. *Polysyndeton* (Ap. 6) in this verse, to emphasise his departure and return, which leads up to what he returned for; also, that he did this without taking the city. Nebuchadnezzar makes no reference to this in his inscription.

38 his sons . . . Esar-haddon. See note on 2 Kings 19. 37.

38. 1 In those days: i.e. Hezekiah's fourteenth year: for fifteen years (603–588 B.C.) are added to his life (*v.* 5), and he reigned twenty-nine years (2 Kings 18. 2); 14 + 15 = 29.

sick. This sickness was therefore during the siege.

the LORD. Heb. Jehovah. Ap. 4. II.

Set thine house in order=Give charge concerning thy house.

die, and not live=thou wilt certainly die. Fig. *Pleonasm* (Ap. 6): by which a thing is put both ways (positive and negative) for emphasis.

2 prayed. As in 37. 4 ("lift up") and *vv.* 14, 15. Contrast 39. 2, where, when the king of Babylon sent letters and he neglected prayer. See the Structure of *C*, p. 974).

3 in truth. See note on 10. 20.

wept sore=wept a great weeping. Fig. *Polyptōton* (Ap. 6), for emphasis. Cp. 2 Kings 20. 3.

38. 4–22 (C^2, p. 974). ISAIAH. ANSWER TO PRAYER. (*Alternation.*)

C^2 | F | 4–6. Jehovah's Message to Hezekiah.
  G | 7, 8. The Sign given.
 F | 9–20. Hezekiah's Prayer to Jehovah.
  G | 21, 22. The Sign asked for.

4 came. The only occurrence of this in the case of Isaiah. Cp. Gen. 15. 1.

5 the God of David. This Divine title reminds and assures Hezekiah that Jehovah would be faithful to His promise made to David in 2 Sam. 7. See Ap. 67. viii, and note on 2 Kings 20. 5.

God. Heb. Elohim. Ap. 4. I.

603-588 have heard thy prayer, I have seen thy tears:
behold, I will add unto thy days °fifteen years.
6 And °I will deliver thee and this city out of
the hand of the king of Assyria: and °I will
°defend this city.

G 7 And this *shall be* °a sign unto thee from
(p. 977) [1]the LORD, that [1]the LORD will do this thing
that He hath spoken;
8 °Behold, I will bring again °the shadow of
the °degrees, which is gone down in the sun
°dial of Ahaz, ten °degrees backward.'"' So
the sun returned ten °degrees, by which °de-
grees it was gone down.

F a 9 °The writing of Hezekiah king of Judah,
(p. 978) when he had been sick, and was recovered of
his sickness:

b 10 I said "in the cutting off of my days, I
shall go to the gates of °the grave: I am deprived of the residue of my years."
11 I said, "I shall not °see °THE LORD, *even*
°THE LORD, °in the land of °the living: I
shall behold °man no more with the inhabitants of °the world.
12 Mine °age is departed, and is removed
from me as a shepherd's tent: I have cut off
°like a weaver my life: He will cut me off
with pining sickness: from day *even* to night
wilt Thou make an end of me."
13 °I reckoned till morning, *that*, °as a lion,
°so will He break all my bones: from day *even*
to night wilt Thou make an end of me.
14 °Like a crane *or* a swallow, so did I chatter:
I did °mourn as a dove: mine eyes fail *with
looking* upward: O °LORD*, I am oppressed;
°undertake for me.
15 What shall I say? He hath both spoken
unto me, and Himself hath done *it:* I shall go
°softly all my years in the bitterness of my °soul.
16 O °LORD*, °by these *things men* live, and
in all these *things is* the life of my °spirit: so
wilt Thou recover me, and make me to live.
17 °Behold, for peace I had great bitterness:
but Thou hast in love to my [15]soul *delivered it*
from the °pit of corruption: for Thou hast cast
all my °sins °behind Thy back.
18 For °the grave cannot praise Thee, death
can °*not* °celebrate Thee: °they that go down
into the pit cannot hope for Thy truth.
19 °The living, the living, He shall praise Thee,
as I *do* this day: °the father to the °children
shall make known Thy truth.
20 [1]The LORD °*was ready* to save me:
a °therefore °we will sing my songs to the stringed
instruments all the days of our life in °the
house of [1]the LORD.

fifteen years. Hence the number of the "Songs of the Degrees". See Ap. 67.

6 I will deliver thee and this city. The city was thus still besieged.

I will. Hezekiah trusted this promise. See Ap. 67. vii.

defend = shield. See note on 31. 5.

7 a sign = the sign. Hezekiah had asked for this sign (see *v.* 22). This shows that *v.* 22 is not "displaced" as alleged. See the Structure on p. 977; and cp. note on 7. 11.

8 Behold. Note Fig. *Asterismos* (Ap. 6) for emphasis.

the shadow of the degrees. It is to these "degrees", or steps of the sundial of Ahaz his father, that Hezekiah refers in the title for "The Songs of the Degrees". See Ap. 67.

degrees = steps. Note the emphasis placed on these by the fivefold repetition of the word.

dial = degrees (making the fifth repetition of the word).

38. 9-20 (*F*, p. 977). HEZEKIAH'S PRAYER TO JEHOVAH. (*Introversion.*)

F | a | 9. The Superscription.
  b | 10-20-. The Prayer.
  a | -20. The Subscription.

9 The writing, &c. Heb. *michtab.* Another spelling of *michtam.* See Ap. 65. xii. This verse is the superscription common to most Psalms, corresponding with the subscription (*v.* -20). See Ap. 65.

10 the grave. Heb. *Sheōl.* Ap. 35. See note on Matt. 16. 18.

11 see THE LORD = appear before Jah. Ref. to Pent. See note on 1. 12; and on "appear" (Ex. 23. 15; 34. 20).

THE LORD. Heb. Jah. Ap. 4. III. Note the emphasis given here by the Fig. *Epizeuxis* (Ap. 6).

in the land of the living. This expression occurs three times with the Art. ("the living") in the Hebrew (viz. here; Job 28. 13; and Ps. 142. 5). Without the Art. it occurs eight times. See note on Ezek. 26. 20.

the living: i.e. alive on the earth. Not *Sheōl*, which is the place of the dead.

man. Heb. *'ādām.* Ap. 14. I.

the world. Heb. *ḥādel* = a quiet land: i.e. when this invasion shall be ended. Some codices read *heled* (transposing the *l* and *d*) = the transitory world: *ḥādel* occurs only here.

12 age. Heb. *dōr* = generation, or succession.

like a weaver. Supply Ellipsis thus: "like a weaver [his thread]." See note on "weave" (19. 9).

13 I reckoned = I waited expectantly.

as a lion = as a lion [awaits his prey].

so will He break. See note on Ps. 22. 16.

14 Like a crane or a swallow: or, like a twittering swallow.

mourn. See note on Ps. 55. 17. Cp. Ezek. 7. 16.

LORD*. This is *Adonai* in the Heb. text, but it is one of the 134 places where it was altered to Adonai, as Jehovah is read in the famous Hillel Codex (A.D. 600), quoted in the *Massōrah*, and followed by A.V. and R.V.

undertake = be a surety. Cp. Job 17. 3 ("put me in surety").

15 softly = slowly. Heb. *dādah.* Only here and in Ps. 42. 4 ("went"). **soul.** Heb. *nephesh.* Ap. 13.

16 LORD* = Jehovah (Ap. 4. II). One of the 134 places where the *Sōpherīm* changed "Jehovah" of the primitive text to "Adonai" (see Ap. 32).

by these, &c. = upon these [Thy doings (*v.* 15) men] revive (Ps. 104. 29, 30), and the reviving of my spirit [is] altogether in them. **spirit.** Heb. *rūach.* Ap. 9.

17 Behold. Fig. *Asterismos.* Ap. 6. **pit of corruption** = pit or corruption. **sins.** Heb. *chāṭā'.* Ap. 44. i. **behind Thy back.** Sins unforgiven are said to be "before His face" (Ps. 109. 14, 15. Jer. 16. 17. Hos. 7. 2). Cp. Mic. 7. 19. Hence the "happinesses" of Ps. 32. 1. **18 the grave.** Heb. *Sheōl.* Ap. 35. Put here by Fig. *Metonymy* (of Subject), Ap. 6, for those who are in it. **not.** Note the Ellipsis of the second negative. See note on Gen. 2. 6, and 1 Kings 2. 9. Cp. for the teaching Pss. 6. 5; 30. 9; 88. 10, 12. Ecc. 9. 10. **celebrate.** See note on "shall not give their light" (13. 10). **they.** Some codices read "and they". **19 The living, the living.** Fig. *Epizeuxis* (Ap. 6), for emphasis, implying that only such are able to praise. **the father to the children.** Note the reference to the Pentateuch (Deut. 4. 9; 6. 7). **children** = sons. **20 was ready.** Supply "was gracious". **therefore, &c.** Note the subscription (*a*) above. **we will sing my songs:** i.e. the "Songs of the Degrees" (Ap. 67). Where are "my songs", and what were they if not the fifteen songs named after the ten degrees by which the shadow of the sun went back on the sundial of Ahaz (*vv.* 7, 8)? **the house of the LORD.** Note Hezekiah's love for this in these songs (Pss. 122. 1, 9; 134. 1, 2). See Ap. 67. xiii.

G 21 For Isaiah had said, "Let them take a lump
(p. 977) of figs, and lay *it* for a plaister upon the boil,
603 and he shall recover."
22 Hezekiah also had said, °"What *is* the
[7]sign that I shall go up to [20]the house of the
LORD?"

Z^3 A^3 **39** °At that time Merodach-baladan, the
(p. 974) son of Baladan, °king of Babylon, sent
°letters and a present to Hezekiah: for he had
heard that he had been sick, and was recovered.

B^3 2 And Hezekiah was °glad of them, °and
shewed them the house of °his °precious things,
°the silver, °and the gold, and the spices, °and
the precious ointment, °and all the house of
°his armour, °and all that was found in °his
°treasures: there was °nothing in °his house,
nor in all °his dominion, that Hezekiah shewed
them not.

C^3 c^1 3 Then came Isaiah the prophet unto king
(p. 979) Hezekiah, and said unto him, "What said
these °men? and from whence came they
unto thee?"

d^1 And Hezekiah said, "They are come from a far
country unto me, *even* from Babylon."

c^2 4 Then said °he, "What have they seen in
thine house?"

d^2 And Hezekiah answered, "All that *is* in mine
house have they seen: there is nothing among
my treasures that I have not shewed them."

c^3 5 Then said Isaiah to Hezekiah, "Hear the
word of °the LORD of Hosts:
6 °'Behold, the days come, that all that *is* in
thine house, and *that* which thy fathers have
laid up in store until this day, shall be carried
to Babylon: nothing shall be left,' saith °the
LORD.
7 'And of °thy sons that shall issue from thee,
which thou shalt beget, shall they take away;
and they shall be °eunuchs in the palace of the
king of Babylon.'"

d^3 8 Then said Hezekiah to Isaiah, °"Good *is* the
word of [6]the LORD which thou hast spoken."
He said moreover, °"For there shall be peace
and truth in my days."

B H **40** °"Comfort ye, °comfort ye My People,"
603-588 °saith your °God.
2 "Speak ye °comfortably to Jerusalem, and
°cry unto her, that her °warfare is accomplished, that her °iniquity is pardoned: for

22 What is the sign . . .? See on 7, 8.

39. 1 At that time: i.e. shortly after the two miracles of the shadow and Hezekiah's recovery from his sickness. Cp. 2 Chron. 32. 31.

king of Babylon. The third king of the Structure *C* on p. 974.

letters and a present. These were more potent than Sennacherib's hosts; just as Ahab's daughter and feast were than his men of war with Jehoshaphat. See 2 Chron. 18. 1-3. Cp. with 2 Chron. 17. 1-3.

2 glad of them. This is further Divine information, given by Him Who knew Hezekiah's heart. 2 Kings 20. 13 records what Hezekiah did: viz. "hearkened unto them". Man could see the *ear*, but only Jehovah could know the *heart*. Hezekiah forgot to pray, as in 37. 4, 14, 15; and 38. 2. Hence his failure.

and. Note the Fig. *Polysyndeton* (Ap. 6), to emphasise and call attention (by five "ands") to every detail.

his. Note the Fig. *Repetitio* (Ap. 6) to mark Hezekiah's ostentation and failure in not giving Jehovah all the glory.

precious things. Hezekiah's possession of these riches, after the depletion of his treasuries in 2 Kings 18. 15, 16, is explained and accounted for by a reference to 2 Chron. 32. 22, 23, 27, and to the spoil of the Assyrians' camp (2 Kings 19. 35).

the silver, and the gold. Ref. to Pent. (Deut. 17. 17).

treasures=treasuries.

nothing. Emphasising the completeness of his act.

39. 3-8 (C^3, p. 974). ISAIAH. HIS MESSAGE.
(*Alternation.*)

C^3 | c^1 | 3-. Isaiah. Question.
  d^1 | -3. Hezekiah. Information.
 c^2 | 4-. Isaiah. Question.
  d^2 | -4. Hezekiah. Ostentation.
 c^3 | 5-7. Isaiah. Denunciation.
  d^3 | 8. Hezekiah. Submission.

3 men. Heb. pl. of *'ĕnōsh*. Ap. 14. III.

4 he: i.e. Isaiah.

5 the LORD of Hosts. See note on 1 Sam. 1. 3.

6 Behold. Fig. *Asterismos* (Ap. 6), for emphasis.

the LORD. Heb. Jehovah. Ap. 4. II.

7 thy sons. Hezekiah had none as yet, and Jehovah's promise to David (2 Sam. 7. 16) seemed in danger of failing. Manasseh was not born till the third of the fifteen added years. Hence his reference to this position in the "Songs of the Degrees". See Pss. 127. 3-5; 128 (quoting in *vv.* 5, 6 the words in Isa. 39. 8). Hezekiah did not marry till after this, and there may be a reference to his marriage to Hephzi-bah in 62. 4, which serves as the basis of the comparison in his prophecy concerning the future blessing of Israel.

eunuchs. See Dan. 1. 3, 4.

8 Good. Hezekiah's submission was like Eli's. Cp. 1 Sam. 3. 18. 2 Kings 20. 19. Job 1. 21; 2. 10. James 5. 10, 11.

For=Nevertheless. The Heb. distinctive accent *mĕyrka* thus marks it.

40. 1-11 (*B*, p. 930). THE VOICE FROM THE WILDERNESS.
THE GATHERING. (*Introversion.*)

B | H | 1, 2. Comfort for Jerusalem. Iniquity gone.
 J | 3-5. The voice. Jehovah's work. Glorious.
 J | 6-8. The voice. Jehovah's word. Eternal.
 H | 9-11. Comfort for Zion. Adonai Jehovah come.

This chapter commences a new Prophecy (see Ap. 82), and follows that in 34. 1—35. 10, after the historic episode of chs. 36—38. It will be seen that it forms an integral part of the prophet Isaiah's book, as this member *B* forms a perfect Correspondence with **B** (ch. 6), and cannot be wrenched from it without destroying the whole. Other evidences may be seen in Ap. 79 and 80. **1 Comfort ye.** Note the Fig. *Epizeuxis* (Ap. 6), for emphasis, and see Ap. 82. **saith.** See note on 1. 11. **God.** Heb. Elohim. Ap. 4. I. **2 comfortably to**=to the heart of: i.e. affectionately. Cp. Gen. 34. 3; 50. 21. Judg. 19. 3. Hos. 2. 14. **cry**=proclaim. Note the same word, and truth, in *v.* 3. **warfare**=hard service or forced service. **iniquity.** Heb. *'āvāh*. Ap. 44. iv.

603-588 she hath received of °the LORD'S hand °double
for all her °sins."

J (p. 979) **3 °The voice of °him that [2]crieth in the wilder-**
ness, "Prepare ye the way of [2]the LORD, make
straight in the desert a °highway for our [1]God.
4 °Every valley shall be exalted, and every
mountain and hill shall be made low: and the
crooked shall be made straight, and the rough
places plain:
5 And the glory of [2]the LORD shall be revealed,
and all °flesh shall see *it* together: for the
mouth of [2]the LORD hath spoken *it*."

J 6 °The voice said, [2]"Cry." And he said,
"What shall I [2]cry?" **"All [5]flesh °*is* grass,**
and all the °goodliness thereof °*is* as the flower
of the field:
7 The grass withereth, the flower fadeth:
because the °spirit of [2]the LORD bloweth upon
it: surely the people [6]*is* grass.
8 The grass withereth, the flower fadeth:
but the word of our [1]God shall °stand for
ever."

H 9 °O Zion, °that bringest °good tidings, get
thee up into the high mountain; °O Jerusalem,
°that bringest °good tidings, lift up thy voice
with °strength; lift *it* up, be not afraid; say
unto the cities of Judah, °"Behold your [1]God!"
10 °Behold, °the Lord GOD will come with
°strong *hand*, and His arm shall rule for Him:
behold, His reward *is* with Him, and His
work before Him.
11 He shall °feed His flock like a shepherd: He
shall °gather the lambs with His arm, and
carry *them* in His bosom, *and* shall gently lead
those that are with young.

A K[1] P[1] (p. 980) 12 °Who hath measured the waters in the
hollow of his hand, and meted out heaven
with the span, and comprehended the dust of
the earth in °a measure, and weighed the
mountains in scales, and the hills in a balance?

the LORD'S. Heb. Jehovah. Ap. 4. II.
double = in full. Put by Fig. *Metonymy* (of Subject), Ap. 6, for that which is complete, thorough, ample. See 61. 7. Gen. 43. 22. Job 11. 6; 41. 13. Jer. 16. 18; 17. 18. Zech. 9. 12. 1 Tim. 5. 17. Cp. Job 42. 10. Gal. 6. 7–9.
sins. Heb. *chāṭā'*. Ap. 44. i.

3 The voice, &c. Quoted in Matt. 3. 3. Mark 1. 3. Luke 3. 4–6. John 1. 23. 1 Pet. 1. 24. Cp. the voice from the temple in ch. 6, concerning the scattering, and this voice outside the land concerning the gathering. The voice was not Isaiah's, but heard by him in vision. John Baptist claims it; but this People would not hear; and He Whom he heralded was crucified and His kingdom was rejected (John 1. 11). The King and the kingdom are therefore alike in abeyance, and the prophecy yet awaits its further fulfilment. Cp. Heb. 2. 8. Rev. 3. 21, 22, &c.
him that crieth = him that proclaimeth. These words are ascribed to Isaiah by the Holy Spirit in Matt. 3. 3, &c. Ch. 42. 1–4 is so ascribed in Matt. 12. 17–21; ch. 53. 1 in John 12. 38. Rom. 10. 16; ch. 53. 4 in Matt. 8. 17; ch. 53. 7, 8 in Acts 8. 32, 33; and 61. 1 in Luke 4. 18, 19. Not to a "second Isaiah". Ap. 79. II.
highway. See note on 7. 3.

4 Every valley, &c. These physical marvels are supernatural, and can never be produced by the *spiritual* and holy living of individual Christians.

5 flesh. Fig. *Synecdoche* (of Genus), Ap. 6, put for all people.

6 The voice = A voice. This is a second "voice": the voice of Jehovah.
is grass. Fig. *Metaphor* (Ap. 6), by which the assertion is boldly made that one thing *is* another (i.e. *represents* it). It differs from the Fig. *Simile* in the next clause, which asserts that one thing only *resembles* another.
goodliness = grace, or loveliness.
is as. Fig. *Simile.* Ap. 6.

7 spirit. Heb. *rūach.* Ap. 9.

8 stand for ever. Cp. 46. 10, 11; 55. 10, 11. Ps. 119. 89–91. Zech. 1. 5. Matt. 5. 18; 24. 35. Mark 13. 31. John 10. 35; 12. 34. 1 Pet. 1. 25.

9 O Zion, that bringest: or, O thou that tellest good tidings to Zion. Cp. 41. 27.
that bringest. This is feminine, personifying the "herald-band". **good** = joyful.
O Jerusalem. See note on "O Zion", above.
strength = power, strength (to endure). Heb. *koaḥ.* Same as in *v.* 31; not the same as in *v.* 10.

Behold your God. See note on the Structure of the four Gospels, which shows this sentence as being applicable to the Gospel by John. **10 Behold.** Fig. *Asterismos.* Ap. 6. **the Lord GOD.** Heb. Adonai Jehovah (Ap. 4). This title is used because of His connection here with the earth. **strong** = mighty strength (to hold fast). Heb. *ḥazaḳ.* Not the same word as in *vv.* 9, 26, 29, 31. **11 feed** His flock. As in the wilderness. See 63. 11. Pss. 77. 20; 78. 52, 53; 80. 1. **gather** = take up.

40. 12–66. 24 (*A*, p. 930). EXHORTATIONS: PROMISSORY AND PROPHETIC.

(*Alternation and Introversion.*)

A | K | 40. 12–31. God's Controversy with the Nations. Vanity of Idols.
  L | M | 41. 1—42. 16. Messiah's Anointing and Mission.
    N | 42. 17—45. 15. Jehovah's Controversy with Israel.
K | 45. 16—47. 15. God's Controversy with the Nations. Vanity of Idols.
  L | *N* | 48. 1–22. Jehovah's Controversy with Israel.
    M | 49. 1—66. 24. Messiah's Mission and Triumph.

40. 12–31 (K, above). GOD'S CONTROVERSY WITH THE NATIONS. VANITY OF IDOLS.

(*Extended and Repeated Alternation.*)

K | O[1] | P[1] | 12. Challenge by Jehovah. Omnipotence.
  Q[1] | 13, 14. Question as to knowledge.
  R[1] | 15–17. Nations insignificant.
O[2] | P[2] | 18–20. Challenge by Jehovah. Comparison.
  Q[2] | 21. Question as to knowledge.
  R[2] | 22–24. Peoples of the earth insignificant.
O[3] | P[3] | 25–27. Challenge by Jehovah. Equality.
  Q[3] | 28. Question as to knowledge.
  R[3] | 29–31. His People. Weakness revived.

These chapters (40. 12—66. 24) form a group corresponding with chs. 1–5; and, like them, consist of exhortations and prophecies, while they are set in contrast with them, being promissory instead of reprehensory. Their subjects, as respectively repeated, will be seen in the Structure of *A*, above. They look beyond the Captivity. **12–14 Who ... Who ... With whom ...?** in *vv.* 12–14 are introductory: while the Fig. *Erotēsis* emphasises the importance of Him Who speaks. **a measure** = a [*Shālīsh*] measure. See Ap. 51. III. 3 (11).

603-588 13 [12] **Who hath directed the [7] Spirit of [2] the**
Q[1] **LORD, or *being* ° His counseller hath ° taught**
(p. 980) **Him?**
14 With whom took He counsel, and *who*
° instructed Him, and [13] taught Him in the
° path of judgment, and [13] taught Him knowledge, and shewed to Him the way of understanding?
R[1] 15 [10] Behold, the nations *are* as a drop ° of a
bucket, and are counted as the small dust of
the balance: [10] behold, He taketh up the ° isles as
a very little thing.
16 And Lebanon *is* ° not sufficient to burn, nor
the beasts thereof sufficient for a burnt offering.
17 All ° nations before Him *are* as ° nothing;
and they are counted to Him less than nothing,
and ° vanity.
O[2] P[2] 18 To whom then will ye liken ° GOD? or
what likeness will ye compare unto Him?
19 The workman ° melteth a ° graven image,
and the goldsmith spreadeth it over with gold,
and casteth silver chains.
20 He that *is* so impoverished that he hath
no oblation ° chooseth a tree *that* will not rot;
he seeketh unto him a cunning workman to
° prepare a ° graven image, *that* shall not be
moved.
Q[2] 21 ° Have ye not known? ° have ye not heard?
hath it not been told you from the beginning?
° have ye not understood from the foundations
of the earth?
R[2] 22 *It is* He That ° sitteth ° upon the ° circle of
the earth, and the inhabitants thereof *are* as
grasshoppers; That stretcheth out the heavens
as a curtain, and spreadeth them out as a tent
to dwell in:
23 That bringeth the princes to nothing; He
maketh the judges of the earth as [17] vanity.
24 Yea, they shall not be planted; yea, they
shall not be sown: yea, their stock shall not
take root in the earth: and He shall also blow
upon them, and they shall wither, and the
whirlwind shall take them away as ° stubble.
O[3] P[3] 25 "To whom then will ye liken Me, or shall I
be equal?" [1] saith the ° Holy One.
26 "Lift up your eyes on high, and behold
Who hath created these *things*, That bringeth
out their host by number: He ° calleth them all
° by names by the greatness of His might, for
that *He is* ° strong in power; not one ° faileth.
27 ° Why sayest thou, O Jacob, and speakest,
O Israel, 'My way is hid from [2] the LORD, and
my judgment is passed over from my [1] God?'
Q[3] 28 ° Hast thou not known? ° hast thou not
heard, *that* the everlasting [1] God, [2] the LORD,
the Creator of the ends of the earth, fainteth
not, neither is weary? ° *there is* no searching
of His understanding.
R[3] 29 He giveth power to the faint; and to *them*
that have no might He increaseth ° strength.
30 Even the youths shall faint and be weary,
and the young men shall ° utterly fall:
31 But they that wait upon [2] the LORD shall
° renew *their* ° strength; they shall ° mount up
with wings as eagles; they shall ° run, and not
be weary; *and* they shall ° walk, and not faint."

13 His counseller = the man (Heb. *'ish*. Ap. 14. II) of His counsel. Note the Fig. *Ellipsis* (Ap. 6) = "[who being] His counseller hath", &c.?
taught Him = made Him know. Heb. *yāda'*.
14 instructed Him = made Him understand.
path. See note on 2. 3.
taught = trained. Heb. *lāmad*.
15 of = on: i. e. hanging from.
isles = maritime countries. See note on 11. 11.
16 not sufficient: i. e. for the wood-offering. Cp. Neh. 10. 39. **17** nations = the nations.
nothing. See note on 5. 8. Not the same word as in following clause.
vanity = a desolation. Heb. *tohū*. Same as "without form" (Gen. 1. 2). See note on 24. 10. Cp. *v.* 23.
18 GOD. Heb. El. Ap. 4. IV.
19 melteth = casteth.
graven. Heb. *peṣel*. Here made by casting.
20 chooseth. See note on 1. 29.
prepare = construct. See note on "the smith", &c., 44. 12.
graven = carved. Same word, but made by cutting.
21 Have ye not . . . ? Fig. *Erotēsis* (Ap. 6), for emphasis.
22 sitteth. Fig. *Anthropopatheia*. Ap. 6.
upon = above.
circle = circuit, or vault: i. e. as far as one can see, around or above. See Job 22. 14. Prov. 8. 27.
24 stubble = straw. Heb. *ḳash*.
25 Holy. See note on Ex. 3. 5.
26 calleth = calleth for, summoneth.
by names. See Ps. 147. 4; and Ap. 12.
strong = strong (for activity in working). Not the same word as in *vv.* 9, 29, 31 (Heb. *'āmaẓ*).
faileth = is missing (when called). Cp. 1 Sam. 30. 19. 2 Sam. 17. 22. See note on 34. 16.
27 Why . . . ? Note the Fig. *Erotēsis* (Ap. 6), to emphasise the conclusion drawn from *v.* 26.
28 Hast . . . ? Fig. *Erotēsis* (Ap. 6), for emphasis.
there is. Some codices, with one early printed edition, Sept., Syr., and Vulg., read "and [so] there is".
29 strength = strength (for defence). Not the same word as in *vv.* 9, 10, 26, 31 (Heb. *'āẓam*).
30 utterly fall. Note Fig. *Epizeuxis* (Ap. 6) for this emphasis. Heb. "they fall, they fall".
31 renew = change. Heb. *ḥalaph*, to change for the better. See note on Lev. 27. 10.
strength = strength (to endure). Same word as in *v.* 9. Not the same as in *vv.* 26, 29.
mount up . . . run . . . walk. Note the Fig. *Catabasis* (Ap. 6), to call attention (by Application) to the progress of experience in grace. At first we fly (cp. Paul, 2 Cor. 11. 5; 12. 11); then we run (cp. Paul, Eph. 3. 8); then we walk (cp. Paul, 1 Tim. 1. 15).

41. 1—42. 17 (M, p. 980). MESSIAH'S ANOINTING AND MISSION. (*Division.*)

M | S[1] | 41. 1-29. Types.
  | S[2] | 42. 1-17. Antitype.

41. 1-29 (S[1], above). TYPES. (*Division.*)

S[1] | T[1] | 41. 1-20. Abraham. From the East (*v.* 2). Past.
  | T[2] | 41. 21-29. Cyrus. From the North (*v.* 25). Future.

41. 1-20 (T[1], above). ABRAHAM AND ISRAEL. (*Extended Alternation.*)

T[1] | U | 1. Islands. Jehovah's call.
  V | 2, 3. Type. Abraham.
  W | 4. Jehovah the Doer.
  U | 5-7. Islands. Answer to Jehovah's call.
  V | 8-19. Type. Israel.
  W | 20. Jehovah the Doer.

1 islands = coast-lands. See note on 11. 11.
renew. Same word as in 40. 31.
strength = strength (to endure); not the same word as in 40. 9, 26, 29, 31. Heb. *koaḥ*.
come near = draw nigh.

S[1] T[1] U **41** Keep silence before me, O ° islands; and
(p. 981) let the people ° renew *their* ° strength: let them ° come near; then let them speak: let
us ° come near together to judgment.

V 603-588 2 Who raised up °the righteous *man* from the east, called him to His foot, gave the nations before him, and made *him* rule over °kings? He gave *them* as the dust to his sword, *and* as driven °stubble to his bow.

3 °He pursued them, *and* passed safely; *even* by the °way *that* he had not gone with his feet.

W 4 Who hath wrought and done *it*, calling the generations from the beginning? **I °the LORD, °the first, and °with the last; °I am He.**

U 5 The [1]isles °saw *it*, and °feared; the ends of the earth were °afraid, °drew near, and came.

6 They helped every °one his neighbour; and *every one* said to his brother, "Be of good courage."

7 So the carpenter encouraged the goldsmith, *and* he that smootheth *with* the hammer him that smote the anvil, saying, "It *is* ready for the sodering:" and he fastened it with nails, *that* it should not be moved.

V e 8 But thou, Israel, *art* °My servant, Jacob whom I have °chosen, the seed of **Abraham °My friend.**

9 *Thou* whom I have taken from the ends of the earth, and called thee from °the chief men thereof, and said unto thee, "Thou *art* [8]My servant; °I have [8]chosen thee, and not cast thee away.

10 °Fear thou not; for I *am* with thee: °be not dismayed; for I *am* thy °God: I will °strengthen thee; yea, I will help thee; yea, I will uphold thee with the right hand of My righteousness.

f 11 °Behold, all they that were incensed against thee shall be ashamed and confounded: they shall be as nothing; and °they that strive with thee shall perish.

12 Thou shalt seek them, and shalt not find them, *even* °them that contended with thee: they that war against thee shall be as °nothing, and as a thing of nought.

e 13 For I [4]the LORD thy [10]God will hold thy right hand, saying unto thee, [10]'Fear not;' I will help thee.

14 [10]Fear not, °thou worm Jacob, *and* ye °men of Israel; I will help thee," saith [4]the LORD, and °thy Redeemer, °the Holy One of Israel.

f 15 [11]"Behold, I will °make thee a new sharp °threshing instrument having teeth: thou shalt thresh the mountains, and beat *them* small, and shalt make the hills as chaff.

16 Thou shalt fan them, and the °wind shall carry them away, and the whirlwind shall scatter them: and thou shalt rejoice in [4]the LORD, *and* shalt °glory in [14]the Holy One of Israel.

17 *When* the °poor and needy seek water, and *there is* none, *and* their tongue °faileth for thirst, I [4]the LORD will °hear them, *I* °the [10]God of Israel will not °forsake them.

18 I will °open rivers in high places, and fountains in the midst of the valleys: I will make the wilderness a pool of water, and the dry land springs of water.

19 I will plant in the wilderness the cedar, the shittah tree, and the myrtle, and the oil tree; I will set in the desert the fir tree, *and* the pine, and the box tree together:

W 20 That they may see, °and know, °and consider, °and understand together, that the hand of the LORD hath done this, and [14]the Holy One of Israel hath created it.

2 the righteous man from the east: i.e. Abraham. Cp. Cyrus raised up from the north, *v.* 25.
kings: i.e. those mentioned in Gen. 14. 1, 8, 9.
stubble=straw. Heb. *kash*, as in 40. 24.
3 He pursued them: i.e. Abraham pursued them unto Dan. Ref. to Pent. (Gen. 14. 14, 15). Ap. 92.
way. See note on "path." Ch. 2. 3.
4 the LORD. Heb. Jehovah. Ap. 4. II.
the first, and . . . last. Occurs here and 44. 6; 48. 12. Thus, three times in Isaiah, and three times in the Apocalypse (Rev. 1. 17; 2. 8; 22. 13).
with the last: i.e. He who called Abraham, the first, will be with the last (Messiah), Who is the subject of this prophecy.
I am He: or, I AM.
5 saw . . . feared . . . afraid . . . drew near. Note the Fig. *Paronomasia* (Ap. 6). Heb. *rā'ū . . . v^eyiyra'ū . . . yeḥĕrādū . . . ḳārbū.*
6 one=man. Heb. *'ish.*

41. 8-19 (*V*, p. 981). **TYPE. ISRAEL.**
(*Alternation.*)

V | e | 8-10. Encouragement. "Fear not".
| f | 11, 12. Ascendency.
| *e* | 13, 14. Encouragement. "Fear not".
| *f* | 15-19. Victory.

8 My servant. See note on 37. 35 for the three "servants" in Isaiah. This was Israel, as the seed of Abraham, not Cyrus (yet). Cp. *vv.* 21-29.
chosen. See note on 1. 29.
My friend. See note on 2 Chron. 20. 7.
9 the chief men=the remote parts.
I have chosen thee. Gen. 12. 1. Josh. 24. 2-4. Neh. 9. 7. Acts 7. 2-7. Ref. to Pent. (Deut. 7. 6; 10. 15; 14. 2). Ap. 92.
10 Fear thou not. Ref. to Pent. (Deut. 31. 6, 8).
be not dismayed=look not around. Some codices, with Syr., read "and be not", &c. It is this that dismays (see notes on Pss. 73 and 77).
God. Heb. Elohim. Ap. 4. I.
strengthen=strength (inherent, for activity). Heb. *'āmaz.* Not the same word as in *vv.* 1 and 21.
11 Behold. Fig. *Asterismos.* Ap. 6.
Behold, all they, &c. Ref. to Pent. (Ex. 23. 22). Ap. 92.
they that strive=the men (Heb. *'ish*, Ap. 14. II) of thy strife: i.e. thine accusers.
12 them that contended=the men (Heb. *'ish*) of thy contention.
nothing. See note on 5. 8.
14 thou worm. To emphasise the weakness of Israel; marked also by the Fig. *Asterismos* (Ap. 6), "Behold".
men. Heb. *m^ethīm.* Ap. 14. V.
thy Redeemer. Ref. to Pent. (Gen. 48. 16. Ex. 6. 6; 15. 13). Ap. 92.
the Holy One of Israel. See note on 1. 4.
15 make thee=set thee for.
threshing instrument. See note on 28. 27.
16 wind. Heb. *rūach.* Ap. 9.
glory. See note on 13. 10.
17 poor=wretched. Heb. *'ānāh.* See note on Prov. 6. 11. **faileth.** See note on 19. 5.
hear=answer.
the God of Israel. See note on 29. 23.
forsake. See note on 1. 4.
18 open rivers, &c. Note that all these physical marvels must be accomplished by the miraculous power of God, not by the spirituality of His People. See note on 35. 1.
20 and. Note the Fig. *Polysyndeton* (Ap. 6) for emphasis.

T² X g (p. 983) 603-588 21 Produce your cause," °saith [4]the LORD; "bring forth your °strong *reasons*," saith °the King of Jacob.

22 "Let them bring *them* forth, and shew Us what shall happen: let them shew the former things, what they *be*, that we may consider them, and know the latter end of them; or declare Us things for to come.

23 Shew the things that are to come hereafter, that We may know that ye *are* gods: yea, do good, or do °evil, that We may be dismayed, and behold *it* together.

h 24 [11]Behold, ye *are* of nothing, and your work of nought: an abomination *is he that* [8]chooseth you.

Y 25 I have °raised up *one* from the north, and he shall °come: from the rising of the sun °shall he call upon °My name:

Y and he shall come upon °princes as *upon* morter, and as the potter treadeth clay.

X g 26 Who hath declared from the beginning, that we may know? and beforetime, that we may say, '*He is* righteous?' yea, *there is* none that sheweth, yea, *there is* none that declareth, yea, *there is* none that heareth your words.

27 °The first *shall say* to Zion, [11]'Behold, °behold them:' and I will give to Jerusalem one that bringeth good tidings.

28 For I beheld, and *there was* no °man; even among them, and *there was* no counseller, that, when I asked of them, could answer a word.

h 29 [11]Behold, they *are* all vanity; their works *are* [12]nothing: their °molten images *are* °wind and °confusion.

S² Z B i **42** **°Behold °My Servant, Whom I uphold; Mine elect, *in Whom* °My soul °delighteth; I have °put °My spirit upon Him: He shall bring forth judgment to the Gentiles.**

2 He shall not °cry, nor lift up, nor cause His voice to be heard in the street.

3 A bruised reed shall He not break, and °the smoking °flax shall He °not quench: He shall bring forth judgment °unto truth.

4 He shall not °fail nor °be discouraged, till He have set judgment °in the earth: and the °isles shall °wait for His °law."

k 5 Thus saith °GOD °the LORD, He That created the heavens, °and stretched them out; He That spread forth the earth, and that which cometh out of it; He That giveth °breath unto the people upon it, and [1]spirit to them that walk therein:

6 "I [5]the LORD have called thee in righteousness, and will hold thine hand, and will keep thee, and give thee for a covenant of the People, for °**a light of the Gentiles**;

7 °To open the blind eyes, to bring out the °prisoners from the prison, *and* them that °sit in darkness out of the prison house.

41. 21-29 (T², p. 981). TYPE. CYRUS.
(*Introversion and Alternation.*)

T² | X | g | 21-23. Challenge as to Prediction.
h | 24. Nothingness.
Y | 25-. Cyrus. Raised up. The act.
Y | -25. Cyrus. Raised up. The purpose.
X | *g* | 26-28. Challenge as to Prediction.
h | 29. Nothingness.

21 saith the LORD. See note on 1. 11.
strong=strong (for weight or importance). Heb. *azam.* Not same word as in *vv.* 1, 10. Heb. *'āmaẓ.*
the King of Jacob. This title occurs only here. Heathen kings were the gods of their people. So Jehovah, the King of Jacob, was the God of Israel.
23 evil. Heb. *rā'a'.* See Ap. 44. viii.
25 raised up one from the north: i.e. Cyrus. See Ap. 57. Cp. Abraham (the other type was "from the east", *v.* 2). This prophecy was made 137 years before its fulfilment. Cp. 44. 28; 45. 1.
come=speed.
shall he call upon My name. This is the counterpart of 45. 3, 4. Cp. Ezra 1. 2 and 2 Chron. 36. 22, 23.
My name=Me (emph.). See note on Ps. 20. 1.
princes. The title of Babylonian governors and prefects of provinces. Heb. *ṣ^eganim.* Used once in Ezra (9. 2, "rulers"); nine times in Nehemiah (2. 16, 16; 4. 14, 19; 5. 7, 17; 7. 5; 12. 40; 13. 11); three times in Jeremiah (51. 23, 28, 57); three times in Ezekiel (23. 6, 12, 23). Always rendered "rulers" except here, which is the only occurrence in Isaiah. Cyrus (the Medo-Persian) did fulfil this on the Babylonian "princes".
27 The first shall say=From the first [I have said].
Behold, behold. Fig. *Epizeuxis* (Ap. 6), for emphasis. See note on 24. 16.
28 man. Heb. *'ish.* Ap. 14. II.
29 molten images. See note on 30. 22.
wind=vanity. Heb. *rūach* (Ap. 9). See note on 57. 6. **confusion.** See note on 24. 10.

42. 1-17 (S², p. 981). ANTITYPE. MESSIAH.
(*Introversion and Alternation.*)

S² | Z | B | i | 1-4. Messiah. Presented.
k | 5-7. Messiah. Addressed.
C | 8. Images.
A | 9. Predictions.
A | 10-12. Praise.
Z | *B* | *i* | 13. Messiah. Presented.
k | 14-16. Messiah. Addressing.
C | 17. Images.

1 Behold. Fig. *Asterismos* (Ap. 6). Quoted in Matt. 12. 17-21.
My Servant: i.e. Messiah. See note on 37. 35.
My soul=I Myself. Heb. *nephesh.* Ap. 13.
delighteth=is well-pleased. **put**=bestowed.
My spirit. Heb. *rūach* (Ap. 9). Here is the doctrine of the Trinity: (1) The Father, the speaker; (2) My "Servant", the Messiah, the Son; and (3) My Spirit. See note on "stretched out" in *v.* 5.
2 cry. See the Divine interpretation "strive" (Matt. 12. 19).
3 the smoking flax: i.e. the wick (made of flax) that is burning dim.
flax. Put by Fig. *Metonymy* (of Cause), Ap. 6, for the wick made of it.
not quench: i.e. not put it out, but trim it and make it burn brightly. This was the servant's work.
unto=in accordance with.
4 fail=go out (as a lamp).
be discouraged=break, or break down.
in=upon.

isles=maritime countries. The Divine interpretation="Gentiles" (Matt. 12. 18-21). See note on 11. 11. **wait.** Ref. to Pent. (Gen. 8. 12 "stayed"). Ap. 92. **law.** See note on 1. 10. **5 GOD.** Heb. El. Ap. 4. IV. **the LORD.** Heb. Jehovah. Ap. 4. II. **and stretched them out**=they that stretched them out. Cp. "us", "our" (Gen. 1. 26). Cp. "image" (singular). **breath.** Heb. *n^eshāmāh* (Ap. 16). See note on 2. 22. **6 a light of the Gentiles.** Quoted in Luke 2. 32. Cp. 49. 6. **7 To open the blind eyes.** Renewing the prophecy of 35. 5. **prisoners.** See 49. 9; 61. 1. **sit.** Put by Fig. *Synecdoche* (of Species) Ap. 6, for being in a permanent condition.

C (p. 983) 603-588 8 °𝔍 *am* [5]the LORD: 𝔱𝔥𝔞𝔱 *is* My name: and My glory °will I not give to °another, neither My °praise to graven images.

A 9 [1]Behold, °the former things are come to pass, and °new things do 𝔍 declare: before they spring forth I tell 𝔶𝔬𝔲 of them.

A 10 °Sing unto [5]the LORD a new song, *and* His praise from the end of the earth, ye that go down to the sea, and all that is therein; the [4]isles, and the inhabitants thereof.

11 Let the wilderness and the cities thereof lift up *their voice*, the villages *that* Kedar doth inhabit: let the inhabitants of the rock sing, let them shout from the top of the mountains.

12 Let them give glory unto [5]the LORD, and declare His praise in the [4]islands.

Z B i (p. 984) 13 [5]The LORD shall °go forth as a °mighty man, He shall °stir up °jealousy like a °man of war: He shall °cry, yea, °roar; He shall prevail against His enemies.

k 14 I have long time holden My peace; I have been still, *and* refrained Myself: *now* will I [13]cry like a travailing woman; I will destroy and devour at once.

15 I will make waste mountains and hills, and dry up all their herbs; and I will make the rivers [4]islands, and I will dry up the pools.

16 And I will bring the blind by a way *that* they knew not; °I will lead them in paths *that* they have not known: I will make darkness light before them, and crooked things straight. °These things °will I do unto them, °and not forsake them.

C 17 They shall be turned back, they shall be greatly ashamed, that °trust in graven images, °that say to the molten images, '𝔜𝔢 *are* our gods.'

N D n (p. 984) 18 °Hear, ye deaf; and look, ye blind, that ye may see.

o 19 Who *is* blind, but °My servant? or deaf, as My messenger *that* I sent? who *is* blind as *he that is* °perfect, and blind as [5]the LORD'S servant?

20 °Seeing many things, but thou observest not; °opening the ears, but °he heareth not."

p 21 [5]The LORD is well pleased for His righteousness' sake; °He will magnify the [4]law, and make *it* honourable.

q 22 But °𝔱𝔥𝔦𝔰 *is* a People robbed and spoiled; *they are* all of them snared in holes, and they are hid in prison houses: they are for a prey, and none delivereth; for a spoil, and none saith, "Restore."

n 23 °Who among you will give ear to this? *who* will hearken and hear for the time to come?

o 24 Who gave °Jacob for a spoil, and °Israel to the robbers? did not [5]the LORD, He against Whom we have °sinned? for they would not walk in His ways,

p neither were they obedient unto His [4]law.

q 25 Therefore He hath poured upon him the fury of His anger, and the °strength of battle: and it hath set him on fire round about, yet he knew not; and it burned him, yet he laid *it* not to heart.

8 𝔍 am. Ref. to Pent. (Ex. 3. 15). Ap. 92.
will I not give. Ref. to Pent. (Ex. 20. 5). Ap. 92.
another: i.e. a strange god.
praise. Heb. *hālal.* Not confined to the "former" part of Isaiah, as alleged. See 13. 10; 38. 18. See Ap. 79. II.
9 the former things, &c. Referring to his prophecies, among others, concerning Sennacherib, chs. 10 and 37.
new things, &c. Thus uniting the predictions of the earlier chapters with the so-called "second" part. See Ap. 79. II. **10 Sing.** Fig. *Pæanismos.* Ap. 6.
13 go forth. This is an enlargement of 41. 15, 16. Still more so in Rev. 6. 2; 19. 11.
mighty man. Heb. *gibbōr.* Ap. 14. iv.
stir up = awaken, incite. See note on Song 2. 7.
jealousy. Ref. to Pent. (Ex. 20. 5). Ap. 92.
man. Heb. *'īsh.* Ap. 14. II.
cry . . . roar. Fig. *Anthropopatheia.* Ap. 6.
16 I will lead = I have led.
I will lead them, &c. Some codices, with Sept., Syr., and Vulg., commence this sentence with "And".
These things, &c. Ref. to Pent. (Deut. 31. 6). Ap. 92.
will I do = have I done. **and not** = and have not.
17 trust = confide. Heb. *bāṭaḥ.* Ap. 69. i.
that say, &c. Ref. to Pent. (Ex. 32. 4). Ap. 92.

42. 18—45. 15 (N, p. 980). JEHOVAH'S CONTROVERSY WITH ISRAEL.
(*Extended Alternation and Introversion.*)

N D | 42. 18-25. Remonstrance. Morals.
E | 43. 1-7. Encouragement. "Fear not." } Israel.
F | 43. 8-13. Witnesses.
G | l | 43. 14-17. Babylon. Destruction.
m | 43. 18-21. Remembrance. Negative.
D | 43. 22-28. Remonstrance. Ceremonials.
E | 44. 1-5. Encouragement. "Fear not." } Israel.
F | 44. 6-20. Witnesses.
G | *m* | 44. 21-23. Remembrance. Positive.
l | 44. 24—45. 15. Jerusalem. Restoration.

42. 18-25 (D, above). REMONSTRANCE. MORALS. (*Extended Alternation.*)

D | n | 18. Call to hear.
o | 19, 20. Israel. "Blind and deaf".
p | 21. The Law magnified by Jehovah.
q | 22. Judgments.
n | 23. Call to hear.
o | 24-. Jacob. "Spoiled and robbed".
p | -24. The Law disregarded by Israel.
q | 25. Judgments.

18 Hear. Note the call to hear in the Structure ("n"), corresponding with the call in "*n*" *v.* 23.
19 My servant. This is Israel. See the Structures of N, p. 980, and D, above; and see note on 37. 35. Not the same "servant" as in *v.* 1.
perfect = an intimate friend or trusted one. Heb. *m^eshullām* (plural of *shālam*), to be at peace with. Cp. 2 Sam. 20. 19. Job 22. 21. Ps. 7. 4. It is from this word we have *Mussulman* and *Moslem.* Israel, in the presence of the foe, was, in Jehovah's sight, thus perfect. See Num. 23. 21.
20 Seeing . . . opening the ears. As Israel had done. Ref. to Pent. (Deut. 29. 1, 2). Ap. 92. But Israel was blind and deaf (*v.* 19). Cp. Jer. 5. 21; 6. 10. Ezek. 12. 2. Matt. 13. 14. John 12. 40.
he. Some codices, with Syr., read "thou" (as in the preceding clause); others read "ye". The pronoun refers to Israel. See *v.* 19.
21 He will magnify the law. Note the correspondence with *v.* 24 ("p" and "*p*" above).
22 𝔱𝔥𝔦𝔰 is a People. Showing most clearly that Israel is the subject of this member (D, above).
23 Who . . . ? The other "call to hear" emphasised by the Fig. *Erotēsis* (Ap. 6).
24 Jacob . . . Israel. See notes on Gen. 32. 28; 43. 6; 45. 26, 28. **sinned.** Heb. *chṭā'.* Ap. 44. i.
25 strength = strength (for prevailing). Not the same word as in 41. 1, 10. Heb. *'azaz*: i.e. battle that prevailed against Israel.

E H (p. 985) 603-588 **43** But now thus saith °the LORD That created thee, O °Jacob, and °He That formed thee, O °Israel,

J r °"Fear not: for I have °redeemed thee, I have called *thee* by thy name; thou *art* Mine.

s **2** °When thou passest through °the waters, I *will be* with thee; and through °the rivers, they shall not overflow thee: when thou walkest through °the fire, thou shalt not be burned; neither shall °the flame °kindle upon thee.

K t **3** For °I *am* [1]the LORD thy °God, °the Holy One of Israel, °thy Saviour:

u I gave °Egypt *for* thy °ransom, °Ethiopia and °Seba for thee.

K t **4** °Since thou wast precious in My sight, thou hast been honourable, and I have loved thee:

u therefore will I give °men for thee, and °people for thy °life.

J r **5** Fear not: for I *am* with thee:

s I will bring thy seed from the °east, and gather thee from the °west;

6 I will say to the °north, 'Give up'; and to the °south, 'Keep not back: bring My sons from far, and My daughters from the ends of the earth;

H **7** *Even* every one that is called by My name: for I have created him for My glory, I have formed him; yea, I have made him.

8 Bring forth °the blind People that have eyes, and the deaf that have ears.

9 Let all the nations be gathered together, and let the [4]people be assembled: who among °them can declare this, and shew us former things? let them bring forth their witnesses, that they may be justified: or let them hear, and say, '*It is* truth.'

F v **10** Ye *are* My witnesses," °saith [1]the LORD, "and °My Servant Whom I have °chosen:

w that ye may know and believe Me, and understand that °I *am* He: before Me there was no °GOD formed, neither shall there be after Me.

11 I, *even* I, *am* [1]the LORD; and beside Me *there is* no saviour.

12 I have declared, and have saved, and I have shewed, when *there was* °no strange *god* among you:

v therefore ye *are* My witnesses," [10]saith [1]the LORD,

w "that I *am* [10]GOD.

13 Yea, before the day *was* I *am* He; and *there is* none that can deliver out of My hand: I will work, and who shall °let it?"

G l (p. 984) **14** Thus saith [1]the LORD, your °Redeemer, [3]the Holy One of Israel; "For your sake I have sent to °Babylon, and have brought down all °their nobles, and the Chaldeans, °whose cry *is* in the ships.

43. 1-7 (E, p. 984). ENCOURAGEMENT. (*Introversion and Alternation.*)

E | H | 1-. Israel created and called.
  J | r | -1. "Fear not".
    s | 2. Preservation.
      K | t | 3-. Jehovah. Israel's Saviour.
        u | -3. Ransom.
      K | *t* | 4-. Jehovah. Israel's Lover.
        u | -4. Ransom.
  J | *r* | 5-. "Fear not".
    s | -5-7-. Restoration.
H | -7. Israel called and created.

1 the LORD. Heb. Jehovah. Ap. 4. II.

the LORD That created thee. This is another Jehovah title (cp. Ap. 4. II.) = Jehovah *Boraăka* = Jehovah thy Creator.

Jacob . . . Israel. See notes on Gen. 32. 28; 43. 6; 45. 26, 28. See 42. 24, above.

He That formed thee = thy Former.

Fear not. Cp. *v.* 5.

redeemed. Heb. *gā'al.* See note on Ex. 6. 6.

2 When thou passest = shouldst thou pass: the habitual sense of *kī* with the Future. Ref. to Pent. (Deut. 31. 6, 8).

the waters . . . the rivers . . . the fire . . . the flame = waters . . . rivers . . . fire . . . flame. A general promise of future deliverance put by Fig. *Metonymy* (of Subject), Ap. 6, for troubles of any and all kinds. This promise refers to Israel's future, and not to the Saxon race, or the Church.

kindle upon thee = pass over thee.

3 I am the LORD thy God = I Jehovah am thy God (Heb. Elohim. Ap. 4. I). Note the three titles. He was Israel's God by covenant (note the others in the next clause):—

the Holy One of Israel, in contrast with all false gods. See note on 1. 4, and Ps. 71. 22.

thy Saviour. This is the third title.

Egypt . . . Ethiopia and Seba = Egypt . . . Nubia (Cush), and Ethiopia. These were given to Persia as ransom-money (as it were) for the release of Israel by Persia through the successors of Cyrus (see Xenophon, *Cyr.* viii. 6, 20; and Herod. i. 153; iii. 25). In the time of Isaiah these three were united under one dynasty.

ransom = atonement price. Heb. *kopher.* See note on Ex. 29. 33.

4 Since thou wast = Ever since thou becamest.

men = a man. Can this refer to Christ? Heb. *'ādām.* Ap. 14. I. **people** = peoples.

life = soul. Heb. *nephesh.* Ap. 13.

5-6 east . . . west . . . north . . . south. This contemplates a wider and greater deliverance than that from Babylon, even from "the ends of the earth".

43. 8-13 (F, p. 984). WITNESSES. (*Alternation.*)

vv. 8, 9. The Challenge.

F | v | 10-. Jehovah's witnesses.
  w | -10-12-. The only God.
  v | -12-. Jehovah's witnesses.
  w | -12, 13-. The only God.

8 the blind People = a blind People: i.e. Israel (see 6. 10; 42. 19, 20. Jer. 5. 21. Ezek. 12. 2. Matt. 13. 14. Acts 28. 26, 27).

9 them. Some codices, with one early printed edition, Syr., and Vulg., read "you".

10 saith the LORD = is Jehovah's oracle.

My Servant: i.e. Israel. See note on 37. 35.

chosen. See note on 1. 29.

I am He: or, "I [am] He [Who is]". Note the Structure, above ("w", and "*w*").

GOD. Heb. El. Ap. 4. IV.

12 no strange god. Ref. to Pent. (Deut. 32. 12, 16). See Ap. 92. **13 let it** = avert it. See Amos 1. 3, 6, 9, 11, 13; 2. 1, 4, 6. **14 Redeemer** = Kinsman-Redeemer. Heb. *Go'el.* See note on Ex. 6. 6. **Babylon.** This is the first occurrence of the name in Isaiah. **their nobles** = all of them in flight. **whose cry is in the ships** = the ships which resound with loud outcries (cp. Lam. 2. 19. Num. 24. 24).

603-588 15 ℑ *am* [1]the LORD, your Holy One, the Creator of Israel, your King."

16 Thus saith [1]the LORD, Which °maketh a way in the sea, and a path in the mighty waters;

17 Which bringeth forth the chariot and horse, the army and the power; "they shall lie down °together, they shall not rise: they are extinct, they are quenched as °tow.

m (p. 984) 18 °Remember ye not the former things, neither consider the things of old.

19 Behold, I will do °a new thing; now it shall spring forth; shall ye not know it? I will even make a way in the wilderness, *and* rivers in the desert.

20 The beast of the field shall honour Me, the dragons and the owls: because °I give waters in the wilderness, *and* rivers in the desert, to give drink to My people, My chosen.

21 °This People have I formed for Myself; they shall shew forth My praise.

D 22 But thou hast not °called upon Me, O Jacob; but thou hast °been weary of Me, O Israel.

23 °Thou hast not brought Me the small cattle of thy burnt offerings; neither hast thou honoured Me with thy sacrifices. I have not caused thee to serve with an offering, nor wearied thee with incense.

24 Thou hast bought Me no sweet cane with money, neither hast thou filled Me with the fat of thy sacrifices: °but thou hast °made Me to serve with thy °sins, thou hast wearied Me with thine °iniquities.

25 ℑ, *even* ℑ, *am* ℌe That blotteth out thy °transgressions °for Mine own sake, and °will not °remember thy [24]sins.

26 Put Me in remembrance: let us plead together: °declare thou, that thou mayest be justified.

27 °Thy first father hath [24]sinned, and thy teachers have [25]transgressed against Me.

28 Therefore I have profaned the °princes of the sanctuary, and have given °Jacob to the curse, and °Israel to reproaches.

E **44** Yet now hear, O Jacob °My servant; and Israel, whom I have °chosen:"

2 °Thus saith °the LORD That made thee, and °formed thee from the womb, *Which* will help thee; "Fear not, O Jacob, [1]My servant; and thou, °Jesurun, whom I have [1]chosen.

3 For °I will pour water upon him that is thirsty, and floods upon the dry ground: I will pour My °spirit upon thy seed, and My blessing upon thine offspring:

4 And they shall spring up *as* among the grass, °as willows by the °water courses.

5 °One shall say, 'ℑ *am* [2]the LORD'S;' and °another shall call *himself* by the name of Jacob; and °another shall subscribe *with* his hand unto [2]the LORD, and surname *himself* by the name of Israel."

F L (p. 987) 6 Thus saith [2]the LORD °the King of Israel, and °his Redeemer °the LORD of hosts; "ℑ

16 maketh a way in the sea. Ref. to Pent. (Ex. 14. 16, 21, 22. Ps. 77. 19). See Ap. 92.

17 together: or, at once.

tow=wick. Heb. flax. Put by Fig. *Metonymy* (of Cause), Ap. 6, for the wick made of it.

18 Remember ye. Note the correspondence of the members "m" and "*m*" (*v.* 18, and 44. 21).

19 a new thing. The future deliverance of Israel will be with greater marvels than at the Exodus.

20 I give waters, &c. Ref. to Pent. (Ex. 17. 6. Num. 20. 11).

21 This People, &c. For Israel (as Birks puts it) "is the keystone of the whole arch of promise". See note on 44. 7.

22 called upon Me. Put by Fig. *Synecdoche* (of Species), Ap. 6, for all that has to do with worship, as developed in *vv.* 23, 24.

been weary of Me. Note the emphasis is on "Me" in these verses (cp. Mic. 6. 3. Mal. 1. 13).

23 Thou hast not brought Me, &c. These verses are quite opposed to the alleged indifference of the prophets to the Divine ritual.

24 but. Note the solemn antithesis.

made Me to serve. Put by Fig. *Metonymy* (of Effect, of the verb), Ap. 6, for the judicial consequences of their sins.

sins. Heb. *chāṭā'*. Ap. 44. i.

iniquities. Heb. *'āvāh*. Ap. 44. iv.

25 transgressions=rebellions. Heb. *pāsha'*. Ap. 44. ix.

for Mine own sake. He does not go out of Himself for the reason which flows from grace.

will not remember. He remembers our infirmities (which man forgets. Ps. 103. 14), but will forget our sins (which man remembers).

remember. Fig. *Anthropopatheia.* Ap. 6.

26 declare=recount [thy works, or sins].

27 Thy first father: i. e. Jacob, as stated in the next verse (cp. Deut. 26. 5. Ezek. 16. 3, 45).

28 princes=priests, whose great duty it was to "teach" the people the Law and Word of God (see notes on Deut. 17. 11; 33. 10).

Jacob . . . Israel. Including the whole Nation: the subject of this prophecy concerning Jehovah's "servant".

44. 1 My servant. The subject of these members "E" and "*E*" (p. 984). See note on 37. 35.

chosen. See note on 1. 29.

2 Thus saith, &c. Jehovah's first controversy with Israel closes with this member "N" (p. 980); and the second closes with "*N*" (p. 984).

the LORD. Heb. Jehovah. Ap. 4. II. Note the Jehovah title, as in 43. 1, in the members "E" and "*E*" (p. 984).

formed=fashioned.

Jesurun. This is a direct reference to the Pentateuch (Deut. 32. 15; 33. 5, 26), the only three places where this name occurs. See notes there and Ap. 92.

3 I will pour, &c. These promises all refer to the day of Israel's future restoration.

spirit. Heb. *rūach.* Ap. 9. For this promise, see Ezek. 36. 25–30; 39. 29. Cp. Isa. 32. 15; 59. 21. Joel 2. 28. Zech. 12. 10. It began at Pentecost (Acts 2. 16); but the kingdom was then rejected (Acts 28. 25, 26), and the promise is now in abeyance. Cp. Joel 2. 28, "afterward".

4 as willows, &c. Ref. to Pent. (Num. 24. 6). Ap. 92.

water courses. See note on "streams", 30. 25.

5 One . . . another . . . another. Heb. *zeh*=this one, that one, &c.

44. 6-20 [For Structure see next page].

6 the King of Israel. Note this title (1) in connection with the O.T. manifestation of the kingdom; (2) the Gospels, the proclamation of the kingdom by the Son (Matt. 27. 42. Mark 15. 32. John 1. 49; 12. 13). All were rejected, and the kingdom therefore is now in abeyance. **his Redeemer**: i. e. his Kinsman-Redeemer. Ref. to Pent. (see note on 41. 14). **the LORD of hosts.** See note on 1 Sam. 1. 3.

603-588 *am* °the first, and **I** *am* the last; and ° beside
Me *there is* no ° God.

M (p. 987) 7 And who, as I, shall call, and shall declare
it, and set it in order for Me, since I °appointed
°the ancient People? and the things that are
coming, °and shall come, let them shew unto
them.

L 8 Fear ye not, neither be afraid: have not I
told thee from that time, and have declared
it? **ye** *are* even °My witnesses. Is there °a **GOD**
beside Me? yea, *there is* °no God; I know not
any.

M N 9 They that °make a graven image *are* all
of them °vanity; and °their °delectable things
shall not profit; and **they** *are* their own witnesses; °they see not, nor know; that they
may be °ashamed.
10 Who hath formed a god, or molten a
graven image *that* is profitable for nothing?
11 Behold, all his fellows shall be [9]ashamed:
and the workmen, **they** *are* of °men: let them
all be gathered together, let them stand up;
yet they shall fear, *and* they shall be [9]ashamed
together.

O x 12 °The smith with the tongs both worketh
in the coals, and fashioneth it with hammers,
and worketh it with the strength of his arms:
y yea, he is hungry, and his strength faileth: he
drinketh no water, and is faint.

x 13 The carpenter stretcheth out *his* rule; he
marketh it out with a line; he fitteth it with
planes, and he marketh it out with the compass,
and maketh it after the figure of a °man, according to the beauty of a °man; that it may
remain in the house.
14 He heweth him down cedars, and taketh
the cypress and the oak, which he strengtheneth
for himself among the trees of the forest: he
planteth an ash, and the rain doth nourish *it.*
15 Then shall it be for a man to burn: for he
will °take thereof, and warm himself; yea, he
kindleth *it,* and baketh bread; yea, he maketh
a god, and worshippeth *it;* he maketh it a
graven image, and falleth down thereto.

y 16 He burneth part thereof in the fire; °with
part thereof he eateth flesh; he roasteth roast,
and is satisfied: yea, he warmeth *himself,* and
saith, 'Aha, I am warm, I have seen the fire:'
17 And the residue thereof he °maketh a god,
even his graven image: he falleth down unto
it, and worshippeth *it,* and prayeth unto it,
and saith, 'Deliver me; for **thou** *art* my god.'

N 18 They have °not known nor understood:
for he hath °shut their eyes, that they cannot
see; *and* their hearts, that they cannot understand.
19 And °none considereth in his heart, neither
is there knowledge nor °understanding to say,
'I have burned part of it in the fire; yea, also
I have baked bread upon the coals thereof;
I have roasted flesh, and eaten *it:* and shall
I make the residue thereof an abomination?
shall I fall down to °the stock of a tree?'
20 He feedeth °on ashes: a deceived heart
hath turned him aside, that he cannot deliver
his °soul, nor say, '*Is there* not °a lie in my
right hand?'

44. 6-20 (*F*, p. 984). WITNESSES.
(*Alternation.*)

F | L | 6. Jehovah. His Own Witness.
| M | 7. Idolaters. Their own witnesses. Ignorance.
| *L* | 8. Jehovah. His Own Witness.
| *M* | 9-20. Idolaters. Their own witnesses. Impotence.

the first, &c. See note on 41. 4. Quoted in Rev. 1. 17, &c.
beside Me. Ref. to Pent. (Deut. 4. 35; 32. 39). Ap. 92.
God. Heb. Elohim. Ap. 4. I.
7 appointed = set, or established.
the ancient People = the everlasting Nation. The nation of Israel is everlasting, like the Covenant. The nations which oppressed Israel (Egypt, Assyria, Babylon, Rome) have passed away; but Israel remains, and, when restored, will remain for ever. Note and cp. the nine everlasting things in Isaiah: (1) covenant (55. 3; 61. 8; cp. note on Gen. 9. 16); (2) kindness (54. 8); (3) salvation (45. 17); (4) excellency (60. 15); (5) joy (51. 11); (6) name (56. 5); (7) light (60. 19, 20); (8) sign (55. 13); and (9) as the pledge of all, "the everlasting God" (40. 28; 63. 12).
and shall come = and [which] shall come.
8 My witnesses. Note the Structures ("L" and "*L*", above).
a GOD. Heb. an Eloah. Ap. 4. V.
no God = no Rock. Ref. to Pent. (Deut. 32. 4. Cp. Isa. 26. 4). Ap. 92.

9-20 (*M*, above). IDOLATERS THEIR OWN WITNESSES. IGNORANCE. (*Introversion.*)

M | N | 9-11. Idolaters. Their stupidity.
| O | 12-17. The smith and the carpenter.
| *N* | 18-20. Idolaters. Their stupidity.

9 make = fashion, or, form.
vanity = emptiness. Heb. *tohū* (without form), as in Gen. 1. 2. See note on 24. 10.
their = the fashioners'.
delectable things. Put by Fig. *Metonymy* (of Adjunct), Ap. 6, for the things they have desired.
they: i.e. the makers and worshippers. See the Structure, above.
ashamed: as the Babylonians were when their city was taken by the Medo-Persians.
11 men. Heb. *'ādām.* Ap. 14. I.

12-17 (O, above). THE SMITH AND THE CARPENTER. (*Alternation.*)

O | x | 12-. The smith and his god.
| y | -12. His own infirmity.
| *x* | 13-15. The carpenter and his god.
| *y* | 16, 17. His own infirmity.

12 The smith with the tongs, &c. "The smith was more or less a sacred person, and the iron foundry was an annex of heathen temples." Mounds of *scoriæ* and iron slag are found near many heathen temples. So writes Prof. Sayce in *The Proceedings of the Society of Biblical Archæology* (1911). Note the contrast exhibited (apparently on purpose) in 1 Kings 6. 7.
13 man. Heb. *'ish.* Ap. 14. II.
15 take thereof = take [of the wood] thereof.
16 with. Some codices in marg., with one early printed edition, Sept., Syr., and Vulg., read "and with".
17 maketh a = maketh into a.
18 not known = not taken note.
shut = smeared.
19 none considereth = none reflecteth; none bringeth back to his heart.
understanding = discernment.
the stock of a tree = a log of wood.
20 on. The A.V. of 1611 had "of".
soul. Heb. *nephesh.* Ap. 13.
a lie: i.e. the maker's vain fancy.

21 Remember these, O Jacob and Israel; for G *m*
thou *art* [1]My servant: I have formed thee; **thou**

603-588 *art* [1]My servant: °O Israel, thou shalt °not be
forgotten of Me.
22 °I have blotted out, as a thick cloud, thy
°transgressions, and, as a cloud, thy °sins:
return unto Me; for I have °redeemed thee.
23 °Sing, O ye heavens; for [2]the LORD hath
done *it:* °shout, ye lower parts of the earth:
°break forth into singing, ye mountains, O
forest, and every tree therein: for [1]the LORD
hath [6]redeemed Jacob, and glorified Himself in
Israel."

l P (p. 988) 24 Thus saith [2]the LORD, thy [6]Redeemer, and
He That [2]formed thee from the womb, "I *am*
[2]the LORD That maketh all *things;* That
stretcheth forth the heavens alone; That
spreadeth abroad the earth by Myself;
25 That frustrateth the °tokens of the °liars,
and maketh °diviners mad; That turneth
°wise *men* backward, and maketh their knowledge foolish;
26 That confirmeth the word of °His Servant,
and performeth the counsel of His messengers;

Q S That saith to °Jerusalem, 'Thou shalt be inhabited'; and to the °cities of Judah, 'Ye shall
be °built, and I will raise up the decayed places
thereof:'
27 That saith to °the deep, 'Be dry, and °I
will dry up thy °rivers:'

T 28 That saith of °Cyrus, '*He is* My shepherd,
and shall perform all My pleasure: °even saying to °Jerusalem, 'Thou shalt be built;' and
to the °temple, 'Thy foundation shall be
laid.'''

45 Thus saith °the LORD to His anointed,
to °Cyrus, whose right hand I have
holden, to subdue nations before him, and I
will °loose the loins of kings; to °open before
him the two leaved gates; and the gates shall
°not be shut;
2 "I will go before thee, and make the
crooked places °straight: I will °break in
pieces the °gates of brass, and °cut in sunder
the bars of iron:
3 And I will give thee the treasures of darkness, and hidden riches of secret places, that
thou mayest know that I, [1]the LORD, Which
°call *thee* by thy name, *am* °the °God of Israel.
4 For Jacob °My servant's sake, and Israel
Mine elect, I have even [3]called thee by thy
name: I have °surnamed thee, °though thou
hast not known Me.
5 I *am* [1]the LORD, and *there is* none else,
there is no [3]God beside Me: I °girded thee,
°though thou hast not known Me:

R 6 That they may know from the rising of the
sun, and from the west, that *there is* °none
beside Me. I *am* [1]the LORD, and *there is*
none else.
7 I form the light, and create darkness: I

21 O Israel. Some codices, with one early printed edition (Rabbinic, 1517), read "And Israel". The reference is to Gen. 32. 26.
not be forgotten. Because of being the "everlasting Nation" (*v.* 7).
22 I have blotted out. See 43. 25.
transgressions=rebellions. Heb. *pāsha'*. Ap. 44. ix.
sins. Heb. *chāṭā'*. Ap. 44. i.
redeemed. Heb. *gā'al.* See note on Ex. 6. 6.
23 Sing . . . shout. Fig. *Pœanismos* (Ap. 6).
break forth into singing. See note on 14. 7.

44. 24—45. 15 (*l*, p. 984). **JERUSALEM RESTORED.**

(*Extended Alternation and Introversion.*)

l | P | 44. 24-26-. Jehovah's attributes.
  Q | S | 44. -26, 27. Jerusalem. Rebuilding.
    T | 44. 28—45. 5. CYRUS.
  R | 45. 6-10. Sovereignty.
| *P* | 45. 11, 12. Jehovah's attributes.
  Q | *T* | 45. 13-. CYRUS.
    S | 45. -13, 14. Jerusalem. Rebuilding.
  R | 15. Inscrutability.

25 tokens=signs. See note on 7. 11.
liars: i.e. the false prophets of the heathen.
diviners: i.e. the astrologers, &c., of Assyria. See note on 47. 13.
wise. Fig. *Antiphrasis* (Ap. 6)=accounted wise.
26 His Servant: i.e. His prophet (Isaiah).
Jerusalem . . . cities, &c. These named first because first built. See *v.* 28. **built**=rebuilt.
27 the deep: i.e. the Euphrates, on which Babylon was built.
I will dry up. Literally fulfilled, at the taking of Babylon, by Cyrus through his general, Gobryas. Cp. Jer. 50. 38; 51. 31, 32, 36.
rivers. Pl. of Majesty for the great river Euphrates.
28 Cyrus. See note on 45. 1.
even saying=and saying: i.e. Jehovah, the Speaker from *v.* 24, and in the preceding clause. It does not mean that Cyrus spoke of rebuilding Jerusalem (for he did not), but it records what Jehovah would say of Cyrus, and what He would say also to Jerusalem. Nehemiah must have obtained a copy of Isaiah on his visit to Jerusalem, or he could not have instructed Cyrus.
Jerusalem. Named before the temple, because the city and its walls were first built, before the temple foundations were laid. See notes on Neh. 7. 4, and on pp. 616-618; also Ap. 57 and 58.
temple. Named after Jerusalem, because the city walls were first built. See note above, and cp. Neh. 7. 4 with Hag. 1. 1-4.

45. 1 the LORD. Heb. Jehovah. Ap. 4. II.
Cyrus. See Ap. 57.
loose the loins. Idiom for weakening. Cp. Job 12. 21. The opposite of "girding" (*v.* 5).
open before him the two leaved gates: i.e. of Babylon, as described by Herodotus. See *Records of the Past*, Part V, p. 162; and cp. Jer. 51. 30, 31.
not be shut. They were found open, and Gobryas and the soldiers of Cyrus entered Babylon without fighting.
2 straight=level.
break in pieces=shiver.
gates of brass. Herodotus (i. 180) tells us that the gates leading to the river were of brass.
cut in sunder=smash.
3 call thee by thy name. Only four named by Divine prophecy before birth: Isaac (Gen. 17. 19); Solomon (1 Chron. 22. 9); Josiah (1 Kings 13. 2); and Cyrus, 137 years before his birth. See Ap. 50, p. 67. **the God of Israel.** See note on 29. 23. **God.** Heb. Elohim. Ap. 4. I. **4 My servant's.** See note on 37. 35. **surnamed.** Cyrus was the additional name divinely given. His Persian name is said to have been Agradates (Strabo, xv. 3, 6). **though thou hast not**=when thou didst not. **5 girded thee.** Contrast "loose" (*v.* 1), and see note on 8. 9. **6 none.** See note on 5. 8.

603-588 make peace, and °create °evil: ℑ [1]the LORD
do all these *things*.
8 Drop down, ye heavens, from above, and let
the skies pour down righteousness: °let the
earth open, and let them bring forth salvation,
and let righteousness spring up together; ℑ
[1]the LORD have created it.
9 Woe unto him that striveth with his Maker!
Let the potsherd *strive* with the potsherds of
the °earth. Shall the clay say to him that
fashioneth it, 'What makest thou?' or thy
work, 'He hath no hands?'
10 Woe unto him that saith unto *his* father,
'What begettest thou?' or to the woman,
'What hast thou brought forth?'"
P (p. 988) 11 Thus saith [1]the LORD, °the Holy One of
Israel, and his °Maker, "Ask Me of things to
come concerning My sons, and concerning the
work of My hands command ye Me.
12 °ℑ have made the earth, and created °man
upon it: ℑ, *even* My hands, have stretched out
the heavens, and all their host have I commanded.
Q T 13 ℑ have °raised him up in righteousness,
and I will direct all his ways:
S °He shall build My city, and he shall let go My
°captives, not for price nor reward," saith
°the LORD of hosts.
14 Thus saith [1]the LORD, "The °labour of
Egypt, and merchandise of Ethiopia and of the
Sabeans, °men of stature, °shall come over
unto thee, and they shall be thine: they shall
come after thee; in chains they shall come
over, and they shall fall down unto thee, they
shall make supplication unto thee, *saying*,
'Surely °GOD *is* in thee; and *there is* none
else, *there is* [6]no [3]God.'"
R 15 Verily Thou *art* a [14]GOD That hidest Thyself, O [3]God of Israel, the Saviour.
U¹ V a (p. 989) 16 They shall be ashamed, and also confounded, all of them: they shall go to confusion
together *that are* makers of °idols.
b 17 *But* Israel shall be saved in [1]the LORD
with an °everlasting salvation: ye shall not
be ashamed nor confounded °world without
end.
c 18 For thus saith [1]the LORD °That created
the heavens; God Himself °That formed the
earth and °made it; He hath established it,
°He created it not °in vain, He formed it to be
inhabited: "ℑ *am* [1]the LORD;
d and *there is* none else.
e 19 I have not spoken in secret, in a dark place
of the earth:
f I said not unto the seed of Jacob, 'Seek ye Me

7 create. Heb. the Poel Participle of the verb *bārā'* (create) which, with "evil", requires the rendering "bring about". Not the same form as in *vv.* 8, 12, or *v.* 18, in connection with the earth. In Jer. 18. 11 the verb is *yāẓar*, to frame, or mould. In Amos 3. 6 it is *'āshah*, to bring about. A word of wide meaning; its sense has to be determined by its context. Here, *disturbance* in contrast with "peace."

evil: never rendered "sin". God brings calamity about as the inevitable consequence of sin. It is rendered "calamity" in Ps. 141. 5; "adversity" in 1 Sam. 10. 19. Ps. 94. 13. Ecc. 7. 14; "grief" in Neh. 2. 10. Prov. 15. 10. Ecc. 2. 17. Jonah 4. 6; "affliction" in Num. 11. 11; "misery" in Ecc. 8. 6; "trouble" in Ps. 41. 1; "sore" in Deut. 6. 22; "noisome" in Ezek. 14. 15, 21; "hurt" in Gen. 26. 29; "wretchedness" in Num. 11. 15; also "harm", "ill", and "mischief". Cp. Jer. 18. 11, and Amos 3. 6. See note on "create", above.

8 let the earth open, &c. When the earth opened before it brought forth destruction (Num. 16. 32; 26. 10 and Ps. 106. 17).

9 earth=ground: i. e. here, clay.

11 the Holy One of Israel. See note on 1. 4.

Maker=Former, or Fashioner.

12 have made, &c. Ref. to Pent. (Gen. 1. 1). Ap. 92.

man. Heb. *'ādām.* Ap. 14. I.

13 raised him up: i. e. raised Cyrus up.

he shall build My city. Nehemiah rebuilt only the walls. See Neh. 7. 4. The city was not rebuilt until after the return under Zerubbabel, and the emancipation by Cyrus. See notes on pp. 616-18, and Ap. 68.

captives. Heb. captivity. Put by Fig. *Metonymy* (of Adjunct), Ap. 6, for the captives in it.

the LORD of hosts. See note on 1 Sam. 1. 3.

14 labour. Put by Fig. *Metonymy* (of Cause), Ap. 6, for that which is produced by it.

men. Heb. pl. of *'ĕnōsh.* Ap. 14. III.

shall come over. Some codices, with five early printed editions (one Rabbinic, in margin, 1517), Sept., Syr., and Vulg., read "and they shall", &c.

GOD. Heb. El. Ap. 4. IV.

45. 16—47. 15 (*K*, p. 980). **GOD'S CONTROVERSY WITH THE NATIONS. VANITY OF IDOLS.**
(*Division.*)

K | U¹ | 45. 16-25. The nations.
  | U² | 46. 1-13. Babylon's idols.
  | U³ | 47. 1-15. Babylon. Doom.

45. 16-25 (U¹, above). **THE NATIONS.**
(*Introversion, and Extended Alternation.*)

U¹ | V | a | 16. Idolaters. Their shame and confusion.
  b | 17. Israel. Saved.
  c | 18-. Earth. Its formation.
  d | -18. None beside Jehovah.
  e | 19-. The oracles of God. Plain.
  f | -19. Call to the seed of Jacob.
 W | 20-. The escaped Nation. Called.
 V | *a* | -20. Idolaters. Their ignorance.
  b | 21. Israel's Saviour.
  c | 22-. Earth. Call to.
  d | -22. "None beside Elohim".
  e | 23. The oath of God. Sure.
  f | 24, 25. Call to the seed of Israel.

16 idols=images. Heb. *ẓīrīm.* Occurs in this sense only here.

17 everlasting salvation. See note on "ancient" people (44. 7). **world without end**=the ages of futurity. **18 That created**=the Creator of. Note how these expressions are heaped together to impress us with the fact that the One Who created all ought to be able to tell us, better than ignorant man, how He created it. **That formed**=The Former of. Heb. *yāẓar*=to fashion. **made**=the Maker of. **He created.** It did not come of itself by evolution (see Ap. 5 and 8). Ref. to Pent. (Gen. 1. 1). **in vain**=*tohū.* The same word as in Gen. 1. 2 ("without form"). Therefore it must have *become tohū*: which is exactly what Gen. 1. 2 declares (see note there). In Gen. 1. 1 we have "the world that then was" (cp. 2 Pet. 3. 6); and in *v.* 2 we have the ruin into which it fell. We are not told how, when, or why, or how long it lasted. When geologists have settled how many years they require, they may place them between *vv.* 1 and 2 of Gen. 1. In Gen. 1. 2—2. 4, we have "the heavens and the earth which are now" of 2 Pet. 3. 7. Both are set in contrast with the "new heavens and the new earth" of 2 Pet. 3. 13.

603-588 °in vain:' I [1]the LORD speak righteousness,
I declare things that are right.

W 20 Assemble yourselves and come; draw near
(p. 989) together, ye *that are* escaped of the nations:
a they have no knowledge that set up the wood
of their graven image, and pray unto a god
that cannot save.
b 21 Tell ye, and bring °*them* near; yea, let
them take counsel together: who hath declared this from ancient time? *who* hath told
it from that time? *have* not I [1]the LORD?
and °*there is* no [3]God else beside Me; a just
[14]GOD and a Saviour; *there is* none beside Me.
c 22 Look unto Me, and be ye saved, all the
ends of the earth:
d for I *am* [14]GOD, and *there is* none else.
e 23 °**I have sworn by Myself, the word is
gone out of My mouth *in* righteousness, and
shall not return, That °unto Me every knee
shall bow, every tongue shall swear.**
f 24 'Surely,' shall *one* say, 'in [1]the LORD have
I righteousness and strength:' *even* to Him
shall °*men* come; and all that are incensed
against Him shall be ashamed.
25 In [1]the LORD shall all the seed of Israel be
justified, and °shall glory.'

U[2] X 46 °Bel boweth down, °Nebo stoopeth,
(p. 990) their idols were upon the beasts, and
upon the cattle: °your carriages °*were* heavy
loaden; °*they are* a burden to the weary *beast*.
2 They stoop, they bow down together; °they
could not deliver the burden, but °themselves
are gone into captivity.
Y g 3 °Hearken unto Me, O °house of Jacob, and
all the remnant of the °house of Israel, °which
are borne *by Me* from the belly, °which are
carried from the womb:
4 And *even* to *your* old age I *am* He; and
even to hoar hairs will I carry *you*: I have
made, and I will bear; °even I will carry, and
will deliver *you*.
h 5 To whom will ye liken Me, and make *Me*
equal, and compare Me, that We may be like?
X 6 They lavish gold out of the bag, and weigh
silver in the balance, *and* hire a goldsmith;
and he maketh it a °god: they fall down, yea,
they worship.
7 They bear him upon the shoulder, they carry
him, and set him in his place, and he standeth;
from his place shall he not remove: yea, *one*
shall cry unto him, yet can he not answer, nor
save him out of his trouble.
Y h 8 °Remember this, and shew yourselves °men:
°bring *it* again to mind, O ye °transgressors.
9 Remember the former things of old: for I
am °GOD, and *there is* none else; *I am* °God,
and *there is* °none like Me,
10 Declaring the end from the beginning, and
from ancient times *the things* that are not *yet*
done, saying, 'My counsel shall stand, and I will
do all My pleasure:'
11 Calling a ravenous bird from the east, °the
man that executeth My counsel from a far
country: yea, I have spoken *it*, °I will also
bring it to pass; I [3]have purposed *it*, I will
also do it.

19 in vain. Heb. *tohû*. Repeated from *v.* 18. Jehovah did not command His People to seek Him in a pathless and trackless waste, where there are no indications of how He is to be found; but in His Word, where He has revealed Himself clearly and distinctly: not "in secret" or "in darkness" (same words as in *v.* 18). Ref. to Pent. (Deut. 30. 11). Ap. 92. See note on 24. 10.

21 them: i.e. the "image" and "god" of *v.* 20.

there is no God. Note the Fig. *Pleonasm* (Ap. 6), by which the same assertion is made in two ways (pos. and neg.) for emphasis. Cp. the Structure "d" and "*d*", p. 989.

23 I have sworn, &c. Quoted in Rom. 14. 11; and Phil. 2. 10. Ref. to Pent. (Gen. 22. 16). Ap. 92.

unto Me. Ascribed to Christ in the quotation above.

24 men come=one come. Heb. text is sing., as in preceding clause; but pl. in *v.* 1.

25 shall glory. See note on "give light" (13. 10).

46. 1-13 (U[2], p. 989). **BABYLON'S IDOLS.**
(*Alternation and Introversion.*)

U[2] | X | 1, 2. Impotence of idols.
  Y | g | 3, 4. Call to hear.
    h | 5. Challenge as to comparison.
  X | 6, 7. Impotence of idols.
  Y | *h* | 8-11. Challenge as to comparison.
    g | 12, 13. Call to hear.

1 Bel. Abbreviation of *Baal*=lord. Here=Zeus, or Jupiter of the Greek and Roman mythology.

Nebo. Answers to the Egyptian Anubis, Greek Hermes, and Roman Mercurius (cp. Acts 14. 12). These gods were indeed brought down. In the *Inscription of Nebuchadonosor*, pp. 15, 21 (Oppert, Rheims, 1866), found at Hillel in 1867 by Sir Hartford Jones, and now in the British Museum, these gods are mentioned, and in this order, with Merodach (Jer. 50. 2). It is a block of black basalt in ten columns, making 620 lines.

your carriages=the things ye carried about: i.e. in procession (Amos 5. 26).

were heavy loaden=are become a burden.

they are a burden=[are even now] loaded on beasts [for exile].

2 they. Aram. and Syr., with five early printed editions, read "and they". But some codices, with two early printed editions, omit "and".

themselves=their soul. Heb. *nephesh*. Ap. 13.

3 Hearken. Note the two calls to hear: here, and *v.* 12 ("g" and "*g*", above). See Ap. 82.

house of Jacob. See note on 2. 5.

house of Israel. See note on 5. 7.

which=who are borne. Ref. to Pent. (Ex. 19. 4. Deut. 1. 31; 32. 11). Ap. 92.

which. Some codices, with two early printed editions, Aram., and Sept., read "and who".

4 even=yea. Some codices, with three early printed editions, Syr., and Vulg., omit "yea".

6 god. Heb. El. Ap. 4. IV.

8 Remember. Ref. to Pent. (Deut. 32. 7). Ap. 92.

men. Heb. *'ish*. Ap. 14. II.

bring it again. The Western reading was "and bring it", &c.

transgressors=rebels. Heb. *pāsha'*. Ap. 44. ix.

9 GOD. Heb. El. Ap. 4. IV.

God. Heb. Elohim. Ap. 4. I.

none. See note on 5. 8.

11 the man that executeth My counsel=the man of My counsel: i.e. Cyrus, a type of Messiah, set apart by God for this special service. See Ap. 57.

I will also bring it to pass. Ref. to Pent. (Num. 23. 19).

13 shall not tarry=will not be too late.

12 Hearken unto Me, ye stouthearted, that *g*
are far from righteousness:
13 I bring near My righteousness; it shall not
be far off, and My salvation °shall not tarry:
and I will place salvation in Zion for Israel My
glory.

U³ Z (p. 991) 603–588
47 Come down, and sit in the dust, O virgin
°daughter of Babylon, sit on the °ground:
°*there is* no throne, O daughter of the Chaldeans: for thou shalt no more be called tender
and delicate.
2 Take the millstones, and °grind °meal: °un-
cover thy locks, °make bare the leg, uncover
the thigh, pass over the rivers.
3 Thy nakedness shall be uncovered, yea, thy
shame shall be seen: I will take vengeance,
and I will °not meet *thee as* a °man.
4 *As for* our Redeemer, °the LORD of hosts
°*is* His name, °the Holy One of Israel.
5 Sit thou silent, and get thee into darkness, O daughter of the Chaldeans: for
thou shalt no more be called, The °lady of
kingdoms.

A i 6 I was wroth with My people, I have polluted
Mine inheritance, and given them into thine
hand: thou didst shew them °no mercy; upon
the °ancient hast thou very heavily laid °thy
°yoke.
7 And thou saidst, 'I shall be [5]a lady for
ever:' *so* that thou didst not lay these *things*
to thy heart, neither didst remember °the latter
end of it.

k 8 Therefore hear now this, *thou that art* given
to pleasures, that dwellest °carelessly, that
sayest in thine heart, '*I am*, and °none else
beside me; I shall not sit *as* a widow, neither
shall I know the loss of °children:'
9 But these two *things* shall come to thee in
a moment in one day, the loss of [8]children, and
widowhood: they shall come upon thee in
their °perfection for the multitude of thy sorceries, *and* for the great abundance of thine
enchantments.

A i 10 For thou hast °trusted in thy °wickedness:
thou hast said, 'None seeth me.' Thy wisdom
and thy knowledge, it hath perverted thee;
and thou hast said in thine heart, '*I am*, and
[8]none else beside me.'

k 11 Therefore shall °evil come upon thee;
thou shalt not know from whence it riseth:
and °mischief shall fall upon thee; thou shalt
not be able to °put it off: and desolation shall
come upon thee suddenly, *which* thou shalt
not know.

Z 12 °Stand now with thine enchantments, and
with the multitude of thy sorceries, wherein
thou hast laboured from thy youth; if so be
thou shalt be able to profit, if so be thou
mayest °prevail.
13 Thou art wearied in the multitude of thy
counsels. Let now the °astrologers, the star-
gazers, °the monthly prognosticators, stand
up, and save thee from *these things* that shall
come upon thee.
14 Behold, they shall be as stubble; the fire
shall burn them; they shall not deliver °them-
selves from the power of the flame: *there shall*
not *be* a coal to warm at, *nor* fire to sit
before it.
15 Thus shall they be unto thee with whom
thou hast laboured, *even* °thy merchants, from
thy youth: °they shall wander every °one to
his quarter; none shall save thee.

47. 1-15 (U³, p. 989). BABYLON. DOOM.
(Introversion and Alternation.)

U³ | Z | 1-5. Call to Babylon. Darkness and silence.
  A | i | 6, 7. Crimination. Cruelty and self-exaltation.
     k | 8, 9. Retribution. Widowhood.
  A | *i* | 10. Crimination. Evil and self-deification.
     k | 11. Retribution. Evil and desolation.
Z | 12-15. Call to Babylon. Impotence.

1 daughter of Babylon. Cp. Tyre (23. 12), and see 37. 22. Ps. 137. 8.
ground=earth. Heb. *'ărez*.
there is no throne=throneless.
2 grind meal: the work of slaves (Ex. 11. 5. Matt. 24. 41).
meal. Put by Fig. *Metonymy* (of Effect), Ap. 6, for the corn from which meal is ground.
uncover thy locks=remove thy veil.
make bare the leg=lift up thy skirts or train.
3 not meet thee as a man=not accept or regard any man. **man.** Heb. *'ādām.* Ap. 14. I.
4 the LORD of hosts. See note on 1 Sam. 1. 3.
the LORD. Heb. Jehovah. Ap. 4. II.
is His name. Ref. to Pent. (Ex. 3. 15; 15. 3). Ap. 92.
the Holy One of Israel. See note on 1. 4.
5 lady of kingdoms=mistress of the kingdoms. The king of Babylon called himself "the King Vicar" (Oppert, *Inscription of Nebuchadonosor*, p. 15). Cp. Ezek. 26. 7. Dan. 2. 37. So the popes name themselves, and are so addressed when crowned. Cp. Rev. 18. 7.
6 no mercy. Cp. 2 Kings 25. 5, 6, 26. Jer. 50. 17; 51. 34.
ancient=elder. Cp. Lam. 4. 16.
thy. In edition of A.V. 1611, "the".
yoke. Cp. Zech. 1. 15.
7 the latter end of it=the issue thereof: but some codices, with one early printed edition (Rabbinic, margin 1517), and Vulg., read "thy latter end". Ref. to Pent. (Deut. 32. 29). Ap. 92.
8 carelessly=confidently.
none else beside me. Babylon and Rome claim the Divine attributes, as used in these chapters. Cp. 45. 6, 14; 46. 9.
none. See note on 5. 8. **children**=sons.
9 perfection=full measure.
10 trusted=confided. Heb. *baṭaḥ.* Ap. 69. i.
wickedness. Heb. *rā'a'.* Ap. 44. viii.
11 evil=calamity. Heb. *rā'a'.* Ap. 44. viii. Cp. 45. 7.
mischief=ruin; especially as prepared for others. Not the same word as in 59. 4. Only here and Ezek. 7. 26.
put it off=expiate it, or charm it away.
12 Stand now with=Persist in.
prevail=strike terror.
13 astrologers. The scientists of Babylon were divided into three classes: writers of (1) charms to be placed on afflicted persons or houses; (2) formulae of incantations; (3) records of observations which mixed up astronomy with astrology, and resulted, in the case of any two successive or concurrent events, in the conclusion that one was the cause of the other; and, the further conclusion was reached by reasoning from the "particular" to the "general".
the monthly prognosticators=they who make known the future by observing new moons. See the fifth "creation tablet" (British Museum).
14 themselves=their souls. Heb. *nephesh.* Ap. 13.
15 thy merchants. Cp. Rev. 18. 11-19.
they shall wander=stagger onward.
one. Heb. *'īsh.* Ap. 14. II.

48. 1-22 [For Structure see next page].

1 house of Jacob. See note on 2. 5.
called by the name of Israel. Ref. to Pent. (Gen. 32. 28; 35. 10). Designates spiritual descent, while "Jacob" denotes natural descent.

48 Hear ye this, O °house of Jacob, which *N* 1¹ (p. 992)
are °called by the name of Israel, and

603–588 are come forth out of the °waters of Judah,
which °swear by the name of °the LORD, and
make mention of °the °God of Israel, *but* not
°in truth, nor in righteousness.
2 For they call themselves of the holy city,
and stay themselves upon [1]the God of Israel;
°The LORD of hosts *is* His name.

m1 (p. 992) 3 I have declared °the former things from
the beginning; and they went forth out of My
mouth, and I shewed them; I did *them* suddenly,
and they came to pass.

l2 4 Because I knew that thou *art* obstinate, and
°thy neck *is* an iron sinew, and thy brow
brass;

m2 5 I have even from the beginning declared *it*
to thee; before it came to pass I shewed *it*
thee: lest thou shouldest say, 'Mine idol hath
done them, and my graven image, and my
molten image, hath commanded them.'

l3 6 Thou hast heard, °see all this; and will not
ye declare *it?*

m3 I have shewed thee new things from this time,
even hidden things, and thou didst not know
them.
7 They are created now, and not from the
beginning; even before the day when thou
heardest them not; lest thou shouldest say,
'Behold, I knew them.'

l4 8 Yea, thou heardest not; yea, thou knewest
not; yea, from that time *that* thine ear was
not opened: for I knew that thou wouldest
deal very treacherously, and wast called a
°transgressor from the womb.

m4 9 For °My name's sake will I defer Mine
anger, and for My praise will I refrain for
thee, that I cut thee not off.
10 Behold, I have refined thee, but not with
silver; I have chosen thee in the furnace of
°affliction.
11 °For Mine own sake, *even* °for Mine own
sake, will I do *it:* for how should [9]*My name*
be polluted? and °I will not give My glory
unto another.

l5 12 Hearken unto Me, O °Jacob and Israel,
My called;

m5 I *am* He; I *am* °**the first,** I **also** *am* °**the last.**
13 Mine hand also hath laid the foundation
of the earth, and My right hand hath °spanned
the heavens: *when* I call unto them, they
°stand up together.

l6 14 All ye, assemble yourselves, and hear;
which among °them hath declared these
things?

m6 [1]The LORD hath loved °him: He will do His
pleasure on Babylon, and His °arm *shall be*
on the Chaldeans.
15 °I, *even* °I, have spoken; yea, I have
called [14]him: I have brought [14]him, and he
shall make his way prosperous.

l7 16 Come ye near unto Me, hear ye this;

m7 I have °not spoken in secret from the beginning; from the time that it was, there *am* I:
and now °the Lord °GOD, °and His °Spirit,
hath sent Me."
17 Thus saith [1]the LORD, thy Redeemer, °the
Holy One of Israel; "I *am* [1]the LORD thy
[1]God Which teacheth thee to profit, Which
leadeth thee by the way *that* thou shouldest go.

l8 18 °O that thou hadst hearkened to My commandments! then had thy °peace been as
°a river, and thy righteousness as the waves
of the sea:
19 Thy seed also had been °as the sand, and

48. 1-22 (*N*, p. 980). GOD'S CONTROVERSY WITH ISRAEL. (*Repeated Alternation.*)

N | l1 | 1, 2. Israel. Call to hear.
m1 | 3. Jehovah. Foreknowledge.
l2 | 4. Israel. Obstinacy.
m2 | 5. Jehovah. Foreknowledge.
l3 | 6-. Israel. Unheedful.
m3 | -6, 7. Jehovah. Foreknowledge.
l4 | 8. Israel. Treachery.
m4 | 9-11. Jehovah. Forbearance.
l5 | 12-. Israel. Call to hear.
m5 | -12, 13. Jehovah. The only God.
l6 | 14-. Israel. Call to assemble and hear.
m6 | -14, 15. Jehovah. Fore-love.
l7 | 16-. Israel. Call to hear.
m7 | -16, 17. Jehovah. The only God.
l8 | 18, 19. Israel. Apostrophe.
m8 | 20, 21. Jehovah. Redeemer and Supplier.
l9 | 22. Israel. Sentence.

waters. Some codices, with three early printed editions, read "days".
swear by the name, &c. Ref. to Pent. (Deut. 6. 13). Ap. 92. **the LORD.** Heb. Jehovah. Ap. 4. II.
the God of Israel. See note on 29. 23.
God. Heb. Elohim. Ap. 4. I.
in truth. See note on 10. 20.
2 The LORD of hosts. See note on 1 Sam. 1. 3.
3 the former things, &c. Such as the birth of Isaac, the Exodus, &c.
4 thy neck, &c. Ref. to Pent. (Ex. 32. 9). Ap. 92.
6 see=look close into.
8 transgressor=rebel. Heb. *pāsha'*. Ap. 44. ix.
9 My name's. See note on Ps. 20. 1.
10 affliction=humiliation, or oppression.
11 For Mine own sake. Note the Fig. *Epizeuxis* (Ap. 6), for great emphasis.
I will not give, &c. Ref. to Pent. (Ex. 20. 5). Cp. 42. 8. Ap. 92.
12 Jacob and Israel: i. e. the natural and spiritual seed. See note on *v.* 1. Some codices, with two early printed editions, read "Jacob my servant"
the first . . . the last. Cp. 41. 4; 44. 6.
13 spanned=stretched out.
stand up. To listen to my words.
14 them. Some codices, with two early printed editions, and Syr., read "you".
him: i. e. Cyrus: 45. 1; 46. 10, 11.
arm. Put by Fig. *Metonymy* (of Cause), Ap. 6, for the judgment inflicted by it. Note also the Fig. *Anthropopatheia* (Ap. 6).
15 I . . . I. Note the Fig. *Epizeuxis.* Ap. 6.
16 not spoken in secret. Ref. to Pent. (Deut. 30. 11). Cp. 45. 19. Ap. 92.
the Lord GOD. Heb. Adonai Jehovah. Ap. 4. VIII (2) and II.
and His Spirit, hath sent Me: or, hath sent both Me and His Spirit: i. e. the prophet, and His Spirit the inspirer of the message sent by Isaiah (cp. Acts 28. 25), "well spake the Holy Ghost by Isaiah", &c. Note the great doctrine of the Trinity.
Spirit. Heb. *rūach.* Ap. 9.
17 the Holy One of Israel. See note on 1. 4.
18 O that thou hadst, &c. Ref. to Pent. (Deut. 5. 29). Cp. Ps. 81. 13. Note Fig. *Œonismos.* Ap. 6 and 92.
peace=well-being, or prosperity. a=the.
19 as the sand. Ref. to Pent. (Gen. 22. 17; 32. 12).

603-588 the offspring of thy bowels like the gravel
thereof; his name should not have been cut off
nor destroyed from before Me.

m[8] (p. 992) 20 Go ye forth of Babylon, flee ye from the
Chaldeans, with a voice of singing declare ye,
tell this, utter it *even* to the end of the earth;
say ye, [1]'The LORD hath redeemed °His servant [1]Jacob.
21 And they thirsted not *when* °He led them
through the deserts: He °caused the waters to
flow out of the rock for them: He clave the
rock also, and the waters gushed out.'

l[9] 22 *There is* °no [18]peace," saith [1]the LORD,
"unto °the wicked.

M B n[1] (p. 993) **49** Listen, O °isles, unto Me; and hearken,
ye °people, from far; °The LORD °hath
called °Me from the womb; from the bowels of
My mother hath He made mention of My name.
2 And He hath made My °mouth like a sharp
°sword; in °the shadow of His °hand hath He
hid Me, and made Me a °polished °shaft; in
His quiver hath He °hid Me;

o[1] 3 And said unto Me, '*Thou art* °My Servant,
O °Israel, in Whom I will be glorified.'

p[1] 4 Then °I said, 'I have laboured in vain,
I have spent My °strength °for nought, and in
vain: *yet* surely My °judgment *is* with [1]the
LORD, and My °work with My °God.'

n[2] 5 And now," °saith [1]the LORD That formed
Me from the womb

o[2] *to be* His Servant, to bring Jacob again to Him,
"Though Israel be °not gathered, yet shall I
be glorious in the eyes of [1]the LORD, and My
[4]God shall be My °strength."
6 And He said, "It is a °light thing that
Thou shouldest be [3]My Servant to raise up
the tribes of Jacob, and to restore the preserved
of Israel: °**I will also give Thee for a light to
the °Gentiles, that °Thou mayest be My °Sal-
vation unto the end of the earth.**"

p[2] 7 Thus saith [1]the LORD, the °Redeemer of
Israel, *and* His Holy One, "to Him °Whom
man despiseth, to Him Whom the °nation
abhorreth, to °a servant of rulers, Kings shall
see and arise, princes also shall worship, because of [1]the LORD That is faithful, *and* °the
Holy One of Israel, and He shall choose
Thee."

n[3] 8 Thus saith [1]the LORD, "**In °an acceptable**

20 His servant. See note on 37. 35.
21 He led them, &c. Ref. to Pent. (Deut. 8. 2).
caused. Ref. to Pent. (Ex. 17. 6. Num. 20. 11). Ap. 92.
22 no peace, &c. Cp. 57. 20.
the wicked = lawless ones: i.e. the wicked in Israel. Heb. *rāsha'*. Ap. 44. x.

49. 1—66. 24 (*M*, p. 980). MESSIAH'S MISSION AND TRIUMPH. (*Introversion and Alternation.*)

M | B | 49. 1-12. The Messiah in Person. His call, qualifications, and mission.
C | 49. 13-26. Zion. Her reconciliation, restoration, and enlargement.
D | 50. 1-11. Sin: the cause of the Separation.
E | G | 51. 1-8. The call to "Hearken".
H | 51. 9—52. 12. The call to Israel ("Awake").
F | 52. 13—53. 12. Messiah's propitiatory work.
E | *G* | 54. 1—56. 8. The call to "Sing" and "Come".
H | 56. 9—58. 14. The call to Israel's enemies ("Devour").
D | 59. 1-21. Sin: the cause of the Separation.
C | 60. 1-22. Zion. Her reconciliation, restoration, and enlargement.
B | 61. 1—66. 24. The Messiah in Person. His anointing, and final victory.

49. 1-12 (B, above). MESSIAH IN PERSON. CALL, QUALIFICATIONS, AND MISSION. (*Repeated and Extended Alternation.*)

B | n[1] | 1, 2. Messiah. Called.
o[1] | 3. Object. Jehovah's glory.
p[1] | 4. Reception.
n[2] | 5-. Messiah. Formed.
o[2] | -5, 6. Object. Jehovah's glory.
p[2] | 7. Reception.
n[3] | 8. Messiah. Given.
o[3] | 9-11. Object. Israel's blessing.
p[3] | 12. Reception.

1 isles = maritime countries. See note on **11. 11.**
people = peoples.
The LORD. Heb. Jehovah. Ap. 4. II.
hath called. Fulfilled in Matt. 1. 18. Luke 1. 28.
Me. The Messiah prophesied of in **7. 14.** Neither Isaiah, nor Israel, nor the Church.
2 mouth . . . the shadow . . . hand. Fig. *Anthropopatheia.* Ap. 6.
sword. Cp. Rev. 1. 16; 2. 12, 16; 19. 15.
polished: or, pointed. **shaft** = arrow.
hid Me. Thirty years at Nazareth.
3 My Servant. See note on 37. 35.
Israel = Prince of GOD. Messiah making this use of, and applying the name to Himself. Israel could not "raise up" Israel (*v.* 6). Christ is called "Israel" in the same way that He is called "David"; and Ps. 24. 6, "Jacob".
4 I said, or thought: i.e. said to Myself.
strength = strength (to endure). Heb. *koaḥ.* Not the same word as in *v.* 5.

for nought. Heb. *tohū.* See note on 24. 10, "confusion". **judgment** = vindication. **work** = recompense. **God.** Heb. Elohim. Ap. 4. I. **5 saith.** Some codices, with Sept. and Syr., read "thus saith". **not.** Heb. text = *l'o* = not; but marked in margin to be read *lō* = to Him, which is confirmed by the list of such readings in the Massōrah. If (in "be not gathered"), the negative be read, then the "though" and the "yet" must be retained; but if the preposition with suffix be read, then the rendering of the clause will be "to bring Jacob again to Him, and that Israel unto Him might be gathered, and I be glorious", &c. Probably both readings may be correct, for Israel was not gathered at His first coming (John 1. 11), but will be at His second coming. **strength** = strength (for victory). Not the same word as in *v.* 4. Heb. *'āzaz.* **6 light** = small. **I will also give, &c.** Quoted in Luke 2. 32. Acts 13. 47. **Gentiles** = nations. Heb. *goyim.* Cp. 42. 6. Therefore not the secret (or Mystery) of the Epistle to the Ephesians. Cp. Gen. 12. 3. Luke 2. 29-32. **Thou.** This cannot be Israel, for it is expressly fulfilled in Christ. **Salvation.** Put by Fig. *Metonymy* (of Effect), Ap. 6, for the Saviour Who wrought salvation. **7 Redeemer** = Kinsman Redeemer. Heb. *go'ēl.* See note on 41. 14 and Ex. 6. 6. **Whom man despiseth** = Whom their (i.e. Israel's) soul (Heb. *nephesh.* Ap. 13) despiseth. Cp. 53. 3. Ps. 42. 5, 6. Matt. 26. 67. 1 Cor. 2. 14. **nation.** Heb. *goi*: i.e. a heathen nation. So called here for its unbelief and rejection of the Messiah. **a servant of rulers.** Cp. Ps. 2. 2. Matt. 27. 41. **the Holy One of Israel.** See note on 1. 4. **8 an acceptable time** = a time of acceptance. Quoted in 2 Cor. 6. 2.

603-588 **time have I °heard Thee, and in a day of salvation have I helped Thee:** and I will preserve Thee, and give Thee for °a covenant of the People, to °establish the earth, to cause to inherit the °desolate heritages;

o³ (p. 993) 9 °That Thou mayest say to the prisoners, °'Go forth;' °to them that *are* in darkness, 'Shew yourselves.' They shall feed in the ways, and their pastures *shall be* in all high places.

10 °**They shall not hunger nor thirst; neither shall the heat nor sun smite them: for He That hath mercy on them shall lead them, even by the springs of water °shall He guide them.**

11 And I will make all My mountains a way, and My °highways shall be exalted.

p³ 12 °Behold, these shall come from far: and, °lo, these from the north and from the west; and these from the land of °Sinim."

C (p. 994) 13 °Sing, O °heavens; and be joyful, O earth; and °break forth into singing, O mountains: for °[1]the LORD hath °comforted His People, and will have mercy upon His afflicted.

J 14 But °Zion said, "[1]The LORD* hath °forsaken me, and °my LORD* hath forgotten me."

K q 15 °Can a woman forget her sucking child, that she should not have compassion on the son of her womb? yea, they may forget, yet °will I not forget thee.

16 [12]Behold, I have °graven thee upon °the palms of *My* hands; thy walls *are* continually before Me.

r 17 Thy °children shall make haste; thy destroyers and they that made thee waste shall go forth of thee.

18 Lift up thine eyes round about, and behold: all these gather themselves together, *and* come to thee. "*As* I live," saith [1]the LORD, "thou shalt surely clothe thee with them all, as with an ornament, and bind them *on thee*, as a °bride *doeth*.

q 19 For thy waste and thy [8]desolate places, and the land of thy destruction, shall even now be too narrow by reason of the inhabitants, and they that swallowed thee up shall be far away.

r 20 The [17]children °which thou shalt have, after thou hast lost the other, shall say again in thine ears, 'The place *is* too strait for me: give place to me that I may dwell.'

21 °Then shalt thou say in thine heart, °'Who hath begotten me these, seeing I have lost my [17]children, and am desolate, a captive, and removing to and fro? and who hath brought up these? °Behold, I was left alone; °these, where °*had they been?*'"

22 Thus saith °the Lord GOD, "Behold, I will °lift up Mine hand to the °Gentiles, and set up My standard to the °people: and they shall bring thy sons in *their* °arms, and thy °daughters shall be carried upon *their* shoulders.

23 And kings shall be thy nursing fathers, and their °queens thy nursing mothers: they shall bow down to thee with *their* face toward the earth, and °lick up the dust of thy feet;

---

heard = answered.
a covenant of the People = the covenant of a People. Cp. 42. 6, 7. Heb. *'âm*, not *goi* as in *v.* 7.
establish the earth = raise up the Land.
desolate. See note on 1. 7.
9 That Thou mayest say. This cannot be the nation, but the Messiah.
Go forth. Cp. 42. 7; 61. 1.
to. Some codices, with two early printed editions, Aram., Sept., Syr., and Vulg., read "and to".
10 They shall not hunger, &c. Quoted in Rev. 7. 16.
shall He guide them = shall He cause them to rest.
11 highways. See note on 7. 3.
12 Behold . . . lo. Fig. *Asterismos* (Ap. 6) for emphasis.
Sinim. Probably = China. Occurs only here.

49. 13-26 (C, p. 993). ZION. RECONCILIATION, RESTORATION, AND ENLARGEMENT. (*Extended Alternation.*)

C | 13. INTRODUCTION. The Call to Rejoice.
J | 14. Zion's despondency.
K | 15-23-. Answer. Promise.
L | -23. Jehovah the only God.
J | 24. Zion's despondency.
K | 25, 26-. Answer. Prophecy.
L | -26. Jehovah the only God.

13 Sing = Shout in triumph. Figs. *Pæanismos* and *Prosopopœia.* Ap. 6.
heavens. A.V. edition, 1611, had "heaven".
break forth into singing. See note on 14. 7.
the LORD. A.V. edition, 1611, had "God".
comforted His People. Cp. 40. 1; 51. 3.
14 Zion said. Fig. *Prolepsis* (Ap. 6). This sets at rest the conflicting interpretations.
forsaken. See note on 1. 4.
my LORD*. One of the 134 places where the Sopherim changed Jehovah of the primitive text to Adonai. Ap. 32.

15-23- (K, above). ANSWER. PROMISE. (*Alternation.*)

K | q | 15, 16. Zion. Not forgotten.
r | 17, 18. Her sons. Returned.
q | 19. Zion. Enlarged.
r | 20-23-. Her sons. Replenished.

15 Can a woman, &c. Figs. *Erotēsis* and *Pathopœia.* Ap. 6.
will I not forget. Fig. *Anthropopatheia.* Ap. 6.
16 graven. Denoting permanence.
the palms, &c. Fig. *Anthropopatheia.* Ap. 6.
17 children = sons.
18 bride. First occurrence in this connection.
20 which thou shalt have . . . other = of thy childlessness, or, of whom thou wast bereaved.
21 Then = And.
Who . . . where? Fig. *Erotēsis.* Ap. 6.
Behold. Fig. *Asterismos.* Ap. 6.
these. Some codices, with Sept. and Vulg., read "and these", or "these therefore".
had they been = were they?
22 the Lord GOD. Heb. Adonai Jehovah. See Ap. 4. VIII (2) and II.
lift up Mine hand. Idiom for "call". Fig. *Anthropopatheia.* Ap. 6.
Gentiles = nations. **people** = peoples.
arms = bosom: the folds of the garment forming a large natural pocket; but children were, and still are, usually carried astride the shoulder as soon as they can sit.
daughters shall be carried. Showing the care they shall receive, for girls are usually left to shift for themselves. See note on 60. 4.
23 queens = princesses.
lick up, &c. Denoting subjection and submission, as in Gen. 3. 14. Cp. Ps. 72. 9 and Mic. 7. 17.

L and °thou shalt know that I *am* [1]the LORD:
(p. 994) for they shall not be ashamed that °wait for
603-588 Me."

J 24 Shall °the prey be taken from the °mighty,
or the lawful captive delivered?

K 25 But thus saith [1]the LORD, "Even the
°captives of the [24]mighty shall be taken away,
and the prey of the °terrible shall be delivered:
for I will contend with him that contendeth
with thee, and I will save thy [17]children.
26 And I will feed them that oppress thee
with their own flesh; and they shall be
drunken with their own blood, as with °sweet
wine:

L and °all flesh shall know that I [1]the LORD °*am*
thy Saviour and thy [7]Redeemer, °the mighty
One of Jacob."

D M[1] s **50** °Thus saith °the LORD, °"Where *is*
(p. 995) °the bill of your mother's °divorcement,
°whom I have °put away?

t or which of My creditors *is it* to whom I have
°sold you? °Behold, for your °iniquities have
ye sold yourselves, and for your °transgressions
is your mother °put away.

t 2 °Wherefore, °when I came, *was there* °no
°man? when I called, *was there* none to
answer?

s °Is My hand shortened at all, that it cannot
°redeem? or have I no power to deliver? [1]behold,
at My rebuke °I dry up the sea, I make
the °rivers a wilderness: °their fish stinketh,
because *there is* no water, and dieth for thirst.
3 I clothe the heavens with blackness, and
I make sackcloth their covering."

M[2] u 4 °The Lord GOD hath given Me the tongue
of the learned, °that I should know how to
speak a word in season to *him that is* weary:
he °wakeneth morning by morning, he °wakeneth
Mine ear °to hear as the °learned.
5 [4]The Lord GOD hath opened Mine ear, and
I was °not rebellious, neither turned away
back.

v 6 °I gave My back to the smiters, and My
cheeks to them that plucked off the hair: I
hid not My face from shame and spitting.

u 7 For [4]the Lord GOD will help Me; therefore
shall I not be confounded: therefore have °I
set My face like a flint, and I know that I shall
not be ashamed.
8 *He is* near That justifieth Me; °who will
contend with Me? let us stand together: °who
is Mine adversary? let him come near to Me.
9 [1]Behold, [4]the Lord GOD will help Me; [8]who
is he *that* shall °condemn Me? lo, they all
shall wax old as a garment; the moth shall
eat them up.

v 10 °Who *is* among you that feareth [1]the LORD,
that obeyeth the voice of His Servant, that

thou shalt know. Ref. to Pent. (Ex. 6. 7). Ap. 92.
wait for me. Ref. to Pent. (same word as in Gen. 49. 18). Ap. 92.

24 the prey. Ref. to Pent. (Num. 31. 11, 12, 26, 27, 32. Occurs elsewhere only in the next verse and Ps. 22. 15.
mighty = a mighty one (sing.). Heb. *gibbōr.* Ap. 14. IV.

25 captives = captivity. Put by Fig. *Metonymy* (of Adjunct), Ap. 6, for "captives".
terrible = tyrant or ruthless one.

26 sweet wine. Heb *'āsīs* = new wine, the product of the same year. Ap. 27. V.
all flesh shall know. Cp. 40. 5; 52. 10.
am thy Saviour: or, am saving thee.
the mighty One of Jacob. Ref. to Pent. (Gen. 49. 24): only here and 60. 16. Nowhere else except Ps. 132. 2, 5. See Ap. 92.

50. 1-11 (D, p. 993). SIN: THE CAUSE OF THE SEPARATION. (*Division.*)

D | M[1] | 1-3. The Breach: caused by Israel's sin.
  | M[2] | 4-11. The Breach: healed by Messiah.

1-3 (M[1], above). THE BREACH: THE CAUSE. (*Introversion.*)

M[1] | s | 1-. Jehovah. Question. Words.
  | t | -1. Not sold by God.
  | *t* | 2-. No help from man.
  | *s* | -2, 3. Jehovah. Question. Power.

1 Thus. Some codices, with two early printed editions, read "For thus".
the LORD. Heb. Jehovah. Ap. 4. II.
Where . . . ? Fig. *Erotēsis.* Ap. 6.
the bill = this bill.
divorcement. Found only here, and in Jer. 3. 8 outside the Pentateuch. See Deut. 24. 1, 3. See Ap. 92.
whom: or, wherewith.
put away . . . sold. Note the *Introversion* of these words in this verse.
Behold. Fig. *Asterismos.* Ap. 6.
sold . . . put away. Note the Introversion.
iniquities. Heb. *'āvāh.* Ap. 44. iv. Cp. 59. 2.
transgressions. Heb. *pāsha'.* Ap. 44. ix.

2 Wherefore . . . ? Fig. *Erotēsis.* Ap. 6.
when I came. Messiah speaks.
no man. See John 1. 11. Cp. Jer. 5. 1. Acts 13. 46; 18. 6; 28. 28.
man. Heb. *'īsh.* Ap. 14. II.
Is My hand shortened . . . ? Ref. to Pent. (Num. 11. 23). Cp. 59. 1. See Ap. 92.
redeem. Heb. *pādāh.* See note on Ex. 13. 13.
I dry up the sea. Ref. to Pent. (Ex. 14. 21). Ap. 92.
rivers. Plural of majesty: i. e. the great river, the Jordan. Ref. to Pent. (Josh. 4. 7, 18). Ap. 92. Cp. Ps. 107. 33.
their fish stinketh. Ref. to Pent. (Ex. 7. 18, 21).

4-11 (M[2], above). THE BREACH: HEALED BY MESSIAH. (*Alternation.*)

M[2] | u | 4, 5. Messiah. Qualified.
  | v | 6. His reception.
  | *u* | 7-9. Messiah. Helped.
  | *v* | 10, 11. His reception.

4 The Lord GOD. Heb. Adonai Jehovah. Ap. 4. VIII (2) and II.
that I should know, &c. He spake none other words than those given Him by the Father. Cp. the seven times this was asserted by Messiah (John 7. 16; 8. 28, 46, 47; 12. 49; 14. 10, 24; 17. 8).
wakeneth = [continually] wakeneth.
to hear as the learned = to hearken as do the instructed.
learned = taught.

5 not rebellious = not perverse or refractory.

6 I gave, &c. Fulfilled in Matt. 26. 67; 27. 26.
7 I set My face like a flint. Note the fulfilment. His death was not an event which happened. He "accomplished" it Himself (Luke 9. 31), and, after saying this, "He steadfastly set His face", as above, "like a flint". He laid down His life Himself: but not till His hour (the right hour) had come (John 10. 15-18).
8 who . . . ? Fig. *Erotēsis.* Ap. 6.
who is Mine adversary? = who can convict Me? Lit. who owneth My sentence?
9 condemn Me = prove Me lawless.
10 Who, &c. These are the words of the prophet in view of Messiah's reception.

603-588 walketh *in* darkness, and hath no light? let
him °trust in the name of [1] the LORD, and stay
upon his °God.

11 [1] Behold, all ye °that kindle a fire, that
°compass *yourselves* about with °sparks:
°walk in the light of °your fire, and in the
°sparks *that* ye have kindled. This shall ye
have of Mine hand; ye shall lie down in
sorrow.

G N^1 w^1 (p. 996) **51** °Hearken to Me, ye that follow after
righteousness, ye that seek °the LORD:
x^1 look unto the rock *whence* ye °are hewn,
and to the °hole of the pit *whence* ye °are
digged.

2 °Look unto °Abraham your father, and
unto °Sarah *that* bare you: for I called him
°alone, and blessed him, and increased him.

y^1 3 For [1] the LORD shall comfort Zion: He will
comfort all her °waste places; and He will
make her wilderness °like Eden, and her
desert °like the garden of [1] the LORD; joy and
gladness shall be found therein, thanksgiving,
and the voice of °melody.

N^2 w^2 4 [1] Hearken unto Me, My People; and give
ear unto Me, O My nation: for a °law shall
proceed from Me, and I will °make My judgment °to rest for a light of °the people.

5 My righteousness *is* near; My salvation is
gone forth, and Mine arms shall judge [4] the
people; the °isles shall °wait upon Me, and
on Mine arm shall they °trust.

x^2 6 Lift up your eyes to the heavens, and look
upon the earth beneath: for the heavens
°shall vanish away like smoke, and the earth
shall wax old like a garment, and they that
dwell therein shall die °in like manner:
y^2 but My salvation shall be for ever, and My
righteousness shall not be abolished.

N^3 w^3 7 [1] Hearken unto Me, ye that °know righteousness, the People in whose heart *is* My [4] law;
fear ye not the reproach of °men, neither be ye
afraid of their revilings.

x^3 8 For the moth shall eat them up like a
garment, and the worm shall eat them like
wool:
y^3 but My righteousness shall be for ever, and
My salvation from generation to generation.

G H O^1 9 °Awake, awake, put on strength, O °arm
of [1] the LORD; awake, as in the ancient days,
in the generations of old. *Art* thou not it that
hath cut °Rahab, *and* wounded the °dragon?

10 *Art* thou not it which hath °dried the sea,
the waters of the great deep; that hath made
the depths of the sea a way for the °ransomed
to pass over?

P^1 11 Therefore the °redeemed of [1] the LORD shall
return, and °come with singing unto Zion;
and everlasting joy *shall be* upon their head:
they shall obtain gladness and joy; *and* sorrow
and °mourning shall flee away.

12 I, *even* I, *am* He That comforteth you:
who *art* thou, that thou shouldest be afraid of
a [7] man *that* shall die, and of the son of °man
which shall be made *as* grass;

13 And forgettest [1] the LORD thy Maker, That

---

10 trust in=confide in. Heb. *bāṭaḥ*. Ap. 69. i.
God. Heb. Elohim. Ap. 4. I.
11 that kindle a fire=that are incendiaries; not the ordinary word for lighting a fire. Only in Deut. 32. 2 (the first occurrence). Jer. 15. 14; 17. 4. Isa. 64. 2.
compass=gird. See note on 8. 9.
sparks=fiery darts.
walk. This is Divine irony (Ap. 6).
your=your own.

51. 1-8 (G, p. 993). THE CALL TO "HEARKEN".
(*Repeated and Extended Alternation.*)

G | N^1 | w^1 | 1-. Hearken unto Me. Righteous.
x^1 | -1, 2. Illustration. Abraham and Sarah.
y^1 | 3. Jehovah. Comfort and Joy.
N^2 | w^2 | 4, 5. Hearken unto Me. People.
x^2 | 6-. Illustration. Heavens and earth.
y^2 | -6. Jehovah. Salvation and Righteousness.
N^3 | w^3 | 7. Hearken unto Me. Righteous.
x^3 | 8-. Illustration. Moth and worm.
y^3 | -8. Jehovah. Righteousness and Salvation.

1 Hearken. Note the call to hear. See Structure, above.
the LORD. Heb. Jehovah. Ap. 4. II.
are=were.
hole of the pit=the hollow of the quarry.
2 Look=Look well: as in *v.* 1. Fig. *Hermeneia* (Ap. 6), by which *v.* 2 interprets *v.* 1.
Abraham . . . Sarah. Ref. to Pent. (Gen. 12, &c.; 24. 36). Ap. 92.
alone. Cp. Ezek. 33. 24. Mal. 2. 15.
3 waste places. Cp. 40. 1; 49. 13.
like Eden. Ref. to Pent. (Gen. 2 and 3). Ap. 92. Elsewhere, only here; Joel 2. 3; and six times in Ezekiel.
like the garden of the LORD. This is a quotation from Gen. 13. 10. Ap. 92.
melody=music or Psalmody.
4 law: i.e. the law of Moses, which was Jehovah's revealed instruction. Cp. Mal. 4. 4.
make . . . to rest=establish.
the people=peoples.
5 isles=maritime countries. See note on 11. 11.
wait. Cp. 42. 4; 60. 9.
trust=hope. Heb. *yaḥal*. Ap. 69. vi. Not the same word as in 50. 10.
6 shall=will have.
in like manner=so. There is no ancient authority for "as a gnat", as some render it.
7 know=take note of.
men=mortal men. Heb. *'ĕnōsh*. Ap. 14. III.

51. 9—52. 12 (H, p. 993). THE CALL TO ISRAEL ("AWAKE"). (*Repeated Alternation.*)

H | O^1 | 51. 9, 10. "Awake, awake". Call to Jehovah.
P^1 | 51. 11-16. Comfort.
O^2 | 51. 17-20. "Awake, awake". Call to Jerusalem.
P^2 | 51. 21-23. Comfort.
O^3 | 52. 1, 2. "Awake, awake". Call to Zion.
P^3 | 52. 3-12. Comfort.

9 Awake. Same word as in 52. 1. Not the same as in *v.* 17. Note the Fig. *Epizeuxis* (for emphasis), Ap. 6.
arm. Fig. *Anthropopatheia*. Ap. 6.
Rahab=Egypt. Cp. Pss. 87. 4; 89. 10.
dragon=crocodile.
10 dried the sea. Ref. to Pent. (Ex. 14. 29).
ransomed=redeemed (by price, or blood). Heb. *ga'al*. Cp. Ex. 6. 6.
11 redeemed=redeemed (by power). Heb. *pādāh*. See note on Ex. 13. 13.
come with singing. Cp. 35. 10.
mourning=sighing. See notes on 21. 2.
12 man. Heb. *'ādām*. Ap. 14. I.

603-588 hath °stretched forth the heavens, and laid the
foundations of the earth; and hast feared continually every day because of the fury of the
oppressor, °as if he were ready to destroy?
and where *is* the fury of the oppressor?
14 The captive exile hasteneth that he may
be loosed, and that he should not die in the
pit, nor that his bread should fail.
15 But I *am* [1]the LORD thy °God, That
°divided the sea, whose waves roared: °The
LORD of hosts *is* His name.
16 And I have °put My words in thy mouth,
and I have covered thee in the shadow of Mine
hand, °that I may plant the heavens, and lay
the foundations of the earth, and say unto
Zion, "Thou *art* My People."

O² **17** °Awake, [9]awake, stand up, O Jerusalem,
(p. 996) which hast drunk at the hand of [1]the LORD the
cup of His fury; thou hast drunken the dregs
of the cup of trembling, *and* wrung *them* out.
18 *There is* none to guide her among all the
sons *whom* she hath brought forth; neither *is*
there any that taketh her by the hand of all
the sons *that* she hath brought up.
19 These two *things* are come unto thee;
°who shall be sorry for thee? desolation, °and
destruction, °and the famine, °and the sword:
by whom shall I comfort thee?
20 °Thy sons have fainted, they lie at the
head of all the streets, as a wild bull in a net:
they are full of the fury of [1]the LORD, the rebuke
of thy [15]God.

P² **21** Therefore hear now this, thou afflicted,
and drunken, but not with °wine:
22 Thus saith °thy LORD [1]the LORD, and thy
[15]God *That* pleadeth the cause of His People,
°"Behold, I have taken out of thine hand the
cup of trembling, *even* the dregs of the cup of
My fury; thou shalt °no more drink it again:
23 But I will put it into the hand of them that
afflict thee; which have said to °thy soul, 'Bow
down, that we may go over:' and thou hast
laid thy body as the ground, and as the street,
to them that went over."

O³ **52** °Awake, awake; put on thy strength,
O Zion; put on thy beautiful garments,
O Jerusalem, °the holy city: for henceforth
there shall no more come into thee the uncircumcised and the unclean.
2 °Shake thyself from the dust; arise, *and*
°sit down, O Jerusalem: loose thyself from
the bands of thy neck, O captive daughter of
Zion.

P³ **3** For thus saith °the LORD, "Ye have sold
yourselves for nought; and ye shall be °re-
deemed °without money."
4 For thus saith °the Lord °GOD, °"My People
went down aforetime into Egypt to sojourn
there; and °the Assyrian °oppressed them
°without cause.
5 Now therefore, °what have I here," saith
[3]the LORD, "that My People °is taken away
for nought? they that rule over them make
them to howl," saith [3]the LORD; "and °**My**
name continually every day *is* blasphemed.
6 Therefore My people shall know My name:
therefore *they shall know* in that day that I
am He That doth speak: behold, *it is* I."
7 °**How beautiful upon the mountains are**
°**the feet of him that bringeth good tidings,**
that publisheth peace; that bringeth good
tidings of good, that publisheth salvation;
that saith unto Zion, "Thy °God reigneth!"
8 Thy watchmen shall lift up the voice; with
the voice together shall they °sing: for they
shall °see eye to eye, when [3]the LORD shall
bring again Zion.

13 stretched forth the heavens. Ref. to Pent. (Gen. 1 and 2). See Ap. 92.
as if he were. A special reading called *Sevīr* (Ap. 34), with some codices, two early printed editions, and Syr., read "who was": referring doubtless to the Antichrist's effort in "the great tribulation".
15 God. Heb. Elohim. Ap. 4. I.
divided the sea. Ref. to Pent. (Ex. 14. 21). Ap. 92.
The LORD of hosts. See note on 1 Sam. 1. 3.
16 put My words in thy mouth. See note on 50. 4 ("that I should know"). Ref. to Pent. (Deut. 18. 18). Ap. 92. **that**: i.e. in order that.
17 Awake = Rouse thee. Not the same form as in *v.* 9 and 52. 1.
19 who . . . ? Fig. *Erotēsis.* Ap. 6.
and. Note the Fig. *Polysyndeton.* Ap. 6.
20 Thy sons have fainted. Note the *Alternation* in this verse. Thus: "fainted at the head", &c., and "they lie as a wild bull", &c.
21 wine. Heb. *yayin.* Ap. 27. I.
22 thy LORD the LORD = thy Adonim Jehovah. See Ap. 4. VIII (3) and II.
Behold. Fig. *Asterismos.* Ap. 6.
no more drink it again. All this refers therefore to the final restoration of Israel.
23 thy soul = thee. Heb. *nephesh.* Ap. 13.

52. 1 Awake. Same form as in 51. 9; not the same as in 51. 17. Fig. *Epizeuxis.* Ap. 6.
the holy city. Heb. "the city of the Sanctuary". See note on Ex. 3. 5.
2 Shake. See note on 33. 9.
sit: i.e. sit as queen. Cp. Rev. 18. 7, for usage.
3 the LORD. Heb. Jehovah. Ap. 4. II.
redeemed. Heb. *gā'al.* See note on Ex. 6. 6.
without money = not with silver. Cp. 1 Pet. 1. 18.
4 the Lord. Heb. Adonai. Ap. 4. VIII (2).
GOD. Heb. Jehovah. Ap. 4. II.
My People went down aforetime. Ref. to Pent. (Gen. 46. 6). See Ap. 92.
the Assyrian. This was "another king" (Acts 7. 18), the first of a new dynasty, the "new king" of Ex. 1. 8, who (of course) "knew not Joseph". See notes on the above passages.
oppressed them. This refers to Ex. 1, and has nothing to do with the later Assyrian carrying away.
without cause = for nothing, groundlessly. This is a Divine comment. See John 15. 25. Heb. *'ephes.* See note on 5. 8.
5 what have I here . . . ? = what do I here? What He did in the circumstances of *v.* 4 we know. What He will do in these new circumstances we are about to be told.
is = hath been.
My name, &c. Quoted in Rom. 2. 24.
7 How beautiful, &c. Quoted in Rom. 10. 15.
the feet. Put by Fig. *Synecdoche* (of Part), Ap. 6, for the whole person of the messenger, that we may not think of him, but of his coming as sent by Jehovah (cp. Nah. 1. 15). Fulfilled partially in John and Christ, both of whom were rejected and slain. There will be other messengers of the future coming, even Elijah and others (Mal. 4. 5). **God.** Heb. Elohim. Ap. 4. I.
8 sing = shout.
see eye to eye = see face to face, and will be face to face with the coming heralds of the King, yea, with the King Himself. This oft misapplied expression has nothing whatever to do with agreement in opinion.

603-588 9 Break forth into joy, [8]sing together, ye
waste places of Jerusalem: for [3]the LORD hath
°comforted His People, He hath [3]redeemed
Jerusalem.
10 [3]The LORD hath made bare His °holy °arm
in the °eyes of all the nations; and all the ends
of the earth shall see the salvation of our [7]God.

**11 °Depart ye, °depart ye, go ye out from
thence, touch no unclean *thing*;** go ye out of
the midst of her; be ye clean, that bear the
vessels of [3]the LORD.

12 For °ye shall not go out with haste, nor
go by flight: for [3]the LORD will go before you;
and °the [7]God of Israel *will be* your °rereward.

F Q T^1 u (p. 998) 13 °Behold, °My Servant shall °deal prudently,
He shall be °exalted and °extolled, and °be very
high.

v 14 °As many were °astonied at Thee; (His
visage was °so marred more than °any man,
and His form more than the sons of °men):

w 15 °So shall He °sprinkle many nations; the
kings shall °shut their mouths at Him: **for
°*that* which had not been told them shall
they see; and °*that* which they had not heard
shall they consider.**

R T^2 *u* **53 °Who °hath believed our °report? and
to whom is the °arm of °the LORD °re-
vealed?**
2 For He shall grow up before °Him as
a °tender plant, and as °a root out of a °dry
ground: He hath no form nor comeliness; and
when °we shall see Him, *there is* no beauty
that we should desire Him.
3 He is °despised and rejected of °men;
a °man of sorrows, and acquainted with grief:
and °we hid as it were *our* faces from Him;
He was despised, and we esteemed Him not.

S *v* **4 Surely °He hath °borne our °griefs, and
°carried our °sorrows:** yet we did esteem Him
stricken, smitten °of °God, and °afflicted.

9 comforted. Cp. 40. 1.

10 holy. See note on Ex. 3. 5.

arm. Put by Fig. *Metonymy* (of Cause), Ap. 6, for the wonders wrought by it. Also Fig. *Anthropopatheia.* Ap. 6.

eyes, &c. = sight, or view. Cp. 40. 5; 49. 26.

11 Depart ye. Note the Fig. *Epizeuxis* (Ap. 6). Cp. Rev. 18. 4. Quoted (in application for us to-day) in 2 Cor. 6. 14–18.

12 ye shall not go out with haste. Ref. to Pent., where it was otherwise (only here, Ex. 12. 33, 39, and Deut. 16. 3). See Ap. 92.

the God of Israel. See note on 29. 23.

rereward = rear-guard. Cp. 58. 8. Ref. to Pent. (Ex. 14. 19). See Ap. 92.

52. 13—53. 12 (F, p. 993). MESSIAH'S PROPITIATORY WORK. (*Introversion.*)

As coming to fulfil the LAW which was in His heart (Ps. 40. 6–8).

F | Q | 52. 13–15. GENESIS. The Divine *counsels* concerning Messiah, summarizing ch. 53 as a whole. The counsel, "Let Us make" (Gen. 1. 26), answering to the counsel here, Let Us redeem.
R | 53. 1–3. EXODUS. Messiah taking His place with the nation.
S | 53. 4–6. LEVITICUS. Messiah's relation to Jehovah. His personal work of atonement, the basis of the whole. Jehovah's dealings with Him in the *Sanctuary.*
R | 53. 7–10–. NUMBERS. Messiah's relation to the earth: finding a grave in it.
Q | 53. –10–12. DEUTERONOMY. The outcome, fulfilling the Divine *counsels* according to the Word.

The first member (GENESIS), Q, is shown to be a summary or epitome of the whole by the following arrangement:—

F | T^1 | u | 52. 13. Messiah's presentation.
v | 52. 14. His sufferings.
w | 52. 15. His reward.
} 52. 13–15.

T^2 | *u* | 53. 1–3. Messiah's reception.
v | 53. 4–10–. His sufferings.
w | 53. –10–12. His reward.
} 53. 1–12.

13 Behold. Fig. *Asterismos* (Ap. 6), to emphasise what is to follow.

My Servant. The Messiah. See note on 37. 35.

deal prudently = prosper. Cp. 1 Sam. 18. 14.

exalted . . . extolled . . . be very high. Fig. *Anabasis* (Ap. 6), for great emphasis = riseth . . . is lifted up . . . becometh very high (cp. Phil. 2. 9–11).

14 As = According as. This corresponds with the "so" of *v.* 15 (not with the "so" in the next clause, which is parenthetic). **astonied**: corresponding with the word rendered "sprinkle" in *v.* 15. From Old French *estonner.* Nine times so spelt, from Wycliff and Geneva Bible. Chaucer spells it "astoned"; Spenser, "astownd". **so marred**: pointing to the depth of the humiliation, as set forth in detail in 53. 4–10–. Cp. Matt. 26. 67, 68; 27. 27–30. **any man.** Heb. *'ish.* Cp. Ps. 22. 6, "I am a worm, and no man". **men.** Heb. *'ādām.* Ap. 14. I. **15 So.** Corresponding with the "As" of *v.* 14. **sprinkle** = cause to leap or spring up for joy. Heb. *nāzāh.* When used of liquids it means to spurt out, as in 63. 3, the only other occurrence in Isaiah, and that in judgment (cp. 2 Kings 9. 33). The usual word for ceremonial sprinkling is *zārak*, not *nāzāh.* The astonishment and the joy of many nations is set in contrast with the astonishment of the many people of *v.* 14. The Sept. reads "shall admire". Moreover, the verb is in the Hiphil conjugation, and we can say "cause to leap up for joy", but not "cause to sprinkle". With this, Gesenius, Fuerst, Lowth, Parkhurst, and others agree. **shut their mouths**: i.e. be dumb with the astonishment. **that which had, &c.** = they to whom it had been told shall see. **that which they, &c.** = they which had not heard shall consider. Quoted in Rom. 15. 21.

53. 1 Who . . . ? Fig. *Erotēsis* (Ap. 6). The questions are asked by the prophet, and the answer is "no one" or few. Quoted in John 12. 38 and Rom. 10. 16. **hath believed** = put faith in. Heb. *'āman.* Ap. 69. III. The tenses are Past (the prophetic Perfect). **report** = hearing. Put by Fig. *Metonymy* (of Adjunct), Ap. 6, for the subject-matter, which was heard. **arm.** Put by Fig. *Metonymy* (of Cause), Ap. 6, for what was wrought by it. Cp. 51. 9; 52. 10. **the LORD.** Heb. Jehovah. Ap. 4. II. **revealed** = made bare: i.e. revealed. **2 Him**: i.e. Jehovah. **tender plant** = a sapling. **a root** = a root-sprout. **dry ground.** The "root" (David) of which He was the offspring was well nigh extinct. **we**: i.e. the people who saw Him. The interpretation is for the Jews of our Lord's day. The application is for us. The nation will yet say it in their confession and weeping. **3 despised and rejected.** Fulfilled in John 1. 10, 11; 8. 48; 10. 20. **men.** Heb. pl. of *'ish.* Ap. 14. II = the chief men. Cp. John 7. 48, 49. **man.** Heb. *'ish.* Ap. 14. II. **we hid.** Cp. 50. 6. Ps. 22. 6, 7; and John 8. 48. Mark 3. 21, 30. John 18. 40. **4 He** [and no one else]. Emphatic. Quoted in Matt. 8. 17. **borne . . . carried** = borne the punishment for. See note on Ezek. 4. 4. Matt. 8. 17. Cp. *vv.* 11, 12. **griefs . . . sorrows.** Put by Fig. *Metonymy* (of Cause), Ap. 6, for the judgment which was brought about by their sins. **of** = by. Gen. of Agent. Ap. 17. **God.** Heb. Elohim. Ap. 4. I. **afflicted** = humbled.

603–588 5 But **He** *was* °wounded for our °transgressions, *He was* bruised for our °iniquities: the chastisement °of our peace *was* upon Him; and °**with His stripes we are healed.**

6 °**All we like sheep have gone astray**; we have turned every one to his own way; and [1]the LORD hath laid on Him the [5]iniquity of us °all.

R (p. 998) 7 He was °oppressed, and **He** was afflicted, yet He °opened not His mouth: °**He is brought as °a lamb to the slaughter, and as a sheep before her shearers is dumb, so He °openeth not His mouth.**

8 **He was taken °from prison and from judgment: and °who shall declare His °generation? for He was °cut off out of the land of the living:** for the [5]transgression of My people was He stricken.

9 And °He °made His °grave with °the wicked, and with °the rich °in His death; because °**He had done no violence, neither *was any* deceit in His mouth.**

10 Yet °it pleased [1]the LORD to bruise Him; He hath put *Him* to grief:

Q w °when thou shalt make °His soul °an offering for °sin, °He shall see *His* seed, He shall prolong *His* days, and the °pleasure of [1]the LORD shall prosper in His hand.

11 He shall see of the travail of [10]His soul, *and* shall be °satisfied: °by His knowledge shall My righteous Servant justify many; for **He** shall bear their [5]iniquities.

12 Therefore will I °divide Him *a portion* °with the great, and He shall divide the spoil with the strong; because He hath °poured out [10]His soul unto death: °**and He was numbered with the °transgressors; and He °bare the °sin of many, and** °made intercession for the [5]transgressors.

E G U[1] (p. 999) **54** °"**Sing, O °barren, thou *that* didst not bear; °break forth into singing, and**

5 wounded=pierced.

transgressions. Heb. *pāsha'*. Ap. 44. ix.

iniquities. Heb. *'āvōn*. Ap. 44. iv.

of=which procured. Gen. of Cause. Ap. 17.

with, &c. Quoted in 1 Pet. 2. 24.

6 All . . . all. Note the Fig. *Epanadiplōsis* (Ap. 6), by which the statement is emphasised as containing the essence of the whole chapter. More noticeable in Heb. *killānū . . . killānū*. Quoted in 1 Pet. 2. 22.

7 oppressed: or, hard pressed.

opened not His mouth. Idiom for silence and submission. Cp. 1 Pet. 2. 22, 23.

He is brought. Quoted in Acts 8. 32, 33.

a lamb. Cp. John 1. 36.

8 from prison and from judgment, &c.=by constraint and by sentence He was taken away.

who shall declare His generation?=as to the men of His age [i.e. His contemporaries], who ponders, or considers as to this seed, seeing He is to be "cut off"? Cp. *v.* 10.

cut off. Cp. Dan. 9. 26. Thus the climax of this prophecy is reached: (1) a hint (42. 4); (2) open lament (49. 4); (3) personal suffering (50. 6); now (4) a violent death (53. 8).

9 He made, &c.=one [or they] appointed, or assigned [His grave]; or, it [His grave] was appointed.

made. Heb. *nāthan* (to give) is rendered "appoint" in Ex. 30. 16. Num. 35. 6. Josh. 20. 7. 2 Kings 8. 6. 1 Chron. 16. 4. Ezra 8. 20. Neh. 9. 17. Ezek. 4. 6; 36. 5; 45. 6; and "assign" in Josh. 20. 8. 2 Sam. 11. 16. Even where it is rendered "to make", it has the force of "appoint" (Gen. 9. 12. Num. 14. 4, &c.). **grave.** Heb. *ķeber*. See Ap. 35.

the wicked=the criminals (pl.). These have a separate part assigned in all Jewish cemeteries.

the rich=a rich [man] (sing.). Cp. Matt. 27. 59, 60. Mark 15. 43, 46. Luke 23. 53. John 19. 40–42.

in His death=when He was dead. Cp. Mark 15. 42–47. John 19. 38, 39.

He had done, &c. Quoted in 1 Pet. 2. 22.

10 it pleased the LORD=Jehovah purposed.

when thou shalt make, &c. This introduces the break in the Dispensations, which is the subject of the rest of the chapter: the "glory which shall follow" the sufferings. See Ap. 71 and 72.

His soul=Himself. Heb. *nephesh*. Ap. 13=life. Cp. John 10. 11, 15, 17, 18.

an offering for sin. Heb. *'ashām*=the trespass offering. See Ap. 43. II. vi and 44. ii. Ref. to Pent., for this is a peculiarly Levitical word (Lev. 14. 12, 21), and cannot be understood apart from it. In Ps. 40 it is the aspect of the whole burnt offering. **He shall see His seed**: "see" corresponding with "see" in 52. 15: i.e. the result, issue, and reward of His sufferings. Cp. Ps. 22. 30; 24. 6; 25. 13. The Chaldee Targum reads, "they (His seed) shall see the kingdom of their Messiah". **pleasure**=purpose. **11 satisfied.** Not disappointed. We have not an impotent Father, or a disappointed Christ, or a defeated Holy Ghost, as is so commonly preached; but an *omnipotent* Father, an *all-victorious* Christ, and an *almighty* Holy Spirit, able to break the hardest heart and subdue the stoutest will. **by His knowledge, &c.** Punctuate: "Satisfied by His knowledge, My righteous Servant shall justify many, for He shall bear", &c. **12 divide**=apportion, or assign. **with**=among. **poured out.** Only here (in the "latter" portion); and 32. 15 (the "former" portion). Ap. 79. II. **and He was numbered.** Quoted in Mark 15. 28. Luke 22. 37. Ap. 79. II. **bare the sin.** Ref. to Pent. (Lev. 10. 17. Num. 9. 13; 18. 32). Cp. *vv.* 4, 11. See Ap. 92. **sin.** Not the same word as in *v.* 10. Heb. *chāṭā'*. **made intercession**=interposed.

54. 1–56. 8 (*G*, p. 993). **THE CALL TO "SING", "COME", &c.**

(*Repeated Alternation.*)

G
- U[1] | 54. 1, 2. Exhortation. "Sing."
  - V[1] | 54. 3. Reason. Fruitfulness.
- U[2] | 54. 4. Exhortation. "Fear not."
  - V[2] | 54. 5–10. Reason. Jehovah's faithfulness.
- U[3] | 54. 11–. Exhortation. Be comforted.
  - V[3] | 54. –11–17. Reason. Jehovah's goodness.
- U[4] | 55. 1–3. Exhortation. "Come."
  - V[4] | 55. 4, 5. Reason. Messiah given.
- U[5] | 55. 6, 7. Exhortation. "Seek."
  - V[5] | 55. 8–13. Reason. Jehovah's gifts.
- U[6] | 56. 1–. Exhortation. "Keep justice."
  - V[6] | 56. –1, 2. Reason. Jehovah's blessing.
- U[7] | 56. 3. Exhortation. Encouragement.
  - V[7] | 56. 4–8. Reason. Jehovah's gathering.

1 Sing=Shout in triumph (52. 8, 9. Zeph. 3. 14). Quoted in Gal. 4. 27. **barren.** Refers to Sarah. **break forth into singing.** See note on 14. 7.

603-588 **cry aloud, thou *that* didst not travail with
**child: for more *are* the °children of the °deso-
late than the °children of the °married wife,"**
saith °the LORD.
2 "Enlarge the place of thy tent, and let them
stretch forth the curtains of thine habitations:
spare not, lengthen thy cords, and strengthen
thy °stakes;

V[1] (p. 999) 3 For thou shalt break forth on the right
hand and on the left; and thy seed shall inherit the °Gentiles, and make the [1]desolate
cities to be inhabited.

U[2] 4 Fear not; for thou shalt not be °ashamed:
neither be thou confounded; for thou shalt not
be put to shame: for thou shalt forget °the
shame of thy youth, and shalt not remember
the reproach of thy widowhood any more.

V[2] W (p. 1000) 5 For thy °Maker *is* thine husband; °the
LORD of hosts *is* His name; and °thy Redeemer
°the Holy One of Israel; °The °God of the
whole earth shall He be called.
6 For [1]the LORD hath called thee as a woman
°forsaken and grieved in °spirit, and a wife of
youth, when thou wast refused," saith thy
[5]God.
7 "For a small moment have I forsaken thee;
but with great mercies will I °gather thee.

X x 8 In °a little wrath °I hid My face from thee
for a moment;

y but with °everlasting kindness will I have
mercy on thee," saith [1]the LORD [5]thy Redeemer.

Y 9 "For this *is as* °the waters of Noah unto Me:

Y for *as* °I have sworn that °the waters of
Noah should no more go over the earth;

X x so have I sworn that I would not be wroth with
°thee, nor rebuke °thee.

y 10 For the mountains shall depart, and the
hills be removed; but My kindness shall not
depart from thee,

W neither shall the covenant of My peace be
removed," saith [1]the LORD That hath mercy
on thee.

U[3] (p. 999) 11 "O thou afflicted, tossed with tempest, *and*
not comforted,

V[3] behold, I will lay thy stones with fair colours,
and lay thy foundations with sapphires.
12 And I will make thy °windows of agates,
and thy gates of carbuncles, and all thy °borders
of pleasant stones.
13 And °**all thy [1]children *shall be* taught** °of
[1]**the LORD**; and great *shall be* the peace of thy
[1]children.
14 In righteousness shalt thou be established:
thou shalt be far from oppression; for thou
shalt °not fear: and from terror; for it shall
not come near thee.
15 Behold, °they shall surely gather together,
but [14]not by Me: whosoever shall gather together against thee °shall fall for thy sake.
16 Behold, °I have created the smith that
bloweth the coals in the fire, and that bringeth
forth an °instrument for his work; and I have
created the waster to destroy.

children = sons. desolate. See note on 1. 7.
married wife = the husbanded one.
the LORD. Heb. Jehovah. Ap. 4. II.
2 stakes = tent-pegs. **3** Gentiles = nations.
4 Fear not . . . ashamed. Ref. to Pent. (Lev. 26. 6). Cp. 44. 16, 17.
the shame of thy youth. Ref. to Israel's days of idolatry. Cp. Jer. 3. 24, 25.

54. 5-10 (V[2], p. 999). REASON. JEHOVAH'S FAITHFULNESS. (*Introversion and Alternation.*)

V[2] | W | 5-7. The Covenant [Marriage] Breach.
X | x | 8-. Wrath overflowing.
y | -8. Everlasting kindness.
Y | 9-. The waters of Noah. Comparison.
Y | -9-. The waters of Noah. Reason.
X | *x* | -9. Wrath restrained.
y | 10-. Everlasting kindness.
W | -10. The Covenant. Breach removed.

5 Maker. Heb. pl. Reference to the triune Jehovah.
the LORD of hosts. See note on 1 Sam. 1. 3.
thy Redeemer = thy kinsman-Redeemer. Ref. to Pent. (Gen. 48. 16. Ex. 6. 6; 15. 13). Ap. 92.
the Holy One of Israel. See note on 1. 4.
The God of the whole earth. This is the title connecting Jehovah with universal dominion. Cp. "The Lord of the whole earth" in Josh. 3. 11, 13. Zech. 6. 5.
God. Heb. Elohim. Ap. 4. I.
6 forsaken. See note on 1. 4.
spirit. Heb. *rūach*. Ap. 9.
7 gather thee = gather thee out.
8 a little wrath = in an overflow of wrath.
I hid My face. Ref. to Pent. (Deut. 31. 17, 18). Cp. Isa. 8. 17; 53. 3; 64. 7. See Ap. 92.
everlasting kindness. See note on "ancient", 44. 7.
9 the waters of Noah. Ref. to Pent. (Gen. 6—9). Ap. 92. Some codices, reading one word instead of two, with Aram., Syr., and Vulg., read "the days of Noah . . . when [I sware, &c.]".
I have sworn = when I sware. Ref. to Pent. (Gen. 6-9). Noah is nowhere else mentioned in the O.T. except in 1 Chron. 1. 4. Ezek. 14. 14, 20. See Ap. 92.
thee. Supply *Ellipsis* (Ap. 6), "thee [for ever]".
12 windows = battlements.
borders = boundaries.
13 all thy children, &c. Quoted in John 6. 45.
of = by. Gen. (of Origin). Ap. 17. 2.
14 not. See note on "no" (5. 8).
15 they: i.e. the enemies of Israel (Ps. 56. 7; 59. 4).
shall fall = shall be overthrown (cp. 8. 14).
16 I have created. Cp. 45. 7, 8.
instrument = weapon.
17 weapon. Same word as instrument (*v.* 16).

55. 1 Ho, &c. This cry heard in Jerusalem to-day. All water has to be bought. Cp. John 4. 14; 7. 37-39.
every one that thirsteth. The invitation is only to these.
come. Fig. *Repetitio* (Ap. 6), for emphasis.
waters: of life (Rev. 22. 17).
wine: of gladness (Ps. 104. 15).
milk: of nourishment (1 Pet. 2. 2).

17 No °weapon that is formed against thee
shall prosper; and every tongue *that* shall
rise against thee in judgment thou shalt condemn. This *is* the heritage of the servants of
[1]the LORD, and their righteousness *is* of Me,"
saith [1]the LORD.

55 °Ho, °every one that thirsteth, °come U[4]
ye to the °waters, and he that hath no
money; °come ye, buy, and eat; yea, °come,
buy °wine and °milk without money and without price.

603-588 2 °Wherefore do ye spend money for *that which is* not bread? and your labour for *that which* satisfieth not? °hearken diligently unto Me, and eat ye *that which is* good, and let your °soul delight itself in fatness.

3 Incline your ear, and come unto Me: hear, and your [2]soul shall live; and I will make an °everlasting covenant with you, *even* °**the sure mercies °of David.**

V^{4} (p. 999) 4 [1]Behold, I have given °Him *for* a Witness to the °people, a Leader and Commander to the °people.

5 [1]Behold, °thou shalt call a nation *that* thou knowest not, and nations *that* knew not °thee shall run unto thee because of °the LORD thy °God, and for °the Holy One of Israel; for He hath glorified thee.

U^{5} 6 Seek ye [5]the LORD while He °may be found, call ye upon Him while He is near:

7 Let the °wicked °forsake his °way, and the °unrighteous °man his °thoughts: and let him return unto [5]the LORD, and He will have mercy upon him; and to our [5]God, for He will °abundantly pardon.

V^{5} 8 For °My °thoughts *are* not °your thoughts, neither *are* your ways My ways," saith [5]the LORD.

9 "For *as* the heavens are higher than the earth, so are My ways higher than your ways, and My thoughts than your thoughts.

10 For °as the rain cometh down, and the snow from °heaven, and returneth not thither, °but watereth the earth, and maketh it bring forth and bud, **that it may give seed to the sower, and bread to the eater:**

11 So shall °My word be that goeth forth out of My °mouth: it shall not return unto Me void, [10]but it °shall accomplish that which I please, and it °shall prosper *in the thing* whereto I sent it.

12 For ye shall °go out with joy, and be led forth with °peace: the mountains and the hills shall °break forth before you into °singing, and all the trees of °the field shall clap *their* hands.

13 Instead of the thorn shall come up the fir tree, and instead of the °brier shall come up the myrtle tree: and it shall be to [5]the LORD for a name, for an °everlasting sign *that* shall not be cut off."

U^{6} **56** Thus saith °the LORD, "Keep ye judgment, and do °justice:

V^{6} for My salvation *is* near to come, and My righteousness to be revealed.

2 Blessed *is* the °man *that* doeth °this, and the son °of man *that* layeth hold on °it; that °keepeth the sabbath from polluting it, and keepeth his hand from doing any °evil.

U^{7} 3 Neither let the son of the °stranger, that hath joined himself to [1]the LORD, °speak, saying, '[1]The LORD hath utterly separated me from His People:' neither let the eunuch say, °'Behold, I *am* a dry tree.'

V^{7} 4 For" thus saith [1]the LORD "unto the eunuchs that [2]keep My sabbaths, and °choose *the things* that please Me, and [2]take hold of My covenant;

5 Even unto them will I give in Mine house and within My walls a °place and a name better than of sons and of daughters: I will give them an [3]everlasting name, that shall not be cut off.

6 Also the sons of the [3]stranger, that join themselves to [1]the LORD, to serve Him, and to

2 Wherefore . . . ? Fig. *Erotēsis* (Ap. 6), to emphasise the universal corruption and practice of the natural man. Cp. John 6. 27.

hearken diligently. Fig. *Epizeuxis* (Ap. 6), for emphasis. Heb. "Hearken a hearkening": i.e. continue to hearken. **soul.** Heb. *nephesh.* Ap. 13.

3 everlasting. See note on "ancient", 44. 7.

the sure mercies of David: i.e. the lovingkindnesses well assured to David, the "everlasting covenant" made with David in 2 Sam. 7. 8-16. Quoted in Acts 13. 34. Assured by oath to David (Ps. 132. 11).

of=pertaining to. Gen. of Relation. Ap. 17. V.

4 Him=Messiah: not David, but David's Son and David's Lord.

people=peoples.

5 thou . . . thee: i.e. Israel, who is addressed here. See Structure, *G*, p. 996.

the LORD. Heb. Jehovah. Ap. 4. II.

God. Heb. Elohim. Ap. 4. I.

the Holy One of Israel. See note on Ps. 71. 22.

6 may be: i.e. letteth Himself be.

7 wicked=lawless man (sing.). Heb. *rāshā'.* Ap. 44. x.

forsake. See note on 1. 4.

way . . . thoughts. Note the *Introversion* of lines in *vv.* 7 and 8:

a | 7-. way.
 b | -7. thoughts.
 b | 8-. thoughts.
a | -8. ways.

unrighteous. Heb. *'āven.* Ap. 44. iii.

man. Heb. *'ish.* Ap. 14. II.

abundantly pardon. Heb. multiply to pardon.

8 My thoughts . . . your thoughts. Note the *Introversion* of the pronouns:

c | My.
 d | your.
 d | your.
c | My.

The contrast thus emphasised is not merely holiness, but vastness.

10 as=according as. **heaven**=the heavens.

but=except it: i.e. until it. Note that the four succeeding tenses are *pasts*, and in the *singular* number. The waters *do* return, as stated in other scriptures (Ps. 135. 7. Jer. 10. 13; 51. 16).

11 My word be that goeth. Ref. to Pent. (Deut. 8. 3; 32. 2).

mouth. Fig. *Anthropopatheia.* Ap. 6.

shall=shall assuredly.

12 go out=go forth: i.e. from the lands of your wandering. **peace**=prosperity.

break forth . . . singing. Fig. *Prosopopœia.* Ap. 6. See note on 14. 7.

the field: i.e. the open country beyond the limits of cultivation.

13 brier: or, nettle.

everlasting. See note on "ancient", 44. 7.

56. 1 the LORD. Heb. Jehovah. Ap. 4. II.

justice=righteousness.

2 man=(mortal) man. Heb. *'ěnōsh.* Ap. 14. III.

this . . . it. This righteousness . . . this salvation. Both Fem.

of man=of Adam. Heb. *'ādām.* Ap. 14. I.

keepeth the sabbath. Ref. to Pent. (Ex. 20. 8-11). Ap. 92. **evil.** Heb. *ra'a'.* Ap. 44. viii.

3 stranger=foreigner. Heb. *nākar.* See Prov. 5. 3.

speak=think. **Behold.** Fig. *Asterismos.* Ap. 6.

4 choose. See note on 1. 29.

5 place: or, trophy. Heb. hand.

603-588 love the name of [1] the LORD, to be His servants,
every one that [2] keepeth the sabbath from polluting it, and taketh hold of My covenant;

7 Even them will I bring °to My °holy mountain, and make them joyful in My °house of prayer: their burnt offerings and their sacrifices °*shall be* accepted upon Mine altar; for °**Mine house shall be called an house of prayer for all °people."**

8 °The Lord GOD Which gathereth the outcasts of Israel saith, "Yet will I gather *others* to him, beside those that are gathered unto him."

H A (p. 1002) 9 All ye beasts of °the field, come to devour, *yea,* all ye beasts in the forest.

B C 10 His watchmen *are* blind: they are all ignorant, they *are* all dumb dogs, they cannot bark; °sleeping, lying down, loving to slumber.

11 Yea, *they are* °greedy dogs *which* can never have enough, and they *are* shepherds *that* cannot understand: they all look to their own way, °every one for his gain, from his quarter.

12 "Come ye," *say they,* "I will fetch °wine, and we will fill ourselves with °strong drink; and to morrow shall be as this day, *and* much more abundant."

D **57** The righteous perisheth, and no °man layeth *it* to heart: and °merciful °men *are* taken away, none considering that the righteous is taken away °from the °evil *to come.*

E 2 °He shall enter into peace: °they shall rest °in their °beds, *each one* walking *in* °his uprightness.

C e 3 But draw near hither, ye sons of the °sorceress, the seed of the adulterer and the whore.

4 Against whom do ye sport yourselves? against whom make ye a wide mouth, *and* draw out the tongue? *are* ye not °children of °transgression, a °seed of falsehood,

f 5 Enflaming yourselves °with idols under every green tree, °slaying the [4] children in the valleys under the clifts of the rocks?

6 Among °the smooth *stones* of the stream *is* °thy portion; they, they *are* thy lot: even to them hast thou poured a °drink offering, thou hast offered a °meat offering. Should °I receive comfort in these?

7 Upon a lofty and high mountain hast thou set thy bed: even thither wentest thou up to offer sacrifice.

8 Behind the doors also and the posts hast thou set up thy °remembrance: for thou hast discovered *thyself to another* than Me, and art gone up; thou hast enlarged thy bed, and made °thee *a covenant* with them; thou lovedst their °bed °where thou sawest *it.*

9 And thou wentest to °the king with ointment, and didst increase thy perfumes, and didst send thy messengers far off, and didst debase *thyself even* unto °hell.

10 Thou art wearied in the greatness of thy way; *yet* saidst thou not, "There is no hope:" thou hast °found the life of thine °hand; therefore thou wast not grieved.

7 to = into. Some codices read "upon".
holy. See note on Ex. 3. 5.
house of prayer. See quotation below.
shall be accepted = for acceptance.
Mine house, &c. Quoted in Matt. 21. 13. Mark 11. 17. Luke 19. 46. Contrast "*your* house" (Matt. 23. 38).
people = peoples.
8 The Lord GOD. Heb. Adonai Jehovah. See Ap. 4. VIII (2), and II.

56. 9—58. 14 (*H*, p. 993). THE CALL TO ISRAEL'S ENEMIES. (*Alternation.*)

H | A | 56. 9. Call to devour.
  B | 56. 10—57. 21. Contrasted characters.
 A | 58. 1. Call to cry aloud.
  B | 58. 2-14. Contrasted conduct.

9 the field. See note on 55. 12.

56. 10—57. 21 (B, above). CONTRASTED CHARACTERS. (*Extended Alternation.*)

B | C | 56. 10-12. The wicked.
  D | 57. 1. The righteous.
   E | 57. 2. Peace.
 C | 57. 3-13-. The wicked.
  D | 57. -13-18. The righteous.
   E | 57. 19-21. Peace.

10 sleeping = dozing, or dreaming.
11 greedy = strong of soul. Heb. *nephesh* (Ap. 13) = strong of appetite: i.e., as well rendered, "greedy".
every one. Heb. *'īsh.* Ap. 14. II.
12 wine. Heb. *yayin.* Ap. 27. I.
strong drink. Heb. *shēkar.* Ap. 27. IV.

57. 1 man. Heb. *'īsh.* Ap. 14. II.
merciful = kind.
men. Heb. pl. of *'ĕnōsh.* Ap. 14. III.
from the evil to come = from the presence of the calamity.
evil = calamity. Heb. *ra'a'.* Ap. 44. viii: i.e. the calamity referred to in Jer. 22. 10. See 2 Kings 22. 16-20.
2 He: i.e. the righteous man.
they: i.e. the men of grace. in = upon.
beds = couches.
his uprightness = his straight path.

57. 3-13- (*C*, above). THE WICKED. (*Alternation.*)

C | e | 3, 4. Inquiry.
  f | 5-10. Crimination.
 e | 11. Inquiry.
  f | 12, 13-. Threatening.

3 sorceress. See note on 2. 6 ("soothsayer").
4 children = offspring.
transgression: i.e. inborn transgression. Heb. *pāsha'.* Ap. 44. ix.
seed of falsehood = false seed. Fig. *Enallagē.* Ap. 6.
5 with idols = with the sacred trees: i.e. the *Ashērahs.* See Ap. 42.
slaying the children. Ref. to Pent. (Lev. 18. 21); to Molech (1 Kings 11. 7. 2 Kings 17. 16, 17); or to Baal (Jer. 19. 5. Ezek. 16. 20; 23. 39. Hos. 13. 1).
6 the smooth stones, &c. = the open places. Judah still in the land. None of the things mentioned in *vv.* 5-7 found in Babylonia.
thy. This and all the Pronouns in *vv.* 6-8 are Fem.
drink offering . . . meat offering. Ref. to Pent. (Ex. 29. 40, 41, &c. Num. 15. 1-10). Cp. 1 Kings 12. 32, 33.
I receive comfort. Fig. *Anthropopatheia.* Ap. 6.
8 remembrance = symbols.
thee. Ed. of A.V. 1611 omits this word "thee".
bed = couch.
where thou sawest it = a hand thou hast seen: as beckoning.
9 the king. Or, the idol, as in 30. 33. 1 Kings 11. 7.
hell. Heb. *Sheōl.* Ap. 35.
10 found . . . hand = found [by the length of thy journeys] a hand to mouth life.

e 11 And of whom hast thou been afraid or
(p. 1002) feared, that thou hast lied, and hast not
603–588 remembered 𝔐𝔢, nor laid *it* to thy heart?
have not 𝔍 held My peace even of old, and
thou fearest 𝔐𝔢 not?

f 12 𝔍 will declare thy righteousness, and thy
works; °for they shall not profit thee.
13 When thou °criest, let °thy companies deliver thee; but the °wind shall carry them all
away; °vanity shall take *them:*

D but he that °putteth his trust in Me shall
possess the land, and shall inherit My °holy
mountain;
14 And shall say, °"Cast ye up, cast ye up,
prepare the way, take up the stumbling block
out of the way of My People."
15 For thus saith the high and °lofty One
°That inhabiteth eternity, Whose name *is*
[13]Holy; "I dwell in the high and [13]holy *place*,
with him also *that is* of a contrite and humble
°spirit, to revive the °spirit of the humble, and
to revive the heart of the contrite ones.
16 For I will not contend for ever, neither will
I be always wroth: for the [15]spirit should fail
before Me, and the °souls *which* 𝔍 have made.
17 For the iniquity of his covetousness was
I wroth, and smote him: °I hid Me, and was
wroth, and he went on frowardly in the way
of his heart.
18 I have seen his ways, and will heal him:
I will °lead him also, and restore comforts unto
him and to his °mourners.

E 19 I create the fruit of the lips; °Peace, peace
to *him that is* far off, and to *him that is* near,"
°saith the LORD; "and I will heal him.
20 But the °wicked *are* like °the troubled sea,
°when it cannot rest, whose waters cast up
mire and dirt.
21 *There is* °no peace," saith °my God, "to
the [20]wicked."

A **58** °Cry aloud, spare not, lift up thy voice
like a trumpet, and shew My People
their °transgression, and °the house of Jacob
their °sins.

B g[1] 2 Yet they seek 𝔐𝔢 daily, and delight to know
(p. 1003) My ways, as a nation that did righteousness,
and °forsook not the ordinance of their °God:
they ask of Me the ordinances of °justice; they
take delight in approaching to °God.
3 °"Wherefore have we fasted," *say they*,
"and Thou seest not? *wherefore* have we
°afflicted our °soul, and Thou takest no knowledge?" °Behold, in the day of your fast ye
find pleasure, and exact all your labours.
4 [3]Behold, °ye fast for strife and debate, and
to smite with the fist of °wickedness: °ye
shall not fast as *ye do this* day, °to make your
voice to be heard on high.
5 Is it such a fast that I have °chosen? a day
for °a man to [3]afflict his °soul? *is it* to bow
down his head as a °bulrush, and to spread
sackcloth and ashes *under him?* wilt thou call
this a fast, and an acceptable day to °the LORD?
6 *Is* not this the fast that I have [5]chosen? to

12 for. Some codices, with two early printed editions, omit "for", and read "and thy works, they will not profit thee".

13 criest. In distress.

thy companies. The paramours of *v.* 8.

wind. Heb. *rûach*. Ap. 9.

vanity. Put by Fig. *Metonymy* (of Adjunct), Ap. 6, for vain men. Cp. Ps. 144. 4. Jas. 4. 14.

putteth his trust=fleeth for refuge to. Heb. *ḥāṣāh*. See Ap. 69. ii.

holy. See note on Ex. 3. 5.

14 Cast ye up=Make a highway. Fig. *Epizeuxis*. Ap. 6. See note on 7. 3.

15 lofty=lifted up. Same word as 6. 1 ("exalted One").

That inhabiteth=inhabiting.

spirit. Heb. *rûach*. Ap. 9.

16 souls=breathing things. Heb. *neshāmāh*. Ap. 16. See note on 2. 22 ("breath").

17 I hid Me. Cp. 45. 15; 59. 2; 64. 7.

18 lead=(gently) lead.

mourners. See note on "mourn" (3. 26).

19 Peace, peace. Fig. *Epizeuxis* (Ap. 6), for great emphasis=perfect peace (as in 26. 3), or great prosperity.

saith the LORD. Heb.=saith Jehovah. Ap. 4. II. The famous Codex *Mugah*, quoted in the *Massōrah*, reads "saith Jehovah my God".

20 wicked=lawless. Heb. *rāshā'*. Ap. 44. x.

the troubled sea=the sea when tossed.

when=for.

21 no peace. Cp. 48. 22.

my God. Heb. Elohim. Ap. 4. I. Some codices read "Jehovah" (Ap. 4. II). Cp. 48. 22. Other codices read "my God", or "Jehovah God" (with Sept. and Vulg.).

58. 1 Cry aloud=Heb. "call with the throat": i.e. deep down as in the oriental throat. It denotes not a wild cry, but solemnity with restraint.

transgression=rebellion. Heb. *pāsha'*. Ap. 44. ix.

the house of Jacob. See note on 2. 5.

sins. Heb. *chāṭā'*. Ap. 44. i.

58. 2-14 (*B*, p. 1002). **CONTRASTED CONDUCT.**
(*Repeated Alternation.*)

B | g[1] | 2-7. Condition. Legal observances.
  h[1] | 8, 9-. Recompense. Illumination.
 g[2] | -9, 10-. Condition. Charity.
  h[2] | -10-12. Recompense. Illumination.
 g[3] | 13. Condition. Legal observance—Sabbath.
  h[3] | 14. Recompense. Ascendancy.

2 forsook. See note on 1. 4.

God. Heb. Elohim. Ap. 4. I.

justice=righteousness. Cp. Ex. 21-23.

3 Wherefore . . . ? Fig. *Erotēsis*. Ap. 6.

afflicted our soul. Ref. to Pent. This is a strictly Levitical technical expression (Lev. 16. 29, 31; 23. 27, 32. Num. 29. 7). This shows that the People were not in exile as alleged, but in the Land. See also the references to other observances below (*v.* 13). Note that in chs. 58 and 59 we have the reference to the Day of Atonement; in chs. 60 and 61, to the Sabbatical and Jubilee years. Ch. 60 refers to the feast of Tabernacles with its "ingathering" (*vv.* 3-5, 13), which followed the Day of Atonement (Lev. 23. 27, 34).

soul. Heb. *nephesh*. Ap. 13. Some codices, with one early printed edition, Aram., Sept., and Vulg., read "souls" (pl.).

Behold. Fig. *Asterismos*. Ap. 6.

4 ye fast. Referring to Day of Atonement, which was still observed; and in the Land, not in exile, as alleged.

wickedness=lawlessness. Heb. *rāshā'*. Ap. 44. x.

ye shall not. Some codices, with two early printed editions, read "and ye shall not".

to make=if ye would make.

5 chosen. See note on 1. 29.

a man. Heb. *'ādām*. Ap. 14. I.

soul. Heb. *nephesh*. Ap. 13.

bulrush. See note on 9. 14.

the LORD. Heb. Jehovah. Ap. 4. II.

603-588 loose the °bands of [4]wickedness, to undo the heavy burdens, and to let the oppressed go free, and that ye break every yoke?

7 *Is it* not °to deal thy °bread to the hungry, and that thou bring the °poor that are cast out to thy house? when thou seest the naked, that thou cover him; and that thou °hide not thyself from °thine own flesh?

h[1] (p. 1003) 8 Then shall thy light break forth as the morning, and °thine health shall spring forth speedily: and thy righteousness shall go before thee; the glory of [5]the LORD shall °be thy °rereward.

9 Then shalt thou call, and [5]the LORD shall answer; thou shalt °cry, and He shall say, "Here I *am*."

g[2] If thou take away from the midst of thee the yoke, the putting forth of the finger, and speaking vanity;

10 And *if* thou °draw out thy [5]soul to the hungry, and satisfy the afflicted [5]soul;

h[2] then shall thy light rise in obscurity, and thy darkness °*be* as the noon day:

11 And [5]the LORD shall °guide thee continually, and satisfy thy [5]soul in °drought, and °make fat thy bones: and thou shalt be like a watered garden, and like a spring of water, whose waters fail not.

12 And *they that shall be* of thee shall °build the old waste places: thou shalt raise up the foundations of many generations; and thou shalt be called, The repairer of the breach, The restorer of paths °to dwell in.

g[3] 13 If thou turn away °thy foot °from the sabbath, *from* doing thy °pleasure on My °holy day; and call the sabbath a delight, the °holy of [5]the LORD, honourable; and shalt honour Him, not doing thine own ways, nor finding thine own °pleasure, nor speaking °*thine own* words:

h[3] 14 Then shalt thou °delight thyself in [5]the LORD; and I will °cause thee to ride upon the high places of the earth, and feed thee with the heritage of Jacob thy father: for the mouth of [5]the LORD hath spoken *it*.

D F (p. 1004) **59** °Behold, °the LORD'S °hand is °not shortened, that it cannot save; neither His ear heavy, that it cannot hear:

G 2 But your °iniquities have separated between you and your °God, and your °sins °have hid *His* face from you, that He will not hear.

3 For your hands are °defiled with blood, and your fingers with [2]iniquity; your lips have spoken lies, your tongue hath muttered perverseness.

4 None °calleth for justice, nor *any* pleadeth °for truth: they °trust in °vanity, and speak °lies; they conceive mischief, and bring forth °iniquity.

5 They hatch °cockatrice' °eggs, and °weave the spider's °web: he that eateth of their eggs dieth, and that which is crushed breaketh out into a °viper.

6 Their [5]webs shall not become garments, neither shall they cover themselves with their works: their works *are* works of [4]iniquity, and the act of violence *is* in their hands.

7 °Their feet run to °evil, and they make haste to shed °innocent blood: their thoughts *are* thoughts of [4]iniquity; wasting and destruction *are* in their °paths.

---

6 bands=pangs. See note on Ps. 73. 4.

7 to deal=to break. The technical term for giving or partaking of food, as in Luke 24. 30, 35. Acts 2. 42, 46; 20. 7, 11; 27. 35. 1 Cor. 10. 16; 11. 24. Cp. Job 42. 11. Lam. 4. 4. Ezek. 18. 7; 24. 17. Hos. 9. 4.

bread. Put by Fig. *Synecdoche* (of Species), Ap. 6, for all kinds of food.

poor. Heb. *'ānāh*. See note on Prov. 6. 11.

hide not. Some codices, with two early printed editions, read "do not thou hide".

thine own flesh. Ref. to Pent. (Gen. 29. 14). Cp. Neh. 5. 1-11. Ap. 92.

8 thine health. Heb. thy healing. Referring to the healing of wounds. **be**=bring up.

rereward=rearguard. Ref. to Pent. (Ex. 14. 19, 20). Cp. 52. 12. **9 cry.** In distress.

10 draw out thy soul. Some codices, with Syr., read "give out thy bread".

be. Supply Ellipsis (of verb "become"). Or we have the Fig. *Oxymoron* (Ap. 6).

11 guide=(gently) guide.

drought. Heb. droughts (pl. of majesty) = great drought. **make fat**=invigorate.

12 build=rebuild. This is still future.

to dwell in: or, leading home.

13 thy foot. Some codices, with one early printed edition, read "thy feet" (pl.).

from the sabbath. Ref. to Pent., as in 56. 2.

pleasure. Some codices, with three early printed editions, read "pleasures" (pl.).

holy. See note on Ex. 3. 5.

thine own words=vain words: or, keep making talk.

14 delight thyself=revel.

cause thee to ride, &c. Ref. to Pent. (Deut. 32. 13; 33. 29).

59. 1-21 (*D*, p. 993). SIN THE CAUSE OF THE BREACH. (*Introversion.*)

D | F | 1. Salvation. Jehovah's power.
  G | 2-8. Israel. Crimination.
  G | 9-15. Israel. Confession.
F | 16-21. Salvation. Jehovah's work.

1 Behold. Fig. *Asterismos.* Ap. 6.

the LORD'S. Heb. Jehovah's. Ap. 4. II.

hand. Fig. *Anthropopatheia.* Ap. 6.

not shortened. Ref. to Pent. (Num. 11. 23). Cp. 50. 2. The phrase occurs nowhere else in the O.T.

2 iniquities. Heb. *'āvāh*. Ap. 44. iv. Same word as in *vv.* 3, 12. Not the same as in *vv.* 6, 7.

God. Heb. Elohim. Ap. 4. I.

sins. Heb. *chāṭā'*. Ap. 44. i.

have hid His face. Cp. 45. 15; 54. 8; 57. 17.

3 defiled. Heb. *gā'al, to redeem*, put for *gā'al, to pollute*, here, and Ezra 2. 62. Neh. 7. 64. Lam. 4. 14. Dan. 1. 8, 8. Zeph. 3. 1. Mal. 1. 7, 12.

4 calleth for justice=sueth in righteousness.

for truth=in truth.

trust=confide. Heb. *bāṭah*. Ap. 69. i.

vanity=confusion. Heb. *tohū*, as in Gen. 1. 2 ("without form"). See note on 24. 10. **lies**=vanity.

iniquity. Heb. *'āven*. Ap. 44. iii. Same word as in *vv.* 6, 7. Not the same as in *vv.* 2, 3, 12.

5 cockatrice'=adders', or vipers'. See note on 11. 8.

eggs . . . web. Note the *Alternation* in *vv.* 5, 6.

weave. See note on 19. 9.

viper. Occurs in Isaiah only here, and in the "former" portion (30. 6). See Ap. 79. II.

7 Their feet=They. Feet being put by Fig. *Synecdoche* (of Part), Ap. 6, for the whole person. Quoted in Rom. 3. 15, 16. **evil.** Heb. *rā'a'*. Ap. 44. viii.

innocent blood. Ref. to Pent. Only here in Isaiah; five times in Deuteronomy (19. 10, 13; 21. 8, 9).

paths=highways. See note on 7. 3.

603-588 8 °**The way of peace they know not**; and *there is* no °judgment in their goings: they have made them crooked paths: whosoever goeth therein shall not know peace.

G i^1 (p. 1005) 9 Therefore is [8]judgment far from us, neither doth °justice overtake us: we wait for light, but behold obscurity; for brightness, *but* we walk in darkness.

k^1 10 °We grope for the wall like the blind, and we grope as if *we had* no eyes: we stumble at noon day as in the °night; *we are* in desolate places as dead *men*.

11 We roar all like bears, and mourn sore like doves:

i^2 we look for [8]judgment, but *there is* none; for salvation, *but* it is far off from us.

k^2 12 For our °transgressions are multiplied before Thee, and our °sins testify against us: for our °transgressions *are* with us; and *as for* our [2]iniquities, we know them;

13 In [12]transgressing and lying against [1]the LORD, and departing away from our [2]God, speaking oppression and revolt, conceiving and uttering from the heart words of falsehood.

i^3 14 And [8]judgment is turned away backward, and [9]justice standeth afar off:

k^3 for truth is fallen in the street, and equity cannot enter.

15 Yea, °truth faileth; and he *that* departeth from °evil °maketh himself a prey:

F l and [1]the LORD saw *it*, and it displeased Him that *there was* no [8]judgment.

16 And He saw that *there was* no °man, and wondered that *there was* no intercessor:

m therefore His °arm brought salvation unto Him; and His righteousness, it sustained Him.

17 For °He put on righteousness as a °breastplate, and an helmet of salvation upon His head; and He put on the garments °of vengeance *for* clothing, and was clad with °zeal as a cloke.

18 According to *their* deeds, accordingly He will repay, fury to His adversaries, recompence to His enemies; to the °islands He will repay recompence.

n 19 So shall they fear the name of [1]the LORD from the west, and His glory from the rising of the sun.

l When the °enemy shall come in °like a flood,

m the °Spirit of [1]the LORD shall °lift up a °standard against him.

20 And °**the Redeemer shall come °to Zion, and unto them that turn from [12]transgression in Jacob, saith [1]the LORD.**

n 21 "**As for Me, this *is* My covenant with them,**" saith [1]the LORD; "My [19]spirit that *is* upon thee, and My words which I have put in thy mouth, shall not depart out of thy mouth, nor out of the mouth of thy seed, nor out of the mouth of thy seed's seed," saith [1]the LORD, "from henceforth and °for ever."

H o p^1 q (p. 1006) **60** °Arise,

r °shine; for °thy light is come,

s and °the glory of °the LORD is risen upon thee.

t 2 For, °behold, the darkness shall cover the earth,

---

8 The way, &c. See Rom. 3. 17.

judgment = righteousness.

59. 9-15 (*G*, p. 1004). CONFESSION.
(*Repeated Alternation.*)

G | i^1 | 9. Justice. Departed.
k^1 | 10, 11-. Condition. Comparisons.
i^2 | -11. Justice. Looked for in vain.
k^2 | 12, 13. Reason.
i^3 | 14-. Justice. Turned away backward.
k^3 | -14, 15-. Reason.

9 justice = righteousness. Same as "judgment", *v.* 8.

10 We grope, &c. Ref. to Pent. (Deut. 28. 29). Idea the same, but word different. The word in Deuteronomy is the same as in Gen. 27. 12, 22; 31. 34, 37. Ex. 10. 21. Job 5. 14; 12. 25. The word in Isaiah occurs nowhere else. Ap. 92.

night. Heb. *nesheph.* A Homonym, with two meanings: (1) *darkness*, as here; Job 24. 15. Prov. 7. 9. 2 Kings 7. 5, 7. Isa. 5. 11; 21. 4. Jer. 13. 16; (2) *daylight*, 1 Sam. 30. 17. Job 7. 4. Ps. 119. 147.

12 transgressions. Heb. *pāsha'.* Ap. 44. ix.

sins. Heb. *chāṭā'.* Ap. 44. i. Note that these three words occur together in Lev. 16. 21.

15 truth faileth = the truth is found missing.

evil. Heb. *rā'a'.* Ap. 44. viii.

maketh himself a prey: i.e. is liable to be despoiled, or outlawed. Rashi says, "is considered mad", as A.V. marg.

59. -15-21 (*F*, p. 1004). SALVATION. JEHOVAH'S WORK. (*Extended Alternation.*)

F | l | -15, 16-. Evil seen by Jehovah.
m | -16-18. Evil removed by Jehovah.
n | 19-. The blessed result.
l | -19-. Evil inflicted by the enemy.
m | -19, 20. Evil removed by Jehovah.
n | 21. The blessed result.

16 man. Heb. *'ish.* Ap. 14. II.

arm. Fig. *Anthropopatheia* (Ap. 6). Put by Fig. *Metonymy* (of Cause), Ap. 6, for the power put forth by it.

17 He put on. Fig. *Anthropopatheia* (Ap. 6). Note that all the armour is for defence.

breastplate = a coat of mail.

of vengeance for clothing = of avenging for clothing. Cp. 61. 2; 63. 4. The Oxf. Gesenius explains it as "of Jehovah as champion of Israel" (p. 528 b).

zeal = jealousy.

18 islands = maritime countries. See note on 11. 11.

19 enemy. Heb. *tzar*, as in *v.* 18.

like a flood = like the flood: the Nile in its overflow.

Spirit. Heb. *rūach.* Ap. 9.

lift up. Fig. *Anthropopatheia.* Ap. 6.

standard: or, banner. Ref. to Pent. (Ex. 17. 15). Heb. *nāṣaṣ.* Ap. 92.

20 the Redeemer = a Redeemer: i.e. the Messiah. Quoted in Rom. 11. 26, 27, showing that the fullness of the Gentiles must be the fullness of the Gentile times.

to = for: i.e. on behalf of. See note on Rom. 11. 26.

21 for ever. This coming deliverance for Israel will be final, and cannot therefore as yet have taken place.

60. 1-22 [For Structure see next page].

1 Arise. Cp. 51. 9, 17, "awake"; 52. 2, "awake"; 60. 1, "arise"; and contrast the cry to Babylon (47. 1), "come down, sit in the dust". See Ap. 82. This refers to the future. **shine.** Cp. 2 Sam. 23. 4.

thy light: i.e. Israel's glory.

the glory of the LORD. Heb. *kābōd.* See 4. 2, 5; 6. 3; 35. 2; 40. 5; 58. 8; **and** *v.* 2 here. Cp. Ps. 106. 20. Jer. 2. 11. Hag. 2. 3, 7, 9.

the LORD. Heb. Jehovah. Ap. 4. II.

2 behold. Fig. *Asterismos* (Ap. 6), to call attention to the condition of the nations just before Israel's future glory shines forth.

t and gross darkness the °people:
(p. 1006) but [1]the LORD shall arise upon thee, and His
s glory shall be seen upon thee.
r 3 And °the Gentiles shall come to thy light,
q and kings to the brightness of thy rising.
p² 4 Lift up thine eyes round about, and see:
°all they gather themselves together, they
come to thee: thy °sons shall come from far,
and thy °daughters shall be °nursed at *thy* side.
5 Then thou shalt see, and °flow together,
and thine heart shall °fear, and °be enlarged;
because the abundance °of the sea shall be
°converted unto thee, the °forces of [3]the Gentiles
shall come unto thee.
6 °The multitude of camels shall cover thee,
the dromedaries of Midian and °Ephah; all they
from °Sheba shall come: they shall bring gold
and incense; and they shall shew forth the
praises of [1]the LORD.
7 All the flocks of °Kedar shall be gathered
°together unto thee, °the rams of °Nebaioth
shall minister unto thee: they shall come up
with acceptance on Mine altar, and I will
°glorify the °house of My glory.
p 8 °Who *are* these *that* fly as a cloud, and as
the doves to their windows?
9 Surely the °isles °shall wait for Me, and
the °ships of Tarshish °first, to bring thy sons
°from far, their silver and their gold with
them, unto the name of [1]the LORD thy °God,
and to °the Holy One of Israel, because He hath
glorified thee.
10 And °the sons of °strangers shall build up
thy walls, and their kings shall minister unto
thee: for °in My wrath I smote thee, but in
My favour have I had mercy on thee.
11 Therefore °thy gates shall be open continually;
they shall °not be shut day nor night;
that *men* may bring unto thee the [5]forces of
the [3]Gentiles, and *that* their kings *may* be
brought.
o 12 For °the nation and kingdom that will
not serve thee °shall perish; yea, *those* nations
shall be utterly wasted.
13 The glory of Lebanon shall come unto
thee, the fir tree, °the pine tree, and the box
together, to beautify the place of My sanctuary;
and I will make °the place of My °feet glorious.
p 14 The sons also of them that °afflicted thee
°shall come bending unto thee; and all they
that despised thee shall bow themselves down
at the soles of thy feet; and they shall call
thee, The city of [1]the LORD, The Zion of [9]the
Holy One of Israel.

60. 1-22 (*C*, p. 993). ZION: RECONCILIATION, RESTORATION, AND ENLARGEMENT. (*Alternation.*)

C | H | 1-16-. Israel's ascendancy.
  J | -16. Jehovah the worker.
 H | 17-22-. Israel's glory.
  J | -22. Jehovah the worker.

60. 1-16- (H, above). ISRAEL'S ASCENDANCY. (*Alternation.*)

H | o | 1-7. Gentiles. Accession.
  p | 8-11. Their ministry.
 o | 12, 13. Gentiles. Subjection.
  p | 14-16-. Their homage.

60. 1-7 (o, above). GENTILES. ACCESSION. (*Division.*)

o | p¹ | 1-3. Israel's rising come.
 | p² | 4-7. Gentiles' attraction to it.

60. 1-3 (p¹, above). ISRAEL'S RISING COME. (*Introversion.*)

p¹ | q | 1-. The rising of Israel.
  r | -1-. The light shining.
   s | -1. The glory of Jehovah.
    t | 2-. Darkness covering the earth.
    t | -2-. Darkness covering the peoples.
   s | -2. The glory of Jehovah.
  r | 3-. The light reflected.
 q | -3. The rising of Israel.

people = peoples.
3 the Gentiles = nations.
4 all they, &c. This is still future.
sons . . . daughters. These are not Gentiles therefore, but true Israelites (Jer. 31. 10). Cp. Ezek. 34. 11-15.
nursed, &c. Carried on the shoulders. So Chald. and Sept. See note on 49. 22.
5 flow together: or, according to the Targum and Syr., "shall be lightened", as in Ps. 34. 5. So in R.V.
fear = praise. Heb. *pāḥad.* A *Homonym*, with two meanings: (1) *to fear*, as in Deut. 28. 66. Job 23. 15; but (2) *to rejoice*, here and Hos. 3. 5 = praise. See note there.
be enlarged = opened as with joy.
of the sea = of the rich seafaring peoples, for which "sea" is put by Fig. *Metonymy* (of Adjunct), Ap. 6.
converted = turned.
forces = fullness, riches, wealth, or resources. This prophecy looks far beyond the return under Ezra-Nehemiah. See *vv.* 12, 15, &c.
6 The multitude = A stream.
Ephah. A Midianite tribe (Gen. 25. 4).
Sheba. Cp. Ps. 72. 10. Both descended from Abraham and Keturah.
7 Kedar. See 21. 16, 17; 42. 11; and cp. Gen. 25. 13. Ps. 120. 5. Song 1. 5. **together** = out.
the. Some codices, with one early printed edition, Sept., and Syr., read "and the".
Nebaioth. A tribe allied to Kedar, descended from Ishmael (Gen. 25. 13). **glorify** = beautify.
house of My glory = My beautiful house.
8 Who are these . . . ? Referring probably to the ships whose sails are compared to wings, developed in next verse.
9 isles = maritime lands. See note on 11. 11.
shall wait. Cp. 42. 4; 51. 5. **ships of Tarshish.** See note on 2. 16. **first** = in the first place, or rank. **from far.** This looks beyond Babylon. **God.** Heb. Elohim. Ap. 4. I. **the Holy One of Israel.** See note on 1. 4. **10 the sons of strangers.** Ref. to Pent. (Ex. 12. 43. Lev. 22. 25). These were expressly excluded. **strangers** = foreigners. **in My wrath.** Cp. 54. 8. Zech. 1. 15. **11 thy gates shall be open.** Heb. they shall keep thy gates open. The word "they" is impersonal: i.e. they who are continually bringing the exiles with their riches. Cp. the same idiom in Luke 12. 20, "they demand thy soul". **not be shut.** These coming times are already being foreshadowed, for this has already been the case for the past few years. This looks beyond the Ezra-Nehemiah period, for see Neh. 13. 19. **12 the nation . . . shall perish.** This is still future. **13 the.** Some codices, with one early printed edition, Sept., and Vulg., read "and the". **the place of My feet:** i.e. the Temple. Cp. 35. 2. Ps. 99. 5; 132. 7. Fig. *Periphrasis.* Ap. 6. **feet.** Fig. *Anthropopatheia.* Ap. 6. **14 afflicted** = oppressed. See 1. 7, 8; 6. 12; 7. 16. **shall come, &c.** Not fulfilled yet. Matt. 8. 11 refers to this. Cp. Mal. 1. 11.

603-588 15 Whereas thou hast been °forsaken and
hated, so that no man went through *thee*, I
will make thee an °eternal excellency, a joy
°of many generations.
16 Thou shalt also suck the milk of [3]the
Gentiles, and shalt suck the breast of kings:
J (p. 1006) and °thou shalt know that I °the LORD *am* thy
Saviour and thy °Redeemer, °the mighty One
of Jacob.

H u (p. 1007) 17 °For brass I will bring gold, and for iron
I will bring silver, and for wood brass, and
for stones iron: I will also make thy officers
peace, and °thine exactors °righteousness.

v 18 °Violence shall no more be heard in thy
land, wasting nor destruction within thy borders;
but thou shalt call thy °walls °Salvation,
and thy gates Praise.

u 19 The sun shall be no more thy light by day;
neither for brightness shall the moon give light
unto thee: but [1]the LORD shall be unto thee an
everlasting light, and thy [9]God thy [7]glory.
20 °Thy sun shall no more °go down; neither
shall thy moon withdraw itself: for [1]the LORD
shall be thine everlasting light, and the days
of thy °mourning shall be ended.

v 21 °Thy People also *shall be* °all righteous:
they shall inherit the land °for ever, the branch
of °My planting, the work of My hands, that
I may be °glorified.
22 °A little one shall become a thousand,
and a small one a strong nation:

J I [1]the LORD will hasten it in °his time.

B K P[1] **61** **°The °Spirit of °the Lord GOD *is* upon
Me; because °the LORD hath °anointed
Me to preach good tidings unto the °meek; He
hath sent Me to °bind up the brokenhearted,
to proclaim liberty to the captives, and °the
opening of the prison to *them that are* bound;**
2 To proclaim °the acceptable year of [1]the
LORD, °and the day of vengeance of our °God;
to comfort all that °mourn;
3 °To appoint unto them that [2]mourn in
Zion, to give unto them °beauty for °ashes, the
oil of joy for mourning, the garment of praise
for the °spirit of heaviness; that they might
be called °trees of righteousness, the planting
of [1]the LORD, that °He might be glorified.

15 forsaken. The type of the forsaken wife is changed to that of the forsaken Land. See note on 1. 4.
eternal. This cannot refer to the prosperity of any past period of Israel's history.
of many generations = of generation after generation.
16 thou shalt know, &c. Ref. to Pent. See notes on 1. 24; 41. 14, &c. Ap. 92.
the LORD am thy Saviour. This constitutes another Jehovah title. Heb. = *Jehovah mōshī'ĕk.*
Redeemer. Cp. 41. 14; 43. 14; 44. 6, 24; 47. 4; 48. 17; 49. 7, 26; 54. 5, 8; 59. 20; 60. 15 (ten times in all, in Isaiah. Cp. Prov. 23. 11.
the mighty One of Jacob. Ref. to Pent. (Gen. 49. 24). Cp. 49. 26. Ps. 132. 2-5. Including the whole natural seed, as well as the spiritual seed of Israel. See notes on Gen. 32. 28; 43. 6; 45. 26, 30. Ap. 92.

60. 17-22 (*H*, p. 1006). ISRAEL'S GLORY. (*Alternation.*)

H | u | 17. Materials.
  v | 18. Evil removed.
 u | 19, 20. Luminaries.
  v | 21, 22-. Good bestowed.

17 For brass. Note the correspondence (by contrast) of this verse with 3. 24 (in A and *A*, p. 930). Cp. also 1. 23-25.
thine exactors = thy tax-gatherers. See Luke 3. 13.
righteousness = righteous. The very opposite to what they have been. Put by Fig. *Metonymy* (of Subject), Ap. 6, for righteous.
18 Violence shall, &c. Cp. Gen. 6. 11, 13. Some codices, with three early printed editions, Sept., and Syr., read "So shall violence", &c. **walls.** Cp. 26. 1.
Salvation: or, Victory.
20 Thy sun . . . go down. }
mourning. See note on 3. 26. } These prophecies yet await fulfilment.
21 Thy People . . . all righteous. }
for ever. This settles the whole question as to any fulfilment in the past.
My planting. Heb. text has "His planting", but "My plantings" in the margin, with some codices, four early printed editions, Aram., Syr., and Vulg.
glorified = get Myself glory.
22 A little one = The little one: i.e. he who has no sons, or few. **his** = its.

61. 1—66. 24 (*B*, p. 993). MESSIAH IN PERSON. (*Alternations.*)

B | K | 61. 1-9. Messiah in Person. Grace.
  L | 61. 10, 11. Joy for present blessings.
   M | N | 62. 1-7. Prayer incited.
     O | 62. 8-12. Answer promised.
 K | 63. 1-6. Messiah in Person. Judgment.
  L | 63. 7-14. Praise for past blessings.
   M | *N* | 63. 15—64. 12. Prayer offered.
     O | 65. 1—66. 24. Answer given.

1-9 (K, above). MESSIAH IN PERSON. (*Division.*)

K | P[1] | 1-3. Messiah. Himself.
 | P[2] | 4-9. Messiah. His People.

1 The Spirit, &c. Quoted in Luke 4. 18, 19. The speaker is therefore the Messiah. **Spirit.** Heb. *rūach.* Ap. 9. **the Lord GOD.** Heb. Adonai Jehovah. See Ap. 4. VIII (2) and II. Some codices, with two early printed editions, Sept., and Vulg., omit "Adonai". **the LORD.** Heb. Jehovah. Ap. 4. II. **anointed.** Matt. 3. 17, with the Divine formula of consecration, "This is My Son", for the office of Prophet; Matt. 17. 5 for the office of Priest; Ps. 2. 7 and Heb. 1. 5, for the office of King. **meek** = oppressed, or lowly ones. **bind up.** Fig. *Anthropopatheia.* Ap. 6. **the opening of the prison** = an opening of the understanding or heart, instead of prison doors. Occurs only here. Heb. *pᵉkah-kōah,* referring to the opening of the vision. **2 the acceptable year** = the year of acceptance, or jubilee year (Lev. 25. 9, 10). We may render:— A year of good-pleasure for Jehovah,
[But] A day of vengeance for our God.
and the day of vengeance. Cp. 59. 17; 63. 4. This is a notable example of how to rightly divide "the Word of truth", when we observe that the Messiah, in quoting this prophecy concerning Himself in Luke 4. 18, 19, "closed the book", and did not go on to quote further in *v.* 20, because the former part of the prophecy referred to the then present time, and not to the future Dispensation of judgment. The Heb. accent separates these two clauses, indicated by "[But]", above. Note that the vengeance is assigned to a "day", in contrast with "year". **God.** Heb. Elohim. Ap. 4. I. **mourn.** See note on 3. 26, and cp. Matt. 5. 4. **3 To appoint** = to set (as a permanent, irrevocable thing). **beauty . . . ashes.** Note the emphasis put on this by the Fig. *Paronomasia,* Ap. 6, *pᵉ'ēr . . . 'ēpher.* **beauty** = an ornament, or nuptial tiara. **ashes:** as put on the head, as a sign of mourning (2 Sam. 13. 19). **spirit of heaviness** = heavy spirit. Heb. *rūach.* Ap. 9. **trees of righteousness.** Ref. to 60. 21. **He.** All is for Jehovah's glory.

P² w a 4 And they shall °build the old °wastes,
(p. 1008) b they shall raise up the former °desolations,
a and they shall repair the °waste cities,
b the °desolations of many generations.

x 5 And °strangers shall stand and feed your flocks, and the sons of °the alien *shall be* your plowmen and your vinedressers.

y 6 But °ye shall be named the Priests of [1]the LORD: *men* shall call you °the Ministers of our [2]God: ye shall eat the riches of °the Gentiles, and in their glory shall ye boast yourselves.

w c 7 For your °shame *ye shall have* °double;
d and *for* °confusion they shall rejoice in their portion:
c therefore in their land they shall possess the double:
d °everlasting joy shall be unto them.

x 8 For I [1]the LORD love °judgment, °I hate robbery for burnt offering; and I will °direct their work °in truth, and I will make an °everlasting covenant with them.

y 9 And their seed shall be known among the [6]Gentiles, and their offspring among the °people: all that see them shall acknowledge them, that they *are* the seed *which* [1]the LORD hath blessed.

L (p. 1007) 10 I will greatly rejoice in [1]the LORD, my °soul shall be joyful in my [2]God; for He hath clothed me with the garments of salvation, He hath covered me °with the robe of righteousness, as °a bridegroom °decketh *himself* with ornaments, and as °a bride adorneth *herself* with her jewels.

11 For as the earth bringeth forth her bud, and as the garden causeth the things that are sown in it to spring forth; so °the LORD* GOD will cause righteousness and praise to spring forth before all the nations.

M N 62 °For Zion's sake will °I not hold My peace, and for Jerusalem's sake I will not °rest, until the righteousness thereof go forth as brightness, and the salvation thereof as a lamp *that* burneth.

2 And °the Gentiles shall see thy righteousness, and all kings thy glory: and thou shalt be °called by a new name, which the mouth of °the LORD shall °name.

3 Thou shalt also be a °crown of °glory in the hand of [2]the LORD, and a royal diadem in the hand of thy °God.

4 Thou shalt no more be termed °Forsaken; neither shall thy land any more be termed °Desolate: but thou shalt be called °Hephzi-bah, and thy land °Beulah: for [2]the LORD delighteth in thee, and thy land shall be married.

5 For *as* a young man marrieth a virgin, *so*

61. 4-9 (P², p. 1007). MESSIAH. HIS PEOPLE.
(*Extended Alternation.*)

P² | w | 4. Israel. Restoration.
x | 5. Gentiles. Gifts.
y | 6. Israel Jehovah's glory.
w | 7. Israel. Restoration.
x | 8. Gentiles. Assistance.
y | 9. Israel Jehovah's glory.

61. 4 (w, above). ISRAEL. RESTORATION.
(*Alternation.*)

w | a | 4-. Wastes. Rebuilt.
b | -4-. Desolations. Raised up.
a | -4-. Wastes. Rebuilt.
b | -4. Desolations. Raised up.

4 build=rebuild. Cp. Amos 9. 11, 12. Acts 15. 16.
wastes=deserted (cities).
desolations=places of silence. See note on 1. 7.
5 strangers=foreigners.
the alien=an unknown people.
6 ye shall be named, &c. Ref. to Pent. (Ex. 19. 6).
the Ministers of our God. Ref. to the technical phrase, common in the Law. See Ex. 28. 35. Num. 16. 9. Deut. 10. 8; 17. 12, &c.
the Gentiles=nations.
7 shame . . . double. Note the Alternation:

61. 7 (*w*, above). ISRAEL. RESTORATION.
(*Alternation.*)

w | c | 7-. Complete compensation.
d | -7-. Rejoicing.
c | -7-. Complete compensation.
d | -7. Rejoicing.

double="double [honour]". Not as in 40. 2. See note there.
confusion=reproach, or disgrace.
everlasting joy. See note on 44. 7.
8 judgment=justice.
I hate robbery, &c. Showing that the sacrificial system was in operation at the time when this prophecy was given.
direct their work=make their recompense.
in truth. See note on 10. 20.
everlasting covenant. See note on "ancient", 44. 7.
9 people=peoples.
10 soul. Heb. *nephesh* Ap. 13.
with the robe. A special various reading called *Sevīr* (Ap. 34), with some codices, one early printed edition, Sept., Syr., and Vulg., read "and with a robe". This necessitates conformity with the Heb. text:—
"With the garments of salvation will He, &c.,
And with a robe of righteousness will He", &c.
a=the.
decketh himself, &c.=adorneth himself (with a turban such as worn by priests).
11 the LORD* GOD=Adonai Jehovah. This is one of the 134 places where the *Sopherīm* changed "Jehovah" of the primitive text to "Adonai"; but both words have been retained instead of the one: viz. Jehovah.

62. 1 For Zion's sake, &c. Not fulfilled, therefore, in the Gospel dispensation; for Zion is still trodden down of the Gentiles (Luke 21. 24).
I. Here we have Messiah's intercession for Israel. See "*B*", p. 1007.
rest. Cp. *vv.* 6, 7.
2 the Gentiles=nations.
called by a new name. As Abraham was (Gen. 17. 5), and Jacob (Gen. 32. 28).
the LORD. Heb. Jehovah. Ap. 4. II.
name=expressly name, or specify.
3 crown=bridal crown. Heb. *'ăṭārāh*, as in 28. 5. 2 Sam. 12. 30. Song 3. 11. **glory**=beauty. **God.** Heb. Elohim. Ap. 4. I. **4 Forsaken.** Heb. *'Ăzūbah*. From *'āzab*. See note on 1. 4. **Desolate.** Heb. *Sh^emāmāh*. See note on 1. 7. **Hephzi-bah.** Heb. *Ḥephẓī-bāh*. Probably a reference to the important marriage of King Hezekiah with Hephzi-bah, which synchronised with this prophecy. See note on 2 Kings 21. 1. **Beulah.** Heb. *B^e'ūlah*=married. See note above. Note the Alternation in this verse.

603-588 shall °thy sons °marry thee: and *as* the bridegroom rejoiceth over the bride, *so* shall thy
[3]God rejoice over thee.
6 I have set watchmen upon thy walls, O
Jerusalem, *which* shall never hold their peace
°day nor night: °ye that make mention of
[2]the LORD, keep not silence,
7 And give Him no °rest, till He establish, and
till He make Jerusalem a praise in the earth.
O (p. 1007) 8 [2]The LORD hath °sworn by His °right hand,
and by the °arm of His strength, "Surely °I
will no more give thy corn *to be* meat for
thine enemies; and the sons of the °stranger
shall not drink thy °wine, for the which thou
hast laboured:
9 But they that have °gathered it shall eat
it, and °praise [2]the LORD; and they that have
°brought it together shall drink it in °the courts
of My holiness."
10 Go through, go through the gates; prepare
ye the way of °the People; °cast up, cast up
the highway; gather out the stones; lift up
a standard for °the People.
11 °Behold, [2]the LORD hath proclaimed unto
the end of the °world, "Say ye to the daughter
of Zion, 'Behold, thy salvation cometh; behold, His reward *is* with Him, and His °work
before Him.'"
12 And they shall call them, The °holy
People, The redeemed of [2]the LORD: and thou
shalt be called, °Sought out, A city °not [4]for-
saken.

K e (p. 1009) 63 °Who *is* °This That cometh from
°Edom, with dyed garments from
°Bozrah?
f This *That is* glorious in His apparel, °travelling
in the greatness of His °strength? I That
speak in righteousness, °mighty to save.
e 2 Wherefore *art Thou* °red in Thine apparel,
and Thy garments like him that treadeth in
the °winefat?
f 3 I have trodden the °winepress alone; and
of °the people *there was* °none with Me: for
I will tread them in Mine anger, and trample
them in My fury; and their °blood °shall be
sprinkled upon My garments, and I will stain
all My raiment.
4 For the °day of vengeance *is* in Mine heart,
and °the °year of My °redeemed is come.
5 And I looked, and *there was* none to help;
and I wondered that *there was* none to uphold:
therefore °Mine own arm brought °salvation
unto Me; and My °fury, it upheld Me.
6 And I will tread down [3]the people in Mine
anger, and °make them drunk in My fury, and
I will bring down their °strength to the earth.
L (p. 1007) 7 I will mention the lovingkindnesses of °the
LORD, *and* the praises of °the LORD, according
to all that °the LORD hath bestowed on us, and
the great goodness toward the °house of Israel,
which He hath bestowed on them according
to His mercies, and according to the multitude
of His lovingkindnesses.
8 For He said, "Surely they *are* My People,
°children *that* will not °lie:" so He was their
Saviour.
9 °In all their affliction He was afflicted, and
°the Angel of His presence saved them: in

5 thy sons marry thee. Note the Fig. *Catachrēsis* (Ap. 6). See note on marry, below.
marry = own, or possess. Heb. *bā'al* = to become an owner, or husband of a wife. See *v.* 4.
6 day nor night. Heb. all the day and all the night.
ye that make mention of = ye that remind.
7 rest = silence, as in *v.* 6.
8 sworn. Fig. *Deēsis.* Ap. 6.
right hand . . . arm. Fig. *Anthropopatheia.* Ap. 6.
I will no more give, &c. Ref. to Pent. (Deut. 28. 30, 31, &c.). Ap. 92.
stranger = foreigner.
wine. Heb. *tīrōsh.* Ap. 27. II.
9 gathered it = gathered it in. Ref. to Pent. (Deut. 20. 6; 28. 30). Cp. Jer 31. 5. Ap. 92.
praise the LORD. Ref. to Pent. (Deut. 14. 23, 26; 16. 11, 14). See note on "shall not" (13. 10).
brought it together = gathered it out. Ref. to Pent. (Deut. 12. 12). Ap. 92.
the courts of My holiness = My holy courts.
10 the People. In 40. 3 the way is to be "prepared" for Messiah: here, for His People.
cast up, cast up the highway. Cp. Figs. *Epizeuxis* and *Polyptōton.* Ap. 6. See note on "highway" (7. 3).
11 Behold. Fig. *Asterismos.* Ap. 6.
world. Heb. earth. Heb. *'ĕretz.*
work = recompense.
12 holy. See note on Ex. 3. 5.
Sought out. Heb. *Derūshah.*
not forsaken. Heb. *L'o-Ne'ezābāh.*

63. 1-6 (*K*, p. 1007). **MESSIAH. IN PERSON. JUDGMENT.** (*Alternation.*)

K | e | 1-. Question.
  f | -1. Answer. Character.
 e | 2. Question.
  f | 3-6. Answer. Work.

1 Who . . . ? Fig. *Erotēsis.* Ap. 6. The prophet's question.
This: i.e. Messiah in the execution of His vengeance in judgment.
Edom = red. } Cp. 34. 5.
Bozrah = vintage. }
travelling = bending forward, as in marching.
strength . . . mighty = strength (for endurance). Heb. *koaḥ.* Not referring to His death, which was in weakness.
2 red = *'ādom.* Hence "Edom" (*v.* 1).
winefat = winepress. Heb. *gath.* Not *yeḳeb*, a wine-vat.
3 winepress = trough. Heb. *pūrah.*
the people = peoples.
none = not a man. Heb. *'īsh.* Ap. 14. II.
blood. Lit. grape-juice, put by Fig. *Metonymy* (of Subject), Ap. 6, for life-blood. All this is in judgment, not redemption. Cp. Rev. 14. 20; 19. 11-21.
shall be sprinkled = will spurt.
4 day . . . year. Cp. 61. 2.
the year of My redeemed. Ref. to Pent. (Deut. 32. 35). Cp. 61. 2.
redeemed = redeemed as by a kinsman (Ex. 6. 6).
5 Mine own arm. Cp. 59. 16.
salvation = victory.
fury = indignation. Some codices, with four early printed editions, read "righteousness". Cp. 59. 18.
6 make them drunk in. Some codices, with one early printed edition, and Aram., read "brake them in pieces with".
strength = life-blood, as in *v.* 3.
7 the LORD. Heb. Jehovah. Ap. 4. II.
house of Israel. See note on 5. 7.
8 children = sons.
lie = deal falsely.
9 In all their affliction He was afflicted. Heb. text reads, "In all their adversity [He was] no adversary". But some codices, with two early printed editions, read as text of A.V.
the Angel of His presence. Ref. to Pent. (Ex. 14. 19; 23. 20, 21; 33. 14). Ap. 92.

603-588 His love and in His pity He °redeemed them;
and He °bare them, and carried them all the
days of old.
10 °But they rebelled, and vexed His °holy
°Spirit: therefore He was turned to be their
enemy, °*and* He fought against them.
11 Then He remembered the days of old,
Moses, *and* His People, *saying,* "Where *is* He
That brought them up out of the sea with the
°shepherd of His flock? where *is* He That °put
His [10] holy [10] Spirit within him?
12 That led *them* by the right hand of Moses
with His glorious °arm, °dividing the water
before them, to make Himself an °everlasting
name?
13 That led them through the deep, as an
horse in the wilderness, *that* they should not
stumble?"
14 °As a beast goeth down into the valley,
the [10] Spirit of [7] the LORD caused him to rest:
so didst Thou lead Thy People, to make Thyself a glorious name.

M N g (p. 1010) 15 Look down from heaven, and behold from
the °habitation of °Thy holiness and of Thy
glory: where *is* Thy zeal and Thy °strength,
the °sounding of Thy bowels and of Thy
mercies toward me? are they restrained?

h 16 Doubtless °Thou *art* our °Father, though
Abraham be ignorant of us, and Israel acknowledge us not: °Thou, O [7] LORD, *art* our Father,
our °Redeemer; Thy name *is* from everlasting.

i 17 O [7] LORD, why hast Thou °made us to err
from Thy ways, *and* °hardened our heart from
Thy fear? °Return for Thy servants' sake,
the tribes of Thine inheritance.

k 18 °The People of [15] Thy holiness have possessed *it* but a little while: our adversaries
have trodden down Thy sanctuary.
19 °We are *Thine:* Thou never barest rule
over them; °they were not called by Thy
name.

g 64 °Oh that Thou wouldest °rend the
heavens, that Thou wouldest come
down, that the mountains might °flow down
°at Thy presence,
2 As *when* the °melting fire burneth, the fire
causeth the waters to boil, to make °Thy name
known to Thine adversaries, *that* the nations
may tremble [1] at Thy presence!
3 °When Thou didst terrible things *which* we
looked not for, Thou camest down, the mountains [1] flowed down [1] at Thy presence.
4 For °since the beginning of the world °*men*
have not heard, °nor perceived by the ear,
neither hath the eye seen, O °God, beside Thee,
***what* He °hath prepared for °him that waiteth**
for Him.
5 °Thou meetest him °that rejoiceth and
worketh righteousness, *those that* remember
Thee in Thy ways: behold, Thou °art wroth;
for we have °sinned: in °those is continuance,
and we shall be saved.

redeemed them. Ref. to Pent. (Ex. 15. 13). Ap. 92.
bare them. Ref. to Pent. (Ex. 19. 4. Deut. 1. 31; 32. 18). Cp. 46. 3, 4. Acts 13. 18. Ap. 92.
10 But they rebelled. Ref. to Pent. (Ex. 15. 24. Num. 14. 11, 34). Ap. 92.
holy. See note on Ex. 3. 5.
Spirit. Heb. *rūach.* Ap. 9.
and He fought = and He Himself fought. Some codices, with three early printed editions, read this "and" in the text.
11 shepherd. Many codices, with five early printed editions (one Rabbinic, 1517), and Vulg., read "shepherds". Referring either to Moses, Aaron, and Joshua; or, the pl. of Majesty, referring to Jehovah their Shepherd. Some codices, with four early printed editions, read "shepherd" (sing.).
put His holy Spirit, &c. Ref. to Pent. (Num. 11. 17). Cp. Ex. 14. 31; 32. 11, 12. Num. 14. 13, 14. Ap. 92.
12 arm. Ref. to Pent. (Ex. 15. 16). Ap. 92.
dividing the water. Ref. to Pent. (Ex. 14. 21, the same word). Ap. 92.
everlasting name. See note on 44. 7.
14 As a beast goeth down = as the cattle go down. Referring to the settlement of Israel in Canaan.

63. 15—64. 12 (*N*, p. 1007). **PRAYER OFFERED.**
(*Extended Alternation.*)

N | g | 63. 15. To look down.
h | 63. 16. "Our Father".
i | 63. 17. Sin.
k | 63. 18, 19. Desolation.
g | 64. 1-7. To come down.
h | 64. 8. "Our Father".
i | 64. 9. Sin.
k | 64. 10-12. Desolation.

15 habitation . . . Thy, &c. See note on "courts" (62. 9).
strength = mighty deeds.
sounding = yearning. Fig. *Anthropopatheia.* Ap. 6.
16 Thou art our Father. Ref. to Pent. (Deut. 32. 6).
Father. A rare word in this connection. Cp. 64. 8.
Redeemer. See note on 60. 16.
17 made us = suffered us.
hardened = let us harden.
Return. Ref. to Pent. (Num. 10. 36). Ap. 92.
18 The People of Thy holiness = Thy holy People. Fig. *Enallage* (Ap. 6). See note on Ex. 3. 5. Ref. to Pent. (Deut. 7. 6; 26. 19).
19 We are [Thine]. There is no word for "Thine" in Heb. text. The Heb. accent (disjunctive) leaves a solemn hiatus between the two clauses; as though, what Israel had become could not be expressed by words: "We are come to this—Thou never barest rule over them"; implying an *Ellipsis* (Ap. 6), to be supplied thus: "We are become [as they]".
they were not called by Thy name = Thy name was not called upon them.

64. 1 Oh, &c. Fig. *Euchē.* Ap. 6. Ch. 64 is joined to ch. 63 by the Massoretic pointing.
rend. A.V., ed. 1611, reads "rent".
flow down = quake. The reference is to Sinai in these verses. Cp. Ps. 68. 7, 8. Judg. 5. 4, 5.
at Thy presence. Note the Fig. *Epistrophē* (Ap. 6), used here for great emphasis.
2 melting. The Heb. word occurs only here, and is plural.
Thy name. See note on Ps. 20. 1.
3 When Thou didst terrible things. Ref. to Pent. (Ex. 34. 10, same word).
4 since the beginning of the world = from of old.
men have not heard. Quoted in 1 Cor. 2. 9. Cp. Ps. 31. 19. **nor.** So, some codices, with two early printed editions, Syr., and Vulg. But others read "have not perceived". **God.** Heb. Elohim. Ap. 4. I. **hath prepared** = could work, or will do. **him that waiteth** = the man who waited. **5 Thou meetest him** = Thou didst meet him. Ref. to Pent. (Gen. 32. 1). Ap. 92. **that rejoiceth** = who was rejoicing, &c. **art wroth** = wert, or wast wroth. **sinned.** Heb. *chāṭā'.* Ap. 44. i. **those is continuance** = those [ways of Thine] is continuance. Same word as "since the beginning" in *v.* 4. Cp. 63. 9, 11, 16, 19.

603-588 6 But we are all as an unclean *thing,* and all our righteousnesses *are* as filthy rags; and we all do fade as a leaf; and our °iniquities, like the °wind, have taken us away.

7 And *there is* none that calleth upon [2]Thy name, that stirreth up himself to take hold of Thee: for Thou °hast hid Thy face from us, and hast consumed us, because of our [6]iniquities.

h (p. 1010) 8 But °now, O °LORD, °Thou *art* our Father; we *are* the clay, and Thou our Potter; and we all *are* the work of Thy °hand.

i 9 °Be not wroth very sore, O [8]LORD, neither °remember [6]iniquity for ever: behold, see, we beseech Thee, we *are* all Thy People.

k 10 Thy °holy cities are a wilderness, Zion is a wilderness, Jerusalem a °desolation.

11 Our [10]holy and our beautiful house, where our fathers °praised Thee, °is burned up with fire: and all our °pleasant things are laid waste.

12 Wilt Thou °refrain Thyself for these *things,* O [8]LORD? wilt Thou hold Thy peace, and afflict us very sore?

O Q (p. 1011) **65** I am sought of *them that* asked not *for Me;* °**I am found of *them that* sought Me not: I said, °"Behold Me, behold Me," unto °a nation *that* was not called by My name.**

2 **I have °spread out My hands all the day unto a rebellious People,** which walketh in a way *that was* not °good, after their own thoughts;

3 A People that °provoketh Me to anger continually to My face; °that sacrificeth in gardens, and °burneth incense °upon altars of brick;

4 Which remain among the °graves, and lodge in the °monuments, which °eat swine's flesh, and °broth of °abominable *things is in* their vessels;

5 Which say, "Stand by thyself, come not near to me; for I am holier than thou." "These *are* a smoke in My °nose, a fire that burneth all the day.

6 °Behold, °*it is* written before Me: I will not keep silence, but °will recompense, even recompense into their bosom,

7 Your °iniquities, and the °iniquities of your fathers together," saith °the LORD, "which have [3]burned incense upon the mountains, and blasphemed Me upon the hills: therefore will I measure their former work into their bosom."

R 8 °Thus saith [7]the LORD, °"As the °new wine is found in the cluster, and *one* saith, 'Destroy it not; for a blessing *is* in it:' so will I do for °My servants' sakes, that I may not destroy them all.

9 And I will bring forth °a seed out of Jacob, and out of Judah an inheritor of My mountains: and Mine elect shall inherit it, and My servants shall dwell there.

10 And °Sharon shall be a fold of flocks, and

6 iniquities. Heb. *'āvāh.* Ap. 44. iv.

wind. Heb. *rūach.* Ap. 9.

7 hast hid=hadst hidden. Cp. 45. 15; 53. 3; 54. 8; 57. 17; 59. 2. Ref. to Pent. (Deut. 31. 17, 18, 20). Ap. 92.

8 now. A special various reading, called *Sevir* (Ap. 34), with some codices, two early printed editions, and Aram., read "Thou".

LORD. Heb. Jehovah. Ap. 4. II.

Thou art our Father. See note on 63. 16.

hand. Some codices, with Sept., Syr., and Vulg., read "hands" (pl.).

9 Be not, &c. Continue not to be, &c.

remember=continue not to remember.

10 holy. See note on Ex. 3. 5.

desolation. Referring to the time of Matt. 23. 38; 24. 2.

11 praised. See note on "shall not", &c. (13. 10).

is burned up with fire. This prayer is proleptic; and is said now by anticipation of the then (and now still future) day of Israel's repentance and return to Jehovah.

pleasant things=goodly places, or vessels. Same word as in 2 Chron. 36. 19.

12 refrain Thyself: i.e. refuse to give way in compassion, &c. Cp. Gen. 43. 1; 45. 1. Isa. 42. 14; 63. 15.

65. 1—66. 24 (*O*, p. 1007). **ANSWER. GIVEN.** (*Extended Alternation.*)

O | Q | 65. 1-7. Contrasted characters.
R | 65. 8-10. Seed promised.
S | 65. 11-16. Threatening.
T | 65. 17-25. New heavens and new earth.
Q | 66. 1-6. Contrasted characters.
R | 66. 7-14. Seed brought forth.
S | 66. 15-18-. Threatening.
T | 66. -18-24. New heavens and new earth.

1 I am found, &c. Quoted in Rom. 10. 20, 21.

Behold Me. Fig. *Epizeuxis.* Ap. 6. See note on 24. 16.

a nation that was not called by My name. Ref. to Pent. (Deut. 32. 21), and to the Dispensation of the Acts. See the Structure of "the Song of Moses", p. 283.

2 spread out, &c. Fig. *Anthropopatheia.* Ap. 6.

good=right. Cp. Ps. 36. 4.

3 provoketh Me to anger. Ref. to Pent. (Deut. 32. 21, the same word, though not the same form). Ap. 92.

that sacrificeth in gardens. Ref. to Pent. (Lev. 17. 5). Cp. 1. 29; 57. 5. Jer. 2. 20. Ap. 92.

burneth. Heb. *kātar.* See Ap. 43. I. vii.

upon altars of brick=upon the bricks: i.e. not on the golden altar of incense.

4 graves=tombs. Heb. *keber.* Ap. 35.

monuments=secret places. Probably in heathen temples.

eat swine's flesh. Ref. to Pent., where this was forbidden (Lev. 11. 7. Deut. 14. 8). Ap. 92. Bones of swine were found at Gezer. See note on 1 Kings 9. 15.

broth. The reference is to a sacrificial feast of unclean food.

abominable things. Ref. to Pent. (Lev. 7. 18; 19. 7). The Heb. word (*piggūl*) is found only in Ezek. 4. 14, beside these passages. Ap. 92.

5 nose. Fig. *Anthropopatheia.* Ap. 6.

6 Behold. Fig. *Asterismos.* Ap. 6.

it is written. Ref. to Pent. (Ex. 32. 35. Lev. 26. Deut. 32). Ap. 92.

will recompense, &c. Ref. to Pent. (Deut. 32. 35, the same word, and is unique in its occurrence). Ap. 92.

7 iniquities. Heb. *'āvāh.* Ap. 44. iv.

the LORD. Heb. Jehovah. Ap. 4. II.

8 Thus saith the LORD. Note the frequent occurrence of this expression in predicting these new things. The first is 42. 5. **As**=According as. **new wine.** Heb. *tīrōsh.* Ap. 27. ii. Here is further reference to the new Israel. See notes on *v.* 1. **My servants' sakes.** Some codices, with one early printed edition, and Sept., read "servant's" (sing.): i.e. Messiah (see note on 37. 35):="for the sake of My servant". **9 a seed.** A further reference to the new Israel of 26. 2; 66. 7, 8. Matt. 21. 43. **10 Sharon.** See note on 33. 9.

603-588 the °valley of Achor a place for the herds to lie
down in, for My People that have sought Me.
S 11 But ye *are* they that °forsake [7]the LORD,
(p. 1011) that forget My °holy mountain, that prepare a
table for °that troop, and that °furnish the
drink offering unto °that number.
12 Therefore will I °number you to the sword,
and ye shall all bow down to the slaughter:
because when I called, ye did not answer;
when I spake, ye did not hear; but did °evil
before Mine eyes, and did °choose *that* wherein
I delighted not."
13 Therefore thus saith °the Lord GOD,
°"Behold, °My servants shall eat, but ye shall
be hungry: °behold, °My servants shall drink,
but ye shall be thirsty: °behold, °My servants
shall rejoice, but ye shall be ashamed:
14 Behold, My servants shall sing for joy of
heart, but ye shall cry for sorrow of heart, and
shall howl for °vexation of °spirit.
15 And ye shall leave your name for a curse
unto My chosen: for [13]the Lord GOD shall slay
thee, and call His servants °by another name:
16 °That °he who blesseth himself in the
earth shall bless himself in the °God of °truth;
and he that sweareth in the earth °shall swear
by the °God of °truth; because the former
troubles are forgotten, and because they are hid
from Mine eyes.
T 17 For, [6]behold, I create °new heavens and a
new earth: and °the former shall not be remembered, nor come into mind.
18 But be ye glad and rejoice °for ever *in that*
which I create: for, behold, I create Jerusalem
a rejoicing, and her People a joy.
19 And I will rejoice in Jerusalem, and joy in
My People: and the voice of weeping shall be
°no more heard in her, nor the voice of crying.
20 °There shall be [19]no more thence an infant
°of days, nor an old man that hath not filled
his days: for the °child shall die an hundred
years old; but the sinner *being* an hundred
years old shall be °accursed.
l 21 And °they shall build houses, and inhabit
them;
m and they shall plant vineyards, and eat the
fruit of them.
l 22 They shall not build, and another inhabit;
m they shall not plant, and another eat: for as
the days of a tree *are* the days of My People,
and Mine °elect shall long enjoy the work of
their hands.
23 °They shall not labour in vain, nor bring
forth for trouble; for they *are* the seed of the
blessed of [7]the LORD, and their offspring with
them.
24 And it shall come to pass, that °before
they call, I will answer; and while they are yet
speaking, I will hear.
25 The °wolf and the lamb shall feed °to-
gether, and the lion shall eat straw like the
bullock: and °dust *shall be* °the serpent's
meat. They shall not hurt nor destroy °in all
My [11]holy mountain," saith [7]the LORD.

valley of Achor. As in Hos. 2. 15. The only two references to the history of Josh. 7.

11 forsake. See note on 1. 4.

holy. See note on Ex. 3. 5.

that troop. Heb. *Gad*, the well-known Syrian god of "Fate".

furnish the drink offering = fill up the mixed wine. Heb. *mimsak*. Ap. 27. vii. Cp. Jer. 7. 18; 44. 17.

that number. Heb. *m^enī*. Same as the god *Manu* (= Destiny) of the Assyrian inscriptions.

12 number = destroy. Heb. *mānīthī*. Fig. *Paronomasia* (Ap. 6), with the name of the god, *M^enī*.

evil. Heb. *rā'a'*. Ap. 44. viii.

choose. See note on 1. 29.

13 the Lord GOD. Heb. Adonai Jehovah. Ap. 4. VIII (2), and II.

Behold, &c. Fig. *Asterismos* (Ap. 6), for emphasis. Fig. *Symplokē*. Ap. 6. Luke 6. 25 refers to the period prophesied here.

My servants. Refers to the new Israel of 26. 2; 66. 7, 8. Matt. 21. 43.

14 vexation = breaking.

spirit. Heb. *rūach*. Ap. 9.

15 by another name: i.e. Hephzi-bah. See 62. 4.

16 That = So that.

he who blesseth, &c. Ref. to Pent. (Gen. 22. 18; 26. 4). Ap. 92. **God.** Heb. Elohim. Ap. 4. I.

truth = faithfulness. Cp. 2 Cor. 1. 20.

shall swear, &c. Ref. to Pent. (Deut. 6. 13). Ap. 92.

17 new heavens, &c.: i.e. new, in respect to the old. Not the "new" of 2 Pet. 3. 13, or Rev. 21. 1. Note the contrast of this with Rev. 21:—

Isa. 65.	**Rev. 21.**
Name, Jerusalem (Hephzibah, *v.* 18).	New Jerusalem (*v.* 2); "great", "holy" (*v.* 10).
Position, on mountain (*v.* 25).	out of heaven (*v.* 2).
Privileges, *vv.* 18–20.	*v.* 4.
Character, sinners there (*v.* 20).	no sinners (*v.* 27).
,, prayer (*v.* 24).	no temple (*v.* 22).
Employment, labour, planting, building (*v.* 21).	already built by God (*vv.* 12–25; 22. 3–5).

the former = viz. those which were, and are now.

18 for ever. Chald. Targum renders it "in the world of worlds": i.e. the most glorious world.

19 no more heard. Therefore not the restoration of Ezra-Nehemiah, or the Church of God now.

20 There. Some codices read "And there".

of days: i.e. of a few days.

child shall die = youth may die: i.e. neither early death, nor premature decay.

accursed = cut off. Cp. Ps. 101. 8.

21 they shall build, &c. Ref. to Pent. (Lev. 26. 16. Deut. 28. 41). Note the *Alternation* in *vv.* 21, 22:—

21 l | 21–. Houses. Build. }
22 m | –21. Vineyards. Plant. } Positive.
l | 22–. Houses. Not build. }
m | –22–. Vineyard. Not plant. } Negative.

22 elect = chosen.

23 They shall not labour in vain. Ref. to Pent. (Deut. 28. 41, reversed). Cp. Lev. 26. 16. Ap. 92.

24 before they call, &c. A reference to 30. 19. The blessing of Messiah (Ps. 21. 3) now extended to the new Israel.

25 wolf, &c. As in 11. 6, 7, 9, which is Millennial, not eternal.

together = as one. Heb. *'echad*. Same word as "one" in Deut. 6. 4: i.e. one of others. Occurs in former part of Isaiah (4. 1; 5. 10; 6. 2, 6; 9. 14; 10. 17; 19. 18; 23. 15; 27. 12; 30. 17, 17; 34. 16; 36. 9); and, in the latter part (47. 9; 51. 2; 65. 25; 66. 8, 8, 17). See Ap. 79. II.

dust. Never was the serpent's food. It is used as a powerful Fig. of Speech, or Idiom, as in Ps. 72. 9. Cp. Prov. 20. 17.

the serpent's, &c. = as for the serpent, dust shall be his food: i.e. the Old Serpent (Rev. 20. 2), who brought in all the sin and misery to the world and to Israel, will then be bound (Rev. 20. 1–3), and he will lick the dust, the symbol of his humiliation, disappointment, and defeat. Referring to the Figs. used in Gen. 3. 14. See Ap. 19.

in all My holy mountain. See note on 11. 9.

Q (p. 1011) 603-588 **66** °Thus saith °the LORD, °"**The heaven *is***
My throne, and the earth *is* My footstool:
where *is* °the house that °ye build unto Me?
and where *is* °the place of My rest?
2 For all those *things* hath Mine hand made,
and all those *things* have been, °saith [1]the
LORD: but to this *man* will I look, *even* to
him that is °poor and of a contrite °spirit, and
°trembleth at My word.
3 He that killeth an ox *is as if* he slew a °man;
he that sacrificeth a lamb, *as if* he °cut off a
dog's neck; he that offereth an °oblation, *as if*
he offered °swine's blood; he that °burneth
incense, *as if* he blessed an idol. Yea, they
have °chosen their own ways,

n (p. 1013) and °their soul delighteth in their abominations.

o 4 I also will [3]choose their delusions, and will
bring their fears upon them;

p because when I called, none did answer;

p when I spake, they did not hear: but they
°did °evil before Mine eyes,

o and [3]chose *that*

n in which I delighted not.
5 Hear the word of [1]the LORD, ye that [2]tremble
at His word; Your brethren that hated you,
that cast you out for My name's sake, said,
'Let [1]the LORD be glorified:' but He shall
appear to your joy, and they shall be ashamed.
6 °A voice of noise from the city, a voice from
the temple, a voice of [1]the LORD That °render-
eth recompence to His enemies.

R (p. 1011) 7 Before she travailed, °she brought forth;
before her pain came, she was delivered of °a
man child.
8 Who hath heard such a thing? °who hath
seen such things? Shall the earth be made to
bring forth in one day? *or* shall °a nation be
born °at once? for as soon as Zion travailed,
she brought forth her °children.
9 Shall I bring to the birth, and not cause to
bring forth?" saith [1]the LORD: "shall I cause
to bring forth, and shut *the womb?*" °saith
thy °God.
10 °"Rejoice ye with Jerusalem, and be glad
with her, all ye that love her: rejoice for joy
with her, all ye that °mourn for her:
11 That ye may suck, and be satisfied with
the breasts of her consolations; that ye may
milk out, and be delighted with the abundance
of her glory.
12 For thus saith [1]the LORD, °Behold, I will
extend °peace to her like a river, and the glory
of the °Gentiles like a flowing stream: °then
shall ye suck, ye shall be borne upon *her* sides,
and be dandled upon *her* knees.
13 As °one whom his mother comforteth, so
will I comfort you; and ye shall be comforted
°in Jerusalem.
14 And °when ye see *this*, your heart shall
rejoice, and your bones shall flourish like an
herb: and the hand of [1]the LORD shall be
known toward His servants, and *His* indignation toward His enemies.

S 15 For, [12]behold, [1]the LORD will come with
fire, and with His chariots like a whirlwind,
to render His anger with fury, and His rebuke
with flames of fire.
16 For by fire and by His sword will [1]the
LORD plead with °all flesh: and the slain of
[1]the LORD shall be many.
17 They that sanctify themselves, and purify
themselves in the °gardens behind °one *tree*
in the midst, eating [3]swine's flesh, °and the

66. 1 Thus saith the LORD. See Ap. 82.
the LORD. Heb. Jehovah. Ap. 4. II.
The heaven, &c. Quoted in Acts 7. 49. Cp. 1 Kings 8. 27. 2 Chron. 6. 18.
the = this. Heb. *zeh*.
ye: i.e. the future builders of the house.
the place of My rest: i.e. rest in satisfaction. The Temple was for sacrifice and atonement (2 Chron. 2. 6), not for dwelling. Cp. Acts 7. 48.
2 saith the LORD = [is] Jehovah's oracle.
poor = wretched, or lowly. Heb. *'ānī*. See note on "poverty", Prov. 6. 11.
spirit. Heb. *rūach*. Ap. 9.
trembleth at = careth anxiously for. Cp. *v.* 5.
3 man. Heb. *'ish*. Ap. 14. II.
cut off = breaketh.
oblation = gift, or meal offering. Heb. *minchah*. Ap. 43. II. iii.
swine's blood. Ref. to Pent. (Deut. 14. 8. Lev. 11. 7). See Ap. 92. Cp. 65. 4.
burneth incense = maketh a memorial of frankincense. Ref. to Pent. (Lev. 2. 2). Ap. 92.
chosen. See note on 1. 29.
their soul = they. Heb. *nephesh*. Ap. 13.
Note the *Introversion* beginning with the last clause of *v.* 3, and including *v.* 4:—

3, 4
n | -3. They delight, &c. } The sin.
o | 4-. I also will choose, &c. }
p | -4-. When I called, &c. } The reason for
p | -4-. When I spake, &c. } the judgment.
o | -4-. They chose, &c. } The sin.
n | -4-. I delighted not. }

4 did = have done.
evil = the evil. Heb. *rā'a'*. Ap. 44. viii.
6 A voice, &c. Cp. Zech. 12. 3-6; 14. 3. Cp. 42. 14.
rendereth recompence. Cp. 65. 6.
7 she brought forth. This is the birth of the new nation. These are the "birth pangs" (or "sorrows") of Matt. 24. 8. In Rev. 12. 1, 2 we have one part of the type in the person of Messiah. Here is the other part of the type.
a man child = a male, as in Rev. 12. 5.
8 who. Some codices, with four early printed editions, Sept., and Vulg., read "and who".
a nation: i.e. the righteous nation of 26. 2. Referred to in *v.* 7. Matt. 21. 43.
at once = at a stroke. **children** = sons.
9 saith thy God. See note on 1. 11.
God. Heb. Elohim. Ap. 4. I.
10 Rejoice ye with Jerusalem. The promises, of 1. 27; 2. 1-5, are now at length to be fulfilled.
mourn. As for one lost, or dead. See note on 3. 26.
12 Behold. Fig. *Asterismos* (Ap. 6), to introduce the Fig. *Syncrisis* (Ap. 6), to increase the emphasis.
peace = prosperity.
Gentiles = nations.
then shall ye suck. The promises of 49. 22 and 60. 4 are again renewed.
13 one = a man. Heb. *'ish*. Ap. 14. II.
in Jerusalem. Not in the Church. Cp. 1. 1.
14 when ye see this = as soon as ye see this.
16 all flesh. Put by Fig. *Synecdoche* (of the Part), Ap. 6, for all mankind.
17 gardens. Cp. 1. 29; 40. 5, and 65. 3.
one tree: i.e. the *Asherah*. See Ap. 42.
and. The Mugah Codex (quoted in the *Massōrah*) and other codices, omit this "and".

603-588 °abomination, and the °mouse, shall °be consumed together, [2] saith [1] the LORD.
18 For I *know* their works and their °thoughts: it shall come,

T (p. 1011) that °I will gather all nations and tongues; and they shall come, and see My glory.
19 And I will set a °sign among them, and I will °send °those that escape of them unto the nations, *to* °Tarshish, °Pul, and °Lud, that draw the bow, *to* °Tubal, and °Javan, *to* the °isles afar off, that have not heard My fame, neither have seen My glory; and they shall declare My glory among the [12] Gentiles.
20 And they °shall bring all your brethren *for* °an offering unto [1] the LORD out of all nations

q upon horses,

r and in chariots, and in litters,

q and upon mules,

r and upon °swift beasts, to My °holy mountain Jerusalem," saith [1] the LORD, °"as the °children of Israel °bring °an offering in a clean vessel into the house of [1] the LORD.
21 And I will also take of °them for °priests °*and* for Levites," saith [1] the LORD.
22 "For as the °**new heavens and the new earth, which I will make**, shall remain before Me, [2] saith [1] the LORD, so shall your seed and your name remain.
23 And it shall come to pass, *that* from one °new moon to another, and from one °sabbath to another, shall [16] all flesh come to worship °before Me, [2] saith [1] the LORD.
24 And they shall go forth, and look upon the carcases of the °men that have °transgressed against Me: for °**their worm shall not die, neither shall their fire be quenched**; and they shall be °an abhorring unto [16] all flesh."

abomination. Heb. *shāḳaẓ.* Ref. to Pent. (Deut. 7. 26). Occurs in Isaiah only here; Leviticus thirteen times (7. 21; 11. 10, 11, 11, 12, 13, 13, 20, 23, 41, 42, 43; 20. 25); and Ezek. 8. 10. Not the same word as in 65. 4. Ap. 92.
mouse. Ref. to Pent., where it is forbidden (Lev. 11. 29). Ap. 92. Elsewhere, only in 1 Sam. 6. 4, 5, 11, 18.
be consumed = come to an end.
18 thoughts = devices.
I will gather. Cp. Joel 3. 2. Zeph. 3. 8.
19 sign. See note on 7. 11.
send: as missionaries.
those that escape: i. e. the remnant of saved Israel.
Tarshish. Put for the far west.
Pul . . . Lud = Phut . . . Lud, put for African peoples. They are mentioned together, as serving in the Egyptian armies (Ezek. 30. 5).
Tubal = the Scythian tribes.
Javan. Put for the Greeks settled in Asia Minor.
isles = maritime countries. See note on 11. 11.
20 shall bring. Not into the Church, but back to the Holy Land.
an offering = a gift offering. Heb. *minchah.* Ap. 43. II. iii.
swift beasts: carriages, as required by the Structure of *v.* 20:—

20 | q | upon horses.
| r | in chariots and litters.
| *q* | upon mules.
| *r* | in carriages.

"Swift beasts" is Heb. *kirkāroth*, from *kārar*, to move in a circle; hence, may mean (like English *car*) any vehicle on wheels. It is never used of animals. There is nothing to suggest "swaying furnaces", as suggested by some, to mean "locomotives".
holy. See note on Ex. 3. 5.
as = according as.
children = sons.
bring an offering, &c. Ref. to Pent. (Lev. 2, &c.). Ap. 92.
21 them, i. e. Israel.
priests and for Levites. Ref. to Pent. (Deut. 17. 9). See notes on Ezek. 43. 19; 44. 10, 13, 15. Ap. 92.
priests. Thus completing the fulfilment of Ex. 19. 6.
and. Some codices, with Aram., Sept., Syr., and Vulg., read this "and" in the text.
22 new heavens, &c. See note on 65. 17.

23 new moon . . . sabbath. Ref. to Pent. and the law concerning them (Num. 10. 10; 28. 11–15). Ap. 92. Cp. Ps. 81. 3, 4. **before Me.** Ref. to Pent., implying centralised worship, as in Ex. 20. 3, 5. Deut. 26. 3, 5. Ap. 92. Cp. 1. 12. **24 men.** Heb. pl. of *'ĕnōsh.* Ap. 14. III. **transgressed.** Heb. *pāsha'.* Ap. 44. ix. **their worm.** Quoted in Mark 9. 44. Referred by our Lord to Gehenna, of which the fires in the valley of Hinnom were an illustration. Heb. *tōlā'*, the maggot bred from putrid substances. See Ex. 16. 20. Deut. 28. 39. Job 25. 6 (second word). Ps. 22. 6. Isa. 14. 11 (second word); 41. 14; 66. 24; and Jonah 4. 7, which are all the occurrences of *tōlā'* in O.T. In the synagogue use, *v.* 23 is repeated after *v.* 24, so that the book may end with comfort. Cp. end of Lamentations, Ecclesiastes, and Malachi. **an abhorring.** The Heb. occurs only here.

THE BOOK OF THE PROPHET

JEREMIAH.

THE STRUCTURE OF THE BOOK AS A WHOLE.

(*Introversion.*)

A | 1. 1-3. INTRODUCTION.
  B | 1. 4-19. JEREMIAH'S COMMISSION GIVEN.
    C | 2. 1—20. 18. PROPHECIES ADDRESSED TO JEWS.
      D | 21. 1—35. 19. HISTORY, &c. JEHOIAKIM. (Not chronological.)
        E | 36. 1-32. BARUCH'S MISSION TO JEHOIAKIM.
      D | 37. 1—45. 5. HISTORY, &c. ZEDEKIAH. (Not chronological.)
    C | 46. 1—51. 64-. PROPHECIES ADDRESSED TO GENTILES.
  B | 51. -64. JEREMIAH'S COMMISSION ENDED.
A | 52. 1-34. CONCLUSION.

For the Canonical order and place of the Prophets, see Ap. 1, and cp. page 1206.
For the Chronological order of the Prophets, see Ap. 77.
For the inter-relation of the prophetic books, see Ap. 78.
For references to the Pentateuch in the Prophets, see Ap. 92.
For the Canonical order of Jeremiah's prophecies, see below.
For the Chronological order of Jeremiah's prophecies, see Ap. 83.
For the Septuagint version of Jeremiah, see Ap. 84.

The prophecies of Jeremiah do not profess to be given in chronological order (see Ap. 83); nor is there any reason why they should be so given. Why, we ask, should modern critics first assume that they ought to be, and then condemn them because they are not?

It is the historical portions, which concern Jehoiakim (**D**) and Zedekiah (***D***), that are chiefly so affected. And, Who was Jehoiakim that his history should be of any importance? Was it not he who "cut up the Word of Jehovah with a penknife, and cast it in the fire"? Why should not his history be "cut up"? Zedekiah rejected the same Word of Jehovah. Why should his history be respected?

Secular authors take the liberty of arranging their own literary matter as they choose; why should this liberty be denied to the sacred writers? The fact that the canonical and chronological portions have each their own particular Structures, and that both are perfect, shows that both orders have the same Divine Author.

Jeremiah's prophecy is dated (1. 2, 3) as being "in the days of Josiah . . . in the thirteenth year of his reign. It came also in the days of Jehoiakim the son of Josiah . . . unto the end of the eleventh year of Zedekiah . . . unto the carrying away of Jerusalem captive in the fifth month."

The 13th year of Josiah was 518 B.C.
The 11th year of Zedekiah was 477 B.C.
Therefore the whole period covered by Jeremiah was 41 years, as shown in Ap. 50, pp. 60, 67, 68, and Ap. 77.

It is highly probable that this period was exactly *forty* years—the last probationary period (see Ap. 10) vouchsafed by Jehovah, before Jerusalem was destroyed and the Temple burnt.* But, as the month in the *thirteenth* year of Josiah, at which the Word first came to Jeremiah, is not stated, the whole period has to be shown as above, viz. 41 years.

Having regard to the *Formulae* of prophetic utterances (see Ap. 82), there appear to be some fifty-one distinct and clearly marked prophecies, commencing with some such formula as "The word of the Lord came", &c. It would have been well if the book could have been divided into fifty-one chapters (instead of fifty-two) so as to coincide with these. They commence as follows :—

I. 1. 4.	XIV. 21. 1.	XXVII. 34. 1.	XL. 45 1.
II. 1. 11.	XV. 24. 4.	XXVIII. 34. 8.	XLI. 46. 1.
III. 1. 13.	XVI. 25. 1.	XXIX. 34. 12.	XLII. 46. 13.
IV. 2. 1.	XVII. 26. 1.	XXX. 34. 1.	XLIII. 47. 1.
V. 3. 6.	XVIII. 27. 1.	XXXI. 35. 12.	XLIV. 48. 1†.
VI. 7. 1.	XIX. 28. 12.	XXXII. 36. 1.	XLV. 49. 1†.
VII. 11. 1.	XX. 30. 1.	XXXIII. 36. 27.	XLVI. 49. 7†.
VIII. 13. 3.	XXI. 32. 1.	XXXIV. 37. 6.	XLVII. 49. 23†.
IX. 13. 8.	XXII. 32. 6.	XXXV. 39. 15.	XLVIII. 49. 28.
X. 14. 1.	XXIII. 32. 26.	XXXVI. 40. 1.	XLIX. 49. 34.
XI. 16. 1.	XXIV. 33. 1.	XXXVII. 42. 7.	L. 50. 1.
XII. 18. 1.	XXV. 33. 19.	XXXVIII. 43. 8.	LI. 51. 59.
XIII. 18. 5.	XXVI. 33. 23.	XXXIX. 44. 1.	

* Like the corresponding period of probation covered by the Acts of the Apostles, before the destruction of the second Temple.

† The Fig. *Ellipsis* (Ap. 6) should be repeated in each of these passages, from 47. 1 ["The word of Jehovah came to Jeremiah the prophet] against", &c.

THE BOOK OF THE PROPHET

JEREMIAH.

A A^1 (p. 1016) 518–500 **1** THE °words of °Jeremiah the son of °Hilkiah, °of the priests that *were* in °Anathoth in the land of Benjamin:

A^2 2 To whom °the ¹word of °the LORD came in the days of °Josiah the son of Amon king of Judah, in the °thirteenth year of his reign.

A^3 3 °It came also in the days of °Jehoiakim the son of Josiah king of Judah, unto the end of the eleventh year of Zedekiah the son of Josiah king of Judah, unto the carrying away of Jerusalem captive in °the fifth month.

B B C a 4 °Then the °word of ²the LORD came unto me, saying,

5 "Before I formed thee in the belly °I knew thee; and before thou camest forth out of the womb I °sanctified thee, *and* I ordained thee a prophet unto °the nations."

6 Then said I, "Ah, °Lord GOD! °behold, °I cannot speak: for I *am* °a child."

7 But ²the LORD said unto me, "Say not, 'I *am* ⁶a child:' for thou shalt go to all that I shall send thee, and °whatsoever I command thee thou shalt speak.

b 8 °Be not afraid of their faces:

D c for I *am* with thee to deliver thee, °saith ²the LORD.

1. 1–3 (**A**, p. 1015). INTRODUCTION.
(*Division.*)

A | A^1 | 1. The Prophet. His Person.
  | A^2 | 2. The Prophet. His Call. Its time.
  | A^3 | 3. The Prophet. His Ministry. Its duration.

1 words: or, prophecies (*vv.* 4, 9; 2. 1, 4, &c.). Cp. 36. 1, 2; but better "words", as the historic portions are also Jehovah's words. Cp. Amos 1. 1.

Jeremiah. Heb. *y'irmᵉyāhū* = whom Jehovah raises up, or launches forth.

Hilkiah. Not the high priest of that name, who was of the line of Eleazar (1 Chron. 6. 4, 13); whereas Anathoth belonged to that of Ithamar (1 Chron. 24. 3, 6). Cp. 2 Chron. 34.

of the priests. Beside Jeremiah, Nathan (1 Kings 4. 5), Ezekiel (1. 3), and probably Zechariah (1. 1) were of priestly origin.

Anathoth. Now *'Anāta*, three miles north-east of Jerusalem. Jeremiah was persecuted there before he prophesied in Jerusalem (11. 21; 12. 6). This prepared him for later conflicts (cp. 12. 5, 6).

2 the word of the LORD came. It is remarkable that, in the four longer prophets, *this formula* is almost entirely confined to the two who were priests (Jeremiah and Ezekiel). See Ap. 82. Cp. Gen. 15. 1. 1 Sam. 9. 27; 15. 10. 2 Sam. 7. 4; 24. 11. 1 Kings 12. 22. 1 Chron. 17. 3; 22. 8. 2 Chron. 11. 2; 12. 7. Ezek. 1. 3; 14. 12. Hos. 1. 1. Joel 1. 1, &c.

the LORD. Heb. Jehovah. Ap. 4. II.

Josiah. Three kings named here and in *v.* 3. Two others not named here (Jehoahaz and Jehoiachin), who reigned only three months each (2 Kings 23. 31; 24. 8).

thirteenth year. A year after Josiah began his reformation (2 Chron. 34. 3). (518 B.C. See Ap. 50. v, p. 60). Sixty-six years after Isaiah ended. For the chronology of Jeremiah, see Ap. 77 and Ap. 83. From 2 Chron. 34. 22, Jeremiah was probably still at Anathoth. **3 It came also in the days.** See note on Gen. 14. 1. **the fifth month.** The month that Jerusalem was destroyed (52. 12. 2 Kings 25. 3, 8). After that, Jeremiah continued in the Land (40. 1; 42. 7); and, later, in Egypt (chs. 43, 44).

1. 4–19 (**B**, p. 1015). JEREMIAH'S COMMISSION GIVEN.
(*Introversions and Alternations.*)

B | B | C | a | 4–7. Commission given.
  | | | b | 8–. "Be not afraid". } Command.
  | | D | c | –8. "I am with thee".
  | | | d | 9, 10. "I have this day", &c. } Encouragement.
  | E | e | 11. Vision (almond tree).
  | | f | 12. Explanation.
  | *E* | *e* | 13. Vision (seething pot).
  | | *f* | 14–16. Explanation. } Mission.
  | *B* | *C* | *a* | 17–. Commission given.
  | | | *b* | –17. "Be not dismayed". } Command.
  | | *D* | *d* | 18, 19–. "I have this day", &c.
  | | | *c* | –19. "I am with thee". } Encouragement.

1. 4–10. Jeremiah's FIRST prophecy (see p. 1015).

4 Then: i.e. in the thirteenth year of Josiah. **word.** Sing., because referring to this special prophecy. **5 I knew.** Put by Fig. *Metonymy* (of Cause), Ap. 6, for choosing. Ref. to Pent. (Ex. 33. 12, 17). Ap. 92. **sanctified thee** = set thee apart, or, hallowed thee. See note on Ex. 3. 5, and cp. John Baptist (Luke 1. 15–17); Paul (Gal. 1. 15, 16); Samson (Judg. 13. 3). **the nations.** This distinguishes Jeremiah from some of the other prophets, and shows that the legend of his martyrdom is only legend. **6 Lord GOD.** Heb. Adonai Jehovah. See Ap. 4. viii (2), and II. **behold.** Fig. *Asterismos.* Ap. 6. **I cannot speak, &c.** Ref. to Pent. (Ex. 4. 10). Ap. 92. This is true of all God's messengers. **a child.** Heb. *na'ar*, a youth. Probably about Josiah's age; for he began to reign at 8 years of age, and 8 + 13 would make him 21. But this refers more to inefficiency than to age. **7 whatsoever I command, &c.** Ref. to Pent. (Num. 22. 20). Ap. 92. **8 Be not afraid, &c.** Ref. to Pent. (Ex. 3. 12; Deut. 31. 6). Ap. 92. Cp. Ezekiel (Ezek. 2. 6); Paul (Acts 26. 17). **saith the LORD** = [is] Jehovah's oracle.

d (p. 1016) 518-500 9 Then [2]the LORD put forth His °hand, and
°touched my mouth. And [2]the LORD said unto
me, "Behold, °I have put My words in thy mouth.
10 See, I have this day °set thee over the
nations and over the kingdoms, °to root out,
°and to pull down, and to destroy, and to
°throw down, to °build, and to plant."

E e 11 °Moreover the [4]word of [2]the LORD came
unto me, saying, "Jeremiah, what seest thou?"
And I said, "I see °a rod of °an almond tree."

f 12 Then said [2]the LORD unto me, "Thou
hast well seen: for °I will hasten My [4]word
to perform it."

E e 13 And the [4]word of [2]the LORD came unto
me the °second time, saying, "What seest
thou?" And I said, "I see °a seething pot;
and the face thereof °*is* °toward the north."

f 14 Then [2]the LORD said unto me, "Out of
the north °an evil shall break forth upon all
the inhabitants of the land.
15 For, °lo, I will call °all the families of the
kingdoms of the north, [8]saith [2]the LORD; and
they shall come, and they shall °set every one
his throne at the entering of the gates of Jerusalem, and against all the walls thereof round
about, and against all the cities of Judah.
16 And I will utter My judgments against
°them touching all their °wickedness, who have
°forsaken Me, and have °burned incense unto
other gods, and worshipped the °works of
their own hands.

C a 17 Thou therefore °gird up thy loins, and
arise, and speak unto them all that I command thee:

b °be not °dismayed at their faces, lest I °con-
found thee before them.

D d 18 For, behold, I have °made thee this day
a defenced city, °and an iron pillar, °and
°brasen walls °against the whole land, °a-
gainst °the kings of Judah, °against °the
princes thereof, °against °the priests thereof,
and °against °the People of the land.
19 And they shall fight against thee; but
they shall not prevail against thee;

c for I *am* with thee, [8]saith [2]the LORD, to deliver thee."

F H K (p. 1018) **2** °Moreover the °word of °the LORD came
to me, saying,

9 hand . . . touched. Fig. *Anthropopatheia* (Ap. 6). Cp. Isaiah (Isa. 6. 6, 7); Ezekiel (Ezek. 2. 8, 9); Daniel (Dan. 10. 16).

I have put My words, &c. This is inspiration. See Deut. 18. 18. Cp. Acts 1. 16. David's "mouth", but not David's "words".

10 set thee = not only appointed, but installed.

to root out = to declare that nations should be rooted out, &c. Fig. *Metonymy* (of Subject), Ap. 6. Note also the Fig. *Polyonymia*, for emphasis.

and to pull down, and to destroy, and to throw down, &c. Note the Fig. *Polysyndeton* (Ap. 6), and see note above.

build, and to plant = to declare that others (Israel and Judah) should be restored. Cp. Ezek. 17. 22-24. A prophecy still future.

Jeremiah's SECOND prophecy.

11 Moreover = And. Another commission introducing two visions.

a rod = a staff for striking. Heb. *makkel*, as in 48. 17 and Gen. 30. 37-41.

a rod of an almond tree. Denotes an almond tree staff, corresponding with a vigilant watchman.

an almond tree. Heb. *shāķēd* = a watcher, or an early waker, because it is the first of the trees to wake from its winter sleep, and is thus what the cock is among birds.

12 I will hasten . . . it = I am watching. Forming the Fig. *Paronomasia* (Ap. 6), "an almond tree (*shāķēd*) . . . I am watching (*shoķēd*)", thus emphasising the certainty.

Jeremiah's THIRD prophecy.

13 second time. In order to complete the sense by explaining that it was the fulfilment of the word of judgment that was to be watched over.

a seething pot = a boiling cauldron. Heb. a pot blown upon: i.e. brought to boiling by blowing the fire.

is. A.V. edition (1611) read "was".

toward the north = from the north: i.e. turned towards the prophet, who saw it from the south. The enemy of which it spoke, though situated on the east, would come round the desert and advance from the north, through Dan, the usual route from Assyria. See *v.* 14.

14 an evil = the calamity. Heb. *rā'a'*. Ap. 44. viii. See note on Isa. 45. 7.

15 lo. Fig. *Asterismos*. Ap. 6.

all. Frequently put (as here) by Fig. *Synecdoche* (of the Whole), Ap. 6, for the principal or greater part.

set, &c. Where the kings of Judah had sat to judge and rule. Fulfilled in 39. 3, for here the setting is hostile.

16 them: i.e. the people of Judah.

wickedness. Heb. *rā'a'*. Ap. 44. viii.

forsaken Me. Ref. to Pent. (Deut. 28. 20). Ap. 92.

burned incense. Heb. *ķatar*. See Ap. 43. I. vii. This includes the burnt offering and parts of the gift offering.

works. Some codices, with one early printed edition, Syr., and Vulg., read "work" (sing.).

17 gird up, &c. See note on 1 Kings 18. 46.

be not dismayed. Note the Fig. *Paronomasia* (Ap. 6), in the alternate words and lines of *C* (p. 1016):—

C | g | 17-. Be not dismayed (*tēḥath*).
  h | -17-. At their faces (*mipp^e nēyhem*).
  g | -17-. Lest I confound thee (*'ăḥit^e kā*).
  h | -17. Before them (*liphnēyhem*).

This may be Englished: "Be not *abashed* . . . Lest I *abash* thee".

18 made thee = give thee [as]. **and.** Note the Fig. *Polysyndeton* (Ap. 6). **brasen walls.** Some codices, with two early printed editions (one in marg.), Targ., Aram., Sept., Syr., and Vulg., read "a wall of bronze" (sing.). **against.** Note the Fig. *Anaphora* (Ap. 6), by which "against" is repeated seven times, in order to emphasise the fact that as man's thoughts and ways are the opposite of Jehovah's (Isa. 55. 8), it is impossible for a prophet who is Jehovah's spokesman to be other than "against" man. See Ap. 49. **the kings of Judah.** See ch. 36. **the princes.** See chs. 37 and 38. **the priests.** See chs. 20 and 26. **the People.** See 34. 19; 37. 2; 44. 21; 52. 6.

2. 1—20. 18 [For Structure see next page].

2. 1—3. 5. Jeremiah's FOURTH prophecy (see p. 1015).

1 Moreover. Ch. 2 is the first chapter of the roll which was re-written after being burned (ch. 36), while ch. 11 is the first of the "many like words" (36. 32) added afterwards. **word.** See note on 1. 1, 4. **the LORD.** Heb. Jehovah. Ap. 4. II.

518-500 2 °"Go and cry in the ears of Jerusalem, saying, 'Thus °saith [1]the LORD; °I remember thee, the kindness of thy °youth, the love of thine espousals, °when thou wentest after Me in the wilderness, in a land *that was* not sown.

3 Israel *was* °holiness unto [1]the LORD, *and* °the firstfruits of His increase: all that °devour him shall °offend; °evil shall come upon them, [2]saith [1]the LORD.

L M O (p. 1018) 4 Hear ye the word of [1]the LORD, O °house of Jacob, and all the families of °the house of Israel:

5 Thus saith [1]the LORD, °What °iniquity have your °fathers found in Me, that they are gone far from Me, and have walked after °vanity, and are °become vain?

6 Neither said they, 'Where *is* [1]the LORD That °brought us up out of the land of Egypt, That °led us through the wilderness, through a land of deserts and of pits, through a land of drought, and of the °shadow of death, through a land that no °man passed through, and where no °man dwelt?'

7 And I brought you into °a plentiful country, to eat the fruit thereof and the goodness thereof; but when ye entered, ye defiled My land, and made Mine heritage an abomination.

8 The priests said not, 'Where *is* [1]the LORD?' and °they that handle the law knew Me not: the °pastors also °transgressed against Me, and the prophets prophesied by Baal, and walked after *things that* °do not profit.

P 9 Wherefore I will yet °plead with you, [2]saith [1]the LORD, and with your °children's children will I plead.

N 10 For pass over the °isles of °Chittim, and see; and send unto °Kedar, and consider diligently, and see if there be such a thing.

11 Hath a nation changed *their* gods, which *are* yet no gods? but My people have changed °their glory for *that which* doth not profit.

12 °Be astonished, O ye heavens, at this, and be horribly afraid, be ye °very desolate, [2]saith [1]the LORD.

13 For My people have committed two °evils; they have forsaken Me the °fountain of living waters, *and* hewed them out °cisterns, broken cisterns, that °can hold no water.

14 *Is* Israel a °servant? *is* he a homeborn °*slave?* why is he °spoiled?

15 The young lions roared upon him, *and* yelled, and made his land waste: his cities are burned without inhabitant.

2 Go and cry. Jeremiah continued to retain his connection with Anathoth (11. 21; 29. 27; 32. 7; 37. 12), though his mission was to Jerusalem.

2. 1–20. 18 (**C**, p. 1015). PROPHECIES ADDRESSED TO JEWS. JOSIAH. (*Alternation.*)

C | F | 2. 1—12. 17. Proclamations.
  G | 13. 1—17. 18. Symbols.
 F | 17. 19–27. Proclamations.
  G | 18. 1—20. 18. Symbols.

2. 1–12. 17 (F, above). PROCLAMATIONS. (*Introversions.*)

F | H | 2. 1—3. 11. To Jerusalem. Espousals.
  J | 3. 12—6. 30. Place. Toward the north.
  J | 7. 1—10. 25. Place. In the Gate of the Temple.
 H | 11. 1—12. 17. To Judah and Jerusalem. Covenant.

2. 1–3. 11 (H, above). TO JERUSALEM. ESPOUSALS. (*Introversions.*)

H | K | 2. 1-3. Espousals.
  L | M | O | 2. 4–8. Call to hear. Remonstrance. Past.
    P | 2. 9. Pleading. Future.
   N | 2. 10–28. Crimination. Idolatry.
  L | *M* | *P* | 2. 29, 30. Pleading. Future.
    O | 2. 31, 32. Call to see. Remonstrance. Past.
   N | 2. 33–37. Crimination. Idolatry.
 K | 3. 1-11. Adultery.

2 saith the LORD. See note on 1. 8.
I remember thee. The expression is used *in good part* Pss. 98. 3; 106. 45; 132. 1. Neh. 5. 19; 13. 14, 22, 31; but *in evil part* Pss. 79. 8; 137. 7. Neh. 6. 14; 13. 29. Probably both senses here: the good on Jehovah's part (*v.* 3. Hos. 11. 1; 2. 19, 20. Amos 2. 10); and the evil on Israel's part, for even in the wilderness Israel was unfaithful (Amos 5. 25, 26. Acts 7. 39–43).
youth. Cp. Ezek. 16. 8.
when. Cp. *v.* 6. Ref. to Pent. (Deut. 2. 7; 8. 2, 15, 16). Cp. Neh. 9. 12–21. Isa. 63. 7–14.
3 holiness unto the LORD. Ref. to Pent. (Ex. 19. 6).
the firstfruits, &c., which were consecrated. Ref. to Pent. (Ex. 23. 19. Deut. 18. 4; 26. 10). Ap. 92.
devour = devoured.
offend = be held guilty. Ref. to Pent. (Lev. 4. 13, 22, 27; 5. 2, 3, 4, 5, 17, 19; 6. 4. Num. 5. 6, 7). Ap. 92.
evil = calamity. Heb. *rā'a'.* Ap. 44. viii. See note on Isa. 45. 7.
4 house of Jacob. Occurs only here, and 5. 20, where it is "in the house of Jacob". The only other passage is Amos 3. 13.
the house of Israel. The *Massōrah* (Ap. 30), records that this expression occurs twenty times in Jeremiah (here; *v.* 26; 3. 18, 20; 5. 11, 15; 9. 26; 10. 1; 11. 10, 17; 13. 11; 18. 6, 6; 23. 8; 31. 27, 31, 33; 33. 14, 17; 48. 13).
5 What iniquity. Ref. to Pent. (Deut. 32. 4). Ap. 92.
iniquity. Heb. *'āvāl.* Ap. 44. iv.
fathers. Not merely recently, but of old (*v.* 7. Judg. 2. 10, &c.).
vanity = the vanity. Put by Fig. *Metonymy* (of Adjunct), Ap. 6, for vain things: i.e. idols. Cp. 10. 3–10, 15; 14. 22; 16. 19, 20. Deut. 32. 21. Acts 14. 15. 1 Cor. 8. 4. **become vain?** Cp. 2 Kings 17. 15. Idolaters always become like the gods they worship. Cp. Pss. 115. 8; 135. 18. **6 brought us up.** Ref. to Pent. (Num. 13. 27; 14. 7, 8. Deut. 6. 10, 11, 18). Ap. 92. **led us.** Ref. to Pent. (Deut. 8. 14–16; 32. 10). Ap. 92. **shadow of death** = deep darkness. **man.** Heb. *'īsh.* Ap. 14. II. **man.** Heb. *'ādām.* Ap. 14. I. **7 a plentiful country** = a country of garden land. Heb. the land of a Carmel. Cp. Isa. 33. 9; 35. 2. **8 they that handle the law.** The law therefore well known, and the priests known as the custodians of it. Ref. to Pent. (Lev. 10. 11. Deut. 17. 11; 33. 10). Ap. 92. **pastors** = shepherds. Used of kings and other leaders of the People. Cp. 17. 16; 23. 1–8. **transgressed** = revolted. Heb. *pāsha'.* Ap. 44. ix. **do not profit.** Fig. *Tapeinosis* (Ap. 6), for emphasis = lead to ruin. **9 plead** = argue, contend. **children's children** = sons' sons. **10 isles** = coastlands, or maritime countries. **Chittim.** See note on Num. 24. 24. **Kedar.** In Arabia. Two names used to represent west and east outlanders. **11 their glory** = His glory. This is one of the emendations of the *Sōpherīm* (Ap. 33), by which the Heb. *k^ebōdī* ("My glory") was changed to *k^ebōdō* ("His glory"), out of a mistaken idea of reverence. **12 Be astonished.** Fig. *Apostrophē.* Ap. 6. **very desolate** = dried up, or, devoid of clouds and vapours. **13 evils.** Heb. *rā'a'.* Ap. 44. viii. **fountain** = a well dug out, but having living water. **cisterns** = a hewn cistern, holding only what it receives. **can hold no water** = cannot hold the waters. **14 servant? . . . slave?** They were treated as such by Assyria, and afterward by Egypt. **spoiled** = become a spoil.

518-500 16 Also the [9]children of °Noph and °Tahapanes have broken the crown of thy head.

17 Hast thou not procured this unto thyself, in that thou hast forsaken [1]the LORD thy °God, when °He led thee by the way?

18 And now what hast thou to do in °the way of Egypt, to drink the waters of °Sihor? or what hast thou to do in the way of Assyria, to drink the waters of °the river?

19 Thine own °wickedness shall correct thee, and thy backslidings shall reprove thee: know therefore and see that *it is* an [13]evil *thing* and bitter, that thou hast forsaken [1]the LORD thy [17]God, and that My fear °*is* not in thee, [2]saith °the Lord GOD of hosts.

20 For of old time I have broken thy yoke, *and* burst thy bands; and thou saidst, °'I will not °transgress;' when upon every °high hill and under every °green tree thou wanderest, playing the harlot.

21 Yet I had planted thee a °noble vine, wholly a right seed: how then art thou turned into the degenerate plant of a °strange vine unto Me?

22 For though thou wash thee with °nitre, and take thee much °sope, *yet* thine °iniquity is °marked before Me, [2]saith [19]the Lord GOD.

23 How canst thou say, 'I am not polluted, °I have not gone after °Baalim?' see thy way in the valley, know what thou hast done: *thou art* a swift dromedary °traversing her ways;

24 A wild ass used to the wilderness, *that* snuffeth up the °wind at °her pleasure; in her occasion who can turn her away? all they that seek her will not weary themselves; in her month they shall find her.

25 Withhold thy foot from being unshod, and thy throat from thirst: but thou saidst, 'There is no hope: no; for I have loved strangers, and after them will I go.'

26 As the thief is ashamed when he is found, so is the house of Israel ashamed; they, °their kings, °their princes, and their priests, and their prophets,

27 Saying to a stock, 'Thou *art* my father;' and to a °stone, 'Thou hast brought me forth:' for they have turned *their* back unto Me, and not *their* face: but in the time of their trouble they will say, 'Arise, and save us.'

28 But °where *are* thy gods that thou hast made thee? let them arise, if they can save thee in the time of thy trouble: °for *according to* the number of thy cities are thy gods, O °Judah.

L M P (p. 1018) 29 Wherefore will ye plead with Me? ye all have [8]transgressed against Me, [2]saith [1]the LORD.

30 In vain have I smitten your [9]children; they received no correction: your own sword hath °devoured your prophets, like a destroying lion.

O 31 O °generation, see ye the word of [1]the LORD. Have I been a wilderness unto Israel? °a land of darkness? wherefore say My People, 'We are lords; we will come no more unto Thee?'

32 Can a maid forget her ornaments, *or* a bride her attire? yet My people have forgotten Me days without number.

33 Why trimmest thou thy way to seek °love? therefore hast thou also taught the [19]wicked °ones thy ways. N

34 Also in thy skirts is found the °blood of the °souls of the °poor innocents: I have not found °it by secret search, but upon all °these.

35 Yet thou sayest, 'Because I am innocent,

16 Noph=Memphis, the capital of Lower Egypt, south of Cairo. Cp. 44. 1. Isa. 19. 13. Ezek. 30. 13, 16; 46. 14, 19.

Tahapanes. The Greek Daphnae, on the Pelusiac branch of the Nile. Cp. 43. 7, 11. See Ap. 87.

17 God. Heb. Elohim. Ap. 4. I.

He led thee. Ref. to Pent. (Deut. 32. 12). Ap. 92.

18 the way of Egypt. Ref. to Pent. (Deut. 17. 16).

Sihor: i.e. the Nile.

the river: i.e. the Euphrates.

19 wickedness. Heb. *rā'a'*. Ap. 44. viii.

is not in thee=should not have pertained to thee.

the Lord GOD of hosts=Adonai (Ap. 4. VIII. 2), Jehovah (Ap. 4. II) of Sebaioth. This title occurs in this book six times (here; 46. 10, 10; 49. 5; 50. 25, 31). Ap. 79. II.

20 I will not transgress. Ref. to Pent. (Ex. 19. 8).

transgress. Heb. *'ābar.* A Homonym. Here=serve; elsewhere=transgress. Ap. 44. vii. Not the same word as in *vv.* 8, 29.

high hill . . . green tree. The places where the Ashērah was worshipped. Ap. 42.

21 noble vine=choice, or precious vine. Heb. *sorēk*, as in Isa. 5. 2. Ref. to Pent. (Gen. 49. 11). Ap. 92.

strange=foreign.

22 nitre: i.e. a mineral alkali. In Palestine a compound of soap.

sope=soap. The A.V., 1611, spelt "sope". Old Eng. spelling. Anglo-Saxon *sāpe*, from Lat. *sapo*, whence Fr. *savon.* Occurs only here, and in Mal. 3. 2.

iniquity. Heb. *'āvōn.* Ap. 44. iv.

marked=graven.

23 I have not gone. Some codices, with four early printed editions (one in marg.), Aram., Sept., and Syr., read, "and I have not gone", &c.

Baalim=lords. Used here for false gods generally, including Moloch. Cp. 7. 31; 19. 5; where Moloch is called Baal.

traversing=entangling.

24 wind. Heb. *rūach.* Ap. 9.

her pleasure=her soul. Heb. *nephesh.* Ap. 13.

26 their kings. Showing that Judah was still in the Land, but in Jehoiakim's reign.

their princes. Some codices, with Sept. and Syr., read "and their princes", perfecting the Fig. *Polysyndeton* (Ap. 6), emphasising all classes.

27 stone. Here fem., to agree with mother.

28 where . . . ? Fig. *Erotēsis.* Ap. 6. Ref. to Pent. (Deut. 32. 37, 38). Ap. 92.

for, &c. Fig. *Epitropē.* Ap. 6.

Judah. Cp. 11. 13.

30 devoured your prophets. See 1 Kings 18. 4, 13. 2 Kings 21. 16. 2 Chron. 24. 21. Cp. Matt. 23. 37. Luke 11. 47. Acts 7. 51, 52. 1 Thess. 2. 15.

31 generation. Once a chosen generation (Pss. 22. 30; 24. 6; 112. 2. Isa. 53. 8); now a perverse generation (7. 29. Deut. 32. 5. Ps. 78. 8). Cp. Matt. 3. 7; 11. 16; 12. 34, 39, 41-45; 16. 4; 17. 17.

a land of darkness: or, Is the land the darkness of Jah?

33 love. Put by Fig. *Metonymy* (of Adjunct), Ap. 6, for the object loved. Cp. *v.* 23.

ones. Here "wicked" is Fem.=wicked women.

34 blood. Put by Fig. *Metonymy* (of the Subject), Ap. 6, for the guilt of bloodshedding.

souls. Heb. *nephesh.* Ap. 13.

poor=helpless. Heb. *'ebyōn.* See note on Prov. 6. 11.

it: i.e. the guilt (of bloodshedding) on the "poor innocents".

these: i.e. these [thy skirts] which evidence it. Note the Fig. *Ellipsis* (Ap. 6), in this verse. Cp. 22. 17.

518-500 surely His anger shall turn from me.' Behold,
I will °plead with thee, because thou sayest,
'I have not °sinned.'
36 Why gaddest thou about so much to change
thy way? thou also shalt be ashamed of Egypt,
°as thou wast ashamed of Assyria.
37 Yea, thou shalt go forth from him, and
°thine hands upon thine head: for [1]the LORD
hath rejected thy confidences, and thou shalt
not prosper in them.

K (p. 1018)
3 °They say, 'If a °man put away his wife,
and she go from him, and become another
man's, shall he return unto her again? shall
not that land be greatly polluted?' 'but thou
hast played the harlot with many lovers; °yet
return again °to Me,' °saith °the LORD.
2 Lift up thine eyes unto the high places,
and see where thou hast not been lien with.
In the ways hast thou sat for them, as the
Arabian in the wilderness; and thou hast
polluted the land with thy whoredoms and
with thy °wickedness.
3 Therefore the °showers have been °with-
holden, and there hath been no latter rain;
and thou hadst a whore's °forehead, thou
refusedst to be ashamed.
4 Wilt thou not from this time cry unto
Me, 'My Father, Thou *art* the °Guide of my
youth?'
5 Will He °reserve °*His anger* for ever? will
He keep *it* to the end? Behold, thou hast
spoken and done °evil things °as thou
couldest.'"
6 [1]The LORD said also unto me °in the days
of Josiah the king, "Hast thou seen *that* which
backsliding °Israel hath done? She is gone
up upon every high °mountain and under
every green °tree, and there hath °played the
harlot.
7 And I said after she had done all these
things, °'Turn thou unto Me.' But she returned not. And her treacherous sister Judah
saw *it.*
8 °And I saw, when for all the causes whereby backsliding [6]Israel committed adultery
I had put her away, and °given her a bill of
divorce; yet her treacherous sister Judah
feared not, but went and [6]played the harlot also.
9 And it came to pass through the lightness
of her whoredom, that she defiled the land, and
committed adultery with °stones and with
°stocks.
10 And yet for all this her treacherous sister
Judah hath not turned unto Me with her whole
heart, but °feignedly, [1]saith [1]the LORD."
11 And [1]the LORD said unto me, "The backsliding Israel hath °justified °herself more
than treacherous Judah.
Q[1] R[1] (p. 1020) 12 Go and proclaim these words °toward the
north, and say, 'Return, thou backsliding Is-
rael, [1]saith [1]the LORD; *and* I will not °cause
Mine anger to fall upon you:
S[1] for I *am* °merciful, [1]saith [1]the LORD, *and* I
will not °keep [5]*anger* for ever.
T[1] 13 °Only acknowledge thine °iniquity, that
thou hast °transgressed against [1]the LORD thy

35 plead=enter into judgment with.
sinned. Heb. *chāṭā'.* Ap. 44. i.
36 as=according as.
37 thine hands upon thine head. The Eastern custom of expressing grief. Cp. 2 Sam. 13. 19.

3. 1 They say=[It is a common] saying. Ref. to Pent. (Deut. 24. 1-4). Ap. 92.
man. Heb. *'ish.* Ap. 14. II.
yet return again to Me=yet [thinkest thou to] return, &c. It was contrary to the law of Deut 24. 1-4. It will be the *new Israel* of Matt. 21. 43 of a yet future day. God never mends what man has marred. This is the lesson of the potter's house. See 18. 1-4.
to Me. See *v.* 7; 4. 1.
saith the LORD=[is] Jehovah's oracle.
the LORD. Heb. Jehovah. Ap. 4. II.
2 wickedness. Heb. *rā'a'.* Ap. 44. viii.
3 showers . . . withholden. Ref. to Pent. (Lev. 26. 19. Deut. 11. 17; 28. 23). Ap. 92.
forehead. Put by Fig. *Metonymy* (of Adjunct), Ap. 6, for impudence. **4 Guide**=Friend.
5 reserve. Heb. *naṭar.* Occurs in Jer. only here and in *v.* 12 ("keep").
His anger. Fig. *Ellipsis* (Absolute). Ap. 6.
evil things=the evil things. Heb. *rā'a',* as in *v.* 2.
as thou couldest: or, hast had thy way.

3. 6—4. 4. Jeremiah's FIFTH prophecy. See p. 1015.
6 in the days of Josiah. This must be noted to understand the context.
Israel. Here refers to the Northern Kingdom. In Jeremiah it usually refers to the whole nation.
mountain . . . tree. Cp. 2. 20, and Hos. 4. 13.
played the harlot. The whole of this refers to idolatry, chiefly because of the uncleanness connected with the phallic worship of the Canaanitish nations.
7 Turn thou unto Me: or, "Unto Me she will return".
8 And I saw. In transcribing from the ancient characters, *Aleph* (א=a) was perhaps taken for *Tau* (ת=t), the two letters differing only in one minute stroke (=א) and (=ת). This shows that the primitive reading was="Though she saw". The Vulg. has preserved the ancient reading, which the R.V. has put in the margin.
given her a bill, &c. Ref. to Pent. (Deut. 24. 1). Ap. 92. Cp. Isa. 50. 1. Mark 10. 4.
9 stones . . . stocks. Put by Fig. *Metonymy* (of Cause), Ap. 6, for the idols made from them.
10 feignedly=in falsehood. The reformation was Josiah's. The People's heart was not changed.
11 justified herself. Cp. Ezek. 16. 51, 52.
herself=her soul. Heb. *nephesh.* Ap. 13.

3. 12—6. 30 (J, p. 1018). **PLACE. TOWARD THE NORTH.** (*Division.*)

J | Q[1] | 3. 12—4. 2. Israel.
  | Q[2] | 4. 3—6. 30. Judah.

3. 12—4. 2 (Q[1], above). **ISRAEL.**
(*Repeated and Extended Alternation.*)

Q[1] | R[1] | 3. 12-. Call to return. } Command.
  S[1] | 3. -12. Reason.
  T[1] | 3. 13. Conditions.
 R[2] | 3. 14-. Call to return.
  S[2] | 3. -14-18. Reason.
  T[2] | 3. 19-21. Conditions.
 R[3] | 3. 22-. Call to return. } Obedience.
  S[3] | 3. -22-25. Return. Reason.
  T[3] | 4. 1, 2. Conditions.

12 toward the north=toward the Northern Kingdom of Israel.
cause Mine anger to fall upon you. Heb. cause My face, or countenance, to fall. Put by Fig. *Metonymy* (of Effect), Ap. 6, for the anger manifested by it. Ref. to Pent. (Gen. 4. 5, 6). **merciful**=gracious, favourable.
keep. See note on "reserve", *v.* 5.
13 Only acknowledge, &c. This, from the first, was, and still is, the one condition of national blessing for Israel. Ref. to Pent. (Lev. 26. 40, 42). Ap. 92.
iniquity. Heb. *'āvōn.* Ap. 44. iv. **transgressed**=rebelled. Heb. *pāsha'.* Ap 44. ix.

518-500 °God, and hast °scattered thy ways to the
°strangers under °every green tree, and ye have
not obeyed My voice, [1]saith [1]the LORD.
R[2] (p. 1020) 14 °Turn, O backsliding children, [1]saith [1]the
LORD;
S[2] i (p. 1021) for I am °married unto you: and I will take
you one of a city, and two of a °family, and I will
bring you to Zion:
15 And I will give you °pastors according to
Mine heart, which shall feed you with knowledge and understanding.
k 16 And it shall come to pass, when ye be
multiplied and increased in the land, °in those
days, [1]saith [1]the LORD, °they °shall say no
more, °'The ark of the covenant of [1]the LORD:'
neither shall it come to mind: neither shall
they remember it; neither shall they °visit *it;*
°neither shall *that* be done any more.
k 17 °At that time they shall °call Jerusalem the
°throne of [1]the LORD; and °all the nations
shall be gathered unto it, to °the name of [1]the
LORD, to Jerusalem: neither shall they walk
any more after the °imagination of their °evil
heart.
i 18 °In those days °the house of Judah shall
°walk with °the house of Israel, °and they shall
°come °together out of the land of the north
to the land that I have given for an inheritance
unto your fathers.
T[2] (p. 1020) 19 But I said, 'How shall I put thee among
the °children, and give thee °a pleasant land,
a goodly heritage of the hosts of nations?' and
I said, 'Thou shalt call Me, My Father; and
shalt not turn away from Me.'
20 Surely *as* a wife treacherously departeth
from her °husband, so have ye dealt treacherously with Me, O [18]house of Israel, [1]saith [1]the
LORD.
21 A voice was heard upon °the high places,
weeping *and* supplications of the [19]children of
Israel: °for they have perverted their way, *and*
they have forgotten [1]the LORD their [13]God.
R[3] 22 Return, ye backsliding [19]children, *and*
I will heal your backslidings."
S[3] °Behold, we come unto Thee: for Thou *art*
[1]the LORD our [13]God.
23 °Truly °in vain *is salvation hoped for*
from the hills, *and from* the multitude of
mountains: °truly in [1]the LORD our [13]God *is*
the salvation of Israel.
24 For °shame hath devoured the °labour of
our fathers from our youth; their flocks and
their herds, °their sons and their daughters.
25 We lie down in our shame, and our confusion covereth us: for we have °sinned against
[1]the LORD our [13]God, we and our fathers, from
our youth even unto this day, and have not
obeyed the voice of [1]the LORD our [13]God.

God. Heb. Elohim. Ap. 4. I.
scattered thy ways=gone hither and thither.
strangers=foreigners.
every green tree. Referring to the worship of the Asherah (Ap. 42).
14- Turn=Return, as in *vv.* 12, 22.

3. -14-18 (S[2], p. 1020). THE REASON. (*Introversion.*)

S[2] i | -14, 15. Restoration.
k | 16. The Symbol. No longer the Ark.
k | 17. The Reality. The Throne.
i | 18. Restoration.

-14 married=am become your husband. This will be the result of the Restoration here promised.
family. Probably a family, or group of cities.
15 pastors. Lit. shepherds; but used in Jeremiah of kings, priests, and prophets, who were the guides of the people. See 2. 8; 3. 15; 10. 21; 23 1, 2, 4; 25. 34; 35. 36.
16 in those days: i.e. the days of the Restoration spoken of in *vv.* -14, 15. Cp. 31. 38-40; 33. 13.
they: i.e. those who return.
shall say no more, 'The ark', &c. The ark was still in the land in the days of this prophecy (2 Chron. 35. 3); but it was to disappear with the broken covenant, of which it was the symbol.
The ark of the covenant of the LORD. Ref. to Pent. (see notes on Ex. 25. 22). Ap. 92. Cp. note on 1 Chron. 13. 3).
visit it. This is conclusive of the fact that it was burnt together with the Temple (as it is not included in the excepted things, in 2 Kings 25. 9, 13-15), notwithstanding the Jewish tradition recorded in 2 Macc. 2. 4-8, and the impossible stories of its being taken over to North Africa, Constantinople, or Ireland.
neither shall that be done, &c.=neither shall it be made any more. It disappeared together with the covenant, of which it was the symbol (8. 19; 12. 7. Ps. 132. 13, 14). The reason follows in *v.* 17. Jehovah's throne will be substituted for it: the reality will take the place of the symbol. Jehovah Himself will take the place of the Shekinah.
17 At that time. Referring to the future Restoration ("*k*" answering to "k" of *v.* 16).
call Jerusalem, &c. Cp. Ps. 87. 2-7. Isa. 60. 1; 65. 18; 66. 7-13, 20.
throne. Cp. 14. 21. 1 Sam. 2. 8. Ps. 47. 8 with Matt 25. 31 and Zeph. 3. 8.
all the nations. This shows that the prophecy refers to the yet future Restoration. Cp. 1. 5, 10.
the name, &c. See note on Ps. 20. 1.
imagination=stubbornness. The word is used eight times by Jeremiah, but is found nowhere else outside the Pentateuch, except in Ps. 81. 12. Cp. 7. 24. The ref. to Pent. is in Deut. 29. 19. See Ap. 92.
evil. Heb. *rā'a'.* Ap. 44. viii.
18 In those days. Still referring to the future Restoration.
the house of Judah. This expression occurs eleven times in this book: here; 5. 11; 11. 10, 17; 12. 14; 13. 11; 22. 6; 31. 27, 31; 33. 14; 36. 3.
walk with=go unto.
the house of Israel. See note on 2. 4.
and they shall=that they may.
come=enter.
together: or, at the same time.
19 children=sons.
a pleasant land. Heb. a land of desire: i.e. to be desired.
20 husband=guide, or friend, as in *v.* 4.
21 the high places=the places where they had sinned. Cp. *v.* 2.
for=because.
22 Behold. Fig. *Asterismos* (Ap. 6), to mark the confession that will be made "in those days".
23 Truly=Thus continuing her confession.
in vain, &c.=as certainly as the hills [have proved] false, and the noisy throng on the mountains [an empty sound], so truly is the salvation of Israel with our God. The "hills" and "mountains" are put by the Fig. *Metonymy* (of Subject), Ap. 6, for the idolatry practised on them. Cp. Ezek. 18. 6, 11, 15.
24 shame=the shameful thing, "shame" being put by Fig. *Metonymy* (of Effect), Ap. 6, for the *Asherah* which put them to shame (*v.* 25). See Ap. 42.
labour. Put by Fig. *Metonymy* (of Cause), Ap. 6, for all that had been produced by labour.
their sons. Some codices, with two early printed editions, Aram., Sept., and Syr., read "and their", thus completing the Fig. *Polysyndeton* (Ap. 6), to emphasise the completeness of the Restoration.
25 sinned. Heb. *chāṭa'.* Ap. 44. i.

T³ (p. 1020) 518–500 4 "If thou wilt °return, O °Israel, °saith
°the LORD, °return unto Me: and if thou
wilt put away thine abominations out of My
sight, °then shalt thou not remove.
2 And °thou shalt swear, ¹The LORD liveth,
°in truth, in judgment, and in righteousness;
and the nations shall bless themselves in Him,
and in Him shall they glory.

Q² U¹ W (p. 1022) 3 For thus saith ¹the LORD to the °men of
Judah °and Jerusalem, Break up your fallow
ground, and sow not among thorns.
4 °Circumcise yourselves to ¹the LORD, and
take away the foreskins of your heart, ye men
of Judah and inhabitants of Jerusalem: lest
My fury come forth like fire, and burn that
none can quench *it*, because of the °evil of
your doings.

X 5 °Declare ye in °Judah, and °publish in Jerusalem; and °say, °'Blow ye the trumpet in the
land:' cry, gather together, and say, 'Assemble yourselves, and let us go into the defenced
cities.'
6 °Set up the °standard toward Zion: °retire,
°stay not: for **I** will bring °evil from the
north, and a great °destruction.
7 °The lion is come up from his thicket, and
the destroyer of the °Gentiles is on his way;
he is gone forth from his place to make thy
land desolate; *and* thy cities shall be laid
waste, without an inhabitant."

W l 8 For this gird you with sackcloth, lament
and howl:

m for the fierce anger of ¹the LORD is not turned
back from us.
9 "And it shall come to pass at that day,
¹saith ¹the LORD, *that* the °heart of the °king
shall perish, °and the °heart of the °princes;
°and the °priests shall be astonished, °and the
°prophets shall wonder."
10 Then said I, "Ah, °Lord GOD! surely
Thou hast °greatly deceived this People and
Jerusalem, saying, 'Ye shall have peace;'
whereas the sword reacheth unto the °soul."
11 At that time shall it be said to this People
and to Jerusalem, "A dry °wind of the high
places in the wilderness toward the daughter
of My People, not to fan, nor to cleanse,
12 *Even* a full ¹¹wind from those *places* shall
come unto Me: now also will **I** give sentence
against °them."
13 Behold, he shall come up as clouds, and
his chariots *shall be* as a whirlwind: his
horses are swifter than eagles. Woe unto us!
for we are spoiled.

l 14 "O Jerusalem, wash thine heart from
°wickedness, that thou mayest be saved.
How long shall thy vain thoughts lodge within thee?

m 15 For a voice declareth °from Dan, and publisheth affliction from °mount °Ephraim.
16 Make ye mention to the nations; behold,
publish against Jerusalem, *that* watchers come
from a far country, and give out their voice
against the cities of Judah.
17 As keepers of a field, are they against her
round about; because she hath been rebellious
against **Me**, ¹saith ¹the LORD.
18 Thy way and thy doings have procured

4. 1 return. Note the Fig. *Cycloides*. Ap. 6.
Israel. Now referring to the northern kingdom.
saith the LORD=[is] Jehovah's oracle.
the LORD. Heb. Jehovah. Ap. 4. II.
then shalt thou not remove=and stray not [from Jehovah]. Cp. 2. 22–26; 3. 2.
2 thou shalt swear. Ref. to Pent. (Deut. 10. 20).
in truth, in judgment, and in righteousness. Fig. *Hendiatris* (Ap. 6)=truly, yea, justly and righteously, the three referring to the one thing, "shalt swear".

4. 3–6. 30 (Q², p. 1020). **JUDAH.**
(*Repeated Alternation.*)

Q² | U¹ | 4. 3–31. Warning. Threatenings. Alarm.
   V¹ | 5. 1–31. Investigation.
 U² | 6. 1–9. Warnings. Threatenings. Alarm.
   V² | 6. 10–21. Investigation.
 U³ | 6. 22–26. Warnings. Threatenings. Alarm.
   V³ | 6. 27–30. Reprobation.

4. 3–31 (U¹, above). **WARNINGS. THREATENINGS. ALARM.** (*Alternation.*)

U¹ | W | 3, 4. Call to repentance.
   X | 5–7. Alarm.
 W | 8–18. Call to repentance.
   X | 19–31. Alarm.

3 men. Heb. *'ish*. Ap. 14. II.
and Jerusalem. Some codices, with Aram., Sept., and Syr., read "and the inhabitants of Jerusalem", as in *v.* 4.
4 Circumcise. Ref. to Pent. (Deut. 10. 16; 30. 6). Ap. 92. Spiritual circumcision in the O.T. is confined to these three passages.
evil. Heb. *rā'a'*. Ap. 44. viii.
5 Declare . . . publish . . . say. Cp. 46. 14; 50. 2.
Judah. Put by Fig. *Synecdoche* (of Part), Ap. 6, for Judah and Benjamin.
Blow ye. Heb. text reads, "And blow ye": but Heb. marg., and some codices, with three early printed editions, Aram., Sept., and Syr., read without the "And". This is followed by A.V. and R.V.
6 Set . . . retire . . . stay. All plural.
standard. A.V. of 1611 had "standards" (pl.).
evil=calamity. Heb. *rā'a'*. Ap. 44. viii.
destruction: or, breaking up.
7 The lion=A lion. Fig. *Hypocatastasis* (Ap. 6), not *Simile* or *Metaphor*. Put thus for the king of Babylon. Contrast 49. 19. See note there.
Gentiles=nations.

4. 8–18 (*W*, above). **CALL TO REPENTANCE.**
(*Alternation.*)

W | l | 8–. Call.
   m | -8–13. Reason.
 l | 14. Call.
   m | 15–18. Reason.

9 heart. Put by Fig. *Metonymy* (of Subject), Ap. 6, for courage.
king . . . princes . . . priests . . . prophets. All had become false and corrupt since Josiah's day.
and. Note the Fig. *Polysyndeton* (Ap. 6), emphasising each of the four.
10 Lord GOD! Heb. Adonai Jehovah. Ap. 4. VIII (2), and II.
greatly deceived. Heb. idiom for declaring that they would be deceived: i.e. by the false prophets who prophesied peace.
soul. Heb. *nephesh*. Ap. 13.
11 wind. Heb. *rūach*. Ap. 9.
12 them. A special various reading called "*Sevir*" (Ap. 34) reads "her".
14 wickedness. Heb. *rāsha'*. Ap. 44. x.
15 from Dan . . Ephraim. The enemy would enter the Land from the north, as he afterward did.
mount=hill country of.

518-500 these *things* unto thee; this *is* thy [14] wickedness, because it is bitter, because it reacheth
unto thine heart."

X (p. 1022) 19 °My bowels, °my °bowels! I am pained
at °my °very heart; my °heart maketh a noise
in me; I cannot hold my peace, because °thou
hast heard, O my [10] soul, the sound of the
trumpet, the alarm of war.
20 Destruction upon destruction is cried; for
the whole land is spoiled: suddenly are my
tents spoiled, *and* my °curtains in a moment.
21 How long shall I see the standard, *and*
hear the sound of the trumpet?
22 For My people *is* foolish, they have not
°known Me; they *are* °sottish °children, and
they have none understanding: they *are* wise
to do °evil, but to do good they have no knowledge.
23 °I beheld the earth, and, °lo, *it was* °with-
out form, and void; and the heavens, and
they *had* no °light.
24 [23] I beheld the mountains, and, lo, they
trembled, and all the hills moved lightly.
25 [23] I beheld, and, lo, *there was* no °man,
and all the birds of the heavens were fled.
26 [23] I beheld, and, lo, the fruitful place *was*
a wilderness, and all the cities thereof were
broken down °at the presence of [1] the LORD,
°*and* by His fierce anger.
27 For thus hath [1] the LORD said, "The
whole land shall be desolate; °yet will I not
make a full end.
28 For this shall the earth mourn, and the
heavens above be black: because I have
spoken *it*, °I have purposed *it*, and will not
repent, neither will I turn back from it.
29 The whole °city shall flee for the noise of
the horsemen and bowmen; they shall go into
thickets, and climb up upon the rocks: °every
city *shall be* forsaken, and not a °man dwell
therein.
30 And *when* °thou *art* spoiled, what wilt
thou do? Though thou clothest thyself with
crimson, though thou deckest thee with ornaments of gold, though thou °rentest thy °face
with painting, in vain shalt thou make thyself
fair; *thy* lovers will despise thee, they will
seek thy °life.
31 For I have heard a voice as of a woman
in travail, *and* the anguish as of her that
bringeth forth her first child, the voice of the
daughter of Zion, *that* bewaileth herself, *that*
spreadeth her hands, *saying*, 'Woe *is* me now!
for my [10] soul is wearied because of murderers.'

V¹ Y¹ (p. 1023) **5** Run ye to and fro through the °streets of
Jerusalem, and see now, and know, and
seek in the °broad places thereof, °if ye can
find a °man, if there be *any* that executeth
judgment, that seeketh the truth; and °I will
pardon it.
2 And though they say, °'The LORD liveth';
surely they swear falsely."
3 O [2] LORD, *are* not Thine eyes upon °the
truth? Thou hast stricken them, but they
°have not grieved; Thou hast consumed
them, *but* they have refused to receive correction: they have made their faces harder than
a rock; they have refused to return.
4 Therefore I said, "Surely these *are* °poor;
they are foolish: for they know not the way
of [2] the LORD, *nor* the °judgment of their °God.
5 I will get me unto the great men, and will
speak unto them; for they have known the way
of [2] the LORD, *and* the judgment of their [4] God:
but these have °altogether broken the yoke,
and burst the bonds.
6 Wherefore a lion out of the forest shall slay Z¹
them, *and* a wolf of the °evenings shall spoil
them, a leopard shall watch over their cities:

19 My bowels. Fig. *Epizeuxis* (Ap. 6), for emphasis. Note the Fig. *Hypotyposis*, *vv.* 19–31 ("*X*"). Put by Fig. *Metonymy* (of Effect), Ap. 6, for the emotions which produce and affect their movement.
bowels . . . very heart . . . heart. Note the Fig. *Anabasis*. Ap. 6. See note below.
my very heart = the walls of my heart.
thou hast. Heb. text reads "I have"; but marg. and some codices, with three early printed editions, and R.V. marg., read "thou hast", as in A.V.
20 curtains. Put by Fig. *Metonymy* (of Cause), Ap. 6, for tents, in which a large proportion of the people lived (2 Sam. 18. 17. 1 Kings 8. 66). Cp. 10. 20.
22 known = acknowledged.
sottish = stupid. Probably from Celtic. Breton *sōt*, or *sōd* = stupid.
children = sons. **evil.** Heb. *rā'a'*. Ap. 44. viii.
23 I beheld. Note the Fig. *Anaphora* (Ap. 6), commencing this and the three following verses.
lo. Fig. *Asterismos*. Ap. 6.
without form, and void. Heb. *tohū va-bohū*. Ref. to Pent. (Gen. 1. 2). Occurs only here. Ap. 92. In Isa. 34. 11, the two words are in another connection. Cp. also Isa. 45. 18. **light** = lights (pl.). Cp. Gen. 1. 14.
25 man. Heb. *'ādām*. Ap. 14. I.
26 at = because of.
and by. Some codices, with five early printed editions, Sept., Syr., and Vulg., read "and because of".
27 yet will I not make a full end. Ref. to Pent. (Lev. 26. 44). Ap. 92. Cp. 5. 10, 18.
28 I have purposed it, and, &c. Ref. to Pent. (Num. 23. 19). Ap. 92.
29 city. Put by Fig. *Metonymy* (of Subject), Ap. 6, for its inhabitants.
every = all, as in preceding clause.
man. Heb. *'īsh*. Ap. 14. II.
30 thou. Fig. *Prosopopœia* (Ap. 6). Put for idolatrous Israel. An adulterous woman.
rentest = enlargest (with paint).
face = eyes. **life** = soul. Heb. *nephesh*. Ap. 13.

5. 1–31 (V¹, p. 1022). **INVESTIGATION.**
(Repeated Alternation.)

V¹ | Y¹ | 1–5. Incrimination.
  Z¹ | 6. Threatening. Invasion. (Fig.)
 Y² | 7, 8. Incrimination.
  Z² | 9. Threatening. Vengeance.
 Y³ | 10–13. Incrimination.
  Z³ | 14–19. Threatening. Invasion. (Lit.)
 Y⁴ | 20–28. Incrimination.
  Z⁴ | 29–31. Threatening. Vengeance.

1 streets = out places, or outskirts.
broad places = market, or open places of concourse.
if ye can find. Ref. to Pent. (Gen. 18. 26, &c.). Ap. 92. Points to reign of Jehoiakim rather than that of Josiah.
man. Heb. *'īsh*. Ap. 14. II.
I will pardon. Ref. to Pent. (Gen. 18. 24–32). Ap. 92.
2 The LORD. Heb. Jehovah. Ap. 4. II.
3 the truth = faithfulness. The same word as in *v* 1.
have not grieved = have felt no pain.
4 poor = become poor, or impoverished, reduced in means. Heb. *dal*. See note on "poverty", Prov. 6. 11.
judgment = justice. **God.** Heb. Elohim. Ap. 4. I.
5 altogether = together, or with one accord.
6 evenings = deserts.

518–500 every one that goeth out thence shall be torn
in pieces: because their °transgressions are
many, *and* their °backslidings are °increased."
Y2 (p. 1023) 7 "How shall I pardon thee for this? thy
°children have °forsaken Me, and °sworn by
them that are no gods: when I had °fed them
to the full, they then °committed adultery, and
assembled themselves by troops in the harlots'
houses.
8 They were *as* fed horses °in the morning:
every one neighed after his neighbour's wife.
Z2 9 °Shall I not visit for these *things?* °saith
[2]the LORD: and shall not °My soul °be
avenged on such a nation as this?
Y3 10 Go ye up upon her walls, and destroy; but
make °not a full end: take away her battlements; for they *are* not [2]the LORD'S.
11 For °the house of Israel and °the house of
Judah have dealt very treacherously against
Me, [9]saith [2]the LORD.
12 They have °belied [2]the LORD, and said,
'*It is* not He; neither shall °evil come upon
us; neither shall we see sword nor famine:
13 And the °prophets shall become °wind,
and the word *is* not in them: thus shall it be
done unto them.
Z3 14 Wherefore thus saith °the LORD God of
hosts, Because ye speak this word, behold,
I will make My words in thy mouth fire, and
this people wood, and it shall devour them.
15 °Lo, °I will bring °a nation upon you
from far, O [11]house of Israel, [9]saith [2]the
LORD: it *is* a mighty nation, it *is* an °ancient
nation, a nation whose language thou knowest
not, neither °understandest what they say.
16 Their quiver *is* as an open sepulchre, they
are all mighty men.
17 And °they shall eat up thine °harvest, and
thy bread, *which* thy sons and thy daughters
should eat: °they shall eat up thy flocks and
thine herds: °they shall eat up thy vines and
thy fig trees: they shall °impoverish thy
fenced cities, wherein thou °trustedst, with the
sword.
18 Nevertheless in those days, [9]saith [2]the
LORD, I will [10]not make a full end with you.
19 And it shall come to pass, when ye shall
say, °'Wherefore doeth [2]the LORD our [4]God
all these *things* unto us?' then shalt thou
answer them, 'Like as ye have [7]forsaken Me,
and served °strange gods in your land, so
shall ye serve °strangers in a land *that is* not
yours.'
Y4 n (p. 1024) 20 °Declare this °in the house of Jacob, and
°publish it in Judah, saying,
21 'Hear now this, O foolish people, and without °understanding; which have eyes, and see
not; which have ears, and hear not:
22 Fear ye not Me? [9]saith [2]the LORD: will
ye not tremble at My presence,
o Which have placed the sand *for* the bound of
the sea by a perpetual decree, that it cannot
pass it: and though the waves thereof toss
themselves, yet can they not prevail; though
they roar, yet can they not pass over it?
p 23 But this People hath a revolting and a
rebellious heart; they are revolted and gone.

transgressions = revolts. Heb. *pāshaʿ*. Ap. 44. ix.
backslidings = apostasies.
increased = strong, or many. **7 children** = sons.
forsaken Me. Ref. to Pent. (Deut. 32. 15, 21). Ap. 92.
sworn. Cp. *v.* 2.
fed them to the full. So in many codices, with two early printed editions, Aram., Sept., Syr., and Vulg.; but some codices, with five early printed editions, read "made them swear".
committed adultery. Ref. to Pent. (Ex. 20. 14. Deut. 5. 18). Ap. 92. The usual formula for idolatry.
8 in the morning: i.e. roaming at large.
9 Shall I not visit . . . ? Fig. *Erotēsis*. Ap. 6.
saith the LORD = [is] Jehovah's oracle.
My soul = I Myself, for emphasis. Heb. *nephesh*. Ap. 13. Fig. *Anthropopatheia*. Ap. 6.
be avenged = avenge herself. Cp. *v.* 29; 9. 9.
10 not a full end. Cp. *v.* 18, and 4. 27.
11 the house of Israel. See note on 2. 4.
the house of Judah. See note on 2. 4.
12 belied = acted deceitfully against. Cp. Josh. 24. 27.
evil = calamity. Heb. *rāʿaʿ*. Ap. 44. viii.
13 prophets: i.e. Jeremiah, and others with him. See one in ch. 26. 20. **wind.** Heb. *rūach*. Ap. 9.
14 the LORD God of hosts. Heb. Jehovah the Elohim of Zebaioth. Occurs in Jeremiah only here, 15. 16; 35. 17; and 49. 5.
15 Lo. Fig. *Asterismos*. Ap. 6.
I will bring. Ref. to Pent. (Deut. 28. 49). Ap. 92.
a nation: i.e. the Chaldeans, but not yet named as such. **ancient.** Cp. Gen. 10. 10.
understandest = hearest. Put by Fig. *Metonymy* (of Cause), Ap. 6, for what is understood. Cp. 1 Cor. 14. 2.
17 they shall eat up. Ref. to Pent. (Lev. 26. 16). Ap. 92. Repeated three times by Fig. *Anaphora* (Ap. 6), for great emphasis.
harvest, &c. Note the similar enumeration in Hab. 3. 17.
impoverish = beat down. Only again in Mal. 1. 4.
trustedst = confidedst. Heb. *baṭaḥ*. Ap. 69. I.
19 Wherefore . . . ? Fig. *Erotēsis*. Ap. 6. Ref. to Pent. (Deut. 29. 24, 25). Ap. 92.
strange . . . strangers = foreign . . . foreigners, or aliens.

5. 20-28 (Y4, p. 1023). **INCRIMINATION.**
(Extended Alternation.)

Y4 | n | 20-22-. Call to fear God.
o | -22. On account of His power.
p | 23. Rebellion in heart.
n | 24-. Call. Refused.
o | -24. Notwithstanding His bounty.
p | 25-28. Rebellion in acts.

20 Declare . . . publish. Cp. 4. 15.
in the house of Jacob. Only here, and Amos 3. 13, with the Prep. "in". See note on 2. 4.
21 understanding. Heb. "heart".
24 That giveth rain. Ref. to Pent. (Deut. 11. 14).
both = even. Some codices omit this word.
the appointed . . . harvest. Ref. to Pent. (Gen. 8. 22).
25 iniquities. Heb. *ʿāvāh*. Ap. 44. iv.
sins. Heb. *chaṭaʾ*. Ap. 44. i. **good** = the good (sing.).
26 wicked. Heb. *rāʿaʿ*. Ap. 44. viii.

24 Neither say they in their heart, 'Let us *n*
now fear [2]the LORD our [4]God,
°That giveth rain, °both the former and the *o*
latter, in his season: He reserveth unto us
°the appointed weeks of the °harvest.'
25 Your °iniquities have turned away these *p*
things, and your °sins have withholden °good
things from you.
26 For among My People are found °wicked
men: they lay wait, as he that setteth snares;
they set a trap, they catch men.

518-500 27 As a cage is full of birds, so *are* their houses full of deceit: therefore they are become great, and waxen rich.

28 They are °waxen fat, they shine: yea, they overpass the deeds of °the wicked: they judge not the cause, the cause of °the fatherless, °yet they prosper; and the right of °the needy do they not judge.

Z[4] (p. 1023) 29 °Shall I not visit for these *things* ?[9] saith [2]the LORD: °shall not [9]My soul [9]be avenged on such a nation as this?

30 °A wonderful and horrible thing is committed in the land;

31 The prophets prophesy falsely, and the priests bear rule °by their means; and My People love *to have it* so: and what will ye do in the end thereof?'' "

U[2] (p. 1022) **6** O ye °children of °Benjamin, gather yourselves to °flee out of the midst of Jerusalem, and °blow the trumpet in °Tekoa, and set up °a sign of fire in °Beth-haccerem: for °evil appeareth out of the °north, and great °destruction.

2 I have likened the °daughter of Zion to a comely and delicate °*woman*.

3 The °shepherds with their flocks shall come unto her; they shall pitch *their* tents against her round about; they shall feed every one in his place.

4 °Prepare ye war against her; arise, and let us go up °at noon. °Woe unto us! for the day goeth away, for the shadows of the evening are stretched out.

5 Arise, and let us go by night, and let us destroy her palaces.

6 For thus hath °the LORD of hosts said, "Hew ye down trees, and °cast a mount against Jerusalem: this *is* the city to be visited; she *is* wholly oppression in the midst of her.

7 As a °fountain casteth out her waters, so she casteth out her °wickedness: violence and spoil is heard in her; before Me continually *is* grief and wounds.

8 Be thou instructed, O Jerusalem, lest °My soul depart from thee; lest I make thee desolate, a land not inhabited."

9 Thus saith [6]the LORD of hosts, "They shall throughly glean the remnant of Israel °as a vine: turn back thine hand as a grapegatherer into the baskets.

V[2] q (p. 1025) 10 To whom shall I speak, and °give warning, that they may hear? °behold, their °ear *is* uncircumcised, and they cannot hearken: behold, the word of [6]the LORD is unto them °a reproach; °they have no delight in it.

r 11 Therefore I am full of the fury of [6]the LORD; I am weary with holding in: I will pour it out upon the °children abroad, and upon the assembly of young men together: for even the husband with the wife shall be taken, the aged with *him that is* full of days.

12 And their houses shall be °turned unto others, *with their* fields and wives together: for I will stretch out My hand upon the inhabitants of the land, °saith [6]the LORD.

28 waxen fat. Ref. to Pent. (the same word as in Deut. 32. 15). Ap. 92.
the wicked = a lawless one. Heb. *rāshaʿ*. Ap. 44. x.
the fatherless = an orphan.
yet they prosper: or, that they [the fatherless] should prosper. Fig. *Ellipsis*. Ap. 6. Ref. to Pent. (Deut. 10. 18; 24. 17; 27. 19). Ap. 92.
the needy = needy ones.
29 Shall I not . . . ? Note the repeated Fig. *Erotēsis*, in the form of Fig. *Anaphora*. Ap. 6.
30 A wonderful = An astounding.
31 by their means. Prophets were raised up when the priests failed in their duty. Now they had become in accord with them. Cp. 23. 25, 26. Ezek. 13. 6, &c.

1 children = sons.
Benjamin. Put by Fig. *Synecdoche* (of the Part), Ap. 6, for the whole of Judah, on account of their close connection with the Gibeathites (Judg. 19. 16. Hos. 9. 9; 10. 9).
flee out. In 4. 6 it was "flee to". Now Jerusalem itself is to be taken.
blow . . . Tekoa. Fig. *Paronomasia* (Ap. 6), for emphasis. Heb. *bithkōʿah . . . tikʿu*.
Tekoa. Now *Khan Tekūʿa*, five miles south of Bethlehem, ten from Jerusalem.
a sign of fire = a fire-signal.
Beth-haccerem = house of the vineyards. Not identified. Conder suggests such a house at *'Ain Karim*.
evil. Heb. *rāʿaʿ*. Ap. 44. viii.
north. Because the armies from Assyria entered the land from the north. See note on 3. 12.
destruction = fracture, or damage, as in *v.* 14.
2 daughter. Put by Fig. *Metonymy* (of Adjunct), Ap. 6, for the helpless inhabitants.
woman. Ref. to Pent. (Deut. 28. 56). Ap. 92.
3 shepherds: i.e. the Chaldean armies. See 3. 15.
4 Prepare, &c. = Prosecute a holy war.
at noon. In the heat of the day, when most are resting. Cp. 15. 8. Song 1. 7. Isa. 32. 2. See 2 Sam. 4. 5.
Woe unto us, &c. See note on 15. 8.
6 the LORD. Heb. Jehovah. Ap. 4. II.
the LORD of hosts = Jehovah *Zebbaioth*, the first of thirty-nine occurrences of this title in Jeremiah (6. 6, 9; 8. 3; 9. 7, 17; 10. 16; 11. 17, 20, 22; 19. 11; 20. 12; 23. 15, 16, 36; 25. 8, 28, 29, 32; 26. 18; 27. 18, 19; 29. 17; 30. 8; 31. 35; 32. 18; 33. 11, 12; 46. 18; 48. 15; 49. 7, 26, 35; 50. 33, 34; 51. 5, 14, 19, 57, 58).
cast a mount = pour out: i.e. the earth from baskets to make a mount.
7 fountain. Heb. *bōr* = a well, bored or hewn out. Cp. 2 Sam. 23. 15, 16. 1 Chron. 11. 17. See note on Gen. 21. 19.
wickedness. Heb. *rāʿaʿ*. Ap. 44. viii.
8 My soul = I myself. Heb. *nephesh*. Ap. 13.
9 as a vine. Here, and in 8. 13, one Codex (Harley, 5720, B.M., Lond.) reads, "on the vine".

6. 10-21 (V^2, p. 1022). **INVESTIGATION.**
(*Extended Alternation.*)

V[2] q | 10. Sin. (Part.) Insensibility.
  r | 11, 12. Threatening. Captivity.
    s | 13-15-. General corruption.
      t | -15. Threatening. Fall.
q | 16, 17. Sin. (Part.) Disobedience.
  r | 18, 19. Threatening. Retribution.
    s | 20. General corruption.
      t | 21. Threatening. Fall.

10 give warning = testify.
behold. Fig. *Asterismos*. Ap. 6.
ear is uncircumcised. Ref. to Pent. (Ex. 6. 12, 30. Lev. 26. 41). Ap. 92. Fig. *Catachresis* (Ap. 6). An ear not brought into the covenant.
a reproach. Note the fate of Jehovah's word in the down-grade of Jeremiah's days. In 6. 10 a reproach; in 8. 9, rejected; in 17. 15, scoffed at; in 23. 36, perverted.
they. So the Mugah Codex quoted in the *Massōrah*. But other codices, with three early printed editions, read "and they". **11 children** = a young child. Heb. *ʿūl*. **12 turned unto others.** Ref. to Pent. (Deut. 28. 30). **saith the LORD** = [is] Jehovah's oracle.

s 13 For from the least of them even unto the
(p. 1025) greatest of them every one *is* given to °covet-
518-500 ousness; and from the prophet even unto the
priest every one dealeth falsely.
14 They have healed also the °hurt °*of the daughter* of My People slightly, saying, °'Peace, peace;' when *there is* no peace.
15 Were they ashamed when they had committed abomination? nay, they were not at all ashamed, neither °could they blush:
t therefore they shall fall among them that fall: at the time *that* I visit them they shall be cast down," saith [6]the LORD.

q 16 Thus saith [6]the LORD, °"Stand ye in the ways, and see, and ask for the °old paths, where *is* the °good way, and walk therein, and ye shall °find rest for °your souls. But they said, 'We will not walk *therein.*'
17 Also I set watchmen over you, *saying,* °'Hearken to the sound of the trumpet.' But they said, 'We will not hearken.'

r 18 Therefore hear, ye nations, and know, O °congregation, what *is* among them.
19 Hear, O earth: behold, I will bring °evil upon this People, *even* the fruit of their thoughts, because they have not hearkened unto My words, nor to °My law, but rejected it.

s 20 To what purpose cometh there to Me °incense from °Sheba, and the sweet cane from a far country? your burnt offerings *are* °not acceptable, nor your sacrifices sweet unto Me.

t 21 Therefore thus saith [6]the LORD, [10]Behold, I will lay stumblingblocks before this people, and the fathers and the sons together shall fall upon them; the neighbour and his friend shall perish.

U³ (p. 1022) 22 Thus saith [6]the LORD, [10]Behold, a people cometh from the north country, and a great nation shall be raised from °the sides of the earth.
23 They shall lay hold on bow and spear; they *are* cruel, and have no mercy; their voice °roareth like the sea; and they ride upon horses, set in array as °men for war against thee, O [2]daughter of Zion."
24 We have heard the fame thereof: our hands wax feeble: anguish hath taken hold of us, *and* pain, as of a woman in travail.
25 Go not forth into the field, nor walk by the way; for the sword of the enemy *and* °fear *is* on every side.
26 O daughter of My people, gird *thee* with sackcloth, °and wallow thyself in ashes: make thee mourning, *as for* an only son, most bitter lamentation: for the spoiler shall suddenly come upon us.

V³ 27 I have set thee *for* a °tower *and* °a fortress among My people, that thou mayest know and °try their °way.
28 They *are* all grievous revolters, walking with slanders: *they are* °brass and iron; they *are* all corrupters.
29 The bellows are burned, the lead is consumed of the fire; the °founder melteth in vain: for the [7]wicked are not plucked away.
30 °Reprobate silver shall *men* call them, because [6]the LORD hath °rejected them.

13 covetousness. Ref. to Pent. (Ex. 18. 21). Ap. 92.
14 hurt. Same word as "destruction" (*v.* 1).
of the daughter. Some codices, with four early printed editions, read these words in the text.
Peace, peace. Fig. *Epizeuxis* (Ap. 6), for emphasis. See note on Isa. 26. 3.
15 could they=knew they how to.
16 Stand ye, &c. A gracious appeal to avoid the threatened calamity, as in 2. 2.
old paths. Cp. 18. 15.
good=right.
find rest. Cp. Matt. 11. 29, 30; where a like invitation and promise is given to those who will "learn". Following likewise on a preceding threatening of judgment. Cp. Deut. 28. 65.
your souls=yourselves (emphatic). Heb. *nephesh.* Ap. 13.
17 Hearken=Give ye heed. Some cod., with two early printed editions, read "And (therefore) give ye heed".
18 congregation=assembly (in its civil aspect). Heb. *'ēdah,* a technical Pentateuchal word. First occurrence in Ex. 12. 3, 6, 19, 47. Used technically of Israel, fifteen times in Exodus; twelve in Leviticus; eighty-three times in Numbers. Found in the prophets only here; 30. 20; and Hos. 7. 12 (ref. to Pent.). Ap. 92.
19 evil=calamity. Heb. *rā'a'.* Ap. 44. viii.
My law. Ref. to Pent. Note that "words" and "law" are put alternatively.
20 incense=frankincense. Put by Fig. *Synecdoche* (of the Part), Ap. 6, for the whole incense of which it was an ingredient.
Sheba. In the south of Arabia.
not acceptable. Cp. Isa. 1. 11-15.
22 the sides, &c. Idiom for a great distance.
23 roareth=will roar. Cp. Isa. 5. 29, 30.
men. Heb. *'ish.* Ap. 14. II.
25 fear is on every side=terror is round about. Cp. 20. 3, 10; 46. 5; 49. 29. Lam. 2. 22.
26 and. Some codices, with five early printed editions, omit this "and".
27 tower=watchtower; or, an assayer.
try=assay (as an assayer of metals).
way. Some codices read "heart".
28 brass and iron. Not silver and gold. Cp. Ezek. 22. 18.
29 founder melteth=refiner refineth.
30 Reprobate . . . rejected. Note the Fig. *Paronomasia* (Ap. 6). Heb. *nim'āṣ . . . mā'aṣ*: i.e. rejected (silver) . . . rejected (them). Cp. Isa. 1. 22. Ezek. 22. 18.

7. 1—10. 25 (*J*, p. 1018). PLACE. IN GATE OF THE TEMPLE. (*Alternation, and Introversion.*)

J | A | C | 7. 1-28. Exhortation.
  | | D | 7. 29—8. 13. Call for lamentation.
  | B | 8. 14—9. 9. Invasion.
  | *A* | *D* | 9. 10-26. Call for lamentation.
  | | *C* | 10. 1-16. Exhortation.
  | *B* | 10. 17-25. Expulsion.

Jeremiah's SIXTH prophecy (see p. 1015).

7. 1-28 (C, above). EXHORTATION. (*Alternation.*)

C | E | 1, 2. Proclamation.
  | F | 3-26. Disobedience.
  | *E* | 27, 28-. Proclamation.
  | *F* | -28. Disobedience.

1 came. The danger attending this message is shown in ch. 26. Cp. 7. 2 with 26. 2; 7. 3 with 26. 13; 7. 12-14 with 26. 4-6. Ch. 26 was in the beginning of the reign of Jehoiakim, probably his fourth year. Ch. 26 is the historical appendix of ch. 7.
the LORD. Heb. Jehovah. Ap. 4. II.

7 The word that °came to Jeremiah from °the LORD, saying, J A C (p. 10

518–500 2 "Stand °in the gate of [1]the LORD'S house, and proclaim there this word, and say, 'Hear the word of [1]the LORD, °all *ye of* Judah, that enter in at these gates to worship [1]the LORD.

$F\ G^1\ H^1$ (p. 1027) 3 Thus saith °the LORD of hosts, the °God of Israel, 'Amend your ways and your doings,

$J^1\ u^1$ and I will cause you to dwell in this place.

v^1 4 °Trust ye not in lying words, saying, °'The temple of [1]the LORD, °The temple of [1]the LORD, °The temple of [1]the LORD, *are* these.'

H^2 5 For if ye throughly amend your ways and your doings; if ye throughly execute judgment between a °man and his neighbour;

$J^2\ v^2$ 6 *If* ye oppress not the °stranger, the fatherless, and the widow, and shed not °innocent blood in this place, neither walk after °other gods to your hurt:

u^2 7 °Then will I cause you to dwell in this place, in the land that I gave to your fathers, °for ever and ever.

H^3 8 °Behold, ye [4]trust in lying words, that cannot profit.

9 Will ye °steal, murder, and commit adultery, and swear falsely, and burn incense unto Baal, and walk after other gods whom ye know not;

$J^3\ v^3$ 10 And °come and stand before Me in this house, °which is called by My name, and say, 'We are delivered to do all these abominations'?

11 °**Is this house, which is called by My name, become a den of robbers** in your eyes? [8]Behold, even I have seen *it,* °saith [1]the LORD.

u^3 12 But go ye now unto My place which *was* °in Shiloh, °where I set My name at the first, and see °what I did to it for the °wickedness of My People Israel.

13 And now, because ye have done all these works, [11]saith [1]the LORD, and I spake unto you, °rising up early and speaking, but ye heard not; and I called you, but ye answered not;

14 Therefore will I do unto *this* house, which is called by My name, wherein ye [4]trust, and unto the place which I gave to you and to your fathers, °as I have done to [12]Shiloh.

15 And I will cast you out of My sight, as I have cast out all your brethren, *even* °the whole seed of Ephraim.'"

16 Therefore pray not thou for this People, neither lift up cry nor prayer for them, neither °make intercession to Me: for I will not hear thee.

H^4 17 Seest thou not what they do in the cities of Judah and in the streets of Jerusalem?

18 The °children gather wood, and the fathers kindle the fire, and the women knead *their* dough, to °make cakes to the °queen of heaven, and to pour out drink offerings unto other gods, that they may provoke Me to anger.

19 Do they °provoke Me to anger? [11]saith [1]the LORD: *do they* not *provoke* themselves to the confusion of their own faces?

$J^4\ v^4$ 20 Therefore thus saith °the Lord °GOD; [8]Behold, Mine anger and My fury shall be poured out upon this place,

u^4 upon °man, and upon beast, and upon the

---

2 in the gate: i.e. in the fore-court. The proclamation has the Temple and its frequenters for its subject.
all ye of Judah = all Judah.

7. 3-26 (F, p. 1026). DISOBEDIENCE.
(Division.)

F | G^1 | 3–20. Incrimination. (Shiloh.)
  | G^2 | 21–26. Incrimination. (Egypt.)

7. 3-20 (G^1, above). INCRIMINATION. (SHILOH.)
(Repeated Alternation and Introversion.)

G^1 | H^1 | 3–. Ways and Doings.
  J^1 | u^1 | –3. Land.
    v^1 | 4. Temple.
 H^2 | 5. Ways and Doings.
  J^2 | v^2 | 6. Temple.
    u^2 | 7. Land.
 H^3 | 8, 9. Ways and Doings.
  J^3 | v^3 | 10, 11. Temple.
    u^3 | 12–16. Land.
 H^4 | 17–19. Ways and Doings.
  J^4 | v^4 | 20–. Temple.
    u^4 | –20. Land.

3 the LORD of hosts, the God of Israel. This title occurs thirty-four times in Jeremiah (7. 3, 21; 9. 15; 16. 9; 19. 3, 15; 25. 15, 27; 27. 4, 21; 28. 2, 14; 29. 4, 8, 21, 25; 31. 23; 32. 14, 15; 35. 13, 18, 19; 38. 17; 39. 16; 42. 15, 18; 43. 10; 44. 2, 11, 25; 46. 25; 48. 1; 50. 18; 51. 33). **God.** Heb. Elohim. Ap. 4. I.

4 Trust = Confide. Heb. *bāṭaḥ*. Ap. 69. I.
The temple of the LORD. Note the Fig. *Epizeuxis* (Ap. 6), for great emphasis, to exhibit the fanaticism common to all idolaters.

5 man. Heb. *'īsh*. Ap. 14. II.

6 stranger, the fatherless, and the widow. Ref. to Pent. (Deut. 24. 17). Ap. 92.
innocent blood. Ref. to Pent. (Deut. 19. 10). Ap. 92. See note on Isa. 59. 7.
other gods. Ref. to Pent. (Ex. 20. 3. Deut. 6. 14; 8. 19, &c.). Ap. 92.

7 Then will I cause, &c. Ref. to Pent. (Deut. 4. 40).
for ever and ever. Put by Fig. *Synecdoche* (of the Whole), Ap. 6, for an age-abiding duration.

8 Behold. Fig. *Asterismos*. Ap. 6.

9 steal, murder, &c. Ref. to Pent. (Ex. 20. 7–15).

10 come = [still] come.
which is called, &c. = whereon My name was called.

11 Is this house . . .? Fig. *Erotēsis*. Ap. 6. This passage used by our Lord, just as Isa. 56. 7 was in Matt. 21. 13. Mark 11. 17. Luke 19. 46.
saith the LORD = [is] Jehovah's oracle.

12 in Shiloh. Now *Seilūn*. Cp. 26. 6, 9; 41. 5.
where I set . . . at the first. Ref. to Pent. (Deut. 12. 5, 11, &c.). Ap. 92. Cp. 1 Sam. 4. 4.
what I did to it. See 1 Sam. 4. 11, and cp. 25. 6.
wickedness. Heb. *rā'a'*. Ap. 44. viii.

13 rising up early and speaking. This phrase is almost peculiar to Jeremiah, where it occurs eleven times (7. 13, 25; 11. 7; 25. 3, 4; 26. 5; 29. 19; 32. 33; 35. 14, 15; 44. 4). Occurs elsewhere only in 2 Chron. 36. 15.

14 as = according as.

15 the whole seed of Ephraim. Put by Fig. *Synecdoche* (of the Part), Ap. 6, for the ten tribes which were already in captivity. The trouble recorded in ch. 27 proves that this prediction was spoken.

16 make intercession. Cp. 11. 14; 14. 11.

18 children = sons. **make**: or, offer.
queen. Some codices, with two early printed editions, read "worship", which is put by Fig. *Metonymy* (of Effect), Ap. 6, for the goddess to whom the worship was offered. See 19. 13; 44. 19; and cp. 2 Kings 21. 3, 5; 23. 12, 13.

19 provoke. Note the Fig. *Ploke* (Ap. 6), by which the one word implies a second meaning. "Do they provoke Me . . .? No: they bring on themselves" the judgments of Jehovah. Ref. to Pent. (Deut. 32. 21).

20 the Lord GOD. Heb. Adonai Jehovah. Ap. 4. viii (2), and II. **man.** Heb. *'ādām*. Ap. 14. I.

518-500 trees of the field, and upon the fruit of the
ground; and it shall burn, and shall not be
quenched."

G[2] w (p. 1028) 21 Thus saith [3] the LORD of hosts, the [3] God
of Israel; °"Put your burnt offerings unto
your °sacrifices, and eat flesh.
22 For °I spake not unto your fathers, nor
commanded them in the day that I brought
them out of the land of Egypt, °concerning
burnt offerings or [21] °sacrifices:

x 23 But °this thing commanded I them, saying,
°'Obey My voice, and I will be your [3] God, and
ye shall be My people: and walk ye in all the
ways that I have commanded you, that it may
be well unto you.'
24 But they hearkened not, nor inclined their
ear, but walked in the counsels *and* in the
°imagination of their evil heart, and went
backward, and not forward.

w 25 Since the day that °your fathers came
forth out of the land of Egypt unto this day
I have even sent unto you all My servants the
prophets, daily [13] rising up early and sending
them:

x 26 Yet they hearkened not unto Me, nor
inclined their ear, but hardened their neck:
they did worse than their fathers.

E (p. 1026) 27 Therefore thou shalt speak all these words
unto them; but they will not hearken to thee:
thou shalt also call unto them; but they will
not answer thee.
28 But thou shalt say unto them,

F 'This *is* °a nation that °obeyeth not the voice
of [1] the LORD their [3] God, nor receiveth °correction:
°truth is perished, and is cut off from
°their mouth.'

D k[1] (p. 1028) 29 °Cut off thine hair, *O* °*Jerusalem*, and
°cast *it* away, and take up a lamentation on
°high places; for [1] the LORD hath rejected and
forsaken the generation °of His wrath.
30 For the [18] children of Judah have done
°evil in My sight, [11] saith [1] the LORD: they
have set their abominations °in the house
°which is called by My name, to pollute it.
31 And they have built the °high places of
°Tophet, which *is* in the valley of the son of
°Hinnom, to °burn their sons and their daughters
in the fire; °which I commanded °*them*
not, neither °came it into My heart.

L[1] M y 32 Therefore, [8] behold, the days come, [11] saith
[1] the LORD, that it shall no more be called
[31] Tophet, nor the valley of the son of [31] Hinnom,
but the valley of °slaughter:

z for they shall bury in [31] Tophet, till there be
no place.

a 33 And °the carcases of this People shall be
meat for the fowls of the heaven, and for the
beasts of the earth; and none shall °fray
them away.

M y 34 Then will I cause to cease from the cities
of Judah, and from the streets of Jerusalem,
°the voice of mirth, and the voice of gladness,
the voice of the bridegroom, and the voice of
the bride:

z °for the land shall be desolate.

7. 21-26 (G[2], p. 1027). INCRIMINATION. (EGYPT.) (*Alternation.*)

G[2] | w | 21, 22. Command.
  x | 23, 24. Disobedience.
  w | 25. Command.
  x | 26. Disobedience.

21 Put=Add.
sacrifices. Heb. *zābach*. Ap. 43. I. iv.
22 I spake not . . . concerning . . . sacrifices. Ref. to Pent. (Ex. 15. 26; 19. 5), which was *before any law was given*. This vindicates the passage from modern criticism. Cp. Lev. 26. 3-13, and 1 Sam. 15. 22, with Ps. 50. 8, 9; 51. 16, 17; Isa. 1. 11-17. Hos. 6. 6. Amos 5. 21-24. Mic. 6. 6-8. Matt. 9. 13; 12. 7; 23. 23.
23 this thing . . . Obey, &c. Ref. to Pent. (Lev. 26. 3-13). Ap. 92.
24 imagination. See note on 3. 17.
25 your fathers came forth, &c. Ref. to Pent. (Ex. 12—15). Ap. 92.
28 a=the. **obeyeth**=hearkeneth to.
correction: or instruction, or discipline.
truth=fidelity, or veracity.
their. The Babylonian Codex reads "your".

7. 29—8. 13 (D, p. 1026). CALL FOR LAMENTATION. (*Repeated Alternation.*)

D | K[1] | 7. 29-31. Incrimination. Pollution of Temple.
  L[1] | 7. 32—8. 3. Threatening. Slaughter.
  K[2] | 8. 4-9. Incrimination. Impenitence.
  L[2] | 8. 10, 11. Threatening. Dispossession.
  K[3] | 8. 12-. Incrimination. Effrontery.
  L[3] | 8. -12, 13. Threatening. Fall. Cast down.

29 Cut off thine hair. A symbol of mourning.
Jerusalem: or, supply "daughter of My People". Cp. 8. 11, 19, 21, 22; 9. 1, 7. The verb is fem. (sing.).
cast it away. Showing the completeness of the operation.
high places. As such. Cp. 3. 21.
of. Gen. of Relation. Ap. 17. 5. Cp. Rom. 8. 36.
30 evil. Heb. *rā'a'*. Ap. 44. viii.
in the house. Note the enormity of the evil.
which is called by My name=whereon My name was called.
31 high places. Idolatrous places. Not the same word as *v.* 29.
Tophet. In the valley of the son of Hinnom (2 Kings 23. 10. Isa. 30. 33. Jer. 19. 6, 11-14).
Hinnom. Now *Wādy er Rabābeh* (Josh. 15. 8; 18. 16. 2 Kings 23. 10. 2 Chron. 28. 3; 33. 6. Neh. 11. 30).
burn. This shows the result of passing them through the fire.
which I commanded them not. Ref. to Pent. (Deut. 17. 3; 18. 10. Lev. 18. 21). Ap. 92. Note the sin of adding to God's commands and words.
them. Some codices, with one early printed edition, Sept., and Syr., read this "them" in the text. Cp. 32. 35.
came=ascended. Put by Fig. *Synecdoche* (of Species), Ap. 6, for coming into the mind.

7. 32—8. 3 (L[1], above). THREATENING. (SLAUGHTER.) (*Extended Alternation.*)

L[1] | M | y | 7. 32-. Cessation of name. } Temple.
  z | 7. -32. Reason.
  a | 7. 33. Carcases unburned.
  M | *y* | 7. 34-. Cessation of joy. } Land.
  z | 7. -34. Reason.
  a | 8. 1-3. Bones unburned.

32 slaughter. Cp. 19. 6; 12. 3. Zech. 11. 4, 7. Occ. only in Jeremiah and Zechariah.
33 the carcases, &c. Ref. to Pent. (Deut. 28. 26).
fray=frighten: from Fr. *effrayer*.
34 the voice of mirth, &c. This refrain is peculiar to Jeremiah. Occurs four times (here; 16. 9; 25. 10; 33. 11) ("joy").
for the land shall be desolate. Ref. to Pent. (Lev. 26. 31, 33, the same word "desolate"). Ap. 92.

a (p. 1028) 518-500 **8** At that time, °saith °the LORD, they shall
bring out the °bones of the kings of Judah,
°and the bones of his princes, °and the bones
of the priests, °and the bones of the prophets,
°and the bones of the inhabitants of Jerusalem, out of their graves:
2 [1]And they shall spread them before the
sun, and the moon, °and all the host of heaven,
whom they have loved, °and whom they have
served, °and after whom they have walked,
°and whom they have sought, °and whom
they have worshipped: they shall °not be
gathered, nor be buried; they shall be for dung
upon the face of the earth.
3 And death shall be chosen rather than life
by all the residue of them that remain of this
°evil family, which remain in all the places
whither I have driven them, [1]saith [1]the LORD
of hosts."

K² b¹ (p. 1029) 4 Moreover thou shalt say unto them, "Thus
saith [1]the LORD; 'Shall they fall, and not
°arise? shall °he turn away, and not return?
5 Why *then* is this People of Jerusalem slidden
back by a perpetual backsliding?
c¹ they hold fast deceit, they refuse to return.
6 I hearkened and heard, *but* they spake not
aright: °no °man repented him of his °wicked-
ness, saying, 'What have I done?' every one
turned to his course, as the horse rusheth into
the battle.
7 Yea, the stork in the heaven °knoweth her
appointed times; and the °turtle and the crane
and the swallow observe the time of their
coming; but My People °know not the judgment of [1]the LORD.
b² 8 How do ye say, 'We *are* wise, and the law
of [1]the LORD *is* with us?'
c² °Lo, certainly in vain made He *it;* the pen of
the scribes *is* in vain.
9 The wise *men* are ashamed, they are dismayed and taken: [8]lo, they have °rejected the
word of [1]the LORD;
b³ and what wisdom *is* in them?

L² (p. 1028) 10 Therefore will I °give their wives unto
others, *and* their fields to them that shall
°inherit *them:* for every one from the least
even unto the greatest is given to covetousness, °from the °prophet even unto the °priest
every one dealeth falsely.
11 For they have healed the °hurt of the
daughter of My people slightly, saying, °'Peace,
peace;' when *there is* no peace.

K³ 12 Were they ashamed when they had committed abomination? nay, they were not at all
ashamed, neither °could they blush:
L³ therefore shall they fall among them that fall:
in °the time of their visitation they shall be
cast down, [1]saith [1]the LORD.
13 I will °surely consume them, [1]saith [1]the
LORD: *there shall be* no grapes °on the vine,
nor figs on the fig tree, and the leaf °shall fade;
and °*the things that* I have given them shall
pass away °from them.'"

B N¹ (p. 1029) 14 °Why do °we sit still? assemble yourselves,
and let us enter into the defenced cities, and let
us be silent there: for [1]the LORD our °God
hath put us to °silence, and given us °water of
gall to drink, because we have °sinned against
[1]the LORD.

8. 1 saith the LORD = [is] Jehovah's oracle.
the LORD. Heb. Jehovah. Ap. 4. II.
bones. Note the Fig. *Repetitio* (Ap. 6), for emphasis.
and. Note the Fig. *Polysyndeton* (Ap. 6), to emphasise each class as responsible for the corruption and apostasy.
2 and. Particularising here the details of the idolatry.
not be gathered. Cp. 2 Sam. 21. 13.
3 evil. Heb. *rā'a'.* Ap. 44. viii.
saith the LORD of hosts. See note on 6. 6. Cp. 1 Sam. 1. 3.

8. 4-9 (K², p. 1028). INCRIMINATION. IMPENITENCE. (*Repeated Alternation.*)

K² | b¹ | 4, 5-. Question.
  c¹ | -5-7. Answer.
 b² | 8-. Question.
  c² | -8-9-. Answer.
 b³ | -9. Question.

4 arise = rise up again.
he turn away, and. The *Massōrah* (vol. II, p. 54, Ginsburg's edition) calls attention to the fact that of the two words represented by "turn" and "and", the first letter of the second word belongs to the first word; so that this latter will read "shall they return [to Him], and He not return [to them]? It is the same word (in Heb.) in both clauses.
6 no man. Fig. *Synecdoche* (of Genus), Ap. 6 = scarcely any. **man.** Heb. *'ish.* Ap. 14. II. Cp. 5. 1.
wickedness. Heb. *rā'a'.* Ap. 44. viii.
7 knoweth. Put by Fig. *Metonymy* (of Cause), Ap. 6, for the effect of acting on the knowledge.
turtle = turtle-dove. **8 Lo.** Fig. *Asterismos.* Ap. 6.
9 rejected. The second of four downward steps. See note on 6. 10.
10 give their wives unto others. Ref. to Pent. (Deut. 28. 30). Ap. 92.
inherit = seize; or, to their dispossessors.
from. Some codices, with two early printed editions, and Syr., read "and from".
prophet . . . priest. The former, raised up on account of the failure of the latter, now of one accord.
11 hurt = breach.
Peace, peace = perfect peace. Fig. *Epizeuxis.* Ap. 6. Cp. 6. 14 and Isa. 26. 3.
12 could they blush. See note on 6. 15.
the time of their visitation. A phrase ("time" or "year") used eight times in Jeremiah (8. 12; 10. 15; 11. 23; 23. 12; 46. 21; 48. 44; 50. 27; 51. 18). Nowhere else, except Isa. 10. 3. Hos. 9. 7. Mic. 7. 4, until our Lord used it in Luke 19. 44.
13 surely consume them. Note the Fig. *Paronomasia* (Ap. 6). Heb. *'āṣōph 'ăsīphēm.*
on the vine. See note on 6. 9.
shall fade = is withered.
the things . . . from them: or, I have appointed them those that shall pass over them.

8. 14—9. 9 (B, p. 1026). INVASION. (*Alternation.*)

B | N¹ | 8. 14-16. The Prophet. Sorrow.
  O¹ | 8. 17. Jehovah. Threatening.
 N² | 8. 18. The Prophet. Sorrow.
  O² | 8. 19. Jehovah. Threatening.
 N³ | 8. 20—9. 9. The Prophet. Sorrow.

14 Why . . .? Fig. *Erotēsis.* Ap. 6. *Vv.* 14-16 spoken by the prophet, not the People. They were being threatened for not doing what is here spoken of, *vv.* 12, 13. Moreover, *v.* 15 is spoken by Jeremiah in 14. 19, which is an earlier passage, chronologically.
we: i.e. the prophet to the People.
God. Heb. Elohim. Ap. 4. I.
silence. Fig. *Ploke* (Ap. 6), the word being used in a different sense.
water of gall = poppy water; = poisoned water.
sinned. Heb. *chāṭā'.* Ap. 44. i.

518-500 15 We looked for peace, but no good *came;* *and* for a time of health, and behold °trouble!

16 The snorting of his horses was heard from °Dan: the whole land trembled at the sound of the neighing of his strong ones; for they are come, and have devoured the land, and all that is in it; the city, and those that dwell therein.

O[1] (p. 1029) 17 "For, °behold, I will send serpents, °cockatrices, among you, which °*will* not *be* charmed, and they shall bite you, [1]saith [1]the LORD."

N[2] 18 (*When* °I would comfort myself against sorrow, my heart *is* faint in me.)

O[2] 19 [17]"Behold the voice of the cry of the daughter of My People because of them that dwell in a far country: *Is* not [1]the LORD in Zion? *is* not her king in her? Why have they °provoked Me to anger with their °graven images, *and* with strange °vanities?"

N[3] P[1] (p. 1030) 20 The harvest is past, the summer is ended, and we are not saved.

21 For the [11]hurt of the daughter of my People am I hurt; I am black; astonishment hath taken hold on me.

22 *Is there* no °balm in °Gilead; *is there* no °physician there? why then is not the health of the daughter of my People recovered?

9 °Oh that my head were °waters, and mine eyes a °fountain of °tears, that I might weep day and night for the °slain of the daughter of my People!

2 Oh that I had in the wilderness a lodging place of wayfaring men; that I might leave my People, and go from them!

P[2] d "for they *be* all adulterers, an assembly of treacherous men.

3 And they °bend their tongues *like* their bow *for* lies: but they are not valiant for the °truth upon the earth; for they proceed from °evil to °evil, and they know not Me, °saith °the LORD.

4 Take ye heed every one of his °neighbour, and °trust ye not in any brother: for °every brother will utterly °supplant, and every °neighbour will walk with slanders.

5 And they will deceive every one his [4]neighbour, and will not speak the truth: they have taught their tongue to speak lies, *and* weary themselves to commit °iniquity.

6 Thine habitation *is* in the midst of deceit; through deceit they refuse to know Me, [3]saith [3]the LORD.

e 7 Therefore thus saith °the [3]LORD of hosts, 'Behold, I will melt them, and try them; for °how shall I do °for the daughter of My People?

d 8 Their tongue *is as* an arrow °shot out; it speaketh deceit: *one* speaketh peaceably to his neighbour with his mouth, but in heart he layeth his wait.

e 9 Shall I not visit them for these *things?* [3]saith [3]the LORD: shall not °My soul be °avenged on such a nation as this?

D f 10 For the mountains will I take up a weeping and wailing, and for the °habitations of the wilderness a lamentation, because they are burned up, so that none can pass through *them;* neither can *men* hear the voice of the cattle; both the fowl of the heavens and the beast are fled; they are gone.

11 And I will make Jerusalem heaps, *and* a den of °dragons; and I will make the cities of Judah desolate, without an inhabitant." g

12 °Who *is* the wise °man, that may understand this? and °*who is he* to whom the h

---

15 trouble = terror.

16 Dan. The Assyrians entered the land from the north.

17 behold. Fig. *Asterismos.* Ap. 6.

cockatrices = adders.

will not be charmed. This shows that the People were not penitent, and *vv.* 14-16 are not their words.

18 I: i.e. the prophet again.

19 provoked . . . vanities. Ref. to Pent. (Deut. 32. 21, same word). Cp. 7. 19. See Ap. 92.

graven images. Ref. to Pent. (Deut. 7. 5, same word). Ap. 92.

8. 20—9. 9 (N[3], p. 1029). THE PROPHET. SORROW. (*Division.*)

N[3] | P[1] | 8. 20—9. 2-. The Prophet's sorrow.
| P[2] | 9. -2-9. The reasons for it.

22 balm . . . physician. The words of the prophet, showing that healing remedies were employed; thus accounting for the silence respecting them. Cp. Isa. 1. 6.

balm = balsam. Cp. 51. 8. Gilead. Cp. 46. 11.

9. 1 Oh that, &c. Fig. *Pathopœia.* Ap. 6.

waters . . . fountain . . . tears. Fig. *Catabasis.* Ap. 6.

slain. Not healed by "balm" or "physician".

-2-9 (P[2], above). THE REASONS FOR THE PROPHET'S SORROW. (*Alternation.*)

P[2] | d | -2-6. Incrimination. Deceit.
| e | 7. Threatening. Trial.
| *d* | 8. Incrimination. Deceit.
| *e* | 9. Threatening. Vengeance.

3 bend: or, prepare. truth = veracity.

evil. Heb. *rā'a'.* Ap. 44. viii.

saith the LORD = [is] Jehovah's oracle.

the LORD. Heb. Jehovah. Ap. 4. II.

4 neighbour = friend.

trust ye not = do not confide. Heb. *bāṭaḥ.* Ap. 69. i.

every brother . . . supplant. Ref. to Pent. (Gen. 25. 26; 27. 36). Ap. 92.

5 iniquity. Heb. *'āvāh.* Ap. 44. iv.

7 the LORD of hosts. See note on 6. 6 and 1 Sam. 1. 3.

how shall = how [else] shall, &c.

for the daughter: or, because of [the wickedness of] the daughter, &c.

8 shot out. Heb. = piercing. But some codices, with two early printed editions, and Syr., read "pointed".

9 My soul = I myself (emphatic). Heb. *nephesh.* Ap. 13. Fig. *Anthropopatheia.* Ap. 6.

avenged. Cp. 5. 9, 29.

9. 10-26 (*D*, p. 1026). CALL FOR LAMENTATION. (*Extended Alternation.*)

D | f | 10. Lamentation.
| g | 11. Threatening. Places.
| h | 12-14. The wise. Call.
| i | 15, 16. Dispersion among the nations.
| *f* | 17-21. Lamentation.
| *g* | 22. Threatening. Persons.
| *h* | 23, 24. The wise. Exhortation.
| *i* | 25, 26. Dispersion with the nations.

10 habitations = pastures.

11 dragons = jackals.

12 Who . . .? Fig. *Erotēsis.* Ap. 6.

man. Heb. *'īsh.* Ap. 14. II.

who . . .? The Ellipsis is thus correctly supplied.

518-500 mouth of [3]the LORD hath spoken, that he may
declare it, for what the land perisheth *and* is
burned up like a wilderness, that none passeth
through?'
13 And [3]the LORD saith, 'Because they have
°forsaken °My law which I °set before them,
and have not obeyed My voice, neither walked
°therein;
14 But have walked after the °imagination
of their own heart, and after Baalim, which
their fathers taught them:
i 15 Therefore thus saith °the LORD of hosts,
p. 1030) the God of Israel; °Behold, I will feed them,
even this people, with °wormwood, and give
them °water of °gall to drink.
16 °I will scatter them also among the °heathen, whom neither they nor their fathers have
known: and I will send a sword after them,
till I have consumed them.'
f 17 °Thus saith [7]the LORD of hosts, 'Consider
ye, and call for the °mourning women, that
they may come; and send for °cunning *women*,
that they may come:
18 And let them make haste, and take up
a wailing for us, that our eyes may run down
with tears, and our eyelids gush out with
waters.
19 For a voice of wailing is heard out of
Zion, °How are we spoiled! we are greatly
confounded, because we have forsaken the land,
°because °our dwellings have cast *us* out.'"
20 °Yet hear the word of [3]the LORD, O ye
°women, and let your ear receive the word of
His mouth, and teach your daughters wailing,
and every one her neighbour lamentation.
21 For death is come up into our windows,
and is entered into our palaces, to cut off the
°children from without, *and* the young men
from the °streets.
g 22 °Speak, "Thus saith [3]the LORD, 'Even the
carcases of °men shall fall as dung upon the
°open field, and as the handful after the harvestman, and °none shall gather *them*.'
h 23 °Thus saith [3]the LORD, °'Let not the
wise *man* glory in his °wisdom, neither °let
the mighty *man* glory in his °might, °let not
the rich *man* glory in his °riches:
24 But °**let him that glorieth glory in this,
that he understandeth and °knoweth Me, that
I *am* the LORD** °Which exercise °lovingkindness, °judgment, and righteousness, in the
earth: for in these *things* I delight, [3]saith
[3]the LORD.
i 25 [15]Behold, the days come, [3]saith [3]the
LORD, that I will punish all *them which are*
°circumcised °with the uncircumcised;
26 Egypt, and Judah, and Edom, and the
°children of Ammon, and Moab, and all °*that
are* in the utmost corners, that dwell in the
wilderness: for all *these* nations *are* °uncircumcised, and all °the house of Israel *are* uncircumcised in the heart.'"

C j 10 Hear ye the word which °the LORD
p. 1032) speaketh unto you, O °house of Israel:

13 forsaken. Ref. to Pent. (Deut. 32. 15, 21). Ap. 92.
My law. Ref. to Pent. (Ex. 20, &c.). Ap. 92.
set before them. Ref. to Pent. (Deut. 4. 8, 44). Ap. 92.
therein. In the law, not the voice.
14 imagination = stubbornness. Ref. to Pent. (see note on 3. 17). Ap. 92.
15 the LORD of hosts, the God of Israel. See note on 7. 3.
Behold. Fig. *Asterismos*. Ap. 6.
wormwood . . . gall. Ref. to Pent. (Deut. 29. 18). Repeated in 23. 15. Occurs also in Lam. 3. 19. Amos 6. 12.
water of gall. Cp. 8. 14.
16 I will scatter. Ref. to Pent. (Lev. 26. 33. Deut. 28. 64). Ap. 92.
heathen = nations.
17 Thus saith, &c. This (*vv.* 17-20) develops the calamity, for which this chapter gives the reason.
mourning women. A class still hired for the purpose. Cp. 2 Sam. 1. 24. 2 Chron. 35. 25. Eccles. 12. 5. Matt. 9. 23. Mark 5. 38.
cunning = skilful (in this business).
19 How . . . ! Supply *Ellipsis*: "[saying], How is it", &c.
because. Some codices, with three early printed editions (one Rabbinic), read "yea, for", or "for indeed".
our dwellings, &c.: or, they have cast down our habitations. Cp. Dan. 8. 11. Job 8. 18. Ezek. 19. 12.
20 Yet: or, For, or Yea.
women. These had been largely the instrumental cause; now they share the calamities.
21 children = infant.
streets . . .
22 Speak. This shows that Jerome's Heb. text was unpointed, for he read d-b-r as *deber* = pestilence, instead of *dābār* = word, or *dabbēr* = speak.
men. Heb. *'ādām* (with Art.). Ap. 14. I.
open field. Some codices, with one early printed edition, read "ground".
none shall gather them. Cp. Ps. 79. 3.
23 Thus saith, &c. The lesson which follows is of universal application.
Let not. Note the Fig. *Symplokē*, or *Anaphora* (Ap. 6), for emphasis.
wisdom . . . might . . . riches. These are the three things which men boast of, and trust in. This was Jerusalem's sin.
let not. Some codices, with six early printed editions (one in margin), Aram., Sept., Syr., and Vulg., read "neither let".
24 let him, &c. Quoted in 1 Cor. 1. 31.
knoweth Me. This lies at the foundation of everything: of all trust in God (for One unknown cannot be trusted at all); of all pleasing (Eph. 1. 17. Col. 1. 9, 10. 1 John 5. 20). The want of it led to Gentile corruption (Rom. 1. 28); to Israel's fall (Isa. 1. 3. Luke 19. 42, 44); and all future blessing is wrapt up in it: for Israel (31. 34. Isa. 54. 13); and for creation (Isa. 11. 9). This is why we have the written Word (2 Tim. 3. 15), and the living "Word" (John 1. 18).
Which exercise, &c. Ref. to Pent. (Ex. 34. 6). Ap. 92.
lovingkindness = favour shown to the unworthy.
judgment = justice to the oppressed. One school of Massorites (Ap. 30) read "and justice", emphasising the statement by the Fig. *Polysyndeton*. Ap. 6.
25 circumcised, &c.: in the flesh, but not in "ears" (6. 10), nor in "heart" (4. 4). Ref. to Pent. (Lev. 26. 41, 42. Deut. 10. 16; 30. 6). Elsewhere only in Ezek. 44. 7, 9.
with the uncircumcised = circumcised in uncircumcision: i. e. "circumcised [externally] who [are yet really] uncircumcised", as explained at the end of the next verse. Hence the contrast with the nations mentioned, which all practised (external) circumcision (Rom. 2. 25-29).
26 children = sons.
that are in the utmost corners: or, all that have the corners of their beard polled. Ref. to Pent. (Lev. 19. 27). Ap. 92. Cp. Jer. 49. 32.
uncircumcised. Supply *Ellipsis* (Ap. 6), from the next clause: "uncircumcised [in heart], and all", &c.
the house of Israel. See note on 2. 4.

10. 1-16 [For Structure see next page].

1 the LORD. Heb. Jehovah. Ap. 4. II.
house of Israel. See note on 2. 4.

518-500 2 "Thus saith [1]the LORD, 'Learn not °the
way of the °heathen, and be not dismayed at
the signs of heaven; for the °heathen are
dismayed at them.
3 For the °customs of the °people *are* °vain:
for °*one* cutteth a tree out of the forest, the
work of the hands of the workman, with the
axe.
4 They deck it with silver and with gold;
they fasten it with nails and with hammers,
that it move not.
5 They *are* °upright as the palm tree, but
speak not: they must needs be °borne, because
they cannot go. Be not afraid of them; for
they cannot do °evil, neither also *is it* in them to
do good.' "
k 6 Forasmuch as °*there is* none like unto Thee,
(p. 1032) O [1]LORD; Thou *art* great, and °Thy name *is*
great in might.
7 °**Who would not fear Thee, O King of
nations?** for to Thee doth it appertain: forasmuch as among all the wise *men* of the nations,
and in all their kingdoms, [6]*there is* none like
unto Thee.
l 8 But they are altogether brutish and foolish:
the stock *is* a doctrine of vanities.
j 9 Silver spread into plates is brought from
°Tarshish, and gold from °Uphaz, the work
of the workman, and of the hands of the
founder: blue and purple *is* their clothing:
they *are* all the work of cunning *men*.
k 10 But [1]the LORD *is* the true °God, He *is*
°the living °God, and an °everlasting king: at
His wrath the earth shall tremble, and the
nations shall not be able to abide His indignation.
11 °Thus shall ye say unto them, "The gods
that have °not made the heavens and the
earth, *even* they °shall perish from the earth,
and from under these heavens.
12 He hath made the earth by His power, He
hath established the °world by His wisdom,
and hath stretched out the heavens by His
°discretion.
13 When He uttereth His voice, *there is*
a multitude of waters in the heavens, and He
causeth the vapours to ascend from the ends
of the earth; He maketh lightnings with rain,
and bringeth forth the °wind out of His
treasures.
l 14 Every °man is brutish in *his* knowledge:
every founder is °confounded by the graven
image: for his molten image *is* falsehood, and
there is no °breath in them.
15 They *are* °vanity, *and* the work of °errors:
in °the time of their visitation they shall
perish.
16 °The Portion of °Jacob *is* not like them:
for He *is* the °Former of all *things;* and Israel
is the rod of His inheritance: °The [1]LORD of
hosts *is* His name."
B 17 °Gather up thy °wares out of the land, O
°inhabitant of the °fortress.
18 For thus saith [1]the LORD, °"Behold, °I
will sling out the inhabitants of the land at
this once, and will distress them, that they
may °find *it so*."
19 Woe is °me for my hurt! my wound is
grievous: but I said, "Truly this *is* °a grief,
°and I must bear it."
20 My °tabernacle is spoiled, and all my
cords are broken: my °children are gone forth
of me, and they *are* not: *there is* none to
stretch forth my tent any more, and to set up
my curtains.
21 For the °pastors °are become brutish, and
have not sought °the LORD: therefore they
shall not prosper, and all their flocks shall be
scattered.

10. 1-16 (*C*, p. 1026). EXHORTATION.
(*Extended Alternation.*)

C | j | 1-5. Idolatry.
  k | 6, 7. Jehovah the true God.
   l | 8. Stupidity of idolaters.
 j | 9. Idolatry.
  k | 10-13. Jehovah the true God.
   l | 14-16. Stupidity of idolaters.

2 the way of the heathen. Ref. to Pent. (Lev. 18. 3; 20. 23). Ap. 92. **heathen** = nations.
3 customs = statutes, or ordinances.
people = peoples. **vain** = a breath.
one cutteth a tree = it [is only] a tree which one cutteth. **5 upright** = stiff.
borne = carried. **evil.** Heb. *rā'a'*. Ap. 44. viii.
6 there is none like, &c. See note on Ex. 15. 11.
Thy name. See note on Ps. 20. 1.
7 Who . . . ? Words quoted in "the song of Moses and the Lamb" (Rev. 15. 3, 4).
9 Tarshish. See note on 1 Kings 10. 22.
Uphaz. Probably = Ophir. Cp. 1 Kings 9. 28; 10. 11.
10 God. Heb. Elohim. Ap. 4. I.
the living God. Both words in plural, referring to the triune God.
everlasting king = king of the ages, or, of eternity.
11 Thus shall ye say, &c. This verse is in Chaldee, to serve as a confession of their faith in their exile.
not made . . . shall perish. Note the Fig. *Paronomasia*. Ap. 6. Heb. *'ābadū ye'badū*.
12 world = the habitable world. Heb. *tēbēl*.
discretion = understanding.
13 wind. Heb. *rūach*. Ap. 9.
14 man. Heb. *'ādām*. Ap. 14. I.
confounded = put to shame.
breath. Heb. *rūach*. Ap. 9.
15 vanity. The common appellative for idols.
errors = mockeries.
the time of their visitation. See note on 8. 12.
16 The Portion of Jacob. Ref. to Pent. (Num. 18. 20. Deut. 32. 9). Ap. 92.
Jacob. Not Israel, because the natural seed is spoken of as in Deut. 32. 9. See notes on Gen. 32. 28; 43. 6; 45. 26, 28. **Former** = Framer.
The LORD of hosts. See note on 6. 6.
17 Gather up = Gather in. Occurs only here.
wares = bundle. For that is all they would be able to take with them.
inhabitant = inhabitress. Put for "the daughter of Zion".
fortress. Put by Fig. *Metonymy* (of Adjunct), Ap. 6, for the city Jerusalem.
18 Behold. Fig. *Asterismos*. Ap. 6.
I will sling. Put by Fig. *Metonymy* (of Adjunct), Ap. 6, for all that is signified by it. Cp. Isa. 22. 17, 18.
find it so = discover the truth of it.
19 me. Zion now speaks in view of the coming deportation; or, Jeremiah voices the calamity.
a grief: or, my affliction. **and I** = but I.
20 tabernacle = tent, or dwelling.
children = sons.
21 pastors = shepherds, or rulers.
are become. This points to Jehoiakim's reign.
the LORD. Heb. Jehovah (with *'eth*) = Jehovah Himself. Ap. 4. II.

518-500 **22** Behold, the °noise of the °bruit is come,
and a great commotion out of the °north
country, to make the cities of Judah desolate,
and a den of °dragons.
23 O [1]LORD, I know that the way of [14]man
°*is* not in himself: °*it is* not in °man that
walketh to °direct his steps.
24 O [1]LORD, correct me, but °with judgment;
not in Thine anger, lest Thou bring me to
nothing.
25 Pour out Thy fury upon the [2]heathen that
know Thee not, and upon the °families that call
not on °Thy name: for they have eaten up
[16]Jacob, and devoured him, and consumed him,
and have made his habitation desolate.

Q O m **11** The °word that came to Jeremiah from
(p. 1033) °the LORD, saying,
2 "Hear ye °the words of °this covenant,
and speak unto the °men of °Judah, and to the
inhabitants of Jerusalem;
3 And say thou unto them, 'Thus saith °the
LORD °God of °Israel; °Cursed *be* the [2]man
that obeyeth not the words of this covenant,
4 Which I commanded your fathers °in the
day *that* I brought them forth out of the land of
Egypt, °from the iron furnace, saying, °'Obey
My voice, and do °them, according to all which
I command you: so shall ye be My People, and
°I will be your [3]God:
5 That I may perform °the oath which I have
sworn unto your fathers, to give them °a land
flowing with milk and honey, as *it is* this
day.'" Then answered I, and said, °"So be
it, O [1]LORD."
6 Then [1]the LORD said unto me, "Proclaim
all these words °in the cities of [2]Judah, and in
the streets of Jerusalem, saying, 'Hear ye the
words of this covenant, and do them.
7 For I earnestly protested unto your fathers
[4]in the day *that* I brought them up out of the
land of Egypt, *even* unto this day, °rising early
and protesting, saying, [4]'Obey My voice.'
8 Yet they obeyed not, nor inclined their ear,
but walked every one in the °imagination of
their °evil heart:

n therefore I will bring upon them all the words
of this covenant, which I commanded *them* to
do; but they did *them* not.'"

m **9** And [1]the LORD said unto me, "A conspiracy
is found among the [2]men of [2]Judah, and among
the inhabitants of Jerusalem.
10 They are turned back to the °iniquities
of their forefathers, which refused to hear My
words; and they °went after other gods to serve
them: °the house of Israel and °the house of
[2]Judah have broken My covenant which I made
with their fathers.

n **11** Therefore thus saith [1]the LORD, °Behold,
I will bring [8]evil upon them, which they shall
not be able to escape; and though they shall
cry unto Me, I will not hearken unto them.
12 Then shall the cities of [2]Judah and inhabitants of Jerusalem °go, and cry unto the gods
unto whom they offer incense: but they shall
not save them at all in the time of their °trouble.
13 For *according to* the number of thy cities
were thy gods, O [2]Judah; and *according to*
the number of the streets of Jerusalem have ye
set up altars to *that* °shameful thing, *even*
altars to burn incense unto Baal.

22 noise = voice.
bruit = rumour. French *bruit*, a voice, from Breton (Celtic) *bruchellein*, to roar (as a lion). Cp. Gr. *bruchaomai*.
north. Cp. 1. 15; 5. 15; 6. 22, &c.
dragons = jackals.
23 is not in = belongs not to.
it is not. Some codices, with two early printed editions, Aram., Sept., Syr., and Vulg., read "nor".
man. Heb. *'ish*. Ap. 14. II.
direct = establish. **24** with = in.
25 families. Some codices read "kingdoms". Cp. Ps. 79. 6.
Thy name = Thee (emphatic). See note on Ps. 20. 1.

11. 1—12. 17 (*H*, p. 1018). PROPHECIES TO JUDAH AND JERUSALEM. (*Alternation.*)

H | Q | 11. 1-14. Against the People.
R | 11. 15-17. The beloved People threatened.
Q | 11. 18—12. 6. Against the men of Anathoth.
R | 12. 7-17. The beloved People threatened.

11. 1-14 (Q, above). PROPHECIES AGAINST THE PEOPLE. (*Alternation.*)

Q | m | 1-8-. Covenant disobeyed.
n | -8. Threatening.
m | 9, 10. Covenant broken.
n | 11-14. Threatening.

Jeremiah's SEVENTH prophecy (p. 1015).

1 word. Sing., indicating this as a special prophecy.
the LORD. Heb. Jehovah. Ap. 4. II.
2 the words. Pl., indicating the many utterances of "this covenant".
this covenant. The old covenant of Exodus had been specially renewed by Judah in Jeremiah's days, under Josiah, in his eighteenth year (2 Kings 23. 1-3).
men. Heb. *'ish*. Ap. 14. II.
Judah. Emphasised by repeated reference here. Cp. *vv.* 2, 6, 9, 10, 12, 13, 17.
3 the LORD God of Israel. This title occurs in Jeremiah fourteen times (11. 3; 13. 12; 21. 4; 23. 2; 24. 5; 25. 15; 30. 2; 32. 36; 33. 4; 34. 2, 13; 37. 7; 42. 9; 45. 2).
the LORD. Heb. Jehovah. Ap. 4. II.
God. Heb. Elohim. Ap. 4. I.
Israel. Still used of Judah as representing the whole nation. See note on 1 Kings 12. 17.
Cursed be the man, &c. Ref. to Pent. (Deut. 27. 26).
4 in the day. See Ap. 18.
from the iron furnace. Ref. to Pent. (Deut. 4. 20).
Obey = Hear, with *Beth* (= ב = B) = Listen or attend to.
Obey My voice. Ref. to Pent. (Ex. 15. 26). Ap. 92.
them: i.e. "the words" of *v.* 3.
I will be your God. Ref. to Pent. (Lev. 26. 3-12).
5 the oath which I have sworn. Ref. to Pent. (Deut. 7. 12). Ap. 92.
a land flowing with milk and honey. Ref. to Pent. (Ex. 3. 8, 17; 13. 5; 33. 3. Lev. 20. 24. Num. 13. 27; 14. 8; 16. 13, 14. Deut. 6. 3; 11. 9; 26. 9, 15; 27. 3; 31. 20). Outside the Pent. it is found only in Josh. 5. 6. Jer. 11. 4; 32. 22; and Ezek. 20. 6, 15; 25. 4). Ap. 92.
So be it, O LORD. Ref. to Pent. (Deut. 27. 15-26: the same word). Ap. 92.
6 in the cities, &c. Cp. 2. 28, and 11. 13.
7 rising early, &c. See note on 7. 13.
8 imagination = stubbornness.
evil. Heb. *ra'a'*. Ap. 44. viii.
10 iniquities. Heb. *'avah*. Ap. 44. iv.
went = are gone.
the house of Israel. See note on 2. 4.
the house of Judah. See note on 3. 18.
11 Behold. Fig. *Asterismos*. Ap. 6.
12 go, and cry, &c. Ref. to Pent. (Deut. 32. 37, 38).
trouble. Same word as evil (*vv.* 8, 15, 17). So in *v.* 14.
13 shameful thing. Heb. "shame": put by Fig. *Metonymy* (of Effect), Ap. 6, for the idol which was the cause of the shame. Cp. 3. 24.

518-500 14 Therefore °pray not thou for this People,
neither lift up a cry or prayer for them: for I
will not hear *them* in the time that they cry
unto Me °for their [12]trouble.
R (p. 1033) 15 What hath My beloved to do in Mine house,
seeing she hath wrought lewdness with many,
and °the holy flesh °is passed from thee? when
thou doest [8]evil, °then thou rejoicest.
16 [1]The LORD called thy name, A green °olive
tree, fair, *and* of goodly fruit: with the noise
of a great tumult He hath kindled fire upon it,
and the branches of it are broken.
17 For °the LORD of hosts, That planted thee,
hath pronounced [8]evil against thee, for the [8]evil
of [10]the house of Israel and of [10]the house of
[2]Judah, which they have °done against themselves to provoke Me to anger in offering incense unto Baal."
Q o (p. 1034) 18 And [1]the LORD °hath given me knowledge
of it, and I °know *it*: then thou shewedst me
their doings.
19 But I *was* °like a lamb *or* an ox *that* is
brought to the slaughter; and I knew not that
they had devised devices against me, °*saying*,
"Let us destroy °the tree with the fruit thereof,
and let us cut him off °from the land of the living,
that his name may be no more remembered."
20 But, O [17]LORD of hosts, That judgest
righteously, That °triest the reins and the
heart, let me see Thy vengeance on them: for
unto Thee have I revealed my cause.
p 21 Therefore thus saith [1]the LORD °of the
°men of Anathoth, that °seek °thy life, saying,
"Prophesy not in the name of [1]the LORD, that
thou die not by our °hand:"
22 Therefore thus saith [17]the LORD of hosts,
[11]"Behold, I will °punish them: the young men
shall die by the sword; their sons and their
daughters shall die by famine:
23 And there shall be no remnant of them: for
I will bring °evil upon the [21]men of Anathoth,
even °the year of their visitation."
o **12** °Righteous *art* Thou, O °LORD, when I
plead with Thee: yet let me talk with
Thee of *Thy* judgments: °Wherefore doth the
way of the °wicked prosper? *wherefore* are
all they happy that °deal very treacherously?
2 Thou hast planted them, yea, they have
taken root: they grow, yea, they bring forth
fruit: Thou *art* °near in their °mouth, and far
from their °reins.
3 But Thou, O [1]LORD, knowest me: Thou
hast seen me, and tried mine heart toward
Thee: pull them out like sheep for the slaughter, and °prepare them for the day of slaughter.
4 °How long shall the land mourn, and the
herbs of every field wither, for the °wickedness
of them that dwell therein? the beasts are
consumed, and the birds; because they said,
"He shall not see our last end."
p 5 If thou hast run with the footmen, and they
have wearied thee, then how canst thou contend with horses? and *if* in the land of peace,
wherein thou °trustedst, *they wearied thee*, then
how wilt thou do in the °swelling of Jordan?
6 For even thy brethren, and the house of thy
father, even they have dealt treacherously with
thee; yea, they have °called a multitude after
thee: believe them not, though they speak fair
words unto thee.

14 pray not, &c. Ref. to Pent. (Ex. 32. 10). Cp. 7. 16; 14. 11. Ap. 92.

for. Some codices, with one early printed edition, Aram., Sept., Syr., and Vulg., read "in the time of", as in *v.* 12.

15 the holy flesh: i.e. the sacrifices. Cp. 7. 21. Hag. 2. 12. Sept. reads, "shall vows (or litanies) and holy flesh", &c.

is passed from thee? = taketh away from thee [thy wickedness]? or, removeth thy evil (i.e. calamity)?

then thou rejoicest: i.e. if such false worship will remove thy calamity, then thou mayest rejoice; but this was impossible.

16 olive tree. The symbol of Israel's religious privileges. See note on Judg. 9. 8-12.

17 the LORD of hosts. See note on 6. 6. 1 Sam. 1. 3.

done = wrought.

11. 18—12. 6 (*Q*, p. 1033). PROPHECIES AGAINST THE MEN OF ANATHOTH. (*Alternation.*)

Q | o | 11. 18-20. The prophet. Prayer.
p | 11. 21-23. Jehovah's answer. Threatening.
o | 12. 1-4. The prophet. Pleading.
p | 12. 5, 6. Jehovah's answer. Threatening.

18 hath given = gave. Jeremiah a type of Messiah. See Ap. 85. **know** = knew.

19 like a lamb. See Ap. 85.

saying. Note the Fig. *Ellipsis* (Ap. 6), as frequently with this verb. See notes on Pss. 109. 5, 6; 144. 12, &c.

the tree with the fruit thereof. Heb. "the dish in his food". Fig. *Hypallage* (Ap. 6), for the food in his dish.

from the land of the living. Jeremiah a type of Christ. See Isa. 53. 8 and Ap. 85.

20 triest the reins and the heart. Cp. 11. 20; 17. 10; 20. 12. Found elsewhere only in Pss. 7. 9; 26. 2. See Ap. 85. **21 of** = concerning.

men. Heb. pl. of *'ĕnōsh.* Ap. 14. III.

seek = are seeking.

thy life = thy soul. Heb. *nephesh.* Ap. 13.

hand. Some codices, with two early printed editions, Sept., Syr., and Vulg., read "hands".

22 punish = visit upon.

23 evil. Heb. *rā'a'.* Ap. 44. viii.

the year of their visitation. See note on 8. 12.

12. 1 Righteous, &c. Fig. *Synchorēsis.* Ap. 6.

LORD. Heb. Jehovah. Ap. 4. II.

Wherefore . . .? Fig. *Erotēsis.* Ap. 6.

wicked = lawless. Heb. *rāsha'.* Ap. 44. x.

deal very treacherously. Fig. *Polyptōton.* Ap. 6. Heb. are traitors of treachery = are utter traitors.

2 near. Anathoth was a city of priests.

mouth. Put by Fig. *Metonymy* (of Cause), Ap. 6, for the words uttered by it.

reins = kidneys. Put by Fig. *Metonymy* (of Subject), Ap. 6, for the affections.

3 prepare = separate, or devote.

4 How long . . .? Fig. *Erotēsis.* Ap. 6.

wickedness = lawlessness. Heb. *rāsha'.* Ap. 44. x.

5 trustedst = confidedst. Heb. *bataḥ.* Ap. 69. i.

swelling. Heb. pride. Put by Fig. *Metonymy* (of Adjunct), Ap. 6, for proud beasts in the undergrowth on the banks of the Jordan. See 49. 19; 50. 44, and cp. Job 41. 34. **6 called** = called loudly.

12. 7-17 (*R*, p. 1033). THE BELOVED PEOPLE THREATENED. (*Division.*)

R | S^1 | 7-13. The beloved People. Themselves.
| S^2 | 14-17. The beloved People. Their enemies.

7 the dearly beloved. Heb. love. Put by Fig. *Metonymy* (of Adjunct), Ap. 6, for one loved.

My soul = I Myself (emphatic). Heb. *nephesh.* Ap. 13. Fig. *Anthropopatheia.* Ap. 6.

7 I have forsaken Mine house, I have left R S^1
Mine heritage; I have given °the dearly beloved
of °My soul into the hand of her enemies.

518-500 8 Mine heritage °is unto Me as a lion in the forest: it crieth out against Me: therefore have I hated it.

9 Mine heritage *is* unto Me *as* a °speckled bird, the birds round about *are* against her; come ye, assemble all the beasts of the field, come to devour.

10 Many °pastors have destroyed My vineyard, they have trodden °My portion under foot, they have made My °pleasant portion a desolate wilderness.

11 They have made it desolate, *and being* desolate it mourneth unto Me; the whole land is made desolate, because no °man layeth *it* to heart.

12 The spoilers are come upon all °high places through the wilderness: for the sword of [1]the LORD shall devour from the *one* end of the land even to the *other* end of the land: no flesh shall have peace.

13 They have sown wheat, but shall reap thorns: they have put themselves to pain, °*but* shall not profit: and they shall be ashamed of your °revenues because of the fierce anger of [1]the LORD.

S[2] (p. 1034) 14 Thus saith [1]the LORD against all Mine evil °neighbours, that touch the inheritance which I have caused My people Israel °to inherit; "Behold, I will pluck them out of their land, and pluck out the house of Judah from among them.

15 And it shall come to pass, after that I have plucked them out I will return, and have compassion on them, and will bring °them again, °every man to his heritage, and °every man to his land.

16 And it shall come to pass, if they will diligently learn the ways of My People, to swear by My name, [1]The LORD liveth; °as they taught My People to swear by Baal; then shall they be °built in the midst of My People.

17 But if they will not °obey, I will utterly pluck up and destroy that nation, °saith [1]the LORD."

T V[1] W (p. 1035) **13** Thus saith °the LORD unto me, "Go and get thee °a linen girdle, and put it upon thy loins, and put it °not in water."

2 So I °got a girdle according to the word of [1]the LORD, and put *it* on my loins.

3 And the word of [1]the LORD came unto me the second time, saying,

4 "Take the girdle that thou hast got, which *is* upon thy loins, and arise, go to °Euphrates, and hide it there in a hole of the rock."

5 So I went, and hid it by Euphrates, °as [1]the LORD commanded me.

6 And it came to pass after many days, that [1]the LORD said unto me, "Arise, go to Euphrates, and take the girdle from thence, which I commanded thee to hide there."

7 Then I went to Euphrates, and digged, and took the girdle from the place where I had hid it:

X q and, °behold, the girdle was marred,

r °it was profitable for nothing.

X q 8 Then the word of [1]the LORD came unto me, saying,

9 "Thus saith [1]the LORD, After this manner will I °mar the pride of Judah, and the great pride of Jerusalem.

r 10 This °evil People, which refuse to hear My words, which walk in the °imagination of their heart, and walk after other gods, to serve them, and to worship them, shall even be as this girdle, which is good for nothing.

W 11 For [5]as the girdle cleaveth to the loins of a °man, so have I caused to cleave unto Me the whole °house of Israel and the whole °house of Judah, °saith [1]the LORD; °that

---

8 is=is become.
9 speckled bird=a bird of prey.
10 pastors. Used of rulers. See note on 2. 8; 3. 15.
My portion. One Codex (Dr. Ginsburg's "G. 1") reads "My possession".
pleasant portion. Heb. portion of desire=my desired portion. **11 man.** Heb. *'īsh.* Ap. 14. II.
12 high=eminent.
13 but. Some codices, with three early printed editions, Syr., and Vulg., read "but" in the text.
revenues=produce.
14 neighbours. Egypt, Edom, Philistia, Ammon, and Moab.
to inherit. Ref. to Pent. (Ex. 32. 13). Ap. 92.
15 them. A.V. 1611 omits this word.
every man. Heb. *'īsh.* Ap. 14. II.
16 as=according as.
built=rebuilt. See note on Num. 13. 22.
17 obey=hearken.
saith the LORD=[is] Jehovah's oracle.

13. 1–17. 18 (G, p. 1018). SYMBOLS.
(*Alternation.*)

G | T | 13. 1–27. Symbolical. Girdle. Bottles.
  | U | 14. 1—15. 21. Literal. Drought.
  | *T* | 16. 1–21. Symbolical. No wife.
  | *U* | 17. 1–18. Literal. Sin of Judah.

13. 1–27 (T, above). SYMBOLS. GIRDLE. BOTTLES. (*Division.*)

T | V[1] | 1–11. The Girdle.
  | V[2] | 12–14. The Bottles.
  | V[3] | 15–27. The Signification.

13. 1–11 (V[1], above). THE GIRDLE.
(*Introversion and Alternation.*)

V[1] | W | 1–7–. The Girdle caused to cleave. }
  | X | q | –7–. Girdle marred. } Symbol.
  | | r | –7. Girdle useless. }
  | *X* | *q* | 8, 9. People marred. }
  | | *r* | 10. People useless. } Signification.
  | *W* | 11. The People caused to cleave. }

1 the LORD. Heb. Jehovah. Ap. 4. II.
a linen girdle. Soft girdles, made of silk or linen, still worn by upper classes. Cp. Ezek. 16. 10. Some embroidered (Dan. 10. 5. Rev. 1. 13; 15. 6).
not in water. So that the cause of its marring be not mistaken. **2 got**=bought.

Jeremiah's EIGHTH Prophecy (p. 1015).

4 Euphrates. On the road to Babylon, this river would be first met with at Carchemish, then held by the Egyptians (46. 2).
5 as=according as.
7 behold. Fig. *Asterismos.* Ap. 6.
it was. Some codices, with one early printed edition, read "and it was".

Jeremiah's NINTH Prophecy (p. 1015).

9 mar the pride, &c. Ref. to Pent. (Lev. 26. 19). Ap. 92.
10 evil. Heb. *rā'a'.* Ap. 44. viii.
imagination=stubbornness.
11 man. Heb. *'īsh.* Ap. 14. II.
house of Israel. See note on 2. 4.
house of Judah. See note on 3. 18.
saith the LORD=[is] Jehovah's oracle.
that they might be unto Me for a people. Ref. to Pent. (Ex. 19. 5). Ap. 92.

490 or 489? they might be unto Me for a People, and for a name, and for a praise, and for a glory: but they would not hear.

V² Y¹ (p. 1036) 12 Therefore thou shalt speak unto them this word; 'Thus saith °the [1]LORD °God of Israel, Every °bottle shall be filled with °wine:' and they shall say unto thee, 'Do we not certainly know that every °bottle shall be filled with °wine?'

Y² 13 Then shalt thou say unto them, 'Thus saith [1]the LORD, [7]Behold, I will fill all the inhabitants of this land, even the kings that sit upon David's throne, and the priests, and the prophets, and all the inhabitants of Jerusalem, with drunkenness.
14 And I will dash them one against another, even the fathers and the sons together, [11]saith [1]the LORD: I will not pity, nor spare, nor have mercy, but destroy them.' "

V³ Z¹ s 15 Hear °ye, and give ear; be not proud: for [1]the LORD °hath spoken.
16 Give glory to [1]the LORD your [12]God, before He cause °darkness, and before your feet stumble upon the dark mountains, and, while ye look for light, He turn it into the shadow of death, *and* make *it* gross darkness.
17 But if ye will not hear it, °my soul shall °weep in secret places for *your* pride; and mine eye shall °weep sore, and °run down with tears,

t because [1]the LORD'S flock is carried away captive.

s 18 Say unto °the king and to the °queen, "Humble yourselves, sit down: for your °principalities shall come down, *even* the crown of your glory.
19 The °cities of °the south shall be shut up, and none shall open *them:* Judah shall be carried away captive all of it, it shall be wholly carried away captive.

t 20 Lift up your eyes, and behold them that come from °the north: where *is* the flock *that* was given thee, thy beautiful flock?

Z² u 21 What wilt thou say when He shall punish thee?

v for thou hast taught them *to be* captains, *and* as chief over thee: shall not sorrows take thee, [5]as a woman in travail?

u 22 And if thou say in thine heart, 'Wherefore come these things upon me?'

v For the greatness of thine °iniquity are thy skirts discovered, *and* thy heels made bare.
23 °Can the Ethiopian change his skin, or the leopard his spots? *then* may ye also do good, that are °accustomed to do °evil.
24 Therefore will I scatter them as the °stubble that passeth away by the °wind of the wilderness.
25 This *is* thy lot, the portion of thy measures from Me, [11]saith [1]the LORD; because thou hast forgotten Me, and °trusted in falsehood.
26 Therefore will I discover thy skirts upon thy face, that thy shame may appear.
27 I have seen thine adulteries, and thy neighings, the lewdness of thy whoredom, *and* thine abominations on the hills in the fields.
Woe unto thee, O Jerusalem! wilt thou not be made clean? °when *shall it* once *be?"*

14 °The word of °the LORD that came to Jeremiah concerning °the dearth. U A¹

---

13. 12-14 (V², p. 1035). THE BOTTLES.
(*Division.*)

V² | Y¹ | 12. Symbol. Bottles filled.
| Y² | 13, 14. Signification. People filled.

12 the LORD God of Israel. See note on 11. 3.
God. Heb. Elohim. Ap. 4. I.
bottle = an earthenware jar: not leathern or skin bottles. **wine.** Heb. *yayin.* Ap. 27. I.

13. 15-27 (V³, p. 1035). THE SIGNIFICATION.
(*Division.*)

V³ | Z¹ | 15-20. Pride.
| Z² | 21-27. Punishment.

13. 15-20 (Z¹, above). PRIDE.
(*Alternation.*)

Z¹ | s | 15-17-. Exhortation.
| t | -17. Jehovah's flock.
| *s* | 18, 19. Exhortation.
| *t* | 20. Jehovah's flock.

15 ye. Now addressing all.
hath spoken. Jehovah's words, not Jeremiah's.
16 darkness. Heb. *nesheph.* A *Homonym*, with two meanings (darkness and daylight). See note on 1 Sam. 30. 17.
17 my soul = Me (emphatic). Heb. *nephesh.* Ap. 13. Fig. *Anthropopatheia.* Ap. 6.
weep . . . weep sore . . . run down. Fig. *Anabasis.* Ap. 6.
run down, &c. Cp. Matt. 26. 38. Luke 19. 41. See Ap. 85.
18 the king and to the queen. This was Jehoiachin, and the queen-mother. See 2 Kings 24. 12, 15. Jehoiachin was only eighteen, so that the queen-dowager would hold a position of some influence (490, or 489 B.C.).
principalities = head-gear.
19 cities. So in Codex "Mugah"; but Codex "Hallel" (both quoted in the *Massōrah*) reads "eyes".
the south = the Negeb. See note on Ps. 126. 4. Cp. Gen. 12. 9; 13. 3.
20 the north. See notes on 1. 13; 3. 12; 6. 1, &c.

13. 21-27 (Z², above). PUNISHMENT.
(*Alternation.*)

Z² | u | 21-. Question. "What . . . ?"
| v | -21. Answer. Reason.
| *u* | 22-. Question. "Wherefore . . . ?"
| *v* | -22-27. Answer. Reason.

22 iniquity. Heb. *'āvāh.* Ap. 44. iv.
23 Can . . . ? Fig. *Erotēsis* and *Parœmia.* Ap. 6.
accustomed = schooled, or trained.
evil. Heb. *ra'a'.* Ap. 44. viii.
24 stubble = (Heb. *kash*), not crushed straw (Heb. *teben*). **wind.** Heb. *rūach.* Ap. 9.
25 trusted = confided. Heb. *bāṭah.* Ap. 69. i.
27 when shall it once be? = how long ere it yet be?

14. 1—15. 21 (U, p. 1035). LITERAL. DROUGHT.

U | A¹ | 14. 1-6. Mourning of Judah.
| A² | 14. 7—15. 21. Intercession.

Jeremiah's TENTH Prophecy (p. 1015).

1 The word, &c. = That which proved to be the word of Jehovah. Not the usual phrase in the Hebrew.
the LORD. Heb. Jehovah. Ap. 4. II.
the dearth. Heb. "*the restraints*": the holding back of rain, put by Fig. *Metonymy* (of Cause), Ap. 6, for the famine caused by it. One of thirteen recorded famines. See Gen. 12. 10. Ref. to Pent. (Deut. 28. 23, 24). Ap. 92. Before the *first* siege (497 B.C.), or before the *third* siege (480 B.C.). See Ap. 83.

97 or 480 2 °Judah mourneth, and the °gates thereof languish; they °are black unto the ground; and the cry of °Jerusalem is gone up.

3 And their nobles have sent their little ones °to the waters: they came to the pits, °*and* found no water; they returned with their vessels empty; they were ashamed and confounded, and °covered their heads.

4 Because the ground is °chapt, for there was no rain in the earth, the plowmen were °ashamed, they [3] covered their heads.

5 °Yea, the hind also calved in the field, and forsook *it*, because there was no grass.

6 And the wild asses did stand in the high places, they snuffed up the °wind like °dragons; their eyes did fail, because *there was* no grass.

A² B (p. 1037) 7 O [1] LORD, though our °iniquities °testify against us, do Thou *it* for Thy name's sake: for our backslidings are many; we have °sinned against Thee.

8 O °the Hope of Israel, the Saviour thereof in time of trouble, why shouldest Thou be as a °stranger in the land, and as a wayfaring man *that* turneth aside to tarry for a night?

9 Why shouldest Thou be as a °man astonied, as a mighty man *that* cannot save? yet Thou, O [1] LORD, *art* °in the midst of us, and °we are called by Thy name; leave us not.

C 10 Thus saith [1] the LORD unto this People, "Thus have they loved to wander, they have not refrained their feet, therefore [1] the LORD doth not accept them; He will now remember their [7] iniquity, and visit their [7] sins."

11 Then said [1] the LORD unto me, °"Pray not for this People for *their* good.

12 When they fast, °I will not hear their cry; and when they °offer burnt offering and an °oblation, °I will not accept them: but I will consume them by the °sword, °and by the °famine, °and by the °pestilence."

D E¹ 13 Then said I, "Ah, °Lord GOD! °behold, the prophets say unto them, 'Ye shall not see the sword, neither shall ye have famine; but I will give you assured peace in this place.'"

E² 14 Then [1] the LORD said unto me, "The prophets prophesy lies in My name: I °sent them not, neither have I °commanded them, neither °spake unto them: they prophesy unto °you a false vision and divination, and a thing of nought, and the deceit of their heart.

15 Therefore thus saith [1] the LORD concerning the prophets that prophesy in My name, and I sent them not, yet they say, 'Sword and famine shall not be in this land;' By sword and famine shall those prophets be consumed.

16 And the People to whom they prophesy shall be cast out in the streets of Jerusalem because of the famine and the sword; and they shall have none to bury them, them, their wives, nor their sons, nor their daughters: for I will pour their °wickedness upon them.

17 Therefore thou shalt say this word unto them; 'Let mine eyes run down with tears night and day, and let them not cease: for the virgin daughter of My People is broken with a great breach, with a very grievous blow.

18 If I go forth into the field, then behold the slain with the sword! and if I enter into the city, then behold them that are sick with famine! yea, both the prophet and the priest go about into a land that they know not.'"

19 °Hast Thou utterly rejected Judah? °hath °Thy soul lothed Zion? why hast Thou smitten us, and *there is* no healing for us? °we looked B

2 Judah . . . Jerusalem. Country and city.

gates. Put by Fig. *Metonymy* (of Adjunct), Ap. 6, for the people assembling there.

are black=sit in black. Cp. 8. 21; 13. 18. Job 2. 8, 13. Isa. 3. 26; 15. 3. Ps. 35. 14.

3 to the waters: i.e. to fetch water.

and. Some codices, with two early printed editions, Aram., Sept., and Syr., read this "and" in the text.

covered their heads. The symbol of mourning (2 Sam. 15. 30; 19. 4. Est. 6. 12).

4 chapt=cleft, cracked, open in slits. From Old Dutch, "koppen", to cut off; "kappen", to cut, or chop (hence Eng. "chops", from Eng. "chapped" and "chip"). Gk. *koptein*, to cut. Heb. here, *ḥāthath*=to be broken.

ashamed. Absence of rain causes to-day great anxiety (Job 29. 23).

5 Yea=For.

6 wind. Heb. *rūach*. Ap. 9.

dragons=jackals.

14. 7—15. 24 (A², p. 1036). INTERCESSION.

(Extended Alternation.)

A² | B | 14. 7-9. Deprecation. Jeremiah.
C | 14. 10-12. Rejection. Jehovah.
D | 14. 13-18. Prophets. (False.)
B | 14. 19-22. Deprecation. Jeremiah.
C | 15. 1-9. Rejection. Jehovah.
D | 15. 10-21. Prophets. (True.)

7 iniquities. Heb. *'āvāh*. Ap. 44. iv.

testify: or, answer. Fig. *Prosopopœia*. Ap. 6.

sinned. Heb. *chāṭā'*. Ap. 44. i.

8 the Hope of Israel. Put by Fig. *Metonymy* (of Adjunct), Ap. 6, for Jehovah, Who was, or should have been, Israel's hope. See 17. 13; 50. 7; and cp. Gen. 49. 18. 1 Tim. 1. 1.

stranger=sojourner.

9 man. Heb. *'ish*. Ap. 14. II.

in the midst. Ref. to Pent. (Ex. 29. 45. Lev. 26. 11, 12). Ap. 92.

we are called, &c.=Thy name was called upon us.

11 Pray not, &c. Ref. to Pent. (Ex. 32. 10). Cp. 7. 16; 11. 14. Ap. 92.

12 I will not, &c. See 7. 16; 11. 14; Ezek. 8. 18. Amos 5. 23. Mic. 3. 4.

offer=offer up.

oblation=a gift offering, or donation. Heb. *minchah*. Ap. 43. II. iii.

sword . . . famine . . . pestilence. Often thus conjoined (after this). Ref. to Pent. (Lev. 26 and Deut. 28). Ap. 92. Cp. 21. 6, 7, 9; 24. 10, &c. See note on 42. 2.

and. Note the Fig. *Polysyndeton* (Ap. 6), to emphasise each particular.

14. 13-18 (D, above). PROPHETS. (FALSE.)

(Division.)

D | E¹ | 13. Jeremiah's complaint.
E² | 14-18. Jehovah's answer. Threatening.

13 Lord GOD. Heb. Adonai Jehovah. Ap. 4. VIII (2) and II.

behold. Fig. *Asterismos*. Ap. 6.

14 sent . . . commanded . . . spake. Cp. 7. 22; 23. 21.

you. Some codices, with two early printed editions, read "them".

16 wickedness=calamity. Heb. *rā'a'*. Ap. 44. viii. Not the same word as *v.* 20.

19 Hast . . . hath . . . ? Fig. *Erotēsis*. Ap. 6.

Thy soul=Thou Thyself (emphatic). Heb. *nephesh*. Ap. 13. Fig. *Anthropopatheia*. Ap. 6.

we looked. Cp. 8. 15; 15. 1, where it has a stronger refusal.

497 or 480 for peace, and *there is* no good; °and for the
time of healing, and behold °trouble!
20 °We acknowledge, O [1] LORD, our °wicked-
ness, *and* the °iniquity of our fathers: for we
have [7] sinned against Thee.
21 Do not abhor *us*, for Thy name's sake, °do
not disgrace the °throne of Thy glory: remember, break not Thy covenant with us.
22 Are there *any* among the °vanities of the
°Gentiles that can cause rain? or can the
heavens give showers? *art* not Thou °He, O
[1] LORD our °God? therefore we will °wait
upon Thee: for Thou hast made all these
things.

C (p. 1037) **15** °Then said °the LORD unto me, "Though
°Moses and °Samuel stood before Me,
yet °My mind *could* not *be* toward this People:
cast *them* out of My sight, and let them go
forth.
2 And it shall come to pass, if they say unto
thee, 'Whither shall we go forth?' then thou
shalt tell them, 'Thus saith [1] the LORD; °Such
as *are* for death, to death; and such as *are* for
the sword, to the sword; and such as *are* for
the famine, to the famine; and such as *are* for
the captivity, to the captivity.'
3 And °I will appoint over them four kinds,
°saith [1] the LORD: the sword to slay, and the
dogs to tear, and the fowls of the heaven, and
the beasts of the earth, to devour and destroy.
4 And I will cause them °to be removed into
all kingdoms of the earth, °because of Manasseh
the son of Hezekiah king of Judah, for *that*
which he did in Jerusalem.
5 For who shall have pity upon thee, O Jerusalem? or who shall bemoan thee? or who
shall go aside to ask °how thou doest?
6 Thou hast forsaken Me, [3] saith [1] the LORD,
thou art gone backward: therefore will I
stretch out My hand against thee, and destroy
thee; I am weary with repenting.
7 And I will fan them with a fan in the °gates
of the land; I will bereave *them* of °children,
I will destroy My People, *since* they return not
from their ways.
8 Their widows are increased to Me °above
°the sand of the seas: I have brought upon
them against the mother of the °young men
a spoiler at noonday: I have caused °*him* to
fall upon it suddenly, °and terrors upon the city.
9 She that hath borne °seven languisheth:
she hath °given up the ghost; her sun is gone
down while *it was* yet day: she hath been
ashamed and confounded: and the residue of
them will I °deliver to the sword before their
enemies, [3] saith [1] the LORD."

D w (p. 1038) 10 Woe is me, my mother, that thou hast
borne me a °man of strife and a °man of contention to the whole earth! I have neither
°lent on usury, nor °men have lent to me on
usury; *yet* every one of them doth curse me.

x 11 °The LORD said, "Verily it shall be well
with °thy remnant; verily I will cause the enemy
to entreat thee *well* in the time of °evil and in
the time of affliction.
12 Shall iron break the northern iron and the
°steel?
13 Thy substance and thy treasures will I
give to the spoil without price, and *that* for all
thy °sins, even in all thy borders.
14 And I will °make *thee* to pass with thine
enemies into a land *which* thou knowest not:
for °a fire is kindled in Mine anger, *which* shall
burn upon you."
15 O [1] LORD, Thou knowest: remember me, w

---

and. Some codices, with three early printed editions and Sept., omit this "and".
trouble = terror. Cp. 8. 15.
20 We acknowledge. These are the prophet's words.
wickedness = lawlessness. Heb. *rāsha'*. Ap. 44. x. Not the same word as in *v.* 16.
iniquity. Heb. *'avōn*. Ap. 44. iv.
21 do not. Some codices, with three early printed editions, Syr., and Vulg., read "neither".
throne of Thy glory. See note on 3. 17.
22 Are there = Exist there. Heb. *yēsh*. See notes on 14. 22. Prov. 8. 21; 18. 24. Luke 7. 25.
vanities = idols. Gentiles = nations.
He. Supply Fig. *Ellipsis* (Ap. 6), "He [That givest rain]". God. Heb. Elohim. Ap. 4. I.
wait upon Thee. Ref. to Pent. (Gen. 49. 18, the first occurrence in this sense). Ap. 92.

15. 1 Then: or, And.
the LORD. Heb. Jehovah. Ap. 4. II.
Moses and Samuel. See Ps. 99. 6 and Ezek. 14. 14 (where other names are thus connected).
Moses. Ref. to Pent. (Ex. 17. 11; 32. 11. Num. 14. 13). Ap. 92.
Samuel. Cp. 1 Sam. 7. 9; 8. 6; 12. 16-23.
My mind = My soul. Heb. My *nephesh*. Ap. 13. Fig. *Anthropopatheia*. Ap. 6.
2 Such as are for death, &c. See notes on 43. 9-11. 2 Sam. 12. 31; 8. 2. Cp. Rev. 13. 10.
3 I will appoint, &c. Ref. to Pent. (Lev. 26. 16).
saith the LORD = [is] Jehovah's oracle.
4 to be removed, &c. Ref. to Pent. (Deut. 28. 25, the same word). Ap. 92.
because of Manasseh. See 2 Kings 21. 3, &c.
5 how thou doest? = of thy welfare?
7 gates. Put by Fig. *Synecdoche* (of Part), Ap. 6, for cities, or for the outlets of the land.
children = sons.
8 above, &c. Fig. *Hyperbole*. Ap. 6.
the sand of the seas. Fig. *Parœmia*. Ap. 6.
young men: choice ones, or warriors.
him to fall upon it . . . and terrors upon the city = I have let fall upon her (the mother), suddenly, anguish and terror. To this, one MS. (Harley, 5720, Brit. Mus.) adds: "Woe unto us! for the day declineth, for the shadows of the evening are stretched out", as in ch. 6. 4.
9 seven = the seven. Not even these will suffice.
given up the ghost = breathed out her soul. Heb. *nephesh*. Ap. 13. deliver = give.

15. 10-21 (*D*, p. 1037). PROPHETS. (TRUE.)
(*Alternation.*)

D | w | 10. Complaint of Jeremiah.
| x | 11-14. Promise of Jehovah.
| *w* | 15-18. Complaint of Jeremiah.
| *x* | 19-21. Promise of Jehovah.

10 man. Heb. *'ish*. Ap. 14. II.
lent on usury. Ref. to Pent. (Ex. 22. 25). Ap. 92.
11 The LORD said = Jehovah said. This formula, as commencing a sentence, occurs only here and 46. 25. It is adopted only in Luke 11. 39; 12. 42; 18. 6; 22. 31.
thy: i. e. Israel's. evil. Heb. *rā'a'*. Ap. 44. viii.
12 steel = bronze. **13 sins.** Heb. *chāṭā'*. Ap. 44. i.
14 make thee to pass with thine enemies into. Some codices, with Sept. and Syr., read "make thee serve with thine enemies in". Cp. 17. 4.
a fire is kindled, &c. Ref. to Pent. (Deut. 32. 22).

497 or 480 and visit me, and °revenge me of my persecutors; take me not away in Thy longsuffering:
know that for Thy sake I have suffered °rebuke.
16 Thy words were °found, and I did eat
them; and Thy word was unto me the joy and
rejoicing of mine heart: for °I am called by Thy
name, °O [1] LORD °God of hosts.
17 I sat not in the assembly of the °mockers,
nor rejoiced; I sat alone because of Thy °hand:
for Thou hast filled me with indignation.
18 Why is my pain perpetual, and my wound
incurable, *which* refuseth to be healed? wilt
Thou be altogether unto me as °a liar, *and as*
waters *that* fail?
x 19 Therefore thus saith [1] the LORD, "If thou
(p. 1038) return, then will I bring thee again, *and* thou
shalt °stand before Me: and if thou °take forth
the precious from the vile, thou shalt be as My
mouth: let them return unto thee; but return
not thou unto them.
20 And °I will make thee unto this People
a fenced brasen wall: and they shall fight
against thee, but they shall not prevail against
thee: for I *am* with thee to save thee and to
°deliver thee,' [3] saith [1] the LORD.
21 'And I will deliver thee out of the hand
of °the wicked, and I will °redeem thee out of
the hand of the terrible."

T F[1] y[1] **16** The word of °the LORD came also unto
(p. 1039) me, saying,
2 "Thou shalt not take thee a wife, neither
shalt thou have sons or daughters in this place.
z[1] 3 For thus saith [1] the LORD concerning the
sons and concerning the daughters that are
born in this place, and concerning their mothers
that bare them, and concerning their fathers
that begat them in this land;
4 They shall die of grievous deaths; they
shall not be lamented; neither shall they be
buried; *but* they shall be as dung upon the
face of the °earth: and they shall be consumed
by the sword, and by famine; and their carcases shall be meat for the fowls of heaven,
and for the beasts of the earth.
y[2] 5 For thus saith [1] the LORD, Enter not into
the house of mourning, neither go to lament
nor bemoan them:
z[2] for I have °taken away My °peace from this
people, °saith [1] the LORD, *even* lovingkindness and °mercies.
6 Both the great and the small shall die in
this land: they shall not be buried, neither
shall *men* lament for them, nor °cut themselves, nor °make themselves °bald for them:
7 Neither shall °*men* tear *themselves* for them
in mourning, to comfort them for the dead; neither shall *men* give them the cup of consolation
to drink for their father or for their mother.
y[3] 8 Thou shalt not also go into the house of
feasting, to sit with them to eat and to drink.
z[3] 9 For thus saith °the [1] LORD of hosts, the °God
of Israel; °Behold, I will cause to cease out
of this place in your eyes, and in your days,
the voice of mirth, and the voice of gladness,
the voice of the bridegroom, and the voice of
°the bride.
F[2] a 10 And it shall come to pass, when thou shalt
shew this People all these words, and they
shall say unto thee, °'Wherefore hath [1] the
LORD pronounced all this great °evil against
us? or what *is* our °iniquity? or what *is* our
°sin that we have committed against [1] the LORD
our [9] God?'

15 revenge = avenge. rebuke = reproach.

16 found = discovered. In the eighteenth year of Josiah, 513 B.C. Heb. *māẓā'*. Not used of revelation. Ref. to 2 Kings 22. 8. 2 Chron. 34. 14, 15.

I am called by Thy name = Thy name was called upon me. Only those thus called feed upon Jehovah's words, and suffer reproach (*v.* 15. Cp. John 17. 14).

O LORD God of hosts. See note on 5. 14, and 1 Sam. 1. 3.

God. Heb. Elohim. Ap. 4. I.

17 mockers = merry-makers.

hand. Put by Fig. *Metonymy* (of Cause), Ap. 6, for guidance.

18 a liar = a deceitful [brook]. The *Ellipsis* (Ap. 6), to be supplied from next clause, as a brook that disappointeth. Cp. Job 6. 20.

19 stand before Me: i.e. as My servant. Cp. 1 Kings 18. 15. 2 Kings 3. 14.

take forth the precious, &c. Ref. to Pent. (Lev. 10. 10). Ap. 92.

20 I will make thee, &c. Cp. 1. 18, 19; 6. 27.

deliver = rescue. Not the same word as in *v.* 9.

21 the wicked = wicked ones. Heb. *rā'īm* (pl.). Ap. 44. viii.

redeem: i.e. by power. Heb. *pādāh*. Ex. 6. 6 and 13 13.

16. 1-21 (*T*, p. 1035). SYMBOLICAL. NO WIFE. (*Division.*)

T | F[1] | 1-9. Symbol. No wife.
| F[2] | 10-21. Signification.

Jeremiah's ELEVENTH Prophecy (p. 1015).

16. 1-9 (F[1], above). SYMBOL. NO WIFE. (*Repeated Alternation.*)

F[1] | y[1] | 1, 2. Prohibition. Not to marry.
| z[1] | 3, 4. Reason.
| y[2] | 5-. Prohibition. Not to mourn.
| z[2] | -5-7. Reason.
| y[3] | 8. Prohibition. Not to feast.
| z[3] | 9. Reason.

1 the LORD. Heb. Jehovah. Ap. 4. II.

4 earth = ground, or soil.

5 taken away. Heb. *'āsaph*. A *Homonym*, with two meanings: (1) to protect, or heal (Num. 12. 14, 15. 2 Kings 5. 6. Ps. 27. 10); (2) to snatch away (Ps. 26 9. Jer. 16. 5). peace: or, blessing.

saith the LORD = [is] Jehovah's oracle.

mercies = compassions, or tender mercies.

6 cut themselves . . . make . . . bald. Ref. to Pent. (Lev. 19. 28; 21. 5. Deut. 14. 1). Cp. 41. 5; 47. 5.

7 men tear themselves = break [bread]. Heb. *pāras*, to break, used of breaking bread, as in Isa. 58. 7. Ezek. 24. 17. Hos. 9. 4, and R.V. The *Ellipsis* (Ap. 6), is wrongly supplied in A.V. See the margin there.

9 the LORD of hosts, the God of Israel. See note on 7. 3. God. Heb. Elohim. Ap. 4. I.

Behold. Fig. *Asterismos*. Ap. 6.

the bride. Cp. 7. 34; 25. 10; 33. 11.

16. 10-21 (F[2], above). SIGNIFICATION. (*Alternation.*)

F[2] | a | 10-13. Threatening. Expulsion.
| b | 14, 15. Promise. Restoration. (Israel.)
| a | 16-18. Threatening. Pursuit.
| b | 19-21. Promise. Restoration. (Gentiles.)

10 Wherefore . . . ? Fig. *Erotēsis*. Ap. 6. Ref. to Pent. (Deut. 29. 24, 25). Cp. 5. 19.

evil = mischief, or calamity. Heb. *rā'a'*. Ap. 44. viii.

iniquity. Heb. *'āvāh*. Ap. 44. iv.

sin. Heb. *chātā'*. Ap. 44. i.

497 or 480 **11 Then shalt thou say unto them, 'Because your fathers have forsaken Me, [5]saith [1]the LORD, and have walked after other gods, and have served them, and have worshipped them, and have forsaken Me, and have °not kept My law;**

12 And ye have done worse than your fathers; for, behold, ye walk every one after the °imagination of his °evil heart, that they may not hearken unto Me:

13 Therefore will I cast you out of this land into a land that ye know not, *neither* ye nor your fathers; and there shall ye °serve other gods day and night; where I will not shew you favour.

b (p. 1039) **14 Therefore, [9]behold, the days come, [5]saith [1]the LORD, that it shall no more be said, [1]'The LORD liveth, That brought up the °children of Israel °out of the land of Egypt;'**

15 But, '[1]The LORD liveth, That brought up the [14]children of Israel from the land of the °north, and from all the lands whither He had driven them:' and I will bring them again into their land that I gave unto their fathers.

a **16 [14]Behold, I will send for °many fishers, [5]saith [1]the LORD, and they shall fish them; and after will I send for many °hunters, and they shall hunt them from every mountain, and from every hill, and out of the holes of the rocks.**

17 For Mine eyes *are* upon all their ways: they are not hid from My face, neither is their [10]iniquity hid from Mine eyes.

18 And first I will recompense their [10]iniquity and their [10]sin °double; because they have defiled My land, they have filled Mine inheritance with the carcases of their detestable and abominable things.'"

b **19 (O [1]LORD, my °Strength, and my Fortress, and my Refuge in the day of affliction, the °Gentiles shall come unto Thee from the ends of the earth, and shall say, Surely our fathers have inherited lies, vanity, and *things* wherein *there is* no profit.)**

20 "Shall a °man make gods unto himself, and they *are* no gods?

21 Therefore, [9]behold, I will this once cause them to know, I will cause them to know Mine hand and My might; and they shall know that °My name *is* [1]The LORD."

U G (p. 1040) **17 The °sin of Judah *is* written with a pen of iron, *and* with the point of a diamond: *it is* graven upon the table of their heart, and upon the horns of °your altars;**

2 Whilst their °children remember their altars and their °groves by °the green trees °upon the high hills.

H J **3 O My °mountain in the field, °I will give thy substance *and* all thy treasures to the spoil, *and* thy high places °for [1]sin, throughout all thy borders.**

4 And thou, even thyself, shalt discontinue from thine heritage that I gave thee; and I will cause thee to serve thine enemies in the land which thou knowest not: for ye have °kindled a fire in Mine anger, *which* shall °burn °for ever."

11 not kept My law. Ref. to Pent. (Ex. 20). Ap. 92.
12 imagination = stubbornness. Ref. to Pent. (see notes on 3. 17; 7. 24; 9. 14; 13. 10). Ap. 92.
evil. Heb. *rā'a'*. Ap. 44. viii.
13 serve other gods. Ref. to Pent. (Deut. 4. 26–28; 28. 36). Ap. 92.
14 children = sons.
out of . . . Egypt. Ref. to Pent. (Ex. 12—15). Ap. 92.
15 north. Babylon on the east; but entrance thence into the Land was by the north.
16 many fishers . . . hunters. Ref. to Judah's enemies. Cp. *v.* 18. Amos 4. 2. Ezek. 12. 13. Hab. 1. 14.
18 double. See note on Isa. 40. 2.
19 Strength = strength (for protection). Heb. *'āzaz*.
Gentiles = nations.
20 man. Heb. *'ādām*. Ap. 14. I.
21 My name. Ref. to Pent. (Ex. 3. 15; 15. 3). Ap. 92.

17. 1-18 (*U*, p. 1035). LITERAL. SIN OF JUDAH.
(*Alternation and Introversion.*)

U | G | 1, 2. Incrimination.
  H | J | 3, 4. Threatening.
    K | 5–8. Trust. False and True.
G | 9, 10. Incrimination.
  H | *K* | 11–14. Trust. False and True.
    J | 15–18. Defiance.

1 sin. Heb. *chāṭā'*. Ap. 44. i.
your. One MS. (Harley, 5720, Brit. Mus.), quotes other MSS. as reading "their" (fol. 240b). So in two early printed editions, Syr., and Vulg.
2 children = sons.
groves = *Asherim* (pl.). See Ap. 42.
the green trees. Some codices, with Aram. and Syr., read "by every green tree".
upon. Some codices, with one early printed edition, Aram., and Syr., read "and upon".
3 mountain in the field. Fig. *Periphrasis* (Ap. 6), put for Jerusalem. Cp. "rock of the plain" (21. 13).
I will give. By Fig. *Hyperbaton* (Ap. 6), these words come at the end of the sentence, to call attention to them.
for sin = in sin: i.e. as a punishment for sin.
4 kindled a fire. Ref. to Pent. (Deut. 32. 22). Cp. 15. 14. **burn.** Cp. Isa. 33. 14.
for ever. Heb. *'ōlām*. See Ap. 150 (Gr. *aiōn*).

17. 5-8 (K, above). TRUST. FALSE AND TRUE.
(*Alternation.*)

K | c | 5. Curse. } False.
  d | 6. Comparison. Heath in desert. } False.
  c | 7. Blessing. } True.
  d | 8. Comparison. Tree in garden. } True.

5 the LORD. Heb. Jehovah. Ap. 4. II.
Cursed, &c. Note the *Alternation* above.
the man = strong man. Heb. *geber*. Ap. 14. IV.
trusteth = confideth. Heb *bāṭaḥ*. Ap. 69. i.
man. Heb. *'ādām*. Ap. 14. I.
6 in. Some codices, with Aram., Sept., Syr., and Vulg., read this word "in" in the text.
7 hope = confidence. Heb. *bāṭaḥ*, as in the preceding line. Not the same word as in *vv.* 13, 17.
8 as a tree. Ref. to an earlier book (Ps. 1. 1-3).

5 Thus saith °the LORD; °"Cursed *be* °the man that °trusteth in °man, and maketh flesh his arm, and whose heart departeth from °the LORD. K c

6 For he shall be like the heath in the desert, and shall not see when good cometh; but shall inhabit the parched places in the wilderness, °*in* a salt land and not inhabited. d

7 Blessed *is* [5]the man that [5]trusteth in [5]the LORD, and whose °hope [5]the LORD is. *c*

8 For he shall be °as a tree planted by the *d*

97 or 480 waters, and *that* spreadeth out her roots by the °river, and shall not see when heat cometh, but her leaf shall be green; and shall not be careful in the year of drought, neither shall cease from yielding fruit.

G (p. 1040) 9 The heart *is* °deceitful above all *things*, and °desperately wicked: °who can know it?

10 °I [5]the LORD search the °heart, *I* try the °reins, °even to give every °man according to his °ways, °*and* according to the °fruit of his doings.

H K e (p. 1041) 11 *As* the partridge sitteth *on eggs*, and hatcheth *them* not;

f *so* he that getteth riches, and not by right, shall leave them in the midst of his °days, and at his end shall be a fool."

f 12 A glorious high throne from the beginning *is* the place of our sanctuary.

13 O [5]LORD, °the Hope of Israel, all that forsake Thee shall be ashamed, *and* they that depart from Me shall be written in the earth,

e because they have forsaken [5]the LORD, the Fountain of living waters.

14 Heal me, O [5]LORD, and I shall be healed; save me, and I shall be saved: for °Thou *art* my Praise.

J (p. 1040) 15 °Behold, they say unto me, °"Where *is* the word of [5]the LORD? let it come now."

16 As for me, I have not hastened from *being* a pastor to follow Thee: neither have I desired the °woeful day; Thou knowest: that which came out of my lips was °*right* before Thee.

17 °Be not a terror unto me: Thou *art* my Hope in the day of °evil.

18 Let them be confounded that persecute me, but let not me be confounded: let them be dismayed, but let not me be dismayed: bring upon them the day of [17]evil, and destroy them with °double destruction.

F g[1] (p. 1041) 19 Thus said [5]the LORD unto me; "Go and stand in °the gate of the [2]children of the People, whereby the kings of Judah come in, and by the which they go out, and in all the gates of Jerusalem;

20 And say unto them, 'Hear ye the word of the LORD, ye kings of Judah, and all Judah, and all the inhabitants of Jerusalem, that enter in by these gates:

21 Thus saith [5]the LORD; Take heed to °yourselves, and °bear no burden on the sabbath day, nor bring *it* in by the gates of Jerusalem;

22 Neither carry forth a burden out of your houses on the sabbath day, neither do ye any work, but hallow ye the sabbath day, °as I commanded your fathers."

h[1] 23 But they °obeyed not, neither inclined their ear, but made their neck stiff, that they might not hear, nor receive instruction.

g[2] 24 "And it shall come to pass, if ye diligently hearken unto Me, [5]saith [5]the LORD, 'to bring in no burden through the gates of this city on the sabbath day, but hallow the sabbath day, to do no work therein;

25 Then shall there enter into the gates of this city kings and princes sitting upon the throne of David, riding in chariots and on °horses, they, and their princes, the °men of Judah, and the inhabitants of Jerusalem: and this city shall remain for ever.

26 And they shall come from the cities of Judah, and from the places about Jerusalem, and from the land of Benjamin, and from °the plain, and from the °mountains, and from °the south, °bringing burnt offerings, and sacrifices, and °meat offerings, and °incense, and bringing

---

river = stream. Heb. *yūbal*, from *yābal*, to flow.

9 deceitful = crooked. Referring to the old nature of the natural man.

desperately wicked = sick unto death = it [is] sick unto death: i.e. it [is] incurable.

who can know it? Fig. *Erotēsis* (Ap. 6), for emphasis.

10 I the LORD. Quoted in Rom. 8. 27. Rev. 2. 23.

heart. Put by Fig. *Metonymy* (of Adjunct), Ap. 6, for the mind, or intellect.

reins. Put by Fig. *Metonymy* (of Adjunct), Ap. 6, for the thoughts, or affections.

even to give = giving. But some codices, with two early printed editions, Sept. reads, "to give", or "that He may give", and Vulg., "who gives".

man. Heb. *'ish*. Ap. 14. II.

ways. Heb. text reads "way" (sing.); but some codices, with two early printed editions, Aram., Sept., Syr., and Heb. text marg., read "ways" (pl.).

and. Some codices, with two early printed editions, Sept., Syr., and Vulg., read this "and" in the text.

fruit of his doings. Cp. 6. 19; 32. 19.

17. 11-14 (*K*, p. 1040). **TRUST. FALSE AND TRUE.** (*Introversion.*)

K | e | 11-. Forsaking. Partridge her eggs.
  f | -11. False trust.
  f | 12, 13-. True trust.
 e | -13, 14. Forsaking. People their God.

11 days = day. But some codices, with one early printed edition, read "days", as A.V. Cp. Luke 12. 20.

13 the Hope of Israel. Put by Fig. *Metonymy* (of Adjunct), Ap. 6, for Jehovah, in Whom Israel hoped.

14 Thou art my praise. Ref. to Pent. (Deut. 10. 21).

15 Behold. Fig. *Asterismos*. Ap. 6.

Where . . . ? Fig. *Erotēsis*. Ap. 6.

16 woeful. Same word as "desperately wicked" (in *v.* 9) = incurable. right. Omit.

17 Be not a terror. Cp. 1. 17.

evil = calamity. Heb. *ra'a'*. Ap. 44. viii.

18 double. Cp. 16. 18, and see note on Isa. 40. 2.

17. 19-27 (*F*, p. 1018). **PROPHECIES.** (*Repeated Alternation.*)

F | g[1] | 19-22. Jehovah. Command.
  h[1] | 23. Disobedience.
 g[2] | 24-26. Jehovah. Promise.
  h[2] | 27-. Disobedience.
 g[3] | -27. Jehovah. Threatening.

19 the gate, &c. Probably the main entrance to the Courts of the Temple. See plan, Ap. 68, p. 105.

21 yourselves = your souls. Heb. *nephesh*. Ap. 13.

bear no burden. Ref. to Pent. (Ex. 20. 8; 23. 12; 31. 13). Ap. 92. Cp. Neh. 13. 15-19.

22 as = according as.

23 obeyed = hearkened.

25 horses. Some codices read "their horses".

men. Heb. *'ish*. Ap. 14. II.

26 the plain. Called *Shephēlah* = Philistia, between Jerusalem and the Mediterranean Sea.

mountains = the central land.

the south = the Negeb. See notes on Gen. 12. 9; 13. 1. Deut. 1. 7. Ps. 126. 4.

bringing burnt offerings, &c. Ref. to Pent. Lev. 1. 1, 2, &c.

meat = meal. Ref. to Pent. (Lev. 2. 1). Ap. 92.

incense = frankincense.

97 or 480 sacrifices of praise, unto the house of [5]the LORD.

h² (p. 1041) 27 But if ye will not hearken unto Me to hallow the sabbath day, and not to bear a burden, even entering in at the gates of Jerusalem on the sabbath day;

g³ then will I °kindle a fire in the gates thereof, and it shall devour the palaces of Jerusalem, and it shall not be quenched.' "

G L (p. 1042) **18** The word which came to Jeremiah from °the LORD, saying,

2 "Arise, and go down to °the potter's house, and there I will cause thee to hear My words."

3 Then I went down to the potter's house, and, behold, he °wrought a work on the wheels.

4 And the vessel that he made of clay was marred in the hand of the potter: so he made it again another vessel, as seemed good to the potter to make *it*.

M 5 Then the word of [1]the LORD came to me, saying,

6 "O °house of Israel, cannot I do with you as this potter? °saith [1]the LORD. °Behold, as the clay *is* in the potter's hand, so *are* ye in Mine hand, O °house of Israel.

N Q¹ i 7 *At what* instant I shall speak concerning a nation, and concerning a kingdom, °to pluck up, and to °pull down, and to destroy *it;*

k 8 If that nation, against whom I have pronounced, turn from their °evil, °I will repent of the °evil that I thought to do unto them.

i 9 And *at what* instant I shall speak concerning a nation, and concerning a kingdom, °to build and to plant *it;*

k 10 If it do [8]evil in My sight, that it obey not My voice, then [8]I will repent of the good, wherewith I said I would benefit them.

Q² l 11 Now therefore go to, speak to the °men of Judah, and to the inhabitants of Jerusalem, saying, 'Thus saith [1]the LORD; [6]Behold, °I frame [8]evil against you, and devise a device against you: return ye now every one from his [8]evil way, and make your ways and your doings good.' "

m 12 And they said, "There is no hope: but we will walk after our own devices, and we will every one do the °imagination of his [8]evil heart."

m 13 Therefore thus saith [1]the LORD; "Ask ye now among the °heathen, who hath heard such things: the virgin of Israel hath done a very horrible thing.

14 °Will *a man* leave the °snow of Lebanon °*which cometh* from the rock of the field? *or* shall the cold flowing waters that come from another place be forsaken?

15 Because My people hath °forgotten Me, they have burned incense to °vanity, and they

27 kindle a fire, &c. Ref. to Pent. (Deut. 32. 22). Ap. 92. Cp. 21. 14. Lam. 4. 11.

18. 1–20. 18 (*G*, p. 1018). SYMBOLS.
(*Extended Alternation.*)

G | L | 18. 1–4. Symbol. Potter's vessel.
  M | 18. 5, 6. Signification. House of Israel.
   N | 18. 7–17. Threatening.
    O | 18. 18. Enemies. Plot.
     P | 18. 19–23. Jeremiah. Prayer.
 L | 19. 1–10. Symbol. Potter's bottle.
  M | 19. 11–13. Signification. People and city.
   N | 19. 14, 15. Threatening.
    O | 20. 1–6. Enemies. Violence.
     P | 20. 7–18. Jeremiah. Prayer.

Jeremiah's TWELFTH Prophecy (p. 1015)

1 the LORD. Heb. Jehovah. Ap. 4. II.

2 the potter's house. Note the lesson, set to Jeremiah there: that Jehovah never *mends* what man has *marred.* He always substitutes something *new.* The *interpretation* belongs to "THE HOUSE OF ISRAEL", and, that being "marred", the new "nation" is to be substituted. See Matt. 21. 43. Cp. Rom. 11. 7. Ezek. 36. 25–28. The *application* belongs to: (1) THE COVENANT (Deut. 6. 25), but it was marred (Jer. 31. 32): for the *New* Covenant, see Heb. 8. 7–13. (2) ORDINANCES, marred (Isa. 1. 11–14); *new* (Heb. 10. 6–9. Col. 2. 14, 17. Gal. 4. 3, 8–11). (3) PRIESTHOOD (Heb. 7. 11–28). (4) KING (2 Sam. 7. 12–16). Cp. Ps. 72. Isa. 9. 6; 11. 1–9; 32. 1–8. Luke 1. 31–33. (5) MAN, marred (Gen. 3. Rom. 8. 7. Jer. 17. 9. Ps. 14. 2; 53. 2. John 3. 6); *new* (2 Cor. 5. 17, 18). (6) THE BODY, marred (Gen. 3. Heb. 9. 27); the *new* (1 Cor. 15. 35, 44, 46, 47). (7) THE HEAVEN AND EARTH, marred (Gen. 3. 2 Pet. 3. 7); the *new* (2 Pet. 3. 13). Ps. 85. 10, 13. Isa. 65. 17, &c. (8) THE CHURCH, marred (2 Tim. 1. 15 (cp. Acts 19. 10; 20. 29); 2. 18; 3. 8; 4. 3, 4); *new* (Eph. 2. 20–22; 4. 4).

wrought = was working.

Jeremiah's THIRTEENTH Prophecy (p. 1015).

6 house of Israel. See note on 2. 4.
saith the LORD = [is] Jehovah's oracle.
Behold. Fig. *Asterismos.* Ap. 6.

18. 7–17 (N, above). THREATENING. (*Division.*)

N | Q¹ | 7–10. Declaration.
  Q² | 11–17. Application.

18. 7–10 (Q¹, above). DECLARATION.
(*Alternation.*)

Q¹ | i | 7. Concerning pulling down.
  k | 8. Condition. Repentance.
 i | 9. Concerning building up.
  k | 10. Condition. Repentance.

7 to pluck up = to declare that it should be plucked up. Heb. idiom. Cp. 1. 10.
pull down. Some codices, with two early printed editions and Syr., read "tear away". Cp. 1. 10.
8 evil = calamity. Heb. *rā'a'.* Ap. 44. viii.
I will repent. Fig. *Anthropopatheia.* Ap. 6.
9 to build, &c. = to declare that it should be built and planted.

18. 11–17 (Q², above). APPLICATION.
(*Introversion.*)

Q² | l | 11. Threatening.
  m | 12. Departure.
  m | 13–16. Departure.
 l | 17. Execution.

11 men. Heb. *'ish.* Ap. 14. II.

I frame = I work (as the potter in *v.* 3). **12 imagination** = stubbornness. **13 heathen** = nations.
14 Will a man leave . . . ? Note the Fig. *Erotēsis* and the Fig. *Ellipsis* (Ap. 6), and render:—
"Will [a man] leave the snow [water] of Lebanon for the rock of the field?
Or shall the cold flowing waters [be forsaken] for strange waters?
snow: i. e. snow [water], used for mixing with wine; or for washing, as in Job 9. 30. **which cometh.** Omit, and supply the word "leave" in the second clause from the first clause. **15 forgotten.** Showing that the emphasis is on the leaving and forsaking of *v.* 14. **vanity.** Used of idols. Fig. *Metonymy* (of Subject), Ap. 6.

97 or 480 have caused them to stumble in their ways
°*from* the °ancient paths, to walk in paths, *in*
°a way not cast up;
16 To make their land desolate, *and* a perpetual °hissing; every one that passeth thereby shall be astonished, and wag his head.
l (p. 1042) 17 I will scatter them °as with an east °wind before the enemy; I will shew them the back, and not the face, °in the day of their calamity."

O 18 Then said they, "Come, and let us devise devices against Jeremiah; for °the law shall not perish from the priest, nor counsel from the wise, nor the word from the prophet. Come, and let us smite him °with the tongue, and let us not give heed to any of his words."

P n (p. 1043) 19 Give heed to me, O [1] LORD, and hearken to the voice of them that contend with me.
20 °Shall [8] evil be recompensed for good? for they have digged a pit for °my soul. Remember that I stood before Thee to speak good for them, *and* to turn away Thy wrath from them.

o 21 Therefore deliver up their °children to the famine, and pour out their *blood* by the force of the sword; and let their wives be bereaved of their °children, and *be* widows; and let their °men be put to death; *let* their young men *be* slain by the sword in battle.
22 Let a cry be heard from their houses, when thou shalt bring a °troop suddenly upon them: for they have digged a pit to take me, and hid snares for my feet.

n 23 Yet, [1] LORD, Thou knowest all °their counsel against me to slay *me:*
o °forgive not their °iniquity, neither blot out their °sin from Thy sight, but let them be overthrown before Thee; deal *thus* with them in the time of Thine anger.

L p **19** Thus °saith °the LORD, "Go and get a potter's earthen °bottle, and °*take* of the °ancients of the people, and of the °ancients of the priests;

q 2 And go forth unto the valley of the son of Hinnom, which *is* by the entry of °the east gate, and proclaim there the words that I shall tell thee,
3 And say, 'Hear ye the word of [1] the LORD, O kings of Judah, and inhabitants of Jerusalem; Thus saith °the [1] LORD of hosts, the °God of Israel; °Behold, I will bring °evil upon this place, the which whosoever heareth, °his ears shall tingle.

r 4 Because they have °forsaken Me, and have estranged this place, and have burned incense in it unto other gods, °whom neither °they nor their fathers °have known, nor the kings of Judah, and have filled this place with the blood of °innocents;

r 5 They have built also the high places of Baal, °to °burn their sons with fire *for* °burnt offerings unto Baal, which I commanded not, nor spake *it,* neither came *it* into °My mind:

q 6 Therefore, [3] behold, the days come, °saith [1] the LORD, that this place shall no more be called °Tophet, nor The valley of the son of °Hinnom, but °The valley of slaughter.
7 And I will make void the counsel of Judah and Jerusalem in this place; and I will cause them to °fall by the sword before their enemies, and by the hands of them that seek their °lives: and their carcases will I give to be

from. Supply the Ellipsis from *vv.* 14, 15 thus: "in that they forsook". **ancient.** Cp. 6. 16.
a way not cast up: i.e. a causeway. Prov. 15. 19. Isa. 57. 14; 62. 10.
16 hissing. Put by Fig. *Metonymy* (of Effect), Ap. 6, for the contempt felt.
17 as. Some codices, with five early printed editions, read "with", instead of "as".
wind. Heb. *rūach.* Ap. 9.
in the day. See Ap. 18.
18 the law, &c. Ref. to Pent. (Lev. 10. 11). Ap. 92.
with the tongue = with hard words. "Tongue" put by Fig. *Metonymy* (of Cause), Ap. 6, for the hard words spoken by it.

18. 19-23 (P, p. 1042). **JEREMIAH. PRAYER.**
(*Alternation.*)

P | n | 19, 20. Complaint.
  o | 21, 22. Imprecation.
  n | 23-. Complaint.
  o | -23. Imprecation.

20 Shall . . . ? Fig. *Erotēsis.* Ap. 6.
my soul = me (emphatic). Heb. *nephesh.* **Ap. 13.**
21 children = sons.
men. Pl. of *'ěnōsh.* Ap. 14. III.
22 troop = marauders.
23 their counsel. See Ap. 85.
forgive not. See Ap. 85.
iniquity. Heb. *'āvōn.* Ap. 44. iv.
sin. Heb. *chāṭā'.* Ap. 44. i.

19. 1-10 (*L*, p. 1042). **THE POTTER'S BOTTLE.**
(*Introversion.*)

L | p | 1. Bottle taken.
  q | 2, 3. Threatening. (General.)
   r | 4. Cause.
   r | 5. Cause.
  q | 6-9. Threatening. (Particular.)
 p | 10. Bottle broken.

1 saith the LORD. Some codices, with two early printed editions, Aram., Sept., and Syr., read "Jehovah said unto me".
the LORD. Heb. Jehovah. Ap. 4. II.
bottle = pitcher. Often seen hanging by a well to this day. Not a leathern wine-skin.
take. The Fig. *Ellipsis* (Absolute), Ap. 6, must be thus supplied. **ancients** = elders.
2 the east gate: i.e. the pottery gate. See Ap. 59. Not from *ḥaraṣ* = east, but from *ḥereṣ* = a potsherd. See note on Isa. 19. 19 and Ap. 81.
3 the LORD of hosts, the God of Israel. See note on 7. 3.
God. Heb. Elohim. Ap. 4. I.
Behold. Fig. *Asterismos.* Ap. 6.
evil = calamity. Heb. *rā'a'.* Ap. 44. viii.
his ears shall tingle. Ref. to earlier books (1 Sam. 3. 11. 2 Kings 21. 12). Cp. the ref. to Samuel in 15. 1.
4 forsaken Me. Ref. to Pent. (Deut. 28. 20; 32. 15). Cp. Jer. 5. 7, 19. Ap. 92.
whom . . . they . . . have known. Ref. to Pent. (Deut. 32. 17). Ap. 92.
innocents = people, not merely babes.
5 to burn = consume. Heb. *sāraph.* Ap. 43. I. viii.
burn their sons, &c. Ref. to Pent. (Lev. 18. 21).
burnt offerings. Cp. 7. 31.
My mind. Heb. My heart. Fig. *Anthropopatheia.* Ap. 6. "Mind" put by Fig. *Metonymy* (of Adjunct), Ap. 6, for the thoughts.
saith the LORD = [is] Jehovah's oracle.
6 Tophet . . . Hinnom. Cp. 7. 31.
The valley of slaughter. Cp. 7. 32.
7 fall by the sword . . . enemies. Ref. to Pent. (Lev. 26. 17. Deut. 28. 25). Ap. 92.
lives = souls. Heb. *nephesh.* Ap. 13.

497 or 480 meat for the fowls of the heaven, and for the
beasts of the earth.
8 And I will make this city °desolate, and
an °hissing; every one that passeth thereby
shall be astonished and hiss because of all the
plagues thereof.
9 And I will cause them °to eat the flesh of
their sons and the flesh of their daughters, and
they shall eat every one the flesh of his friend
in the siege and straitness, wherewith their
enemies, and they that seek their [7] lives, shall
straiten them.'
p 10 Then shalt thou break the [1] bottle in the
(p. 1043) sight of the °men that go with thee,
M 11 And shalt say unto them, 'Thus saith °the
(p. 1042) [1] LORD of hosts; Even so will I break this
People and this city, °as *one* breaketh a potter's vessel, that cannot be made whole again:
and they shall bury *them* in [6] Tophet, till *there*
be no place to bury.
12 Thus will I do unto this place, [6] saith [1] the
LORD, and to the inhabitants thereof, and
even make this city as [6] Tophet:
13 And the houses of Jerusalem, and the
houses of the kings of Judah, shall be defiled
as the place of [6] Tophet, because of all the
houses °upon whose roofs they have burned
incense unto all the host of heaven, and have
poured out drink offerings unto other gods.'"
N 14 Then came Jeremiah from [6] Tophet, whither [1] the LORD had sent him to prophesy;
and he stood in the court of [1] the LORD'S
house; and said to all the People,
15 "Thus saith [3] the [1] LORD of hosts, the [3] God
of Israel; [3] 'Behold, I will bring upon this city
and upon all her towns all the [3] evil that I have
pronounced against it, because they have hardened their necks, that they might not hear
My words.'"

O s **20** Now °Pashur the son of °Immer °the
(p. 1044) priest, who *was* also °chief governor
497 in the house of °the LORD, heard that Jeremiah °prophesied these things.
2 Then [1] Pashur °smote Jeremiah the prophet, and put him in the stocks that *were* in
the °high gate of Benjamin, which *was* by
the house of [1] the LORD.
3 And it came to pass on the morrow, that
[1] Pashur brought forth Jeremiah out of the
stocks.
t Then said Jeremiah unto him, [1] "The LORD
hath °not called thy name [1] Pashur, but °Ma-
gor-missabib.
4 For thus saith [1] the LORD, °'Behold, I will
make thee a terror to thyself, and to all thy
friends: and they shall fall °by the sword of
their enemies, and thine eyes shall behold *it*:
and I will give all Judah into the hand of
°the king of Babylon, and he shall carry them
captive into Babylon, and shall slay them with
the sword.
t 5 Moreover I will deliver all the °strength of
this city, and all the labours thereof, and all
the precious things thereof, and all the treasures of the kings of Judah will I give into the
hand of their enemies, which shall spoil them,
and take them, and carry them to Babylon.
s 6 And thou, [1] Pashur, and all that dwell in
thine house shall go into captivity: and thou
shalt come to Babylon, and there thou shalt
die, and shalt be buried there, thou, and all thy
friends, to whom thou hast prophesied lies.'"
7 O [1] LORD, Thou hast °deceived me, and I P R u
was °deceived: Thou art °stronger than I,
and hast prevailed:

8 desolate . . . hissing. See note on 18. 16.
9 to eat the flesh, &c. Ref. to Pent. (Lev. 26. 29. Deut. 28. 53-57). Cp. Lam. 2. 20; 4. 10.
10 men. Heb. pl. of *'ĕnōsh.* Ap. 14. III.
11 the LORD of hosts. See note on 6. 6.
as = according as.
13 upon whose roofs. Cp. 32. 29.

20. 1-6 (*O*, p. 1042). ENEMIES. VIOLENCE.
(*Introversion.*)

O | s | 1-3-. Pashur's violence.
t | -3, 4. Pashur and Judah: captives.
t | 5. Pashur and Judah: spoils.
s | 6. Pashur's end.

1 Pashur = most noble. The first person named in this book, beside Jeremiah. Not the Pashur of ch. 21. This incident is in the third year of Jehoiakim, just before Nebuchadnezzar comes for the first time. Ch. 21 is in the latter part of Zedekiah's reign, nineteen years later.
Immer. The ancestor of the sixteenth order of priests (1 Chron. 24. 14). **the priest**: i.e. Immer.
chief governor: i.e. Pashur.
the LORD. Heb. Jehovah. Ap. 4. II.
prophesied = was prophesying.
2 smote. Perhaps according to Deut. 25. 3.
high = upper. Probably north of the Temple, which looked toward the gate of Benjamin.
3 not called thy name Pashur. *Pashḥūr* is the foreign Aramaic name, given by his parents. Jeremiah takes this Aramaic name and interprets it in Hebrew (as Isaiah had done in 8. 1, 3). *Pash* = to stay (or remain on), *gūr* = to sojourn or wander about in a strange land. Aram. *seḥōr* = Heb. *ṣābīb*. Hence, "Thy name is not *staying on*, but *wandering about.*" Cp. *v.* 3 with *v.* 6. The opposite of Isa. 8. 1, 3.
Magor-missabib. Heb. *Māgōr-missābīb* = terror-round-about, or fear on every side. Cp. *v.* 10; 6. 25; 46. 5, &c.
4 Behold. Fig. *Asterismos.* Ap. 6.
by the sword. Some codices, with two early printed editions, add "at the hand of".
the king of Babylon. This is the first occurrence in Jeremiah.
5 strength = power, or might. Heb. *ḥāṣen.* Not the same word as in *v.* 7. Put by Fig. *Metonymy* (of Effect), Ap. 6, for the wealth acquired by strength.

20. 7-18 (*P*, p. 1042). JEREMIAH. PRAYER.
(*Introversion.*)

P | R | 7-12. Complaint.
S | 13-. Praise to Jehovah.
S | -13. Praise. Reason for it.
R | 14-18. Complaint.

20. 7-12 (R, above). COMPLAINT.
(*Introversion.*)

R | u | 7-. Jehovah. Commission.
v | -7, 8. Jeremiah. Derision of.
w | 9-. Jehovah's word. Resolve made.
w | -9. Jehovah's word. Resolve useless.
v | 10. Jeremiah. Conspiracy against.
u | 11, 12. Jeremiah. Support.

7 deceived = induced, or persuaded. Heb. *pāthāh*, in a good sense: Gen. 9. 27 ("enlarge"). Prov. 25. 15 ("persuade"). Hos. 2. 14 ("allure"). The adjective *pethī* means *persuasible*, and generally in a good sense: Ps. 19. 7; and is rendered "simple": (Ps. 19. 7; 116. 6; 119. 130. Prov. 1. 4; 8. 5; 21. 11, &c.)
stronger = stronger (to hold fast). Heb. *ḥazak.* Not the same word as in *v.* 5.

v I am in derision daily, every one °mocketh
(p. 1044) me.
497 8 For since I spake, I cried out, I cried violence and spoil; because the word of [1]the
LORD was made a reproach unto me, and a
derision, daily.

w 9 Then I said, "I will not make mention of
Him, nor speak any more in His name."
w But *His word* °was in mine heart as a burning
fire shut up in my bones, and I was weary with
forbearing, and I could not *stay*.

v 10 For I heard the defaming of many, °fear
on every side. "Report," *say they,* "and we
will report it." All my °familiars watched for
my halting, *saying,* "Peradventure he will be
°enticed, and we shall prevail against him,
and we shall take our revenge on him."

u 11 But [1]the LORD *is* with me as a mighty
terrible One: therefore my persecutors shall
stumble, and they shall not prevail: they shall
be greatly ashamed; for they shall not prosper: *their* everlasting confusion shall never
be forgotten.
12 But, O °LORD of hosts, That °triest °the
righteous, *and* seest the °reins and the °heart,
let me see Thy vengeance on them: for unto
Thee have I opened my cause.

S 13 Sing unto [1]the LORD, praise ye [1]the LORD:
S for He hath delivered the °soul of the °poor
from the hand of °evildoers.

R 14 Cursed *be* the day wherein I was born:
°let not the day wherein my mother bare me
be blessed.
15 Cursed *be* the °man who brought tidings
to my father, saying, "A °man child is born
unto thee;" making him very glad.
16 And let that [15]man be °as the cities which
[1]the LORD overthrew, and repented not: and
let him hear the °cry in the morning, and the
°shouting at noontide;
17 Because he slew me not from the womb;
or that my mother might have been my grave,
and her womb *to be* always great *with me.*
18 °Wherefore came I forth out of the womb
to see labour and sorrow, that my days should
be consumed with shame?

D T x **21** The word which came unto Jeremiah
(p. 1045) from °the LORD, when king Zedekiah
479 °sent unto him °Pashur the son of Melchiah,
and °Zephaniah the son of Maaseiah the
priest, saying,
2 "Enquire, I pray thee, of °the LORD for
us; for °Nebuchadrezzar king of Babylon
maketh war against us; if so be that [1]the
LORD will deal with us according to all His
wondrous works, that he may °go up from
us."
3 Then said Jeremiah unto them, "Thus
shall ye say to °Zedekiah:
4 'Thus saith °the LORD °God of Israel;
°Behold, I will turn back the weapons of war
that *are* in your hands, wherewith ye fight
against the king of Babylon, and *against* the
Chaldeans, which besiege you without the
walls, and I will assemble them into the midst
of this city.
5 And I Myself will fight against you with an

mocketh = is laughing at. See Ap. 85.
9 was = became.
10 fear on every side. Heb. *māgōr-missābīb*, as in *v.* 3. Cp. 6. 25; 46. 5, &c.
familiars = those whom I am wont to salute. See Ap. 85.
enticed = induced, or persuaded. Heb. *pāthāh*, *v.* 7.
12 LORD of hosts. See note on 6. 6, and 1 Sam. 1. 3.
triest = testest. the righteous = a righteous one.
reins = kidneys. Put by Fig. *Metonymy* (of Subject), Ap. 6, for thoughts.
heart. Put by Fig. *Metonymy* (of Subject), Ap. 6, for the affections. **13** soul. Heb. *nephesh.* Ap. 13.
poor = helpless. Heb. *'ebyōn.* See note on Prov. 6. 11.
evildoers. Heb. *rā'a'.* Ap. 44. viii.
14 let not the day, &c. Fig. *Pleonasm.* Ap. 6.
15 man. Heb. *'ish.* Ap. 14. II.
man child = a son, a male. Cp. Rev. 12. 5.
16 as the cities, &c. Ref. to Pent. (Gen. 19. 24).
cry: of the besieged for help. } Cp. Ex. 32. 17, 18.
shouting: of the besiegers for victory. }
18 Wherefore . . . ? Fig. *Erotēsis.* Ap. 6. Cp. Job 3.

21. 1—35. 19 (**D**, p. 1015). HISTORY, ETC. JEHOIAKIM. (NOT CHRONOLOGICAL.) (*Introversion.*)

D | T | 21. 1-14. Defeat and Captivity proclaimed.
  U | 22. 1—23. 8. Promise of THE BRANCH.
    V | 23. 9-40. Whirlwind. False Prophets. Rejection.
      W | 24. 1-10. Captives. Remnant. (Fig.)
        X | 25. 1-11. Time. Seventy years.
          Y | 25. 12-38. Nations. The Cup.
            Z | 26. 1-24. Proclamation in Temple.
          Y | 27. 1-22. Nations. Bonds and Yoke.
        X | 28. 1-17. Time. Two years.
      W | 29. 1-32. Captives and Remnant. (Fig.)
    V | 30. 1—31. 40. Whirlwind. Book. Restoration.
  U | 32. 1—33. 26. Promise of THE BRANCH.
T | 34. 1—35. 19. Defeat and Captivity proclaimed.

21. 1-14 (T, above). DEFEAT AND CAPTIVITY PROCLAIMED. (*Alternation.*)

T | x | 1-7. To the king.
  y | 8-10. To the People of the city.
  x | 11, 12. To the king's house.
  y | 13, 14. To the People in the city.

Jeremiah's FOURTEENTH Prophecy, 21. 1-10, and a new division of the book (see **D**, p. 1015).

Note the reigns: ch. 21. Zedekiah (the last king of Judah). Ch. 22. His three predecessors, Shallum (or Jehoahaz), Jehoiakim, and Coniah (or Jechoniah, or Jehoiachin). Chs. 25, 26, 27. Jehoiakim. Ch. 28. Zedekiah again, and the last days of Jerusalem. This order is logical, which is more important than chronological, for the severity of ch. 21 is shown to be justified by the chapters which follow. Cp. 25. 3-5, and see Ap. 83.
1 the LORD. Heb. Jehovah. Ap. 4. II.
sent unto him. Contrast the mission of Hezekiah to Isaiah (2 Kings 19. 2. Isa. 37. 2).
Pashur. Not the Pashur of 20. 1. This prophecy is nineteen years later; the deportation in the reign of Jehoiachin had taken place, and a worse set of men were the rulers. This Pashur was a priest, if Melchiah is the same Melchiah as in 1 Chron. 9. 12.
Zephaniah, &c. He is mentioned again (29. 25; 37. 3; 52. 24). The Heb. accents read "Zephaniah the priest, the son of Maaseiah."
2 the LORD. Heb. Jehovah. Ap. 4. II.
Nebuchadrezzar. First occurrence in Jeremiah.
go up from us: i. e. raise the siege.
3 Zedekiah. The last king of Judah.
4 the LORD God of Israel = Jehovah the Elohim of Israel. See note on 11. 3, and Ap. 4. II and I.
Behold. Fig. *Asterismos.* Ap. 6.

479 °outstretched hand and with a °strong arm,
even in anger, °and in fury, and in great
wrath.
6 And I will smite the inhabitants of this
city, both °man and beast: they shall die of
a great pestilence.
7 And afterward, °saith [2]the LORD, I will
deliver Zedekiah king of Judah, and his servants, and the People, and such as are left in
this city from the pestilence, °from the sword,
and from the famine, into the hand of Nebuchadrezzar king of Babylon, [5]and into the
hand of their enemies, [5]and into the hand of
those that seek their °life: [5]and he shall
smite them with the edge of the sword; °he
shall not spare them, neither have pity, nor
have mercy.

y (p. 1045) 8 And unto this People thou shalt say, Thus
saith [2]the LORD; [4]Behold, °I set before you
the way of °life, and the way of °death.
9 He that abideth in this city shall die by the
sword, and by the famine, and by the pestilence: but °he that goeth out, and °falleth to
the Chaldeans that besiege you, °he shall live,
and his [7]life shall °be unto him for a prey.
10 For °I have set My face against this city
for °evil, and not for good, saith [2]the LORD:
[7]it shall be given into the hand of the king of
Babylon, and he shall burn it with fire.

x 11 And touching the house of the king of Judah, *say,* Hear ye the word of [2]the LORD;
12 O °house of David, thus saith [2]the LORD;
Execute judgment °in the morning, and deliver *him that is* spoiled out of the hand of the
oppressor, lest My fury go out like fire, and
burn that none can quench *it,* because of the
°evil of °your doings.

y 13 Behold, I *am* against thee, O °inhabitant
of the valley, *and* °rock of the plain, [7]saith
[2]the LORD; which say, 'Who shall come
down against us? or who shall enter into our
habitations?'
14 But I will punish you according to the
fruit of your doings, [7]saith [2]the LORD: and
I will °kindle a fire in °the forest thereof, and
°it shall devour all things round about it.

U A^1 B a (p. 1046) 489 **22** Thus saith °the LORD; °Go down to
the house of the °king of Judah, and
speak there this word,
2 And say, 'Hear the word of [1]the LORD, O
[1]king of Judah, that sittest upon the throne of
David, thou, and thy servants, and thy People
that enter in by these gates:
3 Thus saith [1]the LORD; °Execute ye
°judgment and righteousness, and deliver the
°spoiled out of the hand of the oppressor: and
do °no wrong, do °no violence to the °stranger,
the °fatherless, °nor the widow, °neither shed
°innocent blood in this place.

b 4 For if ye do this thing indeed, then shall
there enter in by the gates of this house kings
sitting °upon the throne of David, riding in
chariots and on horses, he, and his °servants,
and his people.
5 But if ye will not hear these words, I swear
by Myself, °saith [1]the LORD, that this house
shall become a desolation.'

5 outstretched hand. Ref. to Pent. (Ex. 6. 6. Deut. 4. 34). Ap. 92.
strong = strong (for holding fast). Heb. *ḥāzaḳ.* Cp. 20. 5, 7.
and. Note Fig. *Polysyndeton.* Ap. 6.
6 man. Heb. *'ādām.* Ap. 14. I.
7 saith the LORD = [is] Jehovah's oracle.
from. Some codices, with Aram., Sept., Syr., and Vulg., read "and from", thus forming the Fig. *Polysyndeton.* Ap. 6. life = soul. Heb. *nephesh.* Ap. 13.
he shall not spare. Ref. to Pent. (Deut. 28. 50).
8 I set before you, &c. Ref. to Pent. (Deut. 30. 19).
life . . . death. Note the *Introversion* in *v.* 9, "die . . . live".
9 he that goeth out, &c. Many acted on this promise (39. 9; 52. 15). falleth = shall fall.
he shall live. Some codices, with two early printed editions, read "then (or so) shall he live".
be unto him for a prey: i.e. he shall save his life, but it will be dearly bought. Cp. 38. 2; 39. 18; 45. 5. The phrase occurs only in Jeremiah.
10 I have set, &c. Ref. to Pent. (Lev. 17. 10). Ap. 92. Cp. Ezek. 15. 7.
evil = calamity. Heb. *rā'a'.* Ap. 44. viii.
12 house of David. Occurs only here in Jeremiah.
in the morning = betimes.
evil. Heb. *rā'a'.* Ap. 44. viii.
your. Some codices, with seven early printed editions, read "their".
13 inhabitant = inhabitress: i.e. Zion.
rock of the plain. Fig. *Periphrasis* (Ap. 6), for Zion.
14 kindle a fire, &c. Ref. to Pent. (Deut. 32. 22). Ap. 92.
the forest thereof = her forest. Put by Fig. *Metonymy* (of Cause), Ap. 6, for the timber from Lebanon used in the buildings. it shall devour. Fulfilled in 52. 13.

22. 1—23. 8 (U, p. 1045). PROMISE OF THE BRANCH. (*Division.*)

U | A^1 | 22. 1–30. Individually.
  | A^2 | 23. 1–8. Collectively.

22. 1-30 (A^1, above). INDIVIDUALLY. (*Alternation.*)

A^1 | B | 1–9. To Jehoiakim.
   C | 10–12. Touching Shallum.
  B | 13–19. To Jehoiakim.
   C | 20–30. Touching Coniah.

22. 1-9 (B, above). TO JEHOIAKIM. (*Alternation.*)

B | a | 1–3. Command.
  b | 4, 5. Consequence.
  a | 6, 7. Address.
  b | 8, 9. Consequence.

1 the LORD. Heb. Jehovah. Ap. 4. II.
Go down. Cp. 36. 12.
king of Judah: i.e. Jehoiakim.
3 Execute ye, &c. See note on 7. 5.
judgment and righteousness. Fig. *Hendiadys* (Ap. 6) = judgment, yea, righteous judgment.
spoiled = robbed.
no . . . nor . . . neither. Note the Fig. *Paradiastolē.* Ap. 6.
stranger = sojourner.
fatherless, nor the widow. Put by Fig. *Synecdoche* (of Species), Ap. 6, for all afflicted ones.
innocent blood. See note on 7. 6.
4 upon the throne of David = for David upon his throne.
servants. Heb. text reads "servant", but some codices, with two early printed editions, read pl., as in A.V.
5 saith the LORD = [is] Jehovah's oracle.
6 house of Judah. See note on 3. 18.

6 For thus saith [1]the LORD unto the king's a
°house of Judah; Thou *art* Gilead unto Me,
and the head of Lebanon: *yet* surely I will
make thee a wilderness, *and* cities *which* are
not inhabited.

489 7 And I will ° prepare destroyers against thee,
every one with his weapons: and they shall
cut down thy choice ° cedars, and cast *them*
into the fire.
b 8 And many nations shall pass by this city,
(p. 1046) and they shall say ° every man to his neighbour,
° 'Wherefore hath [1] the LORD done thus unto
this great city?'
9 Then they shall answer, 'Because they
have forsaken the covenant of [1] the LORD their
° God, and worshipped other gods, and served
them.'
C 10 Weep ye not for ° the dead, neither bemoan
° him: *but* ° weep sore for him that goeth away:
for he shall return no more, nor see his native
country.
500 11 For thus saith [1] the LORD touching ° Shallum the son of Josiah king of Judah, which
reigned instead of Josiah his father, which
went forth out of this place; He shall not
return thither any more:
12 But he shall ° die in the place whither they
have led him captive, and shall see this land
no more.
B 13 Woe unto him that buildeth his house by
unrighteousness, and his ° chambers ° by wrong;
that ° useth his neighbour's service without
wages, and giveth him not for his ° work;
14 That saith, 'I will build me a wide house
and ° large chambers,' and cutteth him out
° windows; and *it is* ° cieled with cedar, and
painted with vermilion.
15 Shalt thou reign, because thou closest
thyself in cedar? did not thy father eat and
drink, and do [3] judgment and ° justice, *and* then
it was well with him?
16 ° He ° judged the cause of the ° poor and
needy; then *it was* well *with him*: *was* not this
to know Me? [5] saith [1] the LORD.
17 ° But thine eyes and thine heart *are* not
but for thy covetousness, and for to [3] shed
innocent blood, and for oppression, and for
violence, to do *it*.
500-489 18 Therefore thus saith [1] the LORD concerning
Jehoiakim the son of Josiah king of Judah;
They shall not lament for him, *saying*, 'Ah
my brother!' or, 'Ah sister!' they shall not
lament for him, *saying*, 'Ah lord!' or, 'Ah his
glory!'
19 He shall be ° buried with the burial of an
ass, ° drawn and ° cast forth beyond the gates
of Jerusalem.
C 20 ° Go up to Lebanon, and ° cry; and lift up
thy voice in Bashan, and cry from ° the passages: for all thy ° lovers are destroyed.
21 I spake unto thee in thy ° prosperity;
but thou saidst, 'I will not hear.' This *hath*
been thy manner from thy youth, that thou
° obeyedst not My voice.
22 The ° wind shall eat up all thy ° pastors,
and thy lovers shall go into captivity: surely
then shalt thou be ashamed and confounded
for all thy ° wickedness.
23 ° O ° inhabitant of ° Lebanon, that makest
thy nest in the cedars, ° how gracious shalt
thou be when pangs come upon thee, the pain
as of a woman in travail!
489 24 *As* I live, [5] saith [1] the LORD, though
° Coniah the son of Jehoiakim king of Judah
were the ° signet upon My ° right hand, yet
would I pluck thee thence;
25 And I will give thee into the hand of them

7 prepare = set apart. Cp. 6. 4; 51. 27, 28.
cedars. Put by Fig. *Metonymy* (of Cause), Ap. 6, for the houses built of cedar.
8 every man. Heb. *'îsh.* Ap. 14. II.
Wherefore . . . ? Ref. to Pent. See note on **16. 10.**
9 God. Heb. Elohim. Ap. 4. I.
10 the dead: i.e. Josiah.
him: i.e. Jehoiachin.
weep sore = weep ye, weep on. Fig. *Polyptōton.* Ap. 6.
11 Shallum the son of Josiah. Josiah had four sons (1 Chron. 3. 15). Shallum had another name—Jehoahaz. Cp. 2 Kings 23. 31, 34. Zedekiah must have been younger than Jehoiakim or Jehoahaz, for he was but twenty-one when he began to reign, and therefore only ten when Jehoiakim began to reign.
12 die in the place, &c., i.e. in Egypt. He was the first king of Israel to do so. 2 Kings 23. 34.
13 chambers = upper chambers.
by wrong = in injustice.
useth his neighbour's service, &c. Ref. to Pent. (Lev. 19. 13). Ap. 92.
work. Put by Fig. *Metonymy* (of Cause), Ap. 6, for the wages earned by his labour = giveth him not [wages] for his work.
14 large = airy, or roomy.
windows = its windows.
cieled = panelled.
15 justice = righteousness, as in *v.* 3.
16 He: i.e. Josiah.
judged the cause. Fig. *Polyptōton.* Ap. 6. Heb. judged the judgment. Fig. *Erotēsis* by *Ellipsis* (Ap. 6) = "[Did he not] judge righteous judgment?" Fig. *Hendiadys*, as in *v.* 3.
poor = wretched. Heb. *'ānāh.* See note on "poverty", Prov. 6. 11.
17 But thine eyes: or, Verily, thou hast neither eyes nor heart save for, &c.
19 buried with the burial of an ass. Note the Fig. *Oxymoron* (Ap. 6), which gives the meaning that he was not buried at all (for asses have no funerals). Jehoiakim is the only king of Judah whose burial is not recorded. See note on 2 Kings 24. 6.
drawn, &c.: i.e. the ass, not Jehoiakim (*v.* 26).
cast forth. Cp. Isa. 26. 19.
20 Go up, &c. Note the Fig. *Eironeia.* Ap. 6.
cry: the cry of distress.
the passages = Abarim: the mountains beyond Jordan, the range of Nebo. Cp. Num. 27. 12; 33. 47, 48. Deut. 32. 49.
lovers: i.e. the neighbouring nations, to whom they looked instead of to God.
21 prosperity. Heb. pl. of majesty = thy great prosperity.
obeyedst not = hearkenedst not to.
22 wind. Heb. *rûach.* Ap. 9.
pastors. Put for rulers of all kinds. See notes on 2. 8; 3. 15, &c.
wickedness. Heb. *rā'a'.* Ap. 44. viii. Put by Fig. *Metonymy* (of Cause), Ap. 6, for the cause of the calamity.
23 O. Fig. *Apostrophe.* Ap. 6.
inhabitant = inhabitress: i.e. Zion.
Lebanon. Fig. *Metalepsis* (Ap. 6): "Lebanon" put for the cedars grown there, then "cedars" put for the houses built of the timber.
how gracious = how greatly to be pitied.
24 Coniah = (by Fig. *Aphaeresis*), Ap. 6, by which the first syllable is cut off. He is called "Jeconiah" (1 Chron. 3. 16), which means "Let Jehovah establish"; but the cutting off of the Divine name "Je" (for Jah or Jehovah) is meant to show the departure of Jehovah from Jeconiah, and that he himself would be cut off.
signet. Cp. Hag. 2. 23.
right hand. Fig. *Anthropopatheia.* Ap. 6.

489 that seek thy °life, and into the hand *of them* whose face thou fearest, even into the hand of Nebuchadrezzar king of Babylon, and into the hand of the Chaldeans.

26 And I will cast thee out, and thy mother that bare thee, into another country, where ye were not born; and there shall ye die.

27 But to the land whereunto they °desire to return, thither shall they not return.

28 *Is* this °man [24]Coniah a despised broken idol? *is he* a vessel wherein *is* no pleasure? wherefore are they cast out, he and his seed, and are cast into a land which they know not?

29 [23]O °earth, earth, earth, hear the word of [1]the LORD.

30 Thus saith [1]the LORD, Write ye this [28]man °childless, °a man *that* shall not prosper in his days: for no [28]man of his seed shall prosper, sitting upon the throne of David, and ruling any more in Judah.

A2 c (p. 1048) 23 Woe be unto °the pastors that destroy and scatter the sheep of My pasture! °saith °the LORD.

2 Therefore thus saith °the [1]LORD °God of Israel against the pastors °that feed My people; Ye have scattered My flock, and driven them away, and have not visited them: °behold, °I will visit upon you the °evil of your doings, [1]saith [1]the LORD.

d 3 And °I will gather the remnant of My flock out of all countries whither I have driven them, and will bring them again to their folds; and they shall be fruitful and increase.

c 4 And I will set up shepherds over them which shall feed them: and they shall fear no more, nor be dismayed, neither shall they be lacking, [1]saith [1]the LORD.

5 [2]Behold, the days come, [1]saith [1]the LORD, that I will raise unto David a righteous °Branch, and a °King shall reign and prosper, and shall execute °judgment and justice in the earth.

6 In his days Judah shall be saved, and °Israel shall dwell safely: and this *is* His name whereby He shall be called, °THE LORD °OUR RIGHTEOUSNESS.

d 7 Therefore, [2]behold, °the days come, [1]saith [1]the LORD, that they shall no more say, [1]'The LORD liveth, °Which brought up the °children of Israel out of the land of Egypt;'

8 But, [1]'The LORD liveth, Which brought up and Which led the seed of °the house of Israel out of the north country, and from all countries whither I had driven them; and they shall dwell in their own °land."

V e 9 °Mine heart within me is broken because of the prophets; all my bones shake; I am like a drunken °man, and like °a man whom °wine hath overcome, because of [1]the LORD, and because of °the words of His holiness.

10 For the land is full of adulterers; for because of swearing the land mourneth; the pleasant places of the wilderness are dried up, and °their course is [2]evil, and °their force *is* not right.

11 For both prophet and priest are profane; yea, in My house have I found their °wickedness, [1]saith [1]the LORD.

25 life = soul. Heb. *nephesh*. Ap. 13.
27 desire to return = are lifting up their soul. Heb. *nephesh*. Ap. 13.
28 man. Heb. *'ish*. Ap. 14. II.
29 earth, earth, earth. Fig. *Epizeuxis* (Ap. 6), for great emphasis.
30 childless: i.e. as to the throne (see last clause). Not one of his seven sons (1 Chron. 3. 17, 18) sat upon his throne.
a man = a strong man. Heb. *geber*. Ap. 14. IV.

23. 1-8 (A2, p. 1046). COLLECTIVELY. (*Alternation*.)

A2 | c | 1, 2. Shepherds. Woe to false.
 d | 3. Restoration. The remnant.
 c | 4-6. Shepherd. The true. The BRANCH.
 d | 7, 8. Restoration. The Nation.

1 the pastors = rulers. See notes on 2. 8; 3. 15, &c.
saith the LORD = [is] Jehovah's oracle.
the LORD. Heb. Jehovah. Ap. 4. II.
2 the LORD God of Israel. See note on 11. 3.
God. Heb. Elohim. Ap. 4. I.
that feed = that are the feeders of. Fig. *Antimereia* (of the Verb). Ap. 6.
behold. Fig. *Asterismos*. Ap. 6.
I will visit, &c. Ref. to Pent. (Ex. 32. 34). Ap. 92.
evil. Heb. *rā'a'*. Ap. 44. viii.
3 I will gather, &c. Cp. 31. 10; 32. 7. Ezek. 34. 13, &c.
5 Branch = Sprout from the root, not from a branch. Cp. Isa. 11. 1; 53. 2. Here, Heb. *zemach*. The name of the brightest star in the Zodiac sign "Virgo". See Ap. 12. See notes on the Structure of the Four Gospels. Cp. 33. 15.
King. See the Structure of the Gospels. Matthew. Cp. Isa. 9. 6, 7. Zech. 6. 12, 13. Ps. 72. 2. Luke 1. 32.
judgment and justice. See note on 22. 3.
6 Israel shall dwell safely. Ref. to Pent. (Lev. 25. 18, 19; 26. 5. Deut. 33. 12, 28. Repeated in 32. 37; 33. 16). Ap. 92.
THE LORD OUR RIGHTEOUSNESS. Heb. *Jehōvah Ẓidkēnū*. See Ap. 4. II. 7. For the reason of the large type in A.V., see Ap. 48.
OUR. Because the gift of God.
7 the days come. Cp. 16. 14, 15.
Which brought up, &c. Ref. to Pent. (Ex. 12—15, &c.). Ap. 92. children = sons.
8 the house of Israel. See note on 2. 4.
land = soil.

23. 9-40 (V, p. 1045). WHIRLWIND. FALSE PROPHETS. REJECTION. (*Alternation*.)

V | e | 9-15. Incrimination.
 f | 16-22. Dehortation.
 e | 23-29. Incrimination.
 f | 30-40. Threatening.

9 Mine heart, &c. Fig. *Pathopœia*. Ap. 6.
man. Heb. *'ish*. Ap. 14. II.
a man = a strong man. Heb. *geber*. Ap. 14. IV.
wine. Heb. *yayin*. Ap. 27. I.
10 their: i.e. the false prophets.
11 wickedness. Heb. *rā'a'*. Ap. 44. viii.
12 the year of their visitation. See note on 8. 12.

12 Wherefore their way shall be unto them as slippery *ways* in the darkness: they shall be driven on, and fall therein: for I will bring [2]evil upon them, *even* °the year of their visitation, [1]saith [1]the LORD.

13 And I have seen folly in the prophets of Samaria; they prophesied in Baal, and caused My People Israel to err.

14 I have seen also in the prophets of Jerusalem an horrible thing: they commit adultery, and walk in lies: they strengthen also the hands of evildoers, that none doth return from

489 his °wickedness: they are all of them unto Me
as °Sodom, and the inhabitants thereof as
Gomorrah.
15 Therefore thus saith °the LORD of hosts
concerning the prophets; [2]Behold, I will feed
them with wormwood, and make them drink
the water of gall: for from the prophets of
Jerusalem is profaneness gone forth into all
the land.

f 16 Thus saith [15]the LORD of hosts, 'Hearken
(p. 1048) not unto the words of the prophets that prophesy unto you: they make you vain: they
speak a vision of their own heart, *and* not out
of the mouth of [1]the LORD.
17 °They say still unto them that despise Me,
[1]'The LORD hath said, 'Ye shall have peace;''
and they say unto every one that walketh
after the °imagination of his own heart, 'No
[2]evil shall come upon you.'
18 For °who hath stood in the °counsel of
[1]the LORD, and hath perceived and heard °His
word? who hath marked His word, and °heard
it?
19 Behold, a whirlwind of [1]the LORD °is gone
forth in fury, even a grievous whirlwind: it
shall °fall grievously upon the head of °the
wicked.
20 The anger of [1]the LORD shall not return,
until He have executed, and till He have performed the thoughts of His heart: in °the
latter days ye shall consider it °perfectly.
21 °I have not sent these prophets, yet they
ran: I have not spoken to them, yet they prophesied.
22 °But if they had stood in My counsel, and
had caused My People to hear My words, then
they should have turned them from their [2]evil
way, and from the [2]evil of their doings.

e 23 °*Am I* a [2]God at hand, [1]saith [1]the LORD,
°and not a [2]God afar off?
24 °Can any hide himself in secret places that
I shall not see him? [1]saith [1]the LORD. °Do
not I °fill heaven and earth? [1]saith [1]the
LORD.
25 I have heard what the prophets said,
that prophesy lies in My name, saying, °'I have
dreamed, I have dreamed.'
26 °How long °shall *this* be in the heart of the
prophets that prophesy lies? yea, *they are*
prophets of the deceit of their own heart;
27 Which think to cause My People to forget My name by their dreams which they tell
[8]every man to his neighbour, °as their fathers
have forgotten My name °for Baal.
28 The prophet that hath a dream, let him
tell a dream; and °he that hath My word, let
him speak My word faithfully. What *is* the
°chaff to the wheat?" [1]saith [1]the LORD.
29 °*Is* not My word like as a fire? [1]saith
[1]the LORD; and like a hammer *that* breaketh
the rock in pieces?

f 30 Therefore, [2]behold, °I *am* against the
prophets, [1]saith [1]the LORD, that steal My
°words every one from his neighbour.
31 [2]Behold, [30]I *am* against the prophets,
[1]saith [1]the LORD, that use their tongues, and
°say, 'He saith.'
32 [2]Behold, I *am* against them that prophesy
false dreams, [1]saith [1]the LORD, and do tell
them, and cause My People to err by their lies,
and by their °lightness; yet I sent them not,
nor commanded them: therefore they shall not
profit this People at all, [1]saith [1]the LORD.
33 And when this People, or the prophet, or
a priest, shall ask thee, saying, 'What *is* the
burden of [1]the LORD?' thou shalt then say
unto them, °'What burden?' I will even °for-
sake you, [1]saith [1]the LORD.
34 And *as for* the prophet, and the priest,
and the People, that shall say, 'The burden of
[1]the LORD,' I will even punish that [8]man and
his house.
35 Thus shall ye say every one to his neighbour, and every one to his brother, 'What hath
[1]the LORD answered?' and, 'What hath [1]the
LORD spoken?'
36 And the burden of [1]the LORD shall ye
mention no more: for every man's word shall
be his burden; for ye have °perverted the words
of °the living God, of [15]the LORD of hosts our
[2]God.

14 wickedness = lawlessness. Heb. *rāshā‘*. Ap. 44. x.

Sodom, &c. Ref. to Pent. (Gen. 19). Cp. Isa. 1. 10.

15 the LORD of hosts = Jehovah Ẓebaiōth. See note on 6. 6 and 1 Sam. 1. 3.

17 They say still. Fig. *Polyptōton.* Ap. 6. Heb. = saying they say = keep on saying.

imagination = stubbornness.

18 who . . .? Fig. *Erotēsis.* Ap. 6. Implying that none hath.

counsel = secret council. Cp. Ps. 25. 14.

His. Heb. text, with R.V., reads "My"; but marg. of Heb. text, the Babylonian Codex, with eight early printed editions, Aram., Syr., and Vulg., read "His" with A.V.

heard: or, announced. Cp. *v.* 22.

19 fall grievously = burst.

the wicked = lawless ones. Heb. *rāshā‘*. Ap. 44. x.

20 the latter days = end of days. Ref. to Pent. (Gen. 49. 1, the same word). Ap. 92.

perfectly. Cp. 30. 24.

21 I have not, &c. Cp. *v.* 32; 14. 14.

22 But if, &c. The Heb. accent requires the rendering: "But, had they stood in My Council: then they would have made My People hear My words, and they would have turned", &c.

23 Am I . . .? Fig. *Erotēsis.* Ap. 6.

and not, &c. Fig. *Pleonasm* (Ap. 6), for emphasis.

24 Can . . .? . . . Do . . .? Fig. *Erotēsis.* Ap. 6.

fill. The Heb. accent ("*Tiphchā*") puts the emphasis on "fill" (not on "earth"), denoting the fulness of the Divine presence which no place can *in*clude, or *ex*clude. A fulness of *grace*, of the prophetic word of judgment, and of promise.

25 I have dreamed. Thus catching the people's ears. Note Fig. *Epizeuxis.* Ap. 6.

26 How long . . .? Fig. *Erotēsis.* Ap. 6.

shall this be = shall this exist. Heb. *yēsh.* See notes on 31. 6, 16, 17. Prov. 8. 21; 18. 24, and Luke 7. 25.

27 as = according as. **for** = in, or through.

28 he that hath, &c. Cp. Ezek. 13. 7.

chaff = crushed, or chopped straw. Heb. *teben.*

29 Is not . . .? Fig. *Erotēsis.* Ap. 6.

30 I am against, &c. Ref. to Pent. (Deut. 18. 20).

words. Edition of A.V., 1611, read "word".

31 say, He saith = uttered it as an oracle. Heb. *ne'ūm.* Ref. to Pent. (Gen. 22. 16. Num. 14. 28; 24. 3, 4, 15, 16). Frequent in the prophets. Ap. 92.

32 lightness = reckless boasting.

33 What burden? Sept., Vulg., and Rashi, read "Ye yourselves are the burden". Cp. *v.* 36.

forsake = reject.

36 perverted. See note on 6. 10.

the living God. Both words are plural.

489 37 Thus shalt thou say to the prophet, 'What
hath [1]the LORD answered thee?' and, 'What
hath [1]the LORD spoken?'
38 But since ye say, 'The burden of [1]the
LORD;' therefore thus saith [1]the LORD;
'Because °ye say this word, 'The burden of
[1]the LORD,' and I have sent unto you, saying,
'Ye shall not say, 'The burden of [1]the
LORD;''
39 Therefore, behold, I, even I, will utterly
forget you, and I will forsake you, and the
city that I gave you and your fathers, *and*
cast you out of My presence:
40 And I will bring an °everlasting reproach
upon you, and a °perpetual shame, which shall
not be forgotten.''

W D (p. 1050) 488 **24** °The LORD °shewed me, and, °behold,
two °baskets of figs *were* set before
°the temple of °the LORD, after that Nebuchadrezzar
king of Babylon had carried away
captive Jeconiah the son of Jehoiakim king of
Judah, and the princes of Judah, with the
°carpenters and smiths, from Jerusalem, and
had brought them to Babylon.

E g 2 One basket *had* very good figs, *even* like
the figs *that are* first ripe:

h and the other basket *had* very °naughty figs,
which could not be eaten, they were so bad.

g 3 Then said [1]the LORD unto me, "What seest
thou, Jeremiah?" And I said, "Figs; the
good figs, very good;

h and the °evil, very °evil, that cannot be eaten,
they are so °evil."

D 4 Again the word of [1]the LORD came unto
me, saying,

E i 5 "Thus saith °the LORD, the °God of Israel;
'Like these good figs, so will I °acknowledge
them that are carried away captive of Judah,
whom I have sent out of this place into the
land of the Chaldeans °for *their* good.

k 6 °For I will set Mine °eyes upon them for
good, and I will bring them again to this land:
and I will °build them, and not pull *them*
down; and I will °plant them, and not pluck
them up.
7 And °I will give them an heart to know
Me, that I *am* [1]the LORD: and °they shall be
My People, and I will be their [5]God: for they
shall return unto Me with their whole heart.

i 8 And as the [3]evil figs, which cannot be
eaten, they are so [3]evil; surely thus saith
[1]the LORD, So will I give Zedekiah the king
of Judah, and his princes, and the residue of
Jerusalem, that remain in this land, and them
that dwell in the land of Egypt:

k 9 And I will deliver them °to °be removed
into all the kingdoms of the earth °for *their*
hurt, °*to be* a reproach and a proverb, °a
taunt and a curse, in all places whither I shall
drive them.
10 And I will send °the sword, °the famine,
and the pestilence, among them, till they be
consumed from off the °land that I gave unto
them and to their fathers.'"

38 ye say = ye keep on saying. Fig. *Polyptōton*. Ap. 6.
40 everlasting . . . perpetual. Put by Fig. *Synecdoche* (of the Whole), Ap. 6, for a part of time = life long. Limited here by the promised Restoration.

24. 1-10 (W, p. 1045). CAPTIVES. REMNANT. (FIGS.) (*Alternations.*)

W | D | 1. Symbol. Two baskets of figs.
  E | g | 2-. Good figs.
    h | -2. Bad figs.
    g | 3-. Good figs.
    h | -3. Bad figs.
  D | 4. Signification of Symbol.
  E | i | 5. Captives. (Good figs.)
    k | 6, 7. For their good.
    i | 8. Remnant. (Bad figs.)
    k | 9, 10. For their evil.

1 The LORD. Heb. Jehovah. Ap. 4. II.
shewed me = made me see.
behold. Fig. *Asterismos*. Ap. 6.
baskets. Heb. *dūdīm*. Still used for fruit in Jerusalem.
the temple. See note on 26. 2.
carpenters and smiths = craftsmen (or artificers) and armourers. **2** naughty = worth naught.
3 evil. Heb. *rā'a'*. Ap. 44. viii. Cp. 29. 17.

Jeremiah's FIFTEENTH Prophecy (see p. 1015).

5 the LORD, the God of Israel = Jehovah Elohim of Israel. See note on 11. 3 and Ap. 4. II and I.
God. Heb. Elohim. Ap. 4. I.
acknowledge = own. Put by Fig. *Metonymy* (of Cause), Ap. 6, for regard, or care for.
for . . . good. Connect this with "acknowledge", not with "sent out".
6 For I will set Mine eyes = And I will set Mine eye. Some codices, with Sept., Syr., and Vulg., read "eyes" (pl.) with A.V.
build . . . plant. Cp. 1. 10; 18. 7-9.
7 I will give, &c. Ref. to Pent. (Deut. 30. 6).
they shall be My People. Ref. to Pent. (Lev. 26. 12).
9 to be removed into = to be tossed to and fro among.
be removed. Ref. to Pent. (Deut. 28. 25). Ap. 92.
for their hurt. Heb. *rā'a'*. Ap. 44. viii. Cp. 25. 6; 38. 4.
to be a reproach = [I will deliver them to be] a reproach.
a taunt. Ref. to Pent. Some codices, with two early printed editions, Aram., Sept., Syr., and Vulg., read "and a", thus completing the Fig. *Polysyndeton* (Ap. 6).
10 the sword, the famine, and the pestilence. Ref. to Pent. (Lev. 26. 25, 26. Deut. 28. 21-24). Ap. 92.
the famine. Some codices, with one early printed edition, Sept., Syr., and Vulg., read "and famine", thus completing the Fig. *Polysyndeton* (Ap. 6).
land = soil, or ground. Heb. *'ădāmāh*.

25. 1-11 (X, p. 1045). TIME. SEVENTY YEARS. (*Introversion.*)

X | n | 1, 2. Time of the prophecy.
  o | 3, 4. Messengers from Jehovah.
    p | 5-7. Disobedience. The cause.
    p | 8. Disobedience. The consequence.
  o | 9-11-. Messengers from Babylon.
n | -11. Duration of the prophecy.

Jeremiah's SIXTEENTH Prophecy (see p. 1015).

1 to. Heb. "upon". Some codices, with two early printed editions, Sept., and Vulg., read "unto".
all the People = the People at large.
the fourth year of Jehoiakim. An important date, being the first year of Nebuchadnezzar. See Ap. 83 and 86.

25 The word that came °to Jeremiah con- X n
cerning °all the People of Judah in °the 496
fourth year of Jehoiakim the son of Josiah

496 king of Judah, that *was* °the first year of
°Nebuchadrezzar king of °Babylon;
2 The which °Jeremiah the prophet °spake
unto [1]all the People of Judah, and [1]to all the
inhabitants of Jerusalem, saying,

o 3 "From the °thirteenth year of Josiah the
(p. 1050) son of Amon king of Judah, even unto this
or 496 day, that *is* °the three and twentieth year, the
word of °the LORD hath come unto me, and
I have spoken unto you, °rising early and
speaking; but ye have not hearkened.
4 And [3]the LORD hath sent unto you all His
servants the prophets, [3]rising early and sending *them;* but ye have not hearkened, nor inclined your ear to hear.

p 5 They said, 'Turn ye again now every one
from his °evil way, and from the °evil of your
doings, and dwell °in the land that [3]the LORD
hath given unto you and to your fathers °for
ever and ever:
6 And go not after other gods to serve them,
and to worship them, and provoke Me not to
anger with the works of your hands; and I
will °do you no °hurt.'
7 Yet ye have not hearkened unto Me, °saith
[3]the LORD; that ye might °provoke Me to
anger with the works of your hands to your
own [6]hurt.

p 8 Therefore thus saith °the LORD of hosts;
'Because ye have not heard My words,

o 9 Behold, I will send and take all the families
of the north, [7]saith [3]the LORD, and Nebuchadrezzar the king of Babylon, °My servant,
and will bring them against this land, °and
against the inhabitants thereof, °and against
all these nations round about, °and will utterly
destroy them, °and make them an °astonish-
ment, and an hissing, °and °perpetual desolations.
10 Moreover °**I will take from them the voice**
of mirth, and the voice of gladness, the voice
of the bridegroom, and the voice of the bride,
the sound of the millstones, and the light of
the °candle.
11 And this whole land shall be a desolation,
°*and* an [9]astonishment;

n and these nations shall serve the king of Babylon °seventy years.

Yq 12 And it shall come to pass, °when [11]seventy
(p. 1051) years are accomplished, *that* I will °punish
the king of Babylon, and that nation, [1]saith
[3]the LORD, for their °iniquity, and the land
of the Chaldeans, and will make °it [9]perpetual
desolations.
13 And I will bring upon that land all My
words which I have pronounced against it,
even all that is written in this book, which
Jeremiah hath prophesied against all the nations.
14 For many nations and great kings shall
serve themselves °of them also: and I will
recompense them according to their deeds,
and according to the works of their own
hands.'

r 15 For thus saith °the LORD God of Israel
unto me; 'Take the °wine cup of this fury at
My hand, and cause all the nations, to whom
I send thee, to drink it.

the first year, &c. See Ap. 86.

Nebuchadrezzar. Cp. 21. 2.

Babylon. Assyria not mentioned, for it had already fallen.

2 Jeremiah the prophet spake. This is the first occurrence of the expression. We find "said" later; and "prophet" in 1. 5; 20. 2; 28. 5, 6, 10, 11, 12, 12, 15; 29. 1, 29; 32. 2; 36. 8, &c., 34. 6; 45. 1.

spake. In ch. 36. 2 he is told to "write", because "Israel" (being dispersed), could not be *spoken* to, as Judah was here.

3 thirteenth year of Josiah. Cp. 1. 2.

the three and twentieth year: i.e. of Jeremiah's prophesying: 18 years under Josiah + 3 months under Jehoahaz + 4 years under Jehoiakim.

the LORD. Heb. Jehovah. Ap. 4. II.

rising early and speaking. See note on 7. 13.

5 evil=calamity. Heb. *rā'a'.* Ap. 44. viii.

in the land=on the soil. Heb. *'ădāmāh.*

for ever and ever=from age to age. This must be read with "given", and refers to God's counsel. See note on Isa. 44. 7 ("ancient").

6 do you no hurt=bring no calamity upon you.

hurt. Heb. *rā'a'.* Ap. 44. viii. Cp. *v.* 5.

7 saith the LORD=[is] Jehovah's oracle.

provoke Me to anger, &c. Ref. to Pent. (Deut. 32. 21).

8 the LORD of hosts. See note on 6. 6, and 1 Sam. 1. 3.

9 My servant. Cp. Isa. 45. 1.

and. Note the Fig. *Polysyndeton.* Ap. 6.

astonishment. Ref. to Pent. (Deut. 28. 37). Cp. *v.* 18; 24. 9.

perpetual=age-abiding. Put by Fig. *Synecdoche* (of the Whole), Ap. 6, for a long time.

10 I will take from them. Quoted in Rev. 18. 23. Cp. 7. 34; 16. 9; 33. 11.

candle=lamp.

11 and. Some codices, with three early printed editions, Syr., and Vulg., read this "and" in the text.

seventy years. From 496 to 426. See the special note on p. 615.

25. 12-38 (Y, p. 1045). NATIONS. THE CUP.
(*Alternation.*)

Y | q | 12-14. Literal.
  | r | 15-29. Symbol. The Cup.
  | *q* | 30-33. Literal.
  | *r* | 34-38. Symbols. Shepherds and Folds.

12 when. No necessary sequence with *v.* 11. Verse 12 commences a fresh paragraph *re* the seventy years.

punish=visit upon, exactly seventy years later.

iniquity. Heb. *'āvāh.* Ap. 44. iv.

t. Heb. masc.=the People rather than the land.

14 of them: i.e. of the Chaldeans.

15 the LORD God of Israel. See note on 11. 3.

wine. Heb. *yayin.* Ap. 27. I.

16 be moved=reel to and fro.

because of the sword, &c. Ref. to Pent. (Lev. 26. 25, 33). Ap. 92.

18 Jerusalem. Comes first (cp. *v.* 29), because of 1 Pet. 4. 17. Amos 3. 2.

and. So some codices, with five early printed editions, Aram., Sept., Syr., and Vulg. Others omit this "and".

as it is this day. Probably added by Jeremiah when this prophecy had been fulfilled.

16 And they shall drink, and °be moved, and
be mad, °because of the sword that I will send
among them.'
17 Then took I the cup at [3]the LORD'S hand,
and made all the nations to drink, unto whom
[3]the LORD had sent me:
18 *To wit,* °Jerusalem, and the cities of Judah, and the kings thereof, °and the princes
thereof, to make them a desolation, an [9]aston-
ishment, an hissing, and a curse; °as *it is*
this day;

496 19 Pharaoh king of Egypt, and his servants,
and his princes, and all his people;
20 And all the °mingled people, and all the
kings of the land of °Uz, and all the kings of
the land of the °Philistines, and °Ashkelon,
and °Azzah, and °Ekron, and the remnant of
°Ashdod,
21 Edom, and Moab, and the °children of
Ammon,
22 And all the kings of Tyrus, and all the
kings of Zidon, °and the kings of the °isles
which °*are* beyond the sea,
23 °Dedan, and °Tema, and Buz, and all
°*that are* in the utmost corners,
24 And all the kings of Arabia, and all the
kings of the [20]mingled people that dwell in the
desert,
25 And all the kings of °Zimri, and all
the kings of Elam, and all the kings of the
Medes,
26 And all the kings of the north, far and
near, one with another, and all the kingdoms
of °the world, which *are* upon the face of °the
earth: and the king of °Sheshach shall drink
after them.
27 Therefore thou shalt say unto them,
Thus saith °the LORD of hosts, the God of
Israel; 'Drink ye, and be drunken, and spue,
and fall, and rise no more, [16]because of the
sword which I will send among you.'"
28 And it shall be, if they refuse to take the
cup at thine hand to drink, then shalt thou
say unto them, 'Thus saith [8]the LORD of
hosts; 'Ye shall certainly drink.
29 For, lo, I begin to bring [5]evil on the city
°which is called by My name, and should ye
be utterly °unpunished? Ye shall not be °unpunished:
for I will call for a sword upon all
the inhabitants of °the earth, [7]saith [8]the LORD
of hosts.'

q (p. 1051) 30 Therefore prophesy thou against them all
these words, and say unto them, [3]'The LORD
shall °roar from on high, and utter His voice
from His °holy habitation; He shall mightily
roar °upon His habitation; He shall give a
shout, as they that tread °*the grapes*, against
all the inhabitants of the earth.
31 A noise shall come *even* to the ends of the
earth; for [3]the LORD hath a controversy with
the nations, He will °plead with all flesh; He
will give them *that are* °wicked to the sword,
[7]saith [3]the LORD.'
32 Thus saith [8]the LORD of hosts, 'Behold,
[5]evil shall go forth from nation to nation, and
a great whirlwind shall be raised up from the
°coasts of the °earth.
33 And °the slain of [3]the LORD shall be at
that day from *one* end of the [32]earth even unto
the *other* end of the earth: they shall not be
lamented, neither gathered, nor buried; they
shall be dung upon the ground.

r 34 Howl, ye °shepherds, and cry; and wallow
yourselves *in the ashes*, ye °principal of the
flock: for the days of your slaughter and °of
your dispersions are accomplished; and ye
shall fall like a °pleasant vessel.
35 And the [34]shepherds shall have no way to
flee, nor the [34]principal of the flock to escape.
36 A voice of the cry of the [34]shepherds, and
an howling of the [34]principal of the flock, *shall
be heard:* for [3]the LORD hath spoiled their
pasture.
37 And the °peaceable habitations are °cut
down because of the fierce anger of [3]the LORD.

20 mingled people. Heb. *'ereb.* Cp. 50. 37. Ezek. 30. 5. Dan. 2. 43. Ezra 9. 2. Ps. 106. 35. In the inscription of Sennacherib (Bellino's *Cylinder*, line 13) the *Urbi* are joined with the Arameans (nomad tribes west of the Euphrates). Sennacherib says that Hezekiah had some "*Urbi*" soldiers with him in Jerusalem.

Uz. Job's country near Idumea (Lam. 4. 21).

Philistines, &c. Cp. ch. 47.

Ashkelon. Now *'Askalan.*

Azzah. Heb. *'Azzāh*=Gaza. Now *Guzzeh.*

Ekron. Now *'Akir.* **Ashdod.** Now *'Esdud.*

21 children=sons.

22 and the kings. So in the Mugah Codex (quoted in the *Massōrah*); but other codices, with one early printed edition, read "and all the kings".

isles=coast-land, or maritime country.

are. Supply "is", referring to coast-land.

23 Dedan. On the borders of Edom (49. 8. Ezek. 25. 13).

Tema, and Buz. The country of Elihu. See Job 32. 2 and note on p. 666.

that are in the utmost corners=all with their hair clipped at the corners.

25 Zimri. Etymology uncertain. Perhaps the country of Zimran, a son of Abraham by Keturah (Gen. 25. 2).

26 the world. Heb. *'erez* (with Art.), the earth.

the earth=the ground, or soil. Heb. *'ădāmāh* (with Art.).

Sheshach. The *Massōrah* explains that this word is "Babel", being a cypher by which the last letter of the alphabet is put for the first, and the next to the last for the second, &c., by which Sh. Sh. Ch. becomes B. B. L. "Babel" (cp. 51. 41, where both words are used). There is another example in 51. 1. See note there. Four classes of nations are to drink of this cup of the fury of Jehovah Elohim of Israel (*v.* 15): (1) Jerusalem and Judah (*v.* 18); (2) Egypt, &c. (*v.* 19); (3) the mingled nations (*vv.* 20–22); and (4) the more distant nations (*vv.* 23–25). Daniel fills in these "times of the Gentiles", which are not within the scope of Jeremiah and Ezekiel. But the point here is that the final judgment of the nations is yet future: when "Great Babylon" comes into remembrance, it will "drink after them". Cp. 49. 12. For this, "Sheshach" must be rebuilt and restored.

the LORD of hosts, the God of Israel. See note on 7. 3.

29 which is called by My name=upon which My name is called.

unpunished=held guiltless. Cp. 1 Pet. 4. 17. Ref. to Pent. (Ex. 20. 7; 34. 7. Num. 14. 18). Ap. 92. Cp. 30. 11; 46. 28; 49. 12.

the earth. Heb. *hā'ārez.* Same word as "the world" in *v.* 26.

30 roar. Cp. *v.* 38, "as a lion".

holy. See Ex. 3. 5.

upon His habitation=against His fold.

the grapes=the winepress. Cp. Isa. 63. 1–6.

31 plead with=judge.

wicked=lawless. Heb. *rāshā'.* Ap. 44. x.

32 coasts=sides: i. e. uttermost parts.

earth. Heb. *'arez.* Cp. *v.* 29.

33 the slain. By the sword. Cp. Isa. 66. 16.

34 shepherds=rulers (of all kinds). Cp. 2. 8; 6. 3. All three had miserable ends: Jehoiakim (22. 18; 36. 30); Jehoiachin, taken to Babylon; and Zedekiah, after his eyes were put out. **principal**=strong ones.

of your dispersions: or, when ye are dispersed. So in the Mugah Codex (quoted in the *Massōrah*), with three early printed editions.

pleasant=precious (i. e. fair, but fragile).

37 peaceable habitations=pastures of peace.

cut down=silenced.

496 38 He hath forsaken His covert, °as the lion: for their land is desolate because of °the fierceness of the oppressor, and because of His fierce anger.'"

Z F s (p. 1053) 498 **26** °In the beginning of the reign of Jehoiakim the son of Josiah king of Judah came this word from °the LORD, saying,

2 "Thus saith [1]the LORD; 'Stand °in the court of [1]the LORD'S house, and speak unto all the °cities of Judah, which come to worship in [1]the LORD'S house, all the words that I command thee to speak unto them; °diminish not a word:

t 3 If so be they will hearken, and turn °every man from his °evil way,

u that I may °repent Me of the °evil, which I purpose to do unto them because of the °evil of their doings.

t 4 And thou shalt say unto them, 'Thus saith [1]the LORD; °'If ye will not hearken to Me, to walk in °My law, which I have set before you,

5 To hearken to the words of My servants the prophets, whom I sent unto you, °both °rising up early, and sending *them*, but ye have not hearkened;

s 6 Then will I make this house like °Shiloh, and will make this city °a curse to all the nations of the earth.'''"

G H 7 So the priests and the prophets and all the people heard Jeremiah speaking these words in the house of [1]the LORD.

8 Now it came to pass, when Jeremiah had made an end of speaking all that [1]the LORD had commanded *him* to speak °unto all the People, that the priests and the prophets and all the People took him, saying, °"Thou shalt surely die.

9 Why hast thou prophesied in the name of [1]the LORD, saying, 'This house shall be like [6]Shiloh, and this city shall be desolate without an inhabitant?'" And °all the People were gathered against Jeremiah in the house of [1]the LORD.

J 10 When the princes of Judah heard these things, then they came up from the king's house unto the house of [1]the LORD, and sat down in the entry of the °new gate of [1]the LORD'S °*house*.

11 Then spake the priests and the prophets unto the princes and to [9]all the People, saying, °"This °man *is* worthy to die; for he hath prophesied against this city, °as ye have heard with your ears."

F 12 Then spake Jeremiah unto all the princes and to all the People, saying, [1]"The LORD sent me to prophesy against this house and against this city all the words that ye have heard.

13 Therefore now amend your ways and your doings, and °obey the voice of [1]the LORD your °God; and [1]the LORD will [3]repent Him of the [3]evil that He hath pronounced against you.

14 As for me, behold, I *am* in your hand: do with me as seemeth good and meet unto you.

15 But know ye for certain, that if ye put me to death, ye shall surely bring °innocent blood upon yourselves, and upon this city, and upon the inhabitants thereof: for of a truth [1]the LORD hath sent me unto you to speak all these words in your ears."

---

38 as the lion. Fig. *Simile* (Ap. 6). Cp. *v.* 30.
the fierceness of the oppressor. Some codices, with one early printed edition, Aram., and Sept., read "the (Sept. "great") sword of oppressors". Cp. 46. 16; 50. 16.

26. 1-24 (Z, p. 1045). **PROCLAMATION IN THE TEMPLE.** (*Alternations.*)

Z | F | 1-6. Jeremiah's mission.
  G | H | 7-9. Opposition.
    J | 10, 11. Defence. Princes.
  F | 12-15. Jeremiah's message.
  G | *H* | 16-23. Contention.
    J | 24. Defence. Ahikam.

26. 1-6 (F, above). **JEREMIAH'S MISSION.** (*Introversion.*)

F | s | 1, 2. Jehovah's house. Message.
  t | 3-. Obedience.
    u | -3. Promise.
  t | 4, 5. Disobedience.
  s | 6. Jehovah's house. Message.

Jeremiah's SEVENTEENTH Prophecy (p. 1015).

1 In the beginning: i.e. before the siege, in the third year of Jehoiakim. See note on 27. 1.
The first edition of the Prophets (Naples, 1485-6), the first edition of the entire Heb. Bible (Soncino, 1488), and the second edition (Naples, 1491-3), introduce the word *ḥăzī* = *half*, here, to indicate that the second half of Jeremiah commences here.
the LORD. Heb. Jehovah. Ap. 4. II.
2 in the court. This was Jeremiah's most public utterance. Cp. 7. 2.
cities. Put by Fig. *Metonymy* (of Subject), Ap. 6, for their inhabitants.
diminish not a word. Ref. to Pent. (Deut. 4. 2; 12. 32). Ap. 92. The importance of this is seen from the note on *v.* 18.
3 every man. Heb. *'ish.* Ap. 14. II.
evil. Heb. *ra'a'.* Ap. 44. viii.
repent Me. Fig. *Anthropopatheia.* Ap. 6.
4 If ye will not hearken. Ref. to Pent. (Lev. 26. 14. Deut. 28. 15). Ap. 92.
My law. Ref. to Pent. (Ex. 20).
5 both = even. Some codices, with one early printed edition, Aram., Sept., Syr., and Vulg., omit this "even".
rising up early, &c. See note on 7. 13.
6 Shiloh. See note on 7. 12.
a curse. Put by Fig. *Metonymy* (of Adjunct), Ap. 6, for the subject of cursing. Cp. 29. 22.
8 unto. One school of Massorites (Ap. 30) reads "concerning".
Thou shalt surely die. This was in accordance with Deut. 18. 20, as they would not believe that Jehovah could send such a message. A ref. to Pent. (Gen. 2. 17). Ap. 92. Jeremiah's danger was very real. Cp. *v.* 20-24.
9 all. Put by Fig. *Synecdoche* (of Genus), Ap. 6, for most of the People.
10 new gate. The Targum takes this to be the east gate.
house. Some codices, with Aram., Syr., and Vulg., read this word "house" in the text.
11 This man is worthy to die = Death's judgment is for this man: "judgment" being put by Fig. *Metonymy* (of the Cause), Ap. 6, for the effect of it: viz. the sentence of death (idiomatically rendered in A.V.). Cp. John 3. 19: where *krisis* is put for the act or process of judging. See Ap. 85.
man. Heb. *'ish.* Ap. 14. II.
as = according as.
13 obey = listen to.
God. Heb. Elohim. Ap. 4. I.
15 innocent blood. Ref. to Pent. (Deut. 19. 10, 13). Ap. 92. Cp. Matt. 27. 4, 25. Luke 23. 13-15. See Ap. 85.

G K (p. 1054) 498 16 °Then said the princes and all the People
unto the priests and to the prophets; °"This
°man *is* not worthy to die: for he hath spoken
to us in the name of [1]the LORD our [13]God."
17 Then rose up °certain of the elders of the
land, and spake to all the assembly of the
People, saying,
L v 18 °"Micah the Morasthite prophesied in the
days of Hezekiah king of Judah, and spake to
all the People of Judah, saying, 'Thus saith
°the LORD of hosts; °'Zion shall be plowed
like a field, and Jerusalem shall become heaps,
and the mountain of the house °as the high
places of a forest.''
w 19 Did Hezekiah king of Judah and all Judah
put him at all to death? did he not fear °the
LORD, and °besought [1]the LORD, and [1]the LORD
°repented Him of the [3]evil which He had
pronounced against them? Thus might we
procure great [3]evil against our °souls.
L v 20 °And there was also a [11]man that prophesied in the name of [1]the LORD, °Urijah the son
of Shemaiah of °Kirjath-jearim, who prophesied against this city and against this land
according to all the words of Jeremiah:
w 21 And when Jehoiakim the king, with all his
°mighty men, and all the princes, heard his
words, °the king sought to put him to death:
but when Urijah heard it, he was afraid, and
fled, and went into Egypt;
22 And Jehoiakim the king sent °men into
Egypt, *namely*, °Elnathan the son of Achbor,
and *certain* °men with him into Egypt.
23 And they fetched forth Urijah out of Egypt,
and brought him unto Jehoiakim the king; who
°slew him with the sword, and cast his dead
body into the graves of the °common People."
K 24 Nevertheless the hand of °Ahikam the son
of °Shaphan was with Jeremiah, that they
should not give him into the hand of the People
to put him to death.

Y M x 498 **27** °In the beginning of the reign of Jehoiakim the son of Josiah king of Judah
°came this word unto Jeremiah from °the
LORD, saying,
2 "Thus saith [1]the LORD to me; 'Make thee
bonds and yokes, and °put them upon thy neck,
3 And send them to the king of Edom, °and
to the king of Moab, °and to the king of the
Ammonites, °and to the king of Tyrus, °and to
the king of Zidon, by the hand of the messengers °which come to Jerusalem °unto Zedekiah
king of Judah;
4 And command them to say unto their masters,
'Thus saith °the LORD of hosts, the °God of
Israel; Thus shall ye say unto your masters;

26. 16-24 (*G*, p. 1053). CONTENTION.
(*Introversion and Alternation.*)

G | K | 16, 17. Defenders. Princes.
  L | v | 18. Case of Micah. } Favourable.
    w | 19. Conduct of Hezekiah. }
  L | *v* | 20. Case of Urijah. } Adverse.
    w | 21-23. Conduct of Jehoiakim. }
K | 24. Defender. Ahikam.

16 Then said the princes, &c. In favour of Jeremiah. Note the Structure "Z", p. 1053; and contrast "G" (*vv.* 7-11) with "*G*" (*vv.* 16-24).
This man, &c. See Ap. 85.
man. Heb. *'ish.* Ap. 14. II.
17 certain = men. Plural of *'ěnōsh.* Ap. 14. III. Some better acquainted with affairs than others.
18 Micah. The prophet whose book is called after his name. Contemporary with Hosea and Amos in Israel, and with Isaiah in Judah. See Ap. 77.
the LORD of hosts. See note on 6. 6. 1 Sam. 1. 3.
Zion shall be plowed, &c. See note on Mic. 3. 12. A prophecy which was wholly fulfilled as to the Jewish Zion (south of Moriah), but not as to the traditional Zion, south-west of Jerusalem. See Ap. 68.
as. The edition of A.V., 1611, omits this "as".
19 the LORD. Heb. *'eth Jehovah* = Jehovah Himself. Ap. 4. II.
besought the LORD = appeased the face of Jehovah. Figs. *Pleonasm* and *Anthropopatheia.* Ap. 6.
repented Him. Fig. *Anthropopatheia.* Ap. 6. Ref. to Pent. (Ex. 32. 14). Ap. 92.
souls. Heb. *nephesh.* Ap. 13.
20 And = But. Said in reply to the friends of Jeremiah by his adversaries. See the Structure above.
Urijah. This incident is not recorded in the historical books, but it illustrates *v.* 5.
Kirjath-jearim. Now *Khan 'Erma*, or *Kuriet el 'Enab*, four miles west of the hill overlooking Beth-shemesh, and about twelve miles from Jerusalem.
21 mighty men. Plural of *geber.* Ap. 14. IV.
the king sought, &c. One of eleven rulers offended with God's messengers. See note on Ex. 10. 28.
22 men. Heb. pl. of *'ěnōsh.* Ap. 14. III.
Elnathan. See 26. 22; 36. 12, 25.
23 slew him with the sword. Cp. Heb. 11. 37.
common People. Heb. sons of the people.
24 Ahikam. The father of Gedaliah, who, when appointed governor by Nebuchadnezzar, stood as the friend of Jeremiah. For a son of Ahikam also befriending Jeremiah, see 40. 6.
Shaphan. See note on 2 Kings 22. 3. See 36. 10 for another son; 29. 3 for another son. Also befriending Jeremiah.

27. 1-22 (*Y*, p. 1045). NATIONS. BONDS AND YOKES. (*Introversion and Alternations.*)

Y | M | x | 1-7-. Nations to serve Babylon.
    y | -7. For a limited time.
  N | z^1 | 8. Exhortation. Nations.
    a^1 | 9-11. Dehortation.
    z^2 | 12, 13. Exhortation. Zedekiah.
    a^2 | 14, 15. Dehortation.
    z^3 | 16-. Exhortation. Priests and People.
    a^3 | -16, 17. Dehortation.
  M | *x* | 18-22-. Remaining vessels to go to Babylon.
    y | -22. For a limited time.

Jeremiah's EIGHTEENTH Prophecy (p. 1015).
Given in reign of Jehoiakim to Jeremiah. Declared, after thirteen years, in fourth year of Zedekiah: i.e. in 485. Cp. *v.* 12. Chs. 27 and 28 were written by Jeremiah, or at his dictation. Cp. "me", 27. 2; 28. 1. Some codices, with Syr., read "Zedekiah", as in *vv.* 3 and 12. **1 In the beginning.** The *Massōrah* (Ap. 30) notes the fact that this expression occurs three times at the commencement of a verse (Gen. 1. 1. Jer. 26. 1; 27. 1). **came.** At the beginning of the reign of Jehoiakim; but it referred to a future time, as shown in *v.* 12. **the LORD.** Heb. Jehovah. Ap. 4. II. **2 put them, &c.** This was literally done, as a prophetic symbol; and at that time prophetic of what was to happen in the reign of Zedekiah, eleven years later. **3 and.** Note the Fig. *Polysyndeton* (Ap. 6), to emphasise each respectively. **which come** = that are coming. Part. *Poel*, as in Gen. 37. 19; 41. 29, 35. Jer. 4. 16; 6. 22; 7. 32; 9. 25; 16. 14; 23. 5, 7; 31. 27, 31, 38; 32. 7; 33. 5, 14, &c. This was to take place eleven years later. **unto Zedekiah.** Then and there we have the fulfilment of this prophecy. **4 the LORD of hosts, the God of Israel.** See note on 7. 3. **God.** Heb. Elohim. Ap. 4. I.

498 5 °'I have made the earth, the °man and the
beast that *are* upon °the °ground, by My °great
power and by My °outstretched arm, and have
given it unto whom it seemed meet unto Me.
6 And now have I given all these lands into
the hand of °Nebuchadnezzar the king of
Babylon, °My servant; and the beasts of the
field have I given him also to serve him.
7 And all nations shall serve °him, and his
son, and his son's son,
y until °the very time of his land come: and
p. 1054) then many nations and °great kings shall
serve themselves of him.
N z[1] 8 And it shall come to pass, *that* the nation
and kingdom which will not serve °the same
[6]Nebuchadnezzar the king of Babylon, and
that will not put their neck under the yoke of
the king of Babylon, that nation will I punish,
°saith [1]the LORD, with the °sword, °and with
the °famine, °and with the °pestilence, until I
have consumed them by his hand.
a[1] 9 Therefore hearken not ye to your prophets,
nor to your °diviners, nor to your dreamers,
nor to your °enchanters, nor to your °sor-
cerers, which speak unto you, saying, 'Ye
shall not serve the king of Babylon':
10 For they prophesy a lie unto you, to remove
you far from your land; and that I should
drive you out, and ye should perish.
11 But the nations that bring their neck under
the yoke of the king of Babylon, and serve
him, those will I let remain still in their own
land, [8]saith [1]the LORD; and they shall till it,
and dwell therein.'''"
z[2] 12 °I spake also °to Zedekiah king of Judah
485 according to all these words, saying, "Bring
your necks under the yoke of the king of
Babylon, and serve him and his people, and live.
13 °Why will ye die, thou and thy People, by
the [8]sword, °by the famine, [8]and by the pestilence, °as [1]the LORD hath spoken against the
nation that will not serve the king of Babylon?
a[2] 14 Therefore hearken not unto the words of
the prophets that speak unto you, saying, 'Ye
shall not serve the king of Babylon:' for they
prophesy a lie unto you.
15 'For I have not sent them,' saith [1]the LORD,
'yet they prophesy a lie in My name; that I
might drive you out, and that ye might perish,
ye, and the prophets that prophesy unto you.'"
z[3] 16 Also I spake °to the priests and to all this
People, saying, "Thus saith [1]the LORD;
a[3] 'Hearken not to the words of your prophets
that prophesy unto you, saying, °'Behold,
°the vessels of [1]the LORD'S house shall now
shortly be brought again from Babylon:' for
they prophesy a lie unto you.
17 Hearken not unto them; serve the king of
Babylon, and live: °wherefore should this city
be laid waste?
M x 18 But if they *be* prophets, and if the word of
[1]the LORD °be with them, let them now make
intercession to °the LORD of hosts, that the
vessels which are left in the house of [1]the
LORD, and *in* the house of the king of Judah,
and °at Jerusalem, go not to Babylon.'
19 For thus saith [18]the LORD of hosts concerning the pillars, and concerning the sea,
and concerning the bases, and concerning the
residue of the vessels that °remain in this °city,
20 Which [6]Nebuchadnezzar king of Babylon
took not, when he carried away captive °Je-
coniah the son of Jehoiakim king of Judah
from Jerusalem to Babylon, and all the nobles
of Judah and Jerusalem;
21 Yea, thus saith [4]the LORD of hosts, the
[4]God of Israel, concerning the vessels that
remain °*in* the house of [1]the LORD, and *in* the
house of the king of Judah and of Jerusalem;
22 'They shall be carried to Babylon, and
there shall they be until the day that I visit
them, [8]saith [1]the LORD;
°then will I bring them up, and restore them y
to this place.'"

5 I have made, &c. Ref. to Pent. (Gen. 1. 1). Ap. 92.
man. Heb. *'ādām.* Ap. 14. I.
the ground. Heb. the face of the ground. Fig. *Pleonasm.* Ap. 6. Some codices read "the face of all the ground". **ground**=earth. Heb. *hā-'ārez.*
great power . . . outstretched arm. Ref. to Pent. (Ex. 6. 6. Deut. 4. 34; 5. 15; 7. 19; 9. 29; 11. 2; 26. 8).
6 Nebuchadnezzar. Some codices spell it "Nebuchadrezzar".
My servant. Cp. 25. 9. See Dan. 2. 37, 38.
7 him, and his son, and his son's son: i.e. Evil Merodach, Nergelissar, and Nabonidus, in whose seventeenth year Babylon was taken by Cyrus. Ap. 57.
the very time=the appointed end.
great kings: i.e. the kings of Persia and Media (Dan. 2. 39). **8 the same**=him.
saith the LORD=[is] Jehovah's oracle.
sword . . . famine . . . pestilence. Ref. to Pent. (Lev. 26. 25, 26. Deut. 28. 21-24). Ap. 92.
and. Note the Fig. *Polysyndeton.* Ap. 6.
9 diviners, &c. These were their heathen guides.
enchanters=observers of the clouds.
sorcerers. These were mediums and necromancers.
12 I spake: i.e. thirteen years after this prophecy came to him. See note on *v.* 1.
to Zedekiah. It is not stated whether he ever addressed the two other kings. Jehoahaz and Zedekiah were the sons of Hamutal; Jehoiakim was the son of the proud Zebudah (2 Kings 23. 36). Cp. 13. 18.
13 Why . . .? Fig. *Asterismos.* Ap. 6.
by. Some codices, with Aram., Syr., and Vulg., read "and by", thus completing the Fig. *Polysyndeton.* Ap. 6. Cp. *v.* 8. **as**=according as.
16 to the priests. Probably in the Temple. Cp. 28. 1.
Behold. Fig. *Asterismos.* Ap. 6.
the vessels: which were taken away by Nebuchadnezzar in the reigns of Jehoiakim and Jeconiah (2 Kings 24. 13. 2 Chron. 36. 7, 10. Dan. 1. 2).
17 wherefore . . .? Fig. *Erotēsis.* Ap. 6.
18 be=exists; or, be and remain. Heb. *yēsh.* Cp. 31. 6, 16, 17, and see notes on Prov. 8. 21; 18. 24.
the LORD of hosts=Jehovah Z^ebaōth. See note on 6. 6. 1 Sam. 1. 3.
at. Some codices, with three early printed editions, omit this "at".
19 remain. Probably because they were too heavy and cumbrous.
city. So the reading of Ben-Asher; but Ben-Naphtali reads "land". These were the two rival critics of the Heb. text in the tenth century A.D. who furnished the vowel-points. Ben-Asher's work was done at Tiberias in 827 "from the destruction of Jerusalem", and is now at Aleppo. Of Ben-Naphtali nothing is known beyond official lists which have come down to us.
20 Jeconiah. Cp. 24. 1.
21 in. Some codices, with three early printed editions, read this "in" in the text.
22 then will I bring them up. Fulfilled by Cyrus (Ezra 1. 7; 5. 13, 14).

X b (p. 1056) 485

28 And it came to pass °the same year, in the beginning of the reign of Zedekiah king of Judah, in the fourth year, *and* in the fifth month, *that* °Hananiah the son of Azur the prophet, which *was* of °Gibeon, spake unto me °in the house of °the LORD, in the presence of the priests and of all the People, saying,

2 "Thus speaketh °the LORD of hosts, the °God of Israel, saying, °'I have broken the yoke of the king of Babylon.

3 Within °two full years will I bring again into this place all the vessels of [1]the LORD'S house, that °Nebuchadnezzar king of Babylon took away from this place, and carried them to Babylon:

4 And I will bring again to this place Jeconiah the son of Jehoiakim king of Judah, with all the °captives of Judah, that went into Babylon, °saith [1]the LORD: for I will break the yoke of the king of Babylon.' "

c 5 Then the prophet °Jeremiah said unto the prophet [1]Hananiah in the presence of the priests, and in the presence of all the People that stood in the house of [1]the LORD,

6 Even the prophet Jeremiah said, °"Amen: [1]the LORD do so: [1]the LORD perform °thy °words which thou hast prophesied, to bring again the vessels of [1]the LORD'S house, and all that is carried away captive, from Babylon into this place.

7 Nevertheless hear thou now this word that I speak in thine ears, and in the ears of all the People;

8 The prophets that have been before me and before thee of old prophesied both against many countries, and against great kingdoms, of war, and of °evil, and of pestilence.

9 The prophet which prophesieth of peace, when the word of the prophet °shall come to pass, *then* shall the prophet be known, that [1]the LORD hath truly sent him."

b 10 Then Hananiah the prophet took °the yoke °from off the prophet Jeremiah's neck, and brake it.

11 And Hananiah spake in the presence of all the people, saying, "Thus saith [1]the LORD; 'Even so will I break the yoke of Nebuchadnezzar king of Babylon from the neck of all nations within the space of two full years.' " And the prophet Jeremiah °went his way.

c 12 °Then the word of [1]the LORD came unto Jeremiah *the prophet,* after that Hananiah the prophet had broken the yoke from off the neck of the prophet Jeremiah, saying,

13 "Go and tell Hananiah, saying, 'Thus saith [1]the LORD; 'Thou hast broken the yokes of wood; but thou shalt make °for them °yokes of iron.

14 For thus saith [2]the LORD of hosts, the [2]God of Israel; °'I have put a yoke of iron upon the neck of all these nations, that they may serve Nebuchadnezzar king of Babylon; and they shall serve him: and I have given him the beasts of the field also.' ' ' "

15 Then said the prophet Jeremiah unto Hananiah the prophet, "Hear now, Hananiah; [1]The LORD hath °not sent thee; but thou makest this people to °trust in a lie.

16 Therefore thus saith [1]the LORD; °'Behold, I will cast thee from off the face of °the earth: this year thou shalt °die, because thou hast °taught °rebellion against [1]the LORD.' "

17 So Hananiah the prophet died the same year in the °seventh month.

29 Now these *are* the °words of the °letter that Jeremiah the prophet sent from Jerusalem unto the °residue of the elders W O (p. 105?) 489-8

---

28. 1-17 (X, p. 1045). TIME. TWO YEARS.
(*Alternation.*)

X | b | 1-4. Hananiah.
 | c | 5-9. Jeremiah.
 | b | 10, 11. Hananiah.
 | c | 12-17. Jeremiah.

1 the same year. As 27. 12, when Jeremiah spoke to Zedekiah; not 27. 1, when he *received* the message which was to be delivered. The same year in which Jeremiah had counselled Zedekiah not to hearken to the false prophets (27. 14).

Hananiah. A false prophet. Cp. 27. 12, 14.

Gibeon. A city of the priests (Josh. 21. 17). Hananiah was therefore probably a priest as Jeremiah was. Now *el Jib*, north of Jerusalem. **in the house.** Cp. 26. 2.

the LORD. Heb. Jehovah. Ap. 4. II.

2 the LORD of hosts, the God of Israel. See note on 7. 3. **God.** Heb. Elohim. Ap. 4. I.

I have broken. This was proved to be a false promise.

3 two full years. Heb. two years in days [measured in] days: i.e. complete years. Cp. Gen. 41. 1. 2 Sam. 13. 23. Not years of days (a day for a year).

Nebuchadnezzar. See note on 27. 6.

4 captives. Heb. captivity. Put by Fig. *Metonymy* (of Subject), Ap. 6, for the people in captivity.

saith the LORD = [is] Jehovah's oracle.

5 Jeremiah. Spelt here, and in this chapter only (except 27. 1. Ezra 1. 1. Dan. 9. 2), in an abbreviated form, "*Yirm^{e}yah*" instead of "*Yirm^{e}yāhū*", as elsewhere. This may be to bring the true prophet into stronger contrast with the false "*Hănan^{e}yah*".

6 Amen. Interpreted in the words which follow.

thy. Edition of A.V., 1611, reads "the".

words. Some codices, with three early printed editions, Aram., and Sept., read "word" (sing.).

8 evil = calamity. Heb. *rā'a'*. Ap. 44. viii. Some codices, with one early printed edition, read "famine". Cp. 27. 8, and 29. 17.

9 shall come to pass. Acc. to the test laid down in Deut. 18. 21, 22 (ref. to Pent.). Ap. 92.

10 the yoke. See 27. 2. Made of wood (*v.* 13).

from off. So that Jeremiah was still wearing it (27. 2).

11 went his way. Having no further word from Jehovah.

Jeremiah's NINETEENTH Prophecy (p. 1015).

12 Then = And. Evidently shortly after this.

13 for = instead of.

yokes of iron. These are never used. No stronger symbol could have been given.

14 I have put, &c. Ref. to Pent. (Deut. 28. 48, the same words). Ap. 92.

15 not sent thee. The test applied (Deut. 18. 21, 22).

trust = confide. Heb. *bātah*. Ap. 69. i.

16 Behold. Fig. *Asterismos.* Ap. 6.

the earth = the ground, or soil. Heb. *hā'ădāmāh.*

die. According to Deut. 18. 20. Ref. to Pent. Ap. 92.

taught = spoken. Ref. to Pent. (Deut. 13. 5). Ap. 92.

rebellion, &c. Zedekiah had taken an oath of allegiance to Nebuchadnezzar (2 Kings 24. 17. 2 Chron. 36. 13. Ezek. 17. 15, 18). So it was a double rebellion.

17 seventh month: i.e. two *months* after, instead of "two *years*" (*v.* 3).

29. 1-32 [For the Structure see next page].

1 words: i.e. prophecies, as in 25. 1; 26. 1; 27. 1; 30. 1, &c. **letter** = writing.

residue of the elders. Cp. Ezek. 8. 1; 14. 1; 20. 1.

489 which were carried away captives, and to the priests, and to °the prophets, and to all the People whom °Nebuchadnezzar had carried away captive from Jerusalem to Babylon;

2 (After that °Jeconiah the king, and °the queen, and the °eunuchs, the princes of Judah and Jerusalem, and the °carpenters, and the smiths, were departed from Jerusalem;)

3 By the hand of Elasah the son of °Shaphan, and Gemariah the son of °Hilkiah, (whom °Zedekiah king of Judah °sent unto Babylon to [1] Nebuchadnezzar king of Babylon) saying,

4 "Thus saith °the LORD of hosts, the °God of Israel, unto all that are carried away captives, whom I have caused to be carried away from Jerusalem unto Babylon;

5 'Build ye houses, and dwell *in them;* and plant gardens, and eat the fruit of them;

6 Take ye wives, and beget sons and daughters; and take wives for your sons, and give your daughters to husbands, that they may bear sons and daughters; that ye may be increased there, and not diminished.

7 And °seek the peace of the city whither I have caused you to be carried away °captives, and pray unto °the LORD for it: for in the peace thereof shall ye have peace.'

P d^{1} 8 For thus saith [4] the LORD of hosts, the [4] God of Israel; 'Let not your prophets and your diviners, that *be* in the midst of you, deceive you, neither hearken to your dreams which ye °cause to be dreamed.

9 For they prophesy falsely unto you in My name: I have not sent them, °saith [7] the LORD.'

e^{1} 10 For thus saith [7] the LORD, 'That after °seventy years be accomplished at Babylon I will visit you, and perform My good word toward you, in causing you to return to this place.

11 For I know the thoughts that I think toward you, [9] saith [7] the LORD, thoughts of peace, and not of °evil, to give you °an expected end.

12 Then shall ye call upon Me, and ye shall go and pray unto Me, and I will hearken unto you.

13 And °ye shall seek Me, and find *Me,* when ye shall search for Me with all your heart.

14 And I will be found of you, [9] saith [7] the LORD: and I will turn °away your °captivity, and I will gather you from all the nations, and from all the places whither I have driven you, saith [7] the LORD; and I will bring you again into the place whence I caused you to be carried away captive.

d^{2} 15 Because ye have said, [7] 'The LORD hath raised us up prophets in Babylon;'

e^{2} 16 *Know* that thus saith [7] the LORD °of the king that sitteth upon the throne of David, and of all the People that dwelleth in this city, *and* of your brethren that are not gone forth with you into captivity;

17 Thus saith °the LORD of hosts; °'Behold, °I will send upon them the sword, °the famine, and the pestilence, °and will make them like °vile figs, that cannot be eaten, they are so [11] evil.

29. 1-32 (*W*, p. 1045). CAPTIVES AND REMNANT. (*Introversion and Repeated Alternation.*)

W | O | 1-7. Letter of Jeremiah to the Captivity.
  | P | d^{1} | 8, 9. Dehortation. False prophets.
  | | e^{1} | 10-14. Prophecy to captives. Good.
  | | d^{2} | 15. Dehortation. False prophets.
  | | e^{2} | 16-19. Prophecy to residue. Evil.
  | | d^{3} | 20-29. Dehortation. False prophets.
  | O | 30-32. Message of Jehovah to the Captivity.

the prophets: i.e. Ezekiel (1. 1); Daniel (1. 6).
Nebuchadnezzar. Same spelling as throughout ch. 28 and *v.* 3 here. Not the same as in *v.* 21.
2 Jeconiah: i.e. Jehoiachin.
the queen = the queen-mother, Nehushta, the wife of Jehoiakim. Cp. 13. 18. See 2 Kings 24. 12, 15.
eunuchs = chamberlains.
carpenters = artificers, smiths. Cp. 24. 1.
3 Shaphan. See note on 2 Kings 22. 3. Cp. 26. 24.
Hilkiah. As in 2 Kings 22. 4.
Zedekiah . . . sent. Cp. 51. 59.
4 the LORD of hosts, the God of Israel. See note on 7. 3.
God. Heb. Elohim. Ap. 4. I.
7 seek the peace = seek the welfare. Cp. Ezra 6. 10.
captives. For sixty-three years. From Jehoiachin's captivity to Cyrus (489 – 426 = 63).
the LORD. Heb. Jehovah. Ap. 4. II.
9 saith the LORD = [is] Jehovah's oracle.
10 seventy years. See special note on p. 615. Cp. 25. 12.
11 evil. Heb. *rā'a'.* Ap. 44. viii.
an expected end. Fig. *Hendiadys.* Ap. 6. Heb. "an end and an expectation" = an end, yea, an end which I have caused you to hope for: i.e. a hoped-for end.
13 ye shall seek Me. Ref. to Pent. (Deut. 4. 29; 30. 2).
14 away = back.
captivity. Put by Fig. *Metonymy* (of Subject), Ap. 6, for captives.
16 of = concerning.
17 the LORD of hosts. See note on 6. 6. 1 Sam. 1. 3.
Behold. Fig. *Asterismos.* Ap. 6.
I will send . . . the sword, &c. Ref. to Pent. (Lev. 26. 25, 26. Deut. 28. 21-24).
the famine. Some codices, with three early printed editions (one in margin), Aram., Syr., and Vulg., read "and famine", thus completing the Fig. *Polysyndeton* (Ap. 6).
and. Note the Fig. *Polysyndeton* in *vv.* 17, 18 (Ap. 6).
vile figs = worthless figs. See 24. 2, &c.
18 with. Some codices, with one early printed edition, read "and with".
removed. Ref. to Pent. (Deut. 28. 25, the same word). Ap. 92. Cp. 24. 9.
19 unto them. Some codices, with four early printed editions, read "unto you".
rising up early, &c. See note on 7. 13.
20 sent. Some codices, with Aram., read "caused to be carried captive". Cp. 24. 5.

18 And I will persecute them with the sword, °with the famine, and with the pestilence, [17] and will deliver them to be °removed to all the kingdoms of the earth, to be a curse, and an astonishment, and an hissing, and a reproach, among all the nations whither I have driven them:

19 Because they have not hearkened to My words, [9] saith [7] the LORD, which I sent °unto them by My servants the prophets, °rising up early and sending *them;* but ye would not hear, [9] saith [7] the LORD.'

20 Hear ye therefore the word of [7] the LORD, all ye of the captivity, whom I have °sent from Jerusalem to Babylon: d^{3}

21 Thus saith [4] the LORD of hosts, the [4] God of

489 Israel, [16]of °Ahab the son of °Kolaiah, and of
°Zedekiah the son of Maaseiah, which prophesy a lie unto you in My name; [17]'Behold,
I will deliver them into the hand of °Nebuchad-
rezzar king of Babylon; and he shall slay them
before your eyes;
22 And of them shall be taken up °a °curse
by all the captivity of Judah which *are* in
Babylon, saying, [7]'The LORD make thee like
Zedekiah and like Ahab, whom the king of
Babylon °roasted in the fire;'
23 Because they have °committed villany
in Israel, and have committed adultery with
their neighbours' wives, and have spoken lying
words in My name, which I have not commanded them; even I know, and *am* a witness, [9]saith [7]the LORD.'
24 *Thus* shalt thou also speak to Shemaiah
the °Nehelamite, saying,
25 'Thus speaketh [4]the LORD of hosts, the
[4]God of Israel, saying, 'Because thou hast sent
letters in thy name unto all the People that *are*
at Jerusalem, and to Zephaniah the son of
Maaseiah the priest, and to all the priests,
saying,
26 [7]'The LORD hath made thee priest in the
stead of Jehoiada the priest, that ye should be
officers in the house of [7]the LORD, for every
°man *that is* °mad, and °maketh himself a
prophet, that thou shouldest put him in prison,
and in the stocks.
27 Now therefore why hast thou not reproved
Jeremiah of Anathoth, which [26]maketh himself
a prophet to you?
28 For therefore he sent unto us *in* Babylon,
saying, 'This *captivity is* long: build ye houses,
and dwell *in them;* and plant gardens, and eat
the fruit of them.''''"
29 And Zephaniah the priest read this letter
in the ears of Jeremiah the prophet.
O 30 Then came the word of [7]the LORD unto
Jeremiah, saying,
31 "Send to all them of the captivity, saying,
'Thus saith [7]the LORD concerning Shemaiah
the [24]Nehelamite; 'Because that Shemaiah
hath prophesied unto you, and I sent him not,
and he caused you to °trust in a lie:
32 Therefore thus saith [7]the LORD; [17]Be-
hold, I will punish Shemaiah the [24]Nehelamite,
and his seed: he shall not have a [26]man to
dwell among this People; neither shall he
behold the good that I will do for My People,
[9]saith [7]the LORD; because he hath taught °re-
bellion against [7]the LORD.''"

V Q U 489 **30** The word that came to Jeremiah from
°the LORD, saying,
2 "Thus speaketh °the LORD °God of Israel,
saying, 'Write thee all the words that I have
spoken unto thee °in a book.
V 3 For, °lo, the days come, °saith [1]the LORD,
that I will bring again the captivity of My
people °Israel and Judah, °saith [1]the LORD:
and I will cause them to return to the land
that I gave to their fathers, and they shall
possess it.'"
U 4 And °these *are* the words that [1]the LORD
spake concerning [3]Israel and concerning Judah.

21 Ahab . . . Zedekiah. These were false prophets whom Nebuchadrezzar treated as stated in *v.* 22.

21, 22 Kolaiah . . . curse . . . roasted. Note the Fig. *Paronomasia* (Ap. 6). Heb. *Kōlāyāh . . . ḳelālāh . . . ḳālām.*

Nebuchadrezzar. Some codices read Nebuchadnezzar. Cp. *v.* 1. **22 a curse** = a curse formula.

23 committed villany = vileness: i.e. worshipped idols. See the first occ. Gen. 34. 7.

24 Nehelamite: or, dreamer.

26 man. Heb. *'ish.* Ap. 14. II.

mad. Cp. John 2. 20; 10. 20, 39. See Ap. 85.

maketh himself a prophet. Cp. Matt. 21. 11. John 8. 53. See Ap. 85.

31 trust = confide. Heb. *baṭaḥ.* Ap. 69. i.

32 rebellion, &c. Ref. to Pent. (Deut. 13. 5). Ap. 92.

30. 1—31. 40 (*V*, p. 1045). BOOK. RESTORATION. (*Alternation and Introversion.*)

V | Q | 30. 1-17. Book.
R | S | 30. 18. City. Rebuilding.
T | 30. 19—31. 1. People. Restoration.
Q | 31. 2-26. Vision.
R | *T* | 31. 27-37. People. Restoration.
S | 31. 38-40. City. Rebuilding.

30. 1-17 (Q, above). BOOK. (*Alternation.*)

Q | U | 1, 2. Words.
V | 3. Restoration. General.
U | 4. Words.
V | 5-17. Restoration. Particular.

Jeremiah's TWENTIETH Prophecy (p. 1015).

1 the LORD. Heb. Jehovah. Ap. 4. II.

2 the LORD God of Israel. See note on 11. 3.

God. Heb. Elohim. Ap. 4. I.

in a book. For abiding comfort and hope in the coming times of trouble. Written before the deportation. Cp. 30. 5-11, 12-24. A dark foreground is shown in 31. 37.

3 lo. Fig. *Asterismos.* Ap. 6.

saith the LORD = [is] Jehovah's oracle.

Israel. As well as Judah.

4 these are the words. This is the introduction to the two chapters.

30. 5-17 (*V*, above). RESTORATION. PARTICULAR. (*Extended Alternation.*)

V | f | 5-7-. Tribulation.
g | -7-10. Restoration.
h | 11. Jehovah the Saviour.
f | 12-15. Tribulation.
g | 16. Retaliation.
h | 17. Jehovah the Healer.

6 a man = a male. Heb. *zakar.*

man = a strong man. Heb. *geber.* Ap. 14. IV.

7 that day. The interpretation here is of the day of Babylon's overthrow. The application is of the yet future Great Tribulation of Matt. 24. This is in contrast with the day of Restoration.

great, &c. = too great to have another like it.

Jacob's. Not Israel's, for it is the natural seed that is here in question, not the spiritual. See notes on Gen. 32. 28; 43. 6; 45. 26, 28.

5 For thus saith [1]the LORD; "We have heard V f
a voice of trembling, of fear, and not of peace.
6 Ask ye now, and see whether °a man doth
travail with child? wherefore do I see every
°man with his hands on his loins, as a woman
in travail, and all faces are turned into paleness?
7 Alas! for °that day *is* °great, so that none
is like it: it *is* even the time of °Jacob's
trouble;
but he shall be saved out of it. g

489 8 For it shall come to pass in that day,
[3]saith °the LORD of hosts, *that* I will °break
his yoke from off thy neck, and will burst thy
bonds, and strangers shall no more serve
themselves of him:
9 But they shall serve [1]the LORD their [2]God,
and °David their king, whom I will raise up
unto them.
10 Therefore °fear thou not, O My servant
[7]Jacob, [3]saith [1]the LORD; neither be dismayed, O Israel: for, lo, I will save thee from
afar, and thy seed from the land of their captivity; and [7]Jacob shall return, and °shall be
in rest, and be quiet, and none shall make *him*
afraid.
h 11 For I *am* with thee, [3]saith [1]the LORD,
to save thee: though I make a full end of all
nations whither I have scattered thee, yet will
I not make a full end of thee: but I will correct
thee °in measure, and will not leave thee
altogether °unpunished.
f 12 For thus saith [1]the LORD, 'Thy bruise *is*
incurable, *and* thy wound *is* grievous.
13 *There is* none to plead thy cause, °that
thou mayest be bound up: thou hast no healing medicines.
14 All thy lovers have forgotten thee; they
seek thee not; for I have wounded thee with
the wound of an enemy, with the chastisement
of a cruel one, for the multitude of thine °ini-
quity; *because* thy °sins were increased.
15 Why criest thou for thine affliction? thy
sorrow *is* incurable for the multitude of thine
[14]iniquity: *because* thy [14]sins were increased,
I have done these things unto thee.
g 16 Therefore °all they that devour thee shall
be devoured; and all thine adversaries, every
one of them, shall go into captivity; and they
that spoil thee shall be a spoil, and all that
prey upon thee will I give for a prey.
h 17 For I will restore health unto thee, and
I will heal thee of thy wounds, [3]saith [1]the
LORD; because they called thee an Outcast,
saying, 'This *is* Zion, whom no man seeketh
after.''
R S 18 Thus saith [1]the LORD; °'Behold, I will
bring again the captivity of [7]Jacob's tents, and
have mercy on his dwellingplaces; and the
city shall be builded °upon her own °heap, and
the °palace shall remain °after the manner
thereof.
T i 19 And out of °them shall proceed thanksgiving and the voice of them that make merry:
and °I will multiply them, and they shall not
be few; I will also glorify them, and they
shall not be °small.
20 Their °children also shall be as aforetime,
and their congregation shall be established
before Me, and I will punish all that °oppress
them.
21 And °their nobles shall be of themselves,
and °their governor shall proceed from the
midst of them; and I will °cause him to draw
near, and he shall approach unto Me: for
°who *is* this that °engaged his heart to approach unto Me? [3]saith [1]the LORD.
k 22 And ye shall be My People, and I will
be your [2]God.

8 the LORD of hosts = Jehovah Ẓ^ebaōth. See note on 6. 6.

break his yoke. Reminding us of 28. 10, 11.

9 David their king. This is yet future. Cp. Ezekiel, Jeremiah's contemporary (Ezek. 34. 23, 24; 37. 24, 25. Isa. 55. 3. Hos. 3. 5) for seven years (484–477). See Ap. 77.

10 fear thou not, &c. Taking up Isa. 41. 10, 13; 43. 5; 44. 2. **shall be in rest** = be [again] in rest.

11 in measure = to the due measure.

unpunished = guiltless. Ref. to Pent. (Ex. 20. 7; 34. 7. Num. 14. 18). Ap. 92.

13 that thou mayest, &c. = for binding thee up.

14 iniquity. Heb. *'āvāh*. Ap. 44. iv.

sins. Heb. *chāṭā'*. Ap. 44. i.

16 all they that devour thee, &c. Ref. to Pent. (Ex. 23. 22). Ap. 92.

18 Behold. Fig. *Asterismos*. Ap. 6.

upon her own heap. This cannot have a spiritual application; still less interpretation. It is literally Zion. This was written in the book, before the siege, which had already been foretold (chs. 7; 19; 21. 10; 34. 2; 37. 10).

heap = ruins. **palace** = fortress.

after the manner thereof: or, upon its own site.

30. 19—31. 1 (T, p. 1058). PEOPLE. RESTORATION. (*Alternation.*)

T | i | 30. 19-21. Blessings.
  | k | 30. 22. People accepted.
  | *i* | 30. 23, 24. Judgment.
  | *k* | 31. 1. People accepted.

19 them: i.e. the restored cities and palaces.

I will multiply. Note the *Alternation*:—

| multiply.
  | not be few.
| glorify.
  | not be despised.

small = small (in number).

20 children = sons.

oppress. First used by God Himself (Ex. 3. 9).

21 their nobles. Heb. his Prince. } i.e. Jacob's.
their governor. Heb. his Ruler. }

cause him to draw near. Ref. to Pent. (Num. 16. 5).

who is this . . . ? Cp. Isa. 63. 1 (in judgment). Matt. 21. 10 (in grace). **engaged** = pledged.

23 continuing whirlwind = a tempest rolling itself upward: i.e. a roaring tempest.

the wicked = lawless ones (pl.). Heb. *rāshā'*. Ap. 44. x.

24 the latter days = the end of the days. Ref. to Pent. (Gen. 49. 1). Cp. 23. 20. Ap. 92.

consider = understand. Cp. 23. 20.

31. 1 At the same time: i.e. in the latter days (30. 24). **saith the LORD** = [is] Jehovah's oracle.

the LORD. Heb. Jehovah. Ap. 4. II.

God. Heb. Elohim. Ap. 4. I.

of = to. **all.** Not Judah alone.

they shall be My People. Ref. to Pent. (Lev. 26. 12). Ap. 92. Cp. 30. 22; 32. 38, &c.

31. 2-26 [For the Structure see next page].

23 Behold, the whirlwind of [1]the LORD goeth i
forth with fury, a °continuing whirlwind: it
shall fall with pain upon the head of °the
wicked.
24 The fierce anger of [1]the LORD shall not
return, until He have done *it*, and until He
have performed the intents of His heart: in
°the latter days ye shall °consider it.

31 °At the same time, °saith °the LORD, k
will I be the °God °of °all the families 489
of Israel, and °they shall be My People.'
2 Thus saith [1]the LORD, 'The People *which* Q l[1]

489 *were* left of the sword found grace in the
wilderness; *even* Israel, °when I went to
cause him to rest.' "
3 [1] The LORD hath appeared of old unto me,
saying, "Yea, I have loved thee with an
°everlasting love: therefore with lovingkindness have I drawn thee.
4 °Again I will build thee, and thou shalt be
built, O virgin of Israel: thou shalt °again be
adorned with thy °tabrets, and shalt go forth
in the dances of them that make merry.
5 Thou shalt yet plant °vines upon the
°mountains of Samaria: the planters shall
plant, and shall °eat *them* as common things.
6 For °there shall be a day, *that* the watchmen upon the °mount Ephraim shall cry,
'Arise ye, and let us go up to Zion unto [1] the
LORD our [1] God.'
7 For thus saith [1] the LORD; 'Sing with
gladness for ° Jacob, and shout among the
chief of the nations: publish ye, praise ye,
and say, 'O [1] LORD, °save Thy People, the
remnant of Israel.'

m¹ 8 °Behold, I will bring them from the north
country, and °gather them from the °coasts of
the earth, *and* with them the blind and the
lame, the woman with child and her that travaileth with child together: a great °company
shall return °thither.

n¹ 9 They shall come with weeping, and with
supplications will I lead them: I will cause
them to walk by the °rivers of waters in a
straight way, wherein they shall not stumble:
for I am a father to Israel, and °Ephraim *is*
My firstborn.' "

l² 10 Hear the word of [1] the LORD, O ye nations,
and declare *it* in the °isles afar off, and say,
°"He that scattered Israel will gather him,
and keep him, as a shepherd *doth* his flock.
11 For [1] the LORD hath °redeemed [7] Jacob,
and °ransomed him from the hand of *him that*
was °stronger than he.
12 Therefore they shall come and sing in the
height of Zion, and shall °flow together to the
goodness of [1] the LORD, for wheat, and for
°wine, and for oil, and for the young of the
flock and of the herd: and their °soul shall be
as a watered garden; and they shall not sorrow any more at all.
13 Then shall the virgin rejoice in the dance,
both young men and old together: for I will
turn their mourning into joy, and will comfort
them, and make them rejoice from their sorrow.
14 And I will satiate the [12] soul of the priests
with fatness, and My people shall be satisfied
with °My goodness, [1] saith [1] the LORD."

m² 15 Thus saith [1] the LORD; °"**A voice was**
heard °in Ramah, lamentation, ***and*** **bitter**
weeping; °Rahel weeping for her °children
refused to be comforted for her °children, °be-
cause they ***were*** **not.**
16 Thus saith [1] the LORD; 'Refrain thy
voice from weeping, and thine eyes from tears:
for thy work °shall be rewarded, [1] saith [1] the
LORD; and they shall °come again from the
land of the enemy.
17 And °there is hope in thine end, [1] saith [1] the
LORD, that thy [15] children shall come again to
their own border.

18 °I have surely heard [9] Ephraim bemoaning n²
himself *thus;* 'Thou °hast chastised me, and
I °was chastised, as a bullock unaccustomed
to the yoke: °turn Thou me, and I shall be
turned; °for Thou *art* [1] the LORD my [1] God.
19 Surely after that I was turned, I repented;
and after that I was instructed, I smote upon

31. 2-26 (*Q*, p. 1058). VISION.
(*Extended and Repeated Alternation.*)

Q | l¹ | 2-7. Joy.
  m¹ | 8. Restoration.
   n¹ | 9. Sorrow ended.
 l² | 10-14. Joy.
  m² | 15-17. Restoration.
   n² | 18-22. Sorrow ended.
 l³ | 23. Blessing.
  m³ | 24. Restoration.
   n³ | 25, 26. Sorrow ended.

2 when I went. Ref. to Pent. (Ex. 3. Num. 10. 33. Deut. 1. 33). Ap. 92.
3 everlasting love. See notes on Isa. 44. 7.
4 Again . . . again, &c. Ap. 92. Fig. *Anaphora.* Ap. 6.
tabrets. See notes on Ex. 15. 20. 1 Sam. 10. 5.
5 vines = vineyards.
mountains. A special reading called *Sevīr* (Ap. 34), reads "cities".
eat them as common things. Ref. to Pent. (Lev. 19. 23-25. Deut. 20. 6; 28. 30). Cp. Isa. 62. 9. Ap. 92.
6 there shall be = there is. Heb. *yēsh.* See note on Prov. 8. 21, and 18. 24. **mount** = hill country.
7 Jacob. Note the frequent use of "Jacob" in these chapters, referring to the natural seed.
save Thy People. Cp. the Heb. *Hosannah.* See Ps. 118. 25, and see note on Matt. 21. 9.
8 Behold. Fig. *Asterismos.* Ap. 6.
gather = gather out.
coasts = borders, or extremities.
company = an organized community.
thither = hither.
9 rivers = streams. Heb. *naḥal* = a wady.
Ephraim is My firstborn. Ref. to Pent. (Ex. 4. 22). Ap. 92. "My firstborn" occ. nowhere else. Cp. Ps. 89. 27. Ephraim is put by Fig. *Synecdoche* (of the Part), Ap. 6, for all the ten tribes.
10 isles = coastlands, or maritime countries.
He that scattered, &c. Ref. to Pent. (Deut. 30. 3).
11 redeemed = liberated, or redeemed (by power). Heb. *pādāh.* See note on Ex. 13. 13.
ransomed = redeemed (by blood) and avenged. Heb. *gā'al.* See note on Ex. 6. 6.
stronger. See note on Ps. 35. 10.
12 flow together. Same word as in 51. 44. Isa. 2. 2. Mic. 4. 1.
wine. Heb. *tīrōsh.* Ap. 27. II.
soul. Heb. *nephesh.* Ap. 13.
14 My. A.V., 1611, omits this "My".
15 A voice was heard, &c. Quoted in Matt. 2. 18. Ref. to Pent. (Gen. 35. 19). Ap. 92.
in Ramah = on the high place. Evidently a "high place" near Bethlehem. A common name in Palestine. The Targum and Vulg. read "in a high place".
Rahel = Rachel. The mother of Joseph and Benjamin (i.e. Ephraim); thus uniting the two kingdoms and the two peoples. Cp. *v.* 9. **children** = sons.
because they were not. Now, another weeping, and other comfort given. Cp. *vv.* 9, 16. Ref. to Pent. (Gen. 42. 36). Ap. 92.
16 shall be rewarded = there exists a reward. Heb. *yēsh.* See note on *v.* 6.
come again: i.e. in resurrection. Cp. *v.* 15.
17 there is = there exists. Heb. *yēsh.* Cp. *v.* 6.
18 I have surely heard, &c. Fig. *Prolepsis.* Ap. 6.
hast chastised = didst chastise.
was chastised = I have been chastised.
turn Thou me = cause Thou me to return.

489 *my thigh*: I was ashamed, yea, even confounded, because I did bear the reproach of
my youth.'
20 *Is* [9] Ephraim My dear son? *is he* a pleasant °child? for since I spake against him,
I do earnestly remember him still: therefore
°My bowels are troubled for him; I will surely have mercy upon him, [1] saith [1] the LORD.
21 °Set thee up waymarks, °make thee °high
heaps: set thine heart toward the highway,
even the way *which* thou wentest: turn again,
O virgin of Israel, turn again to these thy cities.
22 How long wilt thou °go about, O thou
backsliding daughter? for [1] the LORD hath
created a °new thing °in the earth, °A woman
shall °compass °a man.

l3 23 Thus saith °the LORD of hosts, the [1] God
(p. 1060) of Israel; 'As yet they shall use this speech
in the land of Judah and in the cities thereof,
when I shall °bring again their captivity;
[1] 'The LORD bless thee, O habitation of justice, *and* mountain of holiness.'

m3 24 And there shall dwell in Judah itself, and
in all the cities thereof together, husbandmen,
and they *that* go forth with flocks.

n3 25 For I have satiated the weary [12] soul, and
I have replenished every sorrowful [12] soul.'"
26 Upon this I awaked, and beheld; and my
sleep was sweet unto me.

T W 27 [8] "Behold, the days come, [1] saith [1] the
(p. 1061) LORD, that I will sow °the house of Israel
and °the house of Judah with the seed of
°man, and with the seed of beast.

X o 28 And it shall come to pass, *that* like as
I have °watched over them, to pluck up, °and
to break down, and to throw down, and to
destroy, and to afflict; so will I watch over
them, to build, and to plant, [1] saith the LORD.

p 29 In those days they shall say no more,
'The fathers have eaten a sour grape, and the
[15] children's teeth are °set on edge.'
30 But every one shall die for his own °ini-
quity: every man that eateth the sour grape,
his teeth shall be set on edge.

X o **31 °Behold, the days come, [1] saith [1] the LORD,**
that °I will make a new covenant with [27] the
house of Israel, and with [27] the house of Judah:
32 Not according to the covenant °that I
made with their fathers in the day *that* °I took
them by the hand to bring them out of the
land of Egypt; which My covenant they brake,
°although I was an husband unto them, [1] saith
[1] the LORD:
33 But this *shall be* the covenant that I will
make with °the house of Israel; After those
days, [1] saith [1] the LORD, I will put My law in
their inward parts, and write it °in their
hearts; °and will be their [1] God, and they shall
be My People.

p **34 And they shall teach no more °every man**
his neighbour, and °every man his brother,
saying, 'Know [1] the LORD:' for °they shall all
°know Me, from the least of them unto the
greatest of them, [1] saith [1] the LORD: for I
will forgive their iniquity, and I will remem-
ber their °sin no more.

W 35 Thus saith [1] the LORD, Which °giveth the
sun for a light by day, *and* the °ordinances of
the moon and of the stars for a light by night,
Which °divideth the sea when the waves
thereof roar; °The LORD of Hosts *is* His
name:

20 child = a young child. Heb. *yālād*.
My bowels are troubled. Fig. *Anthropopatheia*. Ap. 6. Ref. to Pent. (Deut. 32. 36). Cp. Luke 15. 20.
21 Set thee up = Erect.
make thee = set up. **high heaps**: i.e. finger posts.
22 go about: i.e. in order to elude by withdrawing. Elsewhere only in Song 5. 6.
new thing. The interpretation must satisfy this condition.
in the earth = in the land. This is another condition.
A woman = A spouse: i.e. Israel shall turn and cleave to the Mighty One. See Gen. 1. 27; 5. 2; 6. 19; 7. 3, 9, 16. Lev. 3. 1, 6; 4. 28; 5. 6, &c. Here, the virgin of Israel.
compass = turn about [so as to return to and seek the favour of] the man. A "new thing" for a woman to become the suitor. See 31. 14 and Deut. 24. 4. Hos. 2. 19, &c. Heb. *ṣabab*, to turn about, used in Ps. 26. 6, "so will I compass Thine altar", not go round it, but keep close to it. Cp. Ps. 7. 7. (Jonah 2. 5, "closed me round"). Instead of "going about", wandering (first line), the virgin of Israel will seek, and cleave close to the Mighty One, even Jehovah, as a girdle cleaves to a man.
a man = a mighty one. Heb. *geber*. Ap. 14. IV.
23 the LORD of hosts, the God of Israel. See note on 7. 3. **bring again.** This cannot be spiritualised.

31. 27-37 (*T*, p. 1058). PEOPLE. RESTORATION (*Introversion and Alternation.*)

T W | 27. Seed. Prophecy.
X | o | 28. Destruction and renovation.
p | 29, 30. Proverb.
X | *o* | 31-33. Old and New Covenant.
p | 34. Teaching.
W | 35-37. Seed. Fulfilment.

27 the house of Israel. See note on 2. 4.
the house of Judah. See note on 3. 18. Here we have the union of the two houses. Israel is always named first, for this was the name of the whole nation, which Judah was not.
man. Heb. *'ādām*. Ap. 14. I.
28 watched. Cp. 1. 12 (same word).
and. Note the Fig. *Polysyndeton* (Ap. 6).
29 set on edge. A proverb, mentioned here for the first time. Here restated, and corrected in *v.* 30.
30 iniquity. Heb. *'āvāh*. Ap. 44. iv.
31 Behold. Fig. *Asterismos*. Ap. 6. Quoted in Heb. 8. 8-12; 10. 16, 17. **I will make.** See Matt. 26. 28.
32 that I made. Ref. to Pent. (Ex. 24. 3-8). Ap. 92.
I took them by the hand, &c. Ref. to Pent. (Ex. 19. 4. Deut. 1. 31; 32. 11, 12). Ap. 92.
although I was an husband unto them. The Heb. *bā'al* is a *Homonym* with two meanings: (1) *to be lord*, or *master*, hence to be a husband; (2) *to disdain*, or *reject*. If it be the latter here, the last clause will read, "and I rejected (or abhorred) them, declareth Jehovah". So the Syr. and other ancient interpreters. Moreover, it is quoted thus in Heb. 8. 9, "and I regarded them not, saith the Lord".
33 the house of, &c. Some codices, with four early printed editions (one in marg.), read "the sons of": i.e. of the whole nation.
in their hearts = on their hearts. Cp. Ezek. 11. 19; 36. 26. Heb. 10. 16.
and will be their God. Cp. 24. 7; 30. 22; 32. 38.
34 every man. Heb. *'īsh*. Ap. 14. II.
they shall all know Me. See note on 9. 24.
know. Put by Fig. *Metonymy* (of Cause), Ap. 6, for all the effects of knowing Jehovah.
sin. Heb. *chāṭā'*. Ap. 44. i.
35 giveth the sun, &c. Ref. to Pent. (Gen. 1. 16).
ordinances = statutes. Ref. to Pent. (Gen. 8. 22). Cp. 33. 20, 25. **divideth** = stirreth up, or exciteth.
The LORD of Hosts. See note on 6. 6, and 1 Sam. 1. 3.

489 36 °'If those [35]ordinances depart from before Me,' [1]saith [1]the LORD, '*then* °the seed of Israel also shall cease from being a nation before Me °for ever.'

37 Thus saith [1]the LORD; °'If heaven above can be measured, and the foundations of the earth searched out beneath, I will also cast off all the seed of Israel for all that they have done,' [1]saith [1]the LORD.

S (p. 1058) 38 [8]Behold, the days °come,' [1]saith [1]the LORD, that the city shall be built to [1]the LORD from °the tower of Hananeel °unto °the gate of the corner.

39 And the measuring line shall yet go forth over against it °upon the hill °Gareb, and shall compass about to °Goath.

40 And the whole valley of the dead bodies, and of the ashes, and all the °fields [38]unto the brook of Kidron, unto the corner of the horse gate toward the east, *shall be* °holy unto [1]the LORD; it shall not be plucked up, nor thrown down any more °for ever.'"

U Y[1] Z[1] (p. 1062) 478 **32** °The word that came to Jeremiah from °the LORD in °the tenth year of Zedekiah king of Judah, which *was* the °eighteenth year of Nebuchadrezzar.

2 For then the king of Babylon's army °besieged Jerusalem: and Jeremiah the prophet was shut up in °the court of the prison, which *was* in the king of Judah's house.

3 For Zedekiah king of Judah °had shut him up, saying, "Wherefore dost thou prophesy, and say, 'Thus saith the LORD, 'Behold, I will give this city into the hand of the king of Babylon, and he shall take it;

4 And Zedekiah king of Judah shall not escape out of the hand of the Chaldeans, but shall surely be delivered into the hand of the king of Babylon, and shall speak with him mouth to mouth, and °his eyes shall behold his eyes;

5 And he shall lead Zedekiah to Babylon, and there shall he be until I visit him, °saith [1]the LORD: 'though ye fight with the Chaldeans, ye shall not prosper.'''"

Z[2] A q 6 And Jeremiah said, "The word of [1]the LORD came unto me, saying,

7 °'Behold, Hanameel the son of Shallum °thine uncle shall come unto thee, saying, 'Buy thee °my field that *is* in Anathoth: for °the right of redemption *is* thine to buy *it*.'''"

r 8 So Hanameel mine uncle's son came to me in the court of the prison according to the word of [1]the LORD, and said unto me, "Buy my field, I pray thee, that *is* in Anathoth, which *is* in the country of Benjamin: for [7]the right of inheritance *is* thine, and the redemption *is* thine; buy *it* for thyself."

q Then I knew that this *was* the word of [1]the LORD.

r 9 And I bought the field of Hanameel my uncle's son, that *was* in Anathoth, and weighed him the money, *even* seventeen °shekels of silver.

10 And I subscribed °the evidence, and sealed *it*, and took witnesses, and weighed *him* the money in the balances.

36 If those ordinances. So sure is the literal fulfilment of these prophecies concerning the literal restoration of Israel.

the seed. Note the Structure ("W" and "*W*" on p. 1061). **for ever**=all the days.

37 If heaven above, &c. Another asseveration as to the literal fulfilment of Israel's restoration.

38 come. This word is not in the Heb. text, but it is in the margin, as well as in some codices, with three early printed editions, Aram., Sept., Syr., and Vulg., which read "Lo, days are coming".

the tower of Hananeel. On the north-east corner.

unto=as far as.

the gate of the corner. At the north-west. Cp. 2 Kings 14. 13.

39 upon=over. A special various reading called *Sevir* (Ap. 34), reads "as far as", with some codices, Aram., and Sept. **Gareb . . . Goath.** Not named elsewhere.

40 fields. Heb. text reads "dry places", but the marg., with some codices and seven early printed editions, A.V. and R.V., read "fields". **holy.** See note on Ex. 3. 5.

for ever=for times age-abiding: for aye.

32. 1–33. 26 (*U*, p. 1045). PROMISE OF THE BRANCH. (*Division.*)

U | Y[1] | 32. 1–44. The *first* "word". Restoration of the Land. (In prison.) Tenth year of Zedekiah.
| Y[2] | 33. 1–26. The *second* "word". Restoration of the People. (In prison.)

32. 1–44 (Y[1], above). THE FIRST WORD. (*Division.*)

Y[1] | Z[1] | 1–5. Question of Zedekiah.
| Z[2] | 6–44. Answer of Jeremiah.

The TWENTY-FIRST Prophecy of Jeremiah (p. 1015).

1 The word that came, &c. This chapter commences an historical part of the book, describing the incidents of the two years preceding the capture of Jerusalem by Nebuchadnezzar. See *v.* 2.

the LORD. Heb. Jehovah. Ap. 4. II.

the tenth . . . eighteenth year. Another contact between Biblical and secular chronology. See Ap. 86.

2 besieged=was besieging.

the court of the prison: to which Jeremiah had access. Cp. *vv.* 8, 12, and 33. 1.

3 had shut him up. One of the eleven rulers who were offended with God's messengers. See note on Ex. 10. 28.

4 his eyes shall behold his eyes: he should go to Babylon (34. 3). Yet Ezekiel (12. 13) declared that he should not "see" Babylon. Both statements were true; for we read that Zedekiah did "see" the king of Babylon at Riblah, but his eyes being put out there (2 Kings 25. 6, 7), he never *saw* Babylon, though he was *led* there. See 52. 10, 11.

5 saith the LORD=[is] Jehovah's oracle.

32. 6–44 (Z[2], above). ANSWER OF JEREMIAH. (*Alternation.*)

Z[2] | A | 6–14. Symbol. Purchase of the field.
| B | 15. Signification. Repossession.
| *A* | 16–35. Symbol. Purchase of the field.
| *B* | 36–44. Signification. Repossession.

32. 6–14 (A, above). SYMBOL. PURCHASE OF THE FIELD. (*Alternation.*)

A | q | 6, 7. The word of Jehovah. Coming.
| r | 8–. The field. Request.
| *q* | –8. The word of Jehovah. Known.
| *r* | 9–14. The field. Compliance.

The TWENTY-SECOND Prophecy of Jeremiah (p. 1015).

7 Behold. Fig. *Asterismos.* Ap. 6.

thine uncle: i.e. Shallum, not Hanameel, who was Jeremiah's cousin. See next verse.

my field. Acc. to Num. 35. 5, this would be within 2,000 cubits of Anathoth.

the right, &c. Ref. to Pent. (Lev. 25. 24, 25, 32). Ap. 92. Cp. Ruth 4. 6. **9 shekels.** See Ap. 51. II. 5.

10 the evidence=the deed.

478 11 So I took [10] the evidence of the purchase,
both that which was sealed ° *according* to the
law and custom, and that which was open:
12 And I gave [10] the evidence of the purchase
unto Baruch the son of Neriah, the son of
Maaseiah, in the sight of Hanameel mine
° uncle's *son*, and in the presence of the witnesses that ° subscribed the book of the purchase, ° before all the Jews that sat in the
court of the prison.
13 And I charged Baruch before them, saying,
14 "Thus saith ° the LORD of hosts, the ° God
of Israel; 'Take these evidences, this [10] evidence of the purchase, both which is sealed,
and this evidence which is open; and put
them in an earthen vessel, that they may continue ° many days.'
B 15 For thus saith [14] the LORD of hosts, the
(p. 1062) [14] God of Israel; 'Houses and fields and vineyards shall be possessed again in this land.'"
A C 16 Now when I had delivered [10] the evidence
(p. 1063) of the purchase unto Baruch the son of Neriah,
I prayed unto [1] the LORD, saying,
17 "Ah ° Lord GOD! [7] behold, ° Thou hast
made the heaven and the earth by Thy great
power and stretched out arm, *and* there is
° nothing too hard for Thee:
D s 18 ° Thou shewest ° lovingkindness unto thousands, and recompensest the ° iniquity of the
fathers into the bosom of their ° children ° after
them: the Great, ° the Mighty ° GOD, ° the
LORD of Hosts, *is* His name,
19 Great in counsel, and mighty in work: for
° Thine eyes *are* open upon all the ways of the
sons of ° men: to give every one according to
his ways, and according to the fruit of his
doings:
20 Which hast set ° signs and wonders in the
land of Egypt, *even* unto this day, and in Israel, and among ° *other* men; and hast ° made
Thee a name, as at this day;
21 And hast brought forth Thy People Israel
out of the land of Egypt with [20] signs, and with
wonders, and ° with a strong hand, and with
a stretched out arm, and with great terror;
22 And hast given them this land, which
Thou didst swear to their fathers to give them,
a land flowing with ° milk and honey;
23 And they came in, and possessed it; but
they obeyed not Thy voice, neither walked in
Thy ° law; they have done nothing of all that
Thou commandedst them to do: therefore Thou
hast caused all this ° evil to come upon them:
t 24 [7] Behold the ° mounts, they are come unto
the city to take it; and the city is given into
the hand of the Chaldeans, that fight against
it, because of the sword, and of the famine,
and of the pestilence: and what Thou hast
spoken is come to pass; and, [7] behold, Thou
seest *it*.
25 And Thou hast said unto me, O [17] Lord
GOD, 'Buy thee the field for money, and take
witnesses; ° for the city is given into the hand
of the Chaldeans.'"
C 26 Then came the word of [1] the LORD unto
° Jeremiah, saying,
D t 27 [7] "Behold, I *am* [1] the LORD, ° the [14] God of
all flesh: is there any thing too hard for Me?
28 Therefore thus saith [1] the LORD; [7] 'Behold, I will give this city into the hand of
the Chaldeans, and into the hand of Nebuchadrezzar king of Babylon, and he shall take
it:
29 And the Chaldeans, that fight against
this city, shall come and set fire on this city,
and burn it with the houses, ° upon whose
roofs they have offered incense unto Baal, and

11 according to the law. See notes on *v.* 7.

12 uncle's son. Heb. text reads "uncle". But some codices, with Sept., Syr., and Vulg., read "uncle's son", as in *vv.* 8, 9.

subscribed. Some codices, with three early printed editions, Aram., Syr., and Vulg., read "who[se names] were written".

before. Some codices, with Sept., Syr., and Vulg., read "and before".

14 the LORD of hosts, the God of Israel. See note on 7. 3.

God. Heb. Elohim. Ap. 4. I.

many days: i.e. the seventy years, of which fifty-two years had yet to run (deducting eighteen years from the fourth of Jehoiakim to the tenth of Zedekiah).

32. 16-35 (*A*, p. 1062). THE SYMBOL.
(*Alternation and Introversion.*)

A | C | 16, 17. Prayer. Omnipotence.
  D | s | 18-23. Past mercies. Remembered.
    t | 24, 25. Invasion.
C | 26, 27. Prayer. Answered. Omnipotence.
  D | t | 28, 29. Invasion.
    s | 30-35. Future judgments. Foretold.

17 Lord GOD=Adonai Jehovah. Ap. 14. VIII (2) and II.

Thou hast made, &c. Ref. to Pent. (Gen. 1). Cp. 27. 5.

nothing too hard for Thee. Ref. to Pent. (Gen. 18. 14). Ap. 92.

18 Thou shewest lovingkindness, &c. Ref. to Pent. (Ex. 20. 6; 34. 7. Deut. 5. 9, 10). Ap. 92.

lovingkindness=grace. Heb. *hesed.*

iniquity. Heb. *'āvāh.* Ap. 44. viii.

children=sons. **after them.** Cp. Ex. 34. 6, 7.

the Mighty. Ref. to Pent. (Deut. 10. 17). Ap. 92. Cp. Isa. 9. 6.

GOD. Heb. El (with Art.). Ap. 4. IV. Occurs in Jeremiah only here and 51. 56.

the LORD of Hosts. See note on 6. 6 and 1 Sam. 1. 3.

19 Thine eyes. Fig. *Anthropopatheia.* Ap. 6.

men. Heb. *'ādām.* Ap. 14. I.

20 signs and wonders. Ref. to Pent. (Ex. 7. 3. Deut. 4. 34; 6. 22; 7. 19; 13. 1, 2; 26. 8; 28. 46; 29. 3; 34. 11). Ap. 92. Elsewhere only in Ps. 78. 43; 105. 27; 135. 9; and Neh. 9. 10.

other men=mankind. Heb. *'ādām.* Ap. 14. I.

made Thee a name. Ref. to Pent. (Ex. 9. 16).

21 with a strong hand, &c. Ref. to Pent. (Ex. 9. 6). Ap. 92. See note on 27. 5.

22 milk and honey. Ref. to Pent. (Ex. 3. 8, 17). See note on 11. 5, and Ap. 92.

23 law. Heb. text has "laws" in marg., with some codices and three early printed editions.

evil. Heb. *rā'a'.* Ap. 44. viii.

24 mounts. Erections of earth raised by the enemy to overtop the walls. Cp. 6. 6, and 33. 4.

25 for the city is given, &c. An expression of surprise at the command to buy the field under such circumstances.

The TWENTY-THIRD Prophecy of Jeremiah (p. 1015).

26 Jeremiah. Sept. reads "me": for Jeremiah's answer to Zedekiah took in not only *vv.* 16-25, but *vv.* 27-44.

27 the God of all flesh. Ref. to Pent. (Num. 16. 22). Ap. 92.

29 upon whose roofs, &c. Cp. 19. 13.

478 poured out drink offerings unto other gods, °to
provoke Me to anger.
s (p. 1063) 30 For the [18]children of Israel and the [18]chil-
dren of Judah have only done °evil before Me
from their youth: for the [18]children of Israel
have only [29]provoked Me to anger with the
work of their hands, [5]saith [1]the LORD.
31 For this city hath been to Me *as* a provocation of Mine anger and of My fury from the
day that they built it even unto this day; that
I should remove it from before My face,
32 Because of all the [23]evil of the [18]children of
Israel and of the [18]children of Judah, which
they have done to provoke Me to anger, they,
their kings, their princes, their priests, and
their prophets, and the °men of Judah, and
the inhabitants of Jerusalem.
33 And they have turned unto Me the back,
and not the face: though I taught them, °rising
up early and teaching *them*, yet they have not
hearkened to receive instruction.
34 But they set their abominations in the
house, °which is called by My name, to defile it.
35 And they built the high places of Baal,
which *are* in the valley of the son of Hinnom,
to cause their sons and their daughters °to
pass through *the fire* unto Molech; which I
commanded them not, neither °came it into
My mind, that they should do this abomination, to cause Judah to °sin.

B u (p. 1064) 36 And now therefore thus saith °the LORD,
the [14]God of Israel, concerning this city,
whereof ye say, 'It shall be delivered into the
hand of the king of Babylon by the sword,
and by the famine, and by the pestilence;'

v 37 [7]'Behold, °I will gather them out of all
countries, whither I have driven them in Mine
anger, and in My fury, and in great wrath;
and I will bring them again unto this place,
and °I will cause them to dwell safely:
38 And they shall be My People, and I will
be their [14]God:
39 And I will give them one heart, and one
way, that they may °fear Me °for ever, for
the good of them, and of their [18]children after
them:
40 And I will make an °everlasting covenant
with them, that I will not turn away from
them, to do them good; but I will put My fear
in their hearts, that they °shall °not depart
from Me.
41 Yea, °I will rejoice over them to do them
good, and I will °plant them in this land assuredly with My whole heart and with My
whole °soul.'

u 42 For thus saith [1]the LORD; 'Like as I
have brought all this great [30]evil upon this
people, so will I bring upon them all the good
that I have promised them.

v 43 And fields shall be bought in this land,
whereof ye say, '*It is* desolate without °man
or beast; it is given into the hand of the Chaldeans.'
44 °Men shall buy fields for money, and subscribe [10]evidences, and seal *them*, and take
witnesses in the land of Benjamin, and in the
places about Jerusalem, and in the cities of
Judah, and in the cities of the °mountains,
and in the cities of the valley, and in the cities
of the south: for I will cause their °captivity
to return, [5]saith [1]the LORD.'"

Y² E¹ w¹ 478 **33** Moreover the word of °the LORD came
unto Jeremiah °the second time, while
he was yet shut up in the court of the prison,
saying,
2 "Thus saith [1]the LORD °the Maker thereof, °the LORD That formed it, to establish it;
°the LORD *is* His name;

---

to provoke Me to anger. Ref. to Pent. (Deut. 4. 25; 9. 18; 31. 29; 32. 21). Ap. 92.

30 evil. Heb. *rā'a'*. Ap. 44. viii.

32 men. Heb. *'ish*. Ap. 14. II.

33 rising up early, &c. See note on 7. 13.

34 which is called by My name = upon which My name is called.

35 to pass through the fire. Ref. to Pent. (Lev. 18. 21).

came it into My mind. Cp. 7. 31; 19. 5.

sin. Heb. *chāṭā'*. Ap. 44. i.

32. 36–44 (*B*, p. 1062). SIGNIFICATION. REPOSSESSION. (*Alternation.*)

B | u | 36. City.
 v | 37–41. Its restoration.
 u | 42. People.
 v | 43, 44. Their repossession.

36 the LORD, the God of Israel. See note on 11. 3.

37 I will gather them out, &c. Ref. to Pent. (Deut. 30. 3, the same word).

I will cause them to dwell safely. *Hiphil* of *yāshab* = to settle down. Ref. to Pent. (Lev. 23. 43). Ap. 92. Cp. Ezek. 36. 11, 33. Hos. 11. 11. Zech. 10. 6.

39 fear = revere. for ever = all the days.

40 everlasting covenant. See note on Gen. 9. 16. Ref. to Pent. (Ap. 92). shall = may.

not depart. This must refer to millennial days: for Israel *did* depart; and that is why the nation is still "scattered", and not yet "gathered".

41 I will rejoice, &c. Ref. to Pent. (Deut. 30. 9).

plant. Cp. 1. 10.

soul. Heb. *nephesh*. Ap. 13. Fig. *Anthropopatheia*. Ap. 6.

43 man. Heb. *'ādām*. Ap. 14. I.

44 Men. Not in Heb. Should be in italic type.

mountains = hill country.

captivity. Put by Fig. *Metonymy* (of Subject), Ap. 6, for captives.

33. 1–26 (Y², p. 1062). SECOND WORD. RESTORATION. (*Division.*)

Y² | E¹ | 1–14. The word of Jehovah.
 E² | 15–18. The Branch of Jehovah.
 E³ | 19–26. The faithfulness of Jehovah.

33. 1–14 (E¹, above). THE WORD OF JEHOVAH. (*Extended and Repeated Alternation.*)

E¹ | w¹ | 1–5. The desolate houses.
 x¹ | 6. Blessings. Health and cure.
 y¹ | 7–9. Restoration. "As at the first."
 w² | 10. The desolate cities. (Judah.)
 x² | 11–. Blessings. Joy and gladness.
 y² | –11. Restoration. "As at the first."
 w³ | 12–. The desolate cities. (Judah and Benjamin.)
 x³ | –12, 13. Blessings. Peace and quietness.
 y³ | 14. Restoration.

The TWENTY-FOURTH Prophecy of Jeremiah (p. 1015).

1 the LORD. Heb. Jehovah. Ap. 4. II.

the second time. See the Structure "*U*", p. 1062.

2 the Maker thereof = the doer thereof: i.e. the accomplisher of His word.

the LORD. This is not found in some codices, nor in the Sept., Syr., and Vulg.

the LORD is His name. The *Massōrah* states that this expression occurs only *four* times (Ex. 15. 3. Jer. 33. 2. Amos 5. 8; 9. 6). Ref. to Pent. (Ex. 15. 3). Ap. 92.

478 3 ‘Call unto Me, and I will answer thee, and
shew thee great and °mighty things, which
thou knowest not.’
4 For thus saith °the LORD, the °God of Israel, concerning the houses of this city, and
concerning the houses of the kings of Judah,
which are °thrown down by the mounts, and
by the sword;
5 °‘They come to fight °with the Chaldeans,
but *it is* to fill them with the dead bodies of
°men, whom I have slain in Mine anger and
in My fury, and for all whose °wickedness
I have hid My face from this city.

x1 6 °Behold, I will bring it health and cure,
(p. 1064) and I will cure them, and will reveal unto
them the abundance of peace and truth.

y1 7 And I will cause the °captivity of Judah
and the °captivity of Israel to return, and will
build them, as at the first.
8 And °I will cleanse them from all their
°iniquity, whereby they have °sinned against
Me; and I will pardon all their °iniquities,
whereby they have °sinned, and whereby they
have °transgressed against Me.
9 And it shall be to Me a name of joy, a
praise and an honour before all the nations of
the earth, which shall hear all the good that
I do unto °them: and they shall fear and tremble for all the goodness and for all the prosperity that I procure unto it.’

w2 10 Thus saith [1]the LORD; ‘Again there shall
be heard in this place, which °ye say *shall be*
desolate without °man and without beast, *even*
in the °cities of Judah, and in the streets of
Jerusalem, that are desolate, without °man,
and without inhabitant, and without beast,

x2 11 °The voice of joy, and the voice of gladness, the voice of the bridegroom, and the
voice of the bride, the voice of them that shall
say, ‘Praise °the LORD of hosts: for [1]the
LORD *is* good; for His °mercy *endureth* °for
ever:’ *and* of °them that shall bring the
°sacrifice of praise into the house of [1]the
LORD.

y2 For I will cause to return the captivity of the
land, °as at the first, °saith [1]the LORD.’

w3 12 Thus saith [11]the LORD of hosts; ‘Again
in this place, which is desolate without [10]man
and without beast, and in all the [10]cities
thereof,

x3 shall be an habitation of shepherds causing
their flocks to lie down.
13 In the cities of the °mountains, in the
cities of the vale, and in the cities of the south,
and in the land of Benjamin, and in the places
about Jerusalem, and in the cities of Judah,
shall the flocks pass again under the hands
of him that telleth *them*, [11]saith [1]the LORD.

y3 14 [6]‘Behold, the days come, [11]saith [1]the LORD,
that I will perform that good thing which
I have promised unto the house of Israel and
to the house of Judah.

E2 a 15 In those days, and at that time, will I
(p. 1065) cause °the Branch of righteousness to grow
up unto David; and °He shall execute judgment and righteousness in the °land.

16 In those days shall Judah be saved, and b
Jerusalem shall dwell safely: and °this *is the*
name wherewith she shall be called, °The
[1]LORD our righteousness.’

17 For thus saith [1]the LORD; ‘David shall *a*
never want a °man to sit upon the throne of
the house of Israel;

18 Neither shall °the priests the Levites want *b*
a [17]man before Me to offer burnt offerings, and
to kindle meat offerings, and to do sacrifice
continually.’”

3 mighty = inaccessible: i.e. too high for Jeremiah to know, apart from revelation.
4 the LORD, the God of Israel. See note on 11. 3.
God. Heb. Elohim. Ap. 4. I.
thrown down, &c.: i.e. demolished to serve as a fence against the mounts and the sword.
5 They come: i.e. the demolished houses are coming to be used for defence, &c. For this sense of "come", see Mark 4. 21 (Gr.).
with. Some codices, with two early printed editions and Sept., read "against".
men = mankind. Heb. *'ādām*. Ap. 14. I.
wickedness = lawlessness. Heb. *rāsha'*. Ap. 44. x.
6 Behold. Fig. *Asterismos*. Ap. 6.
7 captivity. As in 32. 44.
8 I will cleanse. This is the foundation of all the blessing.
iniquity. Sing. = the principles. Heb. *'āvāh*. Ap. 44. iv.
sinned . . . sinned. Heb. *chāṭā'*. Ap. 44. i.
iniquities. Pl. = the acts. Heb. *'āvāh*. Ap. 44. iv.
transgressed = rebelled. Heb. *pāsha'*. Ap. 44. ix.
9 them. The Severus Codex (Ap. 34) reads "it".
10 ye say. Jeremiah had been saying this.
man. Heb. *'ādām*. Ap. 14. I.
cities. See the Structure ("w2", "w3"), p. 1064.
11 The voice of joy, &c. Cp. 7. 34; 16. 9; 25. 10.
the LORD of hosts = Jehovah (with *'eth*) Zebaōth. See note on 6. 6, and 1 Sam. 1. 3.
mercy = lovingkindness, or grace. Not the same word as in *v.* 26.
for ever = age-abiding. Therefore the fulfilment is still future.
them that shall bring. Implying a settled order of worship.
sacrifice of praise = thank-offering, or confession (of praise).
as at the first. Note the Structure ("y1"), p. 1064.
saith the LORD = [is] Jehovah's Oracle.
13 mountains = hill country.

33. 15-18 (E2, p. 1064). **THE BRANCH OF JEHOVAH.** (*Alternation.*)

E2 | a | 15. The Branch raised up.
  b | 16. Blessing. Salvation brought.
 a | 17. Heir of David not lacking.
  b | 18. Blessing. Worship secured.

15 the Branch of righteousness. Cp. 23. 5. Isa. 61. 11.
He shall execute, &c. As David is more than once said to have done. Some codices, with three early printed editions and Syr., read:—
"And a King will reign, and prosper,
And will execute", &c.
land. Heb. *'āretz* = earth, or land.
16 this is the name, &c.: or, "this is that which shall be proclaimed to her [as her name]."
The LORD our righteousness. The term is here applied to the city, which has been applied to the king in 23. 6.
17 man. Heb. *'īsh*. Ap. 14. II.
18 the priests the Levites. Ref. to Pent. (Deut. 17. 9, Num. 25. 10-13). Ap. 92. Mal. 2. 5.

E[3] c[1] (p. 1066) 478 19 And the word of [1]the LORD came unto Jeremiah, saying,

20 "Thus saith [1]the LORD; 'If ye can break °My covenant of the day, and My covenant of the night, and that there should not be day and night in their season;

d[1] 21 *Then* may also °My covenant be broken with David My servant, that he should not have a son to reign upon his throne; and with the Levites [18]the priests, My ministers.

c[2] 22 As °the host of heaven cannot be numbered, neither °the sand of the sea measured:

d[2] so will I multiply the seed of David My servant, and the Levites that minister unto Me.'"

c[3] 23 Moreover the word of [1]the LORD came to Jeremiah, saying,

24 "Considerest thou not what this People have spoken, saying, 'The two families which [1]the LORD hath chosen, He hath even cast them off'? thus they have despised My People, that they should be no more a nation before them.

25 Thus saith [1]the LORD; °'If My covenant *be* not with day and night, *and if* I have not appointed the ordinances of heaven and earth;

d[3] 26 Then will I cast away the seed of Jacob, and David My servant, *so* that I will not take *any* of his seed *to be* rulers over the seed of °Abraham, Isaac, and Jacob: for I will cause their [7]captivity to return, and have °mercy on them.'"

T F[1] e (p. 1066) 479 **34** °The word which came unto Jeremiah from °the LORD, when °Nebuchadnezzar king of Babylon, and all his army, and all the kingdoms of the earth of his dominion, and all the people, °fought against Jerusalem, and against all the cities thereof, saying,

2 "Thus saith °the LORD, the °God of Israel; 'Go and speak to Zedekiah king of Judah, and tell him, 'Thus saith [1]the LORD; °'Behold, I will give this city into the hand of the king of Babylon, and he shall burn it with fire:

f 3 And thou shalt not escape out of his hand, but shalt surely be taken, and delivered into his hand; and °thine eyes shall behold the eyes of the king of Babylon, and he shall speak with thee mouth to mouth, and thou shalt go to Babylon.

f 4 Yet hear the word of [1]the LORD, O Zedekiah king of Judah; Thus saith [1]the LORD of thee, Thou shalt not die by the sword:

5 *But* thou shalt die in peace: and °with the burnings of thy fathers, the former kings which were before thee, so shall they °burn *odours* for thee; and they will lament thee, *saying*, 'Ah lord!' for I have pronounced the word, °saith [1]the LORD.'''

e 6 Then Jeremiah the prophet spake all these words unto Zedekiah king of Judah in Jerusalem,

7 When the king of Babylon's army [1]fought against Jerusalem, and against all the cities of Judah that were left, against °Lachish, and against °Azekah: for these defenced cities remained of the cities of Judah.

G H g 8 *This is* the word that came unto Jeremiah from [1]the LORD, after that the king Zedekiah had made °a covenant with all the People

33. 19-26 (E[3], p. 1064). THE FAITHFULNESS OF JEHOVAH. (*Repeated Alternation.*)

E[3] | c[1] | 19, 20. Tokens. Day and night.
d[1] | 21. Covenant with David.
c[2] | 22-. Tokens. Stars and sand.
d[2] | -22. Seed of David.
c[3] | 23-25. Tokens. Day and night.
d[3] | 26. Union of Israel and Judah.

The TWENTY-FIFTH Prophecy of Jeremiah (p. 1015).

20 My covenant of the day, &c. Ref. to Pent. (Gen. 8. 22). Ap. 92. Cp. 31. 35.

21 My covenant . . . with David. Wholly unconditional. Cp. 2 Sam. 7. 12, &c. Cp. Pss. 89. 3, 4, 20-37, and 132. 11, with Jer. 31. 35-37, and 33. 17-26.

22 the host of heaven. Ref. to Pent. (Gen. 15. 3; 22. 17). Cp. Jer. 31. 37. Ap. 92.

the sand of the sea. Ref. to Pent. (Gen. 13. 19).

The TWENTY-SIXTH Prophecy of Jeremiah (p. 1015).

25 If My covenant, &c. Ref. to Pent. (Gen. 8. 22).

26 Abraham, Isaac, and Jacob. See note on Gen. 50. 24.

mercy = compassion. Heb. *rāḥam*. Not the same word as in *v.* 11.

34. 1—35. 19 (*T*, p. 1045). DEFEAT AND CAPTIVITY OF ZEDEKIAH PROCLAIMED. (*Alternations.*)

T | F[1] | 34. 1-7. Threatening to Zedekiah.
G | H | 34. 8-16. Illustration. (Negative.) Covenant of king and princes broken.
J | 34. 17-. Incrimination of People.
F[2] | 34. -17-22. Threatening to the nation.
G | *H* | 35. 1-11. Illustration. (Positive.) Command of Jonadab to Rechabites kept.
J | 35. 12-16. Incrimination of people.
F[3] | 35. 17-19. Threatening to the nation.

34. 1-7 (F[1], above). THREATENING TO ZEDEKIAH. (*Introversion.*)

F[1] | e | 1, 2. City and cities given to Nebuchadnezzar.
f | 3. Zedekiah. Captivity.
f | 4, 5. Zedekiah. Death.
e | 6, 7. City and cities besieged by Nebuchadnezzar.

The TWENTY-SEVENTH Prophecy of Jeremiah (p. 1015).

1 The word. This chapter is ch. 32. 1-5, told over again more fully.

the LORD. Heb. Jehovah. Ap. 4. II.

Nebuchadnezzar. Not that he was necessarily present.

fought = were fighting, or about to fight.

2 the LORD, the God of Israel. See note on 11. 3.

God. Heb. Elohim. Ap. 4. I.

Behold. Fig. *Asterismos*. Ap. 6.

3 thine eyes shall behold, &c. See note on 32. 4.

5 with. Some codices, with Sept., Syr., and Vulg., read "like".

burn odours. Cp. 2 Chron. 16. 14, and observe the word is *sāraph* (Ap. 43. I. viii), not *ḳāṭar* (Ap. 43. I. vii).

saith the LORD = [is] Jehovah's oracle.

7 Lachish. Now *Tell el Hesy*, south of Eglon, ten and a half miles from Eleutheropolis.

Azekah. Now *Tell Zakariya*, in the valley of Elah.

34. 8-16 (H, above). ILLUSTRATION. (NEGATIVE). COVENANT OF ZEDEKIAH AND PRINCES. BROKEN. (*Alternation.*)

H | g | 8-10. Covenant of Zedekiah and princes with servants.
h | 11. Breach of the covenant by king and princes.
g | 12-15. Covenant of Jehovah with the nation.
h | 16. Breach of the covenant by the nation.

The TWENTY-EIGHTH Prophecy of Jeremiah (p. 1015).

8 a covenant. Note the illustration of the two covenants, "g" (*vv.* 8-10) and "*g*" (*vv.* 12-15), and compare with the other illustration in "*H*" (35. 1-11).

479 which *were* at Jerusalem, °to proclaim liberty
unto them;

9 That °every man should let his manservant,
and °every man his maidservant, *being* an
Hebrew or an Hebrewess, °go free; that none
should °serve himself of them, *to wit*, of a Jew
his brother.

10 Now when all the princes, and all the People, which had entered into the covenant,
heard that °every one should let his manservant, and °every one his maidservant, go free,
that none should serve themselves of them
any more, then they obeyed, and let *them* go.

h (p. 1066) 11 But afterward they turned, and caused the
servants and the handmaids, whom they had
let go free, to return, and brought them into
subjection for servants and for handmaids.

g 12 Therefore the word of [1] the LORD came to
Jeremiah from [1] the LORD, saying,

13 "Thus saith [2] the LORD, [2] the God of Israel;
'I made a covenant with your fathers °in the
day that I brought them forth out of the land
of Egypt, out of the house of °bondmen, saying,

14 'At the end of seven years let ye go
[9] every man his brother an Hebrew, which
hath been sold unto thee; and when he
hath served thee six years, thou shalt let
him go free from thee:' but your fathers
hearkened not unto Me, neither inclined their
ear.

15 And ye were now turned, and had done
right in My sight, in proclaiming liberty [9] every
man to his neighbour; and ye had made a
covenant before Me in the house °which is
called by My name:

h 16 But ye turned and °polluted My name,
and caused [9] every man his servant, and [9] every
man his handmaid, whom °he had set at liberty °at their pleasure, to return, and brought
them into subjection, to be unto you for servants and for handmaids.'

J 17 Therefore thus saith [1] the LORD; 'Ye have
not hearkened unto Me, in proclaiming °liberty, every one to his brother, and [9] every man
to his neighbour:

F² i (p. 1067) [2] behold, I proclaim a °liberty for you, [5] saith
[1] the LORD, to the sword, °to the pestilence,
and to the famine; and I will °make you to be
removed into all the kingdoms of the earth.

k 18 And I will give the °men that have °transgressed My covenant, which have not performed the words of the covenant which they
had made before Me, when they °cut the calf
in twain, and °passed between the parts thereof,

19 The princes of Judah, and the princes of
Jerusalem, the eunuchs, and the priests, and
all the People of the land, which passed between the parts of the calf;

20 I will even give them into the hand of their
enemies, and into the hand of them that seek
their °life: and their dead bodies shall be for
meat unto the fowls of the heaven, and to the
beasts of the earth.

k 21 And Zedekiah king of Judah and his
princes will I give into the hand of their enemies, and into the hand of them that seek
their [20] life, and into the hand of the king of
Babylon's army, °which are gone up from you.

22 Behold, I will command, [5] saith [1] the LORD, *i*
'and cause them to return to this city; and
they shall fight against it, and take it, and
burn it with fire: and I will make the cities of
Judah °a desolation without an inhabitant.'"

35 The word which °came unto Jeremiah G H l
from °the LORD °in the days of Jehoiakim the son of Josiah king of Judah, saying, 496

---

to proclaim liberty, &c. Ref. to Pent. (Ex. 21. 2. Lev. 25. 10, 39-46. Deut. 15. 12). Ap. 92. Outside the Pent. the word occurs only in Isa. 61. 1, and Ezek. 46. 17.

9 every man. Heb. *'ish.* Ap. 14. II.

go free. See note on *v.* 8, and cp. *vv.* 21, 22, which show that this covenant was made during a temporary withdrawal of the besiegers, on account of the Egyptians (37. 5).

serve himself of them = use them as bondservants.

The TWENTY-NINTH Prophecy of Jeremiah (p. 1015).

10 every one = *'ish*, as in *v.* 9.

13 in the day = when. See Ap. 18.

bondmen = slaves.

15 which is called by My name = upon which My name is called.

16 polluted My name. Ref. to Pent. (Lev. 19. 12, the same word). Ap. 92. **he** = every man.

at their pleasure = for their own soul. Heb. *nephesh* (Ap. 13): "soul" being put for the affections of the person.

17 liberty . . . liberty. Fig. *Antanaclasis* (Ap. 6), by which the same word is used in two different senses in the same sentence.

34. -17-22 (F², p. 1066). THREATENING OF THE PEOPLE. (*Introversion.*)

F² | i | -17. The people.
  | k | 18-20. The princes.
  | *k* | 21. The king.
  | *i* | 22. The people and cities.

-17 to. Some codices, with three early printed editions, Aram., Sept., and Syr., read "and to", completing the Fig. *Polysyndeton* (Ap. 6).

make you to be removed. Ref. to Pent. (Deut. 28. 25, 64). Ap. 92. Cp. 24. 9.

18 men. Heb. pl. of *'ĕnōsh.* Ap. 14. III.

transgressed. Heb. *'ābar.* Ap. 44. vii.

cut the calf in twain. Cp. Gen. 15. 9, 10.

passed between, &c. Ref. to Pent. (Gen. 15. 10-17).

20 life = soul. Heb. *nephesh.* Ap. 13.

21 which are gone up from you. See note on *v.* 9.

22 a desolation, &c.: or, too desolate to have an inhabitant; or, desolate through having no inhabitant.

35. 1-11 (*H*, p. 1066). ILLUSTRATION. (POSITIVE.) COMMAND OF JONADAB TO HIS SONS. KEPT. (*Alternation.*)

H | l | 1, 2. Command of Jehovah to Jeremiah.
  | m | 3-5. Obedience of Jeremiah.
  | *l* | 6, 7. Command of Jonadab to Rechabites.
  | *m* | 8-11. Obedience of Rechabites.

The THIRTIETH Prophecy of Jeremiah (p. 1015).

1 came. Jeremiah goes back here to insert a preceding event (see 25. 1; 26. 1), in order to complete the correspondence by introducing the second illustration, as shown in the Structure, "H" (34. 8-16) and "*H*" (35. 1-11).

the LORD. Heb. Jehovah. Ap. 4. II.

in the days, &c. Immediately before Nebuchadnezzar's advance, in his fourth year.

496 2 "Go unto the °house of the °Rechabites, and speak unto them, and bring them into the house of [1]the LORD, into °one of the chambers, and give them °wine to drink."

m (p. 1067) 3 Then I took Jaazaniah the son of Jeremiah, the son of Habaziniah, and his brethren, and all his sons, and the whole house of the Rechabites;

4 And I brought them into the house of [1]the LORD, into the chamber of the sons of Hanan, the son of °Igdaliah, °a man of °God, which *was* by the chamber of the princes, which *was* above the chamber of °Maaseiah the son of Shallum, the °keeper of the door:

5 And I set before the sons of the house of the Rechabites °pots full of [2]wine, and cups, and I said unto them, "Drink ye [2]wine."

l 6 But they said, "We will drink no [2]wine: for Jonadab the son of Rechab our father commanded us, saying, 'Ye shall drink no [2]wine, *neither* ye, nor your sons °for ever:

7 Neither shall ye °build house, nor sow seed, nor plant vineyard, nor have *any:* but all your days ye shall dwell in tents; that ye may °live many days °in the land where ye *be* strangers.'

m 8 Thus have we obeyed the voice of Jonadab the son of Rechab our father in all that he hath charged us, to drink no [2]wine all our days, we, our wives, our sons, nor our daughters;

9 Nor to [7]build houses for us to dwell in: neither have we vineyard, nor field, nor seed:

10 But we have dwelt in tents, and have obeyed, and done according to all that Jonadab our father commanded us.

11 But it came to pass, °when Nebuchadrezzar king of Babylon came up into the land, that we said, 'Come, and let us go to Jerusalem for fear of the army of the Chaldeans, and for fear of the army of the °Syrians:' so we dwell at Jerusalem."

J n^1 (p. 1068) 12 Then came the word of [1]the LORD unto Jeremiah, saying,

13 "Thus saith °the LORD of hosts, the [4]God of Israel; 'Go and tell the °men of Judah and the inhabitants of Jerusalem, 'Will ye not receive instruction to hearken to My words? °saith [1]the LORD.

o^1 14 The words of Jonadab the son of Rechab, that he commanded his sons not to drink wine, are performed; for unto this day they drink none, but obey their father's commandment:

n^2 notwithstanding I have spoken unto you, °rising early and speaking;

o^2 but ye hearkened not unto Me.

n^3 15 I have sent also unto you all My servants the prophets, [14]rising up early and sending *them,* saying, 'Return ye now °every man from his °evil way, and amend your doings, and go not after other gods to serve them, and ye shall dwell [7]in the land which I have given to you and to your fathers:'

o^3 but ye have not inclined your ear, nor hearkened unto Me.

n^4 16 °Because the sons of Jonadab the son of Rechab have performed the commandment of their father, which he commanded them;

but this People hath not hearkened unto Me: o^4

17 Therefore thus saith °the LORD God of F^3 *p*

2 house. Put by Fig. *Metonymy* (of Adjunct), Ap. 6, for the descendants of Rechab, through Jonadab his son, who became their chieftain and lawgiver. Cp. *v.* 6.

Rechabites. They were descended from Hobab, the brother-in-law of Moses. A Kenite tribe, who migrated with Israel to Canaan. Cp. Num. 10. 29 with Judg. 1. 16; 4. 11–17; 5. 24. 1 Sam. 15. 6. They were proselytes, not idolaters; inhabiting the wilderness south of Judah.

one of the chambers. There were many, for various purposes of the Temple worship. Cp. 36. 10 with 1 Kings 6. 5. 1 Chron. 9. 27. Neh. 13. 4–12.

wine. Heb. *yayin.* Ap. 27. I.

4 Igdaliah. See note on Ps. 90, Title.

a man of God = the man (Heb. *'ish*, Ap. 14. II) of God (Heb. Elohim, Ap. 4. I): i.e. a prophet. See Ap. 49.

Maaseiah, &c. He was the deputy of the High Priest. Cp. 52. 24. 2 Kings 25. 18. Probably the same whose son Zephaniah, after the carrying away of Maaseiah with Jehoiachin (29. 1), held office under Zedekiah (21. 1; 29. 5; 37. 3).

keeper of the door = keeper of the threshold. There were three. See 2 Kings 25. 18. 2 Chron. 31. 14.

5 pots = bowls.

6 for ever = unto times age-abiding.

7 build. This was as essential as the former injunction.

live many days, &c. Ref. to Pent. (Ex. 20. 12). Ap. 92.

in the land = on the soil.

11 when, &c. They explain why they did not carry out the latter part of their vow (*v.* 7).

Syrians. This is the only place where they are mentioned with the Chaldeans. They had been made subject to Assyria long before; (Isa. 9. 12). After the fall of Nineveh they came under the yoke of Babylon.

35. 12–16 (*J*, p. 1066). INCRIMINATION OF THE PEOPLE. (*Repeated Alternation.*)

J | n^1 | 12, 13. Incrimination.
o^1 | 14–. Obedience of the Rechabites.
n^2 | –14–. Incrimination.
o^2 | –14. Disobedience of the nation.
n^3 | 15–. Incrimination.
o^3 | –15. Disobedience of the nation.
n^4 | 16–. Incrimination.
o^4 | –16. Disobedience of the nation.

The THIRTY-FIRST Prophecy of Jeremiah (p. 1015).

13 the LORD of hosts, the God of Israel. See note on 7. 3.

men. Heb. *'ish.* Ap. 14. II.

saith the LORD = [is] Jehovah's oracle.

14 rising early and speaking. See note on 7. 13.

15 every man. Heb. *'ish.* Ap. 14. II.

evil. Heb. *rā'a'.* Ap. 44. viii.

16 Because, &c. They are praised for their *obedience,* without reference to the nature of the command. Jonadab is not justified by this for imposing his will on all his posterity.

35. 17–19 (F^3, p. 1066). THREATENING OF THE NATION. (*Alternation.*)

F^3 | *p* | 17–. Threatening to the nation.
q | –17. Cause. Disobedience to Jehovah.
p | 18–. Blessing of the Rechabites.
q | –18, 19. Cause. Obedience to Jonadab.

17 the LORD God of hosts, the God of Israel = Jehovah Elohim Zebā'ōth, Elohim of Israel. See Ap. 4. This is the fullest (and therefore the most solemn) use of this Divine title. Occurs in this book only three times (here, 38. 17, and 44. 7).

496 hosts, the [4]God of Israel; °'Behold, I will bring
upon Judah and upon all the inhabitants of
Jerusalem all the °evil that I have pronounced
against them:
q (p. 1068) because I have spoken unto them, but they
have not heard; and I have called unto them,
but they have not answered.'"'
p 18 And Jeremiah said unto the house of the
Rechabites, "Thus saith [13]the LORD of hosts,
the [4]God of Israel;
q 'Because ye have obeyed the commandment
of Jonadab your father, and kept all his precepts, and done according unto all that he hath
commanded you:
19 Therefore thus saith [13]the LORD of hosts,
the [4]God of Israel; Jonadab the son of Rechab
shall not want a [13]man to stand before Me °for
ever.'"

E K M (p. 1070) 496 **36** And it came to pass in °the fourth year
of Jehoiakim the son of Josiah king of
Judah, *that* this word came unto Jeremiah
from °the LORD, saying,
2 "Take thee a °roll of a book, and write
therein all the °words that I have spoken unto
thee against °Israel, and against Judah, and
against all the nations, from the day I spake
unto thee, °from the days of Josiah, even unto
this day.
3 It may be that the house of Judah will hear
all the °evil which I purpose to do unto them;
that they may return °every man from his °evil
way; that I may forgive their °iniquity and
their °sin."
N 4 Then Jeremiah called °Baruch the son of
Neriah: and Baruch wrote from the mouth of
Jeremiah all the words of [1]the LORD, which He
had spoken unto him, upon a roll of a book.
M 5 And Jeremiah commanded Baruch, saying,
"I *am* °shut up; I cannot go into the house
of [1]the LORD:
6 Therefore go thou, and read in the roll,
which thou hast written from my mouth, the
words of [1]the LORD in the ears of the People
in [1]the LORD'S house upon °the fasting day:
and also thou shalt read them in the ears of
all Judah that come out of their cities.
7 It may be they will present their supplication before [1]the LORD, and will return every
one from his [3]evil way: for great *is* the anger
and the fury that [1]the LORD hath pronounced
against this People."
N 8 And [4]Baruch the son of Neriah did according to all that Jeremiah the prophet commanded him, reading in the book the words of
[1]the LORD in [1]the LORD'S house.
495 9 And it came to pass in °the fifth year of
Jehoiakim the son of Josiah king of Judah, in
the °ninth month, *that* °they proclaimed a
fast before [1]the LORD to all the People in Jerusalem, and to all the People that came from
the cities of Judah unto Jerusalem.
10 Then read Baruch in the book the words
of Jeremiah in the house of [1]the LORD, in the
chamber of °Gemariah the son of °Shaphan
°the scribe, in the higher court, at the entry of
the new gate of [1]the LORD'S house, in the ears
of all the People.

Behold. Fig. *Asterismos.* Ap. 6. Used to emphasise further what follows.
evil. Heb. *rā'a'.* Ap. 44. viii.
19 for ever=all the days.

36. 1-32 (E, p. 1015). BARUCH. MISSION TO JEHOIAKIM. (*Introversions and Alternations.*)

E | K | M | 1-3. Command of Jehovah. ⎫
N | 4. Obedience of Jeremiah. ⎬ The first Scroll.
M | 5-7. Command of Jeremiah. ⎪
N | 8-10. Obedience of Baruch. ⎭
L | r | 11-13. Scroll reported to princes.
s | 14. Roll brought.
t | 15. Roll read.
u | 16. Fear.
v | 17, 18. Jeremiah and Baruch.
w | 19. Their concealment.
L | *r* | 20. Scroll reported to the king.
s | 21-. Roll brought.
t | -21-23. Roll destroyed.
u | 24, 25. No fear.
v | 26-. Jeremiah and Baruch.
w | -26. Their concealment.
K | O | 27, 28. Jeremiah. Command. ⎫
P | 29. Jehoiakim. Incrimination. ⎬ The second Scroll.
P | 30, 31. Jehoiakim. Threatening. ⎪
O | 32. Jeremiah. Obedience. ⎭

The THIRTY-SECOND Prophecy of Jeremiah (p. 1015).

1 the fourth year of Jehoiakim. This was after Nebuchadnezzar had left Jerusalem with his band of young captives, including Daniel. See Ap. 86. The city had become quieted down again.
the LORD. Heb. Jehovah. Ap. 4. II.
2 roll=a writing scroll. Heb. *m^egillāh.* Occurs twenty-one times (fourteen times in this chapter. Ps. 40. 7. Ezek. 2. 9; 3. 1, 2, 3. Zech. 5. 1, 2). The name given to the five books called the *m^egilloth* (Song of Solomon, Ruth, Lamentations, Ecclesiastes, and Esther).
words. Pl. Cp. "word" (sing.) (*v.* 1).
Israel. These words were now to be *written* because Israel had been already in dispersion 114 years, and could not be *spoken*, as they were when Judah alone was concerned. Cp. 25. 2.
from the days of Josiah. See 1. 1-3. Not only what is recorded in ch. 25, but what Jehovah had spoken to him for the past twenty-three years.
3 evil=calamity. Heb. *rā'a'.* Ap. 44. viii.
every man. Heb. *'ish.* Ap. 14. II.
iniquity. Heb. *'āvōn.* Ap. 44. iv.
sin. Heb. *chāṭā'.* Ap. 44. i.
4 Baruch=Blessed. The first mention of him chronologically. Other references to him in 32. 12; 43. 3, 6; 45. 1-5. He was brother to Seraiah. Cp. 32. 12 with 51. 59.
5 shut up. Not in prison (for cp. *v.* 19), but in hiding, or from some unexplained reason.
6 the fasting day=a fast day. Being in the ninth month (*v.* 9), it was not that prescribed in the Law, which was in the seventh month (Lev. 16. 29; 23. 27).
9 the fifth year. The reading was deferred for some months.
ninth month. Our December. See Ap. 51. V.
they proclaimed, &c.=all the People of Jerusalem, and all the People who were coming in and out of the cities of Jerusalem, had proclaimed a fast before Jehovah.
10 Gemariah. He was brother of Ahikam (26. 24), and not the Gemariah of 29. 3, who was Hilkiah's son.
Shaphan. See note on 2 Kings 22. 3.
the scribe: i.e. Shaphan (not Gemariah), who was the scribe in Josiah's days. See 2 Kings 22. 3, 8, 9, 10, 12. At the time of this history Elishama was the scribe (unless there were more than one). See *vv.* 12, 20, 21.
11 of=from.

11 When Michaiah the son of [10]Gemariah, the L r
son of Shaphan, had heard out °of the book
all the words of [1]the LORD,

495 12 Then he °went down into the king's
house, into the scribe's chamber: and, lo, all
the princes sat there, *even* Elishama the
scribe, and Delaiah the son of Shemaiah,
and °Elnathan the son of Achbor, and [10]Ge-
mariah the son of Shaphan, and Zedekiah the
son of Hananiah, and all the princes.
13 Then Michaiah declared unto them all the
words that he had heard, when [4]Baruch read
°the book in the ears of the People.

s (p. 1069) 14 Therefore all the princes sent Jehudi the
son of Nethaniah, the son of Shelemiah, the
son of Cushi, unto [4]Baruch, saying, "Take in
thine hand the [2]roll wherein thou hast read in
the ears of the People, and come." So [4]Ba-
ruch the son of Neriah took the [2]roll in his
hand, and came unto them.

t 15 And they said unto him, °"Sit down now,
and read it in our ears." So [4]Baruch read *it*
in their ears.

u 16 Now it came to pass, when they had heard
all °the words, they were afraid both one and
other, and said unto [4]Baruch, °"We will surely tell the king of all these words."

v 17 And they asked [4]Baruch, saying, "Tell us
now, How didst thou write all these words at
his mouth?"
18 Then [4]Baruch answered them, "He pronounced all these words unto me with his
mouth, and I wrote *them* with ink in the book."

w 19 Then said the princes unto Baruch, "Go,
hide thee, thou and Jeremiah; and let no °man
know where ye be."

L r 20 And they went in to the king into the
court, but they laid up the [2]roll in the chamber
of Elishama the scribe, and told all the words
in the ears of the king.

s 21 So the king sent Jehudi to fetch the roll:
and he took it out of Elishama the scribe's
chamber.

t And Jehudi read it in the ears of the king, and
in the ears of all the princes which °stood beside the king.
22 Now the king sat in the winterhouse in
the [9]ninth month: and *there was a fire* °on
the hearth burning before him.
23 And it came to pass, *that* when Jehudi
had read three or four °leaves, °he °cut it with
the °penknife, and cast *it* into the fire that
was on the hearth, until all the roll was consumed in the fire that *was* on the hearth.

u 24 Yet they were °not afraid, nor rent their
garments, *neither* the king, nor any of his servants that heard all these words.
25 °Nevertheless [12]Elnathan and Delaiah and
[10]Gemariah had °made intercession to the
king that he would not burn the roll: but he
would not hear them.

v 26 But the king commanded Jerahmeel the
son of °Hammelech, and Seraiah the son of
Azriel, and Shelemiah the son of Abdeel, to take
[4]Baruch the scribe and Jeremiah the prophet:

w but [1]the LORD hid them.

K O 27 Then the word of the LORD °came to
Jeremiah, after that the king had burned °the
roll, and the words which [4]Baruch wrote at
the mouth of Jeremiah, saying,
28 "Take thee again °another roll, and write
in it all the former words that were in the first
roll, which Jehoiakim the king of Judah hath
burned.

29 And °thou shalt say to Jehoiakim king of P
Judah, 'Thus saith [1]the LORD; 'Thou hast
burned this roll, saying, 'Why hast thou written therein, saying, 'The king of Babylon
shall certainly come and destroy this land, and
shall cause to cease from thence °man and
beast?''

30 Therefore thus saith [1]the LORD °of Je- *P*
hoiakim king of Judah; He shall have °none
to sit upon the throne of David: and his dead
body shall be cast out in the day to the heat,
and in the night to the frost.
31 And I will °punish him and his seed and
his servants for their [3]iniquity; and I will
bring upon them, and upon the inhabitants of
Jerusalem, and upon the [19]men of Judah, all

12 went down. Cp. 22. 1.
Elnathan. The king's emissary against Urijah (26. 22).
13 the=in the.
15 Sit down now. Cp. "stood" (*v.* 21). Showing that these princes were favourable to Jeremiah.
16 the words. Some codices, with two early printed editions, read "these words".
We will surely tell. Showing their earnestness and sincerity in the matter.
19 man. Heb. *'īsh.* Ap. 14. II.
21 stood. See note on *v.* 15.
22 on the hearth=in the brasier: i.e. the vessel into which the burning charcoal was put from the hearth in houses of the better sort.
23 leaves=columns. **he**: i.e. the king.
cut it=cut it up into fragments.
penknife=a scribe's knife. The words of Jehovah are cut up to-day, not with a scribe's knife, but with scribe's pens in the hands of the modern critics. Yet they are "not afraid".
24 not afraid. The courtiers were less open to holy fear than the People were. See note on *v.* 9. Contrast Jehoiakim's father, king Josiah (2 Kings 22. 11). Contrast also the sentence pronounced on them (2 Kings 22. 18–20 with *v.* 30, below on "him").
25 Nevertheless=Moreover.
made intercession. Showing that Elnathan was less hostile than we might perhaps have concluded from 26. 22 and 2 Kings 24. 8.
26 Hammelech=the king. Cp. 38. 6. 1 Kings 22. 26. 2 Kings 11. 1, 2. Zeph. 1. 8.
The THIRTY-THIRD Prophecy of Jeremiah (p. 1015).
27 came. The word of the LORD was "not bound". Cp. 2 Tim. 2. 9.
the roll, and the words. Note the Fig. *Hendiadys* (Ap. 6)="the roll, yea, the very words of Jehovah written therein".
28 another roll. See the Structure, "K" and "*K*" (p. 1069). We are not told what became of this, so it may have got, later, into the hands of Nehemiah, when he visited the Temple ruins.
29 thou shalt say. Not verbally to Jehoiakim, but in the other scroll.
man. Heb. *'ādām.* Ap. 14. I.
30 of=concerning.
none to sit, &c.=none sitting, &c. Heb. *yāshab*, implying permanence. His son Jehoiachin reigned only three months, and then only on sufferance (2 Kings 24. 6–8). See note on 22. 30. See Ap. 99.
31 punish him=visit upon him. Ref. to Pent. (Ex. 32. 34). Ap. 92.

495 the [3]evil that I have pronounced against them; but they hearkened not.' "

O (p. 1069) 32 Then took Jeremiah [28]another roll, and gave it to [4]Baruch the scribe, the son of Neriah; who wrote therein from the mouth of Jeremiah all the words of the book which Jehoiakim king of Judah had burned in the fire: and there were added besides unto them many °like words.

D Q U X (p. 1071) 478 **37** And king Zedekiah the son of Josiah reigned instead of °Coniah the son of Jehoiakim, °whom Nebuchadrezzar king of Babylon made king in the land of Judah.

2 But neither he, nor his servants, nor the People of the land, did hearken unto the °words of °the LORD, which He spake by the prophet Jeremiah.

Y x 3 And Zedekiah the king sent Jehucal the son of Shelemiah and Zephaniah the son of Maaseiah the priest to the prophet Jeremiah, saying, "Pray now unto [2]the LORD our °God for us."

y 4 Now Jeremiah came in and went out among the People: for they had not put him into prison.

z 5 Then °Pharaoh's army was come forth out of Egypt: and when the Chaldeans that besieged Jerusalem heard tidings of them, they departed from Jerusalem.

X 6 Then came the word of [2]the LORD unto the prophet Jeremiah, saying,

7 "Thus saith °the [2]LORD, the [3]God of Israel; 'Thus shall ye say to the king of Judah, that sent you unto Me to enquire of Me; °'Behold, [5]Pharaoh's army, which is come forth to help you, shall return to Egypt into their own land.

8 And the Chaldeans shall come again, and fight against this city, and take it, and burn it with fire.' '

9 Thus saith [2]the LORD; 'Deceive not °yourselves, saying, 'The Chaldeans shall surely depart from us:' for they shall not depart.

10 For though ye had smitten the whole army of the Chaldeans that fight against you, and there remained *but* wounded °men among them, *yet* should they rise up °every man in his tent, and burn this city with fire.' "

Y z 11 And it came to pass, that when the army of the Chaldeans was broken up from Jerusalem for fear of [5]Pharaoh's army,

12 Then Jeremiah went forth out of Jerusalem °to go into the land of Benjamin, °to separate himself thence °in the midst of the People.

13 And when he was in °the gate of Benjamin, a captain of the ward *was* there, whose name *was* Irijah, the son of Shelemiah, the son of °Hananiah; and he took Jeremiah the prophet, saying, "Thou fallest away to the Chaldeans."

14 Then said Jeremiah, "*It is* false; I fall not away to the Chaldeans." But he hearkened not to him: so Irijah took Jeremiah, and brought him to the °princes.

y 15 Wherefore the princes were wroth with Jeremiah, and °smote him, and °put him °in prison in the house of Jonathan the scribe: for they had made that °the prison.

x 16 °When Jeremiah was entered into the

---

32 like words=like unto them. They are preserved to us in this book to a large extent.

37. 1—45. 5 (*D*, p. 1015). HISTORY, ETC. ZEDEKIAH. (*Introversion.*)

D | Q | 37. 1—38. 28. Jeremiah. Persecution and deliverance.
R | 39. 1-9. City taken.
R | 39. 10—44. 30. People taken, and left.
Q | 45. 1-5. Jeremiah. Prophecy to Baruch. (Sorrow and assurance.)

37. 1—38. 28 (Q, above). JEREMIAH, ETC. (*Introversion and Alternation.*)

Q | S | U | 37. 1-20. Public message.
V | 37. 21. In court of the prison.
T | W | 38. 1-6. Accusation. } Persecutors
W | 38. 7-13. Defence. } of Jeremiah.
S | *U* | 38. 14-27. Private conference.
V | 38. 28. In court of the prison.

37. 1-20 (U, above). PUBLIC MESSAGE. (*Alternation and Introversion.*)

U | X | 1, 2. Words of Jeremiah. Disobedience.
Y | x | 3. Message from Zedekiah to Jeremiah.
y | 4. Jeremiah: not in prison.
z | 5. Departure of Chaldeans.
X | 6-10. Words of Jeremiah. Threatening.
Y | *z* | 11-14. Departure of Chaldeans.
y | 15. Jeremiah in prison.
x | 16-20. Message from Jeremiah to Zedekiah.

The history in chs. 37 and 38 reverts to the last two years of Zedekiah's reign, and the actual siege of Jerusalem. It is a new and independent section. See *D*, above.

1 Coniah: i.e. Jeconiah, called also Jehoiachin.
whom: i.e. Zedekiah.

2 words=prophecies.
the LORD. Heb. Jehovah. Ap. 4. II.

3 God. Heb. Elohim. Ap. 4. I.

5 Pharaoh's: i.e. Pharaoh Hophra's. Cp. 44. 30. The Apries of Herodotus, and fourth successor of Psammeticus on the throne of Egypt. He came to help Zedekiah (Ezek. 17. 15-17), but was defeated by the Chaldeans, and Egypt subdued. Cp. 2 Kings 24. 7. Ezek. 29. 1-16, and chs. 30-33. Also Jer. 43. 9-13. Cp. *Encyclopædia Britannica*, eleventh new Cambridge edition (vol. ii, p. 230).

The THIRTY-FOURTH Prophecy of Jeremiah (p. 1015).

7 the LORD, the God of Israel. See note on 11. 3.
Behold. Fig. *Asterismos*. Ap. 6.

9 yourselves=your own souls. Heb. *nephesh*. Ap. 13.

10 men. Heb. pl. of *'ĕnōsh*. Ap. 14. III.
every man. Heb. *'īsh*. Ap. 14. II.

12 to go, &c. Probably to Anathoth.
to separate himself thence=to assign [himself] his portion there (i.e. at Anathoth, in Benjamin, three and a half miles north-east of Jerusalem), where he drew his living.
in the midst: for safety, and to avoid detection.

13 the gate of Benjamin: i.e. the northern gate, called also "the gate of Ephraim" (2 Kings 14. 13. Neh. 8. 16), leading to Anathoth.
Hananiah. Perhaps the false prophet mentioned in 28. 1-17.

14 princes. Named in 38. 1; none of whom had been favourable to Jeremiah in the days of Jehoiakim (26. 16).

15 smote=scourged.
put him in prison. Note Jeremiah's prison experiences: (1) put in on false charge (37. 11-15); (2) released, but confined in the court of the prison; (3) imprisoned again in Malchiah's miry dungeon (38. 1-6); (4) released again as before (38. 13-28); (5) carried away in chains by Nebuchadnezzar, but released at Ramah (40. 1-4).
in prison=in the house of bonds.
the prison=the house of detention.

16 When, &c.=For Jeremiah [actually] entered, &c.

478 °dungeon, and into the °cabins, and Jeremiah
had °remained there many days;

17 Then Zedekiah the king sent, and took
him out: and the king asked him secretly in
his house, and said, °"Is there *any* word from
[2]the LORD?" And Jeremiah said, °"There
is: for," said he, "thou shalt be delivered into
the hand of the king of Babylon."

18 Moreover Jeremiah said unto king Zedekiah, "What have I °offended against thee, or
against thy servants, or against this people,
that ye have put me in °prison?

19 Where *are* now °your prophets which
prophesied unto you, saying, 'The king of
Babylon shall not come against you, nor
against this land?'

20 Therefore hear now, I pray thee, O my
lord the king: let my supplication, I pray
thee, be accepted before thee; that thou cause
me not to return to the house of Jonathan the
scribe, lest I die there."

V 21 Then Zedekiah the king commanded that
(p. 1071) they should commit Jeremiah into the court
of the °prison, and that they should give him
daily a °piece of bread out of the bakers'
street, until all the bread in the city were
spent. Thus Jeremiah [16]remained in the
court of the °prison.

T W a **38** Then Shephatiah the son of Mattan,
(p. 1072) and Gedaliah the son of Pashur, and
478 Jucal the son of Shelemiah, and °Pashur the
son of Malchiah, heard the words that Jeremiah had spoken unto all the people, saying,

2 "Thus saith °the LORD, 'He that remaineth in this city shall die by the sword, by the
famine, and by the pestilence: but he that
°goeth forth to the Chaldeans shall live; for he
shall have his °life for a prey, and shall live.'

3 Thus saith [2]the LORD, 'This city shall
surely be given into the hand of the king of
Babylon's army, which shall take it.'"

4 Therefore the princes said unto the king,
"We beseech thee, let this °man be put to
death: for thus he weakeneth the hands of the
°men of war that remain in this city, and the
hands of all the People, in speaking such words
unto them: for this °man seeketh not the °wel-
fare of this People, but the hurt."

b 5 Then Zedekiah the king said, "Behold, he
is in your hand: for the king *is* not *he that*
can do *any* thing against you."

c 6 Then took they Jeremiah, and cast him into
the °dungeon of Malchiah the son of °Ham-
melech, that *was* in the court of the °prison:
and they let down Jeremiah with cords.

d And in the dungeon *there was* no water, but
mire: so Jeremiah °sunk in the mire.

W a 7 Now when °Ebed-melech the Ethiopian,
one of the eunuchs which was in the king's
house, heard that they had put Jeremiah in
the [6]dungeon; the king then sitting in the
gate of Benjamin;

8 °Ebed-melech went forth out of the king's
house, and spake to the king, saying,

9 "My lord the king, these [4]men have done
evil in all that they have done to Jeremiah the
prophet, whom they have cast into the [6]dun-
geon; and he is like to die for hunger in the
place where he is: for *there is* no more bread
in the city."

10 Then the king commanded [7]Ebed-melech b
the Ethiopian, saying, "Take from hence
°thirty [4]men with thee, and take up Jeremiah
the prophet out of the [6]dungeon, before he die."

11 So Ebed-melech took the [4]men with him, c
and went into the house of the king under the
treasury, and took thence °old cast °clouts
and old rotten rags, and let them down by cords
into the dungeon to Jeremiah.

12 And [7]Ebed-melech the Ethiopian said unto
Jeremiah, "Put now *these* [11]old cast clouts and
rotten rags under thine °armholes under the
cords." And Jeremiah did so.

13 So they drew up Jeremiah with cords, and *d*
took him up out of the [6]dungeon: and Jeremiah
°remained in the court of the [6]prison.

14 °Then Zedekiah the king sent, and took *U* A

---

dungeon = house of the pit. Heb. *bōr*. See notes on Gen. 21. 19 ("well"). Isa. 14. 19 ("pit").
cabins = cells.
remained = abode. Note the Fig. *Cycloides* (Ap. 6), marking the refrain, which is repeated in *v.* 21, and in 38. 13, 28; as shown in the Structure.

17 Is there . . . There is = Does there exist . . . ? . . . There does exist. Heb. *yēsh* . . . *yēsh*. See notes on Prov. 8. 21; 18. 24; and Luke 7. 25.

18 offended = sinned. Heb. *chāṭā'*. Ap. 44. i.
prison = the house of detention. See *v.* 16.

19 your prophets. Not Jehovah's. From the beginning they had prophesied falsely. See 6. 14; 27. 16; 28. 2.

21 prison = guard-house. Not the same word as in *v.* 15.
piece = a cake. Cp. 52. 6. Three were reckoned as a meal (Luke 11. 5); a soldier's ration at that time.

38. 1-13 (T, p. 1071). PERSECUTION OF JEREMIAH. (*Extended Alternation.*)

T | W | a | 1-4. Jeremiah. Accusation by princes.
      b | 5. Zedekiah. Permission for imprisonment.
        c | 6-. The dungeon.
          d | -6. Sinking in the mire.
  W | *a* | 7-9. Jeremiah. Defence by Ebed-melech.
      b | 10. Zedekiah. Command for release.
        c | 11, 12. The dungeon.
          d | 13. Drawing out of the mire.

1 Pashur. See note on 20. 1.

2 the LORD. Heb. Jehovah. Ap. 4. II.
goeth forth. Some codices add "and falleth".
life = soul. Heb. *nephesh*. Ap. 13.

4 man. Heb. *'ish*. Ap. 14. II.
men. Heb. pl. of *'ĕnōsh*. Ap. 14. III.
welfare = peace.

6 dungeon. See note on 37. 16.
Hammelech = the king. See note on 36. 26.
prison = house of detention.
sunk in the mire. To be preferred to the moral sinking of Zedekiah in *v.* 22.

7 Ebed-melech the Ethiopian. See 39. 16; and cp. Acts 8. 27-38.

8 Ebed-melech. Some codices add "the Ethiopian".

10 thirty. The king knew the danger. No need to suppose that "thirty" is a copyist's error for "three"!

11 old cast = cast-off clothes.
clouts = patches. Ang.-Sax. *clūt* = a patch.

12 armholes = armpits.

13 remained. See note on 37. 18.

38. 14-27 (*U*, p. 1071). PRIVATE CONFERENCE. (*Introversion.*)

U | A | 14. Conference.
  B | 15. Jeremiah. Stipulation with king.
  B | 16. Jeremiah. King's agreement.
A | 17-27. Conference.

14 Then, &c. This is the last picture of Zedekiah, and of the house of Judah.

478-477 Jeremiah the prophet unto him into the °third
entry that *is* in the house of [2]the LORD: and
the king said unto Jeremiah, "I will ask thee
a thing; hide nothing from me."

B 15 Then Jeremiah said unto Zedekiah, "If I
(p. 1072) declare *it* unto thee, wilt thou not surely put
me to death? and if I give thee counsel, °wilt
thou not hearken unto me?"

B 16 So °Zedekiah the king sware secretly unto
Jeremiah, saying, °"*As* [2]the LORD liveth, That
made us this °soul, I will not put thee to death,
neither will I give thee into the hand of these
[4]men that seek thy [2]life."

A e 17 Then said Jeremiah unto Zedekiah, "Thus
(p. 1073) saith °the [2]LORD, °the °God of hosts, the °God
of Israel; 'If thou wilt assuredly go forth unto
the king of Babylon's princes, then thy [16]soul
shall live, and this city shall not be burned
with fire; and thou shalt live, and thine house:
18 But if thou wilt not go forth to the king of
Babylon's princes, then shall this city be given
into the hand of the Chaldeans, and they shall
burn it with fire, and thou shalt not escape out
of their hand.'"

f 19 And Zedekiah the king said unto Jeremiah,
"I am °afraid of the Jews that are fallen to the
Chaldeans, lest they deliver me into their hand,
and they mock me."

e 20 But Jeremiah said, "They shall not deliver
thee. Obey, I beseech thee, the voice of [2]the
LORD, which I speak unto thee: so it shall be
well unto thee, and thy [16]soul shall live.
21 But if thou refuse to go forth, this *is* the
word that [2]the LORD hath shewed me:
22 And, behold, all the women that are left
in the king of Judah's house *shall be* brought
forth to the king of Babylon's °princes, and
those *women* shall say, 'Thy friends have °set
thee on, and have prevailed against thee: thy
feet are °sunk in the mire, *and* they are turned
away back.'
23 So they shall bring out all thy wives and
thy °children to the Chaldeans: and thou shalt
not escape out of their hand, but shalt be taken
by the hand of the king of Babylon: and °thou
shalt cause this city to be burned with fire."

f 24 Then said Zedekiah unto Jeremiah, "Let
no [4]man know of these words, and thou shalt
not die.
25 But if the princes hear that I have talked
with thee, and they come unto thee, and say
unto thee, 'Declare unto us now what thou
hast said unto the king, hide it not from us,
and we will not put thee to death; also what
the king said unto thee:'
26 Then thou shalt say unto them, 'I presented
my supplication before the king, that
he would not cause me to return to Jonathan's
house, to die there.'"
27 Then came all the princes unto Jeremiah,
and asked him: and °he told them according to
all these words that the king had °commanded.
So they left off speaking with him; for the
matter was not perceived.

V 28 So Jeremiah °abode in the court of the
(p. 1071) [6]prison until the day that Jerusalem was taken:
and he was *there* when Jerusalem was taken.

14 third entry. Probably the innermost entrance, for secrecy.

15 wilt thou not . . . me?=thou wilt not. This second clause is not a question in the Hebrew text.

16 Zedekiah. Omitted in edition of A.V., 1611.

As the LORD liveth=By the life of Jehovah.

soul. Heb. *nephesh* (Ap. 13): i.e. May He Who gave us both our life, take mine away if I take thine, or give thee, &c.

38. 17-27 (*A*, p. 1072). CONFERENCE. (*Alternation.*)

A | e | 17, 18. Alternatives.
 f | 19. Fear of the People. Expressed.
 e | 20-23. Alternatives.
 f | 24-27. Fear of the princes. Implied.

17 the LORD, the God of hosts, the God of Israel. See note on 35. 17.

the God of hosts. Some codices, with Aram., Sept., Syr., and Vulg., omit "God", and read "Jehovah Z baioth, God of Israel".

God. Heb. Elohim. Ap. 4. I.

19 afraid=apprehensive.

22 princes. Showing that Nebuchadnezzar himself was not there. Cp. 39. 1.

set thee on=persuaded thee. See note on 20. 7.

sunk in the mire. The moral sinking of Zedekiah far worse than Jeremiah's physical sinking.

23 children=sons.

thou shalt cause this city to be burned. Heb. thou wilt burn. Note the idiom by which the *act* is put for the *declaration* that it should be done. Cp. 1. 10.

27 he told them, &c. In Holy Scripture we have an inspired *record* of what was said and done by others, but it does not follow that all that was so said and done was inspired.

commanded. Some codices, with Sept., Syr., and Vulg., add "him".

28 abode. See the note on 37. 16.

39. 1-9 (R, p. 1071). THE CITY TAKEN. (*Alternation.*)

R | g | 1. Nebuchadnezzar.
 h | 2. Taking of the city.
 g | 3. Nebuchadnezzar's princes.
 h | 4-9. Taking of Zedekiah.

1 ninth year. Cp. Ezek. 24. 1, 2.

tenth month. Ch. 52. 4 supplies a further date: viz. "in the tenth day of the month".

2 broken up. Cp. ch. 52. 6; which explains that provisions had failed before then.

3 Sarsechim. Some codices, with four early printed editions, read "Sar-ṣechim". It is the pl. of the Akkadian Sar-sak=king's son.

Rab-saris=chief of the chamberlains. Cp. 2 Kings 18. 17. Dan. 1. 3, 7.

Nergal-sharezer, Rab-mag=Nergal-sharezer, chief of the physicians (or magi). Only four names of persons in this verse, not six.

4 men. Heb. pl. of *'ĕnōsh*. Ap. 14. III.

39 In the °ninth year of Zedekiah king of R g
Judah, in the °tenth month, came Nebu- (p. 1073)
chadrezzar king of Babylon and all his army 479
against Jerusalem, and they besieged it.

2 *And* in the eleventh year of Zedekiah, in h
the fourth month, the ninth *day* of the month, 477
the city was °broken up.[6]

3 And all the princes of the king of Babylon *g*
came in, and sat in the middle gate, *even*
Nergal-sharezer, Samgar-nebo, °Sarsechim,
Rab-saris, °Nergal-sharezer, Rab-mag, with
all the residue of the princes of the king of
Babylon.

4 And it came to pass, *that* when Zedekiah *h*
the king of Judah saw them, and all the °men
of war, then they fled, and went forth out of

477 the city by night, by the way of the king's
garden, °by the gate betwixt the two walls:
and he went out the way of °the plain.
5 But the Chaldeans' army pursued after
them, and overtook Zedekiah in the plains of
°Jericho: and when they had taken him, they
brought him up to Nebuchadnezzar king of
Babylon to °Riblah in the land of Hamath,
where he °gave judgment upon him.
6 Then the king of Babylon slew the sons of
Zedekiah in Riblah °before his eyes: also the
king of Babylon slew all the nobles of Judah.
7 Moreover he °put out Zedekiah's eyes, and
bound him °with chains, °to carry him to
Babylon.
8 And °the Chaldeans burned the king's
house, and the houses of the People, with fire,
and brake down the walls of Jerusalem.
9 Then °Nebuzar-adan the captain of °the
guard carried away captive into Babylon the
remnant of the People that remained in the city,
and those that fell away, that fell to him, with
the rest of the People that remained.
R C 10 But Nebuzar-adan the captain of [9]the
(p. 1074) guard left of the °poor of the People, which had
nothing, in the land of Judah, and gave them
vineyards and fields at the same time.
D 11 Now Nebuchadrezzar king of Babylon
gave charge concerning Jeremiah °to Nebuzar-
adan the captain of [9]the guard, saying,
12 "Take him, and °look well to him, and do
him no harm; but do unto him even as he
shall say unto thee."
13 So Nebuzar-adan the captain of [9]the guard
sent, and Nebushasban, [3]Rab-saris, and [3]Ner-
gal-sharezer, Rab-mag, and all the king of
Babylon's princes;
14 Even they sent, and took Jeremiah out of
the court of the °prison, and committed him unto
°Gedaliah the son of Ahikam the son of °Sha-
phan, that he should °carry him home: °so
he dwelt among the People.
E 15 Now the word of °the LORD came unto
478 Jeremiah, while he was shut up in the court
of the [14]prison, saying,
16 °"Go and speak to Ebed-melech the Ethiopian, saying, 'Thus saith °the [15]LORD of hosts,
the °God of Israel; °'Behold, I will bring My
words upon this city for °evil, and not for
good; and they shall be *accomplished* in that
day before thee.
17 But I will deliver thee in that day, °saith
[15]the LORD: 'and thou shalt not be given into
the hand of the [4]men of whom thou *art* afraid.
18 For I will surely deliver thee, and thou
shalt not fall by the sword, but thy °life shall
be for °a prey unto thee: because thou hast
°put thy trust in Me, [17]saith [15]the LORD.'"

D **40** The word that came to Jeremiah from
477 °the LORD, after that Nebuzar-adan
the captain of the guard had let him go from
Ramah, when he had taken him being bound
in °chains among all that were carried away
captive of Jerusalem and Judah, which were
carried away captive unto Babylon.
2 And the captain of °the guard took Jeremiah, and °said unto him, [1]"The LORD thy
°God hath pronounced this °evil upon this place.

by the gate. On the south corner of Ophel See Ap. 68.

the plain. To avoid the Jordan.

5 Jericho. Thus, Jericho was the scene of Israel's *first* victory (Josh. 6), and *final* defeat.

Riblah. Now *Ribleh*, on the east bank of the Orontes, thirty-five miles north-east of Baalbek, the base and head-quarters of Nebuchadnezzar. Some twenty-two years before, Jehoahaz was put in bonds here by Pharaoh-nechoh, to be led captive to Egypt. See 2 Kings 23. 33.

gave judgment = pronounced sentence: i.e. for his perjury. See 2 Chron. 36. 10, 13. Ezek. 17. 15, 18.

6 before his eyes. A specimen of the inhumanity of those days.

7 put out Zedekiah's eyes. So that Ezekiel was quite correct when he said that Zedekiah should be taken to Babylon, though he should not see it (Ezek. 12. 13).

with chains = with two fetters.

to carry him. Ch. 52. 11, and 2 Kings 25. 7, show that this purpose was executed. It was not so with Jehoiakim (2 Chron. 36. 6).

8 the Chaldeans burned, &c. On the tenth day of the fifth month. Cp. 52. 12, 13. The same day as the capture of the city by the Romans in A.D. 69.

9 Nebuzar-adan = the prince favoured by Nebo.

the guard = the executioners (2 Kings 25. 8). Cp. Gen. 37. 36; 39. 1.

39. 10—44. 30 (*R*, p. 1071). THE PEOPLE TAKEN, AND LEFT. (*Introversion.*)

R | C | 39. 10. The poor of the People.
  D | 39. 11–14. Jeremiah. Liberation commanded.
    E | 39. 15–18. Promise to Ebed-melech.
  D | 40. 1–6. Jeremiah. Liberation effected.
C | 40. 7—44. 30. The poor of the People.

10 poor. Heb. *dal.* See note on "poverty", Prov. 6. 11.

11 to = to the hand of, or through.

12 look well to him. Not the first, rejected by the Jews, who was honoured by the Gentiles.

14 prison = house of detention: as in 38. 6, 13, 28.

Gedaliah. See note on Ahikam, 26. 24. Cp. 40. 6.

Shaphan. See note on 2 Kings 22. 3.

carry him home. Some codices, with one early printed edition (Rabbinic), read "out of the [prison] house". From the next chapter we learn that he was taken north to Ramah with other captives, and from that place was set free, and went to Gedaliah to Mizpah (40. 6). This verse (*v.* 14) is only a brief summary.

so = and.

The THIRTY-FIFTH Prophecy of Jeremiah (p. 1015).

15 the LORD. Heb. Jehovah. Ap. 4. II.

16 Go and speak. Not to interrupt the history, this incident as to Ebed-melech is reserved till now.

the LORD of hosts, the God of Israel. See note on 7. 3. **God.** Heb. Elohim. Ap. 4. I.

Behold. Fig. *Asterismos.* Ap. 6.

evil = calamity. Heb. *rā'a'.* Ap. 44. viii.

17 saith the LORD = [is] Jehovah's oracle.

18 life = soul. Heb. *nephesh.* Ap. 13.

a prey: i.e. he should save it. Cp. 21. 9.

put thy trust = confided. Heb. *bāṭah.* Ap. 69. i.

The THIRTY-SIXTH Prophecy of Jeremiah (p. 1015).

40. 1 the LORD. Heb. Jehovah. Ap. 4. II.

chains = the two fetters, as in 39. 7.

2 the guard. See note on 39. 9.

said. Nebuzar-adan takes all the credit to himself. Cp. 39. 11.

God. Heb. Elohim. Ap. 4. I.

evil = calamity. Heb. *rā'a'.* Ap. 44. viii.

3 because ye have sinned, &c. Ref. to Pent. (Deut. 29. 24, 25). Ap. 92. **sinned.** Heb. *chāṭā'.* Ap. 44. i.

3 Now [1]the LORD hath brought *it*, and done
according as He hath said: °because ye have
°sinned against [1]the LORD, and have not

477 obeyed His voice, therefore this thing is come upon you.
4 And now, °behold, I loose thee this day from the [1]chains which *were* upon thine °hand. If it seem good unto thee to come with me into Babylon, come; and I will look well unto thee: but if it seem ill unto thee to come with me into Babylon, forbear: °behold, all the land *is* before thee: whither it seemeth good and convenient for thee to go, thither go."
5 °Now while he was not yet gone back, *he said,* "Go back also to °Gedaliah the son of Ahikam the son of °Shaphan, whom the king of Babylon hath made governor over °the cities of Judah, and dwell with him among the People: or go wheresoever it seemeth convenient unto thee to go." So the captain of [2]the guard gave him victuals and a °reward, and let him go.
6 Then went Jeremiah unto [5]Gedaliah the son of Ahikam to °Mizpah; and dwelt with him among the People that were left in the land.

C F¹ G (p. 1075) 7 Now when all the captains of the forces which *were* in the fields, *even* they and their °men, heard that the king of Babylon had made [5]Gedaliah the son of Ahikam °governor in the land, and had committed unto him men, and women, and °children, and of the °poor of the land, of them that were not carried away captive to Babylon;

H J 8 Then they came to [5]Gedaliah to [6]Mizpah, even °Ishmael the son of Nethaniah, and Johanan and Jonathan the °sons of Kareah, and Seraiah the son of Tanhumeth, and the sons of Ephai the °Netophathite, and Jezaniah the son of a Maachathite, they and their men.

K 9 And [5]Gedaliah the son of Ahikam the son of [5]Shaphan sware unto them and to their men, saying, "Fear not to serve the Chaldeans: dwell in the land, and serve the king of Babylon, and it shall be well with you.
10 As for me, [4]behold, I will dwell at Mizpah, to serve the Chaldeans, which will come unto us: but ye, gather ye °wine, and °summer fruits, and oil, and put *them* in your vessels, and dwell in your cities that ye have taken."

G 11 Likewise when all the Jews that *were* in Moab, and among the Ammonites, and in Edom, and that *were* in all the countries, heard that the king of Babylon had left a remnant of Judah, and that he had set over them [5]Gedaliah the son of Ahikam the son of [5]Shaphan;

H K 12 Even all the Jews returned out of all places whither they were driven, and came to the land of Judah, to [5]Gedaliah, unto [6]Mizpah, and gathered [10]wine and [10]summer fruits very much.

J L¹ i 13 Moreover Johanan the [8]son of Kareah, and all the captains of the forces that *were* in the °fields, came to [5]Gedaliah to [6]Mizpah,
14 And said unto him, "Dost thou certainly know that Baalis the king of the Ammonites hath sent Ishmael the son of Nethaniah to °slay thee?"

k But Gedaliah the son of Ahikam believed them not.

4 behold. Fig. *Asterismos*. Ap. 6.
hand. Some codices, with eight early printed editions, Sept., Syr., and Vulg., read "hands".
5 Now while he was not yet gone back = And ere yet he could make reply.
Gedaliah. See note on 26. 24, and cp. 39. 14.
Shaphan. See note on 2 Kings 22. 3.
the cities. The A.V. edition, 1611, reads "all the cities".
reward = present.
6 Mizpah. North of Jerusalem, near Anathoth. Cp. 41. 5–9. Josh. 18. 26. 1 Sam. 7. 16; 10. 17, and 1 Kings 15. 22. The scene of the following events: here had been Asa's fortress (41. 9); here Sennacherib and Nebuchadnezzar and Titus got their first view of Jerusalem.

40. 7—44. 30 (*C*, p. 1074). THE POOR OF THE PEOPLE. (*Division.*)

C | F¹ | 40. 7—41. 15. Under GEDALIAH in the land.
  | F² | 41. 16—43. 7. Under JOHANAN in the land.
  | F³ | 43. 8—44. 30. Under JOHANAN in Egypt.

40. 7—41. 15 (F¹, above). UNDER GEDALIAH IN THE LAND. (*Alternation and Introversion.*)

F¹ | G | 40. 7. Gedaliah. Administration.
   H | J | 40. 8. Ishmael's visit.
       K | 40. 9, 10. Invitation of Gedaliah.
   G | 40. 11. Gedaliah. Administration.
   H | *K* | 40. 12. Invitation. Accepted.
       J | 40. 13—41. 15. Ishmael's treachery.

7 men. Heb. pl. of *'ĕnōsh*. Ap. 14. III.
governor. No more attempts to make a king, after Zedekiah's perjury. See Ezek. 17. 15–19.
children = young children.
poor. Heb. "poverty", put by Fig. *Metonymy* (of Adjunct), Ap. 6, for poor people. See Prov. 6. 11.
8 Ishmael. The Massorites (Ap. 30) set their hand to obliterate the Divine names in the case of men who had served to disgrace it. One is *'ēl*, in the compound "Ishmael", which means "whom my El heareth". It is used of five different men, and occurs forty-eight times: twenty times of Hagar's son; twenty-three times of Nethaniah's son in this history; and five times of the other three. On account of his horrible treachery, the memory of which is perpetuated by the fast of the seventh month (Zech. 7. 5; 8. 9), the vowel points were changed to obliterate the Divine Name (El): viz. *yishmā'ēl*, instead of *yishmā''ēl*, which is not observable in the ordinary English spelling.
sons. Some codices, with Aram. and Sept., read "son", as in *v.* 13.
Netophathite = a man of Netophah, now *Khan Umm Tōbah*, north of Bethlehem (1 Chron. 2. 54. Ezra 2. 22. Neh. 7. 26).
10 wine. Heb. *yayin*. Ap. 27. I.
summer fruits. Heb. "summer". Put by Fig. *Metonymy* (of Adjunct), Ap. 6, for the fruits gathered in summer.

40. 13—41. 15 (*J*, above). ISHMAEL'S TREACHERY. (*Division.*)

J | L¹ | 40. 13–16. Treachery. Discovered.
    | L² | 41. 1–15. Treachery. Avenged.

40. 13-16 (L¹, above). TREACHERY. DISCOVERED. (*Alternation.*)

L¹ | i | 13, 14–. Johanan reveals the plot to Gedaliah.
     k | –14. Gedaliah's disbelief.
   i | 15. Johanan's advice to Gedaliah.
     k | 16. Gedaliah's disapproval.

13 fields = field (sing.).
14 slay thee = strike thy soul. Heb. *nephesh*. Ap. 13.
15 man. Heb. *'īsh*. Ap. 14. II.

15 Then Johanan the son of Kareah spake to Gedaliah in Mizpah secretly, saying, "Let me go, I pray thee, and I will [14]slay Ishmael the son of Nethaniah, and no °man shall know *it*: i

477 wherefore should [14]he slay thee, that all the
Jews which are °gathered unto thee should be
scattered, and the remnant in Judah perish?"

k (p. 1075) 16 But [5]Gedaliah the son of Ahikam said
unto Johanan the son of Kareah, "Thou shalt
not do this thing: for thou speakest falsely of
°Ishmael."

L[2] l (p. 1076) 477 **41** Now it came to pass in the seventh
month, *that* Ishmael the son of Nethaniah the son of °Elishama, of the seed royal,
and the princes of the king, °even ten °men
with him, came unto °Gedaliah the son of
Ahikam to °Mizpah; and there they did eat
bread together in °Mizpah.

2 Then arose °Ishmael the son of Nethaniah, and the ten [1]men that were with him, and smote [1]Gedaliah the son of Ahikam the son of Shaphan with the sword, and slew him, whom the king of Babylon °had made governor over the land.

3 [2]Ishmael also slew all the Jews that were with him, *even* with [1]Gedaliah, at [1]Mizpah, and the Chaldeans that were found there, °*and* the [1]men of war.

4 And it came to pass the second day after he had slain Gedaliah, and no °man knew *it*,

5 That there came certain from Shechem, from °Shiloh, and from Samaria, *even* fourscore [1]men, having their beards shaven, and their clothes rent, and having cut themselves, with °offerings and incense in their hand, to bring *them* °to the house of °the LORD.

6 And [2]Ishmael the son of Nethaniah went forth from [1]Mizpah to meet them, °weeping all along as he went: and it came to pass, as he met them, he said unto them, "Come to [1]Gedaliah the son of Ahikam."

7 And it was *so*, when they came into the midst of the city, that [2]Ishmael the son of Nethaniah slew them, *and cast them* into the midst of the pit, he, and the [1]men that *were* with him.

8 But ten [1]men were found among them that said unto [2]Ishmael, "Slay us not: for we have °treasures in the field, of wheat, and of barley, and of oil, and of honey." So he forbare, and slew them not among their brethren.

9 Now °the pit wherein [2]Ishmael had cast all the dead bodies of the [1]men, whom he had slain °because of Gedaliah, °*was* it which Asa the king had made for fear of Baasha king of Israel: *and* [2]Ishmael the son of Nethaniah filled it with *them that were* slain.

m 10 Then [2]Ishmael carried away captive all
the residue of the People that *were* in [1]Mizpah, *even* °the king's daughters, and all the People that remained in [1]Mizpah, whom °Nebuzar-adan the captain of °the guard had committed to [1]Gedaliah the son of Ahikam: and Ishmael the son of Nethaniah carried them away captive,

n and departed to go over to the Ammonites.

l 11 But when Johanan the son of Kareah, and
all the captains of the forces that *were* with him, heard of all the °evil that [2]Ishmael the son of Nethaniah had done,

12 Then they took all the [1]men, and went to fight with [2]Ishmael the son of Nethaniah, and found him by the great waters that *are* in °Gibeon.

13 Now it came to pass, *that* when all the m
People which *were* with Ishmael saw Johanan the son of Kareah, and all the captains of the forces that *were* with him, then they were glad.

14 So all the People that [2]Ishmael had carried away captive from [1]Mizpah °cast about and returned, and went unto Johanan the son of Kareah.

15 But [2]Ishmael the son of Nethaniah escaped from Johanan with °eight [1]men, and n
went to the Ammonites.

16 Then took Johanan the son of Kareah, F[2] M
and all the captains of the forces that *were* with him, all the remnant of the People whom he had recovered from [2]Ishmael the son of

---

gathered = gathered out.

41. 1-15 (L[2], p. 1075). TREACHERY. AVENGED.
(*Extended Alternation.*)

L[2] | l | 1-9. Ishmael's treachery.
  m | 10-. Captives taken.
    n | -10. Ammonites.
l | 11, 12. Ishmael's treachery.
  m | 13, 14. Captives rescued.
    n | 15. Ammonites.

1 Elishama. A seal has been found with his name on it. **even** = and.

men. Heb. pl. of *'ĕnōsh.* Ap. 14. III.

Gedaliah. See note on 26. 24; and cp. 39. 14, and 40. 5.

Mizpah. See note on 40. 6.

2 Ishmael. See note on 40. 8.

had made. Cp. 40. 5.

3 and. Some codices, with Vulg. and three early printed editions, read this "and" in the text.

4 man. Heb. *'īsh.* Ap. 14. II.

5 Shiloh. The last of five references to Shiloh in Jeremiah. Cp. 7. 12, 14; 26. 6, 9.

offerings. These would be meal-offerings, according to Lev. 2. 1. Flesh sacrifices were now impossible. Ref. to Pent. (Lev. 2. 1). Probably for the feast of the fifteenth (Lev. 23. 23, 34. Num. 29. 12. Deut. 16. 13).

to the house, &c. Still recognised as the place which Jehovah had chosen.

the LORD. Heb. Jehovah. Ap. 4. II.

6 weeping all along as he went = going on and on weeping.

8 treasures = hidden [treasures, or stores].

9 the pit: or, cistern. Not mentioned elsewhere, but see 1 Kings 15. 22 and 2 Chron. 16. 6.

because of = besides.

was it. By regrouping the letters, this reads "[was] a large pit which", &c.

10 the king's daughters. See note on 43. 7.

Nebuzar-adan. See note on 39. 9.

the guard = the executioners (2 Kings 25. 8). Cp. Gen. 37. 36; 39. 1.

11 evil = calamity. Heb. *rā'a'.* Ap. 44. viii.

12 Gibeon. Now *el Jib*, about five miles north of Jerusalem, where Joab treacherously slew Amasa (2 Sam. 20. 8, 10). **14 cast about** = turned round.

15 eight. Two had been slain in the encounter above.

41. 16—43. 7 (F[2], p. 1075). UNDER JOHANAN IN THE LAND. (*Introversion and Alternation.*)

F[2] | M | 41. 16-18. Intention to go to Egypt.
  N | O | 42. 1-3. Supplication to Jeremiah.
    P | 42. 4. Jeremiah. Answer promised.
  N | *O* | 42. 5, 6. Supplication to Jeremiah.
    P | 42. 7-22. Jeremiah. Answer given.
M | 43. 1-7. Intention carried out.

477 Nethaniah, from [1] Mizpah, after *that* he had slain [1] Gedaliah the son of Ahikam, *even* mighty [1] men of war, and the women, and the °children, and the eunuchs, °whom he had brought again from [12] Gibeon:

17 And they departed, and dwelt in the °habitation of Chimham, which is by Beth-lehem, to go to enter into Egypt,

18 Because of the Chaldeans: for they were afraid of them, because [2] Ishmael the son of Nethaniah had slain [1] Gedaliah the son of Ahikam, °whom the king of Babylon made governor in the land.

N O (p. 1076) 477 **42** Then all the captains of the forces, and Johanan the son of Kareah, and °Jezaniah the son of Hoshaiah, and all the People from the least even unto the greatest, came near,

2 And said unto Jeremiah the prophet, "Let, we beseech thee, our supplication be accepted before thee, and pray for us unto °the LORD °thy °God, *even* for all this remnant; (for we are left *but* °a few of many, °as thine eyes do behold us:)

3 That [2] the Lord °thy [2] God may shew us the way wherein we may walk, and the thing that we may do."

P 4 Then Jeremiah the prophet said unto them, "I have heard *you;* °behold, I will pray unto [2] the LORD your [2] God according to your words; and it shall come to pass, *that* whatsoever thing [2] the LORD shall answer you, I will declare *it* unto you; I will keep nothing back from you."

N O 5 Then they said to Jeremiah, [2] "The LORD be a true and faithful Witness between us, if we do not even according to all things for the which [2] the LORD thy [2] God shall send thee to us.

6 Whether *it be* good, or whether *it be* °evil, we will obey the voice of [2] the LORD our [2] God, to Whom we send thee; °that it may be well with us, when we obey the voice of [2] the LORD our [2] God."

P Q (p. 1077) 7 And it came to pass after ten days, that the word of [2] the LORD came unto Jeremiah.

8 Then called he Johanan the son of Kareah, and all the captains of the forces which *were* with him, and all the people from the least even to the greatest,

9 And said unto them, "Thus saith °the [2] LORD, the [2] God of Israel, unto Whom ye sent me to present your supplication before Him;

R n 10 'If ye will still abide in this land, then will I °build you, and not °pull *you* down, and I will °plant you, and not °pluck *you* up: for °I repent Me of the [6] evil that I have done unto you.

o 11 Be not afraid of the king of Babylon, of whom ye are afraid; be not afraid of him, °saith [2] the LORD: for °I *am* with you to save you, and to deliver you from his hand.

12 And I will shew mercies unto you, that he may have mercy upon you, and cause you to return to your own °land.

R n 13 But if ye say, 'We will not dwell in this land, neither obey the voice of [2] the LORD your [2] God,'

14 Saying, 'No; but we will go into the land of Egypt, where we shall see no war, nor hear the sound of the trumpet, nor have °hunger of bread; and there will we dwell:'

15 °And now therefore hear the word of [2] the LORD, ye remnant of Judah; Thus saith °the [2] LORD of hosts, the [2] God of Israel; If ye °wholly set your faces to enter into Egypt, and go to sojourn there; *o*

16 Then it shall come to pass, *that* the sword, which ye feared, shall overtake you there in the land of Egypt, and the famine, whereof ye were °afraid, shall follow close after you °there in Egypt; and there ye shall die.

17 So shall it be with all the °men that set their faces to go into Egypt to sojourn there; they shall die by the sword, by the famine, and by the pestilence: and none of them shall remain or escape from the [6] evil that I will bring upon them.'

18 For thus saith [15] the [2] LORD of hosts, the [2] God of Israel; 'As Mine anger and My fury hath been poured forth upon the inhabitants

---

16 children=young children.

17 habitation=*Khan*, or inn. Heb. *gērūth*. Occurs only here. Probably erected by Barzillai (2 Sam. 19. 31-40). Near here was the inn where Joseph and Mary could find no room (Luke 2. 7).

whom, &c. See 40. 5.

42. 1 As ch. 41 records the infamous treachery of Ishmael, so ch. 42 records the obstinate disobedience of Johanan. These incidents are recorded (instead of many others) because they show us something of the moral character of the People; and thus furnish us with the reasons for the calamities which overtook them.

Jezaniah. In 43. 2 he has a second name, "Azariah". The Sept. reads this name here.

2 the LORD. Heb. Jehovah. Ap. 4. II.

thy. A special various reading, called *Sevīr* (Ap. 34), reads "our", as in *v.* 20.

God. Heb. Elohim. Ap. 4. I.

a few. Ref. to Pent. (Lev. 26. 22). Ap. 92.

as=according as.

3 thy. See note on *v.* 2; but here the reading "our" is supported by several codices and one early printed edition. **4 behold.** Fig. *Asterismos*. Ap. 6.

6 evil=ill. Heb. *rā'a'*. Ap. 44. viii.

that it may be well, &c. Ref. to Pent. (Deut. 6. 3).

42. 7-22 (*P*, p. 1076). JEREMIAH. ANSWER GIVEN. (*Introversion.*)

P | Q | 7-9. Supplication made.
  R | n | 10. Abiding.
    o | 11, 12. Promise.
  R | *n* | 13, 14. Departing.
    o | 15-18. Warning.
Q | 19-22. Supplication answered.

The THIRTY-SEVENTH Prophecy of Jeremiah (p. 1015).

9 the LORD, the God of Israel. See note on 11. 3.

10 build . . . pull you down . . . plant . . . pluck you up. Cp. 1. 10.

I repent Me. Ref. to Pent. (Gen. 6. 6. Deut. 32. 36).

11 saith the LORD=[is] Jehovah's oracle.

I am with you. See the Structure "*o*", above.

12 land=soil.

14 hunger of bread. Which they had experienced.

15 And now=Now.

the LORD of hosts, the God of Israel. See note on 7. 3. The same in *v.* 18.

wholly set your faces. Ref. to Pent. (Deut. 17. 16).

16 afraid=apprehensive.

there. The 1611 edition of the A.V. does not read this word. **17 men.** Pl. of *'ĕnōsh*. Ap. 14. III.

477 of Jerusalem; so shall My fury be poured forth
upon you, when ye shall enter into Egypt:
and ye shall be an execration, and an astonishment, and a curse, and a reproach; and ye
shall see this place no more.'"

Q p 19 [2]The LORD hath said concerning you, "O
(p. 1078) ye remnant of Judah; °Go ye not into Egypt:"
q know certainly that I have °admonished you
[21]this day.

r 20 For °ye dissembled in your °hearts, when
ye sent me unto [2]the LORD your [2]God, saying,
"Pray for us unto [2]the LORD our [2]God; and
according unto all that [2]the LORD our [2]God
shall say, so declare unto us, and we will do *it*."

q 21 And *now* I have °this day declared *it* to
you; but ye have not obeyed the voice of [2]the
LORD your [2]God, nor any *thing* for the which
He hath sent me unto you.

p 22 Now therefore know certainly that ye
shall die °by the sword, by the famine, and
by the pestilence, in the place whither ye desire
to go *and* to sojourn.

M s **43** And it came to pass, *that* when Jere-
477 miah had made an end of speaking unto
°all the People all the words of °the LORD
their °God, for which °the LORD their °God
had sent him to them, *even* all these words,
2 Then spake Azariah the son of Hoshaiah,
and Johanan the son of Kareah, and [1]all the
proud °men, saying unto Jeremiah, "Thou
speakest falsely: [1]the LORD our [1]God hath not
sent thee to say, 'Go not into Egypt to sojourn
there:'
3 But °Baruch the son of Neriah setteth thee
on against us, for to deliver us into the hand
of the Chaldeans, that they might put us to
death, °and carry us away captives into
Babylon."

t 4 So Johanan the son of Kareah, and all the
captains of the forces, and [1]all the People,
obeyed not the voice of [1]the LORD, to dwell in
the land of Judah.

s 5 But Johanan the son of Kareah, and all
the captains of the forces, took [1]all the remnant
of Judah, that were returned from [1]all nations,
°whither they had been driven, to dwell in
the land of Judah;
6 *Even* °men, and women, and °children,
and the king's daughters, and every °person
that Nebuzar-adan the captain of the guard
had left with °Gedaliah the son of Ahikam the
son of Shaphan, and Jeremiah the prophet,
and Baruch the son of Neriah.

t 7 So they came into the land of Egypt: for
they obeyed not the voice of [1]the LORD: thus
came they *even* to °Tahpanhes.

F[3] S U 8 °Then came the word of [1]the LORD unto
Jeremiah in [7]Tahpanhes, saying,
9 "Take great stones in thine hand, and hide
them in the clay in °the brickkiln, which *is* at
the entry of Pharaoh's house in [7]Tahpanhes,
in the sight of the [2]men of Judah;
10 And say unto them, 'Thus saith °the
[1]LORD of hosts, the [1]God of Israel; °'Behold, I
will send and take °Nebuchadrezzar the king
of Babylon, My servant, and will set his throne
upon these stones that I have hid; and he
shall spread his royal pavilion over them.

42. 19-22 (*Q*, p. 1077). SUPPLICATION. ANSWERED. (*Introversion.*)

Q p | 19-. Prohibition.
q | -19. Admonition.
r | 20. Incrimination.
q | 21. Declaration.
p | 22. Threatening.

19 Go ye not into Egypt. This had ever been a standing command for Israel (Deut. 17. 16. Isa. 31. 1. Ezek. 17. 15). **admonished** = testified against.

20 ye dissembled, &c. None but Jehovah could know this. Cp. 41. 17. Ps. 139. 2. John 1. 48; 2. 24, 25. **hearts** = souls. Heb. *nephesh*. Ap. 13.

21 this day declared = declared this day. See note on Deut. 4. 26.

22 by the sword, &c. Ref. to Pent. (Lev. 26. 6, 25, 33, 36. Deut. 28. 22). Ap. 92.

43. 1-7 (*M*, p. 1076). INTENTION CARRIED OUT. (*Alternation.*)

M s | 1-3. Johanan. Contradiction. Words.
t | 4. The People. Disobedience.
s | 5, 6. Johanan. Disobedience. Action.
t | 7. The People. Disobedience.

1 all. Put by Fig. *Synecdoche* (of the Whole), Ap. 6, for the greater part, not all without exception.
the LORD. Heb. Jehovah. Ap. 4. II.
God. Heb. Elohim. Ap. 4. I.

2 men. Pl. of *'ěnōsh*. Ap. 14. III.

3 Baruch. A man of noble family (32. 12) suspected here. The reason may be found in 45. 1-5.

5 whither, &c. Cp. 40. 12.

6 men. Heb. pl. of *geber*. Ap. 14. IV.
children = young children.
person = soul. Heb. *nephesh*. Ap. 13.
Gedaliah. See note on 41. 1.

7 Tahpanhes. An Egyptian fortress on the eastern or Syrian frontier of Lower Egypt (cp. 2. 16), where the Pharaoh had his palace. See *v.* 9. Now *Tell Defenneh*; where Petrie discovered (in 1886) a ruin called *Kasr el Bint Yehudi* = the palace of the daughter of Judah, assigned doubtless to the daughters of king Zedekiah. See *v.* 6, above; and 41. 10. See Ap. 87.

43. 8—44. 30 (F[3], p. 1075). UNDER JOHANAN IN EGYPT. (*Introversion and Alternations.*)

F[3] S U | 43. 8-10. Sign. Great stones.
V | 43. 11-13. Threatening.
T W | 44. 1-14-. Idolatry. Declaration.
X | 44. -14. Escape of remnant.
T *W* | 44. 15-27. Idolatry. Discussion.
X | 44. 28. Escape of remnant.
S *U* | 44. 29. Sign. Punishment.
V | 44. 30. Threatening.

The THIRTY-EIGHTH Prophecy of Jeremiah (p. 1015).

8 Then = And. The Structure shows that a new member commences here.

9 the brickkiln = the brick pavement before the royal palace. Laid bare in 1886 by Flinders Petrie. See note on 2 Sam. 12. 31. There could be no "brickkiln" close to the entrance of the palace. But such a platform is seen to-day outside all great, and most small, houses in Egypt. It is called *mastaba*, and is kept clean, and swept. Often made of beaten clay, edged with bricks. For this particular brickwork pavement, see Ap. 87. See note on *v.* 7.

10 the LORD of hosts, the God of Israel. See note on 7. 3. The longer title is used to show the solemnity of the utterance.
Behold. Fig. *Asterismos*. Ap. 6.
Nebuchadrezzar . . . will set, &c. This was fulfilled to the letter. Josephus records it (*Ant.* x. 9, 10), but Egyptian history is naturally silent. It took place five years after his destruction of Jerusalem.

V u (p. 1079) 477 11 And when he cometh, he shall smite the land of Egypt, *and deliver* °such *as are* for death to death; and such *as are* for captivity to captivity; and such *as are* for the sword to the sword.

v 12 And I will kindle a fire in the houses of the gods of Egypt; and he shall burn them, and carry them away captives:

u and he shall array himself with the land of Egypt, °as a shepherd putteth on his garment; and he shall go forth from thence in peace.

v 13 He shall break also the °images of °Beth-shemesh, °that *is* in the land of Egypt; and the houses of the gods of the Egyptians shall he burn with fire.' ' '

T W Y[1] 477 **44** The word that came to Jeremiah concerning all the Jews °which dwell in the land of Egypt, which dwell at °Migdol, and at °Tahpanhes, and at °Noph, and in the country of °Pathros, saying,

2 " Thus saith °the LORD of hosts, the °God of Israel; 'Ye have seen all the °evil that I have brought upon Jerusalem, and upon all the cities of Judah; and, behold, this day they *are* a desolation, and no man dwelleth therein,

Z w 3 Because of their °wickedness which they have committed to provoke Me to anger, in that they went to burn incense, *and* to °serve other gods, whom they knew not, *neither* they, ye, nor your fathers.

x 4 Howbeit I sent unto you all My servants the prophets, °rising early and sending *them*, saying, 'Oh, do not this abominable thing that I hate.'

y 5 But they hearkened not, nor inclined their ear to turn from their [3] wickedness, to burn no incense unto other gods.

Y[2] 6 Wherefore My fury and Mine anger was poured forth, and was kindled in the cities of Judah and in the streets of Jerusalem; and they are wasted *and* desolate, as at this day.'

7 Therefore now thus saith °the [2] LORD, the °God of hosts, the [2] God of Israel;

Z w 'Wherefore commit ye *this* great [2] evil °against your °souls, to cut off from you °man and woman, °child and suckling, °out of Judah, to leave you none to remain;

8 In that ye provoke Me unto wrath with the °works of your hands, burning incense unto other gods in the land of Egypt, whither ye be °gone to °dwell, that ye might cut yourselves off, and that ye might be a curse and a reproach °among all the nations of the earth?

x 9 Have ye forgotten the °wickedness of your fathers, and the °wickedness of the kings of Judah, and the °wickedness of °their wives, and your own °wickedness, and the °wickedness of your wives, which they have committed in the land of Judah, and in the streets of Jerusalem?

y 10 They are not °humbled *even* unto this day, neither have they feared, nor walked in My law, nor in My statutes, that I set before you and before your fathers.'

43. 11-13 (V, p. 1078). THREATENING.
(*Alternation.*)

V | u | 11. Land of Egypt.
  v | 12-. Gods of Egypt.
  u | -12. Land of Egypt.
  v | 13. Gods of Egypt.

11 such as are, &c. See note on 2 Sam. 12. 31.
12 as=according as.
13 images=standing images, or obelisks. Probably *Asherim*. See Ap. 42.
Beth-shemesh. Heb.=House (or Temple) of the Sun; Greek, "Heliopolis"; Egyptian, "On"; about ten miles north-east of Cairo.
that is in the land of Egypt. This is to distinguish it from the Beth-shemesh of Josh. 15. 10. Judg. 1. 33. 1 Sam. 6. 9, 19. See note on Isa. 19. 19; and Ap. 81.

44. 1-14- (W, p. 1078). IDOLATRY. DECLARATION. (*Repeated and Extended Alternation.*)

W | Y[1] | 1, 2. Infliction. Past. Jehovah, &c.
  Z | w | 3. Provocation. Incense.
    x | 4. Remonstrance.
    y | 5. Disregard.
  Y[2] | 6, 7-. Infliction. Past. Jehovah, &c.
  Z | *w* | -7, 8. Provocation. Incense.
    x | 9. Remonstrance.
    y | 10. Disregard.
  Y[3] | 11-14. Infliction. Future.

The THIRTY-NINTH Prophecy of Jeremiah (p. 1015).

This was Jeremiah's THIRTY-NINTH and latest prophecy (p. 1015) relating to Israel. Chs. 46-51 relate to the Gentiles.

1 which dwell, &c. See longer note on p. 1096.
Migdol. See note on Ex. 14. 2.
Tahpanhes. See note on 43. 7.
Noph. A contraction of the Egyptian *Manufr*=the abode of the good. Heb. *Moph* in Hos. 9. 6; afterward=Memphis; now *Abu Sīr*. Cp. 2. 16; 46. 14, 19.
Pathros. A part of Upper Egypt, south of Memphis. Cp. Isa. 11. 11. Ezek. 29. 14; 30. 14.
2 the LORD of hosts, the God of Israel. See note on 7. 3.
the LORD. Heb. Jehovah. Ap. 4. II.
God. Heb. Elohim. Ap. 4. I.
evil=calamity. Heb. *rā'a'*. Ap. 44. viii.
3 wickedness. Heb. *rā'a'*. Ap. 44. viii.
serve other gods. Ref. to Pent. (Deut. 13. 6; 32. 17).
4 rising early, &c. See note on 7. 13.
7 the LORD, the God of hosts, the God of Israel. See note on 35. 17.
God. Some codices, with two early printed editions, Sept., Syr., and Vulg., omit "the God".
against your souls. Ref. to Pent. (Num. 16. 38).
souls. Heb. *nephesh*. Ap. 13.
man. Heb. *'ish*. Ap. 14. II. **child**=little one.
out of Judah=out of the midst of Judah.
8 works. Some codices, with five early printed editions (one, marg.), and Syr., read "work" (sing.).
gone=come. **dwell**=sojourn.
among. Some codices, with three early printed editions, Sept., and Vulg., read "to".
9 wickedness=wickednesses, or wicked ways. Heb. *rā'a'*. Ap. 44. viii. Note the Fig. *Repetitio* (Ap. 6), used for great emphasis. **their wives.** See *v*. 15.
10 humbled=contrite.
11 Behold. Fig. *Asterismos*. Ap. 6.
I will set My face, &c. Ref. to Pent. (Lev. 17. 10; 20. 3, 5, 6). Ap. 92.
evil. Heb. *rā'a'*. Ap. 44. viii.

11 Therefore thus saith [2] the LORD of hosts, the [2] God of Israel; °'Behold, °I will set My face against you for °evil, and to cut off all Judah. Y[3]

12 And I will take the remnant of Judah, that have set their faces to go into the land of

477 Egypt to sojourn there, and they shall all be consumed, *and* fall in the land of Egypt; they shall *even* be consumed ° by the sword *and* by the famine: they shall die, from the least even unto the greatest, by the sword and by the famine: and they shall be an execration, *and* an astonishment, and a curse, and a reproach.

13 For I will punish them that dwell in the land of Egypt, ° as I have punished Jerusalem, [12]by the sword, by the famine, and by the pestilence:

14 So that none of the remnant of Judah, which are gone into the land of Egypt to sojourn there, shall escape or remain, that they should return into the land of Judah, to the which they ° have a desire to return to dwell there:

X (p. 1078) for none shall return but such as shall escape.' "

T W a (p. 1080) 15 Then ° all the ° men which knew that [9]their wives had burned incense unto other gods, and all the women that stood by, a great ° multitude, even all the People that [8]dwelt in the land of Egypt, in [1]Pathros, answered Jeremiah, saying,

16 "*As for* the word that thou hast spoken unto us in the name of [2]the LORD, we will not hearken unto thee.

17 But we will certainly do ° whatsoever thing goeth forth out of our own mouth, to burn incense unto the queen of heaven, and to pour out drink offerings unto her, as we have done, we, and our fathers, our kings, and our princes, in the cities of Judah, and in the streets of Jerusalem:

b for *then* had we plenty of ° victuals, and were well, and saw no [2]evil.

18 But since we left off to burn incense to the queen of heaven, and to pour out drink offerings unto her, we have wanted all *things*, and have been consumed [12]by the sword and by the famine.

19 And when we burned incense to the queen of heaven, and poured out drink offerings unto her, did we make her cakes to worship her, and pour out drink offerings unto her, without our [15]men?"

a 20 Then Jeremiah said unto [15]all the People, to the ° men, and to the women, and to [15]all the People which had given him *that* answer, saying,

21 "The incense that ye burned in the cities of Judah, and in the streets of Jerusalem, ye, and your fathers, your kings, and your princes, and the People of the land, did not [2]the LORD remember ° them, and came ° it *not* ° into His mind?

22 So that [2]the LORD could no longer ° bear, because of the [2]evil of your doings, *and* because of the abominations which ye have committed; therefore is your land a desolation, and an astonishment, and a curse, without an inhabitant, as at this day.

23 Because ye have burned incense, and because ye have ° sinned against [2]the LORD, and have not obeyed the voice of [2]the LORD, nor walked in His law, nor in His statutes, nor in His testimonies; therefore this [2]evil is happened unto you, as at this day."

24 Moreover Jeremiah said unto all the People, and to all the women, "Hear the word of [2]the LORD, all Judah that *are* in the land of Egypt:

25 Thus saith [2]the LORD of hosts, the [2]God of Israel, saying; 'Ye and your wives have both spoken with your mouths, and fulfilled with your hand, saying, 'We will surely perform our vows that we have vowed, [3]to burn incense to the queen of heaven, and to pour out drink offerings unto her:' ye will surely accomplish your vows, and surely perform your vows.'

26 Therefore hear ye the word of [2]the LORD, *b*
[15]all Judah that dwell in the land of Egypt; [11]Behold, ° I have sworn by My great name, ° saith [2]the LORD, that My name shall no more be named in the mouth of any [7]man of Judah in all the land of Egypt, saying, ° 'The Lord GOD liveth.'

27 [11]Behold, ° I will watch over them for [2]evil, and not for good: and all the [7]men of Judah that *are* in the land of Egypt shall be consumed [12]by the sword and by the famine, until there be an end of them.

28 Yet a small number that escape the sword *X*
° shall return out of the land of Egypt into the *(p. 1078)*
land of Judah, and all the remnant of Judah, that are gone into the land of Egypt to sojourn there, shall know whose words shall stand, Mine, or theirs.

29 And this *shall be* a sign unto you, [26]saith *S U*
[2]the LORD, that I will punish you in this place, that ye may know that My words shall surely stand against you for [2]evil:'

30 Thus saith [2]the LORD; [11]'Behold, I will *V*
give Pharaoh-hophra king of Egypt into the

---

12 **by the sword, &c.** Ref. to Pent. (Lev. 26. 6, 25, 33, 36. Deut. 28. 22). Ap. 92. Cp. 42. 22.

13 **as** = according as.

14 **have a desire** = lift up their soul. Heb. *nephesh.* Ap. 13.

44. 15-27 (*W*, p. 1078). IDOLATRY. DISCUSSION. (*Alternation.*)

W | a | 15-17-. Answer of the People.
| b | -17-19. Reason.
| *a* | 20-25. Answer. Jeremiah's reply.
| *b* | 26, 27. Reason.

15 **all.** Put by Fig. *Synecdoche* (of the Whole), Ap. 6, for the specified part.

men. Heb. pl. of *'ĕnōsh.* Ap. 14. III: i.e. the husbands.

multitude = assembly.

17 **whatsoever thing goeth forth, &c.** Ref. to Pent. (Num. 30. 12. Deut. 23. 23). Ap. 92.

victuals. Heb. "bread". Put by Fig. *Synecdoche* (of the Part), Ap. 6, for all kinds of food.

20 **men.** Heb. pl. of *geber.* Ap. 14. IV.

21 **them**: i.e. your fathers.

it: i.e. the incense.

into His mind = upon His heart. Fig. *Anthropopatheia.* Ap. 6.

22 **bear** = forbear.

23 **sinned.** Heb. *chāṭa'.* Ap. 44. i.

26 **I have sworn, &c.** Ref. to Pent. (Gen. 22. 16).

saith the LORD = [is] Jehovah's oracle.

The Lord GOD. Heb. Adonai Jehovah. Ap. 4. VIII (2) and II.

28 **shall return, &c.** So that the king's daughters either returned to Judah or remained in Egypt.

477 hand of his enemies, and into the hand of
°them that seek his °life; °as I gave Zedekiah
king of Judah into the hand of Nebuchadrezzar
king of Babylon, his enemy, and that sought
his °life.' "

Q c[1] **45** The word that Jeremiah the prophet
(p. 1081) spake unto °Baruch the son of Neriah,
496 when he had °written these words in a book
at the mouth of Jeremiah, in °the fourth year
of Jehoiakim the son of Josiah king of Judah,
saying,
2 "Thus saith °the LORD, the °God of Israel,
unto thee, O [1] Baruch;
d[1] 3 'Thou didst say, 'Woe is me now! for [2] the
LORD hath added grief to my sorrow; I fainted
in my sighing, and I find no rest.' '
c[2] 4 Thus shalt thou say unto him, [2] 'The LORD
saith thus; °'Behold, *that* which I have °built
will I °break down, and that which I have
°planted I will °pluck up, even this whole land.
d[2] 5 °And seekest thou great things for thyself?
seek *them* not:
c[3] for, behold, I will bring °evil upon all flesh,
°saith [2] the LORD: but thy °life will I give unto
thee °for a prey in all places whither thou
goest.' ' "

C A E **46** The word of °the LORD °which came
to Jeremiah the prophet °against °the
°Gentiles;
2 [1] Against °Egypt, against the army of
Pharaoh-necho king of Egypt, which was by
the river Euphrates in °Carchemish, which
Nebuchadrezzar king of Babylon smote in °the
496 fourth year of Jehoiakim the son of Josiah
king of Judah.
F e 3 °"Order ye the buckler and shield, and draw
near to battle.
4 Harness the horses; and get up, ye horsemen, and stand forth with *your* helmets; fur-
bish the spears, *and* put on the °brigandines.
f 5 Wherefore have I seen them dismayed *and*
turned away back? and their mighty ones are
°beaten down, and are °fled apace, and look
not back: *for* °fear *was* round about, °saith
[1] the LORD.

them. Not Nebuchadnezzar; but, as the monuments now tell us, the soldiers who revolted against Hophra. He was delivered into their hands, as Zedekiah had already been delivered into the hands of Nebuchadnezzar. **life** = soul. Heb. *nephesh*. Ap. 13.
as = according as.

45. 1-5 (*Q*, p. 1071). BARUCH.
(*Repeated Alternation.*)

Q | c[1] | 1, 2. Word of Jehovah to Baruch.
d[1] | 3. What Baruch had said.
c[2] | 4. Word of Jehovah to Baruch.
d[2] | 5-. What Baruch sought.
c[3] | -5. Word of Jehovah to Baruch.

The FORTIETH Prophecy of Jeremiah (p. 1015).

1 Baruch. He was the grandson of Maaseiah, governor of Jerusalem in Josiah's reign (2 Chron. 34. 8), and brother of Seraiah, chief chamberlain (51. 59).
written these words, &c. See ch. 36.
the fourth year, &c. See Ap. 86.
2 the LORD. Heb. Jehovah. Ap. 4. II.
the LORD, the God of Israel. See note on 11. 3.
God. Heb. Elohim. Ap. 4. I.
4 Behold. Fig. *Asterismos*. Ap. 6.
built . . . break down . . . planted . . . pluck up. See note on 1. 10.
5 And seekest, &c. = Wouldst thou seek to secure great things for thyself?
evil. Heb. *rā'a'*. Ap. 44. viii.
saith the LORD = [is] Jehovah's oracle.
life = soul. Heb. *nephesh*. Ap. 13.
for a prey. Cp. 39. 18.

The FORTY-FIRST Prophecy of Jeremiah (p. 1015).

46. 1—51. 64- (*C*, p. 1015). PROPHECIES ADDRESSED TO GENTILES. (*Introversion.*)

C | A | 46. 1-28. Egypt. South.
B | 47. 1-7. Philistines. West.
C | 48. 1—49. 6. Moab and Ammon. East and South.
D | 49. 7-22. Edom. South.
D | 49. 23-27. Damascus. North.
C | 49. 28-33. Kedar and Hazor. North.
B | 49. 34-39. Elam. East.
A | 50. 1—51. 64-. Babylon. East.

46. 1-28 (A, above). EGYPT. (*Introversion.*)

A | E | 1, 2. Egypt. Proclamation.
F | 3-12. Its overthrow.
F | 13-26. Means employed.
E | 27, 28. Israel. Encouragement.

1 the LORD. Heb. Jehovah. Ap. 4. II.
which came. For the most part in the fourth year of Jehoiakim (see Ap. 86), and may have been included in the roll of ch. 36. This section may be compared with Isaiah's "burdens" and "woes" (cp. p. 930), and Ezekiel (25—32), and Amos (1. 1, 2).

against = concerning. Cp. 49. 1. **the.** Some codices, with six early printed editions (one Rabbinic), read "all the". **Gentiles** = nations. **2 Egypt.** Comes first because most important in connection with Judah, as well as coming second to Babylon at that time (with which it corresponds in position in the Structure above). Judah was indeed, then subject to Egypt. The policy of Judah's rulers was to lean on Egypt instead of heeding Jeremiah. These prophecies are designed to assure the nation that it could not rely on Gentile powers to thwart God's word by Jeremiah. **Carchemish.** Cp. 2 Chron. 35. 20-24. The *Gargamish* of the Inscriptions, now known as *Jerablūs*, or *Membij*, &c. **the fourth year of Jehoiakim.** A critical era in the history of Egypt, Babylon, Judah, and the world. See Ap. 86. Four years before, Pharaoh-necho, on his way to Carchemish, had defeated and slain Josiah at Megiddo, and afterward taken his son Shallum as a vassal to Egypt, and set up Jehoiakim (2 Kings 23. 29-35).

46. 3-12 (F, above). EGYPT. ITS OVERTHROW.
(*Extended Alternation.*)

F | e | 3, 4. Call to battle.
f | 5, 6. Dismay of Egypt.
g | 7, 8. Boast of Egypt.
e | 9. Call to battle.
f | 10. Vengeance of Jehovah.
g | 11, 12. Fall of Egypt.

3 Order ye = Prepare ye, or Put in order. **4 brigandines** = coats of mail. **5 beaten down** = crushed. **fled apace.** Fig. *Polyptōton* (Ap. 6). Heb. fled a flight. Well rendered "fled apace". **fear was round about.** Heb. *māgōr missābīb* = terror round about. See note on 6. 25. **saith, &c.** See note on 45. 5.

496 6 Let not the swift flee away, nor the °mighty man escape; they shall stumble, and fall toward the north by the river Euphrates.

g (p. 1081) 7 Who *is* this *that* cometh up °as a flood, whose waters are moved as the rivers?

8 [2] Egypt riseth up like a flood, and *his* waters are moved like the rivers; and he saith, °'I will go up, *and* will cover the earth; I will destroy the city and the inhabitants thereof.'

e 9 °Come up, ye horses; and rage, ye chariots; and let the [6] mighty men come forth; °the Ethiopians and °the Libyans, that handle the shield; and °the Lydians, that handle *and* bend the bow.

f 10 For this *is* the day of °the Lord GOD of hosts, °a day of vengeance, that He may avenge Him of His adversaries: and the sword shall devour, and it shall be satiate and °made drunk with their blood: for °the Lord GOD of hosts °hath a sacrifice in the north country by the river Euphrates.

g 11 °Go up into °Gilead, and °take balm, O virgin, the daughter of Egypt: in vain shalt thou use many medicines; °*for* thou shalt not be cured.

12 The nations have heard of thy shame, and thy cry hath filled the °land: for the [6] mighty man hath stumbled against the mighty, *and* they are fallen both together."

F G (p. 1082) 13 The word that [1] the LORD spake to Jeremiah the prophet, how Nebuchadrezzar king of Babylon should come *and* smite the land of [2] Egypt.

14 "Declare ye in Egypt, and publish in °Migdol, and publish in °Noph and in °Tahpanhes: say ye, 'Stand fast, and prepare thee; for the sword shall devour round about thee.'

H 15 Why are thy °valiant *men* °swept away? °they stood not, because [1] the LORD °did drive °them.

16 He made many to °fall, yea, °one fell upon another: and they said, 'Arise, and let us go again to our own people, and to the land of our nativity, from the oppressing sword.'

17 They did cry there, 'Pharaoh king of Egypt *is but* a °noise; he hath °passed the time appointed.'

G 18 *As* I live, °saith the King, Whose name *is* °the [1] LORD of hosts, "Surely as Tabor *is* among the mountains, and as Carmel by the sea, *so* shall he come.

19 O thou daughter °dwelling in [2] Egypt, °furnish thyself to go into captivity: for [14] Noph shall be waste and desolate without an inhabitant.

H h 20 [2] Egypt *is like* a very fair °heifer, *but* °destruction cometh; it °cometh out of °the north.

i 21 Also her hired men *are* in the midst of her like fatted bullocks; for they also are turned back, *and* are fled away together: °they did not stand, because the day of their calamity was come upon them, *and* the time of their visitation.

k 22 The voice thereof shall go like a serpent; for they shall march with an army, and come against her with axes, as hewers of wood.

23 They shall cut down her forest, [5] saith [1] the LORD, though it cannot be °searched; because they are more than the °grasshoppers, and *are* innumerable.

---

6 mighty man. Heb. *geber*. Ap. 14. iv.

7 as a flood = as the river: i.e. the Nile, in flood.

8 I will go up. Egypt at this time was so strong that Jeremiah's prophecy seemed most unlikely to come to pass.

9 Come up, &c. Fig. *Eironeia*. Ap. 6. Cp. *v.* 11.

the Ethiopians = Cush. Mercenaries, forming the chief part of the Egyptian forces.

the Libyans. Heb. Phut. Cp. Ezek. 27. 10; 30. 5; and Acts 2. 10.

the Lydians. Not those in Western Asia (Gen. 10. 22). All belonging to Africa.

10 the Lord GOD of hosts. Heb. Adonai Jehovah Zbaōth. Ap. 4. VIII (2) and II. See note on 2. 19.

a day of vengeance. On the Egyptians.

made drunk = bathed. Ref. to Pent. (Deut. 32. 42).

hath a sacrifice. Cp. Isa. 34. 6. Ezek. 39. 17.

11 Go up, &c. Fig. *Eironeia* (Ap. 6), as shown by the rest of the verse.

Gilead. Cp. 8. 22. **take** = fetch.

for thou shalt not be cured = healing there is none for thee. Cp. 8. 22; 51. 8. **12 land** = earth.

46. 13-26 (*F*, p. 1081). MEANS EMPLOYED.
(*Alternation.*)

F | G | 13, 14. Proclamation. Prepare.
  H | 15-17. Fall.
  G | 18, 19. Proclamation. Prepare.
  H | 20-26. Fall.

The FORTY-SECOND Prophecy of Jeremiah (p. 1015).

14 Migdol . . . Noph . . . Tahpanhes. See note on 44. 1.

15 valiant men. Some codices, with two early printed editions, Sept., and Vulg., read "one" (sing.), perhaps referring to *Apis* their sacred bull.

swept away = laid prostrate (sing.). Cp. 1 Sam. 5. 3.

they stood not = he made no stand.

did drive them = had driven him back.

them = him. **16 fall** = be stumbling.

one . . . upon another. Ref. to Pent. (Lev. 26. 37).

17 noise = sound.

passed = let pass over. Cp. 2 Sam. 20. 5.

18 saith the King = [is] the King's oracle. Cp. 48. 15.

the LORD of hosts. See note on 6. 6.

19 dwelling in = inhabitress of. Probably = the Jews, as in Ezek. 12. 2. Jer. 48. 18.

furnish thyself to go into captivity = baggage for captivity prepare thee.

46. 20-26 (*H*, above). FALL OF EGYPT.
(*Extended Alternation.*)

H | h | 20. The north.
  i | 21. Mercenaries.
  k | 22, 23. Enemies.
  h | 24. The North.
  i | 25. Multitudes.
  k | 26. Enemies.

20 heifer. Probably an allusion to *Apis*, the sacred bull.

destruction = piercing. Heb. *kerez*. Occurs only here. R.V. margin suggests gadfly. If it be so, the attack is on the heifer.

cometh. Some codices, with two early printed editions, Aram., Sept., Syr., and Vulg., read "attacketh her".

the north. Though Babylon was on the east, the entry through Palestine was from the north, as Abraham entered it.

21 they did not stand = they made no stand. Some codices, with two early printed editions, Syr., and Vulg., read, "and they have made", &c.

23 searched = reconnoitred.

grasshoppers = locusts.

h 24 The daughter of [2] Egypt shall be con-
(p. 1082) founded; she shall be delivered into the hand
496 of the people of the north."

i 25 ° The [1] LORD of hosts, the ° God of Israel,
saith; ° " Behold, I will punish the ° multitude
of No, and Pharaoh, and [2] Egypt, with their
gods, and their kings; even Pharaoh, and *all*
them that ° trust in him:

k 26 And I will deliver them into the hand of
those that seek their ° lives, and into the hand
of Nebuchadrezzar king of Babylon, and into
the hand of his servants: and afterward it
shall be inhabited, as in the days of old, [5] saith
[1] the LORD.

E l 27 But fear not thou, O My servant ° Jacob,
(p. 1083) and be not dismayed, O Israel:

m for, [25] behold, I will save thee from afar off,
and thy seed from the land of their captivity;
and ° Jacob shall return, and be in rest and at
ease, and none shall make *him* afraid.

l 28 ° Fear thou not, O [27] Jacob My servant,
[5] saith [1] the LORD:

m for I *am* with thee; for I will make ° a full end
of all the nations whither I have driven thee:
but I will not make ° a full end of thee, but correct thee in measure; yet will I ° not leave
thee wholly unpunished."

B J **47** The word of ° the LORD that came to
478 Jeremiah the prophet ° against the
Philistines, ° before that ° Pharaoh smote ° Gaza.

K[1] n[1] 2 Thus saith [1] the LORD; ° " Behold, ° waters
rise up out of ° the north, and shall be an overflowing flood, and shall overflow the land, and
all that is therein; the city, and them that
dwell therein:

o[1] then the ° men shall cry, and all the inhabitants of the land shall howl.

K[2] n[2] 3 At the noise of the stamping of the hoofs of
his ° strong *horses*, at the ° rushing of his chariots, *and at* the rumbling of his wheels,

o[2] the fathers shall not look back to *their* ° children for feebleness of hands;

K[3] n[3] 4 Because of ° the day that cometh to spoil all
the Philistines, *and* to cut off from ° Tyrus
and Zidon every helper that remaineth: for
[1] the LORD will spoil the Philistines, the remnant of ° the country of ° Caphtor.

o[3] 5 ° Baldness is come upon [1] Gaza;

J ° Ashkelon is cut off *with* the remnant of ° their
valley: how long wilt thou cut thyself?"
6 O thou ° sword of [1] the LORD, how long *will
it be* ere thou be quiet? put up thyself into
thy scabbard, rest, and be still.
7 ° How can it be quiet, seeing [1] the LORD hath
given it a charge against Ashkelon, and against
the sea shore? there hath He appointed it.

C L[1] M **48** ° Against ° Moab ° thus saith ° the LORD
of hosts, the God of Israel;

25 The LORD of hosts, the God of Israel. See note on 7. 3.

God. Heb. Elohim. Ap. 4. I.

Behold. Fig. *Asterismos* (Ap. 6), to add to the emphasis of the Divine title employed.

multitude of No: or Amōn of Thebes (an Egyptian idol). **trust**=confide. Heb. *bāṭaḥ*. Ap. 69. I.

26 lives=souls. Heb. *nephesh*. Ap. 13.

46. 27, 28 (*E*, p. 1081). ISRAEL. ENCOURAGEMENT. (*Alternation*.)

E | l | 27-. Encouragement.
  m | -27. Reason.
  l | 28-. Encouragement.
  m | -28. Reason.

27 Jacob. Referring to the natural seed; i.e. the whole nation. See notes on Gen. 32. 28; 43. 6; 45. 26, 28.

28 Fear thou not. Cp. 30. 10, 11. Ref. to Pent. (Gen. 26. 24. Cp. Deut. 31. 8). Ap. 92.

a full end. Cp. 10. 24; 30. 11.

not leave thee wholly unpunished=not hold thee guiltless. Ref. to Pent. (Ex. 20. 7; 34. 7. Num. 14. 18).

47. 1-7 (B, p. 1081). THE PHILISTINES. (*Introversion and Repeated Alternation*.)

B | J | 1. The word of the LORD against the Philistines.
  K[1] | n[1] | 2-. Invasion.
    o[1] | -2. Effect. Mourning.
  K[2] | n[2] | 3-. Invasion.
    o[2] | -3. Effect. Feebleness.
  K[3] | n[3] | 4. Invasion.
    o[3] | 5-. Effect. Mourning.
  J | -5-7. The sword of the LORD against the Philistines.

The FORTY-THIRD Prophecy of Jeremiah (p. 1015).

1 the LORD. Heb. Jehovah. Ap. 4. II.

against=concerning. Cp. 48. 1; 49. 1, 7, 23.

before. To show that this prophecy was not the anticipation of human foresight.

Pharaoh. Pharaoh-necho, after his victory over Josiah (2 Kings 23. 29. 2 Chron. 35. 20).

Gaza. Heb. *'azzāh* (with *'eth*). Now *Ghŭzzeh*. Still standing at the time of this prophecy (the fourth year of Jehoiakim). Not Carchemish, for cp. 2 Kings 24. 7.

2 Behold. Fig. *Asterismos*. Ap. 6.

waters. The symbol of the Chaldean armies.

the north. Cp. 46. 20.

men. Heb. *'ādām*. Ap. 14. I.

3 strong horses. Cp. 8. 16.

rushing=rattling. **children**=sons.

4 the day that cometh. Cp. 46. 10.

Tyrus and Zidon. The same origin as the Philistines. **the country**=the sea coast.

Caphtor. Not identified. Perhaps Crete, whence the Philistines emigrated (Gen. 10. 14. Deut. 2. 23. Amos 9. 7).

5 Baldness=the sign of mourning. Cp. 16. 6.

Ashkelon. Now *'Askalān*.

their valley. Sept. reads "Anakim" instead of *'imḳām*.

6 sword of the LORD. Ref. to Pent. (Deut. 32. 41).

7 How . . . ? Fig. *Erotēsis*. Ap. 6.

48. 1—49. 6 (C, p. 1081). MOAB AND AMMON. (*Division*.)

C | L[1] | 48. 1-47. Moab. } The sons of Lot.
  L[2] | 49. 1-6. Ammon. }

48. 1-47 (L[1], above). MOAB. (*Introversion*.)

L[1] | M | 1-. Introduction.
  N | -1-46. The present state.
  N | 47-. The latter state.
  M | -47. Conclusion.

The FORTY-FOURTH Prophecy of Jeremiah (p 1015, note †).

1 Against=concerning. **Moab.** Always hostile to Israel. Cp. Judg. 3. 12, 28. 1 Sam. 14. 47. 2 Sam. 8. 2. 2 Kings 1. 1; 3. 4-27; 13. 20. In the reign of Jehoiakim they joined with the Chaldeans. **thus saith.** As in Num. 21. 28, 29; 24. 17 (cp. *vv.* 45, 46), and Amos 2. 2 (cp. *vv.* 24, 41, p. 1085) and Zeph. 2. 8, 9 (cp. *vv.* 26, 42, p. 1085). **the LORD of hosts, the God of Israel.** See note on 7. 3. **the LORD.** Heb. Jehovah. Ap. 4. II.

N O p (p. 1084) "Woe unto °Nebo! for it is spoiled: °Kiria-
thaim is confounded *and* taken: °Misgab is
confounded and dismayed.
2 *There shall be* no more praise of [1] Moab:
in °Heshbon they have °devised °evil against
it; come, and let us cut it off from *being* a nation. Also thou shalt °be cut down, O °Mad-
men; the sword shall pursue thee.
3 A voice of crying *shall be* from °Horonaim,
spoiling and great destruction.
4 [1] Moab is destroyed; her little ones have
caused a cry to be heard.
5 For in the going up of °Luhith continual
weeping shall go up; for in the going down of
[3] Horonaim the enemies have heard a cry of
destruction.
q 6 Flee, save your °lives, and be like °the
heath in the wilderness.
7 For because thou hast trusted in thy works
and in thy treasures, °thou shalt also be taken:
and °Chemosh shall go forth into captivity
with his priests and his princes together.
8 And the spoiler shall come upon every city,
and no city shall escape: the valley also shall
perish, and the plain shall be destroyed, as
[1] the LORD hath spoken.
9 Give wings unto Moab, that it may flee and
get away: for the cities thereof shall be desolate, without any to dwell therein.
10 Cursed *be* he that doeth the work of [1] the
LORD °deceitfully, and cursed *be* he that keepeth back his sword from blood.
P Q 11 Moab °hath been at ease from his youth,
and he hath settled on his lees, and hath not
been emptied from vessel to vessel, neither
hath he gone into captivity: therefore his
taste °remained in him, and his scent is not
changed.
R T 12 Therefore, °behold, the days come, °saith
[1] the LORD, that I will send unto him °wan-
derers, that shall cause him to wander, and
shall empty his vessels, and break their bottles.
13 And [1] Moab shall be ashamed of [7] Chemosh,
°as °the house of Israel was ashamed of °Beth-
el their confidence.
U r 14 How say ye, '*We are* mighty and strong
°men for the war?'
s 15 [1] Moab is spoiled, and °gone up *out of* her
cities, and his chosen young men are gone
down to the slaughter, °saith the King, Whose
name *is* °the [1] LORD of hosts.
16 "The calamity of [1] Moab *is* near to come,
and his affliction °hasteth fast.
t 17 All ye that are about him, bemoan him;
and all ye that know his name, say, 'How is
the strong staff broken, *and* the beautiful rod!'
18 Thou daughter that dost inhabit °Dibon,
come down from *thy* glory, and sit in thirst;
for the spoiler of [1] Moab shall come upon thee,
and he shall destroy thy strong holds.
r 19 O °inhabitant of °Aroer, stand by the
way, and espy; ask him that fleeth, and her
that escapeth, *and* say, 'What is done?'
s 20 [1] Moab is confounded; for it is broken
down:
t howl and cry; tell ye it in °Arnon, that [1] Moab
is spoiled,

48. -1-46 (N, p. 1083). MOAB'S (THEN) PRESENT STATE. (*Introversion and Alternation.*)

N | O | p | -1-5. Threatening.
| | q | 6-10. Flight.
| P | 11-28. Condition.
| *P* | 29-39. Character.
| *O* | *p* | 40-43. Threatening.
| | *q* | 44-46. Flight.

Nebo. Not the mountain, but formerly a Reubenite possession (Num. 32. 37, 38), now belonging to Moab.

Kiriathaim. Now probably *el Kŭreiyăt*, between Medeba and Dibon.

Misgab. Probably = the high fort.

2 Heshbon. Now *Hesbān*. The capital of Sihon king of the Amorites. Rebuilt by Reubenites (Num. 32. 37. Cp. Josh. 13. 17).

devised = counselled. Note Fig. *Paronomasia* (Ap. 6). *Heshbōn, hāshbū*.

evil. Heb. *rā'a'*. Ap. 44. viii.

be cut down = be reduced to silence.

Madmen. Now *Umm Deineh*, a town in Moab twelve miles N.E. of Dibon.

3 Horonaim. Probably near Zoar. Cp. Isa. 15. 5.

5 Luhith. Now *Tal'at el Heith*, one mile west of Mount Nebo. **6 lives** = soul. Heb. *nephesh*. Ap. 13.

the heath = naked trees. Cp. 17. 6.

7 thou shalt also = thou too shalt.

Chemosh shall go forth into captivity. Ref. to Pent. (Num. 21. 29). Ap. 92. See Ap. 54, and cp. Judg. 11. 24. 1 Kings 11. 7. 2 Kings 23. 13.

10 deceitfully = negligently: i.e. this work of judgment.

48. 11-28 (P, above), **29-39** (*P*, above). MOAB'S CONDITION AND CHARACTER. (*Extended Alternation and Introversion.*)

P | Q | 11. At ease.
| R | T | 12, 13. Places.
| | U | 14-25. Judgments.
| | S | 26-28. Consequences.
P | *Q* | 29. In pride.
| *R* | *U* | 30, 31. Judgments.
| | *T* | 32-36. Places.
| | *S* | 37-39. Consequences.

11 hath been at ease. Since Moab had driven out the Emims (Deut. 2. 10). **remained** = stood.

12 behold. Fig. *Asterismos*. Ap. 6.

saith the LORD = [is] Jehovah's oracle.

wanderers, that shall cause him to wander = tilters that shall tilt him. Keeping up the symbol of a wine-jar (*v.* 11). **13 as** = according as.

the house of Israel. See note on 2. 4. The last occurrence in Jeremiah.

Beth-el. Ref. to the calves of Jeroboam (1 Kings 12. 29. Hos. 10. 5).

48. 14-25 (U, above). JUDGMENTS. (*Extended Alternation.*)

U | r | 14. Question.
| s | 15, 16. Answer.
| t | 17, 18. Lamentation.
| *r* | 19. Question.
| *s* | 20-. Answer.
| *t* | -20-25. Lamentation.

14 men. Heb. pl. of *'ĕnōsh*. Ap. 14. III.

15 gone up . . . her cities = her cities have gone up, or ascended in burning.

saith the King = [is] the King's oracle. Cp. 46. 18.

the LORD of hosts. See note on 6. 6.

16 hasteth fast. Ref. to Pent. (Deut. 32. 35). Ap. 92.

18 Dibon. Now *Dhībān*. Ruins north of the river Arnon. Cp. *v.* 22.

19 inhabitant = inhabitress. Ref. to "daughter" (*v.* 18).

Aroer. Now *'Ar'air*, on the north bank of *Wādy Mōjib* (Arnon).

20 Arnon. Now *Wādy Mōjib*, on the east side of the Dead Sea.

21 And judgment is come upon the plain country; upon °Holon, and upon °Jahazah, and upon °Mephaath,

22 And upon °Dibon, and upon [1]Nebo, and upon °Beth-diblathaim,

23 And upon [1]Kiriathaim, and upon °Beth-gamul, and upon °Beth-meon,

24 And upon °Kerioth, and upon °Bozrah, and upon all the cities of the land of [1]Moab, far or near.

25 The horn of [1]Moab is cut off, and his arm is broken, [12]saith [1]the LORD.

S (p. 1084) 26 Make ye him drunken: for he magnified *himself* against [1]the LORD: Moab also shall °wallow in his vomit, and he also shall be in derision.

27 For was not Israel a derision unto thee? was he found among thieves? for °since thou spakest of him, thou °skippedst for joy.

28 O ye that dwell in [1]Moab, leave the cities, and dwell in the rock, and be like the dove *that* maketh her nest in the sides of the hole's mouth.

PQ 29 We have heard the °pride of [1]Moab, (he is exceeding proud) his loftiness, and his arrogancy, and his pride, and the haughtiness of his heart.

RU 30 I know his wrath, [12]saith [1]the LORD; but *it shall* not *be* so; his lies shall not so effect *it*.

31 Therefore will I howl for [1]Moab, and I will cry out for all [1]Moab; °*mine heart* shall mourn for the [14]men of °Kir-heres.

T 32 O vine of °Sibmah, I will weep for thee with the weeping of °Jazer: thy °plants are gone °over the sea, they reach *even* to the sea of °Jazer: the spoiler is fallen upon thy summer fruits and upon thy vintage.

33 And joy and gladness is taken from the plentiful field, and from the land of [1]Moab; and I have caused °wine to fail from the winepresses: none shall tread with shouting; *their* shouting *shall be* no shouting.

34 °From the cry of [2]Heshbon *even* unto °Elealeh, *and even* unto °Jahaz, have they uttered their voice, from °Zoar *even* unto [3]Horonaim, °*as* an heifer of three years old: for the waters also of °Nimrim shall be desolate.

35 Moreover I will cause to cease in Moab, [12]saith [1]the LORD, him that offereth in the °high places, and him that burneth incense to his gods.

36 Therefore Mine heart shall sound for Moab °like pipes, and Mine heart shall sound °like pipes for the [14]men of [31]Kir-heres: because the riches *that* he hath gotten °are perished.

S 37 For °every head *shall be* °bald, and every beard clipped: upon all the hands *shall be* cuttings, and °upon the loins sackcloth.

38 *There shall be* lamentation generally upon all °the housetops of [1]Moab, and in the °streets thereof: for I have broken [1]Moab like a vessel wherein *is* no pleasure, [12]saith [1]the LORD.

39 They shall howl, *saying*, 'How is it broken down! how hath [1]Moab turned the back with shame!' so shall [1]Moab be a derision and a dismaying to all them about him.

21 Holon. Now probably *'Aleiyan* (not Holon or Hilen in Judah).

Jahazah . . . Mephaath. Not yet identified. Cp. Isa. 15. 4. **22 Dibon.** See *v.* 18.

Beth-diblathaim. Also Almon-diblathaim (Num. 33. 46, 47). Now probably *Khan Deleyāt* = house of the two disks, mentioned on the Moabite stone. Ap. 54.

23 Beth-gamul. Now *Khan Jemail*, east of Dibon.

Beth-meon. Now *Tell M'aīn.* Cp. Josh. 13. 17.

24 Kerioth. Probably the same as Kiriathaim (*v.* 1).

Bozrah. Now *el Buseirah*, in Edom, south-east of the Dead Sea.

26 wallow in = stagger or splash into.

27 since = as often as, or whenever.

skippedst for joy = didst shake thyself in excitement, or wag thy head.

29 pride = arrogance. Note the Fig. *Synonymia* (Ap. 6): six expressions, for the sake of emphasis.

31 mine heart shall mourn = must one mourn. So the St. Petersburg Codex (A.D. 916), with note that the Eastern Massorites read "I shall mourn".

Kir-heres. Now *Kerak*, the fortified town east of southern end of the Dead Sea.

32 Sibmah. Now probably *Sūmia*, east of Jordan. Cp. Num. 32. 38.

Jazer. Now *Beit Zer'ah*, east of Jordan. Cp. 1 Chron. 26. 31. **plants** = branches.

over the sea. Probably the Dead Sea.

33 wine. Heb. *yayin.* Ap. 27. I.

34 From the cry, &c. Or, on hearing Heshbon's mournful cry.

Elealeh. Now *el 'Al*, a ruin near Heshbon.

Jahaz. A town in Reuben. Not yet identified.

Zoar. Now *Tell esh Shughūr*, on the south side of *Wādy Heshbān.* Originally "Bela".

as an heifer of three years old: or, the third Eglath (to distinguish it from two other Eglaths), or Eglath-Shelishiyah.

Nimrim. Now *Wādy Nīmrīm*, near the south end of the Dead Sea.

35 high places. See note on 1 Kings 3. 3.

36 like pipes. Used in mourning at funerals. Cp. Matt. 9. 23.

are. The 1611 edition of the A.V. reads "is".

37 every head. Some codices, with four early printed editions (one marg.), read "For upon every head".

bald = baldness. The symbol of mourning. Cp. 47. 5.

upon the loins. Some codices, with three early printed editions, Sept., and Vulg., read "and upon all loins".

38 the housetops. Where they prayed to their gods. Cp. 19. 13. **streets** = broadways.

40 he = one (not named): Nebuchadnezzar understood.

shall fly. Codex Oriental, 2091 (British Museum), reads "shall ascend"; but the *Massōrah* (Ap. 30) has a note, saying "according to other codices, it is fly" (fol. 167a).

as an eagle. Ref. to Pent. (Deut. 28. 49). Ap. 92.

41 mighty men's. Heb. *geber.* Ap. 14. IV.

43 Fear = Terror.

Fear, and the pit, and the snare. Note the Fig. *Paronomasia* (Ap. 6). Heb. *paḥad, vapaḥath, vāpaḥ.*

and. Note the Fig. *Polysyndeton.* Ap. 6.

40 For thus saith [1]the LORD; [12]'Behold, °he °shall fly °as an eagle, and shall spread his wings over [1]Moab. Op

41 [24]Kerioth is taken, and the strong holds are surprised, and the °mighty men's hearts in Moab at that day shall be as the heart of a woman in her pangs.

42 And [1]Moab shall be destroyed from *being* a people, because he hath magnified *himself* against [1]the LORD.

43 °Fear, °and the pit, and the snare, *shall be* upon thee, O inhabitant of [1]Moab, [12]saith [1]the LORD.

q (p. 1084) **44** He that fleeth from °the fear shall fall into °the pit; and he that getteth up out of °the pit shall be taken °in the snare: for I will bring upon it, *even* upon [1]Moab, °the year of their visitation, [12]saith [1]the LORD.

45 "They that fled °stood under the shadow of [2]Heshbon because of the force: but °a fire shall come forth out of [2]Heshbon, and a flame from the midst of Sihon, and shall °devour the °corner of Moab, and the crown of the head of the °tumultuous ones.

46 °Woe be unto thee, O [1]Moab! °the people of Chemosh °perisheth: for thy sons are taken °captives, and thy daughters °captives.

N (p. 1083) **47** Yet will I °bring again the captivity of Moab in °the latter days, [12]saith [1]the LORD.'"

M Thus far *is* the judgment of [1]Moab.

L² V¹ W u (p. 1086) **49** °Concerning the °Ammonites, thus saith °the LORD; "Hath Israel no sons? hath he no heir? why *then* doth their king inherit °Gad, and his people dwell in his cities?

v **2** Therefore, °behold, the days come, °saith [1]the LORD, that I will cause an alarm of war to be heard in °Rabbah of the Ammonites; and it shall be a desolate °heap, and her °daughters shall be burned with fire: then shall Israel be heir unto them that were his heirs, °saith [1]the LORD.

X **3** Howl, O °Heshbon, for °Ai is spoiled: °cry, ye daughters of [2]Rabbah, gird you with sackcloth; lament, and run to and fro by the °hedges; for their king shall go into captivity, *and* his priests and his princes together.

W u **4** °Wherefore gloriest thou in the valleys, °thy flowing valley, O backsliding daughter? that °trusted in her treasures, °*saying*, °'Who shall come unto me?'

v **5** [2]Behold, I will bring a fear upon thee, [2]saith °the Lord GOD of hosts, from all those that be about thee; and ye shall be driven out °every man right forth; and none shall gather up him that wandereth.

V² **6** And afterward I will °bring again the captivity of the °children of [1]Ammon, [2]saith [1]the LORD."

D w **7** [1]Concerning °Edom, thus saith °the [1]LORD of hosts; °"*Is* °wisdom no more in °Teman? is counsel perished from the prudent? °is their wisdom vanished?

x **8** Flee ye, turn back, °dwell deep, O inhabitants of °Dedan; for I will bring the calamity of Esau upon him, the time *that* I will visit him.

9 If °grapegatherers come to thee, would they not leave *some* gleaning grapes? if thieves by night, they will destroy till they have enough.

10 °But I have made Esau bare, I have uncovered his secret places, and he shall not be able to hide himself: his seed is spoiled, and his brethren, and his neighbours, and he *is* not.

44 the fear . . . the pit . . . the pit . . . in the snare. Note the Fig. *Paronomasia* (Ap. 6). Heb. *happaḥad . . . happaḥath . . . happaḥath . . . b^epaḥ.*
the year of their visitation. See note on 8. 12.
45 stood . . . because of the force=stood strengthless; or, halted.
a fire shall come forth out of Heshbon, &c. Ref. to Pent. (Num. 21. 28). Ap. 92.
devour. Ref. to Pent. (Num. 24. 17). Ap. 92.
corner: or, flank.
tumultuous ones=sons of tumult.
46 Woe, &c. Fig. *Maledictio.* Ap. 6.
the people of Chemosh. Ref. to Pent. (Num. 21. 29).
perisheth. Same word as "undone" in Num. 21. 29.
captives=in the captivity (masc.).
captives. Fem.
47 bring again the captivity. Note the Fig. *Paronomasia* (Ap. 6). Heb. *v^eshabtî 'eth-sh^ebûth.*
the latter days=in the end, or afterpart of the days.

49. 1-6 (L², p. 1083). **AMMON.**
(*Division.*)

L² | V¹ | 1-5. The former state.
  | V² | 6. The latter state.

49. 1-5 (V¹, above). **THE FORMER STATE.**
(*Introversion and Alternation.*)

V¹ | W | u | 1. Question. Incrimination.
  v | 2. Answer. Threatening.
  X | 3. Lamentation.
  W | *u* | 4. Question. Incrimination.
  v | 5. Answer. Threatening.

The FORTY-FIFTH Prophecy of Jeremiah (p. 1015).

1 Concerning, &c. Supply the Ellipsis, from 47. 1.
Ammonites=sons of Ammon, north of Moab. When the tribes east of Jordan were carried away by Tiglath-pileser (2 Kings 15. 29), Ammon supplanted Gad. This is the sin dealt with here.
the LORD. Heb. Jehovah. Ap. 4. II.
Gad. The 1611 edition of the A.V. reads "God".
2 behold. Fig. *Asterismos.* Ap. 6.
saith the LORD=[is] Jehovah's oracle.
Rabbah. Now *'Ammān*, on the highlands of Gilead. A large Roman city was built there four centuries later, called "Philadelphia". Its ruins yet remain.
heap=*tel.*
daughters: i.e. villages, or smaller dependent towns.
3 Heshbon. Cp. 48. 2.
Ai. An Ammonite town, not yet identified.
cry=cry sadly. **hedges**=fences.
4 Wherefore . . .? Who . . .? Fig. *Erotēsis.* Ap. 6.
thy flowing valley=thy valley flowing [with blood].
trusted=confided. Heb. *bāṭaḥ.* Ap. 69. i.
saying. Some codices, with three early printed editions, read "she who is saying in her heart".
5 the Lord GOD of hosts. See note on 2. 19.
every man. Heb. *'ish.* Ap. 14. II.
6 bring again, &c. See note on 48. 47.
children=sons. Not the same word as *v.* 11.

49. 7-22 (D, p. 1081). **EDOM.**
(*Extended Alternation.*)

D | w | 7. The procuring cause. Wisdom.
  x | 8-13. Desolation.
  y | 14, 15. Instrumentality.
  w | 16. The procuring cause. Pride.
  x | 17, 18. Desolation.
  y | 19-22. Instrumentality.

The FORTY-SIXTH Prophecy of Jeremiah (p. 1015).

7 Edom. From Esau. Judgment for his unbrotherly conduct to Israel. Cp. Ps. 137. 7. Isa. 63. 1. Ezek. 25. 12-14; and Obadiah. **the LORD of hosts.** See note on 6. 6. **Is . . .? is . . .?** Fig. *Erotēsis.* Ap. 6. **wisdom . . . Teman?** A grandson of Esau. See notes on p. 666. **Teman.** A town in Edom. Not yet identified. Cp. Job 2. 11. Amos 1. 12. Obad. 9. Hab. 3. 3. **8 dwell deep**: i.e. in out of the way recesses. **Dedan.** Not identified. He was a grandson of Abraham (Gen. 25. 1-3). Cp. Isa. 21. 13. Ezek. 25. 13. A tribe descended from Abraham by Keturah (Gen. 25. 3). **9 grapegatherers.** Cp. Obad. 5. **10 But.** Supply the Ellipsis thus: But [not so I], for I have laid Esau bare, &c.

11 Leave thy fatherless °children, I will preserve *them* alive; and let thy widows °trust in Me."

12 For thus saith [1]the LORD; [2]"Behold, they whose judgment *was* not to drink of °the cup have assuredly drunken; and *art* thou he *that* shall altogether go unpunished? thou shalt not go unpunished, but thou shalt surely drink *of it*.

13 For °I have sworn by Myself, [2]saith [1]the LORD, that °Bozrah shall become a desolation, a reproach, a waste, and a curse; and all the cities thereof shall be perpetual wastes."

y (p. 1086) 14 I have heard a rumour from [1]the LORD, and an ambassador is sent unto the °heathen, *saying*, "Gather °ye together, and come against her, and rise up to the battle."

15 For, lo, I will make thee small among the [14]heathen, *and* despised among °men.

w 16 Thy °terribleness hath deceived thee, *and* the °pride of thine heart, O thou that dwellest in the clefts of °the rock, that holdest the height of the hill: though thou shouldest make thy °nest as high as the °eagle, I will bring thee down from thence, [2]saith [1]the LORD.

x 17 Also Edom shall be °a desolation: every one that goeth by it shall be astonished, and shall hiss at all the plagues thereof.

18 As in °the overthrow of Sodom and Gomorrah and the neighbour *cities* thereof, [2]saith [1]the LORD, no °man shall abide there, neither shall a son of [15]man dwell in it.

y 19 [2]Behold, °he shall come up °like a lion from the °swelling of Jordan against the habitation of °the strong: °but I will suddenly make °him run away °from her: and who *is* °a chosen *man, that* I may appoint °over her? for °who *is* like Me? and who will °appoint Me the time? and who *is* that °shepherd that will stand before Me?

20 Therefore hear the °counsel of [1]the LORD, that He hath °taken against Edom; and His purposes, that He hath purposed against the inhabitants of [7]Teman: Surely the least of the flock shall °draw them out: surely He shall make their °habitations desolate with them.

21 The earth is moved at the noise of their fall, at the [3]cry °the noise thereof was heard °in the Red sea.

22 Behold, he shall come up and °fly as the [16]eagle, and spread his wings over [13]Bozrah: and at that day shall the heart of the °mighty men of [7]Edom be as the heart of a woman in her pangs."

D a (p. 1087) 23 [1]Concerning °Damascus. °"Hamath is confounded, and °Arpad: for they have heard °evil tidings: they are fainthearted; *there is* °sorrow on the sea; it cannot °be quiet.

24 Damascus is waxed feeble, *and* turneth herself to flee, and fear hath seized on *her*: anguish and °sorrows have taken her, as a woman in travail.

b 25 How is the city of praise °not left,

b the city of my joy!

a 26 Therefore her young men shall fall in her streets, and all the °men of war shall be cut off in that day, [2]saith [7]the LORD of hosts.

27 And I will kindle a fire in the wall of [23]Damascus, and it shall consume the palaces of °Ben-hadad."

11 children = young children. Not the same word as in *v.* 6.
trust = confide. Heb. *bāṭah*. Ap. 69. I.
12 the cup. Put by Fig. *Metonymy* (of Subject), Ap. 6, for its contents. See 25. 15.
13 I have sworn. Ref. to Pent. (Gen. 22. 16). Ap. 92.
Bozrah. Now *el Buseirah*, south-east of the Dead Sea. Not the Bozrah of 48. 24.
14 heathen = nations.
ye together = yourselves out [to war].
15 men. Heb. *'ādām* (with Art.). Ap. 14. I.
16 terribleness = monstrous thing: i.e. an Edomite *Ashērah*. Ap. 42. pride = insolence.
the rock. Probably *Sela*.
nest. Cp. Obad. 4. eagle = vulture.
17 a desolation = an astonishment.
18 the overthrow, &c. Ref. to Pent. (Gen. 19. 25. Deut. 29. 23). Ap. 92. A word almost restricted to that event. man. Heb. *'ish*. Ap. 14. II.
19 he. Nebuchadnezzar. See note on 48. 40.
like a lion. Fig. *Simile*. Ap. 6. Contrast 4. 7, where the assault is against Zion and the feelings are more deeply stirred.
swelling. Heb. pride. Put by Fig. *Metonymy* (of Adjunct), Ap. 6, for the proud beasts in the undergrowth of its banks. See 12. 5; 50. 44. Cp. Job ch. 41.
the strong = a strong one.
but = for. him: i.e. Edom.
from her: i.e. from Idumea.
a chosen man: i.e. Nebuchadnezzar.
over her = over the pasturage.
who is like Me? Cp. note on Ex. 15. 11.
appoint Me the time? i.e. who will summon or arraign Me? shepherd = ruler.
20 counsel. Referring to Teman's wisdom. Cp. *v.* 7.
taken = counselled. Fig. *Polyptōton*. Ap. 6.
draw them out. As a dog drags away and tears a dead body. habitations: or, folds.
21 the noise thereof. Heb. = its sound. Some codices, with eight early printed editions and Aram., read "at their noise" (pl.). in = at.
22 fly as the eagle. Ref. to Pent. (Deut. 28. 49). Ap. 92. Cp. Jer. 48. 40.
mighty men. Heb. *geber*. Ap. 14. IV.

49. 23-27 (*D*, p. 1081). **DAMASCUS.**
(*Introversion.*)

D a | 23, 24. Dismay.
b | 25-. City of praise. } Exclamation.
b | -25. City of joy. }
a | 26, 27. Destruction.

The FORTY-SEVENTH Prophecy of Jeremiah (p. 1015).
23 Damascus. The prophecy concerns Syria generally, of which Damascus was the principal city.
Hamath. Now *Hama*, in the valley of the Orontes, north of Damascus.
Arpad. Now *Tell Erfād*, thirteen miles north of Aleppo. Cp. 2 Kings 18. 34; 19. 13. Isa. 10. 9; 36. 19; 37. 13.
evil tidings = calamitous report. Heb. *rā'a'*. Ap. 44. viii.
sorrow = anxiety, or trouble. Heb. *rā'a'*. Ap. 44. viii. Not the same word as in *v.* 24.
be quiet = rest.
24 sorrows = pangs. Heb. *hēbel*, as in 13. 21.
25 not left = not restored, strengthened, or fortified. A *Homonym*. Here the meaning is as in Neh. 3. 8. See notes on Ex. 23. 5. Deut. 32. 36. 1 Kings 14. 10. 2 Kings 14. 26. Jer. 49. 25. Not its other meaning, to leave or forsake, as in Gen. 2. 24; 39. 6. Neh. 5. 10. Ps. 49. 10. Mal. 4. 1 (Heb. = ch. 3. 19).
26 men. Heb. pl. of *'ĕnōsh*. Ap. 14. III.
27 Ben-hadad. Three kings of Damascus bore this official name. See 1 Kings 15. 18. 2 Kings 13. 3, 25.

C Y c (p. 1088) 28 [1]Concerning °Kedar, and concerning the kingdoms of °Hazor, which Nebuchadrezzar king of Babylon shall smite, thus saith [1]the LORD; "Arise ye, go up to °Kedar, and spoil the °men of the east.

d 29 Their tents and their flocks shall they take away: they shall take to themselves their curtains, and all their vessels, and their camels; and they shall cry unto them, °'Fear *is* on every side.'

Z 30 Flee, get you far off, [8]dwell deep, O ye inhabitants of Hazor, [2]saith [1]the LORD;

Z for Nebuchadrezzar king of Babylon hath [20]taken [20]counsel against you, and hath °conceived a purpose against you.

Y c 31 Arise, get you up unto the wealthy nation, that dwelleth without care, [2]saith [1]the LORD, "which have neither gates nor bars, °*which* dwell alone.

d 32 And their camels shall be a booty, and the multitude of their cattle a spoil: and I will scatter into °all °winds them *that are* °in the utmost corners; and I will bring their calamity from all sides thereof, [2]saith [1]the LORD.

33 And [28]Hazor shall be a dwelling for °dragons, *and* a desolation for ever: there shall no [18]man abide there, nor *any* son of [15]man dwell in it."

B A[1] e 487 34 The word of [1]the LORD that came to Jeremiah the prophet against °Elam in the beginning of the reign of Zedekiah king of Judah, saying,

35 "Thus saith [7]the LORD of hosts; 'Behold, I will break the bow of Elam, the chief of their might.

f 36 And upon Elam will I bring the °four [32]winds from the °four quarters of heaven, and will scatter them toward all those [32]winds; and there shall be no nation whither the outcasts of [34]Elam shall not come.

e 37 For I will cause [34]Elam to be dismayed before their enemies, and before them that seek their °life: and I will bring [23]evil upon them, *even* My fierce anger, [2]saith [1]the LORD; and I will send the sword after them, till I have consumed them:

f 38 And I will set My throne in Elam, and will destroy from thence the king and the princes, [2]saith [1]the LORD.

A[2] 39 But it shall come to pass in °the latter days, *that* I will °bring again the captivity of [34]Elam, [2]saith [1]the LORD.'"

A B **50** The word that °the LORD spake against Babylon °*and* against the land of the Chaldeans °by Jeremiah the prophet.

C[1] D[1] 2 "Declare ye among the nations, and °publish, and °set up a standard; °publish, *and* °conceal not: say, °'Babylon is taken, °Bel is confounded, °Merodach is broken in pieces; her idols are confounded, her °images are broken in pieces.

49. 28-33 (*C*, p. 1081). KEDAR AND HAZOR.
(*Introversion and Alternation.*)

C | Y | c | 28. Command. Invasion.
d | 29. Property. Tents, &c.
Z | 30-. Advice.
Z | -30. Reason.
Y | c | 31. Command. Invasion.
d | 32, 33. Property. Camels, &c.

The FORTY-EIGHTH Prophecy of Jeremiah (p. 1015).

28 Kedar. Name of the Bedouin dwelling in tents (2. 10), east of Palestine.
Hazor. Near the Euphrates and the Persian Gulf.
men = sons.
29 Fear is on every side. Heb. *māgōr missabib.* Cp. 6. 25; 20. 3, 10; 46. 5. Lam. 2. 22.
30 conceived a purpose = devised a device. Fig. *Polyptōton.* Ap. 6.
31 which dwell alone. Ref. to Pent. (Num. 23. 9. Deut. 33. 28). Ap. 92.
32 all winds = all quarters.
winds. Heb. *rūach.* Ap. 9.
in the utmost corners = have the corners of their hair or beards polled. Cp. 9. 26.
33 dragons = jackals.

49. 34-39 (*B*, p. 1081). ELAM.
(*Division.*)

B | A[1] | 34-38. The former state.
A[2] | 39. The latter state.

49. 34-38 (A[1], above). THE FORMER STATE.
(*Alternation.*)

A[1] | e | 34, 35. Debilitation.
f | 36. Dispersion.
e | 37. Dismay.
f | 38. Destruction.

The FORTY-NINTH Prophecy of Jeremiah (p. 1015).

34 Elam. The country east of the Tigris. Cp. Dan. 8. 1, 2. Its subjugation by Nebuchadnezzar (25. 25). Cp. Hab. 2. 8.
36 four. The number connected with the earth (Ap. 10). **37 life** = soul. Heb. *nephesh.* Ap. 13.
39 the latter days. The end or afterpart of the days.
bring again, &c. See note on 48. 47. Cp. Deut. 30. 3.

50. 1—51. 64- (*A*, p. 1081). BABYLON.
(*Introversion and Alternations.*)

A | B | 50. 1. The word of Jehovah to Jeremiah. Declaration.
C[1] | D[1] | 50. 2, 3. Babylon.
E[1] | 50. 4-7. Israel and Judah.
C[2] | D[2] | 50. 8-16. Babylon.
E[2] | 50. 17-20. Israel.
C[3] | D[3] | 50. 21-32. Babylon.
E[3] | 50. 33, 34. Israel and Judah.
C[4] | D[4] | 50. 35—51. 4. Babylon.
E[4] | 51. 5. Israel and Judah.
C[5] | D[5] | 51. 6-18. Babylon.
E[5] | 51. 19. Judah. (Portion.)
C[6] | D[6] | 51. 20-33. Babylon.
E[6] | 51. 34-58. Zion and Jerusalem.
B | 51. 59-64-. The Word of Jeremiah to Seraiah. Ratification.

The FIFTIETH Prophecy of Jeremiah (p. 1015).

1 the LORD. Heb. Jehovah. Ap. 4. II.
and. Some codices, with three early printed editions, Aram., Syr., and Vulg., read this "and" in the text.
by. Heb. idiom = by the hand of; "hand" being put by Fig. *Metonymy* (of Cause), Ap. 6, for the instrumentality or agency, especially in the inspiration of the written words. See note on Zech. 7. 12.
2 publish . . . conceal not. Not now using symbols as in 25. 15. Cp. 4. 5, 6; 46. 14. **set up** = lift up.
Babylon is taken. Cp. Rev. 14. 8; 18. 6, 10, 21: showing that this prophecy is still future.
Bel. Contracted from the Aramaic form of *Ba'al*, the national god of Babylon. See Isa. 46. 1. **Merodach.** Another name for Bel (= Baal), Babylon's god. **images** = manufactured gods. Cp. Lev. 26. 30.

496 ? 3 For out of °the north there cometh up a nation against her, which shall make her land desolate, and °none shall dwell therein: they shall remove, they shall depart, both °man and beast.'

C[1] E[1] g (p. 1089) 4 °In those days, and in that time, °saith [1]the LORD, the °children of Israel shall come, they and the °children of Judah °together, °going and °weeping: they shall go, and seek °the LORD their °God.

h 5 They shall ask the way to Zion with their faces °thitherward, *saying*, 'Come, and let us join ourselves to [1]the LORD in a °perpetual covenant *that* shall not be forgotten.'

i 6 My People hath been °lost sheep: their °shepherds have caused them to go astray, °they have turned them away *on* the mountains: they have gone from mountain to hill, they have forgotten their restingplace.

7 All that found them have devoured them: and their adversaries said, °'We °offend not, because they have °sinned against [1]the LORD, the °Habitation of °justice, even [1]the LORD, °the Hope of their fathers.'

D[2] F 8 Remove out of the midst of Babylon, and °go forth out of the land of the Chaldeans, and be as the he goats before the flocks.

G j 9 For, lo, I will raise and cause to come up against Babylon an °assembly of °great nations from [3]the north country: and they shall set themselves in array against her; from thence she shall be taken: their arrows *shall be* as of a °mighty °expert man; none shall return in vain.

10 And Chaldea shall be a spoil: all that spoil her °shall be satisfied, [4]saith [1]the LORD.

k 11 Because ye were glad, because ye rejoiced, O °ye destroyers of Mine heritage, because ye are grown fat as the heifer at grass, and bellow as bulls;

12 Your mother shall be sore confounded; she that bare you shall be ashamed: °behold, °the hindermost of the nations *shall be* a wilderness, a dry land, and a desert.

13 Because of the wrath of [1]the LORD it shall °not be inhabited, but it shall be wholly desolate: every one that goeth by Babylon shall be astonished, and hiss at all her plagues.

G j 14 Put yourselves in array against Babylon round about: all ye that bend the bow, shoot at her, spare no arrows: for she hath [7]sinned against [1]the LORD.

15 Shout against her round about: she hath °given her hand: her foundations are fallen, her walls are thrown down:

k for it *is* the vengeance of [1]the LORD: take vengeance upon her; °as she hath done, do unto her.

F 16 Cut off the sower from Babylon, and him that handleth the sickle in the time of harvest: for fear of the oppressing sword they shall turn °every one to his people, and they shall flee °every one to his own land.

C[2] E[2] *i* 17 °Israel *is* a scattered sheep; the lions have driven *him* away: first the king of Assyria hath devoured him; and °last this Nebu-

3 the north. Referring to Medo-Persia, which was on the north-west of Chaldea. But a future enemy is foretold.

none shall dwell therein. Showing that the fulfilment is still future.

man. Heb. *'ādām*. Ap. 14. I.

50. 4-7 (E[1], p. 1088), **17-20** (E[2], p. 1088). ISRAEL AND JUDAH. (*Introversion.*)

C[1] | E[1] | g | 4. Repentance.
h | 5. Return.
i | 6, 7. Sheep. Lost.
D[2] | 8-16. Babylon. [See below.]
C[2] | E[2] | *i* | 17, 18. Sheep. Scattered.
h | 19. Restoration.
g | 20. Pardon.

4 In those days. This prophecy awaits its fulfilment. The conquest by Medo-Persia did not exhaust it.

saith the LORD = [is] Jehovah's oracle.

children = sons.

together. Another proof that this prophecy refers to the future. Never yet fulfilled.

going and weeping. Heb. = weeping as they travel, so shall they journey on.

weeping. For their past sins. Cp. 31. 9, 18. Joel 2. 12. Zech. 12. 10-14. Rev. 1. 7.

the LORD. Heb. Jehovah (with *'eth*). Ap. 4. II.

God. Heb. Elohim. Ap. 4. I.

5 thitherward. Heb. = hitherward. Jeremiah was therefore not in Babylon, but in Egypt.

perpetual. Another evidence that this prophecy refers to the future covenant. Cp. 3. 18—4. 2; 11. 1-6; 31. 31.

6 lost sheep. Cp. Matt. 10. 6; 15. 24.

shepherds: i.e. rulers.

they have turned them away on the mountains = on the mountains they seduced them: i.e. by the idolatrous worship practised there.

7 We offend not, &c. Cp. *vv.* 15, 23, 29; 2. 3; 25. 14, 15; 51. 11, 24, 56. Isa. 10. 5-7, 12, &c.; 54. 15-17. Zech. 1. 14-16.

offend. Heb. *'āshām*. Ap. 44. ii.

sinned. Heb. *chāṭā*. Ap. 44. i.

Habitation = pasturage. Cp. 31. 23.

justice = righteousness. In ch. 31. 23 this is applied to Jerusalem. Here Jehovah Himself is the pasturage in which His People find rest.

the Hope of their fathers. Put by Fig. *Metonymy* (of Adjunct), Ap. 6, by which "hope" is put for the God in Whom their fathers hoped. Cp. 1 Tim. 1. 1.

50. 8-16 (D[2], p. 1088). BABYLON. (*Introversion and Alternation.*)

D[2] | F | 8. Removal.
G | j | 9, 10. Invasion.
k | 11-13. Cause.
G | *j* | 14, 15-. Invasion.
k | -15. Cause.
F | 16. Flight.

8 go forth. Heb. text reads "they will go forth"; but margin, with some codices and two early printed editions, reads "go ye forth". Cp. 51. 4, 6. Rev. 18. 4.

9 assembly = a gathered host, or convocation.

great nations. Cp. Isa. 13. 3, 4.

mighty . . . man. Heb. *gibbōr*. Ap. 14. IV.

expert = successful. Cp. 10. 21; 23. 5.

10 shall be satisfied. Cp. 49. 9.

11 destroyers = spoilers, or plunderers.

12 behold. Fig. *Asterismos*. Ap. 6.

the hindermost = the last. Cp. *v.* 17; 25. 26.

13 not be inhabited. Not yet fulfilled. Cp. 1 Pet. 5. 13.

15 given her hand. Put by Fig. *Metonymy* (of Adjunct), Ap. 6, for what is done by it. Here the token of submission. Cp. Lam. 5. 6. Ezek. 17. 18.

as = according as. Cp. Rev. 18. 6, 7.

16 every one. Heb. *'ish*. Ap. 14. II.

17 Israel. Now a united nation. See note on *v.* 4.

last. See note on "hindermost", *v.* 12.

496 ? chadrezzar king of Babylon hath broken his bones."

18 Therefore thus saith °the [1] LORD of hosts, the [4] God of Israel; [12] "Behold, I will punish the king of Babylon and his land, as I have punished the king of Assyria.

h (p. 1089) 19 And I will bring Israel again to his habitation, and he shall feed on Carmel and Bashan, and his °soul shall be satisfied upon °mount Ephraim and Gilead.

g 20 [4] In those days, and in that time, [4] saith [1] the LORD, the °iniquity of [17] Israel shall be sought for, and *there shall be* none; and the [7] sins of Judah, and they shall not be found: for I will pardon them whom I reserve.

D³ l (p. 1090) 21 Go up against the land of °Merathaim, *even* against it, and against the inhabitants of °Pekod: waste and utterly °destroy after them, [4] saith [1] the LORD, and do according to all that I have commanded thee.

22 A sound of battle *is* in the land, and of great °destruction.

23 How is the hammer of the whole earth cut asunder and broken! how is Babylon become a desolation among the nations!

24 I have laid a snare for thee, and thou art also taken, O Babylon, and thou wast not aware: thou art found, and also caught, because thou hast striven against [1] the LORD.

25 [1] The LORD hath opened °His armoury, and hath brought forth the weapons of His indignation: for this *is* the work of °the Lord GOD of hosts in the land of the Chaldeans.

26 Come against her °from the utmost border, open her storehouses: cast her up as heaps, and [21] destroy her utterly: let nothing of her be left.

27 Slay all her bullocks; let them go down to the slaughter: woe unto them!
m for their day is come, the time of their °visitation.

l 28 The voice of them that flee and escape out of the land of Babylon, to declare in Zion the vengeance of [1] the LORD our [4] God, the °vengeance of His temple.

29 Call together the archers against Babylon: all ye that bend the bow, camp against it round about; let none thereof escape: °recompense her according to her work; °according to all that she hath done, do unto her: for she hath been proud against [1] the LORD, against °the Holy One of Israel.

30 Therefore shall her young men fall in the streets, and all her °men of war shall be cut off in that day, [4] saith [1] the LORD.

m 31 [12] Behold, I *am* against thee, *O thou* most proud, [4] saith [25] the Lord GOD of hosts: for thy day is come, the time *that* I will visit thee.

32 And the most proud shall stumble and fall, and none shall raise him up: and I will kindle a fire in his cities, and it shall devour all round about him."

E³ (p. 1088) 33 Thus saith °the [1] LORD of hosts; "The [4] children of Israel and the [4] children of Judah *were* oppressed [4] together: and all that took them captives held them fast; they refused to let them go.

18 the LORD of hosts, the God of Israel. See note on 7. 3.
19 soul. Heb. *nephesh*. Ap. 13.
mount = the hill country of.
20 iniquity. Heb. *'āvāh*. Ap. 44. iv.

50. 21-32 (D³, p. 1088). BABYLON. (*Alternation.*)

D³ | l | 21-27-. Invasion.
| m | -27. Day of visitation.
| *l* | 28-30. Invasion.
| *m* | 31, 32. Day of visitation.

21 Merathaim = double rebellion. So called, here, because the empire was founded in a double rebellion. See Prideaux, *Connection*, vol. i, p. 1. A symbolic name for Babylon, as Pekod is also (below) and Sheshach (25. 26; 51. 41).
Pekod = Visitation: i.e. in judgment.
destroy = devote to extermination. Heb. *ḥāram*. The same word as *v.* 26; not the same as *vv.* 11, 22.
22 destruction = smash; or, breaking down. Heb. *shābar*. Not the same word as in *vv.* 11, 21, 26.
25 His armoury. Fig. *Anthropopatheia*. Ap. 6.
the Lord GOD of hosts. Heb. Adonai Jehovah of hosts. See note on 2. 19.
26 from the utmost border = from the farthest parts, or every quarter.
27 visitation. See note on "Pekod", *v.* 21.
28 vengeance = avenging. So 51. 11. Cp. Dan. 5. 3.
29 recompense her. See Rev. 18. 6.
according to. See note on "as", *v.* 15. Cp. Rev. 18. 6.
the Holy One of Israel. See note on Ps. 71. 22.
30 men. Heb. pl. of *'ĕnōsh*. Ap. 14. III.
33 the LORD of hosts. See note on 6. 6. 1 Sam. 1. 3.
34 Redeemer = Kinsman-Redeemer. Heb. *gā'al*. See notes on Isa. 60. 16, and Ex. 6. 6.
strong = strong (to hold fast). Heb. *ḥāzaḳ*. Not the same word as in *v.* 44.

50. 35—51. 4 (D⁴, p. 1088). BABYLON. (*Introversion.*)

D⁴ | n | 50. 35-38. Sword and drought.
| o | 50. 39, 40. Depopulation.
| p | 50. 41-43. Invasion. Behold.
| *p* | 50. 44. Invasion. Behold.
| *o* | 50. 45, 46. Desolation.
| *n* | 51. 1-4. Wind and winnowers.

35 A sword. Note the Fig. *Anaphora* (Ap. 6) in five successive sentences.
36 liars = praters.
dote = be shown to be foolish.
37 the mingled people = the rabble.
38 idols = horrors.

34 Their °Redeemer *is* °strong; [33] the [1] LORD of hosts *is* His name: He shall throughly plead their cause, that He may give rest to the land, and disquiet the inhabitants of Babylon.

35 °A sword *is* upon the Chaldeans, [4] saith D⁴ n
[1] the LORD, and upon the inhabitants of (p. 1090)
Babylon, and upon her princes, and upon her wise *men*.

36 [35] A sword *is* upon the °liars; and they shall °dote: [35] a sword *is* upon her [9] mighty men; and they shall be dismayed.

37 [35] A sword *is* upon their horses, and upon their chariots, and upon all °the mingled people that *are* in the midst of her; and they shall become as women: [35] a sword *is* upon her treasures; and they shall be robbed.

38 A drought *is* upon her waters; and they shall be dried up: for it *is* the land of graven images, and they are mad upon *their* °idols.

39 Therefore the wild beasts of the desert o

496 ? with the wild beasts of the islands shall dwell
there, and the owls shall dwell therein: and it
shall be °no more inhabited for ever; neither
shall it be dwelt in from generation to generation.
40 As [4]God °overthrew Sodom and Gomorrah
and the neighbour *cities* thereof, [4]saith [1]the
LORD; *so* shall no °man abide there, neither
shall any son of [3]man dwell therein.
p 41 [12]Behold, a people shall come from the
(p. 1090) north, and °a great nation, and many kings
shall be raised up from the °coasts of the earth.
42 They shall hold the bow and the lance:
they *are* cruel, and will not shew mercy: their
voice shall roar like the sea, and they shall
ride upon horses, *every one* put in array, like
a [40]man to the battle, against thee, O daughter
of Babylon.
43 The king of Babylon hath heard the report
of them, and °his hands waxed feeble: anguish
took hold of him, *and* pangs as of a woman in
travail.
p 44 Behold, he shall come up °like a lion from
the swelling of Jordan unto the habitation of
the strong: but I will make them suddenly run
away from her: and who *is* a chosen *man*,
that I may appoint over her? for who *is* like
Me? and who will appoint Me the time? and
who *is* that shepherd that will stand before Me?
o 45 Therefore hear ye the counsel of [1]the LORD,
that He hath °taken against Babylon; and
His purposes, that He hath purposed against
the °land of the Chaldeans: Surely the least of
the flock shall draw them out: surely He shall
make *their* habitation desolate with them.
46 At the noise of the taking of Babylon the
earth is moved, and the cry is heard among
the nations."

n **51** Thus saith °the LORD; °"Behold, I will
raise up against Babylon, and against
them that dwell in the midst of them that rise
up against °Me, a °destroying °wind;
2 And will send unto Babylon °fanners, that
shall °fan her, and shall empty her land: for
in the day of trouble they shall be against her
round about.
3 °Against *him that* bendeth let the archer
bend his bow, and against *him that* lifteth
himself up in his °brigandine: and spare ye not
her young men; °destroy ye utterly all her host.
4 Thus the slain shall fall in the land of the
Chaldeans, and *they that are* thrust through
in her streets.
E[4] 5 For °Israel *hath* not *been* forsaken, nor
(p. 1088) °Judah of his °God, of °the [1]LORD of Hosts;
though their land was filled with °sin against
°the Holy One of Israel.
D[5] H 6 Flee out of the midst of Babylon, and de-
(p. 1091) liver °every man his °soul: be not cut off in
her °iniquity; for this *is* the time of [1]the LORD'S
vengeance; He will render unto her a recompence.
J q 7 Babylon *hath been* a golden cup in [1]the
LORD'S hand, that °made all the earth drunken:
the nations have drunken of her °wine; therefore the nations are mad.

39 no more inhabited, &c. Therefore the fulfilment is still future.
40 overthrew, &c. Ref. to Pent. (Gen. 19. 25). Ap. 92. Cp. 49. 18.
man. Heb. *'ish*. Ap. 14. II.
41 a great nation: i.e. Medo-Persia.
coasts = sides: i.e. remote parts.
43 his hands, &c. See fulfilment in Dan. 5. 6.
44 like a lion, &c. See note on 49. 19 for this verse and *v.* 45, there spoken of Edom.
45 taken = counselled.
land. Some codices, with three early printed editions and Aram., read "inhabitants of the land".

51. 1 the LORD. Heb. Jehovah. Ap. 4. II.
Behold. Fig. *Asterismos*. Ap. 6.
Me. A Massoretic note (Ap. 30) says that this is a cryptogram (Heb. "*Casdīm*"), meaning "the Chaldees". See note on *v.* 41; 25. 26.
destroying = laying waste. Heb. *shaḥath*. The same word as in *vv.* 11, 20, 25. Not the same as in *vv.* 3, 8, 54, 55.
wind. Heb. *rūach*. Ap. 9.
2 fanners . . . fan = winnowers . . . winnow. Fig. *Polyptōton*. Ap. 6.
3 Against him that bendeth, &c. The *Massōrah* (Ap. 30), instead of cancelling the repeated word "against . . . and against" (*'el*), directs the substitution of *'al*, "not . . . and not". The verse will then read, "Let not the archer bend his bow, nor let him lift himself up in his coat of mail" (i.e. in defence of Babylon). This is so read in two early printed editions, Chald., Syr., Vulg., and R.V.
brigandine = coat of mail.
destroy = break down. Heb. *ḥāram*. Same word as *v.* 54. Not the same as *vv.* 1, 8, 11, 20, 25, 25, 54, 55.
5 Israel . . . Judah. Now one People again.
God. Heb. Elohim. Ap. 4. I.
the LORD of Hosts. See note on 6. 6, and 1 Sam. 1. 3.
sin. Heb. *chāṭā*. Ap. 44. i.
the Holy One of Israel. See note on Ps. 71. 22.

51. 6-18 (D[5], p. 1088). BABYLON.
(*Alternation and Introversion.*)

D[5] | H | 6. Injunction to flee from her.
  J | q | 7. Idolatry. (Symbolic.)
    r | 8, 9-. Fall.
  H | -9, 10. Injunction to forsake her.
  J | *r* | 11-16. Fall.
    q | 17, 18. Idolatry. (Literal.)

6 every man. Heb. *'ish*. Ap. 14. II.
soul. Heb. *nephesh*. Ap. 13.
iniquity. Heb. *'āvāh*. Ap. 44. iv. Put by Fig. *Metonymy* (of Cause), Ap. 6, for the judgment brought down by it. Cp. Rev. 18. 4.
7 made all the earth drunken. Cp. Rev. 17. 4.
wine. Heb. *yayin*. Ap. 27. I.
8 is suddenly, &c. This must refer to a future fulfilment, for the present condition came gradually. See Isa. 21. 9; 47. 9, 11. Cp. Rev. 14. 8; 18. 8, 10, 17, 19.
destroyed = broken down. Heb. *shābar*. Not the same as in *vv.* 1, 3, 11, 20, 25, 25, 55.
take balm = fetch balsam. Cp. 8. 22; 46. 11.
9 We. Note this remarkable pronoun.
every one. Heb. *'ish*. Ap. 14. II.
is lifted up = mounteth.

8 Babylon °is suddenly fallen and °destroyed: r
howl for her; °take balm for her pain, if so be
she may be healed.
9 °We would have healed Babylon, but she is
not healed: forsake her, and let us go °every
one into his own country:

for her judgment reacheth unto heaven, and *H*
°is lifted up *even* to the skies.
10 [1]The LORD hath brought forth our righteousness: come, and let us declare in Zion the
work of [1]the LORD our [5]God.

J r (p. 1091) 496 ? 11 Make bright the arrows; gather the
shields: [1]the LORD hath raised up the °spirit
of the kings of °the Medes: for His device *is*
against Babylon, to [1]destroy it; because it *is*
the °vengeance of [1]the LORD, the °vengeance
of His temple.
12 Set up the standard upon the walls of
Babylon, °make the watch strong, set up the
°watchmen, prepare the ambushes: for [1]the
LORD hath both devised and done that which
He spake against the inhabitants of Babylon.
13 O thou that dwellest °upon many waters,
abundant in treasures, thine end is come, *and*
the measure of thy °covetousness.
14 [5]The [1]LORD of hosts hath sworn °by Himself, *saying*, "Surely I will fill thee with men,
as with °caterpillers; and °they shall lift up
a shout against thee."
15 He hath °made the earth by His power,
He hath established the world by His wisdom,
and hath stretched out the heaven by His
understanding.
16 When He uttereth *his* voice, *there is*
a °multitude of waters in the heavens; and
He causeth the vapours to ascend from the
ends of the earth: He maketh °lightnings with
rain, and bringeth forth the [1]wind out of His
treasures.
q 17 Every man °is brutish by *his* knowledge;
every founder is °confounded by the graven
image: for his molten image *is* falsehood, and
there is no °breath in them.
18 They *are* vanity, the work of errors: in °the
time of their visitation they shall perish.
E5 (p. 1088) 19 °The Portion of Jacob *is* not like them;
for He *is* the °Former of all things: and °*Israel*
is the rod of his inheritance: [5]the [1]LORD of
hosts *is* His name.
D6 s1 (p. 1092) 20 "Thou *art* °My battle axe *and* weapons of
war: for °with thee will I break in pieces the
nations, and °with thee will I destroy kingdoms;
21 And [20]with thee will I break in pieces the
horse and his rider; and [20]with thee will I
break in pieces the chariot and his rider;
22 [20]With thee also will I break in pieces
°man and woman; and [20]with thee will I
break in pieces old and young; and [20]with thee
will I break in pieces the young man and the
maid;
23 I will also break in pieces [20]with thee the
shepherd and his flock; and [20]with thee will I
break in pieces the husbandman and his yoke
of oxen; and [20]with thee will I break in pieces
captains and rulers.
24 And I will render unto Babylon and to all
the inhabitants of Chaldea all their °evil that
they have done in Zion in your sight, °saith
[1]the LORD.
t1 25 [1]Behold, I *am* against thee, O [1]destroying
mountain, [24]saith [1]the LORD, which [1]destroyest all the earth: and I will stretch out Mine
hand upon thee, and roll thee down from the
rocks, and will make thee a burnt mountain.
26 And they shall °not take of thee a stone
for a corner, nor a stone for foundations; but
thou shalt be desolate °for ever, [24]saith [1]the
LORD."
s2 27 Set ye up a standard in the land, blow the
trumpet among the nations, °prepare the nations against her, call together against her the
kingdoms of Ararat, °Minni, and Ashchenaz;
appoint a °captain against her; cause °the
horses to come up as the rough [14]caterpillers.
28 Prepare against her the nations with the
kings of [11]the Medes, °the captains thereof,
and all the rulers thereof, and all the land of
his dominion.
29 And the land shall tremble and sorrow:
for every purpose of [1]the LORD shall be performed against Babylon,
to make the land of Babylon a desolation °without an inhabitant. t2

---

11 spirit. Heb. *rūach*. Ap. 9.
the Medes. In the person of Cyrus and others (Ap. 57). Here the then immediate calamity is referred to.
vengeance = avengement.
12 make the watch, &c. Cp. Isa. 21. 5, 6.
watchmen. The 1611 edition of the A.V. reads "watchman".
13 upon many waters. Cp. *v.* 42, and 50. 38; also Rev. 17. 1, 15.
covetousness = dishonest or unrighteous gain.
14 by Himself = by His soul. Heb. *nephesh*. Ap. 13. Fig. *Anthropopatheia*. Ap. 6.
caterpillers = locusts. Cp. Joel 2. 2. Nah. 3. 15.
they: i.e. the assailants.
15 made the earth, &c. Ref. to Pent. (Gen. 1). Ap. 92. Cp. 10. 12, &c. *vv.* 15–19 are repeated from 10. 12–16.
16 multitude = noise.
lightnings, &c. Cp. 10. 13.
17 is brutish by, &c. = is become too brutish to know.
confounded = put to shame.
breath. Heb. *rūach*. Ap. 9.
18 the time of their visitation. See note on 8. 12.
19 The Portion of Jacob, &c. Note the *Alternation* in *v.* 19:—

| Not such as these is Jacob's Portion: (Deut. 32. 9. Ps. 16. 5).
| For [the] Former of all things is He:
| And the Sceptre of his (Israel's) inheritance:
| The LORD of hosts is His Name (Deut. 10. 9).

51. 20–33 (D6, p. 1088). **BABYLON.**
(*Repeated Alternation.*)

D6 | s1 | 20–24. Invasion. Battle-axe.
t1 | 25, 26. Desolation.
s2 | 27–29–. Invasion. Standard.
t2 | –29. Desolation.
s3 | 30–32. Invasion. Unassisted.
t3 | 33. Desolation.

20 My battle axe: or, My hammer, i.e. Cyrus. Fig. *Anthropopatheia*. Ap. 6.
with thee will I break in pieces = with thee will I beat down. Note the Fig. *Anaphora* (Ap. 6), by which ten successive sentences commence with these words. This is for special emphasis.
22 man. Heb. *'ish*. Ap. 14. II.
24 evil. Heb. *rā'a'*. Ap. 44. viii.
saith the LORD = [is] Jehovah's oracle.
26 not take of thee . . for ever. This again must refer to a future fulfilment. The two destructions are intertwined. Cp. *v.* 62.
for ever. See Ap. 151.
27 prepare = set apart, or sanctify.
Minni. Frequently mentioned in the inscriptions, the Assyrians having been compelled to quell revolts there.
captain = muster-master or marshal, like the Assyrian *dupsarru*, or tablet-writer. Heb. *ṭiphsar*. Occurs only here and Nah. 3. 17.
the horses. The 1611 edition of the A.V. reads "her horses".
28 the Some codices, with three early printed editions, read "and the".
29 without an inhabitant. This must be yet future.

s[3] 30 °The mighty men of Babylon have forborn
(p. 1092) to fight, they have remained in *their* holds:
496? their might hath failed; they became as women:
they have burned °her dwellingplaces; her bars
are broken.
31 One °post shall run to meet another, and
one messenger to meet another, to shew the
king of Babylon that his city is taken °at *one*
end,
32 And that the °passages are °stopped, and
the reeds they have burned with fire, and the
°men of war are affrighted.

t[3] 33 For thus saith °the [1]LORD of hosts, the
[5]God of Israel; "The daughter of Babylon *is*
like a threshingfloor, *it is* time to thresh her:
yet a little while, and the time of her harvest
shall come."

E[6] K 34 "Nebuchadrezzar the king of Babylon
(p. 1093) hath devoured me, he hath crushed °me, he
hath made me an empty vessel, he hath swallowed me up like a dragon, he hath filled his
belly with my delicates, he hath cast me out.
35 The violence done to [34]me and to my flesh
be upon Babylon," shall the °inhabitant of
Zion say; "and my blood °upon the inhabitants of Chaldea," shall Jerusalem say.

L 36 Therefore thus saith [1]the LORD; [1]"Behold, I will plead thy cause, and take vengeance for thee; and I will °dry up her °sea,
and make her springs dry.
37 And Babylon shall become heaps, a dwellingplace for °dragons, an astonishment, and
an hissing, °without an inhabitant.
38 They shall roar together like lions: they
shall °yell as lions' whelps.

M 39 In their heat I will make their °feasts, and
I will make them drunken, that they may rejoice, and sleep a perpetual sleep, and not
wake, [24]saith [1]the LORD.

N 40 I will bring them down like lambs to the
slaughter, like rams with he goats.
41 How is °Sheshach taken! and how is the
praise of the whole earth surprised! how is
Babylon become an astonishment among the
nations!
42 The sea is come up upon Babylon: she is
covered with the multitude of the waves thereof.
43 Her cities are a desolation, a dry land, and
a wilderness, a land wherein °no [22]man dwelleth, neither doth *any* son of °man pass thereby.

K 44 And I will punish [1]Bel in Babylon, and
I will bring forth out of his mouth that which
he hath swallowed up: and the nations shall
not flow together any more unto him: yea,
°the wall of Babylon shall fall.

L u 45 My People, go ye out of the midst of her,
and deliver ye [6]every man his °soul from the
fierce anger of [1]the LORD.
46 And lest your heart faint, and ye fear for
the rumour that shall be heard in the land;
a rumour shall both come *one* year, and after
that in *another* year *shall come* a rumour,
and violence in the land, ruler against ruler.

v 47 Therefore, [1]behold, the days come, that
I will °do judgment upon the graven images
of Babylon: and her whole land shall be confounded, and all her slain shall fall in the
midst of her.
48 Then °the heaven and the earth, and °all
that *is* therein, °shall sing for Babylon: for the
spoilers shall come unto her from the north,"
[24]saith [1]the LORD.
49 As Babylon *hath caused* the slain of Israel to fall, so at Babylon shall fall the slain
of °all the earth.
50 Ye that have escaped the sword, go away, *u*

30 The mighty men. Heb. pl. of *gibbōr*. Ap. 14. IV.
her. The 1611 edition of the A.V. reads "their".
31 post = runner.
at one end. Supply the *Ellipsis* by the word "each", instead of "one" = "at [each] end". This will accord with the history; for Herodotus says the Babylonians retired to the city, and "remained in their holds". Cyrus, having turned the waters of the Euphrates, entered the city, by the bed of the river, *at each end* (see Herod. 1. § 191). Cp. Dan. 5. 3, 4, 23, 30. The R.V., "on every quarter", quite misses the point. This passage, therefore, belongs to the past fulfilment; while others still await a future fulfilment.
32 passages = fords. **stopped** = seized.
men. Heb. pl. of *'ĕnōsh*. Ap. 14. III.
33 the LORD of hosts, the God of Israel. See note on **7. 3.**

51. 34-58 (E[6], p. 1088). ZION AND JERUSALEM. (*Extended Alternation.*)

E[6] K | 34, 35. Babylon. Zion's incrimination of.
L | 36-38. Zion. Jehovah's advocacy of.
M | 39. Babylon made drunk.
N | 40-43. Inundation.
K | 44. Babylon. Jehovah's judgment of.
L | 45-56. Zion. Jehovah's avengement of.
M | 57. Babylon made drunk.
N | 58. Conflagration.

34 me. Here, and in *v.* 35, the Heb. text reads "us"; but the margin, and some codices, with two early printed editions, read "me", which is followed by the A.V.
35 inhabitant = inhabitress.
upon. Heb. text reads "against", but a special various reading called *Sevīr* (Ap. 34) has "upon", with some codices, one early printed edition, Aram., Sept., Syr., and Vulg., which are followed by A.V.
36 dry up. Referring to the act of Cyrus (by Gobryas). Cp. *v.* 31, above.
sea = the river Euphrates. So called from its breadth.
37 dragons = jackals.
without an inhabitant. This carries us on to the future again. Cp. 1 Pet. 5. 13.
38 yell: or, shake themselves.
39 feasts = banquets.
41 Sheshach. See note on 25. 26.
43 no man dwelleth. Still future.
man. Heb. *'ādām*. Ap. 14. I.
44 the wall of Babylon. Now recently laid bare by excavations.

51. 45-56 (*L*, above). ZION. JEHOVAH'S AVENGEMENT OF. (*Alternation.*)

L u | 45, 46. Command to go forth from Babylon.
v | 47-49. Judgments on images.
u | 50, 51. Command to go forth from Babylon.
v | 52-56. Judgments on images.

45 soul. Heb. *nephesh*. Ap. 13.
47 do judgment upon = visit upon.
48 the heaven . . . shall sing. Fig. *Pæanismos* and *Prosopopœia* (Ap. 6).
all that is therein. Cp. Rev. 19. 1-3.
49 all the earth. Cp. Isa. 14. 16, 17.

496? stand not still: remember °the LORD afar off,
and let Jerusalem come into your mind."

51 We are confounded, because we have heard reproach: shame hath covered our faces: for strangers are come into the sanctuaries of [1]the LORD'S house.

v (p. 1093) 52 "Wherefore, [1]behold, the days come, [24]saith [1]the LORD, that I will [47]do judgment upon her graven images: and through all her land the wounded shall groan.

53 Though Babylon should °mount up to heaven, and though she should fortify the height of her strength, *yet* from Me shall spoilers come unto her, [24]saith [1]the LORD."

54 A sound of a cry *cometh* from Babylon, and great [8]destruction from the land of the Chaldeans:

55 Because [1]the LORD hath spoiled Babylon, and °destroyed out of her the great voice; when her waves do roar like great waters, a noise of their voice is uttered:

56 Because the spoiler is come upon her, *even* upon Babylon, and her [30]mighty men are taken, every one of their bows is broken: for [1]the LORD °GOD of recompences shall surely requite.

M 57 "And I will make drunk her princes, and her wise *men*, her captains, and her rulers, and her [30]mighty men: and they shall sleep a perpetual sleep, and not wake, [24]saith the King, Whose name *is* [5]the [1]LORD of hosts.

N 58 Thus saith [5]the [1]LORD of hosts; "The broad °walls of Babylon shall be utterly broken, and her high gates shall be burned with fire; and the °people shall labour in vain, and the folk in the fire, and they shall °be weary."

B w (p. 1094) 484 59 The word which Jeremiah the prophet commanded °Seraiah the son of Neriah, the son of Maaseiah, °when he went with Zedekiah the king of Judah into Babylon in the fourth year of his reign. And *this* Seraiah *was* a °quiet prince.

60 So Jeremiah °wrote in a book all the °evil that should come upon Babylon, *even* all these words that are written against Babylon.

x 61 And Jeremiah said to [59]Seraiah, "When thou comest to Babylon, °and shalt see and shalt read all these words;

y 62 Then shalt thou say, 'O [1]LORD, Thou hast spoken against this place, to cut it off, that none shall remain in it, neither man nor beast, but that it shall be °desolate [26]for ever.'

x 63 And it shall be, when thou hast made an end of reading this book,

w *that* thou shalt bind a stone to it, and cast it into the midst of Euphrates:

64 And thou shalt say, 'Thus shall Babylon sink, and shall not rise from the °evil that I will bring upon her: and they shall be weary.'"

B (p. 1015) Thus far *are* the words of Jeremiah.

A O (p. 1094) 488–477 **52** °Zedekiah *was* one and twenty years old when he began to reign, and he reigned eleven years in Jerusalem. And his mother's name *was* Hamutal the daughter of Jeremiah of Libnah.

50 the LORD. Heb. Jehovah (with *'eth*). Ap. 4. II.

53 mount up, &c. Cp. Isa. 14. 12–15.

55 destroyed = caused to perish. Heb. *'ābar*. Not the same as in *vv.* 1, 3, 8, 11, 20, 25, 54.

56 GOD. Heb. El. Ap. 4. IV. The Heb. reads "El of recompences, Jehovah".

58 walls. Some codices, with two early printed editions, Sept., and Vulg., read "wall".
people = peoples. be weary = faint.

51. 59–64– (*B*, p. 1088). WORD OF JEREMIAH TO SERAIAH. (RATIFICATION.)
(*Introversion.*)

B | w | 59, 60. The book sent.
  x | 61. Reading begun.
   y | 62. Words spoken.
  x | 63–. Reading ended.
 w | –63, 64–. The book sunk.

The FIFTY-FIRST Prophecy of Jeremiah (p. 1015).

59 Seraiah. The brother of Baruch (32. 12. Cp. 45. 1).
when he went, &c. Probably to renew his oath of allegiance. Cp. 27. 1; 28. 1.
quiet prince. Probably chief chamberlain. R.V. marg., "quartermaster." Heb. = quiet resting-place (Isa. 32. 18). Probably his office was to prepare the night's camping place during the journey to Babylon.

60 wrote in a book = wrote in one scroll.
evil = calamity. Heb. *rā'a'*. Ap. 44. viii.

61 and shalt see, &c. = then shalt thou look out and read.

62 desolate for ever = age-abiding desolations, showing that this prophecy must wait a future fulfilment.

64 evil. Heb. *rā'a'*. Ap. 44. viii.

52. 1–34 (*A*, p. 1015). APPENDIX.
(*Introversion.*)

A | O | 1–3. Zedekiah and Nebuchadnezzar.
  P | 4–27. Captivity. The great one.
  P | 28–30. Captivities. The three lesser.
 O | 31–34. Jehoiakim and Evil-Merodach.

Similar to ch. 39, but with additional details.

1 Zedekiah. Cp. 2 Kings 24. 18–20. Reigned from 489 to 477 B.C. **2** evil. Heb. *rā'a'*. Ap. 44. viii.
the LORD. Heb. Jehovah. Ap. 4. II.

52. 4–27 (P, above). CAPTIVITY: THE GREAT.
(*Alternations and Introversion.*)

P | Q | a | 4, 5. Jerusalem besieged.
   b | 6. Consequence. Famine.
  a | 7–. Jerusalem taken.
   b | –7. Consequence. Flight.
    R | 8–11. Executions at Riblah.
 Q | c | 12–14. The Temple burned.
   d | 15. The poor taken.
   d | 16. The poor left.
  c | 17–23. The Temple spoiled.
 R | 24–27. Executions at Riblah.

4 ninth year. Cp. 2 Kings 25. 1–21.

2 And he did *that which was* °evil in the eyes of °the LORD, according to all that Jehoiakim had done.

3 For through the anger of [2]the LORD it came to pass in Jerusalem and Judah, till He had cast them out from His presence, that Zedekiah rebelled against the king of Babylon.

4 And it came to pass in the °ninth year of P Q a 479
his reign, in the tenth month, in the tenth *day* of the month, *that* Nebuchadrezzar king of Babylon came, he and all his army, against Jerusalem, and pitched against it, and built forts against it round about.

5 So the city was besieged unto the eleventh 477
year of king Zedekiah.

b 6 And in the fourth month, in the ninth *day*
477 of the month, °the famine was sore in the city,
so that there was no bread for the People of
the land.

a 7 Then the city was broken up,
(p. 1094) b and all the °men of war °fled, and went forth
out of the city by night by the way of the gate
°between the two walls, which *was* by °the
king's garden; (now the Chaldeans *were* by
the city round about:) and they went by the
way of the plain.

R 8 But the army of the Chaldeans pursued
after the king, and overtook Zedekiah in the
plains of Jericho; and all his army was scattered from him.

9 Then they took the king, and carried him
up unto the king of Babylon to °Riblah in the
land of Hamath; where he gave judgment
upon him.

10 And the king of Babylon slew the sons of
Zedekiah before his eyes: he slew also all the
princes of Judah in [9]Riblah.

11 Then he °put out the eyes of Zedekiah;
and the king of Babylon bound him in chains,
and carried him to Babylon, and put him in
prison till the day of his death.

Q c 12 Now in the fifth month, in the °tenth *day*
of the month, which *was* the nineteenth year
of Nebuchadrezzar king of Babylon, came Nebuzar-adan, captain of the guard, *which* served
the king of Babylon, °into Jerusalem,

13 And burned the house of [2]the LORD, and
the king's house; and all the houses of Jerusalem, and all the houses of the great *men*,
burned he with fire:

14 And all the army of the Chaldeans, that
were with the captain of the guard, brake
down all the walls of Jerusalem round about.

d 15 Then Nebuzar-adan the captain of the
guard carried away captive *certain* of °the
poor of the People, and the residue of the People that remained in the city, and those that
fell away, that fell to the king of Babylon, and
the rest of the multitude.

d 16 But Nebuzar-adan the captain of the guard
left *certain* of [15]the poor of the land for vinedressers and for husbandmen.

c 17 Also the °pillars of brass that *were* in the
house of [2]the LORD, and the bases, and the
brasen sea that *was* in the house of [2]the LORD,
the Chaldeans brake, and carried all the brass
of them to Babylon.

18 The caldrons also, and °the shovels, and
the snuffers, and the °bowls, and the spoons,
and all the vessels of brass wherewith they
ministered, took they away.

19 And the basons, and the °firepans, and
the bowls, and the caldrons, and the °candlesticks, and the spoons, and the cups; *that*
which *was* of gold *in* gold, and *that* which *was*
of silver *in* silver, took the captain of the
guard away.

20 The two pillars, one sea, and twelve brasen
bulls that *were* °under the bases, which king
Solomon had made in the house of [2]the
LORD: the brass of all these vessels was without weight.

21 And *concerning* the °pillars, the height of
one pillar *was* eighteen °cubits; and a fillet of
twelve °cubits did compass it; and the thickness thereof *was* four fingers: *it was* hollow.

22 And a °chapiter of brass *was* upon it;
and the height of one chapiter *was* five cubits, with network and pomegranates upon
the chapiters round about, all *of* brass. The
second pillar also and the pomegranates *were*
like unto these.

23 And there were °ninety and six pomegranates °on a side; *and* all the pomegranates
upon the network *were* an hundred round
about.

24 And the captain of the guard took °Seraiah the chief priest, and Zephaniah the R
second priest, and the three keepers of the
°door:

25 He took also out of the city an eunuch,
which had the charge of the [7]men of war; and
°seven [7]men of them that were near the king's
person, which were found in the city; and the
principal scribe of the host, who mustered the
People of the land; and threescore °men of
the People of the land, that were found in the
midst of the city.

26 So Nebuzar-adan the captain of the guard
took them, and brought them to the king of
Babylon to Riblah.

27 And the king of Babylon smote them, and
put them to death in [9]Riblah in the land of
Hamath. Thus Judah was carried away captive out of his own °land.

28 This *is* the people whom Nebuchadrezzar P
carried away captive: in °the seventh year 490
three thousand Jews and three and twenty:

---

6 the famine. Described in the Lamentations of Jeremiah. See note on Gen. 12. 10.

7 men. Heb. pl. of *'ĕnôsh*. Ap. 14. III.

fled, &c. Cp. 2 Kings 25. 4.

between the two walls . . . king's garden. See Ap. 68.

9 Riblah. Now *Ribleh*. On the east bank of the Orontes, thirty-five miles north-east of Baalbek.

11 put out the eyes. See note on 32. 4. Cp. 2 Kings 25. 6, 7. Ezek. 12. 13. Hence, Zedekiah never *saw* Babylon, though he was taken thither.

12 tenth day. In 2 Kings 25. 8 it says "seventh day", but that was "[to] Jerusalem". This is "into Jerusalem". **into**=in.

15 the poor of the people. This is supplemental to 2 Kings 25. 12. Heb. *dal*=impoverished. See note on "poverty", Prov. 6. 11. Cp. Neh. 1. 3.

17 pillars of brass. Cp. 27. 19.

18 the shovels, &c. Ref. to Pent. (Ex. 27. 3, &c.). **bowls**=bowls for sprinkling.

19 firepans=censers. **candlesticks**=lamps.

20 under=beneath.

21 pillars. Cp. 1 Kings 7. 15. 2 Kings 25. 17.

cubits. See Ap. 51. III. 2 (1).

22 chapiter=capital.

23 ninety and six. There were 100 "round about"; Cp. 2 Chron. 3. 16; 4. 13; with 1 Kings 7. 20.

on a side. Heb. *rūach*. See Ap. 9. ix= towards the air, or open air. The other four being behind, out of sight.

24 Seraiah. See 2 Kings 25. 18. 1 Chron. 6. 14. Cp. 51. 59. **door**=threshold.

25 seven. In 2 Kings 25. 19 "five"; but the greater includes the lesser. **men.** Heb. *'īsh*. Ap. 14. II.

27 land=soil.

28 the seventh year. This was at the beginning of Nebuchadrezzar's second siege, the year before Jehoiachin's captivity, 490 B.C.

478 29 In °the eighteenth year of Nebuchadrezzar
he carried away captive from Jerusalem eight
hundred thirty and two °persons:
473 30 In the °three and twentieth year of Nebuchadrezzar Nebuzar-adan the captain of the
guard carried away captive of the Jews seven
hundred forty and five [29] persons: all the
[29] persons *were* four thousand and six hundred.

0 (p. 1094) 31 And it came to pass in the °seven and
452 thirtieth year of the captivity of °Jehoiachin
king of Judah, in the twelfth month, in the
°five and twentieth *day* of the month, *that*
°Evil-merodach king of Babylon in the *first*
year of his reign °lifted up the head of °Jehoi-
achin king of Judah, and brought him forth
out of prison,
32 And spake °kindly unto him, and set his
throne above the throne of the kings that
were with him in Babylon,
33 And changed his prison garments: and he
did continually eat °bread before him all the
days of his life.
34 And *for* his diet, there was a continual
diet given him of the king of Babylon, every
day a portion °until the day of his death, all
the days of his life.

29 the eighteenth year of Nebuchadrezzar was the second year of his third and last siege, or 478 B.C.
persons = souls. Heb. *nephesh*. Ap. 13.
30 three and twentieth year. Four years after the fall of Jerusalem. Another contact of Bible and secular chronology, 473 B.C. See Ap. 86.
31 seven and thirtieth year. Cp. 2 Kings 25. 27-30. See Ap. 50, pp. 60, 67, and throughout.
Jehoiachin. Elsewhere in this book called "Jeconiah" (24. 1; 29. 2), or "Coniah" (22. 24, 28).
five and twentieth. The order given then, but probably not carried out till the "seven and twentieth", according to 2 Kings 25. 27.
Evil-merodach. The son of Nebuchadnezzar.
lifted up the head. Heb. idiom for releasing. Ref. to Pent. (Gen. 40. 13, 20). Ap. 92.
32 kindly unto him = good things with him.
33 bread. Put by Fig. *Synecdoche* (of the Part), Ap. 6, for all kinds of food.
34 until, &c. Note the items above, which are supplemental to 2 Kings 25.

LONGER NOTE ON JEREMIAH 42—44.

"THE JEWS WHICH DWELL IN THE LAND OF EGYPT" (Jer. 44. 1).

As the end of the kingdom of Judah drew near, many of the Jews were determined to go into Egypt; and this in spite of the warning given by Jehovah through Jeremiah.

In Jer. 44 we have the latest prophecy concerning those who had gone thither; which declared that they should not escape, but should be consumed there (44. 27, &c.). This prophecy must have been fulfilled concerning that generation; but their successors, or others that subsequently followed, continued there a little longer, until the time came for Egypt itself to fall into the hands of Babylon.

Recent discoveries of *Papyri* in the ruins of *Elephantine* (an island in the Nile, opposite Assouan), dating from the fifth century B.C., bear witness to two great facts:—

(1) That Jews were then dwelling there (in 424-405 B.C.).

(2) That they were observing the Feast of the Passover, "as it is written in the law of Moses".

The importance of these *Papyri* lies in the fact that modern critics confidently assert and assume that the greater part of the Pentateuch was not written till after the Exile; and even then neither collectively as a whole, nor separately in its distinctive books.

In Ap. 92 it is shown that all through the prophets (who lived at the time of the kings in whose reigns they prophesied) there is a constant reference to the books of the Pentateuch, which conclusively proves that their contents were well known both to the prophets themselves and those whom they addressed.

The Pentateuch, being full of legal expressions, technical ceremonial terms, and distinctive phraseology, affords abundant evidence of the above fact, and makes it easy to call continuous attention to it in the notes of *The Companion Bible*.

But there is further evidence found in the *Papyri* now discovered in the ruins at *Elephantine* in Upper Egypt.

They show that the Jews who dwelt there had a temple of their own and offered up sacrifices therein. That once, when this their temple was destroyed by the Egyptians, they appealed to the Persian governor of Judah, asking permission to restore it (*Papyrus* I).

There is a list preserved, registering the contributions towards the upkeep of the temple (containing the names of many ladies).

But the most interesting and important of these *Papyri* is one dated in the year 419 B.C., which is a Passover "announcement" of the approaching feast, such as were made from the earliest times to the present day (see Neh. 8. 15), containing a brief epitome of its laws and requirements. This particular announcement shows that the following passages were well known: Ex. 12. 16. Lev. 23. 7, 8. Num. 9. 1-14. Deut. 16. 6.

This *Papyrus* has been recently published by Professor Edward Sachau, of Berlin: *Aramäische Papyrus und Ostraka aus einer jüdischen Militärkolonie zu Elephantine. Altorientalische Sprachdenkmäler des 5. Jahrhunderts vor Chr., mit 75 Lichtdrucktafelein.* Leipzig, 1911. A small edition (texts only) by Professor Ungnad, of Jena, is published also under the title of *Aramäische Papyrus aus Elephantine.*

Nearly 2,400 years, since this announcement by Hananjah to the Jews in Egypt, have gone by. Elephantine is now a heap of ruins. The colony of Jews has passed away (unless the "Falashas" of Abyssinia are their descendants), but the Jewish nation still exists, and continues to keep the Passover, a standing witness to their truth of holy Scripture.

THE LAMENTATIONS OF JEREMIAH.

THE STRUCTURE OF THE BOOK AS A WHOLE.

(*Extended Alternations and Introversion.*)

A[1] | A[1] | 1. 1-7. JUDGMENTS. (*Aleph* (א = A) to *Zayin* (ז = Z).)

  B[1] | D[1] | 1. 8-11. ZION. CONFESSION. (*Cheth* (ח = Ḥ) to *Kaph* (כ = K).)

    E[1] | 1. 12, 13. APPEAL TO PASSERS BY. (*Lamed* (ל = L) to *Mem* (מ = M).)

   D[2] | 1. 14-18-. ZION. CONFESSION. (*Nun*) (נ = N) to *Tzaddi* (צ = Ẓ).)

    E[2] | 1. -18, 19. APPEAL TO PASSERS BY. (*Koph*, ק = Ḳ.)

  C[1] | 1. 20-22. PRAYER. (*Resh* (ר = R) to *Tau* (ת = T).)

A[2] | A[2] | 2. 1-13. THE JUDGE. (*Aleph* (א = A) to *Mem* (מ = M).)

  B[2] | D[3] | 2. 14. ZION. SIN UNCONFESSED. (*Nun*, נ = N.)

    E[3] | 2. 15-17. RECRIMINATION OF PASSERS BY. (*Samech* (ס = S) to *Pe* (פ = P).)

  C[2] | 2. 18-22. PRAYER. (*Tzaddi* (צ = Z) to *Tau* (ת = T).)

A[3] | A[3] | 3. 1-21. THE JUDGE. (*Aleph* (א = A) to *Zayin* (ז = Z).)

  B[3] | E[4] | 3. 22-36. REMEMBRANCE OF JEHOVAH'S MERCIES. (*Cheth* (ח = Ḥ) to *Lamed* (ל = L).)

   D[4] | 3. 37-51. ZION. SIN CONFESSED. (*Mem* (מ = M) to *Pe* (פ = P).)

  C[3] | 3. 52-66. PRAYER. (*Tzaddi* (צ = Ẓ) to *Tau* (ת = T).)

A[4] | A[4] | 4. 1-12. JUDGMENTS. (*Aleph* (א = A) to *Lamed* (ל = L).)

  B[4] | D[5] | 4. 13-20. ZION. CONFESSION. (*Mem* (מ = M) to *Resh* (ר = R).)

    E[5] | 4. 21, 22. RETRIBUTION OF JEHOVAH. (*Shin* (ש = S) to *Tau* (ת = T).)

  C[4] | 5. 1-22. PRAYER.

For the place of Lamentations in the Hebrew Canon, see Ap. 1, where it is found to be the central book of the five *M^egillōth* (or scrolls).

The book consists of five Elegies on the destruction of Jerusalem; and not, as Josephus supposed, on the death of Josiah (*Ant. Jud.* L. x, c. 5, § 1), basing his opinion on 2 Chron. 35. 25.

This book is appropriately read on the Fast of the ninth day of the fifth month (Ab, our August. See Ap. 51. V). For on that day are still commemorated the five great calamities which befell the nation, viz.:—

1. The return of the twelve spies, and the decree of the forty years' wanderings in consequence of the rebellion of the People.
2. The destruction of the first Temple by Nebuchadnezzar.
3. The destruction of the second Temple by the Romans under Titus.
4. The taking of Bether by the Romans under Hadrian, when 580,000 were slain.
5. The ploughing of Zion like a field, in fulfilment of Jer. 26. 18, &c. and Micah 3. 12.

The five Elegies are arranged in a remarkable manner:—

The *first two* (chapters 1 and 2) consist of twenty-two long verses of three lines each, each verse respectively commencing with the successive letters of the alphabet.

The *third* (chap. 3) consists of sixty-six verses (3 × 22), each triad of verses commencing with the same letter: e.g. the first three lines commence with א (*Aleph*), the next three with ב (*Beth*), and so on through the twenty-two letters of the alphabet.

The *fourth* (chap. 4) is arranged in twenty-two long verses of two lines each, also arranged acrostically.

The *fifth* (chap. 5) Lamentation is resolved into a prayer, and the acrostic arrangement gives way before the outburst of emotion. The only connection with the alphabet is that the number of the verses corresponds with the number of letters (twenty-two).

The Septuagint (followed by the Arabic and Vulgate versions) prefaces its version with these words: "It came to pass that, after Israel was taken captive and Jerusalem was made desolate, Jeremiah sat weeping, and lamented with this lamentation over Jerusalem, and said . . ."

The Arabic *Targum* begins its paraphrase thus: "Jeremiah the prophet, and great priest, said . . ."

THE °LAMENTATIONS OF JEREMIAH.

A[1] A[1] (p. 1097) **1** (א) °HOW doth the city sit °solitary, *that was* full of people! *how* is she become as a widow! she *that was* great among the nations, *and* princess among the provinces, *how* is she become tributary!

2 (ב) She °weepeth sore in the night, and her tears *are* on her cheeks: among all her °lovers she hath none to comfort *her:* all her friends have dealt treacherously with her, they are become her °enemies.

3 (ג) Judah is gone into captivity because of affliction, and because of great servitude: she dwelleth °among the °heathen, she findeth no rest: all her °persecutors overtook her °between the straits.

4 (ד) °The ways of Zion do °mourn, because none come to the °solemn feasts: all her gates are desolate: her priests sigh, her virgins are afflicted, and she *is* in °bitterness.

5 (ה) Her adversaries °are the chief, her enemies prosper; for °the LORD hath afflicted her for the multitude of her °transgressions: her °children are gone into captivity before the enemy.

6 (ו) And from the daughter of Zion all her beauty is departed: her princes are become °like harts *that* find no pasture, and they are gone without strength before the pursuer.

7 (ז) Jerusalem remembered in the days of her affliction and of her miseries all her °pleasant things that she had in the days of old, when her People fell into the hand of the enemy, and none did help her: the adversaries saw her, *and* did mock at her °sabbaths.

B[1] D[1] 8 (ח) Jerusalem hath °grievously °sinned; therefore she °is removed: all that honoured her despise her, because they have seen her nakedness: yea, she sigheth, and turneth backward.

9 (ט) Her filthiness *is* in her skirts; she °remembereth not her °last end; therefore she came down °wonderfully: she had no comforter. O [5] LORD, °behold my affliction: for the enemy hath magnified *himself.*

10 (י) The adversary hath spread out his hand upon all her [7] pleasant things: for she hath seen *that* the heathen °entered into her sanctuary, whom Thou didst command *that* they should not enter into Thy °congregation.

11 (כ) All her People sigh, they seek bread; they have given their [7] pleasant things for meat to relieve the °soul: see, O [5] LORD, and consider; for I am become vile.

E[1] 12 (ל) *Is it* nothing to you, all ye that pass by? °behold, and see if there °be any °sorrow like unto my sorrow, which is °done unto me, wherewith [5] the LORD hath afflicted *me* in the day of His fierce anger.

13 (מ) From above hath He sent fire into my bones, and it prevaileth against them: He hath spread a net for my feet, He hath turned

---

TITLE. In the Hebrew text the name of the book is its first word, *'Ēykah* = ALAS! The Talmud (Tract, *Baha Bathra*, fol. 14b) calls it *Ḳīnōth* = dirges or elegies. The Sept. has *Thrēnoi*, with the same meaning. The Vulg. has *Threni*, i.e. *Lamentationes* and *Lamenta*.

1 How = Alas! or, O how! Heb. *'ēykah* = an exclamation of pain and grief, a wailing cry (preserved in Eng. "*jackal*"). The *Massōrah* (Ap. 30) points out that this exclamation is used by three prophets, concerning Israel: (1) by Moses in her multiplication (Deut. 1. 12. Cp. *v.* 11); (2) by Isaiah in her dissipation (Isa. 1. 21); (3) by Jeremiah in her desolation (Lam. 1. 1). This word "How" is to be supplied at the beginning of *vv.* 2 and 3 by Fig. *Ellipsis* (Ap. 6). Cp. also 2. 1; 4. 1; and Isa. 14. 12.

solitary: i.e. empty; referring to the houses and streets.

2 weepeth sore. Note Fig. *Polyptōton* (Ap. 6). The Heb. = a weeping she weepeth. Thus well rendered. See note on Gen. 26. 28; and note the Fig. *Prosopopœia* (Ap. 6).

lovers: i.e. allies, whom she had preferred to Jehovah. See Jer. 2. 17, 27, 36, 37; 4. 30; 22. 22. Ezek. 23; and 29. 6, 7, 16.

enemies. Especially the Edomites and Ammonites. Cp. Jer. 12. 14.

3 among the heathen. Ref. to Pent. (Deut. 28. 64, 65).

heathen = nations.

persecutors = pursuers.

between the straits. Like a hunted animal driven where there is no escape. Same word as in Pss. 116. 3; 118. 5. Occurs only in these three places. Cp. *v.* 6.

4 The ways. Not streets in the city, but the roads leading thereto.

mourn. Fig. *Prosopopœia.* Ap. 6.

solemn feasts = appointed feasts. See note on Ps. 74. 8 (same word).

bitterness = bitter for her. Instead of festal joy. Cp. Jer. 7. 34; 16. 9; 25. 10; 31. 13; 33. 11.

5 are the chief = are the head. Ref. to Pent. (Deut. 28. 13, 44), the same word. Ap. 92.

the LORD. Heb. Jehovah. Ap. 4. II.

transgressions = rebellions. Heb. *pāsha'*. Ap. 44. ix.

children = young children, as in 2. 11, 19, 20; and 4. 4. Not "sons". **6 like harts.** See note on *v.* 3.

7 pleasant things. Heb. = things of desire. Put by Fig. *Metonymy* (of Adjunct), Ap. 6, for the things she used to enjoy.

sabbaths: or, sabbath-keepings; which she had herself profaned. See Jer. 17. 21–23. Ezek. 22. 8, 26; 23. 38.

8 grievously sinned. Note the Fig. *Polyptōton* (Ap. 6). Heb. = sinned a sin. Thus well rendered. See note on "weepeth sore" (*v.* 2).

sinned. Heb. *chāṭā'*. Ap. 44. i.

is removed = separated as unclean.

9 remembereth = remembered.

last end = hereafter.

wonderfully. Heb. pl. "wonders" = a great wonder.

behold = see, behold. Same word as in *vv.* 18, 20. Not the same word as in *v.* 12.

10 entered into her sanctuary. Ref. to Pent. (Deut. 23. 3), a technical expression. Ap. 92.

congregation = convocation, or assembly.

11 soul. Heb. *nephesh.* Ap. 13.

12 behold = look attentively. Not the same word as in *vv.* 9, 18, 20. **be** = exists. Heb. *yēsh.* See Gen. 18. 24. Prov. 8. 21; 18. 24, &c. **sorrow** = pain.

done unto me. Cp. *v.* 22; 3. 15.

me back: He hath made me desolate *and*
faint all the day.
D² (p. 1097) 14 (נ) °The yoke of my [5]transgressions is
bound by His hand: they are °wreathed, *and*
come up upon my neck: °He hath made my
strength to °fall, °the LORD* hath delivered
me into *their* hands, *from whom* I am not able
to rise up.
15 (ס) [14]The LORD* hath trodden under foot
all my °mighty *men* in the midst of me: He
hath °called °an assembly against me to
crush my young men: [14]the LORD* hath trodden the virgin, the daughter of Judah, *as* in
a °winepress.
16 (ע) For these *things* I [2]weep; °mine eye,
mine eye runneth down with water, because
the comforter that should °relieve my [11]soul
is far from me: my °children are desolate, because the enemy prevailed.
17 (פ) Zion spreadeth forth her hands, *and*
there is none to comfort her: [5]the LORD hath
commanded concerning °Jacob, *that* his adversaries *should be* round about him: Jerusalem is as a menstruous woman among them.
18 (צ) [5]The LORD °is righteous; for I have
rebelled against His commandment:
E² hear, I pray you, all °people, and [9]behold my
[12]sorrow: my virgins and my young men are
gone into captivity.
19 (ק) I [15]called for my [2]lovers, *but* they deceived me: my priests and mine elders °gave up
the ghost in the city, while they sought their
meat to relieve their [11]souls.
C¹ 20 (ר) °Behold, O [5]LORD; for I *am* in distress: my bowels are troubled; mine heart is
turned within me; for I have grievously rebelled: °abroad the sword bereaveth, at home
there is as death.
21 (ש) They have heard that I sigh: *there is*
none to comfort me: all mine enemies have
heard of my trouble; they are glad that Thou
hast done *it:* Thou wilt bring °the day *that* Thou
hast [15]called, and they shall be like unto me.
22 (ת) °Let all their °wickedness come before
Thee; and do unto them, °as Thou hast [12]done
unto me for all my °transgressions: for my
sighs *are* many, and my heart *is* faint.

A² A² **2** (א) How hath °the LORD* covered the
daughter of Zion with a cloud in His
anger, *and* cast down from heaven unto the
earth °the beauty of °Israel, and remembered
not °His footstool in the day of His anger!
2 (ב) [1]The LORD* hath °swallowed up all the
°habitations of Jacob, and hath not pitied: He
hath thrown down in His wrath the strong
holds of the daughter of Judah; He hath
brought *them* down to the ground: He hath
polluted the kingdom and the princes thereof.
3 (ג) He hath cut off in *His* fierce anger all the
°horn of Israel: He hath drawn back His
°right hand from before the enemy, and He
burned against Jacob like a flaming fire, *which*
devoureth round about.
4 (ד) He hath bent °His bow like an enemy:
He stood with His right hand as an adversary, and slew °all *that were* pleasant to the
°eye in the °tabernacle of the daughter of
°Zion: He poured out His fury like fire.
5 (ה) [1]The LORD* was as an enemy: He hath
swallowed up Israel, He hath swallowed up
all °her palaces: He hath destroyed His strong
holds, and hath increased in the daughter of
Judah °mourning and lamentation.
6 (ו) And He hath violently taken away His
°tabernacle, °as *if it were of* a garden: He
hath destroyed His places of the assembly:
°the LORD hath caused the °solemn feasts and

14 The yoke, &c. Ref. to Pent. (Deut. 28. 48), the same words. Ap. 92. **wreathed** = intertwined.
He: or, It: i.e. the yoke. **fall** = stumble.
the LORD*. One of the 134 places where the *Sōpherim* say they changed Jehovah to Adonai. See Ap. 32.
15 mighty men = valiant ones. Heb. *'abīr*. Not the same word as in 3. 1, 27, 35, 39.
called = proclaimed. Same word as in *vv.* 19, 21.
an assembly = a festal gathering. Now that Israel's feasts had ceased, there was another of a different nature and with a different object.
winepress. Heb. *gath*, where the grapes were trodden. Not the vat (*yekeb*) into which the juice was received.
16 mine eye, mine eye. Fig. *Epizeuxis* (Ap. 6), for emphasis. It is not repeated in the Sept.
relieve my soul = bring me back to life. Cp. *v.* 19.
children = sons. Not the same word as in 2. 11, 19, 20 and 4. 4.
17 Jacob. Referring to the natural seed. See notes on Gen. 32. 28; 43. 6; 45. 26, 28. Cp. 2. 1.
18 is. Heb. = He [is]. **people** = peoples.
19 gave up the ghost = expired, or breathed their last.
20 Behold. Here begins the prayer. See the Structure C¹, on p. 1097.
abroad the sword. Ref. to Pent. (Deut. 32. 25).
21 the day: i.e. the day of vengeance of Jer. 25. 17–26.
22 Let all, &c. This prayer is in accordance with that Dispensation. Not with this. See Ap. 63. IX.
wickedness. Heb. *rā'a'*. Ap. 44. viii.
as = according as.
transgressions = rebellions. Heb. *pāsha'*. Ap. 44. ix. Cp. 3. 42.

2. 1 the LORD*. One of the 134 places where the *Sōpherīm* say they altered "Jehovah" of the primitive text to "Adonai". See Ap. 32.
the beauty of Israel. Probably referring to the Temple (Isa. 64. 11), or the heroic defenders of Jerusalem (2 Sam. 1. 19).
Israel. Referring to the spiritual seed. See note on 1. 17.
His footstool. Probably referring to the ark of the covenant (1 Chron. 28. 2), or the sanctuary (Pss. 99. 5; 132. 7. Isa. 60. 13).
2 swallowed up: i.e. as by an earthquake.
habitations = the open villages of the shepherds, in contrast with the strongholds of the next lines.
3 horn. Put by Fig. *Metonymy* (of Cause), Ap. 6, for the self-protection afforded by it.
right hand. Fig. *Anthropopatheia.* Ap. 6.
4 His bow. Fig. *Anthropopatheia.* Ap. 6.
all that were pleasant to the eye. Heb. = all the desires of the eye; "eye" being put by Fig. *Metonymy* (of the Adjunct), Ap. 6, for the things desired by it.
eye. Transfer here the colon which is wrongly placed after Zion.
tabernacle = tent. Heb. *'ohel.* Ap. 40. 3.
Zion: place this colon after "eye" in preceding line, and connect Zion with the verb which follows.
5 her. Ginsburg thinks it should be "His".
mourning and lamentation. Note the Fig. *Paronomasia* (Ap. 6). Heb. *taănīyyāh vaănīyyah.*
6 tabernacle = dwelling, or pavilion. Heb. *sok.* Occurs only here.
as if it were of a garden: or, as [a booth in] a garden [is destroyed]. See note on Isa. 1. 8. Sept. reads "like a vine". Ginsburg thinks "like a thief".
the LORD. Heb. Jehovah. Ap. 4. II.
solemn feasts = appointed seasons.

sabbaths to be forgotten in Zion, and hath despised in the indignation of His anger the king and the priest.

7 (ז) [1] The LORD* hath cast off His altar, He hath abhorred His sanctuary, He hath given up into the hand of the enemy the walls of her palaces; they have made a noise in the house of [6] the LORD, as in the day of a [6] solemn feast.

8 (ח) [6] The LORD hath purposed to destroy the wall of the daughter of Zion: He hath stretched out a line, He hath not withdrawn His hand from °destroying: therefore He made the rampart and the wall to lament; they languished together.

9 (ט) Her gates are sunk into the °ground; He hath destroyed and broken her bars: °her king and her princes *are* among the °Gentiles: °the law *is* no *more;* her prophets also find no vision from [6] the LORD.

10 (י) The elders of the daughter of Zion sit upon the [9] ground, *and* keep silence: they have cast up dust upon their heads; they have °girded themselves °with sackcloth: the virgins of Jerusalem hang down their heads to the ground.

11 (כ) Mine eyes do fail with tears, my bowels are °troubled, my °liver is poured upon the earth, for the destruction of the daughter of my People; because the °children and the sucklings swoon in the streets of the city.

12 (ל) They say to their mothers, "Where *is* corn and °wine?" when they swooned as the wounded in the streets of the city, when their °soul was poured out into their mothers' bosom.

13 (מ) What thing shall I take to witness for thee? what thing shall I liken to thee, O daughter of Jerusalem? what shall I equal to thee, that I may comfort thee, O virgin daughter of Zion? for thy breach *is* great like the sea: who can heal thee?

B^2 D^3 (p. 1097) 14 (נ) Thy °prophets have seen vain and foolish things for thee: and they have not discovered thine °iniquity, to °turn away thy captivity; but have seen for thee false °burdens and °causes of banishment.

E^3 15 (ס) All that °pass by clap *their* hands at thee; they hiss and wag their head at the daughter of Jerusalem, °*saying*, °"*Is* this the city that *men* call The perfection of beauty, The joy of the whole earth?"

16 (פ) °All thine enemies have opened their mouth against thee: they hiss and gnash the teeth: they say, "We have swallowed *her* up: certainly this *is* the day that we looked for; we have found, we have seen *it*."

17 °(ע) [6] The LORD hath done *that* which He had °devised; He hath fulfilled His word that He had commanded in the days of old: He hath thrown down, and hath not pitied: and He hath caused *thine* enemy to rejoice over thee, He hath set up the horn of thine adversaries.

C^2 18 (צ) Their heart °cried unto [1] the LORD*, O wall of the daughter of Zion, let tears run down like a river day and night: give thyself no rest; let not the apple of thine eye cease.

19 (ק) Arise, cry out in the night: in the beginning of the watches pour out thine heart like water before the face of °the [1] LORD*: lift up thy hands toward Him for the °life of thy young [11] children, that faint for hunger in the top of every street.

20 (ר) Behold, O [6] LORD, and °consider to whom Thou hast done this. °Shall the women eat their fruit, *and* [11] children of a °span long? shall the priest and the prophet be slain in the sanctuary of [1] the LORD*?

21 (ש) The young and the old lie on the ground in the streets: my virgins and my young men are fallen by the sword; Thou hast slain *them* in the day of Thine anger; Thou hast killed, *and* not pitied.

22 (ת) Thou hast called as in a °solemn day my °terrors round about, so that in the day of [6] the LORD'S anger none escaped nor remained: those that I have swaddled and brought up hath mine enemy consumed.

---

8 destroying = swallowing up.
9 ground = earth.
her king, &c. Ref. to Pent. (Deut. 28. 36). Ap. 92.
Gentiles = nations.
the law is no more: i.e. is no longer known and obeyed. Cp. Neh. 13. 1, and Esdras 14. 20, 21.
10 girded . . . with sackcloth. The outward symbol of mourning.
11 troubled = moved, or in ferment.
liver. Fig. for the seat of the emotions. Cp. Job 16. 13.
children = babes.
12 wine. Heb. *yayin.* Ap. 27. I.
soul. Heb. *nephesh.* Ap. 13.
14 prophets, &c. Cp. Ezek. 12. 24; 13. 1-16, 23; 21. 29; 22. 28.
iniquity. Heb. *'āvāh.* Ap. 44. iv.
turn away thy captivity = cause thy captives to return. See note on Deut. 30. 3.
burdens = oracles.
causes of banishment. Here, the Fig. *Metonymy* (of Effect), Ap. 6, is translated. Heb. = expulsions, which is put for the effect of listening to those who brought about the expulsion (Jer. 2. 8; 5. 31; 14. 14; 23. 16).
15 pass by = pass by the way.
saying. Note the *Ellipsis* of this verb, which is very frequent in Hebrew. See Pss. 109. 5; 144, 12, &c.
Is . . . ? Fig. *Erotēsis.* Ap. 6.
16 All, &c. In some Codices, with Syr., *vv.* 16 and 17 are transposed to bring the letters *Ayin* (ע = ') and *Pe* (פ = *P*) into alphabetical order. The Sept. leaves the verses, but transposes the letters. This is done because it is supposed to be a mistake. But it cannot be, because the same order appears in chs. 3 and 4, and in the former case it occurs three times, although the subject-matter allows no such break. It is easier to believe that the outward artificial form is sacrificed to call our attention to the greater importance of the utterance. In *v.* 16 we learn what the enemy thought and said; but, as the *Ayin* (ע) really precedes the *Pe* (פ), so we are reminded that this was only owing to Jehovah's purpose which had been revealed centuries before. See note on *v.* 17.
17 For the transposition of the Hebrew alphabet here, see note on *v.* 16, above.
devised. Ref. to Pent. (Lev. 26. 16, 17. Deut. 28. 15).
18 cried = cried (distressfully).
19 the LORD*. This is the reading in some Codices, with one early printed edition.
life = soul. Heb. *nephesh.* Ap. 13.
20 consider. Put a colon after "consider", and an "?" after "this".
Shall . . . ? Fig. *Erotēsis.* Ap. 6. Ref. to Pent. (Lev. 26. 29. Deut. 28. 53). Ap. 92.
span. See Ap. 51. III. 2 (4).
22 solemn day = day of assembly.
terrors round about. Cp. Jer. 6. 25; 20. 3, 10; 46. 5; 49. 29.

A³ A³ (p. 1097) 3 (א) ° I *am* the ° man *that* hath seen ° affliction by the rod of His wrath.
2 (א) He hath led me, and brought *me into* darkness, but not *into* light.
3 (א) Surely against me is He turned; He turneth his hand *against me* all the day.
4 (ב) My flesh and my skin hath He made old; He hath broken my bones.
5 (ב) He hath ° builded against me, and compassed *me* with ° gall and ° travel.
6 (ב) He hath ° set me in dark places, ° as *they that be* dead of old.
7 (ג) He hath hedged me about, that I cannot get out: He hath made my ° chain heavy.
8 (ג) Also when I cry and shout, He shutteth out my prayer.
9 (ג) He hath inclosed my ways with hewn stone, He hath made my paths ° crooked.
10 (ד) He *was* unto me *as* a bear lying in wait, *and* ° *as* a lion in secret places.
11 (ד) He hath turned aside my ways, and pulled me in pieces: He hath made me desolate.
12 (ד) He hath bent ° His bow, and set me as a mark for the arrow.
13 (ה) He hath caused the ° arrows of His quiver to enter into my reins.
14 (ה) I was a ° derision to ° all my People; *and* their ° song all the day.
15 (ה) He hath filled me with bitterness, He hath made me drunken with wormwood.
16 (ו) He hath also broken my teeth with gravel stones, He hath covered me with ashes.
17 (ו) And Thou hast removed my ° soul far off from peace: I forgat prosperity.
18 (ו) And I said, "My ° strength and my hope is perished from ° the LORD:"
19 (ז) ° Remembering mine affliction and my misery, the wormwood and the gall.
20 (ז) ° My [17] soul hath *them* still in remembrance, and is humbled in me.
21 (ז) This I recall to my ° mind, therefore have I ° hope.

B² E⁴ 22 (ח) *It is of* [18] the LORD'S ° mercies that we are not consumed, ° because His compassions fail not.
23 (ח) *They are* ° new ° every morning: great *is* Thy faithfulness.
24 (ח) [18] "The LORD *is* my portion," saith my [17] soul; "therefore will I hope in Him."
25 (ט) [18] The LORD *is* good unto them that ° wait for Him, to the [17] soul *that* seeketh Him.
26 (ט) *It is* good that *a man* should both hope and ° quietly wait for the salvation of [18] the LORD.
27 (ט) *It is* good for a [1] man that he bear the yoke in his youth.
28 (י) He sitteth alone and keepeth silence, because he hath borne *it* upon him.
29 (י) He putteth his mouth in the dust; if so be there may ° be hope.
30 (י) He ° giveth *his* cheek to him that smiteth him: he is filled full with reproach.
31 (כ) For ° the LORD* will not cast off for ever:
32 (כ) But though He cause grief, yet will He have compassion according to the multitude of His [22] mercies.
33 (כ) For He doth not afflict ° willingly nor grieve the ° children of ° men.
34 (ל) To crush under His feet all the prisoners of the earth,
35 (ל) To ° turn aside the right of a [1] man before the face of ° the MOST HIGH,
36 (ל) To subvert a ° man in his cause, [31] the LORD* approveth not.

3. 1 This chapter contains twenty-two verses: each verse having three lines: each line beginning with the same letter: and so, onward to the end of the alphabet.

I am the man. The prophet is representative of the nation, and speaks in the name of the whole. He is also typical and prophetical of Another, Who, in after years, took on Himself and bore the nation's sin. Ap. 85. The chapter must be read in connection with the Passion Psalms (Pss. 22, 69, 88). The Fig. is *Prosopopœia* (Ap. 6), by which the nation speaks as one man.

man = strong man. Heb. *geber*. Ap. 14. IV.

affliction: or, humiliation.

5 builded against = built up against.

gall. Cp. *v.* 19, and Ps. 69. 21, with Matt. 27. 34.

travel = travail, or labour. This line probably is put for the fortifications and the trench.

6 set me = made me to dwell.

as they, &c. = like the age-long dead.

7 chain = iron, or bronze. Put by Fig. *Metonymy* (of Cause), Ap. 6, for the fetters made of it. Cp. Judg. 16. 21 and 2 Kings 25. 7. 2 Chron. 33. 11; 36. 6. Jer. 39. 7; all of distinguished men.

9 crooked = to turn or wind back.

10 as a lion. See note on Ps. 22. 16.

12 His bow. Fig. *Anthropopatheia*. Ap. 6.

13 arrows = sons. Fig. *Hypocatastasis*. Ap. 6. As "sparks" are called "sons of the flame".

14 derision. Cp. Jer. 20. 8.

all my People. A special various reading called *Sevīr* (Ap. 34), with some codices, and Syr., read "all peoples".

song = mocking-song. Cp. *v.* 63 and Ps. 69. 12.

17 soul. Heb. *nephesh*. Ap. 13.

18 strength = strength (for endurance). Heb. *nēzaḥ*. See notes on Isa. 40. 9, 10, 26, 29, 31.

the LORD. Heb. Jehovah. Ap. 4. II.

19 Remembering = Remember.

20 My soul. The primitive reading was "Thy soul", which the *Sopherīm* have recorded, and state that they altered it to "My soul" (see Ap. 33), considering it an offensive *anthropomorphism*. By so doing they destroyed the logical sequence and deep pathos of the primitive text. The three verses (19, 20, 21) retranslated will show this:—

19 "Remember my humiliation and my misery,
The wormwood and the gall.
20 Yea, verily, Thou wilt remember,
And Thy soul will mourn over me.
21 This I bring back to my heart,
Therefore I shall have hope."

21 mind = heart.

hope = expectation.

22 mercies = lovingkindnesses.

because = verily. **23 new** = fresh.

every morning. Put by Fig. *Synecdoche* (of the Part), Ap. 6, for always and continually.

25 wait for Him. Ref. to Pent. (Gen. 49. 18, same word).

26 quietly wait = wait, and be silent.

29 be. See note on 1. 12.

30 giveth his cheek. Cp. Isa. 50. 6.

31 the LORD*. One of the 134 places where the *Sōpherīm* say they altered "Jehovah" of the primitive text to "Adonai". See Ap. 32. Here some codices, with two early printed editions, also read "Jehovah".

33 willingly = from His heart.

children = sons.

men. Heb. *'īsh* (sing.). Ap. 14. II.

35 turn aside, &c. Ref. to Pent. (Deut. 16. 19; 24. 17; 27. 19, same word). Ap. 92.

the MOST HIGH. Heb. *'Elyōn*. Ap. 4. VI.

36 man. Heb. *'ādām*. Ap. 14. I.

D⁴ (p. 1097) 37 (מ) Who *is* he *that* saith, and it cometh to pass, *when* [31]the LORD* commandeth *it* not?
38 (מ) Out of the mouth of [35]the MOST HIGH proceedeth not °evil and good?
39 (מ) Wherefore doth a living [36]man complain, a [1]man for the punishment of his °sins?
40 (נ) Let us search and try our ways, and turn again to [18]the LORD.
41 (נ) Let us lift up our heart with *our* hands unto °GOD in °the heavens.
42 (נ) We have °transgressed and have rebelled: Thou hast not pardoned.
43 (ס) Thou hast covered with anger, and °persecuted us: Thou hast slain, Thou hast not pitied.
44 (ס) Thou hast covered thyself with a cloud, that *our* prayer should not pass through.
45 (ס) Thou hast made us *as* the offscouring and refuse in the midst of the °people.
46 (פ) °All our enemies have °opened their mouths against us.
47 (פ) °Fear and a snare is come upon us, desolation and destruction.
48 (פ) °Mine °eye runneth down with rivers of water for the destruction of the daughter of my people.
49 (ע) Mine eye trickleth down, and ceaseth not, without any intermission,
50 (ע) Till [18]the LORD look down, and behold from heaven.
51 (ע) Mine eye affecteth °mine heart because of all the daughters of my city.
C³ 52 (צ) Mine enemies chased me sore, like a bird, without cause.
53 (צ) They have cut off my life in the °dungeon, and cast a stone upon me.
54 (צ) Waters flowed °over mine head; *then* I said, °"I am cut off."
55 (ק) I called upon °Thy name, O [18]LORD, out of the low [53]dungeon.
56 (ק) Thou hast heard my voice: hide not Thine ear °at my breathing, °at my cry.
57 (ק) Thou drewest near in the day *that* I called upon Thee: Thou saidst, "Fear not."
58 (ר) O [31]LORD*, Thou hast pleaded the causes of [20]my soul; Thou hast °redeemed my life.
59 (ר) O [18]LORD, Thou hast seen my wrong: judge Thou my cause.
60 (ר) Thou hast seen all their vengeance *and* all their imaginations against me.
61 (ש) Thou hast heard their reproach, O [18]LORD, *and* all their imaginations against me;
62 (ש) The °lips of those that rose up against me, and their °device against me all the day.
63 (ש) Behold their sitting down, and their rising up; I *am* °their musick.
64 (ת) °Render unto them a recompence, O [18]LORD, according to the work of their hands.
65 (ת) °Give them °sorrow of heart, Thy curse unto them.
66 (ת) [43]Persecute and destroy them in anger from under the heavens of [18]the LORD.

A⁴ A⁴ **4** (א) How is the °gold °become dim! *how* is the °most fine gold °changed! the stones of the sanctuary are °poured out in the top of every street.
2 (ב) The precious sons of Zion, comparable to °fine gold, how are they esteemed °as

38 evil. Heb. *rā'a'*. Ap. 44. viii.
39 sins. Heb. *chāṭā'*. Ap. 44. i.
41 GOD. Heb. El. Ap. 4. IV.
the heavens. Supply the *Ellipsis* thus: "the heavens [saying], We have", &c.
42 transgressed = revolted. Heb. *pāsha'*. Ap. 44. ix. Cp. 1. 22.
43 persecuted = pursued. Cp. Ps. 35. 6.
45 people = peoples.
46 All our enemies, &c. Here again, as in 2. 16 and 17, the letters *Pe* (פ = P) and *Ayin* (ע) are transposed; not from any "mistake" or "forgetfulness", but to call our attention to the truth which might otherwise have been overlooked: viz. the sorrow, on account of the destructive work of the enemies (*vv.* 46–48), which would have been averted by true sorrow for the sins which caused it (*vv.* 49–51).
opened their mouths. Cp. Ps. 22. 13.
45 people = peoples.
47 Fear and a snare. Note the Fig. *Paronomasia* (Ap. 6). Heb. *pāchad vāpachath*. Cp. Isa. 24. 17. Jer. 48. 43. In English, "Scare and snare".
48 Mine eye runneth down. Cp. Luke 19. 41. Ap. 85.
eye = tears: "eye" being put by Fig. *Metonymy* (of Adjunct), Ap. 6, for the tears which flow from it.
51 mine heart = my soul. Heb. *nephesh*. Ap. 13.
53 dungeon = pit. Cp. Jer. 38. 6; and Ps. 88. 6.
54 over mine head. Cp. Ps. 69. 2.
I am cut off. Cp. Ps. 88. 5.
55 Thy name = Thee, or Thy attributes. See note on Ps. 20. 1.
56 at my breathing. See note on Mal. 3. 16.
at my cry. Some codices, with Vulg., read "and at my cry" (or outcry).
58 redeemed. Heb. *gā'al*. See note on Ex. 6. 6.
62 lips. Cp. Ps. 22. 7. Ap. 85.
device = meditation. Heb. *Higyon*. See Ap. 66. I.
63 their musick = their mocking song, as in *v.* 14.
64 Render, &c. Cp. Ps. 69. 22.
65 Give them sorrow of heart = Thou wilt suffer them a veiling (or obstinacy) of heart. See Isa. 6. 9, 10.
sorrow = covering, or veiling.

4. 1 This chapter, like chs. 1 and 2, is an acrostic: the twenty-two verses commencing successively with the twenty-two letters of the Hebrew alphabet.
gold . . . most fine gold . . . fine gold. Fig. *Anabasis* (Ap. 6), which is lost in A.V. rendering, which should be "gold . . . fine gold . . . pure gold".
become dim . . . changed . . . poured out. Note the Fig. *Catabasis* (Ap. 6).
2 fine gold = pure gold. See note above.
as earthen pitchers. The comparison is both in the material and in the workmanship. Cp. Jer. 18. 1-6; 19. 1-10.
3 sea monsters. R.V. = jackals (Jer. 9. 11).
ostriches. Cp. Job 39. 13-17.
5 embrace. Cp. Job 24. 8. **6** For = And.
punishment of the iniquity. This is the full translation of the Fig. *Metonymy* (of Effect), Ap. 6: the "iniquity" being put for its consequent punishment.
iniquity. Heb. *'āvāh*. Ap. 44. iv.

earthen pitchers, the work of the hands of the potter!
3 (ג) Even the °sea monsters draw out the breast, they give suck to their young ones: the daughter of My people *is become* cruel, like the °ostriches in the wilderness.
4 (ד) The tongue of the sucking child cleaveth to the roof of his mouth for thirst: the young children ask bread, *and* no man breaketh *it* unto them.
5 (ה) They that did feed delicately are desolate in the streets: they that were brought up in scarlet °embrace dunghills.
6 (ו) °For the °punishment of the °iniquity of

the daughter of my People is greater than the °punishment of the sin of Sodom, that was °overthrown as in a moment, and no hands °stayed on her.

7 (ז) Her Nazarites were purer than snow, they were whiter than milk, they were more ruddy in body than rubies, their polishing *was* of sapphire:

8 (ח) Their visage is blacker than a coal; they are not °known in the streets: their skin °cleaveth to their bones; it is withered, it is become like a stick.

9 (ט) *They that be* slain with the sword °are better than *they that be* slain with hunger: for these pine away, stricken through for *want of* the fruits of the field.

10 (י) The hands of the °pitiful women °have sodden their own °children: they were their meat in the destruction of the daughter of my People.

11 (כ) °The LORD hath accomplished His fury; He hath poured out His fierce anger, and hath °kindled a fire in Zion, and it hath devoured the foundations thereof.

12 (ל) The kings of the earth, and all the inhabitants of the world, would not have believed that the adversary and the enemy should have entered into the gates of Jerusalem.

B⁴ D⁵ (p. 1097) 13 (מ) For the [6]sins of her prophets, *and* the [6]iniquities of her priests, that have shed the blood of the °just in the midst of her,

14 (נ) They have wandered *as* blind *men* in the streets, they have °polluted themselves °with blood, so that men could not touch their garments.

15 (ס) They cried unto them, °"Depart ye; *it is* unclean; depart, depart, touch not:" when they fled away and wandered, they said among the °heathen, "They shall no more sojourn *there*."

16 (פ) The °anger of [11]the LORD hath divided them; He will no more regard them: they respected not the °persons of the priests, they favoured not the elders.

17 (ע) As for us, our eyes as yet failed for our vain help: in our watching we have watched for a nation *that* could not save *us*.

18 (צ) They hunt our steps, that we cannot go in our streets: our end is near, our days are fulfilled; for our end is come.

19 (ק) Our °persecutors are °swifter than the eagles of the heaven: they pursued us upon the mountains, they laid wait for us in the wilderness.

20 (ר) The °breath of our nostrils, °the anointed of [11]the LORD, was taken in their °pits, of whom we said, "Under his shadow we shall live among the [15]heathen."

E⁵ 21 (שׁ) °Rejoice and be glad, O daughter of Edom, that dwellest in °the land of Uz; the cup also shall pass through unto thee: thou shalt be drunken, and shalt make thyself °naked.

22 (ת) The [6]punishment of thine [6]iniquity is °accomplished, O daughter of Zion; He will no more carry thee away into captivity: He will °visit thine [6]iniquity, O daughter of Edom; He will discover thy [6]sins.

C⁴ **5** Remember, O °LORD, what is come upon us: consider, and behold our reproach.

2 Our °inheritance is turned to strangers, our houses to aliens.

3 We are orphans and fatherless, our mothers *are* as widows.

4 We have drunken our water for money; our wood is sold unto us.

5 °Our necks *are* under °persecution: we labour, °*and* °have no rest.

6 We have °given the hand *to* the Egyptians, *and to* the Assyrians, to be satisfied with bread.

7 Our fathers have °sinned, *and are* not; and we have °borne their °iniquities.

8 Servants have ruled over us: *there is* none that doth deliver *us* out of their hand.

9 °We gat our bread with *the peril of* our °lives because of the °sword of the wilderness.

---

punishment of the sin. This is the full translation of the Fig. *Metonymy* (of Effect), Ap. 6, the Heb. *chāṭā'* (sin) being put for the consequent punishment.

overthrown, &c. Ref. to Pent. (Gen. 19. 25). Ap. 92.

stayed = travailed on her: i.e. brought it about; for the overthrow was direct from God.

8 known = recognised.

cleaveth. Heb. occurs only here.

9 are = have proved.

10 pitiful = tender-hearted.

have sodden, &c. Ref. to Pent. (Deut. 28. 56, 57). Ap. 92. Cp. 2 Kings 6. 29. **children** = babes.

11 The LORD. Heb. Jehovah. Ap. 4. II.

kindled a fire. Ref. to Pent. (Deut. 32. 22). Ap. 92.

13 just = righteous ones. Cp. Matt. 23. 31, 37.

14 polluted . . . with blood. Ref. to Pent. (Num. 19. 11, 16). Ap. 92.

15 Depart ye, &c. Ref. to Pent. (Lev. 13. 45). Ap. 92.

heathen = nations.

16 anger = face. Put by Fig. *Metonymy* (of Effect), Ap. 6, as manifesting the anger felt.

persons = face. Put by Fig. *Synecdoche* (of the Part), Ap. 6, for the whole person.

19 persecutors = pursuers.

swifter than the eagles. Ref. to Pent. (Deut. 28. 49).

20 breath. Heb. *rūach*. Ap. 9.

the anointed: i.e. Zedekiah was still Jehovah's "anointed", even as Saul was (1 Sam. 26. 9, 11, 16, 23. 2 Sam. 1. 14, 16).

pits = toils. Occurs only here and Ps. 107. 20. Heb. *shīchīth*. Cp. Jer. 2. 6; 18. 20, 22.

21 Rejoice, &c. Said in solemn irony.

the land of Uz. See notes on p. 666, and Ap. 62.

naked. Between *vv.* 21 and 22 lies the whole of this present Dispensation. See Ap. 63. IX and 72.

22 accomplished = completed.

visit = punish, as in *v.* 6. See note there.

5. 1 The acrostic gives way before the outburst of emotion in prayer. The only connection with it is the number of the verses (twenty-two, corresponding with the letters of the Hebrew alphabet).

LORD. Heb. Jehovah. Ap. 4. II.

2 inheritance: i.e. Canaan.

5 Our necks are under persecution = Our pursuers are upon our necks. **persecution** = pursuers.

and. Some codices, with two early printed editions and Syr., read this "and" in the text.

have no rest = no respite was granted us.

6 given the hand. Put by Fig. *Metonymy* (of the Adjunct), Ap. 6, for voluntary submission.

7 sinned. Heb. *chāṭā'*. Ap. 44. i.

borne. As a burden. The same word as in Isa. 53. 4, 11. **iniquities.** Heb. *'āvāh*. Ap. 44. iv.

9 We gat our bread = We brought home our bread.

lives = souls. Heb. *nephesh*. Ap. 13. Some codices, with one early printed edition, read "souls".

sword of the wilderness. "The sword" is put, by Fig. *Metonymy* (of Cause), Ap. 6, for the raids and fightings of the inhabitants of the wilderness.

10 Our °skin was black like an oven because of the terrible famine.
11 They ravished the °women in Zion, *and* the maids in the cities of Judah.
12 Princes are hanged up by their hand: the °faces of elders were not honoured.
13 They took the young men °to grind, and the °children °fell °under the wood.
14 The elders have ceased from the gate, the young men from their musick.
15 The joy of our heart is ceased; our dance is turned into mourning.
16 The crown is fallen *from* our head: woe unto us, that we have [7]sinned!
17 For °this our heart is faint; for °these *things* our eyes are dim.
18 Because of the mountain of Zion, which is desolate, the °foxes walk upon it.
19 Thou, O [1]LORD, °remainest for ever; Thy throne from generation to generation.
20 Wherefore °dost Thou forget us for ever, *and* forsake us so long time?
21 °Turn Thou us °unto Thee, O [1]LORD, and we shall be turned; renew our days as of old.
22 But Thou hast utterly rejected us; Thou °art very wroth against us.

11 women = wives.
12 faces. Put by Fig. *Synecdoche* (of the Part), Ap 6, for the whole person.
13 to grind: i.e. to do women's work.
children = young children, youths.
fell = staggered.
under the wood: i.e. under [the weight or load] of the wood (they were compelled as bond-slaves to carry).
17 this: i.e. this sin.
these things: i.e. loss of king, country, possessions, and liberties. **18** foxes = jackals.
19 remainest = sittest: i.e. as king.
20 dost = wilt.
21 Turn Thou us. National repentance was the one abiding condition of national blessing, and this must be Jehovah's own work.
unto Thee = unto Thyself. **22** art = hast been.
In the public reading of the Hebrew text *v.* 21 is repeated after *v.* 22, so that the book may end with comfort. The same is the case with Ecclesiastes, Isaiah, and Malachi. The synagogue use appoints this book to be read on the Fast of Ab, which commemorates the destruction of Jerusalem.

THE BOOK OF THE PROPHET EZEKIEL.

THE STRUCTURE OF THE BOOK AS A WHOLE.

(Introversion and Extended Alternation.)

A | 1. 1—12. 28. THE DESOLATION.
  B | 13. 1-23. PROPHETS AND PROPHETESSES.
    C | D | 14. 1-11. ELDERS.
        E | 14. 12—15. 8. THE LAND AND CITY. (JUDGMENTS.)
          F | 16. 1-63. JERUSALEM. (DESERTED INFANT.)
            G | 17. 1-24. BABYLONIAN WAR. (PARABLE.)
              H | 18. 1-32. THE PEOPLE. PROVERB. (SOUR GRAPES.)
                J | 19. 1-14. THE PRINCES OF ISRAEL.
    C | D | 20. 1-44. ELDERS.
        E | 20. 45—22. 31. THE LAND AND CITY. (JUDGMENTS.)
          F | 23. 1-49. JERUSALEM. (TWO SISTERS.)
            G | 24. 1—32. 32. BABYLONIAN WAR. (PARABLE.)
              H | 33. 1-22. THE PEOPLE. SIGN. (WATCHMAN.)
                J | 33. 23-33. THE INHABITANT OF THE WASTES.
  B | 34. 1-31. SHEPHERDS AND FLOCK.
A | 35. 1—48. 35. THE RESTORATION.

NOTES ON THE STRUCTURE OF THE BOOK OF EZEKIEL (p. 1104).

For the Canonical order and place of the Prophets, see Ap. 1 and p. 1206.
For the Chronological order of the Prophets, see Ap. 77.
For the Inter-relation of the Prophetical Books, see Ap. 78.
For the Formulæ of Prophetic utterances, see Ap. 82.
For the Chronological order of Ezekiel's prophecy, see below.
For the References to the Pentateuch in the Prophetical Books, see Ap. 92.
For the Plan of Ezekiel's temple, see Ap. 88.

The Canonical order of Ezekiel's prophecies is *Logical*, but not strictly *Chronological*. Later utterances and visions are recorded in their logical connections rather than in their historical sequence. This latter is noted, so that we may make no mistake. When this fact is observed, and the records discriminated, the meaning becomes perfectly clear. See the table below.

They may be set out as follows :—

THE DATED YEARS IN EZEKIEL.

These are *thirteen* in number, and cover a period of twenty-one years (a period of three sevens) : viz. from 484-3 to 463-2 B.C.

Arranged chronologically, the *seventh* stands in the centre, with six on either side.

Reckoning the three in the 11th year as one year, and the three in the 12th year as one year, we have *nine* several years : viz. the 5th, 6th, 7th, 9th, 10th, 11th, and 12th (*seven*) : and then, after a break of thirteen years, we have *two* : viz. the 25th and 27th.

	Year of the Captivity of Jehoiachin.	Month.	Day.	Chapters.	B.C.
All these prophecies were uttered before the fall of Jerusalem.	5th	4th Thammuz (July)	5th	1. 1, 2	484
	5th	4th Thammuz (July)	12th	3. 16	484
	6th	6th Elul (Sept.)	5th	8. 1	483
	7th	5th Ab (Aug.)	10th	20. 1	482
	9th	10th Tebeth (Jan.)	10th	24. 1	480
	10th	10th Tebeth (Jan.)	12th	29. 1	479
	11th	1st Abib, or Nisan (April)[1]	1st	26. 1	
	11th	1st Abib, or Nisan (April)	7th	30. 20	478
These prophecies were uttered at and after the fall of Jerusalem.	11th	3rd Sivan (June)	1st	31. 1	
	12th	12th Adar (March)	1st	32. 1	
	12th	12th Adar (March)[2]	15th	32. 17	477
	12th	10th Tebeth (Jan.)	5th	33. 21	
	25th	1st Abib, or Nisan (April)	10th	40. 1	465
	27th	1st Abib, or Nisan (April)	1st	29. 17	463

The 30th year of 1. 1, 2 cannot be in succession to the 27th year of ch. 29. 17-21, because the visions of chs. 1 and 10 had already been seen, and the one recorded in ch. 10 is said to have been similar to that already seen in ch. 1. Moreover, if it be in succession to the 27th year, why is it brought into the very beginning of the book without any reason being assigned, or hint given?

The 30th year of 1. 1 cannot have anything to do with Ezekiel's age, or with the commencement of his service as a priest; for this is to misread Num. 4. 3, which states that "all that enter into the host, to do the work in the tabernacle", were taken after the end of the 29th year, "from thirty years old and upward, even until fifty years". Moreover, this thirty years' rule was abrogated by Divine direction to David in 1 Chron. 23. 24-27 (cp. 2 Chron. 31. 17), and changed to "twenty years old and upward".

The 30th year cannot be fitted into any sequence of dates commencing with the fifth year of Jehoiachin's captivity (1. 2), which, in 33. 21 and 40. 1, he speaks of as "our captivity".

It must therefore be a cross-date to some unnamed *terminus à quo*, thirty years before the 5th year of the Captivity. This fixes it as being that epoch-making year 513 B.C., which was the year of Josiah's great Passover, and of the finding the Book of the Law in the 18th year of King Josiah. From 513 B.C. to 484 B.C. is exactly twenty-nine complete years. So also reckons the learned Prideaux (*Connection*, vol. i, p. 71, McCaul's ed., 1845)

[1] No month is named ; but, by comparing 30. 20, it must be the 1st month.
[2] No month is named ; but it was probably the same as in *v.* 1.

THE BOOK OF THE PROPHET

°EZEKIEL.

A A C G (p. 1106) 484 1 °Now it came to pass in the °thirtieth year,
in the °fourth *month,* in the °fifth *day* of the
month, as I *was* among the °captives by the
river of °Chebar, *that* the heavens were opened,
and I saw visions °of °God.
2 In the [1]fifth *day* of the month, which *was*
the °fifth year of king °Jehoiachin's captivity,
3 The word of °the LORD came °expressly
unto °Ezekiel °the priest, the son of Buzi, in
the land of the Chaldeans by the river [1]Chebar;
and °the hand of °the LORD °was there upon
him.

H a 4 And I looked, and, °behold, a °whirlwind
came °out of the north, a great cloud, and a
fire °infolding itself, and a brightness *was*
about it, and out of the midst thereof as the
°colour of °amber, °out of the midst of the fire.

b 5 Also out of the midst thereof *came* the likeness of °four living creatures. And this *was*
their appearance; they had the likeness of a
man.
6 And every one had four faces, and every
one had four wings.
7 And their feet *were* °straight feet; and the
sole of their feet *was* like the sole of a calf's
foot: and they sparkled like the colour of
burnished brass.
8 And *they had* the °hands of a man under
their wings on their four sides; and they four
had their faces and their wings.
9 Their wings *were* joined one to another;
they turned not when they went; they went
every one straight forward.
10 As for the likeness of their °faces, they
four had the face of a °man, and the face of
a lion, on the right side: and they four had
the face of an ox on the left side; they four
also had the face of an eagle.

Ezekiel. In Heb. Y *ḥezē'el* = *y*e*ḥazzeḳ-'ēl* = El is strong, or El strengthens (cp. Isra-el, Gen. 32. 28).

Of the four greater prophets, Ezekiel and Daniel (who prophesied in Babylonia) are compounded with "El" (Ap. 4. IV); while Isaiah and Jeremiah (who prophesied in the land) are compounded with "Jah".

Ezekiel was a priest (1. 3), carried away eleven years before the destruction of the city and temple (1. 2; 33. 21. 2 Kings 24. 14). He dwelt in his own house (8. 1. Cp. Jer. 29. 5). He was married; and his wife died in the year when the siege of Jerusalem began.

1. 1—12. 28 (**A**, p. 1104). THE DESOLATION. (*Alternation.*)

A | A | 1. 1—3. 27. First Vision (by Chebar).
B | 4. 1—7. 27. Signs.
A | 8. 1—11. 24. Second Vision (at Jerusalem).
B | 12. 1-28. Signs.

1. 1—3. 27 (A, above). FIRST VISION (AT CHEBAR). (*Extended Alternation.*)

A | C | 1. 1-28-. The Cherubim.
D | 1. -28. Prostration of Ezekiel.
E | 2. 1, 2. Raised by the Spirit.
F | 2. 3—3. 9. Mission of Ezekiel.
C | 3. 10-23-. The Cherubim.
D | 3. 23. Prostration of Ezekiel.
E | 3. 24-. Raised by the Spirit.
F | 3. -24-27. Mission of Ezekiel.

1. 1-28- (C, above). THE CHERUBIM (FIRST VISION). (*Introversion and Alternation.*)

C | G | 1-3. Visions of God.
H | a | 4. The cloud.
b | 5-21. The living creatures.
H | *a* | 22. The firmament.
b | 23-28-. The living creatures.
G | -28-. Glory of Jehovah.

1 Now = And. This is a link in the prophetic chain. Cp. 1 Pet. 1. 10-12. 2 Pet. 1. 21. Ezekiel had doubtless received and seen the letter sent by Jeremiah (Jer. 29. 1-32).

thirtieth . . . fourth. See notes on p. 1105.

fifth day. Dates in Ezekiel are always of the *month,* not of the week (1. 1; 8. 1; 20. 1; 24. 1; 26. 1; 29. 1; 30. 20; 31. 1; 32. 1; 40. 1). **captives.** Heb. captivity. Put by Fig. *Metonymy* (of Adjunct), Ap. 6, for "captives", as translated. Cp. 3. 15. **Chebar.** Now Khabour. Probably the same as Chebor or Habor (2 Kings 17. 6; 18. 11. 1 Chron. 5. 26), falling into the Euphrates about forty-five miles north of Babylon. On the Inscription it is called *nār Kabari* = great river, or "Grand Canal", cut between the Tigris and the Euphrates. In ch. 3. 15, it is not the same "Chebar" as in 1. 1, but the Chebar to which Ezekiel was sent ("go, get thee", 3. 4). The "Chebar" of 1. 1 was where he dwelt; that of 3. 15 where he was sent. **of** = from. Gen. of Origin or Efficient Cause. Ap. 17. 2. **God.** Heb. Elohim. Ap. 4. I. **2 fifth year.** B.C. 484. Cp. 2 Kings 24. 12, 15. **Jehoiachin.** Called also Jeconiah, and Coniah. Cp. 2 Kings 24. 17-20; 25. 1-21. **3 the LORD.** Heb. Jehovah. Ap. 4. II. **expressly** = in very deed, or in reality. **Ezekiel.** See the Title. **the priest:** and called, as Jeremiah was, to the office of prophet as well. **the hand.** Fig. *Anthropopatheia.* Ap. 6. **was** = became. Cp. Elijah (1 Kings 18. 46); Elisha (2 Kings 3. 15); Daniel (Dan. 10. 10, 18); and John (Rev. 1. 17). **4 behold.** Fig. *Asterismos.* Ap. 6. **whirlwind.** Heb. *rūach* = spirit, but it came to be rendered "storm or whirlwind". Note the three symbols of Jehovah's glory, Storm, Cloud, and Fire. Cp. Nah. 1. 3. Rev. 4. 5. **out of the north.** See note on Ps. 75. 6, and Isa. 14. 13. **infolding itself** = taking hold of itself. R.V. marg., "flashing continually". Human and finite language is unable to find words to express infinite realities. It may mean spontaneous ignition: i.e. without the application of external fire. Cp. Ex. 9. 24. **colour.** Heb. "eye". Put by Fig. *Metonymy* (of Adjunct), Ap. 6, for colour. **amber:** or, glowing metal. **out of:** or, in. **5 four living creatures.** These are "the Cherubim". See Ap. 41. The *zōa* of Rev. 4. 6. **7 straight:** i.e. unjointed. The living creatures did not move by walking. **8 hands.** Heb. text reads "hand". Some codices, with two early printed editions and Heb. text marg., read "hands" (pl.), followed by A.V. and R.V. The sing. is to be preferred, and is so rendered in 10. 7. Why not here? **10 faces.** See Ap. 41. **man.** Heb. *'ādām.* Ap. 14. I.

484 11 Thus *were* their faces: and their wings *were* °stretched upward; two *wings* of every one *were* joined one to another, and two covered their bodies.

12 And they went every one straight forward: whither the °spirit was to go, they went; *and* they turned not when they went.

13 As for the likeness of the living creatures, their appearance *was* like burning coals of fire, *and* like the appearance of °lamps: it went up and down among the living creatures; and the fire was bright, and out of the fire °went forth lightning.

14 And the [5]living creatures °ran and returned as the appearance of a flash of lightning.

15 Now as I beheld the living creatures, °behold one wheel upon the earth by the living creatures, with his four faces.

16 °The appearance of the wheels and their work *was* like unto the colour of a beryl: and they four had one likeness: and their appearance and their work *was* as it were a wheel in the middle of a wheel.

17 When they went, they went upon their four sides: *and* they °turned not when they went.

18 As for their rings, they were so °high that they were dreadful; and their rings *were* full of eyes round about them four.

19 And when °the living creatures went, the wheels went by them: and when °the living creatures were lifted up from the earth, the wheels were lifted up.

20 Whithersoever the [12]spirit was to go, they went, thither *was their* [12]spirit to go; and the wheels were lifted up over against them: for the [12]spirit of [19]the living creature *was* in the wheels.

21 When those went, *these* went; and when those stood, *these* stood; and when those were lifted up from the earth, the wheels were lifted up over against them: for the [12]spirit of [19]the living creature *was* in the wheels.

H a (p. 1106) 22 And the likeness of the °firmament upon the heads of the living creature *was* as the colour of the terrible crystal, °stretched forth over their heads °above.

b 23 And under the [22]firmament *were* their wings °straight, the one toward the other: every one had two, which covered on this side, and every one had two, which covered on that side, their bodies.

24 And when they went, I heard the °noise of their wings, like the noise of great waters, as the °voice of °THE ALMIGHTY, the °voice of speech, as the noise of an host: when they stood, they let down their wings.

25 And there was a [24]voice from the [22]firmament that *was* over their heads, when they stood, *and* had let down their wings.

26 And above the [22]firmament that *was* over their heads *was* the likeness of a throne, as the appearance of a sapphire stone: and upon the likeness of the throne *was* the likeness as the appearance of a °man above upon it.

27 And I saw as the colour of [4]amber, as the appearance of fire round about within it, from the appearance of his loins even upward, and from the appearance of his loins even downward, I saw as it were the appearance of fire, and it had brightness round about.

11 stretched upward=divided or spread out from above. **12 spirit.** Heb. *rūach*. Ap. 9.
13 lamps=the lamp; or, torch (sing.).
went forth=kept going forth.
14 ran and returned: or kept running and returning. The Heb. is Inf. by *Heterosis* (of Mood), Ap. 6.
15 behold. Fig. *Asterismos*. Ap. 6.
16 The. Some codices, with one early printed edition, Sept., Syr., and Vulg., read "And the".
17 turned. The 1611 edition of the A.V. reads "returned". **18 high.** In the sense of sublimity.
19 the living creatures=the living ones. Cp. *vv.* 21, 22; 9. 3; 10. 15, 20. The four were one.
22 firmament=expanse, as in Gen. 1. 6.
stretched forth=spread out.
above=upward. **23 straight**=level.
24 noise. Heb. "voice", as in the next clause=any noise. Articulate speech not mentioned till *v.* 28 and 2. 1. **voice**=noise, as above.
THE ALMIGHTY. Heb. Shaddai. Ap. 4. VII.
voice of speech=noise of tumult.
26 man. Heb. *'ādām*. Ap. 14. I. Cp. Dan. 7. 13.
28 the bow . . . in the cloud. Ref. to Pent. (Gen. 9. 16). Ap. 92. The only allusion to it in O.T. after Genesis. In N.T. cp. Rev. 4. 3; 10. 1.
the glory, &c. Cp. 3. 12, 23; 8. 4; 9. 3; 10. 4, 18, 19; 11. 22, 23; 43. 2, 4, 5; 44. 4.
I fell upon my face. Ref. to Pent. (Num. 14. 5; 16. 4, 22, 45). Ap. 92.

2. 1 He said. See 1. 28: i.e. He Who was enthroned (*v.* 26).
Son of man=son of Adam. Heb. *ben 'ādām*. Ap. 14. I. Used of Ezekiel (exactly one hundred times) by Jehovah, always without the Article. In N.T. used by Christ (of Himself) eighty-six times in A.V. (eighty-three times in R.V., omitting Matt. 18. 11; 25. 13. Luke 9. 56). Used by others of Christ twice (John 12. 34), making the A.V. total eighty-eight, and the R.V. total eighty-five. Always with the Article in N.T. See notes on Ps. 8. 4, Matt. 8. 20, and Rev. 14. 14. *Without* the Article it denotes a human being, a natural descendant of Adam. In Ezekiel it is used in contrast with the celestial living creatures (ch. 1). *With* the Article (as used of Christ) it denotes "the second Man", "the last Adam", taking the place, dispensationally, which "the first man" had forfeited, and succeeding, therefore, to the universal dominion over the earth which had been committed to Adam (Gen. 1. 26. Ps. 8. 4–8). In the N.T., outside the Four Gospels, it is used only in Acts 7. 56. Heb. 2. 6. Rev. 1. 13; 14. 14. And, beside Ezekiel, it is used in O.T. only of Daniel (Dan. 8. 17).
stand, &c. Cp. Dan. 10. 11. Rev. 1. 17. Reminding us that he was not a false prophet, or self-called and sent. Such spake "out of their own heart" (13. 2, 3). Cp. Jer. 23. 16.
2 the spirit entered . . . He spake. Entered with the word. Cp. Gen. 1. 2, 3. The Divine summons is accompanied by Divine preparation. Cp. 3. 24. Rev. 1. 17.
spirit. Heb. *rūach*. Ap. 9.
I heard. This is ever the Divine qualification.

28 As the appearance of °the bow that is in the cloud in the day of rain, so *was* the appearance of the brightness round about. *b*

This *was* the appearance of the likeness of °the glory of [3]the LORD. *G*

And when I saw *it*, °I fell upon my face, and I heard a [24]voice of One That spake. D

2 And °He said unto me, °"Son of man, °stand upon thy feet, and I will speak unto thee." E

2 And °the °spirit entered into me when He spake unto me, and set me upon my feet, that °I heard Him That spake unto me.

F J c (p. 1108) 484 3 And He said unto me, [1]"Son of man, °I send thee to the °children of Israel, to a °rebellious °nation that hath °rebelled against Me: they and their fathers have °transgressed against Me, *even* unto this very day.

4 For *they are* °impudent [3]children and °stiffhearted. I do send thee unto them; and thou shalt say unto them, 'Thus saith °the Lord GOD.'

d 5 And they, °whether they will hear, or whether they will °forbear, (for they *are* a °rebellious house,) yet shall know that there hath been a prophet among them.

e 6 And thou, [1]son of man, be not afraid of them, neither be afraid of their words, though °briers and thorns *be* with thee, and thou dost dwell among °scorpions: be not afraid of their words, nor be dismayed at their looks, though they *be* a [5]rebellious house.

7 And thou shalt speak °My words unto them, [5]whether they will hear, or [5]whether they will forbear: for they *are* most [5]rebellious.

8 But thou, [1]son of man, hear what I say unto thee; Be not thou [5]rebellious like that [5]rebellious house:

K open thy mouth, and °eat that I give thee."

L 9 And when I looked, °behold, an hand *was* sent unto me; and, °lo, °a roll of a book *was* therein;

L 10 And He spread it before me; and it *was* written °within and without: and *there was* written therein °lamentations, and mourning, and woe.

K **3** Moreover He said unto me, °"Son of man, °eat that thou findest; eat this roll, and go speak unto °the °house of Israel."

2 So I opened my mouth, and He caused me to eat that roll.

3 And He said unto me, [1]"Son of man, cause thy belly to eat, and fill thy bowels with this roll that I give thee." °Then did I eat *it;* and it was in my mouth °as honey for sweetness.

J c 4 And He said unto me, [1]"Son of man, go, get thee unto [1]the house of Israel, and °speak with My words unto them.

5 For thou *art* not sent to a people of a strange speech and of an hard language, *but* to [1]the house of Israel;

6 Not to many °people of a strange speech and of an hard language, whose words thou canst not understand. Surely, had I sent thee to them, they would have hearkened unto thee.

d 7 But [1]the house of Israel will not °hearken unto thee; for they °will not hearken unto Me: for all [1]the house of Israel °*are* °impudent and hardhearted.

e 8 °Behold, I have made thy face °strong against their faces, and thy forehead °strong against their foreheads.

9 As an adamant °harder than flint have I made thy forehead: fear them not, neither be dismayed at their looks, though they *be* °a rebellious house."

2. 3—3. 9 (F, p. 1106). MISSION OF EZEKIEL.
(*Introversion and Extended Alternation.*)

F | J | c | 2. 3, 4. People. Their character. } Mission.
  | | d | 2. 5. Reception. }
  | | e | 2. 6–8–. Encouragement. }
  | K | 2 –8. Command to eat.
  | L | 2. 9. The Roll. Sent.
  | *L* | 2. 10. The Roll. Contents.
  | *K* | 3. 1–3. Command to eat.
  | *J* | *c* | 3. 4–6. People. Their language. } Mission.
  | | *d* | 3. 7. Reception. }
  | | *e* | 3. 8, 9. Encouragement. }

3 I send=I am sending. **children**=sons.

rebellious . . . rebelled=revolting (against lawful authority), contumacious. Heb. *marad.* Not the same word as in *vv.* 5, 6, 7, 8. Occurs again in 17. 15; 20. 38.

nation=nations (pl. of Majesty)=the whole nation, Israel and Judah. Hence, the great rebellious nation like the heathen.

transgressed=revolted. Heb. *pāsha'.* Ap. 44. ix.

4 impudent . . . stiffhearted. Ref. to Pent. A reproach brought against Israel eight times in Exodus and Deuteronomy (Ex. 32. 9; 33. 3, 5; 34. 9. Deut. 9. 6, 13; 10. 16; 31. 27). Ap. 92. Cp. Judg. 2. 19, and Isa. 48. 4.

impudent=hard of face. Heb. *ḳāshah.*

stiffhearted=stubborn of heart. Heb. *ḥazaḳ.*

the Lord GOD. Heb. Adonai Jehovah. Ap. 4. VIII (2), and II. This title is characteristic of the prophecies of Ezekiel, being used 214 times. Very rarely in the other prophets. Ezekiel is in exile. This title is to remind him that Jehovah is still the sovereign Lord over all the earth, though Israel be "Lo-ammi"=not My People.

5 whether they will hear, or . . forbear. The latter is evidently assumed, and to be expected; as in 2 Tim. 4. 3. But no alternative is given. "My words" correspond with "preach the word" (2 Tim. 4. 2).

forbear=abstain, or refuse to hear.

a rebellious house. Heb. a house of rebellion. Not the same word as in *v.* 3. Heb. *m^erī*, from *mārāh*, to be bitter, perverse, refractory. Ref. to Pent. (Num. 17. 10. Deut. 31. 27). Elsewhere only in 1 Sam. 15. 23. Neh. 9. 17. Job 24. 13. Prov. 17. 11. Isa. 30. 9). The Verb occurs forty-three times in O.T. The Noun occurs sixteen times in Ezekiel (2. 5, 6, 7, 8, 8; 3. 9, 26, 27; 12. 2, 2, 3, 9, 25; 17. 12; 24. 3; 44. 6).

6 briers and thorns . . . scorpions. Put by Fig. *Hypocatastasis* (Ap. 6), for the rebellious.

7 My words. Nothing less, nothing more, nothing different. Cp. Gen. 3. 2, 3, and 2 Tim. 4. 2, under a similar warning in the following verse. Cp. *v.* 5, note.

8 eat. See 3. 1–3. Cp. Rev. 10. 9, 10.

9 behold . . . lo. Fig. *Asterismos.* Ap. 6.

a roll of a book=a scroll. Cp. Jer. 36. 2. Ps. 40. 7.

10 within and without. Contrary to the usual custom (within only), to show the abundance and completeness of his prophecies. Cp. Rev. 5. 1.

lamentations. Aram. and Sept. read "lamentation" (sing.).

3. 1 Son of man. See note on 2. 1.

eat. Cp. *v.* 10. Also Job 23. 12, Ps. 119. 103, and Jer. 15. 16.

the house of Israel. See note on Ex. 16. 31.

house. Some codices, with one early printed edition, Syr., and Vulg., read "sons".

3 Then did I eat. Cp. Rev. 10. 10.

as honey, &c. Cp. Pss. 19. 10; 119. 103. Jer. 15. 16.

4 speak with My words. This is inspiration. See note on 2. 5, 7. Ezekiel's voice and pen, but Jehovah's words. **6 people**=peoples.

7 hearken=be willing to hearken.

will not hearken=are not willing to hearken.

are=they [are].

impudent, &c. Ref. to Pent. See note on 2. 4.

8 Behold. Fig. *Asterismos.* Ap. 6.

strong=strong, or hard (for endurance). Heb. *ḥazaḳ.* Same as "harder" (*v.* 9). Cp. the name Ezekiel in Title.

9 harder. Same as "strong" (*vv.* 8, 14).

rebellious house. See note on 2. 5.

C M f (p. 1109) 484 10 Moreover He said unto me, [1]"Son of man,
°all My words that I shall speak unto thee re-
ceive in thine heart, and hear with thine ears.
11 And go, get thee to them of the °captivity,
°unto the °children of thy People, and speak
unto them, and tell them, 'Thus saith °the
Lord GOD;' °whether they will hear, or
whether they will forbear."

g 12 Then the °spirit °took me up, and I heard
°behind me a °voice of a great rushing, °*saying*, "Blessed *be* the glory of °the LORD from
His place."
13 *I heard* also the noise of the wings of the
living creatures that touched one another, and
the noise of the wheels over against them,
and a noise of a great rushing.
14 So the [12]spirit °lifted me up, and took me
away, and I went in bitterness, in the heat of
my [12]spirit; but the hand of [12]the LORD was
[8]strong upon me.

N 15 Then I came to them of the captivity at
Tel-abib, that dwelt by the river of °Chebar,
and I °sat where they °sat, and remained there
astonished among them seven days.
12th Thammuz 16 And it came to pass at the end of seven
days, that the word of [12]the LORD came unto
me, saying,
17 [1]"Son of man, I have °made thee a
°watchman unto [1]the house of Israel: therefore hear the word at My mouth, and °give
them warning from Me.
18 When I say unto the °wicked, 'Thou
°shalt surely die;' and thou givest him not
warning, nor speakest to warn the °wick-
ed from his °wicked way, to save °his life;
the same °wicked *man* shall die in his °ini-
quity; but his blood will I require at thine
hand.
19 Yet if thou warn the [18]wicked, and he
turn not from his [18]wickedness, nor from his
[18]wicked way, he shall die in his [18]iniquity;
but thou hast delivered °thy soul.
20 Again, When a righteous *man* doth turn
from his °righteousness, and commit [18]ini-
quity, and I lay a stumblingblock before him,
he shall die: because thou hast not given him
warning, he shall die in his °sin, and his
righteousness which he hath done shall not be
remembered; but his blood will I require at
thine hand.
21 Nevertheless if thou warn the righteous
man, that the righteous [20]sin not, and he doth
not [20]sin, he °shall surely live, because he °is
warned; also thou hast delivered [19]thy soul."

M g 22 And the hand of [12]the LORD was there
upon me; and He said unto me,

f "Arise, go forth into the °plain, and I will
there talk with thee."

N 23 Then I arose, and went forth into the
[22]plain: and, °behold, °the glory of [12]the LORD
stood there, as the glory which I saw by the
river of [15]Chebar:

D (p. 1106) and I fell on my face.

E 24 Then the [12]Spirit entered into me, and set
me upon my feet, and spake with me, and said
unto me,

F "Go, shut thyself within thine house.
25 But thou, O [1]son of man, [23]behold, they
shall put bands upon thee, and shall bind thee
with them, and thou shalt not go out among
them:
26 And I will make thy tongue cleave to the
roof of thy mouth, that thou shalt be dumb,
and shalt not be to them °a reprover: for they
are a [9]rebellious house.
27 But when I speak with thee, I will open

3. 10-23- (*C*, p. 1106). THE CHERUBIM.
(*Alternation and Introversion.*)

C | M | f | 10, 11. Command.
  g | 12-14. The hand of Jehovah.
    N | 15-21. Obedience.
M | g | 22-. The hand of Jehovah.
  f | -22. Command.
    N | 23-. Obedience.

10 all My words. See note on 2. 7.
11 captivity. Put by Fig. *Metonymy* (of Adjunct), Ap. 6, for captives.
unto the children of. The 1611 edition of the A.V. omits these words.
children=sons.
the Lord GOD. Heb. Adonai Jehovah. Ap. 4. VIII (2) and II.
whether, &c. See note on 2. 7.
12 spirit. Heb. *rūach*. Ap. 9. See notes on 8. 3.
took me up=laid hold of me.
behind me. Therefore the prophet must have been facing south, as the glory appeared from the north (1. 4).
voice=sound.
saying, &c. By reading *b^erūm* (arose) instead of *barūk* (Blessed), Ginsburg thinks the meaning should be "[when] the glory of Jehovah arose (or was lifted up) from its place" (cp. 10. 4, 17, 19): i.e. when the vision was withdrawn.
the LORD. Heb. Jehovah. Ap. 4. II.
14 lifted me up, &c. Cp. Acts 8. 39, 40. 2 Cor. 12. 4. Rev. 1. 10. Cp. Obadiah's fear (1 Kings 18. 12).
15 Chebar. Not the Chebar of 1. 3. That was where he dwelt. This was the Chebar whither he was sent. See note on 1. 3; the modern *Khabour*, a tributary of the Euphrates, forty-five miles from Babylon.
sat=dwelt; as in the preceding clause.
17 made=given. God's prophets and ministers were His "gifts" (Eph. 4. 11).
watchman=one who looks out or views from a height, with the object of warning. Heb. *zāphah*. Cp. 33. 2, 6, 7. Isa. 52. 8; 56. 10. Jer. 6. 17. Not *shāmar*, to keep in view with the object of guarding, as in Song 3. 3; 5. 7. Isa. 21. 11; 62. 6. These are the two spheres of the pastoral office.
give them warning. Heb. *zāhar*, to give a signal by a beacon or other fire (Jer. 6. 1). Occurs fourteen times in Ezekiel in connection with the prophet's or pastor's care. Cp. *vv.* 18, 18, 19, 20, 21; 33. 3, 4, 5, 5, 6, 7, 8, 9, 9.
18 wicked=lawless. Heb. *rāshā'*. Ap. 44. x.
shalt surely die. Note the Fig. *Polyptōton*, Ap. 6 (Inf. with Fut.), for emphasis. Heb. "dying, thou wilt die". See notes on Gen. 2. 17; 26. 28.
his life=himself alive.
iniquity. Heb. *'āval*. Ap. 44. vi.
19 thy soul=thyself. Heb. *nephesh*. Ap. 13.
20 righteousness. Heb. is plural in marg., but some codices, with one early printed edition, read "righteous deeds" (pl.) in text and marg.
sin. Heb. *chāṭā'*. Ap. 44. i.
21 shall surely live. See note on "shall surely die" (*v.* 18).
is warned=took warning.
22 plain=valley.
23 behold. Fig. *Asterismos*. Ap. 6.
the glory, &c. See note on 1. 28.
26 a reprover=a man of reproof.

484 °thy mouth, and thou shalt say unto them,
'Thus saith [11]the Lord GOD; He that °heareth,
°let him hear; and he that °forbeareth, °let
him forbear:' for they *are* a [9]rebellious house.

B O Q (p. 1110) **4** Thou also, °son of man, take thee a °tile,
and °lay it before thee, and °pourtray upon
it the city, *even* Jerusalem:
2 And [1]lay siege against it, and build a °fort
against it, and cast a °mount against it; set
the camp also against it, and set *battering*
rams against it round about.
3 Moreover take thou unto thee an iron °pan,
and set it *for* a wall of iron between thee and
the city: and °set thy face against it, and it
shall be besieged, and thou shalt lay siege
against it. This *shall be* a sign to °the house
of Israel.
R h 4 Lie thou also upon thy left side, and °lay the
°iniquity of [3]the house of Israel upon it: °*according*
to the number of the days that thou
shalt lie upon it thou shalt °bear their °iniquity.
i 5 For I have [1]laid upon thee the years of their
844-454 [4]iniquity, according to the number of the days,
°three hundred and ninety days: so shalt thou
[4]bear the [4]iniquity of [3]the house of Israel.
R h 6 And when thou hast accomplished them, lie
°again on thy right side,
i and thou shalt [4]bear the [4]iniquity of the house
495-4 of Judah °forty days: I have °appointed thee
455-4 each day for a year.
Q 7 Therefore thou shalt set thy face toward
°the siege of Jerusalem, and thine arm *shall
be* uncovered, and thou shalt prophesy against
it.
8 And, °behold, I will [1]lay bands upon thee,
and thou shalt not turn thee from one side to
another, till thou hast ended the days of thy
siege.
P j 9 Take thou also unto thee wheat, and barley,
and beans, and lentiles, and millet, and °fitches,
and put them in one vessel, and make thee
bread thereof, *according* to the number of the

27 thy mouth. Cp. 24. 27; 29. 21; 33. 22.
heareth = is minded to hear.
let him = will.
forbeareth = is minded to forbear.

4. 1—7. 27 (B, p. 1106). SIGNS. (*Introversion.*)

B | O | 4. 1-8. The city.
  | P | 4. 9-17. Food.
  | *P* | 5. 1-17. Hair.
  | *O* | 6. 1—7. 27. The mountains.

4. 1-8 (O, above). THE CITY. THE SIEGE. (*Introversion and Alternation.*)

O | Q | 1-3. The city. Siege.
  | R | h | 4. Sign. Left side.
  | | i | 5. Signification.
  | *R* | *h* | 6-. Sign. Right side.
  | | *i* | -6. Signification.
  | *Q* | 7, 8. The city. Siege.

1 son of man. See note on 2. 1.
tile: or, brick. A Babylonian brick, as used for inscription, was about 14 inches by 12.
lay = give, or take, as in *vv.* 1, 2, 5, 8; not *v.* 4. Heb. *nāthan*, rendered "appointed" in *v.* 6.
pourtray = grave.
2 fort = a siege tower, or bulwark.
mount = embankment.
3 pan = a flat plate, as used for baking.
set thy face. Ref. to Pent. (Lev. 17. 10; 20. 3, 5, 6; 26. 17). Ap. 92. Cp. Jer. 21. 10; 44. 11.
the house of Israel. See note on Ex. 16. 31. To be carefully distinguished here from Judah.
4 lay = set, or place. Heb. *sūm*. See note on *v.* 1.
according to the number, &c. Ref. to Pent. (Num. 14. 34). This is no evidence that in prophetic scriptures there is a "year-day" theory. These exceptions prove the opposite rule. In all of them "day" means "day", and "year" means "year".
bear their iniquity. A technical expression belonging to the Pentateuch = to endure the punishment due to iniquity, or sin. See Ex. 28. 38, 43. Lev. 5. 1, 17; 7. 18; 10. 17; 16. 22; 17. 16; 19. 8; 20. 17, 19, 20 (sin); 22. 9 (sin), 16; 24. 15 (sin). Num. 5. 31; 9. 13 (sin); 14. 33 (whoredoms), 34; 18. 1, 1, 22 (sin), 23, 32 (sin); 30. 15. Outside the Pentateuch, only in Ezek. 4. 4, 5, 6; 16. 54 (shame); 18. 19, 20, 20; 23. 49 (sin); 32. 24 (shame), 25 (shame), 30 (shame); 44. 10, 12; and in Isa. 53. 4, 11, 12, where the verb is *sabal* (not *nāsā*, as in Pentateuch), and Lam. 5. 7.
iniquity. Heb. *'avōn*. Ap. 44. iii. Put by Fig. *Metonymy* (of Cause), Ap. 6, for the punishment brought about in consequence of it.

5 three hundred and ninety days. These were to be literal "days" to Ezekiel, and were to represent 390 literal "years". The date of the command is not material to the understanding of this prophecy. The meaning of the expression "bear their iniquity" (see note on *v.* 4) determines the interpretation as referring to the duration of the *punishment*, and not to the period of the iniquity which brought it down. The 390 days stand for 390 years, and the 40 days for 40 years, the duration of the punishment of Israel and Judah respectively. As this has to do with the city Jerusalem (*vv.* 1-3), the periods must necessarily be conterminous with something that affects the ending of its punishment. This was effected solely by the decree for the restoration and rebuilding of Jerusalem in 454 B.C. (Ap. 50, p. 60). Three hundred and ninety years take us back to the sixteenth year of Asa, when Baasha made war on Judah (844 B.C. 2 Chron. 16. 1. Ap. 50, p. 57); which was followed by the solemn announcement by the prophet Jehu against Baasha of the quickly coming punishment of Israel (1 Kings 16. 1, &c.). The punishment of Judah, in like manner, began forty years before (455-4 B.C.): viz. in 495-4 B.C.; 495 (his fifth year), being the year of Jehoiakim's burning of the roll. The prophecy of this punishment was given in his fourth year (Jer. 25. 1, 9-11), and the execution of it speedily followed. This symbolical action of Ezekiel shows us how long Jerusalem's punishment lasted, and when it ended. **6 again** = a second time, showing that they are not necessarily consecutive or continuous, but are conterminous, though not commencing at the same time. **forty days.** See note on *v.* 4. **appointed** = given. Same word as "lay", *vv.* 1, 2, 5, 8. **7 the siege of Jerusalem.** This is the point which determines the interpretation, as do *vv.* 1-3. **8 behold.** Fig. *Asterismos*. Ap. 6.

4. 9-17 (P, above). FOOD. (*Alternation.*)

P | j | 9-12. Sign. Food.
  | k | 13. Signification.
  | *j* | 14, 15. Sign. Food.
  | *k* | 16, 17. Signification.

9 fitches, in English, is another spelling of *vetches*, a plant having tendrils. But the Heb. = *kussemeth* is defined as *triticum spelta*, or spelt, a kind of corn, always distinguished from wheat, barley, &c. Cp. Ex. 9. 32. Isa. 28. 25. Here, in plural.

484 days that thou shalt lie upon thy side, three
hundred and ninety days shalt thou eat thereof.
10 And thy meat which thou shalt eat *shall*
be by weight, twenty °shekels a day: from
time to time shalt thou eat it.
11 Thou shalt drink also water by measure,
the sixth part of an °hin: from time to time
shalt thou drink.
12 And thou shalt eat it *as* barley cakes, and
thou shalt °bake it with dung that cometh out
of °man, in their sight."
k 13 And °the LORD said, "Even thus shall the
(p. 1110) °children of Israel eat their defiled bread
among the °Gentiles, whither I will drive
them."
j 14 Then said I, "Ah °Lord GOD! [8]behold,
my °soul hath not been polluted: for from my
youth up even till now have I not eaten of
°that which dieth of itself, or is torn in pieces;
neither came there °abominable flesh into my
mouth."
15 Then He said unto me, °"Lo, I have
°given thee cow's dung for man's dung, and
thou shalt prepare thy bread °therewith."
k 16 Moreover He said unto me, [1]"Son of man,
[8]behold, °I will break the staff of bread in Jerusalem: and they shall eat bread by weight,
and with care; and they shall drink water by
measure, and with astonishment:
17 That they may want bread and water, and
be astonied one with another, and °consume
away for their [4]iniquity.

P S 1 5 And thou, °son of man, take thee a sharp
°knife, °take thee a barber's rasor, and
cause *it* to pass upon thine head and upon thy
beard: then take °thee balances to weigh, and
divide the *hair*.
m 2 Thou shalt burn with fire a third part °in
the midst of the city, when the days of the
siege are °fulfilled: and thou shalt take a third
part, *and* smite about it with °a [1]knife: and
a third part thou shalt scatter °in the °wind;
and I will °draw out a °sword after them.
n 3 Thou shalt also take thereof a few in number, and bind them in thy skirts.
4 Then take of them again, and cast them into
the midst of the fire, and burn them in the fire;
for thereof shall a fire come forth into all °the
house of Israel."
S l 5 Thus saith °the Lord GOD; °"This *is* Jerusalem: I have set it in the midst of the nations
and countries *that are* round about her.
6 And she hath °changed My judgments into
°wickedness more than the nations, and My
statutes more than the countries that *are* round
about her: for °they have refused My judgments and My statutes, °they have not walked
in them."
7 Therefore thus saith [5]the Lord GOD; "Because ye °multiplied more than the nations
that *are* round about you, *and* have not walked
in My °statutes, °neither have kept My judgments, °neither have done according to the
judgments of the nations that *are* round about
you;
8 Therefore" thus saith [5]the Lord GOD; °"Behold, I, even I, *am* against thee, and will
execute judgments in the midst of thee in the
sight of the nations.
9 And I will do in thee that which I have not
done, and whereunto I will not do any more
the like, because of all thine abominations.
10 Therefore °the fathers shall eat the sons
in the midst of thee, and the sons shall eat
their fathers; and I will execute judgments in
thee, and the whole remnant of thee will I
scatter into all the [2]winds.
11 Wherefore, °*as* I live, °saith [5]the Lord

10 shekels. See Ap. 51. II. 5.
11 hin. See Ap. 51. III. 3 (8).
12 bake it with = bake it upon. Cp. *v.* 15.
man. Heb. *'ādām*. Ap. 14. I.
13 the LORD. Heb. Jehovah. Ap. 4. II.
children = sons. **Gentiles** = nations.
14 Lord GOD. Heb. Adonai Jehovah. See Ap. 4. VIII (2) and II.
soul. Heb. *nephesh*. Ap. 13.
that which dieth of itself. Ref. to Pent. (Ex. 22. 31. Lev. 11. 39, 40; 17. 15). Ap. 92.
abominable flesh. Ref. to Pent. (Lev. 7. 18; 19. 7). Elsewhere, only in Isa. 65. 3. Ap. 92.
15 Lo. Fig. *Asterismos*. Ap. 6.
given. Same word as "appointed", *v.* 6.
therewith: or, thereupon. Cp. *v.* 12.
16 I will break. Ref. to Pent. (Lev. 26. 26). Occurring again in 5. 16; 14. 13; but nowhere else in O.T.
17 consume away, &c. Ref. to Pent. (Lev. 26. 39). Cp. 24. 23; 33. 10 ("pine away"). Ap. 92.

5. 1-17 (*P*, p. 1110). HAIR. (*Extended Alternation.*)

P | S | l | 1. Shaving. (The fourth sign.)
  m | 2. Third part. Burning, &c.
  n | 3, 4. Binding in skirts.
} The sign.
S | *l* | 5-11. Judgments.
  m | 12. Third part. Death, &c.
  n | 13-17. Anger accomplished.
} Signification.

1 son of man. See note on 2. 1.
knife = sword, as in *v.* 12, and 11. 8, 10.
take thee a barber's rasor = as a barber's rasor shalt thou take it. This is the sign of the Assyrian army (Isa. 7. 20).
thee. The 1611 edition of the A.V. reads "the".
2 in the midst of the city. Which he had graven on the brick. See the signification in *v.* 12.
fulfilled = completed. Cp. 4. 8.
a = the. Cp. *v.* 1. **in** = to.
wind. Heb. *rūach*. Ap. 9.
draw out a sword, &c. Ref. to Pent. (Lev. 26. 33).
sword. Same word as "knife" (*v.* 1). Ap. 92.
4 the house of Israel. As in 4. 3.
5 the Lord GOD = Adonai Jehovah. As in 2. 4.
This is Jerusalem. Cp. 4. 1.
6 changed = rejected, or rebelled against. Cp. 20. 8, 13, 21. Num. 20. 24; 27. 14. Heb. *marah*. Occurs forty-two times in O.T., and rendered "changed" only here. See notes on 2. 3, 5.
wickedness. Heb. *rāshā'*. Ap. 44. x.
they: i.e. the nations and the countries.
7 multiplied = rebelled.
statutes. See notes on Gen. 26. 5. Deut. 4. 1.
neither have kept = and have not kept.
neither have done, &c.: or, "and according to the statutes of the nations which are round about you have not done". Some codices, with two early printed editions and Syr., omit this "not". Cp. 11. 12.
8 Behold. Fig. *Asterismos*. Ap. 6.
10 the fathers shall eat, &c. = fathers shall eat, &c. (no Art.). Ref. to Pent. (Lev. 26. 29. Deut. 28. 53).
11 as I live. Figs. *Deēsis* and *Anthropopatheia*. Ap. 6.
saith the LORD = [is] Jehovah's oracle.

484 GOD; Surely, because thou °hast defiled My
sanctuary with all thy destestable things, and
with all thine abominations, therefore will I
also °diminish *thee;* neither shall °Mine eye
spare, neither will I have any pity.

m 12 °A third part of thee shall die with the
(p. 1111) °pestilence, and with famine shall they be consumed in the midst of thee: and a third part
shall fall by the [2]sword round about thee; and
I will scatter a third part into °all the [2]winds,
and I will [2]draw out a [2]sword after them.

n 13 Thus shall Mine anger be accomplished,
°and I will cause My fury to rest upon them,
°and °I will be comforted: and they shall know
that I °the LORD have spoken *it* in My °zeal,
when I have accomplished My fury in them.
14 Moreover °I will make thee waste, and a
reproach among the nations that *are* round
about thee, in the sight of all that pass by.
15 So it shall °be a reproach and a taunt, an
instruction and an astonishment °unto the
nations that *are* round about thee, when I
shall execute judgments in thee in anger and
in fury and in furious rebukes. I [13]the LORD
have spoken *it.*
16 When °I shall send upon them the evil
arrows of famine, °which shall be for *their*
destruction, *and* which I will send to destroy
you: and I will increase the famine upon you,
and will °break your staff of bread:
17 °So will I send upon you famine and evil
beasts, and they shall bereave thee; and pestilence and blood shall pass through thee; and
°I will bring the sword upon thee. I [13]the
LORD have spoken *it.*"

O T o 6 And the word of °the LORD came unto me,
(p. 1112) saying,
2 °"Son of man, set thy face toward °the
mountains of Israel, and prophesy against
them,
3 And say, 'Ye mountains of Israel, hear the
word of °the Lord GOD; Thus saith °the Lord
GOD to the mountains, and to the hills, to the
°rivers, and to the valleys; °'Behold, I, *even* I,
will °bring a sword upon you, and I will °de-
stroy your high places.
4 And your altars shall be desolate, and your
°images shall be broken: and I will cast down
your slain *men* before your °idols.
5 And I will lay the dead carcases of the
°children of Israel before °their [4]idols; and I
will scatter your bones round about your altars.
6 In all your dwellingplaces the cities shall be
laid °waste, and the high places shall be desolate; that your altars may be laid waste and
made desolate, and your [4]idols may be broken
and cease, and your images may be cut down,
and your works may be abolished.
7 And °the slain shall fall in the midst of you,
and °ye shall know that I *am* [1]the LORD.

p 8 Yet will I leave a remnant, that °ye may
have *some* that shall escape the sword among
the nations, when ye shall be scattered through
the countries.
9 And they that escape of you shall remember
Me among the nations whither they shall be
carried captives, because °I am broken with
their °whorish heart, which hath departed

hast defiled. This charge is substantiated in ch. 8.

diminish thee. So the Western codices. Heb. *'egra'* (with *Resh*=r). But the Eastern codices read *'egda'* (with *Daleth*=d)="I shall cut off", with the former reading in margin. But some codices, with two early printed editions, read "cut off" in the text.

Mine eye, &c. Fig. *Anthropopatheia.* Ap. 6. Ref. to Pent. (Deut. 13. 8). Cp. 7. 4; 8. 18; 9. 10. Ap. 92.

12 A third part, &c. This is the signification of the sign (*vv.* 1–4).

pestilence, and with famine. Cp. Josephus, *Ant.* x. 8. i.

all the winds=all quarters. Fig. *Metonymy* (of Adjunct), Ap. 6.

13 and. Note the Fig. *Polysyndeton* (Ap. 6).

I will be comforted. Ref. to Pent. (Deut. 32. 36). Cp. Isa. 1. 24. Ap. 92.

the LORD. Heb. Jehovah. Ap. 4. II.

zeal=jealousy.

14 I will make thee waste. Ref. to Pent. (Lev. 26. 31, 32). Ap. 92.

15 be a reproach and a taunt, &c. Ref. to Pent. (Deut. 28. 37: the words being different). Ap. 92.

unto. Some codices, with one early printed edition, Sept., and Vulg., read "in", or "among".

16 I shall send, &c. Ref. to Pent. (Deut. 32. 23, 24).

which: or, who.

break your staff of bread, &c. Ref. to Pent. (Lev. 26. 26). Ap. 92. Cp. 4. 16.

17 So will I send, &c. Ref. to Pent. (Lev. 26. 22. Deut. 32. 24).

I will bring the sword, &c. Ref. to Pent. (Lev. 26. 25). Ap. 92. Cp. 6. 3; 11. 8; 14. 17; 29. 8; 33. 2. Not used elsewhere in O.T.

6. 1—7. 27 (*O*, p. 1110). **THE MOUNTAINS.**
(*Extended Alternation.*)

O | T | o | 6. 1–7. The mountains of Israel.
p | 6. 8–10. The remnant.
q | 6. 11–. Sign. Smiting.
r | 6. -11-14. Signification.
T | o | 7. 1–15. The Land of Israel.
p | 7. 16–22. The remnant.
q | 7. 23–. Sign. A chain.
r | -7. 23–27. Signification.

1 the LORD. Heb. Jehovah. Ap. 4. II.

2 Son of man. See note on 2. 1.

the mountains. Specially defiled by the high places. Cp. *v.* 13.

3 the Lord GOD. Heb. Adonai Jehovah. See note on 2. 4.

rivers: or, ravines. Cp. 36. 4, 6. Heb. *aphîkîm.* See note on "channels", 2 Sam. 22. 16.

Behold. Fig. *Asterismos.* Ap. 6.

bring a sword. See note on 5. 17.

destroy your high places. Ref. to Pent. (Lev. 26. 30).

4 images=sun-images. Ref. to Pent. (Lev. 26. 30). Ap. 92. Cp. 2 Chron. 14. 5; 34. 4, 7. Isa. 17. 8; 27. 9.

idols=manufactured gods. **5 children**=sons.

their. Some codices, with Vulg., read "your".

6 waste. Ref. to Pent. (Lev. 26. 31). Ap. 92.

7 the slain=a slain one.

ye shall know that I am the LORD. This formula occurs twenty-one times in Ezekiel: five times at the beginning of a verse (6. 13; 11. 12; 20. 42, 44; 37. 13); five times in the middle of a verse (7. 9; 15. 7; 17. 21; 22. 22; 37. 14); and eleven times at the end of the verse (6. 7; 7. 4; 11. 10; 12. 20; 13. 14; 14. 8; 20. 38; 25. 5; 35. 9; 36. 11; 37. 6). In two instances, which are thus safeguarded (see Ap. 93), the verb is fem. (13. 21, 23). Outside Ezekiel it occurs only twice (Ex. 10. 2. 1 Kings 20. 28). See Ginsburg's *Massōrah,* vol. i, pp. 467, 468, §§ 122, 123. For another formula, see note on *v.* 10; and 13. 9.

8 ye. The 1611 edition of the A.V. reads "he": i.e. Israel.

9 I am broken with. Aram., Syr., and Vulg. read "I have broken".

whorish: i.e. idolatrous.

484 from Me, and with their eyes, which go a whoring after their [4]idols: and they shall lothe themselves for the °evils which they have committed in all their abominations.

10 And °they shall know that I *am* [1]the LORD, *and that* I have not said in vain that I would do this [9]evil unto them.'

q 11 Thus saith [3]the Lord GOD; 'Smite with
(p. 1112) thine hand, and stamp with thy foot, and say,
r 'Alas for all the [10]evil abominations of °the house of Israel! for they shall fall by the sword, by the famine, and by the pestilence.

12 He that is far off shall die of the pestilence; and he that is near shall fall by the sword; and he that remaineth and is besieged shall die by the famine: thus will I accomplish My fury upon them.

13 Then shall [7]ye know that I *am* [1]the LORD, when their slain *men* shall be among their [4]idols round about their altars, upon every high hill, in all the tops of the mountains, and under every green tree, and under every thick oak, the place where they did offer °sweet savour to all their idols.

14 °So will I °stretch out My hand upon them, and make the land desolate, yea, more desolate than the wilderness toward °Diblath, in all their habitations: and [10]they shall know that I *am* [1]the LORD.' ' "

T o **7** Moreover the word of °the LORD came unto me, saying,

2 "Also, thou °son of man, thus saith °the Lord GOD unto °the land of Israel; °'An end, °the end is come upon the four corners of °the land.

3 Now *is* °the end *come* upon thee, and I will send Mine anger upon thee, and will judge thee according to thy ways, and will recompense upon thee all thine abominations.

4 And °Mine eye shall not spare thee, neither will I have pity: but I will recompense thy ways upon thee, and thine abominations shall be in the midst of thee: and °ye shall know that I *am* [1]the LORD.'

5 Thus saith [2]the Lord GOD; °'An °evil, °an °only °evil, °behold, is come.

6 °An end is come, °the end is come: °it watcheth for thee; [5]behold, °it is come.

7 °The morning is come unto thee, O thou that dwellest in [2]the land: the time is come, the day of trouble *is* near, and not the °sounding again of the mountains.

8 Now will I shortly pour out My fury upon thee, and accomplish Mine anger upon thee: and I will judge thee according to thy ways, and will recompense thee for all thine abominations.

9 And [4]Mine eye shall not spare, neither will I have pity: I will recompense thee according to thy ways and thine abominations *that* are in the midst of thee; and [4]ye shall know that I *am* [1]the LORD That smiteth.

10 [5]Behold the day, [5]behold, it is come: [7]the morning is gone forth; °the rod hath blossomed, °pride hath budded.

11 Violence is risen up into °a rod of °wickedness: none of them *shall remain*, nor of their multitude, nor of any of theirs: °neither *shall there be* wailing for them.

12 The time is come, the day draweth near: let not the buyer rejoice, nor the seller mourn: for wrath *is* upon all the multitude thereof.

13 For the seller shall not return °to that which is sold, °although they were yet alive: for °the vision *is* touching the whole multitude thereof, *which* shall not return; neither shall any °strengthen himself in the °iniquity of his life.

14 °They have blown the trumpet, even to make all ready; but none goeth to the battle: for My wrath *is* upon all the multitude thereof.

evils. Heb. *rā'a'*. Ap. 44. viii.

10 they shall know that I am the LORD. This expression occurs again in *v.* 14; 12. 15; 20. 26; 30. 8; 32. 15. Other similar passages outside Ezekiel are, first, Ex. 7. 5. Lev. 23. 43 (ref. to Pent.); then 1 Sam. 17. 46, 47. 1 Kings 8. 43; 18. 37. 2 Chron. 6. 33. Pss. 59. 13; 83. 18; 109. 27. Isa. 19. 12; 41. 20; 45. 6. Jer. 31. 34. See Ginsburg's *Massōrah*, vol. i, §§ 118, 134, 135, 137.

11 the house of Israel. See note on Ex. 16. 31.

13 sweet savour = savour of appeasement, or, rest.

14 So will I: or, And I will.

stretch out My hand. Ref. to Pent. (Ex. 7. 5, &c.).

Diblath = Diblathaim (Num. 33. 46. Jer. 48. 22). A Massoretic note records the fact that some MSS. read "Riblah"; but many codices, with ten early printed editions, Aram., Sept., Syr., and Vulg., read "Diblah".

7. 1 the LORD. Heb. Jehovah. Ap. 4. II.

2 son of man. See note on 2. 1.

the Lord GOD = Adonai Jehovah. See note on 2. 4.

the land of Israel = the soil or ground of Israel. *'Admath* Israel, not *'eretz*, as in the next clause. See note on 11. 17.

An end . . . the end . . . the end. The Fig. *Repetitio* for emphasis. Cp. *vv.* 2, 3. See Ap. 6.

the land. Heb. *'eretz.*

4 Mine eye. Fig. *Anthropopatheia.* Ap. 6.

ye shall know, &c. See note on 6. 7.

5 An evil, an only evil. Fig. *Epizeuxis.* Ap. 6.

evil = calamity. Heb. *rā'a'*. Ap. 44. viii.

only = sole. Some codices, with four early printed editions and Aram., read "calamity after calamity", reading *'aḥar* (after) instead of *'aḥad* (i.e. ר = R for ד = D).

behold. Fig. *Asterismos.* Ap. 6.

6 An end . . . the end . . . it watcheth. Fig. *Paronomasia.* Ap. 6. Heb. *ḳēz . . . haḳēz . . . heḳez.*

it = she. Note the sudden change of gender, referring to "the morning" of *v.* 7.

7 The morning is come = The turn (or circle) hath come round.

sounding again. Occurs only here.

10 the rod hath blossomed: i.e. Nebuchadnezzar's sceptre is ready.

pride = insolence, or presumption: i.e. Israel's sin, which has called for the judgment.

11 a rod of wickedness: i.e. a rod to punish the wickedness. Genitive of Relation. Ap. 17. 5.

wickedness = lawlessness. Heb. *rāshā'*. Ap. 44. x.

neither shall there be wailing for them. Some codices, with four early printed editions, Syr., and Vulg., read "no rest for them".

13 to that: i.e. to the possession.

although they were yet alive: i.e. at the time of the redemption, when, at the jubilee, the property sold would come back to the seller. Ref. to Pent. (Lev. 25). Ap. 92.

the vision: or, indignation, if *cḥarān* is read for *chazān*, "wrath"; i.e. ר = R for ד = D, as in *vv.* 12 and 14.

strengthen himself in the iniquity of his life: or, no man by his iniquity shall strengthen his life.

iniquity. Heb. *'āvāh.* Ap. 44. iv.

14 They have blown. Some codices, with Sept., and Vulg., read "Blow ye".

484 15 °The sword *is* without, and the pestilence and the famine within: he that *is* in the field shall die with the sword; and he that *is* in the city, famine and pestilence shall devour him.

p 16 But they that escape of them shall escape,
(p. 1112) and shall be on the mountains like doves of the valleys, all of them mourning, every one for his °iniquity.

17 All hands shall be feeble, and all knees shall be weak *as* water.

18 They shall also gird *themselves* with sackcloth, and horror shall cover them; and shame *shall be* upon all faces, and °baldness upon all their heads.

19 They shall cast their silver in the streets, and their gold shall be removed: their silver and their gold shall not be able to °deliver them in the day of the wrath of [1]the LORD: they shall not satisfy their °souls, neither fill their bowels: because it is the stumblingblock of their [13]iniquity.

20 As for the beauty of His ornament, He set °it in majesty: but they made the images of their abominations °*and* of their detestable things therein: therefore have I set it far from them.

21 And I will give it into the hands of the °strangers for a prey, and to the °wicked of the earth for a spoil; and they shall °pollute it.

22 My face will I turn also from them, and they shall [21]pollute My secret *place*: for the robbers shall enter into it, and defile it.

q 23 °Make a chain:

r for the land is full of °bloody crimes, and the city is full of violence.

24 Wherefore I will bring the worst of the °heathen, and they shall possess their houses: I will also make the pomp of °the strong to cease; and their °holy places shall be defiled.

25 °Destruction cometh; and they shall seek peace, and *there shall be* none.

26 °Mischief °shall come upon °mischief, and °rumour shall be °upon °rumour; then shall °they seek a vision of the prophet; but °the law shall perish from the priest, and counsel from the °ancients.

27 The king shall mourn, and the prince shall be clothed with °desolation, and the hands of the People of the land shall be troubled: I will do unto them after their way, and according to their °deserts will I judge them; and °they shall know that I *am* [1]the LORD.'"

A U s **8** And it came to pass in °the sixth year, in
(p. 1114) the sixth *month*, in the °fifth *day* of the
483 month, *as* I sat in mine house, and °the elders of Judah sat before me, that °the hand of °the Lord GOD fell there upon me.

t 2 Then I beheld, and °lo a likeness as the appearance of °fire: from the appearance of His loins even downward, fire; and from His loins even upward, as the appearance of brightness, as the colour of amber.

s 3 And He put forth the form of an hand, and took me by a lock of mine head; and °the spirit lifted °me up between the earth and the heaven, and brought °me in °the visions of °God °to Jerusalem, to the °door of the inner

15 The sword. Put by Fig. *Metonymy* (of Adjunct), Ap. 6, for war.

The sword is without. Ref. to Pent. (Deut. 32. 25).

16 iniquity. As in *v.* 13: but here is put by Fig. *Metonymy* (of Effect), Ap. 6, for the judgment which was the consequence of it.

18 baldness. A sign of mourning.

19 deliver=rescue.

souls=cravings of their animal nature. Heb. *nephesh.* Ap. 13.

20 it: i.e. His Sanctuary, or His holy city Jerusalem.

and. Some codices, with Syr. and Vulg., read this "and" in the text="and their".

21 strangers=foreigners.

wicked=lawless. Heb. *rāshā'*. Ap. 44. x.

pollute=profane.

23 Make a chain. The sign of captivity, answering to the other sign in *v.* 11- ("q").

bloody crimes=crimes of bloodshed: i.e. capital crimes.

24 heathen=nations.

the strong. The Sept. evidently read *'uzzam*, instead of *'uzzīm* ("the fierce ones"). Cp. 24. 21.

holy. See note on Ex. 3. 5.

25 Destruction: or, Cutting off.

26 Mischief=Calamity. Heb. *chavah.*

shall come. Ref. to Pent. (Deut. 32. 23).

rumour=hearing. Put by Fig. *Metonymy* (of Adjunct), Ap. 6, for what is heard.

upon=after; but a special reading called *Sevīr* (Ap. 34), reads "upon". This is followed by A.V. and R.V.

they seek. But in vain. See *v.* 25.

the law. This was the special province of the priest (Deut. 17. 8-13; 33. 10), as the vision was that of the prophet, and counsel that of elders. Cp. Jer. 18. 18.

ancients=elders.

27 desolation. Put by Fig. *Metonymy* (of Subject), Ap. 6, for rent garments, which were the outward expression of inward grief.

deserts=judgments. Cp. *v.* 23.

they shall know, &c. See note on 6. 10.

8. 1—11. 24 (*A*, p. 1106). SECOND VISION. IN JERUSALEM. (*Introversion and Alternation.*)

A | U | 8. 1-4. The beginning of the Vision.
  V | W | 8. 5—9. 11. Sins and Punishments.
    X | 10. 1-22. Cherubim.
  V | *W* | 11. 1-21. Sins and Punishments.
    X | 11. 22-23. Cherubim.
U | 11. 24, 25. The end of the Vision.

8. 1-4 (U, above). THE BEGINNING OF THE VISION. (*Alternation.*)

U | s | 1. Place. "Mine house."
  t | 2. Vision.
  s | 3. Place. Jerusalem.
  t | 4. Vision.

1 the sixth year, &c. See table on p. 1105.

fifth. Some codices read "first".

the elders of Judah: i.e. of the Jewish colony at Tel-Abib (3. 15).

the hand. Fig. *Anthropopatheia.* Ap. 6.

the Lord GOD. Heb. Adonai Jehovah. See note on 2. 4.

2 lo. Fig. *Asterismos.* Ap. 6.

fire=a man. So the Sept., reading *'īsh* (Ap. 14. II) instead of *'ēsh*=fire.

3 the spirit. Probably an angel. See below. Heb. *rūach.* Ap. 9.

me. Emph.: i.e. Ezekiel himself, as Philip. Cp. 1 Kings 18. 12. 2 Kings 2. 16. Acts 8. 39. 2 Cor. 12. 2, 4. Rev. 1. 10; 4. 2; 17. 3; 21. 10. Cp. 11. 24, 25; 40. 2, 3.

the visions of God: i.e. the visions given him by God. The Gen. of Origin (Ap. 17. 2).

God. Heb. Elohim. Ap. 4. I.

to Jerusalem: i.e. to the actual city itself, not a vision of it.

door=entrance.

483 gate that looketh toward the north; where
was the seat of the image of °jealousy, which
°provoketh to °jealousy.

t 4 And, °behold, °the glory of °the [3]God of Israel *was* there, according to the vision that I
°saw in the plain.

Y^1 Z^1 u^1 (p. 1115) 5 Then said He unto me, °"Son of man, lift
up thine eyes now the way toward the north."
So I lifted up mine eyes the way toward the
north,

v^1 and [4]behold northward at the gate of the altar
this image of [3]jealousy in the entry.

w^1 6 He said furthermore unto me, [5]"Son of
man, °seest thou what they do? *even* the great
°abominations that °the house of Israel committeth here, that °I should go far off from My
sanctuary?

x^1 but turn thee yet again, *and* thou shalt see
greater °abominations."

Z^2 u^2 7 And He brought me to the [3]door of the
court; and when I looked, behold °a hole in
the wall.

v^2 8 Then said He unto me, [5]"Son of man, dig
now in the wall:" and when I had digged in
the wall, behold [7]a [3]door.
9 And He said unto me, "Go in, and behold
the wicked [6]abominations that they do here."
10 So I went in and saw; and [4]behold every
form of creeping things, and °abominable
°beasts, and all the °idols of [6]the house of Israel, pourtrayed upon the wall round about.
11 And there stood before them °seventy
°men of the °ancients of [6]the house of Israel,
and in the midst of them stood °Jaazaniah
the son of Shaphan, with every man his censer in his hand; and a thick cloud of incense
went up.

w^2 12 Then said He unto me, [5]"Son of man,
hast thou seen what the [11]ancients of the
house of Israel do °in the dark, every man in
the chambers of his imagery? for they say,
°'The LORD seeth us not; °the LORD hath
forsaken the earth.'"

x^2 13 He said also unto me, "Turn thee yet
again, *and* thou shalt see greater [6]abomina-
tions that they do."

Z^3 u^3 14 Then He brought me to the [3]door of the
gate of [12]the LORD'S house which *was* toward
the north;

v^3 and, [4]behold, there sat women weeping for
°Tammuz.

w^3 15 Then said He unto me, "Hast thou [6]seen
this, O [5]son of man?

x^3 turn thee yet again, *and* thou shalt see greater
[6]abominations than these."

Z^4 u^4 16 And He brought me into the inner court
of [12]the LORD'S house, and, [4]behold, at the
[3]door of the temple of [12]the LORD, °between
the porch and the altar,

v^4 *were* about °five and twenty men, with °their
backs toward the temple of [12]the LORD, and
their faces toward the east; and they °wor-
shipped the sun toward the east.

jealousy. Put by Fig. *Metonymy* (of Effect), Ap. 6, for the effect produced by it, as explained in the next clause. Ref. to Pent. (Deut. 4. 16). Ap. 92. Elsewhere only in 2 Chron. 33. 7, 15.

provoketh to jealousy. Ref. to Pent. (Ex. 20. 5. Deut. 32. 16). Ap. 92.

4 behold. Fig. *Asterismos.* Ap. 6.

the glory, &c. See note on 1. 28.

the God of Israel. See note on Isa. 29. 23.

plain = valley.

8. 5—9. 11 (W, p. 1114). SINS AND PUNISHMENTS. (*Division.*)

W | Y^1 | 8. 5–17. The Sins of the People.
  | Y^2 | 8. 18—9. 11. The Punishments.

8. 5-17 (Y^1, above). THE SINS OF THE PEOPLE. (*Extended and Repeated Alternations.* Like their sins.)

Y^1 | Z^1 | u^1 | 5–. Place. The North.
v^1 | –5. Abomination. Image of Jealousy.
w^1 | 6–. Appeal to Ezekiel.
x^1 | –6. Announcement of greater.
Z^2 | u^2 | 7. Place. Entrance of the Court.
v^2 | 8–11. Abomination. Chamber of Imagery.
w^2 | 12. Appeal to Ezekiel.
x^2 | 13. Announcement of greater.
Z^3 | u^3 | 14–. Place. Entrance of North Gate.
v^3 | –14. Abomination. Women weeping for Tammuz.
w^3 | 15–. Appeal to Ezekiel.
x^3 | –15. Announcement of greater.
Z^4 | u^4 | 16–. Place. The Inner Court.
v^4 | –16. Abomination. Worshipping the Sun.
w^4 | 17–. Appeal to Ezekiel.
x^4 | –17. Announcement of greatest.

5 Son of man. See note on 2. 1.

6 seest thou . . .? Fig. *Erotēsis.* Ap. 6.

abominations. Put by Fig. *Metonymy* (of Cause), Ap. 6, for the idols and the sin of idolatry which Jehovah abominated.

the house of Israel. See note on Ex. 16. 31.

I should go far off. Lit. to a removal far away: i.e. that they (or I) should remove, &c.

7 a = one: i.e. a single, or certain; as though it were mysterious or remarkable.

10 abominable. Ref. to Pent. (Lev. 7 and 11). Elsewhere only in Isa. 66. 17. Ap. 92.

beasts. This animal-worship was part of Egyptian idolatry. idols = manufactured gods.

11 seventy. The number of the elders. See Num. 11. 16. 2 Chron. 19. 8. Jer. 26. 17.

men. Heb. *'ish.* Ap. 14. II.

ancients = elders. Contrast Ex. 24. 1, &c.

Jaazaniah. His father, Shaphan, had taken part in Josiah's reformation (2 Kings 22. 8, &c.). Two of his sons were friendly to Jeremiah (*Ahikam,* Jer. 26. 24; and *Gemariah,* 36. 10, 25). Another Jaazaniah is mentioned in 11. 1.

12 in the dark. This was a special feature of this animal idolatry.

The LORD seeth us not: or, there is no Jehovah seeing us. Cp. 9. 9. the LORD. Heb. Jehovah. Ap. 4. II.

14 Tammuz. With Art. An idol personifying vegetable and animal life, worshipped in Phœnicia and Babylonia.

16 between the porch and the altar. The place appointed for the priests.

five and twenty. The number of the heads of the twenty-four courses of the priests.

their backs toward the temple. Because their faces were toward the sun-rising.

worshipped the sun. This form of idolatry seen as early as Job 31. 26, 27; and foreseen in Deut. 4. 19; adopted as early as Asa (2 Chron. 14. 5); abolished by Josiah (2 Kings 23. 5, 11).

17 Then He said unto me, "Hast thou [6]seen w^4
this, O [5]son of man? Is it a light thing to the

483 house of Judah that they commit °the [6] abominations which they commit here?
x[4] (p. 1115) for they have filled the land with violence, and have returned to [3] provoke Me to anger: and, °lo, they put °the branch to °their nose.

Y[2] A C (p. 1116) 18 Therefore will I also deal in fury: °Mine eye shall not spare, neither will I have pity: and though they cry in °Mine ears with a loud voice, *yet* will I not hear them."

D E y **9** °He cried also in mine ears with a loud voice, saying, "Cause them that have charge over the city to draw near, even °every man *with* his °destroying °weapon in his hand."

2 And, °behold, °six °men came from the way of the higher gate, which lieth toward the north, and [1] every man a slaughter °weapon in his hand;

z and one °man among them *was* clothed with linen, with a °writer's inkhorn by his side: and they went in, and stood beside the brasen altar.

z 3 And °the glory of °the °God of Israel was gone up from the °cherub, whereupon °He was, to the threshold of °the house. And He called to °the [2] man clothed with linen, which *had* the [3] writer's inkhorn by his side;

4 And °the LORD said unto him, "Go through the midst of the city, through the midst of Jerusalem, and °set a °mark upon the foreheads of [2] the men that sigh and that cry for all the abominations that be done in the midst thereof."

y 5 And to the others He said in mine hearing, "Go ye after him through the city, and smite: let not your eye °spare, neither have ye pity:

6 Slay utterly old *and* young, both maids, and little children, and women: but come not near any [1] man upon whom *is* the mark; and °begin at My sanctuary."

F Then they began at the °ancient [2] men which *were* before the house.

E 7 And He said unto them, "Defile the house, and fill the courts with the slain: go ye forth."

F And they went forth, and slew in the city.

B 8 And it came to pass, while they were slaying them, and I was left, that °I fell upon my face, and cried, and said, °"Ah °Lord GOD! wilt Thou destroy all the residue of Israel in Thy pouring out of Thy fury upon Jerusalem?"

A C 9 Then said He unto me, "The °iniquity of the house of Israel and Judah *is* °exceeding great, and the land is full of blood, and the city full of perverseness: for they say, [4] 'The LORD °hath forsaken the earth, and [4] the LORD seeth not.'

10 And as for Me also, °Mine eye shall not spare, neither will I have pity, *but* I will recompense their way upon their head."

D 11 And, [2] behold, the [1] man clothed with linen, which *had* the [2] inkhorn by his side, reported the matter, saying, "I have done °as Thou hast commanded me."

---

17 the. Some codices, with three early printed editions, read "all the".

lo. Fig. *Asterismos.* Ap. 6.

the branch = the Asherah (Ap. 42), represented by a branch cut to a certain shape.

their. This is one of the eighteen emendations of the *Sopherim* (Ap. 33), by which they record their change of *'aphphi* (My nostrils) of the primitive text, to *'aphphām* (their nostrils), in order to remove what was thought to be an indelicate and derogatory *Anthropomorphism.*

18 Mine eye . . . Mine ears. Ref. to Pent. (Deut. 13. 8). Ap. 92. See 5. 11; 7. 4, 9; 9. 5; and cp. Jer. 21. 7. Fig. *Anthropopatheia.* Ap. 6.

8. 18—9. 11 (Y[2], p. 1115). THE PUNISHMENTS. (*Introversion and Alternation.*)

Y[2] | A | C | 8. 18. Jehovah. Threatening.
  D | 9. 1-7. Punishment. Commanded.
 B | 9. 8. Ezekiel. Deprecation.
 A | *C* | 9. 9, 10. Jehovah. Threatening.
  D | 9. 11. Punishment executed.

9. 1-7 (D, above). PUNISHMENT COMMANDED. (*Alternation.*)

D | E | 1-6-. Command to slay. (The Agents.)
 F | -6. Obedience.
 E | 7-. Command to defile. (The Agents.)
 F | -7. Obedience.

9. 1-6- (E, above). COMMAND TO SLAY. (THE AGENTS.) (*Introversion.*)

E | y | 1, 2-. Six men.
 z | -2. One man.
 z | 3, 4. One man.
 y | 5, 6. The others.

1 He cried, &c. Contrast "though they cry", &c. (8. 18).

every man. Heb. *'ish.* Ap. 14. II.

destroying = dashing (in pieces).

weapon. A various reading called *Sevīr* (Ap. 34), with some codices, four early printed editions, Sept., and Syr., reads "weapons" (pl.).

2 behold. Fig. *Asterismos.* Ap. 6.

six men. Evidently supernatural. Angels are often called "men".

men. Heb. pl. of *'ĕnōsh.* Ap. 14. III.

man. Heb. *'ish.* Ap. 14. II.

weapon. A various reading called *Sevīr,* with some codices, one early printed edition, and Syr., reads weapons (pl.).

a writer's inkhorn. See *v.* 11. Seen in use in the East to this day.

3 the glory, &c. See note on 1. 28.

the God of Israel. See note on Isa. 29. 23.

God. Heb. Elohim. Ap. 4. I.

cherub. Sing., as in 1. 20. **He**: or, It.

the house: i.e. the Temple building.

the man clothed with linen. Cp. Dan. 10. 5, 6. Rev. 1. 13.

4 the LORD. Heb. Jehovah. Ap. 4. II.

set a mark. Cp. Rev. 7. 3; 9. 4; 13. 16, 17; 20. 4.

mark. Heb. Occurs elsewhere only in Job 31. 35.

5 spare = shield.

6 begin at My sanctuary. Cp. Isa. 10. 12. Jer. 25. 29; 49. 12. Mal. 3. 5. 1 Pet. 4. 17.

ancient = elders.

8 I fell upon my face. See note on 1. 28.

Ah. Fig. *Ecphōnēsis.* Ap. 6.

Lord GOD. Heb. Adonai Jehovah. Ap. 4. VIII (2) and II. See note on 2. 4.

9 iniquity. Heb. *'āvāh.* Ap. 44. iv.

exceeding great. Fig. *Epizeuxis.* Ap. 6. Heb. = "great, by degree, degree".

hath forsaken. See 8. 12.

10 Mine eye, &c. See note on 5. 11; 7. 4; 8. 18.

11 as = according as. Some codices, with three early printed editions, read "according to all which".

X G1 H a (p. 1117) 483 **10** Then I looked, and, °behold, in the °firmament that was above the head of the cherubims there appeared over them as it were °a sapphire stone, as the appearance of the likeness of a throne.

b 2 And He spake unto the °man clothed with linen, and said, "Go in °between °the wheels, *even* under the cherub, and fill thine hand with coals of fire from between the cherubims, and °scatter *them* over the city." And he went in in my sight.

I 3 Now the cherubims stood on the right side of the house, when the [2]man went in; and °the cloud filled the inner court.

4 Then °the glory of °the LORD went up from the cherub, *and stood* over the threshold of the house; and the house was °filled with the cloud, and the court was full of the brightness of °the LORD'S glory.

5 And the °sound of the cherubims' wings was heard *even* to the outer court, as the voice of the °ALMIGHTY GOD when He speaketh.

H b 6 And it came to pass, *that* when He had commanded the [2]man clothed with linen, saying, "Take fire from between [2]the wheels, from between the cherubims;" then he went in, and stood beside °the wheels.

7 And °*one* cherub stretched forth his hand from between the cherubims unto the fire that *was* between the cherubims, and took *thereof,* and put *it* into the hands of *him that was* clothed with linen: who took *it,* and went out.

a 8 And there appeared in the cherubims the form of a °man's hand under their wings.

9 And when I looked, [1]behold the four [-6]wheels by the cherubims, one [-6]wheel by one cherub, and another [-6]wheel by another cherub: and the appearance of the [-6]wheels *was* as the colour of a °beryl stone.

10 And *as for* their appearances, they four had one likeness, as if a [-6]wheel had been in the midst of a [-6]wheel.

11 When they went, they went upon their four sides; they turned not as they went, but to the place whither °the head looked they followed it; they turned not as they went.

12 And their whole body, and their backs, and their hands, and their wings, and the [-6]wheels, *were* full of eyes round about, °*even* the [-6]wheels that they four had.

13 As for the [-6]wheels, it was cried unto them in my hearing, °"O [2]wheel."

14 And every one had four faces: the first face *was* the face of °a cherub, and the second face *was* the face of a [8]man, and the third the face of a lion, and the fourth the face of an eagle.

15 And the °cherubims were °lifted up. This *is* the °living creature that I saw by the river of Chebar.

16 And when the [15]cherubims went, the [6]wheels went by them: and when the cherubims lifted up their wings to mount up from the earth, the same [-6]wheels also turned not from beside them.

17 When they stood, *these* stood; and when they were lifted up, *these* [15]lifted up themselves *also:* for the °spirit of the [15]living creature *was* in them.

I 18 Then the glory of [4]the LORD °departed from °off the threshold of the house, and stood over the [15]cherubims.

19 And the [15]cherubims lifted up their wings, and mounted up from the earth in my sight: when they went out, the [-6]wheels also *were* beside them, and *every one* stood at the door of the east gate of [4]the LORD'S house; and [4]the glory of °the °God of Israel *was* over them above.

20 This *is* the [15]living creature that I saw under [19]the [19]God of Israel by the river of Chebar; and I knew that they *were* °the cherubims. G2

---

10. 1-22 (X, p. 1114). THE CHERUBIM.
(Division.)

X | G1 | 1-19. Particular.
  | G2 | 20-22. General.

10. 1-19 (G1, above). PARTICULAR.
(Alternation and Introversion.)

G1 | H | a | 1. Appearance of the Throne.
   | | b | 2. Fire. Ignition. Command.
   | I | 3-5. Position of the Glory.
   | *H* | *b* | 6, 7. Fire. Ignition. Obedience.
   | | *a* | 8-17. Appearance of the Cherubim.
   | *I* | 18, 19. Position of the Glory.

1 behold. Fig. *Asterismos.* Ap. 6.
firmament = expanse. Cp. 1. 22.
a sapphire stone. Cp. 1. 26. Ex. 24. 10.
2 man. Heb. *'ish.* Ap. 14. II. Not the same word as in *vv.* 8, 14, 21. *'Ish* is used of the man clothed with linen. **between** = amid.
the wheels = the whirling [wheels]. The word here and in *vv.* 6-, 13 is *galgal.* Not the same word as in *vv.* -6, 9, 10, 12, 13-, 16, 19, and chs. 1. 15 and 11. 22. In these it is *'ōphan,* from *'āphan,* to turn round: as in Ex. 14. 25, &c. *Galgal* occurs in Pss. 77. 18 (in the heaven); 83. 13. Ecc. 12. 6. Isa. 5. 28; 17. 13. Jer. 47. 3; and Ezek. 23. 24; 26. 10. Dan. 7. 9 (Chaldean). **scatter** = toss.
3 the cloud, &c. It was here as in Ex. 19. 9; 24. 15, 16, 18. Num. 9. 19; 12. 10. 1 Kings 8. 10.
4 the glory, &c. See note on 1. 28.
the LORD. Heb. Jehovah. Ap. 4. II.
filled, &c. As in 1 Kings 8. 10, 11.
5 sound: i.e. their movement, as though about to depart in flight. Cp. *v.* 18.
ALMIGHTY GOD. Heb. *'El Shaddai.* Ap. 4. VII.
6 the wheels = the wheel. Heb. *'ōphan.* See note on *v.* 2. **7 one:** or, the.
8 man's = human. Heb. *'ādām.* Ap. 14. I. The same word as in *vv.* 14, 21. Not the same as in *vv.* 2, 3, 6.
9 beryl stone = stone of Tarshish.
11 the head = one head (sing.).
12 even the wheels, &c.: or, to the four of them belonged their wheels.
13 O wheel: or, Roll, roll; as implying urgency and celerity for the accomplishment of all that was symbolized by the imagery of this chapter. Same word as in *v.* 2. See note.
14 a cherub = the cherub, identifying it with that of *v.* 7.
15 cherubims. Heb. *sherubim,* pl.; Eng. pl. = cherubs.
lifted up. To bear away the symbol of the Divine presence. **living creature.** Singular.
17 spirit. Heb. *rūach.* Ap. 9.
18 departed. This is what is signified by this chapter. In 43. 1-7, &c., it is seen to return when Israel shall again be restored. The latter will be as literal as the former.
off = over.
19 every one: or [the whole].
the God of Israel. See note on Isa. 29. 23.
God. Heb. *Elohim.* Ap. 4. I.
20 the cherubims: i.e. which he had seen in ch. 1.

483 21 Every one had four faces apiece, and every
one four wings; and the likeness of the hands
of a [8] man *was* under their wings.
22 And the likeness of their faces *was* the
same faces which I saw by the river of Chebar,
their appearances and themselves: they went
°every one straight forward.

V W J (p. 1118) 11 Moreover the °spirit lifted me up, and
brought me unto °the east gate of °the
LORD'S house, which looketh eastward: and
behold at the °door of the gate °five and twenty
°men; among whom I saw °Jaazaniah the son
of Azur, and Pelatiah the son of Benaiah, princes
of the people.
2 Then said He unto me, °"Son of man, these
are the °men that devise °mischief, and give
°wicked counsel in this city:
3 Which say, '*It is* not near; let us build
houses: °this *city is* the caldron, and we *be* the
flesh.'
K c 4 Therefore °prophesy against them, °pro-
phesy, O [2] son of man."
d 5 And the [1] Spirit of [1] the LORD fell upon me,
and said unto me, "Speak; Thus saith [1] the
LORD; 'Thus have ye said, O house of Israel:
for I know the things that come into your
°mind, *every one of* them.
6 Ye have multiplied your slain in this city,
and ye have filled the streets thereof with the
slain.'
7 Therefore thus saith °the Lord GOD; 'Your
slain whom ye have laid in the midst of it,
they *are* the flesh, and [3] this *city is* the caldron:
°but I will bring you forth out of the midst
of it.
8 °Ye have feared the sword; and °I will
bring a sword upon you, °saith [7] the Lord
GOD.
9 And I will bring you out of the midst thereof, and deliver you into the hands of °strangers,
and will execute judgments among you.
10 Ye shall fall by the sword; I will judge
you °in the border of Israel; and °ye shall
know that I *am* [1] the LORD.
11 [3] This *city* shall not be your caldron,
neither shall ye be the flesh in the midst thereof; *but* I will judge you [10] in the border of
Israel:
12 And [10] ye shall know that I *am* [1] the LORD:
for ye have not walked in My °statutes, neither
executed My °judgments, but °have done after
the manners of the °heathen that *are* round
about you.'"

c 13 And it came to pass, when I prophesied,
that Pelatiah the son of Benaiah died.
d Then °fell I down upon my face, and cried
with a loud voice, and said, °"Ah [7] Lord GOD!
wilt Thou make °a full end of °the remnant
of Israel?"

J 14 Again the word of [1] the LORD came unto
me, saying,
15 [2] "Son of man, °thy brethren, *even* °thy
brethren, the [2] men of thy °kindred, and all
the house of Israel wholly, *are* they unto
whom the inhabitants of Jerusalem have said,
'Get you far from [1] the LORD: unto us is this
land given in possession.'

22 every one. Heb. *'ish* (Ap. 14. II), as in *vv.* 2, 3, 6.

11. 1-21 (*W*, p. 1114). **SINS AND PUNISHMENTS.** (*Alternation.*)

W | J | 1-3. Sin. Security.
  K | 4-13. Prophecy. Judgment.
 J | 14, 15. Sin. Security.
  K | 16-21. Promise. Restoration.

1 spirit. As in 2. 2. Heb. *rūach.* Ap. 9. See note on 8. 3.
the east gate. Cp. 43. 1.
the LORD'S. Heb. Jehovah's. Ap. 4. II.
door = entrance.
five and twenty men. These are not the same as in 8. 16, but were princes of the People, a title never given to priests, who were called "princes of the sanctuary" (Isa. 43. 28). They were probably those referred to in Jer. 38. 4.
men. Heb. *'ish.* Ap. 14. II.
Jaazaniah. Not the same as in 8. 11.
2 Son of man. See note on 2. 1.
men. Pl. of Heb. *'ĕnōsh.* Ap. 14. III.
mischief = vanity. Heb. *'āven.* Ap. 44. iii.
wicked = evil. Heb. *rā'a'.* Ap. 44. viii.
3 this city = it (or she), as in *vv.* 7, 11.

11. 4-13 (K, above). **PROPHECY.** (*Alternation.*)

K | c | 4. Prophecy. Command.
  d | 5-12. Threatening.
 c | 13-. Prophecy. Event.
  d | -13. Deprecation.

4 prophesy . . . prophesy. Fig. *Epizeuxis* (Ap. 6), for emphasis.
5 mind = spirit. Heb. *rūach.* Ap. 9.
7 the Lord GOD. Heb. Adonai Jehovah. See note on 2. 4.
but I will bring you forth. A special various reading called *Sevîr* (Ap. 34), with some codices and two early printed editions (one Rabbinic), read "when I take you".
8 Ye have feared, &c. Cp. Jer. 42. 16.
I will bring a sword, &c. See note on 5. 17.
saith the LORD = [is] Adonai Jehovah's oracle.
9 strangers = foreigners.
10 in the border of Israel: i.e. at Riblah, in the extreme north of the land (2 Kings 25. 18-21. Jer. 52. 24-27). Cp. *v.* 11.
ye shall know, &c. See note on 6. 7.
12 statutes . . . judgments. See note on Deut. 4. 1.
have done after the manners, &c. Ref. to Pent. (Lev. 18. 3, 4. Deut. 12. 30, 31). Ap. 92.
heathen = nations.
13 fell I down, &c. See note on 1. 28.
Ah. Fig. *Ecphōnēsis.* Ap. 6.
a full end. Cp. Jer. 4. 27; 5. 10, 18.
the remnant of Israel. Cp. 9. 8.
15 thy brethren . . . thy brethren. Fig. *Epizeuxis.* Ap. 6. **kindred** = redemption.

11. 16-21 (*K*, above). **PROMISE.** (*Alternation.*)

K | e | 16, 17. Restoration.
  f | 18. Evil. Removal.
 e | 19, 20. Conversion.
  f | 21. Evil. Recompense.

16 I have scattered, &c. Cp. Jer. 30. 11; 31. 10, &c.
will I be = I will become.
as a little sanctuary = a sanctuary for a little while.
sanctuary = as a holy place, or asylum, as in Isa. 8. 14.

16 Therefore say, 'Thus saith [7] the Lord GOD; K e
'Although I have cast them far off among the
heathen, and although °I have scattered them
among the countries, yet °will I be to them °as
a little °sanctuary in the countries where they
shall come.'
17 Therefore say, 'Thus saith [7] the Lord GOD;

483 °‘I will even gather you from the °people, and
assemble you out of the countries where ye
have been scattered, and I will give you °the
land of Israel.

f (p. 1118) 18 And they shall come thither, and they shall
take away all the detestable things thereof and
all the abominations thereof from thence.

e 19 And °I will give them one heart, and I will
put a new [1] spirit within you; and I will take
the stony heart out of their flesh, and will give
them an heart of flesh:
20 °That they may walk in My statutes, and
keep Mine ordinances, and do them: and they
shall be My People, and I will be their °God.

f 21 But *as for them* whose heart walketh after
the heart of their detestable things and their
abominations, I will recompense their way upon
their own heads, [8] saith [7] the Lord GOD.”

X (p. 1114) 22 Then did the cherubims lift up their wings,
and the wheels beside them; and °the glory of
°the [20] God of Israel *was* over them above.
23 And [22] the glory of [1] the LORD went up
from the midst of the city, and stood upon the
mountain which *is* on the east side of the city.

U 24 Afterwards the [1] spirit took me up, and
brought me in a vision by the [1] Spirit of [20] God
into Chaldea, to them of the captivity. So the
vision that I had seen went up from me.
25 Then I spake unto them of the captivity
all the things that [1] the LORD had shewed me.

B L g (p. 1119) 12 The word of °the LORD also came unto
me, saying,
2 °“Son of man, thou dwellest in the midst of
a °rebellious house, which have eyes to see, and
see not; they have ears to hear, and hear not:
for they *are* a °rebellious house.
3 Therefore, thou [2] son of man, prepare thee
°stuff for °removing, and remove by day in
their sight; and thou shalt remove from thy
place to another place in their sight: it may be
they will consider, though they *be* a [2] rebellious
house.
4 Then shalt thou bring forth thy [3] stuff by
day in their sight, as [3] stuff for removing: and
thou shalt go forth °at even in their sight, as
they that go forth into captivity.
5 °Dig thou through the wall in their sight,
and carry out thereby.
6 In their sight shalt thou bear *it* upon *thy*
shoulders, *and* carry *it* forth in the °twilight:
thou shalt °cover thy face, that thou see not
°the ground: for I have set thee *for* °a sign
unto the house of Israel.”
7 And I did so °as I was commanded: I
brought forth my [3] stuff by day, as [3] stuff for
°captivity, and in the even I [5] digged through
the wall with mine hand; I brought *it* forth in
the [6] twilight, *and* I bare *it* upon *my* shoulder
in their sight.

h 8 And in the morning came the word of [1] the
LORD unto me, saying,
9 [2] “Son of man, hath not the house of Israel,
the [2] rebellious house, said unto thee, ‘What
doest thou?’
10 Say thou unto them, ‘Thus saith °the Lord
GOD; ‘This °burden *concerneth* the prince in
Jerusalem, and all the house of Israel that *are*
among them.”
11 Say, ‘I *am* your [6] sign: like as I have done,
so shall it be done unto them: they shall remove *and* go into captivity.
12 And the prince that *is* among them shall
bear upon *his* shoulder in the [6] twilight, and
shall go forth: they shall dig through the wall
to carry out thereby: he shall [6] cover his face,
that he see not [6] the ground with *his* eyes.
13 °My net also will I spread upon him, and
he shall be taken in My snare: and I will bring
him to Babylon *to* [6] the land of the Chaldeans;
yet shall he °not see it, though he shall die
there.
14 And I will scatter toward every °wind all
that *are* about him to help him, and all his

17 I will even gather you. Cp. Jer. 31. 10. Ref. to Pent. (Deut. 30. 3). Ap. 92. **people**=peoples.

the land of Israel. Here, “the land”, in Heb. is *’admath* (*’ădāmāh*)=the soil of Israel. This expression occurs seventeen times in Ezekiel (11. 17; 12. 19, 22; 13. 9; 18. 2; 20. 38, 42; 21. 3 (Heb.=*v.* 8); 25. 3, 6; 33. 24; 36. 6; 37. 12; 38. 18, 19; “unto the land” (with ל), 7. 2; 21. 3 (Heb. *v.* 8). The three occurrences of the expression, with *’eretz* instead of *’admath*, are thus safeguarded by the *Massōrah*: viz. 27. 17; 40. 2; 47. 18. (See Ginsburg’s *Massōrah*, vol. i, p. 107, § 1100) and Ap. 93.

19 I will give, &c. Cp. 36. 25-27; and Jer. 32. 39.

20 That they may walk, &c. Ref. to Pent. (Deut. 12. 30, 31). Ap. 92.

God. Heb. Elohim. Ap. 4. I.

22 the God of Israel. See note on Isa. 29. 23.

12. 1-28 (*B*, p. 1106). SIGNS. (*Alternation.*)

B | L | g | 1-7. Signs. Removal.
h | 8-16. Signification.
g | 17, 18. Sign. Eating and drinking.
h | 19, 20. Signification.
L | i | 21, 22. Proverb.
k | 23-25. Explanation.
i | 26, 27. Saying.
k | 28. Explanation.

1 the LORD. Heb. Jehovah. Ap. 4. II.

2 Son of man. See note on 2. 1.

rebellious=perverse. See note on 2. 3.

3 stuff=vessels, or baggage.

removing: i.e. for captivity.

4 at even. The sign (*v.* 11) that the prince (Zedekiah) would try to escape by night (2 Kings 25. 4. Jer. 39. 4).

5 Dig thou through the wall. The sign (*v.* 11) that Zedekiah would do this “betwixt the walls” (2 Kings 25. 4. Jer. 39. 4).

6 cover thy face. The sign (*v.* 11) that Zedekiah would disguise himself.

the ground=the land: i.e. the land Zedekiah was going forth from and would never see again. Heb. *’eth hā-ērez.*

a sign. Heb. *’ōth.* Cp. Gen. 1. 14. Divine portents as to things that were to come.

7 as=according as.

captivity. See notes on *v.* 3.

10 the Lord GOD. Heb. Adonai Jehovah. See note on 2. 4.

burden concerneth the prince (i.e. Zedekiah). Note the Fig. *Paronomasia* (Ap. 6), for emphasis. Heb. *hannasī’ hammassā’.* Eng. “this grief [concerneth] the chief”.

13 My net, &c.: i.e. the Chaldean army which overtook Zedekiah.

not see it. The Fig. *Amphibologia*, or *Ænigma* (Ap. 6), as in Jer. 34. 3. The explanation is given in 2 Kings 25. 7, and Jer. 39. 7; 52. 11. Zedekiah was taken to Babylon, but he never saw it, though he died there.

14 wind. Heb. *rūach.* Ap. 9.

483 bands; and I will °draw out the sword after
them.
15 And °they shall know that I *am* [1]the LORD,
when °I shall scatter them among the nations,
and disperse them in the countries.
16 But °I will leave a few °men of them from
the sword, °from the famine, and from the
pestilence; that they may declare all their
abominations among the °heathen whither
they come; and [15]they shall know that I *am*
[1]the LORD.' "

g (p. 1119) 17 Moreover the word of [1]the LORD came to
me, saying,
18 [2]"Son of man, eat thy bread with quaking,
and drink thy water with trembling and with
carefulness;
h 19 And say unto the People of [6]the land, 'Thus
saith [10]the Lord GOD °of the inhabitants of
Jerusalem, *and* of °the land of Israel; 'They
shall eat their bread with carefulness, and drink
their water with astonishment, that °her [6]land
may be desolate from all that is therein, because
of the violence of °all them that dwell therein.
20 And °the cities that are inhabited °shall be
laid waste, and [6]the land shall be desolate; and
°ye shall know that I *am* [1]the LORD.' ' "

L i 21 And the word of [1]the LORD came unto me,
saying,
22 [2]"Son of man, °what *is* that °proverb *that*
ye have in [19]the land of Israel, saying, 'The
days are °prolonged, and every vision faileth?'
k 23 Tell them therefore, 'Thus saith [10]the
Lord GOD; 'I will make this proverb to cease,
and they shall no more use it as a proverb in
Israel; but say unto them, 'The days °are at
hand, and the °effect of every vision.'
24 For there shall be no more any °vain vision
nor flattering divination within the °house of
Israel.
25 For I *am* [1]the LORD: I will speak, and
the word that I shall speak shall come to pass;
it shall be no more °prolonged: for in your
days, O [2]rebellious house, will I say the word,
and will perform it, °saith [10]the Lord GOD."

i 26 Again the word of [1]the LORD came to me,
saying,
27 [2]"Son of man, °behold, *they of* the house
of Israel say, 'The vision that he seeth *is* for
many days *to come*, and he prophesieth of the
times *that are* far off.'
k 28 Therefore say unto them, 'Thus saith [10]the
Lord GOD; 'There shall none of My words be
[25]prolonged any more, but the word which I
have spoken shall be done, [25]saith [10]the Lord
GOD.' "

B M p. 1120) 13 And the word of °the LORD came unto
me, saying,
2 °"Son of man, prophesy °against °the prophets of Israel that prophesy, and say thou
unto them that prophesy out of their own
hearts,
N O 'Hear ye the word of [1]the LORD;
3 Thus saith °the Lord GOD; 'Woe unto the
°foolish prophets, that follow °their own °spirit,
and have seen nothing!
4 O Israel, thy prophets are like the °foxes in
the °deserts.
5 Ye have not gone up into the °gaps, neither
made up the °hedge for the house of Israel to
stand in the battle in the day of [1]the LORD.
6 They have seen vanity and lying divination,
°saying, [1]'The LORD saith:' and [1]the LORD
hath not sent them: and they have made
others to hope that °they would confirm the
word.
7 Have ye not seen a vain vision, and have
ye not spoken a lying divination, whereas ye
say, [6]'The [1]LORD °saith *it*;' albeit I have not
spoken?

draw out the sword, &c. See note on 5. 2, 17.
15 they shall know. See note on 6. 10.
I shall scatter them. Ref. to Pent. (Lev. 26. 33. Deut. 4. 27; 28. 64). Ap. 92.
16 I will leave, &c. Ref. to Pent. (Deut. 4. 27).
men. Heb. pl. of *'ěnōsh*. Ap. 14. III.
from. Some codices, with four early printed editions, Sept., Syr., and Vulg., read "and from", which emphasises the Fig. *Polysyndeton* (Ap. 6), to enhance the completeness of the enumeration.
heathen = nations.
19 of the inhabitants = to the inhabitants.
the land, &c. = concerning the land, &c. Heb. *'ădmath*. See note on 11. 17.
her. Some codices, with one early printed edition, read "their".
all. The 1611 edition of the A.V. omitted this "all".
20 the cities . . . shall be laid waste. Ref. to Pent. (Lev. 26. 31). Ap. 92.
ye shall know, &c. See note on 6. 7.
22 what . . . ? Fig. *Erotēsis*. Ap. 6.
proverb. See the Structure, "i", on p. 1119.
prolonged: i. e. protracted, or postponed.
23 are at hand. The fulfilment took place five years later.
effect = word: i. e. the [fulfilled] word, meaning, or purpose. **24 vain vision.** Cp. Lam. 2. 14.
house. Some codices, with one early printed edition (Rabbinic in marg.), Aram., Sept., Syr., and Vulg., read "sons". **25 prolonged**: i. e. delayed, or deferred.
saith the LORD = [is] Adonai Jehovah's oracle.
27 behold. Fig. *Asterismos*. Ap. 6.

13. 1-23 (B, p. 1104). PROPHETS AND PROPHETESSES. (*Alternation and Introversion.*)

B | M | 1, 2-. Prophets.
  N | O | -2-7. Lies.
    P | 8, 9. Divine hostility.
      Q | 10-16. Symbols.
  M | 17. Prophetesses.
  N | *Q* | 18, 19. Symbols.
    P | 20, 21 Divine hostility.
      O | 22, 23. Lies.

1 the LORD. Heb. Jehovah. Ap. 4. II.
2 Son of man. See note on 2. 1.
against = concerning. Some codices, and the special reading called *Sevīr* (Ap. 34), with Aram., Sept., and Syr., read "against".
the prophets. See the Structure, "M", above. The ref. is to the false prophets of Israel. Cp. Jer. 5. 30, 31; 23. 9-32; 27. 14; 29. 8, 9, 22, 23.
3 the Lord GOD. Heb. Adonai Jehovah. See note on 2. 4. **foolish.** Heb. *nābēl*. See note on Prov. 1. 7.
their own spirit. Not the Holy Spirit.
spirit. Heb. *rūach*. Ap. 9. **4 foxes** = jackals.
deserts = ruins. **5 gaps** = breaches.
hedge = fence or wall of a vineyard (Num. 22. 24. Ps. 80. 12. Isa. 5. 5).
saying, 'The LORD saith' = saying [it] is Jehovah's oracle.
they would confirm the word = their word would be confirmed.
7 saith it; albeit, &c. A solemn warning as to some of the changes made in the Vulgate versions. Cp. 2. 5-7. Jer. 23. 21.

P 8 Therefore thus saith °the Lord GOD; 'Be-
(p. 1120) cause ye have spoken vanity, and seen lies,
483 therefore, behold, I *am* against you, °saith [3]the
Lord GOD.
9 'And Mine hand shall be upon the prophets that see vanity, and that divine lies:
they shall not be in the °assembly of My People, neither shall they be written in the °writing
of the house of Israel, neither shall they enter
into the °land of Israel; and °ye shall know
that I *am* [3]the Lord GOD.

Q R 10 °Because, even because they have seduced
My People, saying, 'Peace;' and *there was* no
peace;

S and °one built up °a wall, and, °lo, °others
°daubed it with °untempered *morter:*

T l 11 Say unto them which [10]daub *it* with [10]un-
tempered *morter,* that it shall fall: there shall
be an overflowing °shower; and ye, O great hailstones, shall fall; and a stormy °wind shall rend *it.*

m 12 [10]Lo, when the wall is fallen, shall it not
be said unto you, 'Where *is* the [10]daubing
wherewith ye have [10]daubed *it?*"

T l 13 Therefore thus saith [3]the Lord GOD; 'I
will even rend *it* with a stormy wind in
My fury; and there shall be an overflowing
[11]shower in Mine anger, and great hailstones
in *My* fury to consume *it.*

m 14 So will I break down the [10]wall that ye
have [10]daubed with [10]untempered *morter,* and
bring it down to the ground, so that the foundation thereof shall be discovered, and °it shall
fall, and ye shall be consumed in the midst thereof: and °ye shall know that I *am* [1]the LORD.

S 15 Thus will I accomplish My wrath upon
the wall, and upon them that have [10]daubed it
with [10]untempered *morter,* and will say unto
you, 'The wall *is* no *more,* neither they that
[10]daubed it;

R 16 *To wit,* the prophets of Israel which prophesy concerning Jerusalem, and which see
°visions of °peace for her, and *there is* no
°peace, [8]saith [3]the Lord GOD.

M 17 Likewise, thou [2]son of man, °set thy face
against the daughters of thy People, which
prophesy out of °their own heart; and prophesy thou against them,

N Q 18 And say, 'Thus saith [3]the Lord GOD;
Woe to the *women* that °sew °pillows to all
°armholes, and °make °kerchiefs upon the
head of every °stature to °hunt °souls! °Will
ye °hunt the °souls of My People, and will ye
save the °souls alive *that come* unto you?
19 And will ye pollute Me among My People
for handfuls of barley and for pieces of bread,
°to slay the [18]souls that should not die, and
°to save the [18]souls alive that should not live,
by °your lying to My People that hear *your* lies?

P 20 Wherefore thus saith [3]the Lord GOD;
°'Behold, I *am* against your [18]pillows, wherewith ye there hunt the [18]souls to make *them*
°fly, and °I will tear them from your arms, and
will let the [18]souls go, *even* the [18]souls that ye
[18]hunt to make *them* °fly.
21 [19]Your [18]kerchiefs also will [20]I tear, and
deliver My People out of your hand, and they
shall be no more in °your hand to be [18]hunted;
and [14]ye shall know that I *am* [1]the LORD.

8 saith the Lord GOD=[is] Adonai Jehovah's oracle.
9 assembly=secret council. **writing**=register.
land=soil. Heb. *'admath.* See note on 11. 17.
ye shall know, &c. This *formula* occurs only here, 23. 49; and 24. 24 (not the same as *v.* 14; 6. 7, &c.)

13. 10-16 (Q, p. 1120). SYMBOLS.
(*Introversion and Alternation.*)

Q | R | 10-. False peace.
S | -10. Wall.
T | l | 11. Storm.
m | 12. Fall.
T | *l* | 13. Storm.
m | 14. Fall.
S | 15. Wall.
R | 16. False peace.

10 Because, even because. Fig. *Epizeuxis.* Ap. 6.
one built=he: i.e. one=a false prophet.
a wall=the outer wall of a house.
lo. Fig. *Asterismos.* Ap. 6.
others: i.e. the false prophets. Cp. *v.* 16.
daubed=coated.
untempered morter=whitewash. Cp. Matt. 23. 29. Acts 23. 3. **11 shower**=rain. Cp. Matt. 7. 25, 27.
wind. Heb. *rūach.* Ap. 9.
14 it. Fem. referring to *ruach* (the wind in *v.* 11).
ye shall know, &c. See note on 6. 7.
16 visions=a vision.
peace. Ref. to meaning of the word Jerusalem.
17 set thy face against, &c. This required Divine courage on the part of Ezekiel. Cp. 14. 8; 20. 46; 21. 2; 29. 2; 38. 2.
their own heart. Cp. *vv.* 2, 3, and a similar transition from men to women in Isa. 3. 16, 17.
18 sew pillows to all armholes=sew together coverings upon all the joints of My hands: i.e. hide from the People the hands of Jehovah lifted up and stretched forth in judgment (Isa. 26. 11; 52. 10).
pillows=coverings for purposes of concealment. Heb. *k^eṣāthōth* (occurs only here and in *v.* 20), from *kāṣāh*, to conceal, to hide. First occ. (of *kāṣāh*) Gen. 7. 19, 20; 9. 23; 18. 17; 24. 65; 37. 26; 38. 14, 15, &c. The object is shown in Isa. 26. 11.
armholes=My hands; referring to the judgments they were to execute (14. 9, 13). Cp. *vv.* 9, 21, 22, 23. The Sept. renders it *proskephalaia*=for the head.
make kerchiefs upon the head of every stature =make mantles to cover the heads (and therefore the eyes) of those on whom the judgments of God's hand were about to fall, lest they should see.
kerchiefs=wraps that cleave close round the head. Heb. *mispāḥōth* (occurs only here), from *ṣaphah*, to join, or cleave closely. *Ṣaphah* occurs 1 Sam. 2. 36 (*put*=attach); 26. 19 (*abiding*=cleaving). Job 30. 7 (*gathered together*). Isa. 14. 1 (*cleave*). Hab. 2. 15 (*puttest*=holdest). The object being to cover the head so that God's hand may not be seen (Isa. 26. 11).
stature=tall figure. Heb. *ḳōmāh*=height. First occ. Gen. 6. 15. Cp. 1 Sam. 16. 7 (his stature); 28. 20, &c. Put, here, for every man of high or lofty station: i.e. for the princes or rulers in Jerusalem, whose eyes were blinded by these false prophetesses.
hunt=harry, or ensnare.
souls. Heb. *nephesh.* Ap. 13. Put here by Fig. *Synecdoche* (of the Part), Ap. 6, for the People.
Will ye . . . ? This is not a question, but a statement.
19 to slay, &c.=to prophesy (falsely) that they should be slain. Fig. *Metonymy* (of Subject), Ap. 6.
to save, &c.=to promise life to those who should not live. Fig. *Metonymy* (of Subject), Ap. 6.
your. Masc. suffix, indicating unwomanly character.
20 Behold. Fig. *Asterismos.* Ap. 6. **fly**=escape.
I will tear. So that these wraps could be torn away.
21 your. Fem. suffix.
22 the righteous=a righteous one.

22 Because with lies ye have made the heart *O*
of °the righteous sad, whom I have not made

483 sad; and strengthened the hands of °the wicked,
that he should not return from °his wicked way,
°by promising him °life:
23 Therefore ye shall see no more vanity, nor
divine divinations: for I will deliver My People
out of your hand: and [14] ye shall know that I
am [1] the LORD.'"

D U (p. 1122) 14 °Then came certain of °the elders of
°Israel unto me, and sat before me.
2 And the word of °the LORD came unto me,
saying,
3 °"Son of man, these °men have set up
their °idols in their heart, and put the stumblingblock of their °iniquity °before their face:
should I be enquired of at all by them?
4 Therefore speak unto *them*, and say unto
them, 'Thus saith °the Lord GOD; °'Every
man of the house of Israel that setteth up his
[3] idols in his heart, and putteth the stumblingblock of his [3] iniquity °before his face, and cometh
to the prophet;
V I [2] the LORD °will answer him that cometh
according to the multitude of his idols;
W 5 That I may take the house of Israel in their
own heart, because they are all estranged from
Me through their [3] idols.''
U 6 Therefore say unto the house of Israel,
'Thus saith [4] the Lord GOD; 'Repent, and
°turn *yourselves* from your [3] idols; and turn
away your faces from all your abominations.
7 For [4] every one of the house of Israel, or of
the stranger that sojourneth in Israel, which
separateth himself from Me, and setteth up his
[3] idols in his heart, and putteth the stumblingblock of his [3] iniquity [4] before his face, and
cometh to a prophet to enquire of him concerning Me;
V I [2] the LORD [4] will answer him by Myself:
8 And °I will set My face against that °man,
and °will make him a sign and a proverb, and °I
will cut him off from the midst of My people;
and °ye shall know that I *am* [2] the LORD.
9 And if the prophet be deceived when he hath
spoken a thing, I [2] the LORD °have deceived
that prophet, and °I will stretch out My hand
upon him, and will destroy him from the midst
of My people Israel.
10 And °they shall bear the punishment of
their [3] iniquity: the punishment of the prophet
shall be even as the punishment of him that
seeketh *unto him*;
W 11 That the house of Israel may go no more
astray from Me, neither be polluted any more
with all their °transgressions; but that they
may be My people, and I may be their °God,
°saith [4] the Lord GOD.'"

E X¹ n¹ 12 The word of [2] the LORD came again to me,
saying,
13 [3] Son of man, when °the land °sinneth
against Me by °trespassing grievously, then
will [9] I stretch out Mine hand upon it, and will

the wicked = a lawless one. Heb. *rāshā'*. Ap. 44. x.
his wicked way = his wrong way. Heb *ra'a'*. Ap. 44. viii.
by . . . life. Here the Figures in *v.* 20 are translated.
life. Continuance in life: i.e. escape from the judgments announced by Jehovah.

14. 1-11 (D, p. 1097). ELDERS.
(Extended Alternation.)

D | U | 1-4-. Sin. Idolaters seeking the Prophet.
  | V | -4. Answer of Jehovah.
  | W | 5. Purpose of His answer.
  | *U* | 6, 7-. Sin. Idolaters seeking the Prophet.
  | *V* | -7-10. Answer of Jehovah.
  | *W* | 11. Purpose of His answer.

1 Then came certain of the elders of Israel. These are to be distinguished from the elders of Judah (8. 1). They had no knowledge (probably) of what was transpiring in Judæa. They had travelled from Tel-abib. **the elders.** See the Structure (p. 1097).
Israel. See 8. 11, 12; 9. 6. In 8. 1 we have Judah's elders. **2 the LORD.** Heb. Jehovah. Ap. 4. II.
3 Son of man. See note on 2. 1.
men. Heb. pl. of *'ĕnōsh*. Ap. 14. III.
idols = manufactured idols.
iniquity = perversity. Heb. *'āvāh*. Ap. 44. iv.
before their face. Instead of God's law, according to Deut. 6. 8; 11. 18; and Prov. 3. 21-23.
4 the Lord GOD. Heb. Adonai Jehovah. See note on 2. 4. **Every man.** Heb. *'īsh, 'īsh*. Ap. 14. II.
before = in front of, or right before.
will answer, &c. = have been replied to for him; he hath come amid [the] multitude of his idols: i.e. he hath answered My claims by classing his idols with Me. The form is *Niphal* which in all its three occ. is rendered Passive, except here and *v.* 7. See Job 11. 2; 19. 7, and Prov. 21. 13. **6 turn yourselves** = turn ye.
7 will answer, &c. = and being replied to for him in Myself: i.e. by his comparing his idols with Me. See note on *v.* 4.
8 I will set My face, &c. Ref. to Pent. (Lev. 17. 10; 26. 17). Ap. 92. **man.** Heb. *'īsh*. Ap. 14. II.
will make him, &c. Ref. to Pent. (Num. 26. 10. Deut. 28. 37). Some codices, with eight early printed editions, read "will make him desolate, for a sign and a proverb".
I will cut him off, &c. Ref. to Pent. (Gen. 17. 14. Ex. 12. 15, 19; 30. 33, 38. Lev. 7. 20, 21, 25, 27; 17. 4, 9; 19. 8; 23. 29. Num. 9. 13, &c.). Ap. 92.
ye shall know, &c. See note on 6. 7.
9 have deceived. Heb. idiom = have permitted him to be deceived: i.e. as a judicial punishment for his own deception of the People.
I will stretch out, &c. Ref. to Pent. (Ex. 3. 20, &c.).
10 they shall bear the punishment, &c. Ref. to Pent. (Ex. 28. 38. Lev. 5. 1, 17. Num. 14. 34, &c.).
11 transgressions = rebellions. Heb. *pāsha'*. Ap. 44. ix. **God.** Heb. Elohim. Ap. 4. I.
saith the Lord GOD = [is] Adonai Jehovah's oracle.

14. 12—15. 8 (E, p. 1097). THE LAND AND CITY. (JUDGMENTS.) *(Division.)*

E | X¹ | 14. 12-23. Literal.
  | X² | 15. 1-8. Symbolical.

14. 12-23 (X¹, above). LITERAL.
(Repeated Alternation.)

X¹ | n¹ | 12, 13. Famine.
   | o¹ | 14. Noah, Daniel, and Job.
   | n² | 15. Beasts.
   | o² | 16. The three men.
   | n³ | 17. Sword.
   | o³ | 18. The three men.
   | n⁴ | 19. Pestilence.
   | o⁴ | 20. Noah, Daniel, and Job.
   | n⁵ | 21. The four sore judgments.
   | o⁵ | 22, 23. A remnant.

13 the land = a land. **sinneth.** Heb. *chāṭā'*. Ap. 44. i. **trespassing.** Heb. *mā'al*. Ap. 44. xi. Note the Fig. *Polyptōton* (Ap. 6). Heb. = to trespass a trespass: i.e. to trespass exceedingly. See note on Gen. 26. 28. Ref. to Pent. (Lev. 5. 15; 6. 2; 26. 40. Num. 5. 6, 12, 27). Ap. 92.

483 °break the staff °of the bread thereof, and will
send famine upon it, and will [8]cut off °man
and beast from it:

o^{1} (p. 1122) 14 Though these °three [8]men, °Noah, °Daniel,
and °Job, were in it, they should deliver *but*
their own °souls by their righteousness, [11]saith
[4]the Lord GOD.

n^{2} 15 °"If I cause °noisome beasts to pass through
the land, and they spoil it, so that it be desolate, that no man may pass through because
of the beasts:

o^{2} 16 *Though* these [14]three [8]men *were* in it, *as* I
live, [11]saith [4]the Lord GOD, they shall deliver
neither sons nor daughters; they only shall be
delivered, but the land shall be desolate.

n^{3} 17 Or °*if* I bring a sword upon that land, and
say, 'Sword, go through the land;' so that I
[8]cut off [13]man and beast from it:

o^{3} 18 Though these [14]three men *were* in it, *as* I
live, [11]saith [4]the Lord GOD, they shall deliver
neither sons nor daughters, but they only shall
be delivered themselves.

n^{4} 19 Or *if* I send a pestilence into that land, and
pour out My fury upon it in blood, to [8]cut off
from it [13]man and beast:

o^{4} 20 Though [14]Noah, Daniel, and Job, *were* in
it, *as* I live, [11]saith [4]the Lord GOD, they shall
deliver neither son nor daughter; they shall *but*
deliver their own [14]souls by their righteousness.

n^{5} 21 For" thus saith [4]the Lord GOD, °"How
much more when I send My four sore judgments upon Jerusalem, the sword, and the
famine, and the [15]noisome beast, and the pestilence, to [8]cut off from it [13]man and beast?

o^{5} 22 Yet, °behold, therein shall be left °a remnant that shall be brought forth, *both* sons
and daughters: °behold, they shall come forth
unto you, and ye shall see °their way and
their doings: and ye shall be comforted concerning the °evil that I have brought upon
Jerusalem, *even* concerning all that I have
brought upon it.
23 And °they shall comfort you, when ye see
their ways and their doings: and [8]ye shall
know that I have not done without cause all
that I have done in it, [11]saith [4]the Lord GOD."

X^{2} p (p. 1123) **15** And the word of °the LORD came unto
me, saying,
2 °"Son of man, What is the vine tree more
than any tree, *or* °*than* a branch which °is
among the trees of the forest?
3 Shall wood be taken thereof to do any work?
or will *men* take a °pin of it to hang any vessel
thereon?
4 °Behold, it is °cast into the fire for fuel; the
fire devoureth both the ends of it, and the midst
of it is burned. °Is it meet for *any* work?

q 5 [4]Behold, when it was whole, it was meet
for no work: how much less shall it be meet
yet for *any* work, when the fire hath devoured
it, and it is burned?

p 6 Therefore thus saith °the Lord GOD; 'As
the vine tree among the trees of the forest,
which I have given to the fire for fuel, °so will
I give the inhabitants of Jerusalem.

7 And °I will set My face against them; they q
shall go out from *one* fire, and *another* fire
shall devour them; and °ye shall know that
I *am* [1]the LORD, when °I set My face against
them.
8 And I will make the land desolate, because
they have °committed a °trespass, °saith [6]the
Lord GOD."

16 Again the word of °the LORD came un- F Y A (p. 1124)
to me, saying,

---

break the staff of the bread. Ref. to Pent. (Lev. 26. 26, &c.). Ap. 92.
of=that is to say. Gen. of Apposition. Ap. 17. 4.
man. Heb. *'ādām.* Ap. 14. I.
14 three men. In Jer. 15. 1, we have two men, "Moses and Samuel", as intercessors. See note there. Here we have "three men", also as intercessors. All three prevailed in saving others. Noah (1 Pet. 3. 20). Daniel (2. 5, 48, 49). Job (42. 8–10).
Noah, Daniel, and Job. This order is determined by the Structure, which is an *Introversion*, in order to separate the true Israelite (of the nation of Israel) from the two who lived before the nation was formed (which is the subject of the book of Exodus).

| NOAH. Earlier than Job, but before Israel was a nation.
| DANIEL. A true Israelite.
| JOB. Later than Noah, but before Israel was a nation.

Noah prevailed in saving others (the whole human race). Gen. 6—9.
Daniel prevailed in saving his fellow wise men (Dan. 2. 24). He is mentioned again in 28. 3. While Ezekiel bears witness to Daniel (already fourteen years in Babylon), Daniel bears witness to Jeremiah (Dan. 9. 2).
souls=soul. Heb. *nephesh.* Ap. 13.
15 If I cause noisome beasts, &c. Ref. to Pent. (Lev. 26. 22). Ap. 92.
noisome=annoying, hurtful.
17 if I bring a sword, &c. Ref. to Pent. (Lev. 26. 25). See Ezek. 5. 17.
21 How much more, &c. National judgments are thus sent for national sins. Cp. *v.* 13.
22 behold. Fig. *Asterismos.* Ap. 6.
a remnant. This is always used in a good sense.
their way, &c.: i.e. their good way and doings.
evil. Heb. *rā'a'.* Ap. 44. viii.
23 they: i.e. the remnant of *v.* 22.

15. 1-8 (X^{2}, p. 1122). SYMBOLICAL. (VINE.)
(*Alternation.*)

X^{2} p | 1–4. Vine. Fit only for fuel. } Symbol.
q | 5. Devoured by fire.
p | 6. Inhabitants of Jerusalem. } Signification.
q | 7, 8. Devoured by another fire.

1 the LORD. Heb. Jehovah. Ap. 4. II.
2 Son of man. See note on 2. 1.
than a. Supply the *Ellipsis* [What is a vine] branch?"
is=hath come to be.
3 pin=peg. **4 Behold.** Fig. *Asterismos.* Ap. 6.
cast into the fire. Cp. John 15. 6.
Is it meet . . . ? Fig. *Erotēsis.* Ap. 6.
6 the Lord GOD. Heb. Adonai Jehovah. See note on 2. 4.
so will I give. Fulfilled in 2 Kings 25. 9.
7 I will set My face. Ref. to Pent. (Lev. 17. 10).
ye shall know, &c. See note on 6. 7.
8 committed a trespass. Fig. *Polyptōton.* Ap. 6. Heb. "trespassed a trespass" for emphasis=committed a great trespass, as in 14. 13.
trespass. Heb. *mā'al.* Ap. 44. xi.
saith the Lord GOD=[is] Adonai Jehovah's oracle.

16. 1-63 [For Structure see next page].

16. 1 the LORD. Heb. Jehovah. Ap. 4. II.

483 2 °"Son of man, cause °Jerusalem to know
her abominations,
3 And say, 'Thus saith °the Lord GOD unto
Jerusalem; 'Thy °birth and thy nativity *is* of
the land of Canaan; °thy father *was* an Amorite, and thy mother an Hittite.
4 And *as for* thy nativity, in the day thou
wast born thy navel was not cut, neither wast
thou washed in water °to supple *thee*; thou
wast not °salted at all, nor swaddled at all.
5 None eye pitied thee, to do any of these
unto thee, to have compassion upon thee; but
thou wast cast out in the open field, to the
lothing of thy °person, °in the day that thou
wast born.
6 And °when I passed by thee, and saw thee
°polluted in thine own blood, I said unto thee
°*when thou wast* in thy blood, 'Live;' yea,
I said unto thee °*when thou wast* in thy blood,
'Live.'
7 I have caused thee to multiply as the bud
of the field, and thou °hast increased and
waxen great, and thou art come to excellent
ornaments: *thy* breasts are °fashioned, and
thine hair is grown, whereas thou *wast* naked
and bare.
8 Now when I passed by thee, and looked
upon thee, °behold, °thy time *was* the time of
love; and °I spread My skirt over °thee, and
covered thy nakedness: yea, I sware unto
°thee, and entered into a covenant with °thee,
°saith [3]the Lord GOD, and thou becamest
Mine.
9 Then washed I thee with water; yea, I
throughly washed away thy blood from thee,
and I anointed thee with oil.

B r 10 I clothed thee also with broidered work,
(p. 1124) and shod thee with °badgers' skin, and I girded
thee about with fine linen, and I covered thee
with silk.
11 I decked thee also with ornaments, and
I put bracelets upon thy hands, and a chain on
thy neck.
12 And I put a jewel °on thy forehead, and
earrings in thine ears, and a beautiful crown
upon thine head.
13 Thus wast thou decked with gold and
silver; and thy raiment *was of* fine linen, and
silk, and broidered work;

s thou didst eat °fine flour, and honey, and oil:
and thou wast °exceeding beautiful, and thou
didst prosper into °a kingdom.

C 14 And thy renown went forth among the
°heathen for thy beauty: for it *was* perfect
through My comeliness, which I had put upon
thee, [8]saith [3]the Lord GOD.

C 15 But thou didst °trust in thine own beauty,
and °playedst the harlot because of thy renown, and pouredst out thy °fornications on
every one that passed by; his it was.

B r 16 And of thy garments thou didst take, and
deckedst thy high places with divers colours,
and [15]playedst the harlot thereupon: °*the like
things* shall not come, neither shall it be *so*.
17 Thou hast also taken thy fair jewels of
My gold and of My silver, which I had given
thee, and madest to thyself images °of men,
and didst commit °whoredom with them,
18 And tookest thy broidered garments, and

16. 1-63 (**F**, p. 1104). JERUSALEM. (DESERTED INFANT.) (*Alternation.*)

F | Y | 1-22. Birth and Education.
  Z | 23-43. Sins.
 Y | 44-46. Birth and Sisterhood.
  Z | 47-63. Sins.

16. 1-22 (Y, above). BIRTH AND EDUCATION. (*Introversion and Alternation.*)

Y | A | 1-9. Birth. Pollution.
  B | r | 10-13-. Garments.
   | s | -13. Food.
    C | 14. Beauty. Renowned.
    C | 15. Beauty. Misused.
  B | *r* | 16-18. Garments.
   | *s* | 19-21. Food.
 | *A* | 22. Birth. Pollution.

2 Son of man. See note on 2. 1.

Jerusalem is the subject of this chapter by *interpretation*. Note the Fig. *Prosōpographia* (Ap. 6). Not the nation as such. By *application*, the reader may, by grace, refer it to himself.

3 the Lord GOD. Heb. Adonai Jehovah. See note on 2. 4.

birth, &c. = excisions and kinships. Cp. Isa. 51. 1. Only other occurrences, 21. 30; 29. 14.

thy father, &c. : i.e. thy founder. This refers to the first builders of Jebus; not to Abraham and his seed. Jebus was a Canaanite city. See Ap. 68. Thus Satan occupied in advance both land and capital as soon as the promise to Abraham was known. See Ap. 23 and 25.

4 to supple = to cleanse.

salted : i.e. rubbed, or washed with salt. This is the custom in the Land to-day.

5 person = soul. Heb. *nephesh.* Ap. 13.

in the day. See Ap. 18.

6 when. This word is not in the Hebrew text.

polluted = trodden under foot. Referring to the city, of course.

when thou . . . blood, &c. Note the Fig. *Epizeuxis* (Ap. 6), for emphasis. Canaanite cities were founded in blood, as proved to-day by human sacrifices discovered on the foundations. See note on 1 Kings 9. 15-17.

7 hast increased = didst increase. This does not refer to the increase in Egypt, but to the city. All the tenses in this verse should be past tenses.

fashioned = developed.

8 behold. Fig. *Asterismos.* Ap. 6.

thy . . . thee : i.e. the city. Not the nation at Sinai.

thy time, &c. Of this covenant nothing has been recorded. The secret is here first revealed.

I spread My skirt, &c. The symbolic act to-day, signifying the taking under one's protection. Common in the East for marrying. Cp. Ruth 3. 9.

saith the Lord GOD = [is] Adonai Jehovah's oracle.

10 badgers' skin. Similarly so used to present day. Ref. to Pent. (Ex. 25. 5; 26. 14. Num. 4. 6). Ap. 92. Occurs elsewhere, only here. No reference to the tabernacle.

12 on thy forehead = in thy nose. Referring to the decorations, &c., of the city after being occupied by David.

13 fine flour, &c. Put by Fig. *Synecdoche* (of the Part), Ap. 6, for all kinds of delicacies.

exceeding beautiful. Heb. *m*e'*od m*e'*od.* Fig. *Epizeuxis* (Ap. 6), thus well rendered.

a kingdom. Hence the expression, "Judah and Jerusalem", the latter being reckoned as a separate kingdom. **14 heathen** = nations.

15 trust = confide. Heb. *bāṭaḥ.* Ap. 69. I.

playedst the harlot. All these expressions that follow are to be interpreted of idolatry, and not to sins of the flesh, to which they are likened.

fornications : i.e. idolatrous acts.

16 the like things. Supply the *Ellipsis* better thus: "thereupon: [saying] they (the curses) come not, and it (the threatened judgment) will not be."

17 of men = of the male: i.e. the *Phallus*, referring to the *Asherah.* See Ap. 42. **whoredom** = idolatry.

483 coveredst °them: and thou hast set Mine oil
and Mine incense before °them.
s (p. 1124) 19 My °meat also which I gave thee, [13]fine
flour, and oil, and honey, *wherewith* I fed thee,
thou hast even set it before them °for a sweet
savour: and °*thus* it was, [14]saith [3]the Lord GOD.
20 Moreover thou hast taken thy sons and
thy daughters, whom thou hast borne unto
Me, and these hast thou °sacrificed unto them
to be devoured. *Is this* of thy °whoredoms
a small matter,
21 That thou hast °slain My °children, and
delivered them to cause them to pass through
the fire for them?
A 22 And in all thine °abominations and thy
[20]whoredoms thou hast not remembered the
days of thy youth, when thou wast naked and
bare, *and* wast °polluted in thy blood.
Z D t (p. 1125) 23 And it came to pass after all thy °wicked-
ness, °(woe, woe unto thee! [14]saith [3]the Lord
GOD;)
24 '*That* thou hast also built unto thee an
°eminent place, and hast made thee an high
place in every street.
25 Thou hast built thy high place at every
head of the way, and hast made thy beauty
to be abhorred, and hast opened thy feet to
every one that passed by, and multiplied thy
[20]whoredoms.
u 26 Thou hast also committed [15]fornication
with the Egyptians thy neighbours, °great of
flesh; and hast increased thy [20]whoredoms, to
provoke Me to anger.
E 27 [8]Behold, therefore °I have stretched out
My hand °over thee, and have diminished thine
°ordinary *food*, and delivered thee unto the
°will of them that hate thee, the daughters of
the Philistines, which are ashamed of thy lewd
way.
D u 28 Thou hast [15]played the whore also with
the Assyrians, because thou wast unsatiable;
yea, thou hast [15]played the harlot with them,
and yet couldest not be satisfied.
29 Thou hast moreover multiplied thy [15]forni-
cation in the land of Canaan °unto Chaldea;
and yet thou wast not satisfied herewith.
t 30 How weak is thine heart, [14]saith [3]the Lord
GOD, seeing thou doest all these *things*, the
work of an °imperious whorish °woman;
31 In that thou buildest thine [24]eminent place
in the head of every way, and makest thine
high place in every street; and hast not been
as an harlot, in that thou scornest °hire;
32 °*But as* a wife that committeth adultery,
which taketh strangers instead of her husband!
33 They °give gifts to all whores: but thou
givest thy °gifts to all thy lovers, and °hirest
them, that they may come unto thee on every
side for thy [20]whoredom.
34 And the contrary is in thee from *other*
women in thy [20]whoredoms, whereas none
followeth thee to commit whoredoms: and in
that thou givest a °reward, and no °reward is
given unto thee, therefore thou art contrary.
E 35 Wherefore, O °harlot, hear the word of
[1]the LORD:'
36 Thus saith [3]the Lord GOD; 'Because thy
°filthiness was poured out, and thy nakedness
discovered through thy [20]whoredoms with thy
lovers, and with all the °idols of thy [22]abomina-
tions, °and by the blood of thy [21]children, which
thou didst give unto them;
37 [8]Behold, therefore I will °gather all thy
lovers, with whom thou hast taken pleasure,
and all *them* that thou hast loved, with all
them that thou hast hated; I will even °gather
them round about against thee, and will discover thy nakedness unto [18]them, that they may
see all thy nakedness.
38 And I will judge thee, °as women that
break wedlock and shed blood are judged; and
I will give thee blood in fury and jealousy.
39 And I will also give thee into their hand,
and they shall throw down thine [24]eminent

---

them = i. e. these images.

19 meat. Put by Fig. *Synecdoche* (of the Part), Ap. 6, for all kinds of food.

for a sweet savour. Ref. to Pent. A legal phrase, found only in Ezekiel outside the Pentateuch. But in Ezekiel four times: viz. 6. 13; 16. 19; 20. 28, 41. See notes on Gen. 8. 21. Lev. 1. 9. Ap. 92.

thus it was = [so] it became.

20 sacrificed, &c. As offerings to idols. Cp. *v.* 36; 20. 26, 31; 23. 39. 2 Kings 16. 3. Ps. 106. 37, 38. Isa. 57. 5. Jer. 7. 31; 32. 35, &c.

whoredoms = idolatries. See notes on *v.* 15.

21 slain My children. See note on *v.* 20, above. Ref. to Pent. (Lev. 18. 21). Ap. 92. children = sons.

22 abominations. Put by Fig. *Metonymy* (of Adjunct), Ap. 6, for that which Jehovah abominated.

polluted = wallowing, or weltering.

16. 23-43 (Z, p. 1124). SINS.
(*Alternation and Introversion.*)

Z | D | t | 23-25. Whoredoms. (Idolatries.)
| | u | 26. Egyptians.
| E | 27. Threatenings.
| *D* | *u* | 28, 29. Assyrians.
| | *t* | 30-34. Whoredoms. (Idolatries.)
| *E* | 35-43. Threatenings.

23 wickedness. Heb. *rā'a'*. Ap. 44. viii.

woe, woe. Note the Figs. *Cataploce* and *Epizeuxis* (Ap. 6), for emphasis.

24 eminent place = brothel house. Put by Fig. *Metonymy* (of Subject), Ap. 6, for the idol's temple.

26 great of flesh = lustful. Referring to their idolatries.

27 I have stretched out My hand, &c. Ref. to Pent. (Ex. 7. 19, &c.). Ap. 92. over = against.

ordinary food = allowance. Referring to food as measured out to captives or slaves.

will = desire. Heb. *nephesh*. Ap. 13.

29 unto Chaldea = Assyrian idolatry as well as Egyptian (*v.* 26). See the Structure, above.

30 imperious = headstrong, or without shame.

woman = wife. Cp. *v.* 32.

31 hire. See note on "reward", *v.* 34.

32 But as = [Thou hast been].

33 give gifts = give fees. gifts = presents.

hirest = bribest.

34 reward = hire. Used especially for the hire of fornication. Heb. *'ethnan*. Ref. to Pent. (Deut. 23. 18). Ap. 92. Used outside the Pentateuch only in 16. 31 (hire), 33, 41. Isa. 23. 17 (hire), 18 (hire). Hos. 9. 1 (reward). Mic. 1. 7 (hire). **35 harlot** = idolatress.

36 filthiness. Heb. = brass. Put by Fig. *Metonymy* (of Adjunct), Ap. 6, for money's worth: i. e. the money of the brothel. See *v.* 31.

idols = manufactured gods.

and by = even as. **37 gather** = gather out.

38 as = with the judgments meted out to: i. e. by death (Lev. 20. 20. Deut. 22. 22. John 8. 5). Cp. Gen. 38. 24.

483 place, and shall break down thy high places: they shall strip thee also of thy clothes, and shall take thy fair jewels, and leave thee naked and bare.

40 They shall also bring up °a company against thee, and they shall stone thee with stones, and thrust thee through with their swords.

41 And they shall burn thine houses with fire, and execute judgments upon thee in the sight of many °women: and I will cause thee to cease from [15]playing the harlot, and thou also shalt give no [31]hire any more.

42 So will I make My fury toward thee to rest, and My jealousy shall depart from thee, and I will be quiet, and will be no more angry.

43 Because thou hast not remembered the days of thy youth, but hast °fretted Me in all these *things*; [8]behold, therefore I also will recompense thy way upon *thine* head, [14]saith [3]the Lord GOD: and °thou shalt not commit this lewdness above all thine [22]abominations.

Y F (p. 1126) 44 [8]Behold, every one that useth proverbs shall use *this* °proverb against thee, saying, 'As *is* the mother, *so is* her daughter.'

G 45 Thou *art* thy mother's daughter, that lotheth her husband and her [21]children;

F and thou *art* the sister of thy sisters, which lothed their husbands and their [21]children: your [3]mother *was* an Hittite, and your father an Amorite.

G H 46 And °thine elder sister

J v *is* Samaria, she and her °daughters

w that dwell at thy left hand:

H and thy °younger sister,

J w that dwelleth at thy right hand,

v *is* Sodom and her °daughters.

Z K M x 47 Yet hast thou not walked after their ways, nor done after their abominations: but, °as *if that were* °a very little *thing*, thou wast corrupted more than they in all thy ways.

y 48 *As* I live, [14]saith [3]the Lord GOD, Sodom thy sister hath not done, she nor her [46]daughters, °as thou hast done, thou and thy daughters.

z 49 [8]Behold, this °was the °iniquity of thy sister Sodom, pride, fulness of bread, and °abundance of idleness was in her and in her daughters, neither did she strengthen the hand of the poor and needy.

50 And they were haughty, and committed abomination before Me: therefore I took them away °as I saw *good.*

y 51 Neither hath Samaria committed half of thy °sins;

x but thou hast multiplied thine abominations more than °they, and hast justified thy sisters in all thine [22]abominations which thou hast done.

52 Thou also, which hast judged thy sisters, bear thine own shame for thy [51]sins that thou hast committed more abominable than they: they °are °more righteous than thou: yea, be thou confounded also, and bear thy shame, in that thou hast justified thy °sisters.

N 53 °When I shall °bring again their captivity, the captivity of °Sodom and her [46]daughters, and the captivity of Samaria and her [46]daughters, then °*will I bring again* the captivity of thy captives in the midst of them:

40 a company=a military host.

41 women: i.e. idolaters, or idolatrous cities.

43 fretted Me=chafed at Me: i.e. at my laws. Aram., Sept., Syr., and Vulg. read "enraged Me".

thou shalt not, &c.: i.e. I will not allow this greatest evil by suffering it to go unpunished, and thus conniving at it (referring to Lev. 19. 29). Ap. 92.

16. 44-46 (*Y*, p. 1124). BIRTH AND SISTERHOOD.
(*Alternation.*)

Y | F | 44. Relations. Mother and daughter.
  G | 45-. Application.
  F | -45. Relations. Mother and sisters.
  G | 46. Application.

44 proverb=derisive proverb. Fig. *Parœmia.* Ap. 6.

16. 46 (*G*, above). APPLICATION.
(*Alternation and Introversion.*)

G | H | And thine elder sister
  J | v | is Samaria, and her daughters
    w | who dwelleth at thy left hand:
  H | and thy younger sister,
  J | *w* | who dwelleth at thy right hand,
    v | is Sodom and her daughters.

46 thine elder: or, thy greater.

daughters. Put by Fig. *Prosopopœia* (Ap. 6), for villages or neighbouring towns. **younger**: or, lesser.

16. 47-63 (*Z*, p. 1124). SINS.
(*Alternation and Introversion.*)

Z | K | M | 47-52. Jerusalem's sins.
    N | 53. Restoration.
    L | 54. Jehovah's purpose.
  K | *N* | 55. Restoration.
    M | 56-62. Jerusalem's sins.
    L | 63. Jehovah's purpose.

16. 47-52 (M, above). JERUSALEM'S SINS.
(*Introversion.*)

M | x | 47. Collectively.
  y | 48. More than Sodom.
  z | 49, 50. Sins of Sodom. } Severally.
  y | 51-. More than Samaria.
  x | -51, 52. Collectively.

47 as if that were . . . thing. The *Ellipsis* is wrongly supplied. See further note.

a very little=a very little time, or quickly. See note on "almost" (Prov. 5. 14).

48 as thou hast done. Sodom does not mean Jerusalem here, but it refers to the Sodom of Gen. 19. Sodom had not Jerusalem's privileges: hence her transgression was less. Cp. *v.* 46, and Matt. 11. 20-24.

49 was=came to be.

abundance of=luxurious: i.e. security of ease. Cp. Deut. 11. 21.

50 as I saw good. Some codices read "when I saw it", with marg. "as thou sawest". Better to omit "good". Cp. Gen. 18. 21. **as**=according to what.

51 sins. Heb. *chāṭā'.* Ap. 44. i.

they: i.e. Samaria and Sodom.

52 are=will prove.

more righteous. See note on *v.* 48.

sisters. Samaria and Sodom.

53 When I: or, When therefore I.

bring again their captivity=restore them; referring not to any return of captives, but to a restoration of prosperity. See notes on Deut. 30. 3. Job 42. 10. Ps. 126. 1.

Sodom. If the waters of the Dead Sea are to be healed, there is no reason why there should not be a restoration as here stated. Cp. 47. 8. Zech. 14. 8.

will I bring again. Aram., Sept., and Vulg. read these words in the text.

L (p. 1126) 54 That thou mayest bear thine own shame,
and mayest be confounded in all that thou
483 hast done, in that thou art a comfort unto
them.

K N 55 When thy sisters, [53]Sodom and her [46]daughters, shall return to their former estate, and Samaria and her daughters shall return to their former estate, then thou and thy [46]daughters shall return to your former estate.

M a 56 For thy sister [53]Sodom was not mentioned
(p. 1127) by thy mouth in the day of thy pride,
57 Before thy [23]wickedness was °discovered,
°as at the time of *thy* reproach of the daughters of °Syria, and all *that are* round about her, the daughters of the Philistines, which despise thee round about.
58 Thou hast borne thy lewdness and thine abominations, [14]saith °the LORD.
59 For thus saith [3]the Lord GOD; 'I will even deal with thee [50]as thou hast done, which hast despised the °oath in breaking the °covenant.

b 60 Nevertheless I will remember My covenant with thee in the days of thy youth, and I will establish unto thee an °everlasting covenant.

a 61 Then thou shalt remember thy ways, and be ashamed, when thou shalt receive thy [46]sisters, thine elder and thy younger: and I will give them unto thee for [46]daughters, but not by thy covenant.

b 62 And I will establish My covenant with thee; and thou shalt know that I *am* [1]the LORD:

L 63 That thou mayest remember, and be con-
(p. 1126) founded, and never open thy mouth any more because of thy shame, when I °am pacified toward thee for all that thou hast done, [14]saith [3]the Lord GOD.'"

G O[1] P[1] **17** And the word of °the LORD came unto
(p. 1127) me, saying,
2 °"Son of man, put forth a °riddle, and speak a °parable unto the house of Israel;
3 And say, 'Thus saith °the Lord GOD; °'A great eagle with great wings, °longwinged, full of °feathers, which had divers colours, came unto Lebanon, and took °the highest branch of the cedar:
4 He cropped off the °top of his young twigs, and carried it into a land of °traffick; he set it in a city of merchants.

Q[1] 5 He took also of °the seed of the land, and planted it in a fruitful field; he placed *it* by great waters, *and* set it *as* a willow tree.
6 And it grew, and became a spreading vine of low stature, whose branches °turned toward him, and the roots thereof were under him: so it became a vine, and brought forth branches, and shot forth sprigs.

R[1] 7 There was also °another great eagle with great wings and many feathers: and, behold, this vine did °bend her roots toward him, and shot forth her branches toward him, that he might °water it by the furrows of her plantation.
8 It was planted in a good °soil by great waters, that it might bring forth branches, and that it might bear fruit, that it might be a goodly vine.''

16. 56-62 (*M*, p. 1126). **JERUSALEM'S SINS.** (*Alternation.*)

M | a | 56-59. Jerusalem's sins.
  | b | 60. Jehovah's covenant remembered.
  | a | 61. Jerusalem's sins.
  | b | 62. Jehovah's covenant established.

57 discovered = unveiled.
as at the time of thy. Sept. and Vulg. read "as now [thou] art". Cp. 23. 43.
Syria. Heb. *'aram.* Some codices, with two early printed editions, read "*'ādām*" = men (ד Daleth = D, being read for ר Resh = R).
58 the LORD. Heb. Jehovah. Ap. 4. II. Some codices, with three early printed editions, read "Adonai". Ap. 4. VIII (2).
59 oath . . . covenant. Ref. to Pent. (Deut. 29. 12, 14). These words are thus found together here, and in 17. 13, 16, 18, 19; but nowhere else in Scripture.
60 everlasting covenant. See notes on Gen. 9. 16 and Isa. 44. 7.
63 am pacified toward thee = have accepted a propitiatory covering for thee.

17. 1-24 (**G**, p. 1104). **BABYLONIAN WAR. PARABLE.** (*Repeated and Extended Alternation.*)

G | O[1] | P[1] | 1-4. Great Eagle. "Topmost branch".
  | | Q[1] | 5, 6. Planting of seed.
  | | R[1] | 7, 8. Another Eagle. (Egypt.)
  | | S[1] | 9, 10. "Shall it prosper?" } The Parable.
  | O[2] | P[2] | 11, 12. King of Babylon.
  | | Q[2] | 13, 14. Planting of seed. (King's.)
  | | R[2] | 15-. Another kingdom. (Egypt.)
  | | S[2] | -15-21. "Shall he prosper?" } The Solution.
  | O[3] | P[3] | 22-. Adonai Jehovah.
  | | Q[3] | -22, 23-. Planting of Messiah.
  | | R[3] | -23. His increase.
  | | S[3] | 24. "It shall prosper." } Future Solution.

This chapter, under a parable, concerns Zedekiah's perfidy and punishment.

1 The LORD. Heb. Jehovah. Ap. 4. II.
2 Son of man. See note on 2. 1.
riddle = enigma. Heb. *chīdāh* = a difficult or perplexing problem put forth for solution. Occ. in Judg. 14. 12, 13, 14, 15, 16, 17, 18, 19 (= riddle). Num. 12. 8. 1 Kings 10. 5. 2 Chron. 9. 1 (= dark sayings). Ps. 49. 4. Prov. 1. 6, &c. Distinct from a "parable". Cp. Ps. 78. 2 (= dark sayings). Dan. 8. 23. Hab. 2. 6 (= "proverb").
parable = the comparing of one thing with another. Not the same as "riddle" (enigma).
3 the Lord GOD. Heb. Adonai Jehovah. See note on 2. 4.
A great eagle. The king of Babylon.
longwinged = long-pinioned, as in *v.* 7.
feathers = plumage.
the highest branch. Jehoiachin (i.e. Jeconiah, or Coniah). See *v.* 12; and Jer. 22. 23, 24.
4 top = topmost. **traffick.** Babylon.
5 the seed of the land. Zedekiah. See *vv.* 6 and 13. Nebuchadnezzar did not set up a Chaldean king over Judah, but nourished Zedekiah, as *vv.* 5, 6 show.
6 turned toward him. Zedekiah being dependent upon Nebuchadnezzar.
7 another great eagle. Pharaoh Hophra, king of Egypt.
bend her roots: i.e. looked for succour to Egypt. Cp. *vv.* 5, 8.
water it. From the Nile.
8 soil = field.

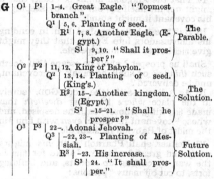

S[1] (p. 1127) 483 9 Say thou, 'Thus saith [3]the Lord GOD;
°'Shall it prosper? shall He not pull up the roots thereof, and cut off the fruit thereof, that it wither? it shall wither in all the leaves of her °spring, even without great power or many people to pluck it up by the roots thereof.

10 Yea, °behold, *being* planted, [9]shall it prosper? shall °it not utterly wither, when the east °wind toucheth °it? °it shall wither in the furrows where it grew.'"

O[2] P[2] 11 Moreover the word of [1]the LORD came unto me, saying,

12 "Say now to the °rebellious house, 'Know ye not what these *things mean?*' tell *them,* [10]Behold, the king of Babylon is come to Jerusalem, and hath taken the king thereof, and the princes thereof, and led them with him to Babylon;

Q[2] 13 And hath °taken of the king's seed, and made a °covenant with him, and hath °taken an °oath of him: he hath also taken the mighty of the land:

14 That the kingdom might be °base, that it might not lift itself up, *but* that by keeping of his covenant it might stand.

R[2] 15 But °he rebelled against him in sending his ambassadors into Egypt, that they might give him horses and much people.

S[2] c (p. 1128) [9]Shall he prosper? shall he escape that doeth such *things?* or shall he break the covenant, and be delivered?

16 *As* I live, °saith [3]the Lord GOD, 'surely in the place *where* the king *dwelleth* that made him king, whose [13]oath he despised, and whose [13]covenant he brake, *even* with him °in the midst of Babylon he shall die.

d 17 Neither shall Pharaoh with *his* mighty army and great °company °make for him in the war, by casting up mounts, and building forts, to cut off many °persons:

d 18 Seeing he despised the [13]oath by breaking the [13]covenant, when, °lo, he had °given his hand, and hath done all these *things,* he shall not escape.

c 19 Therefore thus saith [3]the Lord GOD; *As* I live, surely Mine oath that he hath despised, and My [13]covenant that he hath broken, even it will I recompense upon his own head.

20 And I will °spread My net upon him, and he shall be taken in My snare, and I will bring him to Babylon, and will °plead with him there for his °trespass that he hath °trespassed against Me.

21 And °all his fugitives with all his bands shall fall by the sword, and they that remain shall be scattered toward all winds: and °ye shall know that I [1]the LORD have spoken *it.*'

O[3] P[3] (p. 1127) 22 Thus saith [3]the Lord GOD; 'I will also take of °the highest °branch of the high cedar, and will set *it;* I will crop off from the top of his young twigs °a tender one,

Q[3] and will plant *it* upon an high mountain and eminent:

23 °In the mountain of the height of Israel will I plant it: and it shall °bring forth boughs, and bear fruit, and be a goodly cedar:

R[3] and under it shall dwell all fowl of every wing; in the shadow of the branches thereof shall they dwell.

S[3] 24 And all the trees of the field shall know that I [1]the LORD have brought down the high tree, have exalted the low tree, have dried up the green tree, and have made the dry tree to flourish: °I [1]the LORD have spoken and have done *it.*'"

H T[1] (p. 112) 18 °The word of °the LORD came unto me again, saying,

2 "What mean ye, that ye use this proverb concerning °the land of Israel, saying, °'The fathers have eaten sour grapes, and the °children's teeth are set on edge?'

---

9 Shall it prosper? &c. This is Jehovah's sentence on the perfidy of Zedekiah in breaking his oath to Nebuchadnezzar. Cp. *v.* 13 and the Structure (S[1], S[2], S[3]). Those who interpret this enigma of Zedekiah's daughters are hereby warned that their interpretation shall not prosper. See notes on *vv.* 22 and 24.
spring=sproutings.
10 behold. Fig. *Asterismos.* Ap. 6.
it: i.e. the vine. **wind.** Heb. *rūach.* Ap. 9.
12 rebellious house. See note on 2. 5.
13 taken, &c. Cp. 2 Kings 24. 17.
covenant . . . oath. See note on 16. 59.
taken an oath. See 2 Chron. 36. 13.
14 base=low.
15 he rebelled, &c. See 2 Kings 24. 20. 2 Chron. 36. 13.

17. -15-21 (S[2], p. 1127). "SHALL HE PROSPER?" (*Introversion.*)

S[2] c | -15, 16. Zedekiah's oath broken. "Yet death in Babylon."
d | 17. No escape through the king of Egypt.
d | 18. No escape from the king of Babylon.
c | 19-21. Jehovah's oath sure. Death in Babylon.

16 saith the Lord GOD=[is] Adonai Jehovah's oracle.
in the midst of Babylon, &c. Cp. 12. 13.
17 company=gathered force.
make for him=help him.
persons=souls. Heb. *nephesh.* Ap. 13.
18 lo. Fig. *Asterismos.* Ap. 6.
given his hand. Put by Fig. *Metonymy* (of Adjunct), Ap. 6, for making a covenant (2 Kings 10. 15. Ezra 10. 19. Jer. 50. 15).
20 spread My net upon him. Cp. 12. 13; 32. 3.
plead=reckon. Cp. 20. 36; 38. 22.
trespass that he hath trespassed. See note on 15. 8.
21 all his fugitives. Cp. 12. 14.
ye shall know, &c. See note on 6. 7.
22 the highest branch. Sets forth the restoration of the kingdom in the Messiah.
branch. Cp. Jer. 23. 5, 6; 33. 15. Zech. 3. 8; 6. 12; and Isa. 4. 2.
a tender one. Cp. Isa. 11. 1; 53. 1, 2. The Chaldee Targum interprets this of the Messiah. Those who interpret this of Zedekiah's "younger daughter" are guilty of substituting her for the Messiah Himself; Whose *future* kingdom is to be "in the mountain of the height of Israel", and not in any other country; or, during the present dispensation. See notes on *vv.* 23, 24.
23 In the mountain, &c. Cp. Isa. 2. 2, 3; 54. 1-17; 62. 1-7. **bring forth boughs**=exalt its branch.
24 I the LORD, &c. He will prosper His work. This is in contrast with *vv.* 9, 10 (S[1]), and *vv.* -15-21 (S[2]), which would not prosper.

18. 1-32 [For Structure see next page].

1 The word=And the word.
the LORD. Heb. Jehovah. Ap. 4. II.
2 the land=the soil. Heb. *'admath.* See note on 11. 17. **The fathers, &c.** Cp. Jer. 31. 29, 30.
children's=sons'.

U1 3 *As* I live, °saith °the Lord GOD, ye shall
(p. 1129) not have *occasion* °any more to use this proverb
483 in Israel.
T2 4 °Behold, all °souls are Mine; as the °soul
of the father, so also the °soul of the son is
Mine: the °soul that °sinneth, it shall °die.
U2 c 5 But if a °man be just, and do that which is
lawful and right,
6 *And* hath not °eaten upon the mountains,
neither °hath lifted up his eyes to the idols
of the house of Israel, neither hath °defiled his
neighbour's wife, neither hath °come near to
a menstruous woman,
7 And °hath not oppressed any, *but* °hath
restored to the debtor his pledge, hath spoiled
none by violence, °hath given his bread to the
hungry, and hath covered the naked with a
garment;
8 He *that* °hath not given forth upon usury,
neither hath taken any increase, *that* hath
withdrawn his hand from °iniquity, °hath executed
true judgment between [5]man and [5]man,
9 °Hath walked in My statutes, and hath
kept My judgments, to deal truly; He *is* just,
°he shall surely °live, [3]saith [3]the Lord GOD.
d 10 If he beget a son *that is* °a robber, °a
shedder of blood, and *that* doeth the like to
any one of these *things*,
11 And that doeth not any of those *duties*, but
even hath [6]eaten upon the mountains, and
[6]defiled his neighbour's wife,
12 [7]Hath oppressed the poor and needy, hath
spoiled by violence, [7]hath not restored the
pledge, and hath lifted up his eyes to the idols,
hath committed abomination,
13 [8]Hath given forth upon usury, and hath
taken increase: shall he then [9]live? he shall not
live: he hath done all these abominations; [9]he
shall surely die; °his blood shall be upon him.
c 14 Now, lo, *if* he beget a son, that seeth all
his father's [4]sins which he hath done, and considereth,
and doeth not such like,
15 *That* hath not [6]eaten upon the mountains,
neither hath lifted up his eyes to the idols of
the house of Israel, °hath not defiled his neighbour's
wife,
16 Neither [7]hath oppressed any, [7]hath not
withholden the pledge, neither [7]hath spoiled by
violence, *but* [7]hath given his bread to the hungry,
and hath covered the naked with a garment,
17 *That* hath taken off his hand from °the
poor, *that* [8]hath not received usury nor increase,
hath executed My judgments, [9]hath walked in
My statutes; he shall not [4]die for the °iniquity
of his father, [9]he shall surely live.
d 18 *As for* his father, because he cruelly
[7]oppressed, spoiled his brother by violence,
and did *that* which *is* not good among his
°people, lo, even he shall [4]die in his [17]iniquity.
T3 19 Yet say ye, 'Why? doth not the son bear
the [17]iniquity of the father?'
U3 When the son hath done that which is lawful
and right, *and* hath kept all My statutes, and
hath done them, he shall surely [9]live.
20 The [4]soul that [4]sinneth, it shall [4]die. °The
son shall not bear the [8]iniquity of the father,
neither shall the father bear the [17]iniquity of
the son: the righteousness of °the righteous
shall be upon him, and the °wickedness of °the
wicked shall be upon him.

18. 1-32 (**H**, p. 1104). PEOPLE. PROVERB. (SOUR GRAPES.) (*Repeated Alternation.*)

H | T1 | 1, 2. Proverb.
U1 | 3. Recrimination.
T2 | 4. Proverb.
U2 | 5-18. Discrimination.
T3 | 19-. Proverb.
U3 | -19-24. Discrimination.
T4 | 25-. Proverb.
U4 | -25-28. Discrimination.
T5 | 29-. Proverb.
U5 | -29-32. Discrimination.

3 saith the Lord GOD = [is] Adonai Jehovah's oracle.
the Lord GOD. See note on 2. 4.
any more. This refers to a future time, which has not yet come (Jer. 31. 29, 30). Till then it is otherwise (21. 3. Lam. 5. 7), and has been since Gen. 3. Cp. Rom. 5. 12-21.
4 Behold. Fig. *Asterismos.* Ap. 6.
souls = persons. Heb. *nephesh.* Ap. 13.
sinneth. Descendants were not punished for the sins of their ancestors, unless they persevered in their ancestors' sins. Cp. Ex. 20. 5. Matt. 23. 30-32. Here Heb. *chāṭā'.* Ap. 44. i.
die. Die and live in this chapter are used in the sense of 3. 18.
5 man. Heb. *'ish.* Ap. 14. II.

18. 5-18 (U2, above). DISCRIMINATION. (*Alternation.*)

U2 | c | 5-9. The righteous.
d | 10-13. The wicked.
c | 14-17. The righteous.
d | 18. The wicked.
(All in the Singular Number.)

6 eaten, &c. Implies sacrificing and partaking of the idolatrous feast. Ref. to Pent. (Deut. 12. 2 compared with *vv.* 11, 15). Ap. 92.
hath lifted up his eyes, &c. Put by Fig. *Metonymy* (of Adjunct), Ap. 6, for worship.
defiled, &c. Ref. to Pent. (Lev. 18. 20; 20. 10).
come near. Ref. to Pent. (Lev. 18. 19; 20. 18).
7 hath not oppressed, &c. Ref. to Pent. (Ex. 22. 21. Lev. 25. 14. Deut. 23. 16). Ap. 92.
hath restored, &c. Ref. to Pent. (Ex. 22. 26. Deut. 24. 6, 10, 12, 13). Ap. 92.
hath given his bread, &c. Ref. to Pent. (Deut. 15. 7, 8).
8 hath not given forth, &c. Ref. to Pent. (Ex. 22. 25. Lev. 25. 36, 37. Deut. 23. 19). Ap. 92.
iniquity = trickery. Heb. *'āval.* Ap. 44. vi. Not the same word as in *vv.* 17, 18, 19, 20, 30.
hath executed, &c. Ref. to Pent. (Lev. 19. 15, 35. Deut. 1. 16, 17; 16. 18-20). Ap. 92.
9 Hath walked, &c. Ref. to Pent. (Lev. 18. 5. Deut. 4. 1; 5. 1; 6. 1, 2; 10. 12, 13; 11. 1).
he shall surely live. Ref. to Pent. (Lev. 18. 5).
live. See note on Lev. 18. 5.
10 a robber. Ref. to Pent. (Ex. 22. 2. Lev. 19. 13).
a shedder of blood. Ref. to Pent. (Gen. 9. 6. Ex. 21. 12. Num. 35. 31). Ap. 92.
13 his blood shall be upon him. Ref. to Pent. (Lev. 20. 9, 11, 12, 13, 16, 27). Ap. 92.
15 hath not, &c. Some codices, with two early printed editions, Aram., Sept., Syr., and Vulg., read "and hath not", &c.
17 the poor = the oppressed. The Sept. reads "injustice", as in *v.* 8.
iniquity. Heb. *'āvāh.* Ap. 44. iv. Not the same word as in *vv.* 8. 24, 26.
18 people = peoples.
20 The son, &c. Ref. to Pent. (Deut. 24. 26). Ap. 92.
the righteous = a righteous one.
wickedness . . . the wicked. Heb. *rāsha'.* Ap. 44. x.
the wicked = a lawless one. Heb. text marg., with some codices and three early printed editions, read "lawless ones".

483 21 But if [20]the wicked will turn from °all his [4]sins that he hath committed, and keep all My statutes, and do that which is lawful and right, he shall surely [9]live, °he shall not [4]die.

22 All his °transgressions that he hath committed, they shall not be °mentioned unto him: in his righteousness that he hath done he shall [9]live.

23 °Have I any pleasure at all that [20]the wicked should die? °saith [3]the Lord GOD: *and* not that he should return from his °ways, and live?

24 But when [20]the righteous turneth away from his righteousness, and committeth [8]iniquity, *and* doeth according to all the abominations that [20]the wicked *man* doeth, shall he [9]live? All his °righteousness that he hath done shall not be [22]mentioned: in his °trespass that he hath °trespassed, and in his [4]sin that he hath [4]sinned, in them shall he die.

T4 (p. 1129) 25 Yet ye say, 'The way of °the LORD* is not °equal.'

U4 Hear now, O house of Israel; Is not My way °equal? are not your ways °unequal?

26 When a righteous *man* turneth away from his righteousness, and committeth [8]iniquity, and dieth in them; for his [8]iniquity that he hath done shall he die.

27 Again, when [20]the wicked *man* turneth away from his [20]wickedness that he hath committed, and doeth that which is lawful and right, he shall save his [4]soul alive.

28 Because he considereth, and turneth away from all his [22]transgressions that he hath committed, he [9]shall surely live, [21]he shall not die.

T5 29 Yet saith the house of Israel, 'The way of [25]the LORD* is not [25]equal.'

U5 O house of Israel, are not My ways [25]equal? are not your ways [25]unequal?

30 Therefore I will judge you, O house of Israel, every one according to his ways, [23]saith [3]the Lord GOD. Repent, and turn *yourselves* from all your [22]transgressions; so [17]iniquity shall not be your ruin.

31 Cast away from you all your [22]transgressions, °whereby ye have [22]transgressed; and make you a new °heart and a new °spirit: for why will ye die, O house of Israel?

32 For °I have no pleasure in the death of him that dieth, [23]saith [3]the Lord GOD: wherefore turn *yourselves,* and live ye.

J V (p. 1130) **19** Moreover take thou up a lamentation for the °princes of °Israel,

W e 2 And say, 'What *is* °thy mother? A lioness: she lay down among lions, she nourished her whelps among young lions.

3 And she brought up °one of her whelps: it became a young lion, and it learned to °catch the prey; it devoured °men.

f 4 The nations also heard of him; he was °taken in their pit, and °they brought him with chains unto the land of Egypt.

e 5 Now when she saw that she had waited, *and* her hope was lost, then she took °another of her whelps, *and* made him a young lion.

6 And he went up and down among the lions, he became a young lion, and learned to catch the prey, *and* devoured [3]men.

7 And he °knew their desolate palaces, and he laid waste their cities; and the land was desolate, and the fulness thereof, by the noise of his roaring.

21 all his sins. Heb. text reads "any sin of his"; but the marg., some codices, and two early printed editions, read "all his sins".

he shall not die. Note the Fig. *Pleonasm* (Ap. 6), here. Some codices, with one early printed edition, Sept., Syr., and Vulg., read "and not die".

22 transgressions. Heb. *pāsha'.* Ap. 44. ix.

mentioned unto = remembered against. No "purgatory" here.

23 Have I any pleasure . . . ? Answered in *v.* 32.

ways. Many codices, with eight early printed editions, read plural; but others, with Aram., Sept., and Syr., read "way" (sing.).

saith the Lord GOD = [is] Adonai Jehovah's oracle.

24 righteousness. So Heb. text; but marg., with some codices and one early printed edition, read pl. = "none of his righteous acts". The Heb. verb is pl.

trespass . . . trespassed. Heb. *mā'al.* Ap. 44. xi.

25 the LORD*. This is one of the 134 places where the *Sopherim* say that they changed "Jehovah" of the primitive text to "Adonai". See Ap. 32.

equal. See note on "pondereth", Prov. 21. 2.

unequal. Note the Fig. *Anticatēgoria* (Ap. 6).

31 whereby, &c. The Sept. reads "which ye have committed against Me".

heart . . . spirit. Put by Fig. *Metonymy* (of Cause), Ap. 6, for all that is of the spirit, and not of the flesh. Cp. Luke 1. 46, 47. John 4. 24. "The flesh profiteth nothing" (John 6. 63).

spirit. Heb. *rūach.* Ap. 9.

32 I have no pleasure. This is the answer to the question in *v.* 23.

19. 1-14 (J, p. 1104). THE PRINCE OF ISRAEL.
(Introversion and Alternation.)

J | V | 1. Lamentation.
  W | e | 2, 3. Young lion.
     f | 4. Taken.
     e | 5-7. Another young lion.
     f | 8, 9. Taken.
  W | g | 10, 11. Vine (planted by waters).
     h | 12. Plucked up.
     g | 13. Vine (planted in desert).
     h | 14-. Devoured.
  V | -14. Lamentation.

1 princes. Sept. reads "prince" (sing.). Here refers to Zedekiah.

Israel. Put here for Judah. See note on 1 Kings 12. 17.

2 thy mother. Probably Hamutal, one of the wives of Josiah, the mother of Shallum (or Jehoahaz) and Zedekiah (2 Kings 23. 31 and 24. 18). The other son of Josiah (Jehoiakim) had a different mother (Zebudah). See 2 Kings 23. 36.

3 one of her whelps. Probably Jehoahaz (i.e. Shallum), the youngest son of Josiah, is intended (1 Chron. 3. 15). **catch** = rend.

men. Heb. *'ādām.* Ap. 14. I.

4 taken in their pit. As a lion is taken (Pss. 35. 7; 94. 13).

they: i.e. Pharaoh-necho (2 Kings 23. 30-34. 2 Chron. 36. 1-4). Jeremiah laments his fate. See Jer. 22. 10-12.

5 another of her whelps. Probably Jehoiakim, another son of Josiah (2 Kings 23. 36. 2 Chron. 36. 5). Hardly Jehoiachin, who reigned only three months (2 Kings 24. 8). But Jehoiakim reigned eleven years, and his character corresponds with *vv.* 7, 8, here. See 2 Kings 23. 36; 24. 1-6. Jer. 22. 11-19.

7 knew their desolate palaces. Aram. and Sept. read "injured or defiled his widows".

knew = knew carnally. See 2 Chron. 36. 8.

f (p. 1130) 483 **8** Then the nations set against him on every
side from the provinces, and spread their net
over him: he was [4]taken in their pit.
9 And they put him °in ward in chains, and
brought him to the °king of Babylon: they
brought him into holds, that his voice should
no more be heard upon the mountains of
Israel.

W g **10** °Thy mother *is* like a vine °in thy
blood, planted by the °waters: she was fruitful and full of branches by reason of many
°waters.
11 And she had strong rods for the sceptres
of them that bare rule, and her stature was
exalted among the thick branches, and she
appeared in her height with the multitude of
her branches.

h **12** But she was plucked up in fury, she was
cast down to the ground, and the east °wind
dried up her fruit: her strong rods were broken
and withered; the fire consumed them.

g **13** And °now she *is* planted in the wilderness,
in a dry and thirsty ground.

h **14** And fire is gone out °of a rod of her
branches, *which* hath devoured her fruit, so
that she hath no strong rod *to be* a sceptre to
rule.

V This *is* a lamentation, and shall be for a lamentation.' "

D X (p. 1131) **20** And it came to pass in °the seventh
year, in the fifth *month*, the tenth *day*
of the month, *that* certain of the elders of
Israel came to enquire of °the LORD, and sat
before me.
2 Then came the word of °the LORD unto me,
saying,
3 °"Son of man, speak °unto °the elders of
Israel, and say unto them, 'Thus saith °the
Lord GOD; 'Are ye come to enquire of Me?
As I live, °saith °the Lord GOD, I will not be
enquired of by you.'
4 °Wilt thou judge them, [3]son of man, °wilt
thou judge *them?* cause them to know the
abominations of their fathers:

Y Z¹ i¹ **5** And say unto them, 'Thus saith [3]the Lord
GOD; 'In the day °when I chose Israel, and
°lifted up Mine hand unto the seed of the house
of Jacob, and °made Myself known unto them
in the land of °Egypt, when I °lifted up Mine
hand unto them, saying, 'I *am* °the LORD
your °God;'
6 In °the day *that* I [5]lifted up Mine hand unto
them, to °bring them forth of the land of
[5]Egypt into a land that I had °espied for
them, °flowing with milk and honey, which
is °the glory of all lands:
7 Then said I unto them, 'Cast ye away
°every man the °abominations of his eyes,
and °defile not yourselves with the °idols of
[5]Egypt: I *am* [5]the LORD your [5]God.'

9 in ward in chains = in a cage with hooks (or hoops), as lions are represented on the monuments. See 2 Chron. 36. 5-7, and Jer. 22. 13-19.
king. Some codices read "land".
10 Thy mother. Another *Simile.* See the Structure (*W*, p. 1130).
in thy blood: or, in thy vineyard (acc. to Dr. C. D. Ginsburg).
waters. Ref. to Pent. (Deut. 8. 7). Ap. 92.
12 wind. Heb. *rūach.* Ap. 9.
13 now, &c. Referring to Jeconiah and Ezekiel's own days (1. 3; and 2 Kings 24. 12-16).
14 of a rod: or, of the rod: i.e. Zedekiah, who by his perjury brought about the destruction of Jerusalem by fire.

20. 1-44 (*D*, p. 1104). **ELDERS.**
(*Introversion.*)

D | X | 1-4. The Elders of Israel.
  Y | 5-22. Rebellions and Causes.
  Y | 23-26. Punishments and Reasons.
X | 27-44. The house of Israel.

1 the seventh year. See the table on p. 1105.
the LORD. Heb. Jehovah, with *'eth* (= Jehovah Himself). Ap. 4. II.
2 the LORD. Heb. Jehovah. Ap. 4. II.
3 Son of man. See note on 2. 1.
unto = with. Some codices, with one early printed edition, Aram., Sept., and Vulg., read "unto".
the elders of Israel. In the Captivity; who were being deceived by false prophets who predicted a speedy return.
saith the Lord GOD = [is] Adonai Jehovah's oracle. See note on 2. 4.
4 Wilt thou . . . wilt thou . . .? Note the Fig. *Epizeuxis* (Ap. 6), for emphasis.

20. 5-22 (Y, above). **REBELLIONS AND CAUSES.**
(*Repeated and Extended Alternations.*)
The Structure is made to correspond with the repeated and extended rebellions.

Y | Z¹ | i¹ | 5-7. Commands.
  k¹ | 8-. Rebellion.
  l¹ | -8. Threatening.
  m¹ | 9, 10. Forbearance.
Z² | i² | 11, 12. Statutes.
  k² | 13-. Rebellion.
  l² | -13. Threatening.
  m² | 14-17. Forbearance.
Z³ | i³ | 18-20. Commands.
  k³ | 21-. Rebellions.
  l³ | -21. Threatening.
  m³ | 22. Forbearance.

5 when I chose Israel, &c. Ref. to Pent. (Ex. 6. 7; 20. 2. Deut. 7. 6). Ap. 92.
lifted up Mine hand. Put by Fig. *Metonymy* (of Adjunct), Ap. 6, for "I sware". Cp. *vv.* 6, 15, 23, 28, 42. Gen. 14. 22. Deut. 32. 40. Used seven times in ch. 20.
made Myself known, &c. Ref. to Pent. (Ex. 6. 3).
Egypt. Ezekiel speaks about Israel in Egypt more than any other prophet. See 23. 8. In this chapter he mentions it seven times (*vv.* 5, 6, 7, 8, 8, 9, 10).
the LORD your God = Jehovah (Ap. 4. II) your Elohim.
God. Heb. Elohim. Ap. 4. I.
6 the = that.
bring them forth, &c. Ref. to Pent. (Ex. 3. 8, 17. Deut. 8. 7, 8, 9). Ap. 92.
espied = looked, or spied out.
flowing with milk and honey. Ref. to Pent. (Ex. 3. 8, 17; 13. 5; 33. 3. Lev. 20. 24. Num. 13. 27; 14. 8; 16. 13, 14. Deut. 6. 3; 11. 9; 26. 9, 15; 27. 3; 31. 20). Beside these passages it is found only in 20. 6, 15. Josh. 5. 6. Jer. 11. 5; 32. 22. **the glory** = the gazelle. Put by Fig. *Metonymy* (of Subject), Ap. 6, for "beauty". Cp. *v.* 15. Ps. 48. 2. **7 every man.** Heb. *'ish.* Ap. 14. II. **abominations.** Put by Fig. *Metonymy* (of Cause), Ap. 6, for that which Jehovah abominated. **defile not yourselves, &c.** Ref. to Pent. (Lev. 18. 3). Ap. 92. **idols** = manufactured gods.

k1 (p. 1131) 482 8 But they °rebelled against Me, and would
not hearken unto Me: they did not [7]every man
cast away the [7]abominations of their eyes,
neither did they forsake [7]the idols of [5]Egypt:
l1 then I said, 'I will °pour out My fury upon
them, to accomplish My anger against them
in the midst of the land of [5]Egypt.'

m1 9 But °I wrought for My name's sake, that it
should not be polluted before the °heathen,
among whom they *were*, in whose sight I made
Myself known unto them, in bringing them
forth out of the land of [5]Egypt.
10 Wherefore °I caused them to go forth out
of the land of [5]Egypt, and brought them into
the wilderness.

Z2 i2 11 And I gave them My °statutes, and shewed
them My °judgments, °which *if* a °man °do, °he
shall even °live in them.
12 Moreover also °I gave them My sabbaths,
to be a sign between Me and them, °that they
might know that I *am* [2]the LORD that sanctify
them.

k2 13 But the house of Israel [8]rebelled against
Me in the wilderness: they walked not in My
[11]statutes, and they despised My [11]judgments,
[11]which *if* a [11]man [11]do, [11]he shall even live
in them; and My sabbaths they greatly polluted:
l2 °then I said, I would pour out My fury upon
them in the wilderness, to consume them.

m2 14 But [9]I wrought for My name's sake, that
it should not be polluted before the [9]heathen,
in whose sight I brought them out.
15 Yet also I [5]lifted up My hand unto them
in the wilderness, that °I would not bring
them into the land which I had given °*them*,
[6]flowing with milk and honey, which *is* [6]the
glory of all lands;
16 Because they despised My [11]judgments,
and walked not in My [11]statutes, but polluted
My sabbaths: for °their heart went after their
[7]idols.
17 Nevertheless Mine eye spared them from
destroying them, neither did I make an end of
them in the wilderness.

Z3 i3 18 But °I said unto their °children in the
wilderness, 'Walk ye not in the °statutes of
your fathers, neither observe their °judgments,
nor [7]defile yourselves with their [7]idols:
19 I *am* [5]the LORD your [5]God; walk in My
statutes, and keep My judgments, and do them;
20 And hallow My sabbaths; and they shall
be a sign between Me and you, that °ye may
know that I *am* [5]the LORD your God.'

k3 21 Notwithstanding the [18]children °rebelled
against Me: they walked not in My [11]statutes,
neither kept My [11]judgments to do them, [11]which
if a [11]man [11]do, [11]he shall even live in them;
°they polluted My sabbaths:

l3 then I said, I would [8]pour out My fury upon
them, to accomplish My anger against them in
the wilderness.

m3 22 Nevertheless I °withdrew Mine hand, and
[9]wrought for My name's sake, that it should
not be polluted in the sight of the [9]heathen, in
whose sight I brought them forth.

8 rebelled. See note on 2. 5.

pour out My fury, &c. Repeated in *vv.* 13, 21, 33, 34. See the Structure, p. 1131.

9 I wrought, &c. Repeated in *vv.* 14, 22, 44. Ref. to Pent. (Ex. 32. 12. Num. 14. 13, &c.). Ap. 92.

heathen = nations.

10 I caused, &c. Ref. to Pent. (Ex. 13, &c.). Ap. 92.

11 I gave them, &c. Ref. to Pent. (Deut. 4. 8).

statutes . . . judgments. Ref. to Pent. (Deut. 4. 1).

which if a man do, &c. Ref. to Pent. (Lev. 18. 5).

man. Heb. *'ādām.* Ap. 14. I.

do = do [them].

he shall . . . live. See note on Lev. 18. 5.

12 I gave them, &c. Ref. to Pent. (Ex. 20. 8; 31. 13).

that they might know. Cp. note on 6. 10.

13 then I said, I would, &c. Ref. to Pent. (Num. 14. 22, 23, 29; 26. 65). Ap. 92.

15 I would not bring them into, &c. Ref. to Pent. (Num. 14. 24-30). Ap. 92. Cp. Ps. 95. 11.

them. Sept., Syr., and Vulg. read "to them" in the text.

16 their heart went, &c. Ref. to Pent. (Ex. 32. 23).

18 I said, &c. Ref. to Pent. (Num. 14. 32, 33; 32. 13-15. Deut. 4. 3-6). Ap. 92.

children = sons.

statutes . . . judgments. Like those of Omri (Mic. 6. 16). Cp. Jer. 16. 13.

20 ye may know. See note on 6. 7.

21 rebelled. Ref. to Pent. (Num. 25. 1, 2. Deut. 9. 23, 24; 31. 27). Ap. 92.

they polluted My sabbaths. Some codices, with four early printed editions, add "even My sabbaths".

22 withdrew, &c. Idiom for a relaxing of anger or refraining from punishment.

20. 23-26 (*Y*, p. 1131). PUNISHMENTS AND REASONS. (*Introversions and Alternation.*)

Y | A | 23. Punishments.
| B | C | n | 24-. Judgments.
| | | o | -24-. Statutes.
| | D | -24. Pollution by People.
| B | C | o | 25-. Statutes.
| | | n | -25. Judgments.
| | D | 26-. Pollution by Jehovah.
| A | -26. Punishment.

(B–D: Reasons.)

23 I. Some codices, with three early printed editions, read "Yet even (or, also) I", as in *v.* 15.

that I would scatter, &c. Ref. to Pent. (Lev. 26. 33. Deut. 28. 64). Ap. 92. Cp. 12. 15.

25 I gave them also statutes, &c. In Heb. idiom = I suffered others to give them statutes, &c.: i.e. in their captivity. Active verbs in Hebrew were used to express not only the doing of the thing, but the permission of the thing which the agent is said to do. The verb *nāthan*, to give, is therefore often rendered *to suffer* in this sense. See Gen. 31. 7. Judg. 15. 1. 1 Sam. 24. 7. 2 Sam. 21. 10. Where not so actually rendered it means *permission*. Cp. 14. 9. Ex. 4. 21; 5. 22. Ps. 16. 10. Jer. 4. 10. The same idiom is used in N.T. (Matt. 6. 13; 11. 25; 13. 11. Rom. 9. 18; 11. 7, 8. 2 Thess. 2. 11).

23 °I lifted up Mine hand unto them also in Y A (p. 1132)
the wilderness, °that I would scatter them among
the [9]heathen, and disperse them through the
countries;

24 Because they had not executed My [11]judg- B C n
ments,

but had despised My [11]statutes, o

and had polluted My sabbaths, and their eyes D
were after their fathers' idols.

25 Wherefore °I gave them also statutes *that* B C o
were not good,

and judgments whereby they should not live; n

D (p. 1132) 482 26 And °I polluted them in their own gifts, in
that they caused to °pass through *the fire* all
that openeth the womb,

A that I might make them desolate, to the end
[12]that they might know that I *am* [2]the LORD."

X p (p. 1133) 27 Therefore, [3]son of man, speak unto the
house of Israel, and say unto them, 'Thus saith
[3]the Lord GOD; 'Yet in this your fathers have
blasphemed Me, in that they have °committed
a °trespass against Me.
28 *For* when I had brought them into the
land, *for* the which I [5]lifted up Mine hand to
give it to them, then they saw every high hill,
and all the thick trees, and they offered there
their sacrifices, and there they presented the
provocation of their offering: there also they
made their sweet savour, and poured out there
their drink offerings.
29 Then I said unto them, °'What *is* the
high place whereunto ye go?' And the name
thereof is called Bamah unto this day.''
30 Wherefore say unto the house of Israel,
'Thus saith [3]the Lord GOD; °'Are ye polluted
after the manner of your fathers? and commit
ye whoredom after their [7]abominations?
31 For when ye offer your gifts, when ye
make °your sons to [26]pass through the fire, ye
pollute yourselves with all your [7]idols, even
unto this day: and shall I be enquired of by
you, O house of Israel? *As* I live, [3]saith [3]the
Lord GOD, I will not be enquired of by you.
32 And that which cometh into your °mind
shall not be at all, that ye say, 'We will be as
the [9]heathen, as the families of the countries,
to serve wood and stone.'

q 33 *As* I live, [3]saith [3]the Lord GOD, surely
°with a mighty hand, and with a stretched
out arm, and with fury poured out, °will I rule
over you:
34 And I will bring you out from the °people,
and will gather you out of the countries wherein ye are scattered, [33]with a mighty hand, and
with a stretched out arm, and with fury poured
out.
35 And I will bring you into °the wilderness
of the [34]people, and there will I plead with you
face to face.
36 °Like as I pleaded with your fathers in
the wilderness of the land of Egypt, so will
I plead with you, [3]saith [3]the Lord GOD.
37 And I will cause you to °pass under the
rod, and I will bring you into the °bond of the
covenant:
38 And I will purge out from among you the
rebels, and them that °transgress against Me:
I will bring them forth out of the country where
they sojourn, and they shall not enter °into
the land of Israel: and °ye shall know that I
am [1]the LORD.

p 39 As for you, O house of Israel,' thus saith
[3]the Lord GOD; °'Go ye, serve ye °every one
his idols, and hereafter *also*, if ye will not
hearken unto Me: °but pollute ye My °holy
name no more with your gifts, and with your
[7]idols.

q 40 For in Mine [39]holy mountain, °in the
mountain of the height of Israel, [3]saith [3]the
Lord GOD, there shall all the house of Israel,
all of them in the land, serve Me: there will
I accept them, and there will I °require your
°offerings, and the °firstfruits of your oblations, with all your [39]holy things.
41 I will accept you with your sweet savour,
when I bring you out from the [34]people, and
gather you out of the countries wherein ye
have been scattered; and I will be sanctified
in you before the heathen.
42 And [38]ye shall know that I *am* [2]the LORD,
when I shall bring you [38]into the land of Israel,
into the country *for* the which I [5]lifted up
Mine hand to give it to your fathers.
43 And there shall ye remember your ways,
and all your doings, wherein ye have been
defiled; and °ye shall lothe yourselves in your
own sight for all your °evils that ye have
committed.

26 I polluted them, &c. See note on *v.* 25. The contrast is with their pollution of God's gifts (*v.* 16).

pass through: or, pass over. The firstborn were to be passed over to Jehovah (Ex. 13. 12); but they passed them (through the fire) over to Moloch (Lev. 18. 21. Deut. 18. 10). Note the refs. to Pent. here. Ap. 92.

20. 27-44 (*X*, p. 1131). **THE HOUSE OF ISRAEL.**
(*Alternation.*)

X | p | 27-32. Incrimination.
| q | 33-38. Threatening.
| *p* | 39. Incrimination.
| *q* | 40-44. Restoration.

27 committed a trespass = trespassed a trespass. Fig. *Polyptōton* (Ap. 6), for emphasis = committed a great trespass.

trespass = treachery. Heb. *mā'al*. Ap. 44. xi. As in 14. 13 and 15. 8.

29 What is the high place . . . ? Note the Fig. *Paronomasia* (Ap. 6). Heb. *māh habbāmāh*, for emphasis, to mark the contrast between this idolatrous high place and Zion the true high and holy mountain (*v.* 40).

30 Are ye . . . ? Fig. *Erotēsis*. Ap. 6.

31 your sons. Some codices, with two early printed editions, read "your sons and your daughters".

32 mind = spirit. Heb. *rūach*. Ap. 9.

33 with a mighty hand, &c. Ref. to Pent. (Deut. 4. 34, &c.). **will I rule** = will I become king.

34 people = peoples.

35 the wilderness of the people. Probably another country which would be to them another wilderness in which they were tested as to whether they would hear.

36 Like as I pleaded, &c. Ref. to Pent. (Num. 14. 21-23, 28, 29). Ap. 92. See also *vv.* 13 and 38.

37 pass under the rod. This was the manner of counting the sheep, which were numbered as they passed under the shepherd's club: implying here that none should be lost (Amos 9. 9), and that the restored nation should be holy to Jehovah (cp. *v.* 40). Ref. to Pent. (Lev. 27. 32). Occurs elsewhere only in Jer. 33. 13).

bond = binding obligation. Occurs only here.

38 transgress. Heb. *pāsha'*. Ap. 44. ix.

into the land of Israel = on the soil of Israel. Thus illustrating *v.* 36. Heb. *'admath*. See note on 11. 17.

ye shall know, &c. See note on 6. 7.

39 Go ye, &c. Fig. *Eironeia*. Ap. 6. Divine irony.

every one = every man, as in *vv.* 7, 8.

but: or, yet. **holy.** See note on Ex. 3. 5.

40 in the mountain: i.e. Moriah and Zion. See Ap. 68. Cp. Isa. 2. 2; 54. 1-7; 62. 1-9; 65. 17-25; 66. 20-23.

require = seek.

offerings = heave offerings. Heb. *terūmāh*. Ap. 43. II. viii.

firstfruits of your oblations: i.e. firstfruit gifts or presents. Heb. *mas'ēth*. Not the same word as in chs. 44, 45, and 48, which is *terūmāh* = heave offering.

43 ye shall lothe yourselves. Cp. 16. 61-63.

evils. Same word as "wicked", *v.* 44.

482 44 And [38] ye shall know that I *am* [2] the LORD,
when [9] I have wrought with you for My name's
sake, not according to your °wicked ways, nor
according to your corrupt doings, O ye house
of Israel, [3] saith [3] the Lord GOD.' "

E G[1] H r (p. 1134) 45 Moreover the word of [2] the LORD came
unto me, saying,
46 [3] "Son of man, set thy face toward °the
south, and drop *thy word* toward °the south,
and prophesy °against the forest of °the south
field;

s 47 And say to the forest of [46] the south, 'Hear
the word of [2] the LORD; Thus saith [3] the Lord
GOD; °'Behold, I will kindle a fire in thee,
and it shall devour every green tree in thee,
and every dry tree: the flaming flame shall
not be quenched, and all faces from the south
to the north shall be burned therein.

t 48 °And all °flesh shall see that I [2] the LORD
have kindled it: it shall not be quenched.' "

I 49 Then said I, "Ah [3] Lord GOD! they say of
me, 'Doth he not speak °parables?' "

H r 21 And the word of °the LORD came unto
me, saying,
2 °"Son of man, set thy face toward Jerusalem,
and drop *thy word* toward the °holy
places, and prophesy against °the land of
Israel,

s 3 And say to [2] the land of Israel, 'Thus saith
[1] the LORD; °'Behold, I *am* against thee, and
will °draw forth My sword out of his sheath,
and will cut off from thee °the righteous and
°the wicked.
4 Seeing then that I will cut off from thee
[3] the righteous and [3] the wicked, therefore shall
My sword go forth out of his sheath against
all flesh from the south to the north:

t 5 That all flesh may know that I [1] the LORD
have [3] drawn forth My sword out of his sheath:
°it shall not return any more.' '

G[2] J 6 Sigh therefore, thou [2] son of man, with the
breaking of *thy* loins; and with bitterness sigh
before their eyes.
7 And it shall be, when they say unto thee,
'Wherefore sighest thou?' that thou shalt
answer, 'For the tidings; because it cometh:
and every heart shall melt, and all hands shall
be feeble, and every °spirit shall faint, and all
knees shall be weak *as* water: [3] behold, it
cometh, and shall be brought to pass, °saith
the Lord GOD.' "

K L 8 Again the word of [1] the LORD came unto
me, saying,
9 [2] "Son of man, prophesy, and say, 'Thus
saith °the LORD; Say, °'A sword, a sword is
sharpened, and also furbished:
10 It is sharpened to °make a sore slaughter;
it is furbished that it may °glitter: °should we
then make mirth?

M °it contemneth the °rod of My son, *as* every
tree.

L 11 And He hath given it to be furbished, that
it may be handled: this sword is sharpened,
and it is furbished, to give it into the hand of
°the slayer.' '

---

44 wicked. Heb. *rā'a'*. Ap. 44. viii.

20. 45—21. 32 (*E*, p. 1104). THE LAND AND THE CITY. (JUDGMENTS.) (*Division.*)

E | G[1] | 20. 45—21. 5. Parable and its Interpretation.
  | G[2] | 21. 6-32. Signs and their Signification.

20. 45—21. 5 (G[1], above). PARABLE AND ITS INTERPRETATION. (*Introversion and Extended Alternation.*)

G[1] | H | r | 20. 45, 46. Subject. Forest of the South.
  s | 20. 47. Fire. Devouring.
  t | 20. 48. All flesh shall see.
  I | 20. 49. Ezekiel. Complaint.
  H | *r* | 21. 1, 2. Subject. Jerusalem and the Land.
  s | 21. 3, 4. Sword. Cutting off.
  t | 21. 5. All flesh shall know.

20. 45—22. 31 (*E*, p. 1104). THE LAND AND THE CITY. (*Alternation.*)

E | E | 20. 45—21. 32. Parables and signs.
  F | 22. 1-16. The City defiled.
  E | 22. 17-22. Symbol. Dross.
  F | 22. 23-31. The Land not cleansed.

46 the south = the *Negeb*. See note on Ps. 126. 4.
against: or, unto. Some codices read "toward".
the south field: i. e. Judah and Jerusalem.
47 Behold. Fig. *Asterismos*. Ap. 6.
48 And all flesh shall see. See the Structure above.
flesh. Put by Fig. *Synecdoche* (of the Part), Ap. 6, for the whole person. All flesh = all people, every one.
49 parables. Thus intended to have the same purpose as the Lord's parables. See Matt. 13. 11.
21. 1 the LORD. Heb. Jehovah. Ap. 4. II.
2 Son of man. See note on 2. 1.
holy. See note on Ex. 3. 5.
the land of Israel = the soil of Israel. Heb. *'admath Israel*. See note on 11. 17.
3 Behold. Fig. *Asterismos*. Ap. 6.
draw forth My sword. See note on 5. 2, 17, and 12. 14.
the righteous, &c. Therefore 18. 2, 3, is not yet fulfilled, but corresponds with the green tree and the dry of 20. 47. **the righteous** = a righteous one.
the wicked = a lawless one. Heb. *rāsha'*. Ap. 44. x.
5 it shall not return, &c.: i. e. until it has executed its mission.

21. 6-32 (G[2], above). SIGNS AND THEIR SIGNIFICATION. (*Alternation.*)

G[2] | J | 6, 7. Ezekiel. First sign. Sighing.
  K | 8-13. Signification of first sign.
  J | 14-17. Ezekiel. Second sign. Smiting.
  K | 18-32. Signification of second sign.

7 spirit. Heb. *rūach*. Ap. 9.
saith the Lord GOD = [is] Adonai Jehovah's oracle. See note on 2. 4.

21. 8-13 (K, above). SIGNIFICATION OF FIRST SIGN. (*Alternation.*)

K | L | 8-10-. The sword of Jehovah.
  M | -10. Its contempt for the sceptre of Judah.
  L | 11, 12. The sword of Jehovah.
  M | 13. Its contempt for the sceptre of Judah.

9 the LORD = Jehovah. Ap. 4. II. Some codices, with three early printed editions (one Rabbinic in marg.), read *Adonai*. Ap. 4. VIII (2).
A sword, a sword. Fig. *Epizeuxis* (Ap. 6), for emphasis = a great or sharp sword.
10 make a sore slaughter. Fig. *Polyptōton* (Ap. 6), for emphasis. Heb. to slay a slaughter.
glitter = flash as lightning.
should we then make mirth? or, "should we flourish [the sceptre of My son (i. e. of Judah)]?"
it, &c.: i. e. "Jehovah's sword despiseth the [wooden] sceptre of My son (i. e. Judah), as [it despiseth] every tree". The Ellipsis is to be thus supplied.
rod = sceptre.
11 the slayer: i. e. the king of Babylon.

482 12 Cry and howl, [2] son of man: for °it shall °be
upon My People, it *shall be* upon all the
°princes of Israel: °terrors by reason of the
sword shall be upon My People: °smite therefore upon *thy* thigh.

M (p. 1134) 13 Because °*it is* a trial, °and what if *the sword* contemn even the [10] rod? °it shall be no *more*, [7] saith [7] the Lord GOD.

J 14 Thou therefore, [2] son of man, prophesy, and °smite *thine* hands together, and let the sword be doubled the third time, the sword of the slain: it *is* the sword of the great *men that are* slain, which entereth into their privy chambers.
15 I have set the point of the sword against all their gates, that *their* heart may faint, and °*their* ruins be multiplied: ah! *it is* made °bright, *it is* °wrapped up for the slaughter.
16 °Go °thee one way or other, *either* on the right hand, *or* on the left, whithersoever °thy face *is* set.
17 °I will also smite Mine hands together, and I will cause My fury to rest: I [1] the LORD have said *it*."

K N (p. 1135) 18 The word of [1] the LORD came unto me again, saying,
19 "Also, thou [2] son of man, appoint thee two ways, °that the sword of the king of Babylon may come: °both twain shall come forth out of one land: and °choose thou a place, choose *it* at the head of the way to the city.
20 Appoint a way, that the sword may come

O u to Rabbath of the Ammonites,

v and to Judah in Jerusalem the defenced.

N 21 For the king of Babylon °stood at the parting of the way, at the head of the two ways, °to use divination: he °made *his* arrows bright, he consulted with °images, he °looked in the liver.
22 At his right hand was the divination for Jerusalem, to °appoint captains, to open °the mouth in the slaughter, to lift up the voice with °shouting, to appoint *battering* rams against the gates, to cast a mount, °*and* to build °a fort.
23 And it shall be unto °them as a false divination in their sight, to °them that have °sworn oaths: but He will call to remembrance the °iniquity, that they may be taken."
24 Therefore thus saith [7] the Lord GOD; "Because ye have made your [23] iniquity to be remembered, in that your °transgressions are discovered, so that in all your doings your °sins do appear; because, *I say*, that ye are come to remembrance, ye shall be °taken with the hand.

O v 25 And thou, °profane °wicked prince of Israel, whose day is come, when °iniquity *shall have* °an end,"
26 Thus saith [7] the Lord GOD; "Remove the diadem, and take off the crown: this *shall* not °*be* the same: exalt *him that is* low, and abase *him that is* high.

12 it: i.e. the sword of Jehovah, the king of Babylon.
princes=leaders.
be=come.
terrors by, &c.=who shall be delivered to the sword with My People.
smite therefore, &c. This was the symbol of grief in man, as beating the breast was in woman.
13 it is a trial=it (Jehovah's sword) has been tried (or proved).
and what, &c.=and what [will happen or be the result] if [Jehovah's sword shall not despise] the [wooden] sceptre?
it shall be no more=it will not [despise it].
saith the Lord GOD=[is] Adonai Jehovah's oracle.
14 smite thine hands together, &c. A sign of disappointment or grief in men. Ref. to Pent. (Num. 24. 10).
15 their ruins=the overthrown. So the Sept. and Syr. Cp. Jer. 18. 23.
bright=bright as lightning.
wrapped up=keen, or sharp.
16 Go thee. Fig. *Apostrophe*. Ap. 6. Addressed to the sword.
thee: i.e. the sword. Not Ezekiel. It is fem., not masc.: = Go to the right, turn to the left: or, One stroke to the right, another to the left, &c.
thy face=thine edge.
17 I will also smite, &c. Fig. *Anthropopatheia*. Ap. 6.

21. 18-32 (*K*, p. 1134). SIGNIFICATION OF SECOND SIGN. (*Alternation and Introversion.*)

K | N | 18-20-. The two ways.
  | O | u | -20-. The Ammonites.
  | | v | -20. Judah and Jerusalem.
  | N | 21-24. The two ways.
  | O | v | 25-27. The wicked prince of Israel.
  | | u | 28-32. The Ammonites.

19 that the sword . . . may come=for the sword . . . to come.
both twain=the two ways.
choose thou a place=grave a hand: i.e. set up a sign-post.
21 stood=hath come to a stand.
to use divination=to divine a divination.
made his arrows bright=hath shaken his arrows. This was one of the modes of divination by which the arrow (marked like a lot), gave the decision.
images=teraphim.
looked in, &c.=inspected the liver; another mode of divination. If healthy or double and the lobes inclined inward, the omen was favourable; but if diseased or too dry, or without a lobe or a band between the parts, the omen was unfavourable.
22 appoint captains=set up battering-rams. Cp. 4. 2.
the mouth in the slaughter=a hole by a breach.
shouting=a war-shout.
and. Some codices, with four early printed editions (one Rabbinic in marg.), Aram., Sept., and Syr., read this "and" in the text.
a fort=a siege wall.
23 them: i.e. Zedekiah and the rulers in Jerusalem.
sworn oaths. Referring to Zedekiah's treacherous breach of faith with the king of Babylon. See 17. 11-21.
iniquity=treachery. Heb. *'āvāh*. Ap. 44. iv.
24 transgressions=rebellion (pl. of Majesty)=great rebellion. Heb. *pāsha'*. Ap. 44. ix.
sins. Heb. *chātā'*. Ap. 44. i. Pl. of Majesty=great sin.
taken with the hand=captured, or made captives.
25 profane=pierced through: i.e. deadly wounded one. Zedekiah a type of the future Antichrist. Cp. Rev. 13 3. **wicked**=lawless. Heb. *rāshā'*. Ap. 44. x. **iniquity . . . an end.** Fig. *Hypallage*. Ap. 6. Heb. "iniquity of the end"=an end of the iniquity. Heb. *'āvāh*, as in *v.* 23. **26 be the same**: or, endure. They might exalt and abase, but Jehovah would not recognise it.

27 I will °overturn, overturn, overturn, it: and it shall be no *more*, °until He come Whose right it is; and I will give it *Him*."

u (p. 1135) 28 And thou, [2]son of man, prophesy and say, "Thus saith [7]the Lord GOD concerning the Ammonites, and concerning °their reproach; even say thou, 'The [9]sword, the sword *is* drawn: for the slaughter *it is* furbished, °to consume because of the glittering:

29 Whiles they see vanity unto thee, whiles they divine a lie unto thee, to bring thee upon the necks of *them that are* slain, of °the wicked, whose day is come, when °their [23]iniquity *shall have* an end.

30 Shall I cause *it* to return into his sheath? I will judge thee in the place where thou wast created, in the land of thy nativity.

31 And I will pour out Mine indignation upon thee, I will blow against thee in the fire of My wrath, and deliver thee into the hand of brutish °men, *and* skilful to destroy.

32 Thou shalt be for fuel to the fire; thy blood shall be in the midst of the land; thou shalt be no *more* remembered: for I [1]the LORD have spoken *it*.'"

F w[1] (p. 1136) 22 Moreover the word of °the LORD came unto me, saying,

2 "Now, thou °son of man, wilt thou °judge, wilt thou judge the °bloody city?

x[1] yea, thou shalt shew her all her °abominations.

3 Then say thou, 'Thus saith °the Lord GOD, 'The city sheddeth blood in the midst of it, that her time may come, and maketh °idols against herself to defile herself.

4 Thou art become guilty in thy [2]blood that thou hast shed; and hast defiled thyself in thine [3]idols which thou hast made; and thou hast caused thy °days to draw near, and art °come *even* unto thy years:

w[2] therefore °have I made thee a reproach unto the °heathen, and a mocking to all countries.

5 °*Those that be* near, and *those that be* far from thee, shall mock thee, *which art* infamous *and* °much vexed.

x[2] 6 °Behold, the °princes of Israel, every one were in thee °to their power to shed blood.

7 In thee have they °set light by father and mother: in the midst of thee have they °dealt by oppression with the stranger: in thee have they °vexed the fatherless and the widow.

8 Thou hast despised Mine °holy things, and hast °profaned My sabbaths.

9 In thee are °men that °carry tales to shed blood: and in thee they eat upon the mountains: in the midst of thee they commit lewdness.

10 In thee have they °discovered their fathers' nakedness: in thee have they humbled her that was °set apart for pollution.

11 And one hath °committed abomination with his neighbour's wife; and another hath °lewdly defiled his daughter in law; and another in thee hath °humbled his sister, his father's daughter.

12 In thee have they °taken gifts to shed blood; thou hast °taken usury and increase, and thou hast greedily gained of thy neighbours by extortion, and °hast forgotten Me, °saith [3]the Lord GOD.

13 'Behold, therefore °I have smitten Mine hand at thy dishonest gain which thou hast made, and at thy blood which hath been in the midst of thee. w[3]

14 Can thine heart endure, or can thine hands be strong, in the days that I shall deal with thee? I [1]the LORD °have spoken *it*, and will do *it*.

15 And °I will scatter thee among the heathen,

---

27 overturn, &c. Fig. *Epizeuxis* (Ap. 6), for great emphasis.

until He come: i.e. the promised Messiah Ref. to Pent. (Gen. 49. 10). Ap. 92. See Isa. 9. 6, 7; 42. 1. Jer. 23. 5; 33. 17. Zech. 6. 12, 13, &c.

28 their reproach. Brought against Jerusalem. See Jer. 49. 1. Zeph. 2. 8.

to consume=that when it beginneth it may flash like lightning. **29 the wicked**=wicked ones (pl.).

their. Refers to "them" (*v.* 23).

31 men. Heb. pl. of *'ĕnōsh*. Ap. 14. III.

22. 1-16 (F, p. 1134). THE CITY DEFILED.
(*Repeated Alternation.*)

F | w[1] | 1, 2-. Judgment. Determined.
x[1] | -2-4-. Abominations. General.
w[2] | -4, 5. Judgment. Declared.
x[2] | 6-12. Abominations. Particular.
w[3] | 13-16. Judgment. Detailed.

1 the LORD Heb. Jehovah. Ap. 4. II.

2 son of man. See note on 2. 1.

judge=pronounce judgment on. See 20. 4; 23. 36.

bloody city=city of bloods: bloods (pl. of Majesty) =much blood. Put by Fig. *Metonymy* (of Subject), Ap. 6, for great bloodshed: referring to those put to death for the truth's sake by the wicked rulers. So in *vv.* 3, 4, 6, 12, 27. **abominations**=idolatries.

3 the Lord GOD. Heb. Adonai Jehovah. See note on 2. 4. **idols**=manufactured gods.

4 days. Put by Fig. *Metonymy* (of Adjunct), Ap. 6, for the judgment inflicted in them.

come even unto. Some codices, with Sept., Syr., and Vulg., read "hast entered the time of".

have I made thee a reproach . . . mocking. Ref. to Pent. (Deut. 28. 37). These words occur nowhere else. Ap. 92. **heathen**=nations.

5 those: i. e. those cities.

much vexed=full of confusion.

6 Behold. Fig. *Asterismos.* Ap. 6.

princes=leaders. **to their**=according to their.

7 set light by, &c. Ref. to Pent. (Deut. 27. 16).

dealt by oppression . . . vexed, &c. Ref. to Pent. (Ex. 22. 21, 22). Ap. 92.

8 holy. See note on Ex. 3. 5.

profaned My sabbaths, &c. Ref. to Pent. (Lev. 19. 30).

9 men. Heb. pl. of *'ĕnōsh.* Ap 14. III. Heb. men of slander.

carry tales, &c. Ref. to Pent. (Lev. 19. 16). Ap. 92.

eat upon the mountains: i. e. the idolatries practised on the mountains. Cp. 18. 6.

10 discovered, &c. Ref to Pent. (Lev. 18. 7, 8, 9; 20. 11, 17). Ap. 92.

set apart, &c. Ref. to Pent. (Lev. 18. 19). Ap. 92.

11 committed abomination, &c. Ref. to Pent. (Lev. 18. 20; 20. 10. Deut. 22. 22). Ap. 92. Cp. 18. 11.

lewdly defiled, &c. Ref. to Pent. (Lev. 18. 15; 20. 12).

humbled his sister. Ref. to Pent. (Lev. 18. 9; 20. 17).

12 taken gifts, &c. Ref. to Pent. (Ex. 23. 8. Deut. 16. 19; 27. 25).

taken usury, &c. Ref. to Pent. (Ex. 22. 25. Lev. 25. 36. Deut. 23. 19). Ap. 92. Cp. 18. 8.

hast forgotten Me. Ref. to Pent. (Deut. 32. 18).

saith the Lord GOD=[is] Adonai Jehovah's oracle.

13 I have smitten Mine hand. See note on 21. 17.

14 have spoken it. Cp. 21. 17; and Num. 23. 19.

15 I will scatter, &c. Ref. to Pent. (Deut. 4. 27; 28. 25, 64). Ap. 92. Cp. 12. 14, 15.

482 and disperse thee in the countries, and will consume thy filthiness out of thee.

16 And thou °shalt take thine inheritance in thyself in the sight of the [4]heathen, and thou shalt know that I *am* [1]the LORD.'"

E P (p. 1137) 17 And the word of [1]the LORD came unto me, saying,

18 [2]"Son of man, the house of Israel is to Me become dross: all they *are* °brass, and tin, and iron, and lead, in the midst of the °furnace; they are *even* the °dross of silver.

Q 19 Therefore thus saith [3]the Lord GOD; 'Because ye are all become dross, [6]behold, therefore I will gather you into the midst of Jerusalem.

R 20 *As* they gather silver, and [18]brass, and iron, and lead, and tin, into the midst of the furnace, to blow the fire upon it, to melt *it*; so will I gather *you* in Mine anger and in My fury, and °I will leave *you there*, and melt you.

Q 21 Yea, I will gather you, and blow upon you in the fire of My wrath, and ye shall be melted in the midst thereof.

P 22 As silver is melted in the midst of the furnace, so shall ye be melted in the midst thereof; and ye shall know that I [1]the LORD have poured out My fury upon you.'"

F S 23 And the word of [1]the LORD came unto me, saying,

T 24 [2]"Son of man, say unto her, 'Thou *art* the land that is °not cleansed, °nor rained upon in the day of indignation.'

U y 25 *There is* a conspiracy of her °prophets in the midst thereof, like a roaring lion ravening the prey; they have devoured °souls; they have taken the treasure and precious things; they have made her many widows in the midst thereof.

z 26 Her [25]priests have violated My law, and have profaned Mine [8]holy things: they have °put no difference between the [8]holy and profane, neither have they shewed *difference* between the unclean and the clean, and have hid their eyes from My sabbaths, and I am profaned among them.

V 27 Her [6]princes in the midst thereof *are* like wolves ravening the prey, to shed blood, *and* to destroy [25]souls, to get dishonest gain.

U y 28 And her [25]prophets have daubed them with untempered *morter*, seeing vanity, and divining lies unto them, saying, 'Thus saith [3]the Lord GOD,' when [1]the LORD hath not spoken.

z 29 The People of the land have used oppression, and exercised robbery, and °have vexed the °poor and needy: yea, they °have oppressed the stranger wrongfully.

T 30 And I sought for a °man among them, that should make up the hedge, and stand in the gap before Me for the land, that I should not destroy it: but °I found none.

S 31 Therefore have I poured out Mine indignation upon them; I have consumed them with the fire of My wrath: their own way have I recompensed upon their heads, [12]saith [3]the Lord GOD.

F W **23** The word of °the LORD came again unto me, saying,

2 °"Son of man, there were °two women, the daughters of one mother:

3 And they committed °whoredoms in °Egypt; they committed °whoredoms in their youth: there were their breasts °pressed, and there they °bruised the teats of their virginity.

4 And the names of them *were* °Aholah the °elder, and °Aholibah her sister: and they were Mine, and they bare sons and daughters. Thus *were* their names; Samaria *is* °Aholah, and Jerusalem °Aholibah.

---

16 shalt take thine inheritance = shalt be profaned in thyself (or on thine own account).

22. 17-22 (*E*, p. 1134). SYMBOL, DROSS. (*Introversion.*)

E | P | 17, 18. Incrimination.
Q | 19. Gathering.
R | 20. Comparison.
Q | 21. Gathering.
P | 22. Incrimination.

18 brass = copper, or bronze.
furnace: or crucible.
dross. Lead put into the crucible with gold or silver causes the baser metals to retire, or form *scoriae* or dross at the sides of the crucible, leaving the pure gold or silver in the middle. But here the silver itself becomes the dross. Cp. *v.* 19.

20 I will leave you there. The letter פ (*Pe*=P) in *v^ehippihti*, in being transferred from the ancient Hebrew into the modern square character, was probably mistaken for the נ (*Nun*=N), being much alike. If so, "I will blow" became "I will leave"; and the words "you there" had to be necessarily supplied. By this change the correspondence of the two verses (20, 21) is restored:—*v.* 20. Gather . . . blow . . . melt: *v.* 21. Gather . . blow . . melt.

22. 23-31 (*F*, p. 1134). LAND NOT CLEANSED. (*Introversion and Alternation.*)

F | S | 23. Jehovah. His word.
T | 24. The Land. Not cleansed.
U | y | 25. The prophets. Conspiracy.
z | 26. The priests. Violated the Law.
V | 27. The princes. Like wolves.
U | *y* | 28. The prophets. Daubed.
z | 29. The People. Violated the Law.
T | 30. The Land. No intercessor.
S | 31. Jehovah. His judgment.

24 not cleansed = not to be rained upon.
nor rained upon = nor to receive fruitful showers.
25 prophets. Note the four classes here enumerated. See the Structure above; and *vv.* 26, 28, 29.
souls. Heb. *nephesh.* Ap. 13.
26 put no difference, &c. Ref. to Pent. (Lev. 10. 10; 11. 47; 22. 22). Ap. 92.
29 have vexed . . . have oppressed, &c. Ref. to Pent. (Ex. 22. 21; 23. 9. Lev. 19. 33, &c.). Ap. 92.
poor. Heb. *'ānī.* See note on Prov. 6. 11.
30 man. Heb. *'ish.* Ap. 14. II.
I found none. Cp. 13. 5, and Jer. 5. 1.

23. 1-49 (*F*, p. 1104). JERUSALEM. (TWO SISTERS.) (*Introversion.*)

F | W | 1-4. Aholah and Aholibah.
X | 5-10. Aholah = Samaria (Israel).
X | 11-35. Aholibah = Jerusalem (Judah).
W | 36-49. Aholah and Aholibah.

1 the LORD. Heb. Jehovah. Ap. 4. II.
2 Son of man. See note on 2. 1.
two women. Two sisters, representing respectively Samaria and Jerusalem.
3 whoredoms = idolatries. **Egypt.** Cp. 20. 7, 8.
pressed = handled, as in *vv.* 8, 21.
bruised = squeezed (in natural use).
4 Aholah. Heb. *'āhālāh* = [She has] her own tent. So named probably because Israel set up her own worship as distinct from Jehovah's.
elder. Refers not to age, but to extent.
Aholibah. Heb. *'āhālībāh* = My tent [is] in her.

X Y A (p. 1138) 5 And [4]Aholah played the harlot when she
was Mine;
482 and she doted on her lovers, on the Assyrians
B *her* neighbours,
6 *Which were* clothed with blue, captains and
rulers, all of them desirable young men, horsemen riding upon horses.
C 7 Thus she committed her [3]whoredoms with
them, with all them *that were* °the chosen men
of Assyria, and with all on whom she doted:
with all their idols she defiled herself.
D 8 Neither left she her [3]whoredoms *brought*
from Egypt: for in her youth they lay with
her, and they [3]bruised the breasts of her virginity, and poured their [3]whoredom upon her.
E 9 Wherefore I have delivered her into the
hand of her lovers, into the hand of the
Assyrians, upon whom she doted.
10 These discovered her nakedness: they took
her sons and her daughters, and slew her with
the sword: and she became °famous among
women; for they had executed judgment upon
her.
Y A 11 And when her sister [4]Aholibah saw *this*,
she was more corrupt in her inordinate love
than she, and in her [3]whoredoms more than
her sister in *her* whoredoms.
B 12 She doted upon the Assyrians *her* neighbours, captains and rulers clothed most gorgeously, horsemen riding upon horses, all of
them desirable young men.
C 13 Then I saw that she was defiled, *that* they
took both one way,
14 And *that* she increased her [3]whoredoms:
for when she saw °men pourtrayed upon the
wall, the images of the Chaldeans pourtrayed
with vermilion,
15 Girded with girdles upon their loins,
exceeding in dyed attire upon their heads, all
of them princes to look to, after the manner of
the Babylonians of Chaldea, the land of their
nativity:
16 And as soon as she saw them with her
eyes, she doted upon them, and sent messengers unto them into Chaldea.
17 And the Babylonians came to her into the
bed of love, and they defiled her with their
[3]whoredom, and she was polluted with them,
and her °mind was alienated from them.
18 So she discovered her [3]whoredoms, and
discovered her nakedness: then °My [17]mind
was alienated from her, °like as °My [17]mind
was alienated from her sister.
D 19 Yet she multiplied her [3]whoredoms, in
°calling to remembrance the days of her youth,
wherein she had played the °harlot °in the
land of [3]Egypt.
20 For she doted upon their paramours, whose
flesh *is as* the flesh of asses, and whose issue
is like the issue of horses.
21 Thus thou [19]calledst to remembrance the
lewdness of thy youth, in °bruising thy teats
by the [3]Egyptians for the paps of thy youth.
E a 22 Therefore, O [4]Aholibah, thus saith °the
Lord GOD; °'Behold, I will raise up thy lovers
against thee, from whom thy [17]mind is alienated, and I will bring them against thee on
every side;
23 The Babylonians, and all the Chaldeans,
°Pekod, and °Shoa, and °Koa, *and* all the Assyrians with them: all of them desirable young
men, captains and rulers, great lords and renowned, all of them riding upon horses.
24 And they shall come against thee with
chariots, °wagons, and wheels, and with °an
assembly of °people, *which* shall set against
thee buckler and shield and helmet round
about: and I will set judgment before them,
and they shall judge thee according to their
judgments.
25 And I will set My jealousy against thee,
and they shall deal furiously with thee: they
shall take away thy nose and thine ears; and
thy remnant shall fall by the sword: they shall
take thy sons and thy daughters; and thy
residue shall be devoured by the fire.
26 They shall also strip thee out of thy
clothes, and take away thy fair jewels.
27 Thus will I make thy lewdness to cease b
from thee, and thy [3]whoredom *brought* from
the land of [3]Egypt: so that thou shalt not lift
up thine eyes unto them, nor remember [3]Egypt
any more.'
28 For thus saith [22]the Lord GOD; [22]'Behold, *a*
I will deliver thee into the hand *of them* whom
thou hatest, into the hand *of them* from whom
thy [17]mind is alienated:

23. 5-35 (X, p. 1137). AHOLAH AND AHOLIBAH.
(*Extended Alternation.*)

X | Y | A | 5-. AHOLAH. (Samaria.)
B | -5, 6. Doting on the Assyrians.
C | 7. Her idolatry with them.
D | 8. Her perseverance.
E | 9, 10. Judgment executed.
Y | *A* | 11. AHOLIBAH. (Jerusalem.)
B | 12. Doting on the Assyrians.
C | 13-18. Her idolatry with them.
D | 19-21. Her perseverance.
E | 22-35. Judgment threatened.

7 the chosen, &c. = the choice of Asshur's sons. So *vv.* 9, 12.

10 famous = a name: i.e. infamous.

14 men. Heb. pl. of *'ĕnōsh.* Ap. 14. III.

17 mind = soul. Heb. *nephesh.* Ap. 13.

18 My mind. Fig. *Anthropopatheia.* Ap. 6.

like as = according as.

19 calling to remembrance. Put by Fig. *Metonymy* (of the Cause), Ap. 6, for the desiring of her former idolatries.

harlot. Put for idolatress.

in. Some codices read "from", as in *vv.* 8 and 27.

21 bruising. Aram. and Syr. read "handling", as in *v.* 3.

23. 22-35 (*E*, above). JUDGMENT THREATENED.
(*Alternation.*)

E | a | 22-26. Enemies.
b | 27. Purpose. (Negative.)
a | 28-34. Enemies.
b | 35. Purpose. (Positive.)

22 the Lord GOD. Heb. Adonai Jehovah. See note on 2. 4.

Behold. Fig. *Asterismos.* Ap. 6.

23 Pekod . . . Shoa . . . Koa. These Eastern peoples are all named in the inscriptions.

24 wagons = chariots.

an assembly = a gathered host. **people** = peoples.

482 29 And they shall deal with thee hatefully,
and shall take away all thy °labour, and shall
leave thee naked and bare: and the nakedness of thy [3]whoredoms shall be discovered,
both thy lewdness and thy [3]whoredoms.
30 I will do these *things* unto thee, because
thou hast gone a [3]whoring after the °heathen,
and because thou art polluted with their °idols.
31 Thou hast walked in the way of thy
sister; therefore will I give her °cup into thine
hand.'
32 Thus saith [22]the Lord GOD; 'Thou shalt
drink of thy sister's [31]cup deep and large: thou
shalt be laughed to scorn and had in derision;
it containeth much.
33 Thou shalt be filled with drunkenness and
sorrow, with the [31]cup of astonishment and desolation, with the [31]cup of thy sister Samaria.
34 Thou shalt even drink it and suck *it* out,
and thou shalt °break the sherds thereof, and
°pluck off thine own breasts: for I have spoken
it, °saith [22]the Lord GOD.
b 35 Therefore thus saith [22]the Lord GOD; 'Be-
(p. 1138) cause thou hast forgotten Me, and cast Me
behind thy back, therefore bear thou also thy
°lewdness and thy [3]whoredoms.'"
W c 36 [1]The LORD said moreover unto me; [2]"Son
(p. 1139) of man, wilt thou judge [4]Aholah and [4]Aholi-
bah? yea, declare unto them their abominations;
37 That they have committed °adultery, and
blood *is* in their hands, and with their [30]idols
have they committed °adultery, and have also
°caused their sons, whom they bare unto Me,
°to pass for °them through *the fire*, to devour
them.
d 38 Moreover this they have done unto Me:
they have °defiled My sanctuary in the same
day, and have °profaned My sabbaths.
39 For when they had slain their °children to
their [30]idols, then they came the same day into
My sanctuary to profane it; and, °lo, thus have
they done in the midst of Mine house.
40 And furthermore, that ye have sent for
°men to come from far, unto whom a messenger
was sent; and, [39]lo, they came: for whom thou
didst °wash thyself, °paintedst thy eyes, and
deckedst thyself with ornaments,
41 And satest upon °a stately bed, and a table
prepared before it, whereupon thou hast set
Mine incense and Mine oil.
42 And a voice of a °multitude being at ease
was °with her: and with the °men of °the
common sort *were* brought °Sabeans from the
wilderness, which put bracelets upon their
hands, and beautiful crowns upon their heads.
43 Then said I unto *her that was* old in
[37]adulteries, 'Will they now commit [3]whore-
doms with her, °and she *with them?*'
44 Yet °they went in unto her, as they go in
unto a woman that playeth the harlot: so went
they in unto [4]Aholah and unto [4]Aholibah, the
lewd women.
c 45 And °the righteous [40]men, they °shall judge
them after the manner of adulteresses, and after
the manner of women that shed blood; because
they *are* adulteresses, and blood *is* in their
hands.
d 46 For thus saith [22]the Lord GOD; 'I will
bring up a °company upon them, and will
give them to be removed and spoiled.
47 And the [46]company shall stone them with
stones, and dispatch them with their swords;
they shall slay their sons and their daughters,
and burn up their houses with fire.
48 Thus will I cause lewdness to cease out
of the land, that all women may be taught not
to do after your lewdness.
49 And they shall recompense your lewdness
upon you, and ye shall bear the °sins of your
[30]idols: and °ye shall know that I *am* [22]the
Lord GOD.'"

24 Again in °the ninth year, in the tenth G F[1] G[1]
month, in the tenth *day* of the month, (p. 1140)
the word of °the LORD came unto me, saying, 480

---

29 labour. Put by Fig. *Metonymy* (of the Cause), Ap. 6, for the product of the labour.
30 heathen=nations.
idols=manufactured gods.
31 cup. Cp. Isa. 51. 17. Rev. 14. 9, 10.
34 break: or, gnaw, lest a drop should be lost.
pluck off=tear out: i. e. destroy the occasions of their idolatry.
saith the Lord GOD=[is] Adonai Jehovah's oracle.
35 lewdness . . . whoredoms. Put here by Fig. *Metonymy* (of the Cause), Ap. 6, for the punishment due to the idolatry.

23. 36-49 (*W*, p. 1137). **AHOLAH AND AHOLIBAH.**
(*Alternation.*)

W | c | 36, 37. Judgment.
  | d | 38-44. Incrimination.
  | *c* | 45. Judgment.
  | *d* | 46-49. Threatening.

37 adultery. Put (like whoredom) for all idolatry, as being unfaithfulness to Jehovah. See note on 16. 15.
caused=set apart.
to pass, &c. Ref. to Pent. (Lev. 18. 21; 20. 2-4).
them. "Them" is masc., and refers to the idols, in the first clause; and so, many codices, with six early printed editions (one Rabbinic). But some codices read fem.=themselves.
38 defiled . . . profaned. Ref. to Pent. (Lev. 19. 31). Ap. 92. Cp. 22. 8.
39 children=sons. **lo.** Fig. *Asterismos.* Ap. 6.
40 men. Pl. of *'ěnōsh.* Ap. 14. III.
wash thyself. Cp. Ruth 3. 3.
paintedst, &c. Cp. 2 Kings 9. 30. Jer. 4. 30.
41 a stately bed. Cp. Prov. 7. 16-18. Isa. 57. 8, 9.
42 multitude, &c.=a careless throng.
with her: or, in her: i.e. in Jerusalem.
men of the common sort=men out of the mass of mankind. **men.** Heb. pl. of *'ěnōsh.* Ap. 14. III.
the common sort. Heb. *'ādām.* Ap. 14. I.
Sabeans. Heb. text reads "drunkards". But marg., and some codices, with three early printed editions, read "Sabeans".
43 and she=even hers. Ginsburg thinks it should read "but so it was". Cp. 16. 15, 19.
44 they went. Heb. text reads "came he". A special various reading called *Sevīr* (Ap. 34), with some codices, Aram., Sept., Syr., and Vulg., read "came they".
45 the righteous . . . shall judge. Ref. to Pent. (Lev. 20. 10). Ap. 92.
46 company=a gathered host.
49 sins. Heb. *chāṭā.* Ap. 44. i.
ye shall know, &c. Occurs only here, 13. 9; and 24. 24. Cp. note on 6. 7.

24. 1-32. 33 [For Structure see next page].
1 the ninth year. Of Jehoiachin's captivity. See the table, p. 1105. Cp. 1. 2.
the LORD. Heb. Jehovah. Ap. 4. II.

2 °"Son of man, write thee the name of the day, *even* of °this same day: the king of Babylon set himself against Jerusalem this same day.

G² H¹ (p. 1140) **3** And utter a parable unto the rebellious house, and say unto them, 'Thus saith °the Lord GOD; 'Set on a °pot, set *it* on, and also pour water into it:

4 Gather the pieces thereof into it, *even* every good piece, the thigh, and the shoulder; fill *it* with the choice bones.

5 Take the choice of the flock, and °burn also the °bones under it, *and* make it boil well, and let °them seethe the bones of it therein.'

J¹ **6** Wherefore thus saith [3]the Lord GOD; 'Woe to °the bloody city, to the [3]pot whose °scum *is* therein, and whose °scum is not gone out of it! bring it out piece by piece; °let no lot fall upon it.

7 For her blood is in the midst of her; she set it upon the top of a rock; she poured it °not upon the ground, °to cover it with dust;

8 That it might cause fury to come up to take vengeance; I have set her blood upon the top of a rock, that it should not be covered.'

9 Therefore thus saith [3]the Lord GOD; 'Woe to [6]the bloody city! I will even make the pile for fire great.

H² **10** Heap on wood, kindle the fire, consume the flesh, and °spice it well, and let the bones be burned.

11 Then set it empty upon the coals thereof, that the °brass of it may be °hot, and may burn, and *that* the filthiness of it may be molten in it, *that* the [6]scum of it may be consumed.

J² **12** She hath wearied *herself* with lies, and her great [6]scum went not forth out of her: her scum °*shall be* in the fire.

13 In thy filthiness *is* lewdness: because I have purged thee, and thou wast not purged, thou shalt not be purged from thy filthiness any more, till I have caused My fury to rest upon thee.

14 I [1]the LORD have spoken *it:* it shall come to pass, and I will do *it;* I will not go back, neither will I spare, neither will I repent; according to thy ways, and according to thy doings, shall they judge thee, °saith [3]the Lord GOD.'"

H³ **15** Also the word of [1]the LORD came unto me, saying,

16 [2]"Son of man, behold, I take away from thee °the desire of thine eyes with a °stroke: yet neither shalt thou mourn nor weep, neither shall thy tears run down.

17 Forbear to cry, make no mourning for the dead, °bind the tire of thine head upon thee, and put on thy shoes upon thy feet, and °cover not *thy* lips, and eat not °the bread of °men."

18 So I spake unto the People in the morning: and at even my wife died; and I did in the morning °as I was commanded.

J³ **19** And the People said unto me, "Wilt thou not tell us what these *things are* to us, that thou doest *so?*"

20 Then I answered them, "The word of [1]the LORD came unto me, saying,

21 'Speak unto the house of Israel, 'Thus saith [3]the Lord GOD; 'Behold, I will profane My sanctuary, the excellency of your strength, the °desire of your eyes, and that which your °soul °pitieth; and your sons and your daughters whom ye have °left shall fall by the sword.

22 And ye shall do as I have done: ye shall not cover *your* lips, nor eat [17]the bread of [17]men.

23 And your tires *shall be* upon your heads, and your shoes upon your feet: °ye shall not °mourn nor weep; but ye shall pine away for your °iniquities, and °mourn one toward another.

---

24. 1—32. 33 (*G*, p. 1104). THE BABYLONIAN WAR. PARABLE. (*Division.*)

G | F¹ | 24. 1-27. Jerusalem.
| F² | 25. 1-17. Ammonites and others.
| F³ | 26. 1—28. 26. Tyre and Sidon.
| F⁴ | 29. 1—32. 32. Egypt.

24. 1-27 (F¹, above). JERUSALEM. (*Division.*)

F¹ | G¹ | 1, 2. Literal.
| G² | 3-27. Symbolical.

2 Son of man. See note on 2. 1.

this same day. Cp. 2 Kings 25. 1. Jer. 39. 1; 52. 4. The captives of Israel thus knew what was going on in Jerusalem.

24. 3-27 (G², above). SYMBOLICAL. (*Repeated Alternation.*)

G² | H¹ | 3-5. Symbol A Pot.
| J¹ | 6-9. Signification.
| H² | 10, 11. Symbol. A Fire.
| J² | 12-14. Signification.
| H³ | 15-18. Symbol. Ezekiel.
| J³ | 19-27. Signification.

3 the Lord GOD. Heb. Adonai Jehovah. See note on 2. 4.

pot: or, caldron, using the words of the scoffers in 11. 3, and cp. Jer. 1. 13.

5 burn=pile up.

bones. Ginsburg thinks we should read "wood".

them. The 1611 edition of the A.V. reads "him".

6 the bloody city. See note on 22. 2.

scum=verdigris. Occurs only in this chapter.

let no lot fall, &c. Signifying that the city was to be destroyed, not lotted out to or by the conquerors.

7 not. The 1611 edition of the A.V. omitted this "not".

to cover it with dust. Ref. to Pent. (Lev. 17. 13).

10 spice it well, &c.: or, boil it down till only the bones are left.

11 brass=copper. **hot**=scorched.

12 shall be in the fire. Ginsburg thinks it should read "with a stench".

14 saith the Lord GOD=[is] Adonai Jehovah's oracle.

16 the desire of thine eyes. Put by the Fig. *Periphrasis* (Ap. 6): for Ezekiel's wife. A symbol of Jerusalem. See *v.* 21. **stroke:** or plague.

17 bind, &c. Ref. to Pent. (Lev. 10. 6; 13. 45; 21. 10).

cover not thy lips. Cp. Mic. 3. 7.

the bread of men: i.e. the bread or food brought to the house of mourners. Cp. Jer. 16. 5-7. Hos. 9. 4.

men. Heb. pl. of *'ĕnōsh.* Ap. 14. III.

18 as=according as.

21 desire . . . pitieth. Note the Fig. *Paronomasia* (Ap. 6), to call attention to the emphasis. Heb. *maḥmad . . . maḥmal.*

soul. Heb. *nephesh.* Ap. 13.

left=left behind.

23 ye shall not. Some codices read "yet shall ye neither".

mourn=moan.

iniquities. Heb. *'āvāh.* Ap. 44. iv.

480 24 Thus Ezekiel is unto you a sign: according
to all that he hath done shall ye do: and when
this cometh, ye shall know that I *am* [3] the Lord
GOD.' ' ' "
25 "Also, thou [2] son of man, *shall it* not *be* ° in
the day when I take from them their strength,
the joy of their glory, [16] the ° desire of their
eyes, and that whereupon they set their ° minds,
their sons and their daughters,
26 *That* ° he that escapeth in that day shall
come unto thee, to cause *thee* to hear *it* with
thine ears?
27 In that day shall thy mouth be opened to
him which is escaped, and thou shalt speak,
and be ° no more dumb: and thou shalt be
a sign unto them; and ° they shall know that I
am [1] the LORD."

F² e¹ (p. 1141) **25** The word of ° the LORD came again
unto me, saying,
2 ° "Son of man, set thy face against the
Ammonites, and prophesy against them;
3 And say unto the ° Ammonites, 'Hear the
word of ° the Lord GOD; Thus saith ° the Lord
GOD; 'Because thou saidst, 'Aha,' against My
sanctuary, when it was profaned; and against
° the land of Israel, when it was desolate; and
against the house of Judah, when they went
into captivity;
f¹ 4 ° Behold, therefore ° I will deliver thee to
° the ° men of the east for a possession, and
they shall set their ° palaces in thee, and make
their dwellings in thee: they shall eat thy fruit,
and they shall drink thy milk.
5 And I will make ° Rabbah a stable for
camels, and the Ammonites a couchingplace
for flocks: and ° ye shall know that I *am* [1] the
LORD.'
e² 6 For thus saith [3] the Lord GOD; 'Because
thou hast clapped *thine* hands, and stamped
with the feet, and rejoiced in ° heart with all
thy despite against [3] the land of Israel;
f² 7 [4] Behold, therefore I will stretch out Mine
hand ° upon thee, and will deliver thee for
a spoil to the ° heathen; and I will cut thee off
from the ° people, and I will cause thee to perish
out of the countries: I will destroy thee; and
° thou shalt know that I *am* [1] the LORD.'
e³ 8 Thus saith [3] the Lord GOD; 'Because that
° Moab and Seir do say, [4] 'Behold, the house of
Judah *is* like unto all the [7] heathen;'
f³ 9 Therefore, [4] behold, I will open the side of
Moab from the cities, from his cities *which are*
on his frontiers, the glory of the country, ° Beth-
jeshimoth, ° Baal-meon, and ° Kiriathaim,
10 Unto the [4] men of the east with the Ammonites, and will give them in possession, that the
Ammonites may not be remembered among the
nations.
11 And I will execute judgments upon Moab;
and ° they shall know that I *am* [1] the LORD.'
e⁴ 12 Thus saith [3] the Lord GOD; 'Because that
° Edom hath dealt against the house of Judah
by taking vengeance, and hath greatly offended,
and revenged himself upon them;
f⁴ 13 Therefore' thus saith [3] the Lord GOD; 'I
will also stretch out Mine hand upon [12] Edom,
and will cut off ° man and beast from it; and I

25 in the day. See Ap. 18. **desire** = delight.
minds = souls. Heb. *nephesh*. Ap. 13.
26 he that escapeth. This we find exactly fulfilled in ch. 33. 21, by the flight, on the fifth day of the tenth month, in the twelfth year.
27 no more dumb: i.e. as regards his nation and his testimony to it. In the interval his prophecies are concerning other nations (chs. 25—32).
they shall know, &c. See note on 6. 10.

25. 1-17 (F², p. 1140). AMMONITES AND OTHER NATIONS. (*Repeated Alternation.*)

F² e¹ | 1-3. Incrimination. } Ammon.
f¹ | 4, 5. Threatening.
e² | 6. Incrimination.
f² | 7. Threatening.
e³ | 8. Incrimination. } Moab and Seir.
f³ | 9-11. Threatening.
e⁴ | 12. Incrimination. } Edom.
f⁴ | 13, 14. Threatening.
e⁵ | 15. Incrimination. } Philistines.
f⁵ | 16, 17. Threatening.

1 the LORD. Heb. Jehovah. Ap. 4. II.
2 Son of man. See note on 2. 1.
3 Ammonites. See 21. 28. Ammon was a party to the plot against Gedaliah, the governor whom Nebuchadnezzar appointed after the destruction of Jerusalem. See Jer. 40. 14; 41. 10, 15.
the Lord GOD. Heb. Adonai Jehovah. See note on 2. 4.
the land of Israel = the soil of Israel. Heb. *'admath.* See note on 11. 17.
4 Behold. Fig. *Asterismos.* Ap. 6.
I will deliver. Josephus (*Ant.* x. 9. 7) tells us that Nebuchadnezzar subdued the Ammonites and Moabites in the fifth year after the destruction of Jerusalem. Cp. Jer. 49. 28.
the men of the east: i.e. the Babylonians. See 21. 19, 20. Jer. 25. 21. **men** = sons.
palaces. Heb. rows: i.e. of tents = encampments.
5 Rabbah. See Deut. 3. 11.
ye shall know, &c. See note on 6. 7.
6 heart. Heb. *nephesh.* Ap. 13.
7 upon. A special various reading called *Sevir* (Ap. 34) reads "against".
heathen = nations. **people** = peoples.
thou shalt know, &c. So in 16. 22; 22. 16; 25. 7; 35. 4.
8 Moab. Descended from Lot, like the Ammonites (Gen. 19. 37). Usually hostile to Israel.
9 Beth-jeshimoth. Now *'Ain Surveimeh*, near the north-east corner of the Dead Sea (Num. 33. 49. Josh. 12. 3; 13. 20).
Baal-meon. Now *Tell M'ain* (Num. 32. 38. 1 Chron. 5. 8), two miles south of Heshbon.
Kiriathaim. Now *el Kŭreīyāt*, between Dibon and Medeba (Jer. 48. 1, 23).
11 they shall know, &c. See note on 6. 10.
12 Edom. Descended from Esau (Gen. 36. 1, 43). For their unbrotherly spirit, see Ps. 137. 7. Lam. 4. 21, 22; and Obad. 10-16.
13 man. Heb. *'ādām.* Ap. 14. I.
Teman. A grandson of Esau (Gen. 36. 11). A town or city in Edom, not yet identified.
14 by the hand, &c. See Num. 24. 17-19.
saith the Lord GOD = [is] Adonai Jehovah's oracle.

will make it desolate from ° Teman; and they
of Dedan shall fall by the sword.
14 And I will lay My vengeance upon [12] Edom
° by the hand of My People Israel: and they
shall do in [12] Edom according to Mine anger
and according to My fury; and they shall
know My vengeance, ° saith [3] the Lord GOD.
15 Thus saith [3] the Lord GOD; 'Because the e⁵
Philistines have dealt by revenge, and have
taken vengeance with a despiteful [6] heart, to
destroy *it* for the old hatred;

f[5] (p. 1141) 480 16 Therefore' thus saith [3]the Lord GOD;
[4]'Behold, I will stretch out Mine hand upon
°the Philistines, and I will °cut off the °Cherethims, and destroy the remnant of the sea coast.
17 And I will execute great °vengeance upon them with furious rebukes; and °they shall know that I *am* [1]the LORD, when I shall lay My °vengeance upon them.'"

F[3] M[1] N (p. 1142) 478 **26** And it came to pass in °the eleventh year, in the first *day* of the month, *that* the word of °the LORD came unto me, saying,
2 "°Son of man, because that °Tyrus hath said against Jerusalem, 'Aha, she is broken *that was* the gates of the °people: °she is turned unto me: I shall be replenished, *now* she is laid waste:'

O g 3 Therefore thus saith °the Lord GOD; °'Behold, I *am* against thee, O [2]Tyrus, and will cause many nations to come up against thee, as the sea causeth his waves to come up.

h 4 And they shall destroy the walls of [2]Tyrus, and break down her towers: I will also scrape her dust from her,

i and make her like °the top of a rock.
5 It shall be *a place for* the spreading of nets in °the midst of the sea: for I have spoken *it*, °saith [3]the Lord GOD: and it shall become a spoil to the nations.
6 And her °daughters which *are* in the field shall be slain by the sword; and they shall know that I *am* [1]the LORD.'

O g 7 For thus saith [3]the Lord GOD; [3]'Behold, I will bring upon Tyrus °Nebuchadrezzar king of Babylon, a king of kings, from the north, with horses, and with chariots, and with horsemen, and °companies, and much people.
8 He shall slay with the sword thy [6]daughters in the field: and he shall make a fort against thee, and cast a mount against thee, and lift up the buckler against thee.

h 9 And he shall set °engines of war against thy walls, and with his °axes he shall break down thy towers.
10 By reason of the abundance of his horses their dust shall cover thee: thy walls shall shake at the noise of the horsemen, and of the wheels, and of the chariots, when he shall enter into thy gates, as men enter into a city wherein is made a breach.
11 With the hoofs of his horses shall he tread down all thy streets: he shall slay thy people by the sword, and thy strong °garrisons shall go down to the ground.
12 And they shall make a spoil of thy riches, and make a prey of thy merchandise: and they shall break down thy walls, and destroy thy pleasant houses: and they shall lay thy stones and thy timber and thy dust in the midst of the water.
13 And I will cause the noise of thy songs to cease; and the sound of thy harps shall be no more heard.

i 14 And I will make thee like [4]the top of a rock: °thou shalt be *a place* to spread nets upon; thou shalt °be built no more: for I °the LORD have spoken *it*, [5]saith [3]the Lord GOD.'

16 the Philistines. Cp. Pss. 60. 8, 9; 108. 9, 10. Isa. 11. 14.

cut off the Cherethims. Note the Fig. *Paronomasia* (Ap. 6), for emphasis. Heb. *hikrattî k^erēthîm*; in Eng. I will cut off the cutters off.

Cherethims. A tribe of the Philistines (1 Sam. 30. 14. Zeph. 2. 5). David's body-guard, drawn partly from them.

17 vengeance. Heb. pl. = great vengeance.

they shall know, &c. See note on 6. 10.

26. 1—28. 26 (F[3], p. 1140). TYRE AND ZIDON. (*Division.*)

F[3] | K[1] | 26. 1—28. 19. Tyre.
| K[2] | 28. 20-26. Zidon.

26. 1—28. 19 (K[1], above). TYRE. (*Division.*)

K[1] | L[1] | 26. 1—27. 36. The City of Tyre.
| L[2] | 28. 1-19. The "Prince" and "King" of Tyre.

26. 1—27. 36 (L[1], above). THE CITY OF TYRE. (*Division.*)

L[1] | M[1] | 26. 1-21. The Destruction of Tyre.
| M[2] | 27. 1-36. The Lamentation of Tyre.

26. 1-21 (M[1], above). THE DESTRUCTION OF TYRE. (*Introversion and Extended Alternation.*)

M[1] | N | 1, 2. Tyre rejoices at Jerusalem's fall.
O | g | 3. Invasion by many nations.
h | 4-. Breaking down.
i | -4-6. Likeness to top of a rock.
O | *g* | 7, 8. Invasion by Babylon.
h | 9-13. Breaking down.
i | 14. Likeness to top of a rock.
N | 15-21. Nations lament at Tyre's fall.

1 the eleventh year. The month not given; but see Jer. 39. 1-7; 52. 4-14. See note on 30. 20. Jerusalem fell probably in the fifth month, after the fall but before the destruction in that year of the Temple (2 Kings 25. 8). Cp. *v.* 2. This prophecy *began* to be fulfilled then, and Tyre was taken by Nebuchadnezzar after a thirteen years' siege (see Isa. 23. 1, and Josephus (*Ant.* x. 11. 1; *cont. Apion*, i. 20); but not completely fulfilled till later. Jehovah sees the end from the beginning, and speaks of it by way of prophetic foreshortening. "The day of Jehovah" (30. 3) looks forward to the end.

the LORD. Heb. Jehovah. Ap. 4. II.

2 Son of man. See note on 2. 1.

Tyrus = Tyre, the city. Now, *es Sûr.* Heb. *tzur* = a rock.

people = peoples.

she is turned: i. e. the tide of her traffic.

3 the Lord GOD. Heb. Adonai Jehovah. See note on 2. 4.

Behold. Fig. *Asterismos.* Ap. 6.

4 the top of a rock = a bare rock.

5 the midst of the sea. Tyre was on a promontory spreading out into the sea.

saith the Lord GOD = [is] Adonai Jehovah's oracle.

6 daughters which are in the field = her daughter cities and towns inland.

7 Nebuchadrezzar. Occurs thus spelt four times in this book (here; 29. 18, 19; and 30. 10). See note on Dan. 1. 1.

companies = a gathered host.

9 engines of war = battering rams. Occurs only here.

axes = weapons.

11 garrisons: or, pillars. Seen in vast numbers in the ruins to-day.

14 thou. The 1611 edition of the A.V. reads "they".

be built no more. Zidon's fate has been different. Its extinction was not prophesied. See 28. 20-26.

the LORD. The Syr. and Vulg., with some codices, and two early printed editions, omit "Jehovah" here.

N (p. 1142) 478 15 Thus saith [3]the Lord GOD to [2]Tyrus;
'Shall not the °isles shake at the sound of thy
fall, when the wounded cry, when the slaughter is made in the midst of thee?
16 Then all the princes of the sea shall come
down from their thrones, and lay away their
robes, and put off their broidered garments:
they shall clothe themselves with °trembling;
they shall sit upon the ground, and shall
tremble at *every* moment, and be astonished
at thee.
17 And they shall °take up °a lamentation for
thee, and say to thee, 'How art thou destroyed,
°*that wast* inhabited of seafaring men, the
renowned city, which wast strong in the sea,
she and her inhabitants, which cause their
terror *to be* on all that haunt it!'
18 Now shall the [15]isles tremble in the day of
thy fall; yea, the [15]isles that *are* in the sea
shall be troubled at thy departure.
19 For' thus saith [3]the Lord GOD; 'When I
shall make thee a desolate city, like the cities
that are not inhabited; when I shall bring up
the deep upon thee, and great waters shall
cover thee;
20 When I shall bring thee down with them
that °descend into the pit, with the people of
old time, and shall set thee in the low parts of
the earth, in places desolate of old, with them
that go down to the pit, that thou be not inhabited; °and I shall set glory °in the land of
the living;
21 I will make thee a terror, and thou *shall*
be no *more:* though thou be sought for, yet
shalt thou never be found again, [5]saith [3]the
Lord GOD.'"

M² j (p. 1143) **27** The word of °the LORD came again
unto me, saying,
2 "Now, thou °son of man, take up a lamentation for °Tyrus;
3 And say unto [2]Tyrus, 'O thou that art
situate at °the entry of the sea, *which art*
a merchant of the °people for many °isles,
Thus saith °the Lord GOD; 'O [2]Tyrus, thou
hast said, 'I *am* of perfect beauty.'
4 Thy borders *are* in the midst of the seas,
thy °builders have perfected thy beauty.
5 They have made all thy °*ship* boards of °fir
trees of °Senir: they have taken cedars from
Lebanon to make masts for thee.
6 *Of* the oaks of Bashan have they made
thine oars; °the company of the Ashurites
have made thy benches *of* ivory, *brought*
out of the isles of °Chittim.
7 Fine linen with broidered work from Egypt
was that which thou spreadest forth to be thy
sail; blue and purple from the isles of °Elishah
was that which covered thee.
8 The inhabitants of Zidon and °Arvad were
thy °mariners: thy wise *men,* O Tyrus, °*that*
were in thee, were thy pilots.
9 The °ancients of °Gebal and the wise *men*
thereof were in thee thy calkers: all the ships
of the sea with their mariners were in thee to
°occupy thy merchandise.
10 They of Persia and of °Lud and of °Phut
were in thine army, thy °men of war: they
hanged the shield and helmet in thee; they set
forth thy comeliness.

15 isles=coastlands, or maritime countries.
16 trembling. Heb. pl.=a great trembling.
17 take up=raise.
a lamentation=a dirge.
that wast inhabited of seafaring men: or, that wast an abode from the seas. The Syr. *kataluō* means *to lodge*, and is the rendering of Heb. *yāshab* in Num. 25. 1.
20 descend into the pit. The people of Tyre are meant, as joining those who were dead and buried.
and I shall set glory. This is either a parenthetical contrast referring to Jerusalem (with which the prophecy begins, *v.* 2), or we may read, with Sept., "nor yet arise", &c., completing the end of Tyre, as in *v.* 21.
in the land of the living. This expression occurs eight times without the Article ("the" living): here; 32. 23, 24, 25, 26, 27, 32; and Ps. 27. 13. It occurs three times with the Article ("the living"). See note on Isa. 38. 11. In each case it refers to the condition of *life,* in contrast with "*Sheōl*", which is the condition of death.

27. 1-36 (M², p. 1142). **THE LAMENTATION OF TYRE.** (*Extended Alternation.*)

M² | j | 1-25. Opulence. Influx.
  k | 26, 27. Ruin.
   l | 28-32. Commiseration.
 j | 33. Opulence. Efflux.
  k | 34. Ruin.
   l | 35, 36. Astonishment.

1 the LORD. Heb. Jehovah. Ap. 4. II.
2 son of man. See note on 2. 1.
Tyrus. See note on 26. 2.
3 the entry, &c. Denoting the insular Tyre.
people=peoples.
isles=coast, or maritime lands.
the Lord GOD. Heb. Adonai Jehovah. See note on 2. 4.
4 builders=sons. Cp. Isa. 62. 5.
5 ship boards=planks.
fir=cypress.
Senir=Mount Hermon (Deut. 3. 9).
6 the company of the Ashurites, &c.=a daughter (or branch) of the Ashurites, &c. Ginsburg thinks this clause should read, "they have made thy benches with ivory [and] box-wood (or cypress)"; reading *bith'ashshurīm* instead of *bath-'ăshshurīm* (=a daughter, or branch of the Ashurites), dividing and pointing the words differently. See note on 31. 3; and cp. Isa. 41. 19; 60. 13.
Chittim. Probably Cyprus.
7 Elishah. Probably the Greek Æolis: i.e. the coasts of Peloponnesus. Mentioned in Gen. 10. 4 with Javan (Ionia).
8 Arvad. Now the island *Er Ruad.* Mentioned in 1 Macc. 15. 23.
mariners=rowers. **that were**=they [were].
9 ancients=elders.
Gebal. Now *Jebeil,* on the coast between Beirūt and Tripolis.
occupy=barter, or trade.
10 Lud . . . Phut. Cp. Gen. 10. 6, 13.
men. Heb. pl. of *'ĕnōsh.* Ap. 14. III.
11 men=sons.
Gammadims: or, valiant men.
12 Tarshish. See note on 1 Kings 10. 22.
fairs. Occurs only in this chapter, and here, seven times: *vv.* 12, 14, 16, 19, 22, 27, 33 ("wares").

11 The °men of [8]Arvad with thine army *were*
upon thy walls round about, and the °Gam-
madims were in thy towers: they hanged their
shields upon thy walls round about; they have
made thy beauty perfect.
12 °Tarshish *was* thy merchant by reason of
the multitude of all *kind of* riches; with silver,
iron, tin, and lead, they traded in thy °fairs.

478 13 °Javan, Tubal, and Meshech, they *were* thy merchants: they traded the °persons of °men and vessels of brass in thy market.

14 They of the °house of °Togarmah traded in thy [12]fairs with horses and horsemen and mules.

15 The °men of Dedan *were* thy merchants; many [3]isles *were* the merchandise of thine hand: they brought thee *for* a present horns of ivory and ebony.

16 Syria *was* thy merchant by reason of the multitude of the wares of thy making: they °occupied in thy [12]fairs with emeralds, purple, and broidered work, and fine linen, and coral, and agate.

17 Judah, and °the land of Israel, they *were* thy merchants: they traded in thy market wheat of °Minnith, and °Pannag, and honey, and oil, and balm.

18 Damascus *was* thy merchant in the multitude of the wares of thy making, for the multitude of all riches; in the °wine of °Helbon, and white wool.

19 °Dan also and [13]Javan °going to and fro [16]occupied in thy [12]fairs: bright iron, cassia, and calamus, were in thy market.

20 Dedan *was* thy merchant in precious clothes for chariots.

21 Arabia, and all the princes of Kedar, they °occupied with thee in lambs, and rams, and goats: in these *were they* thy merchants.

22 The merchants of Sheba and Raamah, they *were* thy merchants: they [16]occupied in thy [12]fairs with chief of all spices, and with all precious stones, and gold.

23 °Haran, and °Canneh, and °Eden, the merchants of Sheba, °Asshur, *and* °Chilmad, *were* thy merchants.

24 These *were* thy merchants in all sorts *of things*, in blue clothes, and broidered work, and in chests of rich apparel, bound with cords, and made of cedar, among thy merchandise.

25 The ships of [12]Tarshish did sing of thee in thy market: and thou wast replenished, and made very glorious in the midst of the seas.

k 26 °Thy rowers have brought thee into great
(p. 1143) waters: the east °wind hath broken thee in the
midst of the seas.

27 Thy riches, and thy [12]fairs, thy merchandise, thy mariners, and thy pilots, thy calkers, and the °occupiers of thy merchandise, and all thy [10]men of war, that *are* in thee, and °in all thy °company which *is* in the midst of thee, shall fall into the midst of the seas in the day of thy ruin.

l 28 The °suburbs shall shake at the sound of the cry of thy pilots.

29 And all that handle the oar, the mariners, *and* all the pilots of the sea, shall come down from their ships, they shall stand upon the land;

30 And shall cause their voice to be heard against thee, and shall cry bitterly, and shall cast up dust upon their heads, they shall wallow themselves in the ashes:

31 And they shall make themselves utterly bald for thee, and gird them with sackcloth, and they shall weep for thee with bitterness of °heart *and* bitter wailing.

32 And in their wailing °they shall take up a lamentation for thee, and lament over thee, *saying*, 'What *city is* like [2]Tyrus, like °the destroyed in the midst of the sea?'

33 When thy °wares went forth out of the seas, thou filledst many [3]people; thou didst enrich the kings of the earth with the multitude of thy riches and of thy merchandise. j

34 °In the time *when* thou shalt be broken by the seas in the depths of the waters thy merchandise and all thy [27]company in the midst of thee shall fall. k

35 All the inhabitants of the [3]isles shall be astonished at thee, and their kings shall be sore afraid, they shall be troubled in *their* countenance. l

36 The merchants among the people shall hiss at thee; thou shalt °be a terror, and never *shalt be* °any more.' ' "

13 Javan = Ionia. Cp. Gen. 10. 4. These are named together in Gen. 10. 2.

persons = souls. Heb. *nephesh*. Ap. 13. Referring to the slave trade. See Rev. 18. 13.

men = mankind. Heb. *'ādām*. Ap. 14. I.

14 house. Put by Fig. *Metonymy* (of Subject), Ap. 6, for descendants.

Togarmah (Gen. 10. 3). Probably Armenia.

15 men = sons.

16 occupied = traded. Cp. "occupy" in Luke 19. 13.

17 the land of Israel. Heb. *'eretz Israel*. One of three occurrences of this expression in this book with Heb. *'eretz* (27. 17; 40. 2; 47. 18), instead of *'admath*, which occurs seventeen times. See note on 11. 17.

Minnith. An Ammonite town not yet identified. *Minyeh*, south of Nebo, is suggested by Conder. Cp. Judg. 11. 33.

Pannag. Some article of merchandise, or name of place, not now known.

18 wine. Heb. *yayin*. Ap. 27. I.

Helbon. Now *Helbōn*, in the mountains, thirteen miles north of Damascus.

19 Dan. Heb. Vedan, or Wedan.

going to and fro. Heb. *Meʿūzzāl*. Marg. *Meʿūzzāl* = from Uzal. Cp. Gen. 10. 27.

21 occupied = were the merchants of thy hand. Cp. *v.* 15.

23 Haran. Now *Harran*, between the Euphrates and the Khabour (Gen. 11. 35).

Canneh. Probably now Calneh, a Babylonian city (Gen. 10. 10).

Eden. In Mesopotamia (2 Kings 19. 12. Isa. 37. 12. Amos 1. 5). Mentioned in the Inscriptions. Some suggest *Aden*, in Arabia. Asshur = Assyria.

Chilmad. Now *Kalwādha*, near Baghdad.

26 Thy rowers. Continuing the symbol of a ship, used of Tyre in this chapter.

wind. Heb. *rūach*. Ap. 9.

27 occupiers = barterers, or traders.

in. A special various reading called *Sevīr* (Ap. 34), with four early printed editions, Aram., Sept., and Syr., omit this word "in".

company = gathered host.

28 suburbs. The root *garash* = to drive out or about. When used of a city it = suburbs; but, when used of the sea, it = the driving and casting about of the waves. Cp. Isa. 57. 20. It means here that the waves of the sea lash themselves at the wailing of the pilots.

31 heart = soul. Heb. *nephesh*. Ap. 13.

32 they. Some codices, with two early printed editions, Sept., and Syr., read "their sons".

the destroyed: or, the silent one.

33 wares. See note on "fairs", *v.* 12.

34 In the time when thou shalt be broken: or, "Now thou art wrecked", with Aram., Sept., Syr., and Vulg. **36** be = become.

any more = for ever. Cp. 26. 21.

L² P Q **28** The word of °the LORD came again
p. 1045) unto me, saying,
478 2 °"Son of man, say unto °the prince of
°Tyrus, 'Thus saith °the Lord GOD;

R T m 'Because °thine heart *is* lifted up, and thou
hast said, 'I *am* a °GOD, I sit *in* the seat °of
God, in the °midst of the seas;' yet thou *art*
°a man, and °not GOD,

n though thou set thine heart as the heart of
°God:

U o 3 °Behold, thou *art* °wiser than °Daniel; there
is no secret that they can hide from thee:
4 With thy wisdom and with thine understanding thou hast gotten thee riches,

p and hast gotten gold and silver into thy treasures:

U o 5 By thy great wisdom

p *and* by thy traffick hast thou increased thy
riches,

T m and thine heart is lifted up because of thy riches:

n 6 Therefore' thus saith ²the Lord GOD; 'Because thou hast set thine heart as the heart
²of God;

S q 7 ³Behold, therefore I will bring °strangers
upon thee, the terrible of the nations: and
they shall draw their swords against the
beauty of thy wisdom, and they shall °defile
thy °brightness.
8 They shall bring thee down to the °pit,

r and thou shalt die the deaths of *them that*
are °slain in the ²midst of the seas.

s 9 Wilt thou yet say before Him That slayeth
thee, 'I *am* °God?'

s but °thou *shalt be* ²a man, and no °GOD, in the
hand of Him That ⁸slayeth thee.

r 10 Thou shalt °die the °deaths of the °uncir-
cumcised

q by the hand of ⁷strangers: for I have spoken
it, °saith ²the Lord GOD.'"

P Q 11 Moreover the word of ¹the LORD came unto me, saying,
12 ²"Son of man, take up a lamentation upon
°the king of ²Tyrus, and say unto him, 'Thus
saith ²the Lord GOD;

R t °'Thou sealest up the sum, full of wisdom, and
perfect in beauty.

28. 1-19 (L², p. 1142). "THE PRINCE" AND "THE KING" OF TYRE. (*Extended Alternation.*)

L² | P | Q | 1, 2-. "The PRINCE of Tyre." Commission to speak.
R | -2-6. Description. Type. A mere man (*vv.* 1, 9).
S | 7-10. Destruction of "the Prince".
P | *Q* | 11, 12-. "The KING of Tyre." Commission to speak.
R | -12-17-. Description. Antitype. Satan.
S | -17-19. Destruction of "the King".

1 the LORD. Heb. Jehovah. Ap. 4. II.

2 Son of man. See note on 2. 1.

the prince of Tyrus. The prince (Heb. *nāgīd*) is to be distinguished as the type (*vv.* 1-10) from the king (*melek*) of Tyre, the antitype (*vv.* 11-19). See the Structure above. He is a mere man, as shown in *v.* 9, where note the emphasis marked by the Fig. *Pleonasm* (Ap. 6). He was Ithobalus II. Heb. *'Ethbaal.* See Josephus (*cont. Apion.* § 21).

Tyrus = Tyre (the city), as in 26. 2.

the Lord GOD. Heb. Adonai Jehovah. See note on 2. 4.

28. -2-6 (R, above). DESCRIPTION OF THE PRINCE. (THE TYPE.) (*Introversion and Alternation.*)

R | T | m | -2-. Thine heart is lifted up.
n | -2. As the heart of God.
U | o | 3, 4-. Thy wisdom.
p | -4. Thy riches. Gotten.
U | *o* | 5-. Thy wisdom.
p | -5-. Thy riches. Increased.
T | *m* | -5. Thine heart is lifted up.
n | 6. As the heart of God.

-2 thine heart. Note the Fig. *Polyptōton* (Ap. 6), by which the word heart is repeated in different inflections for emphasis. "Thine heart . . . in the heart (midst) . . . thine heart . . . the heart."

GOD. Heb. *'El* (sing.). Ap. 4. IV.

of God. Heb. Elohim (pl.). Ap. 4. I.

midst = heart (as in ch. 27 throughout).

a man. Heb. *'ādām.* Ap. 14. I.

a man, and not GOD ('El). Note the Fig. *Pleonasm* (Ap. 6), by which the same thing is put in two ways (first pos. and then neg.) to emphasise the fact that the "prince" here spoken to (*vv.* 2-10) is purely human (*'ādām*), and therefore not "the king" spoken to in *vv.* 11-19. **not GOD** = not *'El.* Ap. 4. IV.

God. Heb. Elohim. Ap. 4. I.

3 Behold. Fig. *Asterismos* (Ap. 6), to attract our attention. **wiser.** In thine own eyes.

Daniel. Here an example of wisdom; as of righteousness in 14. 14, 20. Cp. Dan. 1. 17.

28. 7-10 (S, above). DESTRUCTION OF "THE PRINCE". (*Introversion.*)

S | q | 7, 8-. Judgment executed by strangers.
r | -8. Thou shalt die the deaths, &c.
s | 9-. I am Elohim.
s | -9. Thou art a man.
r | 10-. Thou shalt die the deaths, &c.
q | -10. Judgment executed by strangers.

7 strangers = aliens, or foreigners: the Babylonians were noted for their barbarity. Cp. 30. 11; 31. 12. Isa. 1. 7; 25. 2). **defile** = profane. **brightness** = splendour: occurs only here, and *v.* 17. See note on Gen. 3. 1 and Ap. 19. **8 pit** = corruption. Heb. *shaḥath.* **slain** = wounded. **9 God.** Heb. Elohim. Ap. 4. I. **thou shalt be** = thou [art]. **GOD.** Heb. 'El. Ap. 4. IV. **10 die . . . uncircumcised:** i.e. come to the miserable end of the ungodly. Cp. 31. 18; 32. 19, 21, 25, 32. The word being used in its moral, not physical sense **deaths.** Pl. = the great, or awful death. **saith the Lord GOD** = [is] Adonai Jehovah's oracle. **12- the king of Tyrus.** Here we have a supernatural being addressed: He of whom the "prince of Tyre" was only a type; He who was using that "prince" as one of his agents to secure the world-power. He is not a mere "man" as "the prince of Tyre" (see *v.* 9). His description (see the Structure, *vv.* -12-17-, below) is superterrestrial, and superhuman, and can refer to no other than Satan himself.

28. -12-17- (*R*, above). DESCRIPTION OF "THE KING". (THE ANTITYPE.) (*Introversion.*)

R | t | -12, 13. His "wisdom" and "beauty".
u | 14, 15-. The covering Cherub.
v | -15. His iniquity.
v | 16-. His sin.
u | -16. The covering Cherub.
t | 17-. His "wisdom" and "beauty".

-12 Thou sealest up the sum = Thou art the finished pattern. Heb. *toknith* = pattern. Occurs only here, and 43. 10.

478 13 Thou °hast been °in Eden °the garden of
[2]God; every °precious stone *was* thy covering, the sardius, topaz, and the diamond, the
beryl, the onyx, and the jasper, the sapphire,
the emerald, and the carbuncle, and gold: the
workmanship of thy °tabrets and of thy pipes
was prepared in thee °in the day that °thou
wast created.

u 14 Thou °*art* °the anointed cherub that cover-
(p. 1145) eth; °and I have set thee *so:* thou wast upon
°the holy mountain of [2]God; thou °hast walked up and down in the midst of the stones of
fire.

15 Thou *wast* °perfect in thy ways from the
day that thou wast °created,

v till °iniquity was found in thee.

v 16 By the multitude of thy °merchandise they
have filled the midst of thee with violence, and
thou °hast °sinned:

u therefore °I will cast thee as profane out of
°the mountain of [2]God: and I will destroy thee,
O °covering cherub, °from the midst of the
stones of fire.

t 17 Thine heart was lifted up because of thy
beauty, thou °hast corrupted thy wisdom by
reason of thy [7]brightness:

S V w °I will cast thee to the °ground, I will lay thee
(p. 1146) before kings,

x that they may behold thee.

W 18 Thou °hast defiled thy °sanctuaries by the
°multitude of thine °iniquities, by the [15]ini-
quity of thy traffick;

W therefore will I bring forth a fire from the
midst of thee, °it shall devour thee,

V w and I will bring thee to ashes upon the earth

x in the sight of all them that behold thee.

19 All they that know thee among the °people
shall be astonished at thee: thou shalt °be a
terror, and never *shalt* thou *be* °any more.' "

K[2] y 20 Again the word of [1]the LORD came unto
me, saying,

21 °"Son of man, set thy face against °Zidon,
and prophesy against it,

z 22 And say, 'Thus saith [2]the Lord GOD;
[3]'Behold, I *am* against thee, O [21]Zidon; and
°I will be glorified in the midst of thee: and
°they shall know that I *am* [1]the LORD, when
I shall have executed judgments in her, and
shall be sanctified in her.

23 For I will send into her pestilence, and
blood into her streets; and the wounded shall

13 hast been = wast.

in Eden. Here is no evidence of a "legend", but a reality. Satan, the *Nachash* or shining one, was there. See notes on Gen. 3. 1, and Ap. 19. Eve was smitten with his beauty as "an angel of light" (2 Cor. 11. 14); and deferred to him as one possessing this "wisdom", and believed his power to make good his promise. Ref. to Pent. No mention of Eden since Gen. 4. 16. Isa. 51. 3, till here; and none after till 31. 9, 16, 18; 36. 35. Isa. 51. 3. Joel 2. 3. Ap. 92.

the garden of God. This is added to leave us in no doubt as to what is meant by Eden, and to show that it was no mere "summer residence" of the "prince" of Tyre, but the "garden" of Gen. 2. 8–15.

precious stone. Referring to Gen. 2. 11, 12.

tabrets = drums. See note on "timbrel" (Ex. 15. 20), and cp. note on 1 Sam. 10. 5.

in the day. See Ap. 18.

thou wast created. Not begotten by man, or born of woman. This can refer only to Satan.

14 art = wast, as in the other verses here.

the anointed cherub that covereth. Cherub can be used only of a supernatural being, overshadowing and protecting "the world that then was" (2 Pet. 3. 6), or the "garden" of *v.* 13.

and I have set thee so, &c.: or, when I appointed thee . . . thou wast.

the holy mountain, &c. See note on *v.* 16, below; and cp. Isa. 14. 12–14.

hast walked up and down = didst walk to and fro, &c.; referring to facts concerning which nothing further is revealed.

15 perfect . . . created. Referring to the period before Satan's fall. See Ap. 19.

iniquity = perversity. Heb. *'āvāl.* Ap. 44. vi.

16 merchandise = traffic, or going about, as in *v.* 18. Hence it meant calumniator (slanderer), in a moral sense. **hast sinned** = didst sin.

sinned. Heb. *chāṭā'.* Ap. 44. i.

I will cast, &c. = I cast thee as profane. Lit. I profaned thee.

the mountain of God. This Hebrew expression (*har ha'ĕlohim*) occurs seven times (28. 16. Ex. 3. 1; 4. 27; 18. 5; 24. 13. 1 Kings 19. 8. Ps. 68. 15). The *Massōrah* gives these to distinguish it from *har Jehovah*, which also occurs seven times (Gen. 22. 14. Num. 10. 33. Ps. 24. 3. Isa. 2. 3; 30. 29. Mic. 4. 2. Zech. 8. 3).

covering cherub. See note on *v.* 14.

from. Contrast this "from" with "in" in *v.* 14; and see the Structure on p. 1145.

17 hast corrupted = didst corrupt. When this took place we are not told. It was before Gen. 3. 1: and the only time seems to have been between *vv.* 1 and 2 of Gen. 1, and may have been the cause of the overthrow: i.e. the *katabolē kosmou.* See note on Matt. 13. 35.

28. -17-19 (*S*, p. 1145). DESTRUCTION OF "THE KING". (*Introversion and Alternation.*)

S | V | w | -17-. Cast to the earth.
| | x | -17. They that behold thee.
| W | 18-. His fall: the cause of it.
| *W* | -18-. His fall: the consequence of it.
| *V* | *w* | -18-. Brought to ashes on the earth.
| | *x* | -18, 19. They that behold thee.

-17 I will cast thee = I did cast thee. **ground** = earth. Heb. *'eretz* (with Art.). **18 hast defiled** = didst defile. **sanctuaries.** Some codices, with six early printed editions, Aram., Syr., and Vulg., read "sanctuary" (sing.). **multitude** = abounding. **iniquities.** Some codices, with three early printed editions, with Aram. and Syr., read "iniquity" (sing.). Heb. *'āvāh.* Ap. 44. iv. **it shall devour thee.** See Rev. 20. 10. **19 people** = peoples. **be** = become. **any more** = for ever.

28. 20-26 (K[2], p. 1142). ZIDON. (*Introversion.*)

K[2] | y | 20, 21. Prophecy of evil for Zidon.
| z | 22, 23. Jehovah known by His judgment on Zidon.
| *z* | 24. Jehovah known by His removal of Zidon.
| *y* | 25, 26. Prophecy of good for Israel.

21 Son of man. See note on 2. 1. **Zidon.** Was not threatened with extinction, as Tyre was. See note on 26. 2. **22 I will be glorified, &c.** Ref. to Pent. (Ex. 14. 4, 17). Ap. 92. **they shall know, &c.** See note on 6. 10.

478 be judged in the midst of her by the sword
upon her on every side; and [22]they shall
know that I *am* [1]the LORD.

z (p. 1146) 24 And there shall be no more °a pricking
brier unto °the house of Israel, nor *any* grieving thorn of all *that are* round about them,
that despised them; and [22]they shall know that
I *am* [2]the Lord GOD.''

y 25 Thus saith [2]the Lord GOD; 'When I shall
have °gathered [24]the house of Israel from the
[19]people among whom they are scattered, and
shall be °sanctified in them in the sight of the
°heathen, °then shall they dwell °in their land
that I have °given to My servant Jacob.
26 And °they shall dwell °safely therein,
and shall °build houses, and plant vineyards;
yea, they shall dwell with confidence, °when
I have executed judgments upon all those that
despise them round about them; and [22]they
shall know that I *am* [1]the LORD their [2]God.' "

F[4] X A a (p. 1147) 479 **29** °In the tenth year, in the tenth *month*,
in the twelfth *day* of the month, the
word of °the LORD came unto me, saying,
2 °"Son of man, set thy face against °Pha-
raoh king of Egypt, and prophesy against
him, and against all Egypt:
3 Speak, and say, 'Thus saith °the Lord
GOD; °'Behold, I *am* against thee, Pharaoh
king of Egypt, °the great dragon that lieth in
the midst of his rivers, which hath said, °'My
river *is* mine own, and °I have made *it* for
myself.'

b 4 But I will put hooks in thy jaws, and I will
cause the °fish of thy rivers to stick unto thy
scales, and I will bring thee up out of the
midst of thy rivers, and all the fish of thy
rivers shall stick unto thy scales.
5 And I will leave thee *thrown* into the wilderness, thee and all the fish of thy rivers: thou
shalt fall upon the open fields; thou shalt not
be brought together, nor gathered: I have
given thee for meat to the beasts of the field
and to the fowls of the heaven.

c 6 And all the inhabitants of Egypt °shall
know that I *am* [1]the LORD, because they have
been °a staff of reed to °the house of Israel.
7 (When they took hold of thee by thy hand,
thou didst break, and rend all their shoulder:
and when they leaned upon thee, thou brakest,
and madest all their loins °to be at a stand).''

a 8 Therefore thus saith [3]the Lord GOD; [3]'Behold, °I will bring a sword upon thee, and cut
off °man and beast out of thee.
9 And the land of Egypt shall be desolate
and waste; and they [6]shall know that I *am*
[1]the LORD: because he hath said, 'The river
is mine, and I have made *it*.'

b 10 [3]Behold, therefore I *am* against thee, and
against thy rivers, and I will make the land
of Egypt utterly waste *and* desolate, °from
°the tower °of Syene even unto the border
of Ethiopia.

24 a pricking brier. Ref. to Pent. (Num. 33. 55). **the house of Israel.** See note on Ex. 16. 31.

25 gathered. Ref. to Pent. (Deut. 30. 3, 4). See also 11. 17; 20. 41; 34. 13; 36. 24; 37. 21; 39. 27. Lev. 26. 44, 45. Ps. 106. 47. Isa. 11. 11, 12, 13; 27. 12, 13. Jer. 30. 18; 31. 8–10; 32. 37. Hos. 1. 11. Joel 3. 7. Amos 9. 14, 15. Obad. 17–21. Zeph. 3. 19, 20. Ap. 92.
sanctified. Cp. *v.* 22; 36. 23; 38. 23. Isa. 5. 16.
heathen = nations.
then shall, &c. Cp. 36. 28; 37. 25. Jer. 23. 8; 27. 11.
in their land = on their soil.
given, &c. See Gen. 28. 13; and cp. note on Gen. 50. 24.

26 they shall dwell. Ref. to Pent. (Lev. 25. 18, 19. Deut. 12. 10; 33. 28). Ap. 92. See also 34. 25–28; 38. 8. Jer. 23. 6–8; 33. 16. Hos. 2. 18. Zech. 2. 4, 5.
safely = with confidence. Cp. 38. 11. Ref. to Pent. (Deut. 33. 28). Ap. 92.
build, &c. Cp. Isa. 65. 21, 22. Jer. 29. 5, 6, 28; 31. 4, 5; 32. 15. Amos 9. 13, 14.
when I, &c. Cp. *v.* 24; chs. 25—32; 35. Isa. 13—21. Jer. 46—51. Zech. 1. 17.

29. 1—32. 32 (F[4], p. 1140). EGYPT. (*Alternation.*)

F[4] | X | 29. 1—30. 26. Destruction.
  Y | 31. 1–18. Perdition.
 X | 32. 1–16. Destruction.
  Y | 32. 17–32. Perdition.

29. 1—30. 26 (X, above). DESTRUCTION.
(*Alternation.*)

X | A | 29. 1–16. Egypt. Pharaoh.
  B | 29. 17–21. Nebuchadnezzar. Wages promised.
 A | 30. 1–19. Egypt. Allies.
  B | 30. 20–26. Nebuchadnezzar. Wages paid.

29. 1-16 (A, above). EGYPT. PHARAOH.
(*Extended Alternation.*)

A | a | 1–3. Incrimination. The River.
  b | 4, 5. Threatening.
   c | 6, 7. Purpose.
 a | 8, 9. Incrimination. The River.
  b | 10–12. Threatening.
   c | 13–16. Purpose.

1 In the tenth year, &c.: i.e. a year and two days after the siege of Jerusalem began (Jer. 39. 1), and six months, less three days, before its fall. See notes on p. 1105. **the LORD.** Heb. Jehovah. Ap. 4. II.

2 Son of man. See note on 2. 1.
Pharaoh. Namely, Pharaoh Hophra, called Apries by the Greeks. Cp. Jer. 44. 30. He besieged and captured Gaza (Jer. 47. 1); attacked Zidon and encountered the prince of Tyre on the sea (Herodotus, ii. 161: cp. 2 Kings 24. 7. Jer. 46. 2); and said, "no god could deprive him of his kingdom" (Herodotus, ii. 169). Zedekiah relied on him. See Jer. 37. 5–8. Egypt was thus the cause of Jerusalem's destruction. See Jer. 44. 30; and cp. Jer. 46. 25, 26.

3 the Lord GOD. Heb. Adonai Jehovah. See note on 2. 4. **Behold.** Fig. *Asterismos.* Ap. 6.
the great dragon = the great crocodile, to which Egypt was likened on Roman coins. Cp. Isa. 51. 9, where "Rahab" is used of Egypt (Isa. 30. 7).
My river = the Nile.
I have made it. Referring probably to the artificial system of canals and water-ways.

4 fish. Symbols of Pharaoh's subjects.

6 shall know. See note on 6. 7.
a staff of reed. This was by inciting Israel to resist and rebel against Assyria by promises of help which failed. See 2 Kings 18. 21. Isa. 20. 5, 6; 30. 6, 7; 31. 3. Jer. 2. 36; 37. 7.
the house of Israel. See note on Ex. 16. 31.

7 to be at a stand = to come to a stand, or to halt. Ginsburg thinks, "to shake" (Ps. 69. 23). **8 I will bring a sword.** This phrase is peculiar to Ezekiel. See 5. 17; 6. 3; 11. 8; 14. 17; 29. 8; 33. 2. In Leviticus it is: "I will draw out the sword after you". Cp. Lev. 26. 33. **man.** Heb. *'ādām.* Ap. 14. I.
10 from the tower of Syene = from Migdol to Syene. Cp. 30. 6. **the tower** = Migdol. See note on Ex. 14. 2 for "Migdol", and cp. Jer. 44. 1. In the north of Egypt. **of Syene** = to Syene. Heb. *S[e]vēnēh.* Now *Assouan,* in the south.

479 11 No foot of [8]man shall pass through it, nor
foot of beast shall pass through it, neither
shall it be inhabited forty years.
12 And I will make the land of Egypt desolate in the midst of the countries *that are*
desolate, and her cities among the cities *that*
are laid waste shall be desolate forty years:
and I will scatter the Egyptians among the
nations, and will disperse them through the
countries.'
c 13 Yet thus saith [3]the Lord GOD; 'At the
(p. 1147) end of forty years °will I gather the E-
gyptians from the °people whither they were
scattered:
14 And I will °bring again °the captivity
of Egypt, and will cause them to return *into*
the land of °Pathros, into the land of their
°habitation; and they shall be there a °base
kingdom.
15 It shall be the °basest of the kingdoms;
neither shall it exalt itself any more above the
nations: for I will diminish them, that they
shall no more rule over the nations.
16 And it shall be no more the confidence of
[6]the house of Israel, which bringeth *their* °ini-
quity to remembrance, when they shall look
after them: but they [6]shall know that ℑ *am*
[3]the Lord GOD.'"
B 17 And it came to pass in °the seven and
463 twentieth year, in the first *month,* in the first
day of the month, the word of [1]the LORD came
unto me, saying,
18 [2]"Son of man, °Nebuchadrezzar king of
Babylon °caused his army to serve a great service against Tyrus: every °head *was* made
bald, and every °shoulder *was* peeled: yet had
he no wages, nor his army, for Tyrus, for the
service that he had served against it:
19 Therefore thus saith [3]the Lord GOD; [3]'Behold, °I will give the land of Egypt unto [18]Ne-
buchadrezzar king of Babylon; and he shall
take her multitude, and take her spoil, and
take her prey; and °it shall be the wages for
his army.
20 I have given him the land of Egypt *for*
his labour wherewith he served against it, because they wrought for Me, °saith [3]the Lord
GOD.
21 In that day will I cause the horn of the
house of Israel to bud forth, and I will give
thee the opening of the mouth °in the midst of
them; and they [6]shall know that ℑ *am* [1]the
LORD."

A d **30** The word of °the LORD came again
(p. 1148) unto me, saying,
2 °"Son of man, prophesy and say, 'Thus
saith °the Lord GOD; 'Howl ye, Woe °worth
the day!
3 For the day *is* near, even °the day of [1]the
LORD *is* near, a cloudy day; it shall be °the
time of the °heathen.
4 And the sword shall come upon Egypt, and
great pain shall be in °Ethiopia, when the
slain shall fall in Egypt, and they shall take
away her multitude, and her foundations shall
be broken down.
e 5 [4]Ethiopia, and °Libya, and °Lydia, and all
the °mingled people, and °Chub, and the °men
of the land that is in league, shall fall with
them by the sword.''
6 Thus saith [1]the LORD; 'They also that
uphold Egypt shall fall; and the pride of her
power shall come down: from °the tower of
Syene shall they fall in it by the sword, °saith
[2]the Lord GOD.
7 And they shall be desolate in the midst of
the countries *that are* desolate, and her cities
shall be in the midst of the cities *that are*
wasted.
8 And they shall know that ℑ *am* [1]the LORD,
when I have set a fire in Egypt, and *when* all
her helpers shall be destroyed.
9 In that day shall messengers go forth °from

13 will I gather. Therefore they could not be the people known as gipsies. **people** = peoples.
14 bring again, &c. = turn the fortunes, &c. See note on Deut. 30. 3.
the captivity of Egypt: or, the Egyptian captives. Note the discrimination shown in these prophecies. Some were never to be restored; others were to be resuscitated.
Pathros = Upper, or Southern Egypt.
habitation = nativity. **base** = low.
15 basest = lowest.
16 iniquity. Heb. *'āvāh.* Ap. 44. iv.
they shall know, &c. See note on 6. 10.
17 the seven and twentieth year. See the table, p. 1105.
18 Nebuchadrezzar . . . caused his army, &c. That this was fulfilled is shown by Prof. Sayce, *The Egypt of the Hebrews* (1896), p. 130, who quotes an inscription which describes this campaign, which took place (it says) in the thirty-seventh year of his reign. He defeated Pharaoh Amasis. For this spelling ("Nebuchadrezzar") see note on 26. 7.
head was made bald. Probably from the helmet worn in so long a war.
shoulder was peeled. From bearing arms so long.
19 I will give. See note on *v.* 18, above.
it shall be the wages. See the Structure on p. 1147.
20 saith the Lord GOD = [is] Adonai Jehovah's oracle.
21 in the midst. Cp. 3. 26, 27; 24. 27.

30. 1-19 (*A*, p. 1147). EGYPT AND HER ALLIES.
(*Alternation.*)

A | d | 1-4. The Sword.
  e | 5-9. The Allies.
 d | 10-12. The Sword.
  e | 13-19. The Allies.

1 the LORD. Heb. Jehovah. Ap. 4. II.
2 Son of man. See note on 2. 1.
the Lord GOD. Heb. Adonai Jehovah. See note on 2. 4.
worth. This is the past tense (*weorth*) of Anglo-Saxon *weorthan*, to become. It means Woe be to the day! Heb. = Alas for the day!
3 the day of the LORD. See notes on Isa. 2. 12; 13. 6; and Rev. 1. 10.
the time of, &c.: i. e. the season in which their power shall be judged and broken. **heathen** = nations.
4 Ethiopia. Heb. Cush, allied with Egypt. Cp. *v.* 9; and Jer. 46. 9. Also resorted to for help by Israel.
5 Libya . . . Lydia. Heb. *Phut . . . Lud.* Cp. 27. 10. Gen. 10. 6. These were an African people. Cp. Jer. 46. 9. Nah. 3. 9.
mingled people = mixed multitude: i. e. the allies of Babylon. Cp. Jer. 25. 20.
Chub. Perhaps *Caba*, in Mauretania, or *Cobē*, in Ethiopia. **men** = sons.
6 the tower, &c. See note on 29. 10.
saith the Lord GOD = [is] Adonai Jehovah's oracle.
9 from Me = from before Me.

483 Me ° in ships to make the careless Ethiopians
afraid, and great pain shall come upon them,
° as in the day of Egypt: for, ° lo, it cometh.'

d (p. 1147) **10** Thus saith [2] the Lord GOD; 'I will also
make the multitude of Egypt to cease by the
hand of ° Nebuchadrezzar king of Babylon.
11 He and his people with him, the terrible of
the nations, shall be brought to destroy the
land: and they shall draw their swords against
Egypt, and fill the land with the slain.
12 And I will make the rivers dry, and sell
the land into the hand of the ° wicked: and I
will make the land waste, and all that is
therein, by the hand of strangers: I [1] the
LORD have spoken *it*.'

e **13** Thus saith [2] the Lord GOD; 'I will also
destroy the ° idols, and I will cause *their* ° images
to cease out of ° Noph; and there shall
be no more a prince of the land of Egypt: and
I will put a fear in the land of Egypt.
14 And I will make ° Pathros desolate, and
will set fire in ° Zoan, and will execute judgments
in ° No.
15 And I will pour My fury upon ° Sin, the
strength of Egypt; and I will cut off ° the
multitude of [14] No.
16 And I will set fire in Egypt: Sin shall
have great pain, and No shall be rent asunder,
and [13] Noph *shall have* distresses daily.
17 The young men of ° Aven and of ° Pi-beseth
shall fall by the sword: and these *cities*
shall go into captivity.
18 At ° Tehaphnehes also the day shall be
darkened, when I shall break there ° the yokes
of Egypt: and the pomp of her strength shall
cease in her: as for her, a cloud shall cover her,
and her daughters shall go into captivity.
19 Thus will I execute judgments in Egypt:
and they shall know that I *am* [1] the LORD.'"

B f (p. 1149) 478 **20** And it came to pass in ° the eleventh year,
in the first *month*, in the seventh *day* of the
month, *that* the word of [1] the LORD came unto
me, saying,
21 [2] "Son of man, I have broken the arm of
Pharaoh king of Egypt; and, [9] lo, it shall not
be bound up to be healed, to put ° a roller to
bind it, to make it strong to hold the sword.
22 Therefore thus saith [2] the Lord GOD;
° 'Behold, I *am* against Pharaoh king of Egypt,
and will break his arms, the strong, and that
which was broken; and I will cause the sword
to fall out of his hand.

g **23** And I will scatter the Egyptians among
the nations, and will disperse them through
the countries.

f **24** And I will strengthen the arms of the king
of Babylon, and put My sword in his hand:
but I will break Pharaoh's arms, and he shall
groan before him with the groanings of a
deadly wounded *man*.
25 But I will strengthen the arms of the king
of Babylon, and the arms of Pharaoh shall fall
down; and ° they shall know that I *am* [1] the
LORD, when I shall put My sword into the
hand of the king of Babylon, and he shall
stretch it out upon the land of Egypt.

g **26** And I will scatter the Egyptians among
the nations, and disperse them among the countries;
and [25] they shall know that I *am* [1] the
LORD.'"

9 in ships. Going up the Nile. The Sept. reads "hastening" or "running"; but note that Ethiopia sent messengers in ships to promise help to Judah, but Jehovah sent His messengers in ships to prophesy her judgment.

as in the day. Many codices (including the Hillel Codex, A.D. 600, quoted in the *Massōrah*), with three early printed editions, Sept., Syr., and Vulg., read "in the day". Other codices, with seven early printed editions and Aram., read "as (or like, or about the time of) the day".

lo. Fig. *Asterismos.* Ap. 6.

10 Nebuchadrezzar. See notes on 26. 7, and 29. 18.

12 wicked. Heb. *rā'a'*. Ap. 44. viii.

13 idols = manufactured gods.

images = things of nought.

Noph = Memphis. Now *Abu Sîr*.

14 Pathros. Upper, or Southern Egypt.

Zoan = Tanis: now *San*; an ancient Egyptian city in Lower Egypt (Num. 13. 22. Ps. 78. 12). See note on Isa. 30. 4.

No. No Ammon. Now Thebes (Nah. 3. 8). Cp. Jer. 46. 25.

15 Sin = Pelusium, in the Egyptian delta. See 29. 10.

the multitude of No. Heb Hamon-No. Cp. *v.* 14.

17 Aven = On, or Heliopolis (Beth-shemesh, city or house of the Sun), north of Memphis.

Pi-beseth. In some codices written as one word; in others as two words: *Pi* being "the" in Coptic, and *Pasht* = the Egyptian goddess *Artemis.* Now *Tel Basta*, in the Delta, north of Memphis.

18 Tehaphnehes. See note on Jer. 43. 7. Greek name *Daphne.* Now *Tel Defenneh.* See Ap. 87.

the yokes of Egypt. The yokes imposed by Egypt on other peoples. Gen. of Origin. See Ap. 17. 2; and cp. 34. 27.

30. 20-26 (*B*, p. 1147). NEBUCHADNEZZAR. WAGES PAID. (*Alternation.*)

B | f | 20–22. Arms of Pharaoh broken.
  | g | 23. Dispersion.
  | *f* | 24, 25. Arms of Nebuchadnezzar strengthened.
  | *g* | 26. Dispersion.

20 the eleventh year. About four months before the fall of Jerusalem. See table on p. 1105.

21 a roller = a bandage.

22 Behold. Fig. *Asterismos.* Ap. 6.

25 they shall know, &c. See note on 6. 10.

31. 1-18 (Y, p. 1147). PERDITION. (*Introversion and Extended Alternation.*)

Y | C | 1. Introduction.
  | D | 2. Question. Likeness, &c.
  | E | h | 3–5. Exaltation. } Former state.
  | | i | 6. Shelter.
  | | k | 7–9. Envy.
  | *E* | *h* | 10–12. Excision. } Latter state.
  | | *i* | 13, 14. Shelter.
  | | *k* | 15–17. Mourning.
  | *D* | 18–. Question. Likeness.
  | *C* | –18. Conclusion.

1 the eleventh year. See note on 30. 20, and p. 1105.

the third month. About two months before the fall of Jerusalem.

the LORD. Heb. Jehovah. Ap. 4. II.

2 Son of man. See note on 2. 1.

31 And it came to pass in ° the eleventh Y C 478
year, in ° the third *month*, in the first
day of the month, *that* the word of ° the LORD
came unto me, saying,

2 ° "Son of man, speak unto Pharaoh king of D
Egypt, and to his multitude; Whom art thou
like in thy greatness?

E h (p. 1149) 478 3 °Behold, °the Assyrian *was* a cedar in Lebanon with fair branches, and with a shadowing °shroud, and of an high stature; and his top was among the thick boughs.
4 The °waters made him great, the °deep set him up on high with her rivers running round about his plants, and sent out her little rivers unto all the trees of the field.
5 Therefore his height was exalted above all the trees of the field, and his boughs were multiplied, and his °branches became long because of the multitude of waters, when he shot forth.

i 6 All the fowls of heaven made their nests in his °boughs, and under his branches did all the beasts of the field bring forth their young, and under his shadow dwelt all great nations.

k 7 Thus was he fair in his greatness, in the length of his branches: for his root was by great waters.
8 The cedars in °the garden of °God could not hide him: the fir trees were not like his [6]boughs, and the chesnut trees were not like his branches; nor any tree in °the garden of °God was like unto him in his beauty.
9 I have made him fair by the multitude of his branches: so that all the trees of °Eden, that *were* in [8]the garden of [8]God, envied him.

E h 10 Therefore °thus saith °the Lord GOD; 'Because °thou hast lifted up thyself in height, and °he hath shot up his top among the thick boughs, and his heart is lifted up in his height;
11 I have therefore delivered him into the hand of the mighty one of the °heathen; he shall surely deal with him: I have driven him out °for his °wickedness.
12 And °strangers, the terrible of the nations, have cut him off, and have left him: upon the mountains and in all the valleys his branches are fallen, and his boughs are broken by all the °rivers of the land; and all the people of the earth are gone down from his shadow, and have left him.

i 13 Upon his ruin shall all the fowls of the heaven remain, and all the beasts of the field shall be upon his branches:
14 To the end that none of all the trees by the waters exalt themselves for their height, neither shoot up their top among the thick boughs, neither their trees stand up in their height, °all that drink water: for they are all delivered unto death, to the nether parts of the earth, in the midst of the °children of °men, with them that go down to the pit.'

k 15 [10]Thus saith [10]the Lord GOD; 'In the day when he went down to °the grave I caused a mourning: I covered the deep for him, and I restrained the floods thereof, and the great waters were stayed: and I caused Lebanon to mourn for him, and all the trees of the field fainted for him.
16 I made the nations to shake at the sound of his fall, when °I cast him down to °hell with them that descend into °the pit: and all the trees of [9]Eden, the choice and best of Lebanon, all that drink water, shall be comforted in the nether parts of the earth.
17 They also went down into [16]hell with him unto *them that be* slain with the sword; °and

3 Behold. Fig. *Asterismos.* Ap. 6.
the Assyrian. Ginsburg thinks this should read *te'ashshur* (= a box-tree) instead of *'ashshūr* (= an Assyrian). There is no article; and Egypt is the subject here, not Assyria. See note on 27. 6, and cp. Isa. 41. 19; 60. 13. The subject is the proud exaltation of Egypt, which is likened to a box or cypress, exalting itself into a cedar of Lebanon. **shroud** = foliage.
4 waters . . . deep: i.e. the water-ways, and the Nile. Cp. *v.* 15.
5 branches. Heb. text reads "branch" (sing.); but margin, with some codices and four early printed editions, read "branches" (pl.). Occurs only in Ezekiel.
6 boughs = arms. Occurs only here and in *v.* 8.
8 the garden of God. Ref. to Pent. (Gen. 2. 8).
God. Heb. Elohim. Ap. 4. I.
9 Eden. Ref. to Pent. (Gen. 2). Cp. 28. 13. Ap. 92.
10 thus saith, &c. See note on 44. 9.
the Lord GOD. Heb. Adonai Jehovah. See note on 2. 4. **thou.** Pharaoh. **he.** Ashur.
11 heathen = nations.
for. Many codices, with five early printed editions, Syr., and Vulg., read "according to", as our text does. Other codices, with four early printed editions and Aram., read "in".
wickedness = lawlessness. Heb. *rāsha'.* Ap. 44. x.
12 strangers = foreigners.
rivers = torrents. Heb. *'aphīkīm.* See note on "channels", 2 Sam. 22. 16.
14 all. All the trees. So in *v.* 16. **children** = sons.
men. Heb. *'ādām.* Ap. 14. I.
15 the grave. Heb. Sheōl. Ap. 35.
16 I cast him down = I caused him to descend.
hell = Sheōl. Same word as "the grave" in *v.* 15.
the pit. Heb. *bōr.* Showing the sense in which Sheōl is used in *vv.* 15 and 16. See notes on "well", Gen. 21. 19; and "pit", Isa. 14. 19.
17 and they that were his arm. Sept. and Syr. read "and his seed".
18 saith the Lord GOD = [is] Adonai Jehovah's oracle.

32. 1-16 (*X*, p. 1147). **DESTRUCTION.**
(*Introversions and Alternation.*)

X | F | 1, 2-. Lamentation.
  G | H | l | -2. Beast. Waters troubled.
     | m | 3. Net.
    | J | 4-10. Destruction.
  G | *H* | *m* | 11, 12. Sword.
     | *l* | 13. Beasts. Waters troubled no more.
    | *J* | 14, 15. Desolation.
 F | 16. Lamentation.

1 the twelfth year. See the table on p. 1105.
twelfth month. About one year and a half after the fall of Jerusalem.
the LORD. Heb. Jehovah. Ap. 4. II.
2 Son of man. See note on 2. 1.

they that were his arm, *that* dwelt under his shadow in the midst of the [11]heathen.
18 To whom art thou thus like in glory and in greatness among the trees of [9]Eden? yet shalt thou be brought down with the trees of [9]Eden unto the nether parts of the earth: thou shalt lie in the midst of the uncircumcised with *them that be* slain by the sword. D

This *is* Pharaoh and all his multitude, °saith [10]the Lord GOD." C

32 And it came to pass in °the twelfth year, in the °twelfth month, in the first *day* of the month, *that* the word of °the LORD came unto me, saying, *X* F (p. 1150) 477
2 °"Son of man, take up a lamentation for Pharaoh king of Egypt, and say unto him,

GHl (p. 1150) 477 °'Thou art like a young lion of the nations,
°and thou *art* as a °whale in the °seas: and
thou camest forth with thy °rivers, and troubledst the waters with thy feet, and fouledst
their °rivers.'

m **3** Thus saith °the Lord GOD; 'I will therefore spread out My net over thee with a °company of °many °people; and they shall bring
thee up in My net.

J **4** Then will I leave thee upon the land, I will cast thee forth upon the open field, and will
cause all the fowls of the heaven to remain upon thee, and I will °fill the beasts of the
whole earth with thee.
5 And I will lay thy flesh upon the mountains, and fill the valleys with thy °height.
6 I will also water with thy blood the land
°wherein thou swimmest, *even* to the mountains; and the °rivers shall be full of thee.
7 And when I shall °put thee out, °I will cover the heaven, and make the stars thereof
dark; I will cover the sun with a cloud, and the moon shall not give her light.
8 All the °bright lights of heaven will I make dark over thee, and set darkness upon
thy land, °saith [3]the Lord GOD.
9 'I will also vex the hearts of many [3]people, when I shall bring thy destruction among the
nations, into the countries which thou hast not known.
10 Yea, I will make many [3]people amazed at thee, and their kings shall be horribly afraid
for thee, when I shall brandish My sword before them; and they shall tremble at *every*
moment, °every man for his own °life, in the day of thy fall.

GHm **11** For' thus saith [3]the Lord GOD; 'The sword of the king of Babylon shall come upon
thee.
12 By the swords of the mighty will I cause thy multitude to fall, the terrible of the nations, all of them: and they shall spoil the
pomp of Egypt, and all the multitude thereof shall be destroyed.

l **13** I will destroy also all the beasts thereof from beside the great waters; neither shall
the foot of °man trouble them any more, nor the hoofs of beasts trouble them.

J **14** Then will I make their waters °deep, and cause their rivers to run like oil, °saith [3]the
Lord GOD.
15 When I shall make the land of Egypt desolate, and the country shall be destitute of
that whereof it was full, when I shall smite all them that dwell therein, then shall they
know that I *am* [1]the LORD.

F **16** This *is* the lamentation wherewith they shall lament her: the daughters of the nations
shall lament her: they shall lament for her, *even* for Egypt, and for all her multitude,'
[8]saith [3]the Lord GOD."

YK (p. 1151) 477 **17** It came to pass also in [1]the twelfth year,
in the fifteenth *day* of °the month, *that* the word of [1]the LORD came unto me, saying,
18 [2]"Son of man, wail for the multitude of Egypt, and °cast them down, *even* her, and the
daughters of the famous nations, unto the
°nether parts of the earth, with them that go down into °the pit.
19 Whom dost thou pass in beauty? go down, and be thou laid with °the uncircumcised.
20 They shall fall in the midst of *them that are* °slain by the sword: she is delivered to
the sword: °draw her and all her multitudes.

21 °The strong among the mighty °shall speak to him out of the midst of °hell with Ln
them that help him: they are gone down, they lie uncircumcised, [20]slain by the sword.

22 °Asshur *is* there and all her company: o
his °graves *are* about him: all of them [20]slain, fallen by the sword:
23 Whose [22]graves are set in the sides of [18]the

Thou art like = Thou hast been likened to.
and thou art = yet art thou. The contrast is between what was noble and less noble.
whale = crocodile.
seas = a collection of waters, like the branches of the Nile. Cp. Isa. 27. 1.
rivers. Heb. *nahar*. Not the same word as in *v.* 6.
3 the Lord GOD. Heb. Adonai Jehovah. See note on 2. 4.
company = gathered host. Cp. 16. 40.
many: or, mighty. people = peoples.
4 fill = satisfy.
5 height = thy high heap: i.e. of thy slain.
6 wherein thou swimmest: or, of thy overflowing.
rivers = torrents, or ravines. Heb. *'aphīkīm*. See note on 2 Sam. 22. 16. Not the same word as in *v.* 2.
7 put thee out = extinguish thee.
I will cover, &c. Cp. Isa. 13. 10; 14. 12. Joel 2. 10; 3. 15. Amos 8. 9. Rev. 6. 12-14.
8 bright lights = light-bearers. Ref. to Pent. (Gen. 1. 14). Ap. 92. Heb. *mā'ōr*.
saith the Lord GOD = [is] Adonai Jehovah's oracle.
10 every man. Heb. *'ish*. Ap. 14. II.
life = soul. Heb. *nephesh*. Ap. 13.
13 man. Heb. *'ādām*. Ap. 14. I.
14 deep = subside.

32. 17-32 (*Y*, p. 1147). PERDITION.
(*Alternation and Introversion.*)

Y | K | 17-20. Fellowship in Sheōl.
  L | n | 21. Pharaoh.
    o | 22-27. Other Kings and nations.
  K | 28. Fellowship in Sheōl.
  L | *o* | 29, 30. Other Kings and nations.
    n | 31, 32. Pharaoh.

17 the month: i.e. the twelfth month. See *v.* 1.
18 cast them down = cause them to descend: i.e. by Heb. idiom = declare (by the dirge) that they shall descend. See note on 14. 8, 9; 20. 25.
nether = lower.
the pit. Heb. *bōr* = a grave dug in the earth. See note on 31. 16, showing the meaning of Sheōl in *v.* 21.
19 the uncircumcised. This word is repeated ten times in this chapter, and always in connection with an ignominious death (*vv.* 19, 21, 24-30, 32). Cp. Jer. 9. 25, 26.
20 slain by the sword. Note the Fig. *Cycloides* (Ap. 6), by which these words occur as a refrain twelve times in the following verses (twelve being the number of governmental perfection or completion. See Ap. 10).
draw her = drag her away: i.e. to the grave.
21 The strong = The strongest, or chiefest.
shall speak, &c. Note the Fig. *Prosopopœia* (Ap. 6), by which dead people are represented as speaking.
hell = the grave. Heb. Sheōl. Ap. 35.
22 Asshur: i.e. the great empire of Assyria.
graves. Heb. *keber* = burying-places, or sepulchres. See Ap. 35. Same word as in *vv.* 23, 25, 26.

477 pit, and her °company is round about her [22]grave: all of them [20]slain, fallen by the sword, which caused terror °in the land of the living.

24 There *is* Elam and all her multitude round about her [22]grave, all of them [20]slain, fallen by the sword, which are gone down [19]uncircumcised into the [18]nether parts of the earth, which caused their terror [23]in the land of the living; yet have they borne their shame with them that go down to [18]the pit.

25 They have set her a bed in the midst of the slain with all her °multitude: her [22]graves *are* round about him: all of them [19]uncircumcised, [20]slain by the sword: though their terror was caused [23]in the land of the living, yet have they borne their shame with them that go down to [18]the pit: he is put in the midst of *them that be* slain.

26 There *is* Meshech, Tubal, and all her multitude: her [22]graves *are* round about him: all of them [19]uncircumcised, [20]slain by the sword, though they caused their terror [23]in the land of the living.

27 And they shall not lie with the mighty *that are* fallen of the [19]uncircumcised, which are gone down to [21]hell °with their weapons of war: and they have laid their swords under their heads, but their °iniquities shall be upon their bones, though *they were* the terror of the mighty [23]in the land of the living.

K (p. 1151) 28 Yea, thou shalt be °broken in the midst of the [19]uncircumcised, and shalt lie with *them that are* [20]slain with the sword.

L o 29 There *is* Edom, her kings, and all her princes, which with their might are laid by *them that were* [20]slain by the sword: they shall lie with the [19]uncircumcised, and with them that go down to [18]the pit.

30 There *be* the princes of the north, all of them, and all the Zidonians, which are gone down with the slain; with their terror they are ashamed of their might; and they lie [19]uncircumcised with *them that be* [20]slain by the sword, and bear their shame with them that go down to [18]the pit.

n 31 Pharaoh shall see them, and shall be comforted over all his multitude, *even* Pharaoh and all his army [20]slain by the sword, [8]saith [3]the Lord GOD.

32 For I have °caused °My terror [23]in the land of the living: and he shall be laid in the midst of the [19]uncircumcised with *them that are* [20]slain with the sword, *even* Pharaoh and all his multitude, [8]saith [3]the Lord GOD."

H M¹ N (p. 1152) **33** Again the word of °the LORD came unto me, saying,

2 °"Son of man, speak to the °children of thy People, and say unto them, 'When I bring the sword upon a land, if the people of the land take °a °man of their °coasts, and set him for their watchman:

O p 3 If when he seeth °the sword come upon the land, he blow the trumpet, and warn the people;

4 Then whosoever heareth the sound of the trumpet, and taketh not warning; if the sword

23 company=gathered host.
in the land of the living. Used here as the opposite of the land of the dead. See note on 26. 20. The expression occurs six times in this chapter.
25 multitude. The 1611 edition of the A.V. reads "multitudes" (pl.).
27 with their weapons of war. This determines the nature of the place here described as "the grave", "the pit", and "Sheōl".
iniquities. Heb. *'āvāh.* Ap. 44. iv.
28 broken: or, overthrown.
32 caused. Heb. *nathan*=given: as distinct from their terror. See note on 20. 25.
My. Heb. text has "His"; marg. "My".

33. 1-22 (*H*, p. 1104). PEOPLE. SIGN. (WATCHMAN.) (*Division.*)

H | M¹ | 1-9. Signification.
| M² | 10-20. Application.
| M³ | 21, 22. Fulfilment.

33. 1-9 (M¹, above). SIGNIFICATION. (*Alternation and Introversion.*)

M¹ | N | 1, 2. Sign. The watchman.
| O | p | 3-5. Warning. Positive.
| | q | 6. Warning. Negative.
| *N* | 7. Sign. Signification. (Ezekiel.)
| *O* | *q* | 8. Warning. Negative.
| | *p* | 9. Warning. Positive.

1 the LORD. Heb. Jehovah. Ap. 4. II.
2 Son of man. See note on 2. 1.
children=sons. **a**=one.
man. Heb. *'ish.* Ap. 14. II.
coasts=borders: i.e. one man out from within the borders of their land.
3 the sword=judgment. Put by Fig. *Metonymy* (of the Effect), Ap. 6, for that which executes the judgment.
4 his own head=himself: "head" being put by Fig. *Synecdoche* (of the Part), Ap. 6, for the whole person.
5 soul. Heb. *nephesh.* Ap. 13.
6 person=soul. Heb. *nephesh.* Ap. 13.
iniquity. Heb. *'āvāh.* Ap. 44. iv. Not the same as in *vv.* 13, 15, 18.
8 wicked=lawless. Heb. *rāsha'.* Ap. 44. x.
iniquity. Heb. *'āvāh.* Ap. 44. iv.
9 in: or, for.

come, and take him away, his blood shall be upon °his own head.

5 He heard the sound of the trumpet, and took not warning; his blood shall be upon him. But he that taketh warning shall deliver his °soul.

6 But if the watchman see the sword come, and blow not the trumpet, and the people be not warned; if the sword come, and take *any* °person from among them, he is taken away in his °iniquity; but his blood will I require at the watchman's hand.' q

7 So thou, O [2]son of man, I have set thee a watchman unto the house of Israel; therefore thou shalt hear the word at My mouth, and warn them from Me. N

8 When I say unto the °wicked, 'O °wicked *man*, thou shalt surely die;' if thou dost not speak to warn the °wicked from his way, that °wicked *man* shall die in his °iniquity; but his blood will I require at thine hand. O q

9 Nevertheless, if thou warn the [8]wicked of his way to turn from it; if he do not turn from his way, he shall die °in his [8]iniquity; but thou hast delivered thy [5]soul. p

M[2] r[1] (p. 1158) 477 **10 Therefore, O thou [2]son of man, speak unto the house of Israel; 'Thus ye speak, saying, 'If our °transgressions and our °sins *be* upon us, and we °pine away in them, how should we then live?'**

11 Say unto them, °'*As* I live, °saith °the Lord GOD, I have no pleasure in the death of the [8]wicked; but that the [8]wicked turn from his way and live: turn ye, °turn ye from your °evil ways; for °why will ye die, O house of Israel?'

s[1] **12 Therefore, thou [2]son of man, say unto the [2]children of thy People, 'The righteousness of the righteous shall not deliver him in the day of his [10]transgression: as for the [8]wickedness of the [8]wicked, he shall not fall °thereby °in the day that he turneth from his [8]wickedness; neither shall the righteous be able to live °for his *righteousness* °in the day that he °sinneth.**

13 When I shall say to the righteous, *that* he shall surely live; if he °trust to his own righteousness, and commit [8]iniquity, all his °righteousnesses shall not be remembered; but °for his °iniquity that he hath committed, he shall die °for it.

14 Again, when I say unto the [8]wicked, 'Thou shalt surely die;' if he turn from his [10]sin, and do °that which is lawful and °right;

15 *If* the [8]wicked °restore the pledge, °give again that he had robbed, walk in the statutes of life, without committing [13]iniquity; °he shall surely live, °he shall not die.

16 None of his °sins that he hath committed shall be mentioned unto him: he hath done that which is lawful and right; he shall surely live.'

r[2] **17 Yet the [2]children of thy People say, 'The way of °the LORD* is not °equal:' but as for them, their way is not °equal.**

s[2] **18 When the righteous turneth from his righteousness, and committeth [13]iniquity, he shall even die °thereby.**

19 But if the [8]wicked turn from his [8]wickedness, and do [14]that which is lawful and [14]right, he shall live [18]thereby.

r[3] **20 Yet ye say, 'The way of °the Lord is not [17]equal.' O ye house of Israel, I will judge you every one after his ways."**

M[3] (p. 1152) **21 And it came to pass in °the twelfth year of our captivity, in the °tenth *month*, in the °fifth *day* of the month, *that* one that had escaped out of Jerusalem °came unto me, saying, "The city is smitten."**

22 Now the hand of [1]the LORD was upon me in °the evening, afore °he that was escaped came; and had opened my mouth, until he came to me in the morning; and °my mouth was opened, and I was °no more dumb.

J P (p. 1153) **23 Then the word of [1]the LORD came unto me, saying,**

24 [2]"Son of man, they that inhabit those °wastes of °the land of Israel speak, saying, 'Abraham was one, and he inherited the land: but we *are* many; the land is given us for inheritance.'

Q **25 Wherefore say unto them, 'Thus saith**

33. 10-20 (M[2], p. 1152). APPLICATION.
(*Repeated Alternation.*)

M[2] | r[1] | 10, 11. The way of Jehovah.
s[1] | 12-16. The righteous and the wicked.
r[2] | 17. The way of Jehovah.
s[2] | 18, 19. The righteous and the wicked.
r[3] | 20. The way of Jehovah.

10 transgressions. Heb. *pāsha'*. Ap. 44. ix.
sins. Heb. *chāṭā'*. Ap. 44. i.
pine away, &c. Ref. to Pent. See notes on 4. 17 and 24. 23.

11 As I live, &c. Fig. *Deisis*. Ap. 6.
saith the Lord GOD=[is] Adonai Jehovah's oracle. See note on 2. 4.
turn ye. Note the Fig. *Epizeuxis*. Ap. 6.
evil. Heb. *rā'a'*. Ap. 44. viii.
why will ye die . . . ? Fig. *Erotēsis*. Ap. 6.

12 thereby: or, therein.
in the day=when. See Ap. 18.
for his righteousness=thereby, or therein, in the day, &c. **sinneth.** Heb. *chāṭa'*. Ap. 44. i.

13 trust=confide. Heb. *baṭah*. Ap. 69. I.
righteousnesses=righteous deeds. In Hebrew text it is sing. ("righteousness"); but the margin, with four early printed editions, reads "righteousnesses" (pl.).
for: or, in. Cp. *v.* 9.
iniquity. Heb. *'āval* Ap. 44. vi. Not the same word as in *v.* 8, but same as in *vv.* 15, 18.
for it=thereby, or therein, as in *v.* 12.

14 that which is . . . right=judgment and righteousness.

15 restore the pledge, &c. Ref. to Pent. (Ex. 22. 26. Lev. 6. 2, 4, 5. Deut. 24. 6, 10-13, 17).
give again. Note the Fig. *Asyndeton* (Ap. 6), hurrying on to the climax at end of verse.
he shall surely live. Ref. to Pent. (Lev. 18. 5).
he shall not die. Note the Fig. *Pleonasm* (Ap. 6), for emphasis.

16 sins. Heb. text reads "sin"; but marg., some codices, and four early printed editions, read "sins" (pl.).

17 the LORD*. One of the emendations of the *Sōpherīm*, by which they say they changed Jehovah of the primitive text to Adonai. See Ap. 32.
equal. See note on "pondereth", Prov. 21. 2.

18 thereby: or, in them: i.e. in those deeds.

20 the Lord. Heb. Adonai. Ap. 4. VIII (2).

21 the twelfth year . . . tenth month . . . fifth day. This is the date of the taking of Jerusalem by Nebuchadnezzar. See 40. 1. The event in the twenty-fifth year is said to be the fourteenth year from the twelfth (i.e. from the *tenth* month of the twelfth year to the *first* month of the twenty-fifth). The prophecies of the preceding chapters were given to Ezekiel in the Land *before* this twelfth year. See the table on p. 1105, and Ap. 50, p. 60). This was the eleventh year of Zedekiah, in the fourth month and ninth day (Jer. 39. 1, 2. 2 Kings 25. 1-4).
came unto me. While still in the Land, probably in hiding.

22 the evening. Doubtless, of the same day of his escape. **he that was escaped.** As foretold in 24. 26.
my mouth was opened. Cp. 24. 27; 29. 21: i.e. in prophecy.
no more dumb: i.e. silent from prophesying. Note the Fig. *Pleonasm* (Ap. 6), to emphasise the fact.

33. 23-33 (*J*, p. 1104). INHABITANTS OF THE WASTES. (*Extended Alternation.*)

J | P | 23, 24. The saying of the People.
Q | 25-28. Threatening.
R | 29. Purpose. "Then shall they know."
P | 30-32. The saying of the People.
Q | 33-. Threatening.
R | -33. Purpose. "Then shall they know."

24 wastes=ruins.
the land of Israel=the soil of Israel. Heb. *'admath.* Not the same word as in *v.* 28, which is *'eretz.* See note on 11. 17.

477 [11]the Lord GOD; °'Ye eat with the blood, and
lift up your eyes toward your °idols, and shed
blood: and °shall ye possess the land?
26 °Ye stand upon your sword, °ye work
abomination, and ye defile every one his neighbour's wife: and [25]shall ye possess the land?''
27 Say thou thus unto them, 'Thus saith
[11]the Lord GOD; [11]'*As* I live, surely they that
are in the [24]wastes shall fall by the sword, and
him that *is* in the open field will I give to the
beasts to be devoured, and they that *be* in the
forts and in the caves shall die of the pestilence.
28 For I will lay °the land most desolate, and
the pomp of her strength shall cease; and the
mountains of Israel shall be desolate, that none
shall pass through.

R 29 Then °shall they know that I *am* [17]the
(p. 1153) LORD*, when I have laid [28]the land most desolate because of all their abominations which
they have committed.''

P 30 Also, thou [2]son of man, the [2]children of
thy People still are talking °against thee by the
walls and in the °doors of the houses, and
speak one to another, every one °to his
brother, saying, 'Come, I pray you, and hear
what is the word that cometh forth from [1]the
LORD.'
31 And they come unto thee °as the People
cometh, and they sit before thee *as* My People,
and they hear thy words, but they will not do
them: for with their mouth they °shew much
love, *but* their heart goeth after their covetousness.
32 And, °lo, thou *art* unto them as °a very
lovely song of one that hath a pleasant voice,
and can play well on an instrument: for they
hear thy words, but they do them not.

Q 33 And when this cometh to pass, ([32]lo, it will
come,)
R then [29]shall they know that a prophet hath
been among them.''

B S U **34** And the word of °the LORD came unto
(p. 1154) me, saying,
2 °"Son of man, prophesy against the °shep-
herds of Israel, prophesy, and say unto them,
'Thus saith °the Lord GOD unto the °shep-
herds; 'Woe *be* to the °shepherds of Israel
that do feed themselves! should not the °shep-
herds feed the flocks?
3 Ye eat the fat, and ye clothe you with the
wool, ye °kill °them that are fed: *but* ye feed
not the °flock.

V t 4 The diseased have ye not strengthened,
°neither have ye healed that which was sick,
°neither have ye bound up *that which was*
broken, °neither have ye brought again that
which was driven away, °neither have ye
sought that which was lost; but with force
and with °cruelty have ye ruled them.

u 5 And they were scattered, °because *there is*
no [2]shepherd: and they became meat to all the
beasts of the field, when they were scattered.
6 My sheep wandered through all the mountains, and upon every high hill: yea, My [3]flock
was scattered upon all the face of the earth,
and none did search or seek *after them.*

U 7 Therefore, ye [2]shepherds, hear the word of
[1]the LORD;

8 °*As* I live, °saith [2]the Lord GOD, surely
because My [3]flock became a prey, and My flock
became meat to every beast of the field, [5]be-
cause *there was* no [2]shepherd, neither did My
[2]shepherds search for My flock, but the [2]shep-
herds fed themselves, and fed not My flock;
9 °Therefore, O ye [2]shepherds, hear the word
of [1]the LORD;'
10 Thus saith [2]the Lord GOD; °'Behold, I
am against the [2]shepherds; and I will require
My [3]flock at their hand, and cause them to
cease from feeding the flock; neither shall the
[2]shepherds feed themselves any more; for I
will deliver My flock from their mouth, that
they may not be meat for them.

Ye eat with the blood = eat over (*'al*) the blood: i.e. over or near (as the heathen in their necromancy). Ref. to Pent. (not to Deut. 12. 16 (where it is *l'o* = not), but to Lev. 19. 26 (where it is *'al* = over), as here, and where it is connected with the idolatrous practices of the heathen.

idols = manufactured gods.

shall ye . . . ? Note the Fig. *Erotēsis* (Ap. 6).

26 Ye: i.e. Ye [men]. The verb is masculine.

Ye stand upon your sword = Ye take your stand (first occurrence Gen. 18. 8, 22), [leaning] upon, &c. The posture assumed by necromancers waiting for the rites.

ye work, &c.: i.e. ye [women] work, &c. The verb is feminine.

28 the land. Heb. *'eretz*. Not the same word as in *v.* 24.

29 shall they know, &c. See note on 6. 10.

30 against = about. **doors** = entrances.

to = with.

31 as the People cometh: or, according as an assembly cometh together.

shew much love: or, counterfeit lovers. Heb. *'ăgābīm*. See note on next verse.

32 lo. Fig. *Asterismos*. Ap. 6.

a very lovely song. Heb. *'ăgābīm* = a song for the pipes. Note the Fig. *Paronomasia* (Ap. 6), with "lovers", in *v.* 31.

34. 1-31 (***B***, p. 1104). SHEPHERDS AND FLOCK.
(*Alternation.*)

B | S | 1-16. False Shepherds.
  T | 17-22. The Flock. False.
S | 23-30. True Shepherds.
  T | 31. The Flock. True.

34. 1-16 (S, above). FALSE SHEPHERDS.
(*Alternation and Introversion.*)

S | U | 1-3. The False Shepherds.
  V | t | 4. Their neglect.
    u | 5, 6. Consequent scattering of Flock.
  U | 7-10. The False Shepherds.
  V | *u* | 11-16-. Subsequent gathering of Flock.
    t | -16. Their punishment.

1 the LORD. Heb. Jehovah. Ap. 4. II.

2 Son of man. See note on 2. 1.

shepherds = rulers.

the Lord GOD. Heb. Adonai Jehovah. See note on 2. 4.

3 kill = kill for sacrifice, and eating. Heb. *zabach*. Ap. 43. I. iv.

them that are fed = the fat ewe.

4 neither. Note the Fig. *Paradiastole* (Ap. 6), emphasising the five counts.

cruelty = rigour. Ref. to Pent. (Ex. 1. 13, 14. Lev. 25. 46, 53, its only other occurrences).

5 because there is no shepherd: or, without a shepherd.

8 As I live. Fig. *Deisis*. Ap. 6.

saith the Lord God = [is] Adonai Jehovah's oracle.

9 Therefore = Therefore [I repeat] O ye, &c.

10 Behold. Fig. *Asterismos*. Ap. 6.

V u 11 For' thus saith [2]the Lord GOD; [10]'Behold,
(p. 1154) °I, *even* I, will both search My sheep, and
477 seek them out.
12 As a shepherd seeketh out his flock °in the
day that he is among his sheep *that are* scattered; so will I seek out My sheep, and will
deliver them out of all places where they have
been scattered in the cloudy and dark day.
13 And I will bring them out from the °people,
and gather them from the countries, and will
bring them to their own °land, and feed them
upon the mountains of Israel by the °rivers,
and in all the inhabited places of the country.
14 I will feed them in a good pasture, and
upon the high mountains of Israel shall their
fold be: there shall they lie in a good fold, and
in a fat pasture shall they feed upon the mountains of Israel.
15 I will feed My [3]flock, and I will cause them
to lie down, [8]saith [2]the Lord GOD.
16 I will seek that which was lost, and
bring again that which was driven away, and
will bind up *that which was* broken, and will
strengthen that which was sick:
t but I will °destroy the fat and the strong;
I will feed them with judgment.
T v[1] 17 And *as for* you, O My [3]flock,' thus saith
(p. 1155) [2]the Lord GOD; [10]'Behold, I judge between
°cattle and cattle, between the rams and the
he goats.
w[1] 18 °*Seemeth it* a small thing unto °you to
have eaten up the good pasture, but ye must
tread down with your feet the residue of your
pastures? and to have drunk of the deep
waters, but ye must foul the residue with your
feet?
19 And *as for* My [3]flock, they eat that
which ye have trodden with °your feet; and
they drink that which ye have fouled with
°your feet.
v[2] 20 Therefore' thus saith [2]the Lord GOD unto
them; 'Behold, [11]I, *even* I, will judge between
the fat cattle and between the lean cattle.
w[2] 21 Because ye have thrust with side and with
shoulder, and pushed all the diseased with
your horns, till ye have scattered them abroad;
22 Therefore will I °save My [3]flock, and they
shall no more be a prey;
v[3] and I will judge between [17]cattle and cattle.
S W x 23 And I will set up °one shepherd over them,
and he shall feed them, *even* °My servant
°David; he shall feed them, and he shall be their
shepherd.
24 And I [1]the LORD will be their °God, and
[23]My servant David a °prince among them;
I [1]the LORD have spoken *it*.
y 25 And I will make with them °a covenant of
peace, and will cause the evil beasts to cease
out of the land: and they shall dwell safely
in the °wilderness, and sleep in the woods.
X a 26 And I will make them and the places round
about My hill a blessing; and I will cause the
shower to come down in his season; there shall
be showers of blessing.
27 And the tree of the field shall yield her
fruit, and the earth shall yield her increase,
and °they shall be °safe °in their [13]land,
and °shall know that I *am* [1]the LORD, °when b
I have broken the bands of their yoke, and
delivered them out of the hand of °those that
served themselves of them.
28 And they shall no more be a prey to the *W y*
°heathen, neither shall the °beast of the °land
devour them; but they shall dwell safely, and
none shall make *them* afraid.
29 And I will raise up for them a °plant °of *x*
renown,
and they shall be no more °consumed with *X a*
hunger in the land, neither bear the shame of
the [28]heathen any more.

---

11 I, even I. Note the Fig. *Epizeuxis* (Ap. 6), for emphasis.
12 in the day. See Ap. 18.
13 people=nations.
land=soil.
rivers=ravines. Heb. *'ăphīkīm.* See note on "channels", 2 Sam. 22. 16.
16 destroy: or, "watch", reading ר (=R) for ד (=D).

34. 17-22 (T, p. 1154). THE FLOCK
(*Repeated Alternation.*)

T | v[1] | 17. "I judge".
  w[1] | 18, 19. Destructiveness.
 v[2] | 20. "I will judge".
  w[2] | 21, 22-. Voracity.
 v[3] | -22. "I will judge".

17 cattle and cattle: i.e. between the sheep and the goats: rams being the sheep, while the he-goats are set in contrast
18 Seemeth it: or, supply "Is it".
you: i.e. ye goats. The verse goes on to describe the evil work of the goats in fouling the pastures of the sheep. There is a solemn application of this to the churches and congregations in the present day.
your: i.e. the goats.
22 save = bring salvation or deliverance to.

34. 23-30 (S, p. 1154). TRUE SHEPHERD.
(*Alternations and Introversion.*)

S | W | x | 23, 24. The true Shepherd.
   y | 25. Security.
  X | a | 26, 27-. Prosperity. (Positive.)
   b | -27. Purpose.
 W | *y* | 28. Security.
   x | 29-. The plant of renown.
  X | *a* | -29. Prosperity. (Negative.)
   b | 30. Purpose.

23 one shepherd=one ruler. Cp. Isa. 40. 11. John 10. 11.
My servant David. Occurs only here, *v.* 24; 37. 24. 1 Kings 11. 32, 34, and 14. 8. Cp. Jer. 30. 9. Hos. 3. 5.
David. Either David the king, or Messiah, of Whom he was the type.
24 God. Heb. Elohim. Ap. 4. I.
prince=a leader. Cp. Isa. 9. 6, 7; 55. 4.
25 a covenant of peace. Cp. 37. 26.
wilderness=a place of pasture. Cp. Ps. 65. 12. Not a barren place or desert, unless so stated or implied.
27 they . . . shall know. See note on 6. 10.
safe=confident. **in**=on.
when I have broken: or, by My breaking.
those, &c.: i.e. the false rulers.
28 heathen=nations.
beast. The 1611 edition of the A.V. reads "beasts".
land: or, earth.
29 plant. Referring to Messiah, as in *vv.* 23, 24.
of renown: for fame.
consumed=pinched [with hunger].

b (p. 1155) 477
30 Thus °shall they know that I [1]the LORD their [24]God *am* with them, and *that* they, *even* the house of Israel, *are* My People, [8]saith [2]the Lord GOD.

T (p. 1154)
31 And ye My °flock, the [3]flock of My pasture, °*are* °men, *and* I *am* °your [24]God, [8]saith [2]the Lord GOD.' "

A Y c[1] (p. 1156)
35 Moreover the word of °the LORD came unto me, saying,
2 °"Son of man, set thy face against °mount Seir, and prophesy against it,
3 And say unto it, 'Thus saith °the Lord GOD; °'Behold, O [2]mount Seir, I *am* against thee, and I will stretch out Mine hand against thee, and I will make thee most desolate.
4 I will lay thy cities waste, and thou shalt be desolate, and °thou shalt know that I *am* [1]the LORD.

d[1]
5 Because thou hast had °a perpetual hatred, and hast shed *the blood of* the °children of Israel °by the force of the sword in the time of their calamity, in the time °*that their* °iniquity *had* an end:

c[2]
6 Therefore, °*as* I live, °saith [3]the Lord GOD, 'I will prepare thee unto blood, and blood shall pursue thee: °sith thou hast not hated blood, even blood shall pursue thee.
7 Thus will I make [2]mount Seir most desolate, and cut off from it him that passeth out and him that returneth.
8 And °I will fill his mountains with his slain *men:* in thy hills, and in thy valleys, and in all thy rivers, shall they fall that are slain with the sword.
9 I will make thee perpetual desolations, and thy cities shall not °return: and °ye shall know that I *am* [1]the LORD.

d[2]
10 Because °thou hast said, 'These °two nations and these °two countries shall be mine, and we will possess °it;' °whereas [1]the LORD °was there:

c[3]
11 Therefore, [6]*as* I live, [6]saith [3]the Lord GOD, 'I will even °do according to thine anger, and according to thine envy which thou hast used out of thy hatred against them; and I will make Myself known among them, when I have judged thee.
12 And [4]thou shalt know that I *am* [1]the LORD, *and that* I have heard all thy blasphemies which thou hast spoken against the mountains of Israel, saying, 'They are laid desolate, they are given us to consume.'
13 Thus with your mouth ye have boasted against Me, and have multiplied your words against Me: I have heard *them*.'
14 Thus saith [3]the Lord GOD; 'When the whole earth rejoiceth, I will make thee desolate.
15 As thou didst rejoice at the inheritance of °the house of Israel, because it was desolate, so will I do unto thee: thou shalt be desolate, O [2]mount Seir, and all °Idumea, *even* all of it: and °they shall know that I *am* [1]the LORD.' "

Z A[1] B e
36 Also, thou °son of man, prophesy unto the °mountains of Israel, and say, "Ye mountains of Israel, hear the word of °the LORD:

---

30 shall they know. See note on 6. 10. Some codices, with three early printed editions, read "shall the nations know".

31 flock. The 1611 edition of the A.V. omitted these two words "flock, the". **are** = ye [are]

men. Heb. *'ādām*, Ap. 14. I: i.e. human beings, not "sheep", as spoken of in this chapter.

your God. Some codices, with Sept., Syr., and Vulg., read "Jehovah your Elohim".

35. 1—48. 35 (*A*, p. 1104). THE RESTORATION. (*Alternation.*)

A | Y | 35. 1–15. Judgments on enemies.
Z | 36. 1—37. 38. Restoration of Israel.
Y | 38. 1—39. 29. Judgments on nations.
Z | 40. 1—48. 35. Restoration of Israel.

35. 1–15 (Y, above). JUDGMENTS ON ENEMIES. (SEIR.) (*Repeated Alternation.*)

Y | c[1] | 1–4. Threatening. Desolation.
d[1] | 5. Reason. Hatred.
c[2] | 6–9. Threatening. Desolation.
d[2] | 10. Reason. Covetousness.
c[3] | 11–15. Threatening. Desolation.

1 the LORD. Heb. Jehovah. Ap. 4. II.

2 Son of man. See note on 2. 1.

mount Seir: i.e. Edom. Cp. 6. 2; 25. 12–14. Ch. 35 is introductory. Cp. 36. 5, preparing the way for the reoccupation by Israel.

3 the Lord GOD. Heb. Adonai Jehovah. See note on 2. 4. **Behold.** Fig. *Asterismos.* Ap. 6.

4 thou shalt know. See note on 6. 7.

5 a perpetual hatred = a hatred of old.

children = sons.

by the force = by the hands of: "hands" being put by Fig. *Metonymy* (of the Effect), Ap. 6, for the slaughter wrought by them.

that their iniquity had an end: or, in the time of the final punishment for their iniquity.

iniquity. Heb. *'āvāh.* Ap. 44. iv.

6 as I live. Fig. *Deisis.* Ap. 6.

saith the Lord GOD = [is] Adonai Jehovah's oracle.

sith = since. **8 I will fill.** Cp. Isa. 34. 1–15.

9 return = be rebuilt, or inhabited.

ye shall know, &c. See note on 6. 7.

10 thou hast said. Cp. Ps. 83. 4, 12.

two: i.e. Israel and Judah.

it. Can this refer to the blessing which Esau sought?

whereas: or, though.

was there. Cp. 36. 2, 5, and 48. 35.

11 do = deal.

15 the house of Israel. See note on Ex. 16. 31.

Idumea = Edom.

they shall know. See note on 6. 10.

36. 1—37. 38 (Z, above). RESTORATION OF ISRAEL. (*Division.*)

Z | A[1] | 36. 1–38. Literal.
A[2] | 37. 1–28. Symbolical.

36. 1–38 (A[1], above). RESTORATION. LITERAL. (*Introversion.*)

A[1] | B | 1–15. The Land.
C | 16–29–. The People. Israel.
B | –29–38. The Land.

36. 1–15 (B, above). THE LAND. (*Alternation.*)

B | e | 1–3. What the enemy said.
f | 4–12. What Jehovah purposed.
e | 13. What the enemy said.
f | 14, 15. What Jehovah purposed.

What now follows refers to the yet future Restoration of the People and Land of Israel and Judah, as shown in the Structure above.

1 son of man. See note on 2. 1.

mountains of Israel. See 6. 1–7; 36. 1.

the LORD. Heb. Jehovah. Ap. 4. II.

477 **2** Thus saith °the Lord GOD; 'Because °the
enemy °hath said against you, 'Aha, even °the
ancient high places are ours in possession:'
3 Therefore prophesy and say, "Thus saith
[2]the Lord GOD; °Because they have made
you desolate, and °swallowed you up on every
side, that ye might be a possession unto the
residue of the heathen, and ye °are taken up
in the lips of talkers, and *are* an °infamy of
the people:
f (p. 1156) **4** Therefore, ye [1]mountains of Israel, °hear
the word of [2]the Lord GOD; Thus saith [2]the
Lord GOD °to the [1]mountains, and to the hills,
to the °rivers, and to the valleys, to the desolate wastes, and to the cities that are forsaken,
which became a prey and derision to the residue of the heathen that *are* round about;
5 Therefore thus saith [2]the Lord GOD;
Surely in the °fire of My jealousy have I
spoken against the residue of the °heathen,
and against all °Idumea, which have appointed My land into their possession with
the joy of all *their* heart, with despiteful
°minds, to cast it out for a prey.'
6 Prophesy therefore concerning °the land of
Israel, and say unto the [1]mountains, and to
the hills, to the rivers, and to the valleys,
'Thus saith [2]the Lord GOD; °Behold, I have
spoken in My jealousy and in My fury, because
ye have borne the shame of the heathen:'
7 Therefore thus saith [2]the Lord GOD; 'I
have °lifted up Mine hand, Surely the °hea-
then °that *are* about you, they shall bear their
shame.
8 But ye, O [1]mountains of Israel, ye shall
shoot forth your branches, and yield your
fruit to My People of Israel; for they are at
hand to come.
9 For, [6]behold, I *am* for you, and I will turn
unto you, and ye shall be tilled and sown:
10 And I will multiply °men upon you, all the
house of Israel, *even* all of it: and the cities
shall be inhabited, and the wastes shall be
builded:
11 And I will multiply upon you [10]man and
beast; and they shall increase and bring fruit:
and I will settle you after your °old estates,
and will do better *unto you* than at your
beginnings: and °ye shall know that I *am*
[1]the LORD.
12 Yea, I will cause [10]men to walk upon you,
even My People Israel; and they shall possess
thee, and thou shalt be their inheritance, and
thou shalt no more henceforth °bereave them
of men.'
e **13** Thus saith [2]the Lord GOD; 'Because they
say unto you, °'Thou *land* devourest up [10]men,
and hast [12]bereaved thy nations;'
f **14** Therefore thou shalt devour [10]men no
more, neither °bereave thy nations any more,'
°saith [2]the Lord GOD.
15 'Neither will I cause *men* to hear in thee
the shame of the [5]heathen any more, neither
shalt thou bear the reproach of °the people any
more, neither shalt thou cause °thy nations to
fall any more, [14]saith [2]the Lord GOD."
C D (p. 1157) **16** Moreover the word of [1]the LORD came
unto me, saying,
17 [1]"Son of man, when the house of Israel
dwelt in their own [6]land, °they defiled it by
their own way and by their doings: their way
was before Me °as the uncleanness of a removed woman.
18 Wherefore °I poured My fury upon them E
for the blood that they had shed upon the
land, and for their °idols *wherewith* they had
polluted it:
19 And °I scattered them among the [5]heathen,
and they were dispersed through the countries:
°according to their way and according to their
doings I judged them.

---

2 the Lord GOD. Heb. Adonai Jehovah. See note on 2. 4.
the enemy. Note the Structure above.
hath said. The 1611 edition of the A.V. reads "had said".
the ancient high places = the everlasting hills, promised to Israel (Gen. 49. 26. Deut. 13. 13; 33. 15).
3 Because = Because, even because. Fig. *Epizeuxis*. Ap. 6.
swallowed you up. Like a beast of prey. Cp. Job 5. 5. Pss. 56. 1, 2; 57. 3. Eccles. 10. 12.
are = have been.
infamy = evil report.
4 hear. Fig. *Apostrophe*. Ap. 6.
to the mountains, &c. Note the Fig. *Merismos* (Ap. 6).
rivers = torrents, or ravines. Heb. *'ăphīkīm*. See note on "channels", 2 Sam. 22. 16.
5 fire of My jealousy. Ref. to Pent. (Deut. 4. 24).
heathen = nations.
Idumea = Edom.
minds = souls. Heb. *nephesh*. Ap. 13.
6 the land of Israel = the soil of Israel. See note on 11. 17.
Behold. Fig. *Asterismos*. Ap. 6.
7 lifted up Mine hand = sworn. Heb. idiom. Ref. to Pent. (Ex. 6. 8. Num. 14. 30. Deut. 32. 40). Cp. Dan. 12. 7. Elsewhere only in Pentateuch. See Gen. 14. 22, and Ezek. 20. 5.
heathen = nations.
that are = which are yours; referring to "ours" in *v.* 2.
10 men. Heb. *'ādām*. Ap. 14. I.
11 old = former.
ye shall know, &c. See note on 6. 7.
12 bereave, &c. = make childless.
13 Thou land devourest, &c. Ref. to Pent. (Num. 13. 32). Ap. 92.
14 bereave. Heb. text reads "cause to fall"; but marg. reads "make childless". Some codices, with three early printed editions, Aram., Sept., Syr., and Vulg., read "make childless" (text and marg.).
saith the Lord GOD = [is] Adonai Jehovah's oracle.
15 the people = peoples.
thy. The 1611 edition of the A.V. reads "the".

36. 16-29-. (C, p. 1156). THE PEOPLE. ISRAEL
(*Introversion and Alternation.*)

C | D | 16, 17. Israel's uncleanness.
  E | 18, 19. "I scattered".
   F | 20. "They profaned".
    G | g | 21-. Jehovah's Name's sake.
      h | -21. Which Israel had profaned.
    G | *g* | 22-. Jehovah's Name's sake.
      h | -22. Which Israel had profaned.
   F | 23. "I will sanctify".
  E | 24. "I will bring".
 D | 25-29. Israel's cleansing.

17 land = soil.
they defiled it, &c. Ref. to Pent. (Lev. 15. 19; 18. 25, 27, 30. Num. 35. 33, 34). Ap. 92.
as the uncleanness, &c. Ref. to Pent. (Lev. 15. 19; 18, 19, &c.).
18 I poured, &c. See 7. 8; 14. 19; 21. 31. Cp. 2 Chron. 34. 21, 25. Jer. 7. 20; 44. 6, &c.
idols = dirty idols.
19 I scattered, &c. See 5. 12; 22. 15. Ref. to Pent. (Lev. 26. 33. Deut. 28. 64). Ap. 92.
according to their way. See 7. 3, 8; 18. 30; 22. 31; 39. 24.

F 20 And when °they entered unto the [5]heathen,
(p. 1157) whither they went, they °profaned My °holy
477 °name, when °they said to them, 'These *are*
the People of [1]the LORD, and are °gone forth
out of His land.'

G g 21 But °I had pity for Mine [20]holy name,

h which the house of Israel had [20]profaned among
the [5]heathen, whither they went.

G g 22 Therefore say unto the house of Israel,
'Thus saith [2]the Lord GOD; 'I do °not *this*
for your sakes, O house of Israel, but for Mine
[20]holy [20]name's sake,

h which ye have [20]profaned among the [5]heathen,
whither ye went.

F 23 And °I will sanctify My great [20]name,
which was [20]profaned among the [5]heathen,
which ye have profaned in the midst of them;
and the [5]heathen °shall know that I *am* [1]the
LORD,' [14]saith [2]the Lord GOD, when I shall be
sanctified °in you before °their eyes.

E 24 For I will take you from among the
[5]heathen, and gather you out of all countries,
and °will bring you °into your own land.

D 25 °Then will I °sprinkle clean °water upon
°you, and °ye shall be clean: from all °your
filthiness, and from all your [18]idols, will I
cleanse you.
26 A °new heart also will I give [25]you, and
a new °spirit will I put within [25]you: and
I will take away the stony heart out of [25]your
flesh, and I will give you an heart of flesh.
27 And I will put My [26]spirit within [25]you,
and cause [25]you to walk in My °statutes, and
[25]ye shall keep My °judgments, and do *them*.
28 And [25]ye shall dwell in the °land that I
gave to [25]your fathers; and °ye shall °be My
People, and I will °be [25]your °God.
29 I will also save [25]you from all your un-
cleannesses:

B H and I will call for °the corn, and will increase
(p. 1158) it, and lay no famine upon [25]you.
30 And I will multiply the fruit of the tree,
and the increase of the field, that ye shall
receive no more °reproach of famine among
the [5]heathen.

J 31 [25]Then °shall ye remember your own °evil
ways, and your doings that *were* not good,
and shall lothe yourselves in your own sight
for your °iniquities and for your °abomina-
tions.

H 32 [22]Not for your sakes do I *this*, [14]saith
[2]the Lord GOD, 'be it known unto you: °be
ashamed and confounded for your own ways,
O house of Israel.
33 Thus saith [2]the Lord GOD; °'In the day
that I shall have cleansed you from all your
[31]iniquities I will also °cause *you* to dwell in
the cities, and the wastes shall be builded.
34 And the desolate land shall be tilled,
whereas it lay desolate in the sight of all that
passed by.
35 And they shall say, 'This land that was
desolate is become °like the garden of Eden;
and the waste and desolate and ruined cities
are become °fenced, *and* are inhabited.'

J 36 Then the [5]heathen that are left round
about you [23]shall know that I [1]the LORD
build the ruined *places, and* plant that that
was desolate: I [1]the LORD have spoken *it*,
and I will do *it*.'
37 Thus saith [2]the Lord GOD; 'I will °yet
for this °be enquired of by the house of Israel,

20 they. Heb. text reads "he", or "it". A special various reading called *Sevīr* (Ap. 34), and some codices, with Aram., Sept., Syr., and Vulg., read "they".
profaned, &c. Ref. to Pent. (Lev. 19. 12, &c.). Ap. 92.
holy. See note on Ex. 3. 5.
name. See note on Ps. 20. 1.
they said to them: i.e. men said of Israel.
gone=come.
21 I had pity, &c. See 20. 9, 14, 22.
22 not . . . for your sakes, &c. Ref. to Pent. (Deut. 7. 7, 8; 9. 5-7). Ap. 92. Cp. Pss. 106. 8; 115. 1, 2.
23 I will sanctify, &c. The opposite of the profanation of *v.* 20.
shall know. See note on 6. 10.
in you. So in the Babylonian Codex; but some codices, with Codex Hillel and three early printed editions (one in marg.), read "in them".
their. The Babylonian Codex, Codex Hillel, and other codices, with nine early printed editions (one Rabbinic, in marg.), read "your".
24 will bring you, &c. Cp. 11. 17; 34. 13; 37. 21, 25; 39. 27, 28, &c. Ref. to Pent. (Deut. 30. 3-5). Ap. 92.
into your own land=on to your own soil. Heb. *'adāmāh*. Not the same word as in *v.* 28.
25 Then. Note the time for the fulfilment of this prophecy. Not now, among the Gentiles; not now, in the Church of God; but, when Israel shall be brought back "into their own land" (*vv.* 16-24). Note the "you . . . ye . . . your", &c., of *vv.* 25-29. Observe the importance of this word "Then" in other passages. See notes on Ex. 17. 8. Mal. 3. 4, 16. Matt. 25. 1. 1 Thess. 4. 17, &c.
sprinkle=throw. See Lev. 1. 5.
water. See Isa. 44. 3.
you . . . ye . . . your. The same People referred to in *vv.* 25-29 as in *vv.* 16, 17. See the Structure, p. 1157.
26 new heart. Not the old heart improved, but a new heart created and "given". The old one "taken away". **spirit.** Heb. *rūach.* Ap. 9.
27 statutes . . . judgments. Ref. to Pent. See note on Deut. 4. 1. Ap. 92.
28 land. Heb. *'eretz.* Not the same word as in *v.* 24.
ye: i.e. the People who are the subject of these verses. See note on "Then", *v.* 25.
be My People=become to Me a people. } Ref. to
be your God=become to you a God. } Pent. (Lev.
God. Heb. Elohim. Ap. 4. I. } 26. 12).

36. -29-38 (*B*, p. 1156). THE LAND.
(*Alternation.*)

B | H | -29, 30. Its Restoration.
  J | 31. The Purpose. (Negative.)
  H | 32-35. Its Restoration.
  J | 36-38. The Purpose. (Positive.)

29 the corn, &c. Pointing to the physical blessings.
30 reproach, &c. Ref. to Pent. (Deut. 29. 23-28). Ap. 92. Cp. Joel 2. 17, 26.
31 shall ye remember. See 6. 9; 16. 61-63; 20. 43.
evil. Heb. *ra'a'.* Ap. 44. viii.
iniquities. Heb. *'āvāh.* Ap. 44. iv.
abominations: i.e. idolatries.
32 be ashamed. Cp. 16. 63.
33 In the day that=When. See Ap. 18.
cause you to dwell, &c.=cause the cities to be inhabited.
35 like the garden of Eden. Ref. to Pent. (Gen. 2. 8-15). See note on 28. 13. **fenced**=fortified.
37 yet . . . be enquired of: i.e. the time shall come when they will ask for what they had in the past despised.

477 to do *it* for them; I will increase them with
[10] men like a flock.
38 ° As the holy flock, as the flock of Jerusalem in her ° solemn feasts; so shall the waste cities be filled with flocks of [10] men: and they [23] shall know that I *am* [1] the LORD.'"

[2] K[1] L N (p. 1159) **37** The hand of ° the LORD was upon me, and carried me out ° in the ° spirit of ° the LORD, and set me down in the midst of the ° valley which *was* full of bones,
2 And caused me to pass by them ° round about: and, ° behold, *there were* very many in the open valley; and, ° lo, *they were* very dry.

O 3 And he said unto me, ° "Son of man, can these bones live?" And I answered, "O ° Lord GOD, Thou knowest."

M l 4 Again he said unto me, "Prophesy ° upon these bones, and say unto them, 'O ye dry bones, hear the word of [1] the LORD.

m 5 Thus saith [3] the Lord GOD unto these bones; [2] 'Behold, I will cause ° breath to enter into you, and ye shall live:
6 And I will lay sinews upon you, and will bring up flesh upon you, and cover you with skin, and ° put [5] breath in you, and ye shall live; and ° ye shall know that I *am* [1] the LORD.'"

n 7 So I prophesied ° as I was commanded:

o and as I prophesied, there was a ° noise, and [2] behold a ° shaking, and the bones came together, bone to his bone.
8 And when I beheld, [2] lo, the sinews and the flesh came up upon them, and the skin covered them above: but *there was* no [5] breath in them.

M l 9 Then said He unto me, "Prophesy ° unto the ° wind, prophesy, [3] son of man, and say to the ° wind,

m 'Thus saith the [3] Lord GOD; 'Come from the four ° winds, O [5] breath, and ° breathe upon these ° slain, that they may live.'"

n 10 So I prophesied [7] as He commanded me,

o and the [5] breath came into them, and they lived, and stood up upon their feet, an exceeding great army.

L N 11 Then He said unto me, [3] "Son of man, these bones ° are ° the whole house of Israel: [2] behold, they say, 'Our bones are dried, and our hope is lost: ° we are cut off for our parts.'

O P 12 Therefore prophesy and say unto them, 'Thus saith the [3] Lord GOD;

Q p [2] 'Behold, O My People, I will open your ° graves, and cause you to come up out of your ° graves,

q and bring you ° into the land of Israel.

r 13 And [6] ye shall know that I *am* [1] the LORD,

Q P ° when I have opened your [12] graves, O My People, ° and brought you up out of your [12] graves,

---

38 As the holy flock = Like a flock of holy offerings.
solemn feasts = appointed seasons.

37. 1-28 (A[2], p. 1156). RESTORATION. SYMBOLICAL. (*Division.*)

A[2] | K[1] | 1-14. The Dry Bones.
| K[2] | 15-28. The Two Sticks.

37. 1-14 (K[1], above). THE DRY BONES.
(*Alternations: Simple and Extended.*)

K[1] | L | N | 1, 2. The Vision shown.
| | O | 3. The Question. Answer of prophet.
| M | l | 4. Command to prophesy *over* (*'al*).
| | m | 5, 6. Words of the prophecy.
| | n | 7-. Obedience of the prophet.
| | o | -7, 8. Result.
| *M* | *l* | 9-. Command to prophecy *unto* (*'el*).
| | *m* | -9. Words of the prophecy.
| | *n* | 10-. Obedience of the prophet.
| | *o* | -10. Result.
| *L* | *N* | 11. The Vision explained.
| | *O* | 12-14. The Question. Answer of Jehovah.

1 the LORD. Heb. Jehovah. Ap. 4. II.
in the spirit = by the spirit. Cp. 1. 1, 3; 8. 3; 11. 24, 25; 40. 2, 3. These expressions show the meaning of Rev. 1. 10. spirit. Heb. *rūach*. Ap. 9.
valley = plain. Same word as in 3. 22, 23; and 8. 4.
2 round about = on every side. Heb. *ṣābīb ṣābīb* = on this side and on that side. Fig. *Epizeuxis* (Ap. 6), for emphasis.
behold . . . lo. Fig. *Asterismos* (Ap. 6), calling special attention to that which was seen.
3 Son of man. See note on 2. 1.
Lord GOD. Heb. Adonai Jehovah. See note on 2. 4.
4 upon = over. Heb. *'al*.
5 breath = spirit. Heb. *rūach*. Ap. 9.
6 put breath, &c. Ref. to Pent. (Gen. 2. 7). Ap. 92.
ye shall know, &c. See note on 6. 7.
7 as = according as.
noise = voice.
shaking = commotion.
9 unto. Heb. *'el*. Cp. *v.* 4, and see the Structure above.
wind = spirit. Same as "breath" in *v.* 5.
breathe = blow. Heb. *naphah*.
slain = dead (by violent death). Sept. renders it *tous nekrous* = corpses, as distinct from *nekrous*, which (without the Article) refers to the dead as having been once alive (cp. Matt. 22. 31. Luke 24. 5. 1 Cor. 15. 29 (first and third words), 35, 42, 52); while, with the Article it denotes corpses. See Deut. 14. 1. Matt. 22. 32. Mark 9. 10. Luke 16. 30, 31; 24. 46. Acts 23. 6; 24. 15; 26. 8. Rom. 6. 13; 10. 7; 11. 15. Heb. 11. 19; 13. 20. 1 Cor. 15. 12, 13, 15, 16, 20, 21, 29 (second word), 32. Especially cp. 1 Pet. 4. 6. See Ap. 139.
11 are = they [are]. Fig. *Metaphor*. Ap. 6.
the whole house. As distinct from "the house".
we are cut off for our parts = as for us, we are quite cut off, or clean cut off.

37. 12-14 (*O*, above). THE QUESTION. ANSWERED BY JEHOVAH.
(*Introversion and Extended Alternation.*)

O | P | 12-. "Thus saith Jehovah".
| Q | p | -12-. "I will open your graves".
| | q | -12. "And bring you into the land".
| | r | 13-. "And ye shall know", &c.
| *Q* | *p* | -13. "When I have opened your graves".
| | *q* | 14-. "And I shall place you in your own land".
| | *r* | -14-. "Then shall ye know", &c.
| *P* | -14. "Saith Jehovah."

12 graves = sepulchres, or burying-places. Heb. *ḳeber*, not Sheōl. See Ap. 35. The repetition of this must include resurrection as well as restoration.

into the land of Israel = upon the soil of Israel. Heb. *'admath*. See note on 11. 17. **13** when I have opened = by My opening. and brought you up = by My causing you to come up.

q 14 And shall [6]put My °spirit in you, and ye
(p. 1159) shall live, and I shall °place you °in your own
477 land:

r then shall [6]ye know that I [1]the LORD have
spoken *it*, and performed *it*,

p °saith [1]the LORD.' "

K^2 R^1 S s 15 The word of [1]the LORD came again unto
(p. 1160) me, saying,
16 "Moreover, thou [3]son of man, take thee
one °stick, and write upon it, For Judah, and
for the °children of Israel his °companions:

t then take another °stick, and write upon it,
For °Joseph, the °stick of Ephraim, and *for*
all the house of Israel °his companions:

T 17 And join them one to another into one
stick; and they shall become one in thine
°hand.

S t 18 And when the [16]children of thy People shall
speak unto thee, saying, 'Wilt thou not shew
us what thou *meanest* by these?'
19 Say unto them, 'Thus saith the [3]Lord
GOD; [2]'Behold, I will take the stick of Joseph,
which *is* in the hand of Ephraim, and the
tribes of Israel his °fellows, and will put them
with °him,

s *even* with the stick of Judah,

T and make them one stick, and they shall be
one in Mine hand.' '

R^2 U^1 u^1 20 And the [16]sticks whereon thou writest
shall be in thine hand before their eyes.
21 And say unto them, 'Thus saith the [3]Lord
GOD; °'Behold, °I will take the [16]children of
Israel from among the °heathen, whither they
be gone, °and will gather them on every side,
and bring them [12]into their own °land:

v^1 22 And I will make them one nation in the
[21]land °upon the °mountains of Israel; and one
king shall be king to them all: and they shall
be no more two nations, neither shall they be
divided into two kingdoms any more at all:

w^1 23 Neither shall they defile themselves any
more with their °idols, nor with their °detestable
things, nor with any of their °transgressions:

U^2 u^2 but I will save them out of all their °dwellingplaces,
°wherein they have °sinned, and will
cleanse them: so shall they be °My People, and
I will be °their °God.

v^2 24 And °David My servant *shall be* king
over them; and they all shall have one °shepherd:

w^2 they shall also walk in My °judgments, and
observe My °statutes, and do them.

U^3 u^3 25 °And they shall dwell in the [12]land that
I have °given unto Jacob My servant, wherein
your fathers have dwelt; °and they shall
dwell therein, *even* they, and their [16]children,
and their [16]children's [16]children for ever:

v^3 and °My servant David *shall be* their prince
for ever.

14 spirit. Heb. *rūach*. Ap. 9. Same word as "breath" and "wind" above. **place** = settle.

in your own land = upon your own soil. Heb. *'ădāmāh*. Cp. *v.* 21, and see note on *v.* 12.

saith the Lord GOD = [is] Adonai Jehovah's oracle.

37. 15-28 (K^2, p. 1159). THE TWO STICKS.
(*Division.*)

K^2 | R^1 | 15-19. The Sign.
R^2 | 20-28. The Signification.

37. 15-19 (R^1, above). THE SIGN.
(*Alternation and Introversion.*)

R^1 | S | s | 15, 16-. The stick for Judah.
t | -16. The stick for Ephraim.
T | 17. Union.
S | *t* | 18, 19-. The stick for Ephraim.
s | -19-. The stick for Judah.
T | -19. Union.

16 stick. Heb. "wood": put by Fig. *Metonymy* (of Cause), Ap. 6, for anything made of it.

children = sons.

companions: i.e. Benjamin and Levi. Heb. text reads "companion" (sing.); but marg., with some codices and one early printed edition, reads "companions" (pl.).

Joseph. Who held the primogeniture of the other tribes (1 Chron. 5. 1), forfeited by Reuben; and was represented by Ephraim, the head of the ten tribes. Cp. 1 Kings 11. 26. Isa. 11. 13. Jer. 31. 6. Hos. 5. 3, 5.

his companions: i.e. the other tribes.

17 hand. Some codices, with three early printed editions, read "hands" (pl.).

19 fellows. Same word as "companions" in *v.* 16, and same note as to the readings.

him: or, it.

37. 20-28 (R^2, above). THE SIGNIFICATION.
(*Repeated and Extended Alternation.*)

R^2 | U^1 | u^1 | 20, 21. Restoration.
v^1 | 22. One Nation.
w^1 | 23-. Conversion.
U^2 | u^2 | -23. Restoration.
v^2 | 24-. One King.
w^2 | -24. Conversion.
U^3 | u^3 | 25-. Restoration.
v^3 | -25. One King.
w^3 | 26-28. Sanctification.

21 Behold . . . heathen; and . . . land. These words were chosen for the legend on the Zionist medal commemorating the National Federation (of 1896), which is a landmark in the history of the Jewish nation.

I = I even I. Fig. *Epizeuxis* (Ap. 6).

heathen = nations.

land. Heb. *'eretz*. Not the same word as in *vv.* 12, 14, 21. **22 upon** = among.

mountains. A special various reading called *Sevir* (Ap. 34) reads "cities".

23 idols = dirty gods.

detestable = abominable. Referring to idolatry, and its accompaniments.

transgressions = rebellions. Heb. *pāsha'*. Ap. 44. ix.

dwellingplaces. Sept. reads "lawlessnesses". Cp. Jer. 2. 19; 3. 22; 5. 6. So Houbigant, Bishops Newcombe and Horsley, with Ginsburg.

wherein = whereby.

sinned. Heb. *chāṭā'*. Ap. 44. i.

My People = to Me a People.

their God = to them a God.

God. Heb. Elohim. Ap. 4. I.

24 David My servant = Heb. My servant David. Occurs five times (34. 23, 24; 37. 24. 1 Kings 11. 32; 14. 8). In *v.* 25 and 2 Sam. 3. 18 t is (in Heb.) "David My servant" (though the A.V. there renders it "My servant David"). **shepherd** = ruler.

judgments . . . statutes. See note on Deut. 4. 1.

25 And they shall dwell. Repeated in middle of the verse by the Fig. *Mesarchia* (Ap. 6), for emphasis.
given unto Jacob. And not any other land. **My servant David.** Here, it is (in Heb.) "David My servant".

w³ (p. 1160) 477 26 Moreover I will make a °covenant of
peace with them; it shall be an °everlasting
covenant with them: and I will [14]place them,
and multiply them, and will set My sanctuary
in the midst of them for evermore.
27 My °tabernacle also shall be with them:
yea, I will be [23]their [23]God, and they shall be
[23]My People.
28 And the [21]heathen °shall know that I
[1]the LORD do sanctify Israel, °when My sanctuary
shall be in the midst of them °for evermore.' ' "

Y V (p. 1161) 38 And the word of °the LORD came unto
me, saying,
2 °"Son of man, set thy face against °Gog,
°the land of Magog, °the chief prince of °Meshech
and Tubal, and prophesy against him,
3 And say, 'Thus saith °the Lord GOD; °'Behold,
I *am* against thee, O [2]Gog, [2]the chief
prince of [2]Meshech and Tubal:

W 4 And I will °turn thee back, and °put hooks
into thy jaws, and I will bring thee forth, and
all thine °army, horses and horsemen, all of
them clothed with all sorts *of armour, even*
a great °company *with* bucklers and shields,
all of them handling swords:
5 Persia, °Ethiopia, and °Libya with them;
all of them with shield and helmet:
6 °Gomer, and all his bands; the house of
°Togarmah of the north quarters, and all his
°bands: *and* many °people with thee.
7 Be thou prepared, and prepare for thyself,
thou, and all thy °company that are assembled
unto thee, and °be thou a guard unto them.

X x 8 °After many days thou shalt be visited: in
°the latter years thou shalt come into the land
that is brought back from the sword, *and is*
gathered out of many [6]people, against the
mountains of Israel, which have been always
waste: but it is brought forth out of the nations,
and they shall dwell °safely all of them.
9 Thou shalt ascend and come like a storm,
thou shalt be like a cloud to cover the land,
thou, and all thy [6]bands, and many [6]people
with thee.'
10 Thus saith [3]the Lord GOD; 'It shall also
come to pass, *that* at the same time shall
°things come into thy mind, and thou shalt
°think an °evil thought:
11 And thou shalt say, 'I will go up to the
land of °unwalled villages; I will go to them
that are at rest, that dwell [8]safely, all of them
dwelling without walls, and having neither
bars nor gates,
12 °To take a spoil, and to take a prey;' to
turn thine hand upon the desolate places *that*

26 covenant of peace. Cp. 34. 25.
everlasting covenant. See notes on Gen. 9. 16, and Isa. 44. 7.
27 tabernacle. Heb. *mishkān*. See Ap. 42. Ref. to Pent. (Lev. 26. 11, 12). Ap. 92.
28 shall know. See note on 6. 10.
when, &c. = by the existence of My sanctuary in, &c.
for evermore. Therefore this prophecy yet awaits its fulfilment.

38. 1—39. 29 (*Y*, p. 1156). JUDGMENTS ON ENEMIES. (GOG.) (*Alternations.*)

Y | V | 38. 1-3. Gog.
W | 38. 4-7. Repulsed.
X | x | 38. 8-16-. Invasion.
y | 38. -16. Purpose.
x | 38. 17-22. Invasion.
y | 38. 23. Purpose.
V | 39. 1. Gog.
W | 39. 2, 3. Repulse.
X | z | 39. 4-6. Fall.
a | 39. 7. Purpose.
z | 39. 8-21. Spoliation.
a | 39. 22-29. Purpose.

1 the LORD. Heb. Jehovah. Ap. 4. II.
2 Son of man. See note on 2. 1.
Gog. A symbolical name for the nations north and east of Palestine, or the nations as a whole. That the prophecies of chs. 38 and 39 are still future is clear from 38. 8, 14, 16; 39. 9, 25, 26; as Israel will have then already been "gathered", and complete restoration enjoyed immediately following the destruction of Gog: "Now will I bring again the captivity of Israel". It must therefore precede the Millennium; and on that account must be distinguished from Rev. 20. 8, 10; and may therefore perhaps be identified with Rev. 16. 14; 17. 14; 19. 17-21. Cp. Matt. 24. 14-30. Zech. 12. 1-4. It marks the climax of Satan's effort to destroy Israel from being a People, and clearly belongs to the close of a yet future kingdom age. See 38. 8, &c., above). The name is connected with "Og" (Deut. 3. 1-13), and "Agag" (Num. 24. 7), where the Samaritan Pent. reads "Agog", and the Sept. reads "Gog". Here the Arabic reads "Agag". The historical interpretation of this prophecy is confessedly impossible.
the land of Magog = of the land of the Magog. If "Gog" denotes and symbolises all that is powerful, gigantic, and proud, then "Magog" is symbolical of the same lands and peoples. Magog was a son of Japheth.
the chief prince = the head, or leader of *Rosh*. Heb. *Ro'sh*, which may point to Russia.
Meshech and Tubal. The Sept. renders these *Mesoch* and *Thobel*: i. e. the *Moschi* and *Tibareni*, occupying regions about the Caucasus. All these are nations distant from Palestine: not near nations, or nations connected by consanguinity. They were also descended from Japheth (Gen. 10. 2).
3 the Lord GOD. Heb. Adonai Jehovah. See note on 2. 4.
Behold. Fig. *Asterismos*. Ap. 6.
4 turn thee back: or, lead thee away enticingly. Cp. Isa. 47. 10 (perverted). Jer. 50. 6. See the Oxford *Gesenius*.
put hooks, &c. Cp. Isa. 37. 29. Heb. "curbs". **army.** Heb. "power"; put by Fig. *Metonymy* (of Adjunct), Ap. 6, for army, as translated. **company** = gathered host. Cp. 16. 40. **5 Ethiopia** = Cush. **Libya** = Phut. Cp. 27. 10; 30. 5. These were descended from Ham (Gen. 10. 6). **6 Gomer.** North of Asia Minor; also descended from Japheth (Gen. 10. 3). **Togarmah** = Armenia. Cp. 27. 14. Also descended from Japheth (Gen. 10. 3). **bands** = hordes. **people** = peoples. **7 company.** So (sing.) in many codices and seven early printed editions; but some codices, with three early printed editions, read pl. See note on *v.* 4. **be thou a guard,** &c. Sept. reads "thou wilt be for Me a guard." **8 After many days.** Pointing to a then, and yet future time, when Israel shall have been recently "gathered", and before the Restoration is perfected. **the latter years.** See notes above and on *v.* 2. **safely** = confidently. **10 things** = words, or matters. **think an evil thought** = devise a mischievous device. Cp. Dan. 11. 44, 45. **evil.** Heb. *rā'a'*. Ap. 44. viii. **11 unwalled villages** = mere hamlets. **12 To take a spoil,** &c. The Heb. exhibits the Fig. *Polyptōton* (Ap. 6) = "To spoil a spoil and to prey a prey". Cp. Ps. 83. 4, &c.

477 *are now* inhabited, and °upon the °People
that are gathered out of the nations, which
have gotten cattle and goods, that dwell in
the °midst of the °land.

13 °Sheba, and Dedan, and the merchants of Tarshish, with all the young lions thereof, shall say unto thee, 'Art thou come to take a spoil? hast thou gathered thy [4]company to take a prey? to carry away silver and gold, to take away cattle and goods, to take a great spoil?''

14 Therefore, [2]son of man, prophesy and say unto [2]Gog, 'Thus saith [3]the Lord GOD; 'In that day when My [12]People of Israel dwelleth [8]safely, °shalt thou not know *it?*

15 And thou shalt come from thy place out of the north parts, thou, and many [6]people with thee, all of them riding upon horses, a great [4]company, and a mighty army:

16 And thou shalt come up against My [12]People of Israel, as a cloud to cover the land; it shall be °in the latter days, and I will bring thee against My land,

y that °the °heathen may know Me, °when I
(p. 1161) shall be sanctified in thee, O [2]Gog, before their
eyes.'

x 17 Thus saith [3]the Lord GOD; '*Art* thou he of whom I have spoken in old time by My servants the prophets of Israel, which prophesied in those days *many* years that I would bring thee against them?

18 And it shall come to pass at °the same time when [2]Gog shall come against °the land of Israel, °saith [3]the Lord GOD, *that* My fury shall come up in My face.

19 For in My jealousy *and* in the fire of My wrath have I spoken, Surely in that day there shall be a great °shaking in [18]the land of Israel;

20 So that the fishes of the sea, and the fowls of the heaven, and the beasts of the field, and all creeping things that creep upon the earth, and all the men that *are* upon the face of the earth, shall [19]shake at My presence, and the mountains shall be thrown down, and the steep places shall °fall, and every wall shall fall to the ground.

21 And I will call for a sword against him throughout all My mountains, [18]saith [3]the Lord GOD: °every man's sword shall be against his brother.

22 And I will plead against him with pestilence and with blood; and I will rain upon him, and upon his bands, and upon the many [6]people that *are* with him, an overflowing rain, and °great hailstones, fire, and brimstone.

y 23 Thus will I magnify Myself, and sanctify Myself; and I will be known in the eyes of many nations, and °they shall know that I *am* [1]the LORD.''

V **39** °Therefore, thou °son of man, prophesy against °Gog, and say, 'Thus saith °the Lord GOD; °Behold, I *am* against thee, O °Gog, the chief prince of Meshech and Tubal:

W 2 And I will °turn thee back, and °leave but the sixth part of thee, and will cause thee to come up from the north parts, and will bring thee °upon the mountains of Israel:

3 And I will smite thy bow out of thy left hand, and will cause thine arrows to fall out of thy right hand.

4 Thou shalt fall [2]upon the mountains of Is- X z
rael, thou, and all thy bands, and the °people that *is* with thee: I will give thee unto the ravenous birds of every sort, and *to* the beasts of the field to be devoured.

5 Thou shalt fall upon the open field: for I have spoken *it*, °saith [1]the Lord GOD.

6 And I will send a fire on Magog, and among them that dwell carelessly in the °isles: and °they shall know that I *am* °the LORD.

7 So will I make My °holy °name known in a
the midst of My People Israel; and I will not *let them* °pollute My °holy name any more: and the °heathen °shall know that I *am* [6]the LORD, the °Holy One in Israel.

8 Behold, it is come, and it is done, [5]saith z
[1]the Lord GOD; this *is* the day whereof I have spoken.

9 And they that dwell in the cities of Israel shall go forth, and shall set on fire and burn the weapons, both the shields and the buck-

upon = against. A special various reading called *Sevir* (Ap. 34) reads "over".
People: i.e. Israel, as in 39. 13; not in *vv.* 6, 8, 9, 15, 22.
midst. Heb. = navel. Put by Fig. *Metonymy* (of Adjunct), Ap. 6, for the middle.
land = earth. Heb. *'eretz*. Cp. *v.* 18. Of which Palestine is in the centre, politically and morally, if not exactly geographically.
13 Sheba, &c. These are some who protest.
14 shalt thou not know it? The Sept. reads "wilt thou not rouse thyself?"
16 in the latter days = in the end of days. Still future. See notes on *vv.* 2 and 8.
the heathen may know, &c. See note on 6. 10.
heathen = nations.
when I shall be sanctified, &c.: or, by My hallowing Myself, &c.
18 the same time = that day.
the land of Israel = on the soil of Israel. Heb. *'admath*. See note on 11. 17.
saith the Lord GOD = [is] Adonai Jehovah's oracle.
19 shaking = trembling. **20 fall** = sink down.
21 every man's. Heb. *'ish*. Ap. 14. II.
22 great hailstones. As in Josh. 10. 11.
23 they shall know, &c. See note on 6. 10.

39. 1 Therefore, &c. See the Structure, p. 1161.
son of man. See note on 2. 1.
Gog, &c. See note on 38. 2.
the Lord GOD. Heb. Adonai Jehovah. See note on 2. 4. Behold. Fig. *Asterismos*. Ap. 6.
2 turn thee back. See note on 38. 4.
leave but the sixth part of thee = and will lead thee on. This being from the root *shāsha* = to lead; not *shesh* = six.
upon the mountains of Israel. The others will be smitten in their own lands.
4 people = peoples. Some codices, with Aram. and Syr., read "many peoples". Cp. 38. 22.
5 saith the Lord GOD = [is] Adonai Jehovah's oracle.
6 isles = coasts, or maritime lands.
they shall know, &c. See note on 6. 10.
the LORD. Heb. Jehovah. Ap. 4. II.
7 holy. See note on Ex. 3. 5.
name. See note on Ps. 20. 1.
pollute = profane. heathen = nations.
shall know, &c. See note on 6. 10.

477 lers, the bows and the arrows, and the handstaves, and the spears, and they shall burn them with fire seven years:

10 So that they shall take no wood out of the field, neither cut down *any* out of the forests; for they shall burn the weapons with fire: and they shall spoil those that spoiled them, and °rob those that robbed them, [5]saith [1]the Lord GOD.

11 And it shall come to pass °in that day, *that* I will give unto [1]Gog a place there of °graves in Israel, the valley of the passengers on the east of the sea: and it °shall stop the *noses* of the passengers: and there shall they bury [1]Gog and all his multitude: and they shall call *it* The valley of °Hamon-gog.

12 And seven months shall the house of Israel be burying of them, that they may cleanse the land.

13 Yea, all the People of the land shall bury *them;* and it shall be to them a renown the day that I shall be glorified, [5]saith [1]the Lord GOD.

14 And they shall sever out °men of continual employment, passing through the land to bury with the passengers those that remain upon the face of the earth, to cleanse it: after the end of seven months shall they search.

15 And the passengers *that* pass through the land, when *any* seeth a °man's bone, then shall he set up a sign by it, till the buriers have buried it in the valley of [11]Hamon-gog.

16 And also the name of the city *shall be* °Hamonah. Thus shall they cleanse the land.''

17 And, thou [1]son of man, thus saith [1]the Lord GOD; 'Speak unto every feathered fowl, and to every beast of the field, Assemble yourselves, and come; gather yourselves on every side to My sacrifice that I do sacrifice for you, *even* a great sacrifice [2]upon the mountains of Israel, that ye may eat flesh, and drink blood.

18 Ye shall eat the flesh of the mighty, and drink the blood of the °princes of the earth, of rams, of lambs, and of goats, of bullocks, all of them fatlings of Bashan.

19 And ye shall eat fat till ye be full, and drink blood till ye be drunken, of My sacrifice which I have sacrificed for you.

20 Thus ye shall be filled at My table with horses and chariots, with mighty men, and with all men of war, [5]saith [1]the Lord GOD.

21 And I will set My glory among the [7]heathen, and all the [7]heathen shall see My judgment that I have executed, and My hand that I have laid upon them.

a (p. 1161) **22** So the house of Israel shall know that I *am* [6]the LORD their °God from that day and forward.

23 And the [7]heathen [7]shall know that the house of Israel went into captivity for their °iniquity: because they °trespassed against Me, therefore hid I My face from them, and gave them into the hand of their enemies: so fell they all by the sword.

24 According to their uncleanness and according to their °transgressions have I done unto them, and hid My face from them.

25 Therefore' thus saith [1]the Lord GOD; °'Now will I bring again the captivity of Jacob, and have mercy upon the whole house of Israel, and will be jealous for My [7]holy [7]name;

26 °After that they have borne their shame, and all their °trespasses whereby they have °trespassed against Me, when they dwelt °safely °in their land, and none made *them* afraid.

27 °When I have brought them again from the [4]people, and gathered them out of their enemies' lands, and am sanctified in them in the sight of many nations;

28 Then [7]shall they know that I *am* [6]the LORD their [22]God, which caused them to be led into captivity among the [7]heathen: but I have gathered them unto their own land, and have left none of them any more there.

29 °Neither will I hide My face °any more from them: for I have °poured out My °spirit upon the house of Israel, [5]saith [1]the Lord GOD.'' ''

40 In °the five and twentieth year of our captivity, in °the beginning of the year, in the tenth *day* of the month, in the Z A C[1] D[1] (p. 1163) 465

---

10 rob = make a prey.

11 in. The 1611 edition of the A.V. reads "at".
graves = sepulture. Sept. and Vulg. read "memorial for burial".
shall stop . . . passengers = obstructeth, or arresteth, the passengers. Probably on account of its depth.
Hamon-gog = the multitude of Gog.

14 men of continual employment = constantly.
men. Heb. pl. of *'ěnōsh.* Ap. 14. III.

15 man's. Heb. *'ādām.* Ap. 14. I.

16 Hamonah = "to the multitude".

18 princes = leaders.

22 God. Heb. Elohim. Ap. 4. I.

23 iniquity. Heb. *'āvāh.* Ap. 44. iv.
trespassed = committed treachery. Heb. *mā'al.* Ap. 44. xi.

24 transgressions = rebellions. Heb. *pāsha'.* Ap. 44. ix.

25 Now: i.e. after the destruction of Gog; i.e. after the "gathering" but before the final "Restoration", and therefore before the Millennium. See note on 38. 2.

26 After, &c. Another note of time, determining the fulfilment of the prophecy concerning Gog.
trespasses = treachery. Heb. *mā'al,* as in *v.* 23.
safely = confidently.
in their land = on their soil.

27 When. Another mark of time.

29 Neither . . . any more. Another mark of time.
poured out, &c. See Joel 2. 28. Another mark of time.
spirit. Heb. *rūach.* Ap. 9.

40. 1—48. 35 (Z, p. 1156). THE RESTORATION.
(*Alternation.*)

Z | A | 40. 1—44. 31. The House.
  B | 45. 1—46. 18. The Land.
 A | 46. 19–24. The House.
  B | 47. 1—48. 35. The Land.

40. 1—44. 31 (A, above). THE HOUSE.
(*Repeated and Extended Alternation.*)

A | C[1] | D[1] | 40. 1–3. Visions of God.
   E[1] | 40. 4. Injunctions.
    F[1] | 40. 5—42. 20. The House. Itself.
 C[2] | D[2] | 43. 1–6. The Glory. Returning.
   E[2] | 43. 7–12. Injunctions.
    F[2] | 43. 13–27. The House. Its altar.
 C[3] | D[3] | 44. 1–4. The Glory. Abiding.
   E[3] | 44. 5–8. Injunctions.
    F[3] | 44. 9–31. The House. Its Ministers.

1 the five and twentieth year. See table on p. 1105.
the beginning. Probably Abib or Nisan.

465 fourteenth year after that °the city was smitten, in the selfsame day °the hand of °the LORD was upon me, and brought me thither.

2 In the °visions of °God brought He me into °the land of Israel, and set me °upon a very high mountain, °by which *was* as the °frame of a city on the south.

3 And He brought me thither, and, °behold, *there was* a °man, whose appearance *was* like the appearance of brass, with a line of flax in his hand, and a measuring °reed; and he stood in the gate.

E[1] (p. 1163) 4 And the [3]man said unto me, °"Son of man, behold with thine eyes, and hear with thine ears, and set thine heart upon all that I shall shew thee; for to the intent that I might shew *them* unto thee *art* thou brought hither: declare all that thou seest to the house of Israel."

F[1] G K[1] (p. 1164) 5 And °behold a wall °on the outside of °the house round about, and in the [3]man's hand a measuring reed of six °cubits *long* by the °cubit and an hand breadth: so °he measured the breadth of the °building, one [3]reed; and the height, one [3]reed.

6 Then came he unto the gate which looketh toward the east, and went up the stairs thereof, and measured the threshold of the gate, *which was* one [3]reed broad; and °the other threshold *of the gate, which was* one [3]reed broad.

7 And *every* °little chamber *was* one [3]reed long, and one [3]reed broad; and between the little chambers *were* five cubits; and the threshold of the gate by the porch of the gate °within *was* one [3]reed.

8 °He measured also the porch of the gate within, one [3]reed.

9 Then measured he the porch of the gate, eight [5]cubits; and the °posts thereof, two [5]cubits; and the porch of the gate *was* °inward.

10 And the [7]little chambers of the gate eastward *were* three on this side, and three on that side; they three *were* of one measure: and the [9]posts had one measure on this side and on that side.

11 And he measured the breadth of the °entry of the gate, ten [5]cubits; *and* the °length of the gate, thirteen [5]cubits.

12 The °space also before the [7]little chambers *was* one [5]cubit *on this side,* and the space *was* one [5]cubit on that side: and the [7]little chambers *were* six [5]cubits on this side, and six [5]cubits on that side.

13 He measured then the gate from the roof of *one* [7]little chamber to the roof of another: the breadth *was* five and twenty [5]cubits, °door against °door.

14 He °made also [9]posts of threescore [5]cubits, even unto the [9]post of the court round about the gate.

15 And from the °face of the gate of the entrance unto the face of the porch of the inner gate *were* fifty [5]cubits.

16 And *there were* °narrow windows to the [7]little chambers, and to their [9]posts within the gate round about, and likewise to the °arches: and windows *were* round about °inward: and °upon *each* [9]post *were* °palm trees.

K[2] L[1] b[1] 17 Then brought he me into the outward

the city was smitten. The fall of Jerusalem is thus fixed as happening in the eleventh year of the captivity. See the table on p. 1105.
the hand. Cp. 3. 14.
the LORD. Heb. Jehovah. Ap. 4. II
2 visions of God. Cp. 1. 1; 8. 3; 43. 3.
God. Heb. Elohim. Ap 4. I.
the land of Israel. One of the three occurrences in Ezekiel with *'eretz* instead of *'admath.* See notes on 27. 17; and cp. note on 11. 17.
upon a very high mountain. Cp. 17. 22, 23. Isa. 2. 2.
by: or, upon. **frame**=fabric, or structure.
3 behold. Fig. *Asterismos.* Ap. 6.
man. Heb. *'ish.* Ap. 14. II.
reed. See Ap. 51. III. 2 (2).
4 Son of man. See note on 2. 1.

40. 5—42. 20 (F[1], p. 1163). **THE HOUSE ITSELF.** (*Extended Alternation.*)

F[1] | G | 40. 5-43. The Inclosures.
H | 40. 44-46. The Priests' rooms.
J | 40. 47. The Court. Its size and shape.
G | 40. 48—41. 26. The Inner House, or Temple.
H | 42. 1-14. The Priests' rooms.
J | 42. 15-20. The outer place. Its size and shape.

40. 5-43 (G, above). **THE INCLOSURES.** (*Division.*)

G | K[1] | 5-16. The Outer Wall and Gates.
K[2] | 17-43. The Outer and Inner Courts.

5 behold. Fig. *Asterismos.* Ap. 6.
on the: or, went on.
the house: i.e. the Temple.
cubits. See Ap. 51. III. 2 (1).
he measured. In all the measurements the unit is one-seventh longer than Solomon's Temple, pointing to the eighth, the day of God. Seven speaks of completion. Eight speaks of a new beginning (see Ap. 10). In "the day of God" all things will be new.
building: i.e. the wall and its contents.
6 the other: viz. that mentioned in *v.* 7.
7 little. This word may well be omitted.
within. R.V.=toward the house.
8 He measured, &c. Verse 8 is not found in the Sept., Syr., or Vulg. It may be the latter clause of *v.* 7 copied again through human infirmity.
9 posts: or projections, coigns or small turrets.
inward=toward [the house].
11 entry=entrance, or doorway.
length=extent, or way.
12 space=barrier, border, or parapet.
13 door=entrance.
14 made: or, measured.
15 face=front.
16 narrow=latticed. Cp. 41. 16, 26. 1 Kings 6. 4.
arches=projections, or porches.
inward: or, within. **upon**=against.
palm trees. Artificial. Cp. 41. 18.

40. 17-43 (K[2], above). **THE OUTER AND INNER COURT.** (*Repeated and Extended Alternation.*)

K[2] | L[1] | b[1] | 17-22-. North Gate.
c[1] | -22. Seven steps.
d[1] | 23. Opposite Inner Gate.
L[2] | b[2] | 24, 25. South Gate.
c[2] | 26. Seven steps.
d[2] | 27. Opposite Inner Gate.
} The Outer Court.
L[3] | b[3] | 28. South Gate.
c[3] | 29, 30. Chambers, &c.
d[3] | 31. Porches. Eight steps.
L[4] | b[4] | 32. East Gate.
c[4] | 33. Chambers, &c.
d[4] | 34. Porches. Eight steps.
L[5] | b[5] | 35. North Gate.
c[5] | 36. Chambers, &c.
d[5] | 37-43. Porches. Eight steps.
} The Inner Court.

465 court, and, °lo, *there were* °chambers, and a
°pavement made for the court round about:
°thirty °chambers *were* upon the °pavement.
18 And the [17]pavement by the °side of the
gates °over against the length of the gates
was the lower pavement.
19 Then he measured the breadth from the
forefront of the lower gate unto the forefront
of the inner court °without, an hundred [5]cubits
eastward and northward.
20 And the gate of the outward court that
looked toward the north, he measured the
length thereof, and the breadth thereof.
21 And the [7]little chambers thereof *were* three
on this side and three on that side; and the
[9]posts thereof and the [16]arches thereof were
after the measure of the first gate: the length
thereof *was* fifty [5]cubits, and the breadth five
and twenty [5]cubits.
22 And their windows, and their [16]arches, and
their [16]palm trees, *were* after the measure of
the gate that looketh toward the east;
c1 and they went up unto it by °seven steps; and
(p. 1164) the [16]arches thereof *were* before them.
d1 23 And the gate of the inner court *was* over
against the gate toward the north, and toward
the east; and he measured from gate to gate
an hundred [5]cubits.
L2 b2 24 After that he brought me toward the south,
and behold a gate toward the south: and he
measured the [9]posts thereof and the [16]arches
thereof according to °these measures.
25 And *there were* windows in it and in the
arches thereof round about, like those windows: the length *was* fifty [5]cubits, and the
breadth five and twenty [5]cubits.
c2 26 And *there were* [22]seven steps to go up to
it, and the arches thereof *were* before them:
and it had [16]palm trees, one on this side, and
another on that side, upon the [9]posts thereof.
d2 27 And *there was* a gate in the inner court
toward the south: and he measured from gate
to gate toward the south an hundred [5]cubits.
L3 b3 28 And he brought me to the inner court by
the south gate: and he measured the south
gate according to [24]these measures;
c3 29 And the [7]little chambers thereof, and the
posts thereof, and the [16]arches thereof, according to [24]these measures: and *there were* windows in it and in the [16]arches thereof round
[16]about: *it was* fifty [5]cubits long, and five and
twenty [5]cubits broad.
30 And the [16]arches round about *were* five
and twenty [5]cubits long, and five cubits broad.
d3 31 And the [16]arches thereof *were* toward the
°utter court; and [16]palm trees *were* upon the
[9]posts thereof: and the °going up to it *had*
°eight steps.
L4 b4 32 And he brought me into the inner court
toward the east: and he measured the gate
according to [24]these measures.
c4 33 And the [7]little chambers thereof, and the
[9]posts thereof, and the [16]arches thereof, *were*
according to [24]these measures: and *there were*
windows therein and in the [16]arches thereof
round about: *it was* fifty [5]cubits long, and five
and twenty [5]cubits broad.
34 And the [16]arches thereof *were* toward the d4
outward court; and [16]palm trees *were* upon (p. 1164)
the [9]posts thereof, on this side, and on that
side: and the going up to it *had* [31]eight steps.
35 And he brought me to the north gate, and L5 b5
measured *it* according to [24]these measures;
36 The [7]little chambers thereof, the posts c5
thereof, and the [16]arches thereof, and the
windows to it round about: the length *was*
fifty [5]cubits, and the breadth five and twenty
[5]cubits.
37 And the [9]posts thereof *were* toward the d5
utter court; and [16]palm trees *were* upon the
[9]posts thereof, on this side, and on that side:
and the going up to it *had* [31]eight steps.
38 And the [17]chambers and the entries thereof
were by the [9]posts of the gates, where they
°washed the °burnt offering.
39 And in the porch of the gate *were* two
tables on this side, and two tables on that side,
to slay thereon the [38]burnt offering and the °sin
offering and the °trespass offering.
40 And at the side without, as one goeth up
to the entry of the north gate, *were* two tables;
and on the other side, which *was* at the porch
of the gate, *were* two tables.
41 Four tables *were* on this side, and four
tables on that side, by the side of the gate;
eight tables, whereupon °they slew *their sacrifices.*
42 And the four tables *were* of °hewn stone
for the [38]burnt offering, of a [5]cubit and an half
long, and a [5]cubit and an half broad, and one
[5]cubit high: whereupon also they laid the instruments wherewith they slew the [38]burnt
offering and the sacrifice.
43 And within *were* °hooks, an hand broad,

17 lo. Fig. *Asterismos*. Ap. 6.
chambers = attachments. Always rendered "chambers", except 1 Sam. 9. 22, where it is "parlour". These chambers or storerooms are for the priests and Levites, and for the tithes and offerings. Not the same word as in *vv.* 7, 7, 10, 12, 12, 13, 16, 21, 29, 33, 36; but the same as *vv.* 38, 44, 45, 46. See note on 41. 5.
pavement. Stones ranged artificially. Probably tesselated. Cp. John 19. 13.
thirty. Probably ten on each of the three sides of the court, in clusters of five on each of the sides of the three gates.
18 side = shoulder. **over against.** Or, all along.
19 without = from without.
22 seven steps. These are the steps to the outer gates, and distinct from the "eight" of the inner court. Neither have anything to do with the fifteen steps of the "Songs of the Degrees". See Ap. 67.
24 these measures. This phrase is repeated in *vv.* 28, 29, 32, 33, 35: showing the conformity of the whole plan.
31 utter = outer. **going up** = ascent.
eight steps. These were in the inner court. See note on "seven", *v.* 22.
38 washed. Or, took out the entrails of.
burnt offering. See Ap. 43. II. ii. See note on "ordinances", 43. 18.
39 sin offering. See Ap. 43. II. v.
trespass offering. See Ap. 43. II. vi.
41 they slew, &c. = their slaying [was done].
42 hewn stone. The other eight (*v.* 41) were probably of wood.
43 hooks = the ranges.

465 fastened round about: and upon the tables *was*
the flesh of the °offering.

H e (p. 1166) 44 And without the inner gate *were* the
[17]chambers of the singers in the inner court,
which *was* at the [18]side of the north gate; and
their prospect *was* toward the south:

f one at the side of the east gate *having* the
prospect toward the north.

e 45 And he said unto me, "This [17]chamber,
whose prospect *is* toward the south, *is* for the
priests, the keepers of the charge of the house.

f 46 And the [17]chamber whose prospect *is* toward the north *is* for the priests, the keepers
of the charge of the altar: *these are* the sons of
°Zadok among the sons of Levi, which come
near to [1]the LORD to minister unto Him."

J (p. 1164) 47 So he measured the court, an hundred
[5]cubits long, and an hundred [5]cubits broad,
°foursquare; and the altar *that was* before the
house.

G M g (p. 1166) 48 And he brought me to the °porch of the
house, and measured *each* [9]post of the porch,
five [5]cubits on this side, and five [5]cubits on
that side: and the breadth of the gate *was*
three [5]cubits on this side, and three [5]cubits on
that side.

49 The length of the porch *was* twenty
[5]cubits, and the breadth eleven [5]cubits; and
he brought me by the steps whereby they
went up to it: and *there were* pillars by the
[9]posts, one on this side, and another on that
side.

h **41** Afterward he brought me to the °tem-
ple, and measured the °posts, six °cubits
broad on the one side, and six °cubits broad on
the other side, °*which was* the breadth of the
°tabernacle.

2 And the breadth of the °door *was* ten
[1]cubits; and the °sides of the °door *were* five
[1]cubits on the one side, and five [1]cubits on
the other side: and he measured the length
thereof, forty [1]cubits: and the breadth, twenty
[1]cubits.

3 Then went he inward, and measured the
[1]post of the door, two [1]cubits; and the [2]door,
six [1]cubits; and the breadth of the [2]door,
seven [1]cubits.

N 4 So he measured the length thereof, twenty
[1]cubits; and the breadth, twenty [1]cubits, before
the [1]temple: and he said unto me, "This *is* °the
most holy *place*."

M g 5 After he measured the wall of the house,
six [1]cubits; and the breadth of *every* °side
chamber, four [1]cubits, round about the house
on every side.

6 And the [5]side chambers *were* three, one
over another, and thirty in order; and they
entered into the wall which *was* of the house
for the [5]side chambers round about, that they
might have hold, but they had not hold in the
wall of the house.

7 And *there was* °an enlarging, and a winding
about still upward to the [5]side chambers: for
the winding about of the house went still upward round about the house: therefore the
breadth of the house *was still* upward, and so

offering = corban.

40. 44-46 (H, p. 1164). THE PRIESTS' ROOMS.
(*Alternation.*)

H | e | 44-. South Prospect. } Situation.
  f | -44. North Prospect.
  e | 45. South Prospect. } Use.
  f | 46. North Prospect.

46 Zadok among = Zadok: those from.

47 foursquare. Cp. 48. 20 and Rev. 21. 16.

40. 48—41. 26 (*G*, p. 1164). THE INNER HOUSE.
(*Alternations.*)

G | M | g | 40. 48, 49. The Porch.
    h | 41. 1-3. The Temple.
  N | 41. 4. The Most Holy Place.
  M | *g* | 41. 5-11. The Porch.
    h | 41. 12-15. The Temple.
  N | 41. 16-26. The Most Holy Place.

48 porch = vestibule.

41. 1 temple = palace. Heb. *heykāl.*
posts = projections. The Sept. reads "post."
cubits. See Ap. 51. III. 2 (1).
which was. Omit these words, and commence *v.* 2
with the clause which follows.
tabernacle = tent. Heb. *'ohel.* See Ap. 40. 3.

2 door = entrance. sides = shoulders.

4 the most holy place = the Holy of Holies.

5 side chamber. Not the same word for "chamber"
as in *v.* 10 and ch. 40. 7, 7, 10, 12, 12, 13, 16, 21, 29, 33, 36
(which is *tā'*); or in 40. 17, 17, 38, 44, 45, 46; or in 42. 1, 4,
5, 7, 7, 8, 9, 10, 11, 12, 13, 13, 13; or in 44. 19; 45. 5; 46. 19
(which is *lishkāh* = a storeroom).

7 an enlarging = a broadening.

8 the height of the house = that the house had an
elevation or platform. reed. See Ap. 51. III. 2 (3).

10 chambers = storerooms. Heb. *lishkāh.* See note
on *v.* 5.

15 galleries. Heb. *'attīḳ.* Occurs only here, *v.* 16,
and 42. 3, 5. Probably from *nataḳ*, to cut away, but in
what sense is obscure. Perhaps balconies.

increased *from* the lowest *chamber* to the
highest by the midst.

8 I saw also °the height of the house round
about: the foundations of the [5]side chambers
were a full °reed of six great [1]cubits.

9 The thickness of the wall, which *was* for
the [5]side chamber without, *was* five [1]cubits:
and *that* which *was* left *was* the place of the
[5]side chambers that *were* within.

10 And between the °chambers *was* the
wideness of twenty [1]cubits round about the
house on every side.

11 And the [2]doors of the [5]side chambers *were*
toward *the place that was* left, one door toward the north, and another [2]door toward the
south: and the breadth of the place that was
left *was* five [1]cubits round about.

12 Now the building that *was* before the *h*
separate place at the end toward the west *was*
seventy [1]cubits broad; and the wall of the
building *was* five [1]cubits thick round about,
and the length thereof ninety [1]cubits.

13 So he measured the house, an hundred
[1]cubits long; and the separate place, and the
building, with the walls thereof, an hundred
[1]cubits long;

14 Also the breadth of the face of the house,
and of the separate place toward the east, an
hundred [1]cubits.

15 And he measured the length of the building over against the separate place which *was*
behind it, and the °galleries thereof on the one

467 side and on the other side, an hundred [1] cubits,
with the inner temple, and the porches of the
court;
N O i (p. 1167) 16 The °door posts, and the °narrow windows, and the [15] galleries round about on their
three stories, over against the [2] door, °cieled
with wood round about, and from the ground
up to the windows, and the windows *were*
covered;
17 To that above the [2] door, even unto the inner house, and without, and by all the wall
round about within and without, °by measure.
k 18 And *it was* made with °cherubims and
°palm trees, so that a °palm tree *was* between
a cherub and a cherub; and *every* cherub had
two faces;
19 So that the face of a °man *was* toward
the palm tree on the one side, and the face of
a young lion toward the palm tree on the other
side: *it was* made through all the house round
about.
20 From the ground unto above the [2] door
were cherubims and palm trees made, °and *on*
the wall of °the temple.
21 The °posts of [20] the temple *were* squared,
and the face of the sanctuary; the appearance
of the one as the appearance *of the other*.
P 22 The altar of wood *was* three [1] cubits high,
and the length thereof two [1] cubits; and the
corners thereof, and the length thereof, and
the walls thereof, *were* of wood: and he said
unto me, "This *is* the table that *is* before °the
LORD."
O *i* 23 And the temple and the sanctuary had
two doors.
24 And the doors had two leaves *apiece*, two
turning leaves; two *leaves* for the one door,
and two leaves for the other *door*.
k 25 And *there were* made on them, on the
doors of the temple, [18] cherubims and [18] palm
trees, like as *were* made upon the walls; and
there were thick planks upon the face of the
porch without.
26 And *there were* [16] narrow windows and
palm trees on the one side and on the other
side, on the [2] sides of the porch, and *upon* the
[5] side chambers of the house, and thick planks.

H Q[1] **42** Then he brought me forth into the °utter court, the way toward the north:
and he brought me into the °chamber that *was*
over against the separate place, and which
was before the building toward the north.
2 Before the length of an hundred °cubits
was the north °door, and the breadth *was* fifty
°cubits.
3 Over against the twenty *cubits* which *were*
for the inner court, and over against the
°pavement which *was* for the [1] utter court,
was °gallery against °gallery in three *stories*.
4 And before the [1] chambers *was* a walk of
ten [2] cubits breadth inward, a way of one [2] cubit; and their doors toward the north.
5 Now the upper [1] chambers *were* shorter: for
the [3] galleries °were higher than these, than
the lower, and than the middlemost of the
building.
6 For they *were* in three *stories*, but had not

41. 16-26 (*N*, p. 1166). THE MOST HOLY PLACE.
(*Introversion and Alternation.*)

N | O | i | 16, 17. Walls.
k | 18-21. Cherubim.
P | 22. Altar of Wood.
O | *i* | 23, 24. Doors.
k | 25, 26. Cherubim.

16 door posts = thresholds.
narrow = latticed. See note on 40. 16.
cieled = overlaid, panelled, or wainscoted.
17 by measure. Showing that every detail, however small, is important.
18 cherubims. See Ap. 41.
palm trees: i. e. artificial palm trees.
19 man. Heb. *'ādām*. Ap. 14. I.
20 and on the wall of the temple. Render: And as for the wall of the temple, the door-posts were squared; and, as for the face of the sanctuary, the appearance, &c. (as in *v.* 20).
the temple. This word has the extraordinary points (Ap. 31), the dots indicating that the word is repeated by mistake from *v.* 20.
21 posts = post. Sing. Only here and 1 Sam. 1. 9.
22 the LORD. Heb. Jehovah. Ap. 4. II.

42. 1-14 (*H*, p. 1164). THE PRIESTS' ROOMS.
(*Division.*)

H | Q[1] | 1-12. The Rooms.
| Q[2] | 13, 14. Their Uses.

1 utter = outer.
chamber = storeroom. Heb. *lishkāh*. See note on 40. 17.
2 cubits. See Ap. 51. III. 2 (1).
door = entrance.
3 pavement. See note on 40. 17.
gallery. See note on 41. 15.
5 were higher than = took away from.
8 lo. Fig. *Asterismos*. Ap. 6.
before the temple = towards the holy place.
9 from under these chambers = underneath were these chambers.
was the entry = the entrance [was].
11 fashions. Place a full stop here, and begin: "And according", &c.

pillars as the pillars of the courts: therefore
the building was straitened more than the
lowest and the middlemost from the ground.
7 And the wall that *was* without over against
the [1] chambers, toward the utter court on the
forepart of the [1] chambers, the length thereof
was fifty [2] cubits.
8 For the length of the [1] chambers that *were*
in the [1] utter court *was* fifty [2] cubits: and, °lo,
°before the temple *were* an hundred [2] cubits.
9 And °from under these [1] chambers °*was*
the entry on the east side, as one goeth into
them from the [1] utter court.
10 The [1] chambers *were* in the thickness of
the wall of the court toward the east, over
against the separate place, and over against
the building.
11 And the way before them *was* like the appearance of the [1] chambers which *were* toward
the north, as long as they, *and* as broad as
they: and all their goings out *were* both according to their °fashions, and according to
their [2] doors.
12 And according to the doors of the [1] chambers that *were* toward the south *was* a [2] door
in the head of the way, *even* the way directly
before the wall toward the east, as one entereth into them.
13 Then said he unto me, "The north [1] chambers *and* the south [1] chambers, which *are* Q[2]

465 before the separate place, they *be* °holy [1] chambers, °where the priests that approach unto
°the LORD shall eat the most °holy things:
there shall they lay the most °holy things, and
the °meat offering, and the °sin offering, and
the trespass offering; for the place *is* °holy.
14 When the priests enter therein, then shall
they not go out of the [13]holy *place* into the
[1]utter court, but there they shall lay their
garments wherein they minister; for they *are*
[13]holy; and shall put on other garments, and
shall approach to *those things* which *are* for
the people."

J l (p. 1168) 15 Now when he had made an end of measuring the inner house, he brought me forth toward the gate whose prospect *is* toward the
east, and measured it round about.

m 16 He measured the east °side with the measuring °reed, five hundred °reeds, with the
measuring °reed round about.

n 17 He measured the north [16]side, five hundred
[16]reeds, with °the measuring [16]reed round about.

n 18 He measured the south [16]side, five hundred
reeds, with the measuring [16]reed.

m 19 He turned about to the °west [16]side, *and*
measured five hundred [16]reeds with the measuring [16]reed.

l 20 He measured it by the four [16]sides: it had
a wall round about, five hundred *reeds* long,
and five hundred broad, to make a separation
between the sanctuary and the profane place.

C[2] D[2] (p. 1163) **43** Afterward he brought me to the gate,
even the gate that looketh toward the
east:
2 And, behold, °the glory of °the °God of Israel came from the way of the east: and His
voice *was* like a noise of many waters: and
the earth shined with His glory.
3 And *it was* according to the appearance of
the vision which I saw, *even* according to the
vision °that I saw when I came °to destroy
the city: and the visions *were* like the vision
that I saw by the river Chebar; and I fell
upon my face.
4 And the glory of °the LORD came into °the
house by the way of °the gate whose prospect
is toward the east.
5 So the °spirit took me up, and brought me
into the inner court; and, behold, [2]the glory
of [4]the LORD filled [4]the house.
6 And I heard *Him* speaking unto me out of
the house; and °the man °stood by me.

E[2] 7 And He said unto me, °"Son of man, °the
place of My throne, and the place of the soles
of My feet, °where °I will dwell in the midst
of the °children of Israel °for ever; and My
°holy name, shall the house of Israel °no more
defile, *neither* they, nor their kings, by their
°whoredom, nor °by the carcases of their
kings °in their high places.
8 In their °setting of their threshold by My
thresholds, and their post °by My posts, °and
the wall between Me and them, they have
even defiled My [7]holy name by their °abomina-
tions that they have committed: wherefore I
have consumed them in Mine anger.
9 Now let them put away their [7]whoredom,
and the carcases of their kings, far from Me,
and I will dwell in the midst of them for ever.
10 °Thou [7]son of man, °shew the house to the
house of Israel, that they may be ashamed of
their °iniquities: and °let them measure the
°pattern.
11 And if they be ashamed of all that they
have done, [10]shew them the form of the house,

13 holy. See note on Ex. 3. 5.
holy chambers = the chambers of the holy place.
where, &c. Ref. to Pent. (Lev. 6. 16, 26; 24. 9). Ap. 92.
the LORD. Heb. Jehovah. Ap. 4. II.
meat offering = the gift offering. Heb. *minchah.* Ap. 43. II. iii. Ref. to Pent. (Lev. 2. 3, &c.). Ap. 92.
sin offering. Heb. *chattath.* Ap. 43. II. v.

42. 15-20 (*J*, p. 1164). THE OUTER PLACE. (*Introversion.*)

J | l | 15. The circumference.
m | 16. East side.
n | 17. North side.
n | 18. South side.
m | 19. West side.
l | 20. The circumference.

16 side = wind. Heb. *rūach.* Ap. 9.
reeds. See Ap. 51. III. 2 (3).
19 west. Heb. "sea", put for the "side" on which the sea was: i.e. the west.

43. 2 the glory. In 11. 23 he had seen this glory quitting the Temple.
the God of Israel. See note on Isa. 29. 23.
God. Heb. Elohim. Ap. 4. I.
3 that I saw. See 1. 28; 3. 23.
to destroy. Heb. idiom, by which the doer is said to do what he declares shall be done. See 9. 1, 5; note on Jer. 14. 8, 9; 20. 25.
4 the LORD. Heb. Jehovah. Ap. 4. II.
the house. Not Solomon's Temple, but the Temple which he had been shown in vision (chs. 41 and 42).
the gate. Not the present gate on the east side of the Temple area, but that of the yet future Temple (40. 6; 42. 15; 44. 1; 46. 1).
5 spirit. See note on 8. 3. Heb. *rūach.* Ap. 9.
6 the man. Heb. *'ish.* Ap. 14. II.
stood = was standing.
7 Son of man. See note on 2. 1.
the place of My throne. The *Ellipsis* must be thus supplied: "[This is] the place", &c. Not the ark, as in Solomon's Temple. There is no ark here.
where I will dwell, &c. See *v.* 9; 37. 26, 28; 48. 35. Pss. 68. 18; 132. 14. Joel 3. 17.
I will dwell, &c. Ref. to Pent. (Ex. 29. 45).
children = sons.
for ever. Showing that this prophecy yet waits for its fulfilment. **holy.** See note on Ex. 3. 5.
no more defile. Cp. 20. 39; 23. 38, 39; 39. 7. Hos. 14. 8. Zech. 13. 2; 14. 20, 21.
whoredom. Always put for idolatry, by the Fig. *Metonymy* (of the Subject), Ap. 6.
by the carcases, &c. Ref. to Pent. (Lev. 26. 30).
in their high places: or, in their death.
8 setting, &c. Cp. 5. 11; 8. 3-16; 23. 39; 44. 7. 2 Kings 16. 14, 15; 21. 4-7; 23. 11, 12. 2 Chron. 33. 4, 7.
by = close by, alongside of.
and the wall: or, "For [there was but a] wall".
abominations = idolatries.
10 Thou. Some codices, with Sept., Syr., and Vulg., read "Thou therefore". This is yet future, and involves the fulfilment of ch. 37, for Ezekiel and for the whole nation.
shew the house . . . let them measure. This will be the evidence, to the new nation, that all this prophecy, and Ezekiel's part in it, is of Jehovah.
iniquities. Heb. *'āvāh.* Ap. 44. iv.
pattern: or, plan, or arrangement.

465 and the fashion thereof, and the °goings out
thereof, and the °comings in thereof, and all
the °forms thereof, and all the ordinances
thereof, and all the °forms thereof, and all
the °laws thereof: and write *it* in their
sight, that they may keep the whole form
thereof, and all the ordinances thereof, and do
them.
12 This °*is* the law of the house; °Upon the
top of the mountain the whole limit thereof
round about *shall be* °most °holy. °Behold,
this °*is* the law of the house.
F² R¹ (p. 1169) 13 And these *are* the measures of °the altar
after the °cubits: The °cubit *is* a °cubit and
an hand breadth; even the bottom *shall be*
a °cubit, and the breadth a °cubit, and the
border thereof by the edge thereof round about
shall be a span: and this *shall be* the °higher
place of °the altar.
14 And from the °bottom *upon* the ground
even to the lower °settle *shall be* two [13]cubits,
and the breadth one [13]cubit; and from the
lesser °settle *even* to the greater °settle *shall
be* four [13]cubits, and the breadth *one* [13]cubit.
15 So °the altar *shall be* four [13]cubits; and
from °the altar and upward *shall be* four
horns.
16 And [15]the altar *shall be* twelve *cubits*
long, twelve broad, square in the four squares
thereof.
17 And the [14]settle *shall be* fourteen *cubits*
long and fourteen broad in the four squares
thereof; and the border about it *shall be* half
a [13]cubit; and the bottom thereof *shall be* a
[13]cubit about; and his °stairs shall look toward
the east."
R² o 18 And he said unto me, [7]"Son of man, °thus
saith °the Lord GOD; 'These *are* °the ordinances of the altar °in the day when they
shall make it, to offer °burnt offerings thereon,
and to °sprinkle blood thereon.
19 And °thou shalt give to °the priests the
Levites that be of the seed of Zadok, which
approach unto Me, to minister unto Me, °saith
[18]the Lord GOD, a young °bullock for a °sin
offering.
20 And thou shalt take of the blood thereof,
and put *it* on the four horns of it, and on the
four corners of the [14]settle, and upon the border
round about: thus shalt thou cleanse and
purge it.
21 Thou shalt take the bullock also of the
[19]sin offering, and °he shall burn it in the
appointed place of the house, without the sanctuary.
p 22 And on the second day thou shalt offer
a kid of the goats without blemish for a [19]sin
offering; and they shall cleanse the altar, as
they did cleanse *it* with the bullock.
23 When thou hast made an end of cleansing
it, thou shalt offer a young bullock without
blemish, and a ram out of the flock without
blemish.
24 And thou shalt offer them before [4]the
LORD, and the priests shall °cast salt upon
them, and they shall offer them up *for* a burnt
offering unto [4]the LORD.
o 25 Seven days shalt thou prepare every day
a goat *for* a [19]sin offering: they shall also pre-

goings out = the exits.
comings in = the entrances.
forms = models, or visible forms. The word is found only in this verse. Heb. text written "form"; but marg. "forms".
laws. Heb. text written "law"; but marg. "laws". Some codices, with four early printed editions, read "laws" both in text and margin.
12 is. Supply "will be".
Upon, &c. Cp. 40. 2; 42. 20. Ps. 93. 5. Joel 3. 17. Zech. 14. 20, 21. Rev. 21. 27.
most holy = the holy of holies.
holy. See note on Ex. 3. 5.
Behold. Fig. *Asterismos* (Ap. 6), for emphasis.

43. 13-27 (F², p. 1163). THE ALTAR, ETC. (*Division.*)

F² | R¹ | 13-17. The Altar. Itself.
| R² | 18-27. The Altar. Its ordinances.

13 the altar. Heb. *mizbeach.* Same word as in *v.* 18; not the same as in *vv.* 15, 16.
cubits. See Ap. 51. III. 2 (1).
higher place = the pit: i.e. the ash-pit. Heb. *gab* = anything curved or convex, from *gabab* = hollow, hollowed out.
14 bottom = hollow.
settle = ledge. The Heb. word in this sense occurs only here, *vv.* 17, 20, and 45. 19. The altar will be thus narrowed at the top (twelve cubits square). The height and breadth will be the same as Solomon's, except that this will have these ledges for the priests to walk round.
15 the altar = the hearth. Heb. *ha harēl* = the mount of El. Not the same word as in *v.* 13.
17 stairs. Steps were forbidden in Ex. 20. 26: but may be permitted here.

43. 18-27 (R², above). THE ALTAR. ITS ORDINANCES. (*Alternation.*)

R² | o | 18-21. First day. } Separate.
| p | 22-24. Second day. }
| *o* | 25, 26. Seven days. } Collective.
| *p* | 27. Eighth day. }

18 thus saith, &c. See note on 44. 9.
the Lord GOD. Heb. Adonai Jehovah. See note on 2. 4.
the ordinances of the altar. Compared with the Mosaic tabernacle, the ritual began with the consecration of the priests (Lev. 8. 1-10); here, they are already consecrated (*vv.* 19, 26). In Lev. 8. 11, the altar was anointed with the holy oil; here no anointing, and the priests are only from Zadok's line (cp. 40. 46; 44. 15). In Ex. 29. 36, a bullock offered on seven successive days; here only once, and on the other days a kid of the goats. The offerings here (*vv.* 18-27) are *National* and *Priestly* (the Priest representing the Nation); not *individual,* for there will be no day of atonement. The sacrifices will not therefore be as when under the law.
in the day. See Ap. 18. This day is yet future.
burnt offerings. See Ap. 43. II. ii.
sprinkle, &c. = dash, or throw. Ref. to Pent. (Lev. 1. 5). This expression is exclusively technical. Ap. 92. For the exceptions see 2 Chron. 34. 4. Job 2. 12. Isa. 28. 5. Cp. Ezek. 10. 2 and Hos. 7. 9.
19 thou. Testifying to the share of Ezekiel "in the day when", &c.
the priests the Levites. Referring to the distinction between the Levitical priests and all other priests (heathen, Israelitish, or tribal). See note on Deut. 17. 9.
saith the Lord GOD = [is] Jehovah's oracle.
bullock. See note on "ordinances", *v.* 18.
sin offering. Ref. to Pent. (Ex. 29. 14). Ap. 92.
21 he shall burn it. Ref. to Pent. (Ex. 29. 14).
24 cast salt. This was not done in this case under the Mosaic law. Cp. Lev. 2. 13. See Ap. 92.

465 pare a young bullock, and a ram out of the
flock, without blemish.
26 Seven days shall they °purge the altar and
purify it; and they shall °consecrate °them-
selves.
p 27 And when these days are expired, it shall
(p. 1169) be, *that* upon the eighth day, and *so* forward,
the priests shall make °your burnt offerings
upon the altar, and your peace offerings; and
°I will accept you, [19] saith [18] the Lord GOD."

C[3] D[3] **44** Then he brought me back the way of
(p. 1163) °the gate of the outward sanctuary
which looketh toward the east; and it *was*
shut.
2 Then said °the LORD unto me; "This gate
shall be shut, it shall not be opened, and no
°man shall enter in by it; because °the LORD,
°the °God of Israel, hath entered in by it, therefore it shall be shut.
3 °*It is* for °the prince; the prince, he shall
sit in it to eat bread before [2] the LORD; he
shall enter by the way of the porch of *that*
gate, and shall go out by the way of the
same."
4 Then brought he me the way of the north
gate before the house: and I looked, and, °be-
hold, the glory of [2] the LORD filled the house
of [2] the LORD: and I fell upon my face.

E[3] 5 And [2] the LORD said unto me, °"Son of
man, °mark well, and behold with thine eyes,
and hear with thine ears all that I say unto
thee concerning all the °ordinances of the house
of [2] the LORD, and all the °laws thereof; and
°mark well the °entering in of the house, with
every °going forth of the sanctuary.
6 And thou shalt say to the °rebellious, *even*
to the house of Israel, 'Thus saith °the Lord
GOD; 'O ye house of Israel, let it suffice you
of all your abominations,
7 In that ye have brought *into My sanctuary*
°strangers, °uncircumcised in heart, and uncircumcised in flesh, to be in My sanctuary, to
°pollute it, *even* My house, when ye °offer My
bread, °the fat and the blood, and °they have
broken My covenant because of all your abominations.
8 And °ye have not kept the charge of Mine
°holy things: but ye have set keepers of My
charge in My sanctuary for °yourselves.'

F[3] S[1] T q 9 °Thus saith [6] the Lord GOD; 'No °stranger,
(p. 1170) [7] uncircumcised in heart, nor uncircumcised in
flesh, shall enter into My sanctuary, of any
°stranger that *is* among the °children of
Israel.
10 And °the Levites that °are gone away far
from Me, when Israel went astray, which went
astray away from Me after their °idols; they
shall even bear their °iniquity.

r 11 °Yet they shall be ministers in My sanctuary, *having* charge at the gates of the house,
and ministering to the house: they shall slay
the burnt offering and the sacrifice °for the
People, and °they shall stand before them to
minister unto them.

U 12 Because they ministered unto them before
their [10] idols, and °caused the house of Israel to
fall into [10] iniquity; therefore have I lifted up
Mine hand against them, °saith [6] the Lord GOD,
and they shall bear their [10] iniquity.

13 And they shall °not come near unto Me, T q

26 purge=atone for.
consecrate. See note on Ex. 28. 41. Lev. 9. 17.
themselves=it.
27 your . . . you: i.e. nationally, not individually. See note on "ordinance", &c., *v.* 18.
I will accept you. Ref. to Pent. (Lev. 22. 27. Deut. 33. 11). Ap. 92.

44. 1 the gate of the outward sanctuary=the outer gate of the sanctuary.
2 the LORD. Heb. Jehovah. Ap. 4. II.
man. Heb. *'ish.* Ap. 14. II. Therefore the prince of *v.* 3 is more than man: either the risen David, or the Messiah Himself.
the God of Israel. See note on Isa. 29. 23.
God. Heb. Elohim. Ap. 4. I.
3 It is for the prince; the prince. Heb. The Prince! as prince: i.e. the risen David, the Vice-regent of the Messiah (34. 23, 24; 37. 24, 25); or, the Messiah Himself. See note on "man", *v.* 2.
4 behold. Fig. *Asterismos.* Ap. 6.
5 Son of man. See note on 2. 1.
mark well=set thine heart.
ordinances=statutes.
laws. Heb. text "law"; but marg. and some codices, with four early printed editions, read "laws".
entering in=entrance. **going forth**=outgoings.
6 rebellious. Heb. rebellion, put by Fig. *Metonymy* (of Adjunct), Ap. 6, for rebellious people.
the Lord GOD. Heb. Adonai Jehovah. See note on 2. 4.
7 strangers=aliens. Heb. "sons of the foreigner".
uncircumcised in heart. Ref. to Pent. (Lev. 26. 41. Deut. 10. 16). Ap. 92. Cp. Jer. 9. 25, 26.
pollute=profane. **offer**=bring near.
the fat and the blood. Ref. to Pent. (Lev. 3. 16, 17).
they. Most of the ancient versions read "ye".
8 ye have not kept, &c. See 40. 46, &c.
holy. See note on Ex. 3. 5.
yourselves: i.e. your own pleasure.

44. 9-31 (F[3], p. 1163). **THE HOUSE. ITS ORDINANCES.** (*Division.*)

F[3] | S[1] | 9-14. The Levites.
 | S[2] | 15-31. The Priests.

44. 9-14 (S[1], above). **THE LEVITES.**
(*Introversion and Alternation.*)

S[1] | T | q | 9, 10. Prohibitions. (Negative.)
 | | r | 11. Ministry. (Positive.)
 | U | 12. Reason.
 | *T* | *q* | 13. Prohibitions. (Negative.)
 | | *r* | 14. Ministry. (Positive.)

9 Thus saith, &c. This emphatic commencement is repeated in 45. 9, 18; 46. 1, 16; 47. 13. Cp. 31. 10, 15; 43. 18.
stranger=foreigner. **children**=sons.
10 the Levites. These are distinguished here from the priests (15-27); see S[1] and S[2], above and consult note on 43. 19; and Deut. 17. 9.
are gone away=went astray.
idols=dirty idols.
iniquity. Put by Fig. *Metonymy* (of Cause), Ap. 6, for the punishment due to it. Heb. *'āvāh.* Ap. 44. iv.
11 Yet. Refers to the portion of service reserved for these Levites.
for the People: i.e. the Nation. See note on "ordinances", 43. 18.
they shall stand. Ref. to Pent. (Deut. 10. 8). Ap. 92. Cp. *v.* 15 and Num. 16. 9.
12 caused, &c.=were to the house of Israel for a stumblingblock of iniquity.
saith the Lord GOD=[is] Adonai Jehovah's oracle.
13 not come near unto Me. This is to be the punishment in the coming future order.

465 to do the office of a °priest unto Me, nor to
come near to any of My [8]holy things, in the
°most holy *place:* but they shall bear their
shame, and their abominations which they
have committed.

r 14 But I will make them keepers of the charge
(p. 1170) of the house, for all the service thereof, and
for all that shall be done therein.

S² V s 15 But [13]the priests the Levites, the sons of
(p. 1171) Zadok, that kept the charge of My sanctuary
when the [9]children of Israel went astray from
Me, they shall come near to Me to minister
unto Me, and [11]they shall stand before Me to
[7]offer unto Me [7]the fat and the blood, [12]saith
[6]the Lord GOD:

16 They shall enter into My sanctuary, and
they shall come near to My table, to minister
unto Me, and they shall keep My charge.

t 17 And it shall come to pass, *that* when they
enter in at the gates of the inner court, °they
shall be clothed with linen garments; and no
wool shall come upon them, whiles they
minister in the gates of the inner court, and
°within.

18 They shall have linen °bonnets upon their
heads, and shall have linen breeches upon
their loins; °they shall not gird *themselves*
°with any thing that causeth sweat.

19 And when they go forth into the °utter
court, *even* into the °utter court to the People,
they shall put off their garments wherein they
ministered, and lay them in the [8]holy °cham-
bers, °and they shall put on other garments;
and they shall not sanctify the People with
their garments.

20 °Neither shall they shave their heads, nor
suffer their locks to grow long; they shall
°only poll their heads.

21 °Neither shall any priest drink °wine,
°when they enter into the inner court.

22 °Neither shall they take for their wives
a widow, nor her that is put away: but they
shall take maidens of the seed of the house of
Israel, or a widow that had a priest before.

W 23 °And they shall teach My People *the difference* between the [8]holy and °profane, and
cause °them to discern between the unclean
and the clean.

24 °And in °controversy they shall stand in
judgment; *and* they shall judge it according
to My judgments: and they shall keep My
laws and My statutes in all Mine °assemblies;
and °they shall hallow My sabbaths.

V t 25 °And they shall come at no dead °person
to defile themselves: but for father, or for
mother, or for son, or for daughter, °for brother, or for sister that hath had no husband,
they may defile themselves.

s 26 °And after he is cleansed, they shall reckon unto him seven days.

27 And °in the day that he goeth into the
sanctuary, unto the inner court, to minister in
the sanctuary, he shall [7]offer his °sin offering,
[12]saith [6]the Lord GOD.

W 28 And it shall be unto them for an inheritance: °I *am* their inheritance: and ye shall
give them no possession in Israel: I *am* their
possession.

29 They shall eat the meat offering, and the
[27]sin offering, and the trespass offering; and
°every dedicated thing in Israel shall be their's.

30 And the °first of all the firstfruits of all
things, and every °oblation of all, of every
sort of your °oblations, shall be the priest's:
ye shall also give unto the priest °the first of
your dough, that he may cause the blessing to
rest in thine house.

31 The priests shall not eat of any thing that
is °dead of itself, or torn, whether it be fowl
or beast.

---

a priest. See note on 43. 19.
most holy place = holy of holies.

44. 15-31 (S², p. 1170). THE PRIESTS.
(*Alternation and Introversion.*)

S² | V | s | 15, 16. Public. } Ceremonial.
| | t | 17–22. Personal. }
| W | 23, 24. Moral.
| V | t | 25. Personal. } Ceremonial.
| | s | 26, 27. Public. }
| W | 28–31. Moral.

17 they shall be clothed, &c. Ref. to Pent. (Ex. 28. 42). Ap. 92.
within = toward [the house].
18 bonnets = head-dresses, or turbans. Ref. to Pent. (Ex. 39. 28). Ap. 92. Cp. 24. 17. Isa. 61. 10.
they. Some codices, with Aram., Sept., and Vulg., read "and they".
with, &c. Heb. = "with sweat"; sweat being put by Fig. *Metonymy* (of Effect), Ap. 6, for that which causes sweat.
19 utter = outer.
chambers = storerooms. Heb. *lishkāh.* See note on 40. 17. Same word as 41 10; but not elsewhere in ch. 41.
and they shall. Heb. text of some codices reads "they shall"; and marg. "and shall". Cp. 42. 14.
20 Neither shall they, &c. Ref. to Pent. (Lev. 21. 5). Ap. 92.
only poll = surely clip.
21 Neither shall any, &c. Ref. to Pent. (Lev. 10. 9).
wine. Heb. *yayin.* See Ap. 27. I.
when, &c. They might do so at other times.
22 Neither shall they, &c. Ref. to Pent. (Lev. 21. 14). Ap. 92.
23 And they shall teach, &c. Ref. to Pent. (Lev. 10. 11). Ap. 92. profane = common.
them. The 1611 edition of the A.V. reads "men".
24 And in controversy, &c. Ref. to Pent. (Deut. 17. 9). Ap. 92. controversy = strife.
assemblies = appointed seasons.
they shall hallow, &c. Ref. to Pent. (Lev. 19. 30).
25 And they shall come, &c. Ref. to Pent. (Lev. 21. 1). Ap. 92.
person = human being. Heb. *'ādām.* Ap. 14. I.
for brother. Some codices, with one early printed edition, read "or for", completing the Fig. *Paradiastole* (Ap. 6).
26 And after he is cleansed . . . seven days. Ref. to Pent. (Num 6. 10, "on the eighth day"). Ap. 92.
27 in the day. See Ap. 18.
sin offering. Ap. 43. II. v.
28 I am their inheritance. Ref. to Pent. (Num. 18. 20. Deut. 10. 9; 18. 1, 2). Ap. 92.
29 every dedicated thing, &c. Ref. to Pent. (Num. 18. 14). A verbal reference. Ap. 92.
30 first of all, &c. Ref. to Pent. (Ex. 13. 2; 22. 29, 30; 23. 19. Num. 3. 13; 18. 12, 13).
oblation = heave offering. Heb. *terūmah.* See note on Ex. 29. 27. The word is often repeated here. See 45. 6, 7, 13, 16; 48. 8–10, 12, 18, 20, 21.
the first of your dough. Ref. to Pent. (Num. 15. 20).
31 dead of itself, &c. Ref. to Pent. (Lev. 22. 8).

B X[1] Y[1] u[1] **45** Moreover, when ye shall divide by lot
(p. 1172) the land for inheritance, ye shall °offer
465 an °oblation unto °the LORD, an °holy portion of the land: the length *shall be* the length of five and twenty thousand *reeds*, and the breadth *shall be* °ten thousand. This *shall be* °holy in all the borders thereof round about.

v[1] 2 Of this there shall be °for the sanctuary five hundred *in length*, with five hundred *in breadth*, square round about; and fifty °cubits round about for the °suburbs thereof.

u[2] 3 And of this measure shalt thou measure the length of °five and twenty thousand, and the breadth of ten thousand:

v[2] and in it shall be the sanctuary *and* the °most holy *place*.

u[3] 4 The [1]holy *portion* of the land °shall be for the priests the ministers of the sanctuary, which shall come near to minister unto °the LORD: and it shall be a place for their houses,

v[3] and an [1]holy place for the sanctuary.

Y[2] 5 And the five and twenty thousand of length, and the ten thousand of breadth, shall also the Levites, the ministers of the house, have for themselves, °for a possession °for twenty chambers.

Y[3] 6 And ye shall appoint the possession of the city five thousand broad, and [3]five and twenty thousand long, over against the [1]oblation of the [1]holy *portion*: it shall be for °the whole house of Israel.

X[2] A w 7 And *a portion shall be* for the prince on the one side and on the other side of the [1]oblation of the [1]holy *portion*, and of the possession of the city, °before the [1]oblation of the [1]holy *portion*, and before the possession of the city, from the west side westward, and from the east side eastward: and the length *shall be* over against one of the portions, from the west border unto the east border.

8 In the land shall be his possession in Israel:

x and My princes shall no more oppress My People;

w and *the rest of* the land shall they give to the house of Israel according to their tribes.'

x 9 °Thus saith °the Lord GOD; 'Let it suffice you, O princes of Israel: remove violence and spoil, °and execute judgment and justice, take away your °exactions from My People, °saith °the Lord GOD.

10 °Ye shall have just balances, and a just °ephah, and a just °bath.

11 The [10]ephah and the [10]bath shall be of one measure, that the bath may contain °the tenth part of an °homer, and the ephah the tenth part of an °homer: the measure thereof shall be after the °homer.

12 °And the °shekel *shall be* twenty °gerahs: twenty °shekels, five and twenty °shekels, fifteen °shekels, shall be your °maneh.

B C[1] 13 This *is* the [1]oblation that ye shall °offer; the sixth part of an [10]ephah of an [11]homer of wheat, and ye shall give the sixth part of an [10]ephah of an [11]homer of barley:

45. 1—46. 18 (B, p. 1163). RESTORATION. THE LAND. (*Division.*)

B | X[1] | 45. 1-6. The Oblation.
  | X[2] | 45. 7—46. 18. The Prince's Portion.

45. 1-6 (X[1], above). THE OBLATION. (*Division.*)

X[1] | Y[1] | 1-4. The Holy Portion. } Persons.
 | Y[2] | 5. The Portion of the Levites. }
 | Y[3] | 6. The Portion of the City. Place.

45. 1-4 (Y[1], above). THE HOLY PORTION. (*Repeated Alternation.*)

Y[1] u[1] | 1. The Holy Portion.
 v[1] | 2. The Sanctuary.
 u[2] | 3-. The Holy Portion.
 v[2] | -3. The Sanctuary.
 u[3] | 4-. The Holy Portion.
 v[3] | -4. The Sanctuary.

1 offer = heave up. See next note.
oblation = a heave offering. See note on **44.** 30.
the LORD. Heb. Jehovah. Ap. **4.** II.
holy. See note on Ex. 3. 5.
ten. The Sept. reads twenty. Cp. Num. 35. 2. Josh. 21. 2.
2 for the sanctuary: i.e. the outer court (42. 15-20).
cubits. See Ap. 51. III. 2 (1).
suburbs = void ground outside the outer court, to prevent contact.
3 five and twenty thousand = about sixty or seventy miles, according to the length of the cubit.
most holy place = holy of holies.
4 shall be = it [shall be].
the LORD. Heb. Jehovah, with *'eth* = Jehovah Himself. Ap. 4. II. **5** for = as.
for twenty chambers: or, of cities to dwell in.
6 the whole house of Israel. Cp. 48. 19.

45. 7—46. 18 (X[2], above). THE HOLY PORTION. (*Introversion.*)

X[2] | A | 45. 7-12. The Prince's Portion.
 | B | 45. 13-25. Ordinances.
 | *B* | 46. 1-15. Ordinances.
 | *A* | 46. 16-18. The Prince's Portion.

45. 7-12 (A, above). THE PRINCE'S PORTION. (*Alternation.*)

A | w | 7, 8-. The Prince.
 | x | -8-. Injunctions to princes.
 | *w* | -8. The Tribes.
 | *x* | 9-12. Injunctions to princes.

7 before = in front of.
9 Thus saith, &c. See note on **44.** 9.
the Lord GOD. Heb. Adonai Jehovah. See note on 2. 4.
and. Some codices, with five early printed editions, omit this "and". exactions = evictions.
saith the Lord GOD = [is] Adonai Jehovah's oracle.
10 Ye shall have, &c. Ref. to Pent. (Lev. 19. 36).
ephah. See Ap. 51. III. 3 (5).
bath. See Ap. 51. III. 3 (1).
11 the tenth part. See the next note.
homer. Heb. *chomer*: not to be confounded with *'omer*. The former contained ten ephahs; the latter was one-tenth of an ephah. Cp. Ex. 16. 16.
12 And the shekel, &c. Ref. to Pent. (Ex. 30. 13. Lev. 27. 25. Num. 3. 47). Ap. 92.
shekel. See Ap. 51. II. 5.
gerahs. See Ap. 51. II. 2.
maneh. See Ap. 51. II. 3.

45. 13-25 (B, above). ORDINANCES. (*Division.*)

B | C[1] | 13-15. The Offerings. (Things, 13, 14. Lamb, 15.)
 | C[2] | 16, 17-. The Offerers. (People, 16 Prince, 17-.)
 | C[3] | -17-25. The Times. (General, -17. Part., 18-25.)

13 offer = offer up.

465 14 Concerning the ordinance of oil, the [10] bath
of oil, *ye shall offer* the tenth part of a [10] bath
out of the °cor, *which is* an [11] homer of ten
[10] baths; for ten [10] baths *are* an [11] homer:
15 And one lamb out of the flock, out of two
hundred, out of the °fat pastures of Israel; for
a °meat offering, and for a °burnt offering,
and for °peace offerings, °to make °reconcilia-
tion for them, [9] saith [9] the Lord GOD.
C² (p. 1172) 16 °All the People of the land shall give this
[1] oblation for the prince in Israel.
17 °And it shall be the prince's part *to give*
[15] burnt offerings, and [15] meat offerings, and
drink offerings,
C³ in the feasts, and in the new moons, and in
the sabbaths, °in all °solemnities of the house
of Israel: °he shall prepare the °sin offering,
and the [15] meat offering, and the [15] burnt offering, and the [15] peace offerings, to make [15] reconciliation °for the house of Israel.'
18 [9] Thus saith [9] the Lord GOD; °'In the first
month, in the first *day* of the month, thou
shalt take a young °bullock without blemish,
and cleanse the sanctuary:
19 And the priest shall take of the blood of
the [17] sin offering, and put *it* upon the posts of
the house, and upon the four corners of the
°settle of the altar, and upon the posts of the
gate of the inner court.
20 And so thou shalt do the seventh *day* of
the °month °for every one that erreth, and for
him that is °simple: so shall ye °reconcile the
house.
21 °In the first *month,* in the fourteenth day
of the month, ye shall have the passover, a
feast of seven days; unleavened bread shall
be eaten.
22 And upon that day shall the prince prepare for himself and °for all the People of the
land a bullock *for* a [17] sin offering.
23 And seven days of the feast he shall prepare a [15] burnt offering to [1] the LORD, seven bullocks and seven rams without blemish daily
the seven days; and a kid of the goats daily
for a [17] sin offering.
24 And he shall prepare a [10] meat offering of
an [10] ephah for a bullock, and an [10] ephah for a
ram, and an °hin of oil for an [10] ephah.
25 °In the seventh *month,* in the fifteenth day
of the month, shall he do the like in the feast
of the seven days, according to the [17] sin offering, according to the [15] burnt offering, and according to the [15] meat offering, and according
to the oil.'

B D¹ a¹ (p. 1173) **46** °Thus saith °the Lord GOD; 'The
gate of the inner court that looketh
toward the east shall be shut the six working
days; but on the sabbath it shall be opened,
and in the day of the new moon it shall be
opened.
2 And the prince shall enter by the way of
the porch of *that* gate without, and shall stand
by the post of the gate, and the priests shall
prepare °his °burnt offering and his °peace
offerings, and he shall worship at the threshold of the gate: then he shall go forth; but
the gate shall not be shut until the evening.
b¹ 3 Likewise °the People of the land shall worship at the °door of this gate before °the LORD
in the sabbaths and in the new moons.
4 And the [2] burnt offering that the prince c¹
shall °offer unto [3] the LORD in the sabbath day
shall be six lambs without blemish, and a ram
without blemish.
5 And the °meat offering *shall be* an °ephah

14 cor. See Ap. 51. III. 3 (4).
15 fat pastures = well-watered land (Sing.). Cp. Gen. 13. 10.
meat offering = gift offering. See Ap. 43. II. iii.
burnt offering. See Ap. 43. II. ii.
peace offerings. See Ap. 43. II. iv.
to make reconciliation. Ref. to Pent. (Lev. 1. 4). The same expression. Ap. 92.
reconciliation = atonement.
16 All the People of the land shall give this = All the People of the land shall be for, &c. The People will not offer individually. The prince will make the national offering for the People or nation as a whole. See note on "ordinances", 43. 18. There is no Hebrew for "give" here.
17 And it shall be the prince's part = But on the prince himself shall rest, &c.
in all. Some codices, with one early printed edition (Rabbinic), Aram., Sept., Syr., and Vulg., read "and in all", thus completing the Fig. *Polysyndeton* (Ap. 6).
solemnities = appointed seasons.
he. The emphasis is thus marked.
sin offering. See Ap. 43. II. v.
for the house of Israel. The People will thus offer through the prince. They are summed up in him.
18 In the first month, in the first day of the month. See note on Gen. 8. 13.
bullock. Ref. to Pent. (Ex. 29. 1-14). Ap. 92.
19 settle = ledge. See note on 43. 14.
20 month. The Septuagint adds "on the first day of the month".
for every one, &c. They do not offer themselves. The sacrifices here are national, not individual. See note on *v.* 17 above, and on "ordinances", 43. 18.
simple = artless, undesigning.
reconcile = make atonement for.
21 In the first month, &c. Ref. to Pent. (Ex. 12. 18). Ap. 92. This is the Feast of the Passover.
22 for all the People. The People will not do it by families as heretofore, but the prince does it for the whole nation. See notes on *vv.* 17, 20, above, and 43. 18.
24 hin. See Ap. 51. III. 3 (8).
25 In the seventh month, &c. This is the Feast of Tabernacles. Ref. to Pent. (Lev. 23. 34). Ap. 92.

46. 1-15 (*B*, p. 1172). **ORDINANCES.**
(*Repeated and Extended Alternation.*)

B | D¹ | a¹ | 1, 2. Prince.
  b¹ | 3. The People. "They".
  c¹ | 4-7. The offerings.
D² | a² | 8. The Prince.
  b² | 9, 10. The People.
  c² | 11. The offerings.
D³ | a³ | 12-. The Prince.
  b³ | -12. Personal.
  c³ | 13-15. The offerings.

1 Thus saith, &c. See note on 44. 9.
the Lord GOD. Heb. Adonai Jehovah. See note on 2. 4.
2 his: i. e. the prince, who offers for the nation. See notes above, on 45. 16, 17, 20, 22.
burnt offering. Ap. 43. II. ii.
peace offerings. Ap. 43. II. iv.
3 the People of the land. They worship only; they do not offer. Cp. 45. 16. **door** = entrance.
the LORD. Heb. Jehovah. Ap. 4. II.
4 offer = bring near. Ap. 43. I. i.
5 meat offering = meal, or gift, offering. Ap. 43. II. iii.
ephah. Ap. 51. III. 3 (5).

465 for a ram, and the °meat offering for the lambs
as he shall be able to give, and an °hin of oil
to an °ephah.

6 And in the day of the new moon *it shall*
be a young bullock without blemish, and six
lambs, and a ram: they shall be without
blemish.

7 And he shall prepare a [5]meat offering, an
[5]ephah for a bullock, and an [5]ephah for a ram,
and for the lambs according as his hand shall
attain unto, and an [5]hin of oil to an [5]ephah.

D[2] a[2] 8 And when the prince shall enter, he shall
(p. 1173) go in by the way of the porch of *that* gate, and
he shall go forth by the way thereof.

b[2] 9 But when [3]the People of the land shall
come before [3]the LORD in the °solemn feasts,
he that entereth in by the way of the north
gate to worship shall go out by the way of the
south gate; and he that entereth by the way
of the south gate shall go forth by the way of
the north gate: he shall not return by the way
of the gate whereby he came in, but shall go
forth over against it.

10 And °the prince in the midst of them,
when they go in, shall go in; and when they
go forth, °shall go forth.

c[2] 11 And in the feasts and in the °solemnities
the [5]meat offering shall be an [5]ephah to a bullock, and an [5]ephah to a ram, and to the lambs
as he is able to give, and an [5]hin of oil to an
[5]ephah.

D[3] a[3] 12 Now when the prince shall prepare a
voluntary [2]burnt offering or [2]peace offerings
voluntarily unto [3]the LORD, °*one* shall then
open him the gate that looketh toward the
east,

b[3] and °he shall prepare his [2]burnt offering and
his [2]peace offerings, °as he did on the sabbath
day: then he shall go forth; and after his
going forth °*one* shall shut the gate.

c[3] 13 Thou shalt °daily prepare a [2]burnt offering unto [3]the LORD *of* a lamb of the first year
without blemish: thou shalt prepare it every
morning.

14 And thou shalt prepare a [5]meat offering
°for it every morning, the sixth part of an
[5]ephah, and the third part of an [5]hin of oil,
to °temper with the fine flour; a [5]meat offering
continually by a perpetual ordinance unto [3]the
LORD.

15 Thus shall they prepare the lamb, and the
[5]meat offering, and the oil, every morning *for*
a continual [2]burnt offering.'

A 16 [1]Thus saith [1]the Lord GOD; 'If the prince
(p. 1172) give a gift unto any of his sons, the inheritance thereof shall be his °sons'; it *shall be*
their possession by inheritance.

17 But if he give a gift of his inheritance to
one of his servants, then it shall be his to °the
year of liberty; after it shall return to the
prince: °but his inheritance shall be his sons'
for them.

18 Moreover the prince shall not take of the
People's inheritance by oppression, to thrust
them out of their possession; *but* he shall give
his sons inheritance out of his own possession:
that My People be not scattered °every man
from his possession.'"

hin. Ap. 51. III. 3 (8).

9 solemn feasts = appointed times.

10 the prince, &c. = As for the prince, when they come in, he shall come in in the midst of them; and when they go forth, he shall go forth.

shall go forth. Heb. text reads "shall they go forth". Some codices read in marg. "he"; other codices, with Sept., Syr., and Vulg., read "he".

11 solemnities = appointed seasons.

12 one. Supply the *Ellipsis*, "[the gatekeeper] shall".

he shall prepare, &c. It will be the prince's duty to offer for the nation. See notes on 45. 16, 17, 20, 22.

as = according as.

13 daily prepare, &c. Ref. to Pent. (Ex. 29. 38. Num. 28. 3). Ap. 92.

14 for it = thereupon.

temper = mix.

16 sons'. The Sept. and Syr. read "son's".

17 the year of liberty = the year of jubilee. Ref. to Pent. (Lev. 25. 10). Ap. 92. This shows that this prophecy will, and must yet, be literally fulfilled. Moreover, the jubilee occurred only twice in a century.

but, &c. = truly, it is his own inheritance; as to his sons, to them it shall go.

18 every man. Heb. *'ish.* Ap. 14. II.

46. 19-24 (*A*, p. 1163). THE HOUSE.
(*Alternation.*)

A | d | 19. Boiling places. In the inner court.
  e | 20. Uses. For the Priests.
d | 21-23. Boiling places. In the outer court.
  e | 24. Uses. For the People.

19 holy. See note on Ex. 3. 5.

chambers = storerooms. Heb. *lishkāh.* See note on 40. 17. **behold.** Fig. *Asterismos.* Ap. 6.

on the two sides = on the farthest side.

20 to sanctify the People. Cp. 44. 19.

21 utter = outer. The boiling places.

22 courts joined = courts covered over, or closed courts, cloisters.

corners. Heb. *m hukẓā'ōth.* This hybrid word has the extraordinary points (Ap. 31) or dots on the top, denoting that it does not properly belong to the primitive text. It is omitted in Sept., Syr., and Vulg. The clause should therefore read: "these four were of the same measure" (see Ginsburg's *Introduction*, pp. 382-3).

23 And there was a row of building = And there was an enclosure. The 1611 edition of the A.V. reads "And there was a new *building*".

19 After he brought me through the entry, *A* d
which *was* at the side of the gate, into the °holy (p. 1174)
°chambers of the priests, which looked toward
the north: and, °behold, there *was* a place °on
the two sides westward.

20 Then said he unto me, "This *is* the place e
where the priests shall boil the trespass offering and the sin offering, where they shall bake
the [5]meat offering; that they bear *them* not
out into the utter court, °to sanctify the
People."

21 Then he brought me forth into the °utter *d*
court, and caused me to pass by the four
corners of the court; and, behold, in every
corner of the court *there was* a court.

22 In the four corners of the court *there were*
°courts joined of forty *cubits* long and thirty
broad: these four °corners *were* of one
measure.

23 °And *there was* a row *of building* round
about in them, round about them four, and *it*
was made with boiling places under the rows
round about.

e (p. 1174) 465 24 Then said he unto me, "These *are* the places of them that boil, where the ministers of the house shall boil the sacrifice of the People."

B E¹ f (p. 1175) **47** Afterward he brought me again unto the °door of the house; and, °behold, waters issued out from under the threshold of the house eastward: for the forefront of the house *stood toward* the east, and the waters °came down °from under from the °right side of the house, at the south *side* of the altar.

2 Then brought he me out of the way of the gate northward, and led me about the way without unto the °utter gate by the way that looketh eastward; and, [1] behold, there ran out waters on the [1] right side.

3 And when the °man that had °the line in his hand went forth eastward, he measured a thousand °cubits, and he brought me through the waters; °the waters *were* to the ancles.

4 Again he measured a thousand, and brought me through the waters; [3] the waters *were* to the knees. Again he measured a thousand, and brought me through; [3] the waters *were* to the loins.

5 Afterward he measured a thousand; *and it was* a river that I could not pass over: for the waters were risen, [3] waters to swim in, a river that could not be passed over.

6 And he said unto me, °"Son of man, hast thou seen *this?*" Then he brought me, and caused me to return to the brink of the river.

g 7 Now when I had returned, behold, at the bank of the river *were* very many °trees on the one side and on the other.

f 8 Then said he unto me, "These waters issue out toward the °east country, and go down into the °desert, and go into the sea: *which being* brought forth into °the sea, the waters shall be healed.

9 And it shall come to pass, *that* every °thing that liveth, which °moveth, whithersoever the rivers shall come, shall live: and there shall be a very great multitude of fish, because these waters shall come thither: for they shall be healed; and every thing shall live whither the river cometh.

10 And it shall come to pass, *that* the fishers shall stand upon it from °En-gedi even unto °En-eglaim; they shall be a *place* to spread forth nets; their fish shall be according to their kinds, as the fish of °the great sea, exceeding many.

11 But the °miry places thereof and the °marishes thereof shall not be healed; they shall be given to salt.

g 12 And by the river upon the bank thereof, on this side and on that side, shall grow all °trees for meat, whose leaf shall not fade, neither shall the fruit thereof be °consumed: it shall bring forth °new fruit according to his months, because their waters they issued out of the sanctuary: and the fruit thereof shall be for meat, and the leaf thereof for °medicine."

E² F¹ G 13 °Thus saith °the Lord GOD; °"This *shall be* the border, whereby ye shall inherit the land according to the twelve tribes of Israel: °Joseph °*shall have two* portions.

47. 1—48. 35 (*B*, p. 1163). THE LAND. (*Division.*)

B | E¹ | 47. 1-12. The Healing of the Land.
  | E² | 47. 13—48. 35. The Restoration of the Land.

47. 1-12 (E¹, above). THE HEALING OF THE LAND. (*Alternation.*)

E¹ | f | 1-6. The water.
   | g | 7. The trees.
   | *f* | 8-11. The water.
   | *g* | 12. The trees.

1 door = entrance.

behold. Fig. *Asterismos*. Ap. 6.

came down = were coming down. Cp. Joel 3. 18; and see Isa. 12. 3; 44. 3. Zech. 14. 8. Rev. 22. 1.

from under = from beneath. Referring to the perennial source which has supplied the fountain of Gihon. See Ap. 68.

right side: i. e. the south side. Cp. *v.* 2.

2 utter = outer.

3 man. Heb. *'ish*. Ap. 14. II.

the line = a measuring line. Heb. *kav*. Only here in Ezekiel. Not the same word as in 40. 3, which is *pāthīl*.

cubits. See Ap. 51. III. 2 (1).

the waters, &c. = waters [reaching] to the ankle. No Art. Heb. "of the ankles". Gen. of Relation. Ap. 17. 5.

6 Son of man. See note on 2. 1.

7 trees. See the Structure above.

8 east country = the eastern *g^elīlah*: i. e. circular border-land. Used of the Jordan in Josh. 22. 11.

desert = plain. Heb. *'arabāh*. See Deut. 3. 17; 4. 49.

the sea. The so-called Salt, or Dead Sea.

9 thing = soul. Heb. *nephesh*. Ap. 13.

moveth = swarmeth.

10 En-gedi. Now the well-known spring, *Ain Jidy*, on the west shore. The original name was Hazazon-tamar (2 Chron. 20. 2).

En-eglaim. Not yet identified. Eusebius places it eight miles south of *'Ar* of Moab. This would probably be *'Ain Hajla*, the ancient Beth Hogla.

the great sea. The Mediterranean.

11 miry places = swamps.

marishes = marshes. Heb. = pools.

12 trees for meat. Heb. "trees of meat". Gen. of Relation. Ap. 17. 5. Cp. Gen. 2. 9.

consumed = fail.

new = ripe.

medicine = healing. The Divine provision for preserving and restoring health in that future day, when this prophecy shall be literally fulfilled. Cp. Rev. 22. 2.

47. 13—48. 35 (E², above). THE RESTORATION OF THE LAND. (*Division.*)

E² | F¹ | 47. 13-23. The Land.
   | F² | 48. 1-29. The Tribes.
   | F³ | 48. 30-35. The City.

47. 13-23 (F¹, above). THE LAND. (*Introversion and Alternation.*)

F¹ | G | 13, 14. Distribution and Boundaries.
   | H | h | 15-17. North border.
   | | i | 18. East border.
   | *H* | *h* | 19. South border.
   | | *i* | 20. West border.
   | *G* | 21-23. Distribution and Boundaries.

13 Thus saith, &c. See note on 44. 9.

the Lord GOD. Heb. Adonai Jehovah. See note on 2. 4.

Joseph. Ref. to Pent. (Gen. 48. 5-22). Ap. 92.

shall have. Supply this *Ellipsis* (Ap. 6), by "shall inherit".

465 14 And ye shall inherit it, one as well as another: *concerning* the which I lifted up Mine
hand °to give it unto your fathers: and this
land shall fall unto you for inheritance.

H h (p. 1175) 15 And this *shall be* the border of the land
toward the north side, from the great sea, the
way of Hethlon, as men go to Zedad;
16 Hamath, Berothah, Sibraim, which *is* between the border of Damascus and the border
of Hamath; Hazar-hatticon, which *is* by the
°coast of Hauran.
17 And the border from the sea shall be Hazar-enan, the border of Damascus, and the
north northward, and the border of Hamath.
And *this is* the north side.

i 18 And the east side ye shall measure from
Hauran, and from Damascus, and from Gilead,
and from °the land of Israel *by* Jordan, from
the border unto the east sea. And *this is* the
east side.

H h 19 And the south side southward, from Tamar *even* to the waters of °strife *in* °Kadesh,
the °river to [10]the great sea. And *this is* the
south side southward.

i 20 The west side also *shall be* [10]the great
sea from the border, till a man come over
against Hamath. This *is* the west side.

G 21 So shall ye divide this land unto you according to the tribes of Israel.
22 And it shall come to pass, *that* ye shall
divide it by lot for an inheritance unto you,
and to the °strangers that sojourn among you,
which shall beget °children among you: and
they shall be unto you as born in the country
among the °children of Israel; they shall have
inheritance with you among the tribes of Israel.
23 And it shall come to pass, *that* in what
tribe the [22]stranger sojourneth, there shall ye
give *him* his inheritance, °saith [13]the Lord
GOD."

F² J (p. 1176) **48** Now °these *are* the names of the
tribes.
K From the north end to the coast of the way
of Hethlon, as one goeth to Hamath, Hazar-
enan, the border of Damascus northward, to
the coast of Hamath; for these are his sides
east *and* west; a *portion for* °Dan.
2 And by the border of Dan, from the east
side unto the west side, a *portion for* Asher.
3 And by the border of Asher, from the east
side even unto the west side, a *portion for*
Naphtali.

L N 4 And by the border of Naphtali, from the
east side unto the west side, a *portion for*
Manasseh.
5 And by the border of Manasseh, from the
east side unto the west side, a *portion for*
Ephraim.

O 6 And by the border of Ephraim, from the
east side even unto the west side, a *portion for*
Reuben.
7 And by the border of Reuben, from the east
side unto the west side, a *portion for* Judah.

M P 8 And by the border of Judah, from the east
side unto the west side, shall be the °offering
which °ye shall °offer of five and twenty
thousand *reeds in* breadth, and *in* length as
one of the *other* parts, from the east side unto
the west side: °and the sanctuary shall be in
the midst of °it.
9 The °oblation that ye shall offer unto °the
LORD *shall be* of five and twenty thousand in
length, and of ten thousand in breadth.

10 And for them, *even* for the priests, shall Q R¹ S¹
be *this* °holy [9]oblation; toward the north five
and twenty thousand *in length,* and toward
the west ten thousand in breadth, and toward
the east ten thousand in breadth, and toward
the south five and twenty thousand in length:
and the sanctuary of [9]the LORD shall be in
the midst thereof.

---

14 to give it, &c. Ref. to Pent. (Gen. 12. 7; 17. 8; 26. 3; 28. 13; 50. 24). Ap. 92.

16 coast = border, or boundary.

18 the land of Israel. One of the three passages in Ezekiel where *'eretz* (land) is used, instead of *'ădāmāh* (soil). See note on 27. 17; and cp note on 11. 17.

19 strife. Heb. *Meribah.* Ref. to Pent. (Num. 20. 1–13).

Kadesh. Now *'Ain Kadēs.* **river** = torrent.

22 strangers = foreign sojourners.

children = sons.

23 saith the Lord GOD = [is] Adonai Jehovah's oracle.

48. 1–29 (F², p. 1175). THE TRIBES.
(*Introversion and Alternation.*)

F² | J | 1–. The Tribes. "These are the names", &c.
  K | –1–3. The Slave Offspring (Bilhah and Zilpah).
    L | N | 4, 5. Rachel. } The Wives' Offspring.
      O | 6, 7. Leah. }
        M | 8–22. THE OBLATION.
    L | *N* | 23. Rachel. } The Wives' Offspring.
      O | 24–26. Leah. }
  K | 27. The Slave Offspring (Zilpah).
J | 28, 29. The Tribes. "This is the Land", &c.

1 these are the names. For the various orderings and groupings of the twelve tribes, see Ap. 45. Cp. Ex. 1. 1.

Dan. Note the different positions, by which the wives' offspring are placed in the centre, nearest to the oblation; while the slave offspring are placed at the extremities farthest from the oblation.

48. 8–22 (M, above). THE OBLATION.
(*Alternation.*)

M | P | 8, 9. The Oblation. Foursquare.
  Q | 10–19. The Inhabitants.
  P | 20. The Oblation. Foursquare.
  Q | 21, 22. The Prince.

8 offering = heave offering. Heb. *terūmah.* (Ap. 43. II. viii). See note on Ex. 29. 27. The same word as "oblation", *v.* 9; the whole area of which is to be considered as the heave offering offered to Jehovah.

ye. The 1611 edition of the A.V. reads "they".

offer = offer up.

and the sanctuary. Note the *Alternation* in *vv.* 8–10.

it = him: i.e. Judah.

9 oblation = heave offering. See note on *v.* 8

the LORD. Heb. Jehovah. Ap. 4. II.

48. 10–19 (Q, above). THE INHABITANTS.
(*Division.*)

Q | R¹ | 10–14. Ecclesiastical.
  R² | 15–19. Civil.

48. 10–14 (R¹, above). ECCLESIASTICAL.
(*Division.*)

R¹ | S¹ | 10–12. The Priests' Portion.
  S² | 13, 14. The Levites' Portion.

10 holy. See note on Ex 3. 5.

465 11 *It shall be* for the priests °that are sanctified of the sons of Zadok; which have kept
My °charge, which went not astray when
the °children of Israel went astray, °as the
Levites went astray.

12 And *this* [9]oblation of the land that is
°offered shall be unto them a thing most [10]holy
°by the border of the Levites.

S² (p. 1176) 13 And over against the border of the priests
the Levites *shall have* five and twenty thousand in length, and ten thousand in breadth:
all the length *shall be* five and twenty thousand, and the breadth ten thousand.

14 And they shall not sell of it, neither exchange, nor alienate the firstfruits of the land:
for *it is* [10]holy unto [9]the LORD.

R² j (p. 1177) 15 And the five thousand, that are left in the
breadth over against the five and twenty
thousand, °shall be a °profane *place* for the
city, for dwelling, and for suburbs:

k and the city shall be in the midst thereof.

k 16 And these *shall be* the measures thereof;
the north side four thousand and five hundred,
and the south side four thousand and five
hundred, and on the east side four thousand
and five hundred, and the west side four thousand and five hundred.

j 17 And the suburbs of the city shall be toward the north two hundred and fifty, and
toward the south two hundred and fifty, and
toward the east two hundred and fifty, and toward the west two hundred and fifty.

18 And the residue in length over against
the oblation of the [10]holy *portion shall be* ten
thousand eastward, and ten thousand westward: and it shall be over against the [9]obla-
tion of the [10]holy *portion;* and the increase
thereof shall be for food unto them that serve
the city.

19 And they that serve the city shall serve it
out of all the tribes of Israel.

P (p. 1176) 20 All the [9]oblation *shall be* five and twenty
thousand by five and twenty thousand: ye
shall [8]offer the [10]holy [9]oblation foursquare, with
the possession of the city.

Q 21 And the residue *shall be* for the prince,
on the one side and on the other of the holy
oblation, and of the possession of the city, over
against the five and twenty thousand of the
oblation toward the east border, and westward over against the five and twenty thousand toward the west border, over against the
portions for the prince: and it shall be the
[10]holy [9]oblation; and the sanctuary of the
house *shall be* in the midst thereof.

22 Moreover from the possession of the Levites, and from the possession of the city, *being*
in the midst *of that* which is the prince's, between the border of Judah and the border of
Benjamin, shall be for the prince.

L N 23 As for the rest of the tribes, from the east
side unto the west side, °Benjamin *shall have*
°a *portion.*

O 24 And by the border of Benjamin, from the
east side unto the west side, Simeon *shall
have* [23]a *portion.*

25 And by the border of Simeon, from the
east side unto the west side, Issachar [23]a *portion.*

26 And by the border of Issachar, from the
east side unto the west side, Zebulun [23]a *portion.*

27 And by the border of Zebulun, from the *K*
east side unto the west side, Gad [23]a *portion.*

28 And by the border of Gad, at the south *J*
side southward, the border shall be even from
Tamar *unto* the waters of °strife *in* Kadesh,
and to the river °toward the great sea.

29 This *is* the land which ye shall divide by
lot unto the tribes of Israel for inheritance,
and these *are* their portions, °saith the Lord
GOD.

30 And these *are* the °goings out of F³ T (p. 1177)
the city U
on the north side, four thousand and five hun- V l
dred measures.

31 And the gates of the city *shall be* after
the names of the tribes of Israel: three gates
northward; one gate of Reuben, one gate of
Judah, one gate of Levi.

32 And at the east side four thousand and m
five hundred: and three gates; °and one gate
of Joseph, one gate of Benjamin, one gate of
Dan.

33 And at the south side four thousand and *V l*
five hundred measures: and three gates; one
gate of Simeon, one gate of Issachar, one gate
of Zebulun.

34 At the west side four thousand and five *m*
hundred, *with* their three gates; one gate of
Gad, one gate of Asher, one gate of Naphtali.

---

11 that are . . . Zadok=the consecrated body of Zadok's sons. **charge**=ordinance.
children=sons.
as=according as.
12 offered=offered up, or heaved. Ap. 43. I. ix.
by=reaching to.

48. 15-19 (R², p. 1176). CIVIL. (*Introversion.*)

R² | j | 15-. The common place.
  k | -15. The City. Its site.
  k | 16. The City. Its measurements.
j | 17-19. The suburbs.

15 shall be=it [shall be].
profane=common.
23 Benjamin. Note the positions of these five tribes in the south. See the Structure (F²), p. 1175.
a=one.
28 strife. Heb. *Meribah.* See note on 47. 19.
toward. Sept. reads "as far as".
29 saith the Lord GOD=[is] Adonai Jehovah's oracle. See note on 2. 4.

48. 30-35 (F³, p. 1175). THE CITY.
(*Introversion and Alternation.*)

F³ | T | 30-. The City. Its exits.
  U | -30-. Its measurements.
   V | l | -30, 31. The North side. (Its Gates.)
     m | 32. The East side. (Its Gates.)
   V | *l* | 33. The South side. (Its Gates.)
     m | 34. The West side. (Its Gates.)
  U | 35-. Its measurements.
T | -35. The City. Its name.

30 goings out=outlets.
32 and one. Some codices, with Aram., Sept., Syr., and Vulg., omit "and".

U **35** *It was* round about eighteen thousand *measures*:
(p. 1177)
T and the name of the city from *that* day *shall*
465 *be*, ° The LORD *is* there.

35 The LORD [is] **there**: denoting the fact that Jehovah has gone thither and rests There, with all the blessing, peace, security, and glory of His abiding presence. Heb. *Jehovah Shammah*. See Ap. 4. II.

Those who read this book, and believe what God has here written for our learning, will not be troubled with all the puerile guesses and trifling comments of the natural man, but understand something of the grand revelations which can be only spiritually discerned (1 Cor. 2. 14).

THE BOOK OF DANIEL.

THE STRUCTURE OF THE BOOK AS A WHOLE.

(*Introversion*.)

A | 1. 1–21. THE CAPTIVITY OF JUDAH. HISTORICAL EVENTS CONNECTED WITH ITS BEGINNING.

B | 2. 1–49. THE DREAM OF NEBUCHADNEZZAR. THE BEGINNING AND DURATION OF GENTILE DOMINION.

C | 3. 1–30. DANIEL'S COMPANIONS. THE "FIERY FURNACE". ANGELIC DELIVERANCE.

D | 4. 1–37. THE FIRST KING OF BABYLON. NEBUCHADNEZZAR'S DREAM OF THE "GREAT TREE", REVEALING HIS TEMPORARY DEPOSITION.

D | 5. 1–31. THE LAST KING OF BABYLON. BELSHAZZAR'S VISION OF THE "HAND", REVEALING HIS FINAL DOOM.

C | 6. 1–28. DANIEL HIMSELF. THE "DEN OF LIONS". ANGELIC DELIVERANCE.

B | 7. 1—8. 27. THE DREAM AND VISION OF DANIEL. THE END OF GENTILE DOMINION.

A | 9. 1—12. 13. THE DESOLATIONS OF JERUSALEM. PROPHETIC ANNOUNCEMENTS CONNECTED WITH THEIR END.

For the CANONICAL Order and Place of the Prophets, see Ap. 1
For the CHRONOLOGICAL Order of the Prophets, see Ap. 77.
For the Inter-relation of the Prophetic Books, see Ap. 78 and Structure on p. 1206.
For References to the Pentateuch in the Prophetic Books, see Ap. 92.
For the Visions of chs. 7—12, see Ap. 89.
For the Numbered "Days" in 8. 14; 12. 7, 11, 12, see Ap. 90.
For the Seventy Weeks of Daniel (9. 25–27), see Ap. 91.

The position of the book in the "Hagiographa", or third division of the Old Testament ("the Psalms", see Ap. 1), rather than in the second division ("the Prophets"), may be explained by the fact that, unlike the other three greater prophets (Isaiah, Jeremiah, and Ezekiel), it stands in relation to them as the Apocalypse of the Old Testament; and as pertaining to what is yet future. And whereas those three greater prophets speak of the future from an Intro-Israelitish standpoint, Daniel has their prophecies as his background; and, instead of looking at Zion and its neighbouring localised peoples, Daniel has universal Monarchies as his perspective; and is therefore separated from them in the Hebrew Canon, becoming to us the "light" or "lamp" of 2 Pet. 1. 19, and the realisation of 1 Pet. 1. 11.

The first part of the book (1. 1—6. 28, **A** to *C*) is *historic*, while the latter half (7. 1—12. 13, *A* and *B*) is *prophetic*.

Moreover, of the former portion, 2. 4—7. 28 is written in Aramaic (or Chaldee), while the latter portion, 8. 1—12. 13, is written in Hebrew. This is to teach us that the *historic* portion is in the Gentile language, because it is concerned with "the times of the Gentiles", and with Gentile supremacy in relation to Israel; while the *prophetic* portion is in Hebrew (the language of Israel), because it is concerned with "the time of the end", and with the events which will lead up to the time when God will "restore again the kingdom to Israel" (Acts 1. 6).

In Hezekiah's day (604 B.C.) Syriac (or Aramaic) was not understood by the Jews (2 Kings 18. 26); but after the Exile, in Ezra's day (426 B.C.), Hebrew had been so far forgotten that it had to be explained (Neh. 8. 8). In Daniel's day (495 B.C.) both languages were generally understood; and both could be, and were, thus used by him. If an impostor had written the book in Hebrew some 250 years later (as alleged by modern critics), why should he have defeated his own object by writing any portion in Aramaic as well, thus proving himself to be a fool as well as a "forger"?

°DANIEL.

A A (p. 1179) 497 **1** °IN the third year of the reign of Jehoiakim king of Judah °came °Nebuchadnez-
zar king of Babylon unto Jerusalem, and besieged it.
2 And °the LORD* °gave Jehoiakim king of
Judah into his hand, with °part of the vessels
of the house of °God: which he carried into
°the land of Shinar to the house of his god;
and he brought the vessels into the treasure
house of his god.

B C **3** And the king spake unto Ashpenaz °the
master of his eunuchs, that he should bring
certain of the °children of Israel, °and of the
king's seed, and of the °princes;

D a **4** °Children in whom *was* no blemish, but
well favoured, and skilful in all wisdom, and
°cunning in knowledge, and understanding
science, and such as *had* ability in them to
stand °in the king's palace, and whom they
might teach the °learning and the °tongue of
the °Chaldeans.

b **5** And the king appointed them a daily provision of the king's °meat, and of the °wine
which he drank: so nourishing them °three
years, that at the end thereof they might
°stand before the king.

DANIEL = GOD [my] Judge, which accords with the character and contents of the book. Daniel was of the seed-royal of Judah. See note on *v.* 3. He is mentioned thrice by Ezekiel, his contemporary (14. 14, 20; 28. 3), and once by our Lord. In Matt. 24. 15 (Mark 13. 14), the Lord referred also to Dan. 8. 13; 9. 27; 11. 31; 12. 11. In Matt. 24. 30; 26. 64. Mark 14. 62. Luke 22. 69, He referred to Dan. 7. 13. In Matt. 24. 15-17, 20-22, He referred to Dan. 12. 1.

1. 1-21 (A, p. 1178). THE CAPTIVITY OF JUDAH. HISTORICAL EVENTS CONNECTED WITH ITS BEGINNING. (*Introversions and Alternation.*)

A | A | 1, 2. The time.
  B | C | 3. Daniel and his companions.
    D | a | 4. Their attainments.
      b | 5. Their provision. (Appointment.)
  B | C | 6, 7. Daniel and his companions.
    D | b | 8-16. Their provision. (Resolve.)
      a | 17-20. Their attainments.
A | 21. The time.

1 In the third year, &c. It was in the third year of Jehoiakim that Nebuchadnezzar set out from Babylon; and Daniel, writing there, speaks of the starting, not of the arrival at Jerusalem. See note on "came", below. In the fourth year Jehovah says by Jeremiah (25. 9), "I will send". The date would be 497 B.C. and Daniel's sixteenth year, he being born probably in 513 B.C. (Josiah's eighteenth year).

came = went, set out, or proceeded. Heb. *bō'*, which means *to go* or *come*, according to the context and the point of view. It is rendered "went" in Gen. 7. 9, 16; 15. 17. Ex. 5. 1. Num. 8. 22; 14. 24. Judg. 6. 19; 18. 18. 1 Sam. 17. 12. 2 Sam. 2. 24; 12. 16; 17. 25; 20. 3, 8. 1 Chron. 2. 21. Ps. 66. 12. Ezek. 36. 20, 21, 22; 41. 3. It is translated "*go*", in the sense of *proceed* or *set out*, in Deut. 4. 1; 6. 18; 8. 1; 11. 8; 12. 26; 22. 13; 26. 3. Josh. 23. 12. Ruth 3. 4. 1 Sam. 25. 5, &c. Jonah 1. 3, &c. It is rendered "*entered*" (of setting out) in 2 Chron. 27. 2. Job 38. 16, 22. Jer. 9. 21; 14. 18; 17. 25; 22. 4; 34. 10; 37. 16. Lam. 1. 10. Ezek. 44. 2; 46. 2. Dan. 11. 40, 41. Amos 5. 5. Obad. 11. Zech. 5. 4. Nebuchadnezzar did set out in Jehoiakim's third year, but was delayed by fighting the battle with Pharaoh-necho at Carchemish. In the next (the fourth) year (Jer. 46. 2), he carried out the object with which he set out. Cp. 2 Kings 24. 1, and 2 Chron. 36. 6, 7. **Nebuchadnezzar.** This name is so spelt (i.e. with "n" instead of "r") by Berosus (who wrote his history from the monuments, *Cent.* 3, B.C.). Both spellings were in vogue. Ezekiel uses the "r"; and Jeremiah uses "r" before ch. 27; and then eight times the "n" (27. 6 where Nebuchadnezzar is once specially called Jehovah's appointed servant, 8, 20; 28. 3, 11, 14; 29. 1, 3); and after that, always with "r" except twice (34. 1; 39. 5). It is spelt with "n" in 2 Kings 24. 1, 10, 11; 25. 1, 8, 22. 1 Chron. 6. 15. 2 Chron. 36. 6, 7, 10, 13. Ezra 1. 7; 2. 1. Neh. 7. 6. Est. 2. 6). **2 the LORD*.** One of the 134 places where the *Sōpherīm* say they altered "Jehovah" of the primitive text to "Adonai". See Ap. 32. **gave.** See Isa. 39. 6, 7. Jer. 25. 8-11. Ezek. 21. 26, 27. **part.** Others were brought later (2 Kings 24. 13. 2 Chron. 36. 10). See Ezra 1. 7 for the subsequent restoration of them by Cyrus. **God.** Heb. Elohim. Ap. 4. I. **the land of Shinar.** Ref. to Pent. (Gen. 10. 10; 11. 2; 14. 1, 9). Ap. 92. Outside the Pentateuch found only in Josh. 7. 21 (Heb. text). Isa. 11. 11. Zech. 5. 11; and here. **3 the master of his eunuchs.** Heb. *rab ṣārīṣāyn* = master or chief of the eunuchs; whence the title "Rab-saris" in 2 Kings 18. 17. See note there. Called "prince" in *v.* 7. **children** = sons. **and** = even, or both. Some codices, with six early printed editions, omit this "and": reading "sons of Israel, of the king's seed" (or "seed-royal"). **princes** = nobles. Heb. *partᵉmīm*, a Persian word, found only here and Est. 1. 3; 6. 9. Not the same word as in *vv.* 7, 8, 10, 11, &c. **4 Children** = Youths. **cunning** = skilful. **in the king's palace.** The Inscriptions show that there was a palace school with elaborate arrangements for special education. See below on "Chaldeans", and notes on 2. 2. **learning** = character, or books. See Prof. Sayce's *Babylonian Literature*: which shows the existence of a huge literature and famous libraries, in which were arrangements for procuring books from the librarian as in our own day. These books related to all subjects, and were classified according to their subjects (pp. 12-14). **tongue.** This was a special and important department. **Chaldeans.** A name not peculiar to Daniel. From Genesis onward it is met with, especially in Jeremiah. They were distinct from the Babylonians (Jer. 22. 25. Ezek. 23. 23), and belonged to South Babylonia. Used here of a special class, well known as such at that time (cp. 2. 2, 4, 5, 10), and distinct also from other learned classes (2. 4). The word (Heb. *Chasdīm*) is used also in the wider sense of a nationality (5. 30). See Dr. Pinches on *The Old Testament*, p. 371; Rawlinson's *History of Herodotus*, vol. i; pp. 255, 256; and Lenormant's *The Ancient History of the East*, i. pp. 493-5. **5 meat** = food. Heb. *pathbag.* A Persian or Aryan word. Occurs only in Daniel. **wine.** Heb. *yayin.* Ap. 27. I. **three years.** Say 497, 496, and 495 B.C. See note on 2. 1. It does not say these years were concluded before the events of ch. 2 took place. **stand before the king.** Ref. to Pent. (Gen. 41. 46).

B C (p. 1179) 497 6 Now among these were of the [3] children of Judah, °Daniel, °Hananiah, °Mishael, and °Azariah:

7 Unto whom the °prince of the eunuchs °gave names: for he gave unto Daniel *the name* of °Belteshazzar; and to Hananiah, of °Shadrach; and to Mishael, of °Meshach; and to Azariah, of °Abed-nego.

D b 8 But Daniel °purposed in his heart that he would not °defile himself with the portion of the king's meat, nor with the [5] wine which he drank: therefore he requested of the [7] prince of the eunuchs that he might not defile himself.

9 Now °God had brought Daniel into favour and °tender love with the [7] prince of the eunuchs.

10 °And the [7] prince of the eunuchs said unto Daniel, "I fear my lord the king, who hath appointed your meat and your drink: for why should he see your faces °worse liking than the [4] children which *are* of °your sort? then shall ye make *me* endanger my head to the king."

11 Then said Daniel to °Melzar, whom the [7] prince of the eunuchs had set over Daniel, Hananiah, Mishael, and Azariah,

12 "Prove thy servants, I beseech thee, ten days; and let them give °us °pulse to eat, and water to drink.

13 Then let our countenances be looked upon before thee, and the countenance of the [4] children that eat of the portion of the king's [5] meat: and as thou seest, deal with thy servants."

14 So he consented to them in this matter, and proved them ten days.

15 And at the end of ten days their countenances appeared fairer and fatter in flesh than all the [4] children which did eat the portion of the king's [5] meat.

16 Thus [11] Melzar took away the portion of their [5] meat, and the [5] wine that they should drink; and gave them [12] pulse.

a 17 As for these four [4] children, [9] God gave them knowledge and skill in all [4] learning and wisdom: and Daniel had °understanding in all visions and dreams.

18 Now at the end of the days that the king had said he should bring them in, then the [7] prince of the eunuchs brought them in before [1] Nebuchadnezzar.

19 And the king communed with them; and among them all was found none like [6] Daniel, [6] Hananiah, [6] Mishael, and [6] Azariah: therefore [5] stood they before the king.

20 And in all matters of wisdom *and* [17] understanding, that the king enquired of them, he found them ten times better than all the °magicians °*and* astrologers that *were* in all his realm.

A 21 And Daniel °continued *even* unto °the first year of king Cyrus.

B E c (p. 1180) 495 **2** °And in °the second year of the reign of °Nebuchadnezzar Nebuchadnezzar dreamed dreams, wherewith his °spirit was troubled, and his sleep °brake from him.

6 Daniel = God is my Judge. See note on the Title.
Hananiah = Jah is gracious; or, graciously given by Jah.
Mishael = who is (or is as) El? Ap. 4. IV.
Azariah = helped of Jah, or Jah has helped.
7 prince = ruler. Heb. *sar*.
gave names. In token of subjection. See 2 Kings 23. 34; 24. 17. Cp. Gen. 41. 45.
Belteshazzar. According to Dr. Pinches, this is an abbreviated form of Balat-su-ūsur = protect thou (O Bel) his life. Many such abbreviations are found in the inscriptions; but cp. "Belshazzar" (5. 1).
Shadrach. According to Delitzsch = Sudur-Aku (= command of Aku, the moon-god).
Meshach. Perhaps Misha-Aku = who is as Aku?
Abed-nego = servant or worshipper of Nego. It is not wise to suppose this to be a corruption of Abed-nebo, while any day the name may be met with in the Inscriptions.
8 purposed in his heart = made up his mind. Cp. Prov. 23. 7.
defile himself, &c. This was because meat was killed with the blood (contrary to Lev. 3. 17; 7. 26; 17. 10–14; 19. 26), and offered to idols (Ex. 34. 15. 1 Cor. 10. 20. Cp. Acts 15. 29). Not because they were acting on vegetarian and temperance principles.
9 God. Heb. Elohim (with Art.) = the [Triune] God. Ap. 4. I.
tender love = compassion.
10 And: or, Yet.
worse liking = sadder: i.e. thin and sad-looking. Cp. Matt. 6. 16.
your sort = your own age.
11 Melzar. Heb. = the *melzar* = the steward or butler, who had charge of the wine, &c.
12 us. The 1611 edition of the A.V. omitted "us".
pulse = vegetable food (to avoid the idol-tainted meat).
17 understanding = discernment.
20 magicians and astrologers. See notes on 2. 2.
and. Some codices, with Sept., Syr., and Vulg., read this "and" in the text.
21 continued = continued in office. See first occ. Ex. 25. 30: also 27. 20; 28. 29, 30, 38; 29. 38, 42; 30. 8: &c. Cp. Ezek. 39. 14, "continual employment".
the first year of king Cyrus: i.e. during the whole period of Babylonian supremacy over Israel for sixty-nine years (495–426 = 69). It does not say that he did not continue longer, but that he lived to see that important epoch. Cp. 10. 1; and see Ap. 57, and 58.

2. 1–49 (B, p. 1178). THE DREAM OF NEBUCHADNEZZAR. THE DURATION OF GENTILE DOMINION. (*Alternations and Introversion.*)

B | E | c | 1–3. Chaldeans brought in. } Chaldeans.
  d | 4–9. King's requisition.
  e | 10, 11. Their inability.
   F | G | f | 12–16. King's resentment. } Suspense.
     g | 17, 18. Daniel and others.
    H | 19–23. Revelation.
 E | *c* | 24, 25. Daniel brought in. } Daniel.
  d | 26, 27. King's requisition.
  e | 28–30. Daniel's ability.
   F | *H* | 31–45. Communication. } Captivity.
    G | *f* | 46–48. King's gratitude.
     g | 49. Daniel and others.

1 And. Thus linking on this chapter of momentous prophecy with ch. 1, which is pure history.
the second year: 495 B.C. (Daniel's eighteenth year). Therefore Jehoiakim's fifth year, the year of the burning of the roll which marked the official rejection of Jehovah. Hence Nebuchadnezzar's dream. Daniel was in Babylon, and writes from that standpoint. The supposed difficulty is a proof of genuineness; for the writer would have been a fool as well as a forger to have left it unexplained. **Nebuchadnezzar.** See note on 1. 1. **spirit.** Heb. *rūach*. Ap. 9. **brake from** = had been upon: i.e. had now gone from.

495 2 Then the king commanded °to call the °magicians, and the °astrologers, and the °sorcerers, and the °Chaldeans, for to shew the king his dreams. So they came and stood before the king.

3 And the king said unto them, °"I have dreamed a dream, and my [1]spirit °was troubled to know the dream."

d 4 Then spake the [2]Chaldeans to the king °in
(p. 1180) Syriack, °"O king, live for ever: tell thy servants the dream, and we will shew the interpretation."

5 The king answered and said to the [2]Chaldeans, "The °thing is °gone from me: if ye will not make known unto me the dream, with the interpretation thereof, ye shall be °cut in pieces, and your houses shall be °made a dunghill.

6 But if ye shew the dream, and the interpretation thereof, ye shall receive of me gifts and °rewards and great honour: therefore shew me the dream, and the interpretation thereof."

7 They answered again and said, "Let the king tell his servants the dream, and we will shew the interpretation of it."

8 The king answered and said, "I know of certainty that ye would °gain the time, because ye see the thing is [5]gone from me.

9 But if ye will not make known unto me the dream, *there is but* one decree for you: for ye have prepared lying and corrupt words to speak before me, till the time be changed: therefore tell me the dream, and I shall know that ye can shew me the interpretation thereof."

e 10 The [2]Chaldeans answered before the king, and said, "There is not a °man upon the °earth that can shew the king's matter: therefore *there is* no king, lord, nor ruler, *that* asked such things at any [2]magician, or [2]astrologer, or [2]Chaldean.

11 And *it is* a rare thing that the king requireth, and there is none other that can shew it before the king, except the gods, whose dwelling is °not with flesh."

F G f 12 For this cause the king was angry and very furious, and commanded to destroy all the °wise *men* of Babylon.

13 And the decree went forth that the [12]wise *men* should be slain; and they sought Daniel and his °fellows to be slain.

14 Then Daniel answered with °counsel and wisdom to °Arioch the captain of the king's °guard, which was gone forth to slay the [12]wise *men* of Babylon:

15 He answered and said to [14]Arioch the king's captain, "Why *is* the decree *so* hasty from the king?" Then [14]Arioch made the thing known to Daniel.

16 Then Daniel went in, and desired of the king that he would °give him time, and that he would shew the king the interpretation.

2 to call, &c. = to send for. This tells us of the religious system of Babylonia, of which subsequent Jewish commentators and Greek translators would know little or nothing. There were six classes of the Chaldean priesthood.

magicians. Heb. *chartummîm.* Connected with the *kharutu* (the sceptre) or rod of office of those who repelled demons and evil spirits by incantations, &c.

astrologers. Heb. *'ashshāphîm* = in Babylonian, *asipi,* prophets who assumed to announce the will of heaven and predict the future. These were a class apart from the others. The inscriptions speak of *bab Assaput* = the gate of the oracle; also of *bit Assaput* = the house of the oracle.

sorcerers. Heb. *m^{e}kashsh^{e}phîm* = wizard (Ex. 7. 11; 22. 18, fem. Deut. 18. 10, fem. Mal. 3. 5, fem.).

Chaldeans. Heb. *Kasdîm.* See note on 1. 4.

3 I have dreamed. Contrast this with Daniel's vision, in the Structure on p. 1178; and note the other recorded dreams (Gen. 20. 3).

was = is.

4 in Syriack. Heb. *'ărāmith* = Aramaic. The insertion of this word here is to call our attention to the fact that what follows is written not in Hebrew, but in Aramaic, as far as the end of ch. 7. See note on the Structure, p. 1178; and note the other Aramaic portions (Ezra 4. 8—6. 18 and 7. 12-26; also Jer. 10. 11. The Syriac and Chaldee are properly Western and Eastern Aramaic.

O king. This is the first Aramaic word so written. Cp. 3. 9; 5. 10; 6. 6, 21. Neh. 2. 3.

5 thing. The dream.

gone from me. Referring to the forgotten dream.

cut . . . made a dunghill. Cp. 3. 29. Ezra 6. 11. A further mode of punishment, from the Medo-Persians, in 6. 7.

6 rewards. Chald. *n^{e}bizbāh* = a present.

8 gain the time = gain time. It may have reference to that day being an unlucky day. Cp. Est. 3. 7.

10 man. Chald. *'ěnāsh.* Ap. 14. III.

earth. Chald. *beshtā'* = dry ground.

11 not. Is emphatic. They held that there were gods who dwelt in men. But these were beyond mortal men altogether.

12 wise men: i.e. the members of all the classes collectively, mentioned in *v.* 2 above. Chald. *chākam,* denoting acquired wisdom.

13 fellows = companions.

14 counsel and wisdom = prudence and discretion.

Arioch. An ancient Babylonian name, preserved and handed down from Gen. 14. 1 = *Iri-Aku.*

guard = executioners. Cp. Gen. 37. 36; 39. 1; 40. 3. 2 Kings 25. 8. Jer. 39. 9.

16 give him time = appoint him a time.

17 Hananiah, &c. See note on 1. 6.

18 mercies = great mercy. Fig. *Heterosis* (of Number), Ap. 6.

of = from before.

the God of heaven. See note on 2 Chron. 36. 23.

God. Chald. *'elāh.* Ap. 4. I.

secret. Chald. *rāz,* which the Sept. renders *mustērion.* Occurs in O.T. only here, in *vv.* 18, 19, 27, 28, 29, 30, 47, 47; and 4. 9. Not the same word as in *v.* 22.

20 answered and said. See note on Deut. 1. 41.

for ever and ever = from age to age. See Ap. 151.

21 He changeth, &c. Cp. *v.* 9; 7. 25. 1 Chron. 29. 30. Job 34. 24-29. Ps. 31. 14, 15. Ecc. 3. 1-8. Jer. 27. 5-7.

17 Then Daniel went to his house, and made the thing known to °Hananiah, Mishael, and Azariah, his companions:

18 That they would desire °mercies °of °the °God of heaven concerning this °secret; that Daniel and his [13]fellows should not perish with the rest of the [12]wise *men* of Babylon.

19 Then was the [18]secret revealed unto Daniel in a night vision. Then Daniel blessed the [18]God of heaven. H

20 Daniel °answered and said, "Blessed be the name of [18]God °for ever and ever: for wisdom and might are His:

21 And °He changeth the times and the

495 seasons: °He removeth kings, and setteth up
kings: °He giveth wisdom unto the wise, and
knowledge to them that know understanding:
22 °He revealeth the deep and °secret things:
°He knoweth what *is* in the darkness, °and
the light dwelleth with Him.
23 I thank Thee, and praise Thee, O Thou
[18]God of my fathers, Who hast given me wisdom and might, and hast made known unto me
now what we desired of Thee: for Thou hast
now made known unto us the king's matter."

E c (p 1180) 24 Therefore Daniel went in unto [14]Arioch,
whom the king had ordained to destroy the
[12]wise *men* of Babylon: he went and said
thus unto him; "Destroy not the [12]wise *men*
of Babylon: bring me in before the king, and
I will shew unto the king the interpretation."
25 Then [14]Arioch broug htin Daniel before
the king in haste, and said thus unto him, "I
have found a °man of the captives of Judah,
that will make known unto the king the interpretation."

d 26 The king answered and said to Daniel,
whose name *was* °Belteshazzar, "Art thou
able to make known unto me the dream which
I have seen, and the interpretation thereof?"

e 27 Daniel answered in the presence of the
king, and said, "The [18]secret which the king
hath demanded cannot the [12]wise *men,* the
[2]astrologers, the [2]magicians, the soothsayers,
shew unto the king;
28 But there is a [18]God in heaven That revealeth [18]secrets, and °maketh known to the
king [1]Nebuchadnezzar what shall be °in the
latter days. Thy dream, and the visions of
thy head upon thy bed, are these;
29 As for thee, O king, thy thoughts °came
into thy mind upon thy bed, what should come
to pass hereafter: and He That revealeth [18]se-
crets maketh known to thee what shall come
to pass.
30 But as for me, this [18]secret is not revealed
to me for *any* wisdom that I have more than
any living, but °for *their* sakes that °shall make
known the interpretation to the king, and that
thou mightest know the thoughts of thy heart.

F H 31 Thou, O king, °sawest, and °behold a great
image. This great image, whose brightness
was excellent, stood before thee; and the
°form thereof *was* terrible.
32 This image's °head *was* of fine °gold, his
breast and his arms of °silver, his belly and his
thighs of °brass,
33 His legs of iron, his feet part of iron and
part of [32]clay.
34 Thou sawest till that °a stone was cut out
°without hands, which smote the image upon
his °feet *that were* of [32]iron and [32]clay, and
°brake them to pieces.
35 Then was the °iron, the °clay, the °brass,
the °silver, and the °gold, [34]broken to pieces
°together, and became like the chaff of the
summer threshingfloors; and the °wind carried them away, that no place was found for
them: and the [34]stone that smote the image
became a great mountain, and °filled the whole
earth.
36 This *is* the dream; and we will tell the
interpretation thereof before the king.

He removeth, &c. Cp. 4. 17, 32. 1 Sam. 2. 7, 8. Job 12. 18. Pss. 75. 6, 7; 113. 7, 8. Prov. 8. 15, 16. Luke 1. 51, 52. Acts 13. 21, 22.

He giveth, &c. Ex. 31. 3, 6. 1 Kings 3. 8–12; 4. 29; 10. 24. 1 Chron. 22. 12. 2 Chron. 1. 10–12. Prov. 2. 6, 7. Luke 21. 15. 1 Cor. 1. 30. Jas. 1. 5, 17; 3. 15–17.

22 He revealeth, &c. Cp. *vv.* 11, 28, 29. Gen. 37. 5–9; 41. 16, 25, 28. Job 12. 22. Ps. 25. 14 Isa. 14. 24, 26; 42. 9. Matt. 11. 25. Rom. 16. 25, 26. Eph. 3. 5. Col. 1. 25–27.

secret=hidden. Chald. *ṣâthar.* Not the same word as in *v.* 18, &c.

He knoweth, &c. Cp. Job 26. 6. Ps. 139. 11, 12. Jer. 23. 24. Luke 12. 2, 3. John 21. 17. 1 Cor. 4. 5. Heb. 4. 13.

and the light, &c. Cp. 5. 11, 14. Pss. 36. 9; 104. 2. John 1. 9; 8. 12; 12. 45, 46. 1 Tim. 6. 16. Jas. 1. 17. 1 John 1. 5.

25 man. Chald. *g^{e}bar.* Ap. 14. IV.

26 Belteshazzar. See note on 1. 7.

28 maketh=hath made. Cp. *v.* 29.

in the latter days. Ref. to Pent. (Gen. 49. 1. Num. 24. 14. Deut. 4. 30; 32. 29). Ap. 92.

29 came=came up.

30 for their sakes . . . interpretation=to the intent that the interpretation. **shall**=should.

31 sawest=wast looking.

behold. Fig. *Asterismos.* Ap. 6.

form=appearance.

32 head. Note the five parts: (1) the head; (2) the breast and arms; (3) the belly and the thighs; (4) the legs; (5) the feet. These five are preserved distinct throughout. Cp. *vv.* 34, 35, and 38–44, and 45.

gold . . . clay (*v.* 33). Note that the most precious metal, and the highest specific gravity was at the top, decreasing with its descent: (1) gold=19. 3; (2) silver =10. 51; (3) brass=8. 5; (4) iron=7. 6; (5) clay=1. 9: so that it was top-heavy from the first.

34 a stone. See note on Ps. 118. 22.

without hands. An expression always emphasising the absence of all human instrumentality and the act of God alone. See *v.* 45; 8. 25. Job 34. 20. Lam. 4. 6. Cp. Acts 7. 48; 17. 24, 25; 19. 26. 2 Cor. 5. 1. Eph. 2. 11. Col. 2. 11. Heb. 9. 11, 24.

feet: i.e. the fifth kingdom. Not the fourth, which was represented by the "legs of iron".

brake them to pieces: or, they were beaten small.

brake=beat small. Chald. *d^{e}ḳaḳ.* Cp. *vv.* 34, 35, 40, 41, 44, 45.

35 iron, the clay, &c. Note the order differently given to distinguish the five (not the four), answering to the five parts of the image in *v.* 32, and the five kingdoms:—

vv. 32, 33.	*v.* 35.	*v.* 45.
gold,	iron,	iron,
silver,	clay,	brass,
brass,	brass,	clay,
iron,	silver,	silver,
iron and clay.	gold.	gold.

together. As united at the time of the end (forming the *sixth* power), the kingdom of the "Beast" (Rev. 13).

wind. Heb. *rûach.* Ap. 9.

filled the whole earth. Thus marking the *seventh* kingdom, that of Messiah.

37 a kingdom. The O.T. is not designed to be a compendium of "ancient history". It is the history of Jehovah's People, Israel; and other nations are referred to only as, and in so far as, they come into connection with Israel. Babylon was the most ancient of kingdoms (Gen. 10. 10). Cp. Deut. 32. 8. Nebuchadnezzar was not the first king; but he was the "head" or beginning of Gentile dominion in the earth when Israel had been "removed" (according to Jer. 15. 4; 24. 9; 29. 18). These successive kingdoms are reckoned only as they obtained possession of Jerusalem. They existed before that; and each, in turn, was absorbed in the one that succeeded.

37 Thou, O king, *art* a king of kings: for
the [18]God of heaven hath given thee °a kingdom, power, and strength, and glory.

495 38 And wheresoever the °children of °men
dwell, the beasts of the field and the fowls of
the heaven °hath He given into thine hand,
and hath made thee ruler over them all. °Thou
°*art* this °head °of gold.
39 And after thee shall °arise °another kingdom °inferior to thee, and another °third
kingdom of brass, which shall bear rule over
all the earth.
40 And °the fourth kingdom shall be °strong
as iron: forasmuch as iron [34] breaketh in
pieces and °subdueth all *things:* and as iron
that °breaketh all these, shall it [34] break in
pieces and °bruise.
41 °And whereas thou sawest the feet and
toes, part of potters' clay, and part of iron, the
kingdom shall be divided; but there shall be
in it of the °strength of the iron, forasmuch
as thou sawest the iron mixed with °miry
clay.
42 And *as* the toes of the feet *were* °part of
iron, and part of clay, *so* the kingdom shall be
°partly strong, and °partly °broken.
43 And whereas thou sawest iron mixed with
[41] miry clay, °they shall mingle themselves
with the seed of [38] men: but they shall not
cleave one to another, even as iron °is not
mixed with clay.
44 And in the days of °these kings shall
the [18] God of heaven set up a kingdom, which
shall never be destroyed: and the kingdom
shall not be left to other people, *but* it shall
[34] break in pieces and consume all these kingdoms, and it shall stand °for ever.
45 Forasmuch as thou sawest that [34] the stone
was cut out of the mountain [34] without hands,
and that it [34] brake in pieces the [35] iron, the
[35] brass, the [35] clay, the [35] silver, and the [35] gold;
the great [18] God hath made known to the king
what shall come to pass hereafter: and the
dream *is* certain, and the interpretation thereof sure."

G f (p. 1180) 46 Then the king [1] Nebuchadnezzar fell upon
his face, and worshipped Daniel, and com-
manded that they should offer an °oblation
and sweet odours unto him.
47 The king answered unto Daniel, and said,
"Of a truth *it is,* that your [18] God °*is* a [18] God
of [18] gods, and a °Lord of kings, and a [22] Revealer of [18] secrets, seeing thou couldest reveal
this [18] secret."
48 Then the king °made Daniel a great man,
and gave him many great gifts, and made him
ruler over the whole province of Babylon, and
chief of the °governors over all the [12] wise *men*
of Babylon.

g 49 Then Daniel requested of the king, and he
set °Shadrach, Meshach, and Abed-nego, over
the affairs of the province of Babylon: °but
Daniel *sat* in the gate of the king.

38 children = sons.

men. Chald. *'ănāshā'.*

hath He given. According to His word (Jer. 27. 6, 7; 28. 14, &c. Cp. 1. 2 and Ezek. 26. 7.

Thou. Nebuchadnezzar.

art = art represented by. Fig. *Metaphor.* Ap. 6.

head: i.e. the first of these five kingdoms, not the first king of Babylon. See note on *v.* 37.

of. Genitive of Material. Ap. 17. 6.

39 arise = stand up. Chald. *ḳūm* = to begin to exist. See note on Ex. 1. 8.

another. The kingdom of Medo-Persia, which succeeded Babylon by occupying Jerusalem (2 Chron. 36. 22).

inferior. As silver is inferior to gold, in value and in specific gravity (see note on *v.* 32) so the second kingdom was inferior to the first. The successive kingdoms are marked by evolution (or rather, devolution). In the first (Babylon) the king possessed absolute power ("whom he would he slew", &c., 5. 19); the second [Medo-Persian] was a government by law which was superior to the king (6. 1, 14, &c.).

third kingdom. This again was "inferior", as being less despotic.

40 the fourth: i.e. Rome (Luke 2 and 3). Observe that it does not say there were "four, and no more", as alleged; but "the fourth". An *ordinal* number, not *cardinal.* The Chald. is *r^ebī'ayā'* (text), or *r^ebī'āh* (margin) = fourth, as in 3. 25; 7. 7, 19, 23. Not *'arba',* which = four. The *fifth* is revealed in *vv.* 41–43. The power which was to succeed Rome in the possession of Jerusalem was to be the Mohammedan power, which was still future when our Lord referred to it in Luke 21. 24; but the Lord does not *name* it, because the condition of Acts 3. 18–26 could not be anticipated, assumed, or forestalled.

strong = hard. This was the character of Rome, both royal, imperial, and republican.

subdueth = crusheth.

breaketh = dasheth, or bringeth to ruin. Chald. *r^e'a'.* Not the same word as in *vv.* 1, 34, 35, 42, 44, 45.

bruise = bring to ruin. Chald. *r^e'a'.* Ap. 44. viii. The same word as "breaketh" earlier in the verse.

41 And whereas, &c. The fifth power is now to be described (the "feet and toes"). It came into possession of Jerusalem in A. D. 636 (Rome having held the city for 666 years: viz., from the battle of Actium, 31 B. C. —A. D. 636). Its character as described in *v.* 41 is exact; and, as represented by the "feet", Jerusalem has indeed been "trodden down" (Luke 21. 24) as was never done by any of the other four powers.

strength = hardness.

miry = muddy. Chald. *tīn.* Same as Heb. *tīt.* Occ. 2 Sam. 22. 43. Job 41. 30 (Heb. *v.* 22). Pss. 18. 42 (Heb. *v.* 43); 40. 2 (Heb. *v.* 3); 69. 14 (Heb. *v.* 15). Isa. 41. 25; 57. 20. Jer. 38. 6. Mic. 7. 10. Nah. 3. 14. Zech. 9. 3; 10. 5. Not the same as that rendered "broken" (= brittle), *v.* 42, as stated by some commentators.

42 part = a portion [of them], or some of them. Chald. *min.*

partly = in part, or at the end. Chald. *ḳ^eẓāth,* as in 4. 29 (Heb. *v.* 26), 34 (Heb. *v.* 31). Occurs only in these three places. Cp. the Heb. *ḳ^eẓāth* (1. 2 with 5, 15, 18).

partly broken = part [of it shall be] broken.

broken = fragile, easily broken. Chald. *t^ebār.* Occurs only here. **43 they**: i.e. the toes. **is not mixed** = mingleth not. **44 these kings.** Represented by the ten toes: i.e. in their days, at the end of the time of the *fifth* power. Cp. Rev. 17. 12–18. That is the moment of the great stone, and of the coming of Messiah. **for ever** = to the ages. See Ap. 151. **46 oblation** = a gift offering. Ap. 43. II. iii. **47 is** = He [is]. **Lord.** Chald. Adonai. Ap. 4. VIII (2). **48 made Daniel a great man** = exalted Daniel. **governors** = prefects, or nobles. Chald. *signīn.* Occurs in Dan. only here, 3. 2, 3, 27; and 6. 7. **49 Shadrach, &c.** See note on 1. 7. **but Daniel sat in the gate, &c.** See note on Est. 2. 19.

C K L N (p. 1184) 475 **3** Nebuchadnezzar the king made an °image of gold, whose °height *was* °threescore °cubits, *and* the °breadth thereof °six °cubits: he set it up in the plain of °Dura, in the province of Babylon.

2 Then Nebuchadnezzar °the king sent °to gather together the °princes, the °governors, and the °captains, the °judges, the °treasurers, the °counsellers, the °sheriffs, and all the °rulers of the provinces, to come to the dedication of the image which Nebuchadnezzar the king had set up.

3 Then the [2] princes, the [2] governors, and [2] captains, the [2] judges, the [2] treasurers, the [2] counsellers, the [2] sheriffs, and all the [2] rulers of the provinces, were gathered together unto the dedication of the [1] image that Nebuchadnezzar the king had set up; and they stood before the [1] image that Nebuchadnezzar had set up.

4 Then an °herald cried aloud, "To you it is commanded, O °people, °nations, and °languages,

5 *That* at what time ye hear the sound of the °cornet, flute, °harp, °sackbut, psaltery, dulcimer, and all kinds of musick, ye fall down and worship the golden image that Nebuchadnezzar the king hath set up:

6 And whoso falleth not down and worshippeth shall the same °hour be cast into the midst of a burning fiery furnace."

O 7 Therefore at that time, when all the people heard the sound of the [5] cornet, flute, [5] harp, sackbut, psaltery, and all kinds of musick, all the [4] people, the [4] nations, and the [4] languages, fell down *and* worshipped the golden [1] image that Nebuchadnezzar the king had set up.

M 8 Wherefore at that time °certain °Chaldeans came near, and accused the Jews.

9 They spake and said to the king Nebuchadnezzar, "O king, live for ever.

10 Thou, O king, hast made a decree, that every °man that shall hear the sound of the [5] cornet, flute, [5] harp, [5] sackbut, psaltery, and dulcimer, and all kinds of musick, shall fall down and worship the golden image:

11 And whoso falleth not down and worshippeth, *that* he should be cast into the midst of a burning fiery furnace.

12 There are [8] certain Jews whom thou hast set over the affairs of the province of Babylon, °Shadrach, Meshach, and Abed-nego; these [10] men, O king, have not regarded thee: they serve not thy °gods, nor worship the golden [1] image which thou hast set up."

K L N 13 Then Nebuchadnezzar in *his* rage and fury commanded to bring [12] Shadrach, Meshach, and Abed-nego. Then they brought these [12] men before the king.

14 Nebuchadnezzar spake and said unto them, "*Is it* °true, O [12] Shadrach, Meshach, and Abed-nego, do not ye serve my [12] gods, nor worship the golden [1] image which I have set up?

15 Now if ye be ready that at what time ye hear the sound of the [5] cornet, flute, [5] harp, [5] sackbut, psaltery, and dulcimer, and all kinds of musick, ye fall down and worship the [1] image which I have made; °*well:* but if ye wor-

3. 1-30 (**C**, p. 1178). DANIEL'S COMPANIONS. THE FIERY FURNACE. (*Alternations.*)

C | K | L | N | 1-6. Command to worship the image.
O | 7. Obedience.
M | 8-12. Accusation of the three.
K | *L* | *N* | 13-15. Command to worship the image.
O | 16-18. Refusal.
M | 19-30. Condemnation of the three.

1 image. This could not have been an image of a human being. The height and breadth are out of all proportion for this; the former being one to ten instead of one to six. A figure drawn on this scale, will at once be seen to be impossible. Having determined that it is a human figure, tradition then assumes it to have been a proportional figure "on a pedestal", or simply "a bust on a pillar". But there is nothing in the text to suggest this. It would exactly suit an *Asherah* (Ap. 42). The Heb. *tzelem* denotes something shaped by cutting or carving. Ezek 16. 17, and 23. 14, practically make this certain. See the verb in Ezek. 7. 20; and cp. what is said in Num. 33. 52.

height . . . breadth. See above note.

threescore . . . six. The numbers of man (Ap. 10). Note the *six* instruments (cp. 5, 7, 10, 15). See note on 1 Sam. 17. 4. **cubits.** See Ap. 51. III. 2 (1).

Dura. Now *Dūair*, twelve miles south-east of Babylon.

2 the king sent. This great Durbar would hardly have taken place till after the campaign referred to in note on "came" (1. 1). It was therefore probably held about 475 B.C., in Daniel's thirty-eighth year, twenty years after Nebuchadnezzar's dream of himself, the "head of gold" (ch. 2).

to gather together, &c. Note the eight technical terms. Well known to Daniel, but difficult for a Jew in Jerusalem 300 years later to enumerate so minutely and so accurately. **princes**=satraps.

governors. See note on 2. 48.

captains=pashas (as in Neh. 5. 14, 18. Hag. 1. 14), the first three being *governmental.*

judges=viziers, or chief judges.

treasurers: these two being *courtiers.*

counsellers=counsellors of State, judges. The same word as in *v.* 3. Not the same word as in *vv.* 24, 27.

sheriffs=lawyers; these two being *legal.*

rulers, &c.=superintendents, being *functional* and general.

4 herald. Chald. *kārōzā'*. Not from the Greek *kērux*, but an old Persian word *khresic'*, a crier, from which comes the Chald. verb *k*e*var*, to make a proclamation, as in 5. 29. **people**=peoples, or nations.

nations=races, or tribes.

languages=tongues. Fig. *Catabasis.* Ap. 6.

5 cornet, &c. These names are supposed to be Greek, or from the Greek; but Athenæus, a Greek grammarian (about A.D. 200-300), says the *sambukē* ("sackbut") was a Syriac invention. Strabo, in his geography (54 B.C.-A.D. 24), ascribes Greek music to Asia, and says: "the Athenians always showed their admiration of foreign customs" (X. C. III. c. 17, 18).

harp. Chald. *kithroṣ*; Greek *kithara.* Terpander, a Greek musician (seventh century B.C.), the father of Greek music, invented the *kithara* with seven strings (Strabo says) instead of four, and one is sculptured on a monument of Assurbanipal (Lenormant, *La Divination chez les Chaldéens*, pp. 190, 191).

sackbut. See note on "cornet", above.

hour=moment. Chald. *shā'āh*, as in *vv.* 3, 6, 15; 4. 33; 5. 5.

8 certain=men: probably our grandees. Pl. of Chald. *g*e*bar.* Ap. 14. iv. **Chaldeans.** See note on 1. 4.

10 man. Chald. *'ĕnāsh.* Ap. 4. III.

12 Shadrach, &c. See note on 1. 7.

men=strong men, or grandees. Pl. of Chald. *g*e*bar.* Ap. 14. IV. **gods.** Chald. *'elah.* Ap. 4. I.

14 true=of set purpose.

15 well. Note the Fig. *Aposiopesis* (Ap. 6). Or, supply [well and good].

475 ship not, ye shall be cast the same hour into
the midst of a °burning fiery furnace; and
who *is* that °God that shall deliver you out of
my hands?"

O 16 [12] Shadrach, Meshach, and Abed-nego,
(p. 1184) °answered and said to the king, "O Nebuchadnezzar, we °*are* not careful to answer thee
in this matter.

17 If it be *so*, our [15] God Whom we serve °is
able to deliver us from the burning fiery furnace, and He will deliver *us* out of thine hand, O king.

18 But if not, be it known unto thee, O king, that we will not serve thy [12] gods, nor worship °the golden [1] image which thou hast set up."

M h 19 Then was Nebuchadnezzar °full of fury,
(p. 1185) and the °form of his °visage was changed
against [12] Shadrach, Meshach, and Abed-nego: *therefore* he spake, and commanded that they should heat the furnace one seven times more than it was wont to be heated.

i 20 And he commanded the °most mighty
[12] men that *were* in his army °to bind [12] Shadrach, Meshach, and Abed-nego, *and* to cast *them* into the burning fiery furnace.

21 Then these [12] men were [20] bound in their °coats, their °hosen, and their °hats, and their *other* garments, and were cast into the midst of the burning fiery furnace.

k 22 Therefore because the king's °command-
ment was urgent, and the furnace exceeding hot, the flame of the fire slew °those [12] men that took up [12] Shadrach, Meshach, and Abed-nego.

l 23 And these three [12] men, [12] Shadrach, Me-
shach, and Abed-nego, fell down [20] bound into the midst of the burning fiery furnace.

h 24 Then Nebuchadnezzar the king was as-
tonied, and rose up in haste, *and* spake, and said unto his °counsellers, "Did not we cast three [12] men [21] bound into the midst of the fire?" They answered and said unto the king, °"True, O king."

25 He answered and said, "Lo, I see four [12] men loose, walking in the midst of the fire, and they have no hurt; and the form of the fourth is like °the son of [15] God."

i 26 Then Nebuchadnezzar came near to the
°mouth of the burning fiery furnace, *and* spake, and said, "Shadrach, Meshach, and Abed-nego, ye servants of the most high [15] God, come forth, and come *hither*." Then Shadrach, Meshach, and Abed-nego, came forth of the midst of the fire.

k 27 And the [2] princes, [2] governors, and [2] cap-
tains, and the king's [24] counsellers, being gathered together, °saw these [12] men, upon whose bodies the fire had no power, nor was an hair of their head singed, neither were their coats °changed, nor the smell of fire had passed on them.

l 28 *Then* Nebuchadnezzar spake, and said,
"Blessed *be* the [15] God of Shadrach, Meshach, and Abed-nego, Who hath sent His angel, and delivered His servants that trusted in Him, and have changed the king's word, and yielded their bodies, that they might not serve nor worship any [15] god, except their own [15] God.

burning. The 1611 edition of the A.V. omits "burning". **God.** Chald. *'ĕlāh*. Ap. 4. I.

16 answered and said. See note on Deut. 1. 41.

are not careful = do not account it needful.

17 is able to deliver us. The Massoretic pointing requires this punctuation: "to deliver us; from the burning fiery furnace He will deliver us".

18 the. The 1611 edition of the A.V. reads "thy".

3. 19-30 (*M*, p. 1184). CONDEMNATION OF THE THREE. (*Extended Alternation.*)

M h | 19. The king enraged.
i | 20, 21. The Three cast into the furnace.
k | 22. Fire. Power over the executioners.
l | 23. Deliverance to the fire. Fall.
h | 24, 25. The king amazed.
i | 26. The Three called forth from the furnace.
k | 27. Fire. No power over the Three.
l | 28-30. Deliverance from the furnace. Promotion.

19 full of = filled with. **form** = appearance.

visage = countenance.

20 most mighty men. Chald. = mighty [ones] of strength.

to bind. Chald. *kᵉphath*. Occ. only here and *vv.* 21, 23, 24.

21 coats = cloaks, or mantles. **hosen** = tunics.

hats = turbans, mantles, or cloaks.

22 commandment = word.

those men = those very men.

24 counsellers: or, ministers [standing near] to him; either to his throne or near at the time. Chald. *haddābrīn*. Not the same word as in *vv.* 2, 3.

True: or, Truth, or, Surely.

25 the son of God = a son of God (no Art.): i.e. a superhuman being, or an angel. Cp. *v.* 28, and see Ap. 23. Nebuchadnezzar could know nothing of N.T. revelation.

26 mouth = door. **27 saw** = kept gazing upon.

changed: or, discoloured.

29 speak, &c. = charge any fault or error.

amiss: or, rash. Cp. 2 Sam. 6. 7, as Nebuchadnezzar himself had done.

cut in pieces, &c. See note on 2. 5. **deliver** = rescue.

4. 1-37 (**D**, p. 1178). NEBUCHADNEZZAR'S DREAM OF THE GREAT TREE. HIS TEMPORARY DEPOSITION. (*Introversion and Repeated Alternation.*)

D P | 1-3. The Proclamation.
Q¹ | 4, 5. The Dream dreamed.
R¹ | 6-9. Interpretation desired.
Q² | 10-17. The Dream recited.
R² | 18. Interpretation required.
Q³ | 19-23. The Dream repeated.
R³ | 24-33. Interpretation given and fulfilled.
P | 34-37. The Proclamation.

1 Nebuchadnezzar. What follows is evidently a proclamation. Given probably in 454 B.C., the last of the seven years of his "madness" (461-454 B.C.), the same year as the decree of Astyages, Daniel being then fifty-nine.

people = the peoples.

nations = races. **languages** = tongues.

29 Therefore I make a decree, That every people, nation, and language, which °speak any thing °amiss against the [15] God of Shadrach, Meshach, and Abed-nego, shall be °cut in pieces, and their houses shall be made a dunghill: because there is no other [15] God that can °deliver after this sort."

30 Then the king promoted [12] Shadrach, Meshach, and Abed-nego, in the province of Babylon.

4 °Nebuchadnezzar the king, unto all °peo- **D** P
ple, °nations, and °languages, that dwell 462-454
in all the earth; "Peace be multiplied unto you.

454 **2** I °thought it good to shew the signs and °wonders that the °HIGH °God hath wrought toward me.

3 °How great *are* His signs! and how mighty *are* His wonders! His kingdom *is* an everlasting kingdom, and His dominion *is* from generation to generation.

Q[1] (p. 1185) **4** I Nebuchadnezzar was at rest in mine house, and flourishing in my palace:

5 I saw a °dream which made me afraid, and the thoughts upon my bed and the °visions of my head troubled me.

R[1] 462 **6** Therefore made I a decree °to bring in all the wise *men* of Babylon before me, that they might make known unto me the interpretation of the dream.

7 Then came in the °magicians, the astrologers, the Chaldeans, and the soothsayers: and I told the dream before them; but they did not make known unto me the interpretation thereof.

8 But at the last Daniel came in before me, whose name *was* °Belteshazzar, according to the name of my °god, and in whom *is* the °spirit of the °holy °gods: and before him I told the [5]dream, *saying*,

9 'O Belteshazzar, °master of the magicians, because I know that the [8]spirit of the [8]holy [2]gods *is* in thee, and no °secret troubleth thee, tell me the visions of my dream that I have seen, and the interpretation thereof.

Q[2] **10** Thus *were* the visions of mine head in my bed; °I saw, and °behold a tree in the midst of the earth, and the height thereof *was* great.

11 The tree grew, and was strong, and the height thereof reached unto heaven, and the sight thereof to the end of all the earth:

12 The leaves thereof *were* fair, and the fruit thereof much, and in it *was* meat for all: the beasts of the field had shadow under it, and the fowls of the heaven dwelt in the boughs thereof, and all flesh was fed of it.

13 [10]I saw in the visions of my head upon my bed, and, [10]behold, °a °watcher and an [8]holy one came down from heaven;

14 He cried aloud, and said thus, 'Hew down the tree, and cut off his branches, shake off his leaves, and scatter his fruit: let the beasts get away from under it, and the fowls from his branches:

15 Nevertheless leave °the stump of his roots in the earth, even with a band of iron and brass, in the °tender grass of the field; and let it be °wet with the dew of heaven, and *let* his portion *be* with the beasts in the grass of the earth:

16 °Let his heart be changed from °man's, and let a beast's heart be given unto him; and let °seven times pass over him.

17 This matter *is* by the decree of the [13]watchers, and the °demand by the word of the [8]holy ones: to the intent that the living may know that the [2]MOST HIGH °ruleth in the kingdom of men, and giveth it to whomsoever He will, and setteth up over it the °basest of men.'

R[2] **18** This [5]dream I king Nebuchadnezzar have seen. Now thou, O [8]Belteshazzar, declare the interpretation thereof, forasmuch as all the wise *men* of my kingdom are not able to make known unto me the interpretation: but thou *art* able; for the [8]spirit of the holy [8]gods *is* in thee.'

19 Then Daniel, whose name *was* [8]Belteshazzar, was °astonied for °one hour, and his Q[3]
thoughts troubled him. °The king spake, and said, [8]'Belteshazzar, let not the dream, or the interpretation thereof, trouble thee.' [8]Belteshazzar °answered and said, 'My lord, the dream *be* to them that hate thee, and the interpretation thereof to thine enemies.

20 The tree that thou sawest, which grew, and was strong, whose height reached unto the heaven, and the sight thereof to all the earth;

21 Whose leaves *were* fair, and the fruit thereof much, and in it *was* meat for all; under which the beasts of the field dwelt, and upon whose branches the fowls of the heaven had their habitation:

22 It *is* thou, O king, that art grown and become strong: for thy greatness is grown, and reacheth unto heaven, and thy dominion to the end of the earth.

23 And whereas the king saw a [13]watcher and an [8]holy one coming down from heaven, and saying, Hew the tree down, and destroy

2 thought = have thought.
wonders = astonishing things.
HIGH = most HIGH.
God. Chald. *'ĕlāhā'* (emphatic). Ap. 4. I.
3 How great, &c. Cp. *v.* 34; 2. 44; 7. 17.
5 dream. One of twenty recorded dreams. See note on Gen. 20. 3.
visions of my head, &c. Cp. *v.* 10, and 2. 28.
6 to bring in all the wise men, &c. Probably done from motives of state policy, or acting on Daniel's own advice. A writer clever enough to be a forger would be wise enough not to leave the loophole alleged.
7 magicians, &c. See note on 1. 2.
8 Belteshazzar. See note on 1. 7.
god. Chald. *'ĕlāh.* Ap. 4. I.
spirit. Heb. *rūach.* Ap. 9.
holy. See note on Ex. 3. 5.
gods. Chald. *'ĕlahīn* (pl.). Ap. 4. I.
9 master of the magicians. Daniel still held the position given him in 2. 48.
secret. Chald. *rāz.* Same word as in ch. 2 (except *v.* 22). See notes on 2. 18, 22.
10 I saw = I was gazing.
behold. Fig. *Asterismos.* Ap. 6.
13 a watcher and an holy one. Fig. *Hendiadys* (Ap. 6) = an holy angel.
watcher. A Chaldee name (*'īr*) for an angelic being, watching over the affairs of men. Cp *vv.* 17, 23. Not the same root as in 9. 14.
15 the stump of his roots = his root-trunk.
tender grass = herbage.
wet = drenched.
16 Let his heart, &c. The figure here changes from a tree to that of a beast, mentioned in *v.* 15.
man's. Chald. *'ănāshā'.* Ap. 14. III.
seven times. The inscriptions state that there were several years in which Nebuchadnezzar did nothing.
17 demand = mandate.
ruleth = hath dominion.
basest = lowest.
19 astonied = astonished.
one hour. Chald. *shā'ah* = a moment, as *v.* 33; 3. 6, 15; 5. 5.
The king spake. Note the change of speakers.
answered and said. See note on Deut. 1. 41.

462 it; yet leave [15] the stump of the roots thereof
in the earth, even with a band of iron and
brass, in the [15] tender grass of the field; and
let it be [15] wet with the dew of heaven, and
let his portion *be* with the beasts of the field,
till [16] seven times pass over him;

R³ 24 This *is* the interpretation, O king, and
this *is* the decree of the [2] MOST HIGH, which is
come upon my lord the king:
25 That they shall ° drive thee from ° men,
and thy dwelling shall be with the beasts of
the field, and they shall ° make thee to eat
grass as oxen, and they shall [15] wet thee with
the dew of heaven, and [16] seven times shall
pass over thee, till thou know that the [2] MOST
HIGH [17] ruleth in the kingdom of men, and giveth it to whomsoever He will.
26 And whereas they commanded to leave
[15] the stump of the tree roots; thy kingdom
shall be sure unto thee, after that thou shalt
have known that ° the heavens do rule.
27 Wherefore, O king, let my ° counsel be
acceptable unto thee, and ° break off thy ° sins
by ° righteousness, and thine ° iniquities by
shewing mercy to the ° poor; if it may be a
lengthening of thy tranquillity.'
28 ° All this came upon the king Nebuchadnezzar.
461 29 At the end of twelve months he walked
in the palace of the kingdom of Babylon.
30 The king ° spake, and said, 'Is not this
° great Babylon, ° that 𝔍 have built for the
° house of the kingdom by the might of my
power, and for the honour of my majesty?'
31 While the word *was* in the king's mouth,
there fell a voice from heaven, *saying*, 'O king
Nebuchadnezzar, to thee it is spoken; The
kingdom is departed from thee.
32 And they shall [25] drive thee from [25] men,
and thy dwelling *shall be* with the beasts of
the field: they shall [25] make thee to eat grass
as oxen, and [16] seven times shall pass over
thee, until thou know that the [2] MOST HIGH
ruleth in the kingdom of [25] men, and giveth it
to whomsoever He will.'
33 The same [19] hour was the thing fulfilled
upon Nebuchadnezzar: and he was driven
from [25] men, and did eat grass as oxen, and
his body was [15] wet with the dew of heaven,
till his hairs were grown like eagles' *feathers*,
and his nails like birds' *claws*.

P 34 And at the end of the days ° 𝔍 Nebuchad-
454 nezzar lifted up mine eyes unto heaven, and
mine understanding returned unto me, and I
blessed ° the [2] MOST HIGH, and ° I praised
and honoured Him That liveth for ever,
Whose dominion *is* an everlasting dominion,
and His kingdom *is* from generation to generation:
35 And ° all the inhabitants of the earth *are*
reputed as nothing: ° and He doeth according
to His will in the army of heaven, and *among*
° the inhabitants of the earth: and ° none can
stay His hand, or say unto Him, ° 'What doest
Thou?'
36 At the same time my reason returned
unto me; and for the glory of my kingdom, mine honour and brightness returned
unto me; and my ° counsellers and my ° lords
sought unto me; and I was established in my
kingdom, and excellent majesty was added
unto me.
37 Now ° 𝔍 Nebuchadnezzar praise and extol
and honour the King of heaven, all Whose
works *are* truth, and His ways judgment:
and those that walk in pride He is able to
abase."

25 drive thee, &c. The mental disease of Nebuchadnezzar is rare. It is called *Lycanthropy* (from Greek, *lukos* = a wolf, and *anthrōpos* = a man), because the man imagines himself to be a wolf, or some other animal.

men. Chald. pl. of *’ănāsh*. Ap. 14. III.

make = suffer.

26 the heavens. Put by Fig. *Metonymy* (of Subject), Ap. 6, for God Who dwells there. Cp. Luke 15. 18.

27 counsel = advice. Not the same word as in 3. 24, 27; 4. 36; 6. 7.

break off. This is rendered in the Vulgate (the Authorised Version of the Church of Rome) by "redeem"; but the Chald. *p^{e}raḳ* = break off. First occ. in Heb. (*pāraḳ*) Gen. 27. 40. Ex. 32. 2, 3, 24, &c. See note on Ps. 136. 24.

sins: *chăṭāi*. Same as Ap. 44. i.

righteousness. This is rendered as "almsgiving" in the Vulg. But Chald. *tzidḳāh* (Heb. *tz^{e}dāḳāh*) = righteousness never signifies alms or almsgiving.

iniquities. Chald. *‘ivyā’*. Same as Ap. 44. iv.

poor = wretched, miserable. Chald. *‘ănāh*. See note on "poverty", Prov. 6. 11. Here referring doubtless to the Jewish captives.

28 All this came. Here the change is to the historical narration.

30 spake = answered.

great Babylon. The German Orient Society's excavations during recent years have shown how "great" it was. See *Records of the Past*, vol. i, p. 160; vol. ii, p. 282; vol. iii, p. 166, &c.; vol. vii, p. 261, &c.

that 𝔍 have built. Everywhere this is repeated by Nebuchadnezzar on bricks, pavements, walls, &c.

house of the kingdom = the royal palace.

34 𝔍 Nebuchadnezzar, &c. Here the king again speaks. This corresponds with the Proclamation (*vv.* 1–3 = P), and is the ground of its being made.

the MOST HIGH. Cp. *vv.* 17, 32.

I praised, &c. Modern critics are stumbled because Nebuchadnezzar should do this while he was an idolater. But surely it is the token that a great change had taken place.

This occurred in 454, just after Astyages (the great king = Artaxerxes) had issued his decree for the rebuilding of Jerusalem; and it was imperative that Nebuchadnezzar should now issue this imperial decree. See Ap. 58.

This year, 454 B. C., is specially marked by the issue of these two momentous proclamations.

When Nebuchadnezzar's madness began, Daniel was fifty-two, and when it ended, he was fifty-nine years old.

35 all, &c. Cp. Job 34. 14, 15, 19–24. Isa. 40. 15–17, 22–24.

and He, &c. Cp. 1 Sam. 3. 18. Job 23. 13. Pss. 33. 9–11; 115. 3; 135. 6. Isa. 14. 24–27; 46. 10, 11.

the inhabitants, &c. Pss. 33. 8, 14; 49. 1. Isa. 26. 9.

none, &c. Cp. Job 9. 4, 13; 34. 29; 40 9–12; 42. 2. Acts 5. 39; 9. 5; 11. 17, &c.

What, &c. Cp. Job 9. 12; 33. 12, 13; 40. 2. Isa. 45. 9–11.

36 counsellers. See note on 3. 24.

lords. See note on 5. 1, and "princes", 5. 2.

37 𝔍 Nebuchadnezzar, &c. This corresponds with *vv.* 1–3. See the Structure, p. 1185.

D S[1] T m (p. 1188) 426 **5** °Belshazzar the king made °a great feast to a thousand of his °lords, and drank °wine before the thousand.

2 [1]Belshazzar, whiles he tasted the [1]wine, commanded to bring the golden and silver °vessels which his °father Nebuchadnezzar had °taken out of the temple which *was* in Jerusalem; that the king, and his °princes, his °wives, and his concubines, might drink therein.

3 Then they brought the golden [2]vessels that were [2]taken out of the temple of the house of °God which *was* at Jerusalem; and the king, and his [2]princes, his wives, and his concubines, drank in them.

4 They drank [1]wine,

n and praised the [3]gods of gold, and of silver, of brass, of iron, of wood, and of stone.

U o 5 °In the same hour came forth fingers of a °man's hand, and wrote over against the °candlestick upon the plaister of the wall of the king's palace: and the king °saw °the part of the hand that wrote.

p 6 Then the king's °countenance was changed, and his thoughts troubled him, so that the joints of his loins were loosed, and his knees smote one against another.

7 The king cried aloud to bring in the °astrologers, the Chaldeans, and the soothsayers. *And* the king spake, and said to the wise *men* of Babylon, "Whosoever shall read this writing, and shew me the interpretation thereof, shall be clothed with °scarlet, and *have* a chain of gold about his neck, and shall °be the third ruler in the kingdom."

8 Then came in all °the king's wise *men*: but they could not read the writing, nor make known to the king the interpretation thereof.

9 Then was king [1]Belshazzar greatly troubled, and his [6]countenance was changed in him, and his [1]lords were °astonied.

10 *Now* °the queen by reason of the words of the king and his [1]lords °came into the banquet house: *and* the queen spake and said, "O king, live for ever: let not thy thoughts trouble thee, nor let thy countenance be changed:

11 There is a °man in thy kingdom, in whom *is* the °spirit of the °holy °gods; and in the days of thy [2]father light and understanding and wisdom, like the wisdom of the °gods, was found in him; whom the king Nebuchadnezzar thy [2]father, the king, *I say*, thy [2]father, °made master of the magicians, [7]astrologers, Chaldeans, *and* soothsayers;

12 Forasmuch as an excellent [11]spirit, and knowledge, and understanding, interpreting of dreams, and shewing of °hard sentences, and dissolving of doubts, were found in the same Daniel, whom the king named °Belteshazzar: now let Daniel be called, and he will shew the interpretation."

13 Then was Daniel brought in before the king. *And* the king spake and said unto Daniel, °"*Art* thou that Daniel, which *art* of the °children of the captivity of Judah, whom the king my father brought out of °Jewry?

14 I have even heard of thee, that the [11]spirit of °the [11]gods *is* in thee, and *that* light and understanding and excellent wisdom is found in thee.

5. 1-31 (*D*, p. 1178). BELSHAZZAR'S VISION OF THE HAND. HIS FINAL DOOM. (*Division.*)

D | S[1] | 1-29. The Prediction.
  | S[2] | 30, 31. The Fulfilment.

5. 1-29 (S[1], above). THE PREDICTION. (BELSHAZZAR'S FEAST.) (*Alternations.*)

S[1] | T | m | 1-4-. Impiety.
    n | -4. Idolatry.
   U | o | 5. The Hand.
    p | 6-15. Interpretation required.
    q | 16. Gifts promised.
 T | *m* | 17-23-. Impiety.
    n | -23. Idolatry.
   U | *o* | 24. The Hand.
    p | 25-28. Interpretation given.
    q | 29. Gifts given.

1 Belshazzar. He was the son of Nabonidus. The inscriptions show that he was made co-regent while he (Nabonidus) went to meet Cyrus. See note on *vv.* 2, 7; 7. 1.

a great feast. The hall in which it was held has lately been excavated. It is 60 feet wide and 172 feet long, the walls being beautifully decorated with painted stucco designs. See *Records of the Past*, vol. i, part v, p. 160. The date was 426 B.C., Daniel being eighty-seven.

lords=great ones, or nobles. Chald. *rabr*^{e}*ban*, same as "princes" in *vv.* 2, 3.

wine. Chald. *chămrā'*. Same as Heb. *chemer*. Ap. 27. III.

2 vessels. Cp. 1. 2; and see 2 Kings 25. 15. 2 Chron. 36. 10. Jer. 52. 19.

father Nebuchadnezzar. No "historical difficulty". Critics should tell us what word Daniel could have used, seeing there is no word in Chaldee or Hebrew for "grandfather". The word "father" is used by Fig. *Synecdoche* (of Species), Ap. 6, for ancestor. Cp. 1 Kings 15. 11-13, where David is called the "father" of Asa, and Maachah is called his mother (cp. 2 Kings 15. 1, 2 with 11-13). In 2 Kings 14. 3 the same is said of Amaziah; and in 2 Chron. 34. 1, 2, of Josiah. Cp. Rom. 9. 10, where Paul speaks of "our father Isaac". But Jer. 27. 7 explains the matter fully: "all nations shall serve him (i. e. Nebuchadnezzar), and his son (Nabonidus), and his son's son (Belshazzar), until the very time of his land come". See note on 7. 1.

taken out=brought forth. Cp. Ezra 1. 7.

princes. Chald. *rabr*^{e}*bān*, as in *v.* 3, same as "lords" in *vv.* 1, 9, 10, 23. Elsewhere, only in this book, in 4. 36, and 6. 17.

wives. Showing that the "queen" mentioned in *v.* 10 must have been his mother.

3 God. Chald. *'ĕlāhā'*. See Ap. 4. I.

5 In the same hour=At the same moment. See note on "hour", 3. 19. **man's.** Chald. *'ĕnāsh*. Ap. 14. III.

candlestick=lampstand. **saw**=was gazing on.

the part=the end: i. e. the fingers.

6 countenance=bright looks.

7 astrologers, &c. See note on 2. 2.

scarlet=purple.

be the third ruler=rule as one of three: i. e. the third: Nabonidus being the first, and Belshazzar the second.

8 the king's. Some codices read "Babylon's".

9 astonied=dumbfoundered.

10 the queen. Nitocris, the daughter in law of Nebuchadnezzar, and mother of Nabonidus.

came into, &c. She was not present among the "wives" of *v.* 2.

11 man: or, grandee. Chald. *g*^{e}*bar*. Same as Ap. 14. IV.

spirit. Chald. *rūach*. Ap. 9.

holy. See note on Ex. 3. 5.

gods. Chald. *'ĕlāhīn* (pl.). Ap. 4. I.

made master of the magicians. See 2. 48. See note on 2. 2; and cp. 4. 9. **12 hard**=dark.

Belteshazzar. See note on 1. 7.

13 Art thou, &c. . . . ? Showing that the king had no personal knowledge of Daniel, or had disregarded him.

children=sons. **Jewry**=Judah.

14 the gods. Some codices, with seven early printed editions, and Syr., read "the holy gods", as in *v.* 11, and 4. 18.

426 15 And now the wise *men*, the [7]astrologers,
have been brought in before me, that they
should read this writing, and make known
unto me the interpretation thereof: but they
could not shew the interpretation of the thing:

q 16 And I have heard of thee, that thou canst
(p. 1188) make interpretations, and dissolve doubts:
now if thou canst read the writing, and make
known to me the interpretation thereof, thou
shalt be clothed with [7]scarlet, and *have* a chain
of gold about thy neck, and shalt be [7]the third
ruler in the kingdom."

Tm 17 Then Daniel answered and said before the
king, "Let thy gifts be to thyself, and give thy
rewards to another; yet I will read the writing
unto the king, and make known to him the
°interpretation.
18 O thou king, °the MOST HIGH [3]God gave
Nebuchadnezzar thy [2]father a kingdom, and
majesty, and glory, and honour:
19 And for the majesty that He gave him, all
°people, nations, and languages, trembled and
feared before him: °whom he would he slew;
and whom he would he kept alive; and whom
he would he set up; and whom he would he
put down.
20 But when his heart was lifted up, and his
°mind hardened in pride, he was deposed from
his kingly throne, and they [31]took his glory
from him:
21 And he was °driven from the sons of [5]men;
and his heart was made like the beasts, and
his dwelling *was* with the wild asses: they
fed him with grass like oxen, and his body was
°wet with the dew of heaven; till he knew
that [18]the MOST HIGH [3]God ruled in the kingdom of [5]men, and *that* He appointeth over it
whomsoever He will.
22 And thou °his son, O Belshazzar, hast not
humbled thine heart, though thou knewest all
this;
23 But hast lifted up thyself against °the
Lord of heaven; and they have brought the
[2]vessels of His house before thee, and thou,
and thy [1]lords, thy [2]wives, and thy concubines,
have drunk [1]wine in them;

n and thou hast praised the [11]gods of silver,
and gold, of brass, iron, wood, and stone,
°which see not, nor hear, nor know: and the
[3]God °in Whose hand thy °breath *is*, °and
Whose *are* all thy ways, hast thou not glorified:

Uo 24 Then was [5]the part of the hand sent from
Him; and °this writing was °written.

p 25 And this *is* the writing that was [24]written,
°MENE, MENE, °TEKEL, °UPHARSIN.
26 This *is* the interpretation of the thing:
[25]MENE; [3]God hath numbered thy kingdom,
and finished it.
27 [25]TEKEL; Thou art weighed in the
balances, and art found wanting.
28 [25]PERES; Thy kingdom is divided, and
given to the Medes and Persians."

q 29 Then commanded Belshazzar, and they
clothed Daniel with [7]scarlet, and *put* a chain
of gold about his neck, and °made a proclamation concerning him, that he should be [7]the
third ruler in the kingdom.

30 In °that night was [1]Belshazzar the king S[4]
of °the Chaldeans °slain. 426
31 And °Darius the Median °took the kingdom, *being* about °threescore and two years
old.

17 interpretation. Sept., Syr., and Vulg. read "interpretation thereof".

18 the MOST HIGH. Same as Heb. *'elyōn*. Ap. 4. VI.

19 people=peoples.

whom he would, &c See note on "inferior" (2. 39).

20 mind=spirit. Chald. *rūach*. Ap. 9.

21 driven, &c. Cp. 4. 32.

wet=drenched.

22 his son. See note on "father", *v.* 2.

23 the Lord. Chald. *mārē'*. The equivalent for the Heb. Adonai. Ap. 4. VIII (2). Cp. *Maran* in "*Maran-atha*" (1 Cor. 16. 22).

which see not, &c. Cp. Pss. 115. 4-8; 135. 15-17. Isa. 37. 19; 46. 6, 7. Hab. 2. 18, 19. 1 Cor. 8. 4.

in Whose hand, &c. Cp. Gen. 2. 7. Job 12. 10; 34. 14, 15. Pss. 104. 29; 146. 4. Isa. 42. 5. Acts 17. 25, 28, 29.

breath. Chald. *nishmā'*. Same as Heb. *neshāmāh*. Ap. 16.

and Whose, &c. Cp. Job 31. 4. Ps. 139. 3. Prov. 20. 24. Jer. 10. 23. Heb. 4. 13.

24 this writing. The Divine prophetic meaning could not be *known* or *understood* till interpreted by Daniel.

written: or graven.

25 MENE, MENE=**NUMBERED, NUMBERED.** Fig. *Epizeuxis* (Ap. 6), for great emphasis. Chald. *menē'*, *menē'*=numbered [yea] ended. See note on Jer. 27. 7.

TEKEL=**WEIGHED.** Chald. *tekēl* (cp. Heb. *shekel*. Ap. 51. II. 5).

UPHARSIN = **AND DIVIDED** (or **BROKEN**). Chald. *ūpharsīn* (the "*u*" being the conjunction=and), from Chald. *paraṣ*=to break. See note on 4. 27. There is a further reference, by the Fig. *Syllepsis* (or combination), Ap. 6, to the *Persians*, by whom the kingdom of Babylon was broken up.

29 made a proclamation. See note on "herald", 3. 4.

30 that night. Cp. *v.* 1.

Belshazzar. See note on *v.* 2.

the Chaldeans. Here spoken of in the national sense, not of a special class. See note on 1. 4.

slain. Either by the Persians, or it may have been by assassination by one of his own followers, or accidentally in the tumult. Chald. *ḳeṭal*, used of a violent death. Cp. *v.* 19. This was on the third of the month Marchesvan. On the eleventh, Belshazzar's wife died, perhaps from grief. See *Encycl. Brit*, vol. iii, p. 711, 712, 11th (Cambridge) edition. See Ap. 57.

31 Darius the Median. Through not noting the fact that "Darius" was an appellative denoting "the Maintainer", and used by Xerxes and others, modern critics have denied the existence of such a king. ASTYAGES was called "Darius". CYRUS (his son) was co-regent. His general GOBRYAS took the city in the name of CYRUS. See Isa. 45. 1. Cp. Jer. 51. 30, 31. See notes there. Consult Ap. 57.

took. Chald. *ḳebal*=to take from another. Cp. 7. 18. Not the same word as in *vv.* 2, 3, which is *nephaḳ*=to take out; or *v.* 20, which is *'ădāh*=remove.

threescore and two. Born 488 B.C. Herodotus states that CYRUS was about forty years of age at the taking of Babylon (in 426 B.C.). At that age his father ASTYAGES ("Darius the Median") was about "threescore and two years old" (5. 31). Cyrus would therefore be just forty, according to the chronology of Ap. 50, having been born in 466 B.C.

C V (p. 1190) 426 **6** It pleased °Darius to set over the kingdom °an hundred and twenty °princes, which should be over the whole kingdom;

2 And over these three °presidents; of whom Daniel *was* first: that the [1]princes might give accounts unto them, and the king should have no damage.

3 Then this Daniel was °preferred above the [2]presidents and [1]princes, because °an excellent °spirit *was* in him; and °the king °thought to set him over the whole realm.

W1 X1 4 Then the [2]presidents and [1]princes sought to find °occasion against Daniel concerning the kingdom; but they could find none occasion nor fault; forasmuch as he *was* faithful, neither was there any error or fault found in him.

5 Then said these °men, "We shall not find any occasion against this Daniel, except we find *it* against him concerning the law of his °God."

6 Then these [2]presidents and [1]princes °assembled together to the king, and said thus unto him, "King Darius, live for ever.

Y1 7 All the [2]presidents of the kingdom, the °governors, and the [1]princes, the °counsellers, and the °captains, have consulted together °to establish a royal statute, and to °make a firm °decree, that whosoever shall °ask a petition of any [5]God or °man for thirty days, save of thee, O king, he shall be cast into the den of lions.

8 Now, O king, establish the [7]decree, and sign the writing, that it be not changed, according to the law of the Medes and Persians, °which altereth not."

9 Wherefore king Darius signed the writing and the [7]decree.

W2 X2 10 Now when Daniel knew that the writing was signed, he went into °his house; and his windows being open in his chamber °toward Jerusalem, he kneeled upon his knees three times a day, and prayed, and gave thanks before his [5]God, as he did aforetime.

11 Then these [5]men [6]assembled, and found Daniel praying and making supplication before his [5]God.

12 Then they came near, and spake before the king concerning the king's [7]decree; "Hast thou not signed a [7]decree, that every [7]man that shall [7]ask *a petition* of any [5]God or [7]man within thirty days, save of thee, O king, shall be cast into the den of lions?" The king answered and said, "The thing *is* true, according to the law of the Medes and Persians, [8]which altereth not."

13 Then answered they and said before the king, "That Daniel, which *is* of the °children of the captivity of Judah, regardeth not thee, O king, nor the [7]decree that thou hast signed, but °maketh his petition three times a day."

Y2 14 Then the king, when he heard *these* words, was sore displeased °with himself, and set *his* heart on Daniel to deliver him: and he °laboured till the going down of the sun to deliver him.

15 Then these [5]men [6]assembled unto the king, and said unto the king, "Know, O king, that the law of the Medes and Persians *is*, That no [7]decree nor statute which the king establisheth may be changed."

6. 1-28 (*C*, p. 1178). DANIEL HIMSELF. THE DEN OF LIONS. (*Alternations.*)

C | V | 1-3. Daniel's prosperity.
W1 | X1 | 4-6. Conspiracy made.
Y1 | 7-9. Decree obtained.
W2 | X2 | 10-13. Conspiracy succeeds.
Y2 | 14-17. Decree enforced.
W3 | X3 | 18-24. Conspiracy fails.
Y3 | 25-27. Decree reversed.
V | 28. Daniel's prosperity.

1 Darius. A careful study of Ap. 57 will show that this "Darius the Median" of 5. 31 is the Artaxerxes (the great king) of Neh. 2. 1 and Ezra 6. 14, and the Ahasuerus of Est. 1. 1. These names are all used of one and the same person; and by comparison of the Median kings, according to Herodotus, compared with the genealogy of Cyrus in his Cuneiform Cylinder, the important fact becomes clear that this man was ASTYAGES; and the names ARSAMES = CAMBYSES, common to Herodotus, the Behistun Rock, and the Cylinder of Cyrus, all refer to one and the same person.

If this be so, and ASTYAGES is to be identified with "DARIUS the Median", then all difficulty vanishes. The Scripture record harmonizes exactly with the accounts given in the three sources named above; and we have the *real* clue to the parentage of Cyrus the Great (Ap. 57, p. 80).

If this be not so, then "Darius the Median" remains an insoluble riddle to history and chronology alike, for there can be found no place for him on the page of history.

an hundred and twenty. Darius Hystaspis, in his inscription on the Behistun Rock (Ap. 57), enumerates twenty-three names. This number was continually altered according to historical changes and conquests. In Est. 1. 10, 13, 14, there were seven when Astyages took the kingdom; but he added 120 more (Dan. 6. 1), and made 127 (Est. 1. 1; 8. 9; 9. 30).

princes = satraps. As in 3. 2.

2 presidents = ministers. Occurs only in this chapter.

3 preferred . . . the king thought. Showing that Daniel was well known to Astyages, and appreciated.

an excellent spirit. Referring to the affectionate regard in which Astyages held Daniel after many years of faithful service.

spirit. Heb. *rūach*. Ap. 9.

thought = purposed. Chald. *'ăshith*. Occurs only here (426 B.C.), Daniel being eighty-seven.

4 occasion = pretext.

5 men. Pl. of Chald. *gebar*, grandees. Same as Ap. 14. IV.

God. Chald. *'ĕlāh*. Same as Heb. *'Ĕlohim*. Ap. 4. I.

6 assembled = came crowding together.

7 governors = deputies.

counsellers. See note on 3. 24.

captains = pashas. See 3. 2, 3, 27. Cp. Est. 3. 12, &c. Neh. 2. 7, &c.; and Ezra 5. 3, &c. Also Hag. 1. 1, 14; 2. 2, 21. Mal. 1. 8.

to establish a royal statute: or, for the king to establish a statute.

make a firm decree: or, confirm a decree. Occurs only in this chapter.

decree = interdict. Chald. *'ĕṣār*. The same word as in *vv.* 8, 9, 12, 13, 15. Not the same as in *v.* 26.

ask a petition = pray a prayer. Fig. *Polyptōton* (Ap. 6), for emphasis. Cp. *v.* 12. Occurs only in this chapter.

man. Chald. *'ĕnāsh*. Same as Heb. *'ĕnōsh*. Ap. 14. III.

8 which altereth not = which changeth not, or passeth not away.

10 his house. Not into a secret, or public place.

toward Jerusalem. Remembering Solomon's prayer (1 Kings 8. 47-50).

13 children of the captivity. The 1611 edition of the A.V. reads "captivity of the children".

children = sons.

maketh his petition = prayeth a prayer. Same as in *v.* 7. **14 with himself** = concerning it.

laboured = was exerting himself

426 16 Then the king commanded, and they
brought Daniel, and cast *him* into the den of
lions. *Now* the king spake and said unto
Daniel, "Thy [5]God Whom thou servest continually, He will deliver thee."
17 And a stone was brought, and laid upon
the °mouth of the den; and the king sealed it
with his own signet, and with the signet of his
°lords; that the purpose might not be changed
concerning Daniel.
W³ X³ (p. 1190) 18 Then the king went to his palace, and
°passed the night fasting: neither were °in-
struments of musick brought before him: and
his sleep went from him.
19 Then the king arose °very early in the
morning, and went in haste unto the den of
lions.
20 And when he came to the den, he cried
with a lamentable voice unto Daniel: *and* the
king spake and said to Daniel, "O Daniel,
servant of the living [5]God, is thy [5]God, Whom
thou servest continually, able to deliver thee
from the lions?"
21 Then said Daniel unto the king, "O king,
live for ever.
22 My [5]God hath °sent His angel, and hath
shut the lions' mouths, that they have not
hurt me: forasmuch as before Him °innocency
was found in me; and also before thee, O
king, have I done no hurt."
23 Then was the king °exceeding glad for
him, and commanded that they should take
Daniel up out of the den. So Daniel was taken
up out of the den, and no manner of hurt was
found upon him, because he °believed in his
[5]God.
24 And the king commanded, and they
brought those [5]men which had °accused
Daniel, and they cast *them* into the den of
lions, them, their [13]children, and their wives;
and the lions had the mastery of them, and
brake all their bones in pieces or ever they
came at the bottom of the den.
Y³ 25 Then king Darius wrote unto all °people,
nations, and languages, that dwell in all the
earth; "Peace be multiplied unto you.
26 I make a °decree, That in every dominion
of my kingdom men tremble and fear before
the [5]God of Daniel: for He *is* the living °God,
and stedfast for ever, and His kingdom *that*
which shall not be destroyed, and His dominion *shall be even* unto the end.
27 He delivereth and rescueth, and He worketh signs and wonders in heaven and in earth,
Who hath delivered Daniel from the °power
of the lions."
V 28 So this Daniel prospered in the reign of
[1]Darius, and in the reign of °Cyrus the
Persian.

Z¹ A¹ C¹ (p. 1192) 7 °In the first year of °Belshazzar king of
Babylon Daniel °had °a dream and vi-
429 sions of his head upon his bed: then °he wrote
the dream, *and* told °the sum of the °matters.

17 mouth=door.
lords=nobles. See note on "lords" (5. 1), and "princes" (5. 2).
18 passed the night fasting. Showing the long-standing affection which Astyages had for Daniel.
instruments of musick. Some understand the word as referring to "tables"; others, women or dancing girls.
19 very early, &c. Another evidence of the king's strong feelings for Daniel.
22 sent His angel. As in 3. 28.
innocency=rectitude, or purity. See the Structure, p. 1178.
23 exceeding glad. Another proof of the long-standing friendship between Astyages and Daniel.
believed in=had trusted. Chald, *'âman.* Same as Ap. 69. iii.
24 accused. Cp. *v.* 12. Est. 7. 10. Ps. 7. 15-17.
25 people=peoples. Cp. 3. 29.
26 decree. Chald. *te'am*=a decision, implying the pleasure or approval with which it was made.
God. Chald. *'ĕlāhā'* (emphatic).
27 power=paw.
28 Cyrus the Persian. The son of Darius the Mede. He is the young Darius, his father Astyages being the old Darius, "Darius" meaning "the Maintainer". Cp. Isa. 45. 1. See Ap. 57.

7. 1—8. 27 [For Structure see next page].
In the first year of Belshazzar. This was 429 B.C. See Ap. 50, pp. 69 and 72. Daniel being eighty-four years old. Three years before the events of ch. 6. Cp. 5. 30, 31, and the notes on the other dates (8. 1; 9. 1; 10. 1; 11. 1, &c.).
This vision (ch. 7) is still in Chaldee (the Gentile language), because it is the continuation of 2. 44, and shows what will take place in "the days of those kings" before the stone strikes the image. It brings us up to the end of Gentile dominion over Israel. Ch. 8 is in Hebrew, because it specially concerns Israel.
It is the writing of "Daniel the prophet" (Matt. 24). This is directly stated by our Lord, Who, seven times in the Gospel of John, declared that what He spake were not His own words, but the Father's (John 7. 16; 8. 28, 40, 47; 12. 49; 14. 10, 24; 17. 8. Cp. Deut. 18. 18 and Isa. 51. 16).
This member ***B*** consists of two visions. Each is distinct and complete in itself (Z¹, 7. 1-28; Z², 8. 1-27).
The dream of Nebuchadnezzar (ch. 2) was interpreted to him by Daniel; while the dream (or vision) of Daniel was interpreted to him by the Angel. The former referred to the *beginning and duration* of Gentile dominion over Israel; the latter concerns the *end* of it. See the Structure, p. 1178.
The second (ch. 8) was given two years later than the first (cp. 7. 1 with 8. 1), and is subsequent to the first, giving further details concerning "the latter time of their dominion" (i.e. that of the four beasts of the first vision in ch. 7). Further details are given in chs. 9, 11, and 12.
The interpretation is given in *vv.* 17, 18; and shows that these visions (chs. 7 and 8) are still future, and are not therefore to be confounded with the dream of ch. 2. See the notes on *vv.* 17, 18, below.
The interpretations given to us of these two separate visions need no further interpretation by us. The source of the dream is the source of the interpretation also. They are for us to understand and to believe. We may *comment* on the interpretations given, but not *interpret* them.
Belshazzar. The last king of Babylon. Until 1854, when Sir H. C. Rawlinson discovered the cuneiform texts, all was speculation. An inscription belonging to the first year of Nabonidus, his father (see notes on 5. 2, and Jer. 27. 7), calls him his "firstborn son" and gives his name *Bel-sarra-uzer*="O Bel defend the king". There are frequent references to him in contracts and similar documents (*Encycl. Brit.*, 11th (Cambridge) ed., vol. iii, p. 711). He was the last king of Babylon (5. 30, 31). See note on 5. 7. **had**=beheld. **a dream.** One of twenty recorded dreams. See note on Gen. 20. 3. **he wrote.** This is to be noted, as it was afterward "told" in speech (*vv.* 1, 2). **the sum**=substance, or the chief of the words. **matters**=words.

429 **2** Daniel °spake and said, °"I saw in my vision °by night, and, °behold, °the four °winds of the heaven °strove upon °the great sea.

3 And °four great beasts came up from the sea, diverse one from another.

4 °The first *was* °like a lion, and had eagle's wings: °I beheld °till the wings thereof were plucked, and it was lifted up from the earth, and made stand upon °the feet as a °man, and a °man's heart was given to it.

5 And [2]behold another beast, a second, like to a bear, and °it raised up itself °on one side, and *it had* °three ribs in the mouth of it between the teeth of it: and they said thus unto it, 'Arise, devour much flesh.'

6 After this [4]I beheld, and °lo another, like a leopard, which had upon the back of it four wings of °a fowl; the beast had also °four heads; and dominion was given to it.

7 After this [2]I saw in the night visions, and [2]behold °a fourth beast, dreadful and terrible, and strong exceedingly; and it had °great iron teeth: it devoured and brake in pieces, and stamped °the residue with the feet of it: and it *was* diverse from all the beasts that *were* °before it; and it had °ten horns.

8 °I considered °the horns, and, [2]behold, there came up among them another °little horn, before whom there were three of the first horns plucked up by the roots: and, [2]behold, in this horn *were* eyes like the eyes of °man, and a mouth °speaking great things.

D[1] (p. 1192) **9** [4]I beheld °till °the thrones were °cast down, and °the Ancient of days °did sit, Whose garment *was* °white as snow, and the hair of His head like the pure wool: His throne *was like* the fiery flame, *and* °his wheels *as* burning fire.

7. 1—8. 27 (*B*, p. 1178). THE DREAM, AND VISIONS OF DANIEL. THE END OF GENTILE DOMINION. (*Division.*)

B | Z[1] | 7. 1-28. The Vision of the FOUR Beasts. (First year.)
| Z[2] | 8. 1-27. The Vision of the Two Beasts. (Third year.)

7. 1-28 (Z[1], above). THE VISION OF THE FOUR BEASTS. (*Repeated Alternations.*)

Z[1] | A[1] | C[1] | 1-8. The Four Beasts. } The Vision.
D[1] | 9-14. The judgment of the Son of Man. } The Vision.
B[1] | 15, 16. Daniel's perturbation and inquiry.
A[2] | C[2] | 17. The Four Beasts. } The Interpretation.
D[2] | 18. The judgment of the Son of Man. } The Interpretation.
B[2] | 19-22. Daniel's inquiry.
A[3] | C[3] | 23-25. The Fourth Beast. } The Interpretation.
D[3] | 26, 27. The judgment of the Son of Man. } The Interpretation.
B[3] | 28. Daniel's perturbation.

2 spake and said. The vision is related in words.
I saw = I was looking.
by = during.
behold. Fig. *Asterismos* (Ap. 6), for emphasis.
the four winds. All blowing at the same time and producing the one result described in *vv.* 3-8.
winds. Chald. *rūach*. Ap. 9.
strove upon = brake or burst forth against; converging on one point.
the great sea: i.e. the Mediterranean Sea, or the sea, denoting the peoples of the earth, as interpreted for us in *v.* 17.
3 four great beasts. These are not the four dominions of ch. 2. They stand up one after the other, and each stands, successively, in the place of the other. These are to arise in "the days of" those last "ten kings" of Dan. 2. 44. These continue the last of Nebuchadnezzar's last dominion, and do exist together. See note on *v.* 12 below.
4 The first, &c. Cannot be Babylon, for this had already arisen, and was within two years of its end (see notes on *v.* 1). Daniel could not see that kingdom arise now. He had said, "Thou art this head of gold" (2. 38); but Nebuchadnezzar himself had been dead twenty-three years, and these are "four kings which shall arise" (*v.* 17). Therefore Babylon is not included. **like.** These descriptions will be easily recognized by those who shall see them arise. **I beheld** = I continued looking, as in *vv.* 6, 9, 11. Same as "I saw" in *vv.* 2, 7, 13. **till** = till that. **the feet** = the two feet. **man.** Chald. *'ănāsh.* Ap. 14. III. **5 it raised up itself**: or, was made to stand. **on one side**: i.e. partially. **three ribs, &c.** This is not interpreted by the angel. The interpretations given by man are diverse, conflicting, and are unnecessary. **6 lo.** Fig. *Asterismos.* Ap. 6. **a fowl** = a bird. **four heads.** These are not interpreted, and will be understood only when they are seen. It will have these four heads at the time of its being seen. **7 a fourth beast.** Not Rome, for it has the "ten horns" when it is first seen. Moreover, these ten horns are not seen till the time of the end. This fourth beast therefore belongs to the time of the end. The beast of Rev. 13. 1-10 combines in himself all these resemblances. See note on *v.* 23. **great iron teeth.** Lit. two (or two rows of) teeth, great ones. **the residue** = the rest: i.e. the other three beasts which will be co-existent. They do not destroy or succeed one another, like the kingdoms in ch. 2; but are trampled on by the fourth beast. See *v.* 12. **before** = in front of, as in *vv.* 10, 13, 20, and 6. 10, 11, 12, 13, 18, 22, 26, &c. Chald. *ḳ*e*dām*, as in Ezra 4. 18, 23; 7. 14, 19; and frequently in Dan. chs. 2, 3, 4, 5. This shows that the three will be co-existent, for this could not be spoken of those who had long passed away. **ten horns.** These are the same as in Rev. 17. 12, and represent the ten contemporaneous kings at the time of the end. See notes on *vv.* 8, 24. **8 I considered** = I was considering. **the horns.** Mentioned in *v.* 7. **little horn** = a horn of small beginnings. This identifies this vision with those of chs. 8, 9, 11, 12. See Ap. 90. The first of twelve titles given to the power commonly known as "the Antichrist": it is used again in 8. 9. Cp. 11. 21-30. Note the other titles: "the king of Babylon" (Isa. 14. 4); "the Assyrian" (Isa. 14. 25); "Lucifer, son of the morning", in opposition to "the bright and morning star" (Isa. 14. 12); "the Prince that shall come" (Dan. 9. 26); "the king of fierce countenance" (Dan. 8. 23); "the vile person" (Dan. 11. 21); "the wilful king" (Dan. 11. 36); "the man of sin" (2 Thess. 2. 3); "the son of perdition" (2 Thess. 2. 3); "that wicked (or lawless) one" (2 Thess. 2. 8. Rev. 13. 18); "the beast with ten horns" (Rev. 13. 1). **man** = a mortal man. Chald. *'ĕnāsh.* Ap. 14. III. **speaking great things.** This is a further development, explained in *vv.* 11, 20, 25; 8. 11; 11. 36, 37. 2 Thess. 2. 3, 4. Rev. 13. 5, 6. **9 till** = till that. **the thrones** = the seats for judgment. **cast down** = set or placed. The seats of Orientals are cushions laid, not "set", but "cast down". The reference is to this, in Rev. 4. 2. Cp. Pss. 9. 7; 29. 10. Isa. 28. 6. **the Ancient of days** = the Everlasting One. Cp. Ps. 90. 2. Rev. 4. 2. **did sit** = took His seat. **white as snow, &c.** Cp. Rev. 1. 4. **his wheels** = the wheels thereof: i.e. of the throne. Cp. Ezek. 1. 15-20, 26-28; 10. 9-13.

429 10 A fiery stream issued and came forth from before Him: thousand thousands °ministered unto Him, and ten thousand times ten thousand °stood before Him: °the judgment °was set, and °the books were opened.

11 [4]I beheld then because of the voice of the great words which °the horn spake: [4]I beheld *even* [9]till °the beast was slain, and his body destroyed, and given to °the burning flame.

12 As concerning °the rest of the beasts, °they had their dominion taken away: yet °their lives were prolonged °for a season and time.

13 [2]I saw in the night visions, and, behold, *one* like °the Son of Man °came with the clouds of heaven, and came to [9]the Ancient of days, and they brought Him near before Him.

14 And °there was given Him dominion, and glory, and a kingdom, that all °people, nations, and languages, should serve Him: His dominion *is* °an everlasting dominion, which shall not pass away, and His kingdom *that* which shall not be destroyed.

B[1] (p. 1192) 15 I Daniel was °grieved in °my spirit in the midst of *my* body, and the visions of my head troubled me.

16 I came near unto one of °them that °stood by, and °asked him the °truth °of all this. So he told me, and made me know the interpretation of the things.

A[2] C[2] 17 °'These great beasts, which are four, *are* four kings, *which* °shall arise out of the earth.

D[2] 18 But °the saints of °the MOST HIGH shall °take the kingdom, and possess the kingdom for ever, even for ever and ever.'

B[2] 19 Then I would know the [16]truth of [7]the fourth beast, which was diverse from all the others, exceeding dreadful, whose teeth *were of* iron, and his °nails *of* brass; *which* devoured, brake in pieces, and stamped [7]the residue with his °feet;

20 And of the [7]ten horns that *were* in his head, and *of* °the other which came up, and [7]before whom three fell; even *of* that horn that had eyes, and a mouth that °spake very great things, whose look *was* more stout than his fellows.

21 [4]I beheld, and °the same horn °made war with [18]the saints, and prevailed against them;

22 Until [9]the Ancient of days came, and °judgment was given to the saints of [18]the Most High; and the time came that the saints possessed the kingdom.

A[3] C[3] 23 °Thus he said, [7]'The fourth beast shall be the fourth kingdom upon earth, which shall be diverse from all kingdoms, and shall devour the whole earth, and shall tread it down, and break it in pieces.

24 And the [7]ten horns out of this kingdom *are* °ten kings *that* shall arise: and another shall rise after them; and °he shall be diverse from the first, and he shall subdue °three kings.

25 And he shall [8]speak *great* words against [18]the MOST HIGH, and shall °wear out the saints of [18]the MOST HIGH, and think to change times and °laws: and they shall be given into his hand until a °time and times and the dividing of time.

10 ministered = were ministering.
stood = were standing. Indicating readiness for service.
the judgment = the Judge; "judgment" being put by Fig. *Metonymy* (of the Subject), Ap. 6, for the Judge Who actually sat.
was set = took His seat.
the books, &c. Lit. "books were opened".
11 the horn spake = the horn kept speaking.
the beast. At length we learn who "the (little) horn" is. See note on *v.* 8 and Rev. 19. 20.
the burning flame. Cp. 2 Thess. 1. 7–10; 2. 8.
12 the rest of the beasts: i.e. the three mentioned in *vv.* 4–7 as co-existing.
they had, &c. = their dominion was caused to pass away.
their lives were prolonged = a lengthening of their life was given to them: i.e. the remaining three after the fourth beast has been destroyed.
for a season and time: i.e. for an appointed season.
13 the Son of Man. See notes on Ps. 8. 4. Matt. 8. 20. Rev. 14. 14.
came = was coming.
14 there was given, &c. = to Him was given, &c.
people = peoples.
an everlasting dominion. See *vv.* 18, 27; 2. 35, 44; 4. 3; 6. 26. Pss. 45. 6; 145. 13; 146. 10. Isa. 9. 7. Obad. 21. Mic. 4. 7. Luke 1. 33. John 12. 34. Heb. 1. 8.
15 grieved. Because he did not understand. Therefore ch. 7 could not be identical with ch. 2, because he had interpreted that already to Nebuchadnezzar.
my spirit = myself. Chald. *rūach*. Ap. 9.
16 them: i.e. the standing ones.
stood = were standing. Cp. *v.* 10.
asked = made exact inquiry.
truth = certainty. Chald. *yaʻīb*.
of = about.
17 These great beasts, &c. In *vv.* 17, 18 we have therefore the interpretation of this vision, which needs no further interpretation by man.
shall arise. The two which had already arisen cannot therefore be included: viz. Babylon and Medo-Persia, which almost (at this time) equalled Babylon in extent. The vision is not continuous history, but the prophecy of a crisis: and refers to the ten toes of the fifth power of Dan. 2. See note on *v.* 12. In this, and in each successive vision we are always directed to the end and consummation. Cp. *v.* 26; 8. 17–19; 9. 26; 11. 40; 12. 4, 9, 13. Matt. 24. 14, 15. See Ap. 90.
18 the saints = the holy ones: i.e. God's People Israel.
the MOST HIGH. Chald. *ʻelyōnīn*. Same as Heb. *ʻelyōn*. Ap. 4. VI. Here pl. = the Messiah Himself in relation to dominion in the earth. Verse 27 shows that a Person is intended, not a place.
take = receive. As in 5. 31; cp. 2. 6.
19 nails = claws, or hoofs. Chald. text is pl.; marg. sing.
feet. Chald. text, pl.; marg. sing.
20 the other: i.e. the little horn of *v.* 8, which is still future. See Ap. 90; and cp. 8. 9–12, 23–25, and note on *v.* 8.
spake. See note on "speaking", *v.* 8.
21 the same horn. Cp. *v.* 8.
made war. This connects "the little horn" with Rev. 13. 7, and shows it to be still future.
22 judgment: or, vindication.
23 Thus he said. Giving an additional interpretation. **24 ten kings.** See note on *v.* 7.
he. The little horn of *vv.* 8, 20.
three kings. See the interpretation of *v.* 8.
25 wear out = afflict.
laws = law.
time and times, &c.: i.e. three and a half years = one half of the "one week" of Dan. 9. 27. It is repeated as forty-two months (Rev. 11. 2), and as 1,260 days (Rev. 11. 3). See Ap. 90 and 91; and cp. 8. 14; 12. 7, 11, 12.

D³ (p. 1192) 429 26 But [10] the judgment °shall sit, and they shall take away his dominion, to consume and to destroy *it* °unto the end.

27 And the kingdom and dominion, and the greatness of the kingdom under the whole heaven, shall be given to the People of [18] the saints of [18] the MOST HIGH, °Whose kingdom *is* [14] an everlasting kingdom, and all dominions shall serve and obey Him.'

B¹ 28 Hitherto *is* the end of the matter. As for me Daniel, my cogitations °much troubled me, and my countenance changed in me: but °I kept the matter in my heart.

Z² E (p. 1194) 426 **8** °In the third year of the reign of king Belshazzar °a vision appeared unto me, *even unto* me Daniel, °after that which appeared unto me at the first.

2 And I saw in [1] a vision; and it came to pass, when I saw, that °I *was* at °Shushan *in* the palace, which *is* in the province of Elam; and I saw in [1] a vision, and I was by the °river of °Ulai.

F H r 3 Then I lifted up mine eyes, and °saw, and, °behold, there stood before the river °a ram which had °*two* horns: and the °*two* horns *were* high; but one *was* °higher than the other, and the higher came up last.

4 I saw the [3] ram °pushing °westward, and northward, and southward; so that no beasts might stand before him, neither *was there any* that could deliver out of his hand; but he did according to his will, and °became great.

s 5 And as I was considering, [3] behold, an °he goat came °from the west °on the face of the whole earth, and touched not the ground:

t and the goat *had* a °notable horn between his eyes.

6 And he came to the [3] ram that had *two* horns, which I had seen standing before the river, and °ran unto him in the fury of his power.

7 And I saw him come close unto the ram, and he °was moved with °choler against him, and smote the ram, and brake his two horns: and there was no power in the ram to stand before him, but he cast him down to the ground, and stamped upon him: and there was °none that could deliver the ram out of his °hand.

26 shall sit = will take His seat.

unto the end. This is the determining factor of the interpretation. Cp. 8. 17-19; 9. 26; 11. 40; 12. 4, 9, 13. Matt. 24. 14. See note on *v.* 17.

27 Whose, &c. This shows that *'elyonin* (in *v.* 18) means a person, and not a place.

28 much troubled me: or, baffled me. See note on "grieved", *v.* 15.

I kept, &c. Cp. Luke 2. 19. Here ends the portion of the book written in the Chaldee (or Gentile) tongue.

8. 1-27 (Z², p. 1192). THE VISION OF THE TWO BEASTS. (*Introversion and Extended Alternation.*)

Z² E | 1, 2. Circumstances.
The Vision.
F | H | r | 3, 4. Ram.
s | 5-. He-goat.
t | -5-7. Great horn.
u | 8-. Great horn broken.
v | -8. Four horns.
w | 9-12. Little horn. (Future.)
J | 13, 14. Time. Number of days.
G | 15, 16. Command to Angel to give the interpretation to Daniel.
G | 17, 19. The command obeyed by the Angel.
The Interpretation.
F | *H* | *r* | 20. Ram.
s | 21-. He-goat.
t | -21. Great horn.
u | 22-. Great horn broken.
v | -22. Four horns.
w | 23-25. Little horn. (Future.)
J | 26. Time. "Many days".
E | 27. Circumstances.

1 In the third year: 426 B.C. (see Ap. 50, pp. 69 and 72), Daniel being eighty-seven.

a vision. Like the vision in ch. 7, this also is complete in itself, but is necessary to contribute its proof of the unity of the book as a whole. This vision (and the rest of the book from here) is written in Hebrew; because its purpose is to show how Gentile dominion (of ch. 2) specially concerns and affects Israel.

after. Two years after. At the end of the Babylonian empire, for Belshazzar reigned little more than two years.

2 I was at = I was in. Daniel may have retired there (during the lycanthropy of Nebuchadnezzar) when Nehemiah and Mordecai were in the court of Astyages (Neh. 1. 1). That Daniel was there employed by Astyages is clear from 8. 27.

Shushan. The chief city of all Persia.

river. Heb. *'ûbal* = a canal. Only here, and in *vv.* 3, 6.

Ulai. The Eulæus canal, near Susa. Now the *Karûn* river. **3 saw** = looked. **behold.** Fig. *Asterismos.* Ap. 6. **a ram.** In *v.* 20 this is interpreted of Persia. A ram is always the symbol of Persia. Found to-day on ancient Persian coins. The king wore a ram's head of gold, and rams' heads are to be seen on the sculptured pillars of Persepolis. **two horns.** In *v.* 20 these are interpreted of the kings of Media and Persia. **higher,** &c. Cyrus (the latter) became greater than his father Astyages. Both were in existence when Daniel saw the vision. Cp. *v.* 20. **4 pushing** = butting: always hostile. **westward** = to the west. Not the same word as in *v.* 5. **became great** = acted proudly. **5 he goat** = a leaper of the goats. The acknowledged symbol of Greece, as the ram was of Persia (see *v.* 3), because the first colony was directed by an oracle to take a goat for a guide and build a city, which they did, and called it Egeæ (from *Aix* = a goat). Figures of a goat are found to-day on ancient Macedonian monuments. **from the west.** Heb. *ma'rāb.* Not the place of origin, but the direction from it. In *v.* 4 the Heb. = to the west. **on** = over. **notable** = conspicuous. **6 ran unto him.** Symbolizing the rapidity of Alexander's conquests, which, in the short space of thirteen years, subdued the world. **7 was moved with choler** = moved himself, or strove violently with. **choler** = bile. Put by Fig. *Metonymy* (of Cause), Ap. 6, for anger or wrath, which was supposed to be due to excess of bile. Greek, *cholos* = bile; whence we have "cholera". **none that could,** &c. = no deliverer for. **hand** = power. Put by Fig. *Metonymy* (of Cause), Ap. 6, for the power put forth by it.

u 8 Therefore the °he goat °waxed °very °great:
(p. 1194) and when he was strong, the great horn was
426 °broken;
v and °for it °came up °four notable ones toward
°the four °winds of heaven.
w 9 And out of °one of them came forth °a little
horn, which °waxed exceeding great, toward
the °south, and toward the °east, and toward
the °pleasant *land*.
10 And it [9]waxed [4]great, °*even* to the °host
of heaven; and it cast down *some* °of the host
and of the stars to the ground, and °stamped
upon °them.
11 Yea, he magnified *himself* even °to °the
°Prince of the [10]host, and °by him the °daily
sacrifice °was taken away, and the place of
His sanctuary was cast down.
12 And °an host °was given *him* against the
[11]daily *sacrifice* °by reason of °transgression,
and °it cast down the °truth to the ground;
and it °practised, °and prospered.
J 13 Then I heard one °saint speaking, and
another °saint said unto °that certain *saint*
which spake, °'How long *shall be* the vision
°*concerning* the [11]daily *sacrifice*, °and the
[12]transgression of desolation, °to give both
the sanctuary and °the host to be trodden
under foot?'
14 And he said unto °me, 'Unto °two thousand and three hundred °days; then shall the
sanctuary be °cleansed.'
G 15 And it came to pass, when I, *even* I
Daniel, had seen the vision, and sought for
the meaning, then, behold, there stood before
me as the appearance of a °man.
16 And I heard a °man's voice between *the
banks of* Ulai, which called, and said, °'Gabriel,
make this *man* to understand the vision.'
G 17 So he came near where I stood: and when
he came, I was afraid, and fell upon my face:
but he said unto me, 'Understand, O °son of
man: for °at the time of the end °*shall be* the
vision.'
18 Now as he was speaking with me, °I was
in a deep sleep on my face toward the ground:
but he touched me, and set me upright.
19 And he said, [3]'Behold, I will make thee
know what shall be in °the last end of the
°indignation: for at the time appointed the
end *shall be*.

8 waxed very great. Referring to the great extent of Alexander's conquests, as "ran" (*v.* 6) refers to the rapidity of them. **very** = exceedingly.
great: or, proud. Cp. *v.* 4.
broken = broken in pieces. **for it** = instead of it.
came up. Sept. adds "afterward".
four notable ones = four conspicuous [ones].
the four winds. See note on 7. 2.
winds. Heb. *rūach.* Ap. 9.
9 one = [the] one.
a little horn. See note on 7. 8: where it is already shown that this name, and these members ("w" and "*w*", *vv.* 9 and 23) belong to the still future time of the end. See Ap. 90.
waxed = grew. Anglo-Saxon, *weaxan* = to grow. Supply the *Ellipsis* (Ap. 6), "grew [and became]".
south: i.e. Egypt.
east: i.e. Babylonia and Persia.
pleasant land = the glory of [gems]: i.e. the land of Israel. Only Ezekiel (20. 6, 15) and Daniel here use this term of the Holy Land. The same land as in 11. 16, 41. Cp. Ps. 106. 24. Jer. 3. 19. Zech. 7. 14.
10 even to = as far as.
host = stars. Cp. Rev. 12. 4.
of the host and of the stars. Fig. *Hendiadys* (Ap. 6), for emphasis = the starry host.
stamped upon them = trampled them under foot. Cp. *v.* 13; 7. 21, 25.
them: i.e. the people symbolized by them.
11 to = against.
the Prince of the host. God Himself, the Creator and Ruler of the starry host. Verses 10, 11 are "difficult" only if Antiochus Epiphanes is assumed to fulfil them. There is no difficulty arising from "the state of the text".
Prince = Ruler. Heb. *sar.* See note on 10. 13.
by him . . . was taken: or, it took away from Him: i.e. God.
daily sacrifice = the continual [burnt offering]: i.e. the morning and evening sacrifice (Num. 28. 3. 1 Chron. 16. 40. 2 Chron. 29. 7). This belongs to the time of the end, and was not fulfilled by Antiochus. His career was a foreshadowing of it, to show that the fulfilment will yet be exhausted by him who is "the little horn". See Ap. 90; and note all the references there given (8. 11, 12, 13; 9. 27; 11. 31; 12. 11). Ref. to Pent. (Ex. 29. 38. Num. 28. 3). Ap. 92.
12 an host. Here the word is used of a military host, in opposition to the "host" of Num. 4. 23, 30, 35, 39, 43; 8. 24, 25.
was given him against = was set over: i.e. war is raised against "the daily sacrifice".
by reason of = by.
transgression. Heb. *pāsha'.* Ap. 44. ix.
it cast down the truth = truth was cast down. The verb is passive.
truth: i.e. the truth of God as revealed in the law and the prophets.
practised = did it with effect. Cp. *v.* 24.
and prospered = and succeeded. **13 saint** = holy [one]. An angelic attendant. Cp. 4. 13. Deut. 33. 2. Job 5. 1; 15. 15. Ps. 89. 5, 7. Zech. 14. 5. **that certain saint** = a certain [unnamed] one, or such an one, as in Ruth 4. 1. Or, a proper name *Palmōnī* = the wonderful one, or the wonderful [numberer], as in Judg. 13. 18. Isa. 9. 6. Ps. 139. 6. **How long . . . ?** Referring to the *duration* of what is said concerning "the daily sacrifice" and the desolation; not the interval before the fulfilment. **concerning, &c.** = of "the daily sacrifice" [as taken away]. **and.** Supply "and [the setting up of] the desolating (or astounding) rebellion. **to give, &c.:** or, after He hath given over the sanctuary, &c. **the host.** Here it is the "host", the technical term for the ministers of the sanctuary. Cp. Num. 4. 23, 30, 35, 39, 43; 8. 24, 25. **14 me.** Sept., Syr., and Vulg. read "him". **two thousand and three hundred days.** See Ap. 91, and note on *v.* 26 below. **days** = evenings and mornings, the times of the offering of the "continual" or daily sacrifice. **cleansed** = vindicated or sanctified: in this form, occurs only here. Cp. 9. 24; and see Ap. 90. **15 man** = a mighty man. Heb. *geber.* Ap. 14. IV. Here it is *Gabriel*, whence his name. **16 man's.** Heb. *'ādām.* Ap. 14. I. **Gabriel.** The first of two angels who are named in Scripture (cp. 9. 21. Luke 1. 19, 26). The second is Michael (10. 13, 21; 12. 1; Jude 9. Rev. 12. 7). **17 son of man.** Only Daniel and Ezekiel so called, beside Messiah. See note on Ps. 8. 4. **at the time of the end.** This gives the time to which this vision refers. See the interpretation in "*H*" (*vv.* 20–25), and especially "*w*" (*vv.* 23–25). See also Ap. 90; and cp. 7. 26; 9. 26; 11. 40; 12. 4, 9, 13; and Matt. 24. 14. **shall be.** Supply the *Ellipsis* (Ap. 6) by reading "[belongeth]". **18 I was in** = I fell into. **19 the last end.** Another indication of the time of the fulfilment of the vision at the time appointed, &c. **indignation** = wrath [of God].

F H r (p. 1124) 20 The [3] ram which thou sawest having *two* horns *are* °the kings of Media and Persia.

s 21 And the rough goat °*is* the °king of
426 °Grecia:
t and the great horn that *is* between his eyes °*is* the first king.

u 22 Now that being broken, whereas [8] four stood up °for it,
v °four kingdoms shall stand up out of °the nation, but °not in his power.

w 23 And in °the latter time of their kingdom, when °the transgressors °are come to the full, °a king of fierce countenance, and °understanding dark sentences, shall stand up.
24 And his power shall be mighty, but °not by his own power: and he shall destroy wonderfully, and shall [12] prosper, and [12] practise, and shall destroy the °mighty and the °holy People.
25 And through his policy also he shall cause °craft to prosper in his hand; and he shall magnify *himself* in his heart, and °by peace shall destroy many: he shall also stand up against °the Prince of princes; but °he shall be broken without hand.

J 26 And the vision of °the evening and the morning which was told °*is* true: wherefore °shut thou up the vision; for °it *shall be* for many days.'

E 27 And I Daniel °fainted, and was sick *certain* days; afterward I rose up, and did °the king's business; and I was °astonished at the vision, but none °understood *it*.

A K (p. 1196) 9 In °the first year of °Darius the son of °Ahasuerus, of the seed of the Medes,
426 which was °made king over the realm of the Chaldeans;
2 In [1] the first year of his reign I Daniel °understood °by books °the number of the years, whereof the word of °the LORD came to °Jere-

20 the kings. Here in *v.* 20 we have the beginning of the interpretation; which commences with past *history* with which the prophecy (which belongs to the future) is linked on. This is to connect the anticipatory and partial, or foreshadowing, fulfilment, which shows how the "little horn" will act, in a similar way as an individual, and not as a series of kings or popes.

21 is=representeth. It is the Fig. *Metaphor* (Ap. 6).
king: or, kingdom.
Grecia=Greece.
is the first king=representeth the first king: i.e. Alexander the Great (*v.* 5).

22 for it=in the place thereof.
four kingdoms. These are said to have been: (1) Ptolemy's (Egypt, Palestine, and some parts of Asia Minor); (2) Cassander's (Macedonia and Greece); (3) Lysimachus's (Bithynia, Thrace, Mysia, &c.); (4) Seleucus's (Syria, Armenia, and territory east of the Euphrates). But the continuity of Alexander's dominion ceased with him, and will not be seen again till "the little horn" arises.
the nation. Sept. and Vulg. read "his nation".
not in his power: i.e. not with Alexander's vigour of action and endurance.

23 the latter time of their kingdom, &c. This is a further indication as to the interpretation of this vision.
the transgressors. The Sept., Syr., and Vulg. read "transgressions". Heb. *pāsha'*, as in *v.* 12=rebellions. Cp. 9. 24.
are come to the full: or, have filled up their measure. Therefore not full yet. This is a blow to all who are vainly trying to make the world better, and to "realize the kingdom of God on earth" now.
a king of fierce countenance=a king of mighty presence. One of the titles of the antichrist. See note on 7. 8.
understanding dark sentences=skilled in dissimulation.

24 not by his own power. We are not told here who is the giver of the power, but we are not left in ignorance. Rev. 13. 2, and 2 Thess. 2. 9, 10, are clear on this point.
mighty=mighty ones.
holy People=People of the holy ones. These are "the holy ones of the Most High" (7. 18, 22).

25 craft=deceit.
by peace=by their prosperity, or careless security.
the Prince of princes: i.e. the Messiah.
he shall be broken without hand. To understand this read Isa. 11. 4. 2 Thess. 2. 8. Rev. 19. 19, 20. Cp. Isa. 10. 12; 14. 25; 31. 8. Mic. 5. 5-7. Zeph. 2. 13. Zech. 10. 11. Nah. 1. 11. **26 the evening and the morning.** See note on "days" (Ap. 90). These are interpreted as being 2,300 days. No one may interpret the interpretation and say they are "years". **is true**=it [is] truth. **shut thou up.** As in 12. 4. **it shall be, &c.** Supply the *Ellipsis* (Ap. 6) thus: "it [belongeth] to many days [to come]": i.e. to a yet future time. **27 fainted.** The Sept. omits "fainted, and". **the king's business.** In Shushan, whither he had gone. See note on *v.* 2. **astonished**=dumb. **understood**=became aware of.

9. 1—12. 13 (*A*, p. 1178). THE DESOLATIONS OF JERUSALEM. (*Extended Alternation.*)

A | K | 9. 1, 2. The time.
L | 9. 3-19. Daniel's Humiliation.
M | 9. 20-23-. The *Hierophant.*
N | 9. -23-27. The Prophecy.
K | 10. 1. The time.
L | 10. 2, 3. Daniel's Humiliation.
M | 10. 4-21. The *Hierophant.*
N | 11. 1—12. 13. The Prophecy.

1 the first year: 426 B.C., Daniel being then eighty-seven. See Ap. 50. **Darius.** This is an appellative, and means the Maintainer or Restrainer: i.e. Cyrus. See Ap. 57; and special note on p. 615. **Ahasuerus,** an appellative=the venerable king Astyages. See Ap. 57. **made king**: i.e. Cyrus was appointed king of Babylon by Astyages his father. **2 understood**=came to an understanding; perceived, or observed. Heb. *bīn*, to separate or distinguish. Implying that he had not known this before. **by books**=by the writings [of Jeremiah]. Jer. 29. 1, 10, as well as 25. 11. Note the definite Article in the Heb. **the number of the years.** Which were now drawing to an end. **the LORD.** Heb. Jehovah. Ap. 4. II. **Jeremiah.** The passage was doubtless 25. 11-14; 29. 10-14.

426 miah the prophet, that He would °accomplish
°seventy years in °the desolations of Jerusalem.
L **3** And I °set my face unto °the LORD* °God,
(p. 1196) °to seek by prayer and supplications, with
fasting, and sackcloth, and ashes:
4 And I °prayed unto [2]the LORD °my God,
and made my confession, and said, °'O [3]LORD*,
the great and dreadful °GOD, keeping °the
covenant and °mercy to them that love Him,
and to them that keep His commandments;
5 °We have °sinned, and have committed
°iniquity, and have done °wickedly, and have
°rebelled, even by departing from Thy precepts and from Thy judgments:
6 Neither have we hearkened unto Thy servants the prophets, which °spake in Thy name
to our kings, our princes, and our fathers, and
to all the People of the land.
7 O °Lord, righteousness *belongeth* unto
Thee, but unto us confusion of faces, as at
this day; to the °men of Judah, and to the inhabitants of Jerusalem, and unto °all Israel,
that are °near, and *that are* far off, through
all the countries whither Thou hast driven
them, because of their °trespass that they
have °trespassed against Thee.
8 O [7]LORD, to us *belongeth* confusion of
face, to our kings, to our princes, and to our
fathers, because we have [5]sinned against Thee.
9 To [3]the LORD* our °God *belong* °mercies
and forgivenesses, though we have [5]rebelled
against Him;
10 Neither have we °obeyed the voice of [2]the
LORD our [3]God, to walk in His laws, which
He set before us °by His servants the prophets.
11 Yea, [7]all Israel have °transgressed Thy
law, even by departing, that they might not
[10]obey Thy voice; °therefore the curse °is
poured upon us, and the oath that *is* written
in the law of °Moses the servant of [3]God, because we have [5]sinned against Him.
12 And He hath °confirmed His °words,
which He spake against us, and against our
judges that judged us, by bringing upon us
a great °evil: for under the whole heaven hath
not been done as hath been done upon Jerusalem.
13 °As °*it is* written in the law of Moses, all
this [12]evil is come upon us: yet made we not
our prayer before [2]the LORD our [3]God, that
we might turn from our [5]iniquities, and understand Thy truth.
14 Therefore hath [2]the LORD °watched upon
the [12]evil, and brought it upon us: for [2]the
LORD our [3]God *is* righteous in all His works
which He doeth: for we [10]obeyed not His voice.
15 And now, O [3]LORD* our [3]God, That °hast
brought Thy People forth out of the land of
Egypt with a mighty hand, and hast °gotten
Thee renown, as at this day; we have [5]sin-
ned, we have done [5]wickedly.
16 O [3]LORD*, according to all Thy righteousness, I beseech Thee, let Thine anger and Thy
fury be turned away from Thy city Jerusalem,
Thy °holy mountain: °because for our [5]sins,
and for the [5]iniquities of our fathers, Jerusalem and Thy People *are* °*become* a reproach
to all *that are* about us.
17 Now therefore, O our [3]God, hear the
prayer of Thy servant, and his supplications,
and °cause Thy face to shine upon Thy sanctuary that is desolate, °for [3]the LORD'S* sake.

accomplish = fulfil [within].
seventy years. Note the bearing of this on *v.* 24.
the desolations of Jerusalem. From 479 to 409 B.C. See note on p. 615. The "desolations" had therefore lasted 42 (6 × 7) years, and had yet 28 (4 × 7) years to run before they were "accomplished". We find the same subdivisions of the "servitude"; for from the first year of Nebuchadnezzar (496) to the decree of Artaxerxes (Astyages) (454) was forty-two years; and from the decree to the end of the servitude was twenty-eight years.

3 set my face. Knowledge of Jehovah's words quickened his spiritual interest in them.
the LORD*. One of the 134 cases in which the *Sōpherim* state that they altered "Jehovah" of the primitive text to "Adonai". See Ap. 32.
God. Heb. Elohim (with Art.) = the (true) God. Ap. 4. I.
to seek = to worship, or to seek [information].

4 prayed. Ref. to Pent. (Lev. 26. 40). Ap. 92.
my God. Heb. Elohim. Ap. 4. I.
O LORD*, the great, &c. Ref. to Pent. (Ex. 20. 6; 34. 6, 7. Num. 14. 18. Deut. 7. 9). Ap. 92.
GOD. Heb. El. Ap. 4. IV.
the covenant. Note the Art. = the covenant [made of old].
mercy = the lovingkindness or grace [promised therein]. Ref. to Pent. (Ex. 20. 6; 34. 6, 7). Ap. 92.

5 We. Note that Daniel associates himself with his People. Cp. Neh. 1.; and 9. 33-38. Ezra 9. 5-15. Note the Fig. *Anabasis* (Ap. 6) in *v.* 5.
sinned. Heb. *chāṭa'.* Ap. 44. i.
iniquity. Heb. *'āvāh.* Ap. 44. iv.
wickedly = lawlessly. Heb. *rāshā'.* Ap. 44. x.
rebelled = revolted. Heb. *mārad.* Usually of revolt against Deity or royalty.

6 spake in Thy name. Cp. Heb. 1. 1. Cp. Ex. 7. 1 with 4. 16, and see Ap. 49.

7 Lord. Heb. Adonai. Ap. 4. VIII (2).
men. Heb. *'ish.* Ap. 14. II.
all Israel. See note on 1 Kings 12. 17.
near, &c. Cp. Deut. 4. 27. 2 Kings 17. 6, 7. Isa. 11. 11. Jer. 24. 9. Amos 9. 9; and see Acts 2. 36.
trespass . . . trespassed. Heb. *mā'al.* Ap. 44. xi.

9 God. Heb. Elohim. Ap. 4. I.
mercies = compassions.

10 obeyed = hearkened to.
by = by the hand of.

11 transgressed. Heb. *'ābar.* Ap. 44. vii.
therefore the curse is, &c. Ref. to Pent. (Lev. 26. 14, &c. Deut. 27. 15, &c.; 28. 15, &c.; 29. 20; 30. 17, 18; 31. 17; 32. 19).
is poured upon = hath come pouring upon.
Moses the servant of God. See note on 1 Chron. 6. 49. Neh. 10. 29. Ap. 92.

12 confirmed His words: i.e. by His prophets since the giving of the law (2 Kings 17. 13. Isa. 44. 26. Lam. 2. 17. Zech. 1. 6).
words. Heb. marg., with some codices, and one early printed edition, read "word" (sing.). Heb. text, with Sept., Syr., and Vulg., read "words" (pl.).
evil = calamity. Heb. *rā'a'.* Ap. 44. viii.

13 As = According as.
it is written, &c. Ref. to Pent. (Lev. 26. 14, &c. Deut. 28. 15, &c., as above). Ap. 92.

14 watched. Cp. Jer. 31. 28; 44. 27.

15 hast brought, &c. Ref. to Pent. (Ex. 6. 1, 6; 12. 41; 14. 18; 32. 11). Ap. 92.
gotten Thee renown = made Thee a Name.

16 holy. See note on Ex. 3. 5.
because for our sins . . . fathers. Ref. to Pent. (Ex. 20. 5). Ap. 92.
become a reproach. Cp. Jer. 24. 9; 29. 18; 42. 18; 44. 8, 12. Ezek. 5. 14, 15; 22. 4.

17 cause Thy face to shine. Ref. to Pent. (Num. 6. 25, 26). Ap. 92.
for the LORD'S* sake. Sept. reads "for Thy servants' sake".

426 18 O my [3] God, incline Thine ear, and hear;
open °Thine eyes, and behold our [2] desolations, and the city °which is called by Thy name: for °we do not present our supplications before Thee for our righteousnesses, but for Thy great [9] mercies.
19 O [3] LORD*, hear; O [3] LORD*, forgive; O [3] LORD*, hearken and °do; defer not, for Thine own sake, O my [3] God: for Thy city and Thy People [18] are called by Thy name.'

M (p. 1190) 20 And whiles I was speaking, and praying,
and confessing my sin and the [5] sin of my People [7] Israel, and presenting my supplication before [2] the LORD my [3] God for the [16] holy mountain of my God;
21 Yea, whiles I *was* speaking in prayer, even the [7] man °Gabriel, whom I had seen in the vision at the beginning, being caused to fly swiftly, touched me °about the time of the evening °oblation.
22 °And he informed *me*, and talked with me, and said, 'O Daniel, I am now come forth °to give thee skill and understanding.
23 At the beginning of thy supplications the commandment came forth, and I am come to shew *thee*; for thou *art* greatly beloved:

N O therefore understand the matter, and consider the vision.

P 24 °Seventy weeks are °determined upon °thy People and upon °thy [16] holy city,

x to °finish the °transgression,

y °and to °make an end of °sins,

z and to °make reconciliation for °iniquity,

x and to bring in everlasting righteousness,

y and to °seal up the vision and °prophecy,

z and to anoint °the most Holy.

O 25 °Know therefore and understand,

P Q *that* °from the going forth of the °commandment to restore and to build °Jerusalem

18 Thine eyes. Fig. *Anthropopatheia.* Ap. 6.
which is called by Thy name: or, upon which Thy name has been called.
we. Others were praying with Daniel.
19 do = perform [it].
21 Gabriel. See note on 8. 16. This prophecy is not given by a "prophet", but by an angel or hierophant (who shows sacred things) to a prophet. It is therefore a most transcendent prophecy.
about the time, &c. Compare similar important occasions: David (2 Sam. 24. 15, note); Elijah (1 Kings 18. 29); Ezra (Ezra 9. 5).
oblation = gift or donation offering. Heb. *minchah.* Ap. 43. II. iii.
22 And he informed me. The Syr. reads "Yea, he came".
to give thee skill, &c. = to teach thee understanding, or to make thee wise as to, &c. Note the special emphasis as to the admonition for ourselves in the Structures below. It is not a vision that requires *interpretation*, but a direct prophecy given in simple words by the angel Gabriel, sent by God for the express purpose of making everything clear, and solving the most weighty problems that perplex the human mind. There is no "difficulty", as supposed. All that is required of us is to understand, and consider, and believe what is thus written for our learning.

9. -23-27 (N, p. 1196). THE PROPHECY.
(*Alternation.*)

N | O | -23. Admonition. "Understand", "Consider".
  P | 24. The Seventy sevens. In whole.
  O | 25-. Admonitions. "Know", "Understand".
  P | -25-27. The Seventy sevens. In their parts.

9. 24 (P, above). THE SEVENTY SEVENS. IN WHOLE. (*Extended Alternation.*)

P | x | To finish the transgression, } Internals.
  y | And to make an end of (*ḥatham*) sin. }
  z | And to make reconciliation for iniquity, }
  x | And to bring in everlasting righteousness, } Externals.
  y | And to seal up (*ḥatham*) the vision and prophecy, }
  z | And to anoint the Most Holy. }

24 Seventy weeks = Seventy sevens: i.e. of years. Not on any "year-day" theory. If "days" had been intended, it would be so expressed, as in 10. 3 (cp. Lev. 25. 8). Moreover, "years" had been the subject of Daniel's prayer (*v.* 2). The last "seven" is "one", and it is divided in half in *v.* 27, and the half is three and a half *years* (7. 25; cp. 8. 11–14; 11. 33). In Rev. 11. 2 this half is expressed by "forty-two months"; and in the next verse as "1,260 days". See Ap. 90. The whole period is therefore 490 years. **determined** = cut off: i.e. divided off from all other years. The verb is in the singular to indicate the unity of the whole period, however it may be divided up. Heb. *ḥāthak.* Occurs only here. **thy People:** i.e. Daniel's People, Israel, with which alone the prophecy is concerned. **thy holy city:** i.e. Jerusalem (*vv.* 2, 7, 16). **finish** = put an end to. **transgression.** Heb. *pāsha'* (with Art.). Ap. 44. vii. Cp. 8. 12, 23. **and.** Note the Fig. *Polysyndeton* (Ap. 6) in this verse, to emphasise each of these six special announcements and their connection with the *whole* period. **make an end of.** Heb. *ḥatham*, as below ("to seal up"). **sins.** Heb. *chāṭā'.* Ap. 44. i. Heb. marg., with four early printed editions, some codices, and Vulg., read "sin" (sing.). **make reconciliation** = make expiation or atonement. **iniquity.** Heb. *'āvāh.* Ap. 44. iv. **seal up, &c.** = make an end of by fulfilling all that has been the subject of prophecy. **prophecy** = prophet. **the most Holy** = a Holy of Holies. Never used of a person. This answers to the cleansing of the sanctuary (8. 14) which immediately precedes "the end". See Ap. 89. **25 Know therefore and understand.** Note this second admonition, as shown in the Structure ("*O*") above.

9. -25-27 (*P*, above). THE SEVENTY SEVENS. IN THEIR PARTS. (*Introversion.*)

P | Q | -25-. The City. Restoration.
  R | -25. Messiah. Coming.
  S | -25. Time. "Unto" seven sevens and sixty-two sevens.
  S | 26-. Time. "After" the sixty-two sevens.
  R | -26-. Messiah. Cut off.
  Q | -26, 27. The City. Destruction.

from the going forth, &c.: i.e. in the twentieth year of Artaxerxes (= the great king: i.e. Astyages), 454 B.C. See notes on Neh. 2. 1; longer note on p. 653. Also Ap. 50 (p. 60) and Ap. 58 (p. 82). **commandment** = word. Heb. *dābār.* Ap. 73. X. Referring to the Divine word rather than to a royal decree. **Jerusalem.** Not the Temple (as in Ezra), but the city (as in Nehemiah), which was the subject of Daniel's prayer, and therefore the answer to it.

426 R (p. 1198) unto the °Messiah °the Prince
S *shall be* °seven weeks, and °threescore and two weeks: °the street shall be built again, and °the wall, even °in troublous times.

S **26** And °after °threescore and two weeks
R shall [25] Messiah be °cut off, °but not for Himself:

Q T a (p. 1199) and °the people of °the [25] prince that shall come °shall destroy the city and the sanctuary; and °the end thereof *shall be* with a flood,
b °and unto the end of the war °desolations are °determined.

U **27** And °he shall confirm °the covenant with °many
V for °one week:
V and in °the midst of the week
U he shall cause °the sacrifice and the oblation to cease,

Messiah = anointed. Only priests and kings were anointed, lepers, and Elisha (1 Kings 19. 16) being the only exceptions.

Messiah the Prince = "Messiah [that is to say] the Prince [of the People]". Messiah is a noun, and is connected with Prince by apposition: i.e. a priest-king. Only one such known to Scripture (Ps. 110. 4. Zech. 6. 13. John 4. 25).

the Prince. Heb. *nāgîd* = a leader and ruler of the People (1 Sam. 9. 16; 10. 1; 13. 14; 18. 13; 25. 30. 2 Sam. 5. 2, &c.). Therefore not Zerubbabel (who was a prince but not a priest); nor Ezra (who was a priest but not a prince); nor Cyrus (who was a king but not a priest, and he only as a type of Messiah, who was both).

seven weeks = forty-nine years (454–405 B.C.). See Ap. 50, p. 60, and Ap. 91.

threescore and two weeks = 434 years (405 B.C.–A.D. 29): the two together being 49 + 434 = 483 years; leaving seven years to make up the full 490 years of *v.* 24. See Ap. 50, p. 61, and Ap. 91.

the street . . . and the wall = open place . . . and close street: implying the completeness of the restoration; which included the places of resort and the thoroughfares leading thereto, like our English "court and alley".

the street = the broadway or open space by the gates or elsewhere.

the wall. Heb. *ḥārūẓ.* Whatever it may mean, it cannot be "wall", for that is *ḥōmah* (that which surrounds). *Ḥārūẓ* = something cut in or dug out; and may well be used of what is narrow, and then that which is narrowed down to a deciding point, a decision or determination, as in 9. 26; 11. 36. Cp. Isa. 10. 22. Job 14. 5, &c. See the Oxford *Gesenius.* **in troublous times:** i.e. the times of Ezra and Nehemiah. This covers the forty-nine years. We know this, not from history profane or Divine, but from the statement here. **26 after threescore and two weeks.** The definite Article here marks this period, as the one just mentioned in *v.* 24: i.e. after the 483 years. How long "after" is not stated; but it must surely be either immediately or very soon after the Messiah was thus presented and proclaimed in and to Jerusalem as the Prince. The decree was issued in the month of Nisan, the same month as the events in Matt. 21. 1—26. 61. Cp. Zech. 9. 9. Luke 19. 41–44 ("this thy day"). **threescore and two:** i.e. the sixty-two sevens (= 434 years). See note on *v.* 25. **cut off:** i.e. in death. Heb. *karath* (Gen. 9. 11. Deut. 20. 20. Jer. 11. 19. Ps. 37. 9). Cp. Heb. *gāzar* (Isa. 53. 8). **but not for Himself** = but no sign of aught for Him: i.e. He shall be rejected and crucified, and shall not then enter on the kingdom for which He came. It will be rejected, and therefore become in abeyance. See John 1. 11.

9. -26, 27 (*Q*, p. 1198). THE CITY. DESTROYED.

(*Introversion and Alternation.*)

Q | T | a | -26-. The Coming Prince. (The Desolator.)
b | -26. The Desolation (*shamēm*) decreed. The end of the Desolation.
U | 27-. His Covenant made.
V | -27-. The Time. One seven (= 7 years).
V | -27-. The Time. The middle of the one seven (= $3\frac{1}{2}$ years).
U | -27-. His Covenant broken (cp. 11. 30, 31).
T | *a* | -27-. The Coming Prince. (The Desolator.)
b | -27. The Desolation (*shamēm*) decreed. The end of the Desolator.

-26 the people: i.e. the Roman people. Cp. Luke 19. 41–44; 21. 20. **the prince that shall come** = a prince, &c. This is "the little horn" of 7. 8, 24–26; 8. 9–12, 23–25. See Ap. 89. **shall destroy the city, &c.** See Matt. 21. 41; 22. 7. This also was "after threescore and two weeks", but not within the last seven; which are confined to the doings of "the prince's people, the people that is coming" ("the little horn") after the doings of "the people" in the destruction of the city, which ends *v.* 26. What "the little horn" will do is stated in the words which follow. Antiochus never did this. He defiled it, but left it uninjured. **the end thereof:** or, his own end [come]: i.e. the end of the desolator looking on to the end of the last seven years. **and unto the end of the war** = up to the full end of the war (i.e. the end of the last seven years). **desolations** = desolate places. Cp. Matt. 23. 38. **determined.** See note on "the wall", *v.* 25. **27 he shall confirm the covenant** = make a firm covenant: i.e. the little horn will do this at the beginning of the last seven years. See note below on "one week". It may even be the beginning of the 2,300 days of 8. 14. Cp. 11. 21–24. **the covenant** = a covenant. **many** = the many. **one week.** This is the last seven years which completes the "seventy" of *v.* 24; the time when action commences in connection with Daniel's "city" and "People" (i.e. Jerusalem and Israel). These have been in abeyance since *v.* 26. Israel is "*Lo-ammi*" (= not my people, Hos. 1. 9, 10). For the present interval between "*R*" and "T", *vv.* 26 and 27, see Luke 4. 18–20; 21. 24. Ap. 50. 11–14 (pp. 42 and 60); also Ap. 63. IX; 72; and 91. This fills the first half of the "week" (see Rev. 11. 3–11). **the midst of the week** = the middle of the week (i.e. at the end of the first three and a half years). **the sacrifice and the oblation to cease** = sacrifice and oblation to cease. This is the action of "the little horn" (see 8. 11, 12, 13; 11. 31; 12. 11). This belongs to the time of the end, and will be accompanied by the setting up of the abomination mentioned below and by our Lord in Matt. 24. 15. See Ap. 89 and 90.

426 *T a* (p. 1199) and °for the overspreading of °abominations he shall make *it* desolate,

b even °until the consummation, and that °determined °shall be poured upon the °desolate.'

K (p. 1096) 424
10 In °the third year of Cyrus king of Persia a °thing was revealed unto Daniel, whose name was called °Belteshazzar; and the °thing *was* true, °but the °time appointed *was* °long: and he understood the °thing, and had understanding of the vision.

L 2 In those days I Daniel was mourning °three full weeks.
3 I ate no °pleasant bread, neither came flesh nor °wine in my mouth, neither did I anoint myself at all, till °three whole weeks were fulfilled.

M W[1] Y[1] (p. 1200) 4 And in °the four and twentieth day of the first month, as I was by the side of the great river, which *is* °Hiddekel;
5 Then I lifted up mine eyes, and looked, and behold a certain °man °clothed in linen, whose loins *were* girded with fine gold of Uphaz:
6 His body also *was* like the beryl, and his face as the appearance of lightning, and his eyes as lamps of fire, and his arms and his feet like in colour to polished brass, and the voice of his words like the voice of a multitude.
7 And I Daniel alone saw the vision: for the °men that were with me saw not the vision; but a great quaking fell upon them, so that they fled to hide themselves.
8 Therefore I was left alone, and saw this great vision, and there remained no strength in me: for my comeliness was turned in me into corruption, and I retained no strength.

Z[1] 9 Yet heard I the voice of his words: and when I heard the voice of his words,

X[1] then °was I in a deep sleep on my face, and my face toward the ground.

W[2] Y[2] 10 And, °behold, an hand touched me, which set me upon my knees and *upon* the palms of my hands.

Z[2] 11 And he said unto me, 'O Daniel, a [5]man greatly beloved, understand the words that I speak unto thee, and °stand upright: for unto thee am I now sent.' And when he had spoken this word unto me, I stood trembling.
12 Then said he unto me, 'Fear not, Daniel: for from °the first day that thou didst set thine heart to understand, and to °chasten thyself before thy °God, thy words were heard, and I am come for thy words.
13 But °the prince of the kingdom of Persia °withstood me °one and twenty days: but, °lo,

for the overspreading of = on the wing, or battlement of; but Ginsburg suggests *'al kannō* (instead of *'al kanaph*) = in its stead [shall be]: i.e. in place of the daily sacrifice. Cp. 11. 7.

abominations he shall make it desolate = the abomination that maketh desolate. See Ap. 90. This is certainly future. See Matt. 24. 15. Our Lord tells us where it will stand "in the holy place": i.e. in the Temple at Jerusalem: and we have the same admonition to "understand" (cp. *vv.* 23, 25, above). Antiochus, the type of "the little horn", defiled the sanctuary, but he did not destroy it. He cannot therefore be the fulfiller of this prophecy, though he forshadowed him.

abominations. Jehovah's name for an "idol", as being what he detests. Heb. *shakaz* = to be abominable. The "of" in this connection being the Genitive (of the Origin), Ap. 17. 2: i.e. which causes the desolation. Cp. 2 Kings 23. 13. Isa. 44. 19, &c. Dan. 12. 11 is conclusive.

until the consummation = unto a full end. The reference is to Isa. 10. 22, 23.

determined. See note on "the wall", *v.* 25 above.

shall be poured upon = shall come pouring upon. For the fulfilment, cp. Rev. 16. 1, 2, 3, 4, 8, 10, 12, 17.

desolate = the causer of desolation. See 12. 11. Then the consummation of *v.* 24 will be fulfilled.

10. 1 the third year of Cyrus. Called by his appellative "Darius" (= the Restrainer, or Maintainer, in 9. 1; 424 B.C.). Two years later than ch. 9. This is Daniel's latest date; which continues to the end of this book, seventy-three years since his deportation: he being now eighty-nine years old.

thing = word, or matter.

Belteshazzar. See 1. 7.

but the time appointed was long = but [concerned] a long warfare.

time appointed. Heb. *tzaba.* Generally rendered "host" or "army" (8. 10, 11, 12). Put by Fig. *Metonymy* (of Adjunct), Ap. 6, for warfare.

long: or, great.

2 three full weeks = three sevens of days. See next verse and *v.* 13, in contrast with 9. 24, 25. Cp. this humiliation with that of 9. 3–19, and see the Structure ("L" and "*L*", p. 1196).

3 pleasant bread = bread of desires: i.e. pleasant food. **wine.** Heb. *yayin.* Ap. 27. I.

three whole weeks = three sevens of days, as in *vv.* 2, 13.

10. 4-21 (*M*, p. 1196). THE HIEROPHANT.
(*Repeated Alternations.*)

M | W[1] | Y[1] | 4–8. The Hierophant.
Z[1] | 9–. His words.
X[1] | –9. Their effect.
W[2] | Y[2] | 10. The Hierophant.
Z[2] | 11–14. His words.
X[2] | 15. Their effect.
W[3] | Y[3] | 16–. The Hierophant.
Z[3] | –16–17–. Daniel's words.
X[3] | –17. Their effect.
W[4] | Y[4] | 18. The Hierophant.
Z[4] | 19–. His words.
X[4] | –19. Their effect.
W[5] | Y[5] | 20–. The Hierophant.
Z[5] | –20, 21. His words.

4 the four and twentieth, &c.: i.e. the twenty-fourth of Nisan (i.e. Abib). **Hiddekel**: i.e. the Tigris. See Gen. 2. 14. **5 man.** Heb. *'īsh.* Ap. 14. II. **clothed, &c.** Cp. the description in Rev. 1. Note the Divine and angelic appearances in this book: 3. 25; 4. 13, 17, 23; 6. 22; 7. 16; 8. 13, 14, 16–26; 9. 21; 10. 4–8, 10, 16, 18, 20; 12. 1, 5, 6. **7 men.** Heb. pl. of *'ĕnōsh.* Ap. 14. III. Cp. Acts 9. 7. **9 was I in a deep sleep, &c.** Cp. 8. 18. **10 behold.** Fig. *Asterismos.* Ap. 6. **11 stand upright.** Note the Fig. *Polyptōton* (Ap. 6), stand upon thy standing: i.e. stand up where thou art. **12 the first day.** See 9. 23. **chasten** = humble. See note on *v.* 3. **God.** Heb. Elohim. Ap. 4. I. **13 the prince** = ruler. Heb. *ṣar* = a ruler (from *ṣarar* = to rule). Hence *Cæsar, Tzar* or *Czar.* Generally rendered "prince" in this book. See 1. 7, 8, 9, 10, 11, 18; 8. 11, 25; 9. 6, 8; 10. 13, 20, 21; 11. 5; 12. 1. The rulers may be good, angelic (good or evil), or the world-rulers of Eph. 6. 12. **withstood** = was standing confronting me. **one and twenty days.** See *vv.* 2, 3. **lo.** Fig. *Asterismos.* Ap. 6.

424 °Michael, one of the chief °princes, came to help me; and °I remained there °with the kings of Persia.

14 Now I am come to make thee understand what shall befall thy People in °the latter days: for yet the vision *is* for *many* days.'

X^2 (p. 1200) 15 And when he had spoken such words unto me, I set my face toward the ground, and I became °dumb.

W^3 Y^3 16 And, [10]behold, *one* like the similitude of the sons of °men touched my lips:

Z^3 then I opened my mouth, and spake, and said unto him that stood before me, 'O my lord, by the vision my sorrows are turned upon me, and I have retained no strength.

17 For how can the servant of this my lord talk with this my lord?

X^3 for as for me, straightway there °remained no strength in me, neither is there °breath left in me.'

W^4 Y^4 18 Then there came again and touched me *one* like the appearance of a [16]man, and he °strengthened me,

Z^4 19 And said, 'O [5]man greatly beloved, fear not: peace *be* unto thee, be [18]strong, yea, be [18]strong.'

X^4 And when he had spoken unto me, I was [18]strengthened, and said, 'Let my lord speak; for thou hast [18]strengthened me.'

W^5 Y^5 20 Then said he,

Z^5 'Knowest thou wherefore I come unto thee? and now will I return to fight with the [13]prince of Persia: and when I am gone forth, [13]lo, the [13]prince of Grecia shall come.

21 But I will shew thee that which is noted in the scripture of truth: and *there is* none that holdeth with me in these things, but [13]Michael your [13]prince.

N A^1 B^1 (p. 1201) **11** (Also I in the first year of °Darius the Mede, *even* I, °stood to confirm and to strengthen °him.)

2 And °now will I shew thee the truth. °Behold, there shall stand up °yet °three kings in Persia; and the fourth shall be far richer than *they* all: and °by his strength through his riches he shall stir up all against the realm of Grecia.

3 And °a mighty king shall stand up, that shall rule with great dominion, and °do according to his will.

B^2 4 And when he shall stand up, his kingdom shall be °broken, and shall be °divided toward the four °winds of heaven; and °not to his posterity, nor according to his dominion which he ruled: for his kingdom shall be plucked up, even for °others beside those.

B^3 C^1 5 And °the king of the °south shall be strong, and °*one* of his princes; and he shall be strong above °him, and have dominion; his dominion *shall be* °a great dominion.

Michael = who is like GOD (Heb. El)? The second angel named in this book. The special angelic ruler for Israel (*v.* 21; 12. 1. Cp. Jude 9, and Rev. 12. 7).

princes. Heb. *sar* = chief. Not the same word as in 11. 8, 18, 22.

I remained = I was superfluous: i.e. not needed. Hence we may render, "I left him there". Not the same word as in *v.* 17. **with** = beside.

14 the latter days. Ref. to Pent. (Gen. 49. 1. Num. 24. 14. Deut. 4. 30; 31. 29). Ap. 92. See note on 2. 28. Note the bearing of this on the prophecy itself, given in 11. 21—12. 3.

15 dumb. Cp. Ps. 139. 2, 9.

16 men. Heb. *'ādām.* Ap. 14. I.

17 remained = continued. Not the same word as in *v.* 13. **breath.** Heb. *n^eshāmāh.* See Ap. 16.

18 strengthened = strengthened (for endurance). Heb. *ḥazak.* Cp. Ps. 27. 14.

11. 1—12. 13 (*N*, p. 1196). **HIS PROPHECY.** (*Division.*)

N | A^1 | 11. 1–20. The Past. (Then Future to Daniel.)
| A^2 | 11. 21—12. 3. The Future. (Still Future to us.)
| A^3 | 12. 4–13. Meanwhile. (As to Daniel himself.)

11. 1–20 (A^1, above). **THE PAST. THEN FUTURE TO DANIEL.** (*Division.*)

A^1 | B^1 | 1–3. The first king of Grecia.
| B^2 | 4. Four contemporary kings.
| B^3 | 5–20. Subsequent kings.

1 This verse is parenthetical, to tell us what the angelic speaker had done two years previously (426 B.C.).

Darius the Mede is the same king as in 9. 1: i.e. Cyrus.

stood = was at my station.

him: i.e. Michael.

2 now. Calling attention to the then present time (424 B.C.) as being distinct from *v.* 1, which refers to what took place two years before.

Behold. Fig. *Asterismos.* Ap. 6.

yet: i.e. in the then immediate future.

three kings in Persia. Cambyses, the pseudo-Smerdis, and Darius Hystaspes. See Ap. 57. But ancient histories "contain much that is admittedly fabulous" (*Encycl. Brit.*, 11th ed., vol. 21, p. 210), and the commentaries based on them differing among themselves are therefore not to be relied on. We know from this verse that there were three, after Cyrus, and a fourth. Whoever he was, he was succeeded by the "mighty king" of *v.* 4 (Alexander the Great).

by his strength through his riches. Some codices, and five early printed editions, read "by strengthening himself in his riches he will stir up", &c.

3 a mighty king. The he-goat's "little horn" (8. 9).

do according to his will. See 8. 4. Cp. *vv.* 16, 36.

4 broken. See 8. 8. **divided.** See 8. 22.

winds. Heb. *rūach.* Ap. 9.

not to his posterity. But to his generals. Cp. "not in his power" (8. 22).

others beside those: i.e. beside those four. See note on 8. 22.

11. 5–20 (B^3, above). **SUBSEQUENT KINGS.** (*Repeated Alternation.*)

B^3 | C^1 | 5. The first king of the South.
| D^1 | 6. The first king of the North.
| C^2 | 7–9. The second king of the South.
| D^2 | 10. The second king of the North.
| C^3 | 11, 12. The second king of the South.
| D^3 | 13–20. The second king of the North.

That there is a break between the past and the future is manifest from 10. 14, of which this chapter is the continuation. Dr. Tregelles prefers to make it at *v.* 5. This would alter the above Structure, and require only two members: A^1, *vv.* 1–4, the past; and A^2, *v.* 5—12. 3, future. Those who take *vv.* 5–20 as belonging to the past do not agree as to the interpretation from history. We give the commonly held view, making the break between *vv.* 20 and 21. **5 the king of the south.** Ptolemy Soter, son of Lagus, king of Egypt (see *v.* 8). He took the title "king"; whereas his father "Lagus" had been only governor. **south.** With reference to Judea. **one of his princes.** Seleucus I (Nicator = conqueror). **him**: i.e. Ptolemy. **a great dominion.** It added Syria to Babylon and Media.

D^1 (p. 1201) 424 6 And °in the end of years they shall °join themselves together; for °the king's daughter of the south shall come to °the king of the °north to °make an agreement: but she shall not retain the power of the arm; neither shall he stand, nor his arm: but she shall be °given up, and they that brought her, and he that begat her, and he that strengthened her in *these* °times.

C^2 7 But out of °a branch of her roots shall *one* stand up °in his estate, which shall come with an army, and shall enter into the fortress of the king of the north, and shall deal against them, and shall prevail:

8 And shall also carry captives into Egypt their gods, with their princes, *and* with °their precious vessels of silver and of gold; and he shall °continue °*more* years than the king of the north.

9 So the king of the south shall come into *his* kingdom, and shall return into his own °land.

D^2 10 But °his °sons shall be stirred up, and shall assemble a multitude of great forces: and *one* °shall certainly °come, and overflow, and pass through: then shall he return, and °be stirred up, *even* to his fortress.

C^3 11 And °the king of the south shall be moved with °choler, and shall come forth and fight with him, *even* with the king of the north: and °he shall set forth a great multitude; but the multitude shall be °given into °his hand.

12 *And* when he hath °taken away the multitude, his heart shall be lifted up; and he shall °cast down *many* ten thousands: but °he shall not be strengthened *by it.*

D^3 13 For °the king of the north shall °return, and shall set forth a multitude greater than the former, and shall certainly °come °after certain years with a great army and with much riches.

14 And in those times there shall many stand up against °the king of the south: also °the robbers of thy People shall exalt themselves °to establish the vision; °but they shall fall.

15 So °the king of the north shall come, and cast up a mount, and take the most fenced cities: and the arms of the south shall not withstand, °neither his chosen people, neither *shall there be any* strength to withstand.

16 But he that cometh against °him shall °do according to his own will, and none shall stand before him: and he shall stand in the glorious land, °which by his hand shall be °consumed.

17 He shall also °set his face to enter with the strength of his whole kingdom, °and upright ones with him; thus shall he do: and he

6 in the end of years. In *v.* 13 this is rendered "after certain years", said to be sixty-three. Cp. 2 Chron. 18. 2, and *v.* 8 below.

join: i.e. in league.

the king's daughter. Berenice, daughter of Ptolemy II (Philadelphus) of Egypt.

the king of the north. Antiochus.

north. With reference to Judea.

make an agreement = do upright things: i.e. to come to terms upon what is equitable between the parties. Here it included her marriage with Antiochus, who divorced his wife (Laodice) and disinherited her son (Seleucus Callinicus).

given = delivered.

times: or, vicissitudes.

7 a branch of her roots. Her brother Ptolemy III (Euergetes), "roots" referring to their father Ptolemy II (Philadelphus).

in his estate = in his stead. Heb. *kannō.* See note on 9. 27 ("for the overspreading"): i.e. in the stead of Philadelphus, who avenged the murder of Berenice and her son by Laodice. Euergetes had been restored. This is the second king of the south.

8 their precious vessels = vessels of desire, said to have been valued at 40,000 talents of silver; and 2,400 images, including Egyptian idols, which Cambyses had taken from Egypt. Hence he was named by the grateful Egyptians "Euergetes" (= Benefactor).

continue = stand.

more years: i.e. four years, reigning forty-six years in all.

9 land = soil.

10 his. Seleucus II (Callinicus).

sons. Heb. text is "son" (sing.). But the Heb. marg., with some codices and one early printed edition, read "sons" (pl.), as here: i.e. Seleucus II (Callinicus) and his brother Antiochus III. See *Encycl. Brit.*, 11th (Cambridge) ed., vol. 24, p. 604.

shall = he shall: i.e. Antiochus III, the second king of the north, his brother having died by a fall from his horse.

come. Some codices, with one early printed edition, and Syr., read "come against him".

be stirred up = will wage war. Defeating Antiochus III.

11 the king of the south. The second, Ptolemy III.

choler. See note on 8. 7.

he: i.e. the king of the north, Antiochus III.

given = delivered.

his hand: i.e. Ptolemy's hand.

12 taken away = subdued.

cast down, &c. = will cause tens of thousands to fall. This occurred at Raphia, south-west of Gaza.

he shall not be strengthened by it. Giving himself up to licentiousness.

13 the king of the north. The second king, Antiochus III. **return** = renew the war.

come. Some codices, with three early printed editions, read "will come against him". Fig. *Polyptōton* = coming he will come. Ap. 6.

after certain years. Heb. at the end of years, as in *v.* 6. This was fourteen years after his defeat at Raphia.

14 the king of the south. This would be the third king, Ptolemy V (Epiphanes), a mere child.

the robbers = sons of the oppressors: i.e. apostate Jews, or turbulent men who defied laws and justice.

to establish the vision: i.e. to help to fulfil prophecy, by taking the side of Syria, so as to make Judea independent. **but they shall fall.** For they indirectly helped to establish Antiochus. See *vv.* 16–19.

15 the king of the north. This is Antiochus III (the Great); and *vv.* 16–19 describe his doings, which were a typical foreshadowing of his antitype, "the little horn", the yet future antichrist, described in in 11. 21—12. 1; which show how the latter portion can be fulfilled by an individual. **neither his chosen people.** Dr. Ginsburg suggests "but his people will flee". **16 him.** Ptolemy V. **do according to his own will.** Thus foreshadowing but not exhausting what is said of "the vile person" in *vv.* 21, 36. **which by his hand shall be consumed** = much wasted in his hand. **consumed** = perfected: i.e. completely desolated. **17 set his face.** The idiom for expressing a fixed purpose. Cp. 2 Kings 12. 17. **and upright ones . . . shall he do** = he will make equitable terms with him (i.e. Ptolemy V). The words which follow tell us what the terms were. With this agree the Sept., Syr., and Vulg.

424 shall give °him °the daughter of °women, corrupting her: but she shall °not stand *on his side,* neither be for him.

18 After this shall he turn his face unto the °isles, and shall take many: but °a prince °for his own behalf shall cause the reproach offered by °him to cease; °without his own reproach he shall cause *it* to turn upon °him.

19 Then he shall turn his face toward the °fort of his own land: but he shall °stumble and fall, and not be found.

20 Then shall stand up [7]in his estate °a raiser of taxes *in* the glory of the °kingdom: but within few days he shall be destroyed, °neither in anger, nor in battle.

A² E (p. 1203) **21** And [7]in his estate shall stand up °a vile person, to whom °they shall not give the °honour of the kingdom: but he shall come in °peaceably, and obtain the kingdom by flatteries.

22 And with the arms of a flood shall they °be overflown from before him, and shall be °broken; °yea, also the prince of the covenant.

23 And after °the league *made* with him he shall work deceitfully: for he shall come up, and shall become strong °with a small people.

24 He shall enter [21]peaceably even upon the fattest places of the province; and he shall do *that* which his fathers have not done, nor his fathers' fathers; he shall scatter among them the prey, and spoil, and riches: *yea,* and he shall °forecast his devices against the strong holds, even for a time.

25 And he shall stir up his power and his courage against the king of the south with a great army; and the king of the south shall be stirred up to battle with a very great and mighty army; but °he °shall not stand: for they shall [24]forecast devices against him.

26 Yea, °they that feed of the portion of his meat shall destroy him, and his army shall overflow: and many shall fall down slain.

27 °And both these kings' hearts *shall be* to do °mischief, and they shall speak lies at one table; but it shall not prosper: for °yet the end *shall be* at the time appointed.

28 Then shall he return into his land with great riches; and °his heart *shall be* against the holy covenant; and he shall °do *exploits,* and return to his own land.

29 At the time appointed he shall return, and come toward the south; but it shall not be as °the former, or as °the latter.

30 For the ships of °Chittim shall come against him: therefore he shall be grieved, and return, and have indignation °against the °holy covenant: so shall he °do; he shall even return, and °have intelligence with them that forsake the holy covenant.

him. Ptolemy V, then only twelve years of age.

the daughter of women: i.e. Cleopatra, his own daughter, then only eleven years of age. The term denotes beauty, &c.

women: i.e. her mother and grandmother, probably still caring for her education, &c.

not stand, &c. She sided with her husband, and defeated her father's plans.

18 isles = coast-lands, or maritime countries.

a prince = a captain or general. Heb. *ḳāẓin.* Occurs only here in this book. He was the Roman general, Scipio (Lucius Scipio).

for his own behalf: i.e. for his own interest.

him. Antiochus III.

without his own reproach: i.e. with untarnished reputation.

19 fort = fortresses.

stumble = stagger. Antiochus III, after his defeat by Scipio at Magnesia (near Smyrna), withdrew to Syria.

20 a raiser of taxes . . . kingdom = one [Seleucus] causing the exactor [Heliodorus] to pass through [Judea], the glorious land (cp. *vv.* 16, 41; 8. 9). Seleucus sent Heliodorus to Jerusalem to plunder the Temple, &c. See 2 Macc. 3. 4, &c. Zech. 9. 8 is in direct contrast with this.

neither in anger. Ginsburg suggests "and not with hands", because it was by poison.

Here ends the historical portion, which has been fulfilled now, but which was then future. Verse 21—12. 3 passes on to the time which is still (1912) future to us.

11. 21—12. 3 (A², p. 1201). **THE FUTURE.**
(STILL FUTURE TO US.) (*Alternation.*)

A² | E | 11. 21-31. "The vile person" ("the little horn").
  F | 11. 32-35. The People. Tried.
 E | 11. 36-45. "The wilful king" ("the little horn").
  F | 12. 1-3. The People. Delivered.

Here begins the portion of this prophecy which is still future to us (1912), "the latter days" of 10. 14.

21 a vile person. One of the twelve titles given to the antichrist. See note on **7.** 8. The prophecy concerning him is *continuous* to the end of the chapter. It is parallel with 7. 8, &c.; 8. 9, &c.; and 9. -26, 27. He is not another successional king of the north, but a totally different and unique personage, still future. He comes in by "flatteries", and in *v.* 40 he is attacked by both a "king of the south" and a "king of the north". Note the parallel exhibited in Ap. 89.

vile = despicable. Cp. Ps. 15. 4.

they shall not give = to whom was not given.

honour = dignity.

peaceably = unexpectedly: i.e. in a time of careless security (cp. 8. 25). Cp. Ezek. 16. 49 ("abundance of idleness"). So the Oxford *Gesenius,* p. 1017.

22 be overflown from = sweep all.

broken = broken in pieces.

yea, also, &c.: i.e. a prince with whom he had made a covenant or league (*v.* 23), and who had hitherto aided him.

23 the league: i.e. the covenant just mentioned (*v.* 22).

with a small people. Hence he is called "the little horn".

24 forecast his devices = devise plots.

25 he: i.e. the king of the south.

shall not stand = will make no stand.

26 they that feed, &c. There will be treachery within, as well as fighting without. **27 And both these kings' hearts, &c.** = Now, as to the two kings, their hearts [will be set] to do, &c. **mischief** = evil. Heb. *rā'a'.* Ap. 44. viii. **yet the end, &c.** Intimating that these things belong to the closing scenes. Cp. *vv.* 35 and 40. **28 his heart, &c.** Showing when the purpose of breaking the covenant was plotted. **do exploits** = act effectively, or accomplish [the purpose of his heart]. **29 the former.** In *vv.* 25, 26. **the latter.** In *vv.* 42, 43. **30 Chittim** = Cyprus, or some European power. See note on Num. 24. 24. Ref. to Pent. (Num. 24. 24). Ap. 92. **against the holy covenant.** Made with the Jews at the beginning of the last seven years, already mentioned in 9. 27. In 11. 28, he had already plotted the breaking of it. **do** = do [so], or accomplish [it]: i.e. he will break it. **holy.** See note on Ex. 3. 5. **have intelligence** = fix his attention on (with a view to co-operation).

424 31 And arms shall stand on his part, and
they shall °pollute the sanctuary of strength,
and shall °take away the daily *sacrifice*,
and they shall °**place the abomination that
maketh desolate.**

F G (p. 1204) 32 And °such as do °wickedly against the
covenant shall he °corrupt by flatteries:

H but the people that do °know their °God shall
°be strong, and °do *exploits*.
33 And they that °understand among the
people shall instruct many: yet they °shall
fall by the sword, and by flame, by captivity,
and by spoil, °*many* days.
34 Now when they [33]shall fall, they °shall be
holpen with a little help:

G but many shall cleave to them with flatteries.

H 35 And *some* of them of [33]understanding
[33]shall fall, to °try them, and to °purge, and
to make *them* white, *even* to °the time of the
end: because *it is* [27] yet for a time appointed.

E J 36 And the king shall °do according to his
will; and °**he shall exalt himself, and magnify
himself above every °GOD**, and shall speak
marvellous things °against the °GOD of
°gods, and shall prosper till °the indignation
be accomplished: for that that is °determined
shall be done.
37 Neither shall he regard the [32]God of his
fathers, nor °the desire of women, nor regard
any °GOD: for he shall magnify himself
above all.
38 But °in his estate shall he honour the
°God of °forces: and a god whom his fathers knew not °shall he honour with gold,
and silver, and with precious stones, and
pleasant things.
39 Thus shall he °do in °the most strong
holds with a strange god, °whom he shall
acknowledge °*and* increase with glory: and
he shall cause them to rule over many, and
shall divide the land for °gain.

K 40 And °at the time of the end shall the king
of the south push at him: and the king of the
north shall come against him like a whirlwind, with chariots, and with horsemen, and
with many ships;

J and °he shall enter into °the countries, and
shall overflow and pass over.
41 He shall enter also into °the glorious land,
and many *countries* shall be overthrown: but
these shall escape out of his hand, *even* Edom,
and Moab, and the chief of the °children of
Ammon.
42 He shall stretch forth his hand also upon
the countries: and the land of Egypt shall not
escape.
43 But he shall have power over the treasures of gold and of silver, and over all the
precious things of Egypt: and the Libyans
and the Ethiopians *shall be* at his steps.

31 pollute the sanctuary. By putting up the "abomination" (the Asherah, Ap. 42), which brings on the judgment of "desolation". The end is marked by the "cleansing of the sanctuary" (8. 14; 9. 24). Ap. 89.

take away the daily sacrifice. This marks the middle of the "week", or the last seven years. See 8. 11, 12; 9. 27; 12. 11; and Ap. 89. From this point he is energized by Satan.

place the abomination, &c. This accompanies the taking away of the daily sacrifice (8. 13; 9. 27; 12. 11; and Ap. 89). Our Lord refers to this verse in Matt. 24. 15.

11. 32-35 (F, p. 1203). THE PEOPLE. TRIED.
(*Alternation.*)

F | G | 32-. The unfaithful.
  H | -32-34-. The faithful.
  G | -34. The unfaithful.
  H | 35. The faithful.

32 such as do wickedly against=them that are ready to deal lawlessly with.

wickedly. Heb. *rāshā'*. Ap. 44. x.

corrupt=make impious or profane.

know their God. Denotes those who have an experimental rather than an intellectual knowledge. Heb. *yāda'*. **God.** Heb. Elohim. Ap. 4. I.

be strong=prove themselves strong. Heb. *ḥazak*= strong for endurance (i. e. for resisting all temptation to apostatize).

do exploits=work effectually.

33 understand=are wise. See *v.* 35 and 12. 3, 10, where it would be well to use the Heb. *Maskīlim*, as a proper name.

shall fall by the sword: i. e. in the great tribulation which is here described, in part.

many. Some codices, with six early printed editions, read this word "many" in the text.

34 shall be holpen, &c.=shall obtain but little help.

35 try=refine. Expulsion of dross.

purge=purify. Separation from dross.

the time of the end. Now near at hand.

11. 36-45 (*E*, p. 1203). "THE WILFUL KING."
(*Alternations.*)

E | J | 36-39. His character.
  K | 40-. His adversaries. Their Assault.
  J | -40-43. His conquests.
  K | 44, 45. His adversaries. Their Victory.

From *vv.* 36-45 we have "the wilful king" in his unhindered course. It cannot be exhaustively interpreted of Antiochus.

36 do according to his will. Cp. 8. 4; 11. 3.

he shall exalt himself, &c. This is quoted in 2 Thess. 2. 3, 4; and referred to in 7. 25; 8. 11, 25. Rev. 13. 5, 6.

GOD. Heb. El. Ap. 4. IV.

against, &c. Cp. 8. 11, 24, 25.

gods. Heb. *'ēlim*.

the indignation, &c. Jehovah's indignation. Cp. 8. 19; 9. 16; and Isa. 10. 23, 25.

determined=decreed.

37 the desire of women. In view of the context this must refer to any gods desired by women: such as *Baaltis*, *Astarte*, or *Mylitta* of the Babylonians; the Persian *Artemis*, or the *Nanæa* of the Syrians; or the "queen of heaven" of Jer. 7. 18; 44. 17, &c.

GOD. Heb. Eloah. Ap. 4. V.

38 in his estate=in its place: i. e. the God of forces on its pedestal.

God of forces. Heb. *Mā'uzzīm*=God of fortresses.

shall he honour, &c. Thus, in secret he is superstitious, though in public he exalts himself above all gods. **39 do**=deal. **the most strong holds**=the strongest fortresses. **whom he shall acknowledge**=whosoever acknowledgeth him. **and increase**=he will increase. **gain**=a price. **40 at the time of the end**: i. e. near the close of the last seven years. **he**: i. e. this "wilful king". **the countries**=the countries [adjoining]. **41 the glorious land.** Cp. *vv.* 16, 45; and 8. 9. **children**=sons.

K (p. 1204) 424 44 But tidings out of the east and out of the north shall trouble him: therefore he shall go forth with great fury to destroy, and utterly to °make away many.

45 And he shall °plant the °tabernacles of his palace between the seas in the glorious holy mountain; yet he shall °come to his end, °and none shall help him.

F (p. 1203) **12** And °at that time shall °Michael stand up, the great prince which standeth for the °children of °thy People: and there shall be °a time of °trouble, such as never was since there was a nation *even* to that same time: and at that time °thy People °shall be delivered, every one that shall be found °written in the book.

2 And many °of them that °sleep in the dust of the °earth °shall awake, °some to °everlasting life, and °some to shame *and* everlasting °contempt.

3 And °**they that be wise shall shine as the brightness of the firmament**; and they that turn many to righteousness as the stars for ever and ever.

A³ L N (p. 1205) 4 But thou, O Daniel, °shut up the words, and seal the book, °*even* to the time of the end: many shall °run to and fro, and °knowledge shall be increased.'

O 5 Then I Daniel looked, and, °behold, there stood other two, the one on this side of the bank of °the river, and the other on that side of the bank of °the river.

6 And *one* said to the °man clothed in linen, which *was* °upon the waters of the river, °'How long *shall it be to* the end of these wonders?'

M a 7 And I heard the [6]man clothed in linen, which *was* [6]upon the waters of [5]the river, when he °held up his right hand and his left hand unto heaven, and sware by Him That liveth for ever

b that *it shall be* for °a time, times, and an half;

c and when °he shall have accomplished to scatter the power of the holy people, all these *things* shall be finished.

L O 8 And I heard, but I understood not: then said I, 'O °MY Lord, °what *shall be* °the end of these °*things?*'

N 9 And he said, 'Go thy way, Daniel: for the words *are* closed up and sealed till the time of the end.

---

11. 44 make away many = devote many [to extermination]. Rev. 13. 7.

45 plant = spread out.

tabernacles, &c. = palatial tent.

come to his end. This could not be said of Antiochus, for he died at Tabæ, in Persia. "The wilful king" comes to his end in Judea, between Jerusalem and the Mediterranean Sea.

and none shall help him. For he is smitten by God Himself. See Isa. 11. 4. Zech. chs. 12 and 14. 2 Thess. 2. 8. Rev. 19. 20. The grave does not receive him (for Isa. 14. 19 is only a comparison "like"), and he is not joined with them in burial. He is cast into the lake of fire.

12 This is not the epilogue to the book. Verses 1-3 are the conclusion of the prophecy given by the hierophant, which commenced at 10. 20.

1 at that time. This fixes the end of the Tribulation. Note the three subjects thus connected with "the time of the end".

Michael. See note on 10. 13.

children = sons.

thy People: i.e. Daniel's People, Israel.

a time of trouble: i.e. the great Tribulation. Cp. 8. 24, 25; 9. 26. Isa. 26. 20, 21. Jer. 30. 7. Matt. 24. 21. Mark 13. 19. Rev. 16. 17-21.

trouble = tribulation.

shall be delivered. Cp. Isa. 11. 11, &c.; 27. 12, 13. Jer. 30. 7. Ezek. 37. 21-28; 39. 25-29. Hos. 3. 4, 5. Joel 3. 16-21. Amos 9. 11-15. Obad. 17-21. Zech. 12. 3-10. Rom. 11. 5, 6, 15, 26.

written in the book. Ref. to Pent. (Ex. 32. 32, 33). Ap. 92. Cp. Pss. 56. 8; 69. 28. Isa. 4. 3. Ezek. 13. 9. Luke 10. 20. Rev. 3. 5; 13. 8; 20. 12, 15.

2 of them = from among them.

sleep, &c. An inspired revelation as to death.

earth = ground.

shall awake. This is bodily resurrection.

some = these (the former).

everlasting life. John 5. 28, 29. Acts 24. 15.

some = those. The latter: i.e. the rest of the dead (Isa. 26. 19, 21; 27. 6. Rev. 20. 5, 6). Cp. 1 Cor. 15. 23. 1 Thess. 4. 16.

contempt = thrusting away.

3 they that be wise = they that make wise. The *Maskīlīm* of *v.* 10; 11. 33, 35.

12. 4-13 (A³, p. 1201). MEANWHILE. AS TO DANIEL HIMSELF. (*Alternations and Introversion.*)

A³ | L | N | 4. The book closed and sealed.
　　　O | 5, 6. Inquiry of the two. "How long?"
　　　　M | a | 7-. The answer.
　　　　　　b | -7-. The times. Three and a half years.
　　　　　　c | -7. The end.
　L | *O* | 8. Inquiry of Daniel. "What?"
　　　N | 9. The book closed and sealed.
　　　　M | *a* | 10. The answer.
　　　　　　b | 11, 12. The times.
　　　　　　c | 13. The end. The 1,290 and 1,335 days (Ap. 90).

4 shut = close up.

even to = until.

run to and fro: or, apostatize. The Heb. *shūt* = to *rove, turn about, despise*. Hence, *to do despite* (Ezek. 16. 57; 28. 24, 26). But if we spell *sūt* with שׂ (=S), instead of with שׁ (=Sh), the meaning is *to swerve, turn aside, apostatize*, "those who turn aside", or revolters (Ps. 101. 3. Hos. 5. 2); as in Ps. 40. 4 (5), "such as turn aside to lies". So the Oxford *Gesenius*, p. 962 (these are the only occurrence of *sūt*, unless Dan. 12. 4 be another). The dots over the letter ש, making it שׂ (Sin = S) and שׁ (Shin = Sh), formed no part of the inspired primitive text, but were added by the Massoretic scribes, and with the vowel points were gradually introduced into the Heb. text. The Sept., Swete's edition, vol. iii, p. 572 (A) reads *heōs an apomanōsin* = "till many shall have gone raving mad".

knowledge: or, calamities, or wickedness. Ginsburg would read *hārā'oth* for *haddā'ath*. The Sept. (A) reads *adikias*, "wickedness" (Swete's edition, vol. iii, p. 572). The Vatican (B), Theodotion's translation, reads "knowledge" (*gnōsis*): Ginsburg's hypothesis for this reading arises from the two letters ר (= R) for ד (= D), being not infrequently mistaken.

5 behold. Fig. *Asterismos*. Ap. 6.

the river. See note on 10. 4.

6 man. Heb. *'īsh*. Ap. 14. II.

upon = above.

How long . . . ? Note the two questions ("O" and "*O*" in the Structure above).

7 held up his right hand, &c. Ref. to Pent. (Deut. 32. 40). Ap. 92.

a time, times, and an half. See Ap. 90 and 91.

he: i.e. the "little horn" or Antichrist.

8 MY Lord. Heb. *Adonī*. See Ap. 4. VIII (1).

what . . . ? Note the correspondence of these two questions in *vv.* 6 and 8.

the end of these things? (i.e. the "wonders" of *v.* 6). The prophecy from 10. 14 is given in view of these questions.

M a (p. 1205) 10 Many shall be purified, and made white, and °tried; but the °wicked shall do °wickedly: and none of the °wicked shall °understand; but [s]the wise shall understand.

b 11 And from the time *that* °the daily *sacrifice* shall be taken away, and **the °abomination that maketh desolate set up**, *there shall be* °a thousand two hundred and ninety days.

12 °Blessed *is* he that °waiteth, and cometh to °the thousand three hundred and five and thirty days.

c 13 But go thou thy way till °the end *be:* for thou shalt °rest, and °stand in °thy lot at [s]the end of the days.'"

10 tried=refined.
wicked . . . wickedly . . . wicked=lawless . . . lawlessness . . . lawless. Heb. *rāshā'*. Ap. 44. x.
understand. The *Maskīlīm* of *v.* 3.
11 the daily sacrifice . . . taken away. See note on 8. 11; and Ap. 89.
abomination, &c. See note on 8. 12; and Ap. 89.
a thousand two hundred and ninety days. See Ap. 90.
12 Blessed=O the blisses! See Ps. 1. 1. The only Beatitude in this book.
waiteth=is steadfast. Cp. Matt. 24. 13. Mark 13. 13. Rev. 2. 26.
the thousand three hundred and five and thirty days. See Ap. 90. The Heb. accent suggests the rendering: "Blessed is he that expecteth and shall reach [the goal: he shall reach] to day, 1335."
13 the end. This is the sole object of the hierophant's words from 10. 14 onward. **rest**: in death. **stand**: i.e. in resurrection. **thy lot.** The 1611 edition of the A.V. reads "the lot".

THE MINOR* PROPHETS.†

THE STRUCTURE OF THE TWELVE BOOKS‡ AS A WHOLE.§

(*Division.*)

A[1] | THREE Prophets: HOSEA, JOEL, AMOS. The first and third dated, as being in the reigns of Kings of Judah, and in that of a King of ISRAEL also.

A[2] | SIX Prophets: OBADIAH, JONAH, MICAH, NAHUM, HABAKKUK, ZEPHANIAH. The third and sixth being dated, as in the reigns of Kings of JUDAH only.

A[3] | THREE Prophets: HAGGAI, ZECHARIAH, MALACHI. The first and second being dated, as in the reigns of Kings of Medo-Persia only; after the Captivity.

THREE PROPHETS.‖ (*Introversion.*)

A[1] | B[1] | HOSEA. Like AMOS (B[2]), dated in the reigns of Kings of Judah, and in that of Jeroboam II, the King of Israel. HOSEA probably belonged (like Amos) to the Ten Tribes (perhaps to Reuben); and prophesied both to the house of Israel, and to the house of Judah apart.

C[1] | JOEL. Undated. General: concerning (1) the Gentile kingdoms, and (2) "the Day of the Lord."

B[2] | AMOS. Like HOSEA (B[1]), dated in the reigns of one King of Judah, and in that of Jeroboam II, one King of Israel. AMOS probably belonged (like Hosea) to the Ten Tribes (perhaps to Asher); and prophesied to the house of Israel and to the house of Judah apart.

SIX PROPHETS.‖ (*Alternation and Introversion.*)

A[2] | D[1] | F[1] | OBADIAH. Like HABAKKUK (F[2]), is undated; and his prophecy is special, concerning EDOM.

G[1] | JONAH. Like NAHUM (G[2]), is undated; and his prophecy is special, concerning NINEVEH. Gentile repentance.

E[1] | MICAH. Like ZEPHANIAH (E[2]), is dated in the reigns of Kings of Judah only; and his prophecy is special, concerning JUDAH.

D[2] | G[2] | NAHUM. Like JONAH (G[1]), is undated; and his prophecy is special, concerning NINEVEH. Gentile destruction.

F[2] | HABAKKUK. Like OBADIAH (F[1]), is undated; and his prophecy is special, concerning the posterity of Nebuchadnezzar.

E[2] | ZEPHANIAH. Like MICAH (E[1]), is dated in the reigns of Kings of Judah only; and his prophecy is special, concerning JUDAH.

THREE PROPHETS.‖ (*Division.*)

A[3] | H[1] | J[1] | HAGGAI. Dated } in the reigns of Medo-Persian Kings. After the Captivity. Special, concerning the Second Temple.
J[2] | ZECHARIAH. Dated }

H[2] | MALACHI. Undated. General. After the Captivity, and after the days of the Second Temple.

NOTES ON THE STRUCTURE OF THE MINOR PROPHETS (Page 1206).

* Called "Minor", not because they are less inspired, or of less importance, but only because the prophecies are *shorter*.

† The Prophets of the Old Testament are divided in the Hebrew Bible into two groups:

I. The "Former" Prophets (Joshua to 2 Kings. Zech. 1. 4; 7. 7, 12). See note on p. 289, and Ap. 1. II; and therefore by inference,

II. The "Latter" Prophets (Isaiah to Malachi) in unbroken sequence (Daniel being by man's arrangement and nomenclature in the *Hagiographa*). See Ap. 1. III.

‡ In all Hebrew manuscripts, and printed Hebrew Bibles, the Twelve Minor (or Shorter) Prophets are written, and printed *in unbroken sequence*; and have always been counted, and have come down to us, as one book.

Just as each Tribe was a separate entity in Israel, and yet all the twelve together formed one Nation, so these Twelve Prophets are combined together to form one book.

As the former (the twelve Tribes) are called "*dōdekaphūlon*" = twelve tribes (from *dōdeka* = twelve, and ***phūlē*** = tribe), Luke 22. 30; Acts 26. 7; and James 1. 1; so the latter (the twelve prophets) are called "***dōdeka prophētōn***" (Ecclesiasticus 49. 10). In his praise of "famous men", the writer (Jesus, the son of Sirach) says: "and of the twelve prophets (*tōn dōdeka prophētōn*) let their memorial be blessed, and let their bones flourish again from out of their place; for they comforted Jacob (i e. the twelve-tribed Nation) and delivered them by assured hope."

The Hebrew text of this twelve-volumed book is divided into twenty-one *Sedarim* (or sections for public reading), and these read on without regard to the beginnings or endings of the separate books, thus showing that the twelve books are to be treated as one book. The twenty-one *Sedarim* are as follows:—

1. Hos. 1. 1 — 5. 15.	8. Amos 7. 15—Obad. 20.	15. Zeph. 3. 20—Hag. 2. 22.
2. ,, 6. 1 —10. 11.	9. Obad. 21—Jonah 4. 11.	16. Hag. 2. 23—Zech. 4. 1.
3. ,, 10. 12—14. 6.	10. Mic. 1. 1—4. 4.	17. Zech. 4. 2 — 6. 13.
4. ,, 14. 7 —Joel 2. 26.	11. ,, 4. 5—7. 19.	18. ,, 6. 14— 8. 22.
5. Joel 2. 27—Amos 2. 9.	12. ,, 7. 20—Nah. 3. 19.	19. ,, 8. 23—11. 17.
6. Amos 2. 10—5. 13.	13. Hab. 1. 1—3. 19.	20. ,, 12. 1 —14. 20.
7. ,, 5. 14—7. 14.	14. Zeph. 1. 1—3. 19.	21. ,, 14. 21—Mal. 4. 6.

From the above twenty-one *Sedarim* it will be noticed that only *four* books begin with a *Seder* (Hosea, Micah, Habakkuk, and Zephaniah); while *seven* others overlap, and include portions of two books (as in the case of Nos. 5, 8, 9, 12, 15, 16, and 21). See notes on pp. 366 and 616.

§ In seeking for the Structure of their Canonical order as a whole, it will be noted that six are *dated* (Hosea, Amos, Micah, Zephaniah, Haggai, and Zechariah), and the other six are *not dated* (Joel, Obadiah, Jonah, Nahum, Habakkuk, Malachi). These twelve are again divided into two groups: *nine* before the Captivity and *three* after it. Of the dated prophecies, two contain the names of a King of Israel; two contain Kings of Judah only; and two contain Kings of Medo-Persia only.

|| Thus, *three* groups are formed, consisting of (1) *three* books ($\mathfrak{A}^1$); *six* books ($\mathfrak{A}^2$); and *three* books ($\mathfrak{A}^3$).

As thus set out on p. 1206, further correspondences will be noted as to the special and general scope of the several prophecies, as indicated by the respective index-letters.

HOSEA.

THE STRUCTURE OF THE BOOK AS A WHOLE.

(*Introversion.*)

B[1] | A | 1. 1. INTRODUCTION.
| B | 1. 2—3. 5. SYMBOLICAL.
| *B* | 4. 1—14. 8. LITERAL.
| *A* | 14. 9. CONCLUSION

For the CANONICAL order and place of the Prophets, see Ap. 1, and pp. 1206 and 1207.
For the CHRONOLOGICAL order of the Prophets, see Ap. 77.
For the Inter-relation of the Prophetic Books, see Ap. 78.
For the *Formulæ* of Prophetic utterance, see Ap. 82.
For the Inter-relation of the Minor (or Shorter) Prophets, see pp. 1206 and 1207.
For References to the Pentateuch by the Prophets, see Ap. 92.

HOSEA was a prophet to the Ten Tribes (or Northern Kingdom), but he had warnings for Judah also, as well as promises of future blessings.

His prophecy is dated as being in the reigns of Uzziah, Jotham, Ahaz, and Hezekiah, Kings of Judah, and in the days of Jeroboam the son of Joash, King of Israel (1. 1).

The period covered must have been about seventy-two years: for JEROBOAM II ended in 687 B.C., in the fourteenth of UZZIAH; UZZIAH died in 649 B.C., a period of thirty-eight years. If we assume that HOSEA prophesied during the last two or three years of JEROBOAM, we have, then, say two years; UZZIAH, thirty-eight years; JOTHAM, sixteen years (647-631 = 16); Ahaz, sixteen years (632-616 = 16), a period of seventy-two years to the commencement of HEZEKIAH (689-617 B.C. = 72). See Ap. 50, pp. 59, 68; and notes on 2 Kings 15. 6, and 17. 13.

The book of HOSEA points to the events immediately preceding the fall of Samaria (the capital of the Ten Tribes), which took place in the *sixth* year of HEZEKIAH; and the last statement, in 13. 16, is a terrible prophecy of Samaria's end. This took place in 611 B.C., and HOSEA's latest date would therefore be 613 B.C., if 13. 16 were, say, two years before Samaria's fall in 611 B.C.

This gives us, for the whole period covered by Hosea's prophecy, some seventy-six or seventy-eight years (from 689-611 B.C.). See Ap. 50. VII (6), p. 68, and Ap. 77.

If Hosea were, say, twenty when he received his mission, he would be ninety-eight years of age at the destruction of the Northern Kingdom, which ended his prophesying—and probably his life too (cp. Eli, 1 Sam. 4. 15).

Hosea is quoted, in the New Testament, in Matt. 2. 15; 9. 13; 12. 7. Rom. 9. 25, 26. 1 Cor. 15. 55. 1 Pet. 2. 5, 10.

HOSEA.

A (p. 1208) 689-611 **1** THE word of °the LORD that came unto
°Hosea, the son of °Beeri, in the days of
°Uzziah, Jotham, Ahaz, *and* Hezekiah, kings
of Judah, and in the days of °Jeroboam the
son of Joash, king of Israel.

B A C a (p. 1209) 2 °The beginning of the word of [1]the LORD
°by [1]Hosea. And [1]the LORD said to [1]Hosea,
"Go, take unto thee °a wife of °whoredoms
°and °children of °whoredoms:

b °for the °land hath committed great °whoredom, °*departing* °from [1]the LORD."

c 3 So he went and took °Gomer the daughter
of °Diblaim; which conceived, and bare him
a son.

D E G^1 4 And [1]the LORD said unto him, "Call his
name °Jezreel;

H^1 for yet °a little *while*, and I °will avenge the
°blood of °Jezreel upon °the house of Jehu, and
will °cause to cease the kingdom of the house
of Israel.
5 And it shall come to pass °at that day, that
I will break the °bow of Israel in the valley of
[4]Jezreel."

G^2 6 And she conceived again, and bare a daughter. And °*God* said unto him, "Call her name
°Lo-ruhamah:

1. 1 the LORD. Heb. Jehovah. Ap. 4. II.
Hosea. Heb. *Hōshēʻaʻ* = Salvation.
Beeri. Jewish tradition identifies *Beʼērī* with *Beʼērah*, of Reuben (1 Chron. 5. 6). Christian tradition makes Hosea of Issachar. Both names are symbolical, like the other names in this book. This clause not "evidently inserted by a later hand", as alleged.
Uzziah. See note on p. 1208.
Jeroboam: i.e. Jeroboam II, the last king but one of the house of Jehu. See note on 2 Kings 10 30; 14. 23-29. This carries us back to the first fourteen years of Uzziah's long reign. See notes on p. 1208, for the significance of Jeroboam's name here.

1. 2—3. 5 (B, p. 1208). SYMBOLICAL.
(*Introversion and Alternations.*)

B | A | C | a | 1. 2-. Symbol. The First Wife. "Go, take."
b | 1. -2. Signification. The Land departs from Jehovah.
c | 1. 3. The Prophet takes Gomer.
D | E | 1. 4-9. The Former State.
F | 1. 10, 11. The Latter State.
B | 2. 1-4. Samaria. Remonstrance.
B | 2. 5-23. Samaria. Reasons.
A | *C* | *a* | 3. 1-. Symbol. The Second Wife. "Go yet, love", &c.
b | 3. -1. Signification. Israel looks to other gods.
c | 3. 2, 3. The Prophet takes a Woman.
D | *E* | 3. 4. The Present State.
F | 3. 5. The Future State.

2 The beginning, &c. This may be understood not merely of Hosea's prophecies, but as referring to the fact that Hosea was the first (canonically) of fifteen prophets included in the Hebrew canon. See Ap. 77. **by** = in, as in Num 12. 6, 8. Hab. 2. 1. Zech. 1. 9: i.e. through. **a wife of whoredoms:** i.e. a woman of the northern kingdom, and therefore regarded as an idolatress. **whoredoms** = idolatries. The one term is used for the other by Fig. *Metonymy* (of the Subject), Ap. 6, because both were characterised by unfaithfulness; the former to a husband, and the latter to Jehovah, Who sustained that relation to Israel (Jer. 31. 32). Cp. 2 Kings 9. 22. 2 Chron. 21. 13. Jer. 3. 2. Ezek. 16. 17-35; 20. 30; 23. 3, 7, 43. Nah. 3. 4. See 4. 2, 12; 5. 3, 4; 6. 10; 7. 4, &c. **and** = and [beget]. **children** = offspring. Heb. *yālad*. The mother is symbolical of the kingdom, and the offspring of the people. **for the land, &c.** Note this reason ("E", above): which explains what is meant by, and gives the interpretation of, "whoredoms". Ref. to Pent. (Ex. 34. 16. Lev. 17. 7; 20. 5. Num. 15. 39. Deut. 31. 16). Ap. 92. **land.** Heb. *'ereẓ* = earth. Put by Fig. *Synecdoche* (of the Whole), Ap. 6, for the land of Israel. Rendered "land" in 4. 1. Cp. Joel 1. 2, &c. **departing, &c.** Cp. 4. 10; 7. 8; 8. 11, 14; 10. 1; 12. 14; 13. 9. **from** = from after.

1. 4-9 (E, above). THE FORMER STATE. (*Repeated Alternation.*)

E | G^1 | 4-. Symbol. Son's name ("Jezreel").
H^1 | -4, 5. Signification, and Reason.
G^2 | 6-. Symbol. Daughter's name (Lo-Ruhamah).
H^2 | -6, 7. Signification, and Reason.
G^3 | 8, 9-. Symbol. Son's name (Lo-Ammi).
H^3 | -9. Signification, and Reason.

3 Gomer = completion (i.e. the filling up the measure of idolatry). **Diblaim** = a double cake of figs, symbolical of sensual pleasure. **4 Jezreel.** Note the Fig. *Paronomasia* (Ap. 6) between Israel (*v.* 1) and Jezreel (Heb. *Yisrā'ēl* and *Yizr'ĕ'l*). The name is prophetic of coming judgment (see *v.* 5) and future mercy. Jezreel is a *Homonym*, having two meanings: (1) may GOD scatter (Jer. 31. 10); and (2) may GOD sow (Zech. 10. 9). These bind up the two prophetic announcements. Jezreel, the fruitful field, had been defiled with blood (2 Kings 9. 16, 25, 33; 10. 11, 14), and Israel shall be scattered, and *sown* among the nations; but, when God's counsels are ripe, Israel shall be resown in their own land (see 2. 22, 23). **a little while.** See the fulfilment in 10. 14. **will avenge** = shall have visited. **blood** = blood-guiltiness. **Jezreel.** Here, it is used of the valley where the blood was shed. **the house of Jehu.** Jehu had carried out the judgment of God on the house of Ahab, because it accorded with his own will; but he was guilty of murder, because it was not executed purely according to the will of God. He would have disobeyed if it had not served his own interest. This is seen from the fact that he practised Jeroboam's idolatries, for which Ahab had been judged. **cause to cease, &c.** This was fulfilled in 611 B.C. (Ap. 50. V, p. 59). See 2 Kings 18. 11. **5 at that day:** i.e. the day of 2 Kings 18. 11. **bow.** Put by Fig. *Metonymy* (of the Adjunct), Ap. 6, for the armies of Israel. **6 God.** Supply "Jehovah" from the preceding verses. **Lo-ruhamah** = not compassionated. Rendered "not beloved" in Rom. 9. 25, and "not having obtained mercy" in 1 Pet. 2. 10. These latter are the Holy Spirit's Divine interpretation of His own prophecy.

H^2 for I will no more have mercy upon the house
(p. 1209) of Israel; but I will utterly °take °them away.
689-611 7 But I will have mercy upon the house of
°Judah, and will save them °by [1]the LORD
their [6]God, and will not save them by bow,
nor by sword, nor by battle, by horses, nor by
horsemen."

G^3 8 Now when she had weaned [6]Lo-ruhamah,
she conceived, and bare a son.
9 Then said [6]*God*, "Call his name °Lo-ammi:
H^3 for ye *are* not My People, and °I will not be
°your *God*.

F J^1 10 Yet °the number of the °children of Israel
(p. 1210) shall be °as the sand of the sea, which °cannot
be measured nor numbered; **and °it shall
come to pass, *that* in the place where it was
said unto them, °'Ye *are* not My People,'
there it shall be said unto them, '*Ye are* the
sons of °the living °GOD.'**

J^2 11 Then shall the [10]children of Judah and the
[10]children of Israel °be gathered together, and
appoint themselves °one head, and they shall
come up out of °the land: for great *shall be*
the day of °Jezreel.

B **2** Say ye unto your brethren, °Ammi; and
to your sisters, °Ruhamah.
2 Plead with °your mother, plead: for she *is*
not My wife, neither *am* °I her husband: let
her therefore put away her °whoredoms out of
her sight, and her °adulteries from °between
her breasts;
3 °Lest I strip °her naked, and set her as °in
the day that she was born, and make her as
a wilderness, and set her like a dry land, and
slay her with thirst.
4 And I will not have mercy upon her °children; for they *be* the °children of [2]whoredoms.

B d 5 For their [2]mother hath °played the harlot:
she that conceived them hath done shamefully: for she said, 'I will go after °my lovers,
that give *me* °my bread and my water, my
wool and my flax, mine oil and my drink.'

e 6 Therefore, °behold, I will °hedge up °thy
way with thorns, and °make a wall, that she
shall not find her paths.
7 And she shall °follow after her lovers, but
she shall not overtake them; and she shall
seek them, but shall not find *them*:

f then shall she say, °'I will go and return to
my °first husband; for then *was it* better with
me °than now.'

take them away. Supply the *Ellipsis*, "take away [the kingdom which belongs] to them".

them. Heb. *lāhem* = to them.

7 Judah. Verse 7 is not an "interpolation", but is a definite and distinctive contrast with the prophecy concerning Israel.

by the LORD their God = by (Jehovah their Elohim: i.e. the Messiah, or the angel of Jehovah. See 2 Kings 19. 35. But it looks forward to the future fulfilment, which will exhaust the prophecy in the destruction of Antichrist (Isa. 11. 4. 2 Thess. 2. 8, &c.).

9 Lo-ammi = Not My people.

I will not be your God = I am not "I am" to you.

your = to you. Heb. *lākem.*

1. 10, 11 (F, p. 1209). THE LATTER STATE. (*Division.*)

F | J^1 | 10. Israel.
  | J^2 | 11. Judah.

10 In the Hebrew text, ch. 2 commences here.

the number, &c. Ref. to Pent. (Gen. 22. 17; 32. 12).

children = sons. Not fulfilled in any other People, now, but will yet be, in the future, of Israel.

as the sand, &c. Fig. *Parœmia.* Ap. 6. See note on Gen. 13. 16.

cannot be measured, &c. Ref. to Pent. (Num. 23. 10).

it shall come to pass, &c. Verse 10 is not "in glaring contradiction" to *v.* 9, but it marks the contrast between the latter (and yet future state), and the past. See the Structure "D" and "*D*", p. 1209.

Ye are not My People = No People of Mine are ye. Heb. *Lo-'ammī 'attem.* Quoted in Rom. 9. 25, not of the Gentiles, but as an illustration of what may be true in their case as it will be in Israel's. In 1 Pet. 2. 10 the address is to the *Diaspora*: i.e. the "scattered strangers" of Israel, who are now afar off". Cp. Dan. 9. 7. Acts 2. 32.

the living GOD. Always used in contrast with false gods, which have no life. Cp. 1 Thess. 1. 9, &c.

GOD. Heb. El. Ap. 4. IV.

11 be gathered together = be gathered out. See Isa. 11. 12, 13. Jer. 3. 18. Ezek. 37. 16-24.

one head. Zerubbabel was only a typical anticipation, for under him only Judah returned. This refers to a future reunion (Jer. 23. 5, 6. Ezek. 34. 23).

one. Heb. *'echad.* See note on Deut. 6. 4.

the land. Supply the *Ellipsis*: "the land [of their dispersion].

Jezreel. Here used in the sense: "GOD will sow". See note on *v.* 4; and cp. 2. 23. Referring to the day of Israel's restoration as being "life from the dead" (Rom. 11. 15). Cp. Jer. 24. 6; 31. 28; 32. 41. Amos 9. 15.

2. 1 Ammi = My People.

Ruhamah = Pitied One.

2 your mother. Gomer (1. 3). The ten tribes personified by their royal capital.

her husband. Cp. Jer. 31. 32.

whoredoms . . . adulteries = idolatries. See note on 1. 2.

between her breasts = her embraces.

3 Lest, &c. Verse 3 refers to Israel's earliest history.

her: i.e. her land, as shown by the words following. Cp. Ezek. 16. 23-43. **in the day.** See Ap. 18.

4 children = sons: i.e. the individual members of the nation collectively.

2. 5-23 (*B*, p. 1209). REASONS. (*Extended Alternation.*)

B | d | 5. Her False Benefactors.
  | e | 6, 7-. Her Punishments.
  | f | -7. Her Return.
  | *d* | 8. Her True Benefactor.
  | *e* | 9-13. Punishments.
  | *f* | 14-23. Her Reception.

5 played the harlot: i.e. practised idolatries. The silence as to details here is eloquent. **my lovers** = my Baals, or lords. Cp. Jer. 44. 17, 18. **my, &c.** Note the three pairs, including food, clothing, and luxuries. All are claimed as hers. **6 behold.** Fig. *Asterismos* (Ap. 6) for emphasis. **hedge up, &c.** Cp. Job 3. 23; 19. 8. Lam. 3. 7, 9. **thy way.** Jehovah had spoken *of* Israel. Now He speaks *to* her. **make a wall** = Heb. wall a (stone) wall. Fig. *Polyptōton* (Ap. 6) for emphasis = rear a stone wall. **7 follow after** = eagerly follow after. **I will go, &c.** Cp. 5. 15. Luke 15. 18. **first husband.** Cp. Ezek. 16. 8. **than.** Supply the *Ellipsis*: "than [it is] now".

d (p. 1210) 689-611 8 For she °did not know °that I gave her corn, and °wine, and oil, and multiplied her silver and gold, °*which* they prepared for Baal.

e 9 Therefore °will I return, and °take away My corn in the time thereof, and °My [8]wine in the season thereof, and will °recover My wool and My flax *given* to cover her nakedness.

10 And now °will I discover her lewdness in the sight of her lovers, and none shall deliver her out of Mine hand.

11 I will also cause all her mirth to cease, °her feast days, her new moons, and her sabbaths, and all her solemn feasts.

12 And I will °destroy her vines and her fig trees, °whereof she hath said, 'These *are* my °rewards that my lovers have given me:' and I will make them a forest, and the beasts of the field shall eat them.

13 And °I will visit upon her °the days of °Baalim, wherein she burned incense to them, and she °decked herself with her earrings and her jewels, and she went after her lovers, and forgat Me, °saith °the LORD.

f 14 °Therefore, [6]behold, °I will allure her, and °bring her into the wilderness, and speak °comfortably unto her.

15 And I will give her her vineyards °from thence, and °the valley of °Achor for a °door of °hope: and she °shall sing °there, °as in the days of her youth, and as [3]in the day °when she came up out of the land of Egypt.

16 And it shall be at that day, [13]saith [13]the LORD, *that* thou shalt call Me Ishi; and shalt call Me no more °Baali.

17 For °I will take away the names of Baalim out of her mouth, and they shall no more be remembered by their name.

18 And °in that day will I °make a covenant for them with the beasts of the field, °and with the fowls of heaven, and *with* the creeping things of the ground: °and I will break the bow and the sword and the battle out of the earth, and will °make them to lie down safely.

19 And °I will betroth thee unto Me for ever; yea, °I will betroth thee unto Me in righteousness, and in judgment, and in lovingkindness, and in mercies.

20 [19]I will even betroth thee unto Me in faithfulness: and °thou shalt know °the LORD.

21 And it shall come to pass [18]in that day, °I will °hear, [13]saith the LORD, I will °hear the heavens, and °they shall hear the earth;

22 And °the earth shall [21]hear the corn, and the [8]wine, and the oil; and they shall [21]hear °Jezreel.

23 And °I will sow her unto Me in the earth; and I °will have mercy upon her that had not obtained mercy; and **I will say to *them which were* °not My People, °'Thou art My People;'** and they shall say, '*Thou art* my °God.'"

8 did not know. Cp. Isa. 1. 3.
that I = that [it was] I Who. Cp. Ezek. 16. 17-19.
wine = new wine. Heb. *tīrōsh*. Ap. 27. II.
which they, &c. = they made offerings to Baal. Cp. 8. 4.
9 will I return. In judgment.
take away = take back. Cp. *v.* 3.
My wine, &c. They were all His, and from Him.
recover = rescue (Gen. 31. 16).
10 will I discover. Cp. Ezek. 16. 37; 23. 29.
11 her feast days. All these are in the sing. here = her feast, her new moon, her sabbath, her every appointed season.
12 destroy = lay waste. Cp. Ps. 105. 33.
whereof. In *v.* 5.
rewards = my hire, or fee. A technical term. Ref. to Pent. (Deut. 23. 18). Ap. 92.
13 I will visit, &c. Ref. to Pent. (Ex. 32. 34). Ap. 92.
the days: i.e. the feast days.
Baalim. (Pl.) including Baal-gad, Baal-Hermon, Baal-zephon, Baal-berith, &c.
decked herself. Cp. Ezek. 23. 40, 42.
saith the LORD = [is] Jehovah's oracle.
the LORD. Heb. Jehovah. Ap. 4. II.
14 Therefore = Nevertheless. Note that the whole of this present dispensation comes between *vv.* 13 and 14. See Ap. 72. **I** = I myself (emphatic).
bring her, &c. Cp. Ezek. 20. 35.
comfortably = to the heart. Cp. Isa. 40. 2.
15 from thence: i. e. [when she cometh] from thence. Ref. to Pent. (Num. 16. 13, 14). Ap. 92.
the valley of Achor. Ref. to Josh. 7. 26. Ap. 92. The events must have been written down at the time and preserved. See Ap. 47.
Achor = trouble. Cp. Josh. 7. 24-26.
door = entrance.
hope = expectation; no longer of trouble.
shall sing there. Ref. to Pent. (Ex. 15. 1). Ap. 92.
there. Where Jehovah allureth, and bringeth, and speaketh.
as in the days, &c. Cp. Jer. 2. 2. Ezek. 16. 8, 22, 60.
when she came up. Ref. to Pent. (Ex. 1. 10; 12. 38; 13. 18, &c.); and when Jehovah said "My son" (Ex. 4. 22). Ap. 92.
16 Ishi = My husband.
Baali = My lord.
17 I will take away, &c. Ref. to Pent. (Ex. 23. 13) Ap. 92. Cp Josh. 23. 7. Ps. 16. 4. Isa. 2. 18. Ezek. 6. 6; 36. 25, 26; 37. 23. Zech. 13. 2.
18 in that day. That yet future day of Israel's restoration.
make a covenant, &c. Cp. Job 5. 23. Isa. 11. 6-9. Ezek. 34. 25.
and. Note the Fig. *Polysyndeton* (Ap. 6) to emphasise each item.
and I will break. Cp. Ps. 46. 9. Isa. 2. 4. Ezek. 39. 9, 10. Zech. 9. 10.
make them to lie down safely. Ref. to Pent. (Lev. 25. 18, 19; 26. 5, 6. Deut. 12. 10; 33. 12, 28). Ap. 92.
19 I will betroth, &c. Ref. to Pent. (Ex. 22. 16. Deut. 20. 7; 22. 23, 25, 27, 28; 28. 30). Ap. 92. Elsewhere only in 2 Sam. 3. 14 ("espouse"). Notice the thrice-repeated word here, and in *vv.* 19, 20.
20 thou shalt know, &c. Ref. to Pent. (Ex. 6. 7, &c.). This is the sign of Israel's blessing (Isa. 11. 9; 54. 13. Jer. 31. 33, 34. John 6. 45). Their evils came from not knowing (Isa. 1. 3. Luke 19. 42, 44).
the LORD. Heb. Jehovah (with *'eth*) = Jehovah Himself. Ap. 4. II.
21 I will hear. The restoration comes from, and begins with, Jehovah.
hear = answer, or respond to (Zech. 8. 12).
they shall hear. Fig. *Prosopopœia*. Ap. 6. **22 the earth.** Note the Fig. *Anadiplosis* (Ap. 6), by which the word at the end of *v.* 21 is repeated at the beginning of *v.* 22. **Jezreel** = the seed of GOD [which He will sow], as stated in *v.* 23. **23 I will sow her:** i. e. the new Israel. **will have mercy, &c.** = have pity; i.e. will [call her] *Ruhamah*. **her that had not obtained mercy** = Lo-Ruhamah (Not pitied). **not My People** = Lo-ammi. **Thou art My People** = Ammi [art] thou. **they shall say** = and he, he shall say, &c.: i. e. the whole nation as one man. Cp. 1. 11. Zech. 13. 9. Rom. 9. 26. 1 Pet. 2. 10. **God.** Heb. Elohim. Ap. 4. I.

A C a (p. 1209) **3** Then said °the LORD unto me, °"Go yet,
°love °a woman beloved of °*her* friend,
°yet an °adulteress,
b °according to the love of [1]the LORD toward
the °children of Israel, who °look to other gods,
and love °flagons of wine."

c 2 So I bought her to me for °fifteen *pieces* of
silver, and *for* an °homer of barley, and an
half homer of barley:
3 And I said unto her, "Thou shalt °abide for
me °many days; thou shalt not play the harlot,
and thou shalt not be for *another* °man: so
will I also °*be* for thee."

D E K[1] 4 For the [1]children of °Israel shall [3]abide
°many days °without a king, °and without a
°prince, and without a °sacrifice, and without
°an image, and without an °ephod, and *without*
°teraphim:

F K[2] 5 °Afterward shall the [1]children of Israel
°return, and °seek [1]the LORD their °God, and
°David their king; and °shall fear [1]the LORD
and His °goodness
K[3] °in the latter days.

B M O R j (p. 1213) **4** Hear the word of °the LORD, ye °children
of Israel:
k for °the LORD hath °a controversy with the
inhabitants of the land, because *there is* no
truth, nor °mercy, nor °knowledge of °God in
the land.
2 °By swearing, and lying, and killing, and
stealing, and committing adultery, they break
out, and °blood toucheth blood.

l 3 °Therefore shall the land mourn, and every
one that dwelleth therein shall languish, with
°the beasts of the field, and with the fowls of
heaven; yea, the fishes of the sea also shall
°be taken away.

---

3. 1 the LORD. Heb. Jehovah. Ap. 4. II.
Go yet = Go again. See notes on 1. 2.
love. Not "take", as in 1. 2, or love again.
a woman. Not "Gomer" (1. 3) again, but another; hence we must believe that Gomer had died; and that this was a second marriage with its own special signification.
her friend: i.e. Hosea himself.
yet, &c. = though [she has become] an adulteress. Referring to Israel's present condition in this Dispensation (Ap. 72).
adulteress: i.e. an idolatress; and denotes only a woman of the northern tribes.
according, &c. This is the manifestation of Divine love.
children = sons.
look to other gods. Ref. to Pent. (Deut. 31. 18, 20).
flagons of wine = cakes of grapes.
2 fifteen pieces of silver = fifteen shekels (Ap. 51. II. 5). The price of the redemption of a slave.
homer. See Ap. 51. III. 3 (9).
3 abide . . . many days. See the signification in *vv.* 4, 5. Cp. Jer. 3. 1, 2.
abide. Ref. to Pent. (Deut. 21. 13). Ap. 92. See the signification of the sign in *vv.* 4, 5, and cp. Jer. 31. 1, 2. Heb. *yāshāb* = to dwell (sequestered). Same word as in Deut. 21. 13. Not the same word as in 11. 6.
many days. In the case of the sign = a full month. The signification is seen now, in the present Dispensation.
man. Heb. *'īsh.* Ap. 14. II. **be.** Supply ["do"].

3. 4, 5 (*D*, p. 1209). **THE PRESENT AND FUTURE STATES.**

(*Alternations.* According to the Heb. text.)

D | *E* | K[1] | 4-. Time. "Many days."
  L | g | -4-. "Shall abide."
   h | -4-. "The children of Israel."
    i | -4. "Without a king", &c. (Neg.)
 } Present.
 F | K[2] | 5-. Time. "Afterward."
  L | *g* | -5-. "Shall return."
   h | -5-. "The children of Israel."
    i | -5-. "Jehovah, and David their king." (Positive.)
  K[3] | -5. Time. "In the latter days."
 } Future.

The above Structure is according to the order of the words in the Heb. text, not the A.V.

4 Israel. Not merely Judah, but the twelve tribes. Not "British" or any other "Israel". **many days.** All the days of the present Dispensation; "many" implying length of time; "days" implying their limitation. **without.** Note the Fig. *Anaphora* (Ap. 6), emphasising each point, now fulfilled before our eyes. **without a king.** Having rejected Messiah (John 19. 15). This cannot therefore be interpreted now of any People which has a king. **and.** Note the Fig. *Polysyndeton* (Ap. 6) strengthening the emphasis on each point. **prince** = ruler. Heb. *sar*, as in 8. 4. **sacrifice.** Heb. *zabach.* Ap. 43. II. xii. Includes all sacrifices where there is shedding of blood. **an image.** Heb. *mazzēbah* = any upright standing image. Cp. Ex. 23. 24; 34. 13. Isa. 19. 19. **ephod.** Put by Fig. *Metonymy* (of Adjunct), Ap. 6, for the priest or person who wears it. Ref. to Pent. (Ex. 28. 4-8). Ap. 92. This was the girdle of the breastplate which contained the "Urim and Thummim", the wearing of which pertained solely to the high priest. Cp. 1 Sam. 22. 18; 23. 9. Ezra 2 63; and Neh. 7. 65. **teraphim** = idols of any kind. In *v.* 3, Jehovah says they shall not "play the harlot": and, now, for (since 426 B.C.) 2,300 years the truth of this has been seen. Ref. to Pent. (Gen. 31. 19, 34, 35). Ap. 92. **5 Afterward, &c.** This mark of time has not yet been reached. It corresponds with the "many days" of *v.* 4. See the Structure above ("K[1]"). **return, &c.**: i.e. return [to Jehovah]. See 5. 15, and 6. 1. **seek.** Cp 5. 6. Jer. 50. 4, 5. **God.** Heb. Elohim. Ap. 4. I. **David.** Cp. Jer. 30. 9. Ezek. 34. 23, 24; 37. 22, 24. Therefore David must rise again, as Abraham, Isaac, and Jacob must; and note the fact of *Israel* seeking *David.* **shall fear** = shall rejoice in, as in Isa. 60. 6. Jer. 33. 9. Heb. *pāḥad*, a *Homonym* with another meaning (to fear, as in Deut. 28. 66. Job 23. 15. See notes there). **goodness.** Heb. *ṭūb*, as in 14. 2 ("graciously") = Gracious One: i.e. the Messiah. Ref. to Pent. (Ex. 33. 19). Ap. 92. See the notes on 8. 3; 14. 2. **in the latter days.** Rabbi Kimchi (A.D. 1160-1235) and other celebrated Jewish commentators writing on Isa. 2. 2, hold that this expression always means "in the days of the Messiah". Cp. Jer. 30. 24. Ezek. 38. 8, 16. Dan. 2. 28. Mic. 4. 1. Ref. to Pent. (Gen. 49. 1. Num. 24. 14. Deut. 4. 30; 31. 29). Ap. 92.

4. 1–14. 8 [For Structure see next page].

4. 1 the LORD. Heb. Jehovah. Ap. 4. II. **children** = sons. **a controversy** = a judicial inquiry and cause. Cp. 12. 2. Isa. 1. 18, with 3. 13, 14. Jer. 25. 31. Mic. 6. 2. **mercy** = lovingkindness, or grace. **knowledge**: or, acknowledgement. See note on 2. 20. Cp. 4. 6; 5. 4. **God.** Heb. Elohim. Ap. 4. I. **2 By swearing, &c.** These are the evils which flow from a want of the knowledge of God. Cp. *v.* 6; 2. 20. Rom. 1. 21. 1 John 2. 3, 4; 4. 7, 8. **blood toucheth blood**: or, murder follows murder; "blood" being put by Fig. *Synecdoche* (of Species), Ap. 6, for bloodshed. **3 Therefore shall the land mourn.** Cp. Jer. 4. 28, and 12. 4. Amos 5. 16, and 8. 8. **the beasts** = the very beasts (*Beth essentiæ*). **be taken away** = be gathered [into the ranks of the mourners].

R j (p. 1213) **4** Yet °let no °man strive, nor reprove
another:
k for thy People *are* as °they that strive with
689-611 the priest.
l **5** Therefore shalt thou °fall °in the day, and
the prophet also shall °fall with thee in the
night, and I will °destroy °thy mother.
P S[1] **6** My °People are [5]destroyed for °lack of
knowledge: because thou hast rejected °know-
ledge, I will also reject thee, that thou shalt
be no priest to Me: seeing °thou hast forgotten
the law of thy [1]God, I will also forget thy
[1]children.
7 As they were increased, so they °sinned
against Me: °*therefore* will I change their
glory into shame.
8 They °eat up the sin of My People, and
they °set their heart on their °iniquity.
9 And there shall be, °like people, like priest:
and I will °punish them for their ways, and
°reward them their doings.
10 For they shall [8]eat, and °not have enough:
they °shall commit °whoredom, and shall not
increase: because they have left off to take
heed to °the LORD.
11 [10]Whoredom and °wine and °new wine
take away the °heart.
S[2] **12** My People °ask counsel at their °stocks,
and their °staff declareth unto them: for the
°spirit of [10]whoredoms hath caused *them* to
err, and they have °gone a whoring °from
under their [1]God.
13 °They sacrifice upon the tops of the mountains, and burn incense upon the hills, under
oaks and poplars and elms, because the shadow
thereof *is* good: therefore your daughters shall
commit [10]whoredom, and your spouses shall
commit adultery.
14 I will not punish your °daughters when
they commit [10]whoredom, nor your spouses
when they commit adultery: for °themselves
are °separated with whores, and they sacrifice with °harlots: therefore the people *that*
doth not understand shall fall.
Q **15** Though thou, Israel, play the °harlot, *yet*
let not °Judah offend; and come not ye unto
°Gilgal, neither go ye up to °Beth-aven, °nor
swear, [1]The LORD liveth.
16 For Israel °slideth back as a backsliding

4. 1—14. 8 (*B*, p. 1208). LITERAL.
(*Alternation.*)

B | M | 4. 1—5. 15. Incriminations and Threatenings.
N | 6. 1-3. Resolve to return.
M | 6. 4—13. 8. Incriminations and Threatenings.
N | 13. 9—14. 8. Invitation to return.

4. 1—5. 15 (M, above). INCRIMINATIONS, ETC.
(*Extended Alternation.*)

M | O | 4. 1-5. Call to Israel. General.
P | 4. 6-14. Incriminations, &c.
Q | 4. 15-19. Warning as to places in Judah.
O | 5. 1, 2. Call to Israel. Particular.
P | 5. 3-7. Incriminations.
Q | 5. 8-15. Warning as to places in Judah.

4. 1-5 (O, above). CALL TO ISRAEL.
(*Extended Alternation.*)

O | R | j | 1-. Call.
k | -1, 2. Reason.
l | 3. Threatening.
R | *j* | 4-. Call.
k | -4. Reason.
l | 5. Threatening.

4 let no man. The reason being given in *v.* -4.
man. Heb. *'ish.* Ap. 14. II.
they that strive with the priest. Ref. to Pent. (Num. 16. 1, &c. Deut. 17. 12). Ap. 92.
5 fall=stumble.
in the day. Cp. Jer. 6. 4, 5 and 15. 8.
destroy=lay prostrate.
thy mother: i.e. the whole nation is referred to, as is clear from *vv.* 3, &c.; 2. 3, 9, 12.

4. 6-14 (P, above). INCRIMINATIONS AND THREATENINGS. (*Division.*)

P | S[1] | 6-11. The Priests.
S[2] | 12-14. The People.

6 People are. Not "is", because the noun though singular is collective, with plural verb.
lack of knowledge. See note on 2. 20.
knowledge=the knowledge [of Me].
thou hast forgotten. Ref. to Pent. (Deut. 32. 18).
7 sinned. Heb. *chāṭā'.* Ap. 44. i.
therefore will I change their glory into shame. The *Sōpherīm* confess (Ap. 33) that they altered thus the primitive Heb. text: which read "My glory have they changed into shame": i.e. they altered the verb *hēmiru* (they have changed) to *'āmīr* (I shall change); and, *k^{e}bōdī* (My glory) to *k^{e}bōdām* (their glory). This alteration was made from a mistaken reverence. It will be seen that the word "therefore" is not required.
8 eat up the sin=the sin-offering. Ref. to Pent. (Lev. 6. 30): i.e. those sin-offerings which should have been wholly burnt, and not eaten. See notes on Lev. 6. 26, 30. Ap. 92.

set their heart=lift up their soul: i.e. desire. Heb. *nephesh.* Ap. 13. **iniquity**=wrong-doing. Heb. *'āvāh.* Ap. 44. iv. **9 like people, &c.** Cp. Isa. 24. 2. Jer. 5. 31. **punish**=visit. Ref. to Pent. (Ex. 20. 5; 32. 34). Ap. 92. **reward**=requite. **10 not have enough.** Ref. to Pent. (Lev. 26. 26). The same words. Ap. 92. **shall commit**=have committed. **whoredom**=idolatry. See note on 1. 2. **the LORD.** Heb. Jehovah (with *'eth*)=Jehovah Himself. Ap. 4. II. **11 wine.** Heb. *yayin.* Ap. 27. I. **new wine.** Heb. *tīrōsh.* Ap. 27. II. **heart.** Put by Fig. *Metonymy* (of Adjunct), Ap. 6, for understanding. See Isa. 28. 6. Cp. Eccles. 7. 7. **12 ask counsel**=inquire of (habitually). Cp. Jer. 2. 27. Hab. 2. 19. **stocks**=idols made of wood. **staff, &c.** Referring to divination by rods. **spirit.** Heb. *rūach.* Ap. 9. Cp. 5. 4. Isa. 44. 20. **gone a whoring:** i.e. gone away into idolatry. Cp. Ezek. 23. 5. **from under**=from under [the authority] of, &c., as Gomer had left Hosea. Cp. Num. 5. 19, 29. Ezek. 27. 5. **13 They sacrifice, &c.** Cp. Isa. 1. 29, and 57. 5, 7. Ezek. 6. 13, and 20. 28. Ref. to Pent. (Deut. 12. 2). **14 daughters:** who became Temple-women. See next verse. **themselves**=[the men] themselves. **separated**=secluded. **harlots.** Heb. *k^{e}dēshāh*=the Temple-women, consecrated to the unclean "worship" of the Canaanites, by which the foulest corruption became a holy duty. Ref. to Pent. Found only here and Gen. 38. 21, 22, and Deut. 23. 17. Ap. 92. **15 harlot**=wanton. Not the same word as in *v.* 14, though the symbol is similar. **Judah.** Cp. 1. 7. **Gilgal.** Jeroboam had erected an idolatrous temple there. See 9. 15; 12. 11. Amos 4. 4; 5. 5. Cp. Judg. 3. 19. There, too, they had rejected Jehovah as king (1 Sam. 7. 16; 10. 8; 11. 14, 15). See note on 9. 15. **Beth-aven**=house of naught. Put for Beth-el (=the house of GOD), now profaned by Jeroboam (1 Kings 12. 28-33; 13. 1. Amos 3. 14). The prophecy fulfilled in Jer. 48. 13. See also 2 Kings 10. 29; 17. 6-23. Amos 7. 13. **nor swear, &c.** Cp. Amos 8. 14. Zeph. 1. 5. **16 slideth back**=hath been stubborn, restive, or intractable, refractory.

689-611 heifer: now [1]the LORD will feed them as °a lamb °in a large place.

17 Ephraim *is* °joined to idols: let him alone.

18 Their drink is °sour: they have committed [10]whoredom continually: her rulers *with* shame do love, °"Give ye."

19 The °wind hath bound her up °in her wings, and °they shall be ashamed because of their sacrifices.

O (p. 1213) **5** °Hear ye this, °O priests; and hearken, ye house of Israel; and give ye ear, O house of the king; for °judgment *is* toward you, because ye have been a snare on °Mizpah, and a net spread upon °Tabor.

2 And the °revolters °are profound to make slaughter, °though I *have been* a rebuker of them all.

P 3 I know °Ephraim, and Israel is not hid from Me: for now, O Ephraim, thou committest °whoredom, *and* Israel is defiled.

4 They will not °frame their doings to turn unto their °God: for °the spirit of [3]whoredoms *is* in the midst of them, and they have °not known °the LORD.

5 And °the pride of Israel doth testify to °his face: therefore shall Israel and Ephraim fall in their °iniquity; Judah also shall fall with them.

6 They shall °go with their flocks and with their herds to °seek °the LORD; but they shall not find *Him;* He hath °withdrawn Himself from them.

7 They have dealt treacherously against [6]the LORD: for they have begotten °strange °children: now shall °a month devour them with their portions.

Q 8 Blow ye the °cornet in °Gibeah, *and* the trumpet in °Ramah: cry aloud *at* °Beth-aven, °after thee, O Benjamin.

9 Ephraim shall be desolate in the day of rebuke: among the tribes of Israel have I made known that which shall surely be.

10 The princes of Judah were like them °that remove the °bound: *therefore* I will pour out My wrath upon them like water.

11 Ephraim *is* °oppressed *and* broken in judgment, because he °willingly °walked after °the commandment.

12 °Therefore *will* I *be* unto Ephraim as a moth, and to the house of Judah as °rottenness.

13 When Ephraim saw his sickness, and Judah *saw* his wound, then went Ephraim to the Assyrian, and sent to °king Jareb: yet

a lamb = a young ram of more than a year old.

in a large place = an uninclosed space: i e. the lands of the heathen. **17 joined** = mated, or united to.

18 sour. Heb. turned, turned back, thrust aside as having turned bad.

Give ye. By the Fig. *Metallagē* (Ap. 6) the fact of continual whoredom (or idolatrous worship) is changed to the new thought of the rulers loving to continually command, "Give ye [sacrifices]", with contempt for the sacrifices Jehovah commanded. See 8. 13. Thus, the verse is not "untranslatable", as alleged.

19 wind, &c. = the spirit of whoredoms (*v.* 12) has bound itself up. Heb. *rūach.* Ap. 9.

in her wings = in her skirts (so as to impede her gait).

they shall be ashamed. Cp. Isa. 1. 29. Jer. 2. 26. This verse is not "in confusion", as alleged.

These verses (16–19) are not "scraps", as alleged, but are closely connected with the context. They are required by the Structure "Q" and "*Q*" on p. 1213.

5. 1 Hear . . . O priests. This is a call to the priests and others, as 4. 1–5 was also a call to Israel. See the Structure, "O" and "*O*", p. 1213.

judgment is toward you = judgment is denounced upon you.

Mizpah. There were five places with this name: (1) Now *Sūf* (Gen. 31. 49. Judg. 10. 17; 11. 11, 29, 34; 20. 1, 3; 21. 1, 5, 8). (2) In Moab (1 Sam. 22. 3), not identified. (3) The land (or valley) of Moab, now *el Bukei'a* (Josh. 11. 3). (4) In Judah, not identified (Josh. 15. 38). (5) In Benjamin, not identified (Josh. 18. 26. Judg. 22. 1–3; 21. 1, 5, 8. 1 Sam. 7. 5–16; 10. 17. 1 Kings 15 22. 2 Kings 25. 23, 25. 2 Chron. 16. 6. Neh. 3. 7, 15, 19. Jer. 40. 6–15; 41. 1–16, and in this passage, Hos. 5. 1). Mizpah was a symbol of *keeping apart*, not of *meeting again*, as erroneously used to-day.

Tabor is on the west of Jordan and not connected with Ephraim; but Tabor means a mound; so that the idolatrous altar may have been called Mizpah, while Tabor was the "mound" of Gen. 31, both belonging to the same district. Hosea is said to have been buried at Mizpah. **2 revolters** = apostates.

are profound to make slaughter = have deeply designed a slaughter.

though I have been, &c. = and I [will denounce] chastisement to them all. The *Ellipsis* thus supplied explains "these difficult words".

3 Ephraim, the largest of the ten tribes, is put by Fig. *Synecdoche* (of the Part), Ap. 6, for the whole.

whoredom = idolatry. See note on 1. 2.

4 frame = fashion. **God.** Heb. Elohim. Ap. 4. I.

the spirit of whoredoms. See note on 4. 12, 19.

spirit. Heb. *rūach.* Ap. 9.

not known. See note on 2. 20.

the LORD. Heb. Jehovah (with *'eth*) = Jehovah Himself. Ap. 4. II.

5 the pride of Israel. An appellation of Jehovah = the excellency, or the glory of Israel. He in Whom Israel should have gloried; so again in 7. 10. Cp. Amos 8. 7, where it is "the Excellency of Jacob".

his: i.e. Ephraim's, or Israel's.

iniquity. Heb. *'āvāh.* Ap. 44. iv.

6 go . . seek the LORD. Ref. to Pent. (Ex. 10. 9). **seek the LORD.** Ref. to Pent. (Deut. 4. 29). Ap. 92. **the LORD.** Heb. Jehovah. Ap. 4. II. **withdrawn Himself.** Heb. *ḥalaz;* not *sūr* ("depart") in 9. 12. **7 strange** = apostates (who had become as foreigners). Heb. *zūr.* See note on Prov. 5. 3. **children** = sons. **a month.** A short time will complete their dispossession. Shallum reigned just a month (2 Kings 15. 13). **8 cornet** = horn. **Gibeah.** Now *Jeb'a,* of Benjamin (Judg. 18—20). **Ramah.** Now, *er-Ram.* Cp. Isa. 10. 29. **Beth-aven.** See note on 4. 15. **after thee,** &c. Apparently a war-cry = "[Look] behind thee, O Benjamin!" Cp. Judg. 5. 14; 20. 40. **10 that remove,** &c. Ref. to Pent. (Deut. 19. 14; 27. 17). Ap. 92. Elsewhere only in Job 24. 2. Prov. 22. 28; 23. 10. **bound** = boundary, or landmark. **11 oppressed and broken.** Ref. to Pent. (Deut. 28. 33). Ap. 92. **willingly** = wilfully. **walked after** = followed (perseveringly). **the commandment.** Note the *Ellipsis*: "the [idolatrous] commandment [of Jeroboam]" (1 Kings 12. 28. 2 Kings 10. 29–31). Cp. Mic. 6. 16. **Aram., Sept., and Syr. read** "falsehood". Vulg. reads "filthiness", reading *ẓō'*, in pl., for *ẓāv.* **12 Therefore will I be** = For I [am]. **rottenness:** or, a worm. **13 king Jareb.** Professor Sayce (*Higher Criticism and the Monuments,* pp. 416, 417) thinks "Jareb" may be the birth-name of the usurper Sargon II, the successor of Shalmaneser. Shalmaneser did not take Samaria, but his successor did, as stated in an inscription found in the palace which he built near Nineveh. This gets rid of several fanciful hypotheses as to the meaning of "Jareb", besides explaining an historical difficulty. Cp. 10. 6.

689-611 could He not heal you, nor cure you of your wound.

14 For I *will be* unto Ephraim as a lion, and as a young lion to the house of Judah: I, *even* I, will tear and go away; °I will °take away, and none shall rescue °*him*.

15 I will go *and* return to My place, °till they acknowledge their offence, and °seek My face: in their affliction they will °seek Me early.

N (p. 1213) **6** "Come, and °let us return unto °the LORD: for He hath torn, and °He will heal us; He hath smitten, and He will bind us up.

2 °After two days will He °revive us: °in the third day He will raise us up, and we shall °live °in His sight.

3 Then shall we know, *if* we follow on °to know [1]the LORD: °His going forth is °prepared as the °morning; and He shall come °unto us °as the rain, as the latter *and* °former rain unto the earth."

M T (p. 1215) 4 O Ephraim, °what shall I do unto thee? O Judah, what shall I do unto thee? °for your °goodness *is* as a morning cloud, and as the early dew it goeth away.

U W 5 °Therefore have I hewed *them* °by the prophets; I have slain them by the words of My mouth: and °thy judgments *are as* °the light *that* goeth forth.

X 6 For °**I desired** °**mercy, and** °**not sacrifice**; and °the knowledge of °God more than burnt offerings.

7 But they °like °men have °transgressed °the covenant: there have they dealt treacherously against Me.

8 °Gilead *is* a city of them that work °iniquity, *and is* °polluted with blood.

9 And as °troops of robbers wait for a °man, *so* the company of priests murder in the way °by consent: for they °commit °lewdness.

10 I have seen an horrible thing in the house of Israel: there *is* the °whoredom of Ephraim, Israel is defiled.

11 Also, O Judah, °He hath set an °harvest °for thee,

W when I °returned the captivity of My People.

14 I will. Some codices read "and I will".
take away = carry off.
him. Omit.
15 till they acknowledge their offence. Ref. to Pent. (Lev. 26. 40-42). National repentance is the condition of Israel's restoration.
seek My face. Ref. to Pent. (Deut. 4. 29). Ap. 92.
seek Me early. This expression, though not found in the Pentateuch, occurs in Job 7. 21; 8. 5; 24. 5. Pss. 63. 1; 78. 34. Prov. 1. 28; 7. 15; 8. 17; 11. 27; 13. 24. Heb. rising up before dawn to seek. Not the same word as in the preceding clause. Supply the ellipsis after "early": "[they shall say]—'Come'", &c.

6. 1 let us return. These are the words of Israel in a yet future day, as already symbolized by the return of Gomer (3. 2, 3), and foretold in 3. 5. See the Structure ("K² and K³", p. 1212, and of "M", p. 1213). This is the acknowledgment referred to in 5. 15. Deut. 32. 39.
the LORD. Heb. Jehovah. Ap. 4. II.
He will heal us. Cp. Jer. 30. 17.
2 After two days: i.e. two days after this national repentance. See 5. 15, "till".
revive us = bring us back to life. **in** = on.
live = live again in resurrection. Referring to the yet future resurrection of the new Israel (Ezek. 37), which will thus resemble the resurrection of Messiah (1 Cor. 15. 20).
in His sight. Heb. = before His face, as their sin had been (7. 2).
3 to know, &c. See note on 2. 20. Cp. 4. 1.
His going forth. Cp. 2 Sam. 23. 4. Mic. 5. 2. John 16. 28. **prepared** = sure, or fixed.
morning = dawn.
unto us. Cp. Ps. 72. 6. Zech. 9. 9, and Mic. 5. 2.
as the rain. Cp. Ps. 72. 6. Job 29. 23.
former rain. Ref. to Pent. (Deut. 11. 14, Heb. *yoreh*). So rendered only there, here, and Jer. 5. 24. Ap. 92.

6. 4—13. 8 (*M*, p. 1213). INCRIMINATION AND THREATENING. (*Extended Alternation.*)

M | T | 6. 4. Divine Forbearance.
  U | 6. 5—10. 15. Incorrigibility.
   V | 11. 1-7. Contrasted Conduct.
 T | 11. 8-11. Divine Forbearance.
  U | 11. 12—12. 14. Incorrigibility.
   V | 13. 1-8. Contrasted Conduct.

4 what . . . ? Fig. *Erotēsis* and *Aporia*. Ap. 6.
for. Some codices, with Syr. and Vulg., read "and".
goodness = piety.

6. 5—10. 15 (U, above). INCORRIGIBILITY. (*Alternation.*)

U | W | 6. 5. Divine Judgments.
  X | 6. 6-11-. Incorrigibility.
 W | 6. -11—7. 1-. Divine Mercy.
  X | 7. -1—10. 15. Incorrigibility.

5 Therefore have I hewed them, &c. = This is why I hewed them. Heb. idiom, by which the declaration that a thing should be done is spoken of the personal act of doing it. See note on Jer. 1. 18; and cp. Jer. 1. 10; 5 14. **by the prophets:** i.e. declared by the prophets. **thy judgments are.** A regrouping of the letters of the Hebrew word agrees with the Aram., Sept., and Syr., and reads "My judgment is". Verse 5 speaks of Jehovah's acts (see Structure, "W", above). Ref. to Pent. (Deut. 33. 2). Ap. 92. **the light** = light. **6 I desired, &c.** Cp. 1 Sam. 15. 22. Ecc. 5. 1. Mic. 6. 8. **mercy** = lovingkindness. Quoted in Matt. 9. 13; 12. 7. **not sacrifice.** Cp. Ps. 50. 8, 9. Prov. 21. 3. Isa. 1. 11. Heb. *zābach*. Ap. 43. II. xii. **the knowledge of God.** Cp. Jer. 9. 23, 24; 22. 16. See note on 2. 20. **God.** Heb. Elohim. Ap. 4. I. **7 like men.** Heb. like Adam. **men.** Heb. *'ādām*. Ap. 14. I. Cp. Job 31. 33. Pss. 49. 12; 82. 7. **transgressed** = rebelled. Heb. *'ābar*. Ap. 44. vii. **the covenant.** See Josh. 24. 1, 25. **8 Gilead.** Probably Ramoth-Gilead, a city of refuge, and of the priests (Josh. 21. 38). **iniquity.** Heb. *'aven* = vanity (Ap. 44. iii). Referring here, to the sin of idolatry. Cp. "Beth-aven", 4. 15. **polluted with** = tracked with heel-marks of. **9 troops** = gangs. **man.** Heb. *'īsh*. Ap. 14. II. **by consent** = towards Sichem, as in Gen. 37. 14. Sichem (like "Gilead", *v.* 8) was a city of priests (Josh. 21. 21). See note on "Gilead", *v.* 8. **commit lewdness:** i.e. practise idolatry. Jeroboam built Shechem (now *Nablous*), and doubtless set up his calf-worship there (1 Kings 12. 25). **lewdness.** Ref. to Pent. (Heb. *zimmāh*, is a Levitical word, found in Lev. 18. 17; 19. 29; 20. 14, 14). Ap. 92. **10 whoredom** = idolatry. See note on 1. 2. **11 he hath set** = there is appointed. **harvest:** i.e. a reaping time of judgment. See Jer. 51. 33. Joel 3. 13; and cp. Prov. 22. 8. Gal. 6. 7, 8. **for thee.** Some codices, with two early printed editions and Aram., read "for her". **returned** = turned again.

689-611 **7** When I would have healed Israel, then
the °iniquity of Ephraim was discovered,
and the °wickedness of Samaria:
X Y¹ for they commit falsehood; and the thief cometh
(p. 1216) in, *and* the troop of robbers °spoileth without.
2 And they °consider not in their hearts
that I remember all their ¹wickedness: now
their own doings have beset them about; they
are before My face.
3 They make the king glad with their ¹wickedness, and the princes with their lies.
4 They *are* °all °adulterers, °as an oven
heated by the baker, *who* °ceaseth from
°raising °after he hath kneaded the dough,
until it be leavened.
5 °In the °day of our king the princes have
made °*him* °sick with bottles of °wine; he
stretched out his hand with scorners.
6 For °they have made ready their heart
like an oven, whiles they lie in wait: °their
baker sleepeth all the night; in the morning
°it burneth as a flaming fire.
7 They are all hot as an oven, and have
devoured their judges; °all their kings are
fallen: °*there is* none among them that
calleth unto Me.
Z¹ 8 Ephraim, he hath mixed himself among the
°people; Ephraim is °a cake not turned.
9 °Strangers have devoured his strength,
and he knoweth *it* not: yea, gray hairs are
°here and there upon him, yet he knoweth
not.
10 And °the pride of Israel testifieth to his
face: and °they do not return to °the LORD
their °God, nor seek Him for all this.
11 Ephraim also is like a °silly dove without
heart: °they call to Egypt, they go to Assyria.
12 °When they shall go, I will spread My
net upon them; I will bring them down as the
fowls of the heaven; I will chastise them, °as
their °congregation hath heard.
13 Woe unto them! for they have fled from
Me: destruction unto them! because they
have °transgressed against Me: though °I
have °redeemed them, yet they have spoken
lies against Me.
14 And °they have not cried unto Me °with
their heart, when they howled upon their
beds: they °assemble themselves for corn and
°wine, *and* they °rebel against Me.
15 °Though I have bound *and* strengthened
their arms, yet do they imagine °mischief
against Me.
16 They return, *but* not °to the Most High:
they are like °a deceitful bow: their princes

7. 1—10. 15 (*X*, p. 1215). INCORRIGIBILITY.
(*Repeated Alternation.*)

X | Y¹ | 7. -1-7. Internal wickedness. Idolatry. } Political.
| Z¹ | 7. 8—8. 3. External trouble. Foreigners.
| Y² | 8. 4-6. Internal wickedness. Idolatry.
| Z² | 8. 7-10. External trouble. Foreigners.
| Y³ | 8. 11—9. 8. Internal wickedness. Idolatry. } Religious.
| Z³ | 9. 9. External trouble. The days of Gibeah.
| Y⁴ | 9. 10—10. 8. Internal wickedness. Idolatry.
| Z⁴ | 10. 9-15. External chastisement. The days of Gibeah.

1 iniquity. Heb. *'āvāh.* Ap. 44. iv.
wickedness. Heb. pl. of *rā'a'.* Ap. 44. viii.
spoileth = strippeth.
2 consider not in = say not to. Some codices, with one early printed edition, Aram., Syr., and Vulg., read "say not in".
4 all = all of them (kings, princes, and People are idolaters). "All" is put by Fig. *Synecdoche* (of Genus), Ap. 6, for the greater part.
adulterers: i.e. idolaters. See note on 1. 2.
as = [hot] like.
ceaseth = leaves off.
raising = stoking it.
after he hath kneaded, &c. = from [the time of] kneading the dough until it is ready for the fire. Then he heats the oven to stop the fermentation. Even so these idolaters. See note on "baker", *v.* 6.
5 In the day of our king. See 2 Kings 15. 10.
day. Perhaps = [feast] day.
him. Supply "themselves" instead of "him".
sick, &c. Sick with the heat of wine.
wine. Heb. *yayin.* Ap. 27. I.
6 they, &c. Like the baker in *v.* 4.
their baker sleepeth = their anger smoketh: reading *ye'shan'apphem* instead of *yāshēn'ophēhem.* Owing to the similarity in pronunciation and in the ancient form of *Ayin* (') and *Aleph* ('), these letters were interchanged. The *Massōrah* contains lists of words where *Aleph* (א = ') stands for *Ayin* (= ') and vice versa (see Ginsburg's *Massōrah*, letter א, vol. i, p. 57, § 514; and letter ע, vol. ii, p. 390, §§ 352, 360, &c.). See notes on Isa. 49. 7. Amos 6. 8. Zeph. 3. 1, &c. The Aram. and Syr. preserve the reading of the primitive text: "their anger smoketh all night" (like the "oven" in *v.* 4).
it: i.e. the oven.
7 all their kings, &c. Cp. 8. 4. Of the two houses of Omri and Jehu:—Nadab, Zimri, Tibni, Jehoram, Zachariah, Shallum, Pekahiah, and Pekah were all slain by their successors, or others.
there is. Some codices, with two early printed editions (one Rabbinic in margin), read "and there".
8 people = peoples, or nations.
a cake not turned: i.e. a thin (pan)cake, burnt one side and moist the other, and therefore uneatable.
9 Strangers = Outsiders. Cp. 8. 7.
here and there = sprinkled.
10 the pride of Israel. See note on 5. 5.
they do not return, &c. Ref. to Pent. (Deut. 4. 29).
the LORD. Heb. Jehovah. Ap. 4. II.
God. Heb. Elohim. Ap. 4. I.
11 silly = harmless, innocent. Ang.-Sax., *saelig*, happy.
they call, &c. See 2 Kings 15. 19; 17. 4-6. Cp. 5. 13; 9. 3; 12. 1. **12 When** = Howsoever. **as their congregation hath heard.** Those who know not the Pentateuch may call this "unintelligible"; but see Lev. 26. 14, 28. Deut. 27. 14-26. **congregation.** Heb. *'ēdah* is a technical Pentateuchal word which occurs in Exodus fourteen times, in Leviticus twelve times, in Numbers over eighty times, in Joshua fifteen times, in Judges four times, and twice in Kings and Jeremiah. Elsewhere used of any multitude only a few times. **13 transgressed** = revolted. Heb. *pāsha'* (Ap. 44. ix), as in 14. 9. Not the same word as in 6. 7, and 8. 1. **I have redeemed them.** Ref. to Pent. (Deut. 7. 8; 9. 26; 15. 15; 21. 8; 24. 18). Heb. *ga'al* is used in Gen. 48. 16. Ex. 6. 6; 15. 13. Ap. 92. Cp. Mic. 6. 4. **redeemed.** Heb. *pādāh.* See note on Ex. 6. 6, and 13. 13. **14 they have not cried.** Cp. Job 35. 9, 10. Ps. 78. 36. Jer. 3. 10. Zech. 7. 5. **with their heart.** They cried with their voice. **assemble themselves.** In their idol temples. **wine** = new wine. Heb. *tīrōsh.* Ap. 27. II. Not the same word as in *v.* 5. **rebel against** = apostatized from. **15 Though I have bound** = Though I, even I, have warned (or instructed). Cp. Pss. 18. 34; 144. 1. **mischief.** Heb. *rā'a'.* Ap. 44. viii. **16 to the Most High** = to Him Who is on high. Cp. 11. 7. **a deceitful bow.** That disappoints the user, and cannot be depended upon. Cp. Ps. 78. 57.

689-611 shall fall by the sword °for the °rage of their
tongue: this *shall be* their °derision °in the
land of Egypt.

8 °*Set* the trumpet to thy mouth. °*He
shall come* °as an eagle against the house
of °the LORD, because they have °transgressed
°My covenant, and °trespassed against °My law.
2 °Israel shall cry unto Me, "My °God, °we
know Thee."
3 Israel hath cast off °*the thing that is* good:
the enemy shall pursue him.
Y² (p. 1216) 4 °They have set up kings, but not by Me:
they have °made princes, and I °knew *it* not:
°of their silver and their gold have they made
them °idols, that °they may be cut off.
5 °Thy calf, O °Samaria, hath cast *thee* off;
Mine anger is kindled against them: how long
will it be ere they °attain to innocency?
6 °For from Israel *was* it also: the workman
made it; therefore it *is* not ²God: but the calf
of Samaria shall °be broken in °pieces.
Z² 7 For they have sown the °wind, and they
shall reap the whirlwind: it hath no stalk:
°the bud shall yield no °meal: if so be it yield,
the °strangers shall swallow it up.
8 °Israel is swallowed up: now shall they be
among the °Gentiles °as a vessel wherein *is*
no pleasure.
9 For they are °gone up to Assyria, °a °wild ass
alone by himself: Ephraim hath °hired lovers.
10 Yea, though they have °hired among the
nations, now will I °gather °them, and they
shall °sorrow °a little for °the burden of the
°king of princes.
Y³ 11 Because Ephraim hath °made many altars
to °sin, altars shall °be unto him to °sin.
12 °I have written to him the °great things
of °My law, *but* they were °counted °as a
strange thing.
13 °They sacrifice flesh *for* the sacrifices of
Mine °offerings, and °eat *it*; °*but* ¹the LORD
accepteth them not; °now will He remember
their °iniquity, and visit their ¹¹sins: °they
shall return to Egypt.
14 For Israel hath °forgotten His Maker, and
°buildeth temples; and Judah hath multiplied
°fenced cities: but I will send a fire upon °his
cities, and it shall devour °the palaces thereof.

for = because of. **derision** = ridicule.
rage = wrath, &c. [against God]. Cp. Ps. 73. 9.
in the land of Egypt. See 9. 3, 6. Cp. Isa. 30. 3, 5.
8. 1 Set the trumpet, &c. See 5. 8. Cp. Isa. 58. 1.
He shall come. Supply the *Ellipsis* (Ap. 6) thus: "[It (i.e. the threatened judgment)] is coming", &c. Ref. to Pent. (Deut. 28. 49). Ap. 92.
as. This is not merely comparison but assertion: i.e. swiftly. It is not the eagle that comes against the Temple. Cp. Jer. 4. 13. Hab. 1. 8.
the LORD. Heb. Jehovah. Ap. 4. II.
transgressed. Heb. *'ābar*. Ap. 44. vii. Same word as in 6. 7; not the same as in 7. 13; 14. 9.
My covenant . . . My law. Ref. to Pent. (Deut. 4. 13), where a like Alternation is found. Ap. 92.
trespassed. Heb. *pāsha'*. Ap. 44. ix.
2 Israel shall cry, &c. Render: "to Me will they cry: 'My God', we know Thee: Israel [knoweth Thee]".
God. Heb. Elohim. Ap. 4. I.
we know Thee. Cp. Matt. 7. 22. John 8. 54, 55. Isa. 29. 13 (Matt. 15. 8).
3 the thing that is good = the Gracious One. Cp. 3. 5; 14. 2.
4 They have set up kings. Cp. 7. 7. See 2 Kings 15. 13, 17, 27 (Shallum, Menahem, Pekah).
made princes = caused [men] to bear rule. Heb. *sārar* = to bear rule. See note on 12. 3.
knew = acknowledged. **idols** = elaborate idols.
of their silver, &c. Cp. 2. 8; 13. 2.
they = he. The nation spoken of as one man. But the Aram., Sept., and Syr. read "they", with the A.V. and R.V.
5 Thy calf, &c. Render: "He [Jehovah] hath rejected thy calf, O Samaria".
Samaria. The capital is put by Fig. *Synecdoche* (of the Part), Ap. 6, for the whole nation.
attain. Note the *Ellipsis* of the infinitive. Supply: "[be able to] attain", &c.
6 For from Israel, &c. Render: "For from Israel! (i.e. from Israel, of all people) [doth this conduct proceed!—and he—! (i.e., and that calf, what is it)]? A craftsman made him, so no God is he". **be** = become.
pieces = fragments, or splinters. Heb. *sh^ebābīm*. Occurs only here. **7 wind.** Heb. *rūach*. Ap. 9.
the bud . . . meal. Note the Fig. *Paronomasia* (Ap. 6), for emphasis. Heb. *zemach . . . kemach*. It may be Englished: "the *flower* will yield no *flour*".
strangers = outsiders. Cp. 7. 9.
8 Israel is swallowed up. See 2 Kings 17. 6.
Gentiles = nations. **as a vessel.** Cp. Jer. 22. 28; 48. 38.
9 gone up. Cp. 5. 13; 7. 11. **a** = [as] a.
wild ass. Cp. Isa. 1. 3. Jer. 2. 24.
hired lovers = paid the love-fee. Comparing idolatry to whoredom. Cp. Ezek. 16. 33, 34; and see 2 Chron. 28. 20, 21. **10 hired** = hired [lovers]. **gather** = gather [against]. **them:** i.e. the nations (Israel's lovers). **sorrow** = be in woe, writhing.
a little = in a little time, speedily; as in Hag. 2. 6. The Hebrew accents indicate that we should render—"and, ere long, they will be writhing under the burden": king [will be writhing], princes [will be writhing].
the burden of the: i.e. the tribute [laid on them]. **king of princes** = king and princes. Cp. Isa. 10. 8.
11 made many = multiplied. Cp. 12. 10. **sin.** Heb. *chāṭā'*. Ap. 44. i. **be unto him** = have become to him. **sin.** The same word, but here put by Fig. *Metonymy* (of Effect), Ap. 6, for the judgments caused by the sin. **12 I have written.** Not Moses: he was only the pen. It was God who "spoke by the prophets" (Heb. 1. 1); by His Son (John 7. 16; 8. 28, 46, 47; 12. 49; 14. 10, 24; 17. 8); by His Spirit (John 16. 13. Cp. Heb. 2. 4); and by Paul, "the prisoner of Jesus Christ" (cp. 2 Tim. 1. 8). Note the ref. to Pent. (Ex. 17. 14; 24. 4, 7; 34. 27. Num. 33. 1, 2. Deut. 4. 6-8, &c.). See Ap. 47, and 92. **great** = weighty. Cp. Matt. 23. 23. Heb. text reads *ribbō* = myriad; but marg. reads *rubbēy* = multitudes, or manifold, with Sept., Syr., and Vulg. **My law.** Not Moses's law. **counted** = accounted. **as a strange thing** = as something alien or foreign, as modern critics do to-day. This verse necessitates the accessibility of the law in a written form, and gives more than a clue to the date of the Pentateuch. See Ap. 47. **13 They sacrifice flesh, &c.** See note on Jer. 7. 21-23. Zech. 7. 6. **offerings** = sacrificial gifts. Heb. *habhābīm*. Occurs only here. **eat it** = that they may eat it [as common food]. **but.** One school of Massorites read this "but" in the text. Cp. 5. 6, and 9. 4. Jer. 14. 10, 12. Amos 5. 22. **now, &c.** Cp. 9. 9. Amos 8. 7. **iniquity.** Heb. *'āvāh*. Ap. 44. iv. **they shall return to Egypt.** Ref. to Pent. (Deut. 28. 68). Ap. 92. Cp. 2. 15; 9. 3, 6; 11. 5. Sept. reads "they have returned", &c. **14 forgotten His Maker.** Ref. to Pent. (Deut. 32. 18). Ap. 92. **buildeth temples.** Cp. 1 Kings 12. 31, and 2 Chron. 24. 7 with 23. 17. **fenced cities** = fortified cities. See 2 Chron. 26. 9, 10. **his cities.** See 2 Kings 18. 13: i.e. Judah's. **the palaces thereof** = her citadels, the fem. suffix agreeing with "cities", which is fem. in Heb. Modern critics regard this verse as "a later addition, perhaps borrowed from Amos", because "palaces or idol temples are not referred to by Hosea"!

689-611 9 Rejoice not, O Israel, for joy, as *other*
°people: for thou hast °gone a whoring
from thy °God, thou hast loved °a reward
upon every cornfloor.
2 The °floor and the °winepress shall not feed
them, and the °new wine shall fail in °her.
3 They shall not dwell in °the LORD'S land;
but Ephraim shall °return to Egypt, and they
shall eat unclean *things* °in Assyria.
4 They shall not offer °wine *offerings* to [3]the
LORD, neither shall they be pleasing unto Him:
their sacrifices *shall be* unto them as the
°bread °of mourners; all that eat thereof shall
be polluted: for their °bread for their °soul
shall not come into the house of [3] the LORD.
5 What will ye do in the solemn day, and in
the day of the feast of [3] the LORD?
6 For, °lo, they are gone °because of destruction:
°Egypt °shall gather them up, °Memphis
shall bury them: the pleasant *places* for their
silver, nettles shall possess them: thorns
shall be in their °tabernacles.
7 °**The days of visitation are come**, the days
of °recompence are come; Israel shall °know
it: "the prophet *is* a fool, the °spiritual °man
is mad," °for the multitude of thine °iniquity,
and the great °hatred.
8 °The °watchman of Ephraim °*was* with
°my [1] God: °*but* °the prophet °*is* a snare of
a fowler in all his ways, *and* [7] hatred in the
house of °his [1] God.
Z3 (p. 1216) 9 They have deeply corrupted *themselves*, as
in °the days of Gibeah: °*therefore* °He will
remember their [7] iniquity, °He will visit their
°sins.
Y4 10 °I found Israel like grapes in the wilderness;
I saw your fathers as the firstripe in the
fig tree at her first time: *but* °they went to
°Baal-peor, and separated themselves unto
°*that* shame; and °*their* abominations were
according as they loved.
11 *As for* Ephraim, their glory shall °fly
away like a bird, °from the birth, and from
the womb, and from the °conception.
12 °Though they bring up their °children,
yet °will I bereave them, *that there shall* not
be a °man *left:* yea, woe also to them °when
I depart from them!
13 Ephraim, °as I saw °Tyrus, *is* planted in
a pleasant place: but Ephraim shall bring
forth his [12] children to the murderer.
14 Give them, °O [3] LORD: °what wilt Thou
give? give them a miscarrying womb and dry
breasts.

9. 1 people=peoples.
gone a whoring: i.e. gone into idolatry. See note on 1. 2.
God. Heb. Elohim. Ap. 4. I.
a reward=a love-fee. Ref. to Pent. (Deut. 23. 18, "hire"). Ap. 92.
2 floor=threshing-floor.
winepress=winefat. Heb. *yekeb*, the wine receptacle; not *gath*, the winepress. See note on Isa. 5. 2.
new wine. Heb. *tīrōsh.* Ap. 27. II. Not same as *v.* 4.
her. A special various reading called *Sevīr* (Ap. 34), with some codices, one early printed edition, Aram., Sept., Syr., and Vulg., give "them"; some give "with her" in marg.
3 the LORD'S. Heb. Jehovah's. Ap. 4. II.
return to Egypt. See 8. 13; 11. 5. Cp. Ezek. 4. 13.
in Assyria. See 2 Kings 17. 6. Hos. 11. 11.
4 wine. Heb. *yayin.* Ap. 27. I. Not same as in *v.* 2.
bread. Put by Fig. *Synecdoche* (of Species), Ap. 6, for all kinds of food.
of mourners. Ref. to Pent. (Deut. 26. 14. Num. 19. 14). Ap. 92. Heb. *'āven.* A *Homonym.* See note on "Benjamin", Gen. 35. 18.
soul. Heb. *nephesh.* Ap. 13.
6 lo. Fig. *Asterismos* Ap. 6.
because of=from.
Egypt=[yet] Egypt. Cp. 7. 16.
shall gather them up=shall rake them out [for manure, or for burning]; not for burial in their own land; this would be *'āsaph.* But here it is *ḳabaz.* (Jer. 8. 2. Ezek. 29. 5.)
Memphis. The capital of Lower Egypt (near Cairo). Now *Mitrahumy*; also called *Noph.*
tabernacles=tents. Heb. *'ohel* (Ap. 40. 3); "tents" being put by Fig. *Metonymy* (of Adjunct), Ap. 6, for the place where their tents were pitched.
7 The days of visitation are come. Ref. to Pent. (Ex. 32. 34). Ap. 92. Cp. Luke 19. 44; 21. 22.
recompence=retribution.
know [it]=discover [her wickedness, when she said].
spiritual man=man of the Spirit: i.e. God's prophet, who is defined as a man in whom the Spirit of God was.
man. Heb. *'īsh.* Ap. 14. II.
for the multitude, &c.=for great is thine iniquity, great is thine enmity.
iniquity=distortion. Heb. *'āvāh.* Ap. 44. iv.
hatred=provocation.
8 The watchman. Note the series of contrasts, what Ephraim had been, and what Ephraim had now become, which commences here; with remarks following each. See *vv.* 10 and 13; 10. 1, 9; 11. 1; 13. 1.
watchman. Used of a true prophet in Isa. 21. 6-11. Jer. 6. 17; 31. 6. Ezek. 3. 17; 33. 7.
was. Render: "Ephraim [was so], e.g. in Joshua's days.
my God: i.e. Hosea's God. **but**=[but now].
the prophet: i.e. Ephraim.
is=is become.
his God. In contrast with Hosea's God.
9 the days of Gibeah. See 10. 9. This implies a common knowledge of the history of Judges 19. 15, &c.
therefore. Some codices, with three early printed editions (one Rabbinic, marg.), read "now will He", &c. **He**: i.e. Jehovah. Ap. 4. II. **He will visit.** Some codices read "that He may visit". Cp. 8. 13. **sins.** Heb. *chātā'.* Ap. 44. i. **10 I found, &c.** Another contrast. See *v.* 8. **they went, &c.** Ref. to Pent. (Num. 25. 3). The history was well known, or this reference to it would be useless. Ap. 92. **Baal-peor.** Ref. to Pent. (Num. 25. 3. Deut. 4. 3). Ap. 92. Elsewhere only in Ps. 106. 28. Cp. Josh. 22. 17. **that shame**=that shameful thing: the *'Ashērah* and its worship. See Ap. 42. **their, &c.** Supply the *Ellipsis*, and render: "became an abomination like their paramour". **11 fly.** The 1611 edition of the A.V. reads "flee". **from the birth, &c.**=no birth, none with child, no conception. **conception.** This particular word *hērāyōn* occurs only here, and Ruth 4. 13. A similar word (Heb. *harōn*) in Gen. 3. 16. **12 Though they bring up, &c.** Not "inappropriate after *v.* 11", but is part of the contrast commenced there. **children** =sons. **will I bereave them.** Ref. to Pent. (Lev. 26. 22. Deut. 28. 41, 62). Ap. 92. **man.** Heb. *'ādām.* Ap. 14. I. **when I depart from them**=when I take command from them. Heb. *sūr*, as in 8. 4, and 12. 3 (see notes there). Not the same word as "withdraw" in 5. 6, which is *ḥālaz.* **13 as I saw Tyrus.** Another contrast. See note on *v.* 8. The verse does not "defy explanation". **as**=according as. **Tyrus.** See Isa. 23. Ezek. 26-28. **14 O LORD.** Note the Fig. *Aposiopesis* (Ap. 6). **what . . . ?** Fig. *Erotēsis.* Ap. 6.

689-611 15 All their °wickedness *is* in °Gilgal: for there °I hated them: °for the °wickedness of their doings I will drive them out of Mine house, I will love them no more: all °their princes *are* revolters.

16 Ephraim is smitten, their root is dried up, they shall bear no fruit: yea, though they bring forth, yet will I slay *even* the beloved *fruit* of their womb.

17 My [1]God will cast them away, because they did not hearken unto Him: and °they shall be wanderers among the nations.

10 Israel *is* °an empty vine, he bringeth forth °fruit °unto himself: °according to the °multitude of his °fruit he hath °increased the altars; according to the °goodness of his land they have made °goodly °images.

2 °Their heart is divided; now shall they be °found faulty: °He shall break down their altars, He shall spoil their [1] images.

3 For now they shall say, "We have no king, because we feared not °the LORD; what then should a king °do to us?"

4 They have spoken words, swearing falsely in making a covenant: thus judgment springeth up as °hemlock °in the furrows of the field.

5 The inhabitants of °Samaria shall fear because of the calves of °Beth-aven: for the people thereof shall mourn over it, and the °priests thereof *that* °rejoiced on it, for the °glory thereof, because it is departed from it.

6 It shall be also carried unto Assyria *for* a present to °king Jareb: Ephraim shall receive shame, and Israel shall be ashamed of his own °counsel.

7 *As for* [5]Samaria, her king is cut off °as the foam upon the water.

8 The high places also of Aven, the °sin of Israel, shall be destroyed: °the thorn and the thistle shall come up on their altars; and **they shall say to the °mountains, "Cover us;" and to the hills, "Fall on us."**

Z[4] (p. 1216) 9 O Israel, thou hast °sinned °from °the days of Gibeah: °there they stood: the battle in Gibeah against the °children of °iniquity °did not overtake them.

10 °*It is* in My desire that I should chastise them; and the °people shall be gathered against them, °when they shall bind themselves in their °two furrows.

11 °And Ephraim *is as* °an heifer *that is* taught, *and* loveth to tread out *the corn;* but I °passed over upon her fair neck: I will make Ephraim to ride; Judah shall plow, *and* °Jacob shall break his clods.

12 Sow to yourselves in righteousness, reap in mercy; break up your fallow ground: for *it is* time °to seek [3]the LORD, till He come and °rain righteousness upon you.

15 wickedness. Heb. *ra'a'.* Ap. 44. viii.
Gilgal. Cp. 4. 15; 12. 11. The place where Jehovah was rejected, and man's king set up; and where, on account of his impatience and disobedience Saul got his first message of his rejection (1 Sam. 13. 4–15), and his second (1 Sam. 15. 12–33). See note on Hos. 4. 15.
I hated them = have I come to hate them.
for the wickedness, &c. Cp. 1. 6.
their princes are revolters. Note the Fig. *Paronomasia* (Ap. 6), for emphasis. Heb. *sārēyhĕm . . . sor^erīm.* It may be Englished by "their rulers are unruly". Cp. Isa. 1. 23, where the same words are used.
17 they shall be wanderers, &c. Ref. to Pent. (Deut. 28. 64, 65). Ap. 92.

10. 1 an empty vine = a productive or luxurious vine. Heb. a vine emptying or yielding its fruit See notes on Judg. 9. 8–13. Heb. *gephen.* Always fem. except here and 2 Kings 4. 39. Here because it refers to Israel: i. e. to the people.
fruit. Note the Fig. *Polyptōton* (Ap. 6) in the varying inflections of the words, "fruit", "multiply", and "good"; and the Fig. *Synonymia* in "altars" and "images"; all to increase the emphasis of the contrast. See note on 9. 8 ("watchman").
unto himself = like himself: i. e. not for Me.
according to. Note the Fig. *Anaphora* (Ap. 6).
multitude . . . increased. The same word.
goodness . . . goodly. Note the Fig. *Polyptōton* (Ap. 6).
images = pillars: i. e. *'Ashērahs* (Ap. 42). Heb. *mazzēbah* = upright (erect) pillars.
2 Their heart is divided. Cp. 1 Kings 18. 21. 2 Kings 17. 32, 33, 41.
found faulty = held guilty. Referring back to 9. 17.
He shall, &c. Ref. to Pent. (Ex. 23. 24; 34. 13. Deut. 7. 5; 12. 3).
3 the LORD. Heb. Jehovah. Ap. 4. II.
do to us: do for us, or, profit us.
4 hemlock = poppy. Ref. to Pent. (Deut. 29. 18; 32. 32, 33). Ap. 92. Elsewhere only in Job, Psalms, Jeremiah, and Amos 5. 7; 6. 12.
in the furrows. Some codices, with four early printed editions (one Rabbinic, marg.), read "all the furrows".
5 Samaria. See *v.* 7; 7. 1; 8. 5, 6; 13. 16.
Beth-aven. See note on 4. 15.
priests. Heb. *k^emarīm* = priests of Baal, or black ones, from *kāmar* = to be black, from the black dress (or cassocks) worn by them. Occurs only here and 2 Kings 23. 5. Zeph. 1. 4.
rejoiced = leap, or exult. Cp. 1 Kings 18. 26.
glory . . . departed. Ref. to the history (1 Sam. 4. 21, 22).
6 king Jareb. See note on 5. 13.
counsel: i. e. the policy of Jeroboam.
7 as the foam, &c. = on the face of the waters. Ref. to Pent. (Gen. 1. 2; 7. 18). Ap. 92.
8 sin. Heb. *chāṭā'.* Ap. 44. i. Put by Fig. *Metonymy* (of Adjunct), Ap. 6, for the idols associated with it. Cp. Deut. 9. 21. 1 Kings 12. 30.
the thorn and the thistle. Ref. to Pent. (Gen. 3. 18). Ap. 92. This combination of words occurs only in these two places. "Thorns" is found in Ex. 22. 6, &c.; "thistles", Heb. *darda,* only here, and Gen. 3. 18. Cp. 9. 6.
mountains. Such was Beth-el in the hill country of Ephraim (Judg. 4. 5). Contrast Gen. 49. 2, 6.
9 sinned. Heb. *chāṭā.* Ap. 44. i. **from:** or, beyond.
the days of Gibeah. See 9. 9 and Judg. 19 and 20. Note the Article.
there they stood. In battle array. **children** = sons.
iniquity. Heb. *'ālvah.* Occurs only here, from Heb. *'āvāh.* Ap. 44. iv. **did not overtake them.** Supply the Ellipsis: [and shall ye escape ?]. **10 It is in My desire, &c.** = I am resolved to. Ref. to Pent. (Deut. 28. 63). Ap. 92. **people** = peoples **when they shall bind** = they being joined (or yoked) [in cohabitation. Put for idolatries] together in committing idolatry. **two furrows.** Put by Fig. *Metonymy* (of Adjunct), Ap. 6, for being yoked together as oxen in committing the same sins of idolatry. See the interpretation in *vv.* 11–13. **11 And Ephraim** = i. e. the land of Ephraim. Here is the contrast. See note on "watchman", 9. 8. **an heifer.** Cp. Jer. 50. 11. Mic. 4. 13. **passed over upon** = put a yoke upon. **Jacob.** Put here by Fig. *Metonymy* (of Adjunct), Ap. 6, for Ephraim. **12 to seek the LORD.** Ref. to Pent. (Deut. 4. 29). Ap. 92. **rain righteousness, &c.** Ref. to Pent. (Deut. 32. 2). Ap. 92.

689-611 13 °Ye have plowed °wickedness, ye have reaped °iniquity; ye have eaten the fruit of lies: because thou didst °trust in thy °way, in the multitude of thy mighty men.
14 Therefore shall a tumult arise among thy [10] people, and all thy fortresses shall be spoiled, as °Shalman spoiled °Beth-arbel in the day of battle: °the mother was dashed in pieces upon *her* [9] children.
15 So shall Beth-el do unto you because of °your great °wickedness: °in a morning °shall the king of Israel utterly be cut off.

V m[1] (p. 1220) **11** When Israel *was* a child, then °I loved him, and °**called My son out of Egypt.**
n[1] 2 *As* °they called them, so they went from °them: °they °sacrificed unto Baalim, and burned incense to graven images.
m[2] 3 °𝔍 taught Ephraim also to °go, °taking them by their arms;
n[2] but they knew not that °I healed them.
m[3] 4 I °drew them with cords of a °man, with bands of love: and I was to them as they that °take off the yoke on their jaws, and °I laid meat unto them.
n[3] 5 He shall °not return into the land of Egypt, but the Assyrian °shall be his king, because they refused to return.
6 And the sword shall abide on his cities, and shall consume his °branches, and devour *them*, because of their own counsels.
7 And My People are °bent to °backsliding from Me: °though they called them to the °Most High, °none at all would exalt *Him*.
T (p. 1215) 8 °How shall I give thee up, Ephraim? *how* shall I deliver thee, Israel? °how shall I make thee as °Admah? *how* shall I set thee as °Zeboim? Mine heart is turned within Me, My °repentings are kindled together.
9 I will not execute the fierceness of Mine anger, I will not return to destroy Ephraim: for °𝔍 *am* °GOD, and not °man; the Holy One °in the midst of thee: and I will not °enter into °the city.
10 They shall °walk after °the LORD: °He shall roar like a lion: when °𝔋𝔢 shall roar, then the °children shall °tremble °from the west.
11 They shall [10] tremble as a bird out of Egypt, and as a dove out of the land of Assyria: and I will place them °in their houses, °saith [10] the LORD.

U A (p. 1221) 12 °Ephraim compasseth Me about with lies,

13 Ye have plowed=Ye have sown. Heb. *ḥarashtem.* Occurs, with this spelling, only here and Judg. 14. 18. The *Massōrah* (Ap. 30 and 93) places it in an alphabetical list of words, occurring twice, with two different meanings (see Ginsburg's *Massōrah*, vol. i, p. 498, § 411). It is therefore a *Homonym* with one meaning: *ye have plowed* (Judg. 14. 18); and another, *ye have sown* (10. 13).
wickedness=lawlessness. Heb. *rāshā'*. Ap. 44. x.
iniquity. Heb. *'āval.* Ap. 44. vi.
trust=confide. Heb. *bāṭaḥ.* Ap. 69. i.
way. Sept. reads "chariots". This corresponds with the next clause.
14 Shalman. Sayce thinks he is Salamanu, king of Moab, a tributary of Tiglath-Pileser III (cp. 1. 1); therefore a contemporary of Hosea.
Beth-arbel. Heb. *Beth-'arbe'ēl*=house of the ambush of GOD (Heb. El. Ap. 4. IV). Heb. marg. reads *Beth-'arbē'l*, so as to disguise the name El and avoid the supposed offensive expression. Probably now *Irbid*, near Pella, in the Ajlūn, east of Jordan.
the mother, &c. Cp. 13. 16.
15 your great wickedness. Heb. "evil of your evil". Note the Fig. *Polyptōton* (Ap. 6). Heb. *rā'a'.*
in a morning. Some codices, with two early printed editions (one Rabbinic, marg.), read "like the dawn".
shall the king of Israel. Cp. *v.* 7. The king referred to may be Hoshea.

11. 1-7 (V, p. 1215). CONTRASTED CONDUCT.
(*Repeated Alternation.*)

V | m[1] | 1. Love.
  n[1] | 2. Ingratitude.
 m[2] | 3-. Love.
  n[2] | -3. Insensibility.
 m[3] | 4. Love.
  n[3] | 5-7. Threatening.

1 I loved him. Cp. Jer. 2. 2. Mal. 1. 2.
called My son, &c.=called to My son. Ref. to Pent. (Ex. 4. 22, 23). Ap. 92. Quoted in Matt. 2. 15.
2 they. The callers: i.e. the prophets, &c. who called to them.
them. The Sept. and Syr. read "Me".
they. Israel.
sacrificed=kept sacrificing. Cp. 2. 13; 13. 2. 2 Kings 17. 16.
3 𝔍 taught, &c. Ref. to Pent. (Deut. 1. 31; 32. 10, 11, 12). Cp. Isa. 46. 3. **go**=walk. See Acts 13. 18 marg.
taking=I used to take.
I healed them. Ref. to Pent. (Ex. 15. 26).
4 I drew=I would draw.
man. Heb. *'ādām.* Ap. 14. I.
take off=lift up, or loosen: viz. the straps which bind the yoke to the neck.
I laid meat=holding out [food] to him I let him eat.
5 not. Connect this with *v.* 4, for he is to return to Assyria (8. 13; 9. 3). **shall be**=𝔋𝔢 [became].
6 branches. Put by Fig. *Metonymy* (of Subject), Ap 6, for "sons", as being the progeny and defenders.
7 bent to backsliding. Cp. 4. 16.
though they called them, &c.=though they call upon the Most High. **Most High.** Heb. *'al.*
none at all would exalt Him=He shall not altogether lift them up.
8 How . . . ? Figs. *Erotēsis* and *Pathopœia.* Ap. 6.

Admah . . . Zeboim. Ref. to Pent. (Gen. 10. 19; 14. 2, 8. Deut. 29. 23). Ap. 92. These places are not mentioned elsewhere. **repentings**=compassions. **9 𝔍 am GOD, and not man.** Fig. *Pleonasm* (Ap. 6): put both ways for emphasis. Ref. to Pent. (Num. 23. 19). Ap. 92. Cp. Isa. 55. 8, 9. Mal. 3. 6. **GOD.** Heb. *'El.* Ap. 4. IV. **man.** Heb. *'īsh.* Ap. 14. II. **in the midst**=[will not come] into the midst. Ref. to Pent. (Ex. 33. 5). Ap. 92. **enter into**=come against: i.e. as an enemy. The verse is not "nonsense", as alleged. The reference is to *v.* 8. **the city**: i.e. as I came against Sodom and Gomorrah. **10 walk after**=return to. The Structure "*T*" (p. 1215) shows that *vv.* 10, 11 are not an "exilic insertion". **the LORD.** Heb. Jehovah. Ap. 4. II. **He shall roar**=[when] He shall summon them with a lion's roar. **children**=sons [of Israel]. **tremble**=come, or hasten, trembling. **from the west.** Cp. Zech. 8. 7. **11 in their houses.** Cp. Ezek. 28. 25, 26; 37. 21, 25. **saith the LORD**=[is] Jehovah's oracle.

11. 12—12. 14 (*U*, p. 1215). [For Structure see next page.]

12 Ephraim compasseth Me, &c. The Structure "*U*" (p. 1221) shows the change of subject in 11. 12—12. 8, which is "incorrigibility". The chapters are badly divided here.

689-611 and the house of Israel °with deceit: but °Ju-
dah yet ruleth with [9]GOD, and is faithful
°with the saints.

12 Ephraim °feedeth on °wind, and °fol-
loweth after the east wind: he °daily
increaseth lies and °desolation; and they do
°make a covenant with the Assyrians, and
°oil is carried into Egypt.
2 °The LORD hath also a controversy with
Judah, and will °punish °Jacob according to
his ways; °according to his doings will He
°recompense him.
B o (p. 1221) 3 °He °took °his brother °by the heel in the
womb, and °by his strength he °had power
with °God:
4 Yea, he [3]had power over °the Angel, and
°prevailed: °he wept, and made supplication
unto Him:
p °He found him °*in* Beth-el, and there °He
spake °with us;
5 °Even [2]the LORD [3]God of hosts; [2]the LORD
is His °memorial.
6 °Therefore turn thou to thy [3]God: keep
°mercy and judgment, and °wait on thy [3]God
continually.
C q 7 °*He is* a merchant, °the balances of deceit
are in his hand: °he loveth to °oppress.
8 And Ephraim said, "Yet I am become
rich, I have found me out substance: *in* all my
°labours they shall find none °iniquity in me
°that *were* °sin."
r 9 °And I *That am* [2]the LORD thy[3] God from the
land of Egypt will yet make thee to °dwell in
°tabernacles, °as in the days of the solemn feast.
10 I have also °spoken by the prophets, and
I have multiplied visions, and used similitudes, by the ministry of the prophets.
A 11 °*Is there* °iniquity *in* °Gilead? surely
they are vanity: they sacrifice bullocks in
°Gilgal; yea, their altars *are* as °heaps in the
furrows of the fields.
B o 12 And [2]Jacob °fled into the country of
°Syria, and °Israel served for a wife, and for
a wife he °kept *sheep*.

11. 12—12. 14 (*U*, p. 1215). INCORRIGIBILITY. (*Extended Alternation.*)

U | A | 11. 12—12. 2. Incrimination. Lies, &c.
  B | o | 12. 3, 4-. Jacob. Personal history.
    p | 12. -4-6. Divine Favour and Communication.
  C | q | 12. 7, 8. Provocation.
    r | 12. 9, 10. Cause.
A | 12. 11. Incrimination. Idolatry.
  B | *o* | 12. 12. Jacob. Personal history.
    p | 12. 13. Divine Favour and Communication.
  C | *q* | 12. 14-. Provocation.
    r | 12. -14. Consequence.

with deceit. See Isa. 29. 13. Ezek. 33. 31. Matt. 15. 8, 9. Mark 7. 6, 7.

Judah yet ruleth, &c. Cp. 2 Chron. 13. 10-12.

with the saints = with the Holy One. Heb. pl.; so used elsewhere. Cp. Josh. 24. 19. Prov. 30. 3.

12. 1 feedeth on wind. Cp. 8. 7.

wind. Heb. *rūach*. Ap. 9. } i.e. seeketh foreign
followeth after = pursueth. } alliances.

daily = all the day long. **desolation** = violence.

make a covenant, &c. Cp. 5. 13; 7. 11.

oil is carried, &c. As a present, to obtain favour and help. Cp. 5. 13. Isa. 30. 2-7; 57. 9. See 2 Kings 17. 4.

2 The LORD. Heb. Jehovah. Ap. 4. II.

punish = visit upon.

Jacob. Put by Fig. *Metonymy* (of Adjunct), Ap. 6, for Israel, especially the natural seed.

according. Some codices, with two early printed editions (one Rabbinic, marg.), Aram., Sept., Syr., and Vulg., read "and according".

recompense = requite, or repay.

3 He took his brother. Ref. to Pent. (Gen. 25. 26).

took . . . by the heel. Heb. *'āḳab*. Hence his name Jacob.

his brother = his very own brother (with *'eth*).

by his strength = in his manhood: i.e. another example, later in life, but of a similar nature.

had power with = contended with (*Oxford Gesenius*, p. 40). Heb. *sārah*. (Hence his name Israel). The event is referred to only here, and Gen. 32. 28. See note there.

God. Heb. Elohim (with *'eth*) = God Himself. Ap. 4. I.

4 the Angel. Defined in *v.* 5.

prevailed = He (the Angel) overcame him (Jacob). See notes on Gen. 32. 28. Hence the change of Jacob's name to "Israel" = God commands.

he wept: i.e. Jacob. This is the Fig. *Hysterēsis* (Ap. 6), by which former histories are supplemented by later Divine inspiration.

He found him: i.e. God found Jacob.

in Beth-el. Ref. to Pent. (Gen. 28. 17, 19). Note the implied contrast, Beth-el being now the seat of idolatry. **He spake** = Jehovah spake. See next verse. **with us.** Aquila, Symmachus, Theodotion, and Syr. read "with him". **5 Even, &c.** Render: "and Jehovah [is] God (*Elohim*) of the Hosts; Jehovah [is] His memorial [Name]." This is for strong confirmation. **memorial.** Ref. to Pent. (Ex. 3. 15). Ap. 92. **6 Therefore, &c.** Cp. 14. 1. **mercy** = lovingkindness, or grace. **wait on thy God** = wait for thy God. Ref. to Pent. (Gen. 49. 18). Cp. Ps. 37. 7. Isa. 25. 9; 26. 8; 33. 2. Mark 15. 43. Luke 2. 25; 23. 51. **7 He is a merchant.** Supply the *Ellipsis* (Ap. 6): [He, Ephraim, is] a merchant. This is the first of two provocations. See the Structure above; and cp. *v.* 14. **the balances of deceit** = unjust balances. Ref. to Pent. (Lev. 19. 36). **he loveth to oppress.** Money was obtained by oppression. Ref. to Pent. (Lev. 6. 2; 19. 13). Ap. 92. **oppress** = defraud. **8 labours** = toils. **iniquity** = perversity. Heb. *'āvāh*. Ap. 44. iv. Not the same word as in *v.* 11. **that were** = which [is]. **sin.** Heb. *chāṭā'*. Ap. 44. i. **9 And I, &c.** These verses (9, 10) correspond with *v.* 14, and give the cause of the provocation. There is an evident *Ellipsis* (Ap. 6), which may be thus supplied: "And [thou forgettest that] I, Jehovah thy Elohim from the land of Egypt, [that I have promised that] I will yet make thee to dwell in tents as in the Feast of Tabernacles". **dwell in tabernacles.** This is again promised in Zech. 14. 16. **tabernacles.** Since the days of Neh. 8. 17, the feast is called *'ōhālīm* (Ap. 40. 4), as here, instead of *ṣukkōth*, booths. Nehemiah's remark is superfluous unless the laws were ancient. **as in the days, &c.** Ref. to Pent. (Lev. 23. 42, 43). Ap. 92. **10 spoken by the prophets.** Cp. 2 Kings 17. 13. Heb. 1. 1. 2 Pet. 1. 21. **11 Is there iniquity** = [Surely Gilead is] iniquity: supplying the *Ellipsis* (Ap. 6) from the next clause. **iniquity.** Heb. *'aven*. Ap. 44. iii. Not the same word as *v.* 8. **Gilead . . . Gilgal . . . heaps.** Heap of testimony . . . heap of heaps . . . heaps. Note the Fig. *Paronomasia* (Ap. 6). Heb. *Gil'ād . . . Gilgāl . . . gallīm.* **12 fled . . . Syria.** Ref. to Pent. (Gen. 28. 5. Deut. 26. 5). Ap. 92. **Syria.** Ref. to Pent. (Deut. 26. 5). Ap. 92. **Israel served, &c.** Ref. to Pent. (Gen. 29. 18). Ap. 92. **kept sheep.** Ref. to Pent. (Gen. 30. 31, the same Heb. word, *shāmar*). Ap. 92. We may supply the connecting thought: "[yet in after days] Israel was brought out of Egypt . . . and preserved [in the wilderness]".

p (p. 1221) 689–611 13 And °by a prophet ²the LORD brought Israel out of Egypt, and by a prophet was he °preserved.

C q 14 °Ephraim provoked *Him* to anger most bitterly:

r therefore shall °He leave his °blood upon him, and °his reproach shall his °LORD return unto him.

V D (p. 1222) **13** When Ephraim °spake °trembling, he °exalted himself in Israel;

E but when he °offended °in Baal, he died.
2 And now they °sin more and more, and have made them molten images of their silver, *and* idols according to their own °understanding, all of it the work of the craftsmen: they say °of them, "Let the men that sacrifice °kiss the calves."

F 3 Therefore they shall be as the morning cloud, and as the early °dew °that passeth away, as the chaff *that* is driven with °the whirlwind out of the °floor, and as the smoke out of the °chimney.

D 4 °Yet I *am* °the LORD thy °God °from the land of Egypt, and thou °shalt know no god but Me: for °*there is* no saviour beside Me.
5 °I did know thee in the wilderness, in °the land of great drought.

E 6 °According to their pasture, so were they filled; °they were filled, and their heart was °exalted; therefore °have they forgotten Me.

F 7 Therefore I will be unto them °as a lion: °as a leopard °by the way °will I observe *them:*
8 I will meet them as a bear *that is* bereaved *of her whelps,* and will rend the °caul of their heart, and there will I devour them like a lion: °the wild beast shall tear them.

N G¹ s¹ 9 O Israel, °thou hast destroyed thyself;

t¹ °but in Me *is* thine help.
10 °I will be thy king: °where *is any other* that may save thee in all thy cities? and thy judges of whom °thou saidst, "Give me a king and princes."

---

13 by a prophet: i.e. Moses. Ref. to Pent. (Ex. 12. 50, 51; 13. 3. Num. 12. 6–8. Ap 92. Cp. Deut. 18. 15).
preserved = kept, as in *v.* 12.
14 Ephraim. As represented by Jeroboam (1 Kings 12. 25—13. 5), and Hoshea (2 Kings 17. 11–23).
He = God.
blood. Put by Fig. *Metonymy* (of Effect), Ap. 6, for blood-guiltiness.
his reproach. Ref. to Pent. (Deut. 28. 37). Ap. 92.
LORD. Heb. *'Adonim.* Ap. 4. VIII (3).

13. 1–8 (*V*, p. 1215). CONTRASTED CONDUCT. (*Extended Alternation.*)

V | D | 1–. Ephraim's eminence.
  E | –1, 2. Ephraim's fall. Idolatry.
   F | 3. Threatening, and Comparisons.
 D | 4, 5. Jehovah the source of Ephraim's eminence.
  E | 6. Ephraim's fall. Forgetting Jehovah.
   F | 7, 8. Threatening, and Comparisons.

1 spake trembling = spake (authoritatively) [there was] attention; as in Joshua's days (Josh. 4. 14). Cp. Job 29. 21–25.
trembling = panic. Heb. *r^etheth.* Occurs only here. Similar to *reṭeṭ*, which occurs only in Jer. 49. 24 ("fear").
exalted himself: carried weight, or was exalted.
offended = trespassed. Heb. *'āsham.* Ap. 44. ii.
in Baal = with Baal: i.e. with the idolatrous worship of Baal, in Ahab's days.
2 sin. Heb. *chāṭā'.* Ap. 44. i.
understanding = notion.
of them = to them: i.e. to the People.
kiss the calves. Kissing was fundamental in all heathen idolatry. It is the root of the Latin *ad-orare* = to [bring something to] the mouth. "A pure lip" (Zeph. 3. 9) implies more than language.
3 dew. Heb. *ṭal* = the night mist. See note on "Zion", Ps. 133. 3.
that. The 1611 edition of the A.V. reads "it".
the = a. **floor** = threshingfloor.
chimney = window, or opening. No word for chimney in Heb.
4 Yet I, &c. Supply the connecting thought: "[Ye worship these calves], yet I, even I", &c. Cp. 12. 9. Isa. 43. 11. **the LORD.** Heb. Jehovah. Ap. 4. II.
God. Heb. Elohim. Ap. 4. I.
from the land of Egypt. Supply the *Ellipsis* (Ap. 6): "[Who brought thee out] from", &c. Ref. to Pent. (Ex. 20. 2, 3). Ap. 92.
shalt know no: i.e. didst not, or oughtest not to know.
there is no saviour, &c. Cp. Isa. 43. 11; 45. 21. Supply: "no saviour [was there] beside Me". Cp. Acts 4. 12.
5 I did know thee, &c. Ref. to Pent. (Deut. 2. 7; 8. 15; 32. 10). Ap. 92. Cp. Amos 3. 2. The Sept. reads "I shepherded, or was shepherd to thee", reading *r^e'ithīka* instead of *y^eda'tīka*: i.e. ר (Resh = R) for ד (Daleth = D).
the land of great drought. Cp. Deut. 8. 15.
6 According to their pasture, &c.: i.e. the more I fed them, the more they kicked against Me.
they were filled. Note the Fig. *Anadiplōsis* (Ap. 6), repeated for emphasis. **exalted.** Note the correspondence ("E" and "*E*"). **have they forgotten Me.** Ref. to Pent. (Deut. 8. 12–14; 32. 15). **7 as a lion.** Ap. 92. Cp. 5. 14. **as a leopard.** Cp. Jer. 5. 6. **by the way.** Some codices, with three early printed editions, Sept., Syr., and Vulg., read "on the way of Assyria". **will I observe** = shall I watch, or lurk. **8 caul** = enclosure (i.e. the pericardium). **the wild beast shall tear them.** Ref. to Pent. (Lev. 26. 22).

13. 9—14. 8 (*N*, p. 1213). INVITATION TO RETURN. (*Division.*)

N | G¹ | 13. 9–16. Revolt.
  | G² | 14. 1–8. Return.

13. 9–16 (G¹, above). REVOLT. (*Repeated Alternation.*)

G¹ | s¹ | 9–. Incrimination.
  t¹ | –9–11. Promise.
 s² | 12, 13. Incrimination.
  t² | 14. Promise.
 s³ | 15, 16. Incrimination.

9 thou hast destroyed thyself = the destruction [which thou art suffering] is all thine own. Ref. to Pent. (Deut. 32. 5. Heb. *shaḥath*, same word as "corrupted"). Ap. 92. **but in Me, &c.** = for I am thy [true] help.
10 I will be thy king = Where is thy king? Heb. *'ĕhī* = where, as in *v.* 14 twice; *'ĕhī* is separated from the following word "king" by the accent *zakēph*, and connected with *'ēphō'* = now. It therefore means "Where now is thy king? (Hoshea)": the answer being "in prison" (see 2 Kings 17. 4). **where is any other that may save thee . . . ?** = to save thee, or that he may save thee. **thou saidst, "Give," &c.** Ref. to 1 Sam. 8. 5, 19.

689-611 11 °I gave thee a king in Mine anger, and
took *him* away in My wrath.
s[2] 12 The °iniquity of Ephraim *is* °bound up;
p. 1222) his [2]sin *is* °hid.
13 The sorrows of a travailing woman °shall
come upon him: he *is* ° an unwise son; for he
should not ° stay long ° in *the place of* the
breaking forth of ° children.
t[2] 14 I will °ransom them °from °the power
of °the grave; I will °redeem them from
death: °**O death, °I will be °thy plagues; O
°grave, °I will be thy destruction:** °repentance
shall be hid from Mine °eyes.
s[3] 15 Though ° he be ° fruitful among *his* brethren,
°an east wind shall come, the °wind of [4]the
LORD shall come up from the wilderness, and
°his spring shall become dry, and his fountain
shall be dried up: °he shall spoil the treasure
of all pleasant vessels.
16 °Samaria shall become desolate; for she
hath rebelled against her [4]God: they shall fall
by the sword: °their infants shall be dashed in
pieces, and their women with child shall be
ripped up.

G[2] H[1] **14** O Israel, °return °unto °the LORD thy
1223) °God; °for thou hast fallen by thine
°iniquity.
2 Take with you °words, and °turn to [1]the
LORD: °say unto Him,
J[1] "Take away all [1]iniquity, and receive *us*
°graciously: °**so will we °render the °calves
of our °lips.**
3 °Asshur shall not save us; °we will not ride
upon horses: neither will we say any more to
°the work of our hands, '*Ye are* our gods:'
°for in Thee °the fatherless °findeth mercy."
H[2] 4 I will heal their °backsliding, I will love
them freely: for Mine anger is turned away
from °him.
5 I will be as °the dew unto Israel: he shall
°grow as the lily, and °cast forth °his roots
°as Lebanon.
6 His branches shall spread, and his beauty
shall be as the olive tree, and °his smell [5]as
Lebanon.

11 I gave thee, &c. Ref. to 1 Sam. 8. 7; 10. 19; 15. 22, 23; 16. 1. Cp. 10. 3. Or lit. "I give . . . and take him away", referring to a continued act, the violent deaths of Israel's then recent kings: Zachariah murdered by Shallum; Shallum by Menahem; Pekahiah by Pekah; and Pekah by Hoshea, who was now a prisoner in Assyria.

12 iniquity = perversity. Heb. *'āvāh.* Ap. 44. iv.
bound up = tied up, as in a bag. Ref. to Pent. (Deut. 32. 32, 35). Ap. 92. **hid** = reserved.

13 shall come, &c. Isa. 13. 8. Jer. 30. 6. Matt. 24. 8.
an unwise son. Note the Fig. *Meiōsis* (Ap. 6), for emphasis, meaning a most foolish son.
stay long = linger.
in the place, &c.: i.e. in the act of being born. Cp. 2 Kings 19. 3. **children** = sons.

14 ransom = redeem (with power). Heb. *pādāh*, to redeem by power in virtue of the legal right. See note on Ex. 13. 13. **from** = out of.
the power = the hand: i.e. Sheōl's power (to keep in its grasp). **the grave** = Sheōl. See Ap. 35.
redeem. Heb. *ga'al*, to redeem by purchase by assertion of the kinship right. Hence the other meaning of avenging. See note on Ex. 6. 6.
O death. Fig. *Apostrophe* (Ap. 6), for emphasis. Quoted in 1 Cor. 15. 54, 55.
I will be = where [are], &c. See note on *v.* 10.
thy plagues. Heb. *deber* = pestilence. Interpreted in 1 Cor. 15. 55 as "sting". First occ. Ex. 5. 3.
repentance = compassion [on them].
eyes. Fig. *Anthropopatheia.* Ap. 6.

15 he: i.e. Ephraim.
fruitful. Used by Fig. *Irony* (Ap. 6), his name being Ephraim = fruitful. Ref. to Pent. (Gen. 41. 52; 48. 19).
an east wind. Heb. *ḳādīm*; not a scorching wind, *shirocco* (Gen. 41. 6. Jer. 18. 17. Ezek. 17. 10; 19. 12).
wind. Heb. *rūach.* Ap. 9.
his spring, &c. Ref. to Pent. (Deut. 33. 28).
he shall spoil = he shall plunder. Fulfilled in Shalmaneser shortly after, and since that day this prophecy stands fulfilled. The book ends with hope, in the final section below. **16 Samaria.** See 2 Kings 17. 6.
their. Some codices, with one early printed edition, Aram., Sept., and Syr., read "and their".

14. 1-8 (G[2], p. 1222). THE RETURN.
(*Repeated Alternation.*)

G[2] | H[1] | 1, 2-. Jehovah. Invitation.
  J[1] | -2, 3. Israel. Confession. Words provided.
 H[2] | 4-7. Jehovah. Promises.
  J[2] | 8-. Israel. Confession. Words used.
 H[3] | -8. Jehovah. Blessing.

1 return. Cp. 12. 6. Joel 2. 13.
unto = quite up to. Heb. *'ad*; not merely "toward", which would be *'el.* **the LORD.** Heb. Jehovah. Ap. 4. II. **God.** Heb. Elohim. Ap. 4. I. **for.** Cp. 13. 9. **iniquity.** Heb. *'āvāh.* Ap. 44. iv. Some codices, with three early printed editions and Sept., read "transgressions" (pl.). **2 words.** Note the correspondence in the Structure ("J[1]" and "J[2]"): confession commanded, and the command obeyed. **turn** = return, or turn back, as in *v.* 1. **say.** Cp. Luke 15. 18, 19. **graciously** = O Gracious One. See notes on 3. 5, and 8. 3. Eminent Jewish commentators take this as a title of the Messiah. There is no "us" in the Heb. **so will we render.** Quoted in Heb. 13. 15. **render** = pay (as vows) by offering what is due (Pss. 66. 13, 14; 116. 14, 18. Jonah 2. 9). **calves** = oxen. Put by Fig. *Metonymy* (of Subject), Ap. 6, for the sacrifices offered (Ps. 51. 17). **lips.** Put by Fig. *Metonymy* (of Cause), Ap. 6, for the confession, &c., made by them. Cp. Pss. 69. 30, 31; 116. 17; 141. 2. Heb. 13. 15. **3 Asshur, &c.** See 5. 13, 12. 1; and cp. Jer. 31. 18. **we will not ride.** Some codices, with four early printed editions and Syr., read "nor upon horses will we ride". Ref. to Pent. (Deut. 17. 16). Cp. Ps. 33. 17. Isa. 30. 2, 16; 31. 1. **the work of our hands.** Put by Fig. *Metonymy* (of Subject), Ap. 6, for idols of all kinds. **for in Thee** = O Thou in Whom. **the fatherless**: i.e. Israel's orphaned folk. Here we have the key to the symbolic names of ch. 1:—

Gomer shows that the measure of iniquity was full.
Jezreel denotes the consequent scattering.
Lo-Ruhamah (the second child, the girl) foreshadows Israel as the unpitied one.
Lo-Ammi (the last child) denotes Israel's present condition.
Ammi represents Israel's yet future position (2. 1).
Ruhamah = pitied, Lo-Ruhamah's new name (2. 23).

findeth mercy = R hamah = pitied. Referring to Israel's final restoration. See note on 2. 23. **4 backsliding.** Cp. 11. 7. Jer. 5. 6; 14. 7. **him**: i.e. Israel. **5 the dew.** See notes on 6. 4; 13. 3. **grow** = blossom. **cast forth** = strike out. **his roots.** The spurs of Lebanon have the appearance of outspreading roots. **as** = like [those of]. **6 his smell** = his fragrance, or be fragrant, like.

689-611 **7 They that dwell under his shadow shall [1]return; they shall revive *as* the corn, and grow as the vine: °the scent thereof *shall be* as the °wine of Lebanon.**

J^2 (p. 1223) **8 Ephraim °*shall say,* "What have I to do any more with idols? °I have heard *Him,* °and observed Him: °I *am* like a green fir tree.**

H^3 **°From Me is °thy fruit found.**

A (p. 1208) **9 °Who *is* °wise, and he shall understand these *things?* °prudent, and he shall know them? for the ways of [1]the LORD *are* °right, and the °just shall walk in them: but the °transgressors shall °fall therein."**

7 the scent thereof = his memory or remembrance [pleasant] as, &c. So the Sept.
wine. Heb. *yayin.* Ap. 27. I.
8 shall say. In obedience to the command in *v.* 1.
I have heard = I have heard and obeyed.
and observed = and regarded. Contrast 13. 7.
I am like: or, I like a green cypress [will overshadow him]. A verb must be supplied. Referring to "shadow" in *v.* 7.
From Me, &c. This member ("H^3") is Jehovah's reply. Note the emphatic "I" repeated. Cp. Jer. 31. 18.
thy fruit found. Fruitfulness provided, as well as protection and grace.
9 Who is wise . . . ? Fig. *Erotēsis.* Ap. 6. Concluding the whole book, like Ps. 107. 43.
wise. Heb. *chākām* (adj.). See note on Prov. 1. 2. Cp. Ps. 107. 43. Jer. 9. 12. Dan. 12. 10.
prudent = [who is] understanding? Heb. *bīnah.* See note on Prov. 1. 2. Here it is the passive = gifted with understanding. **right** = upright. Ref. to Pent. (Deut. 32. 4). Cp. Job 26. 14; 36. 23. Pss. 18. 30; 77. 19; 145. 17. Prov. 10. 29. Dan. 4. 37. **just** = righteous. **transgressors.** Heb. *pāsha'.* Ap. 44. ix. **fall therein** = stumble in them. Cp. Ps. 119. 165. Prov. 4. 19; 10. 29; 11. 5; 15. 9. Mic. 2. 7. Nah. 3. 3. 1 Cor. 1. 23, 24. 1 Pet. 2. 7, 8.

JOEL.

THE STRUCTURE OF THE BOOK AS A WHOLE.

(*Alternation.*)

1. 1. THE TITLE.

C^1 | A | 1. 2, 3. CALL TO HEAR.
B | 1. 4–13. JUDGMENTS. INFLICTED.
A | 1. 14—2. 17. CALL TO REPENT.
B | 2. 18—3. 21. JUDGMENTS. REMOVED.

For the Canonical order and place of the Prophets, see Ap. 1, and p. 1206.
For the Chronological order of the Prophets, see Ap. 77.
For the *Formulæ* of Prophetic utterance, see Ap. 82.
For the Inter-relation of the Prophetic Books, see Ap. 78.
For the Inter-relation of the Minor (or Shorter) Prophets, see p. 1206.
For the References to the Pentateuch by the Prophets, see Ap. 92.

Joel's prophecy is undated. No references are made to *time,* because it looks onward to the time of the end, and to the events that will usher in "the Day of the Lord".

As Hosea was sent to guilty Israel, so Joel was sent to guilty Judah. Hosea's "burden" relates to the end of the Northern Kingdom; Joel's prophecy relates to the end of the Kingdom of Judah, and probably covers the last seven years of Zedekiah. In that case he would commence in the fifth year of Jehoiachin's captivity, the very year that Ezekiel begins, and 100 years after Isaiah ends. If "Joel completed his prophecy before Amos collected his" (as alleged), then, in the period of Uzziah-Jeroboam II, which ended in 687 B.C., there is no historical background for Joel's burning words concerning Judah and the great "Day of the Lord".

Similar passages in Joel 3. 16 and Amos 1. 2 no more prove that Amos quoted from Joel than they prove that Joel quoted from Amos. The same may be said of Joel 1. 15 and Isa. 13. 6.

In Joel's summons to fasting and prayer, many as are the classes invited, no mention is made of the royal house; and, throughout his prophecy, no king of Judah is mentioned later than Jehoshaphat, and then only in connection with his "valley".

But if the period covered by Joel be taken as from 488 to 477 B.C., then we have, as contemporaries :—

Jeremiah	in Jerusalem;	All prophesying together during the last seven years of the kingdom of Judah.
Joel	in Judah;	
Daniel	in Babylon;	
Ezekiel	in Babylonia and in the Land.	

JOEL.

TITLE 388-477? 1 °THE word of °the LORD that came to
°Joel °the son of Pethuel.
A (p. 1224) 2 °Hear this, °ye °old men, and give ear, all
ye inhabitants of the land. °Hath this been in
your days, or even in the days of your fathers?
3 °Tell ye your °children of it, and *let* your
°children *tell* their °children, and their °chil-
dren another generation.
B A^1 (p. 1225) 4 °That which the °palmerworm hath left
hath the °locust eaten; and that which the
locust hath left hath the °cankerworm eaten;
and that which the cankerworm hath left hath
the °caterpiller eaten.
A^2 B a 5 Awake, ye drunkards, and weep; and howl,
all ye drinkers of °wine,
b because of the °new wine; for it is cut off from
your mouth.
6 For °a nation is come up upon °My land,
strong, and without number, whose teeth *are*
the teeth of a lion, and he hath the cheek teeth
of a great lion.
7 °He hath laid °My vine waste, and °barked
°My fig tree: he hath made it clean bare, and
cast *it* away; the branches thereof are made
white.
C c 8 °Lament like a virgin girded with sackcloth
for the husband of her youth.
d 9 The °meat offering and the °drink offering
is cut off from the house of [1]the LORD; the
priests, [1]the LORD'S °ministers, mourn.
10 The °field is °wasted, the °land mourneth;
for the corn is wasted: the °new wine is dried
up, the oil languisheth.
B a 11 Be ye ashamed, O ye husbandmen; howl,
O [2]ye vinedressers,
b for the wheat and for the barley; because the
harvest of the field is perished.
12 The [7]vine is dried up, and the [7]fig tree
languisheth; the pomegranate tree, the palm
tree also, and the apple tree, *even* all the
trees of the field, are withered: because joy is
withered away from the sons of °men.
C c 13 Gird yourselves, and lament, ye priests:
howl, [2]ye °ministers of the altar: come, °lie
all night in sackcloth, ye ministers of my °God:
d for the [9]meat offering and the [9]drink offering
is withholden from the house of your °God.

1 TITLE. The word of the LORD. Therefore not Joel's. This is the Divine key to the book: Joel's pen, but not Joel's words. Cp. Acts 1. 16 for a similar fact concerning David.

the LORD. Heb. Jehovah. Ap. 4. II.

Joel = Jehovah [is] GOD.

the son of Pethuel. This does not imply that Pethuel was a prophet. It merely distinguishes this Joel from others of the same name.

2 Hear. Note this indication of the formula of Joel's prophetic utterances. See Ap. 82.

ye. Heb. has no proper vocative. The simple Noun with the Article takes its place.

old men. Not official elders, but those whose memory goes back farthest.

Hath . . . ? Fig. *Erotēsis* (Ap. 6), for emphasis. Cp. 2. 2.

3 Tell ye your children. Ref. to Pent. (Deut. 4. 9; 6. 6, 7; 11. 19). Ap. 92. Cp. Ps. 78. 3–8.

children = sons. Note the Fig. *Climax* (Ap. 6).

1. 4-13 (B, p. 1224). JUDGMENTS. INFLICTED. (*Division.*)

B | A^1 | 4. The Destroyers. Symbolical and General.
| A^2 | 5–13. The Destruction. Literal and Particular.

4 That which, &c. Ref. to Pent. (Deut. 28. 38). Cp. 2. 25. The English of this verse is beautifully idiomatic, but twelve Hebrew words condense the whole. See below.

palmerworm. This is named first of four different stages of the locust. English = hairy caterpiller; Heb. *gāzām*, or the gnawer. The *pupa* stage.

locust. Heb. *'arbeh* = the swarmer. The *imago* stage.

cankerworm. Heb. *yeleḳ* = the devourer.

caterpiller. Heb. *ḥasil* = the consumer. The *larva* stage. Cp. 2. 25, and Nah. 3. 15, 16.

These four words show the completeness of the destroying agencies. The Heb. reads:—

"Gnawer's remnant,
Swarmer eats:
Swarmer's remnant,
Devourer eats;
Devourer's remnant,
Consumer eats."

1. 5-13 (A^2, above). THE DESTRUCTION. LITERAL AND PARTICULAR. (*Alternations.*)

A^2 | B | a | 5–. PEOPLE. Call to Awake and Howl.
b | –5-7. Reason. Vine and Fig. Laid waste.
C | c | 8. LAND. Call to Lament.
d | 9, 10. Reason. Offerings cut off.
B | *a* | 11–. PEOPLE. Call to be Ashamed and Howl.
b | –11, 12. Reason. Corn and Wine perished.
C | *c* | 13–. PRIESTS. Call to Lament.
d | –13. Reason. Offerings withholden.

5 wine. Heb. *yayin*. Ap. 27. I.

new wine. Heb. *'āsis*. Ap. 27. V.

6 a nation. See 2. 20; and cp. Dan. 11. Put for the great destroying powers which are symbolized in *v.* 4 by the locusts. Cp. 2. 2, 11, 25. Rev. 9. **My land.** So called because Jehovah is about to put in His claim. The end-time is here referred to, when He will do this: "the day of the LORD". See *v.* 15, and 2. 1, &c. **7 He.** The nation of *v.* 6. **My vine . . . My fig tree.** Note this "My", for Jehovah is about to recover His People Israel, as the issue of "the day of the LORD". Cp. Ps. 80. 8, 14. Isa. 5. 1–6; 27. 2. Hos. 10. 1. Also for the fig-tree cp. Hos. 9. 10. Matt. 21. 19. Luke 13. 6, 7. **barked** = reduced to splinters or chips. Heb. *ḳeẓāphāh*. Occurs only here. The root is connected with foam, cp. Hos. 10. 7. **8 Lament.** Fem. agreeing with "land", *v.* 6. **9 meat offering** = the meal or gift offering. Heb. *minchāh*. See Ap. 43. II. iii. Ref. to Pent. (Lev. 2). Ap. 92. Cp. 2. 14. **drink offering.** Ref. to Pent. (Ex. 29. 40. Lev. 23. 13. Num. 15. 3–10) and Ap. 92. See Ap. 43. II. x. **ministers.** Ref. to Pent. (Num. 3. 6, &c.). Ap. 92. **10 field . . . wasted.** Note the Fig. *Paronomasia* (Ap. 6). Heb. *shuddad . . . sādeh*. **land** = soil. Heb. *'ădāmāh*. Not the same word as in *vv.* 2, 6, 14, &c., in this book; but the same as in 2. 21. Verses 10–12 show why the offerings cannot be brought. **new wine.** Heb. *tīrōsh*. Ap. 27. II. Same word as in 2. 19, 24. Not the same as in *v.* 5 and 3. 18. **12 men.** Heb. *'ādām*. Ap. 14. I. **13 ministers of the altar.** Ref. to Pent. (Ex. 30. 20). Ap. 92. **lie all night, &c.** The symbol of mourning; cp. 2 Sam. 12. 16. **God.** Heb. Elohim. Ap. 4. I.

A D F (p. 1226) 488-477 14 Sanctify ye a fast, call °a solemn assembly, °gather the elders *and* all the inhabitants of the land *into* the house of [1]the LORD your [13]God, and cry unto [1]the LORD,

G 15 Alas for the day! for °the day of [1]the LORD *is* at hand, and as a °destruction from °the ALMIGHTY shall it come.

H 16 °Is not the meat cut off before our eyes, *yea,* °joy and gladness from the house of our [13]God?

17 °The seed is rotten under their clods, the garners are laid desolate, the barns are broken down; for the corn is withered.

18 How do °the beasts groan! the herds of cattle are perplexed, because they have no pasture; yea, the flocks of sheep are made desolate.

19 O [1]LORD, °to Thee will I cry: for °the fire hath devoured the pastures of the °wilderness, and the flame hath burned all the trees of the field.

20 The beasts of the field cry also unto Thee: for the °rivers of waters are dried up, and the fire hath devoured the pastures of the [19]wilderness.

E J **2** Blow ye the trumpet in °Zion, and °sound an alarm in °My °holy mountain: let all the inhabitants of the land tremble:

K for °the day of °the LORD cometh, for *it is* nigh at hand;

L 2 °A day of darkness and of gloominess, a day of clouds and of thick darkness, as the °morning spread upon the mountains: °a great people and a strong; there hath not been ever the like, neither shall be any more after it, *even* to the years of many generations.

3 °A fire devoureth before °them; and behind them a flame burneth: the land *is* as °the garden of Eden before them, and behind them °a desolate wilderness; yea, and nothing shall escape them.

4 °The appearance of them *is* as the appearance of horses; and as °horsemen, so shall they run.

5 °Like the noise of chariots °on the tops of mountains shall they °leap, like the noise of a flame of fire that devoureth the stubble, °as a strong people set in battle array.

6 Before their face the °people shall be much pained: all faces shall gather °blackness.

7 They shall run like mighty men; they shall climb the wall like °men of war; and they shall march every one on his ways, and they shall not break their ranks:

8 Neither shall one °thrust another; they shall °walk every one in his path: and *when* they fall upon the °sword, °they shall not °be wounded.

1. 14—3. 27 (*A*, p. 1224). CALL TO REPENTANCE. (*Simple and Extended Alternations.*)

A | D | F | 1. 14. Call to Fast.
G | 1. 15. Reason.
H | 1. 16-20. Consequences.
E | J | 2. 1-. Call to Blow the Trumpet.
K | 2. -1. Reason.
L | 2. 2-11. Consequences. } People.
D | F | 2. 12-13-. Call to Fast.
G | 2. -13. Reason.
H | 2. 14. Consequences.
E | J | 2. 15-17-. Call to Blow the Trumpet.
K | 2. -17. Reason.
L | 2. 18—3. 21. Consequences. } Priests.

14 a solemn assembly = a day of restraint. Heb. *'ăzārāh.* Occurs only here, in 2. 15; 2 Kings 10. 20; and Isa. 1. 13. Ref. to Pent. (Lev. 23. 36. Num. 29. 35. Deut. 16. 8) where the fem. form *'ăzereth* is used (Ap. 92). It is found also in 2 Chron. 7. 9. Neh. 8. 18.

gather the elders. There being no mention of a king in this book is held by some as pointing to the time of Athaliah's usurpation. But see notes on p. 1224, and Ap. 77.

15 the day of the LORD. See note on Isa. 2. 12. This is the great subject of Joel's prophecy, already then "at hand".

destruction from the ALMIGHTY. Note the Fig. *Paronomasia* (Ap. 6). Heb. *k^e shod mishshaddai* = mighty destruction from the ALMIGHTY. Cp. Isa. 13. 6.

the ALMIGHTY = the All-bountiful. Heb. *Shaddai.* Ap. 4. VII. In this connection it is similar to "the wrath of the Lamb" (Rev. 6. 16, 17) in its violent contrast. **16 Is not . . . ?** Fig. *Erotēsis.* Ap. 6.

joy and gladness. Ref. to Pent. (Deut. 12. 6, 7; 16. 11, 14, 15).

17 The seed, &c. Note the Fig. *Anabasis* (Ap. 6) in this verse. **18 the beasts.** Cp. Hos. 4. 3.

19 to Thee will I cry. Cp. Ps. 50. 15.

the fire. Cp. 2. 3.

wilderness = common land.

20 rivers = waters of the *Aphīḳim.* See note on "channels", 2 Sam. 22. 16.

2. 1 Zion. See Ap. 68.

sound an alarm. Ref. to Pent. (Num. 10. 5, 9). Ap. 92.

My. Note the Pronoun, and see notes on 1. 6, 7.

holy mountain = mountain of My sanctuary.

holy. See note on Ex. 3. 5.

the day of the LORD. See notes on 1. 15. This is the subject of the book. Cp. Obad. 15. Zeph. 1. 14, 15.

the LORD. Heb. Jehovah. Ap. 4. II.

2 A day, &c. Cp. Amos 5. 18, 20.

morning = blackness, or darkness. Heb. *shaḥar.* A *Homonym* with two meanings: (1) *to be black* or *dark* (Job 30. 30). Hence put for seeking in the early morning while yet dark (Pss. 78. 34; 63. 1. Prov. 1. 28. Isa. 26. 9. Hos. 5. 15, &c.); (2) *dawn* or *morning* (Gen. 19. 15; 32. 24, 26. Josh. 6. 15. Hos. 6. 3; 10. 15, &c.).

a great people. Symbolized by the locusts in 1. 4.

3 A fire, &c. Cp. 1. 19, 20.

them. The northern army (*v.* 11) symbolized by the locusts of 1. 4.

the garden of Eden. Ref. to Pent. (Gen. 2. 8; 13. 10). Ap. 92. Cp. Isa. 51. 3. Ezek. 36. 35.

a desolate wilderness. Cp. 3. 19. Ps. 107. 34.

4 The appearance of them: i.e. the army of *v.* 20, symbolized by the locusts of 1. 4. Cp. Rev. 9. 7. **horsemen** = war-horses (Hab. 1. 8). **5 Like the noise, &c.** Cp. Rev. 9. 9. Connect this with the end of *v.* 4. **on the tops, &c.** The Heb. accents connect this with the leaping, not with the chariots. **leap** = rattle along. **as a strong people.** Cp. *v.* 2. Not locusts. The symbol must not be confused with what is symbolized. **6 people** = people's. **blackness** = paleness. **7 men.** Heb. pl. of *'ĕnōsh.* Ap. 14. III. **8 thrust** = jostle, or press. **walk** = march, as in *v.* 7. **sword** = weapons. Heb. *shelach* = missiles, supposed to be "a late word" because not used earlier than 2 Chron. 23. 10; 32. 5. Neh. 4. 17, 23; but it is used in Job 33. 18; 36. 12. Song 4. 13. **they shall not, &c.** Cp. Rev. 9. The whole scene belongs to "the day of the LORD". Only confusion arises from not keeping the symbol distinct from what is symbolized. **be wounded** = stop.

488-477 9 They shall °run to and fro °in the city;
they shall run upon the wall, they shall °climb
up upon the houses; they shall °enter in at the
windows °like a thief.

10 The earth shall quake before [3]them; the
heavens shall tremble: °the sun and the moon
shall be dark, and the stars shall withdraw
their shining:

11 And [1]the LORD shall utter His voice before
His army: for His camp *is* very great: for *He*
is strong that executeth His word: for [1]the day
of [1]the LORD *is* °great and very terrible; and
°who can abide it?

D F 12 °Therefore also now, °saith [1]the LORD,
(p. 1226) °turn ye *even* °to Me °with all your heart,
°and with fasting, and with weeping, and with
mourning:

13 And °rend your heart, and not °your garments, and [12]turn unto [1]the LORD your °God:

G for °He *is* gracious and merciful, slow to anger,
and of great °kindness, and °repenteth Him of
the °evil.

H 14 °Who knoweth *if* He will °return and
[13]repent, and leave °a blessing behind Him;
even a °meat offering and a drink offering
unto [1]the LORD your [13]God?

E J 15 [1]Blow the trumpet in Zion, sanctify a fast,
call °a solemn assembly:

16 °Gather the People, °sanctify the congregation, assemble the elders, °gather the children,
and those that suck the breasts: let the bridegroom go forth of his chamber, and the bride
out of her °closet.

17 Let °the priests, the ministers of [1]the
LORD, weep °between the porch and the altar,
and let them say, °"Spare Thy People, O
[1]LORD, and give not °Thine heritage to
reproach, that the °heathen should rule over
them:

K °wherefore should they say among the °people,
'Where *is* their [13]God?'"

L M¹ 18 Then will [1]the LORD be °jealous for His
(p. 1227) land, and pity His people.

19 Yea, [1]the LORD will answer and say unto
His People, °"Behold, I will send you °corn,
and °wine, and oil, and ye shall be satisfied
therewith: and I will no more °make you a
reproach among the [17]heathen:

N¹ 20 But I will remove far off from you °the
northern *army*, and will drive him into a land
barren and desolate, with his face toward °the
east sea, and his hinder part toward °the utmost sea, and his °stink shall come up, and his
ill savour shall come up, because °he °hath
done great things.

9 run . . . in the city . . . climb . . . enter, &c. These are put for the acts of men.

like a thief. A thief is a man (not an insect); so are these. Cp. Matt. 24. 43, 44. Luke 12. 39. 1 Thess. 5. 2. 2 Pet. 3. 10.

10 the sun and the moon shall be dark. Another proof of what is signified; and that this prophecy concerns what is future. Cp. 3. 15. See Matt. 24. 29. Cp. Isa. 13. 10. Ezek. 32. 7, 8. Acts 2. 20. Rev. 6. 12.

11 great, &c. Cp. *v.* 31. Jer. 30. 7. Amos 5. 18. Zeph. 1. 15.

who can abide it? Ref. to Pent. (Num. 24. 23). Ap. 92. Cp. Jer. 10. 10. Zeph. 1. 14. Mal. 3. 2.

12 Therefore, &c. Another call ("*F*", *v.* 12, corresponding with "F", *v.* 1). See the Structure, p. 1226.

saith the LORD=[is] Jehovah's oracle.

turn ye=turn ye back, or return.

to=quite up to, as in Hos. 14. 1.

with all your heart. Ref. to Pent. (Deut. 6. 5).

and. Some codices, with one early printed edition, Syr., and Vulg., omit this "and".

13 rend your heart. Cp. Pss. 34. 18; 51. 17.

your garments. Ref. to Pent. (Gen. 37. 34). Ap. 92.

God. Heb. Elohim. Ap. 4. I.

He is gracious, &c. Ref. to Pent. (Ex. 34. 6, 7. Num. 14. 18). Ap. 92. Cp. 2 Chron. 30. 9. Neh. 9. 17, 31. Pss. 86. 5, 15; 103. 8; 145. 8.

kindness=grace.

repenteth. Fig. *Anthropopatheia.* Ap. 6.

evil. Heb. *rā'a'.* Ap. 44. viii.

14 Who knoweth . . . ? That this refers to Jehovah is clear from Jonah 3. 9.

return=turn away from [His fierce anger], as in Jonah 3. 9, where it is ascribed to "God". Same word as in *v.* 12.

a blessing: i. e. a new harvest. Cp. Isa. 65. 8.

meat . . . drink offering, &c. See note on 1. 9, 13.

15 a solemn assembly=a day of restraint. See note on 1. 14.

16 Gather=Gather in.

sanctify the congregation=hallow a convocation. Ref. to Pent. (Ex. 19. 10, 22). Ap. 92.

gather=gather out.

closet=bridal canopy. See notes on Ps. 19. 5 and Isa. 4. 5. The only three occurrences of Heb. *chuppāh.*

17 the priests, the ministers of the LORD. See note on 1. 9.

between, &c. Cp. Ezek. 8. 16.

Spare Thy People, &c. Ref. to Pent. (Ex. 32. 11, 12. Deut. 9. 26, 29). Ap. 92. Cp. Neh. 13. 22.

Thine heritage. Ref. to Pent. (Deut. 32. 9). Ap. 92.

heathen=nations.

wherefore . . . ? Fig. *Erotēsis.* Ap. 6. Ref. to Pent. (Deut. 9. 26–29). Ap. 92. Cp. Pss. 42. 10; 79. 10; 115. 2. Mic. 7. 10.

people=peoples.

2. 18—3. 21 (*L*, p. 1226). CONSEQUENCES.
(*Repeated Alternation.*)

L M¹ | 2. 18, 19. Good bestowed. Land and People.
N¹ | 2. 20. Evil removed. Enemy cut off.
M² | 2. 21–32. Good bestowed. Land and People.
N² | 3. 1–16–. Evil removed. Enemy cut off.
M³ | 3. –16–18. Good bestowed. Land and People.
N³ | 3. 19. Evil removed. Enemies cut off.
M⁴ | 3. 20, 21. Good bestowed. Land and People.

18 jealous for His land, &c. Ref. to Pent. (Deut. 32. 36–43). Ap. 92. These remind us of the concluding words of the "Song of Moses", and sum up the object and outcome of all the events which go to make up "the day of the LORD". **19 Behold.** Fig. *Asterismos* (Ap. 6), to call attention to the "blessing" mentioned in *v.* 14. **corn, &c.** Cp. 1. 10; Mal. 3. 11, 12. The Article is used with each of these in the Hebrew text. **wine.** Heb. *tīrōsh.* Ap. 27. II. **make you a reproach.** See note on "rule", *v.* 17. **20 the northern army.** This is what the "locusts" of 1. 4 are the symbol of. The prophet does not "forget for a moment" the locusts of 1. 4; but, here explains the symbol. Locusts do not come from the north. The armies of Rev. 9, Dan. 11 do. **the east sea**: i. e. the Dead Sea. Cp. Ezek. 47. 18. Zech. 14. 8. **the utmost sea**=the Great Sea. Ref. to Pent. (Deut. 11. 24; 34. 2). Ap. 92. Cp. "hinder" in Zech. 14. 8. **stink shall come up.** Referring to the destruction of Isa. 66. 24. **he.** The invader, the antichrist or beast of Dan. 7 and 8. **hath done great things**=he magnified himself to do great things. Cp. Dan. 8. 9–11; 11. 36, and notes there. This is quite inapplicable to locusts.

M[2] O[1] P[1] (p. 1228) 21 °Fear not, O °land; be glad and rejoice:
Q[1] for [1]the LORD °will do great things.
P[2] 22 °Be not afraid, ye beasts of the field: for
488-477 the °pastures of the wilderness do spring,
Q[2] for the tree beareth her fruit, the fig tree and
the vine do yield their °strength.
P[3] 23 °Be glad then, ye °children of Zion, and
rejoice in [1]the LORD your [13]God:
Q[3] for He hath given you the former rain °moder-
ately, and He will cause to come down for you
the rain, the former rain, and the latter rain
°in the first *month.*
24 And the °floors shall be full of °wheat,
and the °fats shall overflow with [19]wine and oil.
25 And I will °restore to you the years that
the °locust hath eaten, the cankerworm, and
the caterpiller, and the palmerworm, °My great
army which I sent among you.
26 And °ye shall °eat in plenty, and be satisfied, and °praise the name of [1]the LORD your
[13]God, That hath dealt wondrously with you:
and My people °shall never be ashamed.
27 And °ye shall know that *I am* in the
midst of Israel, and *that I am* [1]the LORD your
[13]God, and none else: and My people [26]shall
never be ashamed.

O[2] R **28 And it shall come to pass °afterward,**
***that* °I will pour out My °spirit upon °all flesh;**
and your sons °and your daughters shall °pro-
phesy, your old men shall dream dreams, your
young men shall see visions:
29 And also upon the °servants and upon the
handmaids in those days will I pour out My
[28]spirit.
S **30 And °I will shew wonders in the heavens**
and in the earth, °blood, and fire, and pillars
of smoke.
31 The [10]sun shall be turned into darkness,
and the moon into blood, before the [11]great
and °the terrible day of [1]the LORD come.
R **32 And it shall come to pass, *that* whosoever**
shall call on the name of [1]the LORD shall be
delivered: for °in mount Zion and in °Jeru-
salem shall be °deliverance, °as [1]the LORD
°hath said, and in the °remnant whom [1]the
LORD °shall call.

2. 21-32 (M[2], p. 1227). GOOD BESTOWED. LAND AND PEOPLE. (*Division.*)

M[2] | O[1] | 21-27. Temporal blessings.
| O[2] | 28-32. Spiritual blessings.

2. 21-27 (O[1], above). TEMPORAL BLESSINGS. (*Repeated Alternation.*)

O[1] | P[1] | 21-. Apostrophe to the Soil.
Q[1] | -21. Reason.
P[2] | 22-. Apostrophe to the Beasts.
Q[2] | -22. Reason.
P[3] | 23-. Apostrophe to the People.
Q[3] | -23-27. Reason.

21 Fear not. Fig. *Apostrophe.* Ap. 6.
land=soil. Heb. *'ădāmāh.* See note on 1. 10.
will do great things. Greater than the foe himself (*v.* 20).
22 Be not afraid, &c. Fig. *Apostrophe* (Ap. 6), as in *v.* 21. Cp. 1. 18, 20.
pastures, &c. Cp. 1. 19.
strength=abundance.
23 Be glad, &c. Fig. *Apostrophe* (Ap. 6), to the people. **children**=sons.
moderately=in due measure. Ref. to Pent. (Lev. 26. 4. Deut. 11. 14; 28. 12). Ap. 92.
in the first month=[as at] the first, or [as] aforetime. Obviously, the two rains do not come in one and the same month.
24 floors=threshing-floors.
wheat=corn.
fats=vats. Anglo-Saxon (northern) *faet,* (southern) *vat*=a vessel, or cask. Lit.=that which contains. Heb. *yeḳeb*=the reservoir for receiving the wine; not *gath,* the press where the grapes are pressed. See note on Isa. 5. 2. **25 restore**: make good.
locust, &c. See note on 1. 4.
My great army. Here the symbol, and what is symbolized, are joined together, and the army of men (*vv.* 11, 20) is implied by the Fig. *Hypocatastasis* (Ap. 6).
26 ye shall eat, &c. Ref. to Pent. (Lev. 26. 5). Ap. 92.
eat=eat on.
praise, &c. Ref. to Pent. (Lev. 19. 24. Deut. 12. 7; 16. 11; 26. 11). Ap. 92.
shall never be ashamed. This is repeated at the end of the next verse by the Fig. *Epistrophe* (Ap. 6) for emphasis. Not "a copyist's error", as alleged.
27 ye shall know, &c. Ref. to Pent. (Lev. 26. 11-13. Deut. 23. 14). Ap. 92. Cp. Ezek. 37. 26-28.

2. 28-32 (O[2], above). SPIRITUAL BLESSINGS. (*Introversion.*)

O[2] | R | 28, 29. Afterward. After the restoration. Gifts from God.
S | 30, 31. Before the day of the LORD.
R | 32. Afterward. After the restoration. Deliverance from God.

28 afterward: i.e. after the "good bestowed" had begun to be enjoyed (2. 21-27, O[2] above): for the nation had been restored under Ezra and Nehemiah; "the light had sprung up" (Isa. 42. 7. Matt. 4. 12-16. Luke 2. 32); "the days of the Son of Man" were then present (Luke 17. 22). "Afterward" would come the days of the Spirit; and "this is that" which was seen on "the day of Pentecost", when Joel 2. 28, 29 began to be fulfilled. Had the nation repented at the summons of Peter in Acts 3. 18-26, "all things which God had spoken by the mouth of all His holy prophets" would have been fulfilled, including Joel 2. 30, 31, and 32 (S and *R*). Mal. 4. 5 also would have been taken of John the Baptist *if they had received it* (Matt. 11. 14): the Heb. *'achărĕi-kēn* always referring to what follows. **I will pour out My spirit.** Note the Fig. *Epanadiplosis* (Ap. 6) used to emphasise the statement included within this sentence, and the repetition of it at the end of *v.* 29. **spirit.** Heb. *rūach.* Ap. 9. This must be put by Fig. *Metonymy* (of Cause), Ap. 6, for the "power from on high", or spiritual gifts. See note on Acts 2. 4. God the Holy Spirit cannot be "poured out". **all flesh.** Put by Fig. *Synecdoche* (of Genus), Ap. 6, for all sorts and conditions of men, as described in the words which follow. **and your daughters.** Women are not excluded from spiritual gifts. **prophesy.** Not necessarily foretelling, but forthtelling, by speaking for God. Only such as were thus called and gifted could be His spokesmen. Cp. Num. 11. 16, 17, 29. See Ap. 78. **29 servants, &c.** Any whom God might call. Elisha was a ploughman, Amos a herdsman. **30 I will shew.** Cp. Matt. 24. 29. Mark 13. 24. **blood, and fire.** These are symbols of Divine judgment; not of salvation by grace. **31 the terrible, &c.** This is the time for the fulfilment of Joel's prophecy. Cp. 2. 1, 11. Mal. 4. 5. **32 in mount Zion.** Cp. Isa. 46. 13; 59. 20. Obad. 17. Zech. 14. 1-5. Rom. 11. 26. **Jerusalem.** As distinct from Mount Zion. See Ap. 68. **deliverance**=a delivered remnant. Cp. 2. 3. **as**=according as. **hath said**: by Joel and other prophets. **remnant**=an escaped set. **shall call**=is going to call.

N^2 T^1 (p. 1229) 488-477 3 °For, °behold, °in those days, and in that
time, when I shall °bring again the cap-
tivity of Judah and Jerusalem,
2 °I will also gather °all nations, and will
bring them down into °the valley of °Jehosha-
phat,

U^1 and °will plead with them there for °My People and *for* °My heritage °Israel, whom they
have scattered among the nations, and parted
My land.
3 And °they have cast lots for My People;
and have given a boy for an harlot, and sold
a girl for °wine, that they might drink.

V^1 4 Yea, and what have ye to do with Me,
O Tyre, and Zidon, and all the °coasts of
°Palestine? will ye °render Me a recompence?
and °if ye recompense Me, swiftly *and* speedily
will I return your recompence upon your own
head;
5 Because ye have taken My silver and My
gold, and have carried into your temples My
goodly °pleasant things:
6 The °children also of Judah and the °chil-
dren of Jerusalem have ye sold unto °the
Grecians, that ye might remove them far from
their border.
7 [1] Behold, °I will raise them out of the place
whither ye have sold them, and will return your
recompence upon your own head:
8 And I will sell your sons and your daughters into the hand of the [6] children of Judah,
and they shall sell them to the °Sabeans, to
a °people far off: for °the LORD hath spoken *it*.

T^2 9 °Proclaim ye this among the °Gentiles;
°Prepare war, wake up the mighty men, let
all the °men of war draw near; let them
come up:
10 °Beat your plowshares into swords, and
your °pruninghooks into spears: let the weak
say, "*I am* strong."
11 °Assemble yourselves, and come, [2] all ye
°heathen, and gather yourselves together
round about: °thither cause °Thy mighty ones
to come down, O [8] LORD.
12 Let the [11] heathen be °wakened, °and come
up to [2] the valley of [2] Jehoshaphat:

U^2 for °there will I sit to judge all the heathen
round about.

V^2 13 °Put ye in the °sickle, for °the harvest is
ripe: come, °get you down; for the °press is
full, the °fats overflow; for °their °wickedness
is great.

T^3 14 °Multitudes, multitudes in the valley of
°decision:

U^3 for °the day of [8] the LORD *is* near in the valley
of °decision.

3. 1-16- (N^2, p. 1227). EVIL REMOVED.
(*Extended and Repeated Alternation.*)

N^2 | T^1 | 1, 2-. Assemblage.
U^1 | -2, 3. Place and Act. "I will plead."
V^1 | 4-8. Judgment. Threatened.
T^2 | 9-12-. Assemblage.
U^2 | -12. Place and Act. "I will judge."
V^2 | 13. Judgment. Executed.
T^3 | 14-. Assemblage.
U^3 | -14. Place and Act. Time.
V^3 | 15, 16-. Judgment. Threatened.

1 For. Binding this portion to what immediately precedes.
behold. Fig. *Asterismos*. Ap. 6.
in those days, &c. The prophecy, instead of contracting, widens out to the final judgment of the nations (Matt. 25. 31-46, "when the Son of Man shall come in His glory . . . and sit upon the throne of His glory"). There is no resurrection in this chapter or in that. Here we have the nucleus of the nations of Rev. 21. 24.
bring again the captivity. The idiom for restoring the fortunes of. Ref. to Pent. (Deut. 30. 3). Ap. 92. Cp. Job 42. 10. Ps. 126. 1, 4. Ezek. 16. 53, &c. Amos 9. 14.
2 I will also gather. Cp. Zech. 14. 2-4.
all nations. Put by Fig. *Synecdoche* (of the Whole), Ap. 6, for representatives or people from all nations.
the valley of Jehoshaphat. Between Jerusalem and the Mount of Olives. The name then existing is still preserved in the village of *Sh'afat*; now the *Wady Sitti Miriam* and *Wady Far'aūn*. Mentioned only here, and in *v.* 12; the event recorded in 2 Chron. 20. 21-26 being typical of this scene of the future judgment of the nations. Note "to this day".
Jehoshaphat = Jehovah hath judged.
will plead with them = will judge them. Note the Fig. *Paronomasia* (Ap. 6) for emphasis. Heb. *yehōshāphāṭ venishpaṭṭi*. Cp. Isa. 66. 16. Ezek. 38. 22.
My. Note the force of this pronoun when Jehovah calls Israel again "*Ammi*" (Hos. 2. 23). The judgment of Matt. 25 turns on how the nations had treated "My brethren", and not upon the grounds of justification by faith.
My heritage. Ref. to Pent. (Deut. 32. 9). Ap. 92.
Israel. Note this; not merely Judah, but the twelve-tribed nation.
3 they have, &c. This describes past sufferings. Cp. Obad. 16. Nah. 3. 11.
wine. Heb. *yayin*. Ap. 27. I.
4 coasts = circuit, or region.
Palestine = Philistia.
render = pay back. Cp. Ezek. 25. 15-17.
if = though.
5 pleasant things = things of desire, or valuable things. Cp. Dan. 11. 38.
6 children = sons.
the Grecians. Heb. the sons of the Greeks.
7 I will raise, &c. Cp. Isa. 43. 5, 6, with 49. 12. Jer. 23. 8.
8 Sabeans. Defined as a distant nation. See note on Job 1. 15.
people = nations.
the LORD. Heb. Jehovah. Ap. 4. II.
9 Proclaim, &c. Cp. Isa. 8. 9, 10. Jer. 46. 3, 4. Ezek. 38. 7. **Gentiles** = nations.
Prepare = Hallow.
men. Heb. pl. of *'ĕnōsh*. Ap. 14. III.
10 Beat your plowshares, &c. This precedes the opposite command to be given after this in Isa. 2. 4 and Mic. 4. 3, when Hos. 2. 18 shall be fulfilled. **pruninghooks:** or, scythes. **11 Assemble yourselves.** Cp. 3. 2. Heb. *'ūshū* = haste ye, as in Sept. and Vulg. Occurs only here. **heathen** = nations. **thither.** To the valley of Jehoshaphat. **Thy mighty ones.** Cp. Ps. 103. 20. Isa. 13. 3. **12 wakened.** Cp. 3. 2. **and come up.** Cp. Pss. 96. 13; 98. 9; 110. 6. Isa. 2. 4; 3. 13. Mic. 4. 3. **there will I sit, &c.** See *v.* 2. **13 Put ye in the sickle.** Cp. Matt. 13. 39. Rev. 14. 15, 18. **sickle** = vintage-knife. Heb. *maggāl*. Occurs only here and Jer. 50. 16. **the harvest** = the vintage. Cp. Jer. 51. 33. Hos. 6. 11. **get you down** = go in: i.e. into the winepress = tread ye. **press.** Heb. *gath*. **fats.** Heb. *yekeb*. See note on 2. 24. **their.** The 1611 edition of the A.V. reads "the". **wickedness.** Heb. *rā'a'*. Ap. 44. viii. **14 Multitudes.** Note the Fig. *Epizeuxis* (Ap. 6), to express "great multitudes". **decision** = threshing: i.e. judgment. Cp. Isa. 41. 15. **the day, &c.** Defining the time as well as the place. Cp. 2. 1.

V[3] (p. 1229) 488-477 15 °The sun and the moon shall be darkened,
and the stars shall withdraw their shining.
16 °The LORD also shall °roar out of Zion,
and utter His voice from Jerusalem; and °the
heavens and the earth °shall shake:

M[3] °but [8]the LORD *will be* the °hope of His People, and the °strength of the [6]children of [2]Israel.

17 °So shall ye know that I *am* [8]the LORD your °God [21]dwelling in Zion, °My holy mountain: then shall Jerusalem be °holy, and there shall °no °strangers pass through her any more.

18 And it shall come to pass in °that day, *that* the °mountains shall °drop down °new wine, and the °hills shall flow with milk, and all the °rivers of °Judah shall flow with waters, and °a fountain shall come forth of the house of [8]the LORD, and shall water the valley of °Shittim.

N[3] 19 Egypt shall be a desolation, and Edom shall be a desolate wilderness, for the °violence *against* the [6]children of Judah, because they have shed °innocent blood in their land.

M[4] 20 But [18]Judah shall °dwell for ever, and Jerusalem from generation to generation.

21 For I will °cleanse their blood *that* I °have not °cleansed: for [8]the LORD °dwelleth in Zion.

15 The sun and the moon, &c. Cp. 2. 10, 31.

16 The LORD = But Jehovah. Ap. 4. II.

roar out of Zion. Cp. Jer. 25. 30. Ezek. 38. 18-22. Amos 1. 2. **roar** = thunder.

the heavens . . . shall shake. Cp. 2. 10. Hag. 2. 6.

but the LORD. Cp. Isa. 51. 5, 6.

hope = refuge.

strength = stronghold.

17 So shall ye know, &c. Cp. 2. 27. See note on Ezek. 6. 7.

God. Heb. Elohim. Ap. 4. I.

My holy mountain. Cp. Dan. 11. 45. Obad. 16. Zech. 8. 3.

holy = holiness. See note on Ex. 3. 5.

no strangers. Cp. Isa. 35. 8; 52. 1. Nah. 1. 15. Zech. 14. 21. Rev. 21. 27. **strangers** = foreigners.

18 that day. Cp. *v.* 1.

mountains . . . hills. Cp. Amos 9. 13.

drop down = distil.

new wine = sweet wine, or mead. Heb. *'asīs.* Ap. 27. V.

rivers. Heb. *'aphīḳīm.* See note on "channels", 2 Sam. 22. 16.

Judah. The country; not the People.

a fountain, &c. Ezek. 47. 1. Zech. 14. 8. Rev. 22. 1. See Ap. 68.

Shittim = the acacias. Ref. to Pent. (Num. 33. 49). Ap. 92.

19 violence against. Genitive of Relation. Ap. 17. 5.

innocent blood. Ref. to Pent. (Deut. 19. 10; 27. 25).

20 dwell = remain, or be established.

21 cleanse . . . cleansed = clear . . . cleared. This could be done only by avenging it; for God will "by no means clear the guilty" (Ex. 34. 7. Num. 14. 18); and Egypt, Edom, &c., were guilty (*v.* 19), and are not to be "cleansed", but punished for shedding Judah's blood. The Heb. *nāḳāh* is not used of cleansing, naturally or ceremonially. Not the same word as Isa. 4. 4. The Sept. and Syr. render it "make inquisition for" in 2 Kings 9. 7; and evidently read *nāḳam* = to avenge (akin to *nāḳah*). This would be a vivid ref. to Pent. in Deut. 32. 42, 43, the parallel event. Cp. Rev. 6. 10, 11. **have not** = had not. **dwelleth in Zion** = is about to make His dwelling in Zion. Thus ending like Ezekiel (Ezek. 48. 35), Jehovah Shammah. Cp. 3. 17. Ps. 87. 3. Rev. 21. 3.

AMOS.

THE STRUCTURE OF THE BOOK AS A WHOLE.

(*Repeated Alternation.*)

1. 1, 2. THE TITLE.

B² A¹ | 1. 3—6. 14. LITERAL. PROPHETIC.

B¹ | 7. 1-9. SYMBOLIC. GRASSHOPPERS. FIRE. PLUMBLINE.

A² | 7. 10-17. LITERAL. PROPHETIC.

B² | 8. 1-3. SYMBOLIC. BASKET OF SUMMER FRUIT.

A³ | 8. 4-14. LITERAL. PROPHETIC.

B³ | 9. 1-4. SYMBOLIC. STRIKING THE LINTEL.

A⁴ | 9. 5-15. LITERAL. PROPHETIC.

For the Canonical order and place of the Prophets, see Ap. 1 and p. 1207.
For the Chronological order of the Prophets, see Ap. 77.
For the Inter-relation of the Prophetic Books, see Ap. 78.
For the Inter-relation of the Minor (or Shorter) Prophets, see p. 1206.
For the Formulae of prophetic utterances. See Ap. 82.
For references to the Pentateuch by the Prophets, see Ap. 92.

Amos corresponds to Hosea, the link being Jeroboam II (2 Kings 14. 27). See p. 1206. A native of Judah, he prophesied *in* Israel (1. 1; 7. 10), and *against* Israel. As Jeroboam II died in the fourteenth year of Uzziah king of Judah, Amos was among the earliest of all the prophets (chronologically). Hence:

The references to Israel's *Religious* History show that the Law and Commandments were known (2. 4) though not kept, but despised (2. 4); that Israel was oppressive (2. 6), impure (2. 7), luxurious (6. 1-6), idolatrous (2. 8); that they had had earlier prophets (2. 11; 7. 14; 8. 11); that Israel alone knew the true God (3. 2); that Beth-el and Gilgal had been places of transgression (3. 14; 4. 4; 5. 5).

The references to Israel's *Internal* History show that the nation had once been one (3. 1); that Joseph's history was well known (6. 6); that the high places of Israel were known (7. 9); as was David (6. 5).

The references to Israel's *External* History show that the Exodus was known (2. 10; 3. 1; 5. 25; 9. 7); that the nation had wandered in the wilderness (2. 10; 5. 25); and were idolaters there (5. 25, 26); that the Amorites had been destroyed (2. 9, 10); that Gilead (1. 13) and Sodom (4. 11) had been destroyed.

The references to the *Ceremonial* Law show that it could not have been written after the days of Amos. Note the references to Burnt offerings (4. 4; 5. 22), and the Altar of Burnt offerings (9. 1); Meal offerings (5. 22); Peace offerings (5. 22); Thank offerings (4. 5); Free-will offerings (4. 5); Feast days (5. 21); Feast of New Moon (8. 5); the Sabbath laws (8. 5); laws as to debt (8. 6); to vows (2. 11, 12); to baldness for the dead (8. 10); to pledges (2. 8), and many other things.

As to the dating of Amos, it is "concerning Israel in the days of Uzziah and Jeroboam II, two years before the earthquake" (1. 1).

Uzziah and Jeroboam II were contemporary from the twenty-seventh year of Jeroboam till his forty-second year: i.e. fourteen years (from 701-687 B.C.). See Ap. 50.

The inference is that the earthquake and Jeroboam's end coincide; and that the "gap" of twenty-four years in the history of Israel (see Ap. 50, p. 59) was caused by, or in some way related to, the earthquake (687 B.C.), and before Zachariah began his reign of six months.

"Two years before the earthquake" would be 689-688 (a jubilee year). *At that time the prophecy of Amos commenced* (689 B.C.). He declared the death of Jeroboam by the sword (7. 11), and the captivity (7. 11), which took place seventy-eight years later (in 611 B.C.).

Possibly he was "chased out" of Israel into Judah by Amaziah the priest of Beth-el, on the charge of treason against Jeroboam (7. 10-17); or he may have remained (most probably) and perished in the earthquake, as there is no reference to that catastrophe, which might be expected, if his prophecies had extended *beyond* that great landmark in the history of Israel. It would, in that case, follow that the period covered by Amos was during those two years, which would be 689-687 B.C.

The death of Jeroboam II presumably took place before, or about the time of, the earthquake.

AMOS.

TITLE 689-687 **1** °THE words of °Amos, who was among
the °herdmen of °Tekoa, °which he °saw
concerning °Israel °in the days of Uzziah king
of Judah, and in the days of °Jeroboam the
son of Joash king of Israel, °two years before
°the earthquake.

A¹ B¹ D¹ a (p. 1232) 2 And °he said, °"The LORD will °roar from
Zion, and °utter His voice from Jerusalem;
and the °habitations of the °shepherds shall
mourn, and the °top of Carmel shall °wither."
3 °Thus saith ²the LORD; "For °three
°transgressions of Damascus, and for four,

b I will not °turn away °*the punishment* thereof;

a because they have °threshed Gilead °with
threshing instruments of iron:

b 4 But °I will send a fire into the house of
°Hazael, which shall devour the °palaces of
°Ben-hadad.
5 I will break also °the bar of Damascus,
and cut off °the inhabitant from the plain of
°Aven, and him that holdeth the sceptre from
°the house of Eden: and the people of Syria
shall go into captivity unto °Kir," saith ²the
LORD.

TITLE. 1 The words of Amos. But the words of Jehovah by Amos. See *v.* 3.

Amos=Burden.

herdmen=shepherds. Heb. *nōḳ'dīm*; so called from a peculiar breed of stunted sheep (with fine wool). Mesha was called a *nōḳēd*, rendered "sheepmaster" (2 Kings 3. 4). See Ap. 54. Occurs only in these two places. But Amos was also a herdman, as is clear from 7. 14; where *bōḳēr* is from *bāḳār*, an ox, and hence is connected with ploughing (1 Kings 19. 19, 21, &c.). See note on 7. 14.

Tekoa. Now *Khan Tekū'a*, five miles south of Beth-lehem, and ten from Jerusalem. Cp. 2 Sam. 14. 2. 2 Chron. 20. 20.

which=which [words].

saw=saw [in a vision]. Cp. Num. 24. 4, 16. Isa. 30. 10. Ezek. 12. 27.

Israel. This gives us the subject of the book.

in the days. Cp. Hos. 1. 1.

Jeroboam. See 7. 10.

two years before the earthquake: i.e. before the one well known and remembered. Cp. Zech. 14. 5.

the earthquake. Fig. *Hysterēsis.* Ap. 6.

2 he said. Thus writing the words down.

The LORD. Heb. Jehovah. Ap. 4. II. This title is not the usual one in this book.

roar=roar as a lion, or thunder. It is always, when predicated of the LORD, connected with the end of Gentile dominion. Cp. Jer. 25. 30. Joel 3. 16.

utter=give out. **habitations**=pastures.

shepherds. Not the same word as in *v.* 1, but the usual word (*rā'āh*=tenders). **top of Carmel.** Mount Carmel in the north, thus embracing the whole land; now *Jebel Kŭrmŭl*; not Carmel in Judah (south of Hebron); now *el Kŭrmŭl.* Cp. 1 Sam. 25. 2. Isa. 33. 9. **wither**=be dried up.

1. 2—6. 14 (**A¹**, p. 1231). LITERAL. PROPHETIC. (*Division.*)

A¹ | A¹ | 1. 2—2. 16. Israel, Judah, and other nations.
| A² | 3. 1—6. 14. Israel alone.

1. 2—2. 16 (A¹, above). ISRAEL, JUDAH, AND OTHER NATIONS. (*Repeated Alternation, and Introversion.*)

A¹ | B¹ | D¹ | 1. 2-5. North. (Damascus.)
E¹ | 1. 6-8. South. (Gaza.)
C¹ | 1. 9, 10. Middle. (Tyre.)
B² | E² | 1. 11, 12. South. (Edom.)
D² | 1. 13-15. North. (Ammon.)
C² | 2. 1-3. Middle. (Moab.)
B³ | E³ | 2. 4, 5. South. (Judah.)
D³ | 2. 6-16. North. (Israel.)

1. 2-5 (D¹, above). NORTH. DAMASCUS. (*Alternation.*)

D¹ | a | 2-. Transgressions. (General.)
b | -3-. Threatening. (Negative.)
a | -3. Transgressions. (Particular.)
b | 4, 5. Threatening. (Positive.)

3 Thus saith the LORD. Jehovah's words: not the words of Amos. The prophetic formula. See Ap. 82. See the twelve with Jehovah, in *vv.* 3, 6, 9, 11, 13; 2. 1, 4, 6; 3. 12; 5. 4; 16; 7. 17; and the two with Adonai Jehovah in 3. 11; 5. 3. **three . . . four.** Hebrew idiom to express several, or many (Job 33. 29, marg.). Cp. Prov. 30. 15, 18, 21, 29. **transgressions.** Heb. *pāsha'.* Ap. 44. ix. **turn away**=turn it back, or avert it. **the punishment thereof.** There is no *Ellipsis* to be supplied, and no separate Heb. word for "thereof". The Heb. is *lo' 'ăshībennū*, I will not cause it to turn back: i.e. I will not avert it. The pronoun "it" is masc., agreeing with and referring to earthquake (*v.* 1), and means that Jehovah would not avert it. So in all the eight occurrences (*vv.* 3, 6, 9, 11, 13; 2. 1, 4, 6). **threshed Gilead.** Cp. Joel 3. 14. The very term used in 2 Kings 13. 7. **with**=[as it were] with. Fig. *Hypocatastasis.* Ap. 6.

4 I will send a fire. Cp. 1. 7, 10, 12; 2. 2, 5. Ref. to Jer. 17. 27; 49. 27; 50. 32. Hos. 8. 14. **Hazael.** Cp. 2 Kings 8. 12; 10. 32, 33; 13. 3. **palaces:** or fortresses. Heb. *'armōn.* Occurs (in pl.) twelve times in Amos (see Ap. 10): 1. 4, 7, 10, 12, 14; 2. 2, 5; 3. 9, 9, 10, 11; 6. 8; seven times with the verb "devour" (Heb. *'ākal*). **Ben-hadad.** An official title of the Syrian kings=son of Hadad: i.e. the sun-god. The Ben-hadad of 2 Kings 13. 3; not of 2 Kings 8. 7-15. **5 the bar.** Note the Fig. *Metalepsis* (Ap. 6), by which "bar" is put by Fig. *Metalepsis*, Ap. 6, for the gates, and then the gates put for defence of the city. Cp. Deut. 3. 5. 1 Kings 4. 13. Jer. 51. 30. Lam. 2. 9. **the inhabitant:** or, him that is seated: i.e. the ruler, corresponding with the next line. **Aven.** Same as Beth-aven, east of Beth-el, belonging to Benjamin. Cp. Hos. 4. 15; 5. 8; 10. 5, 8. **the house of Eden**=Beth-eden. **Kir.** So in 9. 7. 2 Kings 16. 9. Isa. 22. 6.

E^1 c 6 [3]Thus saith [2]the LORD; "For [3]three
(p. 1233) [3]transgressions of °Gaza, and for four,
689-687
d [3]I will not turn away [3]*the punishment* thereof;
c because they carried away captive °the whole
°captivity, to deliver *them* up to Edom:
d 7 But I will send a fire on the °wall of [6]Gaza,
which shall devour the [4]palaces thereof:
8 And I will cut off [5]the inhabitant from
°Ashdod, and him that holdeth the sceptre
from °Ashkelon, and I will turn Mine hand
against °Ekron: and the remnant of the
Philistines shall perish, °saith °the Lord GOD.
C^1 e 9 Thus [3]saith [2]the LORD; "For [3]three
[3]transgressions of °Tyrus, and for four,
f [3]I will not turn away [3]*the punishment* thereof;
e because they delivered up [6]the whole captivity
to Edom, and remembered not °the brotherly
covenant:
f 10 But [4]I will send a fire on the [7]wall of Tyrus,
which shall devour the [4]palaces thereof."
B^2 E^2 g 11 [3]Thus saith [2]the LORD; "For [3]three
[3]transgressions of °Edom, and for four,
h [3]I will not turn away [3]*the punishment* thereof;
g °because he did pursue °his brother with the
sword, and did cast off all pity, and his anger
did °tear perpetually, and °he kept his wrath
for ever:
h 12 But [4]I will send a fire upon °Teman,
which shall devour the [4]palaces of °Bozrah."
D^2 i 13 [3]Thus saith [2]the LORD; "For [3]three
[3]transgressions of the °children of °Ammon,
and for four,
k [3]I will not turn away [3]*the punishment* thereof;
i because they have °ripped up the women with
child of Gilead, °that they might enlarge their
border:
k 14 But I will kindle a fire in the [7]wall of
°Rabbah, and it shall devour the [4]palaces
thereof, with °shouting in °the day of battle,
with a tempest in the day of the whirlwind:
15 And their king shall go into captivity, °he
and his princes together, [8]saith the LORD.

C^2 l **2** °Thus saith °the LORD; "For °three
°transgressions of °Moab, and for °four,
m °I will not turn away °*the punishment* thereof;
l °because he burned the bones of the king of
Edom into lime:

1. 6-8 (E^1, p. 1232). SOUTH. GAZA.
(*Alternation.*)

E^1 | c | 6-. Transgressions. (General.)
| d | -6-. Threatening. (Negative.)
| *c* | -6. Transgressions. (Particular.)
| *d* | 7, 8. Threatening. (Positive.)

6 Gaza. Now *Ghŭzzeh*, in Philistia.
the whole captivity = a wholesale captivity.
captivity = captives. Put by Fig. *Metonymy* (of Adjunct), Ap. 6, for a whole body of captives. See Jer. 13. 19. Cp. Jer. 47. 1. 2 Chron. 21. 16, 17; 28. 17.
7 wall. Put by Fig. *Synecdochē* (of Part), Ap. 6, for the whole city.
8 Ashdod. Afterward called by the Greeks, "Azotus". Now *Esdūd*, in the plain of Philistia, thirty-five miles north of Gaza.
Ashkelon. Now *'Askalān*, on the coast of Philistia.
Ekron. Afterward, Greek, "Accaron" (1 Macc. 10. 89). Now *'Akir*, six miles west of Gezer. For "Gezer" see note on 1 Kings 9. 15-17.
saith = hath said.
the Lord GOD. Heb. Adonai Jehovah. Ap. 4. VIII (2) and II. This Divine title occurs twenty-one times (7 × 3. See Ap. 10) in this book (1. 8; 3. 7, 8, 11, 13; 4. 2, 5; 5. 3; 6. 8; 7. 1, 2, 4, 4, 5, 6; 8. 1, 3, 9, 11; 9. 5, 8). For "thus hath said Adonai Jehovah" see 3. 11.

1. 9, 10 (C^1, p. 1232). MIDDLE. TYRE.
(*Alternation.*)

C^1 | e | 9-. Transgressions. (General.)
| f | -9-. Threatening. (Negative.)
| *e* | -9. Transgressions. (Particular.)
| *f* | 10. Threatening. (Positive.)

9 Tyrus. Now *es Sūr.* See notes on Isa. 23. Jer. 25. 22; 47. 4. Also Ezek. 26-28. Joel 3. 4, 5.
the brotherly covenant = a covenant of brethren. Cp. 2 Sam. 5. 11. 1 Kings 5. 1; 9. 11-14.

1. 11, 12 (E^2, p. 1232). SOUTH. EDOM.
(*Alternation.*)

E^2 | g | 11-. Transgression. (General.)
| h | -11-. Threatening. (Negative.)
| *g* | -11. Transgression. (Particular.)
| *h* | 12. Threatening. (Positive.)

11 Edom. Cp. Isa. 21. 11; 34. 5. Jer. 49. 8, &c. Ezek. 25. 12-14; 35. 2, &c. Joel 3. 19. Obad. 1. Mal. 1. 4.
because, &c. Ref. to Pent. (Gen. 27. 41. Cp. Deut. 23. 7). Ap. 92. Cp. Mal. 1. 2.
his brother. Ref. to Pent. (Gen. 25. 24-26).
tear perpetually: or, tear [his prey] perpetually. Ginsburg thinks = kept his grudge. Cp. 2 Chron. 28. 17.
he. The 1611 edition of the A.V. omits "he".
12 Teman. Cp. Jer. 49. 7. Obad. 9. Hab. 3. 3. Eliphaz was a Temanite (Job 2. 11, &c.).
Bozrah. Now *el Buseirah*, south-east of the Dead Sea.

1. 13-15 (D^2, p. 1232). NORTH. AMMON.
(*Alternation.*)

D^2 | i | 13-. Transgressions (General.)
| k | -13-. Threatening. (Negative.)
| *i* | -13. Transgressions. (Particular.)
| *k* | 14, 15. Threatening. (Positive.)

13 children = sons.
Ammon. Cp. 1 Sam. 11. 1. **ripped up, &c.** Foretold in Hos. 13. 16. 2 Kings 8. 12; 15. 16. **that they might, &c.** Cp. Jer. 49. 1. **14 Rabbah.** Now *'Amman* (on the highlands of Gilead), "the city of waters", twenty-five miles north of the Dead Sea. Cp. 2 Sam. 11. 1, and 12. 26, 27. Jer. 49. 2. Ref. to Pent. (Deut. 3. 10, 11). Ap. 92. **shouting** = a great war-cry. **the day of battle**: i.e. the day of their foe's tumultuous assault. **15 he.** Ginsburg thinks it = his priests, with Sept.

2. 1-3 (C^2, p. 1232). MIDDLE. MOAB. (*Alternation.*)

C^2 | l | 1-. Transgressions. (General.)
| m | -1-. Threatening. (Negative.)
| *l* | -1. Transgressions. (Particular.)
| *m* | 2, 3. Threatening. (Positive.)

1 Thus saith the LORD. See note on 1. 3. **the LORD.** Heb. Jehovah. Ap. 4. II. **three . . . four.** See note on 1. 3. **transgressions.** See note on 1. 3. **Moab.** Cp. Isa. 15 and 16. Jer. 48. Ezek. 25. 8-11. Zeph. 2. 8. **I will not, &c.** See note on 1. 3. **the punishment thereof.** See note on 1. 3. **because he, &c.** Cp. 2 Kings 3. 27.

m 2 But I will send a fire upon [1] Moab, and it
(p. 1233) shall devour the ° palaces of ° Kirioth: and
689-687 Moab shall die with tumult, with ° shouting,
and with the sound of the ° trumpet:
3 And I will cut off the ° judge from ° the
midst thereof, and will slay all the princes
thereof with him," saith [1] the LORD.

B³ E³ n 4 [1] Thus saith [1] the LORD; "For [1] three
[1] transgressions of Judah, and for four,
o [1] I will not turn away [1] *the punishment* thereof;
n ° because they have despised the law of [1] the
LORD, and have not kept His ° commandments, and ° their lies caused them to err,
after the which their fathers have walked:
o 5 But I will send a fire upon Judah, and it
shall devour the [2] palaces of Jerusalem."

D³ p 6 [1] Thus saith [1] the LORD; "For [1] three
[1] transgressions of Israel, and for four,
q I will not [1] turn away [1] *the punishment* thereof;
p because ° they sold ° the righteous for silver,
and ° the poor for ° a pair of shoes;
7 That ° pant after the dust of the earth on
the head of ° the poor, and ° turn aside the way
of ° the meek: and ° a man ° and his father
will go in unto the *same* ° maid, ° to profane My
° holy name:
8 And they ° lay *themselves* down upon
clothes laid to pledge by ° every altar, and
they drink the ° wine ° of the condemned *in* the
house of their god.
9 ° Yet destroyed I ° the Amorite before
° them, whose ° height *was* like the height of
the cedars, and he *was* strong as the oaks; yet
I destroyed his fruit from above, and his roots
from beneath.
10 Also ° I brought you up from the land of
Egypt, ° and led you forty years through the
wilderness, to possess the land of the Amorite.
11 And ° I raised up of your sons for prophets,
and of your young men ° for Nazarites. ° *Is it*
not even thus, O ye ° children of Israel?
° saith [1] the LORD.
12 But ° ye gave the Nazarites wine to
drink; and commanded the prophets, saying,
'Prophesy not.'
q 13 Behold, I am pressed under you, ° as a cart
is pressed *that is* full of sheaves.
14 Therefore the flight shall perish from the
swift, and the strong shall not strengthen his
force, neither shall the mighty deliver ° himself:
15 Neither shall he stand that handleth the
bow; and *he that is* swift of foot shall not deliver *himself*: neither shall he that rideth the
horse deliver [14] himself.
16 And *he that is* ° courageous among the
mighty shall flee away ° naked in that day,
[11] saith [1] the LORD.

2 palaces. See note on 1. 4.
Kirioth: or, his cities. Now *el Kŭreiyat*, or Kiriathaim, between Dibon and Medeba. Mentioned by Mesha on the Moabite Stone. See Ap. 54.
shouting = war-cry. Cp. 1. 14.
trumpet. Heb. *shophar.*
3 judge = sceptre-holder (Num. 24. 17).
the midst thereof = her midst. Fem. to agree with *'erez* (understood) = the midst of her [land].

2. 4, 5 (E³, p. 1232). SOUTH. JUDAH. (*Alternation.*)

E³ | n | 4–. Transgressions. (General.)
  o | –4–. Threatening. (Negative.)
 n | –4. Transgressions. (Particular.)
  o | 5. Threatening. (Positive.)

4 because . . . despised, &c. Ref. to Pent. (Lev. 26. 14, 15, 43). Ap. 92.
commandments = statutes.
their lies = their idols. Cp. 2 Kings 17. 15. Ps. 40. 4. Isa. 28. 15. Jer. 16. 17–20.

2. 6-16 (D³, p. 1232). NORTH. ISRAEL. (*Alternation.*)

D³ | p | 6–. Transgressions. (General.)
  q | –6–. Threatening. (Negative.)
 p | –6–12. Transgressions. (Particular.)
  q | 13–16. Threatening. (Positive.)

6 they sold. Ref. to Pent. (Lev. 25. 39. Deut. 15. 12). Ap. 92. A Hebrew might sell himself, but not his brother or an insolvent debtor (2 Kings 4. 1. Neh. 5. 5).
the righteous = a righteous one.
the poor = a needy one. Heb. *'ebyōn.* See note on "poverty", Prov. 6. 11.
a pair of shoes. Put by Fig. *Metonymy* (of Adjunct), Ap. 6, for the title-deeds of which it was the token. Cp. Ruth 4. 7.
7 pant = crush. Heb. *shā'aph.* A *Homonym*, meaning (1) to gasp or long for (Job 7. 2; 36. 20. Ps. 119. 131. Ecc. 1. 5. Jer. 2. 24; 14. 6); (2) to crush (like *shūph* in Gen. 3. 15). Rendered "swallow up" in 8. 4. Job 5. 5. Pss. 56. 1, 2; 57. 3. Ezek. 36. 3. So here it = crush. See Oxford *Gesenius*, p. 983, col. 2. Render: "crush the head of the poor ones in the dust of the earth".
the poor = impoverished ones. Heb. *dal* (pl.). See note on "poverty", Prov. 6. 11. Not the same word as in *v.* 6.
turn aside the way = pervert their whole way.
the meek = humble ones. Heb. pl. of *'anī.* See note on "poverty", Prov. 6. 11.
a man. Heb. *'īsh.* Ap. 14. II.
and his father. This was done in the Canaanite idolatry, with the women of the temples, called *Ḳadēshōth* (fem.) and *Ḳadēshīm* (masc.).
maid = a young person (male or female). So called because of youthful vigour.
to profane, &c. This marks the result, not the intention, and shows the enormity of the sin in Jehovah's sight. Ref. to Pent. (Lev. 18. 21; 20. 3). Ap. 92. Cp. Isa. 48. 11. Ezek. 20. 9, 14; 36. 20–23. Rom. 2. 24. 1 Cor. 5. 1.
holy. See note on Ex. 3. 5.
8 lay themselves down, &c. Ref. to Pent. (Ex. 22. 26. Deut. 24. 12). Ap. 92.
every altar. The sin lay in the fact that the law of the one altar had been known as an ancient commandment as well as the law concerning the restoration of pledged garments.
wine. Heb. *yayin.* Ap. 27. I.
of the condemned: or, exacted wine.

9 Yet. Former blessings now cited to heighten the crime of their fivefold rebellion. **the Amorite.** Ref. to Pent. (Num. 21. 24. Deut. 2. 32–34). Ap. 92. Cp. Josh. 24. 8. These being the descendants of the *Nephīlīm* were all to have been destroyed, with the other Canaanite nations, by the sword of Israel. See Ap. 23 and 25. **them.** Some codices, with three early printed editions, read "you". **height.** Ref. to Pent. (Num. 13. 32, 33). Ap. 92. **10 I brought, &c.** Ref. to Pent. (Ex. 12. 51. Deut. 4. 47 (Sihon)). Ap. 92. **and led you, &c.** Ref. to Pent. (Deut. 2. 7; 8. 2). Ap. 92. **11 I raised up, &c.** Not till the priests had failed in their duty to teach the law. See Lev. 10. 8, 11. Deut. 33. 8, 10. Prophets were not provided originally. **for Nazarites.** Ref. to Pent. (Num. 6. 2). Ap. 92. **Is it not . . . ?** Fig. *Erotēsis.* Ap. 6. **children** = sons. **saith the LORD** = [is] Jehovah's oracle. **12 ye gave, &c.** Ref. to Pent. (Num. 6. 2, 3). Ap. 92. **13 as a cart** = according as [a full] cart. **14 himself** = his soul. Heb. *nephesh.* Ap. 13. **16 courageous** = stout in heart. Ap. 92. **naked**: or, armourless.

A² F¹ G (p. 1235) 689-687 **3** Hear this word that °the LORD hath
spoken against you, O °children of Israel,
against the whole family which °I brought
up from the land of Egypt, saying,

H **2** °"You only have I known of all the families of the °earth:

J therefore I will °punish you for all your °ini-
quities.

G **3** °Can two walk together, except they °be
agreed?
4 °Will a lion roar in the °forest, when he
hath no prey? will a young lion cry out of his
den, if he have taken nothing?
5 [3]Can a bird fall in a °snare upon the earth,
where no °gin *is* for him? shall *one* take up
a °snare from the earth, and have taken nothing at all?
6 °Shall a °trumpet be blown in the city, and
the people °not be afraid? °shall there be °evil
in a city, °and [1]the LORD hath not °done *it?*
7 °Surely °the Lord GOD °will do nothing, but
He °revealeth His °secret unto His servants
the prophets.
8 °The lion hath roared, who will not fear? [7]the
Lord GOD hath spoken, °who can but prophesy?
9 Publish in the °palaces at Ashdod, and in
the °palaces in the land of Egypt, and say,
'Assemble yourselves upon the mountains of
Samaria, and behold the great tumults in the
midst thereof, and °the oppressed in the midst
thereof.'

H **10** For °they know not to do °right, °saith
[1]the LORD, who store up violence and robbery in their [9]palaces.'

J **11** Therefore °thus saith [7]the Lord GOD; °"An
adversary *there shall be* even round about the
land; and he shall bring down thy strength
from thee, and thy [9]palaces shall be spoiled."
12 °Thus saith [1]the LORD; °"As the shepherd °taketh out of the mouth of the lion two
legs, or °a piece of an ear; so shall the [1]chil-
dren of Israel be taken out that dwell in Samaria in the corner of a bed, and in Damascus
°*in* a couch.
13 Hear ye, and testify in °the house of Jacob, °saith [7]the Lord GOD, the God of hosts,
14 That °in the day that I shall visit the
transgressions of Israel upon him I will also
visit the altars of Beth-el: and the horns of
the altar shall be cut off, and fall to the
°ground.
15 And I will smite the °winter house with
the °summer house; and the °houses of ivory
shall perish, and °the great houses shall have
an end, [10]saith [1]the LORD.

3. 1—6. 14 (A², p. 1232). ISRAEL ALONE. (*Division.*)

A² | F¹ | 3. 1-15. The whole family from Egypt.
  | F² | 4. 1-13. The Northern Kingdom. (Kine of Bashan.)
  | F³ | 5. 1—6. 14. Lamentations. "Woe, Woe."

3. 1-15 (F¹, above). THE WHOLE FAMILY FROM EGYPT. (*Extended Alternation.*)

F¹ | G | 1. Call to Hear.
  | H | 2-. Jehovah. "I have known."
  | J | -2. Threatening.
  | *G* | 3-9. Call to Answer.
  | *H* | 10. Israel. "They know not."
  | *J* | 11-15. Threatening.

1 the LORD. Heb. Jehovah. Ap. 4. II.
children = sons. Some codices, with one early printed edition, Aram., and Sept., read "house". Either reading shows that these chapters relate to the twelve-tribed nation (see p. 1206).
I brought up, &c. Ref. to Pent. (Ex. 12. 51, &c.).
2 You only have I known, &c. See the Structure above. Ref. to Pent. (Deut. 7. 6). Ap. 92. Cp. Ps. 147. 19, 20. **earth** = soil. Heb. *'ădāmāh.*
punish you = visit upon you, as in *v.* 14. Ref. to Pent. (Ex. 32. 34). Ap. 92.
iniquities. Heb. *'āvāh.* Ap. 44. iv.
3 Can two . . .? Fig. *Erotēsis* (in neg. affirmation). Ap. 6. This is the first of five parables. The answer to each is self-evident.
be agreed = have met together by appointment [of time and place]. **4 Will . . .?** Fig. *Erotēsis.* Ap. 6.
forest = thicket. **5 snare** = net. Heb. *phah.*
gin = a snare, or trap. Gin is short for the Old French *engin,* which is from Latin *ingenium*; hence, something *ingenious.* **6 Shall . . .?** Fig. *Erotēsis.* Ap. 6.
trumpet. Heb. *shophar.*
not be afraid = not run together.
evil = calamity; as in 5. 13. Ps. 141. 5. Heb. *ră'a'.* Ap. 44. viii. = evil: not moral evil, but evil inflicted in judgment, as in 5. 13. Isa. 45. 7. Jer. 18. 11. Lam. 3. 38.
and the LORD hath not done it? With the true meaning of "evil" there is no need to do violence to the Heb. to defend Jehovah's righteous dealings.
done = inflicted.
7 Surely = [No:] for. Cp. Job 31. 18. Mic. 6. 4. The reason follows and is explained.
the Lord GOD. See note on 1. 7.
will do = doeth. Heb. *'āsah* = work, execute (Ex. 12. 12. Num. 5. 30; 33. 4. Deut. 10. 18; 33. 21, &c.).
revealeth. As He did to Abraham, His "prophet" (Gen. 20. 7) in Gen. 18. 17, &c., and has since done by His prophets. Cp. Gen. 6. 13. Ps. 25. 14. John 15. 15.
secret = secret counsel. Heb. *ṣōd.* Cp. Job 15. 8; 29. 4. Prov. 3. 32.
8 The lion hath roared. Fig. *Hypocatastasis.* Ap. 6.
the Lord GOD hath spoken. Fig. *Hermeneia.* Ap. 6. Explaining the Fig. *Hypocatastasis* in the preceding line.
who can but prophesy? Fig. *Erotēsis.* Ap. 6. Some modern critics alter the Heb. to "be frightened", not seeing that it is through the prophets that God speaks (Heb. 1. 1). **9 palaces.** See note on 1. 4.
the oppressed = oppressive acts. Heb. *'ăshūkim* = oppressed by violent and forcible exactions. Occurs only here; Job 35. 9; and Ecc. 4. 1. Ref. to Pent. (Lev. 19. 13. Deut. 24. 14). Ap. 92. **10 they know not.** Marking the Structure. **right** = straightforward. Heb. *nākaḥ.* A rare word. Occurs only in 2 Sam. 15. 3. Prov. 8. 9 ("plain"); 24. 26. Isa. 26. 10 ("uprightness"); 30. 10 ("right things"); 57. 2 ("uprightness"); 59. 14 ("equity"). **saith the LORD** = [is] Jehovah's oracle. **11 thus saith the Lord GOD.** The first of three occurrences of this formula in Amos. See note on 1. 3. **An adversary** = An adversary [shall come]. Fig. *Ellipsis.* Ap. 6. Cp. 2 Kings 17. 3, 6; 18. 9, 10, 11. **12 Thus saith the LORD.** See note on 1. 3. **As** = Just as, or according as. **taketh** = rescueth, like a brand plucked from the burning. **a piece** = the tip. **in a couch** = [in the corner of] a couch: i.e. luxuriously. Cp. 6. 1-4. *Ellipsis* (of Repetition). Ap. 6. **13 the house of Jacob**: i.e. the whole of the natural seed. See note on *v.* 1. **God.** Heb. *Elohim.* Ap. 4. I. **saith the Lord GOD, the God of hosts** = [is] the oracle of Adonai Jehovah, the Elohim of Zebaioth. **14 in the day that, &c.** Ref. to Pent. (Ex. 32. 34). Ap. 92. **ground** = earth. Heb. *'erez.* **15 winter house.** Cp. Jer. 36. 22. **summer house.** Cp. Judg. 3. 20. **houses of ivory.** Put by Fig. *Synecdoche* (of the Whole), Ap. 6, for the parts inlaid, panelled, or overlaid with ivory. Cp. 1 Kings 22. 39. Ps. 45. 8. **the great** = many.

F² K (p. 1236) 689-687 **4** °Hear this word, ye °kine of Bashan, that *are* in the °mountain of Samaria, which °oppress °the poor,

L which crush °the needy, which °say to °their masters, 'Bring, and let us drink.'

M **2** °The Lord GOD hath °sworn by His holiness, that, °lo, the days shall come upon you, that He will take you away with °hooks, and °your posterity with fishhooks.
3 And ye shall go out at the breaches, every °*cow* °*at that which is* °before her; and °ye shall cast *them* into the palace, °saith °the LORD.

K **4** °Come to Beth-el, and °transgress; at °Gilgal multiply °transgression; and bring your sacrifices every morning, *and* your tithes °after three years:
5 And °offer a sacrifice of thanksgiving °with leaven, and proclaim *and* publish the °free offerings: for °this liketh you, O ye °children of Israel, °saith ²the Lord GOD.

L r¹ **6** And I also have given you °cleanness of teeth in all your cities, and want of bread in all your places:

s¹ °yet have ye not returned unto Me, ³saith ³the LORD.

r² **7** And also °I have withholden the rain from you, when *there were* yet three months to the harvest: and I caused it to rain upon one city, and caused it not to rain upon another city: one °piece was rained upon, and the °piece whereupon °it rained not withered.
8 So two *or* three cities wandered unto one city, to drink water; but they were not satisfied:

s² ⁶yet have ye not returned unto Me, ³saith ³the LORD.

r³ **9** °I have smitten you with blasting and mildew: when your gardens and your vineyards and your fig trees and your olive trees increased, °the palmerworm devoured *them:*

s³ ⁶yet have ye not returned unto Me, ³saith ³the LORD.

---

4. 1-13 (F², p. 1235). THE NORTHERN KINGDOM. (THE KINE OF BASHAN.) (*Extended Alternation.*)

F² K | 1-. Call to Hear.
  L | -1. Judgments deserved.
    M | 2, 3. Threatening.
K | 4, 5. Call to Come.
  L | 6-11. Judgments inflicted.
    M | 12, 13. Threatening.

1 Hear . . . ye. Masc.
kine = heifers: the women. Cp. Ps. 22. 12 (masc.). Ezek. 39. 18 (masc.). **mountain** = hill country.
oppress. Heb. *'āshak*, as in 3. 9 (fem.). Ref. to Pent. (Lev. 19. 13. Deut. 24. 14). Cp. 1 Sam. 12. 3, 4.
the poor = exhausted ones. Heb. *dal* (masc.). See note on "poverty", Prov. 6. 11.
the needy = needy ones. Heb. *'ebyōn* (masc.). See note on "poverty", Prov. 6. 11.
say (fem.). **their** (masc.).
2 The Lord GOD. See note on 1. 7.
sworn by His holiness. Ref. to Pent. (Gen. 22. 16).
lo. Fig. *Asterismos.* Ap. 6.
hooks. In the Assyrian monuments we see the captives with literal "hooks" in their noses. Cp. 2 Chron. 33. 11. Job 40. 24; 41. 2. Isa. 37. 29. Ezek 29. 4.
your posterity = the remnant of you. Heb. *'aḥarīth*, as in Ezek. 23. 25. Not posterity.
3 cow: i. e. woman.
at that which is before her = each woman through the breach [in the wall of Samaria].
before her: i. e. without turning to the left or right. Cp. Josh. 6. 5, 20.
ye shall cast them into the palace. Palace, Heb. *harmōn* (see note on 1. 4). Here it is *haharmōnah*, which forms the Fig. *Paronomasia* (Ap. 6) with *'armōn* (3. 11). The clause is to be interpreted by 3. 11, 12, and 5. 27, and would then read:—"ye shall be cast forth toward *Ha-Harmon*". The place is not known, but it may mean "ye women who are at ease in your palaces" (*'armōn*, 3. 11, 12) will be cast forth into *Ha-Harmōnah*: i. e. into exile. The text is not necessarily "corrupt" because we do not happen to know a place of that name.
saith the LORD = [is] Jehovah's oracle.
the LORD. Heb. Jehovah. Ap. 4. II.
4 Come to Beth-el, &c. Here we have Divine irony, as though it meant "Fill up the measure of your iniquity". Cp. Matt. 23. 32.
transgress . . . transgression. Heb. *pāsha'.* Ap. 44. ix.
Beth-el . . . Gilgal. Cp. 3. 14; 5. 5. Hos. 4. 15; 9. 15; 12. 11.
after three years. The ref. is to the Pent. (Num. 28. 3. Deut. 14. 28), Ap. 92; not to "days", or to modern "Mohammedan pilgrimages".
5 offer a sacrifice = offer as incense. Heb. *ḳatar.* Ap. 43. I. vii. Ref. to Pent. (Lev. 7. 13; 23. 17). Ap. 92. Cp. Ps. 56. 12. Jer. 17. 26; 33. 1. Heb. 13. 15.

with leaven. Leavened bread might be eaten by the offerer, but *not consumed on the altar* (Lev. 2. 11, 12). Leaven is mentioned five times in Exodus; four in Leviticus; one in Deuteronomy; *and not elsewhere.* The Mosaic law was well known. Ap. 92. There was no "historic growth" of the Pentateuch. **free offerings.** Ref. to Pent. (Lev. 22. 18, 21. Deut. 12. 6). Ap. 92. **this liketh you** = so ye have loved [to have it]. **children** = sons. **saith the Lord GOD** = [is] Adonai Jehovah's oracle.

4. 6-11 (*L*, above). JUDGMENTS INFLICTED.
(*Repeated Alternation.*)

L | r¹ | 6-. Judgment. (Famine.)
  s¹ | -6. Impenitence.
r² | 7, 8-. Judgment. (Drought.)
  s² | -8. Impenitence.
r³ | 9-. Judgment. (Blasting.)
  s³ | -9. Impenitence.
r⁴ | 10-. Judgment. (Pestilence.)
  s⁴ | -10. Impenitence.
r⁵ | 11-. Judgment. (Overthrow.)
  s⁵ | -11. Impenitence.

6 cleanness of teeth. Put by Fig. *Metonymy* (of Adjunct), Ap. 6, for famine. **yet have ye not, &c.** Note the Structure above, showing the Fig. *Amœbæon* (Ap 6). Cp. Isa. 26. 11. Jer. 5. 3. Hag. 2. 17.
7 I have withholden, &c. Ref. to Pent. (Deut. 28. 22-24). **piece** = portion of land. **it.** Ginsburg thinks this should be "I". **9 I have smitten, &c.** Ref. to Pent. (Deut. 28. 22). Ap. 92. Cp. Hag. 2. 17. **the palmerworm** = the gnawer. Heb. *gāzām.* See note on Joel 1. 4.

r[4] (p. 1236) 689-687 10 °'I have sent among you °the pestilence
°after the manner of Egypt: your young men
have I slain with the sword, and have °taken
away your horses; and °I have made the
stink of your camps to come up unto your
nostrils:

s[4] [6]yet have ye not returned unto Me, [3]saith
[3]the LORD.

r[5] 11 I have overthrown *some* of you, °as
°God overthrew Sodom and Gomorrah, and
°ye were as a firebrand plucked out of the
burning:

s[5] [6]yet have ye not returned unto Me, [3]saith
[3]the LORD.

M 12 Therefore thus will I do unto thee, O Israel: *and* because I will do this unto thee,
°prepare to meet thy [11]God, O Israel.
13 For, [2]lo, He That formeth the mountains,
and °createth the °wind, and °declareth unto
°man what *is* his thought, °That maketh the
morning darkness, °and treadeth upon the
high places of the earth, [3]The LORD, The
[11]God of hosts, °*is* His name.

F[3] N (p. 1237) 5 Hear ye this word which I °take up
against you, *even* a °lamentation, O
°house of Israel.
2 The °virgin of Israel is fallen; °she shall
no more rise: she is forsaken upon her °land;
°*there is* none to raise her up.

O[1] t[1] 3 For thus saith °the Lord GOD; 'The city
that °went out °*by* a thousand shall leave an
hundred, and that which went forth °*by* an
hundred shall leave ten, °to the house of
Israel.'

u[1] 4 For °thus saith °the LORD unto the [1]house
of Israel, °'Seek ye Me, and °ye shall live:
5 But seek not °Beth-el, nor enter into °Gilgal,
and °pass not to °Beer-sheba: for °Gilgal shall
surely go into °captivity, and °Beth-el shall
come to nought.
6 [4]Seek [4]the LORD, and [4]ye shall live;

t[2] lest He break out like fire in the house of
°Joseph, and devour *it*, and *there be* none to
quench *it* in Beth-el.

O[2] t[3] 7 Ye who turn judgment to °wormwood, and
°leave off righteousness °in the earth,

u[2] 8 [4]*Seek Him* That maketh °the seven stars
and °Orion, and turneth °the shadow of death
into the morning, and °maketh the day dark

10 I have sent, &c. Ref. to Pent. (Lev. 26. 25. Deut. 28. 21, 27, 60). Ap. 92.

the pestilence = a pestilence. Put by Fig. *Metonymy* (of Cause), Ap. 6, for the death resulting from it. Sept. renders it "death". See note on 6. 10.

after the manner, &c. Ref. to Pent. (Ex. 9. 3, 6; 12. 29. Deut. 28. 27). Ap. 92. Cp. Ps. 78. 50. Isa. 10. 24, 26.

taken away, &c. Cp. 2 Kings 13. 7.

I have made, &c. Cp. Joel 2. 20.

11 as God overthrew, &c. Ref. to Pent. (Gen. 19. 24, 25. Deut. 29. 23). Ap. 92. Cp. Isa. 13. 19. Jer. 49. 18.

God. Heb. Elohim. Ap. 4. I.

ye were as a firebrand, &c. Cp. Zech. 3. 2. Jude 23.

12 prepare to meet, &c.: i.e. in judgment. Cp. Ezek. 13. 5; 22. 30. Verses 11 and 12 are not "out of place" or an "interpolation", but are required by the Structure, "*M*", p. 1236.

13 createth. Some modern critics allege that this word (Heb. *bārā*, Gen. 1. 1) was not used before the time of Jeremiah; but it is used, besides the Pentateuch, in Pss. 51. 10; 89. 12, 47; 102. 18; 104. 30; 148. 5. Eccles. 12. 1; and in Isaiah frequently.

wind. Heb. *rūach.* Ap. 9.

declareth unto man, &c. Cp. Ps. 139. 2. Dan. 2. 28.

man. Heb. *'ādām.* Ap. 14. I.

That maketh, &c. Cp. 5. 8; 8. 9.

and treadeth, &c. Ref. to Pent. (Deut. 32. 13; 33. 29). Ap. 92. Cp. Mic. 1. 3.

is His name. Ref. to Pent. (Ex. 15. 3). Ap. 92. Cp. 5. 8; 9. 6. Isa. 47. 4. Jer. 10. 16.

5. 1—6. 14 (F[3], p. 1235). **LAMENTATIONS.**
(*Introversions.*)

F[3] | N | 5. 1, 2. Lamentation.
  O[1] | t[1] | 5. 3. Threatening.
    u[1] | 5. 4-6-. Exhortation. "Seek Him."
  t[2] | 5. -6. Threatening.
  O[2] | t[3] | 5. 7. Incrimination.
    u[2] | 5. 8, 9. Exhortation. "Seek Him."
  t[4] | 5. 10, 11-. Incrimination.
  O[3] | t[5] | 5. -11-13. Threatening.
    u[3] | 5. 14, 15. Exhortation. "Seek Good."
  t[6] | 5. 16, 17. Threatening.
N | 5. 18—6. 14. Lamentation.

1 take up = lift up as a burden.

lamentation = dirge.

house of Israel. See note on 3. 1.

2 virgin. Put by Fig. *Metonymy* (of Adjunct), Ap. 6, for the house of Israel, a young girl who is beloved, as in Hosea. Cp. Isa. 37. 22; 47. 1. Jer. 14. 17; 46. 11, &c.

she. Some codices, with one early printed edition, Syr. and Vulg., read "and shall not": i. e. cannot rise again. **land** = soil. Heb. *'ădāmāh.*

there. Some codices read "and [there]".

3 the Lord GOD. Heb. Adonai Jehovah. Ap. 4. VIII (2) and II. **went out** = goeth out [to war].

by a thousand = a thousand strong. Ref. to Pent. (Deut. 32. 30). Ap. 92.

by an hundred = a hundred strong.

to = [belonging] to.

4 thus saith. Note the prophetic formula (see Ap. 82), introducing the exhortation, and emphasising it.

the LORD. Heb. Jehovah. Ap. 4. II. **Seek ye Me, &c.** Note this word "seek" in the several exhortations ("u[1]", "u[2]", and "u[3]"). Ref. to Pent. (Deut. 12. 5). Ap. 92. As in Ps. 9. 10. Isa. 9. 13. Jer. 10. 21. Hos. 10. 12. Zeph. 1. 6. **ye shall live.** Ref. to Pent. (Lev. 18. 5, see note there. Deut. 30. 19). Ap. 92. Cp. Isa. 55. 3. **5 Beth-el . . . Gilgal . . . Beer-sheba.** Cp. Hos. 4. 15; 10. 8. These were the seats of Israel's idolatrous worship. **pass not** = pass not through; which was necessary in order to get from the north to Beer-sheba in the south. Cp. 4. 4; 8. 14. **Gilgal shall surely go into captivity.** Note the Fig. *Paronomasia* (Ap. 6), for emphasis. Heb. *Gilgal gālōh yigleh* = *The Roller, rolling, shall roll away*: i. e. be utterly removed. This is emphasised by the Fig. *Polyptōton* (Ap. 6). **6 Joseph.** Put by Fig. *Synecdoche* (of the Part), Ap. 6, for the whole Northern Kingdom. **7 wormwood.** Ref. to Pent. (Deut. 29. 18). Ap. 92. **leave off . . . in** = cast down . . . to. **8 the seven stars.** Heb. *kīmah* = cluster. Modern name, the Pleiades. See notes on Job 9. 9; 38. 31, 32. Cp. Isa. 13. 10; and see Ap. 12. **Orion.** Heb. *kesel* = rigidity, strength; from *kesālīm* = loins (Job 15. 27): hence, "confidence" derived from strength (Job 8. 14; 31. 24, where the Sept. has *ischun* = strength. Ps. 78. 7. Prov. 3. 26). In the Denderah Zodiac his name is *oar*, from Heb. root *'Or* = light: hence, the glorious One. See Ap. 12. p. 17. Cp. Job 9. 9; 38. 31. **the shadow of death.** Heb. *tzalmāveth.* Not "a late word". We find it ten times in Job; four times in the Psalms. Isa. 9. 2. Jer. 2. 6; 13. 16. **maketh the day, &c.** Cp. Ps. 104. 20.

689-687 with night: °That °calleth for the waters of
the sea, and poureth them out upon the face
of the earth: [4] The LORD °*is* His name:
9 [8] That °strengtheneth the spoiled against
the strong, °so that the spoiled shall come
against the fortress.

t[4] (p. 1237) 10 °They hate °him that rebuketh °in the
gate, and they abhor him that speaketh °uprightly.
11 Forasmuch therefore as your treading *is*
upon °the poor, and ye take from him °burdens
of wheat:

O[3] t[5] °ye have built houses of hewn stone, but ye
shall not dwell in them; ye have planted
°pleasant vineyards, but ye shall not drink
°wine of them.
12 For I know your manifold °transgressions
and your mighty °sins: °they afflict °the just,
they °take a bribe, and they °turn aside °the
poor [10] in the gate *from their right.*
13 °Therefore the prudent shall keep silence
in that time; for it *is* °an evil time.

u[3] 14 °Seek good, and not [13] evil, that [4] ye may
live: and so [4] the LORD, the °God of hosts,
shall be with you, °as ye have spoken.
15 °Hate the [13] evil, and love the good, and
establish judgment [10] in the gate: °it may be
that [4] the LORD [14] God of hosts will be gracious
unto the remnant of °Joseph.'

t[6] 16 Therefore [4] the LORD, the [14] God of hosts,
°the LORD*, saith thus; 'Wailing *shall be* in
all °streets; and they shall say in all the highways,
'Alas! alas!' and they shall call the
husbandman to mourning, and such as are
°skilful of lamentation to wailing.
17 And in all vineyards *shall be* wailing: for
I will °pass through thee," saith the LORD.

N P[1] w (p. 1238) 18 °'Woe unto you that desire °the day of
[4] the LORD! to what end *is* it for you?

x °the day of [4] the LORD [8] *is* °darkness, and not
light.
19 [14] As if a °man did flee from °a lion, and
°a bear met him; or went into the house, and
leaned his hand on the wall, and a serpent bit
him.
20 °*Shall* not [18] the day of [4] the LORD *be*
[18] darkness, and not light? even very dark,
°and no brightness in it?

w 21 °'I hate, I despise your feast days, and °I
will not smell in your °solemn assemblies.
22 Though ye °offer Me °burnt offerings and
your °meat offerings, °I will not accept *them*:
neither will I regard the °peace offerings of
your fat beasts.
23 °Take thou away from Me the noise of
thy songs; for I will not hear the melody of
thy °viols.

That = [Seek Him] That.
calleth, &c. Cp. 9. 6. Job 38. 34. Isa. 48. 13.
is = it [is].
9 strengtheneth the spoiled against the strong = that makes destruction to come suddenly to flash upon the strong.
so that the, &c. = and destruction will come upon the fortress.
10 They hate, &c. The connection is not "difficult". The Structure is the commentary. Cp. Isa. 29. 21.
him that rebuketh, &c. = the reprover.
in the gate: i.e. before the judge.
uprightly = truthfully.
11 the poor = an impoverished one. Heb. *dal*. See note on "poverty", Prov. 6. 11.
burdens = exaction. Sing.
ye have built, &c. Ref. to Pent. (Deut. 28. 30, 39).
pleasant vineyards = vineyards of desire.
wine. Heb. *yayin*. Ap. 27. I.
12 transgressions. Heb. *pāsha'*. Ap. 44. ix.
sins. Heb. *chāṭā'*. Ap. 44. i.
they afflict = oppressors [as ye are] of.
the just = a righteous one.
take a bribe. Ref. to Pent. (Num. 35. 31, 32, the same word). Ap. 92.
turn aside. Ref. to Pent. (Ex. 23. 6. Deut. 16. 19; 24. 17. The same Heb. word in all three cases). Ap. 92. Cp. Isa. 29. 21. Mal. 3. 5.
the poor = needy ones. Heb. *'ebyōn*. See note on "poverty", Prov. 6. 11. Cp. 2. 7. Isa. 29. 21.
13 Therefore, &c. Cp. Prov. 28. 12, 28.
an evil time = a time of calamity. Heb. *rā'a'*. Ap. 44. viii. See note on 3. 6.
14 Seek good. Note the Structure ("u[1]", "u[2]", "u[3]", p. 1237). **God.** Heb. Elohim. Ap. 4. I.
as = according as. Cp. Mic. 3. 11.
15 Hate the evil, &c. Cp. Pss. 34. 14; 97. 10. Rom. 12. 9. This concludes the last of the three exhortations.
it may be. Heb. *'ulay*. The whole verse is the exhortation: but the Heb. accent marks off this sentence, calling attention, not to *uncertainty* on the part of Jehovah, but to the *difficulty* on Israel's part; and this in order to stimulate obedience to the exhortation. Cp. Ex. 32. 30. 2 Kings 19. 4. Joel 2. 14.
Joseph. Put by Fig. *Synecdoche* (of the Part), Ap. 6, for the whole of the Northern Kingdom.
16 the LORD*. One of the 134 places where the *Sōpherim* say they altered "Jehovah" (Ap. 4. II) of the primitive text to "Adonai" (Ap. 4. VIII (2)). See Ap. 32.
streets = open places.
skilful of lamentation: i.e. the professional mourners. Cp. 2 Chron. 35. 25. Ecc. 12. 5. Jer. 9. 17.
17 pass through. Ref. to Pent. (Ex. 12. 12). Ap. 92.

5. 18—6. 14 (*N*, p. 1237). **LAMENTATION.**
(*Division.*)

N | P[1] | 5. 18-27. The First Woe. Presumption, &c.
| P[2] | 6. 1-14. The Second Woe. Security, &c.

5. 18-27 (P[1], above). **THE FIRST WOE.**
(*Alternation.*)

P[1] | w | 18-. Incrimination. Presumption.
| x | -18-20. Threatening. Darkness.
| *w* | 21-26. Incrimination. Idolatry.
| *x* | 27. Threatening. Captivity.

18 Woe. The first woe. See the Structure above.
the day of the LORD. See notes on Isa. 2. 12; 13. 6. Joel 2. 1. **darkness, and not light.** Note the Fig. *Pleonasm* (Ap. 6) for emphasis. Cp. Jer. 30. 7. Joel 2. 2. Zeph. 1. 15. **19 man.** Heb. *'ish*. Ap. 14. II. **a lion.** Heb. the face of a lion. A special various reading called *Sevīr* (Ap. 34) reads "the mouth of a lion". **a bear.** The Syrian bear is fiercer than a lion (Dan. 7. 5. Cp. 2 Kings 2. 24. Lam. 3. 10). **20 Shall not . . . ?** Fig. *Erotēsis* (Ap. 6), for emphasis. **and no brightness.** Note the Figs. *Pleonasm* and *Erotēsis* (Ap. 6). Some codices omit "and". **21 I hate, &c.** Cp. Prov. 21. 27. Isa. 1. 11-14. Jer. 6. 20. **I will not smell, &c.** Ref. to Pent. (Lev. 26. 31). Ap. 92. **solemn assemblies.** Ref. to Pent. (Lev. 23. 36. Num. 29. 35. Deut. 16. 8). Ap. 92. **22 offer** = offer up. **burnt offerings . . . meat offerings.** See Ap. 43. II, and III. **I will not accept, &c.** Ref. to Pent. (Lev. 1. 4). Ap. 92. **peace offerings.** See Ap. 43. II. iv. **23 Take thou away, &c.** Cp. Isa. 1. 13. **viols** = lutes.

689-687 24 But let judgment °run down as waters,
and righteousness as a °mighty °stream.
25 °Have ye offered °unto Me sacrifices and
offerings in the wilderness forty years, O
[1]house of Israel?
26 But °ye have borne the °tabernacle of
your Moloch and °Chiun your images, °the
star of your god which ye made to yourselves.
x (p. 1238) **27 Therefore will I cause you to go into**
captivity °beyond Damascus," °saith the LORD,
Whose name *is* The [14] God of Hosts.

P[2] y[1] (p. 1239) 6 °Woe to °them *that are* °at ease in Zion,
and °trust in the mountain of Samaria,
°*which are* named °chief of the nations, to
whom °the house of Israel °came!
2 °Pass ye °unto °Calneh, and °see; and from
thence go ye to °Hamath the great: then go
down to °Gath of the Philistines: °*be they*
better than °these kingdoms? °or their border
greater than °your border?
3 Ye that °put far away °the evil day, and
cause the °seat of violence to come near;
4 That lie upon beds of ivory, and stretch
themselves upon their couches, and eat the
lambs out of the flock, and the calves out of
the midst of the stall;
5 That °chant to the sound of the viol, *and*
invent to themselves °instruments of musick,
°like David;
6 That drink °wine in °bowls, and anoint
themselves with the chief ointments: but they
°are not grieved for the °affliction of °Joseph.
z[1] 7 Therefore now shall they go captive with
the first that go captive, and the banquet of
them that stretched themselves shall be removed.
y[2] 8 °The Lord GOD hath °sworn °by Himself, °saith °the LORD the °God of Hosts, °I
abhor the °excellency of Jacob, and hate his
palaces:
z[2] therefore will I deliver up the city with °all
that is therein.
9 And it shall come to pass, if there °remain
ten °men in one house, that they shall °die.
10 And °a man's uncle shall take °him up,
and he that °burneth him, to bring out the

24 run down=roll on. Ref. to "Gilgal". **mighty**=inexhaustible. **stream.** Heb. *naḥal*=a wady, or intermittent stream; not *nahar*, a constant-flowing river.

25 Have ye offered, &c. . . ? Fig. *Erotēsis*. Ap. 6. This is a question in some codices and three early printed editions; but other codices, and four early printed editions, read it as an affirmative statement. If a question, the answer is No. See Deut. 32. 17. Josh. 5. 5-7. Jer. 7. 22, 23. Ezek. 20. 8, 16, 24.

unto Me. Not "unto demons". Ref. to Pent. (Lev. 17. 7. Deut. 32. 17). Ap. 92. Cp. Ps. 106. 37. 1 Cor. 10. 7.

26 ye have borne=borne aloft. Fig. *Hysterēsis*. Ap. 6. **tabernacle**=booth. Heb. *ṣikkuth*.

Chiun. The Egyptian or Greek equivalent was *Remphan* (Sept. *Raiphan*; another spelling preserved in the Sept. and in Acts 7. 43). Proper names frequently differ in spelling: e.g. Ethiopia is the Heb. *Kūsh*; Egypt is *Mizraīm*; Mesopotamia and Syria is *'Ăram*, or *'Aram-nahărāīm*, &c.

the star of your god: or, your star-god.

27 beyond Damascus. In Acts 7. 43 beyond Babylon, which was of course "beyond Damascus", and included it, showing what was in the Divine purpose in the words of Jehovah (*v.* 27) by Amos. Moreover, the road to Assyria lay through Damascus. Cp. 2 Kings 15. 29; 16. 9. Isa. 8. 4. Amos 3. 12. May not the Holy Spirit quote and adapt His own words as He pleases?

saith=hath said.

6. 1-14 (P[2], p. 1238). THE SECOND WOE. SECURITY. (*Repeated Alternation.*)

P[2]
- y[1] | 1-6. Incrimination. Security.
- z[1] | 7. Threatening. Captivity.
- y[2] | 8-. Incrimination. Pride.
- z[2] | -8-11. Threatening. Depopulation.
- y[3] | 12, 13. Incrimination. Injustice.
- z[3] | 14. Threatening. Invasion.

1 Woe. The second woe. See 5. 18.

them: i.e. the nobles of Judah, in comparison with the nobles of Israel (in Samaria) in the next clause.

at ease=careless, secure, or easy-going.

trust=confide. Heb. *bāṭaḥ*. Ap. 69. i. Here Part. =them that confide.

which are named=[the men of] name. Cp. Num. 1. 17.

chief of the nations: i.e. Israel. Ref. to Pent. (Ex. 19. 5). Ap. 92.

the house of Israel: i.e. the Northern Kingdom=the People of Israel.

came. Supply the *Ellipsis*: "came [for judgment and justice]", as shown by the rest of this member ("y[1]").

2 Pass=Pass over: i.e. the Euphrates. Cp. Jer. 2. 10.

unto Calneh. The sequence of these cities is logical rather than geographical.

Calneh. On the Tigris. Built by Nimrod (Gen. 10. 10). Called Calno (Isa. 10. 9); Canneh (Ezek. 27. 23).

see=consider [its fate]. So in the next two clauses. **Hamath.** On the north. Now called *Hama*, on the Orontes, north of Damascus. Ref. to Pent. (Gen. 10. 18. Num. 34. 7, 8). Cp. *v.* 14. Ap. 92. **Gath.** Now *Tell es Sāfi*, in the south. See 1 Sam. 5. 8. **be they better:** i.e. these nobles and chief men. **these kingdoms:** which have been overthrown. **or their border**=or [is] their border or boundary greater? &c. **your:** i.e. the borders of Israel and Judah. Supply the logical *Ellipsis*: "[yet I overthrew them; how much more shall I judge you!]". **3 put**=thrust. **the evil day**=the day of calamity. Heb. *rā'a'*. Ap. 44. viii. Cp. 3. 6; 5. 13; 9. 10. **seat:** or, throne. **5 chant**=break out [in song]. Heb. *pāraṭ*. Occurs only here. **instruments of musick.** Heb. *kelai shīr*=instruments of song. **like David**=as David did. **6 wine.** Heb. *yayin*. Ap. 27. I. **bowls**=sacred bowls; not in goblets. **are not grieved**=do not afflict themselves. **affliction**=breach: i.e. the breach of the two kingdoms (1 Kings 12). Cp. Isa. 30. 26. Jer. 6. 14. **Joseph.** Put by Fig. *Synecdoche* (of the Part), Ap. 6, for the whole of the ten tribes. A reference to the Patriarch, by application. **8 The Lord GOD.** Heb. Adonai Jehovah. Ap. 4. VIII (2) and II. See note on 1. 8. **sworn, &c.** Ref. to Pent. (Gen. 22. 16). Cp. Jer. 51. 14. **by Himself**=by His soul. Heb. *nephesh*. Ap. 13. **saith the LORD the God of Hosts**=[is] the oracle of Jehovah, the God of Hosts. **the LORD.** Heb. Jehovah. Ap. 4. II. **God.** Heb. Elohim. Ap. 4. I. **I abhor.** Heb. *tāab*, a *Homonym*, with two meanings. Here, to abhor. In Ps. 119. 20, 40, 174, to desire or long for. **excellency.** Fig. *Ampliatio*. It was once such (cp. 8. 7. Ps. 47. 4. Ezek. 24. 21), but is now no longer so. **all that is therein**=the fulness thereof. **9 remain:** i.e. survive after the siege. **men.** Pl. of *'enōsh*. Ap. 14. III. **die:** i.e. by pestilence. **10 a man's uncle**=a relative. **him:** i.e. the corpse. **burneth.** See note on 4. 10. Here, and 1 Sam. 31. 12 are the only two places where burning of corpses is mentioned. Both are exceptional cases, but it was a common practice of the Horites (cp. Gen. 14. 6. Deut. 2. 12, 22), whose remains were found in the excavations at Gezer. See note on 1 Kings 9. 15-17.

689-687 °bones out of the house, and shall say unto
°him that *is* °by the sides of the house, '*Is
there* yet °*any* with thee?' and he shall say,
'No.' Then shall he say, °'Hold thy tongue:
for we may not °make mention of the name of
[8]the LORD.'
11 For, °behold, [8]the LORD commandeth, and
He will smite the great house with breaches,
and the little house with clefts.

y^3 (p. 1239) 12 °Shall horses run upon the rock? °will
one plow °*there* with oxen? °for ye have
turned judgment into gall, and the fruit of
righteousness into °hemlock:
13 Ye which rejoice in a thing of nought,
which say, 'Have we not taken to us °horns
by our own strength?'

z^3 14 But, [11]"behold, °I will raise up against
you a nation, O house of Israel, saith [8]the
LORD the [8]God of hosts; and °they shall
afflict you °from the entering in of °Hemath
°unto °the river of °the wilderness."

B^1 Q^1 a^1 (p. 1240) 7 Thus hath °the Lord GOD shewed unto
me; and, °behold, He °formed °grass-
hoppers in the beginning of the shooting up
of the latter growth; and, °lo, *it was* the
latter growth after °the king's mowings.

b^1 2 And it came to pass, *that* when they had
made an end of eating the grass of the land,
then I said, [1]"O Lord GOD, forgive, I beseech
Thee: °by whom shall °Jacob arise? for he *is*
small."

c^1 3 °The LORD °repented for this: "It shall
not be," saith °the LORD.

Q^2 a^2 4 Thus hath [1]the Lord GOD shewed unto me:
and, behold, [1]the Lord GOD °called to contend
by fire, and it devoured the great deep, and
°did eat up °a part.

b^2 5 Then said I, "O [1]Lord GOD, cease, I beseech Thee: [2]by whom shall [2]Jacob arise? for
he *is* small."

c^2 6 [3]The LORD [3]repented for this: "This also
shall not be," saith [1]the Lord GOD.

Q^3 a^3 7 Thus He shewed me: and, [1]behold, °the
LORD* stood upon a wall °*made* by a °plumb-
line, with a °plumbline in His hand.

b^3 8 And [3]the LORD said unto me, °"Amos,
what seest thou?" And I said, "A [7]plumb-
line."

c^3 Then said [7]the LORD*, "Behold, I will °set
a plumbline in the midst of My People Israel:
I will not again °pass by them any more:
9 And the °high places of °Isaac shall be
desolate, and the sanctuaries of °Israel shall
be laid waste; and °I will rise against the
house of °Jeroboam with the sword."

A^2 R (p. 1241) 10 Then Amaziah °the priest of °Beth-el sent
to Jeroboam king of Israel, saying, "Amos
hath °conspired against thee °in the midst of
the house of Israel: the land is not able to
°bear all his words.

bones: i.e. one reduced to a mere skeleton. Cp. Job 7. 15; 19. 20.
him that is, &c.: i.e. the survivor.
by the sides of = in the midst of, or hinder part.
any: i.e. any alive or dead.
Hold thy tongue = Hush!
make mention of = call upon, or invoke. Cp. Isa. 26. 13; 49. 1; 62. 6.
11 behold. Fig. *Asterismos*. Ap. 6.
12 Shall horses . . . ? will . . . ? Fig. *Erotēsis*. Ap. 6.
there: or, supply "[the sea]".
for. Supply "[with equal madness]".
hemlock. Ref. to Pent. (Deut. 29. 18, same word as "wormwood"). Ap. 92.
13 horns = powers. "Horns" put by Fig. *Metonymy* (of Cause), Ap. 6, for the power put forth by them.
14 I will raise up, &c. Ref. to Pent. (Deut. 28. 49).
they shall afflict you. Ref. to Pent. (Ex. 3. 9; Deut. 26. 7).
from . . . unto: i.e. through the length and breadth of the land.
Hemath. Same as Hamath (*v.* 2), in the north.
the river. Heb. *naḥal* = torrent, or wady.
the wilderness. Heb. *hā'ărābāh* = the '*Arābāh*: i.e. the plain, south of Judah. Ref. to Pent. (Deut. 1. 1, &c.).

7. 1-9 (B^1, p. 1231). SYMBOLIC.
(Repeated Alternation.)

B^1 | Q^1 | a^1 | 1. SYMBOL. Grasshoppers.
b^1 | 2. Signification. Deprecated.
c^1 | 3. Judgment averted.
Q^2 | a^2 | 4. SYMBOL. Fire.
b^2 | 5. Signification. Deprecated.
c^2 | 6. Judgment averted.
Q^3 | a^3 | 7. SYMBOL. Plumbline.
b^3 | 8-. Signification. Deprecated.
c^3 | -8, 9. Judgment averted.

1 the Lord GOD. Heb. Adonai Jehovah. Ap. 4. VIII (2) and II.
behold . . . lo. Fig. *Asterismos*. Ap. 6.
formed = was forming.
grasshoppers = locusts. Cp. Nah. 3. 17.
the king's mowings. Exacted by the king from the People (1 Kings 4. 7; 18. 5). These are the symbols of the army of 6. 14.
2 by whom shall Jacob arise? Fig. *Erotēsis*. Ap. 6. Some codices, with Sept., Syr., and Vulg., read "who shall raise up Jacob?"
Jacob. Put by Fig. *Metonymy* (of the Subject), Ap. 6, for the whole nation
3 The LORD. Heb. Jehovah. Ap. 4. II.
repented. Fig. *Anthropopatheia*. Ap. 6 Ref. to Pent. (Deut. 32. 36). Ap. 92. Cp. Jonah 3. 10.
4 called, &c. = was calling for fire, to contend [with Israel].
did eat up a part = would have eaten up the land.
a part. Heb. *haḥēleḳ*, with *'eth* = the very portion [of the earth given to Israel]. Cp. Mic. 2. 4.
7 the LORD*. One of the 134 passages in which the *Sōpherim* say they altered Jehovah of the primitive text to Adonai (Ap. 32).
made, &c.: i.e. [made perpendicular] by a plummet.
plumbline = plummet. Occurs only here.
8 Amos. Note this personal touch.
set, &c.: i.e. measure [the doings of Israel] with the plummet of righteousness and judgment. Cp. 2 Kings 21. 13. Isa. 28. 17; 34. 11. Lam. 2. 8, &c.
pass by them = forgive them.
9 high places. Used for idolatrous altars, &c.
Isaac . . . Israel. Used only by Amos in this sense. Put by Fig. *Metonymy* (of Adjunct), Ap. 6, for the nation of Israel. Cp. Ps. 105. 9, 10. Jer. 33. 26, &c.
I will rise against, &c. Fulfilled in 2 Kings 15. 10.
Jeroboam. Cp. Hos. 1. 4.

7. 10-17 [For Structure see next page].

10 the priest. The idolatrous priest.

Beth-el. Cp. 3. 14; 4. 4; 5. 5, 6. conspired = formed a conspiracy; the calves being connected with Israel's state policy (1 Kings 12. 26-33). in the midst, &c.: i.e. openly. Cp. *v.* 8. bear = endure.

689-687 11 For thus Amos saith, °'Jeroboam shall
die by the sword, and [9]Israel shall surely be
led away captive out of their own land.'"

S d 12 Also Amaziah said unto Amos, "O thou
(p. 1241) seer, go, flee thee away °into the land of
°Judah, and there eat bread, and prophesy
there:

e 13 But prophesy not again any more at
[10]Beth-el: for it *is* the king's °chapel, and it
is the king's °court."

S d 14 Then answered Amos, and said to Amaziah, "I *was* no prophet, neither *was* I °a
prophet's son; but I *was* an °herdman, and
a °gatherer of sycomore fruit:
15 And [3]the LORD °took me °as I followed
the flock, and [3]the LORD said unto me, 'Go,
prophesy unto My People Israel.'

e 16 Now therefore hear thou the word of [3]the
LORD: Thou sayest, 'Prophesy not against
Israel, and °drop not *thy word* against the
house of [9]Isaac.'
17 Therefore °thus saith [3]the LORD; 'Thy
wife shall °be an harlot in the city, and thy
sons and thy daughters shall fall by the sword,
and thy °land shall be °divided by line; and
thou shalt die °in a polluted land:

R and Israel shall surely go into captivity °forth
of his land.'"

B[2] T[1] **8** Thus hath °the Lord GOD shewed unto
me: and behold a basket of °summer
fruit.
2 And He said, °"Amos, what seest thou?"
And I said, "A basket of °summer fruit."

T[2] Then said °the LORD unto me, °"The end is
come upon My People of Israel; I will not
again °pass by them any more.
3 And the songs of the °temple shall °be
howlings in that day, °saith [1]the Lord GOD:
there shall be many °dead bodies in every
place; they shall °cast *them* forth °with
silence.

A[3] U 4 Hear this, O ye that °swallow up °the
needy, even to °make °the poor of the land
°to fail,
5 Saying, 'When will °the new moon be
gone, that we may sell corn? and °the sabbath,
that we may °set forth wheat, making the
°ephah small, and the °shekel great, and falsifying the balances by deceit?
6 That we may °buy °the poor for silver, and
°the needy for a pair of shoes; *yea,* and °sell
the refuse of the wheat?'

V 7 [2]The LORD °hath sworn by °the Excellency
of Jacob, Surely I will never forget any of
their works.
8 Shall not the land tremble for this, and
every one mourn that dwelleth therein? and
it shall rise up wholly as a °flood; and it shall
be cast out and °drowned, as *by* the °flood of
Egypt.

7. 10-17 (**A**[2], p. 1231). LITERAL. PROPHETIC.
(*Introversion and Alternation.*)

A[2] | R | 10, 11. Threatening. Captivity.
S | d | 12. Rejection by Amaziah.
e | 13. Prophecy rejected.
S | *d* | 14, 15. Justification by Amos.
e | 16, 17-. Prophecy repeated.
R | -17. Threatening. Captivity.

11 Jeroboam shall die, &c. This charge was not true. Cp. Acts 17. 6, 7; 24. 5. Note what Amaziah omitted to repeat.

12 into . . . Judah. Though belonging to Judah (1. 1) Amos was a prophet to Israel.

13 chapel = sanctuary. **court**: or, palace.

14 a prophet's son. Prophets were not hereditary as priests were. Cp. Heb. 1. 1.

herdman. See notes on 1. 1. **gatherer** = preparer.

15 took me: i.e. called me. Prophets were called by Jehovah; not born prophets, or made prophets by man. See notes on 1 Sam. 10. 5. Heb. 1. 1.

as I followed, &c. Cp. Ps. 78. 70, 71.

16 drop not, &c. Ref. to Pent. (Deut. 32. 2). Ap. 92. Cp. Ezek. 20. 46; 21. 2. Mic. 2. 6, marg.

17 thus saith the LORD. See note on 1. 3.

be an harlot: i.e. become a victim to the lust of the invader. **land** = soil. Heb. *'ădāmāh.*

divided, &c.: i.e. partitioned.

in a polluted land = on polluted (i.e. heathen) soil.

forth of = from upon.

8. 1-3 (**B**[2], p. 1231). SYMBOLICAL.
(*Division.*)

B[2] | T[1] | 1, 2-. The Symbol. Basket of Summer Fruit.
| T[2] | -2, 3. The Signification.

1 the Lord GOD. Heb. Adonai Jehovah. See note on 1. 8.

summer fruit. Heb. *kāyitz* = ripe: "summer" being put by Fig. *Metonymy* (of Adjunct), Ap. 6, for ripe fruits characterizing the summer. Cp. 2 Sam. 16. 2. Jer. 40. 12.

2 Amos. See note on 7. 8.

summer fruit . . . The end. Note the Fig. *Paronomasia* (Ap. 6), for emphasis. Cp. Jer. 1. 11, 12. Heb. *kāyitz hakkētz,* meaning that *ripe* was the fruit; *ripe* will be the time.

the LORD. Heb. Jehovah. Ap. 4. II.

The end. See note above.

pass by = forgive, as in 7. 8.

3 temple. The 1611 edition of the A.V. reads "temples". **be** = become.

saith the Lord GOD = [is] Adonai Jehovah's oracle.

dead bodies = corpses. See notes on 6. 9, 10.

cast them forth: i.e. and burn them.

with silence = with "Hush!" as in 6. 10.

8. 4-14 (**A**[3], p. 1231). LITERAL.
(*Alternation.*)

A[3] | U | 4-6. Incrimination.
V | 7-13. Threatening. Mourning.
U | 14-. Incrimination.
V | -14. Threatening. Fall.

4 swallow up = devour.

the needy = a needy one. Heb. *'ebyōn.* See note on "poverty", Prov. 6. 11.

make . . . to fail = destroy, or cause to cease.

the poor = meek ones. Heb. *'ānāh.* See note on "poverty", Prov. 6. 11.

5 the new moon. Ref. to Pent. (Num. 10. 10, &c.).

the sabbath. Ref. to Pent. (Ex. 20. 10). Ap. 92. Stopping their business for a day.

set forth wheat. Heb. = wheat market: "wheat" being put by Fig. *Metonymy* (of Adjunct), Ap. 6, for the place where it is kept = open granaries, or sell grain.

ephah. Measuring the goods. See Ap. 51. III. 3 (5).

shekel. Weighing the money. See Ap. 51. II. 5. **6 buy the poor, &c.** See note on 2. 6. **the poor** = impoverished ones. Heb. *dal* (pl.). See note on "poverty", Prov. 6. 11. **the needy** = a needy one. Heb. *'ebyōn,* as in *v.* 4. **sell** = sell [as good wheat]. **7 hath sworn, &c.** See note on 6. 8. **the Excellency of Jacob**: i.e. by Himself, as in 6. 8. Ref. to Pent. (Ex. 15. 7). Ap. 92. Cp. 4. 2; 6. 8. Hos. 5. 5; 7. 10. **8 flood.** Heb. *'ōr.* Referring to the overflowing of the Nile. **drowned** = subside.

689-687 9 And it shall come to pass in that day,
[3]saith [1]the Lord GOD, that I will °cause the
sun to go down at noon, and I will darken the
earth in the clear day:
10 And I will turn °your feasts into mourning,
and all your songs into lamentation; and I
will bring up °sackcloth upon all loins, and
°baldness upon every head; and I will make
°it as the mourning of an only *son,* and [2]the
end thereof as a bitter day.
11 °Behold, the days come, [3]saith [1]the Lord
GOD, that I will send a famine in the land,
not a famine of bread, nor a thirst for water,
but °of hearing the °words of [2]the LORD:
12 And they shall °wander from sea to sea,
and from the north even to the east, they shall
run to and fro to seek the [11]word of [2]the LORD,
and shall not find *it.*
13 In that day shall the fair °virgins and
young men faint for thirst.

U (p. 1241) 14 They that swear by the °sin of Samaria,
and say, 'Thy god, O °Dan, liveth;' and, 'The
°manner of °Beer-sheba liveth;'
V even °they shall fall, and never rise up
again."

B³ W¹ (p. 1242) **9** I saw °the LORD* standing °upon °the
altar: and He said, "Smite the °lintel of
the door, that the posts may shake: and cut
them in the head, all of them;
W² °and I will slay °the last of them with the
sword: he that fleeth of them shall not flee
away, and he that escapeth of them shall not
be delivered.
2 °Though they dig into °hell, thence shall
Mine hand take them; though they °climb up
to heaven, thence will I bring them down:
3 And though they hide themselves in the
top of Carmel, I will search and take them
out thence; and though they be hid from My
sight in the bottom of the sea, thence will I
command the serpent, and he shall bite them:
4 And though they go into captivity before
their enemies, thence will I °command the
sword, and it shall slay them: and °I will set
Mine eyes upon them for °evil, and not for
good.

A⁴ X 5 And °the Lord GOD of hosts *is* He That
toucheth the land, and it shall melt, and all
that °dwell therein shall mourn: and it shall
rise up wholly like a °flood; and shall be
drowned, as *by* the °flood of Egypt.
6 *It is* He That buildeth His °stories in the
heaven, and hath founded His °troop °in the
earth; He that °calleth for the waters of the
sea, and poureth them out upon the face of
the earth: °The LORD °*is* His name.

Y 7 *Are* ye not as °children of the Ethiopians
unto Me, O °children of Israel? °saith [6]the
LORD. Have not I °brought up Israel out of
the land of Egypt? and the Philistines from
°Caphtor, and the Syrians from °Kir?"
8 °Behold, the eyes of [5]the Lord GOD *are*
upon the °sinful kingdom, and "I will destroy
it from off the face of the °earth; saving that
I will not utterly destroy the house of Jacob,
[7]saith [6]the LORD.
9 For, °lo, I will command, and I will sift

9 cause the sun. This determines the time of the fulfilment of this "threatening". See Isa. 13. 10; 59. 9, 10. Jer. 15. 9. Joel 2. 2; 3. 15. Mic. 3. 6. Can this refer to the earthquake of 1. 1?

10 your feasts. Ref. to Pent. (Ex 12. 14; 23. 15, 16. Lev. 23). Ap. 92.

sackcloth . . . baldness. The outward symbols of mourning. Cp. *v.* 3. Isa. 15. 2. Ezek. 7. 18.

it: i.e. the land.

11 Behold. Fig. *Asterismos.* Ap. 6.

of hearing, &c. Cp. 1 Sam. 3. 1. Ps. 74. 9. Ezek. 7. 26.

words. With *'eth* = the very words. Some codices, with Aram., Sept., Syr., and Vulg., read "word" (sing.).

12 wander. Heb. go tottering, or staggering.

13 virgins. Heb. *bethūlah* (pl.). See note on Gen. 24. 43.

14 sin = guilt, trespass. Heb. *'āshām.* Ap. 44. ii. Put by Fig. *Metonymy* (of Cause), Ap. 6, for the idol itself.

Dan . . . Beer-sheba. The two places where the calves were set up (1 Kings 12. 26–30).

manner = mode [of worship]; Acts 9. 2. So used in Acts 16. 17; 18. 25, 26; 19. 9, 23; 24. 14.

they: i.e. the two calves, or "they that swear".

9. 1-4 (**B³**, p. 1231). SYMBOLIC.
(*Division.*)

B³ | W¹ | 1–. Symbol. Striking the lintel.
| W² | –1-4. Signification.

1 the LORD*. One of the 134 places where the *Sōpherīm* say they altered "Jehovah" of the primitive text to "Adonai" (Ap. 32). See Ap. 4. VIII (2) and II. Here it is combined with *'eth* = Jehovah Himself.

upon = beside, or by.

the altar. Probably the same altar at Beth-el where Jeroboam had once stood (1 Kings 13. 1). Cp. 7. 13.

lintel = capital. Render: "smite the capital, shake the foundations, cut them off [i.e. the pillars] by the head, all of them".

and I will slay. This is the signification of the symbolical act.

the last of them: i.e. the remnant of the People.

2 Though they dig, &c. Note the Fig. *Catabasis* (Ap. 6).

hell. Heb. Sheōl = THE grave. Ap. 35. Cp. Ps. 139. 8, &c.

climb up. Cp. Job 20. 6. Jer. 51. 53. Obad. 4.

4 command the sword. Ref. to Pent. (Lev. 26. 33. Deut. 28. 25). Ap. 92. Cp. Ezek. 5. 12.

I will set Mine eyes, &c. Ref. to Pent. (Lev. 17. 10; 20. 5). Ap. 92. Cp. Jer. 44. 11.

evil = calamity. Heb. *rā'a'.* Ap. 44. viii. Cp. 3. 6.

9. 5-15 (**A⁴**, p. 1231). LITERAL.
(*Alternation.*)

A⁴ | X | 5, 6. The Land. Touched.
| Y | 7–10. Exile from it.
| *X* | 11–13. The Land. Blessed.
| *Y* | 14, 15. Restoration to it.

5 the Lord GOD. Heb. Adonai Jehovah. Ap. 4. VIII (2) and II. See note on 1. 8.

dwell. The 1611 edition of the A.V. reads "dwelleth".

flood. See notes on 8. 8.

6 stories = chambers above. Cp. Ps. 104. 3, 13.

troop = band: i.e. the blue vault.

in = over.

calleth. Cp. 5. 8.

The LORD. Heb. Jehovah. Ap. 4. II.

is His name. Ref. to Pent. (Ex. 15. 3). Ap. 92.

7 children = sons.

saith the LORD = [is] Jehovah's oracle.

brought up Israel. Ref. to Pent. (Ex. 13. 3, 9, 14, 16; 33. 1. Deut. 5. 15; 6. 21, &c.). Ap. 92.

Caphtor = Crete. Ref. to Pent. (Deut. 2. 23). Ap. 92.

Kir. Supposed to be Lower Mesopotamia.

8 Behold. Fig. *Asterismos.* Ap. 6.

sinful. Heb. *chātā'.* Ap. 44. i.

earth = ground, or soil. Heb. *'ădāmāh.*

9 lo = behold. Fig. *Asterismos.* Ap. 6.

689-687 the house of Israel among all nations, like as
corn is sifted in a sieve, yet shall not °the
least grain fall upon the °earth.
10 All the °sinners of My People shall die by
the sword, which say, 'The evil shall not
overtake nor °prevent us.'

X (p. 1242) **11 °In that day will I raise up the tabernacle °of David that is fallen, and close up
the breaches thereof; and I will raise up his
ruins, and I will build it as in the days of old:
12 That they °may possess the remnant of
°Edom, and of all the °heathen, °which are
called by My °name, [7]saith [6]the LORD That
doeth this.**
13 [8]Behold, the days come, [7]saith [6]the
LORD, that °the plowman shall overtake the
reaper, and the treader of grapes him that
soweth seed; and °the mountains shall drop
°sweet wine, and all the hills shall °melt.

Y 14 And °I will bring again the °captivity of
My People of Israel, and °they shall build the
waste cities, and inhabit *them;* and °they shall
plant vineyards, and drink the °wine thereof;
they shall also make gardens, and eat the
fruit of them.
15 And °I will plant them upon °their land,
and they shall °no more be pulled up out of
their land °which I have given them, °saith
[5]the LORD thy God.

the least grain. Heb. *tzᵉrōr.* A usage common to-day with the *fĕllahheen* (see James Niel's ***Palestine Explored***, p. 250).

earth. Heb. *'eretz.* Not the same word as in *v.* 8.

10 sinners. Heb. *chāṭā,* as in *v.* 8.

prevent = surprise.

11 In that day. Passing to the subject of the future restoration (see the Structure). Quoted in **Acts 15.** 14-18.

of David. Erected on Zion by David (2 Sam. 6. 17. Cp. 7. 6) before the Temple was built on Moriah by Solomon. In 7. 7-9, it was seen to be "out of plumb", therefore on the point of falling. Here it is fallen down: hence the prophecy here given. In Acts 15 the time had come, had the People obeyed Peter's call in Acts 3. 18-21. But it was finally rejected (Acts 28. 25-28), and this prophecy, therefore, yet awaits its fulfilment.

12 may possess = may take possession of.

Edom. Cp. Num. 24. 18. 2 Sam. 8. 14.

heathen = nations.

which are called, &c.: or, on whom My name is called.

name: i.e. Israel.

13 the plowman, &c. This shows that the fulfilment of this prophecy is yet in abeyance, for these temporal blessings were postponed on the rejection of the call to repentance in Acts 3. 18-26. Cp. Acts 28. 25-28. Note the ref. to Pent. (Lev. 26. 5). Ap. 92.

the mountains, &c. Cp. Joel 3. 18.

sweet wine = new wine. Heb. *'āṣīṣ.* See Ap. 27. V.

melt: i.e. dissolve into wine and oil. Fig. ***Hyperbole*** (Ap. 6), for emphasis.

14 I will bring again. Ref. to Pent. (Deut. 30. 5). Ap. 92. Cp. 5. 11. Ps. 53. 6. Jer. 30. 3, 18; 31. 23. Ezek. 16. 53; 39. 25. Joel 3. 1, 2.

captivity = the captives. Put by Fig. *Metonymy* (of Adjunct), Ap. 6, for captives. **they shall build.** Cp. Isa. 61. 4; 65. 21. Jer. 30. 18; 31. 38-40. Ezek. 36. 33-36; 37. 25-28. **they shall plant.** Cp. 5. 11. Isa. 62. 8, 9; 65. 21. Ezek. 28. 26. Hos. 2. 21-23. Joel 3. 18, &c. **wine.** Heb. *yayin.* Ap. 27. I. **15 I will plant.** Ref. to Pent. (Lev. 25. 18, 19; 26. 5). Ap. 92. **their land.** Ref. to Pent. (Gen. 13. 15, &c.). Ap. 92. Cp. Isa. 60. 21. Jer. 24. 6; 32. 41. Ezek. 34. 28; 37. 25. Joel 3. 20. Mic. 4. 4. **no more be pulled up.** Cp. Jer. 32. 41, marg. **which I have given them.** This is the ground of all the blessing. Ref. to Pent. (Num. 32. 7, 9. Deut. 3. 18; 26. 15; 28. 52). Ap. 92. Cp. Josh. 2. 6, 15; 18. 3; 23. 13, 15. Jer. 25. 5. The so-called "Priests' Code", according to most modern critics, was compiled by the priests in Babylon, and most of the Pentateuch is "post-exilic" (see *Encycl. Brit.*, eleventh (Cambridge) edition, vol. 3, p. 852, col. 1). Yet it was well known to Amos (cent. 7 B.C.). Cp. 2. 4, 7, 8, 12; 4. 4, 5; 5. 12, 21, 22; 9. 4, &c. **saith** = hath said.

OBADIAH.

THE STRUCTURE OF THE BOOK AS A WHOLE.

(*Division.*)

D[1]	F[1]	A[1]	1-16. EDOM. DESTRUCTION.
		A[2]	17-21. ISRAEL. RESTORATION.

For the CANONICAL order and place of the Prophets, see Ap. 1, and p. 1206.
For the CHRONOLOGICAL order of the Prophets, see Ap. 77.
For the Inter-relation of the Prophetic Books, see Ap. 78.
For the *Formulæ* of Prophetic utterance, see Ap. 82.
For References to the Pentateuch by the Prophets, see Ap. 92.
For the Inter-relation of the Minor (or Shorter) Prophets, see pp. 1206 and 1207.

The Minor Prophets do not profess to be chronological. The order seems to be logical; hence, Obadiah corresponds with Joel, and takes up Joel's theme, and shows (by contrast) what Joel's "day of the LORD" shall be for Israel's enemies. See pp. 1206-7. Edom is the one enemy in Joel (3. 19) as in Obadiah: indeed, from the first, Gen. 27. 39, 40 was fulfilled (see notes on 1 Kings 22. 47 and 2 Kings 8. 20-22. 2 Chron. 21. 8-10). After that we find prophecies against Edom (Isa. 34. 5-17. Jer. 49. 17-22. Ezek. 25. 12-14; 35; and Obadiah).

The correspondence between Jer. 49 and Obadiah may be thus shown:

Obad. 1-	= Jer. 49.	7-.	Obad. -5	= Jer. 49.	9-.
" -1, 2	= "	14, 15.	" 6	= "	10.
" 3, 4	= "	16.	" 8	= "	-7.
" 5-	= "	-9.	" 9	= "	22.

The two prophecies are independent and original. There is no need to discuss which of the two quoted the other, or whether both refer to an earlier prophet. All beyond the Scripture record is conjecture.

That Obadiah gives details which are complementary may well be explained by the Fig. *Hysterēsis* (Ap. 6).

For the partial fulfilment of the prophecy, see the notes.

The prophecy of Obadiah is undated; but, from the internal evidence, referred to above, it was almost certainly subsequent to the captivity of Jehoiachin (489-8 B.C.), or to the destruction of Jerusalem by Nebuchadnezzar, and the end of Judah. This would bring it to either 482 B.C. or 472 B.C.

OBADIAH.

A[1] A a 1 THE vision of °Obadiah. °Thus saith
(p. 1245) °the Lord GOD °concerning Edom; °"We
82 or 472 have heard °a rumour from °the LORD, °and
an ambassador is sent among the °heathen,
°Arise ye, and let us rise up against her °in
battle."
2 °Behold, I have made thee small among
the [1]heathen: thou art greatly despised.
b 3 The pride of thine heart hath deceived
thee, thou that dwellest in °the clefts of the
rock, whose habitation *is* high; that saith in
his heart, 'Who shall bring me down to the
ground?'
4 °Though thou exalt *thyself* as the eagle,
and though thou °set thy nest °among the
stars, thence will I bring thee down, °saith
[1]the LORD.
B 5 °If thieves came to thee, if robbers by
night, (°how art thou cut off!) would they not
have stolen till they had enough? °if the
grapegatherers came to thee, °would they not
leave *some* grapes?
6 °How are *the things* of Esau °searched
out! *how* are his hidden things sought up!
A b 7 All the °men of thy °confederacy have
brought thee *even* to the border: °the men
that were at peace with thee have deceived
thee, °*and* prevailed against thee; °*they that
eat* thy bread have laid a °wound under thee:
there is none °understanding in him.
8 Shall I not in °that day, [4]saith [1]the LORD,
even destroy the wise *men* out of Edom, and
understanding out of the °mount of Esau?
9 And thy mighty *men*, O °Teman, shall be
dismayed, to the end that every one of the
[8]mount of Esau may be cut off by slaughter.
a 10 For °*thy* violence against thy brother
Jacob shame shall cover thee, and thou shalt
be cut off for ever.
11 °In the day that thou stoodest on the other
side, °in the day that the °strangers carried
away captive his forces, and foreigners entered
into his °gates, and cast lots upon Jerusalem,
even thou *wast* as one of them.
12 But °thou shouldest not have looked on
the day of thy brother [11]in the day that he became a [11]stranger; neither shouldest thou
have rejoiced over the °children of Judah [11]in
the day of their destruction; neither shouldest
thou have °spoken proudly [11]in the day of
distress.
13 [12]Thou shouldest not have entered into
the gate of My people [11]in the day of their
calamity; yea, thou shouldest not have looked
on their affliction [11]in the day of their calamity,
nor have laid *hands* on their substance [11]in the
day of their calamity;
14 Neither shouldest thou have °stood in the
°crossway, to cut off those of his that did escape; neither shouldest thou have delivered
up those of his that did remain [11]in the day of
distress.

1-16 (**A[1]**, p. 1244). EDOM. DESTRUCTION.
(*Alternation and Introversion.*)

A[1] | A | a | 1, 2. Remote Cause. Jehovah's Purpose.
  b | 3, 4. Deceived by Self.
 B | 5, 6. Devastation.
 A | b | 7-9. Deceived by Others.
  a | 10-14. Immediate Cause. Edom's Sin.
 B | 15, 16. Extermination.

1 Obadiah = Servant of Jehovah. Cp. 1 Kings 18. 3.
Thus saith, &c. The words of this prophecy, therefore, are not Obadiah's, but Jehovah's. Cp. *vv.* 8, 18.
the Lord GOD. Heb. Adonai Jehovah. Ap. 4. VIII (2) and II.
concerning Edom. See notes on p. 1244.
We have heard. The rhetorical difficulty may be removed by regarding these words as the words of Edom's foes. **a rumour** = tidings.
the LORD. Heb. Jehovah. Ap. 4. II. Supply the logical *Ellipsis* (Ap. 6): "from Jehovah [that Edom is to be attacked]". **and**: or, and [already].
heathen = nations.
Arise ye. These are the words of the embassage.
in battle = the war.
2 Behold. Fig. *Asterismos.* Ap. 6. Calling attention to the words of Jehovah.
3 the clefts, &c. Referring to the natural position of the Edomites. Cp. 2 Kings 14. 7.
4 Though, &c. The words of Jehovah.
set thy nest. Ref. to Pent. (Num. 24. 21). Ap. 92. Cp. Hab. 2. 9.
among the stars. Fig. *Hyperbole.* Ap. 6.
saith the LORD = [is] Jehovah's oracle.
5 If . . . ? Fig. *Erotēsis.* Ap. 6.
how. Fig. *Ejaculatio,* or *Erotesis.* Ap. 6.
if the grapegatherers. Some codices, with Aram., Sept., and Syr., read "or if", &c.
would they not . . . ? Ref. to Pent. (Deut. 24. 21). Ap. 92. Cp. Isa. 17. 6; 24. 13.
6 How . . . ! Fig. *Erotēsis.* Ap. 6.
searched out: i.e. discovered by the enemies. Ginsburg thinks it should be read "stripped bare".
7 men. Pl. of *'ĕnōsh.* Ap. 14. III.
confederacy. See Ps. 83. 5-8.
the men, &c. = the men who were wont to salute thee.
and. Some codices, with three early printed editions and Syr., read this "and" in the text.
they that eat. The *Ellipsis* is thus correctly supplied.
wound = snare.
understanding in him: or, no discernment of it: in spite of their renown for wisdom. Cp. *v.* 8. Jer. 49. 7.
8 that day: i.e. the day of the fulfilment of the prophecy. Cp. 15, 16, and Isa. 63. 1-6. Jer. 49 13.
mount = hill country.
9 Teman. Cp. Jer. 49. 7.
10 thy violence, &c. Ref. to Pent. (Gen. 27. 41-44. Deut. 23. 7). Ap. 92.
11 in the day. See Ap. 18. Note the Fig. *Repetitio* (Ap. 6) in *vv.* 12, 13, 14. **strangers** = aliens.
gates. Heb. text = gate; but Heb. marg., with some codices and two early printed editions, read "gates" (pl.).
12 thou shouldest not have looked on, &c. All these are Prohibitives in Heb.: i.e. they are addressed to Edom as from a spectator looking on and saying; "Look not thou," &c. **children** = sons.
spoken proudly. Heb. enlarged thy mouth [with laughter]. Cp. Ps. 35. 21. Isa. 57. 4. Ezek. 35. 13.
14 stood in the crossway. Referring to some antecedent event by Fig. *Hysterēsis* (Ap. 6).
crossway = fork of the roads, or a mountain pass.

B (p. 1245) 482 or 472 **15 For °the day of [1]the LORD *is* near upon all the [1]heathen: °as thou hast done, it shall be done unto thee: thy reward shall return upon thine own head.**

16 For [15]as ye have drunk upon My °holy mountain, *so* shall all the heathen drink °continually, yea, they shall drink, and they shall °swallow down, and they shall be °as though they had not been.

A² C (p. 1246) **17 But °upon mount Zion °shall be °deliverance, °and there shall be holiness;**

D **and the house of Jacob °shall possess their possessions.**

E **18 And the house of Jacob shall be a fire, and the house of Joseph a flame, and the house of Esau for stubble, and they shall kindle in them, and devour them; and °there shall not be °*any* remaining of the house of Esau; for [1]the LORD hath spoken *it*.**

D **19 And *they of* °the south shall possess the [8]mount of Esau; and *they of* °the plain the Philistines: and °they shall possess the °fields of Ephraim, and the °fields of Samaria: °and Benjamin *shall possess* Gilead.**

20 And the °captivity of °this host of the [12]children of Israel °*shall possess* that of the Canaanites, °*even* unto °Zarephath; and the °captivity of Jerusalem, which *is* in °Sepharad, shall possess °the cities of [19]the °south.

C **21 And °saviours shall come up on mount Zion to judge the mount of Esau; and °the kingdom shall be [1]the LORD'S."**

15 the day of the LORD. See note on Isa. 2. 11, 17. The prophecy is now enlarged, and includes all the nations who were Israel's enemies.

as=according as. This prophecy was fulfilled, so far as Edom was concerned, later on (see 1 Macc. 5. 4, 65. Josephus, *De Bell.* iv. 5); likewise will the judgment on "all the nations" be literally fulfilled.

16 holy. See note on Ex. 3. 5.

continually. Some codices, with four early printed editions (one Rabbinic in marg.), read "round about".

swallow down: or, stagger. Only elsewhere in Job 6. 3.

as though, &c. Solemn and noteworthy words.

17-21 (A², p. 1244). ISRAEL. RESTORATION.

(*Introversion.*)

A² | C | 17-. Deliverance.
  D | -17. Possession.
    E | 18. Victory.
  D | 19, 20. Possession.
C | 21. Deliverers.

17 upon mount Zion. Cp. Isa. 46. 13. Joel 2. 32.

shall be. Cp. Jer. 46. 28. Joel 3. 16. Amos 9. 8.

deliverance=a delivered remnant. Cp. Joel 2. 32.

and there shall be, &c. Cp. Isa. 1. 26; 4. 3, 4. Joel 3. 17.

shall possess, &c. Ref. to Pent. (Num. 24. 18, 19). Ap. 92. Cp. Isa. 14. 1, 2. Joel 3. 19-21. Amos 9. 11-15.

18 there shall not be. Cp. *vv.* 9, 10, 16.

any remaining=him that remaineth. Twenty-four centuries ago this prophecy was written, and to-day no Edomites can be identified. Cp. *v.* 14, and Num. 24. 19 (the same word). There will be a restored Edom, "in that day", or Isa. 63. 1-6. Jer. 49. 7-22 could not be fulfilled.

19 the south=the south [country], the Negeb. See note on Ps. 126. 4. Cp. Amos 9. 12.

the plain=the lowlands, the Shephelah [shall possess]. Cp. Zeph. 2. 7.

they=they [of the mountain], or [of the centre]. **fields**=territory. **and Benjamin**=and [they of] Benjamin. **20 captivity**=the captives: "captivity" being put by Fig. *Metonymy* (of Adjunct), Ap. 6, for the captives. **this host**: i.e. the whole of the twelve tribes. **shall possess.** Supply the *Ellipsis* thus: "they who are scattered among [the Canaanites]". **even, &c.** Supply "[shall possess] as far as". **Zarephath**=Sarepta, belonging to Sidon and Tyre. **Sepharad** is mentioned with Ionia and Greece (in the west) in the inscriptions of *Behistun*, col. 1, line 15. See Ap. 57, p. 81. Jews were sold as slaves, and were taken to Spain by the Phoenicians to work in the mines near the great city of Ampuria, now being unearthed, near Figueras, in the province of Gerona. The "Jews' houses" are still shown at Besalu. **the cities, &c.** Jewish tradition declares for Spain. **south.** After *v.* 20, supply the logical *Ellipsis* of thought thus: "[yea, My People shall enlarge their borders on all sides], and saviours", &c. **21 saviours**=deliverers: i.e. earthly and human, as in Judges 3. 9, 15. Cp. Mic. 5. 4, 5. See the Structure ("C" and "*C*"), above. **the kingdom shall be the LORD'S.** Cp. Ps. 22. 28. Dan. 2. 44; 7. 14, 27. Zech. 14. 9. Rev. 11. 15; 19. 6.

JONAH.

THE STRUCTURE OF THE BOOK AS A WHOLE.

(*Extended Alternation.*)

𝔊¹ **A** | 1. 1. THE WORD OF JEHOVAH.
  B | 1. 2. MISSION TO NINEVEH.
    C | 1. 3. JONAH. DISOBEDIENCE.
      D | 1. 4—2. 10. CONSEQUENCES. RESURRECTION OF JONAH.
A | 3. 1. THE WORD OF JEHOVAH.
  B | 3. 2. MISSION TO NINEVEH.
    C | 3. 3, 4-. JONAH. OBEDIENCE.
      D | 3. -4—4. 11. CONSEQUENCES. CORRECTION OF JONAH.

NOTES ON THE STRUCTURE OF JONAH (PAGE 1246).

For the CANONICAL order and place of the Prophets, see Ap. 1, and p. 1206.

For the CHRONOLOGICAL order of the Prophets, see Ap. 77.

For the Inter-relation of the Prophetic Books, see Ap. 78.

For the *Formulæ* of prophetic utterance, see Ap. 82.

For References to the Pentateuch by the Prophets, see Ap. 92.

For the Inter-relation of the Minor (or Shorter) Prophets, see pp. 1206–7.

The clue to the date is given in 1. 1: which, by comparison with 2 Kings 14. 25, falls within the time of Jeroboam II and the earlier years of Uzziah: therefore about 690 B.C. (see Ap. 50, p. 59).

Modern critics are practically unanimous in declaring that the book is a "combination of allegory and myth". But the fact that Jonah the prophet was a historic personage is settled by 2 Kings 14. 25. And the fact that the prophecy, with its great miracle, was referred to by Christ as a type of Himself, places the book in as high a position as any other prophecy.

The Century Bible says that "we are not to conclude that the literal validity of the history of Jonah is established by this reference" (note on Matt. 12. 40, p. 206). But, apart from the fact that the Lord referred to the Queen of Sheba in the very next sentence, and thus places Jonah on the same level of "literal validity", the question is placed beyond all controversy by the further fact that seven times in John's Gospel the Lord declared that every one of His words that He uttered was given Him to speak by the Father (see below). Those who strike at these words of Christ are striking at God Himself, and are making the whole of Divine Revelation of none effect. All the puerile and fanciful assumptions used for arguments are swept away with one stroke, and are overwhelmed by this decisive and conclusive fact. Modern critics must now perforce find the answers to their own objections. We need not be at the pains to repeat the refutation of their assumption, that, because certain words have not been required or necessitated by the subjects of the earlier Scriptures, therefore such words did not exist before, and are thus evidences of the book's being written at a later period of time. Only a mind already hostile could invent such a proposition, and only those who are ignorant of "the laws of evidence" could make use of it.

The prophecy of Jonah is literal history, and is besides a twofold type.

(1) He was a type of the death, burial, and resurrection of our Lord: see Matt. 12. 40, where the "as" and the "so" are sufficient to show us that a man's being miraculously *kept alive* for a particular period can be no type of another's being *dead and buried* for the same period.

As our Lord was raised from the dead at the end of that period (see Ap. 156), so Jonah must have been, as miraculously, *raised from the dead.*

Jonah's prayer could have been uttered in the last few moments of life. In any case the words of the prayer were not written down till after he had been vomited up alive (Jonah 2. 1–10).

(2) "As Jonah was a sign unto the Ninevites, so shall also the Son of Man be to this generation" (Luke 11. 30).

That generation were as grieved and angry at the faith and repentance of those to whom the resurrection of our Lord was proclaimed, as Jonah was at the repentance of the Ninevites.

Both these types were hidden in the history by the One Who knew the end from the beginning, and are declared to be so by Him of Whom Jehovah said, "I will put My words in His mouth".

Seven times in John's Gospel our Lord testified to the fulfilment of that promise:—

"My doctrine (i.e. teaching) is not Mine, but His that sent Me" (7. 16).

"As My Father hath taught Me, I speak these things" (8. 28).

"Why do ye not believe Me? He that is of God heareth God's words: ye therefore hear them not, because ye are not of God" (8. 46, 47).

"I have not spoken of (or from) Myself; but the Father which sent Me, He gave me a commandment, what I should say, and what I should speak" (12. 49).

"The words that I speak unto you I speak not of (i.e. from) Myself: but the Father that dwelleth in Me" (14. 10).

"The word which ye hear is not Mine, but the Father's Which sent Me" (14. 24).

"I have given unto them the words which Thou [the Father] gavest Me" (17. 8).

The Century Bible (Jonah; Introduction, p. 200) may say: "It is humiliating for a commentator to collect doubtful stories of sailors swallowed by sharks and vomited out alive." There is truth in this. But if we recognise the fact that the word "alive", includes the thought of *resurrection*, then we have ample evidence that this is conveyed and taught by the "as" and "so" in Matt. 12. 40. In any case we have to remember the words of Jehovah in Deut. 18. 18, 19: "I will put My words in His mouth, and He shall speak unto them all that I shall command Him. And it shall come to pass, that whosoever will not hearken to My words which He shall speak in My name, I will require it of him." We leave the question with these solemn words: "I will require it of him."

The notes will show us Jonah, not as a wayward, thoughtless child, but as a "man of God", willing to sacrifice himself (mistakenly, of course) in order to save his nation. He knew that Assyria at that time was in great difficulties. There is a silence of eighteen years in Assyrian history at that time, and the surrounding nations were beginning to assert themselves. Jonah had just been commissioned to encourage Israel to a restored position (2 Kings 14. 25, 26). He must have known also that Nineveh (Assyria) was to be Jehovah's rod of judgment for Israel. He knew the well-known character of Jehovah, and feared that if he made Jehovah's proclamation Nineveh might repent, and her overthrow be averted. See Jehovah's words (4. 2).

If, however, for the sake of his nation, he did not make the proclamation at all, Nineveh might be overthrown and Israel saved. He was mistaken, and had to be corrected (ch. 4. 4–11).

The great lesson of the book is—not "Jehovah's care for children and cattle", &c., but that the devices of man shall not frustrate His purpose, and that what He hath said shall surely come to pass.

That is the lesson which gives to the book a dignity and importance which is worthy of it, and of its place in the Word of God.

JONAH.

690 A (p. 1248) **1** NOW ° the word of ° the LORD came unto
° Jonah ° the son of ° Amittai, saying,

B **2** ° "Arise, go to ° Nineveh, that great city,
and ° cry against it; for ° their ° wickedness is
come up before Me."

C **3** But [1] Jonah ° rose up to flee unto ° Tarshish
° from the presence of [1] the LORD, and went
down to ° Joppa; and he found a ° ship going
to ° Tarshish: so ° he paid the fare thereof,
and went down into it, to go with them unto
Tarshish ° from the presence of [1] the LORD.

D A D F **4** But [1] the LORD sent out a great ° wind into
the sea, and there was a mighty tempest in
the sea,

G so that the [3] ship ° was like to be broken.

E H **5** Then the ° mariners were afraid, and ° cried
° every man unto his god, and cast forth the
° wares that *were* in the [3] ship into the sea, to
lighten *it* of them. But Jonah was gone down
° into the sides of the ° ship; and he lay, and
was fast asleep.
6 So the ° shipmaster came to him, and said
unto him, "What meanest thou, O sleeper?
arise, call upon thy ° God, if so be that ° God
will think upon us, that we perish not."

1. 1 the word of the LORD came. This statement is unanswerable, and covers the truth of the whole contents of this book. This, or a like expression occurs *seven* times in Jonah (1. 1; 2. 10; 3. 1, 3; 4. 4, 9, 10).

the LORD. Heb. Jehovah. Ap. 4. II.

Jonah is the prophet named and described in 2 Kings 14. 25. He was a native of Gath-hepher, now *el Meshhed*, three miles north-east of Nazareth. Nazareth was in Galilee (see Ap. 169). The statement of the Pharisees in John 7. 52 was not true.

the son of Amittai. See 2 Kings 14. 25.

Amittai = the truth of Jehovah.

2 Arise, go. Contrast "rose up to flee" (*v.* 3).

Nineveh. Cp. Gen. 10. 11, 12. Mentioned again in 3. 2, 3; 4. 11. The capital of Assyria, on the left bank of the Tigris. Called first Nina, from the patron goddess of the city; of Babylonian origin; founded by a colony from Nina in South Babylonia (see *Records of the Past*, vol. iv, part ii, p. 61). Khammurabi, 1915 B.C. (on *Companion Bible* dating), code iv, pp. 60–62, spells it *Ni-nu-a*. Excavations reveal "the mound of *Nebi-Yunus* crowned by the tomb of Jonah, which could not then be explored" (see Art. "Nineveh" in the *Encycl. Brit.*, 11th (Cambridge) edition, 1911).

cry against it. Not whisper or speak softly, but cry, as making a general proclamation. Heb. *ḳara'*. Cp. Judg. 7. 3, 20. Isa. 58. 1. Joel 3. 9. Amos 4. 5, &c. Cp. also *vv.* 2, 6; 3. 2.

their wickedness. Nineveh was noted for violence and cruelty of all kinds, recorded in its own *bas-reliefs*, &c. (see Nah. 2. 8–13). Ref. to Pent. (Gen. 18. 20, 21).

wickedness. Heb. pl. of *rā'a'*. Ap. 44. viii.

3 rose up to flee. Jonah knew that Assyria was to be God's sword of judgment against Israel. If Nineveh perished, Israel might be saved. God's mercy might arrest this overthrow of Nineveh. Was this why Jonah would sacrifice himself to save his nation? This would explain his flight here, and his displeasure, as clearly stated in 4. 1–3. When he said (*v.* 12), "Take me up", &c., he had counted the cost. He confesses to the men (*vv.* 9, 10), but not to God. He gave his life to save his People. The type of Christ may have begun here. See Gal. 3. 13; and cp. Rom. 9. 1–3. **Tarshish.** See note on 1 Kings 10. 22. **from the presence of the LORD.** Ref. to Pent. (Gen. 4. 16). Ap. 92. **Joppa.** Now Jaffa. Cp. Josh. 19. 46. 2 Chron. 2. 16. Acts 9. 36. **ship.** Heb. *'ănīyāh* = any large merchant ship. Not the same word as in *v.* –5. **he paid the fare:** and counted the cost of his flight. See notes on the Structure, p. 1247.

1. 4–2. 10 (**D**, p. 1246). CONSEQUENCES. RESURRECTION OF JONAH. (*Extended Alternation.*)

D | A | 1. 4–15. Jonah's Punishment.
  B | 1. 16. Sacrifice and Vows of Mariners.
   C | 1. 17. The Fish. Preparation and Reception.
 A | 2. 1–7. Jonah's Prayer and Thanksgiving.
  B | 2. 8, 9. Sacrifice and Vow.
   C | 2. 10. The Fish. Ejection.

1. 4–15 (A, above). JONAH'S PUNISHMENT. (*Alternation and Introversion.*)

A | D | F | 4–. The Tempest.
  G | –4. Danger.
 E | H | 5, 6. Prayer of Mariners.
  J | 7–12. Jonah. Self-sacrifice.
D | *G* | 13–. Danger.
  F | –13. The Tempest.
 E | *H* | 14. Prayer of Mariners.
  J | 15. Jonah. Death.

4 wind. Heb. *rūach*. Ap. 9. **was like** = thought. Fig. *Prosōpopœia*. Ap. 6. **5 mariners** = salts. Heb. *mallāch* = salt. **cried** = cried in prayer. Heb. *ze'aḳ*. Not the same word as in *vv.* 2, 14. **every man.** Heb. *'īsh*. Ap. 14. II. **wares** = tackling. Heb. *kᵉli* = implements. **into the sides** = below deck, or cabins. Cp. Ezek. 32. 23. Amos 6. 10. **ship** = the deck, or covered part. Heb. *ṣᵉphīnah*. A genuine Heb. word, borrowed by inland people, (Syrians, Chaldeans and Arabians), from a maritime people; not vice versa. Heb. root *ṣaphan* = to cover (Deut. 33. 21 (marg. ceiled). 1 Kings 6. 9; 7. 3, 7. Jer. 22. 14. Hag. 1. 4). English "deck" is from Dutch *dekken*. **6 shipmaster** = chief of the rope. Phœnician for captain. Heb. *rab hachobēl*. Not a "later word", because a "captain" is not mentioned earlier. *Rab* = captain, or head. See 2 Kings 25. 8. Est. 1. 8. Dan. 1. 3. *Chobēl* occurs in Ezek. 27. 8, 27, 28, 29, where it is rendered "pilot". **God.** Heb. Elohim (with *'eth*) = the true God. With *'eth*, in the second occurrence. Ap. 4. I.

J a[1] (p. 1249) 690 7 And they said every one to his fellow, "Come, and let us cast lots, that we may know for whose cause this °evil *is* upon us."

b[1] So they cast lots, and the lot fell upon [1] Jonah.

a[2] 8 Then said they unto him, "Tell us, we pray thee, °for whose cause this [7] evil *is* upon us; What *is* thine occupation? and whence comest thou? what *is* thy country? and of what people *art* thou?"

b[2] 9 And °he said unto them, "I *am* an °Hebrew; and I fear [1] the LORD, °the God of heaven, °Which hath made the sea and the dry *land*."

a[3] 10 Then were the °men °exceedingly afraid, and said unto him, °"Why hast thou done this?" For the °men knew that he fled [3] from the presence of [1] the LORD, because he had told them.

11 Then said they unto him, "What shall we do unto thee, that the sea may be calm unto us?" for the sea °wrought, and was tempestuous.

b[3] 12 And he said unto them, °"Take me up, and cast me forth into the sea; so shall the sea be calm unto you: for °I know that for my sake this great tempest *is* upon you."

D G (p. 1248) 13 Nevertheless the [10] men °rowed hard to °bring *it* to the land; but they could not:

F for the sea [11] wrought, and was tempestuous against them.

E H 14 Wherefore they [2] cried unto [1] the LORD, and said, "We beseech Thee, O [1] LORD, we beseech Thee, let us not perish for this °man's °life, and lay not upon us innocent blood: for Thou, O [1] LORD, hast done °as it pleased Thee."

J 15 So they °took up Jonah, and °cast him forth into the sea: and the sea °ceased from her raging.

B 16 Then the [10] men feared [1] the LORD exceedingly, and °offered a sacrifice unto [1] the LORD, and made vows.

C 17 Now [1] the LORD had °prepared a °great fish to °swallow up [1] Jonah. And [1] **Jonah °was in the °belly of the fish °three days and three nights.**

A K (p. 1250) 2 °Then Jonah prayed unto °the LORD his °God out of the fish's °belly,

2 And said, "I °cried by reason of mine affliction unto [1] the LORD, and He °heard me;

L c out of the belly of °hell °cried I, *and* Thou °heardest my voice.

1. 7-12 (J, p. 1248). JONAH. SELF-SACRIFICE.
(*Repeated Alternation.*)

J | a[1] | 7-. Mariners. Counsel. Casting of lots.
  | b[1] | -7. Jonah taken.
  | a[2] | 8. Mariners. Inquiry.
  | b[2] | 9. Jonah. Confession.
  | a[3] | 10, 11. Mariners. Fear.
  | b[3] | 12. Jonah. Determination.

7 evil = calamity: as in Amos 3. 6. Heb. *ra'a'*. Ap. 44. viii.

8 for whose cause, &c. = for what cause. The lot had told them the person, but not the "cause". So they appeal to Jonah.

9 he said, &c. He does not tell them all. We find the real reason in 4. 1-3.

Hebrew. Referring to the language spoken. A title used in relation to foreigners (Gen. 40. 15. Ex. 3. 18, &c.).

the God of heaven. The title in relation to the Creator's creatures. See note on 2 Chron. 36. 23.

Which hath made, &c. Ref. to Pent. (Gen. 1. 1, 10).

10 men. Heb. pl. of *'ĕnōsh*. Ap. 14. III.

exceedingly afraid. Fig. *Polyptōton* (Ap. 6) = feared a great fear.

Why . . . ? They knew the *fact* of his flight, but not the *reason*, which is not revealed till 4. 1-3. This is not therefore "a later addition", as alleged.

11 wrought, &c. = grew more and more tempestuous. Heb. "was going on and raging".

12 Take me up . . . I know. He had counted the cost.

13 rowed hard. The tackling had gone. See note on "wares", *v.* 5. **bring it** = bring it back.

14 man's. Heb. *'īsh*. Ap. 14. II.

life = soul. Heb. *nephesh*. Ap. 13.

as = according as. Cp. Ps. 115. 3.

15 took up = took up with reverence or care: as in Gen. 47. 30. Ex. 28. 12, 29, &c. Heb. *nāsā'*.

cast him, &c. Why are we to *assume* that the result was different in this case from that in every other, unless so stated? It must have been death. See note on p. 1247.

ceased, &c. Cp. Ps. 89. 9. Luke 8. 24.

16 offered, &c. = sacrificed: i.e. they vowed that they would offer [when they landed]. Heb. *zebach*. Ap. 43. I. iv, and II. xii.

17 prepared = appointed, or assigned. From Heb. *mānāh*, to number. Hence, to appoint, as in Job 7. 3. Dan. 1. 5, 10, 11; and Chald. *menah* (Dan. 5. 25, 26). Cp. 4. 6-8. Never means to create.

great fish. Large enough to swallow him. In Matt. 12. 40, Greek *kētos* = any large marine monster; whence *Cetaceæ* = the mammalian order of fish. No need for any name. Cp. Matt. 12. 20; 16. 4. Luke 11. 30.

swallow up . . . belly. Not therefore kept alive in the fish's *mouth*, as some imagine. When thus swallowed up, Jonah must have died, and thus became a type of Christ. The "as" and "so" in Matt. 12. 40 require Jonah's death. He would have been no type if he had been miraculously kept alive. See further notes below.

was = came to be. **belly** = bowels.

three days and three nights. The Heb. idiom "three days" can be used for parts of "three days" (and even of years): but not when the word "nights" is added. See Matt. 12. 40, and note the force of "as". See App. 144, and 156.

2. 1-7 [For Structure see next page].

1 Then = And. See note on *v.* 10. **the LORD.** Heb. Jehovah. Ap. 4. II. **God.** Heb. Elohim. Ap. 4. I. **belly** = bowels. Cp. 1. 17.

Note the Fig. *Exergasia* (Ap. 6), as shown by the *Alternation* in *v.* 2.

v. 2 | *e* | I cried, &c. Jonah's affliction.
  | f | And He heard Jonah's request.
  | *e* | Cried I, &c.
  | *f* | And Thou heardest.

2 cried = cried out. Not the same word as in next clause, or in 1. 5; but the same as in 1. 2, 5, 14. **heard** = answered. Heb. *'ānāh*. Not the same word as in the next clause. **hell.** Heb. *Sheōl*. Ap. 35. Cp. Ps. 18. 5; 116. 3. **cried** = cried for help in distress. Not the same word as in preceding clause, or in 1. 2, 5, 14. **heardest** = gavest heed to. Heb. *shāma'*. Not the same word as in preceding clause.

690 3 For Thou °hadst cast me into the deep, in
the °midst of the seas; and the °floods compassed me about: °all Thy billows and Thy
waves passed over me.
4 °Then I said, 'I am cast out of Thy sight;
d yet I will look again °toward Thy °holy tem-
(p. 1250) ple.'
L c 5 The °waters compassed me about, *even* to
the °soul: the °depth closed me round about,
the °weeds were wrapped about my head.
6 I went down to the °bottoms of the mountains; °the earth with her bars °*was* about
me °for ever:
d yet hast Thou °brought up my life from °cor-
ruption, O [1]LORD my [1]God.
K 7 When my [5]soul °fainted within me I remembered °the LORD: and my prayer came
in unto Thee, into Thine [4]holy temple.
B 8 They that °observe °lying vanities °for-
(p. 1248) sake their own °mercy.
9 But I will sacrifice unto Thee with the
voice of thanksgiving; I will pay *that* that I
have vowed. °Salvation *is* °of [1]the LORD."
C 10 °And [1]the LORD spake unto the fish, and
it vomited out Jonah upon the dry *land*.

A **3** And °the word of °the LORD came unto
(p. 1246) Jonah the second time, saying,
B 2 "Arise, go unto Nineveh, °that great city,
and °preach unto it the preaching that I bid
thee."
C 3 So Jonah arose, and went unto Nineveh,
according to the word of [1]the LORD. Now
Nineveh was an exceeding [2]great city of
°three days' journey.
4 And Jonah began to enter into the city
°a day's journey, and he °cried, and said,
D M[1] i "Yet °forty days, and Nineveh shall be over-
(p. 1251) thrown."
k 5 So the °people of Nineveh °believed °God,
and °proclaimed a fast, and put on sackcloth,
from the greatest of them even to the least of
them.
l 6 For word came unto the king of Nineveh,

2. 1-7 (*A*, p. 1248). JONAH'S PRAYER AND THANKSGIVING. (*Introversion and Alternation.*)

A | K | 1, 2-. Affliction.
L | c | -2-4-. Place. Sheōl.
d | -4. Deliverance. Jonah's words.
L | *c* | 5, 6-. Place. The Deep.
d | -6. Deliverance. Jehovah's deeds.
K | 7. Affliction.

Note the Fig. *Exergasia* (Ap. 6), as shown by the *Introversion* in *v.* 3.

v. 3 | *g* | "The deep" as a whole.
h | The seas which make it up.
h | The floods which make it up.
g | The deep as a whole. "All".

3 hadst cast=castedst, or didst cast.
midst=heart.
floods: or, tides. Heb. *nahar.* (Sing.)
all Thy billows, &c. Cp. Ps. 42. 7.
4 Then I said, &c. Cp. Ps. 31. 22.
toward, &c. Cp. 1 Kings 8. 38.
holy. See note on Ex. 3. 5.
5 waters. Cp. Ps. 69. 1.
soul. Heb. *nephesh.* Ap. 13.
depth=an abyss.
weeds=floating sea-weeds.
6 bottoms=roots.
the earth, &c.=as for the earth, her bars, &c. Some codices, with one early printed edition, and Syr., read "and as to the earth".
was. Substitute "were".
for ever. The thought of a drowning man.
brought=didst bring.
corruption=the pit or grave, the place of corruption. Heb. *shachath.*
7 fainted=swooned, or became unconscious to all else. Cp. Ps. 77. 3. Lam. 2. 12. From *'ataph*, to cover or involve in darkness.
the LORD. Heb. Jehovah (with *'eth*)=Jehovah Himself. Ap. 4. II.
8 observe=regard, or heed.
lying=empty.
forsake their own mercy=do not heed their chastisement.
forsake=not to heed. Heb. *'āzab.* Cp. Gen. 2. 24.
mercy. Heb. *hesed.* A *Homonym*, with two meanings: (1) lovingkindness, as in Gen. 24. 12. 2 Sam. 7. 15. 1 Chron. 19. 2. 2 Chron. 6. 14. Ps. 103. 4, 8, 11, 17, &c.; (2) correction, or chastisement (Lev. 20. 17, a wicked thing bringing down punishment). Job 37. 13 (mercy=chastisement, synonymous with "correction" in preceding clause (marg. *rod*)). Prov. 25. 10 (put to shame: i. e. by correction).
9 Salvation is of=Salvation [belongeth] to: as in Ps. 3. 8. The prayer (*vv.* 2-9).
of=to.

10 And, &c. Jonah's rapid thoughts and words before he died were subsequently written down by him; for all the verbs are in the past tense, not the present. Cp. *v.* 6, "didst bring", &c. See notes on p. 1247.

3. 1 the word of the LORD. See note on 1. 1. **the LORD.** Heb. Jehovah. Ap. 4. II. **2 that great city.** Cp. 1. 1, 2; 4. 11. Diodorus Siculus (cent. 1 B.C.), ii. 3, and Herodotus (cent. 4 B.C.), v. 53, both say it was about sixty miles in circuit and about twenty miles across. We must remember that such cities included large areas for cultivation and pasturage. Cp. "much cattle", 4. 11. **preach**=proclaim. Heb. *karā'*=to cry aloud: as in *vv.* 4, 5, 8; 1. 2, 6, 14. **3 three days', &c.**: i. e. in circuit. See note above. **4 a**=one. **cried.** See note on "preach", *v.* 2.

3. -4–4. 11 [For Structures see next page].

-4 forty. The number of probation. See Ap. 10. **5 people**=men. Heb. pl. of *'ĕnōsh.* Ap. 14. III. **believed.** Heb. *'āman.* Ap. 69. III. **God.** Heb. Elohim. Ap. 4. I. **proclaimed a fast.** Professor Rawlinson has shown that just at this time Nineveh was in a time of trouble, and Assyrian history was "shrouded in darkness for forty years" (*Ancient Monarchies*, vol. ii. pp. 379, 380). Hope was given to all the neighbouring countries which were asserting their independence. This explains the readiness of Nineveh to hearken and obey, as was done on another occasion when the prophets of Nineveh declared it needful (see Professor Sayce, *The Higher Criticism and the Monuments*, pp. 489, 490); by the Persians in a national trouble; in Greece, a fast which included cattle (Herodotus, ix. 24); and by Alexander the Great (Plutarch, *Pelop.* §§ 33, 34). This decline of Nineveh gave hope to Israel: which hope had been encouraged by the prophet Jonah himself (2 Kings 14. 25-27). This may have been the reason for Jonah's not wishing to avert the overthrow (*v.* 4) of Nineveh, by giving it the opportunity to repent and thus secure Jehovah's favour (Joel 2. 14). See notes on p. 1247. We thus have veritable history, and not allegory.

690 and he arose from his throne, and he laid his robe from him, and covered *him* with sackcloth, and sat in ashes.

k (p. 1251) 7 And he caused *it* to be proclaimed and published through Nineveh by the decree of the king and his °nobles, saying, "Let neither °man nor beast, °herd nor flock, taste any thing: let them not feed, nor drink water:

8 But let [7]man and beast be covered with sackcloth, and cry mightily unto [5]God: yea, let them turn every one from his °evil way, and from the violence that *is* in their hands.

9 °Who can tell °*if* [5]God will turn and repent, and turn away from His fierce anger, that we perish not?"

i 10 And [5]God saw their works, that they turned from their [8]evil way; and [5]God °repented °of the [8]evil, that He had said that He would do unto them; and He did *it* not.

M² N m **4** But it °displeased Jonah exceedingly, and he was very angry.

n 2 And he prayed unto °the LORD, and said, "I pray thee, O °LORD, *was* not this my saying, when I was yet in my country? °Therefore I fled before unto Tarshish: for °I knew that Thou *art* a gracious °GOD, and merciful, slow to anger, and of great kindness, and repentest Thee of the °evil.

3 Therefore now, O [2]LORD, take, I beseech Thee, my °life from me; for *it is* better for me to die than to live."

O 4 Then said [2]the LORD, "Doest thou well to be angry?"

P Q o 5 So Jonah went out of the city, and sat on the east side of the city, and there °made him a °booth, and sat under it in the shadow, till he might see what would °become of the city.

p 6 And [2]the LORD °God °prepared a °gourd, and made *it* to come up over Jonah, that it might be a °shadow over his head, °to deliver him from his °grief.

R So Jonah °was exceeding glad of the gourd.

P Q p 7 But [6]God [6]prepared a °worm when the morning rose the next day, and it smote the [6]gourd that it withered.

o 8 And it came to pass, when the sun did arise, that [6]God [6]prepared a °vehement °east °wind; and the sun beat upon the head of Jonah, that he fainted,

R and wished °in himself to die, and said, "*It is* better for me to die than to live."

O 9 And [6]God said to Jonah, "Doest thou well to be angry for the [6]gourd?"

N m And he said, °"I do well to be angry, *even* unto death."

n 10 Then said [2]the LORD, "Thou °hast had

---

3. -4—4. 11 (*D*, p. 1246). CONSEQUENCES. CORRECTION OF JONAH. (*Division.*)

D | M¹ | 3. -4–10. Pardon of Nineveh.
| M² | 4. 1–11. Correction of Jonah.

3. -4-10 (M¹, above). PARDON OF NINEVEH. (*Introversion.*)

M¹ | i | -4. Jehovah. Proclamation.
k | 5. People.
l | 6. King. } Repentance.
k | 7–9. People. }
i | 10. Jehovah. Pardon.

7 nobles=great ones.

man. Heb. *'ādām.* Ap. 14. I.

herd nor flock. See note on "that great city", *v.* 2; and "much cattle", 4. 11.

8 evil=wicked. Heb. *rā'a'.* Ap. 44. viii.

9 Who can tell . . . ? Cp. "Who knoweth . . . ?" 2 Sam. 12. 22. Joel 2. 14. Jonah, for one, thought Jehovah might do so. Hence his reluctance to give Nineveh the opportunity to repent.

if=[but that].

10 repented. Fig. *Anthropopatheia.* Ap. 6.

of=concerning.

4. 1-11 (M², above). CORRECTION OF JONAH. (*Introversions and Alternations.*)

M² | N | m | 1. Jonah's anger.
n | 2, 3. Jonah's complaint to Jehovah.
O | 4. Jehovah's question. "Doest thou well?"
P | Q | o | 5. East side.
p | 6–. Gourd. Comes up.
R | -6. Jonah's gladness.
P | *Q* | *p* | 7. Gourd smitten.
o | 8–. East wind.
R | -8. Jonah's sorrow.
O | 9–. Jehovah's question. "Doest thou well?"
N | *m* | -9. Jonah's answer.
n | 10, 11. Jonah's correction by Jehovah.

1 displeased = vexed. Not the waywardness of a child, but the displeasure of a man of God, for great and sufficient reason to him. Now that Nineveh was spared, it might after all be used as God's rod for Israel, and thus destroy the hope held out by him to Israel in 2 Kings 14. 25–27. See note on 3. 5 and p. 1247.

2 the LORD. Heb. Jehovah. Ap. 4. II.

Therefore I fled=hasted to flee. The reason follows, as explained in note on *v.* 1.

I knew. This was well known, from Jehovah's revelation of Himself. Jonah knew, and referred to the Pent. (Ex. 34. 6. Num. 14. 18, 19). David knew (Ps. 86. 5). Hosea knew (Hos. 11. 8, 9). Joel knew (Joel 2. 13). Micah knew (Mic. 7. 18). Jonah's knowledge explains his flight (1. 3). No one could tell us this but himself.

GOD. Heb. El. Ap. 4. IV.

evil. Heb. *rā'a.* Ap. 44. viii.

3 life=soul. Heb. *nephesh.* Ap. 13.

5 made him=made for himself.

booth=hut.

become of=happen to. Hoping for its overthrow.

6 God. Heb. Elohim (as Creator). Ap. 4. I.

prepared=appointed: as in *vv.* 7, 8; 1. 17.

gourd. Heb. *ḳīḳāyōn.* An Egyptian word.

shadow . . . to deliver him. Note the Fig. *Paronomasia* (Ap. 6). Heb. *tzēl . . . l^ehatztzēl.*

grief=evil, or evil case. Heb. *rā'a'.* Ap. 44. viii.

was exceeding glad. Note the Fig. *Polyptōton* (Ap. 6), for emphasis. Heb.=rejoiced with great rejoicing.

---

7 worm. Put by Fig. *Synecdoche* (of the Part), Ap. 6, for a blight of such; as in Deut. 28. 39. They were appointed during the night, and came at sunrise. **8 vehement**=silent, still. Hence, sultry. Occurs only here. Not a "late" word, but not required to be used before this. **east wind**=hot wind. Heb. *ḳādīm*, cognate of "vehement" (Heb. *ḥărīthim*), both words referring to heat. East wind not the same kind as in western climes. Ref. to Pent. (Ex. 10. 13, 19). Ap. 92. **wind.** Heb. *rūach.* Ap. 9. **in himself**=in his soul. Heb. *nephesh.* Ap. 13. **9 I do well.** Supply "I do well [it is right]". **10 hast had pity on**: or, wouldst have spared: same word as in *v.* 11.

690 **pity on the [6]gourd, for the which thou hast not laboured, neither madest it grow; which °came up in a night, and °perished in a night:**
11 And °should not I spare Nineveh, that great city, wherein °are more than sixscore thousand persons °that cannot discern between their right hand and their left hand; and *also* °much cattle?"

came up in a night=was the son of a night.
perished in a night=perished as the son of a night.
11 should not I . . . ? Fig. *Erotēsis* (Ap. 6), no answer being required.
are=exist. Heb. *yĕsh*. See note on Prov. 8. 21.
that cannot discern, &c. Put by Heb. Idiom (Ap. 6), for little children; a similar idiom in Deut. 1. 39. Ap. 92
much cattle. See notes on "great city", 3. 2; and "herd and flock", 3. 7. Nineveh's walls included large areas for pasturage and cultivation. In speaking of the innocent ones in the city these are naturally included. Thus the book suddenly ends; and we are left with the solemn reflection that, Nineveh being spared, the way was thus open for the execution of Jehovah's judgment on Israel by the sword of Assyria, which took place in due time.

MICAH.

THE STRUCTURE OF THE BOOK AS A WHOLE.

(*Alternation.*)

1. 1. THE TITLE.

E[1] | **A** | 1. 2—3. 12. THREATENING.
| **B** | 4. 1—5. 15. CONSOLATION.
| *A* | 6. 1—7. 10. THREATENING.
| *B* | 7. 11-20. CONSOLATION.

For the Canonical order and place of the Prophets, see Ap. 1, and p. 1206-7.

For the Chronological order of the Prophets, see Ap. 77.

For the Inter-relation of the Prophetic Books, see Ap. 78.

For the *Formulæ* of Prophetic Utterance, see Ap. 82.

For References to the Pentateuch by the Prophets, see Ap. 92.

For the Inter-relation of the Minor (or Shorter) Prophets, see p. 1206.

The Prophecy of Micah is dated as being given "in the days of Jotham, Ahaz, and Hezekiah, kings of Judah".

Micah begins, apparently, a year or two before the end of Jotham's reign. Isaiah, in that case, had already been prophesying some seventeen or eighteen years.

By comparing 4. 10 with Isaiah 39. 6, we have another case of similar words occurring in two different prophets; and some, having concluded that one prophet copied from another, have built upon this, certain theories as to dates, &c. But no valid argument can be based on such coincidences: for the simple reason that we are not dealing with the words of the Prophets, but with the words which God spake by them (Heb. 1. 1, &c.). Surely God may speak the same message, even in identical words, by two, three, or more of His prophets. If the need were the same, why should not the words be the same?[1]

In this case, the period covered by Micah and Isaiah was almost exactly the same (cp. Mic. 1. 1 with Isa. 1. 1; and see Ap. 77). It is no wonder that the circumstances did call for similar utterances, constituting a confirmation of the Word of Jehovah "by the mouth of two or three witnesses". Both were independent, without any idea of "copying" one from the other, as is alleged by the writer in *The Encyclopædia Britannica*, eleventh (Cambridge) edition, 1910, 1911, vol. xviii, p. 357, who says: "it is impossible that much, if any, of these chapters (Mic. 4–7) can be ascribed to Micah himself". This is said in face of the fact that Jeremiah (26. 16–19) definitely quotes and refers to Micah.

Having regard to Mic. 1. 1, we see he must have been a contemporary of Isaiah for nine-and-twenty, or thirty years (Isaiah continuing for another seventeen or eighteen years if he died in the Manassean persecution. See Ap. 50, p. 68, and Ap. 77). We may thus date Micah as from 632 to 603 B.C.

[1] In connection with this we may well compare other passages as follows:—

Mic. 1. 9–16.	Isa. 10. 28–32.	Mic. 3. 12.	Isa. 32. 14.	Mic. 5. 6.	Isa. 14. 25.
,, 2. 1, 2.	,, 5. 8.	,, 4. 1.	,, 2. 2.	,, 6. 6–8.	,, 58. 6, 7.
,, 2. 6, 11.	,, 30. 10, 11.	,, 4. 4.	,, 1. 20.	,, 7. 7.	,, 8. 17.
,, 2. 11.	,, 28. 7.	,, 4. 7.	,, 9. 7.	,, 7. 12.	,, 11. 11.
,, 2. 12.	,, 10. 20–23.	,, 4. 10.	,, 39. 6.		
,, 3. 5–7.	,, 29. 9–12.	,, 5. 2–4.	,, 7. 14.		

MICAH.

TITLE (p. 1252) 632–603 **1** °THE word of °the LORD that came to
°Micah the °Morasthite in the days of
Jotham, Ahaz, *and* Hezekiah, kings of Judah,
°which he saw °concerning Samaria and Jerusalem.

A A C (p. 1253) 2 °Hear, °all ye °people; hearken, O earth,
and °all that therein is: and °let °the Lord
°GOD be witness against you, °the LORD*
°from His °holy temple.
3 For, °behold, [1]the LORD cometh forth out
of His place, and will come down, and °tread
upon the high places of the earth.
4 And °the mountains shall be molten under
Him, and the valleys shall be cleft, as wax
before the fire, *and* as the waters *that are*
poured down a steep place.

D¹ a¹ 5 For the °transgression of Jacob *is* all this,
and for the °sins of the house of Israel. °What
is the °transgression of Jacob? °*is it* not
Samaria? and °what *are* the °high places of
Judah? °*are they* not Jerusalem?

b¹ 6 Therefore I will make Samaria as an heap
of the field, *and* as plantings of a vineyard:
and I will pour down the stones thereof into
the valley, and I will °discover the foundations
thereof.
7 And all the °graven images thereof shall be
beaten to pieces, and all the °hires thereof
shall be burned with the fire, and all the idols
thereof will I lay desolate: for she gathered
it of the °hire of an harlot, and °they shall
return to the °hire of an harlot.

c¹ 8 Therefore I will °wail and howl, I will go
stripped and naked: I will make a °wailing
like the °dragons, and mourning as the °owls.
9 For her °wound *is* incurable; for °it is come
unto Judah; °he is come unto °the gate of My
people, *even* to Jerusalem.
10 °Declare ye *it* not at °Gath, weep ye not

1. 1 The word of the LORD. The only occurrence of this expression in this book: bidding us to receive it from Jehovah, not Micah, and to note Micah's pen but Jehovah's words.

the LORD. Heb. Jehovah. Ap. 4. II.

Micah = Who is like Jehovah? An abbreviated form of *Micaiah* (2 Chron. 18. 7, &c.); it is used in Jer. 26. 18 (in the Heb.). Cp. 7. 18.

Morasthite: Mareshah (*v.* 15) or Moresheth-gath (*v.* 14); now *Tel Sandahanna*, in the Shephelah, or plain, between Judea and Philistia. In the excavations at Sandahanna the ancient name is seen as *Marissa*. *Marissa* was a Sidonian colony (cent. 3 B.C.), and was afterward used as the capital of Idumea by the Edomites during the captivity of Judah (see *Records of the Past*, vol. iv, part x, pp. 291–306).

which he saw. Cp. Isa. 1. 1. Obad. 1. Nah. 1. 1.

concerning, &c. This furnishes the subject.

1. 2—3. 12 (**A**, p. 1252). THREATENING.
(*Alternation.*)

A | A | 1. 2—2. 13. The People.
B | 3. 1–4. The Rulers.
A | 3. 5–8. The False Prophets.
B | 3. 9–12. The Rulers.

1. 2—2. 13 (A, above). THE PEOPLE.
(*Introversion and Extended Alternation.*)

A | C | 1. 2–4. The coming of Jehovah.
D¹ | a¹ | 1. 5. Incrimination.
b¹ | 1. 6, 7. Threatening.
c¹ | 1. 8–16. Lamentation.
D² | a² | 2. 1, 2. Incrimination.
b² | 2. 3. Threatening.
c² | 2. 4, 5. Lamentation.
D³ | a³ | 2. 6–. Incrimination.
b³ | 2. –6. Threatening.
c³ | 2. 7–11. Lamentation.
C | 2. 12, 13. The coming of Jehovah.

2 Hear, all ye people. Micah begins by taking up the concluding words of the other Micah or Micaiah (1 Kings 22. 28), and recurs to them in 3. 1, 9; 6. 1, 2. Five times, not three, as some say; and forms no part of the Structure of the whole book. Ref. to Pent. (Deut. 32. 1). Ap. 92.

all ye = ye peoples, all of them.

people = peoples. Including ourselves. **all that therein is** = her fulness. **let the Lord GOD be witness.** Ref. to Pent. (Gen. 31. 50). **the Lord.** Heb. Adonai. Ap. 4. VIII (2). **GOD.** Heb. Jehovah. Ap. 4. II. **the LORD*.** One of the 134 places where the *Sopherim* say they altered "Jehovah" of the primitive text to "Adonai". See Ap. 32. **from His holy temple.** Cp. Ps. 11. 4. Jonah 2. 7. Hab. 2. 20. **holy.** See note on Ex. 3. 5. **3 behold.** Fig. *Asterismos.* Ap. 6. **tread upon, &c.** Ref. to Pent. (Deut. 32. 13; 33. 29). Ap. 92. Cp. Amos 4. 13. **4 the mountains, &c.** This verse foretells the calamities of 2 Kings 17 and 25. **5 transgression** = rebellion. Heb. *pāsha'*. Ap. 44. ix. **sins.** Heb. *chāṭā'*. Ap. 44. i. Aram. and Syr. read sing. **What** = Whose. **is it not Samaria?** = is it not Samaria's [idolatry]? Fig. *Erotēsis.* Ap. 6. **high places.** Cp. 1 Kings 12. 31; 14. 23. Ezek. 6. 6. These existed in Jerusalem (Jer. 32. 35); hence the mention of them in the further question. Fig. *Erotēsis.* Ap. 6. Cp. 2 Kings 16. 4. **are they not Jerusalem?** = is it not Jerusalem's [idol altars]? **6 discover, &c.** This has now recently (1911) been done in the unearthing of Ahab's wine-cellars. **7 graven images.** Heb. *pᵉsilim.* Ref. to Pent. (Ex. 20. 4). Ap. 92. **hires.** The technical Pentateuchal word for a harlot's hire, to which idolatry is compared. Cp. Hos. 8. 9, 10; 9. 1. Ref. to Pent. (Deut. 23. 18). Ap. 92. **they shall return, &c.:** i.e. the wealth gained by idolatry shall be taken away by the Assyrian idolaters. **8 wail** = lament. Cp. the Structure above; and note weight of the prophetic "burden". **dragons** = jackals. **owls.** Heb. daughters of a doleful cry. **9 wound** = stroke. Heb. *makkah* (fem.). **it.** Aram. and Syr. read "she". Referring to her stroke, which is fem. **he** = he, referring to some unnamed foe. Aram. and Syr. read "she", referring to the "stroke" of judgment. **the gate.** Cp. Obad. 11, 13. **10 Declare ye it not at Gath.** Cp. 2 Sam. 1. 20. **Gath.** Now *Tell es Ṣâfi* (Josh. 11. 22, &c.).

632-603 °at all: °in the house of Aphrah roll thyself in the dust.

11 °Pass ye away, thou inhabitant of °Saphir, having thy shame naked: the °inhabitant of Zaanan came not forth °in the mourning of Beth-ezel; °he shall receive of you his standing.

12 For the inhabitant of °Maroth waited carefully for good: but °evil came down from °the LORD unto °the gate of Jerusalem.

13 O thou °inhabitant of °Lachish, bind the chariot to the °swift beast: °she *is* the beginning of the [5]sin to the daughter of *Zion*: for the [5]transgressions of Israel were found in thee.

14 Therefore shalt thou °give presents to [1]Moresheth-gath: the houses of °Achzib *shall be* °a lie to the kings of Israel.

15 Yet will I bring °an heir unto thee, O inhabitant of [1]Mareshah: °he shall come unto Adullam the glory of Israel.

16 °Make thee bald, and poll thee for thy delicate °children; enlarge thy baldness as the eagle; for they are gone into captivity from thee.

D² a² (p. 1253) **2** Woe to them that devise °iniquity, and °work °evil upon their beds! when the morning is light, they practise it, because it °is °in the power of their hand.

2 And they °covet fields, and take *them* by violence; and houses, and take *them* away: so °they oppress a °man and his house, °even a °man and his heritage.

b² 3 Therefore thus saith °the LORD; °"Behold, against °this family do °I devise an °evil, from which ye shall not remove your necks; neither shall ye go haughtily: for this time *is* °evil.

c² 4 In that day shall *one* °take up a parable against you, and °lament with a doleful lamentation, *and* say, 'We be utterly spoiled: he hath °changed the portion of my People: how hath he removed *it* from me! °turning away he hath divided our fields.'

5 Therefore thou shalt have none that shall °cast a cord by lot in the °congregation of [3]the LORD."

D³ a³ 6 °"Prophesy ye not," °*say they to them that* prophesy:

b³ °they shall not prophesy to °them, °*that* they shall not take shame.

at all. Heb. *bakkō*, written *defectively* for *beʿakkō*. Note the Fig. *Paronomasia* (Ap. 6). Heb. *bakko 'al tibkū* = "[in] *Weep*-town *weep* not".

in . . . Aphrah roll thyself in the dust. Note the Fig. *Paronomasia* (Ap. 6). Heb. in *ʿaphrah . . . ʿāphār*. English, "in *Dust-house* roll thyself in *dust*."

11 Pass ye away: i.e. go into exile.

Saphir, having thy shame, &c. Here we have contrast. Saphir = Beauty-town, with beauty shamed; now *es Sûâfîr*.

inhabitant of Zaanan came not forth. Heb. not gone forth hath . . . Zaanan. Heb. Fig. *Paronomasia* (Ap. 6): *lo yatz'āh . . . tz'ănān* = not gone out [to weep] hath the inhabitant of Outhouse.

in the mourning . . . his standing. Commence a fresh sentence here; thus: "The trouble of Beth-ezel (Neighbour-town) shall be a useless neighbour". Or, "the Bystander's house will, from you, get its standing-room".

he shall receive, &c.: or, he will take from you its support.

12 Maroth waited carefully. The inhabitress of Bitter town bitterly grieved for her goods [taken from her]. **evil** = calamity. Heb. *rāʿaʿ*. Ap. 44. viii.

the LORD. Heb. Jehovah. Ap. 4. II. Not by chance.

the gate of Jerusalem. In Taylor's Cylinder, Sennacherib mentions his breaking of this gate (col. iii, lines 22, 23). **13 inhabitant** = inhabitress.

Lachish . . . swift beast. Note the Fig. *Paronomasia* (Ap. 6). Heb. *lārekesh . . . lākīsh* = [bind the chariot] to the horse, O inhabitress of Horse-town.

Lachish. Now *Ummtum Lākis*, or *Tell el Hesy*. See notes on 2 Kings 14. 19; 19. 8.

She. Evidently Samaria. Cp. *vv.* 5, 9; 6. 16.

14 give presents to = give up possessions at.

Achzib . . . a lie. Note the Fig. *Paronomasia* (Ap. 6) = the houses of False-town (*'Akzib*) shall prove false (*l'akzāb*).

Achzib. Now *es Zib* (Josh. 15. 44; 19. 29. Judg. 1. 31).

15 an heir . . . Mareshah. Heb. the possessor (*hayyorēsh*) . . . O Possession (*Mārēshāh*). The possessor whom Jehovah would bring was Assyria.

he shall come, &c. The glory: i.e. the nobility (Isa. 5. 13) of Israel shall go (or flee) unto [the cave] Adullam; as David had done (1 Sam. 22. 1).

16 Make thee bald, &c. The signs of mourning. Cp. Job 1. 20. Isa. 15. 2; 22. 12. Jer. 7. 29; 16. 6; 47. 5; 48. 37). This is addressed to Judah. It was forbidden under the law (Deut. 14. 1). Judah had become as the heathen: let them mourn as the heathen.

children = sons.

2. 1 iniquity. Heb. *'āven*. Ap. 44. iii. Not the same word as in 3. 10. Note the incrimination in *vv.* 1, 2. See the Structure, p. 1253. **work** = plan.

evil = wickedness. Heb. *raʿaʿ*. Ap. 44. viii.

is = exists. Heb. *yēsh*. See note on Prov. 8. 21.

in the power of their hand. A Pentateuchal idiom. Ref. to Pent. (Gen. 31. 29). Cp. Prov. 3. 27. Neh. 5. 5. Does not occur elsewhere.

2 covet fields. Ref. to Pent. (Lev. 6. 4. Deut. 5. 21). Ap. 92.

they oppress, &c. Ref. to Pent. (Lev. 19. 13, where the words are the same). Ap. 92. **man** = a human being. Heb. *geber*. Ap. 14. IV. **even.** So in some codices, with four early printed editions; but many codices, with six early printed editions, Aram., Sept., and Vulg., omit the word "even". **man.** Heb. *'īsh*. Ap. 14. II. **3 the LORD.** Heb. Jehovah. Ap. 4. II. **Behold.** Fig. *Asterismos.* Ap. 6. **this family.** Cp. Amos 3. 1. **I devise.** The contrast to *v.* 1. **evil** = calamity. Heb. *rāʿaʿ*. Ap. 44. viii. **4 take up a parable.** Ref. to Pent. (Num. 23. 7, 18; 24. 3, 15, 20, 23). Twice in Job (Job 27. 1; 29. 1); once in Isaiah (Isa. 14. 4); once in Habakkuk (Hab. 2. 6). Not elsewhere. Ap. 92. Note the Fig. *Chleuasmos* (Ap. 6). **lament with a doleful lamentation.** Note the Figs. *Polyptōton* and *Paronomasia* (Ap. 6), for emphasis. Heb. *venāhāh nehī nihyāh* = wail a wailing of woe. **changed** = changed [for the worse]. Heb. *mūr*; not *ḥalaph* = changed [for the better]. See note on Lev. 27. 10. **turning away** = to a heathen: i.e. our enemy the Assyrian. **5 cast a cord by lot.** Referring to the custom, by which, round every village in Palestine, the land was divided by lot every year to the various families; hence, the expression in Ps. 16. 6: "cord" being put by Fig. *Metonymy* (of Cause), Ap. 6, for the portion of land marked out by it. It therefore = divide your inheritances. Ref. to Pent. (Num. 26. 55, 56). Ap. 92. **congregation** = assembly. Cp. Deut. 23. 1-3, 8. **6 Prophesy** = Do not sputter. **say they to them that prophesy** = so they sputter. **they shall not prophesy.** Not the usual word for prophesy, but Heb. *nātaph*. **they**: i.e. these false prophets. **them** = as to these things: i.e. these doings of Jehovah. **that, &c.** Supply, "[saying], must He put away these suppressers".

c3 (p. 1253) 632-603 7 O *thou that art* named the house of °Jacob, °is the °Spirit of [3]the LORD straitened? *are* these His doings? °do not °My words °do good to him that walketh uprightly?

8 °Even of late My People is risen up as an enemy: ye pull off the robe with the garment from them that pass by securely as men averse from war.

9 The women of My People have ye cast out from their pleasant houses; from their children have ye taken away My glory °for ever.

10 °Arise ye, and depart; for °this *is* not *your* rest: because °it is polluted, °it shall destroy *you*, even with a sore destruction.

11 If a °man walking in the [7]spirit and falsehood do lie, *saying*, 'I will [6]prophesy unto thee of °wine and of °strong drink;' he shall even be the °prophet of this people.

C (p. 1253) 12 °I will surely assemble, O [7]Jacob, all of thee; °I will surely gather the remnant of °Israel; °I will put them together as the sheep °of Bozrah, as the flock in the midst of their fold: they shall °make great noise by reason of *the multitude of* °men.

13 °The breaker is come up before them: they have °broken up, and have passed through the gate, and are °gone out by it: and their king °shall pass before them, and [3]the LORD °on the head of them."

B **3** And I said, °"Hear, I pray you, O heads of Jacob, and ye °princes of the house of Israel; *Is it* not for you to know judgment?

2 Who hate the good, and love the °evil; who pluck off their skin from off them, and their flesh from off their bones;

3 Who also eat the flesh of My People, and flay their skin from off them; and they break their bones, and °chop them in pieces, as for the pot, and as flesh within the caldron.

4 Then shall they cry unto °the LORD, but He will not °hear them: He will even °hide His face from them at that time, as they have behaved themselves ill in their doings."

A 5 Thus saith [4]the LORD concerning the prophets that make My People °err, that °bite with their teeth, and cry, "Peace;" °and he that putteth not into their mouths, they even prepare °war against him.

6 "Therefore night *shall be* unto you, that ye shall not have a vision, and it shall be dark unto you, °that ye shall not divine; and the sun shall go down over the prophets, and the day shall be dark over them.

7 Then shall the seers be ashamed, and the diviners confounded: yea, they shall all cover their lips; for *there is* no answer of °God."

8 But truly I am full of power by the °Spirit of [4]the LORD, and of judgment, and of might, to declare unto °Jacob his °transgression, and to °Israel his °sin.

B 9 [1]Hear this, I pray you, ye heads of the house of [8]Jacob, and princes of the house of [8]Israel, that abhor judgment, and pervert all equity.

10 They build up Zion with blood, and Jerusalem with °iniquity.

11 The heads thereof °judge for reward, and the priests thereof teach for hire, and the prophets thereof divine for money: yet will they lean upon [4]the LORD, and say, "*Is* not [4]the LORD among us? none [2]evil can come upon us."

---

7 Jacob. See notes on Gen. 32. 28; 43. 6; 45. 26, 28.

is the Spirit, &c.? Ref. to Pent. (Num. 11. 23: the same word). Ap. 92.

Spirit. Heb. *rūach.* Ap. 9. **do not**=are not?

My. Sept. reads "His", as in preceding clause: or =are not My words pleasant [saith Jehovah]?

do good=pleasant.

8 Even of late=Only yesterday, or recently: this highway robbery was a new and recent evil.

9 for ever: i.e. not to be restored for the rest of their lives.

10 Arise ye, &c. Usually misquoted in a good sense; but the Structure shows it to be part of the lamentation ("c3", p. 1253).

this=this [land]. Ref. to Pent. (Deut. 12. 9). Ap. 92.

it: i.e. this [land].

it is polluted. Ref. to Pent. (Lev. 18. 27, 28, the same word). Ap. 92.

it shall destroy. Ref. to Pent. (Lev. 18. 28; 20. 22; 26. 38). Ap. 92. Cp. Ezek. 36. 12–14.

11 man. Heb. *'ish.* Ap. 14. II.

wine. Heb. *yayin.* Ap. 27. I.

strong drink. Heb. *shēkār.* Ap. 27. IV.

prophet=sputterer; as in *v.* 6. Lit. dropper [of words].

12 I will, &c. See the Structure, p. 1253.

Israel. See note on Gen. 32. 28; 43. 6; 45. 26, 28.

of Bozrah: or, with Sept., in tribulation. The member "*C*" (*vv.* 12, 13) does not speak of mercy, but of judgment, corresponding with the member "C" (1. 2–4). Not "a complete change", and no "promise to a remnant". Cp. Isa. 34. 6. Amos 1. 12.

make great noise=be in commotion.

men=human beings. Heb. *'ādām.* Ap. 14. I.

13 The breaker=One making a breach. The Assyrian. Heb. *pāratz,* as in Ex. 19. 22, 24. 2 Sam. 5. 20. 1 Chron. 14. 11; 15. 13. Generally in a bad sense.

broken up=broken in.

gone out=gone forth . . . [into captivity].

shall pass=hath passed through.

on=at: for it is Jehovah's judgment. Cp. 1. 2–4.

3. 1 Hear. This is no indication of Structure. It is a continuation of the threatening against the rulers (see "B", 3. 1–4, p. 1253, corresponding with "*B*", 3. 9–12, below). **princes**=judges.

2 evil. Heb. *rā'a'.* Ap. 44. viii.

3 chop them in pieces, as for the pot=spread them out, as flesh for the pot.

4 the LORD. Heb. Jehovah. Ap. 4. II.

hear=answer.

hide His face. Ref. to Pent. (Deut. 31. 17; 32. 20). Ap. 92. Cp. Isa. 59. 1–15. Jer. 33. 5.

5 err=go astray.

bite with their teeth. Alluding to the idolatrous practices of the heathen round the altars of Baal, biting an olive in their mouths and crying "peace", of which the olive was the symbol (Gen. 8. 11). Cp. Zech. 9. 7.

and he, &c.=but against him that putteth not [the olive] into his mouth they declare war.

war=crusade.

6 that ye shall not divine. Ref. to Pent. (Deut. 18. 10, 14. Num. 22. 7; 23. 23). Ap. 92.

7 God. Heb. Elohim. Ap. 4. I.

8 Spirit. Heb. *rūach.* Ap. 9.

Jacob . . . Israel. Cp. 1. 5. See note 2. 7.

transgression. Heb. *pāsha'.* Ap. 44. ix.

sin. Heb. *chāṭā'.* Ap. 44. i.

10 iniquity=deceit. Heb. *'āval.* Ap. 44. vi. Not the same word as in 2. 1.

11 judge for reward, &c. Ref. to Pent. (Ex. 23. 8. Deut. 10. 17; 16. 19; 27. 25. The same word in all these passages). Ap. 92.

632-603 12 Therefore shall °Zion for your sake °be
plowed *as* a field, and °Jerusalem shall become
°heaps, and °the mountain of the house as
°the high places of the forest.

B E[1] (p. 1256) 4 But °in the last days it shall come to
pass, *that* °the mountain of the house of
°the LORD shall be °established in the top of
the mountains, and it shall be exalted above
the hills; and °people shall flow unto it.
2 And many nations shall °come, and say,
°"Come, and let us go up to the mountain of
[1]the LORD, and to the house of °the °God of
Jacob; and He will teach us of His ways, and
we will walk in His paths:" for °the law shall
go forth of Zion, and the word of [1]the LORD
from Jerusalem.
3 And °He shall judge among many [1]people,
and rebuke strong nations afar off; and they
shall beat their swords into °plowshares, and
their spears into °pruninghooks: °nation shall
not lift up a sword against nation, neither
shall they learn war any more.
4 But they shall °sit °every man °under his
vine and under his fig tree; and none shall
make *them* afraid: for the mouth of [1]the °LORD
of hosts hath spoken *it*.
5 For all [1]people will walk [4]every one in
the name of his god, and we will walk in the
name of [1]the LORD our [2]God for ever and ever.

E[2] F H 6 °"In that day, °saith [1]the LORD, will I
assemble her that °halteth, and I will °gather
her that is driven out, and her that I have
afflicted;
7 And I will make her that °halted °a remnant,
and her that was cast far off a strong nation:
and [1]the LORD °shall reign over them °in
mount Zion from henceforth, even for ever."

J d 8 °And thou, O °tower of the flock, °the strong
hold of the daughter of Zion, unto thee shall
it come, even the °first dominion; the kingdom
shall come to the daughter of Jerusalem.

e 9 Now °why dost thou cry out aloud? *is there*
no king in thee? is thy counseller perished?
for pangs have taken thee as a woman in
travail.
10 Be in pain, and labour to bring forth, O
daughter of Zion, like a woman in travail:

f for °now shalt thou go forth out of the city,
and thou shalt dwell in the field, and thou
shalt go °*even* to °Babylon;

g °there shalt thou be delivered; °there [1]the
LORD shall °redeem thee from the hand of
thine enemies.

12 Zion. See Ap. 68.

be plowed as a field. This is true of the site on Ophel, but not true of the traditional site south-west of Jerusalem. See Ap. 68. I. Cp. 1. 6. Jer. 26. 18.

Jerusalem. The city proper, on Mount Moriah.

heaps = ruins. Note the Fig. *Paronomasia* (Ap. 6). Heb. *yirūshālaim 'iyyin*. Cp. 1. 6.

the mountain of the house. Moriah and the Temple. See Ap. 68.

the high places of the forest = a height of a jungle.

4. 1—5. 15 (B, p. 1252). CONSOLATION.
(Division.)

B | E[1] | 4. 1-5. General. The end.
| E[2] | 4. 6—5. 15. Particular. The means.

1 in the last days = at the end of the days. Here we are carried forward to a yet future day. Ref. to Pent. (Gen. 49. 1: the same phrase. Num. 24. 14). Ap. 92. Cp. Isa. 2. 2, &c. Ezek. 38. 8, 16. Hos. 3. 5.

the mountain, &c. Cp. 3. 12; and see Isa. 2. 2-4. Both prophecies are independent, and complementary (see Ps. 24. 3. Ezek. 28. 16).

the LORD. Heb. Jehovah. Ap. 4. II.

established: abidingly: not merely for a time.

people = peoples.

2 come = go. **Come** = Come ye.

the God of Jacob. See notes on Ps. 20. 1.

God. Heb. Elohim. Ap. 4. I.

the law. As contained in the Pentateuch. Ap. 92.

3 He shall judge = He shall rule (Pss. 2. 5, 9; 72. 8, 11; 82. 8; 96. 13; 98. 9; 110. 5, 6. Isa. 11. 3-5; 51. 5. Matt. 25. 31, 32). **plowshares.** Cp. Isa. 2. 4. Joel 3. 10.

pruninghooks: or, scythes.

nation. Some codices, with four early printed editions (one Rabbinic, marg.), Sept., and Syr., read "and nation".

4 sit = dwell. **every man.** Heb. *'īsh*. Ap. 14. II.

under, &c. Cp. 1 Kings 4. 25. Zech. 3. 10.

LORD of hosts. See note on 2 Sam. 1. 3.

4. 6—5. 15 (E[2], above). PARTICULAR. THE MEANS. *(Alternation.)*

E[2] | F | 4. 6—5. 8. Good supplied.
| G | 5. 9. Enemies cut off.
| *F* | 5. 10-14. Evil removed.
| *G* | 5. 15. Enemies cut off.

4. 6—5. 8 (F, above). GOOD SUPPLIED.
(Introversion and Extended Alternation.)

F | H | 4. 6, 7. The Remnant gathered out.
| J | d | 4. 8. The Kingdom. "But thou" (*ve'attāh*).
| e | 4. 9, 10-. Travail.
| f | 4. -10-. Departure.
| g | -10. Deliverance.
| K | 4. 11. Hostility.
| L | 4. 12, 13. Victory.
| *K* | 5. 1. Hostility.
| *J* | *d* | 5. 2. The King. "But thou" (*ve'attāh*).
| *e* | 5. 3-. Travail.
| *f* | 5. -3-6-. Return.
| *g* | 5. -6. Deliverance.
| *H* | 5. 7, 8. The Remnant gathered in.

6 In that day: i.e. the day of *v.* 1.

saith the LORD = [is] Jehovah's oracle. **halteth** = is lame. **gather** = gather out. Cp. Ps. 147. 2. Ezek. 34. 13; 37. 21. **7 halted** = was lame. **a remnant.** Cp. 2. 12; 5. 3, 7, 8; 7. 18. **shall reign.** Cp. Isa. 9. 6; 24. 23. Dan. 7. 14, 27. Obad. 21. Luke 1. 33. Rev. 11. 15. **in mount Zion.** Contrast 3. 12. Ps. 2. 6. Isa. 24. 23. **8 And thou.** Cp. this with 5. 2 in the Structure above ("d" and "*d*"). *Ve'attāh* in both members. **tower of the flock.** Heb. tower of *'Ēder*. Ref. to Pent. (Gen. 35. 21; nowhere else). Used here of Bethlehem (cp. Gen. 35. 19 with Mic. 5. 2). Ap. 92; coupled here with "Ophel" in next clause, "David's birth-place" and "David's city". **the strong hold.** Heb. *'Ophel*. See Ap. 68. I and Ap. 54, line 21, "citadel", p. 78. See note on 2 Chron. 27. 3. **first** = former. For this rendering cp. Ex. 34. 1 (tables). Num. 21. 26 (kings). Deut. 4. 32; 10. 10, &c. (days). 2 Chron. 9. 29; 16. 11; 20. 34 (acts). Ezra 3. 12. Ps. 89. 49 (loving-kindnesses). Isa. 9. 1 (time). Hag. 2. 3, 9 (glory). Zech. 1. 4; 7. 7, 12 (prophets). **9 why dost thou cry...?** This refers to the birth-pangs of the new nation which will be brought forth in that day and at that time. Cp. Isa. 13. 8; 21. 3; 26. 17; 41. 14. Jer. 22. 23; 30. 6; 50. 43. Hos. 13. 13. Matt. 24. 8. **10 now** = meanwhile: i.e. before that day. Cp. *v.* 11 and 5. 1. **even to** = as far as. Cp. Isa. 39. 7; 43. 14. **Babylon.** May "not have been on Micah's political horizon", but it was on Jehovah's. Cp. Amos 5. 25-27. Acts 7. 42, 43. **there . . . there.** Note the repetition for emphasis: i.e. there and then in that future day. **redeem** = redeem [as a kinsman]. Heb. *gā'al*. See note on Ex. 6. 6.

K (p. 1256) 632-603 11 °Now also °many nations are gathered against thee, that say, "Let her be defiled, and let our °eye look upon Zion."

L 12 But °they know not the °thoughts of [1]the LORD, neither understand they His °counsel: °for He shall gather them as the sheaves into the °floor.

13 Arise and °thresh, O daughter of Zion: for I will make thine °horn iron, and I will make thy °hoofs brass: and thou shalt beat in pieces many people: and °I will °consecrate their gain unto [1]the LORD, and their substance unto °THE LORD of the whole earth.

K **5** °Now °gather thyself in troops, O daughter of troops: °he hath laid siege against °us: they shall smite °the judge of Israel with a °rod upon the cheek.

J d 2 °**But thou, °Beth-lehem Ephratah, *though* thou be °little among the °thousands of Judah, *yet* out of thee shall He °come forth °unto me *That is* to be ruler in Israel**; Whose goings forth *have been* from of old, from °everlasting.

e 3 Therefore will he give them up, °until the time *that* °she which travaileth hath brought forth:

f then the remnant of his brethren shall return unto the °children of Israel.

4 And °He shall stand and °feed in the strength of °the LORD, in the majesty of the name of °the LORD His °God; and °they °shall abide: for now °shall He be great unto the ends of the earth.

5 And °this *Man* shall be the peace, when the °Assyrian shall come into our land: and °when he shall tread in our palaces, °then shall we raise against him °seven shepherds, and eight principal °men.

6 And they shall °waste the land of Assyria with the sword, and °the land of Nimrod in the °entrances thereof:

g thus shall He deliver *us* from the Assyrian, °when He cometh into our land, and °when he treadeth within our borders.

H 7 And the remnant of Jacob shall be in the midst of many people °as °a dew from °the LORD, as the showers upon the grass, that tarrieth not for °man, nor waiteth for the sons of [5]men.

8 And the remnant of Jacob °shall be among the Gentiles in the midst of many °people °as a lion among the beasts of the forest, as a young lion among the flocks of sheep: who, if he go through, both treadeth down, and teareth in pieces, and none can deliver.

11 Now = Meanwhile: as in *v.* 10; 5. 1. Referring to the then immediately impending hostility.

many nations. Cp. Isa. 33. 3. Lam. 2. 16. Obad. 11-13.

eye. So some codices, with two early printed editions, Aram., Syr., and Vulg.; but Heb. text reads "eyes". Cp. Ps. 54. 3.

12 they know not. Cp. Isa. 55. 8. Jer. 29. 11.

thoughts = purposes, or plans: i.e. for Israel in purging him of idolatry by his tribulation.

counsel: i.e. with regard to themselves. The reason follows.

for: or, that. **floor** = threshing-floor.

13 thresh = tread as oxen.

horn . . . hoofs. Referring to the strength of the oxen, and to the completeness of the destruction. Ref. to Pent. (Deut. 25. 4). Ap. 92. Cp. Isa. 41. 15. Jer. 51. 33.

I will. Aram., Sept., Syr., and Vulg. read "thou shalt".

consecrate = devote; as in Josh. 6. 19, 24. Cp. Zech. 14. 14. Ref. to Pent. (Lev. 27. 28).

THE LORD. Heb. *'Adōn*. The Divine title, relating to dominion in the earth. See Ap. 4. VIII (1).

5. 1 Now = Meanwhile; as in 4. 10, 11. Showing that 5. 1 relates to the interval between the then present time and "that day" of 4. 1, 6. Cp. the members "K" and "*K*".

gather thyself, &c.: or, thou shalt have sore tribulation [for thy sins], thou daughter of affliction.

he: i.e. the enemy. The Assyrian.

us. The prophet includes himself.

the judge. Or, the then ruler (cp. 1 Kings 22. 24. Lam. 3. 30; 4. 20; 5. 8, 12), who would thus be the type of the Messiah (Matt. 27. 30).

rod = sceptre. Heb. *shēbet* = the club (of defence), as in 7. 14; hence, of office; not *matteh*, the rod or staff (of support), as in 6. 9. See note on Ps. 23. 4.

2 But thou. This marks out the Structure. Cp. 4. 8 ("d") with 5. 2 ("*d*"). Quoted in Matt. 2. 5, 6. John 7. 42.

Beth-lehem Ephratah. The full name given, as in Gen. 35. 19, thus connecting Gen. 35. 21 with Mic. 4. 8.

little = too little [to rank among]. Cp. 1 Cor. 1. 27-29.

thousands = districts (1 Sam. 23. 23). Like our old English divisions, called "hundreds". Cp. Ex. 18. 25. Ref. to Pent. (Ex. 18. 25).

come forth. Note the difference between Heb. here (*yātzā'*) and *bō'* = come unto, in Zech. 9. 9. All the events between these two make up the period we call "the first Advent", and thus are typical of the "second Advent"; the *coming forth* being 1 Thess. 4. 16, and the *coming unto* being 1 Thess. 5. 2, 3, and 2 Thess. 2. 8: the former being in grace, the latter in judgment. A similar period may elapse in the antitypical comings as in the typical comings of 5. 2, and Zech. 9. 9.

unto = for.

everlasting. Cp. Ps. 90. 2. Prov. 8. 22, 23. John 1. 1, 2.

3 until the time: i.e. the end of the "meanwhile" (*v.* 1).

she which travaileth. Cp. 4. 9, 10- ("e"), above, and note there; also John 16. 21, 22, and Rev. 12. 1-6.

children = sons.

4 He: i.e. the Shepherd of Israel. Ref. to Pent. (Gen. 49. 24). Ap. 92. Cp. Ps. 80. 1. Jer. 31. 10. Ezek. 34. 23.

feed = tend, or shepherd (as a flock). Cp. 7. 14. Isa. 40. 11; 49. 10.

the LORD. Heb. Jehovah. Ap. 4. II.

God. Heb. Elohim. Ap. 4. I. **they.** Israel, His flock. **shall abide.** In everlasting security. **shall He be great.** Cp. Pss. 22. 27; 72. 8; 98. 1. Isa. 49. 5, 7; 52. 13. Zech. 9. 10. Luke 1. 32. Rev. 11. 15. **5 this Man, &c.** = this [great Shepherd of Israel]. Cp. Ps. 72. 7. Isa. 9. 6, 7. Zech. 9. 10. **Assyrian.** This is emphatic in Heb. **when, &c.** Cp. Isa. 7. 20; 8. 7-10; 37. 31-36. **then, &c.** Cp. Isa. 44. 28; 59. 19. Zech. 1. 18-21; 9. 13; 10. 3; 12. 6. **seven shepherds . . . men.** When that time comes the meaning of this will be seen. **men.** Heb. *'ādām*. Ap. 14. I. **6 waste** = eat up. **the land of Nimrod.** Ref. to Pent. (Gen. 10. 8-10). Ap. 92. The name occurs elsewhere only in 1 Chron. 1. 10. **entrances** = passes. Cp. Nah. 3. 13. **when.** See note on *v.* 5. **7 as a dew, &c.** Ref. to Pent. (Deut. 32. 2, the same verbal idiom). Ap. 92. **a dew** = a night mist. See note on Ps. 133. 3. **the LORD.** Heb. Jehovah. Ap. 4. II. **man.** Heb. *'ish*. Ap. 14. II. **8 shall be, &c.** This refers to restored Israel "in that day"; not to any other people now. **people.** Heb. = peoples. **as a lion, &c.** Ref. to Pent. (Num. 23. 24; 24. 9). Ap. 92.

G (p. 1256) 632-603 9 Thine hand shall be lifted up upon thine adversaries, and all thine enemies °shall be cut off.

F h (p. 1258) 10 "And it shall come to pass °in that day, °saith [4]the LORD, that °I will cut off thy horses out of the midst of thee, and I will destroy thy chariots:

i 11 And [10]I will cut off the cities of thy land, and throw down all thy strong holds:

h 12 And [10]I will cut off °witchcrafts out of thine °hand; and thou shalt have no *more* °soothsayers:

13 Thy °graven images also will [10]I cut off, and thy °standing images out of the midst of thee; and thou shalt no more worship the work of thine hands.

14 And I will °pluck up °thy groves out of the midst of thee:

i so will I destroy °thy cities.

G 15 And I will execute vengeance in anger and fury upon the °heathen, such as they have not heard."

A M **6** °Hear ye now what °the LORD saith; "Arise, contend thou before the mountains, and let the hills hear thy voice.

2 °Hear ye, O mountains, [1]the LORD'S controversy, and ye strong foundations of the earth:

N for [1]the LORD hath a controversy with His People, and He will plead with Israel.

O P 3 O My People, what have I done unto thee? and wherein have I wearied thee? °testify against Me.

Q 4 For °I brought thee up out of the land of Egypt, °and redeemed thee out of the °house of servants; and °I sent before thee Moses, Aaron, and °Miriam.

5 O My People, °remember now what °Balak king of Moab consulted, and what °Balaam the son of Beor answered him from Shittim unto Gilgal; that ye may know the °righteousness of [1]the LORD."

P 6 °Wherewith shall I come before [1]the LORD, *and* bow myself before °the °high °God? shall I come before Him with °burnt offerings, with calves °of a year old?

7 °Will [1]the LORD be pleased with thousands of rams, *or* with ten thousands of rivers of oil? °shall I give my firstborn *for* my °transgression, °the fruit of my body *for* the °sin of my °soul?

Q 8 He hath shewed thee, O °man, what *is* good; and what doth [1]the LORD require of thee, but to do justly, and to love °mercy, and to °walk humbly with thy [6]God?

M 9 [1]The LORD'S voice crieth unto the °city,

---

9 shall be cut off. Note the Fig. *Anaphora* (Ap. 6), in the repetition, "cut off", four times in *vv.* 9-13. All this refers eventually to restored Israel.

5. 10-14 (*F*, p. 1256). EVIL REMOVED.
(*Alternation.*)

F | h | 10. Evil people, &c. Military.
  i | 11. Cities.
 h | 12-14-. Evil people, &c. Idolaters, &c.
  i | -14. Cities.

10 in that day. The Structure connects 5. 10-14 ("*F*") with 4. 6—5. 8 ("F"), and shows it to be the same, and yet future time, called in 4. 1 "the last days".

saith the LORD =[is] Jehovah's oracle.

I will cut off, &c. See note on *v.* 9. Ref. to Pent. (Deut. 17. 16). Ap. 92. Cp. Isa. 2. 7. Zech. 9. 10.

12 witchcrafts = sorceries. Ref. to Pent. (Ex. 22. 18. Lev. 19. 26. Deut. 18. 10). Ap. 92.

hand. Some codices, with Sept., and Syr., read "hands".

soothsayers: i.e. users of secret or occult arts.

13 graven images. See 1. 7, the same word.

standing images = pillars. Probably = *'Ashērahs.* See Ap. 42. Cp. "groves", *v.* 14. Ref. to Pent. (Ex. 23. 24; 34. 13. Deut. 7. 5). Ap. 92.

14 pluck up = root up, or tear down.

thy groves = thine *'Ashērahs.* Ap. 42. Ref. to Pent. (Ex. 34. 13. Deut. 7. 5; 12. 3). Ap. 92.

thy cities. Ginsburg thinks "thine idols". A.V. marg. suggests "enemies". **15 heathen** = nations.

6. 1—7. 10 (*A*, p. 1252). THREATENING.
(*Extended Alternation.*)

A | M | 6. 1, 2-. Call to hear. Mountains.
  N | 6. -2. Controversy.
   O | 6. 3-8. Expostulation.
 M | 6. 9. Call to hear. City.
  N | 6. 10-16. Controversy.
   O | 7. 1-10. Lamentation.

1 Hear ye. Fig. *Apostrophe.* Ap. 6.

the LORD. Heb. Jehovah. Ap. 4. II.

2 Hear ye, &c. Ref. to Pent. (Deut. 32. 1). Ap. 92.

6. 3-8 (O, above). EXPOSTULATION.
(*Alternation.*)

O | P | 3. Questions of Jehovah.
  Q | 4, 5. Jehovah's Answer. What He had done.
 P | 6, 7. Questions of Jehovah.
  Q | 8. Jehovah's Answer. What Israel should do.

3 testify = answer.

4 I brought thee up, &c. Ref. to Pent. (Ex. 12. 51; 14. 30; 20. 2. Deut. 4. 20). Ap. 92.

and redeemed thee. Ref. to Pent. (Ex. 6. 6; 13. 13-16).

house of servants = house of bondage. Ref. to Pent. (Ex. 13. 3, 14; 20. 2. Deut. 5. 6; 6. 12; 7. 8). Ap. 92.

I sent before . . . Miriam. Ref. to Pent. (Ex. 15. 20, 21. Num. 12. 4, 10, 15; 20. 1; 26. 59). Miriam not mentioned after Deut. 24. 9, except 1 Chron. 6. 3.

5 remember now, &c. Ref. to Pent. (Num. 22. 5; 23. 7; 24. 10, 11; 25. 1; 31. 16. Deut. 23. 4, 5). Ap. 92.

Balak. Not mentioned since Judges 11. 25.

Balaam. Not mentioned since Josh. 24. 9, 10, except in Neh. 13. 2. Cp. 2 Pet. 2. 15, and Jude 11. Rev. 2. 14.

righteousness = righteous acts.

6 Wherewith . . .? Fig. *Erotēsis.* Ap. 6.

the high God = God on high.

high. Heb. *marōm*; not *Elyōn.*

God. Heb. Elohim. Ap. 4. I.

burnt offerings. See Ap. 43. II. ii.

of a year old. Ref. to Pent. (Lev. 9. 3). Ap. 92. **7 Will . . .? shall I . . .?** Fig. *Erotēsis.* Ap. 6. **transgression** = rebellion, insubordination. Heb. *pāsha'.* Ap. 44. ix. **the fruit of my body** = my firstborn. **sin.** Heb. *chāṭā'.* Ap. 44. i. **soul.** Heb. *nephesh.* Ap. 13. **8 man.** Heb. *'ādām.* Ap. 14. I. **mercy** = lovingkindness, or grace. **walk humbly.** The Heb. expression (*hatz^enē' leketh*) occurs only here. This verse embodies the principles governing Jehovah's administration under the Law, but not under the Gospel. Now, He requires faith in the Substitute Whom He has provided for the sinner; and His righteousness must be imputed in grace. See Ap. 63. IX: and 72. Cp. also Rom. 3. 23, 24. Eph. 2. 3-9. Titus 3. 5-8, &c. **9 city.** Put by Fig. *Metonymy* (of the Subject), Ap. 6, for the inhabitants.

632-603 (and °*the man of* °wisdom shall see °Thy
name: hear ye the °rod, and who hath appointed it.
N j 10 Are there yet the treasures of °wickedness
[p. 1259) in the house of the °wicked, and °the scant
°measure *that is* °abominable?
11 Shall I count °*them* pure with °the [10]wicked
balances, and with the bag of deceitful
weights?
12 For the rich men thereof are full of violence, and the inhabitants thereof have spoken
lies, and their tongue *is* deceitful in their
mouth.
k 13 Therefore also °will I make *thee* sick in
smiting thee, in making *thee* desolate because
of thy °sins.
14 °Thou shalt eat, but not be satisfied; and
°thy casting down °*shall be* in the midst of
thee; and thou shalt °take hold, but shalt not
deliver; and *that* which thou deliverest will
I give up to the sword.
15 °Thou shalt sow, but thou shalt not reap;
thou shalt tread the olives, but thou shalt not
anoint thee with oil; and °sweet wine, but
shalt not drink °wine.
j 16 For °the statutes °of Omri are °kept, and
all the works of °the house of Ahab, and ye
walk in their counsels;
k °that I should make thee a desolation, and the
inhabitants thereof an hissing: therefore ye
shall bear the reproach of My people.

O R **7** Woe is me! for I am as when they have
gathered the summer fruits, as the grape-
gleanings of the vintage: *there is* no cluster
to eat: my °soul desired the firstripe fruit.
2 The °good *man* is perished out of the earth:
and *there is* none upright among °men: they
all lie in wait for blood; they hunt °every
man his brother with a net.
3 That they may do °evil with both hands
earnestly, the prince °asketh, and °the judge
°*asketh* for a °reward; and the great *man*, he
uttereth °his mischievous desire: so °they
°wrap °it up.
4 The best of them *is* as a brier: the most
upright *is sharper* than a thorn hedge: °the
day of thy watchmen *and* thy visitation cometh; now shall be their perplexity.
S 5 °Trust ye not in a friend, °put ye not confidence in a guide: keep the °doors of thy
mouth from her that lieth in thy bosom.
**6 For the son °dishonoureth the father, the
daughter riseth up against her mother, the
daughter in law against her mother in law;
a °man's enemies *are* the °men of his own
house**

the man of wisdom shall see Thy name = [such as would have] true stability (or safety) will regard Thy name. The Mugah Codex, quoted in the *Massōrah* (Ap. 30), reads: "such as revere".

wisdom. Heb. *tushīyah.* See note on Prov. 2. 7.

Thy. The Sept. reads: "and He (the LORD) will save such as revere His name".

rod. Heb. *matteh* = staff (for support or chastisement). Not the same word as in 5. 1; 7. 14. Either put by Fig. *Metonymy* (of Cause), Ap. 6, for the chastisement inflicted, or supply the *Ellipsis* thus: "hear ye the rod, and [Him] Who hath appointed [the chastisement]." The suffix of the verb, "it", is fem.; while "rod" is masc. Therefore we may supply "chastisement" (Heb. *tōkahath*), which is fem.

6. 10-16 (*N*, p. 1258). CONTROVERSY.
(*Alternation.*)

N | j | 10-12. Incrimination. Fraud and Deceit.
  k | 13-15. Judgment. Desolation.
  j | 16-. Incrimination. Omri and Ahab.
  k | -16. Judgment. Desolation.

10 wickedness . . . wicked = lawlessness . . . lawless. Heb. *rāshā'.* Ap. 44. x.

the scant measure, &c. Note the word "abominable" below. In this form, only in Prov. 22. 14.

measure = ephah. See Ap. 51. III. 3 (5).

abominable. Ref. to Pent. Out of six words thus rendered, Heb. *zā'am* is chosen in Num. 23. 7, 8, 8, "defied" = abhorred. It occurs only eight times elsewhere. Ap. 92.

11 them. Supply [her]: i.e. the wicked city.

the wicked balances. Heb. balances of wickedness. Ref. to Pent. (Deut. 25. 13-16). Ap. 92.

13 will I make thee sick. Ref. to Pent. (Lev. 26. 16).

sins. Heb. *chātā'.* Ap. 44. i.

14 Thou shalt eat, &c. Ref. to Pent. (Lev. 26. 26).

thy casting down = thy dissatisfaction or emptiness. Heb. *yeshach.* Occurs only here.

shall be in the midst of thee = [shall remain] in thee.

take hold. Some codices, with one early printed edition (Rabbinic, marg.), read "take possession".

15 Thou shalt sow, &c. Ref. to Pent. (Deut. 28. 38-40).

sweet wine. Heb. *tīrōsh.* Ap. 27. II.

wine. Heb. *yayin.* Ap. 27. I.

16 the statutes. Heb. *hukkōth* = in a religious sense (Lev. 20. 8. 2 Kings 17. 34. Jer. 10. 3).

of Omri. Cp. 1 Kings 16. 31, 32, as to the worship of Baal. **kept** = strictly kept. Cp. Hos. 5. 4.

the house of Ahab. Cp. 1 Kings 16. 30, &c.; 21. 25, 26. 2 Kings 21. 3. See Ap. 55.

that I should make, &c. Ref. to Pent. (Deut. 28. 37).

7. 1-10 (*O*, p. 1258). LAMENTATION.
(*Introversion.*)

O | R | 1-4. Evils lamented.
  S | 5, 6. Remedies. Vain.
  S | 7. Remedy. True.
  R | 8-10. Evils endured.

1 soul. Heb. *nephesh.* Ap. 13.

2 good = gracious.

men = mankind. Heb. *'ādām.* Ap. 14. I.

every man. Heb. *'īsh.* Ap. 14. II.

3 evil. Heb. *rā'a'.* Ap. 44. VIII.

asketh = asketh [for a reward]. Ref. to Pent. (Deut. 16. 19). Ap. 92. Cp. 3. 11. Hos. 4. 18.

the judge asketh = the judge [judgeth], &c. Fig. complex *Ellipsis.* Ap. 6. Cp. 3. 11. Isa. 1. 23. **reward** = bribe. **his mischievous desire** = the mischief of his soul. Heb. *nephesh.* Ap. 13. Cp. 3. 9-11. **they**: i.e. the prince and the judge. **wrap it up** = weave it together. Occurs only here. **it.** Heb. suffix is fem., so we must supply a fem. noun: e.g. *zimmāh* = wicked purpose, or mischievous device. Isa. 32. 7. **4 the day of thy watchmen.** Put by Fig. *Metonymy* (of Adjunct), Ap. 6: i.e. the day [of punishment] foretold by thy watchmen. **5 Trust ye not** = Put ye no faith in. Heb. *'āman.* See Ap. 69. III. **put ye not confidence in.** Heb. *batah.* See Ap. 69. I. So the Western Massorites. The Eastern, with three early printed editions, Sept., Syr., and Vulg., read "neither put", &c. Quoted in Matt. 10. 35, 36; Luke 12. 53. **doors** = entrances, or openings. **6 dishonoureth, &c.** Ref. to Pent. (Ex. 20. 12. Deut. 5. 16). Ap. 92. **man's.** Heb. *'īsh.* Ap. 14. II. **men.** Heb. pl. of *'ĕnōsh.* Ap. 14. III. Verse 6 does not end "abruptly", nor does there "yawn a century". Verse 7 gives the true remedy ("*S*") in contrast with the vain remedies of *vv.* 5, 6 ("S").

S (p. 1259) 632–603 7 Therefore I will look unto °the LORD; I
will wait for the °God of my salvation: my
°God will hear me.
R 8 Rejoice not against me, O mine enemy:
°when I fall, I shall arise; when I sit in darkness, [7]the LORD *shall be* a light unto me.
9 I will bear the °indignation of [7]the LORD,
because I have °sinned against Him, until He
plead my cause, and execute judgment for me:
He will bring me forth to the light, *and* I shall
°behold °His righteousness.
10 °Then *she that is* mine enemy shall see
it, and shame shall cover her which said unto
me, °"Where is [7]the LORD thy [7]God?" mine
eyes shall [9]behold her: now shall she be trodden down as the mire of the streets.
B T (p. 1260) 11 *In* the day that thy walls are to be built, *in*
that day shall the °decree °be far removed.
12 *In* that day *also* °he shall °come even to
thee from °Assyria, and *from* °the fortified
cities, and from the fortress even to °the river,
and from sea to sea, and *from* mountain to
mountain.
13 °Notwithstanding °the land shall be desolate because of them that dwell therein, for
the fruit of their doings.
U 14 °Feed Thy People with Thy °rod, the
flock of Thine heritage, °which dwell °soli-
tarily *in* the wood, in the midst of Carmel: let
them feed *in* Bashan and Gilead, °as in the
days of old.
T 15 °According to the days of thy coming out
of the land of Egypt °will I shew unto him marvellous *things.*
16 The nations shall see and be confounded
at all their might: they shall °lay *their* hand
upon *their* mouth, °their ears shall be deaf.
17 They shall °lick the dust like a serpent,
they shall °move out of their °holes like
°worms of the earth: they shall be afraid of
[7]the LORD our [7]God, and shall fear because of
Thee.
U 18 °Who *is* a °GOD like unto Thee, That
°pardoneth °iniquity, and passeth by the
°transgression of the remnant of His heritage?
He retaineth not His anger for ever, because
He delighteth *in* °mercy.
19 He °will turn again, He will have compassion upon us; He will subdue our [18]iniqui-
ties; and Thou wilt cast all their °sins into the
depths of the sea.
20 °Thou wilt perform the truth to Jacob,
***and* the [18]mercy to Abraham, which Thou hast**
°sworn unto our fathers from the days of old.

7 the LORD. Heb. Jehovah. Ap. 4. II. See the Structure.

God. Heb. Elohim. Ap. 4. I.

8 when I fall: i.e. into calamity; not into sin. Lit. I have fallen, I have arisen; though I should sit in darkness, Jehovah, &c.

9 indignation. Put by Fig. *Metonymy* (of Cause), Ap. 6, for the punishment which was the result of it.

sinned. Heb. *chata'.* Ap. 44. i.

behold = look unto.

His righteousness: i.e. His righteous vindication.

10 Then she, &c. So shall she [who had been] mine enemy: i.e. Assyria (in *v.* 12).

Where . . . ? Fig. *Erotēsis.* Ap. 6. Cp. Ps. 42. 2, 10.

7. 11–20 (*B*, p. 1252). CONSOLATION.
(Alternation.)

B | T | 11–13. Restoration of Israel.
U | 14. Prayer.
T | 15–17. Subjugation of Israel's enemies.
U | 18–20. Pardon.

11 decree = prescribed limit or boundary. So the Oxford *Gesenius*, p. 349. Cp. Job 26. 10; 38. 10. Prov. 8. 29. Isa. 24. 5. Jer. 5. 22. Heb. *chok.*

be far removed = become distant: i.e. extended. See the Oxford *Gesenius*, p. 935. Heb. *rachak*, as in Isa. 26. 15. Note the Fig. *Paronomasia* (Ap. 6), *yir'chok.*

12 he = one. But a special various reading called *Sevīr* (Ap. 34), reads "they": i.e. thine exiles.

come = come home; as in 1 Sam. 11. 5. Ps. 45. 15. Prov. 2. 10: or, into blessing; as in Ps. 69. 27. Nothing has "fallen out" of the text!

Assyria. See the "enemy", *v.* 10.

the fortified cities = the cities of *Matzor* (i.e. the fortress) put for Egypt. Cp. Isa. 19. 6; 37. 25.

the river. Put by Fig. *Synecdoche* (of Genus), Ap. 6, for the Euphrates. Also the Fig. *Antonomasia* (Ap. 6).

13 Notwithstanding: i.e. But first, or before this.

the land, &c. Ref. to Pent. (Lev. 26. 33, the same word).

14 Feed, &c. Note here, the prayer of Micah. Supply the *Ellipsis*: "[Then Micah prayed, and said: O Jehovah] Feed Thy People", &c. Feed = shepherd Thou (masc.).

rod. Heb. *shēbet*, as in 5. 1; not as in 6. 9. Here it is the token of rule.

which dwell, &c. = dwell thou (fem.): i.e. the "flock". Heb. *tz'on* (com. gender).

solitarily = alone. Ref. to Pent. (Num. 23. 9. Deut. 33. 28). Ap. 92.

as in the days of old = as in the age-past times: so shall be the yet future day of Israel's consolation; not Micah's day, when Israel was in possession of Bashan, &c. No ground, therefore, for dating this prayer in "the latest period of Israel's history, the days of Haggai and Zechariah", as alleged.

15 According, &c. Verses 15–17 are Jehovah's answer as to the subjugation of Israel's enemies. Ref. to Pent. See note on 6. 4. Ap. 92. Not the continuation of Micah's prayer.

will I shew unto him. Ref. to Pent. (Ex. 34. 10).

16 lay their hand, &c. Put by Fig. *Metonymy* (of Adjunct), Ap. 6, for silence, of which it was the token and sign. See Job 21. 5; 29. 9; 40. 4.

their ears. Some codices, with four early printed editions, read "and their".

17 lick the dust. Put by Fig. *Metonymy* (of Adjunct), Ap. 6, for the utmost humiliation, as in Gen. 3. 14. Cp. Ps. 72. 9. Isa. 49. 23.

move = come quaking.

holes = fastnesses. Heb. *misgereth.* See the Oxford *Gesenius*, p. 689.

worms. Ref. to Pent. (Deut. 32. 24, the same word). Occurs only in these two places.

18 Who is a GOD like . . . ? Fig. *Erotēsis.* Ap. 6. Cp. the meaning of "Micah", 1. 1. Ref. to Pent. (Ex. 15. 11. See note there).

GOD. Heb. El. Ap. 4. IV.

pardoneth iniquity. Ref. to Pent. (Ex. 34. 7). Ap. 92.

iniquity = perverseness. Heb. *'āvah.* Ap. 44. iv.

transgression. Heb. *pāsha'.* Ap. 44. ix.

mercy = lovingkindness, or grace.

19 will turn again. Cp. Hos. 14. 8.

sins. Heb. *chata'.* Ap. 44. i.

20 Thou wilt perform, &c. Quoted in Luke 1. 72, 73.

sworn unto our fathers. Ref. to Pent. (Gen. 50. 24, &c.). Ap. 92. See Ps. 105. 9, 10, 42.

NAHUM.

THE STRUCTURE OF THE BOOK AS A WHOLE.

(Division.)

1. 1. THE TITLE.

B[2] | A[1] | 1. 2-8. JEHOVAH'S ATTRIBUTES DECLARED.
| A[2] | 1. 9—3. 19. JEHOVAH'S JUDGMENTS FORETOLD.

For the Canonical order and place of the Prophets, see Ap. 1, and pages 1206 and 1207.

For the Chronological order of the Prophets, see Ap. 77.

For the *Formulæ* of Prophetic utterance, see Ap. 82.

For the Inter-relation of the Prophetical Books, see Ap. 78.

For the Relation of Nahum to the twelve Minor (or Shorter) Prophets, see p. 1206.

For the References to the Pentateuch, see Ap. 92.

Nahum concludes the seven pre-captivity Prophets, being the last of the second group of three; and corresponding with Jonah, which also has Nineveh for its subject. See the Structure (p. 1206).

Some eighty-seven years before, Jonah had proclaimed Jehovah's favour to Nineveh, which had prolonged its existence till now, when Nahum's prophecy of coming judgment was fulfilled without further delay.

Nahum is undated; but, if 1. 11 refers primarily to the Rab-shakeh (as we believe it does) of 2 Kings 18. 26-28, then we have a clue of great importance, for that speaks of the fourteenth year of Hezekiah, and gives us the date as 603 B.C.

The Rab-shakeh = the chief of the captains, was apparently a renegade Jew, and a "counsellor" high in favour with the Assyrian king (Sennacherib). He was apparently, as to office, similar to our "Political Officer" in the Indian Frontier campaigns. He insisted on speaking to the common People on the wall in the Jews' language; indicating a freedom in the use of Hebrew that would scarcely be possessed by an Assyrian ambassador.

The Rab-shakeh's words certainly show a deadly animosity towards Jehovah; which is borne out by Nah. 1. 11, and Pss. 120. 2; 123. 3. See Ap. 67.

If this be correct, then we may date Nahum as living and prophesying in 603 B.C.

NAHUM.

TITLE 603 **1** THE °burden of °Nineveh. The book of
the °vision of °Nahum the °Elkoshite.

A[1] A (p. 1262) 2 °GOD *is* °jealous, and °the LORD °re-
vengeth; °the LORD revengeth, and °*is* furi-
ous; °the LORD will °take vengeance on His
adversaries, and He reserveth °*wrath* °for His
enemies.

B 3 [2]The LORD *is* °slow to anger, and °great in
power, and °will not at all °acquit *the wicked*:

C [2]the LORD *hath* His way in the whirlwind
and in the storm, and the clouds *are* the dust
of His feet.
4 °He rebuketh the sea, and maketh it dry,
°and drieth up all the rivers: Bashan languisheth, and Carmel, and the flower of Lebanon languisheth.
5 °The mountains quake at Him, and the hills
melt, and the earth is °burned at His presence,
yea, the °world, and all that dwell therein.

C 6 Who can stand before His indignation?
and who can °abide in the fierceness of His
anger? His fury is poured out like fire, and
the rocks are thrown down by Him.

B 7 [2]The LORD *is* °good, a °strong hold in the
day of trouble; and °He knoweth them that
°trust in Him.

A 8 °But with an overrunning flood He will
make an utter end of °the place thereof, °and
darkness shall pursue His enemies.

A[2] D 9 What do ye °imagine against [2]the LORD?
He will make an utter end: °affliction shall
not rise up °the second time.
10 For while *they be* °folden together *as*
°thorns, and while they are drunken *as* drunkards, they shall be devoured as stubble fully
dry.
11 There is *one* come out °of °thee, that [9]im-
agineth °evil against [2]the LORD, °a wicked
counsellor.
12 Thus saith [2]the LORD; "Though *they be*
°quiet, and likewise many, yet thus shall they
be °cut down, °when he shall pass through.

1. 1 **burden.** Cp. Isa. 13. 1—27. 13. See the Structure, p. 930), and Habakkuk. = A prophetic oracle: or, the prophetic doom of Nineveh, written about ninety (603–514 = B.C.) years before Nineveh's doom; and while the Assyrian Empire was at its height. The doom of Nineveh came therefore 176 years after Jonah's mission. The prophecy was addressed to Nahum's own People, but as a menace to Nineveh.

Nineveh. This heading is not "undoubtedly by a later hand", as alleged. The words "the place thereof" (*v.* 8) would be unintelligible without it. Nineveh is not mentioned again until 2. 8; and is only hinted at elsewhere (3. 1, 18). The Structure below is the best commentary.

vision. Like Isaiah, always one whole. Not written before or separately from, its deliverance.

Nahum = the compassionate, or consoler. The name refers back to Jehovah's compassion connected with Jonah's mission eighty-seven years before. Nothing is known of Nahum beyond his book.

Elkoshite. Heb. *'Elkoshī.* A village of this name exists to-day, twenty-four miles north of Nineveh (now *Konyunjik*). See Layard's *Nineveh and its Remains*, i, p. 233.

1. 2-8 (**A**[1], p. 1261). JEHOVAH'S ATTRIBUTES DECLARED. (*Introversion.*)

A[1] | A | 2. Vengeance.
  B | 3-. Long-suffering.
    C | -3-5. Power. Unequalled.
    C | 6. Power. Irresistible.
  B | 7. Goodness.
A | 8. Vengeance.

2 **GOD.** Heb. El. Ap. 4. IV.

jealous. Ref. to Pent. (Ex. 20. 5-7. Deut. 4. 24). Ap. 92. See the Structure, and note the subjects of "A" and "*A*"; "B" and "*B*"; "C" and "*C*".

the LORD. Heb. Jehovah. Ap. 4. II. Note the Fig. *Epizeuxis* (Ap. 6), for great emphasis.

revengeth = avengeth.

is furious = a possessor of wrath. Heb. "lord of wrath". **take vengeance on** = be an Avenger to.

wrath. Fig. *Ellipsis* (Absolute). Ap. 6.

for = against.

3 **slow to anger** = long-suffering. Ref. to Pent. (Ex. 34. 6, 7). Ap. 92. Heb. "long of anger". The opposite of Prov. 14. 17. Cp. Jonah 4. 2.

great. Cp. Job 9. 4; and see the Structure "C", above.

will not, &c. Ref. to Pent. (Ex. 34. 7. Num. 14. 18).

acquit = clear, or hold guiltless.

4 **He rebuketh the sea.** Ref. to Pent. (Ex. 14.) Cp. Ps. 106. 9. Ap. 92.

and drieth up, &c. Cp. Josh. 4. 23. Ps. 74. 15. **5** **The mountains quake, &c.** Cp. Mic. 1. 3, 4. **burned** = upheaved. **world.** Heb. *tēbēl* = the world as inhabited. **6** **abide** = stand up. Cp. Jer. 10. 10. Mal. 3. 2. **7** **good.** See the Structure "*B*", above. Cp. 1 Chron. 16. 34. Ps. 100. 5. Jer. 33. 11. Lam. 3. 25. **strong hold** = a place of safety. **He knoweth, &c.** Cp. Ps. 1. 6. 2 Tim. 2. 12. **trust in** = flee for refuge to. Heb. *ḥāṣāh.* Ap. 69. II. **8** **But, &c.** Note the transition in *v.* 8, which is explained by the Structure "*A*", above. **the place thereof.** Heb. her place: i.e. Nineveh's. See note on title above (*v.* 1). **and darkness, &c.**: or, "as for His foes, darkness shall pursue [them]".

1. 9—3. 19 (**A**[2], p. 1261). JEHOVAH'S JUDGMENTS FORETOLD. (*Introversion.*)

A[2] | D | 1. 9-12-. Destruction of Nineveh.
  E | 1. -12-15. Deliverance of Judah.
D | 2. 1—3. 19. Destruction of Nineveh.

9 **imagine** = devise. Cp. Ps. 2. 1. **affliction** = distress, or trouble; Heb. *ẓārar*, as in *v.* 7: i.e. the trouble that now threatens Nineveh. **the second time.** Referring to the rising up after Jonah's proclamation. Cp. "rise", Jer. 51. 64. Same word as "abide", *v.* 6, above. **10** **folden** = entangled. **thorns.** The emblem of hostile armies (Isa. 10. 17; 27. 4). **11** **of.** Gen. of Origin. Ap. 17. 2. **thee**: i.e. Nineveh (fem.). **evil.** Heb. *rā'a'.* Ap. 44. viii. **a wicked counsellor** = a counsellor of Belial. The counsellor probably = Rabshakeh; and Belial = Sennacherib. See note on p. 1261. **12** **quiet** = secure. **cut down** = cut down (like dry stubble). **when he, &c.** Ref. to Pent. (Ex. 12. 12). Cp. Isa. 8. 8. Dan. 11. 10.

E F¹ (p. 1263) ° Though I have afflicted °thee, I will afflict
thee no more.
603 13 For now ° will I break ° his yoke from off
[12] thee, and will burst thy bonds in sunder.
14 And [2] the LORD hath given a commandment concerning thee, *that* ° no more of thy
name be sown: out of the house of thy gods
will I cut off the graven image and the molten
image: I will ° make thy ° grave; for thou art
° vile.
F² 15 ° Behold upon the mountains the feet of
him that bringeth good tidings, that publisheth peace! O Judah, ° keep thy solemn feasts,
perform thy vows: for ° the wicked shall no
more pass through thee; he is utterly cut off.

D G K **2** ° He that ° dasheth in pieces is come up before thy face: ° keep the munition, watch
the way, ° make *thy* loins strong, ° fortify *thy*
power mightily.
2 For ° the LORD ° hath turned away ° the excellency of ° Jacob, ° as the excellency of Israel: for the emptiers have emptied them out,
and marred their vine branches.

L N 3 The shield of his ° mighty men is ° made red,
the valiant ° men ° *are* in scarlet: ° the chariots
shall be with flaming ° torches in the day of his
preparation, and the ° fir trees shall be terribly
shaken.
4 The chariots shall ° rage in the streets,
they shall ° justle one against another in the
broad ways: ° they shall seem like torches,
they shall ° run like the lightnings.
5 ° He shall ° recount his ° worthies: they shall
stumble ° in their walk; they shall make
haste to ° the wall thereof, ° and ° the defence
shall be prepared.
6 The ° gates of ° the rivers shall be ° opened,
and the palace shall ° be dissolved.

O 7 And ° Huzzab shall be led away captive,
she shall be brought up, and her maids shall

1. -12-15 (E, p. 1262). DELIVERANCE OF JUDAH.
(*Division.*)

E | F¹ | -12-14. Evil removed.
  | F² | 15. Good bestowed.

-12 Though, &c. = And [now, O Judah], &c. Through not seeing the Structure and the change of subject at "E", modern critics say "the first part of this verse is certainly more or less corrupt"; and they alter the Heb. text to make it agree with the last clause ("F¹"), the subject changing there to the removal of evil from Judah. **thee**: i. e. Judah (*v.* 13).

13 will I break, &c. Ref. to Pent. (Gen. 27. 40). Ap. 92.

his yoke. Some codices read "his rod".

14 no more of thy name, &c.: i.e. the dynasty of Nineveh should end.

make = make [it]: i.e. "the house of thy gods".

grave = sepulchre. Heb. *ḳeber.* See note on Gen. 23. 4. Ap. 35.

vile = despicable. Cp. Isa. 37. 37, 38.

15 Behold. Fig. *Asterismos* (Ap. 6), for emphasis, calling attention to the ref. to Isa. 52. 7, the hypothetical second Isaiah, 100 years before he is supposed by modern critics to have lived.

keep thy solemn feasts. Fig. *Polyptōton.* Ap. 6. Heb. "feast thy solemn feasts": used for great emphasis. Ref. to Pent. (Deut. 16. 16, &c.; 23. 21, &c.). Ap. 92.

the wicked. Heb. [the man of] *Belial.* See note on *v.* 11.

2. 1—3. 19 (*D*, p. 1262). DESTRUCTION OF NINEVEH. (*Introversion and Extended Alternation.*)

D | G | K | 2. 1, 2. Jehovah's defiance.
   L | 2. 3-10. Judgment. Invasion.
   M | 2. 11—3. 7. Causes.
   H | 3. 8-10. Examples. Citation.
   H | 3. 11-13. Examples. Application.
G | *K* | 3. 14. Jehovah's defiance.
   L | 3. 15-17. Judgment. Devastation.
   M | 3. 18, 19. Causes.

1 He that dasheth, &c.: i.e. Cyaxares and Nabopolassar (*Herod.* i. 106). A reference or type of the future destruction of Antichrist.

dasheth, &c.: or, the breaker (Heb. *mēphīẓ* = battle-axe, or hammer (Prov. 25. 18)). Cp. Jer. 23. 29; 51. 20. Ezek. 9. 2, marg. Mic. 2. 13.

keep the munition. Fig. *Homœopropheron* (Ap. 6), in the Heb. In English, keep the keeps, or fortify the fortress, or fence the defences. **make thy loins strong**: i. e. be courageous. Cp. Job 40. 7. Jer. 1. 17. **fortify, &c.** = strengthen [thee] with power mightily. Cp. Prov. 24. 5. **2 the LORD.** Heb. Jehovah. Ap. 4. II. The verse not "misplaced", as alleged. See the Structure above. **hath turned away** = restoreth, or is on the way to bring back. **the excellency** = pre-eminence. Used in good, or bad sense according to the context. **Jacob.** Put here for the natural seed, and Judah in contrast with Israel; cp. Gen. 32. 28; 43. 6; 45. 26, 28. **as** = as [He will restore] the excellency, &c.

2. 3-10 (L, above). JUDGMENT. INVASION.
(*Alternation.*)

L | N | 3-6. Nineveh. Assaulted.
  O | 7, 8. Captured.
  N | 9. Nineveh. Spoiled.
  O | 10. Dismayed.

3 mighty men = mighty ones, or warriors. Cp. 2 Sam. 23. 8. 1 Kings 1. 8, 10. **made red** = reddened [with blood]. **men.** Heb. pl. of *'ěnōsh.* Ap. 14. III. **are in scarlet** = [are clad] in scarlet, as were the armies of the Persians. **the chariots shall be . . . torches**: or, with the flashing of steel the chariots [glitter]. **fir trees.** Put by Fig. *Metonymy* (of Cause), Ap. 6, for the spears or lances made from them. **4 rage** = rave [as though mad]. Heb. *hālal.* **justle.** From Old French *jouster,* to tilt; from Low Latin *juxtare,* to approach (as in tilting). Jostle = to push against, a frequentative form; but the Heb. (*shāḳaḳ*) means to run to and fro, as in Isa. 33. 4. Joel 2. 9. **they shall seem** = their appearance is. **run** = rush, or flash. Heb. *rūẓ.* **5 He.** The king of Assyria (3. 18). **recount** = bethink himself of. **worthies** = nobles, who may assemble their troops; as in 3. 18. Judg. 5. 13. 2 Chron. 23. 20. **in their walk** = as they march. **the wall thereof** = her wall: i. e. the wall of Nineveh. **and** = yet. **the defence** = the mantelet, or portable storming cover [of the besiegers]. **6 gates** = flood-gates, or sluices. **the rivers.** Nineveh lay on the east (or left) bank of the Tigris. The Khusur (a perennial stream) ran through it; also a canal from it to the Tigris ran through the city. **opened**: i. e. by the enemy. **be dissolved** = melt away [in fear], or was in dismay. **7 Huzzab.** The words which follow show that the queen or queen-mother is meant: or, *Huzzab* may be taken as a verb (dual of *nāẓah*), and the "and" as = though (like "but" in *v.* 8). In that case read: "though firmly established, she shall be dishonoured and taken captive"; the city being thus personified.

603 °lead *her* as with the voice of doves, °tabering
upon their °breasts.
8 °But Nineveh °*is* of old like a pool of
water: yet °they shall °flee away. Stand,
stand, *shall* °*they cry;* but none shall look
back.
N 9 Take ye the spoil of silver, °take the spoil
(p. 1263) of gold: for *there is* °none end of the store
and glory out of all the pleasant furniture.
O 10 She is °empty, °and void, °and °waste:
and the heart melteth, and the knees smite
together, and much pain *is* in all loins, and
°the faces of them all gather blackness.
M P 11 °Where *is* the dwelling of the °lions, and
(p. 1264) the feedingplace of the young lions, where the
lion, *even* the °old lion, walked, *and* the lion's
whelp, and none made *them* afraid?
12 The lion °did tear in pieces enough for his
whelps, and strangled for his lionesses, and
filled his holes with prey, and his dens with
ravin.
Q 13 °"Behold, I *am* against thee, °saith °the
LORD of hosts, and I will burn her chariots
°in the smoke, and the sword shall devour thy
young lions: and I will cut off thy prey from
the earth, and the voice of thy °messengers
shall no more be heard.

P **3** Woe to the °bloody city! it *is* all full of
lies *and* robbery; the prey °departeth
not;
2 °The noise of a whip, °and the noise of the
rattling of the wheels, and of the pransing
horses, and of the °jumping chariots.
3 The horseman lifteth up both the °bright
sword and the °glittering spear: and *there is*
a multitude of slain, and a great number of
carcases; and *there is* none end of *their*
corpses; °they stumble °upon their corpses:
Q 4 °Because of the multitude of the °whore-
doms of the wellfavoured harlot, °the mistress
of °witchcrafts, that selleth nations through
her °whoredoms, and families through her
°witchcrafts.
5 °Behold, I *am* against thee, °saith the
LORD of hosts; ²and °I will discover thy
skirts upon thy face, ²and °I will shew the nations thy nakedness, and the kingdoms thy
shame.
6 And I will cast abominable filth upon thee,
and °make thee vile, and will set thee as a
gazingstock.
7 And it shall come to pass, *that* all they that
look upon thee shall flee from thee, and say,
'Nineveh is laid waste: who will bemoan
°her?' whence shall I seek comforters for
thee?
H 8 Art thou °better than °populous No, that
(p. 1263)

lead her = mourn for, or bemoaning.

tabering = drumming [with their fingers] incessantly. Heb. *taphaph*, from *toph* = a drum. See note on Ex. 15. 20. 1 Sam. 10. 5.

breasts = hearts. Some codices read "heart" (sing.); but others, with eight early printed editions, read "hearts" (pl.).

8 But = Though, to answer to the "yet" of the next line.

is of old, &c. Read "hath been from of old [filled with men] as a pool [is full] of water".

they: i.e. the defenders.

flee away. Before their besiegers.

they: i.e. the captains.

9 take the spoil. Note the Fig. *Epizeuxis* (Ap. 6), for emphasis.

none end, &c. = [there are] treasures without end, [and] stores of all covetable vessels.

10 empty . . . void . . . waste. Note the Fig. *Paronomasia* (Ap. 6), for emphasis. Heb. *būḳāh ūmbūḳāh ūmᵉbullāḳāh.*

and. Note the Fig. *Polysyndeton* (Ap. 6), for emphasis.

the faces of them all, &c. Only here, and in Joel 2. 6. The reference is to Joel 2. 6 (as 1. 15 is to Isa. 52. 7); not vice versa.

2. 11—3. 7 (M, p. 1263). **CAUSES.**
(*Alternation.*)

M | P | 2. 11, 12. Jehovah. Defiance.
  | Q | 2. 13. The cause. Hostility.
  | *P* | 3. 1-3. Jehovah. Defiance.
  | *Q* | 3. 4-7. The cause. Hostility.

11 Where . . . ? Fig. *Erotēsis* (Ap. 6), for emphasis.

lions. Note the Fig. *Synonymia* (Ap. 6), for emphasis. This is Jehovah's answer to Sennacherib's taunt in 2 Kings 18. 34, looking back after the fulfilment of this prophecy.

old lion = lioness.

12 did tear = was tearing. Nineveh again personified in *vv.* 11, 12.

13 Behold. Fig. *Asterismos.* Ap. 6.

saith the LORD of Hosts = [is] the oracle of Jehovah Sabaioth.

the LORD. Heb. Jehovah, as in *v.* 2. The full expression, "Jehovah of hosts", occurs only here in Nahum ("Q") and in the corresponding member ("*Q*", 3. 5). See note on 1 Sam. 1. 3.

in the smoke = into smoke.

messengers = ambassadors. Cp. 2 Kings 18. 17, 19; 19. 9, 23.

3. 1 bloody city = city of great bloodshed (Ezek. 22. 2, 3; 24. 6, 9. Hab. 2. 12).

departeth not = will not be lacking. Captive princes were exposed to public contumely in cages, &c.

2 The noise, &c. Between *vv.* 1 and 2 supply the logical *Ellipsis* (Ap. 6), thus: "is not released. [Hark! the enemy is within thy gates!] The noise of a whip . . . chariot".

and. Note the Fig. *Polysyndeton* (Ap. 6), for emphasis.

jumping = bumping, or sounding.

3 bright = gleaming. **glittering** = flashing.

they: i.e. the slayers. Heb. text margin, with some codices, and four early printed editions, reads "so that they stumble", &c. **upon** = over.

4 Because, &c. Note the Structure, which shows that here, in the member "*Q*" (*vv.* 4-7), we have the *cause*, corresponding with "Q" (2. 13).

whoredoms = idolatries.

the mistress of witchcrafts. Ref. to Pent. (Ex. 22. 18. Deut. 18. 10). Ap. 92. **witchcrafts** = sorceries. Cp. Isa. 47. 9. **5 Behold.** Fig. *Asterismos* (Ap. 6), for emphasis. **saith the LORD of Hosts** = [is] the oracle of Jehovah Sabaioth. See note on 2. 13. **I will discover.** Carrying out the symbol of whoredom for idolatry. Cp. 2. 13; 3. 5. **I will shew, &c.** (Isa. 47. 2, 3. Jer. 13. 22, 26. Ezek. 16. 37). **6 make thee vile** = disgrace thee. **7 her.** Some codices, with two early printed editions, Aram., Syr., and Vulg., read "thee"; but the Codex "Mugah", quoted in the *Massōrah* (Ap. 30), reads "her". **8 better** = situated better. **populous No** = *N'o-'Āmōn.* *'Āmōn* is not a Heb. word meaning "multitude", but an Egyptian word meaning the Egyptian god "*'Āmōn*". *No* = the Egyptian *net*, meaning the city; now known as "Thebes". (Cp. Jer. 46. 25. Ezek. 30. 14, 15, 16).

603 was situate among °the rivers, *that had* the
waters round about it, whose rampart *was*
° the sea, and her wall *was* ° from ° the sea?
9 Ethiopia °and Egypt *were* her strength,
and *it was* °infinite; °Put and °Lubim were
thy helpers.
10 ° Yet *was* ° she carried away, she went into
captivity: her young children also were dashed
in pieces at the top of all the streets: and they
cast lots for her honourable men, and all her
great men were bound in chains.

H 11 °Thou also shalt °be drunken: thou shalt
(p. 1263) °be hid, thou also shalt seek °strength because
of the enemy.
12 All thy strong holds *shall be like* fig trees
with the firstripe figs: if they be shaken, they
shall even fall into the mouth of the eater.
13 [5]Behold, thy people in the midst of thee
are women: the gates of thy land shall be set
wide open unto thine enemies: the fire shall
devour thy bars.

G K 14 °Draw thee waters for the siege, fortify
thy strong holds: °go into clay, and °tread
the morter, make strong °the brickkiln.

L 15 There shall the fire devour thee; the
sword shall cut thee off, it shall eat thee up
like the °cankerworm: °make thyself many
as the °cankerworm, °make thyself many as
the °locusts.
16 °Thou hast multiplied thy merchants
above the stars of heaven: the [15]cankerworm
°spoileth, and fleeth away.
17 °Thy °crowned *are* as the locusts, and
thy °captains as the great grasshoppers,
which camp in the °hedges in the cold day, *but*
when the sun ariseth they °flee away, and
their place is not known where they *are*.

M 18 Thy °shepherds slumber, O king of Assyria: thy nobles shall °dwell *in the dust:*
thy people is scattered upon the mountains,
and °no man gathereth *them*.
19 *There is* no °healing of thy °bruise; thy
wound is grievous: all that hear the °bruit of
thee shall clap the hands over thee: for °upon
whom hath not thy °wickedness passed continually?"

the rivers = the Nile streams. Heb. *ye'orim*, the regular word for the Nile and its canals, &c. First occurrence Gen. 41. 1; rendered "flood" (Jer. 46. 7, 8. Amos 8. 8; 9. 5); "brooks" (Isa. 19. 6, 7, 8); "streams" (Isa. 33. 21).

the sea. The Nile so called in Job 41. 31. Isa. 18. 2; 19. 5.

from = of: i. e. consisted of.

9 and. Some codices, cited in the *Massōrah* (Ap. 30), omit this word "and"; in which case we should render the clause: "Ethiopia strengthened her; Egypt [defended her with countless hosts (or hosts without end)]".

infinite. Heb. = and there is no end. See the above note; and cp. 2. 9; 3. 3. Isa. 2. 7.

Put. Gen. 10. 6, the third son of Ham, next to *Cush* (Ethiopia) and *Mizraim* (Egypt). Put was among the mercenaries of Tyre (Ezek. 27. 10). Cp. Jer. 46. 9.

Lubim = Lybians. Cp. 2 Chron. 12. 3. Dan. 11. 43.

10 Yet was she, &c. The cuneiform monuments tell us that Thebes, the old capital of Egypt, was destroyed by Assyria about 663 B.C. Assurbanipal has recorded his conquest. Nahum, writing about 603 B.C., refers to this as a well-known event, and likely to be remembered. Nineveh fell later, just as Nahum had foretold. See note on 1. 1. Yet Nahum refers to the Pentateuch! See Ap. 92. **She**: i. e. Thebes.

11 Thou: i. e. Nineveh.

be drunken: i. e. drink of the cup [of judgment]; or, be stupefied by thy calamity.

be hid = hide thyself.

strength = strength [for defence]; hence = "thou shalt seek a stronghold, or refuge [in vain]".

14 Draw thee = Draw for thyself.

go . . . tread, &c.: i. e. make plenty of bricks [for the strongholds].

the brickkiln = the brick-work [= fortifications, or walls] built with bricks. Heb. *malben*. See notes on 2 Sam. 12. 31. Jer. 43. 9; and Ap. 87.

15 cankerworm = the young locust. Heb. *yelek*. See note on Joel 1. 4.

make thyself many = [though thou be] numerous. Fig. *Irony* (Ap. 6).

locusts = the young locust. Heb. *'arbeh*. See note on Joel 1. 4.

16 Thou = [Though] thou, &c.

spoileth = stript itself, or cast off the skin.

17 Thy. The 1611 edition of the A.V. reads "The".

crowned = mercenary crowds. Heb. *minzārim*. Occurs only here. See Fuerst, *Lex.*, p. 832.

captains = muster-masters, or marshals. Heb. *tiphsar*. Occurs only here, and Jer. 51. 27. Like the Assyrian *dupsarru* = a tablet-writer.

hedges = loose stone walls.

flee away = are in flight.

18 shepherds = leaders, or rulers. Here = generals. **dwell** = lie down: i. e. in death. **no man gathereth them.** Ref. to Pent. (Deut. 30. 4). Ap. 92. **19 healing** = alleviation. **bruise** = breaking, or breach: i. e. ruin. **bruit** = report, tidings. Heb. *shēma'*. The English "bruit" = rumour; from the French *bruire*, to make a noise. **upon** = over. Fig. *Erotēsis*. Ap. 6. **wickedness** = cruelty. Heb. *rā'a'*. Ap. 44. viii.

HABAKKUK.

THE STRUCTURE OF THE BOOK AS A WHOLE.

(Division.)

J² | A¹ | 1. 1—2. 20. THE BURDEN OF HABAKKUK.
   | A² | 3. 1–19. THE PRAYER OF HABAKKUK.

For the CANONICAL order and place of the Prophets, see Ap. 1, and pp. 1206 and 1207.

For the CHRONOLOGICAL order of the Prophets, see Ap. 77.

For the Inter-relation of the Prophetic Books, see Ap. 78.

For the *Formulæ* of Prophetic Utterance. See Ap. 82.

For References to the Pentateuch by the Prophets, see Ap. 92.

For the Inter-relation of the Minor (or Shorter) Prophets, see pp. 1206 and 1207.

Of Habakkūk (pronounced *Ḥabaḳ'-ḳūḳ*) nothing can be really known beyond what he says of himself. From this it is clear that he lived in evil days, and was perplexed with the silence and forbearance of a holy God in permitting the evil to continue. Cp. Ps. 73.

His prophecy takes the form of a colloquy with Jehovah; and Jehovah answers his cry by revealing the fact that a time will come when the evil will be visited upon Judah by the Chaldæan successors of Assyria (1. 6), and by the Dispersion of Judah (1. 5–11).

The prayer in chap. 3 is very important as being a summary of Jehovah's dealings with His People from the passage of the Red Sea to the prophet's own time.

The prayer is important also, as being the model (together with Isa. 38), outside the Psalter, of the proper construction of a Psalm, with (1) the *super*-scription, (2) the text, and (3) *sub*-scription (see Ap. 65); and also, of the meaning and use of the word "Selah" (Ap. 66. II).

The prophecy is undated; but we have a clue afforded in 1. 5, 6. It is given to Habakkuk *before* the fall of Nineveh, which placed Babylon at the head of the Gentile world. According to traditional or "received" dating, this took place in 625 B.C., but, according to the chronology given in Ap. 50, it was 515 B.C., or 110 years later.

If the hints given in 1. 3, 11 are to be accepted on the above lines, we may date the prophecy of Habakkuk as being given (as a whole), or at any rate commenced, in the year with which Jeremiah begins: viz. in the thirteenth year of Josiah, 518 B.C., i.e. three years before the destruction of Nineveh.

In this case, supposing one among those Habakkuk addressed to be twenty years old, he would be forty-two in Jehoiakim's fourth year and Nebuchadnezzar's first. At the carrying away to Babylon he would be forty-nine; and at the destruction of Jerusalem he would be sixty-one.

HABAKKUK.

A¹ A (p. 1267) 518 **1** THE °burden which Habakkuk the prophet °did see.
2 O °LORD, how long shall I °cry, and Thou
wilt not hear! *even* °cry out unto Thee *of*
violence, and Thou wilt not save!
3 Why dost Thou shew me °iniquity, and
cause *me* to behold °grievance? for spoiling
and violence *are* before me: and °there are
that raise up °strife and contention.
4 Therefore the law is °slacked, and °judg-
ment doth never go forth: for °the wicked
doth compass about °the righteous; therefore
°wrong judgment °proceedeth.

B **5** **°Behold ye among the °heathen, and °re-**
gard, and °wonder marvellously: for *I* will
work a work in your days, °*which* ye will not
believe, though it be told *you*.
6 For, °lo, °I raise up the Chaldeans, *that*
bitter and hasty nation, which shall march
through the breadth of the land, to possess the
dwellingplaces *that are* not °theirs.
7 °They *are* terrible and dreadful: [6]their
°judgment and [6]their °dignity shall proceed
of °themselves.
8 [6]Their horses also are swifter than the
leopards, and are °more fierce than the evening
wolves: and [6]their horsemen shall spread
[7]themselves, and [6]their horsemen shall come
from far; [7]they °shall fly as the eagle *that*
hasteth to eat.
9 [7]They shall come °all for violence: [6]their
°faces shall °sup up *as* the east wind, and
[7]they shall gather the captivity °as the sand.
10 And [7]they shall scoff at the kings, and
the princes shall be a scorn unto °them: [7]they
shall deride every strong hold; for [7]they shall
°heap dust, and °take it.
11 Then shall *his* °mind change, and he shall
pass °over, and offend, *imputing* this his power
unto his °god.

A **12** °*Art* Thou not from everlasting, O [2]LORD
my °God, mine Holy One? °we shall not die.
O [2]LORD, Thou hast ordained [10]them for judgment; and, °O mighty God, Thou hast established [10]them for correction.

1. 1—2. 20 (A¹, p. 1266). THE BURDEN OF HABAKKUK. (*Alternation.*)

A¹ | A | 1. 1-4. The prophet's cry.
| B | 1. 5-11. Jehovah's answer.
| *A* | 1. 12—2. 1. The prophet's cry.
| *B* | 2. 2-20. Jehovah's answer.

1 burden. See note on Nah. 1. 1.

did see. The Heb. accent places the chief pause on this verb, to emphasise the fact that the *giving* of the vision was of more importance than what was revealed by it. A second and lesser pause is placed on "burden", leaving "Habakkuk" as being less important. The verse therefore should read, "The burden which he saw, Habakkuk the prophet".

2 LORD. Heb. Jehovah. Ap. 4. II.

cry=cry for help in distress; as in Pss. 18. 6, 41; 22. 24. Cp. Job 19. 7. Jer. 20. 8. Showing that the cry is not personal, but made in the name of all who suffered from the evil times.

cry out=cry with a loud voice, implying the complaint.

3 iniquity. Heb. *'aven* (Ap. 44. iii)=trouble, having special reference to the nature and consequences of evil-doing.

grievance = oppression, or injustice. Heb. *'āmāl.* Ap. 44. v.

there are that raise up. A reading is found in some codices (named in the *Massōrah*), "I had to endure".

strife and contention. There should not be a comma after "strife", as in the R.V. The Heb. accents indicate the one act, "and contention rising up", like "spoiling and violence are before me" in the preceding clause.

4 slacked=benumbed.

judgment=justice.

the wicked=a lawless one: looking forward from the Chaldeans to the future Antichrist. Heb. *rāsha'.* Ap. 44. x.

the righteous=the just one (Art. with Heb. *'eth*)

wrong=perverted.

proceedeth=goeth forth.

5 Behold=Look ye. For emphasis, introducing the change to Jehovah's answer. Quoted in Acts 13. 41. Cp. Isa. 29. 14.

Behold . . . regard . . . wonder. Note the Fig. *Anabasis* (Ap. 6).

heathen=nations.

which ye will not believe. Some codices read "yet ye will not believe".

6 lo. Fig. *Asterismos.* Ap. 6.

I raise up, &c. Ref. to Pent. (Deut. 28. 49, 50). Ap. 92.

theirs. Heb. his; and so throughout this chapter.

7 They=It. **judgment**=decision. **dignity**=elevation. **themselves**=itself. Cp. Isa. 10. 8-11, 13, 14. **8 more fierce**=keener. **shall fly as the eagle.** Ref. to Pent. (Deut. 28. 49, 50). Ap. 92. **9 all for violence**: i.e. not for conquest, but for destruction. **faces**=aspect, intent, or eagerness. **sup up, &c.**=swallow up (as in Job 39. 24), as the Palestine burning east wind withers up and destroys all green things. **as the sand.** Fig. *Parœmia.* Ap. 6. **10 them**=it, as above (*v.* 6). **heap dust**=heap up mounds. **take it**=capture it: i.e. every stronghold. **11 mind**=spirit. Heb. *rūach.* Ap. 9. **over**=through. **god.** Heb. *'eloah* (Ap. 4. V): i.e. his object of worship. **12 Art Thou not . . . ?** Note the change of subject, as shown in the Structure above ("*A*"). **God.** Heb. Elohim. Ap. 4. I. **we shall not die.** This is one of the eighteen emendations of the *Sōpherim* (see Ap. 33), which they say they made because it was considered offensive to say this of Jehovah; hence, the one word of the primitive text "who diest not" was changed to "who die not" (rendered in A.V., R.V., and American R.V., "we shall not die"). This is the only one of the eighteen emendations which the R.V. and American R.V. notice, and speak of it in the margin as "an ancient Jewish tradition", whereas a list of such emendations is given in the *Massōrah.* The change from the second person to the first did more than avoid the supposed irreverent expression; it transferred to mortal men the truth which, apart from resurrection, pertains to God alone, "Who only hath immortality" (1 Tim. 6. 16). Cp. 1 Cor. 15. 53, 54. **O mighty God**=O Rock. Cp. Deut. 32. 4, 15, 18, 30. 1 Sam. 2. 2. 2 Sam. 23. 3. Pss. 18. 2, 31, 46; 19. 14, &c.

518 13 ° *Thou art* of purer eyes than to behold
° evil, and canst not look on ° iniquity: wherefore lookest Thou upon them that deal treacherously, *and* holdest Thy tongue when ° the
wicked devoureth *the man that is* more righteous than he?
14 And makest ° men as the fishes of the sea,
as the creeping things, *that have* no ruler
over them?
15 [7] They take up all of [10] them with the
° angle, [7] they catch them in [6] their net, and
gather [10] them in [6] their ° drag: therefore [7] they
rejoice and are glad.
16 Therefore [7] they sacrifice unto [6] their net,
and burn incense unto [6] their [15] drag; because
by them [6] their portion *is* ° fat, and [6] their meat
° plenteous.
17 Shall [7] they therefore empty [6] their net,
and not spare continually to slay the nations?

2 I will stand upon my ° watch, and ° set me
upon the ° tower, and will ° watch to see
what He will say ° unto me, and what I shall
° answer when I am reproved.
B C¹ a¹ (p. 1268) 2 And ° the LORD answered me, and said,
° "Write ° the vision, and make *it* plain ° upon
tables, ° that he may run that readeth it.
b¹ 3 For the vision *is* ° yet for an ° appointed
time, but at the end it shall speak, ° and not
lie: though it tarry, wait for it; because it will
surely come, ° it will not tarry."
D¹ c¹ 4 ° Behold, ° his ° soul *which* is lifted up is not
upright in him:
d¹ but ° **the just shall ° live by his faith.**
C² a² 5 Yea also, because he ° transgresseth by
° wine, *he is* a proud ° man, neither keepeth at
home, who enlargeth his ° desire as ° hell, and
° *is* as death, and cannot be satisfied, but gathereth unto him all nations, and heapeth unto him
all ° people:
6 Shall not all these take up a ° parable against
him, and a taunting ° proverb against him, and
say, ° "Woe to him that increaseth *that which*
is not his! ° how long? and to him that ladeth
himself with ° thick clay!"
7 Shall they not rise up suddenly that shall
° bite thee, and awake that shall ° vex thee,
and thou shalt be for booties unto them?
b² 8 Because thou hast spoiled many nations,
all the remnant of the [5] people shall spoil thee;
because of ° men's blood, and *for* the violence
of the land, of the city, and of all that dwell
therein.
D² c² 9 [6] Woe to him that ° coveteth an ° evil ° covet-

13 Thou art, &c. Note the Fig. *Synchoresis* (Ap. 6).
evil. Heb. *rā'a'*. Ap. 44. viii.
iniquity = perverseness, or wrong. Heb. *'āmāl*. Ap. 44. v. Not the same word as in *v.* 3, or 2. 12.
the wicked = a lawless one. Heb. *rāshā'*. Ap. 44. x. Looking forward to the Antichrist.
14 men. Heb. *'ādām*. Ap. 14. I.
15 angle = hook.
drag = a fish-net. Occurs only here (*vv.* 15, 16) and in Isa. 19. 8. Greek *sagēnē*. See Ap. 122. 3. Italian *seine sagena*, whence (with a different vowel) the Greek verb *sageneuō* = to sweep [a country] clear.
16 fat = fertile, or rich. plenteous = fat.

2. 1 watch = watch-tower; referring to the place.
set me = take my station. tower = fortress.
watch = look out; referring to the act = keep outlook.
unto: or, in.
answer when I am reproved: or, get back because of my complaint.

2. 2-20 (*B*, p. 1267). JEHOVAH'S ANSWER.
(*Repeated Alternation.*)

B | C¹ | a¹ | 2. Command to write.
b¹ | 3. Reason. That the reader may flee.
D¹ | c¹ | 4-. Incrimination. Pride.
d¹ | -4. Contrast. Jehovah's reward.
C² | a² | 5-7. Incrimination. Greed.
b² | 8. Reason. Retaliation.
D² | c² | 9-13. Incrimination. Covetousness.
d² | 14. Contrast. Jehovah's glory.
C³ | a³ | 15, 16. Incrimination. Drunkenness.
b³ | 17. Reason. Retaliation.
D³ | c³ | 18, 19. Incrimination. Idolatry.
d³ | 20. Contrast. Jehovah's exaltation.

2 the LORD. Heb. Jehovah. Ap. 4. II.
Write, &c. Ref. to Pent. (Deut. 27. 8). Ap. 47. and 92.
the vision. Supply the logical *Ellipsis* (Ap. 6): "[which I am about to reveal to thee]". Cp. 1. 1.
upon tables: i. e. boxwood tables smeared with wax. Cp. Luke 1. 63.
that he may run that readeth it = that he that readeth it may flee. Heb. *rūz* = to run as a messenger (Job 9. 25. Jer. 23. 21; 51. 31. Zech. 2. 4); or, to flee for refuge (Ps. 18. 10), as in Hag. 1. 9.
3 yet = deferred.
appointed: i. e. fixed by Jehovah for its fulfilment.
and not lie. Fig. *Pleonasm* (Ap. 6), for emphasis.
it will not tarry. Some codices, with five early printed editions (one Rabbinic, marg.), Aram., Sept., Syr., and Vulg., read "and will not tarry".
4 Behold. Fig. *Asterismos* (Ap. 6), emphasising the twofold answer to the prophet's prayer: the fate of the wicked in the coming judgment, and the preservation and eternal lot of the righteous. Supply the *Ellipsis*: "Behold [the proud one]".
his: i. e. the Chaldean's of ch. 1; or the lawless one described in ch. 1 and in the verses which follow.
soul. Heb. *nephesh*. Ap. 13.
the just = a righteous one. Quoted in Rom. 1. 17 and Gal. 3. 11. Cp. Heb. 10. 38.

live: i. e. live for ever in resurrection life. See notes on Lev. 18. 5. The wicked go on living, without faith, if it refers to *this* life; therefore "live" must refer to a future life. The Heb. accents place the emphasis on "shall live"; not "the just by his faith", but "a just one, by his faith, will live", and make the contrast not between faith and unbelief, but between the fate of each—perishing and living for ever. In Rom. 1. 17 the context places the emphasis on "*the righteous*"; in Gal. 3. 11 it is placed on "*faith*". **5** transgresseth = is transgressing, or is acting deceitfully. wine. Heb. *yayin*. Ap. 27. I. man = strong man. Heb. *geber*. Ap. 14. IV. desire = soul. Heb. *nephesh*. Ap. 13. hell = Sheōl. See Ap. 35. Cp. Isa. 5. 14. is = he [is]. people = peoples. **6** parable. Heb. *māshāl*. proverb = enigma. Heb. *ḥīdāh*, as in Ps. 78. 2. Woe. Note the five woes in *vv.* 6, 9, 12, 15, 19. how long? i. e. for his time is short. thick clay = pledges. Ref. to Pent. Ap. 92. Occurs in this form only here. Cp. other forms in Deut. 15 and 24, where it occurs nine times with a cognate meaning, and in Joel 2. 7. **7** bite: or, exact usury. vex = shake. **8** men's. Heb. *'ādām*. Ap. 14. I. **9** coveteth . . . covetousness = extorteth a gain. Fig. *Paronomasia*. Ap. 6. Heb. *bozea' . . . beẓa'*. evil. Heb. *rā'a'*. Ap. 44. viii.

518 ousness to his house, that he may °set his
nest on high, that he may be delivered from
the °power of °evil!
10 Thou hast °consulted °shame to thy house
by cutting off many [5]people, and hast °sinned
against thy [4]soul.
11 For the stone shall cry out of the wall, and
the beam out of the timber shall answer it.
12 [6]Woe to him that buildeth a town with
blood, and stablisheth a city by °iniquity!
13 [4]Behold, *is it* not of °the LORD of hosts
that the [5]people shall labour in the very fire,
and the [5]people shall weary themselves for
very vanity?
d² 14 For °**the earth shall be filled with the**
(p. 1268) **knowledge of the °glory of [2]the LORD, as the**
waters cover the sea.
C³ a³ 15 [6]Woe unto him that giveth his neighbour
drink, °that puttest thy bottle to *him*, and
°makest *him* drunken also, that thou mayest
look on their nakedness!
16 Thou art filled with shame for glory:
drink thou also, and °let thy foreskin be uncovered: the cup of [2]the LORD'S right hand
shall be turned unto thee, and shameful spew-
ing *shall be* on thy glory.
b³ 17 For the °violence of Lebanon shall cover
thee, and the spoil of beasts, °*which* made them
afraid, because of [8]men's blood, and for the
violence of the land, of the city, and of all
that dwell therein.
D³ c³ 18 What profiteth the graven image that the
maker thereof hath graven it; the molten
image, and a teacher of lies, that the maker of his
work °trusteth therein, to make °dumb idols?
19 °Woe unto him that saith to the wood,
"Awake;" to the dumb stone, "Arise, it shall
teach!" [4]Behold, it *is* laid over with gold and
silver, and *there is* no °breath at all in the
midst of it.
d³ 20 But [2]the LORD *is* in His °holy temple: let
all the earth °keep silence before Him.

A² E (p. 1269) **3** A prayer of Habakkuk the prophet upon
°Shigionoth.
F G 2 O °LORD, I have °heard Thy °speech, *and*
was °afraid: O °LORD, °revive Thy °work in the
midst of the °years, °in the midst of the years
°make known; in °wrath remember °mercy.
H J¹ 3 °GOD °came from °Teman, and the Holy

set his nest on high. Ref. to Pent. (Num. 24. 21).

power = hand. Put by Fig. *Metonymy* (of Cause), Ap. 6, for the power exercised by it.

evil. Heb. *rā'a'*. Ap. 44. viii.

10 consulted = counselled, or devised.

shame = a shameful thing.

sinned against thy soul. Ref. to Pent. (Num. 16. 38).

sinned. Heb. *chāṭā'*. Ap. 44. i.

12 iniquity. Heb. *'āval*. Ap. 44. vi. Not the same word as in 1. 3, 13.

13 the LORD. Heb. Jehovah (with *'eth*) = Jehovah of Hosts Himself. Ap. 4. II. See note on 1 Sam. 1. 3.

14 the earth shall be filled, &c. Ref. to Pent. (Num. 14. 21). Ap. 92. This is the fifth and last occ. of this wondrous prophecy:—Num. 14. 21. Ps. 72. 19. Isa. 6. 3 (= shall be); 11. 9, and Hab. 2. 14.

glory. Cp. Isa. 66. 18, 19. Ezek. 28. 22; 39. 13, 21.

15 that puttest thy bottle to him = that addest (or pourest) thy fury or venom (Heb. construct form of *ḥēmāh* = heat, wrath; not of *ḥēmeth* = bottle) thereto. See Oxford *Gesenius*, p. 705, under *sāphaḥ*.

makest him drunken, &c. Ref. to Pent. (Gen. 9. 22).

16 let thy foreskin be uncovered: i.e. be as one uncircumcised: i.e. uncovenanted.

17 violence of Lebanon: i.e. violence [done to] Lebanon by felling its trees.

which made them afraid: or, shall make thee afraid.

18 trusteth = confideth. Heb. *bāṭaḥ*. Ap. 69. I.

dumb idols. Note the Fig. *Paronomasia* (Ap. 6). Heb. *'ĕlīlīm illemīm* = nothings [that] say nothing. Cp. Jer. 14. 14.

19 Woe unto him, &c. "The sequence of thought" would not be *improved*, as suggested, by making *v.* 19 precede *v.* 18. See the Structure above.

breath = spirit. Heb. *rūach*. See Ap. 9. Cp. Pss. 115. 4-7; 135. 17. Jer. 10. 14.

20 holy. See note on Ex. 3. 5.

keep silence = Hush! Be still! So Zeph. 1. 7. Zech. 2. 13.

3. 1-19 (**A**², p. 1266). THE PRAYER OF HABAKKUK. (*Introversion and Alternation.*)

A² | E | 1. The Superscription.
  F | G | 2. "I have heard." Consequent effect, "fear".
      H | 3-15. Salvation. Jehovah's doings. The Giving of *the Law*.
  F | *G* | 16. "I have heard." Consequent effect, "trembling".
      H | 17-19-. Salvation. Jehovah's character. The Sending of *Grace*.
E | -19. The Subscription.

1 Shigionoth. The pl. of *Shiggaion* (cp. Ps. 7), a crying aloud. See Ap. 65. XX.

2 LORD. Heb. Jehovah. Ap. 4. II.

heard Thy speech = heard Thy hearing. Fig. *Polyptōton*. Ap. 6.

speech = hearing. Put by Fig. *Metonymy* (of Subject), Ap. 6, for what was heard. Here = Thy fame, as in Num. 14. 15. 1 Kings 10. 1. Isa. 66. 19. **afraid.** In awe; as in Ex. 14. 31. **revive** = renew, in the sense of repeating, doing over again. **work.** Some codices, with Aram., Sept., and Syr., read "works": i.e. doings. **years.** Put by Fig. *Metonymy* (of Adjunct), Ap. 6, for the afflictions suffered in them, or "wrath" manifested in them. **in the midst, &c.** Out of 273 occurrences, this is the only place where it refers to *time*. Had Habakkuk learnt, like Daniel? Note the Fig. *Anadiplosis* (Ap. 6), for emphasis. **make known** = make [Thyself] known. The Heb. accent places the logical pause on this verb: i.e. by repeating now what Thou hast done in the past. **wrath.** As manifested in present affliction; showing what is meant by "years", above. **mercy** = compassion. Supply here the logical *Ellipsis* (Ap. 6): "[I will meditate on Thy doings of old:—]".

3. 3-15 (H, above). SALVATION. JEHOVAH'S DOINGS. (*Repeated Alternation.*)

H | J¹ | 3-5. His comings.
   K¹ | 6-11. His doings.
  J² | 12, 13. His going.
   K² | 14. His doings.
  J³ | 15. His going.

3 GOD. Heb. Eloah. Ap. 4. V. Occurs in the prophets only here, and Isaiah, and Daniel. **came from Teman.** Ref. to Pent. (Deut. 33. 2). Ap. 92. **Teman . . . Paran.** Embraces the whole district south of Judah, including Sinai. Cp. Gen. 21. 21. Num. 12. 16; 13. 26. Deut. 33. 2. Ap. 92.

518 One from mount °Paran. °Selah. °His glory covered the heavens, and the earth was full of His praise.

4 And *His* brightness was as the light; He had °horns °*coming* out of His hand: and there *was* °the hiding of His power.

5 °Before Him went the pestilence, and °burning coals went forth at His feet.

K^1 e^1 6 He stood, and °measured the earth: He °beheld, and °drove asunder the nations; and the everlasting mountains were °scattered, the °perpetual hills did bow: His ways *are* everlasting.

f^1 7 I saw the tents of Cushan °in affliction: *and* the °curtains of the land of Midian did tremble.

e^2 8 °Was [2]the LORD displeased against the rivers? °*was* Thine anger against the rivers? °*was* Thy wrath against the sea, that °Thou didst ride upon Thine °horses °*and* Thy chariots of salvation?

f^2 9 °Thy bow was made quite °naked, °(*according* to the oaths of the tribes, *even* *Thy* °word). °Selah. Thou didst cleave the earth °with rivers.

10 °The mountains saw Thee, *and* they trembled: °the overflowing of the water passed by: °the deep °uttered his voice, *and* °lifted up °his hands on high.

e^3 11 °The sun *and* moon stood still in their habitation: °at the light of Thine arrows they went, °*and* at the shining of Thy glittering spear.

J^2 g 12 Thou didst march through the land in indignation, Thou didst °thresh the °heathen in anger.

h 13 Thou wentest forth for the salvation of Thy People, *even* for salvation with Thine °anointed;

g Thou °woundedst the head °out of the house of °the wicked, °by discovering the foundation unto the neck. °Selah.

K^2 14 Thou didst °strike through with °his staves the °head of his °villages: °they came

Selah. Connecting His coming forth with the glorious effects of it. See Ap. 66. II. Note the three "Selahs" in *vv.* 3, 9, 13. **His glory.** Cp. Isa. 6. 3.

4 horns=power. Put by Fig. *Metonymy* (of Effect), Ap. 6, for the power put forth by them. Heb. dual=two rays.

coming out of=from: i. e. power from [His] hands [is] His.

the hiding, &c.=hiding (or concealing) of His [full] power.

5 Before Him went, &c. Supply the logical *Ellipsis* (Ap. 6): "[As He went forth to conquer for His People] before Him went", &c. See Ex. 23. 27. Ps. 68. 1, 2.

burning coals: or, lightning. Cp. Ps. 18. 8; 76. 3; 78. 48.

3. 6-11 (K^1, p. 1269). HIS DOINGS.
(*Repeated Alternations.*)

K^1 | e^1 | 6. At, and after Creation.
f^1 | 7. Among Israel's enemies.
e^2 | 8. At the Exodus.
f^2 | 9, 10. In Israel's Deliverances.
e^3 | 11. At the Conquest of Canaan.

6 measured the earth: or, caused the earth to tremble. So the Targum and the requirement of the "correspondence" with the next line.

beheld=looked.

drove asunder the nations=caused the nations to shake, or start. **scattered**=shattered.

perpetual=ancient, or primeval.

7 in affliction=[brought low] by affliction.

curtains=hangings. Put by Fig. *Metonymy* (of Cause), Ap. 6, for the tents formed by them.

8 Was . . . ? Fig. *Erotēsis.* Ap. 6. Rightly supplied in following clauses.

Thou didst ride. Ref. to Pent. (Deut. 33. 26, 27).

horses=horses [of power].

and. Some codices, with three early printed editions (one Rabbinic), Sept., Syr., and Vulg., read this "and" in the text.

9 Thy bow=[Nay] Thy bow, &c. **naked**=bare.

according to the oaths of the tribes . . . Selah. This second "Selah" (see Ap. 66. II) is to connect the remarkable parenthetic statement with the continuation of the details of Israel's deliverances, which it interrupts, and might otherwise have disturbed. The text of this clause is not "corrupt", as alleged by some modern critics. The oaths are the promises sworn to the fathers or the tribes [of Israel] when still in the loins of the patriarchs.

with rivers=[and the waters gushed out] with rivers. See Pss. 74. 15; 78. 15, 16; 105. 41.

10 The mountains saw Thee. Ref. to Pent. (Ex. 19. 18). Ap. 92. Cp. Ps. 114. 4.

the overflowing, &c. Referring to the Jordan. Cp. Josh. 3. 15, 16.

the deep, &c. Ref. to Pent. (Ex. 14. 22). Ap. 92.

uttered his voice, i. e. [at Thy presence]. **lifted up, &c.**=lifted up his hands [in amazement and submission]. Not a "corruption", but the Fig. *Prosopopœia* (Ap. 6). "The walls" of Ex. 14. 22 compared to its hands. **his hands**=its [walls like] hands. **11 The sun and moon, &c.** Ref. to Josh. 10. 12, 13. **at the light, &c.**=like light Thine arrows flew. **and at the shining, &c.**=like lightning was Thy glittering spear.

3. 12, 13 (J^2, p. 1269). JEHOVAH'S GOINGS. (*Introversion.*)

J^2 | g | 12. For the subduing of Israel's enemies.
h | 13–. For the salvation of Israel.
g | –13. For the subduing of Israel's enemies.

12 thresh=tread down. Cp. Judg. 5. 4. Ps. 68. 7. **heathen**=nations: i. e. the nations of Canaan. **13 anointed:** i. e. for the salvation of Jehovah's anointed People (sing.). See Ps. 105. 15. **woundedst**=dashest in pieces. **out of**=from. **the wicked**=[the] lawless one. Heb. *rāsha'.* Ap. 44. viii. Looking forward to the final destruction of Israel's enemy in the person of the Antichrist. The Targum (or Paraphrase) of Jonathan is remarkable: "the kingdom of Babylon will not remain, nor exercise dominion over Israel. The *Romans* will be destroyed, and not take tribute from Jerusalem; and therefore, on account of the marvellous deliverance which Thou wilt accomplish for Thine Anointed, and for the remnant of Thy People, they will praise the LORD". **by discovering, &c.:** i. e. overturning the house from the top (the neck) so completely as to lay bare the foundations. Such will be the final overthrow of Israel's great enemy. **Selah.** This third Selah connects this final overthrow and its magnitude, when contrasted with the enemy's previous proud boasting and exaltation in *v.* 14. It connects Jehovah's doings also ("K^2", *v.* 14) with Jehovah's goings ("J^3", *v.* 15). See Ap. 66. II. **14 strike through**=pierce. **his staves**=his own weapons. Cp. Judg. 7. 22. **head**=chief. **villages**=leaders. Heb. text="leader" (sing.); but margin "leaders" (pl.), with some codices and five early printed editions. **they came out, &c.**=[when] they came forth.

518 out as a whirlwind to scatter °me: their °re-
joicing *was* °as to devour the °poor secretly.
J[3] 15 Thou didst walk through the sea with
Thine [8]horses, *through* the °heap of great
waters.
F G 16 °When I heard, my °belly trembled; my
lips quivered at the °voice: °rottenness entered
into my bones, and I trembled in °myself, °that
I might rest in the day of trouble: when °he
cometh up °unto the people, °he will invade
them with his troops.
H 17 °Although the °fig tree °shall not °blos-
som, neither *shall* fruit *be* in the °vines; the
labour of the °olive shall fail, and the fields
shall yield no meat; the flock shall be cut off
from the fold, and *there shall be* no herd in
the stalls:
18 Yet I will rejoice in [2]the LORD, I will joy
in the °God of my salvation.
19 [2]The LORD °God *is* my °strength, and He
°will make my feet like hinds' *feet*, and °He
will make me to walk upon mine high places.
E °To the chief singer on °my stringed instruments.

me: i.e. me [who am Thy People].
rejoicing. Cp. Ps. 10. 8, 9.
as=in very deed. *Kaph* (כ=K) *veritatis*.
poor. Heb. *'ānāh*. See note on "poverty", Prov. 6. 11.
15 heap=foaming.
16 When I heard. See the Structure ("*G*", p. 1269).
belly=body.
voice=voice [saying].
rottenness=decay. Some codices, with Aram., Sept., and Syr., read "restlessness".
myself. Place a full stop here, and commence a new sentence.
that I might=O that I might find (or be at) rest, &c.
he: i.e. the invader.
unto=against.
he will invade=he will overcome. Heb. *gūd*. Occurs only here, and Gen. 49. 19.
17 Although. Heb. *kī*, as in 2 Sam. 23. 5; but must be understood not as being hypothetical, but as bringing out the antithesis with *v.* 18 (cp. Job 8. 7).
fig tree . . . vines . . . olive. See note on Judg. 9. 8–12.
blossom. The edible fig, which is the blossom: i.e. the receptacle containing a large number of minute unisexual flowers growing to a succulent. The Heb. text therefore and the A.V. rendering are both scientifically correct.
18 God. Heb. Elohim. Ap. 4. I.
God of my salvation. Cp. Pss. 18. 46; 24. 5; 25. 5; 27. 9. Isa. 17. 10, &c.
19 God. Heb. Adonai. Ap. 4. VIII (2). **strength**=might, or force. Cp. Ps. 18. 32. **will make, &c.** Cp. 2 Sam. 1. 23; 23. 24. 1 Chron. 12. 8. Ps. 18. 33. **He will make me, &c.** Ref. to Pent. (Deut. 32. 13; 33. 29). Ap. 92. Cp. Amos 4. 13. Mic. 1. 3. **To the chief singer.** See Ap. 64. The same word here. **my stringed instruments.** Heb. *neginōth*. Referring to the smitings of Jehovah on the enemies of Israel (*v.* 16). See Ap. 65. XV.

ZEPHANIAH.

THE STRUCTURE OF THE BOOK AS A WHOLE.

E[2] | A[1] | 1. 1—3. 8. MINATORY.
| A[2] | 3. 9–20. PROMISSORY.

For the Canonical order and place of the Prophets, see Ap. 1, and pp. 1206 and 1207.
For the Chronological order of the Prophets, see Ap. 77.
For the Inter-relation of the Prophetic Books, see Ap. 78.
For the *Formulæ* of Prophetic Utterance, see Ap. 82.
For References to the Pentateuch by the Prophets, see Ap. 92.
For the Inter-relation of the Minor (or Shorter) Prophets, see pp. 1206 and 1207.

The last of the Prophets immediately preceding the Captivity.

Unlike all the other Prophets, Zephaniah's genealogy is traced back for four generations; and, as Hezekiah of Prov. 25. 1 and Hizkiah of Zeph. 1. 1 are the same word in Hebrew as Hezekiah King of Judah, he was not improbably his great-great-grandson.

Zephaniah's prophecy is dated in 1. 1, as being given "in the days of Josiah". In ch. 2. 13 he says that Assyria shall be destroyed, and Nineveh made a desolation. Therefore it was before the fall of Nineveh, 515 B.C. according to *The Companion Bible* dating (Ap. 50), or 625 B.C. (according to "received" dating).

Zephaniah was the contemporary of Jeremiah. By a comparison with 2 Kings 23, which records the destruction of "the *remnant* of Baal" (Zeph. 1. 4), Josiah's reformation had not been completed. The prophecy may therefore be dated as coming between the twelfth and the eighteenth year of Josiah—say 518 B.C., or about three years before the fall of Nineveh.

ZEPHANIAH.

A A (p. 1272) 518 **1** °THE word of °the LORD which °came
unto °Zephaniah the son of Cushi, the son
of Gedaliah, the son of Amariah, the son of
°Hizkiah, in the days of Josiah the son of
Amon, king of Judah.
2 "I will °utterly °consume °all *things* from
off °the °land, °saith [1] the LORD.
3 °I will [2] consume °man and beast; I will
[2] consume the fowls of the heaven, °and the
fishes of the sea, °and the °stumblingblocks
°with °the wicked; and I will cut off °man
from off the [2] land, [2] saith [1] the LORD.

D 4 I will also stretch out °Mine hand upon
Judah, and upon all the inhabitants of Jerusalem; and I will cut off the °remnant of Baal
from this place, °*and* the name of the °Che-
marims with the priests;
5 And them that °worship the host of heaven
upon the housetops; and them that worship
and that swear by [1] the LORD, and that swear
by °Malcham;
6 And them that are turned back °from [1] the
LORD; and *those* that have not °sought °the
LORD, nor °enquired for Him.

B E G 7 °Hold thy peace at the presence of °the
Lord °GOD: for the day of [1] the LORD *is* at
hand: for [1] the LORD hath prepared °a sacrifice, He hath °bid his guests.

H J 8 And it shall come to pass in °the °day of
[1] the LORD'S sacrifice, that I will °punish the
princes, and the king's °children, and all such
as are clothed with °strange apparel.

K 9 In the same day also will I punish all
°those that leap °on the threshold, which fill
their masters' houses with °violence and
deceit.

J 10 And it shall come to pass in that day,

1. 1—3. 8 (A[1], p. 1271). MINATORY.
(*Alternations and Introversion.*)

A[1] | A | C | 1. 1-3. Judgments. General. The Land.
D | 1. 4-6. Judah and Jerusalem.
B | E | 1. 7-18. The Day of Jehovah.
F | 2. 1-3. Call to Repentance.
A | *C* | 2. 4-15. Judgments. General. Nations.
D | 3. 1-5. Jerusalem.
B | *F* | 3. 6, 7. Charge of Impenitence.
E | 3. 8. The Day of Jehovah.

1 The word, &c. Cp. Hos. 1. 1. Joel 1. 1. Mic. 1. 1.
the LORD. Heb. Jehovah. Ap. 4. II.
came = became: i.e. came to, or was communicated. Cp. Luke 3. 2. See Ap. 82.
Zephaniah = hidden of Jehovah, or he whom Jehovah hath hidden (Pss. 27. 5; 31. 19, 20; 83. 3). For the connection see 2. 3.
Hizkiah = Hezekiah.
2 utterly consume. Note the Fig. *Paronomasia* (Ap. 6), for emphasis. Heb. *'āsoph 'āsēph* = to end, I end.
consume = take away, or make an end of.
all. Omit "things". = All; as in Job 42. 2. Ps. 8. 6. Isa. 44. 24.
the land. Fig. *Pleonasm* (Ap. 6) = the face of the land.
land = soil, or ground.
saith the LORD = [is] Jehovah's oracle.
3 I will consume. Note the Fig. *Anaphora* (Ap. 6). Three times repeated.
man. Heb. *'ādām* with *'eth* = humanity. Ap. 14. I.
and. Note the Fig. *Polysyndeton* (Ap. 6), for emphasis.
stumblingblocks = ruin. Occurs only here, and Isa. 3. 6. Fig. *Metalepsis.* Ap. 6. "Stumblingblocks" put first for the idols and idolatry, and then idolatry put for the ruin brought about by them.
with = together with. Heb. *'eth.*
the wicked = the lawless ones. Heb. *rāshā'.* Ap. 44. x.
4 Mine hand. Fig. *Anthropopatheia.* Ap. 6.
remnant. Sept. reads "names", reading *shēm* instead of *sh*e*'ār*, as in the next clause.
and. Some codices, with three early printed editions, Aram., Sept., Syr., and Vulg., read this "and" in the text.
Chemarims = *K*e*marīm* = black-robed, or cassocked. From Heb. *Kāmar*, to be black. Used of idolatrous priests because so clothed; not *Kohēn*, as appointed by Jehovah. Occurs only here; 2 Kings 23. 5, and Hos. 10. 5.
5 worship the host of heaven. Ref. to Pent. (Deut. 4. 19; 17. 3). Ap. 92. Cp. 2 Kings 23. 11, 12. Jer. 19. 13.
Malcham = king-god, or king-idol. Syr. and Vulg. read "Milcom".
6 from = from after.
sought . . . enquired. Ref. to Pent. (Deut. 4. 29, where the two Heb. verbs are in the same order, and are rendered "seek . . . seek"). Ap. 92.
LORD. Heb. Jehovah (with *'eth*) = Jehovah Himself.

1. 7-18 (E, above). THE DAY OF JEHOVAH. (*Alternation.*)

E | G | 7. Its nearness.
H | 8-13. Judgments.
G | 14-16. Its nearness.
H | 17, 18. Judgments.

7 Hold thy peace, &c. See Amos 6. 10. Hab. 2. 20. Zech. 3. 13.
the Lord. Heb. Adonai. Ap. 4. VIII (2).
GOD. Heb. Jehovah. Ap. 4. II.
a sacrifice. Sept. reads "His sacrifice".
bid = separated. Heb. sanctified. See note on Ex. 3. 5.

1. 8-13 (H, above). JUDGMENTS. (*Alternation.*)

H | J | 8. Princes.
K | 9. People.
J | 10, 11. Merchants.
K | 12, 13. People.

8 the day of the LORD'S sacrifice. See notes on Isa. 2. 12; 13. 6.
day. Put by Fig. *Metonymy* (of Adjunct), Ap. 6, for the judgments executed in it.
punish = visit upon. Ref. to Pent. (Ex. 32. 34). Ap. 92. Cp. Jer. 9. 25; 11. 22; 13. 21, &c.
children = sons: i.e. the royal house. Cp. 1 Kings 22. 26. 2 Kings 11. 2. Jer. 36. 26; 38. 6, &c.
strange = foreign.
9 those that leap, &c. No reference to idolatrous practice, as in 1 Kings 18. 26; but to the servants of rulers sent to enter the houses of others and steal. Fig. *Periphrasis* (Ap. 6), for robbers.
on = over.
violence and deceit. Put by Fig. *Metonymy* (of Cause), Ap. 6, for the booty procured.

518 [2]saith [1]the LORD, *that there shall be* °the
noise of a cry from the fish gate, and an howling from °the second, and a great crashing
from the hills.
11 Howl, ye inhabitants of °Maktesh, for all
the merchant people are °cut down; all they
that bear silver are cut off.

K 12 And it shall come to pass at that time,
(p. 1272) *that* I will search Jerusalem with °candles,
and punish the °men that are settled on their
lees: that say in their heart, [1]'The LORD will
not do good, neither will He do °evil.'
13 Therefore their goods shall become a
booty, and their houses a desolation: °they
shall also build houses, but not inhabit *them;*
and they shall plant vineyards, but not drink
the °wine thereof.

G 14 °The great [8]day of [1]the LORD °*is* near, *it*
is near, and hasteth greatly, *even* the voice of
[8]the [8]day of [1]the LORD: the °mighty man
shall cry there bitterly.
15 That [8]day *is* a day of °wrath, a day of
°trouble [3]and distress, a day of wasteness [3]and
desolation, a day of darkness [3]and gloominess,
a day of clouds [3]and thick darkness,
16 A day of °the trumpet and alarm against
the fenced cities, and against the high °towers.

H 17 And I will bring distress upon [3]men, that
°they shall walk like blind men, because they
have °sinned against [1]the LORD: and their
blood shall be poured out as dust, and their
flesh as the dung.
18 Neither their silver nor their gold shall be
able to deliver them in the day of [1]the LORD'S
wrath; but the whole °land shall be devoured
by the fire of His jealousy: °for He shall make
even a speedy riddance of all them that dwell
in the °land."

F **2** °Gather yourselves together, yea, °gather
together, O nation °not desired;
2 Before the decree bring forth, *before* the
°day pass as the chaff, before the fierce anger
of °the LORD come upon you, before the day
of °the LORD'S anger come upon you.
3 °Seek ye [2]the LORD, all ye meek of the
earth, which have wrought His °judgment;
°seek righteousness, °seek meekness: it may
be °ye shall be hid in the [2]day of the [2]LORD'S
anger.

A C L[1] 4 °For °Gaza shall be °forsaken, and °Ash-
(p. 1273) kelon a °desolation: they shall drive out
°Ashdod °at the noon day, and °Ekron shall
be °rooted up.
5 Woe unto the inhabitants of the °sea coast,
the nation of the Cherethites! the word of [2]the
LORD *is* against you; O Canaan, the land of
the Philistines, I will even destroy thee, that
there shall be no inhabitant.
6 And the [5]sea coast shall be °dwellings *and*
°cottages for shepherds, and folds for flocks.
7 And the coast shall °be for the remnant of
the house of Judah; they shall feed thereupon:
in the houses of [4]Ashkelon shall they lie down
in the evening: for [2]the LORD their °God
°shall visit °them, and turn away their captivity.

L[2] 8 °"I have heard the reproach of °Moab, and

---

10 the noise of a cry. Fig. *Pleonasm.* Ap. 6.
the second = the new city. See note on 2 Kings 22. 14.

11 Maktesh = the mortar. Probably the local name of the merchants' quarter in the Tyropœon valley, west of Zion. Ap. 68, p. 100. So called from its basin-like shape.
cut down = laid low.

12 candles = lamps.
men. Heb. pl. of *'ĕnōsh.* Ap. 14. III.
evil = harm. Heb. *rā'a'.* Ap. 44. viii.

13 they shall also build, &c. Ref. to Pent. (Deut. 28. 30, 39). Ap. 92. Cp. Amos 5. 11. Mic. 6. 15; and contrast Isa. 65. 21. Amos 9. 14.
wine. Heb. *yayin.* Ap. 27. I.

14 The great day, &c. Cp. Isa. 22. 5. Joel 2. 1, &c.
is near, &c. Heb. [is] near, near. Fig. *Epizeuxis* (Ap. 6), for emphasis: i. e. very near.
mighty man. Heb. *gibbōr.* Ap. 14. IV.

15 wrath . . . trouble, &c. Note the Fig. *Synonymia* (Ap. 6).

16 the trumpet and alarm = an alarming trumpet. Fig. *Hendiadys* (Ap. 6) = a trumpet, yea, a trumpet [call] "to arms"! Cp. 2. 2.
towers. Heb. corners. Put by Fig. *Metonymy* (of Adjunct), Ap. 6, for the towers usually fixed there.

17 they shall walk, &c. Ref. to Pent. (Deut. 28. 29).
sinned. Heb. *chāṭā'.* Ap. 44. i.

18 land. Not the same word as in *vv.* 2, 3.
for. Ginsburg thinks this should be "yea".

2. 1 Gather = Collect. Heb. *kāshash.* Occurs only in Ex. 5. 7, 12. Num. 15. 32, 33. 1 Kings 17. 10, 12. It is not the same word as in 3. 8, 18; or in 3. 19, 20. See the notes there.
not desired = not desirable. Fig. *Antimereia* (of Verb), Ap. 6.

2 day = judgment. See note on 1. 8.
the LORD. Heb. Jehovah. Ap. 4. II.

3 Seek . . . seek. Ref. to Pent. (Deut. 4. 29), as in 1. 6.
judgment = ordinances; as in Isa. 58. 2. Jer. 8. 7.
ye shall be hid. Referring to Isa. 26. 20, and the meaning of the name Zephaniah.

2. 4-15 (*C*, p. 1272). **JUDGMENTS. GENERAL. NATIONS.** (*Division.*)

C | L[1] | 4-7. Gaza. West.
| L[2] | 8-11. Moab and Ammon. East.
| L[3] | 12. Ethiopians. South.
| L[4] | 13-15. Assyria. North.

4 For Gaza. Supply the logical *Ellipsis* (Ap. 6), here, and in *vv.* 8, 12, 13; 3. 1, thus: "[Mine anger shall be upon Gaza, saith the LORD], For", &c.
Gaza . . . forsaken. Note the Fig. *Paronomasia* (Ap. 6), for emphasis. Heb. *'azzāh . . . 'ăzūbah.*
Ashkelon. Now *'Askalan,* on the coast of Philistia.
desolation = ruin. Long since fulfilled.
Ashdod. Now *Esdūd.* The same as Azotus in Acts 8. 40.
at the noon day: i.e. during the noon day siesta.
Ekron . . . rooted up. Note the Fig. *Paronomasia* (Ap. 6), for emphasis. Heb. *'eḳrōn . . . te'aḳer.*

5 sea coast: or, country by the sea.

6 dwellings = pastures.
cottages = pens.

7 be for. Supply the *Ellipsis* (Ap. 6) = "be for [a possession] to".
God. Heb. Elohim. Ap. 4. I.
shall visit them. Ref. to Pent. (Gen. 50. 24. Ex. 3. 16). Ap. 92.
them: i. e. the remnant of Judah.

8 I have heard. Supply the logical *Ellipsis* (Ap. 6): "[My judgment shall come upon Moab], for I have heard", &c., as in *v.* 8, &c.
Moab. Cp. Isa. 15 and 16. Jer. 48. Amos 2. 1-3.

518 the revilings of the °children of °Ammon,
whereby they have °reproached My People,
and magnified *themselves* against their border.
9 Therefore *as* I live, °saith °the LORD of
hosts, °the [7]God of Israel, Surely [8]Moab
°shall be as Sodom, and the [8]children of
Ammon as Gomorrah, *even* °the breeding of
nettles, and saltpits, and a perpetual desolation:
the residue of My People shall spoil
them, and the remnant °of My °People shall
°possess them.
10 This shall they have for their pride, because
they have [8]reproached and magnified
themselves against the People of [9]the LORD of
hosts.
11 [2]The LORD *will be* terrible unto them: for
He will °famish all the gods of the earth; and
men shall worship Him, every one from his
place, *even* all °the °isles of the °heathen.
L3 12 °Ye Ethiopians also, ye *shall be* slain by
(p. 1273) My sword.
L4 13 °And He will °stretch out His hand against
°the north, and destroy Assyria; and will
make Nineveh a desolation, *and* dry like a
wilderness.
14 And flocks shall lie down in the midst of
her, °all the beasts of the nations: both the
cormorant and the bittern shall lodge in the
°upper lintels of it; *their* voice shall sing in
the windows; desolation *shall be* in the thresholds:
for He shall uncover the °cedar work.
15 This *is* the rejoicing city that dwelt carelessly,
that said in her heart, 'I *am*, and *there*
is none beside me:' how is she become a desolation,
a place for beasts to lie down in! every
one that passeth by her shall hiss, *and* °wag
his hand."

D 3 °Woe to °her that is °filthy and °polluted,
(p. 1272) to the oppressing city!
2 She obeyed not the voice; °she received
not °correction; she °trusted not in °the LORD;
°she drew not near to her °God.
3 Her princes within her *are* roaring lions;
her judges *are* evening wolves; they °gnaw
not the bones till the morrow.
4 Her prophets *are* °light *and* °treacherous
persons: her priests have °polluted the sanctuary,
they have °done violence to the law.
5 The just [2]LORD *is* °in the midst thereof;
He will not do °iniquity: °every morning doth
He bring His judgment to light, He faileth
not; but the °unjust knoweth no shame.
B F 6 I have cut off the nations: their °towers are
desolate; I made their streets waste, that none
passeth by: their cities are destroyed, so that
there is no man, that there is none inhabitant.
7 I said, "Surely thou wilt fear Me, thou wilt
receive instruction; so their dwelling should
not be cut off, howsoever I punished them:
but they rose early, *and* °corrupted all their
doings.
E 8 °Therefore wait ye °upon Me, °saith [2]the
LORD, until the day that I rise up °to the
prey: for My determination *is* to °gather the
nations, that I may °assemble the kingdoms, to
pour upon them Mine indignation, *even* all My
fierce anger: °for all the earth shall be devoured
with °the fire of My jealousy.

children = sons.
Ammon. Cp. Jer. 49. 1-6. Amos 1. 13-15.
reproached. See Judg. 11. 12-28.
9 saith the LORD of hosts = [is] the oracle of Jehovah of hosts, the God of Israel. See note on 1 Sam. 1. 3.
the God of Israel. See note on Isa. 29. 23.
shall be as Sodom. Ref. to Pent. (Gen. 19. 24, 25). Ap. 92.
the breeding of nettles, &c. Ref. to Pent. (Deut. 29. 23, &c.). Ap. 92.
of My People. Some codices, with two early printed editions (one Rabbinic), read "of the nations".
People = nation.
possess = inherit.
11 famish = cause to waste away.
the isles of the heathen = the coast-lands of the nations. Ref. to Pent. (Gen. 10. 5). Ap. 92. The phrase occurs nowhere else.
isles = coast-lands. **heathen** = nations.
12 Ye. See note on "For", *v.* 4.
13 And He. See note on "For", *v.* 4.
stretch out His hand. Idiom for executing judgment.
the north: i.e. against Assyria, because although west of Canaan, the road and entrance was by the north.
14 all = all kinds of. Fig. *Synecdoche* (of Genus), Ap. 6.
upper lintels = chapiters, or carved capitals.
cedar work: i.e. the wainscotting.
15 wag his hand. Idiom expressive of derision.

3. 1 Woe = Alas for! See note on "For", 2. 4.
her: i.e. Jerusalem. See the Structure, p. 1272.
filthy = rebellious.
polluted. Heb. *gā'al*, (1) to redeem: (2) to make or deem common or unclean. A *Homonym*, with two meanings. Not the same word as in *v.* 4.
2 she received not. Some codices, with two early printed editions, Aram., Syr., and Vulg., read "neither hath she accepted". **correction** = discipline.
trusted = confided. Heb. *baṭaḥ*. Ap. 69. I. Not the same word as in *v.* 12.
the LORD. Heb. Jehovah. Ap. 4. II.
she drew not near, &c. Some codices, with one early printed edition, Aram., Sept., and Syr., read "neither unto her God hath she drawn near".
God. Heb. Elohim. Ap. 4. I.
3 gnaw not: or, reserve not.
4 light = reckless.
treacherous persons = men (Heb. *'ěnōsh*, Ap. 14. III) of treacheries; placing the emphasis on the treachery.
polluted = profaned. Heb. *ḥālal*. Not the same word as in *v.* 1. Ref. to Pent. (Lev. 19. 8; 21. 23; 22. 15. Num. 18. 32). Ap. 92.
done violence, &c. Cp. Jer. 2. 8. Ezek. 22. 26.
5 in the midst thereof. Ref. to Pent. (Num. 5. 3. Deut. 7. 21). Ap. 92. Cp. *v.* 15.
iniquity. Heb. *'āvāh*. Ap. 44. vi.
every morning = morning by morning. See Ps. 101. 8.
unjust = perverse. Heb. *'āvāl*. See Ap. 44. vi.
6 towers. See note on 1. 16.
7 corrupted, &c. Ref. to Pent. (Gen. 6. 12, same word). Ap. 92.
8 Therefore, &c. The *Massōrah* (Ap. 30 and 93) calls attention to the fact that this verse (*v.* 8) contains all the letters of the Heb. alphabet, including the five final letters. This implies that the verse takes in the whole purpose of Jehovah concerning Israel.
upon: or, for.
saith the LORD = [is] Jehovah's oracle.
to the prey. Sept. and Syr. read "as a witness", reading *'ēd* instead of *'ad*. Cp. Mic. 2. 2.
gather = gather in. Not the same word as in 2. 1.
assemble = gather out.
for all the earth. See 1. 18; and cp. the Structure ("E" and "*E*"), p. 1272.
the fire of My jealousy. Ref. to Pent. (Deut. 4. 24).

A² M P (p. 1275) 518 9 For °then will I turn to the °people °a °pure language, °that they may all call upon the name of [2]the LORD, to serve Him with one °consent.

10 From beyond the rivers of Ethiopia My °suppliants, *even* °the daughter of My dispersed, shall bring Mine offering.

Q 11 In that day shalt thou not be ashamed for all thy doings, wherein thou hast °transgressed against Me: for then I will take away out of the midst of thee them that rejoice in thy pride, and thou shalt no more be haughty °because of °My holy mountain.

12 I will also leave in the midst of thee an afflicted and poor People, and they shall °trust in °the name of [2]the LORD.

13 The remnant of Israel shall not do [5]iniquity, nor speak lies; neither shall a deceitful tongue be found in their mouth: °for they shall feed and lie down, and none shall make *them* afraid."

N R 14 °Sing, O daughter of Zion; shout, O Israel; be glad and rejoice with all the heart, O daughter of Jerusalem.

S 15 [2]The LORD hath taken away thy judgments, He hath cast out thine °enemy: the king of Israel, *even* [2]the LORD, *is* °in the midst of thee:

O thou shalt not °see °evil any more.

N R 16 In that day it shall be said to Jerusalem, °"Fear thou not:" *and to* Zion, "Let not thine hands °be slack."

S 17 [2]The LORD thy [2]God [5]in the midst of thee °*is* mighty; He will save, °He will rejoice over thee with joy; He °will rest in His love, He will joy °over thee with singing.

M P 18 "I will [8]gather *them that are* °sorrowful for the °solemn assembly, *who* are of thee, *to whom* the reproach of it *was* °a burden.

19 °Behold, at that time I will °undo all that afflict thee: and I will save her that halteth, and °gather her that was driven out; and °I will get them praise and fame in every land where they have been put to shame.

20 At that time will I bring you *again*, even in the time that I [19]gather you: °for I will make you a name and a praise among all people of the earth,

Q when I °turn back your captivity before your eyes, °saith [2]the LORD.

3. 9-20 (**A²**, p. 1271). PROMISSORY.

(*Introversion and Alternations.*)

A² | M | P | 9, 10. Good bestowed. Gentiles and Israel. Conversion.
    Q | 11-13. Evil removed.
  N | R | 14. Zion and Jerusalem to praise. (Positive.)
      S | 15-. Jehovah in the midst.
    O | -15. Evil no more seen.
  N | *R* | 16. Zion and Jerusalem. Not to Fear. (Negative.)
      S | 17. Jehovah in the midst.
 M | *P* | 18-20-. Good bestowed. Israel and Gentiles. Restoration.
    Q | -20. Evil removed.

9 then: i.e. after all that is implied in *v.* 8. Note the order of the blessings in "P": Gentiles first, and Israel after; but in "*P*", Israel first, and Gentiles after.

people = peoples.

a pure language = a lip purified: i.e. a clean lip in contrast with "unclean" lips (Isa. 6. 5).

pure = separated from that which is impure or unclean. Heb. *bārar*, as in Ezek. 20. 38. Isa. 52. 11. Dan. 11. 35; 12. 10. The reference is, to being made fit for the worship of Jehovah, as the next clause shows. Cp. 1. 4, 5.

that they may. Some codices, with Syr., and Vulg., read "and may".

consent. Heb. shoulder. Put by Fig. *Metonymy* (of Adjunct), Ap. 6, for the service rendered by it. It is not the Fig. *Metaphor* as alleged.

10 suppliants = worshippers. Heb. *'āthār.* Occurs in this sense nowhere else. From *'āthar* = to burn incense (Ezek. 8. 11); hence to pray or worship.

the daughter of My dispersed: i.e. My dispersed People [Israel].

11 transgressed. Heb. *pāsha'.* Ap. 44. ix.

because of = in.

My. The 1611 edition of the A.V. reads "Mine".

12 trust = flee for refuge to. Heb. *ḥasah.* Ap. 69. II. Not the same word as in *v.* 2.

the name. See note on Ps. 20. 1.

13 for they shall feed, &c. Ref. to Pent. (Lev. 26. 5, 6). Ap. 92.

14 Sing, &c. Fig. *Pœonismus.* Ap. 6.

15 enemy. Some codices, with Aram., Sept., Syr., and Vulg., read "foes" (pl.).

in the midst, &c. Ref. to Pent. (Deut. 7. 21).

see. The Codex Hillel, quoted in the *Massōrah*, (Ap. 30 and 93) with some codices, three early printed editions (one Rabbinic, marg.), Aram., and Vulg., read, 'fear"; but other codices, with nine early printed editions, Sept. (?), and Vulg., read "see", as in A.V.

evil = calamity. Heb. *rā'a'.* Ap. 44. viii.

16 Fear thou not. Ref. to Pent. (Deut. 7. 21). Ap. 92.

be slack = hang down.

17 is mighty; He will save. The Heb. accents place the chief pause or emphasis on "save", implying not that He will save at some future time, but that He is an ever-present Saviour. Read "Jehovah thy Elohim is in the midst of thee, mighty to save [at all times]". Ref. to Pent. (Deut. 10. 17). Ap. 92. **He will rejoice, &c.** Ref. to Pent. (Deut. 30. 9). Ap. 92. **will rest.** Heb. will be silent. Sept. reads "will renew thee", reading ר (= D) instead of ר (= R). **over thee.** The Heb. accent places the emphasis on these two words. **18 sorrowful for.** Supply the *Ellipsis* (Ap. 6) = "sorrowful for [the cessation of]". **solemn assembly** = appointed season. **a burden.** Some codices, with one early printed edition (Rabbinic, marg.), Aram., and Syr., read "a burden on thee". **19 Behold.** Fig. *Asterismos.* Ap. 6. **undo** = deal with. **gather** = gather out, bring together what has been dispersed. Heb. *ḳabaẓ*, as in *v.* 20. Not the same word as in *vv.* 8, 18, or as in 2. 1. Ref. to Pent. (Deut. 30. 3, 4). Ap. 92. **I will get them, &c.** Ref. to Pent. (Deut. 26. 19). Ap. 92. **20 for I will make you, &c.** Ref. to Pent. (Deut. 26. 19). Ap. 92. **turn back your captivity.** Heb. pl. Idiom for restoring blessings as aforetime. See note on Deut. 30. 3. **saith** = hath said.

HAGGAI.

THE STRUCTURE OF THE BOOK AS A WHOLE.

(*Extended Alternation.*)

3[1] | **A** | 1. 1-4. DISAPPROBATION AT NEGLECT.
B | 1. 5-11. PUNISHMENT. SCARCITY.
C | 1. 12—2. 5. OBEDIENCE AND ENCOURAGEMENT.
D | 2. 6-9. "I WILL SHAKE", &c.
} The first and second messages.

A | 2. 10-14. DISAPPROBATION AT NEGLECT.
B | 2. 15-17. PUNISHMENT. SCARCITY.
C | 2. 18, 19. OBEDIENCE AND ENCOURAGEMENT.
D | 2. 20-23. "I WILL SHAKE", &c.
} The third and fourth messages.

For the CANONICAL Order and place of the Prophets, see Ap. 1, and p. 1206.
For the CHRONOLOGICAL Order of the Prophets, see Ap. 77.
For the Inter-relation of the Prophetic Books, see Ap. 78.
For the *Formulæ* of Prophetic Utterance, see Ap. 82.
For References to the Pentateuch by the Prophets, see Ap. 92.
For the Inter-relation of the Minor (or Shorter) Prophets, see pp. 1206 and 1207.

Between ZEPHANIAH and HAGGAI lay the seventy years' captivity in Babylon.

Haggai was the first prophet by whom "God spake" after the Return. Heb. 1. 1, and Ap. 95.

His prophecy is dated "in the second year of Darius" (Hystaspis), sixteen years after the decree of Cyrus, see Ap. 57; and therefore in the year 410 B.C., from the sixth to the ninth month; covering a period of about four months. See Ap. 50, p. 67, and Ap. 77.

There were four distinct messages :—

1. The *first*, on the first day of the sixth month, 1. 1-11.
2. The *second*[1], on the twenty-first day of the seventh month, 2. 1-9.
3. The *third*, on the twenty-fourth day of the ninth month, 2. 10-19.
4. The *fourth*, on the same day as the third, 2. 20-23.

ZECHARIAH'S prophecy began midway between Haggai's second and third messages. See Zech. 1. 1.

[1] The message in 1. 13 is not a dated message, but it refers to the time when Jehovah stirred up the spirit of obedience in Zerubbabel, recorded in *v.* 14, twenty-three days after the delivery of Haggai's first message; nearly a month before the second message (2. 1-9).

HAGGAI.

3[1] **A** A
p. 1277)
410

1 °IN the second year of °Darius °the king, in the °sixth month, in °the first day of the month, came the word of °the LORD °by °Haggai the prophet unto °Zerubbabel the °son of °Shealtiel, °governor of Judah, and to °Joshua the son of °Josedech, the high priest, saying,

B 2 "Thus speaketh °the LORD of hosts, saying, °'This People say, 'The °time is °not come, the °time that [1]the LORD'S house should be built.'"

A 3 Then came the word of [1]the LORD [1]by Haggai [1]the prophet, saying,

B 4 "*Is it* [2]time for °you, O ye, to dwell in your °cieled houses, and this house *lie* waste?

B C 5 Now therefore thus saith [2]the LORD of hosts; °'Consider °your ways.

D 6 °Ye have sown much, and bring in little; ye eat, but ye °have not enough; ye drink, but ye are not filled with drink; ye clothe you, but there is none warm; and he that earneth wages earneth wages *to put it* into a bag with holes.'

C 7 Thus saith [2]the LORD of hosts; [5]'Consider [5]your ways.

8 Go up to the °mountain, and bring wood, and build the house; and I will °take pleasure in it, and °I will be glorified, °saith [1]the LORD.

D 9 Ye looked for much, and, lo, *it came* to little; and when ye brought *it* home, I did blow upon it. Why? °saith [2]the LORD of hosts. Because of Mine house that *is* waste, and ye run °every man unto his own house.

10 Therefore °the heaven over you is stayed from °dew, °and the earth is stayed *from* her fruit.

1. 1-4 (A, p. 1276). DISAPPROBATION AT NEGLECT. (*Alternation.*)

A | A | 1. The word of Jehovah.
B | 2. The People's saying. Cited by Jehovah.
A | 3. The word of Jehovah.
B | 4. The People's saying. Reply of Jehovah.

1 In the second year. See note on p. 1276.

Darius = Darius (Hystaspis). See Ap. 57; and notes on Ezra and Nehemiah.

the king. In Aramaic and later books these words follow the name. In the earlier O.T. books they nearly always precede it. Cp. "king David", "king Hezekiah", &c.

sixth month. Elul, our August–September.

the first day, &c. Therefore the feast-day or Sabbath of the full moon.

the LORD. Heb. Jehovah. Ap. 4. II.

by = by the hand of. The Heb. idiom for God speaking "by the prophets". Ref. to Pent., where the expression occurs thirteen times (Ex. 9. 35; 35. 29. Lev. 8. 36; 10. 11; 26. 46. Num. 4. 37, 45; 9. 23; 10. 13; 15. 23; 16. 40; 27. 23; 36. 13). Cp. the five occurrences in Joshua (14. 2; 20. 2; 21. 2, 8; 22. 9). Judg. 3. 4. 2 Sam. 12. 25. 1 Kings 8. 53, 56; 12. 15; 14. 18; 15. 29; 16. 7; 17. 16. 2 Kings 14. 25. 2 Chron. 10. 15; 23. 18; 29. 25. Neh. 9. 14. Isa. 20. 2. Jer. 37. 2, &c.

Haggai. Heb. *Ḥaggai*; from *Ḥag* = feast, or festival.

Zerubbabel. Heb. = sown in Babylon; because he was of the royal seed of Judah born (or seed sown) in Babylon. Cp. 1 Chron. 3. 19. Ezra 2. 2; 3. 2. See Ap. 99.

son. Put by Fig. *Synecdoche* (of Genus), Ap. 6, for grandson.

Shealtiel. Heb. = asked for from God. The son of Jeconiah (= Jehoiachin), who was taken captive to Babylon (2 Kings 24. 15. 1 Chron. 3. 17). Cp. Ezra 3. 2, 8; 5. 2. Neh. 12. 1. Matt. 1. 12. Luke 3. 27. See Ap. 99.

governor. Ruling Judea as a Persian province, with a Persian title *pechāh*, from which we have the modern *pasha* = prefect, or satrap.

Joshua. The first high priest after the return. See 1. 12, 14; 2. 2, 4. Zech. 3. 1, 3, 8, 9; 6. 11. Spelt "Josuah" in the 1611 edition of the A.V.

Josedech. Heb. = Jehovah is righteous.

This People. Not Zerubbabel or Joshua. **time.**

2 the LORD of hosts. See note on 1 Sam. 1. 3. Repeated here and in *v.* 4 for emphasis. **not.** Sept. reads "not yet". **4 you, O ye.** Heb. Fig. *Epizeuxis* (Ap. 6), for emphasis = you, even you, or that ye yourselves. **cieled** = panelled. Used of the lining of an arched roof. Occurs in 1 Kings 6. 9; 7. 3, 7. Jer. 22. 14. Showing that their houses were not only roofed, but wainscotted or decorated. Heb. = "in your houses [and that too] panelled". Cp. David (2 Sam. 7. 2. Ps. 132. 3). This proves that the Temple had not then been commenced. Cp. *v.* 9. See notes on Neh. 7. 4, and longer note on p. 653. Also Ap. 58.

1. 5-11 (B, p. 1276). PUNISHMENT. SCARCITY. (*Alternation.*)

B | C | 5. Call to consider.
D | 6. Scarcity.
C | 7, 8. Call to consider.
D | 9–11. Scarcity.

5 Consider = Set your heart on, or give your attention to. Occurs five times in this book (1. 5, 7; 2. 15, 18, 18). Cp. Job 1. 8; 2. 3. Isa. 41. 22. **your ways**: i. e. the ways in which ye have been led, your experiences which are detailed in the next verse. **6 Ye have sown, &c.** Ref. to Pent. (Deut. 28. 38, 39). Ap. 92. **have not enough** = are not satisfied. Ref. to Pent. (Lev. 26. 26). Ap. 92. **8 mountain** = hill country. **take pleasure** = be pleased therewith. **I will be glorified** = I will get Me honour. Heb. text has *'ekkābdā*. This is one in a list of twenty-nine words which are without the letter *He* (ה = H) at the end (see Ginsburg's *Massōrah*, vol. i, p. 281). Ap. 30. This letter ה = five (Ap. 10), and later Talmudists regard it as betokening the fact that five things were lacking in the second Temple, viz.: (1) the ark; (2) the sacred fire; (3) the Shekinah; (4) the Urim and Thummim; and (5) the spirit of prophecy. This list is to safeguard (Ap. 93) the other occurrences of the word, which have this letter at the end, among them being Ex. 14. 4, 17. These constitute a ref. to Pent. with Lev. 10. 3 (which, like Hag. 1. 8, is without the ה). Ap. 92. **saith the LORD** = hath said Jehovah. **9 saith the LORD of hosts** = [is] the oracle of Jehovah Sabaioth. **every man.** Heb. *'ish.* Ap. 14. II. **10 the heaven, &c.** Ref. to Pent. (Lev. 26. 19. Deut. 28. 23). Ap. 92. **dew.** See note on Ps. 133. 3. **and.** Note the Fig. *Polysyndeton* (Ap. 6), emphasising each item which is particularised here, and in *v.* 11.

410 11 [10]And I called for a drought upon the land,
[10]and upon the mountains, [10]and upon the
corn, [10]and upon the °new wine, [10]and upon
the oil, [10]and upon °*that* which the ground
bringeth forth, [10]and upon °men, [10]and upon
cattle, [10]and upon all the labour of the hands.'"

C E (p. 1278) 12 Then [1]Zerubbabel the son of [1]Shealtiel,
and [1]Joshua the son of [1]Josedech, the high
priest, with all °the remnant of the People,
obeyed the voice of [1]the LORD their °God,
and the words of [1]Haggai [1]the prophet, °as
[1]the LORD their °God had °sent him, and the
People did fear before [1]the LORD.

F 13 Then spake [1]Haggai °the LORD'S messenger in [1]the LORD'S °message unto the People, saying, "*I am* with you, [9]saith [1]the
LORD."

E 14 And [1]the LORD stirred up the °spirit of
Zerubbabel the son of [1]Shealtiel, [1]governor of
Judah, and the °spirit of [1]Joshua the son of
[1]Josedech, the high priest, and the °spirit of
all [12]the remnant of the People; and °they
came and did work in the house of [2]the LORD
of hosts, their [12]God,
15 °In the four and twentieth day of the
sixth month, in the second year of [1]Darius the
king.

F **2** °In the seventh *month*, in the one and
twentieth *day* of the month, came the
word of °the LORD °by the prophet °Haggai,
saying,
2 "Speak now to °Zerubbabel the son of
°Shealtiel, governor of Judah, and to
°Joshua the son of °Josedech, the high priest,
and to °the residue of the people, saying,
3 °'Who *is* left among you that saw °this
house in her °first glory? and how do ye see it
now? *is it* not in your eyes in comparison of
it as nothing?
4 Yet now be strong, O [2]Zerubbabel, °saith
[1]the LORD; and be strong, O [2]Joshua, son of
[2]Josedech, the high priest; and be strong, all
ye People of the land, °saith the LORD, and
work: for *I am* with you, °saith the LORD of
hosts:
5 *According to* the word that °I covenanted
with you °when ye came out of Egypt, °so
My °Spirit °remaineth among you: fear ye
not.'

D G1 6 For thus °saith [4]the LORD of hosts; '**Yet
°once, it *is* a little while, and °I will shake
the heavens, °and the earth,** °and the sea,
°and the dry *land*;
7 [6]And I will shake all nations,
G2 and °the desire of all nations °shall come:

11 new wine. Heb. *tīrōsh*. Ap. 27. II.
that which. Some codices, with Aram. and Syr., read "all which".
men. Heb. *'ādām*. Ap. 14. I.

1. 12—2. 5 (**C**, p. 1276). OBEDIENCE AND ENCOURAGEMENT. (*Alternation.*)

C | E | 1. 12. Obedience.
  F | 1. 13. Encouragement.
E | 1. 14, 15. Obedience.
  F | 2. 1-5. Encouragement.

12 the remnant: which had returned from Babylon. Cp. *v.* 14; 2. 2, &c.
God. Heb. Elohim. Ap. 4. I.
as=according as. Some codices, with a special various reading called *Sevir* (Ap. 34), one early printed edition, and Syr., read "with which".
sent him. Some codices, with Sept., Syr., and Vulg., read "sent him unto them". Cp. Jer. 43. 1.
13 the LORD'S messenger, &c.=the messenger of Jehovah in the message of Jehovah.
message. Heb. word occ. only here.
14 spirit. Heb. *rūach*. Ap. 9. Put by Fig. *Metonymy* (of Adjunct), Ap. 6, for the state of mind and feeling, &c. Cp. 1 Chron. 5. 26. 2 Chron. 21. 16; 36. 22 (=Ezra 1. 1). Jer. 51. 11.
they came. See Ezra 3. 1, &c.
15 In the, &c. This reads on from *v.* 14, giving the date when Haggai's message took effect about three weeks later. It is not the commencement of another message, as some have supposed. See note on p. 1276.

2. 1 In the seventh month. See note on p. 1276.
the LORD. Heb. Jehovah. Ap. 4. II.
by. See note on 1. 1.
Haggai. See note on 1. 1.
2 Zerubbabel . . . Shealtiel, governor . . . Joshua . . . Josedech. See notes on 1. 1.
the residue=the remnant.
3 Who is left . . . ?=Who is there among you, the remnant? Evidently there were some present who had seen it. Cp. Ezra 3. 12.
this house. The Temple is regarded as one throughout.
first=primitive.
4 saith the LORD of hosts=[is] the oracle of Jehovah Sabaioth. See note on 1 Sam. 1. 3.
5 I covenanted with you: or, supply the *Ellipsis* thus: "[I remember", or "Remember ye] the word which I", &c. Ref. to Pent. (Ex. 29. 45, 46). Ap. 92.
when ye came, &c. Ref. to Pent. (Ex. 12. 51). Ap. 92.
so My Spirit, &c.: i.e. speaking by the prophets. Cp. Neh. 9. 20. Isa. 63. 10-14.
Spirit. Heb. *rūach*. Ap. 9.
remaineth: or, abideth.

2. 6-9 (**D**, p. 1276). "I WILL SHAKE", ETC. (*Division.*)

D | G1 | 6, 7-. Threatening.
  | G2 | -7-9. Promise.

6 saith=hath said.
once=first; as in 1. 1 and 2. 1. Heb. *'chād*=one of several. See note on Deut. 6. 4. There had been shakings before; but this one would be extreme and final. Quoted in Heb. 12. 26, 27. Greek *hapax*=once for all: i.e. first, before the fulfilment of the promise given in the clause which follows. It is fem. here, and cannot agree with "little" (one little, or a little) because *me'at* is masculine. **I will shake.** See the Structure "***D***", below (*v.* 21). Not "convert"; but shake violently, as in Pss. 46. 3; 77. 18. Jer. 10. 10, &c. **and.** Note the Fig. *Polysyndeton* (Ap. 6): emphasising the universality of this last shaking, in contrast with all former shakings. It refers to the great tribulation (Matt. 24. 29, 30). Cp. Isa. 13. 13; 24. 18. **7 the desire.** Put by Fig. *Metonymy* (of the Adjunct), Ap. 6, for the object of desire, which cannot be "things", for *hemdath* is fem. sing., and refers to Him Who alone can satisfy the desire of all nations. Cp. 1 Sam. 9. 20. 2 Chron. 21. 20. **shall come.** The verb is plural: hence some would refer it to the treasures of "silver and gold" of *v.* 8. But when two nouns stand together (as here) the verb may agree in *number* with either noun. Here it agrees with "nations" in number, but with the object desired in reality. The Sept. reads "the elect of all the nations".

410 and I will fill this house with °glory, [6]saith
[4]the LORD of hosts.
8 °The silver *is* Mine, and the gold *is* Mine,'
[4]saith [4]the LORD of hosts.
9 The [7]glory of this °latter house shall be
greater than of the former, [6]saith [4]the LORD of
hosts: and in this place will I give °peace,
[4]saith [4]the LORD of hosts."

A H 10 °In the four and twentieth *day* of the
(p. 1279) ninth *month,* in the second year of Darius,
came the word of [1]the LORD °by [1]Haggai
[1]the prophet, saying,

J a 11 "Thus saith [4]the LORD of hosts; °'Ask
now the priests *concerning* the law, saying,
12 'If one bear °holy flesh in the °skirt of his
garment, and with his skirt do touch bread,
°or pottage, or °wine, or oil, or any meat,
°shall it be °holy?'"

b "And the priests answered and said, °"No."

J a 13 Then said Haggai, "If *one that is* unclean °by a °dead body touch any of these,
[12]shall it be °unclean?"

b And the priests answered and said, "It
[12]shall be °unclean."

H 14 °Then answered Haggai, and said, "So
is this People, and so *is* this nation before Me,
[4]saith [1]the LORD; and so *is* every work of
their hands; and that which they offer °there
is unclean.

B K 15 And now, I pray you, °consider °from this
day and °upward, from before a stone was
laid upon a stone in the temple of [1]the LORD:

L 16 Since those *days* were, when *one* came to
an heap of twenty °*measures,* °there were
but ten: when *one* came to the pressfat for to
draw out fifty °*vessels* out of the press, there
were *but* twenty.
17 °I smote you with blasting and with mildew and with hail in all the labours of your
hands;

M yet ye *turned* not to Me, [4]saith [1]the LORD.

C K 18 °Consider now °from this day and [15]up-
ward, from the four and twentieth day of the
ninth *month, even* from the day that the
foundation of [1]the LORD'S temple was laid,
°consider *it*.

L 19 °Is the seed yet in the barn? °yea, as yet
the vine, and the fig tree, and the pomegranate, and the olive tree, hath not brought forth:

M °from this day will I bless °*you*."

D N^1 20 And °again the word of [1]the LORD came

glory. This refers to the future millennial Sanctuary of Ezekiel (Ap. 88), as it follows after the great shaking of this verse and Rev. 6. 12–17. Moreover this "glory" is connected with the final peace (*v.* 9. Isa. 9. 6; 60. 18). The second Temple was connected with "grace", not "glory", and was followed by wars, not peace (Matt. 10. 34; 24. 6–8. Luke 12. 51).

8 The silver, &c. Cp. Isa. 2. 7; 60. 9–17; 61. 6.

9 latter house, &c. Render: "Greater shall be the last glory of this house than the first". Ezek. 43. 2, 4, 5; 44. 4.

peace. Cp. Isa. 9. 6. Mic. 5. 5. Zech. 9. 9, 10.

2. 10–14 (*A*, p. 1276). DISAPPROBATION.
(Introversion and Alternation.)

A | H | 10. The word of Jehovah by Haggai.
  J | a | 11–12–. Question *re* uncleanness.
    b | –12. Answer.
  J | *a* | 13–. Question *re* uncleanness.
    b | –13. Answer.
 H | 14. The word of Jehovah by Haggai.

10 In the, &c. Nearly two months after the preceding message. See note on p. 1276.

by. Many codices, with eight early printed editions, Sept., and Vulg., read "unto"; but in Codex Hillel (quoted in the *Massōrah*, Ap. 30) and others, with two early printed editions, Aram., and Syr., read "by the hand of", as elsewhere in this book. See note on 1. 1.

11 Ask now, &c. Ref. to Pent. (Lev. 10. 10, 11. Deut. 17. 11; 33. 10). Ap. 92. Supply the *Ellipsis*: "Ask now [direction]", &c.

12 holy. See note on Ex. 3. 5.

holy flesh: i. e. the flesh of a sacrifice. Cp. Jer. 11. 15.

skirt = wing. See note on Ruth 3. 9.

or. Note the Fig. *Paradiastolē* (Ap. 6).

wine. Heb. *yayin.* Ap. 27. I. **shall** = will.

holy. See note on Ex. 3. 5.

No. Ref. to Pent. (Lev. 6. 27). Ap. 92.

13 by = by [touching].

dead body = soul. Heb. *nephesh.* See Ap. 13. ix, where see thirteen passages in which *nephesh* is used of a "dead soul" in distinction from a "living soul", as in Gen. 2. 7. Ref. to Pent. Ap. 92.

unclean. Ref. to Pent. (Lev. 22. 4, 6). Ap. 92.

14 Then, &c. This is the application of *vv.* 11–13.

there. Referring to the altar which was set up before the building of the Temple. See *v.* 15. Cp. Ezra 3. 2, 3, with *v.* 6.

2. 15–19 (*B* and *C*, p. 1276). PUNISHMENT AND ENCOURAGEMENT. *(Extended Alternation.)*

B | K | 15. Consider. Past time: "before".
  L | 16, 17–. After the Ingathering.
   M | –17. Impenitence.
C | *K* | 18. Consider. Subsequent time.
  L | 19–. Before the Ingathering.
   M | –19. Beneficence.

15 consider. See note on 1. 5.

from this day. The day of the prophet's message.

upward = above, as to place; backward, as regards time; as explained. Referring to past time, before the foundation was laid. See the Structure ("K" and "*K*"); and note on *v.* –19.

16 measures. Supply "sheaves".

there = and there. **vessels.** Omit "vessels". Heb. *pūrāh* = a winepress. Occurs only here, and Isa. 63. 3. Hence used of a wine measure. **17 I smote you, &c.** Ref. to Pent. (Deut. 28. 22). Ap. 92. **18 Consider . . . consider.** Fig. *Anadiplōsis.* Ap. 6. **from this day:** i.e. from the day the foundation of the Temple was laid. From this time, subsequently, things would be different, and Jehovah would bless them, as promised in *v.* –19. **19 Is the seed . . . ?** The answer is no. It was sown. **yea, as yet** = howbeit, though at present. See notes on p. 618, and Ap. 58. **from this day** = from this very day. Referring to their obedience in building. **you.** Omit; and take "bless" absolutely.

2. 20–23 (*D*, p. 1276). I WILL SHAKE.
(Division.)

D | N^1 | 20–22. Threatening.
  | N^2 | 23. Promise.

20 again. On the same day: i.e. a second time.

410 unto [1]Haggai in the four and twentieth *day* of the month, saying,
21 "Speak to [2]Zerubbabel, °governor of Judah, saying, °'𝔍 will shake °the heavens and the earth;
22 And I will overthrow the throne of kingdoms, and I will destroy the strength of the kingdoms of the °heathen; and I will overthrow the chariots, and those that ride in them; and the horses and their riders shall come down, every one by the sword of his brother.

N[2] (p. 1279) 23 In that day, [4]saith [4]the LORD of hosts, will I take thee, O [2]Zerubbabel, My servant, the son of [2]Shealtiel, [4]saith [1]the LORD, and will make thee °as a signet: for I have °chosen °thee, [4]saith [4]the LORD of hosts.'"

21 governor. See note on 1. 1.
𝔍 will shake. Cp. the Structure ("**D**" and "***D***"), p. 1276; and note on 2. 6. Heb. I am shaking, or about to shake. Referring to a nearer shaking than 2. 6.
the heavens and the earth. See note on Deut. 4. 26.
22 heathen = nations.
23 as a signet. Cp. Song 8. 6. Jer. 22. 24. See also, for this honour, Zech. 4. 7–10; 6. 13; and cp. Gen. 41. 42. Est. 3. 10.
chosen thee. As David and others were chosen (1 Kings 8. 16; 11. 34, &c.).
thee. This must refer to the true prince and governor of Isa. 9. 6, 7.

ZECHARIAH.

THE STRUCTURE OF THE BOOK AS A WHOLE.

(*Introversions.*)

𝔍[2] | A[1] | B[1] | 1. 1–6. LITERAL PROPHECY. DATED (THE SECOND YEAR OF DARIUS).
C[1] | 1. 7—6. 15. PROPHECIES WITH SYMBOLS. EIGHT VISIONS.
B[2] | 7. 1—8. 23. LITERAL PROPHECY. DATED (THE FOURTH YEAR OF DARIUS).
A[2] | B[3] | 9. 1—10. 12. LITERAL PROPHECIES. FIRST BURDEN.
C[2] | 11. 1–17. PROPHECY WITH SYMBOLS.
B[4] | 12. 1—14. 21. LITERAL PROPHECIES. SECOND BURDEN.

For the CANONICAL Order and Place of the Prophets, see Ap. 1, and pp. 1206 and 1207.
For the CHRONOLOGICAL Order of the Prophets, see Ap. 77.
For the Inter-relation of the Prophetic Books, see Ap. 78.
For the *Formulæ* of Prophetic utterance, see Ap. 82.
For References to the Pentateuch by the Prophets, see Ap. 92.
For the Inter-relation of the Minor (or Shorter) Prophets, see pp. 1206 and 1207.

ZECHARIAH's first prophecy is dated (1. 1) "in the eighth month in the second year of Darius" (Hystaspis) (410 B.C.); sixteen years after the Decree of Cyrus. It thus comes midway between Haggai's second and third messages. See notes on p. 1277.

His last date is in the fourth year of Darius (7. 1).

The Temple was completed in the sixth year of Darius, and was dedicated in Adar (Ap. 51), 405 B.C. The first Passover, and the last Feast of Tabernacles were in 404 B.C. (see p. 617, Ap. 58, and Neh. 9). This marks the close of ZECHARIAH's dated Prophecies; but, as ZECHARIAH really closes the O.T. (see Ap. 77. 9), his prophecies would extend to and cover the *latest date* in the O.T., which is the *eighth* year of Darius Hystaspis in the year 403 B.C. (see Ezra 10. 17 and Ap. 58). The whole period therefore covered by the book of ZECHARIAH is seven years, 410–403 B.C. (Ap. 77).

ZECHARIAH.

A[1] B[1] (p. 1280) 410-407 1 ° IN the eighth month, in the second year
of ° Darius, came the word of ° the LORD
unto ° Zechariah, the son of ° Berechiah, the
° son of ° Iddo the prophet, saying,
2 [1] "The LORD hath been ° sore displeased
with ° your fathers.
3 Therefore say thou unto them, 'Thus ° saith
° the LORD of hosts; ° 'Turn ye unto Me,
° saith ° the LORD of hosts, and I will turn unto
you, ° saith ° the LORD of hosts.
4 Be ye not as [2] your fathers, unto whom ° the
former prophets have cried, saying, 'Thus ° saith
[3] the LORD of hosts; [3] Turn ye now from your
° evil ways, and *from* your ° evil doings:' but
they did not hear, nor hearken unto Me, ° saith
[1] the LORD.
5 [2] Your fathers, ° where *are* they? and the
prophets, do they live for ever?
6 But My words and My statutes, which I
commanded My servants [1] the prophets, did
they not ° take hold of your fathers? and they
returned and ° said, 'Like as [3] the LORD of hosts
thought to do unto us, according to our ways,
and according to our doings, so hath He dealt
with us.'"

A C F[1] 7 ° Upon the four and twentieth day of the
° eleventh month, which *is* the month Sebat,
in the second year of [1] Darius, came the word
of [1] the LORD unto [1] Zechariah, the son of
[1] Berechiah, the son of [1] Iddo the prophet,
saying,
8 ° I saw by night, and behold a ° man riding
upon a red horse, and he stood ° among the
myrtle trees that *were* in the ° bottom; and
behind him *were there* red ° horses, ° speckled,
and white.
F[2] a 9 Then said I, "O ° my lord, what *are* these?"
(p. 1282) b And the ° angel that talked with me said unto
me, "I will shew thee what these ° be."
10 And the [8] man that stood among the
myrtle trees answered and said, "These *are
they* whom [1] the LORD hath sent to walk to
and fro through the earth."
11 And they answered the angel of [1] the
LORD that stood among the myrtle trees, and
said, "We have walked to and fro through the
earth, and, ° behold, all the earth sitteth still,
and is at rest."

1. 1 In the eighth month, &c. See note on p. 1280. Modern critics first assume that the day ought to be named, and then further assume that it has "fallen out accidentally"!

Darius. Darius (Hystaspis). See Ap. 57.

the LORD. Heb. Jehovah. Ap. 4. II.

Zechariah = Remembered of Jehovah.

Berechiah = Blessed of Jehovah. Cp. Matt. 23. 35. This prophet would be the one referred to by the Lord, unless the father of the Zechariah of 2 Chron. 24. 20, 21 had more than one name, which was sometimes the case. See Esau's wives (Gen. 26. 34; 28. 9; 36. 2, 3). The latter would be the last (and Abel the first in the O.T.), according to the place of Chronicles in the Heb. Canon (see Ap. 1).

son. Put by Fig. *Synecdoche* (of Species), Ap. 6, for descendant. **Iddo.** See Ezra 5. 1; 6. 14. Neh. 12. 4, 16.

2 sore displeased. Heb. displeased with a displeasure. Fig. *Polyptōton*. Ap. 6. See note on Gen. 26. 28. **your fathers.** Cp. *vv.* 4, 6.

3 saith = hath said.

the LORD of hosts. Heb. *Jehovah Ẓebai'ōth*. Ap. 4. II. This title occurs fifty-three times in this book, forty-four times in chs. 1-8, and nine times in chs. 9-14. It is characteristic of this book: twenty-nine times it is with the verbs saith or speaketh. All are referred to in the notes.

Turn = Return. Note the Fig. *Epimonē* (Ap. 6), in *vv.* 3-6, in which the fact is emphasised by *dwelling* upon it as the cause of all Jehovah's displeasure.

saith the LORD of hosts = [is] the oracle of Jehovah Sabaioth.

4 the former prophets: i.e. Joshua to 2 Kings. See Ap. 1 and 78. **evil** = wicked. Heb. *rā'a'*. Ap. 44. viii.

saith = hath said.

saith the LORD = [is] Jehovah's oracle.

5 where are they? This in contrast with the words of Jehovah, which endure for ever (*v.* 6). Fig. *Erotēsis*. Ap. 6.

6 take hold of = overtake. Cp. Deut. 28. 15, 45.

said. See Lam. 1. 18.

1. 7—6. 15 (C[1], p. 1280). PROPHECIES WITH SYMBOLS. (*Alternation and Introversion.*)

C[1] | A | C | 1. 7-17. First Vision. Invisible Agencies. Horses.
D | 1. 18-21. Second Vision. External enemies. Horns.
E | 2. 1-13. Third Vision. Jehovah's Purpose. Man, &c.
B | 3. 1-10. Fourth Vision. Joshua. The BRANCH.
A | *E* | 4. 1-14. Fifth Vision. Jehovah's Purpose. Lampstand.
D | 5. 1-4 and 5-11. Sixth and Seventh Visions. External enemies. Flying Roll, and Ephah.
C | 6. 1-8. Eighth Vision. Invisible Agencies. Horses.
B | 6. 9-15. Joshua. The BRANCH.

1. 7-17 (C, above). FIRST VISION. INVISIBLE AGENCIES. HORSES. (*Division.*)

C | F[1] | 7, 8. Vision. Horses and Horsemen.
F[2] | 9-17. Signification.

7 Upon, &c. See note on p. 1280. **eleventh month.** Three months after *v.* 1. **8 I saw, &c.** In this first of the eight visions (1. 8—6. 15) Israel is in dispersion; the Gentiles are in possession at the time of the end. Jehovah is about to interfere on behalf of Jerusalem (*vv.* 16, 17. Isa. 40. 1-5). **man.** Heb. *'īsh*. Ap. 14. II. This man is the "Adonai" of *v.* 9, and "the angel of Jehovah" of *vv.* 11, 12, as the prophet discovers from the "man's" answer. The riders of *v.* 8 report to the angel (*v.* 11). **among** = between. **bottom** = the shade: i.e. between the two mountains of 6. 1. **horses.** Representing all earthly dynasties. **speckled** = bay.

1. 9-17 [For Structure see next page].

9 my lord. Heb. Adonai. Ap. 4. VIII. 2. **angel.** See *vv.* 11, 12, 13, 14, 19; 2. 3, 3; 4. 1, 5; 5. 10; 6. 4, 5. **be** = are. **11 behold.** Fig. *Asterismos*. Ap. 6.

a (p. 1282) 410-407 **12** Then the [9]angel of [1]the LORD answered and said, "O [3]LORD of hosts, how long wilt Thou not have °mercy on °Jerusalem and on the cities of Judah, against which Thou hast had indignation these °threescore and ten years?"

b **13** And [1]the LORD °answered the [9]angel that talked with me *with* good words *and* comfortable words.

14 So the [9]angel that communed with me said unto me, "Cry thou, saying, 'Thus [3]saith [3]the LORD of hosts; I am jealous for [12]Jerusalem and for Zion with a great jealousy.

15 And I am very [2]sore displeased with the °heathen *that are* °at ease: for I was but a little displeased, and they helped forward the °affliction.

16 Therefore thus [3-]saith [1]the LORD; I am returned to [12]Jerusalem with [12]mercies: My house °shall be built in it, [-3]saith [3]the LORD of hosts, and °a line shall be stretched forth upon [12]Jerusalem.'

17 Cry yet, saying, 'Thus [3-]saith [3]the LORD of hosts; My cities through prosperity shall yet be spread abroad; and [1]the LORD shall yet °comfort Zion, and shall yet choose [12]Jerusalem.'"

D c **18** Then lifted I up mine eyes, and saw, and [11]behold four °horns.

d e **19** And I said unto the [9]angel that talked with me, "What *be* these?"

f And he answered me, "These *are* the [18]horns which have scattered °Judah, Israel, and Jerusalem."

c **20** And [1]the LORD °shewed me four °carpenters.

d e **21** Then said I, "What come these to do?"

f And °he spake, saying, "These *are* the horns which have scattered Judah, so that no [8]man did lift up his head: but °these are come to °fray °them, to cast out the horns of the °Gentiles, which lifted up *their* horn over the land of Judah to scatter it."

E G[1] **2** I lifted up mine eyes again, and looked, and °behold a °man with °a measuring line in his hand.

2 Then said I, "Whither goest thou?" And he said unto me, "To measure °Jerusalem, to see what *is* the breadth thereof, and what *is* the length thereof."

G[2] H **3** And, behold, the °angel that talked with me °went forth, and another °angel went out to meet him,

4 And said unto him, "Run, speak to °this young man, °saying, 'Jerusalem shall be inhabited *as* towns °without walls for the multitude of °men and cattle therein:

J **5** For I, °saith the LORD, will be unto her

1. 9-17 (F[2], p. 1281). SIGNIFICATION.
(*Alternation.*)

F[2] | a | 9-. Question of the prophet.
  b | -9-11. Answer of the angel.
 a | 12. Question of the angel.
  b | 13-17. Answer of Jehovah.

12 mercy=compassion, or pity. Cp. 7. 9. Ps. 102. 13. Isa. 14. 1; 49. 13.

Jerusalem. Not the "Church".

threescore and ten. See Dan. 9. 2, and notes on p. 615.

13 answered. See note on Deut. 1. 41. Jehovah Himself now speaks.

15 heathen=nations.

at ease=indifferent (Isa. 32. 9, 11. Amos 6. 1).

affliction=calamity. Heb. *rāʿaʿ*. Ap. 44. viii. Cp. Isa. 47. 11. Jer. 44. 11.

16 shall be built in it. The Temple therefore had not yet been commenced.

a line shall be stretched, &c.: i.e. a measuring-line. Put by Fig. *Metonymy* (of Adjunct), Ap. 6, for the whole work of building. Cp. 2. 1, 2.

17 comfort = pity, or have compassion on; as "mercy" in *v.* 12.

1. 18-21 (D, p. 1281). SECOND VISION.
EXTERNAL ENEMIES. (*Alternations.*)

D | c | 18. Four Horns.
  d | e | 19-. Question.
   f | -19. Answer.
 c | 20. Four Smiths.
  d | *e* | 21-. Question.
   f | -21. Answer.

18 four horns: "horns" being put by Fig. *Metonymy* (of Adjunct), Ap. 6, for the Gentile (*v.* 21) powers signified by them.

19 Judah, Israel, and Jerusalem. With *'eth* prefixed to the first two (not Jerusalem) for emphasis, so that we may not confuse them with the Church or with Gentile peoples. There is no "gloss", as alleged.

20 shewed me. This is part of the second vision.

carpenters=(iron)smiths.

21 he: i.e. the angel.

these: i.e. these four smiths (or it may denote the supernatural princes over the kingdoms). They represent the Divine agencies raised up, by which Jehovah will overthrow them.

fray. Short for *affray*=to terrify; hence English, afraid and affright. So the Heb. *ḥārad*=terrify, put in consternation (Heb. *Hiphil*, causative). Cp. Zeph. 3. 13.

them: i.e. the kingdoms represented by the horns.

Gentiles=nations.

2. 1-13 (E, p. 1281). THIRD VISION. JEHOVAH'S PURPOSE.

E | G[1] | 1, 2. Symbol. Man with measuring line.
 | G[2] | 3-13. Signification.

1 behold. Fig. *Asterismos*. Ap. 6.

man. Heb. *'ish*. Ap. 14. II. Either the same or another angel.

a measuring line. See note on 1. 16; and cp. *v.* 2.

2 Jerusalem. With *'eth*. See note on 1. 19.

2. 3-13 (G[2], above). THE SIGNIFICATION.
(*Extended Alternation.*)

G[2] | H | 3, 4. Jerusalem. Security.
  J | 5. Reason. Jehovah's presence.
   K | 6, 7. Calls to Zion to escape.
    L | 8, 9. Reason. Jehovah's love.
 H | 10-. Zion. Rejoicing.
  J | -10-12. Reason. Jehovah's presence. (Cp. J.)
   K | 13-. Call to enemies to let Zion escape.
    L | -13. Reason. Jehovah's interposition.

3 angel. See note on 1. 9. **went forth:** or, came forward. **4 this young man:** i.e. the man of *v.* 1. **saying.** Supply the logical *Ellipsis* (Ap. 6), "saying [Stop !]", for the reason given implies that measuring will be useless, owing to the overflow of inhabitants. **without walls.** Cp. Isa. 33. 20; 54. 2. Ezek. 38. 11. **men.** Heb. *'ādām*. Ap. 14. I. **5 saith the LORD**=[is] Jehovah's oracle. Ap. 4. II.

410-407 a °wall of fire round about, and will be the
glory °in the midst of her.
K (p. 1282) 6 °Ho, ho, °*come forth,* and flee from the
land of the north, [5]saith [5]the LORD: for °I
have °spread you abroad °as the four °winds
of the heaven, [5]saith [5]the LORD.
7 °Deliver thyself, O Zion, that dwellest
with the daughter of Babylon.
L 8 For thus saith °the LORD of hosts; °After
the glory hath He sent me unto the nations
which spoiled you: for °he that toucheth you
toucheth the apple of °His eye.
9 For, [1]behold, I will shake Mine hand upon
them, and they shall be a spoil to °their servants: and ye shall know that [8]the LORD of
hosts hath sent me.
H 10 Sing and rejoice, O daughter of Zion:
J for, °lo, I come, and °I will dwell [5]in the
midst of thee, [5]saith [5]the LORD.
11 And °many nations shall be joined to [5]the
LORD in that day, and shall be My People:
and [10]I will dwell [5]in the midst of thee, and
thou shalt know that [8]the LORD of hosts hath
sent me unto thee.
12 And [5]the LORD °shall inherit Judah °His
portion in the °holy land, and shall choose
Jerusalem °again.
K 13 °Be silent, O all flesh, before [5]the LORD:
L for He °is raised up out of °His [12]holy habitation.

B M[1] (p. 1283) **3** And he °shewed me °Joshua the high
priest °standing before °the angel of °the
LORD, and °Satan standing °at his right
hand °to resist him.
2 And [1]the LORD said unto [1]Satan, [1]"The
LORD °rebuke thee, O [1]Satan; even [1]the
LORD That °hath chosen Jerusalem rebuke
thee: °*is* not this °a brand plucked out of the
fire?"
3 Now [1]Joshua °was clothed with °filthy garments, and stood before the angel.
M[2] N 4 And He answered and spake unto °those
that stood before him, saying, "Take away the
[3]filthy garments from him." And unto him He
said, °"Behold, I have caused thine °iniquity to
pass °from thee, and °I will clothe thee with
°change of raiment."
5 °And I said, °"Let them set a °fair °mitre
upon his head." So they set a °fair °mitre
upon his head, and clothed him with garments.
And [1]the angel of [1]the LORD °stood by.
O 6 And [1]the angel of [1]the LORD °protested
unto Joshua, saying,
7 "Thus saith °the LORD of hosts; 'If thou
wilt walk in My ways, and °if thou wilt keep
My charge, then thou shalt also °judge My

wall of fire. Like the watch-fires seen round Bedaween camps, which have no walls. Cp. Isa. 26. 1; 33. 21; 60. 18. **in the midst.** Cp. *vv.* 10, 11 ("*J*").

6 Ho, ho. Fig. *Epizeuxis* (Ap. 6), for emphasis.
come forth: or, supply the Ellipsis "[escape]".
I have spread. Ref. to Pent. (Deut. 4. 27; 28. 64).
spread = scattered.
as. Some codices, with five early printed editions, and Syr., read "by", or "throughout". Vulg. reads "into".
winds. Heb. *rūach.* Ap. 9.
7 Deliver. Heb. Ho! Rescue, &c., as in *v.* 6.
8 the LORD of hosts. See note on 1. 3.
After the glory = For His own glory.
he that, &c. Ref. to Pent. (Deut. 32. 10). Ap. 92.
His eye. The primitive text read "Mine eye"; but the *Sōpherim* say (Ap. 33) that they altered this to "His", regarding it as derogatory to Jehovah to read aloud such pronounced anthropomorphic expressions.
9 their servants = their own slaves.
10 lo. Fig. *Asterismos.* Ap. 6.
I will dwell, &c. Ref. to Pent. (Ex. 29. 45, 46. Lev. 26. 11, 12). Ap. 92.
11 many nations, &c. Ref. to Pent. (Ex. 12. 49. Num. 9. 14). Ap. 92.
12 shall inherit . . . His portion. Ref. to Pent. (Deut. 32. 9). Ap. 92. **holy.** See note on Ex. 3. 5.
again = yet; as in 1. 17. Not make a new choice, but demonstrate again His old choice in actual experience.
13 Be silent, &c. Cp. Hab. 2. 20. Zeph. 1. 7.
is raised up = hath roused Himself up. Cp. Ps. 78. 65.
His holy habitation. Ref. to Pent. (Deut. 26. 15).

3. 1-10 (B, p. 1281). **JOSHUA. THE BRANCH.**
(Division.)

B | M[1] | 1-3. Symbol. Joshua.
  | M[2] | 4-10. Signification.

1 shewed me. This is the fourth of the eight visions. See the Structure, p. 1281.
Joshua. See note on Hag. 1. 1.
standing. Put by Fig. *Metonymy* (of Adjunct), Ap. 6, for ministering. **the angel.** See note on 1. 9.
the LORD. Heb Jehovah. Ap. 4. II.
Satan . . . to resist him. Note the Fig. *Paronomasia* (Ap. 6). Heb. *hassātān . . . l^esiṭnō* = the Adversary . . . to be an adversary; or, the Accuser . . . to accuse him, &c.
Satan = Accuser, or Opposer. See Num. 22. 22, 32. 1 Chron. 21. 1. Job 1. 6, 7, 8, 12, &c.
at his right hand. Cp. Ps. 109. 6. Job 30. 12.
to resist him = to be his adversary. Cp. Num. 22. 32, marg. 1 Sam. 29. 4. 2 Sam. 19. 22. 1 Kings 5. 4; 11. 14, 23, 25.
2 rebuke thee. Cp. Jude 9.
hath chosen = hath now and heretofore chosen.
is not this . . . ? i. e. have I not plucked, &c. Fig. *Erotēsis.* Ap. 6. **a brand, &c.** Cp. Amos 4. 11.
3 was = had come to be. Cp. Gen. 1. 2.
filthy. A symbol of the defiling nature of sin. Cp. Prov. 30. 12. Isa. 4. 4, &c.

3. 4-10 (M[2], above). **THE SIGNIFICATION.**
(Alternation.)

M[2] | N | 4, 5. Removal of the iniquity of Joshua.
  | O | 6-8. Promise of access. The BRANCH of Jehovah.
  | *N* | 9. Removal of the iniquity of the Land.
  | *O* | 10. Promise of security. The Word of Jehovah.

4 those that stood, &c.: i. e. the ministering spirits who waited on Him. Cp. Deut. 1. 38. 1 Sam. 16. 21. 1 Kings 10. 8. **Behold.** Fig. *Asterismos.* Ap. 6. **iniquity.** Heb. *'āven.* Ap. 44. iii. **from thee** = from upon thee, or from off thee. Cp. 2 Sam. 12. 13; 24. 10. Job 7. 21. **I will clothe** = I have caused thee to be clothed. **change of raiment** = rich or costly garments: i. e. robes of state, or of righteousness. **5 And I said** = Then said I (i. e. the prophet); but some codices, with Syr. and Vulg., read "then said He". **Let them set.** Ref. to Pent. (Ex. 29. 6). Ap. 92. **fair** = clean, or pure. **mitre** = turban. See Ex. 28. 37. **stood by**: i. e. while this was being done. **6 protested** = solemnly affirmed, or testified. Ref. to Pent. (Gen. 43. 3. Deut. 8. 19). Ap. 92. Cp. Jer. 11. 7. **7 the LORD of hosts.** See note on 1. 3 and on 1 Sam. 1. 3. **if thou wilt keep, &c.** Ref. to Pent. (Lev. 8. 35). Ap. 92. **judge My house, &c.** = govern My house. Ref. to Pent. (Deut. 17. 9). Ap. 92.

410-407 house, and shalt also keep My courts, and
I will give thee °places to walk among °these
that stand °by.
8 Hear now, O [1]Joshua the high priest, thou,
and thy °fellows that sit before thee: for they
are °men wondered at: for, [4]behold, I will
bring forth °My Servant °the °BRANCH.

N (p. 1283) 9 For [4]behold the stone that I have laid
before Joshua; °upon °one stone *shall be*
°seven eyes: [4]behold, I will engrave the
graving thereof, °saith [7]the LORD of hosts,
and I will remove the [4]iniquity of that land
°in one day.

O 10 In °that day, [9]saith [7]the LORD of hosts,
shall ye °call °every man his neighbour under
°the vine and under °the fig tree."

E P g (p. 1284) **4** And the °angel that talked with me came
again, and waked me, as a °man that is
wakened out of his sleep,
2 And said unto me, °"What seest thou?" And
°I said, "I have looked, and °behold, a °candle-
stick all *of* gold, with a bowl upon the top of
it, °and his seven lamps thereon, and °seven
pipes to the seven lamps, which *are* upon the
top thereof:"

h 3 And two olive trees by it, one upon the
right *side* of the bowl, and the other upon the
left *side* thereof.

P g 4 So I answered and spake to the [1]angel that
talked with me, saying, "What *are* these, °my
lord?"
5 Then the [1]angel that talked with me answered and said unto me, "Knowest thou not
what these be?" And I said, "No, [4]my lord."
6 Then he answered and spake unto me,
saying, "This *is* the word of °the LORD unto
Zerubbabel, saying, 'Not by °might, °nor by
°power, °but by My °Spirit, saith °the LORD
of hosts.
7 Who *art* thou, °O great mountain? before
Zerubbabel *thou shalt become* a plain: and he
shall bring forth the headstone *thereof with*
shoutings, *crying*, 'Grace, grace unto it.'"
8 Moreover the word of [6]the LORD came unto
me, saying,
9 °"The hands of Zerubbabel have laid the
foundation of this house; his hands shall also
finish it; and °thou shalt know that [6]the LORD
of hosts hath sent me unto you.
10 For who hath despised the day of small
things? for they shall rejoice, and shall see
the °plummet in the hand of Zerubbabel °*with*
those seven; they *are* the eyes of [6]the LORD,
which run to and fro through the whole earth."

h 11 Then answered I, and said unto him, "What
are these two [3]olive trees upon the right *side*
of the [2]candlestick and upon the left *side*
thereof?"
12 And I answered again, and said unto him,
"What *be these* two [3]olive branches which
through the two golden pipes °empty the
golden *oil* out of themselves?"
13 And he answered me and said, "Knowest
thou not what these *be*?" And I said, "No,
[4]my lord."
14 Then said he, "These *are* °the two anointed
ones, that stand by °the Lord of the whole earth."

places to walk = free access, or right of way.
these that stand by: i.e. the attendant angels of Ps. 103. 21. Cp. 1 Kings 22. 19. 1 Tim. 5. 21.
by: i.e. in My presence.
8 fellows = colleagues.
men wondered at = men of sign: i.e. men to serve as signs [of One greater].
men. Heb. pl. of *'ĕnōsh*. Ap. 14. III.
My Servant the BRANCH: i.e. Messiah.
the BRANCH. Cp. Isa. 4. 2. Jer. 23. 5, 6; 33. 15. Zech. 6. 12. Heb. *zemah*. Not the same word as in Isa. 11. 1, or Ps. 80. 15, 17. See notes on p. 1304.
BRANCH. See Ap. 48.
9 upon = fixed upon; as in Deut. 11. 12. Cp. 1 Kings 9. 3. Ezra 5. 5.
one stone: or, every stone.
seven eyes = seven pairs of eyes. Watching and caring for. Cp. 4. 10.
saith the LORD of hosts = [is] the oracle of Jehovah Sabaioth.
in one day. Cp. Isa. 66. 5-9.
10 that day: i.e. the day of Messiah.
call = call in . . . under: i.e. invite to sit down and feast.
every man. Heb. *'ish*. Ap. 14. II.
the = his own; as in Mic. 4. 4.

4. 1-14 (*E*, p. 1281). JEHOVAH'S PURPOSE. (*Alternation.*)

E P g	1, 2. The Lampstand.	The Sign.
h	3. The Two Olive trees.	
P g	4-10. The House of Jehovah.	The Signification.
h	11-14. The Two Witnesses.	

1 angel. See note on 1. 9.
man. Heb. *'ish*. Ap. 14. II.
2 What seest thou? The fifth vision.
I said. Heb. text reads "he". Some codices, with four early printed editions, are without the Heb. margin, "I".
behold. Fig. *Asterismos*. Ap. 6.
candlestick = a single seven-branched lampstand, as in the Tabernacle and in the second Temple (1 Macc. 1. 21; 4. 49; as seen in the Arch of Titus, in Rome). The ref. is to the Pent. (Ex. 25. 31); not to Solomon's Temple, in which there were ten separate lampstands (1 Kings 7. 49). Cp. Jer. 52. 19. Ap. 92.
and his seven lamps. Ref. to Pent. (Ex. 25. 37).
seven pipes. This looks forward to the future, as described in Rev. 11. 3-12.
4 my lord. Heb. *'ădōn*. See Ap. 4. VIII (1).
6 the LORD. Heb. Jehovah. Ap. 4. II.
might = might [of man].
nor = and not.
power = power [of flesh].
but by, &c.: i.e. as in the lampstand the oil flowed silently, without help from man.
Spirit. Heb. *rūach*. Ap. 9.
the LORD of hosts. See note on 1. 3.
7 O great mountain? Add, by supplying the Ellipsis (Ap. 6), "[that standest in the way of Zerubbabel?]"
9 The hands, &c. Here is the explanation of the vision.
thou shalt know. Some codices, with Aram., Syr., and Vulg., read "ye shall know".
10 plummet. Heb. stone of tin = tin weight used as a plummet.
with those seven = these seven [lamps which thou seest] these [are] the eyes", &c.; as in 3. 9.
12 empty the golden oil out of themselves = empty out of themselves [and fill] the golden [bowls].
14 the two anointed ones. Heb. the two sons of oil; looking forward again to the future, to "the two witnesses" of Rev. 11. 3-13.
the Lord of the whole earth. The Heb. *'ădōn*, Ap. 4. VIII (1), is here specially associated with Messiah's dominion *in the earth*. Cp. 6. 5; 14. 9. Josh. 3. 11-13. Ps. 8. 1, 6, 9; 97. 5. Mic. 4. 13.

D Q j (p. 1285) 410-407 **5** Then I turned, and lifted up mine eyes,
and °looked, and behold a flying °roll.
2 And he said unto me, "What seest thou?"
And I answered, "I see a flying roll; the length
thereof *is* twenty °cubits, and the breadth
thereof ten °cubits."

k 3 Then said he unto me, "This *is* °the curse
that °goeth forth over the face of the whole
°earth:

l for every one that °stealeth °shall be cut off *as*
on this side according to it; and every one
that °sweareth shall be cut off *as* on that side
according to it.
4 °I will bring it forth, °saith °the LORD of
hosts, and it shall °enter into the house of the
thief, and into the house of him that sweareth
falsely by °My name: and it shall °remain in
the midst of his house, and °shall consume it
with the °timber thereof and the stones thereof."

Q j 5 Then the °angel that talked with me went
forth, and said unto me, "Lift up now thine
eyes, and °see what *is* this that [3] goeth forth."

k 6 And I said, "What *is* it?" And he said,
°"This *is* an °ephah that [3] goeth forth." He
said moreover, °"This *is* their °resemblance
through all the earth."
7 And, °behold, there was lifted up a °talent
of lead: and this *is* a woman that sitteth in
the midst of the [6] ephah.
8 And he said, [6] "This *is* °wickedness." And
he cast °it into the midst of the [6] ephah; and
he cast the °weight of lead upon the mouth
thereof.

l 9 Then lifted I up mine eyes, and looked, and,
behold, there came out °two women, and the
°wind *was* in their wings; for they had wings
°like the wings of a °stork: and they lifted up
the [6] ephah between the earth and the heaven.
10 Then said I to the [5] angel that talked with
me, "Whither do these bear the ephah?"
11 And he said unto me, "To build °it an house
in °the land of Shinar: and °it shall be established, and °set there upon her own °base."

C R m **6** And I turned, and lifted up mine eyes,
°and looked, and, behold, there came four
chariots out from between °two mountains; and
the mountains *were* mountains of °brass.

5. 1-11 (*D*, p. 1281). EXTERNAL ENEMIES. THE SIXTH AND SEVENTH VISIONS.
(*Extended Alternations.*)

D | Q | j | 1, 2. Sixth Vision. The Flying Roll.
k | 3-. Signification. The curse.
l | -3, 4. Destination. General. "The whole earth" (*v.* 3).
Q | *j* | 5. Seventh Vision. The Ephah and Flying Women.
k | 6-8. Signification. Iniquity.
l | 9-11. Destination. Special. "The Land of Shinar."

1 looked. This is the sixth vision. See the Structure on p. 1281.
roll = scroll. Hence our word "volume". Cp. Ezek. 2. 9—3. 11.
2 cubits. See Ap. 51. III. 2 (1).
3 the curse. Ref. to Pent. (Lev. 26 and Deut. 28).
goeth forth. Cp. *vv.* 5, 6. Heb. *yāẓ'ā* = to go forth on business, or on an errand. Same word as in 14. 2, 3, 8, &c. (not 14. 16, 18). **earth**: or, land.
stealeth . . . sweareth, &c. Ref. to Pent. (Lev. 19. 12). Ap. 92.
shall be cut off = hath been let off, or declared innocent; as in Num. 5. 31, Ps. 19. 12, 13. Jer. 2. 35: or goeth unpunished; as in Jer. 49. 12. This is always the sense of Heb. *nāḳāh*. Render the passage: "for 'every one that stealeth hath been let off' [is written] on the one side, according to it (the curse or scroll); and 'every one that sweareth (falsely) hath been let off' [is written] on the other side, according to it. Therefore have I brought it (the curse or scroll) forth".
4 I will bring = I have brought.
saith the LORD of hosts = [is] the oracle of Jehovah of hosts. See note on 1 Sam. 1. 3.
enter into = lodge, or abide in.
My name. Emphatic for "Me Myself". See note on Ps. 20. 1. **remain** = lodge, or roost.
shall consume it = shall destroy it, or bring it to an end. Heb. *kālāh*. Not the same word as in 14. 12. Ref. to Pent. (Lev. 14. 45). Ap. 92.
timber = timbers (pl.). **5 angel.** See note on 1. 9.
see. This is the seventh vision. See the Structure on p. 1281. **6 This.** Heb. *z'oth*. Fem. sing.
ephah. See Ap. 51. III. 3 (5).
resemblance = aspect. Heb. eye. Put by Fig. *Metonymy* (of Adjunct), Ap. 6, for their look: i. e. appearance, or colour, as in Lev. 13. 55. Num. 11. 7. Ezek. 10. 9. Cp. Ezek. 1. 4, 7, 16, 27. Dan. 10. 6, &c. Sept. and Syr. read "iniquity" (Ap. 44. iii): i. e. ו (*Vau* = v) instead of י (*Yod* = y).
7 behold = lo. Fig. *Asterismos*. Ap. 6.
talent. See Ap. 51. II. 6 (1). Heb. *kikkār*, a round disk, evidently fitting the ephah like a lid.
8 wickedness = the lawless [one]. Heb. *rāshā'*, Ap. 44. x. Adj. fem. sing. = the embodiment of the principle of lawlessness. The religious aspect of 2 Thess. 2. 8-12. Rev. 17. **it**: i. e. the talent, which had been "lifted up" for the prophet to see, and then cast back "into" the ephah. **weight** = stone; i. e. weight. This was "upon" the ephah, and is to be distinguished from the "talent", which was within. **9 two women.** Perhaps denoting two nations. **wind.** Heb. *rūach*. Ap. 9. **like the wings of a stork.** Evidently a symbol of velocity rather than of character. **stork.** An unclean bird, fond of its young, and a bird of passage. **11 it** = for her. Heb. fem. sing. **the land of Shinar** = Babylonia. Ref. to Pent. (Gen. 10. 10; 11. 2; 14. 1, 9). Ap. 92. Outside the Pentateuch only in Josh. 7. 21. Isa. 11. 11. Dan. 1. 2. **it shall be established** = it (i. e. the house, Heb. masc. sing.) shall be ready (or prepared). R.V. = when it is prepared. **set there** = fixed, or settled. Sept., and Syr., read "they (i. e. the two women) shall settle her there". **base** = fixed resting-place. The interpretation must refer to what is yet future. It cannot refer to the going into captivity; for the People had just returned, and Zechariah had been raised up for their comfort and encouragement. When the time comes, it will be marked by commerce (ephah), false religion (the woman), speedy accomplishment (the wings of a stork), and a spirit in their wings. This will be preparatory to the final judgment of Rev. 18.

6. 1-8 (*C*, p. 1281). INVISIBLE AGENCIES. HORSES. (*Alternation.*)

C | R | m | 1. Symbols. Four chariots.
n | 2, 3. Colours. (General.)
R | *m* | 4, 5. Signification. Four spirits. (Angels.)
n | 6-8. Colours. (Particular.)

1 and looked. This is the eighth vision. See the Structure, p. 1281. **two mountains.** Cp. 1. 8 and 4. 7. **brass** = copper, or bronze. Cp. Deut. 8. 9.

n (p. 1285) 410–407 2 In the first chariot *were* °red horses; and in
the second chariot black horses;
3 And in the third chariot white horses; and
in the fourth chariot °grisled and °bay horses.
R m 4 Then I answered and said unto the °angel
that talked with me, "What *are* these, °my
lord?"
5 And the [4] angel answered and said unto me,
°"These *are* °the four °spirits of the heavens,
which go forth °from standing before °the
Lord of all the earth.
n 6 The black horses which *are* therein go forth
into the north country; and the white go forth
°after them; and the grisled go forth toward
the south country."
7 And the bay went forth, and sought to go
that they might walk to and fro through the
earth: and °he said, "Get you hence, walk to
and fro through the earth." So they walked
to and fro through the earth.
8 Then °cried he °upon me, and spake unto me,
saying, "Behold, these that go toward the
north country have °quieted my °spirit in the
north country."

B S o (p. 1286) 9 And the word of °the LORD came unto me,
saying,
10 "Take of *them of* the °captivity, *even* of
Heldai, of Tobijah, and of Jedaiah, which are
come from Babylon, and come thou the same
day, and °go into the house of Josiah the son
of Zephaniah;
p 11 °Then take silver and gold, and make
°crowns, and set *them* upon the head of °Joshua
the son of °Josedech, the high priest;
T 12 And speak unto him, °saying, 'Thus speaketh °the LORD of hosts, saying, Behold the
°Man Whose name *is* The °BRANCH; and
He shall °grow up out of His place, and He
shall build the temple of [9] the LORD:
13 °Even He °shall build the temple of [9] the
LORD; and He °shall bear the glory, and shall
sit and rule upon His throne; and He shall °be
a priest upon His throne: and the counsel of
peace shall be between them °both.'
S p 14 And the [11] crowns shall °be
o to °Helem, and to Tobijah, and to Jedaiah,
and to °Hen the son of Zephaniah, °for a
memorial in the temple of [9] the LORD.
T 15 And °they *that are* far off °shall come and
build in the temple of [9] the LORD, and ye shall
know that [12] the LORD of hosts hath sent me
unto you. °And *this* shall come to pass,

2 red. The colours are not explained by the angel as having any significance. They are not explained in *v.* 5, probably because then already gone forth.

3 grisled = speckled, or dappled: i.e. like hail. Cp. Gen. 31. 10, 12. Grisled (now spelt grizzled) is from the French *gris* = iron-grey.

bay = strong. Heb. *'ămuzzim.* Occ. only here, and *v.* 7. The fem. noun "strength" only in 12. 5.

4 angel. See note on 1. 9.

my lord. Heb. *'ădōn.* Ap. 4. VIII (1).

5 These are, &c. This is the angel's interpretation, and needs no further explanation. It is for our faith; not for our reason.

the four spirits: or, the four angels. Cp. Rev. 7. 1-3; 9. 14, 15. They thus have to do with the time of the end. Their ministry is earthward, and has to do with judgment.

spirits. Heb. *rūach.* Ap. 9. The world rulers. Referred to in Dan. 10. 13, 20, 21, &c.

from standing, &c. Some codices, with Sept. and Vulg., read "[each] to take their stand before", &c.

the Lord of all the earth. See note on 4. 14.

6 after them: or, to the west of them.

7 he. A special various reading called *Sevīr* (Ap. 34), reads "they".

8 cried . . . upon. An almost obsolete idiom. To "cry upon" meant to *call to*, or *appeal to*, and is still used in this sense in Scotland. It comes to us through the Genevan Bible (1560), from the Great Bible (1539), and Coverdale (1534). It is the sense of the Heb. *z'ak* here. See Judg. 4. 10, 13. Jonah 3. 7, &c.

quieted = caused [mine anger] to rest upon. This is the force of the Heb. *Hiphil.*

spirit. Heb. *rūach.* Ap. 9. Put by Fig. *Metonymy* (of Cause), Ap. 6, for the manifestation of it in feeling: here, anger, wrath. Cp. Judg. 8. 3.

6. 9-15 (*B*, p. 1281). JOSHUA. THE BRANCH.
(*Alternation and Introversion.*)

B | S | o | 9, 10. Heldai and others.
    | | p | 11. Crowns.
    | | T | 12, 13. The Builder. The BRANCH.
    | *S* | *p* | 14-. Crowns.
    | | *o* | -14. Helem and others.
    | *T* | 15. The Builders.

9 the LORD. Heb. Jehovah. Ap. 4. II.

10 captivity: or exile, being a deputation. Heb. *gōlāh.* The special word for the Jews captive in Babylonia (2 Kings 24. 15, 16. Ezra 1. 11; 2. 1, &c. Neh. 7. 6. Est. 2. 6. Jer. 28. 6. Ezek. 1. 1, &c.). Put here by Fig. *Metonymy* (of Adjunct), Ap. 6, for the returned exiles themselves.

go. Supply the Ellipsis (Ap. 6), thus: "come [with them]".

11 Then take, &c. This is another verse, noted in the *Massōrah* (Ap. 30) as being one of twenty-six verses each of which contains all the letters of the Heb. alphabet. Cp. Zeph. 3. 8.

crowns. Heb. pl., referring to the several circlets forming one composite crown. Cp. *v.* 14, where it is used with a verb in the sing.

Joshua . . . Josedech. See note on Hag. 1. 1. **12 saying.** Some codices, with Sept. and Syr., omit this verb; but in that case the Ellipsis (Ap. 6), must be supplied in italics. See note on Ps. 109. 5. **the LORD of hosts.** See note on 1. 3. **Man . . . BRANCH.** Heb. *'īsh.* Ap. 14. II. See the Structure and note on the four Gospels as a whole, p. 1304. **grow up** = sprout forth. Note the Fig. *Paronomasia* (Ap. 6). Heb. *zemach . . . yizmach* = a branch shall branch forth. **13 Even** = Yea. Omitted in some codices; in which case, note the Fig. *Anadiplosis* (Ap. 6). Note the emphatic pronouns (= He, even He, and none other), pointing to the Messiah, and the typical character of the whole proceeding, viz. exiles bringing their gifts to restore Jehovah's house. Their crowns were to be kept as a token of this future hope. Cp. *v.* 14. **shall build.** Compare *vv.* 12, 13 ("T") with *v.* 15 ("*T*"), above. **shall bear, &c.**: i.e. the glory and majesty of royalty. Cp. Matt. 16. 27; 24. 30; 25. 31. **be** = become. **both**: i.e. two offices, priest and king, will be combined in one person, Messiah. **14 be to** = belong to. **Helem.** Syr. reads "Heldai". Cp. *v.* 10. **Hen.** This is either a proper name, or else an abbreviation. It may be also a common noun = "and for the favour (or courtesy) of the son of Zephaniah", &c. **for a memorial.** Ref. to Pent. (Ex. 12. 14, the same word). Ap. 92. **15 they . . . shall come**: i.e. those future builders, of whom these were the type. Cp. Isa. 60. 10. **And this, &c.** = And it shall come to pass: i.e. the promise and prophecy in the former part of the verse.

410-407 °if ye will diligently obey the voice of [9]the
LORD your °God."

B[2] U W[1] (p. 1287) 407 **7** And it came to pass in °the fourth year of
°king Darius, *that* the word of °the LORD
came unto Zechariah in the fourth *day* of the
ninth month, *even* in °Chisleu;
2 When °they had sent unto the house of
°GOD °Sherezer and Regem-melech, and their
°men, to °pray before [1]the LORD,
3 *And* to °speak unto the priests which *were*
in the house of °the LORD of hosts, and to the
prophets, saying, "Should I weep °in the fifth
month, separating myself, °as I have done
°these so many years?"

W[2] X 4 Then came the word of [3]the LORD of hosts
unto me, saying,
5 "Speak unto all the People of the land, and
to the priests, saying, 'When ye fasted and
mourned °in the fifth and °seventh *month*,
°even those seventy years, did ye at all fast
unto Me, *even* to Me?
6 And °when ye did eat, and when ye did
drink, did not ye eat *for yourselves*, and drink
for yourselves?

Y 7 °*Should ye* not *hear* the words which [1]the
LORD hath cried °by °the former prophets,

Z when Jerusalem was inhabited and in prosperity, and the cities thereof round about her,
when *men* inhabited °the south and °the
plain?'"

X 8 And the word of [1]the LORD came unto
Zechariah, saying,
9 "Thus speaketh [3]the LORD of hosts, saying,
°Execute true °judgment, and shew °mercy and
compassions °every man to his brother:
10 And °oppress not the widow, °nor the
fatherless, °the stranger, °nor the poor; and
let none of you imagine °evil against his brother
in your heart."

Y 11 °But they °refused to hearken, °and °pulled
away the shoulder, °and stopped their ears,
that they should not hear.
12 Yea, they made their hearts *as* an adamant
stone, lest they should hear °the law, and the
words which [3]the LORD of hosts hath sent
°in His °spirit [7]by [7]the former prophets:

Z therefore came a great wrath from [3]the LORD
of hosts.
13 "Therefore it is come to pass, *that* [3]as He
cried, and they would not hear; so they cried,
and I would not hear," saith [3]the LORD of
hosts:
14 "But °I scattered them with a whirlwind

if ye will, &c. This condition was not fulfilled; for the command to "repent" (the one condition of national restoration), given by John the Baptist (Matt. 3. 1, 2); Messiah (Matt. 4. 17); and Peter (Acts 2. 38; 3. 19), was not obeyed: and this promise therefore remains for an obedience that is yet future. The verse therefore is not "left unfinished" as alleged.

God. Heb. Elohim. Ap. 4. I.

7. 1—8. 23 (**B[2]**, p. 1280). LITERAL PROPHECIES. DATED. (*Alternation.*)

B[2] | U | 7. 1-14. Fasts.
  V | 8. 1-17. Restoration of Jerusalem.
  U | 8. 18, 19. Feasts.
  V | 8. 20-23. Accession of Nations.

7. 1-14 (U, above). FASTS. (*Division.*)

U | W[1] | 1-3. Question.
  W[2] | 4-14. Answer.

1 the fourth year. Two years later than the first literal prophecy in 1. 1.

king Darius. Darius (Hystaspis). See Ap. 57.

the LORD. Heb. Jehovah. Ap. 4. II.

Chisleu. Corresponding with our December. See Ap. 51. V.

2 they had sent unto the house of GOD, &c.: or, "when Sherezer had sent (and Regem-melech and his men) to Bethel", &c. Beth-el had already been occupied by exiles returned from Babylon. See Ezra 2. 28. Neh. 7. 32; 11. 31. **GOD.** Heb. El. Ap. 4. IV.

Sherezer. Probably born in exile, as he bears an Assyrian name.

men. Heb. pl. of *'enōsh.* Ap. 14. III.

pray before the LORD = entreat Jehovah's favour by prayer (Ex. 32. 11. 1 Kings 13. 6; Jer. 26. 19); or by sacrifice (1 Sam. 13. 12).

3 speak unto the priests, &c. Ref. to Pent. (Deut. 17. 9; 33. 10). Ap. 92.

the LORD of hosts. See note on 1. 3.

in the fifth month. See note on *v.* 5.

as = according as.

these so many years = now so many years. Some codices read "seventy years", as in *v.* 5.

7. 4-14 (W[2], above). ANSWER. (*Extended Alternation.*)

W[2] | X | 4-6. Fasting and Mourning. Formal.
  Y | 7-. The former prophets.
  Z | -7. Disobedience. Prosperity.
  X | 8-10. Fasting and Mourning. True.
  Y | 11, 12-. The former prophets.
  Z | -12-14. Disobedience. Adversity.

5 in the fifth . . . month. The month Ab (our August, Ap. 51. V). The fast had already then been instituted to commemorate the destruction of Jerusalem on the tenth of Ab (Jer. 52 12, 13).

seventh month. The month Tisri (our October). The fast had already then been instituted, on the third of Tisri, to commemorate the murder of Gedaliah by Ishmael, the son of Nethaniah. See Jer. 40. 8; 41. 1-3, 15-18. See further notes on 8. 19.

even. Some codices omit this word.

---

6 when ye did eat, &c. Or, was it not ye that were the eaters, and ye the drinkers? **for yourselves.** Not "before the Lord" or for His glory. See Deut. 12. 7; 14. 26. 1 Chron. 29. 22; and cp. 1 Cor. 10. 31. Col. 3. 17. **7 Should ye not hear . . . ?** Supply the Ellipsis (Ap. 6) better by "[Should ye not have obeyed ?]" or, ["Are not these] the very words?" **by** = by the hand of: "hand" being put by Fig. *Metonymy* (of Cause), Ap. 6, for the agency. **the former prophets.** See note on 1. 4. **the south** = the Negeb. Cp. Gen. 13. 1. Deut. 1. 7: and see note on Ps. 126. 4. **the plain** = the lowland. Heb. *shephēlah.* Cp. Deut. 1. 7. Judg. 1. 9, &c. **9 Execute . . . judgment.** Note the Fig. *Polyptōton* (Ap. 6). Heb. *mishpaṭ . . . shephotū* = true judgment judge ye. Cp. Isa. 58. 6, 7. **mercy** = lovingkindness. **every man.** Heb. *'īsh.* Ap. 14. II. **10 oppress not the widow . . . stranger.** Ref. to Pent. (Ex. 22. 21, 22. Deut. 24. 17). Ap. 92. **nor** = and. **evil.** *rā'a'.* Ap. 44. viii. **11 But they.** Some codices, with four early printed editions, read "and ye", showing the Fig. *Polysyndeton* (Ap. 6). **refused, &c.** Cp. 1. 4. Jer. 6. 10, 17, 19, &c. **and.** Note the Fig. *Polysyndeton* (Ap. 6), for emphasis. **pulled away, &c.** Turning aside from the one who speaks. **12 the law.** Ref. to Pent. (Ex. 20, &c.), Ap. 92. **in** = by. **spirit.** Heb. *rūach.* Ap. 9. **14 I scattered them with a whirlwind.** Not the usual verb, to scatter; but *ṣā'ar* = to drive with a tempest. Occurs only seven times (2 Kings 6. 11 ("sore troubled"). Isa. 54. 11. Hos. 13. 3. Jonah 1. 11, 13. Hab. 3. 14).

407 among all the nations whom they knew not.
Thus °the land was desolate °after them, that
no man passed through nor returned: for they
laid the °pleasant land desolate."

V A (p. 1288) **8** Again the word of °the LORD of hosts
came °*to me*, saying,
2 °"Thus °saith [1]the LORD of hosts; °'I was
jealous for Zion with great jealousy, and °I was
jealous for her with great fury.'
3 [2]Thus °saith °the LORD; 'I am returned unto
Zion, and °will dwell in the midst of Jerusalem: and Jerusalem shall be called °a city
of °truth; and the mountain of [1]the LORD of
hosts °the °holy mountain.'

B C 4 [2]Thus [2]saith [1]the LORD of hosts; 'There
shall °yet old men and old women °dwell in
the °streets of Jerusalem, and °every man
with his staff in his hand °for very age.
5 And the [4]streets of the city shall be full of
boys and girls playing in the [4]streets thereof.'

D 6 [2]Thus [2]saith [1]the LORD of hosts; 'If it be
marvellous in the eyes of °the remnant of this
People in these days, °should it also be marvellous in °Mine eyes?' °saith [1]the LORD of hosts.

C 7 [2]Thus saith [1]the LORD of hosts; '°Behold,
I will save My People °from the east country,
and from the west country;
8 And I will bring them, and they shall dwell
in the midst of Jerusalem: and °they shall be
My people, and I will be their °God, in truth
and in righteousness.'

D q 9 [2]Thus [2]saith [1]the LORD of hosts; 'Let your
hands be strong, ye that hear in these days
these words by the mouth of °the prophets,
which *were* °in the day *that* the foundation of
the house of [1]the LORD of hosts was laid, °that
the temple might be built.

r 10 For before °these days there was no °hire
for °man, nor any hire for beast; neither *was*
there any peace to him that went out or came
in because of the affliction: for I °set all °men
°every one against his neighbour.

q 11 But °now I *will* not *be* unto the residue of
this People as in the former days,' [6]saith [1]the
LORD of hosts.

r 12 'For °the seed *shall be* prosperous; the vine
shall give her fruit, °and the °ground °shall
give her increase, and the heavens shall give
their dew; and I will cause [6]the remnant of
this People to possess all these *things*.

A 13 And it shall come to pass, *that* °as ye were
a curse among the °heathen, O house of Judah,
and °house of Israel; so will I save you, and
°ye shall be a blessing: fear not, *but* let your
hands be strong.'
14 For [2]thus [2]saith [1]the LORD of hosts; [13]'As
I thought to °punish you, when your fathers
provoked Me to wrath, saith [1]the LORD of
hosts, and I repented not:
15 So again have I thought in these days to
do well unto Jerusalem and to the house of
Judah: fear ye not.

the land was desolate. Ref. to Pent. (Lev. 26. 22).
after them: i.e. when they had left it.
pleasant = desirable. Dan. 8. 9.

8. 1-17 (V, p. 1287). RESTORATION OF JERUSALEM. (*Alternation.*)

V | A | 1-3. Displeasure and Reconciliation.
  B | 4-12. Inhabitants. Privileges.
 A | 13-15. Displeasure and Reconciliation.
  B | 16, 17. Inhabitants. Duties.

1 the LORD of hosts. See note on 1. 3.
to me. Some codices, with three early printed editions, Aram., and Syr., read these words in the text.
2 Thus saith, &c. There is a decalogue of prophecies concerning Jerusalem and its inhabitants in this member ("V", see p. 1287). See *vv.* 2, 3, 4, 6, 7, 9, 14, 19, 20, 23. All refer to the future, and await their fulfilment in millennial days. **saith** = hath said.
I was = I was and still am.
3 the LORD. Heb. Jehovah. Ap. 4. II.
will dwell in the midst, &c. Ref. to Pent. (Ex. 29. 45). Ap. 92.
a city of truth = a city of fidelity.
truth = the truth. Cp. Isa. 1. 21, 26.
the holy mountain. Cp. Isa. 2. 2. Jer. 31. 23. Ezek. 40. 2. Mic. 4. 1. **holy.** See note on Ex. 3. 5.

8. 4-12 (B, above). INHABITANTS. PRIVILEGES. (*Alternation.*)

B | C | 4, 5. Inhabitants. Ages.
  D | 6. Address to the Remnant.
 C | 7, 8. Inhabitants. Condition.
  D | 9-12. Address to the Remnant.

4 yet. In the days of the future fulfilment.
dwell = sit. **streets** = broad or open places.
every man. Heb. *'ish.* Ap. 14. II.
for very age = for multitude of days.
6 the remnant. The exiles who had then returned. Cp. Hag. 1. 12, 14.
should it also be marvellous, &c. Ref. to Pent. (Gen. 18. 14, where the verb is the same). Ap. 92.
Mine eyes. Add by Fig. *Ellipsis* (Ap. 6), from preceding clause: "[in those future days]" of which He was speaking.
saith the LORD of hosts = [is] the oracle of Jehovah of hosts.
7 Behold, I will, &c. = Behold Me saving, &c.
from the east country, &c. Cp. Isa. 43. 5. Note the Fig. *Synecdoche* (of the Part), Ap. 6, for the whole earth. See Pss. 50. 1; 113. 3. Isa. 59. 19. Mal. 1. 11, &c.
8 they shall be, &c. Ref. to Pent. (Ex. 6. 7). Ap. 92.
God. Heb. Elohim. Ap. 4. I.

8. 9-12 (*D*, above). ADDRESS TO THE REMNANT. (*Alternation.*)

D | q | 9. Encouragement.
  r | 10. Past Adversity.
 q | 11. Promise.
  | *r* | 12. Future Prosperity.

9 the prophets. See Hag. 1. 6-11; 2. 15-19.
in the day that: i.e. two years before (Hag. 1. 14, 15; 2. 18. Cp. Ezra 5. 1). Ap. 18.
that the temple = even the temple, that it.
10 these = those. **hire** = wages.
man. Heb. *'ādām.* Ap. 14. I.
men. Heb. *'ādām.* Ap. 14. I.
every one. Heb. *'ish.* Ap. 14. II.
set = sent.
11 now. In contrast with the former days.
12 the seed shall be, &c. Ref. to Pent. (Deut. 28. 3-12). Ap. 92.
and. Note the Fig. *Polysyndeton* (Ap. 6), combined with Fig. *Anabasis* (Ap. 6). **ground** = earth.
shall give, &c. Ref. to Pent. (Lev. 26. 4, 20. Deut. 11. 17). Ap. 92. Cp. Pss. 67. 6; 78. 46; 85. 12. Ezek. 34. 27. **13 as** = according as. **heathen** = nations. **house of Israel.** Looking on to the future fulfilment, which rests on the condition of *v.* 8. **ye shall be a blessing.** Ref. to Pent. (Gen. 12. 2). Ap. 92. **14 punish** = bring calamity upon. Heb. *rā'a'.* Ap. 44. viii.

B 16 These *are* the things that ye shall do;
p. 1288) °Speak ye °every man the truth to his neigh-
407 bour; °execute the judgment of truth and peace
in your gates:
17 And let none of you imagine °evil in your
hearts against his neighbour; and °love no
false oath: for °all these *are things* that I
hate, [6]saith [3]the LORD.'"
U 18 And the word of [1]the LORD of hosts came
(p. 1287) unto me, saying,
19 [2]"Thus °saith [1]the LORD of hosts; 'The fast
of °the fourth *month*, and the fast of °the fifth,
and the fast of °the seventh, and the fast of
°the tenth, shall be to the house of Judah joy
and gladness, and cheerful °feasts; therefore
love the truth and peace.'
V E[1] 20 [2]Thus [19]saith [1]the LORD of hosts; '*It shall*
(p. 1289) yet *come to pass*, that there shall come
°people, and the inhabitants of many cities:
21 And the inhabitants of one *city* shall go to
another, saying, °'Let us go speedily °to pray
before [3]the LORD, and to seek °the LORD of
hosts: I will go also.'
22 Yea, many people and strong nations shall
come to seek [21]the LORD of hosts in Jerusalem,
and [21]to pray before the LORD.
E[2] 23 [2]Thus [19]saith [1]the LORD of hosts; 'In
°those days °*it shall come to pass*, that ten
°men shall take hold out of all languages of the
nations, even shall take hold of the skirt of him
that is a Jew, saying, 'We will go with °you:
for we have heard °*that* [8]God *is* with you.'"'

B[3] F 9 The °burden °of the word of °the LORD
407-403 °in the land of °Hadrach, and Damascus
shall be °the rest thereof: °when the eyes of
°man, as of all the tribes of Israel, *shall be*
toward °the LORD.
2 And °Hamath also °shall border thereby;
Tyrus, and Zidon, °though it be very wise.
3 And °Tyrus did build herself a °strong
hold, and heaped up silver °as the dust, and
fine gold °as the mire of the streets.
4 °Behold, °the LORD* will °cast her out, and
He will smite her power in the sea; and she
shall be devoured with fire.
5 °Ashkelon shall °see *it*, and °fear; °Gaza
also *shall see it*, and be very sorrowful, and
°Ekron; for her expectation shall be ashamed;
and the king shall perish from °Gaza, and
°Ashkelon shall °not be inhabited.
6 And a °bastard shall °dwell in °Ashdod, and
I will cut off the pride of the Philistines.
7 And I will take away his °blood out of his

16 Speak, &c. Cp. *v.* 19; 7. 9.
every man. Heb. *'îsh*. Ap. 14. II.
execute, &c. See note on 7. 9.
17 evil. Heb. *rā'a'*. Ap. 44. viii.
love no false oath. Ref. to Pent. (Lev. 6. 3; 19. 12).
all these are things that I hate. Some codices, with Sept. and Syr., read "all these things do I hate".
19 saith = hath said.
the fourth month. The ninth of Tammuz (Jer. 52. 6, 7), when the city was broken up; hence called "the fourth fast".
the fifth. On the tenth of Ab, when the Temple and the houses were burnt (Jer. 52. 12, 13).
the seventh. The third of Tisri, when Gedaliah was slain by Ishmael, the son of Nethaniah (Jer. 40. 8; 41. 1-3, 15-18).
the tenth. On the tenth of Tebeth, when the king of Babylon set his face against Jerusalem (Ezek. 24. 1, 2). So *The Talmud, Rosh Hashanah*, fol. 18 B.
feasts = appointed seasons. These fasts were appointed by man. The feasts were "feasts of Jehovah" because appointed by Him. Ref. to Pent. (Lev. 23. 2-44). Ap. 92. Cp. Zeph. 3. 17.

8. 20-23 (*V*, p. 1287). **ACCESSION OF NATIONS.** (*Division.*)

V	E[1]	20-22. To Jehovah's House.
	E[2]	23. To Jehovah's People.

20 people = peoples. Some codices, with Sept., read "many peoples".
21 Let us go speedily. Fig. *Polyptōton*. Ap. 6. Heb. a going, let us go = Let us by all means go: or, speedily, as in A.V. See note on Gen. 26. 28. Cp. Isa. 2. 3. Mic. 4. 2. **to pray, &c.** See note on 7. 2.
the LORD, &c. Heb. (with *'eth*) = Jehovah of hosts Himself.
23 those days. The fulfilment of this is still future.
men. Heb. pl. of *'ĕnōsh*. Ap. 14. III.
you: i.e. with God's People Israel.
that. Some codices, with Aram., Sept., Syr., and Vulg., read "that" in the text. Supply the Ellipsis :— "[will be the time] that."

9. 1—10. 12 (**B[3]**, p. 1280). **LITERAL PROPHECY. THE FIRST BURDEN.** (*Introversion.*)

B[3]	F	9. 1-7. Deliverance from Enemies. Promised.		
		G	9. 8. Jehovah. Israel's Defence.	
			H	9. 9. Zion's King. First Coming. Salvation.
			H	9. 10, 11. Zion's King. Second Coming. Dominion.
		G	9. 12-17. Jehovah. Israel's Defence.	
	F	10. 1-12. Deliverance from Enemies. Accomplished.		

The use of a varied vocabulary is no proof of a different authorship. It is necessitated by the changes of subject.
1 burden = Divine declaration. Heb. *massa'*. Cp. Isa. 13. 1. Nah. 1. 1.
of = that is to say. Gen. of Apposition. See Ap. 17. 4.
the LORD. Heb. Jehovah. Ap. 4. II.
in: or, on: i.e. resting on.
Hadrach. A country in the neighbourhood of Damascus and Hamath (*v.* 2), &c., mentioned in the Assyrian Inscriptions, with the *'arka* of Gen. 10. 17. **the rest thereof** = its resting-place: i.e. the burden will rest upon it. **when the eyes, &c.** Render: "for Jehovah [will look] in mankind's eye, as well as to all the tribes of Israel's". Cp. Jer. 32. 19, 20: i.e. to render to all according to their doings. **man.** Heb. *'ādām*. Ap. 14. I. **the LORD.** Heb. Jehovah. Ap. 4. II. **2 Hamath.** Now *Hamā*. **shall border thereby** = [which] bordereth thereon: i.e. on the land of Hadrach. **though** = because. **3 Tyrus . . . strong hold.** Note the Fig. *Paronomasia* (Ap. 6). Heb. *ẓōr māẓōr*, which cannot be reproduced in English. **as** = like. **4 Behold.** Fig. *Asterismos*. Ap. 6. **the LORD*.** One of the 134 places where the *Sōpherim* say they altered "Jehovah" to "Adonai". See Ap. 32; and cp. Ap. 4. II and VIII (2). **cast her out** = dispossess her. **5 Ashkelon . . . Gaza . . . Gaza . . . Ashkelon.** Note the Fig. *Antimetabolē* (Ap. 6), for emphasis. **Ashkelon.** Now *'Askalān*. **see . . . fear.** Note the Fig. *Paronomasia* (Ap. 6). Heb. *terā' . . . v[e]tîrā'*. May be Englished by "shall *gaze* . . . and be *amazed* (or be *dazed*)": or "shall peer and fear". **Gaza.** Now *Ghuzzeh*. **Ekron.** Now *'Akir*. **not be inhabited** = have none to sit [on the throne]. **6 bastard** = half-breed, or mongrel. **dwell** = sit [as king]. **Ashdod.** Now *Esdūd*. **7 blood.** Heb. bloods. Put by Fig. *Metonymy* (of Adjunct), Ap. 6, for the sacrifices (which were, of course, eaten).

407-403 mouth, and his °abominations from between
his teeth: but °he that remaineth, °even He,
°*shall be* for our °God, and he shall be as
a °governor in Judah, and °Ekron as a °Jebusite.
G (p. 1289) 8 And I will encamp about Mine house °because
of the army, °because of him that °passeth
by, and °because of him that returneth: °and
no °oppressor shall pass through them any
more: for now have I °seen with Mine eyes.
H 9 °**Rejoice greatly, O daughter of Zion;**
shout, O daughter of Jerusalem: [4]**behold, thy
King °cometh unto thee:** °He *is* °just, and
°having salvation; **lowly, and °riding upon
an ass, and upon a colt the foal of an ass.**
H 10 And °I will cut off the chariot from
Ephraim, and the horse from Jerusalem, and
the battle bow shall be cut off: and °He shall
speak peace unto the °heathen: and His
dominion *shall be* °from sea *even* to sea, and
from °the river *even* to the ends of the earth.
11 As for °thee also, by °the blood of thy
covenant I °have sent forth thy prisoners °out
of the pit wherein *is* no water.
G 12 °Turn you to the °strong hold, ye prisoners
of °hope: even to day do I declare *that* I will
render °double unto thee;
13 When I have bent Judah for Me, °filled
the bow with Ephraim, and raised up thy
sons, O Zion, against °thy sons, O °Greece,
and made thee as the sword of a mighty man.
14 And [1]the LORD shall be seen over them,
and °His arrow shall go forth as the lightning:
and °the Lord °GOD shall blow the trumpet,
and shall go with whirlwinds of the south.
15 °The LORD of hosts shall °defend them;
and they shall °devour, and °subdue with
sling stones; and they shall drink, °*and* °make
a noise as through °wine; and they shall be
°filled like bowls, *and* °as the corners of the altar.
16 And [1]the LORD their [7]God shall save them
in that day as the flock of His People: for *they
shall be as* the °stones of a °crown, °lifted up
as an ensign upon His °land.
17 For how great *is* His goodness, and how
great *is* His beauty! corn shall make the young
men °cheerful, and °new wine the maids.

F J (p. 1291) **10** Ask ye of °the LORD °rain in the time
of the latter rain; °*so* °the LORD °shall
°make bright clouds, °and give °them showers
of rain, to every one grass in the field.

abominations: i.e. the idolatrous sacrifices.
he that remaineth: i.e. the remnant of them.
even He = he also.
shall be for. Supply the *Ellipsis* thus: "[shall be subject unto]". **God.** Heb. Elohim. Ap. 4. I.
governor = chieftain, or duke.
Ekron. Put by Fig. *Synecdochē* (of the Part), Ap. 6, for Philistines.
Jebusite. Put by Fig. *Metonymy* (of the Adjunct), Ap. 6, for bondservant. (1 Kings 9. 20, 21. Isa. 11. 14.)
8 because of = against.
passeth by . . . returneth: i.e. marcheth to and fro.
and: or, so that.
oppressor. Heb. *nāgas* = to press hard, as a task-master (Ex. 5. 6), or as a foreign oppressor (Isa. 9. 4; 14. 2, 4), or as an exactor (2 Kings 23. 35).
seen. Supply the *Ellipsis*: "seen [the affliction of My People] with Mine eyes".
9 Rejoice, &c. Fig. *Paeanismos.* Ap. 6. This verse foretells the first coming of Messiah, recorded in the Gospels.
cometh unto = will come unto. See note on Mic. 5. 2, where we have the *going forth* from Bethlehem (Matt. 2. 1). Here we have the coming unto Jerusalem (Matt. 21. 5). Between these lay all the events which we call "the first advent". So will it be at "the second advent" with its many events, before *v.* 10 is fulfilled. See notes on Matt. 21. 1-10, and Luke 19. 29-44; Ap. 107 and 156.
He is, &c. Note the four features of Messiah's character and condition at His first advent.
(1) **just** = righteous, as being justified or vindicated. Cp. Isa. 45. 21; 53. 11. Jer. 23. 5, 6.
(2) **having salvation.** Heb. *nōshāʻ* is the Niphal participle, which, though it may be *reflexive*, is never active. He was heard and delivered (Ps. 22. 20, 21. Heb. 5. 7), referring to His own sufferings and death out of (Gr. *ek*, Ap. 104. VII), which He was delivered (Ps. 16. 10. Acts 2. 24), and by which He becomes the Saviour of others (Isa. 53. 8, 10, 11).
(3) **lowly** = afflicted, or oppressed. Same word (*ʻānī*; see note on "poverty", Prov. 6. 11) as in Ps. 22. 24. Isa. 53. 4, 7.
(4) **riding upon an ass, &c.** Fulfilled (1) in Matt. 21. 1-11, and from two days afterward (2) in Mark 11. 8-10. Luke 19. 36-40. John 12. 12-19. See Ap 156. A mark of His lowliness.
Note the above four characteristics.
10 I will cut off. Sept. reads "and He will cut off". This refers to the yet future second coming; the present dispensation (Ap. 71 and 72) lying between *vv.* 9 and 10.
He shall speak peace, &c. Cp. Pss. 46. 9; 47. 3. Isa. 2. 4; 9. 6, 7. Mic. 5. 5.
heathen = nations.
from sea . . . to sea. Cp. Ps. 72. 8.
the river: i.e. the Euphrates.
11 thee = thee [O Zion] (fem.; agreeing with Zion), which is also fem. in *vv.* 9, 13.
the blood of thy covenant: or, thy covenant of blood. Ref. to Pent. (Ex. 24. 5-8). Ap. 92. Cp. Heb. 13. 20.
have sent forth = i.e. sent forth [from their captivity].
out of the pit, &c. Ref. to Pent. (Gen. 37. 24). Ap. 92. **12 Turn** = Return. **strong hold.** Heb. *bizzārōn* (from *bāzar*, to cut off) = a safe because inaccessible place. Occurs only here. **hope** = the hope: i.e. which God had given, and on which He had caused them to hope (Ps. 119. 49). **double**: i.e. a prosperity and blessing double what was possessed before. The firstborn's share. Cp. Isa. 61. 7. **13 filled** = grasped. **thy sons, O Greece.** Sept. reads "the sons of Greece". **Greece.** Heb. *Yavan.* Cp. Gen. 10. 2, 4. Isa. 66. 19. Ezek. 27. 13. Dan. 8. 21; 11. 2. Joel 3. 6. **14 His arrow.** Fig. *Anthropopatheia.* Ap. 6. **the Lord.** Heb. *Adonai.* Ap. 4. VIII (2). **GOD.** Heb. Jehovah. Ap. 4. II. **15 The LORD of hosts.** See note on 1. 3. **defend.** See note on Isa. 31. 5. **devour** = devour [their enemies]. **subdue with sling stones**: or, trample on their weapons. **and.** Some codices, with three early printed editions, read this "and" in the text. **make a noise** = shout. **wine.** Heb. *yayin.* Ap. 27. I. **filled**: i.e. filled [with wine] like. **as, &c.** = as the sacrificial bowls [are filled with blood, which are tossed against] the corners (or horns) of the altar. **16 stones** = gems. **crown** = diadem. **lifted up** = conspicuous, or sparkling. **land** = soil. **17 cheerful** = flourish. **new wine.** Heb. *tīrōsh.* Ap. 27. II.

10. 1-12 [For Structure see next page].

1 the LORD. Heb. Jehovah. Ap. 4. II. **rain, &c.** Ref. to Pent. (Deut. 11. 14) = rain of rain = copious rains. Ap. 92. **so, &c.** Render: "[of] Jehovah Who maketh . . . and giveth". **shall make** = Who maketh. **and give** = and giveth. **them.** Some codices, with Syr., read "you".

K 2 For the °idols have spoken °vanity, and the
(p. 1291) diviners have seen a lie, and have told false
407-403 dreams; they comfort in vain: therefore they
went their way as °a flock, they were troubled,
because *there was* no shepherd.
K 3 Mine anger was kindled against the shepherds, and I °punished the goats:
J L for °the LORD of hosts hath visited His flock
the house of Judah, and hath made *them* as His
°goodly horse in the battle.
4 Out of °him °came forth °the corner, out of
him the °nail, out of him °the battle bow, out
of him every °oppressor together.
M 5 And they shall be as mighty *men*, which
tread down *their enemies* in the mire of the
°streets in the battle: and they shall fight,
because [1]the LORD *is* with them, and the
riders on horses shall be confounded.
N 6 And I will strengthen the house of Judah,
and I will save the house of Joseph, and I will
bring them again to place them;
L for I have mercy upon them: and they shall
be as though I had not cast them off: for *I am*
[1]the LORD their °God, and will °hear them.
7 And °*they of* Ephraim shall be like a mighty
man, and their heart shall rejoice °as through
°wine: yea, their °children shall see *it*, and be
glad; their heart shall rejoice in [1]the LORD.
8 I will °hiss for them, and gather them; for
I have redeemed them: and they shall increase
as they °have increased.
9 And I will °sow them among the °people:
and °they shall remember Me in far countries;
and they shall °live with their [7]children, and
°turn again.
10 °I will bring them again also out of the
land of Egypt, and gather them out of Assyria; and I will bring them into the land of
Gilead and Lebanon; and °*place* shall not be
found for them.
M 11 °And °he shall pass through the sea °with
affliction, and shall smite the waves in the
sea, and all the deeps of °the river shall dry
up: and the pride of Assyria shall be brought
down, and the sceptre of Egypt shall depart
away.
N 12 And I will strengthen them in [1]the LORD;
and they shall °walk up and down in His name,
°saith [1]the LORD.

C[2] O **11** °Open thy doors, O Lebanon, that the
fire may devour thy cedars.
2 Howl, °fir tree; °for the cedar is fallen;
because °the °mighty are spoiled: howl, O ye
oaks of Bashan; for the °forest of the vintage
is come down.
3 *There is* a voice of the howling of the
°shepherds; for their glory is spoiled: a voice
of the roaring of °young lions; for the pride of
Jordan is spoiled.
P s 4 °Thus saith °the LORD my °God; °"Feed the
flock °of the slaughter;

10. 1-12 (*F*, p. 1289). DELIVERANCE FROM ENEMIES. ACCOMPLISHED. (*Introversion.*)

F | J | 1. The Flock. The Promise made.
  K | 2. False Shepherds. Incrimination.
  K | 3-. False Shepherds. Punishment.
| *J* | -3-12. The Flock. The Promise fulfilled.

2 idols. Heb. *teraphim*, or household gods. These cannot give rain (Jer. 14. 22). **vanity** = trash.
a flock = he-goats: i.e. bell-wethers. Cp. Isa. 14. 9. Jer. 51. 40.
3- punished = shall visit upon.

10. -3-12 (*J*, above). THE PROMISE FULFILLED. (*Repeated Alternation.*)

J | L | -3, 4. Visitation. } House of Judah.
  M | 5. Victory.
  N | 6-. Jehovah's Strengthening.
| *L* | -6-10. Restoration. } House of Joseph.
  M | 11. Victory.
  N | 12. Jehovah's Strengthening.

-3 the LORD of hosts. See note on 1. 3.
goodly horse = majestic war-horse.
4 him: i.e. Judah (*v.* 3). Cp. Jer. 30. 21.
came forth = went forth.
the corner = the corner-stone (Matt. 21. 42) = Messiah.
nail = tent-pin, or peg. Cp. Isa. 22. 23.
the battle bow. Put by Fig. *Synecdoche* (of the Part), Ap. 6, for all kinds of weapons.
oppressor = governor, or ruler.
5 streets = lanes, or out-places.
6 God. Heb. Elohim. Ap. 4. I. **hear** = answer.
7 they. A special various reading called *Sevîr* (Ap. 34), reads "he".
they of Ephraim, &c. = they (or he) shall be as a mighty one (or warrior) of Ephraim.
as through wine = as wine [maketh the heart to rejoice]. Ps. 104. 15.
wine. Heb. *yayin.* Ap. 27. I. **children** = sons.
8 hiss: or, signal. The figure is borrowed from bee-keepers (Isa. 5. 26; 7. 18).
have increased = did increase [before]. Cp. Ex. 1. 7.
9 sow. Cp. Hos. 2. 23. **people** = peoples.
they shall remember Me. Ref. to Pent. (Deut. 30. 1).
live with, &c. = live, and return with.
turn = return.
10 I will bring them again, &c. Ref. to Pent. (Deut. 30. 3, 5). Ap. 92.
place. Supply: "[the necessary room]".
11 And = Though. **he.** Sept. reads "they".
with = of. Gen. of Apposition. Ap. 17. 4.
the river: i.e. the Nile.
12 walk up and down, &c. = walk (habitually). Ref. to Pent. (Gen. 5. 24; 6. 9; 17. 1). Ap. 92. Cp. Mic. 4. 5; 6. 8.
saith the LORD = [is] Jehovah's oracle.

11. 1-17 (C[2], p. 1280). PROPHECY. WITH SYMBOLS. (*Introversion with Alternations.*)

C[2] | O | 1-3. Threatening.
  P | s | 4, 5. Command.
    t | 6. Reason.
    Q | u | 7-9. Flock. Symbol. "Staves" and "Bands".
      v | 10, 11. "Beauty". "Cut asunder."
    Q | *u* | 12, 13. Flock. Symbol. "Price".
      v | 14. "Bands". "Cut asunder".
  P | *s* | 15. Command.
    t | 16. Reason.
| *O* | 17. Threatening.

1 Open, &c. Fig. *Apostrophe.* Ap. 6.
2 fir = cypress.
for. If the cedar is fallen, how much more the cypress.
the. The 1611 edition of the A.V. reads "all the".
mighty = honourable, or majestic ones. **forest of the vintage** = the inaccessible forest. **3 shepherds** = the rulers of the State. **young lions.** The rapacious nobles. **4 Thus saith** = Thus hath said **the LORD.** Heb. Jehovah. Ap. 4. II. **God.** Heb. Elohim. Ap. 4. I. **Feed** = Tend. Zechariah is to represent a good shepherd, and is sent to shepherd the People whose rulers destroyed them (*vv.* 5, 16). **of** = exposed to, or destined for slaughter. Genitive of Relation. Ap. 17. 5. Cp. Rom. 8. 36.

407-403 5 Whose possessors slay them, and hold themselves not guilty: and they that sell them say, 'Blessed *be* [4]the LORD; for I °am rich:' and their own [3]shepherds pity them not.

t (p. 1291) 6 For I will no more pity the inhabitants of the land, °saith [4]the LORD: but, lo, I will deliver the °men °every one into his neighbour's hand, and into the hand of his king: and they shall smite the land, and out of their hand I will not deliver *them*.

Q u 7 °And I will [4]feed the flock [4]of slaughter, °*even* you, O poor of the flock." And °I took unto me two °staves; the one I called °Beauty, and the other I called °Bands; and I [4]fed the flock.

8 Three shepherds also I °cut off in one month; and my °soul lothed them, and their °soul also abhorred me.

9 Then said I, "I will not feed you: °that that dieth, let it die; and that that is to be cut off, let it be cut off; and let the rest °eat every one the flesh of another."

v 10 And [7]I took my staff, *even* [7]Beauty, and cut it asunder, that I might break my covenant which I had made with all the °people.

11 And it was broken in that day: and so °the poor of the flock that °waited upon me knew that it *was* the word of [4]the LORD.

Q u 12 And I said unto them, "If ye think good, give *me* my °price; and if not, forbear." So they weighed for my °price °thirty *pieces* of silver.

13 And [4]the LORD said unto me, °"Cast it °unto the °potter: a °goodly [12]price that I was °prised at °of them." And [7]I took the [12]thirty *pieces* of silver, and cast them to the °potter °in the house of [4]the LORD.

v 14 Then I cut asunder mine other staff, *even* [7]Bands, that I might break the brotherhood between Judah and Israel.

P s 15 And [4]the LORD said unto me, [7]"Take unto thee yet the °instruments of a °foolish shepherd.

t 16 For, °lo, I will raise up a shepherd in the land, *which* shall not visit °those that be cut off, neither shall seek °the young one, nor heal °that that is broken, nor °feed that °that standeth still: but he shall eat the flesh of the fat, and tear their claws in pieces.

o 17 Woe to the °idol shepherd that leaveth the flock! the sword *shall be* upon his arm, and upon his right eye: his arm shall be °clean dried up, and his right eye shall be utterly °darkened."

B[4] R U (p. 1293) **12** The °burden of the word of °the LORD °for Israel, °saith °the LORD, °Which stretcheth forth the heavens, °and layeth the foundation of the earth, and °formeth the °spirit of °man within him.

2 °"Behold, I will make Jerusalem a cup of trembling unto all the °people round about,

---

5 am rich = am become rich, [and therefore can sell them cheaply].

6 saith the LORD = [is] Jehovah's oracle.

men. Heb. *'ādām.* Ap. 14. I.

every one. Heb. *'ish.* Ap. 14. II.

7 And I will feed = So I [Zechariah] tended.

even you, O poor of the flock. Reading the two words (in Heb.) as one word (with the Sept.) it should be: "for the sheep-traffickers", as in 14. 21 ("Canaanite").

I took. Cp. *vv.* 7, 10, 13, 15 with 6. 10, 11.

staves. Which shepherds use; the crook or staff, and the club. See note on Ps. 23. 4.

Beauty = Graciousness. **Bands** = Union.

8 cut off = sent off. They are unnamed.

soul. Heb. *nephesh.* Ap. 13.

9 that, &c. = the dying will die.

eat every one, &c.: i.e. destroy one another.

10 people = peoples: i.e. here, tribes.

11 the poor of the flock = the sheep-traffickers; as in *v.* 7.

waited upon = were watching me (1 Sam. 1. 12; 19. 11. Ps. 59, title).

12 price = wage.

thirty pieces of silver. The damages for injury done to a servant. Ref. to Pent. (Ex. 21. 32). This is not the passage referred to in Matt. 27. 9. See Ap. 161. *That* was "spoken" by Jeremiah; *this* was *written* by Zechariah.

13 Cast it. As in Gen. 21. 15. 2 Chron. 24. 10.

unto the potter. The Syr. reads "into the treasury".

potter = fashioner. The material cast to, so as to be used by, the fashioner determines the meaning of the word (Heb. *yāzar*). If *clay*, then a potter (Jer. 18. 4; 19. 1). If *stone*, then a jeweller, or mason (Ex. 28. 11. 2 Sam. 5. 11. 1 Chron. 22. 15). If *wood*, then a carpenter (2 Sam. 5. 11. 2 Kings 12. 11. 1 Chron. 14. 1. Isa. 44. 13). If *iron*, then a smith (2 Chron. 24. 12. Isa. 44. 12). If *gold*, then a goldsmith (Hos. 8. 6). If *silver*, then a silversmith (Hos. 13. 2). The casting of silver to a potter was as incongruous as casting clay to a silversmith. See Ap. 161.

goodly = ample. Used of a wide garment. There is no evidence of irony here or elsewhere in Zechariah. The Heb. *'eder* denotes size and amplitude, as in Jonah 3. 6 and Mic. 2. 8. **prised** = priced.

of them: i.e. by them. But some codices read "by you".

15 instruments = implements.

foolish = worthless. Judah and Israel had rejected these, and later on they rejected Messiah the good Shepherd; hence the threatening in *vv.* 16, 17.

16 lo. Fig. *Asterismos.* Ap. 6. This looks forward to the Antichrist; for one of his titles is "the idol shepherd" of *v.* 17.

those that be cut off = the perishing.

the young one = the straying.

that that is broken = the wounded.

feed = nourish.

that standeth still = the weak.

17 idol = idol's. For the sequel to this prophecy see 13. 7-9.

clean dried up = withered.

darkened = blinded.

12. 1-14. 21 [For Structure see next page].

1 burden = oracle. Cp. 9. 1, and the Structure on p. 1280.

the LORD. Heb. Jehovah. Ap. 4. II.

for = upon: i.e. concerning Israel's affliction and final deliverance.

saith the LORD = [is] Jehovah's oracle.

Which stretcheth forth, &c. The omnipotence of Jehovah is the guarantee that His word will be carried out. Cp. Isa. 42. 5; 44. 24; 45. 12, 18; 48. 13.

and layeth, &c. Cp. Ps. 24. 2; 102. 25; 104. 2-5. Amos 4. 8, 13. Note the Fig. *Polysyndeton.* Ap. 6. **formeth, &c.** Ref. to Pent. (Gen. 2. 7. Num. 16. 22). Ap. 92. **spirit.** Heb. *rūach.* Ap. 9. **man.** Heb. *'ādām.* Ap. 14. I. **2 Behold.** Fig. *Asterismos.* Ap. 6. **people** = peoples.

407-403 when they shall be in the siege both against
Judah *and* against Jerusalem.
3 °And in that day will I make Jerusalem °a burdensome stone for all [2]people: all that °burden themselves with it shall be °cut in pieces, though all the [2]people of the earth be gathered together against it.
4 In that day, [1]saith the LORD, I will smite every horse with °astonishment, and his rider with madness: and I will °open Mine eyes upon the house of Judah, and will smite every horse of the [2]people with blindness.

V (p. 1293) 5 And the governors of Judah shall say in their heart, The inhabitants of Jerusalem *shall be* my °strength in °the LORD of hosts their °God.

W 6 In that day will I make the governors of Judah like an °hearth of fire among the wood, and like a torch of fire in a sheaf; and they shall devour all the [2]people round about, on the right hand and on the left:

X and Jerusalem shall be inhabited again in her own place, °*even* in Jerusalem.

W 7 [1]The LORD also shall save the tents of Judah °first, that the glory of the house of David and the glory of the inhabitants of Jerusalem do not magnify *themselves* against Judah.

V 8 In that day shall [1]the LORD defend the inhabitants of Jerusalem; and he that is °feeble among them at that day shall be as David; and the house of David *shall be* as [5]God, as the angel of [1]the LORD before them.

U 9 And it shall come to pass in that day, *that* I will seek to destroy all the nations that °come against Jerusalem.

S Y^1 Z^1 10 And I will pour upon the house of David, and upon the inhabitants of Jerusalem, the [1]spirit of grace and of supplications: and **they shall °look °upon °Me °Whom they have °pierced**, and they shall mourn for Him, as one mourneth for *his* only *son*, and shall be in bitterness for Him, as one that is in bitterness for *his* firstborn.
11 In that day °shall there be a great °mourning in Jerusalem, as the °mourning of °Hadadrimmon in the valley of Megiddon.
12 And the land shall [11]mourn, every family apart; the family of the house of David apart, and their °wives apart; the family of the house of °Nathan apart, and their °wives apart;
13 The family of the house of Levi apart, and their [12]wives apart; the family of °Shimei apart, and their [12]wives apart;
14 All the families that remain, every family apart, and their [12]wives apart.

Z^2 **13** °In that day there °shall be °a fountain °opened to the house of David and to the inhabitants of Jerusalem °for °sin and for uncleanness.

---

12. 1—14. 21 (B^4, p. 1280). LITERAL PROPHECY. (*Introversion.*)

B^4
- R | 12. 1-9. Threatening. Man's day.
  - S | 12. 10—13. 5. Israel. Conversion. (Future.)
    - T | 13. 6, 7-. My Shepherd. (Sword.)
    - *T* | 13. -7-. My Fellow. (Smitten.)
  - *S* | 13. -7-9. Israel. Purified. (Future.)
- *R* | 14. 1-21. Threatening. The Lord's day.

12. 1-9 (R, above). THREATENING AGAINST ENEMIES. (MAN'S DAY.) (*Introversion.*)

R
- U | 1-4. Nations to be cut off.
  - V | 5. Jehovah the Defence of Jerusalem's inhabitants.
    - W | 6-. Judah's leaders.
      - X | -6. Rehabitation of Jerusalem.
    - *W* | 7. Judah's tents.
  - *V* | 8. Jehovah the Defence of Jerusalem's inhabitants.
- *U* | 9. Nations to be cut off.

3 And = And it shall come to pass that in that day, &c.
a burdensome stone. A stone difficult to lift or to move; not a stone to throw. Occurs only here.
burden, &c.: i.e. seek to lift it.
cut in pieces = lacerated. Assyria, Persia, Rome, Greece, Egypt of old, and in later days Spain, Portugal, and Russia have been so lacerated on account of their treatment of the Jews.
4 astonishment = the panic. Cp. Deut. 28. 28.
open Mine eyes upon = regard with favour.
5 strength. See note on 6. 3.
the LORD of hosts. See note on 1. 3.
God. Heb. Elohim. Ap. 4. I.
6 hearth = chafing dish. Cp. 1 Sam. 2. 14.
even in = as.
7 first. Some codices, with Sept., Syr., and Vulg., read "as at the first".
8 feeble = tottering.
9 come. Some codices read "come to make war".

12. 10—13. 5 (S, above). ISRAEL. CONVERSION. FUTURE. (*Division.*)

S
- Y^1 | 12. 10—13. 1. Good bestowed.
- Y^2 | 13. 2-5. Evil removed.

12. 10—13. 1 (Y^1, above). GOOD BESTOWED. (*Division.*)

Y^1
- Z^1 | 12. 10-14. Spirit of grace poured out.
- Z^2 | 13. 1. Fountain opened.

10 look = look attentively with hope and concern; as in Gen. 19. 17, 26. Quoted in Matt. 24. 30. John 19. 37. Cp. the first occ. (Gen. 15. 5), and Ex. 33. 8. This is the effect of the gift of the Spirit. **upon** = unto.
Me. Western codices read "Me"; but the Eastern read "Him", with one early printed edition.
Whom they have pierced. See John 19. 34, 37. Rev. 1. 7.
pierced. Heb. *dākar.* Occurs eleven times, and always means thrust through. Cp. 13. 3.
11 shall there be a great mourning: or, the wailing shall be great.
Hadadrimmon. Now *Rummaneh*, west of Esdraelon, near Megiddo, where king Josiah was slain, and where the mourning was unprecedented (2 Chron. 35. 22-25).
12 wives = women.
Nathan. See 2 Sam. 5. 14. All these names are mentioned in the genealogy of Luke 3.
13 Shimei. See Num. 3. 18.

13. 1 In that day. The future day, when this prophecy shall come to pass.
shall be. This is not the simple future tense, but the verb *hāyah*, with the Participle, meaning that the fountain shall be permanently opened.
a fountain. This waits for a literal fulfilment, and is not an intangible one as in the present day.
opened: i.e., set open. The only occ. of this participle in the O.T.: and the last occ. of the verb itself. Cp. the first in Gen. 7. 11. **for** = for [the expiation of] sin, &c. **sin.** Heb. *chāṭā'.* Ap. 44. i.

Y² A¹ 407–403 2 And it shall come to pass in that day, °saith °the LORD of hosts, *that* I will °cut off the names of the idols out of the land, and they shall no more be remembered:
A² and also I will cause the prophets and the unclean °spirit to pass out of the land.
3 And °it shall come to pass, *that* when any shall yet prophesy, then his father and his mother that begat him shall say unto him, 'Thou shalt not live; for thou speakest lies in the name of °the LORD:' and his father and his mother that begat him °shall thrust him through when he prophesieth.
4 And it shall come to pass in that day, *that* the prophets shall be ashamed °every one of his vision, when he hath prophesied; neither shall they °wear a rough garment to deceive:
5 But he shall say, '**I** *am* no prophet, **I** *am* an husbandman; for °man taught me to keep cattle from my youth.'
T (p. 1293) 6 And °*one* shall say unto °Him, 'What *are* these wounds °in Thine hands?' Then He shall answer, '*Those* with which I was wounded *in* the house of °My friends.'
7 °Awake, O sword, against My Shepherd,
T and against the °Man *That is* My °Fellow, [2]saith [2]the LORD of hosts: °**smite the Shepherd,**
S **and the sheep shall be scattered**: and I will °turn Mine hand upon the °little ones.
8 And it shall come to pass, *that* in all the land, °saith [3]the LORD, two parts therein shall be cut off *and* die; but the third shall be left therein.
9 And I will bring the third part through the fire, and will refine them as silver is refined, and will try them as gold is tried: **they** shall call on My name, and **I** will °hear **them**: I will say, °'**It** *is* My People:' and **they** shall say, [3]'The LORD *is* my °God.'

R B (p. 1294) **14** °Behold, °the day of °the LORD cometh, and °thy spoil shall be divided in the midst of thee.
C 2 For °I will gather all nations against Jerusalem to °battle; and the city shall be taken, and the houses rifled, and the women ravished; and half of the city shall go forth into captivity, and the residue of the People shall not be cut off from the city.
B D¹ 3 Then shall [1]the LORD go forth, and fight against those nations, °as when He °fought in the day of °battle.
E¹ 4 And His feet shall stand in that day °upon the mount of Olives, which *is* before Jerusalem on the east, and the mount of Olives shall cleave in the midst thereof toward the east and toward the west, *and there shall be* a very great °valley; and half of the mountain shall remove toward the north, and half of it toward the south.
5 And ye shall flee *to* the [4]valley of °the mountains; for the [4]valley of the mountains shall reach unto °Azal: yea, ye shall flee, like as ye fled from before °the earthquake in the days of Uzziah king of Judah:

13. 2-5 (Y², p. 1293). EVIL REMOVED. (*Division.*)

Y² | A¹ | 2-. Idols cut off.
| A² | -2-5. False prophets removed.

2 saith the LORD of hosts = [is] the oracle of Jehovah of hosts. See note on 1. 3.
cut off the names. Ref. to Pent. (Ex. 23. 13). Ap. 92.
spirit. Heb. *rūach*. Ap. 9.
3 it shall come to pass. In that yet future day.
the LORD. Heb. Jehovah. Ap. 4. II.
shall thrust him through. Ref. to Pent. (Deut. 13. 6-11; 18. 20). Ap. 92.
4 every one. Heb. *'īsh*. Ap. 44. II.
wear = put on. Some codices, with four early printed editions, and Aram., add "any more".
5 man. Heb. *'ādām*. Ap. 14. I.
6 one shall say unto Him. Messiah is here spoken of, in contrast with these prophets. Spoken in the yet future time, and referring to His past rejection, and to the time when His wounds had been received.
Him. Messiah, Whom they will have already looked upon (12. 10), and now inquire of for explanation.
in = within, or between: i.e. in the palms.
My friends. Typical of His own who received Him not (Mark 3. 21; cp. *vv.* 31, 34, 35. John 1. 11).
7 Awake, &c. This verse stands wholly unconnected, unless we regard it as looking back from the yet future glory to the time of His rejection, when Isa. 53. 5-10 was fulfilled. Cp. 11. 16, 17.
Man = mighty One. Heb. *geber*. Ap. 14. IV.
Fellow. Of none but Messiah could Jehovah say this.
smite the Shepherd. Quoted of Messiah by Messiah, in Matt. 26. 31. Mark 14. 27: showing that the words cannot possibly refer to any "high priest" as alleged.
turn Mine hand upon: i.e. for care and protection.
little = feeble of the flock. Cp. John 18. 8.
8 saith the LORD = [is] Jehovah's oracle.
9 hear = answer.
It is My People. Ref. to Pent. (Lev. 26. 12). Ap. 92.
God. Heb. Elohim. Ap. 4. I.

14. 1-21 (*R*, p. 1293). THREATENING. AGAINST ENEMIES. THE LORD'S DAY. (*Alternation.*)

R | B | 1. Jehovah's day. Coming.
| C | 2. Nations gathered.
| *B* | 3-11. Jehovah's day. Going forth.
| *C* | 12-21. Nations smitten.

1 Behold. Fig. *Asterismos*. Ap. 6.
the day of the LORD. See note on Isa. 2. 11, 12; 13. 6.
the LORD. Heb. Jehovah. Ap. 4. II.
thy (fem.). Referring to Jerusalem.
2 I will gather, &c. Referring to the yet future and final siege of Jerusalem. See Ap. 53.
battle = war. Not the same word as in *v.* 3.

14. 3-11 (*B*, above). JEHOVAH. GOING FORTH. (*Repeated Alternation.*)

B | D¹ | 3. Jehovah. Going forth.
| E¹ | 4, 5-. Events and Consequences.
| D² | -5. Jehovah. Coming.
| E² | 6-8. Events and Consequences.
| D³ | 9. Jehovah. Reigning.
| E³ | 10, 11. Events and Consequences.

3 as = just as. **fought.** Cp. Josh. 10. 14.
battle = close conflict. Not the same word as in *v.* 2. Heb. *ḳerāb*. First occ. 2 Sam. 17. 11.
4 upon the mount of Olives. This precludes the possibility of any reference to what is past. No amount of "poetical imagery" can rob this plain statement of the yet future literal interpretation of this prophecy.
valley. Between the northern and southern half of Olivet. See Ap. 88, p. 127.

5 the mountains = My mountains. So called because of the physical change which HE will yet bring about, in the two new mounts formed out of the one. **Azal.** A new place, yet to have this name, at one extremity of the valley. **the earthquake.** Referred to in Amos 1. Fig. *Hysteresis*. Ap. 6.

D^{2} and [1] the LORD my °God shall come, °*and* all
407–403 °the °saints with °Thee.
E^{2} 6 And it shall come to pass in that day, *that*
the light shall not be °clear, *nor* °dark:
7 But it shall be °one day which shall be
°known to [1] the LORD, °not day, nor night:
but it shall come to pass, *that* at evening time
it shall be light.
8 And it shall be in that day, *that* °living
waters shall go out from Jerusalem; half of
them toward the °former sea, and half of
them toward the °hinder sea: in °summer and
in °winter shall it be.
D^{3} 9 And [1] the LORD shall be °King over all the
(p. 1294) earth: in that day shall there be °one [1] LORD,
and His name °one.
E^{3} 10 All the land shall be turned as °a plain
from °Geba to °Rimmon south of Jerusalem:
and it shall be lifted up, and °inhabited in her
place, from °Benjamin's gate unto the place of
the first gate, unto the °corner gate, and *from* the
°tower of Hananeel unto the king's winepresses.
11 And *men* shall dwell in it, and there shall
be no more utter °destruction; but Jerusalem
°shall be safely inhabited.
C F 12 °And this shall be the plague wherewith
(p. 1295) [1] the LORD will smite all the °people that have
fought against Jerusalem; Their flesh shall
consume away while they stand upon their
feet, and their eyes shall consume away in
their holes, and their tongue shall consume
away in their mouth.
13 And it shall come to pass in that day, *that*
a great °tumult from [1] the LORD shall be
among them; and they shall lay hold °every
one on the hand of his neighbour, and his hand
shall rise up against the hand of his neighbour.
14 And Judah also shall fight at Jerusalem;
and the wealth of all the °heathen round
about shall be gathered together, gold, and
silver, and apparel, in great abundance.
15 And so shall be the plague of the horse, of
the mule, of the camel, and of the ass, and of
all the beasts that shall be in these °tents, °as
this plague.
G 16 And it shall come to pass, *that* every one
that is left of all the nations which came
against Jerusalem shall even go up from year
to year to worship °the King, °the LORD of
hosts, and to keep °the feast of tabernacles.
F 17 And it shall be, *that* whoso will not come
up of *all* the families of the earth unto Jerusalem to worship [16] the King, [16] the LORD of
hosts, even upon them shall be no °rain.
18 And if the family of Egypt go not up, and
come not, °that *have* no [17] *rain;* there shall be
the plague, wherewith [1] the LORD will smite
°the °heathen that come not up to keep the
feast of tabernacles.
19 This shall be the °punishment of Egypt,
and the °punishment of all nations that come
not up to keep the feast of tabernacles.
G 20 In that day shall there °be upon the bells
of the horses, °HOLINESS UNTO [1] THE
LORD; and the pots in [1] the LORD'S house
shall be like the bowls before the altar.
21 Yea, every pot in Jerusalem and in Judah
shall be [20] holiness unto [16] the LORD of hosts:
and all they that sacrifice shall come and take
of them, and °seethe therein: and in that day
there shall be no more the °Canaanite in the
house of [16] the LORD of hosts."

God. Heb. Elohim. Ap. 4. I.
and. Some codices, with Aram., Sept., Syr., and Vulg., read this "and" in the text.
the. Some codices, with Aram. and Syr., read "his".
saints = holy ones: i.e. angels; as in Job 5. 1. Ps. 89. 5, 7. Dan. 4. 13; 8. 13. Matt. 24. 30, 31; 25. 31. Jude 14. Cp. Deut. 33. 2, 3.
Thee. Some codices, with Aram., Sept., Syr., and Vulg., read "Him". This takes us on to the Second Advent. No "flight to Pella" can be accepted as a fulfilment, in any sense.
6 clear = light. **dark** = dense.
7 one day = one [continuous] day, or one day by itself, unique. Cp. Ps. 118. 24.
known to the LORD. This forbids our assumptions, and should restrain our curiosity.
not day, nor night. Answering to "not bright, nor dense" in *v.* 6.
8 living waters = fresh, running, or perennial waters. These are the waters of Ezek. 47.
former = eastern: i.e. the Dead Sea.
hinder = western: i.e. Mediterranean Sea.
summer. Not dried up by heat.
winter. Not congealed by frost.
9 King over all the earth. Cp. 4. 14; 6. 5. Rev. 11. 15.
one. Heb. *'ehād.* See note on Deut. 6. 4. **10 a** = the.
Geba. Now *Jeb'a*, six miles north of Jerusalem.
Rimmon. Now *Khan Umm er Rūmāmīn* (Neh. 11. 29).
inhabited = be inhabited.
Benjamin's gate. See Jer. 20. 2; 37. 13; 38. 6.
corner gate. Cp. 2 Chron. 26. 9.
tower. Jer. 31. 38. See Ap. 59.
11 destruction. Cp. Mal. 4. 6, i.e. Anathema.
shall be, &c. = shall abide in security. Ref. to Pent. (Lev. 26. 5). Ap. 92. Cp. Jer. 23. 6. Ezek. 28. 26; 34. 25, 28, &c.

14. 12–21 (*C*, p. 1294). NATIONS SMITTEN.
(*Alternation.*)

C | F | 12–15. Plague.
  G | 16. Worship.
 F | 17–19. Plague.
  G | 20, 21. Worship.

12 And this shall be, &c. The subject now returns to the smiting of the nations. See the Structure, *C*, p. 1294. **people** = peoples.
13 tumult = panic. **every one.** Heb. *'īsh.* Ap. 14. II.
14 heathen = nations. **15 tents** = camps.
as = like. Some codices read "with".
16 the King. As in *v.* 9. Jehovah will then be the universal Sovereign.
the LORD of hosts. See note on 1. 3.
the feast of tabernacles. Ref. to Pent. (Lev. 23. 34, 43. Deut. 16. 16). Ap. 92. **17 rain** = the [periodic] rain.
18 that have no rain. This read with *v.* 17 makes no sense. Modern critics (with R.V. margin) at once say "the text is probably corrupt". The *Ellipsis* must be supplied by repeating the words from the end of *v.* 17 thus: "if . . . come not, [not upon them shall be no rain, but] upon them there shall be the plague" (as aforesaid in *v.* 12). Egypt has no rain; hence this elliptical expression. Ref. to Pent. (Deut. 11. 10). Ap. 92.
the. Some codices, with five early printed editions (one Rabbinic, in marg.), Sept., Syr., and Vulg., read "all the".
heathen = nations. Some codices read "peoples".
19 punishment. Heb. sin (*chāṭā*, Ap. 44. i). Put by Fig. *Metonymy* (of Cause), Ap. 6, for the punishment brought down by it.
20 be upon = be [inscribed] upon.
HOLINESS UNTO THE LORD. Ref. to Pent. (Ex. 28. 36; 39. 30). Ap. 92. For the large type see Ap. 48.
21 seethe = boil. Ref. to Pent. (Lev. 6. 28). Ap. 92. Cp. 1 Sam. 2. 13. 2 Chron. 35. 13. Ezek. 46. 20, 24. **the** = a.
Canaanite. This is the word which, divided into two in 11. 7, 11, is rendered "the poor of the flock". As one word it means merchant, or trafficker; but it is also used as typical of what is unclean. Cp. Zeph. 1. 11. Matt. 21. 12.

MALACHI.

THE STRUCTURE OF THE BOOK AS A WHOLE.

(Division.)

𝔇[2]	A[1] | 1. 1-5.	NATIONAL ELECTION.
	A[2] | 1. 6—4. 6.	NATIONAL REJECTION.

For the CANONICAL order and place of the Prophets, see Ap. 1, and pp. 1206 and 1207.
For the CHRONOLOGICAL order of the Prophets, see Ap. 77.
For the Inter-relation of the Prophetic Books, see Ap. 78.
For the *Formulæ* of Prophetic utterance, see Ap. 82.
For References to the Pentateuch by the Prophets, see Ap. 92.
For the Inter-relation of the Minor (or Shorter) Prophets, see pp. 1206 and 1207.

Malachi is one of the six undated Minor (or Shorter) Prophets. His book shows that the Temple-worship, with its sacrifices, &c., had been fully restored; but the ceremonial formalism and hypocrisy, which culminated in the days of our Lord's ministry, are seen actively at work.

No sooner were the restraining influences of Ezra and Nehemiah removed, than the corruption began; and went on apace, as evidenced by Mal. 1. 7, 8; 3. 8, &c.

From the "Restoration" and the First Passover to the birth of Messiah was exactly 400 years, the last great period of Probation (40 × 10; see Ap. 10). It was the great testing-time given to the Nation *in the Land.*

If we take the date of Malachi as being 400 years before the anointing of Messiah and the commencement of His Ministry (A.D. 26), then we have, reckoning back from A.D. 26, the year 374 B.C. This gives *thirty years* from the Restoration to the condition of the Nation described in this prophecy, and twenty-nine clear years from Ezra's last date (1st Nisan, 403 B.C.): a period amply sufficient for the terrible declension of which Malachi speaks. Milner, in his valuable Church History, remarks that great reformations seldom seem to last in their purity more than thirty years.

If this be so, then Malachi may be dated as about 374 B.C., thirty years after the commencement of the Temple-worship, which marked the beginning of the 400 years till the birth of THE Messenger (John the Baptist), and of THE MESSIAH. (See Ap. 77. 9.)

MALACHI.

A^1 A^1 (p. 1297) 374 **1** THE °burden of the word of °the LORD °to
Israel °by °Malachi.
2 °"I have loved you, °saith [1]the LORD.
B^1 Yet ye say, 'Wherein hast Thou loved us?'
A^2 *Was* not °Esau °Jacob's brother? °saith [1]the
LORD: yet **I loved °Jacob,**
3 **And I hated [2]Esau,** and laid his mountains
and his heritage waste for the °dragons of
the wilderness.
B^2 4 Whereas Edom saith, 'We are °impover-
ished, but we will return and build the desolate
places;'
A^3 thus °saith °the LORD of hosts, They shall
build, but I will throw down; and they shall
call them, The °border of °wickedness, and,
The people against whom [1]the LORD hath
indignation for ever.
5 And your eyes shall see, and ye shall say,
[1]'The LORD will be magnified from the [4]border
of Israel.'
^{2} C F^1 H 6 °A son honoureth *his* father, and a servant
his °master: °if then I *be* a Father, where *is*
Mine honour? and if I *be* a Master, where *is*
My fear? [4]saith [4]the LORD of hosts unto you,
O priests, that despise °My name. And ye say,
'Wherein have we despised Thy name?'
7 °Ye °offer polluted bread upon Mine altar;
and ye say, 'Wherein have we polluted Thee?'
In that ye say, 'The table of [1]the LORD °*is*
contemptible.'
8 And °if ye [7]offer the blind for sacrifice, [7]*is*
it not °evil? and if ye [7]offer the lame °and sick,
[7]*is it* not °evil? [7]offer it now unto thy governor;
will he be pleased with thee, or accept thy
person? saith [4]the LORD of hosts.
9 And now, °I pray you, beseech °GOD that
He will be gracious unto us: °this hath been
°by your means: will He °regard your persons? [4]saith [4]the LORD of hosts.
10 Who *is there* even among °you that
would shut the doors *for nought?* neither do
ye kindle *fire* on Mine altar for nought. I have
no pleasure in you, [4]saith [4]the LORD of hosts,
neither will I accept an °offering at your hand.
J 11 °For from the rising of the sun even unto
the going down of the same My name *shall be*
great among the °Gentiles; and in every place
incense *shall be* [7]offered unto My name, and
a pure [10]offering: for My name *shall be* great
among the °heathen, [4]saith [4]the LORD of hosts.
G H 12 But ye have profaned °it, in that ye say,

1. 1-5 (**A^1**, p. 1296). NATIONAL ELECTION.
(*Repeated Alternation.*)

A^1 | A^1 | 1, 2-. Words of Jehovah to Israel: of His love.
  B^1 | -2-. Israel's answer.
 A^2 | -2, 3. Words of Jehovah to Israel: of His love.
  B^2 | 4-. Edom's answer.
 A^3 | -4, 5. Words of Jehovah to Israel: of His love.

1 burden. See note on Isa. 13. 1; and cp. Zech. 9. 1; 12. 1, &c. **the LORD.** Heb. Jehovah. Ap. 4. II. **to.** Not "concerning". **by** = by the hand of. **Malachi.** Heb. = My messenger, relating to the five messengers in this book: see Ap. 10. (1) Malachi himself (1. 1); (2) the true Priest (2. 7); (3) John the Baptist (3. 1-); (4) the Messiah Himself (3. -1-3); (5) Elijah (4. 5). This last prophecy introduces the great fulfilment of Jehovah's prophecy by Moses, the first prophet to Israel, in Deut. 18. 15-19. Cp. Acts 3. 18-26; 7. 37.

2 I have loved you. Ref. to Pent. (Deut. 7. 8; 10. 15; 33. 3). **saith** = hath said. Quoted in Rom. 9. 13. **Esau Jacob's.** Put by Fig. *Metonymy* (of Adjunct), Ap. 6, for their posterities. Quoted in Rom. 9. 13. **saith the LORD** = [is] Jehovah's oracle.

3 dragons = jackals. Cp. Isa. 13. 22; 34. 13. Jer. 9. 11; 10. 22; 49. 33; 51. 37.

4 impoverished: or, beaten down. **saith** = hath said. **the LORD of hosts.** This expression occurs twenty-four times in this prophecy, and gives its character to the whole, as in Zechariah. **border:** or, territory. **wickedness** = lawlessness. Heb. *rāshā'.* Ap. 44. x.

1. 6—4. 6 (**A^2**, p. 1296). NATIONAL REJECTION.
(*Extended Alternation.*)

A^2 | C | 1. 6—2. 16. Israel's *deeds* reproved.
  D | 2. 17. Israel's *words* reproved.
   E | 3. 1-6. Jehovah's Messenger. Purging all.
 C | 3. 7-12. Israel's *deeds* reproved.
  D | 3. 13—4. 4. Israel's *words* reproved.
   E | 4. 5, 6. Jehovah's Messenger. Restoring all.

1. 6—2. 16 (C, above). ISRAEL'S *DEEDS* REPROVED. (*Division.*)

C | F^1 | 1. 6-14. Priests and People. Ceremonial.
 | F^2 | 2. 1-16. Priests and People. Moral.

1. 6-14 (F^1, above). PRIESTS AND PEOPLE. CEREMONIAL. (*Alternation.*)

F^1 | G | H | 6-10. Sinful offerings. Priests.
  | J | 11. Jehovah will yet be honoured by a pure offering.
 G | *H* | 12-14-. Sinful offerings. People.
  | *J* | -14. Jehovah will yet be great among the peoples.

6 A son, &c. Ref. to Pent. (Ex. 20. 12), Ap. 92. Note the Fig. *Anacoenōsis* (Ap. 6). An appeal to opponents as having a common interest. Cp. Isa. 5. 4. Luke 11. 19. Acts 4. 19. 1 Cor. 4. 21; 10. 15; 11. 13, 14. Gal. 4. 21. **master.** The Heb. accents place the chief pause here, where the statement ends on which the appeal is based. **if then I, &c.** These two appeals are marked off by minor accents. **My name:** which is again marked off for special emphasis. (1) The argument is based on natural reverence; (2) the breach is shown in the case of Israel (Isa. 41. 8. Hos. 11. 1); (3) the conclusion being that the priests were the guilty cause. **7 Ye offer, &c.** Ref. to Pent. (Deut. 15. 21). Ap. 92. **offer** = bring nigh. Heb. *nāgash.* Ap. 43. I. ii. **is** = it [is]. **8 if ye offer the blind, &c.** Ref. to Pent. (Lev. 22. 22. Deut. 15. 21). Ap. 92. **and sick, is it not** = and sick [saying], it is not evil. **evil.** Heb. *rā'a'.* Ap. 44. viii. **9 I pray you, &c.** Fig. *Irony.* Ap. 6. **GOD.** Heb. El. Ap. 4. IV. **this hath been** = this hath come to pass. **by your means** = at your hands. **regard** = accept. **10 you.** Emph. i. e. you [priests]. **offering** = a gift-offering. Heb. *minchāh.* Ap. 43. II. iii. **11 For.** See the Structure ("J" and "*J*", above) for the commentary. **Gentiles** = nations. **heathen** = nations, or Gentiles. **12 it** = Me. "Me" was the reading in the primitive text; but the *Sōpherīm* state that they altered *'ōthī* (Me) to *'ōthō* (him, or it) out of a (mistaken) sense of reverence. See Ap. 33. Cp. 3. 9; and Ezek. 13. 19.

374 '**The** °table of °the LORD*[7] *is* polluted; and
the fruit thereof, *even* his meat, *is* contemptible.'
13 Ye said also, °'Behold, what a weariness
is it!' °and ye have °snuffed at °it, [4]saith [4]the
LORD of hosts; °and ye brought *that which
was* torn, and the lame, and the sick; thus ye
brought an [10]offering: °should I accept this of
your hand? [4]saith [1]the LORD.
14 But cursed *be* the deceiver, which °hath
in his flock a male, and voweth, and sacrificeth
unto [12]the LORD* a corrupt thing:
J for I *am* a great King, [4]saith [4]the LORD of hosts,
and My name *is* dreadful among the [11]heathen.

F² K¹ L N (p. 1298) **2** And now, O ye °priests, °this commandment *is* for you.
2 °If ye will not hear, and if ye will not lay *it*
to heart, to give glory unto °My name, °saith
°the LORD of hosts,
O I will even °send a curse upon you, and I
will °curse your blessings: yea, I have cursed
them already, because ye do not lay *it* to heart.
3 °Behold, I will °corrupt your seed, and
spread °dung upon your faces, *even* the °dung
of your solemn °feasts; and *one* shall take you
away with °it.
4 And ye shall know that I have sent this
commandment unto you, that My covenant
might °be with Levi, [2]saith [2]the LORD of hosts.
M **5** °My covenant was with him of life and
peace; and °I gave them to him *for* the fear
wherewith he feared Me, and °was afraid before
My name.
6 The law of truth was °in his mouth, °and
iniquity was not found in his lips: he walked
with Me in peace and equity, and did turn
many away °from iniquity.
7 For °the priest's lips should keep °knowledge,
and °they should seek the law at his mouth: for
he *is* the messenger of [2]the LORD of hosts.
L N **8** But ye are departed out of the way; ye have
caused many to stumble at the law; ye have
°corrupted the covenant of Levi, [2]saith [2]the
LORD of hosts.
O **9** "Therefore have I also made you contemptible and base before all the °People,
°according as ye have not kept My ways, but
have °been partial °in the law."
K² P¹ **10** °Have we not all one Father? hath not one
°GOD created us? why do we deal °treacherously °every man against his brother, by
profaning the covenant of our fathers?
11 °Judah hath dealt [10]treacherously, and an
abomination is committed in Israel and in
Jerusalem; for Judah hath profaned the °holiness of °the LORD °which He loved, and hath
married the daughter of a °strange [10]GOD.

table: i.e. the altar.
the LORD* = Jehovah (Ap. 4. II). Heb. *Adonai*. Ap. 4. VIII (2). But this is one of the 134 places which the *Sōpherīm* say they altered Jehovah to "Adonai".
13 Behold. Fig. *Asterismos*. Ap. 6.
and. Note the Fig. *Polysyndeton* (Ap. 6).
snuffed = puffed. "Snuffed" is an archaism for "sniffed" = complained by snivelling: i.e. pooh-poohed.
it = My altar. See note on *v.* 12.
should I accept, &c. Ref. to Pent. (Lev. 22. 20). Ap. 92.
14 hath. Heb. *yēsh*. See note on Lam. 1. 12.

2. 1-16 (F², p. 1297). PRIESTS AND PEOPLE. MORAL. (*Division.*)

F² | K¹ | 1-9. The Priests reproved.
K² | 10-16. The People reproved.

2. 1-9 (K¹, above). THE PRIESTS REPROVED (*Introversion and Alternation.*)

K¹ | L | N | 1, 2-. Commandment given.
O | -2-4. Punishment threatened.
M | 5-7. Covenant with LEVI.
L | *N* | 8. Commandment disobeyed.
O | 9. Punishment administered.

1 priests. See the Structures, above.
this commandment. As to reformation.
2 If ye will not hear. Ref. to Pent. (Lev. 26. 14. Deut. 28. 15). Ap. 92.
My name. See note on Ps. 20. 1.
the LORD of hosts. See note on 1. 4.
saith = hath said.
send a curse = send the curse. Ref. to Pent. (Deut. 28. 20). Ap. 92.
curse your blessings. Ref. to Pent. (Deut. 28. 2).
3 Behold. Fig. *Asterismos*. Ap. 6.
corrupt = rebuke; as in 3. 11. Ps. 106. 9. Isa. 17. 13. Heb. *gā'ar*. Occurs fourteen times. Always rendered "rebuke" except here, and Jer. 29. 27 ("reproved").
dung = refuse; always sacrificial. Occ. seven times.
feasts. Put by Fig. *Metonymy* (of Adjunct), Ap. 6, for the sacrifices offered at the feasts.
it: i.e. the refuse. **4 be** = continue.
5 My covenant was with him. Ref. to Pent. (Num. 25. 10-13. Deut. 33. 8, 9, 10). Ap. 92.
I gave them, &c.: I gave this "life" and "peace" to him [Levi] as an awe-inspiring, reverend characteristic; because he stood in awe of Me. There seems to be a distinct ref. to Phineas (see the refs. above). But there seems to be a distinct ref. to Levi also (Ex. 32. 26-29), in the first place, at any rate. Heb. *mōrā'* = that which makes awe felt.
was afraid before = abased himself.
6 in his mouth: i.e. for teaching.
and iniquity. Heb. *'āval*. Ap. 44. iv.
from iniquity. Heb. *'āvah*. Ap. 44. vi.
7 the priest's lips, &c. This was the first duty of the priests, and was more important than their ceremonial duties. Ref. to Pent. (Lev. 10. 11. Deut. 17. 11; 33. 10). Ap. 92. **knowledge**: i.e. esp. of the law.
they: i.e. the People; according to Deut. 17. 9-11.
8 corrupted = made void.
9 People = peoples: i.e. the tribes.
according as = because, or, in so far as.
been partial = had respect of persons. Cp. Jas. 2. 4.
in = in [administering] the law.

2. 10-16 (K², above). THE PEOPLE REPROVED. (*Repeated Alternation.*)

K² | P¹ | 10, 11. Judah's treachery.
Q¹ | 12. Jehovah's warning.
P² | 13-15-. Judah's treachery.
Q² | -15. Jehovah's warning.
P³ | 16-. Judah's treachery.
Q³ | -16. Jehovah's warning.

10 Have we not all . . . created us? = [Ye say] Have we not, &c., as in *v.* 14. Fig. *Parœmia*. Ap. 6. See John 8. 33, 39, 41, &c. **GOD.** Heb. El. Ap. 4. IV. **treacherously**: or, faithlessly. Used of faithlessness to the marriage bond. **every man.** Heb. *'ish*. Ap. 14. II. **11 Judah, &c.** See Jer. 3. 7, 8, 20; 5. 11, &c. **holiness** = Holy Place, or Sanctuary. **the LORD.** Heb. Jehovah. Ap. 4. II. **which**: i.e. the Sanctuary. **strange** = foreign: i.e. a woman temple-worshipper of a foreign god.

Q[1] (p. 1298) 374 12 [11]The LORD will cut off the °man that
doeth this, °the master and the °scholar, out
of the °tabernacles of Jacob, and him that
°offereth an °offering unto [2]the LORD of hosts.
P[2] 13 And this have ye done again, covering the
altar of [11]the LORD with °tears, with °weeping,
and with °crying out, insomuch that He regardeth not the [12]offering any more, or receiveth *it* with good will at your hand.
14 Yet ye say, °"Wherefore?" Because [11]the
LORD hath been witness between thee and
the wife of thy youth, against whom thou hast
dealt [10]treacherously: yet *is* she thy °com-
panion, and the wife of thy covenant.
15 And did not He °make one? °Yet had He
the residue of the °spirit. °And wherefore
°one? That he might seek a godly seed.
Q[2] Therefore °take heed to °your °spirit, and let
none deal [10]treacherously against the wife of
his youth.
P[3] 16 °For [11]the LORD, the °God of Israel, °saith
°that He hateth °putting away: "for *one*
covereth violence °with his garment," saith
[2]the LORD of hosts:
Q[3] therefore take heed to your [15]spirit, that ye
deal not [10]treacherously."
D (p. 1297) 17 Ye have wearied [11]the LORD with your
words. Yet ye °say, "Wherein have we
wearied *Him*?" When ye say, °"Every one
that doeth °evil *is* good in the sight of [2]the
LORD, and He delighteth in them;" or, "Where
is the [16]God of judgment?"

E R (p. 1299) 3 °"**Behold, I will send °My messenger,**
and he shall °prepare the way before Me:
and °the Lord, Whom ye seek, shall °suddenly
come to His temple, even the messenger of
the covenant, whom ye delight in: °behold,
He shall come, °saith °the LORD of hosts.
2 But °who may °abide the day of His
coming? and who shall stand when He
appeareth?
S for He *is* like a refiner's fire, and like fullers' °sope:
3 And He shall sit *as* a refiner and purifier of
silver: and °He shall purify the sons of Levi,
and purge them as gold and silver, that they
may °offer unto °the LORD an °offering in
righteousness.
4 °Then shall the °offering of Judah and
Jerusalem be °pleasant unto [3]the LORD, as in
the °days of old, and as in °former years.
R 5 And I will come near to you to judgment;
and °I will be a swift witness against °the
sorcerers, °and against the °adulterers, °and
against °false swearers, °and against those
that °oppress the hireling in *his* wages, the
widow, °and °the fatherless, °and that turn

12 man. Heb. *'ish.* Ap. 14. II.
the master and the scholar = wakener and answerer. Referring to the Temple watchers (Ps. 134. 1).
tabernacles = tents.
offereth = bringeth near. Heb. *nāgash*, as in 1. 7, 8, 11; 3. 3. Ap. 43. I. ii.
offering = a meal-offering. Heb. *minchāh.* Ap. 43. II. iii.
13 tears . . . weeping . . . crying out: i.e. of the wronged wives and children.
14 Wherefore? Supply the *Ellipsis*: "Wherefore [doth He not accept it]?"
companion = consort, or mate.
15 Modern critics pronounce this as being "a difficult and certainly corrupt passage"; but it is only elliptical.
make one? = make [of twain] one flesh? Ref. to Pent. (Gen. 2. 24). Ap. 92.
Yet had He, &c. And therefore could have made more than one wife for Adam.
spirit. Heb. *rūach.* Ap. 9.
And wherefore one? = And what [did] that one [Abraham] who [was] seeking a seed of (or from) God? Heb. *zera'* (as in Gen. 21. 12; see note there). The logical *Ellipsis* must be further supplied: "Was Abraham faithless to Sarah and did he ill-treat her when he took an additional wife? How much more ought ye to be faithful to your wives?"
one. Refers to Abraham. See Isa. 51. 2. Ezek. 33. 24. Supply the verb "do", as in Ecc. 2. 12, and as in Judg. 18. 8, from *v.* 18. **take heed** = be watchful over.
your = your own.
16 For, &c. = For [as] hating putting away, hath Jehovah, Israel's God, spoken; and [as hating him that] hath carried violence concealed in his clothing, hath Jehovah Sabaioth spoken, therefore, &c.
God. Heb. Elohim. Ap. 4. I. **saith** = hath said.
that He hateth, &c. = I hate.
putting away = divorce. Ref. to Pent. (Deut. 24. 1).
with his garment. Cp. Pss. 73. 6; 109. 18, 29. Prov. 28. 13. Isa. 30. 1. **17 say** = have said.
Every one, &c. Some codices read "All who do wrong are", &c.
evil = violence. Heb. *rā'a'.* Ap. 44. viii.

3. 1-6 (E, p. 1297). **JEHOVAH'S MESSENGER. PURGING ALL.** (*Alternation.*)

E | R | 1, 2–. His coming.
  S | –2–4. The Reason. "For".
  R | 5. His coming.
  S | 6. The Reason. "For".

1 Behold, I will send, &c. = Behold Me sending, &c. Quoted in Matt. 11. 10. Mark 1. 2. Luke 1. 76; 7. 27. Not to that then present generation, but to the "generation" of our Lord's day. See note on Matt. 11. 18. This is the answer to the question "Where?" in 2. 17.
My messenger. John the Baptist (Matt. 3. 3; 11. 10. Mark 1. 2, 3. Luke 1. 76; 3. 4; 7. 26, 27. John 1. 23). Cp. Matt. 22. 2, 3. Isa. 40. 3–5.
prepare. By removing obstacles from the way. Cp. Isa. 40. 3; 62. 10.
the Lord. Heb. *hā-'Adōn.* Ap. 4. VIII (1). This refers to Messiah. Ref. to Pent. (Ex. 23. 20; 33. 14, 16). Ap. 92. **suddenly** = unexpectedly.
behold Fig. *Asterismos* (Ap. 6), for emphasis.
said = hath said.
the LORD of hosts. See note on 1. 4.

2 who may abide . . . ? Cp. Joel 2. 11. Fig. *Erotēsis.* Ap. 6. **abide** = endure. **sope** = lye; as in Job 9. 30: i e. water mixed with the ashes of certain plants containing alkali. Cp. Mark 9. 3. Occurs only here, and Jer. 2. 22. **3 He shall purify.** Judgment begins at the house of God. See 1 Pet. 4. 17. **offer** = bring near. Heb. *nāgash*, as in 1. 7, 8, 11. Ap. 43. I. ii. **the LORD.** Heb. Jehovah. Ap. 4. II. **offering** = a gift-offering. Heb. *minchah.* Ap. 43. II. iii. Not the same word as in *v.* 8. **4 Then.** When Jehovah shall have sent His messenger (Messiah), and He is accepted. **offering.** The 1611 edition of the A.V. reads "offerings". Same word as in *v.* 3. **pleasant** = acceptable. **days of old** = age-past times. **former** = ancient. **and** Note the Fig. *Polysyndeton.* Ap. 6. **5 I will be, &c.** Cp. Mic. 1. 2. **the sorcerers.** Ref. to Pent. (Ex. 22. 18. Deut. 18. 10). Ap. 92. **adulterers.** Ref. to Pent. (Ex. 20. 14. Lev. 20. 10). Ap. 92. **false swearers** = them that swear to a falsehood. Ref. to Pent. (Lev. 6. 3–5; 19. 12). Ap. 92. **oppress, &c.** Ref. to Pent. (Ex. 22. 21. Deut. 24. 14). Ap. 92. **the fatherless, &c.** Ref. to Pent. (Ex. 22. 22 Deut. 14. 29; 16. 11, 14; 24. 17). Ap. 92.

374 aside the stranger *from his right*, °and °fear
not Me, [1]saith [1]the LORD of hosts.

S 6 °For I *am* [3]the LORD, °I change not;
(p. 1299) therefore ye sons of Jacob are not consumed.

C T V 7 Even from the days of your fathers ye are
(p. 1300) gone away from Mine °ordinances, and have
not kept *them*.

W Return unto Me, and I will return unto you,"
saith [1]the LORD of hosts.

U But ye said, 'Wherein shall we return?

T V 8 Will a °man °rob °God? Yet ye °have
robbed Me. But ye say, 'Wherein °have we
robbed Thee?' In °tithes and °offerings.
9 Ye °*are* cursed with a curse: for ye have
[8]robbed Me, *even* °this whole nation.

W 10 Bring ye °all the [8]tithes into the storehouse, that there may be °meat in Mine
house, and prove Me now herewith, [1]saith
[1]the LORD of hosts, if I will not °open you
the windows of heaven, and °pour you out
a blessing, that *there shall* not *be room*
enough *to receive it*.
11 And I will rebuke °the devourer °for your
sakes, and he shall not destroy the fruits of
your ground; neither shall your vine cast her
fruit before the time in the field, [1]saith [1]the
LORD of hosts.
12 And all nations shall call you blessed:
for ye shall be °a delightsome land, [1]saith [1]the
LORD of hosts.

D X 13 Your words have been °stout against
Me, [1]saith [3]the LORD. Yet ye say, 'What
have we spoken *so much* against Thee?'
14 Ye have said, 'It *is* vain to serve [8]God:
and what profit *is it* that we have kept His
°ordinance, and that we have °walked °mourn-
fully before [1]the LORD of hosts?
15 °And now °we call the proud happy; yea,
°they that work °wickedness °are set up;
°yea, *they that* °tempt [8]God are even delivered.'"

Y 16 °Then they that °feared [3]the LORD °spake
often °one to another: °and [3]the LORD °heark-
ened, °and heard *it*, °and a book of °remem-
brance was written before Him for them that
feared [3]the LORD, and that °thought upon His
name.
17 And they shall be Mine, [1]saith [1]the LORD
of hosts, in that day when °I make up

and. See note above. **fear**=revere.

6 For, &c. Render, according to the Structure,

a | For I [am] Jehovah;
b | I have not changed;
a | And ye [are] Jacob's sons;
b | Ye have not failed.

I change not. Ref. to Pent. (Num. 23. 19). Ap. 92. Not in Himself, nor in His purpose, to change His dealings on the condition stated.

3. 7-12 (*C*, p. 1297). ISRAEL'S *DEEDS* REPROVED. (*Introversion and Alternation.*)

C | T | V | 7-. Sin. Backsliding.
W | -7-. Command. "Return unto ME." Conditional Promise.
U | -7. Israel's reply. "Wherein?"
T | *V* | 8, 9. Sin. Defrauding.
W | 10-12. Command. "Prove ME." Conditional Promise.

7 ordinances=statutes. Heb. *ḥok*. Referring to particular ritual observances. Not the same word as in *v.* 14. **8 man.** Heb. *'ādām*. Ap. 14. I.

rob=defraud. A rare word. Occurs only here, *vv.* 8, 9; and Prov. 22. 23. **God.** Heb. Elohim. Ap. 4. I.

have robbed=are defrauding.

tithes. Ref. to Pent. (Lev. 27. 30-33. Num. 18. 21-32. Deut. 12. 17, &c.; 14. 22-29). Ap. 92.

offerings=heave offerings. Lit., in the tithe and the heave offering. Heb. *terūmāh*. Ap. 43. II. viii. Not the same word as in *vv.* 3, 4; 1. 10, 11, 13; 2. 12, 13.

9 are cursed with a curse. The primitive text read, "ye have cursed Me with a curse". The *Sōpherīm* say (Ap. 33) that they altered the letter מ (Mem=M) into נ (Nun=N), thus making it passive instead of active, and detaching it from the rest of the sentence. This was done to avoid a supposed irreverence.

this whole nation=the nation, the whole of it.

10 all=the whole; implying that a part had been withheld.

meat=prey: i.e. animals for sacrifice. Not put by Fig. *Metonymy* (of Adjunct), Ap. 6, for food; but put by Fig. *Synecdoche* (of Species), Ap. 6, for sacrificial animals.

open you the windows, &c. Ref. to Pent. (Gen. 7. 11; 8. 2). Ap. 92.

pour you out=empty you out.

11 the devourer=the eater: i.e. the locust. Cp. Joel 1. 4. Amos 4. 9.

for your sakes=for you (the Dative of Reference).

12 a delightsome land. Cp. Isa. 62. 4. Dan. 8. 9.

3. 13—4. 4 (*D*, p. 1297). ISRAEL'S *WORDS* REPROVED. (*Alternation.*)

D | X | 3. 13-15. The Proud. Incrimination.
Y | 3. 16-18. The Reverers of Jehovah. Remembrance and Blessing.
X | 4. 1. The Proud. Destruction.
Y | 4. 2-4. The Reverers of Jehovah. Blessing and Remembrance.

13 stout=hard, or bold.

14 ordinance=charge. Heb. *mizvāh*. Not the same word as in *v.* 7. Referring to general religious duties. **walked mournfully before**=gone off mournfully from the presence of Jehovah of hosts. **15 And now.** Cp. 1. 9; 2. 1. **we.** Emphatic. **they that work wickedness**=the workers of lawlessness. **wickedness**=lawlessness. Heb. *rāshā'*. Ap. 44. x. **are set up**=prosper, or are successful. Lit. are built up. Put by Fig. *Metonymy* (of Subject), Ap. 6, for being prospered. Cp. Job 22. 23. Jer. 12. 16. **yea**=yea, [they, proud ones]. Marking a climax. **tempt**=have tempted. Same as "prove" in *v.* 10; but here in a bad sense, as though to challenge or put to the proof. **16 Then**: i.e. when Malachi had spoken thus unto them, and at a time of such apostasy, showing us what is possible and practicable in these like days and "perilous times" which are closing this present Dispensation. **feared**=revered. **spake.** As in *v.* 13. **one to another.** Each one with his friend. **and.** Note the Fig. *Polysyndeton*. Ap. 6. **hearkened, and heard.** As He heard the *groaning* of Israel (Ex. 2. 23, 24); Moses, *without words* (Ex. 14. 15); and Nehemiah (Neh. 2. 4); Hannah, *without words* (1 Sam. 1. 13); Jeremiah, his *breathing* (Lam. 3. 55, 56); Jonah, when *dying* (Jonah 2. 2); the disciples, *their thoughts* (Luke 24. 15, 38). **and a book of remembrance was written.** Some codices, with Syr., read "a record was written in a book of remembrance". **remembrance.** Ref. to Pent. (Ex. 28. 29. Num. 10. 10, the same word). Ap. 92. **thought.** Precious comfort for those now who cannot speak. We can *walk* with God (like Enoch, in the darkest days), and *think* of Him with these God-reverers now, in these similar days. **17 I make up, &c.**=I am preparing.

374 °My jewels; and I will spare them, °as a
°man spareth his own son that serveth him.
18 Then shall ye return, and discern between
°the righteous and °the wicked, between him
that serveth [8] God and him that serveth Him
not.

X (p. 1300) **4** For, °behold, the day cometh, that shall
burn as an oven; and all the proud, yea,
and °all that do °wickedly, shall be stubble:
and the day that cometh shall burn them up,
°saith °the LORD of hosts, that it shall °leave
them neither root nor branch.

Y 2 But unto you that °fear My name shall the
°Sun °of righteousness arise with healing in
His °wings; and °ye shall go forth, and °grow
up °as calves of the stall.
3 And ye shall tread down °the wicked; for
they shall be ashes under the soles of your
feet °in the day that °I shall do *this*, [1] saith
[1] the LORD of hosts.
4 Remember ye °the law of °Moses My
servant, °which I commanded unto him in
Horeb for all Israel, *with* the °statutes and
judgments.

E (p. 1297) 5 [1] Behold, I will send you °Elijah the prophet before the coming of the great and dreadful °day of °the LORD:
6 And he shall turn the heart of the fathers
to the °children, and the heart of the °children
to their fathers, lest I come and smite the
earth with a curse."

My jewels=A peculiar treasure. Heb. *segullāh*=acquired property; hence the word "peculiar"=one's own, and "peculate", to appropriate as one's own; the root being the Latin *pecus*, cattle, of which property originally consisted, and this from Sanskrit *paçu*, that which is fastened up, the root being PAK. The Heb. *segullāh* occurs only eight times (Ex. 19. 5. Deut. 7. 6; 14. 2; 26. 18. 1 Chron. 29. 3. Ps. 135. 4. Ecc. 2. 8. Mal. 3. 17). Ref. to Pent. (Ex. 19. 5. Deut. 7. 6; 14. 2; 26. 18). Ap. 92.

as=according as.

man. Heb. *'ish.* Ap. 14. II.

18 the righteous=a righteous one.

the wicked=a lawless one. Heb. *rāshā'.* Ap. 44. x.

4. 1 behold. Fig. *Asterismos.* Ap. 6.

all that do. Heb.=every one who doeth. But some eighty codices, with four early printed editions, Targum, Aram., Sept., Syr., and Vulg., read "all who work".

wickedly=lawlessness. Heb. *rāshā'.* Ap. 44. x.

saith=hath said.

the LORD of hosts. See note on 1. 4.

leave. A *Homonym.* See notes on Gen. 39. 6. Ex. 23. 5.

2 fear=revere. See the Structure "Y" and "*Y*", p. 1300.

Sun. Here the word "Sun" is fem., as in Gen. 15. 17. Jer. 15. 9. Nah. 3. 17, &c.; and is connected with "righteousness" (which is also fem.), which Messiah, the righteous One, alone can bring.

of. In this case "of" would be the Genitive of Apposition. See Ap. 17. 4.

wings=beams, or rays.

ye. The 1611 edition of the A.V. omits this "ye".

grow up=leap for joy, or frisk. **as**=like.

3 the wicked=lawless ones. Heb. *rāshā'.* Ap. 44. x.

in the day. See Ap. 18.

I shall do this=that I am preparing; as in 3. 17. **4 the law of Moses.** Ref. to Pent. (Ex. 20. 3, &c.). Ap. 92. **Moses My servant.** Ref. to Pent. (Num. 12. 7; see note there). Ap. 92. **which I commanded, &c.** Ref. to Pent. (Deut. 1. 6; 4. 10). Ap. 92. **statutes and judgments.** Ref. to Pent. (Deut. 4. 1. See note there). Ap. 92. **5 Elijah the prophet.** Called thus, only here, and in 2 Chron. 21. 12. Elsewhere, always "Elijah the Tishbite", to indicate his own person; but here "Elijah the prophet" because had Israel received Messiah, John the Baptist would have been reckoned as Elijah (see notes on Matt. 17. 9-13. Mark 9. 11-13): and, at His last supper, the wine, representing His blood, would have been (as it will yet be) reckoned as "the blood of the (New) Covenant", as foretold in Jer. 31. 31-34. Heb. 8. 8-13; 10. 15-17; 12. 24). **day of the LORD.** See note on Isa. 2. 12, 17; 13. 6, &c. **the LORD.** Heb. Jehovah. Ap. 4. II. **6 children**=sons.

THE NEW TESTAMENT*

* For the Greek Text of the New Testament, see Ap. 94.

For the New Testament and the order of its books, see Ap. 95.

THE INTER-RELATION OF THE FOUR GOSPELS.*

THEIR STRUCTURE AS A WHOLE.

GOD SPEAKING "BY HIS SON" (Heb. 1. 2).†

THE PROCLAMATION OF THE KING AND THE KINGDOM.

THE REJECTION OF THE KINGDOM AND THE CRUCIFIXION OF THE KING.

(*Alternation.*)

A[1] | **MATTHEW.** The Lord presented as Jehovah's KING. "Behold THY KING" (Zech. 9. 9). "Behold . . . I will raise unto David a Righteous BRANCH,‡ and a KING shall reign and prosper" (Jer. 23. 5,6 ; 33. 15). Hence the *royal* genealogy is required from Abraham and David downward (1. 1-17): and He is presented as what He is—before MAN (relatively)—the highest earthly position, the King.

B[1] | **MARK.** The Lord presented as Jehovah's SERVANT. "Behold MY SERVANT" (Isa. 42. 1). "Behold, I will bring forth My Servant THE BRANCH"‡ (Zech. 3. 8). Hence NO genealogy is required: and He is presented as what He is—before GOD (relatively)—the lowest earthly position, the ideal Servant.

A[2] | **LUKE.** The Lord presented as Jehovah's MAN. "Behold THE MAN Whose name is THE BRANCH"‡ (Zech. 6. 12). Hence the *human* genealogy is required upward to Adam (Luke 3. 23-38): and He is presented as what He is—before MAN (intrinsically)—the ideal man.

B[2] | **JOHN.** The Lord presented as JEHOVAH HIMSELF. "Behold YOUR GOD" (Isa. 40. 9). "In that day shall Jehovah's BRANCH‡ (i.e. Messiah) be beautiful and glorious" (Isa. 4. 2). Hence NO genealogy is required; and He is presented as what He is—before GOD (intrinsically)—Divine.

* For the order of the Gospels and the other books of the N.T., see Ap. 95. II.

† For the "sundry times" and "divers manners" in which God has spoken to mankind, see Ap. 95. I.

‡ There are twenty-three Hebrew words translated "Branch" in the Old Testament. This word (*zemach*) occurs twelve times (see Ap. 10); but in the passages here quoted it refers specially to the Messiah, and forms a link which connects the four characteristics of "the Branch" with the four presentations of the Messiah, as set forth in the subject-matter of each of the four Gospels respectively.

In Jer. 23. 5, 6, and 33. 15, Christ is presented as "the Branch", the KING *raised up* to rule in righteousness. This forms the subject-matter of MATTHEW'S Gospel.

In Zech. 3. 8, Christ is presented as "the Branch," the SERVANT *brought forth* for Jehovah's service. This forms the subject-matter of MARK'S Gospel. He is seen as Jehovah's servant, entering at once on His ministerial work without any preliminary words.

In Zech. 6. 12, Christ is presented as "the Branch" *growing up* out of His place. This is the characteristic of LUKE'S Gospel, in which this *growing up* forms the subject-matter of the earlier (and separate) portion of the Gospel, and brings out the perfections of Christ as "perfect man".

In Isa. 4. 2, Christ is presented as "the Branch of Jehovah" in all His own intrinsic beauty and glory. This is the great characteristic of the subject-matter of JOHN'S Gospel.

The Four Gospels thus form one complete whole, and are not to be explained by any "*synoptic*" arrangement.

The four are required to set forth the four aspects of the LIFE of Christ, as the four great offerings are required to set forth the four aspects of His DEATH.

No one Gospel could set forth the four different aspects of the life and ministry of the Lord Jesus, as no one offering could set forth all the aspects of His death.

Hence, it is the Divine purpose to give us, in the four Gospels, four aspects of His life on earth.

God has so ordered these that a "Harmony" is practically impossible; and this is the reason why, out of more than thirty attempts, there are scarcely two that agree, and not one that is satisfactory.

The attempt to make *one*, is to ignore the Divine purpose in giving *four*.

No one view could give a true idea of any building; and no one Gospel "Harmony" can include a complete presentation of the Lord's life on earth.

See further on "the Diversity" and "the Unity" of the Four Gospels in Appendixes 96 and 97.

Through failure to recognize this fourfold Divine presentation of the Lord, the term "*Synoptic* Gospels" has been given to the first three, because they are supposed to take one and *the same point of view*, and thus to differ from the fourth Gospel: whereas the difference is caused by the special object of John's Gospel, which is to present the Lord from the Divine standpoint. John's Gospel is thus seen from the Structure above to be essentially one of the *four*, and not one standing apart from the *three*.

THE GOSPEL
ACCORDING TO
MATTHEW.
THE STRUCTURE OF THE BOOK AS A WHOLE.

"BEHOLD THY KING" (Zech. 9. 9).

(*Introversion.*)

A¹ | A | 1. 1—2. 23. PRE-MINISTERIAL.

B | 3. 1-4. THE FORERUNNER.

C | 3. 5-17. THE BAPTISM: WITH WATER.

D | 4. 1-11. THE TEMPTATION: IN THE WILDERNESS.

E | F | 4. 12—7. 29. THE KINGDOM } PROCLAIMED. } THE FOURFOLD MINISTRY OF THE LORD.

G | 8. 1—16. 20. THE KING } PROCLAIMED.

G | 16. 21—20. 34. THE KING } REJECTED.

F | 21. 1—26. 35. THE KINGDOM } REJECTED.

D | 26. 36-46. THE AGONY: IN THE GARDEN.

C | 26. 47—28. 15. THE BAPTISM: OF SUFFERING (DEATH, BURIAL, AND RESURRECTION, 20. 22).

B | 28. 16-18. THE SUCCESSORS.

A | 28. 19, 20. POST-MINISTERIAL.

For the New Testament, and the order of the Books, see Ap. 95.
For the Diversity of the Four Gospels, see Ap. 96.
For the Unity of the Four Gospels, see Ap. 97.
For the Fourfold Ministry of the Lord, see Ap. 119.
For words peculiar to Matthew's Gospel, see some 110 recorded in the notes.

NOTES ON MATTHEW'S GOSPEL.

The Divine purpose in the Gospel by MATTHEW is to set forth the Lord as Jehovah's KING. Hence those events in His ministry are singled out and emphasized which set forth His claims as the Messiah—sent to fulfil all the prophecies concerning Him.

Compared with Mark and Luke, Matthew has no less than thirty-one sections which are peculiar to his Gospel; and all more or less bearing on the King and the Kingdom, which are the special subjects of this Gospel

I. Four events connected with His infancy:

The Visit of the Wise Men (2. 1-15).
The Massacre at Bethlehem (2. 16-18).
The Flight into Egypt (2. 19-22).
The Return to Nazareth (2. 23).

II. Ten Parables:

The Tares (13. 24-30).
The Hid Treasure (13. 44).
The Pearl (13. 45).
The Drag-net (13. 47).
The Unmerciful Servant (18. 23-35).
The Labourers in the Vineyard (20. 1-16).
The Two Sons (21. 28-32).
The Marriage of the King's Son (22. 1-14).
The Ten Virgins (25. 1-13).
The Talents (25. 14-46).

III. Two Miracles:

The Two Blind Men (20. 30-34).
The Coin in the Fish's Mouth (17. 24-27).

IV. Nine Special Discourses:

The Sermon on the Mount (5-7).
The Invitation to the Weary (11. 28-30).
Idle Words (12. 36, 37).
The Revelation to Peter (16. 17-19). See Ap. 147.
Humility and Forgiveness (18. 15-35).
His Rejection of that Generation (21. 43).
The Eight Woes (23. See Ap. 126).
The Prophecy on Olivet (24. 1—25. 46). See Ap. 155.
The Commission and Promise (28. 18-20). See Ap. 167.

V. Six events in connection with His Passion:

The Conspiracy and Suicide of Judas (26. 14-16; 27. 3-11).
The Dream of Pilate's Wife (27. 19).
The Resurrection of Saints after His Resurrection (27. 52, 53).
The suggested Plot about His Body (27. 62-64).
The Watch at the Sepulchre (27. 65, 66).
The Earthquake on the Resurrection Morning (28. 2).

Most of these have to do with the special object of this Gospel. The words and expressions peculiar to this Gospel have the same purpose: such as "the kingdom of heaven", which occurs thirty-two times, and not once in any other Gospel; "Father in heaven", which occurs fifteen times in Matthew, only twice in Mark, and not once in Luke*; "son of David", ten times in Matthew, three in Mark, and three in Luke; "the end of the age", only in Matthew; "that it might be fulfilled which was spoken", nine times in Matthew, and nowhere else; "that which was spoken", or "it was spoken", fourteen times in Matthew, and nowhere else.† Altogether, Matthew has sixty references to the Old Testament, for the Law and the Prophets were fulfilled in the coming of the Messiah. The verb *rheō* occurs twenty times in Matthew (fourteen times of the prophets, and six times in the Sermon on the Mount, rendered "say", Matt. 5. 21, 27, 31, 33, 38, 43).

The question of modern critics as to the source whence the Evangelists got their material does not arise; for, as in the case of Luke (1. 3), it was revealed to them "from above" (Gr. *anōthen*); see note there. Hence the Divine purpose in Luke is to present the Lord not merely as "perfect God" (as in Luke 1. 32-35 and in John); but as "perfect man", full of human tenderness and compassion. Hence also the early chapters concerning His birth and infancy in Luke's Gospel.

---

* Luke 11. 2, "which is in heaven", being omitted by all the critical texts. See Ap. 94. VII.
† Mark 13. 14, "spoken of by Daniel the prophet", being omitted by all the critical texts. See Ap. 94. VII.

°THE °GOSPEL

°ACCORDING TO

°MATTHEW.

A A C a (p. 1307) 1 ° THE ° book of the ° generation of ° Jesus
Christ,
b ° the Son of David,
c ° the Son of Abraham.
D 2 °Abraham ° begat Isaac; and Isaac ° begat
° Jacob; and Jacob ° begat ° Judas ° and his
brethren;
3 And [2] Judas [2] begat ° Phares and Zara of
° Thamar; and Phares [2] begat ° Esrom; and
Esrom [2] begat °Aram;
4 And Aram [2] begat °Aminadab; and Aminadab [2] begat ° Naasson; and Naasson [2] begat
° Salmon;
5 And Salmon [2] begat ° Booz of ° Rachab;
and Booz [2] begat ° Obed of Ruth; and Obed
[2] begat ° Jesse;
6 And Jesse [2] begat ° David the king;

TITLE. The. The titles of the N.T. books in the A.V. and R.V. form no part of the books themselves in the original text.

Gospel. Anglo-Saxon Godspell = a narrative of God: i.e. a life of Christ. The English word "Gospel" has no connection with the Greek *euaggelion*, which denotes good news, and was in use as = joyful tidings, &c., B.C. 9, in an inscription in the market-place of Priene (now *Samsun Kalē*, an ancient city of Ionia, near Mycale), and in a letter (papyrus) 250 years later; both are now in the Royal Library in Berlin.

according to = i.e. recorded by. Gr. *kata*. Ap. 104. x. The title "Saint", as given in the A.V. and R.V., is a mistranslation of the headings found only in the later MSS., which are derived from Church lectionaries; and should have been rendered "THE HOLY GOSPEL ACCORDING TO MATTHEW". The R.V. reads "The Gospel according to Matthew"; L Tr. T and WH read "according to Matthew"; B omits the word *hagion* = holy.

Matthew. See Ap. 141.

1. 1—2. 23 (**A**, p. 1305). PRE-MINISTERIAL. (*Alternation.*)

A | A | 1. 1-17. Concerning others. Ancestors.
  B | 1. 18-25. Concerning Jesus Christ. Birth in the Land.
  A | 2. 1-12. Concerning others. The Wise Men.
  B | 2. 13-23. Concerning Jesus Christ. Flight from the Land.

1. 1-17 (A, above). CONCERNING OTHERS. ANCESTORS. (*Introversion.*)

A | C | a | 1-. Jesus Christ. } In Sum. Ascent.
  b | -1-. David.
  c | -1. Abraham.
    D | 2-6-. The Lay Ancestors: Abraham to David (1 Sam. 16. 13). Fourteen Generations (*v.* 17). } In Detail.
      E | -6-11. The Royal, or Crowned, Ancestors: David (2 Sam. 5. 3-5) to Josiah. Fourteen Generations (*v.* 17).
    D | 12-16. The Lay Ancestors: Jeconiah to Christ. Fourteen Generations (*v.* 17).
  C | *c* | 17-. Abraham. } In Sum. Descent.
  b | -17-. David.
  a | -17. Jesus Christ.

1 The. No Art. in the Greek, but required in English. **book** = scroll, as in Gen. 5. 1 (Sept.). See notes on Gen. 2. 4, and 5. 1; and on the Structure of Genesis, p. 1. Occurs only in connection with the first man and the second man (Gen. 5. 1 and Matt. 1. 1). **generation** = genealogy or pedigree. See Ap. 99. The same meaning as the Heb. expression (Gen. 5. 1). **Jesus Christ:** i.e. the humbled One now exalted. See Ap. 98. XI. **the Son of David.** Because promised directly to David (2 Sam. 7. 12, 16). The expression occurs nine times of Christ in Matt. (1. 1; 9. 27; 12. 23; 15. 22; 20. 30, 31; 21. 9, 15; 22. 42). Cp. Ps. 132. 11. Isa. 11. 1. Jer. 23. 5. Acts 13. 23. Rom. 1. 3. David, heir to the throne. Ap. 98. XVIII. The name of David is in the commencement of the N.T. and in the end also (Rev. 22. 16). **the Son of Abraham.** Because promised to him (Luke 1. 73), and received with joy by him as by David (John 8. 56. Matt. 22. 43). Cp. Gen. 12. 3; 22. 18. Gal. 3. 16. Heir to the land (Gen. 15. 18). Ap. 98. XVII. **2 Abraham.** Gen. 21. 2, 3. Rom. 9. 7, 9. **begat.** Gr. *gennaō*. When used of the father = *to beget* or *engender*; and when used of the mother it means *to bring forth into the world*; but it has not the intermediate sense, *to conceive.* In *vv.* 2-16- it is translated *begat*, and should be so in *vv.* -16 and 20 also. In 1. 1 the noun *genesis* means birth. **Jacob.** Gen. 25. 26. **Judas** = Judah. Gen. 29. 35; 49. 10. **and his brethren.** Because the promise was restricted to the house of Judah; not extended to the whole house of Abraham or of Isaac. **3 Phares and Zara.** Heb. Pharez and Zarah. Twins. Gen. 38. 29, 30. **Thamar.** Gen. 38. 11-30. The first of four women in this genealogy. The other three were Rahab, *v.* 5; Ruth, *v.* 5; Bathsheba, *v.* 6. Note the *Introversion*:—Hebrew, Gentile; Gentile, Hebrew: showing the condescension of Christ in taking our nature. **Esrom.** Heb. Hezron. 1 Chron. 2. 4, 5. **Aram.** Heb. Ram. Ruth 4. 19. 1 Chron. 2. 11. **4 Aminadab** = Amminadab. Ruth 4. 19. 1 Chron. 2. 10. **Naasson.** Heb. Nahshon. Ruth 4. 20. Ex. 6. 23. **Salmon.** Heb. Salma. **5 Booz.** Heb. Boaz. Ruth 4. 21. 1 Chron. 2. 12. **Rachab.** Eng. Rahab. Josh. 2. 1; 6. 25. See note on Thamar, *v.* 3. **Obed of Ruth.** Ruth 4. 21. 1 Chron. 2. 12. **Jesse.** Ruth 4. 22. 1 Chron. 2. 12. **6 David the king.** Ruth 4. 22. This addition to the name of David is because of the object of Matthew's Gospel. See the Structure on p. 1305. Luke 1. 32.

E (p. 1307) and David °the king [2] begat ° Solomon of ° her
that had been the wife of ° Urias ;
7 And Solomon [2] begat ° Roboam ; and Roboam [2] begat °Abia ; and Abia [2] begat ° Asa ;
8 And Asa [2] begat °Josaphat ; and Josaphat
[2] begat ° Joram ; and Joram [2] begat ° Ozias ;
9 And Ozias [2] begat °Joatham ; and Joatham
[2] begat °Achaz ; and Achaz [2] begat ° Ezekias ;
10 And Ezekias [2] begat ° Manasses ; and Manasses [2] begat °Amon ; and Amon [2] begat °Josias ;
11 And Josias [2] begat ° Jechonias and his
brethren, about the time °they were carried
away to Babylon :

D 12 And after ° they were brought to Babylon,
° Jechonias [2] begat ° Salathiel ; and Salathiel
[2] begat ° Zorobabel ;
13 And Zorobabel [2] begat Abiud ; and Abiud
[2] begat Eliakim ; and Eliakim [2] begat Azor ;
14 And Azor [2] begat Sadoc ; and Sadoc [2] begat Achim ; and Achim [2] begat Eliud ;
15 And Eliud [2] begat Eleazar ; and Eleazar
[2] begat Matthan ; and Matthan [2] begat Jacob ;
16 And Jacob [2] begat Joseph the husband of
Mary, °of whom was °born °Jesus, Who is
called °Christ.

C c 17 °So °all °the generations from [1] Abraham
to [1] David *are* °fourteen generations ;

b and from [1] David until the [11] carrying away
into Babylon *are* fourteen generations ;

a and from the carrying away into Babylon
unto [16] Christ *are* fourteen generations.

B F (p. 1308) 5 B.C. 18 ° Now the °birth of °Jesus Christ was °on
this wise : When as His mother ° Mary °was
espoused to Joseph, °before they °came together, she was found with child of °the Holy
Ghost.

the king. Omitted by all the critical Greek texts enumerated and named in Ap. 94. VII.

Solomon. 2 Sam. 12. 24. The line in Matthew is the regal line through Solomon, exhausted in Joseph. The line in Luke is the legal line through Nathan, an elder brother (2 Sam. 5. 14), exhausted in Mary. If Christ be not risen, therefore, all prophecies must fail.

her, &c. See note on Thamar, *v.* 3.

Urias = Uriah (2 Sam. 12. 24).

7 Roboam = Rehoboam (1 Kings 11. 43). Note that in this case and in the three following :—Rehoboam (a bad father) begat a bad son (Abijah) ; Abijah (a bad father) begat a good son (Asa) ; Asa (a good father) begat a good son (Jehoshaphat) ; Jehoshaphat (a good father) begat a bad son (Jehoram).

Abia = Abijam (1 Kings 14. 31) ; Abijah (2 Chron. 12. 16). See note on *v.* 7.

Asa. 1 Kings 15. 8.

8 Josaphat = Jehoshaphat (2 Chron. 17-18).

Joram = Jehoram (2 Kings 8. 16. 2 Chron. 21. 1). Three names are omitted here. All are not necessary in a royal genealogy. In *v.* 1 three names are sufficient. The four names are : 1. Ahaziah (2 Kings 8. 27. 2 Chron. 22. 1-9). 2. Joash or Jehoash (2 Kings 11. 2—12. 20. 2 Chron. 24. 1-25). 3. Amaziah (2 Kings 14. 8-20. 2 Chron. 25. 1, 8). 4. Jehoiakim (2 Kings 23. 36—24. 6. 2 Chron. 36. 5-8).

Ozias = Uzziah (2 Chron. 26. 1), or Azariah (2 Kings 14. 21).

9 Joatham = Jotham (2 Kings 15. 7. 2 Chron. 26. 23).

Achaz = Ahaz (2 Kings 15. 38. 2 Chron. 27. 9).

Ezekias = Hezekiah (2 Kings 16. 20. 2 Chron. 28. 27).

10 Manasses = Manasseh. (2 Kings 20. 21. 2 Chron. 32. 33.)

Amon. (2 Kings 21. 18. 2 Chron. 33. 20.)

Josias = Josiah (2 Kings 21. 24. 2 Chron. 33. 25).

11 Jechonias = Jehoiachin (2 Kings 24. 8).

they were carried away = removed. Gk. *metoikesia* = the Babylonian transference. A standing term. Occurs only in Matt. It began with Jehoiakim, was continued in Jechoniah, and completed in Zedekiah (2 Kings 24 and 25. 2 Chron. 36).

12 they were brought = the carrying away, as in *v.* 11. Jechonias, Jer. 22. 30, does not say "no sons"; but, "no sons to sit on the throne of David". **Salathiel** = Shealtiel, the real son of Assir ; and hence was the grandson of Jeconiah (1 Chron. 3. 17-19), born "after" (see *v.* 12). **Zorobabel.** The real son of Pedaiah (1 Chron. 3. 19), but the legal son of Salathiel (cp. Deut. 25. 5). See Ezra 3. 2 ; 5. 2. Neh. 12. 1.

16 of whom. Gr. *ex hēs*, fem. [Mary]. **born** = brought forth. Gr. *gennaō*. Spoken, here, of the mother. See note on "begat" (*v.* 2). **Jesus.** See Ap. 98. X. **Christ** = Anointed. Heb. Messiah. See Ap. 98. IX.

17 So. Verse 17 is the Fig *Symperasma*. Ap. 6. **all the generations.** See the Structure D, E, *D*, above. The *first* begins with the call of Abraham, and ends with the call of David the layman (1 Sam. 16. 13). The *second* begins with the building of the Temple, and ends with the destruction of it. The *third* begins with the nation under the power of Babylon, and ends with it under the power of Rome (the first and fourth of the world-powers of Dan. 2). **the** : i. e. the generations given above, not all recorded in the O.T. **fourteen.** It is not stated that there were forty-two, but three fourteens are reckoned in a special manner, as shown in the Structure above. Note the three divisions of the whole period, as in the seventy weeks of Daniel (Dan. 9. Ap. 91).

1. 18-25 (B, p. 1307). CONCERNING JESUS CHRIST. HIS BIRTH. (*Introversion.*)

B | F | 18, 19. Begetting.
  G | 20. The angel of Jehovah.
    H | 21. Prophecy delivered.
    H | 22, 23. Prophecy quoted.
  G | 24. The angel of Jehovah.
F | 25. Birth.

18 Now : or, But, in contrast with those mentioned in *vv.* 2-16. Render : "The begetting, then, of Jesus Christ was on this wise (for after His mother was espoused to Joseph, she was found with child) of *pneuma hagion*". See Ap. 101. II. 14. **birth** = begetting. Gr. *gennēsis.* Occ. only here and Luke 1. 14, used of the Father. This verse is quoted by Irenæus (A. D. 178). **Jesus** (Om. by Tr. [WH] Rm.) **Christ.** Heb. Messiah. So translated in John 1. 41 ; 4. 25. See Ap. 98. XI. **on this wise** : i. e. not begotten, as in the cases recorded in *vv.* 2-16. **Mary.** See Ap. 100 for the six of this name in N.T. **was espoused** = had been betrothed. By divine ordering, so that the two lines, through Solomon and Nathan, might be united and exhausted in Messiah. **before.** Gr. *prin.* Occ. seven times (26. 34, 75. Mark 14. 72. Luke 22. 61. John 4. 49 ; 8. 58 ; 14. 9) ; *prin ē*, occ. seven times (Matt. 1. 18. Mark 14. 30. Luke 2. 26 ; 22. 34. Acts 2. 20 ; 7. 2 ; 25. 16). In eleven of the fourteen passages where this word occurs the events *did take place.* In the other three, one was miraculously prevented (John 4. 49) ; the day of the Lord is absolutely certain (Acts 2. 20) ; the other was legally imperative (Acts 25. 16). **came together** : as in 1 Cor. 7. 5. **the Holy Ghost.** Gr. *pneuma hagion* = holy spirit : i. e. power from on high. Not "the Holy Spirit". See Ap. 101. III. 14.

5 B.C. 19 Then Joseph her husband, °being a just *man,* °and °not °willing to °make 𝔥𝔢𝔯 a publick example,° was minded to °put her away °privily.

G (p. 1308) 20 But while °he thought on °these things, °behold, °the °angel of °the LORD °appeared unto him in °a dream, saying, "Joseph, thou [1]son of David, °fear [19]not to take unto thee Mary thy wife: for That Which is °conceived in her is of [11]the Holy Ghost.

H 21 And she shall °bring forth a Son, and thou shalt call °His name °JESUS: for °𝔥𝔢 shall save His People from their °sins."

H 22 Now °all this was done, that it might be °fulfilled which was °spoken °of [20]the LORD °by the prophet, saying,

23 [20]"**Behold, °a virgin shall be with child, and shall [21]bring forth a Son, and they shall call [21]His name °Emmanuel,** which being interpreted is, °**God with us.**"

G 24 Then Joseph being raised from sleep did as [20]the angel of [20]the LORD had bidden him, and took unto him his wife:

F 25 And °knew her °not °till she had [21]brought forth °her firstborn Son: and °he called [21]His name [21]JESUS.

A J (p. 1309) 4 B.C. 2 Now when °Jesus was born °in °Bethlehem of Judæa °in the days of °Herod the king, °behold, there came °wise men from the °east °to Jerusalem,

19 being a just man = though he was a just man (i.e. desirous of obeying the Law).
and = yet. **not.** Gr. *mē.* Ap. 105. II.
not willing = not wishing. Gr. *thelō.* See Ap. 102. 1.
to make 𝔥𝔢𝔯 a publick example = to expose her to shame. L T Tr. A WH read *deigmatizō* instead of *paradeigmatizō.* Occurs only here and in Col. 2. 15. This exposure would have necessitated her being stoned to death, according to the Law (Deut. 22. 22). Cp. John 8. 5.
was minded = made up his mind, or determined. Gr. *boulomai.* See Ap. 102. 2.
put her away = divorce her according to the Law (Deut. 24. 1).
privily = secretly. By putting a "bill of divorcement into her hand" (Deut. 24. 1).
20 he thought: i.e. pondered about or contemplated this step. This was Satan's assault, as he had assaulted Abraham before (Gen. 12. 11-13). See Ap. 23.
these things. The two courses open to him in *v.* 19.
behold. Fig. *Asterismos.* Ap. 6.
the angel of the LORD. The first of three appearances to Joseph in these chapters, G and *G*, p. 1308 (1. 20, 24; 2. 13, 19).
angel = messenger. The context must always show whether human or Divine.
the LORD = Jehovah. No Art. See Ap. 98. VI. i. *a* 1. B. b.
appeared. Gr. *phainō.* See Ap. 105. I.
a dream. Gr. *onar.* Occurs only in Matt. (here; 2. 12, 13, 19, 22; and 27. 19). Only six dreams mentioned in N.T. To Joseph (Matt. 1. 20; 2. 13, 19, 22); to the wise men (Matt. 2. 12); and to Pilate's wife (Matt. 27. 19).
fear not = Be not afraid. This shows his condition of mind.
conceived = begotten. Gr. *gennaō,* as in *vv.* 2, 16, 18.
21 bring forth. Not the same word as in *vv.* 2, 16, 20. Gr. *tiktō.* Not "of thee" as in Luke 1. 35, because not Joseph's son. **His name.** Fig. *Pleonasm.* Ap. 6 = Him. **JESUS.** For this type see Ap. 48. The same as the Heb. Hoshea (Num. 13. 16) with Jah prefixed = God [our] Saviour, or God Who [is] salvation. Cp. Luke 2. 21. See Ap. 98. X. **𝔥𝔢** = He, and none other, or He is the One Who (emph.). **sins.** Gk. *hamartia.* See Ap. 128. II. i. **22 all** = the whole of. **fulfilled.** See Ap. 103 for the first fulfilment of prophecy in the N.T. **spoken.** Gr. *to rhēthen.* By Isaiah to Ahaz (Isa. 7. 13-16), but afterwards written. **of** = by. Gr. *hupo.* Ap. 104. xviii. 1. **by** = through, or by means of. Gr. *dia.* Ap. 104. v. 1. **23 a virgin.** Quoted from Isa. 7. 13-15. See the notes there. Gr. *parthenos,* which settles the meaning of the word in Isa. 7. 14. See Ap. 103, and 107. I. i. **Emmanuel.** Occurs only in Matt. See Ap. 98. VII. **God.** See Ap. 98. I. **25 knew her.** Heb. idiom, and Fig. *Metonymy* (of Adjunct) for cohabitation. Note the imperfect tense = was not knowing. See Ap. 132. I. ii. **not.** Gr. *ou.* Ap. 105. I. **till.** Matt. 12. 46-50; 13. 55, 56, clearly show that she had sons afterwards. See the force of this word *heōs* in Matt. 28. 20, "unto". **her firstborn Son.** These words are quoted by Tatian (A.D. 172) and twelve of the Fathers before cent. 4; and are contained in nearly all MSS. except the Vatican and Sinaitic (cent. 4). All the Texts omit "her firstborn" on this weak and suspicious evidence. But there is no question about it in Luke 2. 7. **he**: i.e. Joseph.

2. 1-12 (*A*, p. 1307). CONCERNING OTHERS. THE WISE MEN.
(*Introversion and Alternation.*)

```
A | J | 1. The Wise Men. Arrival.
  |   K | 2. The Star. Notification.
  |     L | 3. Herod hears of the Wise Men.
  |       M | d | 4. His Question to Rulers. "Where?"
  |         |   e | 5, 6. Their Answer.
  |       M | d | 7-. His Question to the Wise Men. "What Time?"
  |         |   e | -7, 8. Their Mission.
  |     L | 9-. Wise Men hear Herod.
  |   K | -9-11. The Star. Guiding.
  | J | 12. The Wise Men. Departure.
```

1 Jesus. See Ap. 98. X. **in.** Gr. *en.* Ap. 104. viii. **Bethlehem** = house of bread. Now *Beit Lahm,* five miles south of Jerusalem. One of the fenced cities of Rehoboam, originally called Ephrath (Gen. 35. 16, 19). **Herod the king.** To distinguish him from other Herods. See Ap. 109. **behold.** Fig. *Asterismos* (Ap. 6), for emphasis. **wise men.** Gr. *magoi.* It nowhere says they were Gentiles, or that there were only three, or whether they were priests or kings. The "adoration of the Magi" must have taken place at Nazareth, for the Lord was presented in the Temple forty-one days after His birth (8 + 33 days. Lev. 12. 3, 4. Cp. Luke 2. 21-24), and thence *returned* to Nazareth (Luke 2. 39). Ap. 169. There, in "the house" (Matt. 2. 11), not "in a stable" at Bethlehem, they found the Lord. They did not return to Jerusalem from Nazareth (Matt. 2. 12); but, being well on their way home, easily escaped from Herod. Herod, having enquired *accurately* as to the time, fixed on "two years" (Matt. 2. 16), which would have thus been about the age of the Lord. After the flight to Egypt, He *returned* once more to Nazareth (Matt. 2. 23). This chapter (Matt. 2) comes between Luke 2. 39 and 40. **east.** North and south are always in Greek only in sing. East and west are relative to the north and therefore occur in the plural also. **to Jerusalem.** The most likely place.

K (p. 1309) 4 B. C. 2 Saying, ° "Where is He That ° is born King of the Jews? for ° we have seen ° His star [1] in the [1] east, and ° are come to ° worship Him."

L 3 ° When [1] Herod the king ° had heard *these things,* he ° was troubled, and ° all Jerusalem with him.

M d 4 And when he had gathered all the ° chief priests and ° scribes of the People together, he ° demanded of them ° where ° Christ should be born.

e 5 And they said unto him, [1] "In [1] Bethlehem of Judæa: for thus it is ° written ° by the prophet,

6 **'And thou [1] Bethlehem, *in* the land of ° Juda, ° art ° not the least ° among the ° princes of ° Juda: for ° out of thee shall ° come a Governor, That shall ° rule My People Israel.'"**

M d 7 Then [1] Herod, when he had ° privily called the [1] wise men,

e ° enquired of them ° diligently ° what time ° the star ° appeared.

8 And he sent them to [1] Bethlehem, and said, "Go and search [7] diligently ° for the ° young Child; and when ye have found *Him,* bring me word again, ° that I may come and [2] worship Him also."

L 9 When they ° had heard the king, they ° departed;

K and, ° lo, the star, which ° they saw [2] in the east, ° went before them, ° till it ° came and stood over where the [8] young Child was.

10 When they ° saw the star, they ° rejoiced with exceeding great joy.

11 And when they were come ° into the house, they saw the [8] young ° Child with ° Mary His mother, and fell down, and [2] worshipped ° Him: and when they had opened their ° treasures, they presented unto Him gifts; ° gold, and frankincense, and myrrh.

J 12 And being ° warned of God ° in ° a dream that they should ° not return ° to [1] Herod, they ° departed [11] into their own country ° another way.

B N[1] f (p. 1311) 13 And when they ° were [12] departed, [1] behold,

2 Where . . . ? This is the first question in the N.T. See note on the first question in the O.T. (Gen. 3. 9).
is born = has been brought forth : see note on 1. 2.
we have seen = we saw : i.e. we being in the east saw.
His star. All questions are settled if we regard this as miraculous. Cp. Num. 24. 15-19.
are come = we came.
worship = do homage. Gr. *proskuneō.* See Ap. 137. i.
3 When = But.
had heard = on hearing.
was troubled. The enemy used this for another attempt to prevent the fulfilment of Gen. 3. 15. See Ap. 23.
all Jerusalem. Fig. *Synecdoche* (of the Whole), Ap. 6. = most of the people at Jerusalem at that time.
4 chief priests, &c.: i.e. the high priest and other priests who were members of the Sanhedrin, or National Council.
scribes of the People = the *Sōpherim,* denoting the learned men of the People ; learned in the Scriptures, and elders of the Sanhedrin. This incident shows that intellectual knowledge of the Scriptures without experimental delight in them is useless. Here it was used by Herod to compass Christ's death (cp. Luke 22. 66). The scribes had no desire toward the person of the "Governor", whereas the wise men were truly wise, in that they sought the person of Him of Whom the Scriptures spoke and were soon found at His feet. Head-knowledge without heart-love may be used against Christ.
demanded = kept enquiring.
where, &c. This was the first of the two important questions : the other being "what time", &c., *v.* 7.
Christ = the Messiah. See Ap. 98. IX.
5 written = standeth written. Not spoken, as in *v.* 23. Quoted from Mic. 5. 2. See Ap. 107. II. 3 b.
by = by means of. Gr. *dia.* Ap. 104. v. 1.
6 Juda = Judah.
art not the least. Fig. *Tapeinōsis* (Ap. 6), in order to magnify the place.
not = by no means. Gr. *oudamōs.* Occurs only here.
among. See Ap. 104. viii. 2.
princes. Put by the Fig. *Metonymy* (of Subject), Ap. 6, for the "thousands" (or divisions) which they led.
out. Gr. *ek.* Ap. 104. vii. See note on Mic. 5. 2.
come = come forth, not "come unto", as in Zech. 9. 9.
rule = shepherd. Rulers were so called because this was their office.
7 privily = secretly.
enquired . . . diligently = enquired . . . accurately. Cp. Deut. 19. 18. Gr. *akriboō.* Occ. only here and in *v.* 16.
what time, &c. This was the second of the two important questions : the other being "where" (*v.* 4). **the star appeared** = the time of the appearing star. **appeared** = shone forth. See Ap. 106. I. i. **8 for** = concerning. **young Child.** Gr. *paidion.* Ap. 108. v. **that I may come** = that I also may come. Not "Him also" as well as others, but "I also" as well as you. **9 had heard** = having heard. **departed :** to Nazareth (not to Bethlehem). Ap. 169. **lo.** Fig. *Asterismos.* Ap. 6 (for emphasis). **they saw.** When in the east. See *v.* 2. **went before** = kept going before (Imperfect). Therefore not an astronomical phenomenon, but a miraculous and Divine act. **till.** Implying both distance and time. **came** = went : i.e. to Nazareth. See *v.* 1. **10 saw the star.** Supply the Ellipsis from *v.* 9 (Ap. 6) = "having seen the star [standing over where the young child was], they rejoiced", &c. **rejoiced with . . . joy.** Fig. *Polyptōton* (Ap. 6), for emphasis. **11 into.** Gr. *eis.* Ap. 104. vi. **into the house.** Not therefore at Bethlehem, for that would have been into the stable. See note on *v.* 1. There is no "discrepancy" here. **Child.** Gr. *paidion.* See Ap. 108. v. **Mary.** See Ap. 100. **Him.** Not Mary. **treasures** = receptacles or treasure cases. **gold, &c.** From *three* gifts being mentioned tradition concluded that there were three men. But it does not say so, nor that they were kings. These presents supplied their immediate needs. **12 warned of God** = oracularly answered, implying a preceding question. Cp. *v.* 22. **in.** Gr. *kata.* Ap. 104. x. 2. **a dream.** Gr. *onar.* See note on Matt. 1. 20. **not.** Gr. *mē.* Ap. 105. II. **to** = unto. Gr. *pros.* Ap. 104. xv. 3. **departed** = returned. **another** = by another, as in *v.* 5.

2. 13-23 [For Structure see next page].

13 were departed = had withdrawn or retired.

4 B. C. °the angel of °the LORD [7]appeareth to Joseph [12]in a dream,

g (p. 1311) saying, "Arise, and °take the [8]young Child and His mother, and flee [11]into Egypt, and be thou there until I bring thee word: for [1]Herod °will seek the [8]young Child to destroy Him."

h 14 When he arose, he °took the [8]young Child and His mother by night, and [13]departed [11]into Egypt:

i 15 And was there until the °death of [1]Herod:

O1 °that it might be fulfilled which was °spoken °of [13]the LORD [5]by the prophet, saying, °"**Out of Egypt °have I called My Son.**"

N2 16 Then [1]Herod, when he °saw that he was °mocked [15]of the wise men, was exceeding °wroth, and sent forth, and slew °all the °children that were [1]in [1]Bethlehem, and [1]in all the °coasts thereof, from °two years old and under, according to the time which he had [7]diligently enquired °of the wise men.

O2 17 Then was fulfilled that which was °spoken °by °Jeremy the prophet, saying,
18 [1]"**In °Rama was there a voice heard, °lamentation, and weeping, and great mourning, Rachel weeping *for* her °children, and would °not be comforted, because they are °not.**"

N3 f 19 But when [1]Herod was dead, behold, an [13]angel of [13]the LORD [7]appeareth [12]in a dream to Joseph [1]in Egypt,

g 20 Saying, "Arise, and [13]take the [8]young Child and His mother, and go [11]into the land of Israel: for °they are dead which sought the [8]young Child's °life."

h 21 And he arose, and [14]took the [8]young Child and His mother, and came [11]into the land of Israel.

i 22 But when he heard that °Archelaus did reign °in Judæa °in the room of his father [1]Herod, he was afraid to go thither: notwithstanding, being [12]warned of God [12]in a dream, he °turned aside [11]into the parts of °Galilee:
23 And he came and °dwelt °in a city called °Nazareth:

O3 °that it might be fulfilled which was °spoken [5]by the prophets, "**He shall be called a Nazarene.**"

B P (p. 1312) Q j A. D. 26 3 °In those days °came °John the Baptist, °preaching °in the °wilderness of Judæa,

2. 13-23 (*B*, p. 1307). CONCERNING JESUS CHRIST. FLIGHT FROM THE LAND.
(*Repeated and Extended Alternation.*)

B | N1 | f | 13-. The Angel. } Event.
g | -13. His Command to Joseph. } Event.
h | 14. Joseph's Obedience. } Event.
i | 15-. Christ's abode. Egypt. } Event.
O1 | -15. Prophecy fulfilled.
N2 | 16. Herod's wrath and crime. Event.
O2 | 17, 18. Prophecy fulfilled.
N3 | *f* | 19. The Angel. } Event.
g | 20. His Command. } Event.
h | 21. Joseph's Obedience. } Event.
i | 22, 23-. Christ's abode. Nazareth. } Event.
O3 | -23. Prophecy fulfilled.

the angel. See note on 1. 20.
the LORD. Here denotes Jehovah. See Ap. 98. VI. i. *a.* 1. B. b, and 4. II. Divine interposition was needed to defeat the designs of the enemy; and guidance was given only as and when needed. Cp. *vv.* 20, 22. See Ap. 23.
take = take with [thee].
will seek = is on the point of seeking.
14 took = took with [him].
15 death = end. Gr. *teleutē.* Occ. only here.
that = in order that.
spoken. As well as written. Cp. *vv.* 5 and 23.
of = by. Gr. *hupo.* See Ap. 104. xviii. 1.
Out of Egypt, &c. Quoted from Hos. 11. 1. See Ap. 107. I. 3.
Out. Ap. 104. vii. **have I called** = did I call.
16 saw. Ap. 133. I. 1.
mocked = deceived.
wroth. Gr. *thumoōmai.* Occ. only here.
all. The number could not have been great.
children = boys. Pl. of *pais.* Ap. 108. iv.
coasts = borders.
two years. Gr. *dietēs.* Occ. only in Matthew. It was now nearly two years since the birth at Bethlehem. Herod had inquired very accurately, *v.* 7. See notes on *vv.* 1 and 11. The wise men found a *pais*, not a *brephos* (see Ap. 108. iv and viii), as the shepherds did (Luke 2. 16).
of = from. Gr. *para.* Ap. 104. xii. 1.
17 spoken. As well as written.
by = by means of. Gr. *hupo* (Ap. 104. xviii), but all the critical texts read *dia.* Ap. 104. v. 1.
Jeremy = Jeremiah. Quoted from Jer. 31. 15. See Ap. 107. i. 3.
18 Rama = Ramah in O.T., now *er-Ram*, five miles north of Jerusalem.
lamentation. Gr. *thrēnos.* Occ. only here.
children. Gr. pl. of *teknon.* Ap. 108. I.
not. Gr. *ou.* Ap. 105. I.
20 they. Note the Fig. *Heterōsis* (of Number), Ap. 6, by which the pl. is put for the sing.: i. e. Herod.
life = the soul. Gr. *ē psuchē.* See Ap. 110. III.
22 Archelaus. See Ap. 109.
in = over. Gr. *epi.* See Ap. 104. ix. 1. L T [Tr.] [A] WH omit *epi.*
in the room of = instead of. Gr. *anti.* Ap. 104. ii.
turned aside = departed, as in *vv.* 12, 13.
Galilee. The region north of Samaria, including the Plain of Esdraelon and mountains north of it. Ap. 169.
23 dwelt = settled. **in.** Gr. *eis.* Ap. 104. vi.
Nazareth. His former residence. Ap. 169. The Aramaic name. See Ap. 94. III. 3. See note on *vv.* 1, 11, 16, and Luke 2. 39. **that** = so that. **spoken.** It does not say "written". It is not "an unsolved difficulty", as alleged. The prophecy had been uttered by more than one prophet; therefore the reference to the Heb. *nēzer* (= a branch) is useless, as it is used of Christ only by Isaiah (Isa. 11. 1; 60. 21), and it was "spoken" by "the prophets" (pl.). Note the Fig. *Hysterēsis.* Ap. 6.

3. 1-4 [For Structure see next page].

1 In = And in. Gr. *en de.* See Ap. 104. viii. 2. **In those days.** Heb. idiom for an indefinite time (Ex. 2. 11, 23. Isa. 38. 1, &c.): while the Lord, being grown up, was still dwelling in Nazareth. Ap. 169. Cp. 2. 23. **came.** Gr. comes: i. e. presenteth himself. **came John, &c.** Because "the word of God" had come to him (Luke 3. 2). **John the Baptist** = John the baptizer. **preaching** = proclaiming as a herald. Ap. 121. 1. **in.** Gr. *en.* Ap. 104. viii. 1. **wilderness** = country parts, which were not without towns or villages. David passed much of his time there. So John, probably in some occupation also; John now thirty years old. He was the last and greatest of the prophets, and would have been reckoned as Elijah himself, or as an Elijah (Matt. 11. 14. Cp. Mal. 3. 1; 4. 5) had the nation obeyed his proclamation.

26 k (p. 1312) **2** And saying, ° "Repent ye: for ° the kingdom ° of ° heaven ° is at hand."

R **3** For this is he that was ° spoken of ° by the prophet ° Esaias,

Q j saying, ° "**The voice of one crying in the [1] wilderness,**

k '**Prepare ye the way of ° the LORD, make His paths straight.'**"

P **4** And the same John ° had his raiment of camel's hair, and a ° leathern girdle about his loins; and his ° meat was ° locusts and wild honey.

C S l **5** Then went out ° to him ° Jerusalem, and ° all ° Judæa, and ° all the region round about Jordan,

m **6** And ° were ° baptized ° of him [1] in Jordan, confessing their ° sins.

T **7** But when he ° saw many of the ° Pharisees and Sadducees ° come ° to his ° baptism, he said unto them, "O ° generation of ° vipers, ° who hath ° warned *you* to flee ° from ° the wrath ° to come?

8 Bring forth therefore fruits ° meet for [2] repentance:

9 And ° think ° not to say ° within yourselves, ° 'We have Abraham to *our* father:' for I say unto you, that ° God is able ° of these stones to raise up ° children unto Abraham.

T n **10** And ° now ° also the ax ° is laid ° unto the root of the trees: therefore every tree which bringeth [9] not forth good fruit ° is hewn down, and cast ° into the fire.

o **11** I indeed [5] baptize you ° with water [10] unto repentance:

p but He That cometh ° after me is mightier than I, Whose ° shoes I am ° not ° worthy to ° bear:

3. 1-4 (**B**, p. 1305). THE FORERUNNER.
(*Introversion and Alternation.*)

B | P | 1-. John. Time.
  Q | j | -1. His Proclamation.
    k | 2. Subject. Repentance.
   R | 3-. Isaiah.
  Q | *j* | -3-. His cry.
    k | -3. Subject. Preparation.
 P | 4. John. Manner.

2 Repent. Gr. *metanoeō*. See Ap. 111. 1.
the kingdom of heaven. See Ap. 114.
of. Gen. of origin = from. Ap. 17. 2.
heaven = the heavens (pl.). See note on 6. 9, 10.
is at hand = had drawn nigh. What draws nigh may withdraw. See 21. 43. Acts 1. 6; 3. 20.
3 spoken. As well as written.
by. Gr. *hupo*. Ap. 104. xviii. 1, but all the Greek texts read "*dia*". Ap. 104. v. 1.
Esaias = Isaiah. The first of twenty-one occurrences of the name in N.T. See Ap. 79.
The voice, &c. Quoted from Isa. 40. 3. See note there. Ap. 107. I. 1.
the LORD = Jehovah in Isa. 40. 3. See Ap. 98. VI. i. *a*. 1. B. b.
4 had his raiment, &c. Cp. 2 Kings 1. 8.
leathern girdle. Worn to-day by peasants in Palestine.
meat = food.
locusts. Locusts form the food of the people to-day; and, being provided for in the Law, are "clean". See Lev. 11. 22.

3. 5-17 (**C**, p. 1305). BAPTISM.
(*Introversion and Alternation.*)

C | S | l | 5. The Coming of the People to John.
   m | 6. Their Baptism.
  T | 7-9. John's Warning.
  T | 10-12. John's Threatening.
 S | *l* | 13. The Coming of Messiah to John.
   m | 14-17. His Baptism.

5 to = unto. Gr. *pros*. Ap. 104. xv. 3.
Jerusalem . . . Judæa. Put by Fig. *Metonymy* (of Subject), Ap. 6, for their inhabitants. **all.** Put by Fig. *Synecdochē* (of Genus), Ap. 6, for the greater part. **all the region.** Put by Fig. *Synecdochē* (of the Whole), Ap. 6, for the greater part of the country. **6 were baptized** = were being baptized. **baptized of.** See Ap. 115. I. vii. **of** = by. Gr. *hupo*. Ap. 104. xviii. 1. **sins.** Gr. *hamartia*. Ap. 128. II. 1. **7 Pharisees and Sadducees.** See Ap. 120. II. **saw.** Ap. 133. I. 1. **come** = coming. **to.** Gr. *epi*. See Ap. 104. ix. 3. **baptism.** See Ap. 115. II. i. **generation** = brood or offspring. **vipers** = serpents. Not ordinary snakes, but venomous vipers. **who . . .?** Fig. *Erotēsis* (Ap. 6), for emphasis. **warned, &c.** = forewarned; or who hath suggested or given you the hint? **from** = away from. Gr. *apo*. Ap. 104. iv. **the wrath to come.** The reference is to Mal. 4. 1. The coming of Messiah was always connected with judgment; which would have come to pass had the nation repented at the preaching of "them that heard Him" (Heb. 2. 3. Cp. 22. 4). The "times of refreshing", and "the restoration of all things" of Acts 3. 19-26, would have followed. Hence 1 Thess. 1. 10; 2. 16; 5. 9. See notes there; and cp. Matt. 10. 23; 16. 28; 24. 34. Luke 21. 22, 23. Acts 28. 25, 28. **to come** = about to come. **8 meet for** = worthy of. **9 think** = think not for a moment (Aorist). This is an idiom to be frequently met with in the Jerusalem Talmud = be not of that opinion. **not.** Gr. *mē*. Ap. 105. II. **within** = among. Gr. *en*. Ap. 104. viii. 2. **We have, &c.** Cp. John 8. 39. Rom. 4. 1-6; 9. 7. Gal. 3. 9. **God.** Ap. 98. I. i. **of** = out of. Gr. *ek*. Ap. 104. vii. **children.** Gr. pl. of *teknon*. Ap. 108. I.

3. 10-12 (*T*, above). JOHN'S THREATENING. (*Introversion.*)

T | n | 10. Warning. The "Ax" and the "Fire".
  o | 11-. John's Baptism.
   p | -11-. Christ and John.
  o | -11. Christ's Baptism.
 n | 12. Warning. The "Fan" and the "Fire".

10 now = already. **also.** Omitted by all the texts (Ap. 94. VII.). **is laid** = is lying at. The Jerusalem Talmud (*Beracoth*, fol. 5. 1) refers Isa. 10. 33, 34 to the destruction of Jerusalem; and argues from Isa. 11. 1 that Messiah would be born shortly before it. **unto** = at. Gr. *pros*. Ap. 104. xv. 3. **is hewn down** = getteth hewn down. **into.** Gr. *eis*. Ap. 104. vi. **11 with.** Gr. *en*. Ap. 104. viii. 1, and Ap. 115. I. iii. The literal rendering of the Heb. ב (*Beth* = B). Matt. 7. 6; 9. 34. Rom. 15. 6. 1 Cor. 4. 21, &c. See Ap. 115. I. iii. 1. a. **shoes** = sandals. **not.** Gr. *ou*. See Ap. 105. i. **worthy** = fit or equal. Not the same word as "meet for" in *v*. 8. **bear** = bring or fetch. Mark: "stoop down and unloose". Luke: "unloose". Prob. repeated often in different forms.

26 °**He** shall °baptize you [11]- with °the Holy Ghost,
and *with* °fire:
n 12 Whose °fan *is* [1] in His hand, and He will
(p. 1312) °throughly purge His °floor, and °gather His
wheat [10] into the garner; but °He will °burn
up the chaff with unquenchable fire."
S l 13 Then [1] cometh °Jesus °from Galilee [7] to
°Jordan [10] unto John, [7] to be [6] baptized [6] of
him.
m 14 But John °forbad Him, saying, "**I** have
need to be [6] baptized [6] of Thee, and comest **Thou**
[5] to me?"
15 And [13] Jesus answering said [10] unto him,
"Suffer °*it to be so* now: for °thus °it becometh
us to fulfil °all righteousness." Then he
suffered Him.
16 And [13] Jesus, when He was [6] baptized, went
up straightway °out of the water: and, °lo,
the heavens were opened unto Him, and °He
[7] saw °the Spirit of °God descending °like a
°dove, and °lighting °upon Him:
17 And [16] lo °a voice °from [2] heaven, saying,
"This is °My beloved Son, °in Whom °I am
well pleased."

D U **4** °Then was °Jesus led up °of °the Spirit
(p. 1313) °into the °wilderness to be °tempted °of
the devil.
2 And when He had fasted °forty days
and forty °nights, He was afterward an
hungred.
3 And °when °the tempter °came to Him, °he
said,

He shall baptize. "He" is emph. = He Himself will, and no other. See Ap. 115. See Acts 1. 4, 5; 2. 3; 11. 15. Is. 44. 3. Cp. Ezek. 36. 26, 27. Joel 2. 28.

baptize . . . with. See Ap. 115. I. iii. 1. c.

the Holy Ghost = *pneuma hagion*, holy spirit, or "power from on high". No Articles. See Ap. 101. II. 14.

fire. See Acts 2. 3. Note the Fig. *Hendiadys* (Ap. 6) = with *pneuma hagion* = yea, with a burning (or purifying) spirit too, separating the chaff from the wheat (*v.* 12), not mingling them together in water. "Fire" in *v.* 11 is symbolic (see Isa. 4. 3. Mal. 3. 1-4; 4. 1. Cp. Ps. 1. 4; 35. 5. Isa. 17. 13; 30. 24; 41. 16. Jer. 51. 2. Hos. 13. 3). In *v.* 12, the "fire" is literal; for destroying, not for purging.

Note the seven emblems of the Spirit (or of *pneuma hagion*) in Scripture. "Fire" (Matt. 3. 11. Acts 2 3); "Water" (Ezek. 36. 25. John 3. 5; 7. 38, 39); "Wind" (Ezek. 37. 1-10); "Oil" (Isa. 61. 1. Heb. 1. 9); a "Seal" (Eph. 1. 13; 4. 30); an "Earnest" (Eph. 1. 14); a "Dove" (Matt. 3. 16).

12 fan = winnowing shovel. God *fans* to get rid of the chaff; Satan *sifts* to get rid of the wheat (Luke 22. 31).

throughly = thoroughly.

floor = threshing-floor.

gather = gather together.

He. The 1611 edition of the A.V. omits "He".

burn up. Gr. *katakaiō* = burn down, or quite up.

13 Jesus. See Ap. 98. X.

from = away from. Gr. *apo.* Ap. 104. iv.

Jordan = the Jordan.

14 forbad = was hindering. Gr. *diakōluō.* Occ. only here.

15 it to be so: or, supply the Ellipsis by "[Me]". The Lord was now, and here, recognized by John (John 1. 31-34).

thus. In fulfilling this duty.

it becometh us. This duty was incumbent on John as the minister of that Dispensation; likewise on the Lord: hence the word "thus". The reason is given in John 1. 31. **all righteousness:** or every claim of righteous duty. This was the anointing of Messiah (see note on *v.* 17), and anointing was accompanied by washing or immersion (Ex. 29. 4-7; 40. 12. Lev. 8. 6). **16 out of** = away from. Gr. *apo.* Ap. 104. iv. **lo.** Fig. *Asterismos* (Ap. 6), for emphasis. **He saw:** i.e. the Lord saw. **the Spirit of God.** Note the Articles, and see Ap. 101. II. 3. **God.** See Ap. 98. I. i. 1. **like** = as if. Gr. *hōsei* = as it were (not *homoios* = resembling in form or appearance): referring to the descent, not to bodily form as in Mark 1. 10. In Luke 3. 22 *hōsei* may still be connected with the manner of descent, the bodily form referring to the Spirit. **dove.** See note on "fire", *v.* 11. **lighting** = coming. **upon.** Gr. *epi.* Ap. 104. ix. 3. **17 a voice.** There were two voices: the first "Thou art", &c. (Mark 1. 11. Luke 3. 22), while the Spirit in bodily form was descending; the second (introduced by the word "lo"), "this is", &c., after it remained ("abode", John 1. 32). This latter speaking is mentioned by John for the same reason as that given in John 12. 30. Only one voice at the Transfiguration. **from** = out of. Gr. *ek.* Ap. 104. vii. **My beloved Son.** Not Joseph's or Mary's son = My Son, the beloved [Son]. See Ap. 99. **in.** See note on "with", *v.* 11. **I am well pleased** = I have found delight. Heb. idiom, as in 2 Sam. 22. 20. Ps. 51. 16. Cp. Isa. 42. 1. Matt. 12. 18. "This is My beloved Son" was the Divine formula of anointing Messiah for the office of Prophet (Matt. 3. 17); also for that of Priest (Matt. 17. 5. See Ap. 149); and "Thou art My Son" for that of King (Ps. 2. 7. Acts 13. 33. Heb. 1. 5; 5. 5).

4. 1-11 (D, p. 1305). THE TEMPTATION. (*Introversion.*)

D | U | 1-3-. Before the Temptation.
  V | -3-10. The Separate Temptations.
 U | 11. After the Temptation.

1 Then. Immediately after His anointing as Messiah, "the second man" (1 Cor. 15. 47), "the last Adam" (1 Cor. 15. 45), must be tried like "the first man Adam" (1 Cor. 15. 45, 47), and in the same three ways (1 John 2. 16. Cp. with Gen. 3. 6). **Jesus.** See Ap. 98. X. **of** = by. Gr. *hupo.* Ap. 104. xviii. 1. **the Spirit.** Ap. 101. II. 3. **into.** Gr. *eis.* Ap. 104. vi. **wilderness.** The first man was in the garden; Messiah's trial was in the wilderness, and His agony in a garden. Contrast Israel: fed with manna and disobedient, Christ hungered and obedient. **tempted** = tried, or put to the test. Gr. *peirazō*; from *peirō*, to pierce through, so as to test. **2 forty.** The number of probation (Ap. 10). **nights.** Joined thus with "days", are complete periods of twenty-four hours. See Ap. 144. **3 when . . . came, &c.** = having approached Him and said. **the tempter** = he who was tempting Him. See Ap. 116. **came to Him:** as to our first parents, Adam and Eve. See Ap. 19. **he said.** See Ap. 116 for the two sets of three temptations, under different circumstances, with different words and expressions; and, in a different order in Matt. 4 from that in Luke 4. It is nowhere said that there were "three" or only three; as it is nowhere said that there were "three" wise men in chap. 2.

V W1 q1 °"If Thou be °the Son of God, °command that
(p. 1314) °these stones °be made °bread."
r1 4 But He answered and [3]said,
s1 °"It is written, **°Man shall not live °by bread**
°alone, but °by every °word that proceedeth
°out of the mouth of °God.'"
W2 q2 5 °Then the devil °taketh Him up [1]into °the
°holy city, and setteth Him °on °a pinnacle
of the °temple,
6 And saith unto Him, [3]"If Thou be [3]the Son
of God, °cast Thyself down: for °it is written,
'He shall give His angels charge °concerning
Thee: and °in *their* hands they shall bear
Thee up, lest at any time Thou dash Thy foot
°against a stone.'"
r2 7 [1]Jesus said unto him, [4]"It is written again,
s2 °**'Thou shalt °not °tempt °the LORD thy**
God.'"
W3 q3 8 °Again, the devil °taketh Him up[1] into an °exceeding high mountain, and sheweth Him all the
°kingdoms of the °world, and the glory of them;
9 And saith unto Him, °"All these things
will I give Thee, °if Thou °wilt fall down and
°worship me."
r3 10 Then saith [1]Jesus unto him, °"Get thee
hence, °Satan:
s3 for [4]it is written, °**'Thou shalt [9]worship [7]the**
LORD thy [4]God, and Him °only shalt thou
serve.'"
U 11 Then the devil leaveth Him, and, °behold,
(p. 1313) °angels came and ministered unto Him.
E F X 12 Now when [1]Jesus had heard that John was
(p. 1315) °cast into prison, He °departed [1]into Galilee;
27

4. -3-10 (V, p. 1313). THE SEPARATE TEMPTATIONS. (*Repeated and Extended Alternations.*)

V | W1 | q1 | -3. Temptation. "If Thou be".
| r1 | 4-. Answer. "It is written".
| s1 | -4. Scripture. Deut. 8. 3.
W2 | q2 | 5, 6. Temptation. "If Thou be".
| r2 | 7-. Answer. "It is written".
| s2 | -7. Scripture. Deut. 6. 16.
W3 | q3 | 8, 9. Temptation. "If Thou wilt".
| r3 | 10-. Answer. "It is written".
| s3 | -10. Scripture. Deut. 6. 13; 10. 20.

If. Gr. *ei*, with the indicative mood, assuming and taking it for granted as an actual fact: "If Thou art?" See Ap. 118. II. 1. Same as in *v.* 6, but not the same as in *v.* 9.
the Son of God. Cp. this with 3. 17, on which the question is based. See Ap. 98. XV.
command that = speak, in order that.
these stones: in this the fourth temptation; but in the first temptation = "this stone" (Luke 4. 3).
be made = become. **bread** = loaves.
4 It is written = It standeth written. This is the Lord's first ministerial utterance; three times. Cp. the last three (John 17. 8, 14, 17). The appeal is not to the spoken voice (3. 17) but to the written Word. Quoted from Deut. 8. 3. See Ap. 107. I. and 117. I.
Man. Gr. *anthrōpos.* Ap. 123. 1.
by = upon. Gr. *epi.* Ap. 104. ix. 2. **alone** = only.
word = utterance.
out of = by means of, or through. Gr. *dia.* Ap. 104. v. 1. Note the connection of the "hunger" and the "forty" days here, and the same in Deut. 8. 3.
God. See Ap. 98. I. i. 1.
5 Then. The fifth temptation. See Ap. 116.
taketh. Gr. *paralambanō.* Cp. *agō*, of Luke 4. 9. See the usage of *paralambanō*, Matt. 17. 1, implying authority and constraint This is the third temptation in Luke (Luke 4. 9), and the difference of the order is explained in Ap. 116. Both Gospels are correct and true.
the holy city. So called in 27. 53. Rev. 11. 2. Neh. 11. 1. Isa. 48. 2; 52. 1. Dan. 9. 24. The Arabs still call it *El Kuds* = the holy place. It was so called on account of the Sanctuary. **holy.** See note on Ex. 3. 5. **on.** Gr. *epi.* Ap. 104. ix. 3. **a pinnacle** = the wing. Gr. *to pterugion*, used of that part of the Temple (or Holy Place) where "the abomination of desolation" is to stand, according to Theodotion (a fourth reviser of the Sept about the middle of cent. 2). See note on Dan. 9. 27; and cp. Luke 4. 9 and Matt. 24. 15. **temple** = the temple buildings; not *naos*, the house itself or Sanctuary. See note on 23. 16. **6 cast Thyself down.** An attempt upon His life. See Ap. 23, and note on 23. 16. **it is written.** Satan can quote Scripture and garble it by *omitting* the essential words "to keep Thee in all Thy ways", and by *adding* "at any time". Quoted from Ps. 91. 11, 12 (not *v.* 13; see note there). **concerning.** Gr. *peri.* Ap. 104. xiii 1. **in** = upon. Gr. *epi*, as "on" in *v.* 5. **against.** Gr. *pros.* Ap. 104. xv. 3. **7 Thou, &c.** Quoted from Deut. 6. 16 (Ap. 107. II. 3. c.). **not.** Gr. *ou.* See Ap. 105. I. **tempt.** Note the words which follow: "as ye tempted Him in Massah". A reference to Ex. 17. 7 shows that there it was to doubt Jehovah's presence and care. It was the same here. **the LORD** = Jehovah. See Ap. VI. 1. *a.* 4. B. a **8 Again, &c** This should be "The devil taketh Him again", implying that he had taken Him there before, as "It is written again" in *v.* 7. See Ap. 117. I. This is the *second* temptation in Luke (Luke 4. 5). **taketh.** As in *v.* 5; not *anagō*, "leadeth up", as in Luke 4. 5. **exceeding.** Not so in Luke 4. 5; because there it is only *oikoumenē*, the inhabited world, or Roman empire (Ap. 129. 2); here it is *kosmos* (Ap. 129. 1). **kingdoms.** See Ap. 112. **world.** Gr. *kosmos*, the whole world as created. See Ap. 129. 1. **9 All these.** Cp. Luke 4. 6 and see Ap. 116. **if.** See Ap. 118. I. 2. Not the same as in *vv.* 3 and 6. **wilt fall down.** Not in Luke. **worship** = do homage. Ap. 137. i. **10 Get thee hence** = Go! This is the end, and the Lord ends it. In Luke 4. 13, after the third temptation, Satan "departed" of his own accord and only "for a season". Here, after the last, Satan is summarily dismissed, not to return. See Ap. 116. **Satan** = the Adversary. Sept. for Heb. *Ṣaṭan.* **Thou shalt, &c.** Quoted from Deut. 11. 3, 4. See Ap. 107. II. 2, and 117. I. **only** = alone, as in *v.* 4. Quoted from Deut. 6. 13; where the possession of the earth (*v.* 10) depends on loyalty to God (*v.* 12), Who gives it (*v.* 10); and on obedience to Him (*vv.* 17, 18). **11 behold.** Fig. *Asterismos* (Ap. 6), for emphasis. **angels came, &c.** Thus closing the whole of the Temptations. No such ministration at the end of the third temptation in Luke 4. 13.

4. 12—26. 35. THE LORD'S FOURFOLD MINISTRY [For Structure see next page].

12 cast into prison = delivered up. There is no Greek for "into" or "prison". No disciples had yet been called (*vv.* 18-22); therefore John could not yet have been in prison; for, after the calling of disciples (John 2. 2, 11) John was "not yet cast into prison" (John 3. 24, *eis tēn phulakēn*). There is no "inaccuracy" or "confusion". *Paradidōmi* is rendered "cast (or put) in prison" only here and Mark 1. 14, out of 122 occurrences. It means "to deliver up", and is so rendered ten times, and "deliver" fifty-three times. Cp. 5. 25; 10. 17, 19, 21; 24. 9, &c. The "not yet" of John 3. 24 (Gr. *oupō.* Ap. 105. I.) implies that previous attempts and perhaps official inquiries had been made, following probably on the unofficial inquiry of John 1. 19-27. John's being "delivered up" may have led to this departure of Jesus (Ap. 98; X, p. 1315) from Judæa. Christ's ministry is commenced at Matt. 4. 12. Mark 1. 14. Luke 4. 14 and John 1. 35, before the call of any disciples. **departed** = withdrew.

27 13 And leaving °Nazareth, He came and
dwelt °in °Capernaum, which is °upon the
sea coast, °in the borders of Zabulon and
Nephthalim:
14 °That it might be fulfilled which was
°spoken °by °Esaias the prophet, saying,
15 °"**The land of Zabulon, and the land of**
Nephthalim, *by* the way of the sea, beyond
Jordan, °Galilee of the °Gentiles;

Y t **16 The People which °sat [13]in darkness °saw**
(p. 1315) **great °light; and to them which °sat [13]in °the**
region and shadow of death °light is °sprung
up."

u 17 °From that time [1]Jesus began to °preach,
and to say, °"Repent: for °the kingdom of
°heaven °is at hand."

Z A v 18 And [1]Jesus, walking °by the sea of Galilee,
[16]saw two brethren, Simon called Peter, and
Andrew his brother, casting °a net [1]into the
sea: for they were fishers.

w 19 And He saith unto them, "Follow Me, and
I will make you °fishers of °men."

x 20 And they straightway left *their* °nets, and
followed Him.

A v 21 And going on from thence, He [16]saw °other
two brethren, °James *the son* of °Zebedee, and
°John his brother, [13]in °a ship °with °Zebedee
their father, °mending their [20]nets;

w and He called them.

x 22 And they immediately left the ship and
their father, and followed Him.

X 23 And [1]Jesus went about °all Galilee, teaching [13]in their °synagogues, and [17]preaching
°the gospel °of [17]the kingdom,

Y u and healing °all manner of sickness and °all
manner of °disease °among the people.

t 24 And His °fame went °throughout all
Syria: and they brought unto Him all sick
people that were taken with divers °diseases
and torments, and those which were possessed

4. 12—26. 35 (**E**, p. 1305). THE LORD'S FOURFOLD MINISTRY. (*Introversion.*) See Ap. 119.

E | F | 4. 12—7. 29. THE FIRST PERIOD. Subject: The Proclamation of THE KINGDOM, and Call to Repentance (4. 17). "Sermon on the Mount" unnamed (5. 1—7. 29). The Laws of the Kingdom.

G | 8. 1—16. 20. THE SECOND PERIOD. Subject: The Proclamation of THE KING. His Person as "Lord" (8. 2, 6, 8) and "Man" (8. 20). Miracles of Creation, manifesting His Deity; and of Compassion, declaring His Humanity.

G | 16. 21—20. 34. THE THIRD PERIOD. Subject: The Rejection of THE KING. Parabolic Miracles (Lunatic, 17. 14; Blind men, 20. 30-34).

F | 21. 1—26. 35. THE FOURTH PERIOD. Subject: The Rejection of THE KINGDOM. Parables and Teaching as to the coming change of Dispensation, while the Kingdom should be in *abeyance*. The Sermon on the Mount (Olives), 24. 1—25. 46. Miracles: Parabolic and Prophetic: Lazarus (John 11), and the withered Fig-tree (Mark 11. 12-14, 20, 21).

4. 12—7. 29 (**F**, above). THE FIRST PERIOD OF THE MINISTRY. PROCLAMATION OF THE KINGDOM.
(*Extended Alternation and Introversion.*)

F | X | 4. 12-15. The Lord. Departure to Galilee.
Y | t | 4. 16. Depth of the great darkness. The People sitting in it.
u | 4. 17. The Kingdom proclaimed. Words.
Z | 4. 18-22. Disciples called.
X | 4. 23-. The Lord. Going about Galilee.
Y | *u* | 4. -23. The Kingdom proclaimed. Works.
t | 4. 24, 25. Fame of the "Great Light". The People following it.
Z | 5. 1—7. 29. Disciples taught.

13 Nazareth. Aramaic. See Ap. 94. III. 3, and 169.
in = at. Gr. *eis*. Ap. 104. vi.
Capernaum. Jewish authorities identify *Kaphir Nakhum* with *Kaphir Temkhum*, since corrupted into the modern *Tell Hum*. Ap. 169. A Synagogue has been discovered in the present ruins. For events at Capernaum see chs. 8, 9, 17, 18. Mark 1.
upon the sea coast. Gr. *parathalassios*. Occ. only here. **in** = in. Gr. *en*. Ap. 104. viii.
14 That = In order that.
spoken. As well as written.
by = by means of. Gr. *dia*. Ap. 104. v. 1. **Esaias** = Isaiah. **15 The land, &c.** Quoted from Isa. 9. 1, 2. See Ap. 107. II. 2. "Land" is nom., not vocative. **Galilee.** See Ap. 169. **Gentiles** = nations. **16 sat** = was sitting. **saw.** Ap. 133. I. 1. **light.** Ap. 130. 1. **the region and shadow, &c.** Fig. *Hendiadys* (Ap. 6) = "darkness, [yea] the dark shadow of death", or death's darkness. **sprung up** = risen for them.

4. 18-22 (Z, above). DISCIPLES CALLED. (*Extended Alternation.*)

Z | A | v | 18. Two Brethren (Peter and Andrew).
w | 19. Their Call.
x | 20. Their Obedience.
A | *v* | 21-. Two Brethren (James and John).
w | -21. Their Call.
x | 22. Their Obedience.

17 From. Gk. *apo*. Ap. 104. iv. **From that time.** Each portion of the Lord's fourfold ministry had a distinct beginning or ending. See the Structure **E** (above). **preach** = proclaim. See Ap. 121. 1. **Repent.** Gr. *metanoeō*. Ap. 111. I. 1. **the kingdom of heaven.** See Ap. 114. **heaven** = the heavens. See notes on 6. 9, 10. **is at hand** = is drawn nigh. **18 by** = beside. Gr. *para*. Ap. 104. xii. 3. **a net** = a large net. Gr. *amphiblēstron*. Not the same word as in *v.* 20, or 13. 47. **19 fishers of men.** A Talmudic expression: "A fisher of the Law" (Maimonides, *Torah*, cap. I). **men.** Gr. pl. of *anthrōpos*. Ap. 123. I. **20 nets.** Pl. of *diktuon*. Not the same word as in *v.* 18, or 13. 47. **21 other.** Gr. *allos*. Ap. 124. 1. **James . . . John.** See Ap. 141. **Zebedee.** Aram. See Ap. 94. III. 3. **a** = the. These calls were to discipleship, not apostleship. **with.** Gr. *meta*. Ap. 104. xi. 1. **mending** = setting in order. See Ap. 125. 8. **23 all** = the whole. Put by Fig. *Synecdochē* (of the Whole) for all parts. Ap. 6. **synagogues.** See Ap. 120. **the gospel** = the glad tidings. **of** = relating to. See Ap. 17. 5. **all manner of** = every. Put by Fig. *Synecdochē* (of the Whole), Ap. 6, for some of all kinds. **disease.** Gr. *malakia*. Occ. only in Matthew: here; 9. 35; 10. 1. **among.** Gr. *en*. Ap. 104. viii. 2. **24 fame** = hearing. Put by Fig. *Metonymy* (of the Adjunct), Ap. 6, for what was heard. **throughout** = unto. Gr. *eis*. Ap. 104. vi. **diseases.** Gr. *nosos*, transl. sickness in *v.* 23.

27 with ° devils, and those which ° were lunatick, and those that had the palsy; and He healed them.

25 And there followed Him great multitudes of people ° from ° Galilee, ° and *from* Decapolis, and *from* Jerusalem, and *from* Judæa, and *from* beyond Jordan.

Z B (p. 1316) **5** And ° seeing the multitudes, He went up ° into ° a mountain: and when He was ° set, His ° disciples came unto Him:

2 And He ° opened His mouth, and ° taught them, saying,

C a 3 ° "Blessed *are* the ° poor in ° spirit: for theirs is ° the kingdom of ° heaven.

b 4 ° Blessed *are* they that mourn: [3] for they shall be comforted.

c 5 [4] Blessed *are* the ° meek: [3] for they shall inherit ° the earth.

d 6 [4] Blessed *are* they which do ° hunger and thirst after righteousness: [3] for they shall be filled.

d 7 [4] Blessed *are* the ° merciful: [3] for they shall obtain ° mercy.

c 8 [4] Blessed *are* the ° pure in heart: [3] for they shall see ° God.

b 9 [4] Blessed *are* the ° peacemakers: [3] for they shall be called the ° children of ° God.

a 10 [4] Blessed *are* they which ° are persecuted ° for righteousness' sake: [3] for theirs is [3] the kingdom of [3] heaven.

11 Blessed are ye, when *men* shall ° revile you, and persecute *you*, and shall say all manner of ° evil ° against you ° falsely, for My sake.

12 ° Rejoice, and be exceeding glad: [3] for great *is* your reward ° in [3] heaven: ° for so persecuted they the prophets which were before you.

devils = demons. Cp. 12. 26, 27. Mark 3. 22, 26.
were lunatick. Gr. *selēniazomai.* Occ. only here, and 17. 15. From *selēnē* = the moon.
25 from. Gr. *apo.* Ap. 104. iv.
Galilee. Ap. 169.
and. Note the Fig. *Polysyndeton.* Ap. 6.

5. 1—7. 29 (*Z*, p. 1315). DISCIPLES TAUGHT. "THE SERMON ON THE MOUNT". (*Introversion.*)

Z | B | 5. 1-2. Introduction.
  C | 5. 3-12. Characters. True Happiness.
   D | 5. 13-16. True Disciples.
    E | 5. 17—7. 12. THE KINGDOM. Its LAWS.
    E | 7. 13, 14. THE KINGDOM. ENTRANCE into it.
   D | 7. 15-23. False Teachers.
  C | 7. 24-27. Characters. True Wisdom.
 B | 7. 28, 29. Conclusion.

1 seeing. Ap. 133. I. 1.
into. Gr. *eis.* Ap. 104. vi.
a mountain = the mountain. Well known and therefore unnamed, but corresponds with the Mount of Olives in the Structure of the Gospel as a whole Cp. **F** and *F*, p. 1315. There is a reference also to Sinai.
set. The posture of the Oriental teacher to-day.
disciples. Note this fact in interpreting the member *Z*.
2 opened His mouth. Heb. idiom. Fig. *Metonymy* (of Adjunct), Ap 6, for speaking (Job 3. 1. Dan. 10. 16. Acts 8. 35).
taught them. See note on 7. 39, and the Structure, above. The Structure is the commentary showing that this teaching is connected with the proclamation of the kingdom (*v.* 3), and is to be interpreted by it. As the kingdom was rejected and is now in abeyance, so likewise this discourse is in abeyance with all its commands, &c., until "the gospel of the kingdom" is again proclaimed, to herald its drawing nigh. Parts of this address were repeated at different times and on different occasions. Luke nowhere professes to give the whole address in its chronological setting or entirety. Only some thirty separate verses are so repeated by Luke out of 107 verses in Matthew. The later repetitions in Luke were given in "a plain" (Luke 6. 17) and *after* the calling of the Twelve (Luke 6. 13); here the whole is given *before* the calling of the Twelve (Matt. 9. 9). These are marks of *accuracy*, not of "discrepancy" as alleged. Modern critics first assume that the two accounts *are identical*, and then say: "No one now expects to find chronological accuracy in the evangelical records"! For the relation of the Sermon on the Mount to Ps. 15, see Ap. 70; and to the seven "woes" of ch. 23, see Ap. 126.

5. 3-12 (C, above). CHARACTERS. (*Introversion.*)

C | a | 3. Heirs of the Kingdom.
  b | 4. Mourners. Reward for Mourners.
   c | 5. Inheritance. Earthly.
    d | 6. True righteousness.
    d | 7. Fruits of righteousness.
   c | 8. Inheritance. Heavenly.
  b | 9. Peacemakers. Reward for Peacemakers.
 a | 10-12. Heirs of the Kingdom.

3 Blessed = Happy, representing the Heb. *'ashrēy* (not *bārūk*, blessed). *'Ashrēy* (Fig. *Beatitudo*, not *Benedictio*) occurs in nineteen Psalms twenty-six times; elsewhere only in eight books (Deut., 1 Kings, 2 Chron., Isa., Prov., Job, Ecc., and Dan.). The *Aramaic* equivalent for *'ashrēy* is *tōb* (sing., pl., or dual). See Ap. 94. III. 3, and Ap. 63. vi. Gr. *makarios* = happy (not *eulogētos*, which = blessed, and is used only of God (Mark 14. 61. Luke 1. 68. Rom. 1. 25; 9. 5; 2 Cor. 1. 3; 11. 31. Eph. 1. 3. 1 Pet. 1. 3). **poor in spirit.** The equivalent for the Aramaic (Ap. 94. III. 3, p. 135) *'ănaiyīm* (Heb. *'ānah.* See note on Prov. 1. 11) = poor in this world (as in Luke 6. 20), in contrast with the promise of the kingdom. Cp. Jas. 2. 5. **spirit.** Gr. *pneuma.* See Ap. 101. II. 8. **the kingdom of heaven.** Then proclaimed as having drawn nigh (3. 2; 4. 17). See Ap. 114. **heaven** = the heavens. See notes on 6. 9, 10. **4 Blessed.** Note the Fig. *Anaphora* (Ap. 6). The eight Beatitudes are to be contrasted with and understood by the eight "woes" of 23. 13-33. See Ap. 126. **5 meek.** Cp. Ps. 37. 11. **the earth:** or, the land. Gr. *gē.* See Ap. 129. 4. **6 hunger and thirst, &c.** The idiom for a strong desire. Cp. Ps. 42. 1, 2; 119. 103. **7 merciful** = compassionate. Cp. Ps. 41. 1. **mercy.** Not merely now, but in the manifestation of the kingdom, Jas. 2. 13 (cp. Heb. 4. 16; 8. 12; 10. 28). **8 pure in heart.** Cp. Ps. 24. 4; 73. 1. **God.** Ap. 98. I. i. 1. **9 peacemakers.** Cp. Ps. 133. 1. Gr. *eirēnopoios.* Occ. only here. **children** = sons. Gr. *huios.*. See Ap. 108. III. **10 are persecuted** = have been persecuted. Cp. Pss. 37, 39, 40. **for** = on account of. **for righteousness' sake.** Not otherwise. **11 revile** = reproach. **evil** = harmful thing. Gr. *ponēros.* Ap. 128. IV. 1. **against.** Gr. *kata.* Ap. 104. x. 1. **falsely.** This is another condition of the happiness of *v.* 3. **12 Rejoice, &c.** See 1 Pet. 4. 13. Cp. Acts 16. 25. **in.** Gr. *en.* Ap. 104. viii. **for** = because. Not the same as in *v.* 3, &c.

D e 13 °Ye °are the °salt of the [5]earth: but °if the
(p. 1317) salt have lost °his savour, wherewith shall it
27 be salted? it is thenceforth good °for nothing,
but to be cast out, and to be trodden under foot
°of °men.

f 14 Ye are the °light of the °world.

e °A city that is set on an hill °cannot be hid.

f 15 °Neither do men light a °candle, and put
it °under °a bushel, but °on °a candlestick;
and it giveth light unto all that are [12]in the
house.

16 Let your [14]light °so shine before [13]men, °that
they may [1]see your good works, and glorify
your Father Which is [12]in [3]heaven.

E F 17 °Think °not that °I am come to °destroy
°the law, or the prophets: I am °not come to
°destroy, but to fulfil.

18 For °verily I say unto you, °Till °heaven
and °earth pass, one °jot or one °tittle shall
°in no wise pass °from [17]the law, till all be
fulfilled.

19 °Whosoever therefore shall break one of
°these least commandments, and shall teach
[13]men so, he shall be called the least [12]in [3]the
kingdom of [3]heaven: but °whosoever shall do
and teach *them*, the same shall be called great
[12]in [3]the kingdom of [3]heaven.

20 For I say unto you, That except your
righteousness shall exceed °*the righteousness*
of the scribes and °Pharisees, ye shall °in no
case enter [1]into [3]the kingdom of [3]heaven.

G H[1] 21 Ye have °heard that °it was said °by
them of old time, **Thou shalt [17]not kill**; and
[19]whosoever shall kill shall be in danger of
the judgment:'

22 But I say unto you, That [19]whosoever is
angry with his °brother °without a cause
shall be °in danger of the °judgment: and

5. 13-16 (D, p. 1316). TRUE DISCIPLES. (*Alternation.*)

D | e | 13. In the earth. Salt.
  f | 14-. The Light.
  e | -14. In the earth. A City.
  f | 15, 16. A Lamp.

13 Ye. Representing the kingdom of *v.* 3 and 4. 17.
are = represent. Fig. *Metaphor.* Ap. 6.
salt. Cp. Mark 9. 50. Luke 14. 34, 35.
if. See Ap. 118. 1 b, expressing a real contingency; for, if the salt is stored on the bare earth, or is exposed to the air or sun, it *does* lose its savour and is fit for no place but the streets (see Thomson's *The Land and the Book*, Lond., 1869, p. 381).
his = its.
for. Gr. *eis.* Ap. 104. vi.
of = by. Gr. *hupo.* Ap. 104. xiii. 1.
of men. Belongs to former clause, as well, by Fig. *Ellipsis*, Ap. 6. men. Pl. of *anthrōpos.* Ap. 123. 1.
14 light. Gr. *phōs* = light. See Ap. 130. 1.
world. Gr. *kosmos.* See Ap. 129. 1.
A city. *Safed*, so placed, was within sight.
cannot. Verb with *ou.* See Ap. 105. I.
15 Neither = and not (Gr. *ou*). Ap. 105. I.
candle = lamp. Gr. *luchnos.* Ap. 130. 5.
under. Gr. *hupo.* Ap. 104. xviii. 2.
a bushel = the measure. Gr. *modion* = a dry measure. See Ap. 51. III. 3. (2): i.e. any measure there may happen to be in the house.
on = upon. Gr. *epi.* Ap. 104. ix. 3.
a candlestick = the lampstand. Gr. *luchnia.* Ap. 130. 5.
16 so = thus. that = so that.

5. 17—7. 12 (E, p. 1316). THE KINGDOM (THE LAWS OF IT). (*Introversion.*)

E | F | 5. 17-20. They fulfil the Law and the Prophets.
  G | 5. 21-48. They transcend the Law of Moses.
  G | 6. 1—7. 11. They excel the Tradition of the Elders.
  F | 7. 12. They fulfil the Law and the Prophets.

17 Think not, &c. = Deem not for a moment. A very necessary warning against making this mount another Sinai, and promulgating the laws of the kingdom proclaimed in and from 4. 17.

not. Gr. *mē.* See Ap. 105. II. I am come = I have come. Implying former existence. Cp. 8. 10. destroy = pull down, as in 26. 61. the law. The first of fifteen refs. to the Law by Christ (5. 17, 18; 7. 12; 11. 13; 12. 5; 22. 40; 23. 23. Luke 10. 26; 16. 16, 17; 24. 44. John 7. 19, 19, 23; 8. 17; 10. 34; 15. 25), five of these coupled with "Moses". not. Gr. *ou.* Ap. 105. I. **18 verily.** Gr. *amēn.* Used only by the Lord. Same as Heb. *'amen*, preserved in all languages. Should be so given at the beginning of sentences. Always (except once) double in John; twenty-five times. See note on John 1. 52. Till. With A.V. implying a possibility, not a certainty. heaven = the heaven. Always in sing. when connected with the earth. (See notes on 6. 9, 10.) earth = the earth. Ap. 129. 4. jot = *yod.* Gr. *iōta.* Occ. only here. The smallest Heb. letter (י = Y). The Massorites numbered 66,420. tittle = the merest ornament. Not the difference between two similar Heb. letters, e. g. ר (*Resh* = R) and ד (*Daleth* = D), or ב (*Beth* = B) and כ (*Kaph* = K), as alleged, but a small ornament placed over certain letters in the Heb. text. See Ap. 93. III. The Eng. "tittle" is diminutive of *title* (Lat. *titulus*) = a small mark placed over a word for any purpose: e. g. to mark an abbreviation. in no wise. Gr. *ou mē.* See Ap. 105. III. 2. from. Gr. *apo.* Ap. 104. iv. **19 Whosoever** = every one that (with Gr. *an.* Supposing the case). See note on "Till", *v.* 18. Note the Fig. *Anaphora* (Ap. 6). these least = these shortest. Referring not to what men might thus distinguish, but to the difference made by the Lord between the whole Law and its *minutiae.* **20 the righteousness.** Supply "[that]". Pharisees. See Ap. 120. II. in no case. See Ap. 105. III. 2.

5. 21-48 (G, above). THEY TRANSCEND THE LAW OF MOSES. (*Division.*)

G | H[1] | 21-26. The Law of Murder. Com. VI.
  H[2] | 27-32. The Law of Adultery. Com. VII.
  H[3] | 33-37. The Law of Perjury. Com. III.
  H[4] | 38-42. The Law of Retaliation. (Ex. 21. 25. Lev. 24. 20. Deut. 19. 21.)
  H[5] | 43-48. The Law of Love. (Lev. 19. 18.)

H[1]. THE LAW OF MURDER.

21 heard. In the public reading of the Law. it was said. Opp. to "I say". Cp. 19. 8, 9, where the "I" is not emphatic (as it is here). See Ex. 20. 13. Deut. 5. 17. Ap. 117. by them = or to them. **22 brother.** An Israelite by nation and blood; while a neighbour was an Israelite by religion and worship (= a Proselyte). Both distinct from the heathen. So the Talmud defines them. without a cause. Omitted by LT [Trm. A], WH R. in danger of = liable to. judgment. The council of three in the local synagogue. See Ap. 120.

27 [19] whosoever shall say to his brother, °'Raca,'
shall be ° in danger of ° the council: but
[19] whosoever shall say, °'Thou fool,' shall be
° in danger ° of ° hell fire.
23 Therefore [13] if thou ° bring thy ° gift ° to
the altar, and there rememberest that thy
[22] brother hath ought [11] against thee;
24 ° Leave there thy [23] gift before the altar,
and go thy way; first ° be reconciled to thy
[22] brother, and then come and offer thy gift.
25 °Agree with thine ° adversary quickly,
whiles thou art [12] in the way ° with him; lest at
any time the ° adversary deliver thee to the
judge, and the judge deliver thee to the ° officer, and thou be cast [1] into prison.
26 [18] Verily I say unto thee, Thou shalt ° by
no means come out thence, till thou hast paid
the ° uttermost ° farthing.

H² 27 Ye have heard that it was said [21] by them
(p. 1317) of old time, °'**Thou shalt [17] not commit adultery:**'
28 But I say unto you, That ° whosoever
° looketh on ° a woman ° to lust after her hath
committed adultery with her already [12] in his
heart.
29 And ° if ° thy right eye ° offend thee, pluck
it out, and cast *it* [18] from thee: for it is profitable for thee that one of thy members should
perish, and [17] not *that* thy whole body should
be cast [1] into [22] hell.
30 And [29] if ° thy right hand [29] offend thee, cut
it off, and cast *it* [18] from thee: for it is profitable for thee that one of thy members should
perish, and [17] not *that* thy whole body should
be cast [1] into [22] hell.
31 ° It hath been said, [28] '**Whosoever shall put
away his wife, let him give her a writing of
divorcement:**'
32 But I say unto you, That [28] whosoever
shall put away his wife, saving for the cause
of fornication, causeth her to commit adultery:
and whosoever shall marry her that is divorced
committeth adultery.

H³ 33 Again, ye have heard that ° it hath been
said [21] by them of old time, ° **Thou shalt [17] not
° forswear thyself, but shalt perform unto ° the
LORD thine oaths:**'
34 But I say unto you, Swear [29] not ° at all;
neither ° by [18] heaven; for it is ° God's throne:
35 Nor [34] by the [5] earth; for it is His footstool: neither ° by Jerusalem; for it is ° the
city of the great King.
36 Neither shalt thou swear [34] by thy head,
because thou canst [17] not make one hair white
or black.
37 But let your ° communication be, ° Yea,
yea; ° Nay, nay, for ° whatsoever is more
than these ° cometh ° of [11] evil.

H⁴ 38 Ye have heard that ° it hath been said,
'**An eye for an eye, and a tooth for a tooth:**'
39 But I say unto you, That ye resist [17] not
[11] evil: but [28] whosoever shall ° smite thee [15] on
thy right cheek, turn to him the ° other also.
40 And ° if any man ° will sue thee at [17] the
law, and take away thy ° coat, let him have
thy ° cloke also.

Raca. In 1611 edition spelt "Racha"; changed in 1638 edition to "Raca". An *Aramaic* word, see Ap. 94. III. 3; not a contumelious epithet, but a contemptuous interjection, expressing the emotion or scorn of a disdainful mind (so Augustine), like Eng. "You!" Cp. Lat. *Heus tu*, Gr. *raka*. Occ. only here.

in danger of = liable to.

the council = the Sanhedrin. The supreme national court. See Ap. 120.

Thou fool. Gr. *mōros*. Heb. *nabal*. Always = a wicked reprobate, destitute of all spiritual or Divine knowledge (cp. John 7. 49).

of = to or unto. Gr. *eis*. Ap. 104. vi.

hell fire = the gehenna of fire, from Heb. *gēy Hinnom* = the valley of Hinnom, profaned by the fires of Moloch worship (2 Chron. 33. 6), and defiled by Hezekiah. Also called "Tophet", Isa. 30. 33. Here the refuse of Jerusalem was continually being burnt up by the perpetual fires (cp. Jer. 7. 31–33. 2 Kings 23. 10. Mark 9. 48. Isa. 66. 24). See Ap. 131. 2.

23 bring = offer, as in *v.* 24. **gift**: i.e. sacrifice.

to = up to. Gr. *epi*. Ap. 104. ix. 3.

24 Leave. An unusual practice.

be reconciled. Gr. *dialattomai*. Occ. only here.

25 Agree = Be well-minded. Gr. *eunoeō*. Occ. only here.

adversary = opponent (in a lawsuit).

with. Gr. *meta*. Ap. 104. xi. 1.

officer. Here = the tax-collector, as shown by the Papyri. See note on Luke 12. 58.

26 by no means. Gr. *ou mē*. Cp. 105. III. 2.

uttermost = last.

farthing: which shows it to be a case of debt. See Ap. 51. I. 2.

H². THE LAW OF ADULTERY.

27 Thou, &c. Quoted from Ex. 20. 14. Deut. 5. 18. Ap. 117.

28 whosoever = every one that.

looketh = keeps looking. See Ap. 133. I. 5.

a woman = a married woman.

to. Gr. *pros to*. Ap. 104. xv. 3.

29 if. Gr. *ei*. Ap. 118. II. 1.

thy right eye: i.e. thy choicest possession. Fig. *Hypocatastasis*. Ap. 6.

offend = causeth thee to stumble (morally). Cp. 18. 6. 1 Cor. 1. 23.

30 thy right. See note on *v.* 29.

31 It hath been said. It was said. See Deut. 24. 1.

H³. THE LAW OF PERJURY.

33 it hath been said = it was said. See Lev. 19. 12; also Ap. 107. II. 2 and 117. I.

Thou shalt not, &c. Quoted from Ex. 20. 7. Num. 30. 2. Deut. 23. 21.

forswear = swear falsely. Gr. *epiorkeō*. Occ. only here.

the LORD. See Ap. 98. VI. i. *a*. 1. A.

34 at all. Fig. *Synecdochē* (of Genus), Ap. 6; i.e. not lightly. The particulars given in *vv.* 35, 36.

by. Gr. *en*. Ap. 104. viii. **God's**. Ap. 98. I. i.

35 by. Gr. *eis*. Ap. 104. vi.

the city of the great King. Only here in N.T. Cp. Ps. 48. 2, referring to Zion. Contrast 2 Kings 18. 19, 28. See note on 4. 5.

37 communication = word. Gr. *logos*. Omit "be".

Yea, yea = Yes, [be] yes. Fig. *Epizeuxis*. Ap. 6.

Nay, nay = Nay, [be] nay.

whatsoever = what. cometh = is.

of = out of. Gr. *ek*. Ap. 104. vii.

H⁴. THE LAW OF RETALIATION.

38 it hath been said = it was said. Quoted from Ex. 21. 24. Cp. Lev. 24. 20. Deut. 19. 21. See Ap. 107. II. 2 and 117.

39 smite. Gr. *rapizō*. Occ. only in Matthew (here and 26. 67). other. Ap. 124. 1. **40** if any man, &c. = to him who, wishing to go to law with thee.

will = wishing. Gr. *thelō*. See Ap. 102. 1. coat = now called the *sŭlta* = an outer jacket or tunic, Gr. *chitōn*.

cloke. The *jibbeh*, *juteh*, or *benīsh*, a long robe or mantle, full, with short sleeves, Gr. *himation*.

27 **41** And [28] whosoever shall °compel thee °to go
°a mile, go [25] with him twain.
42 Give to him that asketh thee, and [18] from
him that °would borrow °of thee turn -[17] not
thou away.
H5 (p. 1317) **43** Ye have heard that °it hath been said,
'**Thou shalt love thy neighbour,**' and 'hate
°thine enemy.'
44 But I say unto you, Love your enemies,
°bless them that curse you, do good to them
that °hate you, and °pray °for them which
despitefully use you, and persecute you;
45 That ye may °be the [9] children of your
Father Which is [12] in [3] heaven: for He maketh His sun to rise [15] on the [11] evil and [15] on the
good, and sendeth rain [15] on the just and on
the unjust.
46 For [13] if ye love them which love you,
°what reward have ye? do °not even the
°publicans the same?
47 And [13] if ye salute your brethren only,
what do ye more *than others?* do [46] not even
the °publicans so?
48 Be ye therefore °perfect, even as °your
Father Which is [12] in [3] heaven is °perfect.

Int. (p. 1319) **6** Take heed that ye do °not your °alms
before °men, °to be °seen °of them: other-
wise ye have °no reward °of your Father
Which is °in °heaven.
G J1 **2** Therefore when thou doest *thine* alms, do
[1] not sound a trumpet before thee, as the
°hypocrites do [1] in the synagogues and [1] in
the streets, °that they may have glory °of
[1] men. °Verily I say unto you, °They have
their reward.
3 But when thou doest alms, let [1] not thy left
hand °know what thy right °hand doeth:
4 [2] That thine alms may be [1] in secret: and
thy Father Which °seeth [1] in secret Himself
shall reward thee °openly.
J2 **5** And when °thou °prayest, °thou shalt °not
be as the [2] hypocrites *are:* for they °love to
°pray standing [1] in the synagogues and [1] in the
corners of the °streets, °that they may °be
seen of [1] men. [2] Verily I say unto you, [2] They
have their reward.
6 But thou, when thou [5] prayest, enter °into
thy °closet, and when thou hast shut thy door,
[5] pray to thy Father Which is [1] in secret; and
thy Father Which [4] seeth [1] in secret shall reward thee [4] openly.
7 But when ye [5] pray, °use [1] not vain repetitions, as the °heathen *do:* for they think that
they shall be heard °for their °much speaking.
8 Be [1] not ye therefore like unto them: for

41 compel thee. Referring to the custom of forced service or transport. See **27.** 32. Mark 15. 21. Cp. Luke 3. 14.
to go: i.e. to carry his baggage. Cp. Luke 3. 14.
a mile. Gr. *milion* (from Lat. *miliarium*). Occ. only here.
42 would = would fain. Gr. *thelō.* Ap. 102. 1.
of = from. Gr. *apo.* Ap. 104. iv.

H5. THE LAW OF LOVE.

43 it hath been said = it was said. Quoted from Lev. 19. 18, see Ap. 117. I.
thine enemy = thy foe. Personal, political, or religious.
44 bless them . . . hate you. This clause is omitted by all the critical Greek texts. See Ap. 94. VII.
pray. Gr. *proseuchomai.* Ap. 134. I. 2.
for = on behalf of. Gr. *huper.* Ap. 104. xvii. 1.
45 be = become.
46 what reward, &c. The Lord varies the wording of this when repeating it later in Luke 6. 35.
not. Gr. *ouchi.* A strengthened form of *ou.* Ap. 105.
publicans = tax-gatherers. Hence, extortioners. Latin = *publicani.*
47 publicans. L. with Vulg. and some codices read "Gentiles". The publican was despised; Gentiles were detested.
48 perfect. In thus acting on the principles of grace, in conformity with the laws of the kingdom here promulgated. Gr. *teleios.* See Ap. 125. 1.
your . . . heaven. All the texts read "your heavenly Father". See note on 6. 14.

6. 1—7. 11 (*G*, p. 1317). THEY EXCEL THE TRADITION OF THE ELDERS.
(*Division.*)

6. 1. INTRODUCTION.

G
- J1 | 6. 2-4. As to Almsgiving.
- J2 | 6. 5-15. As to Prayer.
- J3 | 6. 16-18. As to Fasting.
- J4 | 6. 19-24. As to Riches.
- J5 | 6. 25—7. 11. As to Cares, &c.

1 not. Gr. *mē.* Ap. 105. II.
alms = an alms. All the critical texts read "righteousness", referring to all the subjects that follow, J1—J5. But this is conjecture, because "alms" is the first subject (*v.* 2). *Dikaiosunē*, "righteousness", was subsequently substituted for *eleēmosunē*, "alms".
men. Gr. *anthrōpos.* Ap. 123. 1.
to = in order to. Gr. *pros to.* Ap. 104. xv. 3.
seen. As in a theatre, so as to be admired. Ap. 133. I. 12. **of** = by (dat. not gen. case).
no. Gr. *ouk.* Ap. 105. I.
of = from. Gr. *para.* Ap. 104. xii. 2.
in. Gr. *en.* Ap. 104. viii.
heaven = heavens (pl.). See note on *vv.* 9, 10.

J1. AS TO ALMSGIVING (*vv.* 2-4).

2 hypocrites = actors: i.e. those who speak or act from under a mask. Used later of actual impiety, to which it led. Cp. 23. 28; 24. 51. Mark 12. 15.
that = so that. **of** = by. Gr. *hupo.* Ap. 104. xviii. 1.
Verily. See note on 5. 18.
They have = They receive. Gr. *apechō.* In the Papyri, (Ap. 94. IV.) used constantly in formal receipts, as = it is received: i.e. those men who desired to be seen of men, were seen, and had received all they looked for. They got their reward, and had nothing more to come. So in *vv.* 5, 16. Luke 6. 24. Cp. Phil. 4. 18. Philem. 15. **3 know** = get to know. Gr. *ginōskō.* Ap. 132. I. ii. **hand.** Omitted in the 1611 edition of the A.V. **4 seeth** = looketh, or observeth. Gr. *blepō.* Ap. 133. I. 5. **openly.** Omitted by all the Gr. texts. Ap. 94. VII.

J2. AS TO PRAYER (*vv.* 5-15).

5 thou prayest, thou. All the critical Gr. texts read "ye pray, ye". **prayest . . . pray.** Gr. *proseuchomai.* See Ap. 134. I. 2. **not.** Gr. *ouk.* Ap. 105. I. **love** = are fond of. Gr. *phileō.* Ap. 135. I. 2. **streets** = open places. **that** = so that. **be seen** = appear. Gr. *phainō.* Ap. 106. I. i. **6 into.** Gr. *eis.* Ap. 104. vi. **closet** = store-chamber. Hence a secret chamber where treasures were stored. Occ. only here, 24. 26, and Luke 12. 3, 24. Cp. Isa. 26. 20. 2 Kings 4. 33. **7 use not vain repetitions** = repeat not the same things over and over; explained in last clause. Gr. *battologeō.* Occ. only here. **heathen** = Gentiles. Gr. *ethnikos.* Occ. only here, and 18. 17. **for** = in. Gr. *en.* Ap. 104. viii. **much speaking.** Gr. *polulogia.* Occ. only here.

27 your Father °knoweth what things ye have
need of, ° before ye ask Him.
9 °After this manner therefore [5] pray ye: °Our
Father ° Which art [1] in °heaven, °Hallowed
be ° Thy name.
10 ° Thy °kingdom ° come. Thy °will °be
done °in °earth, as *it is* [1] in °heaven.
11 Give us this day our ° daily bread.
12 And forgive us °our debts, as ° we °forgive
our debtors.
13 And °lead us [1] not [6] into °temptation, but
°deliver us °from °evil: °For Thine is the
[10] kingdom, and the power, and the glory, °for
ever. Amen.
14 For °if ye forgive [1] men their °trespasses,
your °heavenly Father will °also forgive you:
15 But [14] if ye forgive [1] not [1] men their [14] trespasses, neither will your Father forgive your
[14] trespasses.
J[3] (p. 1319) 16 Moreover when ye fast, °be [1] not, as the
[2] hypocrites, of a sad countenance: for they
°disfigure their faces, that they may °appear
unto [1] men to fast. [2] Verily I say unto you,
[2] They have their reward.
17 But thou, when thou fastest, anoint thine
head, and ° wash thy face;
18 That thou [16] appear [1] not unto [1] men to fast,
but unto thy Father Which is [1] in secret: and
thy Father, Which [4] seeth [1] in secret, shall
reward thee [4] openly.
J[4] 19 °Lay [1] not up for yourselves treasures
°upon [10] earth, where moth and rust doth °cor-
rupt, and where thieves break through and steal:
20 But [19] lay up for yourselves treasures [1] in
[10] heaven, where neither moth nor rust doth
corrupt, and where thieves do [5] not break
through nor steal:
21 For where your treasure is, there will your
°heart be also.
22 The °light of the body is the eye: [14] if
therefore thine eye be °single, thy whole body
shall be full of light.
23 But [14] if thine eye be [13] evil, thy whole body
shall be full of darkness. °If therefore the
light that is [1] in thee °be darkness, how great *is*
that darkness!
24 °No man °can °serve two °masters: for
either he will °hate the one, and love the °other:
or else he will hold to the one, and despise the
°other. Ye °cannot serve °God and °mammon.

8 knoweth. Gr. *oida.* See Ap. 132. I. 1. Very significant in this connection.

before. Gr. *pro.* Ap. 104. xiv.

9 After, &c. Cp. "When". Luke 11. 2-4.

Our Father. See Ex. 4. 22. Deut. 32. 6, &c. The idolater could say to his idol "Thou art my father", so Israel was bound to do so (Isa. 63. 16; 64. 8). The Talmud so teaches. **Which** = Who.

heaven = heavens. See note on *v.* 10.

Hallowed = Sanctified.

Thy. Note that the first three petitions are with respect to God, while the next four concern those who pray. God is to be put first in all prayer.

10 Thy kingdom come. This is the great subject of the first period of the Lord's ministry. See Ap. 119, also Ap. 112, 113, 114, and the Structure on pp. 1304, 1305, and 1315. **kingdom.** See Ap. 112.

come. It was then being proclaimed, but was afterward rejected, and is now in abeyance. See App. 112-114, and cp. Ap. 63. ix. Hence this same petition is *now* correct, not the usual prayers for the "increase" or "extension" of it. **will** = desire. Gr. *thelō.* See Ap. 102. 1.

be done = be brought to pass, come to pass, be accomplished. Gr. *ginomai.* Cp. 26. 42.

in = upon. Gr. *epi.* Ap. 104. ix. 4.

earth = the earth. Gr. *gē.* Ap. 129. 4. All the texts (Ap. 94. VII.) omit the article.

heaven. Here it is sing. because it is in contrast with *earth.* Had it been sing. in *v.* 9, it would have implied that our Father was in heaven, but not on earth. In the Gr. the two clauses are reversed: "as in heaven [so] upon earth also".

11 daily. Gr. *epiousios.* A word coined by our Lord, and used only here and Luke 11. 3, by Him. Compounded from *epi* = upon (Ap. 104. ix.), and *ousios* = coming. This is derived from *eimi* = to come or go, which has the participle *epiousa* (not from *eimi* = to be, which would make the participle = *epousa*). Therefore it means *coming* or *descending upon*, as did the manna, with which it is contrasted in John 6. 32, 33. It is the true bread from heaven, by which alone man can live—the Word of God, which is prayed for here. *Epiousion* has the article and is separated from "this day" by the words "give to us"; "daily" here is from the Vulgate. *Epiousios* has been found in the *Papyri* (*Codd. Sergii*), but as these are, after all, not Greek (as shown by Prof. Nestlé in 1900) but *Armenian*; the evidence for the word being Greek is still wanting.

12 our debts. Sin is so called because failure in the obligation involves expiation and satisfaction.

we = we also = that is only what *we* mortals do. "We" is thus emphatic ("also" is ignored by the A.V.).

forgive. All editions read "have forgiven". That prayer and plea was suited for that dispensation of the kingdom, but is *reversed* in this present dispensation. See Eph. 4. 32. *Then,* forgiveness was conditioned; *now,* we forgive because we have been forgiven on account of Christ's merits. **13 lead** = bring. Not the same word as in 4. 1. **temptation** = trial. Cp. Jas. 1. 12, 13. **deliver** = rescue. **from** = away from. Gr. *apo.* Ap. 104. iv. **evil** = the evil [one]. See Ap. 128. IV. 1. **For, &c.** All the critical texts wrongly omit this doxology; for, out of about 500 codices which contain the prayer, only eight omit it. It is found also in the Syriac, Æthiopic, Armenian, Gothic, Sclavonic, and Georgian Versions. **for ever.** Gr. *eis tous aiōnas.* Ap. 151. II. A. 7. a. **14 if.** Implying a contingency. Gr. *ean* (with Subj.). See Ap. 118. I. b. Forgiveness was conditional in that dispensation of the kingdom. **trespasses** = lapses, varying in degree. Gr. pl. of *paraptōma.* Ap. 128. II. 4. **heavenly.** Here the emphasis is on Father, the adj. *ouranios* being used, instead of the noun, in regimen. It occ. only here, *vv.* 26, 32; 15. 13. Luke 2. 13. Acts 26. 19; and in the critical texts, additional in 5. 48; 18. 35; 23. 9. **also forgive you** = forgive you also (emph. on "you").

J[3]. AS TO FASTING (*vv.* 16-18).

16 be = become. **disfigure . . . appear.** Note the Fig. *Paronomasia* (Ap. 6), *aphanizousin . . . phanōsin.* **appear.** Ap. 106. I. **17 wash.** Gr. *niptō.* Ap. 136. i.

J[4]. AS TO RICHES (*vv.* 19-24).

19 Lay . . . up = Treasure . . . up. In the Elephantinē *Papyri* = establish a credit (*J. of Bib. Lit.*, 1912, p. 27). **upon.** Gr. *epi.* Ap. 104. ix. 1. **corrupt** = cause to vanish. **21 heart be also** = heart also be. **22 light** = lamp. Gr. *luchnos.* Ap. 130. 4. **single** = clear. **23 If.** Assuming it as a fact. Ap. 118. 2. a. **be** = is. **24 No man** = No one. Gr. *oudeis.* See Ap. 105. I. **can** = is able to. **serve.** As a bondservant. **masters.** Gr. *kurios.* See Ap. 98. VI. i. *a.* 4. B. **hate:** or care not for. **other.** Gr. *heteros.* See Ap. 124. 2. **cannot** = are not (Ap. 105. I) able to. **God.** Ap. 98. I. i. 1. **mammon** = riches. An Aramaic word. See Ap. 94. III. 3. Luke 16. 13.

J[5] (p. 1319) 27 25 °Therefore I say unto you, °Take °no thought for your °life, what ye shall eat, or what ye shall drink; nor yet for your body, what ye shall put on. Is [5]not the °life °more than meat, and the body than raiment?

26 °Behold the fowls °of the °air: for they sow not, neither do they reap, nor gather [6]into barns; yet °your [14]heavenly Father feedeth them. Are ye not much better than they?

27 Which °of you by [25]taking thought can °add one °cubit °unto his °stature?

28 And why [25]take ye thought °for raiment? °Consider the lilies of the field, how they grow; they °toil [5]not, neither do they °spin:

29 And yet I say unto you, That even Solomon [1]in all his glory was [5]not arrayed like one of these.

30 Wherefore, °if God so clothe the grass of the field, which to day is, and to morrow is cast [6]into the oven, *shall He* [5]not much more *clothe* you, °O ye of little faith?

31 Therefore [25]take [25]no thought, saying, 'What shall we eat?' or, 'What shall we drink?' or, 'Wherewithal shall we be clothed?'

32 (For after all these things do the °Gentiles seek:) for [14]your heavenly Father knoweth that ye have need of all these things.

33 But seek ye first °the kingdom of God, and °His righteousness; and all these things °shall be added unto you.

34 [25]Take therefore [25]no thought for the morrow: for the morrow °shall take thought for °the things of itself. °Sufficient unto the day °*is* the [23]evil thereof.

7 Judge °not, that ye be °not judged.

2 For °with what judgment ye judge, ye shall be judged: and °with what measure ye mete, it shall be measured to you °again.

3 And why °beholdest thou the °mote that is °in thy °brother's eye, but °considerest °not the °beam that is °in thine own eye?

4 Or how wilt thou say to thy [3]brother, 'Let me pull out the [3]mote °out of thine eye;' and, °behold, a [3]beam *is* [3]in thine own eye?

5 Thou hypocrite, first cast out the [3]beam °out of thine own eye; and then shalt thou see clearly to cast out the [3]mote °out of thy [3]brother's eye.

6 Give [1]not that which is holy unto the °dogs, neither cast ye your pearls before swine, lest °they °trample them °under their feet, °and °turn again and rend you.

7 °Ask, and it shall be given you; seek, and ye shall find; knock, and °it shall be opened unto you:

8 For every one that [7]asketh receiveth; and he that seeketh findeth; and to him that knocketh [7]it shall be opened.

9 Or what °man is there [5]of you, whom °if his son [7]ask bread, will he give him a stone?

10 Or °if he [7]ask °a fish, will he give him a serpent?

11 °If ye then, being °evil, °know how to give

J[5]. AS TO CARES, ETC. (6. 25—7. 11).

25 Therefore = On account of this (Gr. *dia*. Ap. 104. v. 2).

Take no thought = Be not careful: i.e. full of care, or over-anxious. Cp. *vv.* 27, 28, 31, 34.

no. Gr. *mē*. Ap. 105. II.

life = soul. Gr. *psuchē*. Ap. 110. III.

more = [worth] more.

26 Behold = Look attentively (*emblepō*, Ap. 133. I. 7) at (*eis*, Ap. 104. vi).

of = which fly in. Gen. of Relation. Ap. 17. 5.

air = the heaven. Sing. in contrast with earth. See note on 6. 9, 10.

your. Speaking to disciples. Contrast "them" with their creator.

27 of = from among. Gr. *ek*. Ap. 104. vii.

add = prolong.

cubit = span. Cp. Luke 12. 26. Put by Fig. *Metonymy* (of Subject), Ap. 6, for a very small thing, as in Ps. 39. 5, where the Gr. *pēchus* is used as the rendering of Heb. *'ammah*. **unto.** Gr. *epi*. Ap. 104. ix. 3.

stature. Used elsewhere of age in John 9. 21, 23. Heb. 11. 11, and of stature in Luke 19. 3. Doubtful in 6. 27. Luke 2. 52. Eph. 4. 13.

28 for = about or concerning. Gr. *peri*. Ap. 104. xiii. 1.

Consider = Consider carefully, so as to learn from. Gr. *katamanthanō*. Occ. only here. **toil not.** As men. **spin.** As women. Consolation for both sexes.

30 if. Assuming the fact. See Ap. 118. 2. a.

O ye of little faith. Note the four occurrences of this word (*oligopistos*). Here, rebuking *care*; 8. 26, rebuking *fear*; 14. 31, rebuking *doubt*; 16. 8, rebuking *reasoning*. Luke 12. 28 is parallel with Matt. 6. 30.

32 Gentiles = nations.

33 the kingdom of God. See Ap. 114. Occurs five times: Matt. 6. 33; 12. 28; 19. 24; 21. 31, 43.

His: i.e. God. L T [A] WH R omit, and read "His righteousness and kingdom".

shall be added. Hebraism = come on afterward, as in Acts 12. 3. Luke 20. 11. Sept. for Heb. *yāsaph*.

34 shall. Hebraism = is sure to, will certainly.

the things of. All the critical texts omit these words.

Sufficient, &c. Prob. the Fig. *Parœmia*. Ap. 6. This verse is not "omitted by Luke"; but it was not included by the Lord when repeated on a later occasion which Luke records. See Ap. 97.

is = be.

7. 1 not. Gr. *mē*. Ap. 105. II. Jewish proverb.

2 with what, &c. Fig. *Parœmia*. Ap. 6.

with. Gr. *en*. Ap. 104. viii.

again. All the critical texts omit. Ap. 94. VII.

3 beholdest. See Ap. 133. I. 5. This is in contrast with "considerest". Jewish proverb.

mote. Anglo-Saxon, *mot* = a particle of dust, something dry: i.e. any dry particle, as wood (splinter), chaff, or dust. **in.** Gr. *en*. Ap. 104. viii.

brother's. See note on 5. 22.

considerest. Gr. *katanoeō*. Stronger than "beholdest" above. See Ap. 133. II. 4.

not. Gr. *ou*. Ap. 105. I. Not the same word as in *v.* 1.

beam. Gr. *dokos*. Sept. for Heb. *ḳōrah* in 2 Kings 6. 2, 5. **4 out of** = from. Gr. *apo*. Ap. 104. iv.

behold. Fig. *Asterismos* (Ap. 6), for emphasis.

5 out of. Gr. *ek*. Ap. 104. vii.

6 dogs. Note the *Introversion* here.

K | g | dogs.
  h | swine.
  h | swine ("they").
 g | dogs (and the dogs).

they: i.e. the swine.

trample. All the critical texts read "shall trample upon". **under** = with. Gr. *en*. Ap. 104. viii. **and** = and [the dogs]. **turn again and** = having turned.

7 Ask. Gr. *aiteō*. Ap. 134. I. 4. **it shall be opened.** This is never done in the East to this day. The one who knocks is always first questioned. L Tr. WHm. read "it is opened" **9 man.** Gr. *anthrōpos*. Ap. 123. 1. **if.** See Ap. 118. 1. b. **10 if he ask.** All read "if he shall ask". **a fish** = a fish also. **11 If.** Ap. 118. 2. a. **evil** = grudging, or harmful. See Ap. 128. IV. i. Scripture thus challenges man, that is why man challenges it. **know.** Gr. *oida*. Ap. 132. I. i.

27 good gifts unto your °children, how much more
shall your Father Which is [3]in °heaven give
°good things to them that ask Him?
F 12 °Therefore all things whatsoever ye °would
(p. 1317) that [9]men should do to you, do ye even so to
them: for this is °the law and the prophets.
E 13 °Enter ye in °at the °strait gate: for °wide
(p. 1316) *is* the gate, and °broad *is* °the way, that °lead-
eth °to destruction, and many there be which
°go in °thereat:
14 °Because [13]strait *is* the gate, and °narrow
is the way, which leadeth °unto °life, and few
there be that find it.
D 15 °Beware °of false prophets, which come
°to you [3]in sheep's clothing, but inwardly
they are ravening wolves.
16 °Ye shall °know them °by their fruits.
°Do [9]men gather grapes [15]of thorns, or figs
[15]of thistles?
17 Even so every good tree bringeth forth
good fruit; but a corrupt tree bringeth forth
[11]evil fruit.
18 A good tree can [3]not bring forth [11]evil
fruit, neither *can* a corrupt tree bring forth
good fruit.
19 Every tree that bringeth [1]not forth good
fruit is hewn down, and cast °into the fire.
20 Wherefore [16]by their fruits [16]ye shall
[16]know them.
21 [3]Not every one that saith unto Me, °'Lord,
Lord,' shall enter into °the kingdom of °hea-
ven; but he that doeth the °will of My Father
Which is [3]in °heaven.
22 Many will say to Me [3]in that day, [21]'Lord,
Lord, °have we [3]not °prophesied [3]in Thy name?
and °in Thy name have cast out °devils? and
°in Thy name done many °wonderful works?'
23 And then will I profess unto them, 'I never
°knew you: depart °from Me, ye that work
°iniquity.'
C 24 Therefore °whosoever heareth these °say-
ings of Mine, and doeth them, I will liken him
unto a °wise °man, which built his house °upon
°a °rock:
25 °And °the rain descended, and the °floods
came, and the °winds blew, and °beat [24]upon
that house; and it fell [3]not: for it °was founded
[24]upon [24]a rock.
26 And every one that heareth these [24]say-
ings of Mine, and doeth them [1]not, shall be
likened unto a foolish [24]man, which built his
house [24]upon the sand:
27 [25]And the [25]rain descended, and the floods
came, and the winds blew, and °beat upon that
house; and it °fell: and great was the fall of it."
B 28 And it came to pass, when Jesus had
°ended these [24]sayings, the °people were
astonished °at His °doctrine:
29 For He °taught them as *one* °having authority, °and [3]not as the scribes.
G L V1 A1 **8** °When He was come down °from the
(p. 1324) mountain, great multitudes followed Him.
2 And, °behold, there came a °leper and

children: pl. of *teknon*. Ap. 108. I.
heaven = the heavens. See notes on 6. 9, 10.
good things. Cp. Ps. 34. 8–10; 84. 11. Luke 11. 13. Jas. 1. 17.
12 Therefore. Summing up all that has been said in *vv.* 1–11. **would** = be willing. See Ap. 102. 1.
the law. See note on 5. 17.
13 Enter ye in, &c. Repeated on a later occasion. Luke 13. 2.
at = through, or by means of. Gr. *dia*. Ap. 104. v. 1.
strait = narrow. **wide**. Gr. *platus*. Occ. only here.
broad = extensive. Gr. *euruchōros*. Occ. only here.
the way. For "the two ways", see Deut. 30. 15. 1 Kings 18. 21. 2 Pet. 2. 2, 15. **leadeth** = leads away.
to = unto. Gr. *eis*. Ap. 104. vi. **go** = enter in.
thereat = through. Gr. *dia*. Ap. 104. v. 1.
14 Because strait. L Tr. R marg. Syr. Vulg. &c., and some fifty codices read "How strait".
narrow = straitened.
unto. Gr. *eis*. Ap. 104. vi. Same as "to", *v.* 14.
life: i. e. the life [eternal]. See note on Lev. 18. 5. Ap. 170. 1. **15 Beware** = Take heed, as in 6. 1.
of = from, or away from. Gr. *apo*. Ap. 104. iv.: i. e. Beware [and keep] away from.
to. Gr. *pros*. Ap. 104. xv. 3.
16 Ye shall know. Note the Fig. *Epanadiplōsis* (Ap. 6). See *v.* –20.
know = fully know and recognize. See Ap. 132. I. iii.
by = from. Gr *apo*. Ap. 104. iv.
Do men, &c. Fig. *Erotēsis* (Ap. 6), for emphasis.
19 into. Gr. *eis*. Ap. 104. vi.
21 Lord, Lord. Note the Fig. *Epizeuxis* (Ap. 6), for emphasis. Ap. 98. VI. i. *a*. 2. B. a.
the kingdom of heaven. See Ap. 114.
heaven = heavens. All the texts read "the heavens". See notes on 6. 9, 10. **will**. Gr. *thelēma*. See Ap. 102.
22 have = did. Note the Fig. *Erotēsis*. Ap. 6.
prophesied = acted as spokesmen. See Ap. 49.
in Thy name = by or through Thy name. Note the Fig. *Anadiplosis*. Ap. 6. **devils** = demons.
wonderful works. Gr. *dunamis* (see Ap. 172. 1); in Sept. in this sense only in Job 37. 16, for Heb. *miphᵉlā'āh*.
23 knew = got to know. Gr. *ginōskō*. See Ap. 132. I. ii. **from** = away from. Gr. *apo*. Ap. 104. iv.
iniquity = lawlessness. See Ap. 128. X. 1.
24 whosoever = every one (as in *v.* 26). Fig. *Synecdochē* (of Genus), Ap. 6.
sayings = words. Gr. pl. of *logos*. See note on Mark 9. 32. **wise** = prudent.
man. Gr. *anēr*. Ap. 123. 2. **upon**. Gr. *epi*. Ap. 104. ix. 3.
a = the. **rock** = rocky ground.
25 And. Note the Fig. *Polysyndeton* (Ap. 6), emphasizing each particular.
the rain descended = down came the rain. Gr. *brochē*. Occ. only here. On the roof.
floods. At the foundation. **winds**. At the sides.
beat = broke upon, dashed against (with great violence), as in Luke 6. 48, in contrast with "beat" in *v.* 27, which is a much weaker word. **was** = had been.
27 beat upon = on the roof; stumbled against, merely impinged, or lightly struck, in contrast with *v.* 25.
fell = *did* fall.
28 ended. This marks the end of the first period and subject of the Lord's ministry. See the Structure, F, p. 1315, and Ap. 119. **people** = multitudes.
at. Gr. *epi*. Ap. 104. ix. 2. **doctrine** = teaching.
29 taught = was continually teaching.
having authority: i. e. possessing Divine authority. Gr. *exousia*. Ap. 172. 5. In the current Heb. literature of that time it denoted the Heb. *mippī hagg'būrah* = from the mouth of God. See notes on Matt. 26. 64. Mark 14. 62, and Heb. 1. 3.
and not. Note the Fig. *Pleonasm* (Ap. 6). Jewish teachers always referred to tradition, or to what some other teacher had said; and do so to this day.

8. 1–16. 13 [For Structure see next page].

1 When = And when. **from** = away from. Gr. *apo*. Ap. 104. iv. **2 behold**. Fig. *Asterismos* (Ap. 6), for emphasis. **leper**. See note on Ex. 4. 6.

27 °worshipped Him, saying, °"Lord, if Thou
wilt, Thou canst make me °clean."
3 And °Jesus put forth *His* hand, and touched
him, saying, °"I will; be thou [2]clean." And
immediately °his leprosy was cleansed.
4 And °Jesus saith unto him, °"See thou tell
°no man; but °go thy way, °shew thyself to
the priest, and offer the gift that °Moses commanded, °for a testimony unto them."
B^1 i 5 And when Jesus was entered °into °Caper-
(p. 1323) naum, °there came unto Him a °centurion, °be-
seeching Him,
6 And saying, [2]"Lord, my °servant °lieth at
home °sick of the palsy, grievously tormented."
7 And [3]Jesus saith unto him, "I will come
and heal him."
k 8 The centurion answered and said, [2]"Lord,
I am °not °worthy that Thou shouldest °come
°under my roof: but speak the word only,
and my [6]servant shall be healed.
9 For °I am °a man [8]under °authority, having
soldiers [8]under °me: °and I say to °this *man*,
'Go,' °and he goeth; and to °another, 'Come,'
and he cometh; and to my °servant, 'Do this,'
°and he doeth *it*."
l 10 When Jesus heard *it*, He °marvelled, and
said to them that followed, °"Verily I say
unto you, I have not found so great faith, °no,
not °in Israel.
11 And I say unto you, That °many shall
come [1]from the east and west, and shall °sit
down °with Abraham, °and Isaac, °and Jacob,
[10]in °the kingdom of heaven.
12 But the °children of [11]the kingdom shall be

8. 1—16. 13 (G, p. 1315). THE SECOND PERIOD OF THE MINISTRY. PROCLAMATION OF THE KING. (*Introversion and Alternations.*)

G | L | 8. 1—9. 38. THE LORD. His Person. Proclaimed as "Lord" and "Son of Man". Witness and Evidences begun. Miracles and Calls.
  M | N | 10. 1-42. Mission of the TWELVE begun.
    O | P^1 | R^1 | 11. 1, 2. Miracles.
        S^1 | 11. 3-6. Effects.
      Q^1 | T^1 | 11. 7-30. Teaching.
        U^1 | 12. 1-8. Results. Opposition of Pharisees.
      P^2 | R^2 | 12. 9-13. Miracles.
        S^2 | 12. 14-50. Effects.
      Q^2 | T^2 | 13. 1-53. Teaching.
        U^2 | 13. 54-58. Results. Opposition of His own kindred.
  M | *N* | 14. 1-12. Mission of JOHN BAPTIST ended.
    O | P^3 | R^3 | 14. 13-36. Miracles.
        S^3 | 15. 1, 2. Effects.
      Q^3 | T^3 | 15. 3-11. Teaching.
        U^3 | 15. 12-20. Result. Opposition of Pharisees.
      P^4 | R^4 | 15. 21-39. Miracles.
        S^4 | 16. 1-4. Effect.
      Q^4 | T^4 | 16. 5-12. Teaching.
        U^4 | 16. 13-16. Result. Opposition complete.
L | 16. 17-20. THE LORD, Messiah. Declared. Witness and Evidences ended.

8. 1—9. 38 (L, above). [For Structure see next page.]
worshipped = did homage. See Ap. 137. i. The variations in Mark 1, and Luke 5, are due to the fact that they do not record the same miracle. See Ap. 97.
Lord. Ap. 98. VI. i. *a*. 3. B. This is the first time that Jesus is called "Lord". In this second period of His ministry, His Person is to be proclaimed as Messiah, both Divine (here), and in *v.* 20 human. When once they begin to call Him "Lord", they continue. Cp. *vv.* 6, &c. **clean.** See note on *v.* 3. Not the same miracle as in Mark 1. 40 and Luke 5. 12. Here both *without* the city (Capernaum, Ap. 169); there, both *within* (prob. Chorazin), for the leper was "full" and therefore "clean" (Lev. 13. 12, 13). Here, the leper *obeys* and is silent; there, he *disobeys*, so that the Lord could no more enter the city (Chorazin). The antecedents were different, and the consequents also, as may be seen from the two records. **3 Jesus.** All the texts (Ap. 94. VII) read "He". **I will** = I am willing. See Ap. 102. 1. **his leprosy was cleansed.** Fig. *Hypallage* (Ap. 6) = he was cleansed of his leprosy. *Katharizō* is found in the Papyri and in Inscriptions in this sense. **4 Jesus.** See Ap. 98. X. **See.** Gr. *horaō*. Ap. 133. I. 8. **no man** = no one. **go.** To Jerusalem. **shew thyself, &c.** See Lev. 14. 4. **Moses.** The *first* of eighty occurrences of "Moses" in the N.T. *Thirty-eight* in the Gospels (see the first occurrence in each Gospel (Matt. 8. 4. Mark 1. 44. Luke 5. 14. John 1. 17); *nineteen* times in Acts (see note on Acts 3. 22); *twenty-two* times in the Epistles (see note on Rom. 5. 14; *once* in Revelation (Rev. 15. 3). See Ap. 117. I. **for.** Gr. *eis*. Ap. 104. vi.

8. 5-13 (B^1, p. 1324). THE PALSY. (*Introversion.*)

B^1 | i | 5-7. Servant sick.
  k | 8, 9. Word. Sufficiency.
    l | 10-12. The Divine Command.
  k | 13-. Word. Efficacy.
i | -13. Servant healed.

5 into. Gr. *eis*. Ap. 104. vi. **Capernaum.** See note on 4. 13, and Ap. 169. **there came, &c.** This is in connection with the same centurion as in Luke 7. 3, 6, but on a prior occasion. See notes there. **centurion.** Commanding 100 men, the sixtieth part of a legion. **beseeching** = appealing to. Gr. *parakaleō*. Ap. 134. I. 6. **6 servant** = young man, in legal relation (like the French *garçon*). Gr. *pais*. See Ap. 108. IV. **lieth** = is thrown down. **sick of the palsy** = paralysed. **8 not.** Gr. *ou*. Ap. 105. I. **worthy** = fit. Not "worthy" (morally), but "fit" socially. **come** = enter. **under.** Gr. *hupo*. Ap. 104. xviii. 2. **9 I** = I also. **a man.** Gr. *anthrōpos*. See Ap. 123. I. **authority.** Gr. *exousia*. Ap. 172. 5. **me** = myself. **and.** Note the Fig. *Polysyndeton* in this verse, Ap. 6. **this man** = this [soldier]. **another**: i.e. of the same rank (see Ap. 124. 1) = another [soldier]. **servant** = bondservant. **10 marvelled.** Only two things that the Lord marvelled at: (1) faith (here); (2) unbelief (Mark 6. 6). **Verily.** Only Matthew uses this Aramaic word here (supplementary). See note on 5. 18. **no, not** = not even. Gr. *oude*. Related to *ou*. Ap. 105. I. **in.** Gr. *en*. Ap. 104. vii. **11 many.** Used by Fig. *Euphēmismos* for *Gentiles* (Ap. 6), to avoid giving offence at this stage of His ministry. **sit down** = recline as guests (in eating, or at a feast). **with.** Gr. *meta*. Ap. 104. xi. 1. **and.** Note the Fig. *Polysyndeton* (Ap. 6). **the kingdom of heaven.** See Ap. 114. **12 children** = sons, Gr. *huios*. Ap. 108. III (and heirs). A Hebraism, denoting those who were related by any ties of friendship: e. g. followers, learners, inhabitants, &c.

27 **cast out [5]into °outer darkness: there shall be °weeping and gnashing of teeth."**

k (p. 1323) **13 And Jesus said unto the centurion, "Go thy way; and as thou °hast believed, *so* be it done unto thee."**

i **And his [6]servant was healed [10]in the °selfsame hour.**

C¹ (p. 1324) **14 And when Jesus was come [5]into °Peter's house, He °saw his wife's mother °laid, and sick of a fever.**

15 And He touched her hand, and the fever left her: and she arose, and ministered unto them.

D¹ **16 °When °the even was come, they brought unto Him many that were possessed with °devils: and He cast out the °spirits °with *His* word, and healed all that were °sick:**

W¹ X¹ **17 °That it might be fulfilled which was spoken °by °Esaias the prophet, °saying, "Himself °took our infirmities, and °bare *our* °sicknesses."**

Y¹ m **18 Now when Jesus [14]saw great multitudes °about Him, He gave commandment to depart °unto the °other side.**

19 And °a certain scribe came, and said unto Him, °"Master, I will follow Thee whithersoever Thou °goest."

n **20 And Jesus saith °unto him, "The foxes have holes, and the birds of the °air *have* °nests; but °the Son of Man hath [8]not where °to lay *His* head."**

m **21 And °another of His disciples said unto Him, °"Lord, °suffer me °first to go and bury my father."**

n **22 But Jesus said unto him, "Follow Me; and °let °the dead bury their dead."**

V² A² o **23 And when He was entered [5]into °a ship, His disciples followed Him.**

24 And, °behold, there arose a great °tempest

8. 1—9. 38 (L, p. 1323). THE LORD. HIS PERSON. PROCLAIMED AS "LORD" AND "SON OF MAN" (8. 20). MIRACLES AND CALLS.

(*Repeated and Extended Alternations and Introversions.*)

L | V¹ | A¹ | 8. 1-4. The Leper.
  B¹ | 8. 5-13. The Palsy.
  C¹ | 8. 14, 15. The Fever.
  D¹ | 8. 16. Many.
} 8. 1-16. Four Miracles.
 W¹ | X¹ | 8. 17. Testimony. (Isaiah.)
  Y¹ | 8. 18-22. Disciples. Waverers.
V² | A² | 8. 23-27. The Storm.
  B² | 8. 28-31. Two Demoniacs.
  C² | 8. 32-34. The Swine.
  D² | 9. 1-8. The Palsy.
} 8. 23—9. 8. Four. Miracles.
 W² | Y² | 9. 9. Disciple. True. (Matthew.)
  X² | 9. 10-17. Testimony. (People.)
V³ | A³ | 9. 18-26. Two Women.
  B³ | 9. 27-31. Two Blind Men.
  C³ | 9. 32-34. Dumb demon.
  D³ | 9. 35. Many.
} 9. 18-35. Four Miracles
 W³ | X³ | 9. 36, 37. Testimony. (His own.)
  Y³ | 9. 38. Disciples. Prayer for.

outer = the outer. Gr. *exōteros.* Occ. only in Matthew (here, and in 22. 13, and 25. 30). Outside the place where the feast was going on in *v.* 11.

weeping and gnashing = the weeping and the grinding. The Articles denoting not a state but a definite occasion and time when this event shall take place. Used by the Lord seven times (Matt. 8. 12; 13. 42; 13. 50; 22. 13; 24. 51; 25. 30. Luke 13. 28). A study of these will show that the occasion is "the end of the age", when "the Lord and His servants shall have come", and when He will deal with the "wicked" and "unprofitable" servants, and sit down with Abraham and Isaac and Jacob in His kingdom.

13 hast believed = didst believe. **selfsame** = that.

14 Peter's house. The Lord was in Capernaum, so that He was probably lodging with Peter. Cp. Mark 1. 29. See Ap. 169. **saw.** Gr. *eidon.* Ap. 133. I. 1. **laid** = laid out for death. A Hebraism.

16 When = And when. **the even.** Probably the Sabbath, for they came straight out of the Synagogue and waited for the end of the Sabbath. **devils** = demons: i.e. evil spirits. Ap. 101. III. 12. **spirits.** Ap. 101. III. 11. **with His word** = by a word. Supply "a" instead of "His". **sick** = in evil case. Ap. 128. IV. 4. **17 That** = So that. **by** = by means of. Gr. *dia.* Ap. 104. v. 1. **Esaias** = Isaiah. See Ap. 79. I. **saying.** Quoted from the Heb. of Isa. 53. 4. Cp. 1 Pet. 2. 24. See Ap. 107. I. 3. **took . . . bare.** The two words together fulfil the sense of the Hebrew (Isa. 53. 4). The Inspirer of Isaiah adapts and deals as He pleases with His own words. **bare** = to take up for one's self; to bear our infirmities as in Luke 14. 27. Rom. 15. 1. Gal. 5. 10; 6. 17. Cp. John 4. 6. **sicknesses.** Gr. *nosos* diseases.

8. 18-22 (Y¹, above). DISCIPLES. WAVERERS. (*Alternation.*)

Y¹ | m | 18, 19. A Scribe. Forwardness.
 n | 20. Discouragement.
 m | 21. A Disciple. Backwardness.
 n | 22. Encouragement.

18 about = around. Gr. *peri.* Ap. 104. xiii. 3. **unto.** Gr. *eis.* Ap. 104. vi. **other side** = farther side, not either of the words in Ap. 124. **19 a** = one. A Hebraism for "a". **Master** = Teacher. Ap. 98. XIV. v. 1. **goest** = mayest go. **20 unto him.** No Preposition. **air** = heaven. **nests** = roosts. **the Son of Man.** He Who has dominion in the earth. The first of eighty-seven occurrences. See Ap. 98. XVI. **to lay** = He may lay. Cp. Rev. 14. 14. **21 another** = a different one: Gr. *heteros.* Ap. 124. 2. i.e. a disciple, not a "scribe" (*v.* 19). Ap. 124. 2. **Lord.** Ap. 98. VI. *a.* 3. A. **suffer me, &c.** = allow me, &c. This was, and is to-day, a polite way of excusing one's self, it being well understood as such, because all knew that the dead are buried on the day of the death, and no one leaves the house. **first.** No! See 6. 33. **22 let** = leave. **the dead** = corpses. Note the well-known Fig. *Antanaclasis* (Ap. 6), by which one word is used twice in the same sentence with two meanings which *clash* against each other: "leave the dead to bury their own corpses". See Ap. 139. I.

8. 23-27 [For Structure see next page].

23 a ship = the ship. Referring to *v.* 18. **24 behold.** Fig. *Asterismos* (Ap. 6), to call attention to another stage of "the great conflict". See Ap. 23, p. 27. This is not the same tempest as that recorded in Mark 4. 37-41, and Luke 8. 23-25. This was *before* the calling of the Twelve: the other was *after* that event. There is no "discrepancy", if we note the differences on p. 1325, and Ap. 97. **tempest** = earthquake. Always so rendered in the other thirteen occurrences. In the later event it was a squall (Gr. *lailaps*).

27 [10]in the sea, insomuch that the ship °was
covered °with the waves:
p but He was °asleep.
(p. 1325)
25 And His disciples came to *Him* and awoke
q Him, saying, [21]"Lord, save us: we °perish."
q 26 And He saith unto them, °"Why are ye
fearful, °O ye of little faith?"
p Then He arose, and rebuked the winds and
the sea;
o and there °was a great calm.
27 But the °men °marvelled, saying, "What
°manner of man is This, that even the winds
and the sea obey Him!"
B² 28 And °when He was come °to the other
(p. 1324) side [5]into the country of the °Gergesenes,
there met Him °two °possessed with devils,
coming °out of the tombs, exceeding fierce, so
that °no man might pass [17]by that way.
29 And, [2]behold, they cried out, saying,
°"What have we to do with Thee, °Jesus,
Thou °Son of God? °art Thou come hither to
torment us °before the time?"
30 And there was a good way off [1]from them
an herd of many swine feeding.
31 So the °devils [5]besought Him, saying,
°"If Thou cast us out, suffer us to go away
[5]into the herd of swine."
C² 32 And He said unto them, °"Go." And when
they were come out, they went [5]into the herd
of swine: and, [2]behold, the whole herd of
swine ran violently °down °a steep place
[5]into the sea, and °perished [10]in the waters.
33 And they that kept them fled, and went
their ways [5]into the city, and told every thing,
and what was befallen to the [28]possessed of
the devils.
34 And, [2]behold, °the whole °city came out
°to meet Jesus: and when they saw Him,
they °besought *Him* that He would depart
°out of their coasts.

D² r **9** And He entered °into °a ship, and passed
(p. 1325) over, and came °into °His own °city.
2 And, °behold, they brought to Him °a man
sick of the palsy, lying °on a °bed: and
Jesus °seeing °their faith said unto the sick
of the palsy;
s °"Son, be of good cheer; thy °sins °be forgiven thee."

8. 23-27 (A², p. 1324). THE STORM. (*Introversion.*)

A² | o | 23, 24-. Tempest arising.
| p | -24. The Lord asleep.
| q | 25. Disciples awakening Him.
| *q* | 26-. Disciples reproached by Him.
| *p* | -26-. The Lord arising.
| *o* | -26. Tempest calmed.

was covered = was getting covered. Hence it was a *decked* boat. In the later miracle it was an *open* boat, "filled". **with** = by. Gr. *hupo*. Ap. 104. xviii. 1.
asleep = sleeping. **25 perish** = are perishing.
26 Why . . . ? Fig. *Erotēsis* (Ap. 6). Here the danger was not so imminent, for He first rebuked the disciples. In the later miracle the danger was greater, and He rebuked the storm first. See Ap. 97.
O ye of little faith. The second occurrence of this word (*oligopistoi*). See note on 6. 30. **was** = became.
27 men. Pl. of *anthrōpos*. Ap. 123. 1.
marvelled. In 14. 33 "worshipped".
manner, &c. = kind of a Being.
28 when He was come. This miracle of the two demoniacs was not the same as that recorded in Mark 5. 1-20 and Luke 8. 26-40. Here, there were *two* men; in the later miracle there was *one*; here, they landed opposite the place whence they set sail (Gergesenes); there, the Gadarenes (not Gadera) not opposite; here, no name is asked; there, the name is "Legion"; here, no bonds used; there, many; here, the two were *not* afterwards used, and the Twelve not yet called; there, the one man *was* used, and the Twelve had been called. The consequents also are different. See Ap. 97.
to = into. Gr. *eis*. Ap. 104. vi.
Gergesenes. Prob. Girgashites, so called from one of the original Canaanite nations (Gen. 10. 16; 15. 21; Deut. 7. 1. Josh. 3. 10; 24. 11. 1 Chron. 1. 14. Neh. 9. 8). Not Gadarenes, as in Mark and Luke. "Gergesenes is the reading of the vast majority of MSS. of both families; of the Coptic, Æthiopic, and Armenian versions". Origen is the great authority; but Wetstein "imagined" that it was Origen's "gratuitous conjecture". Critics have followed Wetstein, but Scrivener is right (as usual) in retaining Gergesenes.
two. In the later miracle only one. Cp. "we", *v.* 29.
possessed with devils: i.e. demoniacs. Gr. *daimonizomai*. **out of.** Gr. *ek*. Ap. 104. vii.
no. Gr. *mē*. Ap. 105. I.
no man might pass = one was not able to pass.
29 What have we to do with Thee? A Hebraism. See note on 2 Sam. 16. 10. Occ. Mark 1. 24; 5. 7. Luke 4. 34; 8. 28; and John 2. 4.
Jesus. All the texts (Ap. 94. VII) omit "Jesus" here.
Son of God. See Ap. 98. XV.
art . . . ? Fig. *Erotēsis*. Ap. 6.
before. Gr. *pro*. Ap. 104. xiv. **31 devils** = demons.
If. See Ap. 118. 2. a. Assuming that He would do so.
32 Go. Gr. *hupagō* = go forth, i. e. *out of* the man.
down. Gr. *kata*. Ap. 104. x. 1.
a = the. Evidently, the well-known precipice.

perished = died. Those who defiled the temple (21. 12, 13. John 2. 14-16) lost their trade; and those who defiled Israel (here) lost their animals. **34 the whole.** Put by Fig. *Synecdochē* (of Genus), Ap. 6, for the greater part. **city.** Prob. Gergasa. See note on *v.* 28. **to meet** = for a meeting with. Gr. *sunantēsis*. Occ. only here, but L T Tr. WH read *hupantēsin*, which occurs also as the same reading in 25. 1 and John 12. 13. **besought.** Same word as in *vv.* 5, 31. See note on Mark 5. 12. **out of** = away from. Gr. *apo*. Ap. 104. iv.

9. 1-8 (D², p. 1324). THE PALSY. (*Introversion.*)

D² | r | 1, 2-. Palsied Man brought.
| s | -2. Forgiveness declared.
| t | 3. Scribes. Evil thoughts entertained.
| *t* | 4. Scribes. Evil thoughts challenged.
| *s* | 5, 6. Forgiveness. Power claimed.
| *r* | 7, 8. Palsied Man healed.

1 into. Gr. *eis*. Ap. 104. vi. **a ship** = the boat. The one already mentioned in ch. 8. **His own.** See note on "private" (2 Pet. 1. 20). **city.** Capernaum. See note on 4. 13, and Ap. 169. **2 behold.** Fig. *Asterismos*. Ap. 6. **a man sick of the palsy** = a paralytic. **on.** Gr. *epi*. Ap. 104. ix. 1. **bed** = couch. **seeing** = on seeing. See Ap. 133. I. 1. **their faith.** Including of course that of the paralytic. **Son** = Child. Gr. *teknon*. See Ap. 108. I. **sins.** Gr., pl. of *hamartia*. Ap. 128. II. 1. **be forgiven** = stand remitted. L T Tr. and WH read the Indicative = "have been and are forgiven", marking the Lord's authority. Not the ambiguous "be forgiven".

t 3 And, [2]behold, certain of the scribes said
(p. 1325) °within themselves, "This *man* blasphemeth."
27 *t* 4 And °Jesus °knowing their thoughts said,
"Wherefore think ye °evil °in your hearts?
s 5 For whether is easier, to say, '*Thy* [2]sins
[2]be forgiven thee'; or to say, 'Arise, and
walk?'
6 But that ye may [4]know that °the Son of
man hath °power [2]on °earth to forgive [2]sins,"
(then saith He to [2]the sick of the palsy,)
"Arise, take up thy [2]bed, and go °unto thine
house."
r 7 And he arose, and departed °to his house.
8 But when the °multitudes [2]saw *it*, they
marvelled, and glorified God, Which had
given such [6]power unto °men.
W[2] Y[2] 9 And as [4]Jesus passed °forth from thence, He
(p. 1324) [2]saw a [8]man, named °Matthew, sitting °at
°the receipt of custom: and He saith unto him,
"Follow Me." And he arose, and followed
Him.
X[2] t 10 °And it came to pass, as [4]Jesus °sat at
(p. 1326) meat °in °the house, [2]behold, many °publi-
cans and °sinners came and °sat down with
Him and His disciples.
11 And when the °Pharisees [2]saw *it*, they
said unto His disciples, "Why eateth your
°Master °with [10]publicans and [10]sinners?"
u 12 But when [4]Jesus heard *that*, He said unto
them, °"They that be °whole need °not a physician, but they that are sick.
v 13 °But °go ye and learn what *that* °mean-
eth, '**I °will have °mercy, and [12]not sacrifice:**'
for °I am [12]not come to call °the righteous, but
[10]sinners °to repentance."
t 14 Then °came to Him the disciples of John,
saying, "Why do we and the [11]Pharisees °fast
oft, but Thy disciples fast [12]not?"
u 15 And [4]Jesus said unto them, °"Can °the
°children of the bridechamber mourn, as long
as the bridegroom is [11]with them? but the
days will come, when the bridegroom shall be
taken °from them, and then °shall they fast.
v 16 °No man putteth a piece of °new cloth
°unto an old garment, for °that which is put
in to fill it up °taketh [15]from the garment, and
°the rent is made worse.
17 Neither do men put °new wine [1]into °old
°bottles: °else the °bottles °break, and the
wine runneth out, and the °bottles °perish:
but they put °new wine [1]into °new °bottles,
and both are °preserved."
A[3] w 18 While He spake these things unto them,
(p. 1327) [2]behold, there came °a certain °ruler, and
°worshipped Him, saying, "My daughter

3 within = among. Gr. *en*. Ap. 104. viii. 2.
4 Jesus. Ap. 98. X.
knowing = perceiving. Gr. *oida*. Ap. 132. I. i. Same word as "seeing" in *v.* 2. Not the same as "know", *v.* 6, or as in *v.* 30.
evil = mischief. Gr. *ponēros*. Ap. 128. III. i.
in, &c. = among [you] in your hearts. Gr. *en*. Ap. 104. viii. 2.
6 the Son of man. See Ap. 98. XVI.
power = authority. See Ap. 172. 5.
earth = the earth. Gr. *gē*. Ap. 129. 4.
unto. Gr. *eis*. Same as "into", *v.* 1.
7 to. Gr. *eis*. Same as "unto", *v.* 6.
8 multitudes = crowds. So *vv.* 33, 36; "people" in *vv.* 23, 25.
men. Gr *anthrōpos*. Ap. 123. 1.
9 forth = along.
Matthew. An Aramaic word. See Ap. 94. III. 3.
at = over. Gr. *epi*. Ap. 104. ix. 3.
the receipt of custom = the custom-house.

9. 10-17 (X[2], p. 1324). TESTIMONY. TWO QUESTIONS. (*Extended Alternation.*)

X[2] | t | 10, 11. Question of Pharisees to His disciples.
  u | 12. Proverb. } Answer.
   v | 13. Application. }
 t | 14. Question of John's disciples to Him.
  u | 15. Proverb. } Answer.
   v | 16, 17. Application. }

10 And it came to pass. A Hebraism: frequent in O.T. See note on Gen. 1. 2.
sat at meat = was reclining.
in. Gr. *en*. Ap. 104. viii. 1.
the house = his house: i.e. Matthew's house. Cp. Luke 5. 29; so in *v.* 28.
publicans = tax-gatherers.
sinners. Especially in a religious sense. This usage is common in the Inscriptions in Asia Minor (Deissmann).
11 Pharisees. See Ap. 120.
Master = Teacher. See Ap. 98. XIV. v. 1.
with. Gr. *meta*. Ap. 104. xi. 1.
12 They that be, &c. Fig. *Parœmia* (Ap. 6). See "u" above.
whole = strong. Eng. "whole" is from Anglo-Saxon *hael* = our "hale", healthy or strong.
not. Gr. *ou*. Ap. 105. I.
13 But, &c. This is the application. Hos. 6. 6 is quoted with evident reference to Hos. 6. 1; 5. 13 and 7. 1. See Ap. 117. I.
go ye. To your teachers.
meaneth = is.
will have = require. See Ap. 102. 1.
mercy = compassion. Gr. *eleos*.
I am not come = I came not.
the righteous = just ones.
to repentance. All the texts omit: also wanting in Syr. and Vulg. both here and in Mark 2. 17.
14 came = come.
fast oft. Cp. Luke 18. 12.
15 Can, &c. Fig. *Parœmia* (Ap. 6). See "*u*" above.
the children, &c. A Hebraism. Used in various connections. Cp. 23. 15. Deut. 13. 13. 1 Sam. 2. 12 (marg.); 20. 31. 2 Sam. 12. 5 (marg.). John 17. 12. Acts 3. 25.
children = sons. Gr. pl. of *huios*. Ap. 108. III.
from. Gr. *apo*. Ap. 104. iv.
shall = will. **16 No man** = No one. **new cloth** = new flannel: i.e undressed or unfulled. In this condition it is less supple and will tear away. **unto** = on or upon. Gr. *epi*. Ap. 104. ix. 2. **that which is put in, &c.** = the insertion: i.e. the patch put on. **taketh** = teareth away. **the rent is made worse** = a worse rent takes place. **17 new** = freshly made: i.e. young. Gr. *neos* = new as to time. **old bottles** = old or dried skins. **bottles** = wine skins. **else** = otherwise. **break** = burst. **perish** = are ruined. **new bottles** = fresh wineskins of newer quality or character. Gr. *kainos*. **preserved** = preserved together.

9. 18-26, A[3], p. 1324 [For Structure see next page].

18 a certain = one. A Hebraism. **ruler** = a civil ruler. Not the same miracle as that in Mark 5. 22, and Luke 8. 41. See Ap. 138. **worshipped** = began doing homage. Ap. 137. I.

27 °is even now dead: but come and lay Thy hand °upon her, and she shall °live."
19 And [4]Jesus arose, and followed him, and so *did* His disciples.

x (p. 1327) 20 (And, [2]behold, °a woman, which was diseased with °an issue of blood twelve years, came behind *Him*, and touched the °hem of His garment:
21 For she °said °within herself, °"If I may but touch His garment, I shall be °whole."

x 22 But [4]Jesus turned Him about, and when He [2]saw her, He said, "Daughter, be of good °comfort; thy faith hath °made thee whole." And the woman was °made whole [15]from that hour.)

w 23 And when [4]Jesus came [1]into the ruler's house, and [2]saw the °minstrels and the °people °making a noise,
24 He said unto them, °"Give place: for the °maid is [12]not dead, but °sleepeth." And they laughed Him to scorn.
25 But when the people were put forth, He went in, and took her by the hand, and the [24]maid arose.
26 And the °fame hereof went abroad [1]into all that land.

B[3] y 27 And when [4]Jesus departed thence, two blind men followed Him, crying, and saying, "*Thou* °Son of David, have [13]mercy on us."

z 28 And when He was come [1]into °the house, the blind men came to Him: and [4]Jesus saith unto them, "Believe ye that I am able to do this?" They °said unto Him, "Yea, °Lord."
29 Then touched He their eyes, saying, °"According to your faith be it unto you."
30 And their eyes were opened;

z and [4]Jesus straitly charged them, saying, "See *that* [16]no man know *it*."

y 31 But they, °when they were departed, °spread abroad His °fame [4]in all that country.

C[3] (p. 1324) 32 °As they went out, [2]behold, they brought to Him a dumb [8]man °possessed with a devil.
33 And when the °devil was cast out, the dumb spake: and the [8]multitudes marvelled, saying, "It was never so seen [4]in Israel."
34 But the [11]Pharisees said, "He casteth °out [32]devils °through the prince of the [32]devils."

D[3] 35 And [4]Jesus went about all the cities and villages, teaching [4]in their °synagogues, and °preaching °the °gospel °of the kingdom, and healing °every °sickness and °every disease °among the People.

W[3] X[3] 36 But when He saw the [8]multitudes, He was moved with compassion °on them, because they °fainted, and were scattered abroad, °as sheep having °no shepherd.
37 Then saith He unto His disciples, "The harvest °truly *is* °plenteous, but the labourers *are* few;

Y[3] 38 °Pray ye therefore °the Lord of the harvest, that He will send forth labourers [1]into His harvest."

9. 18-26 (A[3], p. 1324). TWO WOMEN.
(*Introversion.*)

A[3] | w | 18, 19. The Ruler's daughter. Dead.
 x | 20, 21. The Woman's faith. Exercised.
 x | 22. The Woman's faith. Rewarded.
 w | 23-26. The Ruler's daughter. Raised.

is even now dead = hath just now died.
upon. Gr. *epi*. Ap. 104. ix. 3.
live = come to life again. Especially to live again in resurrection. See Mark 16. 11. Luke 24. 5, 23. John 11. 25, 26. Acts 1. 3; 9. 41; 25. 19. Rom. 6. 10. 2 Cor. 13. 4. Rev. 1. 18; 2. 8; 13. 14; 20. 4, 5.
20 a woman, &c. Not the same miracle as in Mark 5. 25 and Luke 8. 43. See Ap. 138.
an issue of blood = a hæmorrhage. Gr. *haimorroeō*. Occ. only here.
hem: the tassel at one of the four corners, to touch which was a mark of profound respect. But see Ap. 138, and cp. Num. 15. 37-41. **21** said = kept saying.
within herself. The second woman seems to have spoken to others. within. Gr. *en*. Ap. 104. viii.
If I may, &c. See Ap. 118. I. b. The condition being quite hypothetical.
whole = saved: i.e. healed. A Hebraism. Cp. Ps. 42. 11; 43. 5; 67. 2 = saving health. Not the same word as in *v.* 12.
22 comfort = courage.
made thee whole = saved. As in *v.* 21.
23 minstrels = flute-players, or pipers.
people = crowd. See *v.* 8.
making a noise = loudly wailing.
24 Give place = Go out [of the room].
maid. Gr. *korasion*. The same as "damsel" in Mark 6. 22, 28: not the same as "damsel" in Mark 5. 39 (Ap. 108. IX), which is *paidion* (Ap. 108. V).
sleepeth. Gr. *katheudō*. Ap. 171. 1.
26 fame hereof = this report.

9. 27-31 (B[3], p. 1324). TWO BLIND MEN.
(*Introversion.*)

B[3] | y | 27. Blind men. Their prayer.
 z | 28-30-. The Lord. Compliance.
 z | -30. The Lord. Command.
 y | 31. Blind men. Their disobedience.

27 Son of David. The second of nine occurrences in Matthew. See notes on 1. 1; 21. 9; 22. 42. See Ap. 98. XVIII.
28 the house, or his house. See note on *v.* 10.
said = say. Lord. Ap. 98. VI. i. *a.* 3. B.
29 According to. Gr. *kata*. Ap. 104. x. 2.
31 when they were departed . . . (**32**) As they went out = when they had gone out . . . but as they were leaving. spread . . . fame = made Him known.
32 As they went = As they were going.
possessed with a devil = a demoniac.
33 devil = demon.
34 out devils. The 1611 edition of the A.V. reads "out the devils".
through = by. Gr. *en*. Ap. 104. viii. See note on "with", 3. 11.
35 synagogues. See Ap. 120.
preaching = heralding. Gr. *kērussō*. See Ap. 121. 1.
the gospel of the kingdom = the glad tidings of the kingdom. See Ap. 140.
gospel = glad tidings, good news.
of = concerning. Genitive of Relation. Ap. 17. 5.
every. Fig. *Synecdoche* (of Genus), Ap. 6. Put for every kind.
sickness. Gr. *malakia*. Occ. only in Matthew (here; 4. 23; 10. 1).
among the People. All omit these words.
36 on = concerning. Gr. *peri*. Ap. 104. xiii. 1.
fainted = were wearied. All the texts (Ap. 94. VII) read "were harassed". as. Fig. *Simile*. Ap. 6.
no. Gr. *mē*. Ap. 105. II. Read this with having = feeling as if they had, &c.
37 truly = indeed. plenteous = great.
38 Pray. Gr. *deomai*. Ap. 134. I. 5.
the Lord. Ap. 98. VI. i. *a.* 1. A. b.

M N E (p. 1328) 27
10 And when He had called unto *Him* ° His
twelve ° disciples, He gave them ° power
° *against* unclean ° spirits, ° to cast them out,
and to heal ° all manner of ° sickness and ° all
manner of disease.
2 Now the names of [1] the twelve ° apostles
are these; The first, Simon, who is called
Peter, and Andrew his brother; James *the*
son of ° Zebedee, and John his brother;
3 Philip, and ° Bartholomew; ° Thomas, and
° Matthew ° the publican; James *the son* of
° Alphæus, and Lebbæus, whose surname was
° Thaddæus;
4 Simon the ° Canaanite, and ° Judas Iscariot,
who ° also ° betrayed Him.

F 5 These [1] twelve Jesus sent forth, and commanded them, saying, ° "Go ° not ° into the
way of the Gentiles, and ° into *any* city of the
Samaritans enter ye ° not:
6 But go rather ° to the ° lost sheep of ° the
house of Israel.

G H 7 And as ye go, ° preach, saying, ° 'The kingdom of ° heaven ° is at hand.'
8 Heal ° the sick, cleanse ° the lepers, raise ° the
dead, cast out ° devils: freely ye have received,
freely give.
9 Provide neither ° gold, nor ° silver, nor ° brass
° in your ° purses,
10 Nor ° scrip ° for *your* journey, neither two
coats, neither ° shoes, nor yet ° staves: for the
workman is worthy of his ° meat.
11 And [5] into whatsoever city or ° town ye
shall enter, enquire who ° in it is worthy; and
there abide till ye go thence.
12 And when ye come [5] into ° an house, ° salute it.
13 And ° if the house be worthy, let your
° peace come ° upon it: but ° if it be not worthy,
let your peace return [6] to you.

J 14 And whosoever shall not receive you, nor
hear your words, when ye depart out of that
house or city, ° shake off the dust of your feet.
15 ° Verily I say unto you, It shall be more
tolerable for the land of Sodom and Gomorrha
[11] in ° the day of judgment, than for that city.

E 16 ° Behold, I send you forth as ° sheep [11] in
the midst of ° wolves:

F ° be ye therefore wise as ° serpents, and ° harmless as ° doves.
17 But beware ° of ° men:

G J K a[1] (p. 1329) for they will deliver ° you up ° to ° the councils,
and they will scourge you [11] in their syna-
gogues;

10. 1-42 (N, p. 1323). MISSION OF THE TWELVE (BEGUN). (*Extended Alternation and Introversion.*)

N | E | 1-4. Mission.
  F | 5, 6. Injunctions.
   G | H | 7-13. Their reception.
     J | 14, 15. Their rejection.
 E | 16-. Mission.
  F | -16, 17-. Injunctions.
   G | J | -17-39. Their rejection.
     H | 40-42. Their reception.

1 His twelve. See Ap. 141. **disciples** = learners.
power = authority. See Ap. 172. 5.
against = over. Gr. Gen. of Relation. Ap. 17. 5.
spirits. Pl. of Gr. *pneuma*. See Ap. 101. II. 12.
to = so as to.
all manner of = every. Put by Fig. *Synecdochē* (of Genus), Ap. 6, for all kinds of, as in 9. 35.
sickness. See note on 9. 35.
2 apostles = those sent forth. See note on Mark 3. 14.
Zebedee. See note on 4. 21.
3 Bartholomew, Thomas, and Matthew . . . Alphæus . . . Thaddæus. These are all Aramaic words. See Ap. 94. III. 3.
the publican = the tax-gatherer. Note the Fig. *Ampliatio.* Ap. 6.
Alphæus. Heb. *ḥalphah*. Same root as Cleophas; and probably the same name, if not the same person, as John 19. 25.
4 Canaanite. The Aramaic word for the Greek *Zēlōtēs* (Luke 6. 15. Acts 1. 13) = Zealot: so called from his *zeal* for the Law. See Ap. 94 III. 3. Josephus (*Bell. Jud.* 4. 3, 9) says the sect of "Zealots" did not arise till just before the fall of Jerusalem.
Judas Iscariot. The only apostle not from Galilee. He belonged to Judah.
also betrayed Him = even betrayed Him.
betrayed = delivered up.
5 Go not = Go not abroad: i. e. from the land.
not. Gr. *mē*. Ap. 105. II. **into.** Gr. *eis*. Ap. 104. vi.
6 to. Gr. *pros*. Ap. 104. xv. 3. [Luke 19. 10.
lost sheep. Cp. Ezek. 34. 16; and Matt. 15. 24; 18. 11.
the house of Israel. A *Hebraism* = the family of Israel. See note on 1 Kings 12. 17.
7 preach = herald. Gr. *kērussō*. See Ap. 121. 1.
The kingdom of heaven. See Ap. 114.
heaven = the heavens. See note on 6. 9, 10.
is at hand = is drawn nigh. Cp. 4. 17.
8 the sick = sick ones. **the lepers** = leprous ones.
the dead = dead people. See Ap. 139. 2.
devils = demons. Cp. *v.* 1.
9 gold . . . silver . . . brass. Put by Fig. *Metonymy* (of Cause), Ap. 6, for the money made from them.
in. Gr. *eis*. Ap. 104. vi.
purses = girdles, some of which contain pockets for money and valuables.
10 scrip = that which is written: then a small wallet that holds such a writing. Gr. *pēra*. Only here, Mark 6. 8. Luke 9. 3; 10. 4; and 22. 35, 36. Not a "purse", because no money: not a "bread bag" because no bread (Luke 9. 4. Deissmann quotes an Inscription at *Kefr-Hauar*, in Syria, in which a slave of a temple, "sent by the lady" on a begging expedition, brought back each journey seventy bags (*pēra*) of money which he had collected. The Lord means they were *not to beg*. **shoes** = sandals (i. e. not a spare pair). **staves** = a staff (for walking), not clubs. See note on 26. 47. **meat.** Put by Fig *Metonymy* (of Adjunct), Ap. 6, for all kinds of food. **11 town** = village, as in 9. 35. **in.** Gr. *en*. Ap. 104. viii. 1. **12 an house** = a man's house. **salute it**: i. e. make your *salaam* = pronounce "peace". **13 if, &c.** See Ap 118. 1 b. **peace.** Referring to the *salaam* of *v.* 12. **upon.** Gr. *epi*. Ap. 104. ix. 3. **if it be not.** See Ap. 118. 2 c. **14 shake off, &c.** Fig. *Parœmia*. Ap. 6. Cp. 18. 17. See Acts 13. 51. **15 Verily, &c.** See note on 5. 18. **the day of judgment.** Which the Lord spoke of as imminent, and coming at the end of that dispensation, had the nation repented. **16 Behold.** Fig. *Asterismos* (Ap. 6), for emphasis. **sheep . . . wolves.** No Art., for *all* sheep are *not* in the midst of wolves. **be ye** = become ye. **serpents . . . doves.** With Art., because all serpents are prudent, and all doves harmless. **harmless** = guileless. **17 of** = away from: i. e. beware [and keep] away from. Gr. *apo*. Ap. 104. iv. **men.** Pl. of *anthrōpos*. Ap. 123. 1.

10. -17-39 [For Structure see next page].

you. This was true of the Twelve ("them that heard Him": Heb. 2. 3) in the dispensation of the Acts. **to** = unto. Gr. *eis*. Ap. 104. vi. **the councils** = councils. Courts of justice.

27 **18 °And ye shall be brought °before governors and kings °for My sake, °for a testimony °against them and the °Gentiles.**

b¹ (p. 1329) **19 But when °they deliver you up, °take no thought how or what ye °shall speak: for it shall be given you [11]in that same hour what ye shall speak.**

20 For it is °not ye that speak, but °the Spirit of your Father Which speaketh [11]in you.

a² **21 And the brother shall deliver up the brother [17]to death, and the father the °child: and the °children shall rise up °against *their* parents, and °cause them to be put to death.**

22 And ye °shall be hated °of °all *men* °for My name's sake:

b² **but he that endureth [17]to the °end °shall be saved.**

a³ **23 But when they persecute you [11]in this city, flee ye [5]into °another:**

b³ **for [15]verily I say unto you, Ye shall °not have °gone over the cities of Israel, °till °the Son of man °be come.**

L c¹ **24 °The disciple is [20]not °above *his* °master, nor the °servant °above his °lord.**

25 It is °enough for the disciple that he °be as his [24]master, and the [24]servant as his [24]lord. °If they °have called the master of the house °Beelzebub, how much more °*shall they call* °them of his household?

d¹ **26 °Fear them [5]not therefore: for there is nothing °covered, that shall [20]not be revealed; and hid, that shall [20]not be known.**

c² **27 What I tell you [11]in °darkness, °*that* speak ye [11]in °light: and what ye °hear °in the ear, *that* [7]preach ye °upon the °housetops.**

d² **28 And °fear [5]not °them which kill the body, but are [5]not able to °kill °the soul: but rather fear Him Which is able to °destroy both soul and body [11]in °hell.**

10. -17-39 (*J*, p. 1328). THEIR REJECTION. (*Alternation.*)

J | *K* | -17-23. Enmity.
  L | 24-33. Encouragement.
 K | 34-36. Enmity.
  L | 37-39. Encouragement.

-17-23 (K, above). ENMITY. (*Repeated Alternation.*)

K | a¹ | -17, 18. Enmity. Men.
  b¹ | 19, 20. Promise. Defence.
 a² | 21-22-. Enmity. Brethren.
  b² | -22. Promise. Endurance.
 a³ | 23-. Enmity. Men.
  b³ | -23. Promise. Endurance.

18 And = Yea and; or And . . . kings also.
before. Gr. *epi.* Ap. 104. ix. 3.
for My sake = on account of Me. Gr. *heneken.*
for = with a view to.
against = unto.
Gentiles = nations.
19 they deliver you up. All texts read "they shall have delivered you up".
take no thought = be not anxious (as in 6. 25, 27, 28, 31, 34). **no.** Gr. *mē.* Ap. 105. II.
shall = should.
20 not. Gr. *ou.* Ap. 105. I.
the Spirit = the Spirit (Himself). See Ap. 101. II. 3.
21 child . . . children. Gr. pl. of *teknon.* Ap. 108. I.
against. Gr. *epi.* Ap. 104. ix. 3. Not the same as in *v.* 18.
cause them to be put to death = will put them to death.
22 shall = will.
of = by. Gr. *hupo.* Ap. 104. xviii. 1.
all. Put by Fig. *Synecdochē* (of Genus), Ap. 6, for the greater part.
for = on account of. Gr. *dia.* Ap. 104. iv.
end. Gr. *telos* (not *sunteleia*). See notes on 24. 3, and Ap. 114): i.e. of that dispensation, which would have thus ended had the nation repented at the call of Peter (Acts 3. 19-26). As it did not repent, this is of course now future. Cp. 1 Cor. 1. 8.
shall be saved = he shall be saved (escape or be delivered). Cp. 24. 4-14.
23 another = into the other: i.e. the next. Gr. *allos* (Ap. 124. 1), but all texts read *heteros.* Ap. 124. 2.
not = by no means; in no wise. Gr. *ou mē.* See Ap. 105. III.
gone over = completed, or finished [going over]. **till.** See the four: 10. 23; 16. 28; 23. 39; 24. 34. **the Son of man.** See Ap. 98. XVI. **be come** = may have come. This is rendered hypothetical by the Particle *an* (which cannot be translated), because His coming depended on the repentance of Israel (Acts 3. 19-26). It would then have been (and will now yet be) the judicial coming of "the Son of Man". Cp. Acts 17. 31.

10. 24-33 (L, above). ENCOURAGEMENT. (*Repeated Alternation.*)

L | c¹ | 24, 25. Encouragement.
  d¹ | 26. "Fear not".
 c² | 27. Encouragement.
  d² | 28. "Fear not".
 c³ | 29, 30. Encouragement.
  d³ | 31. "Fear not".
 c⁴ | 32, 33. Encouragement.

24 The disciple = a pupil. **above.** Gr. *huper.* Ap. 104. xvii. 2. **master** = teacher. Ap. 98. XIV. v. 4. **servant** = bondservant. **lord** = master. Ap. 98. VI. i. *a.* 4. A. **25 enough** = sufficient. **be** = become. **If, &c.** See Ap. 118. 2 a. **have called.** All the texts read "have surnamed". **Beelzebub.** Aramaic, *Beelzeboul.* Ap. 94. III. 3. Beelzebub = the lord of flies (2 Kings 1. 2), was the god of the Ekronites. It was changed in contempt by the Israelites to Baalzebel = lord of the dunghill, and thence used of the prince of the demons. **shall they call.** These italics are unnecessary. **them of his household.** Gr. *oikiakos.* Occ. only here, and *v.* 36. **26 Fear . . . not** = Ye should not fear. **covered** = concealed. **27 darkness** = the darkness. **that.** For this word italics are not needed. **light** = the light. **hear in the ear.** A Hebraism. Fig. *Polyptōton.* Ap. 6. Cp. Gen. 20. 8; 23. 16. Ex. 10. 2. Isa. 5. 9. Acts 11. 22. **in** = into. Gr. *eis.* Ap. 104. vi. **upon.** Gr. *epi.* Ap. 104. ix. 1. **housetops.** The usual place of proclamation. **28 fear not.** Heb. *yārē' min.* Deut. 1. 29; 5. 5. Ps. 3. 6; 27. 1. **them** = [and flee] from them. Gr. *apo.* Ap. 104. iii. **kill.** Man causes the loss of life, but he cannot kill: i.e. "destroy" it. Only God can do that. **the soul.** Gr. *psuchē.* See Ap. 110. III. **destroy.** Note the difference. Not "kill" merely. Cp. Luke 12. 4, 5. **hell.** Gr. *geénna.* See note on 5. 22, and Ap. 131. I.

c3 (p. 1329) 27 29 °Are not two sparrows sold °for a farthing? and one °of them shall [20] not fall °on the ground °without your Father.

30 But the very °hairs of your head are all °numbered.

d3 31 [28] Fear ye [5] not therefore, ye are of more value than many sparrows.

c4 32 Whosoever therefore shall °confess Me before [17] men, him will °I confess also before My Father Which is [11] in heaven.

33 But whosoever shall deny Me before [17] men, him will I also deny before My Father Which is [11] in heaven.

K 34 Think [5] not that °I am come to °send peace [29] on °earth: I came [20] not to °send peace, but a °sword.

35 For [34] I am come to °set a [17] man at variance °against his father, and °**the daughter °against her mother, and the daughter in law °against her mother in law.**

36 And a [17] man's foes *shall be* [25] they of his own household.

L 37 He that °loveth father or mother °more than Me is [20] not worthy of Me: and he that °loveth son or daughter more than Me is [20] not worthy of Me.

38 And he that taketh [20] not his °cross, and followeth after Me, is [20] not worthy of Me.

39 °He that findeth his °life shall lose it: and he that °loseth his °life °for My sake shall °find it.

H (p. 1328) 40 He that receiveth °you °receiveth Me, and he that °receiveth Me receiveth Him That sent Me.

41 He that receiveth °a prophet °in the name of a prophet shall receive a prophet's reward; and he that receiveth a righteous man °in the name of a righteous man shall receive a righteous man's reward.

42 And whosoever shall give to drink unto one of °these little ones a cup °of cold *water* only [27] in the name of a disciple, [15] verily I say unto you, he shall °in no wise lose his reward."

O P1 R1 (p. 1323) **11** And it came to pass, when °Jesus had made an end of commanding His twelve disciples, He departed thence to teach and to °preach °in their cities.

2 Now when John had °heard [1] in the prison the works of °Christ, °he sent °two of his disciples,

S1 3 And said unto Him, "Art Thou °He That should come, or °do we look for °another?"

4 °Jesus °answered and said unto them, "Go and °shew John °again those things which ye do hear and °see:

29 are not. See Ap. 105. I a.

for a farthing. Gr. *assarion.* Cp. Luke 12. 6, "five sold for two *assarions*" is not the same; but the difference may arise from the market price, which varied from time to time. Deissmann tells us that a fragment of a papyrus was discovered at Aegira (in Achaea, on the Corinthian gulf), in 1899, containing part of a market tariff of Diocletian (third century, A.D.), showing that sparrows were sold in *tens.* The tariff fixed the *maximum* price of ten for sixteen *denarii* (about 3½*d.* Eng. In our Lord's day, therefore, the market value would be nearly 1*d.* Eng.). See Ap. 51. I. 2 (2).

of=from among. Gr. *ek.* Ap. 104. vii.

on. Gr. *epi.* Ap. 104. ix. 3.

without your Father: i.e. without His knowledge or will.

30 hairs . . . numbered. Note the Fig. *Parēchēsis.* Ap. 6. In Aramaic, hairs=*mene.*

numbered=*mana.*

32 confess Me. Gr. confess in (*en.* Ap. 104. viii) Me. Aramaic idiom.

I confess also=I also confess. Cp. *v.* 33.

34 I am come=I came. Cp. *v.* 6, and 15. 24.

send=cast, as seed. Cp. Mark 4. 26.

earth. Gr. *gē.* See Ap. 129. 4.

sword. Put by Fig. *Metonymy* (of Cause), Ap. 6, for "war" or "fightings".

35 set . . . at variance. Gr. *dichazō.* Occ. only here. Quoted from Mic. 7. 6.

against. Gr. *kata.* Ap. 104. x. 1.

the daughter, &c. See Ap. 117. II.

37 loveth=is fonder of. See Ap. 135. 2.

more than=above. Gr. *huper.* Ap. 104. xvii. 2.

38 cross. Gr. *stauros.* See Ap. 162. All criminals bore their own cross (John 19. 17). Cp. 16. 25.

39 He that findeth=He that has found. Note the *Introversion* in this verse (find, lose; lose, find).

life=soul. See Ap. 110. III. **loseth**=has lost.

for My sake=on account of Me. Luke 14. 14; 20. 35, 36. John 5. 29; 11. 25.

find it. In resurrection. Cp. 1 Pet. 4. 19.

40 you. Those to whom the Lord spoke cannot be excluded.

receiveth. Note the Fig. *Anadiplosis* (Ap. 6), in *vv.* 40, 41.

41 a prophet. See Ap. 49.

in the name of: i.e. because he is. A Hebraism (*b'shem*). Ex. 5. 23. Jer. 11. 21.

in. Gr. *eis.* As in *v.* 27.

42 these little ones: i.e. the Twelve. Cp. 18. 6.

of=full of or containing. Gen. of the contents. Ap. 17. 7. **in no wise.** See Ap. 105. III.

11. 1 Jesus. Ap. 98. X.

preach=proclaim. Ap. 121. 1. Continuing His mission (4. 17).

in. Gr. *en.* Ap. 104. viii. 1.

2 heard in the prison. John's arrest had been mentioned in 4. 12.

Christ=the Messiah. See Ap. 98. XI.

he sent. Gr. *pempō.* Sent as envoys. See notes on Luke 7. 3 and 6. This is not the same mission as that in Luke 7. (1) In this (the former) no number of those sent is given (see note on "two" below): in the latter there were "two" (Luke 7. 19). The antecedents and consequents are different. (2) In the former, the Twelve had just been appointed, which may have raised questions in John's mind; in the latter, the antecedent was the raising of the widow's son, *before* the calling of the Twelve. (3) In the former case, the Lord called them to see and note what He *was then doing,* "which ye are hearing and seeing" (*v.* 4). (NB., the tenses are all *Present.* See *v.* 5.) In the latter case, they are to tell John "what ye have seen and heard" (*v.* 22). The consequents are *repetitions* suited to the different circumstances. See Ap. 97. **two.** All the texts read *dia*=by means of (Ap. 104. v. 1), instead of *duo*=two, as in Luke 7. 18. **3 He That should come**= He Who cometh, or the coming One: i.e. He Who was expected to come. Cp. 3. 11; 21. 9; 23. 39. John 3. 31. Ps. 118. 26. Gen. 49. 10. Isa. 35. 4. Ezek. 21. 27. Zech. 9. 9. **do we look for**=are we to expect. **another**=a different [one]. Gr. *heteros.* Ap. 124. 2. **4 Jesus**=And Jesus. Ap. 98. X. **answered and said.** A Hebraism. See note on Deut. 1. 41. **shew**= report. **again.** Not in the Greek. **see.** Gr. *blepō.* Ap. 133. I. 5. Not the same word as in *vv.* 7, 8.

27 5 °The blind receive their sight, and the lame walk, the lepers are cleansed, and the deaf hear, °the dead are °raised up, and the poor °have the gospel preached to them.

6 And °blessed is *he*, whosoever shall °not be offended [1]in °Me."

Q^1 T^1 M^1 (p. 1331) 7 And as they °departed,[1]Jesus began to say unto the multitudes °concerning John, °"What went ye out °into the wilderness °to see? A reed shaken °with the wind?

8 But [7]what went ye out °for to see? A °man clothed [1]in °soft raiment? °behold, they that wear °soft *clothing* are [1]in kings' houses.

9 But [7]what went ye out [8]for to see? A °prophet? yea, I say unto you, and °more than a °prophet.

N^1 10 For this is *he*, °of whom °it is written, '**Behold, °I send My °messenger °before Thy face, which shall prepare Thy way before Thee.**'

M^2 11 °Verily I say unto you, °Among them that are °born of women there hath °not risen a greater than John the Baptist: notwithstanding he that is °least [1]in °the kingdom of °heaven is greater than °he.

12 °And °from the days of John the Baptist until now [11]the kingdom of [11]heaven °suffereth violence, and °the violent °take it by force.

13 For °all the prophets and °the law prophesied °until John.

N^2 14 And °if ye °will °receive *it*, °this °is °Elias, which °was for to come.

15 °He that hath ears to hear, let him hear.

M^3 16 But whereunto shall I liken °this generation? It is like unto °children sitting [1]in the markets, and calling unto their °fellows,

17 And saying, 'We have piped unto you, and ye °have [11]not °danced; we have mourned unto you, and ye °have [11]not °lamented.'

5 The blind=Blind (no Art. in this verse, because only some of each kind are meant. Not all the blind, &c.). These were the miracles foretold of Him (Isa. 35. 5, 6; 61. 1). No others (*quâ* miracles) would have sufficed as His credentials.

the dead=dead (persons). No Art. See Ap. 139. 2.

raised up=raised to life.

have the gospel preached to them. This is one word in the Greek (*euangelizō*)=are told the good news or glad tidings (Isa. 61. 1).

6 blessed=happy. See note on 5. 3.

not. Gr. *mē*. See Ap. 105. 2.

not be offended=find nothing to stumble at.

Me: i.e. in My Person, My teachings, My grace, &c.; as many did. Cp. Luke 4. 22 with 28.

11. 7-30 (T^1, p. 1323). TEACHING.

(*Repeated Alternation.*)

T^1 | M^1 | 7-9. Ministry of John.
  N^1 | 10. Word of God. Fulfilment of "Messenger".
 M^2 | 11-13. Ministry of John.
  N^2 | 14, 15. Word of God. Fulfilment of Elijah.
 M^3 | 16-24. Ministry of Messiah.
  N^3 | 25-30. Will of God. Rest in.

7 departed=were going forward. See note on *v.* 1.

concerning. Gr. *peri*. Ap. 104. xiii. 1.

What . . . ? Fig. *Erotēsis* (Ap. 6), and *Anaphora*. See *vv.* 8, 9. **into.** Gr. *eis*. Ap. 104. vi.

to see=to gaze on. Gr. *theaomai*. Ap. 133. I. 12.

with=by. Gr. *hupo*. Ap. 104. xviii. 1.

8 for to see=to see. Gr. *eidon*. Ap. 133. I. 1.

man. Gr. *anthrōpos*. Ap. 123. 1.

soft raiment=soft, or effeminate [raiment]. Mantles are meant, made of silk or linen, as worn by the *effendis* or gentry, in the East, to-day.

behold. Fig. *Asterismos*. Ap. 6.

9 prophet. See Ap. 49.

more than=far more than.

10 of=concerning. Gr. *peri*, as in *v.* 7.

it is written=it standeth written.

I send, &c. Quoted from Mal. 3. 1. See Ap. 107. I. 1 and 117. I. Cp. Mark 1. 2. Luke 1. 17, 76; 7. 27.

messenger=angel. Gr. *angelos*.

before. Gr. *pro*. Ap. 104. xiv.

11 Verily. See note on Matt. 5. 18.

Among. Gr. *en* with pl. Ap. 104. viii. 2.

born of women=brought forth by women (see note on Matt. 1. 2, 16, 18). A Hebraism (*yelūd 'ishshah*). See Job 14. 1; 15. 14; 25. 4. **not.** Gr. *ou*. Ap. 105. I. **least**=less: i.e. younger, meaning Himself. **the kingdom.** John was only proclaiming it (but not "in" it). The kingdom was rejected both as announced by John (3. 2), by Christ (4. 17), and by Peter (Acts 2. 38; 3. 19-26); and, since its final rejection in Acts 28. 25, 26, is postponed, and is now in abeyance. See Heb. 2. 8 ("not yet"). The possessor is greater than the proclaimer. **the kingdom of heaven.** See Ap. 114. **heaven**=the heavens (pl.). See notes on 6. 9, 10. **he**: i.e. John. **12 And**=But. **from.** Gr. *apo*. Ap. 104. iv. **suffereth violence**=forceth itself upon men's attention. Gr. *biazomai*. Occ. only here and Luke 16. 16. Supposed to be only passive (as rendered here), but this agrees neither with the facts nor with the context. Deissmann (*Bib. Stud.*, p. 258) tells of the discovery of an inscription of Xanthus the Lycian, found near Sunium (E. Attica), containing the regulations as to approaching the healing divinity of the sanctuary of *Men Tyrannos*: "If any one *forces himself in*, his offering was not acceptable." Those who fulfilled the conditions had the founder's good wishes. This last clause is conclusive and agrees with Luke 16. 16. **the violent**=forceful ones. No Art. Gr. *biastēs*. Occ. only here. **take it by force**=lay hold of it. **13 all the prophets.** See Acts 3. 21. **the law.** See note on 5. 17. **until John.** And all would have been fulfilled then had the nation repented. **14 if, &c.** Assuming it as a fact. See Ap. 118. II. 1, as in *vv.* 21, 23. **will**=are willing. Gr. *thelō*. Ap. 102. 1. **receive**=to receive. Cp. Acts 2. 41. **this is**=he represents. Had the nation repented, John would have been reckoned as Elijah. **is**=represents. Fig. *Metaphor*. Ap. 6. **Elias**=Elijah. **was for to come**=is about to come. See Mal. 4. 5, and Luke 1. 17. **15 He that hath ears to hear.** A Hebraism. Fig. *Polyptōton*. Ap. 6. Used only by the Lord, and marking a dispensational crisis (as this was) on fourteen different occasions. See Ap. 142. **16 this generation?** A significant expression, occurring sixteen times (11. 16; 12. 41, 42; 23. 36; 24. 34. Mark 8. 12, 12; 13. 30. Luke 7. 31; 11. 30, 31, 32, 50, 51; 17. 25; 21. 32). Characterized by other epithets, "evil" and "adulterous" (12. 39, 45; 16. 4. Mark 8. 38. Luke 11. 29); "faithless and perverse" (17. 17. Mark 9. 19. Luke 9. 41); "untoward" (Acts 2. 40). All this because it was the particular generation that rejected the Messiah. **children**=little children. Dim. of *pais*. Ap. 108. iv. **fellows**=companions. Gr. *hetairos*. Some of the texts read "others" (i.e. *heteros* for *hetairos*). Occ. only here; 20. 13; 22. 12; and 26. 50 ("friend"). **17 have not**=did not. **danced . . . lamented.** Fig. *Paronomasia* (Ap. 6) in the Gr. *ōrchēsasthe . . . ekopsasthe*; but Fig. *Parēchēsis*, also (Ap. 6) in Aramaic = *rakkedtōn . . . arkkedtōn*. In Eng. "ye did not leap . . . did not weep"; or "stept not . . . wept not". A common custom to this day; such response on the part of the audience being greatly appreciated.

27 18 For John °came neither °eating nor drinking, and they say, 'He hath a °devil.'
19 °The Son of man [18]came [18]eating and
drinking, and they say, [8]'Behold a man
gluttonous, and a °winebibber, a friend of
publicans and sinners.' °But Wisdom is
justified °of her °children."
20 °Then began He to upbraid the °cities
°wherein most of His °mighty works °were
done, because they °repented [11]not:
21 °"Woe unto thee, °Chorazin! woe unto
thee, °Bethsaida! for [14]if the [20]mighty works,
which were done [1]in you, had °been done [1]in
°Tyre and °Sidon, they would have [20]repented
long ago [1]in sackcloth and ashes.
22 But I say unto you, It shall be more tolerable for [21]Tyre and [21]Sidon °at °the day of
judgment, than for you.
23 And thou, °Capernaum, which °art exalted
unto °heaven, shalt be brought down to °hell:
for [14]if the [20]mighty works, which have [21]been
done [1]in thee, had been done [1]in Sodom, it
would have remained until this day.
24 But I say unto you, That it shall be more
tolerable for the land of Sodom [1]in the day of
judgment, than for thee."

N³ O¹ 25 [22]At °that °time [1]Jesus °answered and
(p. 1332) said, °"I thank Thee, O °Father, °Lord of
[23]heaven and °earth, because Thou °hast hid
these things [12]from °the wise and °prudent,
and hast °revealed them unto babes.
26 Even so, [25]Father: for so it °seemed good
in Thy sight.
27 All things °are delivered unto Me °of My
[25]Father: and °no man °knoweth the Son,
but the [25]Father; neither °knoweth any man
the [25]Father, save the Son, and *he* to whomsoever the Son °will [25]reveal *Him*.

O² P 28 °Come °unto Me, °all *ye* that °labour and
are °heavy laden,
Q and I will °give you rest.
R 29 Take My yoke upon you, and learn [19]of
R Me; for I am °meek and lowly in heart:
Q and ye shall find °rest unto °your °souls.
P 30 For My yoke *is* easy, and My burden is
light."

U¹ 12 °At that °time °Jesus went on the °sab-
bath day °through the °corn; and his
disciples were an hungred, and began to pluck
the ears of corn, and to eat.

18 came. In the Greek this is the Fig. *Hyperbaton* (put out of its place by commencing the verse), causing the Fig. *Anaphora* (Ap. 6).

eating nor drinking. Supply the *Ellipsis* (Ap. 6), eating nor drinking [with others]. **devil** = demon.

19 The Son of Man. See Ap. 98. XVI.

winebibber = drinking to excess.

publicans and sinners. See notes on 5. 46; 9. 10

But = And: i.e. And [for all that] Wisdom was [in each case] vindicated by her children; so with Messiah (the Wisdom of God. 1 Cor. 1. 24, 30. Cp. Matt. 23. 34 with Luke 11. 49). **of** = by. Gr. *apo*. Ap. 104. iv.

children. Ap. 108. I. Tr. reads "work".

20 Then. Marking another stage of His rejection. Fig. *Chronographia*. Ap. 6.

cities. Put by Fig. *Metonymy* (of Subject) for their inhabitants. Ap. 6.

wherein = in which. Gr. *en*, as in *v.* 1.

mighty works. Gr. pl. of *dunamis* (Ap. 172. 1). See note on John 2. 18. **were done** = had taken place.

repented. Gr. *metanoeō*. Ap. 111. 1.

21 Woe, &c. Fig. *Maledictio*. Ap. 6. A testimony as to His rejection.

Chorazin. Not named elsewhere, and no miracles recorded as performed there, or at Bethsaida. See Ap. 169.

Bethsaida. Aramaic. Ap. 94. III. 3. Now *et Tell*; then a fishing suburb of Capernaum; Roman name, *Julias*. **been done** = taken place.

Tyre and Sidon. No mention of the Lord's having been there. **Tyre.** Now *es Sūr*.

Sidon. The Zidon of the O.T.; now *Saida*, twenty-five miles south of *Beirout*. **22 at** = in, as in *v.* 1.

the day, &c. Now drawing near. See note on 16. 23.

23 Capernaum. See note on 4. 13, and Ap. 169.

art = wast.

heaven = the heaven. Sing. because in contrast with the earth. See note on 6. 9, 10. **hell.** Gr. *Hades*. See Ap. 131. 2.

11. 25-30 (N³, p. 1331). THE WILL OF GOD. REST IN. (*Division.*)

N³ | O¹ | 25–27. Rest. Christ's rest: found.
   | O² | 28–30. Rest. Our rest: given and found.

25 that time. Of His rejection. Fig. *Chronographia* (Ap. 6), emphasising the lesson. **time** = season.

answered and said = prayed and said. A Hebraism. See note on Deut. 1. 41.

I thank Thee = I openly confess to Thee.

Father. See Ap. 98. IV.

Lord. See Ap. 98. VI. i. *a*. 4. B. b.

earth = the earth. Ap. 129. 4. **hast hid** = didst hide.

the wise = wise ones (no Art.).

prudent = prudent ones: i.e. in their own eyes.

26 seemed good = became well-pleasing. Occ. with *ginomai*, only here and Luke 10. 21.

27 are delivered = were [at some definite time] delivered. **of** = by. Gr. *hupo*. Ap. 104. xviii. 1.

no man = no one. Gr. *oudeis*, or compound of. Ap. 105. I.

knoweth = fully knoweth. See Ap. 132. I. 3.

will reveal = intendeth (Gr. *boulomai*. Ap. 102. 2) to reveal.

reveal = unveil. Gr. *apokaluptō*.

11. 28-30 (O², above). REST. OURS. GIVEN AND FOUND. (*Introversion.*)

O² | P | 28–. Our burden heavy.
  Q | –28. His rest given.
    R | 29–. Command. "Take", &c.
    R | –29–. Command. Reason, "for".
  Q | –29. Our rest found.
P | 30. His burden light.

28 Come, &c. Here Christ refers, not to sins, but to service; not to guilt, but to labour; not to the conscience, but to the heart; not to repentance, but to learning; not to finding forgiveness, but to finding rest. **unto.** Gr. *pros*. Ap. 104. xv. 3. **all.** Here limited to those seeking "rest". **labour** = toil. **heavy laden** = burdened. **give.** His rest is *given*. Ours must be found in His gift. We have none to give. **29 meek . . . rest.** Note the Fig. *Parēchēsis* (Ap. 6). In the Aramaic or Syriac (Peshito) we have *nīcḥ . . . nᵉyāchāʿ*, but in the Lewis Codex it is better still: *nīcḥ . . . vᵉēnichkōn*. **your souls** = your own selves (emph.). Ap. 110. IV. **souls.** Gr. pl. of *psuchē*. Ap. 110. IV.

12. 1 At. Gr. *en*. Ap. 104. viii. **time** = season. **Jesus.** Ap. 98. X. **sabbath.** See Luke 6. 1. Gr. *sabbata*, Aram. See Ap. 94. III. 3. **through.** Gr. *dia*. Ap. 104. v. 1. **corn** = cornfields.

27 2 But when °the Pharisees °saw *it,* they said
unto Him, °"Behold, Thy disciples do that
which is °not lawful to do °upon the sabbath
day."
3 But He said unto them, °"Have ye [2]not
read °what David did, when he was an hungred, and they that were °with him;
4 How he entered °into °the house of God,
and did eat °the shewbread, °which was [2]not
lawful for him to eat, neither for them which
were [3]with him, °but only for the priests?
5 Or [3]have ye [2]not read °in the law, how that
on °the [1]sabbath days the priests [1]in the
temple °profane °the [1]sabbath, and are
°blameless?
6 But I say unto you, That °in this place is
One °greater than the temple.
7 But °if ye °had known what *this* °mean-
eth, °'**I will have °mercy, and [2]not sacrifice,**'
ye would [2]not have condemned the °guiltless.
8 For °the Son of man is °Lord °even °of the
sabbath day."

P^2 R^2 e (p. 1333) 9 And when He was departed thence, He
went [4]into °their °synagogue:
10 And, [2]behold, there was a °man which
had *his* hand withered.

f And they asked Him, saying, "Is it lawful to
heal °on the [1]sabbath days?"

g °that they might accuse Him.

f 11 °And He said unto them, "What [10]man
shall there be °among you, that shall have
one sheep, and °if it fall [4]into a pit on the
[1]sabbath day, will he °not lay hold on it,
and lift *it* out?
12 °How much then is a [10]man better than
a sheep? Wherefore it is lawful to do °well
on the [1]sabbath days."

e 13 Then saith He to the [10]man, "Stretch
forth thine hand." And he stretched *it* forth;
and it was restored whole, like as the °other.

S^2 S 14 °Then [2]the Pharisees went out, and °held
a council °against Him, how they might
destroy Him.

T 15 But when Jesus [7]knew *it,* He withdrew
Himself °from thence: and great multitudes
followed Him, and He healed them all;
16 And charged them [10]that they should
°not make Him °known:
17 °That it might be fulfilled which was
°spoken °by °Esaias the prophet, saying,

2 the Pharisees. See Ap. 120.
saw. Gr. *eidon.* Ap. 133. I. 1.
Behold. Fig. *Asterismos.* Ap. 6.
not. Gr. *ou.* Ap. 105. I.
upon. Gr. *en.* Ap. 104. viii. 1.
3 Have ye not read...? This question was asked by the Lord on six different occasions, and referred to seven different books of the O.T., and to ten distinct passages. See Ap. 143.
what David did. Ref. to 1 Sam. 21. 6. Ap. 117. I.
with. Gr. *meta.* Ap. 104. xi. 1.
4 into. Gr. *eis.* Ap. 104. vi.
the house of God: i.e. the tabernacle.
the shewbread. See Ex. 25. 30. Lev. 24. 5-8.
which was... but only, &c. See Lev. 24. 9.
5 in the law. See note on 5. 17. Cp. Num. 28. 9, 10 and Ap. 143. **in.** Gr. *en.* Ap. 104. viii.
the sabbath. (Num. 28. 9, 10. Cp. Neh. 13. 17. Ezek. 24. 21. John 7. 22, 23.) There were more sacrifices on the sabbath than on any other day.
profane. Our Eng. word "profane" = far from the temple. The Greek word here = to trample down and thus treat as common. Cp. Acts 24. 6.
blameless = guiltless, as in *v.* 7. Gr. *anaitios.* Occ. only here and *v.* 7. **6 in this place** = here.
greater than the temple. Cp. *v.* 41, a greater prophet; and *v.* 42, a greater king; who can be only God Himself.
7 if, &c. Implying that it was not the fact. See Ap. 118. 1 a. Not the same condition as in *vv.* 11, 26, 27, 28.
had known = were aware of. Gr. *ginōskō.* Ap. 132. I. ii.
meaneth = is.
I will = I desire. Gr. *thelō.* Ap. 102. I. Quoted from Hos. 6. 6. See Ap. 107. II. 1.
mercy = lovingkindness, or grace.
guiltless. Gr. *anaitios.* See note on blameless, *v.* 5.
8 the Son of man. See Ap. 98. XVI.
Lord. See Ap. 98. VI. i. *a.* B. a.
even. All the texts omit this word.
of the sabbath. As the Son of man. Cp. *v.* 6, Lord of the Temple as the Son of God.
9 their. Probably inhabitants of Tiberias. For, in Mark 3. 6, the Pharisees conferred with the Herodians, so that the Lord was in Herod's jurisdiction.
synagogue. See Ap. 120.

12. 9-13 (R^2, p. 1323). **MIRACLES.**
(*Introversion.*)

R^2 | e | 9, 10-. Withered hand.
  f | -10-. Question of the enemies.
    g | -10. Purpose. Accusation.
  f | 11, 12. Questions of the Lord.
e | 13. Withered hand.

10 man. Gr. *anthrōpos.* Ap. 123. 1.
on the sabbath days. This was the first of seven miracles wrought on the sabbath. See Mark 1. 21-31. Luke 13. 11; 14. 2. John 5. 8, 9; 9. 14.
that = in order that.
11 And = But.
among = of. Gr. *ek.* Ap. 104. vii.
if...? The condition is hypothetical. Ap. 118. 1 b.
not. Gr. *ouchi.* Ap. 105. I (a).
12 How much? Fig *Erotēsis*, for emphasis. Ap. 6. **well:** i.e. a good deed. **13 other.** Gr. *allos.* Ap. 124. I.

12. 14-50 (S^2, p. 1323). **EFFECTS.**
(*Introversion.*)

S^2 | S | 14. Proposed destruction of the Lord by enemies.
  T | 15-21. The Word of God. Fulfilled.
    U | 22. Miracle (demoniac) wrought.
    U | 23-37. Miracle. Consequences.
  T | 38-45. The Word of God. Better than a sign.
S | 46-50. Proposed capture by kindred.

14 Then = But. **held a council.** Occ. only in 22. 15; 27. 1, 7; 28. 12. Mark 3. 6; 15. 1. **against.** Gr. *kata.* Ap. 104. x. 1. **15 from thence** = thence, as in *v.* 9. **16 not.** Gr. *mē.* Ap. 105. II. **known** - publicly known. Gr. *phaneros.* Cp. Ap. 106. I. v. **17 That** = To the end that. **spoken.** As well as written. **by** = by means of. Gr. *dia.* Ap. 104. v. 1. **Esaias** = Isaiah (Ap. 79. I). Quoted from Isa. 42. 1-4. See Ap. 107. II. 1. From the Hebrew direct; but the last clause differs, because the Holy Spirit is recording the act of *fulfilment*, and varying it by way of Divine comment.

27 18 °"Behold My °Servant, Whom I have °chosen; My Beloved, °in Whom °My soul °is well pleased: I will put My °spirit °upon Him, and He shall °shew judgment to the °Gentiles.

19 He shall [2]not °strive, nor °cry; neither shall any man hear His voice [5]in the streets.

20 A bruised reed shall He [2]not break, and °smoking flax shall He [2]not quench, till He °send forth [18]judgment °unto victory.

21 And °in °His name shall the [18]Gentiles °trust."

U (p. 1333) 22 Then was brought unto Him °one possessed with a devil, blind, and dumb: and He healed him, °insomuch that the blind and dumb both spake and saw.

U V^1 (p. 1334) 23 And all the °people were amazed, and said, °"Is [16]not This °the son of David?"

V^2 W^1 h 24 But when the °Pharisees heard *it*, they said, °"This *fellow* doth [2]not cast out °devils, °but °by °Beelzebub the prince of the °devils."

25 And °Jesus [7]knew their thoughts, and said unto them, "Every kingdom divided [14]against itself is brought to desolation; and every city or house divided [14]against itself °shall [2]not stand:

26 And [11]if Satan cast out Satan, he is divided °against himself; how [25]shall then his kingdom stand?

i 27 And [11]if I [24]by [24]Beelzebub cast out [22]devils, [24]by whom do your °children cast *them* out? °therefore they shall be your judges.

28 But [11]if I cast out [22]devils by °the Spirit of God, °then °the kingdom of God is come °unto you.

h 29 Or else how can one enter [4]into a °strong man's house, and °spoil his goods, except he first bind the °strong man? and then he will °spoil his house.

i 30 He that is [16]not [3]with Me is [14]against Me; and he that gathereth [16]not [3]with Me scattereth abroad.

W^2 X 31 °Wherefore I say unto you, All manner of °sin and °blasphemy [25]shall be forgiven unto [10]men: but the blasphemy °*against* the *Holy* Ghost shall [2]not be forgiven °unto [10]men.

32 And whosoever speaketh a word [14]against [8]the Son of man, it shall be forgiven him: but whosoever speaketh [14]against °the Holy Ghost, it shall [2]not be forgiven him, neither [5]in this °world, neither [5]in °the *world* to come.

18 Behold, &c. Quoted from Isa. 41. 8; 42. 1. See Ap. 107. I. 1. **Servant.** Gr. *pais.* See Ap. 108. iv.
chosen. Gr. *hairetizo.* Occ. only here.
in. Gr. *eis* (Ap. 104. vi); but L A WH omit. Tr. reads *en* (Ap. 104. viii).
My soul = I (emph.). Heb. *nephesh.* Ap. 9. Gr. *psuchē.* Ap. 110. IV.
is well pleased = hath found delight.
spirit. See Ap. 101. III. 8.
upon. Gr. *epi.* Ap. 104. ix. 3.
shew = declare. **Gentiles** = nations.
19 strive = contend. Gr. *erizō.* Occ. only here.
cry = make outcry or clamour.
20 smoking. Gr. *tuphoomai.* Occ. only here. 1 Tim. 3. 6; 6. 4. 2 Tim. 3. 4.
send forth = bring forth (what was before hidden), as in *v.* 35 and 13. 52. Cp. Deut. 32. 34.
unto. Gr. *eis.* Ap. 104. vi.
21 in. All omit this, and read "on".
His name. A Hebraism. See note on Ps. 20. 1.
trust = hope. Cp. Isa. 41. 8; 42. 1. One of eighteen passages where "trust" should be thus rendered.
22 one possessed with a devil = a demoniac. Gr. *daimonizomai.* **insomuch that** = so that.

12. 23-37 (*U*, p. 1333). MIRACLE. CONSEQUENCES. (*Division.*)

U	V^1	23. People. Amazement.
	V^2	24-37. Pharisees. Blasphemy.

23 people = multitude.
Is not This . . . ? The 1611 edition of the A.V. reads "Is This?" = May not This be? Since 1638 it reads "Is not This".
the son of David. The third of nine occurrences of this Messianic title in Matthew. See Ap. 98. XVIII.

12. 24-37 (V^2, above). PHARISEES. BLASPHEMY. (*Division.*)

V^2	W^1	24-30. Confutation.
	W^2	31-37. Condemnation.

12. 24-30 (W^1, above). CONFUTATION. (*Alternation.*)

W^1	h	24-26. Illustration. Divided kingdom.
	i	27, 28. Application.
	h	29. Illustration. Strong man's house.
	i	30. Application.

24 Pharisees. See Ap. 120.
This fellow = this [man]. Not emphatic.
devils = demons. **but** = except.
by = in [the power of]. Gr. *en.* Ap. 104. viii.
Beelzebub. See note on 10. 25.
25 Jesus = He. All texts omit "Jesus" here.
shall = will. **26 against.** Gr. *epi.* Ap. 104. ix. 3.
27 children = sons: i.e. disciples. The Pharisees believed in and practised exorcism. See Josephus (*Ant.* viii. 2-5), and cp. Acts 19. 13.
therefore = on account of this. Gr. *dia touto.* Ap. 104. iv. 2.
28 the Spirit. There is no Art. Gr. *pneuma* (Ap. 101. III. 4) = by God's *pneuma*, put for Divine power. In Luke 11. 20 God's "finger" put for the power exercised by it by Fig. *Metonymy* (of Cause). So in Ex. 8. 19. **then** = it follows that. **the kingdom of God.** The second of five occurrences in Matthew. See note on 6. 33 and Ap. 114. **unto** = upon. Gr. *epi.* Ap. 104. ix. 3. **29 strong man's** = the strong [one's]. **spoil** = plunder.

12. 31-37 (W^2, above). CONDEMNATION. (*Introversion.*)

W^2	X	31, 32. Words. Forgiven and unforgiven.
	Y	33. Illustration. Trees.
	Z	34-. Expostulation.
	Z	-34. Reason.
	Y	35. Illustration. Characters.
	X	36, 37. Words. Justified and condemned.

31 Wherefore = On this account. Gr. *dia touto*, same as "therefore", *v.* 27. **sin.** Gr. *hamartia.* See Ap. 128. II. 1. **blasphemy** = impious or evil speaking. **against the Holy Ghost** = [concerning] the Spirit. Gr. *pneuma* with Art. See Ap. 101. III. 3. **unto men.** Omit LT Tr. [A] WH R. **32 the Holy Ghost** = the Spirit, the Holy [Spirit], emph. Ap. 101. III. 3. **world** = age, age-time, or dispensation. Gr. *aiōn.* Ap. 129. 2. It must refer to one age-time in contradistinction to another, called "the coming age". Cp. Heb. 1. 2 and see note on Heb. 11. 3. **the world to come** = [the age] about to be. Ap. 129. 2.

Y (p. 1334) 27 33 Either make the tree good, and °his fruit
good; or else make the tree corrupt, and his
fruit corrupt: for the tree °is known °by *his*
fruit.

Z 34 O °generation of vipers, how can ye, being
°evil, speak good things?

z for °out of the °abundance of the heart the
mouth speaketh.

Y 35 °A good [10]man [34]out of the good °treasure
of °the heart bringeth forth good things: and
°an [34]evil [10]man [34]out of the [34]evil treasure
bringeth forth [34]evil things.

X 36 But I say unto you, That every °idle °word
°that [10]men shall speak, they shall °give
account °thereof [5]in the day of judgment.
37 For [33]by thy °words thou shalt be justified,
and [33]by thy °words thou shalt be condemned."

T A (p. 1335) 38 Then certain of the scribes and of the
[24]Pharisees answered, saying, °"Master, we
°would °see °a sign °from Thee."
39 But He answered and said unto them,
"An [34]evil and °adulterous °generation °seeketh
after a sign; and there shall no sign be given
to it, but the sign of the prophet °Jonas:
40 For °as [39]**Jonas was °three days and**
°three nights [5]in °the whale's belly; so shall
[8]the Son of man be three days and °three
nights [5]in °the heart of the °earth.

B j 41 The °men of Nineveh shall °rise [5]in °judg-
ment [3]with this [39]generation, and shall condemn it:

k because they °repented °at the °preaching of
[39]Jonas;

l and, [2]behold, a °greater than [39]Jonas *is* here.

j 42 °The queen of the south shall °rise up [5]in
the judgment [3]with this [39]generation, and shall
condemn it:

k for °she came °from the uttermost parts of the
earth to hear the wisdom of Solomon;

l and, behold, a [41]greater than Solomon *is* here.

A m (p. 1336) 43 °When °the unclean °spirit °is gone °out
of °a [10]man,

n °he °walketh [1]through °dry places, seeking
rest, and °findeth none.

33 his=its.
is known=getteth known. Gr. *ginōskō*. Ap. 132. I. ii.
by=from. Gr *ek*. Ap. 104. vii.

34 generation=offspring or brood. Cp. 3. 7; 23. 33.
evil. See Ap. 128. IV. 1. **out of**. Gr. *ek*. Ap. 104. vii.
abundance: or overflow.

35 A=The. **treasure**=treasury.
the heart. All the texts omit "the heart". **an**=the.

36 idle=careless or useless. Cp. 20. 3. 1 Tim. 5. 13. Tit. 1. 12. 2 Pet. 1. 8.
word=saying. Not the same as in *v.* 37. **that**=which.
give account thereof=suffer its consequences. A Hebraism. **thereof**=concerning (Ap. 104. xiii. 1) it.

37 words. Gr. pl. of *logos*. Not the same as in *v.* 36. See note on Mark 9. 32. "Words" are reckoned as "deeds" (2 Cor. 5. 10). See Ap. 121. 10.

12. 38-45 (*T*, p. 1333). THE WORD OF GOD. BETTER THAN A SIGN. (*Alternation*.)

T | A | 38-40. Sign given. Asked for. (Historic.)
  B | 41, 42. Application.
A | 43-45-. Sign given. Unasked. (Experimental.)
  B | -45. Application.

38 Master=Teacher. See Ap. 98. XIV. v. 1.
would=desire. Gr. *thelō*. Ap. 102. 1.
see=to see. Gr. *eidon*. Ap. 133. I. 1.
a sign. The first of *six* "signs" asked for. Cp. 16. 1; 24. 3. Luke 11. 16. John 2. 18; 6. 30.
from. Gr. *apo*. Ap. 104. iv.

39 adulterous. Spiritually. See Jer. 3. 9. Ezek. 23. 37, &c.
generation. Gr. *genea*. Not the same as in *v.* 34. See note on 11. 16. **seeketh**: or, is for ever seeking.
Jonas=Jonah. See Ap. 117. I.

40 as=just as. The Lord was dead, therefore Jonah must have been. Nothing is said about his being "preserved alive". That "sign" would have had no relation to what is here *signified*. See notes on Jonah.
three nights. Apart from these words, "three days" might mean any portion of a day. But "three nights" forbids this interpretation. See Ap. 144 and 156. Quoted from Jonah 1. 17.
the whale's. Gr. *kētos*. Occ. only here. There is nothing about "a whale" either in the Heb. of Jonah (1. 17) or in the Greek here. The "great fish" was specially "prepared" by its Creator. See Jon. 1. 17.
the heart of the earth=in the earth: i.e. the sepulchre, or tomb, 27. 60. Mark 15. 46. Luke 23. 53. John 19. 40. Acts 13. 29. It is the Fig. *Pleonasm* (a Hebraism), Ap. 6,=the midst, or "in". See Ex. 15. 8. Ps. 46. 2. 2 Sam. 18. 14. Deut. 4. 11. In any case it is not "the centre", any more than the heart is in the centre of the body, instead of near the top. We are to conclude that the Lord establishes "the literal validity of the history of Jonah", inasmuch as He spoke "not His own words but only the words of the Father" (see John 7. 16; 8. 28, 46, 47; 12. 49; 14. 10, 24; 17. 8); so that the assertions of modern critics are perilously near blasphemy against God Himself. **earth**. Gr. *gē*. Ap. 129. 4.

12. 41, 42 (B, above). APPLICATION. (*Extended Alternation*.)

B | j | 41-. Persons. Ninevites ("rise").
  k | -41-. Reason. Proclamation of Jonah.
    l | -41. Greater reason.
j | 42-. Person. Queen of the South ("rise").
  k | -42-. Reason. Wisdom of Solomon.
    l | -42. Greater reason.

41 men. Gr. No Art., pl. of *anēr*. Ap. 123. 2. **rise**=stand up. Not the same word as in *v.* 42. **judgment**=the judgment, as in *v.* 42. Cp. Ps. 1. 5. **repented**. The last reference to repentance in Matthew. See Ap. 111. II. 1. **preaching**=proclamation. Cp. Ap. 121. I. **at**. Gr. *eis*. Ap. 104. vi. **greater**. See note on *v.* 6. **42 The queen**=A queen. **rise up**. In resurrection. Not the same word as "rise" in *v.* 41. **she came**. See 1 Kings 10. 1, &c. **from**=Out of. Gr. *ek*. Ap. 104. vii.

12. 43-45- [For Structure see next page].

43 When=But when. Introducing the allegory. **the**=an. The Art. being inclusive and hypothetic as "a man", which also has the Art. and is rendered "a". **spirit**. Gr. *pneuma*. See Ap. 101. XII. **is gone out**. If of its own accord, it have gone out, it returns (*v.* 44). But not when it is "bound" and cast out, as in *v.* 29. **out of**=away from (Gr. *apo*. Ap. 104. iv) temporarily, as at the proclamation of John. **a**=the. **he**=it. **walketh**=roameth. Cp. Acts 8. 4. **dry**=waterless: i.e. where no human beings are. **findeth none**=findeth [it] not; has no respite. Gr. *ou*, as in *v.* 2.

o (p. 1336) **44** Then [43]he saith, 'I will return [4]into my house °from whence I came out;'

p and when [43]he is come, he findeth *it* empty,
27 swept, and °garnished.

m **45** Then goeth [43]he,

n and taketh with °himself seven other [43]spirits °more wicked than °himself,

o and they enter in and dwell there:

p and °the last *state* of that [10]man °is worse than the first.

B (p. 1335) Even so shall it be °also unto °this °wicked [39]generation."

S C q (p. 1336) **46** While He yet °talked to the °people, [2]behold, *His* mother and His brethren °stood without, °desiring to speak with Him.

r **47** Then one said unto Him, [2]"Behold, Thy mother and Thy brethren °stand without, [46]desiring to speak with Thee."

D **48** But He answered and said unto him that told Him, "Who is My mother? and who are My brethren?"

C q **49** And He °stretched forth His hand °toward His disciples, and said, "Behold My mother and My brethren!

r **50** For °whosoever shall °do the will of My Father Which is [5]in °heaven, °the same is My brother, and sister, and mother."

T[2] E[1] **13** °The same day went °Jesus °out of °the house, and °sat °by the sea °side.
2 And great multitudes were °gathered together °unto Him, so that He went °into °a ship, and sat; and the whole multitude stood °on the shore.

F G **3** And He spake °many things °unto them °in °parables, saying, °"Behold, °a sower went forth to sow;

12. 43-45- (*A*, p. 1335). SIGN GIVEN. UNASKED.
(*Extended Alternation.*)

A | m | 43-. The going out of an unclean spirit.
  n | -43. Action. Seeking rest.
   o | 44-. Return. Purposed.
    p | -44. Condition of house.
 m | 45-. The going out of an unclean spirit.
  n | -45-. Action. Seeking other spirits.
   o | -45-. Return. Effected.
    p | -45. Condition of house.

44 from whence = whence.
garnished = decorated. **45 himself** = itself.
more wicked. Showing that there are degrees of wickedness among spirits and demons. See 17. 21. Acts 16. 16, 17, &c.
the last state. See Dan. 9. 27; 11. 21, 23, &c. Rev. 13; and cp. John 5. 43. **is** = becometh.
also . . . generation = generation also.
this = this [present].
wicked. Gr. *ponēros.* Ap. 128. IV. 1.
wicked generation. See notes on 11. 16; 23. 35; 24. 34. Mark 13. 30. Luke 21. 32. Acts 2. 40.

12. 46-50 (*S*, p. 1333). PROPOSED CAPTURE BY KINDRED.
(*Introversion and Alternation.*)

S | C | q | 46. Mother and brethren. (Natural.) "Without".
   r | 47. Their will. Reported (Mark 3. 21-31).
  D | 48. The Lord's Question.
 C | *q* | 49. Mother and brethren. (Spiritual.) "Within".
   r | 50. God's will. Declared.

46 talked = was talking.
people = multitudes. **stood** = were standing.
desiring to speak = seeking to speak. Their *avowed* purpose. But in Mark 3. 21, 31 their *real* purpose was to "lay hold on Him", and the reason is given: "for they said 'He is beside Himself'". This accounts for the Lord's answer.
47 stand without = are standing without. The reason for not going in is obvious.
49 stretched forth His hand toward = He pointed to.
toward. Gr. *epi.* Ap. 104. ix. 1.
50 whosoever. Fig. *Synecdochē* (of Genus), Ap. 6, defined by obedience, and made an hypothesis by the particle "*an*". **do** = have done.
heaven = [the] heavens. Plural, because there is no contrast with the "earth". See note on 6. 9, 10.
the same = he.

13. 1-53 (T[2], p. 1323). TEACHING. (*Alternation and Introversion.*)

T[2] | E[1] | 1, 2. Place. Departure. "Out of the house".
  F | G | 3-9. ONE Parable. (The Sower.)
    H | 10-23. Question *of* Disciples. Answer *not* understood.
     J | 24-33. THREE Parables. "Another", "Another", "Another".
      K | 34, 35. Multitudes.
 E[2] | 36-. Place. Departure. "Into the house".
  F | *K* | -36-43. Disciples.
     J | 44-50. THREE Parables. "Again", "Again", "Again".
    H | 51. Question *to* Disciples. Answer understood.
    G | 52. ONE Parable. (The Scribe.)
 E[3] | 53. Place. Departure. "Thence".

1 The same day. Gr. *en* (Ap. 104. viii). The day referred to in 12. 46-50. **Jesus.** Ap. 98. X. **out of the house.** The teaching from *vv.* 3-35 was public; from *vv.* 36-52 was within the house, in private. **out of.** Gr. *apo,* as in 12. 43. But Tr. reads [*ek*] and *apo* in marg. WH omit *apo* and read *ek* in marg. L and T read *ek* (104. vii.) in text. **the house**: or His house, at Capernaum (9. 28). Ap. 169. **sat** = was sitting. **by . . . side** = beside. Gr. *para.* Ap. 104. xii. 3. **2 gathered together.** Not the same as in *vv.* 28, 29, 30, 40, 41, 48, but same as in *vv.* 30, 47. **unto.** Gr. *pros.* Ap. 104. xv. 3. **into.** Gr. *eis.* Ap. 104. vi. **a** = the. See notes on 4. 21; 8. 23. **on.** Gr. *epi.* Ap. 104. ix. 3. **3 many things.** Some of these parables were repeated (and varied) on other occasions. There are no "discrepancies". **unto.** Gr. *pros.* Ap. 104. xv. 3. **in** = by. Gr. *en.* Ap. 104. viii. **parables.** Here, *eight* (not "seven" as sometimes alleged) are selected for the special purpose of the Holy Spirit in this Gospel. See Ap. 96 and 145. **Behold.** Fig. *Asterismos.* Ap. 6. **a sower** = the sower. As these eight parables relate to "the Kingdom of the Heavens" (Ap. 114), the sowing must relate to the proclamation of it (*v.* 19): (1) by John, "the wayside", 3. 2, 5, 6; (2) by Christ, the Twelve, and the Seventy, "the stony ground", 4. 12—26. 35; (3) by the Twelve in the land, and Paul in the synagogues of the Dispersion (the Acts); (4) still future (Matt. 24. 14) and on "good", because prepared ground. See Ap. 140. I. 1, and 145.

27 4 And °when he sowed, °some *seeds* fell [1]by
the °way side, and the °fowls came and devoured them up:
5 °Some fell °upon °stony places, where they
had °not much earth: and °forthwith they
sprung up, °because they had °no deepness of
earth:
6 And when the sun was up, they were
scorched; and [5]because they had [5]no root, they
withered away.
7 And some fell °among thorns; and the
thorns sprung up, and choked them:
8 But other fell °into °good ground, and
°brought forth fruit, some an hundredfold,
some sixtyfold, some thirtyfold.
9 °Who hath ears to hear, let him hear."

H L¹ M (p. 1337) 10 And the disciples came, and said unto Him,
"Why speakest Thou unto them [3]in parables?"
N 11 °He answered and said unto them, "Because it °is given unto you °to know °the mysteries °of the kingdom of °heaven, but to
them °it is [5]not given.
12 For °whosoever hath, to him shall be given,
and he shall °have more abundance: but whosoever hath [5]not, °from him shall be taken
away even that he hath.
M 13 °Therefore speak I to them [3]in parables:
N s because they °seeing see [5]not; and °hearing
they °hear [5]not, neither do they understand.
t 14 And °in them is °fulfilled the prophecy of
°Esaias, which saith, **'By °hearing ye shall
[13]hear, and shall °not understand; and [13]seeing
ye shall °see, and shall °not perceive:**
**15 For this people's heart is °waxed gross,
and *their* ears are dull of hearing, and their
eyes they have closed; lest at any time they
should °see with *their* eyes, and hear with
their ears, and should understand with *their*
heart, and should °be converted, and I should
heal them.'**
s 16 But °blessed *are* °your eyes, for they [13]see:
and °your ears, for they hear.
t 17 For °verily I say unto you, That many
prophets and righteous *men* °have desired °to
see *those things* which °ye see, and °have
[5]not °seen *them;* and to hear *those things*
which ye hear, and °have [5]not heard *them*.
L² O u 18 Hear ye therefore the parable of the sower.
19 When any one heareth °the °word of the
kingdom, and understandeth *it* °not, then

4 when he sowed = in (as in *v.* 3): in his sowing.
some = some indeed.
way side. The part of the field beside the way.
fowls = birds.
5 Some = And some.
upon. Gr. *epi.* Ap. 104. ix. 3.
stony places = rocky or broken land.
not. Gr. *ou.* Ap. 105. I.
not much earth. Not depth enough of earth.
forthwith = immediately.
because = through (Gr. *dia.* Ap. 104. v. 1) not (Ap. 105. II) having depth of earth. **no.** Gr. *mē.* Ap. 105. II.
7 among = upon. Gr. *epi.* Ap. 104. ix. 3.
8 into = upon. Gr. *epi.* Ap. 104. ix. 3.
good ground = the ground, the good [ground]. Good, because *prepared.*
brought forth. All the verbs are in past tenses.
9 Who: i. e. Him who hears.

13. 10-23 (H, p. 1336). QUESTION OF DISCIPLES. (*Division.*)

H | L¹ | 10-17. Colloquy.
  | L² | 18-23. Interpretation of Parable.

13. 10-17 (L¹, above). COLLOQUY. (*Alternation.*)

L¹ | M | 10. Question of Disciples. Put.
   | N | 11, 12. Answer. Reason. "Because".
   | *M* | 13-. Question of Disciples. Answered.
   | *N* | -13-17. Answer. Reason. "Because".

11 He = And He.
is given = hath been given: i. e. is permanently given.
to know = to get to know. Gr. *ginōskō.* Ap. 132. I. ii.
the mysteries = the secrets; or the things hitherto kept secret.
of = belonging to. Gen. of Relation. Ap. 17. 5.
the kingdom of heaven. See Ap. 114.
heaven = the heavens (pl.). See notes on 6. 9, 10.
it is not given = it hath not been given.
12 whosoever. Fig. *Synecdochē* (of Genus).
whosoever hath, &c. Fig. *Parœmia.* Ap. 6. Cp. 25. 29.
have more abundance = be made to abound.
from. Gr. *apo.* Ap. 104. iv.

13. -13-17 (*N*, above). ANSWER. REASON. (*Alternation.*)

N | s | -13. Condition of the People. Apathy.
    | t | 14, 15. Prophet. Isaiah. Foreseen.
    | *s* | 16. Condition of Disciples. Happy.
    | *t* | 17. Prophets. Desired to see and hear.

13 Therefore = On this account. Gr. *dia touto.* See Ap. 104. v. 2.
seeing see . . . hearing . . . hear. Fig. *Polyptōton.* Ap. 6.
14 in = upon. Gr. *epi.* Ap. 104. ix. 2.
fulfilled = is fulfilling. See Ap. 107. I. 1; II. 3; and 117. Isa. 6. 9. Cp. John 12. 40. Acts 28. 26.
Esaias = Isaiah. Quoted from Isa. 6. 9, 10. Cp. the other two: John 12. 39. Acts 28. 25-27.
hearing . . . hear . . . seeing . . . see. Fig. *Polyptōton.* Ap. 6.

not = by no means. Gr. *ou mē.* See Ap. 105. III. **see.** Gr. *blepō.* Ap. 133. I. 5. **be converted** = be turned to [the Lord]. **15 waxed gross** = grown fat. **16 blessed** = happy, as in 5. 3, &c. **your eyes . . . your ears** = ye. "Eyes" and "ears" being put by Fig. *Synecdochē* (of the Part), Ap. 6, for the persons themselves. **17 verily.** See note on 5. 18. **have desired** = desired [earnestly]. **to see** = to get a sight of. Gr. *eidon.* Ap. 133. I. 1. **ye see** = ye are seeing. Gr. *blepō.* Ap. 133. I. 5. **have not seen** = never saw. **seen.** Gr. *eidon.* Ap. 133. I. 1. **have not heard** = never heard.

13. 18-23 (L², above). INTERPRETATION OF THE SOWER. (*Introversion and Alternation.*)

L² | O | u | 18, 19-. Interpretation.
   | | v | -19. Wayside.
   | | *v* | 20-. Stony ground.
   | | *u* | -20, 21. Interpretation.
   | *O* | w | 22-. Thorns.
   | | x | -22. Interpretation.
   | | *w* | 23-. Good ground.
   | | *x* | -23. Interpretation.

19 the word of the kingdom: i. e. the proclamation of its having drawn nigh, as in 3. 2; 4. 17. Acts 2. 28; 3. 19-26. **word.** Gr. *logos.* See note on Mark 9. 32. **not.** Gr. *mē.* Ap. 105. II.

27 cometh °the wicked *one*, and catcheth away that which was sown [3]in his heart.

v (p. 1337) This is he which °received seed [1]by the way side. •

v 20 But he that [19]received the seed [8]into stony places,

u the same is he that heareth the [19]word, and °anon °with joy receiveth it;

21 Yet hath he [5]not root [3]in himself, °but dureth for a while: for when tribulation or persecution ariseth [5]because of the [19]word, °by and by he °is offended.

O w 22 He also that [19]received seed °among the thorns

x °is he that heareth the [19]word; and the care of this °world, and the deceitfulness of riches, choke the [19]word, and °he becometh unfruitful.

w 23 But he that [19]received seed [8]into the good ground

x [22]is he that heareth the [19]word, and understandeth *it*; °which also beareth fruit, and bringeth forth, °some an hundredfold, °some sixty, °some thirty."

J (p. 1336) 24 °Another parable put He forth unto them, saying, °"The kingdom of °heaven is likened unto a °man which sowed good seed [3]in his field:

25 But while [24]men °slept, his enemy came and °sowed °tares °among the wheat, and °went his way.

26 But when the blade was sprung up, and brought forth fruit, then °appeared the [25]tares also.

27 So the °servants of the °householder came and said unto him, °'Sir, didst °not thou sow good seed [3]in thy field? from whence then hath it [25]tares?'

28 °He said unto them, °'An enemy °hath done this.' The servants said unto him, °'Wilt thou then that we go and °gather them up?'

29 But he said, °'Nay; lest while °ye [28]gather up the [25]tares, ye root up also the wheat with them.

30 Let both °grow together until the harvest: and [3]in the time of harvest I will say to the °reapers, [28]'Gather ye together first the [25]tares, and bind them °in °bundles °to burn them: but [2]gather the wheat [2]into my barn.'"

31 [24]Another parable put He forth unto them, saying, [24]"The kingdom of [24]heaven is like to a grain of mustard seed, which a [24]man took, and sowed [3]in his field:

32 Which indeed is °the least °of all seeds: but when °it is grown, it is °the greatest among herbs, and becometh a tree, so that the birds of °the air come and °lodge [3]in the branches thereof."

33 [24]Another parable spake He unto them; [24]"The kingdom of [24]heaven is like unto °leaven

the wicked one = the evil [one]. See Ap. 128. IV. 1.

received. Cp. Acts 2. 41. 1 Thess. 2. 13. Not the same word in Greek, but the same truth.

20 anon = immediately. The same word as "by and by" in *v.* 21. **with.** Gr. *meta.* Ap. 104. xi. 1.

21 but dureth for a while = but is temporary, or endureth but for a season.

by and by = immediately. Same word as "anon", *v.* 20. The offence is as immediate as the joy.

is offended = stumbles.

22 among. Gr. *eis.* Ap. 104. vi. Not the same word as in *v.* 5. **is he** = this is he.

world = age. Gr. *aiōn.* See Ap. 129. 2. **he** = it.

23 which also = who indeed.

and bringeth forth = produceth also.

some = some indeed.

some = but other.

24 Another. Gr. *allos.* Ap. 124. 1. The parables spoken outside (*v.* 1) are introduced thus; those within the house by the word "again" (*v.* 36): marking off the Structure *J*, p. 1336; and Ap. 144.

The kingdom of heaven. See Ap. 114.

heaven = the heavens. See note on 6. 9, 10.

man. Gr. *anthrōpos.* Ap. 123. 1.

25 slept. Ap. 171. 1.

sowed = sowed upon [and therefore among]. Gr. *epispeirō* = sowed. Occ. only here. All the texts read "sowed over".

tares. Gr. *zizania* (occ. only in this chapter, *vv.* 25, 36.) Not "darnel" (the *Lolium temulentum* of naturalists), but *zewan* as known to-day in Palestine. While growing it looks like wheat, but when full grown the ears are long and the grains almost black. Each grain of *zewan* must be removed before grinding wheat, or the bread is bitter and poisonous. Wheat is golden; but tares show their true colour as they ripen.

among = in (Gr. *ana*, Ap. 104. i) the midst.

went his way. He had no doubt as to the result. Nor should those have doubt who sow "the good seed" of the Word of God. They should have as much confidence in their sowing as the "enemy" had in his; and go their way, and sow more.

26 appeared. Gr. *phainō.* Ap. 106. I. i.

27 servants = bondservants.

householder = master of the house. See Ap. 98. XIV. iii.

Sir. Gr. *kurios.* Ap. 98. VI. i. *a.* 4. B.

not. Gr. *ouchi*, a strengthened form of *ou.* See Ap. 105. I (*a*).

28 He = And he.

An enemy = A man an enemy. Fig. *Pleonasm* (Ap. 6), for emphasis. **hath done** = did.

Wilt. Gr. *thelō.* See Ap. 102. 1.

gather them up? = collect them together?

29 Nay. Gr. *ou.* Ap. 105. I.

ye gather up = [while] gathering them together.

30 grow together. Gr. *sunauxanomai.* Occ. only here.

reapers. Gr. *theristēs.* Occ. only here, and in *v.* 39.

in = into. Gr. *eis.* Ap. 104. vi.

bundles. Gr. *desmē.* Occ. only here, in this form.

to. Gr. *pros.* Ap. 104. xv. 3.

to burn = in order to burn.

32 the least = less indeed.

of all seeds. Supply the Ellipsis from *v.* 31 = "than all the seeds [that a man sows in his field]".

it is grown = it shall or may have grown. This growth is contrary to nature: to show that it symbolizes an unnatural result, with its consequences.

the greatest among herbs = greater than [garden] herbs.

the air = the heaven (sing.). **lodge** = perch.

33 leaven = sour dough. Always used in a bad sense, as meal is in a good sense: therefore the common interpretation as to the Gospel's improving the world is the exact contrary of the leaven corrupting the whole of the meal. The same is true of the symbol of the "woman", see below. The Lord mentions *three* kinds of leaven, all of which were evil in their working: the leaven (1) of the Pharisees = hypocrisy or formalism (Luke 12. 1); (2) of the Pharisees and Sadducees = evil doctrine or teaching (Matt. 16. 11, 12); (3) of Herod = political religion, or worldliness (Mark 8. 15). Cp. also Gen. 19. 3. 1 Cor. 5. 6-8. Matt. 23. 14, 16, 23-28.

27 ven, which °a woman took, and °hid [30]in three °measures of meal, till the whole was °leavened."

K (p. 1336) **34** All these things spake [1]Jesus unto the °multitude [3]in parables; and without a parable °spake He [5]not unto them:

35 °That it might be °fulfilled which was spoken °by the prophet, saying, "**I will open my mouth [3]in parables; I will °utter things which have been kept secret [12]from the °foundation of the °world.**"

E² (p. 1339) **36** Then °Jesus sent the [34]multitude away, and °went [2]into °the house:

F K y and His disciples came unto Him, saying,

z °"Declare unto us the parable of the [25]tares of the field."

y **37** He answered and said unto them,

z "He That soweth the good seed is °the Son of man;

38 The field is the [35]world; the good seed °are the °children of the kingdom; but the [25]tares are the °children of [19]the wicked *one;*

39 The enemy that sowed them is the devil; the harvest is °the °end of the [22]world; and the [30]reapers are °the angels.

40 As therefore the [25]tares are [28]gathered and burned [3]in the fire; so shall it be [3]in [39]the [39]end of °this [22]world.

41 [37]The Son of man shall send forth His angels, and they shall [28]gather °out of His kingdom all things that °offend, and them which do °iniquity;

42 And shall cast them [2]into °a furnace of fire: there shall be °wailing and °gnashing of teeth.

43 Then shall the righteous °shine forth as the sun [3]in °the kingdom of their °Father. °Who hath ears to hear, let him hear.

J (p. 1336) **44** °Again, [24]the kingdom of heaven is like unto treasure °hid [3]in a field; the which when a [24]man hath found, he hideth, and °for joy thereof goeth and selleth all that he hath, and °buyeth that field.

45 [44]Again, [24]the kingdom of [24]heaven is like unto °a merchant [24]man, seeking goodly pearls:

46 Who, when he had found one pearl of great price, °went and sold all that he had, and [44]bought it.

47 [44]Again, [24]the kingdom of [24]heaven is like unto °a net, that was cast [2]into the sea, and [2]gathered °of every kind:

48 Which, when it was full, they °drew °to shore, and sat down, and [28]gathered the good [2]into vessels, but cast °the bad °away.

49 So shall it be °at [39]the [39]end of the [22]world: the angels shall °come forth, and °sever the °wicked °from among the °just,

50 And shall cast them [2]into the furnace of fire: there shall be [42]wailing and [42]gnashing of teeth."

H **51** °Jesus saith unto them, "Have ye understood all these things?" They say unto him, "Yea, °Lord."

---

a woman. A common symbol of evil in the moral or religious spheres. See Zech. 5. 7, 8. Rev. 2. 20; 17. 1-6.
hid. Cp. *v.* 44, and see the Structure. Ap. 145.
measures. Gr. *saton.* See Ap. 51. III. 3 (ii) (9).
leavened = corrupted.
34 multitude = multitudes (pl.).
spake He not = was He not speaking.
35 That = So that.
fulfilled. Quoted from Ps 78. 2. See Ap. 107. I. 3, and 117.
by = by means of. Gr. *dia.* Ap. 104. v. 1.
utter = pour forth. Gr. *ereugomai.* Occ. only here.
from the foundation of the world. Note the *seven* occurrences of this expression (here; 25. 34. Luke 11. 50. Heb. 4. 3; 9. 6. Rev. 13. 8; 17. 8). Contrast "before the overthrow", &c. (John 17. 24. Eph. 1. 4. 1 Pet. 1. 20).
foundation = overthrow. See Gen. 1. 2. Ap. 146.
world. Gr. *kosmos.* Ap. 129. 1.

13. 36-43 (*K*, p. 1336). DISCIPLES.
(*Alternation.*)

K | y | 36-. Disciples come.
  z | -36. Explanation requested.
 y | 37-. The Lord's answer.
  z | -37-43. Explanation given (*vv.* -37-39). Application made (*vv.* 40-43).

36 went into the house. This determines the Structure E², on p. 1336. the house. Peter's house.
Declare = Expound. Gr. *phrazō.* Occ. only here, and in 15. 15.
37 the Son of man. See Ap. 98. XVI. Cp. 8. 20.
38 are = these are: i. e. represent. Fig. *Metaphor.* Ap. 6.
children = sons. Ap. 108. III.
39 the end of the world = the end of the age, age-time, or dispensation. The expression occurs six times (here, *vv.* 40, 49; 24. 3; 28. 20. Heb. 9. 26), always in this sense. See Ap. 129. II; 151.
end. Gr. *sunteleia* (not "*telos*") = closing time, denoting the joining of two age-times: i.e. the closing time of one leading on to the other. The *sunteleia* mark the closing period, while *telos* marks the actual and final end.
the angels = angels. In *v.* 41 "His angels".
40 this world = this [present] age-time (cp. *vv.* 22, 39).
41 out of. Gr. *ek.* Ap. 104. vii.
offend = cause offence, or stumbling.
iniquity = lawlessness. See Ap. 128. X. 1.
42 a furnace = the furnace, as in *v.* 50.
wailing and gnashing. See note on 8. 12.
gnashing = the grinding.
43 shine forth. Gr. *eklampō.* Occ. only here.
the kingdom, &c. See Ap. 112. 3.
Father. Ap. 98. III.
Who hath, &c. See note on 11. 15. See Ap. 142.
44 Again. This word marks and links together the last three parables. See the Structure "*J*", p. 1336 (Ap. 145), and note on "another", *v.* 24.
hid = lying hidden. Cp. *vv.* 33 and 35.
for = from. Gr. *apo.* Ap. 104. iv.
buyeth. Not the word for "redeem". See note on 2 Pet. 2. 1.
45 a merchant man = a man, a merchant. Cp. *v.* 28, "an enemy".
46 went. The 1611 edition of the A.V. reads "he went".
47 a net = a drag-net, or seine. Gr. *sagēnē.* Occ. only here. of = out of. Gr. *ek.* Ap. 104. vii.
48 drew = drew up. Gr. *anabibazō.* Occ. only here.
to shore = upon (Gr. *epi.* Ap. 104. ix. 3) the shore.
the bad = the useless: i. e. the cat-fish, plentiful in the Sea of Galilee.
away = out.
49 at = in, as in *v.* 3.
come forth = go out. The Lord was speaking on earth.
sever = separate.
wicked = evil ones. Gr. pl. of *ponēros.* Ap. 128. IV. i.

from among. Gr. *ek.* Ap. 104. vii. just = righteous ones. **51** Jesus saith unto them. All the texts omit this clause. Lord. Ap. 98. VI. i. *a.* 4. B. All the texts omit "Lord" here.

G 52 Then said He unto them, [13]"Therefore
(p. 1336) every scribe *which is* °instructed °unto [24]the
27 kingdom of heaven is like unto a [24]man *that*
is °an householder, which bringeth forth [41]out
of his treasure *things* °new and old."

E3 53 And it came to pass, *that* when [1]Jesus had
°finished these parables, He °departed thence.

U2 P a 54 And when He was come [2]into His own
(p. 1340) country,
b He °taught them [3]in their °synagogue,
Q insomuch that they were astonished, and said,
R "Whence hath °this *man* this wisdom, and
these °mighty works?
S c 55 Is [5]not [54]This the carpenter's son?
d is [27]not His mother called Mary?
S c °and His brethren, James, °and Joses, °and
Simon, °and Judas?
d 56 And His sisters, are they [27]not all °with
us?
R Whence then hath [54]this *man* all these
things?"
Q 57 And they were °offended °in Him.
P a But [1]Jesus said unto them, "A prophet is [5]not
without honour, save [3]in his own country, and
[3]in °his own house."
b 58 And He did [5]not many [54]mighty works
there [5]because of their unbelief.

M N T **14** °At that °time °Herod the °tetrarch
°heard of the °fame of °Jesus,
2 And said unto his °servants, "This is John
the Baptist; he is risen °from °the dead; and
°therefore °mighty works do shew forth
themselves °in him."
U V e 3 For °Herod had laid hold on John, and
bound him, and °put *him* [2]in prison °for Herodias' sake, his brother °Philip's °wife.
f 4 For John °said unto him, "It is °not lawful
for thee to have her."
e 5 And °when he would have put him to
death, he feared the multitude,
f because they °counted him as a prophet.

52 instructed = discipled, or initiated as a disciple.
unto. All the texts omit *eis* (Ap. 104. vi). L reads *en* (Ap. 104. viii), reading "in the kingdom", for "unto the kingdom".
an householder = a man a householder. Fig. *Pleonasm* (Ap. 6), for emphasis. See *v.* 27.
new = new (in character). Gr. *kainos*; not *neos*, which = new (in time). See notes on 9. 17; 26. 28, 29.
53 finished. Thus marking the end of this special collocation of parables, showing them to be one whole.
departed. Gr. *metairō*. Occ. only here and 19. 1; referring probably to His going by water.

13. 54-58 (U2, p. 1323). RESULTS. OPPOSITION OF HIS OWN KINDRED. (*Introversion and Alternation.*)

U2 | P | a | 54-. "His own country."
  | b | -54-. His words.
 Q | -54-. Effect of His teaching. "Astonished".
  R | -54. Question. "Whence", &c.
   S | c | 55-. Father. (Male.)
     d | -55-. Mother. (Female.)
   S | c | -55. Brethren. (Males.)
     d | 56-. Sisters. (Females.)
  R | -56. Question. "Whence", &c.
 Q | 57-. Effect of His teaching. "Offended".
P | *a* | -57. "His own country."
  b | 58. "His works."

54 taught = was teaching.
synagogue. See Ap. 120. **this** = this [fellow].
mighty works. Pl. of *dunamis.* Ap. 172. 1. Cp. John 2. 18. Heb. 2. 4, &c.
55 and. Note the Fig. *Polysyndeton* (Ap 6), emphasising each one individually.
56 with. Gr. *pros.* Ap. 104. xv. 3.
57 offended = stumbled.
in = at. Gr. *en.* Ap. 104. viii.
his own house. His own family: "house" being put by Fig. *Metonymy* (of Adjunct), Ap. 6, for the family dwelling within it.

14. 1-12 (*N*, p. 1323). MISSION OF JOHN BAPTIST. ENDED. (*Introversion.*)

N | T | 1, 2. Herod hearing of John.
 U | 3-11. John's death.
 U | 12-. John's burial.
T | -12. Jesus hearing of Herod.

1 At = In. Gr. *en.* Ap. 104. vii.
time = season.
Herod = Herod Antipas. Son of Herod the Great by Malthace. See Ap. 109.
tetrarch. The Greek word transliterated = a governor over the *fourth* part of any region; but the word subsequently lost its strict etymological meaning, and came to denote any petty prince not ruling over an entire country. So called from *tetartos* = fourth. **heard of the fame.** Fig. *Polyptōton.* Ap. 6. Gr. *ēkousen . . . akoēn.* **fame** = hearing, or report. **of** = concerning. Gen. (of Relation). Ap. 17. 5. **Jesus.** Ap. 98. X. **2 servants** = young men or courtiers. Gr. *pais.* Ap. 108. iv. **from.** Gr. *apo.* Ap. 104. iv. **the dead.** With Art. See Ap. 139. 1. **therefore** = on this account. Gr. *dia* (Ap. 104. v. 2) *touto.* **mighty works.** See note on 13. 54, above. **in.** Gr. *en.* Ap. 104. viii.

14. 3-11 (U, above). JOHN'S DEATH. (*Introversion and Alternations.*)

U | V | e | 3. Herod's imprisonment of John (from enmity). } John's death desired.
  f | 4. Reason. John's reproof.
  e | 5-. Herod's imprisonment of John (from fear).
  f | -5. Reason. People's opinion.
 W | 6. Opportunity given.
V | g | 7. Herod's promise to Herodias. Made. } John's death effected.
  h | 8. John's head asked.
  g | 9, 10. Herod's promise to Herodias. Kept.
  h | 11. John's head given.

3 Herod. One of eleven rulers offended with God's reprovers. See note on Ex. 10. 28. **put**: i. e. had him put. **for . . . sake** = on account of. Gr. *dia.* Ap. 104. v. **Philip's** = Philip I, son of Herod the Great and Mariamne II. See Ap. 109. **wife**: i. e. widow. **4 said** = used to say. **not.** Gr. *ou.* Ap. 105. I. **5 when he would have put him to death** = wishing (Ap. 102. 1) to kill him. **counted** = held. Cp. 21. 26, 46.

W 6 But when Herod's birthday was °kept, °the
(p. 1340) daughter of °Herodias danced °before them,
27 and pleased [1] Herod.

Vg 7 Whereupon he promised °with an oath to
give her whatsoever she would ask.

h 8 And she, being °before instructed °of her
mother, said, "Give me here John Baptist's
head °in a °charger."

g 9 And the king was sorry: nevertheless [3]for
°the oath's sake, and them which sat with
him at meat, he commanded *it* to be given *her*.
10 And he sent, and beheaded John [2] in the
prison.

h 11 And his head was brought [8] in a [8] charger,
and given to the °damsel: and she brought *it*
to her mother.

U 12 And his disciples came, and took up the
°body, and buried it,

T and went and told [1] Jesus.

R³ X 13 When [1] Jesus heard *of it*, He °departed
(p. 1341) thence °by ship °into a desert place apart:

Y Z i and when the °people had heard *thereof*,
28 they followed Him on foot °out of the cities.

k 14 And [1] Jesus °went forth, and saw a great
multitude, and was moved with compassion
°toward them, and He healed their sick.

A l 15 And when it was evening, His disciples
came to Him, saying, "This is a desert place,
and the °time is °now past; send the multitude away, that they may go [13] into the villages, and buy themselves victuals."

m 16 But [1] Jesus said unto them, "They need
[4] not depart; give ye them to eat."

n 17 °And they say unto Him, "We °have here
but five loaves, and two fishes."

n 18 He said, "Bring them hither to Me."
19 And He commanded the multitude to sit
down °on the grass, and took the five loaves,
and the two fishes, and looking up °to °heaven,
He blessed, and °brake,

m and gave the loaves to *His* disciples, and the
disciples °to the multitude.

l 20 And they did all eat, and were °filled:
and they took up of the fragments that remained twelve °baskets full.
21 And they that had eaten were about five
thousand °men, beside women and children.

X 22 And °straightway [1] Jesus constrained His
disciples to get [13] into °a ship, and to go before
Him °unto the other side, while °He sent the
multitudes away.
23 And when He had sent the multitudes
away, He went up [13] into [22] a mountain apart
to pray: and when the evening was come, He
was there alone.

Y A B 24 But the ship was now in the midst of the
(p. 1343) sea, tossed °with °waves:

C for the wind was contrary.

D o 25 And in °the fourth watch of the night
[1] Jesus went °unto them, walking [19] on the
sea.

6 kept = being celebrated.
the daughter. Salome (Josephus, *Ant.* xviii. 5. 4).
Herodias. See Ap. 109.
before them = in the midst of them: i.e. in public.
7 with. Gr. *meta.* Ap. 104. xi. 1.
8 before instructed = prompted, or instigated.
of = by. Gr. *hupo.* Ap. 104. xviii. 1.
in = upon. Gr. *epi.* Ap. 104. ix. 2.
charger = a wooden trencher, or dish. Gr. *pinax.* Occ. only here, *v.* 11. Mark 6. 25, 28 and Luke 11. 39 ("platter"). The Eng. is from the French *charger* = to load. Then by Fig. *Metonymy* (of the Subject) Ap. 6, put for *what is laden*; hence, used of a horse, as well as a dish.
9 the oath's = his great or solemn oath.
11 damsel. Gr. *korasion.* Ap. 108. ix.
12 body. Mark 6. 29 reads *ptōma* = corpse.

14. 13-36 (R³, p. 1323). MIRACLES.
(*Alternations and Introversion.*)

R³ | X | 13–. Departure from the people.
  Y | Z | i | –13. Concourse.
      k | 14. Many Miracles.
    A | 15–21. One Miracle. Feeding the Five Thousand.
 X | 22, 23. Departure from the people.
  Y | *A* | 24–33. One Miracle. Walking on the Sea.
    Z | *i* | 34, 35–. Concourse.
       k | –35–36. Many Miracles.

13 departed = withdrew.
by = in. Gr. *en.* Ap. 104. viii.
into. Gr. *eis.* Ap. 104. vi. **people** = multitudes.
out of = from. Gr. *apo.* Ap. 104. iv.
14 went forth. From His solitude, *v.* 13.
toward. Gr. *epi.* Ap. 104. ix. 3.

14. 15-21 (A, above). ONE MIRACLE. FEEDING THE FIVE THOUSAND. (*Introversion.*)

A | l | 15. Multitudes. Hungry.
  m | 16. "Give ye them".
   n | 17. Supply. Insufficient.
   n | 18, 19–. Supply. Sufficient.
  m | –19. "He gave".
 l | 20, 21. Multitudes. Filled.

15 time = hour. **now** = already. **17 And** = But.
have here but = have not (Gr. *ou*, as in *v.* 4) here [anything] except.
19 on = upon. Gr. *epi.* Ap. 104. ix. 3.
to = into. Gr. *eis.* Ap. 104. vi.
heaven = the heaven (sing.). See note on 6. 9, 10.
brake = after breaking. The bread was made in thin cakes, which had to be broken (not cut) before they could be eaten. Hence the idiom "to break bread" means to eat bread, as in Luke 24. 35; Acts 27. 35. See notes on Num. 18. 19, and Isa. 58. 7. Put by Fig. *Metonymy* (of the Adjunct). Ap. 6.
to = [gave] to. The Ellipsis must be thus supplied from the preceding clause. **20 filled** = satisfied.
baskets. Gr. *kophinos.* A small wicker hand-basket.
21 men = males. Gr. pl. of *anēr.* See Ap. 123. 2.
22 straightway = immediately, as in *v.* 31.
a = the.
unto. Gr. *eis.* Ap. 104. vi.
He sent, &c. This was a miracle in itself.

14. 24-33 (*A*, above). ONE MIRACLE. WALKING ON THE SEA. (*Extended Alternation.*)

A | B | 24–. The ship.
  C | –24. The wind. Contrary.
   D | 25–31. The miracle. Wrought.
  B | 32–. The ship.
  C | –32. The wind. Ceased.
   D | 33. The miracle. Effect.

24 with = by. Gr. *hupo.* Ap. 104. xviii. 1.
waves = the waves.

14. 25-31 [For Structure see next page].

25 the fourth watch. See Ap. 51. III. 4. (6).
unto. Gr. *pros.* Ap. 104. xv. 3.

p 26 And when the disciples saw Him walking
(p. 1342) [19]on the sea, they were troubled, saying, "It is
28 °a spirit;" and they cried out °for fear.
q 27 But [22]straightway [1]Jesus spake unto them,
saying, "Be of good cheer; °it is I; be °not
afraid."
o 28 And Peter answered him and said, °"Lord,
°if it be Thou, bid me come [25]unto Thee [19]on
the water."
29 And He said, "Come." And when Peter
was come down [13]out of the ship, he walked
[19]on the water, to go °to [1]Jesus.
p 30 But when °he saw the wind boisterous, he
was afraid; and beginning to °sink, he cried,
saying, [28]"Lord, save me."
q 31 And immediately [1]Jesus stretched forth
His hand, and caught him, and said unto him,
°"O thou of little faith, °wherefore didst thou
°doubt?"
B 32 And when they were come [13]into the ship,
C the wind ceased.
D 33 Then they that were [2]in the ship came and
worshipped Him, saying, "Of a truth Thou
art °the Son of God."
Z i 34 And when they were gone over, they
(p. 1341) came [13]into the land of °Gennesaret.
35 And when the [21]men of that place °had
knowledge of Him, they sent out [13]into all
that country round about,
k and brought unto Him all that were diseased;
36 And besought Him that they might only
touch the °hem of His garment: and as many
as touched were °made perfectly whole.

S^3 15 Then °came to °Jesus °scribes and °Pha-
(p. 1323) risees, which were °of °Jerusalem, saying,
2 "Why do Thy disciples °transgress the
tradition of °the elders? for they °wash °not
their hands when they eat °bread."
T^3 r 3 But He answered and said unto them,
(p. 1342) "Why do °ye °also transgress the commandment of °God °by your tradition?
s 4 For [3]God °commanded, saying, '**Honour thy
father and mother:**' and, '**He that curseth
father or mother, °let him die the death.**'
t 5 But [3]ye say, 'Whosoever shall say to *his*
father or *his* mother, °'*It is* °a gift, by whatsoever °thou mightest be °profited °by °me;'
6 °And honour °not his father or his mother,
°*he shall be free.*' Thus have ye made the
commandment of [3]God of none effect [3]by your
tradition.
r 7 *Ye* hypocrites, well did °Esaias prophesy
°of you, saying,
s 8 °'**This people draweth nigh unto Me with**

14. 25-31 (D, p. 1341). THE MIRACLE WROUGHT. (*Extended Alternation.*)

D | o | 25. The Lord walking on the sea.
p | 26. Disciples troubled.
q | 27. Be not afraid.
o | 28, 29. Peter essaying to walk, &c.
p | 30. Peter afraid.
q | 31. Wherefore didst thou doubt?

26 a spirit=a phantom. Gr. *phantasma*. Occ. only here and Mark 6. 49.
for=from. Gr. *apo*. Ap. 104. iv.
27 it is I=I am [He].
not. Gr. *me*. Ap. 105. II.
28 Lord. Gr. *Kurios*. Ap. 98. VI. i. α. 3. A.
if, &c. See Ap. 118. 2 a. Assuming it as a fact.
29 to. Gr. *pros*. Ap. 104. xv. 3.
30 he saw the wind boisterous. He looked at the circumstances instead of the Lord. This was the secret of his (and of our) failure.
sink=be overwhelmed in the sea. Gr. *katapontizomai*. Occ. only here and 18. 6.
31 O thou of little faith. See note on 6. 30.
wherefore=why, or for what. Gr. *eis* (Ap. 104. vi.) *ti*.
doubt=waver, or hesitate. Gr. *distazō*. Occ. only here and 28. 17.
33 the Son of God=God's Son (no Art.). Ap. 98. XV.
34 Gennesaret. It was at the northern end of the lake and to the west of the Jordan (Ap. 169). The Talmud identifies it with Chinnereth of the O.T. Josephus says it was about four miles long by two and a half broad.
35 had knowledge of=having recognized.
36 hem=border, or fringes. Cp. 9. 20.
made perfectly whole=completely saved or healed. Gr. *diasōzō*=to save throughout. Occ. eight times (here; Luke 7. 3. Acts 23. 24; 27. 43, 44; 28. 1, 4. 1 Pet. 3. 20). All are interesting and used of bodily saving.

15. 1 came=come.
Jesus. See Ap. 98. X.
scribes, &c.=the scribes. Note the four parties addressed in this chapter: (1) scribes, &c. from Jerusalem, *vv.* 1-9; (2) the multitudes, *vv.* 10, 11; (3) the disciples, *vv.* 12-14; (4) Peter, *vv.* 15-20.
Pharisees. See Ap. 120. II.
of=away from. Gr. *apo*. Ap. 104. iv.
Jerusalem. The seat of authority in these matters.
2 transgress. Gr. *parabainō*. Ap. 128. VII. 1.
the elders. Gr. *presbuteroi*. Always used in the Papyri officially, not of age (old men), but of communal officers and heathen priests.
wash not. To wash before eating is still a rigorous custom in Palestine. See Ap. 136.
not. Gr. *ou*. Ap. 105. I.
bread. Put by Fig. *Synecdoche* (of Species), Ap. 6, for all kinds of food.

15. 3-11 (T^3, p. 1323). TEACHING. (*Extended Alternation.*)

T^3 | r | 3. Pharisees. Transgression.
s | 4. God's Commandment.
t | 5, 6. "Ye say".
r | 7. Pharisees. Hypocrisy.
s | 8, 9. God's Word.
t | 10, 11. "I say".

3 ye. Emphatic. Note the Fig. *Anteisagōge*. Ap. 6.
also. Connect "also" with "ye", not with "transgress".
God. Ap. 98. I. i. 1.
by=on account of. Gr. *dia*. Ap. 104. v. 2.

4 commanded. Quoted from Ex. 20. 12; 21. 17. Ap. 117. I. **let him die the death**=he shall surely die. Fig. *Polyptōton*. Ap. 6. See Ex. 21. 17. Lev. 20. 9. Deut. 5. 16; 27. 16. Prov. 30. 17. **5 It is.** Supply ["Be that"] instead of "It is". **a gift**=dedicated to God. **thou**: i.e. the parent. **profited**=helped. **by**=of. Gr. *ek*. Ap. 104. vii. **me**: i.e. the son. **6 And**=And [in consequence of this evasion]. **not**=you certainly do not. Gr. *ou me*=by no means, in no wise. Ap. 105. III. **he shall be free.** There is no *Ellipsis* here if it be supplied as in *v.* 8. **7 Esaias**=Isaiah. See Ap. 79. I. **of**=concerning. Gr. *peri*. Ap. 104. xiii. 1. **8 This people.** Quoted from Isa. 29. 13. See Ap. 107. I. 3 and 117. I.

28 **their mouth, and honoureth Me with *their***
lips; but their heart °is far °from Me.
9 But in vain they do worship Me, °teaching
***for* doctrines the commandments of °men.'"**
t 10 And He °called °the multitude, and said
(p. 1342) unto them, "Hear, and understand:
11 [2]Not that which goeth °into the mouth
defileth °a °man; but that which cometh °out
of the mouth, this defileth °a °man."

U^3 u 12 Then °came °His disciples, and said unto
(p. 1343) Him, "Knowest Thou that the Pharisees were
°offended, after they heard this °saying?"

v 13 But He answered and said, °"Every °plant,
which My °heavenly Father hath [2]not planted,
shall be rooted up.
14 Let them alone: °they be blind leaders of
the blind. And °if the blind lead the blind,
both shall fall [11]into the ditch."

u 15 Then answered °Peter and said unto Him,
°"Declare unto us this parable."

v 16 And [1]Jesus said, "Are [3]ye [3]also °yet without understanding?
17 Do not ye yet understand, that whatsoever entereth °in at the mouth goeth
[11]into the belly, and is cast out [11]into the
°draught?
18 °But those things which proceed [11]out of
the mouth come forth °from the heart; and
they defile the [11]man.
19 For [11]out of the heart proceed °evil
°thoughts, murders, adulteries, fornications,
thefts, °false witness, blasphemies:
20 These are *the things* which defile [11]a man:
but to eat with unwashen hands defileth [2]not
[11]a man."

R^4 E^1 21 Then [1]Jesus went thence, and departed
[11]into the °coasts of Tyre and Sidon.

F^1 w^1 22 And, °behold, a woman of Canaan came
°out of °the same °coasts, and cried unto
Him, saying, °"Have mercy on me, O °Lord,
Thou °Son of David; my daughter is °grievously °vexed with a devil."

x^1 23 °But He answered her [2]not a word.

w^2 And His disciples came and besought Him,
saying, "Send her away; for she crieth after
us."

x^2 24 But He answered and said, °"I am [2]not
sent °but °unto the °lost sheep of °the house of
Israel."

w^3 25 Then came she and °worshipped Him,
saying, °[22]"Lord, help me."

x^3 26 But He answered and said, "It is [2]not

is far = keepeth far distant.
from = away from. Gr. *apo*. Ap. 104. iv.
9 teaching for doctrines. Gr. teaching teachings. Fig. *Polyptōton*. Ap. 6.
men. See Ap. 123. 1.
10 called = called to [Him].
the multitude. See note on "scribes", *v.* 1.
11 into. Gr. *eis*. Ap. 104. vi.
a = the. **man.** Ap. 123. 1.
out of. Gr. *ek*. Ap. 104. vii.

15. 12-20 (U^3, p. 1323). RESULT. OPPOSITION OF THE PHARISEES. (*Alternation.*)

U^3 | u | 12. Disciples. Report. Opposition of Pharisees.
v | 13, 14. The Lord. Explanation of opposition.
u | 15. Disciples. Peter's request.
v | 16-20. The Lord. Explanation of statement.

12 came = came unto [Him].
His disciples. See note on "scribes", *v.* 1.
offended = stumbled.
saying. Gr. *logos*. See note on Mark 9. 32.
13 Every plant. Implying the scribes, &c., by the Fig. *Hypocatastasis*. Ap. 6. See note on "dogs", *v.* 26, and on "leaven" (16. 6).
plant. Gr. *phuteia*. Occ. only here.
heavenly. Gr. *ouranios*. See note on 6. 14.
14 they be, &c. Fig. *Parœmia*. Ap. 6.
if, &c.: i.e. experience will show it. Ap. 118. 1 b.
15 Peter. See note on "scribes", &c., *v.* 1.
Declare = Expound. See note on 13. 36.
16 yet = still. Gr. *akmēn*. Occ. only here.
17 in at = into. Gr. *eis*. Ap. 104. vi.
draught = sewer, or sink. Gr. *aphedrōn*, a Macedonian word.
18 But those, &c. Fig. *Epimonē*, *vv.* 18-20.
from = out of. Gr. *ek*, as in preceding clause.
19 evil. Gr. *ponēros*. Ap. 128. IV. 1.
thoughts = reasonings.
false witness. Gr. *pseudomarturia*. Occ. only in Matthew (here, and 26. 59).

15. 21-39 (R^4, p. 1323). MIRACLES. (*Repeated Alternation.*)

R^4 | E^1 | 21. Departure.
F^1 | 22-28. Miracle. Woman of Canaan.
E^2 | 29. Departure.
F^2 | 30-38. Miracle. The Four Thousand.
E^3 | 39. Departure.

21 coasts = parts. Tyre. See Ap. 169.

15. 22-28 (F^1, above). MIRACLE. WOMAN OF CANAAN. (*Repeated Alternation.*)

F^1 | w^1 | 22. Woman. Her Prayer. "Have mercy".
x^1 | 23-. The Lord. No answer. No claim.
w^2 | -23. Woman. Disciples' prayer. "Send her away."
x^2 | 24. The Lord. Answer. Explanation of silence.
w^3 | 25. Woman. Prayer. "Lord, help."
x^3 | 26. The Lord. Answer delayed.
w^4 | 27. Woman. Plea. Confession. I have no claim.
x^4 | 28. The Lord. Answer. Healing given.

22 behold. Fig. *Asterismos*. Ap. 6.
out of = from. Gr. *apo*. Ap. 104. iv.
the same = those.
coasts = borders.

Have mercy = Pity. **Lord.** Gr. *Kurios*. Ap. 98. VI. i. *a*. 3. B. **Son of David.** The fourth of nine occurrences of this title (Ap. 98. XVIII). The woman (a "dog" of the Gentiles) had no claim on the "Son of David". Hence the silence of the Lord. **grievously** = miserably. **vexed with a devil** = possessed by a demon; Gr. *daimonizomai*. **23 But, &c.** Because a Gentile had no claim on the Son of David. Fig. *Accismus*. Ap. 6. **24 I am, &c.** = I was. **but** = except. **unto** = to. Gr. *eis*. Ap. 104. vi. **lost.** Because being without a shepherd. But see note on 1 Kings 12. 17. **the house of Israel.** Therefore it was still represented by those in the Land. See note on and cp. Acts 2. 14, 22, 36. **25 worshipped Him** = threw herself at His feet [and remained there]. Imperfect tense. Cp. John 9. 38. See Ap. 137. 1. **Lord, help me.** This was a better plea, but there was no definition of the "me", as with the publican: "me, a sinner" (Luke 18. 13).

28 °meet to take °the °children's [2]bread, and to
cast *it* to °dogs."
w^{4} 27 And she said, °"Truth, [22]Lord: °yet the
(p. 1343) [26]dogs eat [1]of the °crumbs which fall [8]from their
masters' table."
x^{4} 28 Then [1]Jesus °answered and said unto her,
°"O woman, °great *is* thy faith: be it unto
thee even as thou wilt." And her daughter
was made whole [8]from that very hour.
E^{2} 29 And [1]Jesus departed from thence, and came
°nigh unto the sea of Galilee; and went up
[11]into °a mountain, and °sat down there.
F^{2} 30 And great multitudes came unto Him,
having °with them *those that were* lame, blind,
dumb, maimed, and many °others, and cast
them down °at [1]Jesus' feet; and He healed
them:
31 Insomuch that the multitude wondered,
when they saw the dumb °to speak, the
maimed °to be whole, the lame °to walk, and
the blind °to see: and they glorified °the God
of Israel.
32 Then [1]Jesus °called His disciples *unto*
Him, and said, "I have compassion °on the
multitude, because they continue with Me °now
°three days, and have °nothing to eat: and °I
will [2]not send them away fasting, lest they
faint °in the way."
33 And His disciples say unto Him, "Whence
should °we have so much bread [32]in °the wilderness, as to °fill so great a multitude?"
34 And [1]Jesus saith unto them, "How many
loaves have ye?" And they said, "Seven,
and a few little fishes."
35 And He commanded the multitude to °sit
down [32]on the ground.
36 And He took the seven loaves and the
fishes, and gave thanks, and °brake *them*, and
gave to His disciples, and the disciples °to the
multitude.
37 And they did all eat, and were [33]filled:
and they took up of the °broken *meat* that was
left seven °baskets full.
38 And they that did eat were four thousand
°men, beside women and children.
E^{3} 39 And He sent away the multitude, and °took
ship, and came [11]into the coasts of °Magdala.
S^{4} y (p. 1344) **16** The °Pharisees also with the °Sadducees
°came, and tempting desired Him that
He would shew them °a sign °from °heaven.
z 2 °He answered and said unto them, "When
it is evening, ye say, °'*It will be* °fair weather:
for °the sky is °red.'
3 And in the morning, '*It will be* °foul weather to day: for [2]the sky is [2]red and lowring.'
z O *ye* hypocrites, ye °can °discern the face of
[2]the sky; but can ye °not *discern* the signs
of the times?
y 4 A °wicked and °adulterous generation °seek-
eth after a sign; and there shall °no sign be
given unto it, but the sign of the prophet
°Jonas." And He left them, and departed.
Q^{4} T^{1} a (p. 1345) 5 And when His disciples were come °to
the other side, they had forgotten to °take
°bread.

26 meet=fair.
the children's bread=the bread of the children, with emphasis on children. Fig. *Enallagē*. Ap. 6.
children's. See Ap. 108. i.
dogs=puppies, or little household dogs; this is true only of such. Dogs are not cared for (in the East) when grown. The Lord used the Fig. *Hypocatastasis* (Ap. 6), implying that she was only a Gentile, and thus had still no claim even on that ground. Gentiles were known as "dogs" by the Jews, and despised as such (7. 6. 1 Sam. 17. 43. 2 Sam. 3. 8; 9. 8. 2 Kings 8. 13. Phil. 3. 2).
27 Truth=Yea.
yet=for even: assenting to the Lord's words, while using them as an additional ground of her plea.
crumbs=scraps.
28 answered and said=exclaimed and said. A Hebraism. See note on Deut. 1. 41.
O woman. Fig. *Ecphonēsis*. Ap. 6.
great is thy faith. Contrast the disciples (16. 8), where the same Fig. *Hypocatastasis* (Ap. 6), is used, and ought to have been understood.
29 nigh unto=beside. Gr. *para*. Ap. 104. xii. 3.
a=the, as in 14. 23.
sat down=was sitting down.
30 with=Gr. *meta*. Ap. 104. xi.
others=differently affected. Gr. *heteros*. Ap. 124. 2.
at=beside. Gr. *para*. Ap. 104. xii. 3.
31 to speak=speaking. **to be whole**=sound.
to walk=walking. **to see**=seeing.
the God of Israel. See Isa. 29. 23.
32 called=called to [Him].
on=upon. Gr. *epi*. Ap. 104. ix. 3.
now=already.
three days=the third day. Observe, not "and nights". See note on 12. 40, and Ap. 144 and 156.
nothing=not (Ap. 105. I.) anything.
I will not=I am not willing. See Ap. 102. 1.
in. Gr. *en*. Ap. 104. viii.
33 we. Emphatic, as are the words which follow.
the wilderness=a desert place. These are emphatic also, in addition to "we". **fill**=satisfy.
35 sit down=recline.
36 brake. See note on 14. 19.
to=[gave] to. Supplying the Ellipsis from the preceding clause.
37 broken meat=fragments, or crumbs.
baskets=large baskets. Gr. *spuris*. Cp. 14. 20. Acts 9. 25. Our modern clothes-basket.
38 men. Ap. 123. 2.
39 took ship=entered into (Gr. *eis*. Ap. 104. vi.) the ship (mentioned above, in 14. 22, &c.).
Magdala. See Ap. 169.

16. 1-4 (S^{4}, p. 1323). **EFFECTS.** (*Introversion.*)

S^{4} y | 1. Sign desired.
  z | 2, 3-. Discernment. (Positive.)
  z | -3. Discernment. (Negative.)
  y | 4. Sign refused.

1 Pharisees . . . Sadducees. See Ap. 120. II.
came=having come to [Him]. **a sign.** Cp. 12. 38.
from=out of. Gr. *ek*. Ap. 104. vii.
heaven=the heaven, or sky (sing.), same as in *vv.* 2, 3.
2 He=And He. **It will be.** Omit.
fair weather. Gr. *eudia*. Occ. only here, and in *v.* 3.
the sky=the heaven (sing.), as in *v.* 1 (see note on 6. 9, 10). This is the point of the question.
red. Gr. *purrazō*. Occ. only here, and in *v.* 3.
3 foul weather=a storm.
can=get to know by experience. Ap. 132. I. ii.
discern. Gr. *diakrinō*. Ap. 122. 4.
not. Gr. *ou*. Ap. 105. I.
4 wicked=evil. Ap. 136. IV. 1. See note on 11. 16.
adulterous: spiritually. See 12. 39. Jer. 3. 9. Ezek. 23. 37. Hos. 1. 2, &c. **seeketh**=is (constantly) seeking.
no. Gr. *ou*. Ap. 105. I. **Jonas**=Jonah. See 12. 39.

16. 5-12 [For Structure see next page].

5 to=unto. Gr. *eis*. Ap. 104. vi.
take=bring. **bread**=loaves.

b (p. 1345) 28 6 Then Jesus said unto them, °"Take heed
and °beware °of the °leaven of the [1]Pharisees
and of the [1]Sadducees."

a 7 And they reasoned °among themselves,
saying, "*It is* because we have [5]taken [4]no
[5]bread."

8 *Which* when Jesus perceived, He said unto
them, °"O ye of little faith, why reason ye
[7]among yourselves, because ye have brought
[4]no [5]bread?

9 Do ye [3]not yet understand, neither remember
the five loaves of the five thousand, and
how many °baskets ye took up?

10 Neither the seven loaves of the four thousand,
and how many °baskets ye took up?

b 11 How is it that ye do [3]not understand that
I spake *it* [3]not to you °concerning [5]bread,
that ye should [6]beware [6]of the [6]leaven [6]of the
[1]Pharisees and [6]of the [1]Sadducees?"

12 Then understood they how that He bade
them [3]not [6]beware [6]of the [6]leaven of bread,
but [6]of the °doctrine of the [1]Pharisees and of
the [1]Sadducees.

U[4] c 13 When Jesus came °into the °coasts of
Cæsarea Philippi, He asked His disciples, saying,
°"Whom do °men say that I °the Son of
man am?"

d 14 And they said, °"Some *say that Thou art*
°John the Baptist: °some, °Elias; and °others,
Jeremias, or one of the prophets."

c 15 He saith unto them, "But [13]whom say ye
that I am?"

d 16 And Simon Peter answered and said,
"Thou art °the Christ, °the Son of the living
God."

L e 17 And Jesus answered and said unto him,
°"Blessed art thou, °Simon °Bar-jona: for
°flesh and blood hath [3]not revealed *it* unto
thee, but My °Father Which is °in °heaven.

f 18 And °I say also unto thee, That °thou art
°Peter,

f and °upon °this °rock I °will build My

16. 5-12 (T[4], p. 1323). TEACHING.
(*Alternation.*)

T[4] | a | 5. Bread. Forgetfulness.
| b | 6. Leaven. Warning.
| *a* | 7-10. Bread. Remembrance.
| *b* | 11, 12. Leaven. Instruction.

6 Take heed=Look well. Gr. *horaō*. Ap. 133. I. 8.
beware of the leaven. Fig. *Hypocatastasis* (Ap. 6), leaven put by implication for "doctrine" (*v.* 12), because of its evil effects. Cp. notes on 15. 26, and 13. 33.
beware=pay attention to, so as to be careful of.
of=from. Here, away from: i.e. beware [and keep] away from, or keep clear of, as in 7. 15. Gr. *apo*. Ap. 104. iv.
leaven. See note on 13. 33.
7 among. Gr. *en*. Ap. 104. viii. 2.
8 O ye of little faith. See note on 6. 30; and cp. 8. 26; 14. 31, and Luke 12. 28.
9 baskets. Gr. *kophinos*. Used in connection with the five thousand and the twelve full baskets left in 14. 20.
10 baskets. Gr. *spuris*. A larger plaited basket or hamper. Used in connection with the seven baskets left in 15. 37.
11 concerning. Gr. *peri*. Ap. 104. xiii. 1.
12 doctrine=teaching. This was the word which the Lord had been *implying* in *v.* 6, using the Fig. *Hypocatastasis*. Ap. 6. The woman of Canaan saw what was *implied* in the word "dog"; and her faith was called "great" (15. 28); the disciples did *not* understand what the Lord implied by the word "leaven", and their faith was "little".

16. 13-16 (U[4], p. 1323). RESULT. OPPOSITION COMPLETED. (*Alternation.*)

U[4] | c | 13. Question. Who say men?
| d | 14. Answer of Disciples.
| *c* | 15. Question. Who say ye?
| *d* | 16. Answer of Peter.

13 into. Gr. *eis*. Ap. 104. vi.
coasts=parts.
Whom=Who. The pronoun being governed by the verb "am", not by the verb "say", it must be "who" as in Acts 13. 25 also.
men. Gr. pl. of *anthrōpos*. Ap. 123. 1.
the Son of man. See Ap. 98. XVI.
14 John. Risen from the dead.
some=others. Gr. *allos*. Ap. 124. 1. **Elias**=Elijah.
others=different ones. Gr. *heteros*. Ap. 124. 2.
16 the Christ=the Messiah. The 1611 edition of the A.V. reads "Thou art Christ".
the Son, &c. See Ap. 98. XV.

16. 17-20 (*L*, p. 1323). JESUS. THE MESSIAH DECLARED. WITNESS AND EVIDENCES. ENDED. (*Introversion.*)

L | e | 17. Divine revelation.
| f | 18-. The Foundation itself. Peter's Confession.
| *f* | -18, 19. The Foundation. To be built on.
| *e* | 20. Divine Injunction.

17 Blessed=Happy. See note on 5. 3. **Simon Bar-jona**=Simon, son of Jonah. The Lord uses his human name and parentage in contrast with the divine origin of the revelation made to him. **Bar-jona.** Aramaic. See Ap. 94. III. 3. 28. Occ. only here. **flesh and blood.** Put by Fig. *Synecdochē* (of the Part), Ap. 6, for a mortal human being in contrast with God the Father in the heavens. See 1 Cor. 15. 50. Gal. 1. 16. Eph. 6. 12. Heb. 2. 14. **Father.** Ap. 98. III. **in.** Gr. *en*. Ap. 104. viii. **heaven**=the heavens (pl.). See note on 6. 9, 10. **18 I say also**=I also say (as well as the Father), looking back to a preceding Agent with Whom the Lord associates Himself. **thou art Peter.** See Ap. 147. **Peter.** Gr. *petros*. A stone (loose and movable), as in John 1. 42. **upon.** Gr. *epi*. Ap. 104. ix. 2. **this.** Very emphatic, as though pointing to Himself. See notes on John 2. 19; 6. 58. One of three important passages where "this" stands for the speaker. See notes on John 2. 19, and 6. 58. **this rock**=Gr. *petra*. *Petra* is Fem., and therefore could not refer to Peter; but, if it refers to Peter's confession, then it would agree with *homologia* (which is Fem.), and is rendered *confession* in 1 Tim. 6. 13, and *profession* in 1 Tim. 6. 12. Heb. 3. 1; 4. 14; 10. 23. Cp. 2 Cor. 9. 13. Whether we are to understand it (with Augustine and Jerome) as implying "thou hast said [it]" (see Ap. 147), or "thou art Peter", most Protestants as well as these ancient "Fathers" agree that Peter's *confession* is the foundation to which Christ referred, and not Peter himself. He was neither the foundation nor the builder—(a poor builder, *v.* 23)—but Christ alone, Whom he had confessed (1 Cor. 3. 11). Thus ends the great subject of this second portion of the Lord's ministry. See Ap. 119. **rock.** Gr. *petra*. A rock (*in situ*) immovable: the Messiah, as being "the Son of the living God", Who is the foretold "foundation-stone" (Isa. 28. 16); and the rejected stone (Ps. 118. 22). **will**=shall. Therefore then future, as in Hos. 1. 10; 2. 23.

28 °church; and °the gates of °hell shall [3] not °prevail against it.

19 And I will give unto thee °the keys of °the kingdom of [17]heaven: °and whatsoever °thou shalt bind °on earth shall be bound [17] in [17] heaven: and whatsoever thou shalt loose °on earth shall be loosed [17] in [17] heaven."

e (p. 1345) 20 Then charged He His disciples that they should tell no man that He was °Jesus °the Christ.

G K Q[1] R g (p. 1346) 21 °From that time forth °began Jesus to shew unto His disciples, how that He °must go °unto Jerusalem, and suffer many things [6] of the elders and chief priests and scribes °and be killed,

h °and °be raised again °the third day.

S 22 Then Peter °took Him, and began to rebuke Him, saying, °"Be it far from Thee, °Lord: this shall °not be unto Thee."

S 23 But He turned, and said unto Peter, °"Get thee behind Me, °Satan: thou art °an offence unto Me: for thou °savourest [3] not the things that °be of °God, but those that be of [13] men."

R g 24 Then said Jesus unto His disciples, °"If any *man* °will °come after Me, let him deny himself, and °take up his °cross, and follow Me.

25 For whosoever °will save °his °life shall lose it: and whosoever will lose °his °life for My sake shall find it.

church = assembly. Defined as "Israel", and the "Remnant" (Rom. 9. 25-27). Not the *ecclesia* of the mystery (or secret) revealed in Ephesians; but that referred to in Ps. 22. 22, 25, &c.

the gates. Put by Fig. *Metonymy* (of Adjunct), Ap. 6, for power.

the gates of hell = the gates of *Hades* (= THE grave), denoting the power of the grave to retain, as in Isa. 38. 10. Job 38. 17 (Sept.). Ps. 9. 13; 107. 18.

hell = THE grave. Gr. *Hades*. See Ap. 131. II.

prevail. Gr. *katischuō*. Occ. only here and Luke 23. 23 = have full strength, to another's detriment: i.e. THE grave shall not have power to retain its captives, because Christ holdeth the keys of those gates, and they shall not be strong enough to triumph (Rev. 1. 18. Cp. Ps. 68. 20). Resurrection is the great truth asserted here. Cp. Ezek. 37. 11-14. Acts 2. 29-31. 1 Cor. 15. 55. Hos. 13. 14.

19 the keys. Put by Fig. *Metonymy* (of Cause), Ap. 6, for the power to open. Christ has the keys of Hades; Peter had the keys of the kingdom. See next note.

the kingdom of heaven = the kingdom of the heavens. See Ap. 112. 1, and 114. This power Peter exercised in Acts 2 in Israel, and Acts 10 among the Gentiles. Not the "Church" of the mystery (Eph. 3).

and. The 1611 edition of the A.V. omits this "and".

thou shalt bind, &c. This power was given to the others (18. 18. John 20. 23), and exercised in Acts 5. 1-11, 12-16. Whatever authority is implied, no power was given to communicate it to others, or to them in perpetuity. Binding and loosing is a Hebrew idiom for exercising authority. To bind = to declare what shall be binding (e.g. laws and precepts) and what shall be not binding. **on.** Gr. *epi*. Ap. 104. ix. 1.

20 Jesus. All the texts omit this, here, with Syr.

the Christ = the Messiah. See Ap. 98. IX.

16. 21—20. 34 (*G*, p. 1305). THE THIRD PERIOD OF THE MINISTRY. THE REJECTION OF THE KING. (*Introversion and Alternation.*)

G | G | K | 16. 21—17. 13. SUFFERINGS. First Announcement.
L | 17. 14-21. Miracle. The lunatic son.
H | M | 17. 22, 23. SUFFERINGS. Second Announcement.
N | 17. 24-27. Gentiles. Authority. Sons free.
J | O[1] | 18. 1-35. Discipleship. Little child.
P[1] | 19. 1-12. Pharisees. Question.
O[2] | 19. 13-15. Discipleship. Little children.
P[2] | 19. 16-26. Certain man. Question.
O[3] | 19. 27—20. 16. Discipleship. Rewards.
H | *M* | 20. 17-19. SUFFERINGS. Third Announcement.
N | 20. 20-27. Gentiles. Authority. Brethren free.
G | *K* | 20. 28. SUFFERINGS. Fourth Announcement.
L | 20. 29-34. Miracle. Blind man.

16. 21—17. 13 (K, above). SUFFERINGS. FIRST ANNOUNCEMENT. (*Division.*)

K | Q[1] | 16. 21-28. The Sufferings and Glory. Foretold.
Q[2] | 17. 1-9. The Glory. Foreshown. (The Transfiguration.)
Q[3] | 17. 10-13. The Sufferings and Glory. Explained.

16. 21-28 (Q[1], above). THE SUFFERINGS AND GLORY. FORETOLD. (*Introversion and Alternation.*)

Q[1] | R | g | 21-. Sufferings. } His Own.
h | -21. Glory. Resurrection. }
S | 22. Peter's rebuke of the Lord.
S | 23. Peter rebuked by the Lord.
R | *g* | 24-26. Sufferings. } His Disciple.
h | 27, 28. Glory. Kingdom. }

21 From that time, &c. This commences the third period of the Lord's ministry, the subject of which is the rejection of Messiah. See Ap. 119. **began, &c.** This is stated four times (here, 17. 22; 20. 17; 20. 28). See the Structure above (K, M, *M*, *K*); each time with an additional feature. See the notes. **must.** Note the necessity (Luke 24. 26). **unto.** Gr. *eis*. Ap. 104. vi. **and.** Note the Fig. *Polysyndeton* (Ap. 6). **be raised again.** Omit "again". Not the same word as in 17. 9, but the same as in 17. 23. **the third day.** The first occurrence of this expression (canonically). See Ap. 148. **22 took Him** = took Him aside. **Be it far from Thee** = "[God] be merciful to Thee". A pure Hebraism. See 1 Chron. 11. 19. **Lord.** Ap. 98. VI. i. *a*. 3. A. **not** = by no means. Gr. *ou mē*. See Ap. 105. III. **23 Get thee ... Satan.** The Lord saw in this a direct assault of Satan himself through Peter. **Satan.** See note on 4. 10. **an offence** = a snare: i.e. an occasion of stumbling. **savourest** = regardest. **be of** = belong to. Gen. of Relation. Ap. 17. 5. **God.** Ap. 98. I. i. 1. **24 If, &c.** Assuming such a case. Ap. 118. 2. *a*. **will** = is willing (Indic.), or desireth. Gr. *thelō*. Ap. 102. 1. All hinges on the will. Cp. John 5. 40. **come** = to come. **take up.** The "cross" was always borne by the one condemned. **cross.** Gr. *stauros*. See Ap. 162. Put by Fig. *Metonymy* (of Adjunct), Ap. 6, for the suffering associated with the burden. **25 will save** = be willing (Subj.) to save, as above. **his life.** Gr. his soul. Should be "soul" here, if "soul" in *v.* 26; or, "life" in *v.* 26, if "life" here. **life** = soul. See note above. Gr. *psuchē*. Ap. 110. III.

28 26 For what is a [13]man profited, °if he shall gain the whole °world, and lose °his own °soul? or what shall a man give in exchange for his °soul?

h (p. 1346) 27 For [13]the Son of man shall come [17]in °the glory of His [17]Father °with His angels; and then He shall °reward every man °according to his °works.

28 °Verily I say unto you, There °be °some standing here, which shall [22]not taste of death, °till they °see [13]the Son of man °coming [17]in His kingdom."

Q² T i (p. 1347) **17** And °after six days °Jesus °taketh °Peter, °James, and John his brother,

k and bringeth them up °into °an high mountain apart,

U l 2 And was °transfigured before them: and His face did shine as the sun, and His raiment °was white as the °light.

m 3 And, °behold, there °appeared unto them °Moses and °Elias °talking °with Him.

V 4 Then answered Peter, and said unto [1]Jesus, °"Lord, it is good for us to be here: °if Thou °wilt, let us make here three °tabernacles; one for Thee, and one for [3]Moses, and one for [3]Elias."

V 5 While he yet °spake, [3]behold, °a bright cloud overshadowed them: and [3]behold a voice °out of the cloud, which said, °"This is My beloved Son, °in Whom I °am well pleased; °hear ye Him."

U l 6 And when the disciples heard *it*, they fell °on their face, and were °sore afraid.

7 And [1]Jesus came and touched them, and said, "Arise, and be °not afraid."

m 8 And when they had lifted up their eyes, they °saw °no man, °save [1]Jesus °only.

T i 9 And as they came down °from the mountain,

k [1]Jesus charged them, saying, "Tell the vision to [8]no man, until °the Son of man °be risen again °from °the dead.

26 if he shall, &c.=if he should. Expressing an impossible condition. Ap. 118. 1. b.

world. Gr. *kosmos.* See Ap. 129. 1.

his own soul=his life, as in *v.* 25.

soul. Gr. *psuchē.* Ap. 110. III. 2.

27 the glory. The sufferings are never mentioned apart from the glory (*v.* 21). See Ap. 71, and cp. 17. 1-9.

with. Gr. *meta.* Ap. 104. xi. 1.

reward=render to.

according to. Gr. *kata.* Ap. 104. x. 2.

works=doing.

28 Verily. See note on 5. 18. **be**=are.

some=some of those.

till. The particle *an*, with the Subjunctive Mood, gives this a hypothetical force. Cp. the four "tills" (10. 23; 16. 28; 23. 39; 24. 34; 26. 29).

see=may have seen. Ap. 133. I. 2. See notes on "*an*" above and below. Gr. *eidon.* Ap. 133. I. 1.

coming, &c. The promise of this coming was definitely repeated later, in Acts 3. 19-26, and was conditional on the repentance of the nation. Hence the particle "*an*", which (though untranslatable) expresses the condition or hypothesis implied. Their continuing to live until Acts 28. 25, 26 was certain; but the fulfilment of the condition was uncertain. No "*an*" after "until" in 17. 9.

17. 1-9 (Q², p. 1346). THE GLORY FORESHOWN. THE TRANSFIGURATION.
(*Introversion and Alternations.*)

Q² | T | i | 1-. The Ascent.
  k | -1. Disciples taken up.
   U | l | 2. The Vision.
    m | 3. The Lord. Accompanied.
     V | 4. Voice. Peter's.
     V | 5. Voice. The Father's.
   U | *l* | 6, 7. The Vision. Ended.
    m | 8. The Lord. Alone.
  T | *i* | 9-. The Descent.
   k | -9. Disciples. Charged.

1 after six days. The Transfiguration (see Ap. 149) is dated in all three Gospels (Mark 9. 2. Luke 9. 28). It was thus connected with the first mention of His sufferings and death (16. 21; 17. 9, 12), and would counteract any doubts that the disclosure might give rise to. By it the *glory* is connected with the sufferings, as it always is (cp. 16. 21 with *v.* 27 and Luke 24. 26, and see Ap. 71. 1 Pet. 1. 11; 4. 13; 5. 1); and it gives a glimpse of His coming (2 Pet. 1. 16-18).

after. Gr. *meta.* Ap. 104. xi. 2.

Jesus. Ap. 98. X.

taketh=taketh [Him aside].

Peter, &c. These three were with Him at the raising of Jairus's daughter (Mark 5. 37), and in Gethsemane (26. 37). **James**=and James. **into.** Gr. *eis.* Ap. 104. vi. **an high mountain.** Not the traditional "Tabor", for it was then inhabited, with a fortress on the top, according to Josephus. More probably Hermon. **2 transfigured.** Gr. *metamorphoomai*=to change the form. Occ. only here, Mark 9. 2, and in Rom. 12. 2, 2 Cor. 3. 18. Marking the change TO a new condition, while *metaschēmatizo*=change FROM a former condition. See note on Phil. 3. 21. **was**=became. **light.** Ap. 130. 1. **3 behold.** Fig. *Asterismos* (Ap. 6), for emphasis. **appeared.** Ap. 106. I. vi. **Moses.** Representing the Law, and those to be raised from the dead. See note on 8. 4. **Elias**=Elijah. Representing those "caught up" without dying. Both mentioned in Mal. 4. 4, 5. **talking**=talking together. In Luke 9. 31 "they spake of His decease". **with.** Gr. *meta.* Ap. 104. xi. 1. **4 Lord.** Ap. 98. VI. i. *a.* 3. A. **if, &c.** See the condition in Ap. 118. II. 1. Not the same as in *v.* 20. **wilt.** Ap. 102. 1. **tabernacles**=booths. **5 spake**=was speaking. **a bright cloud.** Was this the *Shekhinah*, the symbol of Jehovah's glory? **out of.** Gr. *ek.* Ap. 104. vii. **This is My beloved Son.** The Divine *formula* of consecration of Messiah as priest; in 3. 17 as prophet. In Ps. 2. 7. Acts 13. 33, and Heb. 1. 5; 5. 5, as king. **in.** Gr. *en.* Ap. 104. viii. **am well pleased**=have found delight. **hear ye Him.** Cp. Deut. 18. 18, 19. **6 on.** Gr. *epi.* Ap. 104. ix. 3. **sore**=exceedingly. **7 not.** Gr. *mē.* Ap. 105. II. **saw.** Ap. 133. I. 1. **8 no man**=no one. **save**=except, used for *alla* (=but). See note on "but", 20. 23. **only**=alone. **9 from**=away from. Gr. *apo.* Ap. 104. iv. **the Son of man.** See Ap. 98. XVI. **be risen again**=have risen. Here, "again" is part of the verb. Not so in *v.* 23, and 16. 21. **from**=from among. Gr. *ek.* Ap. 104. vii. The first occ. of *ek* in this connection: Always associated with Christ and His People (not with the wicked dead). See all the other occurrences: Mark 6. 14; 9. 9, 10; 12. 25. Luke 9. 7; 16. 31; 20. 35; 24. 46. John 2. 22; 12. 1, 9, 17; 20. 9; 21. 14. Acts 3. 15; 4. 2, 10; 10. 41; 13. 30, 34; 17. 3, 31. Rom. 4. 24; 6. 4, 9, 13; 7. 4; 8. 11, 11; 10. 7, 9; 11. 15. 1 Cor. 15. 12, 20. Gal. 1. 1. Eph. 5. 14. Phil. 3. 11 (see note). Col. 1. 18; 2. 12. 1 Thess. 1. 10. 2 Tim. 2. 8. Heb. 13. 20. 1 Pet. 1. 3, 21. On the other hand, with *apo* (Ap. 104. iv) see 14. 2; 27. 64; 28. 7. Cp. Luke 16. 30, 31. In all other cases it is used simply of a resurrection of dead bodies, or of dead people. **the dead**=dead people (no Art.). See Ap. 139. 2.

Q³ n (p. 1348) 28 10 And His disciples asked Him, saying, "Why then say the scribes that [3] Elias must first come?"

o 11 And [1] Jesus answered and said unto them, "Elias truly °shall first come, and °restore all things.

o 12 But I say unto you, That [3] Elias is come already, and they °knew him °not, but °have done °unto him whatsoever they °listed. Likewise shall °also [9] the Son of man suffer °of them."

n 13 Then the disciples understood that He spake unto them °of John the Baptist.

L p 14 And when they were come °to the multitude, there °came to Him °a *certain* man, kneeling down to Him, and saying,

15 [4] "Lord, have °mercy on my son: for °he is lunatick, and °sore vexed: for ofttimes he falleth [1] into the fire, and oft [1] into the water.

q 16 And I brought him to Thy disciples, and they °could [12] not cure him."

r 17 Then Jesus answered and said, "O °faithless and °perverse °generation, °how long shall I be [3] with you? °how long shall I °suffer you?

p bring him hither to Me."

18 And [1] Jesus rebuked °the devil; and °he departed °out of him: and the °child was cured [9] from that very hour.

q 19 Then came the disciples to [1] Jesus apart, and said, °"Why could [12] not we cast him out?"

r 20 And [1] Jesus said unto them, °"Because of your °unbelief: for °verily I say unto you, °If ye have faith as a grain of mustard seed, ye shall °say unto this mountain, 'Remove hence °to yonder place;' and it shall remove; and nothing shall be impossible unto you.

21 Howbeit °this kind goeth [12] not out °but °by °prayer and fasting."

H M (p. 1346) 22 And while they abode [5] in °Galilee, [1] Jesus said unto them, [9] "The Son of man °shall be °betrayed [1] into the hands of [14] men:

23 And they °shall kill Him, and °the third day He shall °be raised again." And they were exceeding sorry.

N s (p. 1348) 24 And when they were come °to Capernaum, they that received °tribute *money* came to Peter, and said, "Doth [12] not your Master pay tribute?"

17. 10-13 (Q³, p. 1346). THE SUFFERINGS AND GLORY. EXPLAINED. (*Introversion.*)

Q³ | n | 10. Disciples. Question, *re* Elijah.
  o | 11. The Lord. Admission.
  o | 12. The Lord. Addition.
n | 13. Disciples. Explanation, *re* John the Baptist.

11 shall first come = cometh first.

restore = will restore. Not the same, but better. The noun occurs only in Acts 3. 21. The verb occurs eight times: 12. 13; 17. 11. Mark 3. 5; 8. 25; 9. 12. Luke 6. 10. Acts 1. 6. Heb. 13. 19.

12 knew = recognised. Gr. *epiginōskō*. Ap. 132. I. iii.

not. Gr. *ou*. Ap. 105. I.

have done = did.

unto him = in his case. Gr. *en*. Ap. 104. viii.

listed = pleased, or willed. Gr. *thelō*. Ap. 102. 1.

shall . . . suffer = is about . . . to suffer. So in *v.* 22 and 20. 22.

also the Son of man. = the Son of man also.

of = through or by. Gr. *hupo*. Ap. 104. xviii. 1.

13 of = concerning. Gr. *peri*. Ap. 104. xiii. 1.

17. 14-21 (L, p. 1346). MIRACLE. THE LUNATIC SON. (*Extended Alternation.*)

L | p | 14, 15. Request made.
  q | 16. Disciples' inability. Complaint.
  r | 17-. Unbelief. Deplored.
 p | -17, 18. Request granted.
  q | 19. Disciples' inability. Inquiry.
  r | 20, 21. Unbelief. Explained.

14 to. Gr. *pros*. Ap. 104. xv. 3.

came = came down, &c. Cp. Mark 9. 14. Luke 9. 37.

a certain man = a man. Gr. *anthrōpos*. Ap. 123. 1.

15 mercy = pity.

he is lunatick = moonstruck: i.e. epileptic, because epilepsy was supposed to be caused by the moon. Gr. *selēniazomai*. Occ. only in Matthew, here, and 4. 24.

sore vexed = suffers miserably.

16 could not cure him = were not able to cure him.

17 faithless = unbelieving.

perverse = perverted.

generation. See note on 11. 16.

how long . . . ? = until when . . . ? Figs. *Erotēsis* and *Ecphōnēsis*. Ap. 6. **suffer** = put up with.

18 the devil = it, or him.

he = it: i.e. the demon.

out of = away from. Gr. *apo*. Ap. 104. iv. Not the same as *v.* 5.

child = boy. Gr. *pais*. Ap. 108. iv.

19 Why could not we cast him out? = Why were not we able to cast it out? See notes on 21. 21, and Luke 17. 5.

20 Because = On account of. Gr. *dia*. Ap. 104. v. 2. See note on Luke 17. 6.

unbelief. All the texts read "little faith", or "littleness of faith". See note on 6. 30.

verily. See note on 5. 18.

If, &c. Denoting a contingent condition. Ap. 118. 1. b.

say. The Rabbins were termed rooters up of mountains, because they were dexterous in removing difficulties. See note on Luke 17. 6.

to yonder place = thither (as though pointing). See note on Luke 17. 6. **21 this kind.** Implying different kinds. See 12. 45. Acts 16. 17. 1 John 4. 1. T Tr. [A] WH R omit this verse; but not the Syr. **but** = except. **by.** Gr. *en*. Ap. 104. viii. **prayer.** Gr. *proseuchē*. See Ap. 134. II. 2. **22 Galilee.** Ap. 169. **shall be** = is about to be. This is the second of the *four* announcements. See the Structure K, M, *M*, *K*, and note on 16. 21. **betrayed** = delivered up. This is added in this the second announcement of His sufferings. Cp. 16. 21. **23 shall** = will. **the third day.** See note on 16. 21; and Ap. 148. **be raised again** = be raised up. Not the same word as in *v.* 9, but the same as in 16. 21.

17. 24-27 (N, p. 1346). GENTILES. AUTHORITY. SONS FREE. (*Introversion.*)

N | s | 24. Tribute inquired about.
  t | 25. Their own exempted.
   u | 26-. But of foreigners.
  t | -26. Their own free.
 s | 27. Tribute paid.

24 to. Gr. *eis*. Ap. 104. vi. Not the same as in *v.* 14. **tribute money** = the *didrachma* = the half-shekels (Ex. 30. 11-16). Occ. only here. See Ap. 51. I. 8. Not the same word as in *v.* 25; 22. 19.

t (p. 1348) 28 25 He saith, °"Yes." And when he was come [1]into the house, [1]Jesus °prevented him, saying, "What thinkest thou, Simon? °of whom do the kings of the °earth take °custom or °tribute? °of their own °children, or °of °strangers?"

u 26 Peter saith unto him, [25]"Of [25]strangers."

t [1]Jesus saith unto him, °"Then are the [25]children free.

s 27 Notwithstanding, °lest we should offend them, go thou [24]to the sea, and cast °an hook, and take up the fish that first cometh up; and when thou hast opened his mouth, thou shalt find °a piece of money: that take, and give unto them °for Me and thee."

O[1] W[1] (p. 1349) **18** °At the same °time came the disciples unto °Jesus, saying, °"Who is the °greatest °in °the kingdom of °heaven?"

2 And [1]Jesus called a °little child unto Him, and set °him [1]in the midst of them,

3 And said, °"Verily I say unto you, °Except ye °be converted, and become as [2]little children, ye shall °not enter °into [1]the kingdom of [1]heaven.

4 Whosoever therefore shall humble himself °as this [2]little child, the same is [1]greatest [1]in [1]the kingdom of [1]heaven.

5 And whoso shall receive one such [2]little child °in My name receiveth Me.

6 But whoso shall °offend one of these °little ones which °believe °in Me, it were better for him that °a millstone were hanged °about his neck, and *that* he were °drowned [1]in °the depth of °the sea.

X[1] 7 Woe unto the °world °because of offences! for it must needs be that offences come; °but woe to that °man °by whom the offence cometh!

8 Wherefore °if thy hand or thy foot °offend thee, cut them off, and cast *them* °from thee: it is °better for thee to enter [3]into °life halt or maimed, rather than having two hands or two feet to be cast [3]into °everlasting fire.

9 And [8]if thine eye [6]offend thee, pluck it out, and cast *it* [8]from thee: it is better for thee to enter [3]into [8]life with one eye, rather than having two eyes to be cast [3]into °hell fire.

W[2] 10 Take heed that ye despise °not one of these [6]little ones; for I say unto you, That [1]in [1]heaven °their angels do always °behold the face of My °Father Which is [1]in [1]heaven.

11 For °the Son of man is come to save °that which was lost.

12 °How think ye? °if a [7]man have an hundred sheep, and one °of them be gone astray, °doth he °not leave the ninety and nine, and

25 Yes. Showing that the Lord did pay. Cp. *v.* 27.
prevented = anticipated: i.e. spoke first, or forestalled. Gr. *prophthanō*. Occ. only here.
of = from. Gr. *apo*. Ap. 104. iv., as in *v.* 9, not in *vv.* 12, 13. **earth.** Gr. *gē*. Ap. 129. 4.
custom = toll, or duty.
tribute = tax. Gr. *kēnsos*, from Lat. *census*, which = registration, which involved taxation.
children = sons. Ap. 108. III. Not the same as *v.* 18.
strangers = those of other families: i.e. not their own sons. Not foreigners. Gr. *allotrios*. Ap. 124. 6.
26 Then = It followeth, then, that.
27 lest we should offend, &c. But, not (Gr. *mē*. Ap. 105. II) to give them an occasion of offence (either by neglecting their duty or by traducing the Lord). See 18. 6.
an hook. A weighted line with several hooks, rapidly drawn through the water, is employed to-day at Tiberias. Gr. *agkistron*. Occ. only here.
a piece of money. Gr. *statēr*: i.e. a shekel. Occ. only here. See Ap. 51. I. 5.
for. Gr. *anti*. Ap. 104. ii.

18. 1-35 (O[1], p. 1346). DISCIPLESHIP. LITTLE CHILD. (*Repeated Alternation.*)

O[1] | W[1] | 1-6. Instruction. Humility.
X[1] | 7-9. Offences. One's self.
W[2] | 10-14. Instruction. Humility.
X[2] | 15-20. Offences. Brethren.
W[3] | 21, 22. Instruction. Forgiveness.
X[3] | 23-34. Offences. Fellow-servants.
W[4] | 35. Application.

1 At = In. Gr. *en*. Ap. 104. viii. **time** = hour.
Jesus. Ap. 98. X. **Who** = Who, then.
greatest = greater. Put by Fig. *Heterōsis* (of Degree) for greatest. See Ap. 6.
in. Gr. *en*. Ap. 104. viii.
the kingdom of heaven. See Ap. 114.
heaven = the heavens (pl.). See note on 6. 9, 10.
2 little child. Gr. *paidion*. Ap. 108. v.
him = it.
3 Verily. See note on 5. 18.
Except = Unless. Lit. "If ye be not". Assuming the possibility. Ap. 118. I. 2.
be converted = be turned: i.e. to God, in repentance.
not = by no means. Gr. *ou mē*. Ap. 105. III.
into. Gr. *eis*. Ap. 104. vi.
4 as this. Not as this little child humbles himself, for no one but the Lord humbles *Himself*. Cp. Phil. 2. 7, 8.
5 in. Gr. *epi*. Ap. 104. ix. 2.
6 offend = cause to offend, as in *vv.* 8, 9, and 16. 27.
little ones. Not the same as in *v.* 2.
believe in. See Ap. 150. I. 1. v (i).
in. Gr. *eis*. Ap. 104. vi.
a millstone = an ass-millstone. *Onikos*. Occ. only here and Luke 17. 2; but frequently in the *Papyri* (see Deissmann, *New Light*, &c., p. 76). Here denoting a great millstone requiring an ass to turn it.
about. Gr. *epi* = upon. Ap. 104. ix. 3. But all the texts read "*peri*" = around. Ap. 104. xiii. 3.
drowned. See note on 14. 30.
the depth = the deep sea (i.e. the sea as to its depth).
the sea = the sea (as to its surface). So in Rev. 18. 17.
7 world. Gr. *kosmos*. Ap. 129. 1.
because of. Gr. *apo*. Ap. 104. iv.
but = yet, or only.
man. Gr. *anthrōpos*. Ap. 123. 1.

by = by means of. Gr. *dia*. Ap. 104. v. 1. **8 if thy hand,** &c. Assuming the condition. See Ap. 118. I. a. **offend** = keepeth on causing thee to offend. **from.** Gr. *apo*. Ap. 104. iv. **better** = good. Fig. *Heterōsis* (of Degree). Ap. 6. **life** = the life: i.e. resurrection life, or life eternal. Gr. *zōē*. Ap. 170. 1. See note on 9. 18 and Lev. 18. 5. Cp. 7. 14. **everlasting.** See Ap. 151. II. B. ii. **9 hell fire** = Gehenna of fire. See note on 5. 22. Occ. elsewhere only in Mark 9. 47. Ap. 131. 1. **10 not.** Gr. *mē*. Ap. 105. II. **their angels.** Their servants (Heb. 1. 14). The tradition of so-called "guardian" angels has no foundation in this. **behold.** Ap. 133. I. 5. **Father.** Ap. 98. III. **11 the Son of man.** See Ap. 98. XVI. **that which was lost.** Cp. 15. 24. **12 How** = What. This parable was repeated later, in another connection. See Luke 15. 4, &c. **if a man,** &c. The condition is not the same as in *v.* 8, but is purely hypothetical = if there should be to any man. See Ap. 118. 1. b. **of.** Gr. *ek*. Ap. 104. vii. **doth he not,** &c.? Or, will he not leave the ninety-nine on the mountain and seek, &c. **not.** Gr. *ouchi*. Ap. 105. I (a).

28 goeth °into the mountains, and seeketh that which is gone astray?

13 And [12]if so be that he find it, °verily I say unto you, he rejoiceth more °of °that *sheep,* than °of the ninety and nine which went [10]not astray.

14 Even so it is °not the °will of °your [10]Father Which is [1]in [1]heaven, that one of these [6]little ones should perish.

X^{2} (p. 1349) 15 Moreover [12]if thy brother shall °trespass °against thee, go and °tell him his fault between thee and him alone: [12]if he shall hear thee, thou hast gained thy brother.

16 But [12]if he will [13]not hear *thee, then* take °with thee one or two more, **that °in the mouth of °two or three witnesses every °word may be established.**

17 And [12]if he shall °neglect to hear them, tell *it* unto the °church: but if he °neglect to hear °the °church, let him be unto thee as °an heathen man and °a publican.

18 [13]Verily I say unto you, °Whatsoever ye shall bind °on °earth shall be bound [1]in °heaven: and whatsoever ye shall loose °on °earth shall be loosed [1]in °heaven.

19 Again I say unto you, That [12]if two of you shall agree [18]on [18]earth °as touching any °thing that they shall °ask, it shall be done for them °of My [10]Father Which is [1]in [1]heaven.

20 For where °two or three are gathered together [6]in My name, there am I [1]in the midst of them."

W^{3} 21 Then came Peter to Him, and said, °"Lord, how oft shall my brother °sin [15]against me, and I forgive him? till seven times?"

22 Jesus saith unto him, "I say [14]not unto thee, Until seven times: but, Until °seventy times seven.

X^{3} Y^{1} v^{1} (p. 1350) 23 °Therefore is [1]the kingdom of [1]heaven likened unto °a certain king, which °would °take account °of his servants.

24 And when he had begun °to reckon, °one was brought unto him, °which owed him ten thousand °talents.

25 But forasmuch as he had [10]not to pay, his °lord commanded him °to be sold, °and his wife, °and °children, °and all that he had, °and payment to be made.

w^{1} 26 The servant therefore fell down, and °worshipped him, saying, [25]'lord, have patience °with me, and I will pay thee all.'

x^{1} 27 Then the [25]lord of that servant was moved with compassion, and °loosed him, and forgave him the °debt.

Y^{2} v^{2} 28 But the same servant went out, and °found one of his fellowservants, which °owed him an hundred °pence: and he °laid hands on him, and °took *him* by the throat, saying, 'Pay me °that thou owest.'

w^{2} 29 And his fellowservant fell down °at his feet, and °besought him, saying, 'Have patience [26]with me, and I will pay thee all.'

x^{2} 30 And he would [14]not: but went and °cast him [3]into prison, till he should pay the debt.

into = upon. Gr. *epi.* Ap. 104. ix. 3.
13 verily. See note on 5. 18.
of = over. Gr. *epi.* Ap. 104. ix. 2.
that sheep = it. **14 not.** Gr. *ou.* Ap. 105. I.
will = desire. Gr. *thelēma,* from *thelo.* Ap. 102. 1.
your. L Tr. WH and Rm read "My".
15 trespass. Gr. *hamartanō.* Ap. 128. I. 1.
against. Gr. *eis.* Ap. 104. vi.
tell him his fault = reprove him.
16 with. Gr. *meta.* Ap. 104. xi. 1.
in = upon. Gr. *epi.* Ap. 104. ix. 1.
two or three. Ref. to Pent. (Deut. 19. 15). Cp. John 8. 17. See Ap. 117. I.
word. Gr. *rhēma* = statement. See note on Mark 9. 32.
17 neglect = fail. Gr. *parakouō.* Occ. only here.
church = assembly. In this case the synagogue, or local court, as in Acts 19. 39. See Ap. 120.
the church = the assembly also.
an heathen = the Gentile. Gr. *ethnikos.* Occ. only here, and 6. 7. a publican = the tax-gatherer.
18 Whatsoever, &c. See 16. 19.
on = upon. Gr. *epi.* Ap. 104. ix. 1.
earth = the earth. Gr. *gē.* Ap. 129. 4.
heaven = the heaven. See notes on 6. 9, 10.
19 as touching = concerning. Gr. *peri.* Ap. 104. xiii. 1.
thing = matter. ask. Gr. *aiteō.* Ap. 134. I. 4.
of = from. Gr. *para.* Ap. 104. xii. 1.
20 two or three. It was believed that "where two are assembled to study the Law, the Shechinah was with them". **21 Lord.** Ap. 98. VI. i. *a.* 3. A.
sin. Gr. *hamartanō.* Ap. 128. I. 1.
22 seventy times. Gr. *hebdomēkontakis.* Occ. only here.

18. 23-34 (X^{3}, p. 1349). **OFFENCE. FELLOW-SERVANTS.**
(Extended and Repeated Alternation.)

X^{3} | Y^{1} | v^{1} | 23-25. Action of King. Debt owing.
w^{1} | 26. Appeal for delay. Granted.
x^{1} | 27. Conduct. Compliance.
Y^{2} | v^{2} | 28. Action of Servant. Debt demanded.
w^{2} | 29. Appeal for delay. Refused.
x^{2} | 30. Conduct. Non-compliance.
Y^{3} | v^{3} | 31. Action of Servant. Reported.
w^{3} | 32, 33. Appeals. Contrasted.
x^{3} | 34. Conduct. Punished.

23 Therefore = On account of this. Gr. *dia* (Ap. 104. v. 1), *touto.*
a certain king = a man (Ap. 123. 1) a king (Hebraism).
would = wished. Gr. *thelō.* Ap. 102. 1.
take account = to compare accounts. Gr. *sunairō.* Occ. only in Matthew (here, *v.* 24, and 25. 19). Said not to be classical Greek: but the colloquial Greek is found in the *Papyri* in Cent. II. in two letters, one from Oxyrhynchus, and the other from Dakkeh in Nubia, dated March 6, 214 A.D. See Deissmann's *Light,* &c., pp. 118, 119.
of = with. Gr. *meta.* Ap. 104. xi. 1.
24 to reckon = to compare accounts, as in *v.* 23. See note above.
one . . . which owed = one debtor. Found in Sophocles and Plato as well as the *Papyri,* though said to be only Biblical.
talents. See Ap. 51. II. 6. Gr. *talanton.* Occ. only in Matthew.
25 lord. Ap. 98. VI. i. *a.* 4. A.
to be sold. Ref. to Pent. (Ex. 22. 3. Lev. 25. 39, 47).
and. Fig. *Polysyndeton* (Ap. 6), for emphasis.
children. Ap. 108. I.
26 worshipped = did homage. See Ap. 134. I. 7 and 137. 1. with. Gr. *epi.* Ap. 104. ix. 2 (Tr. reads 3).
27 loosed = released.
debt = loan. Gr. *daneion.* Occ. only here.
28 found = sought and found. owed = was owing.
pence. Gr. *dēnaria.* See Ap. 51. I. 4.
laid hands on = seized.
took him by the throat = began throttling him. that = what. **29 at.** Gr. *eis.* Ap. 104. vi.
besought = kept beseeching (imperfect). Ap. 134. I. 6. **30 cast him into prison.** The *Papyri* show that this was a widespread Græco-Roman-Egyptian custom.

Y[3] v[3] (p. 1350) 28 31 So when his fellowservants °saw what °was done, they were °very sorry, and came and °told unto their [25]lord all that was done.

w[3] 32 Then his [25]lord, after that he had called him, said unto him, 'O thou °wicked servant, I forgave thee all that debt, because thou °desiredst me:

33 °Shouldest [14]not thou also have °had compassion on thy fellowservant, °even as I had pity on thee?'

x[3] 34 And his [25]lord was wroth, and delivered him to the °tormentors, till he should pay all that was due unto him.

W[1] (p. 1349) 35 So likewise shall My °heavenly [10]Father do also unto you, [12]if ye [8]from your hearts forgive [13]not every one his brother their °trespasses."

P[1] A (p. 1351) **19** °And it came to pass, *that* when °Jesus had finished these °sayings, He °departed °from Galilee, and came °into the °coasts of Judæa °beyond Jordan;

2 And great multitudes followed Him; and He healed them there.

B y 3 The °Pharisees also came unto Him, °tempting Him, and saying unto Him, "Is it lawful for a man to put away his wife °for every cause?"

z 4 And He answered and said unto them, °"Have ye °not read, that He Which made *them* °at °the beginning made them °male and female,

5 And said, [3]'**For this cause shall a man leave father and mother, and shall cleave to his wife: °and °they twain shall be one °flesh?**'

6 Wherefore they are no more [5]twain, but one [5]flesh. °What therefore °God °hath joined together, let °not °man put asunder."

B y 7 They say unto Him, °"Why did °Moses then °command to **give a °writing of divorcement, and to put her away?**"

z 8 He saith unto them, [7]"Moses °because of the hardness of your hearts °suffered you to put away your wives: but [1]from [4]the beginning it °was [4]not so.

9 °And I say unto you, Whosoever shall put away his wife, except *it be* °for fornication, and shall marry another, committeth adultery: and whoso marrieth her which is put away doth commit adultery."

A 10 His disciples say unto Him, °"If the °case of °the [6]man be so °with *his* wife, it is [4]not °good to marry."

11 But He said unto them, °"All *men* cannot receive this [1]saying, save *they* to whom it °is given.

12 For there are some eunuchs, which were so °born °from *their* mother's womb: and there are some eunuchs, which were °made eunuchs °of [6]men: and there be eunuchs, which have made themselves eunuchs °for °the kingdom of °heaven's sake. He that is able °to receive *it*, °let him receive *it*."

31 saw. Ap. 133. I. 1.
was done = had taken place.
very = exceedingly.
told = narrated (gave an exact account). Gr. *diasapheō*. Occ. only here.
32 wicked. Gr. *ponēros*. Ap. 128. IV. 1.
desiredst = besoughtedst. Same word as in *v.* 29.
33 Shouldest, &c. = Was it not binding on thee?
had compassion = pitied, as in the next clause. Same word. even as I = as I also.
34 tormentors: or jailors. Gr. *basanistēs*. Occ. only here. Imprisonment was called in Roman law-books *cruciatus corporis*.
35 heavenly. Gr. *epouranios*. Elsewhere Gr. *ouranios*. See 6. 14, 26, 32; 15. 13. Luke 2. 13. Acts 26. 19.
trespasses. See Ap. 128. II. 4.

19. 1-12 (P[1], p. 1346). **PHARISEES. QUESTION.**
(*Introversion and Alternation.*)

P[1] | A | 1, 2. The Cause. Miracles wrought.
  B | y | 3. Inquiry. To tempt.
    z | 4-6. Answer. Original purpose.
  B | *y* | 7. Inquiry. To tempt further.
    z | 8, 9. Answer. Mosaic sufferance.
A | 10-12. The Consequence. Disciples instructed.

1 And it came to pass. A Hebraism.
Jesus. Ap. 98. X.
sayings = words. Gr. *logos*. See note on "saying", Mark 9. 32.
departed = withdrew (by sea).
from. Gr. *apo*. Ap. 104. iv.
into. Gr. *eis*. Ap. 104. vi. coasts = borders.
beyond Jordan. Perea, east side of Jordan, from the Sea of Galilee to the Dead Sea.
3 Pharisees. See Ap. 120.
tempting Him = trying Him. See note on Luke 16. 18.
for = on account of. Ap. 104. x. 2.
4 Have ye not read . . ? See Ap. 143.
not. Gr. *ou*. Ap. 105. I.
at = from. Gr. *apo*. Ap. 104. iv.
the beginning. See note on John 8. 44.
male and female = a male and a female. Ref. to Pent. (Gen. 1. 27). This settles the theory of evolution.
male. Gr. *arsēn*. Ap. 123. 5.
5 and they twain. This is added by the Lord to Gen. 2. 24. See Ap. 107. II. 2, and 117. I.
they twain = the two.
flesh. Fig. *Synecdochē* (of the Part), put for the whole person. Ap. 6.
6 What = The unity, not "those" (the persons).
God. Ap. 98. I. i. 1.
hath joined together, &c. = joined together, &c. The converse is true also. See note on Phil. 1. 10.
not. Gr. *mē*. Ap. 105. II.
man. Gr. *anthrōpos*. Ap. 123. 1.
7 Why? Why then? Moses. See note on 8. 4.
command, &c. Not till the close of the forty years.
writing. A bill. Ref. to Pent. (Deut. 24. 1). See Ap. 117. I.
8 because of = in view of, or having regard to. Gr. *pros*. Ap. 104. xv. 3. suffered = allowed.
was not so: i. e. from the first constitution down to Moses.
9 And = But. for. Gr. *epi*. Ap. 104. ix. 2.
10 If the case, &c. The condition is hypothetical. See Ap. 118. I. 1. case = cause, as in *v.* 3.
the man. Put by Fig. *Synecdochē* (of Genus), Ap. 6, for a husband. with. Gr. *meta*. Ap. 104. xi. 1.
good = profitable.
11 All men cannot = not (as in *v.* 4) all men can.
is = has been.
12 born. See note on "begat", 1. 2.
from. Gr. *ek*. Ap. 104. vii.
made eunuchs. The verb occ. only here.
of = by. Gr. *hupo*. Ap. 104. xviii. 1.
for . . . sake. Gr. *dia*. Ap. 104. v. 2.
the kingdom of heaven's. See Ap. 114. heaven's = the heavens'. Pl. as in *v.* 14. Not Sing. as in *v.* 21. to receive . . . let him receive. Fig. *Polyptōton*. Ap. 6.

O² a (p. 1352) 13 Then were there brought unto Him ° little
children, that He ° should put *His* hands on
28 them, ° and pray:
b and the disciples ° rebuked them.

b 14 But [1] Jesus said, "Suffer [13] little children,
and ° forbid them [6] not, to come ° unto Me: for
° of such is [12] the kingdom of [12] heaven."

a 15 And He laid *His* hands on them, and departed thence.

P² c¹ 16 And, ° behold, one came and said unto
Him, ° "Good ° Master, what good thing shall
I do, that I may have ° eternal life?"

d¹ 17 And He said unto him, ° "Why callest
thou Me good? *there is* none good but One,
that is, [6] God: but [10] if thou ° wilt enter [1] into
° life, keep the ° commandments."

c² 18 He saith unto Him, ° "Which?" ° Jesus
said,

d² ° "**Thou shalt do ° no murder, Thou shalt [4] not
commit adultery, Thou shalt [4] not steal, Thou
shalt [4] not bear false witness,**
19 **Honour thy father and *thy* mother: and,
° Thou shalt love thy neighbour as thyself."**

c³ 20 The young man saith unto Him, ° "All
these things have I kept [12] from my youth up:
what lack I yet?"

d³ 21 [1] Jesus said unto him, [10] "If thou ° wilt be
perfect, go *and* sell ° that thou hast, and give
to the ° poor, and thou shalt have treasure ° in
° heaven: and come *and* follow Me."

c⁴ 22 But when the young man heard that [1] saying, he went away ° sorrowful: for he had
° great possessions.

d⁴ 23 Then said [1] Jesus unto His disciples,
° "Verily I say unto you, That a rich man
shall ° hardly enter [1] into [12] the kingdom of
[12] heaven.
24 And again I say unto you, It is easier for
a ° camel to ° go ° through ° the eye of a needle,
than for a rich man to enter [1] into ° the kingdom
of [6] God."

c⁵ 25 When His disciples heard *it,* they were
exceedingly amazed, saying, "Who ° then can
be saved?"

d⁵ 26 But [1] Jesus ° beheld *them,* and said unto
them, ° "With [6] men this is impossible; but
° with [6] God ° all things are possible."

O³ C¹ e¹ (p. 1353) 27 Then answered Peter and said unto Him,
[16] "Behold, we have forsaken all, and followed
Thee; what shall we have therefore?"

19. 13-15 (O², p. 1346). DISCIPLESHIP. LITTLE CHILDREN. (*Introversion.*)

O² | a | 13-. Request for His hands to be laid.
  | b | -13. Rebuked by Disciples.
  | *b* | 14. Encouraged by Christ.
| *a* | 15. Request granted.

13 little children = young children. Gr. pl. of *paidion.* Ap. 108. v. Cp. Mark 10. 13-15. Luke 18. 16, 17.
should put = should lay, as in *v.* 15.
and pray = and should pray. Gr. *proseuchŏmai.* Ap. 134. I. 2
rebuked = reprimanded.
14 forbid = hinder.
unto. Gr. *pros.* Ap. 104. xv. 3.
of such is: or, to such belongeth (in Eng. idiom): so Tyndale.

16-26 (P², p. 1346). A CERTAIN MAN. QUESTION. (*Repeated Alternation.*)

P² | c¹ | 16. Young Man. Question. "What?" &c.
  | d¹ | 17. The Lord. Answer. "Keep", &c.
| c² | 18-. Young Man. Question. "Which?"
  | d² | -18, 19. The Lord. Answer. All. (Tenth omitted.)
| c³ | 20. Young Man. Question. "What?" &c.
  | d³ | 21. The Lord. Answer. The Tenth enforced.
| c⁴ | 22. Young Man. Went away.
  | d⁴ | 23, 24. The Lord. Application.
| c⁵ | 25. Disciples. Question. "Who then?" &c.
  | d⁵ | 26. The Lord. Answer. God.

16 behold. Fig. *Asterismos.* Ap. 6.
Good. All the texts omit. The accounts here (*vv.* 16-27, Mark 10. 17-28, and Luke 18. 18-28) are partly identical and partly complementary.
Master = Teacher. Gr. *Didaskalos.* See Ap. 98. XIV. v. 1.
eternal life = life age-abiding. Gr. *zōē aiōnios.* Ap. 170. 1 and 151. II. B. i. This was to be gained by "doing" in that Dispensation and since the Fall. Cp. Lev. 18. 5. Now all is "done", and "eternal life is the *gift* of God" (Rom. 6. 23. 1 John 5. 11, 12).
17 Why . . .? Note the several questions. See the Structure above.
wilt enter = desirest (Ap. 102. 1) to enter.
life. Gr. *zōē.* Ap. 170. 1.
commandments. All of them (5. 19. Jas. 2. 10, 11. Deut 27. 26 (Sept.). Gal. 3. 10).
18 Which? The Lord, in reply, recites five (the sixth, seventh, eighth, ninth, and fifth), but omits the tenth in order to convict him out of his own mouth when he says he has kept "all these". See Ap. 117. I.
Jesus = And Jesus. Ap. 98. X.
Thou shalt do, &c. Quoted from Ex. 20. 12-16.
no. Gr. *ou.* Ap. 105. I.
19 Thou shalt love thy neighbour as thyself. Quoted from Lev. 19. 18.
20 All these. Yes, but not the tenth. Hence the Lord's answer "go and sell", which brought conviction.
21 wilt be = art willing to be. Ap. 102. 1.
that thou hast = thy property or possession. Same word (but not the same form) as "is" in Phil. 3. 20 = exists as a possession.
poor. Ap. 127. 1.
in. Gr. *en.* Ap. 104. viii. **heaven.** Sing.; not pl., as in *vv.* 12, 14, i.e. not on earth. See notes on 6. 9, 10.
22 sorrowful = grieving. **great** = many. **23 Verily.** See note on 5. 18. **hardly** = with difficulty. **24 camel.** With its burden. Not a cable, as some suggest. **go** = pass. **through.** Gr. *dia.* Ap. 104. v. 1. **the eye.** Gr. *trupēma.* Occ. only here. **the eye of a needle.** A small door fixed in a gate and opened after dark. To pass through, the camel must be unloaded. Hence the difficulty of the rich man. He must be unloaded, and hence the proverb, common in the East. In Palestine the "camel"; in the Babylonian Talmud it is the elephant. **the kingdom of God.** The third of five occurrences in Matthew. See note on 6. 33, and Ap. 114. **25 then** = it followeth. **26 beheld.** Gr. *emblepō.* Ap. 133. 7. Not the same as *vv.* 16, 27. **With.** Gr. *para.* Ap. 104. xii. 2. **all things are possible.** For eternal life is now "the gift of God" (cp. Rom. 6. 23). See also Gen. 18. 14. Job 42. 2 (marg.). Zech. 8. 6 (Sept.). Luke 1. 37.

19. 27—20. 16 [For Structure see next page].

f[1] (p. 1353) 28 **28 And [1]Jesus said unto them, [23]"Verily I say unto you, That °ye which have followed Me, [21]in °the regeneration when °the Son of man °shall sit °in °the throne of His glory, °ye also shall sit °upon twelve thrones, judging °the twelve tribes of Israel.**

g[1] **29 And every one that hath forsaken houses, °or brethren, °or sisters, °or father, °or mother, °or wife, °or children, °or lands, for My name's sake, shall receive an hundredfold, and shall inherit °everlasting °life.**

D[1] **30 But °many *that are* first shall be last; and the last *shall be* first.**

C[2] e[2] **20 For °the kingdom of °heaven is like unto °a man *that is* an householder, which went out °early in the morning °to hire labourers °into his °vineyard.**

f[2] **2 And when he had agreed °with °the labourers °for a °penny a day, he sent them [1]into his [1]vineyard.**

g[2] **3 And he went out °about °the third hour, and saw °others standing idle °in the marketplace,**
4 And said unto them; 'Go ye also [1]into the [1]vineyard, and whatsoever is °right I will °give you.' And they went their way.
5 Again he went out [3]about °the sixth and °ninth °hour, and did likewise.
6 And [3]about °the eleventh hour he went out, and found others standing idle, and saith unto them, 'Why stand ye here all the day idle?'
7 They say unto him, 'Because °no man hath [1]hired °us.' He saith unto them, 'Go ye also [1]into the [1]vineyard; and whatsoever is [4]right, *that* shall ye receive.'

D[2] **8 So when °even was come, the °lord of the [1]vineyard saith unto his steward, 'Call the labourers, and [4]give them *their* hire, beginning °from the last unto the first.'**

C[3] g[3] **9 And when they came that *were hired* [3]about [6]the eleventh hour, they received °every man a penny.**

f[3] **10 But when the first came, they °supposed that they should have received more; and they likewise received [9]every man a [2]penny.**

e[3] **11 And when they had received *it,* they murmured °against the °goodman of the house,**

19. 27—20. 16 (O[3], p. 1346). DISCIPLESHIP. REWARDS.

(Extended and Repeated Alternation with Introversion.)

O[3] | C[1] | e[1] | 19. 27. The first chosen (John 15. 16). The Twelve. Inquiry. "We".
f[1] | 19. 28. Agreement with them. Twelve thrones.
g[1] | 19. 29. Others.
D[1] | 19. 30. Prophecy. First, last; last, first.
C[2] | e[2] | 20. 1. The servants first hired. The Twelve. The Parable.
f[2] | 20. 2. Agreement with them.
g[2] | 20. 3–7. Others. (Third, sixth, ninth, and eleventh hours.)
D[2] | 20. 8. Prophecy fulfilled.
C[3] | g[3] | 20. 9. Others. The last called. Rewarded first.
f[3] | 20. 10. Agreement with the first chosen.
e[3] | 20. 11–15. The first chosen. Their complaint.
D[3] | 20. 16. Prophecy fulfilled. The "many" are first (in order). The few are last (in order).

28 ye. The answer to Peter's "we", *v.* 27.
the regeneration=the making of all things new. The restoration of Acts 3. 21=the "when" of the next clause. In Mark 10. 30 we have the synonymous expression "the coming age": thus referring to the future time of reward, and not to the then present time of their following; the word *palingenesia* occurs only here, and in Titus 3. 5. The Syr. reads "in the new world" (i.e. age).
the Son of man. See Ap. 98. XVI.
shall sit=shall have taken His seat.
in=upon. Ap. 104. ix. 1.
the throne of His glory=His glorious throne.
upon. Gr. *epi.* Ap. 104. ix. 3.
the twelve tribes of Israel. This can have nothing to do with the Church of the Mystery as revealed in the prison epistles.
29 or. Note the Fig. *Paradiastolē.* Ap. 6.
everlasting. Gr. *aiōnios.* See Ap. 151. II. B. ii.
life. Gr. *zōē.* Ap. 170. 1.
30 many. Connected with "last" as well as "first". Omit the italics "that are", and connect this verse with 20. 1 as evidenced by the word "For" (20. 1) and "So" in *v.* 16.

20. 1 the kingdom of heaven. See Ap. 114. This parable occurs only in Matthew, and is called forth by Peter's question in 19. 27.
heaven=the heavens. See note on 6. 9, 10.
a man that is an householder=a man a householder. A Hebraism=master of a house.
early in the morning=together with the dawn.
to hire. Gr. *misthoomai.* Occ. only here, and *v.* 7.
into=for. Gr. *eis.* Ap. 104. vi.
vineyard. See Isa. 5. 1–7. Ps. 80. 8, 9. Israel was in question, not the Church. See 19. 28.
2 with. Gr. *meta.* Ap. 104. xi. 1.
the labourers: i.e. the twelve Apostles (the first called). **for.** Gr. *ek.* Ap. 104. vii; *ek*=out of, or from [the bargain] a penny a day. **penny.** Gr. *dēnarion* (Ap. 51. I. 4)=a day's wage at that time (Luke 10. 35=two days'). Came to be used for any coin, as in English we "turn an honest penny". The initial of *dēnarius* came to be our "d" for pence. **3 about.** Gr. *peri.* Ap. 104. xiii. 3. **the third hour**=9 a.m. The hour named in connection with Pentecost (Acts 2. 15). **others.** Not there at the first hour. Other labourers were then engaged (Acts 4. 36; 6. 1, 5; 8. 4, 12; 9. 10, 25, 27, 30). **in.** Gr. *en.* Ap. 104. viii. **4 right**=just. **give**=pay. **5 the sixth . . . hour.** The hour of the vision when Peter was sent to the Gentiles at Cæsarea (Acts 10. 9). **ninth hour.** The hour when the angel appeared to Cornelius (Acts 10. 3), and others became labourers (Acts 21. 16). **6 the eleventh hour.** The Art. is emphatic, as with the "third". See note on "even" (*v.* 8). It was immediately before the end. **7 no man**=no one. **us.** These were the heralds of the gospel of the kingdom, immediately before the close of the dispensation of the Acts. See Acts 17. 34; 18. 2, 8, 10, 18, 24; 19. 6–8, 20; 20. 1, 4, 17; 21. 8, 16. But, as the Nation refused the call to repent (Acts 28. 25, 26), "the eleventh hour" is still future, awaiting the proclamation foretold in 24. 14. **8 even.** Even Bengel held that this refers to "the last judgment". And it is clearly the time of reckoning and of the reward spoken of in 19. 29, when all will be justly rewarded. **lord.** Ap. 98. VI. i. *a.* 4. A. **from.** Gr. *apo.* Ap. 104. iv. **9 every man**=each. **10 supposed**=reckoned according to law. See note on Luke 3. 23. **11 against.** Gr. *kata.* Ap. 104. x. 1. **goodman**=the master of the house.

28 12 Saying, °'These last °have wrought *but*
one hour, and thou hast °made them equal
unto us, which have borne the burden and
°heat of the day.'
13 But he answered °one of them, and said,
°'Friend, I do thee °no °wrong: didst °not
thou agree with me for a [2] penny?
14 °Take °*that* thine *is*, and go thy way: °I
°will [4] give unto this last, °even as unto thee.
15 Is it °not lawful for me to do what I [14] will
°with °mine own? Is °thine eye °evil, because
°I am °good?'

D[3] (p. 1353) 16 °So the last shall be first, and the first
last: for many be called, but few chosen."

H M (p. 1346) 17 And °Jesus going up °to Jerusalem took
the twelve disciples apart [3] in the way, and
said unto them,
18 °"Behold, we go up [17] to Jerusalem; and
°the Son of man shall be °betrayed unto the
chief priests and unto the scribes, and they
shall °condemn Him to death,
19 And shall °deliver Him [17] to the Gentiles
[17] to mock, and [17] to scourge, and [17] to crucify
Him: and °the third day He shall rise again."

N h (p. 1354) 20 Then °came to Him °the mother of
°Zebedee's °children [2] with her °sons, °wor-
shipping *Him*, and °desiring a certain thing
°of Him.
21 And He said unto her, "What [14] wilt thou?"
She saith unto Him, °"Grant that these my
two [20] sons may sit, the one °on Thy right hand,
and the other °on °the left, [3] in Thy kingdom."

i 22 But [17] Jesus answered and said, °"Ye °know
[15] not what ye °ask. Are °ye able to drink of
°the cup that [15] I °shall drink of, and to be
°baptized with the °baptism that I am °bap-
tized with?" They say unto Him, "We are
able."
23 And He saith unto them, [22] "Ye °shall
drink indeed of My cup, and be [22] baptized
with the [22] baptism that I am [22] baptized with:
but to sit [21] on My right hand, and [21] on My
left, is [15] not Mine to give, °but *it shall be
given to them* for whom it is °prepared °of My
°Father."

k 24 And when the ten heard *it*, they were
°moved with indignation °against the two
brethren.

i 25 But [17] Jesus called them *unto Him*, and said,
[22] "Ye know that the princes of the Gentiles
°exercise dominion over them, and °they that
are great °exercise authority upon them.

12 These = That these. Gr. *hoti*, putting their words between quotation marks. See note on Luke 23. 43.

have wrought but one hour = made one hour. A Hebraism. Cp. Ruth 2. 19, "Where wroughtest thou to-day?" (Heb. *'ānāh 'āsīthā*). So, in the sense of making or spending time (Acts 15. 33; 18. 23. 2 Cor. 11. 25); used for continuing, as suggested in A.V. marg. But it is the same word rendered "made" in the next clause.

made them = done to them.

heat = scorching heat.

13 one. Representing the whole body, as Peter was the "one" in 19. 27.

Friend. Gr. *Hetairos* = Comrade, more distant than *philos* (= beloved). Occ. only in Matthew (here; 11. 16; 22. 12; 26. 50).

no. Gr. *ou.* Ap. 105. 1.

wrong = injustice.

not. Gr. *ouchi.* Ap. 105. I. a.

14 Take = Take up.

that thine is = thine own.

I will give = for I will (Ap. 102. 1) to give.

will = wish, or desire. See Ap. 102. 1.

even as unto thee = as to thee also.

15 not. Gr. *ou.* Ap. 105. I.

with = in. Gr. *en.* Ap. 104. viii.

mine own. Plural = mine own [affairs].

thine eye evil. A Hebraism. Ref. to Pent. (Deut. 15. 9). Ap. 117. I.

evil = grudging. Gr. *poneria.* Ap. 128. IV. 1.

I. Emphatic.

good = generous.

16 So, &c. See note on 19. 30, which precedes the parable, as this concludes it.

17 Jesus. Ap. 98. X.

17 to. Gr. *eis.* Ap. 104. vi. 1.

18 Behold. Fig. *Asterismos.* Ap. 6.

the Son of man. See Ap. 98. XVI.

betrayed, &c. = delivered up, as in *v.* 19. These are the additional features of this third announcement (see note on 16. 21); the second and fourth being 17. 22 and 20. 28.

condemn. Gr. *katakrinō.* Ap. 122. 7.

19 deliver Him = deliver Him up, as in *v.* 18.

the third day. See Ap. 148.

20. 20-27 (*N*, p. 1346). GENTILES. AUTHORITY. BRETHREN FREE. (*Introversion.*)

N | h | 20, 21. Pre-eminence sought for two brethren.
  i | 22, 23. Pre-eminence. Refusal.
    k | 24. Indignation of the ten.
  i | 25, 26-. Pre-eminence. Instruction. For Gentiles, not for brethren.
h | -26, 27. True pre-eminence defined.

20 came. With her sons. Mark 10. 35 "came [with their mother]".

the mother. *Salomē.* Cp. 27. 56 with Mark 15. 40.

Zebedee's. See note on 4. 21.

children = sons. Ap. 108. iii. The two sons (James and John) acted with their mother (prompting her). Cp. "Ye" (*v.* 22, and Mark 10. 35). Mark's account is supplementary. **sons.** Implies what Mark says. All three came together. **worshipping** = prostrating herself. Gr. *proskuneō.* Ap. 137. 1. **desiring** = asking. **of** = from. Gr. *para.* Ap. 104. xii. 1. **21 Grant** = Bid, as in 4. 3; or 23. 3 ("bid"). **on.** Gr. *ek.* Ap. 104. vii. **the left** = [Thy] left. **22 Ye.** Ye two. **know not** = have no idea. Gr. *oida.* Ap. 132. I. 1. **ask** = ask for. Ap. 134. I. 4. **the cup.** Which would be at His right hand. A symbol of participation. Jer. 25. 15; 49. 12. Ezek. 23. 33. **shall drink of** = am about to drink of. **baptized.** Ap. 115. I. i. **baptism.** Ap. 115. II. i. **23 shall** = shall indeed. James (Acts 12. 2), and John martyred, according to tradition. **but it shall be given to them for whom, &c.** Omit all these italics, and read "but [to those] for whom". Cp. Mark 10. 40. **prepared**: or, destined. **of** = by. Gr. *hupo.* Ap. 104. xviii. 1. **Father.** Ap. 98. III. **24 moved with indignation** = took great umbrage. **against** = about, or with respect to. Gr. *peri.* Ap. 104. xiii. 1. **25 exercise dominion** = lord it over. **they that are great** = the great ones. **exercise authority upon.** The Prep. *kata* (= down. Ap. 104. x. 1) in the verb implies a bad sense and = oppress them. Cp. Luke 22. 25; where the verb is not the same. See note there.

28 26 °But it shall [15] not be so °among you:
h °but whosoever [14] will be great °among you,
(p. 1354) let him be your °minister;
27 And whosoever [14] will be °chief [26] among
you, let him be your °servant:
G K 28 Even as [18] the Son of man came [15] not °to
(p. 1346) be ministered unto, but °to minister, and to
give His °life a °ransom °for many."

L 1 29 And as they °departed [8] from Jericho, a
(p. 1355) °great multitude followed Him.
30 And, [18] behold, °two blind men °sitting
°by the way side,

m when they heard that [17] Jesus °passed by,
cried out, saying, "Have °mercy on us, O
°Lord, *Thou* °Son of David."

n 31 And the multitude °rebuked them, because
they should hold their °peace:

n but they °cried °the more, saying, "Have
[30] mercy on us, O [30] Lord, *Thou* °Son of David."

m 32 And [17] Jesus stood still, and °called them,
and said, "What [14] will ye that I °shall do
°unto you?"
33 They say unto Him, [30] "Lord, that our eyes
may be opened."
34 So [17] Jesus had compassion *on them,* and
touched their eyes: and immediately their
eyes °received sight,

l and °they followed Him.

F E[1] o **21** And °when they drew nigh °unto Jeru-
29 salem, and °were come °to °Bethphage,
°unto the mount of Olives, then sent °Jesus
two °disciples,

p 2 Saying unto them, °"Go °into the village
°over against you, and °straightway ye shall
find an °ass tied, and a °colt °with her: loose
them, and bring *them* unto Me.

26 But=However. **among.** Gr. *en.* Ap. 104. viii.
minister=servant (in relation to *activity*).
27 chief=first.
servant=bond-servant (in relation to servitude).
28 The fourth announcement of His sufferings. See note on 16. 21.
to be ministered unto=to be served.
to minister=to serve.
life=soul. See Ap. 110. III. 1.
ransom=redemption price. Ref. to Pent. (Num. 35. 31). Ap. 117. I.
for=in the stead of. Gr. *anti.* Ap. 104. ii.

20. 29-34 (*L*, p. 1346). MIRACLE. TWO BLIND MEN. (*Introversion.*)

L | l | 29, 30-. The two blind men. Sitting.
m | -30. Request, and cry for healing.
n | 31. Rebuke of multitude.
n | -31. Rebuke useless.
m | 32-34-. Request granted. Healing given.
l | -34. The two blind men. Following.

29 departed=not approaching, as in Luke 18. 35; or arriving and leaving, as in Mark 10. 46.
great multitude. The population was about 100,000, doubtless with many blind about the gates.
30 two blind men. There are no "discrepancies" between this account and those of Mark 10. 46 and Luke 18. 35. They describe three miracles on four blind men: one on approaching Jericho; one on leaving; two after He had left. See Ap. 152.
sitting. Not "begging", as in Luke 18. 35.
by=beside. Gr. *para.* Ap. 104. xii. 3. The others were at each gate.
passed by=is passing by. **mercy**=pity.
Lord. Ap. 98. VI. i. *a.* 3. B. a.
Son of David. Therefore Israelites, having a claim on Him as such. The fifth of nine occurrences of this title in Matthew. See note on 1. 1, and Ap. 98. XVIII.
31 rebuked . . . peace=charged them to be silent.
cried=kept crying.
the more. Gr. *meizon.* (Adv.) Occ. only here.
Son of David. The sixth of nine occurrences in Matthew. See note on 1. 1.
32 called them. In the other cases He commanded them to be "called" (Mark 10. 49), and "led" (Luke 18. 40). Ap. 152. **shall**=should.
unto=for. **34 received**=regained.
they followed. As in Mark 10. 52, and Luke 18. 43.

21. 1—26. 35 (*F*, p. 1305). THE FOURTH PERIOD. THE KINGDOM REJECTED. (*Repeated and Extended Alternation.*)

F | E[1] | 21. 1-7. Bethphage. Arrival and Departure.
F[1] | 21. 8-11. Jerusalem. The first entry into.
G[1] | 21. 12-16. In the temple. Cleansing.
E[2] | 21. 17. Bethany. Return to.
F[2] | 21. 18-22. Jerusalem. Return to.
G[2] | 21. 23—25. 46. In the temple and on Olivet. Prediction.
E[3] | 26. 1-17-. Bethany. Return to.
F[3] | 26. -17-29. Jerusalem. The Last Supper.
G[3] | 26. 30-35. In the Mount of Olives. Prediction.

21. 1-7 (E[1], above). BETHPHAGE. ARRIVAL AND DEPARTURE. (*Introversion.*)

E[1] | o | 1. Mission of Two Disciples. Begun.
p | 2, 3. Commission given.
q | 4, 5. Fulfilment of Prophecy.
p | 6. Commission carried out.
o | 7. Mission of Two Disciples. Ended.

1 when they drew nigh. There were *two* entries: the first in Matthew 21: the second on "the first day" of the following week (Mark 11. 1-3. Luke 19. 28-31. John 12. 12-15). See Ap. 153 and 156. **unto . . . to.** Gr. *eis.* Ap. 104. vi. **were come**=had arrived. **Bethphage**=House of Figs. Now *Kefr et Tor.* According to the Talmud Bethphage consisted of some buildings and the space of ground extending from the wall of Jerusalem about a mile (or half-way) toward the town of Bethany (now *el 'Azarîyeh*). See Ap. 153 and 156. **unto**=toward. Gr. *pros.* Ap. 104. xv. 3. All the texts read "*eis*" as in the preceding clause. **Jesus.** Ap. 98. X. **disciples.** Not Apostles. **2 Go**=go forward. **into.** Gr. *eis,* as above. **over against**=or just off the high road. Gr. *apenanti*=facing you. In Mark and Luke *katenanti*=opposite and below, preferred, here, by all the texts. But the text may have been altered to *make* Matt. agree with Mark and Luke. **straightway**=immediately. **ass . . . colt.** Here the *two* are sent for, because Zech. 9. 9 was to be fulfilled. In Mark, and Luke, only *one* (only one being necessary to fulfil the part of Zechariah quoted by John 12. 14, 15). **with.** Gr. *meta.* Ap. 104. xi. 1.

29 3 And °if any *man* say ought unto you, ye
shall say, °'The Lord hath need of them;'
and [2]straightway he will send them."
q 4 All this °was done, that it might be °fulfilled
(p. 1355) which was °spoken °by the prophet, saying,
5 °"**Tell ye the daughter of Sion, °Behold,
thy King cometh unto thee, meek, and sitting
°upon an [2]ass, and a [2]colt the foal of °an ass.**"
p 6 And the disciples went, and did as [1]Jesus
commanded them,
o 7 And °brought the [2]ass, and the [2]colt, and
°put on them their °clothes, and °they set
Him °thereon.
F[1] r 8 And °a very great multitude spread their
(p. 1356) garments °in the way; others cut down
branches °from the trees, and °strawed *them*
°in the way.
s 9 And the multitudes that went before, and
that followed, cried, saying, °"**Hosanna to °the
Son of David: Blessed *is* He That cometh [8]in
the name of °the LORD; °Hosanna [8]in the highest.**"
s 10 And when He was come [2]into Jerusalem,
all the city was °moved, saying, °"Who is
This?"
r 11 And the multitude said, "This is [1]Jesus the
Prophet °of °Nazareth of Galilee."
G[1] t 12 And [1]Jesus went [2]into °the temple of °God,
and cast out all them that sold and bought [8]in
°the temple, and overthrew the tables of °the
moneychangers, and the seats of them that
sold °doves,
u 13 And said unto them, °"It is written, °'**My
house shall be called the house of prayer;**
but ye have made it **a den of °thieves.**'"
t 14 And the blind and the lame came to Him
[8]in [12]the temple; and He healed them.
15 And when the chief priests and scribes
saw the °wonderful things that He °did, and
the °children crying [8]in the temple, and saying,
[9]"**Hosanna to °the Son of David;**" they were
sore displeased,
16 And said unto Him, "Hearest thou what
these °say?"
u And [1]Jesus saith unto them, "Yea; °have ye
never read, °'**Out of the mouth of babes and
sucklings Thou hast °perfected praise**'?"
E[2] 17 And He left them, and went °out of the
(p. 1355) city [2]into Bethany; and He °lodged there.
F[2] 18 Now °in the morning as He returned [2]into
the city, He hungered.

3 if . . . &c. Expressing the condition simply. Ap. 118. 1. b. **The Lord.** Ap. 98. VI. i. *a*. 2. A. 2.
4 was done=came to pass.
fulfilled. Cp. Luke 21. 24 and 32.
spoken. As well as written.
by=through. Gr. *dia*. Ap. 104. v. 1.
5 Tell ye, &c. Quoted from Zech. 9. 9. See Ap. 107. I. 1, and II. 4. Cp. Isa. 62. 11. Ap. 117. I.
Behold. Fig. *Asterismos*. Ap. 6.
upon. Gr. *epi*. Ap. 104. ix. 3.
an ass=a beast of burden. Not the same word as in the preceding clause. **7 brought**=led.
put on . . . clothes. Cp. 2 Kings 9. 13 (a mark of respect). **clothes**=outer garments.
they set Him. "He took His seat". Gr. *epikathizō*. Occ. only here.
thereon=upon them: i.e. the garments.

21. 8-11 (F[1], p. 1355). JERUSALEM. FIRST ENTRY. (*Introversion.*)

F[1] | r | 8. Action.
| s | 9. Cry. Made.
| *s* | 10. Cry. Effect.
| *r* | 11. Action.

8 a very great multitude=the greater part of the crowd: referring to the proportionate part, not to the actual size. **in.** Gr. *en*. Ap. 104. viii.
from. Gr. *apo*. Ap. 104. iv.
strawed=were strewing. Same word as "spread" in preceding clause. Eng. "straw"=to scatter straw. Here used of branches of trees.
9 Hosanna=Save now. Aramaic *Hōshi'ān-na'*=Help now. See Ap. 94. III. 3. Quoted from Ps. 118. 25, 26. At the later entry (Luke 19. 38) the cry was different in words, but similar in intent. For the order of events of these last six days, see Ap. 156.
the Son of David. Ap. 98. XVIII. The seventh of nine occ. of this title in Matthew. See note on 1. 1.
the LORD=Jehovah. Ap. 98. VI. i. *a*. 1. B. a.
10 moved=agitated. Same word as "quake" (27. 51) and "shake" (28. 4. Heb. 12. 26. Rev. 6. 13).
Who is This? The city was evidently taken by surprise at this first entry; but the second entry (Mark 11. 1-11. Luke 19. 29-44) was known, and the people "met Him" (John 12. 18), hence, there was no surprise.
11 of=from. Gr. *apo*. Ap. 104. iv.
Nazareth. See note on 2. 23. Ap. 169.

21. 12-16 (G[1], p. 1355). IN THE TEMPLE. CLEANSING. (*Alternation.*)

G[1] | t | 12. Miracle. Cleansing.
| u | 13. Scripture fulfilled.
| *t* | 14-16-. Miracle. Healing.
| *u* | -16. Scripture fulfilled.

12 the temple. Gr. *hieron*, the temple courts. Not the *naos*. See note on 23. 16. **God.** Ap. 98. I. i. 1.
the moneychangers. The half-shekel had to be paid on the 15th of the month Adar, by every Israelite (even the poorest). In every city collectors sat to receive it. On the 25th day (18 or 19 days before the Passover) they began to sit in the temple; and then they distrained if not paid. Change was given at a profit for the moneychangers. (So Maimonides, quoted by Lightfoot, vol. iii, p. 45, Pitman's edn.) **doves.** Required for the Temple offerings. **13 It is written**=It standeth written. **My house, &c.** A composite quotation from Isa. 56. 7, and Jer. 7. 11. See Ap. 107. II. 4, and 117. I. **thieves**=robbers. Same word as in 27. 38, 44. **15 wonderful things**=the wonders. Occ. only here. These were the Lord's final miracles, wrought at this crisis, and must have been very special in character. **did**=wrought. **children.** Gr. *pais*. See Ap. 108. iv. **the Son of David.** The eighth of nine occ. in Matthew. See note on 1. 1. **16 say**=are saying. **have ye never read . . . ?** See Ap. 143. 4. **Out of.** Gr. *ek*. Ap. 104. vii. See Ap. 107. I. 1, and 117. I. **Out of the mouth, &c.** Quoted from Ps. 8. 2. **perfected**=prepared. Gr. *katartizō*=to perfect by preparing. See Ap. 125. 8. **17 out of**=without, outside. Not the same word as in *v*. 16. **lodged**=passed the night (in the open air). Occ. only here, and in Luke 21. 37.

21. 18-22 (F[2], p. 1355). JERUSALEM. RETURN TO. (*Introversion.*)

F[2] | v | 18, 19-. Words of the Lord. Curse.
| w | -19. Miracle. Fig-tree withered.
| *w* | 20. Miracle. Marvel of Disciples.
| *v* | 21, 22. Words of the Lord. Faith.

18 in the morning=early in the morning. See Ap. 97.

29 **19** And when He saw ° a fig tree ° in the way,
He came ° to it, and ° found nothing thereon,
but leaves only, and said unto it, "Let no fruit
grow ° on thee henceforward ° for ever." And
° presently the fig tree withered away.
20 And when the disciples saw *it*, they marvelled, saying, ° "How soon is the fig tree
withered away!"
21 [1] Jesus answered and said unto them,
° "Verily I say unto you, ° If ye have faith, and
° doubt ° not, ye shall not only do this *which
is done* to the fig tree, but also if ye shall say
unto this mountain, ° 'Be thou removed, and
be thou cast [2] into the sea;' it shall be done.
22 And all things, whatsoever ye shall ° ask
[3] in prayer, believing, ye shall ° receive."
G[2] H K x (p. 1357) **23** And when He was come [2] into the ° temple,
the chief priests and the elders of the People
came unto Him as He was teaching, and said,
° "By ° what ° authority doest Thou these things?
and who gave Thee this ° authority?"
y **24** And [1] Jesus answered and said unto them,
"I also will ask you one ° thing, which ° if ye
tell Me, ° I in like wise will tell you [23] by what
authority I do these things.
25 The ° baptism of John, whence was it?
° from ° heaven, or ° of men?"
z And they reasoned ° with themselves, saying,
[24] "If we shall say, ° 'From heaven;' He will say
unto us, 'Why did ye ° not then believe him?'
26 But [24] if we shall say, [25] 'Of men;' we fear
the ° people;
z for ° all hold John as a prophet."
y **27** And they answered [1] Jesus, and said, "We
° cannot ° tell."
x And He said unto them, "Neither tell I you
[23] by what authority I do these things.
L N[1] a[1] **28** But what think ye?
b[1] ° A *certain* man had two ° sons; and he came
to the first, and said, ° 'Son, ° go work to day
[8] in my vineyard.'
29 He answered and said, ° 'I will [25] not:' but
afterward he ° repented, and went.
30 And he came to ° the second, and said
likewise. And he answered and said, 'I *go*,
° sir:' and went [25] not.

19 a = one (single).
in = on. Gr. *epi*. Ap. 104. ix. 1.
to = up to. Gr. *epi*. Ap. 104. ix. 3.
found nothing. See notes on Mark 11. 13.
on. Gr. *ek*. Ap. 104. vii.
for ever = for the age (see Ap. 151. II. A. ii. 4. a.), i.e. to the end of that Dispensation. The fig tree represents the national privilege of Israel (see notes on Judges 9. 10), and that is to be restored (Rom. 11. 2, 26).
presently = at once, on the spot; Gr. *parachrēma*, rendered "soon" in *v.* 20. See note on "immediately", Luke 1. 64.
20 How soon, &c. Fig. *Erotēsis* (in wonder). Ap. 6.
21 Verily. See note on 5. 18.
If ye have faith, &c. This is the *third* occasion that this was repeated. The first was in 17. 20; Mark 11. 23; and the second in Luke 17. 6. The condition is quite hypothetical. See Ap. 118. 1. b.
doubt. Ap. 122. 4. not. Gr. *mē*. Ap. 105. II.
Be thou removed, &c. It was a common proverb to say of a great teacher, who removed difficulties, that he was "a rooter up of mountains". See note on Luke 17. 6.
22 ask. Gr. *aiteō*. Ap. 134. I. 4.
receive. Supply the Ellipsis: "[it, if it be His will]", from 26. 39-44. Jas. 5. 14, 15. 1 John 5. 14, 15. This is the one abiding condition of all prayer; and this Ellipsis must always be supplied.

21. 23—25. 46 (G[2], p. 1355). IN THE TEMPLE. TEACHING. (*Alternation*.)

G[2] | H | 21. 23—22. 46. Priests and Elders. Controversy.
  J | 23. 1-12. Teaching. Crowds and Disciples. Moral.
 H | 23. 13-39. Scribes and Pharisees. Denunciation.
  J | 24. 1—25. 46. Teaching. Disciples. Prophetic.

21. 23—22. 46 (H, above). PRIESTS AND ELDERS. CONTROVERSY IN TEMPLE. (*Introversion*.)

H | K | 21. 23-27. Questions. Chief Priests and Elders.
  L | 21. 28-44. Parables. Two Sons and Vineyard.
   M | 21. 45. Conviction.
   M | 21. 46. Conspiracy.
  L | 22. 1-14. Parable. Marriage of King's Son.
 K | 22. 15-46. Questions. Pharisees and Sadducees.

21. 23-27 (K, above). QUESTIONS. CHIEF PRIESTS AND ELDERS. (*Introversion*.)

K | x | 23. Their question. Put.
  y | 24, 25-. His question. Put.
   z | -25, 26-. Their reasoning.
   z | -26. Their reason.
  y | 27-. His question. Unanswered.
 x | -27. Their question. Answered.

23 temple = the Temple courts. Gr. *hieron*. See note on 23. 16.
By. Gr. *en*. Ap. 104. viii. what = what kind of. authority. Gr. *exousia*. Ap. 172. 5.
24 thing = question. Gr. *logos* = word, or matter. if. The condition being quite dependent on a contingency. Ap. 118. 1. b. I in like wise = I also. Note the Fig. *Anteisagōge*. Ap. 6. **25** baptism. Ap. 115. II. 1. from. Gr. *ek*. Ap. 104. vii. 1. heaven. Put by Fig. *Metonymy* (of Subject), Ap. 6, for "God", sing. of = from. Same word as "from" in preceding clause. with. Gr. *para*. Ap. 104. xii. 2. not. Gr. *ou*. Ap. 105. I. **26** people = crowd. all. Put by Fig. *Synecdoche* (of Genus), Ap. 6, for the greater part. **27** cannot tell = do not (Ap. 105. I) know. tell = know. Gr. *oida*. Ap. 132. I. i.

21. 28-44 (L, above). PARABLES. (*Division*.)

L | N[1] | 28-32. The Two Sons. Disobedience.
 | N[2] | 33-44. The Husbandmen. Rebellion.

21. 28-32 (N[1], above). THE TWO SONS. DISOBEDIENCE. (*Repeated Alternation*.)

N[1] | a[1] | 28-. Appeal for opinion.
  b[1] | -28-30. The Two Sons. Contrasted.
 a[2] | 31-. Appeal for decision.
  b[2] | -31-. The Two Sons. Answer.
 a[3] | -31, 32. Application.

28 A certain man, &c. Here follow three parables spoken in the Temple. sons = children. Gr. *teknon*. Ap. 108. i. Go work to day = Go to-day, work. **29** I will not = I do not choose [to go]. Ap. 102. 1. repented. Gr. *metamelomai*. See Ap. 111. I. 2. **30** the second. Tischendorf reads "the other" (Gr. *heteros*, Ap. 124. 2). sir. Gr. *kurios*. Ap. 98. VI. i. *a*. 4. B.

a² 29 31 ° Whether [25] of them twain did ° the will of
his father ? "
b² They say unto him, " The first."
(p. 1357) a³ [1] Jesus saith unto them, [21] " Verily I say unto
you, That the ° publicans and the harlots ° go
[2] into ° the kingdom of [12] God ° before you.
32 For John came [2] unto you [8] in the way of
righteousness, and ye believed him [25] not: but
the [31] publicans and the harlots believed him:
and **ye**, when ye had seen *it*, [29] repented [25] not
afterward, that ye might believe him.
N² O c (p. 1358) 33 Hear ° another parable: There was a certain ° householder, which planted a vineyard,
and ° hedged it round about, and digged a
° winepress [8] in it, and built a ° tower, and ° let
it out to husbandmen, and ° went into a far
country:
d 34 And when the ° time of the fruit drew
near, he sent his servants ° to the [33] husbandmen, that they might receive the fruits of it.
35 And the husbandmen took his servants,
and ° beat one, ° and killed ° another, ° and
stoned ° another.
36 Again, he sent ° other servants ° more
than the first: and they did unto them ° likewise.
37 But ° last of all he sent [1] unto them ° his
son, saying, 'They will ° reverence my son.'
38 But when the husbandmen saw the son,
they said ° among themselves, 'This is the
heir; come, let us kill him, and let us ° seize
on his inheritance.'
39 And they caught him, and cast *him* ° out
of the vineyard, and slew *him*.
c 40 ° When ° the lord therefore of the vineyard
° cometh, what will he do unto those husbandmen ? "
d 41 They say unto him, " He will ° miserably
destroy those ° wicked men, and will let out
his vineyard unto [36] other husbandmen,
° which shall render him the fruits [8] in their
seasons."
P 42 [1] Jesus saith unto them, ° " Did ye never
read [8] in the scriptures, °' **The Stone Which the
builders rejected, the same is become the head
of the corner: this is ° the LORD'S doing, and it
is marvellous [8] in our eyes ?'**
O 43 Therefore say I unto you, [31] The kingdom
of [12] God shall be taken [8] from you, and ° given to
a nation bringing forth the fruits thereof.
P 44 And whosoever shall fall ° on this Stone
shall be broken: but ° on whomsoever It shall
fall, It will ° grind him to powder."
M (p. 1357) 45 And when the chief priests and Pharisees
had heard His parables, they ° perceived that
He spake of them.
M 46 But when they sought to lay hands on
Him, they feared the ° multitude, because they
° took Him ° for a prophet.

---

31 Whether of them twain = Which of the two.
the will = the desire. Gr. *thelēma* (the Noun of Ap. 102. I).
publicans = tax-gatherers.
go into . . . before = go before you into.
the kingdom of God. See Ap. 114. The fourth of five occurrences in Matthew. See note on 6. 33.

21. 33-44 (N², p. 1357). THE HUSBANDMEN. REBELLION. (*Alternation.*)

N² | O | 33-41. The Parable. Given.
  P | 42. The Scripture cited (Ps. 118. 22).
 O | 43. The Parable. Its application.
  P | 44. The Scripture cited (Isa. 8. 14).

21. 33-41 (O, above). THE PARABLE GIVEN. (*Alternation.*)

O | c | 33. The Owner making His Vineyard.
  d | 34-39. The Husbandmen. Conduct.
 c | 40. The Owner coming to His Vineyard.
  d | 41. The Husbandmen. Judgment.

33 another. Gr. *allos.* Ap. 124. 1: i.e. a similar. The second parable spoken in the Temple.
householder = master of a house.
hedged it round about = placed about it a fence.
winepress. Sept. for Heb. *gath*, the press, not the vat. Isa. 5. 2.
tower. For the watchmen. See Isa. 1. 8; 5. 2; 24. 20. Job 27. 18.
let it out. There were three kinds of leases: (1) where the labourers received a proportion of the produce for their payment; (2) where full rent was paid; (3) where a definite part of the produce was to be given by the lessees, whatever the harvest was. Such leases were given by the year, or for life, or were even hereditary. From *v.* 34 and Mark 12. 2 the word "of" shows that the latter kind of lease is referred to in this parable.
went into a far country = went abroad, or journeyed. As in 25. 14, 15. Mark 12. 1; 13. 34. Luke 15. 13; 20. 9.
34 time = season. **to.** Gr. *pros.* Ap. 104. xv. 3.
35 beat one, &c. = one they beat, and one they killed, and one they stoned.
and. Note the Fig. *Polysyndeton*, Ap. 6.
another = one.
36 other. Gr. *allos.* Ap. 124. 1.
37 last of all = at last.
his son = his own son. Here is the real answer to *v.* 23.
reverence = stand in awe of.
38 among. Gr. *en.* Ap. 104. viii. 2.
seize on = hold on to, or hold fast. See note on 2 Thess. 2. 6, "withholdeth": which should be rendered as here.
39 out = without, outside (as in Heb. 13. 12).
40 the lord. Ap. 98. VI. i. *a.* 4. A.
cometh = shall have come.
41 miserably . . . wicked. Note the Fig. *Paronomasia* (Ap. 6). Gr. *kakous kakōs.* In Eng. "miserably destroy those miserable [men]" (R.V.); or, "those wretches he will put to a wretched death".
which = of such character that they.
42 Did ye never read, &c.? See Ap. 117. I. and 143. 4.
The Stone, &c. Quoted from Ps. 118. 22. Cp. Acts 4. 10-12. See Ap. 107. I. 1.
the LORD'S = Jehovah's. Ap. 98. VI. i. *a.* 4. B. a. Lit. "from (Ap. 104. xii. 1) Jehovah".
43 given to a nation. The new Israel, as prophesied in Isa. 66. 7-14.
44 on = upon. Gr. *epi.* Ap. 104. ix. 3.
grind him to powder. Supposed to mean winnow or scatter as dust. But in a *Papyrus* (Fayyūm, second or third cent. A.D.) it is used for *ruining* a thing in some way. This supplies the contrast here. Occ. elsewhere only in Luke 20. 18; Sept. (Theodotion) for utter destruction, in Dan. 2. 44. Cp. Job 27. 21. **45 perceived** = got to know. Gr. *ginōskō.* Ap. 132. I. ii. **46 multitude** = crowds. **took Him, &c.** = were holding Him as a prophet. **for.** Gr. = as; but all the texts read "*eis*" = for. Ap. 104. vi.

L Q[1] e (p. 1359) 29
22 And ° Jesus answered and spake unto them again ° by ° parables, and said,
2 °"The kingdom of ° heaven is like unto a certain king, which made a ° marriage for his son,
3 And ° sent forth his servants to call them that ° were bidden ° to the ° wedding:

f and they ° would ° not come.

e 4 Again, he [3] sent forth ° other servants, saying, 'Tell them which ° are bidden, °'Behold, I have prepared my ° dinner: my oxen and *my* ° fatlings *are* killed, and all things *are* ready: come ° unto the [2] marriage.''

f 5 But they ° made light of *it*, and ° went their ways, one [3] to ° his farm, another [3] to his ° merchandise:
6 And the remnant took his servants, and ° entreated *them* spitefully, and ° slew *them*.
7 But when the king heard ° *thereof*, he was wroth: and he sent forth ° his armies, and destroyed those murderers, and ° burned up their city.

Q[2] g 8 ° Then saith he to his servants, 'The [3] wedding is ready, but they which [3] were bidden were [3] not worthy.

h 9 ° Go ye therefore ° into ° the highways, and as many as ye shall find, bid [5] to the [2] marriage.'

h 10 So those servants ° went out ° into [9] the highways, and gathered together all as many as they found, both ° bad and good: and the [3] wedding ° was furnished with guests.

g 11 And when the king came in ° to see the guests, ° he saw there a ° man which had [3] not on ° a [3] wedding garment:
12 And he saith unto him, °'Friend, how camest thou in hither ° not having [11] a [3] wedding garment?' And he was ° speechless.
13 Then said the king to the servants, 'Bind him hand and foot, and take him away, and cast *him* [10] into ° outer darkness; there shall be ° weeping and gnashing of teeth.'
14 ° For many are called, but few *are* chosen."

K R T (p. 1360) 15 Then ° went ° the Pharisees, and took counsel how they might ° entangle Him ° in *His* talk.

22. 1-14 (*L*, p. 1357). PARABLES. MARRIAGE OF KING'S SON. (*Division.*)

L | Q[1] | 1-7. The bidden Guests.
  | Q[2] | 8-14. The substituted Guests.

22. 1-7 (Q[1], above). THE BIDDEN GUESTS. (*Alternation.*)

Q[1] | e | 1-3-. Call to those bidden. First call.
  | f | -3. Servants sent. Refused.
  | *e* | 4. Call to those bidden. Second call.
  | *f* | 5-7. Servants sent. Ill treated.

1 Jesus. See Ap. 98. X.
by=in. Gr. *en.* Ap. 104. viii.
parables. This was the third of the three spoken in the Temple. Cp. 21. 28, 33.
2 The kingdom of heaven. See Ap. 114.
heaven=the heavens. See notes on 6. 9, 10.
marriage=marriage or wedding feast. See Ap. 140. II. 2.
3 sent forth, &c. John, the Lord, and the Twelve.
were bidden=those who had been bidden. This bidding had been done by the prophets. For the custom of such a later "sending" cp. Est. 5. 8 with 6. 14.
to. Gr. *eis.* Ap. 104. vi.
wedding=wedding feast, as "marriage" in *v.* 2.
would not come=wished not to come. Ap. 102. 1.
not. Gr. *ou.* Ap. 105. I.
4 other servants. Peter and "them that heard Him" (Heb. 2. 3), as recorded in the Acts.
are bidden=had been bidden, as in *v.* 3.
Behold. Fig. *Asterismos* (Ap. 6).
dinner=breakfast, or luncheon. Not *deipnon*, which is supper.
fatlings=fatted beasts. Gr. *sitistos.* Occ. only here.
unto. Gr. *eis.* Ap. 104. vi.
5 made light of it=gave no heed [to it].
went their ways=went away.
his=his own; "our own" being emphatic for contrast. Cp. 1 Chron. 29. 16.
merchandise=commerce. Gr. *emporia.* Occ. only in Matthew.
6 entreated, &c. As in Acts 4. 1-3; 5. 40, 41; 11. 19.
slew them. Acts 7. 54-60; 8. 1; 12. 2-5.
7 thereof. See the varied supply of the Ellipsis after "heard" in *vv.* 7, 22, and 33.
his armies. The Roman armies.
burned up their city. Gr. *emprēthō.* Occ. only here. This refers to the destruction of Jerusalem, which took place shortly after the close of the Acts Dispensation.

22. 8-14 (Q[2], above). THE SUBSTITUTED GUESTS. (*Introversion.*)

Q[2] | g | 8. The bidden Guests. Not worthy.
  | h | 9. Other Guests to be substituted.
  | *h* | 10. Other Guests substituted.
  | *g* | 11-14. The intruding Guest. Detected.

8 Then, &c. This, as to time, leaps over the present Dispensation, and takes up the yet future preaching of 24. 14, for it has to do with the same people. **9 Go ye therefore, &c.** After the present Dispensation. **into**=upon. Gr. *epi.* Ap. 104. ix. 3. **the highways**=the public roads, or cross-roads. Gr. *diexodos.* Occ. only here. **10 went out**=having gone out. **into.** Gr. *eis.* Ap. 104. vi. **bad.** Gr. *ponēros.* Ap. 128. III. 1. **was furnished**=became filled. **11 to see**=to gaze upon, view as a spectacle, or inspect. Ap. 133. I. 12. **he saw**=he beheld. Ap. 133. I. 1. **man.** Gr. *anthrōpos.* Ap. 123. 1. **a wedding garment.** As prescribed by Eastern etiquette. **12 Friend.** Gr. *hetairos.* Occ. only in Matthew (here; 11. 16; 20. 13; 26. 50). **not.** Gr. *mē.* Ap. 105. II. Not the same word as in *v.* 11, because this refers to the man's subjective consciousness of the omission when he entered, not to the mere forgetfulness of the fact. **speechless.** There was no excuse for the insult implied in the negative *mē*, above. **13 outer**=the outer. Gr. *exōteros.* Occ. only in Matt. 8. 12; 22. 13; and 25. 30. **weeping, &c.** The weeping and the grinding. See note on 8. 12. **14 For, &c.** Cp. 20. 16.

22. 15-46 (*K*, p. 1357). QUESTIONS. PHARISEES AND SADDUCEES. (*Alternation.*)

K | R | 15-22. The Pharisees' Question. Civil.
  | S | 23-33. The Sadducees' Question. Religious.
  | *R* | 34-40. The Pharisee's Question. Moral.
  | *S* | 41-46. The Lord's Question and Answer.

22. 15-22 [For Structure see next page].

15 went=came: as in *v.* 23. A threefold temptation. See R, S, and *R*, above. **the Pharisees.** See Ap. 120. II. **entangle**=entrap. Gr. *pagideuō.* Occ. only here. **in.** Gr. *en.* Ap. 104. viii.

U 16 And they sent out unto Him ° their dis-
(p. 1360) ciples ° with the ° Herodians, saying, ° "Master,
29 ° we know that Thou art true, and teachest
the way of ° God [15] in truth, ° neither carest
Thou ° for any *man*: for Thou ° regardest [3] not
the person of [11] men.
17 Tell us therefore, What thinkest Thou?
Is it lawful to give ° tribute unto Cæsar, or
[3] not?"

V i 18 ° But [1] Jesus ° perceived their ° wickedness,
and said, "Why tempt ye Me, *ye* hypocrites?
19 Shew Me the [7] tribute ° money."
k And they ° brought unto Him a ° penny.

V i 20 And He saith unto them, "Whose *is* this
° image and ° superscription?"

k 21 They say unto Him, "Cæsar's."
U Then saith He unto them, "Render therefore
unto Cæsar the things which are Cæsar's;
and unto [16] God the things that are [16] God's."

T 22 When they had heard ° *these words*, they
marvelled, and left Him, and went their way.

S l 23 ° The same day came to Him ° the Sadducees, which say that there ° is ° no resurrection, and asked Him,

m 24 Saying, [16] "Master, ° Moses said, ° **'If a man**
° die, having [23] no ° children, his brother shall
° marry his wife, and raise up ° seed unto his
brother'.
25 Now there were ° with us seven brethren:
and the first, when he had married a wife,
deceased, and, having [23] no ° issue, left his wife
unto his brother:
26 Likewise the second also, and the third,
unto the seventh.
27 And ° last of all ° the woman died also.
28 Therefore [15] in the resurrection whose wife
shall she be of the seven? for they all had
her."

l 29 ° Jesus answered and said unto them, "Ye
do err, ° not knowing the scriptures, nor the
power of [16] God.

m 30 For [15] in the resurrection they neither
marry, nor are given in marriage, but are as
the angels of [16] God [15] in ° heaven.
31 But as ° touching the resurrection ° of the
dead, ° have ye [3] not read that which was
spoken unto you ° by [16] God, ° saying,
32 ° **'I am the [16] God of Abraham, ° and the**
God of Isaac, ° and the [16] God of Jacob?' [16] God is
[3] not the [16] God of ° the dead, but of ° the living."
33 And when the multitude heard ° *this*, they
were astonished at His ° doctrine.

R n 34 But when [15] the Pharisees had heard that
(p. 1361) He had put [23] the Sadducees to silence, they
were gathered together.

22. 15-22 (R, p. 1359). THE PHARISEES' QUESTION. (*Introversion and Alternation.*)

R | T | 15. Counsel taken.
  U | 16, 17. Their Question as to Tribute.
    V | i | 18, 19-. His demand.
      k | -19. Their compliance.
    V | *i* | 20. His Question.
      k | 21-. Their Reply.
  (V lines: The Argument.)
  U | -21. Their Question answered.
T | 22. Departure taken.

16 their=their own.

with. Gr. *meta.* Ap. 104. xi. 1.

Herodians. It is uncertain whether this refers to Herod's servants, officers, household, or to a political party. Prob.=courtiers.

Master=Teacher. Ap. 98. XIV. v. 1.

we know. Gr. *oida.* See Ap. 132. 1.

God. Ap. 98. I. i. 1.

neither carest=there is no (Gr. *ou.* Ap. 105. I.) care with Thee.

for=about. Gr. *peri*=concerning. Ap. 104. xiii. 1.

regardest not=lookest not on. Gr. *eis.* Ap. 104. vi.

17 tribute. This was the poll-tax paid in Roman money by each person who was enrolled in the census. See note on 17. 25. Occ. only there, here, and Mark 12. 14.

18 perceived. Gr. *ginōskō.* Ap. 132. I. 2.

wickedness. Gr. *ponēria.* Ap. 128. III (1).

19 money=coin. Gr. *nomisma.* Occ. only here.

penny=a *dēnarius.* See note on 20. 2 and Ap. 51. I. 4.

20 image. Therefore not a Jewish or Herodian coin, but a Roman.

superscription=inscription.

22 these words. See note on "thereof", *v.* 7.

22. 23-33 (S, p. 1359). THE SADDUCEES' QUESTION. (*Alternation.*)

S | l | 23. Sadducees' error. Denial of Resurrection.
  m | 24-28. Resurrection. Questioned.
  l | 29. Sadducees' error. Ignorance of Scripture.
  m | 30-33. Resurrection. Proved.

23 The same day=On (Gr. *en.* Ap. 104. viii) that same day.

the Sadducees. No Article. See Ap. 120. II.

is no resurrection=is not a resurrection.

no. Gr. *mē.* Denying subjectively not the fact, but asserting their disbelief of the fact.

24 Moses. See note on 8. 4.

If a man die, &c. An hypothetical case. See Ap. 118. I. b. Quoted from Deut. 25. 5. See Ap. 107. II. 2.

die=should die.

children. Gr. *teknon,* here put for son. So Deut. 25. 5.

marry. Gr. *epigambreuō.* Occ. only in Matthew. Used here because it specially refers to a marriage between relatives.

seed=issue, as in *v.* 25.

25 with. Gr. *para.* Ap. 104. xii. 2.

issue. Same as "seed" in *v.* 24.

27 last of all=at last, as in 21. 37.

the woman died also=the woman also died.

29 Jesus=But Jesus (Ap. 98. X).

not knowing. Note the negative, implying their unwillingness to know, not stating the mere fact. See Ap. 105. II. All are sure to err who do not know the Scriptures.

30 heaven. Singular. See note on 6. 9, 10.

31 touching=concerning. Gr. *peri.* Ap. 104. xiii. 1. **of the dead**=of dead bodies, with Art. See Ap. 139. 1. **have ye not read . . .**=Did ye never read . . . See Ap. 143. **by.** Gr. *hupo.* Ap. 104. xviii. 1. **saying.** See Ap. 107. II. 1. **32 I am, &c.** Quoted from Ex. 3. 6. See Ap. 117. I. **and.** Note the Fig. *Polysyndeton* (Ap. 6). **the dead**=dead people. See Ap. 139. 2 (without the Article). **the living**=living people. The only conclusion being that they must rise and live again in resurrection in order that He may be their God. This is what the Lord set out to prove (in *v.* 31) "concerning the resurrection". Gr. *zaō.* See note on 9. 18. **33 this.** See note on "thereof" (*v.* 7). **at.** Gr. *epi.* Ap. 104. ix. 2. **doctrine**=teaching.

22. 34-40 [For Structure see next page].

29 35 Then one °of them, *which was* °a lawyer, asked *Him a question,* tempting Him, and saying,
36 [16]"Master, °which °*is* the great commandment [15]in the law?"
o 37 [1]Jesus said unto him, °"**Thou shalt love °the LORD thy [16]God °with all thy heart, and °with all thy °soul, and °with all thy mind.**
(p. 1361) 38 This is the first and great commandment.
o 39 And °the second *is* like unto it, [37]**Thou shalt love thy neighbour as thyself.**
n 40 °On these two commandments hang °all the law and the prophets."
S W p 41 While the °Pharisees were gathered together, [1]Jesus asked them,
42 Saying, °"What think ye °of °Christ? whose Son is He?"
q They say unto Him, °"*The Son* of David."
X 43 He saith unto them, "How then doth David °in °spirit call Him Lord, saying,
44 °'**The LORD said unto My °Lord, 'Sit Thou °on My right hand, °till I make Thine enemies Thy footstool?'**'
W p 45 If David then call Him °Lord, how is He his Son?"
q 46 And °no man was able to answer Him °a word, neither durst any *man* °from that day forth ask Him any more *questions.*

J r[1] **23** Then spake °Jesus to the °multitude, and to His disciples,
2 Saying, "The scribes and the °Pharisees °sit °in °Moses' seat:
s[1] 3 °All therefore whatsoever they bid you observe, °*that* °observe and °do; °but do °not ye °after their works: for °they say, and do °not.
4 °For they bind heavy burdens and grievous to be borne, and lay *them* °on °men's shoulders;

22. 34-40 (*R*, p. 1359). THE PHARISEES' QUESTION. (*Introversion.*)

R | n | 34-36. The Great Commandment. Question.
o | 37, 38. Answer. The First: Love of God. } Severally.
o | 39. Answer. The Second: Love of Neighbour. }
n | 40. The Great Commandment. Jointly.

35 of. Gr. *ek.* Ap. 104. vii.
a lawyer=a teacher of the law.
36 which, &c.=what kind of commandment?
is the great=is great. The Scribes divided them all up: 248 affirmative ones (the number of the members of the body): 365 negative (the number of days in the year): 248+365=613 =the number of letters in the Decalogue. Some were great and some were small (or heavy and light). The question was as to great and small (as in *v.* 38); not the greatest and least.
37 Thou shalt love, &c. Quoted from Deut. 6. 5; 10. 12; 30. 6.
the LORD=Jehovah. Ap. 98. VI. i. *a.* A. *a.*
with. Gr. *en.* Ap. 104. viii.
soul. Gr. *psuchē.* Ap. 110. V.
39 the second, &c. Quoted from Lev. 19. 18.
40 On=In. Gr. *en.* Ap. 104. viii. **all**=the whole.

22. 41-46 (*S*, p. 1359). THE LORD'S QUESTION AND ANSWER. (*Introversion.*)

S | W | p | 41, 42-. His Question: "Whose Son is Messiah?"
q | -42. Their Answer: "The Son of David."
X | 43, 44. David's Words.
W | *p* | 45. His Question: "How is He his Son?"
q | 46. Their Answer: not given.

41 Pharisees. See Ap. 120. II.
42 What think ye of Christ? See Ap. 154.
of=concerning. Gr. *peri,* as in *v.* 16 ("for").
Christ=the Messiah (with Art.).
The Son of David. Lit. David's Son. The last of nine occ. of this title in Matthew. See note on 1. 1, and Ap. 98. XVIII. **43 in**=by, as in *v.* 1.
spirit. Gr. *pneuma.* Ap. 101. II. 3.
44 The LORD said, &c.=Jehovah said unto Adonai. Quoted from Ps. 110. 1. See Ap. 4. II. and VIII (2); Ap. 98. VI. i. *a.* 1. A. *a.* For the principle underlying the form of quotation, see Ap. 107. 1. i and 117. I.
Lord. Ap. 98. VI. i. *a.* 2. A. *a.* **on.** Gr. *ek.* Ap. 104. vii. **till, &c.**=until I shall have (Gr. *an*) set Thine enemies as a footstool for Thy feet. The first of seven references to Ps. 110. 1 in the N.T. (here; Mark 12. 36. Luke 20. 42. Acts 2. 34. 1 Cor. 15. 25. Heb. 1. 13; 10. 13). All refer to Messiah's session on the Father's throne until His enemies shall be placed "as a footstool for His feet", except 1 Cor. 15. 25, where they are at length put in subjection to the Son (Adonai) "*under* His feet." In all the six, the enemies are placed as a footstool by Jehovah, but in 1 Cor. 15. 25 they are placed "under" by Adonai Himself. This was subject to Israel's repentance. See notes on 10. 23; 16. 28; 23. 39; 24. 34. Acts 3. 19-26; 28. 25-26.
45 Lord. Ap. 98. i. *a.* 1. B. b. **46 no man**=no one. Gr. *ou deis.* See Ap. 105. I. **a word.** Gr. *logos.* See note on Mark 9. 32. **from.** Gr. *apo.* Ap. 104. iv.

23. 1-12 (J, p. 1357). TEACHING. IN THE TEMPLE. MULTITUDES AND DISCIPLES. (MORAL.) (*Repeated Alternation.*)

J | r[1] | 1, 2. Self-exaltation. Scribes. (Session.)
s[1] | 3, 4. "Do not ye" what they bid.
r[2] | 5-7. Self-exaltation. Scribes. (Works.)
s[2] | 8-11. "Be not ye" like them.
r[3] | 12. Self-exaltation. Scribes. (Application.)

1 Jesus. Ap. 98. X. **multitude**=crowds. Note the Structure (J[1], p. 1357). **2 Pharisees.** See Ap. 120. II. The Sadducees had their own "leaven" (16. 6) but not this. **sit**=have taken [their] seat. **in**=upon. Gr. *epi.* Ap. 104. ix. 1. **Moses'.** See note on 8. 4. **3 All**=All things. This shows that the words following are not a command, for the whole chapter is taken up with a denunciation of the very things that they thus bade. Later (27. 20-23) they "bade" the People to ask Barabbas and destroy Jesus. **that.** Omit this word as not being in the Greek, or required by the Fig. *Ellipsis.* **observe and do**=ye observe and do. The second person plural is exactly the same in the Indicative and Imperative, and nothing can determine which is the Mood but the context; and the Structure determines its meaning. **observe.** Inwardly. **do.** Outwardly. **but.** Marking the contrast between "ye do" and "do ye not". **not.** Gr. *mē.* Ap. 105. II. **after**=according to. Gr. *kata.* Ap. 104. x. 2. **they say**=they say [ought to be done], but they do not do the works themselves. **not.** Gr. *ou.* Ap. 105. I. Note the difference between the two negatives in this verse.
4 For they bind, &c. By what they "bid you observe". A further proof that "observe and do" is not the Lord's command to carry these many burdens "grievous to be borne". **on**=upon. Gr. *epi.* Ap. 104. ix. 3. **men's.** Gr. *anthrōpos.* Ap. 123. 1.

29 but they *themselves* °will °not °move them
with one of °their fingers.

r² (p. 1361) 5 But all their works they do °for to be
seen of ⁴men: they make broad their °phy-
lacteries, and enlarge °the borders of their
garments,
6 And °love the °uppermost rooms °at feasts,
and the °chief seats °in the synagogues,
7 And °greetings ⁶in the markets, and to be
called °of ⁴men, °Rabbi, Rabbi.

s² 8 But be °not ye called Rabbi: for One is
your °Master, °*even* °Christ; and all ye are
brethren.
9 And call °no *man* your °father °upon the
earth: for One is your °Father, Which is ⁶in
°heaven.
10 Neither be ye called ⁸masters: for One is
your ⁸Master, ⁸*even* ⁸Christ.
11 But °he that is greatest among you shall
be your servant.

r³ 12 And whosoever shall exalt himself shall
be °abased; and he that shall humble himself
shall be exalted.

H Y¹ A t (p. 1362) 13 But °woe unto you, ²scribes and ²Pharisees, hypocrites! for ye °shut up °the king-
dom of °heaven °against ⁴men: for ye °neither
go in *yourselves,* °neither suffer ye them that
are entering to go in.

u 14 ¹³Woe unto you, scribes and ²Pharisees,
hypocrites! for ye devour widows' houses,
and for a pretence °make long prayer:

u °therefore ye shall receive the °greater °dam-
nation.

t 15 ¹³Woe unto you, scribes and ²Pharisees,
hypocrites! for ye compass sea and °land to
make one °proselyte, and when he °is made,
ye make him twofold more °the child of °hell
than yourselves.

B 16 ¹³Woe unto you, *ye* blind guides, which
say, 'Whosoever shall swear °by °the Temple, it is ⁴nothing; but whosoever shall swear
°by the gold of °the Temple, he is a °debtor!'
17 *Ye* fools and blind: for whether is greater,
the gold, or ¹⁶the Temple that sanctifieth the
gold?
18 And, 'Whosoever shall swear ¹⁶by the
altar, it is nothing; but whosoever sweareth
¹⁶by the gift that is upon it, he is ¹⁶guilty.'
19 *Ye* fools and blind: for whether *is* greater,
the gift, or the altar that sanctifieth the gift?
20 Whoso therefore shall swear ¹⁶by the
altar, sweareth ¹⁶by it, and ¹⁶by all things
thereon.
21 And whoso shall swear ¹⁶by ¹⁶the Temple,
sweareth ¹⁶by it, and ¹⁶by Him That dwelleth
therein.

will not move = do not choose to touch.
will. See Ap. 102. 1.
not. Gr. *ou.* Ap. 105. I.
move. Much less bear.
their = their own.
5 for to be seen = to be gazed upon as a spectacle. Same word as "see" in 22. 11.
for = for the purpose. Gr. *pros.* Ap. 104. xv.
phylacteries. Gr. *phulaktērion.* Occ. only here. See notes, &c., on Ex. 13. 9. Deut. 6. 8. Ref. to Pent. Ap. 92 and 117. I.
the borders = the fringes. Ref. to Pent. (Num. 15. 37-41. Deut. 22. 12). Originally a mark of separation between Israel and the surrounding nations. Cp. Luke 8. 44.
6 love = are fond of. Gr. *phileō.* Ap. 135. I. 2.
uppermost rooms = the first place, as in next clause.
at = in. Gr. *en.* Ap. 104. viii.
chief seats = first seats, as in preceding clause.
in. Gr. *en.* Ap. 104. viii.
7 greetings = the formal salutations.
of = by. Gr. *hupo.* Ap. 104. xviii.
Rabbi = my Master. Cp. *v.* 8. Note the Fig. *Epizeuxis* for Emph. (Ap. 6).
8 not. Gr. *mē.* Ap. 105. II.
Master = Leader, Guide, or Director. Gr. *kathēgētēs.* Occ. only here and in *v.* 10. All the texts read *didaskalos,* Teacher.
even Christ. All the texts omit, with Syr.; but, Scrivener thinks, on insufficient authority.
Christ. See Ap. 98. IX.
9 no. Gr. *mē.* Ap. 105. II.
father. This is against those who loved to be so called.
upon. Gr. *epi.* Ap. 104. ix. 1.
Father. See Ap. 98. III.
heaven = the heavens. See note on 6. 9, 10.
11 he that is greatest among you = the greater of you.
12 abased = humbled, as in next clause.

23. 13-39 (*H*, p. 1357). SCRIBES AND PHARISEES. (*Division.*)

H | Y¹ | 13-33. Denunciation. The Eight Woes.
| Y² | 34-39. Prophecy.

13-33 (Y¹, above). DENUNCIATION. THE EIGHT WOES. (*Introversion.*)

Y¹ | A | 13-15. Their treatment of the living.
B | 16-22. False swearing.
C | 23. Hypocrites.
C | 24. Blind guides.
B | 25-28. False cleansing.
A | 29-33. Their treatment of the dead.

13-15 (A, above). THEIR TREATMENT OF THE LIVING. (*Introversion.*)

A | t | 13. Proselytes. The honest hindered.
u | 14-. Incrimination.
u | -14. Condemnation.
t | 15. Proselytes. Those made, made worse.

13 woe. The first of eight woes in Y¹ (*vv.* 13-33). Cp. 5. 3; and see Ap. 126. All the texts (with Syr.) transpose *vv.* 13 and 14.
shut up. Cp. 5. 3.
the kingdom of heaven. See Ap. 114.
heaven = the heavens. See note on 6. 9, 10.
against = before: i.e. in men's faces.
neither = not, as in *v.* 4.
14 Woe, &c. Cp. 5. 4; and see Ap. 126.

make long prayer = praying at great length. **therefore** = on this account. Gr. *dia* (Ap. 104. v. 2). **greater** = more abundant. **damnation** = judgment or condemnation. **15 woe, &c.** Cp. 5. 5, and see Ap. 126. **land** = dry [land]. **proselyte.** The Greek is transliterated, and means a comer over to. Used of a Gentile who came over to the Jews' religion. Occ. only here; and Acts 2. 10; 6. 5; 13. 43. **is made** = becomes [one]. **the child of hell** = a son of Gehenna. A Hebraism = Gehenna's people. See Ap. 131. I; and note on 5. 22. **16 by.** Gr. *en.* Ap. 104. viii. **the Temple** = the Sanctuary: i.e. the *Naos,* or actual Temple building, consisting of the Holy Place and the Holy of Holies. Spelt in *The Companion Bible* with a capital "T", to distinguish it from *hieron,* the whole of the Temple courts, but translated temple also: this is spelt with a small "t" in *The Companion Bible.* **debtor** = is bound [to fulfil the oath]. In *v.* 18 rendered "guilty"; whereby there is (in Eng.) the Fig. *Parēchesis* = guilty [and must pay the *geld,* i.e. the penalty]. See Ap. 6.

29 **22 And he that shall swear [16] by °heaven, sweareth [16] by the throne of °God, and [16] by Him That sitteth thereon.**

C (p. 1362) **23 °Woe unto you, scribes and Pharisees, hypocrites! for ye °pay tithe of mint and °anise and °cummin, and have omitted the weightier *matters* of the law, judgment, mercy, and °faith: these ought ye to have done, and [8] not to leave the other undone.**

C **24 *Ye* blind guides, °which °strain °at °a °gnat, and °swallow °a °camel.**

B **25 °Woe unto you, scribes and Pharisees, hypocrites! for ye °make clean the outside of the cup and of the °platter, but within they are full of °extortion and °excess.**

26 *Thou* blind Pharisee, cleanse first °that *which is* within the cup and platter, that the outside of them may °be °clean also.

27 °Woe unto you, scribes and Pharisees, hypocrites! for ye °are like unto °whited sepulchres, which indeed °appear beautiful outward, but are within full of °dead *men's* bones, and of all uncleanness.

28 Even so ye also °outwardly [27] appear righteous unto [4] men, but within ye are full of hypocrisy and °iniquity.

A **29 °Woe unto you, scribes and Pharisees, hypocrites! because ye build the °tombs of the prophets, and °garnish the °sepulchres of the righteous,**

30 And say, °'If we had been [6] in the days of our fathers, we would [4] not have been partakers with them [6] in the blood of the prophets.'

31 °Wherefore ye be witnesses unto yourselves, that ye are the °children of them which killed the prophets.

32 °Fill ye up then the measure of your fathers.

33 *Ye* serpents, *ye* °generation of vipers, how can ye °escape the [14] damnation of [15] hell?

Y² v (p. 1363) **34 °Wherefore, °behold, I send °unto you prophets, and wise men, and scribes: and *some* °of them ye shall kill and crucify; and *some* °of them shall ye scourge [6] in your synagogues, and persecute *them* °from city °to city:**

w **35 °That °upon you may come all the righteous °blood shed [9] upon the earth, [34] from the blood of °righteous Abel unto the °blood of °Zacharias son of Barachias, whom °ye slew between [16] the Temple and the altar.**

x **36 °Verily I say unto you, All these things shall come [35] upon °this generation.**

22 heaven. Sing. See notes on 6. 9, 10.
God. Ap. 98. I. i. 1.
23 Woe, &c. Cp. 5. 7, and see Ap. 126.
pay tithe=tithe, or take tithes. Eng. tithe=tenth; hence, a district containing *ten* families was called a tithing.
anise=dill. Occ. only here.
cummin. Heb. *kumin.* Gr. *kuminon.* (Occ. only here.) Germ. *kümmel.*
faith. Or, faithfulness, as in Rom. 3. 3. Gal. 5. 22.
24 which, &c. Fig. *Parœmia.* Ap. 6.
strain=habitually filter out. Gr. *diulizō.* Occ. only here.
at. A mistake perpetuated in all editions of the A.V. All "the former translations" had "out".
a=the: which makes it read like a proverb.
gnat. Gr. *kōnōps.* Occ. only here.
swallow=gulp down: Eng. drink up.
camel. An unclean animal. See Lev. 11. 4.
25 Woe, &c. Cp. 5. 8, and see Ap. 126.
make clean=cleanse ceremonially.
platter=dish: i.e. a side dish. Gr. *paropsis.* Occ. only in these verses.
extortion=plunder.
excess=incontinence.
26 that which is within=the inside of.
be=become.
clean also. The "also" must be connected with outside: "that the outside also may become clean".
27 Woe, &c. Cp. 5. 9, and see Ap. 126.
are like unto. Gr. *paromoiazō.* Occ. only here.
whited. Sepulchres were whitened a month before the Passover, to warn off persons from contracting uncleanness (Num. 19. 16).
appear. Ap. 106. I. 1.
dead men's bones=bones of dead people. See Ap. 139. 2.
28 iniquity=lawlessness. Ap. 128. III. 4.
29 Woe, &c. Cp. 5. 9, and see Ap. 126.
tombs. Gr. *taphoi.* There are four at the base of Olivet: those of Zechariah, Absalom, Jehoshaphat, and St. James; but there is no authority for these names.
garnish=adorn or decorate. Perhaps being whitened just then, before the Passover.
sepulchres=*mnemia*=monuments.
30 If, &c. The condition being assumed as an actual fact. See Ap. 118. 2. a.
31 Wherefore=so that.
children=sons. Ap. 108. III.
32 Fill ye up=And ye, fill ye up.
33 generation=offspring, or brood. Pl. as in 3. 7; 12. 34; and Luke 3. 7.
escape=escape from (Gr. *apo*). Ap. 104. iv.

23. 34-39 (Y², p. 1362). **PROPHECY.**
(*Extended Alternation.*)

Y² | v | 34. Prophets. Future sending.
  w | 35. Result.
   x | 36. "I say unto you".
 v | 37. Prophets. Past sending.
  w | 38. Result.
   x | 39. "I say unto you".

34 Wherefore=Because of this. Gr. *dia* (Ap. 104. v. 2) *touto.* **behold.** Fig. *Asterismos.* Ap. 6. **unto.** Gr. *pros.* Ap. 104. xv. 3. **of.** Gr. *ek.* Ap. 104. vii. **from**=away from. Gr. *apo.* Ap. 104. iv. **to.** Gr. *eis.* Ap. 104. vi. **35 That**=So that. **upon.** Gr. *epi.* Ap. 104. ix. 3. **blood.** Put by Fig. *Metonymy* (of the Subject) for blood-guiltiness (Ap. 6). **righteous Abel**=Abel the righteous [one], Gen. 4. 4. Cp. Heb. 11. 4. **Zacharias son of Barachias.** Not the son of Jehoiada (2 Chron. 24. 20, 21) but Zechariah the prophet (Zech. 1. 1, 7), who, we here learn (by Fig. *Hysterēsis*, Ap. 6) was killed in the same way. And why not? Are there not many examples of historical coincidences? Why should the Lord single out "Zacharias the son of Jehoiada" then nearly 800 years before, instead of the later Zacharias (the prophet) some 400 years before? And why may it not be prophetic of another "Zechariah, the son of Baruch" who was thus martyred some thirty-six years after? See Josephus (*Wars*, iv. 5. 4). **ye slew.** This may be taken as the Fig. *Prolēpsis* (Ampliatio), Ap. 6, speaking of future things as present. See 26. 2. Ps. 93. 1; 97. 1; 99. 1. Isa. 37. 22; 48. 5-7. Luke 3. 19, 20. Cp. Matt. 11. 2, &c. **36 Verily.** See note on 5. 18. **this generation.** See note on 11. 16; 24. 34.

v 37 O ° Jerusalem, ° Jerusalem, *thou* that kill-
29 est the prophets, and stonest them which are
sent [34] unto thee, how often would I have
gathered thy ° children together, even as a
hen gathereth her ° chickens ° under *her*
wings, and ye ° would ° not!

w 38 [34] Behold, ° your ° house ° is left unto ° you
° desolate.

x 39 For I say unto you, Ye shall ° not ° see Me
henceforth, ° till ye shall say, °' **Blessed *is* He**
That cometh [6] in the name of ° the LORD.'"

J D (p. 1364) **24** And ° Jesus ° went out, and departed ° from ° the temple:

E and His disciples came to *Him* for to shew
Him ° the buildings of ° the temple.

F 2 And [1] Jesus said unto them, ° "See ye ° not
all these things? ° verily I say unto you,
There ° shall not be left here one stone ° upon
another, that ° shall not be thrown down."

D 3 And as He sat ° upon the mount of Olives,

E the disciples came unto Him ° privately, saying, "Tell us,

G1 when shall these things be

G2 and what *shall be* the sign of Thy ° coming,

G3 and of ° the end of the ° world?"

F H1 y 4 And [1] Jesus answered and said unto them,
° "Take heed that ° no man ° deceive you.

z 5 For many shall come ° in My name, saying,
'I am ° Christ;' and shall [4] deceive many.

z 6 And ye ° shall hear of wars and rumours
of wars: ° see that ye be ° not troubled:

y for ° all ° *these things* ° must ° come to pass,
but ° the end is not yet.

37 Jerusalem. Note the Fig. *Epizeuxis* (Ap. 6), for emphasis. Put by Fig. *Metonymy* (of Adjunct), Ap. 6, for the inhabitants.

children. Pl. of *teknon.* Ap. 108. I.

chickens = brood. Gr. *nossia.* Occ. only here.

under. Gr. *hupo.* Ap. 104. xviii.

would not = were not willing. Ap. 102. 1.

not. Gr. *ou* (Ap. 105. I), denying as a matter of fact.

38 your . . . you. Very emphatic. At the beginning of the Lord's ministry it was "My Father's house" (John 2. 16); but at the end, after His rejection, it was "your house".

house: i.e. the Temple, where He was speaking.

is left = is being left. See 24. 1.

desolate. Every "house" and every place is "desolate" where Christ is not.

39 not = by no means, in no wise. Gr. *ou mē*, Ap. 105. III. **see** = behold. Ap. 133. I. 1.

till. With *an*, implying uncertainty. The *not seeing* was certain: their *saying* it at that time was uncertain. Cp. the four "untils" with *ou mē*: 10. 23; 16. 28; 23. 39; 24. 34.

Blessed, &c. Quoted from Ps. 118. 26; cp. Matt. 21. 9. See Ap. 117. II.

the LORD. Ap. 98. VI. i. *a.* 1. B. a.

24. 1—25. 26 (*J*, p. 1357). TEACHING. DISCIPLES. PROPHETIC. (*Extended Alternation.*)

J | D | 24. 1-. Place. Departure from the Temple.
  E | 24. -1. Disciples come to show.
   F | 24. 2. Prophecy. General.
 D | 24. 3-. Place. Arrival at the Mount of Olives.
  E | 24. -3. Disciples come to ask.
   F | 24. 4—25. 26. Prophecy. Particular.

1 Jesus. Ap. 98. X.

went out, &c. Thus marking this (see Mark 13. 1) as the second of the two prophecies: the former (Luke 21) being spoken "in the Temple". See Ap. 155.

from = away from. Gr. *apo.* Ap. 104. iv.

the temple = the Temple courts, the sacred enclosure. See note on 23. 35.

the buildings, &c. These consisted of the courts, halls, colonnades, towers, and "wings". In Luke 21 "some" spake of its adornment with goodly stones and gifts.

2 See = Behold, look on. Ap. 133. I. 5. Not the same word as in *vv.* 6, 15, 30, 33. **not.** Gr. *ou.* Ap. 105. I. **verily.** See note on 5. 18. **shall not** = shall by no means. Very emphatic, because certain. Gr. *ou mē.* Ap. 105. III. **upon.** Gr. *epi.* Ap. 104. ix. 3. **shall not.** All the texts omit the "*mē*", and read simply "*ou*" as in the first clause. **3 upon.** Gr. *epi.* Ap. 104. 1. **privately** = apart. Luke 21 was spoken publicly.

-3 (*E*, above). DISCIPLES COME TO ASK. (*Division.*)

E | G1 | -3-. First Question: WHEN shall these things (*v.* 2) be?
  | G2 | -3-. Second Question: WHAT the sign of Thy *Parousia*?
  | G3 | -3. Third Question: WHAT [the sign] of the consummation of the Age?

coming = presence. Gr. *parousia.* This is the first of twenty-four occurrences of this important word (Matt. 24. 3, 27, 37, 39. 1 Cor. 15. 23; 16. 17. 2 Cor. 7. 6, 7; 10. 10. Phil. 1. 26; 2. 12. 1 Thess. 2. 19; 3. 13; 4. 15; 5. 23. 2 Thess. 2. 1, 8, 9. Jas. 5. 7, 8. 2 Pet. 1. 16; 3. 4, 12. 1 John 2. 28). The *Papyri* show that "from the Ptolemaic period down to the second century A.D. the word is traced in the East as a technical expression for the arrival or the visit of the king or the emperor", also of other persons in authority, or of troops. (See Deissmann's *Light*, &c., pp. 372-8, 441-5). It is not therefore a N.T. word, as some have supposed. **the end of the world.** See Ap. 129. 2. **the end** = the *sunteleia. Sunteleia* = meeting together of all that marks the consummation of the age; not *telos* = the actual end, *vv.* 6, 13, 14. **world.** See Ap. 129. 2.

24. 4—25. 26 (*F*, above). PROPHECY. PARTICULAR. (*Division.*)

F | H1 | 24. 4-6. Answer to the First Question.
  | H2 | 24. 7-28. Answer to the Second Question.
  | H3 | 24. 29—25. 26. Answer to the Third Question.

24. 4-6 (H1, above). ANSWER TO THE FIRST QUESTION. (*Introversion.*)

Read with Mark 13. 5-7. Luke 21. 8, 9.

H1 | y | 4. Warning. The beginning.
   | z | 5. Many Antichrists. } FIRST SIGN.
   | z | 6-. Rumours of Wars. }
   | y | -6. Warning. Not the end.

4 Take heed. Gr. *blepō.* Ap. 133. I. 5. **no man** = not (*mē.* Ap. 105. II) any one. **deceive** = lead astray. **5 in** = upon: trading upon. Gr. *epi.* Ap. 104. ix. 2. **Christ** = the Messiah. Ap. 98. IX. **6 shall hear** = will be about to hear. **see.** Gr. *horaō.* Ap. 133. I. 8. Not the same word as in *vv.* 2, 15, 30. **not.** Gr. *mē.* Ap. 105. II. **must** = it is necessary [for them to]. **come to pass** = arise (as in *v.* 34). **the end.** Gr. *telos.* Not the same as in *v.* 3. This marks the beginning, not the end. The "many Christs" would be the very first sign. See note on 1 John 2. 18.

H² J (p. 1365) 29 7 °**For nation shall rise °against nation, and kingdom against kingdom**: and there shall be °famines, and pestilences, and earthquakes, °in divers places.

8 All these *are* °the beginning of °sorrows.

K a 9 Then shall they deliver you up °to be afflicted, and shall kill you: and ye shall be hated °of all nations °for My name's sake.

b 10 And then **shall many °be offended**, and °shall betray one another, and shall hate one another.

c 11 And many false prophets shall rise,

c and shall [4]deceive many.

b 12 And °because °iniquity shall °abound, the love of °many shall °wax cold.

a 13 But he that °shall endure °unto °the end, the same shall be °saved.

14 And this °gospel °of the kingdom shall be °preached °in all the °world °for a witness unto all °nations; and then shall [13]the end come.

J d 15 When ye therefore shall °see °**the abomination °of desolation**, spoken of °by Daniel the prophet, stand [14]in °the holy place, (whoso readeth, let him °understand:)

e 16 Then let them which be [14]in Judæa flee °into the mountains:

17 Let him which is °on the housetop [6]not come down to take °any thing °out of his house:

18 Neither let him which is [14]in the field return back to take his clothes.

d 19 And woe unto them that are with child, and to them that give suck [14]in those days!

e 20 But pray ye that your flight °be [6]not in the winter, neither °on the sabbath day:

K f 21 For then °**shall be great tribulation, such as °was [2]not °since °the beginning of the °world to this time, °no, °nor ever shall be**.

22 And except those days should be °shortened, there should [21]no flesh be saved: but [9]for the elect's sake those days shall be shortened.

g 23 Then °if any man shall say unto you, 'Lo, here *is* °Christ,' or 'there;' believe *it* [6]not.

h 24 For there shall arise false Christs, and

24. 7-28 (H², p. 1364). ANSWER TO THE SECOND QUESTION. (*Alternation.*)

H² | J | 7, 8. The Tribulation. The birth-pangs. Read this with Mark 13. 8, and Luke 21. 10, 11.
   K | 9-14. Tribulation. General. } Read this with Mark 13. 9-23, not Luke 21.
 J | 15-20. The Second Sign.
   K | 21-28. The Great Tribulation.

7 For nation, &c. See Ap. 117. II. Quoted from Isa. 19. 2. **against.** Gr. *epi.* Ap. 104. ix. 3.
famines, and pestilences. Fig. *Paronomasia* (Ap. 6). Gr. *limoi kai loimoi.* Eng. dearths and deaths.
in divers = Gr. *kata* (Ap. 104. x. 2) = in [different] places.
8 the = a. **sorrows** = birth-pangs.

24. 9-14 (K, above). TRIBULATION. GENERAL. (*Introversion.*)

K | a | 9. Proclamation. The Gospel of the Kingdom.
  b | 10. Consequences. Stumbling.
   c | 11-. False Prophets. Arising.
   c | -11. False Prophets. Deception.
  b | 12. Consequence. Coldness.
 a | 13, 14. Promise. The Gospel of the Kingdom.

9 to be afflicted = unto tribulation.
to = unto. Gr. *eis.* Ap. 104. vi.
of = by. Gr. *hupo.* Ap. 104. xviii. 1.
for = on account of. Gr. *dia.* Ap. 104. v. 2.
10 be offended = stumble. See Ap. 117. I, II. Quoted from Isa. 8. 15.
shall betray = will deliver up, as in *v.* 9.
12 because = on account of. Gr. *dia*, as in *v.* 9.
iniquity = lawlessness. Ap. 128. III. 4.
abound = be multiplied. Cp. Acts 6. 1, 7; 7. 17; 9. 31.
many = the many.
wax = grow. Anglo-Saxon *weaxen*, to grow.
wax cold. Gr. *psuchomai.* Occ. only here.
13 shall endure = shall have endured.
unto. Gr. *eis*, Ap. 104. vi.
the end. Gr. *telos*, the actual end. Not the *sunteleia* (*v.* 3), but the same as in *vv.* 6 and 14.
saved = delivered (1 Thess. 1. 10).
14 gospel of the kingdom. See Ap. 140.
of = concerning. Gen. of Relation. Ap. 17. 5.
preached = proclaimed. Ap. 121. 1.
in. Gr. *en.* Ap. 104. viii.
world = the (then) habitable world. Gr. *oikoumenē.* See Ap. 129. 3. The civilised as distinct from barbarian. Not the same word as in either *vv.* 3 and 21.
for = to, or with a view to. Gr. *eis.* Ap. 104. vi.
nations = the nations.

24. 15-20 (*J*, above). THE SECOND SIGN. (*Alternation.*)

J | d | 15. Warning. The Second Sign.
  e | 16-18. Direction. Flight.
 d | 19. Commiseration.
  e | 20. Direction. Prayer and Flight.

15 see. Gr. *eidon.* Ap. 133. I. 1. Not the same word as in either *vv.* 2, 6, 30.
the abomination, &c. Ref. to Dan. 12. 11. See Ap. 117. I and II, and notes on Dan. 9. 27; 11. 31; 12. 11. Used as the equivalent for a special idol. Deut. 7. 26. 1 Kings 11. 7. 2 Kings 23. 13. Cp. 2 Thess. 2. 4. **of.** Gen. of Cause, that which brings on God's desolating judgments. **by** = by means of, or through. Gr. *dia.* Ap. 104. v. 1. **the holy place.** See note on "pinnacle", 4. 5. **understand** = observe attentively. **16 into** = upon. Gr. *epi.* Ap. 104. ix. 3. L Tr. WH read "*eis*". Ap. 104. vi. **17 on.** Gr. *epi.* Ap. 104. ix. 1. **any thing.** All the texts read "the things". **out of.** Gr. *ek.* Ap. 104. vii. **20 be** = happen. **on.** Gr. *en.* Ap. 103. viii.

24. 21-28 (*K*, above). THE GREAT TRIBULATION. (*Introversion.*)

K | f | 21, 22. The Great Tribulation. Beginning.
  g | 23. Warning. "If they shall say".
   h | 24-. False Messiahs and false prophets.
   h | -24. Their object.
  g | 25, 26. Warning. "If they shall say".
 f | 27, 28. The Great Tribulation. The End.

21 shall be, &c. See Ap. 117. II. Quoted from Dan. 12. 1. **was not** = has not arisen, or happened; same as "fulfilled", *v.* 34. **since** = from, as in *v.* 1. **the beginning.** See note on John 8. 44. **world.** Gr. *kosmos* Ap. 129. 1. **no.** Gr. *ou.* Ap. 105. I. **nor ever** = *ou mē.* Ap. 105. III; i. e. shall *by no means* happen. **22 shortened** = curtailed. See Ap. 90. **23 if . . . &c.** The condition is hypothetical. Ap. 118. 1. b. **Christ** = the Messiah. Ap. 98. IX.

29 false prophets, and shall °shew great signs and wonders;

h °insomuch that, °if *it were* possible, they shall
(p. 1365) [4]deceive the very elect.

g 25 Behold, I have told you before.

26 Wherefore [23]if they shall say unto you, 'Behold, He is [14]in the desert;' go [6]not forth: 'behold, *He is* [14]in the °secret chambers;' believe *it* [6]not.

f 27 For °as the lightning cometh °out of the east, and shineth even unto the west; so shall °also °the coming of °the Son of man be.

28 For wheresoever the °carcase is, there will the °eagles be °gathered together.

H[3] L N i 29 °Immediately °after the tribulation of
(p. 1366) those days °**shall the sun be darkened,** °**and the moon shall** [2]**not give her light,** °**and the stars shall fall** [1]**from** °**heaven,** °**and** °**the powers of** °**the heavens shall be shaken:**

k 30 And then shall °appear °the sign of [27]the Son of man [14]in [29]heaven:

i [29]and °**then shall all the tribes of the** °**earth mourn,**

k [29]and °they shall see [27]**the Son of man coming** °**in the clouds of** [29]**heaven** °with power and great glory.

O 31 And He shall send His angels [30]**with** °**a great sound of a trumpet, and** °**they shall gather together** °**His elect** °**from the four winds,** [1]**from one end of** °**heaven to the other.**

M P l 32 Now learn °a parable °of the fig tree; When °his branch °is °yet tender, and putteth forth leaves, ye °know that summer *is* nigh:

m 33 So °likewise ye, when ye [6]shall see all these things, [32]know that °it is near, *even* °at the doors.

n 34 [2]Verily I say unto you, °This generation shall °not pass, °till all these things °be fulfilled.

24 **shew**=give. **insomuch that**=so as to, &c. **if it were possible.** The condition involves no doubt as to its being *impossible.* See Ap. 118. 2. a.

26 secret chambers. See note on 6. 6. Gr. *tameion.* Occ. only there, here, and Luke 12. 3, 24.

27 as=just as. **out of**=from. Gr. *apo.* Ap. 104. iv. **also.** All the texts omit "also". **the coming**=the *parousia*, or presence. See note on *v.* 3. **the Son of man.** See Ap. 98. XVI.

28 carcase. Gr. *ptōma.* **eagles**=vultures. **gathered together.** See Job 39. 30: which shows the true interpretation.

24. 29—25. 46 (H[3], p. 1364). THE ANSWER TO THE THIRD QUESTION. (*Introversion and Alternations.*)

H[3] | L | N | 24. 29, 30. The Son of man. Shining forth. The THIRD SIGN.
  O | 24. 31. The gathering of the elect (Israel).
   M | P | 24. 32-41. PARABLES and TYPE. The Fig-tree, and Noah.
    Q | 24. 42-44. Warning. "Watch therefore".
     R | 24. 45-51. Servants. Parable. } General.
   M | *P* | 25. 1-12. PARABLE. The Ten Virgins.
    Q | 25. 13. Warning. "Watch therefore".
     R | 25. 14-30. Servants. Parable. } Particular.
 L | *N* | 25. 31. The Son of man. On His throne.
  O | 25. 32-46. The gathering of the nations (Gentiles).

24. 29-30 (N, above). THE SON OF MAN. SHINING FORTH. THE THIRD SIGN. (*Alternation.*)

Read this with Mark 13. 24-27. Luke 21. 25-28.

N | i | 29. Heaven. Sun darkened.
  k | 30-. The Son of man. The Third SIGN.
 i | -30-. Earth. Mourning.
  k | -30. The Son of man. Himself.

29 Immediately after. No room therefore for a Millennium before His coming. It must follow it. **after.** Gr. *meta.* Ap. 104. xi. 2. **shall the sun, &c.** Ap. 117. II. Quoted from Isa. 13. 10; 34. 4. **and.** Note the Fig. *Polysyndeton* (Ap. 6), to emphasise each particular. **heaven**=the heaven (Sing.). See note on 6. 9, 10. **the powers, &c.** See Isa. 13. 10, 11; 34. 4. Probably referring to the evil "principalities and powers" of Eph. 1. 21; 6. 12. Col. 1. 16; 2. 10, 15. **the heavens.** Pl. See note on 6. 9, 10. **30 appear**=shine forth. Gr. *phainō.* Ap. 106. I. i. **the sign.** As asked in *v.* 3. **then shall, &c.** Quoted from Zech. 12. 12. **earth**=land. Gr. *gē.* Ap. 129. 4. **they shall see.** Gr. *opsomai.* Ap. 133. 8. a. **in**=[seated] upon. Gr. *epi.* Ap. 104. ix. 1. **with.** Gr. *meta.* Ap. 104. xi. 1. Quoted from Dan. 7. 13. **with power and great glory**=with power, yea, with great and glorious power. Fig. *Hendiadys.* Ap. 6. **31 a great sound of a trumpet.** Gr. "a trumpet and a great sound"=a trumpet, yea, a great sounding trumpet. Fig. *Hendiadys* (Ap. 6); not two things, but one. **they shall gather, &c.** Quoted from Deut. 30. 4. See 1 Thess. 4. 16, 17. **His elect.** Who "received the Word". Acts 2. 41. 1 Thess. 2. 13. **from**=out of. Gr. *ek.* Ap. 104. vii. **heaven**=heavens. Pl. See note on 6. 9, 10.

24. 32-41 (P, above). PARABLES AND TYPE. (*Extended Alternation.*)

P | l | 32. PARABLE. The Fig-tree.
 m | 33. The application.
  n | 34. Time. Nearness.
   o | 35, 36. Divine certainty. Creature ignorance.
 l | 37. TYPE. The days of Noah.
  m | 38. The application.
   n | 39-. Time. Suddenness.
    o | -39-41. Divine certainty. Creature ignorance.

32 a=the. Referring probably to a well-known saying. **of**=from. Gr. *apo.* Ap. 104. iv. **his**=its. **is yet**=shall have become already. **know**=get to know. Gr. *ginōskō.* Ap. 132. I. ii. The same word as in *vv.* 33, 39, 43 ("know"). **33 likewise ye**=ye also. **it is near**=He is near. **at.** Gr. *epi.* Ap. 104. ix. 2. **34 This generation.** See note on 11. 16. **not**=by no means. Gr. *ou mē.* Ap. 105. III. **till.** Here with Gr. "*an*", and the Subj. Mood, marking the uncertainty, which was conditional on the repentance of the nation. Note the four "tills" (10. 23; 16. 28; 23. 39; 24. 34), and cp. what is certain with what is uncertain. **be fulfilled**=may have begun to arise, or take place: referring specially to the *first* "sign" in *v.* 4, in response to the first question in *v.* 3; not the same word as in Luke 21. 24, but the same as in *v.* 32.

o 35 [29] Heaven and earth shall pass away, but
p. 1366) My ° words shall [34] not pass away.
29 36 But ° of that day and hour ° knoweth [2] no
man, no, not the angels of [29] heaven, but My
° Father ° only.

l 37 But [27] as the days of Noe *were,* so ° shall
° also ° the coming of [27] the Son of man be.

m 38 For [27] as [14] in the days that were ° before the
flood they were eating and drinking, marry-
ing and giving in marriage, until the day
that ° Noe entered ° into the ark,

n 39 And [32] knew [2] not ° until the flood came, and
took them all away;

o so [37] shall [37] also the coming of [27] the Son of man
be.
40 Then [37] shall two be [14] in the field; ° the one
° shall be ° taken, and the other ° left.
41 Two ° *women shall be* grinding ° at ° the
mill; the one [37] shall be [40] taken, and the other
[40] left.

Q S p 42 ° Watch therefore:
p. 1367)
q for ye [36] know [2] not what hour your ° Lord doth
come.

T 43 But [32] know this, that [24] if the ° goodman
of the house had [36] known in what watch the
thief ° would come,

T he would have watched, and would [2] not have
suffered his house to be broken up.

S p 44 ° Therefore ° be ye also ready:

q for in such an hour as ye think [2] not [27] the Son
of man cometh.

R r 45 Who then is a faithful and wise servant,
s whom his lord hath made ruler ° over his
household, to give them ° meat [14] in due season?

t 46 ° Blessed *is* that servant, whom his lord
when he cometh shall find so doing.

u 47 [2] Verily I say unto you, That he shall
make him ruler ° over all his ° goods.

r 48 ° But and [23] if that ° evil servant shall say
[14] in his heart, "My lord delayeth ° his coming";

s 49 And shall begin to smite *his* fellowservants, and to eat and drink [30] with the drunken;

t 50 The lord of that servant shall come [14] in
a day when he looketh [2] not for *him,* and [14] in
an hour that he is [2] not ° aware of,

u 51 And shall cut him asunder, and appoint
him his portion [30] with the hypocrites: there
shall be ° weeping and gnashing of teeth.

P U W v **25** ° Then ° shall ° the kingdom of ° heaven
p. 1368) be likened unto ten virgins, which took
their ° lamps, and went forth ° to meet the
bridegroom.

---

35 words. Pl. of *logos.* See note on Mark 9. 32.
36 of = concerning. Gr. *peri.* Ap. 104. xiii. 1.
knoweth = has any intuitive knowledge. Gr. *oida.* Ap. 132. I. i. The same word as in *vv.* 42, 43 ("known"); not the same as in *vv.* 32, 33, 39, 43 ("known").
Father. Ap. 98. III.
only = alone. Not the Lord as "the Son of man", though surely as "the Son of God".
37 shall = will.
also the coming = the *parousia* (or presence) also.
the coming = the *parousia.* See note on *v.* 3.
38 before. Gr. *pro.* Ap. 104. xiv.
Noe = Noah.
into. Gr. *eis.* Ap. 104. vi.
39 until. Ref. to Pent. (Gen. 7-11).
40 the one shall be taken, &c. 1 Thess. 4. 15, 16 refers to this, for it is the same *parousia.*
shall = is. So in *v.* 41.
taken = taken to one's side, in peace and for blessing, as in 1. 20, 24; 17. 1. Luke 9. 10; 18. 31; John 14. 3 ("receive").
left. For judgment; as in 13. 30 ("let"); 15. 14 ("let alone"); 19. 27, 29 ("forsaken"); 23. 38; 26. 56, &c.
41 women. Grinding was and is woman's work in the East, and is done in the morning.
at = in. Gr. *en.* Ap. 104. viii.
the mill. Gr. *mulōn.* Occ. only here.

24. 42-44 (Q, p. 1366). WARNING. "WATCH THEREFORE". (*Introversion.*)

Q | S | p | 42-. Warning. "Watch".
q | -42. Reason.
T | 43-. Thief. Knowledge of. } Com-
T | -43. Thief. Action against. } parison.
S | *p* | 44-. Warning. "Be ready".
q | -44. Reason.

42 Watch. As in 1 Thess. 5. 6 and 10 ("wake").
Lord. Ap. 98. VI. i. *a.* 2. B. a.
43 goodman of the house = master of the house.
would come = is coming.
44 Therefore = on this account. Gr. *dia touto.* Ap. 104. v. 2. **be** = become.

24. 45-51 (R, p. 1366). SERVANTS. PARABLE. (*Extended Alternation.*)

R | r | 45-. The faithful and wise servant.
s | -45. His duties performed.
t | 46. His lord's coming.
u | 47. His reward.
r | 48. The evil servant.
s | 49. His duties neglected.
t | 50. His lord's coming.
u | 51. His punishment.

45 over = at the head of. Gr. *epi.* Ap. 104. ix. 1.
meat = their food. "Meat" being put by Fig. *Metonymy* (of Adjunct) for all kinds of food (Ap. 6).
46 Blessed = Happy. As in 5. 3.
47 over = in charge of. Gr. *epi.* Ap. 104. ix. 2.
goods = substance, or property.
48 But and if = But if. As in *v.* 23.
evil. Gr. *kakōs.* Ap. 128. iv. 2.
his coming = to come.
50 aware of = knoweth, as in *v.* 32, 33, 39.
51 weeping and gnashing. See note on 8. 12.

25. 1-12 [For Structure see next page].

1 Then = At that point in a then future time. The Structure of P (p. 1366) shows that this parable formed the closing part of the Lord's teaching on the Mount of Olives (see 24 1, 3); and was designed to illustrate and enforce His teaching as to watchfulness, in view of the then immediate *parousia,* conditional on the repentance of that generation in response to the ministry of Peter and the Twelve, beginning at Pentecost, proclaimed and formulated in Acts 3. 19-26. See the Structure of H^3 (p. 1366). The Parable has nothing to do with the Church to-day as to *interpretation,* though there is the same solemn *application* as to watchfulness. **shall** = will. **the kingdom of heaven.** See Ap. 114. **heaven** = the heavens. Cp. 6. 9, 10. **lamps** = torches. See Ap. 130. 6. **to.** Gr. *eis.* Ap. 104. vi. **to meet** = for the meeting (of two parties from opposite directions): i.e. the meeting and returning with. Gr. *apanantēsis.* Occ. only here, *v.* 6, Acts 28. 15, and 1 Thess. 4. 17. But all the texts read *hupantēsis,* as in John 12. 13.

29 2 And five of them were °wise, and five *were* foolish.

w (p. 1368) 3 They that *were* foolish took their [1]lamps, and took °no oil °with them:

x 4 But the [2]wise took oil °in their °vessels [3]with their lamps.

X y 5 While the bridegroom tarried,

z they all °slumbered and °slept.

V 6 And at midnight °there was a cry made, °'Behold, the bridegroom cometh;

V go ye out [1]to meet him.'

U W v 7 Then all °those virgins arose, and trimmed their [1]lamps.

w 8 And the foolish said unto the [2]wise, 'Give us °of your oil; for our lamps °are gone out.'

x 9 But the wise answered, saying, °'*Not so*; lest there be °not enough for us and you: but go ye rather °to them that sell, and buy for yourselves.'

X y 10 And while they °went to buy, the bridegroom came; and they that were ready went in [3]with him [1]to the °marriage: and the door was shut.

z 11 Afterward °came also the other virgins, saying, °'lord, lord, open to us.'
12 But he answered and said, °'Verily I say unto you, °I know you [9]not.'

Q (p. 1366) 13 °Watch therefore, for ye [12]know °neither the day nor the hour °wherein °the Son of man cometh.

R Y (p. 1368) 14 For °*the kingdom of heaven is* as a °man °travelling into a far country, *who* called his own servants, and delivered unto them his goods.
15 And unto one he gave five °talents, to another two, and to another one; to °every man °according to °his several ability; and straightway °took his journey.

Z 16 Then he that had received the five [15]talents went and °traded with the same, and °made *them* other five [15]talents.
17 And likewise °he that *had received* two, he also gained other two.
18 But he that had received one °went and digged [4]in the °earth, and hid his °lord's money.

Y 19 °After a long time the [18]lord of those servants cometh, and °reckoneth [3]with them.

Z A[1] a[1] (p. 1369) 20 And so he that had received five [15]talents came and brought other five [15]talents, saying, 'Lord, thou deliveredst unto me five [15]talents: [6]behold, I have gained °beside them five [15]talents more.'

b[1] 21 His lord said unto him, 'Well done, *thou* good and faithful servant: thou hast been faithful °over a few things,

c[1] I will °make thee ruler °over many things: °enter thou °into °the joy of thy [18]lord.'

25. 1-12 (*P*, p. 1366). PARABLE. THE TEN VIRGINS. (*Introversion and Alternations.*)

P | U | W | v | 1, 2. The ten.
w | 3. The five foolish.
x | 4. The five wise.
X | y | 5-. The Bridegroom tarrying.
z | -5. The ten sleeping ones.
V | 6-. The Cry.
V | -6. The Call.
U | *W* | *v* | 7. The ten.
w | 8. The five foolish.
x | 9. The five wise.
X | *y* | 10. The Bridegroom coming.
z | 11, 12. The five foolish ones.

2 wise = prudent.
3 no. Gr. *ou.* Ap. 105. I.
with. Gr. *meta.* Ap. 104. xi.
4 in. Gr. *en.* Ap. 104. viii.
vessels. Containing oil, to pour on the torches. Gr. *angeion.* Occ. only here, and 13. 48.
5 slumbered = became drowsy. Gr. *nustazō.* Occ. only here and 2 Pet. 2. 3.
slept = went to sleep (and continued asleep). Gr. *katheudō.* Ap. 171. 1.
6 there was a cry made = there arose a cry.
Behold. Fig. *Asterismos.* Ap. 6.
7 those = those former ones.
8 of. Gr. *ek.* Ap. 104. vii.
are gone out = are going out.
9 Not so. Or, supply the Ellipsis thus: "[we must refuse] lest there be not enough", &c.
not. Gr. *ou.* Ap. 105. I. But all the texts read "*ou mē*". Ap. 105. III. **to.** Gr. *pros.* Ap. 104. xv. 3.
10 went: were on their way.
marriage = marriage, or wedding feast; as in 22. 2, 3, 4.
11 came also the other virgins = "came the other virgins also".
lord, lord. Fig. *Epizeuxis*, Ap. 6, for emph., denoting urgency. Ap. 98. VI. i. *a.* 4. B.
12 Verily. See note on 5. 18.
I know you not. Gr. *oida.* Ap. 132. I. 1.
13 Watch. This is the great lesson of the parable. See Q and *Q* (p. 1366).
neither = not. Gr. *ou*, as in *v.* 6.
wherein = in (Gr. *en.* Ap. 104. viii) which.
the Son of man. See Ap. 98. XVI.

25. 14-30 (*R*, p. 1366). SERVANTS. PARABLE. THE MASTER. (*Alternation.*)

R | Y | 14, 15. The Master. Departure. Commission.
Z | 16-18. Servants. Conduct. Described.
Y | 19. The Master. Return. Reckoning.
Z | 20-30. Servants. Conduct. Judged.

14 the kingdom of heaven. Or supply the Ellipsis from *v.* 13: "[the coming of the Son of man]".
man. Gr. *anthrōpos.* Ap. 123. 1.
travelling, &c. See note on "went", &c., 21. 33.
15 talents. Gr. *talanton.* Occ. only here, and in 18. 24. See Ap. 51. II. 6. (2). Hence the word comes to be used now of any gift entrusted to one for use.
every man = each one.
according to. Gr. *kata.* Ap. 104. x. 2.
his several ability = his own peculiar capacity.
took his journey. Same as "travelling" in *v.* 14.
16 traded with = trafficked or wrought in (Gr. *en.* Ap. 104. viii). The virgins *wait*: the servants *work*.
made them. Put by Fig. *Metonymy* (of Cause), Ap. 6, for "gained". **17 he** = he also.
18 went = went off.
earth = ground. Gr. *gē.* Ap. 129. 4.
lord. Ap. 98. VI. i. *a.* 4. A.
19 After. Gr. *meta.* Ap. 104. xi. 2.
reckoneth = compareth accounts. Gr. *sunairō.* Occ. only here, and in 18. 23, 24.

25. 20-30 [For Structure see next page].

20 beside = upon. Gr. *epi.* Ap. 104. ix. 2. **21 over.** Gr. *epi.* Ap. 104. ix. 3 and 1. **make** = set. **enter ... joy.** He enters into joy, and joy enters into him. **the joy** = the [place of] joy. **into.** Gr. *eis.* Ap. 104. vi.

A² a² (p. 1369) 29 22 He also that had received two [15]talents came and said, [11]'Lord, thou deliveredst unto me two [15]talents: [6]behold, I have gained two other [15]talents [20]beside them.'

b² 23 His [18]lord said unto him, 'Well done, good and faithful servant; thou hast been faithful [21]over a few things

c² I will [21]make thee ruler [21]over many things: [21]enter thou [21]into the joy of thy [18]lord.'

A³ a³ 24 °Then he which °had received the one [15]talent came and said, [11]'Lord, °I knew thee that thou art an hard [14]man, reaping where thou °hast [9]not sown, and gathering where thou °hast [9]not strawed:

25 And I was afraid, and went and hid thy talent [4]in the earth: °lo, *there* thou hast °*that is* thine.'

b³ 26 His [18]lord answered and said unto him, '*Thou* °wicked and slothful servant, °thou knewest that I reap where I sowed [9]not, and gather where I have [9]not [24]strawed:

27 Thou oughtest therefore to have put my money to the °exchangers, and *then* at my coming I should have received mine own with °usury.

c³ 28 Take therefore the [15]talent °from him, and give *it* unto him which hath ten [15]talents.

29 For unto every one that hath shall be given, and he shall have abundance: but [28]from him that hath °not shall be taken away even that which he hath.

30 And cast ye the unprofitable servant [21]into °outer darkness: there shall be °weeping and gnashing of teeth.'

L N (p. 1366) 31 °When [13]the Son of man °shall come [18]in His glory, and all the [3]holy angels with Him, then shall He sit °upon °the throne of His glory:

O B (p. 1369) 32 And before Him °shall be gathered all nations: and He shall separate °them one [28]from another, as a shepherd divideth *his* sheep [28]from the °goats:

C d 33 And He shall set the sheep on His right hand, but the goats on the left.

e 34 Then shall the King say unto them [33]on His right hand, 'Come, ye blessed of My °Father, inherit the kingdom prepared for you [28]from °the foundation of the world:

f 35 For I was °an hungred, and ye gave Me meat: I was thirsty, and ye gave Me drink: I was a stranger, and ye took Me in:

36 °Naked, and ye clothed Me: I was sick, and ye visited Me: I was [4]in prison, and ye came °unto Me.'

g 37 °Then shall the righteous answer Him, saying, °'Lord, when saw we Thee [35]an hungred, and fed *Thee?* or thirsty, and gave *Thee* drink?

25. 20–30 (*Z*, p. 1368). SERVANTS. CONDUCT. JUDGED. (*Repeated and Extended Alternation.*)

Z A¹ a¹ | 20. Reckoning.
b¹ | 21–. Commendation.
c¹ | –21. Reward.
A² a² | 22. Reckoning.
b² | 23–. Commendation.
c² | –23. Reward.
A³ a³ | 24, 25. Reckoning.
b³ | 26, 27. Condemnation.
c³ | 28–30. Punishment.

24 Then he=He also.

had received. Note the change from the Aorist to the Perf. He had received it, and it remained with him.

I knew thee=I got to know thee. Gr. *ginōskō*. Ap. 132. I. ii. Not the same as *vv.* 12, 13, 26.

hast not sown=didst not sow.

hast not strawed=didst not scatter.

25 lo, there. Fig. *Asterismos.* Ap. 6.

that is thine=thine own.

26 wicked. Gr. *ponēros.* Ap. 128. IV. 1.

thou knewest. Gr. *oida.* Ap. 132. I. i.

27 exchangers=bankers. So called from the tables or counters at which they sat. Gr. *trapezitēs.* Occ. only here.

usury=interest. Ref. to Pent. (Deut. 23. 19, 20). Cp. Ps. 15. 5. Hebrews were forbidden to take it from Hebrews, but allowed to take it from foreigners.

28 from=away from. Gr. *apo.* Ap. 104. iv.

29 not. Gr. *mē.* Ap. 105. II. Not the same word as in *vv.* 9, 12, 24, 26, 43, 44, 45.

30 outer=the outer. Gr. *exōteros.* Occ. only in Matthew (here, 8. 12, and 22. 13).

weeping and gnashing. See note on 8. 12.

31 When the Son of man. See the Structure (p. 1366).

shall come=shall have come.

upon. Gr. *epi.* Ap. 104. ix. 1.

the throne. Luke 1. 32. Cp. Ps. 47. 8. Jer. 3. 17; 14. 21. Zeph. 3. 8.

25. 32–46 (*O*, p. 1366). THE GATHERING OF THE NATIONS (GENTILES). (*Introversion and Extended Alternation.*)

O B | 32. The Gathering.
C d | 33. Stationing.
e | 34. Right hand. Blessed.
f | 35, 36. Reason.
g | 37–39. Inquiry.
h | 40. Answer.
C d | 41–. Stationing.
e | –41. Left hand. Cursed.
f | 42, 43. Reason.
g | 44. Inquiry.
h | 45. Answer.
B | 46. The Separation.

32 shall be gathered all nations. There is no resurrection here. Therefore no ref. to Rev. 20. The gathering is to be on earth (Isa. 34. 1, 2. Joel 3. 1, 2, 11, 12). There are three classes, not two. The test is not even "works", but the treatment of the "brethren" by the other two. No believer, i. e. those who "received the word" (Acts 2. 41. 1 Thess. 2. 13): for these were (and will yet be) "taken out of all nations", Acts 15. 14: Israel not gathered here, because "not reckoned among the nations" (Num. 23. 9). The Church of the Mystery (Eph. 3) not here, because the reward here is "from the foundation (Ap. 146) of the world" (*v.* 34); while the Church was chosen "before" that (Eph. 1. 4). The "throne" is that of David (Luke 1. 32).

all nations=all the nations. **them.** Refers to individuals, because it is Masc., while "nations" are Neuter, and therefore are regarded collectively. **goats.** Gr. *eriphion.* Occ. only here. **34 Father.** Ap. 98. III. **the foundation, &c.** See Ap. 146. **35 an hungred**=hungry. **36 Naked**=Scantily clothed. Fig. *Synecdochē* (of the Whole), Ap. 6. **unto.** Gr. *pros.* Ap. 104. xv. 3. **37 Then shall the righteous answer, &c.** Fig. *Dialogismos.* Ap. 6. **Lord.** Ap. 98. VI. i. *a.* 2. B. b.

29 38 When saw we Thee a stranger, and took *Thee* in? or [36] naked, and clothed *Thee?*
39 Or when saw we Thee sick, or [4] in prison, and came [36] unto Thee?'

h (p. 1369) 40 And the King shall answer and say unto them, [12] 'Verily I say unto you, Inasmuch as ye have done *it* unto one of °the least of these My brethren, ye have done *it* unto Me.'

C d 41 Then shall He °say also unto them [33] on the left hand,

e 'Depart [23] from Me, °ye cursed, [21] into °everlasting fire, prepared for the devil and his angels:

f 42 For I was [35] an hungred, and ye gave Me [3] no meat: I was thirsty, and ye gave Me [3] no drink:
43 I was a stranger, and ye took Me [9] not in: [36] naked, and ye clothed Me [9] not: sick and [18] in prison, and ye visited Me [9] not.'

g 44 Then shall they also answer Him, saying, [11] 'Lord, when saw we Thee [35] an hungred, or athirst, or a stranger, or [36] naked, or sick, or [18] in prison, and did [9] not minister unto Thee?'

h 45 Then shall He answer them, saying, [12] 'Verily I say unto you, Inasmuch as ye did *it* [9] not to one of [40] the least of these, ye did *it* [9] not to Me.'

B 46 And these shall go away [21] into °everlasting °punishment: but the righteous [21] into life eternal."

E³ D (p. 1370) **26** And it came to pass, when °Jesus had °finished all these °sayings, He said unto His disciples,
2 °"Ye know that °after two days °is *the feast of* the °passover, and °the Son of man is °betrayed °to be °crucified."

E 3 Then assembled together the chief priests, and the scribes, and the elders of the people, °unto the °palace of the high priest, who was called Caiaphas,
4 And consulted °that they might °take [1] Jesus by °subtilty, and kill *Him.*
5 But they said, °"Not °on the feast *day*, lest there be an uproar among the People."

F G 6 Now when [1] Jesus °was °in °Bethany, °in the house of °Simon °the leper,
7 There came unto Him °a woman having an alabaster °box of °very precious ointment, and poured it °on °His head, as He °sat *at meat.*

H i 8 But when °His disciples saw *it*, they had indignation, saying, [2] "To what purpose *is* this waste?

k 9 For this ointment might have been sold for much, and given to the poor."

40 the least. Emph. = even the least.

41 say also unto them = say unto them also.

ye cursed = that are abiding under a curse.

everlasting fire = the fire, the age-abiding [fire]. See Ap. 151.

46 everlasting. Gr. *aiōnion.* Ap. 151. B. ii. In the same sense as in Heb. 5. 9 (Isa. 45. 17); 6. 2; 9. 12. 2 Thess. 1. 9. (Cp. Ps. 52. 5; 92. 7.) The eternal result must be the same as in the next clause.

punishment. Gr. *kolasis.* According to Aristotle *kolasis* has regard to him who suffers it, while *timōria* has regard to the satisfaction of him who inflicts it. (Occ. only in Heb. 10. 29. The verb *timōreō* only in Acts 22. 5, and 26. 11.) *Kolasis* occ. only here, and 1 John 4. 18 (the verb *kolazomai* only in Acts 4. 21; 2 Pet. 2. 9). What this *kolasis* is must be learnt from 25. 41. Cp. 3. 12, and note on Luke 3. 17.

26. 1-35 (E³, p. 1355). **BETHANY. RETURN TO.**
(*Introversion.*)

E³ | D | 1, 2. The Passover. Two days before.
 E | 3-5. Conspiracy of Chief Priests, Scribes, and Elders.
  F | 6-13. The second Anointing.
 E | 14-16. Conspiracy of Judas Iscariot.
D | 17-35. The Passover. One day before.

1 Jesus. Ap. 98. X.

finished. Cp. 7. 28. Marking an epoch. As in 11. 1; 13. 53; 19. 1. See Ap. 156.

sayings. Pl. of *logos.* See note on Mark 9. 42.

2 Ye know. Gr. *oida.* Ap. 132. I. i.

after. Gr. *meta.* Ap. 104. xi.

after two days, &c. See Ap. 156.

is = takes place, or cometh. Gr. *ginomai.* See note on "fulfilled", Luke 21. 32.

passover. Gr. *pascha*, an Aramaic word. Heb. *peṣach.* Ap. 94. III. 3.

the Son of man. See Ap. 98. XVI.

betrayed = delivered up. The Present Tense is the Fig. *Prolepsis* (Ap. 6). See note on "ye slew", Matt. 23. 35.

to = for: i.e. for the purpose of. Gr. *eis.* Ap. 104. vi.

crucified = hung upon a stake. Gr. *stauros* was not two pieces of wood at any angle. It was an upright pale or stake. Same as *xulon*, a piece of timber (Acts 5. 30; 10. 39. Gal. 3. 13. 1 Pet. 2. 24). Even the Latin *crux* means a mere stake, or stave (cp. *vv.* 47, 55, &c.); while *stauroō* (here) means to drive stakes. See Ap. 162.

3 unto. Gr. *eis.* Ap. 104. vi.

palace = court, with access from the street. Should be so rendered in *vv.* 58, 69. Mark 14. 54, 66; 15. 16. Luke 11. 21; 22. 55. John 18. 15, as it is in Rev. 11. 2. It is rendered "hall" in Mark 15. 16. Luke 22. 55.

4 that = to the end that.

take = seize. **subtilty** = guile.

5 Not. Gr. *mē.* Ap. 105. II. Not the same as in *vv.* 11, 24, 29, 35, 39, 40, 42, 53, 70, 72, 74.

on = during. Gr. *en.* Ap. 104. viii. The same as "among" in the next clause.

on the feast day = during the feast.

26. 6-13 (F, above). **THE SECOND ANOINTING.**
(*Introversion and Alternation.*)

F | G | 6, 7. The woman. Historic.
 H | i | 8. Indignation.
  k | 9. Reasoning.
 H | *i* | 10. Reprehension.
  k | 11. Reasoning.
G | 12, 13. The woman. Prophetic.

6 was = came to be, as in *v.* 20. Gr. *ginomai.* **in.** Gr. *en.* Ap. 104. viii. **Bethany.** Note this return to Bethany from Jerusalem after His first entry in Matt. 21. 1-11, &c., and before His triumphal entry in Mark 11. 1-10, Luke 19. 29-38, and John 12. 12-19. See Ap. 156. **Simon.** Showing this to be a second anointing, later than that of John 12. 2-8. See Ap. 158. **the leper.** Fig. *Ampliatio* (Ap. 6). So called after his healing, as Matthew was still called "the tax-gatherer". See note on Ex. 4. 6. **7 a woman.** Unnamed. In the former anointing it was Mary. See Ap. 158, and note on 1 Sam. 3. 1. **box** = flask. **very precious.** Gr. *barutimos.* Occ. only here. **on** = upon. Gr. *epi.* Ap. 104. ix. 3 (all the texts read ix. 2), as in *vv.* 39, 50. **His head.** In the former anointing, by Mary, it was His feet. See Ap. 158. **sat** = reclined [at table]. **8 His disciples.** In the former case it was Judas Iscariot. Ap. 158.

H i 10 When [1] Jesus °understood *it,* He said unto
(p. 1370) them, "Why trouble ye the woman? for she
29 hath wrought a °good work °upon Me.
k 11 For ye have the poor always °with you;
but Me ye have °not always.
G 12 For [6] in that she hath poured this ointment
°on My body, she did *it* °for My °burial.
13 °Verily I say unto you, Wheresoever °this
gospel shall be °preached [6] in the whole
°world, *there* shall °also this, that this woman
hath done, be told °for a memorial of her."
E 14 Then one of the twelve, called Judas Iscariot, went °unto the chief priests,
15 And said *unto them,* "What °will ye give
me, and I will deliver Him unto you?" And
they °covenanted with him for °thirty pieces
of silver.
16 And °from that time he sought opportunity to [2] betray Him.
D 17 Now °the first *day* of the *feast of* unleavened bread the disciples came to [1] Jesus,
saying unto Him,
F[3] K[1] l °"Where [15] wilt Thou that we prepare for
(p. 1371) Thee to eat the [2] passover?"
m 18 And He said, "Go °into the city °to °such
a man, and say unto him, 'The °Master saith,
'My time is at hand; I will keep the [2] passover °at thy house [11] with My disciples.'"
m 19 And the disciples did as [1] Jesus °had appointed them;
l and they made ready the [2] passover.
K[2] n 20 Now when the even was come, °He sat
down [11] with the twelve.
21 And °as they did eat, He said, [13] "Verily
I say unto you, that one °of you shall °betray
Me."
o 22 And they were exceeding sorrowful, and
began °every one of them to say unto Him,
°"Lord, is it I?"
p 23 And He answered and said, "He that
°dippeth *his* hand [11] with Me [6] in the dish, the
same shall [2] betray Me.
n 24 °The Son of man goeth as it °is written
°of Him: but woe unto that man °by whom
°the Son of man is [2] betrayed! °it had been
good for that man °if he had [11] not been born."
o 25 Then Judas, which [2] betrayed Him,
answered and said, °"Master, is it I?"
p He said unto him, °"Thou hast said."
K[3] 26 And as they were eating, [1] Jesus took
°bread, and blessed *it,* and brake *it,* and gave
it to the disciples, and said, "Take, eat; °this
is My body."
27 And He took the cup, and gave thanks,

10 understood = got to know. Gr. *ginōskō.* Ap. 132. I. ii. Not the same word as in *vv.* 2, 70, 72, 74.
good excellent.
upon = toward. Gr. *eis.* Ap. 104. vi.
11 with. Gr. *meta.* Ap. 104. xi. 1.
not. Gr. *ou.* Ap. 105. i. Not the same as in *vv.* 5, 29, 35; but the same as in *vv.* 24, 39, 40, 42, 53, 70, 72, 74.
12 on. Gr. *epi.* Ap. 104. ix. 1.
for. Gr. *pros.* Ap. 104. xv. 4.
burial = embalming. Cp. John 19. 40. Should be the same as in Mark 14. 8. John 12. 7. It is the Sept. for Heb. *ḥānaṭ,* in Gen. 50. 2.
13 Verily. See note on 5. 18.
this gospel = the good news.
preached = proclaimed. Ap. 121. 1.
world. Gr. *kosmos.* Ap. 129. 1.
also this, that = this also which.
for. Gr. *eis.* Ap. 104. vi.
14 unto. Gr. *pros.* Ap. 104. xv. 3.
15 will ye give . . . ? = what are ye willing to give?
will. Gr. *thelō.* Ap. 102. 1.
covenanted with him = they placed for him [in the balance]: i. e. they weighed to him.
thirty pieces of silver. See Ap. 161. These were shekels of the Sanctuary. Ap. 51. I. 6. This was the price of an ox which had gored a servant (Ex. 21. 32). It was here destined for the purchase of sacrifices.
16 from. Gr. *apo.* Ap. 104. iv.

26. -17-29 (F[3], p. 1355). **JERUSALEM. THE LAST SUPPER.** (*Division.*)

F[3] | K[1] | -17-19. The preparation.
K[2] | 20-25. The Supper. Prediction. Betrayal.
K[3] | 26-29. The New Covenant.

-17-19 (K[1], above). **THE PREPARATION.** (*Introversion.*)

K[1] | l | -17. Preparation. Inquiry.
m | 18. Command.
m | 19-. Obedience.
l | -19. Preparation. Effected.

17 the first day. The eating of the Passover took place on the *fourteenth* of Nisan. See Ex. 12. 6, 8, 18. Lev. 23. 5. Num. 9. 3; 28. 16. The *fifteenth* was the high sabbath, the first day of the feast. See Num. 28. 17.
Where . . . ? This question shows that the date was the fourteenth of Nisan.
18 into. Gr. *eis.* Ap. 104. vi, as in *vv.* 30, 32, 41, 45, 52, 71.
to. Gr. *pros.* Ap. 104. xv. 3.
such a man = a certain one. Gr. *deina.* Occ. only here in N.T.
Master Teacher. Ap. 98. XIV. v. 3.
at thy house = with (Ap. 104. xv. 3) thee.
19 had appointed. Gr. *suntassō.* Occ. only here, and 27. 10.

20-25 (K[2], above). **THE SUPPER. PREDICTION. BETRAYAL.** (*Extended Alternation.*)

K[2] | n | 20, 21. Prediction. Betrayal.
o | 22. Question of all.
p | 23. Answer.
n | 24. Prediction.
o | 25-. Question of one.
p | -25. Answer.

20 He sat down. Thus showing us that this could not be the Passover lamb, which must be eaten *standing.* See Ex. 12. 11.
21 as they did eat. This had been preceded by John 13. 1-30. It was the Passover feast, but not the Passover lamb, which followed it. See *v.* 2, and Ap. 156 and 157. **of.** Gr. *ek.* Ap. 104. vii. **betray Me** = deliver Me up. **22 every** = each. One after the other. **Lord.** Ap. 98. VI. i. *a.* 3. A. Lit., "Not I, is it, Lord?" **23 dippeth** = dipped. **24 The Son of man.** See Ap. 98. XVI. **is written** = hath been (or standeth) written. **of** = concerning. Gr. *peri.* Ap. 104. xiii. 1. **by** = by means of. Gr. *dia.* Ap. 104. v. 1. Not the same word as in *v.* 63. **it had been good.** Fig. *Parœmia.* Ap. 6. **if, &c.** Assuming the condition as a fact. See Ap. 118. 2. a. **25 Master** = Rabbi. Ap. 98. XIV. vii, as in *v.* 49; not the same as in *v.* 18. Lit., "Not I, is it, Master?" **Thou hast said** = Thou thyself hast said [it]. **26 bread** = a hard biscuit, which required to be broken. **this is** = this represents. See Ap. 159 and Ap. 6, Fig. *Metaphor.*

29 and gave *it* to them, saying, "Drink ye all
[21] of it;
28 For this is °My blood of °the °new °testa-
ment, which °is shed for many °for the remission of sins.
29 But I say unto you, I will °not drink
henceforth [21] of °this fruit of the vine, until
that day when I drink it [28] new [11] with you [6] in
My °Father's kingdom."

G³ q (p. 1372) 30 And when they had sung an °hymn,
°they went out [18] into the mount of Olives.
31 Then saith [1] Jesus unto them, 'All ye shall
°be offended °because of Me °this night: for °it
is written, °**'I will smite the shepherd, and the**
sheep of the flock shall be scattered abroad.'
32 But [2] after I am risen again, °I will go before you [18] into °Galilee."

r 33 °Peter answered and said unto Him,
°"Though all *men* shall [31] be offended [31] because of Thee, *yet* will I never [31] be offended."

q 34 [1] Jesus said unto him, [13] "Verily I say unto
thee, °That [31] this night, °before °the cock
crow, thou °shalt deny Me °thrice."

r 35 Peter said unto Him, °"Though I should
die °with Thee, yet will I [29] not deny Thee."
Likewise °also said all the disciples.

D J 36 °Then cometh [1] Jesus [11] with them [3] unto
a °place called °Gethsemane, and saith unto
the disciples,

K "Sit ye here, while I go and °pray yonder."
37 And He took with Him °Peter and the
two sons of °Zebedee, and began to be °sor-
rowful and very heavy.
38 Then saith He unto them, "My °soul is
°exceeding sorrowful, even unto death: tarry
ye here, and watch [11] with Me."

K 39 And He went a little farther, and fell [7] on
His face, and [36] prayed, saying, "O My [29] Father,
[24] if it be possible, let this cup pass [16] from Me:
nevertheless [11] not as I °will, but as Thou
wilt."

28 My blood. No covenant could be made without shedding of blood (Ex. 24. 8. Heb. 9. 20); and no remission of sins without it (Lev. 17. 11).

the new testament=the New Covenant. This can be nothing else than that foretold in Jer. 31. 31. If not made then, it can never now be made, for the Lord has no blood to shed (Luke 24. 39). This is the ground of the proclamation of "them that heard Him" (Heb. 2. 3). See Acts 2. 38, and 3. 19, &c. See also Ap. 95. I.

new. Gr. *kainos*. New as to quality and character; not fresh made. Cp. 27. 60. Mark 1. 27.

testament. Gr. *diathēkē*. This is the first occurrence in the N.T. It is an O.T. word, and must always conform to O.T. usage and translation. It has nothing whatever to do with the *later* Greek usage. The rendering "testament" comes from the Vulg. "testamentum". See Ap. 95. I. *Diathēkē* occurs in N.T. thirty-three times, and is rendered *covenant* twenty times (Luke 1. 72. Acts 3. 25; 7. 8. Rom. 9. 4; 11. 27. Gal. 3. 15, 17; 4. 24. Eph. 2. 12. Heb. 8. 6, 8, 9, 9, 10; 9. 4, 4; 10. 16, 29; 12. 24; 13. 20); and *testament* thirteen times (here, Mark 14. 24. Luke 22. 20. 1 Cor. 11. 25. 2 Cor. 3. 6, 14. Heb. 7. 22; 9. 15, 15, 16, 17, 20. Rev. 11. 19). It should be always rendered "covenant". See notes on Heb. 9. 15–22, and Ap. 95.

is. Used by the Fig. *Prolepsis*. Ap. 6.

for the remission of sins. See Acts 2. 38; 3. 19.

29 not=by no means. Gr. *ou mē*. Ap. 105. III. This might have been soon verified, had the nation repented at the proclamation of Peter (Acts 3. 19–26). But now it is postponed.

this fruit of the vine. Fig. *Periphrasis*. Ap. 6.

Father's. Ap. 98. III, and 112. 3.

26. 30–35 (G³, p. 1355). **THE FIRST PREDICTION OF PETER'S DENIALS.**
(*Alternation*.)

G³ | q | 30–32. The Stumbling of all.
  r | 33. The disclaimer of Peter.
  q | 34. The Denial of one.
  r | 35. The disclaimer of all.

30 hymn=Psalm. Probably the second part of "the great *Hallel*" (or Hallelujah), Pss. 115, 116, 117, 118.

they went out. Another proof that this was not the Passover lamb. Cp. Ex. 12. 22. See note on *v.* 20.

31 be offended=stumble.

because of=in. Gr. *en*. Ap. 104. viii.

this night=in or during (Gr. *en*. Ap. 104. viii) this very night.

it is written=it standeth written.

I will smite, &c. Ref. to Zech. 13. 7. See Ap. 107. I. 1 and 117. I and II. **32 I will go before you.** Cp. John 10. 4. **Galilee.** Ap. 169. **33 Peter**=But Peter. **Though.** Gr. Even if. Same condition implied as in *vv.* 24, 39, 42. **34 That.** Gr. *hoti*. Separating what was said from the time when it was said. See note on Luke 23. 43. **before.** See note on 1. 18. **the**=a: i.e. one of other cocks. **shalt**=wilt. **thrice**: i.e. three denials and a cock-crow; then three more and a second cock-crow; not three cock-crows. This prophecy was uttered three times: (1) John 13. 38, relating to fact, not to time; (2) Luke 22. 34, in the supper room; (3) and last, Matt. 26. 34 (Mark 14. 30), on the Mount of Olives. See Ap. 156 and 160. **35 Though I should die**=Even if (as in *v.* 24) it be necessary for me to die. **with**=together with. Gr. *sun*. Ap. 104. xvi. **also said . . . disciples**=said . . . disciples also.

26. 36–46 (*D*, p. 1305). **THE AGONY.** (*Introversion*.)

D | J | 36–. Arrival.
  K | –36–38. Purpose. Stated.
  K | 39–45. Purpose. Effected.
  J | 46. Departure.

36 Then cometh, &c. The Structure **D** and *D* (p. 1305) shows the correspondence between the Temptation in the Wilderness (4. 1–11) and the Agony in the Garden (26. 36–46). That both were an assault of Satan is shown in Luke 22. 53, John 14. 30; and by the fact that in each case angelic ministration was given. Cp. 4. 11 with Luke 22. 43. **place.** Not the usual word, or the same as in *v.* 52, but Gr. *chōrion*=field, or farmstead; used as "place" is in Eng. of a separated spot, in contrast with the town. Cp. its ten occurrences (here, Mark 14. 32. John 4. 5. Acts 1. 18, 19, 19; 4. 34; 5. 3, 8; 28. 7). **Gethsemane.** An Aramaic word. See Ap. 94. III. 3. **pray.** Gr. *proseuchomai*. Ap. 134. I. 2. As in *vv.* 39, 41, 42, 44. Not the same as in *v.* 53. **37 Peter, &c.**: i.e. Peter, James, and John. **Zebedee.** See note on 4. 21. **sorrowful and very heavy**=full of anguish and distress. Gr. *adēmoneō*=very heavy: only here, Mark 14. 33, and Phil. 2. 26. **38 soul.** Gr. *psuchē*. See Ap. 110. IV. 1. **exceeding sorrowful**=crushed with anguish. So the Sept. Ps. 42. 5, 11; 43. 5. **39 will**=am willing. See Ap. 102. 1.

29 40 And He cometh [14] unto the disciples, and findeth them °asleep, and saith unto Peter, "What, could ye [11] not watch [11] with Me one hour?

41 Watch and [36] pray, °that ye enter [5] not [18] into temptation: the °spirit indeed *is* °willing, but the flesh *is* weak."

42 He went away again the second time, and [36] prayed, saying, "O My [29] Father, [24] if this cup may [11] not pass away [16] from Me, except I drink it, °Thy [39] will be done."

43 And He came and found them asleep again: for their eyes were heavy.

44 And He left them, and went away again, and [36] prayed the third time, saying the same words.

45 Then cometh He [18] to His disciples, and saith unto them, "Sleep on °now, and take *your* rest: behold, °the hour is at hand, and °the Son of man is [2] betrayed [18] into the hands of sinners.

J (p. 1372) 46 Rise, let us be °going: [45] behold, he is at hand that doth [2] betray Me."

L[1] P U (p. 1373) 47 And while He yet spake, °lo, Judas, °one of the twelve, came, and [11] with him a great °multitude [11] with swords and °staves, [16] from the chief priests and elders of the People.

V 48 Now he that [2] betrayed Him °gave them a sign, saying, "Whomsoever I shall kiss, that same is He: °hold Him fast."

49 And forthwith he came to [1] Jesus, and said, °"Hail, [25] Master"; and °kissed Him.

50 And [1] Jesus said unto him, °"Friend, °wherefore art thou come?" Then came they, and laid hands [7] on [1] Jesus, and °took Him.

51 And, [45] behold, one of them which were [11] with [1] Jesus stretched out *his* hand, and drew his °sword, and struck °a servant of the high priest's, and smote off °his ear.

52 Then said [1] Jesus unto him, "Put up again thy sword [18] into his °place: for all they that °take the sword °shall perish °with the sword.

53 Thinkest thou that I °cannot °now °pray to My [29] Father, and He shall °presently °give Me more than °twelve °legions of angels?

54 But how then shall the scriptures be fulfilled, that thus it must °be?"

U 55 [6] In that same hour said [1] Jesus to the [47] multitudes, "Are ye come out as °against °a thief [11] with swords and [47] staves for to take Me? °I sat daily °with you teaching [6] in the temple, and ye °laid °no hold on Me.

56 But all this °was done, [41] that the scriptures of the prophets might be fulfilled."

V Then all the disciples forsook Him, and fled.

40 asleep. Intentionally. Ap. 171. 1.

41 that = to the end that.

spirit. Gr. *pneuma.* Ap. 101. II. 8.

willing = ready.

42 Thy will be done. The very words of 6. 10.

45 now = afterward. Not "now", for see *v.* 46. If taken as meaning "henceforth" it must be a question, as in Luke 22. 46.

the hour is at hand. See note on John 7. 6.

the Son of man. See Ap. 98. XVI.

46 going. To meet Judas; not to attempt flight.

26. 47—28. 15 (*C*, p. 1305). **THE BAPTISM OF SUFFERING** (20. 22, 23). (*Division.*)

C | L[1] | 26. 47—27. 34. The Betrayal.
| L[2] | 27. 35–54. The Crucifixion.
| L[3] | 27. 55–66. The Burial.
| L[4] | 28. 1–15. The Resurrection.

26. 47—27. 54 (L[1], above). **THE BETRAYAL.** (*Introversions and Alternations.*)

L[1] | M | N | P | 26. 47–56. Judas. Treachery.
Q | 26. 57. The Lord. Led to Caiaphas.
R | 26. 58. Peter. Following.
O | S | 26. 59–66. The Lord before Caiaphas.
T | 26. 67, 68. Personal abuse.
M | *N* | *R* | 26. 69–75. Peter. Denial.
Q | 27. 1, 2. The Lord. Delivered to Pilate.
P | 27. 3–10. Judas. Remorse.
O | *S* | 27. 11–26. The Lord before Pilate.
T | 27. 27–34. Personal abuse.

26. 47–56 (P, above). **JUDAS. TREACHERY.** (*Alternation.*)

P | U | 47. Judas with the crowd.
V | 48–54. Acts of two disciples. Treachery and zeal.
U | 55, 56–. The Lord to the multitudes.
V | –56. Act of all the disciples. Desertion.

47 lo. Fig. *Asterismos.* Ap. 6.

one of the twelve. So in all three Gospels. Had probably become almost an appellative by the time the Gospels were written (as "he that betrayed Him" had).

multitude = crowd.

staves = clubs. As in *v.* 55 and Mark 14. 43, 48. Luke 22. 52. Not "staves", which is pl. of *rabdos* = a staff for walking, as in 10. 10. Mark 6. 8. Luke 9. 3 and Heb. 11. 21.

48 gave = had given.

hold Him fast = seize Him.

49 Hail = Gr. *Chaire.* An Aramaic salutation, like the Greek "Peace". Occ. only here; 27. 29; 28. 9; Mark 15. 18. Luke 1. 28. John 19. 3. 2 John 10. 11.

kissed Him = ostentatiously embraced Him.

50 Friend = Comrade. Gr. *hetairos.* Occ. only in Matthew (here; 11. 16; 20. 13; 22. 12).

wherefore, &c. This is not a question, but an elliptical expression: "[Do that] for which thou art here", or "Carry out thy purpose".

took = seized.

51 sword. See Luke 22. 36.

a servant = the bondservant; marking a special body-servant of the high priest, by name "Malchus" (John 18. 10).

his ear = the lobe of his ear. **52 place:** i.e. its sheath. Gr. *topos.* Not the same word as in *v.* 36. **take the sword, &c.:** i.e. on their own responsibility (Rom. 13. 4). **shall perish.** Cp. Gen. 9. 6. **with** = by. Gr. *en.* Ap. 104. viii. **53 cannot** = am not able. **now** = even now. T Tr. WH R read this after "give Me". **pray** = call upon. Gr. *parakaleō.* Ap. 134. I. 6. **presently** = instantly. **give** = send, or furnish. **twelve legions:** i.e. for Himself and the eleven apostles. **legions.** A legion consisted of 6,000 (6,000 × 12 = 72,000). Cp. 2 Kings 6. 17. **54 be** = come to pass. **55 against.** Gr. *epi.* Ap. 104. ix. 3. Not the same word as in *v.* 50. **a thief** = a robber. As in 27 38, 44. (Not "thief", as in 6. 19, 20; 24. 43; or "malefactor", as in Luke 23. 39–43.) **I sat** = I used to sit; or, was accustomed to sit. Imperf. Tense. **with.** Gr. *pros.* Ap. 104. xv. 3. L [Tr.] A WH, omit "with you". **laid no hold on Me** = ye did not (Gr. *ou.* Ap. 105. I) seize me. **no.** Gr. *ou.* Ap. 105. I. **56 was done** = is come to pass.

Q (p. 1373) 29 57 And they that had °laid hold on [1]Jesus led *Him* away [18]to Caiaphas the high priest, where the scribes and the elders °were assembled.

R 58 But Peter followed Him °afar off °unto the high priest's [3]palace, and went °in, and sat [11]with the °servants, to see the end.

S W (p. 1374) 59 Now the chief priests, and elders, and all the °council, °sought °false witness °against [1]Jesus, °to put Him to death;
60 But found °none: yea, though many false witnesses came, °*yet* found they °none.
°At the last came °two false witnesses,
61 And said, "This *fellow* said, °'I am able to destroy the °Temple of °God, and to build it °in three days.'"

X s 62 And the high priest arose, and said unto Him, "Answerest Thou °nothing? what *is it which* these witness against Thee?"

t 63 But [1]Jesus °held His peace.

s And the high priest answered and said unto Him, °"I adjure Thee °by the living [61]God that Thou tell us °whether Thou be °the Christ, °the Son of God."

t 64 [1]Jesus saith unto him, °"Thou hast said: °nevertheless I say unto you, °Hereafter °shall ye see °**the Son of man sitting** °**on the right hand** °**of** °**power, and coming** °**in the clouds of** °**heaven.**"

W 65 Then the high priest rent his °clothes, saying, "He hath spoken blasphemy; what further need have we of witnesses? [45]Behold, now ye have heard His blasphemy.
66 What think ye?"

X They answered and said, "He is °guilty of death."

T (p. 1373) 67 Then did °they spit °in His face, and °buffeted Him; and others °smote *Him* with the palms of their hands,
68 Saying, °"Prophesy unto us, Thou [63]Christ, Who is he that smote Thee?"

R Y^1 u^1 (p. 1374) 69 °Now Peter °sat without [6]in the [3]palace: and °a damsel came unto him, saying, "Thou also wast [11]with [1]Jesus of Galilee."

---

57 laid hold on = seized.
were assembled = had gathered together.
58 afar off = from (Gr. *apo.* Ap. 104. iv) afar.
unto = even to. in = within [the court].
servants = officers.

26. 59-66 (S, p. 1373). THE LORD BEFORE CAIAPHAS. (*Alternation.*)

S | W | 59-61. False witnesses. Sought.
  X | 62-64. Examination.
  W | 65-66-. False witnesses. Superseded.
  X | -66. Condemnation.

59 council = Sanhedrin.
sought = were seeking.
false witness. Gr. *pseudomarturia.* Occ. only in Matthew, here, and 15. 19.
against. Gr. *kata.* Ap. 104. x. 1. Not the same word as in *v.* 55.
to put = so that they might put, &c.
60 none = not [any]. Gr. *ou.* Ap. 105. I.
yet found they none. All the texts omit these words; but Scrivener thinks on insufficient authority.
At the last = But at last.
two. Cp. Deut. 19. 15.
61 I am able to destroy. This was "false". He said "Destroy ye". The false witnesses helped to fulfil it.
Temple. Gr. *naos,* the shrine. See note on 23. 16.
God. Ap. 98. I. i. 1.
in. Gr. *dia.* Ap. 104. v. 1. Perhaps better "within". See Mark 2. 1. Acts 24. 17. Gal. 2. 1.

26. 62-64 (X, above). EXAMINATION (*Alternation.*)

X | s | 62. Question.
  t | 63. Silence.
  s | -63. Adjuration.
  t | 64. Speech. Answer.

62 nothing. Gr. *ouden.* Related to *ou.* Ap. 105. I.
63 held = continued holding.
I adjure Thee = I put Thee on Thine oath. Gr. *exorkizō.* Occ. only here.
by. Gr. *kata.* Ap. 104. x. 1.
whether = if, &c. Throwing no doubt on the assumption: as in *vv.* 24, 39, 42.
the Christ = Messiah. Ap. 98. VIII and IX.
the Son of God. See Ap. 98. XV.
64 Thou hast said = Thou thyself hast said [it].
nevertheless = moreover, or however.
Hereafter, or Later on.
shall ye see. See Ap. 133. I. 8. a.
the Son of man. As in *vv.* 2, 24, 45. This is the last occurrence in Matthew. See Ap. 98. XVI and 117. I. and II. Quoted from Ps. 110. 1. Dan. 7. 13.
on. Gr. *ek.* Ap. 104. vii. (Not the same word as in *v.* 18.) "On" here is not the same as in *vv.* 5, 7, 12, 39, 50. of. Gen. (of Origin). Ap. 17. 2. power. See note on 7. 29. in = upon. Gr. *epi.* Ap. 104. ix. 1. heaven = the heavens. See note on 6. 9, 10. **65** clothes = robe. **66** guilty = deserving or subject to; "guilty" is obsolete in this sense Gr. *enochos,* as in Mark 14. 64. 1 Cor. 11. 27. Jas. 2. 10. **67** in = on to. Gr. *eis.* Ap. 104. vi. buffeted = cuffed, or slapped. smote . . . hands. One word in the Gr. Not necessarily implying "rods". See 5. 39. Mark 14. 65. John 18. 22; 19. 3. Cp. Isa. 50. 6 (Sept.) and Hos. 5. 1; 11. 4 (Symmachus). Gr. *rapizō.* Occ. only in Matthew, here and 5. 39.
68 Prophesy = Divine. Refers to the past, not to the future.

26. 69-75 (*R*, p. 1373). PETER. DENIAL. (*Repeated Alternation.*)

R | Y^1 | 69-74-. Peter. Three denials.
  Z^1 | -74. A cock crowing.
  Y^2 | 75-. Peter. Denial. Remembered.
  Z^2 | -75-. A cock crowing. (The word of the Lord.)
  Y^3 | -75. Peter. Repentance.

26. 69-74- (Y^1, above). PETER. THREE DENIALS. (*Repeated Alternation.*)

Y^1 | u^1 | 69. First challenge. A maid.
  v^1 | 70. First denial.
  u^2 | 71. Second challenge. Another [maid].
  v^2 | 72. Second denial.
  u^3 | 73. Third challenge. Bystanders.
  v^3 | 74-. Third denial.

69 Now Peter, &c. See Ap. 160 on Peter's denials. sat = was sitting. a damsel. Gr. one damsel. Because another is to be mentioned (*v.* 71).

v1 (p. 1374) 70 But he °denied before *them* all, saying,
[2] "I know [11] not what thou sayest."

u2 71 And when he was °gone out [18] into the
29 porch, °another *maid* saw him, and said unto
them that were there, "This °*fellow* was also
[11] with [1] Jesus of Nazareth."

v2 72 And again he [70] denied [11] with an oath, "I
do [11] not [2] know °the man."

u3 73 And [2] after a while came unto *him* they
that stood by, and said to Peter, "Surely thou
also art *one* [21] of them; for thy speech bewrayeth thee."

v3 74 Then began he to °curse and to swear,
saying, "I [2] know [11] not the man."

Z1 And immediately °the cock crew.

Y2 75 And Peter remembered the °word of [1] Jesus, °which °said unto him,

Z2 [34] "Before [34] the cock crow, thou shalt deny Me
[34] thrice."

Y3 And he went out, and wept bitterly.

Q (p. 1373) **27** When the morning was come, all the
chief priests and elders of the People
took counsel °against °Jesus °to put Him to
death:

2 And when they had bound Him, they led
Him away, and delivered Him to Pontius Pilate the governor.

P A w (p. 1375) 3 Then Judas, °which had betrayed Him,
when he saw that He was condemned, °repented himself, and brought again °the thirty
pieces of silver to the chief priests and elders,

x 4 Saying, "I have °sinned in that I have
betrayed °the °innocent °blood." And they
said, °"What *is that* °to us? °see thou *to
that.*"

w 5 And he cast down the pieces of silver °in
the °Temple, and departed,

x and went and °hanged himself.

A y 6 And the chief priests took the silver pieces,
and said, "It is °not lawful for to put them
°into the treasury, °because it is the price of
blood."

z 7 And they took counsel, and °bought °with
them the potter's °field, °to bury strangers in.
8 Wherefore that [7] field was called, "The [7] field
of blood", unto this day.

y 9 Then was fulfilled that which was °spoken
°by °Jeremy the prophet, saying, "**And they
took the thirty pieces of silver, (the price of
Him That was valued, Whom they °of the
°children of Israel did value);**

z 10 **And gave them °for the potter's field, °as
°the Lord °appointed me.**"

S B (p. 1376) 11 And [1] Jesus stood before the governor:

70 denied. See Ap. 160.

71 gone out. To avoid further questioning.

another. Another [maid]; fem. See Ap. 124. I.

This fellow was also = This [man] also was.

72 the man. Not even His name.

74 curse: i.e. to call down curses on himself if what he said were not true. Gr. *katanathematizō.* Occ. only here. See Ap. 160.

the = a. No Art. See note on *v.* 34 and Ap. 160.

75 word = saying. Gr. *rhēma.* See note on Mark 9. 32.

which = Who.

said = had said.

27. 1 against. Gr. *kata.* Ap. 104. x. 1.

Jesus. Ap. 98. X.

to put Him, &c. = so that they might put Him, &c.

27. 3-10 (*P*, p. 1373). **JUDAS. REMORSE.**

(*Alternations.*)

P A | w | 3. Remorse.
| x | 4. Confession.
| *w* | 5-. Restoration.
| *x* | -5. Suicide.
} Money returned.

A | y | 6. Price of blood.
| z | 7, 8. Purchase.
} Fulfilment.
| *y* | 9. Price of blood.
| *z* | 10. Purchase.
} Prophecy.
} Money spent.

3 which had betrayed Him = that delivered Him up.

repented himself. Gr. *metamelomai.* Ap. 111. I. 2.

the thirty pieces, &c. Cp. 26. 15.

4 sinned. Ap. 128. I. 1. Lit. "I sinned".

the innocent. (No Art.) The innocence of the Lord affirmed by six witnesses, three in Matthew and three in Luke: 1. Judas (27. 4); 2. Pilate (27. 24); 3. Pilate's wife (27. 19); 4. Herod (Luke 23. 15); 5. the malefactor (Luke 23. 41); 6. the Roman centurion (Luke 23. 47).

innocent. Gr. *athōos.* Occ. only here, and *v.* 24.

blood. Put by Fig. *Synecdochē* (of the Part), Ap. 6, for the whole person, with a latent ref. to *v.* 6. Cp. *vv.* 24, 25. Ps. 94. 21. Prov. 1. 11.

What . . . &c. Ignoring both the Lord's innocence and Judas's guilt. **to.** Gr. *pros.* Ap. 104. xv. 3.

see thou to that = thou wilt see [to it].

see. Ap. 133. I. 8.

5 in. Gr. *en.* Ap. 104. viii. But all the texts read *eis* = into (vi) the Sanctuary, over the barrier *into* the Sanctuary.

Temple = the Sanctuary. Gr. *naos.* See note on 23. 16.

hanged himself. Gr. *apagchomai.* Occ. only here. Acts 1. 18 describes what took place, in consequence, afterward. He must have been hanging before he could "fall forward". See note there. Gr. *apagchō.* Occ. only here (Matt. 27. 5) in N.T. Sept. for *ḥānak*. 2 Sam. 17. 23, only of Ahithophel, the type of Judas (Ps. 55. 14, 15). See note on Acts 1. 18.

6 not. Gr. *ou.* Ap. 105. I.

into. Gr. *eis.* Ap. 104. vi.

because = since.

7 bought = purchased with money in the market. In Acts 1. 18, the word is not *agorazo*, as here, but *ktaomai* = acquired as a possession by purchase. Acts 1. 18 refers to quite another transaction. See Ap. 161. I. There is no "discrepancy" except that which is created by inattention to the Greek words used.

with = out of. Gr. *ek.* Ap. 104. vii.

field. Gr. *agros*, not *chōrion* = a small holding, as in Acts 1. 18.

to bury strangers in = for (Gr. *eis.* Ap. 104. vi) a burying ground (Gr. *taphē.* Occ. only here) for foreigners.

9 spoken. Not "written", either by Jeremiah or Zechariah, but "spoken" by Jeremiah. Gr. *to rhēthen,* not *ho gegraptai.* See Ap. 161. **by** = by means of, or by [the mouth of]. Gr. *dia.* Ap. 104. v. 1. **Jeremy** = Jeremiah. **of** = from. Gr. *apo.* Ap. 104. iv. **children** = sons. Ap. 108. III. **10 for.** Gr. *eis.* Ap. 104. vi. **as** = according to what. Gr. *katha.* Occ. only here. **the Lord.** Ap. 98. VI. i. a. 1. B. b. **appointed.** Gr. *suntassō.* Occ. only in Matthew (here and 26. 19).

27. 11-26 [For Structure see next page].

C D^1 (p. 1376) and the governor asked Him, saying, "Art Thou the King of the Jews?"
E^1 And [1] Jesus said unto him, °"Thou sayest."
D^2 12 And when He was accused °of the chief
29 priests and elders,
E^2 He answered °nothing.
D^3 13 Then °said Pilate unto Him, "Hearest Thou [6] not how many things they witness against Thee?"
E^3 14 And He answered him to °never a °word; insomuch that the governor marvelled greatly.
D^4 F a 15 Now °at *that* feast the governor was wont to release unto the °people a prisoner, whom they °would.
16 And they had then a notable prisoner, called °Barabbas.
b 17 Therefore when they were gathered together, Pilate said unto them, "Whom °will ye that I release unto you? [16] Barabbas, or °Jesus Which is called °Christ?"
18 For he °knew that °for envy they had delivered Him.
c 19 When he was set down °on the judgment seat, his wife sent °unto him, saying, "Have thou nothing to do with that just Man: for °I have suffered many things this day °in °a dream °because of Him."
F a 20 But the chief priests and elders °persuaded the °multitude that they should °ask [16] Barabbas, and destroy [1] Jesus.
b 21 The governor answered and said unto them, "Whether [9] of the twain [17] will ye that I release unto you?" They said, [16] "Barabbas."
22 Pilate °saith unto them, "What shall I do then with [1] Jesus Which is called [17] Christ?" *They* all °say unto him, "Let Him be °crucified."
23 And the governor said, "Why, what °evil hath He done?" But they °cried out the more, saying, "Let Him be [22] crucified."
c 24 When Pilate saw that he could prevail nothing, but *that* rather a tumult °was made, he took water, and °washed *his* hands before the [20] multitude, saying, "I am °innocent °of the °blood of this just °Person: °see ye *to it.*"
25 Then answered all the People, and said, "His [24] blood *be* °on us, and °on our °children."
B 26 Then released he [16] Barabbas unto them: and when he had °scourged [1] Jesus, he °delivered *Him* to be [22] crucified.
T G 27 Then the soldiers of the governor took [1] Jesus [6] into the °common hall, and gathered °unto Him the whole °band *of soldiers.*

27. 11-26 (*S*, p. 1373). THE LORD BEFORE PILATE. (*Introversion and Alternation.*)

S | B | 11-. The Lord before the Governor.
C | D^1 | -11-. Pilate. Question.
E^1 | -11. The Lord. Answer.
D^2 | 12-. Rulers. Accusation.
E^2 | -12. The Lord. Silence.
D^3 | 13. Pilate. Question of the Lord.
E^3 | 14. The Lord. Silence.
D^4 | 15-25. Pilate. Remonstrance with the People.
B | 26. The Lord delivered by the Governor.

11 Thou sayest = Thou thyself sayest [it]. A Hebraism.
12 of = by. Gr. *hupo.* Ap. 104. xviii. 1. Not the same as in *vv.* 9, 21.
nothing. Note the occasions of the Lord's silence and speech.
13 said. The 1611 edition of the A.V. reads "saith".
14 never = not one.
word. Gr. *rhēma.* See note on Mark 9. 32.

27. 15-25 (D^4, above). PILATE. REMONSTRANCE WITH THE PEOPLE. (*Repeated Alternation.*)

D^4 | F | a | 15, 16. Release of one. Customary.
b | 17, 18. Question as to preference.
c | 19. Advice of Pilate's wife to Pilate.
} Custom existing.
F | *a* | 20. Release of Barabbas. Persuasion.
b | 21-23. Question as to preference.
c | 24, 25. Advice of Pilate to the people.
} Custom acted on.

15 at. Gr. *kata.* Ap. 104. x. 2.
people = crowd. would. Gr. *thelō.* Ap. 102. I.
16 Barabbas. Aramaic. See Ap. 94. III. 3.
17 will = choose. Ap. 102. 1.
Christ = Messiah. Ap. 98. IX.
18 knew = was aware. Gr. *oida.* Ap. 132. I. i.
for = on account of. Gr. *dia.* Ap. 104. v. 2.
19 on = upon. Gr. *epi.* Ap. 104. ix. 1. Not the same as in 25, 30.
unto. Gr. *pros.* Ap. 104. xv. 3. Not the same word as in *vv.* 27, 33; but same as in *v.* 62.
I have suffered = I suffered.
in. Gr. *kata.* Ap. 104. x. 2.
a dream. Gr. *onar.* See note on 1. 20.
because of. Gr. *dia.* Ap. 104. v. 2.
20 persuaded. See Ap. 150. I. 2.
multitude = crowds.
ask = ask for (themselves).
22 saith . . . say. The 1611 edition of the A.V. reads "said . . . said". crucified. See Ap. 162.
23 evil. Gr. *kakos.* Ap. 128. IV. 2.
cried = kept crying.
24 was made = arose, or was brewing.
washed. Gr. *aponipto.* Occ. only here. See Ap. 136. ii. innocent = guiltless.
of = from. Gr. *apo.* Ap. 104. iv. Same as in *vv.* 9, 57. Not the same as in *vv.* 12, 29, 48.
blood. Put by Fig. *Synecdochē* (of Species), Ap. 6, for murder, as in 23. 35. Deut. 19. 12. Ps. 9. 12. Hos. 1. 4. Person = [One].
see ye = ye will see. Gr. *opsomai.* Ap. 133. I. 8. a.
25 on. Gr. *epi.* Ap. 104. ix. 3. Not the same as *vv.* 19, 30.
children = offspring. Gr. pl. of *teknon.* Ap. 108. I.
26 scourged. Gr. *phragelloō.* Occ. only here, and Mark 15. 15. delivered Him = handed Him over.

27. 27-34 (*T*, p. 1373). PERSONAL ABUSE. (*Alternation.*)

T | G | 27. Place. Prætorium.
H | 28-32. Treatment. Crown and Cross.
G | 33. Place. Golgotha.
H | 34. Treatment. The bitter cup.

27 common hall = Prætorium. In Mark 15. 16 it is called the *aulē*, or open courtyard (cp. Matt. 26. 3). In John 18. 28, 33; 19. 9, it is Pilate's house, within the *aulē*. unto = against. Gr. *epi.* Ap. 104. ix. 3. Not the same as in *vv.* 19, 33, 45, 62. band. Render "cohort" and omit "of soldiers". The cohort contained about 600 men.

H d (p. 1377) **28 And they stripped Him, and put on Him a °scarlet °robe.**

e **29 And when they had platted a °crown °of**
29 **thorns, they put *it* °upon His head, and a reed °in His right hand: and they bowed the knee before Him, and °mocked Him, saying, °"Hail, King of the Jews!"**

30 And they spit °upon Him, and took the reed, and °smote Him °on the head.

d **31 And after that they had [29] mocked Him, they took the robe off from Him, and put His own raiment on Him, and led Him away °to [22] crucify *Him*.**

e **32 And as they came out, they found a man of Cyrene, Simon by name: °him they °compelled to bear His cross.**

G (p. 1376) **33 And when they were come °unto a place called °Golgotha, that is to say, a place of a skull,**

H **34 °They gave Him °vinegar to drink mingled °with gall: and when He had °tasted *thereof*, °He would [6] not drink.**

L[2] J[1] f (p. 1377) **35 And they [22] crucified Him, and °parted His garments, casting lots: that it might be fulfilled which was spoken °by the prophet,**

g **°"They parted My garments among them, and upon My vesture did they cast lots."**

f **36 And sitting down they °watched Him there;**

g **37 And °set up °over His head His accusation written, °THIS IS [1] JESUS THE KING OF THE JEWS.**

J[2] h **38 °Then were there two °thieves [22] crucified °with Him, °one on the right hand, and another °on the left.**

27. 28-32 (H, p. 1376). TREATMENT. (*Alternation.*)

H | d | 28. Clothing. Changed.
e | 29, 30. Crown and Sceptre.
d | 31. Clothing. Re-changed.
e | 32. Cross.

28 scarlet=purple.
robe. Gr. *chlamus.* Occ. only here, and *v.* 31.
29 crown. Gr. *stephanos* (used by kings and victors); not *diadēma*, as in Rev. 12. 3; 13. 1; 19. 12.
of. Gr. *ek.* Ap. 104. vii.
upon. Gr. *epi.* Ap. 104. ix. 3.
in. Gr. *epi.* Ap. 104. ix. 3. But all the texts read *in* (as in *vv.* 5, 60).
mocked Him: as foretold by Him in 20. 17-19, but they were only ignorantly fulfilling His own word, as well as the Father's purpose. **Hail ... !** Cp. 28. 9.
30 upon=at. Gr. *eis.* Ap. 104. vi.
smote=kept beating.
on. Gr. *eis.* Same word as "upon", *v.* 30.
31 to=for to. Gr. *eis* (with Inf.). Ap. 104. vi.
32 him=this [man].
compelled. See note on 5. 41.
33 unto. Gr. *eis.* Ap. 104. vi. Not the same word as in *vv.* 19, 27, 45, 62.
Golgotha. An Aramaic word, from the Heb. *Gulgoleth* (see Ap. 94. III. 3. Judg. 9. 53. 2 Kings 9. 35). Nothing is said about a "green hill". But an elevation, which we speak of as being a "head", "shoulder", or "neck". The Latin is *calvaria*=a skull. Hence Eng. Calvary.
34 They gave Him ... drink. Note the five occasions on which this was done; and observe the accuracy of what is said, instead of creating "discrepancies": 1. On the way to Golgotha (Mark 15. 23=were offering, Imperfect Tense), He did not drink. 2. When they arrived there (Matt. 27. 33), He tasted it, but would not drink. 3. Later, by the soldiers after He was on the cross (Luke 23. 36), probably at their own meal. 4. Later still, a proposal made by some and checked by others, but afterward carried out (Matt. 27. 48). 5. The last about the ninth hour, in response to the Lord's call (John 19. 29).
vinegar. In the first case, it was wine (Gr. *oinon*) drugged with myrrh (see Mark 15. 22, 23). 2. In the second case, it was "vinegar (Gr. *oxos*) mingled with gall" (Gr. *cholē*) (Matt. 27. 33). 3. In the third case, it was "sour wine" (Gr. *oxos*), (Luke 23. 36). 4. In the fourth case it was also "sour wine" (Gr. *oxos*), (Matt. 27. 48, as in *v.* 34). 5. In the fifth case it was the same (Gr. *oxos*), (John 19. 28). These then were the *five* occasions and the three kinds of drink. **with.** Gr. *meta.* Ap. 104. xi. 1. **tasted.** See notes above. **He would not.** Gr. *thelō.* See Ap. 102. 1.

27. 35-54 (L[2], p. 1373). THE CRUCIFIXION. (*Division.*)

L[2] | J[1] | 35-37. The parting of the garments.
J[2] | 38-44. After the parting of the garments.
J[3] | 45-54. The three hours' darkness.

27. 35-37 (J[1], above). THE PARTING OF THE GARMENTS. (*Alternation.*)

J[1] | f | 35-. The crucifixion.
g | -35. God's writing fulfilled.
f | 36. The watching.
g | 37. Man's writing put up.

35 parted His garments. This fulfilled Ps. 22. 18; and marks a fixed point in the series of events, which determines the time of others. **by.** Gr. *hupo.* Ap. 104. xviii. 1. **36 watched**=were keeping guard over. (Note the Imperf. Tense.) **37 set up over His head.** This is not therefore the inscription written by Pilate and put upon the cross before it left Pilate's presence (John 19. 19); this was brought after the dividing of the garments; and was probably the result of the discussion of John 19. 21, 22. See Ap. 163. **over.** Gr. *epanō*=up over. See note "upon", 28. 2. **THIS, &c.** For these capital letters see Ap. 48.

27. 38-44 (J[2], above). AFTER THE PARTING OF THE GARMENTS. (*Introversion.*)

J[2] | h | 38. The two *lēstai* (robbers). Brought.
i | 39, 40. The Reviling of the Passers-by
i | 41-43. The Mocking of the Rulers.
h | 44. The two *lēstai* (robbers). Reviling.

38 Then. After the parting of the garments. See Ap. 163. **two thieves**=two robbers. Gr. *lēstai.* Therefore not the two "malefactors" (Gr. *kakourgoi*) of Luke 23. 32, who "were led with Him to be put to death", and came to Calvary and were crucified with Him (Luke 23. 33). These two "robbers" were brought later. Note the word "Then" (*v.* 38). See Ap. 164. **with**=together with: i. e. in conjunction (not association). Gr. *sun.* Ap. 104. xvi. **one on, &c.** See Ap. 164. **on.** Gr. *ek.* Ap. 104. vii.

i (p. 1377) 39 And they that °passed by reviled Him, wagging their heads,

29 40 And saying, °"Thou That destroyest the [5]Temple, and buildest *it* [29]in [5]three days, save Thyself. If Thou be °the Son of God, come down °from the cross."

i 41 Likewise °also the chief priests mocking *Him,* [34]with the scribes and elders, °said,

42 °"He saved °others; Himself He °cannot save. °If He be the King of Israel, let Him now come down [40]from the cross, and we will believe Him.

43 He °trusted [29]in °God; let Him deliver Him now, °if He [17]will have Him: for He said, 'I am [40]the Son of God.'"

h 44 The [38]thieves also, which were crucified with Him, °cast the same in His teeth.

J[3] K l (p. 1378) 45 Now [40]from °the sixth hour °there was darkness over all the °land °unto °the ninth hour.

m 46 And °about [45]the ninth hour [1]Jesus cried with a loud voice, saying, °"**Eli, Eli, lama sabachthani?**" that is to say, "**My [43]God, My [43]God, why hast Thou forsaken Me?**"

L n 47 Some of them that stood there, when they heard *that,* said, "This *man* calleth for °Elias."

o 48 And straightway one [29]of them ran, and took a spunge, and filled *it* with °vinegar, and put *it* on a reed, and °gave Him to drink.

n 49 The rest [41]said, "Let be, let us see whether [47]Elias °will come to save him."

K m 50 [1]Jesus, when He had cried again with a loud voice, yielded up the °ghost.

l 51 And, °behold, °the veil of the [5]Temple was rent °in twain °from the top to the bottom; °and the earth did quake, and the rocks °rent;

52 And the °graves were opened; and many bodies °of the saints which slept °arose,

53 And came °out of the [52]graves °after His °resurrection, and went [6]into °the holy city, and °appeared unto many.

L 54 Now when the centurion, and they that were [34]with him, watching [1]Jesus, °saw the earthquake, and those things that were done, they feared greatly, saying, "Truly This was [40]the Son of God."

L[3] M[1] N (p. 1379) 55 And many women were there °beholding °afar off, °which followed [1]Jesus [40]from °Galilee, ministering unto Him:

39 passed = were passing. Another indication that it was not the Passover day. See Ap. 156.

40 Thou that, &c. Perverting the Lord's words (John 2. 19). Cp. 6. 18.

the Son of God. Ap. 98. XV.

from = off. Gr. *apo.* Ap. 104. iv. Same as in *vv.* 42, 45, 55, 64.

41 also the chief priests = the chief priests also.

said = kept saying.

42 He saved. Note the Alternation here, in the Greek. In Eng. it is an *Introversion.*

j | Others
 k | He saved;
j | Himself
 k | He cannot save.

others. Ap. 124. 1.

cannot = is not (Gr. *ou,* as in *v.* 6) able to.

If he be, &c. The condition is assumed. See Ap. 118. 2. a. All the texts omit "if", and read "he is" (in irony).

43 trusted. See Ap. 150. I. 2. Quoted from Ps. 22. 8.

God. Ap. 98. I. i. 1.

if He will. The condition assumed, as in *v.* 42. Cp. Ps. 18. 19; 41. 11.

44 cast . . . teeth = kept reviling Him. *Both* the robbers reviled; but only *one* of the malefactors (Luke 23. 39, 40). See Ap. 164.

27. 45-54 (J[3], p. 1377). THE THREE HOURS' DARKNESS. (*Alternation and Introversion.*)

J[3] | K | l | 45. Sign in heaven. Darkness.
 m | 46. Cry. "Eli, Eli".
 L | 47-49. Misunderstanding of Bystanders.
 K | *m* | 50. Cry. Repeated.
 l | 51-53. Signs on earth. Veil, earthquake, &c.
 L | 54. Understanding of Centurion and others.

45 the sixth hour. Noon. See Ap. 165.

there was darkness. No human eyes must gaze on the Lord's last hours.

over. Gr. *epi.* Ap. 104. ix. 3.

land. Gr. *gē.* Ap. 109. 4. **unto** = until. See Ap. 165.

the ninth hour. 3 p.m. See Ap. 165.

46 about. Gr. *peri.* Ap. 104. xiii. 3.

Eli, Eli, lama sabachthani. The English transliteration of the Greek, which is the Greek transliteration of the Aram. *'ēlī, 'ēlī, lamah 'ăzabthānī.* The whole expression is Aramaic. See Ap. 94. III. 3. Words not reported in Luke or John. Quoted from Ps. 22. 1. See the notes there. Thus, with the Lord's last breath He gives Divine authority to the O.T. See Ap. 117. I. Note the "seven words" from the cross: (1) Luke 23. 34; (2) Luke 23. 43; (3) John 19. 26, 27; (4) Matthew 27. 46; (5) John 19. 28; (6) John 19. 30; (7) Luke 23. 46.

27. 47-49 (L, above). MISUNDERSTANDING OF BYSTANDERS. (*Introversion.*)

L | n | 47. The Call, *'Elī, 'Elī.* Misunderstood.
 o | 48. Giving to drink.
 n | 49. The Response. Waited for.

47 Elias. Greek for Elijah. Mistaken by the hearers for the Heb. (or Aramaic) *'ēliy-yāh.* **48 vinegar.** Gr. *oxos.* See notes on *v.* 34. **gave** = was offering. **49 will come** = is coming. Ref. to Mal. 4. 5. **50 ghost** = spirit. Gr. *pneuma.* See Ap. 101. II. 6. **51 behold.** Fig. *Asterismos.* Ap. 6. **the veil.** Gr. *katapetasma* = that which is spread out downward, or that which hangs down. Sept. for Heb. *māsāk* (Ex. 26. 37; 35. 12; 40. 5). Occ. only here; Mark 15. 38. Luke 23. 45. Heb. 6. 19; 9. 3; 10. 20. Not the same word as in 1 Cor. 11. 15, or as in 2 Cor. 3. 13-16 (Ex. 34. 33, &c). **in** = into. Gr. *eis.* Ap. 104. vi. Not the same word as in *vv.* 5, 19, 29, 40, 43, 59, 60. **from the top** = from above, as in Luke 1. 3. See note there. Gr. *anōthen.* First of thirteen occurrences. **and.** Note the Fig. *Polysyndeton* in *vv.* 51-53. **rent** = were rent. **52 graves** = tombs. **of the saints.** The 1611 edition of the A.V. had incorrectly "of saints". **arose** = were waked. All the texts read "were raised". Is this the resurrection referred to in Rom. 1. 3? See notes there. Gr. *egersis* = awaking, rousing up, or arising. Occ. only here. Cp. John 12. 24. They thus fulfilled the Lord's word in John 5. 25. **53 out of.** Gr. *ek.* Ap. 104. vii. **after.** Gr. *meta.* Ap. 104. xi. 2. **resurrection** = arising He rose: they were raised. **the holy city.** See note on 4. 5. **appeared:** privately. Gr. *emphanizō.* See Ap. 106. I. iv. **54 saw** = having seen.

27. 55—28. 15 [For Structure see next page].

55 beholding. Gr. *theōreō.* Ap. 133. I. 11. **afar off** = from (Gr. *apo.* Ap. 104. iv) afar. **which** = who: i. e. such as. **Galilee.** Ap. 169.

29 56 °Among °which was Mary Magdalene, and Mary the mother of James and Joses, and the mother of °Zebedee's [9] children.

O p 57 When the even was come, there came a
(p. 1379) rich man [21] of Arimathæa, named Joseph, who °also himself °was [1] Jesus' disciple:

q 58 °He went to Pilate, and begged the body of [1] Jesus.

r Then Pilate commanded the body to be °delivered.

s 59 And when Joseph had taken the body, he wrapped it in a clean linen cloth,

60 And °laid it [5] in his own °new °tomb, which he had hewn out [5] in the rock: and he rolled a great stone to the door of the °sepulchre, and °departed.

M² N 61 And there was °Mary Magdalene, and the other °Mary, sitting over against the °sepulchre.

O p 62 Now the next day, °that followed °the day of the preparation, the chief priests and Pharisees came together [19] unto Pilate,

q 63 Saying, °"Sir, we °remember that that °deceiver said, while He was yet alive, °'After three days I will rise again.'

64 Command therefore that the [61] sepulchre be °made sure until °the third day, lest His disciples come by night, and steal Him away, and say unto the People, 'He is risen [40] from °the dead:' so the last °error shall be worse than °the first."

r 65 Pilate said unto them, °"Ye have °a watch: go your way, [64] make *it* as sure as ye °can."

s 66 So they went, and made the [61] sepulchre sure, sealing the stone, °and setting [65] a watch.

L⁴ M² P **28** °In °the end of °the sabbath, as it began to dawn °toward the first *day* of the week, came °Mary Magdalene and °the other Mary °to see the °sepulchre.

Q t 2 And, °behold, there °was a great earthquake:

u for the angel of °the LORD descended °from °heaven, and came and °rolled back the stone °from the door, and °sat °upon it.

27. 55—28. 15 (L³, p. 1373). BURIAL AND RESURRECTION. (*Division.*)

L³ | M¹ | 27. 55-66. Burial.
L⁴ | M² | 28. 1-15. Resurrection.

27. 55-66 (M¹, above). BURIAL. (*Alternations.*)

M¹ | N | 55, 56. The Women. Mary and the others.
O | p | 57. Joseph of Arimathæa.
q | 58-. His application to Pilate.
r | -58. Pilate's compliance.
s | 59, 60. Tomb. Body placed.
M² | *N* | 61. The Women. Mary and the others.
O | *p* | 62. Chief Priests and Pharisees.
q | 63, 64. Their application to Pilate.
r | 65. Pilate's compliance.
s | 66. Tomb secured.

56 Among. Gr. *en.* Ap. 104. viii. 2.
which. Denoting a class: referring to 27. 55.
Zebedee's. See note on 4. 21.
57 also himself=himself also.
was, &c.=had been discipled to Jesus.
58 He=This [man]. The Lord was thus buried by two secret disciples. See John 19. 38, 39. Cp. Mark 15. 42, 43. Luke 23. 50-53.
delivered=given up. Cp. 18. 25-34.
60 laid it. See note on Isa. 53. 9.
new=Gr. *kainos.* See note on 9. 17; 26. 28, 29. Here=not newly hewn, but fresh; i.e. unused and as yet undefiled by any dead body.
tomb=monument. Gr. *mnēmeion.*
sepulchre=tomb, as above. Not the same word as in *v.* 61.
departed. When Joseph rolled the stone against the door he departed; when the angel rolled it away, he "sat upon it" (Matt. 28. 2).
61 Mary . . . Mary. See Ap. 100.
sepulchre. Gr. *taphos*=burying-place. Not the same word as in *v.* 60.
62 that followed. This was the "high Sabbath" of John 19. 42, not the weekly Sabbath of 28. 1. See Ap. 156.
the day of the preparation. See Ap. 156 and 166.
63 Sir. See Ap. 98. VI. i. *a.* 4. B.
remember=[have been] reminded.
deceiver=impostor.
After three days. They had heard the Lord say this in 12. 39, 40. This is how they understood the "three days and three nights". See Ap. 144, 148, and 166; cp. "after" in *v.* 53.
64 made sure=secured.
the third day. See Ap. 148.
the dead. See Ap. 139. 1. error=deception.
the first. They do not say what the first was. It may be the crucifixion itself.
65 Ye have. Or, Ye may have.

a watch=a guard: the word being a transliteration of the Latin *custodia,* consisting of four soldiers (Acts 12. 4). See note there. Gr. *koustōdia.* Occ. only in Matthew (here, and in 28. 11). can=know [how]. Gr. *oida.* Ap. 132. I. i. **66 and setting a watch**=with (Gr. *meta,* as in *vv.* 34, 41, 54. Not as in *vv.* 7, 38) the watch: i.e. in the presence of the watch, leaving them to keep guard.

28. 1-15 (L⁴, above). RESURRECTION. (*Alternation.*)

L⁴ | P | 1. The Women. Seeing.
Q | 2-4. Events at the Sepulchre.
P | 5-10. The Women. Seeking.
Q | 11-15. Events in the city.

1 In, &c. For the sequence of events connected with the resurrection see Ap. 166. In. Gr. *en.* Ap. 104. viii. the end of=late on, &c. the sabbath. The weekly sabbath. The seventh day; not the high sabbath of *v.* 62 or John 19. 42, because that was the first day of the feast (following the "preparation day"). See Ap. 156. toward. Gr. *eis.* Ap. 104. vi. Mary . . . the other Mary. See Ap. 100. to see=to gaze upon. Gr. *theōreō.* Ap. 133. I. 11. Not the same as in *vv.* 6, 7, 10, 17. sepulchre. Gr. *taphos.* As in 27. 61, 64, 66. Not the same as in "tomb" (27. 60).

28. 2-4 [For Structure see next page].

2 behold. Fig. *Asterismos.* Ap. 6. was=happened. the LORD=Jehovah (Ap. 4. II). See Ap. 98. VI. i. *a.* 1. B. b. from=out of. Gr. *ek.* Ap. 104. vii. heaven. Sing. See note on 6. 9, 10. rolled back=had rolled back. from=away from. Gr. *apo.* Cp. 27. 37. Ap. 104. iv. sat upon it. See note on 27. 60. Sat that it might be known by what power it was rolled back. upon. Gr. *epanō.*

u 3 His °countenance was °like lightning, and
(p. 1380) his raiment white as snow:
29 t 4 And °for fear of him the keepers did shake,
and became as °dead *men*.
P R v 5 And the angel answered and said unto the
women, "Fear °not ye: for °I know that ye
seek °Jesus, Which was crucified.
6 He is °not here: for He is risen, °as He
said. Come, °see the place where °the Lord °lay.
w 7 And go quickly, and tell His disciples that
He is risen [2] from °the dead; and, [2] behold,
He goeth before you °into °Galilee; there
shall ye °see Him: lo, I have told you."
S x 8 And they departed quickly [2] from the sepulchre °with fear and great joy;
y and did run to bring His disciples °word.
R v 9 And as they °went to tell His disciples, [2] behold, [5] Jesus °met them, saying, "All hail."
And they came and °held Him by the feet,
and °worshipped Him.
10 Then said [5] Jesus unto them, "Be [5] not
afraid:
w go tell My brethren that they go [7] into Galilee,
and there shall they [7] see Me."
Q z 11 Now when they were going, [2] behold, some
of °the watch came [7] into the city, and °shewed
unto the chief priests all the things that °were
done.
a 12 And when they were assembled [8] with the
elders, and had taken counsel, they gave
°large money unto the soldiers,
z 13 °Saying, "Say ye, 'His disciples came by
night, and stole Him *away* while we slept.'
14 And °if this come °to the governor's ears,
we will °persuade him, and °secure you."
a 15 So they took the money, and did as they
were taught: and this °saying °is commonly
reported °among the Jews until this day.
B 16 Then the eleven disciples went away [7] into
(p. 1305) Galilee, [7] into °a mountain where [5] Jesus had appointed them.
17 And when they [6] saw Him, they [9] worshipped Him: but some °doubted.
18 And [5] Jesus °came and °spake unto them,
°saying, "All °power °is given unto Me °in
°heaven and °in earth.
A 19 °Go ye therefore, and °teach all °nations,
°baptizing them °in °the name of the °Father,
and of the Son, and of °the Holy Ghost:
20 Teaching them to observe all things whatsoever I have commanded you: and, °lo, I am
[8] with you °alway, *even* °unto °the end of the
°world." Amen.

28. 2-4 (Q, p. 1379). EVENTS AT THE SEPULCHRE.
(*Introversion.*)

Q | t | 2-. Effect. Earthquake.
u | -2. Cause. Action. } The Angel.
u | 3. Cause. Appearance. } The Angel.
t | 4. Effect. Terror of the Watch.

3 countenance = general appearance. Gr. *idea*. Occ. only here. **like lightning**: in effulgence.
4 for = from. Gr. *apo*. Ap. 104. iv.
dead men. See Ap. 139. 2.

28. 5-10 (*P*, p. 1379). THE WOMEN. SEEKING.
(*Introversion and Alternation.*)

P | R | v | 5, 6. Words of the angel.
w | 7. Their Commission.
S | x | 8-. Their departure. } The Women.
y | -8. Their mission. } The Women.
R | *v* | 9, 10-. Words of the Lord.
w | -10. His Commission.

5 not. Gr. *mē*. Ap. 105. II.
I know. Gr. *oida*. See Ap. 132. 1.
6 not. Gr. *ou*. Ap. 105. I. a. **as** = according as.
see. Gr. *eidon*. Ap. 133. I. 1.
the Lord. Ap. 98. VI. i. *a*. 4. B. 2.
lay = was (lately) lying.
7 the dead. See Ap. 139. 4. (Pl.)
into = unto. Gr. *eis*. Ap. 104. vi. **Galilee.** Ap. 169.
see. Gr. *opsomai*. Ap. 133. I. 8. a.
8 with. Gr. *meta*. Ap. 104. xi. 1.
9 went = were going.
met = confronted. As from an opposite direction. Cp. the noun (25. 1, 6. Acts 28. 15. 1 Thess. 4. 17).
held Him by the feet = seized Him by the feet.
worshipped = prostrated themselves before. See Ap. 137. 1.

28. 11-15 (*Q*, p. 1379). EVENTS IN THE CITY.
(*Alternation.*)

Q | z | 11. The Watch. Their report.
a | 12. Bribe offered.
z | 13, 14. The Watch. Report falsified.
a | 15. Bribe accepted.

11 the watch. See note on 27. 65, 66.
shewed = told. See *vv.* 8, 9, 10.
were done = had come to pass.
12 large = sufficient: i.e. to bribe them with.
13 Saying, Say ye = Telling them to say.
14 if this come, &c. = Should this come, &c. A condition of uncertainty. Ap. 118. 1 b.
to. Gr. *epi*. Ap. 104. ix. 1.
persuade = satisfy: i.e. bribe. Cp. Gal. 1. 10. See Ap. 150. II.
secure you = free you from care: i.e. make you safe, or screen you. Cp. 1 Cor. 7. 32.
15 saying = story. Gr. *logos*. See note on Mark 9. 32.
is = has been.
among. Gr. *para*. Ap. 104. xii. 2.
16 a = the.
17 doubted = hesitated. Gr. *distazō*. Occ. only in Matthew (here and in 14. 31). The Gr. aorist may be so rendered, especially in a parenthesis; and is so rendered in 16. 5. Luke 8. 29. John 18. 24: it should be in 26. 48 and in Luke 22. 44 also.
18 came = approached (as in *v.* 9).

spake . . . saying. "Spake" referring to the act, and "saying" referring to the substance. **power** = authority. Gr. *exousia*. Ap. 172. 5. **is given** = has (just, or lately) been given. **in.** Gr. *en*. Ap. 104. viii. **heaven.** Sing. See note on 6. 9, 10. **in** = upon. Gr. *epi*. Ap. 104. ix. 1. **19 Go ye, &c.** See Ap. 167. **teach** = disciple. Not the same word as in *v.* 20. **nations** = the nations. **baptizing . . . in.** See Ap. 115. I. iv. 4. Tr. and WH m. read "having baptized". **in** = into. Ap. 104. vi. Denoting object and purpose. Cp. 3. 11. Acts 2. 38. **the name.** Sing. Not "names". This is the final definition of "the Name" of the One true God. **Father.** Ap. 98. III. **the Holy Ghost** = the Holy Spirit. Gr. *pneuma*. See Ap. 101. II. 3. **20 lo.** Fig. *Asterismos*. Ap. 6. **alway** = all the days. **unto** = until. **the end of the world** = the completion, or consummation, of the age: i.e. that then current dispensation, when this apostolic commission might have ended. See Ap. 129. 2, and note on 13. 39. But as Israel did not then repent (Acts 3. 19-26; 28. 25-28), hence all is postponed till Matt. 24. 14 shall be taken up and fulfilled, "then shall the end (*telos*) of the *sunteleia* come". This particular commission was therefore postponed. See Ap. 167. **world** = age. Gr. *aiōn*. Ap. 129. 2.

THE GOSPEL

ACCORDING TO

MARK.

THE STRUCTURE OF THE BOOK AS A WHOLE.

"BEHOLD MY SERVANT" (Isa. 42. 1).

(*Introversion.*)

B[1] (p. 1304)
A | 1. 1-8. THE FORERUNNER.
B | 1. 9-11. THE BAPTISM: WITH WATER.
C | 1. 12, 13. THE TEMPTATION: IN THE WILDERNESS.
D | E | 1. 14-20. THE KINGDOM } PROCLAIMED. } THE FOURFOLD MINISTRY OF THE LORD.
F | 1. 21—8. 30. THE KING } PROCLAIMED.
F | 8. 31—10. 52. THE KING } REJECTED.
E | 11. 1—14. 25. THE KINGDOM } REJECTED.
C | 14. 26-42. THE AGONY: IN THE GARDEN.
B | 14. 43—16. 14. THE BAPTISM: OF SUFFERING (DEATH, BURIAL, AND RESURRECTION).
A | 16. 15-20. THE SUCCESSORS.

For the New Testament and the order of the Books, see Ap. 95.
For the Inter-relation of the Four Gospels, see the Structure on p. 1304.
For the Diversity of the Four Gospels, see Ap. 96.
For the Unity of the Four Gospels, see Ap. 97.
For the Fourfold Ministry of the Lord, see Ap. 119.
For words used only in Mark, see some 70 recorded in the notes.

Mark is a Roman (Latin) surname. His Hebrew forename was John (Acts 12. 12). He was a cousin of Barnabas (Col. 4. 10). His mother's name was "Mary" (Acts 12. 12; see Ap. 100). What may be gathered of his history can be learnt only by the Scripture references to him (cp. Acts 4. 36; 12. 12; 13. 5, 13; 15. 37-39. Col. 4. 10. 2 Tim. 4. 11. Philem. *v.* 24. 1 Pet. 5. 13).

Mark was not the young man mentioned in ch. 14. 51, 52. See the notes there. His Gospel was not derived, as alleged, from any human sources; such assertions are at the best only conjectures. It was given to him, as Luke's Gospel was given to him, "from above" (Luke 1. 3). This precludes all theories about "copying" and human "inditing" and "transcribing". There are other reasons for the omission and inclusion of certain events, which depend on, and are to be gathered from, the Divine perfections of the Word of God. Such omissions and inclusions are to be explained by the special presentation of the Lord as Jehovah's Servant and not by the conflicting and uncertain speculations as to the "sources" of this Gospel.

To this special presentation of the Lord, in Mark, is due the fact that while He is addressed as "Lord" in the other three Gospels 73 times; by His disciples 37 times, and by others 36 times (5 of which are rendered "Sir"); He is addressed as such in the Gospel of Mark, *only twice*; once by the Woman (a Greek or Gentile), 7. 28, where it should be rendered "Sir"; and 9. 24, where "Lord" is omitted by all the critical texts (see Ap. 94. VI) as well as by the ancient Syriac Version (see Ap. 94, p. 136, note 3). Moreover, He is spoken of as such by the Holy Spirit through the Evangelist *only twice* (16. 19, 20), but that was *after His ascension into heaven.*

To this presentation of the Lord in this Gospel as Jehovah's servant, are due also the minute references to His activities, not only to what He said, but how He said it; what He did, and how He did it. These are not due to any "peculiarity" of the human writer, but to the Divine supplements of the Holy Spirit. Hence we are told:—

How the disciples were sent forth "two and two" (6. 7);
How the centurion "stood by, over against" the Lord (15. 39);
How the people were made to sit "in ranks" (6. 40);
How the Lord went to pray (1. 35);
How He withdrew "to the sea" (3. 7); and how He "sat in the boat, on the sea" (4. 1);
How He was in the stern, asleep "on a pillow" (4. 38); how He sat (12. 41; 13. 3).

We are told also of the fear, astonishment, and sore amazement of the disciples (4. 41; 6. 51; 10. 24, 26); and of the effect of the Lord's words and works on the People (2. 2; 3. 10, 20; 4. 1; 5. 21, 31; 6. 31, 33; 8. 1).

The activities and movements of "Jehovah's Servant" are always prominent, from the very "beginning"; which, without any preface, introduces the public ministry of the Lord, setting forth on the one hand the very height of His Divine power (1. 27, 31; 2. 12; 3. 10; 5. 29; 6. 56; 7. 37); and on the other the depth of His feelings as man—His fatigue, &c. (4. 38; 11. 12; 14. 36); His sympathies and compassion (6. 34; 8. 2); His love (10. 21); His composure (4. 38-40; 15. 5); His seeking solitude (1. 35; 6. 30-32); His wonder (6. 6); His grief (3. 5); His sighing (7. 34; 8. 12); His anger and displeasure (3. 5; 10. 14). See note on "immediately" (1. 12).

The four Gospels are treated in *The Companion Bible* not as four culprits brought up on a charge of fraud, but as four witnesses whose testimony is to be received.

THE GOSPEL

ACCORDING TO

MARK.

A A
(p. 1382)
A. D. 26

1 °THE beginning of the °gospel of °Jesus
Christ, °the Son of God;
2 °As °it is written °in the °prophets, "**Behold, I send My °messenger °before Thy face,
°which shall prepare Thy way °before Thee.**
**3 The voice of one crying [2]in the wilderness,
'Prepare ye the way of °the LORD, make His
paths straight.'"**

B 4 °John °did °baptize [2]in the wilderness,
and °preach the baptism °of °repentance °for
the remission of °sins.
5 And there °went out °unto him °all °the
°land of Judæa, and they of Jerusalem, and
were all [4]baptized °of him [2]in °the river of
Jordan, °confessing °their [4]sins.

B 6 And John was clothed with °camel's hair,
and with a girdle of a skin °about his loins;
and he did eat °locusts and °wild honey;

A 7 And [4]preached, saying, °"There cometh
One mightier than I °after me, the °latchet of
Whose °shoes I am °not °worthy to °stoop
down and unloose.
8 I indeed have [4]baptized you °with water:
but He shall [4]baptize you °with °the Holy
Ghost."

B C 9 And °it came to pass [2]in those days, that
°Jesus came °from °Nazareth of Galilee, and
was [4]baptized [5]of John °in Jordan.

D 10 And °straightway coming up °out of the
water, He saw the °heavens °opened,

D and °the Spirit °like a dove descending °upon
Him:

C 11 And there came a voice °from [10]heaven,
saying, "Thou art °My beloved Son, [2]in Whom
°I am well pleased."

1. 1-8 (A, p. 1381). THE FORERUNNER.
(*Introversion*.)

A | A | 1-3. Prophecy. By God, of John.
| B | 4, 5. John. His mission.
| *B* | 6. John. His person.
| *A* | 7, 8. Prophecy. By John, of Christ.

1 The beginning of the gospel. A Hebraism. No Article. Cp. Hos. 1. 2, "[The] beginning of the word of Jehovah by Hosea". It is the beginning, not of the book, but of the facts of the good news. See note on 8. 11.
gospel = glad tidings. See note on Matthew (Title).
Jesus Christ. See Ap. 98. XI.
the Son of God. See Ap. 98. XV.
2 As. T Tr. WH R read "According as".
it is written = it has been written; i.e. it standeth written. **in.** Gr. *en*. Ap. 104. viii.
prophets. Pl. because it is a composite quotation Mal. 3. 1. Isa. 40. 3. See Ap. 107. II. 4.
messenger = *angelos*.
before Thy face. A pure Hebraism (cp. Amos 9. 4, &c.). Unknown to pure Greek.
before. Gr. *pro*. Ap. 104. xiv. **which** = who.
before Thee. Omitted by L T Tr. WH R.
3 the LORD. Ap. 98. VI. i. α. 1. A. a.
4 John. Cp. Matt. 3. 1-6. Luke 3. 1-4.
did baptize = it came to pass John [was] baptizing.
baptize. See Ap. 115. I.
preach = was proclaiming, or heralding. Ap. 121. 1.
of. Gen. of Relation and Object. Ap. 17. 5.
repentance. See Ap. 111. II. 1.
for = resulting in. Gr. *eis*. Ap. 104. vi.
sins. See Ap. 128. II. 1.
5 went out = kept going out. Imperf. Tense.
unto. Gr. *pros*. Ap. 104. xv. 3.
all. Put by Fig. *Synecdochē* (of the Whole), Ap. 6, for all parts.
the land = country, or territory. Put by Fig. *Metonymy* (of Subject), Ap. 6, for the inhabitants.
of = by. Gr. *hupo*. Ap. 104. xviii. 1.
the river of Jordan. Occ. only in Mark.
confessing. See Matt. 3. 6. **their** = their own.
6 camel's hair. Not a skin, but a garment woven with camel's hair. Cp. 2 Kings 1. 8. **about.** Gr. *peri*. Ap. 104. xiii. 1. **locusts.** See note on Matt. 3. 4. **wild honey.** Plentiful then, and now. **7 There cometh One** = He Who cometh [is]. **after** = behind; as to time. Not the same as in *v.* 14. **latchet** = thong. **shoes** = sandals. To unloose the sandals of another was a proverbial expression. Fig. *Parœmia* (Ap. 6). Supplemental to "bear" in Matt. 3. 11. **not.** Gr. *ou*. Ap. 105. I. **worthy** = fit. **stoop down.** A Divine supplement. Occ. only here. **8 with.** Gr. *en*, as in *v.* 2. **the Holy Ghost.** Gr. *pneuma hagion* (without Articles) = "power from on high". See Ap. 101. II. 14.

1. 9-11 (B, p. 1381). THE BAPTISM: WITH WATER. (*Introversion*.)

B | C | 9. The Lord. His coming to John.
| D | 10-. Seen. The heavens opening.
| *D* | -10. Seen. The Dove descending.
| *C* | 11. The Lord. The Voice coming to Him.

9 it came to pass. A pure Hebraism. **Jesus.** Ap. 98. X. **from.** Gr. *apo*. Ap. 104. iv. Not the same as in *v.* 11. **Nazareth.** See Ap. 94. III. 3, and Ap. 169. **in** = into. Gr. *eis*. Ap. 104. vi. Not the same as in *vv.* 2, 3, 4, 5, 11, 13, 19, 20, 23, 39, 45. **10 straightway** = immediately. See note on *v.* 12. **out of** = away from. Gr. *apo*. Ap. 104. iv. But all the texts read *ek* = out of (Ap. 104. vii). **heavens.** Plural. See note on Matt. 6. 9, 10. **opened** = parting or rending asunder. **the Spirit.** Gr. *pneuma*. With Art. See Ap. 101. II. 3. **like** = as. **upon.** Gr. *epi*. Ap. 104. ix. 3. **11 from** = out of. Gr. *ek*. Ap. 104. vii. **My beloved Son** = My Son, the beloved. As in Matthew and Luke. **I am well pleased** = I have [ever] found delight.

C E (p. 1383) 12 And °immediately [10]the Spirit °driveth Him °into the wilderness.

F 13 And He was there [2]in the wilderness forty days, °tempted [5]of Satan;

F and was °with the wild beasts;

E and °the angels °ministered unto Him.

D E G[1] A. D. 27 14 Now °after that John was °put in prison, [9]Jesus came [12]into °Galilee, [4]preaching the [1]gospel of °the kingdom of God,
15 And saying, "The °time is fulfilled, and [14]the kingdom of God °is at hand: °repent ye, °and °believe °the [1]gospel."

G[2] a 16 Now as He °walked °by the sea of [14]Galilee, He saw °Simon and °Andrew his brother °casting a net °into the sea: for they were fishers.

b 17 And [9]Jesus said unto them, °"Come ye [7]after Me, and I will make you °to become fishers of men."

c 18 And [10]straightway they forsook their nets, and followed Him.

a 19 And when He had gone °a little farther °thence, He saw °James the *son* of °Zebedee, and °John his brother, who also were [2]in the ship °mending their nets

b 20 And [10]straightway °He called them:

c and they left their father [19]Zebedee [2]in the °ship [13]with the hired servants, and went [7]after Him.

F H[1] K[1] 21 And they went [12]into °Capernaum; and

1. 12, 13 (C, p. 1381). THE TEMPTATION: IN THE WILDERNESS. (*Introversion.*)

C | E | 12. The Spirit. Compulsion.
  F | 13-. Satan. Temptations.
  F | -13-. Wild beasts. Companionship.
  E | -13. The Angels. Ministration.

12 immediately. A word characteristic of this Gospel, setting forth as it does the activities of "Jehovah's Servant". The Greek words which it represents (in this and other renderings of *eutheōs* and *euthus*) are used (in Mark) twenty-six times directly of the Lord and His acts; while in Matthew they occur only five times, in Luke once, and in John twice.

driveth Him = driveth Him out. Divine supplemental information as to the character of the *leading* of Matthew and Luke.

into. Gr. *eis.* Ap. 104. vi. Not the same word as in *v.* 16.

13 tempted = being tempted.

with the wild beasts. A Divine supplementary particular. Occ. only here.

with. Gr. *meta.* Ap. 104. xi. 1.

the angels, &c. See note on Matt. 4. 11, and Ap. 116.

ministered = were ministering.

1. 14—14. 25 (D, p. 1381). THE LORD'S FOUR-FOLD MINISTRY. (See Ap. 119.) (*Introversion.*)

D | E | 1. 14–20. THE FIRST PERIOD. Subject: The Proclamation of THE KINGDOM.
  F | 1. 21—8. 30. THE SECOND PERIOD. Subject: The Proclamation of THE KING. His Person.
  F | 8. 31—10. 52. THE THIRD PERIOD. Subject: The Rejection of THE KING.
  E | 11. 1—14. 25. THE FOURTH PERIOD. Subject: The Rejection of THE KINGDOM.

1. 14-20 (E, above). THE FIRST PERIOD OF THE MINISTRY. THE KINGDOM PROCLAIMED. (*Division.*)

E | G[1] | 14, 15. The Proclamation of the Kingdom.
  G[2] | 16–20. The Calling of Four Disciples.

14 after. Gr. *meta.* Ap. 104. xi. 2. This commences the first subject of the Lord's ministry, which occupies in Mark only six verses. See Ap. 119. **put in prison** = was delivered up. **Galilee.** Ap. 169. **the kingdom of God.** See Ap. 114. **15 time** = season. **is at hand** = has drawn near (for the setting up of the kingdom). Cp. Gal. 4. 4. **repent.** See Ap. 111. I. 1. **and believe the gospel.** A Divine supplement to Matt. 4. 17. **believe.** See Ap. 150. I. v. (ii). Here followed by the Gr. Prep. *en.* Ap. 104. viii. **the** = in the.

1. 16-20 (G[2], above). THE CALLING OF FOUR DISCIPLES. (*Extended Alternation.*)

G[2] | a | 16. Two brethren. Simon and Andrew.
  b | 17. Their call.
  c | 18. Their obedience.
  a | 19. Two brethren. James and John.
  b | 20-. Their call.
  c | -20. Their obedience.

16 walked = was walking. **by** = beside. Gr. *para.* Ap. 104. xii. 3. **Simon and Andrew.** See Ap. 141. **casting a net.** The word "net" is included and implied in the Verb. All the texts omit the Noun. **into** = in. Gr. *en*, as in *v.* 2. **17 Come.** This call explains Acts 1. 21, 22. The official mission comes later, in 3. 17, &c. **to become fishers of men.** The likeness is not conveyed by the Fig. *Similē*, or stated by *Metaphor*, but is implied by the Fig. *Hypocatastasis.* See Ap. 6. **19 a little farther.** A Divine supplement, here. **thence.** Omitted by [L] T Tr. A WH R. **James . . . John.** See Ap. 141. **Zebedee.** Aramaic. Ap. 94. III. 3. **mending.** See note on Matt. 4. 21. **20 He called.** See note on "Come" (*v.* 17). **ship** = boat. **with the hired servants.** A Divine supplement in Mark. **21 Capernaum.** See Ap. 169.

1. 21—8. 30 (F, above). THE SECOND PERIOD OF THE LORD'S MINISTRY: THE PROCLAMATION OF THE KING. HIS PERSON. (See Ap. 119.) (*Repeated Alternation.*)

F | H[1] | 1. 21—2. 12. Teaching and Miracles.
  J[1] | 2. 13–22. Call of Levi.
  H[2] | 2. 23—3. 12. Teaching and Miracles.
  J[2] | 3. 13–19-. Calling of the Twelve.
  H[3] | 3. -19—6. 6. Teaching and Miracles.
  J[3] | 6. 7–30. Mission of the Twelve.
  H[4] | 6. 31—8. 30. Teaching and Miracles.

1. 21—2. 12 (H[1], above). TEACHING AND MIRACLES. (*Repeated Alternation.*)

H[1] | K[1] | 1. 21, 22. Teaching. With authority as Lord.
  L[1] | 1. 23–34. Miracles: Unclean spirit (23–28); Fever (29–31); Many (32–34).
  K[2] | 1. 35–39. Teaching, and exercising authority.
  L[2] | 1. 40–45. Miracle: The Leper.
  K[3] | 2. 1, 2. Teaching. The Word of God.
  L[3] | 2. 3–12. Miracle: Palsy, and Divine Act. Forgiveness of sins.

A. D. 27 [10]straightway on the sabbath day He entered
[12]into the synagogue, and °taught.
22 And they were astonished °at His doctrine: for °He taught them as one that had
authority, and [7]not as the scribes.

L[1] (p. 1383) 23 And there was [2]in their °synagogue a
°man [8]with an unclean °spirit; and he °cried
out,
24 Saying, "Let *us* alone; °what have we
to do with Thee, Thou [9]Jesus °of Nazareth?
art Thou come to destroy us? °I know Thee
Who Thou art, °the Holy One of God."
25 And [9]Jesus rebuked him, saying, °"Hold
thy peace, and come °out of him."
26 And when the unclean [23]spirit had °torn
him, and °cried with a loud °voice, he came
[25]out of him.
27 And they were all amazed, insomuch that
they questioned °among themselves, saying,
"What thing is this? what °new °doctrine *is*
this? for °with authority commandeth He
even the unclean [23]spirits, and they do obey
Him."
28 And [12]immediately His °fame spread
abroad °throughout all the region round about
[14]Galilee.
29 And °forthwith, when they were come
[25]out of the [23]synagogue, they entered [12]into
the house of Simon and Andrew, [13]with James
and John.
30 But Simon's wife's mother °lay sick °of
a fever, and °anon they tell Him °of her.
31 And °He came and °took her by the hand,
and lifted her up; and [12]immediately the fever
left her, and she °ministered unto them.
32 And at even, °when the sun did set, they
°brought [5]unto Him all °that were diseased,
and them that were °possessed with devils.
33 And °all the city °was gathered together
°at the door.
34 And He healed many that were sick of
divers diseases, and cast out many °devils;
and suffered [7]not the °devils to speak, because
they [24]knew Him.

K[2] 35 And in the morning, rising up °a great
while before °day, He went out, and departed
[12]into °a solitary place, and there °prayed.
36 And Simon and they that were [13]with
Him °followed after Him.
37 And when they had found Him, they said
unto Him, [33]°"All *men* °seek for Thee."
38 And He said unto them, "Let us go [12]into
the °next °towns, that I may [4]preach there
also: for °therefore °came I forth."
39 And He [4]preached °in their synagogues
°throughout all [14]Galilee, and cast out [34]devils.

L[2] 40 And there came °a leper °to Him, beseeching Him, and kneeling down to Him, and saying unto Him, °"If Thou °wilt, Thou canst
make me clean."
41 And [9]Jesus, °moved with compassion, put
forth *His* hand, and touched him, and saith
unto him, "I [40]will; be thou °clean."
42 And as soon as He had spoken, [12]imme-
diately the leprosy departed [9]from him, and he
was cleansed.
43 And He °straitly charged him, and [29]forth-
with sent him away;
44 And saith unto him, °"See thou say no-

taught = began teaching.
22 at. Gr. *epi*. Ap. 104. ix. 2.
He taught. Referring to the character of His teaching as setting Him forth as Divine. See note on Matt. 7. 29.
23 synagogue. See Ap. 120. I.
man. Gr. *anthrōpos*. Ap. 123. 1.
spirit. Gr. *pneuma*. See Ap. 101. II. 12.
cried = shouted.
24 what have we to do with Thee? See note on 2 Sam. 16. 10.
of Nazareth = [the] Nazarene. Ap. 94. III. 3, and 169.
I know. Gr. *oida*. Ap. 132. I. i. The man said this, the evil spirit moving him.
the Holy One of God. Thus again the Person of the Lord is declared. Cp. Ps. 16. 10. Luke 1. 35.
25 Hold thy peace = Be silent. Cp. Matt. 22. 12.
out of. Gr. *ek*. Ap. 104. vii.
26 torn him = thrown him into convulsions.
cried . . . voice. A Divine supplement, here.
27 among. Gr. *pros*. Ap. 104. xv. 3.
new. New in character, not in time. Gr. *kainos*. See notes on Matt. 9. 17; 26. 29; 27. 60.
doctrine = teaching.
with. Gr. *kata*. Ap. 104. x. 2. Not the same word as in *vv.* 8, 13, 20, 23, 29, 36.
28 fame = hearing, or report. Put by Fig. *Metonymy* (of the Effect), Ap. 6, for what was heard.
throughout = into. Gr. *eis*. Ap. 104. vi.
29 forthwith = immediately, as in *vv.* 12, 28, 31, 42. See note on *v.* 12.
30 lay = was lying.
of, &c. = in a fever.
anon = immediately, as "forthwith" (*v.* 29), above.
of = about. Gr. *peri*. Ap. 104. xiii. 1.
31 He came. On the same sabbath.
took her by the hand. A Divine supplement, here.
ministered = began ministering.
32 when the sun did set. A Divine supplement, here.
brought = kept bringing.
that were diseased. Cp. Matt. 4. 23, 24.
possessed with devils = possessed with demons. Gr. *daimonizomai*. Derivation uncertain. See note on Matt. 8. 16, 28.
33 all. Put by Fig. *Synecdochē* (of Genus), Ap. 6, for the greater part.
was gathered, &c. A Divine supplement, here.
at = to. Gr. *pros*. Ap. 104. xv. 3.
34 devils = demons. See note on *v.* 32.
35 a great . . . day = while yet night. Gr. *ennuchon*. A Divine supplement, here.
a solitary place = a desert place.
prayed = was praying.
36 followed after. Gr. *katadiōkō*. A Divine supplement, here.
37 All, &c. A Divine supplement, here.
seek = are seeking.
38 next = neighbouring.
towns = country towns, or villages.
therefore = for (Gr. *eis*. Ap. 104. vi) this.
came I forth = am I come forth.
39 in. Gr. *en*. Ap. 104. viii. 3.
throughout = in. Gr. *eis*. Ap. 104. vi.
40 a leper. See note on Ex. 4. 6.
to. Gr. *pros*. Ap. 104. xv. 3.
If Thou wilt. A condition of uncertainty with probability. Ap. 118. 1. b.
wilt. Gr. *thelo*. Ap. 102. 1.
41 moved with compassion. A Divine supplement, here.
clean = cleansed.
43 straitly = strictly.
44 See. Ap. 133. I. 8.

A. D. 27 thing to any man: but go thy way, °shew
thyself to the °priest, and offer °for thy cleansing those things which °Moses commanded,
[4]for a testimony unto them."
45 But he went out, and began to °publish *it*
much, and to blaze abroad the matter, insomuch that [9]Jesus °could no more openly enter
[12]into °the city, but was without °in desert
places: and they °came [40]to Him from every
quarter.

K[3] (p. 1383)
2 And again He entered °into Capernaum
°after *some* days; and it was °noised
°that He was °in the house.
2 And °straightway many were gathered together, insomuch that there was °no room to
receive *them*, °no, not so much as °about the
door: and He °preached the word unto them.
L[3] 3 And they come °unto Him, bringing one
°sick of the °palsy, which was borne °of four.
4 And when they °could °not °come nigh
unto Him °for the °press, they °uncovered the
roof where He was: and when they had °bro-
ken *it* up, they let down the °bed °wherein the
[3]sick of the palsy lay.
5 When °Jesus °saw °their faith, He said unto
[3]the sick of the palsy, °"Son, °thy °sins be
forgiven thee."
6 But there were certain of the scribes sitting
there, and reasoning °in their hearts,
7 "Why doth this *man* thus speak blasphemies? who can forgive [5]sins °but °God
only?"
8 And °immediately when [5]Jesus °perceived
°in His spirit that they so reasoned °within
themselves, He said unto them, "Why reason
ye these things [6]in your hearts?
9 °Whether is it easier to say to [4]the sick of
the palsy, '*Thy* [5]sins be forgiven thee'; or to
say, 'Arise, and take up thy [4]bed, and walk?'
10 But that ye may °know that °the Son of
man hath °power °on earth to forgive [5]sins,"
(He saith to [3]the sick of the palsy,)
11 "I say unto thee, Arise, and take up thy
[4]bed, and go thy way [1]into thine house."
12 And [8]immediately he arose, took up the
[4]bed, and went forth before them all; insomuch that they were all amazed, and glorified [7]God, saying, "We never [5]saw it on this
fashion."
J[1] M[1] (p. 1385) 13 And He went forth again °by the sea
side; and all the multitude °resorted [3]unto
Him, and He °taught them.
14 And as He passed by, He [5]saw °Levi °the
son of °Alphæus sitting °at the receipt of custom, and said unto him, "Follow Me." And
he arose and followed Him.
M[2] d (p. 1386) 15 °And it came to pass, that, as [5]Jesus °sat
at meat [6]in °his house, many °publicans and

shew . . . priest. Ref. to Pent. (Lev. 14. 1-32). Ap. 117. I.
for = concerning. Gr. *peri*. Ap. 104. xiii. 1.
Moses. Occ. eight times in Mark: 1. 44; 7. 10; 9. 4, 5; 10. 3, 4; 12. 19, 26. See note on Matt. 8. 4.
45 publish = proclaim. Same word as "preach" in *vv.* 4, 7, 14, 38, 39. See Ap. 121. 1.
could no more = was no longer able to.
the city = any city.
in. Gr. *en*, as in *v.* 2. But T Tr. WH read *epi*. Ap. 104. ix. 2.
came = kept coming.

2. 1 into. Gr. *eis*. Ap. 104. vi.
after. Gr. *dia*. Ap. 104. v. 1.
noised = reported.
that He was in the house = "He is [gone] into the house [and is there]".
in. Gr. *eis* (as above).
2 straightway = immediately. See note on 1. 12. Omitted by [L Tr.] T WH R.
no room = no longer any room.
no . . . about = no, not even (*mēde mēketi*) at (Gr. *pros*. Ap. 104. xv. 3) the door.
preached = was speaking (when what follows took place).
3 unto. Gr. *pros*. Ap. 104. xv. 3.
sick . . . palsy = a paralytic.
of = by. Gr. *hupo*. Ap. 104. xviii. 1.
4 could not = were not able to.
not. Gr. *mē*. Ap. 105. II.
come nigh unto. Gr. *proseggizō*. Occ. only here in N.T.
for the press. The 1611 edition of the A.V. reads "for press".
for = on account of. Gr. *dia*. Ap. 104. v. 2.
press = crowd.
uncovered. Easily done in an Eastern house. Occ. only here in N.T. [Gal. 4. 15.
broken it up. Gr. *exorussō*. Occ. only here and
bed = couch, or pallet. Gr. *krabbaton*, a Latin word. A poor man's bed. Not the same word as in 4. 21.
wherein = on which. Gr. *epi*. Ap. 104. ix. 2.
5 Jesus. Ap. 98. X.
saw. Gr. *eidon*. Ap. 133. I. 1.
their faith. We cannot exclude the faith of the paralytic himself, who had doubtless persuaded the four to do this for him.
Son. Gr. *teknon*. See Ap. 108. i.
thy sins be forgiven thee. Thus proclaiming His Deity, being the second subject of His Ministry. See Ap. 119.
sins. See Ap. 128. II. 1.
6 in. Gr. *en*. Ap. 104. viii. 1.
7 but God only = except One [that is] God.
God. Ap. 98. I. i. 1.
8 immediately. A key-word of this Gospel, to mark the activities of Jehovah's Servant. See note on 1. 12.
perceived. Gr. *epiginōskō*. Ap. 132. I. 3.
in His spirit = in Himself. Gr. *pneuma*. See Ap. 101 II. 9.
within = or among. Gr. *en*. Ap. 104. viii. 2.
9 Whether is it . . . ? = Which is . . . ?
10 know = see. Ap. 133. I. 1.
the Son of man. See Ap. 98. XVI. Thus setting forth His Person, which is the subject of this second period. See **F**, p. 1383; and Ap. 119. Cp. Matt. 8. 20. The first occurrence of this title in Mark. Cp. the last (14. 62).
power = authority. Ap. 172. 5.
on. Gr. *epi*. Ap. 104. ix. 1.

2. 13-22 (J[1], p. 1383). THE CALL OF LEVI. *(Division.)*

J[1]	M[1]	13, 14.	The Lord's Call.
	M[2]	15-22.	Levi's feast.

13 by = beside. Gr. *para*. Ap. 104. xii. 3.
resorted . . . taught = kept coming . . . kept teaching.
14 Levi. Probably his former name before changing it to "Matthew" = the gift of God (Matt. 9. 9).
the son of Alphæus. Occ. only here (i. e. in connection with Levi) in N.T.
Alphæus. Aramaic. See Ap. 94. III. 3.
at = in charge of. Gr. *epi*. Ap. 104. ix. 3.

2. 15-22 [For Structure see next page].

15 And it came to pass. A Hebraism.
sat at meat = reclined [at table].
his house: i.e. Levi's. Not the Lord's. Cp. Matt. 8. 20.
publicans = tax-gatherers.

A.D. 27 °sinners sat also together with [5]Jesus and His disciples: for there were many, and they followed Him.

16 And when the scribes °and Pharisees [5]saw Him °eat °with [15]publicans and [15]sinners, they °said unto His disciples, °"How is it that He eateth and drinketh °with [15]publicans and [15]sinners?"

e (p. 1386) 17 When [5]Jesus heard *it*, He saith unto them, "They that are °whole have °no need of °the physician, but they that are sick: I came °not to call °the righteous, but [15]sinners °to repentance."

d 18 And the disciples of John and of the [16]Pharisees °used to fast: and they come and say unto Him, "Why do the disciples of John and of the [16]Pharisees fast, but Thy disciples fast [17]not?"

e 19 And [5]Jesus said unto them, "Can the °children of the bridechamber fast, while the °bridegroom is [16]with them? as long as they have the bridegroom [16]with them, they °cannot fast.

20 But the days will come, when the [19]bridegroom shall be taken °away from them, and then shall they fast [6]in those days.

21 [17]No man also °seweth a piece of °new cloth °on an old garment: else the °new piece that filled it up taketh away from the old, and the rent is made worse.

22 And [17]no man putteth °new wine [1]into old °bottles: else the °new wine doth burst the °bottles, and the wine is spilled, and the °bottles will be °marred: but °new wine must be put [1]into [21]new °bottles."

N^1 f 23 [15]And it came to pass, that He went °through the corn fields °on the sabbath day;

g and His disciples began, °as they went, °to pluck the ears of corn.

g 24 And the [16]Pharisees [16]said unto Him, °"Behold, why do they [23]on the sabbath day that which is [17]not lawful?"

f 25 And He said unto them, °"Have ye °never read what David did, when he °had need, and was an hungred, he, and they that were [16]with him?

26 How he went [1]into the house of [7]God °in the days of °Abiathar the high priest, and did eat °the shewbread, which is [17]not lawful to eat °but for the priests, and °gave also to them which were °with him?"

27 And He said unto them, "The °sabbath °was made [4]for °man, °and [17]not °man [4]for the °sabbath:

2. 15-22 (M^2, p. 1385). LEVI'S FEAST.
(*Alternation.*)

M^2 | d | 15, 16. Question of Pharisees.
  e | 17. Answer. Proverb.
  d | 18. Question of John's disciples.
  e | 19–22. Answer. Proverbs.

sinners. Gr. pl. of *hamartōlos.* Cp. Ap. 128. I. 1.
sinners sat also = sinners also sat.
16 and Pharisees. L and Tr. read "of the Pharisees". Ap. 120. II.
eat = eating.
with. Gr. *meta.* Ap. 104. xi. 1.
said = kept saying.
How is it . . . ? = Why [doth] . . . ?
17 whole = strong, or able.
no. Gr. *ou.* Ap. 105. I. The emph. is on "no need".
the = a.
not. Gr. *ou*, as above.
the righteous = righteous ones.
to = for. Gr. *eis.* Ap. 104. vi.
18 used to fast = were fasting: i.e. were then observing a fast. It is not the custom that is referred to, but the fact.
19 children, &c. = sons, &c. Ap. 108. iii. A Hebraism, referring to the guests, not to the "friends" (or groomsmen) of John 3. 29.
bridegroom. The Lord, here, refers to Himself.
cannot = are not (as in *v.* 17) able to.
20 away from. Gr. *apo.* Ap. 104. iv.
21 seweth . . . on. Gr. *epirraptō.* Occ. only here.
new = unfulled.
on = upon. Gr. *epi.* Ap. 104. ix. 2.
new = new (in character). Gr. *kainos.* See note on Matt. 9. 17.
22 new = fresh made. Gr. *neos.* See note on Matt. 26. 28, 29.
bottles = wine-skins.
marred = destroyed.

2. 23—3. 12 (H^2, p. 1383). TEACHING AND MIRACLES. (*Division.*)

H^2 | N^1 | 2. 23–28. Teaching. } "Lord of the Sabbath."
  N^2 | 3. 1–12. Miracles. }

2. 23-28 (N^1, above). TEACHING.
(*Introversion.*)

N^1 | f | 23–. The Sabbath Day.
  g | –23. Disciples. Action of.
  g | 24. Disciples. Objection to.
  f | 25–28. The Sabbath Day.

23 through. Gr. *dia.* Ap. 104. v. 1.
on = in, or during. Gr. *en.* Ap. 104. viii. 1.
as they went. Gr. to make their way. A Hebraism. See Judg. 17. 8 (marg.): = as they journeyed; not to make a path by destroying the stalks of corn, but only plucking "the ears".
to pluck, &c. Ref. to Pent. (Deut. 23. 25). Cp. Ap. 92. A recognised custom to this present day, not only for travellers, but for their horses. So with grapes (Deut. 23. 24).
24 Behold = Look. Ap. 133. I. 3.
25 Have ye never read . . . ? = Did ye never read . . . ? See Ap. 143. Fig. *Anteisagogē*, Ap. 6.
never = not (as in *v.* 17).
had need. A Divine supplement to "was hungry" (Matthew and Luke). Occ. only in Mark. "Had need" is *generic*, and "was hungered" is *specific* (explaining the need). **26 in the days of.** Gr. *epi.* Ap. 104. ix. 1. **Abiathar.** Called Ahimelech in 1 Sam. 21. 1; 22. 9, 11, 20; and Ahiah in 1 Sam. 14. 3. The father and his son Abiathar must have had two names, as was frequently the case. And why not, as in our own day? In 2 Sam. 8. 17, and 1 Chron. 18. 16, we have Ahimelech the son of Abiathar; and in 1 Sam. 22. 20 Abiathar is the son of Ahimelech (who was the son of Ahitub). There is no "confusion in the Heb. text". The Lord's enemies are the best witnesses of this, for they would not have missed such an opportunity of effective reply (see 3. 6). *They* knew what modern critics do not know. **the shewbread.** Ref. to Pent. (Ex. 25. 30; 35. 13; 39. 36. Lev. 24. 5–9). Cp 2 Chron. 13. 11. See Ap. 92 and 117. I. **but** = except. To eat this was the priest's first duty *on the Sabbath.* **gave also** = gave to them also. **with.** Gr. *sun.* Ap. 104. xvi. **27 sabbath.** Note the Figure *Antimetabolē* (Ap. 6), "sabbath . . . man . . . man . . . sabbath". **was made** = came into being. **man.** Gr. *anthrōpos.* Ap. 123. 1. **and.** All the texts omit "and". In that case, note the Fig. *Asyndeton* (Ap. 6).

A. D. 27 28 °Therefore [10]the Son of man °is °Lord also of the sabbath."

N² O (p. 1387) 3 °And He entered °again °into the °synagogue; and there was a °man there which had °a withered hand.

P 2 And they °watched Him, °whether He would heal him on the sabbath day; °that they might accuse Him.

Q 3 And He saith unto the [1]man which had [1]the withered hand, °"Stand forth."
4 And He saith unto them, "Is it °lawful to do good on the sabbath days, or to °do evil? to save °life, or to kill?" But they held their peace.
5 And when He had °looked round about on them °with anger, °being grieved °for the °hardness of their hearts, He saith unto the [1]man, "Stretch forth thine hand." And he stretched *it* out: and his hand was restored whole as the °other.

P 6 And the Pharisees went forth, and °straightway °took counsel [5]with the °Herodians °against Him, how they might destroy Him.

O h 7 But °Jesus °withdrew Himself [5]with His disciples °to the sea:

i and a °great multitude °from °Galilee followed Him, and °from Judæa,
8 And [7]from Jerusalem, and [7]from °Idumæa, and *from* beyond Jordan; and they °about Tyre and Sidon, a [7]great multitude, when they had heard what great things He °did, came °unto Him.

h 9 And He spake to His °disciples, that a small ship should wait on Him

i °because of the °multitude, °lest they should throng Him.
10 For He had healed many; insomuch that they °pressed upon Him °for to touch Him, as many as had plagues.
11 And unclean °spirits, when they °saw Him, fell down before Him, and °cried, saying, °"Thou art °the Son of God."
12 And He straitly °charged them that they should °not make Him °known.

J² j (p. 1388) 13 And He goeth up [1]into °a mountain, and calleth *unto Him* whom °He °would: and they °came [8]unto Him.

k 14 And He °ordained twelve, °that they should °be [5]with Him,

k and that He °might °send them forth to °preach,

---

28 Therefore = So then.
is Lord. Ap. 98. VI. i. *α*. 2. B. a. This is the subject of this second period of the Lord's ministry. See Ap. 119.
Lord also of the sabbath = Lord of the Sabbath also. Occ. only here.

3. 1-12 (N², p. 1386). MIRACLE. (*Introversion.*)

N² | O | 1. Miracle of the hand withered.
  P | 2. | Enemies watching.
   Q | 3-5. The hand healed.
  P | 6. Enemies plotting.
 O | 7-12. Miracles. Many.

1 And. Note the Fig. *Polysyndeton* in *vv.* 1-4. Ap. 6.
again: i. e. on another Sabbath. Prob. the next.
into. Gr. *eis*. Ap. 104. vi.
synagogue. See Ap. 120.
man. Gr. *anthrōpos*. Ap. 123. 1.
a withered hand = his hand withered. Cp. Matt. 12. 10.
2 watched = were watching.
whether = if. Implying that they had no doubt about it. Ap. 118. 2. a. **that** = in order that.
3 Stand forth = Rise up [and come] into (as in *v.* 1) the midst.
4 lawful = more lawful. Fig. *Heterōsis* (of Degree), Ap. 6.
do evil. Gr. *kakopoieō*. Cp. Ap. 128. II. 2. and III. 2.
life = soul. Gr. *psuchē*. See Ap. 110. III. 1.
5 looked round. Noting the minutest action of Jehovah's Servant. **with.** Gr. *meta*. Ap. 104. xi. 1.
being grieved. Implying sadness accompanying the anger. A Divine supplement, here.
for = at. Gr. *epi*. Ap. 104. ix. 2.
hardness = hardening. Gr. *pōrōsis*. Occ. only here, Rom. 11. 25, and Eph. 4. 18.
other. Gr. *allos*. Ap. 124. 1.
6 straightway = immediately. See note on 1. 12.
took counsel. See note on Matt. 12. 14.
Herodians. Occ. only here and 12. 13 in Mark, and in Matt. 22. 16. **against.** Gr. *kata*. Ap. 104. x. 1.

3. 7-12 (*O*, above). MIRACLES. MANY. (*Alternation.*)

O | h | 7-. The Sea. Withdrawal to.
  i | -7, 8. Multitudes following.
 h | 9-. The Ship. Order concerning.
  i | -9-12. Multitudes healed.

7 Jesus. Ap. 98. X.
withdrew. Note other withdrawals in Mark (3. 7; 6. 31, 46; 7. 24, 31; 9. 2; 10. 1; 14. 32). Not the same verbs.
to = toward. Gr. *pros*. Ap. 104. xv. 3. L T Tr. m. read "unto". (Gr. *eis*. Ap. 104. vi.)
great. Emph. on "great". Cp. *v.* 8.
from = away from. Gr. *apo*. Ap. 104. iv.
Galilee. See Ap. 169.
8 Idumæa. South of Judæa and Dead Sea.
about. Gr. *peri*. Ap. 104. xiii. 3.
did = was doing. **unto.** Gr. *pros*. Ap. 104. xv. 3.
9 disciples. See note on 6. 30.
because of = on account of. Gr. *dia*. Ap. 104. v. 2.
multitude = crowd. Not the same word as in *vv.* 7, 8.
lest they should = that they might not. Gr. *hina mē*. Ap. 105. II.
10 pressed upon = were besetting.
for to touch = that they might touch.
11 spirits. Gr. pl. of *pneuma*. See Ap. 101. II. 11, or 12.
saw = beheld. Ap. 133. I. 11. **cried** = cried out.
Thou art, &c. A Divine supplement, here, because agreeing with the second subject of the Lord's ministry. See Ap. 119. **the Son of God.** Ap. 98. XV. **12 charged.** Under penalty. **not.** Gr. *mē*. Ap. 105. II. **known** = manifest. Gr. *phaneros*. See Ap. 106. I. viii.

3. 13-19 [For Structure see next page.]

13 a = the. Some well-known resort. **He** = He Himself. **would** = willed. Gr. *thelō*. Ap. 102. 1. Cp. John 15. 16. **came** = went, leaving all. **14 ordained** = made, or appointed. In the sense of Heb. *'āsāh*, in 1 Sam. 12. 6 ("advanced"). **that** = in order that. **be with Him.** This is the first great qualification for any thus called and sent. (1) Like Abel, to have "peace with God"; then (2) like Enoch, to "walk with God", and (3) like Noah, to witness for God (Heb. 11. 4-7). **might** = should. **send them forth** = Gr. *apostellō*. This is the second great qualification here. For the others, see above and Acts 1. 22. **preach.** Ap. 121. 1.

A. D. 27 15 And to have °power to heal sicknesses,
and to cast out °devils:
j 16 And Simon He °surnamed °Peter;
(p. 1388) 17 And James the *son* of °Zebedee, and John
the brother of James; and He [16]surnamed
them °Boanerges, which is, The °sons of
°thunder:
18 And °Andrew, and Philip, and °Bartholomew, and °Matthew, and °Thomas, and
James the *son* of Alphæus, and °Thaddæus,
and Simon the °Canaanite,
19 And Judas Iscariot, which °also betrayed
Him:

H³ R T and they went [1]into an house.

U 20 And the [9]multitude cometh together °again,
so that they °could °not so much as eat bread.

V W Y h 21 And when His °friends heard *of it,*

i they °went out to lay hold on Him: for °they
said,

Z "He is °beside Himself."

X j 22 And the °scribes which came down [7]from
Jerusalem said,

k "He hath °Beelzebub, and °by the prince of
the devils casteth He out [15]devils."

X k 23 And He called them *unto Him,* and °said
unto them °in parables, "How can Satan cast
out Satan?
24 And °if a kingdom be divided °against
itself, that kingdom °cannot stand.
25 And [24]if a house be divided [24]against itself,
that house [24]cannot stand.
26 And °if Satan °rise up [24]against himself,
and be divided, he [24]cannot stand, but °hath
an end.

3. 13-19- (J², p. 1383). THE MISSION OF THE TWELVE. (*Introversion.*)

J² | j | 13. The Twelve. Their Calling.
  k | 14-. To be with Him. } The purpose.
  k | -14, 15. To be sent forth. }
j | 16-19-. The Twelve. Their naming.

15 power = authority. Ap. 172. 5.
devils = demons.
16 surnamed = added [the] name. See Ap. 141.
Peter. Only his *naming* given here; not his *appointment.* In Mark; Peter, James, and John are kept in a group. In Matthew and Luke, Andrew is placed between.
17 Zebedee. See note on 1. 19.
Boanerges. Occ. only in Mark. Aramaic. See Ap. 94. III. 3.
sons of. A pure Hebraism, used with reference to origin, destination, or characteristic. Sparks are "sons of fire" (Job 5. 7); threshed corn is "a son of the floor" (Isa. 21. 10); Judas "a son of perdition" (John 17. 12); sinners' natural condition "sons of disobedience" (Eph. 2. 2; 5. 6).
thunder. The name is Aramaic (Ap. 94. III. 3), allied to Heb. In Heb. "thunder" is *kōl* = voice: i. e. the voice of God (Ex. 9. 23. Ps. 29. 3. Jer. 10. 13).
18 Andrew. A name of Gr. origin = manly. The first called. See Matt. 4. 18, 20. John 1. 40, 41.
Bartholomew. One (Aramaic. Ap. 94. III. 3) of two names, the other being Nathanael (John 1. 45-51). John connects Philip with Nathanael; in the other Gospels, with Bartholomew. Bartholomew is not mentioned in John 21. 2, Nathanael is. The other Gospels mention Bartholomew but not Nathanael.
Matthew. Aramaic. Ap. 94. III. 3.
Thomas. Aramaic. Ap. 94. III. 3. In Gr. = *Didymos* (John 11. 16).
Thaddæus (or Lebbæus as in Matt. 10. 3). He is the Judas of John 14. 22, both words having the same meaning = beloved child. Aramaic. Ap. 94. III. 3.
Canaanite = Canaanæan or Zealot = one who regarded the presence of the Romans as treason against Jehovah.
19 also betrayed Him = even delivered Him up.

3. -19-6. 6 (H³, p. 1383). TEACHING AND MIRACLES. (*Introversion.*)

H³ | R | 3. -19—4. 34. Teaching.
  S | 4. 35—5. 43. Miracles.
R | 6. 1-6. Teaching.

3. -19—4. 34 (R, p. 1388). TEACHING. (*Extended Alternation.*)

R | T | 3. -19. Place. In the house.
  U | 3. 20. Concourse.
  V | 3. 21-33. The Lord with friends and enemies.
T | 4. 1-. Place. By the seaside.
  U | 4. -1. Concourse.
  V | 4. 2-34. The Lord with His disciples.

20 again. Referring back to *v.* 7. **could not** = found themselves unable. **not.** Gr. *mē.* Ap. 105. II.

3. 21-33 (U, above). THE LORD WITH FRIENDS AND ENEMIES. (*Introversions and Alternation.*)

V | W | Y | h | 21-. His kinsfolk. Hearing report.
  i | -21-. Their setting out. Object.
  Z | -21. Their disparagement of Him.
X | j | 22-. First charge. } The Scribes:
  k | -22. Second charge. } their charge.
X | *k* | 23-27. Second charge. } The Lord:
  j | 28-30. First charge. } His reply.
W | *Y* | *i* | 31-. Their arrival.
  h | -31, 32. His kinsfolk. Sending message.
  Z | 33-35. His disparagement of them.

21 friends = kinsfolk. "His brethren, and His mother" (see *v.* 31). **went out** = set out. **they said** = they were saying (Imperf. Tense): i. e. maintained (as we say). **beside Himself** = out of His senses. **22 scribes.** Others also came, with hostile intent. **Beelzebub.** See note on Matt. 10. 25. **by.** Gr. *en.* Ap. 104. viii. 1. **23 said** = began saying. **in.** Gr. *en.* Ap. 104. viii. 1. **24 if a kingdom, &c.** Implying what experience shows (Ap. 118. 1. b). **against.** Gr. *epi.* Ap. 104. ix. 3. **cannot** = is not (Gr. *ou.* Ap. 105. I) able to. **26 if Satan, &c.** Assuming such a case. Ap. 118. 2. a. **rise up** = hath risen up. **hath an end.** A Divine supplement. Occ. only in Mark.

A. D. 27 27 °No man can enter [1]into °a strong man's
house, and °spoil his °goods, except he will
first bind the strong man; and then he will
°spoil his house.

j (p. 1388) 28 °Verily I say unto you, All °sins shall be
forgiven unto °the sons of [1]men, and blasphemies wherewith soever they shall blaspheme:
29 But he that shall blaspheme °against °the
Holy Ghost hath °never forgiveness, but is in
danger of °eternal °damnation:"
30 °Because [21] they said, "He hath an unclean
[11]spirit."

W Y i 31 There came then °His brethren °and His
mother,

h and, standing °without, sent [8] unto Him, calling
Him.
32 And the [9] multitude °sat [8] about Him, and
they said unto Him, °"Behold, Thy mother
and Thy brethren without seek for Thee."

Z 33 And He answered them, saying, "Who is
My mother, or My brethren?"
34 And He °looked round about on them
which °sat [8] about Him, and said, °"Behold
My mother and My brethren!
35 For whosoever shall °do °the will of °God,
the same is My brother, [31] and My sister, [31] and
mother."

T **4** °And He began °again to teach °by the
sea °side:

U and there was gathered °unto Him a great
°multitude, so that He entered °into °a ship,
and sat °in the sea; and the whole °multitude
was °by the sea °on the land.

V A C (p. 1389) 2 And He °taught them many things °by
parables, and said unto them in His °doctrine,

D l 3 "Hearken;

m °Behold, °there went out [1] a sower to sow:
4 And °it came to pass, °as he sowed, some
fell [1] by the way [1] side, and the fowls of the
air came and devoured it up.
5 And some fell °on °stony ground, where
it had °not much °earth; and °immediately
it sprang up, °because it had °no depth of
°earth:
6 But °when the sun °was up, it was scorched;
and [5] because it had [5] no root, it withered away.
7 And some fell °among thorns, and the
thorns grew up, and °choked it, and °it yielded
°no fruit.
8 And other fell °on °good °ground, and did
yield fruit that sprang up and increased; and
brought forth, some thirty, and some sixty,
and some an hundred.

27 No man can = No one is any wise able to. No. Gr. *ou.* Ap. 105. I. **a** = the.
spoil = plunder.
goods = vessels (of gold or silver), &c.
28 Verily. See note on Matt. 5. 18.
sins. See Ap. 128. I. ii. 2, and note on Matt. 12. 31.
the sons of men. See note on *v.* 17.
29 against: i. e. ascribe the Holy Spirit's work, or Christ's work, to Satan. This is the unpardonable sin. Gr. *eis.* Ap. 104. vi.
the Holy Ghost. Gr. *pneuma.* See Ap. 101. II. 3.
never = not (Gr. *ou.* Ap. 105. I) to the age (Gr. *eis ton aiōna*). Ap. 151. II. A. ii. 4. b.
eternal. Gr. *aiōnios.* Ap. 151. II. B. i.
damnation = judgment.
30 Because. This is the reason given.
31 His brethren and His mother: i.e. the kinsfolk of *v.* 21.
and. Note the Fig. *Polysyndeton* (Ap. 6), in *vv.* 31-35.
without. That they might more easily seize Him (*v.* 21).
32 sat = was sitting.
Behold. Fig. *Asterismos.* Ap. 6. Gr. *idou.* Ap. 133. I. 2.
34 looked round about = after casting His glance round. A Divine supplemental detail. Occ. only in Mark.
sat = were sitting. **Behold.** Gr. *ide.* Ap. 133. I. 3.
35 do = have done.
the will. Gr. *to thelēma.* See Ap. 102. 3.
God. Ap. 98. I. i. 1.

4. 1 And. Note the Fig. *Polysyndeton* (Ap. 6), in *vv.* 1-9.
again. He had taught there before. Cp. 3. 7-9.
by . . . side = beside. Gr. *para.* Ap. 104. xii. 3.
unto. Gr. *pros.* Ap. 104. xv. 3.
multitude = crowd.
into. Gr. *eis.* Ap. 104. vi. **a** = the.
in: i. e. in the ship on the sea. Gr. *en.* Ap. 104. viii.
by = toward: i.e. facing. Gr. *pros*, as "unto", above.
on = upon. Gr. *epi.* Ap. 104. ix. 1.

4. 2-34 (*U*, p. 1388). THE LORD WITH HIS DISCIPLES. (*Alternation and Introversion.*)

V | A | C | 2. Parabolic instruction.
D | 3-9. Parable. The Sower.
B | 10-25. Alone with disciples. Expounding.
A | D | 26-32. Parable. The Seeds.
C | 33, 34-. Parabolic instruction.
B | -34. Alone with disciples. Expounding.

2 taught = was teaching.
by = in. Gr. *en.* Ap. 104. viii. Not the same word as in *vv.* 31, 38. **doctrine** = teaching.

4. 3-9 (D, above). PARABLE. THE SOWER. (*Introversion.*)

D | l | 3-. Call to hearken.
m | -3-8. The Parable.
l | 9. Call to hearken.

3 Behold. Fig. *Asterismos* (Ap. 6), for emphasis. Gr. *idou.* Ap. 133. I. 2.
there went out. This parable is repeated in Luke 8. 4 under different circumstances from those in Matt. 13. 3, which accounts for the variation of wording. The *antecedents* in Matthew and Mark are the visit of His kinsfolk, 3. 31-34 (which is a *consequent* in Luke 8. 4). The *consequent* in Matthew and Mark is the question of the Twelve concerning others who asked the meaning. In Luke the *consequent* is the question of the Twelve as to its meaning (thus hearing it for the first time), followed by the visit of His kinsfolk. Why should not a parable be repeated several times? Why need they be identical? and why should not two accounts of the same be supplementary? **4 it came to pass.** A Hebraism. **as he sowed** = in (Gr. *en*, as in *v.* 2) his sowing. **5 on.** Gr. *epi.* Ap. 104. ix. 3. Not the same word as in *v.* 8. **stony ground** = the rocky (place understood). **not.** Gr. *ou.* Ap. 105. I. Not the same word as in *v.* 12. **earth** = soil. Gr. *gē.* Ap. 129. 4. **immediately.** See note on 1. 12. **because, &c.** = on account of its having. Gr. *dia.* Ap. 104. v. 2. **no.** Gr. *mē.* Ap. 105. II. Not the same word as in *vv.* 7, 17, 40. **6 when . . . was up** = having risen. **7 among** = into. Gr. *eis.* Ap. 104. vi. **choked.** The Gr. *sun*, in *sumpnigō*, denotes suffocation by compression. **it yielded no fruit.** A Divine supplement. Occ. only here. **no.** Gr. *ou.* Ap. 105. I. Not the same word as in *v.* 5, but the same as in *vv.* 17, 40. **8 on** = into. Gr. *eis.* Ap. 104. vi. **good.** Because prepared. **ground.** Same word as "earth" in *v.* 5.

l A. D. 27 9 And He said unto them, °"He that hath ears to hear, let him hear."

B E n (p. 1390) 10 And when He °was alone, °they that were °about Him °with the twelve asked of Him the parable.

11 And He said unto them, "Unto you it °is given to °know the °mystery of °the kingdom of God: but unto them °that are without, all *these* things are °done [1] in parables:

o **12 °That °seeing they may °see, and °not °perceive; and °hearing they may °hear, and °not understand; lest at any time they should °be converted, and *their* °sins should °be forgiven them."**

13 And He said unto them, °"Know ye [5] not this parable? and how then will ye [11] know all °parables?

F 14 The sower soweth the °word.

15 And these are they [1] by the way [1] side, where the [14] word is sown; but when they have heard, Satan cometh [5] immediately, and taketh away the [14] word that was sown [1] in their hearts.

16 And these are they likewise which are sown [5] on stony ground; who, when they have heard the [14] word, [5] immediately receive it °with gladness;

17 And have [7] no root [1] in themselves, °and so endure but for a time: afterward, when °affliction or persecution ariseth °for the [14] word's sake, [5] immediately they °are offended.

18 And these are they which are sown [7] among thorns; such as hear the [14] word,

19 And the °cares of this °world, and the deceitfulness of riches, and the lusts °of other things entering in, [7] choke the [14] word, and it becometh unfruitful.

20 And these are they which are sown [5] on good [8] ground; such as hear the [14] word, and receive *it*, and bring forth fruit, some thirtyfold, some sixty, and some an hundred."

E n 21 And He said unto them, °"Is [1] a °candle °brought °to be put °under [1] a °bushel, or °under [1] a °bed? °and [5] not to be set [5] on [1] a °candlestick?

22 For there is °nothing hid, which shall not be °manifested; neither °was any thing kept secret, but that °it should come abroad.

o 23 °If any man have [9] ears to hear, [9] let him hear."

24 And He said unto them, °"Take heed °what ye hear: °with what measure ye mete, it shall be measured °to you: and unto you that hear °shall more be given.

25 For he that hath, to him shall be given: and he that hath [5] not, °from him shall be taken even that which he hath."

D G p q (p. 1391) 26 And He said, °"So is [11] the kingdom of God, as °if °a man °should cast °seed °into the [8] ground;

---

9 He that hath, &c. See Ap. 142.

4. 10-25 (B, p. 1389). ALONE WITH DISCIPLES. ANSWERING.

(*Introversion and Alternation.*)

B | E | n | 10, 11. Hearers. Discrimination.
o | 12, 13. Hearing and not understanding.
F | 14-20. Interpretation of Parable.
E | *n* | 21, 22. Teachers. Discrimination.
o | 23-25. Hearing and understanding.

10 was = came to be.

they that were about Him . . . asked. Occ. only in Mark. Showing that this parable was spoken after that in Luke 8. See note on *v.* 3, above.

about = around. Gr. *peri.* Ap. 104. xiii. 3.

with = in conjunction with. Gr. *sun.* Ap. 104. xvi. Not the same word as in *vv.* 16, 24, 30, 36.

11 is = hath been.

know = get to know. Gr. *ginōskō.* Ap. 132. I. ii. Cp. 1 Cor. 2. 14. All the texts omit "to know" and read "has been given the secret" of the Kingdom, &c.

mystery = secret. Not before made known: i. e. its proclamation would be received only by a few.

the kingdom of God. See Ap. 114.

that are without = outside (that circle). Occ. only in Mark. Cp. 1 Cor. 5. 12, 13. 1 Thess. 4. 12. In Matt. "to them", In Luke "to others".

done = come to be (spoken).

12 That, &c. Quoted from Isa. 6. 9, 10. See Ap. 107. I. 1.

seeing . . . see. Fig. *Polyptōton* (Ap. 6). Gr. *blepō.* Ap. 133. I. 5.

not. Gr. *mē.* Ap. 105. II.

perceive = see. Ap. 133. 1.

hearing . . . hear. Fig. *Polyptōton.* Ap. 6.

be converted = return [to the Lord].

sins. Ap. 128. I. ii. 2.

be forgiven. See Isa. 6. 10.

13 Know ye not . . . ? = Have ye no intuitive knowledge of? Gr. *oida.* Ap. 132. I. i. A Divine supplement, here.

parables = the parables.

14 word. Gr. *logos.* See note on 9. 32.

16 with gladness. This effect of thus hearing has the "immediate" ending described in *v.* 17.

with = in association with. Gr. *meta.* Ap. 104. xi. 1.

17 and . . . for a time = but are temporary.

affliction = tribulation.

for . . . sake = on account of. Gr. *dia.* Ap. 104. v. 2.

are offended = stumble. The stumbling is as immediate as the "gladness" of *v.* 16.

19 cares = anxieties.

world = age. Gr. *aiōn.* Ap. 129. 2.

of = concerning. Gr. *peri.* Ap. 104. xiii. 3.

21 Is . . . brought = Doth . . . come. Fig. *Prosopopœia.* Ap. 6.

candle = the lamp. Gr. *luchnos.* Ap. 130. 4.

to be put = in order to be placed.

under. Gr. *hupo.* Ap. 104. xviii. 3.

bushel = the measure.

bed. Gr. *klinē.* Not the same word as in 2. 4.

and not to be = [Is it] not [brought] in order that it may be. **candlestick** = the lampstand.

22 nothing = not (Gr. *ou.* Ap. 105. I) anything.

manifested. Gr. *phaneroō.* Ap. 106. I. v.

was any thing kept secret = does a secret thing take place.

it should come abroad = it may come into (Gr. *eis.* Ap. 104. vi) [the] light (Ap. 130. 8).

23 If, &c. Assuming the hypothesis as a fact. Ap. 118. 2. a. On the former occasion the Lord said "how" (Luke 8. 18). **shall more be given** = to you, and that with interest.

24 Take heed. Ap. 133. I. 5. **what.** **with.** Gr. *en.* Ap. 104. viii. **to you . . .**

25 from. Gr. *apo.* Ap. 104. iv.

4. 26-32 [For Structure see next page].

26 So = Thus. **if.** A contingent hypothesis. Ap. 118. 1. b. **a man.** Gr. *anthrōpos.* Ap. 123. 1. **should cast** = should have cast. **seed** = the seed. **into** = upon. Gr. *epi.* Ap. 104. ix. 1.

A. D. 27 27 And °should sleep, and rise night and day,
and the seed should °spring and °grow up, he
°knoweth [5]not how.
28 For the [5]earth bringeth forth fruit °of herself; first °the blade, then °the ear, after that
°the full corn [1]in the ear.

r (p. 1391) 29 But when the fruit °is brought forth, [5]immediately he °putteth in the sickle, because
the harvest °is come."

G p 30 And He said, "Whereunto shall we liken
[11]the kingdom of God? or [24]with what °comparison °shall we compare it?

q 31 *It is* like a grain of mustard seed, which,
when it is sown °in the [5]earth, is less than all
the seeds °that be °in the [5]earth:

r 32 But when it is sown, it °groweth up, and
becometh greater than all herbs, and °shooteth
out great branches; so that the fowls of °the
air may lodge [21]under the shadow of it."

C (p. 1389) 33 And with many such parables °spake He
the [14]word unto them, °as they were able to
hear *it*.
34 But without a parable [33]spake He [5]not
unto them:

B and when they were alone, He °expounded all
things to His disciples.

S H L (p. 1391) 35 °And °the same day, when the even was
come, He saith unto them, "Let us pass over
°unto the other side."
36 And when they had sent away the [1]multitude, they took Him even as He was [1]in the
ship. And there were °also [16]with Him °other
little °ships.

M s 37 And there arose a great °storm of wind,
and the waves °beat [1]into the ship, so that it
was now °full.
38 And He was °in the hinder part of the
ship, °asleep [5]on °a pillow:

t and they awake Him, and say unto Him,
°"Master, carest Thou [5]not that we °perish?"

s 39 And He arose, and rebuked the wind,
and said unto the sea, "Peace, be still." And
the wind ceased, and there °was a great calm.

t 40 And He said unto them, "Why are ye °so
fearful? how is it that ye have [7]no faith?"
41 And they °feared exceedingly, and said
one °to another, °"What manner of Man is
This, that even the wind and the sea obey
Him?"

4. 26-32 (*D*, p. 1389). PARABLES. THE SEEDS.
(*Extended Alternation.*)

D | G | p | 26-. The kingdom of God. } The seed
q | -26-28. Seeds. General. } growing
r | 29. Fruit brought forth. } secretly.
G | p | 30. The kingdom of God. } The
q | 31. Seed. Particular. } mustard
r | 32. The tree grown up. } seed.

27 should sleep, and rise. These Present Tenses, following the Past in *v.* 26, indicate the continued rising and sleeping after the seed was sown.
spring = sprout.
grow up = lengthen.
knoweth = has no intuitive knowledge. Gr. *oida*. Ap. 132. I. i.
28 of herself. Gr. *automatē* = automatically. The word occurs only here and Acts 12. 10. Galen (quoted by Wetstein) says it means "Not as being without a cause, but without a cause proceeding from us". "God clothes the grass". The explanation is in 1 Cor. 3. 6, 7.
the . . . the = a . . . a.
the full corn = full corn.
29 is brought forth = delivers itself up.
putteth in = sendeth forth. Gr. *apostellō*. Ap. 174. 1. Cp. John 4. 38.
30 comparison = parable.
shall we = are we to.
31 in = upon. Gr. *epi*. Ap. 104. ix. 1.
that be in the earth. } Divine supplements, here.
32 groweth up. }
shooteth out = makes.
the air = the heaven. Sing. See note on Matt. 6. 9, 10. Occ. only in Mark.
33 spake = was He speaking.
as they were able to hear. Occ. only in Mark.
34 expounded = kept expounding. Cp. Luke 24. 27 and 2 Pet. 1. 20.

4. 35—5. 43 (S, p. 1388). MIRACLES.
(*Introversion and Alternation.*)

H | L | 4. 35, 36. Departure to east side.
M | 4. 37-41. Miracle. Tempest stilled.
J | N | 5. 1. Landing.
O | 5. 2-10. Miracle. Demoniac.
K | 5. 11-13. The Swine. Demons. First Prayer.
K | 5. 14-17. The inhabitants. Second Prayer.
J | *N* | 5. 18-. Embarkation.
O | 5. -18-20. Miracle. Demoniac. Third Prayer.
H | *L* | 5. 21. Return to west side.
M | 5. 22-43. Miracles: Jairus' daughter, and Woman.

35 And the same day. This miracle is not the same as that recorded in Matt. 8. 23-27, but is the same as that in Luke 8. 22-25.
unto. Gr. *eis*. Ap. 104. vi.
36 also . . . ships = boats also. Occ. only in Mark.
other. Gr. pl. of *allos*. Ap. 124. 1.

4. 37-41 (M, above). MIRACLE. TEMPEST STILLED. (*Alternation.*)

M | s | 37, 38-. Storm arising.
t | -38. Disciples alarmed.
s | 39. Storm calmed.
t | 40, 41. Disciples reproved.

37 storm = squall. The earlier storm in Matthew was caused by an earthquake (Gr. *seismos*). That storm was *before* the calling of the Twelve (Matt. 8. 24 and 10. 1). This storm was *subsequent* (cp. 3. 13). **beat** = were beating. Therefore an open boat. **full** = filling. In the earlier storm it was getting *covered*. **38 in** = on. Gr. *epi*. Ap. 104. ix. 2. All the texts prefer Gr. *en* = in (Ap. 104. viii). **asleep** = sleeping (soundly). Ap. 171. 1. **a pillow** = the [wooden] seat [with its leathern covering or cushion]. **Master** = Teacher. Ap. 98. XIV. v. 1. **perish** = are perishing. **39 rebuked the wind** first, and then the disciples, because the danger was greater. In the earlier storm, He rebuked the disciples first, and the storm after, for the opposite reason. **was** = became. **40 so** = thus. **41 feared exceedingly** = feared with a great fear. Fig. *Polyptōton*. Ap. 6. **to.** Gr. *pros*. Ap. 104. xv. 3. **What manner of Man . . . ?** = Who then is this One . . . ?

J N (p. 1391) A. D. 27 **5** And they came over °unto the other side of the sea, °into the country of the °Gadarenes.

O u (p. 1392) 2 And when He was come °out of the °ship, °immediately there °met Him °out of the tombs a °man °with an unclean °spirit,

v 3 Who had *his* °dwelling °among the tombs;

w and °no man could bind him, °no, not with chains:

x 4 °Because that he had been often bound with fetters

y and chains,

y and the chains had been plucked asunder °by him,

x and the fetters broken in pieces:

w °neither could any *man* tame him.

v 5 And always, night and day, he was °in the mountains, and °in the tombs, °crying, and cutting himself with stones.

u a 6 But when he °saw °Jesus °afar off, he °ran and °worshipped Him,

7 And [5]cried with a loud voice, and said, °"What have I to do with Thee, [6]Jesus, *Thou* Son °of the Most High °God? I adjure Thee by °God, that Thou torment me °not."

b 8 For He said unto him, "Come [2]out of the [2]man, *thou* unclean [2]spirit."

b 9 And He asked him, "What *is* thy name?" And he answered, saying, "My name *is* °Legion: for we are many."

a 10 And he °besought Him much that He would [7]not send them away out of the country.

K c 11 Now there was there °nigh unto the mountains a great herd of swine feeding.

d 12 And all the °devils [10]besought Him, saying, "Send us °into the swine, that we may enter °into them."

13 And °forthwith [6]Jesus gave them leave.

d And the unclean [2]spirits went out, and entered [12]into the swine: and the herd °ran violently °down a steep place [12]into the sea, (they were about two thousand;)

c and were choked [5]in the sea.

K e 14 And they that fed the swine fled, and told *it* °in the city, °and °in the country.

f And they went out to [6]see what it was that was °done.

15 And they come °to [6]Jesus, and °see him that was °possessed with the devil, and had the [9]legion, sitting, and °clothed, and in his right mind: and they were °afraid.

5. 1 unto. Gr. *eis*. Ap. 104. vi.
into = unto. Gr. *eis*, as above.
Gadarenes. In the earlier miracle it was Gergesenes (Matt. 8. 28).

5. 2-10 (O, p. 1391). MIRACLE. THE DEMONIAC. (*Introversion.*)

O | u | 2. The meeting.
  v | 3-. Abode. Among the tombs.
    w | -3. None could bind him.
      x | 4-. Fetters often used.
        y | -4-. And chains also.
        y | -4-. But chains broken.
      x | -4-. Fetters broken in pieces.
    w | -4. None could tame him.
  v | 5. Abode. Among the tombs.
u | 6-10. The meeting.

2 out of. Gr. *ek*. Ap. 104. vii. **ship** = boat.
immediately. See note on 1. 12.
met = confronted.
man. Gr. *anthrōpos*. Ap. 123. 1. In the *earlier* miracle there were "two men" (Matt. 8. 28).
with = in [the power of]. Gr. *en*. Ap. 104. viii. 1.
spirit. Gr. *pneuma*. See Ap. 101. II. 12.
3 dwelling. Gr. *katoikēsis*. A Divine supplement, here. **among.** Gr. *en*. Ap. 104. viii. 2.
no man . . . no, not = no one . . . not even. Gr. *oudeis . . . oude*. Compounds of *ou*. Ap. 105. I.
4 Because. Gr. *dia to*. Ap. 104. v. 2.
by. Gr. *hupo*. Ap. 104. xviii. 1.
neither could any man tame him = and no (Ap. 105. I) man was strong enough to master him.
5 in. Gr. *en*. Ap. 104. viii. **crying** = crying out.

5. 6-10 (*u*, above). THE MEETING. (*Introversion.*)

u | a | 6, 7. Worship.
  b | 8. Unclean spirit. Command.
  b | 9. Unclean spirit. Name.
a | 10. Prayer.

6 saw. Gr. *eidon*. Ap. 133. I. 1. Not the same word as in *vv.* 15, 31, 38. **Jesus.** Ap. 98. X.
afar off = from (Gr. *apo*. Ap. 104. iv) afar.
ran. The 1611 edition of the A.V. reads "came".
worshipped = did homage [by prostration]. Ap. 137. 1.
7 What, &c. A Hebraism. See note on 2 Sam. 16. 10.
of the Most High God. A Divine supplement, here. Demons knew Him, if the people were blinded.
God. Ap. 98. I. i. 1. **not.** Gr. *mē*. Ap. 105. II.
9 Legion. A Roman legion was about 6,000 men.
10 besought. Note the three prayers in this chapter: (1) the unclean spirits: Answer "Yes" (*vv.* 10, 12, 13); (2) the Gadarenes: Answer "Yes" (*v.* 17); (3) the healed man: Answer "No" (*vv.* 18, 19). "No" is often the most gracious answer to *our* prayers.

5. 11-13 (K, p. 1391). THE SWINE. (*Introversion.*)

K | c | 11. Swine feeding.
  d | 12, 13-. The demons. Prayer made.
  d | -13-. The demons. Prayer answered.
c | -13. Swine choked.

11 nigh unto = just at. Gr. *pros*. Ap. 104. xv. 3.
12 devils = demons. **into.** Gr. *eis*. Ap. 104. vi.
13 forthwith = immediately, as in *v.* 2.
ran violently = rushed.
down. Gr. *kata*. Ap. 104. x. 1.

5. 14-17 (*K*, p. 1391). THE INHABITANTS. PRAYER. (*Alternation.*)

K | e | 14-. Report of the swineherds.
  f | -14, 15. Citizens. Observation made.
  e | 16. Report of the hearers.
  f | 17. Citizens. Prayer made.

14 in = to. Gr. *eis*. Ap. 104. vi. **and** = as well as. **done** = come to pass. **15 to.** Gr. *pros*. Ap. 104. xv. 3. **see** = gaze upon. Gr. *theōreō*. Ap. 133. I. 11. **possessed with the devil.** Gr. *daimonizomai*. **clothed** = provided with clothes. Cp. Luke 8. 27, where he had for a long time worn none. Gr. *himatizomai*. Occ. only here and Luke 8. 35 in the N.T.; but is found in the *Papyri*, where an apprentice is to be provided with clothes. **afraid** = alarmed.

e (p. 1392) A.D. 27 16 And they that [6]saw *it* °told them how it befell to him that was [15]possessed with the devil, [14]and *also* °concerning the swine.

f 17 And they began to °pray Him to depart °out of their °coasts.

J N (p. 1391) 18 And °when He was come [12]into the [2]ship,

O he that had been [15]possessed with the devil [17]prayed Him that he might be °with Him.

19 Howbeit [6]Jesus suffered him °not, but saith unto him, "Go °home [15]to thy friends, and tell them how great things °the Lord hath done for thee, and hath had compassion on thee."

20 And he departed, and began to publish [5]in Decapolis how great things [6]Jesus had done for him: and all *men* did marvel.

H L 21 And when [6]Jesus was passed over again °by [2]ship [1]unto the other side, °much people gathered °unto Him: and He was °nigh unto the sea.

M P g (p. 1393) 22 And, °behold, there cometh one of the rulers of the °synagogue, °Jairus by name; and when he [6]saw Him, he fell °at His feet,

h 23 And [10]besought Him greatly, saying, °"My little daughter lieth at the point of death: *I pray Thee,* come and °lay Thy hands on her, °that she may be healed; and she shall live."

Q i 24 And *Jesus* went [18]with him; and [21]much people °followed Him, and °thronged Him.

k 25 And a certain woman, °which had an issue of blood twelve years,

26 And had suffered many °things °of many physicians, and had spent all that she had, and was nothing bettered, but rather grew worse,

27 When she had heard °of [6]Jesus, came [5]in the °press behind, and touched His garment.

28 For she said, °"If I may touch but His clothes, I shall be whole."

l 29 And °straightway the fountain of her blood was dried up; and she °felt in *her* body that she was healed °of that plague.

i 30 And [6]Jesus, [2]immediately °knowing [5]in Himself °that virtue had gone [2]out of Him, turned Him about [5]in the [27]press, and said, "Who touched My clothes?"

31 And His disciples °said unto Him, "Thou °seest the °multitude thronging Thee, and sayest Thou, 'Who touched Me?'"

32 And He °looked round about to [6]see her that had done this thing.

k 33 But the woman fearing and trembling, °knowing what was done in her, came and fell down before Him, and told Him all the truth.

l 34 And He said unto her, "Daughter, thy faith hath °made thee °whole; go [14]in peace, and be whole [29]of thy plague."

P g 35 While He °yet spake, there °came °from the ruler of the [22]synagogue's *house certain* which said, "Thy daughter is dead: why troublest thou the °Master any further?"

h 36 °As soon as [6]Jesus °heard the word that

16 told = detailed.
concerning. Gr. *peri.* Ap. 104. xiii. 1.
17 pray. See note on "besought", *v.* 10, and cp. *v.* 18.
out of = away from. Gr. *apo.* Ap. 104. iv.
coasts = borders.
18 when He was come = while He was in [the act of] embarking.
with. Gr. *meta.* Ap. 104. xi. 1.
19 not. Gr. *ou.* Ap. 105. I.
home = to (Ap. 104. vi) thy house.
the Lord. Ap. 98. VI. i. *a.* 1. A. b.
21 by ship = in (Gr. *en.* Ap. 104. viii) the ship.
much people = a vast crowd.
unto. Gr. *epi.* Ap. 104. ix. 3.
nigh unto = beside. Gr. *para.* Ap. 104. xii. 3.

5. 22-43 (*M*, p. 1391). MIRACLES.
(*Alternations.*)

M | P | g | 22. Jairus.
h | 23. His assurance expressed.
Q | i | 24. The throng.
k | 25–28. The Woman's action.
l | 29. The Lord. Miracle.
i | 30–32. The throng.
k | 33. The Woman's confession.
l | 34. The Lord. Approval.
(The Woman.)
P | *g* | 35. Jairus. Messengers from house.
h | 36. His encouragement received.
Q | m | 37. Those accompanying. Apostles.
n | 38, 39–. Into the house.
o | –39. The Lord. Declaration.
p | 40–. Derision.
m | –40–. Those accompanying. Relations.
n | –40. Into the chamber.
o | 41, 42–. The Lord. Miracle.
p | –42, 43. Astonishment.
(Jairus's daughter.)

22 behold. Fig. *Asterismos.* Ap. 6.
synagogue. Ap. 120. I.
Jairus. The Jair of the O.T. See Num. 32. 41. Deut. 3. 14. Judg. 10. 3. Est. 2. 5. 1 Chron. 20. 5.
at. Gr. *pros.* Ap. 104. xv. 3.
23 My little daughter. The Dim. only in Mark.
lay Thy hands, &c. For this action, cp. 6. 5; 7. 32; 8. 23, 25; 16. 18. Acts 9. 17; 28. 8. Heb. 6. 2.
that = so that.
24 followed = was following.
thronged = were thronging.
25 which had = being in (Gr. *en.* Ap. 104. viii).
26 things = treatments.
of = under (Gr. *hupo.* Ap. 104. xviii. 1) many physicians.
27 of = concerning. Gr. *peri.* Ap. 104. xiii. 1.
press = crowd.
28 If, &c. Expressing a contingency. Ap. 118. I. b.
29 straightway = immediately. See note on 1. 12.
felt = knew [by Divine power]. Gr. *ginōskō.* Ap. 132. I. ii.
of = from. Gr. *apo.* Ap. 104. iv.
30 knowing = perceiving thereupon. Gr. *epiginōskō.* Ap. 132. I. iii.
that virtue = that [inherent] power (Ap. 172. 1) from Him had gone forth.
31 said = kept saying.
seest. Gr. *blepō.* Ap. 133. I. 5.
multitude = crowd.
32 looked = was looking.
33 knowing = knowing [intuitively]. Gr. *oida.* Ap. 132. I. i.
34 made . . . whole = saved. Gr. *sōzō.*
35 yet spake = was yet speaking.
came = come.
from = away from. Gr. *apo.* Ap. 104. iv.
Master = Teacher. Ap. 98. XIV. v. 3.
36 As soon as = Immediately. See note on 1. 12.
heard. T Tr. A WH R (not Syr.) read *parakousas* (instead of *akousas,* which A translates "overheard".

A.D. 27 was spoken, He saith unto the ruler of the
22 synagogue, "Be [7] not afraid, only ° believe."

Q m (p. 1393) 37 And He ° suffered no man to follow Him, save Peter, and James, and John the brother of James.

n 38 And He cometh ° to the house of the ruler of the [22] synagogue, and [15] seeth the tumult, and them that wept and ° wailed greatly.
39 And when He was come in,

o He saith unto them, "Why make ye this ado, and weep? the ° damsel ° is [19] not dead, but ° sleepeth."

p 40 And they ° laughed Him to scorn.

m But when He had ° put them all out, He taketh the father and the mother of the [39] damsel, and them that were [18] with Him,

n and entereth in where the [39] damsel was lying.

o 41 And He took the [39] damsel by the hand, and said unto her, ° "Talitha cumi;" which is, being interpreted, ° "Damsel, I say unto thee, arise."
42 And [29] straightway the [41] damsel arose, and ° walked; for she was *of the age* of twelve years.

p And they were ° astonished with a great ° astonishment.
43 And He charged them ° straitly that ° no man should ° know it; and commanded that something should be given her to eat.

R R q (p. 1394) 6 And He went out from thence, and came ° into His own ° country; and His disciples follow Him.

r 2 And when the sabbath day was come, He began to teach ° in the synagogue:

S s and many hearing *Him* were astonished, saying, "From whence hath this *man* these things? and what wisdom *is* this which is given unto him, that even such ° mighty works are ° wrought ° by his hands?

t 3 Is ° not This ° the carpenter, the son of Mary, the brother of James, and Joses, and of Juda, and Simon? and are ° not His sisters here ° with us?"

s And they ° were offended ° at Him.

R q 4 But ° Jesus said unto them, ° "A prophet is [3] not without honour, ° but [2] in his own [1] country, and ° among his own kin, and [2] in his own house."

r 5 And He ° could there do no [2] mighty work, ° save that He laid his hands upon a few ° sick folk, and healed *them.*
6 And He ° marvelled ° because of their unbelief. And He went round about the villages, teaching.

J[3] T W u (p. 1395) 7 And He ° called *unto Him* the twelve, and began to send them forth by ° two and two;

v and gave them ° power over unclean ° spirits;

X w 8 And ° commanded them that they should

---

believe = go on believing.
37 suffered no man = suffered not (Gr. *ou.* Ap. 105. I) any one.
38 to. Gr. *eis*, as in *v.* 1.
wailed. Crying *al-a-lai, al-a-lai*, from the Greek verb *alalazō.* Jewish mourning cries. Occ. elsewhere only in 1 Cor. 13. 1.
39 damsel = child. Ap. 108. v.
is not dead = has not died.
sleepeth. Gr. *katheudō.* See notes on 1 Thess. 4. 13 and 5. 6. Ap. 171. 1.
40 laughed Him to scorn = began laughing at Him.
put them all out. He acted, as well as spoke, with "authority".
41 Talitha cumi. *Aramaic* (Ap. 94. III. 3). Talitha = Aramaic *ṭalīthā'* (= maid. Lat. *puella*) *kūmī* (Imperat. of *kūm*) = arise. Occ. only here. Not "got from Peter", but from the Holy Spirit. Ap. 94. III. 3.
Damsel. Gr. *korasion.* Found only here, and *v.* 42; 6. 22, 28, and Matt. 9. 24, 25; 14. 11. Not the same word as in *vv.* 39, 40, 41-. See Ap. 108. ix.
42 walked = began walking.
astonished . . . astonishment. Fig. *Polyptōton* (Ap. 6), for emphasis. See Gen. 26. 28. Gr. *existēmi* = to be put out [of one's mind]. Noun, *ekstasis*; hence, Eng. *ecstasy* = entrancement, implying bewilderment. See 16. 8. Luke 5. 26. Acts 3. 10. Used of a trance, Acts 10. 10; 11. 5; 22. 17. Hence, Eng. entrancement.
43 straitly = much. **no.** Gr. *mē.* Ap. 105. II.
know = get to know. See Ap. 132. I. ii.

6. 1-6 (*R*, p. 1388). TEACHING.
(*Introversion and Alternation.*)

R | R | q | 1. His own country.
r | 2-. Teaching. (Positive.)
S | s | -2. Astonished.
t | 3-. His kindred.
s | -3. Stumbled.
R | *q* | 4. His own country.
r | 5, 6. Mighty works. (Negative.)

1 into. Gr. *eis.* Ap. 104. vi. Not the same as *v.* 53.
His own country = His native country: i.e. Galilee, Ap. 169. This was His second visit (Matt. 13. 54).
country. Gr. *patris.*
2 in. Gr. *en.* Ap. 104. viii. 1. Not the same word as in *vv.* 8, 25, 55.
mighty works = miracles. One of the renderings of *dunamis* (pl.). Ap. 172. 1.
wrought = come to pass.
by = by means of. Gr. *dia.* Ap. 104. v. 1.
3 not. Gr. *ou.* Ap. 105. 1. Not the same word as in *vv.* 9, 11, 34, 50.
the carpenter = the workman. Such terms used only by His rejecters. Occ. only here and Matt. 13. 35.
with. Gr. *pros.* Ap. 104. xv. 3.
were offended = stumbled. Gr. *scandalizō.*
at = in. Gr. *en.* Ap. 104. viii. 1.
4 Jesus. Ap. 98. X.
A prophet, &c. Fig. *Parœmia.* Ap. 6.
but = except.
among. Gr. *en.* Ap. 104. viii. 2.
5 could there do no = was not (as in *v.* 3) able to do any there. Nazareth saw most of the Lord, but profited least. Ap. 169.
save = except. **sick** = infirm.
6 marvelled because of, &c. Occ. only in Mark.
because of = on account of. Gr. *dia.* Ap. 104. v. 2.

6. 7-30 [For Structure see next page].

7 called. The 1611 edition of the A.V. reads "calleth".
two and two. Gr. *duo duo.* Modern critics object that it is not good Greek to repeat the cardinal number for a distributive numeral. But it is found in Aeschylus and Sophocles, and in the *Oxyrhynchus Papyri* (Nos. 121 and 886). See Deissmann's *Light*, pp. 124, 125. **power** = authority. Ap. 172. 5.
spirits. Gr. pl. of *pneuma.* See Ap. 101. II. 12.
8 commanded = charged. See Matt. 10. 5, &c.

A.D. 27 °take nothing °for *their* journey, save a °staff
only; °no °scrip, °no bread, °no °money °in
their °purse:
9 But *be* shod with sandals; and °not put on
two coats.

x 10 And He said unto them, °"In what place
(p. 1395) soever ye enter [1]into an house, there abide till
ye depart °from that place.

X x 11 And °whosoever shall [9]not receive you,
nor hear you,

w when ye depart thence, °shake off the dust
under your feet [8]for a testimony against them.
Verily I say unto you, It shall be more tolerable for Sodom and Gomorrha [2]in the day of
judgment, than for that city."

W u 12 And they went out, and °preached that
men should °repent.

v 13 And they cast out many °devils, and
°anointed with oil many that were [5]sick, and
healed *them*.

U 14 And king °Herod heard *of Him;* (for His
name was spread abroad:) and he said, that
John the Baptist °was risen °from °the dead,
and °therefore [2]mighty works do shew forth
themselves [2]in him.

V 15 Others °said, That it is °Elias. And others
°said, That it is a prophet, or as one of the
prophets.

V 16 But when [14]Herod heard *thereof,* he said,
"It is John, whom I beheaded: he is risen
[14]from the dead."

U Y y 17 For [14]Herod himself had sent forth and
laid hold upon John,

z and bound him [2]in °prison °for Herodias' sake,
his brother Philip's wife: for he had married
her.
18 For John °had said unto Herod, "It is [3]not
lawful for thee to have thy brother's wife."

Z a 19 Therefore Herodias °had a quarrel against
him, and °would have killed him; but she
[5]could [3]not:

b 20 For [14]Herod feared John, °knowing that he
was a just man and an holy, and °observed
him; and when he heard him, he °did many
things, °and heard him gladly.

Z b 21 And °when a °convenient day was come,
that [14]Herod on his °birthday made a supper to
his °lords, °high captains, and °chief *estates*
of Galilee;
22 And when the daughter of °the said
Herodias came in, and danced, and pleased
[14]Herod and them that sat with him, the king
said unto the °damsel, "Ask of me whatsoever
thou °wilt, and I will give *it* thee."
23 And he sware unto her, "Whatsoever
thou shalt ask of me, I will give *it* thee, unto
the half of my kingdom."

6. 7-30 (J³, p. 1383). MISSION OF THE TWELVE BEGUN, AND JOHN'S ENDED.
(*Introversion and Alternation.*)

J³ T | 7-13. Mission of the Twelve begun.
  U | 14. Herod hears of the Lord.
    V | 15. John. Opinion of others.
    V | 16. John. Opinion of Herod.
  U | 17-29. Herod beheads John.
T | 30. Mission of the Twelve reported.

(U–*U*: Mission of John ended.)

6. 7-13 (T, above). MISSION OF THE TWELVE BEGUN. (*Introversions.*)

T W u | 7-. The Twelve called and sent.
    v | -7. Authority given.
  X w | 8, 9. Journey:
    x | 10. Reception:
  X *x* | 11-. Rejection:
    w | -11. Departure:
W *u* | 12. The Twelve going and proclaiming.
    v | 13. Authority exercised.

(X–*X*: Instructions.)

8 take=take up (as luggage).
for=with a view to. Gr. *eis*. Ap. 104. vi.
staff. See note on Matt. 10. 10.
no. Gr. *mē*. Ap. 105. II.
scrip. See note on Matt. 10. 10.
money. The only coins minted in Palestine then were copper. Cp. Matt. 10. 9 for a Divine supplement.
in. Gr. *eis*. Ap. 104. vi. Not the same as in *vv.* 2, 4, 11, 25, 27, 28, 29, 47, 48, 55, 56.
purse=belt or girdle. Occ. only here, and in Matt. 3. 4; 10. 9. Mark 1. 6; 6. 8. Acts 21. 11. Rev. 1. 13; 15. 6.
9 not. Gr. *mē*. Ap. 105. II.
10 In what place soever=Wherever.
from that place=thence.
11 whosoever=whatever people.
shake off. Fig. *Parœmia*. Ap. 6.
12 preached=proclaimed. See Ap. 121. 1.
repent. See Ap. 111. I. 1.
13 devils=demons.
anointed with oil. Then a common practice. See Jas. 5. 14.
14 Herod. See Ap. 109.
was risen=had been raised.
from=out from. Gr. *ek*. Ap. 104. vii. See Matt. 17. 9.
the dead. No Art. See Ap. 139. 2.
therefore=on account of (Ap. 104. v. 2) this.
15 said=were saying.
Elias=Elijah.

6. 17-29 (*U*, above). HEROD BEHEADS JOHN.
(*Introversions.*)

U Y y | 17-. Herod. Apprehension of John.
  z | -17, 18. Reason. For the sake of Herodias.
    Z a | 19. Herodias's quarrel.
      b | 20. Her failure.
    Z *b* | 21-23. Her opportunity.
      a | 24, 25. Herodias's quarrel.
  Y *z* | 26. Reason. For the sake of his promise.
    y | 27-29. Herod. Execution of John.

17 prison=the prison.
for . . . sake=on account of. Gr. *dia*. Ap. 104. v. 2.
18 had said=kept saying.
19 had a quarrel=kept cherishing a grudge.
would have=was desiring to. See Ap. 102. 1.
20 knowing. Gr. *oida*. Ap. 132. I. 1. Not the same as in *vv.* 33, 38.
observed=kept him (John) safe [from her]: or, protected him; i.e. for the reason given. Occ. only here, and Matt. 9. 17. Luke 2. 19; 5. 38.
did many things. T Trm. WH and R read "was at a loss [what to do]", or hesitated, or was much perplexed, reading *ēporei* instead of *epoiei*. Not the Syr. and=and [yet]. **21 when a convenient day was come**=a convenient day being come, when, &c. convenient=opportune. Only in Mark, and Heb. 4. 16. birthday. The notice of the banquet and guests is a Divine supplement. lords=great men. Occ. only here, Rev. 6. 15, and 18. 23. high captains=chiliarchs (commanders of 1,000 men). chief estates=the first, or leading [men]. **22 the said Herodias**=of Herodias herself. damsel. Gr. *korasion*, as in 5. 41, 42. wilt. See Ap. 102. 1.

a (p. 1395) A.D. 27 24 And she went forth, and said unto her mother, "What shall I ask?" And she said, "The head of John the Baptist."

25 And she came in °straightway °with haste °unto the king, and asked, saying, °"I will that thou give me °by and by °in °a charger the head of John the Baptist."

Y z 26 And the king °was °exceeding sorry; *yet* [17] for his oath's sake, and for their sakes which sat with him, he °would [3] not reject her.

y 27 And °immediately the king sent °an executioner, and commanded his head to be brought: and he went and beheaded him [2] in the prison,

28 And brought his head [25] in [25] a charger, and gave it to the [22] damsel: and the [22] damsel gave it to her mother.

29 And when his disciples heard *of it*, they came and took up his corpse, and laid it [2] in °a tomb.

T 30 And the °apostles gathered themselves together [25] unto [4] Jesus, and °told Him all things, both what they had done, and what they had taught.

H⁴ A¹ y¹ (p. 1396) A.D. 28 31 And He said unto them, °"Come ye yourselves °apart [1] into a desert place, and rest a while:"

z¹ for there were many coming and going, and they had no leisure so much as to eat.

y² 32 And they departed [1] into a desert place by ship privately.

z² 33 And the °people °saw them departing, and many °knew Him, and ran afoot thither °out of all cities, and outwent them, and came together [25] unto Him.

y³ 34 And [4] Jesus, when He came out, [33] saw much people, and was moved with compassion °toward them, because they were as sheep [9] not °having a shepherd: and He began to teach them many things.

B¹ C¹ c¹ 35 And when the day °was now far spent, His disciples came unto Him, and said, "This is a desert place, and now the time *is* °far passed:

36 Send them away, that they may go [1] into the country round about, and into the villages, and °buy themselves bread: for they have °nothing to eat."

d¹ 37 °He answered and said unto them, °"Give ye them to eat."

c² And they say unto Him, °"Shall we go and buy two hundred °pennyworth of bread, and °give them to eat?"

38 [37] He saith unto them, "How many loaves have ye? go and [33] see." And when they °knew, they say, "Five, and two fishes."

d² 39 And He commanded them to make all sit down °by companies °upon the °green grass.

25 straightway = immediately. See note on 1. 12.
with. Gr. *meta*. Ap. 104. xi.
with haste. Note how the opportunity was eagerly seized. See *v.* 19.
unto. Gr. *pros*. Ap. 104. xv. 3. Not the same as in *v.* 23, but the same as in *vv.* 30, 33, 45, 48, 51.
I will = I wish. See Ap. 102. 1.
by and by = instantly.
in = upon. Gr. *epi*. Ap. 104. ix. 2.
a charger = a large flat dish. See note on Matt. 14. 8, 11.
26 was = became.
exceeding. This Divine supplement occurs only here.
would not = was unwilling to. Ap. 102. 1.
27 immediately. See note on 1. 12.
an executioner. Gr. *spekoulatōr*. Occ. only here. A Latin word (*speculator*) = a man who spies out; used of the Roman emperor's body-guard (an armed detective body) round the emperor at banquets, &c. Herod adopted Roman customs.
29 a tomb = the tomb. See note on Matt. 27. 60.
30 apostles. First occurrence in Mark.
told = reported to.

6. 31—8. 30 (H⁴, p. 1383). TEACHING AND MIRACLES. (*Repeated Alternation.*)

H⁴ | A¹ | 6. 31-34. Teaching. Multitudes.
  B¹ | 6. 35-56. Miracles.
 A² | 7. 1-23. Teaching. Pharisees.
  B² | 7. 24—8. 9. Miracles.
 A³ | 8. 10-21. Teaching. Pharisees.
  B³ | 8. 22-26. Miracle.
 A⁴ | 8. 27-30. Teaching. Disciples.

6. 31-34 (A¹, above). TEACHING. MULTITUDES. (*Repeated Alternation.*)

A¹ | y¹ | 31-. Concourse. Proposal.
  z¹ | -31. Reason of Proposal.
 y² | 32. Concourse. Proposal attempted.
  z² | 33. Reason of Failure.
 y³ | 34. Concourse. Teaching.

31 Come . . . apart. See note on "withdrew" (3. 7).
33 people = crowds.
saw. Gr. *eidon*. Ap. 133. I. 1.
knew = recognised. Gr. *epiginōskō*. Ap. 132. I. iii.
out of = from. Gr. *apo*. Ap. 104. iv Not the same word as in *v.* 54.
34 toward = upon. Gr. *epi*. Ap. 104. ix. 2.
having = conscious of (not) having.

6. 35-56 (B¹ above). MIRACLES. (*Alternations.*)

B¹ | C¹ | 35-44. Miracle. Feeding the Five Thousand.
  D¹ | a | 45. Departure.
   b | 46, 47. Alone.
 C² | 48-52. Miracle. Walking on the Sea.
  D² | *a* | 53. Departure.
   b | 54. Recognized.
 C³ | 55, 56. Miracles. Many.

6. 35-44 (C¹, above). MIRACLE. FEEDING THE FIVE THOUSAND. (*Repeated Alternation.*)

C¹ | c¹ | 35, 36. Disciples. "Send them away to buy."
  d¹ | 37-. The Lord. "Give ye."
 c² | -37, 38. Disciples. "Shall we buy?"
  d² | 39-42. The Lord. "Gave them".
 c³ | 43, 44. Disciples. Gathering up twelve baskets.

35 was = had become already.
far passed = advanced.
36 buy. This was their highest thought. Note the answer ("Give").
nothing = not (Ap. 105. I) anything.

37 He = But He. **Give.** This is the Lord's higher thought. **Shall we go, &c.** This question and Christ's answer are a Divine supplement only here. **pennyworth.** See Ap. 51. I. 4. **38 knew** = found out. Gr. *ginōskō*. Ap. 132. I. ii. **39 by companies** = in table-parties: i.e. arranged in three sides of a square, as in a Jewish or Roman dining-room; the guests being seated on the outside and served from the inside. These were arranged in companies of 50 and of 100. Gr. *sumposia sumposia*. Fig. *Epizeuxis* (Ap. 6). **upon.** Gr. *epi*. Ap. 104. ix. 2. **green.** This is a Divine supplement only here.

A. D. 28 40 And they sat down ° in ranks, ° by hundreds, and ° by fifties.
41 And when He had taken the five loaves
and the two fishes, He ° looked up ° to ° heaven,
and blessed, and ° brake the loaves, and ° gave
them to His disciples to set before them;
and the two fishes divided He among them
° all.
42 And they did all eat, and were ° filled.
c³ (p. 1396) 43 And they took up twelve ° baskets full of
the fragments, and ° of the fishes.
44 And they that did eat of the loaves were
about five thousand ° men.
D¹ a 45 And [25] straightway He constrained His
disciples to get [1] into the ° ship, and to go ° to
the other side before [25] unto ° Bethsaida, while
He sent away the people.
b 46 And when He had sent them away, He
departed [1] into ° a mountain ° to pray.
47 And when even was come, the [45] ship was
[2] in the midst of the sea, and He alone ° on the
land.
C² e 48 And ° He [33] saw them ° toiling [2] in rowing;
for the wind was contrary unto them:
f and ° about ° the fourth watch of the night He
cometh [25] unto them, walking ° upon the sea,
and ° would have passed by them.
49 But when they [33] saw Him walking [48] upon
the sea, they supposed it had been ° a spirit,
and cried out:
50 For ° they all [33] saw Him, and were troubled.
And [27] immediately He ° talked [25] with them,
and saith unto them, "Be of good cheer: it is
I; be [9] not afraid."
51 And He went up [25] unto them [1] into the
ship;
e and the wind ° ceased:
f and they were ° sore amazed [2] in themselves
° beyond measure, and wondered.
52 ° For they considered [3] not ° *the miracle* ° of
the loaves: for their heart was ° hardened.
D² *a* 53 And when they had passed over, they
came ° into the land of Gennesaret, and ° drew
to the shore.
b 54 And when they were come ° out of the
[47] ship, [25] straightway they ° knew Him,
C³ 55 And ran through that whole region
round about, and began to carry about [25] in
° beds those that were sick, where they heard
He was.
56 ° And whithersoever He entered, [1] into villages, or cities, or ° country, they laid the sick
[2] in ° the streets, and ° besought Him that they
might touch if it were but the ° border of His
garment: and as many as touched Him were
° made whole.

A² E¹ g (p. 1398) **7** Then came together ° unto Him the ° Pharisees, and certain of the scribes, which
came ° from ° Jerusalem.
2 And when they ° saw some of His disciples
eat bread with ° defiled, ° that is to say, with
unwashen, hands, they found fault.
h (3 ° For the [1] Pharisees, and all the Jews,

40 in ranks = in divisions (like garden beds).
by. Gr. *ana*. Ap. 104. i. All the texts read *kata*. Ap. 104. x. 2.
41 looked up. Ap. 133. III. i.
to = unto. Gr. *eis*. Ap. 104. vi.
heaven = the heaven. Sing. See Matt. 6. 9, 10.
brake . . . gave. The former is the Aorist tense, recording the *instantaneous* act; the latter is the Imperfect tense, describing the *continuous* giving. This shows that the miraculous power was in the hands of Christ, between the breaking and the giving.
all. This is Divine supplement, only in Mark.
42 filled = satisfied. Cp. Matt. 5. 6.
43 baskets. Gr. *kophinos* = a Jewish wicker travelling basket. The same word as in 8. 19; not the same word as in 8. 8, 20.
of = from. Gr. *apo*. Ap. 104. iv.
of the fishes. Only mentioned here.
44 men. Gr. *anēr*. See Ap. 123 2. Not generic, but lit. men (not women). See Matt. 14. 21.
45 ship = boat.
to = unto. Gr. *eis*. Ap. 104. vi (as in preceding clause).
Bethsaida. Ap. 94. III. 3, and Ap. 169.
46 a = the; denoting the well-known mountain.
to pray. See Ap. 134. I. 2.
47 on. Gr. *epi*. Ap. 104. ix. 1.

6. 48-52 (C², p. 1396). MIRACLE. WALKING ON THE SEA. (*Alternation.*)

C² | e | 48-. The wind contrary.
| f | -48-51-. Miracle. Wrought.
| *e* | -51-. The wind. Ceased.
| *f* | -51, 52. Miracle. Effect.

48 He saw = He having seen. Ap. 133. I. 1.
toiling = distressed. Gr. *basanizō*, translated "torment" (5. 7. Matt. 8. 6, 28. Luke 8. 28. Rev. 9. 5; 11. 10; 14. 10; 20. 10. Cp. Matt. 4. 24).
about. Gr. *peri*. Ap. 104. xiii. 3. Not the same word as in *v.* 44.
the fourth watch. See Ap. 51. iv (18).
upon. Gr. *epi*. Ap. 104. ix. 1.
would have passed by = wished (Ap. 102. 1) to pass by. Only here.
49 a spirit. Gr. *phantasma* = a phantom. Cp. Matt. 14. 26.
50 they all saw Him. A Divine supplement, here.
talked with them = spake with them. Matthew and John = to them.
51 ceased = dropped. Cp. 4. 39.
sore = exceedingly.
52 For, &c. Verse 52 is a Divine supplement, here.
the miracle of the loaves = concerning (Gr. *epi*. Ap. 104. ix. 2) the loaves.
hardened. Referring to the habitual state.
53 into = upon. Gr. *epi*. Ap. 104. ix. 3.
drew to the shore. A Divine supplement, here.
54 out of. Gr. *ek*. Ap. 104. vii.
knew = recognised. Ap. 132. I. iii. The result of 5. 20.
55 beds = mats, or mattresses. See note on 2. 4.
56 And, &c. Verse 56 is a Divine supplement, here.
country = country places.
the streets = the market-places. Cp. Matt. 11. 16.
besought. Ap. 134. I. 6.
border. See Matt. 9. 20.
made whole = healed. Gr. *sozō* = to save. Cp. Luke 7. 50.

7. 1-23 [For Structure see next page].

1 unto. Gr. *pros*. Ap. 104. xv. 3.
Pharisees. See Ap. 120. II.
from = away from. Gr. *apo*. Ap. 104. iv.
Jerusalem. Their head-quarters. Cp. Matt. 15. 1.
2 saw. Gr. *eidon*. Ap. 133. I. 1.
defiled = not ceremonially cleansed.
that is to say. Explanation for Gentile readers.
3 For, &c. Verses 3 and 4 are interposed by the Fig. *Parembole* (Ap. 6).

A.D. 28 except they ° wash *their* hands ° oft, eat ° not,
° holding the tradition of the ° elders.
4 And ° *when they come* [1] from the market,
except they ° wash, they eat [3] not. And many
other things there be, which they have received to [3] hold, *as* the ° washing of cups, and
° pots, brasen vessels, ° and of tables.)
h (p. 1398) 5 Then the [1] Pharisees and scribes asked
Him, "Why walk [3] not Thy disciples ° according to the tradition of the [3] elders, but eat
bread with unwashen hands?"
g 6 He answered and said unto them, "Well
hath ° Esaias prophesied ° of you ° hypocrites,
as ° it is written, ° '**This People honoureth Me
with *their* lips, but their heart is far** [1] **from Me.**
7 **Howbeit in vain do they** ° **worship Me, teaching *for* doctrines the** ° **commandments of
° men.'**
8 For ° laying aside the commandment of ° God,
ye [3] hold the tradition of [7] men, *as* the [4] washing of [4] pots and cups: and many ° other such
like things ye do."
9 And He said unto them, ° "Full well ye
° reject the commandment of [8] God, that ye may
° keep your own tradition.
10 For ° Moses said, ° '**Honour thy father and
thy mother;**' and, '**Whoso curseth father or
mother, let him** ° **die the death:**'
11 But ye say, ° 'If a [7] man shall say to his
father or mother, *'It is* ° Corban, (that is to
say, a gift), by whatsoever thou mightest be
profited ° by me;' *he shall be free.'*
12 And ye suffer him no more to do ought for
his father or his mother;
13 ° Making ° the word of [8] God ° of none effect
through your tradition, which ° ye have delivered: and many such like things do ye."
E² i 14 And when He had called all the ° people
unto him, He said unto them, "Hearken unto
Me ° every one *of you,* and understand:
k 15 There is nothing from without a [7] man,
that entering ° into him ° can defile him:
k but the things which come out ° of him, those
are they that defile the [7] man.
i 16 ° If any man have ears to hear, let him
hear."
E³ F (p. 1399) 17 And when He was entered [15] into the
° house [1] from the [14] people, ° His disciples ° asked
Him ° concerning the parable.

7. 1-23 (A², p. 1396). TEACHING. PHARISEES. (*Division.*)

A²	E¹	1-13. Pharisees. Condemnation.
	E²	14-16. People. Proclamation.
	E³	17-23. Disciples. Instruction.

7. 1-13 (E¹, above). PHARISEES. CONDEMNATION. (*Introversion.*)

E¹	g		1, 2. Cavil of Pharisees. Made.
		h	3, 4. Their Question. Reason.
		h	5. Their Question. Asked.
	g		6-13. Cavil of Pharisees. Answered.

3 wash. Gr. *niptō.* Ap. 136. i.
oft = diligently. Gr. *pugmē* = with the fist. T reads *pukna* = often. Syr. reads "carefully".
not. Gr. *ou.* Ap. 105. I.
holding = holding fast or firmly. Cp. Heb. 4. 14. Rev. 2. 25. Implying (here) determined adherence to.
elders. Always denoting in the *Papyri* an official class, whether sacred or secular.
4 when they come. Fig. *Ellipsis* (absolute). Ap. 6. I. 1.
wash = wash themselves (ceremonially). Gr. *baptizō.* WH R marg. read *rhantizō* = sprinkle (ceremonially). See Ap. 136. vii and ix.
washing. The ceremonial cleansing effected by means of water (Num. 8. 6, 7). Gr. *baptismos* = the act of cleansing: not *baptisma* = the rite or ceremonial of baptism, which is the word in all the other passages, except *v.* 8, and Heb. 6. 2; 9. 10. See Ap. 115. II. i. and ii.
pots. Gr. *xestēs.* A Latin word (*sextarius*); a pitcher of any kind, holding about a pint.
and of tables = and of couches. So Syr.
5 according to. Gr. *kata.* Ap. 104. x. 2.
6 Esaias = Isaiah. See Ap. 79. I.
of = concerning. Gr. *peri.* Ap. 104. xiii. 1.
hypocrites. The definition of the word follows.
it is written = it standeth written.
This People, &c. Quoted from Isa. 29. 13. See Ap. 107. I. 3.
7 worship. Gr. *sebomai.* Ap. 137. 2.
commandments = injunctions.
men. Gr. pl. of *anthrōpos.* Ap. 123. 1.
8 laying aside = having forsaken. Same word as in 1. 18, 20. **God.** Ap. 98. I. i.
other. Gr. *allos.* Ap. 124. 1.
9 Full well. Same as "Well" in *v.* 6.
reject = set aside. **keep** = observe.
10 Moses. See note on 1. 44.
Honour, &c. Quoted from Ex. 20. 12; 21. 17.
die the death = surely die.
11 If. The condition being purely hypothetical. See Ap. 118. 1 b.
Corban = a gift dedicated to God. A Divine supplement, giving the word and then translating it. See notes on Matt. 15. 5. Lev. 1. 2. Ezek. 40. 43.
by = from. Gr. *ek.* Ap. 104. vii.
13 Making . . . of none effect = Making void, or annulling. Cp. Matt. 15. 6.
the word of God. Notice the Lord's claim here for the Mosaic Law. Gr. *logos.* See note on 9. 32.
ye have delivered. Note the Past Tense, thus identifying them with their forefathers. Cp. Matt. 23. 35, "ye slew".

7. 14-16 (E², above). PEOPLE. PROCLAMATION. (*Introversion.*)

i		14. Call to hearken.
	k	15-. Defilement is not from without.
	k	-15. Defilement is from within.
i		16. Call to hearken.

14 people = crowd. **every one of you** = all. But there are many to-day who neither "hear" nor understand. **15 into.** Gr. *eis.* Ap. 104. vi. **can defile** = is able to defile. **of** = away from. Gr. *apo.* Ap. 104. iv. **16 If any man** = If any one. See Ap. 118. 2. a. and Ap. 142. Assuming the hypothesis, the result being yet unfulfilled. T WH R omit *v.* 16. Tr. and A put it in brackets. But the Structure requires it; and the Syr. has it.

7. 17-23 [For Structure see next page].

17 house. Supply the Ellipsis thus: "house [away] from". **His disciples.** The third of the three parties addressed in this chapter. See *vv.* 1, 14, 17. **asked** = began asking. **concerning.** Gr. *peri.* Ap. 104. xiii. 1, as in *v.* 6.

G l (p. 1399) A. D. 28 18 And He saith unto them, "Are ye °so without understanding °also? Do ye [3]not perceive, that °whatsoever thing from without entereth [15]into the [7]man, *it* °cannot defile him;

m 19 Because it entereth [3]not [15]into his heart, but [15]into the belly, and goeth out [15]into the °draught," °purging all meats?

G l 20 °And He said, "That which °cometh °out of the [7]man, that defileth the [7]man.

m 21 For from within, [20]out of the heart of [7]men, proceed °evil °thoughts, adulteries, fornications, murders,

22 Thefts, °covetousness, °wickedness, °deceit, °lasciviousness, an °evil eye, °blasphemy, °pride, foolishness:

F 23 All these [22]evil things °come from within, and defile the [7]man."

B² H¹ 24 And from thence He arose, and °went [15]into the borders of Tyre and Sidon, and entered [15]into an house, and °would have °no man °know *it:* but He could [3]not be hid.

J¹ n¹ 25 °For a *certain* woman, whose °young daughter had an unclean °spirit, heard [6]of Him, and came and fell °at His feet:

26 °The woman was a °Greek, a °Syrophenician by nation; and she °besought Him that He would cast forth °the devil [20]out of her daughter.

o¹ 27 But °Jesus said unto her, °"Let the °children first be filled: for it is [3]not °meet to take the °children's bread, and to cast *it* unto the °dogs."

n² 28 And she °answered and said unto Him, "Yes, °Lord: yet the [27]dogs °under the table eat [15]of the °children's crumbs."

o² 29 °And He said unto her, °"For this saying go thy way; [26]the devil is gone [20]out of thy daughter."

n³ 30 And when she was come °to her house, she found [26]the devil °gone out, and °her daughter °laid °upon the bed.

H² 31 And again, departing °from the °coasts of Tyre and Sidon, He came [1]unto the sea of °Galilee, through the midst of the °coasts of Decapolis.

7. 17-23 (E³, p. 1398). DISCIPLES. INSTRUCTION.
(*Introversion and Alternation.*)

E³ | F | 17. Question asked.
  G | l | 18. Defilement is not from without.
    m | 19. Reason.
  G | *l* | 20. Defilement is from within.
    m | 21, 22. Reason.
 F | 23. Question answered.

18 so . . . also = even so.
whatsoever thing from without = all [counted unclean] from without.
cannot = is not (Ap. 105. I) able to.
19 draught = sewer. Syr. reads "digestive process".
purging all meats. Supply the Ellipsis thus (being the Divine comment on the Lord's words): "[this He said], making all meats clean", as in Acts 10. 15. The Syr. reads "carrying off all that is eaten": making it part of the Lord's parable.
20 And He said, &c. Note the Fig. *Epimonē.* Ap. 6.
cometh = issueth.
out of. Gr. *ek.* Ap. 104. vii.
21 evil. Ap. 128. III. 2. Note the Figure *Asyndeton*, leading up to the climax in *v.* 23. Note that in the Greek the first seven are plural, and the other six singular. **thoughts** = reasonings.
22 covetousness = covetous desires.
wickedness = wickednesses. Ap. 128. II. 1.
deceit = guile.
lasciviousness = licentiousness.
evil. Ap. 128. III. 1.
evil eye. Fig. *Catachrēsis.* Ap. 6. Denoting envy, which proceeds out of the heart.
blasphemy = evil speaking in general. Matt. 27. 39. Rom. 3. 8; 14. 16. 1 Pet. 4. 4.
pride = haughtiness. Cp. Prov. 16. 5. Rom. 12. 16. 1 Tim. 3. 6.
23 come = issue. A Divine supplement, here.

7. 24—8. 9 (B², p. 1396). MIRACLES.
(*Repeated Alternation.*)

B² | H¹ | 7. 24. Place.
  J¹ | 7. 25-30. Miracle. Syrophenician Woman.
 H² | 7. 31. Place.
  J² | 7. 32-37. Miracle. Deaf and Dumb Man.
 H³ | 8. 1. Time and Place.
  J³ | 8. 2-9. Miracle. Feeding the Four Thousand.

24 went = went away. See note on "withdrew", 3. 7; 6. 31.
would = wished to. Ap. 102. 1.
no man = no one.
know = get to know. Gr. *ginōskō.* Ap. 132. I. ii.

7. 25-30 (J¹, above). MIRACLE. THE SYROPHENICIAN WOMAN. (*Repeated Alternation.*)

J¹ | n¹ | 25, 26. The Woman. Coming.
  o¹ | 27. The Lord. Delay.
 n² | 28. The Woman. Understanding.
  o² | 29. The Lord. Healing.
 n³ | 30. The Woman. Returning.

25 For, &c. Connect this with *v.* 24, as being an evidence why He could not be hid. **young daughter.** Gr. *thugatrion* = little daughter (Dim.). See ch. 5. 23. **spirit.** Gr. *pneuma.* See Ap. 101. II. 12. Cp. *v.* 26. **at** = towards. Gr. *pros.* Ap. 104. xv. 3. **26 The woman** = But (or Now) the woman. **Greek** = Gentile. Gr. *Hellēnis.* Used in a general sense for non-Jewish. **Syrophenician.** Phenicia in Syria, to distinguish it from Phenicia in North Africa (Libyo-Phenicia). **besought.** Ap. 134. I. 3. Not the same word as in *v.* 32. **the devil** = the demon: the spirit of *v.* 25. **27 Jesus.** Ap. 98. X. **Let the children first be filled.** This is a summary of Matt. 15. 23, 24, and a Divine supplement, here. **children.** Gr. Pl. of *teknon.* See Ap. 108. i. Not the same word as in *v.* 28. **meet** = good. **dogs** = little or domestic dogs. Gr. *kunarion.* Dim. of *kuōn.* Occ. only here and Matt. 15. 26, 27. These were not the pariah dogs of the street, but domestic pets. **28 answered and said.** See notes on Deut. 1. 41 and on Matt. 15. 26, &c. **Lord.** Ap. 98. VI. i. *a.* 3. B. **under the table.** A Divine supplement, here. **children's.** See Ap. 108. v. Not the same word as in *v.* 27. **29 And, &c.** Verses 29, 30 are a Divine supplement, here. **For** = Because, or on account of. Gr. *dia.* Ap. 104. v. 2. **30 to** = into. Gr. *eis.* Ap. 104. vi. **gone out:** i. e. permanently (Perf. Tense). **her** = the. **laid** = thrown; by the convulsion. Cp. 1. 26; 9. 20. **upon.** Gr. *epi.* Ap. 104. ix. 1. **31 from** = out of. Gr. *ek.* Ap. 104. vii. **coasts** = borders. **Galilee.** See Ap. 169.

J² p (p. 1400) A. D. 28 32 ° And they bring unto Him one that was
° deaf, and had an ° impediment in his speech;
and they ° beseech Him to ° put His hand upon
him.
q 33 And He took him aside [1] from the ° multitude, and ° put His fingers [15] into his ears,
° and He spit, and touched his tongue;
34 And looking up [30] to ° heaven, He ° sighed,
and saith unto him, ° "Ephphatha," that is,
"Be opened."
35 And ° straightway his ears were opened,
and the ° string of his tongue was ° loosed, and
he ° spake ° plain.
p 36 And He charged them that they should
tell no man:
q but the more He charged them, so much the
more a great deal they ° published *it;*
37 And were beyond measure astonished,
saying, "He hath done all things well: He
maketh both the deaf to hear, and the dumb
to speak."

H³ (p. 1399) **8** ° In those days the ° multitude being very
great, and having ° nothing to eat, ° Jesus
called His disciples *unto Him,* and saith unto
them,
J³ r¹ (p. 1400) 2 "I have compassion ° on the [1] multitude, because they have now been with Me three days,
and have ° nothing to eat:
3 And ° if I send them away fasting ° to their
own houses, they will faint ° by the way: for
° divers of them came from far."
s¹ 4 And His disciples answered Him, "From
whence can a man satisfy these *men* with
bread here ° in the wilderness?"
r² 5 And He ° asked them, "How many loaves
have ye?"
s² And they said, "Seven."
r³ 6 And He commanded the ° people to sit down
° on the ground: and He took the seven
loaves, and gave thanks, and ° brake, and
° gave to His disciples to set before *them;* and
they did set *them* before the ° people.
7 And they had a few small fishes: and He
blessed, and commanded to set them also before *them.*
s³ 8 So they did eat, and were filled: and they
took up of the broken *meat* that was left
seven ° baskets.
9 And they that had eaten were about ° four
thousand: and He sent them away.

A³ K (p. 1400) 10 And ° straightway He entered ° into ° a ship
° with His disciples, and came ° into the parts
of ° Dalmanutha.
L t 11 And the ° Pharisees came forth, and ° began
to question with Him,
u seeking ° of Him ° a sign ° from ° heaven, tempting Him.
t 12 And He ° sighed deeply in His ° spirit, and
saith, ° "Why doth this generation ° seek after
[11] a sign? ° verily I say unto you,

7. 32-37 (J², p. 1399). MIRACLE. THE DEAF AND DUMB MAN. (*Repeated Alternation.*)

J² | p | 32. The people. Beseeching.
  q | 33-35. Compliance.
 p | 36-. The people. Enjoined.
  q | -36, 37. Non-compliance, and astonishment.

32 And, &c. *Vv.* 32-37 are a Divine supplement, here.

deaf . . . impediment. Not born deaf, and dumb in consequence; but the impediment may have come through subsequent deafness. He could speak, but with difficulty, through not being able to hear his own voice. Cp. *v.* 35.

beseech. Ap. 134. I. 6; not the same word as in *v.* 26.

put=lay. Not the same word as in next verse.

33 multitude=crowd, same as "people" in *v.* 14.

put=thrust. Not the same word as in *v.* 32.

and. Note the Fig. *Polysyndeton* (Ap. 6), particularising each act.

34 heaven=the heaven. Sing. See note on Matt. 6. 9, 10.

sighed=groaned.

Ephphatha. An Aramaic word. See Ap. 94. III. 3.

35 straightway=immediately. See note on 1. 10, 12.

string=band. Not a physiological or technical expression, but the bond of demoniac influence which is thus indicated. The *Papyri* contain detailed prescriptions for "binding" a man; and cases are particularly common in which a man's *tongue* is specially to be *bound.* See Prof. Deissmann's *Light from the Ancient East,* pp. 306-310. The Lord alludes to this in Luke 13. 16.

loosed. The demoniac's fetters were loosed, and the work of Satan was undone.

spake=began speaking.

plain=correctly. Denoting the *fact* of articulation, not the words spoken.

36 published=kept proclaiming. See Ap. 121. 1.

8. 1 In. Gr. *en.* Ap. 104. viii. 1.

multitude=crowd, as in 7. 33.

nothing=not (Gr. *mē.* Ap. 105. II) anything.

8. 2-9 (J³, p. 1399). MIRACLE. FEEDING THE FOUR THOUSAND. (*Repeated Alternation.*)

J³ | r¹ | 2, 3. The Lord. Compassion.
  s¹ | 4. Disciples. Question.
 r² | 5-. The Lord. Question.
  s² | -5. Disciples. Answer.
 r³ | 6, 7. The Lord. Miracle.
  s³ | 8, 9. People. Filled.

2 on. Gr. *epi.* Ap. 104. ix. 3.

nothing=not (Gr. *ou.* Ap. 105. I) anything.

3 if. An hypothetical condition. Ap. 118. 1. b.

to=into. Gr. *eis.* Ap. 104. vi.

by=in. Gr. *en.* Ap. 104. viii. 1.

divers, &c.=some of them are come from far. A Divine supplement, here.

4 in=on. Gr. *epi.* Ap. 104. ix. 1.

5 asked=began asking.

6 people=crowd.

on=upon. Gr. *epi.* Ap. 104. ix. 1.

brake. See notes on Matt. 14. 19. Isa. 58. 7.

gave=kept giving.

8 baskets. Gr. pl. of *spuris,* a large basket or hamper. Occ. only here and in *v.* 20, Matt. 15. 37; 16. 10; and Acts 9. 25.

9 four thousand. Matt. 15. 38 adds a Divine supplement: "beside women and children".

8. 10-21 [For Structure see next page].

10 straightway. See notes on 1. 10, 12.

into. Gr. *eis.* Ap. 104. vi.

a ship=the boat.

with=in company with. Gr. *meta.* Ap. 104. xi. 1. Same word as in *vv.* 14, 38. Not the same as in *v.* 34.

Dalmanutha. Ap. 169.

11 Pharisees. Ap. 120. II.

began. The beginnings of things are very often thus emphasised in Mark. See 1. 1, 45; 4. 1; 5. 17, 20; 6. 2, 7, 34, 55; 8. 11, 31, 32; 10. 28, 32, 41, 47; 11. 15; 12. 1; 13. 5; 14. 19, 33, 65, 69, 71; 15. 8, 18.

of. Gr. *para.* Ap. 104. xiii. 1.

a sign. Cp. Matt. 12. 38.

from. Gr. *apo.* Ap. 104. iv.

heaven. Sing. See notes on Matt. 6. 9, 10.

12 sighed deeply in His spirit. A Divine supplement, here.

spirit. Gr. *pneuma.* See Ap. 101. II. 9.

Why, &c. Fig. *Erotēsis* (Ap. 6). See note on *v.* 17.

seek=repeatedly seek.

12 verily=indeed. See note on Matt. 5. 18.

u °'There shall no sign be given unto this generation.'"
A.D. 28

K (p. 1401) 13 And He left them, and entering [10]into the [10]ship again departed [3]to the other side.

L v 14 °Now *the disciples* had forgotten to take bread, °neither had they [1]in the [10]ship [10]with them more than °one loaf.

w 15 And He °charged them, saying, "Take heed, beware °of °the leaven of the [11]Pharisees, and *of* the leaven of °Herod."

v 16 And they °reasoned °among themselves, saying, "*It is* because we have °no bread."

w 17 And when [1]Jesus °knew *it*, He saith unto them, °"Why reason ye, because ye have [16]no bread? perceive ye not yet, neither understand? have ye your heart yet hardened?

18 °**Having eyes, °see ye °not? and having ears, hear ye °not?** and do ye °not remember?

19 When I brake the five loaves °among °five thousand, how many °baskets full of fragments took ye up?" They say unto him, "Twelve."

20 "And °when the seven [19]among °four thousand, how many °baskets full of fragments took ye up?" And they said, "Seven."

21 And He said unto them, °"How is it that ye do [18]not understand?"

B³ M x 22 °And He cometh [3]to °Bethsaida; and they bring a blind man unto Him, and besought Him to touch him.

y 23 And He °took the blind man by the hand, and led him °out of the town;

N z and when He had spit °on his eyes, and °put His hands upon him, He °asked him °if he [18]saw ought.

a 24 And he °looked up, and said, °"I [18]see °men as trees, walking."

N z 25 After that He [23]put *His* hands again °upon his eyes, and °made him [24]look up:

a and he was restored, and °saw °every man °clearly.

M x 26 And He sent him away [3]to his house, saying,

y °"Neither go [10]into the town, nor tell *it* to any [1]in the town."

A⁴ b¹ (p. 1402) 27 And [1]Jesus went out, and His disciples, [1]into the towns of Cæsarea Philippi: and [3]by the way He asked His disciples, saying unto them, "Whom do [24]men say °that I am?"

---

8. 10-21 (A³, p. 1396). TEACHING. PHARISEES AND DISCIPLES. (*Alternations.*)

A³ | K | 10. Departure to Dalmanutha.
  L | t | 11-. The Lord. Questioned. } Pharisees.
    u | -11. Pharisees. Sign sought.
    t | 12-. The Lord. Troubled.
    u | -12. Pharisees. Sign refused.
 K | 13. Return to the other side.
  L | v | 14. Disciples. Forgetfulness. } Disciples.
    w | 15. Leaven. Warning.
    v | 16. Disciples. Reasoning.
    w | 17-21. Leaven. Instruction.

There shall no sign be, &c. = If there shall be a sign given, &c. A Heb. idiom; = ye will see a sign; but the sentence is left unfinished by the Fig. *Aposiōpēsis* (Ap. 6). The word "if" implies that there is no doubt about it. See Ap. 118. 2. a. Cp. Gen. 21. 23. Deut. 1. 35. 1 Kings 1. 51.

14 Now, &c. See Matt. 16. 5, &c.
neither had they = and they had not (Ap. 105. I).
one loaf. A Divine supplement, here.
15 charged = was charging.
of = [and keep away] from. Gr. *apo.* Ap. 104. iv.
the leaven. Note the Fig. *Hypocatastasis* (Ap. 6), by which the word "doctrine" is implied. Cp. Matt. 16. 6.
Herod. See 3. 6 and Ap. 109.
16 reasoned = were reasoning.
among = one with (Gr. *pros.* Ap. 104. xv. 3) another.
no. Gr. *ou.* Ap. 105. I.
17 knew. Ap. 132. I. ii.
Why reason ye . . . ? Note the Fig. *Erotēsis* (Ap. 6), emphasizing the seven questions of *vv.* 17, 18. Cp. *vv.* 12 and 21.
18 Having eyes, &c. Quoted from Jer. 5. 21.
see. Gr. *blepō.* Ap. 133. I. 5.
not. Gr. *ou.* Ap. 105. I.
19 among = to; or [and gave] to. Gr. *eis.* Ap. 104. vi. Not the same word as in *v.* 16. **five** = the five.
baskets. Gr. *kophinos* = a Jewish wicker travelling hand-basket, of a definite capacity. From this comes our Eng. "coffin". Occ. Matt. 14. 20; 16. 9. Mark 6. 43; 8. 19. Luke 9. 17. John 6. 13. Not the same word as in *v.* 20.
20 when = when [I brake]. Supply the Ellipsis from *v.* 19. **four** = the four.
baskets. Gr. *spuris*, a large basket, or hamper. See note on *v.* 8, 19.
21 How is it . . . ? Fig. *Erotēsis* (Ap. 6). See notes on *vv.* 12, 17.

8. 22-26 (B³, p. 1396). MIRACLE. BLIND MAN. (*Introversion and Alternation.*)

B³ | M | x | 22. Blind man brought.
    y | 23-. Town (Bethsaida) avoided.
  N | z | -23. First application.
     a | 24. Partial restoration.
  N | z | 25-. Second application.
     a | -25. Perfect restoration.
 M | x | 26-. Blind man dismissed.
    y | -26. Town (Bethsaida) to be avoided.

---

22 And He cometh, &c. This miracle is a Divine supplement in this Gospel. The second part of the Lord's ministry was drawing to a close. The proclamation of His Person was reaching a climax (*vv.* 27-30). Note the character of "this generation" brought out by the Fig. *Erotēsis* (Ap. 6) in *vv.* 12, 17, 18, 21; the unbelief of Bethsaida (Matt. 11. 21), is symbolized by this, the last miracle of that period, which that town was not allowed to witness or be told of. Note also the seeming difficulty and the two stages of the miracle, as though symbolic of *vv.* 17, 18. **Bethsaida.** Where most of His miracles had been wrought. A town on the west shore of Galilee. See Ap. 94. III. 3 and 169. **23 took** = took hold of. (So Tyndale.) **out of** = outside of. **on** = into. Gr. *eis.* Ap. 104. vi. **put** = laid. **asked** = was asking. (Imperf.) **if he saw** = can you see . . . ? Present Tense. **24 looked up.** Ap. 133. I. 6. **I see men, &c.** = I see the men [men they must be] for [I see them] as trees, walking. **men.** Gr. *anthrōpos.* Ap. 123. 1. **25 upon.** Gr. *epi.* Ap. 104. ix. 3. **made him look up.** T Tr. A WH and R read "the man looked steadily". **saw.** Gr. *emblepō.* Ap. 133. I. 7. **every man.** L T Tr. A WH R read "everything". **clearly** = distinctly; implying at a distance. Gr. *tēlaugōs* (from *tēle*, far, as in our telescope, telegram, &c.). **26 Neither go, &c.** Note the determination of the Lord not to give Bethsaida any further evidence.

8. 27-30 [For Structure see next page].

27 that I am. The second subject of the Lord's ministry (see the Structure on p. 1383 and Ap. 119), as to His Person, was thus brought to a conclusion; as in Matt. 16. 13-20.

c1 (p. 1402) A. D. 28 28 And they answered, "John the Baptist: °but some *say*, Elias; and others, One of the prophets."

b2 29 And °He saith unto them, "But whom say ye that I am?"

c2 And Peter answereth and saith unto Him, "Thou art °the Christ."

b3 30 And He °charged them that they should tell no man °of Him.

F R X1 Y d 31 And °He [11] began to teach them, that °the Son of man °must suffer many things, and be rejected °of the elders, and *of* the chief priests, and scribes, and be killed,

e and °after three days rise again.

Z 32 And He spake that saying °openly. And Peter took Him, and [11] began to °rebuke Him.

Z 33 But when He had turned about and °looked on His disciples, He rebuked Peter, saying, °"Get thee behind Me, Satan: for thou °savourest [18] not the things that be of °God, but the things that be of [24] men."

Y d 34 °And when He had called the people *unto Him* °with His disciples also, He said unto them, "Whosoever °will come after Me, let him deny himself, and take up his cross, and °follow Me.

35 For whosoever [31] will save his °life shall lose it; but whosoever shall lose his °life for My sake °and the gospel's, the same shall save it.

36 For what shall it profit a [24] man, °if he shall gain the whole °world, and lose his own °soul?

37 Or what shall a [24] man give °in exchange for his [36] soul?

38 °Whosoever therefore shall be ashamed of Me and of °My words [1] in °this adulterous and sinful generation;

e of °him also shall [31] the Son of man be ashamed, when He °cometh [1] in the glory of His °Father [10] with the holy angels."

9 And He °said unto them, °"Verily I say unto you, That there be some of them that stand here, which shall °not taste of death, °till

8. 27-30 (A4, p. 1396). TEACHING.
(*Repeated Alternation.*)

A4 | b1 | 27. The Lord. Question: "Who say men?"
  c1 | 28. Disciples. Answer.
 b2 | 29-. The Lord. Question: "Who say ye?"
  c2 | -29. Disciples. Answer (Peter).
 b3 | 30. The Lord. Charge.

28 but some=and others. Gr. *alloi*. Ap. 124. 1.
29 He saith unto them=He was further saying.
the Christ=the Messiah. Ap. 98. VIII and IX.
30 charged=strictly charged. This second subject of His ministry is thus closed. Sufficient testimony had been given to that generation, as to His Person.
of=concerning. Gr. *peri*. Ap. 104. xiii. 1.

8. 31—10. 52 (*F*, p. 1381). THE THIRD PERIOD OF THE LORD'S MINISTRY: THE REJECTION OF THE KING. (*Introversion and Alternations.*)

F | O | R | 8. 31—9. 13. SUFFERINGS. First Announcement.
  S | 9. 14-29. Miracle. Demoniac.
 P | T | 9. 30-32. SUFFERINGS. Second Announcement.
  U | 9. 33-50. Discipleship.
   Q | V | 10. 1-12. Question. Pharisees.
    W | 10. 13-16. Discipleship.
   Q | *V* | 10. 17-25. Question. Rich young man.
    W | 10. 26-31. Discipleship.
 P | *T* | 10. 32-34. SUFFERINGS. Third Announcement.
  U | 10. 35-44. Discipleship.
O | *R* | 10. 45. SUFFERINGS. Fourth Announcement.
  S | 10. 46-52. Miracle. Blind man.

8. 31—9. 13 (R, above). SUFFERINGS. FIRST ANNOUNCEMENT. (*Division.*)

R | X1 | 8. 31—9. 1. Sufferings and glory. Foretold.
 X2 | 9. 2-10. Sufferings and glory. Foreshown.
 X3 | 9. 11-13. Sufferings and glory. Explained.

8. 31—9. 1 (X1, above). SUFFERINGS AND GLORY. FORETOLD.
(*Introversion and Alternation.*)

X1 | Y | d | 8. 31-. Sufferings. } His own.
  e | 8. -31. Glory. }
   Z | 8. 32. Peter. Rebukes the Lord.
   Z | 8. 33. Peter. Rebuked by the Lord.
 Y | *d* | 8. 34-38-. Sufferings. } His disciples.
  e | 8. -38—9. 1. Glory. }

31 He began. The third period and subject of His ministry: the rejection of Himself as King. See Ap. 119, and notes on Matt. 16. 21-28; Luke 24. 26.
the Son of man. See Ap. 98. XVI.

must. For this necessity see Acts 3. 18. **of.** Gr. *apo*, as in *v.* 15. But all the texts read *hupo*=at the hands of. Ap. 104. xviii. 1. **after.** Gr. *meta.* Ap. 104. xi. 2. See Ap. 148. **32 openly**: i.e. publicly: not as in John 2. 19-21, or John 3. 14, in the earlier portion of His ministry. **rebuke**=remonstrate with. **33 looked, &c.**=saw (Ap. 133. I. 1) His disciples, who might easily have been led astray by Peter's remonstrance. **Get thee behind, &c.** Cp. Matt. 4. 10: regarding it as a Satanic temptation. **savourest**=mindest. **God.** Ap. 98. I. i. 1. **34 And when, &c.** The Lord now speaks to all who follow Him. **with**=in association with. Gr. *sun.* Ap. 104. xvi. Not the same word as in *vv.* 10, 14, 38. **will come**=is willing to come. **will.** Gr. *thelō.* Ap. 102. 1. **follow**: i.e. habitually follow. **35 life.** Gr. *psuchē.* Ap. 110. III. 1. But here correctly rendered "life". See *v.* 36. **and the gospel's.** A Divine supplement, here. **36 if he shall gain, &c.** See Ap. 118. 1. b. **world.** Gr. *kosmos.* Ap. 129. 1. **soul**=life. Same word as "life" in *v.* 35. See Matt. 16. 26. **37 in exchange**=[as] an equivalent. **38 Whosoever therefore**=For whosoever. **My words.** Not of Christ only, but of His words. See note on 9. 32. **this . . . generation.** A Divine supplement, here. Note the frequent refs. to "this generation" as sinful above all others, and as being different from all others: *vv.* 12; 9. 19; 13. 30. See note on Matt. 11. 16. **him also.** The "also" must be after "the Son of man", not after "him". **cometh**=may have come. **Father.** See Ap. 98. III.

9. 1. said=continued to say. **Verily I say unto you.** See the four similar asseverations, Matt. 10. 23; 16. 28; 23. 36; 24. 34. **Verily**=Amen. See note on Matt. 5. 18: not the same word as in *v.* 12. **not**=in no wise, or by no means. Gr. *ou mē.* Ap. 105. III. This solemn asseveration was not needed for being kept alive six days longer. It looked forward to the end of that age. **till.** Gr. *eōs an.* The Particle "*an*" makes the clause conditional: this condition being the repentance of the nation at the call of Peter. Acts 3. 19-26 and cp. 28. 25, 26.

A. D. 28 they °have seen °the kingdom of God °come °with power."

X² f (p. 1403) 2 And °after six days °Jesus taketh *with Him* Peter, and James, and John, and leadeth them up °into an high mountain apart by themselves:

g and He was °transfigured before them.
3 And His raiment became °shining, exceeding white as °snow; °so as °no fuller °on °earth °can white them.
4 And there appeared unto them °Elias °with °Moses: and they were talking with [2] Jesus.

h 5 And Peter °answered and said to [2] Jesus, °"Master, it is good for us to be here: and let us make three tabernacles; one for Thee, and one for [4] Moses, and one for [4] Elias."
6 For he °wist °not what to say; for they were sore afraid.

h 7 And there was a cloud that overshadowed °them: and a voice came °out of the cloud, saying, "This is °My beloved Son: °hear Him."

g 8 And °suddenly, when they had looked round about, they [1] saw [3] no man any more, save [2] Jesus only °with themselves.

f 9 And as they °came down °from the mountain, He charged them that they should °tell °no man what things they had [1] seen, till °the Son of man °were risen °from °the dead.
10 And they °kept that saying °with themselves, questioning one [8] with another what the rising [9] from [9] the dead °should mean.

X³ A 11 And they asked Him, saying, °"Why say the scribes that [4] Elias must °first come?"

B i 12 And He answered and told them, [4] "Elias °verily cometh [11] first, and restoreth all things;

k and how °it is written °of [9] the Son of man, that He °must suffer many things, and be set at nought.

B i 13 But I say unto you,

k That [4] Elias °is indeed °come, and they °have done unto him whatsoever they °listed,

A as it is written [12] of him."

S C l (p. 1404) 14 And when He came °to *His* disciples, He [1] saw a great °multitude °about them, and °the scribes questioning with them.
15 °And °straightway all the °people, when they °beheld Him, °were greatly amazed, and running to *Him* saluted Him.
16 And He asked the scribes, "What question ye [10] with them?"

m 17 And one °of the [14] multitude [5] answered and

have seen = may have seen. Gr. *eidon*. Ap. 133. I. i.
the kingdom of God. See Ap. 114.
come = actually come.
with = in. Gr. *en*. Ap. 104. viii. Not the same word as in *vv.* 4, 8, 10, 16, 19, 24.

9. 2-10 (X², p. 1402). SUFFERINGS AND GLORY. FORESHOWN. (*Introversion.*)

X² | f | 2-. Ascent. Disciples taken up.
  g | -2-4. Vision. The Lord, Moses, and Elijah.
    h | 5, 6. Voice of Peter.
    h | 7. Voice of the Father.
  g | 8. Vision ended. The Lord alone.
f | 9, 10. Descent. Disciples charged.

2 after. Gr. *meta*. Ap. 104. xi. 2. Exclusive reckoning. Cp. Luke 9. 2 (inclusive).
Jesus. See Ap. 98. X. **into.** Gr. *eis*. Ap. 104. vi.
transfigured = transformed.
Gr. *metamorphoō*. To change the form or appearance. Occ. only here, Matt. 17. 2; Rom. 12. 2; and 2 Cor. 3. 18. Contrast *metaschēmatizō*, to transfigure, change the *figure*, shape, mien, &c. (1 Cor. 4. 6. 2 Cor. 11. 13, 14, 15. Phil. 3. 21). See Ap. 149.
3 shining = gleaming. Gr. *stilbō*. Occ. only here.
snow. The whiteness of *nature*.
so as no fuller, &c. A Divine supplement, here.
no. Gr. *ou*. Ap. 105. I.
on. Gr. *epi*. Ap. 104. ix. 1.
earth. Gr. *gē*. Ap. 129. 4.
can white them = is able to whiten them. The whiteness of *art*. **4 Elias** = Elijah. Cp. Mal. 4. 4, 5.
with = together with. Gr. *sun*. Ap. 104. xvi. Not the same word as in *vv.* 8, 10, 19, 24, 50.
Moses. See note on 1. 44.
5 answered and said. See note on Deut. 1. 41.
Master = Rabbi. Ap. 98. XIV. vii. Not the same word as in *v.* 17. **6 wist** = knew. Gr. *oida*. Ap. 132. I. i.
not. Gr. *ou*. Ap. 105. I. Same word as in *vv.* 18, 28, 30, 37, 38, 40, 44, 46, 48. Not the same as in *vv.* 1, 39, 41.
7 them: i.e. Moses and Elijah.
out of = out from. Gr. *ek*. Ap. 104. vii.
My beloved Son = My Son, the beloved.
hear = hear ye. Cp. Deut. 18. 19.
8 suddenly. Gr. *exapina*. Occ. only here in N.T.
with = in company with. Gr. *meta*. Ap. 104. xi. 1.
9 came = were coming.
from = away from. Gr. *apo*. Ap. 104. iv.
tell = relate to. **no man** = no one.
the Son of man. See Ap. 98. XVI.
were = should have.
from = out from. Gr. *ek*. Ap. 104. vii.
the dead. No Art. See Ap. 139. 2.
10 kept = laid hold of and kept.
with = to. Gr. *pros*. Ap. 104. xv. 3.
should mean = is: i.e. "What is the rising from among [other] dead [people]?"

9. 11-13 (X³, p. 1402). SUFFERINGS AND GLORY. EXPLAINED. (*Introversion and Alternation.*)

X³ | A | 11. What the Scribes were saying.
  B | i | 12-. The Lord. Admission.
      k | -12. Prophecy concerning Himself.
  B | *i* | 13-. The Lord. Addition.
      k | -13-. Prophecy concerning Elijah.
A | -13. What is written in the Scripture.

11 Why say the scribes . . . ? = The scribes say, &c. Gr. *men*. Not the same as in *v.* 1. Ap. 104. ix. 3. Not the same as in *v.* 17. has . . . come. **first.** See Mal. 4. 5, 6. **12 verily** = indeed. **it is written** = it standeth written. **of** = upon. Gr. *epi*. **must suffer.** See note on 8. 31. **13 is . . . come** = has . . . come. **have done** = did. **listed** = desired, or liked. Gr. *thelō*. Ap. 102. 1.

9. 14-29 [For Structure see next page].

14 to. Gr. *pros*. Ap. 104. xv. 3. **multitude** = crowd. **about** = around. Gr. *peri*. Ap. 104. xiii. 3. **the scribes.** This particularizing the scribes as questioners is a Divine supplement, here. **15 And, &c.**: *vv.* 15 and 16 are also a Divine supplement, here. **straightway.** See notes on 1. 10, 12. **people** = crowd. Same word as in *v.* 14. **beheld** = saw, as in *v.* 14. **were greatly amazed.** Gr. *ekthambeomai* = to be greatly astonished. Occ. only here; and 14. 33; 16. 5, 6. **17 of** = from among. Gr. *ek*. Ap. 104. vii.

A. D. 28 said, ° "Master, I have brought ° unto Thee my son, which hath a dumb ° spirit;
18 And wheresoever ° he taketh him, ° he teareth him: ° and he ° foameth, ° and ° gnasheth with his teeth, and pineth away: ° and I spake to Thy disciples that they should cast him out; ° and they ° could [6] not."

D n[1] (p. 1404) 19 He [5] answereth him, and saith, "O ° faithless ° generation, how long shall I be [10] with you? how long shall I ° suffer you? bring him [17] unto Me."

o[1] 20 And they brought him [17] unto Him: and ° when he [1] saw Him, [15] straightway the [17] spirit ° tare him; and he fell [3] on the ground, and ° wallowed [18] foaming.

n[2] 21 ° And He asked his father, "How long is it ago since this came unto him?"

o[2] And he said, ° "Of a child.
22 And ofttimes it hath cast him [2] into the fire, and [2] into the waters, ° to destroy him: but ° if Thou canst do any thing, have ° compassion ° on ° us, and help ° us."

n[3] 23 [2] Jesus said unto him, ° "If thou canst ° believe, ° all things *are* possible to him that believeth."

o[3] 24 And [15] straightway the father of ° the child ° cried out, ° and said [8] with tears, ° "Lord, I believe; help Thou mine unbelief."

n[4] 25 When [2] Jesus [1] saw that the [15] people came running together, He rebuked the ° foul [17] spirit, saying unto him, "*Thou* dumb and deaf [17] spirit, I ° charge thee, come [7] out of him, and enter no more [2] into him."
26 And *the spirit* ° cried, and ° rent him sore, and came out of him: and he was ° as one [9] dead; insomuch that many ° said, "He is dead."
27 But [2] Jesus took him by the hand, and lifted him up; and he arose.

C *l* 28 And when He was come [2] into ° the house, His disciples asked Him privately, "Why could [6] not we cast ° him out?"

m 29 And He said unto them, ° "This kind can come forth ° by nothing, but ° by prayer ° and fasting."

P T (p. 1402) 30 And they departed thence, and ° passed ° through Galilee; and He ° would [6] not that any man should know *it*.
31 For ° He taught His disciples, and ° said unto them, ° "The Son of man ° is delivered [2] into the hands of men, and they shall kill Him; and after that He is killed, He shall rise the third day."
32 But they understood not that ° saying, and were afraid to ask Him.

U E G (p. 1405) 33 ° And He came ° to Capernaum: and being ° in the house He asked them, "What was it that ye ° disputed ° among yourselves [29] by the way?"

9. 14-29 (S, p. 1402). MIRACLE. DEMONIAC.
(*Introversion and Alternations.*)

S | C | l | 14-16. Inquiry by the Lord. Of the Scribes.
    m | 17, 18. Inability of Disciples. Complaint.
  D | n[1] | 19. The Lord. Complaint and Command.
      o[1] | 20. Father. Obedience.
    n[2] | 21-. The Lord. Question.
      o[2] | -21, 22. Father. Answer.
    n[3] | 23. The Lord. Question.
      o[3] | 24. Father. Answer.
    n[4] | 25-27. The Lord. Miracle.
  C | *l* | 28. Inquiry by the Disciples. Of the Lord.
    m | 29. Inability of Disciples. Explained.

Master = Teacher. Ap. 98. XIV. v. 1. Not the same word as in *v.* 5.
unto. Gr. *pros.* Ap. 104. xv. 3.
spirit. Gr. *pneuma.* Ap. 101. II. 12.
18 he taketh = it seizeth hold of.
he teareth him = it dasheth him down.
and. Note the Fig. *Polysyndeton*, Ap. 6, emphasizing each detail.
foameth = foameth [at the mouth].
gnasheth = grindeth. This and "pineth away" are a Divine supplement, here.
could not = had not [the] power to.
19 faithless = without faith; not treacherous, but unbelieving.
generation. See note on Matt. 11. 16.
suffer = bear with.
20 when he saw Him. A Divine supplement, here.
tare = convulsed.
wallowed foaming. These details are Divine supplements, here.
wallowed = began to roll about.
21 And He asked, &c. *Vv.* 21-27 are a Divine supplement, here. **Of a child** = From childhood.
22 to = in order to; or, that it might.
if Thou canst. No doubt is implied. See Ap. 118. 2. a.
compassion. Relying on this rather than on the Lord's power. **on.** Gr. *epi.* Ap. 104. ix. 3.
us. Note the tender sympathy of the father.
23 If thou canst. Note how the Lord gives back the father's question, with the same condition implied.
believe. Omitted by T Tr. [A] WH R; not by the Syr.
all things. Fig. *Synecdochē* (Ap. 6). All things included in the promise.
24 the child. Gr. *paidion.* Ap. 108. v.
cried out. Inarticulate.
and said = began to say. Articulate.
Lord. Ap. 98. VI. i. *a.* 3. B. a.
25 foul = unclean. **charge** = command.
26 cried = cried out.
rent him = threw him into convulsions.
as one = as though. **said, He is** = said that he was.
28 the = a. **him** = it.
29 This kind. Showing that there are different kinds of spirits. **by.** Gr. *en.* Ap. 104. vi.
and fasting. Omitted by LT [Tr.] A WH R; not by the Syr.
30 passed through = were passing along through.
through: i. e. not through the cities, but passed along through Galilee past them. Gr. *dia.* Ap. 104. v. 1.
would = wished. Ap. 102. 1.
31 He taught = He began teaching (Imperf.). The continuation of 8. 31.
said unto them = said unto them that.
The Son of man. See Ap. 98. XVI. This was the *second* announcement. See the Structure, "T", p. 1402.
is = will be: or, is to be. Fig. *Heterōsis* (of Tense), Ap. 6.

32 saying. Gr. *rhēma* (the first time it is thus rendered). *Rhēma* denotes *a word, saying,* or sentence in its outward form, as made up of words (i. e. Parts of Speech): whereas *logos* denotes *a word* or saying as the expression of thought: hence, the thing spoken or written, the account, &c., given.

9. 33-50 [For Structure see next page].

33 And He came, &c. *Vv.* 33-35 a Divine supplement, here. **to** = into. Gr. *eis.* Ap. 104. vi. **in.** Gr. *en.* Ap. 104. viii. Same as in *vv.* 36-, 41, 50; not the same as in *vv.* 37, 39, 42. **disputed** = were discussing. **among.** Gr. *pros.* Ap. 104. xv. 3.

H 34 But they held their peace: for [29] by the
(p. 1405) way they °had disputed [33] among themselves,
A. D. 28 who *should be* the °greatest.
F 35 And He °sat down, and °called the twelve,
and saith unto them, °"If any man °desire to
be first, *the same* °shall be last of all, and
°servant of all."
F 36 And He took a [24] child, and set him [33] in
the midst of them: and °when He had taken
him in His arms, He said unto them,
37 "Whosoever shall receive one of such
[24] children °in My name, receiveth Me: and
whosoever shall receive Me, receiveth [6] not
Me, but Him That sent Me."
E G 38 And °John answered Him, saying,
[17] "Master, we [8] saw one casting out °devils in
Thy name, and he followeth [6] not us: and we
forbad him, because he followeth [6] not us."
H J p 39 But [2] Jesus said, "Forbid him °not: for
there is [3] no man which shall do a miracle [37] in
My name, that can lightly speak evil of Me.
40 For he that is [6] not °against us is °on our
part.
q 41 For whosoever shall give you a cup of
water to drink [33] in My name, because °ye
belong to °Christ, [1] verily I say unto you, he
shall [1] not lose his reward.
42 And whosoever °shall offend one of *these*
little ones that °believe in Me, it is °better for
him °that °a millstone were hanged [14] about
his neck, and he were cast [2] into the sea.
K¹ 43 And °if thy hand °offend thee, cut it off:
it is [42] better for thee to enter [2] into °life maimed,
than having two hands to go [2] into °hell, [2] into
°the fire that never shall be quenched:
**44 Where their °worm dieth [6] not, and [43] the
fire is [6] not quenched.**
K² 45 And [43] if thy foot [43] offend thee, cut it off:
it is better for thee to enter °halt [2] into [43] life,
than having two feet to be cast [2] into [43] hell,
[2] into [43] the fire that never shall be quenched:
**46 Where their [44] worm dieth [6] not, and [43] the
fire is [6] not quenched.**
K³ 47 And [43] if thine eye [43] offend thee, pluck it out:
it is [42] better for thee to enter [2] into °the kingdom
of God with one eye, than having two eyes to
be cast [2] into °hell fire:
**48 °Where their [44] worm dieth [6] not, and [43] the
fire is [6] not quenched.**
J p 49 For °every one shall be salted with fire,
and °every sacrifice shall be salted with salt.
50 Salt *is* good: °but [43] if the salt have °lost
his saltness, °wherewith will ye °season it?
q Have salt °in yourselves, and have peace
°one with another."

Q V L **10** And He arose from thence, and cometh
p. 1406) °into the °coasts of Judæa °by the
°farther side of Jordan: and the °people resort

9. 33-50 (U, p. 1402). DISCIPLESHIP.
(*Introversion and Alternation.*)

U | E | G | 33. Event. Disciples. Disputing.
  H | 34. Silence and Reason.
  F | 35. Instruction.
  F | 36, 37. Illustration.
E | *G* | 38. Event. A disciple rebuking.
  H | 39-50. Speech. Answer and Reason.

34 had disputed = had been discussing.
greatest = greater.
35 sat down = took His seat (as Teacher).
called. Denoting solemnity in so doing.
If any man, &c. The condition is assumed as a fact. Ap. 118. 2. a. **desire.** Gr. *thelō.* Ap. 102. 1.
shall be = will be.
servant. Gr. *diakonos*, a voluntary servant. Cp. Eng. "deacon".
36 when He had taken him in His arms. This is all one verb (*enankalisamenos*), and occ. only here.
37 in. Gr. *epi.* Ap. 104. ix. 2.
38 John answered. His conscience was touched; for he remembered what he had done, and confessed it.
devils = demons.

9. 39-50 (*H*, above). SPEECH. ANSWER AND REASON. (*Introversion and Alternation.*)

H | J | p | 39, 40. General.
  q | 41, 42. Particular.
  K¹ | 43, 44. Hand.
  K² | 45, 46. Foot. } Stumbling-blocks.
  K³ | 47, 48. Eye.
J | *p* | 49, 50-. General.
  q | -50. Particular.

39 not. Gr. *mē.* Ap. 105. II.
40 against. Gr. *kata.* Ap. 104. x. 1.
on our part = for (*huper* = on our behalf. Ap. 104. xvii. 1) us.
41 ye belong to Christ = ye are Christ's.
Christ. Ap. 98. IX.
42 shall offend = shall have caused to stumble.
believe in. See Ap. 150. I. 1. v (i). **better** = good.
that = if. A simple hypothesis. Ap. 118. 2. a.
a millstone = a great millstone (turned by an ass). Cp. Matt. 18. 6; Luke 17. 2. A Greek and Roman punishment: not Jewish.
43 if. A contingent hypothesis. Ap. 118. 1. b.
offend = (constantly) cause thee to stumble. Not the same word as in *v.* 42.
life. Gr. *zōē* (Ap. 170. 1). With Art.: i.e. into resurrection life, or life eternal. See note on Matt. 9. 18.
hell. Gr. *Geenna.* See Ap. 131. I.
the fire that never shall be quenched = the fire, the unquenchable. Gr. *to pūr to asbeston.* Cp. Matt. 3. 12.
44 worm. See Isa. 66. 24, and cp. Ex. 16. 20. Job 7. 5; 17. 14; 19. 26; 21. 26; 24. 20. Isa. 14. 11. This verse and *v.* 46 are omitted by T [Tr.] WH R, not the Syriac.
45 halt = lame.
47 the kingdom of God. See Ap. 114.
hell fire = the *Geenna* of fire. See note on *v.* 43.
48 Where, &c. This is included in all the texts; and is quoted from Isa. 66. 24.
49 every one shall be salted with fire. Occ. only here in N.T.
every sacrifice, &c. Some texts omit this clause, but not the Syr. Ref. to Pent. (Lev. 2. 13). This is introduced by "For", as a reason why the lesser (finite and temporal) evil is "good" compared with the greater (and final) evil. Every sacrifice is salted (to assist the burning), Deut. 29. 23. It is better therefore to endure the *removal* of the stumbling-block now, than to be altogether destroyed for ever. **50 but if, &c.** Fig. *Parœmia* (Ap. 6). **lost his saltness** = become saltless. **wherewith** = with (Gr. *en.* Ap. 104. viii) what. Cp. Matt. 5. 13; Luke 14. 34. **season it?** = restore it? **in** = within. Gr. *en* (Ap. 104. viii). **one with another** = among (Gr. *en.* Ap. 104. viii) yourselves. This refers the whole of *vv.* 43-50 back to *vv.* 34, 35; and shows that the stumbling-blocks mentioned in *vv.* 43-47 are the things that destroy peace among brethren.

10. 1-12 [For Structure see next page].

1 into. Gr. *eis.* Ap. 104. vi. **coasts** = confines, or borders. **by.** Gr. *dia.* Ap. 104. v. 1.
farther side = other side. **people** = crowds.

A. D. 28 °unto Him again; and, as He was wont, He
°taught them again.
M 2 And the °Pharisees came to Him, and asked
(p. 1406) Him,
N °"Is it lawful for °a man to put away *his*
wife?" tempting Him.
O 3 And He °answered and said unto them,
"What did °Moses command you?"
O 4 And they said, [3]"Moses °suffered to write
°**a bill of divorcement, and to put *her* away."**
N 5 And °Jesus answered and said unto them,
°"For the hardness of your heart °he wrote
°you this °precept.
6 But °from °the beginning of the creation
°**God made them male and female.**
7 °**For this cause shall °a man °leave his
father and mother, and °cleave °to his wife;**
8 **And they °twain shall be °one flesh:** so
then they are °no more °twain, but one flesh.
9 °What therefore [6]God hath joined together,
let °not man put asunder."
M 10 And °in the house His disciples asked Him
again °of the same *matter*.
L 11 And He saith unto them, "Whosoever
°shall put away his wife, and marry another,
committeth adultery °against her.
12 And °if a woman shall put away her husband, and be married to another, she committeth adultery."
W r 13 And they °brought young °children to
Him, that He should touch them:
s and *His* disciples °rebuked those that brought
them.
s 14 But when [5]Jesus saw *it*, He was °much displeased, and said unto them, "Suffer the
little [13]children to come [1]unto Me, and forbid
them [9]not: for of such is °the kingdom of God.
15 °Verily I say unto you, Whosoever shall
[9]not receive [14]the kingdom of God as [13]a little
[13]child, he shall °not enter °therein."
r 16 And °He took them up in His arms, put
His hands °upon them, and °blessed them.
V P t 17 And when He was gone forth [1]into the
(p. 1407) way, there came one °running, and °kneeled
to Him, and asked Him, "Good °Master, °what
shall I do that I may inherit °eternal °life?"
u 18 And [5]Jesus said unto him, °"Why callest
thou Me good? *there is* °none good but one,
that is, [6]God.

10. 1-12 (V, p. 1402). QUESTION. PHARISEES. (*Introversion.*)

V | L | 1. The Lord. Teaching.
  M | 2-. Question of Pharisees.
   N | -2. Temptation.
    O | 3. What did Moses say?
    O | 4. What Moses said.
   N | 5-9. Confutation.
  M | 10. Question of Disciples.
L | 11, 12. The Lord. Teaching.

unto. Gr. *pros.* Ap. 104. xv. 3.
taught=began teaching.
2 Pharisees. Ap. 120. II.
Is it lawful . . . ?=If it is lawful . . . ? Putting the condition as a simple hypothesis. Ap. 118. 2. a.
a man=a husband. Gr. *anēr.* Ap. 123. 2. Not the same word as in *v.* 7.
3 answered and said. See note on Deut. 1. 41.
Moses. See note on 1. 44. **4 suffered**=allowed.
a bill of divorcement. Ref. to Pent. (Deut. 24. 1).
a bill. Gr. *biblion* (Dim.), a little book or scroll. Latin *libellus*, whence our "libel"=a written accusation.
5 Jesus. Ap. 98. X.
For=In view of. Gr. *pros.* Ap. 104. xv. Not the same word as in *vv.* 22, 27, 45.
he wrote. See Ap. 47.
you=for you. **precept**=(authoritative) mandate.
6 from the beginning of the creation. Therefore there could have been no creation of "man" before Adam. See note on John 8. 44.
God made them. Therefore no evolution. See Gen. 1. 27. **God, &c.** Ap. 98. 1. i. 1.
7 For this cause, &c.=On account of this, &c. Quoted from Gen. 2. 24.
a man. Gr. *anthrōpos.* Ap. 123. 1. Not the same word as in *v.* 2.
leave. Gr. *kataleipō*=to leave utterly, forsake. Not the same word as in *v.* 29. **cleave**=shall be joined.
to. Gr. *pros.* Ap. 104. xv. 3. Same word as in *v.* 50. Not the same as in *vv.* 32-, 33, 46.
8 twain=two. Anglo-Saxon *twegen* (=twain) is masc., *twā* is fem., and *twa*, or *tu*, is neut. So that "twain" is better, as the Masc. takes precedence of Fem.
one=for, or unto. Gr. *eis.* Ap. 104. vi. Not "become one" (as R.V.); but=shall be, or stand for one flesh.
no more=no longer. Gr. *ouketi.* Compound of *ou.* Ap. 105. I.
9 What, &c. Regarding the two as one. The converse is true: what God hath divided, let not man join together. Note the bearing of this on 2 Tim. 2. 15.
not. Gr. *mē.* Ap. 105. II.
10 in. Gr. *en.* Ap. 104. viii. (All the texts read *eis*=into. Ap. 104. vi.) Same word as in *vv.* 21, 30, 32, 37, 52. Not the same as in *v.* 24.
of=concerning. Gr. *peri.* Ap. 104. xiii. 1.
11 shall=shall have.
against. Gr. *epi.* Ap. 104. ix. 3.
12 if a woman, &c. Condition being problematical, because not acc. to Jewish law; it was Greek and Roman law. See Ap. 118. 1. b.

10. 13-16 (W, p. 1402). DISCIPLESHIP. CHILDREN BROUGHT. (*Introversion.*)

W | r | 13-. Request. Made.
  s | -13. Rebuke of Disciples.
  s | 14, 15. Encouragement of the Lord.
r | 16. Request. Complied with.

13 brought=were carrying. Imperf. tense: i. e. as He went on His way. **children.** Gr. *paidia.* Ap. 108. v. **rebuked**=were reprimanding. Imperf. tense: i. e. as they were successively brought. **14 much displeased**=indignant. **the kingdom of God.** See Ap. 114.
15 Verily. See note on Matt. 5. 18. **not**=by no means. See Ap. 105. III. **therein**=into (as in *v.* 1, &c.) it. **16 He took, &c.**=He kept taking, &c. A Divine supplement, here. Cp. Matt. 19. 13 and Luke 18. 15. **upon.** Gr. *epi.* Ap. 104. ix. 3. **blessed**=kept blessing. The word occ. only here in the N.T. in this Tense.

10. 17-24 [For Structure see next page].

17 running=running up. A Divine supplement, here. **kneeled**=kneeling down. A Divine supplement, here. **Master**=Teacher. Ap. 98. XIV. v. **what shall I do . . . ?** Ever the question of the natural man, from Gen. 4. 3 onward. **eternal.** Ap. 151. II. B. 1. **life.** Gr. *zōē.* Ap. 170. 1. **18 Why callest, &c. . . . ?** Note the Fig. *Anteisagōgē*, Ap. 6. **none.** The 1611 edition of the A.V. reads "no man". Compound of Ap. 105. I.

Q v 19 Thou °knowest °the commandments, °**Do**
(p. 1407) [9]**not commit adultery, Do** [9]**not kill, Do** [9]**not**
A. D. 28 **steal, Do** [9]**not bear false witness,**°**Defraud** [9]**not,**
Honour thy father and mother."
w 20 And he answered and said unto Him,
[17]"Master, °all these have I °observed °from
my youth."
Q v 21 Then [5]Jesus °beholding him °loved him,
and said unto him, "One thing thou lackest:
go thy way, °sell whatsoever thou hast, and
give to the poor, and thou shalt have treasure
[10]in °heaven: and come, °take up the cross,
and follow Me."
w 22 And he was sad °at that saying, and
went away grieved: for he had °great possessions.
P u 23 And [5]Jesus looked round about, and saith
unto His disciples, "How °hardly shall they
that have riches enter [1]into [14]the kingdom
of God!"
t 24 And the disciples were astonished [22]at
His words. But [5]Jesus answereth again, and
saith unto them, °"Children, °how hard is it
for them that °trust °in riches to enter [1]into
[14]the kingdom of God!
25 °It is easier for a camel to go °through the
eye of a needle, than for a rich man to enter
[1]into [14]the kingdom of God."
W x 26 And they were astonished out of measure,
saying °among themselves, °"Who then can
be saved?"
y 27 And [5]Jesus looking upon them saith, °"With
°men *it is* °impossible, but °not °with [6]God: for
with [6]God all things are possible."
x 28 Then Peter °began to say unto Him, °"Lo,
we have left all, and have followed Thee."
y 29 And [5]Jesus answered and said, [15]"Verily
I say unto you, There is [18]no man that hath
°left house, °or brethren, or sisters, or father,
or mother, or wife, or [24]children, or lands for
My sake, and the gospel's,
30 But he shall receive an hundredfold now
[10]in this °time, °houses, °and brethren, and
sisters, and mothers, and [24]children, and lands,
°with persecutions; and [10]in °the world to
come [17]eternal [17]life.
31 But many *that are* first shall be last; and
the last first."
T a 32 And they were in the way going up °to
A. D. 29 Jerusalem; and [5]Jesus °went before them: and
they °were amazed; and as they followed,
they were afraid.
b And He °took °again the twelve, and began
to tell them what things should happen unto
Him,

10. 17-24 (*V*, p. 1402). QUESTION. THE RICH YOUNG MAN. (*Introversion and Alternation.*)

V | P | t | 17. Question of one to the Lord.
  u | 18. Question of the Lord.
   Q | v | 19. Answer of the Lord. "Do all."
    w | 20. Young man. Response.
   Q | *v* | 21. Answer of the Lord. Do these.
    w | 22. Young man. Effect.
 P | *u* | 23. Comment of the Lord.
  t | 24. Answer of the Lord to Disciples.

19 knowest. Ap. 132. I. i.
the commandments, &c. If it is a matter of *doing*, ALL must be done. Jas. 2. 10, 11. The Lord cites only some, and these not in order, to convict the questioner more readily: the seventh, sixth, eighth, ninth, and fifth.
Do not, &c. Quoted from Deut. 5. 17-20.
Defraud not. This is a summary of what precedes. Cp. Rom. 13. 7-10.
20 all these. Not so. The command which follows convicts him of a breach of the tenth.
observed=been on my guard against.
from. Gr. *ek.* Ap. 104. vii.
21 beholding=looking upon, as in *v.* 27. Gr. *emblepō.* Ap. 133. I. **loved.** Gr. *agapaō.* Ap. 135. 1.
sell, &c. This was the tenth commandment. This command was suitable for the period prior to the rejection of the kingdom (see *v.* 23), for the King Himself was present, and what could any of His subjects lack? Cp. Ps. 145. 13-16.
heaven. Sing. See note on Matt. 6. 9, 10.
take up the cross. [L] T Tr. WH R omit these words.
22 at=upon [hearing]. Gr. *epi.* Ap. 104. ix. 2.
great=many.
23 hardly=difficultly. Because of their own reluctance to part with riches: not from denial of God's mercy.
24 Children. Gr. pl. of *teknon.* Ap. 108. I.
how hard, &c.=how difficult: or, how hard [a struggle] it is, &c.
trust in=rely upon. Referring to feeling rather than to faith.
in=upon. Gr. *epi.* Ap. 104. ix. 2.
25 It is easier, &c. See notes on Matt. 19. 24.
through. Gr. *dia.* Ap. 104. v. 1.

10. 26-31 (*W*, p. 1402). DISCIPLESHIP. (*Alternation.*)

W | x | 26. Disciples. Question: "Who?" asked.
 y | 27. The Lord. Answer: Possible and Impossible.
 x | 28. Disciples. Question: [What?] (implied).
 y | 29-31. The Lord's Answer.

26 among=to. Gr. *pros.* Ap. 104. xv. 3. Not the same word as in *v.* 43.
Who then . . . ? Expressing astonishment. Fig. *Erotēsis.*
27 With. Gr. *para.* Ap. 104. xii. 2.
men. Ap. 123. 1.
impossible. See Matt. 19. 26.
not. Gr. *ou.* Ap. 105. I.
28 began. See note on 1. 1.
Lo. Fig. *Asterismos.* Ap. 6.
29 left. Gr. *aphiēmi*=to leave behind, let go, disregard. Not the same word as in *v.* 7.
or. Fig. *Paradiastolē*, Ap. 6, particularising each. **30 time**=season. **houses, &c.** These details are a Divine supplement, here. **and.** Note the Fig. *Polysyndeton.* Ap. 6. **with**=in association with (Gr. *meta.* Ap. 104. xi. 1). **with persecutions.** Note this Divine supplement, here. **the world to come**=the coming age (Gr. *aiōn*). See Ap. 129. 2 and 151. II. A. i. 3.

10. 32-34 (*T*, p. 1402). SUFFERINGS. THIRD ANNOUNCEMENT. (*Alternation.*)

T | a | 32-. Jerusalem.
 b | -32. Announcement.
 a | 33-. Jerusalem.
 b | -33, 34. Announcement.

32 to=unto. Gr. *eis.* Ap. 104. vi. **went**=was going on. **were amazed.** This sudden awe is a Divine supplement, here. **took**=took aside. **again.** This was the third announcement of His sufferings. For the others see 8. 31; 9. 31; and 10. 45.

a (p. 1407) A.D. 29 33 *Saying,* °"Behold, we °go up [32] to Jerusalem; °and °the Son of man shall be delivered unto the chief priests, and unto the scribes;

b °and they shall °condemn Him to death, °and shall °deliver Him to the Gentiles:

34 °And they shall °mock Him, °and shall scourge Him, °and shall spit upon Him, °and shall kill Him: °and °the third day He shall rise again."

U c[1] (p. 1408) 35 And James and John, °the sons of Zebedee, come unto Him, saying, [17] "Master, we °would that Thou shouldest do for us whatsoever we shall °desire."

d[1] 36 And He said unto them, "What [35] would ye that I should do for you?"

c[2] 37 They said unto Him, "Grant unto us that we may °sit, one °on Thy right hand, and the other °on Thy left hand, [10] in °Thy glory."

d[2] 38 But [5] Jesus said unto them, "Ye know [27] not what ye ask: °can ye drink of °the cup that I drink of? and be baptized with °the baptism that I am baptized with?"

c[3] 39 And they said unto Him, °"We can."

d[3] And [5] Jesus said unto them, "Ye shall indeed drink of the cup that I drink of; and with the baptism that I am baptized withal shall ye be baptized:

40 But to sit [37] on My right hand and [37] on My left hand is [27] not Mine to give; °but *it shall be given to them* for whom it is prepared."

c[4] 41 And when the ten heard *it,* they began to be °much displeased °with James and John.

d[4] 42 But [5] Jesus called them *to Him,* and saith unto them, °"Ye know that they which are °accounted to rule over the Gentiles exercise lordship over them; and their great ones exercise authority upon them.

43 But so shall it [27] not be °among you: but whosoever °will °be great °among you, shall be your °minister:

44 And whosoever of you [43] will [43] be the °chiefest, shall be °servant of all.

O R (p. 1402) 45 For even [33] the Son of man came [27] not °to be ministered unto, but to minister, °and to give His °life a ransom °for many."

S e (p. 1408) 46 And they came [32] to °Jericho: and °as He went out °of Jericho with His disciples and a great number of people, °blind °Bartimæus, the son of Timæus, °sat °by the highway side begging.

f 47 And when he heard that it was [5] Jesus of Nazareth, he began to cry out, and say, [5] "Jesus, *Thou* °Son of David, have °mercy on me."

48 And many °charged him that he should hold his peace: but he °cried the more a great deal, "*Thou* [47] Son of David, have [47] mercy on me."

33 Behold. Fig. *Asterismos* (Ap. 6), for emphasis.
go up = are going up.
and. Fig. *Polysyndeton.* Ap. 6.
the Son of man. See Ap. 98. XVI.
condemn. Gr. *katakrinō.* Ap. 122. 7.
34 And. Fig. *Polysyndeton,* continued.
mock Him. This is a Divine supplement, here.
the third day. See Ap. 144, 148, and 156.

10. 35-44 (*U,* p. 1402). DISCIPLESHIP.
(*Repeated Alternation.*)

U c[1] | 35. Disciples. Request of Two.
d[1] | 36. The Lord. Inquiry.
c[2] | 37. Disciples. Definition by the Two.
d[2] | 38. The Lord. Answer and Question.
c[3] | 39-. Disciples. Answer of the Two.
d[3] | -39, 40. The Lord. Answer. Non-compliance.
c[4] | 41. Disciples. The Ten. Indignation.
d[4] | 42. The Lord. Teaching and Illustration.

35 the sons = the [two] sons.
would = desire. Gr. *thelō.* Ap. 102. 1.
desire = ask. Ap. 134. I. 4. **37 sit** = sit (in state).
on = at. Gr. *ek.* Ap. 104. vii.
Thy glory. Wondrous faith, coming immediately after the third announcement of His sufferings and resurrection. It was not a "Jewish notion" that the kingdom which had been proclaimed was a grand reality. It was a revealed truth.
38 can ye drink . . . ? = are ye able to drink . . . ?
the cup. Denoting the inward sufferings. Cp. Matt. 26. 39.
the baptism. Denoting the outward suffering.
39 We can = We are able. And they were able, by grace. James (Acts 12. 2); and John, if, according to tradition, he died in boiling oil.
40 but, &c. = but it is theirs for whom it is already prepared. Cp. Matt. 20. 23.
41 much displeased = indignant.
with = concerning. Gr. *peri.* Ap. 104. xiii. 1. Not the same word as in *vv.* 27, 30.
42 Ye know. Gr. *oida.* Ap. 132. I. 1.
accounted to rule = deemed rulers.
43 among. Gr. *en.* Ap. 104. viii. 2. Not the same word as in *v.* 26. **will** = desires. Gr. *thelō.* Ap. 102. 1.
be = to become.
minister. Gr. *diakonos,* a free servant. Not the same word as in *v.* 44. Cp. 9. 35. **44 chiefest** = first.
servant = bondsman. Not the same word as in *v.* 43. Note the Fig. *Epitasis.* Ap. 6.
45 to be ministered unto = to be served. Gr. *diakonizō.*
and to give. This is the fourth announcement of His sufferings. See the Structure *F,* p. 1402.
life = soul. See Ap. 110. III. 1.
for = instead of. Gr. *anti.* Ap. 104. ii.

10. 46-52 (*S,* p. 1402). MIRACLE. BLIND MAN.
(*Introversion.*)

S e | 46. Blind man sitting by the way.
f | 47, 48. Request for healing.
g | 49-. Command.
h | -49-. Encouragement from the Lord.
h | -49. Encouragement from the people.
g | 50. Obedience.
f | 51, 52-. Compliance and healing.
e | -52. Blind man following in the way.

46 Jericho. This is the second mention in N.T. Cp. Matt. 20. 29, the first. Over 100,000 inhabitants (acc. to Epiphanius, Bishop of Cyprus, 368-403. Works: vol. i. 702).
as He went out = as He was going out. The three cases of healing here were: (1) as He drew near (Luke 18. 35); (2) "as He was going out"; and (3) after He had left "two" (not beggars) who sat by the wayside. See Ap. 152. **of** = from. Gr. *apo.* Ap. 104. iv.
blind. The wonder is, not that there were four, but that there were only four. Blindness and eye-diseases are very common in the East; said to be one in five. **Bartimæus.** Aramaic for "son of Timæus", as explained. See Ap. 94. III. 3. **sat** = was sitting. **by** = beside. Gr. *para.* Ap. 104. xii. 3.
47 Son of David. See Ap. 98. XVIII. and note on Matt. 15. 22. **mercy** = pity. **48 charged him, &c.** = were reprimanding him, and told him to hold his tongue. **cried** = kept crying.

g **49 And [5]Jesus °stood still, and °commanded**
(p. 1408) **him to be called.**
A.D. 29
h **And they call the blind man, saying unto him, "Be of good °comfort, rise; He calleth thee."**

g **50 And he, °casting away his garment, rose, and came [7]to [5]Jesus.**

f **51 And [5]Jesus answered and said unto him, "What °wilt thou that I should do °unto thee?" The blind man said unto Him, °"Lord, that I might °receive my sight."**

52 And [5]Jesus said unto him, "Go thy way; thy faith hath °made thee whole."

e **And °immediately he received his sight, and followed °Jesus [10]in °the way.**

R^1 S^1 i **11 °And when they °came nigh °to Jeru-**
(p. 1409) **salem, °unto °Bethphage and Bethany,**
13th Nisan **°at the mount of Olives, He °sendeth forth two**
of His °disciples,

k **2 And saith unto them, "Go your way °into the village °over against you: and °as soon as ye be entered °into it, ye shall find a °colt tied, °whereon °never °man sat; loose him, and °bring *him*.**

3 And °if any man say unto you, 'Why do ye this?' say ye that °the Lord hath need of him; and °straightway he will send him hither."

k **4 And they went their way, and found °the [2]colt tied °by °the door without °in °a place where two ways met; and they loose him.**

5 And certain of them that stood there said unto them, °"What do ye, loosing [4]the [2]colt?"

6 And they said unto them even as °Jesus had commanded: and they let them go.

i **7 And they °brought the [2]colt °to [6]Jesus, and cast their garments on °him; and He sat °upon °him.**

T^1 l **8 And many spread their garments °in the**
(p. 1410) **way: and others °cut down °branches °off the trees, and strawed *them* °in the way.**

m **9 And they that went before, and they that followed, cried, saying, °"HOSANNA; BLESSED *is* HE THAT COMETH °IN THE NAME OF °THE LORD:**

49 stood still=stopped.

commanded him, &c. Note the differences with the other cases. See Ap. 152.

comfort=courage.

50 casting away=casting aside. Cp. Rom. 11. 15.

51 wilt=desirest, as in *vv.* 43, 44.

unto=for. (Dat. case.)

Lord. *Rabboni.* Cp. Ap. 98. XIV. viii. Aram. for "my Master", as in John 20. 16. See Ap. 94. III. 3.

receive=regain.

52 made thee whole=saved thee.

immediately. See notes on 1. 10, 12.

Jesus=Him. According to all the texts, and Syr.

the way. Towards Jerusalem. Cp. *v.* 32.

11. 1—14. 25 (*E*, p. 1381). THE FOURTH PERIOD OF THE LORD'S MINISTRY. REJECTION OF THE KINGDOM. (*Repeated Introversions.*)

E | R^1 | S^1 | 11. 1-7. Bethphage. Arrival. Without.
T^1 | 11. 8-11-. In Jerusalem. Entry. } Within.
T^2 | 11. -11-. In the Temple. Observation. } Within.
S^2 | 11. -11. Bethany. Arrival. Without.
R^2 | S^3 | 11. 12-14. Bethany. Return from. Without.
T^3 | 11. 15-. In Jerusalem. } Within.
T^4 | 11. -15-18. In the Temple. Cleansing. } Within.
S^4 | 11. 19. Out of the City. Bethany. Without.
R^3 | S^5 | 11. 20-26. Bethany. Return from. Without.
T^5 | 11. 27-. In Jerusalem. } Within.
T^6 | 11. -27—12. 44. In the Temple. } Within.
S^6 | 13. 1—14. 25. Return to Bethany.

11. 1-7 (S^1, above). BETHPHAGE. ARRIVAL. (*Introversion.*)

S^1 | i | 1. The Two Disciples. Mission.
k | 2, 3. Command.
k | 4-6. Obedience.
i | 7. The Two Disciples. Return.

1 And=And [on the morrow]. Cp. John 12. 12.

came nigh=drew near; from Bethany to the boundary of Bethphage and Bethany, which were quite distinct. Cp. Luke 19. 29, and John 12. 12-19.

to . . . unto. Gr. *eis.* Ap. 104. vi.

Bethphage. Aramaic. Ap. 94. III. 3. Now *Kefr et Tōr.*

at=towards. Gr. *pros.* Ap. 104. xv. 3.

sendeth forth, &c. Gr. *apostello* (at the first entry, *poreuomai*=Go forward. Matt. 21. 6). This was on the fourth day before the Passover, and is not parallel with Matt. 21. 1-17. This is the second entry, from Bethany (not from Bethphage). The former (on the sixth day before the Passover) was unexpected (Matt. 21. 10, 11). This was prepared for (John 12. 12, 13).

disciples. Not apostles.

2 into. Gr. *eis.* Ap. 104. vi.

over against=below and opposite (*katenanti*). At the former entry it was *apenanti*=right opposite (Matt. 21. 2).

as soon as=immediately. See notes on 1. 10, 12.

colt tied. At the former entry "an ass tied and a colt with her" (Matt. 21. 2). An untamed colt submits to the Lord. Not so His People to whom He was coming (John 1. 11).

whereon. =upon (Gr. *epi.* Ap. 104. ix. 3) which.

never man=no one (Gr. *oudeis.* See Ap. 105. I) of men.

man. Gr. *anthrōpos.* Ap. 123. 1.

bring him=lead it.

3 if any man=if any one. The contingency being probable. See Ap. 118. 1. b. The same word as in *vv.* 31, 32; not the same as in *vv.* 13, 25, 26.

the Lord. Ap. 98. VI. i. a. 2. A. a.

straightway. See note on 1. 12.

4 the=a. According to all the texts.

by=at. Gr. *pros.* Ap. 104. xv. 3. Not the same word as in *vv.* 28, 29, 33.

in=on, or upon. Gr. *epi.* Ap. 104. ix. 1.

a place where two ways met=in that quarter [where the Lord had said]. Gr. *amphodos.* The regular word in the *Papyri* to denote the "quarter" or part (Lat. *vicus*) of a city. Occ. only here in N.T. But Codex *Bezae* (Cambridge), cent. 5 or 6, adds (in Acts 19. 28) after "wrath", "running into that quarter".

5 What do ye . . . ?=What are you doing?

6 Jesus. Ap. 98. X.

7 brought=led.

to. Gr. *pros.* Ap. 104. xv. 3. Not the same word as in *vv.* 1, 13, 15.

him=it.

upon. Gr. *epi.* Ap. 104. ix. 2.

11. 8-11- [For Structure see next page].

8 in=on. Gr. *eis.* Ap. 104. vi. Matthew and Luke have "in". Gr. *en.* Ap. 104. viii.

cut=were cutting.

branches off. The 1611 edition of the A.V. reads "branches of".

branches. Matthew, Mark, and John have each a different word. Each is a Divine supplement to the other two. All three were cut and cast. Matthew, pl. of *klados*=branches; Mark, pl. of *stoibas*=litter, made of leaves from the fields (occ. only here); John 12. 13, has pl. of *baion*=palm branches.

off=out of. Gr. *ek.* Ap. 104. vii.

in=on. Gr. *eis.* Ap. 104. vi.

9 Hosanna, &c. Quoted from Ps. 118. 25, 26. See note on Matt. 21. 9.

in. Gr. *en.* Ap. 104. viii.

the LORD. Ap. 98. VI. i. a. 1. B. a.

m (p. 1410) A.D. 29 10 Blessed *be* °the kingdom of our father
David, that cometh [9]in the name of [9]the LORD:
[9]**Hosanna** [9]**in the highest."**

l 11 And [6]Jesus entered [2]into Jerusalem,

T^2 (p. 1409) and [2]into the °temple: and °when He had
looked round about upon all things,

S^2 and °now the eventide was come, He went
out [1]unto Bethany °with the twelve.

R^3 S^3 12th Nisan 12 And on the morrow, when they were come
°from Bethany, He was hungry:
13 And °seeing °a fig tree afar off °having
leaves, He °came, °if haply He might find any
thing thereon: (and °when He came °to it, He
found nothing but leaves); for °the time of figs
was °not *yet*.
14 And [6]Jesus °answered and said unto it,
°"No man eat fruit °of thee hereafter °for ever."
And °His disciples heard *it*.

T^3 15 And they come [1]to Jerusalem:

T^4 n (p. 1410) and [6]Jesus went [2]into the [11]temple, and °began
°to cast out them that sold and bought [9]in
the [11]temple, and overthrew the tables of the
moneychangers, and the seats of them that
sold doves;
16 °And would [13]not suffer that any man
should carry *any* °vessel °through the
[11]temple.

o 17 And He taught, saying unto them, °"Is it
[13]not written, '**My house shall be called** °**of all**
°**nations the house of** °**prayer?**

o but ye have made it **a den of** °**thieves.'**

n 18 And the scribes and chief priests heard *it*,
and °sought how they might destroy Him: for
they feared Him because all the people was
astonished °at His °doctrine.

S^1 19 And when even was come, He °went °out
of the city.

R^3 S^5 p 13th Nisan 20 °And [8]in the morning, as they passed by,
they [13]saw the fig tree dried up °from the
roots.

q 21 And Peter calling to remembrance saith
unto Him, °"Master, °behold, the fig tree
which Thou cursedst is °withered away."

r 22 And [6]Jesus [14]answering saith unto them,
°"Have faith in °God.

q 23 For °verily I say unto you, That whosoever shall say unto °this mountain, 'Be thou

11. 8-11- (T^1, p. 1409). IN JERUSALEM. ENTRY. (*Introversion.*)

T^1 | l | 8. Action. The Multitude.
  m | 9. Cry. The King.
  m | 10. Cry. The Kingdom.
 l | 11-. Action. The Lord.

10 the kingdom. Note the Structure "m" and "*m*".

11 temple. Gr. *hieron*: i.e. the temple courts. Not the *naos*. See note on Matt. 23. 16.

when He had looked round about upon. Therefore not the same entry as in Matt. 21. 12-16. Cp. *vv.* 15, 16.

now the eventide was come=the hour already being late.

with=in company with. Gr. *meta*. Ap. 104. xi. 1.

12 from=away from. Gr. *apo*. Ap. 104. iv. Not the same word as in *vv.* 20, 30, 31.

13 seeing. Gr. *eidon*. Ap. 133. I. 1.

a fig tree. The symbol of Israel as to national privilege.

having leaves. Cp. 13. 28. Summer was not near. Symbolical of Israel at that time.

came=went.

if haply=if after all. Ap. 118. 2. a. As in *v.* 26. Not the same as in *vv.* 3, 31, 32. He had reason to expect fruit, as figs appear before or with the leaves.

when He came=having come.

to=up to. Gr. *epi*. Ap. 104. ix. 3.

the time, &c.=it was not the season, &c. A Divine supplement, here.

not. Gr. *ou*. Ap. 105. I. The same word as in *vv.* 16, 17, 26, 31, 33. Not the same as in *v.* 23.

14 answered and said. Heb. Idiom. See note on Deut. 1. 41.

No man=No one.

of. Gr. *ek*. Ap. 104. vii.

for ever. Gr. *eis ton aiōna*. See Ap. 151. II. A. ii. 4. a.

His disciples heard. A Divine supplement, here. They heard also the Lord's teaching as to the symbol. See *vv.* 20-26.

11. -15-18 (T^4, p. 1409). IN THE TEMPLE. (*Introversion.*)

T^4 | n | -15, 16. Action of the Lord.
  o | 17-. Teaching. What the Temple was for.
  o | -17. Incrimination. What it had become.
 n | 18. Action of the Rulers.

15 began. See note on 1. 1.

to cast out. This was a further cleansing than that in Matt. 21.

16 And would not suffer, &c. This was not done at the former cleansing in Matt. 21. 12-16.

vessel. Gr. *skeuos*. See note on 3. 27. Used of vessels in general for non-sacred purposes.

through. Gr. *dia*. Ap. 104. v. 1. As if through a street.

17 Is it not written . . . ?=Doth it not stand written that, &c. The composite quotation is from Isa. 56. 7 and Jer. 7. 11. See Ap. 107. II. 4.

of=for.

nations=the nations. See Ap. 107. II. 1.

prayer. Ap. 134. II. 2.

thieves=robbers, or brigands. Gr. *lēstēs*. Cp. Matt. 21. 13; 26. 55. John 10. 1, 8. Not *kleptēs*=a thief.

18 sought=began to seek.

at. Gr. *epi*. Ap. 104. ix. 2.

doctrine=teaching.

19 went=was going (i.e. where He was wont).

out of=without. Doubtless to Bethany, as before. Cp. *v.* 20, and see Ap. 156.

11. 20-26 (S^5, p. 1409). BETHANY. RETURN FROM. (*Introversion.*)

S^5 | p | 20. Fig-tree withered. Nation cut off.
  q | 21. The Lord's word remembered.
   r | 22. God the only source of restoration.
  q | 23, 24. The Lord's word to be believed.
 p | 25, 26. National blessing dependent on national repentance and forgiveness.

20 And in the morning, &c. Verses 20-26 are a Divine supplement of details, here.

from=out of. Gr. *ek*. Ap. 104. vii. Not the same word as in *v.* 12.

21 Master=Rabbi. See Ap. 98. XIV. vii.

behold=see. Fig. *Asterismos*. Ap. 6 and 133. I. i.

withered away. Symbolical as to the national existence and privilege of Israel.

22 Have faith in God. He and He alone can restore it to life—yea, "life from the dead". See Rom. 11. 15.

God. Ap. 98. I. i. 1.

23 verily. See note on Matt. 5. 18.

this mountain. Referring, and probably pointing to Olivet. Cp. Matt. 17. 20; 21. 21; and see note on Luke 17. 6.

A. D. 29 removed, and be thou cast [2]into the sea;' and
shall °not °doubt [9]in his heart, but shall believe
that those things which he saith shall come
to pass; °he shall have whatsoever he saith.
24 °Therefore I say unto you, What things
soever ye desire, when ye °pray, believe that ye
receive *them*, and °ye shall have *them*.

p (p. 1410) 25 And when ye stand [24]praying, forgive, [13]if
ye have ought °against any: that your °Father
also Which is [9]in °heaven may forgive you
your °trespasses.
26 °But [13]if ye do [13]not forgive, neither will
your [25]Father Which is [9]in [25]heaven forgive
your [25]trespasses."

T5 27 And they come again [1]to Jerusalem:

T6 U A (p. 1411) and as He was °walking [9]in the [15]temple,
there come [7]to Him the chief priests, and the
scribes, and the elders,
28 And say unto Him, °"By °what °authority
doest Thou these things? and who gave Thee
°this °authority °to do these things?"

B 29 And [6]Jesus [14]answered and said unto
them, °"I will also ask of you one question,
and answer Me, and I will tell you [28]by what
[28]authority I do these things.
30 The baptism of John, was *it* [20]from
°heaven, or [14]of [2]men? answer Me."

C 31 And they reasoned °with themselves, saying, [3]"If we shall say, [20]'From [30]heaven;' He
will say, 'Why then did ye [13]not believe
him?'
32 But [3]if we shall °say, [14]'Of [2]men;'" they
feared the people: for all *men* counted John,
that he was a prophet indeed.

B 33 And they answered and said unto [6]Jesus,
°"We cannot tell."

A And [6]Jesus answering saith unto them, "Neither do I tell you [28]by what [28]authority I do
these things."

V W D **12** And He °began to speak unto them °by
parables.

E "A *certain* °man planted a vineyard, and
°set an hedge about *it*, and digged *a place for*
the °winefat, and built a °tower, and °let it
out to °husbandmen, and °went into a far
country.

F p1 (p. 1412) 2 And °at the season he sent °to the husbandmen a °servant, that he might receive
°from the husbandmen °of the fruit of the
vineyard.

q1 3 And they °caught *him*, and beat him, and
sent *him* away empty.

not. Gr. *mē*. Ap. 105. II. Not the same word as in *vv.* 13, 16, 17, 26, 31, 33.
doubt. Gr. *diakrinō*. Ap. 122. 4.
he shall have, &c. = there shall be to him.
24 Therefore = On account of (Ap. 104. v. 2) this.
pray. Ap. 134. I. 2.
ye shall have them. [They] shall be to you.
25 against. Gr. *kata*. Ap. 104. x. 2.
Father. Ap. 98. III.
heaven = the heavens. Pl. as in *v.* 26, but Sing. in *v.* 30. See notes on Matt. 6. 9, 10.
trespasses = falling aside. Gr. *paraptōma*. Ap. 128. II. 4.
26 But if, &c. Verse 26 is omitted by T Tr. WH R; but not by the Syr.

11. -27—13. 2 (T6, p. 1409). IN THE TEMPLE (*Introversion and Alternation.*)

T6 | U | 11. -27-33. Authority questioned.
  V | W | 12. 1-11. Teaching. Parable.
    X | 12. 12. Enemies. Conspiracy.
      Y1 | 12. 13-17. Question. Pharisees, &c. Political.
      Y2 | 12. 18-27. Question. Sadducees. Doctrinal.
      Y3 | 12. 28-34. Question. A Scribe. Moral.
  V | *W* | 12. 35-37. Teaching. Question.
    X | 12. 38-40. Enemies. Condemnation.
U | 12. 41-44. Authority exercised.

11. -27-33 (U, above). AUTHORITY QUESTIONED. (*Introversion.*)

U | A | -27, 28. Enemies' question. Asked.
  B | 29, 30. The Lord's question. In answer.
    C | 31, 32. Enemies' reasoning.
  B | 33-. The Lord's question unanswered.
A | -33. Enemies' question. Unanswered.

27 walking. A Divine supplement, here.
28 By. Gr. *en*. Ap. 104. viii. Same word as in *vv.* 29, 33. Not the same as in *v.* 4.
what = what kind (or sort) of.
authority. Gr. *exousia*. Ap. 172. 5.
this = this particular.
to do = that Thou shouldest do.
29 I will also ask, &c. Note the use of the Fig. *Anteisagōgē* (Ap. 6), answering one question by asking another.
30 heaven. Singular. See note on Matt. 6. 9, 10.
31 with. Gr. *pros*. Ap. 104. xv. 3. Not the same word as in *v.* 11.
32 say, Of men. Supply the logical Ellipsis, thus: "Of men [it will not be wise]; for they feared the people", &c.
33 We cannot tell = We do not (Gr. *ou*. Ap. 105. I) know (Gr. *oida*. Ap. 132. I. 1).

12. 1-11 (W, above). TEACHING. PARABLE OF THE VINEYARD. (*Introversion.*)

W | D | 1-. The Lord. Teaching.
  E | -1. Vineyard. Hired to husbandmen.
    F | 2-8. Conduct of husbandmen.
  E | 9. Vineyard. Given to others.
D | 10, 11. The Lord. Application.

1 began. See note on 1. 1.
by = in. Gr. *en*. Ap. 104. viii, as in *v.* 36.
man. Gr. *anthrōpos*. Ap. 123. 1.

set an hedge = placed a fence. **winefat.** Occ. only here in N.T. = a wine-vat. "Fat" is from A.S. *fæt* = a vessel (cp. Dutch *vatten* = to catch). Northern Eng. for *vat*. **tower** = watch-house. See note on Matt. 21. 33. **let it out, &c.** See note on Matt. 21. 33. **husbandmen** = vine-dressers. **went into a far country** = went abroad. See note on Matt. 21. 33.

12. 2-8 [For Structure see next page].

2 at the season. The fourth year after planting it; no profit till then. See Lev. 19. 23, 24. **to.** Gr. *pros*. Ap. 104. xv. 3. **servant** = bond-servant. **from.** Gr. *para*. Ap. 104. xii. 1. Not the same word as in *vv.* 25, 34. **of** = from. Gr. *apo*. Ap. 104. iv. 1. Same word as in *v.* 38; not the same as in *v.* 44. This shows that part of, or the whole rent was to be paid in kind. See note on "let it out", Matt. 21. 33. **3 caught** = took.

p² (p. 1412) 4 And again he sent ° unto them ° another servant;

A. D. 29

q² and ° at him they cast stones, and wounded *him* in the head, and ° sent *him* away shamefully handled.

p³ 5 And again he sent [4] another;

q³ and him they killed,

p⁴ and ° many [4] others;

q⁴ ° beating some, and killing some.

p⁵ 6 Having yet ° therefore one son, ° his ° wellbeloved, he sent him also ° last [4] unto them, saying, 'They will ° reverence my son.'

q⁵ 7 But those husbandmen ° said ° among themselves, ° 'This is the heir; come, let us kill him, and the inheritance shall be ours.'

8 And they took him, and ° killed *him*, and cast *him* ° out of the vineyard.

E (p. 1411) 9 What ° shall therefore ° the lord of the vineyard do? he will come and destroy the husbandmen, and will give the vineyard ° unto ° others.

D 10 And ° have ye ° not read this scripture; ° '**The Stone Which the builders rejected ° is become the head of the corner:**

11 ° **This was ° the LORD'S doing, and it is marvellous ° in our eyes'** "?

X 12 And they sought to lay hold on Him, but feared the people: ° for they ° knew that He had spoken the parable ° against them: and they left Him, and went their way.

Y¹ r (p. 1412) 13 And they send [4] unto Him certain of the ° Pharisees and of the Herodians, ° to ° catch Him in *His* ° words.

s 14 And when they were come, they say unto Him, ° "Master, ° we know that Thou art true, and carest ° for ° no man: ° for Thou ° regardest ° not the person of [1] men, but teachest the way of ° God ° in truth: Is it lawful to give ° tribute to Cæsar, or ° not?

15 ° Shall we give, or shall we ° not give?"

t But He, knowing their hypocrisy, said unto them, "Why tempt ye Me? bring Me a ° penny, that I may see *it*."

t 16 And they brought *it*.

s And He saith unto them, "Whose *is* this ° image and superscription?" And they said unto Him, "Cæsar's."

r 17 And ° Jesus ° answering said unto them, "Render to Cæsar the things that are Cæsar's, and to [14] God the things that are [14] God's." And they ° marvelled at Him.

12. 2-8 (F, p. 1411). CONDUCT OF HUSBANDMEN. (*Repeated Alternation.*)

F p¹ | 2. A servant sent.
q¹ | 3. His treatment.
p² | 4-. Another servant sent.
q² | -4. His treatment.
p³ | 5-. Another servant sent.
q³ | -5-. His treatment.
p⁴ | -5-. "Many others" sent.
q⁴ | -5. Their treatment.
p⁵ | 6. The only Son sent.
q⁵ | 7, 8. His treatment.

4 unto. Gr. *pros.* Ap. 104. xv. 3. As in *vv.* 6, 13, 18.

another. Gr. *allos.* Ap. 124. 1.

at him, &c. = him they stoned. This word "stoned" is omitted by all the texts.

sent him away shamefully handled. L T Tr. WH R with Syr. read "insulted him".

5 many others. All these were "His servants the prophets" up to John the Baptist. Supply the Ellipsis from *v.* 4 thus: "Many others [He sent, whom they used shamefully], beating some and killing some".

beating = scourging.

6 therefore. Omitted by [L] T Tr. A WH R with Syr.

his = his own.

wellbeloved = beloved. Ap. 135. III.

last. A Divine supplement, here.

reverence = have respect to.

7 said . . . This = said that (Gr. *hoti*) this is, &c.

among = to. Gr. *pros.* Ap. 104. xv. 3.

8 killed him. As the Lord had already revealed to the disciples (10. 32-34). **out** = outside.

9 shall = will.

the lord. Implying and leading up to the interpretation. Ap. 98. VI. i. a. 4. A.

unto others. The new Israel, as foretold in Isa. 66. 7-14. **others.** Gr. Pl. of *allos.* Ap. 124. 1.

10 have ye not read . . . ? See Ap. 143.

not = not even. Gr. *oude.* Compound of *ou.* See Ap. 105. I.

The Stone, &c. Quoted from Ps. 118. 22. Cp. Acts 4. 10-12. See Ap. 107. I. 1. **is** = this is.

11 This was, &c. = this was from Jehovah (Gr. *para.* Ap. 104. xii. 1).

the LORD'S = Jehovah's. Ap. 98. VI. i. a. 1. B. a.

in. Gr. *en.* Ap. 104. viii. Same word as in *vv.* 23, -25, 26-, 35, 38, 39. Not the same as in *vv.* 14, -26.

12 for = because.

knew = came to know, or perceived. Gr. *ginōskō.* See Ap. 132. I. ii. Not the same word as in *vv.* 14, 15, 24.

against. Gr. *pros.* Ap. 104. xv. 3.

12. 13-17 (Y¹, p. 1411). QUESTION OF THE PHARISEES. (POLITICAL.) (*Introversion.*)

Y¹ r | 13. Their design planned.
s | 14, 15-. Question *re* Tribute.
t | -15. Request of the Lord.
t | 16-. Request complied with.
s | -16. Question and Answer *re* Tribute.
r | 17. Their design defeated.

13 Pharisees. Ap. 120. II.

to catch = that they might catch.

catch. Gr. *agreuō* = to take in hunting: hence, to ensnare. In Matt. 22. 15 it is *pagideuō* = to ensnare ("entangle"). Both are Divine supplementary renderings of the same Aramaic word: Matt. giving the result of the hunting. Neither of the two words occ. elsewhere.

words = discourse. Gr. *logos.* See note on 9. 32. **14 Master.** Teacher. As in *vv.* 19, 32. Ap. 98. XIV. v. 1. **we know.** Gr. *oida.* See Ap. 132. I. i. **for** = about, or concerning. Gr. *peri.* Ap. 104. xiii. 1. **no man** = no one. Gr. *oudeis,* a compound of *ou.* Ap. 105. I. **for** = because. **regardest not** = lookest (Ap. 133. I. 5) not (Gr. *ou.* Ap. 105. I) on (Gr. *eis.* Ap. 104. vi). **God.** Gr. *Theos.* Ap. 98. I. i. 1. **in** = with. Gr. *epi.* Ap. 104. ix. 1. **tribute.** Occ. only here and in Matt. 17. 25 and 22. 17, 19. See notes there. **not.** Gr. *ou.* Ap. 105. I. Not the same word as in *vv.* 10, 15. **15 Shall we give, &c.** A Divine supplement, here. **not.** Gr. *mē.* Ap. 105. 2. Same word as in *v.* -24. Not the same as in *vv.* 10, 14, 24-, 26, 27, 34. **penny** = *dēnarion.* See note on Matt. 22. 19. Ap. 51. I. 4. **16 image, &c.** See note on Matt. 22. 20. **17 Jesus.** Ap. 98. X. **answering said.** Heb. idiom. See note on Deut. 1. 41. **marvelled** = were wondering. T WH R read "wondered beyond measure" (*exethaumazon,* instead of *ethaumasan,* with A.V. L Tr. A and Syr.).

Y² G (p. 1413) A. D. 29 18 Then come [4] unto Him the °Sadducees, °which say there is °no resurrection; and they °asked Him, saying,

H 19 [14] "Master, °Moses wrote unto us, °'**If a man's brother die, and leave *his* wife *behind him*, and leave [18] no children, that his brother should take his wife, and raise up seed unto his brother.**'

20 Now there were seven brethren: and the first took a wife, and dying left °no seed.

21 And the second took her, and died, °neither left he any seed: and the third likewise.

22 And the seven had her, and left [20] no seed: last of all the °woman died also.

23 [11] In the resurrection therefore, when they shall rise, whose wife shall she be of them? [14] for the seven °had her to wife."

G 24 And [17] Jesus [17] answering said unto them, °"Do ye [14] not °therefore err, °because ye °know [15] not the scriptures, °neither the °power of [14] God?

H 25 [14] For when they shall rise °from °the dead, they [24] neither marry, nor are given in marriage; but are as the angels which are [11] in heaven.

26 °And as touching °the dead, that they rise: [10] have ye not read [11] in the book of [19] Moses, how °in the bush [14] God spake unto him, saying, °'**I *am* the [14] God of Abraham, °and the [14] God of Isaac, °and the [11] God of Jacob?**'

27 He is [14] not the [14] God of °the dead, but the [14] God of °the living: °ye therefore do greatly err."

Y³ u 28 And one of the scribes °came, and having heard them reasoning together, and °perceiving that He had answered them °well, °asked Him,

v °"Which is °the first commandment of all?"

w 29 And [17] Jesus answered him, "The first of all the commandments *is*, °'**Hear, O Israel; °The LORD our [14] God is °one [11] LORD:**

30 And thou shalt °love the [11] LORD thy [14] God °with °all thy heart, °and °with °all thy °soul, °and °with °all thy mind, °and °with °all thy strength:' °this *is* the first commandment.

w 31 And the second *is* like, *namely* this, °'**Thou shalt [30] love thy °neighbour as thyself.**' There is °none other commandment greater than these."

v 32 °And the scribe said unto Him, °"Well, [14] Master, Thou hast said °the truth: °**for °there is one [14] God; and there is [31] none other °but He:**

33 [30] And to [30] love Him [30] with [30] all the heart, [30] and [30] with [30] all the °understanding, and [30] with [30] all the [30] soul, and [30] with [30] all the strength, and to [30] love *his* neighbour as himself, is °more than all whole burnt offerings and sacrifices."

u 34 And when [17] Jesus [15] saw that he answered

12. 18-27 (Y², p. 1411). QUESTION OF THE SADDUCEES (DOCTRINAL). (*Alternation.*)

Y² | G | 18. Their error. Denial of Resurrection.
  H | 19-23. The Doctrine questioned.
 G | 24. Their error. Ignorance of Scripture.
  H | 25-27. The Doctrine proved.

18 Sadducees. (No Article.) See Ap. 120. II.

which=they who. Gr. *hoitines*, marking them as a class characterized by this denial.

no. Gr. *mē*. Ap. 105. II. As in *v.* 19; not the same as in *vv.* 20, 22, i.e. they denied it subjectively.

asked=questioned.

19 Moses. See note on 1. 44 and Matt. 8. 4.

If, &c. Deut. 25. 5, 6. Assuming a simple hypothesis. See Ap. 118. 1. b.

20 no. Gr. *ou*. Ap. 105. I. Same as in *v.* 22; not the same as in *vv.* 18, 19.

21 neither. Compound of *ou*. Ap. 105. I.

22 woman died also=woman also died.

23 had=gat.

24 Do ye not...? Fig. *Erotēsis* (Ap. 6), for emphasis.

therefore=on account of (*dia*. Ap. 104. v. 2) this; referring to the reasons about to be stated in the next two clauses.

know. Gr. *oida*. Ap. 132. I. i.

neither. Gr. *mēde*. A compound of *mē*. Ap. 105. II.

power=(inherent) power. Ap. 172. 1.

25 from=from among. Gr. *ek*. Ap. 104. vii.

the dead. No Art. See Ap. 139. 3.

26 And as touching = But concerning. Gr. *peri*. Ap. 104. xiii. 1.

the dead=dead bodies, or corpses. With Art. See Ap. 139. 4. Not the same as in *v.* 27.

in the bush=at (Gr. *epi*. Ap. 104. ix. 1) the place concerning the bush: i.e. the passage about it in Ex. 3. 6. Cp. Rom. 11. 2 "in Elijah"; see note there.

I am, &c. Quoted from Ex. 3. 2-6.

and. Note the Fig. *Polysyndeton*. Ap. 6.

27 the dead=dead people. Not the same as in *v.* 26. No Art. See Ap. 139. 2.

the living: i.e. those who live again in resurrection. See note on Matt. 9. 18. Therefore they must rise. This is the only logical conclusion of the Lord's argument. The whole subject is resurrection.

ye. Note the emphasis on this pronoun. This clause is a Divine supplement, here.

12. 28-34 (Y³, p. 1411). QUESTION OF A SCRIBE. (MORAL.) (*Introversion.*)

Y³ | u | 28-. Perception of the Lord by the Scribe.
 v | -28. Scribe. Inquiry.
  w | 29, 30. The Lord. Answer. The First Com.
  w | 31. The Lord. Answer. The Second Com.
 v | 32, 33. Scribe. Conviction.
u | 34. Perception of the Scribe by the Lord.

28 came=came up; or came to [Him].

perceiving. Gr. *oida*. Ap. 132. I. i.

well=admirably, finely.

asked=questioned.

Which=Of what nature.

the first, &c.=the first of all the commandments.

29 Hear, O Israel, &c. Quoted from Deut. 6. 4, 5.

The LORD ... LORD=Jehovah ... Jehovah. Ap. 98. VI. i. α. 1. B. a.

one. See note on Deut. 6. 4.

30 love. See Ap. 135. I. 1.

with=out of, or from. Gr. *ek*. Ap. 104. vii.

all thy=thy whole.

and. Note the Fig. *Polysyndeton*. Ap. 6.

soul. Gr. *psuchē*. Ap. 110. V. **this [is] the first commandment.** Note (in the Gr.) the Fig. *Homœoteleuton* (Ap. 6), for emphasis: *hautē, prōtē, entolē*. **31 Thou shalt, &c.** Quoted from Lev. 19. 18. **neighbour**=the one near. Cp. Matt. 5. 43. Luke 10. 27, 29, 36. **none, &c.**=not (Gr. *ou*. Ap. 105. 1) another commandment greater. **32** Verses 32-34 are a Divine supplement, here. **Well**="Right", or as we say "Good". **the truth**=according to (Gr. *epi*. Ap. 104. ix. 1) the truth: i.e. truthfully. Ap. 175. 1. **for**=that. **there is one God.** All the texts read "that He is One" (omitting the word "God"). **but He**=besides Him. **33 understanding**=intelligence. Gr. *sunesis*=a putting together. Not the same word as in *v.* 30, which is *dianoia*=mind, the thinking faculty. **more, &c.** Cp. 1 Sam. 15. 22.

A.D. 29 °discreetly, He said unto him, "Thou art
[14]not far °from °the kingdom of God." And
[14]no man after that durst ask Him *any*
question.

V W x (p. 1414) 35 And [17] Jesus [17] answered and said, °while
He taught [11] in the temple,

y "How say the scribes that °Christ is °the son
of David?

z 36 [14] For °David himself °said [1] by °the Holy
Ghost, [29] '**The LORD said to °my Lord, "Sit
Thou °on My right hand, °till I °make Thine
enemies Thy footstool."**'

y 37 [36] David therefore himself calleth Him
°Lord; and whence is He *then* his son?"

x And °the common people heard Him gladly.

X a 38 And He said unto them [11] in His °doctrine,
°"Beware °of the scribes,

b which °love to °go [11] in °long clothing, and
love salutations [11] in the marketplaces,
39 And the °chief seats [11] in the synagogues,
and the °uppermost rooms °at feasts:

b 40 Which °devour widows' houses, and for
a pretence make long prayers:

a these shall receive °greater damnation."

U c 41 And [17] Jesus sat over against °the treasury,
and °beheld how the people °cast
°money °into °the treasury: and many that
were rich °cast in °much.

d 42 And there came °a certain poor widow,
and she °threw in two °mites, which make
°a farthing.

d 43 And He called *unto Him* His disciples,
and saith unto them, °"Verily I say unto you,
That °this poor widow hath cast more in,
than all they which have cast into [41] the treasury:

c 44 [14] For all *they* did cast in °of their abundance;
but she °of her °want did cast in °all
°that she had, *even* °all her °living."

S[6] J[1] K (p. 1415) **13** And as He went °out of the °temple,
one of His disciples saith unto Him,
°"Master, °see what manner of °stones and
what buildings *are here!*"

34 discreetly = judiciously. Gr. *nounechōs.* Occ. only here in N.T.
from = away from. Gr. *apo.* Ap. 104. iv.
the kingdom of God. See Ap. 114.

12. 35-37 (*W*, p. 1411). TEACHING. QUESTION. (*Introversion.*)

W | x | 35-. The Lord. Teaching. The Place.
  y | -35. His question *re* Scribes' teaching.
   z | 36. The Holy Spirit's Words.
  y | 37-. His question *re* Scribes' teaching.
 x | -37. The Lord. Teaching. The People.

35 while He taught in the temple. See Ap. 156.
Christ = the Messiah. (With Art.) See Matt. 1. 1. Ap. 98. IX. **the son of David.** See Ap. 98. XVIII.
36 David himself. These are the Lord's words. He did not "accept the current view", but He spake from the Father Himself. See Deut. 18. 18. John 7. 16; 8. 28; 8. 46, 47; 12. 49; 14. 10, 24; 17. 8. This settles the authorship of Ps. 110.
said. Quoted from Ps. 110. 1. Midway between Abraham and Messiah, this Psalm was given to David.
the Holy Ghost. See Ap. 101. II. 3.
my Lord. Ap. 98. VI. i. *a.* 2. A. a. The same as Heb. *Adonai.* See Ap. 4. VIII (2).
on = at. Gr. *ek.* Ap. 104. vii.
till I make. See note on Matt. 22. 44.
make = shall have set.
37 Lord. Ap. 98. VI. i. a. 2. B. b.
the common people = the great crowd. Indicating numerical, not social, distinction.

12. 38-40 (*X*, p. 1411). ENEMIES. CONDEMNATION. (*Introversion.*)

X | a | 38-. Warning.
  b | -38, 39. Enemies. Character.
  b | 40-. Enemies. Actions.
 a | -40. Condemnation.

38 doctrine = teaching.
Beware = take heed. Ap. 133. I. 5.
of = away from (Gr. *apo.* Ap. 104. iv.): i.e. take heed [and keep] away from. Not the same word as in *v.* 44.
love = desire, or will to. Gr. *thelō.* Ap. 102. 1.
go = walk about. **long clothing** = robes. Gr. *stolais.*
39 chief seats. See note on Matt. 23. 6.
uppermost rooms = first couches or places.
at = in. Gr. *en.* Ap. 104. viii. Not the same as in *v.* 17.
40 devour = eat up. Being occupied in making wills and conveyances of property, they abused their office.
greater damnation = heavier judgment.

12. 41-44 (*U*, p. 1411). AUTHORITY EXERCISED. (*Alternation.*)

U | c | 41. The many, casting in.
  d | 42. The widow. Her act.
  d | 43. The widow. The Lord's commendation.
 | c | 44. The many and the widow.

41 *Vv.* 41-44 are parallel with Luke 21. 1-4. See notes there. **the treasury.** Situated in the women's court, occupying about 200 feet square, and surrounded by a colonnade. Inside, against the wall, were thirteen receptacles, called "trumpets" (from their shape): nine being for legal dues, and four for voluntary contributions. All labelled for their special objects. **beheld** = observed thoughtfully. Gr. *theōreō.* Ap. 133. I. 11. **cast** = are casting. **money** = copper money; called *prutah*, two of which made a farthing. **into.** Gr. *eis.* Ap. 104. vi. **cast in** = were casting [in] (as He looked on). **much** = many [coins]. Referring to number, not to value. **42 a certain poor widow** = one poor widow. **threw** = cast, as above. **mites.** Pl. of *lepton* = the small thin Jewish copper coin (from *leptos* = peeled, or pared down). Occ. only here, and Luke 12. 59; 21. 2. See Ap. 51. I. 3. **a farthing.** Gr. *kodrantēs.* A [Roman] *quadrans*; i.e. a fourth, being a fourth of the Roman "*as*". Hence a *fourthing* = our farthing. Occ. only here, and Matt. 5. 26. See Ap. 51. I. 2. **43 Verily.** See note on Matt. 5. 18. **this poor widow** = this widow; and she a poor one. **44 of** = out of. Gr. *ek.* Ap. 104. vii. **want** = destitution. **all** = the whole. **that** = as much as. **living** = life. Put by Fig. *Metonymy* (of Effect), Ap. 6, for the means whereby her life was supported: i.e. her livelihood. Gr. *bios.* See Ap. 170. 2.

13. 1—14. 25 [For Structure see next page].

1 out of the temple. As in Matt. 24. 1, marking this as the latter of two prophecies; the former (Luke 21. 1, 37) being spoken "in the temple". **out of.** Gr. *ek.* Ap. 104. vii. **temple.** Gr. *hieron.* See notes on Matt. 4. 5; 23. 16. **Master** = Teacher. Ap. 98. XIV. v. 1. **see.** Gr. *ide.* Ap. 133. I. 3. Not the same as in *vv.* 2, 26. **stones.** There are some measuring 20 to 40 feet long, and weighing over 100 tons.

L 2 And °Jesus answering said unto him,
p. 1415) °"Seest thou these great buildings? there
A.D. 29 shall °not be left one stone °upon another,
that shall °not be thrown down."
K M[1] 3 And as He sat °upon °the mount of Olives
over against the [1]temple, Peter and James
and John and Andrew asked Him privately,
4 "Tell us, °when shall these things be?
M[2] and °what *shall be* the °sign when all these
things shall be fulfilled?"
L N[1] e 5 And [2]Jesus answering them °began to say,
"Take heed lest any *man* deceive you:
f 6 °For many shall come °in My name, saying,
°'I am *Christ;*' and shall deceive many.
e 7 And when ye shall hear of wars and rumours
of wars, be ye °not troubled:
f for *such things* must needs °be; but the end
shall not *be* yet.
[2] O[1] P g 8 °**For nation shall rise °against nation, °and
kingdom °against kingdom**: and there shall
be earthquakes °in divers places, and there
shall be famines °and troubles: these *are* °the
beginnings of °sorrows.
h 9 But take heed to yourselves: [6]for they
shall deliver you up °to councils; and °in °the
synagogues ye shall be beaten: and ye shall be
brought °before rulers and kings °for My sake,
i °for a testimony °against them.
10 And the °gospel must first be °published
°among all °nations.
h 11 But °when they shall °lead *you*, and deliver
you up, °take °no thought beforehand
what ye shall speak, neither do ye premeditate:
but whatsoever shall be given you °in
that hour, that speak ye: [6]for it is °not ye
that speak, but °the Holy Ghost.
12 Now the brother shall betray the brother
[9]to death, and the father the °son; and °**children
shall rise up [8]against *their* parents**, and
shall °cause them to be put to death.

13. 1—14. 25 (S[6], p. 1409). RETURN TO BETHANY. (*Division.*)

S[6] | J[1] | 13. 1-37. On leaving the Temple. The second great Prophecy on the Mount of Olives.
| J[2] | 14. 1-25. On arrival at Bethany. The second Supper and second Anointing.

13. 1-37 (J[1], above). ON LEAVING THE TEMPLE. (*Alternation.*)

J[1] | K | 1. The Disciples' remark.
| L | 2. The Lord's reply. Prediction.
| *K* | 3, 4. The Disciples' Two Questions.
| *L* | 5-37. The Lord's reply. Prophecy.

2 Jesus. See Ap. 98. X.
Seest. Gr. *blepō.* Ap. 133. I. 5.
not = by no means. Gr. *ou mē* (Ap. 105. III), denoting absolute certainty. The same word as in *vv.* 30, 31; not the same as in *vv.* 7, 11, 14, 15, 16, 19, 21, 24, 33, 35.
upon. Gr. *epi.* Ap. 104. ix. 2.

13. 3, 4 (*K*, above). THE DISCIPLES' TWO QUESTIONS. (*Division.*)

K | M[1] | 3, 4-. "WHEN shall these things be?" (*pote*).
| M[2] | -4. "WHAT shall be the sign?" (*ti*).

3 upon. Gr. *eis.* Cp. 104. vi.
the mount of Olives. The former prophecy being in the Temple. See Ap. 155.
4 when. Note the first question (M[1]).
what . . . sign. The second question (M[2]).

13. 5-37 (*L*, above). THE LORD'S REPLY. PROPHECY. (*Division.*)

L | N[1] | 5-7. Answer to the first Question (M[1]).
| N[2] | 8-37. Answer to the second Question (M[2]).

13. 5-7 (N[1], above). ANSWER TO THE FIRST QUESTION. (*Alternation.*)

N[1] | e | 5. Warning. "Be not deceived."
| f | 6. Reason. Things seen.
| *e* | 7-. Warning. "Be ye not troubled."
| *f* | -7. Reason. Things heard.

5 began. See note on 1. 1. *Vv.* 5, 7, 11, parallel with Matt. 24. 4-6. Luke 21. 8, 9. Ap. 155.
6 For = Because.
in = upon (= trading upon, as the basis of their claims). Gr. *epi.* Ap. 104. ix. 2. Not the same word as in *vv.* 8, 9, 11, 14, 16, 24, 25, 26, 32. **I** = that I am [He].
7 not. Gr. *mē.* Ap. 105. II. Not the same word as in *vv.* 2, 11, 14, 19, 24, 30, 31, 33, 35.
be = come to pass.

13. 8-37 (N[2], above). ANSWER TO THE SECOND QUESTION. (*Division.*)

N[2] | O[1] | 8-27. Prophecy. Instruction.
| O[2] | 28-37. Parables. Warnings.

13. 8-27 (O[1], above). PROPHECY. INSTRUCTION. (*Introversion.*)

O[1] | P | 8-13. Time. Beginning.
| Q | 14-20. Sign. The Abomination of desolation. Flight.
| *Q* | 21-23. Sign. False Christs. Disbelief.
| *P* | 24-27. Time. The end.

13. 8-13 (P, above). TIME. BEGINNING. (*Introversion.*)

P | g | 8. The beginning.
| h | 9-. Persecution.
| i | -9, 10. Testimony and Reason.
| *h* | 11-13-. Persecution.
| *g* | -13. The end.

8 For nation, &c. Quoted from Isa. 19. 2. **against** = upon. Gr. *epi.* Ap. 104. ix. 3. **and.** Fig. *Polysyndeton,* Ap. 6. **in.** Gr. *kata.* Ap. 104. x. 2. **the beginnings** = a beginning. See Ap. 155. **sorrows** = birth-pangs. **9 to** = unto. Gr. *eis.* Ap. 104. vi; not the same word as in *vv.* 27, 34. **in** = unto. Gr. *eis,* as above. **the synagogues** = synagogues. **before.** Gr. *epi.* Ap. 104. ix. 1. **for** = with a view to. Gr. *eis.* Ap. 104. vi. **against** = to. **10 gospel** = glad tidings [of the kingdom], as in Matt. 24. 14. See Ap. 112, 113, 114. **published** = proclaimed. Gr. *kērussō.* See Ap. 121. 1. **among** = unto. Gr. *eis.* Ap. 104. vi. **nations** = the nations. **11 when** = whenever. **lead** = may be leading. **take no thought** = be not full of care beforehand. See note on Matt. 6. 25. **no.** Gr. *mē.* Ap. 105. II. **in.** Gr. *en.* Ap. 104. viii. Not the same word as in *vv.* 6, 9, 16. **not.** Gr. *ou.* Ap. 105. I. Not the same word as in *vv.* 2, 7, 15, 16, 21, 30, 31. **the Holy Ghost.** See Ap. 101. II. 3. **12 son** = child. Gr. *teknon.* Ap. 108. i. **children.** Pl. of *teknon,* above. Quoted from Mic. 7. 6. **cause them, &c.** = put them, &c.

A.D. 29 13 And ye shall be hated °of all *men* °for
My name's °sake:
g but he that shall endure °unto °the end, the
(p. 1415) same shall be saved.

Q j 14 But when ye shall °see °**the abomination**
of desolation, °spoken of °by Daniel the prophet, standing where it ought [11]not, (°let him
that readeth understand,) then let them that be
[11]in Judæa flee [11]to the mountains:
15 And let him that is °on °the housetop [7]not
go down °into the house, neither enter *therein,*
to take any thing [1]out of his house:
16 And let him that is [9]in the field [7]not turn
back again for to take up his garment.
17 But woe to them that are with child, and
to them that give suck [11]in those days!

k 18 And °pray ye that your flight be [7]not in
the winter.

j 19 [6]For *in* those days shall be °**affliction, such**
as °was [11]not °from °the beginning of the
creation which °God created unto this time,
°**neither shall °be.**

k 20 And except that °the LORD had °shortened
those days, °no flesh °should be saved: but
[13]for the °elect's sake, whom He hath chosen,
°He hath shortened the days.

Q l 21 And then °if any man shall say to you,
°'Lo, here *is* °Christ;' or, °'lo, *He is* there;'
m believe *him* [7]not:

l 22 [6]For false [21]Christs and false °**prophets**
shall rise, and shall °shew signs and wonders,
°to seduce, °if *it were* possible, even the elect.

m 23 But take ye heed: [21]behold, I have foretold you all things.

P n 24 °**But [11]in those days, °after that tribulation,**
the sun shall be darkened, and the moon shall
[11]not give her °light,
25 And the stars °of heaven °shall fall, °and
the powers that are [11]in °heaven shall be
shaken.

o 26 And then °shall they see °**the Son of man**
coming [11]in the clouds °with °great °power and
glory.

o 27 And then shall He send His angels,

n and shall gather together °His elect °from
the four winds, [19]from the uttermost part of
the earth to the uttermost part [25]of heaven.

O² R p 28 Now learn °a parable °of the fig tree;
(p. 1417) When her °branch °is yet tender, and putteth
forth °leaves, ye °know that summer is near:

13 of = by. Gr. *hupo*. Ap. 104. xviii. 1. Not the same word as in *vv.* 28, 32.
for . . . sake = on account of. Gr. *dia*. Ap. 104. v. 2. Not the same word as in *v.* 9.
unto. Gr. *eis*. Ap. 104. vi. the end. See Ap. 155.

13. 14-20 (Q, p. 1415). SIGN. THE ABOMINATION, ETC FLIGHT. (*Alternation.*)

Q | j | 14-17. Flight.
  | k | 18. Commiseration.
  | *j* | 19. Flight.
  | *k* | 20. Commiseration.

14 see. Gr. *eidon*. Ap. 133. I. 1, as in *v.* 29; not the same word as in *vv.* 1, 2, 26.
the abomination of desolation. See Matt. 24. 22. Quoted from Dan. 9. 27; cp. 12. 11; and Ap. 89, 90, 91.
spoken of by Daniel the prophet. Om. by [L] T Tr. A WH R, but not the Syr.
by. Gr. *hupo*. Ap 104. xviii. 1.
let him, &c. Heb. idiom (later usage) = let him who reads and comments on these words in the assembly, &c. Cp. 1 Tim. 4. 13.
15 on = upon. Gr. *epi*. Ap. 104. ix. 1.
the housetop. Cp. Matt. 24. 17.
into. Gr. *eis*. Ap. 104. vi.
18 pray ye. Gr. *proseuchomai*. Ap. 134. I. 2.
19 affliction = tribulation. As in *v.* 24. Quoted from Dan. 12. 1. was not = has not been the like.
from the beginning of the creation which God created. Note the emphasis of this peculiar amplification, giving the Divine condemnation of "Evolution". Cp. in *v.* 20, "the chosen whom He chose". See note on John 8. 44. God. Ap. 98. I. i. 1.
neither = nor by any means. Gr. *ou mē*. Ap. 105. III.
be = come to pass.
20 the LORD. Ap. 98. VI. i. *a*. B. b.
shortened. See on Matt. 24. 22.
no flesh. Not (as in *v.* 11) any flesh.
should be = should have been.
elect's sake. See note on *v.* 19, above.
He hath shortened. See note on Matt. 24. 22, and Ap. 90.

13. 21-23 (*Q*, p. 1415). SIGN. THE FALSE CHRIST. (*Alternation.*)

Q | l | 21-. False Christs.
  | m | -21. Warning. Believe not.
  | *l* | 22. False Christs.
  | *m* | 23. Warning. Take ye heed.

21 if any man, &c. The condition of probable contingency. Ap. 118. 1. b. Not the same word as in *v.* 22.
Lo. Fig. *Asterismos*. Ap. 6.
Christ = the Messiah. Ap. 98. IX.
22 prophets, &c. Quoted from Deut. 13. 1.
shew = give. But T and A read "work", not Syr.
to. Gr. *pros*. Ap. 104. xv. 4.
if, &c. Quite a hypothetical condition; so much so that no verb is expressed. Ap. 118. 2. a. Not the same word as in *v.* 21.

13. 24-27 (*P*, p. 1415). TIME. THE END. (*Introversion.*)

P | n | 24, 25. Signs in heaven.
  | o | 26. The coming of the Son of man.
  | *o* | 27-. The sending of His angels.
  | *n* | -27. Signs on earth.

24 But, &c. Quoted from Isa. 13. 10. after. Gr. *meta*. Ap. 104. xi. 2. light. See Ap. 130. 7.
25 of heaven = of the heaven. Sing. with Art. As in *vv.* 31, 32; not as in *v.* 25-. See note on Matt. 6. 9, 10.
shall fall = shall be falling out; implying continuousness. and the powers, &c. Quoted from Isa. 34. 4.
heaven = the heavens. Pl. with Art. Not the same as in *vv.* 25-, 31, 32. See note on Matt. 6. 9, 10. **26** shall they see. Gr. *opsomai*. Ap. 133. I. 8. a. the Son of man. See Ap. 98. XVI. Quoted from Dan. 7. 13. Cp. Joel 2. 31. with. Gr. *meta*. Ap. 104. xi. 1. great = much. power. See Ap. 172. 1. **27** His elect. Referring to Israel. See *vv.* 20, 22. Isa. 10. 20-22; 11. 11-16; 27. 6; 65. 9, 15, 22; Jer. 31. 36-40; 33. 17-26. Ezek. 36. 8-15, 24; 37. 21-28; 39. 25-29. Amos 9. 11-15. Obad. 17, 21. Zeph. 3. 20. from = out of. Gr. *ek*. Ap. 104. vii.

13. 28-37 [For Structure see next page].

28 a parable = the parable. See Matt. 24. 32. of = from. Gr. *apo*. Ap. 104. iv. Not the same word as in *vv.* 13, 32. branch. Gr. *klados*. See note on 11. 8. is yet = shall have already become; as in Matt. 24. 32. leaves = its leaves. know = get to know. Gr. *ginōskō*. Ap. 132. I. ii.

q 29 So ° ye in like manner, when ye shall [1] see
(p. 1417) these things ° come to pass,
A. D. 29 r [28] know that it is nigh, *even* ° at the doors.
S 30 ° Verily I say unto you, that ° this generation shall [2] not pass, till all these things ° be done.
31 ° Heaven and earth shall pass away: but My words shall [2] not pass away.
32 But ° of that day and *that* hour ° knoweth no man, ° no, not the angels which are [11] in [31] heaven, neither ° the Son, but the ° Father.
33 ° Take ye heed, ° watch and pray: [6] for ye [32] know [11] not when the ° time is.
Rp 34 *For the Son of man is* as ° a man ° taking a far journey, ° who left his house, and gave authority to his ° servants, and to ° every man his work, ° and commanded the porter ° to watch.
q 35 [34] Watch ye therefore: [6] for ye [32] know [11] not when the ° master of the house cometh, at even, or at midnight, or at the cockcrowing, or in the morning:
r 36 Lest coming suddenly he find you ° sleeping.
S 37 And what I say unto you I say unto all, [34] Watch."

J² T **14** ° After two days was *the feast of* the ° passover, and of unleavened bread:
U and the chief priests and the scribes ° sought how they might ° take Him ° by craft, and put *Him* to death.
2 But they said, ° "Not ° on the feast *day*, lest there be an ° uproar of the People."
V W 3 ° And being ° in Bethany ° in ° the house of Simon ° the leper, as He sat at meat,
X there came ° a woman having an alabaster ° box of ointment of ° spikenard ° very precious; and she ° brake the ° box, and ° poured *it* ° on His head.
Y s 4 And there were ° some that had indignation ° within themselves, and said, "Why ° was this waste of the ointment ° made?

13. 28-37 (O², p. 1415). PARABLES. WARNING.
(*Alternations.*)

O² | R | p | 28. Parable. The Fig-tree.
q | 29-. Application.
r | -29. Nearness.
S | 30-33. Watch.
R | *p* | 34. Parable. The Householder.
q | 35. Application.
r | 36. Suddenness.
S | 37. Watch!

29 ye in like manner = ye also.
come = taking place. **at.** Gr. *epi.* Ap. 104. ix. 2.
30 Verily. See note on Matt. 5. 18.
this generation. See note on Matt. 11. 16.
be done = may have taken place. See note on Matt. 24. 34; where the Gr. particle, *an*, with the Subjunctive Mood, marks it as being conditional on the repentance of the nation (Acts 3. 18-26).
31 Heaven = the heaven. Sing. See note on Matt. 6. 9, 10.
32 of = concerning. Gr. *peri.* Ap. 104. xiii. 1.
knoweth. Gr. *oida.* Ap. 132. I. i.
no, not = not even. Gr. *oude.* Compound of *ou.* Ap. 105. I.
the Son: i.e. as "the Son of man". See *v.* 26.
Father. Ap. 98. III.
33 Take ye heed. Gr. *blepō.* Ap. 133. I. 5.
watch = lie sleepless. Not the same word as in *vv.* 34, 35, 37. **time** = season, or crisis.
34 a man. Gr. *anthrōpos.* Ap. 123. 1.
taking a far journey. See note on Matt. 21. 33.
who left = leaving. **servants** = bond-servants.
and commanded the porter = commanded the porter withal.
to watch = to keep awake. Not the same word as in *v.* 33. Note the Fig. *Epanadiplōsis* (Ap. 6), *vv.* 34 and 37.
35 master = lord. Gr. *kurios.* Ap. 98. VI. 4. A.
36 sleeping = composing yourselves for sleep (voluntarily). Gr. *katheudō.* See notes on 1 Thess. 4. 14, and 5. 6. Not *koimaomai* = to fall asleep involuntarily (as in death). See Ap. 171. 1.

14. 1-25 (J², p. 1415). ARRIVAL AT BETHANY.
(*Introversion.*)

J² | T | 1-. Two days before the Passover.
U | -1, 2. Conspiracy of the Rulers.
V | 3-9. The second Supper, and second Anointing.
U | 10, 11. Conspiracy of Judas.
T | 12-25. One day before the Passover.

1 After two days. See Ap. 156. Cp. Matt. 26. 2.
After = Gr. Now after. Cp. *v.* 12. Gr. *meta.* Ap. 104. xi. 2. As in *vv.* 28, 70.
passover. Aramaic. Ap. 94. III. 3. See note on Matt. 26. 2. **sought** = were seeking. **take Him** = get hold of Him. **by.** Gr. *en.* Ap. 104. viii. Not the same word as in *vv.* 19, 21. **2 Not.** Gr. *mē.* Ap. 105. II. Not the same word as in *vv.* 7, 29, 36, 37, 49, 56, 68, 71. **on** = in; i.e. during. Gr. *en.* Ap. 104. viii. Not the same word as in *vv.* 3, 6, 35, 46, 62. **uproar** = tumult.

14. 3-9 (V, above). THE SECOND SUPPER, AND SECOND ANOINTING.
(*Introversion and Alternation.*)

V | W | 3-. The Feast.
X | -3. The woman.
Y | s | 4. Indignation. Some.
t | 5. Reason.
Y | *s* | 6. Reprehension. The Lord.
t | 7. Reason.
X | 8. The woman.
W | 9. The Prophecy.

3 And being. Parallel with Matt. 26. 6-13. **in.** Gr. *en.* Ap. 104. viii. Not the same word as in *vv.* 20, 60, 62. **the house, &c.** Not therefore the first supper (John 12. 1, &c.), as that was in the house of Lazarus, six days before the Passover. See Ap. 156, 157, and 158. **the leper.** Note the Fig. *Ampliatio* (Ap. 6), by which Simon still retained the name describing what he had once been. **a woman.** Not Mary; the second occasion being quite different. See Ap. 158. **box** = flask. **spikenard** = pure nard. Liquid, because it was poured. **very precious** = of great price. **brake.** Alabaster being brittle it was easily done. A Divine supplement, here. **poured.** Gr. *katacheō.* Occ. only here and in Matt. 26. 7; not in John 12. 3. **on.** Gr. *kata.* Ap. 104. x. 1. Not the same word as in *vv.* 2, 35, 46. **4 some.** At the first anointing it was only one, Judas (John 12. 4). **within.** Gr. *pros.* Ap. 104. xv. 3. Not the same word as in *v.* 58. **was . . . made** = is come to pass.

t (p. 1417) A.D. 29 5 °For it might have been sold for more
than three hundred °pence, and have been
given to the poor." And they °murmured
against her.

Y s 6 And °Jesus said, "Let her alone; why trouble ye her? she hath °wrought a °good work
°on Me.

t 7 [5]For ye have the poor °with you always,
and °whensoever °ye will ye °may do them
°good: but °Me ye have °not always.

X 8 °She hath done what she could: she is
come aforehand °to anoint My body °to the
°burying.

W 9 °Verily I say unto you, °Wheresoever this
°gospel shall be °preached °throughout the
whole °world, *this* also that she hath done
shall be spoken of °for a memorial of her."

U 14th Nisan 10 And Judas Iscariot, one of the twelve,
°went °unto the chief priests, °to betray Him
unto them.
11 And when they heard *it*, they °were glad,
and promised to give him money. And he
°sought how he might conveniently °betray
Him.

T Z[1] u (p. 1418) 12 And °the first day of unleavened bread,
when they °killed °the [1]passover, His disciples
said unto Him, "Where wilt thou that we go
and prepare that Thou mayest eat °the [1]pass-
over?"

v 13 And He sendeth forth two of His disciples,
and saith unto them, "Go ye °into the city,
and there shall meet you °a °man bearing a
pitcher of water: follow him.
14 And wheresoever he shall go in, say ye to
the °goodman of the house, °'The Master
saith, 'Where is the guestchamber, where I
shall eat [12]the [1]passover [7]with My disciples?'
15 And °he will shew you a large upper room
°furnished *and* prepared: there make ready
for us."

v 16 And His disciples went forth, and came
[13]into the city, and found °as He had said unto
them:

u and they made ready [12]the [1]passover.

Z[2] w 17 And °in the evening He cometh [7]with
the twelve.
18 And as they sat and did eat, [6]Jesus said,
[9]"Verily I say unto you, One °of you which
eateth [7]with Me shall [10]betray Me."

x 19 And they °began to be sorrowful, and to
say unto Him one °by one, "*Is* it I?" and
another *said*, "*Is* it I?"

5 For. Gr. *gar*, giving the reason.
pence. See Ap. 51. I. 4.
murmured = deeply moved. Occ. only in 1. 43, Matt. 9. 30, and John 11. 33, 38.
6 Jesus. Ap. 98. X.
wrought. The object had been accomplished. In John 12. 7 (on the former occasion) it was to be reserved for the burial.
good = happy, excellent, appropriate. Not the same word as in *v.* 7.
on. Gr. *eis.* Ap. 104. vi. Not the same word as in *vv.* 2, 3, 35, 46.
7 with = in company with. Gr. *meta.* Ap. 104. xi. 1. Not the same word as in *v.* 49.
whensoever ye will. A Divine supplement, here.
ye will = ye wish. Gr. *thelō.* Ap. 102. 1.
may = can.
good. Not the same word as in *v.* 6.
Me ye have not always. Transubstantiation is incompatible with this.
not. Gr. *ou.* Ap. 105. I. Not the same word as in *v.* 2.
8 She hath done what she could = What she had [to do] she did. A Divine supplement, here.
to anoint = to anoint [beforehand]. Occ. only here.
to = for, or unto. Gr. *eis.* Ap. 104. vi.
burying = embalming. See note on Matt. 26. 12.
9 Verily. See note on Matt. 5. 18.
Wheresoever. With *an*, with the Subjunctive, marking the phrase as being hypothetical. See note on Matt. 10. 23.
gospel = glad tidings.
preached = proclaimed. Gr. *kērussō.* Ap. 121. 1.
throughout. Gr. *eis.* Ap. 104. vi.
world. Gr. *kosmos.* Ap. 129. 1.
for. Gr. *eis.* Ap. 104. vi. Not the same word as in *v.* 24.
10 went = went off (smarting under the rebukes of *vv.* 6–9).
unto. Gr. *pros.* Ap. 104. xv. 3. Not the same word as in *v.* 34.
to betray = to the end that he might deliver up.
11 were glad = rejoiced.
sought = kept seeking; i.e. busied himself continuously. This is the sense of the Imperf. Tense here.
betray = deliver up.

14. 12–25 (*T*, p. 1417). ONE DAY BEFORE THE PASSOVER. (*Division.*)

T | Z[1] | 12–16. Preparation.
| Z[2] | 17–21. Prediction.
| Z[3] | 22–25. Celebration.

14. 12–16 (Z[1], above). PREPARATION. (*Introversion.*)

Z[1] | u | 12. Preparation. Inquiry.
| v | 13–15. Directions. Given.
| *v* | 16–. Directions. Carried out.
| *u* | –16. Preparation effected.

12 the first day of unleavened bread. This was the 14th of Nisan; the first day of the Feast, the 15th of Nisan, was the "high day": the great sabbath. See Ap. 156. Moreover, "the preparation" had not yet been made. See note on Matt. 26. 17.
killed = were wont to kill.
the passover. *Pascha*, Aramaic. Ap. 94. III. 3. Put by Fig. *Metonymy* (of Adjunct), Ap. 6, for the lamb. It was this that was killed and eaten. **13 into.** Gr. *eis.* Ap. 104. vi. **a man.** Gr. *anthrōpos.* Ap. 123. 1. **man bearing a pitcher.** Most unusual, for women carry pitchers, and men carry skin bottles. **14 goodman of the house** = the master of the house. **The Master** = The Teacher. Ap. 98. XIV. v. 3. **15 he** = he himself. **furnished** = spread with couches and other necessaries. **16 as** = just as.

14. 17–21 (Z[2], above). PREDICTION. (*Introversion.*)

Z[2] | w | 17, 18. Betrayal. The first Prediction.
| x | 19. Question of the Disciples.
| *x* | 20. Answer of the Lord.
| *w* | 21. Betrayal. The second Prediction.

17 in the evening = the evening having come. **18 of** = from among. Gr. *ek.* Ap. 104. vii. Not the same word as in *v.* 21. **19 began.** See note on 1. 1. **by.** Gr. *kata.* Ap. 104. x. 1.

x 20 And He answered and said unto them,
p. 1418) "*It is* one [18] of the twelve, that dippeth [7] with
A. D. 29 Me °in the dish.

w 21 °The Son of [13] man indeed goeth, [16] as it
°is written °of Him: but woe to °that [13] man
°by whom °the Son of man is [10] betrayed!
[6] good were it for that man °if he had °never
been born."

Z[3] 22 And as they °did eat, [6] Jesus took bread,
and blessed, and brake *it*, and gave to them,
and said, "Take, °eat: this °is My body."
23 And He took the cup, and when He had
given thanks, He gave *it* to them: and they
all drank [18] of it.
24 And He said unto them, "This [22] is °My
blood of the °new testament, which °is shed
°for many.
25 [9] Verily I say unto you, °'I will drink °no
more [18] of the fruit of the vine, until that day
°that I drink it °new [3] in °the kingdom of God.'"

C A[1] y 26 And when they had °sung an hymn, they
p. 1419) went out [13] into the mount of Olives.
27 And [6] Jesus saith unto them, "All ye
°shall be offended °because of Me °this night:
°for °it is written, '**I will smite the shepherd,
and the sheep shall be scattered.**'
28 But [1] after that °I am risen, I will °go before you [13] into Galilee."

z 29 But Peter said unto Him, °"Although
all shall be offended, yet *will* [7] not I."

y 30 And [6] Jesus saith unto him, [9] "Verily I say
unto thee, °That this day, *even* [3] in this night,
before °the cock crow °twice, thou °shalt
deny Me thrice."

z 31 But he °spake the more °vehemently, °"If
I should die with Thee, I will °not deny Thee
°in any wise." Likewise °also said they all.

A[2] a 32 And they °came [8] to a place which was
named °Gethsemane:

b and He saith to His disciples, "Sit ye here,
while I shall °pray."
33 And He taketh [7] with °Him Peter and
James and John, and [19] began to be °sore
amazed, and to be °very heavy;
34 And saith unto them, "My °soul is exceeding sorrowful °unto death: tarry ye here,
and °watch."

b c[1] 35 And He went forward a little, and fell °on
the °ground, and °prayed that, [21] if it were
possible, the °hour might pass °from Him.

20 in=into. Gr. *eis*. Ap. 104. vi. As in *v.* 60. Not the same word as in *vv.* 3, 25, 30, 49, 62.

21 The Son of man. See Ap. 98. XVI.

is written=it standeth written.

of=concerning. Gr. *peri*. Ap. 104. xiii. 1. Not the same word as in *vv.* 18, 20, 23, 25, 69, 70.

that man. Emphatic.

by=by means of. Gr. *dia*. Ap. 104. v. 1. Not the same word as in *v.* 1.

if, &c. Assuming the condition as an actual fact. Ap. 118. 2. a. **never**=not. Gr. *ou*. Ap. 105. I.

22 did eat=were eating. All that happened before and at this third supper is not given in Mark.

eat. All the texts omit this word.

is=represents. Fig. *Metaphor*. See Ap. 6.

24 My blood. No covenant could be made without blood. See note on Matt. 26. 28.

new testament=new covenant. See note on Matt. 26. 28, and Ap. 95. I. Cp. Jer. 31. 31.

is shed=is being, or is about to be shed. Fig. *Heterōsis* (of Tense), Ap. 6, or Fig. *Prolēpsis*, Ap. 6.

for=concerning. Gr. *peri*. Ap. 104. xiii. But all the texts read *huper*. Ap. 104. xvii.

25 I will=that I will. After the verb "to say" the conj. *hoti* marks off the words spoken. Cp. Matt. 14. 26; 16. 18; 20. 12; 21. 3; 26. 34; 27. 47. Mark 1. 40; 6. 14, 15, 16, 18, 35; 9. 26; 14. 57, 58. See note on Luke 23. 43, and Ap. 173.

no more=not any more, in any wise. Gr. *ouketi, ou mē*. Ap. 105. III. **that**=when.

new=fresh. See note on Matt. 26. 29.

the kingdom of God. See Ap. 114.

14. 26-42 (*C*, p. 1381). THE AGONY.
(*Division.*)

C	A[1]	26-31. The Mount of Olives.
	A[2]	32-42. Gethsemane.

14. 26-31 (A[1], above). THE MOUNT OF OLIVES.
(*Alternation.*)

A[1] y | 26-28. The stumbling of all.
z | 29. Peter's disclaimer.
y | 30. The denial of one.
z | 31. Peter's vehement disclaimer.

26 sung an hymn. See Matt. 26. 30.

27 shall be offended=will stumble.

because of=in, or at. Gr. *en*. Ap. 104. viii.

this night=in (Gr. *en*) this night. But all the texts omit "because . . . night". ([L].) **for**=because.

it is written=it standeth written. Quoted from Zech. 13. 7. **28 I am risen**=My being raised.

go before. Cp. Matt. 26. 32.

29 Although=Even if all, &c. Throwing no doubt on the hypothesis. Ap. 118. 2. a.

30 That this day. The conj. *hoti* makes "this day" part of what He said. See note on Luke 23. 43, and *v.* 25 above. We have the same construction in Luke 4. 21; 19. 9, but not in Matt. 21. 28; Luke 22. 34; 23. 43.

the cock=a cock. See Ap. 160.

twice. A Divine supplement, only here. See Ap. 160.

shalt=wilt. **31 spake**=kept saying.

vehemently=of (Gr. *ek*. Ap. 104. vii) excess. **If I should die, &c.**=If it were needful for me to die, &c. The condition being uncertain, and the result remaining to be seen. Ap. 118. 1. b. **not . . . in any wise.** Gr. *ou mē*. Ap. 105. III. **also said**=said they all also: i. e. all as well as Peter.

14. 32-42 (A[2], above). GETHSEMANE. (*Introversion.*)

A[2] | a | 32-. Departure.
| b | -32-34. Purpose stated.
| *b* | 35-41. Purpose effected.
| *a* | 42. Departure.

32 came=come. **Gethsemane.** See note on Matt. 26. 36. **pray.** Gr. *proseuchomai*. Ap. 134. I. 2.
33 Him=Himself. **sore amazed.** Gr. *ekthambeō*. A Divine supplement, here, 9. 15, and 16. 5, 6.
very heavy=deeply weighed down, or depressed. **34 soul.** Gr. *psuchē*. See Ap. 110. IV.
unto=even to. Gr. *heōs*. **watch**=keep awake. As in *vv.* 37, 38; and in 13. 34, 35, 37.

14. 35-41 [For Structure see next page].

35 on=upon. Gr. *epi*. Ap. 104. ix. 1. **ground.** Gr. *gē*. Ap. 129. 4. **prayed**=was praying; as in *v.* 32. Here in the Imperf. Tense. **hour.** Put by Fig. *Metonymy* (of Adjunct), Ap. 6, for what is done in that time. **from**=away from. Gr. *apo*. Ap. 104. iv. As in *vv.* 36 and 52; not the same as in *v.* 43.

A. D. 29 36 And He said, ° "Abba, ° Father, all things
are possible unto Thee; take away this cup
[35]from Me: nevertheless [7]not what I ° will,
but what Thou ° wilt."
37 And He cometh, and findeth them ° sleeping,
and saith unto Peter, ° "Simon, ° sleepest
thou? ° couldest [7]not thou [34] watch one hour?
38 [34]Watch ye and pray, ° lest ye enter [13] into
temptation. The ° spirit truly *is* ° ready, but
the flesh *is* weak."
c² (p. 1420) 39 And again He went away, and [35] prayed,
and ° spake the same words.
40 And when He returned, He found them
[37]asleep again, ([5]for their eyes were heavy,)
° neither ° wist they what to answer Him.
c³ 41 And He cometh the third time, and saith
unto them, [37]"Sleep on ° now, and take *your*
rest: ° it is enough, ° the hour is come; behold,
[21]the Son of man ° is [10] betrayed [13] into the
hands of ° sinners.
a 42 Rise up, let us go; ° lo, he that [10] betrayeth
Me ° is at hand."
B B¹ C 43 And immediately, while He yet spake,
cometh Judas, ° one of the twelve, and [7] with
him a great ° multitude [7] with swords and
° staves, ° from the chief priests and the scribes
and the elders.
J N P 44 And he ° that [10] betrayed Him had given
them a ° token, saying, "Whomsoever I shall
kiss, that same is He; ° take Him, and lead
Him away ° safely."
45 And as soon as he was come, he ° goeth
straightway to Him, and saith, ° "Master,
Master;" and ° kissed Him.
46 And they laid their hands ° on Him, and
[44]took Him.
Q 47 And ° one of them that stood by ° drew
a sword, and smote ° a servant of the high
priest, and cut off his ° ear.

14. 35-41 (*b*, p. 1419). PURPOSE EFFECTED.
(*Division*.)

b | c¹ | 35-38. The First Prayer.
  | c² | 39, 40. The Second Prayer.
  | c³ | 41. The Third Prayer.

36 Abba. Aramaic for Father. Occ. only here, Rom. 8. 15, and Gal. 4. 6. See Ap. 94. III. 3. (Heb. *'ab.*)
Father. Ap. 98. III.
will . . . wilt. Gr. *thelō*. Ap. 102. 1.
37 sleeping . . . sleepest. Having composed themselves for sleep. Gr. *katheudō*; not *koimaomai*. See notes on 1 Thess. 4. 14 and 5. 6.
Simon. The name a Divine supplement, here.
couldest not thou = wast thou not able.
38 lest ye enter, &c. = that ye may not (Gr. *mē*, as in *v.* 2) enter, &c.
spirit. Gr. *pneuma*. Ap. 101. II. 8.
ready = prompt, or willing. Occ. only here, Matt. 26. 41, and Rom. 1. 15.
39 spake the same words. A Divine supplement, here.
40 neither wist they = and they knew not (Gr. *ou*. Ap. 105. I).
wist = knew. Gr. *oida*. Ap. 132. I. i. "Wist" is the Past Tense of Anglo-Saxon *witan* = to know.
41 now = the remaining time.
it is enough = he is receiving [the money, *v.* 11]. The verb *apechō*, in the *Papyri*, is the technical word for *giving a receipt*. See the notes on Matt. 6. 2, 5, 16. Cp. Luke 6. 24. Phil. 4. 18. Philem. *v.* 15. The Lord knew that at that moment Judas had received the promised money, and that the moment had come; just as He knew that Judas was near at hand (*v.* 42).
the hour is come. See note on John 7. 6.
is betrayed = is [on the point of being] delivered up.
sinners = the sinners.
42 lo. Fig. *Asterismos* (Ap. 6); same word as "behold" in *v.* 41.
is at hand = is drawn near. If the Lord knew this, He knew that Judas had received the money (*v.* 41).

14. 43—16. 14 (***B***, p. 1381). THE BAPTISM OF SUFFERINGS. (*Division*.)

B | B¹ | 14. 43—15. 39. Death.
  | B² | 15. 40—16. 8. Burial.
  | B³ | 16. 9-13. Resurrection.

14. 43—15. 39 (B¹, above). DEATH. (*Introversions and Alternations.*)

B¹ | C | 14. 43. The Arrival of Judas.
  D | E | G | J | 14. 44-52. Conspiracy. (Judas.)
      K | 14. 53. The Lord led to Caiaphas.
    H | 14. 54. Peter. Following.
    F | L | 14. 55-64. The Lord before Caiaphas.
      M | 14. 65. Personal abuse.
  D | *E* | *H* | 14. 66-72. Peter. Denial.
      G | *J* | 15. 1-. Conspiracy. (Rulers.)
        K | 15. -1. The Lord led to Pilate.
    F | *L* | 15. 2-15. The Lord before Pilate.
      M | 15. 16-23. Personal abuse.
C | 15. 24-39. The Crucifixion of the Lord.

14. 44-52 (J, above). CONSPIRACY. (JUDAS.) (*Introversion.*)

J | N | P | 44-46. Betrayal. By one.
    Q | 47. The zeal of one. Peter defending.
  O | 48. The Lord. Appeal to multitude.
  O | 49. The Lord. Reason of the Appeal.
  N | *P* | 50. Desertion. By all.
    Q | 51, 52. The zeal of one. Lazarus following.

43 one = being one. See note on Matt. 26. 47. **multitude** = crowd. **staves**: or clubs. Gr. *xulon* = wood, timber. Put by Fig. *Metonymy* (of Cause), Ap. 6, for weapons made from timber. **from** = from beside. Gr. *para*. Ap. 104. xii. 1. **44 that betrayed Him** = that was delivering Him up. **token** = a concerted sign. Gr. *sussēmon*, a compound of the Gr. *sun* (= in conjunction with. Ap. 104. xvi) and *sēmeion* = a sign. **take** = seize. **safely** = secured assuredly. Occ. only here, Acts 2. 36; 16. 23. **45 goeth** = cometh up. **Master, Master** = Rabbi, Rabbi. Fig. *Epizeuxis* (Ap. 6) = great Rabbi. Note that Judas never spoke of or to Him as "Lord". Cp. 1 Cor. 12. 3. **kissed** = effusively kissed. See note on Matt. 26. 49. **46 on.** Gr. *epi*. Ap. 104. ix. 3. **47 one of them, &c.** This was Peter (not named in Matthew, Mark, or Luke, but only in John 18. 10). **drew a sword.** Cp. Luke 22. 35-38. **a servant** = the servant. See note on Matt. 26. 51. **ear.** Gr. *ōtion*; but all the texts read *ōtarion*. See note on Matt. 26. 51.

O (p. 1420) A.D. 29 48 And [6]Jesus °answered and said unto them,
"Are ye come out, as °against a °thief, [7]with
swords and *with* [43]staves to take Me?

O 49 I was daily °with you [3]in the temple
teaching, and ye took Me [7]not: °but the scriptures must be fulfilled."

NP 50 And they all °forsook Him, and fled.

Q 51 °And there °followed Him °a certain young
man, having a °linen cloth °cast °about *his*
°naked *body;* and °the young men laid hold
on him:
52 And he °left °the linen cloth, and fled
[35]from them naked.

K 53 And they led [6]Jesus away °to the high
priest: and °with him were assembled all the
chief priests °and the elders and the scribes.

H 54 And Peter followed him °afar off, °even
[13]into the °palace of the high priest: and °he
sat [7]with the °servants, and °warmed himself
°at the °fire.

F L R (p. 1421) 55 And the chief priests and °all the °council
°sought for witness °against [6]Jesus to put Him
to death; and °found none.
56 [5]For many °bare false witness [55]against
Him, but their °witness °agreed [7]not together.
57 And there arose certain, and [56]bare false
witness [55]against Him, °saying,
58 "We heard Him say, 'I will destroy this
°Temple that is °made with hands, and °within
three days I will build °another °made without hands.'"
59 But neither so did their witness agree
together.

S d 60 And the high priest °stood up [20]in the
midst, and °asked [6]Jesus, saying, "Answerest
Thou nothing? what *is it which* these witness
against Thee?"

e 61 But He held His peace, and answered
nothing.

d Again the high priest asked Him, and said
unto Him, "Art Thou °the Christ, the Son of
°the Blessed?"

e 62 And [6]Jesus said, °"I am: and ye shall
°see °the Son of man sitting °on the right
hand of °power, and coming °in the clouds of
°heaven."

48 answered and said. See note on Deut. 1. 41.
against=upon. Gr. *epi.* Ap. 104. ix. 3.
thief=robber, as in 15. 27. See note on Matt. 26. 55.
49 with. Gr. *pros.* Ap. 104. xv. 3.
but=but [this is done] to the end that, &c. Luke 22. 37; 24. 44. Cp. Zech. 13. 7; Isa. 53. 7, &c.
50 forsook Him, and fled=leaving Him, fled.
51 And there followed, &c. This is a Divine supplement, peculiar to Mark's Gospel.
followed=was following.
a certain young man=one particular young man. That this might be Lazarus, is probable: (1) because the Lord had returned to Bethany each preceding night of that week; (2) because Lazarus would be looking out; (3) because of the linen robe, betokening his social position; (4) and especially because he was wanted: "The chief priests consulted that they might put Lazarus also to death" (John 12. 10). None of the apostles was arrested. Peter (though suspected) and another (John 18. 15) were unmolested; (5) his name is not given here by Divine guidance, because Lazarus was probably still alive, and therefore in danger.
linen cloth. Gr. *sindōn*=a linen cloak (so called probably from *Indos*=Indian).
cast about=having clothed [himself]; as in Matt. 6. 29 (arrayed), 31; 25. 36, 38, 43. Mark 16. 5. Luke 12. 27; 23. 11. John 19. 2. Acts 12. 8.
about=upon. Gr. *epi.* Ap. 104. ix. 1.
naked. Without waiting to put on all his robes.
the young men: i.e. the soldiers; as in 2 Sam. 2. 14. Gen. 14. 24. **52 left, &c.**=leaving behind...fled.
the linen cloth=the *sindōn.*
53 to. Gr. *pros.* Ap. 104. xv. 3.
with him=to him: i.e. by his order or edict.
and. The Fig. *Polysyndeton* (Ap. 6) emphasizes each class.
54 afar off=from (Gr. *apo.* Ap. 104. iv) afar.
even=as far as within.
palace=court. See note on Matt. 26. 3.
he sat=he was sitting, and continued to sit.
servants=officers. **warmed**=was warming.
at. Gr. *pros.* Ap. 104. xv. 3.
fire. Gr. light; put by Fig. *Metonymy* (of Adjunct), Ap. 6, for fire, because it was the light that led to his recognition, *v.* 66.

14. 55-64 (L, p. 1420). THE LORD BEFORE CAIAPHAS. (*Alternation.*)

L | R | 55-59. Witnesses sought.
   S | 60-62. Examination.
   R | 63. Witnesses superseded.
   S | 64. Condemnation.

55 all the=the whole. **council**=Sanhedrin.
sought for witness against=were seeking, &c. This was contrary to their rule: "In judgments against the life of any man, they begin first to transact about quitting the party who is tried, and they begin not with those things which make for his condemnation". *Sanhedr.* cap. 4 (cited by Lightfoot, Pitman's ed., xi. 442). See the new edition of *The Babylonian Talmud*, vol. viii, p. 100. N. Talmud Pub. Co., N.Y., U.S.A. **against.** Gr. *kata.* Ap. 104. x. 1. As in *vv.* 56, 57. **found none**=did not (Ap. 105. I) find [any]. **56 bare**=were bearing. **witness**=testimonies. **agreed not**=were not alike. A Divine supplement, here. **57 saying**=saying that. See note on *v.* 25. **58 Temple.** Gr. *naos.* See Matt. 23. 16. **made with hands...made without hands.** A Divine supplement, here. **within.** Gr. *dia.* Ap. 104. v. 1. Not the same word as in *v.* 4. **another.** Gr. *allos.* See Ap. 124. 1.

14. 60-62 (S, above). EXAMINATION. (*Alternation.*)

S | d | 60. Question of High Priest.
   e | 61-. The Lord. Silent.
   d | -61. Adjuration of High Priest.
   e | 62. The Lord. Assent.

60 stood up in the midst=stood up [and came down] into the midst. Showing that this was not a formal judicial trial, but only to get sufficient evidence to send the Lord to Pilate (15. 1). **asked**=further asked. **61 the Christ**=the Messiah. Ap. 98. IX. **the Blessed.** Used by the Jews instead of the name, Jehovah. **62 I am**=I am [He]. See John 4. 26; 8. 28, 58; each time followed by extraordinary effects. See John 18. 6. **see.** Gr. *opsomai.* Ap. 133. I. 8. a. **the Son of man.** The last occ. of this title (Ap. 98. XVI) in Mark. The first is 2. 10. **on**=at. Gr. *ek.* Ap. 104. vii. Not the same word as in *vv.* 2, 3, 6, 35, 46. **power.** Gr. *dunamis.* Ap. 172. 1. Put by Fig. *Metonymy* (of Adjunct), Ap. 6, for Jehovah Who exercises it, and that in judgment. **in**=amid. Gr. *meta.* Ap. 104. xi. 1. Not the same word as in *vv.* 3, 20, 25, 30, 49, 60, 66. **heaven**=the heavens. See note on Matt. 6. 9, 10.

R (p. 1421) A.D. 29 63 Then the high priest °rent his clothes, and saith, "What need we any further witnesses?

S 64 Ye have heard the blasphemy: what think ye?" And they all °condemned Him to be °guilty of death.

M 65 And some [19] began to spit on Him, and to cover His face, and to °buffet Him, and to say unto Him, "Prophesy:" and the [54] servants °did strike Him °with the palms of their hands.

H f[1] (p. 1422) 66 And as Peter was beneath [3] in the [54] palace, there cometh one of the maids of the high priest:
67 And when she saw Peter [54] warming himself, she °looked upon him, and said, "And thou also wast [7] with [6] Jesus of Nazareth."
68 But °he denied, saying, "I °know [7] not, neither °understand I what thou sayest."

g[1] And he went out [13] into °the porch; and °the cock crew.

f[2] 69 And °a maid saw him again, and [19] began to say to them that stood by, "This is *one* [18] of them."
70 And [68] he denied it again. And a little [1] after, they that stood by said again to Peter, "Surely thou art *one* [18] of them: for thou art a Galilæan, and thy speech agreeth *thereto*."
71 But he [19] began °to curse and to swear, *saying*, [68] "I know [7] not this [21] Man of Whom ye speak."

g[2] 72 And the second time [68] the cock crew.

f[3] And Peter called to mind the °word that [6] Jesus said unto him, °"Before [68] the cock crow twice, thou °shalt deny Me thrice." And when he thought thereon, he wept.

E G J (p. 1420) **15** And °straightway °in the morning the chief priests °held a consultation °with the elders °and scribes °and the whole council, °and bound °Jesus, and °carried *Him* away,

K and delivered *Him* to Pilate.

F L h (p. 1422) 2 And °Pilate asked Him, "Art Thou the King of the Jews?" And He °answering said unto him, °"Thou sayest *it*."
3 And the chief priests °accused Him °of many things: but He answered °nothing.
4 And Pilate asked Him again, saying, "Answerest Thou [3] nothing? behold how many things they witness against Thee."
5 But Jesus °yet answered °nothing; so that Pilate marvelled.

i 6 Now °at °*that* feast °he released unto them one prisoner, whomsoever they desired.
7 And there was *one* named °Barabbas, *which lay* bound [1] with them that had °made insurrection with him, °who had committed murder °in the insurrection.
8 And the °multitude °crying aloud °began to

63 rent his clothes. This was strictly forbidden. See Lev. 10. 6; 21. 10.
64 condemned. Gr. *katakrinō*. Ap. 122. 7.
guilty = liable to.
65 buffet = cuff. See note on Matt. 26. 67.
did strike = kept striking.
with the palms of their hands. Gr. *rapisma* = with smart blows. Occ. only here and in John 18. 22; 19. 3.

14. 66-72 (*H*, p. 1420). PETER. DENIALS. (*Repeated Alternation.*)

H | f[1] | 66-68-. Peter. Denial.
| g[1] | -68. A cock crowing.
| f[2] | 69-71. Peter. Denials.
| g[2] | 72-. A cock crowing.
| f[3] | -72. Peter. Repentance.

67 looked upon. See Ap. 133. I. 7.
68 he denied. See Ap. 160.
know. Gr. *oida*. Ap. 132. I. i.
understand. Gr. *epistamai*. Ap. 132. I. v.
the porch = the vestibule. Gr. *proaulion*. Occ. only here in N.T.: = the vestibule leading from the outer gate to the court. **the** = a. See Ap. 160.
69 a maid = the maid. See Ap. 160.
71 to curse and to swear = cursing and swearing. The verb *anathematizō* is not peculiar to Biblical Greek, as alleged; for Deissmann shows, from the *Papyri*, that it is of pagan origin, first coined by Greek Jews. (See *Light from the Ancient East*, pp. 92, 93.)
72 word = saying. Gr. *rhēma*. See note on Mark 9. 32.
Before = that (*hoti*) before. See note on *v.* 25.
shalt = wilt.
15. 1 straightway. See notes on 1. 10, 12.
in. Gr. *epi*. Ap. 104. ix. 3. Not the same word as in *vv.* 7, 29, 38, 41, 46.
in the morning = any time before sunrise, while yet dark. Cp. 1. 35; 16. 2, 9. John 20. 1. The Lord must have been led to Pilate before our midnight, because it was "about the sixth hour" of the night when Pilate said "Behold your king" (John 19. 14). It was therefore in the night, at which time it was unlawful to try a prisoner. See the *Talmud*, Sanhedrin, cap. 4. It was also unlawful on the eve of the Sabbath, and this was the eve of the High Sabbath. See Ap. 165.
held a consultation = having formed a council. See note on Matt. 12. 14.
with = in association with. Gr. *meta*. Ap. 104. xi. 1. Same as in *vv.* 7, 28, 31. Not the same as in *v.* 27.
and. Note the Fig. *Polysyndeton* (Ap. 6) to emphasize the fact that it was the act of the whole council.
Jesus. Ap. 98. X.
carried Him away. Matt. 27. 2 has *apēgagon* = *to lead away* what is alive (in contrast with *pherein*, which is generally used of what is inanimate). Luke has *ēgagon* = they led (Luke 23. 1). Mark has *apēnegkan* = carried, as though from faintness.

15. 2-15 (*L*, p. 1420). THE LORD BEFORE PILATE. (*Introversion.*)

L | h | 2-5. Pilate and the Lord.
| i | 6-13. Pilate and the People.
| *i* | 14-. Pilate and the Multitude.
| *h* | -14, 15. Pilate and the Lord.

2 Pilate asked Him. Matthew and Mark carefully distinguish between this interview with the Lord and the rulers alone, and a subsequent interview with the multitude (Luke 23. 4).
answering said. See note on Deut. 1. 41.
Thou sayest = Thou thyself sayest [it].
3 accused = kept accusing.
of many things = urgently.
nothing = not (Gr. *ou*. Ap. 105. I.) anything. All the texts omit this clause.

5 yet . . . nothing = not anything any longer (Gr. *ouden ouketi*). **6 at.** Gr. *kata*. Ap. 104. x. 2. **that feast** = a feast: i. e. any of the three great feasts. **he released** = he used, or was wont, to release. Imperf. Tense. **7 Barabbas.** Aramaic. Ap. 94. III. 3. **made &c.** = been fellow insurgents. **who.** Denoting a class of criminals. **in.** Gr. *en*. Ap. 104. viii. As in *vv.* 29, 41, 46: not the same as in *vv.* 1, 38. **8 multitude** = crowd. **crying aloud.** All the texts read "having gone up". **began.** See note on 1. 1.

A. D. 29 desire °*him to do* °as he had °ever done unto them.

9 But Pilate answered them, saying, °"Will ye that I release unto you the King of the Jews?"

10 For °he knew that the chief priests had °delivered Him °for envy.

11 But the chief priests °moved the °people, that he should rather release [7]Barabbas unto them.

12 And Pilate [2]answered and said again unto them, "What [9]will ye then that I shall do *unto Him* Whom ye call the King of the Jews?"

13 And they cried out again, °"Crucify Him."

i 14 Then Pilate said unto them, "Why, what
(p. 1422) °evil °hath He done?"

h And they cried out the more exceedingly, [13]"Crucify Him."

15 And *so* Pilate, °willing °to content the people, released [7]Barabbas unto them, and delivered [1]Jesus, when he had scourged *Him*, to be crucified.

M j 16 And the soldiers led Him away °into °the
(p. 1423) hall, called Prætorium; and they call together the whole °band.

k 17 And they clothed Him with °purple, and platted a crown of thorns, and put it about His *head*,

18 And [8]began to salute Him, °"Hail, King of the Jews!"

19 And they °smote Him on the head with a reed, and °did spit upon Him, and bowing *their* knees °worshipped Him.

20 And when they had mocked Him, they took off the purple from Him, and put His own clothes on Him, and led Him out °to crucify Him.

21 And they °compel one Simon a Cyrenian, who °passed by, coming °out of °the country, the father of Alexander and °Rufus, to bear His cross.

j 22 And they bring Him °unto the place °Golgotha, which is, being interpreted, "The place of a skull."

k 23 And °they gave Him to drink wine mingled with myrrh: but He received *it* °not.

C T l 24 And °when they had crucified Him, they °parted His garments, casting lots °upon them, what every man should take.

---

him to do. Note the Ellipsis thus properly supplied.
as = according as. **ever.** Om. by T. WH R.
9 Will ye . . . ? Are ye willing . . . ? Gr. *thelō.* See Ap. 102. 1.
10 he knew = he was beginning to know. Gr. *ginōskō.* Ap. 132. I. 2.
delivered Him = delivered Him up.
for = on account of. Gr. *dia.* Ap. 104. v. 2.
11 moved = vehemently stirred up (as by an earthquake). Gr. *anaseiō*, connected with *seismos*, an earthquake.
people = crowd, as in *v.* 8.
13 Crucify Him. Stoning was the proper Jewish death for blasphemy. Cp. John 18. 31, 32. Crucifixion was the Roman punishment for *treason*. Note the addresses of Pilate:

To the Council.	To the People.	To the Priests (specially).
MATTHEW.	MARK.	LUKE.
	15. 8–11.	
27. 17–20.		
		23. 13–19.
,, 21–23.		
		,, 20, 21.
	,, 12–14.	
		,, 22, 23.
,, 24, 25.		

Then Pilate's final attempt to rescue the Lord.

Matt. 27. 26.	Mark 15. 15.	Luke 23. 24, 25.

14 evil. Gr. *kakos.* Ap. 128. IV. 2.
hath He done = did He do (at any time). Aorist.
15 willing = determining. Gr. *boulomai.* See Ap. 102. 2.
to content the people = to satisfy the crowd. This is the motto of the present day, but it always ends in judgment. See and cp. Ex. 32. 1 with 26, 27. Acts 12. 3 with 23. 2 Tim. 4. 3 with 1 and 8. So here.

15. 16–23 (*M*, p. 1420). PERSONAL ABUSE. (*Alternation.*)

M | j | 16. Place. Prætorium.
  k | 17–21. Treatment. Mockery.
 j | 22. Place. Golgotha.
  k | 23. Treatment. Bitter draught.

16 into = within.
the hall = the court. See Matt. 26. 3.
band. Gr. *speira* = a company bound or assembled round a standard: Lat. *manipulus* = a handful of hay or straw twisted about a pole as a standard: and, by Fig. *Metonymy* (of Adjunct), Ap. 6, put for the men-at-arms gathered round it.
17 purple. See Matt. 27. 28.
18 Hail. See note on Matt. 26. 49.
19 smote = kept smiting.
did spit = kept spitting.
worshipped = did homage to. Ap. 137. 1.
20 to = to the end that they might.
21 compel. See note on Matt. 27. 32.
passed by = was passing by.
out of = away from. Gr. *apo.* Ap. 104. iv. Not the same word as in *v.* 46. **the country** = a field. **Rufus.** This may be the Rufus of Rom. 16. 13.
22 unto. Gr. *epi.* Ap. 104. ix. 3. As in *v.* 46. Not the same word as in *vv.* 41, 43. **Golgotha.** See note on Matt. 27. 33. **23 they gave,** &c. = they were offering. See notes on Matt. 27. 34, 48. **not.** Gr. *ou.* Ap. 105. I.

15. 24–39 (*C*, p. 1420). THE CRUCIFIXION. (*Introversion and Alternation.*)

C | T | l | 24. The soldiers. Parting of garments.
  m | 25. Time. Event at third hour (9 a.m.).
   U | n | 26. The Indictment.
    o | 27, 28. The two Robbers. Brought.
   U | *n* | 29–32–. The Indictment.
    o | –32. The two Robbers. Reviling.
 T | *m* | 33–38. Time. Events at sixth and ninth hours (noon to 3 p.m.).
  l | 39. A soldier.

24 when they had, &c. The two robbers of *v.* 27, and Matt. 27. 38, not yet brought. See Ap. 164. **parted** = divided. **upon.** Gr. *epi.* Ap. 104. ix. 3.

m (p. 1423) 25 And it was °the third hour, and they crucified Him.

U n 26 And the °superscription of His accusation
A.D. 29 was °written over, °THE KING OF THE JEWS.

o 27 And °with Him °they crucify two °thieves; the °one °on His right hand, and °the other on His left.

28 And °the scripture was fulfilled, which saith, "**And He was numbered** [1]**with the** °**transgressors.**"

U n 29 And they that passed by °railed on Him, wagging their heads, and saying, °"Ah, Thou That °destroyest the °Temple, and buildest *it* [7]in three days,

30 Save Thyself, and °come down °from the cross."

31 Likewise °also the chief priests mocking °said °among themselves [1]with the scribes, "He saved °others; Himself He °cannot save.

32 Let °Christ °the King of Israel °descend now [30]from the cross, that we may °see and °believe."

o And °they that were crucified with Him °reviled Him.

T m 33 And when °the sixth hour was come, there °was darkness °over the whole land until °the ninth hour.

34 And at [33]the ninth hour [1]Jesus cried with a loud voice, saying, °"**Eloi, Eloi, lama sabachthani?**" which is, being interpreted, "**My God, My God, why hast Thou forsaken Me?**"

35 And some of them that stood by, when they heard *it*, said, °"Behold, He calleth °Elias."

36 And one ran and filled a spunge full of vinegar, and put *it* on a reed, and °gave Him to drink, saying, "Let alone; let us see whether Elias will come to take Him down."

37 And [1]Jesus °cried with a loud voice, and °gave up the ghost.

38 And the °veil of the [29]Temple was rent °in °twain [30]from °the top to the bottom.

l 39 And when the centurion, °which stood over against Him, saw that He so cried out, and [37]gave up the ghost, he said, "Truly this Man was °the Son of God."

B² V p (p. 1425) 40 There were °also women looking on °afar off: °among whom was Mary °Magdalene, and Mary the mother of James °the less and of Joses, and °Salome;

41 (Who °also, when He was [7]in Galilee, °followed Him, and °ministered unto Him;) and many [31]other women which came up with Him °unto Jerusalem.

25 the third hour. Of the day (John 11. 9), i.e. 9 a.m. No discrepancy; for the sixth hour of John 19. 14 was the sixth hour of the night (from about sunset), viz. "about" midnight (in the midst of the trial), when Pilate said "Behold your King". The context there and here explains and settles the matter. Here, the trial was over; in John 19. 14 the trial was going on. See Ap. 156 and 165. It was the hour of the morning sacrifice.

26 superscription, &c. = inscription of His indictment. Not the writing put "over His head" (Matt. 27. 37). See Ap. 163.

written over = written down (or inscribed, as in Acts 17. 23. Heb. 8. 10; 10. 16). Gr. *epigraphō*. Occ. elsewhere only in Rev. 21. 12. See Ap. 163.

THE KING, &c. See Ap. 163 for the "inscriptions on the cross", and Ap. 48 for the difference of types.

27 with = together with. Gr. *sun*. Ap. 104. xvi.

they crucify. Present Tense, describing what was done *then* (*after* the dividing of the garments), not when they put the Lord on the cross in *v.* 24.

thieves = robbers, not malefactors as in Luke 23. 32, who were "led with Him". See Ap. 164.

one on His right hand, &c.: i.e. outside the two "malefactors" of Luke 23. 32. See Ap. 164, and note on John 19. 18. **on** = at. Gr. *ek*. Ap. 104. vii.

the other = one.

28 the scripture. Isa. 53. 12. See Ap. 107. I. 1.

transgressors = lawless ones. Ap. 128. VIII. 2.

railed on = were blaspheming.

29 Ah, or Aha. **destroyest.** As in 13. 2.

Temple = *Naos*. See notes on Matt. 4. 5; 23. 16.

30 come down. See note on "descend", *v.* 32.

from = off. Gr. *apo*. Ap. 104. iv. As in *v.* 32.

31 also the chief priests = the chief priests also (as well as the passers by). **said** = kept saying.

among themselves = to (Gr. *pros*. Ap. 104. xv. 3) each other. **others.** Gr. *allos*. Ap. 124. 1.

cannot = is not (*v.* 23) able to.

32 Christ = the Messiah. Ap. 98. IX.

the King of Israel. Referring to the confession in *v.* 2. **descend.** Same as "come down" in *v.* 30.

see (Ap. 133. I. 1).

believe (Ap. 150. I. 1. i). Vain promise. For they did not believe, though He *came up* from the grave.

they that were . . . reviled Him. Both the "robbers", but only one of the "malefactors", reviled (Luke 23. 39).

33 the sixth hour of the day. (John 11. 9.) From sunrise: i.e. noon. See note on *v.* 25, and Ap. 165.

was = became.

over. Gr. *epi*. Ap. 104. ix. 3.

the ninth hour. The hour of offering the evening sacrifice: i.e. 3 p.m. So that the darkness was from noon till 3 p.m. See Ap. 165.

34 Eloi, &c. Quoted from Ps. 22. 1. See note on Matt. 27. 46.

35 Behold. Fig. *Asterismos*. Ap. 6.

Elias = Elijah.

36 gave Him = was giving. See note on Matt. 27. 34.

37 cried with a loud voice, and = having uttered a loud cry, He

gave up the ghost = expired. Gr. *ekpneō* = to breathe out, or expire. Occ. only here, *v.* 39, and Luke 23. 46.

38 veil. See note on Matt. 27. 51.

in = into. Gr. *eis*. Ap. 104. vi. **twain** = two.

the top = above. Gr. *anōthen*, as in Luke 1. 3. See note there. **39 which** = who.

the Son of God = a Son of God: i.e. a supernatural or Divine being. Ap. 98. XV. Found frequently in the Fayyûm *Papyri* as a title of the Emperor Augustus, in Latin as well as Greek inscriptions.

15. 40—16. 8 [For Structure see next page].

40 also women = women also. **afar off** = from (Gr. *apo*. Ap. 104. iv) afar. **among.** Gr. *en*. Ap. 104. viii. 2. **Magdalene.** See Matt. 27. 56. **the less** = junior. Divinely supplied only in Mark to distinguish him from James the Apostle (cp. Matt. 13. 55, and 27. 56). See also Acts 12. 17; 15. 13; 21. 18. Gal. 2. 12. **Salome.** See Matt. 27. 56. **41 also, when He was in Galilee** = when He was in Galilee also. **followed . . . ministered** = used to follow and minister. **unto.** Gr. *eis* Ap. 104. vi. Not the same word as in *vv.* 22, 43, 46.

q (p. 1425) A.D. 29 **42** And now °when the even was come, because it was °the preparation, that is, °the day before the sabbath,

W X **43** Joseph °of Arimathæa, an °honourable °counsellor, °which also waited for °the kingdom of God, came, and °went in boldly °unto Pilate, and °craved the body of [1]Jesus.

44 And Pilate °marvelled °if He were already dead: and calling *unto him* the centurion, he asked him whether He had been °any while dead.

45 And when he °knew *it* [43]of the centurion, he °gave the °body to Joseph.

Y r **46** And he bought °fine linen, and took Him down, and wrapped Him in the linen,

s and laid Him [7]in a °sepulchre which was hewn °out of a °rock,

t and rolled °a stone [22]unto the door of the °sepulchre.

V p **47** And Mary Magdalene and Mary *the mother* of Joses °beheld where He was laid.

q 7thNisan W Y r **16** And °when the sabbath was past, Mary Magdalene, and Mary the *mother* of James, and Salome, °had bought °sweet spices, that they might come and anoint Him.

s 8thNisan **2** And very early in the morning the °first *day* of the week, they °came °unto the °sepulchre °at the rising of the sun.

t **3** And they said °among themselves, °"Who °shall °roll us away the stone °from the door of [2]the sepulchre?"

4 And when they °looked, they °saw that the stone °was rolled away: for it was very great.

X **5** And entering °into [2]the sepulchre, they °saw a young man sitting °on the right side, clothed in a °long white °garment; and they were °affrighted.

6 And he saith unto them, "Be °not [5]affrighted: Ye seek °Jesus of Nazareth, °Which was crucified: He is risen; He is °not here: °behold the place where they laid Him.

7 But go your way, tell His disciples °and Peter that He goeth before you [5]into Galilee: there shall ye °see Him, °as He said unto you."

8 And they went out quickly, and fled °from [2]the sepulchre; for they trembled and were amazed: neither said they any thing to any *man*; for they were afraid.

---

15. 40—16. 8 (B[2], p. 1420). THE BURIAL.

(*Alternations and Introversion.*)

B[2] | V | p | 15. 40, 41. Women. Several.
  q | 15. 42. Before the High Sabbath.
    W | X | 15. 43-45. The Body obtained.
      Y | r | 15. 46-. Fine linen bought.
        s | 15. -46-. Laid in the sepulchre.
        t | 15. -46. The stone rolled to the door.
 V | p | 15. 47. Women. Two.
  q | 16. 1-. After the High Sabbath.
    W | Y | r | 16. -1. Spices bought.
        s | 16. 2. Came to the sepulchre.
        t | 16. 3, 4. The stone rolled away from the door.
      X | 16. 5-8. The Body sought.

42 when the even was come=evening already having come. Cp. Matt. 27. 57.

the preparation: i. e. the 14th of Nisan, the day before the Passover (on the 15th), which took place on the 14th at even, and ushered in the High Sabbath, which commenced after sunset on the 14th.

the day before the sabbath: i. e. the day before the High Sabbath. See Ap. 156.

43 of=he from. Gr. *ho apo*. Ap. 104. iv.

honourable=honourable (in rank), as in Acts 13. 50; 17. 12.

counsellor. A member of the Sanhedrin. See Luke 23. 51.

which also waited=who himself also was waiting.

the kingdom of God. See Ap. 114.

went in boldly=took courage and went in; i. e. braving all consequences.

unto=to. Gr. *pros*. Ap. 104. xv. 3. Not the same word as in *vv.* 22, 41, 46.

craved the body. Because in the usual course the Lord would have been buried with other criminals. See note on Isa. 53. 9.

44 marvelled=wondered. This verse and the next are a Divine supplement, peculiar to Mark.

if He were, &c. Implying a hypothesis which he did not yet expect. Ap. 118. 2. a. **any while**=long.

45 knew=having got to know. Gr. *ginōskō*. See Ap. 132. I. ii.

gave=made a gift of (Gr. *dōreō*). Occ. only here and 2 Pet. 1. 3, 4.

body. Gr. *sōma*=body. But all the texts read *ptōma* =corpse.

46 fine linen. Gr. *sindōn*. See note on 14. 51, 52.

sepulchre=memorial tomb.

out of. Gr. *ek*. Ap. 104. vii. Not the same word as in *v.* 21. **rock.** Gr. *petra*, as in Matt. 16. 18.

a stone. See note on Matt. 27. 60.

47 beheld=were (attentively) looking on so as to see exactly. Gr. *theōreō*, Ap. 133. I. 11.

16. 1 when the sabbath was past: i. e. the weekly sabbath. This was three nights and three days from the preparation day, when He was buried. See Ap. 156.

had bought. Before the weekly sabbath (Luke 23. 56; 24. 1). **sweet spices**=aromatics.

2 first (day) of the week. Gr. the first of the Sabbath. **came**=come. **unto**=up to. Gr. *epi*. Ap. 104. ix. 3. **sepulchre.** See 15. 46. **at the rising, &c.**=the sun having risen. **3 among**=to. Gr. *pros*. Ap. 104. xv. 3. **Who shall roll, &c.?** That was their only difficulty; therefore they could not have heard about the sealing and the watch. This is a Divine supplement, peculiar to Mark. **shall**=will. **roll us away.** The ground being on an incline (sideways), therefore the door was more easily closed than opened. **from**=out of (Gk. *ek*. Ap. 104. vii): out of the bottom of the incline. Not the same word as in *v.* 8. L and Tr. read *apo* (Ap. 104. iv), away from, as in *v.* 8. **4 looked**=looked up. Gr. *anablepo*. Ap. 133. I. 6. **saw**=see (implying attention, surprise, and pleasure). Gr. *theōreō*. Ap. 133. I. 11. **was**=had been. **5 into**=Gr. *eis*. Ap. 104. vi. **saw.** Ap. 133. I. 1. **on**=in. Gr. *en*. Ap. 104. viii. Not the same word as in *v.* 18. **long . . . garment.** Gr. *stolē*=a long outer robe of distinction. **affrighted**=amazed. **6 not.** Gr. *mē*. Ap. 105. II. Not the same as in the next clause and *vv.* 14, 18. **Jesus.** Ap. 98. X. **Which was crucified**=Who has been crucified. Note the Fig. *Asyndeton* (Ap. 6), leading up breathlessly to the climax—"there shall ye see Him". Thus the passage is emphasized; and the "sudden reduction of 'ands'" is *not* "an internal argument against genuineness"! **not.** Gr. *ou*. Ap. 105. I. **behold**=look. Gr. *ide*. Ap. 133. I. 3. **7 and Peter.** A Divine supplement, here. **see.** Gr. *opsomai*. Ap. 133. I. 8. a. **as**=even as. **8 from**=away from. Gr. *apo*. Ap. 104. iv.

B³ u (p. 1426) A. D. 29 **9 °Now when *Jesus* was risen °early the first *day* of the week, He °appeared first to Mary Magdalene, °out of whom He had cast seven °devils.**

v **10 *And* she went and told them that had been °with Him, as they mourned and wept.**

w **11 And they, when they had heard that He °was alive, and had been °seen °of her, °believed not.**

u **12 °After °that He °appeared °in °another form unto two °of them, °as they walked, and went [5]into the country.**

v **13 And they went and told *it* unto the residue:**
w **neither believed they them.**

A Z **14 °Afterward He [12]appeared unto the eleven as they sat at meat, and °upbraided them with their unbelief and hardness of heart, because they believed [-6]not them which had [11]seen Him after He was risen.**

A **15 And °He said unto them, "Go ye [5]into all the °world, and °preach °the gospel to °every creature.**
16 He that °believeth and is °baptized shall be saved; but he that °believeth not shall be °damned.
17 And °these signs shall follow °them that [16]believe; °In My name °shall they cast out [9]devils; they shall °speak with °new tongues;
18 °They shall °take up serpents; and °if they °drink any deadly thing, it shall °not hurt them; they shall °lay hands on the sick, and they shall recover."

Z **19 So then [12]after °the Lord had spoken unto them, He was received up [5]into °heaven, and sat °on the right hand of °God.**

A **20 And they went forth, and [15]preached °every where, °the LORD working with *them*, and °confirming the °word °with °signs following. Amen.**

16. 9-13 (B³, p. 1420). RESURRECTION.
(*Repeated Alternation.*)

B³ | u | 9. His appearance to Mary.
v | 10. Her report.
w | 11. Disciples' unbelief.
u | 12. His appearance to two disciples.
v | 13-. Their report.
w | -13. Disciples' unbelief.

9 Now when Jesus was risen, &c. For the sequence of events after the Resurrection, see Ap. 166. For the genuineness of these last twelve verses (9-20) of Mark, see Ap. 168.

early: i.e. any time after sunset on our Saturday, 6 p.m. See Ap. 165.

appeared. Gr. *phainō*. Ap. 106. I. i. Not the same word as in *v.* 12.

out of=from. Gr. *apo*. Ap. 104. iv.

devils=demons.

10 with=in company with. Gr. *meta*. Ap. 104. xi. 1. Not the same word as in *v.* 20.

11 was alive=is alive [again from the dead]. See note on *zaō*. Matt. 9. 18.

seen. Gr. *theaomai*. Ap. 133. I. 12.

of=by. Gr. *hupo*. Ap. 104. xviii. 1.

believed not=disbelieved [it].

12 After. Gr. *meta*. Ap. 104. xi. 2.

that=these things.

appeared =was manifested. Gr. *phaneroo*. Ap. 106. I. v. Not the same word as in *v.* 9.

in. Gr. *en*. Ap. 104. viii.

another=different. Gr. *heteros*. Ap. 124. 2.

of=out of. Gr. *ek*. Ap. 104. vii.

as they walked, &c. See Luke 24. 13-35.

16. 14-20 (*A*, p. 1381). THE SUCCESSORS.
(*Alternation.*)

A | Z | 14. After the Lord had risen.
A | 15-18. Commission.
Z | 19. After the Lord had ascended.
A | 20. Obedience.

14 Afterward, &c.=Later. Gr. *husteron*. A Divine supplement, here.

upbraided=reproached.

15 He said. Probably some time after *v.* 14, on the eve of the Ascension.

world=*kosmos*. Ap. 129. 1.

preach=proclaim. Gr. *kērussō*. Ap. 121. 1.

the gospel=the glad tidings.

every creature=all the creation. Put by Fig. *Synecdochē* (of Genus), Ap. 6, for all mankind. Fulfilled during "that generation". See Col. 1. 6, 23.

16 believeth. See Ap. 150. I. 1. i. **baptized.** See Ap. 115. I. 1. **believeth not**=disbelieveth. **damned**=condemned. Gr. *katakrinō*. Ap. 122. 7. **17 these signs shall follow**=these signs shall attend, or follow close upon. See Ap. 167 and Heb. 2. 3, 4, and the fulfilment in Acts 3. 7, 8; 5. 16; 6. 8; 9. 34, 40, &c. They were limited to the dispensation covered by the Acts of the Apostles. See Heb. 2. 3, 4; 6. 1-6; and cp. 1 Cor. 13. 8-10. **them that believe.** Not merely the Apostles, therefore. See Ap. 168. **In**=Through. Gr. *en*. Ap. 104. viii. **In My name.** Note the Fig. *Asyndeton*, Ap. 6. **shall they cast out devils.** See Acts 8. 7; 16. 18; 19. 11-16. **speak with new tongues.** See Acts 2. 4-11 (as foretold by Joel 2. 28, 29); 10. 46; 19. 6. 1 Cor. 12. 28; and ch. 14. **new**=different in character. Gr. *kainos*, not *neos*. See notes on Matt. 9. 17; 26. 28, 29. **18 They shall take up serpents.** See Acts 28. 5. Cp. Luke 10. 19. **if they drink, &c.** The condition to be seen by the result. Ap. 118. 1. b. **drink, &c.** Eusebius (iii. 39) records this of John and of Barsabas, surnamed Justus. **not**=by no means. Gr. *ou mē*. Ap. 105. III. **lay hands on** (Gr. *epi*. Ap. 104. ix. 3) **the sick.** See Acts 3. 7; 19. 11, 12; 28. 8, 9. 1 Cor. 12. 9, 28. James 5. 14. **19 the Lord.** Ap. 98. VI. i. *a*. 3. C. The contrast is between the Lord of *v.* 19, and the disciples of *v.* 20. **heaven**=the heaven. Sing. See notes on Matt. 6. 9, 10. **on**=at. Gr. *ek*. Ap. 104. vii. **God.** See Ap. 98. I. i. 1. **20 every where.** See Col. 1. 6, 23. **the LORD**=Jehovah (Ap. 89. VI. i. *a*. 1. A. b). The witness of "GOD" is distinguished (in Heb. 2. 4) from the testimony of His SON (Heb. 2. 3), and from the gifts of the SPIRIT (*pneuma hagion*, Ap. 101. II. 14) (Heb. 2. 4). **confirming, &c.** See Heb. 2. 4. **the word.** Gr. *logos*. See note on 9. 32. **with**=by means of. Gr. *dia*. Ap. 104. v. 1.

THE GOSPEL

ACCORDING TO

LUKE.

THE STRUCTURE OF THE BOOK AS A WHOLE.

"BEHOLD THE MAN" (Zech. 6. 12).

(*Introversion*.)

𝔄[2] **A** | 1. 1—2. 52. PRE-MINISTERIAL. THE DESCENSION.

B | 3. 1-20. THE FORERUNNER.

C | 3. 21-38. THE BAPTISM: WITH WATER.

D | 4. 1-14-. THE TEMPTATION: IN THE WILDERNESS.

E **F** | 4. -14—5. 11. THE KINGDOM } PROCLAIMED.

G | 5. 12—9. 21. THE KING } PROCLAIMED.

G | 9. 22—18. 43. THE KING } REJECTED.

F | 19. 1—22. 38. THE KINGDOM } REJECTED.

(E: THE FOURFOLD MINISTRY OF THE LORD.)

D | 22. 39-46. THE AGONY: IN THE GARDEN.

C | 22. 47—24. 12. THE BAPTISM: OF SUFFERING (DEATH, BURIAL, AND RESURRECTION).

B | 24. 13-49. THE SUCCESSORS.

A | 24. 50-53. POST-MINISTERIAL. THE ASCENSION.

For the New Testament, and the order of the Books, see Ap. 95.
For the Inter-relation of the Four Gospels, see the Structure on p. 1304.
For the Diversity of the Four Gospels, see Ap. 96.
For the Unity of the Four Gospels, see Ap. 97.
For the Fourfold Ministry of the Lord, see Ap. 119.
For the words, &c., peculiar to Luke's Gospel, see some 260 words recorded in the notes.

NOTES ON LUKE'S GOSPEL.

The Divine purpose in the Gospel by LUKE is to set forth the Lord not so much as the Messiah, "the King of Israel", as in Matthew's Gospel, or as Jehovah's servant, as in Mark; but as what He was in Jehovah's sight, as the ideal MAN—"the Man Whose name is the BRANCH" (Zech. 6. 12). See the Structure of the Four Gospels on p. 1304.

In Luke, therefore, the Lord is specially presented as "the Friend of publicans and sinners"—the outcasts of society (Luke 5. 29, &c.; 7. 29, 34, 37, &c.; 15; 18. 9, &c.; 19. 7, &c.; 23. 39, &c.); as manifesting tenderness, compassion, and sympathy (7. 13; 13. 1, &c.; 19. 41, &c.; 23. 28, &c.), which went beyond the limits of national prejudice (6. 6, 27, &c.; 10. 30, &c.; 11. 41, &c.; 13. 1, &c.; 14. 1, &c.; 17. 11, &c.). Hence Luke alone gives the parable of the good Samaritan (10. 30, &c.); and notes that the one leper who gave thanks to God was a Samaritan (17. 16, 18).

Hence also many references to women, who, so alien to Jewish custom, find frequent and honourable mention: Elisabeth, Anna, the widow of Nain (7. 11–15); the penitent woman (7. 37, &c.); the ministering women (8. 2, &c.); the "daughters of Jerusalem" (23. 27, &c.); Martha (10. 38–41) and Mary, of Bethany (10. 39, 42); Mary Magdalene (24. 10).

As the ideal Man, the Lord is presented as dependent on the Father, in prayer (3. 21; 5. 16; 6. 12; 9. 18, 29; 11. 1; 18. 1; 22. 32, 41; 23. 34, 46). On six definite occasions the Lord is shown in prayer; and no less than seven times "glorifying God" in praise is mentioned (2. 20; 5. 25; 7. 16; 13. 13; 17. 15; 18. 43; 23. 47).

The Four Hymns are peculiar to LUKE: the *Magnificat* of Mary (1. 46–55); the *Benedictus* of Zacharias (1. 68–79); the *Nunc Dimittis* of Simeon (2. 29–32); and the *Gloria in Excelsis* of the angels (2. 14).

The six Miracles peculiar to LUKE (all characteristic of the presentation of the Lord in Luke) are:—

1. The Draught of Fishes (5. 4–11).
2. The Raising of the Widow's Son at Nain (7. 11–18).
3. The Woman with a Spirit of Infirmity (13. 11–17).
4. The Man with the Dropsy (14. 1–6).
5. The Ten Lepers (17. 11–19).
6. The Healing of Malchus (22. 50, 51).

The eleven Parables peculiar to LUKE (all having a like significance) are:—

1. The Two Debtors (7. 41–43).
2. The Good Samaritan (10. 30–37).
3. The Importunate Friend (11. 5–8).
4. The Rich Fool (12. 16–21).
5. The Barren Fig-tree (13. 6–9).
6. The Lost Piece of Silver (15. 8–10).
7. The Lost Son (15. 11–32).
8. The Unjust Steward (16. 1–12).
9. The Rich Man and Lazarus (16. 19–31).
10. The Unjust Judge and Importunate Widow (18. 1–8).
11. The Pharisee and the Publican (18. 9–14).

Other remarkable incidents and utterances peculiar to LUKE may be studied with the same object and result (3. 10–14; 10. 1–20; 19. 1–10, 41–44; 22. 44; 23. 7–12; 23. 27–31; 23. 34; 23. 40–43; 24. 50–53).

As to LUKE himself: his name (Gr. *Loukas*) is probably an abbreviation of the Latin *Lucanus*, *Lucilius* or *Lucius*.* While he was the author of the Acts of the Apostles, he does not once name himself; and there are only three places where his name is found: Col. 4. 14. 2 Tim. 4. 11. Philem. 24.

From these and the "we" portions of the Acts (16. 10–17; 20. 5–15; 21. 1–18; 27. 1—28. 16) we may gather all that can be *known* of LUKE. We first hear of him at Troas (Acts 16. 10), and from thence he may be followed through the four "we" sections. See the notes on the Structure of the Acts as a whole.

It will be noted in the Structure of this Gospel as a whole that, while in JOHN there is no Temptation, and no Agony, in LUKE we not only have these, but the Pre-Natal Section (1. 5—2. 5, A^2, p. 1430) as well as the Pre-Ministerial, which is common to all the four Gospels.

* It was held till recently that *Loukas* never represented the Latin *Lucius*; but Sir W. Ramsay saw, in 1912, an inscription on the wall of a temple in Antioch in Pisidia, in which the names *Loukas* and *Loukios* are used of the same person. See *The Expositor*, Dec. 1912.

THE GOSPEL

ACCORDING TO

LUKE.

A A[1] B **1** °FORASMUCH as many
C D a °have taken in hand
b °to set forth in order °a declaration
c °of those °things °which are most surely believed °among us,
E d 2 Even as they delivered them unto us,
e which °from the beginning °were °eyewitnesses, and °ministers of the word;
B 3 It seemed good to me also,
C E e °having had perfect understanding of °all things °from the very first,
d to write unto thee
D a °in order, °most excellent °Theophilus,
b 4 °That thou °mightest know
c the certainty of those °things, °wherein °thou hast been instructed.

A[2] F H f 5 °THERE was °in the days of °Herod, °the
5 B.C. king of Judæa, a certain priest named Zacharias, °of the course of °Abia: and his wife *was* °of °the daughters of Aaron, and her name *was* °Elisabeth.

1. 1—2. 52 (**A**, p. 1427). PRE-MINISTERIAL. THE DESCENSION. (*Division.*)

A | A[1] | 1. 1-4. Introduction.
| A[2] | 1. 5—2. 5. Pre-Natal.
| A[3] | 2. 6-52. Pre-Ministerial.

1. 1-4 (A[1], above). INTRODUCTION.
(*Alternations and Introversions.*)

A[1] | B | 1-. Other writers. Many.
C | D | a | -1-. Their undertaking. To draw up. } Their writing. } Work of others.
b | -1-. Their object. Declaration.
c | -1. Their matter. Things believed.
E | d | 2-. Recipients. "Us". } Its delivery.
e | -2. Authority. Eye-witnesses.
B | 3-. The writer. One (Luke).
C | *E* | *e* | -3-. Authority. Revelation. } Its delivery. } Luke's work.
d | -3-. Recipient. "Thee".
D | *a* | -3. Luke's undertaking. To write. } Luke's writing.
b | 4-. His object. To give knowledge.
c | -4. His matter. Things taught.

1 Forasmuch as=Since, as is well known indeed. Gr. *epeidēper*. Occ. only here in N.T. **have taken in hand.** Implying previous non-success (Acts 19. 13). Elsewhere only in Acts 9. 29. A medical word. Cp. Col. 4. 14. **to set forth in order**=to draw up. **a declaration**=a narrative. Gr. *diēgēsis*. Occ. only here in N.T., used by Galen of a medical treatise. **of**=concerning. Gr. *peri*. Ap. 104. xiii. 1. Not the same word as in *vv.* 5, 27, 35, 61. **things**=matters, or facts. **which are most surely believed**=which have been fully accomplished; i. e. in fulfilment of prophetic announcement. **among.** Gr. *en*. Ap. 104. viii. 2. As in *vv.* 25, 28, 42. **2 from.** Gr. *apo*. Ap. 104. iv. **from the beginning.** Gr. *ap' archēs*; i. e. from the birth or ministry of the Lord. Cp. John 15. 27. Acts 1. 1, 21, 22. **were**=became. **eyewitnesses.** Gr. *autoptai*. Occ. only here. Not the same word as in 2 Pet. 1. 16. A medical word (Col. 4. 14). Cp. our *autopsy*. **ministers**=attendants. A technical word, often translated "officer". **3 having had perfect understanding**=having followed up accurately. **all.** The 1611 edition of the A.V. omitted this "all". **from the very first**=from above. Gr. *anōthen*. As in Matt. 27. 51 (the top, Mark 15. 38). John 3. 3, 7 (again), 31 (from above); 19. 11, 23. James 1. 17; 3. 15, 17. It may mean from the beginning, as in Acts 26. 5, but there is no need to introduce that meaning here, as it is already in *v.* 2. Moreover, having understood them "from above", he necessarily understood them from the very beginning, as well as perfectly, or accurately. The greater includes the less. **in order**=with method. **most excellent.** A title of social degree, not of moral quality. See Acts 23. 26; 26. 25. **Theophilus.** A common Roman name=beloved of God. **4 That**=in order that. **mightest know**=get to have full knowledge. Gr. *epiginōskō*. Ap. 132. I. iii. Not the same word as in *vv.* 18, 34. **things**=words. **wherein**=concerning (Gr. *peri*. Ap. 104. xiii. 1) which. **thou hast been instructed**=thou wast [orally] taught. Gr. *katēcheō*. See Acts 18. 25. 1 Cor. 14. 19. Gal. 6. 6.

1. 5—2. 5 [For Structure see next page].

5 There was=There came to be. A Hebraism, cp. *v.* 8, and see on 2. 1. **in.** Gr. *en*. Ap. 104. viii. Not the same word as in *vv.* 15, 20, 44-, 47. **in the days.** A Hebraism. See Matt. 2. 1. Cp. Est. 1. 1. **Herod.** See Ap. 109. **the king.** This title had been conferred by the Roman Senate on the recommendation of Antony and Octavius. **of**=out of. Gr. *ek*, Ap. 104. vii. **Abia** is named in 1 Chron. 24. 10, and Neh. 12. 17. Out of the *four* who returned from Babylon twenty-four courses were formed (by lot) with the original names. See Ap. 179. III. **the daughters of Aaron.** The female descendants of Aaron always married priests. **Elisabeth.** Aaron's wife, Elisheba (Ex. 6. 23) is spelt *Elizabeth* in the Sept.

5 B.C. 6 And they were both righteous °before °God,
walking [5]in all the commandments and °ordi-
nances of °the LORD blameless.
7 And they had °no °child, °because that
Elisabeth was barren, and they both were *now*
°well stricken [5]in years.

g 8 And °it came to pass, that °while he executed the priest's office before [6]God [5]in the
order of his course,
9 °According to the custom of the priest's
office, °his lot was °to burn °incense °when he
went °into °the Temple of [6]the LORD.

J h 10 And the whole multitude of the people
were °praying without °at the time of incense.

i 11 And there °appeared unto him °an angel
of [6]the LORD standing °on °the right side of
°the altar of incense.

K j 12 And when Zacharias °saw *him*, he was
troubled, and fear fell °upon him.

k 13 But the [11]angel said °unto him, "Fear
°not, Zacharias: °for thy °prayer °is heard;
and thy wife Elisabeth shall °bear thee a son,
and thou shalt call his name °John.
14 And thou shalt have °joy and gladness;
and many shall rejoice °at his °birth.
15 For he shall be great °in the sight of [6]the
LORD, and °shall drink neither wine nor
°strong drink; and he °shall be filled with
°the Holy Ghost, even °from his mother's
womb.
16 And many of the °children of Israel shall
he turn °to °the LORD their [6]God.
17 And he shall °go [6]before Him [5]in °the
spirit and power of °Elias, °**to turn the hearts
of the fathers [16]to the children**, and the °dis-
obedient °to the °wisdom of the just; **to
make ready a people prepared for [16]the LORD.**"

K j 18 And Zacharias said [13]unto the angel,
°"Whereby shall I °know this? °for I am
an old man, and my wife [7]well stricken [5]in
years."

k 19 And the [11]angel °answering said unto him,

1. 5—2. 5 (A[2], p. 1429). PRE-NATAL.
(*Alternation.*)

A[2] | F | 1. 5-25. John. Conception.
  G | 1. 26-56. The Holy Family.
  F | 1. 57-80. John. Circumcision.
  G | 2. 1-5. The Holy Family.

1. 5-25 (F, above). JOHN. CONCEPTION.
(*Introversions and Alternations.*)

F | H | f | 5-7. Barrenness. Experienced.
    g | 8, 9. Ministration of Zacharias.
  J | h | 10. The people. Praying.
    i | 11. The Vision.
      K | j | 12. Zacharias. Trouble.
        k | 13-17. Angel. Promise.
      K | *j* | 18. Zacharias. Doubt.
        k | 19, 20. Angel. Penalty.
  J | *h* | 21. The people. Marvelling.
    i | 22. The Vision.
  H | *g* | 23. Ministration of Zacharias.
    f | 24, 25. Barrenness. Removed.

6 before. The Texts read *enantion*, not *enōpion* (=in the presence of, as *v.* 19). Both are found in the Papyri in this sense. **God.** Ap. 98. I.
ordinances=legal requirements. Gr. pl. of *dikaiōma*, which should always be so rendered in its other nine occurrences (Rom. 1. 32; 2. 26; 5. 16, 18; 8. 4; Heb. 9. 1, 10; Rev. 15. 4; 19. 8). Cp. Num. 36. 13. Sometimes rendered "judgments" (Ex. 21. 1; 24. 3), where LXX has *dikaiōma*.
the LORD. Must here and elsewhere be often rendered Jehovah. See Ap. 98. VI. i. *a*. 1. A. b.
7 no. Gr. *ou*. Ap. 105. I.
child. Gr. *teknon*. See Ap. 108. 1.
because that=inasmuch as.
well stricken=advanced.
8 it came to pass. A Hebraism. See note on *v.* 5.
while he executed, &c.=in (Gr. *en*. Ap. 104. viii) executing. Gr. *hierateuō*, to act as a priest. Not peculiar to Biblical Greek, but found often in the Papyri.
9 According to. Gr. *kata*. Ap. 104. x. 2.
his lot was=it fell to him by lot.
to burn incense. Gr. *thumiaō*. Occ. only here in N.T.
incense. The first recorded use of incense by man began in *disobedience* (Num. 16. 6), and the last ended in *unbelief* (*v.* 20). **when he went**=going.
into. Gr. *eis*. Ap. 104. vi.
the Temple=The *Naos*, or Shrine; i.e. "the Holy Place". Not *hieron* (the Temple courts). See note on Matt. 23. 16.
10 praying. See Ap. 134. I. 2.
at the time=at the hour. This was the signal.

11 appeared. Ap. 106. I. 6. **an angel.** For the frequent refs. to angels in Luke, see *v.* 26; 2. 9, 13, 21; 12. 8; 15. 10; 16. 22; 22. 43; 24. 4, 23. Also frequently in Acts. **on**=at. Gr. *ek*. Ap. 104. vii. **the right side**=the propitious side. Cp. Matt. 25. 33. Mark 16. 5. John 21. 6. **the altar of incense.** See Ex. 30. 1-10; 37. 25-28. 1 Kings 7. 48. **12 saw.** Gr. *eidon*. Ap. 133. I. 1. **upon.** Gr. *epi*. Ap. 104. ix. 3. As in *v.* 35. Not the same word as in *v.* 58. **13 unto**=to. Gr. *pros*. Ap. 104. xv. 3. Not the same word as in *v.* 26. **not.** Gr. *mē*. Ap. 105. II. As in *vv.* 20-, 30, not as in *vv.* -20, 22, 34. **for**=because. **prayer**=a definite petition. **is heard**=was heard: i.e. not now, or recently. Evidently the prayer for offspring, which was now no longer offered. **bear thee**=bring forth to thee. **John**=Jehovah sheweth favour. **14 joy and gladness.** Fig. *Hendiadys* (Ap. 6)=joy, yea exultant joy. **at**=upon [the occasion of]. Gr. *epi*. Ap. 104. ix. 2, as in *v.* 29. **birth**=bringing forth. Gr. *gennaō*, used of the mother. See note on Matt. 1. 2. **15 in the sight of**=before. See note on "before", *v.* 6. **shall drink neither**=shall in no wise (Gr. *ou mē*. Ap. 105. III) drink. **strong drink.** Gr. *sikera*, any intoxicating drink not from grapes. **shall be filled.** Verbs of filling take the Gen. of what the person or vessel is filled with. See Ap. 101. II. 14. note. Here *pneuma hagion* is in the Genitive case. **the Holy Ghost**=holy spirit. Gr. *pneuma hagion*, or "power from on high". See Ap. 101. II. 14. **from.** Gr. *ek*. Ap. 104. vii; i.e. before birth. Cp. *v.* 44. **16 children**=sons. See Ap. 108. iii. **to**=towards. Gr. *epi*. Ap. 104. ix. 3. **Lord.** Gr. *kurios*. Ap. 98. vi. i. *a*. 1. B. b. **17 go**=go forth. **the spirit and power.** Fig. *Hendiadys* (Ap. 6)=the spirit—yea, the powerful spirit (Mal. 4. 5). **Elias**=Elijah. **to turn, &c.** Ref. to Mal. 3. 1 and 4. 5, 6. See Ap. 107. II. 4. **disobedient**=unbelieving. **to**=in. Gr. *en*. Ap. 104. viii. **wisdom.** Gr. *phronēsis* (not *sophia*)=understanding. Occ. only here, and Eph. 1. 8=the product of *sophia*. See notes on Job 28. 28; 40. 4. **18 Whereby**=According to (Gr. *kata*, as in *v.* 9) what [sign]. **know**=get to know. Gr. *ginōskō*. Ap. 132. I. ii. **for I am an old man.** To Zechariah the promise seemed to come too late; to Mary (*v.* 34) too early. **19 answering said.** See note on Deut. 1. 41.

5 B. C. "I am °Gabriel, that stand °in the presence of
God; and °am sent to speak [13]unto thee, and
to °shew thee these glad tidings.
20 And, °behold, °thou shalt be dumb, and
[13]not able to speak, until the day that these
things shall °be performed, because thou °be-
lievest °not my words, °which shall be fulfilled °in their season."

J h 21 And the people °waited for Zacharias, and
°marvelled that he tarried so long [5]in [9]the
Temple.

i 22 And when he came out, he could [-20]not
°speak unto them: and they °perceived that
he °had seen a vision [5]in [9]the Temple: for he
°beckoned unto them, and remained speechless.

H g 23 And [8]it came to pass, that, as soon as the
°days of his °ministration were accomplished,
he departed °to his own house.

f 24 And °after those days his wife Elisabeth
SIVAN °conceived, and °hid herself five months,
°saying,
25 "Thus hath [6]the LORD dealt with me [5]in
the days wherein He °looked on *me*, °to take
away my reproach [1]among men."

G L[1] M 26 And [5]in °the sixth month the [11]angel
[19]Gabriel was sent °from God °unto a city of
°Galilee, named °Nazareth,
27 °To a °virgin °espoused to a °man
whose name was Joseph, [5]of the house of David; and the °virgin's name *was* °Mary.
28 And the [11]angel came in [13]unto her, and
said,

N[1] l[1] °"Hail, °*thou that art* highly favoured, [6]the
LORD *is* °with thee: °blessed *art* thou [1]among
°women."

m[1] 29 And °when she [12]saw *him*, she was troubled [14]at his saying, and °cast in her mind
what manner of salutation this should be.

N[2] l[2] 30 And the [11]angel said unto her, "Fear
[13]not, [27]Mary: for thou hast °found °favour
°with God.

TEBETH 31 And, [20]behold, °thou shalt conceive [5]in
thy womb, °and bring forth a Son, °and shalt
call His name °JESUS.

Gabriel = the mighty man of GOD. The messenger of the Restoration (*v.* 26; Dan. 8. 16; 9. 21), as Michael is the messenger of Israel's deliverance from judgment (Dan. 10. 13, 21; 12. 1. Jude 9; and Rev. 12. 7). Prob. two of the "seven" angels of Rev. 1. 4; 3. 1; 4. 5; 5. 6; 8. 2, 6; 15. 1, 6, 7, 8; 16. 1; 17. 1; 21. 9.
in the presence. Same as "before", *v.* 6.
am = was. **shew** = announce.
20 behold. Fig. *Asterismos.* Ap. 6.
thou shalt be dumb. The finite Verb and Participle denote continuous silence.
be performed = come to pass.
believest not = didst not believe. Ap. 150. I. 1. ii. Note the Negative. **not.** Gr. *ou.* Ap. 105. I.
which = which are of a kind which. Gr. *hoitines,* denoting a class, or kind of words.
in = up to. Gr. *eis.* Ap. 104. vi. Marking the process continuing up to the end.
21 waited for = were looking for. The finite Verb and Participle denoting protracted waiting.
marvelled. Because such waiting was usually short.
22 speak: i.e. pronounce the usual blessing (Num. 6. 24).
perceived = clearly perceived, or recognised. Gr. *epiginōskō.* Ap. 132. I. iii.
had seen. Gr. *horaō.* Ap. 133. I. 8.
beckoned = kept making signs. **23 days** = week.
ministration = public service. Gr. *leitourgia.* Hence Eng. "liturgy". **to** = unto. Gr. *eis.* Ap. 104. vi.
24 after. Gr. *meta.* Ap. 104. xi. 2.
conceived. Gr. *sullambanō.* A medical word, used in this sense in Luke and in James 1. 15. See Ap. 179. III.
hid = completely secluded. Probably to avoid all possibility of uncleanness, as in Judges 13. 4, 5, 7, 12–14. Occ. only here in N.T.
saying = saying that (Gr. *hoti*); giving the words.
25 looked on. Gr. *epeidon.* Ap. 133. II. 1. Occurs only in Luke here, and Acts 4. 29.
to take away my reproach. Cp. Gen. 30. 23. 1 Sam. 1. 6–10. Hos. 9. 14. Contrast 23. 29.

1. 26–56 (G, p. 1430). THE HOLY FAMILY.
(*Division.*)

G | L[1] | 26–38. Visit of Gabriel to Mary.
  | L[2] | 39–56. Visit of Mary to Elisabeth.

1. 26–38 (L[1], above). VISIT OF GABRIEL TO MARY. (*Introversion, and Repeated Alternation.*)

L[1] | M | 26–28–. Mission of the Angel.
  | N[1] | l[1] | –28. Angel. Salutation.
  | | m[1] | 29. Mary. Troubled.
  | N[2] | l[2] | 30–33. Angel. Promise.
  | | m[2] | 34. Mary. Inquiry.
  | N[3] | l[3] | 35–37. Angel. Answer.
  | | m[3] | 38–. Mary. Content.
  | *M* | –38. Departure of the Angel.

26 the sixth month. After the vision of Zachariah. This (cp. *v.* 36) is the passage which gives John's age as six months older than the Lord's. See Ap. 179. **from.** Gr. *hupo.* Ap. 104. xviii. 1. **unto.** Gr. *eis.* Ap. 104. vi. **Galilee.** One of the four Roman divisions of Palestine, comprising Zebulun, Naphtali, and Asher. Cp. Matt. 4. 13. **Nazareth.** Now *en-Nāzirah.* Aram. See Ap. 94. III. 3. See on Matt. 2. 23. **27 To.** Gr. *pros.* Ap. 104. xv. 3. **virgin.** This settles the meaning of the Heb. *'almāh* in Isa. 7. 14. There is no question about the Gr. *parthenos.* **espoused** = betrothed. A year before marriage. See Matt. 1. 18. **man** = husband. Gr. *anēr.* Ap. 123. 2. **Mary** = the Heb. *Miriam.* Ex. 15. 20. See Ap. 100. 1. **28 Hail.** See note on Matt. 26. 49. **thou that art highly favoured** = [thou] having been graced [by God] = endued with grace. Occ. only here, and Eph. 1. 6 = accepted through grace. "Grace" does not occur in Matthew or Mark. **with** = in association with. Gr. *meta.* Ap. 104. xi. 1. Not the same word as in *vv.* 30, 37, 51, 56. **blessed . . . women.** Omitted by T [Tr.] A WH R. Prob. brought here from *v.* 42, where it is unquestioned. **29 when she saw him.** Omitted by all the texts. **cast in her mind** = began to reason, or was reasoning. Imperfect Tense. **30 found.** Put by Fig. *Synecdochē* (of Species), Ap. 6, for "received". **favour** = grace: which is favour to the unworthy, as patience is favour to the obstinate, as mercy is favour to the miserable, as pity is favour to the poor, &c. **with** = from. Gr. *para.* Ap. 104. xii. 2. **31 thou shalt conceive**: i.e. forthwith conceive. The Tense marks a future action, the beginning of which in relation to future time is past, but the consequences of which still continue. **and.** Note the Fig. *Polysyndeton* in *vv.* 31, 32, emphasizing each detail. Note the four statements of the angel, combining the four key-texts of the four Gospels shown on page 1304:

(1) **Thou shalt . . . bring forth a Son**: "Behold the Man".
(2) **Thou shalt call His name Jesus**: "Behold My Servant".
(3) **He shall be great . . . the Son of the Highest** (*v.* 32): "Behold your God".
(4) **He shall reign, &c.** (*v.* 33): "Behold thy King".

JESUS. See note on Matt. 1. 21 and Ap. 48 and 98. X.

5 B.C. 32 °He shall be great, [31]and shall be called the Son of °the Highest: [31]and [6]the LORD [6]God shall give unto Him the throne of His father David:

33 [31]And He shall reign °over the house of °Jacob °for ever; [31]and of His kingdom there shall be [7]no end."

m[2] 34 Then said Mary [13]unto the angel, "How shall this be, °seeing I °know [-20]not a [27]man?"

N[3] l[3] 35 And the angel answered and said unto her, [15]"The Holy Ghost shall come [12]upon thee, and the power of [32]the Highest °shall overshadow thee: °therefore also °that holy Thing Which shall be born [5]of thee shall be called °the Son of [6]God.

36 And, [20]behold, thy °cousin Elisabeth, °she hath also conceived a son [5]in her old age: and this is [26]the sixth month with her, who was called barren.

37 For [30]with God °nothing shall be impossible."

m[3] 38 And Mary said, °"Behold the °handmaid of the LORD; be it unto me [9]according to thy °word."

M And the angel departed [2]from her.

L[2] O 39 And Mary arose [5]in those days, and went [9]into the hill country [28]with haste [9]into a city of Juda;

40 And °entered [9]into the house of Zacharias, and saluted Elisabeth.

P Q[1] n[1] 41 And [8]it came to pass, that, when Elisabeth heard the salutation of Mary,

o[1] the babe °leaped [5]in her womb; and Elisabeth was filled with [15]the Holy Ghost:

n[2] 42 And she °spake out with a loud voice, and said,

Q n[3] "Blessed *art* thou [1]among women, and blessed *is* the fruit of thy womb.

43 And whence *is* this to me, that the mother of my Lord should come [27]to me?

o[2] 44 For, °lo, as soon as the voice of thy salutation °sounded [20]in mine ears, the babe [41]leaped [5]in my womb °for joy.

n[4] 45 And °blessed *is* she that believed: for there shall be a °performance of those things which were told her °from the LORD."

P R p 46 And °Mary said, °"My soul doth magnify the LORD,

---

32 He shall be great, &c. Marks the break in the Dispensations, *vv.* 32, 33 being yet future.

the Highest = the Most High. Gr. *hupsistos.* Occ. seven times in Luke (1. 32, 35, 76; 2. 14 (pl.); 6. 35; 8. 28; 19. 38 (pl.); and twice in Acts (7. 48; 16. 17). Elsewhere, only four times (Matt. 21. 9 (pl.). Mark 5. 7; 11. 10 (pl.); and Heb. 7. 1).

33 over. Gr. *epi.* Ap. 104. ix. 3.

Jacob. Put for all the natural seed of the twelve tribes.

for = unto. Gr. *eis.* Ap. 104. vi.

for ever = unto the ages. See Ap. 151. II. A. ii. 7. a. See Ps. 45. 6. Dan. 7. 13, 14, 27. Mic. 4. 7. 1 Cor. 15. 24–28. Heb. 1. 8. Rev. 11. 15.

34 seeing, &c. = since, &c. Mary's answer shows how she understood the angel's promise. She does not question the *fact*, as Zacharias did (*v.* 18), but only inquires as to the *mode.* To Mary the promise seems too early, to Zacharias too late.

know = come to know. Gr. *ginōskō.* Ap. 132. I. ii.

35 shall overshadow. Cp. Ex. 33. 22. Mark 9. 7.

therefore = wherefore.

that holy Thing. See Heb. 7. 26. 1 Pet. 2. 22, and note on Matt. 27. 4.

the Son of God = God's Son. Ap. 98. XV.

36 cousin = kinswoman.

she hath also conceived = she also hath conceived.

37 nothing = not (Gr. *ou.* Ap. 105. I) any word. Gr. *rhēma.* See note on Mark 9. 32.

38 Behold. Gr. *idou.* Ap. 133. I. 2.

handmaid = bondmaid.

word. See note on *v.* 37. Same word.

1. 39–56 (L[2], p. 1431). VISIT OF MARY TO ELISABETH. (*Introversion.*)

L[2] | O | 39, 40. Mary. Journey.
  P | 41–45. Blessing of Mary.
  P | 46–55. Hymn of Mary.
 O | 56. Mary. Return.

40 entered. A detail, to emphasize the fact, by which she recognized the truth of the sign of *v.* 36.

1. 41–45 (P, above). BLESSING OF MARY. (*Introversions.*)

P | Q | n[1] | 41–. Hearing.
   o[1] | –41. Exultation of Babe.
  n[2] | 42–. Speaking.
 Q | n[3] | –42, 43. Benediction.
   o[2] | 44. Exultation of Babe.
  n[4] | 45. Beatitude.

41 leaped. Gr. *skirtaō.* Only used in N.T. here, *v.* 44, and 6. 23. Cp. Gen. 25. 22. Sept. has the same word.

42 spake out = cried out. Gr. *anaphōneō.* Occ. only here. A medical word. See Col. 4. 14.

43 to. Gr. *pros.* Ap. 104. xv. 3.

44 lo. Fig. *Asterismos.* Ap. 6.

sounded in = came into.

for joy = in (Gr. *en.* Ap. 104. viii) exultation.

45 blessed = happy. Not the same word as in *v.* 42.

performance = fulfilment. **from.** Gr. *para.* Ap. 104. xii. 1.

1. 46–55 (*P*, above). HYMN OF MARY. (*Alternation.*)

P | R | 46–49. Favours to herself. Condescension.
 S | 50. Mercy to all that fear Him.
 R | 51–53. Favours to others. Discrimination.
 S | 54, 55. Mercy remembered to Israel.

1. 46–49 (R, above). FAVOURS TO HERSELF. (*Alternation.*)

R | p | 46, 47. Mary rejoicing.
  q | 48–. Reason.
 p | –48. All rejoicing.
  q | 49. Reason.

46 Mary. From a common practice of transcribers in replacing a pronoun by the corresponding proper noun, or name, some have thought that this hymn is a continuation of Elisabeth's words. And the Structure favours this idea. But there is no MS. evidence for it. **My soul** = I myself. For emphasis. See Ap. 110. IV. 1.

5 B.C. 47 And °my spirit hath °rejoiced °in °God my Saviour.

q 48 For He hath °regarded the low estate of His [38]handmaiden:

p for, [20]behold, [2]from henceforth all generations shall call me [45]blessed.

q 49 For °He That is mighty hath done to me great things; and holy *is* °His name.

S 50 And His °mercy *is* on them that °fear Him °from generation to generation.

R 51 He hath shewed strength °with °His arm; He hath scattered the proud in the imagination of their hearts.

52 He hath °put down the mighty [2]from *their* °seats, and exalted °them of low degree.

53 He hath filled the hungry with good things; and the rich He hath sent empty away.

S 54 He hath °holpen His servant Israel, °in remembrance of *His* [50]mercy;

55 °As He spake [27]to °our fathers, to Abraham, and to his seed °for ever."

O 56 And Mary abode °with her about three months, and °returned [23]to her own house.

F T¹ U 4 B.C. NISAN 57 Now Elisabeth's °full time came that she should be delivered; °and she °brought forth a son.

V 58 And her neighbours and her [36]cousins heard how [6]the LORD had °shewed great mercy °upon her; and they rejoiced with her.

U r 59 And [8]it came to pass, that °on the eighth day they came to circumcise the °child; and °they called him Zacharias, °after the name of his father.

s 60 And his mother answered and said, °"Not *so*; but he shall be called John."

r 61 And they said [13]unto her, °"There is none °of thy kindred °that is called by this name."

s 62 And they °made signs to his father, how he °would have him called.

63 And he asked for a °writing table, and °wrote, saying, "His name is °John."

V And they marvelled all.

T² W¹ 64 And his mouth was opened °immediately, and his tongue *loosed*, and he °spake, and praised [6]God.

65 And fear came °on all that dwell round

47 my spirit. See Ap. 101. II. 9.
rejoiced = exulted.
in. Gr. *epi.* Ap. 104. ix. 2.
God my Saviour. Note the Article = the God [Who is] the Saviour [of me]. See Sept. Deut. 32. 15. Ps. 24. 5; 25. 5; 95. 1.
48 regarded = looked (Gr. *epiblepō.* Ap. 133. III. 4) upon (Gr. *epi.* Ap. 104. ix. 3). See James 2. 3, and cp. 1 Sam. 1. 11. Ps. 33. 14; 119. 132 (Sept.).
49 He That is mighty = the Mighty One.
His name. See note on Ps. 20. 1.
50 mercy = pity. Gr. *eleos.* See *vv.* 54, 58, 72, 78. Not the same word as in *v.* 30. **fear** = reverence.
from generation, &c. = unto (Gr. *eis.* Ap. 104. vi) generations of generations.
51 with. Gr. *en.* Ap. 104. viii.
His arm. Fig. *Anthrōpopatheia.* Ap. 6. Cp. Isa. 52. 10; 59. 1, 16.
52 put down the mighty. Amaziah (2 Kings 14. 10); Uzziah (2 Chron. 26. 16); Nebuchadnezzar (Dan. 5. 20); Belshazzar (Dan. 5. 23, 30).
seats = thrones.
them of low degree = the lowly.
54 holpen = laid hold of [for help], or taken by the hand. Cp. Isa. 41. 8, 9.
in remembrance = [in order] to remember.
55 As = according as.
our fathers. Cp. Mic. 7. 20. Gal. 3. 16. Acts 2. 39.
for ever = unto the age. See Ap. 151. II. A. ii. 4. a.
56 with = in fellowship with. Gr. *sun.* Ap. 104. xvi. Not the same word as in *vv.* 28, 30, 37, 39, 51, 66.
returned = returned back. Gr. *hupostrephō.* Almost peculiar to Luke. Occ. only in Mark 14. 40. Gal. 1. 17. Heb. 7. 1, outside Luke and Acts.

1. 57-80 (*F*, p. 1430). JOHN. (*Division.*)

F T¹ | 57-63. John. Birth and Circumcision.
T² | 64-79. Zacharias. Prophecy: Fulfilled and Renewed.
T³ | 80. John. Growth till manifestation.

1. 57-63 (T¹, above). JOHN. BIRTH AND CIRCUMCISION. (*Alternation.*)

T¹ | U | 57. John. Birth.
V | 58. Neighbours. Congratulations.
U | 59-63-. John. Circumcision.
V | -63. Neighbours. Wonder.

57 full time = fulfilled time.
and. Note the Fig. *Polysyndeton* (Ap. 6) throughout the passage *vv.* 57-67, eighteen "ands".
brought forth. Gr. *gennaō.* Correctly rendered here, of the mother. Used of the father it = beget. See note on Matt. 1. 2.
58 shewed great mercy = magnified His mercy. A Hebraism. Cp. Gen. 19. 19. 2 Sam. 22. 51, Sept.
upon = with. Gr. *meta.* Ap. 104. xi. 1. Not the same word as in *vv.* 12, 35.

1. 59-63 (*U*, above). JOHN. CIRCUMCISION. (*Alternation.*)

U | r | 59. Neighbours. Name Zacharias.
s | 60. Mother. "John".
r | 61. Neighbours. Name Zacharias.
s | 62, 63. Father. "John".

59 on = in. Gr. *en.* Ap. 104. viii. Not the same word as in *v.* 65. **on the eighth day.** Gen. 17. 12. Lev. 12. 3. Phil. 3. 5. **child.** Gr. *paidion.* Ap. 108. v. **they called.** Imperf. Tense = were for calling. **after.** Gr. *epi.* Ap. 104. ix. 2. Not the same word as in *v.* 24. **60 Not so** = No. Gr. *ouchi.* Ap. 105. I. **61 There is** = That there is. **of** = among. Gr. *en.* Ap. 104. viii. 2. **that is** = who is. **62 made signs.** Imperf. Tense = were consulting him by signs; i.e. while the colloquy was going on. **would** = wished to. Gr. *thelō.* Ap. 102. 1. **63 writing table** = writing tablet. Table was used for tablet in 1611. Used by medical writers in Luke's day. **wrote, saying.** A Hebraism. Cp. 2 Kings 10. 6. **"John"** = the grace of Jehovah, was thus the first written word of that dispensation.

1. 64-79 (T², above). ZACHARIAS. PROPHECY: FULFILLED AND RENEWED. (*Division.*)

T² | W¹ | 64-67. Prophecy. Given of Zacharias.
W² | 68-79. Prophecy. Given by Zacharias.

64 immediately = at once. Gr. *parachrēma.* Occ. nineteen times. All in Luke or Acts, except Matt. 21. 19, 20. A medical word (see Col. 4. 14), used thirteen times in connection with disease or healing. Rendered "straightway" in 8. 55. Acts 5. 10. **spake** = began to speak. Imperf. Tense. **65 on** = upon. Gr. *epi.* Ap. 104. ix. 3.

4 B.C. about them: and all these °sayings °were
noised abroad °throughout all the hill country
of Judæa.
66 And all they °that heard *them* laid *them*
up [5] in their hearts, saying, "What manner of
[59] child shall this be!" And the hand of [6] the
LORD was [28] with him.
67 And his father Zacharias was filled with
[15] the Holy Ghost, and prophesied, saying,

W^2 t 68 °"Blessed *be* [6] the LORD °God of Israel; for
He hath °visited and °redeemed His people,

u 69 And hath raised up °an horn of salvation
for us [5] in the house of °His servant David;

v 70 [55] As He spake °by the mouth of His holy
prophets, which have been °since the world
began:

w 71 That we should be saved [2] from our enemies, and [2] from the hand of all that hate us;

x 72 To perform the mercy *promised* °to our
fathers, and to remember His holy covenant;

x 73 °The oath which He sware [27] to our father
Abraham,

w 74 That He would grant unto us, that we
being delivered °out of the °hand of our enemies might °serve Him without fear,
75 [5] In °holiness and °righteousness [6] before
Him, all the days of our life.

v 76 And thou, [59] child, shalt be called the prophet of [32] the Highest: for thou shalt go °before the face of [6] the LORD to prepare His
ways;

u 77 To give °knowledge of salvation unto His
people °by the remission of their sins,

t 78 °Through the °tender mercy of our God;
°whereby the °dayspring [15] from °on high
hath [68] visited us,
79 To °give light to them that sit [5] in darkness and *in* °the shadow of death, to °guide
our feet [9] into the way of peace."

T^3 80 And the [59] child grew, and °waxed strong
[5] in °spirit, and was [5] in °the deserts till the
day of his °shewing [13] unto Israel.

A^3 *G* (p. 1430) **2** And °it came to pass °in those days, that
there went out °a decree °from Cæsar
Augustus, that °all the °world should be °taxed.
2 (*And* °this taxing was first made when
°Cyrenius was governor of Syria.)
3 And all went to be [1] taxed, °every one °into
his own city.

sayings. Gr. pl. of *rhema*. See note on Mark 9. 32.
were noised abroad = were talked of.
throughout all = in (Gr. *en*. Ap. 104. viii) the whole.
66 that heard. The 1611 edition of the A.V. reads "that had heard".

1. 68-79 (W^2, p. 1433). PROPHECY. GIVEN BY ZACHARIAS. (*Introversion.*)

W^2
- t | 68. Visitation.
  - u | 69. Salvation.
    - v | 70. Prophets.
      - w | 71. Enemies.
        - x | 72. The Covenant.
        - *x* | 73. The Covenant.
      - *w* | 74, 75. Enemies.
    - *v* | 76. Prophet.
  - *u* | 77. Salvation.
- *t* | 78, 79. Visitation.

68 Blessed. Hence the name "Benedictus" given to Zacharias's prophecy. **God** = the God.
visited = looked on. Not the same word as in *v.* 48. See Ap. 133. III. 5.
redeemed = wrought a ransom for. Cp. Titus 2. 14.
69 an horn of salvation. A Hebraism. See Ps. 132. 17. 1 Sam. 2. 1, 10. Ezek. 29. 21.
His servant David. See Ps. 132. 10.
70 by = through. Gr. *dia.* Ap. 104. v. 1.
since the world began = from [the] age: i. e. of old. See Ap. 151. II. A. ii. 1.
72 to = with. Gr. *meta.* Ap. 104. xi. 1.
73 The oath, &c. See Gen. 12. 3; 17. 4; 22. 16, 17.
74 out of = from. Gr. *ek.* Ap. 104. vii.
hand. The 1611 edition of the A.V. reads "hands".
serve: or worship. **75 holiness.** Toward God.
righteousness. Toward men. Cp. 1 Thess. 2. 10. Eph. 4. 24.
76 before. Gr. *pro.* Ap. 104. xiv.
77 knowledge. Gr. *gnōsis.* Ap. 132. II. i.
by = for. Gr. *en.* Ap. 104. viii.
78 Through = On account of. Gr. *dia.* Ap. 104. v. 2.
tender mercy = bowels of compassion. Fig. *Anthrōpopatheia* (Ap. 6).
whereby = in (Gr. *en.* Ap. 104. viii) which.
dayspring. Gr. *anatolē.* Heb. *ẓemach* = branch (see page 1304), is rendered *anatolē* in Jer. 23. 5 and Zech. 3. 8, because of its springing up. Both meanings (branch and light) are here combined. Cp. Ezek. 16. 7; 17. 10.
on high. Gr. *hupsos.* Occ. five more times: 24. 49. Eph. 3. 18; 4. 8. James 1. 9. Rev. 21. 16.
79 give light to = shine upon.
the shadow of death. A Hebraism. *Ẓalmaveth.* Job 10. 21; 38. 17. Ps. 23. 4; 107. 10. Isa. 9. 2. Matt. 4. 16, &c.
guide = direct. Wycliffe has "dress", through the O. French *dresser* = to arrange, still preserved as an English military term.
80 waxed strong = grew and was strengthened.
spirit. Gr. *pneuma.* See Ap. 101. II. 10.
the deserts. The Art. indicating a well-known part.
shewing = public or official inauguration. Gr. *anadeixis.* Only occ. here. The verb *anadeiknumi* occ. 10. 1. See note there.

1 it came to pass in those days. The seventh and last occurrence of this ominous phrase. See note on Gen. 14. 1. **it came to pass.** A Hebraism, frequent in Luke. Cp. 1. 8. **in.** Gr. *en.* Ap. 104. viii. **a decree** = an edict. **from.** Gr. *para.* Ap. 104. xii. 1. **all.** Fig. *Synecdochē* (of the whole) for a part of the whole; i. e. the Roman Empire. **world.** Gr. *oikoumenē.* See Ap. 129. 3. Cp. Acts 11. 28. **taxed** = enrolled, or registered. **2 this taxing was first made** = this was the first registration to be made. A second is recorded in Acts 5. 37. **Cyrenius.** Gr. for the Latin *Quirinus.* His full name was Publius Sulpicius Quirinus. **3 every one,** &c. A Papyrus (in British Museum), being a rescript of the Prefect Gaius Vibius Maximus (A. D. 103–4), shows that Herod must have been acting under Roman orders. Vib. Max. was Præfect of Egypt, and wrote: "The enrolment by households being at hand, it is necessary to notify all who for any cause soever are outside their homes to return to their domestic hearths, that they may accomplish the customary dispensation of enrolment, and continue steadfastly in the husbandry that belongeth to them." There is a large number of Papyri relating to these enrolments. See Deissmann's *Light from the Ancient East*, pp. 268, 269. **into** = unto. Gr. *eis.* Ap. 104. vi.

4 B.C. **4 And Joseph also °went up °from Galilee,**
°out of the city of °Nazareth, [3] into Judæa,
°unto °the city of David, which is called
°Bethlehem; °(because he was °of the house
and °lineage of David:)
5 To be [1] taxed °with Mary his °espoused
wife, being °great with child.

A^3 X^1 **6 And °so it was, that, °while they were**
there, the days were accomplished that she
should be delivered.

15th Tisri First Day of Feast of Tabernacles. **7 And she brought forth °her firstborn Son,**
and °wrapped Him in swaddling clothes, and
laid Him [1] in °a °manger; because there was
°no room for them [1] in °the inn.

Y^1 A C **8 And there were [1] in the same °country**
shepherds abiding in the field, keeping watch
°over their flock by night.

D E **9 And, °lo, °the angel of °the LORD °came**
upon them, and °the glory of °the LORD shone
round about them: and they °were sore
afraid.

F y **10 And the angel said unto them, "Fear °not:**
for, °behold, °I bring you good tidings of
great joy, °which shall be to all °people.

z **11 °For unto you °is born this day**

z **[1] in the city of David**

a^1 **°a Saviour,**

a^2 **which is °Christ**

a^3 **°the Lord.**

y **12 And this *shall be* a sign unto you; Ye**
shall find °the Babe [7] wrapped in swaddling
clothes, lying [1] in [7] a [7] manger."

D E **13 And suddenly there was [5] with the angel**

4 went up: literally true, the ascent from Nazareth to Jerusalem being at least 1,500 feet.
from = away from. Gr. *apo*. Ap. 104. iv.
out of. Gr. *ek*. Ap. 104. vii.
Nazareth. Aram. See note on 1. 26. = Branch-Town, where He, Jehovah's "Branch" (Zech. 3. 8; 6. 12), was brought up (4. 16).
unto. Gr. *eis*. Ap. 104. vi. Not the same word as in *vv.* 15-, 20, 48, 49.
the city of David. 1 Sam. 20. 6. Zion also so called, 2 Sam. 5. 9; 6. 10, 12, 16. 1 Kings 2. 10, &c.
Bethlehem = the house of bread. Cp. Gen. 35. 19; 48. 7. Ps. 132. 6. Now *Beit Lahm*, about five miles south of Jerusalem.
because he was = on account of (*dia*. Ap. 104. v. 2) his being.   **of.** Gr. *ek*. Ap. 104. vii.
lineage: i.e. the family.
5 with = in conjunction with. Gr. *sun*. Ap. 104. xvi. Not the same word as in *vv.* 36, 51, 52.
espoused = married. Not merely "betrothed" (Matt. 1. 20, 24, 25). See note on Matt. 1. 18. Cp. Deut. 22. 23, 24.
great with child. Cp. 1. 24. Gr. *enkuos*. Occ. only here in N.T.

2. 6-52 (A^3, p. 1429). PRE-MINISTERIAL.
(Repeated Alternation.)

A^3 | X^1 | 6, 7. The Holy Child. Birth.
      Y^1 | 8-20. Attestations. (Heavenly.)
   X^2 | 21-24. The Holy Child. Presentation.
      Y^2 | 25-38. Attestations. (Earthly.)
   X^3 | 39-52. The Holy Child. Growth.

6 so it was = it came to pass; as in *v.* 1.
while = in (Gr. *en*. Ap. 104. viii) the time.
7 her firstborn Son = her son, the firstborn. Ap. 179. II.
wrapped . . . swaddling clothes. Gr. *sparganoō* = to swathe. Occ. only here and *v.* 12. A medical term = bandage. See Col. 4. 14. Eng. "swathe". Anglo-Saxon *swathu* = as much grass as is mown at one stroke of the scythe. From Low Germ. *swade* = a scythe. Hence a shred, or slice, then a bandage. Cp. Ezek. 16. 4.
a = the. But all the Texts omit the Art.
manger. Gr. *phatnē* (from *pateomai*, to eat). Occ. only in *vv.* 12, 16, and 13. 15. Sept. for Heb. *'ēbus*. Prov. 14. 4.   **no.** Gr. *ou*. Ap. 105. I.
the inn = the *Khan*. Not "guestchamber", as in 22. 11 and Mark 14. 14, its only other occurrences.

2. 8-15 (Y^1, above). ATTESTATIONS. (HEAVENLY.) *(Alternation.)*

Y^1 | A | 8-15. Angelic Message. Given.
   B | 16. The Shepherds. Departure.
   A | 17-19. Angelic Message. Reported.
   B | 20. The Shepherds. Return.

2. 8-15 (A, above). ANGELIC MESSAGE. *(Introversion and Alternation.)*

A | C | 8. The Shepherds. Watch.
   D | E | 9. One Angel.
      F | 10-12. His Message. News.
   D | *E* | 13. The Heavenly Host.
      F | 14. Their Message. Praise.
   C | 15. The Shepherds. Resolve.

8 country = region where David fed his father's sheep, when sent for by Samuel (1 Sam. 16. 11, 12). **over.** Gr. *epi*. Ap. 104. ix. 3.   **9 lo.** Fig. *Asterismos* (Ap. 6), to call attention to the wondrous event. **the angel** = an angel. No Art. See note on 1. 11. Ap. 179. II. 2.   **the LORD** = Jehovah (Ap. 98. VI. *a*. 1. B. b). **came upon** = stood by. Gr. *ephistēmi*. Used eighteen times by Luke. Cp. 24. 4. Acts 12. 7; 23. 11.   **the glory**: the *Shekinah*, which symbolized the Divine presence. See Ex. 24. 16. 1 Kings 8. 10. Isa. 6. 1-3. Acts 7. 55.   **were sore afraid** = feared a great fear. Fig. *Polyptōton*. Ap. 6. See note on Gen. 26. 28.

2. 10-12 [For Structure see next page].

10 not. Gr. *mē*. Ap. 105. II.   **behold.** Fig. *Asterismos*. Ap. 6.   **I bring you good tidings.** Gr. *euangelizomai* = I evangelize (announce) to you great joy.   **which.** Denoting the class or character of the joy.   **people** = the People [of Israel].   **11 For** = That: meaning "born to-day"; not "I announce to-day". See note on Luke 23. 43.   **is born** = was born, or brought forth.   **a Saviour.** Not a helper: for a Saviour is for the lost.   **Christ the Lord** = Heb. *Mashiah Jehovah*, i.e. Jehovah's Anointed. 1 Sam. 24. 6. Ap. 98. XIII.   **the Lord.** Ap. 98. VI. *a*. 3. B. a. The Lord of all power and might. Therefore able to save. Cp. Rom. 14. 9. 1 Cor. 8. 6; 12. 3. 2 Cor. 4. 5. Phil. 2. 11. These three words define and contain the "Gospel" as being good news as to a PERSON; and as being Christianity as distinct from Religion, which consists of Articles, Creeds, Doctrines, and Confessions; i.e. all that is outward. Cp. Phil. 3. 4-7, 9, 10, 20, 21. Note that in the Gr. the words, "in the city of David", come last. Hence the z and *z* correspond in the Structure, p. 1436.   **12 the Babe** = a babe.

4 B.C. **a multitude of the °heavenly °host praising °God, and saying,**

F G b **14 °"Glory**

H **to [13]God**

c **[1]in the highest,**

G c **and °on earth**

b **peace,**

H **°good will °toward men."**

C **15 And [1]it came to pass, as the angels were gone away [4]from them [3]into °heaven, the shepherds said one °to another, °"Let us now go even °unto Bethlehem, and °see this °thing which °is come to pass, which [9]the LORD hath °made known unto us."**

B **16 And they came with haste, and °found °Mary, and Joseph, and the Babe lying [1]in [7]a manger.**

A **17 And when they had [15]seen *it*, they made known abroad the °saying which was told them °concerning this °Child.**

18 And all they that heard *it* wondered °at those things which were told °them °by the shepherds.

19 But Mary °kept all these [15]things, °and pondered *them* [1]in her heart.

B **20 And the shepherds returned, glorifying and praising [13]God °for all the things that they had heard and [15]seen, °as it was told °unto them.**

X² **21 And when °eight days were °accomplished for the circumcising of the [17]Child, °His name was called °JESUS, Which was so named °of the angel °before He was conceived [1]in the womb.**

22 And when °the days of °her purification °according to °the law of Moses were [21]accomplished, they °brought Him °to Jerusalem, to °present *Him* to [9]the LORD;

23 [20](As it is written [1]in [22]the law of [9]the LORD, °Every male that openeth the womb shall be called °holy to [9]the LORD;)

24 And to offer a sacrifice [22]according to that which is said [1]in [22]the law of the LORD, °A pair of turtledoves, or two young pigeons.

Y² I **25 And, [10]behold, there was a °man [1]in Jerusalem, whose name *was* °Simeon; and the same °man *was* just and °devout, °waiting for**

2. 10-12 (F, p. 1435). HIS MESSAGE. NEWS.
(*Introversion, in the order of the Greek words.*)

F | y | 10. The Announcement.
  z | 11-. The Time.
    a¹ | -11-. A Saviour. }
    a² | -11-. Christ. } The Gospel. A Person.
    a³ | -11. The Lord. }
  z | -11-. The Place.
y | 12. The Sign.

13 heavenly host = host of heaven. So Tr. WH marg. **host** = the *Sabaiōth* of the O.T. Cp. Dan. 8. 10. Rom. 9. 29. Jas. 5. 4. Rev. 5. 11, 12. **God.** Ap. 98. I. i. 1.

14. (*F*, p. 1435). THEIR MESSAGE. PRAISE.
(*Alternation and Introversion, according to the Greek.*)

F | G | b | 14-. Glory.
    c | -14-. Sphere: "in the Highest".
  H | -14-. To God.
G | c | -14-. Sphere: "on Earth".
  b | -14-. Peace.
  H | -14. [From God] among [favoured] men.

14 Glory. Supply the Ellipsis: [be] to God. Cp. 19. 38. **on earth peace.** But man murdered "the Prince of peace", and now vainly talks about "Peace". **on.** Gr. *epi.* Ap. 104. ix. 1. **earth.** Gr. *gē.* Ap. 124. 4. **good will toward men.** All the texts read "among men of good pleasure", reading *eudokias* instead of *eudokia.* But the sense is the same, as the "good pleasure" is that of Jehovah alone = among men of [His] good pleasure: see 12. 32, "It is your Father's good pleasure to give you the kingdom". But it was man's bad pleasure to *reject* the kingdom. See the Structure (*F*). **toward** = among. Gr. *en.* Ap. 104. viii. 2. **15 heaven** = the heaven. Sing. with Art. **to.** Gr. *pros.* Ap. 104. xv. 3. **Let us now go** = [Come now], let us go through. **unto** = as far as. **see.** Gr. *eidon.* Ap. 133. I. i. **thing** = word, or saying. Gr. *rhēma.* See note on Mark 9. 32. **is** = has. **made known:** i.e. the saying of *v.* 12. Gr. *gnōrizō.* Cp. *gnōsis.* Ap. 132. II. i. **16 found** = discovered, after search, or in succession. Gr. *aneuriskō.* Occ. only here and in Acts 21. 4. **Mary, and Joseph, and the Babe.** Each has the Art. with conj. emphasizing the several parties referred to. **17 saying.** Gr. *rhēma*, as in *v.* 15. **concerning.** Gr. *peri.* Ap. 104. xiii. 1. **Child.** As in 1. 59. **18 at** = concerning, as in *v.* 17. **them** = to (Gr. *pros*, as in *v.* 15-) them. **by.** Gr. *hupō.* Ap. 104. xviii. 1. **19 kept** = kept within herself.

and pondered = pondering; i.e. weighing them. Cp. Gen. 37. 11. **20 for** = on. Gr. *epi.* Ap. 104. ix. 2. **as** = according as. **unto.** Gr. *pros.* Ap. 104. xv. 3. **21 eight days, &c.:** i.e. on the last and great day of the Feast of Tabernacles (John 7. 37). **accomplished** = fulfilled. See Lev. 12. 3. **His name.** Supply the logical Ellipsis thus: "[Then they circumcised Him] and called His Name", &c. Only four named before birth: Ishmael, Isaac, John, and the Lord. **JESUS.** See note on Matt. 1. 21. Ap. 98. X. **of** = by. Gr. *hupo*, as in *v.* 18. **before.** Gr. *pro.* Ap. 104. xiv. **22 the days:** i.e. forty days after the birth of a son (eighty after a daughter). See Lev. 12. 2-4. **her** = their. So all the texts; i.e. Joseph and Mary. **according to.** Gr. *kata.* Ap. 104. x. 2. See Ex. 13. 12; 22. 29; 34. 19. Num. 3. 12, 13; 18. 15. **the law.** Mentioned five times in this chapter, oftener than all the rest of Luke, to show the truth of Gal. 4. 4. **brought Him** = brought Him up. **to.** Gr. *eis.* Ap. 104. vi. **present, &c.** Ex. 13. 2. Num. 18. 15, 16. **23 Every male, &c.** Quoted from Ex. 13. 2. Num. 18. 15. **holy.** See note on Ex. 3. 5. **24 A pair, &c.** Lev. 12. 2, 6.

2. 25-38 (Y², p. 1435). ATTESTATIONS. (EARTHLY.) (*Alternation.*)

Y² | I | 25-27. Simeon.
  J | 28-35. His testimony.
I | 36, 37. Anna.
  J | 38. Her testimony.

25 man. Gr. *anthrōpos.* See Ap. 123. 1. **Simeon.** In Heb. *Shimeʿōn* = hearing. Cp. Gen. 29. 33. Possibly the father of Gamaliel (Acts 5. 34). **devout.** Gr. *eulabēs.* Used only by Luke = taking hold of well; i.e. careful and circumspect in observing the Law. Cp. Acts 2. 5; 8. 2. The kindred word *eulabeia*, rendered "godly fear", occurs twice (Heb. 5. 7; 12. 28). **waiting for.** Cp. Gen. 49. 18. Isa. 49. 23; and see Ap. 36. Joseph of Arimathæa was another who thus waited. Mark 15. 43. Cp. *v.* 38; 3. 15; 24. 21.

4 B.C. °the consolation of Israel: and °the Holy
Ghost was °upon him.
26 And °it was revealed unto him [18]by °the
Holy Ghost, that he should [10]not [15]see death,
°before he had [15]seen °the LORD'S Christ.
27 And he came °by °the Spirit [3]into °the
temple: and when the parents brought [1]in
[17]the Child Jesus, to do °for Him °after the
custom of [22]the law,
J 28 Then °took He Him up °in his arms, and
blessed God, and said,
29 °"Lord, now lettest Thou Thy servant
depart [1]in peace, [22]according to Thy °word:
30 For mine eyes have [15]seen °Thy salvation,
31 Which Thou hast prepared °before the
face of all °people;
32 **A light °to lighten °the Gentiles,** and the
°glory of thy people Israel."
33 And °Joseph and His mother °marvelled
°at those things which were spoken °of Him.
34 And [25]Simeon blessed them, and said
[20]unto Mary His mother, [10]"Behold, this *Child*
is °set °for the °fall and °rising again of many
[1]in Israel; and °for a sign which shall be
°spoken against;
35 °(Yea, a °sword shall °pierce through
thy own °soul also,) that the °thoughts [4]of
many hearts may be °revealed."
I 36 And there was one °Anna, a °prophetess,
the daughter [4]of Phanuel, of the tribe of °Aser:
She was of a great age, and had lived °with
an husband seven years [4]from her virginity;
37 And She *was* a widow of about fourscore
and four years, which departed °not [4]from the
[27]temple, but °served *God* with fastings and
prayers night and day.
J 38 And She °coming in °that instant gave
°thanks likewise unto °the LORD, and spake
[33]of Him to all them that °looked for °redemption
[1]in Jerusalem.
X³ K d 39 And when they had °performed all things
[22]according to [22]the law of [9]the LORD, they
returned [3]into Galilee, [22]to their own city
°Nazareth.
e 40 And [17]the Child grew, and waxed strong
°in spirit, filled with wisdom: and °the grace
of [13]God was [13]upon Him.
L M P 41 Now His parents went [22]to Jerusalem
every year at the feast of the °passover.

the consolation of Israel. Cp. Acts 28. 20 and Isa. 40. 1. "May I see the consolation of Israel!" was a Jewish formula of blessing; and an adjuration also: "May I not see it, if I speak not the truth!"
the Holy Ghost = *pneuma hagion* = a spiritual gift. See Ap. 101. II. 14.
upon. Gr. *epi.* Ap. 104. ix. 3.
26 it was revealed. Gr. *chrēmatizō.* Occ. nine times; seven times of a Divine communication; here, Matt. 2. 12, 22. Acts 10. 22; 11. 26. Rom. 7. 3. Heb. 8. 5; 11. 17; 12. 25.
the Holy Ghost. The Person being the revealer (with Articles). Not the same as in *v.* 25. See Ap 101. II. 3.
before. Gr. *prin.* See note on "Till", Matt. 1. 25.
the Lord's Christ = Jehovah's Anointed. See note on *v.* 11. Ap. 98. VI. i. *a.* B. b. and XIII.
27 by = in. Gr. *en.* Ap. 104. viii.
the Spirit. The Holy Spirit Himself. See Ap. 101. II. 3.
the temple = the Temple courts. Gr. *hieron.* See notes on Matt. 4. 5; 23. 16.
for = concerning. Gr. *peri.* Ap. 104. xiii. 1.
after = according to. As in *v.* 22.
28 took = received. **in** = into, as in *v.* 3.
29 Lord = Master. Gr. *Despotēs.* Ap. 98. XIV. ii. Occurs ten times in N.T. (here; Acts 4. 24. 1 Tim. 6. 1, 2. 2 Tim. 2. 21. Tit. 2. 9. 1 Pet. 2. 18. 2 Pet. 2. 1. Jude 4. Rev. 6. 10). **word** = saying. See *v.* 26.
30 Thy salvation. Gr. *to sōtērion* (not the usual *sōtēria*). Used of Jehovah Himself (not merely of salvation as such). See Isa. 62. 11. Cp. Luke 3. 6.
31 before. Gr. *kata.* Ap. 104. x. 2.
people = the peoples.
32 A light. Gr. *phōs.* See Ap. 130. 1. Quoted from Isa. 42. 6.
to lighten = for (Gr. *eis,* as in *v.* 34) a revelation of. Gr. *apokalupsis* = a revelation by unveiling and manifesting to view. The first of eighteen occurrences. All noted in Ap. 106. II. i. Cp. Ps. 98. 2, 3. Isa. 42. 6; 49. 6; 52. 10, &c. **the Gentiles.** See Isa. 25. 7.
glory. The special blessing for Israel. Israel has had the "light". She is yet to have the glory.
33 Joseph. Most of the texts (not the Syriac) read "His father". **marvelled** = were marvelling.
at. Gr. *epi.* Ap. 104. ix. 2. Not the same word as in *v.* 18.
of = concerning. Gr. *peri.* Ap. 104. xiii. 1. Not the same word as in *vv.* 4, 35, -36.
34 set = destined.
for. Gr. *eis.* Ap. 104. vi. Not the same word as in *vv.* 10, 11, 20, 27, 30.
fall: i. e. a stumbling-block. See Isa. 8. 14, and cp. Matt. 21. 42, 44. Acts 4. 11. Rom. 9. 33. 1 Cor. 1. 23.
rising again = rising up. Matt. 11. 5. Ap. 178. II. 1.
spoken against. See Acts 28. 22. Not a prophecy, but describing its character.
35 Yea = And thee.
sword. Gr. *rhomphaia.* Occ. only here and Rev. 1. 16; 2. 12, 16; 6. 8; 19. 15, 21. Sept. for Zech. 13. 7.
pierce, &c. When on the Cross.
soul. Gr. *psuchē.* Ap. 110. v. 1.
thoughts = reasonings. Cp. 5. 22. Matt. 15. 19. John 9. 16. 1 Cor. 11. 19. 1 John 2. 19. **revealed** = unveiled. Gr. *apokaluptō.* Ap. 106. I. ix. **36 Anna.** Heb. Hannah, as in 1 Sam. 1. 20 = He was gracious. **prophetess.** Only here and Rev. 2. 20. **Aser** = Asher; thus Anna of Israel united with Simeon of Judah. **37 not.** Gr. *ou.* Ap. 105. I. **served.** Same as 1. 74. **38 coming in** = standing by. **that instant** = at the same time (or hour). **thanks** = praise. **the Lord.** All the texts read "God". **looked** = waited. **redemption.** See notes on *v.* 24; 24. 21. Mark 15. 43.

2. 39-52 (X³, p. 1435). THE HOLY CHILD. GROWTH. (*Introversion and Alternation.*)

X³ | K | d | 39. Return to Galilee.
    | | e | 40. The Lord. Growth.
    | | L | 41-50. The Feast of the Passover.
    | *K* | *d* | 51. Return to Nazareth.
    | | *e* | 52. The Lord. Increase.

39 performed = ended. **Nazareth.** See note on Matt. 2. 23. **40 in spirit.** All the texts omit this. Ap. 101. vi. Matt. 2 comes in here. **the grace, &c.** Cp. John 1. 14. Isa. 11. 2, 3.

2. 41-50 [For Structure see next page].

41 passover. See Ap. 94. III. 3.

A.D. 8 **42** And when He was °twelve years old, they went up [22] to Jerusalem [27] after the custom of the feast.

Q **43** And when they had fulfilled the days, °as they returned, °the Child Jesus tarried behind [1] in Jerusalem; and °Joseph and His mother °knew [37] not *of it.*

R S f **44** But they, °supposing Him to have been [1] in °the company,

g went °a day's journey; and they °sought Him °among *their* kinsfolk °and acquaintance.

T **45** And when they found Him [10] not,

S f they turned back again [22] to Jerusalem,

g °seeking Him.

46 And [1] it came to pass, that °after three days

T they found Him [1] in [27] the temple,

N °sitting [1] in the midst of the °doctors, both hearing them, and asking them questions.

O **47** And all that heard Him were astonished [33] at His understanding and answers.

M P **48** And when they [15] saw Him, they were amazed: and His mother said [20] unto Him,

Q °"Son, why hast Thou thus dealt with us?

R [10] behold, °Thy father and I have [41] sought Thee sorrowing."

49 And He said [20] unto them, "How is it that ye sought Me?

N °wist ye [37] not that I °must be about My Father's business?"

O **50** And they °understood [37] not the [17] saying which He spake unto them.

K d **51** And He went down [36] with them, and came [22] to [4] Nazareth, and was °subject unto them: but His mother kept all these [17] sayings [1] in her heart.

e **52** And Jesus °increased °in wisdom and °stature, and in favour °with God and °man.

B U
A.D. 26 **3** Now °in the °fifteenth year of the °reign of °Tiberius Cæsar, °Pontius Pilate being °governor of Judæa, and °Herod being tetrarch of Galilee, and his brother °Philip

2. 41-50 (L, p. 1437). THE FEAST OF THE PASSOVER. (*Extended Alternations.*)

L | M | P | 41, 42. Parents at Jerusalem.
Q | 43. The Child. Tarrying behind.
R | 44-46-. Parents' search.
N | -46. The Child. Employment.
O | 47. Effect. Astonishment.
M | *P* | 48-. Parents at Jerusalem.
Q | -48-. The Child. Questioned.
R | -48, 49-. Parents. Search.
N | -49. The Child. Employment.
O | 50. Effect. Unintelligent.

42 twelve years old: when every Jewish boy becomes "a son of the law". If they performed "*all things*" acc. to the Law, Joseph had paid the five shekels redemption money (Num. 3. 47; 18. 16), which gave Joseph the *legal right* to be reckoned the "father", claiming the obedience shown in *v.* 51. See notes on *v.* 48, and 3. 23, which thus explain the genealogy there.

43 as they returned = in (Gr. *en.* Ap. 104. viii) their returning.

the Child. Now the Gr. is *pais* = the youth as becoming Jehovah's servant. See Ap. 108. iv.

Joseph and His mother. All the Texts read "His parents".

knew not = did not get to know of it. Gr. *ginōskō.* Ap. 132. I. ii.

2. 44-46- (R, above). PARENTS' SEARCH. (*Alternations.*)

R | S | f | 44-. Journey from Jerusalem.
g | -44. Search.
T | 45-. Unsuccessful.
S | *f* | -45-. Journey back to Jerusalem.
g | -45, 46-. Search.
T | -46-. Successful.

44 supposing = surely reckoning. See note on 3. 23.

the company: i. e. in the caravan.

a day's journey. Probably to *Beerōth,* about six miles north of Jerusalem. Now *Bireh.*

sought = searched up and down.

among. Gr. *en.* Ap. 104. viii. 2. **and** = and among.

45 seeking = searching (all the way they went). Gr. *anazēteō,* as in *v.* 44.

46 after = with. Gr. *meta.* Ap. 104. xi. 2.

sitting. This was strictly according to rule.

doctors = teachers: i. e. Rabbis.

48 Son. Gr. *teknon* = child. See Ap. 108. i.

Thy father. This was legally correct on the part of Mary. (See note on *v.* 42, above.) But not truly so; therefore the Lord's correction, "MY Father's business", *v.* 49.

49 wist ye not = knew ye not. Gr. *oida.* See Ap. 132. I. i.

must. These are the first recorded words of the Lord. The reference is to Ps. 40. 5-11. John 4. 34. Hence the Divine necessity. Cp. Matt. 16. 21; 26. 54. Mark 8. 31. Luke 4. 43; 9. 22; 13. 33; 24. 7, 26, 46. John 3. 14; 4. 4; 12. 34, &c. The last-recorded words as the Son of man were, "It is finished": i. e. the Father's business which He came to be about. Compare His first and last ministerial or official words. See note on Matt. 4. 4, "It is written". **50 understood not.** Cp. 9. 45; 18. 34. Mark 9. 32. John 1. 10, 11; 10. 6. **51 subject.** See note on *v.* 42. **52 increased** = advanced. **in wisdom.** See Ap. 117. **stature** = maturity in all respects. **with** = from beside. Gr. *para.* Ap. 104. xii. 2. **man** = men. Gr. *anthrōpos.* Ap. 123. 1.

3. 1-20 (**B**, p. 1427). THE FORERUNNER. (*Introversion and Alternation.*)

B | U | 1, 2-. Herod the Tetrarch.
V | W | -2. The Word of God. Coming to John.
X | 3. John proclaiming.
V | *W* | 4-6. The Word of God fulfilled by John.
X | 7-18. John proclaiming.
U | 19, 20. Herod the Tetrarch.

1 in. Gr. *en.* Ap. 104. viii. **fifteenth . . . Tiberius.** See Ap. 179. I, note 2. Augustus died in A.D. 14, but Tiberius was associated with him for two or three years. This would make Tiberius's fifteenth year A.D. 26. **reign** = government. Gr. *hegemonia* (not *basileia* = kingdom). **Pontius Pilate.** First mention. Appointed sixth Procurator of Judaea, A.D. 25. After his deposition, he went to Rome, and (according to Eusebius) committed suicide in A.D. 36. **governor.** Cognate word with "reign" above. **Herod . . Philip.** See Ap. 109. Herod Antipas, half-brother of Philip I, who abducted Philip's wife, Herodias, and married her. This was the Herod to whom the Lord was sent for trial.

A. D. 26 tetrarch of Ituræa and of the region of Trachonitis, and Lysanias the tetrarch of Abilene,

2 °Annas and Caiaphas being the high priests,

V W °the word of God came °unto °John the son of Zacharias [1]in °the wilderness.

X 3 And he °came °into all the country about Jordan, °preaching the °baptism of °repentance °for °the remission of °sins;

V W 4 As it is written [1] in the book of °the words of °Esaias the prophet, saying, "**The voice of one crying [1] in the wilderness, 'Prepare ye the way of °the LORD, make His °paths straight.**

5 Every valley shall be filled, and every mountain and hill shall be brought low; and the crooked shall be made straight, and the rough ways *shall be* made smooth;

6 And all °flesh shall °see the salvation of °God.'"

X Y h 7 °Then said he to the °multitude that came forth to be °baptized °of him, "O °generation of vipers, who hath °warned you to flee °from the wrath °to come?

8 Bring forth therefore fruits worthy of °repentance, and begin °not to say °within yourselves, 'We have Abraham to *our* °father': for I say unto you, That God is able °of °these stones to raise up °children unto Abraham.

i 9 And °now also the axe is laid °unto the root of the trees:

k every tree therefore which bringeth [8]not forth good fruit is hewn down, and cast [3]into the fire."

Z l^1 10 And the people asked him, saying, "What shall we do then?"

m^1 11 He °answereth and saith unto them, "He that hath two °coats, let him impart to him that hath °none; and he that hath °meat, let him do likewise."

l^2 12 Then came °also publicans to be °baptized, and said [9]unto him, °"Master, what shall we do?"

m^2 13 And he said [9]unto them, "Exact °no more °than that which is appointed you."

l^3 14 And °the soldiers likewise demanded of him, saying, "And what shall we do?"

m^3 And he said [9]unto them, °"Do violence to no man, neither °accuse *any* falsely; and be content with your wages."

Y h 15 And as the people were °in expectation, and all men °mused [1]in their hearts °of John, whether he were °the Christ, or not;

2 Annas. See Ap. 94. III. 3. 5.

Annas and Caiaphas being the high priests. Caiaphas was the High Priest as successor of Aaron; while Annas was the *Nasi*, or head of the Sanhedrin (as successor of Moses), and thus associated with Caiaphas in government. This explains John 18. 13, 24, and Acts 4. 6.

the word of God came, &c. See Ap. 82. Cp. Jer. 1. 2. Ezek. 6. 1, &c. John was the last and greatest of the prophets.

unto=upon. Gr. *epi*. Ap. 104. ix. 3. Not the same word as in *vv.* 9, 12, 13, 14.

John the son of Zacharias. In Matthew, John the Baptist.

the wilderness: i.e. in the cities and towns of the open country. See *v.* 4; Josh. 15. 61, 62; and 1 Sam. 23. 14, 24.

3 came=went. **into.** Gr. *eis*. Ap. 104. vi.

preaching=proclaiming. See Ap. 121. 1.

baptism. See Ap. 115. II. i. 2.

repentance. See Ap. 111. II. 1.

for=with a view to. Gr. *eis*. Ap. 104. vi.

the remission=remission. A medical word (see Col. 4. 14). Used by Luke ten times. Rest of N.T. only seven times. See 4. 18. **sins.** Ap. 128. I. ii.

4 the words, &c. See notes on Isa. 40. 3, and Mal. 3. 1. See Ap. 107. II. 4. **Esaias**=Isaiah. See Ap. 79. I.

the LORD=Jehovah. Ap. 4. II and 98. VI. i. *a*. 1. B. a.

paths=beaten tracks.

6 flesh. Put by Fig. *Synecdochē* (of Genus), Ap. 6, for people. **see.** Gr. *opsomai*. Ap. 133. I. 8 (a).

God. Ap. 98. I. i. 1.

3. 7-18 (*X*, p. 1438). JOHN PROCLAIMING.

(*Introversion and Alternations: Extended and Repeated.*)

X | Y | h | 7, 8. The people. Baptism.
i | 9-. The Axe.
k | -9. The Trees.
Z | l^1 | 10. The people. Question.
m^1 | 11. John's answer.
l^2 | 12. The publicans. Question.
m^2 | 13. John's answer.
l^3 | 14-. The soldiers. Question.
m^3 | -14. John's answer.
Y | *h* | 15, 16. The people. Baptism.
i | 17-. The Fan.
k | -17, 18. The Wheat and Chaff.

7 Then said he=He said therefore.

multitude=crowds. **baptized.** Ap. 115. I. vii.

of=by. Gr. *hupo*. Ap. 104. xviii. 1. Not the same word as in *vv.* 8, 15.

generation=offspring, or brood.

warned=forewarned; implying secrecy.

from=away from. Gr. *apo*. Ap. 104. iv. Not the same word as in *v.* 22.

to come=about to come. Quite true; for, had the nation repented, all that the prophets had foretold, both as to the sufferings and following wrath and glory, would have been fulfilled.

8 repentance=the repentance which has been demanded, and which you profess.

not. Gr. *mē*. Ap. 105. II. Not the same word as in *v.* 16.

within=among. Gr. *en*. Ap. 104. viii. 2.

father. Emphatic, by the Fig. *Hyperbaton* (Ap. 6), being put in the Greek as the first word of the sentence. See John 8. 33, 53.

of=out of. Gr. *ek*. Ap. 104. vii. Not the same word as in *v.* 7. **these stones.** Cp. 19. 40; Matt. 3. 9. **children.** Ap. 108. i. **9 now also the axe is laid**=already even the axe lies; or, and even the axe lies. Referring to *national* privileges. **unto.** Gr. *pros*. Ap. 104. xv. 3. **11 answereth and saith.** See note on Deut. 1. 41. **coats**=tunics (cp. Matt. 5. 40). One kind of garment, put by Fig. *Synecdochē* (of Species) for a garment of any kind. **none**=not, as in *v.* 8. **meat**=food, or victuals. **12 also publicans**=the tax-farmers also. **baptized.** Ap. 115. I. 1. **Master**=Teacher. Ap. 98. XIV. v. 1. **13 no**=nothing. Gr. *mēden*. **than**=beside. Gr. *para*. Ap. 104. xii. 3. **14 the soldiers**=some soldiers (no Art.) going on service. Not the Noun, but the Participle=men under arms. Josephus (*Ant.* xviii. 5, §§ 1, 2) tells us that Herod Antipas (*v.* 1) was engaged in a war with Aretas his father-in-law, a petty king in Arabia Petrea, at this very time, and his soldiers were passing from Galilee through the very country where John was proclaiming. **Do violence**=terrify with a view to extortion. Occ. only here in the N.T. **accuse any falsely.** See note on 19. 8. **15 in expectation.** See notes on 2. 25, 38; 24. 21. Mark 15. 43. **mused**=reasoned. **of**=concerning. Gr. *peri*. Ap. 104. xiii. 1. **the Christ**=the Messiah. Ap. 98. IX.

A.D. 26 16 John answered, saying unto *them* all, "I indeed °baptize you with water; but °One mightier than I cometh, the °latchet of Whose °shoes I am °not °worthy to unloose: He shall °baptize you °with the Holy Ghost and °with fire:

i 17 Whose °fan *is* [1] in His hand, and He will throughly purge His °floor, and will gather the wheat [3] into His garner;

k but the chaff He will °burn with fire unquenchable."

18 And many °other °things in his exhortation °preached he unto the people.

U 19 But °Herod the tetrarch, being reproved °by him °for Herodias his brother Philip's wife, and °for all the °evils which Herod had done,

20 °Added °yet this °above all, that he shut up John [1] in °prison.

C A 21 Now when all the people were baptized, °it came to pass, that Jesus also being baptized, and °praying, °the heaven was opened,

B 22 And °the Holy Ghost descended °in a bodily shape like a dove °upon Him, and a voice came °from heaven, which said, "Thou art °My beloved Son; [1] in Thee °I am °well pleased."

A 23 And Jesus Himself °began to be about thirty years of age,

B being (°as was supposed) the Son of °Joseph, °which was °*the son* of Heli,

24 Which was *the son* of Matthat, which was *the son* of Levi, which was *the son* of Melchi, which was *the son* of Janna, which was *the son* of Joseph,

25 Which was *the son* of Mattathias, which was *the son* of Amos, which was *the son* of Naum, which was *the son* of Esli, which was *the son* of Nagge,

26 Which was *the son* of Maath, which was *the son* of Mattathias, which was *the son* of Semei, which was *the son* of Joseph, which was *the son* of Juda,

27 Which was *the son* of Joanna, which was *the son* of Rhesa, which was *the son* of Zorobabel, which was *the son* of Salathiel, which was *the son* of Neri,

28 Which was *the son* of Melchi, which was *the son* of Addi, which was *the son* of Cosam, which was *the son* of Elmodam, which was *the son* of Er,

29 Which was *the son* of Jose, which was *the son* of Eliezer, which was *the son* of Jorim, which was *the son* of Matthat, which was *the son* of Levi,

30 Which was *the son* of Simeon, which was *the son* of Juda, which was *the son* of Joseph, which was *the son* of Jonan, which was *the son* of Eliakim,

31 Which was *the son* of Melea, which was *the son* of Menan, which was *the son* of Mattatha, which was *the son* of °Nathan, which was *the son* of David,

32 Which was *the son* of Jesse, which was *the son* of Obed, which was *the son* of °Booz, which was *the son* of Salmon, which was *the son* of °Naasson,

16 baptize. Ap. 115. I. ii and iii. b.
One = the One: i.e. He that is mightier.
latchet = thong, or lace.
shoes = sandals. A well-known proverb. Fig. *Parœmia.* Ap. 6.
not. Gr. *ou.* Ap. 105. I. **worthy** = fit.
with the Holy Ghost = with holy spirit. Gr. *pneuma hagion*: i.e. power from on high, or with spiritual gifts. See Ap. 101. II. 4.
with fire. Because this was foretold as being among the things which were about to be fulfilled, had the nation repented. "This (Acts 2. 16) is that (Joel 2. 30)." It symbolizes the judgments included in that day.
17 fan = winnowing-fan.
floor = threshing-floor.
burn = burn up. Gr. *katakaiō* = to consume entirely. Cp. Matt. 3. 12. Heb. 13. 11.
18 other = different. See Ap. 124. 2.
things = things therefore.
preached = announced the glad tidings. Gr. *euangelizō.* See Ap. 121. 4. Not the same word as in *v.* 3.
19 Herod. See Matt. 14. 3. Ap. 109.
by. Gr. *hupo.* Ap. 104. xviii. 1.
for = concerning. Gr. *peri.* Ap. 104. xiii. 1. Not the same word as in *vv.* 3.
evils. Gr. *ponēra* (pl.). Ap. 128. IV. 1.
20 Added. Gr. *prostithēmi.* A medical word in the sense of apply or administer, used by Luke thirteen times; in the rest of the N.T. five times.
yet this = this also.
above = to. Gr. *epi.* Ap. 104. ix. 2.
prison. The fortress of Machærus, on the borders of Arabia north of the Dead Sea (Josephus, *Ant.* bk. xviii. ch. v. § 2).

3. 21-38 (C, p. 1427). THE BAPTISM. WITH WATER. (*Alternation.*)

C | A | 21-. The Baptism of the Lord.
  | B | -21, 22. Genealogy. Divine.
  | *A* | 23-. The Age of the Lord.
  | *B* | -23-38. Genealogy. Human.

21 it came to pass. As in *v.* 1. The 1611 edition of the A.V. reads "and it came to pass".
praying. Note the occasions of the Lord's praying: here; 5. 16; 6. 12; 9. 18, 28; 11. 1; 22. 41-44.
the heaven. Sing. See notes on Matt. 6. 9, 10.
22 the Holy Ghost = the Spirit the Holy [Spirit]. See Ap. 101. II. 3.
in a bodily shape. Peculiar to Luke.
upon. Gr. *epi.* Ap. 104. ix. 3.
from = out of. Gr. *ek.* Ap. 104. vii.
My beloved Son = My Son, the beloved [Son].
I am well pleased = I have found delight.
23 began = when He began [His ministry?] He was about thirty years of age.
as was supposed = as reckoned by law. Gr. *nomizō* = to lay down a thing as law; to hold by custom, or usage; to reckon correctly, take for granted. See Matt. 20. 10. Luke 2. 44. Acts 7. 25; 14. 19; 16. 13, 27.
Joseph was begotten by Jacob, and was his natural son (Matt. 1. 16). He could be the legal son of Heli, therefore, only by marriage with Heli's daughter (Mary), and be reckoned so *according to law* (Gr. *nomizō*). It does not say "begat" in the case of Heli.
which = who. So throughout *vv.* 24-38.
the son of Heli. The genealogy of the ideal man begins from his father, and goes backward as far as may be. That of a king begins at the source of his dynasty and ends with himself. Cp. that of Matthew with Luke, and see Ap. 99.
31 Nathan. This is the natural line through Nathan. In Matthew 1. 6, the regal line is shown through Solomon. Thus both lines became united in Joseph; and thus the Lord being raised from the dead is the one and only heir to the throne of David. For the two lines see Ap. 99.
32 Booz = O.T. Boaz.
Naasson = O.T. Nahshon.

A. D. 26 33 Which was *the son* of °Aminadab, which was *the son* of °Aram, which was *the son* of °Esrom, which was *the son* of °Phares, which was *the son* of °Juda,

34 Which was *the son* of Jacob, which was *the son* of Isaac, which was *the son* of Abraham, which was *the son* of °Thara, which was *the son* of °Nachor,

35 Which was *the son* of °Saruch, which was *the son* of °Ragau, which was *the son* of °Phalec, which was *the son* of °Heber, which was *the son* of °Sala,

36 Which was *the son* of °Cainan, which was *the son* of Arphaxad, which was *the son* of °Sem, which was *the son* of °Noe, which was *the son* of Lamech,

37 Which was *the son* of °Mathusala, which was *the son* of Enoch, which was *the son* of Jared, which was *the son* of °Maleleel, which was *the son* of Cainan,

38 Which was *the son* of Enos, which was *the son* of Seth, which was *the son* of Adam, which was °*the son* of God.

D C n **4** And °Jesus being °full of °the Holy Ghost returned °from Jordan, and was led °by °the Spirit °into °the wilderness,

o 2 Being °forty days °tempted °of °the devil. And °in those days He did eat °nothing:

D^1 p^1 and when they were ended, He afterward hungered.

q^1 3 And the devil said °unto Him, °"If Thou be °the Son of God, command °this stone that it be made bread."

r^1 4 And [1]Jesus answered °him, saying, °"It is written, That °**man shall °not live °by bread alone, but °by every °word of °God.**"

D^2 p^2 5 And the devil, °taking Him up [1]into an high mountain, shewed °unto Him all the kingdoms of °the world °in a moment of time.

q^2 6 And the devil said [3]unto Him, "All this °power will I give Thee, and the glory of them: °for that is delivered unto me; and to whomsoever °I will I give it.

7 °If Thou therefore wilt °worship me, all shall be Thine."

r^2 8 And [1]Jesus answered and said [3]unto him, °"Get thee behind Me, Satan: for °it is written, '**Thou shalt [7]worship °the LORD thy [4]God, and Him only shalt thou serve.**'"

D^3 p^3 9 And he °brought Him °to Jerusalem, and set Him °on a °pinnacle of the °temple,

q^3 and said [3]unto Him, [3]"If Thou be [3]the Son of God, cast Thyself down °from hence:

---

33 Aminadab = O.T. Amminadab. **Aram** = O.T. Ram. **Esrom** = O.T. Hezron. **Phares** = O.T. Pharez. **Juda** = O.T. Judah. **34 Thara** = O.T. Terah. **Nachor** = O.T. Nahor. **35 Saruch** = O.T. Serug. **Ragau** = O.T. Reu. **Phalec** = O.T. Peleg. **Heber** = O.T. Eber. **Sala** = O.T. Salah. **36 Cainan.** See Ap. 99, note. **Sem** = O.T. Shem. **Noe** = O.T. Noah. **37 Mathusala** = O.T. Methuselah. **Maleleel** = O.T. Mahalaleel. **38 the son of God.** Because *created* by God; the angels are so called, for the same reason. See Ap. 23.

4. 1-14- (D, p. 1427). THE TEMPTATION.
(*Introversion and Alternations.*)

D | C | n | 1. Return from Jordan, filled with *pneuma hagion*.
o | 2-. Time. Duration.
D^1 | p^1 | -2. The Occasion. Hunger.
q^1 | 3. The First Temptation.
r^1 | 4. The Answer.
D^2 | p^2 | 5. The Occasion. Vision.
q^2 | 6, 7. The Second Temptation.
r^2 | 8. The Answer.
D^3 | p^3 | 9-. The Occasion. Station.
q^3 | -9-11. The Third Temptation.
r^3 | 12. The Answer.
C | *o* | 13. Time. Intermission.
n | 14-. Return in the power of the Spirit.

1 Jesus. Ap. 98. X.
full. Used of *pneuma hagion* only when without the Art. See Ap. 101. II. 14, and Acts 6. 3; 7. 55; 11. 24.
the Holy Ghost. No Art. Gr. *pneuma hagion*, or "power from on high". See above.
from = away from. Gr. *apo*. Ap. 104. iv.
by. Gr. *en*. Ap. 104. viii. Not the same word as in *v.* 4.
the Spirit. With Art. = the Holy Spirit Himself.
into. Gr. *eis*. Ap. 104. vi. All the texts read *en*. The Spirit not only led Him "into" the wilderness but guided Him when there.
the wilderness. Supply the *Ellipsis* (Ap. 6) thus: "the wilderness, [and was there in the wilderness,] being tempted", &c.
2 forty. See Ap. 10. Cp. Ex. 34. 28. Num. 14. 34. 1 Kings 19. 8. Read, as in R.V., "forty days, being", &c.
tempted = troubled and tried.
of = by. Gr. *hupo*. Ap. 104. xviii. 1. Not the same word as in *vv.* 14, 25.
the devil. Here named because these three temptations came before the three recorded in Matthew 4. There it is *ho peirazōn* = "he who was tempting Him". See Ap. 116.
in. Gr. *en*. Ap. 104. viii.
nothing = not (Gr. *ou*. Ap. 105. I) anything.
3 unto = to.
If Thou be, &c. Gr. *ei*, with Ind. Ap. 118. 2. a. Assuming the fact. Same word as in *v.* 9; not the same word as in *v.* 7.
the Son of God. Referring to 3. 22. Ap. 98. XV.
this stone; "these stones" in Matt. 4. 3. Repeated under different circumstances. Ap. 116.
4 him = to (Gr. *pros*. Ap. 104. xv. 3) him.
It is written = It standeth written. In Deut. 8. 3. See Ap. 107. See note on Matt. 4. 4.
man. Gr. *anthrōpos*. Ap. 123. 1.
not. Gr. *ou*. Ap. 105. 1.
by = upon. Gr. *epi*. Ap. 104. ix. 2.
word = saying. Cp. Matt. 4. 4, and see Ap. 116.
God. Gr. *Theos*. Ap. 98. I. 1.
5 taking. Gr. *anagō* = leading. Not *paralambanō* = taking with. As in Matt. 4. 5. See Ap. 116.
the world. Gr. *oikoumenē*. See Ap. 129. 3. Not *kosmos*, as on a subsequent occasion (Matt. 4. 8). See Ap. 116.
in a moment of time. Occurs only here.
6 power = authority. Ap. 172. 5. In Matthew "these things". See Ap. 116.
for that, &c. This was not repeated on the subsequent occasion (Matt. 4. 9).
I will. Gr. *thelō*. See Ap. 102. 1.
7 If Thou therefore, &c. Ap. 118. 1. b. The condition hypothetical.
worship me = worship before me. See Ap. 137. 1. See note on "before", 1. 6.
8 Get thee, &c. But the devil did not do so yet. He left of his own accord (*v.* 12). See Ap. 116. Most of the texts omit this.
it is written, &c. In Deut. 6. 13; 10. 20. Ap. 107. I. 1.
the LORD = Jehovah. Ap. 4. II and 98. i. *a.* 1. B. a.
9 brought = led. Gr. *agō*, not *paralambano*, as in Matt. 4. 5 (on a subsequent occasion). See Ap. 116.
to = unto. Gr. *eis*. Ap. 104. vi.
on. Gr. *epi*. Ap. 104. ix. 3.
pinnacle. See note on Matt. 4. 5.
temple. Gr. *hieron*. See note on Matt. 23. 16.
from hence = hence. In the subsequent temptation (Matt. 4. 6) = "down".

A. D. 26 10 For °it is written, '**He shall give His angels charge °over thee, °to keep thee:**

11 **And °in *their* hands they shall bear thee up, lest at any time thou dash thy foot °against a stone.'**"

r[3] 12 And [1]Jesus answering said unto him, "It °is said, '**Thou shalt [4]not tempt [8]the LORD thy [4]God.**'"

C o 13 And when the devil had ended °all the temptation, he °departed [1]from Him °for a season.

n 14 And [1]Jesus returned [2]in the °power of [1]the

A. D. 27 Spirit [1]into Galilee:

E F E[1] F and °there went out a °fame °of Him °through all the region round about.

15 And °He taught [2]in their °synagogues, being glorified °of all.

G H[1] K 16 And He came [9]to °Nazareth, where He had been brought up: and, °as His custom was, He went [1]into the [15]synagogue °on the sabbath day, and °stood up for °to read.

L 17 And °there was delivered unto Him the book of the prophet °Esaias. And when He had °opened the book, He °found the place where °it was written,

K 18 °"**The Spirit of [8]the LORD *is* °upon Me, °because He hath °anointed Me to °preach the gospel to the °poor; He hath °sent Me °to heal**

10 it is written. In Ps. 91. 11, 12. See Ap. 107.
over=concerning. Gr. *peri.* Ap. 104. xiii. 1.
to keep. Gr. *diaphulassō*=thoroughly protect. Occ. only here in N.T.
11 in=on. Gr. *epi.* Ap. 104. ix. 1.
against. Gr. *pros.* Ap. 104. xv. 3.
12 is said=hath been said, &c. Deut. 6. 16.
13 all=every.
departed. Of his own accord. See note on Matt. 4. 10, and Ap. 116.
for a season=until a convenient time. See Matt. 4. 11. Returning again and repeating the three temptations in a different order and under different circumstances. See Ap. 116.
14 power. Gr. *dunamis.* Ap. 172. 1.

4. -14—22. 38 (**E**, p. 1427). THE LORD'S FOUR-FOLD MINISTRY. (*Introversion.*)

E | **F** | 4. -14—5. 11. THE FIRST PERIOD. Subject: THE KINGDOM. Its Proclamation.
  | **G** | 5. 12—9. 21. THE SECOND PERIOD. Subject: THE KING. Proclaimed. His Person. Teaching and Miracles.
  | ***G*** | 9. 22—18. 43. THE THIRD PERIOD. Subject: the Rejection of THE KING.
  | ***F*** | 19. 1—22. 38. THE FOURTH PERIOD. Subject: the Rejection of THE KINGDOM. Parables, revealing the coming change of dispensation in which the Kingdom would be in ABEYANCE.

4. -14—5. 11 (**F**, above). THE FIRST PERIOD OF THE MINISTRY. PROCLAMATION OF THE KINGDOM. (*Division.*)

F | E[1] | 4. -14-30. Nazareth. Proclamation.
  | E[2] | 4. 31-44. Capernaum. Miracles.
  | E[3] | 5. 1-11. Gennesaret. Call of Peter.

4. -14-30 (E[1], above). NAZARETH. PROCLAMATION. (*Introversion.*)

E[1] | F | -14, 15. Return to Galilee.
  | G | 16-27. Proclamation.
  | *G* | 28, 29. Rejection.
  | *F* | 30. Departure from Nazareth.

14 there went out a fame, &c. In Luke (as in the other Gospels) only those events are selected which tend to illustrate the special presentation of the Lord and His ministry. Cp. the commencing events of each: Matt. 4. 13. Mark 1. 14. Luke 4. -14-30, and John 1. 19-43. For this fourfold ministry, see Ap. 119. Thus this first period commences and its subject, as stated more precisely in *vv.* 43, 44. **fame**=report. Gr. *phēmē.* Not the same word as in *v.* 37. **of**=concerning. Gr. *peri.* Ap. 104. xiii. 1. **through.** Gr. *kata.* Ap. 104. x. 1. **15 He**=He Himself. **synagogues.** Ap. 120 **of**=by. Gr. *hupo.* Ap. 104. xviii. 1.

4. 16-27 (G, above). PROCLAMATION. (*Repeated Alternation.*)

G | H[1] | 16-20-. Prophecy. Given.
  | J[1] | -20. Effect. Attention.
  | H[2] | 21. Prophecy. Fulfilment.
  | J[2] | 22. Effect. Wonder.
  | H[3] | 23-27. Prophecy. Application.

4. 16-20- (H[1], above). PROPHECY. GIVEN. (*Alternation.*)

H[1] | K | 16. Reading. Intention.
  | L | 17. Book given.
  | *K* | 18, 19. Reading. Act.
  | *L* | 20-. Book returned.

16 Nazareth=the (or, that) Nazareth thus defined. Aram. See Ap. 94. III. 3. 36. See Ap. 169. **as His custom was**=according to (Gr. *kata.* Ap. 104. x. 2) custom. **on.** Gr. *en.* Ap. 104. viii. **stood up.** Being summoned by the superintendent (*v.* 17). This incident (*vv.* 16-31) is peculiar to Luke. **to read.** Gr. *anaginōskō.* Later usage=to read aloud (as here, 2 Cor. 3. 15. Col. 4. 16. 1 Thess. 5. 27). But in the Papyri generally=to read. (See Milligan, *Selections*, pp. 39, 112.) The Lord *preached* in other synagogues, but *read* only here in Nazareth, which shows that He owned, and was owned, to be a member of this. **17 there was delivered, &c.**=there was further delivered: i. e. the prophets (the *Haphtorah*), the second lesson after another had read the Law (the *Parashah* or first lesson). This delivery was made by the *chazan*=overseer, or *Sheliach tzibbor*, angel of the congregation. See Rev. 2. 1, 8, 12, 18; 3. 1, 7, 14. **Esaias**=Isaiah. For the occ. of his name in the N.T. see Ap. 79. I. **opened**=unrolled. This word and "closed" (*v.* 20) occ. only here in the N.T. Cp. Neh. 8. 5. **found the place.** Isa. 61. 1, 2. Doubtless the *Haphtorah* or second lesson for the day. **it was written**=it stood written. See Ap. 107. I. 1 and II. 1. **18 The Spirit.** The Article is understood, in English. See *v.* 1. **upon.** Gr. *epi.* Ap. 104. ix. 3. **because**=on account of which. **anointed Me.** Hence His name "Christ". Cp. Acts 10. 38. **preach the gospel**=announce the glad tidings (see *vv.* 43, 44). See Ap. 121. 4. Note the sevenfold Prophecy (Ap. 10). **poor.** Ap. 127. 1. **sent.** Ap. 174. 1. **to heal the broken-hearted.** All the texts omit this clause.

A.D. 27 the brokenhearted, °to preach °deliverance to
the captives, and recovering of sight to the
blind, °to set at liberty them that are bruised,
19 -18 To preach °the acceptable year of [8] the
LORD."

L 20 And He °closed the book, and He gave *it*
again to °the minister, and °sat down.

J[1] And the eyes of all them that were in the
[15] synagogue °were fastened on Him.

H[2] 21 And He began °to say °unto them, "This
day is °this scripture fulfilled [2] in your ears."

J[2] 22 And all bare Him witness, and wondered
°at °the gracious words which proceeded °out
of His mouth. And they said, "Is [4] not This
°Joseph's Son?"

H[3] M[1] 23 And He said [21] unto them, "Ye will °surely
say [3] unto Me this °proverb, °'Physician, heal
Thyself:' whatsoever we have heard °done [2] in
°Capernaum, do °also here [2] in Thy country."
24 And He said, °"Verily I say unto you,
°No prophet is °accepted [2] in his own °country.

M[2] s 25 But I tell you °of a truth, many widows
were [2] in Israel [2] in the days of °Elias, when
°the heaven was shut up °three years °and six
months, °when great famine was °throughout
all the land;

t 26 °But [21] unto none of them was [25] Elias
sent, °save °unto °Sarepta, *a city* of Sidon,
[21] unto a woman *that was* a widow.

s 27 And many lepers were [2] in Israel °in the
time of °Eliseus the prophet;

t and none of them was cleansed, saving °Naaman the Syrian."

G 28 And all they [2] in the [15] synagogue, when
they heard these things, were filled with
wrath,
29 And rose up, and °thrust Him °out of the
city, and led Him unto °the brow of the hill
whereon their city was built, °that they might
°cast Him down headlong.

F 30 But He °passing °through the midst of
them °went His way,

E[2] N 31 °And came down [9] to °Capernaum, a city
of °Galilee, and °taught them [16] on the sabbath days.

---

to preach = to proclaim. See Ap. 121. I.
deliverance. Gr. *aphesis.* Cp. 3. 3.
to set at liberty . . . bruised = to send away in discharge (*en aphesei*) the oppressed, or broken. Occurs only here. This is added from Isa. 58. 6, making the quotation "compound". See Ap. 107. II. 4. This form of reading was allowed and provided for.
19 the acceptable year = the welcome year. Either the Jubilee year (Lev. 25. 8-17), or on account of the Lord's ministry commencing then.
20 closed = rolled up. Cp. *v.* 17. Because it was not yet manifest whether the King and the Kingdom would be received or rejected. See Ap. 72.
the minister = the servant (or "verger"), who put it away. Not the President, who first received it from the servant (Heb. *chazan*) and "delivered" it to the reader.
sat down: i. e. to teach.
were fastened = continued fixed. Almost peculiar to Luke. See 22. 56, and ten times in Acts. Elsewhere only in 2 Cor. 3. 7, 13.
21 to say unto them, &c. = to say to them *that* (Gr. *hoti*) This day, &c. Note the force of "that", and see note on 19. 9. Mark 14. 30 (where *hoti* is used), and contrast 22. 34, and Matt. 21. 28 (where *hoti* is absent).
unto. Gr. *pros.* Ap. 104. xv. 3.
this scripture. Not the next clause of Isa. 61. 2, which He did not read. That was then doubtful, and is now postponed.
22 at. Gr. *epi.* Ap. 104. ix. 2.
the gracious words = the words of grace. See note on 1. 30. Gen. of character, Ap. 17. 1.
out of. Gr. *ek.* Ap. 104. vii.
Joseph's Son. See note on 3. 23.

4. 23-27 (H[3], p. 1442). PROPHECY. APPLICATION. (*Division.*)

H[3] | M[1] | 23, 24. Declaration.
| M[2] | 25-27. Illustration.

23 surely = doubtless.
proverb = parable. Fig. *Parœmia.* Ap. 6.
Physician, &c. Peculiar to Luke. See Col. 4. 14.
done = being done.
Capernaum. See Ap. 169. First occ. in Luke. Silence there is no proof of ignorance.
also here = here also.
24 Verily. See note on Matt. 5. 18.
No = That no. Gr. *hoti oudeis.* See note on "say", *v.* 21.
accepted; or, welcome. As in *v.* 19.
country. Cp. Matt. 13. 57 (later).

4. 25-27 (M[2], above). ILLUSTRATION. (*Alternation.*)

M[2] | s | 25. Israel. } Widows.
| t | 26. Sidon. }
| *s* | 27-. Israel. } Lepers.
| *t* | -27. Syria. }

25 of a truth = in (as in *v.* 11) truth. **Elias** = Elijah. See 1 Kings 17. 1, 8, 9; 18. 1. James 5. 17. **the heaven.** Sing. with Art. See note on Matt. 6. 9, 10. Rev. 11. 12, 13; 13. 6. **three years and six months.** An ominous period. Cp. Dan. 12. 7. Rev. 11. 2, 3; 13. 5; and Ap. 89, 90. **and six months.** Not "a Jewish tradition", but a well-known fact. See notes on 1 Kings 17. 1 and 18. 1. **when, &c.** = and there arose. **throughout** = over. Gr. *epi.* Ap. 104. ix. 3. **26 But** = And. **save** = but. Used, not in the sense of *limitation*, but of *exclusion*, as in Gal. 2. 16. Supply the *Ellipsis* (Ap. 6) = "[but he was sent] to Sarepta". **unto.** Gr. *eis.* Ap. 104. vi. **Sarepta.** Heb. *Zarephath* (1 Kings 17. 9), now *Surafend*, in ruins. **27 in the time of.** Gr. *epi.* Ap. 104. ix. 1. **Eliseus** = Elisha. **Naaman.** See 2 Kings 5. **29 thrust** = cast. **out** = without, outside. **the brow** = an overhanging brow. Gr. *ophrus.* Occ. only here in N.T. A medical word (cp. Col. 4. 14), used of the eyebrows because of their hanging over. At Nazareth it is not beneath, but hangs *over* the town about forty feet. All the texts omit "the". **that they might, &c.** See Ap. 23. **cast Him down headlong.** Gr. *katakrēmnizō.* Occ. only here in N.T., and in the Sept. only in 2 Chron. 25. 12. **30 passing through.** Doubtless the eyes of the people were holden. See 24. 16. Cp. John 8. 59; 10. 39, 40 (cp. Pss. 18. 29; 37. 33). **through.** Gr. *dia.* Ap. 104. v. 1. **went His way** = went away. Probably never to return.

4. 31-44 [For Structure see next page].

31 And, &c. Fig. *Polysyndeton* (Ap. 6) in *vv.* 31-37. Cp. Mark 1. 21-28. **Capernaum.** The second place of His ministry. See the Structure (E[2], p. 1442). See Ap. 169. **Galilee.** See Ap. 169. **taught** = was teaching (i. e. continuously).

O u 32 And they were °astonished [22] at His °doctrine:
A.D. 27
v for His word was °with °power.
P 33 And [2] in the synagogue there was a °man, which had a °spirit °of an °unclean °devil, and cried out with a loud voice,
34 Saying, °"Let *us* alone; °what have we to do with Thee, *Thou* °Jesus of Nazareth? art Thou come °to destroy us? °I know Thee Who Thou art; °the Holy One of [4] God."
35 And [1] Jesus rebuked him, saying, °"Hold thy peace, and come °out of him." And when the [33] devil °had thrown him °in the midst, he came °out of him, and °hurt him °not.
O u 36 °And they were all °amazed, and spake °among themselves, saying, °"What a word *is* this!
v for °with °authority and [14] power He commandeth the [33] unclean [33] spirits, and they come out."
N 37 And the °fame [14] of Him went out [1] into every place of the country round about.
P w 38 °And He °arose [22] out of the [15] synagogue, and entered [1] into Simon's house. And Simon's wife's mother was °taken with a °great fever; and they °besought Him °for her.
x 39 And He °stood over her, and °rebuked the fever; and it left her: and °immediately she arose and ministered unto them.
40 Now °when the sun was setting, all they that had any sick with divers diseases brought them [21] unto him; and He °laid His hands on every one of them, and healed them.
41 And devils also came [35] out of many, °crying out, and °saying, "Thou art °Christ [3] the Son of God." And He rebuking *them* suffered them [4] not to speak: for they [34] knew that He was °Christ.
w 42 °And when it was day, He departed and went [1] into a desert place: and the people °sought Him, and came °unto Him, and °stayed Him, that He should °not depart [1] from them.
x 43 And He °said [21] unto them, "I must [18]-preach °the kingdom of God to °other cities also: °for °therefore am I sent."
44 And He °preached [2] in the synagogues of °Galilee.

E[3] y **5** °And °it came to pass, that, as the people pressed upon Him °to hear the word of °God, *He* °stood °by °the lake of Gennesaret,

4. 31-44 (E[2], p. 1442). CAPERNAUM. MIRACLES.
(*Introversion and Alternation.*)

E[2] | N | 31. The Lord's fame.
O | u | 32-. Its Effect. Astonishment.
v | -32. Reason. Power.
P | 33-35. Miracle. Demoniac.
O | *u* | 36-. Its Effect. Amazement.
v | -36. Reason. Authority.
N | 37. The Lord's teaching.
P | 38-44. Miracles. Various.

32 astonished. Cp. Matt. 7. 28.
doctrine = teaching. **with.** Gr. *en.* Ap. 104. viii.
power = authority, as in *v.* 6.
33 man. Gr. *anthrōpos.* Ap. 123. 1.
spirit = Gr. *pneuma.* Ap. 101. II. 12.
of. Gen. of Apposition. Ap. 17. 4.
unclean. Occurs thirty times, of which twenty-four apply to demons. **devil** = demon.
34 Let us alone = Ah!
what have, &c. See note on 2 Sam. 16. 10.
Jesus. Demons and Gadarenes, and His enemies could thus irreverently use this name, but His disciples with true reverence called Him "Master", or "Lord" (John 13. 13). **to destroy us.** Cp. James 2. 19.
I know, &c. Gr. *oida.* Ap. 132. I. 1. Note the Sing.
the Holy One of God. Cp. 1. 35. Ps. 16. 10.
35 Hold thy peace = Be muzzled, as in 1 Cor. 9. 9. Cp. Matt. 22. 12, 34. Mark 1. 25.
had thrown, &c. Gr. *rhiptō,* the medical word for convulsions. Occ. only here, 17. 2. Matt. 9. 36; 15. 30; 27. 5; and Acts 22. 23; 27. 19, 29.
in = into. Gr. *eis.* Ap. 104. vi.
out of = away from. Gr. *apo.* Ap. 104. iv. 1.
hurt. Gr. *blaptō.* A medical word, opposed to *ōpheleō* = to benefit. Occ. only here and Mark 16. 18.
not = in no possible manner. Gr. *mēden.* Compound of *mē.* Ap. 105. II.
36 And they were all amazed = Astonishment came upon (Gr. *epi.* Ap. 104. ix. 3) all.
amazed. Gr. *thambos* = astonishment. Peculiar to Luke.
among = to (Gr. *pros.* Ap. 104. xv. 3) one another.
What a word is this! What is this word, that?
with. Gr. *en.* Ap. 104. viii.
authority. Same word as power in *v.* 6.
37 fame = noise, or ringing in the ears. Gr. *ēchos.* Not the same word as in *v.* 14. Occurs only here, Acts 2. 3 and Heb. 12. 19. The verb *ēcheō* occurs in 21. 25 and 1 Cor. 13. 1. A medical word (see Col. 4. 14).

4. 38-44 (*P*, above). MIRACLES. VARIOUS.
(*Alternation.*)

P | w | 38. Place. Simon's house.
x | 39-41. Miracle.
w | 42. Place. Desert.
x | 43, 44. Proclamation.

38 And He arose, &c. Cp. Matt. 8. 14-17. Mark 1. 29-34.
arose out of = arose [and went] out of.
taken = pressed, or oppressed. Cp. Acts 28. 8. Almost peculiar to Luke, who uses the word nine times; only three times elsewhere, Matt. 24. 4. 2 Cor. 5. 14. Phil. 1. 23 (being in a strait). **great.** Peculiar to Luke, in this connection. **besought.** Aorist Tense; implying a single act. Not the Imperfect, as generally used. **for** = concerning. Gr. *peri.* Ap. 104. xiii. 1. **39 stood over her.** A medical reference. Peculiar to Luke. **rebuked.** Peculiar to Luke. **immediately.** Gr. *parachrēma.* See 1. 64. **40 when the sun, &c.** They waited for the end of the Sabbath. **laid His hands, &c.** Peculiar to Luke. **41 crying out** = screaming (inarticulately). **saying, Thou** = saying that Thou. See note on *v.* 34. **Christ.** All the texts omit this. **Christ** = the Messiah. Ap. 98. IX. **42 And when, &c.** Fig. *Polysyndeton* in *vv.* 42-44. Cp. Mark 1. 35-39. **sought Him.** All the texts read "were seeking after Him". **unto** = up to. Gr. *heōs.* **stayed Him** = held Him fast. Gr. *katechō.* See note on 2 Thess. 2. 6. **not.** Gr. *mē.* Ap. 105. II. **43 said . . . I, &c.** said . . that I must. See note on *vv.* 21, 24. **the kingdom of God.** See Ap. 114. **other** = different. See Ap. 124. 2. **for** = because. This is the subject of the First Period of His ministry. See 4. -14, and Ap. 119. **therefore** = for (Gr. *eis.* Ap. 104. vi) this. **44 preached** = was proclaiming, as in *vv.* -18, 19. Not the same word as in *v.* 43. **Galilee.** See Ap. 169. A Trm WH Rm. read Judæa.

5. 1-11 [For Structure see next page].

1 And, &c. *Vv.* 1-11. **it came to pass.** See 1. 8. **to hear** = and heard. So all the texts. **God.** Ap. 98. I. 1. **He.** Emphatic, to distinguish Him from the crowds. **stood** = was standing. **by** = beside. Gr. *para.* Ap. 104. xii. 3. **the lake, &c.** See Ap. 169. Matthew, Mark, and John call it "sea".

z 2 And °saw °two °ships °standing by the
A.D. 27 lake: but °the fishermen were gone °out of
them, and were °washing *their* °nets.
3 And He entered °into one of the [2]ships,
which was Simon's, and °prayed him that he
would °thrust out a little °from the °land.
And He °sat down, and °taught the people °out
of the [2]ship.

a 4 Now °when He had left speaking, He said
°unto Simon, °"Launch out [3]into the deep,
and °let down your [2]nets °for a °draught."
5 And Simon answering said °unto Him,
°"Master, we have toiled °all the night, and
have taken nothing: nevertheless °at Thy
word I will [4]let down the [2]net."
6 And when they had this done, they inclosed
a great °multitude of fishes: and their [2]net
°brake.
7 And they beckoned [5]unto *their* partners,
which were °in the °other [2]ship, that they
should come and help them. And they came,
and filled both the [2]ships, so that they °began
to sink.

a 8 When Simon Peter [2]saw *it,* he fell down at
°Jesus' knees, saying, "Depart [3]from me; for
°I am °a sinful man, O °Lord."
9 For °he was astonished, and all that were
°with him, [5]at the [4]draught of the fishes which
they had taken:
10 And so *was* °also James, and John, the
sons of °Zebedee, which were partners with
Simon. And [8]Jesus said [4]unto Simon, "Fear
°not; [3]from henceforth thou shalt °catch
°men."

z 11 And when they had brought their ships
°to [3]land,

y they °forsook all, and followed Him.

G Q[1] S 12 And [1]it came to pass, °when He was [7]in
°a certain °city,

T U °behold a [8]man °full of leprosy: who [2]seeing
[8]Jesus fell °on *his* face, and °besought Him,
saying, °"Lord, °if Thou °wilt, Thou canst
make me °clean."
13 And He put forth *His* hand, and °touched
him, saying, "I [12]will: °be thou clean." And
immediately the leprosy departed [3]from him.

5. 1-11 (E[3], p. 1442). GENNESARET.
(*Introversion.*)

E[3] | y | 1. People. "Pressed upon Him."
| z | 2, 3. Ships. Standing.
| a | 4-7. Miracle.
| *a* | 8-10. Effects.
| *z* | 11-. Ships. Landing.
| *y* | -11. Disciples. "Followed Him."

2 saw. Ap. 133. I. 1. Not the same word as in *v.* 27.
two ships. At that time there were about 4,000 on the lake. **ships** = boats.
standing: i. e. at anchor. Eng. idiom is "lying".
the fishermen. This call was not that of Mark 1. 16-20. When the Lord said "Let us go", &c. (Mark 1. 38), they perhaps did not go with Him, but returned to their ships. But from this second call they never left Him. See *v.* 11, below.
out of = away from. Gr. *apo.* Ap. 104. iv, as in *v.* 36. Not the same word as in *vv.* 3, 17.
washing. Gr. *apoplunō.* Ap. 136. vi. At the first call they were casting their net (*amphiblēstron*). Here they were washing their nets.
nets. Gr. pl. of *diktuon.* Cp. John 21. 6-11.
3 into. Gr. *eis.* Ap. 104. vi. Not the same word as in *v.* 16.
prayed = asked. See Ap. 134. 3. Not the same word as in *v.* 16. **thrust out** = push off. A nautical word.
from = away from. **land.** Gr. *gē.* Ap. 129. 4.
sat down. The attitude for teaching. See note on 4. 20.
taught = was teaching. Imperf. Tense.
out of. Gr. *ek.* Ap. 104. vii. Not the same as in *vv.* 2, 36.
4 when He had left speaking. The Aorist Tense implies the immediate succession of the events.
unto. Gr. *pros.* Ap. 104. xv. 3. The same word as in *v.* 10.
Launch out. Same as "thrust out" in *v.* 3. Addressed to one (Peter).
let down = let ye down: addressed to all. Occ. seven times; five of these by Luke, here, *v.* 5; Acts 9. 25; 27. 17, 30. The other two are Mark 2. 4. 2 Cor. 11. 33.
for = with a view to. Gr. *eis.* Ap. 104. vi. Not the same word as in *v.* 14-. Same as in *v.* -14.
draught = haul. Used of what is drawn, from Anglo-Saxon *drag-an.* **5 unto** = to.
Master. Gr. *Epistatēs.* A word peculiar to Luke, implying knowledge and greater authority than *Rabbi,* or Teacher. Occ. seven times (5. 5; 8. 24, 24, 45; 9. 33, 49; 17. 13, and nowhere else). See Ap. 98. XIV. iv.
all = all through. Gr. *dia.* Ap. 104. v. 1.
at = upon, or [relying] upon. Gr. *epi.* Ap. 104. ix. 2. As in *v.* 9. Not with the same case as in *v.* 27.
6 multitude = shoal.
brake = were beginning to break. Imperf. Tense. Occ. 8. 29 and Acts 14. 14. Elsewhere only in Matt. 26. 65. Mark 14. 63 ("rent").

7 in. Gr. *en.* Ap. 104. viii. Not the same as in *vv.* 18, 19. **other** = different = another of two. See Ap. 124. 2. **began to sink** = are now sinking. **8 Jesus.** Ap. 98. X. **I am a sinful man.** True conviction has regard to what one *is,* not to what one *has done.* Cp. Manoah (Judg. 13. 22), Israel (Ex. 20. 19), men of Beth-shemesh (1 Sam. 6. 20), David (2 Sam. 12. 13), Job (Job 40. 4; 42. 2-6), Isaiah (Isa. 6. 5). **a sinful man** = a man (Ap. 123. 2) a sinner. Emphasizing the individual. **Lord.** Not "Jesus", as in 4. 34. Ap. 98. VI. i. *a.* 3 A. **9 he was astonished** = astonishment laid hold of him. **with** = united with. Gr. *sun.* Ap. 104. xvi. **10 also James** = James also. **Zebedee.** Aram. Ap. 94. III. 3. **not.** Gr. *mē.* Ap. 105. II. **catch** = be capturing (alive), used of taking captives. Gr. *zōgreō.* Occ. only here, and 2 Tim. 2. 26. **men.** Ap. 123. 1. **11 to.** Gr. *epi.* Ap. 104. ix. 3. **forsook all** = let go all. Not the same word as in *v.* 28. Cp. 18. 28-30. Mark 10. 29, 30. See note on *v.* 2.

5. 12—9. 20 [For Structure see next page].

12 when He was = in (Gr. *en,* as in *v.* 7) His being. **a certain city** = one of the cities. Prob. one in which "most of His mighty works were done", viz. Chorazin or Bethsaida. When named together these are always in this order. By comparing 5. 18 and Mark 1. 45 with 5. 29, Matt. 9. 10 and Mark 2. 15, it seems clear that that certain city was not Capernaum. The attempts to "touch" the Lord were all in that city or neighbourhood (6. 19. Matt. 9. 20; 14. 36. Mark 3. 10; 6. 56. Cp. 5. 15). Hence this city was probably Chorazin. **behold.** Fig. *Asterismos.* Ap. 6, and 133. I. 2. **full of leprosy.** "Full", in this connection, is a medical word. Cp. Col. 4. 14. See note on Ex. 4. 6. **on.** Gr. *epi.* Ap. 104. ix. 3. Not the same case as in *v.* 24. **besought.** Gr. *deomai.* Ap. 134. I. 5. **Lord.** Now being proclaimed as to His person: the King, Lord of all and yet (*v.* 24) the Son of man. Cp. Matt. 8. 2, 6, 8, 20. **if.** Denoting a contingent probability. See Ap. 118. I. b. **wilt.** Gr. *thelō.* Ap. 102. 1. **clean.** The sick are healed: lepers are cleansed. **13 touched.** See note on "city", *v.* 12. **be thou clean** = be thou made clean (Passive).

A.D. 27 **14 And He °charged him to tell °no man:
°but °"go, and shew thyself to the priest, and
offer °for thy [12]cleansing, according as °Moses
commanded, [4]for a testimony unto them."
15 But so much the more went there a °fame
abroad °of Him: and great multitudes °came
together to hear, and to be healed °by Him
°of their infirmities.**

V **16 And He °withdrew himself °into the wilderness, and °prayed.**

S **17 And [1]it came to pass °on °a certain day,**
T V **as He was teaching, °that there were Pharisees and °doctors of the law sitting by, which
were come [3]out of every town of °Galilee,
and °Judæa, and °Jerusalem: and the
power of °the LORD was *present* °to heal
°them.**

U W b **18 And, [12]behold, [8]men °brought °in a °bed
a [10]man which was °taken with a palsy: and
they sought *means* to bring him in, and to
°lay *him* before Him.
19 And when they could [10]not find °by what
way they might bring him in °because of the
multitude, they went °upon the housetop, and
let him down °through the tiling [9]with *his*
couch [3]into the midst before [8]Jesus.**

c **20 And when He [2]saw °their faith, He said
unto him, [10]"Man, thy sins °are forgiven thee."**

X **21 And the scribes and the Pharisees began
to reason, saying, "Who is This Which speaketh blasphemies? Who °can forgive sins, but
°God alone?"**

W c **22 But when Jesus °perceived their °thoughts,
He °answering said [4]unto them, "What reason ye [7]in your hearts?
23 Whether is easier, to say, 'Thy sins °be
forgiven °thee'; or to say, 'Rise up and walk?'
24 But °that ye may °know that °the Son
of man hath °power °upon °earth to forgive
sins," (He said [5]unto the sick of the palsy,) "I
say [5]unto thee, 'Arise, and take up thy couch,
and go [3]into thine house.'"**

b **25 And °immediately he rose up before them,
and took up that °whereon he lay, and departed
°to his own house, glorifying [21]God.**

X **26 And °they were all °amazed, and they**

5. 12—9. 21 (**G**, p. 1427). THE SECOND PERIOD OF THE LORD'S MINISTRY. PROCLAMATION OF THE KING. (*Repeated Alternation.*)

G | Q¹ | 5. 12–26. Tour. Miracles.
| R¹ | 5. 27–39. Disciples. Call of Levi.
| Q² | 6. 1–11. Tour. Sabbaths.
| R² | 6. 12–16. Disciples. Call of the Twelve.
| Q³ | 6. 17—8. 56. Tour. Healing and Teaching.
| R³ | 9. 1–10–. Disciples. Mission of the Twelve, and return.
| Q⁴ | 9. –10–17. Tour. Miracle.
| R⁴ | 9. 18–21. Disciples. Confession of Messiah.

5. 12-26 (Q¹, above). TOUR. MIRACLES. (*Extended Alternation and Introversion*).

Q¹ | S | 12–. A certain city.
T | U | –12–15. Miracle. Leper. "Lord".
V | 16. Prayer.
S | 17–. A certain day.
T | *V* | –17. Teaching.
U | 18–26. Miracle. Paralytic. "Son of man".

14 charged. A military word. Also used of a physician, "prescribe".
no man=no one. Compound of *mē*. Ap. 105. II; i. e. no one whom he might happen to meet.
but=but [said].
go . . . shew, &c. See Lev. 14. 1–32.
for=concerning. Gr. *peri*. Ap. 104. xiii. 1.
Moses. See note on Matt. 8. 4. The first of ten occ. in Luke; 2. 22; 5. 14; 9. 30, 33; 16. 29, 31; 20. 28, 37; 24. 27, 44.
15 fame=report. Gr. *logos*.
of=concerning. Gr. *peri*. Ap. 104. xiii. 1.
came together=kept coming together.
by. Gr. *hupo*. Ap. 104. xviii. 1. All the texts omit "by Him".
of=from. Gr. *apo*. Ap. 104. iv.
16 withdrew=continued withdrawn. Peculiar to Luke here, and 9. 10.
into=in. Gr. *en*. Ap. 104. viii.
prayed. Gr. *proseuchomai*. Ap. 134. I. 2. The second recorded occasion in Luke; see 3. 21.
17 on=in. Gr. *en*. Ap. 104. viii. See the Structures "S" and "*S*".
a certain day=in one of the days.
that=and.
doctors, &c.=teachers of the law. Gr. *nomodidaskalos*. Occ. only here, Acts 5. 34, and 1 Tim. 1. 7.
Galilee, . . . Judæa, . . . Jerusalem. Palestine was divided into the three districts (mountain, sea-shore, and valley). Cp. Acts 1. 8; 10. 39
the LORD=Jehovah. Ap. 98. VI. i. *a*. 1. B. b.
to=for, or with a view to. Gr. *eis*. Ap. 104. vi.
them. T Trm. A WH R. read "him" instead of "them". If so, then the clause reads, "the power of Jehovah was [present] for Him to heal", but miracles were few "because of their unbelief", Matt. 13. 58.

5. 18-26 (*U*, above). MIRACLE. THE PARALYTIC. (*Alternation and Introversion.*)

U | W | b | 18, 19. The Paralytic. Brought.
c | 20. Forgiveness. Declared.
X | 21. Effect. Enemies Reasoning.
W | *c* | 22–24. Forgiveness. Bestowed.
b | 25. The Paralytic. Healed.
X | 26. Effect. People Glorifying.

18 brought=carrying. **in**=upon. Gr. *epi*. Ap. 104. viii. **bed**=couch. Gr. *klinē*; not the poor man's bed, *krabbaton*. John 5. 10. **taken with a palsy**=paralysed. Gr. *paraluomai*. Not the same word as in 4. 38. Luke always uses the Verb, not the Adj. (contrast Matt. 4. 24; 8. 6. Mark 2. 3–10). Cp. Acts 8. 7. Strictly medical usage. Cp. Col. 4. 14. **lay**=place. **19 by.** Gr. *dia*. All the texts omit. **because**=on account of. Gr. *dia*. Ap. 104. v. 2. **upon.** Gr. *epi*. Ap. 104. ix. 3. **through.** Gr. *dia*. Ap. 104. v. 1. **20 their faith.** Why exclude the man himself, as is generally done? **are**=have been. **21 can forgive**=is able to forgive. **God.** Ap. 98. I. 1. **22 perceived**=well knowing. Gr. *epiginōskō*. Ap. 132. I. iii. **thoughts**=reasonings. **answering said.** See note on Deut. 1. 41, and Ap. 122. 3. **23 be**=have been. **thee**=to thee. **24 that**=in order that. **know.** Gr. *oida*. Ap. 132. I. 1. **the Son of man.** Ap. 98. XVI and 99. First occ. in Luke; cp. twenty-sixth, 24. 7. **power**=authority. Ap. 172. 5. **upon.** Gr. *epi*. Ap. 104. ix. 1. **earth.** Gr. *gē*. Ap. 129. 4. **25 immediately.** Gr. *parachrēma*. See 1. 64; 4. 39. Outside Luke and Acts it occurs only in Matt. 21. 19, 20. **to**=into, as in *v*. 24, above. **26 they . . . amazed**=amazement seized them all.

A. D. 27 glorified [21] God, and were °filled with fear, °saying, "We have °seen °strange things to day."

R[1] Y 27 And °after these things He went forth, and °saw a °publican, named °Levi, sitting °at °the receipt of custom: and He said [5] unto him, "Follow Me."

Z 28 And he °left all, rose up, and followed Him.

Y 29 And [27] Levi made Him a great °feast [7] in his own house: and there was a great company of [27] publicans and of °others that sat down °with them.

Z A 30 But °their scribes and Pharisees murmured °against His disciples, saying, "Why do ye eat and drink [29] with °publicans and sinners?"

B 31 And [8] Jesus answering said [4] unto them, "They that are °whole need °not a physician; but they that °are °sick.
32 °I came [31] not to call °the righteous, but sinners °to °repentance."

A 33 And they said [4] unto Him, "Why do the disciples of John fast °often, and °make °prayers, and likewise *the disciples* of the Pharisees; but Thine °eat and drink?"

B C[1] 34 And He said [4] unto them, °"Can ye make the °children of the bridechamber fast, °while the bridegroom is [29] with them?
35 But °the days will come, °when the bridegroom °shall be taken away [3] from them, and °then shall they fast [7] in those days."

C[2] 36 And He spake °also a parable [4] unto them; °"No man putteth a piece of a °new garment [19] upon an old; °if otherwise, then °both the °new maketh a rent, and the piece that was *taken* [2] out of the °new °agreeth [31] not with the old.

C[3] 37 And [36] no man putteth °new wine [3] into old °bottles; else the °new wine will burst the °bottles, and °be spilled, and the °bottles shall perish.
38 But [37] new wine must be put [3] into [37] new [37] bottles; and both are preserved.

C[4] 39 No man also having drunk old *wine* straightway desireth [37] new: for he saith, 'The old is °better.'"

filled with = filled of. Cp. 1. 15; 4. 28; 6. 11. Matt. 22. 10 (furnished). Acts 5. 17, &c.
saying = saying that. See 4. 21, 24, 41; 23. 43, &c.
seen. Ap. 133. I. 1.
strange things = paradoxes, i.e. contrary to what is generally seen.

5. 27-39 (R[1], p. 1446). DISCIPLES. CALL OF LEVI. (*Alternation.*)

R[1] | Y | 27. Levi. His call.
  Z | 28. His obedience.
 Y | 29. Levi. His feast.
  Z | 30-39. His instruction.

27 after. Gr. *meta.* Ap. 104. xi. 2.
saw = viewed with attention. Gr. *theaomai.* Ap. 133. I. 12.
publican = toll-collector, or tax-gatherer. See on 3. 12.
Levi. There can be no doubt about Levi and Matthew being different names for the same person (Matt. 9. 9. Mark 2. 14). For similar changes, at epochs in life, cp. Simon and Peter, Saul and Paul. Matthew is an abbreviation of *Mattathias* = Gift of God, and he is so called after this. "Sitting" shows he was a custom-house officer.
at. Gr. *epi.* Ap. 104. ix. 3.
the receipt of custom = the toll office.
28 left = left behind. Not the same word as "forsook" in *v.* 11.
29 feast = reception (banquet). Gr. *dochē.* Occ. only here and 14. 13. **others.** See Ap. 124. 1.
with = in company with. Gr. *meta.* Ap. 104. xi. 1.

5. 30-39 (*Z*, above). HIS INSTRUCTION. (*Alternation.*)

Z | A | 30. Scribes and Pharisees. Question.
  B | 31, 32. The Lord's Answer.
 A | 33. Scribes and Pharisees. Question.
  B | 34-39. The Lord's Answer.

30 their scribes and Pharisees = the scribes and Pharisees among them: "their" referring to Galilean scribes, as distinguished from those of Jerusalem (Matt. 15. 1). Note the same distinction as to synagogues in Matt. 4. 23; 9. 35, &c.
against. Gr. *pros.* Ap. 104. xv. 3.
publicans = the publicans. See *v.* 27.
31 whole = in health (Matt. and Mark have "strong"). This (*hugiainō*) is the medical word (Col. 4. 14), as in 7. 10; 15. 27. 3 John 2. Paul uses it in a moral sense (1 Tim. 1. 10; 6. 3. 2 Tim. 1. 13; 4. 3. Tit. 1. 9, 13; 2. 1, 2).
not. Gr. *ou.* Ap. 105. 1.
are = have themselves.
sick = sickly, in an evil condition. Gr. *kakōs.* Adv. of *kakos.* Ap. 128. III. 2.
32 I came = I have come.
the righteous = righteous ones.
to = unto, with a view to. Gr. *eis.* Ap. 104. vi. **repentance.** Ap. 111. II. 1. **33 often.** Gr. *pukna.* Occ. only here and in Acts 24. 26. 1 Tim. 5. 23. **make prayers.** Note this as distinguished from *praying.* **prayers** = petitions, or supplications. Not used in the other Gospels. See Ap. 134. II. 3. **eat and drink.** Like ordinary people, without making it a part of their religion.

5. 34-39 (*B*, above). THE LORD'S ANSWER. (*Division.*)

B | C[1] | 34, 35. The Sons of the Bridechamber.
 | C[2] | 36. Old and New Garments.
 | C[3] | 37, 38. Old and New Wine-skins.
 | C[4] | 39. Old and New Wine.

34 Can ye make = Ye surely cannot (Gr. *mē.* Ap. 105. II), can ye? **children, &c.** = sons (Ap. 108. iii). Heb. idiom for the bridal party. **while** = in (Gr. *en.* Ap. 104. viii) the time when. **35 the days will come** = there will come days [for those]. **when.** All the texts read "and when", following up the Fig. *Aposiopēsis* (Ap. 6), as though the time for revealing the fact of His crucifixion had not yet come. **shall be taken away.** Gr. *apairō.* Occ. only here, and the parallels (Matt. 9. 15. Mark 2. 20) implying a violent death; as "lifted up" in John 3. 14. **then shall they fast.** As they did (Acts 13. 2, 3). **36 also a parable** = a parable also. **No man, &c.** = that no one (Gr. *oudeis.* Ap. 105. I), [having rent a piece] from a new garment, putteth it upon an old. **new.** Gr. *kainos.* See note on Matt. 9. 17. **if.** Ap. 118. 2. a. **both, &c.** = he will both rend the new, and the new will not agree with the old. **agreeth** = harmonizeth. Gr. *sumphōneō.* **37 new** = fresh made. Gr. *neos.* See note on Matt. 9. 17. **bottles** = wine-skins. **be spilled** = it will be poured out. **39 better** = good. So all the texts.

Q² D¹ A. D. 27 **6** And °it came to pass °on °the second
sabbath after the first, that He °went
°through the °corn fields; and His disciples
plucked the ears of corn, and °did eat, rubbing
them in *their* hands.
2 And certain of the Pharisees said unto
them, "Why do ye that which is °not lawful
to do [1]on the sabbath days?"
3 And °Jesus °answering °them said, °"Have
ye °not read so much as this, °what David
did, when himself was an hungred, and they
which were °with him;
4 How he went °into the house of God, and
°did take and eat the shewbread, and gave
°also to them that were [3]with him; which it is
[2]not lawful to eat but for the priests alone?"
5 And he said unto them, That °the Son of
man is Lord °also of the sabbath.

D² E d 6 And [1]it came to pass °also [1]on another
sabbath, that He entered [4]into the synagogue
and taught: and there was a °man °whose
right hand was °withered.

e 7 And the scribes and Pharisees °watched
Him, °whether He would °heal [1]on the sabbath day;

f °that they might °find an accusation against
Him.

E d 8 But He °knew their °thoughts, and said to
the [6]man which had the withered hand, "Rise
up, and stand forth °in the midst." And he
arose and stood forth.
9 Then said [3]Jesus °unto them, °"I will ask
you one thing; Is it lawful on the sabbath
days to do good, or to do evil? to save °life,
or to destroy *it*?"
10 And °looking round about upon them all,
He said unto the [6]man, "Stretch forth thy
hand." And he did so: and his hand was
restored °whole as the °other.

e 11 And they were °filled with °madness;

f and °communed one °with another what they
might do to [3]Jesus.

R² F 12 And [1]it came to pass °in those days, that
He went out [4]into °a mountain °to pray, and
°continued all night

G in °prayer to God.

F 13 And when it °was day, He called *unto*
Him His disciples: and °of them He chose
twelve, whom °also He named apostles;

G 14 Simon, (whom He °also named Peter,) and
Andrew his brother, James and John, Philip
and °Bartholomew,

6. 1-11 (Q², p. 1446). TOUR. SABBATHS. (*Division*.)

Q² | D¹ | 1-5. One Sabbath. The Corn-fields.
| D² | 6-11. Another Sabbath. The Synagogue.

1 it came to pass. A Hebraism.
on. Gr. *en.* Ap. 104. viii. Not the same word as in *vv.* 20, 39, 49.
the second sabbath after the first. All this represents only one word in the Greek (*deuteroprōtos*), i.e. the second-first. Occ. only here in the N.T. The first and second sabbaths can occur only in the week of the three great Feasts. The first day of these feasts is a Sabbath "high day" (Heb. *yōm tōv*), and is the "first" or great sabbath, whatever day of the week it falls on (see Lev. 23. 7, 24, 35), the weekly sabbath then becomes the "*second*".

This "second sabbath" was therefore the ordinary *weekly sabbath*, as is clear from Matt. 12. 1. Not seeing this the current Greek texts solve the difficulty by omitting the word altogether! L Trm. WH R.

went=was going. **through.** Gr. *dia.* Ap. 104. v. 1. **corn fields.** See Matt. 12. 1. **did eat**=were eating.
2 not. Gr. *ou.* Ap. 105. I. Not the same word as in *vv.* 29, 30, 37, 39, 49.
3 Jesus. Ap. 98. X.
answering . . . said. See note on Deut. 1. 41.
them=to (Gr. *pros.* Ap. 104. xv. 3) them.
Have ye not read. See Ap. 143.
not=not so much as. Gr. *ouden*, compound of *ou.* Ap. 105. I.
what David did. See notes on Matt. 12. 4.
with=in company with. Gr. *meta.* Ap. 104. xi. 1.
4 into. Gr. *eis.* Ap. 104. vi.
did take. Peculiar to Luke.
also to them=to them also.
5 the Son of man. See Ap. 98. XVI.
also of the sabbath=of the sabbath also.

6. 6-11 (D², above). ANOTHER SABBATH. THE SYNAGOGUE. (*Repeated and Extended Alternation.*)

D² | E | d | 6. Withered hand.
| | e | 7-. Enemies. Watching.
| | f | -7. Purposed Accusation.
| *E* | *d* | 8-10. Withered hand. Healed.
| | *e* | 11-. Enemies. Madness.
| | *f* | -11. Purposed Machination.

6 also on another sabbath=on another sabbath also. Cp. Matt. 12. 9-14. Mark 3. 1-6.
man. Gr. *anthrōpos.* Ap. 123. 1.
whose right hand=his hand, the right [one].
withered. See on Mark 3. 1.
7 watched=kept watching. Imperf. Tense. Cp. Mark 3. 2.
whether=if, &c. Assuming the possibility of the condition. Ap. 118. 2. a. **heal.** See *v.* 18.
that=in order that. **find.** Peculiar to Luke.
8 knew=all along knew. Imperf. Tense. Gr. *oida.* Ap. 132. I. 1. Not the same word as in *v.* 44.
thoughts=reasonings (cp. Matt. 15. 19. James 2. 4).
in. Gr. *eis.* Ap. 104. viii. Not the same word as in *vv.* 12, 17, 23, 41, 42.

9 unto. Gr. *pros.* Ap. 104. xv. 3. Not the same word as in *v.* 35. **I will ask.** All the texts read, "I ask", i.e. "I further ask". **life**=a soul. See Ap. 110. III. 1. **10 looking round, &c.** Mark's Divine supplement is "with anger", &c. **whole**=healed. **other.** See Ap. 124. 1. **11 filled with**=filled of. See note on 5. 26. **madness**=senseless rage. **communed**=began to discuss. **with**=[saying] one to. Gr. *pros.* Ap. 104. xv. 3.

6. 12-16 (R², p. 1446). DISCIPLES. CALL OF THE TWELVE. (*Alternation.*)

R² | F | 12-. Time. Night.
| G | -12. Act. Prayer.
| *F* | 13. Time. Days.
| *G* | 14-16. Act. Calling of the Twelve.

12 in. Gr. *en.* Ap. 104. viii. Not the same word as in *vv.* 8, 17, -23. **a**=the. **to pray.** The third of seven such occasions in Luke. See note on 3. 21. **continued all night.** Peculiar to Luke. A medical word. Cp. Matt. 14. 23. **prayer to God.** Gr. prayer of God. Gen. of Relation. Ap. 17. 5. **13 was**=became. **of**=from. Gr. *apo.* Ap. 104. iv. Not the same word as in *vv.* 34, 44, 45. **also He named apostles**=He named apostles also. Peculiar to Luke. **14 also named**=named also. See Ap. 141. **Bartholomew.** Ap. 94. III. 3.

A.D. 27 15 °Matthew and °Thomas, James the *son* of
°Alphæus, and Simon called Zelotes,
16 And Judas *the brother* of James, and Judas Iscariot, which °also was the traitor.
Q³ H K¹ 17 And He came down ³with them, and °stood
°in °the plain, and °the company of His disciples, and a great multitude of people °out of
all Judæa and Jerusalem, and from the sea
coast of Tyre and Sidon, which came to hear
Him, and to be °healed ¹³of their diseases;
18 And they that were °vexed °with unclean
°spirits: and they were °healed.
19 And the whole multitude °sought to touch
Him: for there °went °virtue °out of Him,
and ¹⁷healed *them* all.
L M g 20 °And He °lifted up His eyes °on His disciples, and said, °"Blessed *be ye* poor: for yours
is °the kingdom of God.
h 21 ²⁰Blessed *are ye* that hunger °now: for ye
shall be filled.
i Blessed *are ye* that weep °now: for ye shall ⁶laugh.
j 22 ²⁰Blessed are ye, when ⁶men shall hate
you, and when they shall °separate you *from
their company,* and shall reproach *you,* and
°cast out your name as °evil, °for °the Son of
man's sake.
23 Rejoice ye ¹²in that day, and leap for joy:
for, °behold, your reward *is* great ¹²in °hea-
ven: for °in the like manner did their fathers
°unto the prophets.
g 24 °But °woe unto you that are rich! for ye
°have received your °consolation.
h 25 ²⁴Woe unto you that °are full! for ye
shall hunger.
i ²⁴Woe unto you that laugh now! for ye shall
mourn and weep.
j 26 ²⁴Woe unto you, when all ⁶men shall
speak well of you! for so did ²³their fathers to
°the false prophets.
N O R T k 27 But I say unto you which hear, °Love
your enemies,
l do °good to them which hate you,

15 Matthew and Thomas . . . Alphæus. All Aramaic. Ap. 94. III. 3.
16 also was the traitor = became even a traitor.

6. 17–8. 56 (Q³, p. 1446). TOUR. HEALING AND TEACHING. (*Introversions.*)

Q³ | H | K¹ | 6. 17–19. Works. Healing.
L | 6. 20–49. Teaching.
K² | 7. 1–17. Works. Miracles.
J | 7. 18–35. Concerning John.
J | 7. 36–47. Concerning the Pharisees.
H | K³ | 7. 48–50. Work. Forgiveness.
L | 8. 1–21. Teaching.
K⁴ | 8. 22–56. Works. Miracles.

17 stood = stopped. **in** = on. Gr. *epi.* Ap. 104. ix. 1. **the plain** = a level [spot]. **the company** = a crowd. **out of** = away from. Gr. *apo.* Ap. 104. iv. **healed.** Gr. *iaomai.* Cp. 5. 17. **18 vexed** = beset. **with.** Gr. *hupo.* Ap. 104. xviii. 1, but the Texts read *apo.* **spirits.** Gr. *pneuma.* See Ap. 101. xi. **healed.** Gr. *therapeuō.* Cp. 5. 15.
19 sought . . went, &c. Both are the Imperf. Tense = all the while were seeking to touch Him, for virtue was going out, &c. **virtue** = power. Ap. 172. 1. **out of** = from (beside). Gr. *para.* Ap. 104. xii. 1.

6. 20–49 (L, above). TEACHING. (*Introversion and Alternation.*)

L | M | 20–26. Blessing and Woe.
N | O | 27–38. Discipleship.
P | 39. Parable.
N | *O* | 40. Discipleship.
P | 41–45. Parable.
M | 46–49. Blessing and Woe. (Stability and Instability.)

6. 20–26 (M, above). BLESSING AND WOE. (*Extended Alternation.*)

M | g | 20. Poor.
h | 21–. Hungry.
i | –21. Weepers.
j | 22, 23. Hated, &c.
} Blessings.
g | 24. Rich.
h | 25–. Full.
i | –25. Laughers.
j | 26. Praised.
} Woes.

20 And, &c. Not "Luke's version" of "the Sermon on the Mount", but a repetition in a different form of certain parts of it on a subsequent occasion. Why create a "discrepancy" by supposing that our Lord never repeated any part of His discourses? Cp. Isa. 28. 9–13. **lifted up His eyes.** Peculiar to Luke. **on** = unto. Gr. *eis.* Ap. 104. vi. **Blessed, &c.** = Happy. See note on Matt. 5. 3. **the kingdom of God.** See Ap. 114. **21 now.** In contrast with the future. In Divine reckoning the best always comes last. Peculiar to Luke. **22 separate you, &c.** = cut you off. **cast out, &c.** Cp. Deut. 22. 19. **evil.** Gr. *ponēros.* Ap. 128. III. 1. **for** = on account of. Gr. *heneka.* **the Son of man.** See Ap. 98. XVI. **23 behold.** Fig. *Asterismos.* Ap. 6. **heaven** = the heavens. See notes on Matt. 6. 9, 10. **in the like manner** = according to (Gr. *kata.* Ap. 104. x. 2) the same things. **unto** = to. **24 But.** Gr. *plēn.* Emphatic. **woe.** This is not a different and discrepant version of the Sermon on the Mount, but a varied repetition of parts of it. **have received** = are receiving. Gr. *apechō.* The common word in the Papyri for a receipt. See note on Matt. 6. 2. **consolation.** Gr. *paraklēsis* = comfort. Akin to "Comforter". John 14. 16, 26, &c. Cp. Luke 2. 25. **25 are full** = have been filled. **26 the false prophets.** Cp. Jer. 5. 31. 1 Kings 18. 19, 22; 22. 11. Isa. 30. 10.

6. 27–38 (O, above). DISCIPLESHIP. (*Introversion.*)

O | R | 27–36. Positive.
S | 37. Negative.
R | 38. Positive.

6. 27–36 (R, above). POSITIVE. (*Extended Alternation and Introversion.*)

R | T | k | 27–. Love to enemies.
l | –27–29. Do good.
m | 30. Give.
} Command.
U | n | 31. Rule. Human.
o | 32–34. Reasons.
T | *k* | 35–. Love to enemies.
l | –35–. Do good.
m | –35–. Lend.
} Command.
U | *o* | –35. Reason.
n | 36. Rule. Divine.

27 Love. Gr. *agapaō.* See Ap. 135. I. **good** = well.

A.D. 27 28 °Bless them that curse you, and °pray °for them which despitefully use you.

29 And unto him that smiteth thee °on the *one* °cheek offer °also the °other; and him that taketh away thy °cloke forbid °not *to take thy* °coat also.

m 30 Give to every man that asketh of thee; and [13] of him that taketh away thy goods ask *them* [29] not again.

U n 31 And °as ye °would that [6] men should do to you, do ye also to them likewise.

o 32 °For °if ye love them which love you, °what °thank have ye? for sinners also love those that love them.

33 And °if ye do good to them which do good to you, [32] what thank have ye? for sinners also do even the same.

34 And [33] if ye lend *to them* °of whom ye hope to receive, [32] what thank have ye? for sinners also lend to sinners, to receive °as much again.

T k 35 But [27] love ye your enemies,

l and do good,

m and lend, hoping for nothing again; and your reward shall be °great, and ye shall be the °children of the Highest:

U o for He is kind °unto the unthankful and *to* the [22] evil.

n 36 °Be ye therefore °merciful, [31] as your Father also is °merciful.

S 37 Judge [29] not, and ye shall °not be judged: condemn [29] not, and ye shall °not be condemned: forgive, and ye shall be forgiven:

R 38 Give, and it shall be given unto you; good measure, pressed down, and shaken together, and running over, shall °men give [4] into your bosom. For with the same measure that ye °mete withal it shall be measured to you again."

P 39 And He spake a parable unto them, °"Can the blind lead the blind? °shall they [2] not both fall [4] into the ditch?

N O 40 The disciple is [2] not °above his °master: but every one that is °perfect shall be as his master.

P 41 And why °beholdest thou the °mote that is [12] in thy brother's eye, but perceivest [2] not the °beam that is [12] in thine own eye?

42 Either how °canst thou say to thy brother, 'Brother, let me pull out the [41] mote that is [12] in thine eye,' when thou thyself [41] beholdest [2] not the [41] beam that is [12] in thine own eye? Thou hypocrite, cast out first the beam °out of thine own eye, and then shalt thou see clearly to pull out the mote that is [12] in thy brother's eye.

43 For a good tree bringeth [2] not forth corrupt fruit; neither doth a corrupt tree bring forth good fruit.

44 For every tree °is known °by °his own fruit. For °of thorns men do [2] not gather figs, nor °of a °bramble bush gather they grapes.

45 A good [6] man [42] out of the good treasure of his heart bringeth forth that which is good; and an [22] evil [6] man [42] out of the [22] evil treasure of his heart bringeth forth that which is [22] evil: for °of the abundance of the heart his mouth speaketh.

46 And why call ye Me, °Lord, Lord, and do not the things which I say? M

47 °Whosoever cometh °to Me, and heareth My °sayings, and doeth them, °I will shew you to whom he °is like:

48 He is like a [6] man which built an house, and °digged deep, and laid the foundation [29] on °a °rock: and when the °flood arose, the

---

28 Bless. Not the same word as in *vv.* 20, 21, 22.
pray. See Ap. 134. I. 2.
for=on behalf of. Gr. *huper.* Ap. 104. xvii. 1.
29 on. Gr. *epi.* Ap. 104. ix. 3. Not the same word as in *vv.* 1, 2, 6, 7, 20. **cheek**=jaw.
also the other=the other also.
other. See Ap. 124. 1.
cloke=mantle. See Matt. 5. 40.
not. Gr. *mē.* Ap. 105. II.
coat=tunic. See Matt. 5. 40. **31 as**=according as.
would=desire. Gr. *thelō.* See Ap. 102. 1.
32 For=And.
if. Assuming the hypothesis. Ap. 118. 2. a.
what=what kind of.
thank. Gr. *charis.* Occ. more than 150 times; eight in Luke, here, *vv.* 33, 34; 1. 30; 2. 40, 52; 4. 22; 17. 9; not once in Matt. or Mark; generally transl. "grace". Ap. 184. I. 1.
33 if ye do good. The condition being quite uncertain, where experience will decide. Ap. 118. 1. b.
34 of=from. Gr. *para.* Ap. 104. xii. 1.
as much again=the like.
35 great. Emph. by Fig. *Hyperbaton.* Ap. 6.
children=sons. Ap. 108. iii.
the Highest. Put by Fig. *Metonymy* (of Adjunct) for Him Who is on high. See note on 1. 32.
unto. Gr. *epi.* Ap. 104. ix. 3.
36 Be ye=Become ye.
merciful=compassionate. Gr. *oiktirmōn.* Occ. only here and James 5. 11.
37 not. Gr. *ou mē.* Ap. 105. III.
38 men=[they] the professional measurers.
mete. Anglo-Saxon=to measure.
39 Can the blind . . . ?=Is a blind [man] able to lead a blind [man]? **shall**=will.
40 above. Gr. *huper.* Ap. 104. xvii. 2.
master=teacher. Gr. *didaskalos.* Ap. 98. XIV. v.
perfect=set to rights (by his instruction being complete). See Ap. 125. 8.
41 beholdest. See Ap. 133. I. 5.
mote . . . beam. See notes on Matt. 7. 3.
42 canst thou . . . ?=art thou able?
out of. Gr. *ek.* Ap. 104. vii. Not the same word as in *vv.* 17, 19.
44 is known=gets to be known. Gr. *ginōskō.* Ap. 132. I. ii. **by.** Gr. *ek.* Ap. 104. vii.
his=its. **of**=from. Gr. *ek.* Ap. 104. vii.
bramble bush. Gr. *batos.* Occ. outside Luke and Acts only in Mark 12. 26. It is the same word in Ex. 3. 2–4 (Sept.).
45 of=out of. Gr. *ek.* Ap. 104. vii. Cp. Isa. 32. 6.
46 Lord, Lord. Fig. *Epizeuxis* (Ap. 6), for emphasis. Ap. 98. VI. i. *a.* 2. B. a.
47 Whosoever=Every one. Fig. *Synecdochē* (of Genus), Ap. 6. Put for those only who come.
to. Gr. *pros.* Ap. 104. xv. 3.
sayings=words. Pl. of *logos.* Not the same word as in 7. 1. See note on Mark 9. 32.
I will shew . . . is like. Peculiar to Luke.
48 digged deep. Gr. digged and deepened. Fig. *Hendiadys* (Ap. 6), for emphasis: i.e. he dug—yea, he dug deep.
a=the. **rock.** Gr. *petra.* As in Matt. 16. 18.
flood, or inundation. Gr. *plēmmura.* Only here in N.T.

A. D. 27 °stream °beat vehemently upon that house, and
could [2]not shake it: °for it was founded °upon
a rock.

49 But he that heareth, and °doeth [29]not, is
like a [6]man that without a foundation built an
house [48]upon the earth; against which the
[48]stream did [48]beat vehemently, and immediately °it fell; and the °ruin of that house was
great."

K² V¹ W **7** Now when He had °ended all His °say-
ings °in the °audience of the people, He
entered °into °Capernaum.

2 And °a certain centurion's °servant, who
was °dear unto him, was sick, and ready to
die.

X¹ p¹ **3** And when he heard °of °Jesus, he °sent
°unto Him °the elders of the Jews, °beseech-
ing Him that He would come and heal his
[2]servant.

q¹ **4** And when they came °to [3]Jesus, they °be-
sought Him °instantly, saying, That he °was
worthy for whom He should do this:

5 "For he °loveth our nation, and °he hath
built °us °a synagogue."

X² p² **6** Then [3]Jesus °went °with them. And when
He was now °not far °from the house, the cen-
turion °sent friends [4]to Him, °saying unto
Him,

q² °"Lord, °trouble °not Thyself: for I am °not
worthy that Thou shouldest enter °under °my
roof:

7 Wherefore neither thought I myself worthy
to come [3]unto Thee: but °say in a word, and
my °servant shall be healed.

8 For °I also am a °man °set [6]under authority, having [6]under °me soldiers, and I say
unto one, 'Go,' and he goeth; and to another,
'Come,' and he cometh; and to my [2]servant,
'Do this,' and he doeth *it*."

X³ p³ **9** When [3]Jesus heard these things, °He marvelled at him, and turned Him about, and said
unto the people that followed Him, "I say
unto you,

q³ I have °not found so great faith, °no, not °in
Israel."

W **10** And they that were [6]sent, returning °to
the house, found the [2]servant °whole °that had
been sick.

stream = river. Gr. *potamos*.
beat vehemently = burst or brake. A medical term for a rupture.
for, &c. All the texts read "on account of (Gr. *dia*) its being well built". **upon.** Gr. *epi*. Ap. 104. ix. 3.
49 doeth not. The Negative expresses the feeling = doth not wish to do them.
it fell. All the texts read *sunepesen* for *epesen*, i.e. it collapsed.
ruin = breaking up. Another medical word.

7. 1-17 (K², p. 1449). WORKS. MIRACLES.
Division.

K² | V¹ | 1-10. The Centurion's Servant healed.
| V² | 11-17. The Widow's Son raised.

7. 1-10 (V¹, above). THE CENTURION'S SERVANT HEALED.
Introversion and Repeated Alternations.

V¹ | W | 1, 2. The Servant dying.
X¹ | p¹ | 3. Centurion hears and sends.
q¹ | 4, 5. The Elders praise.
X² | p² | 6-. Centurion comes.
q² | -6-8. His own dispraise.
X³ | p³ | 9-. The Lord hears the Centurion.
q³ | -9. The Lord's praise.
W | 10. The Servant healed.

1 ended = completed, or finished.
sayings. Gr. pl. of *rhēma*. Not the same word as in 6. 47. See note on Mark 9. 32.
in = into. Gr. *eis*. Ap. 104. vi.
audience = hearing. Gr. "ears". Put by Fig. *Metonymy* (of Adjunct), Ap. 6, for hearing.
into. Gr. *eis*. Ap. 104. vi.
Capernaum. See Ap. 169.
2 a certain centurion: viz. the same that the Lord had blessed before (Matt. 8. 5-13); i.e. before the calling of the twelve, Matt. 10. 1, &c. This second healing of the centurion's *bondman* took place *after* the calling of the twelve (6. 13-16). Note the different words and incidents.
servant = bondman. Gr. *doulos*, not "*pais*" as in Matt. 8. 6 (Ap. 108. iv) and in *v.* 7 here, for the "*pais*" might be a "*doulos*", while the "*doulos*" need not be a "*pais*". "*Pais*" relates to origin, "*doulos*" to condition, when used of the same person.
dear = esteemed, or honoured. Not said of the "*pais*", and more suitable to "*doulos*".
3 of = about. Gr. *peri*. Ap. 104. xiii. 1. Not the same word as in *vv.* 21-, -30, 35. **Jesus.** Ap. 98. X.
sent = sent away (the sender remaining behind). Gr. *apostellō*. Ap. 174. 1.
unto. Gr. *pros*. Ap. 104. xv. 3.
the elders = some of [the] elders.
beseeching = asking. Not the same word as in *v.* 4. Ap. 134. I. 3. **4 to.** Gr. *pros*. Ap. 104. xv. 3.
besought. Stronger word than in *v.* 3. Ap. 134. I. 6.
instantly = pressingly, or urgently.
was = is: giving the exact words.
5 loveth. Gr. *agapaō*. Ap. 135. I. 1. **he** = he himself.

us = for us. **a synagogue** = the synagogue. The Lord knew all the synagogues in Capernaum; so that this must have been some special synagogue, probably a new one, built since the event of Matt. 8. 5-13. **6 went** = was going. **with** = in conjunction or fellowship with. Gr. *sun*. Ap. 104. xvi. **not far.** In the former case, the Lord did not go; being prevented by the centurion. **not.** Gr. *ou*. Ap. 105. 1. **from.** Gr. *apo*. Ap. 104. iv. **sent.** Gr. *pempō* (Ap. 174. 4) = to send with; the envoy being accompanied by an escort. **saying.** He himself was present, and was the speaker. **Lord.** Ap. 98. VI. i. *a*. 3. B. a. The Person of the Lord is the subject of this second period of His ministry. See Ap. 119. **trouble not Thyself.** This second and similar address shows a greater depth of humility, prob. grown since the former healing, of which the synagogue may have been a votive token. **not.** Gr. *mē*. Ap. 105. II. Not the same word as in preceding and following clause. **not worthy.** Gr. *ou*. As in first clause. **under.** Gr. *hupo*. Ap. 104. xviii. 2. **my.** Emphatic by position in the sentence. Fig. *Hyperbaton*. Ap. 6. **7 say in a word** = say by, or with a word. Dative case. **servant.** Here, it is Gr. *pais*. Ap. 108. iv. See note on *v.* 2. **8 I also am, &c.** = I also, a man, am appointed under (or, obedient to) authority. **man.** Gr. *anthrōpos*. Ap. 123. I. **set** appointed. **me** = myself. **9 He marvelled, &c.** The only other instance of the Lord's marvelling is at their *unbelief* (Mark 6. 6). **not. . . no, not** = not even. Gr. *oude*. **in.** Gr. *en*. Ap. 104. viii. **10 to** = unto. Gr. *eis*. Ap. 104. vi. **whole** = in good health. A medical word. See note on 5. 31. **that had been sick.** Omitted by L T Tr. [A] WH R. Thus the antecedents and consequents, and subjects of the two miracles differ in important details.

V² Y r 11 °And °it came to pass the day after, that
A.D. 27 He went [1] into a city called °Nain;
s °and many of His disciples went with Him,
°and much people.
Z t 12 Now when He came nigh to °the gate of
the city, °behold, there was °a dead man carried out, the only son of his mother,
u [11] and she was a widow: [11] and much people of
the city was [6] with her.
A v 13 [11] And when °the Lord °saw her, He had
°compassion °on her,
w [11] and said unto her, "Weep °not."
A v 14 [11] And He °came [11] and °touched the °bier:
[11] and they that bare *him* °stood still.
w [11] And He said, °"Young man, I say unto thee,
°Arise."
Z t 15 [11] And °he that was dead °sat up, [11] and
began to speak.
u [11] And He delivered him to his mother.
Y s 16 [11] And there came a fear on all: [11] and they
glorified God, saying, That °a great prophet
°is risen up °among us; [11] and, That God °hath
visited His People.
r 17 [11] And this °rumour [3] of Him went forth
°throughout all Judæa, [11] and °throughout all
the region round about.
J B¹ x 18 And the disciples of John °shewed him
[3] of all these things.
y 19 And John calling *unto him* °two of his
disciples sent *them* to °Jesus, saying, "Art
Thou °He That should come? or °look we for
°another?"
x 20 When the °men were come [3] unto Him,
they said, "John Baptist hath sent us [3] unto
Thee, saying, 'Art Thou [19] He That should
come? or [19] look we for [19] another?'"
y 21 And [9] in that °same hour He °cured many
°of *their* °infirmities and °plagues, and of
°evil °spirits; and unto many *that were* blind
He gave sight.
22 Then °Jesus answering said unto them,
"Go your way, and tell John what things ye
have °seen and heard; how that °the blind
°see, °the lame walk, °the lepers are cleansed,
°the deaf hear, °the °dead are [16] raised, °to the
poor the gospel is preached.
23 And °blessed is *he*, whosoever shall °not
be offended [9] in Me."

7. 11-17 (V², p. 1451). THE WIDOW'S SON RAISED. (*Introversions and Alternations.*)

V² | Y | r | 11-. The Lord. Entering into Nain.
  s | -11. The people with the Lord.
   Z | t | 12-. The dead man.
    u | -12. His mother.
     A | v | 13-. Compassion. } To the Mother. } The Lord.
      w | -13. Words.
     A | *v* | 14-. Acts. } To her Son.
      w | -14. Words.
   Z | *t* | 15-. The dead man.
    u | -15. The mother.
 Y | *s* | 16. The people with the Lord.
  r | 17. The Lord. His praise going out from Nain.

11 Verses 11-17 peculiar to Luke. Selected because it is connected with the Lord's Person as God—raiser of the dead; and as Man—full of compassion.

And. Note the Fig. *Polysyndeton* (Ap. 6), the "many ands" in these verses (11-17) emphasizing every detail. The "ands" in the English do not always agree with those in the Greek.

it came to pass. A Hebraism. See note on 1. 8.

Nain. Now, *Nein*. Occ. only here in N.T. The ruins are on the slope of Little Hermon, west of Endor.

12 the gate. All funerals were outside.

behold. Fig. *Asterismos.* Ap. 6. To call attention to the two great crowds meeting.

a dead man. Gr. *ho nekros.* Ap. 139. 1.

13 the Lord. This Divine title more frequent in Luke than in any of the other Gospels. See *vv.* 19, 31; 10. 1; 11. 1; 12. 42; 17. 5, 6; 19. 8; 22. 61. Ap. 98. VI. i. *a.* 3. A.

saw. Gr. *eidon.* Ap. 133. I. 1. Not the same word as in *v.* 24.

compassion. See on *v.* 11 the reason for the selection of this miracle, here. **on.** Gr. *epi.* Ap. 104. ix. 2.

not. Gr. *mē.* Ap. 105. II. **14 came** = came up.

touched. Without defilement. Another remarkable fact, emphasized by the "and".

bier. Probably of wicker-work.

stood still. Another remarkable particular.

Young man. Ap. 108. x. **Arise.** Ap. 178. I. 4.

15 he that was dead = the corpse. See Ap. 139. 1.

sat up. A medical word (Col. 4. 14). Gr. *anakathizō.* Occurs only here and Acts 9. 40. Common in medical writings; and found also in the Papyri, in a letter from a Christian servant to his absent master about the illness of his mistress (Milligan's *Selections*, p. 130).

16 a great prophet. See 9. 8, 19.

is risen up. Ap. 178. I. 4.

among. Gr. *en.* Ap. 104. viii. 2.

hath visited. Cp. 1. 68. John 3. 2.

17 rumour = report. Gr. *logos.*

throughout = in. Gr. *en.* Ap. 104. viii.

7. 18-35 (J, p. 1449). CONCERNING JOHN. (*Division.*)

J | B¹ | 18-23. John's Second Mission concerning the Lord.
  B² | 24-35. The Lord's testimony concerning John.

7. 18-23 (B¹, above). JOHN'S SECOND MISSION CONCERNING THE LORD. (*Alternation.*)

B¹ | x | 18. Disciples of John. Report to him.
  y | 19. John. Question sent to the Lord.
 x | 20. Disciples of John. Report to the Lord.
  y | 21-23. John. Answer sent to John.

18 shewed him = brought word. This became the occasion of John's second mission. If the Lord could raise the dead, why was he languishing in prison? **19 two** = a certain two. The mission in Matt. 11. 1, &c., was earlier than this. See notes on Matt. 11. 2. No number named there. See note on "two" there. **Jesus.** All the texts read "the Lord". See note on *v.* 13. **He That should come** = the coming [Messiah]. **look we** = do we look. **another.** Gr. *allos.* Ap. 124. 1. But Tr. and WH read "*heteros*". Ap. 124. 2. **20 men.** Gr. pl. of *anēr.* Ap. 123. 2. **21 same.** Omit. No equivalent in the Greek. **cured** = healed. **of** = from. Ap. 104. iv. **infirmities** = diseases (chronic). **plagues** = scourges (acute). Medical terms (Col. 4. 14). **evil.** Gr. *ponēros.* Ap. 128. III. 1. **spirits.** See Ap. 101. II. 12. **22 Jesus.** Omit [L] T Tr. A WH R. **seen and heard.** The evidence was not that they were miracles (*qua* miracles), but that the miracles were those that had been prophesied. See Isa. 29. 18; 35. 4-6; 60. 1-3. Had the Lord worked miracles far more extraordinary they would have been no evidence at all as to His claims. **the . . . the, &c.** No articles in the Greek. **see** are seeing again. Ap 133. I. 6. **dead** = dead people. No Art. See Ap. 139. 2. **to the poor the gospel is preached:** lit. the poor (Ap. 127. 1) are being evangelized (Ap. 121. 4). **23 blessed** = happy. **not be offended** = find not (Gr. *mē.* Ap. 105. II) anything to stumble at.

B² C a 24 And when the messengers of John were
A.D. 27 departed, He began to speak [3]unto the people
°concerning John, "What °went ye out [1]into
the wilderness °for to see? A reed shaken
°with the °wind?
25 But what [24]went ye out °for to see? A
[8]man clothed [9]in °soft raiment? [12]Behold,
they which °are gorgeously apparelled, and
live °delicately, are [9]in °kings' courts.
26 But what [24]went ye out [25]for to see? °A
prophet? Yea, I say unto you, and much more
than a prophet.
27 This is *he*, [3]of whom °it is written, [12]'**Be-**
hold, I send My messenger °before Thy face,
which shall °prepare Thy way °before Thee.'
28 For I say unto you, [16]Among those that
are °born of women there is °not a greater
prophet than John the Baptist: but he that is
°least [9]in °the kingdom of God is greater
than he."

b 29 And all the people that heard *Him*, and
the °publicans, °justified God, being baptized
with the baptism of John.

C b 30 But the Pharisees and lawyers °rejected
the °counsel of God °against themselves, being
[6-]not baptized °of him.

a 31 °And the Lord said, "Whereunto then
shall I liken the [8]men of °this generation?
and to what are they like?
32 They are like unto °children sitting [9]in
°the marketplace, and calling one to another,
and saying, °'We have piped unto you, and
ye °have [-6]not danced; °we have mourned to
you, and ye °have [-6]not wept.'
33 For John the Baptist came neither °eating
°bread nor °drinking °wine; and ye say, 'He
hath a °devil.'
34 °The Son of man °is come [33]eating and
[33]drinking; and ye say, [25]'Behold a gluttonous [8]man, and a winebibber, a friend of
[29]publicans and sinners!'
35 °But °wisdom is justified [21-]of all her
°children."

J D F¹ 36 °And one of the Pharisees °desired Him
that He would eat °with him. And He went
[1]into the Pharisee's house, and °sat down to
meat.

7. 24–35 (B², p. 1452). THE LORD'S TESTIMONY CONCERNING JOHN. (*Introversion.*)

B² | *C* | a | 24–28. Commendation of John. } People.
| | b | 29. Effect on the People. }
| *C* | b | 30. Effect on the Pharisees. } Pharisees.
| | a | 31–35. Crimination of Pharisees. }

24 concerning. Gr. *peri.* Ap. 104. xiii. 1.
went ye out=have ye gone out (perf.). All the texts, however, read "went ye out" (aor.).
for to see=to look at. Gr. *theaomai.* Ap. 133. I. 12.
with=by. Gr. *hupo.* Ap. 104. xviii. 1.
wind. Gr. *anemos.*
25 for to see=to see. Gr. *eidon.* Ap. 133. I.
soft. See Matt. 11. 8. A contrast to "camel's hair".
are=are existing. Same word as "was" in Rom. 4. 19; "being" in Phil. 2. 6; and "is" in Phil. 3. 20.
delicately=luxuriously. The Herods were noted for this (Acts 12. 21. Mark 6. 21. Josephus, *Bel. Jud.*, 1. 20, § 3; *Ant.* xix. 8. 2).
kings' courts=royal palaces. Gr. pl. of *basileion.* Occ. only here in N.T.
26 A prophet. See Ap. 49. One who spoke *for* God. Not necessarily beforehand. Cp. Ex. 4. 16; 7. 1.
27 it is written=it standeth written. Quoted from Mal. 3. 1. See Ap. 107.
before. Gr. *pro.* Ap. 104. xiv.
prepare. See note on 1. 17.
before. Gr. *emprosthen*=in the presence of.
28 born=brought into the world. Gr. *gennaō*, used of the mother. See note on Matt. 1. 2.
not. Gr. *oudeis*=no one. Cp. 5. 36.
least. See note on Matt. 11. 11. John only proclaimed it. But had the nation then accepted the Lord, it would have been realized.
the kingdom of God. See Ap. 114.
29 publicans=toll collectors. See on Matt. 5. 46.
justified God. A Hebraism=declared God to be just, by submitting to John's baptism.
30 rejected=set aside, or annulled, by the interpretation they put upon it. Cp. Gal. 2. 21. Prov. 1. 24.
counsel. Gr. *boulē.* See Ap. 102. 4, and cp. Eph. 1. 9, 11. See also Acts 2. 23; 4. 28, &c.
against=as to. Gr. *eis.* Ap. 104. vi.
of=by. Gr. *hupo.* Ap. 104. xviii.
31 And the Lord said. All the texts omit these words.
this generation. See note on Matt. 11. 16.
32 children=little children. Ap. 108. v.
the=a.
We have piped=We piped: i. e. played at being at a wedding.
have not danced=danced not.
we have mourned=we mourned: i. e. we played at being at a funeral.
have not wept=wept not. Cp. 6. 21.

33 eating . . . drinking. Heb. idiom for ordinary living. Cp. 1. 15. Matt. 3. 4. **bread . . . wine.** Peculiar to Luke. **devil**=demon. Later, they said the same of the Lord. John 7. 20; 10. 20.
34 The Son of man. See Ap. 98. XVI. **is**=has. **35 But**=And yet. **wisdom.** See note on Matt. 11. 19. **children:** i. e. those produced by her. See Ap. 108. i.

7. 36–50 (*J*, p. 1449). CONCERNING THE PHARISEES. (*Introversion and Repeated Alternation.*)

J | D | F¹ | 36. The Pharisee.
| | G¹ | 37, 38. The Woman.
| | F² | 39. The Pharisee.
| E | H | c | 40–. Proposal. }
| | | d | –40. Assent. }
| | J | 41–42. Parable. } The Lord.
| | *H* | c | 43–. Supposition. }
| | | *d* | –43. Confirmation. }
| *D* | F³ | 44–46. The Pharisee.
| | G² | 47, 48. The Woman.
| | F⁴ | 49. The Pharisees.

36 And one, &c. Verses 36–50 peculiar to Luke. Not to be identified with Simon (Mark 14. 3). All the circumstances are different. Simon was one of the commonest names. There are nine mentioned in the N.T., and two among the Twelve. **desired**=asked, or invited. Ap. 134. I. 3. **with**=in company with. Gr. *meta.* Ap. 104. xi. 1. **sat down to meat**=reclined [at table].

G1 37 And, [12]behold, °a woman [9]in °the city,
A. D. 27 °which °was a sinner, °when she knew that
°*Jesus* [36]sat at meat [9]in the Pharisee's house,
brought an °alabaster box of ointment,
38 °And stood °at His feet behind *Him*
weeping, °and began to °wash His feet with
tears, °and °did wipe *them* with the hairs of
her head, °and °kissed His feet, °and anointed
them with the ointment.

F2 39 Now when the Pharisee which had °bid-
den Him [13]saw *it*, he spake °within himself,
saying, "This Man, °if He were a prophet,
would have °known who and what manner of
woman *this is* °that toucheth Him: for she is
a sinner."

E H c 40 And Jesus °answering said [3]unto him,
°"Simon, I have somewhat to °say [3]unto thee."

d And he saith, °"Master, °say on."

J 41 °"There was a certain creditor which
had two debtors: the one owed five hundred
°pence, and the °other fifty.
42 And °when they had nothing to pay, he
frankly forgave them both. Tell Me therefore, which of them will [5]love him °most?"

H c 43 Simon answered and said, °"I suppose
that *he*, to whom he forgave [42]most."

d And He said unto him, "Thou hast rightly
°judged."

D F3 44 And He turned [4]to the woman, and said
unto Simon, °"Seest thou this woman? I entered [1]into thine house, °thou gavest me °no
water °for My feet: but °she hath [38]washed My
feet with tears, and wiped *them* with the hairs
of her head.
45 Thou gavest Me [44]no kiss: but °this
woman °since the time I came in hath -[6]not
°ceased to kiss My feet.
46 My head with oil thou didst [32]not anoint:
but [45]this woman hath anointed My feet with
ointment.

G2 47 °Wherefore I say unto thee, her °sins,
which are many, are forgiven; °for she [5]loved
much: but to whom little is forgiven, *the same*
[5]loveth little."
48 And He said °unto her, "Thy [47]sins are
forgiven."

F4 49 And they that [36]sat at meat with Him
°began to say [39]within themselves, °"Who is
This That forgiveth [47]sins also?"

*H K*3 50 And He said [4]to the woman, "Thy faith
(p. 1449) hath saved thee; go [1]in peace."

L K **8** And °it came to pass °afterward, that He
°went throughout °every city and village,
°preaching and °shewing the glad tidings of
°the kingdom of God:

L and the twelve °*were* °with Him,
2 And °certain women, which had been
°healed °of °evil °spirits and infirmities, Mary
called Magdalene, °out of whom °went seven
°devils,

37 a woman. Not to be identified with Mary Magdalene: it is a libel on her to do so, and quite arbitrary. Cp. Matt. 21. 32.
the city. That it was Magdala is a pure assumption.
which = who: i. e. ref. to a class.
was, &c. All the texts read "which was in the city, a sinner".
when she knew = having got to know. Gr. *ginōskō*. Ap. 132. I. ii. **Jesus** = He.
alabaster. See Matt. 26. 7. Mark 14. 3.
38 And. Note the Fig. *Polysyndeton*. Ap. 6.
at = beside. Gr. *para*. Ap. 104. xii. 3.
wash = bedew. **did wipe** = was wiping.
kissed = was ardently kissing. Cp. Acts 20. 37.
39 bidden = invited.
within. Gr. *en* = in. Ap. 104. viii.
if, &c. Assuming and believing the fact. Ap. 118. 2 a.
known = got to know, as in *v.* 36.
that. Same as "which" in *v.* 36.
40 answering: i. e. his secret doubt.
Simon. See note on *v.* 36.
say unto thee. You have been condemning Me!
Master = Teacher. Ap. 98. XIV. v. **say on** = say it.
41 There was, &c. Gr. "There were two debtors to a certain money-lender".
pence = denarii. See Ap. 51. I. 4.
other = a different one. Gr. *heteros*. See Ap. 124. 2.
42 when they had nothing = not (Gr. *mē* as in *v.* 13) having anything. **most** = more.
43 I suppose = I take it. Gr. *hupolambanō*, used only by Luke; here, 10. 30. Acts 1. 9; 2. 15. Medical use, to check (a disease). **judged.** Ap. 122. 1.
44 Seest thou = Dost thou mark. Gr. *blepō*. Ap. 133. I. 5. The Lord calls Simon's attention to *her works*, but He calls the woman's attention (*v.* 47) to *His own grace* towards her.
thou gavest, &c. Cp. Gen. 18. 4; 19. 2. Judg. 19. 21. 1 Tim. 5. 10. **no.** Gr. *ou*. Ap. 105. 1.
for = upon. Gr. *epi*. Ap. 104. ix. 3.
She. Emphatic. **45 this woman** = she (emph.).
since the time = from (Gr. *apo*) the time when.
ceased = been intermittent. A medical word. Occ. only here in N.T.
47 Wherefore = for which cause, or because her sins are forgiven. **sins.** Ap. 128. I. ii.
for = that. This could be seen; and was the sign, not the cause or consequence.
48 unto her. Note the change.
49 began. Noting the uprising of the thought.
Who is This . . . ? This incident chosen because it sets forth the Lord's Person as God. The subject of this Second Period of His ministry. See Ap. 119.

8. 1-21 (*L*, p. 1449). TEACHING.
(*Alternation.*)

L | K | 1-. Proclaiming.
  L | -1-3. Comparing.
K | 4-18. Teaching.
  L | 19-21. Kindred.

1 it came to pass. Note the Hebraism, here and in chs. 5. 1; 6. 1, &c. Verses 1-3 are peculiar to Luke.
afterward. No longer confining Himself to Capernaum. **went throughout** = journeyed through.
every city and village = by city and village.
preaching = proclaiming. See Ap. 121. 1.
shewing the glad tidings. Gr. *euangelizō* = announcing, &c. Ap. 121. 4.
the kingdom of God. Ap. 114.
were. Substitute *went*.
with = together with. Gr. *sun*. Ap. 104. xvi. Not the same word as in *vv.* 13, 14, 15, 45.
2 certain women. Allusions to "women" in Matt. only in 27. 55, 56, and in Mark 15. 40, but mentioned prominently in Luke. See note on p. 1428.
healed. See 6. 18.
of = from. Gr. *apo*. Ap. 104. iv.

evil. Gr. *ponēros*. Ap. 128. III. 1. **spirits.** Gr. pl. of *pneuma*. Ap. 101. II. 12. **out of** = away from. Gr. *apo*. Ap. 104. iv. Not the same word as in *v.* 37. **went** = had gone out. **devils** = demons.

A.D. 27 3 And Joanna °the wife of Chuza Herod's
steward, and Susanna, and many °others,
°which ministered unto Him °of their °sub-
stance.

K M e 4 And when much people were gathered together, and °were come °to Him out of every
city, He spake °by a parable:
5 °"A sower went out to sow °his seed: and
°as he sowed, some °fell °by the way side;
and it was trodden down, and the °fowls of
the °air devoured it.
6 And °some [5]fell °upon °a rock; and as soon
as it was °sprung up, it withered away, °be-
cause it lacked °moisture.
7 And [6]some [5]fell °among °thorns; and the
thorns °sprang up with it, and °choked it.
8 °And [3]other [5]fell °on good ground, °and
[6]sprang up, °and bare fruit an hundredfold."
f °And when He °had said these things, He
cried, °"He that hath ears to hear, let him
hear."

N g 9 And His disciples asked Him, saying,
°"What might this parable be?"
h 10 And He said, "Unto you it °is given to
°know the °mysteries of [1]the kingdom of
God: but to °others °in parables; °**that °see-
ing they might °not °see, and hearing they
might °not understand.**

M e 11 Now the parable °is this: The seed °is the
°word of °God.
12 Those [5]by the way side are they that
hear; then cometh the devil, and °taketh
away the [11]word [2]out of their hearts, °lest they
should believe and be saved.
13 They [8]on the rock *are they*, which, when
they hear, receive the [11]word °with joy; and
these have °no root, which °for a °while believe, and [10]in time of °temptation fall away.
14 And that which [5]fell °among thorns are
they, which, when they have heard, °go
forth, and are °choked °with cares and riches
and pleasures of °*this* life, and bring [13]no fruit
to perfection.
15 But that °on the good ground are they,
°which [10]in an honest and good heart, having
°heard the [11]word, °keep *it*, and bring forth
fruit °with °patience.

f 16 °No man, when he hath lighted a °candle,
covereth it with a vessel, or putteth *it* under
a °bed; but setteth *it* °on a °candlestick, that
they which enter in may [10]see the light.
17 For °nothing is °secret, that shall °not

3 the wife. She may have been the cause of Herod's interest. Mark 6. 14–16. Luke 23. 8.
others. Gr. pl. of *heteros*. Ap. 124. 2. See Matt. 27. 55.
which. Marking a class.
of = from. *apo* as in *v.* 2, but all the texts read *ek*.
substance = property.

8. 4–18 (*K*, p. 1454). TEACHING.
(*Introversion and Alternations.*)

K | M | e | 4–8–. Parable. Sower. } The Lord.
| | f | –8. Call to hear. }
| N | g | 9. Question. } The Disciples.
| | h | 10. Answer. }
| *M* | e | 11–15. Parable. Interpretation. } The Lord.
| | *f* | 16–18. Caution to hearers. }

4 were come = kept coming.
to. Gr. *pros*. Ap. 104. xv. 3. Not the same word as in *vv.* 27, 39.
by. Gr. *dia*. Ap. 104. v. 1. Not the same word as in *vv.* 5, 12.
5 A sower. Gr. "the sower". The first utterance of the parable, which was repeated (and varied) and combined with seven other parables, later on, after the arrival of His kindred. This (in Luke) was given before the arrival, and was consequent on a lengthened tour ending in Capernaum. The consequent here is the inquiry of the Twelve ("What", Luke 8. 9); the consequent in Matthew and Mark (which are identical) is another inquiry ("Why", Matt. 13. 10). In the later repetition, the interpretation *after* the inquiry (Matt. 13. 18. Mark 4. 10); in Luke, it follows the parable immediately.
his seed. Peculiar to this first giving of the parable.
as he sowed = in (Gr. *en*. Ap. 104. viii) his sowing.
fell. It was not sown on the way side.
by = beside. Gr. *para*. Ap. 104. xii. 3. **fowls** = birds.
air = sky. Gr. the heaven (Sing.). See notes on Matt. 6. 9, 10. **6 some** = other. Gr. *heteros*, as in *v.* 3.
upon. Gr. *epi*. Ap. 104. ix. 3. Not the same word as in *v.* 43.
a rock = the rock. Gr. *petra*. As in Matt. 16. 18.
sprung up. Gr. *phuō*. Occ. only here, *v.* 8, and Heb. 12. 15.
because it lacked = on account of (Gr. *dia*. Ap. 104. v. 2) its not (Gr. *mē*. Ap. 105. II) having.
moisture. Gr. *ikmas*. Occ. only here in N.T.
7 among = in (Gr. *en*. Ap. 104. viii) the midst of.
thorns = the thorns.
sprang up with it = sprang up together. Gr. *sumphuō*. Occ. only here in N.T. A medical word, used of bones uniting and wounds closing.
choked = stifled, as in *v.* 33. Elsewhere only in Matt. 13. 7.
8 And. Note the Fig. *Polysyndeton* (Ap. 6) in *v.* 8.
on. Gr. *epi*. Same as "upon" (*v.* 6).
had. The 1611 edition of the A.V. omits "had".
He that hath ears, &c. See note on Matt. 11. 15 and Ap. 142.
9 What . . . ? See note on *v.* 5. Not the same word as on the later occasion (Matt. 13. 10), which was "Why". They knew "what", but desired further information.
10 is = has been.
know = get to know. See Ap. 132. I. ii.

mysteries = secrets. **others** = the rest. Gr. *hoi loipoi*. Cp. Acts 5. 13. Rom. 11. 7. Eph. 2. 3. 1 Thess. 4. 13. Rev. 20. 5. **in.** Gr. *en*. Ap. 104. viii. **that** = in order that. Quoted from Isa. 6. 9, 10. See Ap. 107. I. 1. **seeing.** Ap. 133. I. 5. **not.** Gr. *mē*. Ap. 105. II. **11 is** = means. Fig. *Metaphor* (Ap. 6): i. e. represents. **word.** Gr. *logos*. **God.** Ap. 98. I. 1. **12 taketh** = snatches. **lest** = in order that . . . not, as in *v.* 10. **13 with** = in association with. Gr. *meta*. Ap. 104. xi. 2. Not the same word as in *vv.* 1, 14, 15, –28, 38. **no.** Gr. *ou*. Ap. 105. I. **for.** Gr. *pros*. Ap. 104. xv. 3. **while** = season. **temptation** = trial. In the second utterance of this parable (see note on *v.* 5), the Lord used the words "tribulation or persecution". **14 among.** Gr. *eis*. Ap. 104. vi. **go forth** = as they go on their way. **choked** = stifled. Gr. *sumpnigō*, as in *v.* 42. Not the same word as in *vv.* 8, 33. **with** = by. Gr. *hupo*. Ap. 104. xviii. 1. **this life.** Gr. *bios* = the life that is lived. Not *zōē*, or *psuchē*. See Ap. 170. 2. **15 on** = in. Gr. *en*. Ap. 104. viii. Not the same word as in *vv.* 8, 13, 16, 23. **which.** Denoting a class. **keep it** = hold it fast.' See note on 2 Thess. 2. 6. Fig. *Tapeinōsis* (Ap. 6), for much more is done beside this. **with** = in. Gr. *en*. Ap. 104. viii. **patience** = patient endurance. **16 No man.** Gr. *oudeis*, compound of *ou*. Ap. 105. I. **candle** = a lamp. See Ap. 130. 4. **bed** = couch. **on** = upon. Gr. *epi*. Ap. 104. ix. 1. **candlestick** = lampstand. **17 nothing** = not (Gr. *ou*. Ap. 105. I) anything. **secret** = hidden. **not.** Gr. *ou*. Ap. 105. I.

A. D. 27 °be made manifest; °neither *any thing* hid,
that shall °not °be [10]known and °come abroad.
18 °Take heed therefore °how ye hear: for
whosoever hath, to him shall be given; and
whosoever hath [10]not, °from him shall be
taken even that which he °seemeth to have."

L 19 °Then came [4]to Him *His* mother and His
brethren, and °could [17]not °come at Him °for
the °press.
20 And it was told Him *by certain* which
said, "Thy mother and Thy brethren °stand
without, °desiring to °see Thee."
21 And He °answered and said °unto them,
"My mother and My brethren are these which
hear the [11]word of [11]God, and °do it."

H K[4]Q[1]R l 22 °Now [1]it came to pass [15]on a certain day,
that He went °into °a ship °with His disciples:

m and He said °unto them, "Let us go over °un-
to the other side of the °lake."

n And they °launched forth.

S o 23 But as they sailed He °fell asleep:

p and there °came down °a storm of wind °on
the lake; and they °were filled *with water*,

q and °were in jeopardy.

S o 24 And they came to Him, and °awoke Him,
saying, °"Master, °master, °we perish." Then
He °arose, and rebuked the wind and the
°raging of the water:

p and they ceased, and there °was a calm.

q 25 And He said unto them, "Where is your
faith?"

R n And they being afraid wondered,

m saying one [4]to another, °"What manner of
°Man is This! for °He commandeth even the
winds and water, and they obey Him."

l 26 And °they arrived °at the country of the
°Gadarenes, which is °over against Galilee.

Q[2]T V A r 27 And when He went forth °to land, there
met Him °out of the city a certain °man, which
had °devils °long time, and °ware [13]no clothes,
neither abode [10]in *any* house, but [10]in the
tombs.

be made = become. **neither.** Gr. *oude*. **not.** Gr. *ou*, as above, but all the texts read *ou mē*. Ap. 105. III. **be** = become. **come abroad** = come to (Gr. *eis*. Ap. 104. vi) light (Gr. *phaneros* = manifestation).

18 Take heed. Gr. *blepō*. See Ap. 133. I. 5. **how.** Contrast "what" on the second occasion (Mark 4. 24). **from** = away from. Gr. *apo*. Ap. 104. iv. **seemeth** = thinketh. Peculiar to Luke.

19 Then came, &c. For the motive, see Mark 3. 21- with 31-35. Cp. Matt. 12. 47. **could not** = were not able to. **come at Him** = fall in with Him. Gr. *suntunchanō*. Occ. only here in N.T. **for** = on account of. Gr. *dia*. Ap. 104. v. 2. **press** = crowd.

20 stand = are standing. **desiring** = wishing. Gr. *thelō*. Ap. 102. 1. **see.** Gr. *eidon*. Ap. 133. I. 1.

21 answered and said. See note on Deut. 1. 41. **unto.** Gr. *pros*. Ap. 104. xv. 3. Not the same word as in *v*. -22. **do** = are doing.

8. 22-56 (*K*[4], p. 1449). WORKS.
(*Alternation and Introversion.*)

K[4] | O | 22-39. Two Miracles.
P | i | 40-. The Lord. Returned.
k | -40. Effect. Waiting.
O | 41-55. Two Miracles.
P | *k* | 56-. Effect. Astonishment.
i | -56. The Lord. Charge.

8. 22-39 (O, above). TWO MIRACLES.
(*Division.*)

O | Q[1] | 22-26. The Tempest stilled.
Q[2] | 27-39. The Demoniac healed.

8. 22-26 (Q[1], above). THE TEMPEST STILLED.
(*Introversions and Alternations.*)

Q[1] | R | l | 22-. Departure.
m | -22-. Words of the Lord.
n | -22. Effect. Obedience.
S | o | 23-. The Lord asleep.
p | -23-. Storm. Dangerous.
q | -23. Disciples. Jeopardy.
S | *o* | 24-. The Lord awakened.
p | -24. Storm rebuked.
q | 25-. Disciples. Rebuked.
R | *n* | -25. Effect. Wonder.
m | -25. Words of the Disciples.
l | 26. Arrival.

22 Now, &c. This is not the same storm as in Matt. 8. 24 (see notes there), but the same as in Mark 4. 37. Matthew's was before the calling of the Twelve; this occurred after that event. The antecedents and consequents differ in both cases. **into.** Gr. *eis*. Ap. 104. vi.

a ship. In Matthew, *the* "boat". **with** = and. **unto them** = to them. Gr. *pros*. Ap. 104. xv. 3. **unto.** Gr. *eis*. Ap. 104. vi. **lake.** See Ap. 169. **launched forth** = put to sea, or set sail. **23 fell asleep** = fell off (Gr. *aphupnoō*) into sleep. Only here in N.T. **came down.** Not rose up, as on the former occasion (Matt. 8. 24). **a storm of wind** = a squall. On the former occasion it was an earthquake (Gr. *seismos*). Here it was *lailaps*. **on** = on to. Gr. *eis*. Ap. 104. vi. **were filled** = were being swamped. Imperf. tense. Hence this was an open boat; in Matthew a decked boat. **were in jeopardy** = were beginning to be in danger. **24 awoke** = roused. Ap. 178. I. 5. **Master.** See note on 5. 5. Note the Fig. *Epizeuxis* (Ap. 6), for emphasis. Not the same word as in *v*. 49. **we perish** = we are perishing: i. e. drowning. **arose** = was aroused. Ap. 178. I. 4. T Tr. WH R have the same word as "awoke" above. **raging.** Gr. *kludōn*. Occ. only here and Jas. 1. 6 ("wave"). **was** = became. **25 What manner ... This!** = Who then is this [man]! **He commandeth.** Peculiar to Luke. **26 they arrived** = they sailed down, or, dropped down. Occ. only here in the N.T. **at** = unto. Gr. *eis*. Ap. 104. vi. **Gadarenes.** See note on Matt. 8. 28. The people were Gadarenes, but the city was not Gadara. See Ap. 169. **over against** = opposite. Gr. *antiperan*. Occ. only here in N.T.; opposite Lower Galilee (not whence they had sailed). See Ap. 169.

8. 27-39 [For Structure see next page].

27 to = on to. Gr. *epi*. Ap. 104. ix. 3. **out of the city.** Connect with the "man", not with "met". **out of.** Gr. *ek*. Ap. 104. vii. Not the same word as in *vv*. 2, 12, 29, 33, 35, 38, 46. **man.** Gr. *anēr*. Ap. 123. 2. **devils** = demons. **long time . . . clothes** = and for a long time was not putting on any mantle, cloak, or outer garment (Sing.) **ware.** And 16. 19. Not a word peculiar to the Bible. It is met with in Josephus, and in an inscription from Delphi (*c*. 154 B. C.). See Deissmann, *Light*, &c., p. 78.

s A. D. 27 **28** When he [20]saw °Jesus, he cried out, and fell down before Him, and with a loud voice said, °"What have I to do with Thee, °Jesus, *Thou* Son of God °most high? I °beseech Thee, torment me [19]not."

B **29** (For °He had commanded the unclean °spirit to come [2]out of the °man.

B For oftentimes °it had caught him: and he was °kept bound with °chains and in fetters; and °he brake the bands, and °was driven °of the °devil [22]into the wilderness.)

A r **30** And [28]Jesus asked him, saying, "What is thy name?" And he said, "Legion:" because °many [27]devils were entered [22]into him.

s **31** And they °besought Him that He would [10]not command them to go out [22]into °the deep.

32 And there was there an herd of many swine feeding [15]on the mountain: and they [31]besought Him that He would suffer them to enter [22]into °them.

W And He suffered them.

33 Then went the [27]devils [2]out of the [29]man, and entered [22]into the swine: and the herd °ran violently °down °a steep place [22]into the lake, and were [7]choked.

U X C t **34** When they that fed *them* [20]saw what °was done, they fled,

u and went and told *it* °in the city and °in the country.

D **35** Then they went out to [20]see what [34]was done; and came [4]to [28]Jesus, and found the [29]man, [2]out of whom the [27]devils were departed, sitting °at the feet of [28]Jesus, clothed, and °in his right mind: and they were afraid.

C t **36** They also which [20]saw *it*

u told them by what means °he that was possessed of the devils was °healed.

D **37** Then the whole multitude of the country of the Gadarenes round about °besought Him to depart [18]from them; for they °were taken with great fear:

Y and He went up [22]into the ship, and returned back again.

T V **38** Now the [27]man [2]out of whom the devils were departed [28]besought Him that he might be [1]with Him:

W but °Jesus °sent him away, saying,

39 "Return °to thine own house, and °shew °how great things God hath done unto thee." And he went his way, °and published [1]throughout the whole city °how great things [28]Jesus had done °unto him.

P i **40** And [1]it came to pass, that, °when [28]Jesus was returned,

k the people *gladly* received Him: for they were all °waiting for Him.

O F v **41** °And, behold, there came a [27]man named

8. 27-39 (Q², p. 1456). THE DEMONIAC HEALED.
(*Introversion and Alternation.*)

Q² T | V | 27-32-. Demons. Petition.
    W | -32, 33. Answer. Consent.
  U | X | 34-37-. People. Petition.
    Y | -37. Answer. Consent.
 T | *V* | 38-. Demoniac. Petition.
    W | -38, 39. Answer. Refusal.

8. 27-32- (V, above). DEMONS. PETITION.
(*Introversion and Alternation.*)

V | A | r | 27. Demons. Description.
    s | 28. Their petition.
   B | 29-. Reason. The Lord's command.
   B | -29. Reason. The Man's condition.
  A | *r* | 30. Demons. Name.
    s | 31, 32-. Their petition.

28 Jesus. Ap. 98. X. Demons irreverently use this sacred name, as is done by so many to-day: but His own disciples called Him "Master" (*v.* 24) and "Lord". See John 13. 13.

What have I, &c. See note on 2 Sam. 16. 10.

most high. The Lord called thus elsewhere only in Mark 5. 7. Cp. 1. 32, 35; 6. 35.

beseech. See Ap. 134. I. 5. Not the same word as in *vv.* 31, 32, 37, 41.

29 He had commanded=He was commanding. Imperfect tense.

spirit. Gr. *pneuma.* See Ap. 101. II. 12.

man. Gr. *anthrōpos.* Ap. 123. 1. Not the same word as in *vv.* 27, 38, 41, but the same as in *vv.* 33, 35.

it had caught=it had seized. Only here and in Acts 6. 12; 19. 29; 27. 15.

kept bound=bound, being guarded.

chains, &c. See notes on Mark 5. 4.

he brake the bands, and=breaking the bands, he.

was driven. Gr. *elaunō.* Occurs five times: here; Mark 6. 48. John 6. 19. James 3. 4, and 2 Pet. 2. 17.

of=by. Gr. *hupo.* Ap. 104. xviii. 1.

devil=demon.

30 many, &c. See note on Mark 5. 9.

31 besought. Gr. *parakaleō.* See Ap. 134. I. 6. Not the same word as in *vv.* 28, 37, 38.

the deep. Gr. *abussos*; not the sea as in 5. 4. Occurs nine times: here, Rom. 10. 7. Rev. 9. 1, 2, 11; 11. 7; 17. 8; 20. 1, 3.

32 them=these.

suffered them=gave them leave. Cp. Mark 5. 13. Acts 21. 39, 40; 27. 3.

33 ran=rushed.

down. Gr. *kata.* Ap. 104. x. 1.

a steep place=the precipice.

8. 34-37- (X, above). PEOPLE. PETITION.
(*Introversion and Alternation.*)

X | C | t | 34-. The Swineherds.
    u | -34. Their report.
   D | 35. The Citizens. Fear.
  C | *t* | 36-. The Swineherds.
    u | -36. Their report.
   D | 37-. The Citizens. Request.

34 was done=had happened.

in=into. Gr. *eis.* Ap. 104. vi.

35 at=beside. Gr. *para.* Ap. 104. xii.

in his right mind=of sound mind.

36 he that was possessed of the devils=the demonized [man].

healed=saved. Same word as in *v.* 12.

37 besought=was asking. Gr. *erōtaō.* Ap. 134. I 3.

were taken. A medical word, as in 4. 38.

38 Jesus. All the texts omit.

sent him away. Note the answers to the three prayers in this chapter, in *vv.* 32, 33, 37, 38, 39.

39 to=unto. Gr. *eis.* Ap. 104. vi. Not the same word as in *vv.* 19, 25, 27, -35. **shew**=tell: tell the whole story. **how great things**=whatsoever. **and published**=proclaiming. See Ap. 121. 1. **unto**=for. **40 when . . . returned**=in (Gr. *en.* Ap. 104. viii) . . . returning. **waiting for**=looking for, as in 1. 21; 3. 15; 7. 19, 20; 12. 46. Acts 3. 5; 10. 24; 28. 6, &c.

8. 41-55 [For Structure see next page].

41 And, behold. Fig. *Asterismos* (Ap. 6). These two miracles are not the same as those recorded in Matt. 9. 18-26, but the same as in Mark 5. 22, &c. See the notes there, and Ap. 138.

A. D. 27 °Jairus, and he °was a ruler of the °synagogue: and he fell down [35] at [28] Jesus' feet, and [31] besought Him that He would come [22] into his house:

w 42 For he had one only daughter, about twelve years of age, and she lay a dying.

G^1 x^1 But °as He went the people °thronged Him.

y^1 43 And a woman °having an issue of blood °twelve years, which had spent all her °living °upon physicians, °neither could be [2] healed °of any,

44 Came behind *Him,* and touched the °border of His garment:

z^1 and immediately her issue of blood °stanched.

G^2 x^2 45 And [28] Jesus said, °"Who touched Me?" When all denied, Peter and they that were [13] with Him said, [24] "Master, the multitude °throng Thee and °press *Thee,* and sayest Thou, °'Who touched Me?'"

46 And [28] Jesus said, "Somebody °hath touched Me: for °I perceive that °virtue is gone [2] out of Me."

y^2 47 And when the woman [20] saw that she was [17] not hid, she came trembling, and °falling down before Him, she declared unto Him before all the people [9] for what cause °she had touched Him, and how she was °healed immediately.

z^2 48 And He said unto her, "Daughter, °be of good comfort: thy faith hath °made thee whole; go [34] in peace."

F v 49 While He yet spake, there cometh one °from the ruler of the [41] synagogue's *house,* saying to him,

w "Thy daughter is °dead; trouble [10] not the °Master."

G^3 x^3 50 But when [28] Jesus heard *it,* He answered him, saying, "Fear [10] not: °believe only, and she shall be [48] made whole."

y^3 51 And when He came [22] into the house, He °suffered no man to go in, °save °Peter, and James, and John, and the father and the mother of the maiden.

z^3 52 And all °wept, and bewailed her: but He said, "Weep [10] not; she is [17] not dead, but °sleepeth."

G^4 x^4 53 And they °laughed Him to scorn, °knowing that she was dead.

y^4 54 And He put them all out, and took her by the hand, and called, saying, °"Maid, arise."

z^4 55 And her °spirit °came again, and she arose °straightway: and He °commanded to give her °meat.

P k 56 And her parents were astonished:

i but He charged them that they should tell °no man what °was done.

R^3 J M c **9** Then He called °His twelve disciples together,

d and gave them °power and °authority °over all °devils, and to °cure diseases.

8. 41-55 (*O*, p. 1456). TWO MIRACLES.
(*Alternations, Simple and Extended.*)

O | F | v | 41. Ruler of Synagogue. Appeal.
  w | 42-. Daughter dying.
    G^1 | x^1 | -42. The Throng.
      y^1 | 43, 44-. The Woman. Action.
        z^1 | -44. Healing effected.
    G^2 | x^2 | 45, 46. The Throng.
      y^2 | 47. The Woman. Confession.
        z^2 | 48. Healing confirmed.
(The Woman.)
  F | *v* | 49-. Ruler of Synagogue. Messenger.
  w | -49. Daughter dead.
    G^3 | x^3 | 50. Belief.
      y^3 | 51. Admission.
        z^3 | 52. Miracle assured.
    G^4 | x^4 | 53. Unbelief.
      y^4 | 54. Exclusion.
        z^4 | 55. Miracle effected.
(The Maid.)

Jairus. An Israelite name, Jair (Num. 32. 41. Josh. 13. 30. Judg. 10. 3). **was a** = held the office of. Gr. *huparchō.*
synagogue. Ap. 120.
42 as He went = in (Gr. *en.* Ap. 104. viii) His going.
thronged = were stifling. Gr. *sumpnigō.* Not the same word as in *vv.* 7, 33, but same as "choked" (*v.* 14).
43 having = being in. Gr. *en,* above.
twelve = from (Gr. *apo.* Ap. 104. iv) twelve.
living. Gr. *bios.* See Ap. 170. 2.
upon. Gr. *eis.* Ap. 104. vi.
neither, &c. = could not . . . by any. Gr. *ou . . . oudeis.*
of. Gr. *hupo,* but all the texts read *apo.*
44 border = hem (Num. 15. 38, 39. Deut. 22. 12).
stanched = stopped. A medical term.
45 Who touched = Who [is it] that was touching.
throng. Gr. *sunechō.* Cp. *v.* 37; 4. 38; 12. 50.
press. Gr. *apothlibō.* Occ. only here.
46 hath touched . . . I perceive = did touch . . . I came to know (Gr. *ginōskō.* Ap. 132. I. ii).
virtue = power (inherent). Gr. *dunamis.* See Ap. 172. 1.
47 falling down = having fallen down. In terror.
she had touched = she touched.
healed. See 6. 17.
48 be of good comfort. All the texts omit.
made thee whole = saved thee, as in *vv.* 12, 36, 50.
49 from. Gr. *para.* Ap. 104. xii. 1.
dead. Emph. by Fig. *Hyperbaton.* Ap. 6.
Master = Teacher. Ap. 98. XIV. v.
50 believe. Ap. 150. I. 1. i.
51 suffered no man = suffered not (Gr. *ou.* Ap. 105. I) any one. **save** = except.
Peter, and James, and John. Cp. Mark 9. 12; 14. 33.
52 wept, and bewailed = were weeping and wailing. Both Imperf. Tense. **sleepeth.** Gr. *katheudō.* Ap. 171. 1.
53 laughed Him to scorn = were deriding Him.
knowing. Gr. *oida.* Ap. 132. I. i.
54 Maid = Child. Gr. *pais.* Ap. 108. iv.
55 spirit. Gr. *pneuma.* Ap. 101. II. 6.
came again. A Hebraism. Cp. 1 Sam. 30. 12.
straightway = immediately. Gr. *parachrēma,* as in *vv.* 44, 47. **commanded** = directed.
meat = [something] to eat
56 no man = no one. Gr. *mēdeis.*
was done = had happened.

9. 1-10- (R^3, p. 1446). DISCIPLES. MISSION OF THE TWELVE, AND RETURN.
(*Introversion and Alternation.*)

R^3 | J | 1-6. The Twelve. Sent out.
  K | a | 7-. Herod. What he heard.
    b | -7-. Perplexity.
      L | -7, 8. Reason.
  K | *a* | 9-. Herod. What he said.
    b | -9. Curiosity.
J | 10-. The Twelve. Return.

9. 1-6 [For Structure see next page].

1 His twelve disciples. Most of the texts omit "His disciples". Hence we must render, "the Twelve". Cp. *v.* 10. **power.** Gr. *dunamis.* Ap. 172. 1. **authority.** Gr. *exousia.* See Ap. 172. 5. **over.** Gr. *epi.* Ap. 104. ix. 3. **devils** = the demons. **cure.** Gr. *therapeuō.* Same as "heal" (*v.* 6).

A.D. 27 **2 And He sent them to °preach °the kingdom of God, and to °heal the sick.**

N e **3 And He said °unto them, "Take nothing °for *your* journey, neither °staves, nor °scrip, neither bread, neither money; neither have two coats apiece.**

f **4 And whatsoever house °ye enter °into, there abide, and thence depart.**

e **5 And whosoever °will °not receive you, when ye go out °of that city, °shake off the very dust °from your feet [3]for a testimony °against them."**

M c **6 And they departed,**

d **and went °through the towns, °preaching the gospel, and [1]healing every where.**

K a **7 Now °Herod the tetrarch heard of all that °was done °by Him:**

b **and he was °perplexed,**

L **°because that it was said °of some, that John was risen °from °the dead;**

8 And [7]of some, that °Elias °had appeared; and of others, that one of the old prophets was risen again.

K a **9 And Herod said, "John have I beheaded: but Who is This, °of Whom I hear such things?"**

b **And he °desired to °see Him.**

J **10 And the °apostles, when they were returned, told Him all that they had done.**

Q[4] O **And He took them, and went aside privately**
A.D. 28 **[4]into a desert place belonging to the city called °Bethsaida.**

P **11 And the people, °when they knew *it*, followed Him: and He received them, and spake unto them [9]of [2]the kingdom of God, and [2]healed them that had need of °healing.**

O **12 And when the day began to °wear away, then came the twelve, and said unto Him, "Send the multitude away, that they may go [4]into the towns and country round about, and °lodge, and get °victuals: for we are here °in a desert place."**

13 But He said [3]unto them, "Give ye them to eat." And they said, "We have °no more but five loaves and two °fishes; °except we should go and buy °meat [3]for all this people."

P **14 For they were about five thousand °men. And He said °to His disciples, "Make them °sit down by fifties in a company."**

15 And they did so, and made them all [14]sit down.

16 Then He took the five loaves and the two fishes, and looking up °to °heaven, He blessed them, and brake, and gave to the disciples to set before the multitude.

17 And they did eat, and were all filled: and there was taken up of fragments that °remained to them twelve °baskets.

9. 1-6 (J, p. 1458). THE TWELVE. SENT OUT.
(*Introversions and Alternation.*)

J | M | c | 1-. The Call.
  d | -1, 2. Power given.
 N | e | 3. Preparation.
  f | 4. Reception. } Directions.
  e | 5. Rejection.
 M | c | 6-. The Departure.
  d | -6. Power exercised.

2 preach=proclaim. Ap. 121. 1.
the kingdom of God. See Ap. 114.
heal. Gr. *iaomai.* Not the same word as in *v.* 1.
3 unto=to. Gr. *pros.* Ap. 104. xv. 3.
for=with a view to. Gr. *eis.* Ap. 104. vi.
staves. See note on Matt. 10. 10.
scrip=a collecting bag (for money). See note on Matt. 10. 10.
4 ye enter=ye may enter. (The force of *an.*)
into. Gr. *eis.* Ap. 104. vi.
5 will not=may not. (The force of *an.*)
not. Gr. *mē.* Ap. 105. II. Not the same word as in *vv.* 27, 40, 49, -50, 53, 55, 56, 58.
of=from. Gr. *apo.* Ap. 104. iv. Not the same word as in *vv.* 7, 8, 9, 11-.
shake off, &c. Fig. *Parœmia.* Ap. 6.
from. Gr. *apo.* Ap. 104. iv. Not the same word as in *v.* 7. **against.** Gr. *epi.* Ap. 104. ix. 3.
6 through the towns=village by (Gr. *kata.* Ap. 104. x. 2) village.
preaching the gospel=announcing the glad tidings. Ap. 121. 4. **7 Herod, &c.** See Ap. 109.
was done=was being done "by Him".
by. Gr. *hupo.* Ap. 104. xviii. 1. [L] T Tr. A WH R omit "by Him".
perplexed=bewildered: i.e. seeing no way out. Gr. *diaporeō.* Used only by Luke, here; 24. 4. Acts 2. 12; 5. 24; 10. 17. **because.** Gr. *dia.* Ap. 104. v. 2.
of=by. Gr. *hupo.* Ap. 104. xviii. 1.
from=out from. Gr. *ek.* Ap. 104. vii.
the dead=dead people. No Art. See Ap. 139. 2.
8 Elias=Elijah.
had appeared: i.e. in fulfilment of Mal. 4. 5. Ap. 106. I. i. Not the same word as in *v.* 31.
9 of=concerning. Gr. *peri.* Ap. 104. xiii. 1.
desired=was seeking. More than desiring.
see. Gr. *eidon.* Ap. 133. I. 1. Not the same word as in *v.* 36.
10 apostles. See the Twelve, *v.* 1.

9. -10-17 (Q[4], p. 1446). TOUR. MIRACLE.
(*Alternation.*)

Q[4] | O | -10. The Twelve. Retirement.
 P | 11. The People. Taught.
 O | 12, 13. The Twelve. Colloquy.
 P | 14-17. The People. Fed.

10 Bethsaida. Peculiar to Luke. See Ap. 169. Aram. Ap. 94. III. 3.
11 when they knew=having got to know it. Ap. 132. I. ii. Not the same word as in *vv.* 33, 55.
healing. Gr. *therapeia.* Cp. *v.* 1.
12 wear away=decline.
lodge. Peculiar to Luke, here. Gr. *kataluō,* to unloose, disband, halt, also destroy, its most frequent meaning. Cp. 19. 7; 21. 6. Matt. 5. 17. Mark 14. 58.
victuals=provisions.
in. Gr. *en.* Ap. 104. viii. Not the same word as in *vv.* 48, 49.
13 no. Gr. *ou.* Ap. 105. 1.
fishes; except. Supply the logical *Ellipsis* (Ap. 6): "fishes, [therefore we are not able to give them to eat] except we should go", &c. **except**=unless indeed.
meat=food.
14 men. Gr. pl. of *anēr.* Ap. 123. 2.
to. Gr. *pros.* Ap. 104. xv. 3. Not the same word as in *vv.* 16, -51, 53, 56, 62. **sit down**=recline.
16 to. Gr. *eis.* Ap. 104. vi. Not the same word as in *vv.* 14, 40, 52, 62. **heaven**=the heaven (Sing.). See notes on Matt. 6. 9, 10. **17 remained**=was over and above. Put a comma after "them". **baskets.** See note on Matt. 14. 20.

R[4] g[1] A. D. 28
18 And °it came to pass, °as He was alone
°praying, His disciples were with Him: and
He asked them, saying, °"Whom say the people that I am?"

h[1] **19** They °answering said, "John the Baptist;
but °some *say*, [8]Elias; and °others *say*, that
one of the old prophets is risen again."

g[2] **20** He said unto them, "But [18]whom say ye
that I am?"

h[2] Peter [19]answering said, °"The Christ of God."

g[3] **21** And He °straitly °charged them, and commanded *them* to tell no man °that thing;

G A L P[1] **22** Saying, °"The Son of man °must °suffer
many things, and °be rejected [5]of the elders
and chief priests and scribes, and be slain, and
be °raised °the third day."
23 And He said [14]to *them* all, °"If any *man*
°will come after Me, let him deny himself, and
°take up his cross °daily, and follow Me.
24 For whosoever °will °save his °life shall
lose it: but whosoever °will lose his °life for
My sake, the same shall °save it.
25 For what is a °man °advantaged, °if he
gain the whole °world, °and lose himself, or
°be cast away?
26 For whosoever °shall be ashamed of Me
and of My words, of °him shall [22]the Son of
man be ashamed, when He shall come [12]in His
own °glory, and *in His* Father's, and of the holy
angels.
27 But I tell you °of a truth, there be °some
standing here, which shall °not °taste of
death, till °they [9]see [2]the kingdom of God."

P[2] **28** And [18]it came to pass °about an eight days
°after these sayings, He took Peter and John
and James, and went up [4]into °a mountain
°to pray.
29 °And °as He [28]prayed, the °fashion of His
°countenance °was altered, and His raiment
was white *and* °glistering.
30 And, °behold, there °talked with Him two
[14]men, °which were °Moses and [8]Elias:
31 Who °appeared [12]in [26]glory, and °spake
of His °decease which He °should °accomplish
°at Jerusalem.
32 But Peter and they that were °with him
were °heavy with sleep: and °when they were
awake, they [9]saw His glory, and the two [14]men
that stood with Him.
33 And [18]it came to pass, °as they °departed
[5]from Him, Peter said [3]unto Jesus, °"Master,
it is good for us to be here: and let us make
three °tabernacles; one for Thee, and one for
Moses, and one for [8]Elias:" [5]not °knowing
what he said.

9. 18-21 (R[4], p. 1446). DISCIPLES. CONFESSION OF MESSIAH. (*Repeated Alternation.*)

R[4] | g[1] | 18. The Lord. Question.
  h[1] | 19. Disciples. Answer.
 g[2] | 20-. The Lord. Question.
  h[2] | -20. Peter. Answer.
 g[3] | 21. The Lord. Charge.

18 it came to pass. See note on 2. 1.
as He was=in (Gr. *en.* Ap. 104. viii) His praying. The fourth of seven such recorded occasions.
praying. Peculiar to Luke, here. Ap. 134. I. 2.
Whom=Who.
19 answering said. See note on Deut. 1. 41.
some=others. Ap. 124. 1.
others. Same as "some" above.
20 The Christ=The Messiah. Ap. 98. IX.
21 straitly=strictly.
charged=charged (under penalty).
that thing=this. Thus closes the second of the four great periods of the Lord's ministry. Enough had been said and done by Him. See Ap. 119.

9. 22—18. 43 [For Structure see next page].

9. 22-36 (L, p. 1461). SUFFERINGS. FIRST ANNOUNCEMENT. (*Division.*)

L | P[1] | 22-27. The Sufferings and Glory. Foretold.
 | P[2] | 28-36. The Sufferings and Glory. Foreshown.

22 The Son of man. See Ap. 98. XVI.
must=it is necessary. See 24. 26. Acts 3. 18.
suffer=to suffer. This is the first mention of His sufferings. See the Structure, and cp. "L", "N", and "*L*", "*N*". Note that these are never mentioned apart from the "glory" (*vv.* 26, 32) in either O.T. or N.T.
be rejected. After trial, therefore trial premeditated, and deliberate, "after three days" (Matt. 27. 63).
raised. Pass. of *egeirō.* Ap. 178. 4.
the third day. But see Ap. 148.
23 If any man, &c. See Ap. 118. 2. a.
will come=desireth (Ap. 102. 1) to come.
take up=let him take up.
daily. Peculiar to Luke, here.
24 will=desireth, or willeth (Ap. 102. 1) to.
save. Gr. *sōzō.* **life**=soul. Gr. *psuchē.* Ap 110. III. 1.
25 man. Gr. *anthrōpos.* Ap. 123. 1.
advantaged=profited.
if he gain=having gained. A mercantile word.
world. Gr. *kosmos.* Ap. 129. 1.
and lose himself=having destroyed himself.
be cast away=suffer loss. Another mercantile word.
26 shall be ashamed of=may (with Gr. *an*) have been ashamed of; implying [before men].
him=this [one].
glory. Often mentioned by itself, but the sufferings never mentioned apart from it.
27 of a truth. Thus emphasizing the coming statement. **some**=some of those.
not=in no wise, or by no means. Gr. *ou mē* (Ap. 105. III). **taste of**=experience [the approach of].
they see=they may possibly (Gr. *an*) have seen.
28 about an eight days. This is *inclusive* reckoning (including parts of two other days), and is exactly the same as the exclusive *six* days of Matt. 17. 1 and Mark 9. 2. **after.** Gr. *meta.* Ap. 104. xi. 2.
a=the (well known).
to pray. Ap. 134. I. 2. This is the fifth of seven such occasions. Peculiar to Luke, here. **29 And**=And it came to pass. **as He prayed**=in (Gr. *en.* Ap. 104. viii) His praying. **fashion**=appearance. **countenance**=face. **was altered**=[became] different. Gr. *heteros.* Ap. 124. 2. **glistering**=effulgent, or lightening forth (as though from internal light). The Eng. "glister" is from the Anglo-Saxon *glisian*=to shine, or glitter. **30 behold.** Fig. *Asterismos* (Ap. 6). **talked**=were talking. **which**=who. **Moses.** See Ap. 149. **31 appeared . . . and**=being seen. See Ap. 106. vi. **spake**=were speaking. Peculiar to Luke, here. **decease.** Gr. *exodos.* See Ap. 149. **should**=was about to. **accomplish.** His death did not merely *happen.* It was He Who Himself accomplished it and fulfilled all the Scriptures concerning it. Cp. *v.* 53 and Isa. 50. 7. **at**=in. Gr. *en.* Not the same word as in *vv.* 43, 61. **32 with.** Gr. *sun.* Ap. 104. xvi. Not the same word as in *v.* 41. **heavy**=oppressed. **when they were awake**=on fully waking up. Gr. *diagrēgoreō.* Occ. only here. **33 as they departed**=in (Gr. *en.* Ap. 104. viii. 1) their departing. Peculiar to Luke, here. The verb *diachōrizomai* occ. only here in N.T. **Master.** Gr. *epistatēs.* Ap. 98. XIV. iv. Used only of Christ, as having authority. **tabernacles.** Cp. Matt. 17. 4. **knowing.** Gr. *oida.* Ap. 132. I. i. Not the same word as in *v.* 11.

A. D. 28 **34 While he thus spake, °there came a cloud, and °overshadowed °them: and they feared °as they entered [10] into the cloud.**

35 And [34] there came a voice °out of the cloud, saying, "This is My beloved Son: °hear Him."

36 And °when the voice was past, Jesus was found alone. And they °kept *it* close, and told °no man [12] in those days any of those things which they had °seen.

M Q i **37 And [18] it came to pass, that °on the next day, when they were °come down [5] from °the hill, much people met Him.**

k **38 And, [30] behold, a [14] man [22] of the company cried out, saying, °"Master, I °beseech Thee, °look °upon my son: for he is mine only child.**

R T l **39 And, °lo, a °spirit taketh him, and he °suddenly crieth out; and it °teareth him °that he foameth again, and °bruising him hardly departeth [5] from him.**

m **40 And I [38] besought Thy disciples to cast °him out;**

U **and they could °not."**

S **41 And Jesus [19] answering said, "O °faithless and °perverse generation, how long shall I be °with you, and °suffer you?**

R T m **Bring thy son hither."**

l **42 And as he was yet °a coming, the °devil °threw him down, and °tare *him*.**

U **And Jesus rebuked the unclean [39] spirit, and [2] healed the °child,**

Q k **and delivered him again to his father.**

i **43 And they were all °amazed °at the °mighty power of God.**

B N **But while they °wondered every one °at all**

9. 22—18. 43 (*G*, p. 1427). THE THIRD PERIOD OF THE LORD'S MINISTRY. THE REJECTION OF THE KING. (*Introversion and Alternations.*)

G | A | L | 9. 22-36. Sufferings. First Announcement.
| | M | 9. 37-43-. Miracle. Lunatic son.
| B | N | 9. -43-45. Sufferings. Second Announcement.
| | O | 9. 46-62. Disciples instructed as to the then *present*.
| C | 10. 1-24. The Kingdom nigh.
| D | 10. 25-37. Demand of Lawyer.
| E | 10. 38-42. Journey.
| F | 11. 1-13. Disciples. Request. Prayer.
| G | 11. 14—13. 9. Miracles, &c.
| H | 13. 10-17. Place. Synagogue. Sabbath. Miracle.
| J | 13. 18-21. The Kingdom. Likeness.
| *J* | 13. 22-35. The Kingdom. Entrance.
| *H* | 14. 1-24. Place. Pharisee's house. Sabbath. Miracle.
| *G* | 14. 25—17. 4. Parables.
| *F* | 17. 5-10. Disciples. Request. Faith.
| *E* | 17. 11-19. Journey.
| *D* | 17. 20-. Demand of Pharisees.
| *C* | 17. -20-24. The Kingdom nigh.
| *B* | *N* | 17. 25. Sufferings. Third Announcement.
| | *O* | 17. 26—18. 30. Disciples instructed as to the *future*.
| *A* | *L* | 18. 31-34. Sufferings: Fourth Announcement.
| | *M* | 18. 35-43. Miracle. The Blind Man.

34 there came = there came to be. **overshadowed** = enveloped. The word occ. only here, 1. 35. Matt. 17. 5. Mark 9. 7. Acts 5. 15. **them:** i. e. the three, not the six, as the Apostles heard the voice "out of" the cloud. **as they entered** = in (Gr. *en*. Ap. 104. viii) their entering. **35 out of.** Gr. *ek*. Ap. 104. vii. Not the same word as in *v.* 5. **hear** = hear ye. **36 when . . . was past**, lit. in (Gr. *en*. Ap. 104. viii) the passing of. **kept it close** = were silent. **no man** = no one. Compound of *ou*. Ap. 105. I. **seen.** Gr. *horaō*. Ap. 133. 8.

9. 37-43- (M, above). MIRACLE. THE LUNATIC SON. (*Introversions.*)

M | Q | i | 37. Much People met the Lord.
| | k | 38. The Father. Plea for his Son.
| R | T | l | 39. Lunatic's seizure.
| | | m | 40-. Father besought Disciples.
| | U | -40. Inability of Disciples.
| | S | 41-. Reproof of Unbelief.
| *R* | *T* | *m* | -41. Father commanded to bring.
| | | *l* | 42-. Lunatic's seizure.
| | *U* | -42-. Ability of the Lord.
| *Q* | *k* | -42. The Father. Son delivered.
| | *i* | 43-. All the People amazed.

37 on. Gr. *en*. Ap. 104. viii. **come down.** Gr. *katerchomai*, only once outside Luke and Acts (in Jas. 3. 15). **the hill** = the mountain, as in *v.* 28. **38 Master** = Teacher. Ap. 98. XIV. v. **beseech.** Ap. 134. I. 5. **look.** Gr. *epiblepō*. Ap. 133. III. 4. **upon.** Gr. *epi*. Ap. 104. ix. 3. **39 lo.** Fig. *Asterismos*. Ap. 6. **spirit.** Gr. *pneuma*. Ap. 101. II. 12: a demon; cp. *v.* 42. **suddenly.** Gr. *exaiphnēs*. Only here, 2. 13. Mark 13. 36. Acts 9. 3; 22. 6, always in connection with supernatural events. **teareth him** = throws him into convulsions. **that he foameth again** = with (Gr. *meta*. Ap. 104. xi. 1) foaming. **bruising him** = making a complete wreck of him. Cp. Mark 5. 4. Rev. 2. 27. **40 him** = it. **not.** Gr. *ou*. Ap. 105. I. **41 faithless** = unbelieving. **perverse** = perverted. **with.** Gr. *pros*. Ap. 104. xv. 3. Not the same word as in *vv.* 32-, 49. **suffer** = bear with. Cp. Acts 18. 14. 2 Cor. 11. 1. **42 a coming** = coming near. **devil** = demon. A spirit, *v.* 39. **threw** = dashed. **tare** = completely convulsed. Gr. *susparassō*. Occ. only here in N.T. **child.** Gr. *pais*. Ap. 108. iv. Not the same word as in *v.* 47. **43 amazed** = astonished. **at.** Gr. *epi*. Ap. 104. ix. 2. Not the same word as in *vv.* 31, 61. **mighty power** = majesty. Occ. only here, Acts 19. 27, and 2 Pet. 1. 16. **wondered** = were wondering.

A. D. 28 things which °Jesus did, He said [3] unto His disciples,

44 "Let these °sayings sink down [10] into your ears: for [22] the Son of man °shall be °delivered [10] into the hands of [25] men."

45 But they °understood not this °saying, and it was °hid [5] from them, that they °perceived it [5] not: and they feared to ask Him [9] of that °saying.

O V¹ n 46 Then there arose a reasoning °among them, °which of them should be °greatest.

o 47 And Jesus, °perceiving the °thought of their heart, took a °child, and set him °by Him,

o 48 And said unto them, "Whosoever shall receive this [47] child °in My name receiveth Me: and whosoever shall receive Me receiveth Him That sent Me:

n for he that °is °least [46] among you all, the same °shall be great."

V² p 49 And John [19] answered and said, [33] "Master, we [9] saw one casting out [42] devils [48] in Thy name; and we forbad him,

q because he followeth [40] not °with us."

p 50 And Jesus said [3] unto him, "Forbid *him* [5] not:

q for he that is [40] not °against °us is °for °us."

V³ r 51 And [1] it came to pass, °when the time was come °that He should be received up, °He stedfastly °set His face to go [16] to Jerusalem,

s 52 And sent messengers °before His face: and they went, and entered [10] into a village of the °Samaritans, to °make ready for Him.

r 53 And they did [40] not receive Him, because His face was as though He °would go [16] to Jerusalem.

s 54 And when His disciples James and John [9] saw *this*, they said, °"Lord, °wilt Thou that we °command fire to come down from °heaven, and consume them, °even as [8] Elias did?"

55 But He turned, and rebuked them, °and said, "Ye [33] know [40] not what manner of °spirit ye are of.

56 For [22] the Son of man °is [40] not come to destroy [25] men's °lives, but to [24] save *them*." And they went [16] to °another village.

V⁴ t¹ 57 And [18] it came to pass, that, °as they went [12] in the way, °a certain *man* said [3] unto Him, °"Lord, I will follow Thee whithersoever Thou goest."

u¹ 58 And Jesus said unto him, "Foxes have

Jesus. Most of the texts omit "Jesus" here.

44 sayings = words. Pl. of *logos*. See note on Mark 9. 32. Not the same word as in *v.* 45.

shall be = is about to be.

delivered = delivered up. The second announcement of His sufferings. See the Structure on p. 1461.

45 understood not = were ignorant of.

saying. Gr. *rhēma*. Not the same word as in *v.* 44. See note on Mark 9. 32. **hid** = veiled.

perceived it not = should not understand it. Not the same word as in *v.* 47.

9. 46–62 (O, p. 1461). DISCIPLES. INSTRUCTED AS TO THE *PRESENT*. (*Division.*)

O | V¹ | 46–48. *Re* Humility. All the Disciples.
  | V² | 49, 50. *Re* Fellowship. One (John).
  | V³ | 51–56. *Re* Forbearance. Two (James and John).
  | V⁴ | 57–62. *Re* Discipleship. Three (unnamed).

9. 46–48 (V¹, above). *Re* HUMILITY. ALL THE DISCIPLES. (*Introversion.*)

V¹ | n | 46. Reasoning.
   | o | 47. Child taken.
   | *o* | 48–. Child received.
   | *n* | –48. Reasoning.

46 among. Gr. *en*. Ap. 104. viii. 2.

which = who. **greatest** = greater.

47 perceiving = having seen. Ap. 133. I. 1. Not the same word as in *v.* 45.

thought = reasoning, as in *v.* 46.

child. Ap. 108. v. Not the same word as in *v.* 42.

by = beside. Gr. *para*. Ap. 104. xii. 2. Not the same word as in *v.* 7.

48 in. Gr. *epi*. Ap. 104. ix. 2.

is = subsists or exists. Gr. *huparchō*, not the verb "to be". See Phil. 2. 6 (being); 3. 20 (is).

least = lowliest.

shall be. All the texts read "is".

9. 49, 50 (V², above). *Re* FELLOWSHIP. ONE (JOHN). (*Alternation.*)

V² | p | 49–. Prohibition. Positive.
   | q | –49. Reason. "Because."
   | *p* | 50–. Prohibition. Negative.
   | *q* | –50. Reason. "For."

49 with = in association with. Gr. *meta*. Ap. 104 xi. 1. Not the same word as in *vv.* 32–, 41.

50 against. Gr. *kata*. Ap. 104. x. 1.

us. All the texts read "you".

for us = on our behalf. Gr. *huper*. Ap. 104. xvii. 1.

9. 51–56 (V³, above). *Re* FORBEARANCE. (*Alternation.*)

V³ | r | 51. The Lord. Purpose. "His face set."
   | s | 52. Disciples. Mission.
   | *r* | 53. The Lord. Purpose. "His face set."
   | *s* | 54–56. Disciples. Resentment rebuked.

51 These verses are peculiar to Luke.

when the time was come = in (Gr. *en*. Ap. 104. viii) the fulfilling of the days. Marking a certain stage of the Lord's ministry.

that He should be received up = for the receiving Him up. Gr. *analēpsis*. Occ. only here in the N.T. The kindred verb *analambanō* is used of the ascension of Elijah in Sept. (2 Kings 2. 11), and of the Lord in Mark 16. 19. Acts 1. 2, 11, 22, and 1 Tim. 3. 16. **He** = He Himself. **set His face.** See note on *v.* 31. Isa. 50. 7. **52 before.** Gr. *pro*. Ap. 104. xiv. **Samaritans.** Cp. 2 Kings 17. 26–33. **make ready** = to prepare [reception]. **53 would go** = was going. **54 Lord.** Ap. 98. VI. i. *a* 3. A. **wilt.** Ap. 102. 1. **command fire** = should call down fire. **heaven** = the heaven (Sing.). See note on Matt. 6. 9, 10. **even as Elias did** = as Elijah also did. See 2 Kings 1. 10. Omitted by T Trm. [A] WH. **55 and said . . . save them** (*v.* 56). This clause is omitted by all the texts. **spirit.** Heb. *pneuma*. See Ap. 101. II. 7. **56 is not come** = came not. **lives** = souls. Ap. 110. III. 1. **another** = different. Ap. 124. 2.

9. 57–62 [For Structure see next page].

57 as they went = in (Gr. *en*. Ap. 104. viii) their going. **a certain man.** A scribe (Matt. 8. 19) **Lord.** Om. L T Tr. [A] WH R.

A.D. 28 holes, and birds of °the air *have* nests; but
[22]the Son of man °hath [40]not where to lay *His*
head."

t² 59 And He said [3]unto [56]another, "Follow
Me." But he said, [54]"Lord, °suffer me first to
go and °bury my father."

u² 60 [43]Jesus said unto him, "Let the dead
[59]bury °their dead: but go thou and °preach
[2]the kingdom of God."

t³ 61 And [56]another also said, "Lord, I will follow Thee; but °let me first go bid them farewell, which are °at home at my house."

u³ 62 And Jesus said [3]unto him, °"No man,
having put his °hand to the plough, and °look-
ing back, is fit for [2]the kingdom of God."

C W **10** °After these things the °Lord °appointed
°other °seventy also, and sent them two
and two °before His face °into every city and
place, whither He Himself °would come.
2 Therefore said He °unto them, "The harvest truly *is* great, but the labourers *are* few:
°pray ye therefore the [1]Lord of the harvest,
that He °would send forth labourers [1]into His
harvest.

X 3 Go your ways: °behold, I send you forth as
lambs °among wolves.
4 Carry °neither °purse, °nor °scrip, °nor
°shoes: and °salute °no man °by the way.

Y v¹ 5 And [1]into whatsoever house °ye enter, first
say, °'Peace *be* to this house.'
6 And °if the son of peace be there, your
peace shall rest upon it: °if °not, it shall turn
°to you again.
7 And °in the same house remain, eating and
drinking such things as °they give: for the
labourer is worthy of his hire. Go °not °from
house °to house.
8 And [1]into whatsoever city °ye enter, and
they receive you, eat such things as are set
before you:
9 And °heal the sick that are °therein,

w¹ and say °unto them, °'The kingdom of God is
°come nigh °unto you.'

v² 10 But [1]into whatsoever city [8]ye enter, and
they receive you [7]not, go your ways out [1]into
the streets of the same, and say,
11 'Even the very dust °of your city, which
°cleaveth on us, we do °wipe off against you:

w² °notwithstanding °be ye sure of this, that [9]the
kingdom of God is [9]come nigh [9]unto you.'

v³ 12 But I say unto you, that it shall be more
tolerable [7]in that day for Sodom, than for that
city.
13 Woe unto thee, °Chorazin! woe unto
thee, °Bethsaida! for [-6]if the °mighty works
had °been done [7]in Tyre and Sidon, which
have °been done [7]in you, they had a great

9. 57-62 (V⁴, p. 1462). *Re* DISCIPLESHIP. THREE (UNNAMED). (*Repeated Alternation.*)

V⁴ | t¹ | 57. Forwardness.
| u¹ | 58. Discouragement.
| t² | 59. Backwardness.
| u² | 60. Encouragement.
| t³ | 61. Undecidedness.
| u³ | 62. Reproof.

58 the air = the heaven, as in *v.* 54.
hath not where, &c. See note on Matt. 8. 20, and cp. Rev. 14. 14.
59 suffer me = allow me.
bury my father. A euphemism for declining an invitation, as the Jews buried within twenty-four hours and did not leave the house for ten days.
60 their = their own.
preach = declare. Gr. *diangellō.* Ap. 121. 6. Occurs elsewhere only in Acts 21. 26 (signify). Rom. 9. 17.
61 let = allow. Verses 61, 62 are peculiar to Luke.
at home at my house = in (Gr. *eis.* Ap. 104. vi) my house, or at home.
62 No man = no one. Compound of *ou.* Ap. 105. I.
hand. Plough always held with one hand.
looking. Ap. 133. I. 5.

10. 1-24 (C, p. 1461). THE KINGDOM NIGH. (*Introversion and Repeated Alternation.*)

C | W | 1, 2. The Seventy. Sent.
| X | 3, 4. The Disciples' danger.
| Y | v¹ | 5-9-. Houses and Cities. Entrance.
| w¹ | -9. Message: Kingdom nigh.
| v² | 10, 11-. Cities. Rejection.
| w² | -11. Message: Kingdom nigh.
| v³ | 12-15. Cities. Retribution.
| *X* | 16. The Disciples' danger.
| *W* | 17-24. The Seventy. Return.

Verses 1-16 are peculiar to Luke.
1 After. Gr. *meta.* Ap. 104. xi. 2.
Lord. Ap. 98. VI.
appointed. Gr. *anadeiknumi.* Occ. only here, and Acts 1. 24 (shew).
other = others, as in 9. 56, 59, 61.
seventy also: i. e. as well as the Twelve.
before. Gr. *pro.* Ap. 104. xiv.
into. Gr. *eis.* Ap. 104. vi.
would come = was about to come.
2 unto. Gr. *pros.* Ap. 104. xv. 3. Not the same word as in *vv.* -9, 11.
pray. Gr. *deomai.* Ap. 134. I. 5. Implying the sense of need.
would = may.
3 behold = lo. Fig. *Asterismos.* Ap. 6.
among = in (Gr. *en.* Ap. 104. viii) the midst.
4 neither = not. Gr. *mē.* Ap. 105. II.
purse. Gr. *balantion.* Peculiar to Luke; only here; 12. 33; 22. 35, 36.
nor. Gr. *mē.*
scrip = a beggar's collecting bag. See on Matt. 10. 10.
nor. Gr. *mēde.*
shoes = sandals: i. e. a second pair or change.
salute = greet. In Luke only here and 1. 40.
no man. Gr. *mēdeis.*
by. Gr. *kata.* Ap. 104. x. 2.
5 ye enter = ye may enter.
Peace, &c. The usual salutation. Cp. Judg. 19. 20.
6 if = if indeed. A condition of uncertainty. Ap. 118. 1 b.
if not. Gr. *ei* (Ap. 118. 2. a) *mēge* (Ap. 105. II).
to. Gr. *epi.* Ap. 104. ix. 3. Not the same word as in *vv.* 7, 15, 30, -34.
7 in. Gr. *en.* Ap. 104. viii.
they give = are with (Gr. *para.* Ap. 104. xii. 1) them.
not. Gr. *mē.* Ap. 105. II.
from = out of. Gr. *ek.* Ap. 104. vii. Not the same word as in *vv.* 21, 30, 42.
to. Gr. *eis.* Ap. 104. vi.
8 ye enter = ye may enter (with Gr. *an*).

9 heal. See on 6. 18. **therein** = in (Gr. *en.* Ap. 104. viii) it. **unto** = to. **The kingdom of God.** See Ap. 114. **come nigh** = drawn nigh. **unto.** Gr. *epi.* Ap. 104. ix. 3. **11 of** = out of. Gr. *ek.* Ap. 104. vii. Not the same word as in *v.* 22. **cleaveth.** A medical term, used of the uniting of wounds. **wipe off.** Gr. *apomassō.* Occ. only here in N.T. All the texts add "the feet" (A, "our feet"). **notwithstanding.** See note on *v.* 20. **be ye sure** = get to know. Gr. *ginōskō.* Ap. 132. I. ii. **13 Chorazin . . . Bethsaida.** See Ap. 169. **Bethsaida.** Aram. Ap. 94. III. 3. **mighty works** = powers. Gr. pl. of *dunamis.* See Ap. 172. 1. **been done** = taken place.

A. D. 28 while ago °repented, sitting [7]in °sackcloth and °ashes.

14 °But it shall be more tolerable for Tyre and Sidon °at the judgment, than for you.

15 And **thou**, °Capernaum, °which art exalted °to °heaven, °shalt be thrust down °to °hell.

X 16 He that heareth you heareth Me; and he that °despiseth you °despiseth Me; and he that °despiseth Me °despiseth Him That °sent Me."

W Z^1 x 17 And °the seventy returned again °with joy,

y saying, "Lord, even the °devils are °subject unto us °through Thy name."

18 And He said unto them, °"I beheld °Satan as lightning °fall [7]from [15]heaven.

19 [3]Behold, °I give unto you °power to tread °on serpents and scorpions, and °over all the °power of the enemy: and °nothing shall by any means hurt you.

x 20 °Notwithstanding [7]in this rejoice [7]not, that the °spirits are [17]subject unto you;

y but rather rejoice, because your names °are written [7]in °heaven."

Z^2 A^1 21 [7]In that hour °Jesus °rejoiced °in spirit, and said, °"I thank Thee, O Father, °Lord of [15]heaven and earth,

A^2 B a that Thou °hast hid these things °from the wise and prudent, and °hast revealed them unto babes:

b even so, Father; for °so it °seemed good °in Thy sight.

C 22 All things °are delivered to Me °of My Father: and °no man °knoweth Who the Son is, °but the Father; and Who the Father is, °but the Son,

C and *he* to whom the Son °will reveal *Him*."

B b 23 And He turned Him [2]unto *His* disciples, and said privately, °"Blessed *are* °the eyes which °see the things that ye °see:

a 24 For I °tell you, that many °prophets and °kings have °desired to °see those things which **ye** [23]see, and have °not °seen *them;* and to hear those things which ye hear, and have °not heard *them*."

repented. See Ap. 111. I. 1.

sackcloth. Gr. *sakkos*, from Heb. *saḳ*=sacking. A coarsely woven material used for sieves and strainers (worn next the skin in mourning), Isa. 3. 24. Job 16. 15. 1 Kings 21. 27. 2 Kings 6. 30; not laid aside at night, 1 Kings 21. 27. Joel 1. 13. Cp. Isa. 20. 2, &c.

ashes. Also a sign of mourning. See 1 Sam. 4. 12. 2 Sam. 1. 2; 13. 19. Job 2. 12. Ezek. 27. 30, &c.

14 But=Howbeit. See note on *v.* 20.

at=in. Gr. *en.* Ap. 104. viii. Not the same word as in *vv.* 32, 39.

15 Capernaum. See Ap. 169.

which art exalted. All the texts read, "shalt thou be exalted?" (with *mē*, Ap. 105. II. Interrog.).

to. Gr. *heōs.* As far as to.

heaven=the heaven (sing). See note on Matt. 6. 9, 10.

shalt, &c.=thou shalt be brought down.

hell. Gr. *Hadēs.* See Ap. 131. 2.

16 despiseth=rejecteth. See 7. 30, and cp. Gal. 2. 21; 3. 15.

sent. Ap. 174. I.

10. 17-24 (*W*, p. 1463). THE SEVENTY. RETURN. (*Division.*)

W | Z^1 | 17-20. The Joy of the Seventy.
| Z^2 | 21-24. The Joy of the Lord.

10. 17-20 (Z^1, above). THE JOY OF THE SEVENTY. (*Alternation.*)

Z^1 | x | 17-. Joy. Manifestation.
| y | -17-19. Cause. Subjection of Spirits.
| *x* | 20-. Joy. Dehortation.
| *y* | -20. Cause. Names written in heaven.

17 the seventy. See note on *v.* 1.

with. Gr. *meta.* Ap. 104. xi. 3. Not the same word as in *v.* 27.

devils=demons.

subject=subdued, put under. Cp. 2. 51. 1 Cor. 15. 27, 28. Eph. 11. 22. Phil. 3. 21.

through. Gr. *en.* Ap. 104. viii.

18 I beheld. Gr. *theōreō.* Ap. 133. I. 11.

Satan. Heb. transliterated=the Adversary. 1 Sam. 29. 4. *Diabolos* is the more frequent term in the N.T. Both are in Rev. 12. 9.

fall=having fallen.

19 I give=I have given. So L m T Tr. A WH R.

power=authority. Gr. *exousia.* Ap. 172. 5.

on. Gr. *epanō*, upon (from above). Not the same word as in *vv.* 34, 35, 37.

over=upon. Gr. *epi.* Ap. 104. ix. 3.

power=might. Gr. *dunamis.* Ap. 172. 1.

nothing . . . by any means. Gr. *ouden . . ou mē.* Ap. 105. I, III.

20 Notwithstanding. Gr. *plēn*, as in *v.* 11; rendered "But" in *v.* 14, an emphatic conjunction.

spirits. Ap. 101. II. 12.

are written=have been written (T Tr. WH R), or inscribed (T WH). See Ex. 32. 32. Ps. 69. 28. Dan. 12. 1. Phil. 4. 3. Heb. 12. 23. Rev. 3. 5; 13. 8; 17. 8; 20. 12; 21. 27; 22. 19.

heaven=the heavens (pl.). See notes on Matt. 6. 9, 10.

10. 21-24 (Z^2, above). THE JOY OF THE LORD. (*Division.*)

Z^2 | A^1 | 21-. Thanksgiving. Expressed.
| A^2 | -21-24. Thanksgiving. Cause: Revelation.

21 Jesus. Om. by all the texts. **rejoiced**=exulted. **in spirit.** Gr. *en* (Ap. 104. viii) *pneuma.* See Ap. 101. II. 8. But all the texts read "by the Spirit, the Holy [Spirit]". Ap. 101. II. 3. **I thank.** See notes on Matt. 11. 25-27. **Lord, &c.** Having therefore absolute power. Ap. 98. VI. i. *a.* 1. B. b.

10. -21-24 (A^2, above). THANKSGIVING. CAUSE: REVELATION. (*Introversions.*)

A^2 | B | a | -21-. Things hidden. (Neg.) } Recipients.
| | b | -21. Things revealed. (Pos.) }
| C | 22-. Revelation. By the Father.
| *C* | -22. Revelation. By the Son.
| *B* | *b* | 23. Things revealed. (Pos.) } Recipients.
| | *a* | 24. Things hidden. (Neg.) }

hast hid=didst hide. **from.** Gr. *apo.* Ap. 104. iv. **hast revealed**=didst reveal. **so**=thus. **seemed good**=was it well-pleasing. **in Thy sight**=before thee. **22 are**=were. **of**=by. Gr. *hupo.* Ap. 104. xviii. 1. **no.** Gr. *ou.* Ap. 105. I. **knoweth**=getteth to know. Gr. *ginōskō.* Ap. 132. I. ii. **but**=except. **will reveal Him**=willeth (Ap. 102. 3) to reveal [Him]. **23 Blessed**= Happy. Fig. *Beatitudo*, not *Benedictio.* **the eyes.** Put by Fig. *Synecdochē*, of the Part (Ap. 6), for the whole person. **see.** Gr. *blepō.* Ap. 133. I. 5. **24 tell you**=say to you. **prophets.** Abraham (Gen. 20. 7; 23. 6), Jacob (Gen. 49. 18; Ap. 36), &c. **kings.** David (2 Sam. 23. 1-5). **desired.** Gr. *thelō.* Ap. 102. 1. **see.** Gr. *eidon.* Ap. 133. I. 1. **not.** Gr. *ou.* Ap. 105. I.

D E[1] c 25 And, [3]behold, a certain °lawyer stood up,
A.D. 28 °and tempted Him, saying, °"Master, what
shall I do to inherit eternal life?"

d 26 He said [2]unto him, °"What is written [7]in
°the law? how readest thou?"

c 27 And he answering said, **"Thou shalt °love
the °LORD thy God °with all thy heart,
°and °with all thy °soul, °and °with all thy
°strength, °and °with all thy mind; °and thy
neighbour as thyself."**

d 28 And He said unto him, "Thou hast answered °right: °this do, and °thou °shalt live."

E[2] F 29 °But he, °willing to justify himself,

G said [2]unto Jesus, "And who is my °neigh-
bour?"

H 30 And Jesus °answering said, "A certain
°*man* went °down [21]from Jerusalem [7]to Jericho, and fell among °thieves, which °strip-
ped him of his raiment, and °wounded *him,*
and °departed, °leaving *him* °half dead.

J[1] c[1] 31 And °by °chance °there came down a certain °priest that way:

d[1] and when he [24-]saw him, he °passed by on the
other side.

J[2] c[2] 32 And likewise a Levite, °when he was °at
the °place,

d[2] came and °looked *on him,* and [31]passed by on
the other side.

J[3] c[3] 33 But a certain Samaritan, as he °journeyed,
°came °where he was:

d[3] e and when he [24-]saw him,
he °had compassion *on him,*

f 34 And went to *him,* and °bound up his
°wounds, °pouring in oil and wine, and set him
°on his own beast, and brought him [7]to an °inn,

e and took care of him.

H 35 And [34]on the morrow when he departed,
he took out two °pence, and gave *them* to °the
host, and said unto him, 'Take care of him;
and °whatsoever thou °spendest more, °when
I come again, °I will repay thee.'

10. 25-37 (D, p. 1461). DEMAND OF LAWYER. (*Division.*)

D | E[1] | 25-28. His first demand. "What?", &c.
 | E[2] | 29-37. His second demand. "Who?", &c.

10. 25-28 (E[1], above). HIS FIRST DEMAND. WHAT? (*Alternation.*)

E[1] | c | 25. The Lawyer. Question: "What shall I do?"
 | d | 26. The Lord. Answered by two other Questions: "What? . . . How?"
 | c | 27. The Lawyer. Answer.
 | *d* | 28. The Lord. Answer.

25 lawyer = doctor or teacher of the Law.
and tempted Him = putting Him to the test.
Master = Teacher. Ap. 98. XIV. v.
26 What is written . . . ? = What standeth written? See Ap. 143.
the law. See note on Matt. 5. 17, and Ap. 117.
27 love. Ap. 135. I. 1.
LORD = Jehovah (Deut. 6. 5; 10. 12. Lev. 19. 18). Ap. 98. VI. i. *a.* 1. B. a. **with** = out of. Gr. *ek.* Ap. 104. vii.
and. Note the Fig. *Polysyndeton.* Ap. 6.
soul. Gr. *psuchē.* Ap. 110. V. 1.
strength. Gr. *ischus.* Ap. 172. 3.
with all thy mind. All the texts read *en* (Ap. 104. viii) instead of *ek* (Ap. 104. vii).
and thy neighbour, &c. Lev. 19. 18.
28 right = rightly, or correctly.
this do. No one ever did it, because the Law was given that, being convicted of our impotence, we might thankfully cast ourselves on His omnipotence. Cp. Rom. 7. 7-13.
thou shalt live. See notes on Lev. 18. 5, and cp. Ezek. 20. 11, 13, 21. But see Rom. 3. 21, 22. This is why Deut. 6. 5 is one of the passages inscribed in the Phylacteries. See Structure of Ex. 13. 3-16, and note on Deut. 6. 4. **shalt** = wilt. Cp. Gal. 3. 22.

10. 29-37 (E[2], above). HIS SECOND DEMAND. WHO? (*Introversion and Repeated Alternation.*)

E[2] | F | 29-. Self-justification.
 G | -29. Question of the Lawyer. "Who?"
 H | 30-. The Traveller. Left for Death.
 J[1] | c[1] | 31-. The Priest.
 d[1] | -31. His conduct.
 J[2] | c[2] | 32-. The Levite.
 d[2] | -32. His conduct.
 J[3] | c[3] | 33-. The Samaritan.
 d[3] | -33, 34. His conduct.
 H | 35. The Traveller. Left for Life.
 G | 36. Question of the Lord. "Which?"
 F | 37. Self-condemnation.

29 But he, &c. Verses 29-37 peculiar to Luke.
willing = desiring, as in *v.* 24.
neighbour. Cp. Matt. 5. 43. Lev. 19. 18.
30 answering = taking him up. Gr. *hupolambanō.* Used only by Luke, here, 7. 43. Acts 1. 9; 2. 15, and in this sense only here = taking [the ground] from under him. **man.** Gr. *anthrōpos.* Ap. 123. 1. **down.** In more senses than one. The road was a steep descent. Cp. 19. 28. **thieves** = robbers, or brigands, as in Matt. 26. 55. John 18. 40. See notes there. **stripped, &c.** Not of his raiment only, but of all he had. **wounded** = inflicted wounds. **departed** = went off. **leaving him.** Supply, with the force of the verb *tunchanō* = leaving him [for all they cared] half dead. **half dead.** Gr. *hēmithanēs.* Occ. only here in N.T. **31 by** = according to. Gr. *kata.* Ap. 104. x. 2. **chance** = coincidence. Occ. only here in N.T. **there came down** = was going down; his duties being over. Jericho was a priestly city. **priest.** Who might become defiled. **passed by on the other side.** One word in Gr. *antiparerchomai.* Occ. only here and *v.* 32 in N.T. **32 when he was** = being. **at.** Gr. *kata.* Ap. 104. x. 2. **place** = spot. **looked on him, and** = seeing (as in *v.* 31) him. **33 journeyed.** Gr. *hodeuō.* Occ. only here. **came where he was.** A beautiful type of the Lord. And the end is seen in John 14. 3. **where he was** = to (*kata,* as above) him.

10. -33, 34 (d[3], above). THE SAMARITAN'S CONDUCT. (*Introversion.*)

d[3] | e | -33. His feeling. Compassion.
 | f | 34-. His conduct. Help.
 | *e* | -34. His feeling. Thoughtful care.

had compassion = was moved with compassion. **34 bound up.** Gr. *katadeō,* a medical word. Occ. only here in N.T. **wounds.** Gr. *trauma.* Occ. only here. **pouring in.** Gr. *epicheō.* Occ. only here. **on** = upon. Gr. *epi.* Ap. 104. ix. 3. **inn.** Gr. *pandocheion* = a *khan.* Occ. only here in N.T. **35 pence** = *denarii.* See Ap. 51. I. 4. Two *denarii* = half a shekel, the ransom money for a life (Ex. 30. 12, 13). **the host.** Gr. *pandocheus.* Cp. "inn", above. **spendest more.** Gr. *prosdapanaō.* Occ. only here. **when I come again** = in (Gr. *en.* Ap. 104. viii) my coming back. **I.** Emph.

G 36 Which °now of these three, °thinkest
A.D. 28 thou, °was[29] neighbour unto him that fell °among
the [30]thieves?"
F 37 And he said, "He that shewed mercy °on
him." Then said Jesus unto him, "Go, and
do thou likewise."
E K^1 38 °Now it came to pass, as they went, that
He entered [1]into a certain village: and a certain woman named °Martha
L^1 received Him [1]into her house.
K^2 39 And she had a sister called °Mary,
L^2 which °also °sat °at °Jesus' feet, and °heard His
word.
K^3 40 But [38]Martha was °cumbered °about much
serving, and °came to Him,
L^3 M g and said,
h °"Lord, °dost Thou [24]not care that my sister
hath left me to serve alone?
i bid her therefore that °she help me."
M g 41 And [39]Jesus answered and said unto her,
°"Martha, [38]Martha, thou art °careful and
°troubled [40]about many things:
h 42 But °one thing is needful:
i and [39]Mary hath chosen that good part, which
shall [24]not be taken away [21]from her."

F N **11** And °it came to pass, that, °as He was
°praying °in a certain place, °when He
ceased, one of His disciples said °unto Him,
O °"Lord, teach us to °pray,
N °as John also taught his disciples."
O P^1 2 And He said unto them, "When ye [1]pray,
say, 'Our Father Which art [1]in °heaven,
°Hallowed be °Thy name. °Thy kingdom
°come. Thy will °be done, as [1]in °heaven, so
°in °earth.
3 Give us °day by day our °daily °bread.
4 And °forgive us our °sins; for we also forgive every one that is indebted to us. And
°lead us °not °into °temptation; but deliver us
°from °evil.'"

36 now = therefore. Om. by [L] T [Tr.] A WH R.
thinkest thou = seems to thee.
was = to have become.
among. Gr. *eis.* Ap. 104. vi.
37 on = with. Gr. *meta.* Ap. 104. xi. 1.

10. 38-42 (E, p. 1461). JOURNEY.
(*Alternation.*)

E | K^1 | 38-. Martha.
  | L^1 | -38. Her reception of the Lord.
  | K^2 | 39-. Mary.
  | L^2 | -39. Her listening to the Lord.
  | K^3 | 40-. Martha.
  | L^3 | -40-42. Her colloquy with the Lord.

38 Now. Verses 38-42 peculiar to Luke.
Martha. Aram. Ap. 94. III. 3.
39 Mary. Ap. 100. 3. **also sat** = sat also.
sat = seated herself. Gr. *parakathizō.* Occ. only here in N.T. Mary always misunderstood, but always found "at the Lord's feet"; (1) her want of care, cp. *v.* 42; (2) her following Martha, John 11. 31; cp. *vv.* 32, 33; (3) her anointing of the Lord's feet, John 12. 3; cp. *vv.* 5, 7.
at = beside. Gr. *para.* Ap. 104. xii. 3. All the texts read *pros* = against. Ap. 104. xv. 3.
Jesus'. All the texts read "the Lord's".
heard = was listening to.
40 cumbered = distracted. Gr. *perispaomai.* Occ. only here.
about = concerning. Gr. *peri.* Ap. 104. xiii. 3.
came = came up.

10. -40-42 (L^3, above). MARTHA. HER COLLOQUY WITH THE LORD.
(*Extended Alternation.*)

L^3 | M | g | -40. Carefulness.
  | | h | -40-. Complaint of Mary.
  | | i | -40. Request.
  | *M* | *g* | 41. Carefulness.
  | | *h* | 42-. Approbation of Mary. } The Lord.
  | | *i* | -42. Refusal. }

-40 Lord. Note the avoidance of the name "Jesus" by His disciples and others. See Ap. 98. VI. i. *a.* 3. A.
dost Thou not care . . . ? = is it no concern to Thee . . . ?
she help me. Gr. *sunantilambanomai.* Occ. only here and Rom. 8. 26 in N.T. Supposed to be only a Biblical word, but it is found in the *Papyri*, and in inscriptions in the sense of taking a mutual interest or share in things.
41 Martha, Martha. Fig. *Epizeuxis.* Ap. 6. See note on Gen. 22. 11. **careful.** See note on Matt. 6. 25.
troubled = agitated. Gr. *turbazomai.* Occ. only here.
42 one thing, &c. = of one of [them] is there need. Not the unspiritual idea of "one dish", as there were not two or more as in our days. The Lord referred not to Martha's serving, but to her over-care.

11. 1-13 (F, p. 1461). DISCIPLES. REQUEST. PRAYER. (*Alternation.*)

F | N | 1-. Occasion. The Lord praying.
  | O | -1-. Request made.
  | *N* | -1. Precedent. John's teaching.
  | *O* | 2-13. Request complied with.

1 it came to pass. A Hebraism. See 2. 1. **as He was praying** = in (Gr. *en.* Ap. 104. viii) His praying. The sixth of seven such occasions. **praying.** Gr. *proseuchomai.* Ap. 134. I. 2. **in.** Gr. *en.* Ap. 104. viii. Not the same word as in *vv.* -2, 6, 7, 33-. **when** = as. **unto** = to. Gr. *pros.* Ap. 104. xv. Not the same word as in *vv.* 24, 51. **Lord.** Note the disciple's form of address. **as** = even as.

11. 2-13 (*O*, above). REQUEST. COMPLIED WITH. (*Division.*)

O | P^1 | 2-4. Example.
  | P^2 | 5-13. Illustration. Parable.

2 heaven = the heavens. See note on Matt. 6. 9, 10. **Hallowed** = Sanctified. **Thy name.** See note on Ps. 20. 1. **Thy kingdom.** See Ap. 111, 112, 113, 114. **come** = Let . . . come. **be done** = come to pass. **heaven** (sing.). See note on Matt. 6. 9, 10. **in** = upon. Gr. *epi.* Ap. 104. ix. 1. **earth.** Gr. *gē.* Ap. 129. 4. **3 day by day** = according to (Gr. *kata.* Ap. 104. x. 2) the day. **daily.** Gr. *epiousios.* See note on Matt. 6. 11. **bread.** Put by Fig. *Synecdochē* (of the Part), Ap. 6, for food in general. **4 forgive.** See note on 3. 3. Jas. 5. 15. **sins.** Trespasses comes from Tyndale's Version. **lead** = bring. **not.** Gr. *mē.* Ap. 105. II. Not the same word as in *vv.* -7, 8, 38, 40, 44, 46, 52. **into.** Gr. *eis.* Ap. 104. vi. **temptation** = trial or testing. **from** = away from. Gr. *apo.* Ap. 104. iv. Not the same word as in *vv.* 16, 31. **evil** = the evil, or, the evil one, denoting active harmfulness.

P² j 5 °And He said [1]unto them, "Which °of
A. D. 28 you shall have a friend, and shall go [1]unto
him at midnight, and say unto him, 'Friend,
°lend me three loaves;
6 °For a friend of mine °in his journey is
come °to me, and I have °nothing to set before
him?'
7 And he from within shall answer and say,
'Trouble me [4]not: the door is °now shut, and
my °children are °with me °in bed; I °cannot
rise and give thee.'
8 I say unto you, Though he will °not rise
and give him, °because he is his friend, yet
°because of his °importunity he will rise and
give him as many as he needeth.
k 9 And I say unto you, °Ask, and it shall be
given you; °seek, and ye shall find; °knock,
and it shall be opened unto you.
10 For every one that asketh receiveth; and
he that seeketh findeth; and to him that knocketh it shall be opened.
j 11 °If a son shall ask bread of °any of you
that is a father, will he give him a stone? or
°if *he ask* °a fish, will he °for a fish give him
a serpent?
12 Or °if he shall ask an egg, will he °offer
him a scorpion?
k 13 [-11]If ye then, being [4]evil, °know how to give
good gifts unto your °children: how much
more shall *your* °heavenly Father give °the
Holy Spirit to them that ask Him?"
G Q 14 And He was casting out a °devil, and it
was dumb. And it came to pass, when the
devil was gone out, °the dumb spake;
R V and the people wondered.
W 15 But some [5]of them said, "He casteth out
[14]devils °through °Beelzebub the chief of the
[14]devils."
16 And °others, [4]tempting *Him*, sought °of
Him a sign °from °heaven.
X Y¹ l 17 But He, [13]knowing their °thoughts, said unto
them, "Every kingdom divided °against itself
is °brought to desolation; and a house *divided*
°against a house falleth.
18 [-11]If Satan also be divided [17]against himself,

11. 5-13 (P², p. 1466). ILLUSTRATION. PARABLE. (*Alternation.*)

P² | j | 5-8. The Friend.
  k | 9, 10. Application.
 j | 11, 12. The Father.
  k | 13. Application.

5 And He said, &c. Verses 5-10 are peculiar to Luke.
of=among. Gr. *ek*. Ap. 104. vii.
lend. Gr. *chraō*. Occ. only here.
6 For=Since. **in**=off. Gr. *ek*. Ap. 104. vii.
to. Gr. *pros*. Ap. 104. xv. 3. Not the same word as in *v.* 37.
nothing to=not (Gr. *ou*. Ap. 105. I) what I may.
7 now=already. The door would on no account be opened to a stranger at night.
children. Gr. *paidion*. Ap. 108. v.
with. Gr. *meta*. Ap. 104. xi. 1. Not the same word as in *vv.* 20, 37. A whole family will sleep in one room, in the garments worn by day, in one large bed.
in. Gr. *eis*. Ap. 104. vi.
cannot=am not (Gr. *ou*. Ap. 105. I) able to.
8 not. Gr. *ou*. Ap. 105. I.
because=on account of. Gr. *dia*. Ap. 104. v. 2.
importunity=shamelessness, impudence. Gr. *anaideia*. Occ. only here in N.T.
9 Ask... seek... knock. Note the Fig. *Anabasis* (Ap. 6).
Ask. Gr. *aiteō*. Always used of an inferior to a superior. Never used of the Lord to the Father.
11 If, &c.=Shall a son ask, &c.
any=which. **if, &c.** Ap. 118. 2. a.
a fish=a fish also **for**=instead. Gr. *anti*. Ap. 104. ii.
12 if. Gr. *ean*. Ap. 118. 1. b. **offer**=give to.
13 know. Gr. *oida*. Ap. 132. I. 1.
children. Ap. 108. i.
heavenly=out of (Gr. *ek*. Ap. 104. viii) heaven.
the Holy Spirit=spiritual gifts. No articles. Gr. *pneuma hagion*. See Ap. 101. II. 4. Note the five contrasts. A loaf, a stone; a fish, a serpent; an egg, a scorpion; temporal gifts, spiritual gifts; earthly fathers, the heavenly Father.

11. 14–13. 9 (G, p. 1461). MIRACLES, &c. (*Introversion and Alternations.*)

G | Q | 11. 14-. Miracle. The Dumb Man.
 R | 11. -14-36. The evil generation.
  S | T | 11. 37. Occasion. In the Pharisee's house.
   U | 11. 38-54. Colloquies.
  S | *T* | 12. 1-. Occasion. The Multitudes without.
   U | 12. -1-59. Addresses.
 R | 13. 1-5. The evil generation.
Q | 13. 6-9. Parable. The Fig-tree.

14 devil=demon.
the dumb spake=the dumb [man] spake.

11. -14-36 (R, above). THE EVIL GENERATION. (*Extended Alternation.*)

R | V | -14. Wonder of the People.
 W | 15, 16. The evil Generation. Manifested.
  X | 17-26. The Lord's answer to their thoughts.
V | 27, 28. Exclamation of the Woman.
 W | 29-. The evil Generation. Exposed.
  X | -29-36. The Lord's answer to their words (*v.* 16).

15 through=by. Gr. *en*. Ap. 104. viii. **Beelzebub.** Aram. See on Matt. 10. 25. Ap. 94. III. 3.
16 others. Gr. pl. of *heteros*. Ap. 124. 2. **of**=from. Gr. *para*. Ap. 104. xii. 1. **from**=out of. Gr. *ek*. Ap. 104. vii. **heaven.** Sing., as in *v.* -2.

11. 17-26 (X, above). THE LORD'S ANSWER TO THEIR THOUGHTS. (*Division.*)

X | Y¹ | 17-23. Confutation. Illustrations.
 | Y² | 24-26. Recrimination. Parable.

11. 17-23 (Y¹, above). CONFUTATION. ILLUSTRATIONS. (*Alternation.*)

Y¹ | l | 17, 18. The divided Kingdom.
 m | 19, 20. Application.
 l | 21, 22. The strong man's house.
 m | 23. Application.

17 thoughts=intents, purposes, or machinations. Gr. *dianoēma*. Occ. only here in N.T. **against.** Gr. *epi*. Ap. 104. ix. 3. **brought to desolation.** Gr. *erēmoō*. Occ. only here, Matt. 12. 25; and Rev. 17. 16; 18. 17, 19.

A.D. 28 how shall his kingdom stand? because ye say
that I cast out devils [15] through °Beelzebub.

m 19 And [-11] if I °by [15] Beelzebub cast out [14] devils,
°by whom do your sons cast *them* out? °there-
fore shall they be your judges.

20 But [-11] if I °with °the finger of God cast
out [14] devils, no doubt °the kingdom of God is
°come upon you.

l 21 When °a strong man °armed °keepeth
°his palace, his °goods are [1] in peace:

22 But °when [21] a stronger than he shall
come upon him, and overcome him, he °taketh
from him °all his armour °wherein he °trusted,
and divideth his °spoils.

m 23 He that is [4] not [7] with Me is against Me:
and he that gathereth [4] not [7] with Me scattereth.

Y² n 24 When the °unclean °spirit is gone out °of
[21] a °man,

o he walketh °through °dry places, seeking rest;
and finding °none,

p he saith, 'I will return °unto my house whence
I came out.'

q 25 And when he cometh, he findeth *it* swept
and °garnished.

n 26 Then goeth he,

o and °taketh *to him* seven °other [24] spirits
more °wicked than himself;

p and they enter in, and °dwell there:

q and the last *state* of that [24] man °is worse than
the first."

V 27 And [1] it came to pass, °as He spake these
things, a certain woman [5] of the °company lifted
up her voice, and said unto Him, °"Blessed
is the womb that bare Thee, and the paps
which Thou °hast sucked."

28 But He said, "Yea rather, [27] blessed *are*
they that hear the word of God, and [21] keep
it."

W 29 °And when the people °were gathered thick
together, He began to say, °"This is an °evil
generation: they seek a °sign;

X Z¹ and there shall °no °sign be given it, but the
sign of °Jonas the prophet.

Z² r¹ 30 For °as [-29] Jonas °was a [29] sign unto °the
Ninevites,

s¹ so shall °also °the Son of man be to °this
generation.

r² 31 °The queen of the south shall °rise up [1] in
the judgment [7] with the °men of [30] this gene-

Beelzebub. Aram., as in *v.* 15. See note on Matt. 10. 25. This is the "unpardonable sin". See Mark 3. 28–30.

19 by. Gr. *en.* Ap. 104. viii.

therefore = on this account. Gr. *dia.* Ap. 104. v. 2.

20 with = by. Gr. *en*, as in *v.* 19. Cp. Matt. 3. 11.

the finger of God. Fig. *Anthropopatheia.* Ap. 6. See Ex. 8. 19. Finger, here, put by Fig. *Metonymy* (of Subject), Ap. 6, for the Holy Spirit Himself.

the kingdom of God. See Ap. 114.

come upon you. With suddenness and surprise. Gr. *phthanō.* Occ. elsewhere: Matt. 12. 28. Rom. 9. 31. 2 Cor. 10. 14. Phil. 3. 16. 1 Thess. 2. 16; 4. 15.

21 a = the.

armed = fully armed: from head to foot. Cp. Matt. 12. 28. Gr. *kathoplizomai.* Occ. only here in N.T.

keepeth = guardeth.

his palace = his own court. Gr. *aulē.* Matt. 26. 3, 58, 69.

goods = possessions.

22 when = as soon as.

taketh = taketh away. Same word as in 8. 12.

all his armour = his panoply. Occ. only here, and Eph. 6. 11, 13.

wherein = on (Gr. *epi.* Ap. 104. ix. 2) which.

trusted = had trusted.

spoils. Cp. Mark 5. 35. Occ. only here.

11. 24–26 (Y², p. 1467). RECRIMINATION. PARABLE. (*Extended Alternation.*)

Y² | n | 24–. Departure.
  o | –24–. Search. For rest.
   p | –24. Return.
    q | 25. Condition.
 n | 26–. Departure.
  o | –26–. Search. For other spirits.
   p | –26–. Return.
    q | –26. Condition.

24 unclean. See 4. 33.

spirit: i. e. demon. See Ap. 101. II. 12.

of = away from. Gr. *apo.* Ap. 104. iv.

man. Gr. *anthrōpos.* Ap. 123. 1. Not the same word as in *vv.* 31, 32.

through. Gr. *dia.* Ap. 104. v. 1.

dry = waterless. Cp. Isa. 13. 21, 22; 34. 14, &c.

none = not (Gr. *mē.* Ap. 105. II) [any].

unto. Gr. *eis.* Ap. 104. vi.

25 garnished = adorned.

26 taketh = taketh to. Cp. Matt. 7. 21.

other = different. Gr. *heteros.* Ap. 124. 2.

wicked. Ap. 128. III. 1.

dwell = settle down. is = becomes.

27 as He spake = in (Gr. *en.* Ap. 104. viii) His speaking. company = crowd.

Blessed = Happy. hast sucked = didst suck.

29 And when, &c. Verses 29–36 peculiar to Luke.

were gathered = were gathering. Occ. only here.

This, &c. See note on Matt. 11. 18.

evil. Gr. *ponēros.* Ap. 128. III. 1. Cp. Matt. 12. 34.

sign. Gr. *sēmeion.* Ap. 176. 3.

11. –29–36 (*X*, p. 1467). THE LORD'S ANSWER TO THEIR THOUGHTS. (*Division.*)

X | Z¹ | –29. The Sign. Jonah.
 Z² | 30–32. The Signification. The Lord.
 Z³ | 33–36. Illustration and Application.

–29 no. Ap. 105. II.

Jonas = Jonah. See notes on p. 1247.

---

11. 30–32 (Z², above). THE SIGNIFICATION. THE SON OF MAN. (*Repeated Alternation.*)

Z² | r¹ | 30–. Jonah the prophet.
  s¹ | –30. The Son of man.
 r² | 31–. The Queen of the South.
  s² | –31. The Son of man.
 r³ | 32–. The Men of Nineveh.
  s³ | –32. The Son of man.

30 as = even as. **was** = became. **the Ninevites.** They must therefore have known of the miracle connected with him. **also the Son of man** = the Son of man also. **the Son of man.** See Ap. 98. XVI. **this generation.** See note on *v.* 29. **31 The queen of the south.** See 1 Kings 10. 1–13. 2 Chron. 9. 1–12. **rise up.** From the dead. **men.** Gr. pl. of *anēr.* Ap. 123. 2.

A. D. 28 ration, and °condemn them: for she came [16]from
the °utmost parts of the [2]earth to hear the
wisdom of Solomon;
s^2 and, °behold, °a greater than Solomon *is* here.
r^3 32 The [31]men of Nineve shall °rise up [1]in the
judgment [7]with [30]this generation, and shall
[31]condemn it: for they °repented °at the °preach-
ing of [29]Jonas;
s^3 and, [31]behold, [31]a greater than Jonas *is* here.
Z^3 A^1 33 °No man, when he hath lighted a °candle,
putteth *it* [7]in a °secret place, neither °under
°a bushel, but °on °a candlestick, that they
which come in may °see the °light.
A^2 B 34 The °light of the body is the °eye:
C t therefore when thine eye is °single,
u thy whole body also is °full of light;
t but when *thine eye* is °evil,
u thy body also *is* °full of darkness.
C v 35 °Take heed therefore that the °light which
is [1]in thee be [4]not darkness.
w 36 [13]If thy whole body therefore *be* [34]full of
light,
v having °no part dark,
w the whole shall be [34]full of light,
B as when °the bright shining of a [33]candle °doth
give thee light."
S T 37 And °as He spake, a certain Pharisee °be-
sought Him °to °dine °with him: and He went
in, and °sat down to meat.
J D^1 E F 38 And when the Pharisee saw *it*, he marvelled
that He had [8]not first °washed °before °dinner.
G x 39 And the Lord said [1]unto him, "Now do
ye Pharisees make °clean the outside of the
cup and the °platter; but your inward part is
full of °ravening and °wickedness.
40 °*Ye* fools, did [8]not He That made that
which is without make that which is within
also?
41 °But rather give alms of °such things as

condemn. Gr. *katakrinō*. Ap. 122. 7.
utmost parts = the ends.
behold. Fig. *Asterismos*. Ap. 6.
a greater = something more. Cp. Matt. 12. 6.
32 rise up = stand up as witnesses. Not the same word as "rise up" in *v.* 31. Ap. 178. I. 1.
repented. See Ap. 111. I. 1.
at. Gr. *eis*. Ap. 104. vi.
preaching = proclamation. See Ap. 121. 3.

11. 33-36 (Z^3, p. 1468). ILLUSTRATION AND APPLICATION. (*Division.*)

Z^3 | A^1 | 33. Illustration. Lamp in the house.
| A^2 | 34-36. Application. Eye in the body.

33 No man, &c. Repeated here from Matt. 5. 15. Gr. *oudeis* = no one, compound of *ou*. Ap. 105. I.
candle = lamp. See Ap. 130. 4.
secret place = cellar, or vault. All the texts read *kruptē* (crypt). **under.** Gr. *hupo*. Ap. 104. xviii. 2.
a bushel = the corn measure. Cp. Matt. 5. 15.
on. Gr. *epi*. Ap. 104. ix. 3.
a candlestick = the lampstand. Ap. 130. 5.
see. Ap. 133. I. 5.
light. Ap. 130. 7. All the texts read 130. 1.

11. 34-36 (A^2, above). APPLICATION. THE EYE IN THE BODY. (*Introversion and Alternations.*)

A^2 | B | 34-. The Lamp.
C | t | -34-. The eye (eyesight).
u | -34-. The body.
t | -34-. The eye (eyesight).
u | -34. The body.
C | v | 35. Darkness.
w | -36-. Light.
v | -36-. Darkness.
w | -36-. Light.
B | -36. The Lamp.

34 light = lamp. Same word as "candle" in *v.* 33. See Ap. 130. 4.
eye. Put by Fig. *Metonymy* (of Subject), Ap. 6, for the eyesight.
single = sound: referring to the eyesight as "good". Occ. only here and Matt. 6. 22.
full of light = illuminated.
evil. Gr. *ponēros*. See Ap. 128. III. 1.
full of darkness = dark.
35 Take heed = Seq. Gr. *skopeō*. Occ. only here; Rom. 16. 17. 2 Cor. 4. 18. Gal. 6. 1. Phil. 2. 4; 3. 17.
light. Gr. *phōs*. See Ap. 130. 1.
36 no. Gr. *mē*. Ap. 105. II.
the bright shining of a candle = the lamp with its brilliance.
doth give thee light = may light thee. Gr. *phōtizō*. Cp. Ap. 130. 1. **37 as He spake** = lit. in (Gr. *en*. Ap. 104. viii) His speaking. **besought** = asked. Ap. 134. I. 3. **to dine** = that he would dine. **dine** = take breakfast. Gr. *aristaō*, not *deipneō*. The morning meal after returning from the synagogue. Occ. (with the noun) only here; 14. 12. Matt. 22. 4. John 21. 12, 15. **with** = beside. Gr. *para*. Ap. 104. xii. 2. **sat down to meat** = reclined Himself.

11. 38-54 (U, p. 1467). COLLOQUIES. (*Division.*)

U | D^1 | 38-52. Particular.
| D^2 | 53, 54. General.

11. 38-52 (D^1, above). PARTICULAR. (*Alternation.*)

D^1 | E | F | 38. The Pharisee offended.
G | 39-44. The Lord's answer.
E | *F* | 45. The Lawyer offended.
G | 46-52. The Lord's answer.

38 washed = performed His ablutions. Ap. 115. I. viii and Ap. 136. vii. **before.** Gr. *pro*. Ap. 104. xiv. **dinner.** Gr. *ariston*. See note on "dine", *v.* 37.

11. 39-44 (G, above). THE LORD'S ANSWER TO THE PHARISEE. (*Introversion*)

G | x | 39-41. Self-deception. Concealed wickedness.
y | 42. Woe. Inconsistency. Tithing.
y | 43. Woe. Pride. Uppermost seats.
x | 44. Self-deception. Concealed defilement.

39 clean: i. e. ceremonially clean. **platter** = dish. See note on Matt. 14. 8. **ravening and wickedness** = wicked greed. Fig. *Hendiadys*. Ap. 6. **wickedness.** Ap. 128. II. 1. **40 Ye fools.** Fools = senseless ones. Gr. *aphrōn*. The first of eleven occ. **41 But rather, &c.** = Nevertheless [ye say] "give alms", &c. This was the great meritorious work, supposed to cleanse or make amends for everything. **such things as ye have** = the things that are within. Gr. *ta enonta*. Occ. only here in N.T.

A.D. 28 ye have; and, [31] behold, all things are clean unto you.

y **42** But woe unto you, Pharisees! for °ye tithe mint and rue and °all manner of herbs, and °pass over °judgment and °the love of God: these °ought ye to have done, and [4] not to °leave the other undone.

y **43** Woe unto you, Pharisees! for ye °love the °uppermost seats [1] in the synagogues, and greetings [1] in the markets.

x **44** Woe unto you, scribes and Pharisees, °hypocrites! for ye are as graves which °appear not, and the [24] men °that walk over *them* are [8] not °aware *of them.*"

E F **45** Then answered one of the °lawyers, and said unto him, °"Master, °thus saying Thou °reproachest us also."

G H a **46** And he said, "Woe unto you also, *ye* [45] lawyers! for ye °lade [24] men with burdens °grievous to be borne,

b and ye yourselves °touch [8] not the burdens with one of your fingers.

J **47** Woe unto you! for °ye build the °sepulchres of the prophets, and your fathers killed them.
48 °Truly ye bear witness °that ye allow the deeds of your fathers: for they indeed killed them, and ye build their sepulchres.

J **49** [19] Therefore also said °the Wisdom of God, °'I will send °them °prophets and apostles, and *some* [5] of them they shall slay and persecute:
50 That the blood of °all the prophets, which was °shed [4] from the °foundation of the °world, may be °required °of °this generation;'
51 [4] From the blood of °Abel unto the blood of °Zacharias, which perished between °the altar and °the temple: °verily I say unto you, It shall be [50] required [50] of [50] this generation.

H b **52** Woe unto you, [46] lawyers! for ye have taken away the °key of knowledge:

a ye entered [8] not in yourselves, and them that were entering in ye °hindered."

D² **53** And as He °said these things [1] unto them, the scribes and the Pharisees began °to urge *Him* vehemently, and to °provoke Him to speak °of °many things:
54 °Laying wait for Him, and seeking to °catch something °out of His mouth, °that they might accuse Him.

S T **12** °In the mean time, when there were gathered together an innumerable multitude of people, insomuch that they °trode one upon another,

U K c He began to say °unto His disciples °first of

---

42 ye tithe = ye tithe, or pay or take tithes. Gr. *apodekatoō*. Occ. only here; 18. 12. Matt. 23. 23; and Heb. 7. 5.
all manner of herbs = every herb. Fig. *Synecdochē* (of the Genus), Ap. 6, for all tithable herbs.
pass over = pass by, as in Mark 6. 48.
judgment. A Hebraism = justice. Ap. 177. 7.
the love of God. Gen. of relation (Ap. 17. 5), meaning the love required by God, as admitted by the lawyer (10. 27).
ought ye to have done = it behoved you to do.
leave . . . undone = leave aside. But most of the texts read "pass by", as in the preceding clause.
43 love. Ap. 135. I. 1.
uppermost. Same as "chief" in Matt. 23. 6.
44 hypocrites. Theodotion's rendering of Job 34. 30, and 36. 13, and Aquila and Theod. in Job 15. 34, and by Aquila, Sym., and Theod. in Prov. 11. 9, Isa. 33. 14, and Sept. in Isa. 32. 6, show that the word had come to mean not merely "false pretence", but positive impiety or wickedness. **appear not** = are unseen.
that walk over them = who walk about above them.
aware = know. Gr. *oida*. Ap. 132. I. 1.
45 lawyers = teachers of the law. Gr. *nomikos*. Not the same as in 5. 17.
Master = Teacher. Ap. 98. XIV. v.
thus = these things. **reproachest** = insultest.

11. 46-52 (*G*, p. 1469). THE LORD'S ANSWER TO THE LAWYER. (*Introversions.*)

G | H | a | 46-. Others laden. (Positive.)
    b | -46. Themselves not helping. (Negative.)
      J | 47, 48. Superstition.
      J | 49-51. Persecution.
  H | b | 52-. Themselves not entering. (Negative.)
    a | -52. Others hindered. (Positive.)

46 lade. Cp. "heavy laden", Matt. 11. 28.
grievous. This refers to the innumerable precepts of the Oral Law, now embodied in the Talmud. Gr. *dusbastaktos*. Occ. only here and Matt. 23. 4 in N.T.
touch. Gr. *prospsauō* = to touch gently. A medical word, used of feeling the pulse or a sore place on the body. Occ. only here.
47 ye build = ye are building.
sepulchres = tombs. See Matt. 23. 29.
48 Truly = So then.
that ye allow = and give your full approval to.
49 the Wisdom of God. This is Christ Himself; for in Matt. 23. 34 this is exactly what He did say. It is not a quotation from the O.T., or any apocryphal book.
I will send, &c. This He did, in and during the dispensation of the Acts. Cp. Matt. 22. 1-7.
them = unto (Gr. *eis*. Ap. 104. vi) them.
prophets and apostles. See note on Eph. 2. 20.
50 all the prophets. Cp. 6. 23.
shed = poured out. Same word as in 22. 20.
foundation, &c. See note on Prov. 8. 22. Matt. 13. 35.
world. Gr. *kosmos*. See Ap. 129. 1.
required. Gr. *ekzēteō*. Occ. also Acts 15. 17. Rom. 3. 11. Heb. 11. 6; 12. 17. 1 Pet. 1. 10.
of. Gr. *apo*. Ap. 104. iv.
this generation. See note on Matt. 11. 16.
51 Abel. Gen. 4. 8. Ap. 117. I.
Zacharias. See note on Matt. 23. 35.

the altar. Of burnt offering. **the temple.** Gr. the house: i. e. the *naos*, or Sanctuary. See note on Matt. 23. 16. **verily.** See note on Matt. 5. 18. **52 key.** Put by Fig. *Metonymy* (of Adjunct), Ap. 6, for entrance to and acquirement of knowledge. Cp. Mal. 2. 8. **hindered** = forbade, as in 9. 49.
53 said = was saying. **to urge Him vehemently** = to urgently press upon Him. **provoke Him to speak.** Gr. *apostomatizō*. Occ. only here. The *Papyri* show that from its original meaning (to dictate what was to be written) it had come to mean "to examine by questioning a pupil as to what he had been taught". Here, therefore, they were not *questioning* for information, but for *grounds of accusation.* **of** = concerning. Gr. *peri*. Ap. 104. xiii. 1. **many** = very many. **54 Laying wait for** = watching. Only here and Acts 23. 21. **catch.** Both are hunting expressions. **out of.** Gr. *ek*. Ap. 104. vii. Not the same word as in *v.* 24. **that, &c.** T [Tr.] WH R omit.

12. 1 In. Gr. *en*. Ap. 104. viii. **trode one upon another** = trampled one another down.

12. -1-59 [For Structure see next page].

unto. Gr. *pros*. Ap. 104. xv. 3. Not the same word as in *v.* 11. **first.** The Structure ("K") on p. 1471 shows that this must be connected with "disciples" and not with what follows.

A.D. 28 all, °"Beware ye °of the °leaven of the Pharisees, °which is °hypocrisy.
2 For there is °nothing °covered, that shall °not °be revealed; neither hid, that shall °not be °known.
3 °Therefore whatsoever ye °have spoken [1]in °darkness shall be heard [1]in the light; and that which ye °have spoken °in the ear [1]in °closets shall be °proclaimed °upon the °housetops.
d 4 And °I say °unto you My friends, °Be °not afraid °of them that kill the body, and °after that have °no more that they can do.
5 But I will °forewarn you whom °ye shall fear: °Fear °Him, which [4]after He hath killed hath °power to cast °into °hell; yea, [4]I say unto you, °Fear Him.
6 Are °not five sparrows sold for °two farthings, and [2]not one °of them is forgotten °before God?
7 But even the very hairs of your head °are all numbered. Fear [4]not therefore: ye are of °more value than many sparrows.
c 8 Also [4]I say unto you, Whosoever °shall confess °Me °before °men, °him °shall °the Son of man also confess before the angels of God:
9 But he that °denieth Me [6]before [8]men [8]shall be °denied [6]before the angels of God.
10 And whosoever shall speak a °word against [8]the Son of man, it shall be forgiven him: but [4]unto him that blasphemeth °against °the Holy Ghost it shall [2]not be forgiven.
d 11 And when they bring you °unto the °synagogues, and *unto* magistrates, and °powers, °take ye [4]no thought how or what thing ye shall °answer, or what ye shall say:
12 For [10]the Holy Ghost [8]shall teach you [1]in the same hour what ye °ought to say."
L e 13 And one [6]of the company said unto Him, °"Master, speak to my brother, that he °divide the inheritance °with me."
14 And He said unto him, [8]"Man, who °made Me a judge or a divider °over you?"
f 15 And He said [1]unto them, °"Take heed, and °beware [1]of °covetousness: for a °man's °life consisteth [2]not [1]in the abundance of the things which he °possesseth."

12. 1-59 (*U*, p. 1467). ADDRESSES. (*Alternation.*)

U | K | 1-12. To the Disciples.
  L | 13-21. To the People.
  K | 22-53. To the Disciples.
  L | 54-59. To the People.

12. 1-12 (K, above). TO THE DISCIPLES. (*Alternation.*)

K | c | 1-3. Hypocrisy.
  d | 4-7. Persecution.
  c | 8-10. Open Confession.
  d | 11, 12. Persecution.

Beware ye = Take heed to yourselves. Cp. Matt. 16. 6, spoken on another occasion. **of.** Gr. *apo.* Ap. 104. iv. **leaven.** See note on Matt. 13. 33. **which.** Denoting a class of things in the category of impiety. **hypocrisy.** See note on "hypocrite" (11. 44).
2 nothing. Gr. *ouden.* Compound of *ou.* Ap. 105. I. **covered** = concealed. Gr. *sunkaluptomai.* Only here in N.T. **not.** Gr. *ou.* Ap. 105. I. Not the same word as in *vv.* 4, 6-, 7, 21, 26, 27-, 29, 32, 33, 47, 48, 59. **be** = become. **revealed** = uncovered. Gr. *apokaluptō.* See Ap. 106. I. ix. **known.** Gr. *ginōskō.* Ap. 132. I. ii.
3 Therefore = Instead of (Gr. *anti.* Ap. 104. ii) which. **have spoken** = spake. **darkness** = the darkness. **in** = to. Gr. *pros.* Ap. 104. xv. 3. **closets** = the chambers. Occ. only here, *v.* 24, and Matt. 6. 6; 24. 26. **proclaimed.** Ap. 121. 1. **upon.** Gr. *epi.* Ap. 104. ix. 1. **housetops.** Cp. Matt. 24. 17.
4 I say unto you. Always introduces an important matter. **unto** = to. **Be not afraid** (*phobēthēte*) . . . **ye shall fear** (*phobēthēte*) (*v.* 5). Note the Fig. *Anadiplōsis* (Ap. 6), by which all the words between are emphasized, by being thus enclosed. **not.** Gr. *mē.* Ap. 105. II. Not the same word as in *vv.* 2, 6, 10, 15, 21, 26, 27, 39, 45, 46, 56, 57, 59. **of** = from [the hands of]. Gr. *apo.* Ap. 104. iv. Cp. Matt. 10. 28. Not the same word as in *vv.* 6, 13, 25, 48, 57. **after.** Gr. *meta.* Ap. 104. xi. 2. **no.** Gr. *ou.*
5 forewarn = shew, or warn; cp. 3. 7. **ye shall fear.** See note on *v.* 4. **Fear.** Note the second *Anadiplōsis.* Ap. 6. **Him, which:** i. e. God Who. **power** = authority. See Ap. 172. 5. **into.** Gr. *eis.* Ap. 104. vi. **hell** = the Gehenna. See note on 2 Kings 23. 10. Matt. 5. 3, and Ap. 131.
6 not. See Ap. 105. I. a. **two farthings** = two *assaria.* See note on Matt. 10. 29. **of** = out of. Gr. *ek.* Ap. 104. vii. **before** = in the sight of. Gr. *enōpion,* as in 1. 15. **7 are** = have been. See note on Matt. 10. 30. Acts 27. 34; and cp. 1 Sam. 14. 45. 1 Kings 1. 52. **more value** = differ from: i. e. excel. **8 shall** = may (with Gr. *an*). **Me** = in (Gr. *en.* Ap. 104. viii.) Me: i. e. in My Name. **before** = in the presence of. Gr. *emprosthen.* **men.** Pl. of *anthrōpos.* Ap. 123. 1. **him** = in him. **shall** = will. **the Son of man.** See Ap. 98. XVI. **9 denieth** = has disowned. **denied** = utterly disowned. **10 word.** Not "blaspheme", as in next clause. **against.** Gr. *eis.* Ap. 104. vi. **the Holy Ghost.** With Art. See Ap. 101. II. 3. As in *v.* 12. **11 unto** = before. Gr. *epi.* Ap. 104. ix. 3. **synagogues.** See Ap. 120. **powers** = authorities. Ap. 172. 5. **take ye no thought** = be not full of care, or anxious. **answer** = reply in defence. See Acts 6. 8, 10. 2 Tim. 4. 17. 1 Pet. 3. 15. Cp. Dan. 3. 16. **12 ought to** = should.

12. 13-21 (L, above). TO THE PEOPLE. (*Introversion.*)

L | e | 13, 14. A Man's request. Made.
  f | 15. Covetousness. Warning.
  f | 16-20. Covetousness. Parable.
  e | 21. The Man's request. Application.

13 Master = Teacher. Ap. 98. XIV. v. **divide.** Cp. Deut. 21. 15-17. **with.** Gr. *meta.* Ap. 104. xi. 1. **14 made** = appointed, or constituted. Cp. Ex. 2. 14. **over.** Gr. *epi.* Ap. 104. ix. 3. Not with the same case as in *vv.* 42, 44. **15 Take heed** = See. Gr. *horaō.* Ap. 133. I. 8. **beware** = keep yourselves from. **covetousness.** All the texts read "all covetousness". **man's** = to any one. **life.** Gr. *zōē.* See Ap. 170. 1. Not so with *bios* (Ap. 171. 2). **possesseth.** Gr. *huparchō.* See Phil. 2. 6 (being); 3. 20 ("is").

f 16 And He spake a parable [1]unto them, saying,
A.D. 28 "The °ground of a certain rich [8]man °brought forth plentifully:

17 And he °thought °within himself, saying, 'What shall I do, because I have °no room where to °bestow my fruits?'

18 And he said, 'This will I do: I will pull down my °barns, and build greater; and there will I [17]bestow all my °fruits and my °goods.

19 And I will say to °my °soul, °'Soul, thou hast much goods °laid up °for many years; take thine ease, eat, drink, *and* be merry.''

20 But God said unto him, '*Thou* °fool, °this night °thy soul °shall be required [1]of thee: then whose shall those things be, °which thou hast °provided?'

e 21 So *is* he that layeth up treasure for himself, and is [4]not rich °toward God."

K O Q 22 And He said [1]unto His disciples, °"Therefore [4]I say unto you, °Take [4]no thought for your °life, what ye shall eat; neither for the body, what ye shall put on.

23 °The [22]life is more than °meat, and the body *is more* than raiment.

R g 24 °Consider the °ravens: for they °neither sow °nor reap; which °neither have °storehouse °nor °barn; and God feedeth them:

h how much more are ye better than the °fowls?

25 And which [6]of you with [22]taking thought can add °to his °stature one cubit?

26 °If ye then be °not able to do that thing which is °least, why take ye thought °for the rest?

R g 27 Consider the lilies how °they grow: they °toil [2]not, they spin [2]not; and yet I say unto you, that °Solomon [1]in all his glory was [2]not arrayed like one of these.

h 28 [26]If then God so clothe the °grass, which is to day [1]in the field, and to morrow is °cast [5]into the oven; how much more *will he clothe* you, °O ye of little faith?

Q 29 And seek [4]not ye what ye shall eat, or what ye shall drink, °neither be ye °of doubtful mind.

30 For all these things do the nations of the °world seek after: and your Father °knoweth that ye have need of these things.

31 But rather seek ye °the kingdom of God; and all these things shall be added unto you.

P 32 Fear [4]not, °little flock; for °it is your Father's good pleasure to give you [31]the kingdom.

O 33 °Sell °that ye have, and give alms; provide yourselves °bags which °wax [4]not old,

16 ground = estate. Gr. *chōra*.
brought forth plentifully. Gr. *euphoreō*. Occ. only here.
17 thought = was reasoning.
within. Gr. *en*. Ap. 104. viii.
no = not. Gr. *ou*. Ap. 105. I.
bestow = gather together, or lay up.
18 barns = granaries.
fruits = produce. Not the same word as in *v.* 17. Tr. WH R read "the corn". **goods** = good things.
19 my soul. Idiom for "myself". Gr. *mou psuchē*. See Ap. 13. VI. 18, Ap. 110, and note on Jer. 17. 21.
soul = *psuchē*. See Ap. 110. IV. 1.
laid up = laid by.
for (Gr. *eis*. Ap. 104. vi) **many years.** Cp. Prov. 27. 1.
20 fool. See note on 11. 40.
this night = this very night.
thy soul = thy life. Ap. 110. III. 2.
shall be required = they demand. Only here and 6. 30. Tr. A WH read "is required". But both are impersonal, referring to some unknown invisible agencies which carry out God's judgments or Satan's will. Cp. Ps. 49. 15. Job 4. 19; 18. 18; 19. 26; 34. 20. In a good sense cp. Isa. 60. 11.
which, &c. In the Gr. this clause is emph., standing before the question "then whose", &c.
provided = prepared.
21 toward. Gr. *eis*. Ap. 104. vi.

12. 22-53 (*K*, p. 1471). TO THE DISCIPLES. (*Alternation.*)

K | O | 22-31. Solicitude. Discouraged. } Negative.
  | P | 32. Fear of Man. Discouraged. }
  | *O* | 33, 34. Liberality. Encouraged. } Positive.
  | *P* | 35-53. Watchfulness for the Lord. }

12. 22-31 (O, above). SOLICITUDE. DISCOURAGED. (*Introversion and Alternation.*)

O | Q | 22, 23. Solicitude. Dehortation.
  | R | g | 24-. Ravens.
  | | h | -24-26. Application.
  | *R* | *g* | 27. Lilies.
  | | *h* | 28. Application.
  | *Q* | 29-31. Solicitude. Dehortation.

22 Therefore = On (Gr. *dia*. Ap. 104. v. 3) this [account].
Take no thought, &c. This saying is repeated from Matt. 6. 25. See note there.
life. Gr. *psuchē*. See Ap. 110. III. 1. It is what can "eat".
23 The. [L] T Tr. A WH R read "For the", &c.
meat = food. Cp. Matt. 6. 25-34.
24 Consider, &c. See note on Matt. 7. 3.
ravens. See Job 38. 41. Ps. 147. 9. Occ. only here in N.T.
neither sow = sow not (Gr. *ou*. Ap. 105. I).
nor. Gr. *oude*. **neither have** = have not, as above.
storehouse. Same as "closet" in *v.* 3.
barn = granary. **fowls** = birds.
25 to. Gr. *epi*. Ap. 104. ix. 3.
stature = age, as in John 9. 21, 23. Heb. 11. 11, referring to fullness of growth, hence rendered "stature" (Luke 19. 3. Eph. 4. 13). A "cubit" could not be "the least" of *v.* 26. It must therefore be put by Fig. *Metonymy* (of Subject), Ap. 6, for *length* generally: either the least measure (an inch) to his height, or a moment to his age (or life). Gr. *hēlikia*. Occ. elsewhere in Luke 2. 52 and Matt. 6. 27.
26 If ye, &c. Assuming the hypothesis as a fact. See Ap. 118. 2 a. **not.** Compound of *ou*. Ap. 105. I. **least.** This determines the meaning of "cubit" in *v.* 25, or it would nullify the Lord's argument. **for.** Gr. *peri*. Ap. 104. xiii. 1. **27 they grow.** T Tr. A WH m. omit, and read "how they toil not", &c. **toil not, they spin not** = neither toil nor spin. T A WH m. read "neither spin nor weave". **Solomon . . . was not** = not even Solomon was. 1 Kings 3. 13; 10. 1-29. Song 3. 6-11. **28 grass, &c.** Cp. Isa. 40. 6. 1 Pet. 1. 24. Jas. 1. 10, 11. **cast:** i. e. for fuel, "oven" being put by Fig. *Metonymy* (of Adjunct), Ap. 6, for the furnace; as we say "the kettle boils" or "light the fire". **O ye of little faith.** Gr. *oligopistos*. See all the five occ. in note on Matt. 6. 30. **29 neither** = and not. Gr. *mē*. Ap. 104. II. **of doubtful mind** = excited. Occ. only here in N.T. **30 world.** Gr. *kosmos*. Ap. 129. 1. **knoweth.** Gr. *oida*. Ap. 132. I. i. **31 the kingdom of God.** See Ap. 114. **32 little flock.** Cp. Ps. 23. 1. Isa. 40. 11. Matt. 26. 31. John 10. 12-16. **it is your Father's good pleasure** = your Father took delight. The King was present: what could He not supply? **33 Sell.** Cp. Acts 2. 44, 45; 4. 37. **that ye have.** Gr. *huparchō*: your possessions. See note on "is", Phil. 3. 20. **bags** = purses. **wax not old** = never wear out.

A. D. 28 a treasure [1]in °the heavens °that faileth not,
where [17]no thief approacheth, neither °moth
°corrupteth.
34 For where your treasure is, there will your
°heart be also.
P S U **35** Let your loins be girded about, and *your*
°lights burning;
36 And ye yourselves like [4]unto [8]men °that
wait for their °lord, °when he °will °return
°from °the wedding; that when he cometh
and knocketh, they may open [4]unto him immediately.
37 °Blessed *are* those °servants, whom the
[36]lord when he cometh shall find °watching:
°verily I say [4]unto you, that he shall gird himself,
and make them to sit down to meat, and
will come forth and serve them.
38 And °if he shall come [1]in the °second
watch, or come [1]in the °third watch, and find
them °so, [37]blessed are those [37]servants.
V **39** And this [2]know, that [26]if the °goodman
of the house had [30]known what hour the thief
would come, he would have [37]watched, and
[2]not have suffered his house to be °broken
through.
40 °Be ye therefore ready also: for [8]the Son
of man cometh at an hour when ye think
[2]not."
W **41** Then Peter said unto him, °"Lord, speakest
Thou this parable [1]unto us, or even °to
all?"
V i **42** And the Lord said, "Who then is °that
faithful and wise steward, whom *his* [36]lord shall
°make ruler °over his household,
k to give *them their* °portion of meat [1]in due
season?
l **43** [37]Blessed *is* that [37]servant, whom his [36]lord
when he cometh shall find so doing.
m **44** Of a truth I say [4]unto you, that he will
make him ruler °over all [33]that he hath.
i **45** But and [38]if that [37]servant say [1]in his
heart, 'My [36]lord °delayeth his coming;
k °and shall begin to beat the °menservants
°and °maidens, °and to eat and drink, °and to
be drunken;
l **46** The [36]lord of that [37]servant will come [1]in a
day when he looketh [2]not for *him*, [45]and °at
an hour when he °is [2]not aware,
m [45]and will °cut him in sunder, [45]and will appoint
him his portion [13]with the °unbelievers.
U **47** °And that [37]servant, which [2]knew his [36]lord's
°will, and prepared [4]not *himself*, neither did
°according to his °will, shall be beaten with
many *stripes*.
48 But he that [2]knew [4]not, and did commit
things worthy of stripes, shall be beaten with
few *stripes*. For [4]unto whomsoever much is
°given, °of him shall be much required: and
to whom men have committed much, of him
they will ask the more.

the heavens. Pl. See notes on Matt. 6. 9, 10.
that faileth not=unfailing.
moth. Cp. Jas. 5. 2.
corrupteth=destroyeth, as in Rev. 8. 9; 11. 18.
34 heart be also=heart also be.

12. 35-53 (*P*, p. 1472). WATCHFULNESS FOR THE LORD. (*Alternation.*)

P | S | 35-48. His Servants.
  T | 49. Effect of His coming. Fire.
 S | 50. His own sufferings.
  T | 51-53. Effect of His coming. Sword.

12. 35-48 (S, above). HIS SERVANTS. (*Introversion.*)

S | U | 35-38. Watchfulness.
  V | 39, 40. Parable. Thief.
   W | 41. Peter's question.
  V | 42-46. Parable. Servants.
 U | 47, 48. Preparedness.

35 lights=lamps. See Ap. 130. 4.
36 that wait for=waiting, or looking, for. Gr. *prosdechomai*, as in 2. 25, 38; 23. 51. Mark 15. 43. Tit. 2. 13.
lord. Ap. 98. VI. i. *a*. 4. A.
when=whensoever.
will. All the texts read "may".
return. Gr. *analuō*. Occ. only here, and Phil. 1. 23, in N.T. In Sept. only in the Apocryphal books, and always in the sense of *returning back*, as in *ana-kamptō* (Heb. 11. 15). See Tobit 2. 9. Judith 13. 1. 1 Esd. 3. 3. Wisd. 2. 1; 5. 12; 16. 14. Ecclus. 3. 15. 2 Macc. 8. 25; 9. 1; 12. 7; 15. 28. The noun *analusis*=a returning back of the body to dust, as in Gen. 3. 19, occurs only once, in 2 Tim. 4. 6.
from=out of. Gr. *ek*. Ap. 104. vii.
the wedding=the marriage feast.
37 Blessed=Happy. **servants**=bondmen.
watching. Gr. *grēgoreō*, as in 1 Thess. 5. 6, 10 (wake).
verily. See note on Matt. 5. 18.
38 if. Gr. *ean*. Ap. 118. 1. b.
second . . . third watch. See Ap. 51. IV (12, 17).
so=thus.
39 goodman=master. Ap. 98. XIV. iii.
broken=dug. Occ. only here; Matt. 6. 19, 20; 24. 43.
40 Be=Become.
41 Lord. Note, not "Jesus". Ap. 98. VI. i. *a*. 3. A.
to. Gr. *pros*. Same as "unto" in preceding clause.

12. 42-46 (*V*, above). PARABLE. SERVANTS. (*Extended Alternation.*)

V | i | 42-. The Steward. Faithful and wise.
  k | -42. Servants. Well-treated.
   l | 43. The Lord's coming.
    m | 44. His reward.
 i | 45-. The Steward. Evil.
  k | -45. Servants. Ill-treated.
   l | 46-. The Lord's enemy.
    m | -46. His punishment.

42 that faithful and wise steward=the faithful steward and prudent [man].
make ruler=set.
over. Gr. *epi*. Ap. 104. ix. 1. Not the same case as in *vv.* 14, 44.
portion of meat=measure of food. Gr. *sitometrion*. Occ. only here. Supposed to be a peculiar N.T. word, but it is found in the Papyri, and the kindred verb in Gen. 47. 12, 14 (Sept.).
44 over. Gr. *epi*. Ap. 104. ix. 2. Not the same case as in *vv.* 14, 42.
45 delayeth. The emphasis is placed on this verb by the Fig. *Hyperbaton* (Ap. 6), because it is this postponement of the reckoning which leads to his evil doing.
and. Note the Fig. *Polysyndeton* (Ap. 6) in *vv.* 45 and 46.
menservants. See Ap. 108. iv.

maidens. Gr. *paidiskē*. See 22. 56. **46 at**=in, as in preceding clause. **is not aware**=knows not. Ap. 132. I. ii. **cut him in sunder.** Cp. Dan. 2. 5. Heb. 11. 37. **unbelievers**=unfaithful. **47 And**=But. **will.** Gr. *thelēma*. See Ap. 102. 2. **according to.** Gr. *pros*. Ap. 104. xv. 3. **48 given**=committed. **of**=from. Gr. *para*. Ap. 104. xii. 1.

T A.D. 28 **49** °I am come to °send °fire °on the °earth; and °what will I, °if it be already kindled?

S **50** But °I have a baptism to be baptized with; and °how am I straitened till it be °accomplished!

T **51** Suppose ye that °I am come °to give peace °on °earth? I tell you, °Nay; but rather °division:

52 For °from henceforth there shall be five [1]in one house divided, three °against two, and two °against three.

53 The father shall be divided [52]against the son, and the son [52]against the father; the mother °against the daughter, and the daughter °against the mother; the mother in law °against her daughter in law, and the daughter in law °against her mother in law."

L **54** And He said °also to the people, "When ye see a cloud rise °out of the west, straightway ye say, 'There cometh a °shower;' and so °it is.

55 And when *ye see* the south wind blow, ye say, 'There will be heat;' and it cometh to pass.

56 *Ye* °hypocrites, ye °can discern the °face of the °sky and of the [49]earth; but how is it that ye do [2]not discern this time?

57 Yea, and why even [4]of yourselves °judge ye [2]not what is right?

58 °When thou goest [13]with thine °adversary °to °the magistrate, *as thou art* °in the way, °give diligence that thou mayest be °delivered [52]from him; lest he °hale thee [41]to the judge, and the judge deliver thee to the °officer, and the °officer cast thee [5]into prison.

59 I tell thee, thou shalt °not depart thence, till thou °hast paid the very last °mite."

R Y n **13** There °were present °at that season some °that told Him °of the °Galilæans, whose blood °Pilate had mingled °with their sacrifices.

o **2** And °Jesus answering said unto them, "Suppose ye that these Galilæans °were °sinners °above all the Galilæans, because they °suffered such things?

p **3** I °tell you, °Nay:

q but, °except ye repent, ye shall all likewise perish.

49 I am come=I came, &c.
send. Gr. *ballō.* In fourteen out of the eighteen occ. in Luke, rendered "cast". See *vv.* 28, 58.
fire. See Joel 2. 30, &c. Had the nation received Him, *all* that the prophets had spoken would have been fulfilled. So would it have been had Peter's proclamation been received (Acts 3. 18–26). See note on *v.* 51.
on=into. Gr. *eis.* Ap. 104. vi. But all the texts read *epi* (Ap. 104. ix. 3). **earth.** Gr. *gē.* Ap. 129. 4.
what will I . . . ?=what do I wish? Fig. *Aposiopesis,* Ap. 6 (no answer being required or given).
if it be, &c. Another *Aposiopesis* (Ap. 6) repeated. The Lord was "straitened" (*v.* 50). The nation had not yet finally rejected Him. Ap. 118. 2. a.
50 I have a baptism, &c. Referring to the sufferings which had to be first accomplished. See 24. 26. Acts 3. 18. Ap. 115. II. i. 1 and I. i.
how am I straitened=how am I being pressed. Gr. *sunechomai,* as in Acts 18. 5 and Phil. 1. 23. The prayer in Gethsemane shows how this was. See 22. 41, 42. Heb. 5. 7.
accomplished. See 9. 31. John 19. 28.
51 I am come=I became present, as in Acts 21. 18.
to give peace. This was the *object* of His coming (Isa. 9. 6, 7): but the *effect* of His presence would bring war. He came not to judge (John 12. 47) as to this *object,* but the *effect* of His coming was judgment (John 9. 39). **on**=in. Gr. *en.* Ap. 104. viii.
earth=the earth. Ap. 129. iv.
Nay. Gr. *ouchi.* See Ap. 105. I. a.
division=disunion. Occ. only here.
52 from henceforth=from (Gr. *apo.* Ap. 104. iv) now: explaining the effect.
against. Gr. *epi.* Ap. 104. ix. 2. Referring to Mic. 7. 6.
53 against. In the last four instances *epi* governs the acc.
54 also to the people=to the crowds also; not "inconsequent". See the Structure ("*L*", p. 1471).
out of=from. Gr. *apo.* Ap. 104. iv.
shower. Occ. only here. **it is**=it happens.
56 hypocrites. See note on 11. 44.
can=know [how to]. Gr. *oida.* Ap. 132. I. 1.
face=appearance.
sky=the heaven. Sing. See notes on Matt. 6. 9, 10.
57 judge ye, &c. Found in an inscription at Amorgus, as pronouncing a just judgment, anticipating *v.* 58.
58 When thou goest=For, when thou art brought. Introducing the reason for this conclusion of the whole argument.
adversary. Shown in the last clause to be the *taxgatherer.*
to=before. Gr. *epi.* Ap. 104. ix. 3. **the**=a.
in the way. Emph. by Fig. *Hyperbaton* (Ap. 6).
give diligence=work hard, or take pains, or do your best. Not a Latinism, but found in the Oxyrhyncus Papyri, second century B.C.
delivered=set free. Occ. only here, Acts 19. 12, and Heb. 2. 15.
hale=haul. Anglo-Saxon *holian.* Occ. only here in N.T.
officer=tax-gatherer: i. e. the adversary of the first clause. Gr. *praktōr*=doer, or executive officer. Thus used in the Papyri. Occ. only here in N.T.; once in LXX, Isa. 3. 12. *He* was the one who could cast a defaulter into prison. **59 not**=by no means. Gr. *ou mē.* Ap. 105. III. **hast paid**=shalt have paid. This verse is repeated from Matt. 5. 25, with a different purpose, and therefore with different words. **mite.** See Ap 51. I. 3.

13. 1-5 (*R,* p. 1467). THE EVIL GENERATION. (*Extended Alternation.*)

R Y | n | 1. Human inflictions.
o | 2. "Suppose ye?"
p | 3-. Nay.
q | -3. Warning to that generation.
Y | *n* | 4-. Natural infliction.
o | -4. "Suppose ye?"
p | 5-. Nay.
q | -5. Warning to that generation.

1 were present=arrived. **at**=in. Gr. *en.* Ap. 104. viii. Not the same word as in *v.* 24. **that told Him**=telling Him. **of**=about. Gr. *peri.* Ap. 104. xiii. 1. **Galilæans . . . Pilate.** Probably the cause of the enmity of 23. 12. **with.** Gr. *meta.* Ap. 104. xi. 1. **2 Jesus** (Ap. 98. X). Read "He" with [L] T Tr. A WH R. **were**=happened to be. **sinners**=defaulters. Connecting it with 12. 58, above. Gr. *para.* Ap. 104. xii. 3. **suffered**=have suffered. **3 tell**=say to. **Nay.** Gr. *ouchi.* Ap. 105. I (a). **except ye repent**=if (Ap. 118. 1. b) ye repent (Ap. 111. 1) not (Ap. 105. II).

Y n 4 Or those eighteen, °upon whom the tower
A. D. 28 °in °Siloam fell, and °slew them,
o think ye that they [2]were [2]sinners [2]above all
°men that dwelt °in Jerusalem?
p 5 I tell you, [3]Nay:
q but, [3]except ye repent, ye shall all likewise
perish."
Q r 6 He spake also °this parable; "A certain
man had °a fig tree planted [4]in his °vineyard;
and he came and sought fruit °thereon, and
found °none.
7 Then said he °unto the °dresser of his vineyard, °'Behold, °these three years I come
seeking fruit °on this [6]fig tree, and find [6]none:
s °cut it down; why °cumbereth it the ground?'
r 8 And he answering said unto him, °'Lord,
let it alone °this year also, till I shall dig
°about it, and °dung *it:*
9 And °if it bear fruit, *well:*
s and °if °not, *then* °after that °thou shalt [7]cut
it down.'"
H t 10 And He was teaching [4]in one of the synagogues
u [7]on the °sabbath.
v 11 And, [7]behold, there was a woman which
had a °spirit °of infirmity °eighteen years,
and was °bowed together, and °could °in no
wise °lift up *herself.*
w 12 And when [2]Jesus °saw her, He called *her*
to Him, and said unto her, "Woman, thou art
°loosed from thine infirmity."
x 13 And He laid *His* hands on her: and immediately she was °made straight, and glorified
God.
t 14 And the ruler of the synagogue answered
with indignation,
u because that [2]Jesus had healed on the sabbath
day, and said unto the people, "There are six
days [4]in which men ought to work: [4]in them
therefore come and be healed, and °not on the
sabbath day."
v 15 The Lord then answered him, and said,
"*Thou* °hypocrite, doth °not each one of you
on the sabbath °loose his ox or *his* ass °from
the stall, and lead *him* away to watering?
w 16 And °ought [15]not this woman, being a
°daughter of Abraham, whom Satan hath
bound, °lo, these [11]eighteen years, be [12]loosed
[15]from this °bond on the sabbath day?"
x 17 And °when He had said these things, all
His adversaries were °ashamed: and all the
people rejoiced °for all the glorious things that
were °done °by Him.

4 upon. Gr. *epi.* Ap. 104. ix. 3.
in. Gr. *en.* Ap. 104. viii. Not the same word as in *v.* 21.
Siloam. See Ap. 68, p. 100. Cp. Neh. 3. 15. Isa. 8. 6. John 19. 7.
slew = killed.
men. Gr. *anthrōpos.* Ap. 123. 1.

13. 6-9 (*Q*, p. 1467). PARABLE. THE FIG-TREE. (*Alternation.*)

Q | r | 6, 7-. Owner to vine-dresser.
  | s | -7. Order. "Cut it down."
  | *r* | 8, 9-. Vine-dresser to owner.
  | *s* | -9. Order. Postponed.

6 this parable. Combining the fig tree and the vineyard. See John 15. 1.
a fig tree. The symbol of Israel's *national* privilege. See notes on Judges 9. 8-12. Here it denotes that special privilege of that generation. Cp. Jer. 24. 3. Hos. 9. 10. Matt. 21. 19.
vineyard. Ps. 80. 8-11. Cp. Isa. 5. 2, &c.
thereon = on (Gr. *en.* Ap. 104. viii) it.
none = not (Ap. 105. I. a) any.
7 unto. Gr. *pros.* Ap. 104. xv. 3.
dresser of vineyard. One word in Gr. Occ. only here.
Behold. Fig. *Asterismos.* Ap. 6.
these three years. Can refer only to the period of the Lord's ministry. The texts add *aph' hou* = from which, or since (three years). **on.** Gr. *en.* Ap. 104. viii.
cut it down = cut it out: i.e. from among the vines.
cumbereth it the ground = injureth it the soil also. The A.V. omits this "also", though it stands in the Greek text.
cumbereth. Gr. *katargeō.* Only here in the Gospels. Twenty-five times in the Epistles in the sense of vitiate. See Rom. 3. 3.
8 Lord. Ap. 98. VI. i. *a.* 4. B.
this: i.e. this third year.
about. Gr. *peri.* Ap. 104. xiii. 2.
dung it = put manure. Gr. *kopria.* Only here, and 14. 35.
9 if, &c. Ap. 118. 1. b.
not. Gr. *mēge,* compound of *mē.* Ap. 105. II.
after that = in (Gr. *eis.* Ap. 104. vi) the future.
thou shalt. Note, not I will.

13. 10-17 (H, p. 1461). PLACE. SYNAGOGUE. MIRACLE.

H | t | 10-. Place. Synagogue. Woman.
  | u | -10. The Sabbath.
  | v | 11. Condition of Woman. Bound.
  | w | 12. Loosing.
  | x | 13. Effect. God glorified.
  | *t* | 14-. Place. Synagogue. Ruler.
  | *u* | -14. The Sabbath.
  | *v* | 15. Condition of Cattle. Bound.
  | *w* | 16. Loosing.
  | *x* | 17. Effect. Adversaries ashamed.

10 sabbath. Pl. See on 24. 1.
11 spirit. Gr. *pneuma.* An evil demon. Ap. 101. 12.
of = causing. Gen. of Origin. Ap. 17. 2.
eighteen years. A type of the condition of the nation. A long-standing case, as "Signs" "C" and "*C*". Ap. 176.

bowed together = bent double. Occ. only here in N.T. **could in no wise lift** = wholly unable to lift, &c. **in no wise.** Not. Gr. *ou mē,* as in *v.* 35; but *mē eis to panteles* = not unto the furthest extent = unable to the uttermost. Occ. only here (complete human inability), and Heb. 7. 25 (complete Divine ability). **lift up.** Occ. only here, 21. 28 and John 8. 7, 10 in the N.T. **12 saw.** Ap. 133. I. 1. **loosed.** Used of disease only here in N.T., because she had been bound with a demoniac band. See note on Mark 7. 35. **13 made straight** = set upright again. Gr. *anorthoō.* Occ. only here, Acts 15. 16. Heb. 12. 12. Cp. *ana* = again, in *analuō* 12. 36 ("return"). **14 not.** Gr. *mē.* Ap. 105. II. **15 hypocrite.** See note on 11. 44. **not.** Gr. *ou.* Ap. 105. I. **loose.** Cp. note on *v.* 12, and see the Structure. **from.** Gr. *apo.* Ap. 104. iv. **16 ought.** The same word as the ruler's, but as an Interrogative. The former was based on ceremonial law; the Lord's, on the necessity of Divine love. **daughter.** Put by Fig. *Synecdochē* (of Species), Ap. 6. for descendant. **lo.** Gr. *idou.* Ap. 133. I. 2. Same as Behold, *v.* 7. **bond.** See note on Mark 7. 35. **17 when He had said** = while He was saying. **ashamed** = put to shame. **for** = at. Gr. *epi.* Ap. 104. ix. 2. **done** = coming to pass. **by.** Gr. *hupo.* Ap. 104. xviii. 1.

J y 18 °Then said He, °"Unto what is °the king-
A. D. 28 dom of God like? and whereunto shall I resemble it?

z 19 It is like a grain of mustard seed, which
a [4]man took, and cast °into his garden; and it
grew, and °waxed a °great tree; and the °fowls
of °the air °lodged [4]in the branches of it."

y 20 And again He said, "Whereunto shall I
liken [18]the kingdom of God?

z 21 It is like °leaven, which a woman took and
hid °in three measures of meal, till the whole
was leavened."

J Z 22 And He went °through the cities and villages, teaching, and °journeying °toward Jerusalem.

A a 23 Then said one unto Him, °"Lord, °are
there few that °be saved?" And He said
[7]unto them,

b 24 °"Strive to enter in °at the °strait °gate:
for many, I say unto you, will seek to enter in,
and shall [15]not be able.

c 25 °When once the °master of the house °is
risen up, and hath °shut to the door, and ye
begin to stand without, and to knock at the
door, saying, °'Lord, Lord, open unto us;'
and He shall answer and say unto you, °'I
know you [15]not °whence ye are:'
26 Then shall ye begin to say, 'We have
eaten and drunk °in Thy presence, and °Thou
hast taught [4]in our streets.'
27 But He shall say, 'I tell you, [25]I know you
[15]not [25]whence ye are; depart [15]from Me, all
ye workers of °iniquity.'
28 There shall be °weeping and gnashing of
teeth, °when ye shall °see Abraham, and Isaac,
and Jacob, and all the prophets, [4]in [18]the kingdom of God, and you *yourselves* °thrust out.

b 29 And °they shall come [15]from the east,
°and *from* the west, °and [15]from the north,
°and *from* the south, °and shall °sit down [4]in
[18]the kingdom of God.

a 30 And, [7]behold, there are last which shall be
first, and there are first which shall be last."

A d 31 °The same °day there came certain °of the
Pharisees, saying unto Him, "Get Thee out,
and depart hence:

e for Herod °will kill Thee."

d 32 And He said unto them, "Go ye, and tell
that °fox, [7]'Behold, I cast out °devils, and I
°do °cures to day and to morrow, and the third
day °I shall be perfected.
33 Nevertheless I must °walk to day, and to
morrow, and the *day* following:

e for °it cannot be that °a prophet perish °out of
Jerusalem.'

Z 34 O °Jerusalem, Jerusalem, which °killest

13. 18-21 (J, p. 1461). THE KINGDOM. LIKENESS. (*Alternation.*)

J | y | 18. Question. "What is it like?"
  | z | 19. Answer. Mustard-seed.
  | *y* | 20. Question. "What is it like?"
  | *z* | 21. Answer. Leaven.

18 Then said He, &c. Repeated with variations from Matt. 13. 31, &c. **Unto what . . . ?** Cp. Isa. 40. 18.
the kingdom of God. Ap. 114.
19 into. Gr. *eis*. Ap. 104. vi.
waxed = became into (Gr. *eis*).
great. Omit [L] T [Tr. A] WH R. **fowls** = birds.
the air = the heaven. Sing. See notes on Matt. 6. 9, 10.
lodged = nested. Gr. *kataskēnoō*. Occ. four times: here; Matt. 13. 32. Mark 4. 32. Acts 2. 26.
21 leaven. See note on Matt. 13. 33.
in. Gr. *eis*. Ap. 104. vi.

13. 22-35 (*J*, p. 1461). THE KINGDOM. ENTRANCE INTO IT. (*Introversion.*)

J | Z | 22. Jerusalem. Journeying toward it.
  | A | 23-30. The Kingdom. Individual entrance.
  | *A* | 31-33. The King. Personal. Departure.
  | *Z* | 34, 35. Jerusalem. Apostrophe to it.

22 through. Gr. *kata*. Ap. 104. x. 2.
journeying = progressing.
toward. Gr. *eis*. Ap. 104. vi.

13. 23-30 (A, above). THE KINGDOM. INDIVIDUAL ENTRANCE. (*Introversion.*)

A | a | 23. Question.
  | b | 24. Explanation. Many will seek.
  | c | 25-28. Reasons.
  | *b* | 29. Explanation. Many will enter.
  | *a* | 30. Answer.

23 Lord. Ap. 98. VI. i. a. 3. A.
are there = if (Ap. 118. 2. a) there are.
be = are being.
24 Strive = Struggle, lit. agonize. Occ. elsewhere only in John 18. 36. 1 Cor. 9. 25. Col. 1. 29; 4. 12. 1 Tim. 6. 12. 2 Tim. 4. 7.
at = through. Gr. *dia*. Ap. 104. v. 1.
strait = narrow.
gate. All the texts read "door", as in *v*. 25. In Matt. 7. 13 it is "gate".
25 When once = From (Gr. *apo*. Ap. 104. iv) whatsoever time. **master of the house.** Ap. 98. XIV. iii.
is risen up = may have risen up (Gr. *an*).
shut to. Occ. only here.
Lord, Lord. Note the Fig. *Epizeuxis* (Ap. 6), for emphasis. See note on Gen. 22. 11.
I know. Gr. *oida*. Ap. 132. I. 1.
whence: i. e. of what family or household.
26 in Thy presence = before Thee.
Thou hast taught, &c. This shows to whom these words are addressed, and thus limits the interpretation to "this generation".
27 iniquity = unrighteousness. Gr. *adikia*. Ap. 128. VII.
28 weeping = the weeping. See note on Matt. 8. 12.
when. Defining the special occasion.
see. Ap. 133. I. 8 (a).
thrust out = being cast outside. This is the occasion referred to.
29 they shall come. A ref. to Isa. 49. 12.
and. Note the Fig. *Polysyndeton*. Ap. 6.
sit down = recline (at table). Cp. 7. 36; 12. 37.

13. 31-33 [For Structure see next page].

31 The same day = In, or on, &c. (Gr. *en*. Ap. 104. viii) = just then. **day.** L T Tr. m. WH R read "hour".
certain of the Pharisees = certain Pharisees.

will = wishes: i. e. means to. See Ap. 102. 1. **32 fox.** Fig. *Hypocatastasis*. Ap. 6. **devils** = demons. **do cures** = perform, or effect cures. **cures.** Occ. only here and Acts 4. 22, 30. **I shall be perfected** = I come to an end [of My work]: viz. by the miracle of John 11. 40-44. Cp. John 19. 30. **33 walk** = journey: i. e. through Herod's country. **it cannot be** = it is not (Ap. 105. I.) fitting. Gr. *endechomai*. Occ. only here in N.T. **a prophet.** See next verse. **out of**: i. e. except in. **34 Jerusalem, Jerusalem.** Fig. *Epizeuxis* (Ap. 6). See note on Gen. 22. 11. Repeated on the second day before the Passover (Matt. 23. 37). See Ap. 156. **killest the prophets.** See 11. 47; 20. 14; 23. 34. Cp. Isa. 1. 21.

A. D. 28. the prophets, and stonest them that are sent [7]unto thee; how often °would I have gathered thy °children together, as a °hen *doth gather* her brood °under *her* wings, and °ye would [15]not!

35 [7]Behold, °your house is left unto you °desolate: and °verily I say unto you, Ye shall °not [12]see Me, °until *the time* come when ye shall say, °'**Blessed *is*** °**He That cometh** [4]**in the name of the** °**LORD.'**"

H B f **14** And °it came to pass, °as He went °into the house of one of the °chief °Pharisees to eat °bread on °the sabbath day, that they °watched Him.

2 And, °behold, there was a certain °man °before Him °which had the dropsy.

g 3 And °Jesus answering spake °unto the °lawyers and Pharisees, saying, "Is it lawful to heal on the sabbath day?"

h 4 And they held their peace.

f And He °took *him*, and healed him, and let him go;

g 5 And °answered them, saying, "Which of you shall have °an ass or an ox fallen [1]into a pit, and will °not °straightway °pull him °out on the sabbath day?"

h 6 And they could [5]not °answer Him again °to these things.

C E 7 And He put forth a parable °to those which were °bidden, when He marked how they °chose out the °chief °rooms; saying [3]unto them,

F i 8 "When thou art [7]bidden °of any *man* °to °a wedding, °sit °not down °in the highest [7]room; lest a more honourable man than thou be [7]bidden °of him;

k 9 And he that [7]bade thee and him come and say to thee, 'Give this man °place';

l and thou °begin °with shame °to take the °lowest °room.

F i 10 But when thou art [7]bidden, go and [8]sit down [8]in the [9]lowest [9]room; that when he that

k [7]bade thee cometh, he may say unto thee, °'Friend, °go up higher':

l then shalt thou have °worship in the presence of them that [8]sit °at meat with thee.

E 11 °For whosoever exalteth himself shall be °abased; and he that humbleth himself shall be exalted."

13. 31-33 (*A*, p. 1476). THE KING. PERSONAL DEPARTURE. (*Alternation.*)

A | d | 31-. Pharisees. Advice given.
  e | -31. Their reason.
 d | 32, 33-. Pharisees. Advice rejected.
  e | -33. The Lord's reason.

would I have gathered=I desired to gather. Cp. *v.* 31. **children.** Ap. 108. i. **hen.** Specially contrasted with "fox", *v.* 32. Cp. Matt. 23. 37. **under.** Gr. *hupo.* Ap. 104. xviii. 2. **ye would not**=ye did not desire it.

35 your house=the Temple. It had been Jehovah's house. Cp. John 2. 16. Now it was no longer owned as His. Cp. Luke 19. 46.

desolate. Every place is "desolate" where Christ is not. **verily.** See note on Matt. 5. 18.

not=by no means. Gr. *ou mē.* Ap. 105. III.

until. Gr. *heōs an* (all the texts omit "*an*", but it does not alter the conditional sense, which is in the verb).

Blessed. Fig. *Benedictio,* as in 1. 42; 19. 38; not *Beatitudo,* as in 12. 37, 38, 43, or 14. 14, 15. Quoted from Ps. 118. 26. Referring to the final and national repentance of Israel, which might have been then (Acts 3. 18-20) near, but Acts 28. 25-28 is yet future, while all blessedness has been postponed.

He That cometh=the coming One.

LORD=Jehovah. Ap. 4. II and Ap. 98. VI. i. *a.* 1. B. a.

14. 1-24 (*H*, p. 1461). PLACE. PHARISEE'S HOUSE. (*Alternation.*)

H | B | 1-6. Healing.
  C | 7-11. Parable. Marriage Feast.
 B | 12-14. Teaching.
  C | 15-24. Parable. The Great Supper.

14. 1-6 (B, above). HEALING. (*Extended Alternation.*)

B | f | 1, 2. Man with dropsy.
  g | 3. Question of the Lord.
   h | 4-. Inability to answer.
 f | -4. Man healed.
  g | 5. Question of the Lord.
   h | 6. Inability to answer.

1 it came to pass. A Hebraism. See on 2. 1.

as He went=in (Gr. *en.* Ap. 104. viii) His going.

into. Gr. *eis.* Ap. 104. vi.

chief Pharisees=rulers of the Pharisees (Ap. 120. II).

bread. Put by Fig. *Synecdochē* (of the Part) for any kind of food.

the sabbath day=a certain Sabbath.

watched=were engaged in watching.

2 behold. Fig. *Asterismos.* Ap. 6.

man (Ap. 123. 1) . . . **which had the dropsy**=dropsical (a medical term). Occ. only here.

before Him. Not one of the guests.

3 Jesus. Ap. 98. X. **unto.** Gr. *pros.* Ap. 104. xv. 3.

lawyers=doctors of the law.

4 took=took hold of. Cp. 20. 20. 1 Tim. 6. 12.

5 answered them=answering unto (Gr. *pros*; as in *v.* 3) them.

an ass. All the texts read *huios*=a son, instead of *onos*=an ass, which latter has no MS. authority. In O.T. always ox and ass. Cp. Ex. 23. 12.

not. Gr. *ou.* Ap. 105. I. Not the same word as in *vv.* 8, 12, 28, 29. **straightway**=immediately. **pull . . . out**=draw . . . up. The Gr. word occ. only here and Acts 11. 10. **6 answer again**=reply. **to**=as to. Gr. *pros.* Ap. 104. xv. 3.

14. 7-11 [For Structure see next page].

7 to. Gr. *pros.* Ap. 104. xv. 3. Not the same word as in *v.* 8. **bidden**=invited or called. Gr. *kaleō.* **chose out**=were picking out. Going on before His eyes. **chief rooms**=first couches. Gr. *prōtoklisia.* Same as "highest room", *v.* 8. Cp. 20. 46. Matt. 23. 6. **8 of**=by. Gr. *hupo.* Ap. 104. xviii. 1. Not the same word as in *vv.* 28, 33. **to.** Gr. *eis.* Ap. 104. vi. **a wedding**=wedding feast. **sit**=recline. **not.** Gr. *mē.* Ap. 105. II. Not the same word as in *vv.* 5, 6, 14, 20, 26, 27, 28, 30. **in.** Gr. *eis.* Ap. 104. vi. **9 place.** Gr. *topos.* **begin.** Cp. Prov. 25. 6, 7. **with.** Gr. *meta.* Ap. 104. xi. **to take**=to take (and keep in it). **lowest**=last. Gr. *eschatos.* **room**=place, as above. Cp. *v.* 22 and 2. 7. **10 Friend.** Gr. *philos,* Noun of *phileō.* Ap. 135. I. 2. **go up**=go up, forward. Occ. only here. **worship**=honour. Gr. *doxa*=glory. **at meat**=at table. **11 For, &c.** This is repeated on two other occasions. Cp. 18. 14 and Matt. 23. 12. **abased**=humbled.

B G m 12 Then said He °also to him that [7]bade
A.D. 28 Him, "When thou makest a °dinner or a °supper,

n °call [8]not thy [10]friends, °nor thy brethren, °neither thy kinsmen, °nor *thy* rich neighbours;

o lest they also °bid thee again, and a recompence °be made thee.

G m 13 But when thou makest a °feast,

n °call °the poor, the °maimed, the lame, the blind:

o 14 °And thou shalt be °blessed; for they °cannot recompense thee: for thou shalt be recompensed °at the °resurrection of the just."

C H r 15 And when one of them that [8]sat [10]at meat with Him heard these things, he said unto Him, [14]"Blessed *is* he that shall eat bread °in °the kingdom of God."

16 Then said He unto him, "A certain [2]man °made a great supper,

s and [7]bade many:

r 17 And °sent his °servant at supper time to say to them that were [7]bidden, 'Come; for all things are now ready.'

s 18 And they all °with one °*consent* began to °make excuse. The first said unto him, 'I have bought °a piece of ground, and I °must needs °go °and see it: °I pray thee °have me excused.'

19 And °another said, 'I have bought five yoke of oxen, and I °go to °prove them: [18]I pray thee °have me excused.'

20 And [19]another said, 'I have married a wife, and °therefore I °cannot come.'

J p 21 So that [17]servant came, and °shewed his °lord these things.

q Then °the master of the house being angry said to his [17]servant, [18]'Go out quickly [1]into the streets and lanes of °the city, and bring in hither °the poor, °and the [13]maimed, °and the °halt, °and the blind.'

J p 22 And the [17]servant said, °'Lord, it is done as thou °hast commanded, and °yet there is [9]room.'

q 23 And the lord said [3]unto the servant, [18]'Go out [1]into the highways and hedges, and °compel *them* to come in, that my house °may be filled.

H 24 For I say unto you, That °none of those °men which were [7]bidden shall taste of my supper.'"

14. 7-11 (C, p. 1477). PARABLE. MARRIAGE FEAST. (*Introversion and Extended Alternation.*)

C | E | 7. Occasion.
F | i | 8. Dehortation. Highest place.
k | 9-. Humiliation.
l | -9. Shame.
F | *i* | 10-. Exhortation. Lowest place.
k | -10-. Exaltation.
l | -10. Honour.
E | 11. Application.

14. 12-14 (*B*, p. 1477). TEACHING. (*Extended Alternation.*)

B | G | m | 12-. Occasion. Dinner or Supper.
n | -12-. Guests. Dehortation.
o | -12. Recompense. Human.
G | *m* | 13-. Occasion. Feast.
n | -13. Guests. Exhortation.
o | 14. Recompense. Divine.

12 also to him = to him also. The host.
dinner . . . supper. See note on Matt. 22. 4.
call. Gr. *phōneō.* Cp. 19. 15.
nor. Fig. *Paradiastolē* (Ap. 6), for emphasis.
neither . . . nor. Gr. *mēde,* compound of *mē.* Ap. 105. II.
bid . . . again. Gr. *antikaleō.* Occ. only here.
be made thee = take place, when such an one asks for gifts, not friends.
13 feast, or reception. Occurs only here and in 5. 29.
call. Same word as bid, *v.* 7.
the poor. Note the Fig. *Asyndeton* (Ap. 6), not emphasizing the particular classes, but hastening us on to the climax in *v.* 14. Note the opposite Figure in *v.* 21.
maimed = crippled. Only here, and *v.* 21.
14 And thou shalt be blessed. This is the climax.
blessed = happy. Fig. *Beatitudo,* not *Benedictio.*
cannot = have not [wherewith to]. Ap. 105. I.
at = in. Gr. *en.* Ap. 104. viii.
resurrection. Ap. 178. II. 1.

14. 15-24 (*C*, p. 1477). PARABLE. THE GREAT SUPPER. (*Introversion and Alternation.*)

C | H | 15-20. First guests invited.
J | p | 21-. Servant. First report.
q | -21. Other guests to be "brought in".
J | *p* | 22. Servant. Second report.
q | 23. Other guests to be constrained.
H | 24. First guests rejected.

14. 15-20 (H, above). THE FIRST GUESTS. (*Alternation.*)

H | r | 15, 16-. Supper prepared.
s | -16. Guests invited.
r | 17. Supper ready.
s | 18. Guests beg off.

15 in. Gr. *en.* Ap. 104. viii.
the kingdom of God. See Ap. 114.
16 made. T Tr. A WH and R read "was making". This parable is in Luke only. For the interpretation, see Ap. 140. II. 3. **17 sent.** According to custom.
servant = bondman.
18 with one consent = from (Gr. *apo.* Ap. 104. iv) one [mind]. **make excuse** = beg off.
a piece of ground = a field.
must needs = have need to.
go = go out (i. e. from the city). Gr. *exerchomai,* as in *vv.* 21, 23. **and see** = to see. Ap. 133. I. 1.
I pray. Ap. 134. I. 3. **have** = consider me.
19 another. Ap. 124. 2.

go = go forth. **prove** = try. **have** = hold. **20 therefore** = on account of (Gr. *dia*) this. **cannot** = am not (Gr. *ou.* Ap. 105. I) able to. **21 shewed** = reported to. **lord.** Ap. 98. VI. i. *a.* 4. A. **the master of the house.** Ap. 98. Note these different titles, appropriate to each case, and see Ap. 140. II. 3. **the city.** Jerusalem. See Ap. 140. II. 3. **the poor.** Note the Fig. *Polysyndeton* (Ap. 6) in this verse, emphasizing each class (with no climax at the end). The opposite of the Fig. in *vv.* 13, 14. **and.** This is the Figure. **halt** = lame. The same word as "lame" in *v.* 13. **22 Lord.** Ap. 98. VI. i. *a.* 4. B. Note the various titles throughout. **hast commanded** = didst command. **yet** = still. **23 compel** = constrain. See all the nine occ.: here; Matt. 14. 22. Mark 6. 45. Acts 26. 11; 28. 19. 2 Cor. 12. 11. Gal. 2. 3, 14; 6. 12. Compulsion necessary, because the "will" is a fallen "will", and therefore no stronger than that of our first parents when unfallen. See Ps. 14. 2. 3; 53. 2, 3. John 5. 40. Rom. 3. 10-18. Man's fallen will has never been used *for* God, without the compulsion of Phil. 2. 13. **may be filled.** Used of loading a ship. **24 none** = not (Gr. *ou.* Ap. 105. I) one. **men.** Ap. 123. 2. Not the same word as in *vv.* 2, 16, 30.

G K M
A.D. 28 25 And there °went great multitudes with Him: and He turned, and said [3] unto them,

N O t 26 °"If any *man* come [7] to Me, and °hate [5] not his father, and mother, and wife, and children, and brethren, and sisters, yea, and his own °life also,

u he [20] cannot be My disciple.

t 27 And whosoever doth [5] not bear °his cross, and come after Me,

u [20] cannot be My disciple.

P 28 For which °of you, °intending to build a tower, sitteth °not down first, and °counteth the °cost, °whether he have °*sufficient* to finish *it?*

29 Lest haply, after he hath laid °the foundation, and is [8] not °able to °finish *it*, all that °behold *it* °begin to mock him,

30 °Saying, °'This [2] man began to build, and was [5] not able to [29] finish.'

31 Or what king, going °to make war against [19] another king, sitteth [28] not down first, and consulteth [28] whether he be able °with ten thousand °to meet him that cometh °against him [9] with twenty thousand?

32 Or else, while the other is [22] yet a great way off, he sendeth an °ambassage, and °desireth °conditions °of peace.

O 33 So likewise, whosoever he be [28] of you that °forsaketh [5] not all that °he hath, he [20] cannot be my disciple.

P 34 °Salt *is* good: but °if the salt have °lost his savour, °wherewith shall it be °seasoned?

35 It is neither fit °for the °land, nor yet °for °the dunghill; *but* men cast it °out.

L °He that hath ears to hear, let him hear."

K M **15** °Then drew near unto Him °all the °publicans and sinners °for to hear Him.

N Q 2 And the °Pharisees and scribes °murmured, saying, "This man receiveth °sinners, and eateth with them."

S U[1] V[1] v[1] 3 And He spake °this parable °unto °them, saying,

14. 25—17. 4 (*G*, p. 1461). PARABLES.
(*Introversion and Alternation.*)

G | K | M | 14. 25. Occasion. Concourse of people.
N | 14. 26-35-. Teaching.
L | 14. -35. Dispensational call.
K | *M* | 15. 1. Occasion. Concourse of people.
N | 15. 2—17. 4. Teaching.

25 went = were going.

14. 26-35- (N, above). TEACHING.
(*Alternation.*)

N | O | 26, 27. Discipleship.
P | 28-32. Parable.
O | 33. Discipleship.
P | 34, 35-. Parable.

14. 26, 27 (O, above). DISCIPLESHIP.
(*Alternation.*)

O | t | 26-. Alternatives.
u | -26. Condition.
t | 27-. Alternatives.
u | -27. Condition.

26 If any. The case being assumed. Ap. 118. 2. a. **hate not.** See Matt. 10. 37. **life** = soul. See Ap. 110. III. 1. **27 his** = his own.

28 of = out of. Gr. *ek.* Ap. 104. vii. Not the same word as in *v.* 8. **intending** = desiring. See Ap. 102. 1. **not.** Ap. 105. I. a. **counteth** = reckoneth, or calculateth. Gr. *psēphizō.* Occurs only here and in Rev. 13. 18 in N.T. It is from *psēphos* = a pebble, with which calculations were made, or votes given. Occurs only in Acts 26. 10. Rev. 2. 17. **cost.** Gr. *dapanē.* Occ. only here. **whether.** Same as "if" in *v.* 26. **sufficient to finish it** = the [means] for (Gr. *pros.* Ap. 104. xv. 3, but the texts read *eis*) [its] completion. Gr. *apartismos.* Occ. only here.

29 the foundation = its foundation. **able** = strong enough. **finish it** = finish it off. Gr. *ekteleō.* Only here and *v.* 30. **behold.** Gr. *theōreō.* Ap. 133. I. 11. **begin.** As they see him nearing the end of his resources.

30 Saying, &c. = Saying that this man, &c. See note on 4. 21; 19. 9. Mark 14. 30, &c.

31 to make war = to encounter for (Gr. *eis.* Ap. 104. vi) war. **with** = in [the midst of]. Gr. *en.* Ap. 104. viii. **to meet.** Gr. *apantaō*, as in Matt. 28. 9. **against.** Gr. *epi.* Ap. 104. ix. 3.

32 Or else = If not. **ambassage** = embassy. Only here and 19. 14. **desireth** = asketh, or seeketh. Ap. 134. I. 3. **conditions** = the [terms]. **of** = for. Gr. *pros.* Ap. 104. xv. 3.

33 forsaketh = taketh leave of. **he hath** = himself possesses.

34 Salt, &c. See note on Matt. 5. 13. **if, &c.** A contingent assumption. Ap. 118. 1. b. **lost his savour** = become tasteless. Cp. Matt. 5. 13. **wherewith** = with (Gr. *en.* Ap. 104. viii) what. **seasoned.** Only here, Mark 9. 50. Col. 4. 6.

35 for. Gr. *eis.* Ap. 104. vi. **land.** Ap. 129. iv. **the dunghill** = manure. **out** = without. **He that hath, &c.** See Ap. 142.

15. 1 Then drew near = Then were drawing near. **all.** Put by Fig. *Synecdochē* (of the Part), Ap. 6, for a large number. **publicans** = tax-gatherers. **for to hear** = to hear.

15. 2—17. 4 (*N*, above). TEACHING. (*Alternations.*)

N | Q | 15. 2. Pharisees. Murmuring.
R | S | 15. 3-32. Address to Pharisees.
T | 16. 1-13. Address to Disciples.
Q | 16. 14. Pharisees. Derision.
R | *S* | 16. 15-31. Address to Pharisees.
T | 17. 1-4. Address to Disciples.

2 Pharisees. See Ap. 120. II. This settles the scope of all that follows. **murmured** = were muttering. The word implies subdued threatening. Occ. only here and 19. 7. **sinners.** See on Matt. 9. 10.

15. 3-32 [For Structure see next page].

3 this parable. It had already been uttered in Matt. 18. 12-14 with another object (*v.* 11), and with a different application (*v.* 14). It is now repeated, later, under different circumstances (Luke 15. 1, 2), in combination with two other similar parables, with quite another application (*vv.* 6, 7; 9, 10; 23, 24). Hence the change of certain words. **unto.** Gr. *pros.* Ap. 104. xv. 3. **them.** This determines the scope of the three parables.

A.D. 28 4 "What °man °of you, having an hundred sheep,
w^1 °if he lose one °of them,
x^1 doth °not leave the ninety and nine °in the °wilderness, and go °after that which is lost, °until he find it?
y^1 5 And °when he hath found *it*, he layeth *it* °on °his shoulders, rejoicing.
z^1 6 And °when he cometh °home, he calleth together *his* friends and neighbours, saying unto them, 'Rejoice °with me; for I have found my sheep which was lost.'
W^1 7 °I say unto °you, that likewise joy shall be [4]in °heaven °over one sinner °that repenteth, more than °over ninety and nine °just persons, which need °no °repentance.
U^2 V^2 v^2 8 °Either what °woman having °ten °pieces of silver,
w^2 °if she lose one piece,
x^2 doth °not light a °candle, and sweep the house, and seek °diligently °till she find *it*?
y^2 9 And [5]when she hath found *it*, she calleth *her* °friends and *her* neighbours together,
z^2 saying, 'Rejoice [6]with me; for I have found °the [8]piece which °I had lost.'
W^2 10 Likewise, [7]I say unto [7]you, there °is joy °in the presence of the angels of °God [7]over one sinner [7]that repenteth."
U^3 V^3 v^3 11 °And He said, "A certain °man had °two sons:
w^3 a 12 And the younger of them said to *his* father, 'Father, °give me °the portion of °goods that °falleth *to me*.' And he divided unto °them *his* °living.

15. 3-32 (S, p. 1479). ADDRESS TO PHARISEES. (*Repeated Alternation.*)

S | U^1 | V^1 | 3-6. The Hundred Sheep.
  W^1 | 7. Application.
U^2 | V^2 | 8, 9. The Ten Drachmas.
  W^2 | 10. Application.
U^3 | V^3 | 11-24. The Two Sons.
  W^3 | 25-32. Application.

15. 3-6; 8, 9; 11-24 [For Structure see below].

4 man. Gr. *anthrōpos.* Ap. 123. 1. Here representing Christ. **of**=from among. Gr. *ek.* Ap. 104. vii. **if he lose**=having lost. **not.** Gr. *ou.* Ap. 105. I. **in.** Gr. *en.* Ap. 104. viii. **wilderness.** A place of wild fertility. Cp. 2. 8. **after.** Gr. *epi.* Ap. 104. ix. 3. **until he find it?** Note the importance of this expression.

5 when he hath found it=having found it. In Matt., "If so be that he find it." For the reason, see note on *v.* 3. **on.** Gr. *epi.* Ap. 104. ix. 3. **his shoulders**=his own shoulders; not those of another.

6 when he cometh=having come. **home**=into (Gr. *eis.* Ap. 104. vi) the house. **with me;** not with the sheep (because of the scope of the parable). See note on *v.* 3. The joy is in heaven (*v.* 7).

7 I: i.e. I who know. John 1. 51. **you.** Murmuring Pharisees. This is the point of the parable. **heaven.** Sing. See notes on Matt. 6. 9, 10. **over.** Gr. *epi.* Ap. 104. ix. 2. **that repenteth**=repenting. Ap. 111. I. 1. **just persons:** i. e. the Pharisees. Cp. *v.* 2; 16. 15; 18. 9. **no.** Gr. *ou.* Ap. 105. I. **repentance.** Ap. 111. II. 1. Cp. Matt. 3. 2.

8 Either. This parable is recorded only in Luke. **woman.** Here representing the Holy Spirit. **ten.** See the Structures of V^2, above. **pieces of silver.** Gr. *drachmas.* Occ. only here, and in *v.* 9. See Ap. 51. I. 6. **if she lose.** An uncertain contingency. Ap. 118. 1. b. **not.** Gr. *ouchi.* Ap. 105. I. a. **candle**=lamp. Ap. 130. 4. **diligently.** A medical word. Used only here. **till.** Same as "until" in *v.* 4. **9 friends.** Female friends (Fem.). **the piece.** Not "my", as in *v.* 6. **I had lost**=I lost. Cp. "was lost" in *v.* 6. **10 is**=becomes, or takes place, or results. Same as "arose" in *v.* 14. **in the presence of**=before. It does not say that the angels rejoice; but it is the divine joy in their presence. **God.** Ap. 98. I. i. 1.

15. 3-6 (V^1); **8, 9** (V^2); **11-24** (V^3). The **100.** The **10.** The **2.** (*Extended Alternation.*)

The Hundred.
V | v^1 | 3, 4-. The Sheep.
w^1 | -4-. One lost.
x^1 | -4. Sought.
y^1 | 5. Found.
z^1 | 6. Joy.

The Ten.
V^2 | v^2 | 8-. The Drachmas.
w^2 | -8-. One lost.
x^2 | -8. Sought.
y^2 | 9-. Found.
z^2 | -9. Joy.

The Two.
V^3 | v^3 | 11. The Sons.
w^3 | 12-16. One lost.
x^3 | 17-20-. Sought.
y^3 | -20-22. Found.
z^3 | 23, 24. Joy.

15. 11-32 (U^3, above). THE TWO SONS. (*Extended Alternation.*)

U^3 | V^3 | a | 12-16. The younger son (cp. V^3, above).
b | 17-20-. His penitence.
c | -20. His father's compassion.
d | 21. The younger son's confession.
e | 22, 23. The father's gifts.
f | 24. The reason. "For", &c.
W^3 | *a* | 25, 27. The elder brother.
b | 28-. His anger.
c | -28. The father's entreaty.
d | 29, 30. The elder son's complaint.
e | 31-32-. The father's gifts.
f | -32. The reason. "For", &c.

11 And He said. This parable is peculiar to this gospel. See note on *v.* 3. **man** (as in *v.* 4). Here representing the Father (God). **two sons.** See the Structure (V^3, above). **12 give me.** Contrast "make me" (*v.* 19). **the portion.** According to Jewish law, in the case of two sons the elder took two-thirds, and the younger one-third of movable property, at the father's death. **goods**=movable property. Gr. *ousia.* Only here and *v.* 13. **falleth to me.** This is the technical term in the *Papyri*, in such cases. See Deissmann's *Light*, &c., p. 152, and *Bib. Stud.*, p. 230. **them.** Including the elder, who did not ask it. **living.** Gr. *bios*, life. Ap. 170. 2. Put by Fig. *Metonomy* (of Effect), Ap. 6, for his means or property which supported his life.

A. D. 28 13 And [4]not many days °after the younger son gathered all together, and °took his journey °into a °far country, and there wasted his °substance °with riotous living.

14 And °when he had spent all, there arose a mighty famine °in that land; and he °began to be in want.

15 And he went and °joined himself to °a citizen of that country; and he sent him [13]into his fields to feed swine.

16 And he °would fain have filled his belly °with the °husks that the swine °did eat: °and °no man gave unto him.

x[3] b 17 And when he °came °to himself, he said, 'How many hired servants of my father's °have bread enough and to spare, and °I perish °with hunger!

18 I will arise and go °to my father, and will say unto him, 'Father, I have °sinned °against °heaven, and °before thee,

19 And °am no more worthy to be called thy son: °make me as one of thy hired servants.''

y[3] 20 And he arose, and °came [18]to °his father.

c But when he was yet a great way off, his father saw him, °and had compassion, °and °ran, °and fell [5]on his neck, °and °kissed him.

d 21 And the son said unto him, 'Father, °I have [18]sinned [18]against [18]heaven, and °in thy sight, and [19]am no more worthy to be called thy °son.'

e 22 But the father said [18]to his °servants, °'Bring forth the °best robe, °and °put *it* on him; °and put a °ring °on his hand, °and °shoes °on *his* feet:

z[3] 23 [22]And bring hither the fatted calf, [22]and °kill *it;* [22]and let us eat, [22]and be merry:

f 24 For this my son °was dead, and is alive again; he °was lost, and °is found.' And they °began to be merry.

W[3] X *a* 25 Now °his elder son was [4]in the field: and as he came and drew nigh to the house, he heard °musick and dancing.

26 And he °called one of the °servants, and °asked what these things °meant.

27 And he said unto him, 'Thy brother °is come; and thy father hath killed the fatted calf, because he hath received him °safe and sound.'

b 28 And °he was angry, and °would [4]not go in:

c therefore came his father out, and °intreated him.

d 29 And he answering said to *his* father, °'Lo,

13 after. Gr. *meta.* Ap. 104. xi. 2. Referring to the rapidity of the fall of Israel.

took his journey = went abroad.

into. Gr. *eis.* Ap. 104. vi.

far country. Cp. Acts 2. 39. Eph. 2. 17.

substance = property. Same word as "goods" in *v.* 12.

with riotous living = living ruinously. Gr. *asōtōs.* Occurs only here. The kindred noun (*asōtia*) occurs only in Eph. 5. 18. Tit. 1. 6. 1 Pet. 4. 4.

14 when he had spent = having spent. Gr. *dapanaō.* Elsewhere only Mark 5. 26. Acts 21. 24. 2 Cor. 12. 15. James 4. 3.

in = throughout. Gr. *kata.* Ap. 104. x. 2. Not the same word as in *vv.* 4, 7, 25.

began to be in want. Contrast "began to be merry" (*v.* 24).

15 joined himself to = cleaved to (Gr. Pass. of *kollaō* = glue together); i. e. he forced himself.

a citizen = one of the citizens. Contrast Phil. 3. 20.

16 would fain have filled = was longing to fill.

with = from. Gr. *apo.* Ap. 104. iv.

husks = pods of the carob tree. Only here in N.T.

did eat = were eating.

and. Note the emphasis of the Fig. *Polysyndeton* (Ap. 6), here. **no man.** Gr. *oudeis*, compound of *ou.* Ap. 105. I.

17 came to himself. Cp. "came to his father" (*v.* 20). **to.** Gr. *eis.* Ap. 104. vi.

have bread enough and to spare, or abound in food. **I perish** = I (emph.) am perishing.

with hunger = from the famine. The texts add *hōde* = here. **18 to.** Gr. *pros.* Ap. 104. xv. 3.

sinned. Ap. 128. I. i. **against.** Gr. *eis.* Ap. 104. vi.

heaven. Sing. with Art. See notes on Matt. 6. 9, 10. "Heaven" put by Fig. *Metonymy* (of Subject), Ap. 6, for God Himself.

before. Gr. *enōpion.* Same word as in *v.* 10, "in the presence of".

19 am no more worthy = I no longer deserve.

make me. Contrast "give me" (*v.* 12).

20 came to his father. Cp. "came to himself" (*v.* 17). **his** = his own.

and. Note the Fig. *Polysyndeton* (Ap. 6).

ran. Cp. Isa. 6. 6, "Then flew". See note on *v.* 21, and cp. Isa. 65. 24.

kissed = fervently kissed. Same word as in Matt. 26. 49.

21 I have sinned = I sinned. Confession of sin is the necessary condition for receiving the blessing. Cp. 2 Sam. 12. 13. Ps. 32. 5. Isa. 6. 5, 6. Luke 5. 8, &c. And so with Israel (Lev. 26. 40-42. Isa. 64. 6, 7. Hos. 5. 15; 14. 1, 2).

in thy sight. Same Greek words as "before thee" in *v.* 18.

son. Note the Fig. *Aposiopēsis* (Ap. 6), for he did not finish what he meant to have said.

22 servants = bond-servants.

Bring forth. L [Tr.] A WH R add "quickly".

best = first. Either the first that comes to hand, or the former robe the son used to wear. See on Gen. 27. 15.

and. Note the Fig. *Polysyndeton* (Ap. 6), emphasizing each particular. **put it on him** = clothe him with it.

ring = a signet-ring. Occ. only here. See Jas. 2. 2, and cp. Gen. 41. 42.

on = for (Gr. *eis.* Ap. 104. vi).

shoes = sandals. The ring and the sandals mark a free man. Servants went barefoot. **23 kill it** = sacrifice it. It was a sacrificial feast. **24 was.** Not the past tense of the verb "die", but of the verb "to be". He had been as a dead man (Gr. *nekros.* Ap. 139. 2) to his father. **is found** = was found; i. e. "when he came to himself" (*v.* 17), which shows that that was the result of the father's seeking. **began, &c.** Contrast "began to be in want" (*v.* 14). **25 his elder son.** This is the point of the parable (cp. *v.* 2). It was addressed "unto them" specially (*v.* 3), as the correction of their murmuring. **musick and dancing.** Gr. symphonies and chorus, i.e. a "choral dance". Both words occ. only here. **26 called** = called to him. **servants** = young men. Gr. *pais.* See Ap. 108. iv. Not the same word as in *vv.* 17, 19, 22. **asked** = began to inquire. Imperf. tense. **meant** = might be. **27 is come . . . safe and sound.** Corresponding with the father's dead and lost . . . alive and found (*v.* 24). **28 he was angry.** Referring to the deep-seated feeling of the Pharisees against Messiah and those who followed Him. This increased steadily (and is seen to-day). Cp. Acts 11. 2, 3, 17, 18; 13. 45, 50; 14. 5, 19; 17. 5, 6, 13; 18. 12, 13; 19. 9; 21. 27-31; 22. 18-22. Gal. 5. 11. 1 Thess. 2. 14-16. **would not go in** = was not willing (Ap. 102. 1) to go in. **intreated.** Gr. *parakaleō.* Ap. 134. I. 6 **29 Lo.** Gr. *idou.* Ap. 133. I. 2. Fig. *Asterismos.* Ap. 6.

A. D. 28 these many years do I serve thee, °neither
transgressed I at any time thy commandment:
and yet thou never gavest me °a kid, that
I might make merry °with my °friends:
30 But as soon as this °thy son °was come,
which hath °devoured °thy [12] living [29] with
°harlots, thou hast [23] killed for him the fatted
calf.'

e 31 And he said unto him, °'Son, thou art °ever
[29] with me, and °all that I have is thine.
32 °It was meet that we should make merry,
and be glad:

f for this °thy brother [24] was dead, and is alive
again; and was lost, and is found.'"

T Y g **16** And He said °also °unto His disciples,
"There was °a certain rich °man, which
had a °steward; and the same °was accused
unto him °that he had wasted his goods.
2 And he called him, and said unto him,
°'How is it that I hear this °of thee? °give
°an account of thy °stewardship; for thou
°mayest be °no longer [1] steward.

h 3 Then the [1] steward said °within himself,
'What shall I do? for my °lord °taketh away
°from me the [2] stewardship: °I cannot dig; to
°beg I am °ashamed.
4 °I am resolved what °to do, that, °when I
am put out of the [2] stewardship,

j °they may receive me °into °their houses.'

h 5 So he °called °every one of his [3] lord's
debtors *unto him*, and said unto the first, 'How
much owest thou unto my [3] lord?'
6 And he said, 'An hundred °measures of oil.'
And he said unto him, °'Take °thy bill, and
°sit down °quickly, and write fifty.'
7 Then said he to °another, °'And how much
owest °thou?' And he said, 'An hundred °mea-
sures of wheat.' And he said unto him, [6] 'Take
[6] thy bill, and write fourscore.'

g 8 And °the [3] lord commended the unjust
[1] steward, because he had done °wisely:

Z j for the °children of this °world are °in °their
generation °wiser °than the °children of light.

k 9 °And I say unto you,

neither transgressed I, &c. This was the Pharisees' claim and boast. Cp. 18. 11, 12 and 18-21.
a kid. In contrast with "the fatted calf" (*v.* 23).
with. Gr. *meta.* Ap. 104. xi. 1.
friends. Contrast with harlots (*v.* 30).
30 thy son. Not "my brother". Contrast with "thy brother" (*v.* 32).
was come = came as though a stranger. Not "returned". devoured = eaten up. Contrast with *v.* 23.
thy. Malignant thought.
harlots. Contrast with "my friends" (*v.* 29).
31 Son = Child. Gr. *teknon.* Affectionately reminding him of his birth. Ap. 108. i.
ever = always. Ap. 151. II. b. ii.
all that I have. See Rom. 9. 4, 5, and cp. Matt. 20. 14.
32 It was meet. Cp. Acts 11. 18.
thy brother. Contrast with "thy son" (*v.* 30).

16. 1-13 (T, p. 1479). ADDRESS TO DISCIPLES. (*Alternation.*)

T | Y | 1-8-. Parable. The Unjust Steward.
  | Z | -8-12. Application: *re* "Mammon".
  | *Y* | 13-. Illustration. Two Masters.
  | *Z* | -13. Application: *re* "Mammon".

16. 1-8- (Y, above). PARABLE. THE UNJUST STEWARD. (*Introversion.*)

Y | g | 1, 2. His master's requirement.
  | h | 3, 4-. The steward's unjust resolution.
  | i | -4. Its object. Subsequent reception.
  | *h* | 5-7. The steward's unjust action.
  | *g* | 8. His master's approbation.

1 also unto His disciples = unto His disciples also. Note the Structure R and *R*, p. 1479, which gives the scope of the two chapters: both peculiar to this gospel.
unto. Gr. *pros.* Ap. 104. xv. 3.
a certain rich man. Cp. *v.* 19.
man. Gr. *anthrōpos.* Ap. 123. 1.
steward. A house manager, or agent, managing the house and servants, assigning the tasks, &c., of the latter. Cp. Eliezer (Gen. 15. 2; 24. 2), Joseph (Gen. 39. 4).
was accused. Gr. *diaballomai.* Occ. only here = to be struck through, implying malice, but not necessarily falsehood. that he had wasted = as wasting.
2 How is it . . . ? = What is this . . . ?
of = concerning. Gr. *peri.* Ap. 104. xiii. 1. Not the same word as in *v.* 9. give = render.
an = the. stewardship = the office of the steward (*v.* 1).
mayest = canst. no. Gr. *ou.* Ap. 105. I.
3 within = in. Gr. *en.* Ap. 104. viii.
lord = master, as in *v.* 13. Ap. 98. VI. i. *a.* 4. A.
taketh away = is taking away.
from. Gr. *apo.* Ap. 104. iv.
I cannot dig, &c. = to dig, I am not (Gr. *ou.* Ap. 105. I) strong enough.
beg. Gr. *epaiteō.* Cp. Ap. 134. I. 4. Occ. only here in A.V., but see 18. 35.

ashamed. Ashamed to beg, but not ashamed to embezzle. **4** I am resolved, &c.; or, I have it! I know, &c. Ap. 132. I. 2. to do = I will do. when I am put out of = when I shall have been removed from. they: i. e. the debtors. into. Gr. *eis.* Ap. 104. vi. their = their own. **5** called. Separately. every = each. **6** measures. Gr. pl. of *batos.* The Heb. *bāth.* Ap. 51. III. 3 (11) (7). Not the same word as in *v.* 7. Take = Take back. thy bill = writings, i. e. agreement. sit . . . write = sitting down, quickly write. quickly. It was a secret and hurried transaction. **7** another. Gr. *heteros.* Ap. 124. 2. thou. Note the emphasis: "And thou, How much owest thou?" measures. Gr. pl. of *koros.* Ap. 51. III. 3 (11) (8). Not the same word as in *v.* 6. **8** the lord = his master. wisely = shrewdly. Occ. only here.

16. -8-12 (Z, above). APPLICATION: *re* MAMMON. (*Introversion.*)

Z | j | -8. Christ's judgment.
  | k | 9-. Do I say? What the steward's master said?
  | l | -9. Object. Subsequent reception.
  | *k* | 10. [Nay, I say], "He that is faithful", &c.
  | *j* | 11, 12. Christ's judgment.

children = sons. Ap. 108. iii. world = age. Ap. 129. 2. in their generation wiser, &c. These two clauses should be transposed. in = to; i. e. with reference to. Gr. *eis.* Ap. 104. vi. their = their own. wiser = more shrewd. than = above. Gr. *huper.* Ap. 104. xvii. 2. children of light. Supply the *Ellipsis*: [are with reference to theirs]. In the former case they are all unscrupulous alike. **9** And = And, Do I say unto you? &c. Is this what I say to you? In *vv.* 10-12 the Lord gives the reason why He does not say that; otherwise these verses are wholly inconsequent, instead of being the true application of *vv.* 1-8 (Z, above). For this punctuation see Ap. 94. V. 3.

l ‘**Make to yourselves friends °of the °mammon**
A. D. 28 **of unrighteousness; that, when °ye fail, they may receive you ⁴into °everlasting °habitations.’**

k **10 °He that is °faithful °in that which is least is °faithful °also °in much: and he that is unjust °in the least is unjust °also °in much.**

j **11 °If therefore ye have °not been ¹⁰faithful ¹⁰in the unrighteous ⁹mammon, who will °commit to your trust the °true *riches?***

12 And ¹¹if ye have ¹¹not been ¹⁰faithful ¹⁰in that which is °another man's, who shall give you that which is °your own?

Y **13 No °servant °can °serve two °masters:**

Z **for either he will hate the one, and love °the other; or else he will hold to the one, and despise °the other. Ye °cannot serve °God and ⁹mammon."**

Q **14 And °the Pharisees also, who °were °covetous, heard all these things: and they °derided Him.**

R S A **15 And He said °unto them, "Ye are they which °justify yourselves before ¹men; but ¹³God knoweth your hearts: for that which is highly esteemed °among ¹men is °abomination °in the sight of ¹³God.**

B **16 °The law and the prophets *were* until John: °since that time °the kingdom of ¹³God is °preached, and °every man °presseth ⁴into it.**

17 And it is easier for °heaven and °earth to pass, than one °tittle of ¹⁶the law to fail.

A C¹ **18 °Whosoever °putteth away his wife, and marrieth ⁷another, committeth adultery: and whosoever marrieth her that is put away ³from *her* husband committeth adultery.**

C² **19 °There was ¹a certain rich ¹man, which °was clothed in purple and fine linen, and fared °sumptuously every day:**

20 And there was a certain °beggar named

of = out of, or by. Gr. *ek*. Ap. 104. vii.

mammon. Aramaic for "riches". See Ap. 94. III. 3. 32.

ye fail. All the texts read "it shall fail".

everlasting = eternal. Gr. *aiōnios*. Ap. 151. II. B. ii.

habitations = tents. Answering to the "houses" of *v.* 4.

10 He that is faithful, &c. This is the Lord's own teaching, which gives the reason why "No!" is the true answer to His question in *v.* 9.

faithful. Ap. 150. III. **in.** Gr. *en*. Ap. 104. viii.

also in much = in much also.

11 If. Assuming it as a fact. Ap. 118. 2. a.

not. Gr. *ou*. Ap. 105. I.

commit to your trust = entrust to you. Ap. 150. I. 1. iv. **true.** Ap. 175. 2.

12 another man's = a foreigner's. Cp. Acts 7. 6 and Heb. 11. 9 ("strange"), and Matt. 17. 25, 26 ("stranger"). Gr. *allotrios* (Ap. 124. 6).

your own. Gr. *humeteros*. But, though all the modern critical texts (except WH and Rm) read it thus, yet the primitive text must have read *hēmeteros* = ours, or our own; for it is the reading of "B" (the Vatican MS.) and, before this or any other Greek MS. extant, Origen (186–253), Tertullian (second cent.), read *hēmon* = ours; while Theophylact (1077), and Euthymius (twelfth cent.), with B (the Vatican MS.) read *hēmeteros* = our own, in contrast with "foreigners" in preceding clause. See note on 1 John 2. 2. This makes true sense; otherwise it is unintelligible.

13 servant = domestic household servant. Gr. *oiketēs*. Occ. only here; Acts 10. 7. Rom. 14. 4. 1 Pet. 2. 18.

can = is able to.

serve = do bondservice. Gr. *douleuō*. As in 15. 29.

masters = lords, as in *vv.* 3, 5, 5, 8.

the other. Same as "another" in *v.* 7.

cannot = are not (Gr. *ou*. Ap. 105. I) able to.

God. See Ap. 98. I. i. 1.

14 the Pharisees. See Ap. 120. II.

were = being then. Gr. *huparchō*, as in *v.* 23, and see on 7. 25.

covetous = money-lovers (referring to *mammon*, *vv.* 11, 13); occ. only here, and 2 Tim. 3. 2.

derided = were turning up their noses at. Occ. only here and 23. 35. Found in the LXX. Pss. 2. 4; 22. 7; 35. 16. This was the immediate cause of the second Parable (*vv.* 19–30), and the solemn application (*v.* 31).

16. 15–31 (*S*, p. 1479). ADDRESS TO THE PHARISEES. (*Alternation.*)

S | A | 15. What the Pharisees esteemed (God's abomination).
  | B | 16, 17. The Law and the Prophets. Proclaimed.
  | *A* | 18–30. What the Pharisees taught (God's abomination).
  | *B* | 31. Moses and the Prophets. Not believed.

15 unto them. Addressed to the Pharisees. See the Structure "R" and "*R*", p. 1479. **justify yourselves.** See notes on 15. 7, 29; and cp. 7. 39. Matt. 23. 25. **among.** Gr. *en*. Ap. 104. viii. **abomination.** In contrast with their derision. **in the sight of.** Same word as "before" in preceding clause. **16 The law.** See note on Matt. 5. 17. **since that time** = since (Gr. *apo*. Ap. 104. iv) then. **the kingdom of God.** See Ap. 114. **preached.** Gr. *euangelizō*. See Ap. 121. 4. **every man.** Gr. *pas*, all. Put by Fig. *Synecdochē* (of the *Genus*), Ap. 6, for many. "But not ye!" **presseth.** See note on Matt. 11. 12. **17 heaven.** Sing. with Art. See note on Matt. 6. 9, 10. **earth.** Gr. *gē*. Ap. 129. 4. **tittle.** See note on Matt. 5. 18 and Ap. 93. III.

16. 18–30 (*A*, above). WHAT THE PHARISEES TAUGHT. (*Division.*)

A | C¹ | 18. Concerning divorce ("the Law").
  | C² | 19–30. Concerning the dead (*v.* 31) ("the Prophets").

18 Whosoever, &c. This verse is not "loosely connected", or "out of any connexion" with what precedes, as alleged. The Structure above shows its true place, in C¹, how the Pharisees made void the law (as to divorce); and C², how they made void the prophets (*vv.* 16, 17) and the rest of Scripture as to the dead (*vv.* 19–23). **putteth away, &c.** The Rabbis made void the law and the prophets by their traditions, evading Deut. 22. 22, and their "scandalous licence" regarding Deut. 24. 1. See John Lightfoot, *Works* (1658), J. R. Pitman's edn. (1823), vol. xi, pp. 116–21 for the many frivolous grounds for divorce. **19 There was, &c.** = But there was. This commences the second part of the Lord's address to the Pharisees, against their tradition making void God's word as to the dead, which may be seen in Pss. 6. 5; 30. 9; 31. 17; 88. 11; 115. 17; 146. 4. Eccles. 9. 6, 10; 12. 7. Isa. 38. 17–19, &c. It is not called a "parable", because it cites a notable example of the Pharisees' tradition, which had been brought from Babylon. See many other examples in Lightfoot, vol. xii, pp. 159–68. Their teaching has no Structure. See C², above. **was clothed** = was habitually clothed. Imperf. tense. See on 8. 27. **sumptuously** = in splendour. Gr. adv. of *lampros*, is transl. "gorgeous" in 23. 11. Only here. **20 beggar** = poor man. Ap. 127. 1.

A. D. 28 °**Lazarus, which was °laid °at his gate, °full**
of sores,
21 And °desiring to be fed °with °the crumbs
which fell [3]from the rich man's table: °more-
over the dogs came and °licked his °sores.
22 And it came to pass, that the [20]beggar
died, and was carried °by °the angels [4]into
°Abraham's bosom: the rich man also died,
°and was buried;
23 And [10]in °hell he °lift up his eyes, °being
[10]in °torments, and °seeth [22]Abraham °afar off,
and Lazarus [10]in his bosom.
24 And °he cried and °said, °'Father [22]Abra-
ham, have mercy on me, and send [20]Lazarus,
that he may dip the tip of his finger in water,
and °cool my tongue; for I am °tormented [10]in
this flame.'
25 But [22]Abraham said, °'Son, remember
that thou in thy °lifetime °receivedst thy good
things, and likewise Lazarus °evil things: but
now he is comforted, and thou art [24]tormented.
26 And °beside all this, between us and you
there °is a great °gulf °fixed: so that they
which °would pass from hence °to you °can-
not; °neither can they pass °to us, that *would*
***come* from thence.'**
27 Then he said, °'I pray thee therefore,
[24]father, that thou wouldest send him °to my
father's house:
28 For I have five brethren; that he may
°testify unto them, °lest they also come [4]into
this place of [23]torment.'
29 [22]Abraham saith unto him, 'They have
°Moses and the prophets; let them hear them.'
30 And he said, °'Nay, [24]father [22]Abraham:
but °if one went [1]unto them °from °the dead,
they will °repent.'
B **31 °And he said unto him, [30]'If they hear**
[11]not [29]Moses and the prophets, neither will
they °be persuaded, °though one rose °from
[30]the dead.'"

T D1 **17 °Then said He °unto °the disciples, "It**
is °impossible but that °offences will
come: but woe *unto him*, °through whom they
come!

Lazarus. A common Talmudic contraction of the Heb. Eleazar; but introduced by the Lord to point to His own closing comment in *v.* 31.
laid = cast down. **at.** Gr. *pros.* Ap. 104. xv. 3.
full of sores. Gr. *helkoō.* Occ. only here.
21 desiring = eagerly desiring; but in vain, as in 15. 16 ("would fain").
with = from. Gr. *apo.* Ap. 104. iv.
the crumbs. Some texts read "the things".
moreover, &c. = but [instead of finding food] even the dogs, &c.
licked = licked off; i.e. licked clean. Gr. *apoleichō.* Occ. only here. The texts read *epileichō*, licked over.
sores. Gr. *helkos* (= ulcer).
22 by. Gr. *hupo.* Ap. 104. xviii. 1.
the angels. The Pharisees taught that there were three sets of angels for wicked men; and others for good men. See *v.* 18; and Lightfoot, *Works*, vol. xii, pp. 159–61.
Abraham's bosom. The Pharisees taught that there were three places: (1) Abraham's bosom; (2) "under the throne of glory"; (3) in the garden of Eden (Gr. Paradise). Speaking of death, they would say "this day he sits in Abraham's bosom". Lightfoot, *Works*, vol. xii, pp. 159–63.
and was buried 23 . . . in hell. Tatian (A.D. 170), the Vulg. and Syr., omit the second "and", and read, "and was buried in Hades".
23 hell. Gr. Hades = the grave. See Ap. 131. II.
lift up = having lifted up. Cp. similar imagery in Judg. 9. 7–15. Isa. 14. 9–11.
being = being there. See note on "were", *v.* 14.
torments. Gr. *basanos.* Occ. only here, *v.* 28, and Matt. 4. 24.
afar off = from (Gr. *apo.* Ap. 104. iv) afar.
seeth . . . Lazarus. The Pharisees taught that in life two men may be "coupled together", and one sees the other after death, and conversations take place. See Lightfoot, quoted above.
24 he cried and said = crying out, he said. The Pharisees gave long stories of similar imaginary conversations and discourses. See Lightfoot, vol. xi, pp. 165–7.
Father Abraham. Cp. Matt. 3. 9. John 8. 39.
cool. Gr. *katapsuchō.* Occ. only here. A medical word.
tormented = distressed. Gr. *odunaomai.* Occ. only in Luke (here, 2. 48, and Acts 20. 38, "sorrowing").
25 Son = Child. Gr. *teknon.* Ap. 108. I.
lifetime = life. Gr. *zōē*, as being the opposite of death. See Ap. 170. 1.
receivedst = didst receive back, or had all.
evil things. See Ap. 128. III. 2.
26 beside. Gr. *epi.* Ap. 104. ix. 2. **is** = has been.
gulf = chasm. A transliteration of the Gr. *chasma*, from *chaskō*, to gape. A medical word for an open wound. **fixed** = set fast, established. Cp. 9. 51 (set His face). Rom. 1. 11. 2 Pet. 1. 12. **would** = desire to. Gr. *thelō.* Ap. 102. 1. **to.** Gr. *pros.* Ap. 104. xv. **cannot** = are not (Gr. *mē.* Ap. 105. II) able. **neither.** Gr. *mēde.* **27 I pray** = I entreat. Gr. *erōtaō.* Ap. 134. I. 3. **to** = unto. Gr. *eis.* Ap. 104. vi. **28 testify** = earnestly testify. **lest they also** = that they also may not (Gr. *mē.* Ap. 105. II). **29 Moses and the prophets.** The latter including the historical books. See Ap. 1. Referring to *v.* 16. Cp. John 1. 45; 5. 39, 46. **Moses.** See note on 5. 14. **30 Nay.** Gr. *ouchi.* Ap. 105. I a. **if.** Implying a contingency. See Ap. 118. 1 a. **from** = away from. Ap. 104. iv. Contrast the Lord's *ek* (Ap. 104. vii. in next clause). **the dead.** No Art. See Ap. 139. 2. **repent.** See Ap. 111. I. 1. **31 And, &c.** The lesson of the parable. From these final words of the Lord (*v.* 31, *B*) Lightfoot says "it is easy to judge what was the design and intention of this parable" (vol. xii, p. 168). The Lord's words were proved to be true, by the results of the resurrection of another Lazarus (John 12. 9), and of Himself (Matt. 28. 11–13). **be persuaded.** Much less "repent", as in *v.* 30. **though** = not even if. **from** = from among. Note the Lord's true word, in contrast with the rich man's in *v.* 30.

17. 1–4 (*T*, p. 1479). ADDRESS TO DISCIPLES. (*Division.*)

T | D1 | 1, 2. Stumbling-blocks introduced.
| D2 | 3, 4. Introducers to be rebuked.

1 Then said He, &c. *Vv.* 1, 2 contain matter which had been spoken by the Lord on a former occasion (Matt. 18. 6, 7. Mark 9. 42) and repeated here with a variation of certain words; *vv.* 3, 4 also had been spoken before, and recorded in Matt. 18. 21, 22 (but not in Mark). The passage here is therefore not "out of its context", but is repeated with special reference to 16. 14–30. See Ap. 97. **unto.** Gr. *pros.* Ap. 104. xv. 3. **the disciples.** All the texts read "His disciples". This is to be noted in contrast with 16. 15. **impossible** = inevitable. Gr. *anendektos.* Occ. only here. **offences** = stumbling-blocks. **through.** Gr. *dia.* Ap. 104. v. 1.

A.D. 28 2 It were °better for him °that a °millstone
were hanged °about his neck, and he °cast
°into the sea, than that he should °offend one
of these little ones.

D^2 3 Take heed to yourselves: °If thy brother
°trespass °against thee, °rebuke him; and °if
he °repent, forgive him.
4 And [3]if he [3]trespass [3]against thee °seven
times in a day, and seven times in a day turn
again °to thee, saying, 'I [3]repent;' thou shalt
forgive him."

F E^1 5 And the apostles said unto °the Lord, °"Increase our faith."

E^2 m 6 And [5]the Lord said, °"If ye had faith as
a grain of mustard seed,
n °ye might say unto °this °sycamine tree, 'Be
thou plucked up by the root, and be thou
planted °in the sea;' and it °should obey you.

m 7 But which °of you, having a °servant plowing or °feeding cattle, will say unto him °by
and by, when he is come °from the field, 'Go
and °sit down to meat?'
8 °And will not rather say unto him, 'Make
ready wherewith I may sup, and gird thyself,
and serve me, °till °I have eaten and drunken;
and °afterward thou shalt eat and drink?'
9 Doth he thank that [7]servant because he
did the things that were commanded him?
°I trow °not.

n 10 °So likewise ye, when ye °shall have
done all those things which are commanded
you, °say, 'We are °unprofitable [7]servants:
we have done that which was our duty to
do.'"

E F^1 11 And °it came to pass, °as He went °to
A.D. 29 Jerusalem, that He passed [1]through °the midst
of Samaria and °Galilee.
12 And as He °entered [2]into a certain village,
there met Him °ten °men that were lepers,
which stood °afar off:
13 And they lifted up *their* voices, and said,
°"Jesus, °Master, have °mercy on us."

F^2 G 14 And when He saw *them*, He said unto
them, "Go shew yourselves unto the priests."

H o And [11]it came to pass, that, °as they went,
they were cleansed.

2 better=well. Gr. *lusiteleō*. Occ. only here.
that=if. Ap. 118. 2. a.
millstone. See note on Matt. 18. 6.
about=round. Gr. *peri*. Ap. 104. xiii. 2.
cast=hurled (with violence).
into. Gr. *eis*. Ap. 104. vi.
offend=be a cause of stumbling to. This was spoken with reference to the traditions of the Pharisees in 16. 15-30.
3 If. Marking a possible contingency (Ap. 118. 1. b). Not the same condition as in *v.* 6.
trespass=sin. Gr. *hamartanō*. Ap. 128. I. i. As the Pharisees did. **against.** Gr. *eis*. Ap. 104. vi.
rebuke him. As the Lord had done (16. 15-31).
repent. See Ap. 111. I. 1.
4 seven. On the former occasion "seventy" (Matt. 18. 21, 22). No discrepancy. See Ap. 97.
to=unto. Gr. *epi*. Ap. 104. ix. 3; but the texts read *pros*.

17. 5-10 (*F*, p. 1461). **APOSTLES' REQUEST.** (*Division.*)

F | E^1 | 5. Request. Faith.
| E^2 | 6-10. Answer. Faith and Duty.

5 the Lord. Ap. 98. VI. i. *a.* 3. A.
Increase our faith=Give us more faith.

17. 6-10 (E^2, above). **ANSWER. FAITH AND DUTY.** (*Alternation.*)

E^2 | m | 6-. Hypothesis.
| n | -6. Result.
| *m* | 7-9. Fact.
| *n* | 10. Application.

6 If. Assuming the condition. See Ap. 118. 2. a.
ye might say=ye might, with Gr. *an*, marking it as being purely hypothetical.
this sycamine tree. On a former occasion (Matt. 17. 20) the Lord said "this mountain" (of the Transfiguration); and also on a later occasion (Mark 11. 23), referring to Olivet. But here, "this tree," because the locality was different. No discrepancy therefore.
sycamine=mulberry. Occ. only here. Not the same as in 19. 4. Both used medicinally.
in. Gr. *en*. Ap. 104. viii.
should. With Gr. *an*, still marking the hypothesis.
7 of=from among. Gr. *ek*. Ap. 104. vii. As in *v.* 15, but not the same as in *vv.* 20-, 25.
servant=bondman.
feeding cattle=shepherding.
by and by . . . Go=Come at once.
from=out of. Gr. *ek*. Ap. 104. vii.
sit down to meat=recline at table.
8 And will not rather=But will he not (Ap. 105. I. a).
till=while. **I have, &c.**=I eat and drink.
afterward=after (Gr. *meta*. Ap. 104. xi. 2) these things.
9 I trow not=I think not.
not. Gr. *ou*. Ap. 105. I.
10 So likewise ye=Thus ye also.
shall=may. **say, We**=say that (Gr. *hoti*) we. **unprofitable**=not needed, no use for. This may be for various reasons. Occurs only here and in Matt. 25. 30, where the reason may be for having done wickedly. Not the same word as in Rom. 3. 12. Tit. 3. 9. Philem. 11. Heb. 13. 17.

17. 11-19 (*E*, p. 1461). **JOURNEY.** (*Division.*)

E | F^1 | 11-13. The Ten Lepers.
| F^2 | 14-19. Their healing.

11 it came to pass. A Hebraism. **as He went**=as He was on (Gr. *en*. Ap. 104. viii) His way. **to**=unto. Gr. *eis*. Ap. 104. vi. **the midst of**: i. e. between them. **Galilee.** See Ap. 169. **12 entered**=was about to enter. **ten.** Cp. 2 Kings 7. 3, and note on Ex. 4. 6. **men.** Gr. pl. of *anēr*. Ap. 123. 2. **afar off.** As required by Lev. 13. 45, 46. The Talmudical law prescribed 100 paces. **13 Jesus.** See Ap. 98. X. **Master.** See Ap. 98. XIV. iv. **mercy**=compassion.

17. 14-19 (F^2, above). **THE HEALING OF THE TEN LEPERS.** (*Introversion and Alternation.*)

F^2 | G | 14-. Command. "Go."
| H | o | -14. Cleansing.
| | p | 15, 16. Return of one.
| *H* | *o* | 17. Cleansing.
| | *p* | 18. Return of the one.
| *G* | 19. Command. "Arise, Go."

14 as they went=in (Ap. 104. viii) their going.

p A. D. 29 15 And one [7]of them, when he saw that he was healed, turned back, and °with a loud voice glorified °God,

16 And fell down °on *his* face °at His feet, giving Him thanks: and he was a °Samaritan.

H o 17 And [13]Jesus answering said, °"Were there not ten cleansed? °but where *are* the nine?

p 18 °There are [9]not found that returned to give glory to [15]God, save this °stranger."

G 19 And He said unto him, "Arise, go thy way: thy faith hath made thee whole."

D 20 And °when He was demanded °of °the Pharisees, when °the kingdom of God °should come,

C J q He answered them and said, °"The kingdom of God cometh [9]not [15]with °observation:

r 21 Neither shall they say, °'Lo, here!' or, °'lo there!'

s for, °behold, [20]the kingdom of God is °within °you."

J q 22 And He said [1]unto °the disciples, "The days will come, when ye shall desire to see °one of the days of °the Son of man, and ye shall [9]not see *it.*

r 23 And they shall say to you, °'See here;' or, °'see there:' °go °not after *them,* °nor follow *them.*

s 24 For as the lightning, that °lighteneth °out of the one *part* °under °heaven, shineth °unto the other *part* °under °heaven; so shall °also [22]the Son of man be [6]in °His day.

B N 25 But °first must He suffer many things, and be °rejected °of °this generation.

O K M 26 And as it °was [6]in °the days of °Noe, so shall it be °also [6]in the days of [22]the Son of man.

27 They did eat, °they drank, they married wives, they were given in marriage, until the day that [26]Noe entered [2]into the ark, and the flood came, and destroyed them all.

28 Likewise °also as it [26]was [6]in °the days of Lot; [27]they did eat, they drank, they bought, they sold, they planted, they builded;

15 with. Gr. *meta.* Ap. 104. xi. 1.
God. Ap. 98. I. i. 1.
16 on. Gr. *epi.* Ap. 104. ix. 3.
at = beside. Gr. *para.* Ap. 104. xii. 3.
Samaritan. See 2 Kings 17. 29–35. Cp. 10. 33.
17 Were there not . . . ? = Were not (Gr. *ouchi.* Ap. 105. I. a.) the ten cleansed? but the nine, where [are they]?
18 There are not = Were there not?
stranger = alien. Gr. *allogenēs* = of another race. Occurs only here, but frequently in the Sept. Used by the Romans in the Inscription discovered by Clermont-Ganneau in 1871 (now in the Imperial New Museum in Constantinople). It was put up on the marble barriers of the inner courts of the Temple to warn off Gentiles. See Deissmann's *Light,* pp. 74, 75. Cp. Acts 21. 28.

17. -20-24 (*C*, p. 1461). THE KINGDOM NIGH.
(*Extended Alternation.*)

C | J | q | -20. It comes not by hostile watching. (Neg.)
  r | 21-. Nor by saying, "Lo here!" &c. (Neg.)
  s | -21. Reason. It is here among you. (Pos.)
J | *q* | 22. It shall not be seen by unhostile desiring. (Neg.)
  r | 23. Nor by saying, "See here", &c. (Neg.)
  s | 24. Reason. It will come suddenly. (Pos.)

20 when He was demanded = having been asked.
of = by. Gr. *hupo.* Ap. 104. xviii. 1.
the Pharisees. Who were watching Him with hostile intent (6. 7; 14. 1; 20. 20. Mark 3. 2).
the kingdom of God. See Ap. 114.
should come = is coming.
observation = hostile watching. Gr. *paratērēsis.* Occurs only here. The verb *paratēreō* is used always in a bad sense; and occurs only in Acts 9. 24, and Gal. 4. 10 (observe), beside the four passages quoted above.
21 Lo. Gr. *idou.* Ap. 133. I. 2.
behold. Fig. *Asterismos* (Ap. 6), for emphasis. Ap. 133. I. 2.
within = in the midst of, or, among: i. e. already there in the Person of the King (whose presence marks a kingdom). Gr. *entos,* the same meaning as Gr. *en* (Ap. 104. viii), with the plural rendered "among" 115 times in N.T. The same meaning as in Matt. 12. 28. John 1. 26.
you = you yourselves. His bitter enemies. Therefore not in their hearts; but the very opposite.
22 the disciples. Note the change.
one of the days, &c. Such as they were then seeing, i. e. have another opportunity.
the Son of man. See Ap. 98. XVI.
23 See. Same as "Lo" in *v.* 21.
go not = go not forth. **not.** Gr. *mē.* Ap. 105. II. **nor.** Gr. *mēde.* **24 lighteneth** = flasheth. Gr. *astraptō.* Occurs only here and in 24. 4. **out of.** Gr. *ek.* Ap. 104. vii. **under.** Gr. *hupo.* Ap. 104. xviii. 2. **heaven.** Sing. without Art. Cp. Matt. 6. 9, 10. **unto.** Gr. *eis.* Ap. 104. vi. **also the Son of man** = the Son of man also. **His day.** Described in the Apocalypse. **25 first must He suffer.** Cp. the *four* announcements: 9. 22, 44; 17. 25; 18. 31–33, and the Structure on p. 1461. **rejected.** This was the subject of the *third* period of the Lord's ministry. See Ap. 119. **of** = on the part of. Gr. *apo.* Ap. 104. iv. Not the same word as in *vv.* 7, 15, 20-. **this generation** = this (present) generation. See note on Matt. 11. 16.

17. 26—18. 30 (*O*, p. 1461). DISCIPLES INSTRUCTED AS TO THE PAST. (*Introversion.*)

O | K | 17. 26–37. The coming of the King. Sudden.
  L | 18. 1–14. Discipleship. Character. Two Parables.
  L | 18. 15–27. Discipleship. Character. Two Examples.
K | 18. 28–30. The rewards of the King. Manifold.

17. 26-37 (K, above). THE COMING OF THE KING, ETC. (*Alternation.*)

K | M | 26–29. Suddenness. Illustration.
  N | 30. That day.
M | 31–33. Suddenness. Direction.
N | 34. That night.

26 was = came to pass, as in *v.* 11, 14. **the days of Noe.** See Gen. 6. 4–7, 11–13. Ap. 117. I, II. **Noe** = Noah. **also in the days** = in the days also. **27 they drank** = they were drinking (and so the Imperfect tense throughout the verse). Note the Fig. *Asyndeton* in this verse (Ap. 6), to emphasize the crisis of the flood. **28 also** = even. **the days of Lot.** See Gen. 19. 15–25. Isa. 13. 19. Ezek. 16. 46–56. Amos 4. 11. Jude 7. Ap. 117. I, II.

A.D. 29 **29** But the same day that Lot went out °of
Sodom it rained fire and brimstone °from [24]hea-
ven, and °destroyed *them* all.
N **30** °Even thus shall it be in the day when
[22]the Son of man is °revealed.
M **31** [6]In that day, he which shall be °upon the
°housetop, and his °stuff [6]in the house, °let
him [23]not °come down to take it away: and
he that is [6]in the field, let him likewise [23]not
return °back.
32 °Remember Lot's wife.
33 Whosoever [10]shall seek to save his °life
shall lose it; and whosoever shall lose °his
life shall °preserve it.
N **34** I tell you, in that night there shall be °two
men °in one bed; the one shall be taken, °and
the °other shall be left.
35 Two *women* shall be °grinding °together;
the one shall be taken, and the [34]other left.
36 °Two *men* shall be [6]in the field; the one
shall be taken, and the [34]other left."
37 And they answered and said unto Him,
°"Where, °Lord?" And He said unto them,
°"Wheresoever the °body *is*, thither will the
°eagles be gathered together."

L O **18** And He spake °a parable unto them
°*to this end*, that men ought °always
to °pray, and °not °to faint;
P t **2** Saying, "There was °in a city a judge,
which feared [1]not °God, °neither °regarded
°man:
u **3** And there was °a widow [2]in that city; and
she °came °unto him, saying, °'Avenge me
°of mine adversary.'
t **4** And he °would °not for a while: but °after-
ward he said °within himself, 'Though I fear
°not [2]God, nor [2]regard [2]man;
u **5** Yet °because this widow troubleth me,
I will [3]avenge her, lest by her °continual
coming she °weary me.'"
Q **6** And the Lord said, "Hear what °the
unjust judge saith.
7 °And shall °not [2]God [3]avenge His own
°elect, which cry day and night [3]unto Him,
though °He bear long °with them?
8 I tell you that °He will [3]avenge them
speedily. Nevertheless when °the Son of man
cometh, shall He find °faith °on °the earth?"
O **9** And He spake this parable [3]unto °certain
which trusted °in themselves that they were
righteous, and °despised °others:

29 of = from. Gr. *apo*. Ap. 104. iv.
from. Gr. *apo*. Ap. 104. iv.
destroyed. Gr. *apollumi*. Cp. 4. 34, &c.
30 Even thus = according to (Gr. *kata*. Ap. 104. x. 2) these things; or, according to the Texts, the same things.
revealed. Gr. *apokaluptō*.
31 upon. Gr. *epi*. Ap. 104. ix. 1.
housetop. Cp. 12. 3; 5. 19.
stuff = vessels, or goods. Cp. Matt. 12. 29. Eng. "stuff" is from Low Latin *stupa* and O. Fr. *estoffe*.
let him not, &c. This was repeated later on the Mount of Olives (Matt. 24. 17-20. Mark 13. 14-16).
come down. By the staircase outside.
back. Gr. *eis ta opisō*. To the things behind.
32 Remember, &c. Fig. *Exemplum*. See Gen. 19. 26, and Ap. 117. I.
33 life. Gr. *psuchē*. See Ap. 110. III. 1.
his life = it.
preserve it = preserve it alive. Gr. *zōogoneō*. Occurs only here and in Acts 7. 19. Repeated from 9. 24, 25. Matt. 10. 39. Mark 8. 35.
34 two men: i. e. two persons.
in = upon. Gr. *epi*. Ap. 104. ix. 1.
and. The 1611 edition of the A.V. omitted this "and".
other. Gr. *heteros*. Ap. 124. 2.
35 grinding, &c. Referring to the morning.
together (Gr. *epi to auto*) = to the same (end). Cp. Matt. 22. 34. Acts 14. 1 (*kata to auto*).
36 Two, &c. The texts omit this verse.
37 Where, Lord? The question repeated in Matt. 24. 28, as well as the answer.
Lord. Ap. 98. vi. i. *a*. 3. A.
Wheresoever, &c. Fig. *Parœmia*. Ap. 6.
body = carcass.
eagles = vultures. See Job 39. 30. Cp. Hab. 1. 8. Hos. 8. 1. Rev. 19. 17-21.

18. 1-14 (L, p. 1486). DISCIPLESHIP. CHARACTER, ETC. TWO PARABLES.
(*Extended Alternation.*)

L | O | 1. First Parable. Perseverance in Prayer.
  P | t | 2. The unjust judge. } Righteous Vindication.
    u | 3. The widow. Plaint.
    t | 4. The unjust judge.
    u | 5. The widow. Redress.
    Q | 6-8. Application *re* the Kingdom.
  O | 9. Second Parable. Self- and true righteousness.
  P | v | 10-. Pharisee. } Righteous Justification.
    w | -10. Publican.
    v | 11, 12. Pharisee.
    w | 13. Publican.
    Q | 14. Application *re* Kingdom.

1 a parable. Both parables peculiar to Luke. Only here that the explanation is put first.
to this end, &c. Gr. *pros* (Ap. 104. xv. 3) *to dein* = to the purport that it is necessary, &c.
always. Fig. *Synecdochē* (of Genus), Ap. 6 = on all occasions, perseveringly.
pray. Gr. *proseuchomai*. Ap. 134. I. 2.
not. Gr. *mē*. Ap. 105. II.
to faint = to lose heart, be discouraged, give in, or give up. Gr. *egkakeō*. **2** in. Gr. *en*. Ap. 104. viii. God. Ap. 98. I. i. 1. neither. Gr. *mē*. Ap. 105. II. regarded. Gr. *entrepomai*. Cp. Matt. 21. 37. man. Gr. *anthrōpos*. Ap. 123. 1. **3** a widow. Widows were specially cared for under the law. See Ex. 22. 22. Deut. 10. 18. Cp. Isa. 1. 17, 23. Mal. 3. 5. Acts 6. 1; 9. 41. 1 Tim. 5. 3, &c. came = kept coming, or repeatedly came. unto. Gr. *pros*. Ap. 104. xv. 3. Avenge me = Do me justice from. Gr. *ekdikeō*. Occ. here, *v.* 5. Rom. 12. 19. 2 Cor. 10. 6. Rev. 6. 10; 19. 2. of = from. Gr. *apo*. Ap. 104. iv. **4** would not = did not wish to. Ap. 102. 1. not. Gr. *ou*. Ap. 105. I. afterward = after (Gr. *meta*. Ap. 104. xi. 2) these things. within = to. Gr. *en*. Ap. 104. viii. **5** because. Gr. *dia*. Ap. 104. v. 2. continual. Gr. *eis telos* = to the end. weary me = pester, lit. give me a blow under the eye. Gr. *hupōpiazō*. Occurs only here and in 1 Cor. 9. 27 ("buffet"). **6** the unjust judge = the judge of injustice. Gr. *adikia*. Ap. 128. VII. 1. **7** And shall not God = And God, shall He not. not. Gr. *ou mē*. Ap. 105. III. elect: i. e. His own people. He bear long = He delayeth. The unjust judge delayed from selfish indifference. The righteous God may delay from a divinely all-wise purpose. with = over. Gr. *epi*. Ap. 104. ix. 2. Not the same word as in *vv.* 11, 27. **8** He will avenge = He will perform the avenging (Gr. *ekdikēsis*. Cp. *v.* 5) of. Cp. Ps. 9. 12. Isa. 63. 4. Heb. 10. 37. the Son of man. Ap. 98. XVI. faith = the faith. on. Gr. *epi*. Ap. 104. ix. 1. the earth. Gr. *gē*. Ap. 129. 4. **9** certain = some also. in. Gr. *epi*. Ap. 104. ix. 2. despised = made nothing of. others = the rest. See 8. 10.

P v
A.D. 29 10 "Two men °went up °into the temple to [1]pray;

w the one a °Pharisee, and the °other a °publican.

v 11 The [10]Pharisee °stood °and [1]prayed °thus °with himself, [2]'God, I thank Thee, that I am [4]not as [9]other [2]men *are*, °extortioners, °unjust, adulterers, or even as this [10]publican.

12 I fast °twice in the week, I give tithes of °all that I °possess.'

w 13 And the [10]publican, °standing °afar off, [4]would °not lift up so much as *his* eyes °unto °heaven, but °smote °upon his breast, saying, [2]'God °be merciful to me °a sinner.'

Q 14 I tell you, this man [10]went down °to his house °justified °*rather* than °the other: °for every one that exalteth himself shall be abased; and he that humbleth himself shall be exalted."

L R x 15 °And they brought unto Him °also °infants, that He would °touch them:

y but when *His* disciples °saw *it*, they rebuked them.

x 16 But °Jesus called them *unto Him*,

y and said, "Suffer °little children to come [3]unto Me, and forbid them [1]not: for of such is °the kingdom of [2]God.

S 17 °Verily I say unto you, Whosoever shall [1]not receive [16]the kingdom of [2]God as a [16]little child shall °in no wise enter °therein."

R 18 °And a certain °ruler asked Him, saying, "Good °Master, what shall I do to inherit °eternal °life?"

19 And [16]Jesus said unto him, °"Why callest thou Me good? none *is* good, save one, *that is*, [2]God.

20 Thou °knowest the commandments, **Do [1]not commit adultery, Do [1]not kill, Do [1]not steal, Do [1]not bear false witness, Honour thy father and thy mother."**

21 And he said, °"All these have I kept from my youth up."

22 Now when [16]Jesus heard these things, He said unto him, °"Yet lackest thou one thing: sell all °that thou hast, and distribute unto °the poor, and thou shalt have treasure [2]in °heaven: and °come, follow Me."

23 And when he heard this, °he was very sorrowful: for he was °very rich.

S 24 And when [16]Jesus °saw that [23]he was very sorrowful, He said, "How °hardly °shall they that have riches enter [10]into [16]the kingdom of [2]God!

25 For it is easier for a °camel to go °through a needle's eye, than for a rich man to enter [10]into [16]the kingdom of [2]God."

10 went up. It was always "up" to the Temple on Mount Moriah. Cp. "went down" (*v.* 14).
into. Gr. *eis*. Ap. 104. vi.
Pharisee. See Ap. 120. II.
other. The different one. Gr. *heteros*. Ap. 124. 2.
publican. See note on Matt. 5. 46.
11 stood=took his stand, or took up his position (by himself).
and prayed=and began to pray.
thus=these things.
with=to. Gr. *pros*. Ap. 104. xv. 3.
extortioners. Like this tax-gatherer.
unjust. Like the judge of *vv.* 2–5.
12 twice in the week. The law prescribed only one in the year (Lev. 16. 29. Num. 29. 7). By the time of Zech. 8. 19 there were *four* yearly fasts. In our Lord's day they were bi-weekly (Monday and Thursday), between Passover and Pentecost; and between the Feast of Tabernacles and the Dedication.
all. The law only prescribed corn, wine, oil, and cattle (Deut. 14. 22, 23. Cp. Matt. 23. 23).
possess=gain, acquire. Not a word about his sins. See Prov. 28. 13.
13 standing: i.e. in a position of humility.
afar off. Cp. Ps. 40. 12. Ezra 9. 6.
not . . . so much as=not even. Gr. *ou* (Ap. 105. I) *oude*.
unto. Gr. *eis*. Ap. 104. vi.
heaven=the heaven. Sing. See note on Matt. 6. 9, 10.
smote, &c.=was smiting, &c., or, began to smite. Expressive of mental grief. Cp. 23. 48. Jer. 31. 19. Nah. 2. 7.
upon. Gr. *eis*; but all the texts omit.
be merciful=be propitiated or reconciled (through the atoning blood sprinkled on the mercy-seat). Gr. *hilaskomai*. Cp. Ex. 25. 17, 18, 21. Rom. 3. 25. Heb. 2. 17. Used in the Sept. in connexion with the mercy-seat (Gr. *hilastērion*). Heb. 9. 5.
a sinner=the sinner (cp. 1 Tim. 1. 15). Gr. *hamartōlos*. Cp. Ap. 128. II. 3.
14 to=unto. Gr. *eis*. Ap. 104. vi.
justified. Reckoned as righteous.
rather than. The texts read "compared with". Gr. *para*. Ap. 104. xii. 2.
the other=that one.
for, &c. Repeated from 14. 11. Cp. Hab. 2. 4.

18. 15–27 (*L*, p. 1486). DISCIPLESHIP. CHARACTER. TWO EXAMPLES. (*Alternation.*)

L | R | 15, 16. Infants brought.
  S | 17. Application.
 R | 18–23. Ruler comes.
  S | 24–27. Application.

18. 15, 16 (R, above). INFANTS BROUGHT. (*Alternation.*)

R | x | 15–. Infants brought.
  y | –15. Rebuke.
 x | 16–. Infants called.
  y | –16. Approbation.

15 And they brought, &c. As in Matt. 19. 13–15, and Mark 10. 13–16. A common custom for mothers to bring their babes for a Rabbi's blessing.
also infants=infants also.
infants=their babes. See Ap. 108. viii.
touch. Supplemental in Luke.
saw. Gr. *eidon*. Ap. 133. I. 1.
16 Jesus. See Ap. 98. X.
little children. Ap. 108. v. the kingdom of God. Ap. 112. II. and 114. **17 Verily.** See note on Matt. 5. 18. in no wise. Gr. *ou mē*. Ap. 105. III. therein=into (Ap. 104. vi) it. **18 And a, &c.** As in Matt. 19. 16–30. Mark 10. 17–31. ruler. Supplemental. Not so described in Matthew or Mark. Master=Teacher. Ap. 98. XIV. v. 1. eternal. See Ap. 151. II. B. i. life. Gr. *zōē*. Ap. 170. 1. **19 Why, &c.** See note on Matt. 19. 17. **20 knowest.** Gr. *oida*. Ap. 132. I. i. **21 All these.** See note on Matt. 19. 20. **22 Yet lackest, &c.**=Still one thing is lacking to thee. that=whatsoever. the poor. Ap. 127. 1. See note on John 12. 8. heaven. No Art. Sing. See note on Matt. 6. 9, 10. come=come hither. **23 he was**=he became. Cp. Mark 10. 22. very rich=rich exceedingly. **24 when Jesus saw that he was**=Jesus seeing (Ap. 133. I. 1) him becoming. hardly=with difficulty. shall they=do they. **25 camel.** See note on Matt. 19. 24. through. Gr. *dia*. Ap. 104. v. 1.

A.D. 29 26 And they that heard *it* said, "Who then °can be saved?"

27 And He said, "The things which are °impossible °with [2]men are °possible °with [2]God."

K a 28 Then Peter said, °"Lo, we °have left °all, and followed Thee."

29 And He said unto them, [17]"Verily I say unto you, There is no man that hath left house, °or parents, °or brethren, °or wife, °or children,

b for [16]the kingdom of [2]God's sake,

a 30 Who shall [7]not receive °manifold more [2]in °this present time,

b and [2]in °the °world to come [8]life °everlasting."

A L 31 °Then He took *unto him* the twelve, and said [3]unto them, °"Behold, we go up [14]to Jerusalem, and all things that °are written °by the prophets °concerning [8]the Son of man shall be accomplished.

32 For He shall °be delivered unto the Gentiles, and shall be mocked, and spitefully entreated, and spitted on:

33 And they shall scourge *Him*, and put Him to death: and the third day He shall °rise again."

34 And they °understood °none of these things: and this °saying was hid °from them, °neither knew they the things which were spoken.

M T 35 °And it came to pass, that °as He was come nigh [13]unto Jericho, °a certain blind man °sat °by the way side °begging:

U 36 And hearing the multitude pass by, °he asked what it meant.

37 And they told him, that [16]Jesus °of Nazareth °passeth by.

T W 38 And he °cried, saying, [16]"Jesus, *Thou* °Son of David, have °mercy on me."

X 39 And they which °went before rebuked him, that he should hold his peace:

W but he °cried so much the more, "*Thou* [38]Son of David, have [38]mercy on me."

X Y 40 And [16]Jesus °stood, and °commanded him °to be °brought [3]unto Him: and when he was °come near, He °asked him,

26 can = is able to.
27 impossible, &c. See note on Matt. 19. 26.
with. Gr. *para*. Ap. 104. xii. 2.
possible. Cp. Job 42. 2. Jer. 32. 17. Zech. 8. 6.

18. 28-30 (*K*, p. 1486). THE REWARDS OF THE KINGDOM. (*Alternation.*)

K | a | 28, 29-. All forsaken.
b | -29. For the kingdom's sake.
a | 30-. More received.
b | -30. In the coming age.

28 Lo. Gr. *idou*. Ap. 133. I. 2. Fig. *Asterismos*. Ap. 6.
have left = left.
all. The critical texts read "our own", marking a particular case (5. 11). Cp. Deut. 28. 8-11.
29 or. Note the Fig. *Paradiastolē* (Ap. 6), for emphasis.
30 manifold more. Gr. *pollaplasiōn*. Occ. only here.
this present time = this very season.
the world to come = the age that is coming.
world = age. See Ap. 129. 2.
everlasting. Ap. 151. II. B. ii.
31 Then, &c. For *vv.* 31-34, cp. Matt. 20. 17-19, and Mark 10. 32-34. The *fourth* announcement of His rejection (see the Structure *G* *A*, p. 1461), containing additional particulars.
Then = And. No note of time.
Behold. Fig. *Asterismos* (Ap. 6). Same word as "Lo", *v.* 28.
are written = have been and stand written.
by = by means of, or through. Gr. *dia*. Ap. 104. v. 1.
concerning = for: i.e. for Him to accomplish.
32 be delivered, &c. These particulars (in *vv.* 32, 33) are supplementary to the former three announcements. See the Structure (p. 1461).
33 rise again. Ap. 178. I. 1.
34 understood none, &c. As in 9. 43-45. Cp. Mark 9. 32. none = nothing. Gr. *oudeis*.
saying. Gr. *rhēma*. See note on Mark 9. 32.
from. Gr. *apo*. Ap. 104. iv.
neither knew they = and they did not (Ap. 105. I) know (Ap. 132. I. ii).

18. 35-43 (*M*, p. 1461). MIRACLE. THE BLIND MAN. (*Alternation.*)

M | T | 35. The blind man. Sitting.
U | 36, 37. The multitudes. Reply.
T | 38-43-. The blind man. Healed.
U | -43. The multitude. Praising God.

35 And it came to pass, &c. Not the same miracle as in Matt. 20. 29-34, or Mark 10. 46-52. See Ap. 152.
as He was come nigh = in (Gr. *en*. Ap. 104. viii) His drawing near. In Mark 10. 46, "as He went out".
a certain, &c. Not the same description as in Matt. 20. 30, or Mark 10. 46. sat = was sitting (as a custom). by = beside. Gr. *para*. Ap. 104. xii. 3. begging. So Bartimæus (Mark 10. 46); but not the two men (Matt. 20. 30). Gr. *prosaiteō*. Occ. only here. Mark 10. 46. John 9. 8, but all the texts read *epaiteō*, as in 16. 3. **36** he asked = he kept asking (Imp.) He knew not; but the other two heard and knew. **37** of Nazareth = the Nazaræan. passeth by = is passing by.

18. 38-43 (*T*, above). THE BLIND MAN. HEALED. (*Alternation.*)

T | W | 38. The blind man. His cry.
X | 39-. Multitude. Rebuke him.
W | -39. The blind man. Cry increased.
X | 40-43. Multitude. Ignored.

38 cried = called out. Son of David. Ap. 98. XVIII. Cp. the call of the other men (Ap. 152). mercy = pity. **39** went before rebuked. Those who go before the Lord (instead of following) are apt to make mistakes. cried = continued calling (Imp.). Not the same word as in *v.* 38.

18. 40-43- (*X*, above). MULTITUDE IGNORED. BLIND MAN HEALED. (*Alternation.*)

X | Y | 40, 41-. The Lord's Command and Question.
Z | -41. The blind man. Answer.
Y | 42. The Lord's Word.
Z | 43-. The blind man. Healed.

40 stood = stopped. commanded . . . brought. The other man the Lord commanded to be "called" (Mark 10. 49). The two were called by Himself (Matt. 20. 32). to be brought unto. Gr. *agō pros*. Used by Luke also in 4. 40; 19. 35. He uses *prosagō* in 9. 41. Acts 16. 20; 27. 27. come near. The one in Mark 10. 50. The two were already near (Matt. 20. 32). asked. Gr. *eperōtaō*. Cp. Ap. 134. I. 3.

A.D. 29 41 Saying, "What °wilt thou that I shall do unto thee?"

Z And he said, °"Lord, that I may receive my sight."

Y 42 And [16] Jesus said unto him, "Receive thy sight: thy faith hath °saved thee."

Z 43 And °immediately he received his sight, and followed Him, glorifying [2] God:

U and all the people, when they [15] saw *it*, gave praise unto [2] God.

F A¹ **19** °And *Jesus* °entered and passed through °Jericho.

B¹ c 2 And, °behold, *there was* a °man °named °Zacchæus, which was the °chief among the publicans, and he was rich.
3 And he °sought to °see °Jesus °who He was; and could °not °for the °press, °because he was °little of °stature.
4 And °he ran before, and climbed up °into a °sycomore tree to [3] see Him: for He °was to pass that *way*.

d 5 And when [3] Jesus came °to the place, °He looked up, and [3] saw him, and said °unto him, °"Zacchæus, make haste, and come down; for to day °I must abide °at thy house."
6 And he made haste, and came down, and received Him joyfully.

e 7 And when they [3] saw *it*, they all °murmured, saying, That He was gone °to be guest °with °a [2] man that is a °sinner.

c 8 °And [2] Zacchæus °stood, and said [5] unto the Lord; [2] "Behold, °Lord, the half of my goods °I give to the °poor; and °if °I have taken any thing from any man by false accusation, I restore *him* °fourfold."

d 9 And [3] Jesus said [5] unto him, °"This day is salvation °come to this °house,

e forsomuch as he also is °a °son of Abraham.
10 For °the Son of man °is come to seek and to save that which was lost."

41 wilt = desirest. See Ap. 102. 1.
Lord. See Ap. 98. VI. i. *a.* 3. B. a.
42 saved = healed. See on 8. 36.
43 immediately. See 1. 64.

19. 1—22. 38 (*F*, p. 1427). THE FOURTH PERIOD OF THE LORD'S MINISTRY. THE REJECTION OF THE KINGDOM. (*Repeated Alternation.*)

F
A¹ | 19. 1. Place. Jericho to Jerusalem.
B¹ | 19. 2-10. Event. Calling of Zacchæus.
A² | 19. 11. Place. Approaching Jerusalem.
B² | 19. 12-27. Event. Parable.
A³ | 19. 28, 29-. Place. Ascending to Jerusalem.
B³ | 19. -29-35. Event. Mission of the Two.
A⁴ | 19. 36, 37-. Place. Descending to Jerusalem.
B⁴ | 19. -37-44. Events. Progress, &c.
A⁵ | 19. 45-. Place. Jerusalem. The Temple.
B⁵ | 19. -45, 46. Event. Cleansing of the Temple.
A⁶ | 19. 47-. Place. Temple. Teaching.
B⁶ | 19. -47, 48. Event. Conspiracy.
A⁷ | 20. 1-. Place. Temple.
B⁷ | 20. -1-47. Event. Confutation of Enemies.
A⁸ | 21. 1-. Place. Temple. Treasury.
B⁸ | 21. -1-4. Event. The poor widow.
A⁹ | 21. 5-. Place. Temple. Remaining in.
B⁹ | 21. -5-36. Event. Prophetic Discourse.
A¹⁰ | 21. 37, 38. Place. Temple and Abode.
B¹⁰ | 22. 1-38. Event. The Last Passover.

1 And, &c. Verses 1-10 are peculiar to Luke.
entered, &c. = having entered . . . was passing through. After the healing of the blind man. Cp. "come nigh" (18. 35).
Jericho. Now *Eriha.* In mediæval times *Riha.* The city of palm trees (Deut. 34. 3. Judg. 1. 16), about eighteen miles from Jerusalem, and six miles from the Jordan. Cp. Josh. 6. 26 with 1 Kings 16. 34. It afterward became a great and wealthy city with some 100,000 inhabitants (cp. Josephus, *Bell. Jud.* iv. 8. Ecclus. 24. 14).

19. 2-10 (B¹, above). EVENT. CALLING OF ZACCHÆUS. (*Extended Alternation.*)

B¹
c | 2-4. Zacchæus. Expectation.
d | 5, 6. The Lord. Detection.
e | 7. Enemies. Objection.
c | 8. Zacchæus. Protestation.
d | 9-. The Lord. Declaration.
e | -9, 10. Enemies. Vindication.

2 behold. Ap. 133. i. 2. Fig. *Asterismos.* Ap. 6.
man. Gr. *anēr.* Ap. 123. 2. **named** = called by name.
Zacchæus. Aramaic, *Zakkai* = pure. Ezra 2. 9. Neh. 7. 14. Ap. 94. III. 3.
chief among the publicans = a chief tax-gatherer. Gr. *architelōnēs.* Occ. only here. See notes on 3. 12 and Matt. 9. 9. **3 sought** = was (busy) seeking. **see.** Ap. 133. I. 1. **Jesus.** Ap. 98. X. **who He was.** Not what kind of a person, but which one of the crowd he was. **not.** Gr. *ou.* Ap. 105. I. **for.** Gr. *apo.* Ap. 104. iv. **press** = crowd. **because** = seeing that. Not the same word as in *vv.* 11-, 44. **little** = small. **stature.** Gr. *hēlikia.* See note on 12. 25. **4 he ran before, and** = having run forward before, he. **into** = on to. Gr. *epi* (Ap. 104. ix. 3). **sycomore.** Occ. only here. Not the same word as "sycamine" in 17. 6, or with our "sycamore", but the Egyptian fig, as in John 1. 49. **was to pass, &c.** = was about to pass through by (or through. Gr. *dia.* Ap. 104. v. 1) that [way]. **5 to** = up to. Gr. *epi.* Ap. 104. ix. 3. **He looked up** = Jesus looked up. Gr. *anablepō.* Ap. 133. III. 1. **unto.** Gr. *pros.* Ap. 104. xv. 3. **Zacchæus.** Cp. John 10. 3. **I must abide.** Adopting the royal mandate. **at** = in. Gr. *en.* Ap. 104. viii. Not the same word as in *vv.* 29, 37. **7 murmured** = began to murmur aloud. **to be guest** = to lodge, or put up. Cp. 2. 7. Mark 14. 14. **with.** Gr. *para.* Ap. 104. xii. 2. **a man that is a sinner** = a sinful man. **sinner.** Gr. *hamartōlos.* Cp. Ap. 128. I. i. ii. 1. 2. **8 And** = But. **stood** = took his stand. See note on 18. 11. **Lord.** Ap. 98. VI. i. *a.* 3. A. a. **I give:** i.e. I now propose to give (present tense). Referring to a present vow, not to a past habit. **poor.** Ap. 127. 1. **if, &c.** Assuming the actual fact, no doubt being thrown on it. Not a mere possible case. Ap. 118. 2. a. **I have taken . . . by false accusation.** Gr. *sukophanteō.* Occurs only here and in 3. 14. It was said to mean informing of a breach of the law which forbade the exportation of figs (prohibited, in time of dearth, by an old Athenian law); but for this there is no authority. Whatever its origin, it came to mean a malicious accuser. Our Eng. word "sycophant" means a toady. The word *sukophantēs* (*sūkon,* a fig; *phaino,* to show) had something to do with figs, but nobody knows what. **fourfold.** This was the restitution required of a sheep-stealer (Ex. 22. 1). **9 This day** = That this day, the Gr. *hoti* placing what was said within quotation marks. Contrast 23. 43, where there is no "*hoti*". **come** = come to pass. **house.** Put by Fig. *Metonymy* (of Subject), Ap. 6, for the household. **a son.** The 1611 edition of the A.V. reads "the son". **son.** Ap. 108. iii. Put by Fig. *Synecdochē* (of Genus), Ap. 6, for a descendant. **10 the Son of man.** See Ap. 98. XVI. **is come** = came.

A^2 A.D. 29 **11 And as they heard these things, He °added and spake a parable, °because He was nigh to Jerusalem, and because they thought °that °the kingdom of God °should °immediately °appear.**

B^2 C F **12 He said therefore, °"A certain °nobleman went °into a °far country**

G **to receive for himself °a kingdom, and to return.**

D H **13 And he called °his ten °servants, and delivered them ten °pounds,**

J **and said [5]unto them, °'Occupy °till I come.'**

E K **14 But his °citizens °hated him,**

L **and sent °a message after him, saying, 'We °will [3]not have this *man* to reign °over us.'**

C F **15 And °it came to pass, that °when he was returned,**

G **having received the [12]kingdom,**

D H **then he °commanded these servants to be called unto him, to whom he had given the money, that he might °know how much every man °had gained by trading.**

J M^1 **16 Then came the first, saying, °'Lord, thy [13]pound °hath gained ten [13]pounds.'**

N^1 **17 And he said unto him, 'Well, thou good [13]servant: [3]because thou hast been faithful °in a very little, °have thou °authority over ten °cities.'**

M^2 **18 And the second came, saying, [16]'Lord, thy [13]pound hath °gained five [13]pounds.'**

N^2 **19 And he said °likewise to him, °'Be thou also over five [17]cities.'**

M^3 **20 And °another came, saying, [16]'Lord, [2]behold, *here is* thy [13]pound, which I °have kept laid up [17]in a °napkin:**

N^3 f **21 For I feared thee, [3]because thou art an °austere °man: °thou takest up that thou layedst [3]not down, and reapest that thou didst [3]not sow.'**

11 added and spake=went on to speak.

because=on account of (Gr. *dia.* Ap. 104. v. 2) [the fact] that. Not the same word as in *v.* 44.

that. Gr. *hoti*, same as "because" in *vv.* 3, 17, 21, 31.

the kingdom of God. See Ap. 114.

should=was about to.

immediately=at the very moment. See 1. 64.

appear=be manifested. Ap. 106. I. ii.

19. 12-27 (B², p. 1490). EVENT. PARABLE. (THE NOBLEMAN.) (*Extended Alternation.*)

B^2 | C | F | 12-. Nobleman. Departure.
G | -12. His object purposed.
D | H | 13-. Servants. Commissioned.
J | -13. Their duty.
E | K | 14-. Citizens. Hatred.
L | -14. Their message.
C | *F* | 15-. Nobleman. Return.
G | -15-. His object attained.
D | *H* | -15. Servants. Summoned.
J | 16-26. Their reckoning.
E | *K* | 27-. Citizens. Hatred.
L | -27. Their execution.

12 A certain nobleman. This parable is peculiar to Luke. The point of it was that Herod the Great and his son Archelaus (Ap. 109) had actually gone from Jericho (where the parable was spoken; and where the latter had just rebuilt his palace. Josephus, *Ant.* xvii. 13. § 1) to Rome to receive the sovereignty (see Josephus, *Ant.* xiv. 14. § 3, 4; xvii. 9. § 4). Herod Antipas (Ap. 109) subsequently did the same thing (Josephus, *Ant.* xviii. 7. § 2).

nobleman=a man (Ap. 123. 1) high born. Gr. *eugenēs.* Elsewhere only in Acts 17. 11. 1 Cor. 1. 26.

into=unto. Gr. *eis.* Ap. 104. vi. As in *vv.* 30, 45; not in *vv.* 4, 23. **far**=distant.

a kingdom=his sovereignty, or sovereign power.

13 his ten servants=ten servants of his.

servants=bond-servants.

pounds. Gr. *mna.* See Ap. 51. II. 4 (2). Archelaus did thus actually leave money in trust with his servants, Philippus being in charge of his pecuniary affairs. Not the same parable as that of the Talents in Matt. 25. 14-30, which was uttered later, on the second day before the last Passover. See Ap. 156. V.

Occupy=Engage in business, or use (as a house where one's business is done). From the Latin *occupare*, and French *occuper.* Gr. *pragmateuomai.* Occ. only here. Cp. Judg. 16. 11. Ps. 107. 23 (P.B.V.).

till I come: i. e. while I go and return. **14 citizens**, or subjects. **hated**=used to hate. **a message**=an embassy (cp. 14. 32). This was actually done in the case of Archelaus (Josephus, *Ant.* xvii. 11. § 1, &c.). The Jews appealed to Augustus, on account of the cruelties of Archelaus and the Herods generally. It led ultimately to his deposition. **will.** Ap. 102. 1. **over.** Gr. *epi.* Ap. 104. ix. 3. **15 it came to pass.** A Hebraism. **when, &c.**=on (Gr. *en.* Ap. 104. viii) his coming back. **commanded**=directed. **know**=get to know. Ap. 132. I. ii. **had gained by trading.** Gr. *diapragmateuomai.* Occurs only here.

19. 16-26 (*J*, above). THEIR RECKONING. (*Repeated Alternation.*)

J | M^1 | 16. First Servant. Gain. Ten pounds.
N^1 | 17. Commendation and Reward.
M^2 | 18. Second Servant. Gain. Five pounds.
N^2 | 19. Reward.
M^3 | 20. Another Servant. Nothing.
N^3 | 21-26. Censure and Punishment.

16 Lord. Ap. 98. VI. i. *a.* 4. B. **hath gained**=hath gained by labour: i. e. made in addition. Occurs only here. **17 in.** Gr. *en.* Ap. 104. viii. **have thou authority, &c.** Exactly what Archelaus had then just done. **authority.** Gr. *exousia.* Ap. 172. 5. **cities.** Evidently in the kingdom to which the nobleman had returned. **18 gained**=made. **19 likewise to him**=to this one also. **Be**=Become. **20 another.** Gr. *heteros.* Ap. 124. 2. **have kept**=was keeping. **napkin**=handkerchief. See on John 11. 44.

19. 21-26 (N^3, above). CENSURE AND PUNISHMENT. (*Alternation.*)

N^3 | f | 21. The servant's excuse.
g | 22, 23. The nobleman's retort.
f | 24, 25. The servant's punishment.
g | 26. The nobleman's reply.

21 austere. Gr. *austēros*=dry, then hard and harsh. Only here, and *v.* 22. **man.** Gr. *anthrōpos.* Ap. 123. 1. **thou takest up, &c.** Typical injustice of those times.

g 22 And he saith unto him, °'Out of thine
A.D. 29 own mouth will I judge thee, *thou* °wicked
[13]servant. °Thou °knewest that I was an
[21]austere [21]man, taking up that I laid [3]not
down, and reaping that I did [3]not sow:
23 Wherefore then gavest [3]not thou my
money [4]into the °bank, that at my coming I
might have required mine own °with °usury?'
f 24 And he said unto them that stood by,
'°Take °from him the [13]pound, and give *it* to
him that hath ten [13]pounds.'
25 (And they said unto him, [16]'Lord, he
hath ten [13]pounds.')
g 26 °'For I say unto you, That unto every
one which hath shall be given; and [24]from
him that hath °not, even that he hath shall
be taken away [24]from him.
E K 27 °But those mine enemies, which °would
[26]not that I should reign [14]over them,
L bring hither, and °slay *them* before me.'"
A[3] 28 And when He had thus spoken, He °went
before, °ascending up °to Jerusalem.
29 °And [15]it came to pass, when He was
come nigh [28]to °Bethphage and °Bethany, °at
the mount called *the mount* of Olives,
B[3] O P °He sent two of His disciples,
Q 30 Saying, °"Go ye [12]into the village °over
against *you;* [17]in the which at your entering
R ye shall find a °colt tied, °whereon yet never
[21]man sat:
S T loose him, and bring *him hither*.
U h 31 And °if °any man ask you, 'Why do ye
loose *him?*' thus shall ye say unto him,
i [3]'Because °the Lord hath need of him.'"
O P 32 And they that were sent went their way,
Q and found even as He had said unto them.
R 33 And as they were loosing the colt,
S U h °the owners thereof said [5]unto them, "Why
loose ye the [30]colt?"
i 34 And they said, [31]"The Lord hath need
of him."
T 35 And they °brought him °to [3]Jesus: and
they cast °their garments °upon the colt, and
they °set [3]Jesus thereon.
A[4] 36 And as He went, they °spread their
clothes [17]in the way.
37 And when He was come nigh, even now
°at °the °descent of the mount of Olives,
B[4] V[1] the whole multitude of the disciples began to
rejoice and praise °God with a loud voice °for
all the °mighty works that they had [3]seen;
38 °Saying, "**Blessed** *be* **the King That
cometh** [17]**in** °**the name of** °**the LORD**: peace [17]in
°heaven, and glory [17]in the highest."
V[2] 39 And some of the °Pharisees °from among
the multitude said [5]unto Him, °"Master, rebuke Thy disciples."

22 **Out of.** Gk. *ek*. Ap. 104. vii.
wicked. Gr. *ponēros*. Ap. 128. III. 1.
Thou knewest. Or, Didst thou know, &c.?
knewest. Gr. *oida*. Ap. 132. I. i.
23 bank = table, of the exchangers.
with. Gr. *sun*. Ap. 104. xvi. usury = interest.
24 Take from him, &c. Cp. Matt. 21. 43.
from = away from. Gr. *apo*. Ap. 104. iv.
26 For I say, &c. This is the Lord's own application.
not. Gr. *mē*. Ap. 105. II.
27 But = But as for.
would not = were unwilling. Ap. 102. 1.
slay them = cut them down. Gr. *katasphazō*. Occ. only here.
28 went before = went on.
ascending. See note on 10. 30, 31.
to = unto. Gr. *eis*. Ap. 104. vi.
29 And, &c. This is the second entry, which was not unexpected as the former was (Matt. 21. 1, &c.), but pre-arranged (John 12. 12, 13). See Ap. 153 and 156.
Bethphage. See note on Matt. 21. 1.
Bethany. Now *el 'Azeriyeh* = The place of Lazarus. See Ap. 156. Bethany was the starting-point of this second entry. See John 12. 1, 12; Mark 11. 1, whereas in Matt. 21. 1 the Lord was at Bethphage. See note there.

19. -29-35 (B[3], p. 1490). EVENT. MISSION OF THE TWO DISCIPLES.
(*Extended Alternation and Introversion.*)

B[3] | O | P | -29. Two disciples sent.
Q | 30-. Ye shall find.
R | -30-. Loose him.
S | T | -30. And bring him.
U | h | 31-. If any object.
i | -31. "The Lord hath need", &c.
O | *P* | 32-. Two disciples go.
Q | -32. They find as was said.
R | 33-. They loose the colt.
S | *U* | *h* | -33. The owners' objection.
i | 34. "The Lord hath need", &c.
T | 35. They bring him.

-29 He sent two. As before (Matt. 21. 1).
30 Go = Withdraw. Not go forward, as in Matt. 21. 2.
over against. Gr. *katenanti*, down and opposite.
colt. On the former entry, *two* animals were sent for. Luke is not "less circumstantial", but more so.
whereon = on (Gr. *epi*. Ap. 104. ix. 3) which.
31 if, &c. The condition probable. Ap. 118. 1. b.
any man = any one.
the Lord. Ap. 98. VI. i. *a*. 2. A. a.
33 the owners. Gr. *kurioi*. See Ap. 98. VI. i. *a*. 4. A.
35 brought = led.
to. Gr. *pros*. Ap. 104. xv. 3.
their = their own.
upon. Gr. *epi*. Ap. 104. ix. 3.
set. Gr. *epibibazō*. Only here, 10. 34, and Acts 23. 24.
36 spread = were strewing under. Gr. *hupostrōnnumi*. Occ. only here.
37 at = to. Gr. *pros*. Ap. 104. xv. 2.
the descent. The second sight of the city after the first, owing to a dip in the route.
descent. Gr. *katabasis*. Occ. only here.

19. -37-44 (B[4], p. 1490). EVENTS. PROGRESS.
(*Division.*)

B[4] | V[1] | -37, 38. Crowds. Acclamation.
V[2] | 39, 40. Enemies. Objection.
V[3] | 41-44. Jerusalem. Commiseration.

-37 God. Ap. 98. I. i. 1.
for = concerning. Gr. *peri*. Ap. 104. xiii. 1.

38 Saying, &c. Quoted from Ps. 118. 26. the name. See note on Ps. 20. 1. the LORD = Jehovah. See Ap. 98. VI. i. *a*. 1. A. a. heaven. Sing. without Art. See note on Matt. 6. 9, 10.
39 Pharisees. Ap. 120. II. 1. from among = from, as in *v*. 24. Master = Teacher. Ap. 98. XIV. v. 1.

A. D. 29 40 And He answered and said unto them, "I tell you that, [31] if these should hold their peace, the stones would immediately cry out."

V[3] j 41 And when He was °come near, He °beheld the city, and °wept °over it,
42 °Saying, °"If thou °hadst [15] known, even thou, at least [17] in this thy °day,

k the things °*which belong* unto thy peace!

l but now they are hid [24] from thine eyes.

k 43 For °the days shall come [35] upon thee, that thine enemies shall cast a °trench about thee, and compass thee round, and keep thee in on every side,
44 And shall °lay thee even with the ground, and thy °children °within thee; and they shall not leave [17] in thee °one stone upon another;

j °because thou [15] knewest [3] not the °time of thy °visitation."

A[5] 45 And He went [12] into °the temple,

B[5] and began °to cast out them that sold °therein, and them that bought;
46 Saying unto them, °"It is written, '**My house is the house of prayer**: but ye have made it °a °den of °thieves.' "

A[6] 47 And He °taught °daily in [45] the temple.

B[6] But the °chief priests and the scribes and the chief of the people sought to destroy Him,
48 And could [3] not find what they might do: for all the people were °very attentive to hear Him.

A[7] **20** And °it came to pass, *that* °on one of °those days, as He °taught the people °in °the temple, and °preached the gospel,

[7] W X[1] m[1] the chief priests and the scribes °came upon *Him* °with the elders,
2 And spake °unto Him, saying, "Tell us, °by °what °authority dost Thou these things?

19. 41-44 (V[3], p. 1492). JERUSALEM. COMMISERATION. (*Introversion.*)

V[3] | j | 41, 42-. "If thou hadst known".
  k | -42-. Jerusalem's day of grace.
   l | -42. Consequence. Now hidden.
  k | 43, 44-. Jerusalem's day of recompense.
 j | -44. "Thou knewest not".

41 come near. Marking the progress.
beheld . . . and = looking on. Ap. 133. I. 1.
wept = wept aloud. Gr. *klaiō* = to wail. Not *dakruō* = to shed silent tears, as in John 11. 35.
over. Gr. *epi.* Ap. 104. ix. 2.
42 Saying, &c. Peculiar to Luke.
If thou, &c. Assuming it as an actual fact. Ap. 118. 2. a. Not the same as in *vv.* 8, 31, 40.
hadst known. Put by Fig. *Metonymy* (of Cause), Ap. 6, for heeding. See note on Isa. 1. 3.
day. Put by Fig. *Metonymy* (of Adjunct), Ap. 6, for the events taking place in it.
which belong unto = for (Gr. *pros.* Ap. 104. xv. 3) thy peace. For these see Isa. 48. 18 and Ps. 122. Note the Fig. *Aposiopēsis* (Ap. 6), denoting that the blessedness involved in this knowledge was overwhelmed by the thought of the tribulation which was to come on account of their ignorance of it.
43 the days = days.
trench = rampart. Gr. *charax.* Occurs only here. Cp. Isa. 29. 3, 4; 37. 33.
44 lay = level (and dash). Cp. Sept., Ps. 137. 9. Hos. 10. 14. **children.** Ap. 108. i.
within. Gr. *en.* Ap. 104. viii.
one stone, &c. = stone upon (Gr. *epi.* Ap. 104. ix. 2) stone.
because = the reason for (*anti.* Ap. 104. ii) which things [is that]. **time** = season.
visitation. As stated in 1. 68 and 78.
45 the temple = the temple courts. Gr. *hieron.* See Matt. 23. 16.
to cast out, &c. This is a repetition of the Lord's act in Matt. 21. 12, but the same as in Mark 11. 15, which has supplementary details. See Ap. 156.
therein = in (Gr. *en*).
46 It is written = It standeth written. Quoted from Isa. 56. 7 and Jer. 7. 11. See Ap. 107. II. 4.
a den of thieves = a robbers' cave.
den = cave. Gr. *spēlaion.* Occ. six times: here; Matt. 21. 13. Mark 11. 17. John 11. 38 (cave), Heb. 11. 38, and Rev. 6. 15.
thieves = robbers, or brigands. As in John 10. 1, 8; 18. 40 and 2 Cor 11. 26, and should be so rendered in Matt. 21. 13; 26. 55; 27. 38, 44, &c. Not *kleptēs* = a thief. **47 taught** = was (or continued) teaching. **daily** = day by day: i. e. on each of these last six days. Cp. 20. 1. See Ap. 156. **chief priests** = high priests. **48 very attentive to hear Him** = hanging on Him, listening.

20. 1 it came to pass. A Hebraism. See note on 2. 1. **on.** Gr. *en.* Ap. 104. viii. **those days.** Those last six days. See Ap. 156. **taught** = was teaching. **in.** Gr. *en.* Ap. 104. viii. **the temple** = the temple courts. See note on Matt. 23. 16. **preached the gospel** = announced the glad tidings. Gr. *euaggelizō.* Ap. 121. 4. Almost peculiar to Luke and Paul. Luke uses it twenty-five times and Paul twenty-four.

20. -1-47 (B[7], p. 1490). EVENTS. CONFUTATION. (*Introversions.*)

B[7] | W | X[1] | -1-8. Enemies. First attack. Authority.
   Y | 9-18. Parable against them.
  X[2] | 19-26. Enemies. Second attack. Tribute money.
 W | X[3] | 27-40. Enemies. Third attack. Resurrection.
   Y | 41-44. Dilemma for them.
  X[4] | 45-47. Enemies. Disciples warned against them.

20. -1-8 (X[1], above). ENEMIES. FIRST ATTACK. AUTHORITY. (*Repeated Alternation.*)

X[1] | m[1] | -1, 2. Enemies. Question. The Lord's authority.
  n[1] | 3, 4. The Lord's Question in reply.
 m[2] | 5, 6. Enemies. Reasoning.
  n[2] | 7. The Lord's Question unanswered.
 m[3] | 8. Enemies. Answer declined.

-1 came upon. Implying suddenness and hostility. See Acts 4. 1; 6. 12; 23. 27. Cp. Mark 11. 27. **with.** Gr. *sun.* Ap. 104. xvi. Not as in *v.* 5. **2 unto.** Gr. *pros.* Ap. 104. xv. 3. **by.** Gr. *en.* Ap. 104. viii. **what** = what kind of; i. e. as Priest, Scribe, Prophet, Rabbi or what? **authority.** Gr. *exousia.* Ap. 172. 5. *v.* 2 in *religious* matters; *v.* 22 in *civil* matters; *v.* 33 in *domestic* matters.

D. 29 or Who is He that gave Thee this °author-
ity?"
n^1 3 And He answered and said [2] unto them, "I
will also ask you one °thing; and answer Me:
4 The °baptism of John, was it °from °heaven,
or °of °men?"
m^2 5 And they °reasoned °with themselves, saying, °"If we shall say, [4]'From [4]heaven;' He
will say, 'Why then °believed ye Him °not?'
6 But and [5]if we say, [4]'Of [4]men;' all the
people °will stone us: for °they be persuaded
that John was a prophet."
n^2 7 And they answered, that they °could not
tell whence *it was.*
m^3 8 And °Jesus said unto them, °"Neither tell I
you [2]by [2]what [2]authority I do these things."
Y o^1 9 °Then began He to speak °to °the people
this parable; "A certain [4]man planted a °vine-
yard, and °let it forth to °husbandmen, and
°went into a °far country for a long time.
p^1 10 And °at the season he sent a °servant [9]to
the husbandmen, that they should give him
°of the fruit of the [9]vineyard: but the husbandmen °beat him, and sent *him* away empty.
11 And °again he sent °another [10]servant:
and they [10]beat him also, and entreated *him*
shamefully, and sent *him* away empty.
12 And [11]again he sent °a third: and they
°wounded him also, and °cast *him* out.
13 Then said °the lord of the vineyard,
°'What shall I do? I will send my °beloved
son: °it may be they will °reverence *him* when
they °see him.'
14 But when the husbandmen [13]saw him,
they °reasoned °among themselves, saying,
'This is the heir: come, let us kill him, that
the inheritance may °be ours.'
15 So they cast him °out of the vineyard, and
killed *him.*
o^2 What therefore shall [13]the lord of the vineyard do unto them?
p^2 16 °He shall come and destroy these husbandmen, and shall give the vineyard to
°others." And when they heard *it,* °they said,
°"God forbid."
o^3 17 And He °beheld them, and said, "What is
this then that °is written, °'**The stone which
the builders rejected, the same is °become
the head of the corner**'?
18 Whosoever shall fall upon that stone shall
be °broken; but on whomsoever it shall fall,
it will °grind him to powder."
X^2 q^1 19 °And the chief priests and the scribes °the
same hour sought to lay hands °on Him; and
they feared the people: for they °perceived
that He had spoken this parable °against
them.

3 I will also = I also will.
thing: or question. Gr. *logos* = word. See note on Mark 9. 32.
4 baptism. Ap. 115. II. i. 2.
from. Gr. *ek.* Ap. 104. vii.
heaven. Sing. See note on Matt. 6. 9, 10.
of = from, as above.
men. Gr. *anthrōpos.* Ap. 123. 1.
5 reasoned. Gr. *sullogizomai.* Occurs only here. It implies close deliberation with one another.
with = among. Gr. *pros.* Ap. 104. xv. 3.
If, &c. Expresses a contingency. Ap. 118. 1. b.
believed. Ap. 150. I. 1. ii.
not. Gr. *ou.* Ap. 105. I. As in *vv.* 26, 38; not as in *v.* 7.
6 will stone us = will stone us to death. Gr. *katalithazō.* Occurs only here.
they be persuaded = it [the people] has been firmly convinced. Implying long settled conviction. Gr. *peithō.* Ap. 150. I. 2.
7 could not tell = did not know. Ap. 132. I. i.
not. Gr. *mē.* Ap. 105. II.
8 Jesus. Ap. 98. X.
Neither. Gr. *oude.*

20. 9-18 (Y, p. 1493). PARABLE AGAINST ENEMIES. (*Repeated Alternation.*)

Y | o^1 | 9. Proprietor of Vineyard. Action.
  p^1 | 10-15-. Husbandmen. Conduct.
 o^2 | -15. Proprietor of Vineyard. Question.
  p^2 | 16. Husbandmen. Destruction.
 o^3 | 17, 18. Proprietor (the Lord). Application.

9 Then began, &c. See Matt. 21. 34, 46 and Mark 12. 1-12. See notes there.
to. Gr. *pros.* Ap. 104. xv. 3.
the people. But still in the hearing of the rulers.
vineyard. See Isa. 5. 1-7. Jer. 2. 21. Ezek. 15. 1-6.
let it forth. See note on Matt. 21. 33.
husbandmen: i. e. Israel.
went . . . far country = left the country. See note on Matt. 21. 33.
10 at. Gr. *en*; but all the texts omit.
servant = bond-servant.
of = from. Gr. *apo.* Ap. 104. iv.
beat. This is supplementary, not contradictory to Matthew and Mark.
11 again he sent = he sent yet. Gr. "added to send". A Hebraism (19. 11. Acts 12. 3. Cp. Gen. 4. 2).
another = a different. Gr. *heteros.* Ap. 124. 2.
12 a. The 1611 edition of the A.V. reads "the".
wounded. Gr. *traumatizō.* Occurs only here and Acts 19. 16. Cp. 10. 34.
cast him out. See 13. 33, 34 and Neh. 9. 26. 1 Kings 22. 24-27. 2 Chron. 24. 19-22. Acts 7. 52. 1 Thess. 2. 15. Heb. 11. 36, 37.
13 the lord. Gr. *ho Kurios.* Ap. 98. VI. i. a. 4. A.
What shall I do? Cp. Gen. 1. 26; 6. 7.
beloved. Gr. *agapētos.* Ap. 135. III.
it may be = surely. Gr. *isōs.* Occurs only here; and only once in O.T. where it is Sept. for Heb. *'ak* (1 Sam. 25. 21).
reverence. See note on Matt. 21. 37.
see. Ap. 133. I. i.
14 reasoned. Not the same word as in *v.* 5.
among. Same as "with" (*v.* 5).
be = become.
15 out of = outside. Cp. Heb. 13. 12, 13. John 19. 27.
16 He shall come = [Some answered] he, &c. Cp. Matt. 21. 41.
others = others (of the same kind); i. e. a new Israel, not a different Gentile nation, which would be *heteros.* Ap. 124. 2.
they said: i. e. others who heard it said.
God forbid = May it never be! Gr. *mē genoito.* Heb. *chalilah* = the opposite of "Amen" (Gen. 44. 7, 17. Josh. 22. 29). Occurs only here in the Gospels, but ten times in Romans.
17 beheld = looked fixedly. Gr. *emblepō.* Ap. 133. I. 7.
is written = has been written. See Ap. 143.
The stone, &c. Quoted from Ps. 118. 22. Cp. 19. 38.
become = become into. Gr. *eis.* Ap. 104. vi.
18 broken = broken to pieces.
grind him to powder. See note on Matt. 21. 44.

20. 19-26 [For Structure see next page].

19 And, &c. Cp. Matt. 22. 15-22. Mark 12. 13-17. See Ap. 156.
the same = in (Gr. *en.* Ap. 104. viii) the same. Not the same as in *v.* 23.
on. Gr. *epi.* Ap. 104. ix. 3.
perceived = got to know. Gr. *ginōskō.* Ap. 132. I. ii.
against. Gr. *pros.* Ap. 134. xv. 3.
against them. Cp. Jer. 18. 18.

A. D. 29 20 And they °watched *Him,* and sent forth
°spies, which should °feign themselves °just
men, that they might take hold of His °words,
°that so they might deliver Him unto the
°power and [2]authority of °the governor.

r1 21 And they °asked Him, saying, °"Master,
°we know that Thou sayest and teachest
rightly, °neither °acceptest Thou the person *of*
any, but teachest the way of °God °truly:
22 Is it lawful for us to give °tribute unto
Cæsar, or °no?"

q2 23 But He °perceived their °craftiness, and
said [2]unto them, "Why tempt ye Me?

r2 24 °Shew me a °penny. °Whose image and
superscription hath it?" They answered and
said, "Cæsar's."

q3 25 And He said unto them, "Render therefore unto Cæsar the things which be Cæsar's,
and unto [21]God the things which be [21]God's."
26 And they could [5]not take hold of His
°words before the people: and they marvelled
°at His answer, and held their peace.

W X3 A 27 °Then came to *Him* certain of the °Sad-
ducees, which °deny that there is any °resur-
rection; and [20]they [21]asked Him,

B s 28 Saying, [21]"Master, °Moses °wrote unto us,
[5]**If any man's brother die, having a wife, and**
he die °without children, that his brother
should take his wife, and °raise up seed unto
his brother.

t 29 There were therefore seven brethren: and
the first took a wife, and died without [28]children.
30 And the second took her to wife, and he
died [28]childless.
31 And the third took her; and in like
manner the seven also: and they left [22]no
°children, and died.

u 32 Last of all °the woman died also.
33 Therefore [1]in the [27]resurrection whose wife
of them °is she? for seven had her °to wife."

B s 34 And [8]Jesus answering said unto them,
t "The °children of this °world marry, and °are
given in marriage:
35 But they which shall be accounted worthy
to °obtain that [34]world, and the [27]resurrection
[4]from °the dead, neither marry, nor [34]are given
in marriage:
36 °Neither can they die any more: for they
are °equal unto the angels; and are the [34]chil-
dren of [21]God, being the [34]children of the
[27]resurrection.

u 37 °Now that °the dead are °raised, even
°Moses °shewed °at the bush, when he calleth
°**the LORD the [21]God of Abraham, °and the**
[21]**God of Isaac, °and the [21]God of Jacob.**

20. 19-26 (X2, p. 1493). ENEMIES. SECOND ATTACK. TRIBUTE MONEY. (*Repeated Alternation.*)

X2 | q1 | 19, 20. Conspiracy made.
r1 | 21, 22. Their question.
q2 | 23. Conspiracy perceived.
r2 | 24. The Lord's question.
q3 | 25, 26. Conspiracy silenced.

20 watched. See on 17. 20. Cp. 6. 7; 14. 1; Mark 3. 2.
spies=secret agents. Gr. *enkathetos*=liers in wait. Josh. 8. 14. Job 31. 9. Occurs only here in N.T.
feign. Gr. *hupokrinomai.* Ap. 122. 9. Occurs only here in N.T.
just=righteous: i.e., here, honest.
words=discourse. Gr. pl. of *logos.* See note on Mark 9. 32.
that so=to (Gr. *eis.* Ap. 104. vi) the end that.
power=rule. The Roman power. Gr. *archē.* Ap. 172. 6.
the governor. Pilate. He alone had the rule as to life and death. So that it was the Lord's life they had in view.
21 asked=questioned.
Master=Teacher. Gr. *didaskalos.* Ap. 98. XIV. v. 1.
we know. Gr. *oida.* Ap. 132. I. i.
neither. Gr. *ou.* Ap. 105. I.
acceptest. See Gal. 2. 6. Jas. 2. 1. It is a Hebraism. See Lev. 19. 15. Mal. 1. 8.
God. Gr. *theos.* Ap. 98. I. i. 1.
truly=with (Gr. *epi.* Ap. 104. ix. 1) truth.
22 tribute. Gr. *phoros*=anything brought. Here the poll-tax, which was disputed by scrupulous legalists. Only here, 23. 2, and Rom. 13. 6, 7.
no. Gr. *ou.* Ap. 105. I.
23 perceived=discerned. Gr. *katanoeō.* Not the same word as in *v.* 19.
craftiness=cunning. Gr. *panourgia.* Used only by Luke (here), and Paul (1 Cor. 3. 19. 2 Cor. 4. 2; 11. 3. Eph. 4. 14).
24 Shew=Exhibit. Not the same word as in *v.* 37.
penny. Gr. *denarius.* Ap. 51. I. 4.
Whose image, &c.? See note on Matt. 22. 20.
26 words. Gr. *rhēma.* See note on Mark 9. 32.
at. Gr. *epi.* Ap. 104. ix. 2.

20. 27-40 (X3, p. 1493). ENEMIES. THIRD ATTACK. RESURRECTION. (*Introversion and Extended Alternation.*)

X3 | A | 27. Sadducees. Questioning.
B | s | 28. Statement of Moses.
t | 29-31. Hypothetical case.
u | 32, 33. Death and Resurrection.
B | *s* | 34-. Statement of the Lord.
t | -34-36. The true case.
u | 37, 38. Death and Resurrection.
A | 39, 40. Sadducees. Silenced.

27 Then came, &c. Cp. Matt. 22. 23-33. Mark 12. 18-27.
Sadducees. See Ap. 120. III.
deny . . . resurrection=say that there is no (Ap. 105. II) resurrection (Ap. 178. II. 1). This is the key to what follows.
28 Moses. See note on 5. 14.
wrote. See Deut. 25. 4.
without children (Gr. *ateknos*)=children. Occ. only here and *vv.* 29, 30.
raise up. Ap. 178. 1. 2.
31 children. Ap. 108. i.
32 the woman died also=the woman also died.
33 is=becomes.
to wife=as wife.
34 children=sons. A Hebraism. Ap. 108. iii.
world=age. Ap. 129. 2. This age as distinguished from the age (or dispensation) that is to come, the age to which resurrection is the door of entrance.

are given, &c. Gr. *ekgamiskomai.* Occ. only here and *v.* 35. **35 obtain**=attain to. **the dead**=dead people: i. e. leaving them for a subsequent resurrection. No Art. See Ap. 139. 3. **36 Neither, &c.**=For neither. Gr. *oute.* No more births, marriages, or deaths. 1 Cor. 15. 52. Rev. 21. 4. **equal unto the angels.** Gr. *isangelloi.* Occurs only here. **37 Now**=But. **the dead**=corpses. See Ap. 139. 1. **are raised.** Gr. *egeirō.* Ap. 178. I. 4. **Moses shewed.** Moses cited because his testimony was in question (*v.* 28). **shewed**=disclosed. Gr. *mēnuō,* originally to disclose something before unknown. Occurs only here, John 11. 57. Acts 23. 30. 1 Cor. 10. 28. **at the bush**=[in the Scripture] on (Gr. *epi.* Ap. 104. ix. 1). Referring to one of the Sections known by that name. See on 2 Sam. 1. 18, "the Bow"; Ezek. 1, "the Chariot". Cp. Rom. 11. 2, "Elijah". Quoted from Ex. 3. 6. **the LORD**=Jehovah. See Ap. 98. VI. i. *a.* 1. B. b. **and.** Note the Fig. *Polysyndeton* (Ap. 6), for emphasis.

A. D. 29 38 For He is [5]not a [21]God of °the dead, but
of °the living: for all °live °unto Him."
A 39 Then certain of the scribes answering
said, [21]"Master, Thou hast well said."
40 And after that they durst °not ask Him
any *question at all*.
Y v 41 °And He said [2]unto them, "How say
they that °Christ is °David's son?
w 42 And °David himself saith [1]in °the book
of Psalms, °**'The LORD said unto my °Lord,**
'Sit Thou °on My right hand,
43 Till I °make Thine enemies °Thy foot-
stool."
w 44 °David therefore calleth Him °Lord,
v how is He then his son?"
X[4] 45 Then °in the audience of all the people
He said unto His disciples,
46 °"Beware [10]of the scribes, which °desire to
walk [1]in long robes, and love °greetings in
the markets, and °the highest seats [1]in the
°synagogues, and the °chief rooms °at feasts;
47 Which °devour widows' houses, and for
a °shew make long prayers: the same shall
receive greater °damnation."

A[8] **21** °And He °looked up,
B[8] C x and °saw the rich men casting their
gifts °into °the treasury.
y 2 And He saw °also a certain °poor widow
casting in thither two °mites.
D 3 And He said, "Of a truth I say unto you, that
this poor widow hath cast in °more than they all:
C x 4 For all these have °of their abundance cast
in °unto the °offerings of °God:
y but she °of her °penury hath cast in all the
°living that she had."
A[9] 5 And as some spake °of °the temple,
B[9] E how it was adorned with goodly stones and
°gifts, He said,

38 the dead = dead [people], as in *v.* 35. Ap. 139. 2.
the living = living [people].
live. In resurrection. See note on Matt. 9. 18.
unto = by. The Dative of the Agent, as in Matt. 5. 21, "by them"; 2 Cor. 12. 20, "by you"; Rom. 10. 20, "of (= by) them"; 2 Pet. 3. 14, "of (= by) Him"; 1 Tim. 3. 16, "of (= by) angels".
40 not = not any more. Gr. *ouketi*. Compound of *ou*, Ap. 105. I.

20. 41-44 (*Y*, p. 1493). DILEMMA FOR THEM. (*Introversion*.)

Y | v | 41. The Lord's question. "How?"
  w | 42, 43. The Scripture.
  w | 44-. The Inference.
  v | -44. The Lord's question. "How?"

41 And He said, &c. Cp. Matt. 22. 41-46, and Mark 12. 35-37.
Christ = the Messiah. Ap. 98. IX.
David's son. See Ap. 98. XVIII.
42 David himself saith, &c. Considering that the Lord spoke only what the Father gave Him to speak (Deut. 18. 18, 19. John 7. 16; 8. 28; 12. 49; 14. 10, 24; 17. 8, 14), it is perilously near blasphemy for a modern critic to say: "nothing can be more mischievous . . . or more irreverent than to drag in the name of our Lord to support a particular view of Biblical criticism." The Lord's name is not "dragged in". It is He Who is speaking. It is He Who declares in the name of Jehovah that "David himself wrote these words "in the book of Psalms". It is the denial of this that must "undermine faith in Christ".
the book, &c. Quoted from Ps. 110. 1.
The LORD = Jehovah. Ap. 98. VI. i. *a*. 1. A. a.
Lord = Heb. Adonai. Ap. 98. VI. i. *a*. 2. A. a.
on. Gr. *ek*. Ap. 104. vii.
43 make = set.
Thy footstool = as a footstool for Thy feet. See note on Matt. 22. 44.
44 David therefore calleth Him Lord. According to the modern critics it was not David but some one else! Lord. Ap. 98. VI. i. *a*. 2. B. 2.
45 in the audience of all the people = as all the people were listening.
46 Beware = Beware [and keep] from, &c.
desire. Gr. *thelō*. Ap. 102. 1.
greetings = salutations. Cp. 11. 43. See note on Matt. 23. 7.
the highest = first, front, or chief.
synagogues. Ap. 120. I.
chief rooms = best seats, or couches. See 14. 7.
at = in. Gr. *en*. Ap. 104. viii. **47** devour = swallow up. shew = pretext. damnation = judgment, or condemnation. Ap. 177. 6. Cp. 10. 14.

21. -1-4 (B[8], p. 1490). EVENT. THE POOR WIDOW.

B[8] | C | x | -1. Rich men. } Their acts.
         y | 2. Poor widow. }
     D | 3. Declaration of the Lord.
     C | *x* | 4-. Rich men. } His words.
          y | -4. Poor widow. }

1 And He looked up, &c. The Lord was still in the Temple, showing that this prophetic discourse is not the same as that spoken later on the Mount of Olives. They are similar to *v.* 11, when the Lord goes back and speaks of what shall happen "before all these things". See Ap. 155. looked up. Gr. *anablepō*. Ap. 133. I. 1. saw. Gr. *eidon*. Ap. 133. I. 1. into. Gr. *eis*. Ap. 104. vi. the treasury. See note on Matt. 24. 1 and Mark 12. 41. Cp. John 8. 20. **2** also a certain poor widow = a certain poor widow also. poor. Gr. *penichros* = one who works for daily bread. Occurs only here. mites. Gr. *lepta*. See Ap. 51. I. 3. **3** more. As a matter of proportion. **4** of = out of. Gr. *ek*. Ap. 104. vii. unto. Gr. *eis*, as in *v.* 1. offerings = gifts. Put by Fig. *Metonymy* (of Adjunct), Ap. 6, for the chest containing them. God. See Ap. 98. I. i. 1. penury = lack, or want. living = livelihood. Gr. *bios*. Ap. 170. 2.

21. -5-36 (B[9], p. 1490). EVENT. PROPHETIC DISCOURSE. (*Alternation*.)

B[9] | E | -5. Remark of some, *re* Temple.
     F | 6. The Lord's answer. Its destruction.
     E | 7. Question of some. "When?", "What Sign?"
     F | 8-36. The Lord's answer.

5 of = about. Gr. *peri*. Ap. 104. xiii. 1. the temple. Gr. *hieron*. See note on Matt. 23. 16. gifts = dedicated gifts. Gr. pl. of *anathēma*. Occurs only here. Cp. Josephus, *Bell. Jud.* V. 5. § 4.

F 6 "*As for* these things which ye °behold, the
A.D. 29 days will come, °in the which there shall not
be left °one stone upon another, that shall °not
be thrown down."

E 7 And °they asked Him, saying, °"Master,
but °when shall these things be? and °what
°sign *will there be* when these things °shall
come to pass?"

F G 8 °And He said, °"Take heed that ye be °not
°deceived: °for many shall come °in My name,
saying, '*I* am *Christ;*' and the °time °draweth
near: go ye °not therefore after them.

H J¹ K¹ 9 But when ye shall hear of wars and °commotions, °be ⁸not terrified:

L¹ for these things must °first come to pass; but
°the end *is* ⁶not °by and by."

J² K² 10 °Then said He unto them, °"**Nation shall
rise °against nation, and kingdom °against
kingdom:**
11 And great earthquakes shall be °in divers
places, and °famines, and pestilences; and
°fearful sights and great °signs shall there be
°from °heaven.

L² 12 But °before all these, they shall lay their
hands °on you, and persecute *you*, delivering
you up °to the synagogues, and into prisons,
being brought °before kings and rulers for My
name's sake.
13 And it shall °turn to you °for °a testimony.
14 Settle *it* therefore °in your hearts, ⁸not to
°meditate before what ye shall °answer:
15 For *I* will give you °a mouth and wisdom,
which all your adversaries shall ⁶not be able
°to gainsay nor resist.
16 And ye shall be °betrayed both °by parents,
°and brethren, °and kinsfolks, °and friends;
°and *some* °of you shall they cause to be put
to death.
17 And ye shall be hated °of all *men* °for My
name's sake.
18 But there shall °not an °hair ⁴of your head
perish.
19 ⁶In your °patience °possess ye your
°souls.
20 And when ye shall ¹see °Jerusalem compassed °with armies, then °know that the
desolation thereof °is nigh.
21 Then let them which are ⁶in Judæa flee
¹²to the mountains; and let them which are
⁶in the midst of °it depart out; and let
⁸not them that are ⁶in the °countries enter
°thereinto.

6 behold = are gazing at. Gr. *theōreō.* Ap. 133. I. 11.
in. Gr. *en.* Ap. 104. viii.
one stone upon another = stone upon (Gr. *epi.* Ap. 104. ix. 2) stone. **not.** Gr. *ou.* Ap. 105. I.
7 they: i.e. "the some" of *v.* 5. Not any of the Apostles. See Ap. 155.
Master = Teacher. See Ap. 98. XIV. v. 1.
when . . . what? Note the two questions here, and the three on the later occasion. See Ap. 155.
sign = the sign. Gr. *to sēmeion.* Ap. 176. 3.
shall come to pass? = may be about to take place?

21. 8-36 (*F*, p. 1496). THE LORD'S ANSWER.
(*Introversion.*)

F | G | 8. Warning.
H | 9-28. Prophecy.
H | 29-33. Illustration (Fig-tree).
G | 34-36. Warning.

8 And He said, &c. See Ap. 155.
Take heed. Gr. *blepō.* Ap. 133. I. 5.
not. Gr. *mē.* Ap. 105. II.
deceived = misled.
for many, &c. This was speedily fulfilled. It was the first sign as to "when" (*v.* 7). Cp. 1 John 2. 18, "the last hour."
in. Gr. *epi.* Ap. 104. ix. 2.
time = season.
draweth = has drawn.

21. 9-28 (H, above). PROPHECY.
(*Repeated Alternation.*)

H | J¹ | K¹ | 9-. The first things.
L¹ | -9. Time. End not yet (then).
J² | K² | 10, 11. The last things. Tribulation.
L² | 12-24. Time. Before these last (*vv.* 10, 11).
J³ | K³ | 25-27. The last things. Great Tribulation. (Details of *vv.* 10, 11.)
L³ | 28. Time. Israel's redemption nigh.

9 commotions = unrest. Occurs only here, and 1 Cor. 14. 33. 2 Cor. 6. 5; 12. 20. Jas. 3. 16.
be not terrified = be not scared. Gr. *ptoeō.* Occurs only here and 24. 37.
first. See the Structure K¹, above.
the end. Gr. *to telos.* Not the sunteleia. Cp. Matt. 24. 3 and 14.
by and by = immediately. As in Matt. 24. 6, "not yet", Mark 13. 7. Cp. 17. 7. Matt. 14. 31. Mark 6. 25. See Ap. 155.
10 Then said He, &c. Matt. 24. 7, 8. Mark 13. 8.
Nation, &c. Quoted from Isa. 19. 2.
against. Gr. *epi.* Ap. 104. ix. 3.
11 in divers. Gr. *kata.* Ap. 104. x. 2.
famines, and pestilences. Gr. *limoi kai loimoi.* Fig. *Paronomasia* (Ap. 6), for emphasis, like Eng. "dearths and deaths".
fearful sights = things that fill with fear. Gr. pl. of *phobētron.* Occurs only here, but in Sept. Isa. 19. 17. In medical language = objects imagined by the sick.
signs. Gr. *sēmeion.* Ap. 176. 3.
from. Gr. *apo.* Ap. 104. iv.
heaven. Sing. No Art. See note on Matt. 6. 9, 10.

12 before all these. The Lord goes back, here, instead of continuing, as in Matt. 24. 8, 9, and Mark 13. 9. See Ap. 155. **before.** Gr. *pro.* Ap. 104. xiv. **on** = upon. Gr. *epi.* Ap. 104. ix. 3. **to** = unto. Gr. *eis.* Ap. 104. vi. **before** = up to. Gr. *epi.* Ap. 104. ix. 3. **13 turn** = turn out. **for.** Gr. *eis.* Ap. 104. vi. **a testimony.** Cp. Phil. 1. 28. 2 Thess. 1. 5. **14 in.** Gr. *eis.* Ap. 104. vi. **meditate.** Cp. 12. 11. Matt. 10. 19, 20. **answer.** Cp. 1 Pet. 3. 15. **15 a mouth and wisdom.** Note the Fig. *Hendiadys* (Ap. 6) = a mouth, yea, a wise mouth. Mouth, too, put by Fig. *Metonymy* (of Adjunct), Ap. 6, for what is spoken by it. Cp. Ex. 4. 11, 12. Jer. 1. 9. Isa. 6. 7. **to gainsay, &c.** See Acts 4. 14; 6. 10. **16 betrayed** = delivered up. **by.** Gr. *hupo.* Ap. 104. xviii. 1. **and.** Note the Fig. *Polysyndeton* (Ap. 6), for emphasis. **of** = from among. Gr. *ek.* Ap. 104. vii. **17 of** = by. Gr. *hupo.* Ap. 104. xviii. 1. **for** = on account of. Gr. *dia.* Ap. 104. v. 2. **18 not** = by no means. Gr. *ou mē.* Ap. 105. III. **hair, &c.** Cp. Matt. 10. 30. **19 patience** = patient endurance. **possess ye** = ye shall possess. Occurs only here, and 18. 12. Matt. 10. 9. Acts 1. 18; 8. 20; 22. 28. 1 Thess. 4. 4. **souls** = lives. Ap. 110. III. 2. **20 Jerusalem.** This is the point of the Lord's prophecy, in Luke. There is nothing of this in Matthew or Mark. See Ap. 155. **with** = by. Gr. *hupo.* Ap. 104. xviii. 1. **know** = get to know. Ap. 132. I. ii. **is nigh** = has drawn near. **21 it** = her. **countries** = fields. **thereinto** = into (Gr. *eis.* Ap. 104. vi) her.

A. D. 29 22 For these be **the days of °vengeance,**
that °all things which °are written may be
°fulfilled.
23 But woe unto them that are with child,
and to them that give suck, [6]in those days!
for there shall be great distress °in the °land,
and °wrath °upon this people.
24 °And they shall fall by the °edge of the
sword, °and shall be °led away captive [1]into
all nations: °and Jerusalem shall be °trodden
down [17]of the °Gentiles, °until °the times of
the °Gentiles be [22]fulfilled.

J[3] K[3] a 25 °And there shall be signs [6]in the sun,
°and in the moon, and in the stars; and °upon
the °earth distress of nations, °with perplexity;
°the sea and the waves roaring;

b 26 °Men's hearts °failing them °for fear, and
for °looking after those things which are
coming on the °earth:

b for °**the powers of** °**heaven** °**shall be shaken.**

a 27 And then shall they °see °**the Son of
man coming** [6]**in a cloud** °with power and
great glory.

L[3] 28 And when these things begin to come to
pass, then °look up, and lift up your heads;
°for your °redemption draweth nigh."

H M 29 And He spake to them a parable; °"Behold the fig tree, and all the trees;

N c 30 When they °now °shoot forth,

d °ye see and [20]know °of your own selves that
summer is °now nigh at hand.

N c 31 °So likewise ye, when ye [1]see these things
°come to pass,

d [20]know ye that °the kingdom of [4]God is nigh
at hand.

M 32 °Verily I say unto you, °This generation
shall [18]not pass away, °till all be fulfilled.
33 °Heaven and [25]earth °shall pass away:
but My °words shall [18]not pass away.

G 34 And take heed to yourselves, lest at any
time your °hearts be °overcharged [25]with

22 vengeance. Quoted from Hos. 9. 7. See Dan. 9. 26, 27; and Josephus, *Bell. Jud.* v. 10.

all things which are written. These and no more nor less. As in Acts 3. 21.

are written = have been, and stand written.

fulfilled. As in *v.* 24. Not the same word as in *v.* 32.

23 in = upon. Gr. *epi.* Ap. 104. ix. 1.

land. Gr. *gē.* Ap. 129. 4.

wrath. See 1 Thess. 2. 16.

upon = among. Gr. *en.* Ap. 104. viii. But all the texts read "to".

24 And. Note the Fig. *Polysyndeton* (Ap. 6), for emphasis. **edge** = mouth (Gen. 34. 26 m.).

led away captive. Josephus speaks of 1,100,000 slain and 97,000 taken away to Egyptian mines and elsewhere (*Bell. Iud.* vi. 9).

trodden down. Not the future tense of the verb (*pateō*), but the future of the verb "to be", with the Pass. Part. of *pateō* = shall be and remain trodden down, in a way that it had never been before. The reference is to the Mohammedan possession since A. D. 636 in succession to the "fourth" or Roman possession. See note on Dan. 2. 40.

Gentiles = nations, as in preceding clause.

until, &c. So that a day is coming when the nations will cease to tread it down, and it will be possessed by its rightful owner—Israel.

the times: i. e. the times of the Gentile possession of Jerusalem.

21. 25-27 (K[3], p. 1497). THE LAST THINGS.
(*Introversion.*)

K[3] | a | 25. Signs. In Heaven and Earth.
  b | 26-. Earth.
  b | -26. Heaven.
 a | 27. Signification.

25 And. Note the Fig. *Polysyndeton* (Ap. 6), for emphasis.

And there shall be, &c. The Lord here passes over the intervening present dispensation, and takes up the yet future time of the end, enlarged on later in Matt. 24. 29-31. Mark 13. 24-27.

upon. Gr. *epi.* Ap. 104. ix. 1.

earth. Gr. *gē.* Ap. 129. 4. Not the same as in *v.* 26; but the same as "land" in *v.* 23.

with. Gr. *en.* Ap. 104. viii.

the sea, &c. Cp. Ps. 46. 3. Isa. 5. 30. Rev. 17. 15.

26 Men's. Gr. *anthrōpos.* Ap. 123. 1.

failing = fainting. Gr. *apopsuchō.* Occurs only here. Luke used three compounds of the simple verb (*psuchō*, Matt. 24. 12), all peculiar to him: e.g. "cool", 16. 24; "gave up the ghost", Acts 5. 5, 10; 12. 23.

for = from. Gr. *apo.* Ap. 104. iv. **looking after** = expectation. Gr. *prosdokia,* from the verb *prosdokeō.* Ap. 133. III. 3. **earth** = the inhabited earth. Gr. *oikoumenē.* Ap. 129. 3. **the powers,** &c. Ap. 172. 1. Probably refers to the angelic world rulers. See notes on Dan. 10. 13. **heaven** = the heavens. See note on Matt. 6. 9, 10. **shall be shaken.** Cp. Matt. 11. 7. Luke 6. 38. Acts 4. 31. Heb. 12. 26, 27. **27 see.** Gr. *opsomai.* Ap. 133. I. 8. a. **the Son of man.** Ap. 98. XVI. **with.** Gr. *meta.* Ap. 104. xi. 1. **28 look up.** Gr. *anakuptō* = watching with outstretched neck. Occurs only here, 13. 11, and John 8. 7, 10. **for** = because. **redemption** = deliverance from the tribulation. See Zech. 14. 1-4.

21. 29-33 (*H*, p. 1497). ILLUSTRATION. FIG TREE. (*Introversion and Alternation.*)

H | M | 29. Sign. Fig tree and all the trees.
 N | c | 30-. Shooting forth of leaves.
  d | -30. Inference. Summer near.
 N | *c* | 31-. Events. "These things" (*vv.* 25-28).
  d | -31. Inference. Kingdom nigh.
 M | 32, 33. Signification. "These things" (*vv.* 9 and 12-24).

29 Behold = Look ye. Ap. 133. I. 1. Fig. *Asterismos.* Ap. 6. **30 now** = already. **shoot forth** = sprout. **ye see and know** = seeing (Gr. *blepō.* Ap. 133. I. 5) ye get to know. Gr. *ginōskō.* Ap. 132. I. ii. **of** = from [experience]. Gr. *apo.* Ap. 104. iv. **31 So likewise ye** = so ye also. **come** = coming. **the kingdom of God.** See Ap. 114. **32 Verily.** See note on Matt. 5. 18. **This generation.** See note on Matt. 11. 16. **till all be fulfilled** = till (Gr. *eōs an*) all may possibly come to pass. (Not the same word as "fulfilled" in *v.* 24.) Had the nation repented at Peter's call, in Acts 2. 38; 3. 19-26, "all that the prophets had spoken" would have come to pass. **33 Heaven** = the heaven. **shall pass away.** Cp. Ps. 102. 26. Isa. 51. 6. 2 Pet. 3. 7, 10. **words** = utterances. Gr. pl. of *logos.* See note on Mark 9. 32. Cp. Isa. 40. 8. **34 hearts.** Put by Fig. *Synecdochē* (of the Part), Ap. 6, for the whole person. **overcharged** = weighed down. Gr. *barunō.* Only here. Cp. 9. 32. 2 Cor. 5. 4.

A. D. 29 °surfeiting, and °drunkenness, and °cares °of
this life, and *so* that day °come °upon you
°unawares.
35 For °as a snare shall it come [12]on all
them that dwell [12]on the face of the whole
[25]earth.
36 °Watch ye therefore, °and pray °always,
that ye may be accounted worthy to escape all
these things that °shall come to pass, and to
°stand before [27]the Son of man."
A10 **37** °And in the day time He was teaching [6]in
the temple; and at night He went out, and
°abode °in the mount that is called *the mount*
of Olives.
38 And all the people °came early in the
morning °to Him [6]in the [5]temple, for to hear
Him.

B10 O1 e **22** °Now the feast of unleavened bread
°drew nigh, which is called the °pass-
over.
f **2** And the chief priests and scribes °sought
how they might °kill Him; °for they feared
the people.
f **3** Then entered °Satan °into °Judas surnamed Iscariot, being of the number °of °the
twelve.
4 And he °went his way, and communed
with the chief priests and °captains, how he
might °betray Him unto them.
5 And they were °glad, and °covenanted to
give him money.
6 And °he promised, and [2]sought °oppor-
tunity to betray Him unto them °in the absence of °the multitude.
e **7** Then °came °the day of unleavened bread,
when the °passover must be killed.
O2 g **8** And He sent Peter and John, saying, "Go
and prepare us the [7]passover, that we may
°eat."
h **9** And they said unto Him, "Where °wilt
Thou that we prepare?"
h **10** And He said unto them, °"Behold, when
ye are entered [3]into the city, there shall a
°man meet you, bearing a pitcher of water;
follow him [3]into the house where he entereth
in.
11 And ye shall say unto the °goodman of the
house, °'The Master saith unto thee, 'Where
is the guestchamber, where I shall eat the
[7]passover °with My disciples?''

surfeiting. Gr. *kraipalē.* A medical word used for the nausea after drunkenness, from which is the Lat. *crapula.* Occurs only here. The Eng. is from the Old French *surfait* or *sorfait*=excess.
drunkenness. Gr. *methē.* Occurs only here, Rom. 13. 13. Gal. 5. 21.
cares. See note on Matt. 6. 25, "drunkenness" of to-day; "cares" for to-morrow.
of this life. Gr. *biōtikos*=of or belonging to *bios.* Ap. 170. 2.
come=should come.
upon. Gr. *epi.* Ap. 104. ix. 3.
unawares=suddenly. Gr. *aiphnidios.* Occurs only here, and 1 Thess. 5. 3.
35 as a snare. Cp. Ecc. 9. 12. Isa. 24. 17.
36 Watch. See on Mark 13. 33.
and pray=praying.
always=in (Gr. *en.* Ap. 104. viii) every season.
shall come to pass=are about to come to pass.
stand. See Ps. 1. 5. Mal. 3. 2.
37 And in the day time=by day. A parenthetic statement referring to His custom during these last six days. See Ap. 156.
abode=used to lodge.
in=into: i. e. into its protecting shelter. Occurs only here, and Matt. 21. 17.
38 came early in the morning. Gr. *ōrthrizō.* Occurs only here. Supply the Relative *Ellipsis* thus: "[rising] early in the morning, came".
to. Gr. *pros.* Ap. 104. xv. 3.

22. 1-38 (B10, p. 1490). EVENT. THE LAST PASSOVER. (*Division.*)

B10 | O1 | 1-7. The Feast. Nigh.
O2 | 8-13. The Feast. Prepared.
O3 | 14-20. The Feast. Partaken of.
O4 | 21-38. The Feast. Events following.

22. 1-7 (O1, above). THE FEAST. NIGH. (*Introversion.*)

O1 | e | 1. The Feast nigh.
f | 2. Conspiracy of chief priests and scribes.
f | 3-6. Subornation of Judas.
e | 7. The Feast arrived.

1 Now, &c. Cp. Matt. 26. 17-19. Mark 14. 12-16.
drew=was drawing.
passover. Aramaic, *pascha.* Ap. 94. III. 3.
2 sought=were seeking. Contemporaneously with the Feast.
kill Him=get rid of, or make away with Him. Gr. *anaireō*=take up and carry off.
for, &c. Therefore their aim was to take Him secretly, and evade a public trial.
3 Satan. See note on Matt. 4. 10.
into. Gr. *eis.* Ap. 104. vi.
Judas . . . the twelve. See Ap. 141.
of. Gr. *ek.* Ap. 104. vii.
4 went his way . . . and=having gone away.
captains=officers of the Levitical Temple guards. Cp. Jer. 20. 1. Acts 4. 1.
betray Him=deliver Him up.
5 glad=rejoiced. Because that promised to solve their difficulty. **covenanted**=agreed. **6 he promised.** For his part. See notes on Prov. 16. 1, 9, 33. **opportunity.** Implying the difficulty. **in the absence of**=without. Gr. *ater.* Occurs only here, and *v.* 35. **the multitude**=a crowd. **7 came**=came near; for the preparation had not yet been made. See Ap. 156. **the day.** The 15th of Nisan. This was only the 10th. **passover.** Put by Fig. *Metonymy* (of Adjunct), Ap. 6, for the Lamb. Aramaic. See note on *v.* 1.

22. 8-13 (O2, above). THE FEAST. PREPARED. (*Introversion.*)

O2 | g | 8. Command. Make ready.
h | 9. Their question. "Where?"
h | 10-12. His answer.
g | 13. Obedience. Made ready.

8 eat=eat [it]: not the Lamb, but the Feast=the *Chagīgah.* **9 wilt.** Gr. *thelō.* Ap. 102. 1. **10 Behold.** Fig. *Asterismos.* Ap. 6. **man.** Gr. *anthrōpos.* Ap. 123. 1. An unusual sight. They might have met many men carrying wine-skins, and women carrying pitchers, but not a *man* carrying a "pitcher". **11 goodman**=the master of the house. Ap. 98. XIV. iii. **The Master**=The Teacher. Ap. 98. XIV. v. 2. **with.** Gr. *meta.* Ap. 104. xi. 1.

A.D. 29 12 And °he shall shew you °a large upper room °furnished: there make ready."

g 13 And they went, and found °as He had said unto them: and they made ready the [7]passover.

O³ P¹ i¹ 14 °And when the hour °was come, He °sat down, and the twelve °apostles °with Him.

15 And He said °unto them, °"With desire I have desired to eat °this [7]passover [11]with you before I suffer:

k¹ 16 For I say unto you, I will °not any more eat °thereof, until °it be fulfilled °in °the kingdom of God."

P² i² 17 And He took the °cup, and gave thanks, and said, "Take this, and divide *it* among yourselves:

k² 18 For I say unto you, I will [16]not drink °of °the fruit of the vine, until [16]the kingdom of God °shall come."

P³ i³ 19 °And He took °bread, and °gave thanks, and brake *it*, and gave unto them, saying,

k³ °"This is My body which °is given °for you: this do °in remembrance of Me."

P⁴ i⁴ 20 Likewise °also the [17]cup °after supper, saying,

k⁴ "This cup *is* the °new °testament [16]in My blood, which is shed °for you.

O⁴ Q 21 But, [10]behold, the hand of him that °betrayeth Me *is* with Me °on the table.

22 And truly °the Son of man goeth, °as it °was determined: but woe unto that [10]man °by whom He is betrayed!"

23 And they began to enquire °among themselves, which [3]of them it was that °should do this thing.

R 24 And °there was °also °a strife °among them, which of them should be accounted the °greatest.

25 And He said unto them, "The kings of the °Gentiles °exercise lordship over them; and they that °exercise authority upon them are called °benefactors.

26 But ye *shall* °not *be* so: but he that is [24]greatest [24]among you, let him be as the younger; and he that °is chief, as he that doth °serve.

27 For whether *is* greater, he that °sitteth at meat, or he that serveth? *is* [26]not he that sitteth at meat? but I am °among you as he that [26]serveth.

28 Ye are they which have continued [11]with Me [16]in My °temptations.

29 And I °appoint unto you a kingdom, °as My °Father hath appointed unto Me;

---

12 he = that one.

a large, &c. Probably the same room of Acts 1. 13 and 2. 1.

furnished = strewed with divans and cushions.

13 as = even as.

22. 14-20 (O³, p. 1499). THE FEAST. PARTAKEN OF. (*Repeated Alternation.*)

O³ | P¹ | i¹ | 14, 15. Desire.
 k¹ | 16. The reason.
 P² | i² | 17. The Cup.
 k² | 18. The reason.
 P³ | i³ | 19-. The Bread.
 k³ | -19. The reason.
 P⁴ | i⁴ | 20-. The Cup.
 k⁴ | -20. The Signification.

14 And when, &c. Cp. Matt. 26. 20. Mark 14. 17.

was come = had come to pass: i. e. had arrived.

sat down (Gr. *anapiptō*) = reclined.

apostles. This is supplementary. Matthew and Mark have "the twelve" only.

with. Gr. *sun.* Ap. 104. xvi. Not the same word as in *vv.* 11, -15, 21, 28, 33, 49, 52, 53, 59; but the same as in *v.* 56.

15 unto. Gr. *pros.* Ap. 104. xv. 3.

With desire I have desired = I have earnestly desired. Fig. *Polyptoton* (Ap. 6). See note on Gen. 26. 28.

this passover. Not the eating of the Lamb, but the *Chagīgah* or feast which preceded it = this [as] a Passover.

16 not = by no means. Gr. *ou mē.* Ap. 105. III.

thereof = of (Gr. *ek.* Ap. 104. vii) it.

it be fulfilled = it may be fulfilled. Which it would have soon been, had the nation repented.

in. Gr. *en.* Ap. 104. viii.

the kingdom of God. See Ap. 114.

17 cup. Put by Fig. *Metonymy* (of the Subject), Ap. 6, for the wine in it.

18 of = from. Gr. *apo.* Ap. 104. iv.

the fruit = the produce: i. e. the wine (*gennēma*, not *karpos* = fruit).

shall come = may have come.

19 And He, &c. Cp. Matt. 26. 26-29. Mark 14. 22-25. 1 Cor. 11. 23-25.

bread. A thin flat hard biscuit, which was broken, and not cut.

gave thanks. Gr. *eucharisteō.*

This is My body. See Ap. 159.

is given = is being given.

for = on your behalf. Gr. *huper.* Ap. 104. xvii. 1.

in = for. Gr. *eis.* Ap. 104. vi.

in remembrance, &c. = for My memorial.

20 also the cup = the cup also.

after. Gr. *meta.* Ap. 104. xi. 2.

new. Gr. *kainē.* See Matt. 9. 16, 17.

testament = covenant. Gr. *diathēkē.* See notes on Heb. 9. 14-23. Blood has nothing to do with a "will" or "testament", but it has with a covenant.

for. Gr. *eis.* Ap. 104. vi.

22. 21-38 (O⁴, p. 1499). THE FEAST. EVENTS FOLLOWING. (*Alternation.*)

O⁴ | Q | 21-23. Prediction. Betrayal. (JUDAS.)
 R | 24-30. Kingdom. Establishment anticipated.
 Q | 31-34. Prediction. Denial. (PETER.)
 R | 35-38. Kingdom. Rejection anticipated.

21 betrayeth Me = is delivering Me up. The first warning. **on.** Gr. *epi.* Ap. 104. ix. 1. **22 the Son of man.** See Ap. 98. XVI. **as** = according as. Gr. *kata.* Ap. 104. x. 2. **was determined** = has been determined. See Acts 2. 23; 3. 18; 4. 27, 28. **by.** Gr. *dia.* Ap. 104. v. 1. **23 among.** Gr. *pros.* Ap. 104. xv. 3. **should do** = was about to do. **24 there was** = there happened. **also a strife** = a strife also. **a strife** = a love of dispute. Gr. *philoneikia.* Occurs only here. **among.** Gr. *en.* Ap. 104. viii. 2. **greatest** = greater. **25 Gentiles** = nations. **exercise lordship** = lord it. Gr. *kurieuō.* **exercise authority.** Gr. *exousiazō.* Cp. Ap. 172. 5. **benefactors.** See note on Matt. 20. 25. **26 not.** Gr. *ou.* Ap. 105. I. **is chief** = the leader. **serve.** See note on "minister" (Matt. 20. 26). Cp. Phil. 2. 7. **27 sitteth** = reclineth. **among** = in the midst of. **28 temptations** = trials. **29 appoint** = assign. **as** = even as. **Father.** Ap. 98. III.

A. D. 29 30 That ye may eat and drink °at My table [16]in My kingdom, and sit [21] on thrones judging the twelve tribes of Israel."

Q 31 And °the Lord said, °"Simon, Simon, [10]behold, °Satan °hath desired *to have* °you, that he may °sift *you* as wheat:

32 But I have °prayed °for °thee, that °thy faith fail °not: and °when thou art converted, °strengthen thy brethren."

33 And he said unto Him, °"Lord, I am ready to go [11]with Thee, both [3]into prison, and °to death."

34 And He said, "I tell thee, °Peter, °the cock shall [16]not °crow °this day, before that thou shalt thrice deny that thou °knowest Me."

R l 35 And He said unto them, °"When I sent you without purse, °and °scrip, °and shoes, lacked ye any thing?" And they said, "Nothing."

m 36 Then said He unto them, °"But now, he that hath a purse, let him take *it*, and likewise *his* [35]scrip: and he that hath °no sword, let him sell his garment, and buy °one.

l 37 For I say unto you, that this that °is written must yet be accomplished [16]in Me, '**And He was reckoned °among the transgressors:**' for the things °concerning Me have an end."

m 38 And they said, [33]"Lord, [10]behold, here *are* two swords." And He said unto them, "It is enough."

D S 39 And He came out, and went, °as He was wont, [33]to the mount of Olives; and His °disciples also followed Him.

40 And when He was [30]at °the place, He said unto them, °"Pray that ye enter [32]not [3]into temptation."

T 41 And °He °was withdrawn °from them about a stone's cast,

U and kneeled down, and [40]prayed,

42 Saying, "Father, °if °Thou be willing, remove this cup [41]from Me: nevertheless [32]not My °will, but Thine, be done."

V 43 And there °appeared °an angel unto Him [41]from °heaven, °strengthening Him.

U 44 And °being [16]in °an agony He [40]prayed °more earnestly: and His sweat °was as it were great drops of blood falling down °to the °ground.

T 45 And when He rose up [41]from prayer, and was come °to His disciples, He found them sleeping °for sorrow,

S 46 And said unto them, "Why sleep ye? rise and [40]pray, lest ye enter [3]into temptation."

W¹XAC 47 And while He °yet spake, [10]behold a

30 at. Gr. *epi*. Ap. 104. ix. 1.

31 the Lord. See Ap. 98. VI. 1. *a*. 3. B. c.

Simon, Simon. The sixth example of this Fig. *Epizeuxis* (Ap. 6). See note on the first (Gen. 22. 11).

Satan. See note on Matt. 4. 10.

hath desired = hath demanded. Gr. *exaiteō*. Occurs only here in N.T. It means to obtain by asking.

you. Plural.

sift. Gr. *siniazō* = to sift (as wheat), to get rid of the corn. Occurs only here. The Lord "winnows" to get rid of the chaff. Cp. Matt. 3. 12. 1 Pet. 5. 8, 9.

32 prayed. Gr. *deomai*. Ap. 134. I. 5. Not the same word as in *vv*. 40, 41, 44, 46.

for = concerning. Gr. *peri*. Ap. 104. xiii. 1.

thee. Simon. **thy faith.** Not Simon himself.

not. Gr. *mē*. Ap. 105. II.

when thou, &c. = thou, when thou hast once turned again.

strengthen = establish. Cp. 1 Pet. 5. 10.

33 Lord. Ap. 98. VI. i. a. 3. A.

to = into. Gr. *eis*, as "into" prison. Ap. 104. vi.

34 Peter. The Lord addressed him as such, only here, and Matt. 16. 18, to remind him of his weakness. See Ap. 147. He mentions him in Mark 16. 7.

the cock = a cock. See Ap. 160.

crow. See Ap. 173, and note on Matt. 26. 34.

this day = to-day. Gr. *sēmeron*.

knowest. Gr. *oida*. Ap. 132. I. i.

22. 35-38 (*R*, p. 1500). KINGDOM. REJECTION ANTICIPATED. (*Alternation*.)

R | l | 35. Time past. Directions connected with the Proclamation.
  m | 36. Time present. New directions given. The former abrogated.
  l | 37. Time past. Reasons for old directions.
  m | 38. Time present. New directions obeyed.

35 When I sent, &c. See on 9. 2, 3.

and. Note the Fig. *Polysyndeton* (Ap. 6).

scrip. See note on Matt. 10. 10.

36 But now, &c. Showing that precepts given when the kingdom was being proclaimed, no longer held good when it had been rejected.

no sword = not [money]. Gr. *mē*. Ap. 105. II.

one = a sword.

37 is written = standeth written. See Isa. 53. 12.

among = with. Gr. *meta*. Ap. 104. xi. 1.

concerning. Gr. *peri*. Ap. 104. xiii. 1.

22. 39-46 (*D*, p. 1427). THE AGONY. (*Introversion*.)

D | S | 39, 40. Prayer. Disciples exhorted to.
  T | 41-. Disciples. Withdrawal from.
   U | -41, 42. Prayer to His Father.
    V | 43. Angelic ministrant.
   U | 44. Prayer to His Father.
  T | 45. Disciples. Return to.
 S | 46. Prayer. Disciples exhorted to.

39 as He was wont = according to (Gr. *kata*. Ap. 104. x. 2) [His] custom. **disciples.** The eleven.

40 the place. *Gethsemanē* = the oil-press.

Pray. Gr. *proseuchomai*. Ap. 134. I. 2. Not the same word as in *v*. 32. **41 He** = He Himself.

was withdrawn = was parted. Gr. *apospaō*. Only here; Matt. 26. 51. Acts 20. 30; 21. 1.

from. Gr. *apo*. Ap. 104. iv.

42 if, &c. See Ap. 118. 2. a.

Thou be willing = it be Thine intention. Cp. Ap. 102. 3.

will = desire. Gr. *thelēma*. Cp. Ap. 102. 2. Verses 43, 44 are omitted or marked as doubtful by most texts, but the Syr. includes them. See Ap. 94. V, note. **43 appeared.** Ap. 106. I. vi. **an angel.** As after the Temptation (Matt. 4. 11). **heaven.** Sing., without the Art. See Matt. 6. 9, 10. **strengthening.** Gr. *enischuō*. Occurs only here, and Acts 9. 19. **44 being** = becoming. Implying increasing intensity. **an agony.** Gr. *agōnia*. Occurs only here. **more earnestly.** Only here. **was** = became. **to** = upon. Gr. *epi*. Ap. 104. ix. 3. **ground** = earth. Gr. *gē*. Ap. 129. 4. **45 to.** Gr. *pros*. Ap. 104. xv. 3. **for** = from. Gr. *apo*. Ap. 104. iv.

22. 47—24. 2 [For Structure see next page].

Verses 47-53. Cp. Matt. 26. 47-56. Mark 14. 43-52. **47 yet spake** = was yet speaking.

A.D. 29 °multitude, and he that was called Judas, one of the twelve, °went before them, and drew near unto °Jesus to kiss Him.

D 48 But [47] Jesus said unto him, "Judas, °betrayest thou [22] the Son of man with a kiss?"

E n 49 When they which were °about Him °saw what °would follow, they said unto Him, [33] "Lord, shall we smite °with the sword?"

o 50 And one [3] of them smote °the servant of the high priest, and cut off his right ear.

E n 51 And [47] Jesus answered and said, "Suffer ye thus far." And He touched his ear,

o and °healed him.

D 52 Then [47] Jesus said [15] unto the °chief priests, and [4] captains of the °temple, and the elders, which were come °to Him, "Be ye come out, as °against °a thief, [11] with swords and staves?
53 When I was daily [11] with you [16] in the [52] temple, ye stretched forth °no hands [52] against Me: but this is °your hour, and the power of darkness."

C 54 Then °took they Him,

B and led *Him*, and brought Him [3] into the high priest's house.

A F1 p1 And Peter °followed afar off.
55 And when they had °kindled a fire [27] in the midst of the °hall, and were set down together, Peter sat down [27] among them.

q1 56 But °a certain maid °beheld him as he sat °by the °fire, and °earnestly looked upon him, and said, °"This man was also [14] with Him."

p2 57 And he denied Him, saying, "Woman, I [34] know Him [26] not."

q2 58 And [20] after a little while °another [49] saw him, and said, °"Thou art also [3] of them."

p3 And Peter said, [10] "Man, I am [26] not."

q3 59 And about the space of one hour after °another confidently affirmed, saying, °"Of a truth this *fellow* also was [11] with Him: for he is a Galilæan."

p4 60 And Peter said, [10] "Man, I [34] know [26] not what thou sayest."

F2 r And °immediately, while he °yet spake, [34] the cock crew.

s 61 And [31] the Lord turned, °and °looked upon Peter.

r And Peter remembered the °word of [31] the Lord, how He had said unto him,

s "Before [34] the cock crow, thou shalt deny Me thrice."

22. 47—24. 12 (*C*, p. 1427). THE BAPTISM OF SUFFERING. (*Division.*)

C | W1 | 22. 47—23. 49. Death, and Events leading up to.
W2 | 23. 50-56. Burial.
W3 | 24. 1-12. Resurrection.

22. 47—23. 49 (W1, above). DEATH, AND EVENTS LEADING UP TO IT. (*Introversion.*)

W1 | X | 22. 47-65. Conspiracy. Effected.
Y | 22. 66—23. 23. Led away to trial.
Z | 23. 24, 25. Pilate's sentence.
Y | 23. 26-32. Led away to death.
X | 23. 33-49. Conspiracy. Completed.

22. 47-65 (X, above). CONSPIRACY. EFFECTED. (*Alternation.*)

X | A | 47-54-. Judas. Treachery and arrest.
B | -54-. In the high priest's house.
A | -54-62. Peter. Denials.
B | 63-65. In the high priest's house.

22. 47-54- (A, above). JUDAS. TREACHERY AND ARREST. (*Introversion and Alternation.*)

A | C | 47. Betrayal.
D | 48. The Lord. Remonstrance to the Betrayer.
E | n | 49. Interposition by Disciples.
o | 50. Ear smitten.
E | *n* | 51-. Interposition by the Lord.
o | -51. Ear healed.
D | 52, 53. The Lord. Remonstrance to the Captors.
C | 54-. Arrested.

multitude = crowd. went = was going.
Jesus. See Ap. 98. X.
48 betrayest thou = deliverest thou up.
49 about = around. Gr. *peri*. Ap. 104. xiii. 2.
saw. Gr. *eidon*. Ap. 133. I. i.
would follow = was about to happen.
with. Gr. *en*. Ap. 104. viii.
50 the servant. The well-known servant Malchus (John 18. 10).
51 healed him. Added by Luke. See on 6. 17.
52 chief priests. The heads of the twenty-four courses.
temple. Gr. *hieron*. See note on Matt. 23. 16.
to = against. Gr. *epi*. Ap. 104. ix. 3.
against. Same as "to", above.
a thief = a brigand, or robber. See note on Matt. 27. 38, and Ap. 164.
53 no = not. Ap. 105. I.
your hour, &c. = your hour [and the hour of] the authority (Ap. 172. 5) of darkness. See Eph. 6. 12. Col. 1. 13; and cp. Heb. 2. 14.
54- took = seized.

22. -54-62 (*A*, above). PETER. DENIALS. (*Division.*)

A | F1 | -54-60-. Peter's Fall.
F2 | -60-62. Peter's Repentance.

22. -54-60- (F1, above). PETER'S FALL. (*Repeated Alternation.*)

F1 | p1 | -54, 55. Peter following.
q1 | 56. Recognition by a maid.
p2 | 57. Peter's denial.
q2 | 58-. Recognition by another.
p3 | -58. Peter's denial.
q3 | 59. Recognition by another.
p4 | 60. Peter's denial.

Verses 54-60. Cp. 26. 57-75. Mark 14. 53-72.
-54 followed = was following. **55** kindled = lighted. Gr. *haptō*. Only in Luke 8. 16; 11. 33; 15. 8. hall = court. **56** a certain maid. See Ap. 160. beheld = saw, as in *v*. 49. by = at. Gr. *pros*. Ap. 104. xv. 3. fire = light. Ap. 130. 1. earnestly looked. Ap. 133. III. 6. This man was also = This one also was. **58** another = different one. Gr. *heteros*. Ap. 124. 2. Thou art also = Thou also art. **59** another = a certain other (Gr. *allos*. Ap. 124. 1). See Ap. 160. Of = Upon. Gr. *epi*. Ap. 104. ix. 1.

22. -60-62 [For Structure see next page].

60 immediately = on the spot. Gr. *parachrēma*. See 1. 64. yet spake = was yet speaking. Ap. 160. **61** and looked. He was bound; and to *speak* aloud was out of the question. looked upon. Gr. *emblepō*. Ap. 133. I. 7. word. Gr. *logos*. See note on Mark 9. 32.

A.D. 29 62 And Peter went °out, and wept bitterly.
B 63 And °the men that held [47]Jesus °mocked Him, °and smote *Him.*
64 And when they had °blindfolded Him, they struck Him on °the face, and °asked Him, saying, "Prophesy, who is it that smote Thee?"
65 And many °other things blasphemously °spake they °against Him.

Y G^1 66 And as soon as it °was day, °the elders of the people °and the chief priests and the scribes came together, and led Him [3]into their °council, saying,

H^1 67 °"Art Thou °the Christ? tell us." And He said unto them, °"If I tell you, ye will [16]not °believe:
68 And [67]if °I also ask *you,* ye will [16]not answer Me, nor let *Me* go.
69 °Hereafter shall [22]the Son of man °sit °on the right hand of the °power of °God."
70 Then said they all, "Art Thou then °the Son of [69]God?" And He said [15]unto them, °"Ye say that I am."
71 And they said, °"What need we any further witness? for we ourselves °have heard [18]of His own mouth."

G^2 **23** And the whole °multitude of them arose, and led Him °unto Pilate.

H^2 2 And they began to accuse Him, saying, °"We found this *fellow* °perverting the nation, and forbidding to give tribute to Cæsar, saying that He Himself is °Christ a King."
3 And Pilate °asked Him, saying, "Art Thou °the King of the Jews?" And He answered him and said, °"Thou sayest *it.*"
4 Then said Pilate °to the chief priests and *to* the °people, °"I find no fault °in this °Man."
5 And they °were the more fierce, saying, "He °stirreth up the people, teaching °throughout all Jewry, beginning °from °Galilee to this place."
6 When Pilate heard °of [5]Galilee, he asked °whether the [4]Man were a Galilæan.

G^3 7 And as soon as he °knew that He °belonged unto Herod's °jurisdiction, he °sent Him [4]to Herod, who himself also was °at Jerusalem at °that time.

H^3 t 8 And when Herod °saw °Jesus, he was exceeding glad: for he was °desirous to see Him °of a long *season,* °because he had heard

22. -60-62 (F^2, p. 1502). PETER'S REPENTANCE. (*Alternation.*)

F^2 | r | -60. Event. A cock crowing.
| s | 61-. The Lord's look.
| *r* | -61-. Event. A cock crowing.
| *s* | -61, 62. The Lord's word.

62 out = outside.
63 the men. Gr. pl. of *anēr.* Ap. 123. 2. Not the same word as in *v.* 10.
mocked = were mocking. Gr. *empaizō.* Cp. 18. 32.
and smote = smiting.
64 blindfolded = covered. Gr. *perikaluptō.* Only here; Mark 14. 65. Heb. 9. 4.
the face. Still covered.
asked = kept asking. Ap. 134. I. 3.
65 other = different. Ap. 124. 2.
spake = said.
against = to. Gr. *eis.* Ap. 104. vi.

22. 66—23. 23 (Y, p. 1502). LED AWAY TO TRIALS. (*Repeated Alternation.*)

Y | G^1 | 22. 66. Led before the Sanhedrin.
| H^1 | 22. 67-71. Examination.
| G^2 | 23. 1. Led before Pilate.
| H^2 | 23. 2-6. Examination.
| G^3 | 23. 7. Sent to Herod.
| H^3 | 23. 8-11-. Examination.
| G^4 | 23. -11, 12. Sent back to Pilate.
| H^4 | 23. 13-23. Compromise proposed.

66 was = became.
the elders = the assembly of the elders, as in Acts 22. 5.
and, &c. Read "both chief priests and scribes". There are no Articles.
council. Gr. *sunhedrion.*
67 Art Thou = If Thou art, &c. The condition assumed. See Ap. 118. 2. a.
the Christ = the Messiah. Ap. 98. IX.
If I tell you. Implying "which I do not". Ap. 118. 1. b.
believe. Ap. 150. I. 1. i.
68 I also ask you = I ask [you] also.
69 Hereafter = From (Gr. *apo.* Ap. 104. iv) henceforth, as in 1. 48; 5. 10. John 1. 51.
sit = be seated.
on = at. Gr. *ek.* Ap. 104. vii.
power. Gr. *dunamis.* Ap. 172. 1.
God. Ap. 98. I. i. 1.
70 the Son of God. Ap. 98. XV.
Ye say, &c. A Hebraism, denoting a strong affirmation.
71 What need, &c. = Why have we still need of testimony?
have heard = heard.

23. 1 multitude. Gr. *plēthos* = number (not *ochlos* = crowd). In the usage of the *Papyri* it denotes an assembly.
unto. Gr. *epi.* Ap. 104. ix. 3.
2 We found. As the result of our examination.
perverting = agitating. Not the same word as in *v.* 14. Cp. 9. 41.
Christ = Messiah. Ap. 98. IX. **3 asked** = questioned. **the King.** Pilate using the Art., as though implying his belief. **Thou sayest.** A Hebraism for a strong affirmation. Cp. 22. 70, &c. **4 to.** Gr. *pros.* Ap. 104. xv. 3. **people** = crowds. **I find no fault, &c.** Cp. Matt. 27. 4. **in.** Gr. *en.* Ap. 104. viii. **Man.** Gr. *anthrōpos.* Ap. 123. 1. **5 were the more fierce** = kept insisting. Gr. *epischuō.* Occurs only here in N.T. **stirreth up** = instigates. Gr. *anaseiō.* Stronger than "pervert" in *v.* 2. Occurs only here, and Mark 15. 11. **throughout.** Gr. *kata.* Ap. 104. x. 1. **from.** Gr. *apo.* Ap. 104. iv. **Galilee.** See Ap. 169. **6 of Galilee** = Galilee [mentioned]. **whether** = if. Ap. 118. 2. a. **7 knew** = got to know. Gr. *ginōskō.* Ap. 132. I. 2. **belonged unto** = was of. Gr. *ek.* Ap. 104. vii. **jurisdiction** = authority. Ap. 172. 5. **sent.** Gr. *anapempō.* Ap. 174. 5, only here; *vv.* 11, 15; Philem. 12; and (acc. to texts) Acts 25. 21. **at** = in Gr. *en.* Ap. 104. viii. **that time** = those days: i. e. of the Feast.

23. 8-11 [For Structure see next page].

8 saw. Gr. *eidon.* Ap. 133. I. i. **Jesus.** Ap. 98. X. **desirous** = wishing. Gr. *thelō.* Ap. 102. 1. **of.** Gr. *ek.* Ap. 104. vii. **because he had heard** = on account of (Gr. *dia.* Ap. 104. v. 2) his hearing.

A. D. 29 many things °of Him; and he °hoped to have seen some °miracle °done °by Him.

u 9 Then he °questioned with Him [4]in many °words;

v but He answered him nothing.

u 10 And the chief priests and scribes °stood and °vehemently accused Him.

t 11 And Herod °with his men of war °set Him at nought, and °mocked *Him*, and arrayed Him in a °gorgeous robe,

G[4] and [7]sent Him again to Pilate.

12 And the same day Pilate and Herod were made friends °together: for before they were [7]at enmity °between themselves.

H[4] w[1] 13 °And Pilate, when he had called together the chief priests and the rulers and the people,

14 Said °unto them, "Ye have brought this [4]Man unto me, as One That °perverteth the people: and, °behold, I, having °examined *Him* before you, have found no fault [4]in this [4]Man touching those things whereof ye accuse Him:

15 °No, nor yet Herod: for I [7]sent you [4]to him; and, °lo, nothing worthy of death °is done °unto Him.

16 °I will therefore °chastise Him, and release *Him*."

17 (For of necessity he must release one unto them °at °the feast.)

x[1] 18 And they cried out °all at once, saying, "Away with this *Man*, and release unto us °Barabbas:"

19 (Who °for a certain °sedition °made [4]in the city, and for °murder, °was cast °into prison.)

w[2] 20 Pilate therefore, °willing to release [8]Jesus, °spake again to them.

x[2] 21 But they °cried, saying, "Crucify *Him*, crucify Him."

w[3] 22 And he °said [14]unto them the third time, "Why, what °evil hath He done? I have found no cause of death [4]in Him: I will therefore chastise Him, and let *Him* go."

x[3] 23 And they °were instant with loud voices, °requiring that He might be crucified. And the voices of them and of the chief priests °prevailed.

Z 24 And Pilate °gave sentence that °it should be as they required.

25 And he released unto them him that [19]for sedition and [19]murder [19]was cast [19]into prison, whom they °had desired; but he delivered [8]Jesus to their °will.

Y y 26 °And as they led Him away, they °laid

23. 8-11- (H[3], p. 1503). EXAMINATION BEFORE HEROD. (*Introversion.*)

H[3] | t | 8. Herod. Curiosity.
  u | 9-. Questioning by Herod.
    v | -9. The Lord. Silence.
  u | 10. Accusation of chief priests and scribes.
t | 11-. Herod. Carelessness.

of = concerning. Gr. *peri*. Ap. 104. xiii. 1.
hoped = was hoping (all that long time).
miracle = sign. See Ap. 176. 3.
done = accomplished.
by. Gr. *hupo*. Ap. 104. xviii. 1.
9 questioned. Gr. *erōtaō*. Ap. 134. 3.
words. Pl. of *logos*. See note on Mark 9. 32.
10 stood = had stood.
vehemently. Gr. *eutonōs*. Occurs only here, and Acts 18. 28. **11 with.** Gr. *sun*. Ap. 104. xvi.
set Him at nought = treated Him with contempt.
mocked. See 22. 63.
gorgeous = resplendent. Cp. Acts 10. 30. Rev. 15. 6.
12 were made = became.
together = with (Gr. *meta*. Ap. 104. xi. 1) one another.
between = with reference to. Gr. *pros*. Ap. 104. xv. 3.

23. 13-23 (H[4], p. 1503). COMPROMISE PROPOSED. (*Repeated Alternation.*)

H[4] | w[1] | 13-17. Pilate's first appeal. "No fault", *vv.* 4, 14.
  x[1] | 18, 19. Demand for the Lord's death (first).
w[2] | 20. Pilate's second appeal.
  x[2] | 21. Demand for the Lord's death (second).
w[3] | 22. Pilate's third appeal. "No cause of death".
  x[3] | 23. Demand for the Lord's death (third).

Verses 13-25. Cp. Matt. 27. 15-26. Mark 15. 6-15.
14 unto. Gr. *pros*. Ap. 104. xv. 3.
perverteth = turneth away. Gr. *apostrephō*. Not the same word as in *v.* 2.
behold. Fig. *Asterismos*. Ap. 6.
examined. Gr. *anakrinō*. Ap. 122. 2.
15 No, nor yet = nor even.
lo. Fig. *Asterismos*. Ap. 6.
is done = has been done. Cp. *v.* 41.
unto Him: i. e. by Him.
16 I will, &c. Probably with his own hands (cp. *v.* 22. Matt. 27. 26. Mark 15. 15) instead of crucifying Him; with the view of releasing Him.
chastise. Cp. Isa. 53. 5.
17 at. Gr. *kata*. Ap. 104. x. 2.
the = a. Most texts omit this verse.
18 all at once = all together, or in a mass. Gr. *pamplēthei*. Occurs only here.
Barabbas. Aramaic (Ap. 94. III. 3) = son of a (distinguished) father. ORIGEN (A. D. 186-253) read "Jesus, Barabbas" in Matt. 27. 17, the choice lying between two of the same name.
19 for = on account of. Gr. *dia*. Ap. 104. v. 3.
sedition = insurrection.
made = which had taken place.
murder. Cp. Acts 3. 14. was = had been.
into. Gr. *eis*. Ap. 104. vi.
20 willing = wishing. Gr. *thelō*. Ap. 102. 1.
spake . . . to = addressed. Gr. *prosphōneō*. Cp. Acts 21. 40; 22. 2.
21 cried = kept shouting. Gr. *epiphōneō*.
22 said = spake. evil. Gr. *kakos*. Ap. 128. III. 2.
23 were instant = were urgent. Gr. *epikeimai*, to press upon. Cp. 7. 4. Judges 16. 16. Acts 26. 7. Rom. 12. 12. 2 Tim. 4. 2.

requiring. Ap. 134. 4. prevailed = had power to bear down (Pilate's remonstrance). **24 gave sentence** = pronounced sentence. Gr. *epikrinō*. Ap. 122. 6. Occurs only here. it, &c. = their request should be carried out. **25 had desired.** Same word as "require" in *v.* 23. will = desire. Gr. *thelēma*. Cp. Ap. 102. 2.

23. 26-32 (*Y*, p. 1502). LED AWAY TO DEATH. (*Alternation.*)

Y | y | 26. The Lord. Led away.
  z | 27. Others. Following.
y | 28-31. The Lord. Final warning.
  z | 32. Others. Led with Him.

26 And as, &c. Cp. Matt. 27. 31-34. Mark 15. 20-23. **laid hold upon.** Cp. Acts 16. 19; 17. 19; 18. 17; 21. 30-33.

A. D. 29 hold upon one Simon, a Cyrenian, coming °out
of °the country, and on him they laid °the
cross, that he might bear *it* after [8]Jesus.
z 27 °And there followed Him a great °com-
pany of people, and of women, which also
°bewailed and lamented Him.
y 28 But [8]Jesus turning [14]unto them said,
°"Daughters of Jerusalem, weep °not °for Me,
but weep °for yourselves, and °for your °chil-
dren.
29 For, [14]behold, the days are coming, [4]in the
which they shall say, °'Blessed *are* the barren,
and the wombs that °never bare, and the paps
which °never gave suck.'
30 Then shall they begin to say to the
mountains, 'Fall °on us;' and to the °hills,
'Cover us.'
31 For °if they °do these things [4]in °a green
tree, what °shall be done [4]in °the dry?"
z 32 And there were °also two °other, °male-
factors, °led [11]with Him to be put to death.
X j a 33 And when they were come [4]to the place,
which is called °Calvary, there they °crucified
Him,
b and the [32]malefactors, one °on the right hand,
°and the other °on the °left.
K c 34 Then said [8]Jesus, °"Father, °forgive them;
for they °know °not what they °do."
d And they parted His raiment, and cast lots.
35 And the people stood °beholding. And
the rulers also with them °derided *Him*, saying, "He saved °others; let Him save Himself,
[31]if °He be °Christ, the chosen of °God."
36 And the soldiers also [11]mocked Him, °com-
ing to Him, and °offering Him vinegar,
37 And saying, [31]"If Thou be the king of the
Jews, save Thyself."
38 And a °superscription also was written
°over Him in letters of Greek, and Latin, and
Hebrew, °THIS IS THE KING OF THE
JEWS.
J b 39 And one of the [32]malefactors which were
hanged °railed on Him, saying, [31]"If Thou be
°Christ, °save Thyself and us."
40 But the [32]other answering rebuked him,
saying, "Dost not thou fear [35]God, seeing thou
art [4]in the same °condemnation?
41 And we indeed justly; for we °receive the
due reward of °our deeds: but this Man °hath
done nothing amiss."
42 And he said unto [8]Jesus, °"Lord, remember
me when Thou °comest °into Thy kingdom."
43 And [8]Jesus said unto him, "Verily °I say
unto thee, °To day shalt thou be °with Me [4]in
°paradise."
a 44 °And it was about the °sixth hour, and

out of. Gr. *apo.* Ap. 104. iv.
the country = a field. **the cross.** See Ap. 162.
27 And there, &c.: *vv.* 27–32, peculiar to Luke.
company = multitude.
bewailed and lamented = were beating their breasts and lamenting.
28 Daughters, &c. Not therefore the women from Galilee of *vv.* 49, 55. **not.** Gr. *mē.* Ap. 105. II.
for = on, or over. Gr. *epi.* Ap. 104. ix. 3.
children. Gr. pl. of *teknon.* Ap. 108. I.
29 Blessed = Happy. See note on Matt. 5. 3, and cp. 11. 27. Hos. 9. 12–16.
never bare = did not (Gr. *ou.* Ap. 105. I) bear.
30 on. Gr. *epi.* Ap. 104. ix. 3.
hills. Gr. pl. of *bounos.* Occurs only here and in 3. 5.
31 if they do. Assuming the case. Ap. 118. 2. a.
do = are doing.
a green tree = the living wood: i. e. the Lord.
shall be done = must happen.
the dry = the dry [wood]: i. e. the nation.
32 also two other = others also, two.
other = different ones. Gr. pl. of *heteros.* Ap. 124. 2.
malefactors = evildoers. Gr. *kakourgoi.* Not *lēstai* = brigands, as in Matt. 27. 38. See Ap. 164.
led with Him. The brigands were brought later.

23. 33–49 (*X*, p. 1502). CONSPIRACY COMPLETED. (*Alternation and Introversion.*)

X | J | a | 33–. Crucifixion. Accompanying facts.
| | b | –33. The two malefactors. Led with the Lord.
| K | c | 34–. The Lord's prayer.
| | d | –34–38. Spectators.
| *J* | *b* | 39–43. The two malefactors. Crucified.
| | *a* | 44, 45. Crucifixion. Accompanying events.
| *K* | *c* | 46. The Lord's cry.
| | *d* | 47–49. Spectators.

33 to. Gr. *epi.* Ap. 104. ix. 3.
Calvary is the Greek for the Heb. *Golgotha* = a skull. Now called "a hill". But see Conder's *Jerusalem*, p. 80.
crucified. See Ap. 162. **on** = at. Gr. *ek.* Ap. 104. vii.
and the other = and one.
left. Gr. *aristeros.* Only here, Matt. 6. 3. 2 Cor. 6. 7. Not the same word as in Matt. 27. 38.
34 Father. See Ap. 98. III.
forgive them. The last of eight recorded occasions of prayer in Luke. See note on 3. 21, and cp. Matt. 27. 46 for the last "seven words" on the cross. Cp. Isa. 53. 12. **know.** Gr. *oida.* Ap. 132. I. i.
not. Gr. *ou.* Ap. 105. I.
do = are doing. Cp. Acts 3. 17. 1 Cor. 2. 8.
35 beholding = looking on, or gazing at. Gr. *theōreō.* Ap. 133. I. 11. Not the same word as in *v.* 29.
derided = were mocking: i. e. turning up their noses at Him. Same word as in 16. 14. Cp. Pss. 2. 4; 22. 7; 35. 16 (LXX).
others. Gr. *allos.* Ap. 124. 1. Not the same word as in *vv.* 32, 40. **He** = This fellow.
Christ = the Messiah. Ap. 98. IX.
God. Ap. 98. I. i. 1. **36 coming** = coming up close.
offering, &c. See note on Matt. 27. 33 and 48.
38 superscription. Not the same word as in Matthew and John. See Ap. 163.
over. Gr. *epi.* Ap. 104. ix. 2.
THIS IS, &c. See Ap. 48 for this type; and Ap. 163 for the words themselves.
39 railed = kept up a railing.

Christ. The Lewis Codex of the Syr. Gospels recently found at Mount Sinai reads "Saviour", not Messiah. **save Thyself and us.** This reads (in the same Codex), "save Thyself alive this day, and us also". **40 condemnation.** Ap. 177. 6. **41 receive** = are receiving. **our deeds** = what we did. **hath done** = did. **42 Lord.** Most Texts omit this, but not the Syr. which reads "my Lord". Ap. 98. VI. i. *a.* 3. A. **comest** = shalt have come. **into** = in (Gr. *en*), but some texts with Syr. read "into": i. e. into possession of. **43 I say unto thee, To day** = "I say unto thee to day". **To day.** Connect this with "I say", to emphasize the solemnity of the occasion; not with "shalt thou be". See the Hebraism in note on Deut. 4. 26. As to the punctuation, see Ap. 94. V. i. 3; and as to the whole clause, see Ap. 173. **with.** Gr. *meta.* Ap. 104. xi. 1. Not the same word as in *vv.* 11, 32, 35. **paradise** = the paradise: i. e. the one well known to Scripture. See note on Ecc. 2. 5. **44 Verses 44–46.** Cp. Matt. 27. 45–50; Mark 15. 33–37. **sixth hour**: i. e. noon. See Ap. 165.

A.D. 29 there °was a darkness °over all °the earth until
the °ninth hour.
45 And the sun was darkened, and °the veil
of °the Temple was rent [4]in the midst.
K c 46 And when [8]Jesus had cried with a loud
voice, He said, [34]"Father, [19]into Thy hands
I °commend My °spirit:" and having said
thus, He °gave up the ghost.
d 47 °Now when the centurion saw what °was
done, he glorified [35]God, saying, "Certainly
this was a righteous [4]Man."
48 And all the °people that came together [33]to
that sight, [35]beholding the things which °were
done, °smote their breasts, and °returned.
49 °And all °His acquaintance, and the
women that °followed Him [5]from °Galilee,
°stood afar off, °beholding these things.
W² L N 50 And, [14]behold, *there was* a °man named
°Joseph, a °counsellor; *and he was* a good
°man, and a just:
51 (The same had [34]not °consented to the
°counsel and deed of them;) *he was* °of Arimathæa, a city of the Jews: who °also himself
waited for °the kingdom of [35]God.
52 This *man* went unto Pilate, and °begged
the body of [8]Jesus.
O e 53 And he took it down, and wrapped it in
°linen,
f and laid it [4]in a °sepulchre that was °hewn in
stone, wherein °never man °before was laid.
M 54 And that day was °the preparation, and
°the sabbath drew on.
L N 55 And the women also, which °came with
Him °from [5]Galilee, °followed after,
O f and °beheld the [53]sepulchre, and how His
body was laid.
e 56 And they [48]returned, and °prepared spices
and ointments;
M and °rested the sabbath day according to the
commandment.

W³ P **24** °Now upon °the first *day* of the week,
°very early in the morning, they came
°unto the °sepulchre, bringing the spices which
they had prepared, and certain *others* °with
them.
Q 2 And °they found the stone rolled away
°from the sepulchre.

was = came to be. **over.** Gr. *epi*. Ap. 104. ix. 3. **the earth** = the land. Gr. *gē*. Ap. 129. 4. **ninth hour**: i.e. 3 p.m. See Ap. 165.

45 the veil. See Lev. 4. 6. Matt. 27. 51. **the Temple** = the *Naos*. See note on Matt. 23. 16.

46 commend = commit, or entrust. Cp. Ps. 31. 5. Acts 7. 59. 1 Pet. 2. 23. **spirit.** Gr. *pneuma*. Ap. 101. II. 6. Cp. 8. 55. **gave up the ghost** = expired, or breathed (His last).

47 Now, &c. Cp. Matt. 27. 51-56. Mark 15. 39-54. **was done** = took place.

48 people = crowds. **were done** = took place. **smote, &c.** = beating... returned. The women "stood". **returned.** Gr. *hupostrephō* = turned back. Occurs thirty-two times in Luke and Acts, and only three times elsewhere in N.T.

49 And = But. Marking the contrast between the people and the women. **His acquaintance** = those who knew (Ap. 132. I. ii) Him. **followed** = followed with. **Galilee.** See Ap. 169. **stood** = continued standing. The crowds turned back. **beholding** = looking on. Gr. *horaō*. Ap. 133. I. 8.

23. 50-56 (W², p. 1502). BURIAL.
(Alternation and Introversion.)

W² | L | N | 50-52. Joseph.
    O | e | 53-. The body honoured.
        f | -53. The body laid.
    M | 54. Time. The high Sabbath drew on.
  L | *N* | 55-. The women.
    O | *f* | -55. The body laid. Beheld.
        e | 56-. The body to be further honoured.
    M | -56. Time. The high Sabbath. Rest.

50 man. Gr. *anēr*. Ap. 123. 2. **Joseph.** One of two secret disciples who buried the Lord: Nicodemus being the other (see John 3. 1, 4, 9; 7. 50; 19. 39). The Eleven had no part in it. **counsellor.** A member of the Sanhedrin.

51 consented = voted with. Gr. *sunkatatithēmi*. Occurs only here. **counsel.** Gr. *boulē*. Ap. 102. 4. **of** = from. Gr. *apo*. Ap. 104. iv. **also himself** = himself also. **the kingdom of God.** See Ap. 114.

52 begged = asked. Gr. *aiteō*. Same word as "require", *v.* 23, and "desire", *v.* 25. Ap. 134. I. 4.

53 linen. Showing he was a rich man. Cp. Matt. 27. 57. Mark 14. 51; 15. 46. **sepulchre** = tomb. **hewn in stone** = hewn in a rock. Gr. *laxeutos*. Occurs only here. **never . . . before.** Gr. *ouk oudepō oudeis*.

54 the preparation. See Ap. 156. **the sabbath.** The high sabbath. See Ap. 156.

55 came = were come with. Only here and Acts 16. 17. **from** = out of. Gr. *ek*. Ap. 104. vii. **followed after.** Gr. *sunakoloutheō*. Only here and Mark 5. 37. **beheld.** Gr. *theaomai*. Ap. 133. I. 12.

56 prepared, &c. These had to be bought (Mark 16. 1) between the two sabbaths. See Ap. 156. **rested.** Gr. *hēsuchazō* = to rest from labour. Occurs only here, and in 14. 4. Acts 11. 18; 21. 14; and 1 Thess. 4. 11. **the commandment.** Lev. 23. 4-7. See Ap. 156.

24. 1-12 (W³, p. 1502). RESURRECTION. *(Extended Alternation and Introversion.)*

W³ | P | 1. The women. Return to the Sepulchre.
  Q | 2-4-. Perplexity experienced.
    R | g | -4-6. The Lord not there.
        h | 7, 8. The Lord's words not believed.
  P | 9, 10-. Women. Return to the Apostles.
  Q | 10. Perplexity reported.
    R | *h* | 11. The women's words not believed.
        g | 12. The Lord not there.

1 Now = But, &c. Cp. Matt. 28. 1. Mark 16. 2-4. See Ap. 166. **the first day of the week.** Our Saturday sunset to Sunday sunset. **very early in the morning.** Gr. *orthros bathus*, lit. at deep dawn. Cp. John 20. 1. **unto** = upon. Gr. *epi*. Ap. 104. ix. 3. **sepulchre** = tomb. **with.** Gr. *sun*. Ap. 104. xvi.

2 they found, &c. See the question they had asked (Mark 16. 3). **from** = away from. Gr. *apo*. Ap. 104. iv. Not the same word as in *vv.* 46, 49.

A.D. 29 3 And they entered in, and found °not the
body of °the Lord °Jesus.
4 °And it came to pass, °as they were much
perplexed °thereabout,
R g °behold, two °men stood by them °in °shining
°garments:
5 And °as they were afraid, and bowed
down *their* faces °to the earth, they said °unto
them, "Why seek ye °the living °among °the
dead?
6 He is [3]not here, but is °risen: °remember
how He spake unto you when He was yet [4]in
°Galilee,
h 7 Saying, °'The Son of man must be delivered °into the hands of °sinful °men, and be
crucified, and the third day rise again.'"
8 And they remembered His °words,
P 9 And returned [2]from the sepulchre, and
told all these things unto the eleven, and to
all the rest.
10 It was °Mary Magdalene, and Joanna, and
Mary *the mother* of James, °and other *women*
that were [1]with them,
Q which told these things [5]unto the apostles.
R h 11 And their [8]words seemed °to them °as °idle
tales, and they °believed them not.
g 12 Then arose Peter, °and ran [1]unto the
sepulchre; and stooping down, he °beheld the
linen clothes °laid by themselves, and °de-
parted, wondering °in himself at that which
was come to pass.
B S[1] T U 13 And, [4]behold, two °of °them °went °that
same day [5]to a village called °Emmaus, which
was [2]from Jerusalem *about* threescore °fur-
longs.
V 14 And they °talked together °of all these
things which had happened.
15 [4]And it came to pass, that, °while they
communed *together* and reasoned, [3]Jesus Himself °drew near, and °went with them.
W 16 But their eyes were holden that they
should °not °know Him.
X Y 17 And He said [5]unto them, "What manner
of °communications *are* these that ye °have
one °to another, as ye walk, °and are sad?"
Z 18 And the one [13]of them, whose name was
°Cleopas, answering said [5]unto Him, "Art
Thou °only a stranger [4]in Jerusalem, °and hast
[3]not °known the things which are come to
pass °there [4]in these days?"

3 not. Gr. *ou.* Ap. 105. I.
the Lord Jesus. See Ap. 98. VI. i. *a.* 3. B. c. The first occurrence of this full expression. Rightly found in this connexion. It is the prelude to some forty occurrences in the Epistles.
Jesus. Ap. 98. X.
4 And it came to pass. A Hebraism.
as, &c. = in (Gr. *en.* Ap. 104. viii) their being, &c.
thereabout = concerning this. Gr. *peri.* Ap. 104. xiii. 1.
behold. Gr. *idou.* Ap. 133. I. 2. Fig. *Asterismos.* Ap. 6.
men. Gr. pl. of *anēr.* Ap. 123. 2. Not the same word as in *v.* -7.
in. Gr. *en.* Ap. 104. viii. Not the same word as in *vv.* 12, 47.
shining = flashing as lightning. Occurs only here, and in 17. 24. **garments** = splendid raiment. Only here.
5 as they were, &c. = becoming filled with fear.
to. Gr. *eis.* Ap. 104. vi.
unto. Gr. *pros.* Ap. 104. xv. 3.
the living = the living One.
among. Gr. *meta.* Ap. 104. xi. 1. Not the same word as in *v.* 47. **the dead.** See Ap. 139. 4.
6 risen. Ap. 178. 4.
remember. The true messenger of the Lord recalls His words. Cp. *v.* 8. **Galilee.** Ap. 169.
7 The Son of man. See Ap. 98. XVI.
into. Gr. *eis.* Ap. 104. vi.
sinful, sinners. Gr. *hamartōlos.* Cp. Ap. 128.
men. Gr. pl. of *anthrōpos.* Ap. 123. 1.
8 words. Gr. pl. of *rhēma.* See note on Mark 9. 32.
10 Mary. See Ap. 100.
and, &c. = and the rest (Ap. 124. 3).
11 to them = in their sight. **as** = like.
idle tales = silly nonsense. Gr. *lēros.* Occurs only here. A medical term for delirium.
believed not = disbelieved. Gr. *apisteō.*
12 and ran. Note the six things Peter did here, "arose", "ran", "stooped", "beheld", "departed", "wondered"; and the one thing he did not do, "believed". **beheld.** Gr. *blepō.* Ap. 133. I. 5.
laid by themselves. Important evidence in view of Matt. 28. 12-15.
departed, &c. = went away to (Gr. *pros.* Ap. 104. xv. 3) his own [house] wondering.

24. 13-49 (*B*, p. 1427). THE SUCCESSORS.
(*Division.*)

B | S[1] | 13-32. Journey to Emmaus.
| S[2] | 33-49. Return to Jerusalem.

24. 13-32 (S[1], above). JOURNEY TO EMMAUS.
(*Extended Alternation.*)

S[1] | T | U | 13. The village. Journeyed to.
V | 14, 15. On the way thither.
W | 16. Their eyes holden.
X | 17-27. The Lord's instruction.
T | *U* | 28. The village. Reached.
V | 29, 30. Within the house.
W | 31. Their eyes opened.
X | 32. The Lord's disappearance.

13 of. Gr. *ek.* Ap. 104. vii. Not the same word as in *vv.* 14, -42. **them.** Not apostles.
went = were going. **that** = in (Gr. *en*) that.
Emmaus. Now *Khan el Khamaseh*, eight miles south-west of Jerusalem (Conder), or *Urtas*, seven miles south (Finn). **furlongs.** See Ap. 51. III. 1. (2). **14 talked together** = were conversing with (Gr. *pros.* Ap. 104. xv. 3) one another. Same as "communed" in *v.* 15. **of** = concerning. Gr. *peri.* Ap. 104. xiii. 1.
15 while, &c. = in (Gr. *en*) their communing, &c. **drew near, and** = having drawn near. **went** = was walking. **16 not.** Gr. *mē.* Ap. 105. II. **know** = recognize. Gr. *epiginōskō.* Ap. 132. I. iii.

24. 17-27 (X, above). THE LORD'S INSTRUCTION. (*Alternation.*)

X | Y | 17. Question of the Lord. "What manner?"
Z | 18. Answer of Cleopas.
Y | 19-. Question of the Lord. "What things?"
Z | -19-27. Answer of Cleopas.

17 communications. Gr. pl. of *logos.* See note on Mark 9. 32. **have** = exchange. Only here in N.T.
to. Gr. *pros.* Ap. 104. xv. 3. **and are sad.** According to T Tr. WH R (not the Syr.) the question ends at "walk", and reads on: "and they stood still, sad in countenance". **18 Cleopas.** Aramaic. See Ap. 94. III. 3. An abbreviation of Cleopatros. Not the same as Clopas of John 19. 25. **only a . . . and hast** = the only . . . who has. **known** = got to know. Ap. 132. I. ii. **there** = in (Gr. *en*) it.

Y 19 And He said unto them, °"What things?"
A.D. 29 And they said unto Him, °"Concerning [3]Jesus
Z of Nazareth, Which was °a prophet mighty
[4]in deed and °word before God and all the
people:
20 And how the chief priests and our rulers
delivered Him [5]to °be condemned to death, and
have crucified Him.
21 But we °trusted that it had been He Which
°should have redeemed Israel: and °beside all
°this, to day is °the third day °since °these
things were done.
22 Yea, and certain women also [13]of our
company made us astonished, which were
early °at the sepulchre;
23 And when they found [16]not His body,
they came, saying, that they had °also °seen
a vision of angels, which said that He °was
alive.
24 And certain of them which were [1]with us
went °to the sepulchre, and found *it* even so as
the women had said: but Him they °saw
[3]not."
25 °Then He said [5]unto them, °"O fools, and
slow of heart to °believe °all that the prophets have spoken:
26 °Ought °not °Christ to have suffered these
things, °and to enter [7]into His glory?"
27 And °beginning °at °Moses and °all the
prophets, He °expounded unto them [4]in all
the scriptures the things [19]concerning Himself.
T U 28 And they drew nigh °unto the village,
whither they °went: and He °made as though
He would have gone further.
V 29 But they °constrained Him, saying, "Abide
°with us: for it is °toward evening, and the day
°is far spent." And He went in to tarry [1]with
them.
30 [4]And it came to pass, °as He °sat at meat
29- with them, He °took °bread, and blessed *it*,
and °brake, and gave to them.
W 31 And their eyes were opened, and they
[16]knew Him; and He °vanished °out of their
sight.
X 32 And they said one [-17]to another, °"Did [26]not
our heart burn °within us, while He °talked
with us °by the way, and while He °opened to
us the scriptures?"
S² A 33 And they rose up the same hour, and
returned [5]to Jerusalem, and found the eleven
°gathered together, and them that were [1]with
them,
B 34 °Saying, °"The Lord °is risen indeed, and
°hath appeared to Simon."
35 And they °told what things *were done* [4]in
the way, and how He °was [18]known of them
[4]in °breaking of bread.
A 36 And as they thus spake, [3]Jesus Himself
stood [4]in the midst of them,
B C E and saith unto them, "Peace *be* unto you."
37 But they were terrified and affrighted, and
supposed that they had °seen a °spirit.

19 What things? = What kind of things?
Concerning. Gr. *peri.* Ap. 104. xiii. 1.
a prophet. See Acts 3. 22.
word. Gr. *logos.* See note on Mark 9. 32.
20 be condemned to = the judgment (Gr. *krima.* Ap. 177. 6) of.
21 trusted = were hoping.
should have redeemed = was about to redeem. In accordance with 2. 38. Cp. Acts 1. 6.
beside = with. Gr. *sun.* Ap. 104. xvi.
this = these things.
the third day. See Ap. 148 and 166.
since = from (Gr. *apo.* Ap. 104. iv) the time when.
22 at. Gr. *epi.* Ap. 104. ix. 3.
23 also. Read "also" after "angels".
seen. Gr. *horaō.* Ap. 133. I. 8.
was alive = is living.
24 to. Gr. *epi*, as above.
saw. Gr. *eidon.* Ap. 133. I. 1.
25 Then = And.
O fools = O dullards. Gr. *anoētos* = without reflection (not *aphrōn* = without mind; or *asophos* = without wisdom); i.e. dull is your heart, and slow in believing.
believe. See Ap. 150. I. v. (iii) 1.
all = on all. Not some. The Jews believed the prophecies of the "glory", but not those of the "sufferings", and cast the Lord out, because they thought He was not good enough for the world. Many to-day do the reverse, and think the world is not yet good enough for Him.
26 Ought not, &c. . . .? Behoved it not?
not. Gr. *ouchi.* Ap. 105. I. a.
Christ = the Messiah. Ap. 98. IX.
and to enter, &c. This, in God's counsels, was to follow immediately on the sufferings, had the nation repented. See Acts 3. 18-26, and cp. 1 Pet. 1. 11; 4. 13; 5. 1. Doubtless this was the subject of Acts 1. 3.
27 beginning at Moses. Cp. Gen. 3. 15; 22. 18. Ex. 12. Lev. 16. Num. 21. 9. Deut. 18. 15. Num. 24. 17; 20. 11.
at = from. Gr. *apo.* Ap. 104. iv.
Moses. See note on 5. 14.
all = from all, &c. Cp. Isa. 7. 14; 9. 6, 7; 40. 10, 11; 50. 6; 53. 4, 5. Jer. 23. 5; 33. 14, 15. Ezek. 34. 23. Mic. 5. 2. Zech. 6. 12; 9. 9; 12. 10; 13. 7. Mal. 3. 1; 4. 2. See also Heb. 1. 1.
expounded = interpreted.
28 unto. Gr. *eis.* Ap. 104. vi.
went = were going.
made, &c. i.e. was going farther (but for their constraint). There was no deception. Lit., added to go. Gr. *prospoieomai.* Only here.
29 constrained. Gr. *parabiazomai.* Occurs only here and Acts 16. 15.
with. Gr. *meta.* Ap. 104. xi. 1.
toward. Gr. *pros.* Ap. 104. xv. 3.
is far spent = has declined.
30 as He sat, &c. = in (Gr. *en*) His sitting down.
sat = reclined.
took bread. He took the part of the host.
bread = the bread.
brake, &c. See note on Matt. 14. 19.
31 vanished = became invisible. Gr. *aphantos.* Only here.
out of their sight = from (Gr. *apo.* Ap. 104. iv) them.
32 Did not, &c. = was not our heart burning.
within = in. Gr. *en.*
talked = was talking.
by = in. Gr. *en.*
opened = was interpreting.
33 gathered = crowded. Only here.

24. 33-49 (S², p. 1507). **RETURN TO JERUSALEM.**
(*Alternation.*)

S² | A | 33. The eleven and others.
  B | 34, 35. The Lord. His doings. Reported.
 A | 36-. The eleven. The Lord in the midst.
  B | -36-49. The Lord. His words.

34 Saying: i.e. the eleven and those with them, being the speakers.
The Lord. Ap. 98. VI. i. *a.* 3. A.
is risen = has risen. Gr. *egeirō.* Ap. 178. I. 4.
hath appeared. Gr. *optomai.* Ap. 106. I. vi.

35 told = related. **was known** = became known. Ap. 132. I. ii. **breaking, &c.** = the breaking of the bread.

24. -36-49 [For Structure see next page].

37 seen. Gr. *theōreō.* Ap. 133. I. 11. **spirit.** Gr. *pneuma.* Ap. 101. II. 11.

F i 38 And He said unto them, "Why are ye
A.D. 29 troubled? and why do °thoughts arise [4]in
your hearts?

k 39 °Behold My hands and My feet, that it is
I Myself: handle Me, and °see; for a [37]spirit
hath [3]not flesh and bones, as ye [37]see Me
have."

40 And when He had thus spoken, He shewed
them *His* hands and *His* feet.

E 41 And while they yet believed not °for joy,
and °wondered,

F i He said unto them, "Have ye here °any
°meat?"

k 42 And they gave Him a piece of a °broiled
fish, and °of an °honeycomb.
43 And He took *it*, and did eat before them.

D G l 44 And He said unto them, "These *are* the
°words which I spake [5]unto you, while I was
yet [1]with you,

m that all things °must be fulfilled, which °were
written [4]in °the Law of [27]Moses, and *in*
the Prophets, and *in* the Psalms, concerning
°Me."

H 45 Then °opened He their understanding,
that they might understand the Scriptures,

G m 46 And said unto them, "Thus it is [44]written,
and thus it behoved [26]Christ to suffer, and to
°rise °from °the dead °the third day:

l 47 And that °repentance and °remission of
°sins should be °preached °in His name
°among all °nations, °beginning °at Jerusalem.

H 48 And ye are °witnesses of these things.

C 49 And, [4]behold, I °send °the promise of
My Father °upon you:

D but tarry ye [4]in the city of Jerusalem, until ye
be endued with °power [46]from on high."

J 50 And °He led them out °as far as [5]to
°Bethany,

K n and He lifted up His hands, and blessed them.

o 51 [4]And it came to pass, °while He blessed
them,

K o He °was parted [2]from them, and carried up
[7]into °heaven.

n 52 And they °worshipped Him,

J and returned [5]to Jerusalem [29]with great joy:
53 And were continually [4]in the °temple,
praising and blessing [19]God. Amen.

24. -36-49 (*B*, p. 1508). THE LORD. HIS WORDS. (*Alternation.*)

B | C | -36-43. Proof. As to the past.
D | 44-48. Instruction.
C | 49-. Promise. As to the future.
D | -49. Command.

24. -36-43 (C, above). PROOF. AS TO THE PAST. (*Alternations.*)

C | E | -36, 37. Feelings. Terror and fright.
F | i | 38. Question. "Why?"
k | 39, 40. The Lord's answer.
E | 41-. Feelings. Joy and wonder.
F | *i* | -41. Question. "Have ye?", &c.
k | 42, 43. Their answer.

38 thoughts = reasonings.
39 Behold. Gr. pl. of *ide*. Ap. 133. I. 3.
see. Same as "behold".
41 for = from. Gr. *apo*. Ap. 104. iv.
wondered = were wondering. **any** = anything.
meat = eatable. Gr. *brōsimos*. Occurs only here.
42 broiled. Gr. *optos*. Occurs only here.
of = from. Gr. *apo*. Ap. 104. iv.
honeycomb. Common fare. Most texts omit from "and" to end of verse.

24. 44-48 (D, above). INSTRUCTION. (*Alternation and Introversion.*)

D | G | l | 44-. Words. Past.
m | -44. To be fulfilled.
H | 45. The Scripture understood.
G | *m* | 46. Fulfilled.
l | 47. Words. Present.
H | 48. The Scriptures testified.

44 words. Pl. of *logos*. See note on Mark 9. 32.
must. Same as "ought" (*v.* 26). Cp. Acts 17. 3.
were written = have been (and stand) written. Cp. *vv.* 26, 27.
the Law, &c. These are the three great divisions of the Hebrew Bible. See Ap. 1 and note on Matt. 5. 17.
Me. Christ is the one great subject of the whole Bible. Cp. Is. 40. 7. John 5. 39. Acts 17. 3. 1 John 5. 20.
45 opened, &c. For this important truth, see Matt. 11. 27; 13. 11; 16. 17. John 16. 13. Acts 16. 14. 1 Cor. 2. 14. Cp. Ps. 119. 18. **46 rise.** Ap. 178. I. 1.
from = out from among. Gr. *ek*. Ap. 104. vii.
the dead. Ap. 139. 3. See note on Matt. 17. 9.
the third day. See Ap. 148 and 156.
47 repentance. Ap. 111. II. 1.
remission of sins. The new Covenant having been made, this could now be proclaimed. Cp. 1. 17. Acts 2. 38; 3. 19; 10. 43; 13. 38, 39. Heb. 9. 22.
sins. Gr. *hamartia*. Ap. 128. I. ii. 1.
preached = proclaimed. Ap. 121. 1.
in = on (the strength, or foundation of). Gr. *epi*. Ap. 104. ix. 2. **among** = to. Gr. *eis*. Ap. 104. vi.
nations = the nations.
beginning at Jerusalem. Cp. Isa. 2. 3. Mic. 4. 2.
at = from. Gr. *apo*. Ap. 104. iv. Cp. Acts 1. 8. This was done by Peter (Acts 1-12).
48 witnesses = witness-bearers. Cp. Acts 1. 8; 2. 32; 3. 15; 4. 33; 5. 30-32, &c.

49 send. Gr. *apostellō*, but T Tr. A WH R read *exapostellō*, send out or forth. Ap. 174. 1. 2. **the promise:** i.e. the gift of *pneuma hagion*. According to Joel 2. 28 (Acts 2. 17, 18). See Isa. 44. 3. Ezek. 36. 26. **upon.** Gr. *epi*. Ap. 104. ix. 3. **power from on high.** This defines the meaning of *pneuma hagion*, which is synonymous with it. See Acts 1. 4, 5.

24. 50-53 (*A*, p. 1427). POST MINISTERIAL. (*Introversions.*)

A | J | 50-. Led out to Bethany.
K | n | -50. His blessing them.
o | 51-. He is separated.
K | *o* | -51. He is carried up.
n | 52-. Their worship of Him.
J | 52, 53. Return to Jerusalem.

50 He led, &c. At the end of the forty days (Acts 1. 3-12). **as far as to.** Until they were at, or opposite to. **Bethany.** Now *el 'Azarîyeh*. **51 while:** i.e. in (Gr. *en*) the act, &c. **was parted** = stood apart. **heaven.** Sing. See note on Matt. 6. 9, 10. **52 worshipped** = having worshipped. Ap. 137. 1. **53 temple** = the Temple courts. See note on Matt. 23. 16. Not offering or eating of the sacrifices there, but at home. See Acts 1. 14; 2. 46; 3. 1; 5. 42. Luke ends his Gospel, and commences the Acts with the Ascension.

THE GOSPEL

ACCORDING TO

JOHN.

THE STRUCTURE OF THE BOOK AS A WHOLE.

"BEHOLD YOUR GOD" (Isa. 40. 9).

(Introversion.)

B² | A | 1. 1-28. THE FORERUNNER.

B | 1. 29-34. THE BAPTISM: WITH WATER.

C | D | 1. 35—4. 54. THE KINGDOM } PROCLAIMED. } THE FOURFOLD MINISTRY OF THE LORD.
E | 5. 1—6. 71. THE KING
E | 7. 1—11. 54-. THE KING } REJECTED.
D | 11. -54—18. 1. THE KINGDOM

B | 18. 2—20. 31. THE BAPTISM: OF SUFFERING (DEATH, BURIAL, AND RESURRECTION).

A | 21. 1-25. THE SUCCESSORS.

For the New Testament and the order of its Books, see Ap. 95.
For the Diversity of the Four Gospels, see Ap. 96.
For the Unity of the Four Gospels, see Ap. 97.
For the Fourfold Ministry of the Lord, see Ap. 119.
For words peculiar to John's writings, see some 84 words recorded in the notes.

The Divine purpose in the Gospel by JOHN is to present the Lord Jesus as GOD. This is the one great feature which constitutes the difference between this Gospel and the other three.

It has already been noted that in the first three Gospels the Lord Jesus is presented respectively as Israel's King, Jehovah's Servant, and the ideal Man; and that those incidents, words, and works are selected, in each Gospel, which specially accord with such presentation.

Thus they present the Lord on the side of His perfect humanity. It is this that links them together, and is the real reason for their being what is called "Synoptic", and for the marked difference between them, taken together, and the fourth Gospel.

It would have been a real marvel had there been perfect similarity between the selected words and works which characterize the first three Gospels and those of the fourth, where the presentation is on the side of His Deity. That would indeed have presented an insoluble problem.

The differences which have been noted are not due to any peculiarity of literary style, or of individual character, but are necessitated by the special presentation of the Lord which is the design of each Gospel.

Hence, in the Structure of the fourth Gospel (above), when compared with the other three, it will be noted that there is no Temptation in the Wilderness, and no Agony in the Garden. The reason for this is obvious, for both would have been entirely out of place, and out of harmony with the purpose of the Gospel as a whole.

For the same reason, while the Transfiguration is recorded in the first three Gospels, no mention is made of it in John, the reason being that it concerned the sufferings and the earthly glory of the Son of man (see Ap. 98. XVI and 149), while in John the presentation of the Son of God (Ap. 98. XV) is concerned with His heavenly and eternal glory.

The only incidents which John records in common with the first three Gospels are seven in number (Ap. 10), viz.:—

The Work of John the Baptist.
The last Supper.
The Anointing at Bethany.
The Passion, and
The Resurrection, and
Two Miracles: the Feeding of the 5,000 and
the Walking on the Sea.

In the other Gospels, miracles are so called, or "mighty works", but in John they are always called "signs" (see Ap. 176), because they are recorded not as to their facts or their effects, but as to their number and signification.

In John it is the Person of the Lord that is presented, rather than His offices; and His ministry is mainly in Jerusalem and Judæa rather than in Galilee.

Hence the Lord's visits to the Feasts find a special place (2. 13—3. 21; 5. 1; 7. 10; 10. 22; 11. 55, &c.); while His ministry in Galilee is constantly assumed, rather than described (6. 1; 7. 1; 10. 40).

These differences are due, not to the conditions of religious thought prevalent in John's day, but to the presentation of the Lord for all time.

NOTES ON JOHN'S GOSPEL.

The purpose of the Holy Spirit by John, in His presentation of the Messiah, is to say to us and to all, "Behold your God"; and His Deity is observed throughout this Gospel. See 1. 3, 14, 33, 34, 49; 3. 13, 14; 5. 23, 26; 6. 51, 62; 8. 58; 13. 33, &c. This is emphasized by the first and last references (1. 1 and 20. 28, 31).

The same purpose and design are seen in the presentation of the Lord as having the Divine attribute of *Omniscience*. This is not entirely absent in the other Gospels; but it pervades the fourth Gospel, and is manifested by much more frequent reference (see the Table below).

In this connexion the presentation of the Lord as God required special words which are not needed and are not found in the other Gospels. Attention is called to some 84 in the notes.

But of important words which are characteristic of this Gospel, and are found in other Gospels, the necessity of their more frequent use will be seen from the following examples which are set out below, and referred to in the notes. In most cases the number of the occurrences is more than in all the other three put together.

The characteristic words are :—	The number of their occurrences. MATT.	MARK	LUKE	JOHN
abide = *menō* [1]	3	2	7	41
believe = *pisteuō*. Ap. 150.	11	15	9	99
the Father = *ho Patēr* (used of God). Ap. 98. III	44	5	17	121
My Father. Used by the Lord [2]	14	—	4	35
finish = *teleioō*	—	—	2	19
flesh = *sarx*	5	4	2	13
glory = *doxa*	8	3	13	19
glorify = *doxazō*	4	1	9	23
Jews = *Ioudaioi* (including Mark 1. 5 and John 3. 22)	5	7	5	71
judge = *krinō*	6	—	6	19
know = *oida*. See Ap. 132. I. i	18	13	14	61
know = *ginōskō*. See Ap. 132. I. ii	20	13	28	56
lay down His life	—	—	—	6
light = *phōs*. See Ap. 130. 1	7	1	6	23
life = *zōē*. See Ap. 170	7	4	6	36
life (give life to) = *zōopoieō*	—	—	—	3
live = *zaō*. See Ap. 170	6	3	8	17
love (Noun) = *agapē*. See Ap. 135. II. 1	1	—	1	7
love (Verb) = *agapaō*. See Ap. 135. I. 1	7	5	13	37
love (Verb) = *phileō*. Ap. 135. I. 2	5	1	2	13
parable = *paroimia*	—	—	—	4
send = *pempō*. See Ap. 174. 4	4	1	10	33
sign = *sēmeion*	13	7	11	17
true (Adj.) = *alēthēs* (faithful). Ap. 175. 1	1	1	—	13
true (Adj.) = *alēthinos* (genuine). Ap. 175. 2	—	—	1	8
truth = *alētheia*	1	3	3	25
truly = *alēthōs*	3	2	3	10
Verily, verily = *Amēn, amēn* [3]	—	—	—	25
witness (bear) = *martureō* [4]	1	—	2	33
witness = *marturia*	—	3	1	14
works = pl. of *ergon*	5	2	2	27
world = *kosmos*. See Ap. 129. 1	9	3	3	79

It is not only the use of certain words that characterizes this special presentation of the Lord, but the absence of others is equally instructive. For, as in Matthew and Luke the Lord is constantly addressed as "Lord", but not often in Mark, where it would not be in keeping with His presentation as Jehovah's *servant*; so in John the Lord is never represented as praying [5] to the Father as in the other Gospels, but always as saying or speaking to Him. This is a special characteristic of the fourth Gospel, wonderfully in harmony with its great design. On the other hand, prayer is specially required on the part of a *king* (as in Matthew) in respect of his delegated authority (Matt. 14. 23; 26. 36, 39, 42, 44); also on the part of a *servant*, in respect of His assumed subjection (Mark 1. 35; 6. 46; 14. 32, 35, 39); and of an ideal *Man* in respect of his dependence upon God at all times (Luke 3. 21; 5. 16; 6. 12; 9. 18, 28, 29; 11. 1; 22. 41, 44, 46).

Thus, while in the first three Gospels the Lord is presented on the side of His humanity, as in prayer on eight occasions, not once is He so presented in John's Gospel.[5] And the reason is obvious. Moreover, He "lays down" His life: no one takes it from Him. This occ. only in John.[6]

[1] *Menō* is rendered (in John): "abide," 22 times; "dwell," 5; "remain," 5; "continue," 3; "endure," 1; "abide still," 1; "tarry," 3; "be present," once. In John's Epistles it occ. 26 times: 67 times in all.

[2] See John 2. 16; 5. 17, 43; 6. 32, 65; 8. 19, 19, 28, 38, 49, 54; 10. 17, 18, 25, 29, 29, 32, 37; 14. 2, 7, 12, 20, 21, 23, 28; 1. 1, 8, 10, 15, 23, 24; 16. 10; 20. 17, 17, 21. On the other hand, the expression "our Father" does not occur at all, and the reason is evident. Nor does the word *huios*=son, as used of believers as being the "sons of God"; but always *teknon*. Paul uses *huios* of believers (Rom. 8. 14, 19. Gal. 4. 7). But he uses *teknon* also (Rom. 8. 16, 17, 21. Phil. 2. 15. Eph. 5. 1). John uses *huios* almost exclusively for the Lord. The reason for this is evident also.

[3] In order to emphasize the greater authority with which the Lord spoke, as God, and as coming with double importance.

[4] This witness was borne *by the Father* (John 5. 32, 37; 8. 18); *by the Son* (8. 14; 18. 37); *by the Holy Spirit* (15. 26; 16. 13, 14); *by the written Word* (1. 45; 5. 39, 46); *by the works* (5. 17, 36; 10. 25; 14. 11; 15. 24); *by the Forerunner* (1. 7; 5. 33, 35); *by His disciples* (15. 27; 19. 35; 21. 24).

[5] True, the English word "pray" is used of the Lord in John 16. 26; 17. 9, 9, 15, 20; but the Greek word is different. It is *erōtaō* = to *ask* (Ap. 134. I. 3), and implies familiarity if not equality. It is not *proseuchomai* (Ap. 134. I. 2), as in the other Gospels. The same is true of *proseuchē*, prayer (Ap. 134. II. 2). [6] See note on 10. 11.

THE GOSPEL

ACCORDING TO

JOHN

A A^1 C^1 1 °IN the beginning °was °the Word, °and
°the Word °was °with °God, and °the
Word °was God.
2 °The same [1]was [1]in the beginning [1]with
[1]God.
3 °All things °were made °by Him; °and
°without Him °was °not any thing made that
°was made.
D^1 E^1 4 [1]In Him [1]was °life; and the life [1]was °the
light of °men.
F^1 5 And [4]the light °shineth [1]in °darkness; and
the darkness °comprehended °it °not.
B^1 G^1 6 °There was a [4]man °sent °from °God,
whose name *was* °John.
H^1 A.D. 26 7 [2]The same came °for a witness, °to bear
°witness °of [4]the Light, °that °all *men* °through
°him might °believe.
8 °He was [5]not °that Light, but °*was sent* [7]to
bear witness [7]of °that Light.

1. 1-28 (A, p. 1510). THE FORERUNNER.
(*Repeated Alternation and Introversion.*)

A | A^1 | C^1 | 1-3. God.
  D^1 | E^1 | 4. Life.
    F^1 | 5. Reception. } THE WORD.
  B^1 | G^1 | 6. Mission.
    H^1 | 7, 8. Witness. } JOHN BAPTIST.
A^2 | D^2 | E^2 | 9. Light.
    F^2 | 10-13. Reception.
  C^2 | 14. Man. } THE WORD.
  B^2 | H^2 | 15-. Witness.
    G^2 | -15. Mission. } JOHN BAPTIST.
A^3 | D^3 | E^3 | 16-. Fullness.
    F^3 | -16, 17. Reception.
  C^3 | 18. Revealer of the Father. } THE WORD.
  B^3 | G^3 | 19-. Mission.
    H^3 | -19-28. Record. } JOHN BAPTIST.

1 In the beginning. Gr. *en* (Ap. 104. viii) *archē*. Occ. *four* times in the N.T. (Cp. Gen. 1. 1). The context will always supply the dependent word (where it is not expressed). Here, and in *v.* 2, supply "[of the *aions*= ages"]; for the *Logos* then "was", and the *aions* were prepared by Him (Heb. 1. 2; 11. 3). In Acts 11. 15 supply "[of our ministry" (2. 4)]. In Phil. 4. 15 supply "[the proclamation of] the Gospel". For the combination of *archē*, with other prepositions, see notes on John 6. 64 ("*ex archēs*"); on John 8. 44 ("*ap' archēs*"); on Heb. 1. 10 ("*kat' archas*"). **was** = was [already pre-existent]. Creation is not mentioned till *v.* 3. "The Word had no beginning". See *v.* 3; 17. 5. 1 John 1. 1. Eph. 1. 4. Prov. 8. 23. Ps. 90. 2. Cp. 8. 58. Not the same "was" as in *v.* 14. **the Word.** Gr. *Logos*. As the spoken word reveals the invisible thought, so the Living Word reveals the invisible God. Cp. *v.* 18. **and.** Note the Fig. *Polysyndeton*. Ap. 6. **with.** Gr. *pros*. Ap. 104. xv. 3. Implying personal presence and relation. Cp. *v.* 18. **God.** With the Art. = the revealed God of the Bible. Ap. 98. I. i. 1. **the Word was God.** This is correct. The Art. designates "the Word" as the subject. The order of the words has to do only with the emphasis, which is thus placed on the predicate, while "the Word" is the subject. **was God.** Here "God" is without the Art., because it denotes the conception of God as Infinite, Eternal, Perfect, Almighty, &c. Contrast 4. 24.
2 The same = This [Word], or He. **3 All things.** Referring to the infinite detail of creation. **were made** = came into being. Not the same word as in *v.* 1. **by** = through. Gr. *dia*. Ap. 104. v. 1. As in Rom. 11. 36. Col. 1. 16. Heb. 1. 2. **and without, &c.** Note the Fig. *Pleonasm*. Ap. 6. **without** = apart from. **was** = came into being. Not the same word as in *v.* 1. **not any thing** = not even one thing. Gr. *oude*, compound of *ou*. Ap. 105. I. **was made** = hath come into being. **4 life.** Gr. *zōē*. Ap. 170. 1: i. e. the fountain of life. Hence 1 John 5. 11, 12, and Ps. 36. 9: manifested (1. 4); obtained (3. 16); possessed (4. 14); sustained (6. 35); ministered (7. 38); abounding (10. 10); resurrection (11. 24, 25). A characteristic word of this Gospel. See note on p. 1511. **the light.** Not a light. Cp. 8. 12. Gr. *phōs*. Ap. 130. 1. A characteristic word of this Gospel. See note on p. 1511. **men.** Gr. pl. of *anthrōpos*. Ap. 123. 1. **5 shineth.** Gr. *phainō*. Ap. 106. I. i. **darkness** = the darkness. Presupposing the Fall. Gen. 3. 19. **comprehended it.** This is direct from the Vulgate. The Gr. *katalambanō* is so rendered only here. It means, overcame or overpowered Him not. See 1 Thess. 5. 4 (overtake). Mark 9. 18. John 8. 3, 4 (take); 12. 35 (come upon hostilely). **it.** Referring grammatically to *phōs*, the light (neuter); but logically to the Word. Quoted by Tatian (A. D. 150-170), *Orat. ad Graecos*, xiii. Note the Fig. *Parechēsis* (Ap. 6) in the Aramaic (not in the Greek or English), "darkness comprehended". Aram. *k'bēl ḳabēl*. **not.** Gr. *ou*. Ap. 105. I. **6 There was** = There arose. Not the same word as in *v.* 1. **sent.** Cp. Mal. 3. 1. Gr. *apostellō* (Ap. 174. 1), whence we have our "Apostle" = one sent. John not only came, but was "sent". **from** = from beside. Gr. *para*. Ap. 104. xii. 1. Not "by", but from. Cp. 15. 26. **God.** No Art. Cp. *v.* -1. Ap. 98. I. i. 1. **John**: i.e. John the Baptist; the John of the narrative, not of the Gospel. Occ. twenty times, and is never distinguished by the title "Baptist", as in Matt., Mark, and Luke. **7 for a witness**: i.e. with a view to bearing witness; not merely to be a witness. That would be *martur* (*martus*, as in Acts 1. 8, 22, &c.). This is *marturia* = a bearing witness. Gr. *eis*. Ap. 104. vi. Not the same word as in *v.* 16. **to bear witness** = in order that (Gr. *hina*) he might bear witness. Gr. *martureō*, a characteristic word of this Gospel. See note on p. 1511. **witness.** Gr. *marturia*, a characteristic word of this Gospel. **of** = concerning. Gr. *peri*. Ap. 104. xiii. 1. **that** = in order that. Gr. *hina*. Often found in John. **all**: i. e. all, without distinction. **through.** Gr. *dia*. Ap. 104. v. 1. **him.** John the Baptist. Cp. 5. 33. Acts 10. 37; 13. 24. **believe.** See Ap. 150. I. 1. i. A characteristic word of this Gospel. See note on p. 1511. **8 He** = That one. Cp. 2. 21. **that Light** = the Light. Cp. 9. 5; 12. 35. **was sent.** Supply "came" from *v.* 7.

A[2] D[2] E[2] **9 °*That* [1]was the °true [4]Light, Which light-**
A. D. 26 **eth °every man that cometh °into the °world.**

F[2] **10 He was [1]in the [9]world, and the [9]world**
°was made [3]by Him, and the [9]world °knew
Him [5]not.
11 °He came °unto °His own, and °His own
°received Him [5]not.
12 But °as many as °received Him, to them
gave He °power to become °the sons of
[6]God, *even* to them that °believe °on °His
name:
13 °Which were °born, [5]not °of °blood, °nor
°of the °will of the °flesh, °nor of the °will of
°man, but of [6]God.

C[2] **14 °And [1]the Word °was made °flesh, and**
°dwelt °among us, °(and we °beheld His °glory,
°the glory °as of °the only begotten °of the
°Father,) °full of °grace and °truth.

B[2] H[2] **15 John [7]bare witness [7]of Him, and °cried,**
saying,

G[2] **"This °was He of Whom I spake, He That**
cometh °after me °is preferred before me: °for
He [1]was °before me."

A[3] D[3] E[3] **16 °And [13]of His °fulness**

F[3] **have °all we received, and °grace °for grace.**
17 [15]For the law was given [3]by °Moses, *but*
°grace and [14]truth came [3]by °Jesus Christ.

9 That, &c. Render: [He] was the true (or very) Light, that which, coming into the world, lighteneth every man (without distinction). We should connect this "coming" with "the Light" (with R.V.): because "coming into the world" is continually associated with the Lord. See 3. 19; 6. 14; 9. 39; 11. 27; 12. 46; 16. 28; 18. 37. Note esp. 3. 19 and 12. 46. Many lamps found in the tombs at Gezer (1 Kings 9. 15–17) have inscribed on them "The light of Messiah shines for all".

true = very. Gr. *alēthinos*. Ap. 175. 2. A characteristic word of this Gospel. See note on p. 1511.

every man: i. e. without distinction, as the sun shines on all (Matt. 5. 45, &c.). Gr. *panta anthrōpon*. Not collectively, but individually and personally. For centuries Israel only had this light, and Gentiles were the exception. Henceforth there was to be no distinction. Gentiles were to be blessed with Abraham's seed in the days of Messiah. Cp. Gen. 12. 3. Rom. 15. 8–12. **into.** Gr. *eis*. Ap. 104. vi.

world. Gr. *kosmos*. Ap. 129. 1. A characteristic word in this Gospel. See note on p. 1511.

10 was made = came into being.

knew. Gr. *ginōskō*. Ap. 132. I. ii. One of the characteristic words of this Gospel. See p. 1511.

11 He came. Denoting the definite historical fact.

unto. Gr. *eis*. Ap. 104. vi.

His own. Neut. pl.: i. e. His own things, or possessions. Supply *ktēmata* (possessions), as in Matt. 19. 22. Cp. Matt. 21. 33–41. What these "possessions" were must be supplied from Matt. 1. 1, viz. the land of Abraham, and the throne of David.

His own. Masc. pl.: i. e. His own People (Israel).

received = received (to themselves).

12 as many as: *v.* 9 is collective; *v.* 12 is individual.

received = accepted (from a giver). Not the same word as in *v.* 11. **power** = authority. Ap. 172. 5. **the sons** = children. Gr. pl. of *teknon*. Not "sons". In John the word *huios* = son, is mostly reserved for the Lord Himself. See note 2, p. 1511. In John *teknon* occ. only here, 8. 39, and 11. 52. Ap. 108. i. Paul uses both "children" and "sons," of believers, but John uses the former only. See note 2 on p. 1511. **believe** = [are] believing. Ap. 150. I. 1. v. (i). See note on *v.* 7. **on.** Gr. *eis*. Ap. 104. vi. **His name**: i. e. Himself. See note on Ps. 20. 1. **13 Which** = Who: i. e. those who believe on His name. But antecedent to any ancient MSS., Irenaeus (A. D. 178), Tertullian (A. D. 208), Augustine (A. D. 395), and other Fathers, read "Who was begotten" (Sing., not Pl.). The "*hos*" (= Who) agreeing with "*autou*" (His name. Gr. *onoma autou*, name of Him). Verse 14 goes on to speak of the incarnation of Him Who was not begotten by human generation. The Latin Codex *Veronensis* (before Jerome's Vulgate) reads, "*Qui . . . natus est*". Tertullian (*De carne Christi*, c. 19) says that "believers" could not be intended in this verse, "since all who believe are born of blood", &c. He ascribes the reading of the Received text to the artifice of the Valentinian Gnostics of the second and third cents.). See *Encyl. Brit.*, eleventh (Camb.) edn., vol. 27, pp. 852–7. **born** = begotten. See note on Matt. 1. 2, and Ap. 179. **of** = out of, or from. Gr. *ek*. Ap. 104. vii. Not the same word as in *vv.* 7, 8, 14, 15, 22, 44, 47. **blood.** It is pl. (bloods) for emphasis, acc. to Heb. idiom, as in 2 Sam. 16. 7, 8. Ps. 26. 9. **nor** = nor yet. Gr. *oude*. **will.** Gr. *thelēma*. Ap. 102. 2. **flesh.** A characteristic word of this Gospel. See p. 1511. **man.** Gr. *anēr*. Ap. 123. 2. **14 And, &c.** Continuing *v.* 13, and showing that *v.* 13 also relates to the Word. **was made** = became, as in *v.* 3. **flesh.** See note on *v.* 13. The new mode of His being. Put by Fig. *Synecdochē* (of the Part), Ap. 6, for His humanity. **dwelt** = tabernacled. Occ. only here, Rev. 7. 15; 12. 12; 13. 6; 21. 3. See Ap. 179. **among.** Gr. *en*. Ap. 104. viii. 2. **and we, &c.** For other similar parenthetical remarks characteristic of this Gospel, see *vv.* 38, 41, 42, 44; 2. 9; 4. 8, 9, 44, 45; 5. 2; 6. 10, 23; 7. 2, 39, 50; 9. 7; 11. 2; 19. 31; 21. 7, 8. **beheld.** Gr. *theaomai*. Ap. 133. I. 12. Not the same word as in *vv.* 29, 36, 42, 47. Cp. Luke 9. 32. 2 Pet. 1. 16. 1 John 1. 1; 4. 14. **glory.** The Shekinah. See Luke 9. 32. 2 Pet. 1. 17. Gr. *doxa*. One of the characteristic words of this Gospel. **the glory** = glory. No Art. Note the Fig. *Anadiplōsis*, Ap. 6. **as of** = exactly like. **the only begotten** = an only begotten [Son]. As applied to Christ it occ. only here, *v.* 18; 3. 16, 18. 1 John 4. 9. But it is used of an earthly relationship in Luke 7. 12; 8. 42; 9. 38. Heb. 11. 17. Sept. for "only One", Ps. 25. 16. See note there. **of** = from beside: i. e. (sent) from beside. Gr. *para*. Ap. 104. xii. 1. Not the same word as in *vv.* 13, 15, 16, 22, 34, 35, 40, 44, 47. **Father.** See Ap. 98. III. A characteristic word of this Gospel. Occ. 121 times. **full** = abounding in. **grace and truth.** A Hebraism for the sum of Divine revelation. Heb. *chesed ve'emeth.* See Gen. 24. 27; 32. 10. Ex. 34. 6. Ps. 40. 10, 11; 61. 7. **truth.** A characteristic word of this Gospel. **15 cried** = hath cried aloud. **was.** As in *v.* 1. **after me.** In the order of ministry. **is preferred before me** = had being before me (as to time). **for** = because. **before me** = first: i. e. (already) before me. **16 And.** The texts read "For", but not the Syr. **fulness.** Gr. *plērōma*. **all we.** The Evangelist speaks here, not the Baptist. **grace for grace** = grace in place of grace; new grace, continuous, and unintermitted. Ever fresh grace according to the need. **for** = over against. Gr. *anti*. Ap. 104. ii. **17 Moses.** The first of 13 occ. in John (1. 17, 45; 3. 14; 5. 45, 46; 6. 32; 7. 19, 22, 22, 23; 8. 5; 9. 28, 29). **grace and truth.** In the days of Moses there was grace (Ex. 34. 6, 7), and the law itself was an exhibition of truth; but when Jesus Christ came, He was Himself the Truth, i. e. the very personification of truth (14. 6), and His life and death were the supreme manifestation of grace. **Jesus Christ.** See Ap. 98. XI.

C[3] 18 °No man °hath seen [6]God at any time; °the
A.D. 26 only begotten Son, °Which is °in the °bosom
[14]of the Father, °He °hath declared *Him.*
B[3] G[3] 19 And this is the °record of John,
H[3] J when °the Jews °sent priests and Levites °from
Jerusalem to °ask him, "Who art thou?"
20 And he confessed, °and °denied [5]not; °but
confessed, "I am [5]not °the Christ."
21 And they [19]asked him, °"What then? Art
thou °Elias?" And he saith, "I am [5]not."
"Art thou °that prophet?" And he answered,
°"No."
22 Then said they unto him, "Who art thou?
[7]that we may give an answer to them that °sent
us. What sayest thou [7]of thyself?"
23 He said, °"I *am* **the voice of one crying**
[1]**in the wilderness, 'Make straight the way of**
°**the LORD,'** as said the prophet °Esaias."
K 24 And they which °were [6]sent were [13]of the
°Pharisees.
J 25 And they [19]asked him, and said unto him,
"Why °baptizest thou then, °if thou be [5]not
[21]that Christ, nor [21]Elias, neither [21]that prophet?"
26 John answered them, saying, "I °baptize
with water: but there standeth One among
you, Whom ye °know [5]not;
27 He it is, Who coming [15]after me [15]is preferred before me, °Whose °shoe's °latchet I
am [5]not worthy to unloose."
K 28 These things were done [1]in °Bethabara
beyond Jordan, where John was [25]baptizing.
B L[1] 29 The next day John °seeth °Jesus coming
°unto him, and saith, °"Behold °the °Lamb
°of [1]God, Which °taketh away the °sin of the
[9]world.
30 This is He °of Whom °I said, After me
cometh a [13]Man Which is preferred before me:
[15]for He was before me.
M a 31 And I [26]knew Him [5]not:
b but [7]that He should be °made manifest to
Israel,
c °therefore am I come [26]baptizing with water."

18 No man: i.e. no human eye. Gr. *oudeis.* Compound of *ou.* Ap. 105. I.
hath seen. Gr. *horaō.* Ap. 133. 8.
the only begotten Son. Lm. Tr. WH. Rm., with the Syr., read "God (i.e. Christ) only begotten". The readings vary between ΥC and ΘC.
Which is = He Who is: like "was" in *v.* 1.
in = into. Gr. *eis.* Ap. 104. vi. This expresses a continued relationship.
bosom. Fig. *Anthropopatheia.* Ap. 6. Cp. 13. 23; 21. 20. **He** = That One.
hath declared = revealed. Gr. *exēgeomai* = to lead the way, make known by expounding. Hence Eng. "exegesis". Only here, Luke 24. 35. Acts 10. 8; 15. 12, 14; 21. 19.

1. -19-28 (H[3], p. 1512). JOHN'S RECORD. (*Alternation.*)

H[3] | J | -19-23. Inquiries and Answers. "Who?"
K | 24. Evangelist's parenthesis.
J | 25-27. Inquiries and Answers. "Why?"
K | 28. Evangelist's parenthesis.

19 record = witness. Gr. *marturia.* See note on *v.* 7.
the Jews. A characteristic expression of this Gospel see note on p. 1511), pointing to the consequences of their rejection of Messiah, when they would be *Lo Ammi* (= not My People): no longer regarded as "Israel", but as "Jews", the name given them by Gentiles.
sent = deputed. Ap. 174. 1.
from = out of. Gr. *ek.* Ap. 104. vii.
ask. Gr. *erōtaō.* Ap. 134. 3.
20 and denied not. Fig. *Pleonasm* (Ap. 6), for emphasis.
denied. Gr. *arneomai.* In John only here, and 18. 25, 27.
but = and. **the Christ** = the Messiah. Ap. 98. IX.
21 What then? = What then [are we to say]?
Elias = Elijah. Referring to Mal. 4. 5.
that prophet = the prophet. Referring to Deut. 18. 18. Cp. Acts 3. 22, 23.
No. Gr. *ou.* Ap. 105. I.
22 sent. Gr. *pempō.* See Ap. 174. 4. A characteristic word in this Gospel. See note on p. 1511
23 I am, &c. Quoting from Isa. 40. 3. See Ap. 107.
the = a. **the LORD.** Ap. 98. VI. i. a. 1. B. a.
Esaias = Isaiah. The first of four occ. of his name in John; and this from the latter part of Isaiah, which modern critics say Isaiah did not write. But see the Structure, p. 930, and Ap. 79. I.
24 were = had been. **Pharisees.** Ap. 120. II.
25 baptizest . . . ? See Ap. 115. I. i. They expected baptism, from Ezek. 36. 25. **if.** Ap. 118. 2. a.
26 baptize with. Ap. 115. I. iii. 1. a.
know. Gr. *oida.* Ap. 132. I. i. A characteristic word of this Gospel. See p. 1511. **27 Whose shoe's latchet** = the thong of whose sandal. **latchet** = a little lace, or thong. O.Fr. *lacet,* a lace; dim. of *lags,* from Lat. *laqueus.* **28 Bethabara.** All the texts read *Bethania* (with the Syr.). Identified by Conder and Wilson with *Makht-Ababarah,* near Jericho. Not uncommon then or now for two or more places to have the same name. See on 11. 3.

1. 29-34 (**B**, p. 1510). BAPTISM: WITH WATER. (*Repeated and Extended Alternations.*)

B | L[1] | 29, 30. John's witness. "The Lamb of God".
M | a | 31-. "I knew Him not".
b | -31-. John's baptism. Purpose stated.
c | -31. Nature of it. "Water".
L[2] | 32. John's witness. "The Spirit".
M | *a* | 33-. "I knew Him not".
b | -33-. Christ's baptism. Sign given.
c | -33. Nature of it. "Spirit".
L[3] | 34. John's witness. "The Son of God".

29 seeth. Gr. *blepō.* Ap. 133. I. 5. **Jesus.** Ap. 98. X. **unto.** Gr. *pros.* Ap. 104. xv. 3. **Behold.** Gr. *ide.* Ap 133. I. 3. Sing Addressed to the whole company. **the Lamb of God.** Referring to "the Lamb" spoken of in Isa. 53. 7, with possible reference to the approaching Passover. This was the title of our Lord for that dispensation. **Lamb.** Gr. *amnos.* Occurs only here, *v.* 36; Acts 8 32; 1 Pet. 1. 19. See 21. 15, where it is *arnion,* which occurs in Revelation twenty-eight times of the Lord, once of the false prophet (13. 11). **of** = provided by. See Gen. 22. 8 and Ap. 17. 2. **taketh away** = taketh [on Himself to bear] away. Gr. *airō.* Cp. Matt. 4. 6 (first occ.). **sin.** Sing. Ap. 128. I. ii. 1. **30 of.** All the texts read *huper* (Ap. 104. xvii. 1), instead of *peri* (xiii. 1). **I said.** See *vv.* 15, 27. **31 made manifest.** Gr. *phaneroō.* Ap. 106. I. v. **therefore** = on account of this. Gr. *dia* (Ap. 104. v. 1). The purpose should be well noted. Cp. Rom. 15. 8.

L[2] **32** And John °bare record, saying, "I °saw
A.D. 26 °the Spirit descending [19]from °heaven °like
a dove, and it °abode °upon Him.
M a **33** And I [26]knew Him [5]not:
b but He That [22]sent me to [26]baptize with
water, the same said unto me, [32]'Upon whom
thou shalt °see [32]the Spirit descending, and
°remaining °on Him,
c the same is He Which [26]baptizeth with °the
Holy Ghost.'
L[3] **34** And °I saw, and °bare record that This
is °the Son [13]of God."
N P[1] Q d[1] **35** Again the next day after John °stood, and
°two [13]of his disciples;
36 And °looking upon [29]Jesus as He °walked,
he saith, [29]"Behold [29]the Lamb of [1]God!"
37 And the two disciples heard him °speak,
and they followed [29]Jesus.
38 Then [17]Jesus °turned, and [32]saw them following, and saith unto them, "What seek
ye?" They said unto Him, °"Rabbi," (which
is to say, being °interpreted, °Master,) "where
°dwellest Thou?"
39 He saith unto them, "Come and °see."
They came and [33]saw where He [38]dwelt, and
abode °with Him that day: for it was about
°the tenth hour.
e[1] **40** One [13]of the [35]two which °heard John
speak, and followed Him, was °Andrew, °Simon
Peter's brother.
d[2] **41** °He °first findeth his own brother Simon,
and saith unto him, "We have found °the
Messias," (which is, being [38]interpreted, the
Christ.
42 And he °brought him °to [29]Jesus. And
when [29]Jesus [36]beheld him, He said, "Thou art
Simon the son of °Jona:
R thou shalt be called °Cephas," (which is by
[38]interpretation, °A stone.)
Q d[3] **43** °The day following [29]Jesus °would go
forth [9]into °Galilee, and findeth °Philip, and
saith unto him, "Follow Me."
e[2] **44** (Now [43]Philip was °of Bethsaida, °the city
of [40]Andrew and Peter.)
d[4] **45** [43]Philip findeth °Nathanael, and saith unto
him, "We have found Him, of Whom [17]Moses
[1]in the °Law, and the Prophets, °did write, [29]Je-
sus of °Nazareth, °the son of Joseph."
46 And [45]Nathanael said unto him, °"Can
there any good thing come °out of [45]Naza-
reth?" [43]Philip saith unto him, "Come and
[33]see."

32 bare record=bare witness. Cp. *v.* 19, and see note on 1. 7.
saw=have beheld. Gr. *theaomai*. Ap. 133. I. 12.
the Spirit. See Ap. 101. II. 3.
heaven. Sing., without Art. See note on Matt. 6. 9, 10. **like**=as it were.
abode. One of the characteristic words of John's Gospel and Epistles. See list and note 1 on page 1511.
upon. Gr. *epi*. Ap. 104. ix. 3.
33 see. Gr. *eidon*. Ap. 133. I. 1.
remaining. Gr. *menō*, *v.* 32.
on=upon, as in *v.* 32.
the Holy Ghost=holy spirit. Gr. *pneuma hagion*. No articles. See Ap. 101. II. 14.
34 I saw=I have seen. Gr. *horaō*. Ap. 133. I. 8.
bare record=have borne witness.
the Son of God. Ap. 98. XV.

1. 35—4. 54 (**D**, p. 1510). THE FIRST PERIOD OF THE LORD'S MINISTRY. SUBJECT: THE PROCLAMATION OF THE KINGDOM. (*Introversion*.)

D | N | 1. 35—2. 12. Galilee.
O | 2. 13—3. 21. Jerusalem.
O | 3. 22—4. 3-. Judea.
N | 4. -3-54. Samaria and Galilee.

1. 35—2. 12 (N, above). GALILEE. (*Division*.)

N | P[1] | 1. 35-51. The first Call. Manifestation of the Lord's grace.
P[2] | 2. 1-12. The first Sign. Manifestation of the Lord's glory.

1. 35-51 (P[1], above). THE FIRST CALL. MANIFESTATION OF THE LORD'S GRACE. (*Alternations*.)

P[1] | Q | d[1] | 35-39. Call of Andrew. "The next day".
e[1] | 40. Parenthetic explanation.
d[2] | 41, 42-. Call of Simon.
R | -42. Characteristic.
Q | d[3] | 43. Call of Philip. "The next day".
e[2] | 44. Parenthetic explanation.
d[4] | 45, 46. Call of Nathanael.
R | 47-51. Characteristic.

35 stood=was standing.
two. One being Andrew (*v.* 40), the other probably John (the Evangelist), as he never mentions himself.
36 looking upon=having fixed his gaze on. Gr. *emblepō*. Ap. 133. I. 7. Occurs in John only here, and *v.* 42.
walked=was walking about.
37 speak=speaking. Gr. *laleō*.
38 turned, and=having turned.
Rabbi. Ap. 98. XIV. vii.
interpreted. Gr. *hermēneuō*. Occ. only here, *v.* 42; 9. 7. Heb. 7. 2. **Master**=Teacher. Ap. 98. XIV. v. 1.
dwellest=abidest. Gr. *menō*, as in *v.* 32.
39 see. Gr. *eidon*. Ap. 133. I. 1, but all the texts read "Ye shall see". Gr. *horaō*. Ap. 133. I. 8 (a).
with. Gr. *para*. Ap. 104. xii. 2.
the tenth hour: i. e. of the day, according to Hebrew reckoning. The context must decide whether of the night or day. Here, therefore, 4 p.m. (cp. the other hours in John: here; 4. 6, 52; 11. 9; 19. 14. See Ap. 165).

40 heard John speak=heard (this) from (Gr. *para*. Ap. 104. xii. 1) John. **Andrew, Simon**. See Ap. 141. **41 He**=This one. **first findeth**. Andrew is the first to find his brother, and afterwards John finds his. The Latin Version (Cod. Vercellensis, Cent. 4) must have read Gr. *prōi*=early [in the morning]; not *prōtos*, as in the Rec. text. Not *primum*=first, as in the Vulgate. **the Messias**=the Messiah. Ap. 98. VIII. Occurs only here, and 4. 25. **42 brought**=led. Gr. *agō*. **to**. Gr. *pros*. Ap. 104. xv. 3. **Jona**. Aramaic for John. Ap. 94. III. 3. **Cephas**. Aramaic. Occurs only in 1 Cor. 1. 12; 3. 22; 9. 5; 15. 5. Gal. 2. 9. **A stone**=Peter=Gr. *Petros*. See note on Matt. 16. 18. **43 The day following**. The last of these four days of John's ministry. (Cp. *vv.* 19, 29, 35, 43.) **would**=desired to. Gr. *thelō*. Ap. 102. 1. **Galilee**. See Ap. 169. **Philip**. Ap. 141. **44 of**=from. Gr. *apo*. Ap. 104. iv. **the city**. Gr. out of (Gr. *ek*. Ap. 104. vii) the city. **45 Nathanael**=the gift of God. Heb. *N^ethan^e'el*; as in Num. 1. 8. 1 Chron. 2. 14. Generally identified with Bartholomew (Aramaic. Ap. 94. III. 3). **Law . . . Prophets**. See notes on Luke 24. 44. **did write**=wrote. See Ap. 47. **Nazareth**. Ap. 169. **the son of Joseph**. The words are Philip's, and expressed the popular belief. Cp. Ap. 99. **46 Can there any, &c.** Fig. *Parœmia*. **out of**. Gr. *ek*. Ap. 104. vii.

R A.D. 26 47 [29]Jesus [33]saw [45]Nathanael coming [42]to Him, and saith [7]of him, [29]"Behold an °Israelite °indeed, [1]in whom is [21]no guile!"

48 [45]Nathanael saith unto Him, "Whence [10]knowest Thou me?" [29]Jesus °answered and said unto him, °"Before that [43]Philip called thee, when thou wast °under the fig tree, I [33]saw thee."

49 [45]Nathanael [48]answered and saith unto Him, [38]"Rabbi, Thou art [34]the Son of God; Thou art °the King of Israel."

50 [29]Jesus [48]answered and said unto him, "Because I said unto thee, I [33]saw thee °under the fig tree, °believest thou? thou shalt °see greater things than these."

51 And He saith unto him, °"Verily, verily, I say unto you, °Hereafter ye shall [50]see °heaven open, and the angels of [1]God ascending and descending [32]upon °the Son of man."

P² S **2** And °the third day there °was a °marriage °in °Cana of Galilee; and the mother of °Jesus °was there:

2 And both [1]Jesus was °called and His °disciples, °to the [1]marriage.

T f 3 And °when they wanted °wine, °the mother of [1]Jesus saith °unto Him, "They have no °wine."

4 [1]Jesus saith unto her, °"Woman, °what have I to do with thee? °Mine hour is not yet come."

g 5 His mother saith unto the °servants, °"Whatsoever He saith unto you, do *it*."

U 6 And there were set there °six °waterpots of stone, °after the manner of the purifying of °the Jews, containing two or three °firkins apiece.

T g 7 [1]Jesus saith unto them, °"Fill the [6]waterpots °with water." And they filled them up to the brim.

8 And He saith unto them, °"Draw out now, and bear unto the °governor of the feast." And they bare *it*.

f 9 When the °ruler of the feast had tasted the water that °was made [3]wine, and °knew °not whence it was: °(but the [5]servants which °drew the water °knew;) the [8]governor of the feast called the bridegroom,

10 And saith unto him, °"Every °man at the beginning doth set forth good [3]wine; and when men have °well drunk, then that which is °worse: *but* thou hast kept the good wine until now."

47 Israelite: i.e. not a "Jacob". See notes on Gen. 32. 28.

indeed = truly. Gr. *alēthōs*. Adv. of No. 1, Ap. 175.

48 answered and said. Heb. idiom. See Deut. 1. 41. Ap. 122. 3. **Before.** Gr. *pro*. Ap. 104. xiv.

under. Gr. *hupo*. Ap. 104. xviii. 2.

49 the King of Israel. Thus proclaiming the Person of the Lord, in connexion with the Kingdom.

50 under = down beneath. Not the same word as in *v.* 48.

believest. Ap. 150. I. 1. i. See 1. 7.

see. Ap. 133. I. 8 (a).

51 Verily, verily. See note on Matt. 5. 18. In John always double. Fig. *Epizeuxis* (Ap. 6), for emphasis, twenty-five times (here, 3. 3, 5, 11; 5. 19, 24, 25; 6. 26, 32, 47, 53; 8. 34, 51, 58; 10. 1, 7; 12. 24; 13. 16, 20, 21, 38; 14. 12; 16. 20, 23; 21. 18). See note 3 on page 1511.

Hereafter = From henceforth. But omitted by all the texts (not the Syr.). It was conditional on the repentance of the nation, and will yet be seen.

heaven = the heaven. Sing., with Art. See note on Matt. 6. 9, 10.

the Son of man. The first occ. in John. Ap. 98. XVI and 99.

2. 1–12 (P², p. 1515). **THE FIRST SIGN. MANIFESTATION OF THE LORD'S GLORY.**
(*Introversions.*)

P² | S | 1, 2. The Sign. Occasion.
  T | f | 3, 4. Need. Manifested.
    g | 5. Servants. Mary's direction.
      U | 6. The vessels.
  T | g | 7, 8. Servants. The Lord's command.
    f | 9, 10. Need. Supplied.
S | 11, 12. The Sign. Explanation.

1 the third day. Of this first week: i.e. the third day after the last event (1. 43–51), i.e. the seventh day. Cp. the 1st (1. 19–28); 2nd (29–34); 3rd (1. 35–42); 4th (1. 43–51). In Genesis, after six days there comes a marriage.

was = took place.

marriage = marriage feast, as in Matt. 22. 2, &c. Sometimes lasting a week.

in. Gr. *en*. Ap. 104. viii.

Cana of Galilee. Now *Kefr Kenna*, on the road from Nazareth to Tiberias. So called to distinguish it from Cana in Asher.

Jesus. Ap. 98. X.

was there: i.e. was already there when the Lord arrived.

2 called = invited.

disciples. Probably six in number: viz. Andrew, Simon, Philip, Nathanael (1. 40–51), with James and John (Mark 1. 16–20). See Ap. 141.

to. Gr. *eis*. Ap. 104. vi.

3 when, &c. = when wine failed. Quite a serious calamity.

wine. Gr. *oinos*. The only word for wine in the N.T. Sept. for Heb. *yayin*. Ap. 27. I. (Also for *Tīrōsh* (Ap. 27. II) in Gen. 27. 28. Judg. 9. 13. Joel 1. 10).

the mother of Jesus. Never called Mary in this Gospel. She became John's "mother" (19. 26, 27).

unto. Gr. *pros*. Ap. 104. xv. 3.

4 Woman. Quite a respectful form of address. Not as in Eng. In Greek authors = Madam. **what, &c.** A Hebraism (2 Sam. 16. 10). **Mine hour, &c.** Marking a crisis, which is noted in *v.* 11. A characteristic expression in this Gospel. See note on 7. 6. **5 servants** = free servants. Gr. *diakonos*. Cp. Matt. 20. 26. Mark 9. 35. **Whatsoever, &c.** Mary's last-recorded words. **6 six waterpots.** See Ap. 176. **waterpots** = jars. Occ. only here, *v.* 7, and 4. 28. **after the manner, &c.** Proportioned to the number of the guests. **after** = according to. Gr. *kata*. Ap. 104. x. 2. **the Jews.** See note on 1. 19. **firkins.** See Ap. 51. III. 3. (6). **7 Fill.** The first sign. Note "Cast", 21. 6, and see the Structure in Ap. 176. **with.** Gr. idiom. See note [1], on Ap. 101. II. 14. **8 Draw out.** Gr. *antleō*. Occ. only here, *v.* 9; 4. 7, 15. **governor, &c.** Occ. only here, and *v.* 9. See Gen. 24. 13, 20. **9 ruler, &c.** Same word as "governor", &c. **was made** = had become. **knew.** Gr. *oida*. Ap. 132. I. i. See note on 1. 26. Not the same word as in *vv.* 24, 25. **not.** Gr. *ou*. Ap. 105. I. **but, &c.** See note on "and we", &c., 1. 14. **drew** = had drawn. **10 Every man, &c.** This is man's way: i.e. to give the good thing first, and the worse thing after. God's way is always the opposite. See note on Ex. 15. 2. **man.** Gr. *anthrōpos*. Ap. 123. 1. **well drunk** = drunk freely. **worse** = inferior.

S 11 This °beginning of °miracles did [1]Jesus
A.D. 26 [1]in [1]Cana of Galilee, and °manifested forth
°His glory; and His °disciples °believed on
Him.
12 °After this He went °down [2]to °Capernaum,
He, °and His mother, and His brethren, °and
His disciples: °and they °continued there [9]not
many days.

O V 13 And °the Jews' °passover was at hand,
and [1]Jesus °went up [2]to Jerusalem,

W h 14 And found [1]in the °temple °those that sold
oxen [12]and sheep and doves, and the °changers
of money sitting:
15 And when He had °made a scourge °of
°small cords, He °drove °them all out °of the
[14]temple, °and the sheep, and the oxen; and
poured out the °changers' °money, and overthrew the tables;
16 And said unto them that sold doves, "Take
these things hence; make °not °My °Father's
house an house of °merchandise."

i 17 And His disciples remembered that °it was
written, °"**The zeal °of Thine house hath eaten
me up.**"

h 18 Then °answered the Jews and said unto
Him, "What °sign shewest Thou unto us,
°seeing that Thou doest these things?"
19 [1]Jesus [18]answered and said unto them,
°"Destroy °this °Temple, and [1]in three days
I will °raise it up."
20 Then said the Jews, °"Forty and six years
was this [19]Temple in building, and wilt Thou
°rear it up [1]in three days?"
21 °But °He °spake °of the [19]Temple °of His
body.

i 22 When therefore He was [19]risen °from °the
dead, His disciples °remembered that He had
°said this unto them; and they °believed °the
scripture, and the °word which [1]Jesus had
°said.

V 23 °Now when He was [1]in Jerusalem °at the
[13]passover, [1]in the feast *day*, many °believed

11 beginning, &c. Our attention is thus called to the order.
miracles = the signs. A characteristic word in this Gospel. See p. 1511, and Ap. 176. 3.
manifested forth. See Ap. 106. I. v. Cp. 21. 1, 14.
His glory. This is the key to the signification of the eight signs of this Gospel (Ap. 176). See note on 1. 14.
disciples believed, &c. Cp. *vv.* 17, 22. Four hundred and fifty years since the Jews had seen a miracle. The last was in Dan. 6.
believed on. See Ap. 150. I. 1. v (i). See note on 1. 7.
12 After. Gr. *meta.* Ap. 104. xi. 2.
down. True geographically. Cp. "up", *v.* 13.
Capernaum. Now *Tell Hûm.*
and. Note the Fig. *Polysyndeton.* Ap. 6.
continued. Gr. *menō.* See note on 1. 32, and p. 1511.

2. 13—3. 21 (O, p. 1515). JERUSALEM. (*Alternation*).

O | V | 2. 13. Passover at hand.
  W | 2. 14–22. Event. Cleansing of the Temple.
 V | 2. 23–25. Passover arrived.
  W | 3. 1–21. Event. Colloquy with Nicodemus.

13. the Jews' passover. After the revival under Ezra and Nehemiah corruption proceeded apace (see notes on p. 1296), and the Lord found the nation as described in Malachi. Hence, what were once "the feasts of Jehovah" are spoken of as what they had then become, "feasts of the Jews" (5. 1; 6. 4; 7. 2; 11. 55; 19. 42). See note on 1. 19.
passover. Gr. *pascha*, Aramaic. See Ap. 94. III, p. 135.
went up. Gr. *anabainō*, same word as "ascending", 1. 51. Cp. "down", *v.* 12.

2. 14-22 (W, above). EVENT. CLEANSING OF THE TEMPLE. (*Alternation.*)

W | h | 14–16. Driving out. Action.
 i | 17. Disciples. Remembrance of Scripture.
 h | 18–21. Driving out. Questioned.
 i | 22. Disciples. Remembrance of Scripture.

14 temple. Gr. *hieron.* See note on Matt. 23. 16.
those. Denoting a class.
changers of money. Gr. pl. of *kermatistēs.* Occ. only here.
15 made a scourge = plaited a whip. Occ. only here.
of = from. Gr. *ek.* Ap. 104. vii. Not the same word as in *vv.* 21, 25.
small cords = rush-ropes. Gr. *schoinion.* Only here and in Acts 27. 32.
drove . . out = cast out. Not the same event as in Matt. 21. 12, 13. Mark 11. 15, 16. Luke 19. 45, 46.
them all = all: i. e. the animals, both the sheep and the oxen and the sellers. **and** = both. **changers.** Gr. *kollubistēs* (from *kollubos*, a small coin). Occ. only here. **money** = small coin. Gr. pl. of *kerma.* Occ. only here. **16 not.** Gr. *mē.* Ap. 105. II. Not the same word as in *vv.* 9, 12, 24, 25. **My Father's house.** This was at the beginning of His ministry. At the end He called it "your house" (Matt. 23. 38). **My Father's.** A characteristic expression in this gospel. Occ. thirty-five times. See p. 1511. **merchandise.** Gr. *emporion* = market-place (not *emporia*, which = the traffic itself). On the later occasion the words naturally differ. Cp. Matt. 22. 5. **17 it was written** = it is (or standeth) written. Cp. 6. 31, 45; 8. 17; 10. 34; 12. 14. **The zeal, &c.** Quoted from Ps. 69. 9. See the rest of the verse in Rom. 15. 3, and other parts of the Ps. in 15. 25 (*v.* 4); 19. 28 (*v.* 21). Rom. 11. 9, 10 (*v.* 22). Acts 1. 20 (*v.* 25). See Ap. 107. **of.** Gen. of Relation. Ap. 17. 5. Cp. 3. 3. **18 answered . . . said.** See note on Deut. 1. 41 and Ap. 122. 3. **sign.** Same as "miracle", *v.* 11. **seeing, &c.** Supply the *Ellipsis* (Ap. 6) = "What sign shewest thou to us [that Thou art the Messiah], seeing that Thou doest these things?" **19 Destroy, &c.** The Lord's enemies remembered His words, and perverted them: saying, "I will destroy", &c. See Matt. 26. 61; Mark 14. 58. **this.** See on Matt. 16. 18. **Temple.** Gr. *naos.* See note on Matt. 23. 16. **raise . . up.** Gr. *egeirō.* Ap. 178. 4. **20 Forty and six years.** Begun B. C. 20. See Josephus, *Wars*, I. xxi. 1. **rear** = raise. **21 But He spake, &c.** Fig. *Epitrechon* (Ap. 6). For other examples, see 7. 39; 12. 33; 21. 19. **He.** Gr. *ekeinos.* Emph. in contrast with "thou" in *v.* 20. See note on 1. 18. **spake** = was speaking. Gr. *legō.* **of** = concerning. Gr. *peri.* Ap. 104. xiii. 1. **of** = that is to say. Gen. of Apposition. Ap. 17. 4. **22 from** = out from. Gr. *ek.* Ap. 104. vii. **the dead.** No Article = dead people. See note on Matt. 17. 9, and Ap. 139. 3. **remembered.** Cp *v.* 17. They remembered it after His resurrection, and believed it. Contrast His enemies. See note on *v.* 19. **said** = spake. Gr. *legō*, as in *v.* 21. **believed.** Ap. 150. I. 1. ii. See note on 1. 7. **the scripture**: i. e. that the scripture was true. Here, probably, Ps. 16. 10. The word *graphē* occ. twelve times in John: here; 5. 39; 7. 38, 42; 10. 35; 13. 18; 17. 12; 19. 24, 28, 36, 37; 20. 9. **word.** Gr. *logos.* See on Mark 9. 32. **said.** Gr. *epō.* **23 Now when, &c.** Note the Fig. *Pleonasm* (Ap. 6) in the triple definitions (for emph.). **at** = in. Gr. *en.* Ap. 104. viii. **believed in.** See Ap. 150. I. 1. v (i). Same as *v.* 11, denoting a definite act.

A.D. 26 °in °His name, °when they saw the [11]miracles
which He °did.
24 °But [1]Jesus did [9]not °commit Himself
unto them, °because °He °knew all *men*,
25 And needed [9]not that any should °testify
[21]of [10]man: for He [24]knew °what was [1]in [10]man.

W X[1] 3 °There was °a °man °of the °Pharisees,
named °Nicodemus, a °ruler of the Jews:
2 The same came °to °Jesus °by night, and
said unto Him, °"Rabbi, we °know that Thou
art a °teacher °come °from °God: for °no man
can do these °miracles that Thou °doest, °except
°God be °with him."

Y[1] 3 [2]Jesus °answered and said unto him,
°"Verily, verily, I say unto thee, [2]Except °a
man be °born °again, he °cannot °see °the
kingdom of [2]God."

X[2] 4 [1]Nicodemus saith °unto Him, °"How can
a [1]man °be born when he is °old? can he enter
the second time °into his mother's womb, and
°be born?"

Y[2] j 5 [2]Jesus answered, [3]"Verily, verily, I say
unto thee, [2]Except [3]a man be [3]born °of water
and *of* the spirit, he [3]cannot °enter [4]into [3]the
kingdom of [2]God.

k 6 °That which is [3]born [1]of the °flesh is flesh;
and that which is [3]born [1]of °the Spirit °is spirit.

j 7 Marvel °not that I said unto thee, Ye must
be [3]born [3]again.

k 8 °The wind °bloweth where °it listeth, and
thou hearest °the sound thereof, but °canst
°not °tell whence it cometh, and whither it
goeth: so is every one that °is born [5]of °the
Spirit."

X[3] 9 [1]Nicodemus [3]answered and said unto Him,
[4]"How can °these things °be?"

in. Gr. *eis*. Ap. 104. vi.
His name = Him (emph.). See note on Ps. 20. 1.
when they saw = beholding. Gr. *theōreō*. Ap. 133. I. 11. did = was doing.

24 But Jesus: i. e. But Jesus [for His part].
commit = trust. Same word as "believed" in *v.* 23, but not the same tense. Here it denotes a continual action or habit. Gr. *pisteuō*. Ap. 150. I. 1. iv. See note on 1. 7.
because. Gr. *dia*. Ap. 104. v. 2. **He** = He Himself.
knew. Gr. *ginōskō*. Ap. 132. I. ii. See note on 1. 10.

25 testify = bear witness. See note on 1. 7.
what was in man. This attribute elsewhere attributed only to Jehovah (Jer. 17. 10; 20. 12). Here this knowledge was *universal* ("all", *v.* 24), and *individual* ("man").

3. 1-21 (*W*, p. 1517). EVENT. COLLOQUY WITH NICODEMUS. (*Repeated Alternation.*)

W | X[1] | 1, 2. Nicodemus. Admission.
  Y[1] | 3. The Lord. Answer. Stated.
 X[2] | 4. Nicodemus. Question. "How?"
  Y[2] | 5-8. The Lord. Answer. Repeated.
 X[3] | 9. Nicodemus. Question. "How?".
  Y[3] | 10-21. The Lord. Answer. Confirmed.

1 There was = Now there was.
a man. With special reference to the last word of ch. 2. **man.** Gr. *anthrōpos*. Ap. 123. 1.
of. Gr. *ek*. Ap. 104. vii. **Pharisees.** Ap. 120. 2.
Nicodemus. Mentioned three times (here, 1, 4, 9; 7. 50; 19. 39). Rabbinical tradition makes him one of the three richest men in Jerusalem. See Lightfoot, vol. xii, p. 252.
ruler. A member of the Sanhedrin, or National Council. See on Matt. 5. 22.

2 to. Gr. *pros*. Ap. 104. xv. 3.
Jesus. Ap. 98. X. **by night.** See 7. 50; 19. 39.
Rabbi. Ap. 98. XIV. vii 1.
know. Gr. *oida*. Ap. 132. I. i.
teacher. Cp. *v.* 10. Gr. *didaskalos*. Ap. 98. XIV. v. 4.
come from God. Render: "Thou art come from God as Teacher". **from.** Gr. *apo*. Ap. 104. iv.
God. Ap. 98. I. i. 1.
no man = no one. Compound of *ou*. Ap. 105. I.
miracles = signs. See note on 2. 11.
doest = art doing.
except = if . . . not. Gr. *ean mē*. Ap. 118. 1. b. and 105. II. **with.** Gr. *meta*. Ap. 104. xi.

3 answered and said. A Hebraism. See note on Deut. 1. 41. Ap. 122. 3. **Verily, verily.** See note on 1. 51. **a man** = any one. **born** = begotten. See note on Matt. 1. 2. **again** = from above. Gr. *anōthen* = from above: i. e. by Divine power, as in *v.* 31; 19. 11, 23. Matt. 27. 51. Mark 15. 38. Luke 1. 3. Jas. 1. 17; 3. 15, 17. The Talmud uses this figure, as applied to proselytes. **cannot** = is not (Gr. *ou*. Ap. 105. I) able to. **see.** Gr. *eidon*. Ap. 133. I. 1. **the kingdom of God.** Ap. 114. Occ. in John only here and in *v.* 5. **4 unto.** Gr. *pros*. Ap. 104. xv. 3. **How . . . ?** Note other such questions, 4, 9. 1 Cor. 15. 35. All answered by "the gift of God" (3. 16; 4. 10. 1 Cor. 15. 38). The question implies a negative answer. **be born.** Nicodemus misunderstands, and uses the Verb *gennaō* of the mother. The Lord uses it of the Father, as meaning *begetting*. **old.** Applying it to his own case. **into.** Gr. *eis*. Ap. 104. vi.

3. 5-8 (Y[2], above). THE LORD. ANSWER. REPETITION. (*Alternation.*)

Y[2] | j | 5. Reference to question.
  k | 6. Explanation.
 j | 7. Reference to question.
  k | 8. Illustration.

5 of water, &c. = of water and spirit. No Art. Fig. *Hendiadys* (Ap. 6). Not two things, but one, by which the latter Noun becomes a superlative and emphatic Adjective, determining the meaning and nature of the former Noun, showing that one to be spiritual water: i. e. not water but spirit. It is to be rendered "of water—yea, spiritual water". Cp. Eph. 5. 26, and see 7. 38, 39 and Ezek. 36. 25-27 for the "earthly things" of *v.* 12. **enter.** Showing what the Lord meant by "see", in *v.* 3. **6 That which is born** = That (Neuter) which has been begotten. Note the difference between this Perfect here and in *v.* 8, and the Aorists in *vv.* 3, 4, 5, 7. **flesh.** See note on 1. 13. **the Spirit**: the Holy Spirit (with Art.). See Ap. 101. II. 3. **is spirit.** This is a fundamental law, both in nature and grace. **7 not.** Gr. *mē*. Ap. 105. II. **8 The wind** = The Spirit. The word *pneuma*, occ. 385 times, and is rendered "wind" only here. It should be trans. Spirit, as at end of verse. "Wind" is *anemos*; occ. 31 times, and is always so rendered. **bloweth** = breatheth. **it listeth** = He willeth. Ap. 102. 1. The Eng. "listeth" is Old Eng. for Anglo-Saxon *lusteth*; i. e. pleaseth or desireth. **the sound thereof** = His voice. **canst not tell** = knowest not. Gr. *oida*. Ap. 132. I. i. **not.** Gr. *ou*. Ap. 105. I. **is born** = has been begotten, as in *v.* 6. **the Spirit**: completing the Fig. *Epanadiplōsis* (Ap. 6), converting this verse into a most solemn and independent statement of facts. **9 these things.** See Jer. 31. 33; 32. 39. Ezek. 11. 19; 18. 31; 36. 25-27. Ps. 51. 10. **be** = come to pass. Ref. to *v.* 4.

Y[3] A 10 [2]Jesus [3]answered and said unto him, °"Art
A.D. 26 thou °a master of Israel, and °knowest [8]not these things?

B 11 [3]Verily, verily, I say unto thee, We speak that we do [2]know, and °testify that °we have °seen; and °ye receive [8]not our °witness.

A 12 °If I have told you °earthly things, and ye °believe [8]not, how shall ye °believe, °if I tell you *of* °heavenly things?

B C[1] D l 13 °And [2]no man °hath °ascended up °to °heaven, °but He That °came down °from °heaven, *even* °the Son of man °Which is °in °heaven.

m 14 [13]And °as °Moses lifted up the serpent [13]in the wilderness, even so °must [13]the Son of man °be lifted up:

n 15 That °whosoever °believeth in Him should [7]not perish, °but have °eternal °life.

D l 16 For [2]God so °loved the °world, that He gave His °only begotten °Son, that [15]whosoever [15]believeth in Him should [7]not perish, [15]but have °everlasting [15]life.

m 17 For [2]God °sent [8]not His [16]Son [4]into the [16]world °to condemn the [16]world;

n but that the [16]world °through Him might be saved.

C[2] o[1] 18 He that [15]believeth on Him is [8]not [17]condemned: but he that [12]believeth [7]not is [17]condemned already,

p[1] because he hath [7]not [15]believed in °the name of °the [16]only begotten °Son of [2]God.

3. 10-21 (Y[3], p. 1518). THE LORD. ANSWER. CONFIRMED. (*Alternation*).

Y[3] | A | 10. Expostulation. Ignorance.
  B | 11. Testimony. The Lord's.
  A | 12. Expostulation. Unbelief.
  B | 13-21. Testimony. The Evangelist's.

10 Art thou . . . ? or Thou art, &c. Not irony.
a master=the (famous) teacher; referring to his official position. Gr. *didaskalos*. See Ap. 98. XIV. v. 4.
knowest not=hast not got to know; or perceivest not. Gr. *ginōskō*. Ap. 132. I. ii. See note on 1. 10.
11 testify=bear witness to. Gr. *martureō*. See notes on 1. 7 and p. 1511.
seen. Gr. *horaō*. Ap. 133. I. 8. Cp. 1. 18; 14. 7, 9.
ye: i.e. ye teachers of Israel.
witness. See note on 1. 7.
12 If I have. Assuming it as a fact. Ap. 118. 2. a.
earthly things. Ezek. 36. 25-27. 1 Cor. 15. 40. Col. 3. 2. 2 Cor. 5. 1. Phil. 2. 10; 3. 19.
believe. Ap. 150. I. 1. i. See note on 1. 7.
if I tell. Supposing I tell. Ap. 118. 1. b.
heavenly=Pl. of *epouranios*. Occ. only here and Matt. 18. 35 in the Gospels. See Eph. 1. 3, 20; 2. 6; 3. 10; 6. 12. Phil. 2. 10, &c.

3. 13-21 (*B*, above). TESTIMONY. THE EVANGELIST'S. (*Division*.)

B | C[1] | 13-17. Salvation.
  C[2] | 18-21. Condemnation.

3. 13-17 (C[1], above). SALVATION. (*Extended Alternation.*)

C[1] | D | l | 13. The Son of Man. His Person.
  m | 14. His lifting up. His death.
  n | 15. Belief. Life through Him.
  D | *l* | 16. The only-begotten Son.
  m | 17-. His mission.
  n | -17. Belief. Salvation through Him.

13 And, &c. The *kai* (=And) here is a Hebraism, and does not mark the actual transition. There is nothing whatever in the context to show where the Paragraph breaks should be in this chapter; either in the MSS., or in the Versions. The A.V. varies in its different editions. The A.V. text in the R.V. *Parallel Bible* has a ¶ at *vv.* 14 and 16. The Camb. Paragraph Bible (Dr. Scrivener) has no break either at *vv.* 14 or 16. The R.V. has a break only at *v.* 16, with WH and Scrivener's Greek Text. *The Companion Bible* makes the important break at *v.* 13: (1) because the Past Tenses which follow indicate completed events; (2) because the expression "only begotten Son" is not used by the Lord of Himself, but only by the Evangelist (1. 14, 18; 3. 16, 18; 1 John 4. 9); (3) because "in the name of" (*v.* 18) is not used by the Lord, but by the Evangelist (1. 12; 2. 23. 1 John 5. 13); (4) because to do the truth (*v.* 21) occ. elsewhere only in 1 John 1. 6; (5) because "Who is in heaven" (*v.* 13) points to the fact that the Lord had already ascended at the time John wrote; (6) because the word "lifted up" refers both to the "sufferings ' (*v.* 14; 8. 28; 12. 32, 34) and to "the glory which should follow" (8. 28; 12. 32. Acts 2. 33; 5. 31); and (7) because the break at *v.* 13 accords best with the context, as shown by the Structure B, above. **hath ascended**=hath gone up (of himself). It does not say: "hath been taken up by God," as Enoch and Elijah. But Christ had "gone up" when the Evangelist wrote these words. **ascended.** Gr. *anabainō*. As in 1. 51; 2. 13; 5. 1; 7. 8, &c. Matt. 20. 17. Mark 6. 51. Rom. 10. 6. **to**=into. Gr. *eis*. Ap. 104. vi. Cp. Deut. 30. 12. Prov. 30. 4. Acts 2. 34. Rom. 10. 6. Eph. 4. 10. **heaven**=the heaven. See note on Matt. 6. 9, 10. **but**=except, lit. if not. Gr. *ei mē*. **came down.** Gr. *katabainō*. The opposite of "gone up". **from**=out of. Gr. *ek*. Ap. 104. vii. Not the same word as in *v.* 2. **the Son of Man.** See Ap. 98. XVI. **Which is, &c**=Who is, &c., and was there when John wrote. This clause is in the Syr., but is omitted by WH, and put by R.V. in the margin. Omit "even". **in.** Gr. *en*. Ap. 104. viii. **14 as**=even as. Ref. to Num. 21. 9. **Moses.** See note on 1. 17 and Matt. 8. 4. **must**=it behoved to, in order to fulfil the prophetic Scripture. See Luke 24. 26, 46. Acts 3. 18; 17. 3, and cp. Heb. 2. 9, 10. **be lifted up.** See note on *v.* 13. **15 whosoever**=every one who. As here defined. **believeth in.** See Ap. 150. I. 1. v (i). (See note on 1. 7.) L reads *epi*; Lm T Tr. A WH and R read *en*. **but have.** Fig. *Pleonasm* (Ap. 6), for emph. The phrases "hath", "have eternal life", are the usual expressions in this Gospel for "live for ever" (Ap. 151. II. A. ii. 4. a). Cp. *vv.* 16, 36; 5. 24; 6. 40, 47, 54. 1 John 3. 15; 5. 11. **eternal.** Gr. *aiōnios*. Ap. 151. II. B. i: i.e. in Him. Cp. 1 John 5. 12. **life.** See note on 1. 4. Ap. 170. 1. **16 loved.** Gr. *agapaō*. Ap. 135. I. 1. A word characteristic of this Gospel. See p. 1511. **world.** Gr. *kosmos*. Ap. 129. 1. See note on 1. 9. **only, &c.** See 1. 14. **Son.** Ap. 108. iii. **everlasting.** Same as "eternal" in *v.* 15. See Ap. 151. II. B. ii. **17 sent.** Gr. *apostellō*. Ap. 174. 1. **to condemn**=to judge. Gr. *krinō*. Ap. 122. 1. A characteristic word of this Gospel. See note on p. 1511. **through.** Gr. *dia*. Ap. 104. v. 1.

3. 18-21 [For Structure see next page].

18 the name: i.e. Him. See note on Ps. 20. 1. **Son of God.** See Ap. 98. XV.

o^3 A.D. 26 19 And °this is the °condemnation, that
°light is come [4]into the [16]world, and °men
[16]loved °darkness rather than °light, because
their °deeds were °evil.

p^2 20 For every one that °doeth °evil hateth the
[19]light, °neither cometh [2]to the [19]light, lest his
[19]deeds should be °reproved.

o^3 21 But he that °doeth °truth cometh [2]to [19]the
light, that His [19]deeds may be °made manifest,
that they °are °wrought [13]in [2]God."

O E 22 °After these things came [2]Jesus and His
disciples [4]into °the °land of Judæa;

F and there He tarried [2]with them, and °baptized.

G 23 And John also was [12]baptizing [13]in °Ænon
near to °Salim, because there was °much water
there: and they came, and were [22]baptized.
24 For John °was °not yet cast [4]into °prison.

G H^1 25 °Then there arose a °question °between
some of John's disciples °and °the Jews °about
°purifying.
26 And they came [4]unto John, and said unto
him "Rabbi, He That was [2]with thee beyond
Jordan, to Whom thou °barest witness, °behold,
the same baptizeth, and °all *men* come [2]to
Him."

H^2 J 27 John [3]answered and said, "A [1]man can
°receive °nothing, except it °be given him
[13]from [13]heaven.

K q 28 Ye yourselves [26]bear me witness, that I
said, I am [8]not °the Christ, but that I am
°sent before Him.

r 29 He that hath the bride is the bridegroom:
but °the friend of the bridegroom, which
standeth and heareth him, °rejoiceth greatly
°because of the bridegroom's voice: this my
joy therefore is fulfilled.

3. 18-21 (C^2, 1519). CONDEMNATION.
(*Repeated Alternation.*)

C^2 | o^1 | 18-. Believeth. Positive.
p^1 | -18. Believeth not. Negative.
o^2 | 19. Loving darkness. Positive and reason.
p^2 | 20. Not coming to the Light. Negative and reason.
o^3 | 21. Doing truth. Positive and reason.

19 this is=this is what it consists in; viz: **condemnation**=judging: i.e. the process rather than the result. Gr. *krisis*. Ap. 177. 7.
light=the light. Ap. 130. 1. See note on 1. 4.
men=the men. As a class. Ap. 123. 1.
darkness=the darkness.
deeds=works. Pl. of *ergon*. A characteristic word of this Gospel. See note on p. 1511.
evil. Gr. *ponēros*=active evil. Ap. 128. III. 1.
20 doeth=practises, or (habitually) does. Gr. *prassō*.
evil. Gr. *phaulos*=worthless, base. Occ. only here; 5. 29. Titus 2. 8. Jas. 3. 16, in Rec. Text, but in Rom. 9. 11. 2 Cor. 5. 10, in most texts for *kakos*. Here, pl.= worthless things.
neither=and . . . not. Gr. *ou*. Ap. 105. I.
reproved=brought home to him. Cp. 16. 8 (convince).
21 doeth. Actively produces, having regard to the object and end of the action. Gr. *poieō*. Cp. the two verbs, *prassō* and *poieō*, in a similar connexion in 5. 29.
truth=the truth. Gr. *alētheia*. Ap. 175. 1. A characteristic word of this Gospel. See note on 1. 14.
made manifest. Gr. *phaneroō*. Ap. 106. I. v.
are=have been, and still continue to be.
wrought in God: i.e. in His fear, or in His strength.

3. 22—4. 2 (*O*, p. 1515). JUDÆA.
(*Introversion.*)

O | E | 3. 22-. Coming into Judæa.
F | 3. -22. The Lord. Baptizing.
G | 3. 23, 24. John. Baptizing.
G | 3. 25-36. John's disciples. Controversy.
F | 4. 1, 2. The Lord. Baptizing.
E | 4. 3-. Departing from Judæa.

22 After=After (Gr. *meta*. Ap. 104. xi. 2) these things. A note of time, frequent in John. See 21. 1.
the land of Judæa: lit. the Judæan land. Phrase only here. **land.** Gr. *gē*. Ap. 129. 4.
baptized=was (engaged in) baptizing. See 4. 2 and Ap. 115. I. i. **23 Ænon**=Springs. Now *Fār'ah*. The springs near *Umm al 'Amdān*, 7½ miles below *Beīsan*. **Salim.** Still so called; east of Shechem. **much water**=many waters (i.e. springs).
24 was=had been. **not yet.** Gr. *oupō*, compound of *ou*. **prison**=the prison. Cp. Matt. 4. 12.

3. 25-36 (*G*, above). JOHN BAPTIST'S DISCIPLES. CONTROVERSY. (*Division.*)

G | H^1 | 25, 26. The questioning.
H^2 | 27-36. The answer.

25 Then=Therefore: i.e. on account of the facts stated in *vv.* 22-24. **question**=questioning. **between some of**=[on the part] of. Gr. *ek*. Ap. 104. vii. **and**=with. Gr. *meta*. Ap. 104. xi. 1. **the Jews.** All the texts read "a Jew". Gr. *Ioudaion*, with Syr. But it has been suggested that *Iou* was the primitive abbreviation for *Iēsou* (=of Jesus), and being repeated (by inadvertence) led to the reading *Iou[daion]* (=a Jew). This would agree better with *vv.* 22-24; with "Therefore" in *v.* 25, and with the action of John's disciples, and John's answer. See the Structure H^2, above. **about**=concerning. Gr. *peri*. Ap. 104. xiii. 1. **purifying**=purification. Cp. 2. 6. Luke 2. 22; 5. 14. **26 barest witness**=hast borne witness. See note on 1. 7. **behold.** Gr. *ide*. Ap. 133. 3. Fig. *Asterismos*. Ap. 6. **all.** This was the gravamen.

3. 27-36 (H^2, above). JOHN'S ANSWER. (*Alternations.*)

H^2 | J | 27. God the Giver of all to men.
K | q | 28. Contrast.
r | 29. His voice.
q | 30. Contrast.
r | 31-34. His words.
J | 35. God the Giver of all to Messiah.
K | s | 36-. Belief on the Son.
t | -36-. Consequence. Everlasting life.
s | -36-. Rebellion against the Son.
t | -36. Consequence. Abiding wrath.

27 receive=take [upon himself]. **nothing.** Gr. *ou ouden*. A double negative. **be given**=have been given. **28 the Christ**=the Messiah. Ap. 98. IX. **sent.** Ap. 174. 1. **29 the friend, &c.** He played a very important part in the wedding ceremonies. **rejoiceth greatly.** Fig. *Polyptōton* (Ap. 6). Gr. *chara chairei*=joyeth with joy. **because of.** Gr. *dia*. Ap. 104. v. 2.

q 30 He [14]must increase, but I *must* decrease.
r 31 He That cometh °from above is above all:
A.D. 26 he that is [1]of the °earth is °earthly, and speaketh [1]of the °earth: He That cometh [13]from
heaven is above all.
32 And what He hath [11]seen and °heard,
that He [11]testifieth; and [2]no man receiveth His
°testimony.
33 He that hath received His [32]testimony hath
set to his seal that [2]God is °true.
34 For He Whom [2]God hath [17]sent speaketh
the °words of [2]God: °for °God giveth [8]not °the
Spirit °by measure *unto Him*.
J 35 °The Father [16]loveth the Son, and hath
given all things °into His hand.
K s 36 He that [15]believeth on the Son
t hath [16]everlasting [15]life:
s and he that °believeth [8]not the Son
t °shall [8]not °see [15]life; but the °wrath of [2]God
°abideth °on him."

F **4** When °therefore °the Lord °knew how
the °Pharisees had heard that °Jesus
°made and °baptized more disciples than John,
2 °(Though [1]Jesus Himself °baptized °not,
but His disciples,)
E 3 He left Judæa,
N L^1 M^1 and departed °again °into °Galilee.
4 And °He must needs °go °through Samaria.
5 °Then cometh He °to a city of Samaria,
which is called Sychar, near to the °parcel of
ground °that Jacob gave to his son Joseph.
6 Now °Jacob's °well was there. [1]Jesus
therefore, being wearied °with *His* journey,
°sat thus °on the °well: *and* it was about
°the sixth hour.
7 There cometh a woman °of Samaria to
draw water:
M^2 N u [1]Jesus saith unto her, °"Give Me to drink."

31 from above. Gr. *anōthen*, same as "again" in *v.* 3. **earth.** Gr. *gē*. Ap. 129. 4.
earthly = of the earth.
32 heard. Not "hath heard".
testimony. Gr. *marturia*. See note on "witness", 1. 7.
33 true. Ap. 175. 1. A characteristic word of this Gospel. See p. 1511.
34 words. Gr. pl. of *rhēma*. See note on Mark 9. 32.
for God, &c. Or "for the Spirit giveth not [the words of God] by measure [unto Him]".
God. [L] T [Tr.] A WH R., not Syr., omit "God" here.
the Spirit. With Art. = the Giver, not the gift. Ap. 101. II. 3. This was by measure unto John, but not unto the Lord. Cp. 15. 26; Matt. 11. 27. What John saw and heard was limited (*vv.* 27–30).
by. Gr. *ek*. Ap. 104. vii.
35 The Father. See note on 1. 14.
into. Gr. *en*. Ap. 104. viii.
36 believeth not = obeyeth not. Gr. *apeitheō*. Cp. Ap. 150. I. 2. See note on 1. 7. Only here in John.
shall not see = will not see. Note the future here, in contrast with "hath".
see. Ap. 133. I. 8. a.
wrath = [permanent] wrath. Gr. *orgē*; as in Matt. 3. 7. Luke 3. 7. 1 Thess. 2. 16, &c. Not *thumos*, which = [temporary] wrath.
abideth. Present tense. See note on 1. 32.
on = upon. Gr. *epi*. Ap. 104. ix. 3.
4. 1 therefore. See 3. 22.
the Lord. Ap. 98. VI. i. *a*. 3. B. c. For the occ. of this absolute title in John, see 6. 23; 11. 2; 20. 20; and cp. 20. 2, 13, 18, 25; 21. 7.
knew = came to know. Gr. *ginōskō*. Ap. 132. I. ii. See note on 1. 10. Cp. 2. 24.
Pharisees. Ap. 120. II (John never refers to the Sadducees by name). Jesus. Ap. 98. X.
made, &c. = is making and baptizing.
baptized. Ap. 115. I. i.
2 Though = And yet.
baptized. It was not the practice of Jesus to baptize. Imperf. Tense.
not. Gr. *ou*. Ap. 105. I. Cp. 3. 22.

4. -3-54 (*N*, p. 1515). GALILEE. (*Division.*)

N | L^1 | -3-27-. The woman of Samaria.
| L^2 | -27-42. The Disciples and the Samaritans.
| L^3 | 43-54. The second sign.

4. -3-27- (L^1, above). THE WOMAN OF SAMARIA. (*Division.*)

L^1 | M^1 | -3-7-. The Circumstances.
| M^2 | -7-27-. The Colloquy.

3 again. See 1. 43. into. Gr. *eis*. Ap. 104. vi. Galilee. See Ap. 169. **4 He must needs** = it was necessary [for] Him. See Josephus, *Life*, § 52. *Ant.* xx. vi. 1. A necessity not only geographical, but including the Divine counsels. go = pass. Gr. *dierchomai*. Cp. 8. 59. through. Gr. *dia*. Ap. 104. v. 1. **5 Then** = Therefore. to. Gr. *eis*. Ap. 104. vi. Sychar. Now *'Askar*. A village on the slope of Mount Ebal and north of Jacob's well. parcel of ground = field or land. that Jacob gave. Cp. Gen. 33. 19; 48. 22. Josh. 24. 32. **6 Jacob's well.** Cp. Gen. 49. 22. well = spring. Gr. *pēgē*. Not the same word as in *vv.* 11, 12, but as in *v.* 14. with = from. Gr. *ek*. Ap. 104. vii. sat = was sitting. on: or by. Gr. *epi*. Ap. 104. ix. 2. Cp. 5. 2. the sixth hour. Of the day, i. e. noon. See on 1. 39, and Ap. 165. **7 of** = out of. Gr. *ek*. Ap. 104. vii.

4. -7-27- (M^2, above). THE COLLOQUY. (*Introversion and Repeated Alternation.*)

M^2 | N | u | -7. The Lord. Request. I.
| v | 8. Disciples. Gone away.
O | w^1 | 9. The woman. "How?"
| x^1 | 10. The Lord. "If thou knewest." II.
| w^2 | 11, 12. The woman. "Whence?"
| x^2 | 13, 14. The Lord. "I will give." III.
| w^3 | 15. The woman. "Give me."
| x^3 | 16. The Lord. "Go, call." IV.
| w^4 | 17-. The woman. "I have no husband.'
| x^4 | -17, 18. The Lord. "Well said." V.
| w^5 | 19, 20. The woman. "Where to worship."
| x^5 | 21-24. The Lord. "Believe Me." VI.
| w^6 | 25. The woman. "Messiah cometh."
N | *u* | 26. The Lord. Declaration. "I am He." VII.
| *v* | 27-. Disciples. Come back.

-7 Give Me, &c. The first word. Note the *seven* (Ap. 10) times the Lord spoke to the woman, and the gradual ascent to the final declaration in *v.* -26.

v 8 °(For His disciples were gone away °unto
A.D. 26 the city °to buy °meat.)
O w[1] 9 Then saith the woman of Samaria unto
Him, °"How is it that Thou, being a Jew,
°askest drink °of me, °which am a woman of
Samaria? [8](for °the Jews °have °no dealings
with the Samaritans.)"
x[1] 10 [1]Jesus °answered and said unto her, °"If
thou °knewest °the gift of God, and Who it is
That saith to thee, 'Give Me to drink;' thou
wouldest have [9]asked of Him, and He would
have given thee °living water."
w[2] 11 The woman saith unto Him, °"Sir, Thou
hast nothing to draw with, and the °well is
°deep: from whence then hast Thou that
[10]living water?
12 °Art Thou greater than our father Jacob,
which gave us the [11]well, and drank °thereof
himself, °and his °children, and his °cattle?"
x[2] 13 [1]Jesus [10]answered and said unto her,
°"Whosoever drinketh [7]of this water °shall
thirst again:
14 But °whosoever drinketh [7]of the water
that I shall give him shall °never thirst; but
the water that I shall give him shall °be °in
him a °well of water °springing up [3]into
°everlasting °life."
w[3] 15 The woman saith °unto Him, [11]"Sir, give
me this water, °that I thirst °not, neither °come
hither to draw."
x[3] 16 [1]Jesus saith unto her, "Go, call thy °hus-
band, and come hither."
w[4] 17 The woman [10]answered and said, "I have
[9]no husband."
x[4] [1]Jesus said unto her, "Thou hast °well said,
'I have [9]no [16]husband':
18 For thou hast had five [16]husbands; and
he whom thou now hast is [2]not thy [16]husband:
°in that saidst thou °truly."
w[5] 19 The woman saith unto Him, [11]"Sir, °I
°perceive that Thou art a °prophet.
20 Our fathers °worshipped [14]in °this mountain; and ye say, that [14]in Jerusalem is the
place where °men ought to °worship."
x[5] 21 [1]Jesus saith unto her, °"Woman, °believe
Me, the hour cometh, when ye shall °neither
[14]in this mountain, °nor yet °at Jerusalem,
[20]worship °the Father.
22 °Ye worship ye [10]know [2]not °what: we
[10]know what we [20]worship: for °salvation is
[7]of the Jews.
23 But the hour °cometh, and now is, when
the °true °worshippers shall [20]worship [21]the
Father [14]in °spirit and °in °truth: for [21]the
Father seeketh such to [20]worship Him.
24 °God *is* °a Spirit: and they that [20]wor-
ship Him °must worship *Him* [14]in spirit and
[23]in [23]truth."
w[6] 25 The woman saith unto Him, "I [10]know

8 For, &c. See note on *v.* 34.
unto. Gr. *eis.* Ap. 104. vi.
to = in order that (Gr. *hina*) they might.
meat. Put by Fig. *Synecdochē* (of the Species), Ap. 6, for all kinds of food.
9 How, &c. See note on 3. 4.
askest. Gr. *aiteō.* Ap. 134. I. 4, as in *v.* 10.
of = from. Gr. *para.* Ap. 104. xii. 1.
which am = being.
the Jews . . . the. No articles.
have . . . dealings = have . . . familiar intercourse. Gr. *sunchraomai.* Occ. only here.
no. Gr. *ou.* Ap. 105. I.
10 answered and said. A Hebraism. See Deut. 1. 41 and Ap. 122. 3.
If thou, &c. Assuming the hypothesis as a fact. Ap. 118. 2 a.
knewest = hadst known. Gr. *oida.* Ap. 132. I. i. See note on 1. 26.
the gift. See note on "How", 3. 4. Gr. *dōrea.* Occ. only here in the Gospels, elsewhere only in Acts 2. 38; 8. 20; 10. 45; 11. 17. Rom. 5. 15, 17. 2 Cor. 9. 15. Eph. 3. 7; 4. 7. Heb. 6. 4. Note the eight gifts in this Gospel (4. 10; 10. 11; 13. 15; 14. 16, 27; 17. 8, 14, 22).
living: i.e. perennial, unfailing. Understood by all Jews, from Jer. 2. 13; 17. 13. Zech. 14. 8. Gr. *zaō*, a word characteristic of this Gospel. See note on p. 1511.
11 Sir. Ap. 98. VI. i. *a.* 3. B. b.
well = a well dug out. Not the same word as in *vv.* 6, 14.
deep. In 1869 it was 105 feet, and had 15 feet of water.
12 Art Thou, &c., or Surely Thou art not (Ap. 105. II).
thereof = out of (Gr. *ek.* Ap. 104. vii) it.
and. Fig. *Polysyndeton.* Ap. 6.
children = sons. Ap. 108. iii.
cattle. Gr. pl. of *thremma.* Occ. only here.
13 Whosoever drinketh = Every one who is in the habit of drinking. **shall** = will.
14 whosoever drinketh = he who may have drunk (Gr. *an*, with Subj. Aor.).
never thirst = by no means (Gr. *ou mē.* Ap. 105. III) thirst for ever (Ap. 151. II. A. ii. 4. b).
be = become. **in.** Gr. *en.* Ap. 104. viii.
well = fountain, as in *v.* 6. Not as in *vv.* 11, 12.
springing up = welling up.
everlasting. Ap. 151. II. B. ii.
life. See note on 1. 4, and Ap. 170. 1.
15 unto. Gr. *pros.* Ap. 104. xv. 3.
that. Gr. *hina.* See 1. 7.
not. Gr. *mē.* Ap. 105. II.
come hither. Some texts read *dierchomai* (as in *v.* 4) = come all the way hither (through, or across the plain).
16 husband. Gr. *anēr.* Ap. 123. 2.
17 well. Cp. 8. 48; 13. 13. Matt. 15. 7. Mark 12. 32. Luke 20. 39. **18 in.** Omit.
truly = true. See note on 3. 33 and Ap. 175. 1.
19 I perceive. Gr. *theōreō.* Ap. 133. I. 11. See *The Didachē* xi. 4. 5; and cp. *v.* 42 here.
prophet. See Ap. 49.
20 worshipped. Ap. 137. 1.
this mountain. Gerizim. The well was at its foot. (See Deut. 27. 12.) **men ought** = it is necessary.
21 Woman. See on 2. 4.
believe Me. Ap. 150. I. 1. ii. See note on 1. 7. This formula occurs only here and 14. 11.
neither . . . nor. Gr. *oute . . . oute.*
at. Gr. *en.* Ap. 104. viii.
the Father. See Ap. 98. III, and note on 1. 14.
22 Ye worship . . . what. See 2 Kings 17. 24–34, esp. *v.* 33.
salvation = the salvation [which the prophets foretold]. Cp. Luke 2. 30.
23 cometh, and now is = is coming, and is now on its way. Its coming depended on the repentance of the nation, when all the prophecies would have been fulfilled. See Acts 3. 18–26. **true** = real. See note on 1. 9. Ap. 175. 2. **worshippers.** Gr. *proskunētēs.* Only here. **spirit.** Ap. 101. II. 8. **in.** No Preposition with the second "in". **truth.** Ap. 175. 1. See note on 1. 14. **24 God.** See Ap. 98. I. i. 1, with Art. Contrast 1. 1. **a Spirit** = spirit: i.e. not flesh, or material substance. Not "a" Spirit. **must.** Note this absolute condition. Cp. *v.* 4; 3. 7, 14, 30; 9. 4; 10. 16; 12. 34; 20. 9, &c.

A.D. 26 that °Messias [23]cometh, Which is called °Christ:
when He °is come, He will °tell us all things."

N u 26 [1]Jesus saith unto her, °"I That °speak
unto thee am *He*."

v 27 And °upon this came His disciples,

L² P and °marvelled that He °talked °with °the
woman: yet no man said, "What seekest
Thou?" or, "Why talkest Thou °with her?"

Q 28 The woman then left her waterpot, and
went her way [3]into the city, and saith to the
°men,

R 29 "Come, °see [28]a Man, Which told me all
things °that ever I did:

S y °is not this the [25]Christ?"

z 30 °Then they went °out of the city, and °came
[15]unto Him.

P 31 [14]In the mean while His disciples °prayed
Him, saying, °"Master, eat."
32 But He said unto them, "I have °meat to
eat that ye [10]know [2]not °of."
33 Therefore said the disciples one °to another,
"Hath any man brought Him *ought* to
eat?"
34 [1]Jesus saith unto them, "My °meat is °to
do the °will of Him That °sent me, and to
°finish His °work.
35 °Say [2]not ye, 'There are yet four months,
and *then* cometh harvest?' °behold, I say unto
you, Lift up your eyes, and °look on the fields;
for they are white °already [33]to harvest.
36 And he that reapeth receiveth wages, and
gathereth fruit [8]unto [14]life °eternal: [15]that both
he that soweth and he that reapeth may rejoice
together.
37 And °herein °is that °saying [23]true, °'One
soweth, and °another reapeth.'
38 I °sent you to reap that whereon ye bestowed
[9]no labour: °other men °laboured, and
ye °are entered [3]into °their labours."

Q 39 And many of the Samaritans [7]of that city
°believed on Him

R °for the [37]saying of the woman, which °testified,
"He told me all [29]that ever I did."

S z 40 So when the Samaritans were come [15]unto
Him, they °besought Him that He would °tarry
°with them: and He °abode there °two days.
41 And many more °believed °because of His
own °word;

y 42 And °said unto the woman, "Now we
[41]believe, °not [41]because of thy saying: for we
have heard *Him* ourselves, and [10]know that
this is °indeed [29]the °Christ, the °Saviour of
°the world."

25 Messias = Messiah. Ap. 98. VIII.
Christ. See Ap. 98. IX.
is come = comes, or shall have come.
tell. Gr. *anangellō*. See 5. 15; 16. 13, 14, 15, 25 (shew). Cp. Ap. 121. 5, 6.
26 I That speak, &c. = I am [He] Who am speaking, &c. This is the seventh and last of the Lord's seven utterances, and marks the climax. See note on *v.* 7, and Ap. 176.
speak = am talking.
27- upon. Gr. *epi*. Ap. 104. ix. 2.

4. -27-42 (L², p. 1521). THE DISCIPLES AND THE SAMARITANS.
(*Extended Alternation and Introversion.*)

L² | P | -27. The disciples. Marvelling. Silent.
  Q | 28. The city. The woman.
   R | 29-. Her testimony.
    S | y | -29. "Is not this the Messiah?"
      z | 30. Samaritans. Coming.
 P | 31-38. The disciples. Instructed. Silenced.
  Q | 39-. The city. The men.
   R | -39. Her testimony.
    S | *z* | 40, 41. Samaritans. Believing.
      y | 42. This is indeed the Messiah.

-27 marvelled. All the texts read "were wondering". Gr. *thaumazō*. First occ. Matt. 8. 10.
talked = was talking.
with. Gr. *meta*. Ap. 104. xi. 1.
the woman = a woman. One of six things forbidden to a Rabbi by the Talmud; and she being a Samaritan caused the greater wonder.
28 men. Gr. pl. of *anthrōpos*. Ap. 123. 1.
29 see. Ap. 133. I. 1.
that ever = whatsoever.
is not this? = can this be?
30 Then. All the texts omit.
out of. Gr. *ek*. Ap. 104. vii.
came = were coming.
31 prayed = were asking. Gr. *erōtaō*. Ap. 134. I. 3.
Master. Gr. *Rabbi*. Ap. 98. XIV. vii. 1.
32 meat. Gr. *brōsis* = eating. Not the same word as in *v.* 34.
of. Omit "of".
33 to. Gr. *pros*. Ap. 104. xv. 3.
34 meat. Put by Fig. *Metonymy* (of Species), Ap. 6, for all kinds of food. Gr. *brōma*. Not the same word as in *v.* 33.
to do = in order to do. Emphasizing the object and end, not the act. Cp. Luke 2. 49; 4. 4.
will. Ap. 102. 2.
sent. Gr. *pempō*. Ap. 174. 4. See note on 1. 22.
finish. Gr. *teleioō*. A characteristic word of this Gospel; here, 5. 36; 17. 4, 23; 19. 28. See p. 1511.
work. A characteristic word of this Gospel, most frequently in pl. See p. 1511.
35 Say not ye. Fig. *Paroemia*. Ap. 6.
behold. Gr. *idou*. Ap. 133. I. 2. Fig. *Asterismos*. Ap. 6.
look on. Gr. *theaomai*. Ap. 133. I. 12.
already. This does not refer to the present mission field, but to the then present expectation of national repentance (on which the glorious harvest was conditional) by the proclamation of the kingdom. See Ap. 119.
36 eternal. Ap. 151. II. B. i.
37 herein = in (Gr. *en*) this.
is = i.e. is [exemplified] the true saying.
saying. Gr. *logos*. See note on Mark 9. 32.
38 sent. Ap. 174. 1.

One . . . another. Gr. *allos*. Ap. 124. 1.
other men. Gr. pl. of *allos*.
laboured = have laboured.
are entered = have entered.
their: i.e. John the Baptist and the Lord.
39 believed on. Ap. 150. I. 1. v (i). See note on 1. 7.
for = on account of. Gr. *dia*. Ap. 104. v. 2.
testified = bore witness. See note on 1. 7.
40 besought = asked. Gr. *erōtaō*. Ap. 134. I. 3.
tarry. Gr. *menō*. See note on "abode", 1. 32.
with. Gr. *para*. Ap. 104. xii. 2.
abode. Gr. *menō*, as above.
two days. See note on *v.* 43.
41 believed. Ap. 150. I. 1. i.
because of. Gr. *dia*. Ap. 104. v. 2.
word. Gr. *logos*. See note on Mark 9. 32.
42 said = were saying: i.e. as one and another spoke.
not = no longer. Gr. *ouketi*.
indeed = truly. Cp. Ap. 175. 1, and p. 1511.
Christ = All the texts omit "the Christ", but not the Syr. See Ap. 94. V, note 3.
Saviour. In John only here, and 1 John 4. 14. See note on Matt. 1. 21.
the world. Gr. *kosmos*. Ap. 129. 1, i.e. of the Gentiles as well as the Jews. See note on 1. 9.

L^3 T A. D. 26 43 Now °after °two days He departed thence,
and went [3]into [3]Galilee.
44 (°For [1]Jesus Himself [39]testified, that °a
prophet hath [9]no honour [14]in °his own country.)
45 Then when He was come [3]into [3]Galilee,
the Galilæans °received Him, having °seen all
the things that He did [21]at Jerusalem [21]at the
feast: [44](for they also went [3]unto the feast).
46 So [1]Jesus came °again [3]into °Cana of
[3]Galilee, where He °made the water wine.

U V a And there was a certain °nobleman, whose son
was sick [21]at °Capernaum.
47 When he heard that [1]Jesus was come
[30]out of Judæa [3]into [3]Galilee, he went [15]unto
Him, and [40]besought Him [15]that He would come
down, and heal his son: for he was °at the
point of death.

b 48 Then said [1]Jesus [15]unto him, °"Except ye
[29]see °signs and wonders, ye will °not [41]be-
lieve."

a 49 The [46]nobleman saith [15]unto Him, [11]"Sir,
come down °ere my °child die."

b 50 [1]Jesus saith unto him, "Go thy way; thy
son °liveth."

W And the [28]man [41]believed the [41]word that
[1]Jesus had spoken unto him, and he went his
way.

U V c 51 °And as he was now going down, his
°servants °met him,

d and told *him*, saying, "Thy °son [50]liveth."

c 52 °Then enquired he [9]of them the hour
°when he began to °amend.

d And they said unto him, "Yesterday at °the
seventh hour the fever left him."

W 53 So the father [1]knew that *it was* [21]at the
same hour, [14]in the which [1]Jesus said unto
him, "Thy [51]son [50]liveth:" and himself [41]be-
lieved, and his whole house.

T 54 This *is* again °the second miracle *that*
[1]Jesus did, when He was come [30]out of Judæa
[3]into [3]Galilee.

$X^1Y^1Z^1e^1$ A. D. 27 **5** °After °this there was °a feast of °the
Jews; and °Jesus went up °to Jerusalem.

e^2 2 Now there is °at Jerusalem °by the sheep

4. 43-54 (L^3, p. 1521). THE SECOND SIGN.
(*Introversion and Alternation.*)

L^3 | T | 43-46-. Departure from Judæa to Galilee.
  U | V | a | -46, 47. The father. Request.
      b | 48. The Lord. Answer.
      a | 49. The father. Request.
      b | 50-. The Lord. Answer.
    W | -50. Belief.
  U | *V* | c | 51-. The father. Return.
      d | -51. Servants' report.
      c | 52-. The father. Inquiry.
      d | -52. Servants' reply.
    W | 53. Belief.
T | 54. Departure from Judæa to Galilee.

43 after two days. See 11. 6, and cp. with the Seventh Sign. Ap. 176. **after.** Gr. *meta.* Ap. 104. xi. 2.
two = the two; viz. those mentioned in *v.* 40.
44 For Jesus, &c. Note the parenthetical explanation, and see note on "and we beheld", 1. 14.
a prophet. Fig. *Parœmia.* Ap. 6.
his own country = his native place. See 7. 41, 42. Which was Galilee (Ap. 169). The Lord had proved the truth of this proverb before He went to Cana (from Nazareth), as recorded in Luke 4. 16-30. See Ap. 97. The Lord went and returned thither, notwithstanding that experience.
45 received. Gr. *dechomai.* Only occ. here in John.
seen. Gr. *horaō.* Ap. 133. I. 8.
46 again . . Cana, &c. Referring to 2. 1.
made. Not the same word as "made" in 2. 9.
nobleman = a royal officer. Prob. belonging to the court of Herod Antipas (Ap. 109). Gr. *basilikos.* Occ. only here; *v.* 49. Acts 12. 20, 21; and Jas. 2. 8.
Capernaum. Ap. 169.
47 at the point of death = about to die. Not the same miracle as that of the centurion's servant recorded in Matt. 8. 5-12 and Luke 7. 1-10. The two miracles differ as to time, place, person, pleading, plea, disease, the Lord's answer, and the man's faith, as may be easily seen by comparing the two as to these details.
48 Except = If not. Gr. *ean mē.* Ap. 118. 1. b. and 105. II. **signs.** See note on 2. 11.
signs and wonders. See Ap. 176.
not = in no wise. Gr. *ou mē.* Ap. 105. III.
49 ere = before. See note on Matt. 1. 18.
child. Gr. *paidion.* Ap. 108. v.
50 liveth. Gr. *zaō.* A word characteristic of this Gospel. See p. 1511, and cp. Ap. 170. 1.
51 And = But already. **servants** = bond-servants.
met. Gr. *apantaō,* but all the texts read *hupantaō.*
son = boy. Gr. *pais.* Ap. 108. iv.
52 Then = Therefore.
when = in (Gr. *en.* Ap. 104. viii) which.
amend = get better. Gr. *kompsoteron echō.* Occ. only here in N.T. **the seventh hour** = 1 o'clock p.m. Cp. Ap. 165. **54 the second miracle** = a second sign. Having thus begun to number the signs in this Gospel, we may continue to do so, and complete the whole (eight). See Ap. 176. See note on 2. 11.

5. 1—6. 71 (**E**, p. 1510). THE SECOND PERIOD OF THE LORD'S MINISTRY. SUBJECT: THE PROCLAMATION OF THE KING. (*Division.*)

E | X^1 | 5. 1-47. In Jerusalem.
  | X^2 | 6. 1-71. In Galilee.

5. 1-47 (X^1, above). IN JERUSALEM. (*Division.*)

X^1 | Y^1 | 1-15. The THIRD Sign. The impotent Man.
  | Y^2 | 16-47. Consequent Conspiracy of, and Colloquy with, the Jews.

5. 1-15 (Y^1, above). THE THIRD SIGN. THE IMPOTENT MAN. (*Division.*)

Y^1 | Z^1 | 1-7. The occasion.
  | Z^2 | 8-15. The sign.

5. 1-7 (Z^1, above). THE OCCASION. (*Division.*)

Z^1 | e^1 | 1. The time.
  | e^2 | 2. The place.
  | e^3 | 3, 4. The people.
  | e^4 | 5-7. The man.

1 After, &c. A phrase common in John. See 21. 1. Ten times in the Revelation. **After.** Gr. *meta.* Ap. 104. xi. 2. **this** = these things. **a feast.** Perhaps Purim, but uncertain. **the Jews.** See note on 2. 13. **Jesus.** See Ap. 98. X. **to.** Gr. *eis.* Ap. 104. vi. **2 at** = in. Gr. *en.* Ap. 104. viii. **by** = upon, or at. Gr. *epi.* Ap. 104. ix. 2.

A. D. 27 °*market* a pool, °(which is called in the Hebrew tongue ° Bethesda, having five °porches).

e[3] 3 °In these lay a great multitude of impotent folk, of blind, °halt, withered, °waiting for the moving of the water.

4 °For an angel went down °at a certain season °into the pool, and °troubled the water: whosoever then first [1] after the °troubling of the water stepped [3] in was made °whole of whatsoever disease °he had.

e[4] 5 °And a certain °man was there, which had an infirmity °thirty and eight years.

6 When [1] Jesus °saw Him lie, and °knew that he had been now °a long time *in that case,* He saith unto him, °"Wilt thou be made [4] whole?"

7 The impotent [5] man answered him, °"Sir, I have °no [5] man, when the water is [4] troubled, °to put me °into the pool: but °while I am coming, °another steppeth down °before me."

Z[2] A f 8 [1] Jesus saith unto him, °"Rise, take up thy °bed, and walk."

g 9 And immediately the [5] man was made [4] whole,

h and took up his [8] bed, and walked:

i and °on °the same day was °the sabbath.

i 10 The Jews therefore said unto him that °was cured, "It is °the sabbath day:

h °it is °not lawful for thee to °carry *thy* [8] bed."

g 11 He answered them, "He That made me [4] whole, °the same said unto me,

f 'Take up thy bed, and walk.'"

B 12 Then °asked they him, °"What [5] man is that Which said unto thee, 'Take up thy [8] bed, and walk?'"

13 °And he that °was healed °wist [10] not who it was: for [1] Jesus had °conveyed Himself away, a °multitude being [3] in ° *that* place.

A 14 °Afterward [1] Jesus °findeth him [3] in the °temple, and said unto him, °"Behold, thou °art made [4] whole: °sin no more, °lest a worse thing °come unto thee."

B 15 The [5] man departed, and told the Jews that it was [1] Jesus, Which had made him [4] whole.

Y[2] C 16 And °therefore °did the Jews °persecute [1] Jesus, and °sought to slay Him, because He had done these things [9] on [9] the sabbath day.

market, or gate. Cp. Neh. 3. 1, 32; 12. 39, and Ap. 68, p. 100. [15. 40.

which is called. Gr. *epilegomai.* Only here and Acts

Bethesda. Aramaic. Ap. 93. III. 3. Cp. Siloam in the sixth sign, Ap. 176.

porches = arches, i.e. a colonnade, or cloister. Gr. *stoa.* Occ. only here, 10. 23. Acts 3. 11; 5. 12. The Eng. "porch" is from the French *porche,* Lat. *porticum* = a gallery or door. All from Lat. *portare* = to carry—the wall being *carried over* by an arch.

3 In. Gr. *en.* Ap. 104. viii.

halt = lame. Eng. from Anglo-Saxon *healt* = stop, because of having to stop frequently from lameness.

waiting. From this word to the end of *v.* 4 is omitted by T Tr. A WH R, but not the Syriac (see Ap. 94. V. ii note 3). If it be an addition it must have been a marginal note to explain the "troubling" of *v.* 7, which gradually got into the text.

4 For an angel. The water was intermittent from the upper springs of the waters of Gihon (see Ap. 68, and 2 Chron. 32. 33, R.V.). The common belief of the man expressed in *v.* 7 is hereby described. All will be clear, if we insert a parenthesis, thus: "For [it was said that] an angel", &c.

at a certain season = from time to time. Gr. *kata* (Ap. 104. x. 2) *kairon.*

into. Gr. *en.* Ap. 104. viii

troubled. Gr. *tarassō.* Cp. 11. 33; 12. 27; 13. 21; 14. 1, 27.

whole = well or sound. Gr. *hugiēs.* Seven times in John. Cp. 7. 23.

he had = held him fast. See note on "withholdeth", 2 Thess. 2. 6.

5 And, &c. See Ap. 176.

man. Gr. *anthrōpos.* Ap. 123. 1.

thirty and eight years. The period of the wanderings. Cp. "from birth", 9. 1.

6 saw = seeing. Ap. 133. I. 1. The Lord, in this and the sixth sign, takes the initiative (9. 1).

knew = knowing. Ap. 132. I. iii. See note on 1. 10. Not the same word as in *v.* 32.

a long time. Cp. 9. 2.

Wilt thou = Desirest thou to. Gr. *thelō.* Ap. 102. 1.

7 Sir. Gr. *kurios.* Ap. 98. VI. i. a. 3. B. b. Supply the *Ellipsis* thus: "Sir [I am indeed willing, but] I have," &c.

no. Gr. *ou.* Ap. 105. I.

to = in order that (Gr. *hina*) he may. [time when.

into. Gr. *eis.* Ap. 104. vi.

while = in (Gr. *en*) the

another. Ap. 124. 1.

before. Gr. *pro.* Ap. 104. xiv.

5. 8-15 (Z[2], p. 1524). THE SIGN. (*Alternation.*)

Z[2] | A | 8-11. The Lord: seeking, and healing.
B | 12, 13. The Jews. Question asked.
A | 14. The Lord: finding, and saving.
B | 15. The Jews. Question answered.

5. 8-11 (A, above). THE LORD: SEEKING AND HEALING. (*Introversion.*)

A | f | 8. "Take up thy bed and walk" (saith).
g | 9-. "The man was made whole."
h | -9-. "And took up his bed and walked."
i | -9. "On the same day was the sabbath."
i | 10-. "It is the sabbath day."
h | -10. "Not lawful to carry thy bed."
g | 11-. "He that made me whole" (said).
f | -11. "Take up thy bed and walk."

8 Rise. Ap. 178. I. 4. The third sign. See Ap. 176. **bed.** A rough cottonwool quilt called to-day *khaf,* the poor man's bed. The Gr. *krabbaton* is a Latin word meaning a "pallet". **9 on.** Gr. *en.* Ap. 104. viii. **the same day . . . sabbath** = that day a Sabbath. Cp. 9. 14 and Ap. 176. This seems to imply that it was not the weekly sabbath, but the same as 19. 31. See Ap. 156. **10 was cured** = had been healed. **the sabbath day** = a sabbath. **it is not lawful.** A forced interpretation of Jer. 17. 21, &c., by the Rabbis, made the carrying of anything from a public place into a private place, or vice versa, unlawful (Talmud, *Sabb.* 6. a). **not.** Gr. *ou.* Ap. 105. I. Not the same word as in *vv.* 23-, 28, 45. **carry** = take up, as in *v.* 8. **11 the same** = that one there. Gr. *ekeinos,* emph. **12 asked.** Gr. *erōtaō.* Ap. 134. 3. **What man . . . ?** = Who is the man . . . ? **13 And** = But. **was healed** = had been healed. **wist** = knew. Ap. 132. I. i. Anglo-Saxon *witan* = to know. **conveyed Himself away** = turned aside, as if to avoid a blow. Gr. *ekneuō.* Occ. only here. **multitude** = crowd. **that** = the. **14 Afterward** = After these things. See note on *v.* 1. **findeth.** Cp. 9. 35. See Ap. 176. **temple** = the temple courts. See note on Matt. 23. 16. **Behold.** Fig. *Asterismos.* Ap 6. **art made** = hast become. **sin, &c.** = continue no longer (Gr. *mēketi*) in sin. **sin.** Gr. *hamartanō.* Ap. 128. I. i. See 9. 24, 25, 31, 34. Ap. 176. **lest** = in order that . . . not Gr. *mē.* Ap. 105. II. **come unto thee** = happen to thee, or befall thee.

5. 16-47 [For Structure see next page].

16 therefore = on account of (Gr. *dia.* Ap. 104. v. 2) this. **did . . . persecute** = began to persecute. Beginning of open hostility. **sought** = were seeking. Most texts, not Syr., omit this clause.

D A.D. 27 17 But [1] Jesus answered them, °"My Father °worketh °hitherto, °and I work."

C 18 [16] Therefore the Jews sought the more °to kill Him, °because He [10] not only °had broken the sabbath, but °said also that °God was °His Father, making Himself equal with °God.

D E 19 °Then answered [1] Jesus and said unto them, °"Verily, verily, I say unto you, The Son can °do °nothing °of Himself, °but what He °seeth °the Father °do: for what things soever He doeth, °these also doeth the Son °likewise.

20 For [19] the Father °loveth the Son, and sheweth Him all things that Himself doeth: and He will shew Him greater °works than these, °that ye may marvel.

F G 21 For as [19] the Father °raiseth up °the dead, and °quickeneth °*them;* even so °the Son °quickeneth whom He [6] will.

H 22 °For [19] the Father °judgeth °no man, but hath °committed all °judgment unto the Son:

23 [20] That all *men* should honour the Son, °even as they honour [19] the Father. He that honoureth °not the Son honoureth [10] not [19] the Father Which hath °sent Him.

H 24 [19] Verily, verily, I say unto you, He that heareth My °word, and °believeth on Him That [23] sent Me, hath °everlasting °life, and shall [10] not come [7] into °condemnation; but °is passed °from death °unto °life.

G j 25 [19] Verily, verily, I say unto you, °The hour is coming, and °now is, when [21] the dead shall hear the voice of °the Son of God: and they that hear °shall live.

26 For °as [19] the Father hath [24] life [3] in Himself; so °hath He given to [21] the Son to have [24] life [3] in Himself;

k 27 And [26] hath given Him °authority to execute [22] judgment also, because He is °the Son of man.

j 28 Marvel [23] not at this: for [25] the hour is coming, [3] in the which all that are [3] in °the graves shall hear His voice,

5. 16-47 (Y², p. 1524). CONSEQUENCES. CONSPIRACY OF, AND COLLOQUY WITH, THE JEWS. (*Alternation.*)

Y² | C | 16. Conspiracy. Made.
   D | 17. Defence. The Father and the Son.
   C | 18. Conspiracy. Increased.
   D | 19-47. Defence. The Father and the Son.

17 My Father. See note on 2. 16.
worketh. Cp. 9. 4, and see Ap. 176.
hitherto = until now; referring to the O.T. Dispensation. Now Jehovah was speaking "by His Son" (Heb. 1. 2).
and I work = I also am working [now].
18 to kill Him. Note three attempts on the Lord's life, all connected with His claim to Deity, here; 8. 58, 59; 10. 30, 31.
because He not only. The 1611 edition of the A.V. reads "not only because He".
had broken = was breaking.
said also that God was His Father = also called God His own Father.
God. Ap. 98. I. i. 1. **His** = His own.

5. 19-47 (*D*, above). DEFENCE. THE FATHER AND THE SON. (*Alternation.*)

D | E | 19, 20. The Son's works are the Father's.
    F | 21-29. Proof. Communication.
  E | 30. The Son's works are the Father's.
    F | 31-47. Proof. Witnesses.

19 Then = Therefore.
Verily, verily. The fifth occ. See note on 1. 51.
do. His works were like His words. See note on 7. 16.
nothing. Gr. *ou ouden.* A double negative.
of = from. Gr. *apo.* Ap. 104. iv.
but = if not. Gr. *ean mē.*
seeth. Gr. *blepō.* Ap. 133. I. 5.
the Father. See note on 1. 14. **do** = doing.
these also. Read "also" after "Son".
likewise = in like manner.
20 loveth. Gr. *phileō.* One of the characteristic words of this Gospel. See page 1511, and Ap. 135. I. 2.
works. See note on 4. 34.
that = in order that. Gr. *hina.*

5. 21-29 (F, above). PROOF. COMMUNICATION. (*Introversion.*)

F | G | 21. Concerning quickening and resurrection.
  H | 22, 23. Concerning judgment.
  H | 24. Concerning judgment.
  G | 25-29. Concerning quickening and resurrection.

21 raiseth = awaketh. Gr. *egeirō.* Ap. 178. I. 4. **quickeneth** = giveth life to. Occ. in John only here, twice, and 6. 63. Then universally believed by the Jews. **the dead** = corpses. See Ap. 139. 1. **them.** Supply the *Ellipsis* (complex, Ap. 6. III. 2), thus: "quickeneth [whom He will]; so the Son also [raiseth the dead, and] quickeneth whom He will." **the Son** = the Son also. **22 For . . . no man** = For not even . . . any one. Gr. *oude oudeis.* A double negative. **judgeth.** One of the characteristic words of this Gospel. See Ap. 122. I and p. 1511. **committed** = given. **judgment.** Gr. *krisis.* Ap. 177. 7. **23 even as.** Gr. *kathōs.* **not.** Gr. *mē.* Ap. 105. II. **sent.** Gr. *pempō.* Ap. 174. 4. One of the characteristic words of this Gospel. See note on 1. 22 and p. 1511. **24 word.** Gr. *logos.* See note on Mark 9. 32. **believeth on.** See Ap. 150. I. ii. **everlasting.** Gr. *aiōnios.* Ap. 151. II. B. ii. **life.** See note on 1. 4. **condemnation** = judgment, as in *v.* 22. **is** = has. **from** = out of. Gr. *ek.* Ap. 104. vii. **unto.** Same as "into", above.

5. 25-29 (*G*, above). CONCERNING QUICKENING AND RESURRECTION. (*Alternation.*)

G | j | 25, 26. Resurrection.
  k | 27. Judgment.
  j | 28, 29-. Resurrection.
  k | -29. Judgment.

25 The hour = An hour. Put by Fig. *Synecdochē* (of the Part), Ap. 6, for a definite and special time. **now is.** Because, had the nation repented, "all that the prophets had spoken" would have been fulfilled according to Acts 3. 21, including the resurrection foretold in Ezek. 37, and Isa. 26. 19, &c. **the Son of God.** Ap. 98. XV. This title is associated with *resurrection*, as in *v.* 27 *judgment* is with the Son of man. **shall live.** See note on 4. 50. **26 as** = even as. Gr. *hōsper.* **hath He given** = He gave (in eternity past). **27 authority.** Gr. *exousia.* See Ap. 172. 5. **the Son of man** (see Ap. 98. XVI). The only occ. in John without the Article (except Rev. 1. 13; 14. 14). Cp. Dan. 7. 13. **28 the graves** = the tombs. Therefore they are not in heaven or hell.

A.D. 27 29 And shall come forth; they that have
°done °good, [24]unto °the °resurrection of [24]life;
k and they that have °done °evil, [24]unto °the °re-
surrection of °damnation.
E 30 I can [19]of Mine own Self do [19]nothing: [26]as
I hear, I [22]judge: and My [22]judgment is just; because I seek [10]not Mine own °will, but the
°will of °the Father Which hath [23]sent Me.
F J 31 °If °I °bear witness °of Myself, My °wit-
ness is [10]not °true.
32 °There is [7]another that [31]beareth witness
[31]of Me; and I °know that the [31]witness which
he [31]witnesseth [31]of Me is [31]true.
33 Ye °sent °unto John, and °he [31]bare witness unto the °truth.
34 But I receive [10]not testimony °from [5]man:
but these things I say, °that ye might be saved.
35 He was °a burning and a shining °light:
and ye [6]were willing °for a °season to rejoice
[3]in his °light.
K 36 But I have °greater [31]witness than *that*
of John: for the [20]works which [19]the Father
[26]hath given Me °to finish, the same [20]works
that I do, [31]bear witness [31]of Me, that [19]the
Father hath [33]sent Me.
37 And [19]the Father Himself, Which °hath
[23]sent Me, °hath [31]borne witness [31]of Me. Ye
have °neither heard His voice at any time, °nor
°seen His °shape.
38 And ye have [10]not His [24]word °abiding [3]in
you: for Whom He °hath [33]sent, Him ye [24]believe
[10]not.
L 39 °Search °the scriptures; for [3]in them ye
think ye have °eternal life: and they are they
which °testify [31]of Me.
40 And ye °will [10]not come °to Me, [20]that ye
°might have [24]life.
K 41 I receive [10]not °honour [34]from [5]men.
42 But I [6]know you, that ye have [10]not the
°love of God [3]in °you.
43 I am come [3]in [17]My Father's name, and
ye receive Me [10]not: [31]if [7]another shall come [3]in
his own name, °him ye will receive.
44 How can ye °believe, which receive
[41]honour °one of another, and seek [10]not °the
[41]honour that *cometh* [34]from °God only?
J 45 Do [23]not think that I will accuse you [40]to
[19]the Father: there is *one* that accuseth you,
even °Moses, °in whom °ye trust.
46 For °had ye [24]believed [45]Moses, ye would
have [24]believed °Me: for he °wrote [31]of °Me.
47 But °if ye [24]believe [10]not his °writings, how
shall ye [24]believe My °words?"

29 done = wrought. Gr. *poieō* = accomplished (referring to the object, aim or end of the act), and generally associated with *good*.
good = good things (Pl.). **the** = a.
resurrection. Gr. *anastasis.* Ap. 178. II. 1.
done (Gr. *prassō.* Cp. 3. 20, 21) = practised (referring to the means by which the object is obtained) and is associated with evil, as are four out of six occurrences of the noun *praxis* (= deed), Matt. 16. 27. Luke 23. 51. Acts 19. 18. Rom. 8. 13; 12. 4. Col. 3. 9.
evil = evil things (pl.). Same word as in 3. 20.
damnation = judgment. Gr. *krisis*, as in *v.* 22.
30 will. Gr. *thelēma.* Ap. 102. 2.
the Father. All the texts read "Him".

5. 31-47 (*F*, p. 1526). PROOF, WITNESSES.
(*Introversion.*)

F | J | 31-35. The witness of John.
K | 36-38. The Father's witness.
L | 39, 40. The testimony of Scripture.
K | 41-44. The Father's witness.
J | 45-47. The witness of Moses.

31 If. Assuming the condition, where experience will decide. Ap. 118. 1. b.
I. Emphatic = I alone.
bear witness. See note on 1. 7.
of = concerning. Gr. *peri.* Ap. 104. xiii. 1. The emphasis being on "Myself". Gr. *emautou.*
witness. See note on 1. 7.
true. Ap. 175. 1. Referring to Deut. 19. 15. Cp. 8. 14. See p. 1511.
32 There is. See *v.* 31 and 7. 28; 8. 26.
know. Gr. *oida.* Ap. 132. I. i.
33 sent = have sent. Gr. *apostellō.* Ap. 174. 1.
unto. Gr. *pros.* Ap. 104. xv. 3.
he bare = he hath borne.
truth. See note on 1. 14.
34 from. Gr. *para.* Ap. 104. xii. 1.
35 a . . . light = the . . . lamp. Gr. *luchnos.* Ap. 130. 4. A common Rabbinic idiom for a famous man. In contrast with Christ (8. 12).
for. Gr. *pros.* Ap. 104. xv. 3.
season. Gr. hour, put by Fig. *Metonymy* (of Subject), Ap. 6, for a brief period. Cp. 12. 23.
light. Gr. *phōs.* Ap. 130. 1.
36 greater witness = the witness, greater.
to finish = in order that I should complete them.
37 hath sent = sent (at a definite time).
hath borne. And still bears.
neither . . . nor. Gr. *oute . . . oute.*
seen. Gr. *horaō.* Ap. 133. I. 8.
shape = form. Gr. *eidos.* Cp. Luke 3. 22; 9. 39.
38 abiding. See note on 1. 32. **hath sent** = sent.
39 Search. Gr. *ereunaō* = to search as a lion or hound tracks by the scent. Not the same word as in Acts 17. 11. Here the Verb may be the imperative or indicative mood; but the indicative never commences a sentence without the pronoun or some other word, while the imperative is so used. See 7. 52; 14. 11 (Believe); 15. 20 (Remember).
the scriptures = the (sacred) writings.
eternal. Ap. 151. II. B. i, as in *v.* 24.
testify. See note on 1. 7.

40 will not come = do not will (*v.* 6) to come. **to.** Gr. *pros.* Ap. 104. xv. 3. **might** = may. **41 honour.** Gr. *doxa* = approval, here, as in *v.* 44; or "praise", as in 9. 24; 12. 43. 1 Pet. 4. 11. See p. 1511. **42 love of God** = love toward God. Gen. of Relation. Ap. 17. 5. Occ. in the Gospels elsewhere only in Luke 11. 42. **you** = yourselves, as in 6. 53. Mark 4. 17. 1 John 5. 10. **43 him, &c.** Cp. 2 Thess. 2. 4. **44 believe.** Ap. 150. I. 1. i. **one of another** = from (Gr. *para.* Ap. 104. xii. I) one another. **the.** Note the Art. here, and not in the preceding clause. **God only** = the only God (Ap. 98. I. i. 1). Cp. 1 Tim. 1. 17. **45 Moses.** See note on 1. 17. **in** = on. Gr. *eis.* Ap. 104. vi. **ye trust** = ye have set your hope. **46 had ye** = if (Ap. 118. 2. a) ye had. **wrote.** See Ap. 47. **Me.** See note on Luke 24. 27. **47 if.** Ap. 118. 2. a. **writings.** Gr. Pl. of *gramma* = letters, used of *written characters*, or of a *document.* For the former, see Luke 23. 38. 2 Cor. 3. 7; or the *letter* of Scripture contrasted with its *spirit* (Rom. 2. 27, 29; 7. 6. 2 Cor. 3. 6). For the latter see Luke 16. 6, 7 (where it is a debtor's account), and Acts 28. 21 (where it is an ordinary letter). In 7. 15 and Acts 26. 24, it is used for learning (cp. Isa. 29. 11, 12. Acts 4. 13). In 2 Tim. 3. 15 it is used for the sacred writings as a whole. Hence the Scribes were called *grammateis.* **words.** Gr. *rhēma* (pl.). See note on Mark 9. 32.

$X^2 M^1$ N P f A.D. 27 **6** °After these things °Jesus °went over the
sea °of Galilee, °which is *the sea* °of
°Tiberias.
2 And a great °multitude °followed Him,
g because they °saw °His °miracles which He
°did °on them that were diseased.
Q **3** And [1]Jesus went up °into °a mountain,
and there He °sat °with His disciples.
A.D. 28 **4** °And the °passover, °a °feast of the °Jews,
was nigh.
O R **5** °When [1]Jesus °then °lifted up *His* eyes, and
°saw °a great °company °come °unto Him, He
saith °unto °Philip, "Whence shall we buy
°bread, °that these may eat?"
S **6** And this He said °to prove him: for He
Himself °knew what He °would do.
R **7** [5]Philip answered Him, "Two hundred
°pennyworth of [5]bread is °not sufficient for
them, [5]that °every one of them may take a
little."
8 One °of His disciples, °Andrew, °Simon
Peter's brother, saith unto Him,
9 "There is °a lad here, which hath °five
°barley loaves, and two °small fishes: °but
what are they °among so many?"
S T **10** And [1]Jesus said, "Make the °men °sit
down." (°Now there was much grass °in the
place.) So the men °sat down, in number about
five thousand.
U **11** And [1]Jesus took the loaves; and when
He had given thanks, He distributed °to the
disciples, and the disciples to them that were
[10]set down; °and likewise of the [9]fishes °as
much as they °would.
T **12** °When they were °filled, He said unto
His disciples, "Gather up the fragments that
°remain, [5]that nothing be lost."
U **13** Therefore they gathered *them* together,

6. 1-71 (X^2, p. 1524). IN GALILEE. (*Division.*)

X^2 | M^1 | 1-15. The FOURTH Sign. (The Feeding of the 5,000.)
M^2 | 16-25. The FIFTH Sign. (The Walking on the Sea.)
M^3 | 26-71. The Signification of the Fourth and Fifth Signs.

6. 1-15 (M^1, above). THE FOURTH SIGN. (*Introversions and Alternation.*)

M^1 | N | P | f | 1, 2-. Crowd. Following.
g | -2. Signs seen.
Q | 3, 4. Departure to the mountain.
O | 5-13. The Fourth Sign. (The Feeding of the 5,000.)
N | *P* | g | 14-. Sign seen.
f | -14. Crowd. Confession.
Q | 15. Departure to the mountain.

1 After these things. This expression occurs seven times in John's Gospel; and "after this" three times. **After.** Gr. *meta.* Ap. 104. xi. 2. Cp. 5. 1.
Jesus. See Ap. 98. X. **went**=went away.
of. The Gen. of Relation. See Ap. 17. 5.
which is the sea of. This is the rendering of the Gen. "of" Tiberias.
Tiberias. The city is still in existence. It was not visited by the Lord, and therefore not guilty of rejecting Him. All the cities which did reject Him have perished.
2 multitude=crowd. **followed**=was following.
saw=beheld. Gr. *horaō.* Ap. 133. I. 8. Not the same word as in *vv.* 5, 14, 19, 22, 24, 26, 30, 40, 62, but same as in *vv.* 36, 46, 46. L Tr. A WH R. read *theōreō*, Ap. 133. I. 11, as in *v.* 19.
His. All the texts omit "His".
miracles=signs. See note on 2. 11. Ap. 176. 3.
did=was doing, or working.
on. Gr. *epi.* Ap. 104. ix. 1.
3 into. Gr. *eis.* Ap. 104. vi.
a mountain=the mountain, i.e. the one overlooking the lake.
sat=was sitting [when He saw the crowds approaching]. **with**=amid. Gr. *meta.* Ap. 104. xi. 1.
4 And=Now.
passover. Gr. *pascha.* Aramaic. Ap. 94. III. 3.
a=the.
feast of the Jews. See note on 2. 13.
Jews. See note on 1. 19.

6. 5-13 (O, above). THE FOURTH SIGN. (The feeding of the 5,000.) (*Alternation.*)

O | R | 5. Question to Philip.
S | 6. Sign purposed.
R | 7-9. Answer of Philip.
S | 10-13. Sign performed.

5 When . . . lifted up=having lifted up. **then**=therefore. Cp. *v.* 15, and see Ap. 176. **saw**=having seen. Gr. *theaomai*, Ap. 133. I. 12. **a great . . . come**=that a great . . . is coming. **company**=crowd, as in *v.* 2. **unto**=toward. Gr. *pros.* Ap. 104. xv. 3. Not the same word as in *vv.* 16, 27. **Philip.** Because Bethsaida (Ap. 169) was a neighbouring town. Cp. 1. 44; 12. 21. See Ap. 141. **bread**=loaves. **that**=in order that. Gr. *hina.* **6 to prove**=proving, i.e. putting him to the test. **knew.** Gr. *oida.* Ap. 132. I. i. See note on 1. 26. **would do**=was about to do. **7 pennyworth.** See Ap. 51. I. 4. **not.** Gr. *ou.* Ap. 105. I. **every . . . little.** Recorded only in John. **8 of.** Gr. *ek.* Ap. 104. vii. **Andrew.** Ap. 141. He appears with Philip in 1. 44; 12. 22. **Simon Peter.** Ap. 141. **9 a lad**=a little boy. Gr. *paidarion.* Ap. 108. vi. The "baker boy", with his basket of barley-loaves, is still to be seen where people congregate. **five.** See Ap. 10. **barley.** Gr. *krithinos.* Occ. only here and *v.* 13. Cp. Judg. 7. 13. 2 Kings 4. 42. Ezek. 13. 19. **small fishes.** Gr. *opsarion.* Occ. only here, *v.* 11, and 21. 9, 10, 13. **among**=for. Gr. *eis.* Ap. 104. vi.

6. 10-13 (*S*, above). SIGN PERFORMED. (*Alternation.*)

S | T | 10. Command to sit down.
U | 11. Distribution.
T | 12. Command to gather.
U | 13. Gathering.

10 men. Ap. 123. 1. **sit down**=recline. **Now, &c.** See note on "and we", 1. 14. **in.** Gr. *en.* Ap. 104. viii. **11 to the disciples, and the disciples.** Om. by all the texts and Syr. **and likewise**=likewise also. **as much as they would.** Recorded only in John. **would**=wished. Ap. 102. 1. **12 When**=But when. **filled.** Not the same word as in *v.* 26. **remain**=remain over, as in *v.* 13.

A. D. 28 and filled °twelve °baskets with the fragments
[8]of the [9]five [9]barley loaves, which [12]remained
over and above °unto them that had °eaten.

NPg 14 °Then °those [10]men, when they had °seen
the [2]miracle that [1]Jesus did, said,

f "This is °of a truth °that prophet that should
come [3]into the °world."

Q 15 When [1]Jesus therefore °perceived that
they °would come and take Him by force, °to
make Him a king, He °departed again [3]into
[3]a mountain Himself alone.

M[2] V j 16 And when °even was *now* come, His disciples went down °unto the sea,

k 17 And entered [3]into °a ship, and °went over
the sea °toward °Capernaum.

W l And it °was °now dark, and [1]Jesus was °not
come °to them.

m 18 And the sea °arose by reason of a great
°wind °that blew.

X n 19 So when they had rowed about °five and
twenty or thirty °furlongs, they °see [1]Jesus
walking [2]on the sea, and drawing nigh unto
the [17]ship:

o and they were afraid.

X n 20 But He saith unto them, °"It is I;

o be °not afraid."

W l 21 [5]Then they °willingly received Him [3]into
the ship:

m °and immediately the [17]ship °was °at the
°land °whither they °went.

V j 22 The day following, when the °people
which stood on °the other side of the sea [14]saw
that there was °none °other °boat there, save
that one °whereinto His disciples were entered,
and that [1]Jesus went [7]not with His disciples
[3]into the °boat, but *that* His disciples °were
gone away alone;
23 °(Howbeit there came [22]other [22]boats °from
[1]Tiberias nigh unto the place where they did
[5]eat bread, after that °the Lord had given
thanks:)
24 When the [22]people therefore [14]saw that
[1]Jesus was [7]not there, neither His disciples,

k °they also °took shipping, and came °to [17]Ca-
pernaum, seeking for [1]Jesus.
25 And when they had found Him on °the
other side of the sea, they said unto Him,
°"Rabbi, when °camest Thou hither?"

M[3] Z[1] A 26 [1]Jesus answered them and said, °"Verily,
verily, I say unto you, Ye seek Me, [7]not because ye [14]saw °the [2]miracles, but because ye
did [5]eat [8]of the loaves, and °were filled.

13 twelve, one for each of the apostles.
baskets. Gr. *kophinos* = a wicker hand-basket, not the same as in Matt. 15. 37. Mark 8. 8.
unto them that had eaten. Recorded only by John.
eaten = fed. Gr. *bibrōskō.* Occ. only here. Root of our "browse", to feed in the open.
14 Then = Therefore. A supplementary note by John.
those = the. **seen.** Gr. *eidon.* Ap. 133. I. 1.
of a truth = truly.
that prophet that should come = the prophet who is coming. See 1. 21. **world.** See note on 1. 9.
15 perceived. See note on 1. 10. Ap. 132. I. ii.
would come = were about to come.
to = in order that (Gr. *hina*) they might.
departed = withdrew. Gr. *anachōreō.* Only here in John.

6. 16-25 (M[2], p. 1528). THE FIFTH SIGN.
(*Introversion and Alternations.*)

M[2] | V | j | 16. At the sea. Disciples.
    k | 17-. A boat (*ploion*).
  W | l | -17. The Lord absent.
    m | 18. Sudden danger.
   X | n | 19-. The Lord seen.
     o | -19. "They were afraid."
   X | *n* | 20-. The Lord heard.
     o | -20. "Be not afraid."
  W | *l* | 21-. The Lord present.
    m | -21. The sudden safety.
 V | *j* | 22-24-. At the sea. Crowd.
   k | -24, 25. The boats (*ploiaria*).

16 even . . . come = it became late.
unto. Gr. *epi.* Ap. 104. ix. 3. Not the same word as in *vv.* 5, 27, 34, 45, -65.
17 a ship = a fishing-smack. Gr. *ploion.* Not *ploiarion*, as in *v.* 22. **went** = were going.
toward. Gr. *eis.* Ap. 104. vi.
Capernaum. See Ap. 169.
was = had become. **now** = already.
not. Gr. *ou*, but all the texts read *oupō*, "not yet".
to. Gr. *pros.* Ap. 104. xv. 3.
18 arose = was rising.
wind. Gr. *anemos.* Only here in John.
that blew = [that was] blowing.
19 five and twenty . . . furlongs (Ap. 51. III. 1 (2)). About half-way.
see. Gr. *theōreō.* Ap. 133. I. 11.
20 It is I = I am [He]. Cp. 4. 26; 8. 24, 28, 58; 13. 19; 18. 5, 6, 8. Mark 13. 6. Luke 21. 8.
not. Gr. *mē.* Ap. 105. II. Same word as in *vv.* 27, 43. Not the same as in *vv.* 7, 17, 22, 24, 26, 32, 36, 38, 42, 46, 56, 64-, 70.
21 willingly received = were willing to receive.
and . . . went. Recorded only by John.
was = became. **at.** Gr. *epi.* Ap. 104. ix. 1.
land, or shore. Gr. *gē.* Ap. 129. 4.
whither = to (Gr. *eis*) which.
went = were bound.
22 people = crowd.
the other side. The eastern. In *v.* 25 the western; cp. *v.* 59. **none.** Gr. *ouk.* Ap. 105. I.
other. Ap. 124. 1.
boat = dinghy. Gr. *ploiarion.* The one belonging to the *ploion* of *v.* 17 (which had gone away). *Ploiarion* occurs only here, *vv.* 23, 24; 21. 8. Mark 3. 9; 4. 36. *Ploion*, here = smack, is the usual word for "ship"; *ploiarion* = the dinghy belonging to it.
whereinto = into (Gr. *eis.* As in *v.* 3) which. **were gone** = went away. **23 Howbeit.** See note on "and we beheld", 1. 14. **from** = out from. Gr. *ek.* Ap. 104. vii. **the Lord.** See Ap. 98. VI. i. *a.* 3. B. c. **24 they** = themselves. Emphatic. **took shipping** = entered into (Gr. *eis*, *v.* 3) the boats (*ploia*), but all the texts read *ploiaria.* **to** = unto. Gr. *eis*, as in *v.* 3. **25 the other side.** The western. In *v.* 22, the eastern. **Rabbi.** See Ap. 98. XIV. vii. **camest Thou hither** = hast Thou got here.

6. 26-71 [For Structure see next page].

26 Verily, verily. The eighth occ. See note on 1. 51. **the miracles** = signs. No Art. **were filled** = satisfied. Not the same word as in *v.* 12.

A.D. 28 27 °Labour [20]not for the °meat which perisheth, °but for that °meat which °endureth °unto
°everlasting °life, which °the Son of man shall
give unto you: for °Him hath °God °the Father
°sealed."

B 28 [5]Then said they [5]unto Him, °"What shall we
do, [5]that we might °work the °works of [27]God?"
29 [1]Jesus °answered and said unto them,
"This is the [28]work of [27]God, [5]that ye °believe
on Him Whom He hath °sent."

A C 30 They said °therefore unto Him, °"What
°sign shewest Thou then, [5]that we may [14]see,
and °believe Thee? °what dost Thou work?
31 °Our fathers did [5]eat °manna [10]in the
desert; °as it is written, °'**He gave them bread**
[23]**from °heaven to [5]eat.'**"

D 32 [5]Then [1]Jesus said unto them, [26]"Verily,
verily, I say unto you, °Moses gave you [7]not
°that bread [23]from [31]heaven; but °My Father
giveth you the °true bread [23]from [31]heaven.
33 For the bread of [27]God is °He Which
cometh down [23]from [31]heaven, and giveth
[27]life unto °the [14]world."

C 34 [5]Then said they [5]unto Him, °"Lord,
°evermore give us this bread."

D 35 And [1]Jesus said unto them, °"I am the
bread of [27]life: he that cometh [17]to Me shall
°never hunger; and he that [29]believeth on Me
shall °never thirst.

B 36 But I said unto you, That °ye also have
°seen Me, °and °believe [7]not.

Z^2 E 37 °All that [27]the Father giveth Me shall
°come [17]to Me; and him that °cometh [17]to
Me I will °in no wise °cast °out.

6. 26-71 (M^3, p. 1528). THE SIGNIFICATION OF THE FOURTH AND FIFTH SIGNS. COLLOQUIES. (*Division.*)

M^3 | Z^1 | 26-36. With unbelievers.
| Z^2 | 37-59. With believers.
| Z^3 | 60-71. With disciples.

6. 26-36 (Z^1, above). COLLOQUY WITH UNBELIEVERS. (*Alternation.*)

Z^1 | A | 26, 27. Bread: earthly.
B | 28, 29. Belief.
A | 30-35. Bread: heavenly.
B | 36. Unbelief.

27 Labour not . . . but = Labour for the latter rather than for the former. Fig. *Heterōsis* (of Degree). Ap. 6.
meat. Gr. *brōsis*, the act of eating (Matt. 6. 19, 20 = "rust"). Not *brōma* = food (4. 34). Cp. also 1 Cor. 8. 4.
endureth. Gr. *menō*. Same as "dwelleth", *v.* 56. See note on "abode", 1. 32. [16, 28, 34, 45, -65.
unto. Gr. *eis*. Ap. 104. vi. Not the same as in *vv.* 5,
everlasting. Gr. *aiōnios*. See Ap. 151. II. B. ii.
life. Gr. *zōē*. See note on 1. 4, and Ap. 170. 1.
the Son of man. See Ap. 98. XVI.
Him hath God the Father sealed = for Him (= this One) the Father, even God, sealed.
God. See Ap. 98. I. i. 1.
the Father. See note on 1. 14.
sealed. The Jews discussed "the seal of God", e. g. "What is the seal of the Holy, Blessed God? Rabbi Bibai answered, 'Truth'. But what is 'truth'? Rabbi Bon saith, 'the living God and King eternal'. Rabbi Chaninah saith . . . 'truth is the seal of God'." *Bab. Talmud*, Sanhedr., quoted by Lightfoot, vol. xii, p. 291 (Pitman's ed.).
28 What shall we do . . . ? = What are we to do . . . ?
work the works. Fig. *Polyptōton*. Ap. 6.
works. See note on 4. 34.
29 answered and said. See Ap. 122. 3, and note on Deut. 1. 41.
believe on. See Ap. 150. I. 1. v (i), and note on 1. 7.
sent. Gr. *apostellō*. Ap. 174. 1.

6. 30-35 (*A*, above). BREAD: HEAVENLY. (*Alternation.*)

A | C | 30, 31. Request of Jews for sign.
D | 32, 33. Answer. Bread from heaven.
C | 34. Request of Disciples for thing signified.
D | 35. Answer. Bread of life.

30 therefore. In consequence of the Lord's claim. **What sign, &c.** The emphasis is on "Thou". **sign** See note on 2. 18. **believe Thee.** See Ap. 150. I. 1. ii, and note on 1. 7. **what . . . ?** = what [sign], &c.? **31 Our fathers, &c.** See Ex. 16. 15. Over half a million able for war; probably three millions in all. Num. 2. 32. **manna** = the manna. **as** = according as. **He gave, &c.** Quoted from Ps. 78. 24. This was their hope and belief; and this was the "sign" looked for in "the days of Messiah". So the *Midrash* (a Commentary on Ecc.): "The former Redeemer [Moses] caused manna to descend for them; in like manner shall our latter Redeemer [Messiah] cause manna to come down, as it is written: 'There shall be a handful of corn in the earth' (Ps. 72. 16)." See *Lightfoot*, vol. xii, p. 293. **heaven.** Singular. See note on Matt. 6. 9, 10. **32 Moses.** The fifth of seven refs. to Moses. See note on 1. 17. The Gemarists affirm that "manna was given for 'the merits of Moses'". **that bread** = the [true] bread. **My Father.** See note on 2. 16. **true.** Gr. *alēthinos*. See note on 1. 9, and Ap. 175. 2. **33 He**, or "That". **the world.** Put by Fig. *Metonymy* (of Subject), Ap. 6, for its inhabitants. Used in John to show that Gentiles will be included in Israel's blessing. **34 Lord.** See Ap. 98. VI. i. a. 3. B. a. **evermore.** Gr. *pantote*, see notes on *v.* 35. **35 I am the bread of life.** A form of expression peculiar to this Gospel. The Fig. *Metaphor* (Ap. 6), which carries over, and asserts that one thing is, i. e. *represents* the other; thus differing from *Similē*, and *Hypocatastasis* (Ap. 6). See Ap. 159, par. 1. Note the seven (Ap. 10) examples in this Gospel: I am the Bread of Life (6. 35, 41, 48, 51); the Light of the world (8. 12; 9. 5); the Door of the sheep (10. 7, 9); the Good Shepherd (10. 11, 14); the Resurrection and the Life (11. 25); the true and living Way (14. 6); the true Vine (15. 1, 5). **never** = in no wise. Gr. *ou mē*. Ap. 105. III. **never thirst** = in no wise at any time (Gr. *ou mē . . . pōpote*) thirst. Or supply the *Ellipsis* by repeating "*pōpote*" after "hunger". Both A.V. and R.V. renderings are inadequate. The A.V. includes the Gr. *pōpote* in the second "never". The R.V. weakens the first "never" by rendering it "not". Neither A.V. nor R.V. give the force of the strong negative *ou mē*. **36 ye also have seen Me** = ye have seen Me also; with emphasis on "seen". **and** = yet. **believe.** Ap. 150. I. 1. i.

6. 37-59 [For Structure see next page].

37 All = Whatever (Neut. sing.). **come . . . cometh.** "come" = reach, denoting arrival; "cometh" denotes the act and process. **in no wise.** Gr. *ou mē*. Ap. 105. III. As "never" in *v.* 35. **cast out.** Referring to the Divine Supplement "send away" in Matt. 14. 15. Put by Fig. *Tapeinōsis* (Ap. 6) for giving blessing to such. **out** = without.

A.D. 28 38 For °I came down [23] from [31] heaven, [7] not
[15] to do Mine own °will, but the °will of Him
That °sent Me.
39 And this is [27] the Father's [38] will Which
hath [38] sent Me, [5] that °of all which He hath
given me I should °lose nothing, but should
°raise it up again °at the last day.
40 And this is the [38] will of Him That [38] sent
Me, [5] that every one which [19] seeth °the Son,
and [29] believeth on Him, °may have [27] everlasting [27] life: °and I will [39] raise him up [39] at
the last day."
F 41 [4] The Jews [5] then °murmured °at Him,
because He said, [35] "I am the bread which
came down [23] from [31] heaven."
42 And °they said, "Is [7] not this [1] Jesus, the
son of Joseph, whose father and mother we
[6] know? how is it [5] then that He saith, [38] 'I
came down [23] from [31] heaven?'"
E 43 [1] Jesus therefore answered and said unto
them, [41] "Murmur [20] not °among yourselves.
44 °No man °can [37] come [17] to Me, °except
[27] the Father Which hath [38] sent Me °draw
him: and I will [39] raise him up [39] at the last
day.
45 °It is written [10] in °the prophets, '**And
they shall be °all °taught of [27] God.**' Every
man therefore that hath heard, and hath
learned °of [27] the Father, [37] cometh [5] unto Me.
46 [7] Not that °any man hath [2] seen [27] the
Father, °save He Which is °of [27] God, He hath
[2] seen [27] the Father.
47 [26] Verily, verily, I say unto you, He that
[29] believeth on Me °hath [27] everlasting [27] life.
F p 48 [35] I am °that bread of [27] life.
49 Your fathers °did [5] eat manna [10] in the
wilderness, and °are dead.
50 This is the bread which cometh down
[23] from [31] heaven, [5] that °a man may eat °there-
of, and [20] not die.
51 [35] I am the °living bread which came
[23] down from heaven:
q °if [46] any man [5] eat [8] of °this bread, °he shall
live °for ever: °and the bread that I will give
is °My °flesh, which °I will give °for the [27] life
of [33] the world."
r 52 [4] The Jews therefore °strove °among themselves, saying, "How [44] can this Man give us
His [51] flesh to [5] eat?"
q 53 [5] Then [1] Jesus said unto them, [26] "Verily,

6. 37-59 (Z^2, p. 1530). COLLOQUY WITH BELIEVERS. (*Alternation*.)

Z^2 | E | 37-40. The Father. His will.
F | 41, 42. The Lord. Bread from heaven. Jews murmuring.
E | 43-47. The Father. His action.
F | 48-59. The Lord. Bread of life. Jews murmuring.
} The Signification of the Fourth Sign.

38 I came down = I am come down.
will. Gr. *thelēma.* Ap. 102. 2.
sent. See note on 1. 22.
39 of all = whatever, as in *v.* 37. Cp. *v.* 44, and 12. 32.
lose nothing = not (Ap. 105. II) lose any of (Gr. *ek.* Ap. 104. vii) it. **raise.** Ap. 178. I. 1.
at the last day. An expression found only in John (five times): here; *vv.* 44, 54; 11. 24; 12. 48. Cp. 1 John 2. 18. It refers to the coming of Messiah, and was used idiomatically for "the age to come", at the end of that dispensation (see *Lightfoot*, vol. xii, p. 294. Pitman's ed.). It would then have taken place had Israel repented. See Acts 3. 19-21. **at** = in. Gr. *en.* Ap. 104. viii.
40 the Son. Cp. 3. 36. **may** = should.
and I will = and (that) I should.
41 murmured = were murmuring. Gr. *gonguzō*, the Sept. word for Israel's murmuring in the wilderness. See 1 Cor. 10. 10. Cp. Jude 16.
at = concerning. Gr. *peri.* Ap. 104. xiii. 1.
42 they said = were saying.
43 among yourselves = with (Gr. *meta.* Ap. 104. xi. 1) one another.
44 No man = No (Ap. 105. I) one.
can come = is able to come (two verbs).
except. Gr. *ean mē.* Ap. 118. 1. b and 105. II.
draw him. Those thus *drawn* are defined in *v.* 37 as "all" those who are *given* (without *exception*). In 12. 32 the "all" are not thus defined, and denote "all" (without *distinction*).
45 It is written = It standeth written.
the prophets. See Isa. 54. 13. Jer. 31. 34.
all. Here it denotes "all" without exception. See note on "draw him", *v.* 44.
taught of God. In 1 Thess. 4. 9 the words are compounded (*theodidaktos*).
of = from. Gr. *para.* Ap. 104. xii. 1, implying close intimacy. See *v.* 46.
46 any man = any one.
save. Gr. *ei mē* = if not. Ap. 118. 2. a and 105. II.
of = from (beside). Gr. *para.* Ap. 104. xii. 1. Implying past and present union. Cp. 7. 29; 9. 16, 33.
47 hath = possesseth. Not, of course, in himself (or he would never die), but by faith in Christ.

6. 48-59 (*F*, above). THE LORD. BREAD OF LIFE. (*Introversion*.)

F | p | 48-51-. The Sign.
q | -51. The Signification.
r | 52. The Jews. Contention.
q | 53-57. The Signification.
p | 58, 59. The Sign.

48 that = the. **49 did eat** = ate. **are dead** = died. **50 a man** = any one: i.e. without distinction. **thereof** = of (Gr. *ek.* Ap. 104. vii) it. **51 living.** See note on 4. 10. **if.** For the condition, see Ap. 118. 1. b. **this bread** = this [One before you]. One of three passages in which "this" indicates the speaker. Cp. 2. 19. Matt. 16. 18. **he shall live**; in and by resurrection. See note on 4. 50, 51, 53. **for ever** = unto the age. See Ap. 151. II. A. ii. 4. a. **and the bread that I will give** = but the bread, moreover, which I will give. The omission of the particle ("*de*") in A.V. hides the line of the discussion: (1) I will give this bread; (2) This bread is My flesh; (3) My flesh is My body which I will give up in death. **My flesh** = Myself. Put by the Fig. *Synecdochē* (of the Part), Ap. 6, for the whole person, as in Gen. 17. 13. Ps. 16. 9 (Acts 2. 26-31). Prov. 14. 30. Matt. 19. 5. Rom. 3. 20. 1 Cor. 1. 29. 2 Cor. 7. 5; and for Christ's own person, 1. 14. 1 Tim. 3. 16. 1 Pet. 3. 18. Heb. 10. 20. 1 John 4. 2. Just as "My soul" is also put for the whole person (Num. 23. 10. Judg. 16. 30. Ps. 3. 2; 16. 10; 33. 19; 103. 1. Isa. 58. 5. Acts 2. 31. Rom. 13. 1). In view of the Jews' unbelief, the Lord used the Fig. *Synecdochē* here. To take a figure of speech literally, and treat what is literal as a figure, is the most fruitful source of error. **flesh.** See note on 1. 13. **I will give.** All the texts omit this, but not the Syr. See Ap. 94. V, note 3. **for.** *Gr. huper.* Ap. 104. xvii. 1. **52 strove** = were contending. Gr. *machomai.* Only here, Acts 7. 26. 2 Tim. 2. 24. James 4. 2. An advance on "murmuring" in *v.* 41. **among themselves** = with (Gr. *pros.* Ap. 104. xv. 3) one another.

A.D. 28 verily, I say unto you, [44]Except ye °eat the
°flesh of [27]the Son of man, and °drink His
°blood, ye have °no [27]life [10]in you.
54 Whoso °eateth My [53]flesh, and [53]drinketh
My [53]blood, hath °eternal [27]life; and I will
[39]raise him up [39]at the last day.
55 For My [51]flesh is meat °indeed, and My
[53]blood is drink °indeed.
56 He that [54]eateth My [51]flesh, and [53]drinketh
My [53]blood, °dwelleth [10]in Me, and I [10]in him.
57 °As the [51]living [27]Father hath [29]sent Me,
and I °live °by [27]the Father: so he that [54]eat-
eth Me, even He shall °live °by Me.
p 58 °This is that bread which came down
[23]from [31]heaven: [7]not [31]as your fathers did
[5]eat manna, and [49]are dead: he that [54]eateth
of [51]this bread shall °live [51]for ever."
59 These things said He [10]in the °synagogue,
as He taught [10]in [17]Capernaum.
Z^3 G s 60 °Many therefore [8]of His disciples, when
they had heard *this*, said, °"This is an hard
°saying; who [44]can hear it?"
t 61 When [1]Jesus [6]knew [10]in Himself that His
disciples [41]murmured [41]at °it, He said unto
them, "Doth this °offend °you?
62 °*What* and [51]if ye shall [19]see [27]the Son of
man °ascend up where He was before?
63 It is °the spirit that °quickeneth; °the
[51]flesh profiteth °nothing: the °words that I
°speak unto you, *they* are °spirit, and *they* are
[27]life.
u 64 But there are some [8]of you that [36]believe
[7]not." For [1]Jesus [6]knew °from the beginning who they were that °believed [20]not, and
who °should betray Him.
65 And He said, °"Therefore said I unto
you, that [44]no man [44]can [37]come [5]unto Me, [44]ex-
cept it were given unto him [8]of [32]My Father."
G s 66 [23]From °that *time* many of His disciples
went °back, and °walked °no more [3]with Him.
t 67 [5]Then said [1]Jesus unto the twelve, °"Will
ye also go away?"
68 [5]Then Simon Peter answered Him, [34]"Lord,
[17]to whom shall we go? Thou hast the
[63]words of [54]eternal [27]life.
69 And we °believe and °are sure that Thou
art °that Christ, °the Son of °the living [28]God."
u 70 [1]Jesus answered them, °"Have [7]not I
°chosen you °twelve, and one [8]of you is a
devil?"

53 eat . . . drink, &c. The Hebrews used this expression with reference to *knowledge* by the Fig. *Metonymy* (of the Subject), Ap. 6, as in Ex. 24. 11, where it is put for being alive; so eating and drinking denoted the operation of the mind in receiving and "inwardly digesting" truth or the words of God. See Deut. 8. 3, and cp. Jer. 15. 16. Ezek. 2. 8. No idiom was more common in the days of our Lord. With them as with us, *eating* included the meaning of *enjoyment*, as in Ecc. 5. 19; 6. 2; for "riches" cannot be *eaten*; and the Talmud actually speaks of *eating* (i.e. enjoying) "the years of Messiah", and instead of finding any difficulty in the figure they said that the days of Hezekiah were so good that "Messiah will come no more to Israel; for they have already devoured Him in the days of Hezekiah" (Lightfoot, vol. xii, pp. 296, 297). Even where *eating* is used of the devouring of enemies, it is the enjoyment of victory that is included. The Lord's words could be understood thus by hearers, for they knew the idiom; but of "the eucharist" they knew nothing, and could not have thus understood them. By comparing *vv.* 47 and 48 with *vv.* 53 and 54, we see that believing on Christ was exactly the same thing as eating and drinking Him.

flesh . . . blood. By the Fig. *Synecdochē* (of the Part), Ap. 6, this idiom is put for the whole Person. See note on "flesh", 1. 13, and cp. Matt. 16. 17. 1 Cor. 15. 50. Gal. 1. 16. Eph. 6. 12. Heb. 2. 14. **no** = not. Ap. 105. I.

54 eateth = feedeth on (so as to enjoy). Gr. *trōgō*, as in *vv.* 56, 57–58. Not the same word as in *vv.* 5, 13, 23, 26, 31, 49, 50, 53, 58–. See the two words in *v.* 58.

eternal. Gr. *aiōnios*. Ap. 151. II. B. i.

55 indeed = truly. Gr. *alēthōs*. All the texts read *alēthēs* (Ap. 175. 1); but not the Syr.

56 dwelleth = abideth. Same as "endureth" in *v.* 27. See note on "abode" in 1. 32.

57 As = According as. See 13. 15. 1 John 2. 6; 4. 17.

live. See note on 4. 50.

by = through. Gr. *dia*. Ap. 104. v 2.

58 This, &c. Cp. *v.* 50, and see on Matt. 16. 18.

live for ever. This is the opposite of death (*v.* 49), and is to be only by and through resurrection (*vv.* 39, 40, 44).

59 synagogue. See Ap. 120. I.

6. 60–71 (Z^3, p. 1530). COLLOQUY: WITH DISCIPLES.

Z^3	G	s	60. Disciples. Murmuring.
		t	61–63. The Lord's expostulation.
		u	64, 65. Some unbelievers. One betrayer.
	G	*s*	66. Disciples. Defection.
		t	67–69. The Lord's expostulation.
		u	70, 71. Twelve chosen. One betrayer.

60 Many. Other than the twelve (*v.* 70).

This is an hard saying. The emphasis is on "hard" by the Fig. *Hyperbaton* (Ap. 6).

saying. Gr. *logos*. See note on Mark 9. 32.

61 it = this. **offend** = cause to stumble.

you? Emph.; i.e. you, as well as those Jews.

62 What and if, &c.? The *Apodosis* which is wanting (by *Ellipsis*) must be supplied thus: "If (as in *v.* 51) therefore ye should behold the Son of man ascending up where He was before [will ye be offended then]?" **ascend** = ascending. **63 the spirit.** Ap. 101. II. 6. **quickeneth** = giveth life. Gr. *zōopoieō*. See note on 5. 21. **the flesh.** See note on 1. 13. **nothing.** Gr. *ouk ouden*. A double negative. **words.** Gr. *rhēma*. See note on Mark 9. 32. **speak** = have spoken, and do speak. **spirit.** See Ap. 101. II. 4. **64 from the beginning.** First occ. of "*ex archēs*" in John. As in 1. 1, the *Ellipsis* of dependent noun must be supplied here, and in the only other occurrence (16. 4): "from the beginning [of the Lord's ministry]". For the occ. of *archē* with other prepositions, see notes on 1. 1; 8. 44, and Heb. 1. 10. **believed not** = would not believe. Note the subjective emphasis of *mē*. Ap. 105. II. See also Ap. 150. I. 1. i. **should** = would. **65 Therefore** = For this cause. Gr. *dia* (Ap. 104. v. 2) *touto*. **66 that time** = this cause. It is the same cause to this day. **back.** Gr. *eis ta opisō*. **walked** = walked about. **no more.** Compound of *ou*. Ap. 105. I. **67 Will ye also go away?** = Surely ye also do not (Gr. *mē*. Ap. 105. II) wish (Ap. 102. 1) to go away? Implying a negative answer. **69 believe** = have believed. Ap. 150. I. 1. i. **are sure** = have got to know. Gr. *ginōskō*. See Ap. 132. I. ii. See note on 1. 10. **that Christ** = the Messiah. Ap. 98. IX. **the Son of . . . God.** Thus, the second portion of the Lord's ministry ends with a similar declaration on the part of Simon Peter, as in Matt. 16. 16: though not the same occasion. So the Syr. reads, showing that the various readings of the Greek need not be heeded. See Ap. 94. V, note 3. **the living God.** This expression always implies the contrast with all other gods. **70 Have not I chosen** = Did I not choose. Cp. 13. 18; 15. 16, 19. Luke 6. 13. **twelve** = the twelve. See Ap. 141.

A.D. 28 71 °He spake of °Judas °Iscariot °*the son* of Simon: for He it was °that should betray Him, being one [8] of the [70] twelve.

E H[1] J **7** °After these things °Jesus °walked °in °Galilee: for He °would °not walk °in °Jewry, because °the Jews °sought °to kill Him.

K L 2 Now °the Jews' feast °of tabernacles was °at hand.

3 °His brethren therefore said °unto Him, "Depart hence, and go °into Judæa, °that Thy disciples also may °see the °works that Thou doest.

4 For *there is* °no man *that* doeth any thing [1] in secret, and he himself seeketh to be known °openly. °If Thou do these things, °shew Thyself to the °world."

M 5 (For °neither did [3] His brethren °believe in Him.)

L N v 6 °Then [1] Jesus said unto them, "My °time is °not yet come:

w but °your °time is alway ready.

O 7 The [4] world °cannot hate you;

O but Me it hateth, because I °testify °of it, that the [3] works thereof are °evil.

N w 8 °Go ye up °unto °this feast:

v I °go [6] not up yet °unto °this feast: for My [2] time °is [6] not yet full come."

J 9 When He had said these °words unto them, He °abode *still* [1] in [1] Galilee.

K 10 But °when [3] His brethren were gone up, then went He also up [8] unto the feast, [1] not openly, but as it were [1] in secret.

H[2] P R[1] 11 [6] Then the Jews [1] sought Him °at the feast, and said, "Where is °He?"

12 And there was much °murmuring °among

71 He spake = But, or Now He was speaking.
Judas. Ap. 141.
Iscariot = a man of Kerioth, which was in Judah (Josh. 15. 25). Kerioth now probably Khan Kureitin.
the son of Simon. So designated only here, 12. 4; 13. 2, 26. The only apostle not a Galilean. Cp. 12. 6.
that should betray Him = [who] was about to betray Him. Note the two verbs. Thus ends the second portion of the Lord's ministry (Ap. 119), and thus is ushered in the third.

7. 1—11. 54- (*E*, p. 1510). THE THIRD PORTION OF THE LORD'S MINISTRY. SUBJECT: THE REJECTION OF THE KING. (*Division.*)

E H[1] | 7. 1-10. In Galilee.
H[2] | 7. 11—11. 54-. In Jerusalem.

7. 1-10 (H[1], above). IN GALILEE. (*Alternation.*)

H[1] J | 1. Galilee. Walk in.
K | 2-8. Feast of Tabernacles.
J | 9. Galilee. Continuance in.
K | 10. Feast of Tabernacles.

1 After these things. See note on 6. 1. Marking a new subject.
Jesus. See Ap. 98. X.
walked = was walking. Gr. *peripateō*. Cp. 6. 19.
in. Gr. *en*. Ap. 104. viii. **Galilee.** Ap. 169.
would not walk = did not desire (Ap. 102. 1) to walk. Note the two verbs.
not. Gr. *ou*. Ap. 105. I.
Jewry. Gr. *Ioudaia*. In Middle Eng. *Jewerie*, from the Old French *Juierie* = "Jewry", a Jews' district. Occ. elsewhere only in Dan. 5 13.
the Jews, i. e. the hostile party. See note on 1. 19.
sought = were seeking to kill Him. Thus is introduced the third subject of the Lord's ministry. Ap. 119.

7. 2-8 (K, above). FEAST OF TABERNACLES. (*Introversion.*)

K | L | 2-4. The Lord's brethren. Their advice given.
M | 5. Parenthetic remark concerning them.
L | 6-8. The Lord's brethren. Their advice rejected.

2 the Jews' feast. See note on 2. 13.
of tabernacles = of booths. Not *skēnē*, as in Sept. (Lev. 23. 34. Deut. 16. 13. 2 Chron. 8. 13. Ezra 3. 4); but *skēnopēgia* = booth-making, as in Deut. 16. 16; 31. 10. Zech. 14. 16, 18, 19. Only direct reference to this feast in N.T. See Ap. 179. II. 4.

at hand = near. **3 His brethren.** Cp. 2. 12 and Mark 3. 21, 31. **unto.** Gr. *pros*. Ap. 104. xv. 3. **into.** Gr. *eis*. Ap. 104 vi. **that** = in order that. Gr. *hina*. **see** = be spectators of. Gr. *theōreō*. Ap. 133. I. 11. **works.** See note on 4. 34. **4 no man** = no one. Gr. *oudeis* (compound of Ap. 105. I). **openly.** Gr. *parrhēsia*, lit. in plain language. **If.** Assuming the fact. Ap. 118. 2. a. Not the same word as in *vv.* 17, 37. **shew.** Gr. *phaneroō*. Ap. 106. I. v. Cp. 1. 31; 2. 11. **world.** Put by Fig. *Metonymy* (of Subject), Ap. 6, for its inhabitants. See note on 1. 9, and Ap. 129. 1. **5 neither** = not even. Gr. *oude*. Ap. 105. I. See note on "And we beheld", &c., 1. 14. **believe in.** Ap. 150. I. 1. v. (i). See note on 1. 12.

7. 6-8 (*L*, above). THE LORD'S BRETHREN: THEIR ADVICE REJECTED. (*Introversions.*)

L | N | v | 6-. Himself.
w | -6. His brethren.
O | 7-. Brethren: not hated.
O | -7. Himself: hated.
N | *w* | 8-. His brethren.
v | -8. Himself.

6 Then = Therefore. Not the same word as in *v.* 10. **time** = seasonable moment. **not yet.** Gr. *oupō*. A compound of *ou* (Ap. 105. I). The Lord's death was accomplished by Himself. See 10. 17, 18. Luke 9 31. Until that hour (the right hour) came, He was immune (*vv.* 8, 30; 8. 20). At length it was "at hand" (Matt. 26. 45); and came, according to His word (12. 23, 27; 13. 1; 17. 1. Cp. Mark 14. 41). **your** = your own. Gr. *humeteros*. Emph. **7 cannot** = is not (Ap. 105. I) able to. **testify** = bear witness See note on 1. 7. **of** = concerning. Gr. *peri*. Ap. 104. xiii. 1 **evil.** Gr. *ponēros*. Ap. 128 III. 1. **8 Go . . . up.** Gr. *anabainō*, the technical word for going up with others as in a caravan. See 11. 55. Matt. 20 17, 18. Mark 10. 32, 33. Luke 2. 42; 18. 31 (cp. *v.* 35); 19 4, 28. John 11. 55 Acts 21. 15. **unto.** Gr. *eis*. Ap. 104. vi. **this** = the. **is not yet full come** = has not yet been fulfilled. Cp. Luke 21. 24. Acts 7. 23. **9 words** = things. **abode.** See note on 1. 32. **10 when.** Not a note of *time* but of *sequence*, as in 2. 9, 23; 4. 1, 40; 6. 12, 16; 11. 6, 32, 38.

7. 11—11. 54- [For Structure see next page].

11 at = in. Gr *en*. Ap. 104. viii. **He** = that man. Emphatic. **12 murmuring.** See note on 6. 41 **among.** Gr. *en*. Ap. 104. viii. 2.

A. D. 28 the °people °concerning Him: for some °said,
"He is a good Man:" others °said, °"Nay;
but He °deceiveth the °people."
13 Howbeit [4]no man spake [4]openly [7]of Him
°for fear of [1]the Jews.

S[1] T[1] 14 Now °about the midst of the feast [1]Jesus
went up [3]into the °temple, and °taught.

U[1] 15 And [1]the Jews °marvelled, saying, "How
°knoweth this Man °letters, having °never
learned?"

T[2] 16 [1]Jesus °answered them, °and said, °"My
°doctrine is [1]not Mine, but His That °sent Me.
17 °If any man °will do His °will, he shall
°know [7]of the [16]doctrine, whether it be °of
God, or *whether* I speak °of Myself.
18 He that speaketh [-17]of himself seeketh
his own °glory: but He That seeketh °His
glory That [16]sent Him, °the same is °true,
and no °unrighteousness is in Him.
19 Did [1]not °Moses give you the law, and
yet none °of you °keepeth the law? Why °go
ye about [1]to kill Me?"

U[2] 20 The [12]people [16]answered and said, "Thou
hast a °devil: who [19]goeth about [1]to kill
Thee?"

T[3] 21 [1]Jesus [16]answered and said unto them,
"I °have done °one [3]work, and ye all
[15]marvel.
22 [19]Moses °therefore gave unto you circumcision; ([1]not because it is [19]of [22]Moses, but [19]of
°the fathers;) and ye °on the sabbath day circumcise a °man.
23 [4]If a [22]man [22]on the sabbath day receive
circumcision, that [19]the law of [22]Moses should
not be broken: °are ye angry at Me, because
I have made a [22]man °every whit °whole [22]on
the sabbath day?
24 °Judge °not °according to the °appear-
ance, but °judge °righteous °judgment."

U[3] 25 [6]Then said some of them [19]of °Jerusalem,
"Is [1]not this He, Whom they °seek [1]to kill?
26 °But, °lo, He speaketh °boldly, and they
say °nothing unto Him. °Do the rulers [17]know
°indeed that this is the °very °Christ?
27 °Howbeit we [15]know °this man whence
He is: but °when [26]Christ °cometh, [4]no man
[17]knoweth °whence He is."

7. 11—11. 54- (H[2], p. 1533). IN JERUSALEM.
(*Alternation.*)

H[2] | P | 7. 11—8. 59. At the Feast of Tabernacles.
Q | 9. 1—10. 21. Subsequent events.
P | 10. 22-38. At the Feast of Dedication.
Q | 10. 39—11. 54-. Subsequent events.

7. 11—8. 59 (P, above). AT THE FEAST OF TABERNACLES. (*Repeated Alternations.*)

P | R[1] | 7. 11-13. The Lord. Immune.
S[1] | 7. 14-30-. Colloquy with Jews.
R[2] | 7. -30, 31. The Lord. Immune.
S[2] | 7. 32-43. Colloquy with Pharisees and others.
R[3] | 7. 44—8. 1. The Lord. Immune.
S[3] | 8. 2-20-. Colloquy with Scribes and Pharisees.
R[4] | 8. -20. The Lord. Immune.
S[4] | 8. 21-59-. Colloquy with Scribes and Pharisees.
R[5] | 8. -59. The Lord. Immune.

people = crowds.
concerning. Gr. *peri*. Ap. 104. xiii. 1.
said = were saying.
Nay. Gr. *ou*. Ap. 105. I.
deceiveth = leadeth astray. Cp. Mark 13 5 6. 1 Tim. 4. 1. Jude 13.
people = crowd.
13 for = on account of. Gr. *dia*. Ap. 104. v. 2.

7. 14-30- (S[1], above). COLLOQUY WITH JEWS.
(*Repeated Alternation.*)

S[1] | T[1] | 14. The Lord. Teaching.
U[1] | 15. Jews. Marvel.
T[2] | 16-19. The Lord. Answer.
U[2] | 20. Jews. Accusation.
T[3] | 21-24. The Lord. Answer.
U[3] | 25-27. Jews. Objection.
T[4] | 28, 29. The Lord. Answer.
U[4] | 30-. Jews. Action.

14 about the midst, &c. Expression occ. only here.
temple. Gr. *hieron*. See note on Matt. 23. 16.
taught = began to teach (Imperf. tense).
15 marvelled = were wondering.
knoweth. Gr. *oida*. Ap. 132. I. i. See note on 1. 26.
letters. Gr. pl. of *gramma*. Put by Fig. *Metonymy* (of Adjunct), Ap. 6, for what is written; e.g. an account (Luke 16. 6, 7); the Pentateuch (John 5. 47); Epistles (Acts 28. 21); the whole Scripture (2 Tim. 3. 15). Hence, used of general literature such as the Talmudical writings (here, and in Acts 26. 24). Cp. our term, "man of letters", and see Acts 4. 13.
never = not. Gr. *mē*. Ap. 105. II.
16 answered . . . and said. See note on Deut. 1. 41 and Ap. 122. 3. The 1611 edition of the A.V. omitted "and said".
My doctrine, &c. The first of seven declarations that the Lord spoke only the Father's words (see 8. 28, 47; 12. 49; 14. 10, 24; 17. 8).

doctrine = teaching. sent. See note on 5. 23. **17** If, &c. For the condition, see Ap. 118. 1. b. will do = desire (Ap. 102. 1) to do. will. Gr. *thelēma*. Ap. 102. 2. know = get to know. Gr. *ginōskō*. Ap. 132. I. ii. See note on 1. 10. of. Gr. *ek*. Ap. 104. vii. of = from. Gr. *apo*. Ap. 104. iv. **18** glory. See note on 1. 14. His glory, &c. = the glory of Him that sent. the same = He. true. See note on 3. 33. unrighteousness. See Ap. 128. VII. 1. **19** Moses. See note on 1. 17. keepeth = doeth. go . . . about = seek. **20** devil = demon. Cp. Matt. 11. 18. **21** have done = did. one. A Heb. idiom for "a". See 1. 3. **22** therefore gave unto you = for this cause (*dia* [Ap. 104. v. 2] *touto*) has given you. circumcision. Moses mentioned the precept only in Exod. 12. 44, 48. Lev. 12. 3. The Law not given by Moses, but based on Gen. 17. 9-14. the fathers. That is, Abraham. on. Gr. *en*. Ap. 104. viii. man. Gr. *anthrōpos*. Ap. 123. 1. **23** are ye angry? Gr. *cholaō* (from *cholē* = bile). Occurs only here. every whit = entirely (in contrast with one member). whole = sound (in contrast with wound). **24** Judge. See note on 5. 22 and Ap. 122. 1. not. Gr. *mē*. Ap. 105. II. according to. Gr. *kata*. Ap. 104. x. 2. appearance = sight; i. e. objective or outward appearance. judge . . . judgment. Fig. *Polyptōton*. Ap. 6. righteous = the righteous. judgment. Ap. 177. 7. **25** Jerusalem. See note on Matt. 15. 1. Cp. Mark 1. 5. seek = are seeking. **26** But = And. lo. Fig. *Asterismos*. Ap. 6. Gr. *ide*. Ap. 133. I. 3. boldly = openly, as in *v.* 4. nothing. Gr. *ouden*. Compound of *ou*. Do the rulers know indeed? = The rulers have not ascertained, have they? indeed. Gr. *alēthōs* = truly or really. very. Same as "indeed" above. All the texts omit "very", but not the Syr. See Ap. 94. V, note 3, p. 136. Christ = the Messiah. See Ap. 98. IX. **27** Howbeit = But, or And yet. this man = this one. when = whenever. cometh = may come. whence He is: i.e. how He may come. The Rabbis taught that He would come from Bethlehem and then be hid, but none knew where. See Lightfoot, vol. xii, pp. 303, 4.

T4 28 [6]Then °cried [1]Jesus [1]in the [14]temple as
A.D. 28 He °taught, saying, "Ye both [15]know Me,
and ye [15]know whence I am: and I am [1]not
come [-17]of Myself, but He That [16]sent Me is
°true, Whom ye [15]know [1]not.
29 But I [15]know Him: for I am °from Him,
and He hath °sent Me."
U4 30 °Then they °sought to °take Him:
R2 but [4]no man laid hands on Him, because His
hour was [6]not yet come.
31 And many [19]of the [12]people [5]believed on
Him, and said, "When [26]Christ °cometh, °will
He do more °miracles than these which this
Man °hath done?"
S2 V1 32 The °Pharisees heard that the [-12]people
°murmured such things [12]concerning Him;
and the °Pharisees and the chief priests [29]sent
°officers °to [30]take Him.
W1 33 [6]Then said [1]Jesus unto them, "Yet a little
while am I °with you, and *then* °I go [3]unto
Him That [16]sent Me.
34 Ye °shall seek Me, and shall [1]not find *Me:*
and where °I am, *thither* ye [7]cannot come."
V2 35 [6]Then said the Jews °among themselves,
"Whither °will He go, that we shall [1]not find
Him? °will He go [8]unto °the °dispersed
°among the °Gentiles, and teach the °Gen-
tiles?
36 What *manner of* °saying is this that He
said, 'Ye shall seek Me, and shall [1]not find
Me: and where I am, *thither* ye [7]cannot
come?'"
W2 37 °In °the last day, °that great *day* of the
feast, [1]Jesus stood and cried, saying, [17]"If
any man thirst, let him come [3]unto Me, and
°drink.
38 °He that [5]believeth on Me, °as the scripture °hath said, °**out of °His °belly °shall flow
°rivers of °living water.**"
39 °(But °this spake He [7]of °the Spirit,
Which they that [5]believe on Him should °re-
ceive: for °the Holy Ghost was not yet
given; because that [1]Jesus was not yet
°glorified.)
V3 40 Many [19]of the [12]people therefore, when
they heard this [36]saying, said, °"Of a truth
this is the Prophet."

28 cried = cried aloud. **taught** = was teaching. **true.** Gr. *alēthinos* (Ap. 175. 2). See note on 1. 9.
29 from = from beside. Gr. *para.* Ap. 104. xii. 1. **sent.** Gr. *apostellō.* Ap. 174. 1. Not the same word as in *vv.* 16, 18, 28–33; but the same word as in *v.* 32.
30 sought = were seeking. **take** = arrest. See in *vv.* 32, 44, and Acts 12. 4. 2 Cor. 11. 32.
31 cometh = shall have come. **will He . . . ?** = He will not (Gr. *mēti*), will He? The texts read *mē.* **miracles** = signs. Gr. *sēmeion.* See note on 2. 11, and Ap. 176. 3. **hath done** = did.

7. 32–43 (S2, p. 1534). COLLOQUY WITH PHARISEES AND OTHERS. (*Repeated Alternation.*)

S2 | V1 | 32. Pharisees. Among themselves.
W1 | 33, 34. The Lord. Answering their thoughts.
V2 | 35, 36. Jews. Among themselves.
W2 | 37–39. The Lord. Anticipating the people's thoughts.
V3 | 40–43. The people. Among themselves.

32 Pharisees. See Ap. 120. II. **that . . . murmured** = murmuring. Gr. *gonguzō.* Occ. elsewhere in John only in 6. 41, 43, 61. **officers, or servants;** as in 18. 36. Cp. 18. 3, 12, 18; 19. 6, and Matt. 26. 58. Mark 14. 54, 65. **to.** See 6. 15.
33 with. Gr. *meta.* Ap. 104. xi. 1. **I go** = I withdraw. Cp. 6. 21, 67.
34 shall = will. **I am.** The formula of Divine and eternal existence. See note on 6. 35, and cp. 8. 58.
35 among = to. Gr. *pros.* Ap. 104. xv. 3. **will He go?** = is He about to go? (Two verbs.) **the dispersed.** Gr. *Diaspora* = the Dispersion. Occurs three times; here, 1 Pet. 1. 1 ("scattered"), and Jas. 1. 1 ("which are scattered abroad"; lit. "in the Dispersion"). **among** = of. **Gentiles.** So called from the Latin *gentes* = nations (as distinguished by race); hence, used of nations, as distinct from the one nation Israel (Gen. 12. 2. Cp. 14. 1, 9); Heb. = *gōyim*: rendered in A.V. "nations" 371 times, "heathen" 143 times, "Gentiles" 30 times, and "people" 11 times. In N.T. days, Greece being the great dominating nation in arms, literature, and language, the word *Hellēnes* became the N.T. word for all non-Jews, *Hellēn,* the son of Deucalion, being the legendary ancestor of the Greek nation (Homer, *Iliad,* ii. 684). *Hellēn* had been already used in the Sept. Version, of the "Philistines" (Isa. 9. 12), and of "the sons of Javan" (Zech. 9. 13. 1 Macc. 8. 18. 2 Macc. 4. 36. Josephus (*Ant.* I. vi. 1). *Hellēnes* in the N.T. never means Jews, but is always distinguished from them. See 12. 20. Acts 14. 1; 16. 1, 3; 18. 4; 19. 10, 17; 20. 21. Rom. 1. 16; 2. 9, 10; 3. 9; 10. 12. 1 Cor. 1. 24; 10. 32. Gal. 2. 3; 3. 28. Col. 3. 11. On the other hand, the Gr. *Hellēnistēs* = Hellenized, and speaking Greek, is used of those who were Jews by birth, but spoke Greek. It occurs three times, and is rendered "Grecians". See Acts 6. 1; 9. 29; 11. 20.
36 saying. Gr. *logos.* See note on Mark 9. 32.
37 In = Now on. Gr. *en,* as in *v.* 1. **the last day.** See Lev. 23. 34–36. **that** = the. **drink** = let him drink.
38 He that = that. Read this in connection with the previous verse: "let him drink that believeth on Me". **as** = according as. **hath said** = hath said [concerning Me]. Ap. 107. II. 3. **out of.** Gr. *ek.* Ap. 104. vii, as in *vv.* 41, 52. Not the same word as in *v.* 42. **His belly.** Put by Fig. *Synecdochē* (of the Part), Ap. 6, for the whole person, for emphasis = Himself. Here referring to Messiah (the Giver), not to the believer. He is, and will be, the Source of all spiritual blessing "as the Scripture hath said": Isa. 12. 3; 55. 1; 58. 11. Ezek 47. 1. Joel 3. 18. Zech. 13. 1; 14. 8. See Ap. 107. **His.** Referring not to the believer (the receiver), but to the Lord (the Giver). **shall flow.** Gr. *rheō* Occ. only here in N.T. **rivers.** This is the emphatic word, by the Fig. *Hyperbaton* (Ap. 6), implying abundance. See Num. 20. 11. 1 Cor. 10 4. **living.** See note on 4. 10.
39 But this, &c. See note on "And we" (1. 14). Here the true interpretation is given. **this spake He of the Spirit.** Not of the believer. **the Spirit.** Referring to the gift of *pneuma hagion* (in the next clause), of which He was the Giver, and believers the recipients. See Ap. 101. II. 14. **receive.** And which would be "in him" (the receiver) "springing up" *in him,* not flowing out as a river *from him,* for the supply of others. See the refs. on *v.* 38. **the Holy Ghost.** Gr. *pneuma hagion.* Ap. 101. II. 14. There are no Articles. It denotes the gift given by the Giver and received by the believer, as promised in Acts 1. 5 and fulfilled in Acts 2. 4. **glorified:** i.e. ascended. Cp. 16. 7, Ps. 68. 18, and Acts 2. 33. One of the characteristic words of this Gospel. See p. 1511.
40 Of a truth. Gr. *alēthōs.* See note on "indeed" (1. 47).

A. D. 28 41 °Others said, "This is the [26]Christ." But
°some said, °"Shall [26]Christ come [38]out of
[1]Galilee?
42 Hath [1]not the scripture said, That
[26]Christ cometh [19]of °the seed of David, and
[28]out of the town of °Bethlehem, where David
was?"
43 °So there °was °a division [12]among the
[12]people °because of Him.
R^3 X 44 And some [19]of them °would have [30]taken
Him; but [4]no man laid hands on Him.
Y^1 x^1 45 [6]Then °came the [32]officers °to the chief
priests and [32]Pharisees;
y^1 and they said unto them, "Why have ye [1]not
brought Him?"
x^2 46 The [32]officers answered, "Never [22]man
spake °like this Man."
y^2 47 [6]Then answered them the [32]Pharisees,
°"Are ye also deceived?
48 °Have any [19]of the °rulers or [19]of the
[32]Pharisees [5]believed on Him?
49 But this [-12]people who [17]knoweth [24]not the
law are °cursed."
x^3 50 °Nicodemus saith [3]unto them, °(he that
came [45]to Jesus by night, being one [19]of them,)
51 "Doth our [19]law [24]judge *any* man, °before
°it hear him, and [17]know what he doeth?"
y^3 52 They [16]answered and said unto him, "Art
thou also [19]of [1]Galilee? °Search, and °look: for
[38]out of [1]Galilee ariseth no prophet."
X 53 °And every man went [8]unto his own
house.

8 °Jesus went °unto the mount of Olives.
S^3 A 2 And °early in the morning He came
again °into the °temple, and all the °people
came °unto Him; and He °sat down, and
°taught them.
B C 3 And the scribes and °Pharisees °brought

41 Others. See Ap. 124. 1.
some=others. As before.
Shall ... come=What, doth Christ come? (Present tense.)
42 the seed of David. Ps. 110; 132. Isa. 11. 1, 10. Jer. 23. 5, &c. Bethlehem. See Mic. 5. 2.
43 So=Therefore. was=arose
a division. The first of three instances. See 9. 16; and 10. 19.
because of Him. Not only in the three cases noted above, but down to the present day.
because of=on account of. Gr. *dia*. Ap. 104. v. 2.

7. 44—8. 1 (R^3, p. 1534). THE LORD. IMMUNE.
(*Introversion and Repeated Alternation.*)

R^3 | X | 44. The Lord. Immune.
  Y^1 | x^1 | 45-. Return of officers.
    y^1 | -45. Pharisees' Question.
    x^2 | 46. Answer of officers.
    y^2 | 47-49. Pharisees' Question.
    x^3 | 50, 51. Protest of Nicodemus.
    y^3 | 52. Pharisees' Question.
  X | 7. 53; 8. 1. The Lord. Immune.

44 would have taken Him=desired to take Him (two verbs). Luke 7. 17. See Ap. 102. 1.
45 came. "Sent", in *v.* 32.
to. Gr. *pros*. Ap. 104. xv. 3.
46 never. Gr. *oudepote*
like=thus, as. Some texts omit this last clause, but not Syr. See note 3, p. 1511. Cp. 4. 29.
47 Are ye, &c.?=Have ye also been led astray (*v.* 12)? Referring to *action* rather than to *thought*.
48 Have ...? Fig. *Erotēsis*. Ap. 6.
rulers. Members of the Sanhedrin.
49 cursed=laid under a curse. Gr. *epikataratos*. Only here and Gal. 3. 10, 13. Found often in the Sept. and in the *Papyri*. See Deissmann's *Light*, &c. p. 93.
50 Nicodemus. See 3. 2 and 19. 39.
he that came. See note on "and we" (1. 14). Some texts omit this clause, but not the Syr. (Ap. 94, note 3, p. 136). **51** before=except (Gr. *ean mē*) first.
it hear=it has heard.
52 Search=Search [the Scriptures], as in 5. 39.
look=see. Ap. 133. I. 3. If they had looked, they would have found that Jonah and Hosea arose out of Galilee, and perhaps Elijah, Elisha, and Amos.
53 And every man, &c. From 7. 53—8. 11 is omitted by L T Tr. [A] WH. The R.V. note questions it. WH place it in double brackets at the end of the Gospel. As to ancient MSS., A (the Alexandrine, London) and C (Ephraemi, Paris), are defective here, so that the oldest omitting it are ℵ (Sinaitic, Cent. v), B (Vatican, Cent. iv). The oldest containing it is D (Bezæ, Cent. vi). It is contained in the Vulgate (383), and Jerome (378-430) testifies (*adv. Pelag.* ii. p. 762) that it is found in many Greek and Latin Codices. It is also found in the Jerusalem Syr. (Cent. v), the Memphitic (Cent. iii or iv), Aethiopic (Cent. iv). Eusebius, Bishop of Cæsarea (315-320), quotes (*Hist. Ecc.* iii. 39) Papias, Bishop of Hierapolis (in Phrygia, 130), as referring to it. Ambrose (374-397) quotes it, as does Augustine (395-430), *de adult. coniugiis* (lib. ii, cap. 7). Though WH omit it, Dean Burgon (1883) quotes: "Drs. W. and H. remark that 'the argument which has always told most in its favour in modern times is its own internal character. The story itself has justly seemed to vouch for its own internal truth, and the words in which it is clothed to harmonize with other Gospel narratives'" (*The Revision Revised*, p. 311, note). We may ask: How is it that all the MSS. which do contain it (including 300 Cursives) agree in placing it here? It was another attempt following on 7. 32, and referred to in 8. 15.

8. 1 Jesus=But Jesus. Connecting 8. 1 with 7. 53. See Ap. 98. X. **unto.** Gr. *eis*. Ap. 104. vi.

8. 2-20- (S^3, p. 1534). COLLOQUY WITH SCRIBES AND PHARISEES. (*Introversion.*)

S^3 | A | 2. Place. The Temple.
  B | 3-11. Scribes and Pharisees. Temptation.
  B | 12-19. Scribes and Pharisees. Their rebuke.
A | -20. Place. The Temple.

2 early in the morning=at dawn. **into**=unto, as in *v.* 1. **temple.** Gr. *hieron*. See note on Matt. 23. 16. **people.** Gr. *laos*. In John's Gospel only here, 11. 50; 18. 14. Not *ochlos*, or *plēthos*. **unto.** Gr. *pros*. Ap. 104. xv. 3. **sat down . . . and**=having sat down. **taught**=was teaching.

8. 3-11 (B, above). SCRIBES AND PHARISEES. TEMPTATION. (*Alternation.*)

B | C | 3. The woman brought.
  D | 4-9-. Condemned.
  C | -9. The woman left.
  D | 10, 11. Uncondemned.

3 Pharisees. See Ap. 120. II. **brought**=bring.

A.D. 28 [2]unto Him a woman °taken °in adultery; and
when they had set her °in the midst,
D E 4 They say unto Him, °"Master, this woman
was taken [3]in adultery, °in the very act.
F a 5 Now °Moses [3]in the law °commanded us,
that such should be stoned: °but what sayest
Thou?"
6 This they said, °tempting Him, °that they
might have to accuse Him.
b But [1]Jesus stooped down, and with *His* finger
wrote °on the ground, °*as though He heard*
them not.
F a 7 So when they continued °asking Him, He
°lifted up Himself, and said [2]unto them, "He
that is °without sin among you, let him first
cast °a stone °at her."
b 8 And again He stooped down, and °wrote
[6]on the ground.
E 9 And they which heard *it*, being °convicted
°by *their own* conscience, went out one by
one, beginning °at the °eldest, *even* °unto the
last:
C and [1]Jesus was left alone, and the woman
standing [3]in the midst.
D 10 When [1]Jesus had lifted up Himself, and
°saw °none °but the woman, He said unto her,
"Woman, where are those thine accusers?
hath °no man °condemned thee?"
11 She said, [10]"No man, °Lord." And [1]Jesus
said unto her, "Neither do I [10]condemn °thee:
go, and °sin no more."
B G^1 12 °Then spake [1]Jesus °again unto them,
saying, °"I am the °light of the °world: he
that followeth Me shall °not walk [3]in darkness, but °shall have the °light of °life."
H^1 13 The [3]Pharisees therefore said unto Him,
"Thou °bearest record °of Thyself; Thy
°record is °not °true."
G^2 14 [1]Jesus °answered and said unto them,
°"Though I [13]bear record [13]of Myself, *yet* My
[13]record is [13]true: for I °know whence I came,
and whither I go; but ye °cannot tell whence
I come, °and whither I go.
15 Ye °judge °after the °flesh; I °judge [10]no
man.
16 And yet °if I [15]judge, My °judgment is
[13]true: for I am [13]not alone, but I and °the
Father That °sent Me.
17 °It is °also written [3]in °your law, that
the °testimony of °two men is [13]true.
18 I am one that °bear witness [13]of Myself,
and [16]the Father That [16]sent Me °beareth
witness [13]of Me."

taken = having been taken. **in.** Gr. *en.* Ap. 104. viii.

8. 4-9- (D, p. 1536). CONDEMNED.
(*Introversion and Alternation.*)

D | E | 4. Accusation.
  F | a | 5, 6-. Question asked.
    b | -6. The Lord. Inattention.
  F | *a* | 7. Question answered.
    b | 8. The Lord. Inattention.
E | 9-. Conviction.

4 Master = Teacher. Ap. 98. XIV. v. 1.
in the very act. Gr. *ep'* (Ap. 104. ix. 2) *autophōrō.* *Autophōros* means self-detected.
5 Moses. See note on 1. 17.
commanded . . . stoned. This law referred only to a "betrothed damsel" (Deut. 22. 24); and to show that the Lord knew their thoughts, and knew also that this was another man's "wife". He complied with the law prescribed in "such" a case (Num. 5. 11-31), and stooped down and wrote the curses (as required in *v.* 23) on the ground. **but** = therefore.
6 tempting = testing. The temptation was in the word "such", and of two cases they mention the punishment without defining what it was: for the one in Deut. 22. 23, 24 (a virgin) the death was stoning; but in the case of a "wife" the punishment was *not* stoning, but required a special procedure (Num. 5. 11-31) which left the punishment with God. **that** = in order that. Gr. *hina.*
on, &c. = into (Gr. *eis.* Ap. 104. vi) [the dust of] the earth (Ap. 129. 4).
as though, &c. This *Ellipsis* (Ap. 6) is wrongly supplied. It was not from inattention, but to call their attention to the fact that the case was "such" as required the fulfilment of Num. 5 and *not* Deut. 22.
7 asking. Ap. 134. I. 3.
lifted up. Gr. *anakuptō.* Only here, *v.* 10. Luke 13. 11; 21. 28.
without sin = sinless. Gr. *anamartētos.* Cp. Ap. 128. I. 1. ii. Occ. nowhere else in the N.T.
a stone = the stone, i.e. the heavy stone for execution. Cp. *v.* 59. **at** = upon. Gr. *epi.* Ap. 104. ix. 2.
8 wrote. The curses, as before.
9 convicted, &c. By the manifestation of the Lord's knowledge of what was in their hearts and of what they were concealing for the purpose of tempting Him. Gr. *elenchō.* Same word as in *v.* 46; 3. 20; 16. 8.
by. Gr. *hupo.* Ap. 104. xviii. 1.
at = from. Gr. *apo.* Ap. 104. iv.
eldest = elders. **unto** = as far as.
10 saw. Ap. 133. I. 12. **none.** Gr. *mēdeis.*
but = except. Gr. *plēn.* **no man** = no one. Gr. *oudeis.*
condemned. Ap. 122. 7.
11 Lord. See Ap. 98. VI. i. *a.* 3. B. a.
thee. He does not say "*thy sin*". He speaks judicially. **sin.** Ap. 128. I. i.

8. 12-19 (*B*, p. 1536). SCRIBES AND PHARISEES. THEIR REBUKE. (*Repeated Alternation.*)

B | G^1 | 12. The Lord. Declaration.
  H^1 | 13. Pharisees. Objection.
G^2 | 14-18. The Lord. Refutation.
  H^2 | 19-. Pharisees. Question.
G^3 | -19. The Lord. Rebuke.

12 Then = Therefore.
again. This section has no necessary connection with 7. 52, but refers to a subsequent occasion in "the Treasury" (*v.* 20). **I am.** See note on 6. 35. **light.** Gr. *phōs* (Ap. 130. 1). Not *luchnos* as in 5. 35 (Ap. 130. 4). One of the characteristic words of this Gospel. See note on 1. 4. **world.** Ap. 129. 1. See note on 1. 9. Put by Fig. *Metonymy* (of the Subject), Ap. 6, for its inhabitants without distinction, implying others than Jews. **not** = in no wise. Gr. *ou mē.* Ap. 105. III. **shall have** = not merely see it, but possess it. **life** = the life. Ap. 170. 1. See note on 1. 4.
13 bearest record. See note on 1. 32. **of** = concerning. Gr. *peri.* Ap. 104. xiii. i. **record.** See note on 1. 19. **not.** Gr. *ou* (Ap. 105. I). **true.** Gr. *alēthēs.* See Ap. 175. 1 and note on 3. 33.
14 answered and said. See Ap. 122. 3 and note on Deut. 1. 41. **Though** = Even if. Ap. 118. 1. b. **know.** Gr. *oida.* Ap. 132. I. i. See note on 1. 26. **cannot tell** = know (Gr. *oida*) not (Ap. 105. I). **and.** All the texts read "or". **15 judge.** See Ap. 122. 1 and note on 5. 22. **after** = according to. Gr. *kata.* Ap. 104. x. 2. **flesh.** See note on 1. 13. **16 if.** Assuming the condition. Ap. 118. 1. b. **judgment.** Ap. 177. 7. **the Father.** See note on 1. 14. **sent.** See Ap. 174. 4 and note on 1. 22.
17 It is . . . written = It has been (and standeth) written. **also . . . law** = law also, *your* law. **your** = your own. Gr. *humeteros.* Emphatic Cp. 7. 49. **testimony.** Gr. *marturia.* See note on "record", *v.* 13. **two.** See Deut. 19. 15. **18 bear witness.** Same as "bear record" in *v.* 13. See note on 1. 7.

H² 19 [12] Then said they unto Him, "Where is
A. D. 28 Thy [16] Father?"
G³ Jesus answered, "Ye °neither [14] know Me, °nor
°My Father: °if ye had [14] known Me, ye
°should have [14] known °My Father also."
A 20 These °words spake [1] Jesus [3] in °the treasury, °as He taught [3] in the [2] temple:
R⁴ and [10] no man °laid hands on Him; for His
hour was °not yet come.
S⁴ c¹ 21 [12] Then said [1] Jesus again unto them, "I
°go My way, and ye °shall seek Me, and shall
die [3] in your °sins: whither I °go, ye °cannot
come."
d¹ 22 [12] Then said the °Jews, °"Will He kill
Himself? because He saith, 'Whither I go,
ye [21] cannot come.'"
c² 23 And He said unto them, °"Ye are °from
beneath; I am °from above: °ye are °of this
[12] world; I am [13] not °of this [12] world.
24 I said therefore unto you, that ye [21] shall
die [3] in your [21] sins: for [16] if ye °believe [6] not
that °I am *He*, ye [21] shall die [3] in your °sins."
d² 25 [12] Then said they unto Him, "Who art
Thou?"
c³ And [1] Jesus saith unto them, °"Even *the same*
that I said unto you °from the beginning.
26 I have many things to say and to [15] judge
[13] of you: but He That [16] sent Me is [13] true; and
I °speak °to the [12] world those things which
I have heard °of Him."
d³ 27 They °understood [13] not that He °spake
to them of [16] the °Father.
c⁴ 28 [12] Then said [1] Jesus unto them, °"When
ye °have °lifted up the °Son of man, °then shall
ye °know that [24] I am *He*, and *that* °I do °no-
thing °of Myself; but as [19] My Father °hath
taught Me, °I [27] speak these things.
29 And He That [16] sent Me is °with Me: [16] the
Father hath [13] not left Me °alone; for °I do
always those things that please Him."
d⁴ 30 As He [27] spake these °words, many °be-
lieved [6] on Him.
c⁵ 31 [12] Then °said [1] Jesus °to those [22] Jews which
°believed on Him, [16] "If ye °continue [3] in °My
word, *then* °are ye My disciples °indeed;
32 And ye shall [28] know the °truth, and the
°truth shall °make you free."
d⁵ 33 They answered Him, "We be Abraham's
seed, and °were never in bondage to °any
man: how sayest Thou, 'Ye shall be made
free?'"

19 neither . . . nor. Gr. *oute*, compound of *ou*. Ap. 105. I. **My Father.** See note on 2. 16.
if. A true hypothesis. Ap. 118. 2. a.
should = would.
20 words. Gr. *rhēma*. See note on Mark 9. 32.
the treasury. A part of the Temple, in the court of the women. Occ. in Mark 12. 41, 43. Luke 21. 1, and John only here. **as He taught** = teaching.
laid hands = arrested. See 7. 30, 32, 44.
not yet come. See note on 7. 6.

8. 21-59- (S⁴, p. 1534). COLLOQUY WITH SCRIBES AND PHARISEES. (*Repeated alternation.*)

S⁴ | c¹ | 21. The Lord. Declaration. "I go".
d¹ | 22. The Jews. Misconception.
c² | 23, 24. The Lord. Declaration.
d² | 25-. The Jews. Question.
c³ | -25, 26. The Lord. Declaration.
d³ | 27. The Jews. Not understanding.
c⁴ | 28, 29. The Lord. Declaration.
d⁴ | 30. The Jews. Result. Many believing.
c⁵ | 31, 32. The Lord. Promise.
d⁵ | 33. The Jews. Assertion.
c⁶ | 34-38. The Lord. Denial.
d⁶ | 39-. The Jews. Assertion.
c⁷ | -39-41-. The Lord. Counter Assertion.
d⁷ | -41. The Jews. Denial.
c⁸ | 42-47. The Lord. Accusation.
d⁸ | 48. The Jews. Counter Accusation.
c⁹ | 49-51. The Lord. Denial and Declaration.
d⁹ | 52, 53. The Jews. Accusation and Question.
c¹⁰ | 54-56. The Lord. Counter Accusation.
d¹⁰ | 57. The Jews. Assertion and Question.
c¹¹ | 58. The Lord. Revelation.
d¹¹ | 59-. The Jews. Hostility.

21 go My way = withdraw Myself.
shall = will.
sins = sin. See Ap. 128. I. ii. 1. The sin of rejecting Him.
cannot = are not (Gr. *ou*) able to.
22 Jews. See note on 1. 19.
Will He kill Himself? = Surely He will not (Gr. *mēti*) kill Himself?
23 Ye are from beneath; i. e. of the earth. See 1 Cor. 15. 47. The phrase occurs only in this Gospel.
from = out from. Gr. *ek*. Ap 104. vii. Cp. 1. 46.
from above. Gr. *ek tōn anō* (pl.) = the heavens. See 3. 13, 31; 6. 33, 38, 42. Col. 3. 1. **of.** Gr *ek*, as above.
24 believe. See note on 1. 7, and Ap. 150. I. 1. i.
I am He = I am. There is no "He" in the Gr. See note on 6. 35. **sins.** Pl. here. See *v.* 21.
25 Even the same that . . . beginning = He Whom I say also to you at the beginning [of this colloquy, *vv.* 12-20]. Cp. Sept., Gen. 43. 18, 20 = at the beginning [of our coming down] = at the first.
from the beginning. There is no "from" in the Gr. See note on *v.* 44.
26 speak. Gr. *legō*. All the texts read "say". Gr. *laleō*.
to = unto. Gr. *eis*. Ap. 104. vi.
of = from [beside]. Gr. *para*. Ap. 104. xii. 1.
27 understood not = did not get to know. Ap. 132. I. ii. See note on 1. 10.
spake = was speaking. Not "saying", as in *v.* 26.
Father. See note on 1. 14.

28 When . . . then. Revealing that, after that, men would believe in the truth of His Deity. **have** = may, or shall have. **lifted up.** Cp. 3. 14; 12. 34. **Son of man.** Ap. 98. XVI. **know.** Ap. 132. I. ii, as in *v.* 27. **I do, &c.** Note the complex *Ellipsis* (Ap. 6) = "Of Myself I do nothing [nor speak]; but according as the Father taught Me, these things I speak [and do them]". **nothing.** Gr. *ouden*. **of** = from. Gr. *apo*. Ap. 104. iv. **hath taught** = taught. **I speak, &c.** See note on "My doctrine", 7. 16. **29 with.** Gr. *meta*. Ap. 104. xi. 1. **alone.** Cp. *v.* 16. **I do always, &c.** = I do the things pleasing to Him always. The last word in the sentence in the Greek emphasized by the Fig. *Hyperbaton* (Ap. 6). **30 words** = things. **believed on.** See note on 1. 7, and Ap. 150. I. 1. v (i). Cp. *v.* 31. **31 said** = spake, as in *v.* 27, -28. **to.** Gr. *pros*. Ap. 104. xv. 3. **believed on** = had believed. Ap. 150. I. 1. ii. Thus distinguishing these Jews from the true believers of *v.* 30. Note the emphatic word "ye" in next clause. **continue** = abide. See note on 1. 32. **My word** = the word which is Mine. Gr. *logos*. See note on Mark 9. 32. **are ye** = ye are. **indeed** = truly. Gr. *alēthōs*. See note on 1. 47. Trusting in Him, not merely admitting His claims. **32 truth.** See note on 1. 14. **make** = set. **33 were never . . any man, &c.** Have been in bondage to no one (Ap. 105. I) at any time. Thus ignoring all historical facts. These were "the Jews" who believed in *v.* 31, and thus proved themselves not "believers indeed".

c6 **34** [1] **Jesus answered them, °"Verily, verily, I**
A.D. 28 **say unto you, °Whosoever °committeth °sin**
is °the servant of °sin.
35 And [34] the servant °abideth [13] not [3] in the
house °for ever: ***but*** **°the Son °abideth °ever.**
36 [16] If [35] the Son therefore shall [32] make you
free, °ye shall be free °indeed.
37 I [14] know that ye are Abraham's seed; but
ye seek to kill Me, because [31] My word °hath
°no place [3] in you.
38 I speak that which I °have seen °with
[19] My Father: and ye do that which °ye have
seen °with your father."
d6 **39 They [14] answered and said unto Him,**
"Abraham is our father."
c7 **[1] Jesus saith unto them, [19] "If ye were Abra-**
ham's °children, ye would do the °works of
Abraham.
40 But now ye seek to kill Me, °a Man That
hath told you the [32] truth, which I have heard
[26] of °God: this did [13] not Abraham.
41 Ye °do the °deeds of your father."
d7 **[12] Then said they to Him, "We °be [13] not born**
[23] of fornication; we have one [16] Father, ***even***
[40] God."
c8 **42 [1] Jesus said unto them, [19] "If [40] God were**
your [16] Father, ye would °love Me: for I pro-
ceeded forth and °came [23] from [40] God; °neither
°came I [28] of Myself, but He °sent Me.
43 Why do ye [13] not °understand My °speech?
even **because ye [14] cannot °hear My °word.**
44 Ye are [23] of ***your*** **father the °devil, and the**
°lusts of your father ye °will do. He was a
°murderer °from the beginning, and °abode
[13] not [3] in the [32] truth, because there is no [32] truth
[3] in him. When he speaketh °a lie, he speaketh
[23] of °his own: for he is a liar, and the father
of it.
45 °And because I °tell ***you*** **the [32] truth, ye**
°believe Me [13] not.
46 °Which [23] of you °convinceth Me [13] of [21] sin?
And [19] if I say the [32] truth, why do ye [13] not
[45] believe Me?
47 °He that is [23] of [40] God [43] heareth [40] God's
°words: ye therefore [43] hear ***them*** **[13] not, be-**
cause ye are not [23] of [40] God."
d8 **48 [12] Then [14] answered the [22] Jews, and said**
unto Him, "Say we [13] not well that thou art
a Samaritan, and hast a °devil?"
c9 **49 [1] Jesus answered, "I have [13] not a [48] devil;**
but I °honour [19] My Father, and ye do dishonour
Me.
50 And I seek not Mine own °glory: there is
One That seeketh and [15] judgeth.
51 [34] Verily, verily, I say unto you, [16] If a man
°keep My °saying, he shall °never °see
death."

34 Verily, verily. Called forth by this manifest misrepresentation of the truth. The twelfth occ. See 1. 51. **Whosoever** = Every one who.
committeth = doeth or practiseth.
sin. Not a single act, but a life of sin itself. Same as "sin" in *v.* 21.
the servant = a bondservant.
35 abideth. See note on 1. 32.
for ever. See Ap. 151. II. A. ii. 4. a. He may be sold or manumitted.
the Son. Gr. *huios.* Ap. 108. iii. Never used of *believers* in this Gospel. This word is reserved for Christ only. See note 2, p. 1511.
ever = for ever, as above.
36 ye shall be free indeed = ye will be really free.
indeed. Gr. *ontōs.* Not the same word as in *v.* 31. Cp. 1 Tim. 6. 19, R.V.
37 hath no place = findeth no entrance. Cp. 1 Thess. 2. 13. **no** = not. Gr. *ou.* Ap. 105. I.
38 have seen. Gr. *horaō.* Ap. 133. I. 8.
with. Gr. *para.* Ap. 104. xii. 2.
ye have seen. All the texts read = ye have heard. But not the Syr. See Ap. 94. v, note 3, p. 136.
39 children. Gr. pl. of *teknon.* Ap. 108. i. See note 2, p. 1511.
works. See note on 4. 34.
40 a Man. Gr. *anthrōpos.* Ap. 123. 1. Used by the Lord of Himself only here, and in contrast with the "manslayer" of *v.* 44. **God.** Ap. 98. I. i. 1.
41 do = are doing. **deeds** = works, as in *v.* 39.
be not born = have not been begotten (see Matt. 1. 2).
42 love. Gr. *agapaō.* Ap. 135. I. 1.
came = am here.
neither = not even. Gr. *oude.*
came I = am I come.
sent. Gr. *apostellō.* Ap. 174. 1.
43 understand = get to know. Ap. 132. I. ii.
speech. Referring to the *form* of the discourse.
hear. Heb. idiom = understand, receive, or believe, as in 9. 27; 10. 3; 12. 47. Acts 3. 22, 23. Gal. 4. 21.
word. Denoting the *subject* of the discourse.
44 devil. Gr. *diabolos.* Thrice in this Gospel: here, 6. 70; 13. 2. Not the same word as in *vv.* 48, 49.
lusts = strong desires of all kinds. Cp. Mark 4. 19. The only occ. of *epithumia* in John's Gospel. Occurs in 1 John 2. 16, 17, and Rev. 18. 14.
will do = will (Ap. 102. 1) to do (two verbs).
murderer = manslayer. Occ. only here and in 1 John 3. 15. Because death came through him. Cp. Heb. 2. 14.
from the beginning. Gr. *ap' archēs.* The expression occurs twenty-one times, and the dependent noun must be supplied. In Matt. 19. 4. 8; 24. 21. Mark 10. 6; 13. 19. 2 Pet. 3. 4, we must supply "from the beginning [of the creation]". Here we must supply "[of the human race]". In Luke 1. 2. John 15. 27. 1 John 1. 1 we must supply "[of the Lord's ministry]". In Acts 26. 4, supply "[of my public life]". 1 John 2. 7, 7 (all the texts, with Syr., omit), 13, 14, 24, 24; 3. 11. 2 John 5, 6, supply "[of your hearing]".
abode not = stood not. His fall must have taken place before Gen. 3. 1. Probably in "the world that then was" (Gen. 1. 1. 2 Pet. 3. 6).
a = the. Cp. 2 Thess. 2. 11.
his own. Cp. 15. 19.
45 And = But. **tell you** = speak.
believe Me. Ap. 150. I. 1. ii. See note on 1. 7.
46 convinceth = convicteth. Cp. *v.* 9; 3. 20; 16. 8 ("reprove"). **47 He that, &c.** Note the Introversion in the structure of *v.* 47:—

e | f | He that is of God
  | g | heareth God's words:
  | g | ye therefore hear them not,
  | f | because ye are not of God.

words = sayings. Gr. *rhēma.* See note on Mark 9. 32. **48 devil** = demon. Gr. *daimonion.* Cp. 7. 20. **49 honour.** Cp. 5. 23. **50 glory.** See note on 1. 14. **51 keep.** Gr. *tēreō,* implying watching rather than guarding. See notes on 17. 12. **saying** = word. Gr. *logos.* See note on Mark 9. 32. **never see death** = by no means (Gr. *ou mē.* Ap. 105. III) see (Ap. 133. I. 11) death for ever (Gr. *eis ton aiōna.* Ap. 151. II. A. ii. 4. b): i. e. eternal death, because he will have part in the "resurrection unto life" as declared by the Lord in 11. 25. See notes there. **see death.** The expression occ. only here in N.T.

d9 52 [12]Then said the [22]Jews unto Him, "Now
A.D. 28 we [28]know that Thou hast a [48]devil. Abraham *is dead, and the prophets; and Thou
sayest, [16]'If a man keep My [51]saying, he shall
[51]never °taste of death.'
53 Art Thou greater than our father Abraham,
which [52]is dead? and the prophets [52]are dead:
whom makest Thou Thyself?"

c10 54 [1]Jesus answered, [16]"If I °honour Myself,
My °honour is [28]nothing: it is [19]My Father
That °honoureth Me; of Whom ye say, that
He is your [40]God:
55 Yet ye have [13]not [28]known Him; but I
[14]know Him: and [16]if I should say, I [14]know
Him [18]not, I shall be a liar like unto you: but
I [14]know Him, and keep His [51]saying.
56 Your father Abraham °rejoiced °to °see
°My day: and °he saw *it*, and °was glad."

d10 57 [12]Then said the [22]Jews [2]unto him, "Thou
art not yet fifty years old, and hast Thou
[38]seen Abraham?"

c11 58 [1]Jesus said unto them, [34]"Verily, verily,
I say unto you, Before Abraham °was, I
am."

d11 59 [12]Then °took they up °stones [56]to cast °at
Him:

R5 but [1]Jesus hid Himself, and °went °out of the
[2]temple, going °through the midst of them,
and so °passed by.

Q J L 9 And °as *Jesus* passed by, °He °saw a
°man °which was blind °from *his* birth.
2 And His °disciples °asked Him, saying,
"°Master, who did °sin, °this man, or his
parents, °that he °was born blind?"

M 3 °Jesus answered, °"Neither hath this man
[2]sinned, °nor his parents: °but [2]that the °works
of °God should be made manifest °in him.
4 °I must °work the [3]works of Him That °sent
Me, while it is day: the night cometh, when no
man °can work.
5 As long as I am [3]in the °world, °I am the
°light of the °world."

L 6 When He had thus spoken, He °spat on the
°ground, and made °clay of the spittle, and He
°anointed the eyes of the blind man with the
°clay.
7 And said unto him, "Go, °wash °in °the
°pool of °Siloam," (°which is by interpretation,
°Sent.) He went his way therefore, and °washed,
and came °seeing.

M N 8 The °neighbours therefore, and they which

52 is dead = died.
taste of death. They altered the Lord's words. Not an O.T. term. Occurs five times: here; Matt. 16. 28. Mark 9. 1. Luke 9. 27. Heb. 2. 9.
54 honour = glorify. Gr. *doxazō*. See p. 1511.
honour = glory. See note on 5. 41.
56 rejoiced = leaped for joy. Gr. *agalliaō*. Cp. 5. 35.
to = in order that (Gr. *hina*) he might.
see. Ap. 133. I. i. Therefore Abraham must have heard of it from Jehovah, for "faith cometh by hearing" (Rom. 10. 17).
My day = the day, Mine; i.e. the day of My promised coming.
he saw = he saw [it, by faith]. Ap. 133. I. i.
was glad = rejoiced. Gr. *chairō*. Cp. 3. 29.
58 was = came into existence: i.e. was born.
I am. See note on 6. 35.
59 took . . . up stones. And thus would murder the great Prophet Himself. Cp. 10. 31, 39 and Matt. 23. 31, 37.
stones, i.e. heavy stones. Cp. *v.* 7. The Temple was not yet finished, and stones would be lying about. Lightfoot, vol. xii, pp. 247–9, 324.
at = upon. Gr. *epi*. Ap. 104. ix. 3.
went = went forth. **out of.** Gr. *ek*. Ap. 104. vii.
through. Gr. *dia*. Ap. 104. v. 1.
passed by. All the texts omit this clause, but not the Syr. See note 3, p. 1511, and on 9. 1.

9. 1—10. 21 (Q, p. 1534). SUBSEQUENT EVENTS. (*Alternation.*)

Q | J | 9. 1–38. The Sixth Sign.
K | 9. 39–41. Charge of the Lord against Pharisees.
J | 10. 1–18. Signification of the Sign.
K | 10. 19–21. Charge of the Jews against the Lord.

9. 1–38 (J, above). THE SIXTH SIGN. (*Alternations.*)

J | L | 1, 2. The Sign. Occasion.
M | 3–5. The Purpose of the Sign.
L | 6, 7. The Sign. Wrought.
M | 8–38. The Consequence of the Sign.

1 as . . . passed by. See 8. 59.
He saw. Cp. 5. 6 and see Ap. 176 (C and *C*, p. 194).
saw. See Ap. 133. I. i.
man. Gr. *anthrōpos*. Ap. 123. 1.
which was. Should be in italics.
from his birth. Gr. *ek* (Ap. 104. vii) *genetēs*. Occurs only here.
2 disciples. Not necessarily the Twelve. See note on "neighbours" (*v.* 8) and Structure "*M*".
asked. Gr. *erōtaō*. Ap. 135. I. 3.
Master. Gr. *Rabbi*. Ap. 98. XIV. vii. 1.
sin. Ap. 128. I. i. The only sign (with the *third*; "C", p. 194) connected with sin. See 5. 14.
this man. The Lord was appealed to as Rabbi to settle a much controverted point as to pre-natal sin; or another question that "there shall be neither merit nor demerit in the days of the Messiah" (Lightfoot, xii, p. 326), referring back to "My day" (8. 56).
that = in order that. Gr. *hina*. **was** = should be.
3 Jesus. See Ap. 98. X.
Neither . . . nor. Gr. *oute . . . oute*.
but that. Supply the *Ellipsis*: but [he was born blind] in order that. Here we have the real answer to the question in *v.* 2. **works.** See note on 4. 34. **God.** Ap. 98. I. i. 1. **in.** Gr. *en*. Ap. 104. viii **4 I must work.** T Tr WH R read "We"; but not the Syr. See Ap. 94. V, note 3, p. 136. **work the works.** Fig. *Polyptōton* (Ap. 6), for emphasis. **sent.** Gr. *pempō*. Ap. 174. 4. See note on 1. 22. Not the same word as in *v.* 7. **can work** = is able to work (two verbs). **5 world.** Ap. 129. 1. See note on 1. 9. **I am.** See note on 6. 35. **light.** Gr. *phōs*. See Ap. 130. 1 and note on 1. 4. **6 spat, &c.** For the signification, see Ap. 176. **ground.** Gr. *chamai*. Occurs only here and in 18. 6. **clay.** Gr. *pēlos*. Occurs only here and in *vv.* 11, 14, 15, and Rom. 9. 21. **anointed the eyes, &c** = applied the clay to (Gr. *epi*. Ap. 104. ix. 3) the eyes. Occurs only here and in *v.* 11. **7 wash.** Gr. *niptō*. Ap. 136. 1. See on 13. 10. **in** = into. Gr. *eis*. Ap. 104. vi. **pool.** Cp. 5. 2. Gr. *kolumbēthra*, a pool for swimming or bathing. Occurs only here, *v.* 11 and 5. 2, 4, 7. **Siloam.** See Ap. 68. III, p. 101. **which, &c.** See note on "and we" (1. 14). **Sent.** So called from the sending forth of the waters, which were intermittent. See Ap. 174 1. Not the same word as in *v.* 4. **seeing.** Gr. *blepō*. Ap. 133. I. 5.

9. 8–38 [For Structure see next page].

8 neighbours. Note the different parties in the Structure on p. 1541.

A.D. 28 before had °seen him that he was blind, said,
"Is °not this he that °sat and begged?"
9 °Some said, "This is he:" °others *said*,
"He is like him:" *but* he said, "I am *he*."
10 Therefore said they unto him, "How were
thine eyes opened?"
11 He °answered and said, "A [1]man That is
called [3]Jesus made [6]clay, and [6]anointed mine
eyes, and said unto me, 'Go °to the [7]pool of
[7]Siloam, and [7]wash:' and I went and [7]washed,
and I °received sight."
12 °Then said they unto him, "Where is he?"
He said, "I °know °not."
O 13 They °brought °to the °Pharisees him
that aforetime was blind.
14 °And it was °the sabbath day when [3]Jesus
°made the [6]clay, and opened his eyes.
15 [12]Then again the [13]Pharisees also [2]asked
him how he had [11]received his sight. He said
unto them, "He put [6]clay °upon mine eyes,
and I [7]washed, and do [7]see."
16 Therefore said some [6]of the [13]Pharisees,
"This [1]man is [12]not °of [3]God, because he
keepeth [12]not the sabbath day." [9]Others said,
"How can a [1]man that is a °sinner do such
°miracles?" And °there was a division °among
them.
17 They say unto the blind man again, "What
sayest thou °of him, that he °hath opened thine
eyes?" He said, "He is a °prophet."
P 18 °But °the Jews did [12]not °believe °concern-
ing him, that he had been blind, and [11]received
his sight, until they called the parents of °him
that had [11]received his sight.
19 And they [2]asked them, saying, "Is this
your °son, °who ye say °was [2]born blind? how
[12]then doth he now [7]see?"
20 His [1]parents [11]answered them and said,
"We [12]know that this is our [19]son, and that
he was [2]born blind:
21 But °by what means he now [7]seeth, we
[12]know [12]not; or who [17]hath opened his eyes,
we [12]know [12]not: he is of age; [2]ask him: he
shall speak °for himself."
22 These *words* spake his parents, because
they feared [18]the Jews: for [18]the Jews had
°agreed already, [2]that °if °any man °did confess that He was °Christ, he should °be °put
out of the synagogue.
23 °Therefore said his parents, "He is of age;
[2]ask him."
O 24 [12]Then °again called they the [1]man that
was blind, and said unto him, °"Give [3]God
the °praise: we [12]know that this [1]man is a
[16]sinner."
25 °He [11]answered and said, °"Whether he be
a [16]sinner *or no*, I [12]know [12]not: one thing I
[12]know, that, whereas I was blind, now I
[7]see."
26 Then said they to him again, "What did
he to thee? how opened he thine eyes?"
27 He answered them, °"I have told you
already, and ye did [12]not °hear: wherefore
°would ye hear *it* again? °will ye also be his
disciples?"
28 [12]Then they °reviled him, and said, "Thou
art °his disciple; but we are °Moses' disciples.
29 We [12]know that [3]God °spake unto [28]Moses:
as for this *fellow*, we [12]know [12]not °from
whence he is."

9. 8-38 (*M*, p. 1540). THE CONSEQUENCE OF THE SIGN. (*Introversion.*)

M | N | 8-12. The neighbours and the man.
O | 13-17. The Pharisees and the man.
P | 18-23. The parents and the man.
O | 24-34. The Pharisees and the man.
N | 35-38. The Lord and the man.

seen. Gr. *theōreō.* Ap. 133. I. 11. Not the same word as elsewhere in this chapter.
not. Ap. 105. I.
sat and begged = was sitting and begging.
9 Some. Gr. *allos.* Ap. 124. 1, as in next clause.
others. See note above.
11 answered and said. See Ap. 122. 3 and note on Deut. 1. 41. **to** = unto. Gr. *eis.* Ap. 104. vi.
received sight = looked up [and saw]. Ap. 133. I. 6.
12 Then = Therefore.
know = have (intuitive) knowledge. Gr. *oida.* Ap. 132. I. i. See note on 1. 26.
not. Gr. *ou.* Ap. 105. I. Not the same as in *v.* 39.
13 brought = bring. **to.** Gr. *pros.* Ap. 104. xv. 3.
Pharisees. See Ap. 120. II.
14 And = Now.
the sabbath day = a sabbath. Cp. 5. 10.
made the clay. Held then to be a breach of the law.
15 upon. Gr. *epi.* Ap. 104. ix. 3.
16 of = from (beside). Gr. *para.* Ap. 104. xii. 1.
sinner. Gr. *hamartōlos.* Cp. Ap. 128. I. i. ii.
miracles = signs. See Ap. 176. 3 and note on 2. 11.
there was, &c. The second of three. See note on 7. 43.
among. Gr. *en.* Ap. 104. viii. 2.
17 of = concerning. Gr. *peri.* Ap. 104. xiii. 1.
hath opened = opened. **prophet.** Cp. 4. 19.
18 But = Therefore.
the Jews. See note on 1. 19. See the Structure "P".
believe. See Ap. 150. I. 1. iii and p. 1511.
concerning. Gr. *peri.* Ap. 104. xiii. 1.
him = the very one.
19 son. Ap. 108. iii.
who = of whom. **was** = that he was.
21 by what means = how.
for = concerning, as in *v.* 18.
22 agreed . . . that = agreed together, to this end that.
if. For the condition see Ap. 118. 1. b. Not the same as *v.* 41. **any man** = any one. Ap. 123. 3.
did confess = should confess. Cp. Matt. 7. 23; 10. 32.
Christ = Messiah. See Ap. 98. IX. No art.
be = become.
put out, &c. Gr. *aposunagōgos.* Occ. only here, 12. 42, and 16. 2 = our Eng. "excommunicated".
23 Therefore = On account of (Gr. *dia.* Ap. 104. v. 2) this.
24 again = of (Gr. *ek.* Ap. 104. vii) a second time.
Give God the praise = Give glory to God, as in Josh. 7. 19. 1 Sam. 6. 5. A form of adjuration.
praise = glory. Gr. *doxa.* See p. 1511.
25 He = Therefore he.
Whether = If. Ap. 118. 2. a.
27 I have told = I told. **hear.** See note on 8. 43.
would ye hear = do ye wish (Ap. 102. 1) to hear (two verbs).
will ye also, &c. = surely ye also do not (Ap. 105. II) wish to become.
28 reviled = railed at. Not merely rebuked, but abused. Elsewhere only in Acts 23. 4. 1 Cor. 4. 12. 1 Pet. 2. 23.
His = that Man's. Spoken with contempt.
Moses'. See note on 1. 17.
29 spake = hath spoken.
from whence = whence. Cp. 7. 27; 8. 14.
30 herein = in (Gr. *en.* Ap. 104. viii) this.
marvellous = wonderful.

30 The [1]man [11]answered and said unto them,
"Why °herein is a °marvellous thing, that ye
[12]know [12]not [29]from whence he is, and *yet*
he [17]hath opened mine eyes.

A.D. 28 31 Now we [12]know that [3]God heareth [12]not
[16]sinners: but [22]if [22]any man be °a worshipper
of God, and doeth His °will, him He heareth.
32 °Since the world began was it [12]not heard
that [22]any man opened the eyes of one that
was born blind.
33 °If this man were °not [16]of [3]God, He
°could do nothing."
34 They [11]answered and said unto him,
"Thou wast °altogether born [3]in °sins, and dost
°thou teach us?" And they °cast him °out.

N 35 [3]Jesus heard that they had [34]cast him out;
and °when He had found him, He said unto
him, °"Dost thou °believe on °the Son of
God?"
36 He [11]answered and said, "Who is He,
°Lord, that I might [35]believe on Him?"
37 And [3]Jesus said unto him, "Thou hast
both °seen Him, and it is He That talketh
°with thee."
38 And He said, [36]"Lord, I °believe." And
he °worshipped Him.

K 39 And [3]Jesus said, °"For °judgment I am
come °into this [5]world, that they which see
[33]not might [7]see; and that they which [7]see
might °be made blind."
40 And °*some* [6]of the [13]Pharisees which
were [37]with Him heard these words, and said
unto Him, °"Are we blind also?"
41 [3]Jesus said unto them, °"If ye were blind,
ye °should have °no [34]sin: but now ye say,
'We [7]see;' therefore your [34]sin °remaineth.

JQS 10 °Verily, verily, I say unto you, He that
°entereth °not °by the door °into °the
sheepfold, but °climbeth up °some other way,
T °the same is a °thief and a °robber.
U 2 But he that [1]entereth in [1]by the door is
°the shepherd of the sheep.
3 To him the °porter openeth; and the sheep
°hear his voice: and he °calleth his own sheep
°by name, and leadeth them out.
4 And when °he putteth forth his own sheep,
he goeth °before them, and the sheep follow
him: °for they °know his voice.
5 And a stranger will they °not follow, but
will flee °from him. [4]for they [4]know °not the
voice of strangers."
R 6 °(This °parable spake °Jesus unto them: but
they °understood [-5]not °what things they were
which He spake unto them.)

31 a worshipper of God = a pious man, or God-fearing [man]. Gr. *theosebēs*. Occ. only here in N.T. Cp. the kindred noun in 1 Tim. 2. 10. In an inscription at Miletus the Jews are called *theosebeioi*. Deissmann, *Light*, &c., Ap. IV, p. 446.

will. Gr. *thelēma*. Ap. 102. 2.

32 Since the world began. Gr. *ek tou aiōnos*. See Ap. 151. II. A. ii. 3. This phrase occ. only here in N.T. See note on 6. 64.

33 If. Ap. 118. 2. a. **not.** Gr. *mē*. Ap. 105. II.

could do nothing = would not (Ap. 105. I) be able to do anything.

34 altogether = wholly. **sins.** Ap. 128. I. ii. 1.

thou. Note the emphasis.

cast him out. Not the same word as in *v.* 22.

out = outside.

35 when He had found him. Cp. 5. 14, and see Ap. 176.

Dost thou believe on, &c. Requiring an affirmative answer. Almost = Surely thou believest, &c. See Ap. 150. I. 1. v. (i), and note on 1. 7.

the Son of God. See Ap. 98. XV.

36 Lord. See Ap. 98. VI. i. *a.* 3. A.

37 seen. Gr. *horaō*. Ap. 133. I. 8.

with. Gr. *meta*. Ap. 104. xi. 1.

38 believe. Ap. 150. I. 1. i.

worshipped. Ap. 137. 1.

39 For judgment I am come. Referring to the *effect* of His coming: 12. 47 refers to the *object* of His coming. **For.** Gr. *eis*. Ap. 104. vi.

judgment. Ap. 177. 6. **into.** Gr. *eis*.

be made = become. **40 some** = [those].

Are we blind also? = Surely we also are not (Gr. *mē*. Ap. 105. II) blind, are we?

41 If ye were blind. Assuming the condition as an actual fact. See Ap. 118. 2. a. **should** = would.

no. Gr. *ou*. Ap. 105. I.

remaineth = abideth. See note on 1. 32.

10. 1-18 (*J*, p. 1540). SIGNIFICATION OF THE SIGN. (*Introversion and Extended Alternation.*)

J | Q | S | 1-. The Door.
    T | -1. The Thief and Robber. } The Parable.
    U | 2-5. The Shepherd.
  R | 6. Parable heard, but not understood.
Q | *S* | 7-9. The Door.
    T | 10. Thieves and Robbers. } The Interpretation.
    U | 11-18. The Good Shepherd.

1 Verily, verily. The fifteenth occ. Connecting the sign with the signification. See note on 1. 51.

entereth = entereth in. Note the Fig. *Parēchēsis* (Ap. 6), the Aramaic (Ap. 94. III) being: *min tar'ā' letīrā'*.

not. Gr. *mē*. Ap. 105. II. As in *vv.* -37, 38. Not the same as in *v.* 5.

by = by means of. Gr. *dia*. Ap. 104. v. 1.

into. Gr. *eis*. Ap. 104. vi.

the sheepfold = the fold (Gr. *aulē*) of the sheep; the two symbols being used separately. See *v.* 16.

climbeth up = mounts up [over the fence].

some other way = from another quarter. The "from" is significant. Gr. *allachothen*. Only here, in N.T. **the same** = that one. **thief.** Who uses craft. Gr. *kleptēs*. Always correctly so rendered. Cp. Ap. 164. **robber.** One who uses violence. Gr. *lēstēs*. As in *v.* 8; 18. 40. 2 Cor. 11. 26. Elsewhere wrongly rendered "thief", as in Matt. 21. 13; 26. 55; 27. 38, 44. Mark 11. 17; 14. 48; 15. 27. Luke 10. 30, 36; 19. 46; 22. 52. **2 the** = a: i.e. one of many. **3 porter** = door-keeper. Gr. *thurōros*. Occ. only here; 18. 16, 17. Mark 13. 34. Cp. Ap. 160. III. **hear** = hear [and understand]. Cp. 8. 43. **calleth.** Gr. *kaleō*. But all the texts read *phōneō*, generally implying a personal address. Cp. 13. 13. **by name** = according to (Gr. *kata*. Ap. 104. x. 2) their name. **4 he putteth forth** = he shall have put forth. **before** = in front of. Not the same as in *v.* 8. **for** = because. **know** = know intuitively. From birth, not from having been taught. Ap. 132. I. i. See note on 1. 26. **5 not** = by no means, or in no wise. Gr. *ou mē*. Ap. 105. III. **from** = away from. Gr. *apo*. Ap. 104. iv. **not.** Gr. *ou*. Ap. 105. 1. **6 This parable.** See note on "and we", &c. (1. 14). **parable** = wayside saying. Gr. *paroimia*. Not parable, which is *parabolē*. *Paroimia* occ. in John, here; and (transl. "proverb") in 16. 25, 25, 29, and 2 Pet. 2. 22. *Parabolē* occurs fifty times, but is not used in John. *Paroimia* is the Sept. word for *māshāl* = proverb in Prov. 1. 1. See note there. **Jesus.** Ap. 98. X. **understood not** = did not get to know. Gr. *ginōskō*. Ap. 132. I. i. See note on 1. 10. **what things they were** = what it was, or what it meant.

Q S A.D. 28 7 °Then said [6]Jesus unto them again, [1]"Verily, verily, °I say unto you, °ℑ am the door °of the sheep.

8 °All that ever came °before Me are [1]thieves and [1]robbers: but the sheep did [-5]not hear them.

9 °ℑ am the door: [1]by Me °if °any man enter in, he shall be saved, and shall go in °and out, and °find pasture.

T 10 The [1]thief cometh [-5]not, °but °for to steal, °and to kill, °and to destroy: °ℑ am come °that they might have °life, and that they °might have *it* °more abundantly.

U V 11 °ℑ am °the good Shepherd: the good Shepherd °giveth His °life °for the sheep.

W 12 But °he that is an °hireling, °and [-5]not the shepherd, whose own the sheep are [-5]not, °seeth the wolf coming, °and leaveth the sheep, °and fleeth: °and the wolf °catcheth them, and scattereth the sheep.

13 °The [12]hireling fleeth, °because he is an [12]hireling, and °careth [-5]not °for the sheep.

X h 14 [11]ℑ am the good Shepherd,

i and °know My *sheep*,

k and °am known °of Mine.

k 15 °As °the Father [14]knoweth Me,

i °even so [14]know ℑ °the Father:

h and I °lay down My [11]life [11]for the sheep.

W 16 And °other sheep I have, which are [-5]not °of this °fold: them also °I must bring, and they °shall hear My voice; and there shall °be one °fold, *and* one Shepherd.

V 17 °Therefore doth °My Father °love Me, [13]because ℑ [15]lay down My [11]life, [10]that I might take it again.

18 °No man taketh it [5]from Me, but ℑ lay it down °of Myself. I have °power [15]to lay it down, and I have °power to take it again. This commandment have I received °of [17]My Father."

K 19 There °was °a division therefore again °among the °Jews °for these °sayings.

7 Then = Therefore.

I say ... ℑ am = I say ... that I am, &c.; *hoti*, putting the words that follow as a quotation. See Ap. 173.

of = for. Of the sheep, not of the fold.

8 All that ever = All whoever.

before. Gr. *pro.* Ap. 104. xiv. The true Shepherd could not come till God's purpose was ripe in the fullness of the times (Gal. 4. 4). Moses and the prophets were not "thieves and robbers". None of them claimed to do more than point, as John the Baptist did, to the coming One. All others were deceivers.

9 ℑ am = I represent. See note on 6. 35.

if, &c. A contingency which would be proved by the result. Ap. 118. 1. b. Not the same word as in *vv.* 24, 35, 37, 38. any man = any one. Ap. 123. 3.

and out = and shall go out. The two expressions being the idiom used for life in general.

find = shall find.

10 but = except. Gr. *ei mē.*

for to steal = in order that (Gr. *hina*) he may steal.

and. Note the Fig. *Polysyndeton* (Ap. 6), for emph.

ℑ am come = I came.

that = in order that (Gr. *hina*).

life. Gr. *zōē.* Ap. 170. 1. See note on 1. 4.

might = may.

more abundantly, i. e. life in abundance.

10. 11-18 (*U*, p. 1542). THE GOOD SHEPHERD. (*Alternation.*)

U | V | 11. Laying down His life.
  W | 12. Other shepherds.
   X | 14, 15. His and His Father's knowledge.
  W | 16. Other sheep.
 V | 17, 18. Laying down His life.

11 ℑ am, &c. See note on 6. 35.

the good Shepherd = the Shepherd—the good [one]. Connect this with *death*, and Ps. 22; connect the "great" Shepherd with *resurrection* (Heb. 13. 20), and Ps. 23; and connect the "chief" Shepherd with *glory* (1 Pet. 5. 4), and Ps. 24.

giveth His life = layeth down His life. The expression is frequent in John. See *vv.* 15, 17, 18; 13. 37, 38; 15. 13. 1 John 3. 16. Agreeing with the presentation in this Gospel. See page 1511. Cp. Matt. 20. 28. Mark 10. 45.

life = soul. Gr. *psuchē.* See Ap. 110. III. 1.

for = on behalf of. Gr. *huper.* Ap. 104. xvii.

12 he that is an hireling = the hired servant. Gr. *misthōtos.* Only here, *v.* 13, and Mark 1. 20.

and not = and not being.

seeth. Gr. *theōreō* = to view [with fixed gaze], i. e. with terror or fascination. See Ap. 133. I. 11.

and. Note the Fig. *Polysyndeton* (Ap. 6), for emph.

catcheth them = catcheth or snatcheth them away. Same as "pluck", *vv.* 28, 29. Cp. Acts 8. 39. 2 Cor. 12. 2, 4. 1 Thess. 4. 17, &c. **13** The hireling fleeth. [L] Tm. Trm. WH R omit, but not the Syr. See Ap. 94. V, note 3, p. 136. because. Gr. *hoti.* Same as "for" in *v.* 4. careth not for = is not himself concerned about. for = concerning. Gr. *peri.* Ap. 104. xiii. 1.

10. 14, 15 (X, above). HIS AND HIS FATHER'S KNOWLEDGE. (*Introversion.*)

X | h | 14-. I am the good shepherd,
  i | -14-. and know My sheep,
   k | -14. and am known of Mine.
   k | 15-. As the Father knoweth Me,
  i | -15-. even so know I the Father:
 h | -15. and I lay down My life for the sheep.

This is the expansion of *v.* 11: the member "*h*" showing *why* the Lord is "the good Shepherd" of "h".

14 know ... am known = get to know ... am known. Gr. *ginōskō.* Ap. 132. I. ii. Not the same as in *vv.* 4, 5. See note on 1. 10. of = by. Gr. *hupo.* Ap. 104. xviii. 1. **15** As = According as. the Father. See note on 1. 14. even so know ℑ = I also know. lay down. Same as "give", *v.* 11. **16** other. Gr. *allos.* See Ap. 124. 1. of = out of. Gr. *ek.* Ap. 104. vii. fold. Gr. *aulē* = a place in the open air, as in *v.* 1, not the same word as in the next clause. I must = it behoves Me. shall = will. be = become. fold = flock. Gr. *poimnē.* Only here, Matt. 26. 31. Luke 2. 8. 1 Cor. 9. 7. **17** Therefore = On account of (Gr. *dia.* Ap. 104. v. 2) this. My Father. See note on 2. 16. love. Gr. *agapaō.* Ap. 135. I. 1. See note on 3. 16. **18** No man = No one. Gr. *oudeis*, i. e. no being, man or devil. Until 1660 the A.V. read "none". of = from. Gr. *apo.* Ap. 104. iv. power = authority. Ap. 172. 5. of = from. Gr. *para.* Ap. 104. xii. 1. **19** was = arose. a division. This was the third of three. See note on 7. 43. among. Gr. *en.* Ap. 104. viii. 2. Jews. See note on 1. 19. for = on account of. Gr. *dia.* Ap. 104. v. 2. sayings = words. Gr. pl. of *logos.* See note on Mark 9. 32.

A.D. 28 20 And many [16]of them said, "He hath a
°devil, and is mad; why hear ye Him?"
21 [16]Others said, "These are [-5]not the °words
of °him that hath a devil. °Can a [20]devil open
the eyes of the blind?"

P l¹ 22 °And it was °at Jerusalem °the feast of the
dedication, and it was winter.
23 And [6]Jesus °walked °in the °temple °in
°Solomon's porch.
24 [7]Then °came the Jews round about Him,
and said unto Him, "How long dost Thou
°make °us to doubt? °If Thou be the °Christ,
tell us °plainly."

m¹ 25 [6]Jesus answered them, "I °told you, and
ye °believed [-5]not: the works that I do [23]in
°My Father's name, they bear witness °of Me.
26 But ye [25]believe [-5]not, because ye are
[-5]not [16]of My sheep, as I said unto you.
27 My sheep [3]hear My voice, °and I [14]know
them, °and they follow Me:
28 [27]And I give unto them °eternal [10]life;
[27]and they shall °never perish, °neither shall
[9]any *man* °pluck them °out of My hand.
29 [17]My Father, which gave *them* Me, is
greater than all; and [18]no *man* is able to
[28]pluck *them* [28]out of [17]My Father's hand.
30 I and [17]*My* Father are °one."

l² 31 Then the Jews took up stones °again °to
stone Him.

m² 32 [6]Jesus answered them, "Many good works
have I shewed you °from [17]My Father; [19]for
which of those works do ye stone Me?"

l³ 33 The Jews answered Him, saying, [13]"For
a good work we stone Thee [-5]not; but [13]for
°blasphemy; and because that Thou, being a
man, makest Thyself °God."

m³ 34 [6]Jesus answered them, "Is it [-5]not written
[23]in your °law, '**I said, 'Ye are °gods?'**
35 [24]If he called them [34]gods, °unto whom the
word of [33]God came, and the scripture °cannot
be °broken;
36 Say ye of Him, Whom [15]the Father hath
°sanctified, and °sent [1]into the °world, 'Thou
blasphemest; because I said, 'I am °the Son
of God?'
37 [24]If I do [-5]not the works of [17]My Father,
°believe Me [1]not.
38 But [24]if I do, °though ye [37]believe [1]not
Me, [37]believe °the works: [10]that ye may [14]know,
and °believe, °that [15]the Father *is* [23]in Me,
and I [23]in Him."

Q Y A 39 Therefore they sought again to °take Him:
but He °escaped [28]out of their hand,

B 40 And °went away again beyond Jordan

20 devil = demon. Gr. *daimonion*. Cp. 8. 48, and Matt. 12. 24.

21 words. Gr. pl. of *rhēma*. See note on Mark 9. 32.

him that hath a devil = one possessed by a demon.

Can a devil . . . ? = Surely a demon is not (Gr. *mē*. Ap. 105. II) able to . . . is he?

10. 22-38 (*P*, p. 1534). AT THE FEAST OF DEDICATION. (*Repeated Alternation.*)

P | l¹ | 22-24. The Jews. Question.
  m¹ | 25-30. The Lord. Answer.
 l² | 31. The Jews. Stoning.
  m² | 32. The Lord. Answer.
 l³ | 33. The Jews. Stoning.
  m³ | 34-38. The Lord. Answer.

22 And. Fig. *Chronographia*. Ap. 6.

at. Gr. *en*. Ap. 104. viii.

the feast of the dedication. Gr. *enkainia* = renewal, from *kainos*, new, i.e. the cleansing of Ezra's temple after its defilement by Antiochus Epiphanes, 25th Chisleu (= December), 164 B.C. Cp. 1 Macc. 4. 52-59.

23 walked = was walking. **in.** Gr. *en*. Ap. 104. viii.

temple. Gr. *hieron*. See note on Matt. 23. 16.

Solomon's porch. According to Josephus (*Ant.* xx. 9, § 7), this was a relic from Solomon's temple (cp. Acts 3. 11; 5. 12).

24 came . . . round about = encircled. Cp. Ps. 88. 17.

make us to doubt? Gr. raise our souls, i.e. hold us in suspense, or excite our expectations.

us = our souls. Ap. 110. IV. 3. **If, &c.** Ap. 118. 2. a.

Christ, i.e. Messiah. Ap. 98. IX.

plainly. Same Gr. word as "openly", 18. 20.

25 told. He had not spoken to them as He did in 4. 26; 9. 35-37, but the works were evidence enough to those who had eyes to see. Cp. 5. 36; 7. 31; 9. 32; 15. 24.

believed. Ap. 150. I. 1. i.

My Father's name. Only occurs here and 5. 43. Cp. Rev. 14. 1.

of = concerning. Gr. *peri*. Ap. 104. xiii. 1.

27 and. Fig. *Polysyndeton*. Ap. 6.

28 eternal. Gr. *aiōnios*. Ap. 151. II. B. i.

never = by no means (Gr. *ou mē*. Ap. 105. III) unto the age (Gr. *eis ton aiōna*. Ap. 151. II. A. ii. 4. b).

neither = and not (Gr. *ou*. Ap. 105. I).

pluck = snatch. See *v.* 12.

out of. Gr. *ek*. Ap. 104. vii.

30 one. Gr. *hen*. Neut., one in essence, not one person which would be *heis*, masc. This is the climax of His claim to oneness with the Father in *vv.* 18, 25, 28, 29. Cp. also *v.* 38; 14. 11. Rev. 22. 3.

31 again. See 8. 59. **to.** Gr. *hina*, as in *v.* 10.

32 from. Gr. *ek*. Ap. 104. vii.

33 blasphemy. See Lev. 24. 16.

God = Jehovah. See Ap. 98. I. i. 1.

34 law. The usual division is "the Law, the Prophets, and the Psalms" (Luke 24. 44). Here the Psalms are included in the Law. Cp. 15. 25.

gods. See Ap. 98. I. i. 4. Quoted from Ps. 82. 6.

35 unto. Gr. *pros*. Ap. 104. xv. 3.

cannot = is not (Gr. *ou*. Ap. 105. I) able to.

broken. Cp. 7. 23.

36 sanctified = set apart for a holy purpose. Cp. 17. 19.

sent. Ap. 174. 1. **world.** Ap. 129. 1.

the Son of God. Ap. 98. XV.

37 believe. Ap. 150. I. 1. ii.

38 though = even if. Gr. *kān* = *kai ean*. Ap. 118. 1. b.

the works. These have a voice of their own. Cp. Ps. 19. 1-4. **believe.** Ap. 150. I. 1. iii. **that, &c.** With this profound statement cp. 14. 10, 11, 20; 17. 11, 21. See also Matt. 11. 27.

10. 39—11. 54- (*Q*, p. 1534). SUBSEQUENT EVENTS. (*Introversion and Alternation.*)

Q | Y | A | 10. 39. Desire to take Him.
   B | 10. 40-42. The Lord escapes.
  Z | 11. 1-46. The SEVENTH Sign. The Raising of Lazarus.
 Y | A | 11. 47-53. Counsel to take Him.
   B | 11. 54-. The Lord escapes.

39 take = arrest. See 7. 30, 32, 44. **escaped** = went forth. Cp. 8. 59 and Luke 4. 30. **40 went away, &c.** This was in December, and He remained away till April, visiting Bethany (11. 1) in the interval, and spending the latter part of the time at the city Ephraim (11. 54).

A. D. 28 [1]into the place °where John at first °baptized;
and there He abode.
41 And many °resorted [35]unto Him, and °said,
"John °did °no °miracle: but all things that
John spake [25]of this Man were °true."
42 And many °believed °on Him °there.

Z C **11** Now a certain *man* °was sick, *named*
°Lazarus, °of Bethany, °the town of °Mary
and her sister °Martha.
2 (°It was *that* [1]Mary which anointed °the
Lord with ointment, and wiped His feet with
her hair, whose brother Lazarus [1]was sick.)

D 3 Therefore his sisters °sent °unto Him,
saying, "°Lord, °behold, he whom Thou
°lovest °is sick."
4 When °Jesus heard *that*, He said, "This
°sickness is °not [3]unto death, but °for °the
°glory of °God, °that °the Son of God might be
glorified °thereby."
5 (Now [4]Jesus °loved [1]Martha, and her sister,
and Lazarus.)

C E[1] F G 6 When He had heard therefore that he [3]was
sick, °He abode two days still °in the same
place where He was.

H 7 °Then °after that saith He to *His* disciples,
"Let us go °into Judæa again."

J 8 *His* disciples say unto Him, °"Master, the
Jews °of late sought to stone Thee; and goest
Thou thither again?"

F G 9 [4]Jesus answered, "Are there [4]not °twelve
hours in the day? °If °any man walk [6]in the
day, he stumbleth [4]not, because he °seeth °the
°light of this °world.
10 But [9]if a man walk [6]in the night, he
stumbleth, because °there is no [9]light [6]in him."

H 11 These things said He: and [7]after that He
saith unto them, "Our °friend [1]Lazarus
°sleepeth; but I °go, [4]that I may °awake him
out of sleep."

where, &c. See 1. 28.
baptized = was baptizing. Ap. 115. I. i.
41 resorted = came. said = kept saying.
did, &c. Miracles were not necessarily the credentials of a prophet (Deut. 13. 1–3). no. Gr. *ouden.*
miracle = sign, a characteristic word in this Gospel. See note on 2. 11, and p. 1511.
true. Gr. *alēthēs.* Ap. 175. 1.
42 believed. See Ap. 150. I. v. (i).
on. Gr. *eis.* Ap. 104. vi.
there. Emphatic, in contrast with His treatment in Jerusalem.

11. 1–46 (Z, p. 1544). THE SEVENTH SIGN. THE RAISING OF LAZARUS. (*Extended Alternation.*)

Z | C | 1, 2. The Sign. Occasion.
  D | 3–5. The purpose. The glory of God.
 C | 6–44. The Sign. Performance.
  D | 45, 46. The Consequences. Belief of some and opposition of others.

1 was sick. Pointing to great weakness and exhaustion, the result of active disease, rather than the disease itself. The verb is used thirty-six times, generally translated in the Gospels "sick", in Paul's Epistles "weak", but in John 5. 3, 7 "impotent".
Lazarus. Same as Eleazar = God helpeth. First occ. Ex. 6. 23. of = from. Gr. *apo.* Ap. 104. iv.
the town = of (Gr. *ek.* Ap. 104. vii) the town, or unwalled village. See Luke 10. 38, which refers to Bethany. Mary. See Ap. 100. 3.
Martha Aramaic. See Ap. 94. III. 3.
2 It was, &c. This is an explanatory statement, anticipating what is related in 12. 3.
the Lord. Gr. *Kurios.* Ap. 98. VI. i. *a.* 3. B. c.
3 sent. Gr. *apostellō.* Ap. 174. 1. If the place of 10. 40 was Bethabara beyond Jordan, and is to be identified with Beth-nimrah (Num. 32. 36) in Peraea, it would be about 25 miles from Jerusalem.
unto. Gr. *pros.* Ap. 104. xv. 3.
Lord. Ap. 98. VI. i. *a.* 3. A.
behold. Gr. *ide.* Ap. 133. I. 3.
lovest. Ap. 135. I. 2.
is sick: lit. is weakening = is sinking.
4 Jesus. Ap. 98. X.
sickness. Gr. *astheneia* = weakness, not *nosos*, active disease. See note on Matt. 4. 23.
not. Gr. *ou.* Ap. 105. I.
for = for the purpose of. Gr. *huper.* Ap. 104. xvii. 1.
the glory, &c. The glory of God and of His Son are one and the same. glory. See p. 1511. God. Ap. 98. I. i. 1. that = in order that. Gr. *hina.* the Son of God. Ap. 98. XV. thereby = through (Gr. *dia.* Ap. 104. v. 1) it. **5** loved. Ap. 135. I. 1. Not the same word as in *vv.* 3, 36.

11. 6–44 (*C*, above). THE SIGN. PERFORMANCE. (*Division.*)

C | E[1] | 6–16. Departure of the Lord.
  | E[2] | 17–44. Arrival of the Lord.

11. 6–16 (E[1], above). DEPARTURE, ETC. (*Extended Alternation.*)

E[1] | F | G | 6. Days (lit.). Abode.
   H | 7. The Lord's proposal. "Let us go."
    J | 8. Disciples. Dissuasion.
  F | *G* | 9, 10. Day (fig.). Work.
   H | 11–15. The Lord's proposal. "Let us go."
    J | 16. Disciples. Acquiescence.

6 He abode . . . still. Gr. *tote men emeinen.* Then indeed He remained. Both A.V. and R.V. omit these important adverbs. in. Gr. *en.* Ap. 104. viii. **7** Then = Afterward. Gr. *epeita.* after. Gr. *meta.* Ap. 104. xi. 2. into. Gr. *eis.* Ap. 104. vi. **8** Master = Rabbi. Ap. 98. XIV. vii. 1. of late sought = just now were seeking. Cp. 8. 59. **9** twelve hours; reckoning from sunrise to sunset, 6 a.m. to 6 p.m. If. Ap. 118. 1 b. any man. Ap. 123. 3. seeth. Ap. 133. I. 5. the light, &c., i.e. the sun naturally, the Sun of righteousness metaphorically. light. Gr. *phōs.* Ap. 130. 1. world. Gr. *kosmos.* Ap. 129. 1. **10** there is no light in him = the light is not (Gr. *ou.* Ap. 105 I) in him. The clauses in *vv.* 9, 10 are strictly antithetical.

Illustration (exoteric). { Walking by day in the light of the sun, a man stumbles not.
Walking by night without that light, he stumbles.

Application (esoteric) { He that hath the Son is walking in the light.
He that hath not the Son walks in darkness.

Cp 8. 12; 12. 35, 36, 46. **11** friend. Gr. *philos,* noun of *phileō, v.* 3. sleepeth = has fallen asleep. Gr. *koimaomai.* Ap. 171. 2. go. Gr. *poreuomai,* to go with a set purpose. Cp. 14. 2, 3, and Matt. 2. 8, 9. Not the same word as in *v.* 8. awake him out of sleep. Gr. *exupnizō.* Occurs only here.

A.D. 28 12 °Then said His disciples, [3]"Lord, °if he
[11]sleep, he °shall do well."
13 (Howbeit [4]Jesus spake °of his death: but
they thought that He had spoken °of taking of
rest in sleep.)
14 °Then said [4]Jesus unto them °plainly,
[1]"Lazarus °is dead.
15 And I am glad °for your sakes that I was
[4]not there, to the intent ye may °believe;
nevertheless let us go [3]unto him."

J 16 [12]Then said °Thomas, which is called
°Didymus, unto his °fellow disciples, "Let us
also go, [4]that we may die °with Him."

E² K L 17 [12]Then when [4]Jesus came, He found that he
had *lain* [6]in the °grave four days already.
18 (Now Bethany was nigh unto Jerusalem,
°about fifteen furlongs off:)

M 19 And many °of the Jews °came °to [1]Martha
and [1]Mary, to °comfort them °concerning
their brother.

N 20 [12]Then [1]Martha, as soon as she heard that
[4]Jesus was coming, °went and met Him: but
[1]Mary °sat *still* [6]in the house.
21 [12]Then said [1]Martha [3]unto [4]Jesus, [3]"Lord,
[12]if Thou hadst been here, my brother had
[4]not died.
22 But I °know, that even now, whatsoever
Thou wilt °ask of [4]God, [4]God will give *it*
Thee."

O P 23 [4]Jesus saith unto her, "Thy brother shall
°rise again."

Q 24 [1]Martha saith unto Him, "I [22]know that
he shall [23]rise again [6]in the °resurrection °at
the °last day."

P R 25 [4]Jesus said unto her, °"I am the [24]resurrection,

S and the °life:

R he that °believeth °in Me, though he were
dead, °yet shall he live:

S 26 And whosoever °liveth and [25]believeth
[26]in Me shall °never die.

Q °Believest thou this?"
27 She saith unto Him, "Yea, [3]Lord: I
[-26]believe that Thou art °the Christ, °the Son
of God, Which should come [7]into the [9]world."

K L 28 And when she had so said, she went her
way, and called [1]Mary her sister °secretly,
saying, °"The Master is come, and calleth
for thee."
29 As soon as she heard *that*, she arose
quickly, and came [3]unto Him.

12 Then=Therefore. **if.** Ap. 118. 2. a.
shall do well=shall be saved. Gr. *sōzō*, as in 10. 9.
13 of=concerning. Gr. *peri*. Ap. 104. xiii. 1.
14 Then said Jesus; lit. Then therefore Jesus said.
plainly. See 10. 24.
is dead=died. Aorist tense. This shows that death had taken place some time before, probably soon after the message was sent by the sisters. Cp. *vv.* 17, 39.
15 for your sakes=on account of (Gr. *dia*. Ap. 104. v. 2) you. **believe.** Ap. 150 I. 1. i.
16 Thomas. Ap. 94. III. 3 and 141.
Didymus=twin, a Greek word with the same meaning as Thomas. Occurs here, 20. 24, and 21. 2.
fellowdisciples. Gr. *summathētēs*. Occurs only here.
with (Gr. *meta*. Ap. 104. xi. 1) **Him**, i.e. the Lord, not with Lazarus. Thomas realized that to return to the neighbourhood of Jerusalem meant certain death.

11. 17-44 (E², p. 1545). THE ARRIVAL, ETC.
(*Extended Alternation.*)

E² | K | L | 17, 18. Arrival near Bethany.
M | 19. The Jews present.
N | 20-22. Martha.
O | 23-27. Resurrection. Promise.
K | *L* | 28-30. Arrival near Bethany.
M | 31. The Jews present.
N | 32. Mary.
O | 33-44. Resurrection. Performance.

17 grave=tomb. Gr. *mnēmeion*. First, a memorial or monument, then a sepulchre. Cp. 5. 28.
18 about, &c.=as it were from (Gr. *apo*. Ap. 104. iv) fifteen furlongs, i. e. 1⅞ miles.
19 of=out of, from among. Gr. *ek*. Ap. 104. vii.
came=had come.
to. Gr. *pros*, as in *v.* 3
comfort. Gr. *paramutheomai*; to speak tenderly, consolingly. Occurs only here; *v.* 31; 1 Thess. 2. 11 and 5. 14.
concerning. Gr. *peri*, as in *v.* 13.
20 went and met=met. The word implies desire to avoid notice.
sat still=was sitting (Gr. *kathezomai*). There is no word for "still", and the A.V. and R.V. insertion of it implies, without warrant, that Mary heard as well as Martha, but nevertheless remained where she was. Compare the other five occurrences of the word, 4. 6; 20. 12. Matt. 26. 55. Luke 2. 46 Acts 6. 15.
22 know. Gr. *oida*. Ap. 132 I. i.
ask. Gr. *aiteō*. Ap. 134. 4. Used of our prayers (Matt. 7. 7, &c.), never of the Lord's address to the Father. Neither Martha, the disciples or the Jews understood the claim of 10. 30.

11. 23-27 (O, above). THE LORD'S PROMISE.
(*Alternation.*)

O | P | 23. The Lord's promise (Lazarus).
Q | 24. Martha (knowledge).
P | 25, 26-. The Lord's promise (all believers).
Q | -26, 27. Martha (belief).

23 rise again. Gr. *anistēmi*. See Ap. 178. I. 1.
24 resurrection. Ap. 178. II. 1.
at=in. Gr. *en*. Ap. 104 viii.
last day. See 6. 39, 40, 44, 54; 12. 48; and cp. Dan. 12. 2, 13.

11. 25, 26- (*P*, above). THE LORD'S PROMISE. (*Alternation.*)

P | R | 25-. Resurrection "I am", &c.
S | -25-. Life.
} Declaration concerning Himself.
R | -25. Resurrection for dead saints.
S | 26-. Life for living ones.
} Declaration concerning His own.

25 I am (emphatic). See note on Exod. 3. 14, and cp. 8. 58. **life.** Gr. *zōē*. Ap. 170. 1. **believeth.** See Ap. 150. I. 1. v. (i). These words refer to 1 Thess. 4. 16. **in.** Gr. *eis*. Ap. 104. vi. **yet shall he live**=shall live. Fig. *Aposiopēsis*. Ap. 6. The word "yet" is not in the Gr., and is unwarrantably introduced by both A.V. and R.V. **26 liveth**=is alive, referring to 1 Thess. 4. 17. **never**=by no means (Gr. *ou mē*. Ap. 105. III) unto the age (Gr. *eis ton aiōna*. Ap. 151. II. A. ii. 4. b). **Believest.** See Ap. 150. I. iii. **27 the Christ**=the Messiah (Ap. 98. IX). **the Son of God** (Ap. 98. XV). Cp. Peter's confession in Matt. 16. 16. **28 secretly, saying**=saying secretly. **The Master.** Gr. *ho didaskalos*. Ap. 98. XIV. v. 3.

A.D. 28 30 Now [4]Jesus was [4]not yet come [7]into the
town, but was [6]in that place where [1]Martha
met Him.

M 31 The Jews [12]then which were [16]with her [6]in
the house, and [19]comforted her, when they
°saw [1]Mary, that she rose up hastily and
went out, followed her, °saying, "She goeth
°unto the grave to °weep there."

N 32 [12]Then when [1]Mary was come where [4]Jesus
was, and [31]saw him, she °fell down °at His
feet, saying unto Him, [3]"Lord, [12]if Thou
hadst been here, my brother had [4]not died."

O T1 n 33 When [4]Jesus therefore [31]saw her [31]weeping,
and the Jews also [31]weeping which came with
her, He °groaned in the °spirit, and °was
troubled,
34 And said, "Where have ye laid him?"

o They said unto Him, "Lord, come and [31]see."

n 35 [4]Jesus °wept.

o 36 [12]Then said the Jews, [3]"Behold how He
[3]loved him!"

U 37 °And some [19]of them said, "Could [4]not
°this man, Which opened the eyes of the
°blind, have caused that even °this man
should °not have died?"

T2 p 38 [4]Jesus therefore again [33]groaning [6]in Himself cometh °to the [17]grave.

q It was a °cave, and a stone lay °upon it.

p 39 [4]Jesus said, "Take ye away the stone."

q [1]Martha, the sister of him that was dead, saith
unto Him, [3]Lord, by this time he stinketh: for
he hath been *dead* °four days."

U 40 [4]Jesus saith unto her, "Said I [4]not unto
thee, that, [9]if thou wouldest [15]believe, thou
shouldest °see °the [4]glory of [4]God?"

T3 r 41 [12]Then they took away the stone *from the
place* where the dead was laid.

s And [4]Jesus lifted up *His* eyes, and said,
°"Father, I thank Thee that Thou °hast
heard Me.
42 And I [22]knew that Thou hearest Me
always: but °because of the people which
stand by I said *it*, [4]that they may [−26]believe
that Thou hast [3]sent Me."

r 43 And when He thus had spoken, He cried
with a loud voice, [1]"Lazarus, °come forth."
44 And °he that was dead came forth, bound
hand and foot with °graveclothes: and his
face was bound about with a °napkin.

s [4]Jesus saith unto them, "Loose him, and let
him go."

D 45 [12]Then many [19]of the Jews which came [19]to
(p. 1545) [1]Mary, and had °seen °the things which [4]Jesus
did, [25]believed on Him.
46 °But some [19]of them °went their ways [19]to
the °Pharisees, and °told them °what things
[4]Jesus had done.

31 saw. Gr. *eidon.* Ap. 133. I. 1.
saying. T Tr. A WH R read, "supposing".
unto. Gr. *eis.* Ap. 104. vi.
weep (Gr. *klaiō*) = to wail. Not the same word as in *v.* 35.
32 fell down. Others who fell down before Him or at His feet were the wise men (Matt. 2. 11), Jairus (Mark 5. 22), the woman (Mark 5. 33), the Syrophenician (Mark 7. 25), Peter (Luke 5. 8), the leper (Luke 5. 12), the Gadarene (Luke 8. 28), and the Samaritan (Luke 17. 16). This makes nine in all. See Ap. 10.
at. Gr. *eis.* Ap. 104. vi.

11. 33-44 (*O*, p. 1546). **RESURRECTION. PERFORMANCE.** (*Alternations.*)

O T1 n | 33, 34-. The Lord. Groaning.
o | -34. The Jews. Answer.
n | 35. The Lord. Weeping.
o | 36. The Jews. Remark.
U | 37. What some said.
T2 p | 38-. The Lord. Groaning.
q | -38. The grave described.
p | 39-. The Lord. Command.
q | -39. The dead described.
U | 40. What the Lord said.
T3 r | 41-. Lazarus. Dead.
s | -41, 42. The Lord. Request.
r | 43, 44-. Lazarus. Called.
s | -44. The Lord. Command.

33 groaned. Gr. *embrimaomai*, to snort as a horse does, from fear or anger; hence, to feel strong emotion, be indignant, &c. Only occurs here, *v.* 38. Matt. 9. 30. Mark 1. 43; 14. 5.
spirit. Ap. 101. II. 9.
was troubled = troubled Himself. Cp. Gen. 6. 6. Judg. 10. 16.
35 wept = shed tears. Gr. *dakruō.* Occurs only here. The noun *dakru* or *dakruon* occurs eleven times, and is always transl. by pl. "tears".
37 And = But.
this man (Gr. *houtos*) = this (One). Cp. Matt. 8. 27.
blind = blind (man). See 9. 1-7.
not. Gr. *mē.* Ap. 105. II.
38 to = unto. Gr. *eis*, as *v.* 31.
cave. Natural or artificial. Cp. Isa. 22. 16.
upon = against. Gr. *epi.* Ap. 104. ix. 2.
39 four days. The Rabbis taught that the spirit wandered about for three days, seeking re-admission to the body, but abandoned it on the fourth day, as corruption began then.
40 see. Ap. 133. I. 8 (a).
the glory of God, i.e. the manifestation of the same glory by which Christ was raised. Cp. Rom. 6. 4.
41 Father. See 1. 14 and Ap. 98. III. Fifteen times the Lord used this term in prayer (omitting parallel passages in brackets): Matt. 11. 25, 26 (Luke 10. 21); 26. 39, 42 (Mark 14. 36. Luke 22. 42). Luke 23. 34, 46. John 11. 41; 12. 27, 28; 17. 1, 5, 11, 21, 24, 25 (15 = 3 × 5. Ap. 6). Next to John 17, this is the longest prayer recorded of our Lord.
hast heard = heardest (Aorist tense). This suggests that the prayer was heard and answered before, perhaps in Peraea. See *v.* 4.
42 because of. Gr. *dia*, as in *v.* 15.
43 come forth; lit. hither, out.
44 he that was dead. Gr. *ho tethnēkōs*, the dead man. Cp. Luke 7. 12.
graveclothes. Gr. *keiriai.* Only used here in N.T. In the Sept. it is used in Prov. 7. 16, as the rendering of the Heb. *marbaddim.* Originally it meant a bed-girth, and so any kind of wrapping. Here, = swathings.
napkin. Gr. *soudarion.* A Latin word, *sudarium*, or sweat-cloth. Used only here, 20. 7. Luke 19. 20, and Acts 19. 12.
45 seen (Gr. *theaomai.* Ap. 133. I. 12) = regarded with wonder.
the things which. Some read "the thing which", referring to this special miracle, or rather these two miracles; for how could Lazarus, when restored to life, come forth, bound, as he was, hand and foot, and his eyes covered, save by a further exercise of Divine power? Thus there was a great increase of disciples, which alarmed the rulers.
46 But some. These were probably temple spies.
went, &c. = went off.
Pharisees. Ap. 120. II.
told = "informed".
what things = the thing which, as in *v.* 45. So L T Tr. WH.

A V 47 [12] Then gathered the chief priests and the
A. D. 28 [46] Pharisees a ° council, and said,
W °"What do we? for ° this man doeth many
° miracles.
48 [9] If we let Him thus alone, all *men* will
[25] believe on Him: and the Romans shall come
and take away both ° our ° place and ° nation."
V 49 And one [19] of them, *named* Caiaphas, being
the high priest ° that same year, said unto them,
W °"Ye [22] know nothing at all,
50 ° Nor consider that ° it is expedient for ° us,
[4] that one [47] man should die [4] for the ° people, and
that the whole [48] nation perish [37] not."
51 And this spake he [4] not [1] of himself: but
being high priest that year, he ° prophesied
that [4] Jesus ° should die [4] for that [48] nation;
52 And [4] not [4] for that [48] nation only, but [4] that
also He should ° gather together [25] in one the
° children of [4] God that ° were scattered abroad.
53 [12] Then ° from ° that day forth they took
counsel together ° for to put Him to death.
B 54 [4] Jesus therefore ° walked [10] no more ° openly
° among the Jews;
D X[1] but went thence [31] unto a country near to the
wilderness, [7] into a city called ° Ephraim, and
there ° continued [16] with His disciples.
Y[1] A[1] 55 And the ° Jews' passover was nigh at
A. D. 29 hand: and many went ° out of the country up
[38] to Jerusalem ° before the passover, ° to ° purify
themselves.
56 Then ° sought they for [4] Jesus, and spake
° among themselves, as they stood [6] in the
° temple, "What think ye, that He will ° not
come [38] to the feast?"
B[1] 57 Now both the chief priests and the Pharisees had given a commandment, [4] that, [9] if ° any
man ° knew where He were, he should ° shew
it, that they might ° take Him.

11. 47-53 (*A*, p. 1544). COUNSEL TO TAKE HIM. (*Alternation.*)

A | V | 47-. The Chief Priests. Council.
  W | -47, 48. Consultation.
 V | 49-. The High Priest (Caiaphas).
  W | -49-53. Decision.

47 council. Gr. *sunedrion.* The Sanhedrin was the supreme national court. See Matt. 5. 22. It consisted of seventy-one members, originating, according to the Rabbis, with the seventy elders, with Moses at their head (Num. 11. 24). Its sittings were held in the "stone chamber" in the temple precincts.

What do we? = What are we about? i. e. something must be done.

this man. See *v.* 37, but "man" (Ap. 123. 1) is expressed here.

miracles = signs (Gr. *sēmeion*). A characteristic word in John's Gospel. See p. 1511 and Ap. 176. 3.

48 our = of us. Gr. *hēmōn.* Both the word and its position are emphatic. They claimed for themselves what belonged to God. Cp. Matt. 23. 38, *your* house. So the feasts of the Lord (Lev. 23. 2), are called in this gospel, feasts of the Jews (*v.* 55; 5. 1; 6. 4; 7. 2).

place (Gr. *topos*). No doubt the temple was meant, the centre and source of all their influence and power. The word is often so used. See 4. 20. Acts 6. 13, 14; 21. 28, 29.

nation. Gr. *ethnos.* "Our" belongs to nation as well as to place. They claimed the nation which they ruled as their own (see Luke 20. 14).

49 that, &c. Caiaphas had been appointed six months before.

Ye know nothing at all = ye know nothing (Gr. *ouk ouden*, a double negative), i. e. you do not grasp the position; you do not see how critical it is.

50 Nor. Gr. *oude.*

it is expedient = it is to our interest.

us. All the texts read "you".

people. Gr. *laos.* The word that expresses their relationship to God (Deut. 14. 2. Matt. 2. 6), as "nation" is a more general term (Luke 7. 5; 23. 2).

51 prophesied. The Jews regarded any *ex cathedra* utterance of the High Priest as inspired. Here Caiaphas was used by God, as Balaam was (Num. 22. 38). See Acts 2. 23; 4. 27, 28. **should die** = was about to die.

52 gather together. Cp. 10. 16 with Jer. 23. 3; 31. 10.

children. Gr. *teknon.* Ap. 108. i.

were scattered abroad = had been scattered. See Lev. 26. 33. Deut. 28. 64. Jer. 9. 16. Ezek. 12. 15; 22. 15, &c. **53 from.** Gr. *apo.* Ap. 104. iv. **that day,** i. e. the day on which the council came to their awful decision. **for to, &c.** = in order that (Gr. *hina*) they might kill Him, i. e. on some *judicial* pretence. The raising of Lazarus, followed, as it was, by so many becoming believers, brought the malignity of the Pharisees to a climax. It was the last of the three miracles that so exasperated them, the others being those on the impotent man, and on the man born blind. See the result in each case (5. 16; 9. 16, 22, 34). **54 walked** = was walking. **openly.** Same as "plainly" in *v.* 14. **among.** Gr. *en.* Ap. 104. viii. **Ephraim.** If it is to be identified with the modern *Ophrah*, it is about 16 miles north-east of Jerusalem. Cp. 2 Chron. 13. 19. **continued** (Gr. *diatribō*) = abode; so transl. in Acts 12. 19; 14. 3, 28; 16. 12; 20. 6. In 3. 22; Acts 25. 6, "tarried".

11. -54—18. 1 (*D*, p. 1510). THE MINISTRY. FOURTH PERIOD. (*Alternation.*)

D | X[1] | 11. -54. Departure. Ephraim.
 Y[1] | 11. 55—12. 19. Hostility manifested.
  Z[1] | 12. 20-36-. Greeks. The hour come. Glorification.
X[2] | 12. -36. Departure. Concealment.
 Y[2] | 12. 37-50. Hostility explained.
  Z[2] | 13. 1—17. 26. Disciples. The hour come. Glorification.
X[3] | 18. 1. Departure. Gethsemane.

11. 55—12. 19 (Y[1], above). HOSTILITY MANIFESTED. (*Alternation.*)

Y[1] | A[1] | 11. 55, 56. Passover. People. Concourse.
 B[1] | 11. 57. Hostility. Chief Priests' command.
A[2] | 12. 1-9. Passover. Bethany. Anointing.
 B[2] | 10, 11. Hostility. Chief Priests' counsel.
A[3] | 12-18. Passover. People. Meeting.
 B[3] | 19. Hostility. Chief Priests' perplexity.

55 Jews' passover. Commencing on the 14th Nisan. See note on 2. 13. **out of.** Gr. *ek.* Ap. 104. vii. **before.** Gr. *pro.* Ap. 104. xiv. **to** = in order to. Gr. *hina.* **purify themselves:** i. e. from Levitical uncleanness. See Num. 9. 10 and Acts 21. 24. **56 sought** = were seeking. **among themselves** = with (Gr. *meta.* Ap. 104. xi. 1) one another. **temple.** Gr. *hieron.* See note on Matt. 23. 16. **not** = in no wise. Gr. *ou mē.* Ap. 105. III. **57 any man** = any one. Gr. *tis.* Ap. 123. 3. **knew** = got to know. Gr. *ginōskō.* Ap. 133. ii. **shew** = disclose. Gr *mēnuō.* Only used here, Luke 20. 37. Acts 23. 30, and 1 Cor. 10. 28. **take** = arrest. Gr. *piazō.* Occurs twelve times, nine times in this sense. The three exceptions are 21. 3, 10. Acts 3. 7.

A² C A.D. 29 10th day of Nisan 12 °Then °Jesus °six days °before the passover came °to Bethany, where °Lazarus was °which had been dead, whom He °raised °from °the dead.
2 There they made Him °a supper; and °Martha °served: but [1]Lazarus was one of them that sat at the table with Him.

D E 3 [1]Then took °Mary a °pound of °ointment of °spikenard, very costly, and °anointed the feet of [1]Jesus, and wiped His feet with her hair: and the house was filled °with the odour of the ointment.

F 4 [1]Then saith one °of His disciples, °Judas Iscariot, °Simon's *son*, which °should betray Him,
5 "Why was °not this ointment sold for °three hundred pence, and given to the °poor?"
6 This he said, [5]not that he cared °for the [5]poor; but because he was a °thief, and had °the bag, and bare what was put therein.

D E 7 [1]Then said [1]Jesus, °"Let her alone: °against the day of My burying hath she kept this.

F 8 For the [5]poor always ye have °with you; but Me ye have [5]not always."

C 9 Much people [4]of the Jews therefore °knew that He was there: and they came [5]not °for [1]Jesus' °sake only, but °that they might °see [1]Lazarus also, whom He had [1]raised [1]from [1]the dead.

B² 10 But the chief priests consulted [9]that they might °put [1]Lazarus also to death;
11 Because that °by reason of him many of the Jews °went away, and °believed on [1]Jesus.

A³ G J 11th day of Nisan 12 °On the next day °much people that were come [1]to the feast, when they heard that [1]Jesus was coming [1]to Jerusalem,
13 Took branches of palm trees, and went forth °to meet Him,

K and °cried, °"Hosanna: **BLESSED *IS* THE KING OF ISRAEL THAT COMETH °IN THE NAME OF THE °LORD."**

12. 1-9 (A², p. 1548). BETHANY.
(*Introversion and Alternation.*)

A² | C | 1, 2. The Lord and Lazarus (*ek nekrōn*).
  D | E | 3. The Anointing. Act.
    F | 4-6. Objection. Made.
  D | *E* | 7. The Anointing. Purpose.
    F | 8. Objection. Refuted.
C | 9. The Lord and Lazarus (*ek nekrōn*).

1 Then = Therefore. **Jesus.** Ap. 98. X.
six days, &c.: i.e. on the ninth day of Nisan; our Thursday sunset to Friday sunset. See Ap. 156.
before. Gr. *pro.* Ap. 104. xiv.
to = unto. Gr. *eis.* Ap. 104. vi.
Lazarus. See note on 11. 1.
which had been dead. [L Tr. A] T WH R and Syr. omit these words. **raised.** Gr. *egeirō.* Ap. 178. I. 4.
from = out of. Gr. *ek.* Ap. 104. vii.
the dead. There is no article. See Ap. 139. 3.
2 a supper. The first of the three suppers. It was on Saturday evening, at the close of the Sabbath, on the tenth day of Nisan. See Ap. 157.
Martha. Aramaic. See Ap. 94. III. 3.
served = was serving. Gr. *diakoneō.* Occurs twenty-two times in the Gospels: thirteen times transl. "minister" (Matt. 4. 11 to Luke 8. 3); nine times "serve" (Luke 10. 40 to John 12. 26). Cp. Luke 10. 40. Same word as in Luke 22. 27.
3 Mary. See Ap. 100. 3.
pound. Gr. *litra* = Lat. *libra* = about 12 oz. Ap. 51. II. 4 (3). Occurs only here and 19. 39.
ointment. Gr. *muron.* Aromatic balsam.
spikenard. See note on Mark 14. 3.
anointed. Three anointings are recorded in the Gospels. The first, probably in Capernaum in the house of Simon the Pharisee (Luke 7. 36-50): a woman anointed His *feet.* The one here was the second, and again His *feet* were anointed. At the third, in the house of Simon the leper, a woman (unnamed) anointed His head. For the last two see Ap. 156, 157, and 158.
with = out of, or from. Gr. *ek.* Ap. 104. vii.
4 of = out of. Gr. *ek.* Ap. 104. vii.
Judas Iscariot. See note on 6. 71.
Simon's son. These words are omitted by T Tr. WH R here, but found in all the texts in 6. 71, 13. 2, and 26. In some places the word Iscariot is made to agree with Simon.
should betray Him = was about to deliver Him up.
5 not. Gr. *ou.* Ap. 105. I.
three hundred pence = about £10. See Ap. 51. I. 4.
poor. See Ap. 127. 1.
6 for = concerning. Gr. *peri.* Ap. 104. xiii. 1.
thief. Gr. *kleptēs.* The same word as in 10. 1, 8, 10. Matt. 6. 19; 24. 43, &c. Not the same as in Matt. 21. 13; 26. 55; 27. 38. Luke 10. 30. That is *lēstēs*, and should be transl. "robber", as in 10. 1, 8; 18. 40. **the bag.** Gr. *glōssokomon.* Only here and 13. 29. Used in the Sept. of the chest made by command of Joash (2 Chron. 24. 8-11). The word means a bag to keep the tongues or reeds of wind instruments, and if Judas was a shepherd (Kerioth being in the hilly district of southern Judah), the bag might be the pouch or wallet for the reeds of the pipes so much used by the eastern shepherd. **7 Let her alone, &c.** L T Tr. A WH R (not the Syriac) read, "Let her alone, in order that she may keep it," &c. **against** = unto. Gr. *eis.* Ap. 104. vi. **8 with you** = among yourselves: i.e. not the outside poor, but the Lord's poor. **with.** Gr. *meta.* Ap. 104. xi. 1. **9 knew** = got to know. Gr. *ginōskō.* Ap. 132. I. ii. **for . . . sake** = on account of. Gr. *dia.* Ap. 104. v. 2. **that** = in order that. Gr. *hina.* **see.** Gr. *eidon.* Ap. 133. I. 1. **10 put . . . to death.** Gr. *apokteinō* = kill. Occurs seventy-five times, and mostly implies violent death, not by judicial execution. Cp. Matt. 14. 5. Luke 9. 22; 20. 14. Acts 3. 15; 7. 52; 23. 12. Rev. 13. 10. **11 by reason of** = on account of. Gr. *dia*, as in *v.* 9. **went away** = withdrew: i.e. from the chief priests' faction. **believed on.** See Ap. 150. I. 1. v (i).

12. 12-18 (A³, p. 1548). PASSOVER. PEOPLE. MEETING. (*Introversion and alternation.*)

A³ | G | J | 12, 13-. People. Meeting.
    K | -13. Praise.
  H | 14. Entry. The Act.
  H | 15, 16. Entry. The Prophecy.
G | *K* | 17. Testimony.
    J | 18. People. Reason of Meeting.

12 On the next day: i.e. the fourth day before the Passover, the 11th of Nisan. Our Saturday sunset to Sunday sunset. See Ap. 156. **much people** a great crowd. **13 to meet** = for (Gr. *eis.* Ap 104. vi) meeting. **cried.** Gr. imp. of *krazō.* Same word as in *v.* 44, but L T Tr. A WH R read imp. of *kraugazō* = were shouting out; used once of the Lord, 11. 43. Other occ.: 18. 40; 19. 6, 15. Matt. 12. 19; 15. 22. Acts 22. 23. In the Sept., only in Ezra 3. 13. **Hosanna, &c.** See note on Matt. 21. 9. **in.** Gr. *en.* Ap. 104. viii. **Lord.** Ap 98 VI. i. a. 1. B. a.

H A. D. 29 14 And [1]Jesus, when He had found a young ass, sat °thereon; as it is °written,

H **15 "Fear °not, daughter of Sion: behold, thy King cometh, sitting °on an ass's colt."**

16 These things °understood [5]not His disciples at the first: but when [1]Jesus was °glorified, then remembered they that these things °were written °of Him, and *that* they °had done these things unto Him.

G K 17 °The people therefore that was [8]with Him when He called [1]Lazarus °out of his °grave, and [1]raised him [1]from [1]the dead, °bare record.

J 18 °For this cause [17]the people also met Him, °for that they heard that He had done this °miracle.

B^3 19 °The Pharisees therefore said °among themselves, °"Perceive ye how ye °prevail °nothing? °behold, the °world is gone after Him."

Z^1 L 12th day of Nisan 20 °And there were certain °Greeks °among them that °came up to °worship °at °the feast:

21 The same came therefore to °Philip, which was °of °Bethsaida of Galilee, and °desired him, saying, °"Sir, °we would see [1]Jesus."

22 [21]Philip cometh and telleth °Andrew: and again °Andrew and [21]Philip tell [1]Jesus.

23 And [1]Jesus answered them, saying, "The hour is come,

M [9]that °the Son of man should be [16]glorified.

N 24 °Verily, verily, I say unto you, °Except °a corn of wheat fall °into the °ground and die, it °abideth alone: but °if it die, it °bringeth forth much fruit.

O 25 He that °loveth his °life shall lose it; and he that hateth his °life [13]in this [19]world shall °keep it °unto °life °eternal.

26 [24]If any man [2]serve Me, let him follow Me; and where I am, there shall also My servant be: [24]if any man [2]serve Me, him will °*My* Father °honour.

L 27 °Now is My °soul °troubled; °and what shall I say? °Father, save Me [1]from this hour: but [18]for this cause came I [25]unto this hour.

M 28 [27]Father, [16]glorify Thy name." [1]Then came there a voice [1]from °heaven, *saying*, °"I have both [16]glorified *it*, and will [16]glorify *it* again."

29 [17]The people therefore, that stood by, and

14 thereon = upon (Gr. *epi*. Ap. 104. ix. 3) it.
written. See Ap. 153. 4. Quoted from Zech. 9. 9.
15 not. Gr. *mē*. Ap. 105. II.
on = upon. Gr. *epi*. Ap. 104. ix. 3.
16 understood = perceived. Gr. *ginōskō*. Ap. 132. I. ii.
glorified. Gr. *doxazō*. One of the characteristic words in John (see p. 1511).
were written = had been written. Cp. 2. 17; 5. 39.
of = about. Gr. *epi*. Ap. 104. ix. 2.
had done = did.
17 The people = The crowd.
out of. Gr. *ek*. Ap. 104. vii.
grave. See note on 11. 17.
bare record = were testifying. See note on 1. 7.
18 For this cause = on account of (Gr. *dia*. Ap. 104. v) this. **for that** = because. Gr. *hoti*, as in *vv.* 6, 11.
miracle = sign. Gr. *sēmeion*. See Ap. 176. 3, and p. 1511.
19 The Pharisees. See Ap. 120. II.
among. Gr. *pros*. Ap. 104. xv. 3.
Perceive. Gr. *theōreō*. Ap. 133. I. 11.
prevail = profit. Gr. *ōpheleō*. Occurs fifteen times, always transl. profit, except here; Matt. 27. 24; Mark 5. 26, and Luke 9. 25.
nothing = nothing at all. Gr. *ouk ouden*, a double negative. **behold.** Fig. *Asterismos*. Ap. 6.
world. Gr. *kosmos*. Ap. 129. 1.

12. 20—36- (Z^1, p. 1548). GREEKS. THE HOUR COME. GLORIFICATION. (*Alternation*.)

Z^1 | L | 20-23-. The hour is come.
  M | -23. Glorification.
    N | 24. Death.
      O | 25, 26. Words to Disciples.
L | 27. The hour is come.
  M 28-31. Glorification.
    N | 32, 33. Death.
      O | 34-36. Words to people.

20 And, &c. This was the third day before the Passover, 12th of Nisan, our Sunday sunset to Monday sunset.
Greeks. Gr. *Hellēnes*: i. e. Gentiles, not Greek-speaking Jews, or Grecians (Acts 6. 1; 9. 29).
among = out of. Gr. *ek*. Ap. 104. vii.
came up = were coming up, according to custom.
worship. Gr. *proskuneō*. Ap. 137. 1. This would be in the outer court of the Temple, called the Court of the Gentiles. Cp. Rev. 11. 2.
at = in. Gr. *en*. Ap. 104. viii.
the feast. They would not be allowed to eat the Passover, unless they were proselytes (Ex. 12. 48).
21 Philip . . . of Bethsaida. See Ap. 141. Probably these Greeks were from Galilee (Ap. 169), and, as Philip bore a Greek name, had some acquaintance with him. **of.** Gr. *apo*. Ap. 104. iv.
desired = prayed. Gr. *erōtaō*. Ap. 134. I. 3.
Sir. Gr. *kurios*. Ap. 98. VI. i. *a*. 4. B.
we would see = we wish (Gr. *thelō*. Ap. 102. i) to see (Gr. *eidon*. Ap. 133. I. 1).
22 Andrew. See Ap. 141. Andrew belonged to the first group of the Apostles, Philip to the second. **23 the Son of man.** Ap. 98. XVI, and 99. **24 Verily, verily.** The seventeenth occ. of this double *amēn*. See note on 1. 51. **Except** = If not. Gr. *ean* (Ap. 118. 1. b) *mē* (Ap. 105. II). **a corn of wheat** = the seed-corn of the wheat. The Gr. word *kokkos* occurs seven times: in Matt. 13. 31; 17. 20. Mark 4. 31. Luke 13. 19; 17. 6 (of mustard seed); here; and 1 Cor. 15. 37. **into.** Gr. *eis*. Ap. 104. vi. **ground.** Gr. *gē*. Ap. 129. 4. **abideth.** Gr. *menō*, one of the characteristic words in this Gospel. See p. 1511. **if.** Gr. *ean*. Ap. 118. 1. b. **bringeth forth** = beareth. **25 loveth.** Gr. *phileō*. Ap. 135. I. 2. **life.** Gr. *psuchē*. Ap. 110. III. 1, and 170. 3. Cp. Matt. 10. 39; 16. 25, 26. Mark 8. 35-37. Luke 9. 24; 17. 33. **keep** = guard, or preserve. Gr. *phulassō*. See note on 17. 12. **unto.** Gr. *eis*. Ap. 104. vi. **life.** Gr. *zōē*. Ap. 170. 1. **eternal.** Gr. *aiōnios*. Ap. 151. II. B. i. **26 My Father.** Gr. the Father. Ap. 98. III. **honour.** Gr. *timaō*, only used by John, here, 5. 23, and 8. 49. **27 Now** = At this moment. Not the "Now" of 11. 1, 5. **soul.** Gr. *psuchē*; here used in the personal sense = *I* myself. Ap. 110. IV. 1. **troubled.** Cp. 11. 33; 13. 21; 14. 1, 27. **and what shall I say?, &c.** Supply the *Ellipses* (Ap. 6) that follow, thus: (Shall I say) "Father, save Me from this hour?" (No!) It is for this cause I am come to this hour. (I will say) "Father, glorify Thy name". **Father.** Ap. 98. III. See 1. 14. **28 heaven** (sing.). See note on Matt. 6. 9, 10. **I have, &c.** The Father's name was glorified in the wilderness by the Son's victory over the "tempter". It was about to be glorified again by the final victory over Satan, in the contest beginning in Gethsemane and ending at the empty tomb.

A.D. 29 **heard *it*, said that it °thundered: others said,
"An angel spake to Him."**
**30 [1] Jesus °answered and said, "This voice
came [5] not °because of Me, but °for your sakes.**
**31 [27] Now is the °judgment of this [19] world:
[27] now shall the °prince of this [19] world be °cast
°out.**

N **32 And I, [24] if I be °lifted up [1] from the °earth,
will °draw °all *men* °unto °Me."**
**33 This He said, signifying °what death He
°should die.**

O **34 The people answered Him, °"We have
heard [17] out of the law that °Christ [24] abideth
°for ever: and how sayest Thou, 'The °Son of
man must be [32] lifted up?' who is °this °Son
of man?"**
**35 Then [1] Jesus said °unto °them, "Yet a
little while is the °light °with you. Walk
°while ye have the °light, °lest darkness °come
upon you: for he that walketh [13] in darkness
°knoweth [5] not whither he goeth.**
**36 [35] While ye have [35] light, [11] believe °in the
[35] light, that ye may °be the °children of [35] light."**

X^2 **These things spake [1] Jesus, and departed, and
°did hide Himself °from °them.**

Y^2 P^1 Q **37 But though He had done so many [18] miracles °before them, yet they [11] believed [5] not [11] on
Him:**

R t^1 **38 That the °saying of °Esaias the prophet
might be °fulfilled, which he spake, [13] "LORD,
who hath °believed our report? and to whom
hath °the arm of the [13] LORD been revealed?"**

u^1 **39 °Therefore they °could [5] not °believe,**
t^2 **because that [38] Esaias said again,**
**40 °"He hath blinded their eyes, and hard-
ened their heart;**
u^2 **that they should [15] not [9] see with *their* eyes, nor
understand with *their* heart, and be converted,
and I should heal them."**

29 thundered, &c. They heard a sound, but could not distinguish what it was. Cp. Acts 9. 4; 22. 9.

30 answered, &c. See Ap. 122. 3.
because of=on account of. Gr. *dia*. Ap. 104. v. 2.
for your sakes=on account of (Gr. *dia*. Ap. 104. v) you.

31 judgment. Gr. *krisis* (Ap. 177. 7); i.e. the crisis reached when the world pronounced judgment against Christ and His claims.
prince=ruler. Gr. *archōn*; applied to Satan as prince of this world (*kosmos*, Ap. 129. 1) three times, here, 14. 30, and 16. 11; as prince of the demons in Matt. 12. 24. Mark 3. 22; and as prince of the power of the air in Eph. 2. 2. The same word used in Rev. 1. 5 of the Lord. The prince of this world was a well-known Rabbinical term (*Sar hā 'ōlām*, prince of the age) for Satan, "the angel", as they say, "into whose hands the whole world is delivered". See Dr. John Lightfoot's *Works*, xii, p. 369.
cast out. Same word as in 9. 34, 35. Matt. 21. 39. Mark 12. 8. Luke 20. 15. Acts 7. 58; 13. 50. In Luke 4. 29, rendered "thrust".
out (Gr. *exō*)=without, outside.

32 lifted up. Gr. *hupsoō*. Occurs twenty times. Always in John refers to the cross; see *v*. 34; 3. 14, 14, and 8. 28. In fourteen other passages (Matt. 11. 23; 23. 12, 12. Luke 1. 52; 10. 15; 14. 11, 11; 18. 14, 14. Acts 2. 33; 5. 31; 13. 17. 2 Cor. 11. 7. 1 Pet. 5. 6) rendered "exalt", and in James 4. 10, "lift up".
earth. Gr. *gē*. Ap. 129. 4.
draw. Gr. *helkuō*. Same word as in 6. 44. Used elsewhere in 18. 10; 21. 6, 11 and Acts 16. 19. The classical form *helkō* occurs in Acts 21. 30. James 2. 6. It was thought the form *helkuō* was peculiar to the N.T. and Sept., but it is found in one of the Oxyrhyncus *Papyri*. See Deissmann, *Light*, &c., pp. 437–9.
all. Cp. 6. 37, 39. **unto.** Gr. *pros*. Ap. 104. xv. 3.
Me=Myself. Gr. *emautou*.

33 what death=what kind of death.
should die=was about to die.

34 We have heard=we heard. The Gr. tense (aorist) refers to a definite time, and may refer to a portion of the law (cp. note on 10. 34) read on the Great Sabbath, two days previously. The quotation is usually referred to Ps. 89. 29, but it may rather be Ps. 92 (see title), which is said to have been read on the Sabbath from the days of Ezra.
Christ. Ap. 98. IX.
for ever=unto the age. Ap. 151. II. A. ii. 4. a.
Son of man. Ap. 98. XVI. **this.** Emphatic; perhaps a reference to the idea that there would be two Messiahs—Messiah Ben-Joseph to suffer, and Messiah Ben-David to reign. **35 unto**=to. **them:** i.e. the people around Him. **light.** Ap. 130. 1. **with.** Gr. *meta*, as in *vv*. 8, 17, but all the texts read *en*, among. **while.** All the texts read "as". **lest darkness**=in order that (Gr. *hina*) darkness may not (Gr. *mē*. Ap. 105. II). **come upon**=seize. Gr. *katalambanō*. Same word as in 1. 5. Mark 9. 18. Phil. 3. 12, 13. 1 Thess. 5. 4. **knoweth.** Gr. *oida*. Ap. 132. 1. **36 in**=on. Gr. *eis*. Ap. 104. vi. **be**=become. **children**=sons. Ap. 108. iii. **did hide Himself**=was hidden. **from**=away from. Gr. *apo*. Ap. 104. iv. **them**: i.e. the Greeks of *v*. 20. Cp. Matt. 10. 5.

12. 37-50 (Y^2, p. 1548). HOSTILITY EXPLAINED. (*Division.*)

Y^2	P^1	37–43. Unbelief and Belief. John's Explanation.
	P^2	44–50. Belief and Unbelief. The Lord's Explanation.

12. 37-43 (P^1, above). UNBELIEF AND BELIEF. (*Introversion and Repeated Alternation.*)

P^1	Q			37. Unbelief.
	R	t^1		38. Isaiah. Citation.
			u^1	39–. Consequence.
		t^2		–39, 40–. Isaiah. Citation.
			u^2	–40. Consequence.
		t^3		41. Isaiah. Occasion.
	Q			42, 43. Belief.

37 before=in the presence of. Cp. 1 Thess. 1. 3; 2. 19. **38 saying.** Gr. *logos*. See note on Mark 9. 32. This is quoted from Isa. 53. 1. See note there. **Esaias.** Greek form of Isaiah. **fulfilled.** Gr. *plēroō*= filled full or accomplished. See 13. 18; 15. 25; 17. 12; 18. 9, 32: 19. 24 36. **believed.** Ap. 150. I. 1. ii. **the arm of the Lord**=Messiah, as the executant of His decrees. Isa. 51. 9; 52. 10. Cp. "polished shaft", Isa. 49. 2. **39 Therefore**=On account of (Gr. *dia*. Ap. 104. v) this: i.e. the unbelief of *v*. 37. **could not**=were not able to. **believe.** Ap. 150. I. 1. i. Judicial blindness follows persistent unbelief. **40 He hath blinded, &c.** Quoted from Isa. 6. 9, 10. See notes there. This was the second occasion of this prophecy being quoted, the first being in Matt. 13. 14 (cp. Mark 4. 12. Luke 8. 10), when the Lord explained why He spoke to the people in parables; the other two being Acts 28. 26, 27 and Rom. 11. 8.

t3 A. D. 29 **41** These things said [38] Esaias, °when he [9] saw His °glory, and spake °of Him.

Q **42** Nevertheless [20] among the chief rulers also many [11] believed [11] on Him; but [30] because of [19] the Pharisees they did [5] not confess *Him*, [35] lest they should °be put out of the synagogue:

43 For they °loved the °praise of °men more than the °praise of °God.

P2 S1 **44** [1] Jesus cried and said, °"He that [11] believeth on Me, [11] believeth [5] not [11] on Me, but [11] on Him That °sent Me.

45 And he that °seeth Me °seeth Him That [44] sent Me.

T1 **46** °I am come a [35] light [24] into the [19] world, that whosoever [11] believeth [11] on Me should [15] not [24] abide [13] in darkness.

S2 **47** And [24] if any man hear My °words, and [39] believe [15] not,

T2 I °judge him [5] not: for I came [5] not to °judge the [19] world, but to save the [19] world.

S3 **48** He that °rejecteth Me, and receiveth [15] not My [47] words,

T3 hath one that [47] judgeth him: the °word that I have spoken, the same shall [47] judge him [13] in °the last day.

S4 **49** For °I have [5] not spoken [4] of Myself; but the [27] Father Which [44] sent Me, He gave me a commandment, what I should °say, and what I should °speak.

50 And I [35] know that °His commandment is [-25] life °everlasting: whatsoever I [49] speak therefore, even as the [27] Father [49] said unto Me, so I [49] speak."

Z2 U1 V Xv 14th day of Nisan **13** °Now °before the °feast of the °passover, °when °Jesus °knew that °His hour was come

w that He should °depart °out of this °world °unto °the Father,

x having °loved His own which were °in the °world, He °loved them °unto the °end.

41 when. Gr. *hote*. All the texts read *hoti*, because.
glory. Gr. *doxa*. One of the characteristic words in John's Gospel. See 1. 14.
of = concerning. Gr. *peri*. Ap. 104. xiii. 1.
42 be put out of the synagogue = become excommunicate (*aposunagōgoi*). See note on 9. 22, and cp. 16. 1.
43 loved. Gr. *agapaō*. Ap. 135. I. 1.
praise = glory. Same word as in *v.* 41.
men. Gr. *anthrōpos*. Ap. 123. 1.
God. Ap. 98. I. i. 1.

12. 44-50 (P2, p. 1551). BELIEF AND UNBELIEF. (*Repeated Alternation.*)

P2 | S1 | 44, 45. Belief in the Son.
T1 | 46. Blessing.
S2 | 47-. Non-belief in the Son.
T2 | -47. Judgment, not of the Son.
S3 | 48-. Rejection of the Son.
T3 | -48. Judgment by the Father.
S4 | 49, 50. Rejection of the Father.

44 He that believeth, &c. Faith in the Lord does not *rest* in Him, but passes on to recognize that He is the manifestation of the Father. Cp. 1. 14, 18; 3. 33.
sent. Gr. *pempō*. Ap. 174. 4.
45 seeth. Gr. *theōreō*. Ap. 133. I. 11.
46 I am come, &c. Cp. 8. 12.
47 words = sayings. Gr. *rhēma*. See note on Mark 9. 32.
judge. Gr. *krinō*. Ap. 122. 1.
48 rejecteth. Gr. *atheteō*. Occ. sixteen times in twelve passages. The others are: Mark 6. 26; 7. 9. Luke 7. 30; 10. 16. 1 Cor. 1. 19. Gal. 2. 21; 3. 15. 1 Thess. 4. 8. 1 Tim. 5. 12. Heb. 10. 28. Jude 8. Often transl. despise. It means to count as nothing. See 1 Cor. 1. 19.
word. Gr. *logos*. Same word as "saying" in *v.* 38. See note on Mark 9. 32.
the last day. The sixth and last occ. of this expression in John. See 6. 39, 40, 44, 54; 11. 24.
49 I have not spoken of Myself: i.e. from Myself. The Lord's constant claim was that His very words were what the Father had given Him to speak. Cp. 3. 34; 7. 16-18; 8. 28, 47; 14. 10, 24; 17. 8, 14.
say. Gr. *eipon*. This has to do with the matter, or subject.
speak. Gr. *laleō*. This word, which is very common in John's Gospel, and occurs eight times in this chapter, refers to the words in which the message was delivered. See note above and next verse.
50 His commandment, &c. Fig. *Ellipsis*. Ap. 6. The result of obeying His commandment is life everlasting. Cp. 1 John 3. 23; 5. 11.
everlasting. Gr. *aiōnios*. Same as "eternal" in *v.* 25. See Ap. 151. II. B. ii.

13. 1-17. 26 (Z2, p. 1548). DISCIPLES. THE HOUR COME. GLORIFICATION. (*Division.*)

Z2 | U1 | 13. 1—16. 33. The Lord. Communication to His Disciples.
U2 | 17. 1-26. The Lord. Prayer to the Father.

13. 1-16. 33 (U1, above). COMMUNICATION TO HIS DISCIPLES. (*Alternation.*)

U1 | V | 13. 1-38. Cleansing. Washing.
W | 14. 1-31. Return to the Father.
V | 15. 1—16. 4. Cleansing. Pruning.
W | 16. 5-33. Return to the Father.

13. 1-38 [For Structure see next page].

13. 1 Now. Not the same word as in 12. 27, 31, expressing a point of time, but a particle (Gr. *de*) introducing a new subject. before. Gr. *pro*. Ap. 104. xiv. The preparation day, the 14th day of Nisan, our Tuesday sunset to Wednesday sunset, the day of the Crucifixion. See Ap. 156. feast. See on Matt. 26. 17 and Num. 28. 17. passover. Aram. *pascha*. See Ap. 94. III. 3. when Jesus knew = Jesus (Ap. 98. X), knowing (Gr. *oida*, Ap. 132. I. 1). His hour. See 2. 4; 7. 30; 8. 20; 12. 23, 27; 17. 1; and contrast Luke 22. 53. depart. Gr. *metabainō* = pass over from one place to another. Used by John in three other places: 5. 24; 7. 3, and 1 John 3. 14. out of. Gr. *ek*. Ap. 104. vii. world. Gr. *kosmos*. Ap. 129. 1. unto. Gr. *pros*. Ap. 104. xv. 3. the Father. Ap. 98. III. See 1. 14. loved. Gr. *agapaō*. Ap. 135. I. 1. in. Gr. *en*. Ap. 104. viii. unto. Gr. *eis*. Ap. 104. vi. end = furthest extent, referring not so much to a period of time, the end of His life, as to His readiness to descend to the humblest service in their behalf.

y 2 And °supper °being ended, °the devil having
A. D. 29 °now put °into the heart of °Judas Iscariot,
Simon's *son*, to betray Him;

Y[1] z[1] 3 [1]Jesus [1]knowing that [1]the Father °had
given all things [2]into His hands, and that He
was °come °from °God, and °went °to °God;
4 He °riseth °from °supper, and laid aside His
°garments; and took a °towel, and girded Himself.
5 °After that He °poureth water [2]into a bason,
and began to °wash the disciples' feet, and to
°wipe *them* with the [4]towel wherewith He was
girded.
6 °Then cometh He [3]to °Simon Peter; and
°Peter saith unto Him, °"Lord, dost °Thou
[5]wash °my feet?"
7 [1]Jesus answered and said unto him, "What
I do Thou knowest °not °now; but thou shalt
°know °hereafter."
8 [6]Peter saith unto Him, "Thou shalt °never
[5]wash my feet." [1]Jesus answered him, °"If I
[5]wash thee °not, thou hast °no part °with Me."
9 [6]Simon Peter saith unto Him, [6]"Lord, [8]not
my feet only, but also *my* hands and *my* head."
10 [1]Jesus saith to him, "He that is °washed
needeth [7]not save to [5]wash *his* feet, but is
°clean every whit:
a[1] and ye are °clean, but [7]not all."
11 For He [1]knew who °should betray Him;
°therefore said He, "Ye are [7]not all [10]clean."

Y[2] z[2] 12 °So after He had [5]washed their feet, and
had taken His [4]garments, and was set down
again, He said unto them, [7]"Know ye °what
I have done to you?
13 Ye °call Me °Master and °Lord: and °ye
say well; for *so* I am.
14 °If I then, °your [13]Lord and [13]Master, have
[5]washed your feet; ye also °ought to [5]wash
one another's feet.
15 For I have given you an °example, that ye
should do as I have done to you.
16 °Verily, verily, I say unto you, The °serv-
ant is [7]not greater than his °lord; °neither °he
that is sent greater than he that °sent him.
17 [14]If ye [1]know these things, happy are ye
[8]if ye do them.

13. 1-38 (V, p. 1552). CLEANSING. WASHING.
(*Alternation and Introversion.*)

V | X | v | 1-. The Hour come.
w | -1-. Return to the Father.
x | -1. Love to His Disciples.
y | 2. Judas. Betrayal.
Y[1] | z[1] | 3-10-. Washing. Act.
a[1] | -10, 11. The Traitor. Knowledge.
Y[2] | z[2] | 12-17. Washing. Example.
a[2] | 18, 19. The Traitor. Communication.
Y[3] | z[3] | 20. Reception.
a[3] | 21-30. The Traitor. Revelation.
X | *v* | 31, 32. The Hour come.
w | 33. Return to the Father.
x | 34, 35. Disciples. Love to one another.
y | 36-38. Peter. Denial.

2 supper. The last supper recorded. See Ap. 157.
being ended. In view of *v.* 26, Alford's transl., "supper having been served," is preferable to A.V. and R.V. renderings. It means "supper being laid". Washing would naturally *precede* the meal. Cp. Luke 7. 44.
the devil. See notes on Matt. 4. 1-11. Luke 4. 1-13, and Ap. 19 and 116. **now** = already.
into. Gr. *eis.* Ap. 104. vi. **Judas.** See 6. 71.
3 had given, &c. These statements of His divine origin, authority, and coming glory, are made so as to enhance the amazing condescension of the service to which He humbled Himself to do the office of a bond-slave.
come = come forth. Cp. 8. 42; 16. 27, 28, 30; 17. 8.
from. Gr. *apo.* Ap. 104. iv.
God. Ap. 98. I. i. 1. **went** = is going away.
to = unto. Gr. *pros.* As in *v.* 1.
4 riseth. Ap. 178. 4. **from.** Gr. *ek.* Ap. 104. vii.
supper = supper table (as we should say), i.e., after they had taken their places.
garments, i.e. the outer garment. Gr. *himation*, transl. "robe" in 19. 2, 5. This was removed for working, and for sleeping was often used as a coverlet. When removed, leaving only the *chitōn* or tunic, the man was said to be naked.
towel. Gr. *lention*, a linen cloth (Lat. *linteum*).
5 After that = Then.
poureth = putteth, same word as in *v.* 2.
wash. Gr. *niptō.* Ap. 136. i. **wipe.** Gr. *ekmassō.* Occ. elsewhere, 11. 2; 12. 3. Luke 7. 38, 44.
6 Then = Therefore. **Simon Peter.** Ap. 141.
Peter. No word for Peter. Some substitute *ekeinos* (*he*, emphatic), but L T Trm. A WH R reject it. **Lord.** Gr. *kurios.* Ap. 98. VI. i. *a*. 3. A. **Thou ... my.** The pronouns are emphatic. **7 not.** Gr. *ou.* Ap. 105. I. **now.** Gr. *arti* = just now. **know** = get to know. Gr. *ginōskō.* Ap. 132. I. ii. **hereafter** = after (Gr. *meta.* Ap. 104. xi. 2) these things. **8 never** = by no means (Gr. *ou mē.* Ap. 105. III) unto the age (Gr. *eis ton aiōna.* Ap. 151. II. A. ii. 4. b). **If.** Gr. *ean*, with subj. Ap. 118. 1. b. **not.** Gr. *mē.* Ap. 105. II. **no** = not (Ap. 105. I) any. **with.** Gr. *meta.* Ap. 104. xi. 1. **10 washed** = bathed. Gr. *louō.* Ap. 136. iii. Note the distinction between washing the whole body, and washing only a part of it. Cp. 1 Cor. 6. 11. **clean.** Gr. *katharos.* Occ. twenty-seven times, transl. ten times "clean", sixteen "pure", and once "clear" (Rev. 21. -18) = free from impurity or dross. Used here of the eleven (cp. 15. 3), but not of Judas into whose heart Satan had "cast" the impure thought of *v.* 2. **11 should betray Him** = the one who is betraying Him. **therefore** = on account of (Gr. *dia.* Ap. 104. v). **12 So after** = When therefore. **what** = what [it is]. **13 call Me** = address Me as. Gr. *phōneō*, always used of calling with the voice (*phōnē*). Cp. 11. 28; 12. 17; and cp. *kaleō*, Luke 6. 46; 15. 19. **Master** (Gr. *didaskalos*) = Teacher. See Ap. 98. XIV. v. and cp. Matt. 26. 25, 49. **Lord.** Ap. 98. VI. i. *a*. 2. A. a. **ye say well.** Would that Christians to-day would treat Him with the same respect which He here commends, instead of calling Him by the name of His humiliation, Jesus, by which He was never addressed by disciples, only by demons (Matt. 8. 29. Mark 1. 24; 5. 6. Luke 8. 28) and those who only knew Him as a prophet (Mark 10. 47. Luke 18. 38). The Holy Spirit uses "Jesus" in the Gospel narratives. **14 If I then** = Therefore if (Ap. 118. 2. a) I. **your** = the. **ought,** &c. By Fig. *Synecdochē* (Ap. 6) the act of feet-washing is put for the whole circle of offices of self-denying love. Literal feet-washing was not known before the fourth cent. A.D. **15 example.** Gr. *hupodeigma.* Occ. Heb. 4. 11; 8. 5; 9. 23, &c. **16 Verily, verily.** The eighteenth occ. of this solemn expression. See 1. 51. Three more occ. in this chapter, *vv.* 20, 21, 38. **servant** = bond-servant. Gr. *doulos.* Once applied to the Lord (Phil. 2. 7). Frequent in Paul's epistles. **lord.** Gr. *kurios.* Ap. 98. VI. i. *a*. 4. A. **neither.** Gr. *oude.* **he that is sent** = an apostle. Gr. *apostolos.* Occ. 81 times, always transl. "apostle", save here, 2 Cor. 8. 23, and Phil. 2. 25. **sent.** Gr. *pempō.* Ap. 174. 4.

a[2] 18 I speak [7]not °of you all: I [1]know whom I
A.D. 29 have chosen: but that the scripture may be fulfilled, °**He that eateth °bread [8]with me hath
lifted up his heel °against me.**
19 °Now I tell you [1]before it come, that, when
it is come to pass, ye may °believe that °I am
He.
Y[3] z[3] 20 [16]Verily, verily, I say unto you, He that
receiveth whomsoever I [16]send receiveth Me;
and he that receiveth Me receiveth Him That
[16]sent Me."
a[3] 21 When [1]Jesus had thus said, He was °trou-
bled in °spirit, and testified, and said, [16]"Verily,
verily, I say unto you, that one °of you shall
betray Me."
22 [6]Then the disciples °looked one °on another,
doubting [18]of whom He °spake.
23 Now there was °leaning °on [1]Jesus' °bosom
one of His disciples, whom [1]Jesus [1]loved.
24 [6]Simon Peter therefore °beckoned to him,
°that he should ask who it should be [18]of whom
He [22]spake.
25 He then °lying °on [1]Jesus' °breast saith unto Him, [6]"Lord, who is it?"
26 [1]Jesus answered, "He it is, to whom I shall
give a °sop, when I have dipped *it.*" And when
He had dipped the °sop, He gave *it* to [2]Judas
Iscariot, *the son* of Simon.
27 And °after the [26]sop °Satan entered [2]into
him. °Then said [1]Jesus unto him, "That thou
doest, do quickly."
28 Now °no man at the table [7]knew °for what
intent He °spake this unto him.
29 For some *of them* °thought, because [2]Judas
had the °bag, that [1]Jesus °had said unto him,
"Buy *those things* that we have need of °a-
gainst °the feast;" or, that he should give
something to the °poor.
30 °He [6]then having received the [26]sop went
°immediately out: and it was °night.
X v 31 °Therefore, when °he was gone out, [1]Jesus
said, °"Now is °the Son of man °glorified,
and [3]God is °glorified [1]in Him.
32 °If [3]God be [31]glorified [1]in Him, [3]God shall
also [31]glorify Him [1]in Himself, and shall
°straightway [31]glorify Him.
w 33 °Little children, yet °a little while I am
[8]with you. Ye shall seek Me: and °as I said
unto °the Jews, Whither I go, ye °cannot come;
so now I say to you.
x 34 A °new commandment I give unto you,
That ye [1]love one another; as I have [1]loved
you, that ye also [1]love one another.
35 °By this shall all *men* [7]know that ye are
My disciples, [8]if ye have °love °one to another."

18 of=concerning. Gr. *peri.* Ap. 104. xiii. 1.
He that, &c. Quoted from Ps. 41. 9.
bread. Gr. the bread, i.e. My bread. In a pastoral letter of an Egyptian bishop about 600 A.D. on a Coptic *ostracon* this verse is quoted from the Sept., "He that eateth *My* bread", &c. (Deissmann, *Light from the Ancient East*, p. 215).
against. Gr. *epi.* Ap. 104. ix. 3.
19 Now=From now. Gr. *ap'* (Ap. 104. iv) *arti.* Cp. 14. 7 and Matt. 26. 29.
believe. Ap. 150. I. 1. iii.
I am. Omit "He", and cp. 8. 28, 58; 18. 5, 6.
21 troubled. See 11. 33. **spirit.** Ap. 101. II. 9.
of=out of. Gr. *ek.* Ap. 104. vii.
22 looked. Gr. *blepō.* Ap. 133. I. 5.
on=towards. Gr. *eis.* Ap. 104. vi.
spake=is speaking.
23 leaning=reclining. Gr. *anakeimai,* generally transl. "sat at meat"; cp. *v.* 28. Reclining on the divan, his head towards the Lord's bosom, John was in the favoured position, on the Lord's right hand, Judas being on His left. **on**=in (Gr. *en,* as in *v.* 1).
bosom. Gr. *kolpos.* Cp. the other five occ.: 1. 18. Luke 6. 38; 16. 22, 23. Acts 27. 39 (creek).
24 beckoned=signed or nodded. Gr. *neuō.* Only here and Acts 24. 10.
that he should ask who it should be. L T Tr. A WH R read, "and saith to him, 'Say who it is'".
25 lying=lying back. Not the same word as "leaning" in *v.* 23. Peter was beyond Judas, and leaning back signed to John behind the Lord.
on. Gr. *epi.* Ap. 104. ix. 3.
breast. Gr. *stēthos.* Not the same word as "bosom" in *v.* 23. Occ. only here; 21. 20. Luke 18. 13; 23. 48. Rev. 15. 6.
26 sop. Gr. *psōmion,* a morsel. Only occ. here and *vv.* 27, 30. It was a mark of honour for the host to give a portion to one of the guests. The Lord had appealed to the conscience of Judas in *v.* 21, now He appeals to his heart.
27 after. Gr. *meta.* Ap. 104. xi. 2.
Satan. The only occ. of this title in John. Before this clause in the Greek is the word *tote,* then, marking the point of time; it is strangely ignored in the A.V. It is significant that the rejection of the Lord's last appeal hardened Judas, so that his heart became open to the entrance of Satan. Up to this moment Judas had been possessed by the evil thought, now he is obsessed by the evil one.
Then=Therefore. The Lord knew what had taken place, and that further appeal was useless. He dismisses him to the work he is set upon. See the terrible words in Ps. 41. 6, "His heart gathereth iniquity to itself; he goeth abroad, he telleth", exactly what Judas did.
28 no man at the table=no one (Gr. *oudeis*) of those reclining (Gr. *anakeimai*). See *v.* 23.
for what intent=with a view to (Gr. *pros.* Ap. 104. xv. 3) what.
spake this unto him=spake to him.
29 thought=were thinking.
bag. See note on 12. 6. **had said**=saith.
against=for. Gr. *eis.* Ap. 104. vi.
the feast: i.e. the feast beginning at the close of Passover, when the high day, 15th of Nisan, began (Ap. 156).
poor. Gr. *ptōchos.* See 12. 8 and Ap. 127. 1.
30 He=That One. Gr. *ekeinos,* emphatic.

immediately. Gr. *eutheōs,* a very common word in Mark's Gospel. Occ. in John only here, 5. 9; 6. 21 and 18. 27. L T Tr. A WH R read *euthus,* as in *v.* 32. **night:** i.e. about the third hour of the night, 9 p.m., Tuesday night. See Ap. 165. **31 Therefore, when**=When therefore. **he was gone out**=he went out. **Now.** Gr. *nun.* See 12. 27. **the Son of man.** Ap. 98. XVI (1). **glorified.** A characteristic word in this Gospel. See 11. 4; 12. 16, 23, 28; 17. 1, &c. **32 If.** Ap. 118. 2. a. [L Tr. A] WH R omit the conditional clause. **straightway.** Gr. *euthus.* See note on *v.* 30. **33 Little children.** Gr. *teknion.* Ap. 108. ii. Only occ. here, Gal. 4. 19 (where the reading is doubtful), and in John's first Epistle. **a little while.** Cp. 7. 33, 34; 14. 19; 16. 16–19. **as**=even as. **the Jews.** The Lord uses this expression only here, 4. 22; 18. 20 and 36. **cannot come**=are not (Gr. *ou.* Ap. 105. I) able to come. The third time He said these words. Cp. 7. 34; 8. 21. **34 new.** Gr. *kainos.* See note on Matt. 9. 17. **35 By**=In. Gr. *en.* Ap. 104. viii. **love.** Gr. *agapē.* Ap. 135. II. 1. **one to another**=among (Gr. *en*) yourselves. Cp. the only other place in the Gospels where *en allēlois* occurs (Mark 9. 50).

y
A.D. 29
36 [6]Simon Peter said unto Him, [6]"Lord, whither goest Thou?" [1]Jesus answered him,
"Whither I go, thou canst [7]not follow Me
[31]now; but thou shalt follow °Me afterwards."
37 Peter said unto Him, [6]"Lord, why [33]cannot
I follow Thee °now? I will °lay down my
°life °for Thy sake."
38 [1]Jesus °answered him, "Wilt thou [37]lay
down thy [37]life [37]for My sake? [16]Verily, verily,
I say unto thee, °The cock shall °not °crow,
till thou hast °denied Me thrice.

W Z^1 B^1 **14** Let °not your heart be °troubled: °ye
°believe °in °God, °believe also °in Me.
C^1 2 °In °My Father's house are many °mansions: °if *it were* [1]not *so*, °I would have told
you. I go to prepare a place for you.
3 And °if I go and prepare a place for you, °I
will come again, and receive you °unto Myself;
°that where I am, *there* °ye may be also.
4 And whither I go ye °know, and the way ye
°know."
5 °Thomas saith °unto Him, °"Lord, we
[4]know °not whither Thou goest; and how
°can we [4]know the way?"
6 °Jesus saith [5]unto him, °"I am the °way,
°the °truth, and the °life: °no man °cometh
[3]unto °the Father, °but °by Me.
7 °If ye had °known Me, ye should have
°known [2]My Father also: and °from henceforth ye °know Him, and have °seen Him."
A^1 D^1 8 °Philip saith [5]unto Him, [5]"Lord, shew us
[6]the Father, and it sufficeth us."
9 [6]Jesus saith [5]unto him, "Have I been °so
long time °with you, and yet hast thou [5]not
[7]known Me, Philip? he that hath [7]seen Me
hath [7]seen [6]the Father; and how sayest thou
then, 'Shew us [6]the Father'?
10 °Believest thou [5]not that I am [2]in [6]the
Father, and [6]the Father [2]in Me? °the °words
that I speak [5]unto you I speak [5]not °of Myself:
but [6]the Father That °dwelleth [2]in Me, He
doeth °the works.
11 °Believe Me that I *am* [2]in [6]the Father, and
[6]the Father [2]in Me: or else °believe Me °for
the °very works' sake.
E^1 12 °Verily, verily, I say [5]unto you, He that

36 Me. All the texts omit.
37 now=just now. Gr. *arti*.
lay down, &c. Cp. 10. 11, 15; 15. 13. 1 John 3. 16.
life. Gr. *psuchē*. Ap. 110. III. 1.
for Thy sake=on behalf of (Gr. *huper*. Ap. 104. xvii. 1) Thee.
38 answered him. All the texts read, "answereth".
The=A.
not=by no means. Gr. *ou mē*. Ap. 105. III.
crow. Gr. *phōneō*. Same word as in *v.* 13.
denied=utterly denied (Gr. *aparneomai*), always of denying a person, as in Matt. 26. 34, 35, 75. Mark 14. 30, 31, 72. Luke 22. 34 61; but L T Tr. A WH R read *arneomai*, the milder form, without the intensive prefix.

14. 1-31 (W, p. 1552). RETURN TO THE FATHER. (*Alternation*.)

W | Z^1 | B^1 | 1. Comfort. Coming again.
  | | C^1 | 2-7. Return to the Father. Purpose.
  | A^1 | D^1 | 8-11. Question and Answer. Manifestation.
  | | E^1 | 12-17. Communications.
  | Z^2 | B^2 | 18. Comfort. Coming again.
  | | C^2 | 19-21. Return to the Father. Promise.
  | A^2 | D^2 | 22-24. Question and Answer. Manifestation.
  | | E^2 | 25-27-. Communications.
  | Z^3 | B^3 | -27, 28-. Comfort. Coming again.
  | | C^3 | -28-31. Return to the Father.

1 not. Gr. *mē*. Ap. 105. II.
troubled. Cp. 11. 33 (Himself); 12. 27 (My soul); 13. 21 (spirit). Here it is the heart. In all cases the whole being is meant. See also Luke 24. 38.
ye believe. There is no reason for translating the two verbs differently. Both are imperative. "Believe in God, and believe in Me".
believe. Ap. 150. I. 1. v (i). **in.** Gr. *eis*.
God. Ap. 98. I. i. 1.
2 In. Gr. *en*. Ap. 104. viii.
My Father's. In John's Gospel the Lord uses this expression thirty-five times, though in a few instances the texts read "the" instead of "My". It is found fourteen times in these three chapters 14-16. It occurs seventeen times in Matthew, six times in Luke (three times in parables), but not once in Mark.
mansions=abiding places. Gr. *monē* (from *menō*, a characteristic word in this Gospel). Occurs only here and in *v.* 23.
if it were not so=if not. Gr. *ei mē*. There is no verb.
I would, &c. All the texts add "that" (*hoti*), and read "would I have told you that I go", &c.
3 if. Ap. 118. 1. b.
I will come, &c.=again I am coming, and I will receive you.

unto. Gr. *pros*. Ap. 104. xv. 3. **that**=in order that. Gr. *hina*. **ye may be also**=ye also may be. **4 know.** Gr. *oida*. Ap. 132. I. 1. Most of the texts omit the second "ye know", and read, "whither, &c., ye know the way." **5 Thomas.** See Ap. 94. III and 141. **unto**=to. **Lord.** Ap. 98. VI. 1. *a*. 3. A. **not.** Gr. *ou*. Ap. 105. I. **can, &c.** The texts read, "know we". **6 Jesus.** Ap. 98. X. **I am.** This affirmation used by our Lord at least twenty-five times in John. See 4. 26; 6. 20 ("It is I". Gr. *Egō eimi*), 35, 41, 48, 51; 8. 12, 18, 23, 24, 28, 58; 10. 7, 9, 11, 14; 11. 25; 13. 19; 15. 1, 5; 18. 5, 6, 8, 37. **way.** Cp. Acts 9. 2; 18. 25, 26; 19. 9, 23; 22. 4; 24. 22. **the truth**=and the truth. Note the Fig. *Polysyndeton* to emphasize the Lord's statement. **truth.** Gr. *alētheia*. Cp. Ap. 175. 1. This word occurs twenty-five times in John, always in the lips of the Lord, save 1. 14, 17 and 18. 38 (Pilate). Only seven times in Matthew, Mark, and Luke. **life.** Ap. 170. 1, a characteristic word in this Gospel, where it occurs thirty-six times. See first occ. (Matt. 7. 14), "the way which leadeth unto life", and cp. 1 John 5. 11, 12, 20. **no man**=no one. Gr. *oudeis*. **cometh.** Cp. 6. 44. **the Father.** See 1. 14. **but**=if not. Gr. *ei mē*. **by**=through. Gr. *dia*. Ap. 104. v. 1. **7 If, &c.** Ap. 118. 2. a. **known.** Ap. 132. I. ii. **from henceforth**=from (Gr. *apo*. Ap. 104. iv) now. **seen.** Ap. 133. I. 8. Cp. 1 John 1. 1. **8 Philip.** See 1. 43-48; 6. 5; 12. 21, 22, and Ap. 141. **9 so long time.** Philip, one of the first called. See 1. 43. **with.** Gr. *meta*. Ap. 104. xi. 1. **10 Believest.** Ap. 150. I. iii. **the words, &c.** Supply the *Ellipsis* (Ap. 6) thus: "The words that I speak, I speak not of Myself, but the Father that dwelleth in Me speaketh them, and the works that I do, I do not of Myself, but the Father that dwelleth in Me doeth them". **words.** Gr. *rhēma*. See Mark 9. 32. **of**=from. Gr. *apo*. Ap. 104. iv. **dwelleth**=abideth. Gr. *menō*. See p. 1511. **the works.** The texts read "His works". **11 Believe Me that, &c.** Ap. 150. I. ii and iii. **believe Me.** Ap. 150. I. ii. **for . . . sake**=On account of. Gr. *dia*. Ap. 104. v. 2. **very works**=works themselves. **12 Verily, verily.** The twenty-second occ. See on 1. 51.

A.D. 29 [1]believeth on Me, °the works that I do shall
°he do also; and °greater *works* than these
shall he do; because I go [3]unto [2]My Father.
13 And whatsoever ye shall °ask [2]in My
°name, that will I do, [3]that [6]the Father may
be °glorified [2]in the Son.
14 [3]If ye shall [13]ask any thing [2]in My [13]name,
I will do *it*.
15 [3]If ye °love Me, °keep My commandments.
16 And I will °pray [6]the Father, and He
°shall give you °another °Comforter, [3]that He
may °abide [9]with you °for ever;
17 *Even* °the Spirit of [6]truth; Whom the
°world °cannot receive, because it °seeth Him
[5]not, neither [7]knoweth Him: but ye [7]know
Him; for He [10]dwelleth °with you, and shall
be [2]in you.

Z² B² 18 I will [5]not leave you °comfortless: I °will
come °to you.

C² 19 Yet °a little while, and the [17]world [17]seeth
Me °no more; but ye [17]see Me: because I live,
ye °shall live also.
20 °At that day ye shall [7]know that I *am* [2]in
[2]My Father, and ye [2]in Me, and °I [2]in you.
21 He that hath My commandments, and keepeth them, he it is that [15]loveth Me: and he that
[15]loveth Me shall be [15]loved °of [2]My Father,
and I will [15]love him, and will °manifest Myself to him."

A² D² 22 °Judas saith [5]unto Him, [5]not Iscariot,
"Lord, °how is it that Thou °wilt [21]manifest
Thyself [5]unto us, and [5]not [5]unto the [17]world?"
23 [6]Jesus °answered and said [5]unto him, [3]"If
°a man [15]love Me, he will keep My °words:
and My Father will [15]love him, and We will
come [3]unto him, and make Our °abode [17]with
him.
24 He that [15]loveth Me [1]not [15]keepeth [5]not
My °sayings: and the word which ye hear is
[5]not Mine, but [6]the Father's °Which sent Me.

E² 25 These things have I spoken [5]unto you, °be-
ing *yet* present [17]with you.
26 But the [16]Comforter, *Which is* °the Holy
Ghost, Whom [6]the Father will send [2]in My
name, °He shall °teach you all things, and
°bring all things to your remembrance, whatsoever I have said unto you.

the works, &c.: i.e. similar works, e.g. Acts 3. 7; 9. 34. **He do also** = he also do.

greater. Not only more remarkable miracles (Acts 5. 15; 19. 12) by the men who were endued with power from on high (*pneuma hagion*, Ap. 101. II. 14), but a more extended and successful ministry. The Lord rarely went beyond the borders of Palestine. He forbade the twelve to go save to the lost sheep of the house of Israel (Matt. 10. 5, 6); after Pentecost they went "everywhere" (Acts 8. 4), and Paul could say, "your faith is spoken of throughout the whole world" (Rom. 1. 8).

13 ask. Ap. 134. I. 4. Cp. Matt. 7. 7.

name. The word occurs first in Matt. 1. 21, associated with Jesus (Ap. 98. X). Cp. Mark 16. 17 with Acts 3. 6, 16; 4. 10, &c. **glorified.** See 12. 16.

15 love. Gr. *agapaō*. Ap. 135. I. 1, and see p. 1511.

keep. Most of the texts read, "ye will keep".

16 pray. Gr. *erōtaō*. Ap. 134. I. 3. Not *aiteō* as in *v.* 13. See 1 John 5. 16, where both words are used.

shall = will.

another. Gr. *allos*. Ap. 124. 1.

Comforter. Gr. *paraklētos*, rendered "Advocate" in 1 John 2. 1. *Paraklētos* and the Lat. *Advocatus* both mean one called to the side of another for help or counsel. The word is only found in John: here; *v.* 26; 15. 26; 16. 7 and 1 John 2. 1. So we have one Paraclete (the Holy Spirit) as here, and another with the Father. The Rabbinical writings often refer to the Messiah under the title *Mᵉnāḥem* (= Comforter), and speak of His days as the days of consolation. Cp. Luke 2. 25. See Dr. John Lightfoot's *Works*, vol. xii, p. 384.

abide. Gr. *menō*. Same as "dwelleth" in *v.* 10. See p. 1511.

for ever. Gr. *eis ton aiōna*. Ap. 151. II. A. 4. a.

17 the Spirit of truth = the Spirit (Ap. 101. II. 3) of the truth. The definite article in both cases.

world. Gr. *kosmos*. Ap. 129. 1.

cannot = is not (Ap. 105. I) able to.

seeth. Gr. *theōreō*. Ap. 133. I. 11.

with = beside. Gr. *para*. Ap. 104. xii. 2.

18 comfortless = orphans. Gr. *orphanos*. Occurs only here and James 1. 27.

will come = am coming. As in *v.* 3.

to. Gr. *pros*. Ap. 104. xv. 3.

19 a little while; i.e. about thirty hours. From the moment the Lord was taken down from the cross and entombed, He disappeared from the eyes of the world. Acts 10. 40. 41. **no more.** Gr. *ouk eti*.

shall live also = also shall live.

20 At = In. Gr. *en*. Ap. 104. viii.

At that day. Referring primarily to the forty days after His resurrection, but this well-known Hebrew term describes the day of the Lord, in contradistinction to this present day of man (1 Cor. 4. 3 marg.). See Isa. 2. 11–17 and Rev. 1. 10.

I in you. Fulfilled primarily at Pentecost, but looking on to the time when He will be among (Gr. *en*. Ap. 104. viii. 2) His people, as Jehovah-Shāmmāh. See Ezek. 43. 7; 48. 35. Zeph. 3. 15–17. **21 of** = by. Gr. *hupo*. Ap. 104. xviii. 1. **manifest.** Gr. *emphanizō*. Ap. 106. I. iv. **22 Judas.** Ap. 141. 10. Brother or son of James (Luke 6. 16, R.V.). Five others of this name. Judas Iscariot; Judas, the Lord's brother (Matt. 13. 55); Judas of Galilee (Acts 5. 37); Judas of Damascus (Acts 9. 11); and Judas Barsabas (Acts 15. 22). This is the only mention of this Judas. **how is it . . . ?** = how comes it to pass? **wilt** = art about to. **23 answered, &c.** See note on Deut. 1. 41 and Ap. 122. 3. **a man** = any one. Gr. *tis*. Ap. 123. 3. **words** = word (sing.). Gr. *logos*: i.e. the commandments of *vv.* 15, 21. **abode.** Same word as "mansions", in *v.* 2. **24 sayings** = words. Gr. *logos*. Same as "word" in the next clause, and in *v.* 23. Cp. 8. 51, 52, 55, and see note on Mark 9. 32. **Which sent Me.** This expression (Gr. *ho pempsas*, Ap. 174. 4), occ. twenty-four times, all in John. See 4. 34; 5. 23, 24, 30, 37; 6. 38, 39, 40, 44; 7. 16, 28, 33; 8. 16, 18, 26, 29; 9. 4; 12. 44, 45, 49; 13. 20; 15. 21; 16. 5. In the third person, "that sent Him", twice, 7. 18; 13. 16. **25 being yet present** = abiding. Gr. *menō*. A characteristic word in John's Gospel. See p. 1511. Same word as "abide", *v.* 16, and "dwell", *vv.* 10, 17. **26 the Holy Ghost** = the Spirit, the Holy. Gr. *to Pneuma to Hagion*. The only place in John where the two articles are found. Elsewhere Matt. 12. 32. Mark 3. 29; 12. 36; 13. 11. Luke 2. 26; 3. 22. Acts 1. 16; 5. 3, 32; 7. 51; 8. 18; 10. 44, 47; 11. 15; 13. 2, 4; 15. 8; 19. 6; 20. 23, 28; 21. 11; 28. 25. Eph. 1. 13; 4. 30. Heb. 3. 7; 9. 8; 10. 15. Twenty-eight times (7 × 4 = 28. Ap. 10). See Ap. 101. II. 3. **He** = that One. Gr. *ekeinos*. **teach.** Gr. *didaskō*. Occ. 97 times, always rendered "teach". Cp. 1 John 2. 27. Other words transl. "teach" are *katangellō*, Acts 16. 21; *katēcheō*, 1 Cor. 14. 19. Gal. 6. 6; *mathēteuō*, Matt. 28. 19. Acts 14. 21; and *paideuō*, Acts 22. 3. Titus 2. 12. **bring, &c.** = put you in mind of. Occ. seven times: here; Luke 22. 61. 2 Tim. 2. 14. Titus 3. 1. 2 Pet. 1. 12. 3 John 10. Jude 5. Cp 2. 17, 22; 12. 16. Luke 24. 6, 8 (a kindred word).

A. D. 29 27 °Peace I leave °with you, °My °peace I give
°unto you: [5]not as the °world giveth, give I
°unto you.
Z^3 B^3 [1]Let [1]not your heart be troubled, °neither let
it °be afraid.
28 Ye °have heard how I said unto you, I go
away, and °come *again* [3]unto you.
C^3 If ye [15]loved Me, ye would rejoice, because °I
said, I go [3]unto [6]the Father: for [2]My Father is
°greater than I.
29 And °now I have told you before it come to
pass, [3]that, when it is come to pass, ye might
°believe.
30 °Hereafter I will [5]not talk much [9]with
you: for the °prince of this [17]world cometh, and
hath °nothing [2]in Me.
31 But °that the [17]world may [7]know that
°I [15]love [6]the Father; and °as [6]the Father
°gave Me commandment, °even so °I do. °Arise, °let us go hence.

V F^1 G^1 b **15** °I am the °true °vine, and °My Father
is the Husbandman.
2 Every °branch °in Me that beareth °not
fruit He °taketh away: and every *branch* that
beareth fruit, He °purgeth it, °that it may
°bring forth more fruit.
3 °Now ye are °clean °through the °word
which I have spoken °unto you.

27 Peace. Fig. *Synecdochē*. Gr. *eirēnē*. Six times in John, always by the Lord. Cp. Dan. 10. 19. **with you**=to you. **My peace.** The Prince of Peace (Isa. 9. 6) alone can give true peace. Cp. 16. 33; 20. 19, 21, 26. Luke 24. 36. **unto**=to. **world.** Gr. *kosmos*. Ap. 129. 1. The world talks of peace, and we have Peace Societies, and Temples of Peace, while the nations are arming to the teeth. The world (Acts 4. 27) slew Him Who came to bring peace, and now talks of creating a "World's Peace" without the Prince of Peace, in ignorance of Ps. 2. 4. Prov. 1. 25–27. 1 Thess. 5. 3. **neither.** Gr. *mēde*. **be afraid**=show cowardice. Gr. *deiliaō*. Occ. only here. The noun *deilia* occ. only in 2 Tim. 1. 7, and the adj. *deilos* in Matt. 8. 26. Mark 4. 40. Rev. 21. 8.

28 have heard=heard (Aor.). **come again**=am coming (omit "again"). **I said.** All the texts omit. **greater.** The Lord was not inferior as to His essential being (see *vv.* 9–11; 10. 30), but as to His office, as sent by the Father. See 1 Cor. 15. 27. Phil. 2. 9–11.

29 now. Gr. *nūn*. See 12. 27. **believe.** Ap. 150. I. 1. i.

30 Hereafter I will not=No longer (Gr. *ouk eti*) will I. **prince.** See 12. 31. **nothing.** Gr. *ouk ouden*, a double negative, for emphasis. No sin for Satan to work upon. Cp. 8. 46. 2 Cor. 5. 21. Heb. 4. 15. 1 Pet. 2. 22, 23. 1 John 3. 5.

31 that=in order that. Gr. *hina*. **I love.** The only place where the Lord speaks of loving the Father. Six times the Father's love to the Son is mentioned, 3. 35; 10. 17; 15. 9; 17. 23, 24, 26. The adj. *agapētos*, beloved, does not occ. in John's Gospel, but nine times in his Epistles. See Ap. 135. III. **as**=even as. **gave . . . commandment**=charged. Cp. Matt. 4. 6; 17. 9, and see notes on Isa. 49. 6–9. **even so.** Cp. 3. 14; 5. 23; 12. 50. Note even as . . . even so. **I do**=I am doing, i. e. carrying it out in obedience to the Father's will. Cp. 4. 34; 5. 30; 6. 38–40. Phil. 2. 8. Heb. 5. 8. **Arise.** Implying haste. Gr. *egeirō*. Ap. 178. I. 4. **let us go.** Cp. 11. 15.

15. 1—16. 4 (*V*, p. 1552). CLEANSING. PRUNING. (*Division.*)

V | F^1 | 15. 1–17. Love manifested and commanded.
| F^2 | 15. 18—16. 4. Hatred foretold and experienced.

15. 1-17 (F^1, above). LOVE MANIFESTED AND COMMANDED. (*Alternation.*)

F^1 | G^1 | b | 1–3. The Vine and its branches. Pruning.
c | 4. Fruitfulness.
b | 5–. The Vine and its branches. Abiding.
c | –5–7. Fruitfulness.
H^1 | 8. Purpose. The Father glorified.
G^2 | d | 9–. The Father's love to the Son.
e | –9–. The Son's love to Disciples.
d | –9, 10–. Disciples abiding in Son's love.
e | –10. Son abiding in Father's love.
H^2 | 11. Purpose. Joy.
G^3 | f | 12–. Command. Love one another.
g | –12, 13. Example.
f | 14. Commands for friends.
g | 15, 16. Proof of friendship.
H^3 | 17. Purpose. Love one another.

1 I am. See on 14. 6. **true**=real. Ap. 175. 2. **vine.** Three trees are used in the N.T. to teach important lessons. The fig is used by our Lord to show the causes of the doom of Israel. In Rom. 11, Paul applies the figure of the olive tree also to Israel, and utters a solemn warning to the Gentiles; i. e. all the Gentiles upon whom My name is called (Acts 15. 17), now grafted in in Israel's place. The vine speaks of Israel's temporal and spiritual blessings (Ps. 80 and Isa. 5). That vine failed. Henceforth there is no blessing for Israel as such till He comes Who is the true Israel (Isa. 49. 3), as He is the true vine. Then shall Isa. 27. 6 be fulfilled. The *interpretation* of this passage is for Israel alone, though many blessed lessons may be drawn from it, by way of application. Through reading the "Church" into these verses, great confusion has resulted and grievous distress been caused to the people of God. **My Father.** See 2. 16. **2 branch.** Gr. *klēma*. Only here, and *vv.* 4, 5, 6. **in.** Gr. *en*. Ap. 104. viii. **not.** Gr. *mē*. Ap. 105. II. **taketh away**=raiseth. Gr. *airō*. Occ. 102 times, and transl. more than forty times, take up, lift up, &c. Take away is a secondary meaning, see the Lexicons. Cp. Matt. 4. 6; 16. 24. Luke 17. 13. Rev. 10. 5; 18. 21, and Ps. 24. 7, 9 (Sept.). **purgeth**=cleanseth. Gr. *kathairō*. Occ. only here, and Heb. 10. 2. Of the two kinds of branches, the fruitless and the fruitful, He raises the former from grovelling on the ground, that it may bear fruit, and cleanses the latter that it may bear more fruit. **that**=in order that. Gr. *hina*. **bring forth**=bear. Same word as in the two previous clauses. **3 Now**=Already. **clean.** Gr. *katharos*. Cp. 13. 10, 11, the only other occ. in John, and the verb *kathairō* in *v.* 2. **through**=on account of. Ap. 104. v. 2. **word.** Gr. *logos*. See on Mark 9. 32. **unto**=to.

c
A. D. 29 4 °Abide [2]in Me, °and I [2]in you. As the
[2]branch °cannot bear fruit °of itself, °except it
°abide [2]in the vine; °no more can ye, °except
ye °abide [2]in Me.

b 5 [1]I am the vine, ye *are* the [2]branches: He
that [4]abideth [2]in Me, and I [2]in him,
c the same [2]bringeth forth much fruit: for °without Me ye can do °nothing.
6 °If a man [4]abide °not [2]in Me, he °is cast
forth as °a [2]branch, and °is withered; and
°men gather them, and cast *them* °into °the
fire, and they are burned.
7 °If ye [4]abide [2]in Me, and My °words [4]abide
[2]in you, °ye shall °ask what ye °will, and it
shall °be done [3]unto you.

H^{1} 8 °Herein °is [1]My Father °glorified, °that ye
bear much fruit; °so shall ye be My disciples.

G^{2} d 9 °As °the Father °hath loved Me,

e so have I °loved you:

d °continue ye [2]in My °love.
10 [7]If ye °keep My commandments, ye shall
[4]abide [2]in My [9]love;

e even as I have °kept [1]My Father's commandments, and [4]abide [2]in His [9]love.

H^{2} 11 These things have I spoken [3]unto you,
[2]that °My joy might °remain [2]in you, and *that*
°your joy °might be full.

G^{3} f 12 This is °My commandment, [2]That ye [9]love
one another,

g °as I °have [9]loved you.
13 Greater [9]love hath °no man than this, [2]that
°a man °lay down his °life °for his °friends.

f 14 Ye are My [13]friends, [7]if ye do °whatsoever
I command you.

g 15 °Henceforth I call you not °servants; for
the °servant °knoweth °not what his °lord
doeth: but I have called you [13]friends; for all
things that I have heard °of [1]My Father I
°have made known [3]unto you.
16 °Ye have [15]not chosen Me, but I °have
chosen you, and °ordained you, [2]that ye should
°go and [2]bring forth fruit, and *that* your fruit
should [11]remain: [2]that whatsoever [7]ye shall
°ask of [9]the Father [2]in My name, He may give
it you.

H^{3} 17 These things I command you, [2]that ye
[9]love one another.

F^{2} J h 18 °If the °world hate you, °ye know that it
°hated Me before *it hated* you.
19 [18]If ye were °of the [18]world, the [18]world
°would love his own: but because ye are [15]not
°of the [18]world, but I °have chosen you °out of
the [18]world, °therefore the [18]world hateth you.

4 Abide. Gr. *menō*. See p. 1511.
and I. Read "I also [abide] in you". Omit the full stop, and supply "for".
cannot=is not (Ap. 105. I) able to.
of. Gr. *apo*. Ap. 104. iv.
except=if . . . not. Gr. *ean mē*. Ap. 118. 1. b and 105. II.
no more=even so neither. Gr. *houtōs oude*.
5 without. Gr. *chōris*, apart from. Cp. 1. 3, and 20. 7 (by itself), the only other occ. in John.
nothing. Gr. *ou ouden*, a double negative.
6 If a man . . . not. Gr. *ean mē tis*. Ap. 118. 1. b and 123. 3. See "except" in *v.* 4. It is no longer "you" or "ye" but "any one", speaking generally.
is cast forth . . . is withered. (Both verbs are in the Aorist)=was cast forth, &c., perhaps referring to the fig-tree (Matt. 21. 19, and Ap. 156). Cp. Matt. 13. 6.
a=the. **men**=they. Cp. Matt. 13. 30, 39, 41.
into. Gr. *eis*. Ap. 104. vi.
the fire. No art. in received text, but added by T Tr. A WH R, making it emphatic. See Matt. 13. 40, 42. Rev. 20. 15.
7 If. Ap. 118. 1. b.
words sayings. Gr. *rhēma*. See Mark 9. 32.
ye shall ask. All the texts read "ask". Cp. 14. 13, 14. Gr. *aiteō*. Ap. 134. I. 4.
will. Gr. *thelō*. Ap. 102. I.
be done=come to pass. Gr. *ginomai*.
8 Herein=In (Gr. *en*. Ap. 104. viii) this.
is . . . glorified=was . . . glorified (Aorist). Gr. *doxazō*. See p. 1511 and cp. 13. 31.
that=in order that (Gr. *hina*), showing the Father's purpose. Cp. 11. 15, 50; 12. 33; 13. 1-3.
so shall ye be=and (that) ye may become. Gr. *ginomai*. See on "done" in *v.* 7.
9 As=Even as. Gr. *kathōs*.
the Father. See on 1. 14.
hath loved=loved. Aor. as in second clause. Ap. 135. I. 1.
continue=abide. Gr. *menō*, as in *v.* 4.
love. Ap. 135. II. 1, and see p. 1511.
10 keep. Gr. *tēreō*. Cp. 8. 51, 52, 55; 14. 15, 21, 23, 24.
11 My joy=the joy that is mine (emph.). Three times in John, here, 3. 29, and 17. 13.
remain=abide. Gr. *menō* as above, but all the texts read "be".
your joy. As He gave them His peace (14. 27), so He seeks to make them partakers of His joy.
might be full=may be fulfilled: i.e. filled full.
12 My commandment. My charge to you. As the Father's charge to Me (*v.* 10) so My charge to you. Cp. 13. 34. **as**=even as.
have loved=loved, as in *v.* 9.
13 no man=no one. Gr. *oudeis*.
a man=one. Gr. *tis*. Ap. 123. 3.
lay down. Gr. *tithēmi*, lit. place; transl. "giveth" in 10. 11; "lay down" in 10. 15, 17, 18; 13. 37, 38. 1 John 3. 16. **life.** Ap. 110. III.
for=in behalf of. Gr. *huper*. Ap. 104. xvii. 1.
friends (Gr. *philos*, noun of *phileō*. Ap. 135. I. 2)=those whom one loves. Cp. 13. 1. Rom. 5. 6-8.
14 whatsoever. The texts read "the things which".
15 Henceforth . . . not=No longer. Gr. *ouketi*, compound of *ou*.
servants=bondservants.
knoweth. Ap. 132. I. 1.
not. Gr. *ou*. Ap. 105. I.

lord. Gr. *kurios*. Ap. 98. VI. i. *a*. 4. A. **of**=with. Gr. *para*. Ap. 104. xii. 1. **have made known**=made known (Aor.). **16 Ye have not, &c.**=Not that ye chose Me, &c. Fig. *Antimetabolē*. Ap. 6. Thus reversing the custom of the Jews for the disciple to choose his own master. See Dr. John Lightfoot, *Works*, vol. iii. p. 175. **have chosen**=chose. **ordained**=placed. Gr. *tithēmi*, as in *v.* 13. Cp. 1 Tim. 1. 12; 2. 7. 2 Tim. 1. 11. Heb. 1. 2. **go**=go forth. **ask of**=ask, as in *v.* 7.

15. 18—16. 4 [For Structure see next page].

18 If. Ap. 118. 2. a. **world.** Gr. *kosmos*. See 14. 17 and Ap. 129. 1. **ye know**=know (imp.). Gr. *ginōskō*. Ap. 132. I. ii. **hated**=hath hated. Therefore continues to hate. **19 of**=out of. Gr. *ek*. Ap. 104. vii. **would love.** Would love and continue loving (Imperfect). Gr. *phileō*. Ap. 135. I. 2. **have chosen**=chose. **out of.** Gr. *ek*, as above. **therefore**=on account of (Gr. *dia*. Ap. 104. v. 2) this.

A.D. 29 20 °Remember the [3]word that I said [3]unto
you, The [15]servant is [15]not greater than his
[15]lord. [18]If they °have persecuted Me, they
will °also °persecute you; [18]if they °have kept
My °saying, they will keep yours also.

i 21 But all these things will they do °unto you
°for My name's sake, because they [15]know
[15]not °Him That sent Me.

h 22 [18]If I °had [2]not come and °spoken [3]unto
them, they °had [15]not had °sin: but °now they
have °no °cloke °for their °sin.
23 He that hateth Me hateth [1]My Father also.
24 [18]If I had [2]not done °among them the
works which °none °other man did, °they had
[15]not had [22]sin: but [22]now have they both
°seen and hated both Me and [1]My Father.

i 25 But *this cometh to pass*, [2]that the [3]word
might be °fulfilled that is written [2]in °their
law, °**They hated Me** °**without a cause.**

K l¹ 26 But when °the Comforter °is come, whom
I will °send [3]unto you °from [9]the Father, *even*
°the Spirit of truth, Which °proceedeth °from
[9]the Father, °He °shall °testify °of Me:

l² 27 And ye also °shall bear witness, because
°ye have been °with Me °from the beginning.

l³ **16** These things have I spoken °unto you,
°that ye should °not be °offended.

J j 2 They °shall °put you out of the synagogues:
yea, the time cometh, [1]that whosoever °killeth
you will think that he °doeth °God °service.

k 3 And these things will they do °unto you,
because they °have °not °known °the Father,
°nor Me.

j 4 But these things have I told you, [1]that when
°the time °shall come, ye may remember that
I told you of them.

k And these things I said [3]not unto you °at the
beginning, because I was °with you.

W L 5 But °now I °go My way °to °Him That
°sent Me;

15. 18—16. 4 (F², p. 1557). HATRED FORETOLD AND EXPERIENCED.
(*Introversion and Alternation.*)

F² | J | h | 15. 18–20. The World's hatred to Disciples.
| | i | 15. 21. Reason.
| | *h* | 15. 22–24. The World's hatred to Christ.
| | *i* | 15. 25. Reason.
| K | l¹ | 15. 26. The Spirit's testimony.
| | l² | 15. 27. The Disciples' testimony.
| | l³ | 16. 1. The Lord's warning.
| *J* | j | 16. 2. The World's hatred manifested.
| | k | 16. 3. Reason.
| | *j* | 16. 4–. The World's hatred foretold.
| | *k* | 16. –4. Reason.

20 Remember. Referring to 13. 16.
have persecuted = persecuted (Aor.). Gr. *diōkō* = to pursue (opp. to *pheugō*, to flee), here with malignant intent. It is transl. thirty-one times "persecute", and thirteen times "follow", &c. in a good sense. Cp. Acts 9. 4. In Luke 11. 49 and 1 Thess. 2. 15 a stronger word, *ekdiōkō*, is used.
also, &c. = persecute you also.
have kept = kept (Aor.).
saying. Gr. *logos.* Same as "word" above, and in *vv.* 3, 25.
21 unto. The received text has the dative, but all the texts read *eis* (Ap. 104. vi).
for My name's sake = on account of (Gr. *dia.* Ap. 104. v. 2) My name. See Acts 4. 7, 17, 18; 5. 40, 41; 9. 14, 16, 21. 1 Pet. 4. 14, 16, where all the texts read "name" instead of "behalf".
Him That sent Me. See on 14. 24.
22 had . . . come, &c. = came and spake.
had not had sin = would not have (imperf.) sin, i.e. in rejecting Him as the Messiah. Fig. *Heterōsis.* Ap. 6.
sin. Ap. 128. I. ii. 1.
now. Gr. *nūn.* See 12. 27.
no = not (Ap. 105. I) any.
cloke = excuse. Gr. *prophasis.* Occurs seven times, rendered "pretence" in Matt. 23. 14. Mark 12. 40. Phil. 1. 18; "shew", Luke 20. 47; "colour", Acts 27. 30, and "cloke", here and 1 Thess. 2. 5.
for = concerning. Gr. *peri.* Ap. 104. xiii.
24 among. Gr. *en.* Ap. 104. viii.
none other man = no one else. Gr. *oudeis allos.* Ap. 124. 1. Cp. 5. 36; 9. 30.
they had not, &c. Same as in *v.* 22. Notice the different negatives *mē* and *ou* in the two clauses of the verse as in *v.* 22. **seen.** Gr. *horaō.* Ap. 133. I. 8.
25 fulfilled. See note on "full" in *v.* 11.
their law. Cp. 8. 17.
They hated, &c. Quoted from Pss. 35. 19 and 69. 4. Cp. also Pss. 109. 3 and 119. 161. **without a cause.** Gr. *dōrean.* Occurs eight times; transl. "freely" in Matt. 10. 8. Rom. 3. 24. 2 Cor. 11. 7. Rev. 21. 6; 22. 17: "in vain", Gal. 2. 21: "for nought", 2 Thess. 3. 8.
26 the Comforter. See 14. 16. **is come** = shall have come. **send.** Gr. *pempō.* Ap. 174. 4. **from.** Gr. *para.* Ap. 104. xii. 1. **the Spirit of truth.** See on 14. 17. **proceedeth** = goeth forth. **He.** Gr. *ekeinos*, as in 14. 26. **shall** = will; one of the many instances where both A.V. and R.V. blur the sense of their translation by the misuse of "shall" and "will". **testify** = bear witness. Gr. *martureō.* See note on 1. 7. **of** = concerning. Gr. *peri.* Ap. 104. xiii. 1. **27 shall bear witness** = testify, or are testifying (present). **ye have been** = ye are. **with.** Gr. *meta.* Ap. 104. xi. 1. **from the beginning.** See note on 8. 44.

16. 1 unto = to. **that** = in order that. Gr. *hina.* **not.** Gr. *mē.* Ap. 105. II. **offended:** lit. scandalized, or caused to stumble. See 6. 61. Matt. 5. 29; 11. 6; 26. 31, 33. Cp. 1 Cor. 1. 23. Gal. 5. 13. The Talmud speaks of Him as "the hung". **2 shall** = will. **put you out, &c.** = make you excommunicate. Gr. *aposunagōgos.* Occurs only here; 9. 22; and 12. 42. Cp. 9. 34, 35. **killeth.** See Acts 7. 59; 12. 2; 23. 12; 26. 10. **doeth, &c.** = is presenting an offering to God. See Acts 26. 9. **God.** Ap. 98. I. i. 1. **service.** Gr. *latreia*, technical word for an "offering". Occurs five times: here; Rom. 9. 4; 12. 1. Heb. 9. 1, 6. In the Sept. five times: Exod. 12. 25, 26; 13. 5. Josh. 22. 27. 1 Chron. 28. 13. **3 unto you.** All the texts omit. **have not known** = knew not (Aor.). **not.** Gr. *ou.* Ap. 105. I **known.** Ap. 132. I. 1. **the Father.** See p. 1511. **nor.** Gr. *oude.* **4 the time.** The texts read "their hour": i.e. the time of the things of *vv.* 2, 3. **shall come** = shall have come. **at the beginning** = from the beginning. Gr. *ex archēs.* See note on 6. 64. **with.** Gr. *meta.* Ap. 104. xi. 1.

16. 5-30 [For Structure see next page].

5 now. Gr. *nun.* See 12. 27. **go My way** = am going away: i.e. withdrawing. **to.** Gr. *pros.* Ap. 104. xv. 3. **Him That sent Me.** See on 14. 24. **sent.** Gr. *pempō.* Ap. 174. 4.

M N A.D. 29 and °none °of you °asketh Me, Whither goest Thou?
6 But because I have said these things [1]unto you, sorrow hath filled your heart.

O 7 °Nevertheless I tell you the °truth; It is °expedient for you that I °go away: for °if I go [1]not away, the °Comforter will [3]not come °unto you; but °if I °depart, I will [5]send Him °unto you.

N 8 °And °when He is come, °He will °reprove the °world °of °sin, and °of righteousness, and °of °judgment:
9 [8]Of [8]sin, °because they °believe [3]not °on Me;
10 [8]Of righteousness, because I go [5]to °My Father, and ye °see Me °no more;
11 [8]Of [8]judgment, because the prince of this [8]world °is judged.

O 12 °I have yet many things to say [1]unto you, but ye °cannot °bear them now.
13 °Howbeit when [8]He, °the Spirit of [7]truth, °is come, He will °guide you °into °all [7]truth: for He shall [3]not speak °of Himself; but °whatsoever He shall hear, *that* °shall He speak; and He will °shew you °things to come.
14 [8]He [13]shall °glorify Me: for He [13]shall receive [5]of Mine, and [13]shall [13]shew *it* [1]unto you.
15 All things that [3]the Father hath are Mine: °therefore said I, that He [13]shall take [5]of Mine, and [13]shall [13]shew *it* [1]unto you.

L 16 °A little while, and ye °shall [3]not [10]see Me: and again, °a little while, and ye shall °see Me, °because I go [5]to [3]the Father."

M P 17 °Then said *some* [5]of His disciples °among themselves, "What is this that He saith unto us, [16]'A little while, and ye shall [3]not [10]see Me: and again, a little while, and ye shall [16]see Me:' and, 'Because I go [5]to [3]the Father?'"
18 They said therefore, "What is this that He saith, 'A little while?' we °cannot tell what He saith."

16. 5-33 (*W*, p. 1552). RETURN TO THE FATHER. (*Alternation.*)

W | L | 5-. Return to the Father.
  M | N | -5, 6. Disciples. Silence and Sorrow.
    O | 7. Promise of Holy Spirit to Disciples.
    N | 8-11. Mission of Holy Spirit to the World.
    O | 12-15. Mission of Holy Spirit to the Disciples. } Explanations.
L | 16. Return to the Father.
  M | P | 17, 18. Disciples. Inquiry.
    Q | 19-28. The Lord's Answer.
    P | 29, 30. Disciples. Certainty.
    Q | 31-33. The Lord's Answer. } Explanations.

none = no one. Gr. *oudeis*.
of = out of. Gr. *ek*. Ap. 104. vii.
asketh. Gr. *erōtaō*. Ap. 134. I. 3. They did not grasp the expediency of His going. So questioning had given place to sorrow. All else was excluded by the distress caused by "the things" foretold.
7 Nevertheless = But.
truth. Gr. *alētheia*. Cp. Ap. 175. 1, and see p. 1511.
expedient = profitable. Gr. *sumpherō*. Cp. Matt. 5. 29, 30. Acts 20. 20. Occurs in John here; 11. 50; and 18. 14. The two last passages indicate what Caiaphas deemed "expedient".
go away: i. e. openly.
if. Ap. 118. 1. b.
Comforter. See on 14. 16.
unto. Gr. *pros*. Same as "to" in *v.* 5.
depart. Gr. *poreuomai*. Same word as in 14. 2. Note the three different words used by the Lord. In this verse, *aperchomai* twice, transl. "go away", expressing the *fact*; *poreuomai*, "depart", describing the change of sphere from earth to heaven, and in *v.* 5 *hupagō*, the *manner*, secretly, viz. by resurrection. It was in this way that Peter could not follow Him *then* (13. 36).
8 And, &c. These four verses exhibit the Fig. *Prosapodosis*, Ap. 6.
when He is come = having come.
He. Gr. *ekeinos*. See 14. 26.
reprove = convict, i. e. bring in guilty. Gr. *elenchō* (Lat. *convinco*). Elsewhere in John 3. 20, "reprove"; 8. 9, "convict"; 8. 46, "convince". Cp. also Titus 1. 9. James 2. 9.
world. Gr. *kosmos*. Ap. 129. 1.
of = concerning. Ap. 104. xiii. 1.
sin. Ap. 128. I. ii. 1.
judgment. Ap. 177. 7.

9 because. The mission of the Holy Spirit was to bring the world in guilty in regard to three things: (1) Sin. In God's sight sin is refusal to believe the Gospel concerning His son (1 John 5. 10). The Jews regarded only moral offences (as men do to-day) and infractions of the ceremonial law and the traditions of the elders (Matt. 15. 2) as sin. (2) Righteousness. Here also God's standard and man's differ. The Jews regarded the punctilious Pharisee (Luke 18. 11, 12) as the ideal. The only righteous One, whose standard was the will of God (8. 29. Heb. 10. 7), was rejected and crucified, and now in righteousness was to be removed from the earth, the seal of the Father's approval being put upon Him by resurrection. In Him Who is made unto us righteousness (1 Cor. 1. 30), the Divine standard is revealed (Rom. 1. 17). (3) Judgment. For the prince of this world has been already judged (12. 31) and sentenced, and ere long the sentence will be executed (Rom. 16. 20). believe ... on. Ap. 150. I. 1. v. (i).
10 My Father. See on 14. 2. see = behold. Ap. 133. I. 11. no more. Gr. *ouketi*. **11 is judged** = has been judged. Ap. 122. 1. **12 I have, &c.** Still there are many things I have. cannot = are not (Ap. 105. I) able. bear. Gr. *bastazō*. Cp. its use in 10. 31; 19. 17. Matt. 20. 12. Acts 15. 10. Gal. 6. 2, 5. Cp. 1 Cor. 3. 2. Heb. 5. 12. 1 Pet. 2. 2. **13 Howbeit** = But. the Spirit of truth. See on 14. 17 and Ap. 101. II. 3. is come = shall have come. guide = lead on the way. Gr. *hodēgeō*. Elsewhere in Matt. 15. 14. Luke 6. 39. Acts 8. 31. Rev. 7. 17. Used in the Sept. for Heb. *nāḥāh*. Neh. 9. 19. Pss. 23. 3; 73. 24; 139. 24, &c. into. Gr. *eis*. Ap. 104. vi. all truth = all the truth: i. e. all the truth necessary for His people from Ascension to Descension; the truth concerning the Pentecostal Church, the blessed hope of His return, and the mystery or secret of the Body of Christ, yet to be revealed to Paul. of = from. Gr. *apo*. Ap. 104. iv. whatsoever = whatsoever things. shall = will. shew = tell or report. See 4. 25; 5. 15. Acts 14. 27; 15. 4; 1 Pet. 1. 12. things to come = the coming things. **14 glorify.** See p. 1511. **15 therefore** = on account of (Gr. *dia*. Ap. 104. v. 2) this. **16 A little while.** See on 13. 33. shall not see Me. Most of the texts read, "see (Ap. 133. 11) Me no more". see. Ap. 133. I. 8. a. Not the same word as in first clause. because, &c. T Tr. A WH R omit this clause. **17 Then** = Therefore. among themselves = to (Gr. *pros*. Ap. 104. xv. 3) one another. **18 cannot tell** = do not (Gr. *ou*. Ap. 105. I.) know. Ap. 132. I. 1.

Q R 19 °Now °Jesus [3]knew that they °were de-
A. D. 29 sirous to [5]ask Him, and said [1]unto them, "Do
ye enquire °among yourselves [8]of that I said,
[16]'A little while, and ye shall [3]not [10]see Me: and
again, [16]a little while, and ye shall [-16]see Me?'
20 °Verily, verily, I say [1]unto you, That ye
[13]shall °weep and °lament, but the [8]world [13]shall
rejoice: and ye shall be sorrowful, but your
sorrow shall be turned [13]into joy.
21 °A woman when she is in travail hath
sorrow, because her hour is come: but as soon
as she is delivered of the °child, she remembereth [10]no more the °anguish, °for joy that a
°man °is born [13]into the [8]world.
22 And ye [5]now therefore have sorrow: but I
will [-16]see you again, and your °heart shall rejoice, and your joy °no man °taketh °from you.
S 23 And °in that day ye shall [5]ask Me °no-
thing. [20]Verily, verily, I say unto you, Whatsoever ye shall °ask [3]the Father °in My name,
He will give *it* you.
24 °Hitherto °have ye [23]asked [23]nothing [23]in
My name: [23]ask, and ye shall receive, [1]that
your joy may be °full.
T 25 These things have I spoken [1]unto you [23]in
°proverbs: °but °the time cometh, when I
[13]shall [10]no more speak [1]unto you [23]in °pro-
verbs,
T but I [13]shall [13]shew you °plainly [8]of [8]the Father.
S 26 °At °that day ye shall [23]ask [23]in My name:
and I say [3]not [1]unto you, that I will °pray
[3]the Father °for you:
27 For [3]the Father Himself °loveth you, because ye have °loved Me, and have °believed
that I came out °from God.
R 28 I came forth [27]from [3]the Father, and am
come [13]into the [8]world: again, I leave the
[8]world, and °go [5]to [3]the Father."
P 29 His disciples °said [1]unto Him, °"Lo, [5]now
(p. 1560) speakest Thou [25]plainly, and speakest °no
[25]proverb.
30 [5]Now °are we sure that Thou knowest
all things, and needest [3]not [1]that any man
should [5]ask Thee: °by this we [27]believe that
Thou camest forth [22]from God."
Q 31 [19]Jesus answered them, "Do ye now °be-
lieve?
32 °Behold, °the hour cometh, yea, is [5]now
come, [1]that ye °shall be scattered, °every man
°to °his own, and shall leave Me alone: °and
yet I am [3]not alone, because [3]the Father is
[4]with Me.
33 These things I have spoken [1]unto you,
[1]that [23]in Me ye might have °peace. [23]In the
[8]world ye shall have °tribulation: but be of
good cheer; I have °overcome the [8]world."

16. 19-28 (Q, p. 1560). THE LORD'S ANSWER.
(*Introversion.*)

Q | R | 19-22. Departure and Return.
S | 23, 24. Their prayer in that day.
T | 25-. Speaking no longer in proverbs. (Neg.)
T | -25. Speaking plainly. (Pos.)
S | 26, 27. Their prayer at that day.
R | 28. First Coming and Departure.

19 Now. All the texts omit.
Jesus. Ap. 98. X.
were desirous = were wishing. Gr. *thelō.* Ap. 102. 1.
among yourselves = with (Gr. *meta.* Ap. 104. xi. 1) one another.
20 Verily, verily. Twenty-third occurrence. See on 1. 51. **weep.** Gr. *klaiō.* See 11. 31, 33.
lament. Gr. *thrēneō* (cp. Engl. *threnody*). See Luke 23. 27, and the other two occ. Matt. 11. 17 and Luke 7. 32 (mourn).
21 A woman = The woman. The article, in conjunction with the Hebraism "in that day", *vv.* 23, 26, indicates *the* woman (wife) of Rev. 12. See Isa. 66. 7-11. Mic. 5. 3. Cp. Ps. 22. 31. Hos. 13. 13. Mic. 4. 9, 10. The time is the time of Jacob's trouble (Jer. 30. 7), the birth-pangs (sorrows, Matt. 24. 8) which will result in the birth of the new Israel, the nation of Isa. 66. 8 and Matt. 21. 43. **child.** Ap. 108. v.
anguish. Gr. *thlipsis,* tribulation. Matt. 24. 21, 29.
for = on account of. Gr. *dia.* Ap. 104. v. 2.
man. Ap. 123. 1. **is born** = was born.
22 heart. Cp. 14. 1.
no man = no one. Gr. *oudeis.*
taketh. Most of the texts read "shall take".
from. Gr. *apo.* Ap. 104. iv.
23 in that day. See 14. 20. The use of this important Hebraism (Isa. 2. 11, 12 and note there) in connexion with the woman of *v.* 21 shows that it refers to Israel and has nothing to do with the Church. The promise as to "asking in My name" was fulfilled as long as the offer of restoration on condition of national repentance continued; when that offer was withdrawn (Acts 28. 28), the promises (and "gifts") were withdrawn also. They will be renewed "in that day".
in. Gr. *en.* Ap. 104. viii.
nothing. A double negative. Gr. *ouk ouden.*
ask. Gr. *aiteō.* Ap. 134. I. 4.
in My name. See on 14. 13. The texts connect "in My name" with "give" instead of "ask".
24 Hitherto = Until now.
have ye asked = asked ye.
full = fulfilled: i.e. filled full.
25 proverbs. Gr. *paroimia,* a wayside saying. Occ. five times: here (twice); *v.* 29; 10. 6 (parable); and 2 Pet. 2. 22. In the Sept. it is found in Prov. 1. 1 and at the title of the book. Elsewhere *parabolē* is used. In N.T. *parabolē* is frequent, rendered "parable", save Mark 4. 30 (comparison); Luke 4. 23 (proverb); and Heb. 9. 9; 11. 19 (figure).
but. Omit. **the time** = an hour.
plainly = in free speech, openly. See 11. 14.
26 At = In. Gr. *en.* Ap. 104. viii.
that day. See *v.* 23.
pray. Gr. *erōtaō.* Same as "ask" in *v.* 5.
for = concerning. Gr. *peri.* Ap. 104. xiii. 1.
27 loveth. Gr. *phileō.* Ap. 135. I. 2.
believed. Ap. 150. I. 1. iii.
from = from beside. Gr. *para.* Ap. 104. xii. 1. Cp. 8. 42; 13. 3; 17. 8. **28 go.** Same word as "depart", *v.* 7. **29 said** = say. The texts omit "unto Him". **Lo.** Gr. *ide.* Ap. 133. I. 3. **no.** Gr. *oudeis.* **30 are we sure** = we know. Gr. *oida.* Ap. 132. I. 1. Same word as "tell" (*v.* 18) and "knowest" in next clause. **by** = in. Gr. *en.* Ap. 104. viii. **31 believe.** Ap. 150. I. 1. i. **32 Behold.** Gr. *idou.* Ap. 133. I. 2. **the hour** = an hour (no art.). All the texts omit "now". **shall be scattered** = should be dispersed. Gr. *skorpizō.* Occ. elsewhere 10. 12. Matt. 12. 30. Luke 11. 23. 2 Cor. 9. 9. A stronger word in 11. 52. Matt. 26. 31. **every man** = each. **to** = unto. Gr. *eis.* Ap. 104. vi. **his own** = his own (home). Gr. *ta idia.* Cp. 1. 11, where it means his own possessions. **and yet** = and. **33 peace.** Gr. *eirēnē.* See 14. 27; 20. 19, 21. 26. **tribulation.** Same as "anguish", *v.* 21. **overcome** = conquered. Gr. *nikaō.* Occ. twenty-eight times. Only here in John's Gospel, but six times in first Epistle. Always transl. "overcome", save in Rev. 5. 5; 6. 2; 15. 2. The noun *nikē* only in 1 John 5. 4, and *nikos* in Matt. 12. 20. 1 Cor. 15. 54, 55, 57.

U² V Y r **17** These °words spake °Jesus, and lifted
A. D. 29 up His eyes °to °heaven, and said, °"Father, the °hour is come; °glorify Thy °Son,
s °that Thy °Son °also may °glorify Thee:

t 2 °As Thou hast given Him °power °over all
°flesh, [1]that He should give °eternal °life °to
as many as Thou hast given Him.

t 3 And °this is [2]life [2]eternal, [1]that they might
°know Thee the only °true °God, and °Jesus
Christ, Whom Thou hast °sent.

s 4 I have [1]glorified Thee °on the °earth: °I
have finished the work which Thou °gavest Me
°to do.

r 5 And °now, O [1]Father, [1]glorify Thou Me
°with Thine own Self with the °glory which
I had °with Thee °before the °world was.

Z m 6 I °have manifested Thy °name °unto the
°men which Thou °gavest Me °out of the
[5]world: Thine they were, and Thou gavest
them Me; and they have °kept Thy °word.

n 7 [5]Now they have [3]known that all things
whatsoever Thou hast given Me are °of Thee.
8 For I have given unto them the °words
which Thou gavest Me; and they °have received
them, and °have [3]known °surely that I came
out °from Thee, and they °have believed that
Thou didst [3]send Me.

W 9 I °pray °for them: I °pray °not °for the
[5]world, but °for them which Thou hast given
Me; for they are Thine.
10 And °all Mine are Thine, and Thine are
Mine; and I °am [1]glorified °in them.
11 And °now I am °no more [10]in the [5]world,
but these are [10]in the [5]world, and I come °to
Thee. °Holy [1]Father, [6]keep °through Thine

17. 1-26 (U², p. 1552). THE LORD'S PRAYER TO THE FATHER. (*Introversion and Alternation.*)

U² | V | Y | 1-5. The Glorification of the Son.
Z | m | 6. I have manifested Thy name.
n | 7, 8. The Son sent by the Father and recognized.
W | 9-11. Disciples. One "as We are".
X | A | 12. "I kept them."
B | o | 13. Purpose of the Lord's words.
p | 14-. Thy Word given.
q | -14. They not of the world.
X | *A* | 15. "Thou . . keep them."
B | *q* | 16. They not of the world.
p | 17. Thy Word. Truth.
o | 18, 19. Purpose of the Lord's work.
W | 20-23. Disciples. Those who believe through them. One "as We are".
V | *Y* | 24. The glory of the Son.
Z | *n* | 25. The Son sent by the Father recognized.
m | 26. I have declared Thy name.

17. 1-5 (Y, above). THE GLORIFICATION OF THE SON. (*Introversion.*)

Y | r | 1-. Glorification of the Son by the Father.
s | -1. Glorification of the Father by the Son.
t | 2. Eternal Life. A Gift.
t | 3. Eternal Life. Its purpose.
s | 4. Glorification of the Father by the Son.
r | 5. Glorification of the Son by the Father.

1 words=things; i.e. from 13. 31 to 16. 33. **Jesus.** Ap. 98. X. **to**=unto. Gr. *eis*. Ap. 104. vi. **heaven**=the heaven (sing.). See on Matt. 6. 9, 10. **Father.** Ap. 98. III. See on 1. 14. **hour.** Cp. 12. 23, 27; 13. 1. **glorify.** See on 12. 16 and p. 1511. **Son.** Ap. 98. XV and Ap. 108. iii. **that**=in order that. Gr. *hina*. **also.** All texts omit. **2 As**=Even as. **power**=authority. Ap. 172. 5. **over all flesh.** Lit. of: i.e. in relation to (Ap. 17. 5) all flesh. Cp. Isa. 40. 5. Luke 3. 6. Acts 2. 17. **eternal.** Ap. 151. II. B. i. **life.** Ap. 170. 1. **to as many, &c.** Lit. everything that Thou hast given Him, to them. Seven times in this prayer His people are said to have been given Him by the Father, *vv.* 2, 6, 6, 9, 11, 12, 24; but see notes on *vv.* 11, 12. **3 this, &c.** Not a definition of eternal life, but the purpose (Gr. *hina*, as in *v.* 1) for which it is given. **know.** Ap. 132. I. ii. **true.** Ap. 175. 2, and p. 1511. **God.** Ap. 98. I. i. 1. **Jesus Christ.** Ap. 98. XI. **sent.** Ap. 174. 1. Christ said to be the sent One six times in this prayer, forty-three times in John; *apostellō*, 17 times; *pempō*, 33 times. **4 on.** Gr. *epi*. Ap. 104. ix. 1. **earth.** Ap. 129. 4. **I have finished.** The texts read "having finished". Cp. 4. 34; 5. 36; 19. 30. **gavest**=hast given. **to do**=in order that (Gr. *hina*, as in *v.* 1) I should do it. **5 now.** Gr. *nun*, as in 13. 31. **with**=beside. Gr. *para*. Ap. 104. xii. 2. **glory.** Gr. *doxa*. See p. 1511. **before.** Gr. *pro*. Ap. 104. xiv. **world.** Ap. 129. 1. **6 have manifested**=manifested. **name.** Cp. *vv.* 11, 12, 26. Exod. 34. 5. Ps. 9. 10; 20. 1 (see note there). **unto**=to. **men.** Ap. 123. 1. **gavest.** Cp. *v.* 2; 6. 37; 12. 32. **out of.** Gr. *ek*. Ap. 104. vii. **kept.** Gr. *tēreō*. This word is used in these chapters twelve times: 14. 15, 21, 23, 24; 15. 10, 10, 20, 20; 17. 6, 11, 12, 15; nine times in reference to the Word, thrice in reference to the disciples. **word.** Gr. *logos*. See Mark 9. 32. Three statements are made by the Lord of His disciples, each three times: their relationship to the Word, *vv.* 6, 7, 8; relationship to the Sent One, *vv.* 8, 18, 25; relationship to the world, *vv.* 14, 14, 16. **7 of**=from. Gr. *para*. Ap. 104. xii. 1. **8 words.** Gr. *rhēma*. See Mark 9. 32. **have received**=received. **have known**=knew. **surely**=truly. Gr. *alēthōs*. Cp. Ap. 175. 1. **from.** Gr. *para*, as in *v.* 7. **have believed**=believed. Ap. 150. I. 1. iii. **9 pray**=ask. Gr. *erōtaō*. Ap. 134. I. 3. The Lord uses this word eight times in these chapters: 14. 16; 16. 5, 23, 26; 17. 9, 9, 15, 20. The word *aiteō*, used of an inferior addressing a superior, occ. 14. 13, 14; 15. 7, 16; 16. 23, 24, 24, 26. Cp. Mark 15. 43 (crave), Luke 23. 52 (beg). **for**=concerning. Gr. *peri*. Ap. 104. xiii. 1. **not.** Gr. *ou*. Ap. 105. I. **10 all Mine are Thine, &c.**=all things that are Mine are Thine, &c. This is a claim of perfect equality. Everything belonging to the Father, from essential being to works, the Son claims as His own. Luther says, "Any man can say 'All mine is Thine', but only the Son can say 'All that is Thine is Mine.'" Cp. 1 Cor. 3. 21-23. **am glorified**=have been glorified. See *vv.* 6-8. **in.** Gr. *en*. Ap. 104. viii. **11 now . . . no more**=no longer. Gr. *ouketi*. **to**=unto. Gr. *pros*. Ap. 104. xv. 3. **Holy Father.** When speaking of Himself, the Lord says, "Father", *vv.* 1, 5, 21, 24; when speaking of His disciples, "Holy Father"; when speaking of the world, "Righteous Father", *v.* 25. The holiness of God has separated the disciples from the world. Cp. 1 John 2. 15, 16. **through**=in. Gr. *en*, as in *v.* 12.

A. D. 29 own [6] name those ° whom Thou hast given Me,
[1] that they may be ° one, as We *are*.
X A **12** ° While I was ° with them ° in the [5] world,
I [6] kept them [10] in Thy name: ° those that Thou
gavest Me I ° have kept, and none ° of them is
° lost, ° but ° the [1] son of ° perdition; [1] that ° the
scripture ° might be ° fulfilled.
B o **13** And [5] now come I [11] to Thee; and these
things I speak [10] in the [5] world, [1] that they might
have My joy [12] fulfilled [10] in themselves.
p **14** I have given them ° Thy [6] word;
q and the [5] world ° hath hated them, because they
are [9] not [12] of the [5] world, even as I am [9] not
[12] of the [5] world.
X A **15** I [9] pray [9] not [1] that Thou shouldest take
them [6] out of the [5] world, but [1] that Thou
shouldest [6] keep them ° from ° the evil.
B q **16** They are [9] not [12] of the [5] world, even as I
am [9] not [12] of the [5] world.
p **17** ° Sanctify them [11] through ° Thy ° truth:
° Thy [6] word is ° truth.
o **18** ° As Thou ° hast [3] sent Me ° into the [5] world,
even so ° have I also [3] sent them ° into the
[5] world.
19 And ° for their sakes ° I [17] sanctify Myself,
[1] that they also ° might be [17] sanctified [11] through
° the [17] truth.
W u **20** ° Neither [9] pray I [9] for these alone, but [9] for
them also which ° shall ° believe on Me ° through
their [6] word.
21 [1] That they all may be [11] one;
v as Thou, [1] Father, *art* [10] in Me, and I [10] in Thee,
w [1] that they also may be [11] one [10] in Us:
x [1] that the [5] world may [8] believe that Thou ° hast
[3] sent Me.
u **22** And the [5] glory which Thou ° gavest Me I
have given them; [1] that they may be [11] one,
v even as We are one:
w **23** I [10] in them, and Thou [10] in Me, [1] that they
may be ° made perfect ° in [11] one,
x ° and [1] that the [5] world may [3] know that Thou
° hast [3] sent Me, and ° hast ° loved them, ° as
Thou ° hast ° loved Me.
V Y **24** [1] Father, I ° will [1] that they also, whom Thou
hast given Me, be [12] with Me where I am; [1] that
they may ° behold My [5] glory, which Thou hast

whom. All the texts read "which", referring to "name": i.e. "Keep them through Thy name which Thou hast given Me." Cp. Exod. 23. 21. Isa. 9. 6. Phil. 2. 9, 10. Rev. 19. 12.

one. Gr. *en.* Neut. as in 10. 30. This request is made five times (Ap. 6) in this chapter: here, *vv.* 21, 21, 22, 23.

12 While = When. **with.** Gr. *meta.* Ap. 104. xi. 1.

in the world. All the texts omit.

those that. As in *v.* 11, all the texts put the relative in the sing., and read "in Thy name that Thou gavest Me, and I kept them".

have kept = kept (Gr. *phulassō*), i.e. guarded. Cp. Luke 2. 8 (keep watch). 1 John 5. 21. Not the same word as in former clause and *v.* 6.

of = out of. Gr. *ek.* Ap. 104. vii.

lost. Gr. *apollumi.* Occ. twelve times in John: 6. 12, 39; 12. 25; 17. 12; 18. 9 (lose); 3. 15, 16; 6. 27; 10. 28; 11. 50 (perish); 10. 10 (destroy); 18. 14 (die). Used of the doom of the sinner. One of the strongest words in the Greek language to express final and irretrievable destruction.

but = except. Gr. *ei mē.*

the son, &c. This expression occ. here and 2 Thess. 2. 3 (the Antichrist). Used in the Sept. in Isa. 57. 4, "children of transgression". Cp. Matt. 9. 15; 13. 38; 23. 15. Luke 16. 8. Acts 13. 10. Eph. 2. 2, in all which passages "child" should be "son".

perdition. Gr. *apōleia,* a kindred word to *apollumi.* Occ. twenty times. Only here in John. First occ. Matt. 7. 13.

the scripture, &c. This expression occ. five times in John, here, 13. 18; 19. 24, 28, 36.

might be = may be, expressing certainty.

fulfilled. See on 15. 11.

14 Thy word. In *v.* 6 the word is "kept", here it is "given"; in *v.* 17 its character is stated, "truth".

hath hated = hated.

15 from = out of. Gr. *ek,* as in the former clause.

the evil = the evil one. See on Matt. 6. 13. Cp. 1 John 5. 19. Three things the Lord requested for His disciples: to be kept from the evil one, to be sanctified through the truth (*v.* 17), and to behold His glory (*v.* 24).

17 Sanctify = Hallow. Gr. *hagiazō.* Separation is the idea of the word "holy". See note on Ex. 3. 5.

Thy. All the texts read "the".

truth. The truth is the great separating force. Cp. Matt. 10. 35.

Thy word, &c. = The word that is Thine is the truth. The Incarnate and revealed Words alike. Cp. 5. 33; 14. 6; 16. 13. Matt. 22. 16. 2 Cor. 6. 7; 13. 8. Gal. 2. 5, 14. Eph. 1. 13.

18 As = Even as. **hast sent** = didst send.

into. Gr. *eis.* Ap. 104. vi.

have . . . sent = sent.

19 for their sakes = on behalf of (Gr. *huper.* Ap. 104. xvii. 1) them.

I sanctify Myself = I dedicate or consecrate Myself. This shows the meaning of sanctify; not making holy as to moral character, but setting apart for God. The Lord was the antitype of all the offerings, which were holy unto Jehovah.

might be = may be. **the truth.** There is no article.

17. 20-23 (*W*, p. 1562). DISCIPLES. THOSE WHO BELIEVE THROUGH THEM. ONE "AS WE ARE". (*Extended Alternation.*)

W | u | 20, 21-. Unity.
  v | -21-. Comparison.
   w | -21-. Unity.
    x | -21. Purpose.
 u | 22-. Unity.
  v | -22. Comparison.
   w | 23-. Unity.
    x | -23. Purpose.

20 Neither = Not. (Gr. *ou.* Ap. 105. I). **shall believe.** All the texts read "believe". **believe on.** Ap. 150. I. 1. v. (i). **through.** Gr. *dia.* Ap. 104. v. **21 hast sent** = didst send (Aor.). **22 gavest.** Here the reading should be "hast given". **23 made perfect** = perfected. Gr. *teleioō.* Same word as "finish" in *v.* 4. **in** = into. Gr. *eis.* Ap. 104. vi. **and.** All omit. **hast sent** = didst send. **hast loved** = lovedst. **loved.** Gr. *agapaō.* See p. 1511. **as** = even as. **24 will.** Gr. *thelō.* Ap. 102. 1. Cp. 12. 21; 15. 7; 16. 19. **behold.** Gr. *theōreō.* Ap. 133. I. 11. Cp. 2. 23.

A.D. 29 given Me: for Thou [23] lovedst Me [5] before °the
foundation of the [5] world.

Z n 25 O °righteous [1] Father, the [5] world °hath
[9] not [3] known Thee: but I °have [3] known Thee,
and these °have [3] known that Thou °hast [3] sent
Me.

m 26 And I °have declared [6] unto them Thy
[6] name, and will declare *it*: [1] that the °love
wherewith Thou °hast [23] loved Me may be [10] in
them, and I [10] in them."

B A[1] B y **18** °When °Jesus had spoken these °words,
He °went forth °with His disciples over
the °brook °Cedron, where was a °garden, °in-
to the which He entered, and His disciples.
2 And Judas also, which betrayed Him, °knew
the place: for [1] Jesus ofttimes resorted thither
°with His disciples.
3 Judas then, having received °a band *of men*
and °officers °from the °chief priests and Pharisees, cometh thither [2] with °lanterns and
°torches and °weapons.

z 4 Jesus therefore, [2] knowing all things that
should come °upon Him, went forth, and said
°unto them, "Whom seek ye?"
5 They answered Him, "Jesus °of Nazareth." Jesus saith [4] unto them, °"I am *He*."
And Judas also, which betrayed Him, stood
[2] with them.
6 As soon then as He had said [4] unto them,
[5] "I am *He*," they went °backward, and fell
°to the ground.
7 Then °asked He them again, "Whom seek
ye?" And they said, [1] "Jesus of [5] Nazareth."
8 [1] Jesus answered, "I have told you that [5] I
am *He*: °if therefore ye seek Me, let these go
their way:"
9 °That the °saying might be °fulfilled, which
He spake, °"Of them which Thou gavest Me
have I lost °none."

y 10 °Then Simon Peter having a °sword °drew
it, and °smote the high priest's °servant, and
cut off his right °ear. The servant's name was
Malchus.

z 11 Then said [1] Jesus [4] unto Peter, "Put up thy
sword [1] into the sheath: °the cup which °My
Father hath given Me, shall I °not drink it?"

the foundation, &c. See Ap. 146.
25 righteous Father. See on *v.* 11.
hath not known Thee=knew Thee not. See 8. 55. Rom. 1. 18-32. 1 Cor. 1. 21; 2. 8.
have known=knew.
hast sent=didst send.
26 have declared=declared: i.e. made known. Gr. *gnōrizō*. See 15. 15, the only other occ. in John. Kindred word to *ginōskō* (Ap. 132. I. ii) and *gnōsis*, knowledge.
love. Gr. *agapē*. Ap. 135. II. 1.
hast loved=lovedst. This whole chapter beautifully illustrates Pss. 119 and 138. 2.

18. 1—20. 31 (*B*, p. 1510). DEATH, BURIAL, AND RESURRECTION. (*Division.*)

B	A[1]	18. 1—19. 30. Death. Events leading up to it.
	A[2]	19. 31-42. Burial.
	A[3]	20. 1-31. Resurrection.

18. 1—19. 30 (A[1], above). DEATH. (*Introversion.*)

A[1]	B		18. 1-11. The Arrest.
		C	18. 12-27. Trial before Annas.
		C	18. 28—19. 16. Trial before Pilate.
	B		19. 17-30. The Crucifixion.

18. 1-11 (B, above). THE ARREST. (*Division.*)

B	y		1-3. Judas. Treachery.
		z	4-9. The Lord. Avowal.
	y		10. Peter. Zeal.
		z	11. The Lord. Resignation.

1 When Jesus, &c.=Jesus, having spoken.
Jesus. Ap. 98. X. **words**=things.
went forth: i.e. from the place where He had been speaking. See 14. 31.
with. Gr. *sun*. Ap. 104. xvi.
brook. Gr. *cheimarros*, a winter torrent. Occurs only here.
Cedron. Called Kidron (2 Sam. 15. 23 and elsewhere in O.T.). David crossed it, when with a few faithful followers he fled from Absalom. The name seems to have been given both to the valley and to the torrent which, in winter, sometimes ran through it. Now Wādy-en-Nār.
garden. Gr. *kēpos*. An orchard or plantation. Cp. Luke 13. 19.
into. Gr. *eis*. Ap. 104. vi.
2 knew. Gr. *oida*. Ap. 132. I. i.
with. Gr. *meta*. Ap. 104. xi.
3 a band=the cohort; the word means the tenth part of a legion, therefore 600 men; but the term was probably used with some latitude.
officers. The Temple guard. Cp. 7. 32, 45, 46.
from. Gr. *ek*. Ap. 104. vii.
chief priests. These were Sadducees (Acts 5. 17). So Sadducees and Pharisees sunk their differences in order to destroy Him, just as Herod and Pilate were made friends (Luke 23. 12) over His condemnation. **lanterns.** Gr. *phanos*. Occurs only here. Cp. Ap. 106. I. i. **torches.** Gr. *lampas*. Generally rendered "lamp" (Matt. 25. 1-8. Rev. 4. 5; 8. 10), but "light" in Acts 20. 8. **weapons.** The swords and staves of Luke 22. 52. **4 upon.** Gr. *epi*. Ap. 104. ix. 3. **unto**=to. **5 of Nazareth**=the Nazarene. For some reason Nazareth had an evil name (see 1. 46), and so Nazarene was a term of reproach. The name has nothing to do with Nazarite (separated) applied to Joseph (Gen. 49. 26), and those like Samson who took the vow of Num. 6. **I am.** Gr. *ego eimi*. These words were used nine times in John, 4. 26; 6. 20; 8. 24, 28, 58; 13. 19, as well as in these verses, 5, 6, 8. Whatever may be said of the first two instances, the others are claims to the Divine title of Ex. 3. 14 (Ap. 98. II). See esp. 8. 58. There are fourteen instances of the metaphorical use of the phrase in connection with "bread", "light", &c. **6 backward.** Gr. *eis* (Ap. 104. vi) *ta opisō*. **to the ground.** Gr. *chamai*. Only here, and 9. 6. **7 asked**=demanded. Gr. *eperōtaō*. A stronger word than *erōtaō* (Ap. 134. I. 3), which occurs in *v.* 19. **8 if.** Ap. 118. 2. a. **9 That**=In order that. Gr. *hina*. **saying.** Gr. *logos*. See Mark 9. 32. **fulfilled.** See 17. 12. **Of**=Out of. Gr. *ek*. Ap. 104. vii. **none**=not one (Gr. *ouk oudeis*), a double negative. **10 Then Simon, &c.**=Simon Peter, therefore. Cp. Luke 22. 49. **sword.** One of the two of Luke 22. 38. **drew.** Gr. *helkuō*. See 12. 32. **smote.** Gr. *paiō*. Only here, Matt. 26. 68. Mark 14. 47. Luke 22. 64. Rev. 9. 5. **servant**=bond-servant. Gr. *doulos*. See 13. 16. In all the four Gospels the definite article is used, *the* servant. Malchus had advanced so as to seize the Lord, and thus became the object of Peter's attack. **ear.** Gr. *ōtion*. Only used in connexion with this incident, and in all four Gospels, the usual word being *ous*. **11 the cup.** Cp. Matt. 20. 22, 23; 26. 39, 42. Rev. 14. 10. **My Father.** See on 2. 16. **not**=in no wise. Gr. *ou mē*. Ap. 105. III.

C D 12 [3]Then the [3]band and the °captain and
A. D. 29 [3]officers of the Jews °took [1]Jesus, and bound
Him,
13 And led Him away °to °Annas first; for he
was father in law to Caiaphas, which was the
high priest that same year.
14 Now °Caiaphas was he, which gave counsel to the Jews, that it was expedient that one
man should die °for the people.

E 15 And Simon Peter °followed [1]Jesus, and *so*
did °another disciple: that disciple was °known
[4]unto the high priest, and went in with [1]Jesus
[1]into the °palace of the high priest.
16 But Peter °stood °at the door without.
[3]Then went out that [15]other disciple, which
was [15]known [4]unto the high priest, and spake
[4]unto °her that kept the door, and brought in
Peter.
17 [3]Then saith the damsel [16]that kept the door
[4]unto Peter, "Art °not thou also *one* [9]of °this
°Man's disciples?" He saith, "I am °not."
18 And the [10]servants and °officers °stood there,
who had made °a fire of coals; for it was cold:
and they °warmed themselves: and Peter
°stood [2]with them, and °warmed himself.

D 19 The high priest [3]then °asked [1]Jesus °of His
disciples, and °of His °doctrine.
20 [1]Jesus answered him, "I °spake °openly to
the °world; I ever taught °in the °synagogue,
and °in the °temple, whither the Jews always
resort; and °in secret °have I said °nothing.
21 Why [7]askest thou Me? [7]ask them which
heard Me, what I °have said unto them: °be-
hold, they [2]know what I said."
22 °And when He had thus spoken, one of the
[3]officers which stood by °struck [1]Jesus °with
the palm of his hand, saying, "Answerest Thou
the high priest so?"
23 [1]Jesus answered him, [8]"If I °have spoken
°evil, bear witness [19]of the °evil: but [8]if well,
why °smitest thou Me?"
24 °Now Annas °had °sent Him bound °unto
Caiaphas the high priest.

E 25 And Simon Peter °stood and warmed himself. They said therefore [4]unto him, "Art
[17-]not thou also *one* [9]of His disciples?" He
°denied *it*, and said, "I am [-27]not."
26 One [9]of the [10]servants of the high priest,
being *his* kinsman whose [10]ear Peter cut off,
saith, "Did [-17]not I °see thee [20]in the garden
[2]with Him?"
27 °Peter [3]then [25]denied again: and °imme-
diately °the cock °crew.

18. 12-27 (C, p. 1564). TRIAL BEFORE ANNAS AND CAIAPHAS. (*Alternation.*)

C | D | 12-14. The Lord led away to Annas.
E | 15-18. Peter. Denial.
D | 19-24. The Lord examined by Annas.
E | 25-27. Peter. Denial.

12 captain. Gr. *chiliarchos* = commander of a thousand. One of the six tribunes attached to a legion. His presence shows the importance attached by the Romans to the arrest, the Jews having represented it as a case of dangerous sedition.

took: i.e. surrounded and seized. Cp. Acts 26. 21.

13 to = unto. Gr. *pros.* Ap. 104. xv. 3.

Annas. He had been deposed in 779 A. U. C., the year our Lord's ministry began (Ap. 179), and three others had been promoted and deposed before Caiaphas was appointed by Valerius Gratus. Our Lord was taken to Annas first, because his experience in the Law would the better enable him to formulate a charge against Him.

14 Caiaphas. See 11. 49-53.

for = in behalf of. Gr. *huper.* Ap. 104. xvii. 1.

15 followed = was following.

another. Gr. *allos.* Ap. 124. 1.

known. Gr. *gnōstos.* Cp. *ginōskō.* Ap. 132. I. ii. That this was John himself is highly improbable. He always designates himself "the disciple whom Jesus loved" (13. 23; 19. 26; 21. 7, 20). It is more probable it was some one of influence, as Nicodemus or Joseph of Arimathæa, both members of the Sanhedrin.

palace = Gr. *aulē.* Originally the court, open to the air, around which the house was built, then the house itself.

16 stood = was standing.

at. Gr. *pros.* Ap. 104. xv. 2.

her that kept the door = doorkeeper. Gr. *thurōros.* Here and in *v.* 17 fem. Occ. elsewhere 10. 3. Mark 13. 34 (masc.). Female porters were not uncommon. Cp. Acts 12. 13. The Sept. reads in 2 Sam. 4. 6, "The porter (fem.) of the house winnowed wheat, and slumbered and slept". Cp. Josephus, *Antiq.*, bk. vii, ch. ii. 1.

17 not. Gr. *mē.* Ap. 105. II.

this Man's = this fellow's. Spoken in contempt.

Man's. Ap. 123. 1. **not.** Gr. *ou.* Ap. 105. I.

18 officers. The Chiliarch and Roman soldiers had gone back to their barracks (Antonia), leaving the Lord in the hands of the Jews.

stood . . . warmed. All these verbs are in the imperfect.

a fire of coals. Gr. *anthrakia.* Only here and 21. 9.

19 asked. Gr. *erōtaō.* Ap. 134. I. 3.

of = concerning. Gr. *peri.* Ap. 104. xiii. 1.

doctrine. To elicit something to be used against Him.

20 spake. The texts read "have spoken".

openly. Gr. *parrhēsia.* Cp. 7. 4.

world. Gr. *kosmos.* Ap. 129. 1.

in. Gr. *en.* Ap. 104. viii.

synagogue. See Ap. 120. Omit "the". It is general, applying to more than one.

temple = temple courts. Gr. *hieron.* See Matt. 23. 16.

have I said = I said.

nothing. Gr. *ouden*, neut. of *oudeis.* **21 have said** = said. **behold.** Gr. *ide.* Ap. 133. I. 3. **22 And when He had thus spoken** = But He having said these things. **struck . . . with the palm, &c.** = gave a blow. Gr. *rapisma.* Only here, 19. 3. Mark 14. 65. This beginning of indignities may have been with or without a weapon. **23 have spoken** = spoke. **evil** = evilly. Gr. *kakōs*, adverb of *kakos* (Ap. 128. III. 2) in next clause. **smitest.** Gr. *derō.* Occ. fifteen times. Transl. "beat" except here, Luke 22. 63, and 2 Cor. 11. 20. It has been alleged against the Lord that He did not carry out His own precept in Matt. 5. 39. But those words were spoken during the first part of His ministry, when the kingdom was being proclaimed. See Ap. 119. This was when the kingdom had been rejected, and the King was about to be crucified. Cp. Luke 22. 35-38. **24 Now.** In the Received text, there is no word for "Now", but most of the critical texts insert *oun*, therefore. **had sent** = sent. Gr. *apostellō.* Ap. 174. 1. This shows that this preliminary inquiry was conducted by Annas. John omits the trial before Caiaphas. **unto.** Gr. *pros.* Ap. 104. xv. 3. **25 stood, &c.** = was standing, &c., as in *v.* 18. **denied.** Gr. *arneomai.* See note on 13. 38. See Ap. 160. **26 see.** Gr. *eidon.* Ap. 133. I. 1. **27 Peter, &c.** = Again therefore Peter denied. **immediately.** Gr. *eutheōs.* See 13. 30. **the** = a. **crew** = crowed. The first of the two cock-crowings. See Ap. 160. The word is *phōneō*, to make a sound with the voice.

C F H[1] 28 °Then led they [1] Jesus °from Caiaphas
A.D. 29 °unto the °hall of judgment: and °it was early;
and they themselves went [−17] not [1] into the
judgment hall, °lest they should be °defiled;
but [9] that they might °eat the passover.
29 Pilate [3] then °went out [24] unto them, and
said, "What °accusation bring ye °against
[17] this [17] Man?"
30 They answered and said [4] unto him, [8] "If
He were [17−] not a °malefactor, we would [−17] not
have delivered Him up [4] unto thee."
31 [3] Then said Pilate [4] unto them, °"Take ye
Him, and °judge Him °according to your law."
The Jews therefore said [4] unto Him, °"It is
°not lawful for us to put °any man to death:"
32 [9] That the [9] saying of [1] Jesus might be [9] fulfilled, which He spake, °signifying what death
He °should die.
J 33 [3] Then Pilate entered [1] into the [28] judgment
hall again, and °called [1] Jesus, and said [4] unto
Him, "Art Thou °the King of the Jews?"
34 [1] Jesus answered him, "Sayest thou this
thing °of thyself, or did °others tell it thee [19] of
Me?"
35 Pilate answered, "Am I a Jew? Thine
own nation and the chief priests have delivered
Thee [4] unto me: what °hast Thou done?"
36 [1] Jesus answered, "My kingdom is [−17] not
[9] of this [20] world: [8] if My kingdom were [9] of this
[20] world, then would My °servants fight, [9] that
I should [17−] not be delivered to the Jews: but
°now is My kingdom [−17] not from hence."
37 Pilate therefore said [4] unto Him, °"Art
Thou a king then?" Jesus answered, "Thou
sayest that I am a king. °To this end was I
born, and °for this cause came I [1] into the
[20] world, [9] that I should °bear witness unto °the
truth. Every one that is [9] of °the truth heareth
°My voice."
38 Pilate saith [4] unto Him, °"What is
[37] truth?"
H[2] And when he had said this, he went out again
[24] unto the Jews, and saith [4] unto them, "I find
[20] in Him °no °fault *at all*.
39 But ye have a °custom, [9] that I should
release [4] unto you one °at the passover: °will
ye therefore that I release [4] unto you °the King
of the Jews?"
40 [3] Then °cried they all again, saying,
[17−] "Not °this Man, but °Barabbas." Now
°Barabbas was a °robber.

G **19** Then Pilate therefore took °Jesus, and
°scourged *Him*.

18. 28—19. 16 (*C*, p. 1564). TRIAL BEFORE PILATE. (*Alternation.*)

C | F | H[1] | 18. 28-32. Pilate and the Jews.
J | 18. 33-38-. Examination by Pilate.
H[2] | 18. -38-40. Pilate. Release proposed.
G | 19. 1-3. Scourging.
F | H[3] | 19. 4-7. Pilate and the Jews. No fault.
J | 19. 8-11. Further examination.
H[4] | 19. 12-14. Pilate. Release sought.
G | 19. 15, 16. Deliverance to death.

28 Then = Therefore. This follows the decision of the Sanhedrin recorded in Matt. 26. 58—27. 2 and parallel passages. See above, *v.* 24.

from = away from. Gr. *apo*. Ap. 104. iv.

unto. Gr. *eis*. Ap. 104. vi.

hall of judgment. Gr. *praitōrion*. Lat. *praetorium*, the house of the Prætor. See Mark 15. 16. Probably connected with the castle of Antonia, built by Herod the Great and named after Mark Antony. It was not Herod's palace, as is clear from Luke 23. 7. Cp. same word in Acts 23. 35. Phil. 1. 13.

it was early: i. e. in the early hours of the Preparation between 11 p.m. and midnight.

lest, &c. = in order that they might not. Gr. *hina mē*.

defiled. Gr. *miainō*. Only here, Tit. 1. 15, 15. Heb. 12. 15. Jude 8.

eat the passover. At the close of this Preparation Day, the 14th Nisan, "at even". See Ap. 156, 165.

29 went out. Gr. *exerchomai*. All the texts add *exō*, outside.

accusation = charge. Gr. *katēgoria*. Cp. Eng. "category". against. Gr. *kata*. Ap. 104. x. 1.

30 malefactor = evildoer. Gr. *kakopoios*. Only here and 1 Pet. 2. 12, 14; 3. 16; 4. 15. Cp. Luke 23. 32. They expected Pilate to take their word for it, and condemn Him unheard. See Acts 25. 16.

31 Take ye Him = Take Him yourselves.

judge. Gr. *krinō*. Ap. 122. 1.

according to. Gr. *kata*. Ap. 104. x. 2.

It is not lawful. For violations of their law they seem to have had the power of stoning to death. See 8. 59; 10. 31. Acts 7. 59. But they feared the people, and so had determined to raise the plea of rebellion against Cæsar and throw the odium of the Lord's death upon Pilate.

not . . . any man. Gr. *ouk oudeis*. A double negative.

32 signifying, &c. See 12. 33.

should die = is about to die.

33 called. Gr. *phōneō*. See *v.* 27.

the King, &c. This shows the malicious charge the Jews had made.

34 of = from. Gr. *apo*. Ap. 104. iv.

others. Gr. *allos*. Ap. 124. 1.

35 hast Thou done? = didst Thou?

36 servants. Gr. *hupēretēs*. Same word as "officer", *v.* 3. now. Gr. *nun*, as in 17. 5.

37 Art Thou a king then? = Is it not then (Gr. *oukoun*. Occ. only here) that Thou art a king? or, So then a king Thou art?

To this end = To (Gr. *eis*. Ap. 104. vi) this, i. e. for this purpose.

for this cause. Exactly the same words, *eis touto*, as in previous clause. bear witness = testify. Gr. *martureō*. See on 1. 7. the truth. See on 14. 6, and p. 1511. My voice. See 8. 47; 10. 3, 4, 16, 27.

38 What is truth? The question of many a man. Pilate was not "jesting", as Lord Bacon says. He was doubtless sick of the various philosophies and religions which contended for acceptance. no. Gr. *oudeis*. fault. Gr. *aitia* (cp. *aiteō*, Ap. 134. I. 4), a charge, accusation; hence a ground of charge. **39** custom. Gr. *sunētheia*. Only here and in 1 Cor. 11. 16. at. Gr. *en*. Ap. 104. viii. will ye . . . ? = do ye wish . . . ? Gr. *boulomai*. Ap. 102. 2. Only occ. of this word in John. the King of the Jews. It was this taunt that led them to retort by the threat of *Læsa majestatis* (high treason) against Pilate himself (19. 12). **40** cried = cried aloud, shouted. Gr. *kraugazō*. Cp. 19. 6, 15. Acts 22. 23. this Man = this fellow. Cp. 7. 27; 9. 29. Barabbas. Aramaic. Ap. 94. III. 3. robber = bandit, highway robber. Gr. *lēstēs*. Cp. Mark 11. 17; 14. 48; 15. 27. Not *kleptēs*, thief. The two words together in 10. 1, 8. They chose the robber, and the robber has ruled over them to this day.

19. 1 Jesus. Ap. 98. X. scourged. Gr. *mastigoō*. Not the same word as in Matt. 27. 26. Mark 15. 15, which is *phragelloō*. Cp. 2. 15. A Florentine Papyrus of A.D. 85 contains the following addressed by a Prefect in Egypt to one Phibion: "Thou wast worthy of scourging . . . but I deliver thee to the people." Deissmann, *Light*, &c., p. 267.

A.D. 29 2 And the soldiers platted a crown °of °thorns,
and put *it* on His head, and they put on Him
a °purple robe,
3 And said, °"Hail, King of the Jews!" and
they °smote Him with their hands.
F H[3] 4 Pilate °therefore went °forth again, and
saith °unto them, °"Behold, I bring Him °forth
to you, °that ye may °know that I find °no
°fault °in Him."
5 °Then came [1] Jesus [4] forth, wearing the
°crown of thorns, and °the purple robe. And
Pilate saith [4] unto them, [4] "Behold the °Man!"
6 When the °chief priests therefore and
°officers °saw Him, they °cried out, saying,
°"Crucify *Him*, °crucify *Him*." Pilate saith
[4] unto them, °"Take ye Him, and °crucify *Him*:
for I find °no [4] fault [4] in Him."
7 The Jews answered him, "We have a law,
and °by °our law He °ought to die, because
He °made Himself the °Son of God."
J 8 When Pilate therefore heard that °saying,
he was °the more afraid;
9 And went again °into the °judgment hall,
and saith [4] unto [1] Jesus, °"Whence art Thou?"
But [1] Jesus gave him [6] no answer.
10 [5] Then saith Pilate [4] unto Him, "Speakest
Thou °not unto me? °knowest Thou °not
that I have °power to [6] crucify Thee, and have
°power to release Thee?"
11 [1] Jesus answered, "Thou couldest have
°no [10] power *at all* °against Me, °except it were
given thee °from above: °therefore °he that
°delivered Me [4] unto thee hath °the greater
sin."
H[4] 12 And °from thenceforth Pilate °sought to
release Him: but the Jews [6] cried out, saying,
°"If thou let this Man go, thou art [10] not
°Cæsar's friend: whosoever maketh himself
a king speaketh against °Cæsar."
13 °When Pilate therefore heard °that [8] saying, he brought [1] Jesus [4] forth, and sat down °in
the °judgment seat °in a place that is called
°the Pavement, but in the Hebrew, °Gab-
batha.
14 And it was °the preparation of the passover, and about °the sixth hour: and °he
saith [4] unto the Jews, [4] "Behold your King!"

2 of = out of. Gr. *ek*. Ap. 104. vii.
thorns. The sign of earth's curse (Gen. 3. 18).
purple. Gr. *porphureos*. The adj. occurs only here, *v.* 5, and Rev. 18. 16.
3 Hail. See on Matt. 27. 29.
smote Him, &c. = gave Him blows. See 18. 22.
4 therefore. All the texts omit.
forth = outside. Gr. *exō*. See 18. 29.
Behold. Gr. *ide*. Ap. 133. I. 3.
that = in order that. Gr. *hina*.
know. Gr. *ginōskō*. Ap. 132. I. ii.
no. Gr. *oudeis*.
fault. See 18. 38.
in. Gr. *en*. Ap. 104. viii. And yet he had scourged Him, illegally, hoping thereby to satiate the blood-thirst of the Jews.
5 Then = Therefore.
crown of thorns; lit. the thorny crown. Not the same expression as in *v.* 2.
the purple robe. To the horrible torture of the flagellum had been added the insults and cruelties of the soldiers. Cp. Isa. 50. 6.
Man. Gr. *anthrōpos*. Ap. 123. 1. Pilate hoped the pitiable spectacle would melt their hearts. It only whetted their appetite.
6 chief priests. These would, no doubt, include Caiaphas.
officers. See 18. 3. These temple guards are conspicuous for their zeal, due perhaps to the Lord's interference with the sellers of Matt. 21. 12-15.
saw. Gr. *eidon*. Ap. 133. I. 1.
cried out. See 18. 40.
Crucify. See Ap. 162. Omit "*Him*" in each case.
Take ye Him = Take Him yourselves.
no = not. Gr. *ou*. Ap. 105. I.
7 by = according to. Gr. *kata*. Ap. 104. x. 2.
our = the.
ought. Gr. *opheilō*. Elsewhere in John only in 13. 14.
made Himself, &c. This was the charge on which the Sanhedrin condemned Him. See Matt. 26. 65, 66. Cp. Lev. 24. 16.
Son of God. Ap. 98. XV.
8 saying. Gr. *logos*. See Mark 9. 32.
the more afraid. A dreadful presentiment was growing in Pilate's mind, due to what he may have heard of the Lord's miracles, to His bearing throughout the trial, and to his wife's message.
9 into. Gr. *eis*. Ap. 104. vi.
judgment hall. See 18. 28.
Whence art Thou? This was Pilate's fifth question of the Lord. See 18. 33, 35, 37, 38. It expressed the fear that was growing within him. Pilate may have been a freethinker (as some infer from 18. 38), but like freethinkers of all ages, he was not free from superstition. Was this Man, so different from all others he had ever seen, really a supernatural Being? **10 not.** Gr. *ou*. Ap. 105. 1. **knowest.** Gr. *oida*. Ap. 132. I. i. **power** = authority. Gr. *exousia*. Ap. 172. 5. **11 no . . . at all.** Gr. *ouk oudeis*. A double negative. **against.** Gr. *kata*. Ap. 104. x. 1. **except.** Gr. *ei mē* = if not. **from above.** Gr. *anōthen*. See on 3. 3. **therefore** = on account of (Gr. *dia*. Ap. 104. v. 2) this. **he that, &c.**: i.e. Caiaphas. Judas had delivered Him to the Sanhedrin, the Sanhedrin to Pilate. **delivered.** See on *v.* 30, "gave up". **the.** Omit "the". **12 from thenceforth** = on (Gr. *ek*. Ap. 104. vii) this. **sought** = was seeking. **If.** Ap. 118. 1. b. **Cæsar.** Gr. *Kaisar*. This title was adopted by the Roman emperors after Julius Cæsar. Frequently found in inscriptions. Deissmann, *Light*, &c., p. 383. Octavius added the title Augustus (Luke 2. 1) = Gr. *Sebastos* (Acts 25. 21, 25). **13 When Pilate, &c.** = Pilate therefore having heard. **that saying.** All the texts read "these words". **in** = upon. Gr. *epi*. Ap. 104. ix. 1. **judgment seat.** Gr. *bēma*: lit. a pace, a step, then a platform or raised place. In this case it was a stone platform with a seat in the open court in front of the Prætorium. Occ. only here in John. **in.** Gr. *eis*. Ap. 104. vi. **the Pavement.** Gr. *lithostrōtos* = strewn with stone: i.e. of mosaic or tesselated work. **Gabbatha.** Aramaic. Ap. 94. III. 3. The meaning of this word is uncertain.
14 the preparation: i.e. the day before the Passover was eaten "at even" on the 14th Nisan. All four Gospels state that our Lord was entombed on the Preparation Day (*vv.* 31, 42. Matt. 27. 62. Mark 15. 42. Luke 23. 54). See Ap. 165. **the sixth hour**: i.e. midnight. The hours in all the Gospels are according to Hebrew reckoning: i.e. from sunset to sunset. See Ap. 156, 165. Some have thought that the events from 13. 1 could not be crowded into so brief a space, but the Jews were in deadly earnest to get all finished before the Passover, and in such a case events move quickly. **he saith, &c.** In irony here, as in pity (*v.* 5). Some have thought that, in *v.* 13, "sat" should be "set Him". Justin Martyr says, "They set Him on the judgment-seat and said, 'Judge us'" (*First Apology*, xxxv). But out of forty-eight occurrences of the verb *kathizō*, only one other (Eph. 1. 20) is, without question, used transitively.

G 15 But they [6]cried out, °"Away with *Him*,
A.D. 29 °away with *Him*, [6]crucify Him." Pilate saith
[4]unto them, °"Shall I [6]crucify your King?"
The chief priests answered, °"We have [6]no
king °but [12]Cæsar."
16 Then °delivered he Him therefore [4]unto
them °to be [6]crucified. And they took [1]Jesus,
and led *Him* away.

B K 17 And He bearing His °cross went forth
[9]into a place called *the place* of a °skull, which
is called in the Hebrew °Golgotha:

L b 18 Where they [6]crucified Him, and °two
°other °with Him, °on either side one, °and
[1]Jesus in the midst.

c 19 °And Pilate °wrote a title, and put *it* °on
the [17]cross. And °the writing was, [1]JESUS °OF
NAZARETH THE KING OF THE JEWS.
20 This title [5]then read many of the Jews:
°for the place where [1]Jesus was [6]crucified was
°nigh to the city: and it was written in Hebrew,
and Greek, *and* Latin.
21 [5]Then said °the chief priests of the Jews to
Pilate, "Write °not, 'The King of the Jews;'
but that °He said, I am King of the Jews."
22 Pilate answered, °"What I have written
°I have written."

c 23 [5]Then °the soldiers, when they had [6]crucified
[1]Jesus, °took His garments, and made
four parts, to every °soldier a part; and also
His °coat: now the °coat was °without seam,
woven [12]from °the top °throughout.
24 They said therefore °among themselves,
"Let us [21]not rend it, but cast lots °for it,
whose it shall be:" [4]that °the scripture might
be fulfilled, which saith, **"They parted My
°raiment among them, and °for My vesture
they did cast lots.°"** These things therefore
the [23]soldiers did.

b 25 °Now there °stood °by the [17]cross of
[1]Jesus His mother, and His mother's sister,
°Mary the *wife* of Cleophas, and °Mary Magdalene.
26 °When [1]Jesus therefore [6]saw His mother,
and the disciple standing by, whom He °loved,
He saith [4]unto His mother, °"Woman, °behold
thy °son!"
27 Then saith He to the disciple, [26]"Behold
thy mother!" And °from that hour that disciple
took her °unto his own *home*.

L d 28 °After this, [1]Jesus, [10]knowing that all

15 Away with. Gr. *airō*. First occ. in John 1. 29. The imperative *aron* is used in exactly the same way in a Papyrus from Oxyrhynchus, in a letter from a boy to his father. Deissmann, *Light*, p. 187.

Shall I . . . ? = Is it your King I am to crucify?

We have, &c. This was their final and deliberate rejection of their King, and the practical surrender of all their Messianic hopes. Cp. 1 Sam. 8. 7.

but. Same as "except" in *v.* 11.

16 delivered, &c.: i.e. to their will (Luke 23. 25). Thus the Lord's execution was in Jewish hands (Acts 2. 23). The centurion and his quaternion of soldiers merely carried out the decision of the chief priests, Pilate having pronounced no sentence, but washed his hands, literally as well as metaphorically, of the matter.

to be = in order that (Gr. *hina*) He might be.

19. 17-30 (*B*, p. 1564). **CRUCIFIXION.**
(*Introversion.*)

B | K | 17. Delivered to death.
  | L | b | 18. Fellow-sufferers.
  | | c | 19-22. Discussion. Pilate and the Jews.
  | | c | 23, 24. Discussion. The soldiers.
  | | b | 25-27. Fellow-sufferers.
  | L | d | 28. Saying. "I thirst."
  | | e | 29. Vinegar. Given.
  | | e | 30-. Vinegar. Received.
  | | d | -30-. Saying. "It is finished."
  | K | -30. Death.

17 cross. Gr. *stauros*. See Ap. 162.

skull. Gr. *kranion*. See Matt. 27. 33.

Golgotha. Aramaic. Ap. 94. III. 3.

18 two other = other two. Ap. 164.

other. Gr. *allos*. Ap. 124. 1.

with. Gr. *meta*. Ap. 104. xi. 1.

on either side one. Gr. *enteuthen kai enteuthen*: lit. hither and thither, i.e. on this side and on that side. This was before the parting of the garments (*v.* 23). See Ap. 164.

and, &c.: lit. and the middle one, Jesus.

19 And = Moreover.

wrote. John alone mentions that Pilate wrote it himself. See Ap. 163. **on.** Gr. *epi*. Ap. 104. ix. 1.

the writing was = it was written.

OF NAZARETH = the Nazarene. See 18. 5.

20 for = because. Gr. *hoti*.

nigh. Probably just outside the north wall, between the Damascus Gate and Herod's Gate, and near the so-called grotto of Jeremiah, about half a mile from the Prætorium. See Conder's *Jerusalem*, p. 151, &c., and Palestine Exploration Society's maps.

21 the chief priests of the Jews. This expression occurs only here. They were no longer God's priests.

not. Gr. *mē*. Ap. 105. II.

He = that fellow. Gr. *ekeinos*. Spoken with contempt.

22 What, &c. Fig. *Amphibologia*. Ap. 6.

I have written. It therefore stands written for ever. Caiaphas as representative of the Jews proclaimed the Lord as Saviour for the world, Pilate fastens upon the Jews the hated name of the Nazarene as their King.

23 the soldiers. These were probably slaves attached to the legion who were employed as executioners. **took** = received. The garments were their perquisite. **coat.** Gr. *chitōn*. A tunic worn next the body, and reaching to the knees. **without seam.** Gr. *arraphos*. Occurs only here. Josephus says one of the high priest's garments was without seam. **the top** = the parts above (Gr. *ta anōthen*). Cp. Matt. 27. 51. Mark 15. 38. **throughout** = through (Gr. *dia*. Ap. 104. v. 1) the whole. **24 among themselves** = to (Gr. *pros*. Ap. 104. xv. 3) one another. **for** = concerning. Gr. *peri*. Ap. 104. xiii. 1. **the scripture, &c.** See 13. 18; 17. 12; 18. 9, 32. The quotation is from Ps. 22. 18. **raiment.** Same word as "garments" in *v.* 23. **for** = upon. Gr. *epi*. Ap. 104. ix. 3. **These things, &c.** = The soldiers therefore indeed did these things. The Gr. particle *men* is ignored both by A.V. and by R.V. It marks a contrast with what follows. **25 Now** = But. **stood** = were standing. **by** = beside. Gr. *para*. Ap. 104. xii. 2. **Mary.** See Ap. 100. John omits the name of his own mother Salome, who was there also (Matt. 27. 56). **26 When, &c.** Read, "Jesus therefore, seeing". **loved.** Gr. *agapaō*. Ap. 135. I. 1. **Woman.** See on 2. 4. **behold.** Gr *idou*. Ap. 133. I. 2; but the texts read *ide*. Ap. 133. I. 3. **son.** Gr. *huios*. Ap. 108. iii. Joseph being evidently dead, and her firstborn son (Matt. 1. 25) dying, there would be no support for Mary. In view of 7. 3-5, it was a befitting arrangement. **27 from.** Gr. *apo*. Ap. 104. iv. **unto his own.** Gr. *eis* (Ap. 104. vi) *ta idia*. This expression occurs in 1. 11; 16. 32. Acts 21. 6. A different phrase in 20. 10. **28 After.** Gr. *meta*. Ap. 104. xi. 2.

A. D. 29 things °were now accomplished, [4]that [24]the scripture might be fulfilled, saith, "I thirst."

e **29** °Now there was set a vessel full of °vinegar: and they filled a spunge with vinegar, and put *it* upon hyssop, and put *it* to His mouth.

e **30** When [1]Jesus therefore °had received the vinegar,

d He said, °"It is finished:"

K and He °bowed His head, and °gave up the °ghost.

A² M **31** The Jews therefore, because it was the [14]preparation, [4]that the bodies should [21]not °remain °upon the [17]cross °on the sabbath day, (for that sabbath day was °an high day,) °besought Pilate [4]that their °legs might be °broken, and *that* they might be °taken away.

N **32** [5]Then came the [23]soldiers, and [31]brake the [31]legs of °the first, and of the [18]other which was °crucified with him.

33 But when they came °to [1]Jesus, and [6]saw that He was dead already, they [31]brake [10]not His [31]legs:

34 But one of the [23]soldiers with a spear °pierced His °side, and °forthwith came there out °blood and water.

35 And he that °saw *it* °bare record, and his °record is °true: and he [10]knoweth that he saith °true, [4]that ye might °believe.

36 For these things were done, [4]that [24]the scripture should be fulfilled, °**"A bone of Him shall [10]not be °broken."**

37 And again °another scripture °saith, **"They shall °look °on Him whom they °pierced."**

M **38** And [28]after °this Joseph °of °Arimathæa, being °a disciple of [1]Jesus, °but secretly °for fear of the Jews, [31]besought Pilate [4]that he might °take away the body of [1]Jesus: and Pilate °gave *him* leave. He came therefore, and °took the body of [1]Jesus.

39 And there came °also °Nicodemus, which at the first came to [1]Jesus °by night, °and brought °a mixture of °myrrh and °aloes, about an hundred °pound *weight.*

were now accomplished = have been already finished. Gr. *teleō*. Not the same word as "fulfilled", which is *teleioō* = consummated. There is a deep significance here. He saw the casting of the lots, and knew that all that the Scripture had foretold of others was finished. There yet remained a prediction for Him to realize, that of Ps. 69. 21. See note on Ps. 69. 1.

29 Now. All the texts omit. **vinegar.** See note [on Matt. 27. 34.

30 had received = received.

It is finished. Gr. *teleō*, as in *v.* 28. Ps. 22 ends with the word "done". Of the seven sayings from the Cross, Matthew (27. 46) and Mark (15. 34) record one (Psalm 22. 1); Luke three (23. 34, 43, 46); and John three (*vv.* 26, 27, 28, 30). It is clear from Luke 23. 44 that the promise to the malefactor was before the darkness. The words of Ps. 22. 1 were uttered at the beginning or during the course of the three hours' darkness. Probably the Lord repeated the whole of Ps. 22, which not only sets Him forth as the Sufferer, but also foretells the glory that is to follow. Perhaps other Scriptures also, as a terrible witness against the chief priests, who were present (Mark 15. 31. Luke 23. 35), and must have heard.

bowed. This suggests that till then He had kept His head erect. He now lays down His life, as He said (10. 18).

gave up. Gr. *paradidōmi*. This word occurs fifteen times in John; transl. nine times "betray", of Judas; five times "deliver", of the chief priests and Pilate.

ghost. Gr. *pneuma*. Ap. 101. II. 6. Matthew says, *aphēke to pneuma*, sent forth His spirit (27. 50); Mark (15. 37) and Luke (23. 46) say, *exepneuse*, breathed out, i. e. drew His last breath. Cp. Gen. 2. 7. Pss. 104. 29, 30; 146. 4. Ecc. 12. 7.

19. 31-42 (A², p. 1564). **BURIAL.** (*Alternation.*)

A² | M | 31. Removal of bodies proposed.
N | 32-37. Bodies dishonoured.
M | 38, 39. Removal of *the* Body effected.
N | 40-42. The Body honoured.

31 remain. Gr. *menō*. See p. 1511. Cp. Deut. 21. 23.
upon. Gr. *epi*. Ap. 104. ix. 1.
on. Gr. *en*. Ap. 104. viii.
an high day. It was the first day of the Feast, the 15th Nisan. See Lev. 23. 6, 7. Our Wednesday sunset to Thursday sunset. See Ap. 156, 165.
besought. Gr. *erōtaō*. Ap. 134. I. 3.
legs. Gr. *skelos*. From the hip downwards. Occ. only in these three verses.
broken. Gr. *katagnumi* = broken in pieces, shattered. Occurs only in these verses and in Matt. 12. 20.
taken away. Same word as in *v.* 15.

32 the first, &c. See Ap. 164. **crucified with.** Gr. *sustauroō*. Only here, Matt. 27. 44. Mark 15. 32. Rom. 6. 6. Gal. 2. 20. **33 to.** Gr. *epi*. Ap. 104. ix. 3. **34 pierced.** Gr. *nussō*. Occurs only here. **side.** Gr. *pleura*. Only here; 20. 20, 25, 27. Acts 12. 7. **forthwith** = immediately. Gr. *euthus*. **blood and water.** The question of the physical cause of the Lord's death has been much discussed; but we need not seek a natural explanation of what John records as a miraculous sign. The blood and water may have been symbolical of the sprinkling with blood and cleansing with water of the Old Covenant. See Heb. 9. 12-14, 19-22. 1 John 5. 6, 8. **35 saw.** Gr. *horaō*. Ap. 133. I. 8. **bare record.** Gr. *martureō*. **record.** Gr. *marturia*. Both these are characteristic words in this Gospel. See note on 1. 7, and p. 1511. **true** = reliable, genuine. See Ap. 175. 2 and p. 1511. **true** = true to fact. See Ap. 175. 1 and p. 1511. **believe.** Ap. 150. I. 1. i. **36 A bone, &c.** This has reference to Ex. 12. 46. Num. 9. 12. Thus in all things He was the antitype of the Passover lamb. **broken.** Gr. *suntribō*. Not the same word as in *vv.* 31, 32. Cp. Ps. 34. 20. **37 another.** Gr. *heteros*. Ap. 124. 2. **saith.** Note the careful discrimination in the words used. The former Scripture was fulfilled, i. e. filled full. This is not fulfilled, but in order to its fulfilment it was necessary that He should be pierced. See Zech. 12. 10. It was fulfilled in the case of those who looked upon Him, but waits for its complete fulfilment when the spirit of grace and supplication is poured out on repentant Israel. **look.** Gr. *opsomai*. Ap. 133. I. 8. a. **on.** Gr. *eis*. Ap. 104. vi. **pierced.** Gr. *ekkenteō*. Only here and Rev. 1. 7 = pierced through. Includes therefore the piercing of the hands and feet. Cp. Ps. 22. 16. **38 this** = these things. **of** = from. Gr. *apo*. Ap. 104. iv. **Arimathæa.** Probably Ramah, where Samuel was born. 1 Sam. 1. 1, 19. Called in the Sept. Armathaim. **a disciple . . . but secretly.** Matthew calls him "a rich man" (27. 57); Mark, "an honourable counsellor" (15. 43); Luke, "a good man and a just" (23. 50). See on 18. 16. **for** = because of. Gr. *dia*. Ap. 104. v. 2. **take away . . . took.** Gr. *airō*. Same word as in *vv.* 15, 31. **gave him leave.** Gr. *epitrepō*. Generally transl. "suffer". Matt. 8. 21, &c. Cp. Acts 21. 39, 40. **39 also Nicodemus.** Read, Nicodemus also. **Nicodemus.** See 3. 1, and 7. 50. **to.** Gr. *pros*. Ap. 104. xv. 3. **by night.** Now he comes openly, as Joseph did. **and brought** = bringing. **a mixture.** Gr. *migma*. Occ. only here. Some read *heligma* = a roll. **myrrh.** Gr. *smurna*. Only here and in Matt. 2. 11. **aloes.** a fragrant aromatic wood. Occurs only here in N.T. Referred to four times in O.T. **pound.** Gr. *litra*. See 12. 3 and Ap. 51. II. 4 (3).

N A.D. 29
40 [5] Then took they the body of [1] Jesus, and
° wound it in ° linen clothes [18] with the spices,
as the manner of the Jews is to ° bury.
41 Now [4] in the place where He was [6] crucified
there was a ° garden; and [4] in the ° garden a
° new ° sepulchre, ° wherein was ° never man
yet laid.
42 ° There laid they [1] Jesus therefore ° because
of the Jews' [14] preparation *day;* for the [41] sepulchre was nigh at hand.

A³ O¹ P 18th day of Nisan
20 ° The first *day* of the week cometh
° Mary Magdalene ° early, when it was
yet dark, ° unto the ° sepulchre, and seeth the
stone ° taken away ° from the ° sepulchre.
2 ° Then she runneth, and cometh ° to Simon
Peter, and ° to the ° other disciple, whom ° Jesus
° loved, and saith ° unto them, "They ° have
[1] taken away ° the Lord ° out of the [1] sepulchre,
and we ° know ° not where they ° have laid
Him."

Q
3 Peter therefore went forth, and that [2] other
disciple, and ° came ° to the [1] sepulchre.
4 So they ° ran both together: and the [2] other
disciple ° did outrun Peter, and came first [3] to
the [1] sepulchre.
5 And he ° stooping down, *and looking in,*
° saw the ° linen clothes lying; ° yet went he
[2] not in.
6 [2] Then cometh Simon Peter following him,
and went ° into the [1] sepulchre, and ° seeth the
[5] linen clothes ° lie,
7 And the ° napkin, that was ° about His head,
[2] not lying ° with the [5] linen clothes, but
° wrapped together ° in ° a place by itself.
8 Then went in ° also that [2] other disciple,
° which came first [3] to the [1] sepulchre, and he
° saw, and ° believed.
9 For ° as yet they [2] knew ° not ° the scripture,
that He ° must ° rise again ° from the dead.
10 [2] Then the disciples went away again ° unto
° their own home.

40 wound. Gr. *deō.* Generally transl. "bind". See 11. 44; 18. 12, 24. The other evangelists use a different word.

linen clothes=linen cloths or bandages. The rolls used for swathing the bodies of the rich (Isa. 53. 9). The Rabbis say criminals were wrapped in old rags.

bury=entomb. Gr. *entaphiazō.* Only here and Matt. 26. 12. The noun *entaphiasmos* occurs in 12. 7 and Mark 14. 8.

41 garden. Gr. *kēpos.* See 18. 1.

new. Gr. *kainos.* See on Matt. 9. 17.

sepulchre=tomb. Gr. *mnēmeion.* Before this in John transl. "grave", 5. 28; 11. 17, 31, 38; 12. 17.

wherein=in (Gr. *en.* Ap. 104. viii) which.

never man yet=not yet any one. Gr. *oudepō oudeis.*

42 There laid they Jesus. Here the body (*v.* 38) is called "Jesus". Cp. 20. 2.

because of=on account of. Gr. *dia.* Ap. 104. v. 2.

20. 1-31 (A³, p. 1564). RESURRECTION.
(*Division.*)

A³ | O¹ | 20. 1-18. Events. Morning.
   | O² | 20. 19-31. Events. Evening.

20. 1-18 (O¹, above). EVENTS. MORNING.
(*Introversion.*)

O¹ | P | 1, 2. Report of Mary.
   | Q | 3-10. Peter and John.
   | *P* | 11-17. Mary alone.
   | *Q* | 18. Report of Mary.

20. 1 The first day of the week=On the first (day) of the Sabbaths (pl.). Gr. *Tē miā tōn sabbatōn.* The word "day" is rightly supplied, as *mia* is feminine, and so must agree with a feminine noun understood, while *sabbatōn* is neuter. Luke 24. 1 has the same. Matthew reads, "towards dawn on the first (day) of the Sabbaths", and Mark (16. 2), "very early on the first (day) of the Sabbaths". The expression is not a Hebraism, and "Sabbaths" should not be rendered "week", as in A.V. and R.V. A reference to Lev. 23. 15-17 shows that this "first day" is the first of the days for reckoning the seven Sabbaths to Pentecost. On this day, therefore, the Lord became the firstfruits (*vv.* 10, 11) of God's resurrection harvest (1 Cor. 15. 23).

Mary. See Ap. 100.

early: i.e. about the ninth or tenth hour (3 to 4 a.m.). See Ap. 165.

unto. Gr. *eis.* Ap. 104. vi.

sepulchre. See 19. 41.

taken away=having been taken away. Gr. *airō.* See 19. 15. **from.** Gr. *ek.* Ap. 104. vii. **2 Then**=Therefore. **to.** Gr. *pros.* Ap. 104. xv. 3. **other.** Gr. *allos.* Ap. 124. 1. **Jesus.** Ap. 98. X. **loved**=used to love (imperf.). Gr. *phileō.* Ap. 135. I. 2. **unto**=to. **have taken**=took. **the Lord.** Gr. *kurios.* Ap. 98. VI. i. *a.* 3. A. **out of.** Gr. *ek.* Ap. 104. vii. **know.** Gr. *oida.* Ap. 132. I. i. **not.** Gr. *ou.* Ap. 105. I. **have laid**=laid. Same word as in 11. 34. Implying care and reverence, and so suggesting that Joseph and Nicodemus had removed Him. **3 came**=were coming. **to**=unto. Gr. *eis.* Ap. 104. vi. **4 ran**=were running. **did outrun**=ran ahead, more quickly than. This affords no ground for the assumption by so many commentators, even Alford, that John was younger than Peter. **5 stooping down.** Gr. *parakuptō.* The word implies bending down to see more clearly. Cp. the other occ.: *v.* 11. Luke 24. 12. James 1. 25. 1 Pet. 1. 12. **saw.** Gr. *blepō.* Ap. 133. I. 5. **linen clothes.** See 19. 40. **yet went he**=however he went. **6 into.** Gr. *eis.* Ap. 104. vi. **seeth**=intently beholdeth. Gr. *theōreō.* Ap. 133. I. 11. **lie**=lying. **7 napkin.** See 11. 44. **about**=upon. Gr. *epi.* Ap. 104. ix. 1. **with.** Gr. *meta.* Ap. 104. xi. 1. **wrapped together**=rolled, or coiled round and round. Gr. *entulissō.* Used elsewhere, only in Matt. 27. 59. Luke 23. 53, of the linen cloth. Here it implies that the cloth had been folded round the head as a turban is folded, and that it lay still in the form of a turban. The linen clothes also lay exactly as they were when swathed round the body. The Lord had passed out of them, not needing, as Lazarus (11. 44), to be loosed. It was this sight that convinced John (*v.* 8). **in**=into. Gr. *eis.* Ap. 104. vi. **a place by itself**=one place apart. **8 also, &c.**=that other disciple also. **which**=who. **saw.** Gr. *eidon.* Ap. 133. I. 1. **believed** (Ap. 150. I. 1. i): i.e. believed that He was risen. All that He had said about rising again the third day had fallen upon dull ears. The chief priests had taken note of His words (Matt. 27. 63), but the disciples had not. **9 as yet . . . not**=not yet. Gr. *oudepō,* as in 19. 41. **the scripture.** Cp. Ps. 16. 10, 11, &c. **must.** Cp. 3. 14; 12. 34. **rise again.** Gr. *anistēmi.* Ap. 178. I. 1. **from the dead.** Gr. *ek nekrōn.* Ap. 139. 3. **10 unto.** Gr. *pros.* Ap. 104. xv. 3. **their own home**=their lodging. Not the same words as in 19. 27. Galilean fishermen, constantly moving about with their Rabbi since the Feast of Tabernacles, six months before, could have had no settled home, as we understand it, in Jerusalem. They had not been there since their Master left it (see 10. 40), till the last few days.

P 11 But [1] Mary stood without °at the [1] sepulchre
A.D. 29 °weeping: °and as she wept, she [5] stooped down,
and looked [6] into the [1] sepulchre,
12 And [6] seeth °two angels °in white °sitting,
the one °at the head, and the other °at the feet,
where the body of [2] Jesus had lain.
13 And they say [2] unto her, °"Woman, why
[11] weepest thou?" She saith [2] unto them, "Because they °have [1] taken away my °Lord, and
I [2] know [2] not where they °have laid Him."
14 And °when she had thus said, she °turned
herself °back, and [6] saw [2] Jesus standing, and
[2] knew [2] not that it was [2] Jesus.
15 [2] Jesus saith [2] unto her, [13] "Woman, why
[11] weepest thou? whom seekest thou?" She,
supposing Him to be the °gardener, saith [2] unto
Him, °"Sir, °if Thou °have borne Him hence,
tell me where Thou °hast laid Him, and I will
[1] take Him away."
16 [2] Jesus saith [2] unto her, [1] "Mary." She
turned herself, and saith [2] unto Him, °"Rabboni;" which is to say, °"Master."
17 [2] Jesus saith [2] unto her, °"Touch Me °not;
°for I am °not yet ascended [2] to °My Father:
but go [2] to °My brethren, and say [2] unto them,
'I °ascend [10] unto °My Father, and °your
Father; and *to* My °God, and your °God.'"

Q 18 Mary Magdalene °came °and told the disciples that she had °seen [2] the Lord, and *that*
He had spoken these things [2] unto her.

O^2 R f 19 [2] Then the same day at evening, being [1] the
first *day* of the week, when the doors were
shut °where the disciples were °assembled °for
fear of the Jews, came [2] Jesus and stood [7] in
the midst, and saith [2] unto them, °"Peace *be*
[2] unto you."

g 20 And when He had so said, He shewed
[2] unto them *His* °hands and His °side. [2] Then
°were the disciples °glad, when they [8] saw
[2] the Lord.

f 21 [2] Then said [2] Jesus to them again, [19] "Peace
be [2] unto you: as °*My* Father hath °sent Me,
°even so °send I you."

g 22 And when He had said this, He °breathed
on *them*, and saith [2] unto them, "Receive ye
°the Holy Ghost:

11 at. Gr. *pros*. Ap. 104. xv. 3.
weeping. Gr. *klaiō*. See on 11. 33.
and = therefore.
12 two angels. Probably Michael and Gabriel. Cp. Dan. 9. 21; 10. 21; 12. 1. Luke 1. 19, 26. The supreme importance of the Lord's resurrection in the Divine counsels demanded the presence of the highest angels.
in. Gr. *en*. Ap. 104. viii.
sitting: i.e. at either end of the rock-cut ledge whereon the Lord had been laid (as the cherubim at either end of the mercy-seat, Ex. 25. 19). They *sit* in the empty tomb who *stand* in the presence of God (Luke 1. 19. Rev. 8. 2). **at.** Gr. *pros*. Ap. 104. xv. 2.
13 Woman. See on 2. 4. **have taken** = took.
Lord. Ap. 98. VI. i. *a*. 3. A. **have laid** = laid.
14 when, &c. = having said these things.
turned . . . back: i. e. turned half round.
back. Gr. *eis* (Ap. 104. vi) *ta opisō*.
15 gardener. Gr. *kēpouros*. Occurs only here.
Sir. Gr. *kurios*. Ap. 98. VI. 1. *a*. 3. B. b.
if. Ap. 118. 2. a. **have borne** = didst bear.
hast laid = didst lay.
16 Rabboni. Ap. 98. XIV. viii. Most of the texts add, before Rabboni, "in Hebrew".
Master. Gr. *didaskalos*. Ap. 98. XIV. v. 1. Cp. 13. 13.
17 Touch Me not = Do not be holding Me. Gr. *haptō*. Only here in John; elsewhere, thirty-nine times. See Matt. 8. 3, 15; 9. 20, 21, 29.
not. Gr. *mē*. Ap. 105. II.
for. This gives the reason for the prohibition. He afterwards allowed the women to hold Him by the feet (Matt. 28. 9). On this day, the morrow after the Sabbath, the high priest would be waving the sheaf of the firstfruits before the Lord (Lev. 23. 10, 11); while He, the firstfruits from the dead (1 Cor. 15. 23), would be fulfilling the type by presenting Himself before the Father.
not yet. Gr. *oupō*; compound of *ou*. Ap. 105. I.
My Father. See on 2. 16.
My brethren. Cp. Matt. 12. 50; 28. 10. Heb. 2. 11.
ascend = am ascending.
My . . . your. This marks the essential difference in His and their relationship with the Father. But because God is the God and Father of our Lord (Eph. 1. 3) He is therefore our God and Father too.
God. Gr. *Theos*. Ap. 98. I. i. 1.
18 came = cometh.
and told = telling. Gr. *apangellō*. See 4. 51. Matt. 2. 8. Cp. Ap. 121. 5. 6. **seen.** Gr. *horaō*. Ap. 133. I. 8.

20. 19-31 (O^2, p. 1570). EVENTS. EVENING.
(Alternation.)

O^2 | R | 19-23. Appearance to the Ten.
  S | 24, 25. Belief that rests on sight.
 R | 26-29. Appearance to the Eleven.
  S | 30, 31. Belief that rests on the Word.

20. 19-23 (R, above). APPEARANCE, ETC. *(Alternation.)*

R | f | 19. Peace.
  g | 20. Gladness.
 f | 21. Peace.
  g | 22, 23. Power.

19 where. Probably the upper room. See Mark 14. 15. Luke 22. 12. Acts 1. 13. **assembled.** All the texts omit. **for** = on account of. Gr. *dia*. Ap. 104. v. 2. **Peace.** Cp. 14. 27; 16. 33. **20 hands . . . side.** Luke says hands and feet. All three were pierced. See on 19. 37. **side.** See 19. 34. **were . . . glad** = rejoiced. **21 My Father** = The Father. See 1. 14. **sent.** Gr. *apostellō*. Ap. 174. 1. **even so** = I also. **send.** Gr. *pempō*. Ap. 174. 4. Note the distinction. The Father sent the Son alone, but the Son sends His disciples with an "escort" or guard, i. e. the Holy Spirit. This is to emphasize the fact that the Lord remains (by the Spirit) with those whom He sends. **22 breathed on.** Gr. *emphusaō*. Only here in N.T., but used in the Sept. in Gen. 2. 7 for the Heb. word *nāphah*, to breathe, or blow with force. The same Lord who, as Jehovah Elohim, breathed into Adam's nostrils the breath of life so that he became a living soul, here breathes upon the apostles that they may receive Divine power. Satan tries to parody the Lord's words and works. In the "Great" Magical Papyrus of about the third century A.D. occurs the following in a spell for driving out a demon: "When thou adjurest, blow (*phusa*), sending the breath from above [to the feet], and from the feet to the face". Deissmann, *Fresh Light*, p. 260. **the Holy Ghost.** Gr. *pneuma hagion* (no art.): i.e. power from on high. See Ap. 101. II. 14. The Firstfruits of the resurrection here bestows the firstfruits of the Spirit, not only on the apostles, but on "them that were with them" (Luke 24. 33, and cp. Acts 1. 14; 2. 1).

A.D. 29 23 Whose soever °sins ye °remit, they are remitted [2]unto them; *and* whose soever *sins* ye retain, they are retained."

S 24 But °Thomas, one °of the twelve, called Didymus, was [2]not [7]with them when [2]Jesus came.

25 The [2]other disciples therefore said [2]unto him, "We have [18]seen [2]the Lord." But he said [2]unto them, °"Except I shall [8]see [12]in His hands the °print of the nails, and °put my finger [6]into the °print of the nails, and °thrust my hand [6]into His [20]side, I will °not [8]believe."

R 26 And °after eight days again His disciples were within, and Thomas [7]with them: *then* came [2]Jesus, °the doors being shut, and stood [7]in the midst, and said, [19]"Peace *be* [2]unto you."

27 Then saith He to Thomas, °"Reach hither thy finger, and °behold My hands; and °reach hither thy hand, and [25]thrust *it* [6]into My [20]side: and °be [17]not °faithless, but °believing."

28 And Thomas answered and said [2]unto Him, °"My [2]Lord and my [17]God."

29 [2]Jesus saith [2]unto him, °"Thomas, because thou hast [18]seen Me, thou hast [8]believed: blessed *are* they °that have [17]not [8]seen, and *yet* have [8]believed."

S 30 °And many other °signs truly did [2]Jesus °in the presence of His disciples, °which are [2]not written [12]in this book:

31 But °these °are written, °that ye °might °believe that [2]Jesus is the °Christ, the °Son of [17]God; and °that [8]believing ye °might have °life °through His °name.

A T1 **21** °After these things °Jesus °shewed Himself again to the disciples °at the sea of Tiberias; and °on this wise °shewed He *Himself*.

U V1 X 2 There were together Simon Peter, and

23 sins. Ap. 128. I. ii. 1.
remit. Gr. *aphiēmi*. Always transl. elsewhere "forgive", when sins or debts are referred to. This authority bestowed upon the apostles and others continued in force with other "gifts" till Acts 28, which records the final rejection of the Kingdom. To suppose that the "Church" of Eph. 1 has any share in them is not rightly to divide the Word of Truth, but to introduce perplexity and confusion. See Mark 16. 17 and Ap. 167.
24 Thomas. The third mention of him in John. See 11. 16; 14. 5.
of=out of. Gr. *ek*. Ap. 104. vii.
25 Except=If . . . not. Gr. *ean mē*. Ap. 118. 1. b, and 105. II.
print. Gr. *tupos*, type. Elsewhere transl. figure, fashion, example, &c.
put. Gr. *ballō*, generally transl. "cast". See 15. 6; 19. 24.
thrust. Gr. *ballō*, as above.
not=by no means. Gr. *ou mē*. Ap. 105. III.
26 after eight days: i.e. a week later, on the day following the second Sabbath of the seven in the reckoning to Pentecost.
after. Gr. *meta*. Ap. 104. xi. 2.
the doors being shut. This shows that the Lord had now the spiritual body, *sōma pneumatikon*, of 1 Cor. 15. 44.
27 Reach hither=Bring here.
behold. Gr. *ide*. Ap. 133. I. 3.
be=become.
faithless. Gr. *apistos*=unbelieving.
believing. Ap. 150. III.
28 My Lord and my God. First testimony to the Deity of the risen Lord. Possibly Thomas was using the words of Ps. 86. 15, which in the Sept. read *Kurie ho Theos*, and claiming forgiveness for his unbelief on the ground of Ex. 34. 6, to which this verse of the Psalm refers.
29 Thomas. All the texts omit.
that, &c.=who saw not and believed. See 4. 48. Matt. 16. 1. 1 Cor. 1. 22. Those who crave for miracles and signs to-day will have them, but they will be Satan's miracles.
30 And many, &c. Therefore many and other (Ap. 124. 1).
signs. See p. 1511 and Ap. 176. 3. These were always in relation to and in proof of His Messiahship.
in the presence of=in the sight of. Gr. *enōpion*. **which are not written.** Here was the opportunity for the writers of the Apocryphal Gospels, &c., of which they were not slow to avail themselves. **31 these.** Emphatic. **are written**=have been (and therefore stand) written. **that**=in order that. Gr. *hina*. **might**=may. **believe.** Ap. 150. I. 1. iii. **Christ.** Ap. 98. IX. **Son of God.** Ap. 98. XV. **life.** Ap. 170. 1. **through**=in. Gr. *en*. Ap. 104. viii. **name.** Cp. 1. 12. Acts 3. 6; 4. 10, 12; 10. 43. 1 Cor. 6. 11. 1 John 5. 13.

21. 1-25 (*A*, p. 1510). THE SUCCESSORS. (*Alternation.*)

A | T1 | 1. Manifestation of the Lord.
| U | 2–13. Miracle.
| T2 | 14. Manifestation of the Lord.
| *U* | 15–23. Ministry.
| T3 | 24, 25. Witness to the Lord.

1 After these things. A note of time frequent in John. See 3. 22; 5. 1, 14; 6. 1; 7. 1; 13. 7; 19. 38. **After.** Gr. *meta*. Ap. 104. xi. 2. **Jesus.** Ap. 98. X. **shewed**=manifested. Gr. *phaneroō*. Ap. 106. I. v; not merely presented Himself, but revealed His power and glory. See 2. 11. Not the same word as 14. 21, 22, which is *emphanizō*. Ap. 106. I. iv. **at**=upon. Gr. *epi*. Ap. 104. ix. 1. **on this wise**=thus.

21. 2-13 (U, above). MIRACLE. (*Division.*)

U | V1 | 2–6. Appearance of the Lord. Unknown.
| V2 | 7–13. Appearance of the Lord. Known.

21. 2-6 (V1, above). APPEARANCE, &c. (*Alternation and Introversion.*)

V1 | X | 2. Disciples. Alone.
| Y | h | 3–. Fishing.
| | i | –3. Failure. "Nothing."
| *X* | 4. Disciples. The Lord present.
| *Y* | *i* | 5. Failure. "No meat."
| | *h* | 6. Fishing.

A. D. 29 Thomas called Didymus, and Nathanael °of Cana in Galilee, and the *sons* of Zebedee, and two °other °of His disciples.

Y h 3 Simon Peter saith °unto them, °"I go a fishing." They say °unto him "We also go °with thee." They went forth, and entered °into °a ship °immediately;

i and °that night they °caught °nothing.

X 4 But when the morning was °now come, [1]Jesus stood °on the shore: but the disciples °knew °not that it was [1]Jesus.

Y i 5 °Then [1]Jesus saith [3]unto them, °"Children, have ye any °meat?" They answered Him, °"No."

h 6 And He said [3]unto them, °"Cast the °net [4]on the right side of the ship, and ye shall find." They °cast therefore, and °now they were not able to °draw it °for the multitude of fishes.

V² Z k 7 Therefore that disciple whom [1]Jesus °loved saith [3]unto Peter, "It is °the Lord." °Now when Simon Peter °heard that it was °the Lord, he °girt °*his* fisher's coat *unto him*, (for he was °naked,) and did cast himself [3]into the sea.

l 8 And the [2]other disciples came in °a little ship; (for they were [4]not far °from °land, but as it were °two hundred cubits,) °dragging °the [6]net with fishes.

A 9 As soon [5]then as they °were come °to [8]land, they °saw a °fire of coals there, and °fish laid thereon, and °bread.

Z l 10 [1]Jesus saith [3]unto them, "Bring [2-]of °the fish which ye have now [3]caught."

11 Simon Peter °went up, and [6]drew the [6]net °to [8]land full of great fishes, an hundred and fifty and three: and for all there were so many, yet was [4]not the [6]net broken.

k 12 [1]Jesus saith [3]unto them, "Come *and* °dine." And °none of the disciples °durst °ask Him, "Who art Thou?" [4]knowing that it was the Lord.

A 13 [1]Jesus °then cometh, and taketh °bread, and giveth them, and °fish likewise.

T² 14 This is °now the third time that [1]Jesus [1]shewed Himself to °His disciples, after that He was °risen °from the dead.

---

2 of = from. Gr. *apo*. Ap. 104. iv.
other. Gr. *allos*. Ap. 124. 1.
of = out of. Gr. *ek*. Ap. 104. vii.
3 unto = to.
I go a fishing = I go forth to fish.
with. Gr. *sun*. Ap. 104. xvi.
into. Gr. *eis*. Ap. 104. vi.
a = the; probably that of Matt. 4. 21, belonging to Zebedee and his sons.
immediately. All the texts omit.
that night = in (Gr. *en*. Ap. 104. viii) that night.
caught. Gr. *piazō*. Used in the Gospels by John only, and always, save here and *v.* 10, of "taking" the Lord (7. 30, 32, 44; 8. 20; 10. 39; 11. 57).
nothing. Gr. *oudeis*, compound of *ou*. Ap. 105. I.
4 now = already.
on. Gr. *eis*. Ap. 104. vi.
knew. Gr. *oida*. Ap. 132. I. i.
not. Gr. *ou*. Ap. 105. I.
5 Then = Therefore.
Children. Gr. *paidion*. Ap. 108. v.
meat. Gr. *prosphagion*. Something to eat with (your bread), a relish. Occ. only here.
No. Gr. *ou*. Ap. 105. I.
6 Cast. Gr. *ballō*, as in 20. 25, 27.
net. A bag or purse net. Gr. *diktuon*, as in Matt. 4. 20. Mark 1. 18. Luke 5. 2. For other words for "net", see Matt. 4. 18; 13. 47.
now they were not = no longer (Gr. *ouketi*) were they.
draw. Gr. *helkuō*. See on 12. 32.
for = from. Gr. *apo*. Ap. 104. iv. This was the eighth sign. See Ap. 176.

21. 7-13 (V², p. 1572). **APPEARANCE, &c.**
(*Alternation and Introversion.*)

V² Z | k | 7. Recognition by John.
     | l | 8. Fish caught.
     | A | 9. Provision made.
  Z | l | 10, 11. Fish brought.
     | k | 12. Recognition by all.
     | A | 13. Provision enjoyed.

7 loved. Gr. *agapaō*. Ap. 135. I. 1.
the Lord. Ap. 98. VI. i. *a*. 3. A.
Now when = Therefore.
heard = having heard.
girt. Gr. *diazōnnumi*. Only here and 13. 4, 5.
his fisher's coat = the upper garment. Gr. *ependutēs*. Only here in N.T. Used in the Sept. for the Heb. *mᵉ'il*, robe, in 1 Sam. 18. 4. 2 Sam. 13. 18.
naked. Gr. *gumnos*. This means he had only his tunic or undergarment on. Cp. Mark 14. 51. Acts 19. 16.
8 a little ship = the boat. Gr. *ploiarion*, dim. of *ploion*, *vv.* 3, 6. Elsewhere in 6. 22, 23 "boat", Mark 3. 9; 4. 36.
from. Gr. *apo*. Ap. 104. iv.
land = the land. Gr. *gē*. Ap. 129. 4.
two, &c. = about (Gr. *apo*. Ap. 104. iv) two, &c.: i.e. one hundred yards. See Ap. 51. III. 2 (1).
dragging. Gr. *surō*. Only here, Acts 8. 3; 14. 19; 17. 6. Rev. 12. 4. Not the same word as in *v.* 6. **the net with fishes** = the net of fishes.
9 were come = went forth. **to** = unto. Gr. *eis*. Ap. 104. vi. **saw** = see. Gr. *blepō*. Ap. 133. I. 5. **fire of coals.** Gr. *anthrakia*. Only here and 18. 18. **fish.** Gr. *opsarion*, dim. of *opson*, cooked meat, eaten as a relish. In 6. 9, 11, the only other passage where it occ., it is in the plural as in *v.* 10 below. Here it probably means a little fish. **bread** = a loaf. One little fish and one loaf to feed eight persons. A beautiful variant of, and supplement to, the widow's handful of meal and cruse of oil (1 Kings 17). It was a type of the food He would supply them with, in the strength of which they would go "many days". **10 the fish.** Here the word is *opsarion* in the plural. But they were *great* fishes (*v.* 11). So it must be used in a general sense. **11 went up** = went back. **to.** Gr. *epi*. Ap. 104. ix. 1, but all the texts read *eis*. **12 dine.** Gr. *aristaō*. Only here, *v.* 15, and Luke 11. 37. The *ariston* was the morning meal, as contrasted with the afternoon meal, which was called *deipnon*, transl. "supper". Cp. Matt. 22. 4. Luke 11. 38; 14. 12. **none** = no one. Gr. *oudeis*. **durst** = ventured to. Contrast their freedom in questioning Him before. It marks the change in their relationship wrought by the resurrection. **ask** = inquire. Only here and Matt. 2. 8; 10. 11. **13 then.** All the texts omit. **bread** = the loaf. **fish** = the fish of *v.* 9. **14 now** = already. **His** = the. **risen.** Gr. *egeirō*. Ap. 178. I. 4. **from the dead.** Gr. *ek nekrōn*. See Ap. 139. 3.

U B[1] C[1] 15 °So when they had [12] dined, [1] Jesus saith
A. D. 29 to Simon Peter, °"Simon, *son* of Jonas, [7] lovest
thou Me °more than these?" He saith [3] unto
Him, "Yea, [7] Lord; Thou [4] knowest that I °love
Thee."

D[1] He saith [3] unto him, °"Feed My °lambs."

C[2] 16 He saith to him again °the second time,
[15] "Simon, *son* of Jonas, [7] lovest thou Me?"
He saith [3] unto Him, "Yea, [7] Lord; Thou [4] knowest that I [15] love Thee."

D[2] He saith [3] unto him, °"Feed My °sheep."

C[3] 17 He saith [3] unto him the third time, [15] "Simon,
son of Jonas, [15] lovest thou Me?" Peter was
°grieved because He said [3] unto him the third
time, [15] "Lovest thou Me?" And he said [3] unto
Him, [7] "Lord, Thou [4] knowest all things; Thou
°knowest that I [15] love Thee."

D[3] Jesus saith [3] unto him, [15] "Feed My [16] sheep.

C[4] 18 °Verily, verily, I say [3] unto thee, When
thou wast °young, thou °girdedst thyself, and
walkedst whither thou °wouldest: but when
thou shalt be old, thou shalt stretch forth thy
hands, and [2] another shall °gird thee, and °carry
thee whither thou °wouldest [4] not."
19 This spake He, signifying by °what death
he should °glorify °God.

D[4] And °when He had spoken this, He saith [3] unto
him, °"Follow Me."

B[2] 20 °Then Peter, °turning about, [9] seeth the
disciple whom [1] Jesus [7] loved [19] following; which
°also leaned °on His breast °at supper, and
said, [7] "Lord, °which is he that °betrayeth
Thee?"
21 Peter °seeing him saith to [1] Jesus, [7] "Lord,
and °what *shall* this man *do?*"
22 [1] Jesus saith [3] unto him, "°If I [18] will that
he °tarry till I come, °what *is that* °to thee?
[19] follow thou Me."
23 [5] Then went this °saying abroad °among
the brethren, that °that disciple °should [4] not
die: yet [1] Jesus said [4] not [3] unto him, "He shall
[4] not die;" but, [22] "If I [18] will that he [22] tarry
till I come, what *is that* [22] to thee?"

T[3] 24 This is the disciple which °testifieth °of
these things, and wrote these things: and we
[4] know that his °testimony is °true.
25 And there are °also many [2] other things
which [1] Jesus did, the which, [22] if they should
be written °every one, °I suppose that °even
the °world itself could °not °contain °the books
that should be written. °Amen.

21. 15-23 (*U*, p. 1572). MINISTRY.
(*Division.*)

U	B[1]	15-19. The future of Peter.
	B[2]	20-23. The future of John.

21. 15-19 (B[1], above). THE FUTURE OF PETER.
(*Repeated Alternation.*)

B[1]	C[1]		15-. Question.
		D[1]	-15. Command.
	C[2]		16-. Question.
		D[2]	-16. Command.
	C[3]		17-. Question.
		D[3]	-17. Command.
	C[4]		18, 19-. Prediction.
		D[4]	-19. Command.

15 So = Therefore.

Simon. Peter was always addressed by the Lord as Simon except in Luke 22. 34. See Ap. 147.

more than these: i.e. than these other disciples do. Referring to his words in Matt. 26. 33, 35.

love. Gr. *phileō.* Ap. 135. I. 2. Note the different words used in these verses. The Lord uses *agapaō* twice and *phileō* once, Peter always *phileō.*

Feed: i.e. provide pasture for. Gr. *boskō.* Save in this passage, always of swine.

lambs. Gr. *arnion,* a diminutive. Only here and in the Revelation, where it occ. twenty-nine times, always of the Lord, except 13. 11. The other word for "lamb", *amnos,* only in 1. 29, 36. Acts 8. 32. 1 Pet. 1. 19.

16 the = a.

Feed = Shepherd. Gr. *poimainō.* Occ. eleven times, transl. "rule" in Matt. 2. 6. Rev. 2. 27; 12. 5; 19. 15. Cp. *poimēn,* 10. 2, 11, 12, 14, 16 (Shepherd); Eph. 4. 11 (pastors). **sheep.** Gr. *probaton.*

17 grieved. Gr. *lupeō.* Elsewhere in John, 16. 20. Cp. 1 Pet. 1. 6. The noun *lupē* occ. in 16. 6, 20, 21, 22. Cp. 1 Pet. 2. 19.

knowest. Gr. *ginōskō.* Ap. 132. I. ii.

18 Verily, verily. Twenty-fifth and last occ. of this double Amen (Ap. 10). See on 1. 51 and p. 1511.

young. Gr. *neōteros,* younger. The positive *neos* applied to any one up to thirty. This and 20. 4 gave rise to the tradition that Peter was a middle-aged man.

girdedst. Gr. *zōnnumi.* Only here.

wouldest. Gr. *thelō.* Ap. 102. 1.

carry = lead. Gr. *pherō.* Cp. Mark 9. 17. Luke 15. 23. Acts 14. 13.

19 what = what kind of.

glorify. Gr. *doxazō.* See p. 1511.

God. Ap. 98. I. i. 1. **when He had** = having.

Follow. Gr. *akoloutheō.* Used of soldiers, servants, and pupils. First occ. in John, 1. 37.

20 Then. All the texts omit.

turning about = having turned round.

also leaned = leaned also.

on. Gr. *epi.* Ap. 104. ix. 3.

at. Gr. *en.* Ap. 104. viii. **which** = who.

betrayeth. See on 19. 30, "gave up".

21 seeing. Gr. *eidon.* Ap. 133. I. 1.

what, &c.: lit. this one, what?

22 If. Ap. 118. 1. b.

tarry. Gr. *menō,* transl. abide, remain, &c. See p. 1511.

what, &c. Peter's curiosity rebuked. Cp. Matt. 17. 4. **to** = with reference to. Gr. *pros.* Ap. 104. xv. 3. **23 saying.** Gr. *logos.* See on Mark 9. 32. **among** = unto. Gr. *eis.* Ap. 104. vi. **that.** Gr. *ekeinos.* **should not die** = is not dying: i.e. is not going to die. **24 testifieth** = beareth witness. Gr. *martureō.* See p. 1511, note 4. **of** = concerning. Gr. *peri.* Ap. 104. xiii. 1. **testimony.** Gr. *marturia.* Cp. 19. 35, and see p. 1511. **true.** Gr. *alēthēs.* Ap. 175. 1. **25 also many, &c.** = many other things also. See 20. 30. **every one** = one by one. Gr. *kath'* (Ap. 104. x. 2) *en.* **I suppose** = I think. Gr. *oimai,* contr. for *oiomai,* which occ. in Phil. 1. 16. James 1. 7. **even . . . not.** Gr. *oude,* compound of *ou.* Ap. 105. I. **world.** Gr. *kosmos.* Ap. 129. 1. **contain.** Gr. *chōreō.* Elsewhere in John: 2. 6; 8. 37 (hath no place). Cp. Matt. 19. 11, 12. **the books, &c.** = the written books. Fig. *Hyperbolē.* Ap. 6. **Amen.** All the texts omit. In that case, only the *double* "verily" found in John. This chapter is a supplement, of the highest value, to the Gospel formally concluded in 20. 31. The use of the first person singular in *v.* 25, contrasted with the Evangelist's modest self-effacement elsewhere, has led some to doubt the Johannine authorship of this chapter. But the evidence of the MSS. and Versions, and the attestation clause at *v.* 24 is so closely allied to that in 19. 35 as to leave little room for doubt. Note further, the use of many characteristic words (see p. 1511), the expression noted in *v.* 1, the double "verily" (*v.* 18), and, above all, the eight signs with their wonderful structure and correspondence (see Ap. 176).

THE ACTS OF THE APOSTLES.

THE STRUCTURE OF THE BOOK AS A WHOLE.

(*Introversion and Extended Alternation.*)

A | 1. 1-3. INTRODUCTION.

B | **C** | 1. 4—2. 13. JERUSALEM. MISSION OF THE HOLY SPIRIT. EQUIPMENT OF THE APOSTLES.

D | 2. 14—8. 1-. THE MINISTRY OF PETER (WITH OTHERS) TO THE NATION IN JERUSALEM AND IN THE LAND.

E | 8. -1—11. 30. PETER'S MINISTRY (WITH OTHERS) IN THE LAND OF ISRAEL.

F | 12. 1-23. JERUSALEM. PETER'S IMPRISONMENT. SUBSEQUENT ABODE (CÆSAREA) AND CLOSE OF MINISTRY.

B | *C* | 12. 24—13. 3. ANTIOCH. MISSION OF THE HOLY SPIRIT. EQUIPMENT OF PAUL AND BARNABAS.

D | 13. 4—14. 28. THE MINISTRY OF PAUL (WITH OTHERS) TO THE DISPERSION. APART FROM JERUSALEM AND THE TWELVE.

E | 15. 1—19. 20. PAUL'S MINISTRY IN ASSOCIATION WITH THE TWELVE.

F | 19. 21—28. 29. EPHESUS AND JERUSALEM. PAUL'S ARREST AND IMPRISONMENT. SUBSEQUENT ABODE (ROME) AND CLOSE OF MINISTRY.

A | 28. 30, 31. CONCLUSION.

For the New Testament and the Order of the Books, see Ap. 95.
For the Chronology of the Acts, see Ap. 180.
For the Dispensational place of the Acts, see Ap. 181.
For words used only by Luke, see some 400 recorded in the Notes as occurring only in Acts, and some 60 which occur both in his Gospel and in Acts. Many are terms employed in medical works.

The writer is, without doubt, Luke. The book has the same introductory address as his Gospel (cp. 1. 1 with Luke 1. 3), and takes up the history where the third Gospel leaves it, giving in greater detail the account of the Ascension, with which that Gospel closes.

It is an expansion, in part at least, of Mark 16. 20, and records the fulfilment of the Lord's promise to send the Holy Spirit (Luke 24. 49), as well as the answer to His prayer on the cross (Luke 23. 34), a prayer which secured to the guilty nation a further respite from the doom He had pronounced (Luke 13. 35).

Throughout the book the millennial kingdom is in view (2. 17-20; 3. 19-21; 8. 12; 14. 22; 20. 25; 28. 23, 31). The question of the Apostles (1. 6) rules the character of the Acts.

The action has Jerusalem as its centre. The Mosaic Law is observed. Peter and the other Apostles are found continually in the Temple. Paul goes first to the Synagogues, because "it was necessary that the word of God should *first* have been spoken to you" (13. 46). He keeps the feasts (18. 21; 20. 16). He has vows (18. 18; 21. 23, 26), and walks orderly, keeping the Law (21. 24). The Gentiles take the second place (26. 22, 23), coming in after the Jew, but no longer as proselytes (10. 44; cp. 11. 3).

Wherever the name "Christ" is used without a qualifying word, "Jesus", or "Lord", it has the definite article, *the* Christ, i.e. the Messiah.

The book naturally divides into two parts which are relative, mainly (1) to the ministry of Peter, John, Stephen, Philip, &c., to the People in the Land, and (2) to the ministry of Paul, Barnabas, Silas, &c., to the Dispersion outside the Land. Fuller details will be found in Ap. 181.

Eighteen speeches or addresses are recorded :—

Seven by Peter :
1. To the assembled believers, 1. 15-22.
2. On the day of Pentecost, 2. 14-40.
3. In the Temple, 3. 12-26.
4. Before the Sanhedrin, 4. 8-12.
5. ,, ,, ,, 5. 29-32.
6. In the house of Cornelius, 10. 28-43.
7. In the council at Jerusalem, 15. 7-11.

One by James : On the same occasion, 15. 13-21.

One by Stephen : Before the Sanhedrin, 7. 2-53.

Seven by Paul :
1. In the Synagogue at Antioch, 13. 16-41.
2. At Lystra, 14. 15-17.
3. On Mars' Hill, 17. 22-31.
4. At Miletus, 20. 18-35.
5. On the stairs before the castle, 22. 1-21.
6. Before Felix, 24. 10-21.
7. Before Agrippa, 26. 2-29.

And those of Gamaliel, 5. 35-39, and Tertullus, 24. 2-8.

Luke nowhere names himself, but what are called the "we" sections (16. 10-17; 20. 5-15; 21. 1-18; 27. 1—28. 16) indicate where he was in the company of the Apostle. Cp. also Philem. 24; 2 Tim. 4. 11.

There is a noteworthy correspondence, or parallelism, between the miracles wrought through Peter and those wrought through Paul. Cp. 3. 2-8 with 14. 8-10; 5. 12, 15, 16 with 19. 11, 12; 9. 36-42 with 20. 9-12.

THE
ACTS OF THE APOSTLES.

A **1** THE °former °treatise °have I made, O
°Theophilus, °of all that °Jesus °began both
to do and teach,
2 Until the day in which He was °taken up,
°after that He °through °the Holy Ghost had
°given commandments unto °the apostles whom
He °had chosen:
3 To whom °also He °shewed Himself alive
°after His passion °by many °infallible proofs,
being °seen of them °forty days, and speaking
of the things °pertaining to °the kingdom of
God:

B C A a 4 And, °being assembled together with *them*,
b °commanded them that they should °not °de-
part °from Jerusalem, but °wait for the
°promise of the Father, "which," *saith He*,
"ye °have heard of Me.
5 °For John truly °baptized with water; but
ye shall °be baptized with ²the Holy Ghost
°not °many days hence."

a 6 When they therefore were come together,
they °asked of Him, saying, "°Lord, °wilt Thou
°at this time °restore again °the kingdom to
Israel?"

b 7 And He said °unto them, "It is ⁵not °for
you to °know °the times or the seasons, which
the Father hath put °in His own °power.
8 But ye shall receive °power, after that °the
Holy Ghost is come °upon you: °and ye shall
be °witnesses °unto Me both ⁷in Jerusalem,
°and ⁷in all Judæa, °and in Samaria, °and
°unto the uttermost part of the °earth."

B 9 And when He had spoken these things,
while they °beheld, He was °taken up; and
°a cloud °received Him °out of their sight.
10 And while they °looked stedfastly °toward
°heaven as He °went up, °behold, two °men
stood by them ⁷in white apparel;

---

1. 1 former. Lit. first. This links the Acts with Luke's Gospel, see p. 1575.
treatise = account. Gr. *logos*. Ap. 121. 10.
have. Omit.
Theophilus. See note on Luke 1. 3.
of = concerning. Gr. *peri*. Ap. 104. xiii. 1.
Jesus. Ap. 98. X.
began. This shows that the Acts records the continuation of the Lord's ministry to the Circumcision (Rom. 15. 8).
2 taken up = received up. Cp. Mark 16. 19.
after that He . . . had = having.
through. Gr. *dia*. Ap. 104. v. 1.
the Holy Ghost = Divine power. Ap. 101. II. 14.
given commandments unto = commanded.
the apostles. See Ap. 189.
had chosen = chose out (Luke 6. 13).
3 also. Read after "Himself".
shewed = presented.
after His passion = after (Gr. *meta*. Ap. 104. xi. 2) that He suffered.
by. Gr. *en*. Ap. 104. viii.
infallible proofs = indubitable evidence. Gr. *tekmērion*. Only here. Cp. 1 John 1. 1, 2.
seen. Gr. *optanomai*. Ap. 133. I. 10. Only here.
forty days = during (Gr. *dia*. Ap. 104. v. 1) forty days. The only reference to the period between the Resurrection and the Ascension.
pertaining to = concerning. Gr. *peri*, as in *v*. 1.
the kingdom of God. Ap. 112. 2 and 114.

1. 4—2. 13 (C, p. 1575). JERUSALEM. MISSION OF THE HOLY SPIRIT. EQUIPMENT OF THE APOSTLES. (*Alternations.*)

C | A | a | 1. 4-. Assembled.
  | | b | -4, 5. Command. Wait.
  | | *a* | 6. Come together.
  | | *b* | 7, 8. Promise given.
  | B | 9-11. Ascension of the Lord.
  | *A* | c | 12, 13. Return.
  | | d | 14. Obedience. Waiting.
  | | *c* | 15-26. Assembled.
  | | *d* | 2. 1-3. Promise fulfilled.
  | *B* | 2. 4-13. The Descent of the Spirit.

4 being assembled together with. Gr. *sunalizomai*. Only here. commanded. Gr. *parangellō*. First occ. Matt. 10. 5. Cp. Ap. 121. 5, 6. Not the same word as in *v*. 2. not. Gr. *mē*. Ap. 105. II. depart = separate themselves. Gr. *chōrizō*. First occ. Matt. 19. 6. from. Gr. *apo*. Ap. 104. iv. wait for. Gr. *perimenō*. Only here. promise of the Father. See Ap. 17. 2. Cp. Luke 24. 49. have heard = heard. **5** For John truly = Because John indeed (Gr. *men*). baptized with. Ap. 115. I. ii. be baptized with. Ap. 115. I. iii. 1. b. not. Gr. *ou*. Ap. 105. I. many days hence = after (Gr. *meta*. Ap. 104. xi. 2) these many days. **6** asked of = were questioning. Gr. *eperōtaō*. Cp. Ap. 134. I. 3. Lord. Ap. 98. VI. i. β. 2. B. wilt Thou. Lit. if (Ap. 118. 2. a) Thou dost. Fig. *Heterōsis* (of Tense). Ap. 6. at = in. Gr. *en*. Ap. 104. viii. restore again = establish or set up. Gr. *apokathistanō*. First occ. Matt. 12. 13. the kingdom: i.e. the Messianic kingdom, which the prophets spoke of, and all Israelites were looking for. Cp. Luke 1. 32, 33; and see App. 112 and 114. **7** unto. Gr. *pros*. Ap. 104. xv. 3. for you = yours. know. Gr. *ginōskō*. Ap. 132. I. ii. the times, &c. = the great time, &c. A Hebraism, pl. of majesty. Fig. *Heterōsis*. Ap. 6. in. Gr. *en*, as *v*. 6. power = authority. Ap. 172. 5. **8** power. Gr. *dunamis*. Ap. 172. 1. the Holy Ghost = the Holy Spirit (with art.). Ap. 101. II. 3. Cp. Luke 24. 49. upon. Ap. 104. ix. 3. and. Fig. *Polysyndeton*. Ap. 6. witnesses. See note on John 1. 7. unto Me. Texts read, "of Me", or "My" witnesses. Cp. Isa. 43. 10, 12; 44. 8. unto = as far as. Gr. *heōs*. earth. Ap. 129. 4. **9** beheld. Ap. 133. I. 5. taken up = lifted up. Gr. *epairō*. First occ. Matt. 17. 8. Always in Gospels, "lift up". a cloud. Not a rain cloud of the earth, but referring to the attendant *angelic* hosts. Cp. Pss. 24. 7-10; 47. 5. Matt. 24. 30; 26. 64. 1 Thess. 4. 17. Rev. 1. 7; 11. 12. received. Gr. *hupolambanō*. Here; 2. 15. Luke 7. 43; 10. 30. out of their sight = from (Ap. 104. iv) their eyes. **10** looked stedfastly = were gazing earnestly. Ap. 133. III. 6. toward = into. Ap. 104. vi. heaven = the heaven (sing.). See note on Matt. 6. 9, 10. went up = was going. behold. Ap. 133. I. 2. men. Ap. 123. 2. These were angels. Cp. 10. 30. John 20. 12.

11 Which °also said, °"Ye [10]men of Galilee, why stand ye °gazing up °into [10]heaven? °this same [1]Jesus, Which is taken up [4]from you °into heaven, shall °so come in like manner as ye °have seen Him °go °into [10]heaven."

4 c **12 Then returned they °unto Jerusalem [4]from the mount called °Olivet, which is °from Jerusalem °a sabbath day's journey.**

13 And when they °were come in, they went up [11]into °an °upper room, where °abode both °Peter, and James, and John, and Andrew, Philip, and Thomas, Bartholomew, and Matthew, James *the son* of Alphæus, and Simon Zelotes, and Judas *the brother* of James.

d **14 These all °continued °with one accord in °prayer and °supplication, °with the women, °and Mary the mother of Jesus, and °with His °brethren.**

c **15 And [7]in those days Peter °stood up [7]in the midst of the °disciples, and said, (the °number of names °together were about °an hundred and twenty,)**

16 °"Men *and* brethren, this °scripture must needs have been °fulfilled, which the Holy °Ghost °by the mouth of °David spake before °concerning Judas, which °was guide to them that °took [1]Jesus.

17 For he was °numbered °with us, and °had obtained °part of this °ministry.

18 °Now °this man °purchased a °field °with the °reward of °iniquity; and falling °headlong, he °burst asunder in the midst, and all his bowels °gushed out.

19 And it was °known °unto all the dwellers at Jerusalem; insomuch as that [18]field is called in their °proper °tongue, °Aceldama, that is to say, The [18]field of blood.

20 For it °is written [7]in °the book of Psalms, 'Let his °habitation be °desolate, and °let no man dwell °therein: and his °bishoprick let °another °take.'

21 Wherefore of these [10]men which have companied with us °all the time that °the Lord [1]Jesus °went in and out °among us,

11 also said=said also.

Ye men of Galilee. Lit. Men, Galileans. The term "men" was usual in addressing a company. Cp. our use of the word, "Gentlemen". This usage is common in Acts: *v.* 16; 2. 14, 22, 29, 37; 3. 12; 5. 35; 7. 2; 13. 15, 16, 26, 38; 15. 7, 13; 17. 22; 19. 35; 21. 28; 22. 1; 23. 1, 6; 28. 17.

gazing up. Ap. 133. I. 7. Some texts read Ap. 133. I. 5.

into. Ap. 104. vi.

this same=this.

so . . . in like manner. The Descent, therefore, will be like the Ascension, actual, literal, visible, unexpected, save by those looking for Him, in the clouds of heaven, and to the same place whence He departed (Zech. 14. 4).

have seen=beheld. Ap. 133. I. 12.

go=going.

12 unto. Ap. 104. vi.

Olivet. Only here in N.T., but found often in the Papyri. The usual expression is the "Mount of Olives".

from=near.

a sabbath day's journey. See Ap. 51. III. 1 (5).

13 were come=entered.

an=the.

upper room. Gr. *huperōon*: here; 9. 37, 39; 20. 8. Not the same word as in Mark 14. 15. Luke 22. 12.

abode=were abiding. Gr. *katamenō*. Only here.

Peter, &c. See Ap. 141.

14 continued=were continuing. Gr. *proskartereō*. In Acts, here; 2. 42, 46; 6. 4; 8. 13; 10. 7.

with one accord=with one mind. Occ. eleven times in Acts, once in Rom. 15. 6. Found in a Papyrus of 117 B.C.

prayer. Ap. 134. II. 2.

supplication. The texts omit.

with. Ap. 104. xvi.

and Mary. The last mention of her, "at prayer".

brethren. Ap. 182.

15 stood up=rose up. Gr. *anistēmi*. Ap. 178. I. 1.

disciples. The texts read "brethren".

number. Gr. *ochlos*, crowd. This is an occ. of the Fig. *Epitrechon*. Ap. 6.

together=to the same (place). Gr. *epi to auto*. See 2. 1, 44; 4. 26. 1 Cor. 7. 5; 11. 20; 14. 23.

an hundred and twenty=three forties. A divinely appointed number during a period of waiting. It was the number of Ezra's great synagogue. See Ap. 10.

16 Men and brethren. Cp. *v.* 11.

scripture. Gr. *graphē*.

fulfilled=filled full. Ap. 125. 7.

Ghost=Spirit. Ap. 101. II. 3.

by=through. Ap. 104. v. 1.

David. Peter asserts that Ps. 69 was written by David, and was the utterance of the Holy Spirit. Cp. 2 Pet. 1. 21. **concerning.** Ap. 104. xiii. 1. **was**=became. **took**=arrested. Gr. *sullambanō*. Cp. Matt. 26. 55. **17 numbered.** Gr. *katarithmeō*. Only here. **with.** Gr. *sun*, as in *v.* 14, but the texts read *en*, among. **had.** Omit. **part**=the lot. Gr. *klēros*. Five times in the Gospels, of the lots cast for the Lord's garments. **ministry.** Gr. *diakonia*. Ap. 190. II. 1. **18 Now**=Therefore. Verses 18, 19 form a parenthesis. **this man**=this one, indeed. **purchased**=caused to be purchased. Fig. *Metonymy* (of Effect). Ap. 6. See Ap. 161. **field**=place, or holding. Gr. *chōrion*. See note on Matt. 26. 36. **with.** Ap. 104. vii. **reward**=pay. Gr. *misthos*. Sin pays its wages (Rom. 6. 23). **iniquity.** Ap. 128. VII. 1. Cp. 2 Pet. 2. 13, where the same Greek words are transl. "wages of unrighteousness". **headlong.** Gr. *prēnēs*. Only here. **burst asunder.** Gr. *lakeō*. Only here. Dr. John Lightfoot (1602–75) writes:—"The devil, immediately after Judas had cast back his money into the temple, caught him up into the air, strangled him, threw him headlong, and dashed him in pieces on the ground". He refers to Tobit 3. 8, and adds, "That this was known to all the dwellers at Jerusalem, argues that it was no common and ordinary event, and must be something more than hanging himself, which was an accident not so very unusual in that nation." *Works*, viii, pp. 366, 367. This requires that Matt. 27. 5 be read, "He was hanged, or strangled", instead of "hanged himself". **gushed out**=were poured out. **19 known.** Gr. *gnōstos*. Cp. Ap. 132. I. ii. This word occ. fifteen times, ten times in Acts. **unto**=to. **proper**=own. Gr. *idios*. **tongue**=dialect. Gr. *dialektos*. Only in Acts: here; 2. 6, 8; 21. 40; 22. 2; 26. 14. **Aceldama.** See Ap. 94. III. 3. 3 and 161. **20 is**=has been. **the**=a: i.e. the second book, in Ps. 69. 25. **habitation**=farm, or country house. Gr. *epaulis*. Only here. **desolate**=desert: i.e. let the place he has thus acquired become a wilderness. **let, &c.** Lit. let there not (Gr. *mē*. Ap. 105. II) be the dweller (*v.* 19). **therein**=in (Gr. *en*. Ap. 104. viii) it. **bishoprick.** Gr. *episcopē*, the office of an *episcopos*, or overseer. Occ. only here; Luke 19. 44. 1 Tim. 3. 1. 1 Pet. 2. 12. Cp. *v.* 17. This is a composite quotation from Pss. 69. 25, and 109. 8. Ap. 107. II. 4. **another.** Gr. *heteros*. Ap. 124. 2. **take**=receive. **21 all**=in (Gr. *en*) all. **the Lord.** Ap. 98. VI. i. *β*. 2. A. **went in and out.** A Hebraism for life in general. Fig. *Synecdochē* (of the Species). Ap. 6. Cp. 9. 28. Deut. 28. 6. John 10. 9. **among**=over. Ap. 104. ix. 3.

22 Beginning [4]from the °baptism of John, [8]unto that same day that He was [2]taken up [4]from us, must °one °be ordained to be a [8]witness [14]with us of His °resurrection."

23 And they °appointed two, Joseph called °Barsabas, who was surnamed Justus, and Matthias.

24 And they °prayed, and said, "Thou, [6]Lord, °Which knowest the hearts of all *men*, °shew °whether °of these two Thou [2]hast chosen,

25 That he may °take part of °this [17]ministry and °apostleship, °from which Judas °by transgression fell, °that he might go °to °his own place."

26 And they gave forth their °lots; and the °lot fell [8]upon Matthias; and he was °numbered °with the eleven [2]apostles.

d **2** And °when the day of °Pentecost was °fully come, they were all °with one accord °in one place.

2 And °suddenly there came a °sound °from [p]heaven as of a °rushing °mighty °wind, and it filled all the house where they were sitting.

3 And there °appeared unto them °cloven tongues like as of fire, and it sat °upon °each of them.

B **4** And they were all filled with °the Holy Ghost, and began to °speak with °other tongues, °as °the Spirit °gave them °utterance.

5 And there were °dwelling °at Jerusalem Jews, °devout °men, °out of every °nation °under [2]heaven.

6 Now °when this was noised abroad, the °multitude came together, and were °confounded, because that °every man heard them [4]speak in his own °language.

7 And they were all °amazed and marvelled, saying °one to another, °"Behold, are °not all these which [4]speak Galilæans?

8 And how hear we [6]every man in our own °tongue, °wherein we were born?

9 °Parthians, and Medes, and Elamites, and the [5]dwellers in Mesopotamia, and in Judæa, and °Cappadocia, in Pontus, and Asia,

10 Phrygia, and Pamphylia, in °Egypt, and in the parts of Libya °about Cyrene, and °strangers of Rome, Jews and °proselytes,

11 °Cretes and Arabians, we do hear them

---

22 baptism. Gr. *baptisma.* Ap. 115. II. i. 2. Put for ministry by Fig. *Synecdochē.* Ap. 6.

one = one of these. **be ordained to be** = become.

resurrection. Gr. *anastasis.* Ap. 178. II. 1. The resurrection is the great subject of the Apostolic witness. Cp. 2. 32; 3. 26; 4. 10; 5. 30; 10. 40; 13. 30; 17. 3, 31, &c.

23 appointed = put forward, or nominated.

Barsabas. Texts read Barsabbas. Ap. 94. III. 3. 11. Cp. 15. 22.

24 prayed. Gr. *proseuchomai.* Ap. 134. I. 2.

Which knowest, &c. Lit. heart-knowing. Gr. *kardiognōstēs.* Only here and 15. 8. Cp. Jer. 17. 10.

shew = shew plainly. Gr. *anadeiknumi.* Only here and Luke 10. 1.

whether of these two. Lit. of these two, the one.

of. Ap. 104. vii.

25 take part = receive the lot. Gr. *klēros.*

this ministry, &c. = this apostolic ministry. Fig. *Hendiadys.* Ap. 6.

apostleship. Gr. *apostolē.* Only here, Rom. 1. 5. 1 Cor. 9. 2. Gal. 2. 8.

from. Ap. 104. vii, but texts read *apo.*

by transgression fell = transgressed. Ap. 128. VI. 1.

that he might = to. **to.** Gr. *eis.* Ap. 104. vi.

his own. Same word as "proper", *v.* 19.

26 lots, lot. Gr. *klēros.* Same word as "part", in *v.* 17.

numbered. Gr. *sunkatapsēphizō.* Only here. See note on Luke 14. 28.

with. Gr. *meta.* Ap. 104. xi. 1.

2. 1 when, &c. Lit. in (Ap. 104. viii) the day ... being completed. The Syriac and Vulgate read "days". This refers to the completion of the seven weeks (fifty days inclusive) from the waving of the sheaf of firstfruits (Lev. 23. 15, 16).

Pentecost = fiftieth (day). Gr. *Pentēkostos.* Only here; 20. 16. 1 Cor. 16. 8.

fully come = being fulfilled. Gr. *sumplēroō.* Only here and Luke 8. 23; 9. 51.

with one accord. See note on 1. 14.

in one place = together. See note on 1. 15.

2 suddenly. Gr. *aphnō.* Only here; 16. 26; 28. 6.

sound. Gr. *ēchos.* Only here; Luke 4. 37. Heb. 12. 19.

from. Ap. 104. vii.

heaven = the heaven (sing.). See Matt. 6. 9, 10.

rushing, &c. = a mighty wind borne along.

rushing. Gr. pass. of *pherō.* Same word as in 2 Pet. 1. 21 (moved).

mighty. Gr. *biaios.* Only here. The noun, *bia* (force), is only found in Acts. See 5. 26.

wind = blast. Gr. *pnoē*, from *pneō*, to breathe, or blow, whence *pneuma.* Only here and 17. 25. In the Sept. twenty-one times, of which fifteen are the rendering of the Heb. *n^eshāmāh.* Ap. 16.

3 appeared unto = were seen by. Gr. *horaō.* Ap. 133. I. 8.

cloven tongues = tongues distributing, or parting themselves.

upon. Gr. *epi.* Ap. 104. ix. 3. **each** = each one. **4 the Holy Ghost** = Holy Spirit. Ap. 101. II. 14. **speak.** Gr. *laleō.* Ap. 121. 7. **other.** Gr. *heteros.* Ap. 124. 2. **as** = even as. **the Spirit.** Ap. 101. II. 3. **gave** = was giving. **utterance** = to utter or speak forth. Gr. *apophthengomai*, here, *v.* 14, and 26. 25. **5 dwelling.** Gr. *katoikeō.* As in 1. 19. Not sojourners for the Feast, but Jews of the dispersion who had taken up their abode at Jerusalem, perhaps because of the expectation of the Messiah. Cp. Luke 2. 25, 38. **at** = in. Ap. 104. viii. **devout** = pious. Gr. *eulabēs.* Only here, 8. 2, and Luke 2. 25. **men.** Ap. 123. 2. **out of.** Gr. *apo.* Ap. 104. iv. **nation.** Gr. *ethnos.* In Acts transl. twelve times, "nation"; thirty times, "Gentiles"; once, "people" (8. 9); and once, "heathen" (4. 25). **under** = of those under. Ap. 104. xviii. 2. **6 when, &c.** Lit. this voice (Gr. *phōnē*) having come. **multitude.** Gr. *plēthos.* Occ. seventeen times in Acts, transl. multitude, save 28. 3, "bundle". **confounded.** Gr. *sunchunō.* Only here, 9. 22; 19. 32; 21. 27, 31. **every man, &c.** = they heard them speaking, each one. **language.** Gr. *dialektos.* See note on 1. 19. **7 amazed** = dumbfounded. Cp. Mark 3. 21. **one to another** = to (Ap. 104. xv. 3) one another. The texts omit, but not the Syriac. **Behold.** Ap. 133. I. 2. Fig. *Asterismos.* Ap. 6. **not.** Ap. 105. I. **8 tongue.** Gr. *dialektos*, as in *v.* 6. **wherein.** In (Ap. 104. viii) which. **9 Parthians, &c** These were Jews of the dispersion. The first four were within the limits of the Persian Empire. Elam is mentioned in Gen. 14. 1. Jer. 49. 34 (note). Dan. 8. 2, &c. Mesopotamia is the same as Padan-Aram (Gen. 24. 10; 28. 2). **Cappadocia, &c.** Provinces of Asia Minor. Asia here means the district comprising Mysia, Lydia, &c., on the Western coast, governed by a Roman pro-consul. Cp. Rev. 1. 4. **10 Egypt, &c.** These were from Africa. **about.** Gr. *kata.* Ap. 104. x. 2. **strangers, &c.** = sojourners from Rome. Gr. *epidēmeō.* Only here and 17. 21. **proselytes.** See note on Matt. 23. 15. **11 Cretes** = Cretans. See Tit. 1. 12.

[4]speak in our tongues the °wonderful works
of °God."
12 And they were all [7]amazed, and °were in
doubt, saying °one to another, °"What meaneth this?"
13 [4]Others °mocking said, °"These men °are
full of °new wine."
C^1 E^1 F^1 14 But Peter, standing up °with the eleven,
lifted up his °voice, and °said °unto them,
°"Ye men of Judæa, and all *ye* that [5]dwell at
Jerusalem, be this °known °unto you, and
°hearken to my °words:
15 For these are [7]not drunken, as ye °suppose,
°seeing it is *but* °the third hour of the day.
G^1 16 But °this is that which was spoken °by
the prophet Joel;
17 'And it shall come to pass °in °the last
days,' saith God, 'I will °pour out °of My
°Spirit [3]upon °all flesh: and your °sons and
your daughters shall prophesy, and your
°young men shall °see °visions, and your old
men shall °dream °dreams:
18 And °on My °servants and °on My °hand-
maidens I will [17]pour out [17]in those days [17]of
My [17]Spirit; and they shall prophesy:
19 And I will °shew °wonders [17]in [2]heaven
above, and °signs °in the °earth beneath;
blood, and fire, and °vapour of °smoke:
20 The sun shall be °turned °into darkness,
and the moon °into blood, before that great
and °notable °day of the °LORD come:
21 And it shall come to pass, *that* whosoever
shall °call on the name of the [20]LORD shall be
saved.'
F^2 22 °Ye men of Israel, hear these °words;
°Jesus °of Nazareth, a °Man °approved °of
[11]God °among you by °miracles and [19]wonders
and [19]signs, which [11]God did [16]by Him [17]in
the midst of you, as ye yourselves °also °know:
23 Him, °being delivered by the °determinate
°counsel and °foreknowledge of [11]God, ye °have
taken, and [16]by °wicked hands °have crucified
and °slain:
24 Whom [11]God hath °raised up, having

wonderful works = great things. Gr. *megaleios*. Only here and Luke 1. 49.
God. Ap. 98. I. i. 1.
12 were in doubt = were perplexed. Occ. here; 5. 24; 10. 17. Luke 9. 7; 24. 4.
one to another. Gr. *allos* (Ap. 124. 1) *pros* (Ap. 104. xv. 3) *allon*.
What meaneth this? = What does this imply? Gr. *thelō*. (Ap. 102. 1.)
13 mocking. Gr. *chleuazō*. Only here and 17. 32. The texts read *diachleuazō*.
These men = They.
are full = have been filled. Gr. *mestoō*. Only here.
new wine. Gr. *gleukos*. Only here. This word and *mestoō* are frequent in medical works.

2. 14—8. 1- (**D**, p. 1575). THE MINISTRY OF PETER (WITH OTHERS) TO THE NATION IN JERUSALEM. (*Repeated Alternation.*)

D | C^1 | 2. 14-47. Among the brethren.
  D^1 | 3. 1—4. 22. Among the people.
 C^2 | 4. 23—5. 11. Among the brethren.
  D^2 | 5. 12-42. Among the people.
 C^3 | 6. 1-7. Among the brethren.
  D^3 | 6. 8—8. 1-. Among the people.

2. 14-47 (C^1, above). AMONG THE BRETHREN. (*Division.*)

C^1 | E^1 | 14-36. Peter's address.
  E^2 | 37-47. Results.

2. 14-36 (E^1, above). PETER'S ADDRESS. (*Repeated Alternation.*)

E^1 | F^1 | 14, 15. Appeal. Men of Judæa.
  G^1 | 16-21. Reference to Joel.
 F^2 | 22-24. Appeal. Men of Israel.
  G^2 | 25-28. Reference to Ps. 16.
 F^3 | 29-33. Appeal. Men and Brethren.
  G^3 | 34-36. Reference to Ps. 110.

14 with. Ap. 104. xvi.
voice. Gr. *phōnē*. See *v.* 6.
said = spoke out. Gr. *apophthengomai*, as in *v.* 4. This was an utterance in the power of the Holy Spirit.
unto = to.
Ye men, &c. Lit. men, Jews, and dwellers at Jerusalem. See note on 1. 11. The ministry of Peter was to the Circumcision. Cp. Matt. 15. 24.
known. See note on 1. 19.
hearken = attend closely. Gr. *enōtizomai*. Only here. Lit. take into the ears.

words = sayings. Gr. *rhēma*. Mark 9. 32. **15 suppose.** Gr. *hupolambanō*. See note on 1. 9. **seeing** = for. **the third hour**: i. e. 9 a.m. Ap. 165. Cp. 1 Thess. 5. 7. **16 this is that, &c.** Quoted from Joel 2. 28-31. See Ap. 183. **by** = through. Ap. 104. v. 1. **17 in.** Ap. 104. viii. **the last days.** See note on Gen. 49. 1. **pour out.** Gr. *ekcheō*. Transl. "shed forth" in *v.* 33. **of.** Ap. 104. iv. **Spirit.** Ap. 101. II. 14. **all flesh.** A Hebraism. Cp. Isa. 40. 5; 66. 24. Luke 3. 6. John 17. 2. **sons.** Gr. *huios*. Ap. 108. iii. **young men.** Ap. 108. x. **see.** Ap. 133. I. 8 (a). **visions.** Gr. *horasis*. Rev. 4. 3; 9. 17. **dream.** Only here and Jude 8. **dreams.** Only here. **18 on.** Gr. *epi*. Ap. 104. ix. 3. **servants.** Gr. *doulos*. Ap. 190. I. 2. **handmaidens** = bondmaids. Gr. *doulē*. **19 shew** = give. **wonders.** Ap. 176. 2. **signs.** Ap. 176. 3. **in.** Ap. 104. ix. 1. **earth.** Ap. 129. 4. Wonders in the heavens, signs upon earth. **vapour.** Only here and Jas. 4. 14. **smoke.** Only here, and twelve times in Revelation. **20 turned** = changed. Only here; Gal. 1. 7. Jas. 4. 9. **into.** Ap. 104. vi. **notable.** Gr. *epiphanēs*. Only here. Same word as in the Sept. Cp. Ap. 106. iii. The kindred noun, *epiphaneia*, is used of the Lord's coming. 2 Thess. 2. 8. 1 Tim. 6. 14, &c. In Joel, the word is "terrible". **day of the Lord.** First occ. of this expression is in Isa. 2. 12. See note there. **Lord.** Ap. 98. VI. i. β. 1. B. a. **21 call, &c.** Gr. *epikaleō*. Cp. 7. 59; 9. 14; 22. 16. Rom. 10. 12-14. 1 Cor. 1. 2. **22 Ye men, &c.** Cp. *v.* 14. **words.** Ap. 121. 10. **Jesus.** Ap. 98. X. **of Nazareth** = the Nazarene. This title occ. seven times in Acts. **Man.** Ap. 123. 2. **approved** = set forth, or commended. Gr. *apodeiknumi*. Only here, 25. 7. 1 Cor. 4. 9. 2 Thess. 2. 4. **of.** Ap. 104. iv. **among** = unto. Ap. 104. vi. **miracles** = powers. Ap. 176. 1. **also.** Omit. **know.** Ap. 132. I. i. **23 being delivered.** Only here. **determinate** = determined. Gr. *horizō*. Here; 10. 42; 11. 29; 17. 26, 31. Luke 22. 22. Rom. 1. 4. Heb. 4. 7. **counsel.** Ap. 102. 4. **foreknowledge.** Gr *prognōsis*. Cp. Ap. 132. I. iv. Only here and 1 Pet. 1. 2. **have taken, and.** The texts omit. **wicked.** Gr. *anomos*. Ap. 128. III. 3. **have crucified** = nailed up to (the cross). Gr. *prospēgnumi*. Only here. In the other forty-five places "crucify" is *stauroō*. **slain** = slew. Gr. *anaireō*, take off, or away. Occ. twenty-three times. All in Luke and Acts, save Matt. 2. 16. Heb. 10. 9. **24 raised up,** Ap. 178. I. 1. Cp. 13. 32, 33.

loosed the °pains of death: because it was [7] not possible that He should be °holden °of it.

G2 25 For °David speaketh °concerning Him, '**I °foresaw the °LORD °always °before my face, for He is °on my right hand, °that I should °not be °moved:**

26 °**Therefore did my heart rejoice, and my tongue °was glad; moreover °also my flesh shall °rest °in hope:**

27 **Because Thou wilt [7] not °leave °my soul °in °hell, °neither wilt Thou °suffer Thine °Holy One to °see °corruption.**

28 **Thou °hast made known to me the ways of °life; Thou shalt make me full of °joy °with Thy countenance.'**

F6 29 °Men *and* brethren, °let me °freely speak °unto you °of the °patriarch David, that he is both dead and buried, and his °sepulchre is °with us °unto this day.

30 Therefore °being a prophet, and [22] knowing that [11] God °had sworn °with an oath to him, that °**of the fruit of his loins, °according to the flesh, He would raise up Christ to sit °on °His throne;**

31 He °seeing this before, [4] spake [29] of the °resurrection of °Christ, that °**His soul was [7] not °left [27] in [27] hell, [27] neither His flesh °did [27] see [27] corruption.**

32 This [22] Jesus °hath [11] God [24] raised up, °whereof we °all are °witnesses.

33 Therefore °being by the right hand of [11] God °exalted, and having received °of the Father the °promise of °the Holy Ghost, He hath °shed forth this, which ye °now °see and hear.

G3 34 For David °is [7] not ascended [20] into °the heavens: but he saith himself, [25] '**The LORD said [14] unto my °Lord, Sit Thou [25] on My right hand,**

35 **Until I make Thy foes °Thy footstool.'**

36 Therefore let °all the house of Israel °know °assuredly, that [11] God hath made that same [22] Jesus, Whom ye °have crucified, both °Lord and [31] Christ."

E2 H e 37 Now when they heard *this*, they were °pricked in their heart, and said [29] unto Peter and to the rest of the °apostles, [29] "Men *and* brethren, what shall we do?"

f 38 Then Peter said [29] unto them, °"Repent, and °be baptized every one of you °in the °name

pains = birth-pangs. Gr. *ōdin.* Only here; Matt. 24. 8. Mark 13. 8. 1 Thess. 5. 3. Used in the Sept. in Ps. 116. 3, where the A.V. reads "sorrows".
holden. Same word as "retain", in John 20. 23.
of = by. Ap. 104. xviii. 1.
25 **David.** Ps. 16. 8.
concerning = with reference to. Ap. 104. vi.
foresaw = saw before (me). Only here and 21. 29. Gr. *proorao.*
Lord. Ap. 98. VI. i. β. 1. A. a.
always = through (Ap. 104. v. 1) every (event).
before my face. Lit. in the eyes of (Gr. *enōpion*) me.
on. Ap. 104. vii.
that = in order that. Gr. *hina.*
not. Ap. 105. II. moved. shaken.
26 Therefore = On account of (Ap. 104. v. 2) this.
was glad = rejoiced exceedingly. See Matt. 5. 12. 1 Pet. 1. 8; 4. 13.
also my flesh = my flesh also.
rest. Lit. tabernacle. Gr. *kataskēnoō.* Here; Matt. 13. 32. Mark 4. 32. Luke 13. 19.
in. Gr. *epi.* Ap. 104. ix. 2.
27 leave = forsake, or abandon. Gr. *enkataleipō.* Occ. nine times. Always transl. "forsake", except here and Rom. 9. 29.
my soul = me. Ap. 110. IV. 1.
in = into. Ap. 104. vi.
hell. Ap. 131. II.
neither. Gr. *oude.* suffer = give.
Holy One. Gr. *hosios.* Here; 13. 34, 35. 1 Tim. 2. 8. Tit. 1. 8. Heb. 7. 26. Rev. 15. 4; 16. 5. Over thirty times in Sept., of which twenty-five are in Psalms. Mostly as rendering of Heb. *ḥā īd* = grace, or favour. See Deut. 33. 8. Pss. 16. 10; 52. 9.
see. Ap. 133. I. 1.
corruption. Gr. *diaphthora.* Only here; *v.* 31; 13. 34–37.
28 hast made known = madest known. Ap. 132. I. ii.
life. Ap. 170. 1.
joy. Gr. *euphrosunē.* Only here and 14. 17.
with. Gr. *meta.* Ap. 104. xi. 1.
29 **Men, &c.** See note on 1. 11.
let me = I may.
freely = with (Ap. 104. xi. 1) frankness.
unto. Ap. 104. xv. 3.
of. Gr. *peri.* Ap. 104. xiii. 1.
patriarch. Occ. here, 7. 8, 9, and Heb. 7. 4. Applied to Abraham and the sons of Jacob, as founders of the nation, and to David, as founder of the monarchy.
sepulchre = tomb, as in Mark 5. 5. Gr. *mnēma.* Cp. 7. 16. Luke 23. 53. The more usual word is *mnēmeion,* as in 13. 29.
with = among. Gr. *en.* Ap. 104. viii. 2.
unto = until. Gr. *achri.*
30 **being.** Gr. *huparchō.* See note on Luke 9. 48.
had sworn = swore. See 2 Sam. 7.
with = by.
of = Gr. *ek.* Ap. 104. vii.

according . . . Christ to sit. The texts read, "He would set (one)". on = Gr. *epi.* Ap. 104. ix. 1. His throne. i.e. God's throne. Cp. 1 Chron. 29. 23, and see Ps. 2. 6. **31** **seeing this before** = fore-seeing (it). Gr. *proeidon.* Here and Gal. 3. 8. resurrection. Gr. *anastasis.* Ap. 178. II. 1. Christ = the Christ. Ap. 98. IX. His soul. Texts read "He". left. Gr. *kataleipō,* but the texts read *enkataleipō,* as in *v.* 27. did see = saw. **32** **hath.** Omit. whereof = of which. all. i.e. the twelve. witnesses. See note on 1. 8. **33** **being . . . exalted.** Gr. *hupsoō.* See note on John 12. 32. of = from beside. Gr. *para.* Ap. 104. xii. 1. promise. See note on 1. 4. the Holy Ghost = the Holy Spirit. Ap. 101. II. 3. shed forth. Same as "pour out" in *vv.* 17, 18. now. Omit. see. Gr. *blepō.* Ap. 133. I. 5. **34** **is not ascended** = went not up. Therefore still sleeping. Cp. 13. 36. the heavens. See note on Matt. 6. 9, 10. Lord. Ap. 98. VI. i. β. 2. A. a. **35** **Thy footstool** = the footstool of Thy feet. Quoted from Ps. 110. 1. See note on Matt. 22. 44. **36** **all the house, &c.** Cp. *v.* 14. know. Gr. *ginōskō.* Ap. 132. I. ii. assuredly. Gr. *asphalōs.* See note on "safely", Mark 14. 44. have crucified = crucified. Gr. *stauroō,* not same word as in *v.* 23. Lord. Ap. 98. VI. i. β. 2 B.

2. 37–47 [For Structure see next page].

37 **pricked** = pierced through. Only here in N.T. In Sept. Gen. 34. 7. Ps. 109. 16, &c. apostles. See Ap. 189. **38** **Repent.** Ap. 111. I. 1. be baptized . . . in. Ap. 115. I. v. For the formula of baptism, see Ap. 185. name. Note the frequent use of "the name" in the Acts. Cp. 3. 6, 16; 4. 10, 12, 17, 18, 30, &c. See also Gen. 12. 8. Ex. 3. 13–15; 23. 21.

of ° Jesus Christ ° for the ° remission of ° sins,
and ye shall receive the ° gift of [33] the Holy
Ghost.
39 For the [33] promise is [14] unto you, and to
your ° children, and to all that are ° afar off,
even as many as [25] the LORD our [11] God shall
° call."
40 And ° with many [4] other [22] words did he
° testify and ° exhort, saying, "Save yourselves
° from this ° untoward generation."
g **41** Then they that ° gladly ° received his [22] word
were ° baptized:
J h and the same day there were added *unto them*
about three thousand ° souls.
i **42** ° And they ° continued stedfastly in the
[37] apostles' ° doctrine and ° fellowship, and in
° breaking of bread, and in ° prayers.
H e **43** [42] And fear came ° upon every [41] soul:
f and many [19] wonders and [19] signs were done
[16] by the [37] apostles.
g **44** [42] And all that ° believed were ° together,
and had all things common;
45 [44] And sold their possessions [44] and goods,
[44] and parted them ° to all *men*, as ° every man
had need.
J i **46** And they, [42] continuing daily [1] with one
accord [17] in the ° temple, and [42] breaking bread
° from house to house, ° did eat their ° meat
° with ° gladness and ° singleness of heart,
47 ° Praising [11] God, and having ° favour ° with
all the ° people.
h And the ° Lord added ° to the church daily
° such as should be saved.

D[1] K k **3** Now ° Peter and John ° went up together
° into the ° temple ° at the hour of ° prayer,
being ° the ninth *hour*.
m **2** And a ° certain ° man ° lame ° from his
mother's womb was carried, whom they ° laid

2. 37-47 (E[2], p. 1579). RESULTS.
(*Alternation and Introversion.*)

E[2] | H | e | 37. Conviction.
  f | 38-40. Apostle's Counsel.
  g | 41-. Converts.
  J | h | -41. Souls added.
  i | 42. Continuance.
H | *e* | 43-. Fear.
  f | -43. Apostles' Miracles.
  g | 44, 45. Converts.
  J | *i* | 46, 47-. Continuance.
  h | -47. Souls added.

Jesus Christ. i. e. Jesus as Messiah. Ap. 98. XI.
for. Gr. *eis*. Ap. 104. vi.
remission = forgiveness. Gr. *aphesis*. Cp. Ap. 174. 12.
sins. Ap. 128. I. ii. 1.
gift = free gift. Gr. *dōrea*. See note on John 4. 10. Always used of divine gifts. The word *dōron* is always used of man's gifts, except in Eph. 2. 8.
39 children. Ap. 108. i.
afar off. Lit. unto (Gr. *eis*) far, i. e. the Dispersion and then the Gentiles. Cp. 22. 21. Eph. 2. 13, 17. Fig. *Euphēmismos*. Ap. 6.
call = call to (Himself).
40 with = by.
testify = earnestly testify. Gr. *diamarturomai*. Occ. fifteen times. Once in Luke 16. 28, nine times in Acts, and five times in Paul's Epistles.
exhort. Ap. 134. I. 6.
from = away from. Gr. *apo*. Ap. 104. iv.
untoward = crooked.
41 gladly. Texts omit.
received = received fully. Gr. *apodechomai*. Only here; 15. 4; 18. 27; 24. 3; 28. 30. Luke 8. 40.
baptized. Ap. 115. I. i.
souls. Ap. 110. II. See Ps. 110. 3.
42 And. This and the "ands" in following verses give the Fig. *Polysyndeton*. Ap. 6.
continued stedfastly. Gr. *proskartereō*. See note on 1. 14.
doctrine = teaching.
fellowship = the fellowship. Cp. *v.* 44.
breaking of bread. This was the common meal. Cp. *vv.* 44, 46 and Matt. 14. 19. Isa. 58. 7.
breaking. Only here and Luke 24. 35.
prayers = the prayers. Ap. 134. II. 2. Cp. 3. 1.
43 upon = to.
44 believed. Ap. 150. I. 1. i.
together. See *v.* 1.
45 to all. i. e. to the believers. **every man** = any one. Ap. 123. 3. **46 temple** = temple courts. Gr. *hieron*. See note on Matt. 23. 16. **from house to house** = at home. **did eat** = were partaking of. **meat** = food. Gr. *trophē*. nourishment. **with.** Gr. *en*. **gladness.** Occ. here; Luke 1. 14, 44. Heb. 1. 9. Jude 24. **singleness.** Gr. *aphelotēs*. Only here. **47 Praising.** Gr. *aineō*. Always used of praising God. Here; 3. 8, 9. Luke 2. 13, 20; 19. 37; 24. 53. Rom. 15. 11. Rev. 19. 5. **favour.** Gr. *charis*. Ap. 186. I. 1. **with** = in regard to. Gr. *pros*. Ap. 104. xv. 3. **people.** Gr. *laos*. **Lord.** Ap. 98. VI. i. β. 1. A. b. **to the church.** The texts omit. **such, &c.** = the saved.

3. 1—4. 22 (D[1], p. 1579). AMONG THE PEOPLE. (*Introversion and Alternation.*)

D[1] | K | 3. 1-11. Miracle. Performed.
  L | M[1] | 3. 12-26. Answer to People.
  N[1] | 4. 1-7. Arrest.
  M[2] | 4. 8-12. Answer to Rulers.
  N[2] | 4. 13-18. Decision.
  M[3] | 4. 19-20. Answer to Rulers.
  N[3] | 4. 21-. Release.
K | 4. -21-22. Miracle. Result.

3. 1-11 (K, above). MIRACLE. PERFORMED. (*Introversion.*)

K | k | 1. In the Temple.
  m | 2. The Beautiful Gate.
  n | 3-9. The Lame Man healed.
  m | 10. The Beautiful Gate.
k | 11. Solomon's Porch.

1 Peter and John. Mentioned together seven times in Acts, John always in subordination to Peter. **went** = were going. **into.** Gr. *eis*. Ap. 104. vi. **temple.** See 2. 46. **at** = upon. Ap. 104. ix. 3. **prayer.** Ap. 134. II. 2. **the ninth hour.** About 3 p.m. See Ap. 165. Cp. Luke 1. 9, 10. **2 certain.** Ap. 123. 3. **man.** Ap. 123. 2. **lame** = being (Gr. *huparchō*. See note on Luke 9. 48) lame. **from.** Gr. *ek*. Ap. 104. vii. **laid** = were laying, i. e. used to lay.

daily °at the gate of the [1]temple which is
called °Beautiful, to °ask °alms °of them that
entered [1]into the [1]temple;

n 3 Who, °seeing [1]Peter and John about to go
[1]into the [1]temple, °asked °an [2]alms.
4 °And [1]Peter, °fastening his eyes °upon
him °with [1]John, said, °"Look °on us."
5 [4]And he °gave heed °unto them, °expecting
to receive something [2]of them
6 Then Peter said, "Silver and gold °have I
none; but such as I have °give I thee: °In °the
name of °Jesus Christ °of Nazareth °rise up
and walk."
7 And he °took him by the right hand, and
°lifted *him* up: and °immediately his °feet and
°ankle bones °received strength.
8 And he °leaping up stood, and walked, and
entered with them [1]into the [1]temple, walking,
and °leaping, and praising °God.
9 And all the °people [3]saw him walking and
praising [8]God:

m 10 And they °knew that it was he which sat
°for [2]alms °at the [2]Beautiful gate of the [1]tem-
ple: and they were filled with wonder and
°amazement °at that which had happened [5]unto
him.

k 11 And as °the lame man which was healed
held [1]Peter and John, all the [9]people ran together °unto them °in the °porch that is called
Solomon's, °greatly wondering.

M[1] O[1] o 12 [4]And when Peter [3]saw *it*, he answered
[11]unto the [9]people, °"Ye men of Israel, why
marvel ye [10]at this? or why °look ye so earnestly °on us, as though by our own °power or
°holiness we had made °this man to walk?

p 13 The [8]God of Abraham, and of Isaac, and
of Jacob, the [8]God of our fathers, hath °glori-
fied His °Son [6]Jesus;

q Whom ye °delivered up, and °denied °Him
°in the presence of Pilate, °when He was determined to °let *Him* go.

q 14 But ye [13]denied °the Holy One and °the
Just, and °desired °a murderer °to be granted
[5]unto you;

at = towards. Ap. 104. xv. 3.
Beautiful. Probably the East gate, which, Josephus says, "was of Corinthian brass and greatly excelled those that were only covered over with silver and gold" (*Wars* 5. § 3).
ask. Ap. 134. I. 4.
alms. Gr. *eleēmosunē.* This was shortened into "*aelmesse*", and then into "alms".
of = from. Gr. *para.* Ap. 104. xii. 1.
3 seeing. Ap. 133. I. 1.
asked. Gr. *erōtaō.* Ap. 134. I. 3.
an alms. Lit. to receive an alms.
4 And = But.
fastening his eyes. Gr. *atenizō.* Ap. 133. III. 6.
upon. Gr. *eis.* Ap. 104. vi.
with. Gr. *sun.* Ap. 104. xvi.
Look. Gr. *blepō.* Ap. 133. I. 5.
on. Same as "upon".
5 gave heed. Gr. *epechō.* Here, 19. 22. Luke 14. 7. Phil. 2. 16. 1 Tim. 4. 16.
unto = to.
expecting. Gr. *prosdokaō.* Ap. 133. III. 3.
6 have I none = belong not (Gr. *ou.* Ap. 105. I). Apart from Peter's lack, it was unlawful by Rabbinical ruling to carry a purse into the Temple.
give, &c. = this I give thee.
In. Gr. *en.* Ap. 104. viii.
the name. See 2. 38.
Jesus Christ. Ap. 98. XI.
of Nazareth = the Nazarene. This title occurs seven times in Acts. See 2. 22; 4. 10; 6. 14; 10. 38; 22. 8; 26. 9.
rise up. Gr. *egeirō.* Ap. 178. I. 4.
7 took. Gr. *piazō.* See note on John 11. 57.
lifted = raised, as in *v.* 6.
immediately. Gr. *parachrēma.* Occ. nineteen times, of which ten are in Luke and seven in Acts.
feet. Gr. *basis,* a step, then that with which one steps, &c. Only here.
ankle bones. Gr. *sphuron.* Only here.
received strength = were strengthened. Gr. *stereoō.* Only here, *v.* 16, and 16. 5.
8 leaping up. Gr. *exallomai.* Only here, a strong form of *hallomai.*
leaping. Gr. *hallomai.* Only here, 14. 10, and John 4. 14. Cp. Isa. 35. 6.
God. Ap. 98. I. i. 1.
9 people. See 2. 47.
10 knew. Gr. *epiginōskō.* Ap. 132. I. iii.
for. Gr. *pros.* Ap. 104. xv. 3.
at. Gr. *epi.* Ap. 104. ix. 2.
amazement. Gr. *ekstasis,* ecstasy. See note on Mark 5. 42.
11 the lame . . . healed. The texts read "he".
unto. Gr. *pros.* Ap. 104. xv. 3. **in.** Ap. 104. ix. 2. **porch, &c.** See note on John 10. 23. **greatly wondering.** Only here. Cp. Mark 14. 33. This miracle was significant of Israel's restoration. Isa. 35. 6. Cp. Matt. 11. 5.

3. 12-26 (M[1], p. 1581). ANSWER TO PEOPLE. (*Division.*)

O[1] | 12-16. Explanation.
O[2] | 17-26. Application.

3. 12-16 (O[1], above). PETER'S EXPLANATION. (*Introversion.*)

O[1] | o | 12. Miracle. Negative. Not by man's power.
  p | 13-. God glorified His servant Jesus.
    q | -13. Ye denied Him.
    q | 14, 15-. Ye killed Him.
  p | -15. God raised Him.
o | 16. Miracle. Positive. By His Name.

12 Ye men of Israel. Lit. Men, Israelites. See note on 1. 11. **look ye so earnestly.** Gr. *atenizō,* Ap. 133. III. 6. **on** = to. **power.** Gr. *dunamis.* Ap. 172. 1. **holiness** = godliness. Cp. Ap. 137. 5. **this man** = him. **13 glorified.** Gr. *doxazō.* See note on p. 1511. **Son** = Servant. Ap. 108. iv. Cp. Isa. 42. 1; 49. 6. Matt. 12. 18. **delivered up.** Gr. *paradidōmi.* See note on John 19. 30. **denied.** Cp. John 19. 15. **Him.** The texts omit. **in.** Gr. *kata.* Ap. 104. x. 2. **when, &c.** Lit. he having decided (Gr. *krinō.* Ap. 122. 1). **let Him go** = to release Him. Gr. *apoluō.* Ap. 174. 11. **14 the Holy One.** Cp. 4. 27, 30. Isa. 29. 23; 43. 3; 49. 7. Fig. *Antonomasia.* Ap. 6. **the Just.** Gr. *dikaios.* Ap. 191. 1. Cp. 7. 52; 22. 14. **desired.** Gr. *aiteō.* Ap. 134. I. 4. **a murderer** = a man (Ap. 123. 2) a murderer. **to be granted.** Gr. *charizomai.* Ap. 184. II. 1.

aside out of the °council, they °conferred °among
themselves,
16 Saying, "What shall we do to these [9]men?
for that indeed a °notable °miracle hath °been
done °by them *is* °manifest to all them that
°dwell in Jerusalem; and we °cannot deny *it*.
17 But °that it °spread °no further °among
the [1]people, let us °straitly °threaten them,
°that they [1]speak henceforth to no [9]man °in
this [10]name."
18 And they called them, and commanded
them °not to °speak °at all °nor teach [17]in the
[10]name of [13]Jesus.
M3 19 But Peter and John °answered and said
[1]unto them, °"Whether it be right in the sight
of [10]God to hearken unto you °more than unto
[10]God, °judge ye.
20 For we [16]cannot °but [1]speak the things
which we °have seen and heard."
N3 21 °So when they had further threatened
them, they °let them go, finding °nothing how
they might punish them, °because of the
[1]people:
K for all *men* °glorified [10]God °for that which
°was done.
22 For the [9]man was above forty years old,
[5]on whom this [16]miracle of healing °was
shewed.
C2 P1 Q 23 And °being [21]let go, they went °to °their
own company, and °reported all that the chief
priests and elders had said [1]unto them.
R t 24 And when they heard that, they lifted up
their voice [23]to [10]God °with one accord, and
said, °"Lord, Thou °*art* God, Which °hast made
[12]heaven, and °earth, and the sea, and all that
[7]in them is:
u 25 Who [16]by the mouth of Thy °servant
David °hast said,
v **'Why did the °heathen °rage, and the [1]people**
°imagine vain things?
26 °The kings of the [24]earth stood up, and
the °rulers were gathered °together °against
the °LORD, and °against His °Christ.'
v 27 For °of a truth °against Thy holy °Child
[13]Jesus, Whom thou °hast anointed, both
Herod, and Pontius Pilate, [13]with the °Gentiles,
and the [1]people of Israel, were gathered together,

15 council = Sanhedrin. Gr. *sunedrion*. See note on Matt. 5. 22.
conferred. Gr. *sumballō*. Only used by Luke, here, 17. 18; 18. 27; 20. 14. Luke 2. 19; 14. 31.
among themselves = towards (Gr. *pros*. Ap. 104. xv. 3) one another.
16 notable. Gr. *gnōstos*, as in *v*. 10.
miracle. Gr. *sēmeion*. Ap. 176. 3.
been done = come to pass.
by. Gr. *dia*. Ap. 104. v. 1.
manifest. Gr. *phaneros*. Ap. 106. I. viii.
dwell in = inhabit. Gr. *katoikeō*. See note on 2. 5.
cannot = are not (Gr. *ou*. Ap. 105. I) able to.
17 that = in order that. Gr. *hina*.
spread. Gr. *dianemomai*. Only here.
no further = not (Gr. *mē*) for (Gr. *epi*) more.
among = unto. Gr. *eis*. Ap. 104. vi.
straitly threaten = threaten with threats. Fig. *Polyptōton*. Ap. 6.
threaten. Gr. *apeileō*. Only here and 1 Pet. 2. 23. The noun *apeilē* occ. here, *v*. 29; 9. 1. Eph. 6. 9.
that they speak, &c. = Lit. no longer to speak to no man. A double negative, for emphasis.
in = Gr. *epi*. Ap. 104. ix. 2.
18 not. Gr. *mē*. Ap. 105. II.
speak = speak forth. Gr. *phthengomai*. Only here, and 2 Pet. 2. 16, 18. Cp. 2. 4.
at all. Gr. *katholou*. Only here.
nor. Gr. *mede*.
19 answered and said. Ap. 122. 3.
Whether = If. Gr. *ei*. Ap. 118. 2. a.
more = rather.
judge. Gr. *krinō*. Ap. 122. 1. Fig. *Anacœnōsis*. Ap. 6.
20 but = not. As *v*. 17.
have seen and heard = saw (Gr. *eidon*. Ap. 133. I. 1) and heard.
21 So when, &c. = But having further threatened. Only here.
let . . . go = Gr. *apoluō*. Ap. 174. 11.
nothing, &c. = no further means of punishing.
because of. Gr. *dia*. Ap. 104. v. 2.
glorified. Gr. *doxazō*. See note on 3. 13.
for. Gr. *epi*. Ap. 104. ix. 2.
was done = had taken place.
22 was shewed = had been wrought.

4. 23—5. 11 (C², p. 1579). AMONG THE BRETHREN. (*Division*.)

C2 | P1 | 4. 23-31. Return of the Apostles.
   | P2 | 4. 32—5. 11. Unity.

4. 23-31 (P¹, above) RETURN OF THE APOSTLES. (*Introversion*)

P1 | Q | 23. Report.
   | R | 24-30. Prayer.
   | *R* | 31-. Answer.
   | *Q* | -31. Testimony.

23 being = having been.
to. Gr. *pros*. Ap. 104. xv. 3.
their own company = their own. Gr. *idios*.
reported. Gr. *apangellō*. Cp. Ap. 121. 5, 6.

4. 24-30 (R, above). PRAYER. (*Introversion*.)

R | t | 24. God's power. Creation.
  | u | 25-. Word by David.
  | v | -25, 26. Man's rage predicted.
  | *v* | 27, 28. Man's rage accomplished.
  | *u* | 29. Word by Apostles.
  | *t* | 30. God's power. Healing.

24 with one accord. See note on 1. 14. **Lord**. Gr. *Despotēs*. Ap. 98. VI. ii. 1. **art God**. The texts omit. **hast made** = madest. **earth**. Gr. *gē*. Ap. 129. 4. **25 servant**. Gr. *pais*. Ap 108 iv. and 190. I. 6. **hast said** = saidst. This quotation is from Ps. 2. 1, 2. See notes there. **heathen** = nations. Gr. *ethnos*. Hence our word "heathen". **rage**. Gr. *phruassō*. Only here in N.T. Used in Sept. of Ps. 2. 1, as transl. of Heb. *rāgash*. **imagine** = meditate. Gr. *meletaō*. Here, Mark 13. 11. 1 Tim. 4. 15. **26 The kings**. i. e. Gentiles. **rulers**. i. e. Jews. **together**. See note on 1. 15. **against**. Gr. *kata*. Ap. 104. x. 1. **Lord**. Ap. 98. VI. i. β. 1. A. *a*. **Christ**. i. e. Messiah. Ap. 98. IX. **27 of a truth**. Lit. upon (Ap. 104. ix 1) truth. The texts add "in this city". **against**. Gr. *epi*. Ap. 104. ix. 3. **Child** = servant. Gr. *pais*, as *v*. 25. Fig. *Catachresis* Ap. 6. **hast anointed** = didst anoint. See note on Luke 4. 18. **Gentiles**. Gr. *ethnos*, as in *v*. 25.

28 For to do whatsoever Thy hand and Thy °counsel °determined before °to be done.

u 29 And °now, °Lord, °behold their [17]threatenings: and °grant [10]unto Thy °servants, that °with all [13]boldness they may [1]speak Thy [4]word,

t 30 [7]By stretching forth Thine hand °to heal; and that °signs and °wonders may be done [16]by the [10]name of Thy holy [27]Child [13]Jesus."

R 31 And °when they had °prayed, the place was °shaken °where they were assembled together; and they were all [8]filled with °the Holy Ghost,

Q and they [1]spake the [4]word of [10]God [29]with [13]boldness.

P^2 S 32 And °the multitude of them that [4]believed were of one heart and of one °soul:

T °neither said °any *of them* that °ought of °the things which he possessed was his own; but they had all things common.

S 33 And with great [7]power °gave the °apostles °witness of the [2]resurrection of °the Lord [13]Jesus: and great °grace was °upon them all.

T U^1 34 °Neither °was there °any [12]among them °that lacked: for as many as °were °possessors of °lands or houses sold them, and brought the prices of the things that were sold,

35 And laid *them* down °at the [33]apostles' feet: and °distribution was made unto every man °according as °he had need.

U^2 V^1 36 And °Joses, who °by the [33]apostles was surnamed °Barnabas, (which is, being interpreted, The °son of °consolation,) a Levite, *and* °of the country of Cyprus,

37 °Having °land sold *it*, and brought the money, and laid *it* [35]at the [33]apostles' feet.

V^2 W x **5** But a °certain °man °named °Ananias, °with Sapphira his wife, sold a possession,

2 And °kept back *part* °of the price, his wife

---

28 counsel. Ap. 102. 4. Cp. 2. 23.
determined before. Gr. *proorizō.* Generally translated "predestinate". See Rom. 8. 29, 30. 1 Cor. 2. 7. Eph. 1. 5, 11.
to be done. Fig. *Hypo-zeugma* (*Zeugma.* 3. Ap. 6). As "hand" could not determine.
29 now = as to the present. Gr. *tanun.* A strong form of *nun.* Only here, 5. 38; 17. 30; 20. 32; 27. 22.
Lord. Ap. 98. VI. i. β. 1. B. b.
behold. Gr. *epeidon.* Ap. 133. II. 1. Only here and Luke 1. 25. **grant** = give.
servants = bond-servants. Ap. 190. I. 2.
with. Ap. 104. xi. 1.
30 to heal = for (Gr. *eis.* Ap. 104. vi) healing.
signs. As in *vv.* 16, 22.
wonders. Gr. *teras.* Ap. 176. 2.
31 when they had = while they.
prayed. Ap. 134. I. 5.
shaken. Gr. *saleuō.* Cp. 16. 26.
where = in (Ap. 104. viii) which.
the Holy Ghost. Ap. 101. II. 14.

4. 32—5. 11 (P^2, 1585). UNITY.
(*Alternation.*)

P^2 | S | 4. 32-. Unity.
 T | 4. -32. Community of goods.
 S | 4. 33. Power and Grace.
 T | 4. 34—5. 11. Community of goods.

32 the multitude, &c. = of the full number (Gr. *plēthos*) of the believing ones.
soul. Ap. 110. V. 1.
neither = and not even. **any** = one.
ought = any one. Gr. *tis.* Ap. 123. 3.
the things which he possessed = his possessions. Gr. *huparchō.* Cp. Luke 9. 48 and 12. 15.
33 gave = were giving forth.
apostles. Ap. 189.
witness = the testimony. Gr. *marturion.* First occ. Matt. 8. 4.
the Lord. Ap. 98. VI. i. β. 2. A.
grace. Ap. 184. I. 1.
upon. Gr. *epi.* Ap. 104. ix. 3.

4. 34—5. 11 (*T*, above). COMMUNITY OF GOODS.
(*Division.*)

T | U^1 | 4. 34, 35. General.
 | U^2 | 4. 36—5. 11. Particular.

34 Neither = For neither.
was = were. Gr. *huparchō.* See note on Luke 9. 48. The texts read *ēn* was. **any.** Ap. 123. 3.
that lacked = in need. Only here. Cp. Ap. 134. I. 5. **were.** Gr. *huparchō.* **possessors.** Gr. *ktētōr.* Only here. **lands.** Gr. *chōrion.* See note on Matt. 26. 36. **35 at.** Ap. 104. xii. 3. **distribution, &c.** = it was distributed. **according as.** Gr. *kathoti,* as in 2. 24, 45. **he** = any one. Gr. *tis,* as in *v.* 34.

4. 36—5. 11 (U^2, above). PARTICULAR. (*Division.*)

U^2 | V^1 | 4. 36-37. Devotedness.
 | V^2 | 5. 1-11. Deceit.

36 The next chapter should begin here. **Joses.** Texts read Joseph, as in 1. 23. **by.** Ap. 104. xviii. 1. **Barnabas.** It is possible that Joseph Barnabas, or Barnabbas, is the same as Joseph Barsabbas of 1. 23, and that he was reserved for a better lot by the Holy Spirit. **son.** Ap. 108. iii. See note on 3. 25. **consolation.** Or, exhortation. Gr. *paraklēsis* has both meanings. See Luke 2. 25; 6. 24. 1 Cor. 14. 3. **of the country of Cyprus** = a Cypriote by race. **37 Having.** Gr. *huparchō.* **land.** Lit. a field, as in Luke 14. 18.

5. 1-11 (V^2, above). DECEIT. (*Extended Alternation.*)

V^2 | W | x | 1, 2. Ananias.
 y | 3, 4. Remonstrance.
 z | 5-. Death.
 X | a | -5. Fear.
 b | 6. Burial.
 W | *x* | 7, 8. Sapphira.
 y | 9. Remonstrance.
 z | 10-. Death.
 X | *b* | -10. Burial.
 a | 11. Fear.

1 certain. Ap. 123. 3. **man.** Ap. 123. 2. **named** = by name. **Ananias.** Ananias and Sapphira, names of grace and beauty attached to persons whose principles were bad. **with.** Ap. 104. xvi. **2 kept back.** Gr. *nosphizomai.* Only here, *v.* 3. Tit. 2. 10. **of** = from. Ap. 104. iv.

also °being privy *to it*, and brought a [1]certain
part, and laid *it* °at the °apostles' feet.

y 3 But Peter said, "Ananias, why hath Satan
filled thine heart to lie to °the Holy Ghost,
and to [2]keep back *part* [2]of the price of the
°land?
4 °Whiles it remained, was it °not thine own?
and after it was sold, °was it not °in thine
own °power? °why °hast thou conceived this
thing °in thine heart? thou hast °not lied
°unto °men, but °unto °God."

z 5 °And Ananias hearing these °words fell
down, and °gave up the ghost:

X a and °great fear came °on all them that heard
°these things.

b 6 [5]And the °young men °arose, °wound him
up, and carried *him* out, and buried *him*.

W x 7 [5]And it was °about the space of three hours
after, °when his wife, °not °knowing what was
done, came in.
8 [5]And Peter °answered [4]unto her, "Tell me
°whether ye sold the [3]land for so much?"
And she said, "Yea, for so much."

y 9 Then Peter said °unto her, °"How is it that
ye °have agreed together to tempt the °Spirit
of the °LORD? °behold, the feet of them which
have buried thy °husband *are* °at the door,
and °shall carry thee out."

z 10 Then fell she down °straightway °at his
feet, and °yielded up the ghost:

X b and the °young men came in, and found her
°dead, and, carrying *her* forth, buried *her* °by
her [9]husband.

a 11 And [5]great fear came °upon all the °church,
and °upon °as many as heard these things.

D[2]Y[1] c[1] 12 [5]And °by the hands of the [2]apostles were
many °signs and °wonders °wrought °among
the °people;

d[1] (and they were all °with one accord [4]in °Solomon's porch.

c[2] 13 [5]And of the rest durst °no man °join himself to them: but the [12]people °magnified them.
14 [5]And °believers were the more added to
the °Lord, °multitudes both of [1]men and °women.)
15 °Insomuch that they brought forth the

being privy to = being conscious of. Gr. *suneidon*. Only here, 12. 12; 14. 6. 1 Cor. 4. 4.
at. Ap. 104. xii. 3.
apostles'. Ap. 189.
3 the Holy Ghost. Two arts. Ap. 101. II. 3: Cp. 1. 16.
land. Gr. *chōrion*, as in 1. 18, 19; 4. 34, not *ktēma* possession, as in *v.* 1; 2. 45. Matt. 19. 22.
4 Whiles . . . power? Lit. Is it not (Gr. *ouchi*. Ap. 105. I. a.) that, remaining, it remained to thee, and sold, it belonged to thy right?
was = belonged. Gr. *huparchō*. See Luke 9. 48.
in. Gr. *en*. Ap. 104. viii.
power. Ap. 172. 5.
why = why is it that.
hast . . . conceived = didst put, implying careful deliberation, not sudden temptation.
not. Ap. 105. I.
unto = to.
men. Ap. 123. 1.
God. Ap. 98. I. i. 3.
5 And = Now, or But.
words. Ap. 121. 10.
gave up the ghost = expired. Only here, *v.* 10; 12. 23. A medical word. Cp. *ekpneō*. Mark 15. 37.
great fear. Cp. "great grace", "great power", in 4. 33.
on = upon. Ap. 104. ix. 3.
these things. The texts omit.
6 young men = younger (men).
arose. Ap. 178. I. 1.
wound . . . up. Gr. *sustellō*. Only here and 1 Cor. 7. 29.
7 about the space . . after = as it were an interval. Gr. *diastēma*. Only here. A medical word.
when = and.
not. Ap. 105. II.
knowing. Ap. 132. I. i.
8 answered. Ap. 122. 3.
whether = if. Ap. 118. 2. a.
9 unto. Gr. *pros*. Ap. 104. xv. 3.
How = Why.
have agreed together = were agreed together. Gr. *sumphōneō*. Here, 15. 15, and four times in the Gospels. Cp. Engl. "symphony".
Spirit. Ap. 101. II. 3.
Lord Ap. 98. VI. i. β. 1. B. b.
behold. Ap. 133. I. 2. Fig. *Asterismos*. Ap. 6.
husband. Ap. 123. 2.
at. Ap. 104. ix. 2.
shall = they shall.
10 straightway. Gr. *parachrēma*. See note on 3. 7.
at. Gr. *para*, as in *v* 2, but the texts read *pros*.
yielded up the ghost. Same as in *v.* 5.
young men. Ap. 108. x. **dead.** Ap. 139. 2.
by. Ap. 104. xv. 3.
11 upon. Gr. *epi*. Ap. 104. ix. 3.
church. Ap. 186.
as many as = all those who.

5. 12-42 (D[2], p. 1579). AMONG THE PEOPLE. (*Division.*)

D[2] | Y[1] | 12-21-. Apostles' Activity.
| Y[2] | -21-42. Rulers' Opposition.

5. 12-21- (Y[1], above). APOSTLES' ACTIVITY. (*Repeated Alternation.*)

Y[1] | c[1] | 12-. Miracles.
| d[1] | -12. In the Temple.
| c[2] | 13-16. Miracles.
| d[2] | 17, 18. In prison.
| c[3] | 19, 20. Miracle.
| d[3] | 21-. In the Temple.

12 by. Ap. 104. v. 1. **signs.** Ap. 176. 3. **wonders.** Ap. 176. 2. **wrought** = being wrought. Cp. Mark 16. 17, 18. **among.** Ap. 104. viii. 2. **people.** Gr. *laos*. See note on 2. 47. **with one accord.** See note on 1. 14. **Solomon's porch.** See note on John 10. 23. **13 no man** = no one. Gr. *oudeis*. **join himself.** Gr. *kollaomai*. See note on Luke 15. 15. **magnified.** Gr. *megalunō*. Cp. Luke 1. 46, 58. **14 believers** = believing (ones). Ap. 150. I. 1. **Lord.** Ap. 98. VI. i. β. 2. A. **multitudes.** Gr. *plēthos*. See note on 2. 6. **women.** Cp. 1. 14. **15 Insomuch that** = So that. This depends upon the first clause of *v.* 12, all that intervenes being in a parenthesis.

°sick °into the streets, and laid *them* °on beds and °couches, °that °at the least the shadow of Peter passing by might °overshadow °some of them.
16 There came °also a [14]multitude *out* of the cities °round about °unto Jerusalem, bringing [15]sick folks, and them which were °vexed °with unclean °spirits: and they were °healed °every one.

d2 17 °Then the °high priest °rose up, and all they that were [1]with him, (which is the °sect of the °Sadducees,) and were filled with °indignation,
18 And laid their hands [5]on the [2]apostles, and put them [4]in the °common °prison.

c3 19 But the angel of the [9]LORD [12]by night opened the °prison doors, and brought them forth, and said,
20 "Go, stand and °speak [4]in the °temple to the [12]people all °the °words of this °life."

d3 21 [5]And when they heard that, they entered °into the [20]temple °early in the morning, and °taught.

Y2 e1 But the [17]high priest came, and they that were [1]with him, and called the °council together, and all the °senate of the °children of Israel,

f1 and °sent °to the °prison to have them brought.
22 But when the °officers came, and found them [4]not [4]in the [19]prison, they returned, and °told,
23 Saying, "The [21]prison °truly found we °shut °with all safety, and the °keepers standing °without °before the doors: but when we had opened, we found [13]no man within."

e2 24 Now when °the high priest and the °captain of the [20]temple and the chief priests heard these °things, they °doubted °of them °whereunto this would grow.
25 Then came °one and [22]told them, saying, [9]"Behold, the [1]men whom ye put [4]in [19]prison are standing [4]in the [20]temple, and teaching the [12]people."

f2 26 Then went the [24]captain [1]with the [22]officers, and brought them °without violence: for they feared the [12]people, °lest they should have been stoned.
27 [5]And when they had brought them, they set *them* °before the [21]council:

e3 and the [17]high priest °asked them,
28 Saying, "Did [4]not we °straitly command you that ye should [7]not teach °in this °name? and, [9]behold, ye have filled Jerusalem with your doctrine, and °intend to °bring °this [4]Man's blood [11]upon us."

f3 29 Then Peter and the *other* [2]apostles [8]an-

---

sick. See note on John 11. 1.
into = along. Ap. 104. x. 2.
on = upon. Ap. 104. ix. 1.
couches. Gr. *krabbatos*. See note on Mark 2. 4.
that = in order that. Gr. *hina*.
at the least = even if (it might be).
overshadow. Gr. *episkiazō*. See note on Luke 9. 34.
some = some one. Ap. 123. 3.
16 also, &c. = a multitude also.
round about. Gr. *perix*. Only here.
unto. Ap. 104. vi.
vexed = beset. Gr. *ochleō*, to crowd. Only here and Luke 6. 18. A medical word.
with = by. Ap. 104. xviii. 1.
spirits. Ap. 101. II. 12.
healed. Gr. *therapeuō*. See note on Luke 6. 17, 18.
every one = all of them.
17 Then = But.
high priest. Gr. *archiereus*.
rose up. Ap. 178. I. 1. See *v*. 6.
sect. Gr. *hairesis* = a choosing, hence "heresy". Occ. here, 15. 5; 24. 5, 14; 26. 5; 28. 22. 1 Cor. 11. 19. Gal. 5. 20. 2 Pet. 2. 1.
Sadducees. Ap. 120. II. 2. Cp. 4. 1.
indignation. Gr. *zēlos*. Only other occ. in Acts in 13. 45. Used in a good sense in John 2. 17. 2 Cor. 11. 2, &c.
18 common = public. Gr. *dēmosios*. Only here, 16. 37; 18. 28; 20. 20.
prison. Same as "hold" in 4. 3.
19 prison. Gr. *phulakē*, the common word for "prison".
20 speak. Ap. 121. 7.
temple. See 2. 46.
the words, &c. = these words of life. Fig. *Hypallagē*. Ap. 6.
words. Gr. *rhēma*. See note on Mark 9. 32.
life. Ap. 170. 1. The life through resurrection so bitterly opposed by the Sadducees. Cp. 13. 26.
21 into. Gr. *eis*. Ap. 104. vi.
early in the morning = towards (Ap. 104. xviii) daybreak. Gr. *tou orthrou*. Cp. Luke 24. 1. John 8. 2.
taught = were teaching.

5. -21-42 (Y2, p. 1587). **RULERS' OPPOSITION.**
(Repeated Alternation.)

Y2
e1 | -21. Assembly.
f1 | -21-23. Apostles sent for.
e2 | 24, 25. Alarm.
f2 | 26, 27. Apostles brought.
e3 | -27, 28. Investigation.
f3 | 29-32. Apostles' Answer.
e4 | 33. Murderous Design.
f4 | 34. Apostles excluded.
e5 | 35-39. Wise counsel.
f5 | 40-42. Apostles released.

-21 council. See note on Matt. 5. 22.
senate = assembly of the elders Only here in N.T. but frequent in Sept. for "elders".
children = sons. Ap. 108. iii.
sent. Ap. 174. 1.
to = unto Ap. 104. vi.
prison = place of bonds. Only here, *v*. 23; 16. 26. Matt. 11. 2. Used in Sept. in Gen. 39. 22, &c.
22 officers. Ap. 190. I. 7. See note on Luke 1. 2. John 7. 32; 18. 3.
told. Same as "reported", 4. 23.
23 truly = indeed.

shut = locked. Gr. *kleiō*. with. Ap. 104. viii and 12. 6, 19. without. The texts omit. keepers = guards. Gr. *phulax*. Only here before. Ap. 104. xiv. **24** the high priest and. The texts omit. captain. See note on 4. 1. things = words. Ap. 121. 10. doubted = were doubting. Gr. *diaporeō*. See note on Luke 9. 7. of. Ap 104. xiii. 1. whereunto, &c. = what this might come to be. **25** one. Ap. 123. 3. **26** without. Lit. not (Ap. 105. I.) with (Ap. 104. xi. 1) violence (Gr. *bia*; here, 21. 35; 24. 7; 27. 41). lest = in order that (Gr. *hina*). **27** before = in. Ap. 104. viii. asked. See note on 1. 6. **28** straitly command. Lit. command with a command. Fig. *Polyptōton*. Ap. 6. A Hebraism. in. Gr. *epi*. Ap. 104. ix. 2. name. See note on 2. 38. intend. Gr. *boulomai*. Ap. 102. 3. bring Gr. *epagō*. Only here and 2 Pet. 2. 1, 5. Cp. their own invocation in Matt. 27. 25. this, &c. = the blood of this Man (Emph.).

swered and said, °"We ought to °obey [4]God
rather than [4]men.
30 The [4]God of our fathers °raised up °Jesus,
Whom ye °slew °and hanged [15]on a °tree.
31 °Him °hath [4]God °exalted °with His right
hand *to be* a °Prince and a °Saviour, for to
give °repentance to Israel, and °forgiveness of
°sins.
32 And we are °His °witnesses of these °things;
and *so is* also °the Holy Ghost, Whom [4]God
°hath given to them that [29]obey Him."

c[4] 33 °When they heard *that*, they were °cut *to*
the heart, and °took counsel to °slay them.

f[4] 34 Then °stood there up [25]one [4]in the [21]coun-
cil, a °Pharisee, named °Gamaliel, a °doctor
of the law, °had in reputation °among all the
[12]people, and commanded to °put the [2]apostles
forth a little space;

e[5] 35 And said [9]unto them, °"Ye [1]men of Israel,
take heed to yourselves what ye °intend to do
°as touching these [4]men.
36 For [23]before these days [17]rose up °Theudas,
°boasting himself to be °somebody; to whom a
number of [1]men, about four hundred, °joined
themselves: who was [33]slain; and all, as
many as °obeyed him, were °scattered, and
°brought [21]to nought.
37 °After °this man [17]rose up °Judas of Galilee [4]in the days of the °taxing, and °drew away
much [12]people °after him: °he also °perished;
and all, *even* as many as [36]obeyed him, were
dispersed.
38 And now I say unto you, °Refrain °from
these [4]men, and let them alone: for °if this
°counsel or this work be °of [4]men, it °will
come to nought:
39 But °if it be [38]of [4]God, ye °cannot °over-
throw it; °lest haply ye be found even °to fight
against God."

f[5] 40 [5]And to him they °agreed; and when they
had called the [2]apostles, and °beaten *them*,
they commanded that they should [7]not [20]speak
[28]in the [28]name of [30]Jesus, and °let them go.
41 °And they departed [38]from the presence of
the [21]council, rejoicing that they were °counted
worthy to °suffer shame °for °His [28]name.
42 And daily [4]in the [20]temple, and °in every
house, they ceased [4]not to teach and °preach
°Jesus Christ.

C[3] Z **6** And °in those days, when the number of
the disciples was multiplied, there arose
a °murmuring of the °Grecians °against the

29 We ought = it is necessary.
obey. Gr. *peitharcheō.* Only here, *v.* 32; 27. 21. Tit. 3. 1.
30 raised up. Gr. *egeirō.* Ap. 178. I. 4.
Jesus. Ap. 98. X.
slew = laid hands on. Gr. *diacheirizomai.* Only here and 26. 21.
and = having. **tree.** Ap. 162.
31 Him = This One. It is emphatic, and so placed first in the sentence. **hath.** Omit.
exalted. Gr. *hupsoō.* See note on John 12. 32.
with = at, or to. See 2. 33.
Prince. Gr. *archēgos.* See note on 3. 15.
Saviour. Gr. *Sōtēr.* Occurs twenty-four times. First occ. Luke 1. 47.
repentance. Ap. 111. II. 1.
forgiveness. Gr. *aphesis.* More frequently transl. "remission". See 2. 38. Luke 4. 18; 24. 47. Cp. Ap. 174. 12.
sins. Gr. *hamartia.* Ap. 128. I. ii. 1.
32 His. Omit.
witnesses. See note on 1. 8.
things = words. Gr. *rhēma,* as in *v.* 20.
the Holy Ghost. Ap. 101. II. 3.
hath given = gave.
33 When, &c. = Now they having heard.
cut to the heart. Gr. *diapriomai.* Only here and 7. 54.
took counsel = were consulting. Gr. *bouleuō.*
slay. Gr. *anaireō.* See note on 2. 23.
34 stood there up = rose up. Gr. *anistēmi.* Ap. 178. I. 1, as in *vv.* 6, 17.
Pharisee. Ap. 120. II.
Gamaliel. The grandson of the famous Hillel. He was Saul's instructor (22. 3), and is said to have died about 52 A.D.
a doctor of the law. See note on Luke 5. 17.
had in reputation = honoured. Gr. *timios.* Generally transl. "precious".
among = by (dat. case).
put . . . forth. Lit. make . . . outside, i.e. put out of court.
35 Ye men of Israel = Men, Israelites. See note on 1. 11. **intend** = are about.
as touching = upon, or in the case of. Ap. 104. ix. 2.
36 Theudas. The name is not uncommon in the Talmud.
boasting, &c. = saying that he was.
somebody. Gr. *tis.* Ap. 123. 3. Fig. *Tapeinōsis.* Ap. 6.
joined themselves. Gr. *proskollaomai.* Only here, Matt. 19. 5. Mark 10. 7. Eph. 5. 31. Cp. *v.* 13.
obeyed. Ap. 150. I. 2.
scattered. Gr. *dialuō.* Only here. A medical word.
brought. Lit. came to be.
37 After. Gr. *meta.* Ap. 104. xi. 2.
this man = this one.
Judas of Galilee. His revolt is recorded by Josephus, *Ant.* xviii. 1. § 1.
taxing. Gr. *apographē.* Only here and Luke 2. 2, which see.
drew away = caused to revolt or apostatize.
after. Gr. *opisō.* **he also.** Ap. 124. 5.
perished. Gr. *apollumi.* Only here in Acts. See note on John 17. 12. **38 Refrain** = Stand away. Gr. Mid. of *aphistēmi* (*v.* 37). **from.** Ap. 104. iv. **if.** Ap. 118. I. b. **counsel.** Gr. *boulē.* Ap. 102. 4. **of** = out of. Gr. *ek.* Ap. 104. vii. **will come to nought** = will be overthrown. Gr. *kataluō,* transl. "dissolve" in 2 Cor. 5. 1. **39 if.** Gr. *ei.* Ap. 118. 2. a. **cannot** = are not (Ap. 105. I.) able to. **overthrow.** Gr. *kataluō,* as in *v.* 38. **lest haply.** Gr. *mēpote,* compound of *mē.* Ap. 105. II. **to fight against God** = God-fighters. Gr. *Theomachos.* **40 agreed,** as *v.* 36. **beaten.** Cp. Deut. 25. 1-3. Mark 13. 9. **let them go.** See on 4. 21. **41 And they** = They indeed therefore. **counted worthy.** Gr. *kataxioomai.* Here, Luke 20. 35; 21. 36. 2 Thess. 1. 5. **suffer shame** = be dishonoured or counted unworthy. Gr. *atimazō.* Here, Luke 20. 11. John 8. 49. Rom. 1. 24; 2. 23. Jas. 2. 6. Fig. *Oxymōron.* Ap. 6. **for.** Ap. 104. xvii. 1. **His** = the. **42 in every house.** Gr. *kat'* (Ap. 104. x. 2) *oikon* = at home. See on 2. 46. **preach.** Ap. 121. 4. **Jesus Christ** = Jesus as the Christ (Ap. 98. XI), the name of *v.* 41.

6. 1-7 [For Structure see next page].

6. 1 in. Ap. 104. viii. **murmuring.** Gr. *gongusmos.* An onomatopœic word. Here, John 7. 12. Phil. 2. 14. 1 Pet. 4. 9. **Grecians** = Greek-speaking Jews. Gr. *Hellēnistēs.* **against.** Ap 104. xv. 3.

Hebrews, because their widows were °neglected °in the °daily °ministration.

A g 2 Then the twelve called the multitude of the disciples *unto them*, and said, "It is °not °reason that we should leave the °word of °God, and °serve °tables.

h 3 Wherefore, brethren, °look ye out °among you °seven °men °of honest report, full of °the Holy Ghost and wisdom, whom we may appoint °over this °business.

A g 4 But we will °give ourselves continually to °prayer, and to the °ministry of the [2]word."

h 5 ¶ And the °saying pleased the whole [2]multitude: and they chose °Stephen, a [3]man full of °faith and of [3]the Holy Ghost, and Philip, and Prochorus, and Nicanor, and Timon, and Parmenas, and Nicolas a °proselyte of °Antioch:

6 Whom they set °before the °apostles: and when they had °prayed, they °laid *their* hands on them.

Z 7 And the [2]word of [2]God increased; and the number of the disciples multiplied [1]in Jerusalem greatly; and a great °company of the priests were obedient to °the [5]faith.

D[3] B[1] 8 And Stephen, full of °faith and °power, did great °wonders and °miracles °among the °people.

C[1] 9 ¶ Then there °arose °certain °of the °synagogue, which is called *the synagogue* of the °Libertines, and Cyrenians, and Alexandrians, and of them °of °Cilicia and of Asia, °disputing with Stephen.

B[2] 10 And they were [2]not °able to °resist the wisdom and the °spirit by which he °spake.

C[2] 11 Then they °suborned [3]men, which said, "We have heard him [10]speak °blasphemous °words °against °Moses, and *against* [2]God."

B[3] 12 And they °stirred up the [8]people, and the °elders, and the scribes, and came upon *him*, and °caught him, and brought *him* °to the °council,

C[3] 13 And set up false °witnesses, which said, "This °man ceaseth [2]not to [10]speak [11]blasphemous [11]words °against this holy place, and the law:

14 For we have heard him say, that this °Jesus °of Nazareth °shall °destroy °this place,

6. 1-7 (C[3], p. 1579). AMONG THE BRETHREN.
(Introversion and Alternation.)

C[3] Z | 1. Disciples multiplied.
  A | g | 2. Apostles' Work. Negative.
      h 3. Appointment proposed.
  A | *g* | 4. Apostles' Work. Positive.
      h | 5, 6. Appointment made.
Z | 7. Disciples multiplied.

neglected = being overlooked. Gr. *paratheōreō*. Cp. Ap. 133. I. 11. Only here.
daily. Gr. *kathēmerinos*. Only here.
ministration = ministering. Ap. 190. II. 1. It was the relief of 2. 44, 45.
2 not. Ap. 105. I.
reason = pleasing. Gr. *arestos*. Occurs also 12. 3. John 8. 29. 1 John 3. 22.
word. Ap. 121. 10.
God. Ap. 98. I. i. 1.
serve. Ap. 190. III. 1.
tables. i. e. the business of distribution. Fig. *Idiōma*. Ap. 6.
3 look ye out. Ap. 133. III. 5.
among = from. Ap. 104. vii.
seven. Ap. 10.
men. Gr. *anēr*. Ap. 123. 2.
of honest report. Lit. witnessed to, or attested. Gr. *martureō*. Cp. Heb. 11. 2, 4, 5, 39, R.V.
the Holy Ghost. Ap. 101. II. 14. The texts omit "Holy". Cp. *v.* 10.
over. Ap. 104. ix. 1.
business = need. Gr. *chreia*, as in 2. 45; 4. 35.
4 give ourselves continually. Gr. *proskartereō*, as in 1. 14.
prayer. Ap. 134. II. 2. **ministry.** Ap. 190. III. 1.
5 saying. Gr. *logos*, as in *v.* 2.
Stephen. Gr. *Stephanos* = a crown. All the names are Greek. These are called the seven deacons, but the word *diakonos* is not used in the Acts. See Ap. 190. I. 1. Besides Stephen, Philip is the only one of whom anything is recorded (8. 5; 21. 8).
faith. Ap. 150. II. 1.
proselyte. See note on Matt. 23. 15.
Antioch. In Syria.
6 before = in the presence of.
apostles. Ap. 189.
prayed. Ap. 134. I. 2.
laid, &c. Cp. Num. 27. 18-23.
7 company = crowd. Gr. *ochlos*.
the faith, i.e. in the Name. Cp. 3. 16.

6. 8—8. 1 (D[3], p. 1579). AMONG THE PEOPLE.
(Alternation.)

D[3] B[1] | 6. 8. Stephen's Miracles.
  C[1] | 6. 9. Opposition.
B[2] | 6. 10. Stephen's Wisdom.
  C[2] | 6. 11. False Witnesses.
B[3] | 6. 12. Stephen's Arrest.
  C[3] | 6. 13, 14. False Witnesses.
B[4] | 6. 15—8. 1. Stephen's Testimony and Martyrdom.

8 faith. The texts read "grace". Ap. 184. I. 1. **power.** Ap. 172. 1. **wonders.** Ap. 176. 2. **miracles** = signs. Ap. 176. 3. **among.** Ap. 104. viii. **people.** See note on 2. 47. **9 arose.** Ap. 178. I. 1. **certain.** Ap. 123. 3. **of** = out of. Ap. 104. vii. **synagogue.** Ap. 120. **Libertines.** During the Civil Wars many Jews had been enslaved, and afterwards set free by their masters. A manumitted slave was called *libertinus*. These were probably the descendants of such freedmen who had returned to Jerusalem, after the decree of Tiberius expelling the Jews from Rome about 20 A.D. **of** = from. Ap. 104. iv. **Cilicia.** A province of Asia Minor, of which Tarsus was the capital. See 21. 39. Probably Saul was one of these disputers. **disputing.** Gr. *suzēteō*, generally transl. "question". Cp. Mark 1. 27; 8. 11; 9. 10, 14, 16. **10 able** = strong enough. See 15. 10. **resist.** Gr. *anthistēmi*. Cp. Luke 21. 15. **spirit.** See note on *v.* 3. **spake.** Ap. 121. 7. **11 suborned.** Gr. *hupoballō*. Only here. **blasphemous.** Gr. *blasphēmos*. Here, *v.* 13. 1 Tim. 1. 13. 2 Tim. 3. 2. 2 Pet. 2. 11. **words.** Gr. *rhēma*. See note on Mark 9. 32. **against.** Ap. 104. vi. **Moses.** See note on 3. 22. Here meaning the Law. **12 stirred up.** Gr. *sunkineō*. Only here. Frequent in medical works. **elders, &c.** See note on 4. 5, and Ap. 189. **caught** = violently seized. Gr. *sunarpazō*. Only here, 19. 29; 27. 15, and Luke 8. 29. **to** = unto. Ap. 104. vi. **council.** See note on 4. 15. **13 witnesses.** Gr. *martur*. See 1. 8. **man.** Ap. 123. 1. **against.** Ap. 104. x. 1. **14 Jesus.** Ap. 98. X. **of Nazareth** = the Nazarene. Cp. 2. 22; 3. 6; 4. 10. **shall** = will. **destroy.** Gr. *kataluō*. Cp. 5. 38, 39. **this place,** i. e. the temple, in one of the courts of which the Sanhedrin was sitting.

and shall °change the °customs which Moses delivered us."

B⁴ D 15 And all that sat [1]in the [12]council, °looking stedfastly °on him, °saw his face °as it had been the face of an angel.

7 Then said the high priest, °"Are these things so?"

E i 2 And he said, "°Men, brethren, and fathers, hearken; The °God of °glory °appeared unto our father Abraham when he was °in Mesopotamia, before he °dwelt °in °Charran,

3 And said °unto him, **'Get thee °out of thy °country, and °from thy °kindred, and °come °into the °land which I shall shew thee.'**

4 Then came he [3]out of the [3]land of the Chaldæans, and [2]dwelt [2]in [2]Charran: and from thence, °when his father was dead, He °removed him [3]into this [3]land, °wherein ye now [2]dwell.

5 And He gave him °none inheritance [2]in it, °no, not *so much as* °to set his foot on: yet He °promised that **He would give it to him °for a °possession, and to his seed °after him,** when *as yet* he had °no °child.

6 And [2]God °spake on this wise, **That his seed should °sojourn [2]in a °strange [3]land; and that they should °bring them into bondage, and °entreat *them* evil °four hundred years.**

7 **'And the °nation °to whom they shall be in bondage will I °judge,'** said [2]God: **'and [5]after °that shall they come forth, and °serve Me [2]in this place.'**

8 And He gave him the °covenant of circumcision: and so *Abraham* begat Isaac, and circumcised him the eighth day; and Isaac *begat* Jacob; and Jacob *begat* the twelve °patriarchs.

j 9 And the [8]patriarchs, °moved with envy, sold Joseph [3]into Egypt: but [2]God was °with him,

10 And °delivered him [3]out of all his °afflictions, and gave him °favour and wisdom °in the sight of Pharaoh king of Egypt; and he made him governor °over Egypt and all his house.

11 Now there came a dearth [10]over all °the land of Egypt and Chanaan, and great [10]affliction: and our fathers found [5]no °sustenance.

12 But when Jacob heard that there was °corn [2]in Egypt, he °sent out our fathers °first.

change. Gr. *allassō*. Here; Rom. 1. 23. 1 Cor. 15. 51, 52. Gal. 4. 20. Heb. 1. 12.

customs. Gr. *ethos*. Hence Engl. "ethics". Occ. twelve times. All in Luke and Acts, except John 19. 40. Heb. 10. 25.

6. 15—8. 1 (B⁴. p. 1590). **STEPHEN'S TESTIMONY AND DEATH.** (*Introversion.*)

B⁴ | D | 6. 15—7. 1. Stephen and the High Priest.
  E | i | 7. 2-8. Abraham. The Land promised.
    j | 7. 9-16. Joseph. Persecuted. Delivered.
     k | 7. 17-31. Moses. Type of the Prophet.
      l | 7. 32-34. The Wilderness a Holy Place.
       m | 7. 35-39. Rejection.
        F | 7. 40-43. Tabernacles of Idols.
        F | 7. 44. Jehovah's Tabernacle.
  E | *i* | 7. 45-. Joshua. The Land possessed.
    j | 7. -45, 46. David. Persecuted. Delivered.
     k | 7. 47. Solomon. Type of the King.
      l | 7. 48-50. All Places Holy.
       m | 7. 51-53. Resistance.
 D | 7. 54—8. 1-. Death of Stephen.

15 looking stedfastly = fastening their eyes. Ap. 133. III. 6. Cp. 1. 10.

on. Gr. *eis*. Ap. 104. vi.

saw. Ap. 133. I. 1. **as it had been** = as if.

7. 1 Are these things so = If (Ap. 118. 2. a) these things are so.

2 Men. Ap. 123. 2. Cp. 1. 11.

God. Ap. 98. I. i. 1.

glory. See p. 1511. This is the genitive of character. Ap. 17. 1. Cp. Ps. 29. 3, and note the seven other similar expressions, "the God of comfort" (Rom. 15. 5. 2 Cor. 1. 3), "hope" (Rom. 15. 13), "love" (2 Cor. 13. 11), "patience" (Rom. 15. 5), "peace" (Rom. 15. 33, &c.), "*all* grace" (1 Pet. 5. 10), and "truth" (Deut. 32. 4, &c.),

appeared unto = was seen by. Gr. *optomai*. Ap. 106. vi.

in. Gr. *en*. Ap. 104. viii.

dwelt = settled. Gr. *katoikeō*. See note on 2. 5.

Charran = Haran (Gen. 11. 31).

3 unto. Gr. *pros*. Ap. 104. xv. 3.

out of. Gr. *ek*. Ap. 104. vii.

country = land. Gr. *gē*. Ap. 129. 4.

from = out of. Gr. *ek*, as above.

kindred. Gr. *sungeneia*. Only here, *v.* 14, and Luke 1. 61.

come = hither. Gr. *deuro*.

into. Gr. *eis*. Ap. 104. vi.

land. Gr. *gē*, as above.

4 when = after that. Gr. *meta*. Ap. 104. xi. 2. It was Abraham, not Terah, who had been called (Gen. 12. 1), and therefore Terah could get no farther than Haran. There was a long sojourn in Haran of twenty-five years. See Ap. 50. pp. 51, 52.

removed him. Gr. *metoikizō* = to cause to change one's abode. Only here and *v.* 43. In the Sept., in 1 Chron. 5. 6. Amos 5. 27, &c. wherein = into (Gr. *eis*. Ap. 104. vi) which, i. e. into which ye came and now dwell there. **5 none** = not (Gr. *ou*. Ap. 105. I) any. no, not, &c. = not even (Gr. *oude*). Fig. *Epitasis*. Ap. 6. to set his foot on = a place (Gr. *bēma*. See note on John 19. 13) for a foot. promised. Ref. to Gen. 13. 15. for. Gr. *eis*. Ap. 104. vi. possession. Gr. *kataschesis*. Only here and *v.* 45. after. Gr. *meta*. Ap. 104. xi. 2. no = not any, as above. child. Gr. *teknon*. Ap. 108. i. **6 spake.** Gr. *laleō*. Ap. 121. 7. Quoted from Gen. 15. 13, 14. sojourn = be a stranger. Gr. *paroikos*. Here, *v.* 29. Eph. 2. 19. 1 Pet. 2. 11. The verb *paroikeō*, only in Luke 24. 18. Heb. 11. 9. strange = foreign. Gr. *allotrios*. Ap. 124. 6. bring them into bondage = enslave them. Gr. *douloō*. Ap. 190. III. 3. entreat them evil = wrong them. Gr. *kakoō*. Cp. Ap. 128. III. 2. Here, *v.* 19; 12. 1; 14. 2; 18. 10. 1 Pet. 3. 13. four hundred years. See note on Ex. 12. 40. **7 nation.** Gr. *ethnos*. See note on 4. 25, 27. to whom, &c. = whom they shall serve. Gr. *douleuō*. Ap. 190. III. 2. judge. Gr. *krinō*. Ap. 122. 1. that = these things. serve = worship. Gr. *latreuō*. Ap. 137. 4. Cp. Ex. 3. 12. **8 covenant.** Gr. *diathēkē*. See note on Matt. 26. 28. patriarchs. See note on 2. 29. **9 moved with envy** = being jealous. Gr. *zēloō*. Cp. the noun *zēlos*, 5. 17. with. Gr. *meta*. Ap. 104. xi. 1. **10 delivered.** Gr. *exaireō*. Here, *v.* 34; 12. 11; 23. 27; 26. 17. Matt. 5. 29; 18. 9. Gal. 1. 4. afflictions = tribulations. Gr. *thlipsis*. Cp. Ps. 105. 17-19. favour = grace. Gr. *charis*. Ap. 184. I. 1. in the sight of = before. Gr. *enantion*. over. Gr. *epi*. Ap. 104. ix. 3. **11 the land of.** Omit. sustenance. Gr. *chortasma*. Only here. Cp. the verb *chortazō* = to fill. First occ. Matt. 5. 6. **12 corn.** Gr. *sita*, an irregular pl. of *sitos*, the word used elsewhere in N.T. and Sept. The texts read *sitia*, from *sition*, a word much used by medical writers. sent out. Gr. *exapostellō*. Ap. 174. 2. first = the first time.

13 And °at the second *time* Joseph was °made known to his brethren; and Joseph's °kindred °was made known °unto Pharaoh.
14 Then °sent Joseph, and °called his father Jacob to *him*, and all his [3]kindred, °threescore and fifteen °souls.
15 So Jacob went down [3]into Egypt, and °died, he, and our fathers,
16 And were °carried over [3]into °Sychem, and laid [2]in the °sepulchre that Abraham °bought for a sum of money °of the °sons of Emmor *the father* of Sychem.

k 17 But °when the time of the °promise drew nigh, which [2]God had sworn to Abraham, the °people grew and multiplied [2]in Egypt,
18 Till °another °king °arose, which °knew °not Joseph.
19 °The same °dealt subtilly with our [13]kindred, and [6]evil entreated our fathers, so that they °cast out their °young children, °to the end they might °not °live.
20 [2]In which time °Moses was born, and was °exceeding °fair, and °nourished up [2]in his father's house three months:
21 And when he was °cast out, Pharaoh's daughter °took him up, and [20]nourished him [5]for °her own [16]son.
22 And [20]Moses was °learned °in all the wisdom of the Egyptians, and was mighty [2]in °words and [2]in °deeds.
23 And when °he was full forty years old, it came °into his heart to °visit his brethren the °children of Israel.
24 And °seeing one *of them* °suffer wrong, he °defended *him*, and °avenged °him that was oppressed, °and smote the Egyptian:
25 For he supposed his brethren °would have understood how that [2]God °by his hand would °deliver them: but they understood [18]not.
26 And the °next day he °shewed himself unto them as they °strove, and °would have set them °at one °again, saying, °'Sirs, ye are brethren; why °do ye wrong one to another?'
27 But he that [26]did his neighbour wrong °thrust him away, saying, '**Who made thee a ruler and a °judge °over us?**
28 °**Wilt thou °kill me, as thou °diddest the Egyptian yesterday?**'
29 Then fled [20]Moses [13]at this °saying, and was a °stranger [2]in the [3]land of °Madian, where he begat two [16]sons.
30 And when forty years were °expired, there [2]appeared to him [2]in the wilderness of mount

13 at = in. Gr. *en*. Ap. 104. viii.
made known. Gr. *anagnōrizomai*. Only here. Cp. Ap. 132. I. ii. **kindred** = race. Gr. *genos*.
was made known = became (Gr. *ginomai*) manifest (Gr. *phaneros*. Ap. 106. I. viii). See Gen. 45. 16.
unto = to.
14 sent. Gr. *apostellō*. Ap. 174. 1.
called . . . to him. Gr. *metakaleomai*. Here, 10. 32; 20. 17; 24. 25. *meta* in composition expresses the idea of change.
threescore, &c. This included Jacob's kindred. See note on Gen. 46. 26.
souls. Gr. *psuchē*. Ap. 110. II.
15 died = came to his end. Gr. *teleutaō*.
16 carried over = removed. Gr. *metatithēmi*. Only here; Gal. 1. 6. Heb. 7. 12; 11. 5, 5. Jude 4.
Sychem = Shechem (Gen. 50. 5). See Ap. 187.
sepulchre. Gr. *mnēma*. See note on 2. 29.
bought. Gr. *ōneomai*. Only here.
of = from. Gr. *para*. Ap. 104. xii. 1.
sons. Gr. *huios*. Ap. 108. iii.
17 when = as soon as.
promise. Gr. *epangelia*. See note on 1. 4.
people. Gr. *laos*. See note on 2. 47.
18 another. Gr. *heteros*. Ap. 124. 2.
king. See Ap. 188.
arose. Gr. *anistēmi*. Ap. 178. I. 1.
knew. Gr. *oida*. Ap. 132. i.
not. Gr. *ou*. Ap. 105. I.
19 The same = This one.
dealt subtilly with. Gr. *katasophizomai*. Only here. In Sept. "deal wisely", Ex. 1. 10.
cast out = caused to be exposed (Gr. *ekthetos*. Only here).
young children = babes. Gr. *brephos*. Ap. 108. viii.
to the end. Gr. *eis*.
not. Gr. *mē*. Ap. 105. II.
live = be born alive, or preserved alive. Gr. *zōogoneō*. Only here and Luke 17. 33. See also 1 Tim. 6. 13. In Sept. in Ex. 1. 17, 18, 22, &c.
20 Moses. See note on 3. 22.
exceeding fair = fair to God. Fig. *Idiōma*. Ap. 6.
fair. Gr. *asteios*. Only here and Heb. 11. 23. The word used in Ex. 2. 2, Sept.
nourished up. Gr. *anatrephō*. Only here, *v.* 21 and 22. 3. A word common in medical writers.
21 cast out. Gr. *ektithēmi*, verb of *ekthetos*, in *v.* 19. Only here, 11. 4; 18. 26; 28. 23.
took . . . up. Gr. *anaireō*. Generally transl. "kill", i. e. take away (by death). See *v.* 28; 2. 23; 5. 33, 36, &c.
her own son = a son for herself.
22 learned = educated. Gr. *paideuō*.
in all, &c. This included the mysteries of the Egyptian religion, as all education was in the hands of the priests.
words. Gr. *logos*. Ap. 121. 10.
deeds = works. Fig. *Syntheton*. Ap. 6.
23 he was, &c. Lit. a period (Gr. *chronos*) of forty years (Gr. *tessarakontaetēs*. Only here and 13. 18) was fulfilled. Gr. *plēroō*. Ap. 125. 7.

into = upon. Gr. *epi*. Ap. 104. ix. 3. **visit.** Gr. *episkeptomai*. Ap. 133. III. 5. **children** = sons. Gr. *huios* as in *v.* 16. **24 seeing.** Gr. *eidon*. Ap. 133. I. 1. **suffer wrong** = being wronged. Gr. *adikeō*. Cp. Ap. 128. VII. 1. **defended.** Gr. *amunomai*. Only here. **avenged** = took vengeance (Gr. *ekdikēsis*. Here, Luke 18. 7, 8; 21. 22. Rom. 12. 19. 2 Cor. 7. 11. 2 Thess. 1. 8. Heb. 10. 30. 1 Pet. 2. 14) for. **him that was oppressed** = the oppressed one. Gr. *kataponeomai*. Only here and 2 Pet. 2. 7. **and smote** = having smitten. **25 would have.** Omit. **by.** Gr. *dia*. Ap. 104. v. 1. **deliver them** = give them salvation. **26 next** = following. Gr. *epeimi*. Only here, 16. 11; 20. 15; 21. 18; 23. 11. See note on Matt. 6. 11. **shewed himself.** Gr. *optomai*, as in *v.* 2. **strove** = fought. Gr. *machomai*. Only here, John 6. 52. 2 Tim. 2. 24. James 4. 2. **would have set them** = was driving them together. Gr. *sunelaunō*. Only here. But the texts read "was reconciling them", Gr. *sunallassō*. **at one** = into (Gr. *eis*. Ap. 104. vi) peace. **again.** Omit. **Sirs** = Men. Gr. *aner*. Ap. 123. 2. The pl. *andres* is transl. "Sirs" six times, all in Acts, here, 14. 15; 19. 25; 27. 10, 21, 25. **do ye wrong one to another** = wrong ye one another. Gr. *adikeō*, as in *v.* 24. **27 thrust him away.** Gr. *apōtheomai*. Only here, *v.* 39; 13. 46. Rom. 11. 1, 2. 1 Tim. 1. 19. **judge.** Gr. *dikastēs*. Only here, *v.* 35. Luke 12. 14. Cp. Ap. 177. 4. **over.** Gr. *epi*. Ap. 104. ix. 1. **28 Wilt thou** = Thou dost not (Ap. 105. II) wish (Ap. 102. 1); *mē* is used with questions, where a negative answer is expected. **kill.** Gr. *anaireō*, as in *v.* 21. **diddest** = killedst. **29 saying.** Gr. *logos*, as in *v.* 22. **stranger.** Gr. *paroikos*. Same as "sojourn" in *v.* 6. **Madian** = Midian. See Ex. 2. 15; 3. 1. **30 expired** = fulfilled. Gr. *plēroō*, as in *v.* 23.

Sina an Angel °of the Lord [2] in a flame °of fire
in a bush.
31 When [20] Moses [24] saw *it*, he wondered at
the °sight: and as he drew near to °behold *it*,
the voice of °the LORD came °unto him,

l 32 *Saying*, '**I *am* the [2] God of thy fathers, the
[2] God of Abraham, and the °God of Isaac, and
the °God of Jacob.**' Then [20] Moses °trembled,
and durst [18] not [31] behold.
33 Then said °the LORD to him, '**Put off °thy
shoes from thy feet: for the place °where thou
standest is holy °ground.**
**34 °I have [24] seen, I have [24] seen the °affliction
of My [17] people which is [2] in Egypt, and I have
heard their °groaning, and am come down to
[10] deliver them. And now [3] come, I [14] will send
thee [3] into Egypt.**'

m 35 This [20] Moses whom they refused, saying,
'**Who made thee a ruler and a [27] judge?**' the
same did [2] God [14] send *to be* a ruler and a °de-
liverer °by the hand of the Angel Which [2] appeared to him [2] in the bush.
36 °He brought them out, after that he had
°shewed °wonders and °signs [2] in the [3] land
of Egypt, and [2] in the Red sea, and [2] in the
wilderness forty years.
37 This is °that [20] Moses, which said [13] unto
the [23] children of Israel, °'**A Prophet shall [30] the
Lord °your [2] God °raise up [13] unto you °of your
brethren, °like unto me; °Him shall ye hear.**'
38 This is he, that was [2] in the °church [2] in
the wilderness [9] with the Angel Which [6] spake
to him [2] in the mount Sina, and *with* our
fathers: who received the °lively °oracles to
give [13] unto us:
39 To whom our fathers °would [18] not °obey,
but [27] thrust *him* °from them, and in their hearts
turned back again [3] into Egypt,

F 40 Saying unto Aaron, '**Make us °gods °to
go before us: for *as for* this [20] Moses, which
brought us [3] out of the [3] land of Egypt, we °wot
[18] not what °is become of him.**'
41 And they °made a calf [2] in those days, and
offered sacrifice [13] unto the °idol, and °rejoiced
[2] in the works of their own hands.
42 Then [2] God turned, and gave them up to
°worship the °host of °heaven: °as it °is written [2] in °the book of the prophets, '**O °ye house
of Israel, °have ye offered to Me °slain beasts
and sacrifices *by the space of* forty years [2] in
the wilderness?
43 °Yea, ye took up the °tabernacle of Moloch,
and the star of your [40] god °Remphan, °figures
which ye made to °worship them: and I will
°carry you away °beyond °Babylon.**'

F 44 Our fathers had the [43] tabernacle of °witness
[2] in the wilderness, [42] as He °had appointed
[6] speaking [13] unto [20] Moses, that he should make
it °according to the °fashion that he had °seen.

of the Lord. The texts omit.
of fire in a bush = of a burning bush. Fig. *Antimereia*. Ap. 6.
31 sight. Gr. *horama*. Occ. twelve times, all in Acts, except in Matt. 17. 9. Always trans. "vision", except here. Not the same word as in 2. 17.
behold = inspect, or consider. Gr. *katanoeō*. Ap. 133. II. 4.
the Lord. Ap. 98. VI. i. *β*. 1. B. a.
unto him. The texts omit. The quotations are from Ex. 3.
32 God. The texts omit the third and fourth occ. of the word in this verse.
trembled = became trembling (Gr. *entromos*. Only here, 16. 29. Heb. 12. 21).
33 the Lord. Ap. 98. VI. i. *β*. 1. A. a.
thy shoes, &c. = the sandal of thy feet.
where = in (Gr. *en*) which, but the texts read *epi*.
ground. Gr. *gē*. Ap. 129. 4.
34 I have seen, I have seen. A Hebraism. Fig. *Polyptōton*. Ap. 6. Lit. Seeing, I saw.
affliction = wrong. Gr. *kakōsis*. Only here. Cp. *kakoō*, *vv.* 6, 19.
groaning. Gr. *stenagmos*. Only here and Rom. 8. 26.
35 deliverer = redeemer. Gr. *lutrōtēs*. Only here. Cp. *lutron*, ransom (Matt. 20. 28. Mark 10. 45); *lutroō*, redeem (Luke 24. 21. Tit. 2. 14. 1 Pet. 1. 18); *lutrōsis*, redemption (Luke 1. 68; 2. 38. Heb. 9. 12).
by = in. Gr. *en*, but the texts read *sun*.
36 He = This one.
shewed. Lit. done. See Deut. 31. 2; 34. 7.
wonders. Gr. *teras*. Ap. 176. 2.
signs. Gr. *sēmeion*. Ap. 176. 3.
37 that = the.
A Prophet. Quoted from Deut. 18. 15. Cp. 3. 22.
your. The texts omit.
raise up. Gr. *anistēmi*. Ap. 178. I. 1.
of. Gr. *ek*. Ap. 104. vii.
like unto = as.
Him shall ye hear. The texts omit, but not the Syriac.
38 church. Ap. 186.
lively = living. Fig. *Idiōma*. Ap. 6.
oracles = utterances. Gr. *logion*. Only here; Rom. 3. 2. Heb. 5. 12. 1 Pet. 4. 11.
39 would. Ap. 102. 1.
obey = be obedient (Gr. *hupēkoos*. Only here; 2 Cor. 2. 9. Phil. 2. 8).
from them = away.
40 gods. Ap. 98. I. i. 5.
to go before. Gr. *proporeuomai*. Only here and Luke 1. 76.
wot = know. Ap. 132. I. i.
is become of = has come (to).
41 made a calf. Gr. *moschopoieō*, a compound word, meaning "were calf-making". Only here.
idol. Gr. *eidōlon*. The first of eleven occ. Only word so rendered.
rejoiced = were rejoicing. Gr. *euphrainō*. Same word as in 2. 26.
42 worship. Same word as "serve" in *v.* 7.
host = army. Gr. *stratia*. Only here and Luke 2. 13.
heaven = the heaven. See note on Matt. 6. 9, 10.
as = even as. **is** = has been.
the = a. **ye.** Omit.
have ye offered = did ye offer. This question is introduced by *mē*, as in *v.* 28.
slain beasts. Gr. *sphagion*. Only here. Cp. *sphagē*, 8. 32.

43 Yea, ye = Ye even. **tabernacle.** Gr. *skēnē*, tent. **Remphan.** See notes on Amos 5. 25-27, from which this quotation is taken. It follows the Sept. very closely. Ap. 107. II. 3 (b). **figures.** Gr. *tupos*. See note on John 20. 25 (print). Rom. 5. 14. **worship.** Gr. *proskuneō*. Ap. 137. 1. **carry . . . away.** Gr. *metoikizo*, as in *v.* 4. **beyond.** Gr. *epekeina*. Only here. **Babylon.** Amos says "Damascus". See note there. The stages of captivity were: Syrian, to Damascus; Assyrian, beyond Damascus to Mesopotamia; Babylonian, to Babylon and beyond, and now they were to be carried to the uttermost parts of the earth. **44 witness** = testimony. Gr. *marturion*, as in 4. 33. See Ex. 25. 16: 26. 33; 30. 6 Rev. 15. 5. **had appointed** = arranged. **according to.** Gr. *kata*. Ap. 104. x. 2. **fashion** Gr *tupos*, as in *v.* 43. **seen.** Gr. *horaō*. Ap. 133. I. 8. Cp. Ex. 26. 30; 27. 8. Heb. 8. 5.

Ei 45 Which °also our fathers that °came after brought in [9]with °Jesus °into the [5]possession of the °Gentiles, whom [2]God °drave out °before the face of our fathers,

j °unto the days of °David;

46 Who found [10]favour °before [2]God, and °desired to find a °tabernacle for the [2]God of Jacob.

k 47 But °Solomon built Him an house.

l 48 °Howbeit °the Most High [2]dwelleth [18]not [22]in °Temples °made with hands; [42]as saith the prophet,

49 [42]**'Heaven *is* My throne, and °earth *is* °My footstool: °what house will ye build Me?' saith [31]the LORD: 'or what *is* the place of My °rest?**

50 **Hath °not My hand made all these things?'**

m 51 Ye °stiffnecked and °uncircumcised in heart and ears, ye do always °resist °the Holy Ghost: as your fathers *did*, so *do* ye.

52 Which of the prophets °have [18]not your fathers persecuted? and they °have slain them which °shewed before °of the °coming of °the Just One; of Whom ye °have been now °the °betrayers and murderers:

53 Who °have received the law °by the °disposition of angels, and °have [18]not kept *it*."

D 54 When they heard these things, they were °cut to the heart, and they °gnashed °on him with *their* teeth.

55 But he, °being full of °the Holy Ghost, °looked up stedfastly [3]into [42]heaven, and [24]saw the [2]glory of [2]God, and °Jesus standing °on the °right hand of [2]God,

56 And said, °"Behold, I °see °the heavens °opened, and the °Son of man standing [55]on the [55]right hand of [2]God."

57 Then they cried out with a °loud voice, and °stopped their ears, and °ran upon him °with one accord,

58 And cast *him* °out of the city, and °stoned *him:* and the °witnesses laid down their clothes °at a °young man's feet, whose name was °Saul.

59 And they [58]stoned Stephen, °calling upon *God*, and saying, °"Lord [55]Jesus, receive my °spirit."

60 And he °kneeled down, and cried with a

45 also. This should be read after "brought in".
came after = received in succession. Gr. *diadechomai.* Only here. R.V. "in their turn".
Jesus = Joshua. Cp. Heb. 4. 8. The Heb. means "Jehovah the Saviour". See note on title, Josh. 1.
into. Gr. *en.* Ap. 104. viii.
Gentiles. Gr. *ethnos*, same as nation, *v.* 7.
drave out = thrust out. Gr. *exōtheō.* Only here and 27. 39. Cp. *v.* 27.
before = from. Gr. *apo.* Ap. 104. iv.
unto = until. Gr. *heōs.*
David. Like Joseph, David was rejected, and tested by affliction before God gave him deliverance.
46 before = in the eyes of. Gr. *enōpion.*
desired = asked. Gr. *aiteō.* Ap. 134. I. 4. See 2 Sam. 7. 2, 3.
tabernacle. Gr. *skēnōma.* Only here and 2 Pet. 1. 13, 14. Not the same as in *v.* 44. R.V. reads "habitation". Cp. Ps. 132. 5.
47 Solomon. Stephen does not enlarge upon the history of either David or Solomon, probably because he saw the gathering storm on the faces of his audience.
48 Howbeit, &c. Read, "But not the Most High in hand-made temples dwelleth". The "not" stands first by Fig. *Anastrophē.* Ap. 6.
the Most High. Gr. *hupsistos.* This, as a title of Deity, occ. nine times. See Luke 1. 32.
Temples. The texts omit.
made with hands. Gr. *cheiropoiētos.* Here, 17. 24. Mark 14. 58. Eph. 2. 11. Heb. 9. 11, 24.
49 earth. Gr. *gē*, as in *v.* 3.
My footstool = the footstool of my feet, as in 2. 35. Cp. Matt. 5. 35, and see note on Matt. 22. 44.
what = what kind of.
rest. Gr. *katapausis.* Only here; Heb. 3. 11, 18; 4. 1, 3, 3, 5, 10, 11.
50 not. Gr. *ouchi.* Ap. 105. I (a). Freely quoted from Isa. 66. 1, 2.
51 stiffnecked. Gr. *sklērotrachēlos.* Only here in N.T., but in Sept. in Ex. 33. 3, 5; 34. 9. Deut. 9. 6, 13. Cp. Deut. 31. 27. 2 Chron. 30. 8. Prov. 29. 1. This is an instance of Fig. *Ecphōnēsis.* Ap. 6.
uncircumcised. Gr. *aperitmētos.* Only here.
resist = fall against. Gr. *antipipto.* Only here.
the Holy Ghost. Ap. 101. II. 3. This verse is quoted in support of the idea that men can successfully withstand the Spirit, instead of stumbling at His words. Cp. Matt. 21. 44.
52 have, &c. = did . . . persecute. **have slain** = slew.
shewed before. Gr. *prokatangellō.* See 3. 18.
of. Gr. *peri.* Ap. 104. xiii. 1.
coming. Gr. *eleusis.* Only here.
the Just One. Gr. *dikaios.* Ap. 191. 1. Cp. 3. 14; 22. 14. 1 John 2. 1.
have been = became. **the.** Omit. **betrayers.** Gr. *prodotēs.* Here, Luke 6. 16. 2 Tim. 3. 4.
53 have. Omit. **by** = unto. Gr. *eis.* Ap. 104. vi. **disposition.** Gr. *diatagē.* Only here and Rom. 13. 2. The Syriac reads, "by the precept". Cp. *v.* 38 and Gal. 3. 19. **have, &c.** = guarded it not.
54 cut. Gr. *diapriomai*, as in 5. 33. **gnashed, &c.** = were gnashing their teeth on him. Gr. *bruchō.* Only here. An onomatopoeic word, like *brugmos.* Matt. 8. 12, &c. Both are medical words. **on.** Gr. *epi.* Ap. 104. ix. 3. **55 being.** Gr. *huparchō.* See note on Luke 9. 48. **the Holy Ghost.** No article. Ap. 101. II. 14. **looked up stedfastly.** Gr. *atenizō.* Ap. 133. III. 6. He was probably in one of the Temple courts, open to the sky. **Jesus.** Ap. 98. X. **on.** Gr. *ek.* Ap. 104. vii. **right hand.** Fig. *Anthrōpopatheia.* Ap. 6. **56 Behold.** Gr. *idou.* Ap. 133. I. 2. Fig. *Asterismos.* Ap. 6. **see** = behold. Gr. *theōreō.* Ap. 133. I. 11. **the heavens.** Pl. See note on Matt. 6. 9, 10. **opened.** Gr. *anoigō*, but the texts read "*dianoigō*", thrown open. **Son of Man.** Ap. 98. XVI. The eighty-fifth occ. Only here in Acts, and the only place where He is so named by man. In John 12. 34, the Lord's own words are repeated in a question. **57 loud** = great, i. e. the shout of the crowd in indignation. **stopped** = held tight. Gr. *sunechō.* See Luke 4. 38. **ran** = rushed. **upon.** Gr. *epi.* Ap. 104. ix. 3. **with one accord.** Gr. *homothumadon.* See note on 1. 14. **58 out of** = without. Gr. *exō.* Cp. Lev. 24. 14. The charge was blasphemy, as in the case of his Master. Cp. Heb. 13. 13. **stoned him** = kept casting stones at him. Gr. *lithoboleō.* Cp. Mark 12. 4. **witnesses.** See note on 1. 8. In accordance with the law they had to cast the first stone (Deut. 17. 7). **at.** Gr. *para.* Ap. 104. xii. 3. **young man.** Gr. *neanias.* Only here, 20. 9; 23. 17, 18, 22. He was probably about thirty-three years of age. *Neanias* was the next period to *neaniskos* (Ap. 108. x), but the limits are very uncertain. **Saul.** Gr. *Saulos.* Cp. 22. 20. **59 calling upon.** There is no Ellipsis of the word God. See R.V. Stephen called upon and invoked the Lord. **Lord.** Ap. 98. VI. i. β. 2. B. **spirit.** Ap. 101. II. 6. **60 kneeled down.** Lit. "placed the knees", an expression used in Luke (22. 41) and Acts (here, 9. 40; 20. 36; 21. 5), and once in Mark (15. 19). In the Epistles we read "bow the knee". Eph. 3. 14.

[57] **loud voice, [59] "Lord, lay [19] not this °sin °to**
their charge." And when he had said this, he
°fell asleep.

8 And Saul was °consenting unto his
°death.
E F^1 **And °at that °time there °was a great perse-**
cution °against the °church which was °at
Jerusalem; and they were all °scattered abroad
°throughout the °regions of Judæa and Sa-
maria, °except °the apostles.
2 And °devout °men °carried Stephen ***to his***
burial, **and made great °lamentation °over him.**
3 °As for Saul, he °made havock of the
[1] **church, entering into °every house, and**
°haling [2] men and °women committed ***them*** **°to**
°prison.
G^1 **4 °Therefore they that were [1] scattered abroad**
°went every where °preaching the °word.
H^1 I^1 J n **5 Then Philip went down [3] to the city of**
Samaria,
o **and °preached °Christ °unto them.**
p **6 And the °people °with one accord °gave heed**
[5] **unto those things °which Philip spake,**
q **°hearing and seeing the °miracles which he**
°did.
7 For unclean °spirits, crying with loud voice,
came out of many that were possessed ***with***
them: **and many °taken with palsies, and**
that were lame, were °healed.
K **8 And there °was great joy °in that city.**
J n **9 But there was a °certain [2] man, °called Simon,**
which °beforetime [8] in the °same city used sor-
cery, °and bewitched the °people of Samaria,
o **°giving out that himself was °some great one:**

sin. Gr. *hamartia.* Ap. 128. I. ii. 1.
to their charge = to them.
fell asleep. Gr. *koimaomai.* Ap. 171. 2.

8. 1 consenting unto = approving of. Gr. *suneudokeō.* Only here, 22. 20. Luke 11. 48. Rom. 1. 32. 1 Cor. 7. 12, 13. Cp. John 16. 2.
death. Gr. *anairesis* = taking off. Only here and 22. 20. Cp. *anaireō,* 2. 23, &c. This clause belongs to the previous chapter.

8. -1—11. 30 (E, p. 1575). MINISTRY OF PETER AND OTHERS IN THE LAND.
(Extended Alternation.)

E | F^1 | 8. -1-3. Persecution in Jerusalem.
  G^1 | 8. 4. Believers scattered.
   H^1 | 8. 5-40. Ministry at Samaria, &c.
 F^2 | 9. 1, 2. Persecution by Saul.
  G^2 | 9. 3-19-. Saul converted.
   H^2 | 9. -19-22. Ministry at Damascus.
 F^3 | 9. 23-30. Persecution of Saul.
  G^3 | 9. 31. Assemblies multiplied.
   H^3 | 9. 32—10. 48. Ministry at Lydda, &c.
 F^4 | 11. 1-17. Dissension in the Assemblies.
  G^4 | 11. 18. Peace restored.
   H^4 | 11. 19-30. Ministry at Phenice, &c.

at = in. Gr. *en.* Ap. 104. viii
time = day. **was** = arose.
against. Gr. *epi.* Ap. 104. ix. 3.
church. Ap. 186.
scattered abroad. Gr. *diaspeirō.* Only here, *v.* 4; 11. 19. Cp. *diaspora.* Jas. 1. 1. 1 Pet. 1. 1.
throughout. Gr. *kata.* Ap. 104. x. 2.
regions = districts. **except.** Gr. *plēn.*
the apostles. They remained at the centre of affairs, to watch over the infant assemblies. Cp. *v.* 14. See Ap. 189.
2 devout. Gr. *eulabēs.* See note on 2. 5.
men. Gr. *anēr.* Ap. 123. 2.
carried . . . to his burial. Lit. carried away together. Gr. *sunkomizō.* Only here.
lamentation. Gr. *kopetos.* Only here.
over. Gr. *epi.* Ap. 104. ix. 2.
3 As for = But.
made havock of. Gr. *lumainomai.* Only here.
every house. Gr. *kata* (Ap. 104. x. 2) *tous oikous* = house by house. **haling** = dragging. Gr. *surō.* See note on John 21. 8. **women.** Cp. 1. 14; 5. 14. **to.** Gr. *eis.* Ap. 104. vi. **prison.** Gr. *phulakē.* See 5. 19. **4 Therefore, &c.** = They therefore indeed. **went every where.** Lit. passed through. Gr. *dierchomai.* Occ. forty-three times, thirty-one times in Luke and Acts. **preaching.** Gr. *euangelizō.* Ap. 121. 4. **word.** Gr. *logos.* Ap. 121. 10.

8. 5-40 (H^1, above). MINISTRY AT SAMARIA, &c. *(Division.)*

H^1 | I^1 | 5-25. Samaria.
 | I^2 | 26-40. In the South.

8. 5-25 (I^1, above). SAMARIA. *(Alternation.*

I^1 | J | n | 5-. Philip.
  o | -5. His message.
   p | 6-. Heed given.
    q | -6, 7. Cause.
     K | 8. Philip's ministry. Result.
 J | *n* | 9-. Simon.
  o | -9. His message.
   p | 10, 11-. Heed given.
    q | -11. Cause.
     K | 12-25. Philip's ministry. Result.

5 preached. Gr. *kērussō.* Ap. 121. 1. **Christ,** i. e. the Messiah. Ap. 98. IX. **unto** = to. **6 people** = crowds. Gr. *ochlos.* **with one accord.** Gr. *homothumadon.* See note on 1. 14. **gave heed.** Same word as "take heed" in 5. 35, and "attended" in 16. 14. **which Philip spake** = spoken by (Gr. *hupo.* Ap. 104. xviii. 1) Philip. **hearing, &c.** Lit. in (Gr. *en.* Ap. 104. viii) that they heard and saw (Gr. *blepō.* Ap. 133. I. 5). **miracles** = signs. Gr. *sēmeion.* Ap. 176. 3. **did** = was doing. **7 spirits.** Ap 101. II. 12. **taken with palsies** = paralytic. Gr. *paraluomai.* Only here, 9. 33. Luke 5. 18, 24. Heb. 12 12. (feeble). **healed.** Gr. *therapeuō.* Ap. 137. 6. **8 was** = came to be. **in.** Gr *en.* Ap 104. viii. **9 certain.** Gr. *tis.* Ap. 123. 3. **called.** Lit. by name. **beforetime . . . used sorcery** Lit before was (Gr. *prouparchō.* Only here and Luke 23. 12) practising magic (Gr *mageuō,* to act as a magos. Only here. Cp. 13. 6, 8. Matt. 2. 1, 7, 16). **same.** Omit. **and bewitched** = bewitching. Gr *existēmi,* to drive out of one's senses. In middle voice, to be amazed. Cp 2. 7, 12. Mark 3. 21. 2 Cor. 5. 13. **people.** Gr. *ethnos,* nation. **giving out** = saying. **some** = a certain. Gr. *tis.* Ap. 123 3

p 10 To whom they all [6]gave heed, °from the °least to the greatest, saying, "°This man is the great °power of °God."

11 And to him they °had regard,

q °because that of long time he had [9]bewitched them with °sorceries.

K r 12 But when they °believed Philip [4]preaching °the things °concerning °the kingdom of [10]God, and the °name of °Jesus Christ, they were °baptized, both [2]men and [3]women.

s 13 Then Simon himself °believed also: and when he was [12]baptized, he °continued with Philip, and °wondered, °beholding the °miracles and °signs which were done.

t 14 Now when the [1]apostles which were [1]at Jerusalem heard that Samaria had received the [4]word of [10]God, they °sent °unto them Peter and John:

r 15 Who, when they were come down, °prayed °for them, that they might receive °the Holy Ghost:

16 (For as yet he was fallen °upon °none of them: only they °were °baptized in the [12]name of the °Lord °Jesus.)

17 Then laid they *their* hands °on them, and they °received [15]the Holy Ghost.

s 18 And when Simon °saw that °through laying on of the [1]apostles' hands °the Holy Ghost °was given, he offered them money,

19 Saying, "Give me also this °power, °that on whomsoever I lay hands, he may receive [15]the Holy Ghost."

20 But Peter said [14]unto him, "Thy money °perish °with thee, because thou hast thought °that the °gift of [10]God may be purchased °with money.

21 Thou hast °neither part °nor °lot [8]in this °matter: for thy heart is °not right °in the sight of [10]God.

22 °Repent therefore °of this thy °wickedness, and °pray °God, °if perhaps the °thought of thine heart °may be °forgiven thee.

23 For I °perceive that thou art °in the °gall of °bitterness, and *in* the °bond of °iniquity."

24 Then °answered Simon, and said, [22]"Pray ye °to °the Lord °for me, that °none of these things which ye have spoken come °upon me."

t 25 °And they, when they had °testified and °preached the [4]word of [24]the Lord, returned

10 from. Gr. *apo*. Ap. 104. iv.
least, &c. Lit. little unto great.
This man = This one.
power. Gr. *dunamis*. Ap. 172. 1.
God. Ap. 98. I. i. 1. He thus assumed to be the Divine Logos. Cp. 1 Cor. 1. 24.
11 had regard. Same word as "gave heed" in *vv.* 6, 10.
because that . . . he had. Lit. because of (Gr. *dia*. Ap. 104. v. 2) their having been bewitched by.
sorceries = magical arts. Gr. *mageia*. Only here. Cp. *mageuō*, *v.* 9.

8. 12-25 (*K*, p. 1595). PHILIP'S MINISTRY. RESULT. (*Alternation.*)

K | r | 12. Baptisms.
  s | 13. Simon's baptism.
   t | 14. Apostles' visit.
 r | 15-17. Holy Spirit given.
  s | 18-24. Simon's offer.
   t | 25. Apostles' return.

12 believed. Ap. 150. I. 1. ii.
the things. The texts omit.
concerning. Gr. *peri*. Ap. 104. xiii. 1.
the kingdom of God. Ap. 112 and 114.
name. Cp. 3. 6.
Jesus Christ. Ap. 98. XI.
baptized. Ap. 115. I. i.
13 believed also = also believed. Ap. 150. I. 1. i.
continued = was continuing. Gr. *proskartereō*. See note on 1. 14.
wondered = was amazed, or dumbfounded. Middle of *existēmi*. Cp. "bewitched", *v.* 9.
beholding. Gr. *theōreō*. Ap. 133. I. 11.
miracles. Gr. *dunamis*. Ap. 176. 1.
signs. Gr. *semeion*. Ap. 176. 3. The A.V. reverses the translation here. "Miracles and signs" should be "signs and powers, or mighty works". The texts add "great".
14 sent. Gr. *apostellō*. Ap. 174. 1.
unto. Gr. *pros*. Ap. 104. xv. 3.
15 prayed. Gr. *proseuchomai*. Ap. 134. I. 2.
for = concerning. Gr. *peri*, as in *v.* 12.
the Holy Ghost = holy spirit. Gr. *pneuma hagion*. No article. Ap. 101. II. 14.
16 upon. Gr. *epi*. Ap. 104. ix. 2.
none = no one. Gr. *oudeis*. There is a double negative in the sentence.
were = had been. Gr. *huparchō*. See Luke 9. 48.
baptized in = baptized into. Ap. 115. I. iv.
Lord. Ap. 98. VI. i. *β*. 2. A.
Jesus. Ap. 98. X. See Ap. 185.
17 on = upon. Gr. *epi*. Ap. 104. ix. 3.
received = were receiving, i.e. continuing to receive.
18 saw. Gr. *theaomai*. Ap. 133. I. 12. The texts read *eidon*. Ap. 133. I. 1.
through. Gr. *dia*. Ap. 104. v. 1.
the Holy Ghost. *to pneuma to hagion*. Both articles, because referring to what has been already spoken of in *v.* 15. was = is. **19** power = authority. Gr. *exousia*. Ap. 172. 5. that = in order that. Gr. *hina*. **20** perish. Lit. be unto (Gr. *eis*) destruction (Gr. *apolēa*). See John 17. 12. Peter's indignant words are an instance of Fig. *Apodioxis*. Ap. 6. with. Gr. *sun*. Ap. 104. xvi. that, &c. = to purchase. gift = free gift. Gr. *dōrea*. See 2. 38. with = through. Gr. *dia*. Ap. 104. v. 1. **21** neither = not. Gr. *ou*. Ap. 105. I. nor. Gr. *oude*. lot. Gr. *klēros*. Cp. 1. 17, 25, 26. matter = reckoning, or account. Gr. *logos*. Ap. 121. 10. not. Gr. *ou*, as above. in the sight of = in the eyes of. Gr. *enōpion*. But the texts read *enanti*, before. **22** Repent. Gr. *metanoeō*. Ap. 111. I. 1. of = from. Gr. *apo*. Ap. 104. iv. wickedness. Gr. *kakia*. Ap. 128. II. 2. pray. Gr. *deomai*. Ap. 134. I. 5. God. Ap. 98. I. i. 1. The texts read "Lord". Ap. 98. VI. i. *β*. 2. A. if. Gr. *ei*. Ap. 118. 2. a. thought. Gr. *epinoia*. Only here. may = shall. forgiven. Gr. *aphiēmi*. Ap. 174. 12. **23** perceive = see. Gr. *horaō*. Ap. 133. I. 8. in. Gr. *eis*. Ap. 104. vi. gall. Gr. *cholē*. Only here and Matt. 27. 34. Cp. Deut. 29. 18. bitterness. Gr. *pikria*. Here, Rom. 3. 14. Eph. 4. 31. Heb. 12. 15. bond. Gr. *sundesmos*. Here, Eph. 4. 3. Col. 2. 19; 3. 14. A medical word for a ligature. iniquity. Gr. *adikia*. Ap. 128. VII. 1. **24** answered, &c. Ap. 122. 3. to. Gr. *pros*. Ap. 104. xv. 3. the Lord. Ap. 98. VI. i. *β*. 2. A. for. Gr. *huper*. Ap. 104. xvii. 1. none = not one. Gr. *mēdeis*. upon. Gr. *epi*. Ap. 104. ix. 3. From this incident comes the term "simony" for traffic in sacred things. **25** And they. Lit. They indeed therefore. testified. Gr. *diamarturomai*, i.e. fulfilled their testimony. Cp. 2. 40. preached = spoke. Gr. *laleō*. Ap. 121. 7.

[3] to Jerusalem, and °preached the gospel in many °villages of the Samaritans.

I² u¹ 26 °And °the angel of °the LORD °spake [14] unto Philip, saying, °"Arise, and go °toward the south °unto the way that goeth down [10] from Jerusalem °unto °Gaza, which is desert."

v¹ 27 And he [26] arose and went: and, °behold, a [2] man of Ethiopia, an eunuch °of great authority °under °Candace °queen of the Ethiopians, who °had the charge of all her °treasure, and had come [3] to Jerusalem for to °worship,
28 Was returning, and sitting °in his chariot read Esaias the prophet.

u² 29 °Then °the Spirit said [5] unto Philip, "Go near, and °join thyself to this chariot."
30 °And Philip °ran thither to *him*, and heard him read the prophet Esaias, and said, °"Understandest thou what thou readest?"

v² 31 And he said, "How can I, °except °some man should °guide me?" And he °desired Philip that he would come up and sit [20-] with him.
32 °The place of the scripture which he read was this, **"He was led as a sheep °to the °slaughter; and like a °lamb °dumb before °his shearer, so opened he [21] not his mouth:**
33 [8] **In his °humiliation his °judgment was taken away: and who shall °declare his °generation? °for his °life is taken [10] from the °earth."**
34 And the eunuch [24] answered Philip, and said, [22] "I pray thee, °of whom speaketh the prophet this? °of himself, or °of °some °other °man?"

u³ 35 °Then Philip °opened his mouth, and began °at °the same scripture, and [5] preached [5] unto him [16] Jesus.

v³ 36 And as they went °on *their* way, they came [26-] unto a [9] certain water; and the eunuch said, °"See, *here is* water; what doth hinder me to be [12] baptized?"
37 And Philip said, [22] "If thou [13] believest °with all thine heart, thou mayest." And he [24] answered and said, "I °believe that [12] Jesus Christ is the °Son of [10] God."
38 And he commanded the chariot to stand still: and they went down both °into the water, both Philip and the eunuch; and he [12] baptized him.

u⁴ 39 And when they were come up °out of the water, [29] the Spirit of [26] the Lord caught away Philip, that the eunuch °saw him °no more: °and he °went on his way °rejoicing.
40 But Philip °was found °at °Azotus: and

preached the gospel in = evangelized. Gr. *euangelizō*. Ap. 121. 4.
villages. Once John had wished to call down fire from heaven on a Samaritan village. Luke 9. 54.

8. 26-40 (I², p. 1595). IN THE SOUTH.
(*Alternation.*)

I² | u¹ | 26. Philip. The Angel's command.
| v¹ | 27, 28. The Eunuch. Reading.
| u² | 29, 30. Philip. The Spirit's command.
| v² | 31-34. The Eunuch. Questions.
| u³ | 35. Philip. Preaching.
| v³ | 36-38. The Eunuch. Baptism.
| u⁴ | 39, 40. Philip. Caught away.

26 And = But.
the = an.
the Lord. Ap. 98. VI. i. *β*. 1. B. b.
spake. Gr. *laleō*, as v. 25.
Arise. Gr. *anistēmi*. Ap. 178. I. 1.
toward = down to. Gr. *kata*. Ap. 104. x. 2.
unto. Gr. *epi*. Ap. 104. ix. 3.
unto. Gr. *eis*. Ap. 104. vi.
Gaza. One of the five cities of the Philistines; destroyed by Alexander.
27 behold. Gr. *idou*. Ap. 133. I. 2.
of great authority = a potentate. Gr. *dunastēs*. Ap. 98. V.
under = of.
Candace. A title of the queens of Ethiopia. Cp. Pharaoh.
queen. Gr. *basilissa*. Only here, Matt. 12. 42. Luke 11. 31. Rev. 18. 7.
had the charge of = was over (Gr. *epi*. Ap. 104. ix. 1).
treasure. Gr. *gaza*. Only here.
worship. Gr. *proskuneō*. Ap. 137. 1.
28 in = upon. Gr. *epi*. Ap. 104. ix. 1.
29 Then = And.
the Spirit, i. e. the angel. Ap. 101. II. 11.
join thyself. Gr. *kollaomai*. See note on 5. 13.
30 And. Same as "Then", v. 29.
ran thither to him, and. Lit. having run up.
Understandest. Gr. *ginōskō*. Ap. 132. I. ii. Fig. *Paregmenon*. Ap. 6. "Read" is *anaginōskō*.
31 except. Lit. If (Ap. 118. 1. b.) . . . not (Ap. 105. II).
some man = some one. Gr. *tis*. Ap. 123. 3.
guide me = lead me in the way. Gr. *hodēgeō*. Only here, Matt. 15. 14. Luke 6. 39. John 16. 13. Rev. 7. 17.
desired = besought. Gr. *parakaleō*. Ap. 134. I. 6.
32 The place = Now the context. Gr. *periochē*. Only here. Quoted from Isa. 53. 7, almost word for word from the Sept.
to. Gr. *epi*. Ap. 104. ix. 3.
slaughter. Gr. *sphagē*. Only here, Rom. 8. 36. Jas. 5. 5.
lamb. Gr. *amnos*. See note on John 1. 29.
dumb. Gr. *aphōnos*, voiceless. Only here, 1 Cor. 12. 2; 14. 10. 2 Pet. 2. 16. The usual word in the Gospels is *kōphos*.
his shearer = the one shearing (Gr. *keirō*) him.
33 humiliation = low estate. Referring to the whole period of His life on earth. Gr. *tapeinōsis*. Only here, Luke 1. 48. Phil. 3. 21. James 1. 10.
judgment. Gr. *krisis*. Ap. 177. 7.
declare = tell. Gr. *diēgeomai*. Only here, 9. 27; 12. 17. Mark 5. 16; 9. 9. Luke 8. 39; 9. 10. Heb. 11. 32.
generation = posterity. Gr. *genea*. Cp. Matt. 1. 17. See also Dan. 9. 26, "have nothing" (R.V.). John 12. 24, "alone". **for** = because. **life.** Gr. *zōē*. Ap. 170. 1. **earth.** Gr. *gē*. Ap. 129. 4. **34 of** = concerning. Gr. *peri*. Ap. 104. xiii. 1. **some . . . man.** Gr. *tis*. Ap. 123. 3. **other.** Gr. *heteros*. Ap. 124. 2. **35 Then** = But. **opened his mouth.** A Hebraism. Fig. *Idiōma*. Ap. 6. **at** = from. Gr. *apo*. Ap. 104. iv. **the same** = this. **36 on** = down. Gr. *kata*. Ap. 104. x. 2. **See** = Behold. Gr. *idou*. Ap. 133. I. 2. **37** Most texts omit this verse. The R.V. puts it in the margin. **with** = out of. Gr. *ek*. Ap. 104. vii. **believe.** Ap. 150. I. 1. iii. **Son.** Gr. *huios*. Ap. 108. iii. See also Ap. 98. XV. **38 into.** Gr. *eis*. Ap. 104. vi. **39 out of.** Gr. *ek*. Ap. 104. vii. **saw.** Gr. *eidon*. Ap. 133. I. 1. **no more.** Gr. *ouk ouketi*, a double negative. **and** = for. Supply *Ellipsis*, taught by the Spirit, he needed him not. **went on his way** = went his way. **rejoicing.** Cp. v. 8. **40 was found** = was carried to, and found. A *constructio prægnans*. **at** = to. Gr. *eis*. Ap. 104. vi. **Azotus.** Ashdod. See Josh. 11. 22.

passing through he [4] preached in all the cities, °till he came [3] to °Cæsarea.

F² (p. 1595) **9 °And Saul, yet °breathing out °threatenings and °slaughter °against the disciples of °the Lord, went °unto the high priest,**
2 And °desired °of him letters °to °Damascus °to the synagogues, that °if he found °any °of this way, °whether they were °men or °women, he might bring them bound °unto Jerusalem.

G² L **3 [1] And °as he journeyed, °he came near [2] Damascus: and °suddenly there °shined round about him a °light °from °heaven:**
4 And he °fell °to the °earth, and heard a °voice saying [1] unto him, °"Saul, Saul, why persecutest thou Me?"

M **5 [1] And he said, "Who art Thou, °Lord?" And °the Lord said, "I am °Jesus Whom thou persecutest: °*it is* hard for thee to kick against the pricks."**
6 And he trembling and astonished said, [5] "Lord, what wilt Thou have me to do?" And [5] the Lord *said* unto him,

N **°"Arise, and go °into the city, and it shall be °told thee what thou must do."**
7 [1] And the [2] men which °journeyed with him stood °speechless, °hearing a [4] voice, but °seeing °no man.

O **8 [1] And Saul °arose [3] from the [4] earth; and when his eyes were opened,**

P **he °saw °no man: but they °led him by the hand, and brought *him* [6] into [2] Damascus.**
9 [1] And he was three days °without sight,

Q **and °neither did eat °nor drink.**

L **10 [1] And there was a °certain disciple °at [2] Damascus, °named Ananias; and °to him said [1] the Lord °in a °vision, "Ananias."**

M **And he said, °"Behold, I *am here*, [5] Lord."**

N **11 [1] And [1] the Lord *said* °unto him, [6] "Arise, and go °into the °street which is called °Straight, and °enquire [10] in the house of Judas for °*one* called Saul, of Tarsus: for, [10] behold, he °prayeth,**

till. Gr. *heōs*.

Cæsarea. Not Cæsarea Philippi (Matt. 16. 13), but the place on the coast, between Carmel and Joppa. It was built by Herod, and called Cæsarea Sebaste, in honour of Augustus (Gr. *Sebastos*) Cæsar. Herod built a mole or breakwater, so as to make a harbour (Josephus, *Ant.* XVI. v. 1). Now a ruin.

9. 1 And = But, or Now.

breathing out. Gr. *empneō*. Only here.

threatenings. Gr. *apeilē*. See 4. 17.

slaughter = murder. Gr. *phonos*. Occ. ten times. Always trans. murder, except here and Heb. 11. 37.

against. Gr. *eis*. Ap. 104. vi.

the Lord. Ap. 98. VI. i. β. 2. A. **unto** = to.

2 desired. Gr. *aiteō*. Ap. 134. I. 4.

of. Gr. *para*. Ap. 104. xii. 1.

to. Gr. *eis*. Ap. 104. vi.

Damascus. Probably the oldest city in the world. First mentioned in Gen. 14. 15. Founded before Baalbec and Palmyra, has outlived them both. In David's time a garrison town (2 Sam. 8. 6). Rebelled against Solomon (1 Kings 11. 24). Many interesting events connected with it. See 2 Kings 8. 7-15; 14. 28; 16. 9, 10. 2 Chron. 24. 23. Isa. 7. 8, &c.

to. Gr. *pros*. Ap. 104. xv. 3.

if. Gr. *ean*. Ap. 118. 1. b.

any. Gr. pl. of *tis*. Ap. 123. 3.

of this way = being of the way. Note the term "the way" to describe the faith of the believers. See 18. 25, 26; 19. 9, 23; 22. 4; 24. 14, 22, and cp. John 14. 6.

whether they were = both.

men. Gr. *anēr*. Ap. 123. 2.

women. Cp. 8. 3. **unto.** Gr. *eis*. Ap. 104. vi.

9. 3-19- (G², p. 1595). **SAUL CONVERTED.**

(*Extended Alternation.*)

G² | L | 3, 4. Call to Saul.
  M | 5, 6-. Response.
   N | -6, 7. Command. Arise.
    O | 8-. Obedience.
     P | -8, 9-. Blindness.
      Q | -9. Fasting.
 L | 10-. Call to Ananias.
  M | -10. Response.
   N | 11-16. Command. Arise.
    O | 17-. Obedience.
     P | -17, 18. Sight restored.
      Q | 19-. Fast ended.

3 as he journeyed. Lit. in (Gr. *en*. Ap. 104. viii) the journeying.

he came near = it came to pass that he drew nigh.

suddenly. Gr. *exaiphnēs*. Occ. here, 22. 6. Mark 13. 36. Luke 2. 13; 9. 39.

shined round about = flashed around. Gr. *periastraptō*. Only here and 22. 6. Compound of *peri*, around, and *astraptō*, to lighten. (See Luke 17. 24; 24. 4. Cp. Matt. 28. 3.) **light.** Gr. *phōs*. Ap. 130. 1. **from.** Gr. *apo*. Ap. 104. iv, but texts read *ek*. **heaven,** sing. See Matt. 6. 9, 10. **4 fell . . . and** = falling. **to.** Gr. *epi*. Ap. 104. ix. 3. **earth.** Gr. *gē*. Ap. 129. 4. **voice.** Gr. *phōnē*. Same as "sound", 2. 6. **Saul, Saul.** Up to 13. 9, the Greek form *Saulos* is used in the narrative, but here, 17; 13. 21; 22. 7, 13; 26. 14, the Hebrew *Saoul* is found. Fig. *Epizeuxis*. Ap. 6. See Gen. 22. 11. **5 Lord.** Ap. 98. VI. i. β. 2. B. **the Lord.** The texts read "He". **Jesus.** Ap. 98. X. **it is hard, &c.** The texts omit "it is hard", &c., to "unto him", in the middle of *v.* 6. The words were probably supplied from the personal narrative in 26. 14. **6 Arise.** Gr. *anistēmi*. Ap. 178. I. 1. **into.** Gr. *eis*. Ap. 104. vi. **told.** Gr. *laleō*. Ap. 121. 7. **7 journeyed with.** Gr. *sunodeuō*. Only here. **speechless.** Gr. *enneos* or *eneos*. Only here in N.T., but found in Sept. Prov. 17. 28 (holdeth his peace) and Is. 56. 10 (dumb). **hearing.** The companions of Saul heard the sound of the voice, but did not distinguish the words spoken. Cp. 22. 9. This is expressed by the word "voice" (*phōnē*) being in the genitive case here, and in the accusative case in *v.* 4. Cp. John 12. 28-30. **seeing.** Gr. *theōreō*. Ap. 133. I. 11. **no man** = no one. Gr. *mēdeis*. **8 arose** = was raised up. Gr. *egeirō*. Ap. 178. I. 4. **saw.** Gr. *blepō*. Ap. 133. I. 5. **no man** = no one. Gr. *oudeis*. The texts read "nothing". **led . . . and** = leading him by the hand. Gr. *cheiragōgeō*. Only here and 22. 11. Cp. 13. 11. **9 without sight** = not (Gr. *mē*) seeing (Gr. *blepō*. Ap. 133. I. 5). **neither** = not. Gr. *ou*. Ap. 105. I. **nor.** Gr. *oude*. **10 certain.** Gr. *tis*. Ap. 123. 3. **at.** Gr. *en*. Ap. 104. viii. **named** = by name. **to.** Gr. *pros*. Ap. 104. xv. 3. **in.** Gr. *en*, as above. **vision.** See note on 7. 31. **Behold.** Gr. *idou*. Ap. 133. I. 2. Fig. *Asterismos*. Ap. 6. **11 unto.** Gr. *pros*. Ap. 104. xv. 3. **into.** Gr. *epi*. Ap. 104. ix. 3. **street** = lane. Gr. *rhumē*. Here, 12. 10. Matt. 6. 2. Luke 14. 21. **Straight.** It ran direct from the W. gate to the E. gate. In oriental cities such would be the bazaar. **enquire** = seek. Gr. *zēteō*. **one, &c.** = a Tarsean, Saul by name. Tarsus was the capital of Cilicia. Saul was doubtless one of those who disputed with Stephen (6. 9). **prayeth.** Gr. *proseuchomai*. Ap. 134. I. 2.

12 And °hath seen [10]in a [10]vision a [2]man
[10]named Ananias coming in, and putting *his*
hand on him, that he might °receive his
sight."
13 Then Ananias answered, [5]"Lord, I have
heard °by many °of this [2]man, °how much evil
he hath done to Thy °saints [10]at Jerusalem:
14 And here he hath °authority °from the
chief priests to bind all that °call on Thy
name."
15 But [1]the Lord said [11]unto him, "Go thy
way: for He is °a chosen vessel °unto Me, to
bear My name °before the °Gentiles, and kings,
and the °children of Israel:
16 For I will °shew him how great things he
must °suffer °for My name's sake."

O 17 [1]And Ananias went his way, and entered
[6]into the house; and putting his hands °on
him said,

P °"Brother °Saul, [1]the Lord, *even* [5]Jesus,
That °appeared unto thee [10]in the way
°as thou camest, hath °sent me, that thou
mightest [12]receive thy sight, and be filled with
°the Holy Ghost."
18 And °immediately there °fell [3]from his eyes
as it had been °scales: and he [12]received sight
°forthwith, and [6]arose, and was °baptized.

Q 19 And when he had received °meat, he was
strengthened.

H² (p. 1595) [1]Then was Saul [10]certain days °with the disciples which were [10]at [2]Damascus.
20 And °straightway he °preached °Christ
[10]in the synagogues, that °He is °the Son of
God.
21 But all that heard *him* °were amazed, and
said; "Is °not this he that °destroyed them
which [14]called on this name [10]in Jerusalem, and
came hither °for that intent, °that he might
bring them bound °unto the chief priests?"
22 But Saul °increased the more in strength,
and °confounded the Jews which °dwelt [10]at
[2]Damascus, °proving that this is °very Christ.

F³ R u 23 [1]And °after that °many days were fulfilled, the Jews °took counsel to °kill him:

v 24 But their °laying await was °known °of

12 hath seen = saw. Gr. *eidon*. Ap. 133. I. 1.
receive his sight. Gr. *anablepō*. Ap. 133. I. 6.
13 by = from. Gr. *apo*. Ap. 104. iv.
of = concerning. Gr. *peri*. Ap. 104. xiii. 1.
how much evil = how many evil things. Gr. *kakos*. Ap. 128. III. 2.
saints = holy, or separated, ones. Gr. *hagios*. Cp. Ps. 116. 15.
14 authority. Gr. *exousia*. Ap. 172. 5.
from. Gr. *para*. Ap. 104. xii. 1.
call, &c. See note on 2. 21.
15 a chosen vessel = a vessel of choice, or election (Gr. *eklogē*). Occ. here, Rom. 9. 11; 11. 5, 7, 28. 1 Thess. 1. 4. 2 Pet. 1. 10. unto = for.
before = in the presence of.
Gentiles = nations. Gr. *ethnos*.
children = sons. Gr. *huios*. Ap. 108. iii. Note the order.
16 shew = forewarn. Gr. *hupodeiknumi*. Occ. elsewhere 20. 35. Matt. 3. 7. Luke 3. 7; 6. 47; 12. 5.
suffer. See 2 Cor. 11. 23-28.
for My name's sake = on behalf of (Gr. *huper*. Ap. 104. xvii. 1) My name. See 22. 14-18.
17 on. Gr. *epi*. Ap. 104. ix. 3.
Brother. Thus recognizing him as a fellow-disciple.
Saul. Gr. *Saoul*, as in *v.* 4.
appeared unto = was seen by. Gr. *optomai*. Ap. 106. I. vi.
as = by which.
sent. Gr. *apostellō*. Ap. 174. 1.
the Holy Ghost. Gr. *pneuma hagion*. Ap. 101. II. 14.
18 immediately = straightway. Gr. *eutheōs*.
fell = fell away. Gr. *apopiptō*. Only here.
scales. Gr. *lepis*. Only here in N.T. In Sept., Lev. 11. 9, 10, &c. Cp. Tobit 11. 13.
forthwith. Gr. *parachrēma*. Cp. 3. 7; 5. 10. The texts omit.
baptized. Ap. 115. I. 1.
19 meat = nourishment. Gr. *trophē*.
with. Gr. *meta*. Ap. 104. xi. 1.
20 straightway. Gr. *eutheōs*, as in *v.* 18.
preached. Gr. *kērussō*. Ap. 121. 1.
Christ. The texts read "Jesus".
He = This One.
the Son of God. Ap. 98. XV.
21 were amazed. Gr. *existēmi*. Cp. 2. 7; 8. 9, 13.
not. Gr. *ou*. Ap. 105. I.
destroyed = devastated. Gr. *portheō*. Same word as in Gal. 1. 13, 23. Not the same as in 8. 3.
for that intent = for (Gr. *eis*. Ap. 104. vi) this.
that = in order that. Gr. *hina*.
unto. Gr. *epi*. Ap. 104. ix. 3.
22 increased . . . in strength = was strengthened. Gr. *endunamoō*. Occ. elsewhere, Rom. 4. 20. Eph. 6. 10. Phil. 4. 13. 1 Tim. 1. 12. 2 Tim. 2. 1; 4. 17. Heb. 11. 34. Cp. Ap. 172. 1.
confounded. See note on 2. 6. dwelt. See note on 2. 5. proving. Gr. *sumbibazō*. Lit. bring together, compare. Here, 16. 10 1 Cor. 2. 16. Eph. 4. 16. Col. 2. 2, 19. very Christ = the Christ, i.e. the Messiah. Ap. 98. IX. Instead of searching the Scriptures to see if these things were so, the Damascenes were occupied with the change in Saul's attitude. Hence we read nothing of believers. Contrast 17. 11, 12. No epistle addressed to them nor any record of a church there.

9. 23-30 (F³, p. 1595). PERSECUTION OF SAUL. (*Alternation and Introversion.*)

F³ | R | u | 23. Plot to kill (*anaireō*).
    v | 24. Plot known.
        x | 25, 26-. Escape to Jerusalem.
            S | y | -26. Suspicion.
                z | 27. Preaching boldly (*parrhēsiazomai*).
            S | *y* | 28. Reception.
                z | 29-. Speaking boldly (*parrhēsiazomai*).
   R | *u* | -29. Plot to slay (*anaireō*).
    v | 30-. Plot known.
        x | -30. Escape to Tarsus.

23 after that = when. many days = the three years of Gal. 1. 18. Cp. 1 Kings 2. 38, 39, where many days also implies three years. took counsel = plotted. Gr. *sumbouleuō*. Occ. elsewhere, Matt. 26. 4. John 11. 53; 18. 14. Rev. 3. 18. kill. See note on "slain", 2. 23. **24** laying await = plot. Gr. *epiboulē*. Occ. elsewhere 20. 3, 19; 23. 30. known. Gr. *ginōskō*. Ap. 132. ii. of = to.

Saul. And they °watched the gates day and
night °to [23] kill him.

x 25 Then the disciples took him by night, and
°let *him* down °by the wall °in a °basket.
26 [1] And when Saul was come °to Jerusalem,
he °assayed to °join himself to the disciples:

S y but they were all afraid of him, °and believed
°not that he was a disciple.

z 27 But °Barnabas °took him, and brought *him*
°to the °apostles, and °declared [1] unto them how
he had [12] seen [1] the Lord [10] in the way, and that
He had °spoken to him, and how he had
°preached boldly [10] at [2] Damascus [10] in the name
of [5] Jesus.

S y 28 And he was [19] with them °coming in and
going out [10] at Jerusalem.

z 29 And he °spake boldly [10] in the name of
[1] the Lord [5] Jesus, and °disputed °against the
°Grecians:

R u but they °went about to °slay him.

v 30 °*Which* when the brethren knew,

x they °brought him down [2] to °Cæsarea, and
°sent him forth [26] to [11] Tarsus.

G3 (p. 1595) 31 °Then had the °churches °rest °throughout
all Judæa and Galilee and Samaria, °and were
edified; and °walking in the fear of [1] the Lord,
and in the °comfort of °the Holy Ghost, °were
°multiplied.

H3 T a 32 [1] And it came to pass, as Peter passed
°throughout all *quarters,* he came down °also
[27] to the [13] saints which [22] dwelt at °Lydda.
33 [1] And there he found a [10] certain °man
[10] named Æneas, °which had kept his bed
°eight years, and was °sick of the palsy.
34 And Peter said [1] unto him, "Æneas,
°Jesus Christ °maketh thee whole: [6] arise, and
°make thy bed." And he [6] arose [18] immediately.

b 35 And all that [22] dwelt at Lydda and Saron
[12] saw him, and °turned [4] to [1] the Lord.

a 36 Now there was [10] at Joppa a [10] certain °disciple
[10] named °Tabitha, which °by interpretation
is called °Dorcas: this woman was full

watched = were watching. Gr. *paratēreō.* See note on Luke 17. 20.

to = that they might. In 2 Cor. 11. 32, Paul says "the governor under Aretas kept the city with a garrison". This Aretas was Herod's father-in-law, upon whom he made war because Herod had abandoned his daughter for his brother Philip's wife, Herodias. Perhaps to do the Jews a pleasure, like Felix, Aretas endeavoured to seize Paul.

25 let him down = sent him down. Gr. *kathiēmi.* Occ. elsewhere, 10. 11; 11. 5. Luke 5. 19.

by = through. Gr. *dia.* Ap. 104. v. 1.

in = lowering (Gr. *chalaō*) him in. See note on Luke 5. 4.

in. Gr. *en.* Ap. 104. viii.

basket. Gr. *spuris.* See note on Matt. 15. 37.

26 to. Gr. *eis.* Ap. 104. vi.

assayed = tried. Gr. *peiraō.*

join. See note on 5. 13.

and believed not = not (Gr. *mē.* Ap. 105. II.) believing, i.e. hesitating to believe. Ap. 150. I. iii.

27 Barnabas. See note on 4. 36.

took = laid hold of. Gr. *epilambanomai.* Occ. twelve times in Luke and Acts. Mostly of helping or arresting.

to. Gr. *pros.* Ap. 104. xv. 3.

apostles. Ap. 189.

declared = related. Gr. *diēgeomai.* See note on 8. 33.

spoken. Gr. *laleō.* Ap. 121. 7.

preached boldly = spoke without reserve. Gr. *parrhēsiazomai.* Occ. elsewhere, *v.* 29; 13. 46; 14. 3; 18. 26; 19. 8; 26. 26. Eph. 6. 20. 1 Thess. 2. 2.

28 coming in and going out. See note on 1. 21.

29 spake boldly. Same word as "preached boldly" in *v.* 27. disputed. Same word as in 6. 9.

against. Gr. *pros.* Ap. 104. xv. 3.

Grecians. See note on 6. 1.

went about = took in hand. Gr. *epicheireō.* Occ. elsewhere, 19. 13. Luke 1. 1. A medical word.

slay. Same word as "kill", *vv.* 23, 24.

30 Which . . . knew = But the brethren having got to know it. Gr. *epiginōskō.* Ap. 132. I. iii.

brought . . . down. Gr. *katagō.*

Cæsarea. See 8. 40.

sent. Gr. *exapostellō.* Ap. 174. 2. See 11. 25.

31 Then, &c. = The church indeed therefore.

churches. Ap. 186.

rest = peace. Gr. *eirēnē.*

throughout. Gr. *kata.* Ap. 104. x. 1.

and were edified = being edified. Gr. *oikodomeō.* Cp. 4. 11; 7. 47, 49.

walking = going. Fig. *Hendiadys.* Ap. 6. Read, "being edified and walking in the fear of the Lord were replenished with".

comfort. Gr. *paraklēsis.* See note on 4. 36.

the Holy Ghost. Ap. 101. II. 3.

were = was. The texts put this verse in the sing. "The church . . . was". multiplied. See note on 6. 1.

9. 32—10. 48 (H3, p. 1595). MINISTRY AT LYDDA, &c. (*Alternation.*)

H3 | T | 9. 32-42. Æneas, &c.
  U | 9. 43. Abode (*menō*).
 T | 10. 1-48-. Cornelius.
  U | -48. Abode (*epimenō*).

9. 32-42 (T, above). ÆNEAS, &c. (*Alternation.*)

T | a | 32-34. Miracle.
  b | 35. Result.
 a | 36-41. Miracle.
  b | 42. Result.

32 throughout = through. Gr. *dia.* Ap. 104. v. 1. also to the saints = to the saints also. Lydda. Ludd, in the plain of Sharon, about a day's journey w. of Jerusalem. See 1 Chron. 8. 12. **33** man. Gr. *anthrōpos.* Ap. 123. 1. which had kept his bed = lying on (Gr. *epi.* Ap. 104. ix. 2) a bed (Gr. *krabbaton.* See note on Mark 2. 4). eight years = from (Gr. *ek.* Ap. 104. vii) eight years. sick of the palsy = paralysed. See note on 8. 7. **34** Jesus Christ. Ap. 98. XI. maketh thee whole = healeth thee. Gr. *iaomai.* See note on Luke 6. 17. make thy bed. Lit. spread for thyself. **35** turned. See 11. 21; 14. 15; 15. 19; 26. 18, 20. **36** disciple. Gr. *mathētria,* the fem. form of *mathētēs.* Only here. Tabitha. Aramaic. Ap. 94. III. 3. 42. The Hebrew for roe or gazelle is Zebee. The fem. is found in 2 Kings 12. 1, there spelt Zibiāh. by interpretation = being interpreted. Gr. *diermēneuō.* Here, Luke 24. 27. 1 Cor. 12. 30; 14. 5, 13, 27. Dorcas. Gr. for antelope, or gazelle.

of good works and °almsdeeds which she
did.
37 [1]And it came to pass [10]in those days, that
she °was sick, and died: whom when they had
°washed, they laid *her* [10]in an °upper chamber.
38 [1]And °forasmuch as Lydda was nigh to
Joppa, and the disciples had heard that Peter
was °there, they [17]sent [11]unto him two [2]men
°desiring *him* that he would [26]not °delay to
come °to them.
39 Then Peter [6]arose and went with them.
When he was come, they brought him [6]into
the [37]upper chamber: and all the widows stood
by him weeping, and shewing the °coats and
garments which Dorcas made, while she was
[19]with them.
40 But Peter put them all °forth, and °kneeled
down, and [11]prayed; and turning *him* [10]to the
body said, "Tabitha, [6]arise." And she opened
her eyes: and when she [12]saw Peter, she sat
up.
41 [1]And he gave her *his* hand, and °lifted her
up, and °when he had called the [13]saints and
widows, presented her alive.
b 42 [1]And °it was °known [31]throughout all Joppa;
and many °believed in [1]the Lord.
U 43 [1]And it came to pass, that he °tarried many
days [10]in Joppa °with °one Simon a °tanner.

TV[1]c **10** There was a °certain °man °in °Cæsarea
°called Cornelius, a °centurion of the
°band called the °Italian *band,*
2 *A* °devout *man,* and one that feared °God
°with all his house, which gave much °alms to
the °people, and °prayed to °God alway.
3 He °saw [1]in a °vision °evidently °about °the
ninth hour of the day an angel of [2]God coming
in °to him, and saying °unto him, "Cornelius."
4 °And when he looked on him, °he was
afraid, and said, "What is it, °Lord?" And
He said [3]unto him, "Thy °prayers and thine
[2]alms are come up °for a °memorial °before
[2]God.
d 5 And now °send [1]men °to Joppa, and °call
for *one* Simon, °whose surname is Peter:
6 °He °lodgeth °with °one Simon a °tanner,
whose house is °by the sea side: °he shall tell
thee what thou oughtest to do."
e 7 °And when the angel which °spake [3]unto
°Cornelius was departed, he called two of his
°household servants, and a [2]devout soldier of
them that °waited on him continually;
8 And °when he had declared all *these* things
[3]unto them,
f he sent them [5]to Joppa.

almsdeeds = alms. Gr. *eleēmosunē*, as in 3. 2.

37 was sick = fell sick. Gr. *astheneō*. Frequent in the Gospels. In Acts, here, 19. 12; 20. 35.

washed = bathed. Gr. *louō*. Ap. 136. iii.

upper chamber = upper room. See note on 1. 13.

38 forasmuch as Lydda was nigh. Lit. Lydda being near.

there = in (Gr. *en*. Ap. 104. viii) it.

desiring = entreating. Gr. *parakaleō*. Ap. 134. I. 6.

delay. Gr. *okneō*. Only here.

to = as far as. Gr. *heōs*.

39 coats. Gr. *chitōn*. = tunic or under-garment.

40 forth = outside. Gr. *exō*. Cp. Mark 5. 40.

kneeled down. Same expression as in 7. 60.

41 lifted her up. Lit. caused her to rise up. Gr. *anistēmi*, as above, *v.* 40.

when he had = having.

42 it was = it came to be.

known. Gr. *gnōstos*. See note on 1. 19.

believed in. Ap. 150. I. 1. V. (iii.) 2.

43 tarried = abode. Gr. *menō*. See note on p. 1511.

with. Gr. *para*. Ap. 104. xii. 2.

one = a certain. Gr. *tis*. Ap. 123. 3.

tanner. Gr. *burseus*. Only here and 10. 6, 32. Perhaps no one else would receive him.

10. 1-48- (*T*, p. 1600). CORNELIUS.
(*Division.*)

T | V[1] | 10. 1-24-. Preparation.
| V[2] | 10. -24-48-. Conference.

10. 1-24- (V[1], above). PREPARATION.
(*Extended Alternation*).

V[1] | c | 1-4. Vision.
d | 5, 6. Command.
e | 7, 8-. Obedience.
f | -8, 9-. Messengers sent.
c | -9-19-. Vision.
d | -19, 20. Command.
e | 21, 22. Obedience.
f | 23, 24-. Messengers received.

10. 1 certain. Gr. *tis*. Ap. 123. 3.

man. Gr. *anēr*. Ap. 123. 2.

in. Gr. *en*. Ap. 104. viii.

Cæsarea. See note on 8. 40.

called = by name.

centurion = a captain over a hundred men. Gr. *hekatontarchēs*. Occ. elsewhere, *v.* 22; 24. 23; 27. 1, 31. In the Gospels and in nine other places in Acts, the form *hekatontarchos* is used.

band = cohort. Gr. *speira*. See Matt. 27. 27.

Italian. It would be one levied in Italy.

2 devout = pious. Gr. *eusebēs*. Here, *v.* 7; 22. 12. 2 Pet. 2. 9. Not the same as in 2. 5; 8. 2.

God. Ap. 98. I. i. 1.

with. Gr. *sun*. Ap. 104. xvi.

alms. Gr. *eleēmosunē*. See note on 3. 2.

people. Gr. *laos*. See note on 2. 47.

prayed. Gr. *deomai*. Ap. 134. I. 5.

3 saw. Gr. *eidon*. Ap. 133. I. 1.

vision. Gr. *horama*, as in 7. 31.

evidently = clearly, i. e. objectively. Gr. *phanerōs*.

about = as if.

the ninth hour = 3 p.m. Ap. 165.

to. Gr. *pros*. Ap. 104. xv. 3. **unto** = to. **4 And when he looked on him** = But gazing at him. Gr. *atenizō*. Ap. 133. III. 6. See note on 1. 10. **he was afraid, and** = and becoming affrighted, he. Gr. *emphobos*. Here, 22. 9; 24. 25. Luke 24. 5, 37. Rev. 11. 13. **Lord.** Gr. *kurios*. Used as in John 4. 11, where it is rendered "Sir". **prayers.** Gr. *proseuchē*. Ap. 134. II. 2. **for.** Gr. *eis*. Ap. 104. vi. **memorial.** Gr. *mnēmosunon*. Here, Matt. 26. 13. Mark 14. 9. **before** = in the sight of. Gr. *enōpion*. **5 send.** Gr. *pempō*. Ap. 174. 4. **to.** Gr. *eis*. Ap. 104. vi. **call for** = send for. Gr. *metapempō*. Ap. 174. 7. **whose surname is** = who is surnamed. **6 He** = This one. **lodgeth.** Gr. pass. of *xenizo*, to receive as a guest. **with.** Gr. *para*. Ap. 104. xii. 2. **one.** Gr. *tis*. Ap. 123. 3. **tanner.** See 9. 43. **by the sea side** = by the side of (Gr. *para*. Ap. 104. xii. 3.) the sea. **he shall, &c.** The texts omit this clause. **7 And** = Now. **spake.** Gr. *laleō*. Ap. 121. 7. **Cornelius.** The texts read "him". **household servants.** Gr. *oiketēs*. Ap. 190. I. 5. **waited.. continually.** Gr. *proskartereō*. See note on 1. 14. **8 when he had declared** = having related. Gr. *exegeomai*. Here, 15. 12, 14; 21. 19. Luke 24. 35. John 1. 18. **sent.** Gr. *apostellō*. Ap. 174. 1.

9 On the morrow, as they °went on their journey, and °drew nigh [3]unto the city,

c Peter went up °upon the °housetop to °pray °about °the sixth hour:

10 [7]And he became °very hungry, and °would have °eaten: but while they made ready, °he fell into a trance,

11 And °saw °heaven opened, and a [1]certain vessel descending °unto him, as it had been a great °sheet °knit at the four corners, and °let down °to the °earth:

12 °Wherein °were °all manner of °fourfooted beasts of the [11]earth, °and wild beasts, and °creeping things, and fowls of the °air.

13 And there came a voice [3]to him, °"Rise, Peter; °kill, and eat."

14 But Peter said, °"Not so, [4]Lord; for I °have °never eaten any thing that is common or °unclean."

15 And the voice *spake* °unto him again °the second time, °"What [2]God hath cleansed, *that* call °not thou common."

16 This was done °thrice: and the vessel was received up again °into [11]heaven.

17 Now while Peter °doubted [1]in himself what this [3]vision which he had [3]seen should °mean, °behold, the [1]men which were [8]sent °from Cornelius °had made enquiry for Simon's house, and stood °before the gate,

18 And called, and °asked °whether Simon, which was surnamed Peter, were [6]lodged there.

19 While Peter °thought °on the [3]vision,

d °the Spirit said [3]unto him, [17]"Behold, three [1]men seek thee.

20 °Arise therefore, and get thee down, and go [2]with them, °doubting °nothing: °for I have [8]sent them."

e 21 Then Peter went down [3]to the [1]men °which were sent unto him from Cornelius; and said, [17]"Behold, I am he whom ye seek: what *is* the cause °wherefore ye °are come?"

22 And they said, "Cornelius the [1]centurion, a °just [1]man, and one that feareth [2]God, and °of good report °among all the °nation of the Jews, was °warned from God °by an holy angel to °send for thee [16]into his house, and to hear °words °of thee."

f 23 Then called he them in, and [6]lodged *them*. And on the morrow Peter went away [2]with them, and [1]certain brethren [17]from Joppa accompanied him.

9 went on their journey. Gr. *hodoiporeō*. Only here.
drew nigh = were drawing near.
upon. Gr. *epi*. Ap. 104. ix. 3.
housetop = house.
pray. Gr. *proseuchomai*. Ap. 134. I. 2.
about. Gr. *peri*. Ap. 104. xiii. 2.
the sixth hour, i. e. midday. Ap. 165.

10 very hungry. Gr. *prospeinos*. Only here.
would have eaten = wished (Gr. *ethelō*. Ap. 102. 1) to eat.
eaten. Gr. *geuomai*, to taste (food understood). Always trans. "taste", except in Acts, here, 20. 11; 23. 14.
he fell, &c. Lit. a trance (Gr. *ekstasis*) fell upon (Gr. *epi*. Ap. 104. ix. 3.) him. The texts read "came upon him". *Ekstasis* is sometimes transl. "amazement", as in 3. 10. It is akin to *existēmi* (2. 7; 8. 9, &c.). This was not an objective vision, as in the case of Cornelius.

11 saw = beheld. Gr. *theōreō*. Ap. 133. I. 11.
heaven = the heaven. Matt. 6. 9, 10.
unto him. The texts omit.
sheet. Gr. *othonē*. Only here and 11. 5.
knit. The texts omit. Read "Let down by the four corners".
let down = sent down. Gr. *kathiēmi*. Occ. elsewhere, 9. 25; 11. 5. Luke 5. 19.
to = upon. Gr. *epi*. Ap. 104. ix. 1.
earth. Gr. *gē*. Ap. 129. 4.

12 Wherein = In (Gr. *en*. Ap. 104. viii) which.
were. Gr. *huparchō*. See note on Luke 9. 48.
all manner of = all.
fourfooted beasts. Gr. *tetrapous*. Here 11. 6. Rom. 1. 23.
and wild beasts. The texts omit.
creeping things. Gr. *herpeton*. Here 11. 6. Rom. 1. 23. James 3. 7.
air = heaven.

13 Rise. Gr. *anistēmi*. Ap. 178. I. 1.
kill = slay. Gr. *thuō*, to slay, or to sacrifice.

14 Not so = By no means. Gr. *mēdamōs*.
have . . . eaten = ate.
never = not even at any time. Gr. *oudepote*.
unclean. Gr. *akathartos*. The previous twenty-one occ. all apply to evil spirits. Here the reference is to the ceremonial uncleanness of the Levitical law.

15 unto. Gr. *pros*. Ap. 104. xv. 3.
the second time. Lit. from (Gr. *ek*. Ap. 104. vii.) a second (time).
What = The things which.
not. Gr. *mē*. Ap. 105. II.

16 thrice. Lit. upon (Gr. *epi*. Ap. 104. ix. 3) thrice.
into. Gr. *eis*. Ap. 104. vi.

17 doubted = was perplexed. Gr. *diaporeō*. See note on Luke 9. 7.
mean = be.
behold. Gr. *idou*. Ap. 133. I. 2.
from. Gr. *apo*. Ap. 104. iv.
had made enquiry . . . and = having inquired carefully. Gr. *dierōtaō*. Compd. of *dia* Ap. 104. v, and *erōtaō* Ap. 134. I. 3. Only here.

before = at. Gr. *epi*. Ap. 104. ix. 3. **18 asked** = inquired. Gr. *punthanomai*. **whether** = if. Gr. *ei*. Ap. 118. 2. a. **19 thought on** = turned over in his mind. Gr. *enthumeomai*. Only here and Matt. 1. 20; 9. 4. The texts read *dienthumeomai*, a stronger word. **on.** Gr. *peri*. Ap. 104. xiii. 1. **the Spirit,** i. e. the angel of *v.* 3. Ap. 101. II. 11. **20 Arise therefore** = But arise. Same as rise *v.* 13. **doubting.** Gr. *diakrinō*. Ap. 122. 4. **nothing.** Gr. *mēdeis*. **for I have sent them.** This proves that it is the angel that is speaking. Cp. *v.* 5. **21 which were sent unto him from Cornelius.** All the texts and Syriac omit. **wherefore** = on account of (Gr. *dia*. Ap. 104. V. 2) which. **are come** = are present. **22 just.** Gr. *dikaios*. Ap. 191. 1. **of good report** = borne witness to. Gr. *martureō*. Same as "of honest report" in 6. 3. **among** = by. Gr. *hupo*. Ap. 104. xviii. 1. **nation.** Gr. *ethnos*. **warned from God.** Gr. *chrēmatizō*. See note on Luke 2. 26. **by.** Gr. *hupo*, as above. **send for.** Gr. *metapempō*, as in *v.* 5. **words.** Gr. *rhēma*. See note on Mark 9. 32. **of** = from. Gr. *para*. Ap. 104. xii. 1.

24 And the morrow after they entered [16]into
[1]Cæsarea.
V² W [7]And Cornelius °waited for them, and had
called together his kinsmen and °near friends.
25 °And as Peter was coming in, Cornelius
°met him, and fell down °at his feet, and °worshipped *him*.
26 But Peter °took him up, saying, °"Stand
up; I myself also am a °man."
27 And °as he talked with him, he went in,
and found many that were come together.

X 28 And he said [15]unto them, "Ye °know how
that it is an °unlawful thing for a [1]man that
is a Jew to °keep company, or come [3]unto °one
of another nation; but [2]God °hath shewed °me
that I should °not call any [26]man common or
[14]unclean.
29 Therefore °came I *unto you* °without gainsaying, as soon as I was [22]sent for: I [18]ask
therefore °for what intent ye °have [22]sent for
me?"

Y 30 And Cornelius said, °"Four days ago °I
was fasting until this hour; and at [3]the ninth
hour I [9]prayed [1]in my house, and, [17]behold,
a [1]man stood [4]before me in °bright clothing,
31 And said, 'Cornelius, thy [4]prayer °is heard,
and thine [2]alms °are had in remembrance °in
the sight of [2]God.
32 [5]Send therefore [5]to Joppa, and °call
hither Simon, [5]whose surname is Peter; he
is [6]lodged [1]in the house of *one* Simon a [6]tanner [6]by the sea side: °who, when he cometh,
shall [7]speak unto thee.'
33 °Immediately therefore I [5]sent [3]to thee;
and thou °hast well done that thou art come.
Now therefore are we all here present [4]before
[2]God, to hear all things that are commanded
thee °of [2]God."

X g¹ 34 Then Peter °opened *his* mouth, and said,
"°Of a truth I °perceive that [2]God is °no °respecter of persons:
35 But [1]in every [22]nation he that feareth
Him, and worketh righteousness, is °accepted
with Him.
36 The °word which *God* [8]sent [3]unto the
°children of Israel, °preaching peace °by Jesus
Christ: °(He is [4]Lord of all:)
37 That [22]word, *I say*, ye °know, which °was
published °throughout all Judæa, and began
[17]from Galilee, °after the °baptism which John
°preached;

10. 24-48- (V², p. 1601). CONFERENCE.
(*Introversion.*)

V² | W | -24-27. Expectation.
  X | 28, 29. Peter.
    Y | 30-33. Cornelius.
  X | 34-43. Peter.
W | 44-48-. Realization.

24 waited = was waiting. Gr. *prosdokaō*. Ap. 133. III. 3.

near = intimate. Gr. *anankaios*. Lit. necessary. First occ. Transl. elsewhere "necessary", "needful", &c.

25 And as, &c. = Now as it came to pass that Peter entered in.

met. Gr. *sunantaō*. Here 20. 22. Luke 9. 37; 22. 10. Heb. 7. 1, 10.

at. Gr. *epi*. Ap. 104. ix. 3.

worshipped = did him homage or reverence. Gr. *proskuneō*. Ap. 137. 1.

26 took him up = raised him up. Gr. *egeirō*. Ap. 178. I. 4.

Stand up = rise up. Gr. mid. of *anistēmi*. Ap. 178. I. 1.

man. Gr. *anthrōpos*. Ap. 123. 1.

27 as he talked with = conversing with. Gr. *sunomileō*. Only here.

28 know. Gr. *epistamai*. Ap. 132. I. v.

unlawful. Gr. *athemitos*. Here and 1 Pet. 4. 3. *Themis* is that which is established by custom or usage.

keep company. Gr. *kollaomai*. See Luke 15. 15.

one of another nation = aliens. Gr. *allophulos* Only here in N.T., but freq. in Sept., where the Heb. reads "Philistines".

hath. Omit.

me. Emphatic because it stands first in the sentence. "Me God shewed".

not call any = call no (Gr. *mēdeis*).

29 came, &c. Read, "without gainsaying also I came".

without gainsaying. Gr. *anantirrhētōs*. Only here.

for what intent = for what word, or reason. Gr. *logos*. Ap. 121. 10.

have. Omit.

30 Four days ago = From (Gr. *apo*. Ap. 104. iv) the fourth day.

I was, &c. The texts omit "fasting", and read "until this hour I was praying".

bright = shining. Gr. *lampros*.

31 is = was.

are had in, &c. = were remembered.

in the sight of. The same as "before", *vv.* 4, 30, 33.

32 call hither. Gr. *metakaleō*. See note on 7. 14.

who, &c. The texts omit.

33 Immediately. Gr. *exautēs*. Here, 11. 11; 21. 32; 23. 30. Mark 6. 25. Phil. 2. 23.

hast well done = didst well. Cp. Phil. 4. 14. James 2. 19. 2 Pet. 1. 19. 3 John 6.

of = by. Gr. *hupo*. Ap. 104. xviii. 1.

10. 34-43 (*X*, above). PETER. (*Alternation.*)

X | g¹ | 34-38. The Lord's Life.
  h¹ | 39-. Witnesses.
g² | -39, 40. The Lord's Death and Resurrection.
  h² | 41. Witnesses.
g³ | 42. The Lord the Judge.
  h³ | 43. Witnesses.

34 opened his mouth. See note on 8. 35. **Of** = Upon. Gr. *epi*. Ap. 104. ix. 1. **perceive.** See note on 4. 13. **no** = not a. Gr. *ou*. Ap. 105. I. **respecter of persons.** Lit. one who takes faces (i. e. persons) into account. Gr. *prosōpolēptēs*. Only here. Cp. James 2. 9. **35 accepted with** = acceptable to. Gr. *dektos*. Here Luke 4. 19, 24. 2 Cor. 6. 2. Phil. 4. 18. **36 word.** Gr. *logos*. Ap. 121. 10. **children** = sons. Gr. *huios*. Ap. 108. iii. **preaching.** Gr. *euangelizō*. Ap. 121. 4. **by** = by means of. Gr. *dia*. Ap. 104. v. 1. **Jesus Christ.** Ap. 98. XI. **He, &c.** Cornelius had no claim on Him as son of David. Cp. Matt. 15. 22-28. **37 know.** Gr. *oida*. Ap. 132. I. i. **was published.** Lit. came to be. **throughout.** Gr. *kata*. Ap. 104. x. 1. **after.** Gr. *meta*. Ap. 104. xi. 2. **baptism.** Ap. 115. II. i. 2. **preached** = proclaimed. Gr. *kērussō*. Ap. 121. 1.

38 ° How [2] God anointed ° Jesus ° of Nazareth with ° the Holy Ghost and with ° power: Who went about ° doing good, and ° healing all that were ° oppressed [33] of the devil; for [2] God was ° with Him.

h1 39 And we are ° witnesses of all things which He did both [1] in the ° land of the Jews, and [1] in Jerusalem;

g2 Whom they ° slew ° and hanged ° on a ° tree:
40 ° Him [2] God ° raised up the third day, and ° shewed Him openly;

h2 41 ° Not to all the [2] people, but [3] unto [39] witnesses ° chosen before [33] of [2] God, *even* to us, who ° did eat and ° drink with Him [37] after He [13] rose ° from the dead.

g3 42 And He ° commanded us to [37] preach [3] unto the [2] people, and to ° testify that it is He Which was ° ordained [33] of [2] God *to be* the ° Judge of ° quick and ° dead.

h3 43 To [40] Him ° give all the prophets witness, that ° through His ° name whosoever ° believeth in Him shall receive ° remission of ° sins."

W 44 While Peter yet [7] spake these [22] words, [38] the Holy Ghost fell ° on all them which heard ° the [36] word.
45 And ° they [1] of the circumcision which ° believed ° were astonished, as many as came with Peter, because that [44] on the ° Gentiles also was poured out the ° gift of [38] the Holy Ghost.
46 For they heard them ° speak with tongues, and ° magnify [2] God. Then ° answered Peter,
47 ° "Can ° any man ° forbid water, that these should [15] not be ° baptized, which have received [38] the Holy Ghost ° as well as we?"
48 And he commanded them to be ° baptized [1] in the name of ° the Lord.

U Then ° prayed they him to ° tarry [1] certain days.

F4 i **11** ° And the ° apostles and brethren that were ° in Judæa heard that the ° Gentiles ° had also received the ° word of ° God.
2 And when Peter was come up ° to Jerusalem, ° they that were ° of the circumcision ° contended ° with him,
3 Saying, "Thou wentest in ° to ° men uncircumcised, and didst ° eat with them."

k 4 But Peter ° rehearsed *the matter* from the beginning, and ° expounded *it* ° by order ° unto them, saying,

38 How, &c. The Gr. reads, "Jesus of Nazareth, how God anointed (see 4. 27) Him".
Jesus. Ap. 98. X.
of = from. Gr. *apo*. Ap. 104. iv.
the Holy Ghost = holy spirit. No art. Ap. 101. II. 14.
power. Gr. *dunamis*. Ap. 172. 1.
doing good. Gr. *euergeteō* = acting as a benefactor. Only here. Cp. Luke 22. 25, and see 4. 9.
healing. Gr. *iaomai*. See note on Luke 6. 17.
oppressed = overpowered. Gr. *katadunasteuō*. Here, James 2. 6. Cp. Luke 13. 16. 2 Cor. 12. 7. Rev. 2. 10.
with. Gr. *meta*. Ap. 104. xi. 1.
39 witnesses. Gr. *martur*. See note on 1. 8.
land = country. Gr. *chōra*.
slew. Gr. *anaireō*. See note on 2. 23.
and hanged = having hanged Him.
on. Gr. *epi*. Ap. 104. ix. 1.
tree. See note on 5. 30.
40 Him = This One.
raised up. Gr. *egeirō*. Ap. 178. I. 4.
shewed Him openly. Lit. gave Him to become manifest, i. e. to be openly seen. Gr. *emphanēs*. Here, Rom. 10. 20. Cp. Ap. 106. I. iv.
41 Not. Gr. *ou*. Ap. 105. I.
chosen before. Gr. *procheirotoneō*. Only here. Cp. 14. 23.
did eat . . . with. Gr. *sunesthiō*. Here, 11. 3. Luke 15. 2. 1 Cor. 5. 11. Gal. 2. 12.
drink with. Gr. *sumpinō*. Only here.
from the dead. Gr. *ek nekrōn*. Ap. 139. 3.
42 commanded = charged.
testify = fully testify. Gr. *diamarturomai*. See note on 2. 40.
ordained. Gr. *horizō*. See note on 2. 23.
Judge. Gr. *kritēs*. Cp. Ap. 122. 1, and 177. 6, 7, 8.
quick = living.
dead = dead persons. Gr. *nekros*. Ap. 139. 2.
43 give . . . witness = testify. Gr. *martureō*, as in *v.* 22.
through. Gr. *dia*. Ap. 104. v. 1.
name. See note on 2. 38.
believeth in. Ap. 150. I. 1. v. (1).
remission = forgiveness. Gr. *aphesis*. See note on 2. 38; 5. 31.
sins. Gr. *hamartia*. Ap. 128. I. ii. 1.
44 on. Gr. *epi*. Ap. 104. ix. 3.
the word, i. e. the gospel message. Fig. *Idioma*. Ap. 6.
45 they, &c., i. e. the Jews. Cp. 11. 2. Rom. 4. 12; 15. 8. Gal. 2. 12. Col. 4. 11. Tit. 1. 10. These were Jewish Christians, called "brethren", *v.* 23, 11. 12.
believed = were faithful. Gr. *pistos*. Ap. 150. III.
were astonished. Gr. *existēmi*. See note on 2. 7.
Gentiles. Gr. *ethnos*. Same as "nation", *vv.* 22, 35.
gift. Gr. *dōrea*. See note on John 4. 10.
46 speak = speaking. Gr. *laleō*, as in *v.* 7.
magnify = magnifying. Gr. *megalunō*, as in 5. 13.
answered. Ap. 122. 3.

47 Can. Gr. *mēti*. Cp. *mē*. Ap. 105. II. any man = any one. Gr. *tis*. Ap. 123. 3. forbid. Same as "hinder" in 8. 36. baptized. Ap. 115. I. i. as well as we = even as we also. **48** baptized in. Ap. 115. I. iii. c. the Lord. Ap. 98. VI. i. β. 2 A. The texts read "Jesus Christ". prayed. Gr. *erōtaō*. Ap. 134. I. 3. tarry. Gr. *epimenō*. See John 8. 7 (continue).

11. 1-17 (F4, p. 1595). DISSENSION IN THE ASSEMBLY (*Introversion.*)

F4 | i | 1-3. Peter blamed.
| k | 4-10. Peter's Vision.
| l | 11, 12. Command.
| *k* | 13, 14. Cornelius' Vision.
| *i* | 15-17. Peter vindicated.

11. 1 And = Now. apostles. Ap. 189. in = throughout. Gr. *kata*. Ap. 104. x. 2. Gentiles. Gr. *ethnos*, as in 10. 45. had. Omit. word. Gr. *logos*. Ap. 121. 10. God. Ap. 98. I. i. 1. **2** to. Gr. *eis*. Ap. 104. vi. they, &c. See note on 10. 45. of. Gr. *ek*. Ap. 104. vii. contended = were contending. Gr. *diakrinō*. Ap. 122. 4. with = against. Gr. *pros*. Ap. 104. xv. 3. **3** to. Gr. *pros*. Ap. 104. xv. 3. men. Gr. *anēr*. Ap. 123. 2. eat with. Gr. *sunesthiō*, as in 10. 41. **4** rehearsed . . from the beginning, and = having begun. expounded = set forth. Gr. *ektithēmi*. See note on 7. 21. by order = in order. Gr. *kathexēs*. See note on 3. 24. unto = to.

5 "I was °in the city of Joppa °praying: and
°in a °trance I °saw a °vision, A °certain
vessel descend, as it had been a great °sheet,
°let down °from °heaven by four corners; and
it came °even to me:
6 °Upon the which °when I had fastened
mine eyes, I °considered, and [5]saw °fourfooted
beasts of the °earth, and °wild beasts, and
°creeping things, and fowls of the °air.
7 [1]And I heard a voice saying [4]unto me,
°'Arise, Peter; °slay and eat.'
8 But I said, °'Not so, °Lord: for °nothing
common or unclean hath at any time entered
°into my mouth.'
9 But °the voice °answered °me °again [5]from
[5]heaven, 'What [1]God hath cleansed, *that* °call
°not thou common.'
10 [1]And this °was done °three times: and all
were °drawn up again [8]into [5]heaven.

l 11 And, °behold, °immediately there °were
three [3]men °already come °unto the house
°where I was, °sent °from °Cæsarea °unto me.
12 [1]And °the spirit bade me go with them,
°nothing °doubting. Moreover these six brethren °accompanied me, and we entered [8]into
the [3]man's house:

k 13 And he °shewed us how he had [5]seen °an
angel [5]in his house, °which stood and said
°unto him, [11]'Send °men [2]to Joppa, and °call
for Simon, °whose surname is Peter;
14 Who shall °tell thee °words, °whereby
thou and all thy house shall be saved.'

i 15 [1]And °as I began to °speak, °the Holy
Ghost fell °on them, °as °on us °at the beginning.
16 Then remembered I the [14]word of [8]the
Lord, how that He said, 'John indeed °baptized
with water; but ye shall be °baptized with °the
Holy Ghost.'
17 °Forasmuch then as [1]God gave them the
like °gift as *He did* [4]unto °us, °who °believed
on °the Lord °Jesus Christ; what was I, that
I °could °withstand [1]God?"

G[4] 18 °When they heard these things, they
(p. 1595) °held their peace, and glorified [1]God, saying,
"Then hath [1]God °also to the [1]Gentiles
°granted °repentance °unto °life."

H[4] Z[1] m[1] 19 °Now they which were °scattered abroad
°upon the °persecution that °arose °about

5 in. Gr. *en.* Ap. 104. viii.
praying. Gr. *proseuchomai.* Ap. 134. I. 2.
trance. Gr. *ekstasis.* See 10. 10.
saw. Gr. *eidon.* Ap. 133. I. 1.
vision = sight. Gr. *horama.* See note on 7. 31.
certain. Gr. *tis.* Ap. 123. 3.
sheet. Gr. *othonē*, as in 10. 11.
let down = sent down, as in 10. 11.
from = out of. Gr. *ek.* Ap. 104. vii.
heaven = the heaven. See Matt. 6. 9, 10.
even to = as far as to. Gr. *achris.*
6 Upon = Unto. Gr. *eis.* Ap. 104. vi.
when I had . . . eyes = having gazed. Gr. *atenizō.* Ap. 133. III. 6. See note on 1. 10.
considered. Gr. *katanoeō.* Ap. 133. II. 4.
fourfooted beasts. Gr. *tetrapous*, as in 10. 12.
earth. Gr. *gē.* Ap. 129. 4.
wild beasts. Gr. *thērion.* Omitted in 10. 12.
creeping things. Gr. *herpeton.* See 10. 12.
air = heaven.
7 arise. Gr. *anistēmi.* Ap. 178. I. 1.
slay. Gr. *thuō*, as in 10. 13.
8 Not so = By no means. Gr. *mēdamōs.*
Lord. Ap. 98. VI. i. β. 2 B.
nothing, &c., never at any time (Gr. *oudepote*) came anything common, &c.
into. Gr. *eis.* Ap. 104. vi.
9 the = a.
answered. Gr. *apokrinomai.* Ap. 122. 3.
me. Omit.
again. Lit. from (Gr. *ek.* Ap. 104. vii) a second (time).
call = make.
not. Gr. *mē.* Ap. 105. II.
10 was done = came to pass.
three times. Lit. upon (Gr. *epi.* Ap. 104. ix) thrice.
drawn up. Gr. *anaspaō.* Only here and Luke 14. 5. Cp. 20. 30.
11 behold. Gr. *idou.* Ap. 133. I. 2.
immediately. Gr. *exautēs*, as in 10. 33.
were . . . come = stood before.
already. Omit.
unto = at. Gr. *epi.* Ap. 104. ix. 3.
where = in (Gr. *en.* Ap. 104. viii) which.
sent. Gr. *apostellō.* Ap. 174. 1.
from. Gr. *apo.* Ap. 104. iv.
Cæsarea. See note on 8. 40.
unto. Gr. *pros.* Ap. 104. xv. 3.
12 the spirit. The angel of 10. 3.
nothing. Gr. *mēdeis.*
doubting. Gr. *diakrinō.* Ap. 122. 4.
accompanied = came with (Gr. *sun.* Ap. 104. xvi).
13 shewed = announced. Gr. *apangellō.* Same as "report", 4. 23, and "tell", 5. 22, 25.
an = the.
which stood and said = standing and saying.
unto him. Omit.
men. All the texts omit.
call for = send for. Gr. *metapempō.* Ap. 174. 7.
whose surname is = who is surnamed.

14 tell thee = speak (Gr. *laleō.* Ap. 121. 7) to (Gr. *pros.* Ap. 104. xv. 3) thee. **words.** Gr. *rhēma.* See note on Mark 9. 32. **whereby** = by (Gr. *en.* Ap. 104. viii) which. **15 as I began.** Lit. in (Gr. *en*) my beginning. **speak.** Gr. *laleō*, as in *v.* 14 (tell). **the Holy Ghost.** Ap. 101. II. 4. **on** = upon. Gr. *epi.* Ap. 104. ix. 3. **as, &c.** = even as on us also. **at the beginning** = in (Gr. *en*) the beginning. Cp. 2. 4 and John 1. 1. **16 baptized.** Ap. 115. I. ii. **baptized.** Ap. 115. I. iii. i. b. **the Holy Ghost.** No art. Ap. 101. II. 14. **17 Forasmuch then** = If (Ap. 118. 2 a) therefore. **gift.** Gr. *dōrea.* Cp. 2. 38 and John 4. 10. **us** = us also. **who** = when we. **believed.** Ap. 150. I. 1. v. (iii) 2. **the Lord.** Ap. 98. VI. i. β. 2. A. **Jesus Christ.** Ap. 98. XI. **could** = was able to. **withstand** = hinder. **18 When they heard** = Now, having heard. **held their peace** = ceased, as in 21. 14. See Luke 14. 4; 23. 56. 1 Thess. 4. 11. **also to the Gentiles** = to the Gentiles also. This and *v.* 3 shows that Cornelius was not a proselyte. **granted** = given. **repentance.** Gr. *metanoia.* Ap. 111. II. 1. **unto.** Gr. *eis.* Ap. 104. vi. **life.** Gr. *zōē.* Ap. 170. 1.

11. 19-30 [For Structure see next page]

19 Now they = They indeed therefore. **scattered abroad.** Gr. *diaspeirō.* See note on 8. 1. **upon** = from. Gr. *apo.* Ap. 104. iv. **persecution.** Gr. *thlipsis.* See note on 7. 10. **arose** = came to pass. **about** = over, or upon. Gr. *epi.* Ap. 104. ix. 2.

Stephen travelled as far as Phenice, and Cyprus, and °Antioch, °preaching the [1]word to °none °but [4]unto the °Jews only.
20 [1]And °some [2]of them were [3]men °of Cyprus and Cyrene, which when they were come [2]to Antioch, [15]spake [11]unto the °Grecians, °preaching [17]the Lord °Jesus.

n1 21 And the hand of [8]the Lord was °with them: and a great number °believed, and turned [11]unto [17]the Lord.

m2 22 Then °tidings °of these things °came [18]unto the ears of the °church which was [5]in Jerusalem: and they °sent forth °Barnabas, °that he should go °as far as Antioch.
23 Who, °when he came, and had [5]seen the °grace of [1]God, was glad, and °exhorted them all, that with °purpose of heart they would °cleave [4]unto [17]the Lord.
24 For he was a good [3]man, and full of [16]the Holy Ghost and of °faith:

n2 and much °people was added [4]unto [17]the Lord.

m3 25 Then departed Barnabas [2]to Tarsus, °for to seek Saul:
26 And °when he had found him, he brought him [18]unto Antioch. [1]And °it came to pass, that a whole year they assembled themselves °with the [22]church, and taught much [24]people. °And the disciples were °called °Christians first [5]in Antioch.

Z2 o 27 And [5]in these days °came prophets [11]from Jerusalem [18]unto Antioch.
28 [1]And there °stood up one [2]of them °named °Agabus, and signified °by °the Spirit that there °should be great °dearth °throughout all the °world:

p which came to pass °in the days of °Claudius Cæsar.

o 29 °Then the disciples, every man according to his ability, °determined to °send °relief [4]unto the brethren which °dwelt [5]in Judæa:

p 30 Which °also they did, °and [11]sent it [8]to the °elders [28]by the hands of Barnabas and Saul.

11. 19-30 (H4, p. 1595). MINISTRY AT PHENICE, &c. (*Division.*)

H4 | Z1 | 19-26. In Spiritual Things.
| Z2 | 27-30. In Carnal Things.

11. 19-26 (Z1, above). IN SPIRITUAL THINGS. (*Alternation.*)

Z1 | m1 | 19, 20. Preaching by Cypriotes, &c.
n1 | 21. Many believers.
m2 | 22-24-. Preaching by Barnabas.
n2 | -24. Much people added.
m3 | 25, 26. Preaching by Barnabas and Saul.

Antioch. The capital of Syria, about sixteen miles from the sea. Seleucia was its port.
preaching = speaking. Gr. *laleō*, as in *vv.* 14, 15.
none = no one. Gr. *mēdeis.*
but = except. Gr. *ei mē.*
Jews = Seed of Abraham.
20 some. Gr. *tis.* Ap. 123. 3.
of Cyprus, &c. Cypriotes and Cyrenians.
Grecians. See note on 6. 1. Most texts read *Hellēnes*, Greeks. There was nothing strange in speaking to the Greek-speaking Jews.
preaching. Gr. *euangelizō.* Ap. 121. 4.
Jesus. Ap. 98. X.
21 with. Gr. *meta.* Ap. 104. xi. 1.
believed, and = having believed. Ap. 150. I. 1. i.
22 tidings = the report, or word. Gr. *logos.* Ap. 121. 10.
of = concerning. Gr. *peri.* Ap. 104. xiii. 1.
came = was heard. **church.** Ap. 186.
sent forth. Gr. *exapostellō.* Ap. 174. 2.
Barnabas. He was himself of Cyprus. Cp. 4. 36, and see *v.* 20.
that he should go. The texts omit.
as far as. Gr. *heōs.*
23 when he came and had = having come, and.
grace. Ap. 184.
exhorted = was exhorting. Gr. *parakaleō.* Ap. 134. 1. 6. Cp. 4. 36.
purpose. Gr. *prothesis*, that which is put before one. The Eng. word is from the Lat. *propositum*, which exactly corresponds to the Greek. The word is used of the shewbread, i. e. the bread of presentation, in Matt. 12. 4. Mark 2. 26. Luke 6. 4. Heb. 9. 2. In its seven other occ. it is rendered as here.
cleave unto = abide with. Gr. *prosmenō.* Here, 18. 18. Matt. 15. 32. Mark 8. 2. 1 Tim. 1. 3; 5. 5.
24 faith. Ap. 150. II. 1.
people. Gr. *ochlos.* Lit. crowd.
25 for to seek. Lit. to seek up and down. Gr. *anazēteō.* Here, Luke 2. 44.
26 when he had = having.
it came to pass. The three clauses which follow are all dependent on "it came to pass". **with.** Gr. *en.* **And** = And that. **called.** Gr. *chrēmatizō.* This word occ. nine times. See note on Luke 2. 26. Generally of a Divine communication. The noun *chrēmatismos* occ. only in Rom. 11. 4. Though the name may have been given at first by Gentiles in mockery, the usage of the word by the Holy Spirit indicates that its real origin was Divine. **Christians.** Here, 26. 28. 1 Pet. 4. 16. Cp. 15. 17. Jews could not have given the name, as *Christos* was a sacred word.

11. 27-30 (Z2, above). IN CARNAL THINGS. (*Alternation.*)

Z2 | o | 27, 28-. Prophecy of Dearth.
p | -28. Fulfilment.
o | 29. Purpose of Relief.
p | 30. Fulfilment.

27 came = came down. **prophets.** Ap. 189. **28 stood up.** Gr. *anistēmi.* Ap. 178. I. 1. **named** = by name. **Agabus.** Cp. 21. 10. **by** = through. Gr. *dia.* Ap. 104. v. 1. **the Spirit.** The article shows that this was the Holy Spirit (Ap. 101. II. 3), speaking through Agabus. Cp. 21. 11. **should be** = was about to be. **dearth.** Gr. *limos.* Occ. twelve times. Cp. 7. 11. Elsewhere transl. "hunger" or "famine". **throughout** = over. Gr. *epi.* Ap. 104. ix. 3. **world.** Gr. *oikoumenē.* Ap. 129. 3. **in the days of.** Gr. *epi.* Ap. 104. ix. 1. A Gr. idiom. **Claudius Cæsar.** The fourth Roman Emperor (A. D. 41-54). Roman historians mention several famines during his reign. See also Josephus, *Ant.* XX. iii. 6. **29 Then, &c.** Lit. But as any one (Gr. *tis*) of the disciples prospered (Gr. *euporeomai.* Only here), they determined, each one of them. **determined.** Gr. *horizō.* See note on 2. 23. **send.** Gr. *pempō.* Ap. 174. 4. **relief** = for (Gr. *eis.* Ap. 104. vi) ministration. Gr. *diakonia.* Ap. 190. II. 1. **dwelt.** See note on 2. 5. **30 also they did** = they did also. **and sent** = sending. **elders.** Gr. *presbuteros.* This is the first time we meet with elders in the Christian churches. Ap. 189. Here elders included the Apostles. Cp. 8. 1. 1 Pet. 5. 1.

F A **12** Now ° about that ° time ° Herod the king
° stretched forth *his* hands to ° vex ° certain ° of ° the church.
2 And he ° killed ° James the brother of ° John
with the ° sword.
B C q 3 And ° because he saw it ° pleased the Jews,
he ° proceeded further to ° take Peter also.
(Then were the days of ° unleavened bread.)
r 4 And when he had ° apprehended him, he
put *him* ° in ° prison, and delivered *him* to four
° quaternions of soldiers to keep him;
D s ° intending ° after ° Easter to ° bring him forth
to the ° people.
t 5 Peter ° therefore was kept ° in [4] prison:
u but ° prayer was made ° without ceasing ° of the
[1] church ° unto ° God ° for him.
v 6 And when Herod ° would have brought him
forth, ° the same night Peter was ° sleeping between two soldiers, bound with two chains:
and the ° keepers ° before the door ° kept the
[4] prison.
7 And, ° behold, the angel of ° the LORD ° came
upon *him*, and a ° light shined [5] in the ° prison:
and he smote ° Peter on the side, and ° raised
him up, saying, ° "Arise up ° quickly." And
his chains fell ° off from *his* hands.
8 And the angel said [5] unto him, ° "Gird thyself, and bind on thy sandals." And so he did.
And he saith ° unto him, "Cast thy ° garment
about thee, and follow me."
9 And he went out, and followed ° him; and
° wist ° not that it was ° true which was done
° by the angel; but ° thought he ° saw a ° vision.
10 ° When they were past the first and the
second ° ward, they came ° unto the iron gate
that leadeth ° unto the city; which ° opened to
them ° of his own accord: and they went out,
and passed on through one ° street,
w and ° forthwith the angel departed ° from him.
D s 11 And ° when Peter was come ° to himself, he
said, "Now I ° know ° of a surety, that [7] the

12. 1-23 (**F**, p. 1575). JERUSALEM. PETER'S IMPRISONMENT. (*Introversion.*)

F | A | 1, 2. Herod. Persecution.
  B | 3-19-. Peter. Imprisonment and Release.
| *A* | -19-23. Herod. Judgment and Death.

12. This chapter is a parenthesis, describing events in A.D. 44.

1 about. Gr. *kata.* Ap. 104. x. 2.
time = season.
Herod. Herod Agrippa I. Ap. 109.
stretched forth his hands = put to his hands. Cp. Luke 9. 62, same phrase.
vex = maltreat. Gr. *kakoō.* See note on 7. 6.
certain. Gr. *tis.* Ap. 123. 3.
of = of those from (Gr. *apo.* Ap. 104. iv).
the church. Ap. 186.
2 killed. Gr. *anaireō.* See note on 2. 23.
James. Ap. 141. 3.
John. Ap. 141. 4. The last historical reference to John.
sword. Death by the sword was regarded by the Rabbis as particularly disgraceful.

12. 3-19- (B, above). PETER. IMPRISONMENT. (*Introversion and Alternation.*)

B | C | q | 3. Herod's base policy.
  r | 4-. Peter guarded.
 D | s | -4. Intention.
  t | 5-. Prison.
  u | -5. Prayer.
  v | 6-10-. Deliverance effected.
  w | -10. Angel's Departure.
 D | *s* | 11. Frustration.
  t | 12-. House.
  u | -12. Prayer.
  v | 13-17-. Deliverance recounted.
  w | -17. Peter's Departure.
 C | *r* | 18. Peter missed.
  q | 19-. Herod's Vengeance.

3 because he saw = seeing. Gr. *eidon.* Ap. 133. I. 1.
pleased = is pleasing to. See note on 6. 2, and Mark 15. 15 (note).
proceeded further = added. A Hebraism. Gr. *prostithēmi.* Cp. Luke 20. 11.
take. See note on 1. 16.
unleavened bread. Lit. the unleavened (things). Leaven in every form was to be put away. Ex. 12. 15, 19. **4 apprehended** = arrested. Gr. *piazō.* See note on John 11. 57. **in** = into. Gr. *eis.* Ap. 104. vi. **prison** = ward. Gr. *phulakē.* **quaternions.** Gr. *tetradion*, a body of four. Only here. There were four soldiers to guard Peter for each of the four watches. The prisoner was chained to two and the other two kept watch. See *v.* 6. **intending.** Gr. *boulomai.* Ap. 102. 3. **after.** Gr. *meta.* Ap. 104. xi. 2. **Easter.** Gr. *to pascha*, the Passover. Easter is a heathen term, derived from the Saxon goddess *Eastre*, the same as Astarte, the Syrian Venus, called Ashtoreth in the O.T. **bring . . . forth** = lead up, i. e. to the judgment seat. Cp. Luke 22. 66. **people.** Gr. *laos.* **5 therefore** = then indeed. **in.** Gr. *en.* Ap. 104. viii. **prayer.** Gr. *proseuchē.* Ap. 134. II. 2. **without ceasing** = intense, Gr. *ektenēs.* Occ. elsewhere only in 1 Pet. 4. 8. The comparative only in Luke 22. 44, and the adverb in 1 Pet. 1. 22. The texts here read the adverb, *ektenōs.* **of** = by. Gr. *hupo.* Ap. 104. xviii. 1. **unto.** Gr. *pros.* Ap. 104. xv. 3. **God.** Ap. 98. I. i. 1. **for** = in behalf of. Gr. *huper.* Ap. 104. xvii. 1, but texts read *peri*, concerning. **6 would have brought** = was about to bring. **the same** = that. **sleeping.** Gr. *koimaomai.* Ap. 171. 2. **keepers** = guards. See 5. 23. **before.** Gr. *pro.* Ap. 104. xiv. **kept** = were keeping. **7 behold.** Gr. *idou.* Ap. 133. I. 2. **the Lord.** Ap. 98. VI. i. β. 2. B. **came upon** = stood over. **light.** Gr. *phōs.* Ap. 130. 1. **prison.** Gr. *oikēma*, dwelling. Only here. The R.V. reads "cell". That was Peter's dwelling-place. The angel of the Lord there. **Peter on the side** = Peter's side. **raised . . . up.** Gr. *egeirō.* Ap. 178. I. 4. **Arise up.** Gr. *anistēmi.* Ap. 178. I. 1. **quickly** = in (Gr. *en*) or with speed. **off from.** Gr. *ek.* Ap. 104. vii. **8 Gird thyself.** Gr. *perizōnnumi.* Occ. elsewhere, Luke 12. 35, 37; 17. 8. Eph. 6. 14. Rev. 1. 13; 15. 6. Texts read *zōnnumi*, as in John 21. 18. **unto** = to. **garment.** Gr. *himation*, the outer garment. **9 him.** The texts omit. **wist** = knew. Gr. *oida.* Ap. 132. I. i. **not.** Gr. *ou.* Ap. 105. I. **true.** Gr. *alēthēs.* Ap. 175. 1. **by** = through. Gr. *dia.* Ap. 104. v. 1. **thought** = was thinking. **saw.** Gr. *blepō.* Ap. 133. I. 5. **vision.** Gr. *horama*, as in 7. 31. **10 When, &c.** Now, having passed through. **ward** = prison. Gr. *phulakē*, as in *vv.* 4, 5, 6, 17. **unto** = upon. Gr. *epi.* Ap. 104. ix. 3. **unto.** Gr. *eis.* Ap. 104. vi. **opened** = was opened. **of his own accord** = automatically. Gr. *automatos.* Elsewhere only in Mark 4. 28. **street.** Gr. *rhumē.* See note on 9. 11. **forthwith** = immediately. Gr. *eutheōs.* **from.** Gr. *apo.* Ap. 104. iv. **11 when, &c.** Peter, having come to be. **to himself** = in (Gr. *en*) himself, i. e. in his right senses. Cp. "out of his senses", or "beside himself". **know.** Gr. *oida*, as in *v.* 9. **of a surety** = truly. Gr. *alēthōs.* Cp. Ap. 175. 1.

Lord °hath sent His angel, and °hath delivered
me °out of the hand of [1]Herod, and *from* all
the °expectation of the [4]people of the Jews."
t 12 And °when he had considered *the thing*,
he came °to the house of °Mary the mother of
°John, whose surname was Mark;
u where many were °gathered together °praying.
v 13 And °as Peter knocked at the door of the
°gate, a °damsel came to °hearken, °named
°Rhoda.
14 And °when she knew Peter's voice, she
opened [9]not the [13]gate °for gladness, but ran
in, and °told how Peter stood [6]before the
[13]gate.
15 And they said [5]unto her, °"Thou art
mad." But she °constantly affirmed that it
was even so. Then said they, "It is his
°angel."
16 But Peter °continued knocking: and when
they had opened *the door*, and [3]saw him, they
°were astonished.
17 But he, °beckoning -[8]unto them with the
hand to °hold their peace, °declared -[8]unto them
how °the Lord °had brought him [11]out of the
[4]prison. And he said, "Go °shew these things
-[8]unto °James, and to the brethren." And he
w departed, and went °into °another place.
Cr 18 Now °as soon as it was day, there was °no
small °stir °among the soldiers, °what was
become of Peter.
q 19 And when [1]Herod had °sought for him,
and found him °not, he °examined the [6]keepers, and commanded that *they* should be °put
to death.
A And he went down [10]from Judæa °to °Cæsarea,
and *there* °abode.
20 And °Herod °was highly displeased with
°them of Tyre and Sidon: but they °came
°with one accord °to him, and having °made
Blastus °the king's chamberlain °their friend,
°desired peace; °because their country was
°nourished °by the °king's *country*.
21 And upon a °set day [1]Herod, arrayed in
°royal °apparel, sat °upon °his throne, and
°made an oration [5]unto them.
22 And the °people °gave a shout, *saying*,
"*It is* the voice of a °god, and [9]not of a °man."
23 And °immediately the [7]angel of [7]the LORD
smote him, °because he gave [9]not [5]God the
glory: and he was °eaten of worms, and °gave
up the ghost.

hath sent = sent. Gr. *exapostellō*. Ap. 174. 2.
hath delivered = delivered. See note on 7. 10.
out of. Gr. *ek*. Ap. 104. vii.
expectation = eager looking. Gr. *prosdokia*. Elsewhere only in Luke 21. 26. Cp. Ap. 133. III. 3.
12 when, &c. = having considered or realized. Gr. *suneidon*. See note on 5. 2.
to. Gr. *epi*. Ap. 104. ix. 3.
Mary. Ap. 100. 5.
John. See 13. 5, 13; 15. 37, 39. Col. 4. 10. 2 Tim. 4. 11.
gathered together. Gr. *sunathroizō*. Elsewhere only in 19. 25. Luke 24. 33.
praying = and praying. Gr. *proseuchomai*. Ap. 134. I. 2.
13 as Peter knocked = Peter, having knocked.
gate. Gr. *pulōn*. Transl. "porch" in Matt. 26. 71.
damsel. Gr. *paidiskē*. Cp. Ap. 108. iv, v, vi.
hearken = answer. Gr. *hupakouō*. Elsewhere transl. "obey", or "be obedient".
named = by name.
Rhoda. Gr. *Rhodē*, rose.
14 when she knew = having recognized. Gr. *epiginōskō*. Ap. 132. I. iii.
for = from. Gr. *apo*. Ap. 104. iv.
told = reported. Gr. *apangellō*. Cp. Ap. 121. 6.
15 Thou art mad. Gr. *mainomai*. Here, 26. 24, 25. John 10. 20. 1 Cor. 14. 23.
constantly affirmed = kept strongly asserting. Gr. *diischurizomai*. Compd. of *dia* and *ischurizomai*. Cp. Ap. 172. 3. Elsewhere only in Luke 22. 59.
angel, i. e. guardian angel, according to Jewish belief. Cp. Matt. 18. 10. Heb. 1. 14.
16 continued. Gr. *epimenō*. See note on 10. 48.
were astonished = were astounded. Gr. *existēmi*. See 2. 7; 8. 9; 9. 21; 10. 45.
17 beckoning. Lit. shaking down. Gr. *kataseiō*. Only in Acts, here, 13. 16; 19. 33; 21. 40. The action suggested he was in haste and must not be interrupted.
hold their peace = be silent.
declared. Gr. *diēgeomai*. See 8. 33.
the Lord. Ap. 98. VI. i. *β*. 2. A.
had. Omit.
shew. Same as "told" in *v.* 14.
James. The Lord's brother. See Gal. 1. 19, and Ap. 182.
into. Gr. *eis*. Ap. 104. vi.
another. Gr. *heteros*. Ap. 124. 2.
18 as soon as, &c. = day having come.
no. Gr. *ou*. Ap. 105. I.
stir = disturbance. Gr. *tarachos*. Here and 19. 23.
among. Gr. *en*. Ap. 104. viii. 2.
what was, &c. Lit. what then Peter had come to be.
19 sought for him = sought him up and down.
not. Gr. *mē*. Ap. 105. II.
examined. Gr. *anakrinō*. Ap. 122. 2.
put to death = led away, i. e. to execution. Gr. *apagō*. Same word as in Matt. 27. 31, &c.
to. Gr. *eis*, as in *v.* 10.
Cæsarea. See 8. 40.
abode. Gr. *diatribō*, to rub away, or spend (time). Occ. John 3. 22; 11. 54, and eight times in Acts.

20 Herod. Texts read "He". **was highly displeased.** Gr. *thumomacheō*, to fight angrily. Only here. **them of Tyre, &c.** = the Tyrians, &c. **came** = were present, or presented themselves. **with one accord.** Gr. *homothumadon*. See note on 1. 14. **to.** Gr. *pros*. Ap. 104. xv. 3. **made . . . their friend** = persuaded, or won over. Gr. *peithō*. Ap. 150. I. 2. **the king's chamberlain** = one who was over (Gr. *epi*. Ap. 104. ix. 1) the bedchamber (Gr. *koitōn*. Only here) of the king. **desired** = were asking for. Gr. *aiteō*. Ap. 134. I. 4. **because.** Gr. *dia*. Ap. 104. v. 2. **nourished.** Cp. 1 Kings 5. 9, 11. Ezek. 27. 17. **by.** Gr. *apo*. Ap. 104. iv. **king's** = royal. Gr. *basilikos*. See note on John 4. 46. **21 set** = appointed. **royal.** Same as "king's", *v.* 20. **apparel.** Josephus (*Ant.* XIX. viii. 2) says it was of silver tissue, and glittered resplendently in the sun. **upon.** Gr. *epi*. Ap. 104. ix. 1. **his throne** = the throne. Gr. *bēma*. Always transl. "judgment seat" save here and 7. 5. Cp. John 19. 13. **made an oration,** i. e. a political oration. Gr. *dēmēgoreō*. Only here. **22 people.** Gr. *dēmos*. The usual word for the populace. Only here, 17. 5; 19. 30, 33. **gave a shout.** Gr. *epiphōneō*. Only here, 22. 24, and Luke 23. 21. **god.** Ap. 98. I. i. 5. **man.** Gr. *anthrōpos*. Ap. 123. 1. **23 immediately.** Gr. *parachrēma*. See note on 3. 7. **because** = the reason for (Gr. *anti*. Ap. 104. ii) which. **eaten of worms.** Gr. *skōlēkobrōtos*. Only here. *skōlēx*, a worm, only in Mark 9. 44-48. **gave up the ghost** = expired. Gr. *ekpsuchō*. Only here and 5. 5, 10.

BC 24 But the °word of [5]God °grew and °multiplied.

25 And Barnabas and Saul returned °from Jerusalem, when they had fulfilled *their* °ministry, and °took with them [12]John whose surname was Mark.

13 Now there were °in the °church that was °at °Antioch °certain °prophets and °teachers; as Barnabas, and Simeon that was called Niger, and Lucius of Cyrene, and Manaen, °which had been brought up with °Herod the °tetrarch, and Saul.

2 As they °ministered to °the Lord, and fasted, °the Holy Ghost said, °"Separate Me Barnabas and Saul °for the work °whereunto I have called them."

3 And °when they had fasted and °prayed, and laid *their* hands on them, they °sent *them* away.

DE 4 So they, being °sent forth °by [2]the Holy Ghost, °departed °unto °Seleucia;

F and from thence they °sailed °to °Cyprus.

5 And when they were [1]at °Salamis, they °preached the °word of °God °in the °synagogues of the Jews: and they had °also John to *their* °minister.

6 And when they had gone through the isle °unto °Paphos, they found a °certain °sorcerer, a °false prophet, a Jew, whose name *was* °Bar-jesus:

7 Which was °with the °deputy of the country, Sergius Paulus, a °prudent °man; °who called for Barnabas and Saul, and °desired to hear the [5]word of [5]God.

8 But °Elymas the sorcerer (for so is his name by interpretation) °withstood them, seeking to °turn away the [7]deputy °from the °faith.

9 Then Saul, (who °also *is called* °Paul,) filled with °the Holy Ghost, °set his eyes °on him,

10 And said, "O full of °all °subtilty and °all

24 word. Gr. *logos.* Ap. 121. 10.
grew = increased.
multiplied. Gr. *plēthunō.* See Matt. 24. 12.
25 from. Gr. *ek.* Ap. 104. vii.
ministry, i. e. of administering the contributions of 11. 30. Gr. *diakonia.* Ap. 190. II. 1.
took with them. Gr. *sumparalambanō.* Only here, 15. 37, 38, and Gal. 2. 1.

13. 1 in. Gr. *kata.* Ap. 104. x. 2.
church. Ap. 186. **at** = in. Gr. *en.* Ap. 104. viii.
Antioch. See note on 11. 19.
certain. Texts omit.
prophets. Ap. 189.
teachers. Gr. *didaskalos.* Occ. forty-eight times in Gospels, transl. "Master" except in Luke 2. 46 (doctor) and John 3. 2 (teacher). Only here in Acts. Always "teacher" in the Epistles, except Jas. 3. 1 (master).
which had been brought up with = foster-brother of. Gr. *suntrophos.* Only here.
Herod. Herod Antipas. Ap. 109.
tetrarch. See Matt. 14. 1. Luke 3. 19; 9. 7.
2 ministered. Gr. *leitourgeō.* Ap. 190. III. 6. Here, Rom. 15. 27. Heb. 10. 11. In the Sept. used of the Levitical service, as in Heb. 10. 11.
the Lord. Ap. 98. VI. i. *β.* 2. A.
the Holy Ghost. Ap. 101. II. 3.
Separate. Cp. Rom. 1. 1. Gal. 1. 15.
for. Gr. *eis.* Ap. 104. vi.
whereunto = to which.
3 when they had = having.
prayed. Gr. *proseuchomai.* Ap. 134. I. 2.
sent . . . away. Gr. *apoluō.* Ap. 174. 11.

13. 4—14. 28 (*D*, p. 1575). THE MINISTRY OF PAUL (WITH OTHERS) TO THE DISPERSION. APART FROM JERUSALEM AND THE TWELVE.

(*Introversion.*)

D E | 13. 4-. Departure from Antioch.
  F | 13. -4-12. Cyprus.
    G | 13. 13. Perga.
      H | 13. 14-50. Antioch (Pisidia).
        I | 13. 51—14. 6-. Iconium.
          J | 14. -6-20-. Lystra.
            K | 14. -20. Derbe.
          J | 14. 21-. Lystra.
        I | 14. -21-. Iconium.
      H | 14. -21-24. Antioch (Pisidia).
    G | 14. 25-. Perga.
  F | 14. -25. Attalia.
E | 14. 26-28. Return to Antioch.

4 sent forth. Gr. *ekpempō.* Ap. 174. 6. **by.** Gr. *hupo.* Ap. 104. xviii. 1. **departed** = went down. **unto.** Gr. *eis.* Ap. 104. vi. **Seleucia.** See on 11. 19. **sailed.** Gr. *apopleō.* Here, 14. 26; 20. 15; 27. 1. **to.** Gr. *eis,* as above. **Cyprus.** Cp. 4. 36. **5 Salamis.** The first port they would reach, at east end of the island. **preached.** Gr. *katangellō.* Ap. 121. 5. **word.** Gr. *logos.* Ap. 121. 10. **God.** Ap. 98. I. i. 1. **in.** Gr. *en.* Ap. 104. viii. **synagogues.** Ap. 120. I. Cp. *v.* 14; 14. 1; 17. 1, 10, 17; 18. 4, 19; 19. 8. **also John** = John also. See 12. 25. **minister.** Gr. *hupēretēs* (Ap. 190. I. 3). He was not included by the Holy Spirit's command, but doubtless came at his kinsman (Col. 4. 10) Barnabas' invitation. **6 unto** = as far as. **Paphos.** The capital and residence of the governor. **certain.** Gr. *tis.* Ap. 123. 3. **sorcerer.** Gr. *magos.* Here, *v.* 8, and Matt. 2. 1, 7, 16. **false prophet.** Gr. *pseudoprophētēs.* Used five times by our Lord. **Bar-jesus.** Ap. 94. III. 3. 8. **7 with.** Gr. *sun.* Ap. 104. xvi. **deputy of the country.** Gr. *anthupatos.* Here, *vv.* 8, 12; 19. 38. This is the Gr. word for proconsul. Cyprus had been an imperial province, governed by a proprætor, but according to Strabo Augustus transferred it to the Senate, and the governor would be now a proconsul. The title "proconsul" has been found on a coin of Cyprus of A. D. 52, and a slab has been discovered at Soli in Cyprus, with the name Paulus, proconsul. One of the proofs of Luke's accuracy. **prudent.** Gr. *sunetos.* Here, Matt. 11. 25. Luke 10. 21. 1 Cor. 1. 19. **man.** Gr. *anēr.* Ap. 123. 2. **who** = he. **desired** = sought earnestly. Gr. *epizēteō.* See 12. 19. **8 Elymas.** The knowing one. Cp. *Ulema,* the corporation of Moslem who interpret the Koran. Arabic *alim,* wise. **withstood.** Gr. *anthistēmi.* First occ. Matt. 5. 39; often transl. "resist". **turn away.** Gr. *diastrephō.* On its other six occ. transl. "pervert" or "perverse", as *v.* 10. **from.** Gr. *apo.* Ap. 104. iv. **faith.** Gr. *pistis.* Ap. 150. II. 1. **9 also, &c.** = is called Paul also. As a Roman citizen he would have a Roman name, as well as his Jewish one. **Paul.** Always so called from this time, except when he refers to his conversion, 22. 7, 13; 26. 14. **the Holy Ghost.** Ap. 101. II. 14. **set his eyes . . . and** = gazing intently. Gr. *atenizō.* Ap. 133. III. 6. This is inconsistent with weak sight. **on.** Gr. *eis.* Ap. 104. vi. **10 all.** Notice the three "alls". **subtilty** = guile. Gr. *dolos.* Cp. Matt. 26. 4. Mark 14. 1. Rev. 14. 5.

°mischief, *thou* °child of the devil, *thou* enemy of all °righteousness, wilt thou °not cease to °pervert the °right ways of °the Lord?
11 And now, °behold, the hand of [2]the Lord *is* °upon thee, and thou shalt be blind, °not °seeing the sun °for a season." And °immediately there fell °on him a °mist and a darkness; and he went about seeking °some to lead him by the hand.
12 Then the [7]deputy, when he °saw what was done, °believed, being °astonished °at the °doctrine of [2]the Lord.

G 13 Now when °Paul and his company °loosed [8]from Paphos, they came [4]to °Perga °in Pamphylia: and John °departing [8]from them returned [4]to Jerusalem.

H L 14 But °when they departed [8]from Perga, they came [4]to °Antioch [13]in Pisidia, and went °into the [5]synagogue on °the sabbath day, and sat down.
15 And °after the °reading of the law and the prophets the °rulers of the synagogue °sent °unto them, saying, "*Ye* °men *and* brethren, °if °ye have any [5]word of °exhortation °for the °people, °say on."

M x 16 Then °Paul °stood up, and °beckoning with *his* hand said, °"Men of Israel, and °ye that fear [5]God, give audience.
17 The [5]God of this [15]people of Israel chose our fathers, and °exalted the [15]people °when they dwelt as strangers [5]in the °land of Egypt, and °with an high arm brought He them °out of it.
18 And °about the time °of forty years °suffered He their manners [5]in the wilderness.
19 And °when He had destroyed °seven °nations [5]in the [17]land of Chanaan, He °divided their [17]land to them by lot.
20 And [15]after °that He gave *unto them*

mischief = wickedness. Gr. *radiourgia.* Only here. Cp. 18. 14.
child = son. Gr. *huios.* Ap. 108. iii. See Matt. 13. 38; 23. 15. John 8. 44; 17. 12. 1 John 3. 10, and cp. "sons of Belial", so frequent in the O.T.
righteousness. Gr. *dikaiosunē.* Ap. 191. 3.
not. Gr. *ou.* Ap. 105. I.
pervert. See *v.* 8. **right** = straight.
the Lord. Ap. 98. VI. i. *β*. 2. B. This rebuke is a case of Fig. *Aganactēsis.* Ap. 6.
11 behold. Gr. *idou.* Ap. 133. I. 2.
upon. Gr. *epi.* Ap. 104. ix. 3.
not. Gr. *mē.* Ap. 105. II.
seeing. Gr. *blepō.* Ap. 133. I. 5.
for = until.
immediately. Gr. *parachrēma,* as in 3. 7.
on. Gr. *epi,* as above.
mist. Gr. *achlus.* Only here. A medical word for incipient blindness.
some to lead, &c. Lit. hand-leaders. Gr. *cheiragōgos.* Only here. Cp. 9. 8.
12 saw. Gr. *eidon.* Ap 133. I. 1.
believed. Ap. 150. I. 1. i.
astonished. Gr. *ekplēssō.* Cp. Matt. 7. 28; 22. 33. Luke 4. 32. **at.** Gr. *epi.* Ap. 104. ix. 2.
doctrine = teaching.
13 Paul and his company. Lit. Those about (Gr. *peri.* Ap. 104. xiii. 2) Paul. A Greek idiom.
loosed = weighed (anchor). Gr. *anagō.* Used in this sense once in Luke (8. 22), and thirteen times in Acts (16. 11; 18. 21, &c.).
Perga. The capital of Pamphylia. A few miles up the Cestrus, which flows into the bay of Attalia. Now a ruin. John's departure may have been due to some difference as to the change of plan, and the proceeding from the lowlands of Pamphylia to the high ground of Antioch may have been on account of Paul's illness, to which he refers in Gal. 4. 13. **in** = of.
departing = having withdrawn. Gr. *apochōreō.* Only here, Matt. 7. 23. Luke 9. 39.

13. 14-50 (H, p. 1609). ANTIOCH (PISIDIA).
(*Alternation.*)

H | L | 14, 15. Synagogue. First Sabbath.
  M | 16-41. Paul. Address.
   N | 42, 43. Effect.
 L | 44, 45. Synagogue. Second Sabbath.
  M | 46, 47. Paul and Barnabas. Appeal.
   N | 48-50. Effect.

14 when they, &c. = having gone through, as *v.* 6. **Antioch.** The capital of Pisidia, and a Roman colony. **in** = of. **into.** Gr. *eis.* Ap. 104. vi. **the sabbath day** = the day of the sabbaths. See note on John 20. 1. This was after Passover A. D. 46, or 47. **15 after.** Gr. *meta.* Ap. 104. xi. 2. **reading.** Gr. *anagnōsis.* Only here, 2 Cor. 3. 14. 1 Tim. 4. 13. See note on Luke 4. 16, 17. **rulers, &c.** Gr. *archisunagōgos.* Here, 18. 8, 17. Mark 5. 22, 35, 36, 38. Luke 8. 49; 13. 14. These rulers were probably the ruler and the angel. Ap. 120. I. 1, 2. **sent.** Gr. *apostellō.* Ap. 174. 1. **unto.** Gr. *pros.* Ap. 104. xv. 3. **men, &c.** See note on 1. 11. **if.** Ap. 118. 2. a. **ye have.** There is among (Gr. *en.* Ap. 104. viii) you. **exhortation.** Gr. *paraklēsis.* See note on 4. 36. **for.** Gr. *pros,* as above. **people.** Gr. *laos.* **say on** = speak. Gr. *legō.*

13. 16-41 (M, above). PAUL. ADDRESS. (*Alternation.*)

M | x | 16-22. Israel's History. David raised up (*ēgeire, v.* 22).
  y | 23. Promise fulfilled (*ēgage*).
   z | 24, 25. Repentance preached.
 x | 26-31. The Lord's Death and Resurrection (*ēgeire, v.* 30).
  y | 32-37. Promises fulfilled (*ēgeire, v.* 37).
   z | 38-41. Forgiveness proclaimed.

16 Paul. From this time Paul takes precedence of Barnabas. **stood up, &c.** = having risen up, and beckoned. **stood up.** Gr. *anistēmi.* Ap. 178. I. 1. **beckoning.** See note on 12. 17. **Men of Israel** = Men, Israelites. See note on 1. 11. **ye that fear God.** Cp. *v.* 26; 10. 2, 22, 35. Luke 1. 50; 12. 5; 23. 40. Rev. 11. 18; 14. 7; 15. 4; 19. 5. Ps. 61. 5, &c. **17 exalted.** Gr. *hupsoō.* See note on John 12. 32. **when they dwelt as strangers** = in (Gr. *en.* Ap. 104. viii) their sojourning. Gr. *paroikia.* Only here and 1 Pet. 1. 17. Cp. 7. 6. **land.** Gr. *gē.* Ap. 129. 4. **with.** Gr. *meta.* Ap. 104. xi. 1. **out of.** Gr. *ek.* Ap. 104. vii. **18 about** = as it were. Gr. *hōs.* **of forty years.** Gr. *tessarakontaetēs.* See 7. 23. **suffered He their manners.** Gr. *tropophoreō,* but many MSS. read *trophophoreō,* bore them as a nurse. Cp. Deut. 1. 31. It is the change of one letter in the Greek. **19 when He had** = having. **seven.** See Deut. 7. 1. **nations.** Gr. *ethnos.* **divided . . . by lot** = gave by lot. Gr. *kataklērodoteō.* Only here. Cp. Sept., Ps. 77. 55. But texts read *kataklēronomeō,* distributed by lot. Freq. in Sept.; e.g. Num. 33. 54. **20 that** = these things.

judges [18]about °the space of °four hundred
and fifty years, °until °Samuel the prophet.
21 And afterward they °desired a king:
and [5]God gave °unto them °Saul the °son of
Cis, a [7]man °of the tribe of Benjamin, °by
[20]the space of °forty years.
22 And [19]when He had °removed him, He
°raised up [21]unto them David °to be their
king; to whom also °He gave testimony, and
said, '**I °have found David the *son* of Jesse, a**
[7]man °after Mine own heart, which °shall
fulfil all My °will.'
y 23 °Of °this man's seed hath [5]God °according
to *His* °promise °raised [21]unto Israel a Saviour,
°Jesus:
z 24 °When John had first preached °before
°His coming the °baptism of °repentance to all
the [15]people of Israel.
25 And as John °fulfilled his °course, he said,
°'Whom °think ye that I am? I am [10]not *He*.
But, [11]behold, there cometh One [15]after me,
Whose shoes of *His* feet I am [10]not worthy to
loose.'
x 26 [15]Men *and* brethren, [10]children of the
°stock of Abraham, and °whosoever among
you feareth [5]God, to you °is the [5]word of this
salvation °sent.
27 For they that °dwell [1]at Jerusalem, and
their rulers, °because they knew °Him not,
°nor yet the voices of the prophets which are
[15]read °every sabbath day, they have [25]fulfilled
them °in condemning *Him*.
28 And °though they found °no °cause of
death *in Him*, yet [21]desired they Pilate that
He should be °slain.
29 And when they had °fulfilled °all that
was written °of Him, they took *Him* down
[8]from the °tree, and laid *Him* °in a °sepulchre.
30 But [5]God [22]raised Him °from the dead:
31 And He was °seen °many days °of them
which °came up with Him [8]from °Galilee [4]to
Jerusalem, who °are His °witnesses [15]unto
the [15]people.
y 32 And we °declare unto you glad tidings,
how that the [23]promise which was made [15]unto
the fathers,
33 [5]God hath fulfilled °the same [21]unto us
their °children, °in that He hath raised up
[23]Jesus again; as °it is also written [5]in the
second psalm, '**Thou art My [21]Son, this day have**
I °begotten Thee.'
34 °And as concerning that He [33]raised Him
up [30]from the dead, *now* °no more to return °to
°corruption, He said °on this wise, '**I will give**
you the °sure °mercies of David.'

the space of. Omit.
four hundred and fifty years. See Ap. 50. iv, and 86. 2.
until. Gr. *heōs*, i. e. the end of Samuel's ministry.
Samuel. See note on 3. 24.
21 desired = asked. Gr. mid. of *aiteō*. Ap. 134. I. 4.
unto = to.
Saul. Gr. *Saoul*. The Hebr. form. Cp. 9. 4.
son. Gr. *huios*. Ap. 108. iii.
of = out of. Gr. *ek*. Ap. 104. vii.
by. Omit.
forty years. See Ap. 10 and 50. V. p. 56.
22 removed = set aside. Gr. *methistēmi*. Only here, 19. 26. Luke 16. 4. 1 Cor. 13. 2. Col. 1. 13.
raised up. Gr. *egeirō*. Ap. 178. I. 4.
to be their king = for (Gr. *eis*. Ap. 104. vi) king.
He gave testimony, and = having testified, (Gr. *martureō*. See p. 1511). He. The quotation is from Ps. 89. 20.
have. Omit.
after = according to. Gr. *kata*. Ap. 104. x. 2.
shall fulfil = will do.
will = wishes, or desires. Pl., as in Eph. 2. 3. Gr. *thelēma*. Ap. 102. 2.
23 Of = From. Gr. *apo*. Ap. 104. iv.
this man's = this one's.
according to. Gr. *kata*, as in *v.* 22.
promise. See 2 Sam. 7. 12-16. Ps. 132. 11.
raised. Gr. *egeirō*, as in *v.* 22. But the texts read *agō*, led or brought. **Jesus.** Ap. 98. X.
24 When John, &c. = John having before proclaimed. Gr. *prokērussō*. See note on 3. 20.
before. Gr. *pro*. Ap. 104. xiv.
His coming. Lit. the face of His entering in (Gr. *eisodos*), i. e. upon public life.
baptism. Ap. 115. II. i. 2.
repentance. Gr. *metanoia*. Ap. 111. II.
25 fulfilled, &c. = was running his race. Cp. 20. 24.
fulfilled. Gr. *plēroō*. Ap. 125. 7.
course. Gr. *dromos*. Only here, 20. 24. 2 Tim. 4. 7.
Whom = Who.
think = suppose. Gr. *huponoeō*. Only here, 25. 18; 27. 27.
26 stock = race. Gr. *genos*.
whosoever, &c. = those among (Gr. *en*. Ap. 104. viii. 2) you who fear. See *v.* 16.
is = was.
sent. Gr. *apostellō*, as in *v.* 15, but the texts read *exapostellō*. Ap. 174. 2.
27 dwell. Gr. *katoikeō*. See note on 2. 5.
because, &c. = being ignorant of.
Him. This word referring to *v.* 26.
nor yet = and.
every sabbath day = throughout (*kata*) every sabbath.
in condemning = having judged. Gr. *krinō*. Ap. 122. 1.
28 though they = having.
no. Gr. *mēdeis*.
cause. Gr. *aitia*. See John 18. 38; 19. 4, 6.
slain. Gr. *anaireō*. See note on 2. 23.
29 fulfilled = ended. Gr. *teleō*.

all that was = all things that were. of = concerning. Gr. *peri*. Ap. 104. xiii. 1. tree. Gr. *xulon*. See 5. 30. in = into. Gr. *eis*. Ap. 104. vi. sepulchre = tomb. Gr. *mnēmeion*. See note on Matt. 27. 60. **30** from the dead. Gr. *ek nekrōn*. Ap. 139. 3. **31** seen. Gr. *optomai*. Ap. 106. I. vi. many days = for (Gr. *epi*. Ap. 104. ix. 3) many days. of = by. came up with Him. Gr. *sunanabainō*. Only here and Mark 15. 41. Galilee. All the Apostles, except Judas, were Galileans. Cp. 1. 11; 2. 7. Luke 23. 49, 55. are. The texts add "now". witnesses. See 1. 8. **32** declare unto you glad tidings = tell you good news. Gr. *euangelizō*. Ap. 121. 4. **33** the same = this. children. Gr. *teknon*. Ap. 108. i. in that he hath . . . again = having raised up. Gr. *anistēmi*. Ap. 178. I. 1. it is also, &c. = it has been written in the second Psalm also. See Ps. 2. 7. Ap. 107. I. 1. begotten Thee = brought Thee to the birth, i. e. in resurrection. **34** And as concerning = But. no more, &c. = being no longer (Gr. *mēketi*. Comp. of *mē*. Ap. 105. II.) about to return. to = unto. Gr. *eis*. Ap. 104. vi. corruption. Gr. *diaphthora*. See note on 2. 27. Here corruption means the place of corruption, i. e. the grave, for He did not see corruption and therefore could not *return* to it. on this wise = thus. sure = assured. Gr. *pistos*. Ap. 150. III. mercies = holy things. Gr. *hosios*. See 2. 27. Same as "holy" in *v.* 35. The sure mercies are the promises faithfully kept by the Almighty. Fig. *Catachresis*. Ap. 6. See Isa. 55. 3.

35 Wherefore He saith °also [5]in °another *psalm,* **'Thou °shalt [10]not °suffer Thine °Holy One to [12]see [34]corruption:'**

36 For °David, °after he had °served his own generation by the °will of [5]God, °fell on sleep, and was laid [15]unto his fathers, and [12]saw [34]corruption.

37 But He, Whom [5]God [22]raised °again, [12]saw °no [34]corruption.

z 38 Be it °known [21]unto you therefore, [15]men *and* brethren, that °through [23]this Man is [5]preached [21]unto you the °forgiveness of °sins:

39 And °by °Him °all that [12]believe are °justified [8]from all things, from which ye °could [10]not be °justified °by the law of °Moses.

40 °Beware therefore, °lest that come °upon you, which is spoken of [5]in the prophets;

41 °**'Behold, ye °despisers, and wonder, and °perish: for I work a work [5]in your days, a work which ye shall °in no wise °believe °though °a man °declare it [21]unto you.'**"

N 42 And when °the Jews were °gone [17]out of the [5]synagogue, °the Gentiles °besought that these °words might be °preached to them °the next sabbath.

43 Now when the °congregation was °broken up, many of the Jews and °religious °proselytes followed Paul and Barnabas: who, °speaking to them, °persuaded them to °continue in the °grace of [5]God.

L 44 And °the next sabbath day °came °almost the whole city together to hear the [5]word of [5]God.

45 But when the Jews [12]saw the °multitudes, they were filled with °envy, and °spake against those things which were spoken [4]by Paul, contradicting and blaspheming.

M 46 Then Paul and Barnabas °waxed bold, and said, "It was necessary that the [5]word of [5]God should first have been °spoken to you: but °seeing ye °put it from you, and °judge yourselves °unworthy of °everlasting °life, °lo, we turn [4]to the °Gentiles.

47 For so hath °the Lord commanded us, *saying,* **'I have set thee [22]to be a °light of the °Gentiles, °that thou shouldest be [2]for salvation °unto the ends of the °earth.'**"

N 48 And when the [46]Gentiles heard this, they were glad, and glorified the [5]word of [2]the Lord: and as many as were °ordained [4]to °eternal [46]life [12]believed.

49 And the [5]word of [2]the Lord was °published °throughout all the °region.

35 also, &c. = in another Psalm also.
another. Gr. *heteros.* Ap. 124. 2. The reference is to Ps. 16. 10. Cp. 2. 27.
shalt = wilt.
suffer = give.
Holy One. Gr. *hosios.* as in *v.* 34.
36 David = David indeed.
after he had = having.
served. Gr. *hupēreteō.* Ap. 190. III. 4.
will. Gr. *boulē.* Ap. 102. 4. Cp. *v.* 22. Only place where *boulē* is transl. "will".
fell on sleep. Gr. *koimaomai.* Ap. 171. 2.
37 again. Omit.
no = not. Gr. *ou.* Ap. 105. I.
38 known. Gr. *gnōstos.* See note on 1. 19.
through. Gr. *dia.* Ap. 104. v. 1.
forgiveness = remission. Gr. *aphesis.* See note on 2. 38; 5. 31.
sins. Gr. *hamartia.* Ap. 128. I. ii. 1.
39 by = in. Gr. *en.* Ap. 104. viii.
Him = This One.
all that believe are = every one who believes is.
justified. Gr. *dikaioō.* Ap. 191. 2.
could not = were not able to.
Moses. See 3. 22.
40 Beware = See. Gr. *blepō.* Ap. 133. I. 5.
lest. Gr. *mē.* Ap. 105. II.
upon. Gr. *epi.* Ap. 104. ix. 3. But the texts omit "upon you".
41 Behold. Gr. pl. of *ide.* Ap. 133. I. 3. The quotation is from Hab. 1. 5. Ap. 107. I. 3.
despisers. Gr. *kataphronētēs.* Only here.
perish = vanish away. Gr. *aphanizō.* Occ. elsewhere, Matt. 6. 16, 19, 20. Jas. 4. 14. Negative of *phainō.* Ap. 106. i. Cp. Luke 24. 31. Heb. 4. 13; 8. 13.
in no wise. Gr. *ou mē.* Ap. 105. III.
believe. Ap. 150. I. 1. ii.
though = (even) if. Ap. 118. 1. b.
a man = one. Gr. *tis.* Ap. 123. 3.
declare. Gr. *ekdiēgeomai.* Only here and 15. 3. A medical word. Cp. *diēgeomai* (8. 33).
42 the Jews. Texts omit.
gone = going forth. Gr. *exeimi.* Only here, 17. 15; 20. 7; 27. 43.
the Gentiles. The texts read "they".
besought = were beseeching. Gr. *parakaleō.* Ap. 134. I. 6.
words. Gr. *rhēma.* See note on Mark 9. 32.
preached = spoken. Gr. *laleō.* Ap. 121. 7.
the next sabbath = on (Gr. *eis.* Ap. 104. vi) the intervening (Gr. *metaxu*) sabbath. One of the weekly gatherings. See Ap. 120.
43 congregation = synagogue.
broken up = released. Gr. *luō,* same word as "loosed" in *v.* 25.
religious = worshipping. Gr. *sebomai.* Ap. 137. 2.
proselytes. See note on Matt. 23. 15.
speaking to = addressing. Gr. *proslaleō.* Only here and 28. 20.
persuaded = were urging. Gr. *peithō.* Ap. 150. I. 2.
continue. Gr. *epimenō.* See note on 10. 48. The texts read *prosmenō,* as in 11. 23. grace. Gr. *charis.* Ap. 184. **44** the next sabbath day = the following sabbath; not the same expression as in *v.* 42. came . . . together = was gathered together. almost. Gr. *schedon.* Here, 19. 26, and Heb. 9. 22. **45** multitudes = crowds. Gr. *ochlos.* envy. Gr. *zēlos.* Cp. 5. 17. spake against. Gr. *antilegō.* Cp. Luke 2. 34. The same word as "contradicting" at the end of the verse. See note on 28. 19. **46** waxed bold, and = speaking boldly. Gr. *parrhēsiazomai.* See note on 9. 27. spoken. Gr. *laleō.* Ap. 121. 7. seeing = since. Gr. *epeidē.* put it from you = thrust it away. Gr. *apōtheomai.* See note on 7. 27. judge. Gr. *krinō.* Ap. 122. 1. unworthy = not (Gr. *ou*) worthy. everlasting. Gr. *aiōnios.* Ap. 151. II. B. ii. life. Gr. *zōē.* Ap. 170. 1. lo = behold. Fig. *Asterismos.* Ap. 6. Gr. *idou.* Ap. 133. I. 2. Gentiles. Gr. *ethnos.* **47** the Lord. Ap. 98. VI. i. β. 1. A. a. light. Gr. *phōs.* Ap. 130. 1. The quotation is from Isa. 49. 6. This commission to Jehovah's Servant is cited as their authority for turning to the Gentiles. that thou shouldest be = to be. unto = as far as. Gr. *heōs.* earth. Gr. *gē.* Ap. 129. 4. **48** ordained = appointed. Gr. *tasso.* Here, 15. 2; 22. 10; 28. 23. Matt. 28. 16. Luke 7. 8. Rom. 13. 1. 1 Cor. 16. 15. eternal. Gr. *aiōnios.* Ap. 151. II. B. i. **49** published. Gr. *diapherō.* Lit. to carry through. throughout. Gr. *dia.* Ap. 104. v. 1. region. Gr. *chōra.* See 8. 1; 16. 6.

50 But the Jews °stirred up the °devout and °honourable women, and the °chief men of the city, and °raised persecution °against Paul and Barnabas, and expelled them °out of their °coasts.

I a 51 But they °shook off the dust of their feet [50]against them, and came [4]unto °Iconium.

52 And the disciples were filled with joy, and with [9]the Holy Ghost.

14 And °it came to pass °in Iconium, that they went °both together °into the °synagogue of the Jews, and so °spake,

b that a great °multitude both of the Jews and also of the °Greeks °believed.

c 2 But the °unbelieving Jews °stirred up the °Gentiles, and °made their °minds evil affected °against the brethren.

a 3 Long time therefore °abode they °speaking boldly °in °the Lord, °Which °gave testimony °unto the °word of His °grace, and °granted °signs and °wonders to be done °by their hands.

b 4 But the [1]multitude of the city was °divided: and °part °held °with the Jews, and °part °with the °apostles.

c 5 And when there was an °assault made both of the [2]Gentiles, and also of the Jews [4]with their °rulers, to °use *them* despitefully, and to stone them,

6 They °were ware of *it*,

J O and fled °unto °Lystra and Derbe, cities of Lycaonia, and unto the °region that lieth round about:

7 And there they °preached the gospel.

P d 8 And there sat a °certain °man °at Lystra, impotent in his feet, °being °a cripple °from his mother's womb, who °never °had walked:

9 °The same °heard Paul [1]speak: who °stedfastly beholding him, and °perceiving that he had °faith to be °healed,

50 stirred up = instigated. Gr. *parotrunō*. Only here.

devout. Gr. *sebomai*, same as "religious" (*v.* 43).

honourable. Gr. *euschēmōn*. Here, 17. 12. Mark 15. 43. 1 Cor. 7. 35; 12. 24.

chief men = first.

raised. Gr. *epegeirō*. Ap. 178. I. 7. Only here and 14. 2.

against. Gr. *epi*. Ap. 104. ix. 3.

out of. Gr. *apo*. Ap. 104. iv.

coasts = borders.

13. 51—14. 6- (I, p. 1609). ICONIUM. (*Alternation.*)

I | a | 13. 51—14. 1-. Preaching.
  b | 14. -1. Result.
   c | 14. 2. Opposition.
 a | 14. 3. Preaching.
  b | 14. 4. Result.
   c | 14. 5, 6-. Opposition.

51 shook off. Gr. *ektinassō*. Only here, 18. 6. Matt. 10. 14. Mark 6. 11. A medical word. Cp. Neh. 5. 13. Fig. *Parœmia*. Ap. 6.

Iconium. Now Konieh, the present (1915) terminus of the Bagdad railway. About 300 miles from Smyrna.

14. 1 it came to pass. See note on 4. 5.

in. Gr. *en*. Ap. 104. viii.

both together. Gr. *kata* (Ap. 104. x. 2) *to auto*. Cp. *epi to auto*. 1. 15, &c.

into. Gr. *eis*. Ap. 104. vi.

synagogue. Ap. 120. I.

spake. Gr. *laleō*. Ap. 121. 7.

multitude. Gr. *plēthos*. See note on 2. 6.

Greeks. These were Gentiles. Gr. *Hellēn*.

believed. Ap. 150. I. 1. i.

2 unbelieving. Gr. *apeitheō*. Cp. Ap. 150. I. 2. This is the second occ. First occ. John 3. 36. Often transl. "disobedient".

stirred up. Gr. *epegeirō*. See note on 13. 50.

Gentiles. Gr. *ethnos*. The Gr. reads, "stirred up and made evil affected the minds of the Gentiles".

made . . . evil affected = embittered, or poisoned. Gr. *kakoō*. See note on 7. 6.

minds = souls. Gr. *psuchē*. Ap. 110. IV. 2.

against. Gr. *kata*. Ap. 104. x. 1.

3 abode. Gr. *diatribō*. See note on 12. 19.

speaking boldly. Gr. *parrhēsiazomai*. See note on 9. 27.

in. Gr. *epi*. Ap. 104. ix. 2. Indicating the subject of their discourse. **the Lord.** Ap. 98. VI. i. *β*. 2. A. **Which** = Who. **gave testimony** = witnessed. Gr. *martureō*. See p. 1511. **unto** = to. **word.** Gr. *logos*. Ap. 121. 10. **grace.** Gr. *charis*. Ap. 184. 1. **granted** = gave. **signs.** Gr. *sēmeion*. Ap. 176. 3. **wonders.** Gr. *teras*. Ap. 176. 2. **by.** Gr. *dia*. Ap. 104. v. 1. **4 divided.** Gr. *schizō*, to rend; hence *schisma*, division. See John 7. 43; 9. 16; 10. 19. **part . . . part** = some indeed . . . but others. **held** = were. **with.** Gr. *sun*. Ap. 104. xvi. **apostles.** Ap. 189. **5 assault** = onset. Gr. *hormē*. Only here and Jas. 3. 4. **rulers,** i. e. of the Jews. **use . . . despitefully** = insult. Gr. *hubrizō*. Occ. Matt. 22. 6. Luke 11. 45; 18. 32. 1 Thess. 2. 2. **6 were ware of it, and** = having considered it. Gr. *suneidon*. See note on 5. 2.

14. -6-20 (J, p. 1609). LYSTRA. (*Alternation and Introversion.*)

J | O | -6, 7. Preaching.
 P | d | 8-10. Miracle. Healing.
   e | 11-13. Deification.
 O | 14-18. Remonstrance.
 P | *e* | 19. Repudiation.
   d | 20-. Miracle. Resurrection.

unto. Gr. *eis*. Ap. 104. vi. **Lystra, &c.** The order in the Gr. is "unto the cities of Lycaonia, Lystra and Derbe". **region, &c.** Gr. *perichōros*. Cp. Matt. 3. 5. Luke 4. 14. **7 preached, &c.** = were preaching the gospel. Gr. *euangelizō*. Ap. 121. 4. They were itinerating to evangelize the whole district. Timothy was one of the converts, as, on the return visit, he is called a disciple (16. 1). **8 certain.** Gr. *tis*. Ap. 123. 3. **man.** Gr. *anēr*. Ap. 123. 2. **at** = in. Gr. *en*. Ap. 104. viii. **being.** Texts omit. **a cripple** = lame. **from.** Gr. *ek*. Ap. 104. vii. **never.** Gr. *oudepote*. **had.** Texts omit. **9 The same** = This one. **heard** = was hearing. **stedfastly beholding** = gazing at. Gr. *atenizō* Ap. 133. III. 6. See note on 1. 10. **perceiving.** Gr. *eidon*. Ap. 133. I. 1. **faith.** Gr. *pistis*. Ap. 150. II. 1. **healed** = saved. Gr. *sōzō*.

10 Said with a loud voice, ° "Stand ° upright
° on thy feet." And he leaped and ° walked.
e **11** And when the ° people ° saw what Paul
° had done, they lifted up their voices, saying
° in the speech of Lycaonia, "The ° gods are
come down ° to us ° in the likeness of ° men."
12 And they called Barnabas, ° Jupiter; and
Paul, ° Mercurius, because he was the ° chief
speaker.
13 Then the priest of Jupiter, ° which was
° before their city, brought ° oxen and garlands
° unto the gates, and ° would have done sacrifice
[4] with the [11] people.
O **14** ° *Which* when the apostles, Barnabas and
Paul, heard *of*, they ° rent their clothes, and
° ran in ° among the [11] people, crying out,
15 And saying, ° "Sirs, why do ye these
things? We also are [11] men ° of like passions
with you, ° and [7] preach unto you ° that ye
should turn ° from these ° vanities [13] unto ° the
living ° God, [3] Which made ° heaven, and
° earth, and the sea, and all things that are
° therein:
16 Who [1] in ° times ° past suffered all ° nations
to walk in their own ways.
17 ° Nevertheless He ° left ° not Himself ° without witness, ° in that He did good, and ° gave
us rain ° from heaven, and ° fruitful seasons,
° filling our hearts with food and ° gladness."
18 And ° with these sayings ° scarce ° restrained they the [11] people, that they had ° not done
sacrifice [3] unto them.
P e **19** ° And there came thither *certain* Jews [15] from
Antioch and Iconium, ° who persuaded the
[11] people, and having ° stoned Paul, ° drew *him*
° out of the city, ° supposing he ° had been dead.
d **20** ° Howbeit, as the disciples ° stood round
about him, he ° rose up, and came [1] into the city:
K and ° the next day he departed [4] with Barnabas
° to Derbe.
J **21** And ° when they had [7] preached the gospel
to that city, and ° had taught many,
they returned again [20] to Lystra,
I and *to* Iconium,
H and Antioch,

10 Stand. Gr. *anistēmi.* Ap. 178. I. 1.
upright = straight. Gr. *orthos.* Only here and Heb. 12. 13.
on. Gr. *epi.* Ap. 104. ix. 3.
walked = began to walk. Cp. Isa. 35. 6.
11 people = crowd. Gr. *ochlos.*
saw. Gr. *eidon.* Same as "perceive" in *v.* 9.
had done = did.
in the speech of Lycaonia. Gr. *Lukaonisti.*
gods. Ap. 98. I. i. 5.
to. Gr. *pros.* Ap. 104. xv. 3.
in the likeness of = likened to.
men. Gr. *anthrōpos.* Ap. 123. 1. The Lycaonians were no doubt familiar with the legend of Jupiter and Mercury's visit in disguise to the aged couple, Philemon and Baucis, the scene of which was laid in the neighbouring province of Phrygia. See Ovid, *Metam.* VIII.
12 Jupiter. Gr. *Zeus.* The father of the gods.
Mercurius. Gr. *Hermēs.* The messenger of the gods.
chief speaker. Lit. the leader of the word (Gr. *logos.* Ap. 121. 10), or message.
13 which, i. e. whose temple.
before. Gr. *pro.* Ap. 104. xiv.
oxen and garlands = garlanded oxen. Fig. *Hendiadys.* Ap. 6.
unto. Gr. *epi.* Ap. 104. ix. 3.
would have, &c. = were desiring (Gr. *ethelō.* Ap. 102. 1) to sacrifice.
14 Which when, &c. = But the apostles, Barnabas and Paul, having heard.
rent. Cp. Matt. 26. 65.
ran in = rushed in. Gr. *eispēdaō.* Only here and 16. 29. The texts read *ekpēdaō,* rushed out. Used by medical writers of a bounding pulse.
among = to. Gr. *eis.* Ap. 104. vi.
15 Sirs. Gr. *andres.* Ap. 123. 2. Cp. 7. 26.
of like passions. Gr. *homoiopathēs.* Only here and Jas. 5. 17.
and preach unto you. Lit. evangelizing you. See *v.* 7. **that ye should** = to.
from. Gr. *apo.* Ap. 104. iv.
vanities = vain things. Gr. *mataios.* Here, 1 Cor. 3. 20; 15. 17. Tit. 3. 9. Jas. 1. 26. 1 Pet. 1. 18. Used in the Sept. 1 Kings 16. 13, 26. Jer. 8. 19. Jonah 2. 9, &c. Fig. *Metonymy* of Adjunct. Ap. 6.
the living God. This notable expression occ. fifteen times in the O.T., on thirteen occasions (2 Kings 19. 4, 16 being the same as Isa. 37. 4, 17), viz. Deut. 5. 26. Josh. 3. 10. 1 Sam. 17. 26, 36. 2 Kings 19. 4, 16. Ps. 42. 2; 84. 2. Isa. 37. 4, 17. Jer. 10. 10; 23. 36. Dan. 6. 20, 26. Hos. 1. 10; and sixteen times in the N.T. Matt. 16. 16; 26. 63. John 6. 69: here, Rom. 9. 26. 2 Cor. 3. 3; 6. 16. 1 Thess. 1. 9. 1 Tim. 3. 15; 4. 10; 6. 17. Heb. 3. 12; 9. 14; 10. 31; 12. 22. Rev. 7. 2. It is noteworthy that it is used twice by Peter, once by Caiaphas, once in the Revelation, and the remaining twelve times by Paul. The Lord once uses the words "the living Father" in John 6. 57. It is of course in contrast with idols. Cp. Deut. 32. 40. **God.** Ap. 98. I. i. 1. **heaven** = the heaven. See Matt. 6. 9, 10. **earth.** Gr. *gē.* Ap. 129. 4. **therein** = in (Gr. *en.* Ap. 104. viii) it. **16 times** = generations. Gr. *genea.* **past** = passed away. Gr. *paroichomai.* Only here. **nations.** Gr. *ethnos.* **17 Nevertheless** = And yet. **left.** Gr. *aphiēmi.* Ap. 174. 12. **not.** Gr. *ou.* Ap. 105. I. **without witness.** Gr. *amarturos.* Only here. **in that He did, &c.** = doing good. Gr. *agathopoieō.* Here, Mark 3. 4. Luke 6. 9, 33, 35. 1 Pet. 2. 15, 20; 3. 6, 17. 3 John 11. **gave** = giving. **from heaven.** Gr. *ouranothen.* An adverb. Only here and 26. 13. **fruitful** = fruit-bearing. Gr. *karpophoros.* Only here. **filling** = satisfying. Gr. *empiplēmi.* Here, Luke 1. 53; 6. 25. John 6. 12. Rom. 15. 24. A medical word. **gladness.** Gr. *euphrosunē.* Only here and 2. 28. **18 with these sayings** = saying these things. **scarce** = with difficulty. Gr. *molis.* **restrained** = made to cease. Gr. *katapauō.* Only here and Heb. 4. 4, 8, 10. **not.** Gr. *mē.* Ap. 105. II. **19 And** = But. **who persuaded** = and having persuaded. Gr. *peithō.* Ap. 150. I. 2. **stoned.** Cp. 2 Cor. 11. 25. **drew** = dragged. Gr. *surō.* See note on John 21. 8. **out of** = outside. Gr. *exō.* **supposing** = reckoning. Gr. *nomizō.* This word, which occ. fifteen times, always means to conclude from custom, law, or evidence, never to imagine. See note on Luke 3. 23. **had been dead** = was dead, as was the fact. **20 Howbeit** = But. **stood round about** = encircled. Gr. *kukloō.* Only here, Luke 21. 20. John 10. 24. Heb. 11. 30. Rev. 20. 9. **rose up, and** = having risen up, i. e. by Divine power. Gr. *anistēmi.* Ap. 178. I. 1. Same word as "stand" in *v.* 10. **the next day** = on the morrow. Cp. Matt. 10. 23. **to** = unto. Gr. *eis.* Ap. 104. vi. **21 when they had** = having. **had taught** = having made disciples of. Gr. *mathēteuō.* Only here, Matt. 13. 52; 27. 57; 28. 19.

22 °Confirming the °souls of the disciples, *and* °exhorting them to °continue in °the faith, and °that we must °through much °tribulation enter [1] into °the kingdom of God.
23 And °when they had °ordained them °elders °in every °church, °and had prayed °with °fasting, they °commended them to the [3] Lord, °on Whom they °believed.
24 And °after they had passed throughout Pisidia, they came [20] to Pamphylia.

G 25 And [23] when they had °preached the [3] word [1] in Perga,

F they went down [1] into °Attalia:

E 26 And thence °sailed [20] to Antioch, from whence they had been °recommended to the °grace of [15] God °for the work which they fulfilled.
27 And °when they were come, and °had gathered the [23] church together, they °rehearsed °all that [15] God °had done [23] with them, and how He had opened °the door of [9] faith [3] unto the [2] Gentiles.
28 And there they [3] abode °long time [4] with the disciples.

E Q U[1] *e* **15** And °certain men which came down °from °Judæa °taught °the brethren, *and said,* °"Except ye be circumcised °after the °manner of °Moses, ye °cannot be °saved."
2 °When therefore Paul and Barnabas had °no small °dissension and °disputation °with them, they °determined that Paul and Barnabas, and [1] certain °other °of them, should go

22 confirming. Gr. *epistērizō*. Only here, 15. 32, 41; 18. 23. The simple verb *stērizō* occ. thirteen times, first occ. Luke 9. 51. The kindred verb *stereoō* only in Acts. See 3. 7.
souls. Gr. *psuchē*. Ap. 110. IV. 1.
exhorting. Gr. *parakaleō*. Ap. 134. I. 6.
continue. Gr. *emmenō*. Only here, Gal. 3. 10. Heb. 8. 9. Compd. of *menō*. See p. 1511.
the faith. Gr. *pistis*. Ap. 150. II. 1. Cp. 6. 7; 13. 8.
that. *Ellipsis* of "saying".
through. Gr. *dia*. Ap. 104. v. 1.
tribulation. Gr. *thlipsis*. See note on 7. 10.
the kingdom of God. Ap. 114.
23 when they had = having.
ordained = chosen. Gr. *cheirotoneō*. Only here and 2 Cor. 8. 19.
elders. Ap. 189. Cp. Tit. 1. 5.
in. Gr. *kata*. Ap. 104. x. 2.
church. Ap. 186.
and had prayed = having prayed. Gr. *proseuchomai*. Ap. 134. I. 2.
with. Gr. *meta*. Ap. 104. xi. 1.
fasting = fastings. Cp. 13. 2.
commended. Gr. *paratithēmi*. Cp. Luke 23. 46.
on. Gr. *eis*. Ap. 104. vi.
believed. Ap. 150. I. 1. v (i).
24 after they had = having.
25 preached = spoken. Gr. *laleō*. Ap. 121. 7.
Attalia. A town on the coast of Pamphylia. Gr. *Attaleia*.
26 sailed = sailed away. Gr. *apopleō*. See note on 13. 4.
recommended = committed. Gr. *paradidōmi*. See note on John 19. 30.
grace. Gr. *charis*. Ap. 184.
for. Gr. *eis*. Ap. 104. vi.
27 when they were = having.
had = having.
rehearsed = recited. Gr. *anangellō*. Cp. Ap. 121. 5, 6. **all that** = whatsoever. **had done** = did. **the** = a. **28 long time** = no (Gr. *ou*. Ap. 105. I) little time. About two years and a half.

15. 1—**19.** 20 (*E*, p. 1575). PAUL'S MINISTRY IN ASSOCIATION WITH THE TWELVE. (*Introversion.*)

E | Q | 15. 1-41. Dissension within.
R | 16. 1-11. Lystra, and extended tour in Asia Minor.
S | 16. 12-40. Philippi.
T | 17. 1-14. Thessalonica and Berea.
S | 17. 15—18. 18-. Athens and Corinth.
R | 18. -18—19. 12. Ephesus, and extended tour in Asia Minor.
Q | 19. 13-20. Opposition without.

15. 1-41 (Q, above). DISSENSION WITHIN. (*Division.*)

Q | U[1] | 1-35. Dissension about Circumcision.
U[2] | 36-41. Dissension about Mark.

15. 1-35 (U[1], above). DISSENSION ABOUT CIRCUMCISION. (*Introversion.*)

U[1] | e | 1, 2. Antioch. Judaizers.
f | 3-5. Appeal to Jerusalem.
g | 6-11. Council. Peter.
h | 12. Paul and Barnabas. Evidence.
g | 13-21. Council. James.
f | 22-29. Answer from Jerusalem.
e | 30-35. Antioch. Progress.

15. 1 certain men. Gr. *tis*. Ap. 123. 3. These men are disavowed by the Apostles (*v.* 24). Cp. Gal. 2. 12. **from.** Gr. *apo*. Ap. 104. iv. **Judæa.** As though from head-quarters. Perhaps some of the priests of 6. 7. Cp. Gal. 2. 4. **taught** = were teaching. **the brethren.** See note on 11. 26. **Except** = If not. Gr. *ean* (Ap. 118. 1. b.) *mē* (Ap. 105. II). **after** = in. **manner** = custom. See note on 6. 14. **Moses.** See notes on 3. 24. Matt. 8. 4, and cp. John 7. 22. **cannot.** Lit. are not (Gr. *ou*. Ap. 105. I) able to. **saved.** Cp. *v.* 11, and 16. 30. **2 When therefore, &c.** Lit. Now no small dissension and disputation having taken place by Paul, &c. **no.** Gr. *ou*. Ap. 105. I. **dissension** = disagreement. Gr. *stasis*, a standing up. The word for sedition. Occ. here, 19. 40; 23. 7, 10; 24. 5. Mark 15. 7. Luke 23. 19, 25. Heb. 9. 8. **disputation.** Gr. *suzētēsis*. Only here, *v.* 7; 28. 29. Texts read *zētēsis*, questioning. Cp. 25. 20. **with** = towards. Gr. *pros*. Ap. 104. xv. 3. **determined** = appointed. Gr. *tassō*. Same as "ordained" (13. 48). **other** = others. Gr. *allos*. Ap. 124. 1. **of.** Gr. *ek*. Ap. 104. vii.

up °to Jerusalem °unto the °apostles and elders
°about this °question.

f 3 °And °being brought on their way °by the
°church, they °passed through °Phenice and
Samaria, °declaring the °conversion of the
°Gentiles: and they caused great joy °unto all
the brethren.
4 And when they were °come [2] to Jerusalem,
they were °received °of the [3] church, and *of*
the [2] apostles and elders, and they °declared
all things that °God had done °with them.
5 But there °rose up [1] certain °of the °sect of
the °Pharisees which °believed, saying, That
it °was needful to circumcise them, and to
command *them* to °keep the law of [1] Moses.

g 6 And the [2] apostles and elders °came together
°for to °consider °of this °matter.
7 And when there had been much °disputing,
Peter °rose up, and said [2] unto them, °"Men
and brethren, ye °know how that °a good while
ago [4] God °made choice °among us, that the
[3] Gentiles °by my mouth should hear the °word
of the gospel, and [5] believe.
8 And [4] God, °Which knoweth the hearts,
°bare them witness, giving them °the Holy
Ghost, °even as He *did* [3] unto us;
9 And °put no difference between us and them,
°purifying their hearts by °faith.
10 Now therefore why °tempt ye [4] God, to
°put a °yoke °upon the neck of the disciples,
which °neither our fathers °nor we °were able
to °bear?
11 But we °believe that °through the °grace
of the °Lord °Jesus Christ we shall be saved,
°even as they."

h 12 Then all the °multitude kept silence, and
°gave audience to Barnabas and Paul, °de-
claring °what °miracles and °wonders [4] God
had wrought [7] among the [3] Gentiles [7] by them.

g 13 And °after they had °held their peace,
°James °answered, saying, [7] "Men *and* brethren, °hearken [3] unto me:
14 °Simeon hath [12] declared how [4] God °at
the first did °visit °the [3] Gentiles, to take °out
of them a °people °for His name.
15 And to this °agree the [7] words of the
°prophets; as it °is written,

to. Gr. *eis*. Ap. 104. vi.
unto. Gr. *pros*. Ap. 104. xv. 3.
apostles and elders. Ap. 189.
about. Gr. *peri*. Ap. 104. xiii. 1.
question. Gr. *zētēma*. Here, 18. 15; 23. 29; 25. 19; 26. 3. Cp. "disputation" above.
3 And = They indeed therefore.
being brought on their way. Gr. *propempō*. Cp. Ap. 174. 4. Here, 20. 38; 21. 5. Rom. 15. 24. 1 Cor. 16. 6, 11. 2 Cor. 1. 16. Tit. 3. 13. 3 John 6. Cp. Gen. 18. 16.
by. Gr. *hupo*. Ap. 104. xviii. 1.
church. Ap. 186.
passed = were passing.
Phenice: i. e. Phenicia. This shows they went by the coast road, as far as Cæsarea.
declaring. See note on 13. 41.
conversion. Gr. *epistrophē*. Only here. For the verb, which occ. thirty-nine times, see *v.* 19 and 3. 19.
Gentiles. Gr. *ethnos*.
unto = to.
4 come. This was Paul's third visit. Not by revelation. No Divine action.
received. Gr. *apodechomai*. See note on 2. 41.
of = by. Gr. *hupo*. Ap. 104. xviii. 1.
declared = related. Gr. *anangellō*. Same as "rehearsed" (14. 27).
God. Ap. 98. I. i. 1.
with. Gr. *meta*. Ap. 104. xi. 1. I. e. as His instrument (*v.* 12).
5 rose up. Gr. *exanistēmi*. Ap. 178. I. 2.
of = of those from (Gr. *apo*. Ap. 104. iv).
sect. Gr. *hairesis*. See note on 5. 17.
Pharisees. Ap. 120. II. 1.
believed. Ap. 150. I. 1. i. I. e. in Jerusalem.
was = is.
keep = observe. Gr. *tēreō*.
6 came together = were gathered together.
for. Omit.
consider = see. Gr. *eidon*. Ap. 133. I. 1.
of = concerning. Gr. *peri*. Ap. 104. xiii. 1.
matter. Gr. *logos*. Ap. 121. 10.
7 disputing. Same as disputation, *v.* 2. Much feeling would be exhibited.
rose up. Gr. *anistēmi*. Ap. 178. I. 1.
Men *and* brethren. See note on 1. 16.
know. Gr. *epistamai*. Ap. 132. I. v.
a good while ago. Lit. from (Gr. *apo*. Ap. 104. iv) early (Gr. *archaios*) days, i. e. about thirteen years before. Ap. 181.
made choice = chose out. Gr. *eklegomai*, as in 1. 2.
among. Gr. *en*. Ap. 104. viii. 2.
by = through. Gr. *dia*. Ap. 104. v. 1. Cp. 10. 44-48.
word. Gr. *logos*. Ap. 121. 10.
8 Which knoweth, &c. = the Heart-searcher. See note on 1. 24. **bare . . . witness.** Gr. *martureō*. See p. 1511. **the Holy Ghost.** Both articles are here, but used grammatically, referring back to 2. 4 (the same gift). Ap. 101. II. 14. **even as, &c.** = as He did to us also. **9 put no difference** = discriminated in nothing. Gr. *diakrinō*. Ap. 122. 4. **purifying** = having cleansed. Gr. *katharizō*. Cp. 10. 15; 11. 9. The Heart-searcher is the Heart-cleanser. **faith** = the faith. Gr. *pistis*. Ap. 150. II. 1. **10 tempt.** Gr. *peira ō*, try, put to the test. Always transl. "tempt" up to this verse, except John 6. 6 (prove). Cp. 5. 9. **put** = lay. **yoke.** Not circumcision only, but obligation to keep the whole law. **upon.** Gr. *epi*. Ap. 104. ix. 3. **neither . . . nor.** Gr. *oute . . . oute*. **were able** = had strength. Gr. *ischuō*. Cp. Ap. 172. 3. **bear** = carry. Gr. *bastazō*. Cp. Matt. 3. 11. **11 believe.** Ap. 150. I. 1. iii. **through.** Gr. *dia*. Ap. 104. v. 1. **grace.** Ap. 184. I. 1. **Lord.** Ap. 98. VI. i. *β*. 2 B. **Jesus Christ.** Ap. 98. XI, but texts omit "Christ". **even as they** = according to (Gr. *kata*. Ap. 104. x. 2) the manner in which they also (will be). These are the last words of Peter recorded in the Acts. See his own argument turned against himself in Gal. 2. 14-21. **12 multitude.** Gr. *plēthos*. See note on 2. 6. **gave audience** = were listening to. **declaring.** Gr. *exēgeomai*. See note on 10. 8. **what** = how many, or how great. Cp. Mark 3. 8. **miracles** = signs. Gr. *sēmeion*. Ap. 176. 3. **wonders.** Gr. *teras*. Ap. 176. 2. **13 after.** Gr. *meta*. Ap. 104. xi. 2. **held their peace.** Same as kept silence in *v.* 12. **James.** See note on 12. 17. **answered.** Ap. 122. 3. **hearken unto** = hear. Same word as "gave audience" in *v.* 12, and "hear", *vv.* 7, 24. **14 Simeon** = Simon. Gr. *Sumeōn*. Cp. 2 Pet. 1. 1. **at the first, &c.** = first visited. Gr. *episkeptomai*. Ap. 133. III. 5. Cp. Luke 1. 68, 78. 7. 16. **the Gentiles, &c.** Read, to receive out from among the Gentiles. **out of.** Gr. *ek*. Ap. 104. vii. **people.** Gr. *laos*. **for.** Gr. *epi*, but texts omit the preposition. **15 agree.** Gr. *sumphōneō*. See note on 5. 9. **prophets.** Only one prophet is quoted (Amos 9. 11 12), but there are many similar predictions in Isaiah and others. See Ap. 107. I. 1. **is** has been.

16 [13] **'After °this I °will °return, and will °build again the °tabernacle of David, which is fallen down; and I will °build again the °ruins thereof, and I will °set it up:**

17 That °the residue of °men might °seek after °the LORD, and °all the [3] Gentiles, °upon whom °My name is called,' saith °the LORD, ° 'Who doeth all these things.'

18 °Known [3] unto [4] God are all His works °from the beginning of the world.

19 Wherefore °my sentence is, °that we trouble °not them, which °from among the [3] Gentiles °are turned °to [4] God:

20 But that we °write [3] unto them, that they °abstain [1] from °pollutions of idols, and *from* °fornication, and *from* things °strangled, and *from* blood.

21 For [1] Moses [2] of °old time hath °in every city them that °preach him, being read °in the °synagogues °every sabbath day."

f 22 Then °pleased it the [2] apostles and elders, °with the whole [3] church, to °send °chosen °men [2] of °their own company [2] to Antioch °with Paul and Barnabas; *namely*, Judas surnamed °Barsabas, and °Silas, °chief °men [7] among the brethren;

23 °And they wrote *letters* [7] by them °after this manner; "The [2] apostles and elders and brethren *send* °greeting [3] unto the brethren which are [2] of the [3] Gentiles °in Antioch and Syria and Cilicia:

24 Forasmuch as we °have heard that [2] certain which went °out from us have troubled you with [7] words, °subverting °your souls, °saying, '*Ye must* be circumcised, and keep the law:' to whom we °gave no *such* commandment:

25 °It seemed good [3] unto us, °being assembled °with one accord, to [22] send [22] chosen [22] men [2] unto you [22] with our beloved Barnabas and Paul,

26 [17] Men °that have hazarded their °lives °for the name of our °Lord [11] Jesus Christ.

16 this = these things.

will return, &c. A Hebraism for "I will build again". Cp. Gen. 26. 18. Num. 11. 4 (marg.).

return. Gr. *anastrephō*. Cp. 5. 22. But elsewhere refers to passing one's life, except John 2. 15 (overthrow). Cp. the noun *anastrophē*. Always transl. "conversation", i. e. manner of life, or behaviour.

build again = build up. Gr. *anoikodomeō*. Only here.

tabernacle = tent. Gr. *skēnē*, as in 7. 43, 44. Not the house or throne. Significant of the lowliness of its condition when He comes to raise it up.

ruins. Lit. things dug down. Gr. *kataskaptō*. Only here and Rom. 11. 3. The texts read "things overturned". Gr. *katastrephō*.

set it up = make upright or straight. Gr. *anorthoō*. Here, Luke 13. 13. Heb. 12. 12.

17 the residue. Gr. *kataloipos*. Only here. It is the faithful remnant.

men. Gr. *anthrōpos*. Ap. 123. 1. The Heb. would be *ādām*, while the A.V. text of Amos 9. 12 is Edom (Hebr. *ĕdōm*), but the consonants are the same, and the only difference is in the pointing. That *ādām*, not Edom, is right can hardly be questioned, or James would not have used it.

seek after = earnestly seek. Gr. *ekzēteō*. Only here, Luke 11. 50, 51. Rom. 3. 11. Heb. 11. 6; 12. 17. 1 Pet. 1. 10. Cp. Jer. 29. 13.

the Lord. Ap. 98. VI. i. β. 1. A. *a*.

all the Gentiles. The Gentiles take the second place. Zech. 8. 23.

upon. Gr. *epi*. Ap. 104. ix. 3.

My name. Cp. Jas. 2. 7. Deut. 28. 10. Jer. 14. 9

Who doeth, &c. Most of the texts read, "Who maketh these things known from the beginning of the world", and omit "unto God are all His works". See R.V. and margin.

18 Known. Gr. *gnōstos*. See note on 1. 19.

from the . . . world = from the age. Gr. *ap' aiōnos*. Ap. 151. II. A. ii. 1.

19 my sentence is = I judge, or decide. Gr. *krinō*. Ap. 122. 1.

that we trouble not = not (Gr. *mē*. Ap. 105. II) to trouble or harass. Gr. *parenochleō*. Only here. Cp. kindred verbs in 5. 16. Heb. 12. 15.

from among. Gr. *apo*. Ap. 104. iv.

are turned = are turning. Gr. *epistrephō*. See *v.* 3, and 9. 35. **to.** Gr. *epi*. Ap. 104. ix. 3.

20 write. Gr. *epistellō*. Only here, 21. 25. Heb. 13. 22.

abstain. Gr. mid. of *apechō*. This form occ. here, *v.* 29. 1 Thess. 4. 3; 5. 22. 1 Tim. 4. 3. 1 Pet. 2. 11. **pollutions.** Gr. *alisgēma*. Only here. Pollution would be caused by eating unclean (forbidden) food. Cp. *v* 29. 1 Cor. 8. The verb *alisgeō* occ. in the Sept. of Dan. 1. 8 and Mal. 1. 7, 12. **fornication.** In many cases the rites of heathenism involved uncleanness as an act of worship. Cp. Num. 25. 1-15. Probably the worship of the golden calf was of that character (Exod. 32. 6, 25). **strangled.** Gr. *pniktos*. Only here, *v.* 29; 21. 25. The verb *pnigō* occ. Matt. 18. 28. Mark 5. 13. In this case the blood remained in the carcase, contrary to Lev. 17. 10-14. **21 old time.** Lit. ancient (Gr. *archaios*, as in *v.* 7) generations. **in every city.** Gr. *kata* (Ap. 104. x. 2) *polin*, i. e. city by city. A similar idiom occ. below, "every Sabbath day". **preach.** Gr. *kērussō*. Ap. 121. 1. The question was whether Gentile converts, entering by the door of faith (14. 27), could be saved by faith alone without the seal of faith (Rom. 4. 11). In other words, whether they could belong to the family of believers (up to this time and later held as a strictly Jewish polity) without formal admission as "strangers" in accordance with Ex. 12. 48, 44. The Epistle to the Hebrews was probably written to make the position clear to Hebrews and converts alike. **in.** Gr. *en*. Ap. 104. viii. **synagogues.** Ap. 120. I. **every, &c.** See above. **22 pleased it** = it seemed (good) to. Gr. *dokeō*. **with.** Gr. *sun*. Ap. 104. xvi. **send.** Gr. *pempō*. Ap. 174. 4. **chosen men** = men chosen out. **men.** Gr. *anēr*. Ap. 123. 2. **their own company** = themselves. **Barsabas** = Barsabbas. Perhaps a brother of Joseph of 1. 23. See *v.* 32. **Silas.** So called in Acts. In the Epistles Silvanus. This was a Latin name, and he was a Roman citizen (16. 37). **chief** = leading. Gr. *hēgeomai*. **23 And they wrote** = Having written. In *v.* 30 it is called "a letter". **after this manner.** The texts omit. **greeting.** Gr. *chairein*. Lit. to rejoice. Fig. *Ellipsis* (Ap. 6). I bid you to rejoice. Cp. Fr. *adieu*, (I commend you) to God. Cp. 23. 26. Jas. 1. 1. **in** = throughout. Gr. *kata*, as in *v.* 21. **24 have.** Omit. **out from.** Gr. *ek*. Ap. 104. vii. **subverting** = unsettling. Gr. *anaskeuazō*. Only here, and not in Sept. **your souls** = you (emph.). Gr. *psuchē*. Ap. 110. IV. 1. **saying . . . law.** The texts omit. **gave no such commandment** = commanded it not (Gr. *ou*. Ap. 105. I). **25 It seemed good.** Same word as "it pleased", *v.* 22. **being assembled** = having come to be. **with one accord.** Gr. *homothumadon*. See note on 1. 14. **26 that have hazarded.** Lit. having given up. Gr. *paradidōmi*. Often transl. "deliver up", or "betray". In *v.* 40 and 14. 26 "recommend". **lives.** Gr. *psuchē*. Ap. 110. III. 1. **for** = in behalf of. Gr. *huper*. Ap. 104. xvii. 1. **Lord.** Ap. 98. VI. i. β. 2. A.

27 We °have sent therefore Judas and Silas, °who shall also tell *you* the same things [7]by °mouth.

28 For [25]it seemed good to °the Holy Ghost, and to °us, to lay upon you °no greater °burden °than these °necessary things;

29 That ye [20]abstain from °meats offered to idols, and from blood, and from things [20]strangled, and from [20]fornication: °from which °if ye keep yourselves, ye shall do well. °Fare ye well."

e **30** So °when they were dismissed, they came [2]to Antioch: and °when they had gathered the [12]multitude together, they delivered the epistle:

31 °*Which* when they had read, they rejoiced °for the °consolation.

32 And Judas and Silas, °being prophets also themselves, °exhorted the brethren °with many [7]words, and °confirmed *them*.

33 And °after they had tarried *there* a space, they °were let go °in peace [1]from the brethren [2]unto the [2]apostles.

°**34** Notwithstanding it pleased Silas to abide there still.

35 °Paul also and Barnabas °continued [21]in Antioch, teaching and °preaching the [7]word of the [26]Lord, [4]with many °others also.

U² **36** And °some days [13]after Paul said [2]unto Barnabas, "Let us go again and [14]visit our brethren [21]in every city °where we °have preached the [7]word of the [26]Lord, *and see* how they °do."

37 And Barnabas °determined to °take with them °John, °whose surname was Mark.

38 But Paul °thought [19]not good to [37]take him with them, who °departed [1]from them [1]from Pamphylia, and went [19]not with them [2]to the work.

39 °And the contention was so sharp between them, °that they °departed asunder °one [1]from the other: and so °Barnabas °took Mark, and °sailed °unto Cyprus;

40 And Paul °chose [22]Silas, and departed, being °recommended [3]by the brethren [3]unto the [11]grace of °God.

41 And he went through Syria and Cilicia, [32]confirming the [3]churches.

Ri **16** Then °came he to °Derbe and Lystra: and, °behold, a °certain disciple was there, °named °Timotheus, the °son of a °certain

27 have sent. Gr. *apostellō*. Ap. 174. 1.
who shall also tell. Lit. themselves also telling. See note on 12. 14.
mouth = word (of mouth). Gr. *logos*. Ap. 121. 10.
28 the Holy Ghost. Ap. 101. II. 3.
us: i. e. the whole church (*v.* 22). no. Gr. *mēdeis*.
burden. Gr. *baros*. Occ. here, Matt. 20. 12. 2 Cor. 4. 17. Gal. 6. 2. 1 Thess. 2. 6. Rev. 2. 24.
than = except.
necessary = compulsory. Gr. *epanankes*. Only here. Circumcision therefore was not compulsory.
29 meats offered to idols. Gr. *eidōlothutos*. Occ. here, 21. 25. 1 Cor. 8. 1, 4, 7, 10; 10. 19, 28. Rev. 2. 14, 20. This explains what the pollutions (*v.* 20) were.
from. Gr. *ek*. Ap. 104. vii.
if ye keep = keeping carefully. Gr. *diatēreō*. Only here and Luke 2. 51.
Fare ye well. Lit. be strong. Gr. *rōnnumi*. Only here and 23. 30. The usual way of ending a letter.
30 when they, &c. = having then been dismissed, i. e. let go. Gr. *apoluō*, as in *v.* 33. Ap. 174. 11.
when they had = having.
31 Which, &c. = And having read *it*.
for. Gr. *epi*. Ap. 104. ix. 2.
consolation. See 4. 36; 13. 15.
32 being prophets also themselves = being themselves also prophets. See Ap. 189.
exhorted. Gr. *parakaleō*. Ap. 134. I. 6.
with = by means of. Gr. *dia*. Ap. 104. v. 1.
confirmed = strengthened. Gr. *epistērizō*. See note on 14. 22.
33 after, &c. = having continued some time. Lit. made time.
were let go. Same as "dismissed" in *v.* 30.
in = with. Gr. *meta*. Ap. 104. xi. 1.
34 This verse is omitted by all the texts. The R.V. puts it in the margin.
35 Paul also = But Paul.
continued. Gr. *diatribō*. See note on 12. 19.
preaching. Gr. *euangelizō*. Ap. 121. 4.
others. Gr. *heteros*. Ap. 124. 2.
36 some days after = after certain (Gr. *tis*. Ap. 123. 3) days.
where = in (Gr. *en*. Ap. 104. viii) which.
have preached = preached. Gr. *katangellō*. Ap. 121. 5. do = fare.
37 determined = purposed. Gr. *bouleuō*. See 5. 33; 27. 39. But the texts read *boulomai*. Ap. 102. 3.
take with them. Gr. *sumparalambanō*. See 12. 25.
John. See note on 12. 12.
whose surname was = who was called.
38 thought . . . good. Gr. *axioō*, to reckon worthy, or right. Here, 28. 22. Luke 7. 7. 2 Thess. 1. 11. 1 Tim. 5. 17. Heb. 3. 3; 10. 29.
departed = fell away. Gr. *aphistēmi*. Cp. Luke 8. 13.
39 And the contention, &c. But there arose a sharp contention. Gr. *paroxusmos*. Only here and Heb. 10. 24. A medical word. The verb occ. in 17. 16.
that = so that. departed asunder = separated. Gr. *apochōrizomai*. Only here and Rev. 6. 14. one from the other = from one another. Barnabas. He here disappears from the history. took . . . and = having taken. sailed = sailed away. Gr. *ekpleō*. Only here, 18. 18; 20. 6. unto. Gr. *eis*. Ap. 104. vi. **40** chose . . . and = having chosen. Gr. *epilegomai*. Only here and John 5. 2 (called). recommended. See *v.* 26. God. The texts read "the Lord".

16. 1-11 (R, p. 1615). LYSTRA, AND EXTENDED TOUR IN ASIA MINOR. (*Introversion.*)

R | i | 1-3. Preparation to go forth (*exelthein*, *v.* 3).
  k | 4. Decrees of Council.
    l | 5. Churches prospering.
  k | 6-9. Decree of the Spirit.
i | 10, 11. Preparation to go forth (*exelthein*, *v.* 10).

1 came . . . to = arrived at. Gr. *katantaō*. Occ. nine times in Acts, four times in Paul's epistles. Always accompanied by *eis*, except 20. 15. Derbe and Lystra. They would reach Derbe first, coming from Cilicia. behold. Gr. *idou*. Ap. 133. I. 2. certain. Gr. *tis*. Ap. 123. 3. named = by name. Timotheus. From this time closely associated with Paul in the ministry (Rom. 16. 21). He was probably one of his converts at his previous visit (14. 7). Cp. my own son in the faith (1 Tim. 1. 2, 18. 2 Tim. 1. 2). In six of Paul's epistles Timothy is joined with him in the opening salutation. His name, which means honour of God, or valued by God (*timē* and *theos*), suggests the important part he was to take in the revelation of God's eternal purpose. son. Gr. *huios*. Ap. 108. iii. certain. Texts omit.

woman, which was a Jewess, °and believed;
but his father *was* a °Greek:
2 Which was °well reported of °by the
brethren that were °at Lystra and Iconium.
3 Him °would Paul have to °go forth °with
him; and took and circumcised him °because
of the Jews which were °in those °quarters:
for they °knew all that his father °was a [1] Greek.
k **4 And as they °went through the cities, they**
delivered them the °decrees for to °keep, that
were °ordained °of the °apostles and elders
which were [2] at Jerusalem.
l **5 °And so were the °churches °established in**
the °faith, and increased in number °daily.
k **6 °Now when they had gone throughout**
Phrygia and °the region of Galatia, and were
°forbidden [4] of °the Holy Ghost to °preach the
°word [3] in °Asia,
7 °After they were come °to Mysia, they
°assayed to go °into °Bithynia: but °the Spirit
suffered them °not.
8 And they passing by Mysia came down [1] to
°Troas.
9 And a °vision °appeared to Paul °in the
night; °There stood a man of Macedonia, and
°prayed him, saying, "Come over °into Mace-
donia, and help us."
i **10 And °after he °had seen the [9] vision,**
immediately °we °endeavoured to go [9] into
Macedonia, °assuredly gathering that °the
Lord had called us °for to preach the gospel
unto them.
11 Therefore °loosing °from Troas, we °came
with a straight course [1] to °Samothracia, and
the °next *day* [1] to °Neapolis;
S V **12 And from thence [1] to °Philippi, which is**
°the chief city of that part of Macedonia, *and*
a °colony: and we were [3] in that city °abiding
[1] certain days.
W m[1] **13 And °on the sabbath we went °out of the**

and believed = a believer. Gr. *pistos.* Ap. 150. III. Eunice (2 Tim. 1. 5), as well as her mother Lois, had instructed Timothy in the Holy Scriptures from his infancy (2 Tim. 3. 15).

Greek: i. e. a Gentile (Gr. *Hellēn*). His influence doubtless prevented Timothy's being circumcised when eight days old.

2 well reported of = borne witness to. Gr. *martureō.* See p. 1511.

by. Gr. *hupo.* Ap. 104. xviii. 1.

at = in. Gr. *en.* Ap. 104. viii.

3 would Paul have = Paul purposed. Gr. *thelō.* Ap. 102. 1.

go forth. Gr. *exerchomai.*

with. Gr. *sun.* Ap. 104. xvi.

because of. Gr. *dia.* Ap. 104. v. 2.

in. Gr. *en.* Ap. 104. viii.

quarters = places.

knew. Gr. *oida.* Ap. 132. I. i.

was = was by race. Gr. *kuparchō.* See note on Luke 9. 48.

4 went through = were going through. Gr. *diaporeuomai.* Occ. elsewhere Luke 6. 1; 13. 22; 18. 36. Rom. 15. 24.

decrees, or edicts. Gr. *dogma.* Occ. also 17. 7. Luke 2. 1. Eph. 2. 15. Col. 2. 14.

keep = observe, or guard. Gr. *phulassō.*

ordained = decided. Gr. *krinō.* Ap. 122. 1.

of = by, as in *v.* 2.

apostles, &c. Ap. 189.

5 And so, &c. = The churches indeed therefore.

churches. Ap. 186.

established. Gr. *stereoō.* See note on 3. 7; 14. 22. A medical word.

faith. Ap. 150. II. 1.

daily. Gr. *kath'* (Ap. 104. x. 2) *hēmeran,* i. e. day by day.

6 Now, &c. The texts read, "They went through".

the region of Galatia = the Galatian country.

forbidden = hindered.

the Holy Ghost. Ap. 101. II. 3.

preach = speak. Gr. *laleō.* Ap. 121. 7.

word. Gr. *logos.* Ap. 121. 10.

Asia. See note on 2. 9.

7 After they were = Having.

to = down to. Gr. *kata.* Ap. 104. x. 2. I.e. to the border of Mysia. R.V. "over against".

assayed = were attempting. Gr. *peirazō.* See 15. 10.

into. Gr. *kata,* as above, but the texts read *eis.* **Bithynia.** The province of Bithynia and Pontus, lying on the S.E. shores of the Propontis (Sea of Marmora), and the south shore of the Pontus Euxinus (Black Sea). **the Spirit** = the Holy Spirit. Ap. 101. II. 3. The texts add "of Jesus", but it was the same Spirit Who sent Paul and Barnabas forth from Antioch (13. 2, 4), and had already hindered Paul and Silas (*vv.* 6, 7). The Spirit promised by the Lord Jesus (2. 33. John 16. 7). **not.** Gr. *ou.* Ap. 105. I. **8 Troas.** Alexandreia Troas, the port on the coast of Mysia, about thirty miles south of the Dardanelles. Now *Eski Stamboul.* **9 vision.** Gr. *horama.* See note on 7. 31. It has been suggested that Paul had met Luke, and that it was he who was seen in the vision. **appeared to** = was seen by. Gr. *horaō.* Ap. 133. I. 8. **in** = through. Gr. *dia.* Ap. 104. v. 1. **There stood, &c.** = A certain (Gr. *tis.* Ap. 123. 3) man (Gr. *anēr.* Ap. 123. 2), a Macedonian, was standing. **prayed** = praying. Ap. 134. I. 6. **into.** Gr. *eis.* Ap. 104. vi. **10 after** = when. **had seen** = saw. Gr. *eidon.* Ap. 133. I. 1. **we.** Here Luke comes upon the scene. **endeavoured** = sought. **assuredly gathering.** Gr. *sumbibazō.* See note on 9. 22. **the Lord.** Ap. 98. VI. i. *β.* 2. A., but the texts read "God". **for to . . . them.** Lit. to evangelize them. Gr. *euangelizō.* Ap. 121. 4. **11 loosing.** See note on 13. 13. **from.** Gr. *apo.* Ap. 104. iv. **came, &c.** = ran direct. Gr. *euthudromeō.* Only here and 21. 1. I. e. ran before the wind. **Samothracia.** The highest in elevation of the northern Ægean islands, midway between Troas and Philippi. **next.** See note on 7. 26. **Neapolis.** The harbour of Philippi, distant about ten miles away. The first European soil trodden by Paul. It had taken two days with a favourable wind. Cp. 20. 6.

16. 12-40 [For Structure see next page].

12 Philippi. The scene of the decisive battle which ended the Roman republic 42 B.C. **the chief city, &c.** Lit. the first of the district, a city of Macedonia, a colony. Amphipolis had been the chief city, and was still a rival of Philippi. **colony.** Gr. *kolōnia.* Only here. A Roman military settlement. The word survives in the names of some places in England, e.g. Lincoln. These coloniæ were settlements of old soldiers and others established by Augustus to influence the native people. Hence the significance of *v.* 37. **abiding.** Gr. *diatribō.* See note on 12. 19. **13 on the sabbath** = on the (first) day of the sabbaths. See note on John 20. 1. **out of.** Gr. *exō,* without.

°city °by a river side, °where °prayer was wont to be made; and we sat down, and °spake °unto the women which °resorted *thither*.

n^1 **14** And a [1]certain woman named Lydia, a °seller of purple, of the city of °Thyatira, °which worshipped °God, °heard *us:* whose heart °the Lord °opened, that she attended [13]unto the things which were [13]spoken [4]of Paul.

o^1 **15** And when she was °baptized, and her household, she °besought *us,* saying, °"If ye have °judged me to be °faithful to [14]the Lord, come [9]into my house, and °abide *there.*" And she °constrained us.

m^2 **16** And it came to pass, as we went [1]to [13]prayer, a [1]certain °damsel °possessed with a °spirit °of divination met us, which brought her °masters much °gain by °soothsaying:

n^2 **17** °The same °followed Paul and us, and °cried, saying, "These °men are the °servants of the °Most High [14]God, which °shew [13]unto °us the way of °salvation."

18 And this °did she °many days. But Paul, being °grieved, turned and said to the [16]spirit, "I °command thee [3]in °the name of °Jesus Christ to come °out of her." And he came out the same hour.

o^2 **19** And when her [16]masters [10]saw that the hope of their [16]gains °was gone, they °caught Paul and Silas, and °drew *them* [9]into the °marketplace °unto the °rulers,

20 And °brought them to the °magistrates, saying, "These [17]men, °being Jews, do °exceedingly trouble our city,

21 And °teach °customs, which °are [7]not lawful for us to °receive, °neither to °observe, °being Romans."

16.12-40 (S, p. 1615). PHILIPPI.
(*Introversion and Alternation.*)

S | V | 12. Abiding in Philippi.
  W | m^1 | 13. Prayer.
      n^1 | 14. Lydia. Heart opened.
        o^1 | 15. Result. Hospitality.
    m^2 | 16. Prayer.
      n^2 | 17, 18. Damsel. Demon cast out.
        o^2 | 19-24. Result. Persecution.
    m^3 | 25, 26. Prayer.
      n^3 | 27-34. Jailor. Conversion.
        o^3 | 35-39. Result. Vindication.
  V | 40. Departure from Philippi.

city. The texts read "gate".

by a river side = beside (Gr. *para.* Ap. 104. xii. 3) the river. No art. because the river (the Gangas) was well known to Luke.

where, &c. The texts read "where we reckoned prayer would be". See note on 14. 19.

prayer. Gr. *proseuchē.* Ap. 134. II. 2. Here a place of prayer.

spake. Gr. *laleō.* Ap. 121. 7. **unto** = to.

resorted thither = came together.

14 seller of purple. Gr. *porphuropōlis.* Only here. The celebrated purple dye was made from the murex, a shell-fish. Referred to by Homer.

Thyatira. On the Lycus in Lydia. Inscriptions of the guild of Dyers at Thyatira.

which worshipped = one worshipping. Gr. *sebomai.* Ap. 137. 2. No doubt a proselyte.

God. Ap. 98. I. i. 1.

heard = was hearing.

the Lord. Ap. 98. VI. i. β. 2. A.

opened = opened effectually. Gr. *dianoigō.* Only here, 17. 3. Mark 7. 34, 35. Luke 2. 23; 24. 31, 32, 45.

15 baptized. Ap. 115. I. i.

besought. Gr. *parakaleō.* Ap. 134. I. 6.

If. Ap. 118. 2. a.

judged. Gr. *krinō.* Ap. 122. 1.

faithful. Gr. *pistos.* Ap. 150. III.

abide. Gr. *menō.* See p. 1511.

constrained. Gr. *parabiazomai.* Only here and Luke 24. 29. Hindered in Asia their first convert is an Asiatic.

16 damsel. Gr. *paidiskē.* See note on 12. 13. **possessed with** = having. Cp. Luke 13. 11. **spirit.** Ap. 101. II. 12. **of divination.** Gr. *Puthōn.* Only here. The texts read "a spirit, a Python". The Python was a serpent destroyed, according to Greek Mythology, by Apollo, who was hence called Pythius, and the priestess at the famous temple at Delph was called the Pythoness. Through her the oracle was delivered. See an instance of these oracular utterances in Pember's *Earth's Earliest Ages,* ch. XII. The term Python became equivalent to a soothsaying demon, as in the case of this slave-girl who had an evil spirit as "control". She would be nowadays called a medium. The Lord's commission in Mark 16 was to cast out demons (*v.* 17). To say that the girl was a ventriloquist, who was disconcerted, and so lost her power, shows what shifts are resorted to in order to get rid of the supernatural. **masters** = owners. Gr. *kurios.* Ap. 98. VI. i. *a.* 4. A. **gain.** Gr. *ergasia* = work; hence, wages, pay. Only here, *v.* 19; 19. 24, 25. Luke 12. 58. Eph. 4. 19. **soothsaying** = fortune-telling. Gr. *manteuomai.* Only here. In Sept. used of false prophets. Deut. 18. 10. 1 Sam. 28. 8, &c. **17 The same** = This one. **followed . . . and** = following persistently. Gr. *katakoloutheō.* Only here and Luke 23. 55. **cried** = kept crying, i.e. the demon in her. Cp. Matt. 8. 29. Luke 4. 33. **men.** Gr. *anthrōpos.* Ap. 123. 1. **servants** = bond-servants. Gr. *doulos.* Ap. 190. I. 2. **Most High God.** See note on Luke 1. 32 and cp. Mark 5. 7. Not necessarily a testimony to the true God, as the term was applied to *Zeus.* **shew** = proclaim. Gr. *katangellō.* Ap. 121. 5. **us.** The texts read "you". **salvation.** Cp. Luke 4. 34, where a demon testifies to the Lord, to discredit Him. **18 did** = was doing. **many** = for (Gr. *epi.* Ap. 104. ix. 3) many. **grieved** = worn out with annoyance. Gr. *diaponeomai.* Only here and 4. 2. **command.** Gr. *parangellō.* See note on 1. 4. **the name.** See note on 2. 38. **Jesus Christ.** Ap. 98. XI. **out of** = out from. Gr. *apo.* Ap. 104. iv. **19 was gone** = came out. Same word as in *v.* 18. Perhaps the demon rent and tore her in coming out, as in Mark 9 26. Luke 9. 42. **caught** = laid hold on. **drew** = dragged. Gr *helkuō.* Cp. 21. 30, where *helkō,* the classical form, is used, and see note on John 12. 32. **marketplace.** Gr. *agora.* Where the courts were held. Lat. *forum.* **unto.** Gr. *epi.* Ap. 104. ix. 3. **rulers** = authorities. Gr. *archōn.* **20 brought.** Gr. *prosagō.* Only here, 27. 27. Luke 9. 41. 1 Pet. 3. 18. **magistrates.** These were Romans. Gr. *stratēgos.* Showing Luke's accuracy. The magistrates of this colony bore the same title as at Rome, prætors, for which *stratēgos* is the Greek rendering, though before this it is applied to the captain of the Temple guard. **being.** Gr. *huparchō.* See note on Luke 9. 48. **exceedingly trouble.** Gr. *ektarassō.* Only here. It suggests that a riot was feared. **21 teach** = proclaim. Same as "shew" (*v.* 17). **customs.** Gr. *ethos.* See note on 6. 14. **are** = it is. **receive.** Gr. *paradechomai.* Only here, 22. 18. Mark 4. 20. 1 Tim. 5. 19. Heb. 12. 6. **neither.** Gr. *oude.* **observe** = do. **being.** Gr. *eimi.* Note the distinction. These men, being Jews to begin with . . . us who are Romans, as is well known.

22 And the °multitude °rose up together
°against them: and the [20]magistrates °rent off
their clothes, and commanded to °beat *them*.
23 And when they had laid many °stripes
upon them, they cast *them* [9]into prison,
°charging the °jailor to °keep them °safely:
24 Who, having received such a charge,
°thrust them [9]into the °inner prison, and
°made their feet fast °in the stocks.

m3 25 And °at °midnight Paul and Silas °prayed,
and °sang praises unto [14]God: and the prisoners °heard them.
26 And °suddenly there was a great °earth-
quake, so that the foundations of the °prison
were °shaken: and immediately all the doors
were opened, and every one's bands were
°loosed.

n3 27 And °the keeper of the prison °awaking
out of his sleep, and [10]seeing the prison doors
open, he °drew out his sword, and °would
have killed himself, °supposing that the prisoners had °been fled.
28 But Paul cried with a loud voice, saying,
°"Do thyself no harm: for we are all here."
29 Then he °called for a °light, and °sprang
in, and °came trembling, and fell down before
Paul and Silas,
30 And brought them °out, and said, °"Sirs,
what must I do °to be saved?"
31 And they said, °"Believe on [10]the Lord
[18]Jesus °Christ, and thou shalt be saved, and
°thy house."
32 And they [13]spake [13]unto him the [6]word of
[10]the Lord, and to all that were [3]in his house.
33 And he took them °the same hour of the
night, and °washed °*their* stripes; and was
[15]baptized, he and all his, °straightway.
34 And when he had °brought them [9]into
his house, he °set meat before them, and °re-
joiced, °believing in [14]God °with all his house.

o3 35 And when it was day, the [20]magistrates
°sent the °serjeants, saying, °"Let those [17]men
go."
36 And the [27]keeper of the prison °told °this
saying °to Paul, "The [20]magistrates have
[35]sent °to [35]let you go: now therefore °depart,
and go [3]in peace."
37 But Paul said °unto them, "They have
°beaten us °openly °uncondemned, [20]being
°Romans, and have [23]cast *us* [9]into prison; and

22 multitude = crowd. Gr. *ochlos*.
rose up together. Gr. *sunephistēmi*. Only here.
against. Gr. *kata*. Ap. 104. x. 1.
rent off. Gr. *perirrēgnumi*. Only here.
beat them = beat them with rods. Gr. *rabdizō*. Only here and 2 Cor. 11. 25. The lictors who attended on the prætors carried rods or staves (*rabdos*) for the purpose, and were called rod-bearers. Gr. *rabdouchos*. See *v.* 35.

23 stripes. Gr. *plēgē*. Four times transl. "wound", five times "stripe", and twelve times "plague".
charging. Same as "command" in *v.* 18.
jailor. Gr. *desmophulax*, i.e. keeper of the prison. Only here and *vv.* 27, 36.
keep. Gr. *tēreō*. Cp. 12. 5, 6.
safely. Gr. *asphalōs*. See note on Mark 14. 44.

24 thrust = cast, as *v.* 23.
inner. Gr. *esōteros*. Comparative of *esō*, within. Only here and Heb. 6. 19.
made . . . fast = made safe. Gr. *asphalizō*. Only here and Matt. 27. 64-66.
in the stocks. Lit. unto (Gr. *eis*. Ap. 104. vi) the wood.

25 at. Gr. *kata*. Ap. 104. x. 2.
midnight. Gr. *mesonuktion*. Only here, 20. 7. Mark 13. 35. Luke 11. 5.
prayed, and = praying. Gr. *proseuchomai*. Ap. 134. I. 2.
sang praises unto. Lit. were hymning. Gr. *humneō*. Here, Matt. 26. 30. Mark 14. 26. Heb. 2. 12. The first two passages refer to the great Hallel. See notes on Matt. 26. 30. Ps. 113. If this were sung by Paul and Silas, note the beautiful significance of Pss. 115. 11; 116. 3, 4, 15, 17; 118. 6, 29, and in the result, Ps. 114. 7. The noun *humnos* (hymn) only in Eph. 5. 19. Col. 3. 16.
heard = were listening to. Gr. *epakroaomai*. Only here. The noun occ. in 1 Sam. 15. 22 (Sept.).

26 suddenly. Gr. *aphnō*. See note on 2. 2.
earthquake. Gr. *seismos*. See note on Matt. 8. 24.
prison. Gr. *desmōterion*. See note on 5. 21. Not the word *phulakē* which occ. *vv.* 23, 24, 27, 37, 40.
shaken. Gr. *saleuō*. See 4. 31.
loosed. Gr. *aniēmi*. Only here, 27. 40. Eph. 6. 9. Heb. 13. 5.

27 keeper of the prison. Same as "jailor" (*v.* 23).
awaking out of his sleep. Lit. becoming awake. Gr. *exupnos*. Only here. The verb *exupnizō* only in John 11. 11.
drew out = drew.
would have killed = was about to kill. Gr. *anaireō*. See note on 2. 23.
supposing. Gr. *nomizō*. See note on 14. 19.
been fled = escaped. Cp. 12. 19; 27. 42. Roman soldiers were responsible with their lives for prisoners in their charge.

28 Do thyself no harm = Do nothing (Gr. *mēdeis*) evil (Gr. *kakos*. Ap. 128. III. 2) to thyself.

29 called for = asked for. Gr. *aiteō*. Ap. 134. I. 4. light. Gr. *phōs*. Ap. 130. 1. sprang in. Gr. *eispēdaō*. Only here and 14. 14. came trembling = becoming (Gr. *ginomai*) in a tremble (Gr. *entromos*). See note on 7. 32. **30** out = outside. Gr. *exō*. Sirs. Gr. *kurios*. Cp. Ap. 98. VI. i. *a*. 4. B. Same as "masters" (*v.* 16). to be = in order that (Gr. *hina*) I may be. This man was under deep conviction of sin, "shaken to his foundations". He was ready to be told of the Lord Jesus Christ. To bid people to believe, who are not under conviction, is vain. **31** Believe. Gr. *pisteuō*. Ap. 150. I. v. (iii.) 2. Christ. The texts omit. Cp. Matt. 1. 21. thy house: i.e. on the same condition of faith. **33** the same = in (Gr. *en*. Ap. 104. viii) the same. washed = bathed them. Gr. *louō*. Ap. 136. iii. their stripes = from (Gr. *apo*. Ap. 104. iv) their wounds. straightway. Gr. *parachrēma*. Same as immediately (*v.* 26). See note on 3. 7. **34** brought. Gr. *anagō*. Same as "loosed", *v.* 11. set meat = placed a table. Cp. Ps. 23. 5. rejoiced. See note on "was glad", 2. 26. believing. Ap. 150. I. 1. ii. with all his house. Gr. *panoiki*, an adverb. Only here. **35** sent. Gr. *apostellō*. Ap. 174. 1. serjeants = lictors. Gr. *rabdouchos*. See *v.* 22. Only here and *v.* 38. Let . . . go = Release. Gr. *apoluō*. Ap. 174. 11. **36** told = reported. Gr. *apangellō*. See note on 4. 23. this saying = these words. Gr. *logos*, as in *v.* 6. to. Gr. *pros*. Ap. 104. xv. 3. to, &c. = in order that (Gr. *hina*) you may be released. depart = come forth. **37** unto. Same as "to" in *v.* 36. beaten. Gr. *derō*, as in 5. 40. openly = publicly. Gr. *dēmosia*. See note on 5. 18. uncondemned = without investigation. Gr. *akatakritos*. Only here and 22. 25. Romans = men (Gr. *anthrōpos*) Romans. The charge was that they were Jews, introducing alien customs, and the magistrates condemned them without inquiry. Cp. 21. 39; 22. 25.

now do they thrust us out °privily? °nay
verily; but let them come themselves and
°fetch us out."
38 And the [35]serjeants [36]told these °words
[13]unto the magistrates: and they °feared,
when they heard that they were Romans.
39 And they came and [15]besought them, and
°brought *them* out, and °desired *them* to depart out of the city.
V 40 And they went °out of the prison, and
entered [9]into *the house of* Lydia: and when
they had [10]seen the brethren, they °comforted
them, and departed.

T X p **17** Now when they had °passed through
°Amphipolis and °Apollonia, they came
°to °Thessalonica, where was a °synagogue
of the Jews:
q 2 And °Paul, as his manner was, went in
°unto them, and °three sabbath days °rea-
soned with them °out of the scriptures,
3 °Opening and °alleging, that °Christ must
needs have suffered, and °risen again °from
the dead; and that °this °Jesus, Whom **I**
°preach °unto you, is °Christ.
r 4 And °some °of them °believed, and °con-
sorted with Paul and Silas; and of the °de-
vout Greeks a great °multitude, and of the
°chief women °not a few.
s 5 But °the Jews which believed not, °moved
with envy, °took unto them °certain °lewd
°fellows °of the baser sort, and °gathered a
company, and °set °all the city on an uproar,
and °assaulted the house of Jason, and °sought
to bring °them out [1]to the °people.
6 And °when they found them not, they
°drew Jason and [5]certain °brethren °unto the
°rulers of the city, crying, "These that have
°turned the °world upside down are come
hither also;

privily = secretly. Gr. *lathra*. Only here, Matt. 1. 19; 2. 7. John 11. 28. Note the contrast, "openly . . . secretly". Fig. *Antithesis*. Ap. 6.
nay verily = no (Gr. *ou*. Ap. 105. I.) indeed.
fetch = lead. Same word as in 5. 19; 7. 36, 40.
38 words. Gr. *rhēma*. See note on Mark 9. 32.
feared = were alarmed. Cp. 22. 29. They had violated the Roman law by which no Roman citizen could be scourged, or put to death, by any provincial governor without an appeal to the Emperor. Cp. 25. 11, 12.
39 brought. Same word as "fetch" (*v.* 37).
desired = were praying. Gr. *erōtaō*. Ap. 134. I. 3.
40 out of. Gr. *ek*. Ap. 104. vii.
comforted = exhorted. Gr. *parakaleō*, as in *vv.* 9, 15, 39. Ap. 134. I. 6.

17. 1-14 (T, p. 1615). THESSALONICA AND BERÆA. (*Extended Alternation.*)

T | X | p | 1. Thessalonica. Synagogue.
q | 2, 3. Reasoning from the Scriptures.
r | 4. Believers.
s | 5-9. Persecution.
X | *p* | 10. Beræa. Synagogue.
q | 11. Searching the Scriptures.
r | 12. Believers.
s | 13, 14. Persecution.

17. 1 passed through. Gr. *diodeuō*. Only here and Luke 8. 1. A medical word.
Amphipolis. About thirty-three miles south-west of Philippi.
Apollonia. Thirty miles further, about midway between Amphipolis and Thessalonica.
to. Gr. *eis*. Ap. 104. vi.
Thessalonica. Now *Salonica* or *Saloniki*. Rose to importance in the time of Cassander, who rebuilt it and called it after his wife. Has been an important city in the past, and also in recent days during the second Balkan war (1913), and seems destined to play an important part in the immediate future.
synagogue. Ap. 120. I.
2 Paul, &c. Lit. according to (Gr. *kata*. Ap. 104. x. 2.) that which was customary (Gr. *ethō*) with Paul, he. This verb *ethō* occ. only here, Matt. 27. 15. Mark 10. 1. Luke 4. 16.
unto. Gr. *pros*. Ap. 104. xv. 3.
three, &c. On (Gr. *epi*. Ap. 104. ix. 3) three sabbath days.
reasoned. Gr. *dialegomai*. Second occ. First, Mark 9. 34. Occ. ten times in Acts. **out of** = from. Gr. *apo*. Ap. 104. iv. **3 Opening.** See note on 16. 14. **alleging.** Lit. setting before them. Gr. *paratithēmi*. See 14. 23; 16. 34; 20. 32. Matt. 13. 24. Mark 8. 6, 7. 1 Cor. 10. 27. **Christ must needs, &c.** Lit. it was necessary that the Messiah (Ap. 98. IX) should suffer and rise. **risen.** Gr. *anistēmi*. Ap. 178. I. 1. **from the dead.** Gr. *ek nekrōn*. Ap. 139. 3. **this, &c.** = this is the Christ, Jesus, Whom I proclaim. **Jesus.** Ap. 98. X. **preach.** Gr. *katangellō*. Ap. 121. 5. **unto** = to. **4 some** = certain. Gr. *tis*. Ap. 123. 3. **of** = out of. Gr. *ek*. Ap. 104. vii. **believed** = were persuaded. Gr. *peithō*. Ap. 150. I. 2. I. e. were convinced, not by persuasive words of Paul's (1 Cor. 2. 4), but by the opening and expounding of the Scriptures. Hence the Thessalonians became a type of all true believers (see 1 Thess. 1. 7; 2. 13). This and *vv.* 11, 12 beautifully illustrate Rom. 10. 17. **consorted with** = cast in their lot with. Gr. *prosklēroomai*. Only here. **devout.** Gr. *sebomai*. Ap. 137. 2. Same as "worshipping" or "religious". Cp. 13. 43, 50; 16. 14; 18. 7. **multitude.** Gr. *plēthos*. See note on 2. 6. **chief** = first. Cp. 13. 50. I. e. women of the best families. **not.** Gr. *ou*. Ap. 105. I. **5 the Jews, &c.** = the unbelieving (Gr. *apeitheō*, as in 14. 2) Jews. **moved with envy** = filled with jealousy. Gr. *zēloō*, as in 7. 9. **took unto them.** Gr. *proslambanō*. See 18. 26; 27. 33, 34, 36. Matt. 16. 22. Mark 8. 32. In 28. 2 and onward it is transl. "receive". **certain.** Same as "some" (*v.* 4). **lewd** = evil. Gr. *ponēros*. Ap. 128. III. 1. Lewd is from A.S. *læwed*, lay. **fellows** = men. Gr. *anēr*. Ap. 123. 2. **of the baser sort.** Lit. belonging to the market. Gr. *agoraios*. Only here and 19. 38. These were idlers, ready for mischief, as we should say "rowdies". **gathered a company.** Gr. *ochlopoieō*, to make a crowd. Only here. **set . . . on an uproar** = were setting, &c. Gr. *thorubeomai*. Occ. here, 20. 10. Matt. 9. 23. Mark 5. 39. Cp. "uproar" (20. 1). **all.** Omit. **assaulted . . . and.** Having attacked. **sought** = were seeking. **them,** i. e. Paul and Silas, who were staying with Jason (*v.* 7). **people.** Gr. *dēmos*. See note on 12. 22. Either the mob or the popular assembly, for Thessalonica was a free city. **6 when, &c.** = not (Gr. *mē*. Ap. 105. II) having found them. **drew** = were dragging. Gr. *surō*. See note on John 21. 8. **brethren.** The believers of *v.* 4. **unto** = before. Gr. *epi*. Ap. 104. ix. 3. **rulers of the city.** Gr. *politarchēs*, compound of *politēs*, citizen, and *archō*, to rule. Only here and *v.* 8. The noun or the corresponding verb is found in many inscriptions in Macedonia, five of them in Thessalonica. One on an arch spanning a street to-day, where seven politarchs are recorded, and amongst them Sosipater, Secundus, and Gaius, names identical with those of Paul's friends (19. 29; 20. 4). **turned . . . upside down.** Gr. *anastatoō*. Only here, 21. 38. Gal. 5. 12. Cp. *anastasis*. Ap. 178. II. 1. **world.** Gr. *oikoumenē*. Ap. 129. 3.

7 Whom Jason hath °received: and these all
°do °contrary to the °decrees of Cæsar, saying that there is °another °king, *one* [3] Jesus."
8 And they °troubled the °people and the
[6] rulers of the city, when they heard these
things.
9 And when they had taken °security °of
Jason, and of °the other, they °let them go.

X p 10 And the brethren °immediately °sent away
Paul and Silas °by night °unto °Berea: who
coming *thither* °went °into the [1] synagogue of
the Jews.

q 11 These were more °noble than those °in
Thessalonica, in that they received the °word
°with all °readiness of mind, and °searched
the scriptures °daily, °whether °those things
were so.

r 12 Therefore many [4] of them °believed; also
of °honourable women which were Greeks,
and of °men, [4] not a few.

s 13 But when the Jews °of Thessalonica °had
knowledge that the [11] word of °God was
°preached °of Paul °at Berea, they came
thither also, °and stirred up the [8] people.
14 And then [10] immediately the brethren °sent
away Paul to go °as it were °to the sea: but
Silas and Timotheus °abode there still.

S t 15 And they that °conducted Paul brought
him °unto Athens: and °receiving a commandment [2] unto Silas and Timotheus °for to come
°to him °with all speed, they °departed.
16 Now while Paul °waited for them [13] at
Athens, his °spirit was °stirred [11] in him,
°when he saw the city °wholly given to
idolatry.

u 17 Therefore °disputed he [11] in the [1] synagogue
with the Jews, and with the [4] devout persons,
and [11] in the market [11] daily °with them that
°met with him.

v 18 Then [5] certain °philosophers of the °Epi-
cureans, and of the °Stoicks, °encountered

7 received, i. e. as guests. Gr. *hupodechomai*. Here, Luke 10. 38; 19. 6. Jas. 2. 25. A medical word.
do = practise. Gr. *prattō*.
contrary to. Gr. *apenanti*. See 3. 16. Matt. 21. 2.
decrees. Gr. *dogma*. See note on 16. 4.
another. Gr. *heteros*. Ap. 124. 2.
king. The same sinister attempt to raise the charge of high treason, as in John 18. 36, 37; 19. 12. Paul, in proclaiming the Messiah, must have spoken of His reign.
8 troubled. Gr. *tarassō*. See note on John 5. 4.
people = crowd. Gr. *ochlos*.
9 security. Gr. *to hikanon*, that which is sufficient, i. e., "substantial bail".
of = from. Gr. *para*. Ap. 104. xii. 1.
the other = the rest (pl.). Ap. 124. 3.
let them go = released them, as in 16. 35.
10 immediately. Gr. *eutheōs*.
sent away. Gr. *ekpempō*. Ap. 174. 6. Only here and 13. 4.
by night = through (Gr. *dia*. Ap. 104. v. 1) the night.
unto. Gr. *eis*. Ap. 104. vi.
Berea. About thirty miles to the W. Now Verria.
went. Gr *apeimi*. Only here. They were not deterred by their treatment at Thessalonica.
into. Gr. *eis* as above.
11 noble. Gr. *eugenēs* = well born. Occ. here, Luke 19. 12. 1 Cor. 1. 26. Hence they were more courteous.
in. Gr. *en*. Ap. 104. viii.
word. Gr. *logos*. Ap. 121. 10.
with. Gr. *meta*. Ap. 104. xi. 1.
readiness of mind. Gr. *prothumia*. Only here, 2 Cor. 8. 11, 12, 19; 9. 2.
searched = examined. Gr. *anakrinō*. Ap. 122. 2. Not the same word as in John 5. 39.
daily. See 16. 5.
whether = if. Ap. 118. 2. b.
those = these.
12 believed. Ap. 150. I. 1. i.
honourable. Gr. *euschēmōn*. See note on 13. 50. Mark 15. 43.
men. Gr. *anēr*. Ap. 123. 2.
13 of = from. Gr. *apo*. Ap. 104. iv.
had knowledge = got to know. Gr. *ginōskō*. Ap. 132. I. ii.
God. Ap. 98. I. i. 1.
preached. Gr. *katangellō*. Ap. 121. 5.
of. Gr. *hupo*. Ap. 104. xviii. 1.
at = in. Gr. *en*.
and stirred up = stirring up. Gr. *saleuō*. Cp. 4. 31; 16. 26. The texts add "and troubling" as in *v.* 8.
14 sent away. Gr. *exapostellō*. Ap. 174. 2.
as it were. Gr. *hōs*, but the texts read *heōs*, as far as.
to. Gr. *epi*. Ap. 104. ix. 3.
abode. Gr. *hupomenō*. Gen. transl. "endure".

17. 15—18. 18—(*S*, p. 1615). ATHENS AND CORINTH. (*Extended Alternation.*)

S t | 17. 15, 16. Athens.
u | 17. 17. Reasoning.
v | 17. 18-21. Philosophers. Questioning.
w | 17. 22-31. Paul's defence.
x | 17. 32-34. Results.
t | 18. 1-3. Corinth.
u | 18. 4, 5. Reasoning and testifying.
v | 18. 6-. Jews. Opposing.
w | 18. -6. Paul's repudiation.
x | 18. 7-18-. Results.

15 conducted. Gr. *kathistēmi*. Only here in this sense. Generally transl. "make", "appoint". Here the brethren made all the arrangements. **unto** = as far as. Gr. *heōs*. **receiving** = having received. **for to** = in order that (Gr. *hina*) they should. **to.** Gr. *pros*. Ap. 104. xv. 3. **with all speed** = as quickly as possible. Gr. *hōs tachista*. Only here. **departed.** Gr. *exeimi*. See 13. 42. **16 waited.** Gr. *ekdechomai*. Here, John 5. 3. 1 Cor. 11. 33; 16. 11. Heb. 10. 13; 11. 10. Jas. 5. 7. 1 Pet. 3. 20. **spirit.** Ap. 101. II. 8. **stirred.** Gr. *paroxunomai*. Only here and 1 Cor. 13. 5. A medical word. Cp. Acts 15. 39. **when he saw** = beholding. Gr. *theōreō*. Ap. 133. I. 11. **wholly, &c.** = full of idols. Gr. *kateidōlos*. Only here. **17 disputed** = was reasoning. Gr. *dialegomai*, as in *v.* 2. **with.** Gr. *pros*. Ap. 104. xv. 3. **met with.** Gr. *paratunchanō*. Only here. **18 philosophers, &c.** = of the Epicurean and Stoic philosophers. Only occ. of *philosophos*. The Epicureans were followers of Epicurus (342-279 B. C.) who held that pleasure was the highest good, while the Stoics were disciples of Zeno (about 270 B. C.) who taught that the supreme good was virtue, and man should be free from passion and moved by neither joy nor grief, pleasure nor pain. They were Fatalists and Pantheists. The name came from the porch (Gr. *stoa*) where they met. **encountered.** Gr. *sumballō*. See note on 4. 15.

him. And [4]some said, "What °will this
°babbler say?" °other some, "He seemeth to
be °a setter forth of °strange °gods:" because
he °preached [3]unto them [3]Jesus, and the
°resurrection.
19 And they °took him, and brought him
[6]unto °Areopagus, saying, °"May we °know
what this °new doctrine, °whereof thou speakest, *is*?
20 For thou bringest [5]certain °strange things
[1]to our °ears: we °would [19]know therefore what
these things °mean."
21 (For all the Athenians and °strangers
which °were there °spent their time °in °no-
thing else, but either to tell, or to hear [4]some
°new thing.)

w 22 Then Paul stood [11]in the midst of °Mars'
hill, and said, °"*Ye* men of Athens, I °perceive
that °in all things ye are °too superstitious.
23 For as I passed by, and °beheld your °de-
votions, I found an °altar °with this inscription,
TO THE °UNKNOWN [13]GOD. °Whom therefore ye °ignorantly °worship, °Him °declare
I [3]unto you.
24 [13]God That made the °world and all
things °therein, °seeing that He is °Lord of
°heaven and °earth, °dwelleth [4]not [11]in °temples
°made with hands;
25 Neither is °worshipped °with °men's hands,
°as though He needed °any thing, °seeing He
giveth to all °life, and °breath, and all things;
26 And hath made [4]of °one blood °all nations
of [25]men for to [24]dwell °on all the face of the
[24]earth, and hath °determined the times °be-
fore appointed, and the °bounds of their
°habitation;
27 °That they should seek °the Lord, °if
°haply they might °feel after Him, and find
Him, though He °be [4]not far °from °every one
of us:
28 For °in Him we live, and move, and

will, &c. = would this babbler wish (Gr. *thelō*. Ap. 102. 1.) to say.

babbler. Gr. *spermologos* = seed-picker. Only here. Used of birds, and so applied to men who gathered scraps of information from others.

other some = and some.

a setter forth = a proclaimer. Gr. *katangeleus*. Cp. Ap. 121. 5. Only here. Cp. the verb in *vv.* 3, 13, 23.

strange = foreign. Gr. *xenos*. An adj., but generally transl. stranger, ("man" understood), as in *v.* 21.

gods = demons. Gr. *daimonion*. Occ. sixty times, fifty-two times in the Gospels. Only here in Acts. Transl. "devils" in A.V. and R.V. (marg. demons) save here.

preached. Gr. *euangelizō*. Ap. 121. 4.

resurrection. Gr. *anastasis*. Ap. 178. II. 1. They were accustomed to personify abstract ideas, as victory, pity, &c., and they may have thought that Jesus and the resurrection were two new divinities. One charge against Socrates was that of introducing new divinities.

19 took. Gr. *epilambanomai*. See note on 9. 27; 23. 19.

Areopagus = the hill of Mars, or the Martian hill. Gr. *Areios pagos*. Cp. *v.* 22. Where the great council of the Athenians was held.

May = Can.

know. Gr. *ginōskō*, as in *v.* 13.

new. Gr. *kainos*. See note on Matt. 9. 17.

whereof, &c. = which is spoken (Gr. *laleō*. Ap. 121. 7) by (Gr. *hupo*. Ap. 104. xviii. 1) thee.

20 strange. Gr. *xenizō*, to treat as *xenos* (*v.* 18), hence to lodge. See 10. 6, 18, 23, 32. 1 Pet. 4. 4, 12.

ears. Gr. *akoē*, hearing.

would = wish to. Gr. *boulomai*. Ap. 102. 3.

mean. Lit. wish (Gr. *thelō*. Ap. 102. 1) to be.

21 strangers. See *vv.* 18, 20.

were there = were dwelling or sojourning. Gr. *epidēmeō*. Only here and 2. 10.

spent their time. Gr. *eukaireō*, to have leisure. Only here, Mark 6. 31. 1 Cor. 16. 12.

in = for. Gr. *eis*. Ap. 104. vi.

nothing else = no other thing. Gr. *oudeis heteros* (Ap. 124. 2).

new thing = newer thing, i. e. the latest idea. Gr. *kainoteros*. Comp. of *kainos* (*v.* 19). Only here.

22 Mars' hill. See *v.* 19.

Ye men of Athens. Gr. *andres Athēnaioi*. See note on 1. 11.

perceive. Same as "saw", *v.* 16. in = according to. Gr. *kata*. Ap. 104. x. 2. too superstitious = more religiously disposed than others. Gr. *deisidaimonesteros*, comparative of *deisidaimōn*, compound of *deidō* (to fear) and *daimōn*. Only here. The noun occ. in 25. 19. The A.V. rendering is too rude, and Paul had too much tact to begin by offending his audience. Fig. *Protherapeia*. Ap. 6. **23** beheld. Gr. *anatheōreō*. Ap. 133. II. 3. devotions = the objects of your worship. Gr. *sebasma*. Only here and 2 Thess. 2. 4. Cp. *sebomai*. Ap. 137. 2. altar. Gr. *bōmos*. Only here. Add "also". with this, &c. = on (Gr. *en*) which had been inscribed. Gr. *epigraphō*. Only here, Mark 15. 26. Heb. 8. 10; 10. 16. Rev. 21. 12. UNKNOWN. Gr. *agnōstos*. Only here. For type see Ap. 48. Public or private calamities would suggest that some god whom they could not identify must be propitiated. Whom. The texts read "what". ignorantly = being ignorant. Gr. *agnoeō*. worship. Gr. *eusebeō*. Ap. 137. 5. Him = This. declare. Same as "preach" (*vv.* 3, 13). Note Paul's skilful use of local circumstances. **24** world. Gr. *kosmos*. Ap. 129. 1. therein = in (Gr. *en*) it. seeing that He is = This One being essentially (Gr. *huparchō*. See note on Luke 9. 48). Lord. Ap. 98. VI. i. *β*. 1. B. b. heaven. No art. See note on Matt. 6. 9, 10. earth. Gr. *gē*. Ap. 129. 4. dwelleth. See note on 2. 5. temples = shrines. Gr. *naos*. See note on Matt. 23. 16. made with hands. See note on 7. 48. This is a direct quotation from Stephen's speech. **25** worshipped. Gr. *therapeuō*. Ap. 137. 6. with = by. Gr. *hupo*. Ap. 104. xviii. 1. men's. Gr. *anthrōpos*. Ap. 123. 1. as though He needed = as needing. Gr. *prosdeomai*. Only here. any thing = something. Gr. *tis*, as *vv.* 4, 5. seeing He giveth = Himself giving. life. Gr. *zōē*. Ap. 170. 1. breath. Gr. *pnoē*. See note on 2. 2. **26** one blood. The texts omit "blood". The "one" here means either Adam, or the dust of which he was formed. One (Gr. *heis*) is sometimes used for a certain one (Gr. *tis*). See Matt. 8. 19; 16. 14. Mark 15. 36. Rev. 18. 21; 19. 17. all nations = every nation (Gr. *ethnos*). on. Gr. *epi*. Ap. 104. ix. 3. determined. Gr. *horizō*. See note on 2. 23. before appointed. Gr. *protassō*. Only here. But the texts read *prostassō*. Cp. 1. 7 and see Ap. 195. bounds. Gr. *horothesia*. Only here. habitation. Gr. *katoikia*. Only here. Cp. "dwellers", 2. 5. **27** That they should seek = To seek. the Lord. Ap. 98. VI. i. *β*. 1. A. b. The texts read "God". if. Ap. 118. 2. b. haply = at least. feel after = grope for. Gr. *psēlaphaō*. Only here, Luke 24. 39. Heb. 12. 18. 1 John 1. 1. be. Gr. *huparchō*. See note on Luke 9. 48. Cp. "seeing" &c., *v.* 24. from. Gr. *apo*. Ap. 104. iv. every = each. Fig. *Association*. Ap. 6. **28** in = by. Gr. *en*. Ap. 104. viii.

°have our being; as [5]certain also of °your
own poets have said, 'For we are °also His
°offspring.'
29 °Forasmuch then as we are the [28]offspring
of [13]God, we ought [4]not to °think that °the
Godhead is like [3]unto gold, or silver, or stone,
°graven °by °art and [25]man's °device.
30 °And the times of this ignorance [13]God
°winked at; but °now °commandeth all [25]men
every where to °repent:
31 Because He °hath appointed a day, [11]in
the which He °will °judge the [6]world [11]in
°righteousness °by °*that* [12]Man Whom He
°hath °ordained; °*whereof* He hath given
°assurance [3]unto all *men*, °in that He hath
[3]raised Him [3]from the dead."

x 32 °And when they heard of the [18]resurrec-
tion °of the dead, some °mocked: and others
said, "We will hear thee again °of this *matter*."
33 So Paul departed °from among them.
34 °Howbeit [5]certain [12]men °clave [3]unto him,
and [12]believed: °among the which *was* °Diony-
sius the °Areopagite, and a woman °named
Damaris, and °others °with them.

t **18** °After these things °Paul °departed
°from Athens, and came °to °Corinth;
2 And °found a °certain Jew °named °Aquila,
°born in Pontus, °lately come °from Italy,
°with his wife °Priscilla; (°because that
°Claudius had commanded all Jews to [1]depart
°from Rome:) and came °unto them.
3 And [2]because he was °of the same craft, he
°abode °with them, and °wrought: for °by
their occupation they were °tentmakers.

have our being = are.

your own poets = the poets with (Gr. *kata*. Ap. 104. x. 2) you. He refers to Aratus, who was a native of Cilicia (abt. 270 B.C.). Cleanthes (abt. 300 B.C.) has almost the same words. Ap. 107. II. 5.

also His offspring = His offspring also.

offspring. Gr. *genos*. Transl. kind, race, nation, kindred, &c. Offspring only here, *v.* 29, and Rev. 22. 16. Adam was by creation son of God. Gen. 1. 27; 2. 7. See Ap. 99 and Luke 3. 38. All mankind are descended from Adam, and in that sense are the posterity or offspring of God. That every child born into the world "comes fresh and fair from the hands of its Maker", and is therefore the direct offspring of God, is emphatically contradicted by John 1. 13, where the One begotten of God is set in opposition to the rest of mankind who are begotten of the flesh and will of man.

29 Forasmuch . . . are = Being then. Gr. *huparchō*, as in *vv.* 24, 27.

think = reckon. Gr. *nomizō*. See note on 14. 19.

the Godhead. Gr. *to theion*. Ap. 98. I. ii. 3.

graven = an engraving, or sculpture. Gr. *charagma*. Only here and eight times in Rev. of the mark of the beast. Cp. *charaktēr*. Heb. 1. 3.

by = of.

art. Gr. *technē*. Only here, 18. 3. Rev. 18. 22.

device = thought. Gr. *enthumēsis*. Only here, Matt. 9. 4; 12. 25. Heb. 4. 12. Cp. 10. 19.

30 And, &c. Lit. The times indeed therefore of ignorance.

winked at; but = having overlooked. Gr. *hupereidon*. Only here.

now. Emphatic. See note on 4. 29.

commandeth. Gr. *parangellō*. See note on 1. 4.

repent. Ap. 111. I. 1. Cp. 2 Cor. 5. 19.

31 hath. Omit.

will = is about to.

judge. Gr. *krinō*. Ap. 122. 1.

righteousness. Gr. *dikaiosunē*. Ap. 191. 3.

by. Gr. *en*. Ap. 104. viii. ***that*** = a.

ordained. Same as "determined", *v.* 26.

***whereof*, &c.** = having afforded. **assurance.** Gr. *pistis*. Ap. 150. II. 1. **in that He hath** = having. **32 And, &c.** = But having heard. **of the dead.** Gr. *nekrōn*. Ap. 139. 2. **mocked** = were mocking. Gr. *chleuazō*. See note on 2. 13. To Epicureans and Stoics alike a resurrection of dead persons was a madman's dream. Only those whose "hearts the Lord opened" (*v.* 34) could receive it. Cp. 16. 14. **of** = concerning. Gr. *peri*. Ap. 104. xiii. 1. **33 from among them** = out of (Gr. *ek* Ap. 104. vii) the midst of them. **34 Howbeit** = But. **clave . . . and** = having joined themselves. Gr. *kollaō*. See note on 5. 13. **among.** Gr. *en*. Ap. 104. viii. 2. **Dionysius** = Dionysius also. **Areopagite.** A member of the Athenian assembly. **named** = by name. **others.** Gr. *heteros*, as in *vv.* 7, 21. **with.** Gr. *sun*. Ap. 104. xvi.

18. 1 After. Gr. *meta*. Ap. 104. xi. 2. **Paul.** Texts read "he". **departed.** See 1. 4. **from.** Gr. *ek*. Ap. 104. vii. **to.** Gr. *eis*. Ap. 104. vi. Probably in spring of A.D. 52. See Ap. 180. **Corinth.** At this time the political capital of Greece and seat of the Roman proconsul (*v.* 12), as Athens was its literary centre. Its situation on an isthmus, with harbours on two seas, Lechaeum and Cenchreae, made it of great commercial importance, goods being transhipped and carried across the isthmus from one harbour to another, as was the case at Suez before the canal was made. Strabo says it was the chief emporium between Asia and Italy. The worship of Aphrodite (Lat. Venus), the same as Ashtoreth (Judges 2. 13), was carried on here, with all the Oriental licentiousness, probably introduced by the Phœnicians (1 Kings 11. 33). Attached to the temple of Venus were one thousand courtesans. The word *korinthiazomai*, to act the Corinthian, was infamous in classical literature. These facts underlie and explain much in the Epistles to the Corinthians, e.g. 1 Cor. 5. 6. 7. 9. 27; as also the fact that the renowned Isthmian games were held in the Stadium attached to the temple of Poseidon (Neptune), a short distance from the city. These games, as well as the temples of Athens, Corinth, and elsewhere, supplied Paul with many of the metaphors with which his writings abound. **2 found** = having found. **certain.** Gr. *tis*. Ap. 123. 3. **named** = by name. **Aquila.** See Rom. 16. 3. 1 Cor. 16. 19. 2 Tim. 4. 19. **born, &c.** = a Pontian by race. **lately.** Gr. *prosphatos*. Only here. The adj. *prosphatos*, found in Heb. 10. 20, was common in medical writers. **from.** Gr. *apo*. Ap. 104. iv. **with.** Read "and". **Priscilla.** Aquila is never mentioned apart from his wife. Both these are Latin names. Their Jewish names are not given. **because.** Gr. *dia*. Ap. 104. v. 2. **Claudius.** This edict was issued early in A.D. 52 in consequence either of disturbances in Rome, caused by Jews, or of Judæa itself being almost in a state of rebellion. **unto** = to. **3 of the same craft.** Gr. *homotechnos*. Only here. A word applied by physicians to one another. The medical profession was called the healing art (Gr. *technē*). **abode** = was abiding. See 16. 15. **with.** Gr. *para*. Ap. 104. xii. 2. **wrought** = was working. Gr. *ergazomai*. **by their occupation** = as to their craft. Gr. *technē*. **tentmakers.** Gr. *skēnopoios*. Only here. They wove the black cloth of goat's or camel's hair of which tents were made. Every Jewish boy was taught some handicraft. Cp. 1 Cor. 4. 12. 1 Thess. 2. 9; 4. 11. 2 Thess. 3. 8. The Rabbis said, "Whoever does not teach his son a trade is as if he brought him up to be a robber."

u 4 And he °reasoned °in the °synagogue °every sabbath, and °persuaded °the Jews and °the °Greeks.

5 °And when Silas and Timotheus °were come [2]from Macedonia, Paul °was pressed in the °spirit, °and testified to the Jews *that* °Jesus °*was* °Christ.

v 6 And when they °opposed themselves, and blasphemed,

w he °shook *his* °raiment, and said °unto them, "Your blood *be* °upon °your own heads; I *am* °clean: [2]from °henceforth I will go °unto the °Gentiles."

x 7 And he departed thence, and entered °into a [2]certain *man's* house, [2]named °Justus, *one* that °worshipped °God, whose house °joined hard to the [4]synagogue.

8 And °Crispus, the °chief ruler of the synagogue, °believed on °the Lord °with all his house; and many of the Corinthians hearing °believed, and were °baptized.

9 Then spake [8]the Lord to Paul [4]in the night °by a °vision, "Be °not afraid, but °speak, and °hold °not thy peace:

10 For I am °with thee, and °no man shall °set on thee to °hurt thee: for I have much °people [4]in this city."

11 And he °continued *there* °a year and six months, teaching the °word of [7]God °among them.

12 [5]And °when Gallio °was the deputy of Achaia, the Jews °made insurrection °with one accord against Paul, and brought him °to the °judgment seat,

13 Saying, °"This *fellow* °persuadeth °men to [7]worship [7]God °contrary to the law."

14 And when Paul was °now about to °open *his* mouth, Gallio said [6]unto the Jews, °"If it were °a matter of wrong or °wicked °lewdness, O *ye* Jews, °reason would °that I should bear with you:

15 But [14]if it be °a question °of °words and names, and *of* °your law, °look ye *to it;* °for I °will be no judge of °such *matters.*"

4 reasoned. Gr. *dialegomai.* See 17. 2, 17.
in. Gr. *en.* Ap. 104. viii.
synagogue. Ap. 120. I. In the museum at Corinth is a fragment of a stone with the inscription, *(suna)gōgē hebr(aiōn)* = synagogue of the Hebrews. The letters in brackets are missing. Its date is said to be between 100 B. C. and A. D. 200.
every sabbath = sabbath by sabbath. Cp. 15. 21.
persuaded = was persuading, or sought to persuade. Ap. 150. I. 2.
the. Omit.
Greeks. Gr. *Hellēn.* See 14. 1.
5 And = Now.
were come = came down.
was pressed, &c. Read, was engrossed with or by (Gr. *en*) the word, i. e. his testimony.
spirit. All the texts read "word" (Gr. *logos.* Ap. 121. 10).
and testified = earnestly testifying. Gr. *diamarturomai.* See note on 2. 40.
Jesus. Ap. 98. X. ***was*** = is.
Christ = the Messiah. Ap. 98. XI. Cp. 1 Cor. 1. 23. This was to the Jews a horrible "scandal".
6 opposed themselves. Gr. *antitassomai,* to set in battle array. Elsewhere transl. "resist". Rom. 13. 2. Jas. 4. 6; 5. 6. 1 Pet. 5. 5.
shook. Gr. *ektinassō.* See note on 13. 51.
raiment = outer garments. Gr. *himation.* Cp. 12. 8.
unto. Gr. *pros.* Ap. 104. xv. 3.
upon. Gr. *epi.* Ap. 104. ix. 3.
your own heads. Fig. *Synecdochē.* Ap. 6. "Head" put for man himself.
clean = pure (Gr. *katharos*), i. e. free from responsibility. Cp. 20. 26. Ezek. 3. 17–21.
henceforth = now. **unto.** Gr. *eis.* Ap. 104. vi.
Gentiles. Gr. *ethnos.* I. e. in Corinth. See next verse. He still continued to go first to the synagogues in other places. See 19. 8 and Ap. 181. 6.
7 into. Gr. *eis.* Ap. 104. vi.
Justus. Some texts read Titus, or Titius, Justus.
worshipped. Gr. *sebomai.* Ap. 137. 2.
God. Ap. 98. I. i. 1.
joined hard. Gr. *sunomoreō.* Only here.
8 Crispus. See 1 Cor. 1. 14.
chief, &c. Gr. *archisunagōgos.* Here and *v.* 17 transl. chief ruler, &c. In all other places, ruler, &c. See note on 13. 15.
believed on. Ap. 150. I. 1. ii.
the Lord. Ap. 98. VI. i. β. 2. A.
with. Gr. *sun.* Ap. 104. xvi.
believed. Ap. 150. I. 1. i.
baptized. Ap. 115. I. i. and 185.

9 by. Gr. *dia.* Ap. 104. v. 1. **vision.** Gr. *horama.* See note on 7. 31. **not.** Gr. *mē.* Ap. 105. II. **speak.** Gr. *laleō.* Ap. 121. 7. **hold . . . thy peace** = be . . . silent. Gr. *siōpaō.* Only here in Acts, ten times in the Gospels. This is the Fig. *Pleonasm.* Ap. 6. **10 with.** Gr. *meta.* Ap. 104. xi. 1. **no man** = no one. **set on thee** = lay (hands) on thee. **hurt thee** = do thee evil. Gr. *kakoō.* See note on 7. 6. **people.** Gr. *laos.* Here used generally. **11 continued.** Lit. "sat". Fig. *Synecdochē* (of species). "Sit" used of a permanent condition. **a year and six months.** In A. D. 52–53. During this period Paul wrote 1 Thess. (A. D. 52) and 2 Thess. (A. D. 53), and probably Hebrews. See introductory notes to these epistles and Ap. 180, 193. **word.** Gr. *logos.* Ap. 121. 10. **among.** Gr. *en.* Ap. 104. viii. 2. **12 when, &c.** Lit. Gallio being proconsul. Another instance of Luke's accuracy. Achaia was a senatorial province under Augustus, imperial under Tiberius, but after A. D. 44 restored by Claudius to the senate and therefore governed by a proconsul. **Gallio.** Brother of Seneca, who was Nero's tutor. Said to be an amiable and gracious man. **was the deputy.** Gr. *anthupateuō.* Lit. holding the office of proconsul (*anthupatos*). Only here. Some of the texts read *anthupatou ontos,* being proconsul. Cp. 13. 7; 19. 38. **made insurrection . . . against** = rose up against. Gr. *katephistēmi.* Only here. The verb *ephistēmi* occ. 17. 5, "assault". **with one accord.** Gr. *homothumadon.* See note on 1. 14. **to.** Gr. *epi.* Ap. 104. ix. 3. **judgment seat.** Gr. *bēma.* See note on John 19. 13. In the Athenian courts there were two other platforms, for the accuser and the accused. **13 This** *fellow* = This one. **persuadeth.** Gr. *anapeithō.* Strong form of *peithō* (Ap. 150. I. 2). Only here. **men.** Gr. *anthrōpos.* Ap. 123. 1. **contrary to** = against. Gr. *para.* Ap. 104. xii. 3. **14 now.** Omit. **open his mouth.** Fig. *Idiōma.* Ap. 6. A Hebraism. **If** = If indeed. Gr. *ei.* Ap. 118. 2. a. **a matter of wrong** = an injustice. Gr. *adikēma.* Ap. 128. VII. 2. **wicked.** Gr. *ponēros.* Ap. 128. III. 1. **lewdness** = recklessness. Gr. *radiourgēma.* Only here. Cp. 13. 10. **reason would** = according to (Gr. *kata.* Ap. 104. x. 2) reason (Gr. *logos.* Ap. 121. 10). **that I should** = I would. **15 a question.** Gr. *zētēma.* See note on 15. 2. The texts read "questions". **of.** Gr. *peri.* Ap. 104. xiii. 1. **words** = a word. Gr. *logos.* Ap. 121. 10. **your law** = the law (that is) with (Gr. *kata.* Ap. 104. x. 2) you. **look, &c.** = look ye yourselves to it. Gr. *opsomai.* Ap. 133. I. 8 (a). **for.** Omit. **will be no judge** = will (Gr. *boulomai.* Ap. 102. 3) not (Gr. *ou.* Ap. 105. I.) be a judge (Gr. *kritēs.* Cp. Ap. 122. 1. and 177. 6, 7, 8). **such** = these.

16 And he °drave them [2] from the [12] judgment seat.
17 Then °all the Greeks took °Sosthenes, the [8] chief ruler of the synagogue, and °beat *him* before the [12] judgment seat. And °Gallio cared for none of those things.
18 And Paul *after this* °tarried *there* yet °a good while,
R Y y and then °took his leave of the brethren, °and sailed thence [7] into Syria, and [8] with him Priscilla and Aquila; having °shorn *his* head [4] in °Cenchrea: for he had a °vow.
z 19 And °he °came [1] to Ephesus, and left them there: but he himself entered [7] into the [4] synagogue, and [4] reasoned with the Jews.
20 When they °desired *him* to °tarry °longer time with them, he °consented °not;
y 21 But °bade them farewell, saying, °"I must by all means keep this feast that cometh in Jerusalem: but I will °return again [6] unto you, °if [7] God will." And he °sailed [2] from Ephesus.
z 22 And °when he had landed °at Cæsarea, and °gone up, and saluted the °church, he went down [1] to Antioch.
23 And °after he had spent °some time *there*, he departed, and went over *all* the °country of Galatia and Phrygia °in order, °strengthening all the disciples.
Z A[1] a 24 [5] And a [2] certain Jew [2] named °Apollos, [2] born at Alexandria, an °eloquent °man, *and* °mighty [4] in the scriptures, [19] came [1] to Ephesus.
b 25 °This man was °instructed °in °the way of [8] the Lord; and being °fervent in the °spirit, he [9] spake and taught °diligently the things °of °the Lord, °knowing only the °baptism of John.

16 drave. Gr. *apelaunō.* Only here. They probably persisted in their charges and so the lictors were ordered to clear the court.
17 all the Greeks. The texts read, "they all". **Sosthenes.** He had apparently succeeded Crispus (*v.* 8). Cp. 1 Cor. 1. 1.
beat. The crowd, to whom the Jews were obnoxious, would be glad to second the work of the lictors.
Gallio, &c. Lit. none (*ouden*) of these things was a concern to Gallio. He refused to interfere in behalf of such troublesome litigants.
18 tarried = stayed on. Gr. *prosmenō.* See note on 11. 23.
a good while = many days.

18. -18—19. 12 (*R*, p. 1615). **EPHESUS, AND EXTENDED TOUR IN ASIA MINOR.** (*Introversion.*)

R | Y | 18. -18-23. Paul. Ministry at Ephesus and elsewhere.
 | Z | 18. 24-28. Apollos. Ministry at Ephesus and in Achaia.
 | *Y* | 19. 1-12. Paul. Ministry at Ephesus.

18. -18-23 (Y, above). **PAUL. MINISTRY AT EPHESUS, &c.** (*Alternation.*)

Y | y | -18. Leaves Corinth (*apotassō*).
 | z | 19, 20. Ministry at Ephesus.
 | *y* | 21. Leaves Ephesus (*apotassō*).
 | *z* | 22, 23. Ministry at Cæsarea, &c.

took his leave = having taken leave. Gr. *apotassō*, to set apart. Mid. withdraw. In N.T. always in Mid. Voice. Here, *v.* 21. Mark 6. 46. Luke 9. 61; 14. 33. 2 Cor. 2. 13.
and sailed = sailed away. See note on 15. 39.
shorn. Gr. *keirō.* Occ. elsewhere, 8. 32, and 1 Cor. 11. 6. In the latter passage *keirō*, which means to "shear", and *xuraō*, which means to "shave", both occur. Cp. 21. 24.
Cenchrea. This was the port east of Corinth whence he would set sail.
vow. Gr. *euchē.* Ap. 134. II. 1. Only here, 21. 23, and Jas. 5. 15. It has been questioned whether these words refer to Paul or to Aquila. The facts point to Paul, for whichever it was, the ceremonies connected with the vow could only be completed at Jerusalem, and while Paul was hastening his journey thither (*v.* 21), Aquila appears to have remained at Ephesus (*v.* 26).
19 he. The texts read "they". **came.** Gr. *katantaō.* See note on 16. 1. **20 desired** = asked. Gr. *erōtaō.* Ap. 134. I. 3. **tarry.** Gr. *menō.* See p. 1511. **longer time** = for (Gr. *epi.* Ap. 104. ix. 3) more time. **consented.** Gr. *epineuō*, to nod towards. Only here. Used in medical works. **not.** Gr. *ou.* Ap. 105. I. **21 bade them farewell.** Gr. *apotassō*, as in *v.* 18, "took his leave." **I must . . . Jerusalem.** The texts omit this clause, but not the Syriac. **return.** Gr. *anakamptō*, bend back (my steps). Only here, Matt. 2. 12. Luke 10. 6. Heb. 11. 15. **if God will** = God being willing (Gr. *thelō.* Ap. 102. 1). **sailed.** Gr. *anagō.* See note on 13. 13. **22 when he had landed** = having come down. **at** = to. Gr. *eis.* Ap. 104. vi. **gone up**, i. e. to Jerusalem. Fig. *Ellipsis.* Ap. 6. **church.** Ap. 186. **23 after, &c.** Lit. having made. See 15. 33. **some time.** Probably three months. It was from Antioch he had gone forth on his first missionary journey; it had happier associations for him than Jerusalem, where they were "all zealous of the law" (21. 20). **country of Galatia.** Not the province, but the district. **in order.** Gr. *kathexēs.* See note on 3. 24. **strengthening.** Gr. *epistērizō.* The texts read *stērizō.* See note on 14. 22.

18. 24-28 (Z, above). **APOLLOS. MINISTRY AT EPHESUS, &c.** (*Division.*)

Z | A[1] | 24-26. Ephesus.
 | A[2] | 27, 28. Achaia.

18. 24-26 (A[1], above). **EPHESUS.** (*Alternation.*)

A[1] | a | 24. Mighty in the Scriptures.
 | b | 25. Teaching accurately.
 | *a* | 26-. Speaking boldly.
 | *b* | -26. Instructed more accurately.

24 Apollos. Shortened form of Apollonius. **eloquent.** Gr. *logios.* Only here. The word may mean either "eloquent", or "learned". The latter idea is expressed in the next phrase. **man.** Gr. *anēr.* Ap. 123. 2. **mighty.** Gr. *dunatos.* Said of Moses (7. 22). **25 This man** = This one. **instructed.** Gr. *katēcheō.* See notes on 21. 21, 24. Luke 1. 4. Rom. 2. 18. Cp. Engl. "catechise". **in** = as to. **the way.** See note on 9. 2. **fervent.** Gr. *zeō*, to boil. Only here and Rom. 12. 11. His was burning zeal. Fig. *Idiōma.* Ap. 6. **spirit.** Ap. 101. II. 8. Fervent in spirit means spiritually fervent, or exceedingly zealous. **diligently** = accurately. Gr. *akribōs.* Here Matt. 2. 8. Luke 1. 3. Eph. 5. 15. 1 Thess. 5. 2. The verb *akriboō* only in Matt. 2. 7, 16. **of** = concerning (Gr. *peri.* Ap. 104. xiii. 1). **the Lord.** The texts read "Jesus". **knowing.** Gr. *epistamai.* Ap. 132. I. v. **baptism.** Gr. *baptisma.* Ap. 115. II. i. 2.

a 26 And °he began to °speak boldly [4]in the [4]synagogue:

b whom when Aquila and Priscilla had heard, they took him unto *them*, and °expounded [2]unto him [25]the way of [7]God °more perfectly.

A² 27 And when he °was disposed to pass [7]into Achaia, the brethren wrote, °exhorting the disciples to °receive him: who, when he was come, °helped them much which had [8]believed °through °grace:

28 For he °mightily °convinced the Jews, *and that* °publickly, shewing [9]by the scriptures that [5]Jesus [5]was [5]Christ.

Y c **19** And it came to pass, that, °while Apollos was °at °Corinth, Paul having passed through the °upper °coasts came °to Ephesus:

d and finding °certain disciples,

e 2 He said °unto them, °"Have ye received °the Holy Ghost °since ye believed?" And they said °unto him, °"We have not so much as heard whether there be any Holy Ghost."

f 3 And he said °unto them, °"Unto what then were ye °baptized?" And they said, °"Unto John's °baptism."

g 4 Then said Paul, "John °verily °baptized with the [3]baptism of °repentance, saying °unto the °people, °that they should °believe °on Him Which should come °after him, that is, °on °Christ Jesus.
5 When they heard *this*, they were [3]baptized °in °the name of °the Lord °Jesus."

g 6 And when Paul had laid *his* hands upon them,

f °the Holy Ghost came °on them;

e and they °spake with tongues, and °prophesied.

d 7 And all the °men were about twelve.

c 8 And he went °into the °synagogue, and °spake boldly °for the space of °three months, °disputing and °persuading the things °concerning the °kingdom of God.
9 But when °divers were °hardened, and °believed not, °but spake evil of °that way

26 he=this one.
speak boldly. Gr. *parrhēsiazomai.* See note on 9. 27.
expounded. Gr. *ektithēmi.* Set out before him. See note on 7. 21.
more perfectly=more accurately. Comp. of *akribōs, v.* 25.
27 was disposed=wished. Gr. *boulomai.* Ap. 102. 3.
exhorting. Gr. *protrepomai.* Only here. According to the order in the Gr. this refers to Apollos, and it should read, "the brethren, having encouraged him, wrote".
receive. Gr. *apodechomai.* See note on 2. 41.
helped. Gr. *sumballō.* See note on 4. 15.
through. Gr. *dia.* Ap. 104. v. 1.
grace. Ap. 184.
28 mightily. Gr. *eutonōs.* Only here and Luke 23. 10. A medical word.
convinced=confuted. Gr. *diakatelenchomai.* Only here.
publickly. Gr. *dēmosia.* See note on 5. 18.

19. 1-12 (*Y*, p. 1627). **PAUL. MINISTRY AT EPHESUS.** (*Introversion.*)

Y c | 1-. Paul's arrival at Ephesus.
d | -1. Certain men. Their character. Disciples.
e | 2. Spiritual gifts. Their ignorance of them.
f | 3. What they had received. John's baptism.
g | 4, 5. What Paul said. Paul's description of John's action.
g | 6-. What Paul did. Luke's description. Paul's action.
f | -6-. What they now received. Spiritual gifts.
e | -6. Spiritual gifts. Their use of them.
d | 7. The men. Their number. About twelve.
c | 8-12. Paul's continuance at Ephesus.

19. 1 while . . . was. Lit. in (Gr. *en*) the being Apollos.
at=in. Gr. *en.* Ap. 104. viii.
Corinth. All the notices of Apollos are connected with Corinth, except Tit. 3. 13, when he was apparently in Crete, or expected to pass through it.
upper. Gr. *anōterikos.* Only here.
coasts=parts, i. e. the highland district, at the back of the Western Taurus range. Paul's route was probably through Derbe, Lystra, Iconium, the Phrygian lake district, and the Lydian part of the Province of Asia. It was about August—September, A. D. 54.
to. Gr. *eis.* Ap. 104. vi.
certain. Gr. *tis.* Ap. 123. 3.
2 unto. Gr. *pros.* Ap. 104. xv. 3.
Have ye received. Lit. If (Ap. 118. 2. a) ye received.

the Holy Ghost. Gr. *pneuma hagion.* No art. Ap. 101. II. 14. **since ye believed**=having believed. Ap. 150. I. 1. i. There is no note of time, or sequence, any more than in Eph. 1. 13, "after." See note there. **We have, &c.** Lit. But not even (Gr. *oude*) heard we if (Ap. 118. 2. a) holy spirit is (given). John taught the coming of the Holy Spirit (Matt. 3. 11), and Paul that no one could believe without the enabling power of the Holy Spirit. Therefore the twelve men could not have questioned the existence of the Holy Spirit, and Paul would have rebuked them if they had. The reference must have been to the promised gifts. **3 unto them.** The texts omit. **Unto.** Gr. *eis.* Ap. 104. vi. **baptized.** Ap. 115. I. iv. **baptism.** Ap. 115. II. i. 2. **4 verily**=indeed. **baptized.** Ap. 115. I. i. **repentance.** Gr. *metanoia.* Ap. 111. II. **unto**=to. **people.** Gr. *laos.* See note on 2. 47. **that**=in order that. Gr. *hina.* **believe.** Ap. 150. I. 1. v. (i). **on.** Gr. *eis.* Ap. 104. vi. **after.** Gr. *meta.* Ap. 104. xi. 2. **Christ Jesus.** Ap. 98. XII. The texts omit "Christ". **5 in**=into. Gr. *eis.* Ap. 104. vi. **the name.** See note on 2. 38. This verse continues Paul's statement of John's action. See the Structure. **the Lord.** Ap. 98. VI. i. *β*. 2. A. **Jesus.** Ap. 98. X. **6 the Holy Ghost.** Both arts. Ap. 101. II. 3. **on.** Gr. *epi.* Ap. 104. ix. 3. **spake.** Gr. *laleō.* Ap. 121. 7. **prophesied.** See Ap. 189. **7 men.** Gr. *anēr.* Ap. 123. 2. **8 into.** Gr. *eis.* Ap. 104. vi. **synagogue.** Ap. 120. I. **spake boldly.** Gr. *parrhēsiazomai.* See note on 9. 27. **for the space of**=for. Gr. *epi.* Ap. 104. ix. 3. **three months.** Sept. to Dec. A. D. 54. **disputing** =reasoning. Gr. *dialegomai.* See 17. 2. **persuading.** Gr. *peithō.* Ap. 150. I. 2. **concerning.** Gr. *peri.* Ap. 104. xiii. 1. **kingdom of God.** Ap. 114. **9 divers**=some. Gr. *tines.* Ap. 124. 4. **hardened.** Gr. *sklērunō.* Rom. 9. 18. Heb. 3. 8, 13, 15; 4, 7. **believed not**=were unbelieving. Gr. *apeitheō.* Cp. 14. 2; 17. 5. **but spake evil**=speaking evil. Gr. *kakologeō.* Here, Matt. 15. 4. Mark 7. 10; 9. 39. **that way**=the way. See note on 9. 2.

before the °multitude, he °departed °from them,
and °separated the disciples, [8]disputing daily
°in the °school of °one °Tyrannus.
10 And this continued °by the space of two
years; so that all °they which dwelt in Asia
heard the °word of [5]the Lord °Jesus, both
Jews and °Greeks.
11 And °God °wrought °special °miracles °by
the hands of Paul:
12 So that [9]from his °body were °brought
°unto the °sick °handkerchiefs or °aprons,
and the °diseases °departed [9]from them, and
the °evil °spirits went out °of them.

Q B[1] h[1] 13 Then [1]certain of the °vagabond Jews,
°exorcists, °took upon them to °call °over
them which had evil [12]spirits the °name of [5]the
Lord [5]Jesus, saying,

i[1] °"We °adjure you by [5]Jesus Whom Paul
°preacheth."

h[2] 14 And there were seven °sons of *one* Sceva,
a Jew, *and* °chief of the priests, °which did so.

i[2] 15 And the [12]evil [12]spirit °answered and said,
[5]"Jesus I °know, and Paul I °know; but who
are ye?"

h[3] 16 And the °man [9]in whom the [12]evil [12]spirit
was °leaped [6]on them, and °overcame °them,
°and prevailed °against them, so that they fled
°out of that house naked and °wounded.

B[2] k 17 And this °was °known to all the Jews and
[10]Greeks also [10]dwelling at Ephesus; and fear
fell [6]on them all, and the [13]name of [5]the Lord
[5]Jesus was °magnified.

multitude. Gr. *plēthos.* See note on 2. 6.
departed = having withdrawn. Gr. *aphistēmi.*
from. Gr. *apo.* Ap. 104. iv.
separated. Gr. *aphorizō.* Cp. 13. 2.
in. Gr. *en.* Ap. 104. viii.
school. Gr. *scholē.* Lit. leisure, then lecture or discussion, then place for such. Only here.
one. The texts omit.
Tyrannus. Evidently a well-known teacher. He may have been a Rabbi, who had become a convert. "In towns where there were many Jews, both in Judea and elsewhere, they had a synagogue and a divinity school." (Dr. John Lightfoot, *Works*, iii. 236.)
10 by the space of = for. Gr. *epi.* Ap. 104. ix. 3.
they which dwelt = the dwellers. Gr. *katoikeō.* See note on 2. 5.
word. Gr. *logos.* Ap. 121. 10.
Jesus. The texts omit.
Greeks. Gr. *Hellēn.* Contrast 2 Tim. 1. 15 with this *v.* 10.
11 God. Ap. 98. I. i. 1.
wrought = was doing.
special. Lit. no (Gr. *ou.* Ap. 105. I) chance, i. e. no ordinary. Gr. *tunchanō* = to happen.
miracles. Gr. *dunamis.* See Ap. 176. 1.
by = through. Gr. *dia.* Ap. 104. v. 1. Paul was only the instrument, God the worker.
12 body = skin. Gr. *chrōs.* Only here. Medical writers used *chrōs* instead of *sōma* for body.
brought. Gr. *epipherō.* Only here, 25. 18. Rom. 3. 5. Phil. 1. 16. Jude 9. The texts read *apopherō*, carry.
unto = upon. Gr. *epi.* Ap. 104. ix. 3.
sick. See John 11. 3, 4.
handkerchiefs. Gr. *soudarion.* See note on John 11. 44.
aprons. Gr. *simikinthion.* Only here. The Lat. *semicinctium* means girding half-way round. These would be the linen aprons used in the craft of tent-making.
diseases. Gr. *nosos.* See note on Matt. 4. 23, 24.
departed. Gr. *apallassō.* Only here, Luke 12. 58 (deliver). Heb. 2. 15 (deliver). **evil** = wicked. Gr. *ponēros.* Ap. 128. III. 1. **spirits.** Ap. 101. II. 12. **of them.** The texts omit.

19. 13-20 (*Q*, p. 1615). OPPOSITION WITHOUT. (*Division.*)

Q | B[1] | 13–16. Exorcists.
  | B[2] | 17–20. Results.

19. 13-16 (B[1], above). EXORCISTS. (*Alternation.*)

B[1] | h[1] | 13–. Exorcists. General.
     | i[1] | –13. Adjuration.
     | h[2] | 14. Exorcists. Special.
     | i[2] | 15. Spirit's answer.
     | h[3] | 16. Exorcists. Discomfiture.

13 vagabond = roving. Gr. *perierchomai.* Only here, 28. 13. 1 Tim. 5. 13. Heb. 11. 37. Cp. Gen. 4. 14. **exorcists.** Gr. *exorkistēs.* Only here. The verb *exorkizō*, to adjure, only in Matt. 26. 63. **took upon them** = took in hand. Gr. *epicheireō.* See note on 9. 29. **call . . . the name** = name. **over.** Gr. *epi.* Ap. 104. ix. 3. To get control over a demon, it was necessary to know its name (cp. Mark 5. 9) or to invoke the name of a superior power or spirit. Josephus (*Ant.* VIII. ii. 5) relates how an exorcist, named Eleazar, when expelling a demon in the presence of Vespasian, invoked the name of Solomon. The great magical Papyrus of the third century, in the Bibliothèque Nationale of Paris, gives spells in which the names of Abraham, Isaac, and Jacob, and of Jesus, God of the Hebrews, are used. **We.** The texts read "I". **adjure.** Gr. *orkizō.* This is the formula for casting out a demon in the above-named Papyrus, where *exorkizō* also is found. **preacheth.** Gr. *kērussō.* Ap. 121. 1. **14 sons.** Gr. *huios.* Ap. 108. iii. **chief of the priests** = a chief priest. Gr. *archiereus.* This word is only used in the Gospels, Acts, and Hebrews. It is used of the High Priest and priestly members of the Sanhedrin. Cp. Matt. 26. 3. Every town with a synagogue had a Sanhedrin of twenty-three members, if there were 120 Jews in the place; of three members, if there were fewer. Sceva was a member of the Sanhedrin at Ephesus. **which did so** = doing this. **15 answered and said.** Ap. 122. 3. **know.** Gr. *ginōskō.* Ap. 132. I. ii. **know.** Gr. *epistamai.* Ap. 132. I. v. In the English there is the Fig. *Epistrophe*, Ap. 6, but not in the Gr. **16 man.** Gr. *anthrōpos.* Ap. 123. 1. **leaped.** Gr. *ephallomai.* Only here. **overcame** = having overpowered. Gr. *katakurieuō.* Here, Matt. 20. 25. Mark 10. 42. 1 Pet. 5. 3. **them.** The texts read "them both". So it would seem only two of them were acting. **and prevailed.** Lit. were strong. Gr. *ischuō.* See note on 15. 10. **against.** Gr. *kata.* Ap. 104. x. 1. **out of.** Gr. *ek.* Ap. 104. vii. **wounded.** Gr. *traumatizō.* Only here and Luke 20. 12.

19. 17-20 [For Structure see next page].

17 was = became. **known.** Gr. *gnōstos.* See note on 1. 19. **magnified.** Gr. *megalunō.* See note on 5. 13.

l 18 And many that [2]believed came, and °confessed, and °shewed their °deeds.

l 19 Many of them also which °used °curious °arts °brought their °books together, °and burned them °before all *men:* and they °counted the price of them, and found *it* fifty thousand *pieces* of silver.

k 20 So °mightily °grew the [10]word of °God and °prevailed.

F C[1] D m 21 °After these things were °ended, Paul °purposed [9]in °the spirit, when he had passed through Macedonia and Achaia, to go [1]to Jerusalem, saying, °"After I have been there, I must °also °see Rome."

22 So he °sent [8]into Macedonia two of them that °ministered [4]unto him, Timotheus and °Erastus; but he himself °stayed [5]in Asia °for a season.

23 And °the same time there arose °no small °stir °about [9]that way.

24 For a [1]certain *man* °named Demetrius, a °silversmith, which made silver °shrines

19. 17-20 (B², p. 1629). RESULTS. (*Introversion.*)

B² | k | 17. The Lord's Name magnified.
  l | 18. Believers confessing.
  l | 19. Magic arts renounced.
  k | 20. The Word of God growing.

18 confessed. Cp. Matt. 3. 6. **shewed**=declared. See note on 15. 4. **deeds**=practices. Gr. *praxis.* Elsewhere, Matt. 16. 27 (works). Luke 23. 51. Rom. 8. 13; 12. 4 (office). Col. 3. 9.

19 used=practised. Gr. *prassō.* **curious arts.** Gr. *periergos.* Only here and 1 Tim. 5. 13. The word means "going beyond that which is legitimate". The kindred verb only in 2 Thess. 3. 11. **arts**=*things.* **brought . . . together**=having collected. **books.** These were either books on magic, or strips of parchment or papyrus, with charms written on them. Many of these have been discovered. The great magical Papyrus referred to above (*v.* 13) contains about 3,000 lines. **and burned them**=burnt them up. **before**=in the presence of. **counted.** Gr. *sumpsēphizō.* Only here.

20 mightily=according to (Gr. *kata.* Ap. 104. x. 2) strength (Gr. *kratos.* Ap. 172. 2) **grew.** Gr. *auxanō.* Cp. 6. 7; 12. 24. **God.** The texts read "the Lord". **prevailed.** Same word as in *v.* 16. This verse is an example of the Fig. *Epicrisis.* Ap. 6.

19. 21—28 (*F*, p. 1575). EPHESUS AND JERUSALEM. PAUL'S APPREHENSION AND IMPRISONMENT. SUBSEQUENT ABODE (ROME), AND CLOSE OF HIS MINISTRY. (*Division.*)

F | C¹ 19. 21—21. 40. Final Ministry and last Missionary Journey.
  | C² | 22. 1—28. 29. Apprehension and Imprisonment.

19. 21—21. 40 (C¹, above). FINAL MINISTRY. (*Introversion.*)

C¹ | D | 19. 21-41. Disturbance at Ephesus.
  E | 20. 1-6. Departure for Macedonia.
  F | 20. 7-12. Troas.
  G | 20. 13-16. Voyage to Miletus.
  G | 20. 17-38. At Miletus.
  F | 21. 1-15-. Journey to Cæsarea.
  E | 21. -15-26. Return to Jerusalem.
  D | 21. 27-40. Disturbance at Jerusalem.

19. 21-41 (D, above). DISTURBANCE AT EPHESUS. (*Introversion and Alternation.*)

D | m | 21-25-. Assembly summoned.
  n | -25-27. Speech of Demetrius.
  o | 28. Outcry.
  H | p | 29-. Confusion.
  q | -29. Gaius and Aristarchus seized.
  I | 30-. Paul's purpose.
  I | -30, 31. Paul restrained.
  H | *p* | 32. Confusion.
  q | 33. Alexander put forward.
  o | 34. Outcry.
  n | 35-40. Town Clerk's speech.
  m | 41. Assembly dismissed.

21 After=As soon as. **ended**=fulfilled or accomplished. Gr. *plēroō.* Frequently used of the O. T. prophecies. Also of any plan being carried out. Cp. Matt. 3. 15. Mark 1. 15. Luke 7. 1. John 7. 8. The reference is not to the affairs at Ephesus only, but to the things recorded in 13. 4–19. 20. Here ends Paul's proclamation of the kingdom, and a further development of God's purpose begins. See the Structure on p. 1575 and Ap. 181. **purposed.** Lit. placed. Gr. *tithēmi.* Occ. more than ninety times. Transl. "lay", more than forty times. Cp. 5. 2. Luke 1. 66; 9. 44; 21. 14. **the spirit**=his spirit. Ap. 101. II. 9. The meaning is that he was firmly resolved. Fig. *Idiōma.* Ap. 6. **after.** Gr. *meta.* Ap. 104. xi. 2. **also see, &c.**=see Rome also. **see.** Gr. *eidon.* Ap. 133. I. 1. **22 sent.** Gr. *apostellō.* Ap. 174. 1. Cp. 1 Cor. 4. 17. **ministered.** Gr. *diakoneō.* Ap. 190. III. 1. **Erastus.** Cp. Rom. 16. 23. 2 Tim. 4. 20. **stayed.** Lit. held on. Gr. *epechō.* See note on 3. 5. **for a season**=a time. **23 the same time**=at (Gr. *kata.* Ap. 104. x. 2) that season. **no.** Gr. *ou.* Ap. 105. I. **stir.** See note on 12. 18. **about**=concerning. Gr. *peri.* Ap. 104. xiii. 1. **24 named**=by name. **silversmith.** Gr. *argurokopos.* Lit. silver-beater. Only here. **shrines.** Gr. *naos.* See note on Matt. 23. 16. Here a shrine meant an image of the goddess and part of the famous temple. These might be large enough to make ornaments for rooms or small enough to be carried as charms. On the reverse of a coin of Ephesus in the British Museum is a facade of the temple with a figure of Artemis in the centre.

°for °Diana, brought [23]no small °gain [4]unto
the °craftsmen;
25 Whom he °called together °with the
°workmen °of like occupation, and said,
n °"Sirs, ye [-15]know that °by this °craft we
have our °wealth.
26 °Moreover ye °see and hear, that °not
alone at Ephesus, but °almost throughout all
Asia, this Paul hath [8]persuaded and °turned
away °much people, saying that they be [23]no
°gods, which are made °with hands:
27 So that [26]not only °this our craft °is in
danger °to be set at nought; but °also that
the °temple of the great °goddess [24]Diana
should be °despised, and her °magnificence
should be °destroyed, whom all Asia and the
°world °worshippeth."

o **28** °And when they heard *these sayings*,
they were full of wrath, and °cried out, saying,
"Great *is* [24]Diana of the Ephesians."

H p **29** And the °whole city was filled with °con-
fusion:
q and having °caught °Gaius and °Aristarchus,
°men of Macedonia, Paul's °companions in
travel, they °rushed °with one accord [8]into
the °theatre.

I **30** And when Paul °would have entered in
[-3]unto the °people,
I the disciples suffered him[26]not.
31 And [1]certain of the °chief of Asia, which
were his friends, °sent [2]unto him, °desiring
him that he would °not °adventure himself
[8]into the [29]theatre.

H p **32** Some therefore cried one thing, and some
another: for the °assembly was °confused;
and the more part °knew [26]not °wherefore they
were come together.

q **33** And they °drew °Alexander [16]out of the
°multitude, the Jews °putting him forward.
And °Alexander °beckoned with the hand, and
°would have °made his defence [4]unto the
[30]people.

o **34** But when they °knew that he was a Jew,

for = of.
Diana. Gr. *Artemis.* Not the chaste huntress of popular mythology, but an Oriental deity who personified the bountifulness of nature. An alabaster statue in the museum of Naples represents her with a castellated crown, and many breasts, with various emblematic figures indicating that she is the universal mother of all creation. Layard, in *Nineveh and its Remains*, gives reasons for identifying her with Semiramis, the Queen of Babylon, from whom all the licentiousness in ancient worship proceeded.
gain. Gr. *ergasia.* See note on 16. 16.
craftsmen. Gr. *technitēs.* Only here, *v.* 38. Heb. 11. 10. Rev. 18. 22. Cp. 18. 3.
25 called together = gathered together. See note on 12. 12.
with = and.
workmen. Gr. *ergatēs.* A general term.
of like occupation. Lit. concerning (Gr. *peri.* Ap. 104. xiii. 2) such things. The shrines were made in terra-cotta, marble, &c., as well as silver. Demetrius was a guild-master of the silversmiths' guild, or trade union, and perhaps the other workmen had their own guilds.
Sirs. Gr. *anēr.* Ap. 123. 2. See note on 7. 26.
by = out of. Gr. *ek.* Ap. 104. vii.
craft. Same as "gain", *v.* 24.
wealth. Gr. *euporia.* Only here. Cp. "ability", 11. 29.
26 Moreover = And.
see = behold. Gr. *theōreō.* Ap. 133. I. 11.
not. Gr. *ou.* Ap. 105. I.
almost. See 13. 44.
turned away. Gr. *methistēmi.* See note on 13. 22.
much people = a great crowd (Gr. *ochlos*).
gods. Ap. 98. I. i. 5.
with = by. Gr. *dia.* Ap. 104. v. 1.
27 this our craft. Lit. this share for us, i. e. our line of trade.
is in danger. Gr. *kinduneuō.* Only here, *v.* 40. Luke 8. 23. 1 Cor. 15. 30.
to be set at nought. Lit. to come into (Gr. *eis*) rejection (Gr. *apelegmos*). Only here.
also. Read after Diana.
temple. Gr. *hieron.* See Matt. 23. 16. The ruins of this temple, one of the wonders of the ancient world, and of the amphitheatre (*v.* 29), still remain.
goddess. Gr. *thea*, fem. of *theos.* Only here, *vv.* 35, 37.
despised = reckoned for (Gr. *eis*) nothing (Gr. *ouden*).
magnificence. Gr. *megaleiotēs.* Only here, Luke 9. 43. 2 Pet. 1. 16.
destroyed. Gr. *kathaireō*; lit. taken down. Cp. 13. 19, 29. Luke 1. 52. 2 Cor. 10. 5.
world. Gr. *oikoumenē.* Ap. 129. 3. **worshippeth.** Gr. *sebomai.* Ap. 137. 2. **28 And when, &c.** = Moreover having heard and become full of wrath, they. **cried out** = were crying out. **29 whole.** Omit. **confusion.** Gr. *sunchusis.* Lit. pouring together. Only here. Cp. *v.* 32. **caught** = seized. Gr. *sunarpazō.* See note on 6. 12. **Gaius.** If a Macedonian, not the same as in 20. 4, nor the one in Rom. 16. 23. 1 Cor. 1. 14. He may have lived in Corinth. **Aristarchus.** See 20. 4; 27. 2. Col. 4. 10. Philem. 24. **men of Macedonia** = Macedonians. **companions in travel** = fellow travellers. Gr. *sunekdēmos.* Only here and 2 Cor. 8. 19. Cp. 2 Cor. 5. 6. **rushed.** Gr. *hormaō.* Only here, 7. 57, and of the swine in Matt. 8. 32. Mark 5. 13. Luke 8. 33. In the Greek these two statements are transposed. See R.V. **with one accord.** See note on 1. 14. **theatre.** Gr. *theatron.* Only here, *v.* 31. 1 Cor. 4. 9. Cp. Ap. 133. I. 12. **30 would** = was wishing. Gr. *boulomai.* Ap. 102. 3. **people.** Gr. *dēmos.* See 12. 22. **31 chief of Asia** = Asiarchs. Gr. *Asiarchēs.* These were persons chosen for their wealth and position to preside over the public festivals and games, and defray the expenses. About this time a decree was passed that the month Artemisius, named after the goddess, should be wholly devoted to festivals in her honour. This decree is extant, and opens with words that sound like an echo of *v.* 35. **sent.** Gr. *pempō.* Ap. 174. 4. **desiring** = exhorting. Gr. *parakaleō.* Ap. 134. I. 6. **not.** Gr. *mē.* Ap. 105. II. **adventure.** Lit. give. Fig. *Idiōma.* Ap. 6. **32 assembly.** Gr. *ekklēsia.* Ap. 186. **confused** = confounded. Gr. *sunchunō.* See note on 2. 6. **knew.** Gr. *oida.* Ap. 132. I. i. **wherefore** = on account of what. **33 drew** = put forward. Gr. *probibazō.* Only here and Matt. 14. 8, which see. The texts read *sumbibazō.* See 9. 22. **Alexander.** Perhaps the same as in 1 Tim. 1. 20. 2 Tim. 4. 14. **multitude.** Same as "people", *v.* 26. **putting . . . forward.** Gr. *proballō.* Only here and Luke 21. 30 **beckoned.** See note on 12. 17. **would have made** = purposed (Gr. *thelō.* Ap. 102. 1) to make his defence (Gr. *apologeomai*, to speak in defence. Occ. here, 24. 10; 25. 8; 26. 1, 2, 24. Luke 12. 11; 21. 14. Rom. 2. 15. 2 Cor. 12. 19. Cp. 22. 1). **34 knew.** Gr. *epiginōskō.* Ap. 132. I. iii.

°all with one voice °about the space of two hours cried out, "Great *is* [24] Diana of the Ephesians."

n 35 And when the °townclerk had °appeased the [26] people, he said, °"*Ye* [7] men of Ephesus, °what [16] man is there that °knoweth [26] not how that the city of the Ephesians is a °worshipper of the °great [27] goddess [24] Diana, and of °the *image* which fell down from Jupiter?

36 Seeing then that these things °cannot be spoken against, °ye ought to °be °quiet, and to do °nothing °rashly.

37 For ye have brought hither these [7] men, which are neither °robbers of churches, nor yet blasphemers of °your [27] goddess.

38 °Wherefore °if Demetrius, and the [24] craftsmen which are °with him, have a °matter °against °any man, the °law is open, and there are °deputies: let them °implead one another.

39 But [38] if ye °enquire [38] any thing [8] concerning °other matters, it shall be °determined [9] in a °lawful [32] assembly.

40 For we are [27] in danger to be °called in question °for this day's °uproar, there [36] being °no °cause °whereby we may give an °account of this °concourse."

m 41 And °when he had thus spoken, he °dismissed the [32] assembly.

E r **20** °And °after the °uproar was ceased, Paul °called unto *him* the disciples, and °embraced *them,* and departed °for to go °into °Macedonia.

s 2 And when he had gone over °those parts, and had °given them much exhortation, he came [1] into Greece,

t 3 And *there* °abode three months. And °when the Jews laid wait for him, as he was about to °sail [1] into Syria,

r °he purposed to return °through Macedonia.

4 And there °accompanied him °into Asia °Sopater of Berea; and of the Thessalonians,

all with one voice . . . out. Lit. one voice came from (Gr. *ek*) all crying out.

about, &c. = as it were for (Gr. *epi*) two hours. Fig. *Battologia.* Ap. 6.

35 townclerk = recorder. Gr. *grammateus.* In all its other sixty-six occ. transl. scribe.

appeased = quieted. Gr. *katastellō.* Only here and *v.* 36.

Ye, &c. = Men, Ephesians. Cp. 1. 11.

what man. The texts read, "who of men."

knoweth. Gr. *ginōskō.* Ap. 132. I. ii.

worshipper. Gr. *neōkoros.* Lit. temple-sweeper. Only here. This very word occ. on coins of Ephesus.

great goddess Diana. The texts read "great Diana".

the *image*, &c. Gr. *Diopetēs.* Only here. Lit. the fallen from Zeus. The lower part of the image in the shrine was a block of wood which was said to have fallen from the sky.

36 cannot be spoken against = are indisputable. Gr. *anantirrhētos.* Only here. The adv. in 10. 29.

ye ought to = it is needful that ye should.

be. Gr. *huparchō.* See note on Luke 9. 48.

quiet = calmed or appeased, as in *v.* 35.

nothing. Gr. *mēdeis.*

rashly = rash, or headstrong. Gr. *propetēs.* Only here and 2 Tim. 3. 4 (heady).

37 robbers of churches = plunderers of temples. Gr. *hierosulos.* Only here.

your goddess. The texts read "our god". Ap. 98. I. i. 5.

38 Wherefore if = If (Ap. 118. 2. a) indeed then.

with. Gr. *sun.* Ap. 104. xvi.

matter = charge. Lit. word. Gr. *logos.* Ap. 121. 10. Fig. *Idiōma.* Ap. 6.

against. Gr. *pros.* Ap. 104. xv. 3.

any man. Gr. *tis.* Ap. 123. 3.

law is open = courts (Gr. *agoraios.* See note on 17. 5) are being held.

deputies = proconsuls. Gr. *anthupatos.* See note on 13. 7. Asia was a pro-consular province, but there was only one proconsul. The townclerk was probably speaking generally.

implead = charge, or accuse. Gr. *enkaleō.* Only here, *v.* 40; 23. 28, 29; 26. 2, 7. Rom. 8. 33.

39 enquire = seek diligently. Same word as in 12. 19; 13. 7.

other. Gr. *heteros.* Ap. 124. 2.

determined = resolved. Gr. *epiluō.* Only here and Mark 4. 34 (expounded).

lawful. Gr. *ennomos,* under laws. Only here and 1 Cor. 9. 21. **40 called in question.** Same as "implead" (*v.* 38). **for** = concerning, as in *v.* 8. **uproar.** Gr. *stasis,* insurrection. **no.** Gr. *mēdeis,* as in *v.* 36. **cause.** Gr. *aition.* Only here and Luke 23. 4, 14, 22. **whereby** = concerning (Gr. *peri,* as in *v.* 8) which. **account.** Gr. *logos.* Ap. 121. 10. **concourse.** Gr. *sustrophē.* Only here and 23. 12. **41 when,** &c. = having said these things. **dismissed** = dissolved. Gr. *apoluō.* Ap. 174. 11.

20. 1-6 (E, p. 1630). DEPARTURE FOR MACEDONIA. (*Extended Alternation.*)

E | r | 1. Departure.
  s | 2. Arrival in Greece.
   t | 3-. Abode. Three months.
  r | -3-5. Return through Macedonia.
   s | 6-. Arrival at Troas.
    t | -6. Abode. Seven days.

20. 1 And = Now. **after.** Gr. *meta.* Ap. 104. xi. 2. **uproar** = din. Gr. *thorubos.* Here, 21. 34; 24. 18. Matt. 26. 5; 27. 24. Mark 5. 38; 14. 2. Cp. 17. 5. **called unto.** The texts and Syriac read comforted, or exhorted. Ap. 134. I. 6. **embraced.** Gr. *aspazomai.* Generally transl. "salute", or "greet". Cp. 2 Cor. 13. 12. **for.** Omit. **into.** Gr. *eis.* Ap. 104. vi. **Macedonia.** Cp. *vv.* 21, 22. **2 those parts.** Doubtless including Philippi, Thessalonica, &c. **given them much exhortation.** Lit. exhorted (Gr. *parakaleō.* Ap. 134. I. 6) them with many a word (Gr. *logos.* Ap. 121. 10). **3 abode three months.** Lit. having done three months. Cp. 15. 33; 18. 23. Fig. *Synecdochē* (of the species). Ap. 6. The whole period covered by *vv.* 1-3 is about nine months. **when,** &c. Lit. a plot (Gr. *epiboulē.* See 9. 24) having been made against him by (Gr. *hupo.* Ap. 104. xviii. 1) the Jews. **sail.** Gr. *anagō.* See note on 13. 13. **he purposed.** Lit. his purpose or judgment was. Gr. *gnōmē.* Ap. 177. 2. **through.** Gr. *dia.* Ap. 104. v. 1. **4 accompanied** = were accompanying. This was their purpose, but they went before and waited at Troas (*v.* 5). Gr. *sunepomai.* Only here. **into** = as far as. **Sopater.** Shortened form of Sōsipater, which is found in Rom. 16. 21, but there is no connexion between the two persons. The texts add "son of Pyrrhus".

°Aristarchus and °Secundus; and °Gaius of
Derbe, and Timotheus; and of Asia, °Tychicus
and °Trophimus.
5 These going before °tarried for us °at
°Troas.
s **6** And we °sailed away °from °Philippi [1] after
the °days of unleavened bread, and came
°unto them °to [5] Troas in °five days;
t where we °abode seven days.
F u **7** [1] And °upon the °first *day* of the week, when
°the disciples °came together to °break bread,
Paul °preached °unto them, °ready to °depart
on the morrow; and °continued °his speech
until midnight.
8 [1] And there were many °lights °in the
°upper chamber, where they were °gathered
together.
v **9** And there °sat °in °a °window a °certain
°young man °named Eutychus, °being fallen
°into °a deep sleep: and as Paul was °long
[7] preaching, he °sunk down °with sleep, and
fell down [6] from the °third loft, and was taken
up °dead.
v **10** And Paul went down, and fell on him, and
°embracing *him* said, °"Trouble °not yourselves; for his °life is [8] in him."
u **11** When he therefore was come up again,
and had [7] broken °bread, and eaten, and °talked
°a long while, even till °break of day, °so he
departed.
12 And they brought the °young man alive,
and were °not °a little °comforted.
G **13** And we went before °to ship, and [3] sailed
°unto Assos, there °intending to °take in
Paul: for so °had he appointed, °minding
himself to °go afoot.
14 And when he °met with us °at Assos, we
[13] took him in, and came [6] to Mitylene.
15 And we °sailed thence, and °came the °next
day °over against Chios; and the °next *day*
we °arrived [14] at Samos, and tarried [5] at
Trogyllium; and the °next *day* we came [6] to
Miletus.

Aristarchus. See 19. 29.
Secundus. Only here.
Gaius. Not the same as in 19. 29.
Tychicus. See Eph. 6. 21. Col. 4. 7. 2 Tim. 4. 12. Tit. 3. 12. He was with Paul in his first and second imprisonments at Rome, and was twice sent by him to Ephesus, which was no doubt his native place, as it was that of Trophimus.
Trophimus. See 21. 29. 2 Tim. 4. 20.
5 tarried = were waiting.
at = in. Gr. *en.* Ap. 104. viii.
Troas. Cp. 16. 8. 2 Cor. 2. 12.
6 sailed away. Gr. *ekpleō.* See note on 15. 39.
from. Gr. *apo.* Ap. 104. iv.
Philippi: i. e. from Neapolis, its port.
days, &c. This was Passover, A. D. 57.
unto. Gr. *pros.* Ap. 104. xv. 3.
to. Gr. *eis,* as in *v.* 1.
five days. Cp. 16. 11.
abode. Gr. *diatribō.* See note on 12. 19.

20. 7-12 (F, p. 1630). **TROAS.**
(Introversion.)

F | u | 7, 8. Preaching.
| v | 9. Eutychus dead.
| *v* | 10. Eutychus restored.
| *u* | 11, 12. Breaking bread, and converse.

7 upon. Gr. *en.* Ap. 104. viii.
first, &c. = first day of the sabbaths, i. e. the first day for reckoning the seven sabbaths to Pentecost. It depended upon the harvest (Deut. 16. 9), and was always from the morrow after the weekly sabbath when the wave sheaf was presented (Lev. 23. 15). In John 20. 1 this was the fourth day after the Crucifixion, "the Lord's Passover." Cp. Ap. 156. This was by Divine ordering. But in A. D. 57 it was twelve days after the week of unleavened bread, and therefore more than a fortnight later than in A. D. 29.
the disciples. The texts read "we".
came together = were gathered together, as in *v.* 8.
break bread. See note on 2. 42.
preached. Gr. *dialegomai.* Often transl. "reason". See note on 17. 2. **unto** = to.
ready = being about. Same as in *vv.* 3, 13, 38.
depart. Gr. *exeimi.* See note on 13. 42.
continued = was extending. Gr. *parateinō.* Only here.
his speech = the word. Gr. *logos,* as in *v.* 2.
8 lights. Gr. *lampas.* Ap. 130. 6.
in. Gr. *en.* Ap. 104. viii.
upper chamber. See note on 1. 13.
gathered together. See note on *v.* 7.
9 sat = was sitting.
in. Gr. *epi.* Ap. 104. ix. 1. **a** = the. **window.** Gr. *thuris.* Only here and 2 Cor. 11. 33. It was an opening with a lattice. Eutychus, being asleep on the window-seat with the lattice open, fell out. **certain.** Gr. *tis.* Ap. 123. 3. **young man.** Gr. *neanias.* See note on 7. 58. **named** = by name. **being fallen** = being borne down. Gr. *katapherō.* Only in this *v.* and 26. 10. "Sunk down" is the same word. **into** = by (dat.). **long.** Lit. for (Gr. *epi.* Ap. 104. ix. 3) more (than usual). **with.** Gr. *apo.* Ap. 104. iv. **third loft** = third storey. Gr. *tristegon.* Only here. **dead** = a corpse. Ap. 139. 2. Gr. *nekros.* **10 embracing.** Gr. *sumperilambanō.* Only here. Cp. 1 Kings 17. 21. 2 Kings 4. 34. **Trouble . . . yourselves.** Gr. *thorubeomai.* See 17. 5. **not.** Gr. *mē.* Ap. 105. II. It was midnight. Any loud outcry would have roused the neighbourhood and caused a scene. **life.** Gr. *psuchē.* Ap. 110. III. 1. and 170. 3. **11 bread.** The texts read "the bread", to support the idea that it was a Eucharistic service, but see note on *v.* 7 and the refs. in 2. 42. **talked.** Gr. *homileō.* Only here, 24. 26. Luke 24. 14, 15. Hence our word "homily", for a solemn discourse. **a long while** = for (Gr. *epi.* Ap. 104. ix. 3) long (time). **break of day.** Gr. *augē.* Only here. **so.** Emph. to call attention to the circumstances attending his departure. **12 young man.** Gr. *pais.* Ap. 108. iv. Not the same as *v.* 9. **not.** Gr. *ou.* Ap. 105. I. **a little** = moderately. Gr. *metriōs.* Only here. Fig. *Tapeinosis.* Ap. 6. **comforted.** Gr. *parakaleō.* Ap. 134. I. 6. See *v.* 2. They were cheered by the miracle and Paul's words. **13 to ship** = on board. Lit. upon (Gr. *epi.* Ap. 104. ix. 3) the ship. **unto.** Gr. *epi,* as above. **intending** = being about. Same as in *vv.* 3, 7, 38. **take in** = receive on board. **had he appointed.** Gr. *diatassō.* See note on 7. 44. **minding** = being about, as above **go afoot.** Gr. *pezeuō.* Only here. The distance was twenty miles. **14 met.** Gr. *sumballō.* See note on 4. 15. **at.** Gr. *eis.* Ap. 104. vi. **15 sailed thence, and** = having sailed away. Gr. *apopleō.* See note on 13. 4. **came** = arrived. Gr. *katantaō.* See note on 16. 1. **next.** Gr. *epeimi.* See note on 7. 26. **over against.** Gr. *antikru.* Only here. **next.** Gr. *heteros.* Ap. 124. 2. **arrived.** Gr. *paraballō.* Only here and Mark 4. 30 (compare, i. e. bring alongside). **next.** Gr. *echomai,* to hold oneself near to. Note the three different words for "next" in this verse.

16 For Paul had °determined to °sail by
Ephesus, °because he would [10]not °spend the
time [8]in Asia: for he °hasted, °if it were
possible for him, to be [14]at Jerusalem the day
of °Pentecost.

G w 17 And [6]from °Miletus he °sent [6]to °Ephesus,
and °called the °elders of the °church.

x 18 And when they were come °to him, he
said °unto them, "Ye °know, [6]from the first
day °that I °came [1]into Asia, °after what
manner I have been °with you °at all seasons,
19 °Serving °the Lord [18]with all °humility of
mind, and with °many tears, and °temptations,
which befell me °by the °lying in wait of the
Jews:
20 *And* how I °kept back °nothing °that was
profitable *unto you,* °but have shewed you,
and have taught you °publickly, and °from
house to house,
21 °Testifying both °to the Jews, and also to
the Greeks, °repentance °toward °God, and
°faith °toward our [19]Lord °Jesus Christ.

K y 22 And now, °behold, I go °bound in the
°spirit [13]unto Jerusalem, [10]not °knowing the
things that shall °befall me there:
23 °Save that °the Holy Ghost °witnesseth
°in every city, saying that bonds and °afflic-
tions °abide me.
24 But °none of these things move me,
°neither °count I my [10]life °dear [7]unto myself,
so that I might °finish my °course [18]with °joy,
and the °ministry, which I have received °of
[19]the Lord °Jesus, to [21]testify °the gospel of
the °grace of [21]God.
25 And now, [22]behold, I [22]know that ye all,
°among whom I have °gone °preaching °the
kingdom of God, °shall see my face °no more.

z 26 Wherefore I °take you to record °this day,
that I *am* °pure [6]from the blood of all *men.*
27 For I °have [12]not shunned °to °declare
[7]unto you all the °counsel of [21]God.

a 28 °Take heed therefore [7]unto yourselves,

16 determined = decided. Gr. *krinō.* Ap. 122. 1. It was a question of taking a ship stopping at Ephesus or Miletus.
sail by. Gr. *parapleō.* Only here.
because . . . would = in order that he might.
spend the time. Gr. *chronotribeō,* wear away the time. Only here.
hasted = was hurrying on.
if. Ap. 118. 2. b.
Pentecost. Cp. *v.* 7.

20. 17-38 (*G*, p. 1630). AT MILETUS.
(*Introversion and Alternation.*)

G | w | 17. Summons.
x | 18-21. Paul's conduct and testimony.
K | y | 22-25. His future.
z | 26, 27. His faithfulness.
a | 28. Charge.
K | *y* | 29-31-. The future of the Ephesians.
z | -31. Paul's earnestness.
a | 32. Commendation.
x | 33-35. Paul's character and conduct.
w | 36-38. Leave-taking.

17 Miletus. A city of great importance, as its remains show.
sent = having sent. Gr. *pempō.* Ap. 174. 4.
Ephesus. The time taken in summoning the elders was much less than he would have had to spend there, besides which there was the danger of a renewal of the rioting.
called. Gr. *metakaleō.* See note on 7. 14.
elders. Gr. *presbuteros.* See Ap. 189.
church. See Ap. 186.
18 to. Gr. *pros.* Ap. 104. xv. 3.
unto = to.
know. Gr. *epistamai.* Ap. 132. I. v.
that = from (Gr. *apo*) which.
came. Gr. *epibainō.* Only here, 21. 2, 6; 25. 1; 27. 2. Matt. 21. 5. Lit. to go upon.
after what manner = how.
with. Gr. *meta.* Ap. 104. xi. 1.
at all seasons = all the time.
19 Serving. Gr. *douleuō.* Ap. 190. III. 2.
the Lord. Ap. 98. VI. i. *β.* 2. A.
humility of mind. Gr. *tapeinophrosunē.* Only here, Eph. 4. 2. Phil. 2. 3. Col. 2. 18, 23; 3. 12. 1 Pet. 5. 5.
many. Omit.
temptations. Gr. *peirasmos.* Always transl. as here, save in 1 Pet. 4. 12. Here it means "trials", as in Luke 22. 28. See 2 Cor. 11. 26. **by** = in. Gr. *en.* Ap. 104. viii. **lying in wait** = plots, as in *v.* 3.
20 kept back. Gr. *hupostellō.* Only here, *v.* 27. Gal. 2. 12. Heb. 10. 38. A medical word, used of withholding food from patients. **nothing.** Gr. *oudeis.* **that was profitable** = of the things profitable. **but have,** &c. Lit. so as not (Gr. *mē*) to shew and teach. **publickly.** Gr. *dēmosia.* See note on 5. 18. **from house to house** in your houses. Gr. *kat' oikon,* as in 2. 46. **21 Testifying** = witnessing. Gr. *diamarturomai.* See note on 2. 40. **to the Jews,** &c. = to Jews and Greeks. **repentance.** Gr. *metanoia.* Ap. 111. II. **toward.** Gr. *eis.* Ap. 104. vi. **God.** Ap. 98. I. i. 1. **faith.** Gr. *pistis.* Ap. 150. II. 1. **Jesus Christ.** Ap. 98. XI. **22 behold.** Gr. *idou.* Ap. 133. I. 2. "And now, behold", repeated *v.* 25. Fig. *Epibolē.* Ap. 6. **bound in the spirit** = firmly resolved. Fig. *Idiōma.* Ap. 6. **spirit.** Ap. 101. II. 9. **knowing.** Gr. *eidon.* Ap. 133. I. 1. **befall** = meet. Gr. *sunantaō.* See note on 10. 25. Not the same word as in *v.* 19. **23 Save** = But only. **the Holy Ghost.** Ap. 101. II. 3. **witnesseth.** Same word as testify, *v.* 21. The texts add "to me". **in every city.** Gr. *kata polin.* Cp. 15. 21. **afflictions.** Gr. *thlipsis.* See note on 7. 10. **abide** = await or remain for. Gr. *menō.* See p. 1511. **24 none,** &c. = I make of no (Gr. *oudeis*) account (Gr. *logos*). **neither.** Gr. *oude.* **count** = hold. **dear** = precious. Gr. *timios.* See note on 5. 34. **finish.** Gr. *teleioō.* Ap. 125. 2. Only here in Acts. Often transl. "perfect". **course.** See note on 13. 25. Ten years were yet to pass before this would be. See 2 Tim. 4. 7, 8. **joy.** All the texts omit "with joy". **ministry.** Gr. *diakonia.* Ap. 190. II. 1. **of** = from. Gr. *para.* Ap. 104. xii. 1. **Jesus.** Ap. 98. X. **the gospel,** &c. Ap. 140. IV. **grace.** Ap. 184. I. 1. **25 among.** Gr. *en.* Ap. 104. viii. 2. **gone.** Gr. *dierchomai.* See note on 8. 4. **preaching.** Gr. *kērussō.* Ap. 121. 1. **the kingdom of God.** Ap. 114. The texts omit "of God". **shall see.** Gr. *opsomai.* Ap. 133. I. 8 (a). **no more** = no longer. Gr. *ouketi.* **26 take you to record** = am witnessed to by you. Gr. *marturomai.* Only here, Gal. 5. 3. Eph. 4. 17. The texts add 26. 22. 1 Thess. 2. 11 for *martureomai.* Fig. *Deisis.* Ap. 6. **this day.** Lit. in (Gr. *en*) the day of to-day. **pure,** &c. Cp. 18. 6. **27 have . . . shunned** = shunned or shrunk. Gr. *hupostellō.* Same as "kept back", *v.* 20. **to.** Lit. not (Gr. *mē*) to. **declare.** Gr. *anangellō.* See note on 14. 27. Same as "shew", *v.* 20. **counsel.** Gr. *boulē.* Ap. 102. 4. All the revealed purpose of God up to that time. The Prison Epistles, containing the final revelation of God's counsel, were not yet written. **28 Take heed.** Gr. *prosechō.* The sixth occ. in Acts. See note on 8. 6, 10, 11.

and to all the °flock, °over the which [23]the
Holy Ghost hath made you °overseers, to
°feed the [17]church of °God, which He hath
°purchased °with His own blood.

K y 29 °For I [22]know °this, that [1]after my
°departing shall °grievous wolves enter °in
among you, [10]not °sparing the [28]flock.
30 °Also °of your own selves °shall °men
°arise, °speaking °perverse things, to °draw
away °disciples °after them.
31 Therefore °watch,

z °and remember, that °by the space of three
years I ceased [12]not to °warn every one night
and day [18]with tears.

a 32 And °now, °brethren, I °commend you to
[21]God, and to the °word of His [24]grace, which
is able to °build you up, and to give °you an
°inheritance [25]among all °them which are
°sanctified.

x 33 I °have coveted °no man's silver, or gold,
or °apparel.
34 Yea, ye yourselves °know, that these hands
°have ministered [7]unto my °necessities, and to
them that were [18]with me.
35 I °have shewed you all things, how that
so °labouring ye ought to °support the °weak,
and to [31]remember the [32]words of [24]the Lord
Jesus, how He said, °'It is more blessed to give
than to receive.'"

w 36 And when he had thus spoken, he °kneeled
down, and °prayed °with them all.
37 And °they all wept sore, and °fell °on
Paul's neck, °and kissed him,
38 °Sorrowing most of all °for °the [32]words
which he spake, that they °should °see his
face [25]no more. And they °accompanied him
[13]unto the ship.

F L **21** And it came to pass, that after we were
°gotten °from them, and had °launched,
we came °with a straight course °unto Coos, and

flock. Gr. *poimnion*, little flock. Only here, *v.* 29. Luke 12. 32. 1 Pet. 5. 2, 3. For *poimnē*, see John 10. 16.

over = in, or on. Gr. *en*. Ap. 104. viii. Out of 2,622 occ. of *en*, it is rendered "over" only here.

overseers. Gr. *episkopos*. Elsewhere transl. "bishop". Phil. 1. 1. 1 Tim. 3. 2. Tit. 1. 7. 1 Pet. 2. 25. They are called "elders", in *v.* 17, which makes it clear that "elders" (*presbuteroi*) and bishops (*episkopoi*) are the same. Ap. 189.

feed = shepherd. Gr. *poimainō*. Occ. eleven times; transl. "feed" seven times; "rule" in Matt. 2. 6. Rev. 2. 27; 12. 5; 19. 15.

God. Some texts read "Lord", but Alford gives good reasons for rejecting the change, due to Arian and Socinian attempts against the Lord's Deity.

purchased = gained possession of, or acquired. Gr. *peripoieomai*. Only here and 1 Tim. 3. 13. Cp. 1 Pet. 2. 9.

with = by means of. Gr. *dia*. Ap. 104. v. 1.

29 For. The texts omit. **this.** Omit.

departing. Gr. *aphixis*. Only here.

grievous = oppressive. Gr. *barus*. Elsewhere 25. 7. Matt. 23. 4, 23. 2 Cor. 10. 10. 1 John 5. 3.

in among = unto. Gr. *eis*. Ap. 104. vi.

sparing. Gr. *pheidomai*. Always transl. "spare" save 2 Cor. 12. 6. No other word for "spare" save Luke 15. 17. This verse is an instance of the Fig. *Hypocatastasis* (Ap. 6), to call attention to the true character of Apostolical succession.

30 Also, &c. = Of your own selves also.

of = out of. Gr. *ek*. Ap. 104. vii.

shall = will. **men.** Gr. *anēr*. Ap. 123. 2.

arise. Gr. *anistēmi*. Ap. 178. I. 1.

speaking. Gr. *laleō*. Ap. 121. 7.

perverse. See note on 13. 8.

draw away. Gr. *apospaō*. Only here, 21. 1. Matt. 26. 51. Luke 22. 41.

disciples = the disciples.

after, i. e. in their train. Gr. *opisō*.

31 watch. Cp. 1 Pet. 5. 8.

and remember = remembering. Gr. *mnēmoneuō*. Always transl. "remember", save Heb. 11. 15, 22.

by the space of three years. Gr. *trietia*. Only here.

warn. Gr. *noutheteō*. Used only by Paul, here and seven times in his epistles.

32 now. See note on 4. 29.

brethren. The texts omit.

commend. Gr. *paratithēmi*. See note on 17. 3.

word. Gr. *logos*. Ap. 121. 10.

build . . . up. Gr. *epoikodomeō*. Only used by Jude (20), and Paul, here and six times in his epistles.

you. The texts omit. **inheritance.** Gr. *klēronomia*. Only word transl. inheritance, save 26. 18. Col. 1. 12. **them which are** = the. **sanctified.** Gr. *hagiazō*. See note on John 17. 17, 19. **33 have coveted** = desired. **no man's.** Gr. *oudeis*. **apparel.** Gr. *himatismos*. The word expresses more stateliness than the common word *himation*. Here, Matt. 27. 35. Luke 7. 25; 9. 29. John 19. 24. 1 Tim. 2. 9. **34 know.** Gr. *ginōskō*. Ap. 132. I. ii. **have ministered** = ministered. Gr. *hupereteō*. Ap. 190. III. 4. See note on 13. 36. **necessities** = needs. Cp. 2. 45. **35 have shewed** = shewed. Gr. *hupodeiknumi*. See note on 9. 16. **labouring** = toiling. Gr. *kopiaō*. Cp. Matt. 6. 28, first occ. **support.** Gr. *antilambanomai*. Only here, Luke 1. 54. 1 Tim. 6. 2. **weak.** Gr. *astheneō*. Often transl. "sick". **It is, &c.** This is one of the *Paroemiae* (Ap. 6) of the Lord, not elsewhere recorded. **36 kneeled down.** See note on 7. 60. **prayed.** Gr. *proseuchomai*. Ap. 134. I. 2. **with.** Gr. *sun*. Ap. 104. xvi. **37 they all, &c.** Lit. there was a great weeping of all. **fell** = having fallen. **on.** Gr. *epi*. Ap 104. ix. 3. **and kissed.** Gr. *kataphileō*. Only here, Matt. 26. 49. Mark 14. 45 (Judas). Luke 7. 38, 45 (the woman); 15. 20 (the father). **38 Sorrowing.** Gr. *odunōmai*. Only here, Luke 2. 48; 16. 24, 25. **for** = upon. Gr. *epi*. Ap. 104. ix. 2. **the words** = the word. Gr. *logos*. Ap. 121. 10. **should** = were about to. **see** = behold. Gr. *theōreō*. Ap. 133. I. 11. **accompanied.** Gr. *propempō*. See note on 15. 3. Cp. Ap. 174. 4.

21. 1-15- (*F*, p. 1630). JOURNEY TO CÆSAREA. (*Alternation.*)

F | L | 1-3. Journey to Tyre.
  M | 4. Prophetic warning.
    N | 5, 6. Departure.
L | 7-9. Journey to Cæsarea.
  M | 10-14. Prophetic warning.
    N | 15-. Departure.

21. 1 gotten = withdrawn Same word as 20. 30. **from.** Gr. *apo*. Ap. 104. iv. **launched.** Gr. *anagō*. See note on 13. 13. **with a straight course.** Gr. *euthudromeō*. See note on 16. 11. **unto.** Gr. *eis*. Ap. 104. vi.

the *day* °following °unto Rhodes, and from
thence °unto Patara:
2 And finding a ship sailing over [1]unto
Phenicia, we °went aboard, and °set forth.
3 Now when we had °discovered °Cyprus, we
left it on the left hand, and °sailed °into Syria,
and °landed °at °Tyre: for °there the ship was
to °unlade her °burden.

M 4 And °finding °disciples, we °tarried there
seven days: who said to Paul °through °the
Spirit, that he should °not °go up °to
Jerusalem.

N 5 °And when we had °accomplished those
days, we departed and went our way; °and
they all brought us on our way, °with wives
and °children, till *we were* out of the city:
and °we kneeled down °on the °shore, °and
prayed.
6 And when we had °taken our leave one of
another, we °took ship; and they returned
°home again.

L 7 And when we had °finished °*our* course
[1]from Tyre, we °came [4]to Ptolemais, and
°saluted the brethren, and °abode °with them
one day.
8 And the °next *day* we that were °of Paul's
company departed, and came [1] unto °Cæsarea:
and we entered [3]into the house of Philip the
evangelist, which was *one* °of °the seven;
and [7]abode [7]with him.
9 And °the same man had four daughters,
virgins, °which did prophesy.

M b 10 And as we [4]tarried *there* many days,
there °came down [1]from Judæa a °certain
°prophet, °named °Agabus.
11 And when he was come °unto us, he took
Paul's girdle, and bound his own hands and
feet, and said, "Thus saith °the Holy Ghost,
'So °shall the Jews °at Jerusalem bind the
°man that owneth this girdle, and °shall
°deliver *him* [3]into the hands of the °Gentiles.'"

c 12 And when we heard these things, both we,
and °they of that place, °besought him [4]not to
[4]go up [4]to Jerusalem.

b 13 Then Paul answered, °"What mean ye to
weep and to °break mine heart? for I °am

following. Gr. *hexēs.* Only in Luke's writings. Here, 25. 17; 27. 18. Luke 7. 11; 9. 37. Note the different expressions for next day used by Luke. Cp. 20. 15.
2 went aboard = having embarked. Gr. *epibainō.* See note on 20. 18.
set forth. Same as launched, *v.* 1.
3 discovered = sighted. Gr. *anaphainomai.* Ap. 106. I. ii. Only here and Luke 19. 11.
Cyprus. The Kittim of the O.T. See Num. 24. 24. Isa. 23. 1, 12. Jer. 2. 10. Ezek. 27. 6. Dan. 11. 30. Cp. 4. 36; 13. 4-12.
sailed. Gr. *pleō.* Only here, 27. 2, 6, 24. Luke 8. 23.
into. Gr. *eis.* Ap. 104. vi.
landed. Gr. *katagō.* Lit. bring down. Occ. elsewhere 9. 30; 22. 30; 23. 15, 20, 28; 27. 3; 28. 12. Luke 5. 11. Rom. 10. 6.
at = into. Gr. *eis.*
Tyre. See Matt. 11. 21.
there. Gr. *ekeise.* Only here and 22. 5.
unlade = unload. Gr. *apophortizomai.* Only here.
burden. Gr. *gomos.* Only here and Rev. 18. 11, 12.
4 finding = having found. Gr. *aneuriskō,* to find by searching. Only here and Luke 2. 16.
disciples = the disciples. Probably few. He no longer seeks the synagogue.
tarried. Gr. *epimenō.* See note on 10. 48.
through. Gr. *dia.* Ap. 104. v. 1.
the Spirit = the Holy Spirit. Ap. 101. II. 3. Cp. *vv.* 11-14 and 1. 2.
not. Gr. *mē.* Ap. 105. II.
go up. Gr. *anabainō,* but the texts read *epibainō,* as in *v.* 2.
to. Gr. *eis.* Ap. 104. vi.
5 And = But it came to pass that.
accomplished = completed. Ap. 125. 9.
and they all, &c. = all with wives and children, bringing us on our way. Gr. *propempō.* See note on 15. 3.
with. Gr. *sun.* Ap. 104. xvi.
children. Gr. *teknon.* Ap. 108. i.
we kneeled down = having kneeled down. See note on 7. 60.
on. Gr. *epi.* Ap. 104. ix. 3.
shore. Gr. *aigialos.* Only here, 27. 39, 40. Matt. 13. 2, 48. John 21. 4.
and prayed = we prayed. Gr. *proseuchomai.* Ap. 134. I. 2.
6 taken our leave. Gr. *aspazomai.* See note on 20. 1.
took ship = embarked (Gr. *epibainō,* as in *v.* 1) on (Gr. *eis*) the ship, i. e. the same ship as *v.* 2.
home. Lit. to (Gr. *eis*) their own (things).
7 finished. Gr. *dianuō.* Only here.
our course = the voyage. Gr. *ploos.* Only here and 27. 9, 10.

came. Gr. *katantaō.* See note on 16. 1. **saluted.** Same as "take leave" in *v.* 6. **abode.** Gr. *menō.* See p. 1511. **with.** Gr. *para.* Ap. 104. xii. 2. **8 next.** Here the common word *epaurion* is used. Cp. "following", *v.* 1. **of Paul's company.** Lit. about (Gr. *peri.* Ap. 104, xiii. 2) Paul. **Cæsarea.** See note on 8. 40. About sixty miles from Tyre by the coast road. **of.** Gr. *ek.* Ap. 104. vii. **the seven.** See 6. 5. **9 the same man** = this one. **which did prophesy.** Gr. *prophēteuō.* They were evangelists, like their father. This is in accord with Joel 2. 28, as quoted in 2. 17. See Ap. 49 and 189.

21. 10-14 (*M*, p. 1635). PROPHETIC WARNING. (*Alternation.*)

M | b | 10, 11. Agabus. Prediction.
c | 12. Disciples. Entreaty.
b | 13. Paul. Devotion.
c | 14. Disciples. Submission.

10 came down. Cæsarea was 2,000 feet below the hill country of Judæa. **certain.** Gr. *tis.* Ap. 123. 3. **prophet.** See Ap. 189. **named** = by name. **Agabus.** See 11. 28. **11 unto.** Gr. *pros.* Ap. 104. xv. 3. **the Holy Ghost** = the Holy Spirit. Ap. 101. II. 3. Both articles here. **shall** = will. **at** = in. Gr. *en.* Ap. 104. viii. **man.** Gr. *anēr.* Ap. 123. 2. **deliver.** Gr. *paradidōmi.* See note on John 19. 30. **Gentiles.** Gr. *ethnos.* **12 they of that place** = the residents, i. e. the believers there. Gr. *entopios.* Only here. **besought** = were beseeching. Gr. *parakaleō.* Ap. 134. I. 6. **13 What mean ye, &c.** Lit. What are ye doing, weeping, &c. **break** = crush. Gr. *sunthruptō.* Only here. **am ready** = hold myself in readiness. This expression occ. also 2 Cor. 12. 14. 1 Pet. 4. 5.

ready °not to be bound only, but °also to die
[3]at Jerusalem °for °the name of °the Lord
°Jesus."
c 14 And when he would [4]not be °persuaded,
we °ceased, saying, "The °will of [13]the Lord
be done."
N 15 And °after those days we °took up our
E d carriages, and [4]went up [4]to Jerusalem.
16 There went [5]with us °also *certain* of the
disciples °of [8]Cæsarea, °and brought °with
them °one °Mnason °of Cyprus, an °old
disciple, [7]with whom we should °lodge.
17 And when we were come [4]to Jerusalem,
the brethren received us °gladly.
18 And the *day* °following Paul °went in
[5]with us [11]unto James; and all the °elders
°were present.
e 19 And when he had [7]saluted them, he
°declared °particularly what things °God
°had wrought °among the [11]Gentiles °by his
°ministry.
f 20 And when they heard *it,* they °glorified
°the Lord, and said °unto him, "Thou °seest,
°brother, how many °thousands of Jews there
are which °believe; and they °are all °zealous
of the law:
g 21 And they °are °informed °of thee, that
thou teachest all the Jews which are °among
the [11]Gentiles °to forsake °Moses, °saying that
they ought [4]not to circumcise *their* °children,
°neither to walk °after the °customs.
22 What is it therefore? °the multitude must
needs come together: for they will hear that
thou art come.
g 23 Do therefore this that we say to thee: We
have four [11]men which have a °vow °on them;
24 Them take, and °purify thyself [5]with them,
and °be at charges °with them, that they may
°shave *their* heads: and all °may °know that
those things, whereof they were [21]informed
°concerning thee, are °nothing;
f but *that* thou thyself also °walkest orderly,
and keepest the law.
e 25 As °touching the [11]Gentiles which
[20]believe, we °have written °*and* concluded

not. Gr. *ou.* Ap. 105. I.
also to die = to die also.
for = in behalf of. Gr. *huper.* Ap. 104. xvii. 1.
the name. See note on 2. 38.
the Lord. Ap. 98. VI. i. *β*. 2. A.
Jesus. Ap. 98. X. Paul's decision was approved (23. 11).
14 persuaded. Gr. *peithō.* Ap. 150. I. 2.
ceased. See note on 11. 18.
will. Gr. *thelēma.* Ap. 102. 2.
15 after. Gr. *meta.* Ap. 104. xi. 2.
took up, &c = having prepared for moving, or packed up. "Carriage" is used in the old sense of that which is carried. Cp. 1 Sam. 17. 22. Gr. *aposkeuazomai.* Only here.

21. -15-26 (*E*, p. 1630). **RETURN TO JERUSALEM.** (*Introversion.*)

E | d | -15-18. Paul and his companions enter the assembly (*eiseei*).
e | 19. God's work among the Gentiles.
f | 20. Zealous of the law.
g | 21, 22. Suspicion of Paul.
g | 23, 24-. To remove suspicion.
f | -24. Keeping the law.
e | 25. Ordinances for the Gentiles.
d | 26. Paul and the seven men enter the Temple (*eiseei*).

16 also, &c. = certain also.
of = from. Gr. *apo.* Ap. 104. iv.
and brought = bringing.
with them. Omit.
one. Gr. *tis.* Ap. 123. 3.
Mnason. Nothing more is known of him.
of Cyprus = a Cypriote, as in 4. 36; 11. 20.
old. Gr. *archaios.* Not referring to his age but to his standing in the Christian assembly. An early disciple.
lodge. Gr. *xenizō.* See note on 10. 6.
17 gladly. Gr. *asmenōs.* Only here and 2. 41.
18 following. Gr. *epeimi.* See note on 7. 26.
went in. Gr. *eiseimi.* Only here, *v.* 26; 3. 3. Heb. 9. 6.
elders. See Ap. 189.
were present = came. Gr. *paraginomai.* Occ. thirty-seven times. Elsewhere transl. "come".
19 declared = related. See note on 10. 8.
particularly. Lit. one by one, each one of the things which.
God. Ap. 98. I. i. 1. See note on 1 Cor. 3. 9.
had wrought = did.
among. Gr. *en.* Ap. 104. viii. (2).
by = through. Gr. *dia.* Ap. 104. v. 1.
ministry. Gr. *diakonia.* Ap. 190. II. 1.
20 glorified = were glorifying. Not a single act, but a continual praising.
the Lord. The texts read "God".

unto = to. **seest.** Gr. *theōreō.* Ap. 133. I. 11. **brother.** Cp. 9. 17 and 2 Pet. 3. 15. **thousands.** Gr. *murias* = myriads. Fig. *Hyperbolē.* Ap. 6. Cp. John 3. 26; 12. 19. **believe** = have believed. Ap. 150. I. 1. i. **are.** Emph. Gr. *huparchō.* See note on Luke 9. 48. **zealous.** Gr. *zēlōtēs.* Properly a noun, meaning zealot, i. e. enthusiast. Occ. here, 22. 3. 1 Cor. 14. 12. Gal. 1. 14. Tit. 2. 14. Also as a title. See Ap. 141. 11. **21 are** = were. **informed** = instructed. See note on 18. 25. **of** = concerning. Gr. *peri.* Ap. 104. xiii. 1. **among.** Gr. *kata.* Ap. 104. x. 2. **to forsake** = apostasy (Gr. *apostasia.* Only here and 2 Thess. 2. 3) from (Gr. *apo*). **Moses.** See note on 3. 22. Matt. 8. 4. Here meaning the law, as in 6. 11; 15. 21. **saying that they ought.** I. e. telling or bidding them. Cp. 2 John 10, 11. **children.** Gr. *teknon.* Ap. 108. i. **neither.** Gr. *mēde.* **after** = by. **customs.** See note on 6. 14. **22 the multitude, &c.** Some texts omit this, and read "they will certainly (Gr. *pantōs*) hear". **23 vow.** Gr. *euchē.* See 18. 18. Ap. 134. II. 1. **on.** Gr. *epi.* Ap. 104. ix. 1. **24 purify.** Gr. *hagnizō.* Cp. John 11. 55. This refers to the ceremonies connected with the Nazirite vow (Num. 6). James, who was probably the speaker, would be glad to find Paul was already under the vow he had taken at Cenchreæ (18. 18), as facilitating the execution of his plan. **be at charges** = pay the expenses of the sacrifices. Gr. *dapanaō.* Here, Mark 5. 26. Luke 15. 14. 2 Cor. 12. 15. Jas. 4. 3. **with** = upon. Gr. *epi.* Ap. 104. ix. 2. **shave.** Gr. *xuraō.* Only here and 1 Cor. 11. 5, 6. See note on *keirō,* 18. 18. **may** = shall. **know.** Gr. *ginōskō.* Ap. 132. I. ii. **concerning.** Same as "of", *v.* 21. **nothing.** Gr. *oudeis.* **walkest orderly.** Gr. *stoicheō* = to walk according to religious observances. Here, Rom. 4. 12. Gal. 5. 25; 6. 16. Phil. 3. 16. **25 touching.** Gr. *peri.* Ap. 104. xiii. 1. **have written** = wrote. *and* **concluded** = having decided. Gr. *krinō.* Ap. 122. 1.

°that they observe no such thing, save only that they keep themselves from °*things* offered to idols, and from blood, and from strangled, and from fornication."

d 26 Then Paul took the [11]men, and the °next day [24]purifying himself [5]with them °entered [3]into the °temple, °to signify the °accomplishment of the days of °purification, until that °an offering should be °offered [13]for °every one of them.

D h¹ 27 And when the seven days were °almost °ended, the Jews which were [16]of Asia, °when they saw him °in the [26]temple, °stirred up all the °people, and laid hands [5]on him,

i¹ 28 Crying out, °"Men of Israel, help: °This is the °man, that teacheth all *men* every where °against the °people, and the law, and °this place: and °further brought °Greeks also [3]into the [26]temple, and hath polluted this holy place."

29 (For they had °seen before [5]with him [27]in the °city Trophimus °an Ephesian, whom they °supposed that Paul had brought [3]into the [26]temple.)

k¹ 30 And °all the city was moved, and °the [28]people ran together: and they °took Paul, and °drew him out of the [26]temple: and °forthwith °the doors were shut.

h² 31 And as they °went about to kill him, °tidings °came [20]unto the °chief captain of the °band, that all Jerusalem °was in an uproar.

32 Who °immediately took °soldiers and °centurions, and °ran down °unto them: and when they °saw the [31]chief captain and the °soldiers, they °left beating of Paul.

i² 33 Then the [31]chief captain °came near, and [30]took him, and commanded *him* to be bound with °two chains; and °demanded who he was, and what he had done.

34 And some °cried one thing, some another, [19]among the °multitude: and when he could [4]not [24]know °the certainty °for the °tumult, he commanded him to be carried [3]into the °castle.

---

that they . . . only. The texts omit.
things **offered, &c.** = that which is offered, &c. Gr. *eidōlothutos.* See note on 15. 29.

26 next. Same as in 20. 15. Gr. *echomai.*
entered. Gr. *eiseimi,* as in *v.* 18.
temple. Gr. *hieron.* See note on Matt. 23. 16.
to signify = declaring. Gr. *diangellō.* Only here, Luke 9. 60. Rom. 9. 17.
accomplishment. Gr. *ekplērōsis.* Only here. Cp. 13. 33.
purification. Gr. *hagnismos.* Only here.
an offering = the offering. See Num. 6. 14–20. Gr. *prosphora.* Only here, 24. 17. Rom. 15. 16. Eph. 5. 2. Heb. 10. 5, 8, 10, 14, 18.
offered. Gr. *prospherō.* First occ. Matt. 2. 11 (presented).
every = each.

21. 27–40 (*D*, p. 1630). **DISTURBANCE AT JERUSALEM.** (*Extended Alternation.*)

D | h¹ | 27. Riot.
  i¹ | 28, 29. Charge.
   k¹ | 30. Paul seized.
 h² | 31, 32. Chief captain interposes.
  i² | 33, 34. Inquiry as to charge.
   k² | 35, 36. Violence of people.
 h³ | 37. Chief captain appealed to.
  i³ | 38, 39. Inquiry about Paul.
   k³ | 40. Silence of people.

27 almost = about to be.
ended. Gr. *sunteleō.* Elsewhere Matt. 7. 28. Mark 13. 4. Luke 4. 2, 13. Rom. 9. 28. Heb. 8. 8.
when they saw = having seen. Gr. *theaomai.* Ap. 133. I. 12.
in. Gr. *en.* Ap. 104. viii.
stirred up = excited. Gr. *suncheō.* This form occ. only here. See note on 2. 6.
people = crowd. Gr. *ochlos.*
28 Men of Israel. See note on 1. 11; 2. 22.
This = This one, this fellow.
man. Gr. *anthrōpos.* Ap. 123. 1.
against. Gr. *kata.* Ap. 104. x. 1.
people. Gr. *laos.* See 2. 47.
this place: i. e. the Temple.
further = moreover.
Greeks. Gr. *Hellēn.*
29 seen before. Gr. *prooraō.* Only here and 2. 25.
city. It was in the city Trophimus was seen in Paul's company, and they came to the conclusion that when they saw Paul in the Temple, Trophimus must be there too.
an = the.
supposed = concluded. Gr. *nomizō.* See note on 14. 19. But the evidence was insufficient. Paul was too well informed not to be aware of the inscription which forbade the entry of any alien within the inner temple under penalty of death. It was on one of the pillars of the balustrade which separated the court of the women, where the Nazirite ceremonies were performed, from the inner sanctuary. The stone bearing this inscription was discovered by M. Clermont Ganneau in 1871. It is as follows: "No alien is to enter within the railing and enclosure round the temple. Whosoever is caught will be responsible to himself for his death which will ensue." **30 all the city** = the whole city. **the people ran, &c.** = there was a running together (Gr. *sundromē.* Only here) of the people. **took.** Gr. *epilambanomai.* See note on 9. 27. **drew** = were dragging. Gr. *helkō.* Only here and Jas. 2. 6. Cp. 16. 19. **forthwith** = immediately. **the doors, &c.** These were the gates leading into the court of the women. Shut by the Levitical door-keepers to prevent profanation by murder. **31 went about** = were seeking. Cp. John 7. 19, 20. **tidings** = a report. Gr. *phasis.* Only here. **came.** Lit. went up, i. e. to the Castle of Antonia, which overlooked the Temple. **chief captain.** Gr. *chiliarchos.* The commander of 1,000 men. See note on John 18. 12. **band** = cohort. Gr. *speira.* See John 18. 3. **was in an uproar** = was in commotion. Gr. *sunchunō.* See notes on *v.* 27; 2. 6; 19. 29. **32 immediately.** Gr. *exautēs.* See note on 10. 33. **soldiers, &c.** From the garrison in Antonia. **centurions.** Gr. *hekatontarchos.* The form used in the Gospels, and in nine places in Acts. Here, 22. 25, 26; 23. 17, 23; 27. 6, 11, 43; 28. 16. **ran down.** Gr. *katatrechō.* Only here. **unto** = upon. Gr. *epi.* Ap. 104. ix. 3. **saw.** Gr. *eidon.* Ap. 133. I. 1. **left beating of Paul** = ceased beating Paul. **33 came near, and** = having drawn near. **two chains**: i. e. either hand chained to a soldier. See note on 12. 6. **demanded.** Gr. *punthanomai.* See note on 4. 7; 10. 18. **34 cried** = were crying out. Gr. *boaō,* as in 17. 6. The texts read *epiphōneō,* as in 12. 22 (gave a shout) and 22. 24. **multitude.** Same as people, *v.* 27. **the certainty** = the sure thing. Gr. *asphalēs.* Adj. meaning "safe" or "sure". Occ. here, 22. 30; 25. 26. Phil. 3. 1. Heb. 6. 19. **for** = on account of. Gr. *dia.* Ap. 104. v. 2. **tumult.** Same as uproar, 20. 1. **castle.** Gr. *parembolē.* Occ. elsewhere, *v.* 37; 22. 24; 23. 10, 16, 32. Heb. 11. 34; 13. 11, 13. Rev. 20. 9.

k[2] 35 And when he came °upon the °stairs, °so
it was, that he was °borne °of the soldiers
[34]for the °violence of the [27]people.
36 For the °multitude of the [28]people followed
after, crying, °"Away with him."

h[3] 37 And as Paul °was to be °led [3]into the
[34]castle, he said [20]unto the [31]chief captain,
°"May I speak [11]unto thee?" °Who said,
°"Canst thou speak °Greek?

i[3] 38 °Art [13]not thou °that Egyptian, which
°before these days °madest an uproar, and
leddest out [3]into the wilderness four thousand
[11]men °that were murderers?"
39 But Paul said, "I am a -[28]man *which am*
a Jew °of Tarsus, *a city* °in Cilicia, a °citizen
of °no °mean city; and, I °beseech thee, suffer
me to °speak [11]unto the [28]people."

k[3] 40 And when he had °given him licence,
Paul °stood [23]on the [35]stairs, and °beckoned
with the hand [20]unto the [28]people. And when
there was made a great silence, he °spake unto
them in the °Hebrew °tongue, saying,

C[2] O R l **22** °"Men, brethren, and fathers, hear ye
my °defence *which I make* now °unto
you."
2 (And when they heard that he °spake in the
°Hebrew °tongue to them, they °kept the more
silence: and he saith,)
3 "I am °verily a °man *which am* a Jew,
born °in Tarsus, *a city* °in Cilicia, yet °brought
up °in this city °at the feet of °Gamaliel, *and*
°taught °according to the °perfect manner of

35 upon. Gr. *epi.* Ap. 104. ix. 3.
stairs. Gr. *anabathmos.* Only here and *v.* 40.
so it was=it befell, as in 20. 16.
borne. Gr. *bastazō,* as in 15. 10.
of=by. Gr. *hupo.* Ap. 104. xviii. 1.
violence. Gr. *bia.* See note on 5. 26.
36 multitude. Gr. *plēthos.* See note on 2. 6.
Away with him. Gr. *airō.* See note on John 19. 15.
37 was=was about.
led=brought.
May I speak. Lit. If (Ap. 118. 2. a) it is permitted me to say something.
Who=But he.
Canst thou speak=Dost thou know. Gr. *ginōskō.* Ap. 132. I. ii.
Greek. Gr. *Hellēnisti.* Only here and John 19. 20.
38 Art not thou=Art thou not then.
that=the.
before. Gr. *pro.* Ap. 104. xiv.
madest an uproar=stirred up to sedition. Gr. *anastatoō.* See note on 17. 6.
that were murderers=of the *Sicarii*, or assassins (Gr. *sikarios.* Only here). The *Sicarii* (a Latin word from *sica*, a curved dagger) were bandits who infested Judæa in the time of Felix, who sent troops against them, though Josephus says it was at the instigation of Felix that they murdered the high priest Jonathan. The Egyptian referred to was a false prophet who led a number of the Sicarii to Jerusalem, declaring that the walls would fall down before them.
39 of Tarsus=a Tarsean. Gr. *Tarseus.* See note on 9. 11.
in=of.
citizen. Gr. *politēs.* Only here and Luke 15. 15; 19. 14.
no. Gr. *ou.* Ap. 105. I.
mean=without mark. Gr. *asēmos.* Only here. Used of disease without definite symptoms. In the medical writer, Hippocrates, the very expression "no mean city" occurs. Fig. *Tapeinosis.* Ap. 6.
beseech. Gr. *deomai.* Ap. 134. I. 5.
speak. Gr. *laleō.* Ap. 121. 7. **40 given him licence.** Same word as "suffer" in *v.* 39. **stood... and**=standing. **beckoned.** See note on 12. 17. **spake unto *them***=addressed (them). Gr. *prosphōneō.* Only here, 22. 2. Matt. 11. 16. Luke 6. 13; 7. 32; 13. 12; 23. 20. **Hebrew.** Gr. *Hebrais.* Only here, 22. 2; 26. 14. **tongue**=dialect. Gr. *dialektos.* See note on 1. 19. There should be no break before ch. 22.

22. 1—28. 29 (C[2], p. 1630). APPREHENSION AND IMPRISONMENT. (*Introversion and Division.*)

C[2] | O | 22. 1—23. 22. Paul and the Jews in Jerusalem. Two addresses.
  P | 23. 23-35. Journey to Cæsarea.
    Q[1] | 24. 1-27. Paul and Felix.
    Q[2] | 25. 1-12. Paul and Festus.
    Q[3] | 25. 13—26. 32. Paul and Agrippa.
  P | 27. 1—28. 16. Journey to Rome.
O | 28. 17-29. Paul and the Jews in Rome. Two addresses.

22. 1—23. 22 (O, above). PAUL AND THE JEWS IN JERUSALEM, &c. (*Alternation.*)

O | R | 22. 1-21. Paul's defence.
  S | 22. 22-30. Events following.
R | 23. 1-10. Paul's defence.
  S | 23. 11-22. Events following.

22. 1-21 (R, above). PAUL'S DEFENCE. (*Alternation.*)

R | l | 1-5. A zealous Jew.
  m | 6-10. Revelation from the Lord.
l | 11-16. A chosen vessel.
  m | 17-21. Revelation from the Lord.

22. 1 Men, &c. See note on 1. 11 and 7. 2. **defence.** Gr. *apologia.* Occ. eight times, here; 25. 16. 1 Cor. 9. 3. 2 Cor. 7. 11. Phil. 1. 7, 17. 2 Tim. 4. 16. 1 Pet. 3. 15. See the verb, 19. 33. **unto.** Gr. *pros.* Ap. 104. xv. 3. **2 spake . . . to**=addressed. Gr. *prosphōneō,* as in 21. 40. **Hebrew.** Gr. *Hebrais,* as in 21. 40. **tongue.** Gr. *dialektos,* as in 1. 19. **kept, &c.**=shewed silence the more. **3 verily.** Texts omit. **man.** Gr. *anēr.* Ap. 123. 2. **in.** Gr. *en.* Ap. 104. viii. **in Cilicia**=of Cilicia. **brought up.** Gr. *anatrephō.* Only here and 7. 20, 21. **at.** Gr. *para.* Ap. 104. xii. 3. **Gamaliel.** See note on 5. 34. Only mentioned in these two places. **taught.** Gr. *paideuō,* to train a child (*pais*), instruct, chastise. See 7. 22. Luke 23. 16, 22. **according to.** Gr. *kata.* Ap. 104. x. 2. **perfect manner.** Lit. accuracy. Gr. *akribeia.* Only here. Much used by medical writers.

the law °of the fathers, °and was °zealous
°toward °God, °as ye all are this day.
4 And I persecuted °this °way °unto °the
death, °binding and °delivering °into prisons
both [3] men and °women.
5 As °also the high priest doth °bear me
witness, and °all the estate of the elders: °from
whom also I received letters [1] unto the °brethren,
and °went °to Damascus, to bring them which
were °there bound °unto Jerusalem, °for to be
punished.

m 6 And it came to pass, that, as I made my
journey, and °was come nigh °unto Damascus
°about °noon, °suddenly there °shone °from
°heaven a great °light °round °about me.
7 And I fell [-5] unto the °ground, and °heard
a voice saying [6] unto me, °'Saul, Saul, why
persecutest thou Me?'
8 And I °answered, 'Who art Thou, °Lord?'
And He said [1] unto me, 'I am °Jesus °of
Nazareth, Whom thou persecutest.'
9 And they that were °with me °saw indeed
the [6] light, °and were afraid; but they °heard
°not the voice of Him That °spake to me.
10 And I said, °'What shall I do, [8] Lord?'
And °the Lord said [1] unto me, °'Arise, and go
[4] into Damascus; and there it shall be °told
thee °of all things which are °appointed for
thee to do.'

11 And when I could [9] not °see °for the °glory
of °that [6] light, being °led by the hand °of
them that °were with me, I came [4] into
Damascus.
12 And °one Ananias, a °devout [3] man
[3] according to the law, °having a good report
[11] of all the Jews which °dwelt *there*,
13 Came [1] unto me, and stood, and said [6] unto
me, 'Brother °Saul, °receive thy sight.' And
the same hour I °looked up °upon him.
14 And he said, 'The [3] God of our fathers hath
°chosen thee, °that thou shouldest °know His
°will, and °see °that Just One, and °shouldest
hear °the voice °of His mouth.
15 For thou shalt be °His °witness [1] unto all
°men of °what thou hast °seen and heard.
16 And now why tarriest thou? [10] arise, and
be °baptized, and °wash away thy °sins,
°calling on °the name of °the Lord.'

of the fathers. Gr. *patrōos*, pertaining to the fathers. Only here, 24. 14; 28. 17.
and was = being. Gr *huparchō*. See note on Luke 9. 48.
zealous. See note on 21. 20.
toward = of, i. e. a zealot in behalf of. Cp. Phil. 3. 5, 6.
God. Ap. 98. I. i. 1.
as ye, &c. This was to conciliate them. Fig. *Protherapeia.* Ap. 6.
4 this. Emph.
way. See 9. 2.
unto = as far as.
the. Omit.
binding. Gr. *desmeuō.* Only here and Matt. 23. 4.
delivering. Same as "commit" in 8. 3.
into. Gr. *eis.* Ap. 104. vi.
women. Cp. 8. 3; 9. 2.
5 also, &c. = the high priest also.
bear . . . witness. Gr. *martureō.* See p. 1511. Same as 15. 8.
all the estate, &c. = the whole presbytery. Gr. *presbuterion.* Only here, Luke 22. 66. 1 Tim. 4. 14.
from. Gr. *para.* Ap. 104. xii. 1.
brethren. This means the Jewish rulers in Damascus.
went = was going.
to = unto. Gr. *eis.* Ap. 104. vi.
there. Gr. *ekeise.* Only here and 21. 3. Add "also".
unto. Gr. *eis*, as above.
for to be punished = in order that (Gr. *hina*) they might be punished. Gr. *timōreō.* Only here and 26. 11.
6 was come nigh = drew near.
unto = to.
about. Gr. *peri.* Ap. 104. xiii. 2.
noon. Gr. *mesēmbria.* Only here and 8. 26 (south).
suddenly. Gr. *exaiphnēs.* See note on 9. 3.
shone . . . round. Gr. *periastraptō.* See note on 9. 3.
from = out of. Gr. *ek.* Ap. 104. vii.
heaven = the heaven. See note on Matt. 6. 9, 10.
light. Gr. *phōs.* Ap. 130. 1.
7 ground. Gr. *edaphos.* Only here.
heard. See note on 9. 4.
Saul, Saul. See note on 9. 4.
8 answered. Gr. *apokrinomai.* Ap. 122. 3.
Lord. Ap. 98. VI. i. β. 2. B.
Jesus. Ap. 98. X.
of Nazareth = the Nazarene. See 2. 22. The Lord Himself uses the despised name.
9 with. Gr. *sun.* Ap. 104. xvi.
saw = beheld. Gr. *theaomai.* Ap. 133. I. 12. It was no mere lightning flash. Cp. "glory", *v.* 11.

and were afraid. Omit. **heard.** See note on 9. 7. **not.** Gr. *ou.* Ap. 105. I. **spake.** Gr. *laleō.* Ap. 121. 7. **10 What shall I do.** This question is only in this account. **the Lord.** Ap. 98. VI. i. β. 2. A. **Arise.** Gr. *anistēmi.* Ap. 178. I. 1. **told.** Gr. *laleō*, as in *v.* 9. **of** = concerning. Gr. *peri.* Ap. 104. xiii. 1. **appointed.** Gr. *tassō.* See note on 13. 48. **11 see.** Gr. *emblepō.* Ap. 133. I. 7. **for** = from. Gr. *apo.* Ap. 104. iv. **glory.** Gr. *doxa.* See note on John 1. 14. Cp. 7. 55. **that.** Emph. **led by the hand.** See note on 9. 8. **of** = by. Gr. *hupo.* Ap. 104. xviii. 1. **were with.** Gr. *suneimi.* Only here and Luke 9. 18. **12 one** = a certain. Gr. *tis.* Ap. 123. 3. **devout.** Gr. *eusebēs.* See note on 10. 2, but the texts read *eulabēs*, as in 2. 5. **having a good report** = borne witness to. Gr. *matureō*, as in *v.* 5. Cp. Heb. 11, 2, 4, &c., R.V. **dwelt.** Gr. *katoikeō.* See note on 2. 5. **13 Saul.** Gr. *Saoul*, as in *v.* 7. **receive thy sight.** Lit. look up. Gr. *anablepō.* Ap. 133. 1. 6. **looked up.** Same word. Gr. *anablepō.* **upon.** Gr. *eis.* Ap. 104. vi. **14 chosen** = destined. Gr. *procheirizomai.* Only here and 26. 16. Not the same as in 1. 2, &c. **that thou shouldest know** = to know. Gr. *ginōskō.* Ap. 132. 1. ii. **will.** Gr. *thelēma.* Ap. 102. 2. **see.** Gr. *eidon.* Ap. 133. I. 1. **that Just One** = the Righteous One. Gr. *dikaios.* Ap. 191. 1. Cp. 3. 14; 7. 52. 1 John 2. 1. Fig. *Antonomasia.* Ap. 6. Paul was thus led to avoid using any term that would excite his hearers. **shouldest hear** = to hear. **the voice of His mouth** = His commands. Fig. *Idiōma.* Ap. 6. Paul thus received his commission direct from the Lord Himself. Cp. Gal. 1. 12. **of** = out of. Gr *ek.* Ap. 104. vii. **15 His witness** = a witness to Him. **witness.** See 1. 8. **men.** Gr. *anthrōpos.* Ap. 123. 1. **what** = the things which. **seen.** Gr. *horaō.* Ap. 133. I. 8. **16 baptized.** Ap. 115. I. i. The verb is in Mid. Voice. **wash away.** Gr. *apolouō.* Ap. 136. iv and 185. **sins.** Gr. *hamartia.* Ap. 128. I. ii. 1. **calling on.** See note on 2. 21. **the name.** See note on 2. 38. **the Lord.** The texts read "of Him", i. e. His name, referring to the Righteous One.

m 17 And it came to pass, that, when I °was
come again [5]to Jerusalem, even while I °prayed
[3]in the °temple, I was [3]in a °trance;
18 And [14]saw Him °saying [6]unto me, 'Make
haste, and get thee °quickly °out of Jerusalem:
for they will [9]not °receive thy °testimony
°concerning Me.'
19 And I said, [8]'Lord, °they °know that I
°imprisoned and °beat °in every synagogue
them that °believed °on Thee:
20 And when the blood of °Thy martyr
Stephen was °shed, I also was standing by,
and °consenting °unto his death, and °kept the
°raiment of them that °slew him.'
21 And He said [1]unto me, 'Depart: for I will
°send thee far hence [5]unto the °Gentiles.'"

S n 22 And they °gave him audience [4]unto this
°word, and *then* °lifted up their voices, and
said, °"Away with such a *fellow* °from the
°earth: for it is [9]not °fit that he should live."
23 And as they °cried out, and °cast off *their*
°clothes, and °threw dust [4]into the air,

o 24 The °chief captain commanded him to be
brought [4]into the °castle, and bade that he
should be °examined by °scourging; °that he
might °know °wherefore they °cried so
°against him.

p 25 And as they °bound him with °thongs,
Paul said [1]unto the °centurion that stood by,
°"Is it lawful for you to °scourge a [15]man that
is a Roman, and °uncondemned?"
26 When the [25]centurion heard *that*, he °went
and °told the [24]chief captain, saying, °"Take
heed °what thou doest: for this [15]man is
a Roman."

p 27 Then the [24]chief captain came, and said
[6]unto him, "Tell me, art thou a Roman?" He
said, "Yea."
28 And the [24]chief captain [8]answered, "With
a great °sum °obtained I this °freedom."
And Paul said, "But I was *free* °born."

o 29 Then °straightway they °departed [22]from
him which °should have [24]examined him: and
the [24]chief captain also was afraid, after he
[24]knew that he was a Roman, and because he
had bound him.

n 30 °On the morrow, °because he would have
[14]known the °certainty wherefore he was

17 was come again=returned. See 9. 26. Gal. 1. 18. Ap. 180.
prayed=was praying. Gr. *proseuchomai*. Ap. 134. I. 2.
temple. Gr. *hieron*. See Matt. 23. 16. A point to weigh with his hearers.
trance. Gr. *ekstasis*. See note on 10. 10.
18 saying. Before "saying" supply ellipsis, "and heard Him".
quickly=with (Gr. *en*. Ap. 104. viii) speed.
out of. Gr. *ek*. Ap. 104. vii.
receive. Gr. *paradechomai*. See note on 16. 21. Fig. *Tapeinosis*. Ap. 6.
testimony. Gr. *marturia*. See note on p. 1511 and cp. 1. 8.
concerning. Gr. *peri*. Ap. 104. xiii. 1.
19 they=they themselves.
know. Gr. *epistamai*. Ap. 132. I. v.
imprisoned=was imprisoning. Gr. *phulakizō*. Only here.
beat=was beating. Gr. *derō*. See note on 5. 40.
in every synagogue. Gr. *kata tas sunagōgas*, synagogue by synagogue. Showing Paul's systematic action.
believed. Gr. *pisteuō*. Ap. 150. I. 1. v. (iii) 2.
on. Gr. *epi*. Ap. 104. ix. 3.
20 Thy martyr Stephen=Stephen Thy witness (Gr. *martur*. See 1. 8).
shed=being poured out. Gr. *ekcheō*, as in 2. 17, 18, 33.
consenting. Gr. *suneudokeō*. See note on 8. 1.
unto his death. The texts omit.
kept=was guarding.
raiment=garments. As in 14. 14.
slew. Gr. *anaireō*. See note on 2. 23.
21 send. Gr. *exapostellō*. Ap. 174. 2.
Gentiles=nations. Gr. *ethnos*.

22. 22-30 (S, p. 1639). EVENTS FOLLOWING.
(*Introversion.*)

S | n | 22, 23. Paul before the people.
  o | 24. Torture ordered.
   p | 25, 26. Rights claimed.
   p | 27, 28. Rights admitted.
  o | 29. Torture abandoned.
 n | 30. Paul before the Council.

22 gave him audience=were listening to him. As in *v.* 7, the verb followed by the gen. case shows that they followed what he was saying.
word. Gr. *logos*. Ap. 121. 10. The thought of Gentiles on an equality with Jews was intolerable.
lifted up, &c. Cp. 2. 14; 14. 11.
Away. See note on John 19. 15.
from. Gr. *apo*. Ap. 104. iv.
earth. Gr. *gē*. Ap. 129. 4.

fit. Gr. *kathēkō*. Only here and Rom. 1. 28. To teach the Gentiles that the Messiah of the Jews was a crucified malefactor was an outrageous offence to the orthodox Jew (1 Cor. 1. 23). **23 cried out**=were crying out. Gr. *kraugazō*. See John 18. 40. **cast off.** Gr. *riptō*. **clothes**=outer garments. Gr. *himation*. Holding them in their hands and tossing them upward. **threw**=were throwing. Gr. *ballō*. Ap. 174. 9. **24 chief captain.** See note on 21. 31. **castle.** See note on 21. 34. **examined.** Gr. *anetazō*. Only here and *v.* 29. **scourging.** Gr. *mastix*. Here and Heb. 11. 36 transl. "scourging"; in the Gospels (Mark 3. 10; 5. 29, 34. Luke 7. 21) transl. "plague". Cp. John 19. 1. **that**=in order that. Gr. *hina*. **know.** Gr. *epiginōskō*. Ap. 132. I. iii. **wherefore**=on account of (Gr. *dia*. Ap. 104. v. 2) what cause. **cried**=were shouting. Gr. *epiphōneō*. See note on 12. 22. **against.** Lit. "at". No preposition. **25 bound.** Gr. *proteinō*, to stretch out or tie up. Only here. **thongs.** Gr. *himas*. Here, Mark 1. 7. Luke 3. 16. John 1. 27. **centurion.** See note on 21. 32. **Is it**=If (Gr. *ei*. Ap. 118. 2. a) it is. **scourge.** Gr. *mastizō*. Only here. The usual word is *mastigoō*. **uncondemned.** Gr. *akatakritos*. See note on 16. 37. **26 went.** The chiliarch having given his orders, had gone to his quarters. **told.** Gr. *apangellō*. See note on 16. 36. **Take heed.** The texts omit. **what thou doest**=what art thou about to do? **28 sum.** Gr. *kephalaion*. Only here and Heb. 8. 1. In Sept. Lev. 6. 4. Num. 4. 2; 5. 7 (principal), &c. **obtained.** Gr. *ktaomai*. See note on 1. 18. **freedom.** Gr. *politeia*=citizenship. Here and Eph. 2. 12. **born**="even born so." **29 straightway.** Gr. *eutheōs*, as in 21. 30 (forthwith). **departed.** See note on 19. 9. **should have, &c.**=were about to examine. **30 On the morrow**=But on the morrow. **because, &c.**=wishing (Gr. *boulomai*. Ap. 102. 3.) to know. **certainty.** See note on 21. 34.

°accused °of the Jews, he loosed him °from *his* bands, and commanded the chief priests and all their °council to °appear, and °brought Paul down, and set him °before them.

R q **23** And Paul, °earnestly beholding the °council, said, °"Men *and* brethren, I have °lived in all good °conscience °before °God until this day."

2 And the high priest °Ananias commanded them that stood by him to smite °him on the mouth.

3 Then said Paul °unto him, [1]"God °shall smite thee, *thou* °whited °wall: for sittest thou °to judge me °after the law, and commandest me to be smitten °contrary to the law?"

4 And they that stood by said, °"Revilest thou [1]God's high priest?"

r 5 Then said Paul, "I °wist °not, brethren, that he was °the high priest: for it °is written, '**Thou shalt °not speak °evil of the ruler of thy °people.**'"

q 6 °But when Paul °perceived that the one part were °Sadducees, and the °other °Pharisees, he cried out °in the [1]council, [1]"Men *and* brethren, I am a Pharisee, the °son of a Pharisee: °of °the °hope and °resurrection °of the dead I am °called in question."

r 7 And when he had °so said, there arose a °dissension °between the Pharisees and the Sadducees: and the °multitude was °divided.

8 For °the Sadducees say that there is °no [6]resurrection, °neither angel, °nor °spirit: but °the Pharisees confess both.

9 And there arose a great °cry: and the scribes *that were* of the Pharisees' part °arose, and °strove, saying, "We find °no °evil [6]in this °man: but °if a [8]spirit or an angel °hath spoken to him, °let us not fight against God."

10 And when there arose a great [7]dissension, the °chief captain, °fearing °lest Paul should have been °pulled in pieces °of them, commanded the °soldiers to go down, and to °take him by force °from among them, and to bring *him* °into the °castle.

S s 11 And the night °following °the Lord stood

accused. Gr. *katēgoreō*. Occ. nine times in Acts.
of. Gr. *para*. Ap. 104. xii. 1, but the texts read *hupo*, xviii. 1.
from *his* bands. The texts omit.
council = the Sanhedrin. See John 11. 47.
appear. The texts read "come together".
brought . . . down. Gr. *katagō*. See note on 21. 3.
before. Gr. *eis*. Ap. 104. vi.

23. 1-10 (*R*, p. 1639). PAUL'S DEFENCE. (*Alternation.*)

R | q | 1. Paul's life.
  r | 5. Dispute with High Priest.
 q | 6. Paul's faith.
  r | 7-10. Dispute between the sects.

23. 1 earnestly beholding. Gr. *atenizō*. Ap. 133. III. 6.
council. See note on 22. 30.
Men *and* brethren. See note on 1. 11.
lived. Gr. *politeuomai*, to live as a citizen. Only here and Phil. 1. 27.
conscience. Gr. *suneidēsis*. Cp. 24. 16.
before = to.
God. Ap. 98. I. i. 1.
2 Ananias. Son of Nedebæus. He was murdered by a band of the Sicarii some years after, being caught in an aqueduct where he had concealed himself (Josephus, *Ant.* XX. v. 2; vi. 2; ix. 2; *Wars*, II. xvii. 9).
him on the = his.
3 unto. Gr. *pros*. Ap. 104. xv. 3.
shall = is about to.
whited = whitewashed. Gr. *koniaō*. Only here and Matt. 23. 27. See note there.
wall. Gr. *toichos*. The wall of a building, not the wall of a city (*teichos*). Only here.
to judge = judging. Gr. *krinō*. Ap. 122. 1.
after = according to. Gr. *kata*. Ap. 104. x. 2.
contrary to the law = acting against law. Gr. *paranomeō*. Only here.
4 Revilest. Gr. *loidoreō*. See note on John 9. 28.
5 wist = knew. Gr. *oida*. Ap. 132. I. i.
not. Gr. *ou*. Ap. 105. I.
the. Omit.
is written = has been written, or standeth written. See Ex. 22. 28.
evil. Gr. *kakōs*. Cp. Ap. 128. III. 2. Cp. John 18. 23. Jas. 4. 3 (amiss).
people. Gr. *laos*. See note on 2. 47.
6 But = Now.
perceived = got to know. Gr. *ginōskō*. Ap. 132. I. ii. Some may have heard Paul's address on the stairs (22. 1-21), and were discussing his statement about the risen Lord, and might have put a question to him.

Sadducees . . . Pharisees. Ap. 120. II. **other.** Gr. *heteros*. Ap. 124. 2. **in.** Gr. *en*. Ap. 104. viii. **son.** Gr. *huios*. Ap. 108. iii. **of** = concerning. Gr. *peri*. Ap. 104. xiii. 1. **the** = a. **hope and resurrection** = resurrection-hope. Fig. *Hendiadys*. Ap. 6. **resurrection.** Gr. *anastasis*. Ap. 178. II. 1. **of the dead.** Gr. *nekrōn*. No art. Ap. 139. 2. **called in question** = judged. Gr. *krinō*, as in *v.* 3. **7 so said** = spoken (Gr. *laleō*. Ap. 121. 7) this. **dissension.** Gr. *stasis*. See note on 15. 2. **between** = of. **multitude.** Gr. *plēthos*. See 2. 6. **divided.** Gr. *schizō*. See note on 14. 4. **8 the.** Omit. **no.** Gr. *mē*. Ap. 105. II. **neither . . . nor.** Gr. *mēte . . . mēte*. **spirit.** Ap. 101. II. 11. **9 cry.** Gr. *kraugē*. Here; Matt. 25. 6. Eph. 4. 31. Heb. 5. 7. Rev. 14. 18; 21. 4. **arose.** Gr. *anistēmi*. Ap. 178. I. 1. **strove** = were earnestly contending. Gr. *diamachomai*. Only here. **no** = nothing. Gr. *oudeis*. **evil.** Gr. *kakos*. Ap. 128. III. 2. **man.** Gr. *anthrōpos*. Ap. 123. 1. **if.** Gr. *ei*. Ap. 118. 2. a. **hath spoken** = spoke. Gr. *laleō*, as in *v.* 7. **let us not, &c.** All the texts omit. They suddenly broke off. Perhaps the Pharisees were afraid to express their thoughts. It is the Fig. *Aposiōpēsis*. Ap. 6. The words in the A.V. were probably added by some copyist from 5. 39, adapting Gamaliel's language. **10 chief captain.** See note on 21. 31. **fearing.** Gr. *eulabeomai*. Only here and Heb. 11. 7. The texts read *phobeomai* (as 22. 29), a much more common word. **lest.** Gr. *mē*. Ap. 105. II. **pulled in pieces** = torn asunder. Gr. *diaspaō*. Only here and Mark 5. 4. **of** = by. Gr. *hupo*. Ap. 104. xviii. 1. **soldiers.** Lit. an army or detachment. Gr. *strateuma*. Here, *v.* 27. Matt. 22. 7. Luke 23. 11. Rev. 9. 16; 19. 14, 19. **take . . . by force.** Gr. *harpazō*. Cp. 8. 39 (caught away). **from among** = out of (Gr. *ek*) the midst of. **into.** Gr. *eis*. Ap. 104. vi. **castle.** See note on 21. 34.

23. 11-22 (*S*, p. 1639). EVENTS FOLLOWING. (*Alternation.*)

S | s | 11. Comfort from the Lord.
  t | 12-15. Conspiracy formed.
 s | 16-19. Consideration from the chief captain.
  t | 20-22. Conspiracy revealed.

11 following. Gr. *epeimi*. See note on 7. 26. **the Lord.** Ap. 98. VI. i. β. 2. A.

by him, and said, ° "Be of good cheer, ° Paul:
for as thou hast ° testified [6] of Me ° in Jerusalem,
so must thou ° bear witness ° also ° at Rome."

t 12 And when it was day, ° certain of the Jews
° banded together, and ° bound themselves
under a curse, ° saying that they would [8] neither
eat [8] nor drink till they had killed Paul.
13 And they were more than forty which had
made this ° conspiracy.
14 And they came to the chief priests and
° elders, and said, ° "We have [12] bound ourselves
under a great ° curse, ° that we will ° eat
° nothing until we have slain Paul.
15 Now therefore ye ° with the [1] council ° signify
to the [10] chief captain that he ° bring him down
° unto you to morrow, as ° though ye would
° enquire ° something ° more perfectly ° concerning him: and we, ° or ever he come near, are
ready to ° kill him."

s 16 And when Paul's sister's [6] son heard of
their ° lying in wait, he ° went and entered
[10] into the [10] castle, and ° told Paul.
17 Then Paul called one of the ° centurions
unto *him*, and said, "Bring this ° young man
[3] unto the [10] chief captain: for he hath ° a
certain thing to [16] tell him."
18 ° So he took him, and brought *him* ° to the
[10] chief captain, and said, ° "Paul the ° prisoner
called me unto *him*, and ° prayed me to bring
this [17] young man [3] unto thee, who hath ° something to ° say ° unto thee."
19 Then the [10] chief captain ° took him by the
hand, and ° went *with him* aside ° privately,
and ° asked *him*, "What is that thou hast to
[16] tell me?"

t 20 And he said, "The Jews ° have agreed to
° desire thee that thou wouldest [15] bring down
Paul to morrow [10] into the [1] council, as [15] though
they would ° enquire ° somewhat [6] of him
[15] more perfectly.
21 But do ° not thou ° yield unto them: for there
° lie in wait for him ° of them more than forty
° men, which have [12] bound themselves with an
oath, that they will [8] neither eat [8] nor drink
till they have [15] killed him: and now are they
ready, ° looking for ° a promise ° from thee."
22 ° So the [10] chief captain *then* ° let the
[17] young man depart, and ° charged *him*, ° "*See thou* tell ° no man that thou hast ° shewed
these things [18] to me."

Pu 23 And ° he called unto *him* ° two [17] centurions,

Be of good cheer = Take courage. Gr. *tharseō*. Here; Matt. 9. 2, 22; 14. 27. Mark 6. 50; 10. 49. Luke 8. 48. John 16. 33.
Paul. The texts omit.
testified. Gr. *diamarturomai.* See note on 2. 40.
in. Gr. *eis.* Ap. 104. vi.
bear witness. Gr. *martureō.* See p. 1511 and note on John 1. 7.
also at Rome = at Rome also.
at. Gr. *eis*, as above.
12 certain of. The texts omit.
banded together = having made a coalition, i. e. of the two sects. Gr. *sustrophē.* See note on 19. 40.
bound . . . curse. Gr. *anathematizō.* Only here, *vv.* 14, 21, and Mark 14. 71, where see note.
saying, &c. Josephus records a vow taken by ten men to kill Herod the Great. In a papyrus from Oxyrhynchus, in the Bodleian Library, there is a letter from an Egyptian boy, threatening that, if his father will not take him to Alexandria, he would neither eat nor drink.
13 conspiracy. Gr. *sunōmosia.* Only here.
14 elders. Ap. 189.
We have bound . . . curse. Lit. we have anathematized ourselves (see Mark 14. 71) with an anathema. A Hebraism. Fig. *Polyptōton.* Ap. 6.
curse. Gr. *anathema.* Here; Rom. 9. 3. 1 Cor. 12. 3; 16. 22. Gal. 1. 8, 9.
that we will = to.
eat = taste. See note on 10. 10.
nothing. Gr. *mēdeis.*
15 with. Gr. *sun.* Ap. 104. xvi.
signify. Gr. *emphanizō.* Ap. 106. I. iv.
bring . . . down. Gr. *katagō.* See note on 21. 3.
unto. The texts read *eis.* Ap. 104. vi.
though ye would = being about to.
enquire. Gr. *diaginōskō.* This is the medical word for making a careful examination. Only here and 24. 22. The noun *diagnōsis* only in 25. 21.
something . . . him = the things concerning him more accurately (Gr. *akribesteron*, comparative of *akribōs*, 18. 25, 26). Occ. 18. 26; 24. 22.
concerning. Gr. *peri.* Ap. 104. xiii. 1.
or ever = before. Gr. *pro.* Ap. 104. xiv.
kill. Gr. *anaireō.* See note on 2. 23. Not the same word as in *vv.* 12, 14.
16 lying in wait. Gr. *enedra.* Only here and 25. 3.
went, &c. This may be rendered "having come in upon (them) and entered", suggesting that he made the discovery accidentally. See R.V. marg. But it was of God. Paul was not to be "cut off" at the will of the enemy, any more than the "seed". See Ex. 2. 6, and Ap. 23.
told = reported (it to). Gr. *apangellō.* See note on 4. 23.
17 centurions. See note on 21. 32.
young man. Gr. *neanias*, but the texts read *neaniskos.* Ap. 108. x.
a certain thing. Gr. *tis.* Ap. 123. 3.
18 So, &c. = He therefore indeed having taken him, brought him.
to. Gr. *pros.* Ap. 104. xv. 3. **Paul the prisoner.** This was a title the apostle cherished as one of honour. See Eph. 3. 1; 4. 1. 2 Tim. 1. 8. Philem. 1, 9. **prisoner.** Gr. *desmios.* **prayed** = asked. Gr. *erōtaō.* Ap. 134. I. 3. **something.** Gr. *tis.* Same as "a certain thing", *v.* 17. **say** = speak. Gr. *laleō.* Ap. 121. 7. **unto** = to. **19 took.** Gr. *epilambanomai.* See note on 9. 27. **went . . . aside** = having withdrawn. Gr. *anachōreō.* Cp. Matt. 12. 15. **privately.** Gr. *kat'* (Ap. 104. x. 2) *idian.* This expression occ. many times in the first three Gospels, transl. apart, aside, &c. **asked** = enquired of. Gr. *punthanomai.* See note on 21. 33. **20 have agreed** = agreed. Gr. *suntithēmi.* Here, 24. 9. Luke 22. 5. John 9. 22. **desire.** Same as "prayed", *v.* 18. **enquire.** Same as "asked", *v.* 19. **somewhat** = something, as in *v.* 18. **21 not.** Gr. *mē.* Ap. 105. II. **yield unto** = be persuaded by. Gr. *peithō.* Ap. 150. I. 2. **lie in wait.** Gr. *enedreuō.* Only here and Luke 11. 54. Cp. *v.* 16. **of.** Gr. *ek.* Ap. 104. vii. **men.** Ap. 123. 2. **looking for.** Gr. *prosdechomai.* Cp. 24. 15. Mark 15. 43 (waited for). **a** = the. This shows that some promise of a further trial of Paul had been given. **from.** Gr. *apo.* Ap. 104. iv. **22 So, &c.** The chief captain indeed then. **let . . . depart** = sent away. Gr. *apoluō.* Ap. 174. 11. **charged** = commanded. Gr. *parangellō.* See note on 1. 4. ***See thou* tell** = to tell. Gr. *eklaleō.* Only here. **no man** = no one. Gr. *mēdeis.* **shewed.** Same as "signify", *v.* 15.

23. 23-35 [For Structure see next page].

23 he called = having called. **two** = certain (Gr. *tis.* Ap. 123. 3) two.

°saying, "Make ready two hundred soldiers to go °to °Cæsarea, and °horsemen threescore and ten, and °spearmen two hundred, °at the third hour of the night;
24 And provide *them* °beasts, °that they may °set Paul on, and °bring *him* safe [3] unto °Felix the °governor."

v 25 °And he wrote a letter °after this manner:
26 °"Claudius Lysias [18] unto the °most excellent [24] governor Felix *sendeth* °greeting.
27 This [21] man °was taken [10] of the Jews, and °should have been [15] killed [10] of them: °then came I [15] with °an army, °and rescued him, having °understood that he was a Roman.
28 And °when I would have °known the cause °wherefore they °accused him, I [15] brought him forth [10] into their council:
29 Whom I °perceived to be [28] accused [6] of °questions of their law, but °to have [11] nothing °laid to his charge worthy of death or of bonds.
30 And when °it was °told me how that °the Jews laid wait °for the [21] man, I °sent °straightway [18] to thee, °and gave commandment to his °accusers also to say °before thee °what *they had* against him. °Farewell."

w 31 °Then the soldiers, °as it was °commanded them, took Paul, and brought *him* °by night °to °Antipatris.
32 On the morrow they °left the [23] horsemen to go [15] with him, and returned [31] to the [10] castle:

v 33 Who, °when they came [31] to [23] Cæsarea, and °delivered the °epistle to the [24] governor, presented Paul also °before him.
34 And °when the [24] governor had read *the letter*, he °asked [21] of what °province he was. And when he °understood that *he was* °of °Cilicia;

u 35 "I will °hear thee," said he, "when thine [30] accusers °are also come." And he commanded him to be °kept [6] in Herod's °judgment hall.

23. 23-35 (P, p. 1639). JOURNEY TO CÆSAREA.

(*Introversion.*)

P | u | 23, 24. Chief captain. Orders.
  v | 25-30. Letter written.
   w | 31, 32. Journey.
  v | 33, 34. Letter received.
 u | 35. Felix. Orders.

saying = he said.

to = as far as. Gr. *heōs*. About seventy miles.

Cæsarea. See note on 8. 40.

horsemen. Gr. *hippeus*. Only here and *v.* 32.

spearmen. Gr. *dexiolabos*. Only here. Some light-armed troops are meant.

at = from. Gr. *apo*. Ap. 104. iv. The third hour of the night was 9 p.m., and no one could pursue till the gates were open at 6 a.m.

24 beasts. Gr. *ktēnos*. Here; Luke 10. 34. 1 Cor. 15. 39. Rev. 18. 13.

that = in order that. Gr. *hina*.

set . . . on. Gr. *epibibazō*. Here, and Luke 10. 34; 19. 35.

bring . . . safe = keep him safe and bring him. Fig. *Ellipsis*. Ap. 6. Gr. *diasōzō*. See Matt. 14. 36.

Felix. Claudius made him Procurator of Judæa in A. D. 52. Josephus gives many details of the stirring times of his rule, and of his cruelty and treachery (*Ant.* XX. vii. 1; viii. 5, 6, 7, &c.).

governor. Gr. *hēgemōn*. The general term for a subordinate ruler, Felix being a lieutenant of the Proprætor of Syria.

25 And he wrote = Having written.

after this manner = having (Gr. *periechō*, but texts read *echō*) this form (Gr. *tupos*, 7. 43).

26 Claudius Lysias. As the Procurator's legate, he was responsible for order in Jerusalem. He had shown promptness and vigour, and, moreover, kindly consideration for his prisoner (*v.* 19), and in his letter puts Paul's case in a favourable light. He certainly claims some credit for himself to which he was not entitled (*v.* 27), and says nothing about his proposing to scourge a Roman citizen. But he stands far above Felix, or even Festus, and is entitled to rank with Julius (27. 3, 43).

most excellent. Gr. *kratistos*. Only occ. here; 24. 3; 26. 25, and Luke 1. 3. It was an official title. Cp. "Excellency". **greeting.** See note on 15. 23. **27 was taken** = having been seized. See note on 1. 16, and cp. John 18. 12. **should have been** = being about to be, or on the point of being. **then came I** = having come. **an army** = the detachment, as in *v.* 10. **and rescued him** = I delivered. Gr. *exaireō*. See note on 7. 10. **understood** = learnt. He did not learn it till he was about to have him scourged. It has been called "a dexterous falsehood". **28 when I would have known** = wishing (Gr. *boulomai*. Ap. 102. 3) to know. **known.** Gr. *ginōskō*. Ap. 132. I. ii, but the texts read *epiginōskō*. Ap. 132. I. iii. **wherefore** = on account of (Gr. *dia*. Ap. 104. v. 2) which. **accused** = were accusing. Gr. *enkaleō*. See note on 19. 38. **29 perceived** = found. **questions.** Gr. *zētēma*. See note on 15. 2. **to have nothing, &c.** = as having no accusation. **laid to his charge.** Gr. *enklēma*. Only here and 25. 16. **30 it was told me, &c.** Lit. a plot was revealed to me as about to be laid against the man. **told** = revealed. Gr. *mēnuō*. See Luke 20. 37 (shewed). **the Jews.** The texts omit. **for** = against. Gr. *eis*. Ap. 104. vi. **sent.** Gr. *pempō*. Ap. 174. 4. **straightway.** Gr. *exautēs*. See note on 10. 33. **and gave commandment** = having commanded, or charged. Gr. *parangellō*. See *v.* 22. **accusers.** Gr. *katēgoros*. Here; *v.* 35; 24. 8; 25. 16, 18. John 8. 10. Rev. 12. 10. **before.** Gr. *epi*. Ap. 104. ix. 1. **what *they had*.** Omit. **Farewell.** Omit. **31 Then** = So then. **as it was** = according to (Gr. *kata*. Ap. 104. x. 2) that which was. **commanded.** Gr. *diatassō*. See note on 7. 44. **by** = through. Gr. *dia*. Ap. 104. v. 1. **to.** Gr. *eis*. Ap. 104. vi. **Antipatris.** A small town in the plain of Sharon, about forty miles from Jerusalem. Built by Herod the Great, and called after his father, Antipater. **32 left.** Gr. *eaō*. Generally transl. "suffer" in the sense of "permit". **33 when they came** = having entered. **delivered** = having delivered. Gr. *anadidōmi*. Only here. **epistle.** Same as letter, *v.* 25. **before** = to. **34 when, &c.** The texts read "when he had read it". **asked** = questioned. Gr. *eperōtaō*. See note on 1. 6. **province.** Gr. *eparchia*. Only here and 25. 1. **understood** = learnt by enquiry. Gr. *punthanomai*. See *vv.* 19, 20. **of** = from. Gr. *apo*. Ap. 104. iv. **Cilicia.** Cilicia was included in the province of Syria, and therefore in the jurisdiction of Felix. **35 hear** = hear fully. Gr. *diakouō*. Only here. **are also come** = also shall have come. **kept** = guarded. **judgment hall.** Gr. *praitōrion*. See note on Matt. 27. 27. John 18. 28. It here means the guard-room attached to Herod's palace.

Q¹T **24** And °after five days °Ananias the high
priest °descended °with °the °elders,
and *with* a °certain °orator *named* Tertullus,
°who °informed the °governor °against Paul.
U V 2 And when he was called forth, Tertullus
began to °accuse *him*, saying, °"Seeing that
°by thee we enjoy °great quietness, and that
°very worthy deeds are done °unto this °nation
°by thy °providence:
3 We °accept *it* °always, and °in all places,
°most noble Felix, ¹with all °thankfulness.
4 °Notwithstanding, °that I °be °not °further
tedious unto thee, I °pray thee °that thou
wouldest hear us °of thy °clemency °a few
words.
W 5 For we have found this °man *a* °pestilent
fellow, and °a mover of °sedition °among all
the Jews °throughout the °world, and a °ring-
leader of the °sect of the °Nazarenes:
6 Who °also °hath gone about to °profane the
°temple: whom we °took, °and °would have
°judged °according to our law.
7 But the °chief captain Lysias came *upon us*,
and ¹with great °violence took *him* away °out
of our hands,
8 °Commanding his °accusers to come °unto
thee: by °examining °of whom thyself °mayest
°take knowledge °of all these things, whereof
we accuse him."
9 And the Jews also °assented, °saying that
these things were so.
V 10 °Then Paul, °after that the ¹governor had
beckoned ²unto him to speak, °answered,
°"Forasmuch as I °know that thou hast been
°of °many years a °judge ²unto this ²nation,
I do °the more cheerfully °answer °for myself:
W x 11 Because that thou °mayest °understand,

24. 1-27 (Q¹, p. 1639). PAUL AND FELIX.
(*Introversion and Alternation.*)

Q¹ | T | 1. Felix. On the judgment seat.
  U | V | 2-4. Tertullus. Introduction.
    W | 5-9. His charges.
  V | 10. Paul. Introduction.
    W | 11-21. His defence.
T | 22-27. Felix. Decision.

24. 1 after. Gr. *meta.* Ap. 104. xi. 2.
Ananias. See note on 23. 2.
descended = came down.
with. Gr. *meta* Ap. 104. xi. 1.
the = certain. Gr. *tis.* Ap. 123. 3.
elders. See Ap. 189.
certain. Gr. *tis*, as above.
orator = advocate. Gr. *rhētōr.* Only here. The adv. in 1 Tim. 4. 1 (expressly).
who. Pl., referring to the Jews (*v.* 9) as well as their spokesman.
informed. Gr. *emphanizō.* Ap. 106. I. iv.
governor. See note on 23. 24.
against. Gr. *kata.* Ap. 104. x. 1.
2 accuse. Gr. *katēgoreō.* See note on 22. 30.
Seeing . . . enjoy = Obtaining (as we do). Gr. *tunchanō*, to obtain, (intr.) to happen. See note on 19. 11.
by = through. Gr. *dia.* Ap. 104. v. 1.
great quietness. Lit. much peace (Gr. *eirēnē*).
very worthy deeds. Gr. *katorthōma*, but the texts read *diorthōma.* Only here. The words are from *orthos* (see 14. 10), and the former means "a right action", the latter, "an amelioration" or "reform".
unto = to. **nation.** Gr. *ethnos.*
providence = provident care, or foresight. Gr. *pronoia.* Only here and Rom. 13. 14.
3 accept = receive. Gr. *apodechomai.* See note on 2. 41.
always = in every case. Gr. *pantē.* Only here.
in all places = everywhere. Gr. *pantachou.*
most noble. Same as "most excellent", in 23. 26.
thankfulness. Gr. *eucharistia.* In the other fourteen occ. rendered "thanksgiving", "thanks", or "giving of thanks".
4 Notwithstanding = But. **that** = in order that. Gr. *hina.* **be . . . tedious unto** = hinder. Gr. *enkoptō.* Occ. here, Rom. 15. 22. Gal. 5. 7. 1 Thess. 2 18. 1 Pet. 3. 7. **not.** Gr. *mē.* Ap. 105. II. **further.** Lit. for (Gr. *epi.* Ap. 104. ix. 3) more (time). **pray.** Gr. *parakaleō.* Ap. 134. I. 6. **that thou wouldest** = to. **of** = in. Dat. case. **clemency.** Gr. *epieikia.* Only here and 2 Cor. 10. 1. **a few words** = concisely. Gr. *suntomōs.* Only here. A medical word. **5 man.** Gr. *anēr.* Ap. 123. 2. **pestilent.** Gr. *loimos*, a plague. Occ. elsewhere. Matt. 24. 7. Luke 21. 11. **a mover of** = stirring up. **sedition.** Gr. *stasis.* See note on 15. 2. The texts read "seditions". **among.** Dat. case. **throughout.** Gr. *kata.* Ap. 104. x. 2. **world.** Gr. *oikoumenē.* Ap. 129. 3. **ringleader.** Gr. *prōtostatēs.* Only here. **sect.** Gr. *hairesis.* See note on 5. 17. **Nazarenes.** Cp. 6. 14. Only here is the term applied to believers. The Jews would not call them Christians (11. 26), as that was derived from the word for Messiah; so Tertullus was instructed to call them Nazarenes. Cp. 22. 8. **6 also.** This should follow "temple". **hath gone about** = attempted. Same as "assayed" (16. 7). **profane** = pollute. Gr. *bebēloō.* See note on Matt. 12. 5, the only other occ. **temple.** Gr. *hieron.* See note on Matt. 23. 16. **took** = seized also. **and would have, &c.** These words and *vv.* 7 and 8, as far as "unto thee", are omitted by the texts, but not by the Syriac. Dean Alford puts the words in brackets and declares himself at a loss to decide respecting them, it being inexplicable that Tertullus should have ended so abruptly. **would have judged** = purposed (Gr. *ethelō.* Ap. 102. 1) to judge. **judged.** Gr. *krinō.* Ap. 122. 1. **according to.** Gr. *kata.* Ap. 104. x. 2. **7 chief captain.** See note on 21. 31. **violence.** Gr. *bia.* See note on 5. 26. **out of.** Gr. *ek.* Ap. 104. vii. **8 Commanding** = Having commanded. Lysias had done this after he had sent Paul to Cæsarea to escape the plot. Hence the bitterness of the Jews against him. It is one of the strongest grounds for the retention of these verses. **accusers.** Gr. *katēgoros.* See note on 23. 30. **unto.** Gr. *epi.* Ap. 104. ix. 3. **examining** = having examined. Gr. *anakrinō.* Ap. 122. 2. **of.** Gr. *para.* Ap. 104. xii. 1. **mayest** = wilt be able to. **take knowledge** = know fully. Gr. *epiginōskō.* Ap. 132. I. iii. **of** = concerning. Gr. *peri.* Ap. 104. xiii. 1. **9 assented** = agreed. Gr. *suntithēmi.* See note on 23. 20. **saying** = affirming. Gr. *phaskō.* Only here; 25. 19. Rom. 1. 22. Rev. 2. 2. **10 Then** = And. **after that, &c.** Lit. the governor having nodded. See note on John 13. 24. **answered.** Gr. *apokrinomai.* Ap. 122. 3. **Forasmuch as, &c.** = Knowing (as I do). **know.** Gr. *epistamai.* Ap. 132. I. v. **of.** Gr. *ek.* Ap. 104. vii. **many years.** About seven; i. e. since A.D. 52. **judge.** See note on 18. 15. **the more cheerfully.** Gr. *euthumoteron.* Only here. The texts read the adverb *euthumōs.* Cp. 27. 22, 36. **answer.** Gr. *apologeomai.* See note on 19. 33. **for, &c.** = in regard to the things concerning (Gr. *peri.* Ap. 104. xiii. 1) myself.

24. 11-21 [For Structure see next page].

11 mayest = canst. **understand.** Gr. *ginōskō.* Ap. 132. I. ii, but the texts read *epiginōskō* (iii).

that there are °yet but °twelve days °since I went up °to Jerusalem °for to °worship.

y **12 And they °neither found me °in the [6]temple °disputing °with °any man, °neither °raising up the people, °neither °in the °synagogues, nor °in the city:**

13 [12]Neither can they °prove the things °whereof they now [2]accuse me.

z **14 But this I confess [2]unto thee, that °after °the way which they call °heresy, so °worship I the °God °of my fathers, °believing all things which °are written °in the law and [12]-in the °prophets:**

15 °And have hope °toward [14]God, which they themselves also °allow, that there shall be a °resurrection °of the dead, both of °the just and °unjust.

16 And °herein do I °exercise myself, to have always a °conscience °void of offence °toward [14]God, and *toward* °men.

x **17 Now °after °many years I came to bring °alms °to my [2]nation, and °offerings.**

18 °Whereupon certain Jews °from Asia found me °purified [12]in the [6]temple,

y **°neither [1]with °multitude, °nor [1]with °tumult.**

19 Who ought to have been here °before thee, and °object, °if they had ought °against me.

20 Or else let these same *here* say, °if they have found °any °evil doing [12]in me, while I stood [19]before the °council,

z **21 Except it be [10]for this one °voice, that I cried standing °among them, °'Touching the [15]resurrection [15]of the dead I am °called in question °by you this day.'"**

Ta **22 °And °when Felix heard these things, °having more perfect knowledge [8]of *that* [14]way, he °deferred them, and said, "When Lysias the [7]chief captain shall °come down, I will °know the uttermost of your matter."**

24. 11-21 (*W*, p. 1645). DEFENCE.
(*Extended Alternation.*)

W x | 11. Admission.
y | 12, 13. Repudiation.
z | 14-16. Confession. Resurrection.
x | 17, 18-. Admission.
y | -18-20. Repudiation.
z | 21. Confession. Resurrection.

yet but = not (Gr. *ou*. Ap. 105. I) more than.
twelve days: i. e. since 21. 17.
since = from (Gr. *apo*. Ap. 104. iv) which.
to. Gr. *en*, but the texts read *eis*, unto.
for. Omit.
worship. Gr. *proskuneō*. Ap. 137. 1.
12 neither. Gr. *oute*.
in, in. Gr. *en*. Ap. 104. viii.
disputing. Gr. *dialegomai*. See note on 17. 2.
with. Gr. *pros*. Ap. 104. xv. 3.
any man = any one. Gr. *tis*. Ap. 123. 3.
neither = or.
raising up the people = making up a seditious gathering (Gr. *episustasis*. Only here and 2 Cor. 11. 28) of the multitude (Gr. *ochlos*).
neither . . . nor. Gr. *oute . . . oute*.
synagogues Ap. 120. I.
in = throughout. Gr. *kata*. Ap. 104. x. 2.
13 prove. Same as "shew" (1. 3). Here = demonstrate.
whereof = concerning (Gr. *peri*. Ap. 104. xiii. 1) which.
14 after = according to. Gr. *kata*. Ap. 104. x. 2.
the way. See note on 9. 2.
heresy. Same word as "sect", *v.* 5.
worship. Gr. *latreuō*. Ap. 137. 4.
God. Ap. 98. I. i. 1.
of my fathers. Gr. *patrōos*. See note on 22. 3.
believing. Gr. *pisteuō*. Ap. 150. I. 1. ii.
are = have been.
in = according to. Gr. *kata*, as above.
prophets. Ap. 189.
15 And have = Having.
toward. Gr. *eis*. Ap. 104. vi.
allow = look for. Gr. *prosdechomai*. See note on 23. 21.
resurrection. Gr. *anastasis*. Ap. 178. II. 1.
of the dead. Ap. 139. 2, but the texts omit, not the Syriac.
the just = righteous. Gr. *dikaios*. Ap. 191. 1.
unjust = unrighteous. Gr. *adikos*. Four times transl. "unrighteous"; eight times "unjust". Cp. Ap. 128. VII. 1. **16 herein** = in (Gr. *en*. Ap. 104. viii) this. **exercise.** Gr. *askeō*, to practise as an art, used of the healing art in medical writings. Only here. **conscience.** Cp. 23. 1. **void of offence.** Gr. *aproskopos*. The verb *proskoptō* means to stumble, and this adj. here means "without stumbling", while in the other two occ., 1 Cor. 10. 32. Phil. 1. 10, it means "not causing to stumble". **toward.** Gr. *pros*. Ap. 104. xv. 3. **men.** Gr. *anthrōpos*. Ap. 123. 1. **17 after.** Gr. *dia*. Ap. 104. v. 1. **many.** Lit. more. It was about five years since his previous visit. See Ap. 180. **alms.** See note on 3. 2. **to.** Gr. *eis*. Ap. 104. vi. **offerings.** Gr. *prosphora*. See note on 21. 26. **18 Whereupon** = In (Gr. *en*) which, i. e. while engaged in the offerings. **from.** Gr. *apo*. Ap. 104. iv. **purified.** Gr. *hagnizō*. See note on 21. 24, 26. **neither** = not. Gr. *ou*. Ap. 105. I. **multitude** = crowd. Gr. *ochlos*, as in *v.* 12. **nor.** Gr. *oude*. **tumult.** Same as "uproar", 20. 1. A Latin MS. of the thirteenth century adds "And they laid hands on me, crying, Away with our enemy". **19 before.** Gr. *epi*. Ap. 104. ix. 1. **object** = accuse, as in *v.* 2. **if.** Gr. *ei*. Ap. 118. 2. b. **against.** Gr. *pros*. Ap. 104. xv. 3. **20 if.** The texts omit. **any** = what. **evil doing.** Gr. *adikēma*. Ap. 128. VII. 2. **council.** Gr. *sunedrion*. See note on Matt. 5. 22. John 11. 47. **21 voice** = utterance. Gr. *phōnē*. **among.** Gr. *en*. Ap. 104. viii. 2. **Touching** = Concerning. Gr. *peri*. Ap. 104. xiii. 1. **called in question** = judged. Gr. *krinō*. Ap. 122. 1. **by.** Gr. *hupo*, but the texts read *epi*, before, as in *vv.* 19, 20.

24. 22-27 (*T*, p. 1645). FELIX. DECISION. (*Alternation.*)

T | a | 22. Adjournment.
b | 23. Paul in custody.
a | 24-26. Conferences.
b | 27. Paul in bonds.

22 And = Now. **when, &c.** = Felix, having heard. **having, &c.** = knowing (Gr. *oida*. Ap. 132. I. i) more perfectly, or accurately. Gr. *akribesteron*. See note on 18. 26; 23. 15. **deferred.** Gr. *anaballō*. Only here. Cp. 25. 17. Much used in medical works. **come down.** Same as "descended", *v.* 1. **know the uttermost, &c.** Lit. investigate thoroughly (Gr. *diaginōskō*, as in 23. 15) the things referring to (Gr. *kata*. Ap. 104. x. 2) you.

23 And he °commanded °a °centurion to °keep
°Paul, and to let *him* have °liberty, and that he
should forbid °none of °his acquaintance to
°minister or come [2]unto him.
a **24** And [1]after [1]certain days, when Felix came
°with his wife °Drusilla, which was a Jewess,
he °sent for Paul, and heard him °concerning
the °faith °in °Christ.
25 And as he °reasoned [8]of °righteousness,
°temperance, and °judgment to come, Felix
°trembled, and [10]answered, "Go thy way °for
this time; when I °have a °convenient season,
I will °call for thee."
26 He hoped also that money °should have
been given °him °of Paul, °that he might loose
him: °wherefore he [24]sent for him °the oftener,
and °communed with him.
b **27** But °after two years °Porcius Festus came
into Felix' room: and Felix, °willing to °shew
the Jews a °pleasure, left Paul bound.

Q² c¹ **25** Now when °Festus °was come °into the
°province, °after three days he ascended
°from °Cæsarea °to Jerusalem.
d¹ **2** Then the °high priest and the °chief of the
Jews °informed him °against Paul, and °be-
sought him,
3 °And desired °favour [2]against him, that he
would °send for him [1]to Jerusalem, °laying wait
°in the way to °kill him.
c² **4** But Festus °answered, that Paul should be
°kept °at [1]Cæsarea, and that he himself would
depart °shortly *thither*.
d² **5** "Let them therefore," said he, "which
°among you are able, °go down with *me*, and
°accuse this °man, °if there be °any wickedness
°in him."

23 commanded. Gr. *diatassō*. See 7. 44.
a = the. Probably the one who had come with him.
centurion. Gr. *hekatontarchēs*. See 10. 1.
keep. Gr. *tēreō*. See 16. 23 and John 17. 6.
Paul. The texts read "him".
liberty = relaxation. Gr. *anesis*. Occ. here; 2 Cor. 2. 13; 7. 5; 8. 13. 2 Thess. 1. 7. Cp. the verb *aniēmi*, 16. 26.
none = no one. Gr. *mēdeis*.
his acquaintance = his own (people).
minister. Ap. 190. III. 4. See 13. 36.
24 with. Gr. *sun*. Ap. 104. xvi.
Drusilla. Ap. 109. She was the daughter of Herod Agrippa I, and had left her first husband, Azizus, king of Emesa, and married Felix. It was no doubt through her that Felix had his knowledge of "the Way" (*v.* 22).
sent for. Gr. *metapempō*. Ap. 174. 7. See note on 10. 5.
concerning. Gr. *peri*. Ap. 104. xiii. 1.
faith. Gr. *pistis*. Ap. 150. II. 1.
in = towards, or with regard to. Gr. *eis*. Ap. 104. vi.
Christ. The texts add "Jesus". Ap. 98. XII.
25 reasoned. Gr. *dialegomai*. See 17. 2.
righteousness. Gr. *dikaiosunē*. See Ap. 191. 3.
temperance = self-control. Gr. *enkrateia*. Only here; Gal. 5. 23, 2 Pet. 1. 6. The adj. *enkratēs* only in Tit. 1. 8, and the kindred verb only in 1 Cor. 7. 9; 9. 25.
judgment. Gr. *krima*. Ap. 177. 6.
trembled and = having become terrified. Gr. *emphobos*. See 10. 4.
for this time = for the present.
have. Gr. *metalambanō*, to partake of, or obtain a share of. Occ. 2. 46 (eat); 27. 33. 2 Tim. 2. 6. Heb. 6. 7; 12. 10.
convenient season = season, or opportunity. Gr. *kairos*. Cp. Gal. 6. 10 Heb. 11. 15.
call for. Gr. *metakaleō*. See 7. 14. The season never came for hearing what Paul had to teach, though he found opportunity to see if he could get a bribe.
26 should = would. **him.** Omit.
of = by. Gr. *hupo*, as in *v.* 21.
that . . . him. The texts omit.
wherefore. Add "also".
the oftener. Gr. *puknoteron*. Comp. of *puknos*, the neut. being used adverbially. See Luke 5. 33. Add "also". **communed** = was communing, or used to talk. Gr. *homileō*. See 20. 11. **27 after two years.** Lit. a space of two years (Gr. *dietia*, only here and 28. 30) having been fulfilled (Gr. *plēroō*. Ap. 125. 7). **Porcius, &c.** Lit. Felix received Porcius Festus as successor (Gr. *diadochos*. Only here. Cp. the verb in 7. 45). **willing** = wishing. Gr. *thelō*. Ap. 102. 1. **shew** = lay up with the Jews. Gr. *katatithēmi*, to deposit. Here; 25. 9. Mark 15. 46. **pleasure.** Gr. *charis*. Ap. 184. I. 1.

25. 1-12 (Q², p. 1639). PAUL AND FESTUS. (*Repeated Alternation.*)

Q² | c¹ | 1. Festus. At Jerusalem.
  d¹ | 2, 3. Paul. Plot against, by Jews.
 c² | 4. Festus. Offer to judge.
  d² | 5. Paul. His accusers.
 c³ | 6. Festus. On the judgment seat.
  d³ | 7, 8. Paul. Accusers refuted.
 c⁴ | 9. Festus. Offer to Paul.
  d⁴ | 10, 11. Paul. Appeal to Cæsar.
 c⁵ | 12. Festus. Decision.

25. 1 Festus. He was procurator only about two years (A. D. 60–62) when he died. Knowing the turbulence of the Jews, he wished to have the support of the priestly party. Hence his favour to them, in seeking to induce Paul to go to Jerusalem for trial, though Festus may not have known the reason of the request. Josephus commends him as a rooter-out of robbers and the Sicarii (21. 38). See *Wars*, II. xiv. 1. **was come.** Gr. *epibainō*. See 20. 18. **into** = to. **province.** See 23. 34. **after.** Gr. *meta*. Ap. 104. xi. 2. **from.** Gr. *apo*. Ap. 104. iv. **Cæsarea.** See 8. 40. **to** = unto. Gr. *eis*. Ap. 104. vi. **2 high priest.** Gr. *archiereus*. The texts read "chief priests". **chief** = first. **informed.** Gr *emphanizō*. See 23. 15 and Ap. 106. I. iv. **against.** Gr. *kata*. Ap. 104. x. 1. **besought** = were beseeching. Gr. *parakaleō*. Ap. 134. I. 6. **3 And desired** = Asking. Gr. *aiteō*. Ap. 134. I. 4. **favour.** Gr. *charis*. Ap. 184. I. 1. **send for.** Gr. *metapempō*. See 10. 5 and Ap. 174. 7. **laying wait.** Lit. making a plot (Gr. *enedra*, as in 23. 16). **in** = along. Gr. *kata*. Ap. 104. x. 2. **kill.** Gr. *anaireō*. See 2. 23. **4 answered.** Ap. 122. 3. **kept.** Gr. *tēreō*. **at** = in. Gr. *eis*. Ap. 104. vi. **shortly.** Lit. in (Gr. *en*) speed. **5 among.** Gr. *en*. Ap. 104. viii. 2. **go down with.** Gr. *sunkatabainō*. Only here. **accuse.** Gr. *katēgoreō*. See note on 22. 30. **man.** Gr. *anēr*. Ap. 123. 2. The texts read, "if there be anything in the man amiss, accuse him." **if.** Gr. *ei*. Ap. 118. 2. a. **any.** Gr. *tis*. Ap. 123. 3. **in.** Gr. *en*. Ap. 104. viii.

c3 6 And when he had °tarried [5]among them °more than ten days, he went down °unto [1]Cæsarea; and °the next day sitting °on the °judgment seat commanded Paul to be °brought.

d3 7 And when he was come, the Jews which °came down [1]from Jerusalem °stood round about, °and laid many and grievous °complaints [2]against Paul, which they °could °not °prove.

8 °While °he answered for himself, °"Neither °against the law of the Jews, °neither °against the °temple, °nor yet °against Cæsar, °have I offended °any thing at all."

c4 9 But Festus, °willing °to do the Jews a pleasure, [4]answered Paul, and said, °"Wilt thou go up [1]to Jerusalem, and there be °judged °of these things °before me?"

d4 10 Then said Paul, "I °stand °at Cæsar's [6]judgment seat, where I ought to be [9]judged: °to the Jews have I done no wrong, as °thou °very well °knowest.

11 °For °if I °be an offender, or have committed [8]any thing worthy of death, I °refuse [7]not to die: but °if there be °none of these things whereof these [5]accuse me, °no man °may °deliver me °unto them. I °appeal unto °Cæsar."

c5 12 Then Festus, when he had °conferred °with the °council, [4]answered, "Hast thou [11]appealed unto [11]Cæsar? °unto [11]Cæsar shalt thou go."

Q3 X e 13 °And °after °certain days °king Agrippa

6 tarried. Gr. *diatribō*. See 12. 19.
more, &c. The texts read, "not (Gr. *ou*) more than eight or ten".
unto. Gr. *eis*. Ap. 104. vi.
the next day = on the morrow.
on = upon. Gr. *epi*. Ap. 104. ix. 1.
judgment seat. Gr. *bēma*. See John 19. 13.
brought = brought forth, as in *vv*. 17, 23.
7 came = had come.
stood round about. Gr. *periistēmi*. Only here; John 11. 42. 2 Tim. 2. 16. Tit. 3. 9.
and laid, &c. The texts read, "bringing against him".
complaints = charges. Gr. *aitiama*. Only here.
could = were . . . able to. See 15. 10.
not. Gr. *ou*. Ap. 105. I.
prove. Gr. *apodeiknumi*. See 2. 22.
8 While, &c. Lit. Paul making his defence. Gr. *apologeomai*. See 19. 33.
he. The texts read "Paul".
Neither. Gr. *oute*.
against. Gr. *eis*. Ap. 104. vi.
temple. Gr. *hieron*. See Matt. 23. 16.
nor yet = neither. Gr. *oute*, as above.
have I offended = did I transgress. Gr. *hamartanō*. Ap. 128. I. i.
any thing at all = any thing. Gr. *tis*. Ap. 123. 3.
9 willing = purposing. Gr. *thelō*. Ap. 102. 1.
to do the Jews a pleasure = to gain favour with the Jews, as in 24. 27.
Wilt thou = Art thou willing to. Gr. *thelō*, as above.
judged. Gr. *krinō*. Ap. 122. 1.
of = concerning. Gr. *peri*. Ap. 104. xiii. 1.
before. Gr. *epi*. Ap. 104. ix. 1.
10 stand = am standing.
at = before. Gr. *epi*, as above.
to, &c. = the Jews I wronged (Gr. *adikeō*. See 7. 24) in nothing (Gr. *oudeis*).
thou = thou also. Festus admitted this in *vv*. 18, 19.
very well. Lit. better (i. e. than others). **knowest** = knowest thoroughly. Gr. *epiginōskō*. Ap. 132. I. iii. **11 For if** = If then indeed. **if.** Ap. 118. 2. a. **be an offender** = am doing wrong. Gr. *adikeō*, as in *v*. 10. **refuse.** Lit. beg off. Gr. *paraiteomai*. See Luke 14. 18. **none** = nothing. Gr. *oudeis*. **no man** = no one. Gr. *oudeis*. **may** = can. See *v*. 7. **deliver.** Lit. grant. Gr. *charizomai*. Ap. 184. II. 1. See 3. 14. **unto** = to. **appeal unto** = call upon, invoke. Gr. *epikaleomai*. See 2. 21. **Cæsar:** i.e. the Emperor before whose tribunal every Roman citizen was entitled to appear. Paul, seeing the desire of Festus to hand him over to the Jews, was constrained to exercise this right. Cp. 16. 37; 22. 25. **12 conferred.** Gr. *sullaleō*. Only here; Matt. 17. 3. Mark 9. 4. Luke 4. 36; 9. 30; 22. 4. **with.** Gr. *meta*. Ap. 104. xi. 1. **council.** See Matt. 12. 14. Gr. *sumboulion*. Not the same word used for "council" elsewhere in Acts, which is *sunedrion*. See 4. 15, &c. It means the assessors of the court, or chief officers of the government. **unto** = before. Gr. *epi*. Ap. 104. ix. 3. One can detect a tone of resentment, since Paul's appeal had baffled the desire of Festus to gain favour with the Jews.

25. 13—26. 32 (Q3, p. 1639). PAUL AND AGRIPPA. (*Alternation and Introversion.*)

Q3 | X | 25. 13-21. Festus consults Agrippa.
  Y | 25. 22. Agrippa desires to hear Paul.
   Z | A | 25. 23-. Court convened.
     B | 25. -23. Paul brought to the bar.
 X | 25. 24-27. Festus opens the case.
  Y | 26. 1-. Agrippa calls on Paul for his defence.
   Z | B | 26. -1-29. Paul's defence.
     A | 26. 30-32. Court rises.

25. 13-21 (X, above). FESTUS CONSULTS AGRIPPA. (*Alternation.*)

X | e | 13-15. The Jews' request.
  f | 16. Festus' reply.
  e | 17-19. The Jews' charges.
  f | 20, 21. Festus' decision.

13 And = Now. **after certain days.** Lit. certain days having passed by. Gr. *diaginomai*. Only here; 27. 9. Mark 16. 1. **certain.** Gr. *tines*. Ap. 124. 4. **king Agrippa.** Agrippa the Second, son of the Herod of ch. 12, and Cypros, grand-niece of Herod the Great. At the death of his father, he was too young to be appointed his successor; but in A.D. 50 Claudius gave him the kingdom of Chalcis, his uncle, the husband of Bernice, who occupied that throne, having died two years before. This was shortly afterwards exchanged for the tetrarchies of Abilene and Trachonitis, with the title of king. His relations with his sister Bernice were the occasion of much suspicion. He was of the Jews' religion, though of Idumaean descent, and well versed in Jewish laws and customs (26. 3). Josephus (*Wars*, II. xvi. 4) records a speech he made to dissuade the Jews from engaging in war with the Romans. He sided with the Romans in the war, and after A.D. 70 retired with Bernice to Rome, where he died about A.D. 100.

and Bernice °came [6]unto Cæsarea to °salute Festus.

14 And when they °had been there many days, Festus °declared °Paul's cause [11]unto the king, saying, "There is a °certain [5]man left °in bonds °by Felix:

15 °About whom, when I °was °at Jerusalem, the [2]chief priests and the °elders of the Jews [2]informed *me,* °desiring *to have* °judgment [2]against him.

f 16 °To whom I [4]answered, 'It is [7]not °the manner of the Romans to [11]deliver °any °man °to die, before that he which is [5]accused have the °accusers °face to face, and °have licence °to answer for himself °concerning the °crime laid against him.'

e 17 Therefore, when they were come hither, °without any delay °on the morrow I sat [6]on the [6]judgment seat, and commanded the [5]man to be brought forth.

18 °Against whom when the [16]accusers stood up, they °brought °none °accusation of such things as I °supposed:

19 But had [14]certain °questions °against him [9]of their own °superstition, and [9]of °one °Jesus, Which was dead, Whom Paul °affirmed to be alive.

f 20 And °because I °doubted °of such manner of °questions, I °asked *him* °whether he °would go [1]to Jerusalem, and there be [9]judged [9]of these matters.

21 But when Paul had [11]appealed to be °reserved [6]unto the °hearing of °Augustus, I commanded him to be °kept till I might °send him [16]to [11]Cæsar."

Y 22 Then Agrippa said °unto Festus, °"I [20]would also hear the [16]man myself." "To morrow," said he, "thou shalt hear him."

Z A 23 °And on the morrow, when Agrippa was come, and Bernice, [12]with great °pomp, and was entered °into the °place of hearing, °with the °chief captains, and °principal [5]men of the city,

B at Festus' commandment Paul was brought forth.

X 24 And Festus said, "King Agrippa, and all [5]men °which are here present with us, ye °see °this man, [15]about whom all the °multitude of the Jews °have dealt with me, both [4]at Jerusalem, and *also* here, °crying that he ought °not to live any longer.

came. Gr. *katantaō.* See 16. 1.
salute. As vassal of Rome, to pay his respects to the procurator, Rome's representative.
14 had been = had tarried, as in *v.* 6.
declared = set forth. Gr. *anatithēmi.* Only here and Gal. 2. 2.
Paul's cause. Lit. the things about (Gr. *kata.* Ap. 104. x. 2) Paul.
certain. Gr. *tis.* Ap. 123. 3.
in bonds = a prisoner. Gr. *desmios,* always rendered "prisoner" save here and Heb. 13. 3.
by. Gr. *hupō.* Ap. 104. xviii. 1.
15 About = concerning. Gr. *peri.* Ap. 104. xiii. 1.
was = was come.
at = to. Gr. *eis.* Ap. 104. vi.
elders. Ap. 189.
desiring *to have* = asking for. Gr. *aiteō.* Ap. 134. I. 4.
judgment. Gr. *dikē.* Ap. 177. 4. The texts read *katadikē* (condemnation), a word found nowhere else in N.T.
16 To. Gr. *pros.* Ap. 104. xv. 3.
the manner = a custom.
any. Gr. *tis.* Ap. 123. 3.
man. Gr. *anthrōpos.* Ap. 123. 1.
to die = unto (Gr. *eis*) destruction (Gr. *apōleia*). Cp. 8. 20. But the texts omit.
accusers. See note on 23. 30.
face to face. Gr. *kata* (Ap. 104. x. 2) *prosōpon.*
have licence = should receive opportunity (lit. place).
to answer, &c. = of defence. Gr. *apologia,* as in 22. 1.
concerning. Gr. *peri.* Ap. 104. xiii. 1.
crime laid against him = charge. Gr. *enklēma,* as in 23. 29.
17 without any delay = having made no (Gr. *mēdeis*) delay (Gr. *anabolē.* Only here. Cp. 24. 22).
on the morrow = the next (day). Gr. *hexēs.* See 21. 1.
18 Against = Concerning. Gr. *peri,* as in *vv.* 9, 15, 16, 19, 20, 24, 26.
brought = were bringing. Gr. *epipherō.* See 19. 12. But the texts read *pherō,* same as in *v.* 7.
none. Gr. *oudeis.*
accusation = charge. Gr. *aitia,* the common word for cause, or charge.
supposed. See 13. 25.
19 questions. Gr. *zētēma.* See 15. 2.
against. Gr. *pros.* Ap. 104. xv. 3.
superstition = religion. Gr. *deisidaimonia.* Cp. 17. 22. Festus would not say "superstition" in speaking to Agrippa, who was himself of the Jews' religion.
one = a certain, as above, *v.* 14.
Jesus. Ap. 98. X.
affirmed = was affirming. Gr. *phaskō.* See 24. 9.
20 because, &c. Lit. I, being at a loss (Gr. *aporeomai.* Only here; John 13. 22. 2 Cor. 4. 8. Gal. 4. 20).
of such manner of questions. Lit. for (Gr. *eis*) the enquiry (Gr. *zētēsis.* Only here; John 3. 25. 1 Tim. 1. 4; 6. 4. 2 Tim. 2. 23. Tit. 3. 9. Cp. *v.* 19) concerning (Gr. *peri*) these things.
asked = said.

whether = if. Ap. 118. 2. b. **would** = would be willing (Gr. *boulomai.* Ap. 102. 3) to. **21 reserved** = kept. Gr. *tēreō.* **hearing** = examination. Gr. *diagnōsis.* Only here. See note on 23. 15. **Augustus.** Gr. *Sebastos.* The Gr. word means "venerable", the same as the Lat. *augustus,* a title first used by Octavianus, the adopted son of Julius Cæsar, and his successor, and by the Emperors succeeding. Cp. the title "Ahasuerus". Ap. 57, p. 80. **kept.** Same as "reserved". **send.** Gr. *pempō.* Ap. 174. 4, but the texts read *anapempō.* Ap. 174. 5. **22 unto.** Gr. *pros.* Ap. 104. xv. 3. **I would also** = I also was wishing to (Ap. 102. 3). **23 And** = Therefore. **pomp.** Gr. *phantasia.* Only here. Cp. the verb in Heb. 12. 21. **into.** Gr. *eis.* Ap. 104. vi. **place of hearing.** Gr. *akroatērion.* Only here. Cp. *akroatēs,* hearer, Rom. 2. 13, &c. **with.** Gr. *sun.* Ap. 104. xvi. **chief captains.** Gr. *chiliarchos.* See 21. 31. **principal men** = men who were of eminence (Gr. *kat'* (Ap. 104. x. 2) *exochēn. Exochē* occ. only here). **24 which are here present with.** Gr. *sumpareimi.* Only here. **see** = behold. Gr. *theōreō.* Ap. 133. I. 11. **this man** = this (one). **multitude.** Gr. *plēthos.* See 2. 6. **have dealt with** = complained to. Gr. *entunchanō.* Lit. to meet with, apply to. Elsewhere transl. "make intercession". Rom. 8. 27, 34; 11. 2. Heb. 7. 25. **crying** = crying out. Gr. *epiboaō.* Only here. The texts read *boaō,* not so strong a word. **not . . . any longer.** Gr. *mē* (Ap. 105. II) *mēketi.* A double negative.

25 But when I °found that he had °committed °nothing worthy of death, and that he himself hath [11] appealed to [21] Augustus, I °have determined to [21] send him.

26 [9] Of whom I have °no °certain thing to write [11] unto my °lord. Wherefore I have brought him forth [9] before you, and specially [9] before thee, O king Agrippa, that, °after °examination had, I might have °somewhat to write.

27 For it seemeth to me °unreasonable to [21] send a prisoner, and [24] not °withal to signify the °crimes *laid* [2] against him."

Y **26** Then Agrippa said °unto Paul, °"Thou art permitted to speak °for thyself."

ZBCg Then Paul stretched forth the hand, and °answered for himself:

2 "I °think myself °happy, king Agrippa, because I °shall [1] answer for myself this day °before thee °touching all the things whereof I am °accused °of the Jews:

3 Especially °*because I know* thee to be expert in all °customs and °questions which are °among the Jews: wherefore I °beseech thee to hear me °patiently.

h 4 My °manner of life °from my °youth, which was °at the first °among mine own °nation °at Jerusalem, °know all °the Jews;

5 °Which knew me °from the beginning, °if they °would °testify, that °after the °most straitest °sect of our °religion I lived a °Pharisee.

h 6 And now I stand and am °judged °for the hope of the promise made [2] of °God °unto our fathers:

7 [6] Unto which *promise* our °twelve tribes, °instantly °serving *God* day and night, hope to °come. °For which hope's sake, °king Agrippa, I am [2] accused [2] of the °Jews.

g 8 Why °should it be thought a thing °incredible °with you, °that [6] God °should raise °the dead?

25 found = perceived. Gr. *katalambanō*. See 4. 13.
committed = done.
nothing. Gr. *mēdeis*.
have determined = decided. Gr. *krinō*. Ap. 122. 1.
26 no = not (Gr. *ou*) any (Gr. *tis*). Ap. 123. 3.
certain = sure. See note on 21. 34.
lord. Gr. *kurios*. Cp. Ap. 98. VI. i. This title was refused by the Emperors, Augustus and Tiberius, but accepted by Caligula and his successors.
after, &c. Lit. examination having taken place.
examination. Gr. *anakrisis*. Only here. Cp. 24. 8.
somewhat. Gr. *tis*.
27 unreasonable. Gr. *alogos*. Only here; 2 Pet. 2. 12. Jude 10 (transl. "brute"). A medical word.
withal, &c. = to signify the charges also.
crimes = charges. Gr. *aitia* as in *v.* 18.

26. 1 unto. Gr. *pros*. Ap. 104. xv. 3.
Thou art permitted. Lit. It is permitted thee. Gr. *epitrepō*. Same word as "suffer" and "give licence" (21. 39, 40).
for = in behalf of. Gr. *huper*. Ap. 104. xvii. 1.

26. -1-29 (*B*, p. 1648). **PAUL'S DEFENCE.**
(*Introversion.*)

B | C | -1-8. Introduction.
  D | 9-23. Statement.
C | 24-29. Conclusion.

26. -1-8 (C, above). **INTRODUCTION.**
(*Introversion.*)

C g | -1-3. Appeal to Agrippa's knowledge.
  h | 4, 5. Paul's life.
  h | 6, 7. Paul's hope.
g | 8. Appeal to Agrippa's reason.

answered, &c. = was making his defence. Gr. *apologeomai*. See 19. 33.
2 think. Gr. *hēgeomai*. This word has two meanings, "to lead" (15. 22) and "hold, or reckon", as here and in nineteen subsequent passages.
happy. Gr. *makarios*. Occ. fifty times. Always transl. "blessed", save here, John 13. 17. Rom. 14. 22. 1 Cor. 7. 40. 1 Pet. 3. 14; 4. 14.
shall = am about to.
before. Gr. *epi*. Ap. 104. ix. 1.
touching = concerning. Gr. *peri*. Ap. 104. xiii. 1.
accused. Gr. *enkaleō*. See 19. 38.
of = by. Gr. *hupo*. Ap. 104. xviii. 1.
3 *because*, &c. Lit. thou being an expert. Gr. *gnōstēs*. Only here. Cp. *gnōstos* (1. 19).

customs. Gr. *ethos*. See 6. 14. questions. Gr. *zētēma*. See 15. 2. among = according to. Gr. *kata*. Ap. 104. x. 2. beseech. Gr. *deomai*. Ap. 134. I. 5. patiently. Gr. *makrothumōs*. Only here. Fig. *Protherapeia*, Ap. 6. **4** manner of life. Gr. *biōsis*. Only here. Cp. Ap. 170. 2. from. Gr. *ek*. Ap. 104. vii. youth. Gr. *neotēs*. Only here; Matt. 19. 20. Mark 10. 20. Luke 18. 21. 1 Tim. 4. 12. at the first = from (Gr. *apo*. Ap. 104. iv) the beginning (Gr. *archē*). Cp. note on John 8. 44. among. Gr. *en*. Ap. 104. viii. nation. Gr. *ethnos*. Generally applied to Gentiles, but to Israel in 10. 22; 24. 2, 10, 17, &c. at = in. Gr. *en*. Ap. 104. viii. know. Gr. *oida*. Ap. 132. I. i. the. Omit. **5** Which knew me = Knowing me before. Gr. *proginōskō*. Ap. 132. I. iv. from the beginning. Gr. *anōthen*. See note on Luke 1. 3. if. Ap. 118. 1. b. would = be willing to. Gr. *thelō*. Ap. 102. 1. testify. Gr. *martureō*. See p. 1511, and note on John 1. 7. after = according to. Gr. *kata*. Ap. 104. x. 2. most straitest = strictest, or most precise. Gr. *akribestatos*. Cp. the adverb *akribōs* and the comparative adj. in 18. 25, 26. A medical word. sect. Gr. *hairesis*. See 5. 17. religion = form of worship. Gr. *thrēskeia*. Only here; Col. 2. 18. Jas. 1. 26, 27. Herodotus uses the word of the ceremonies of the Egyptian priests. Used also in the Papyri. Pharisee. See Ap. 120. II. **6** judged. Gr. *krinō*. Ap. 122. 1. for = upon (the ground of). Gr. *epi*. Ap. 104. ix. 2. God. Ap. 98. I. i. 1. unto. The texts read *eis*. Ap. 104. vi. **7** twelve tribes. Gr. *dōdekaphulon*. Only here. This single word to denote the whole twelve tribes shows that Paul regarded them as one. To him there were no "lost" tribes as fondly imagined to-day. instantly = in (Gr. *en*) intensity. Gr. *ekteneia*. Only here. Cp. the adj. *ektenēs* (12. 5). serving. Gr. *latreuō*. Ap. 137. 4 and 190. III. 5. come = arrive. Gr. *katantaō*. See 16. 1. For which hope's sake = On account of (Gr. *peri*. Ap. 104. xiii. 1) which hope. king Agrippa. The texts omit. Jews. The texts add, "O king". **8** should it be thought = is it judged. Gr. *krinō*, as in *v.* 6. incredible. Gr. *apistos*. Only occ. in Acts. Elsewhere transl. "faithless", "unbelieving", &c. with. Gr. *para*. Ap. 104. xii. 2. that = if. Ap. 118. 2. a. should raise = raises. Gr. *egeirō*. Ap. 178. I. 4. the dead = dead persons. Gr. *nekros*. Ap. 139. 2. Cp. *v.* 23.

D E 9 I °verily thought with myself, that I ought
to do many things contrary °to °the name of
°Jesus °of Nazareth.

F i 10 Which thing I °also did °in Jerusalem:
and many of the °saints did I °shut up in
prison, having received °authority °from the
°chief priests; and when they were °put to
death, I °gave my °voice against *them*.
11 And °I punished them oft °in every °syna-
gogue, and °compelled *them* to blaspheme;
and being °exceedingly °mad against them,
I persecuted *them* even [7] unto °strange cities.

k 12 °Whereupon as I °went °to Damascus
°with [10] authority and °commission [10] from the
[10] chief priests,

G 13 At midday, O king, I °saw °in the way
a °light °from heaven, °above the °brightness
of the sun, °shining round about me and them
which journeyed °with me.
14 And when we were all °fallen [12] to the
°earth, I heard a voice °speaking [1] unto me,
°and saying in the °Hebrew °tongue, °'Saul,
Saul, why persecutest thou Me? °*it is* hard for
thee to °kick °against the °pricks.'
15 And I said, 'Who art Thou, °Lord?' And
He said, 'I am [9] Jesus Whom thou persecutest.

H 16 But °rise, and °stand °upon thy feet:

J for I °have appeared unto thee °for this purpose, to °make thee a °minister and a °witness
both of these things which thou hast [13] seen,
and of those things in the which I will °appear
unto thee;

K l 17 °Delivering thee [4] from the °people, and
from the °Gentiles, [7] unto whom °now I °send
thee,

m 18 To open their eyes, °*and* to °turn *them*
°from darkness [12] to [13] light, and *from* the °power
of Satan °unto [6] God, that they may receive
°forgiveness of °sins, and °inheritance [4] among
°them which are sanctified by °faith that is
°in Me.'

E 19 Whereupon, O king Agrippa, I was °not
°disobedient °unto the °heavenly °vision:

26. 9-23 (D, p. 1650). STATEMENT.
(*Extended Alternation and Introversion.*)

D | E | 9. Opposition.
F | i | 10, 11. Persecution. Jerusalem, &c.
k | 12. Persecution. Damascus.
G | 13-15. Jesus the Persecuted.
H | 16-. Stand (Gr. *histēmi*).
J | -16. Witness.
K | l | 17. The People and the Gentiles.
m | 18. Light.
E | 19. Obedience.
F | *k* | 20-. Preaching. Damascus.
i | -20. Preaching. Jerusalem, &c.
G | 21. Paul the persecuted.
H | 22-. Continue (Gr. *histēmi*).
J | -22, 23-. Witness.
K | *m* | -23-. Light.
l | -23. The People and the Gentiles.

9 verily = therefore indeed.
to = unto. Gr. *pros*. Ap. 104. xv. 3.
the name. See 2. 38.
Jesus. Ap. 98. X.
of Nazareth = the Nazarene. See 2. 22. This is the seventh and last occ. of the title in Acts.
10 also did = did also. He not only thought, but acted. **in.** Gr. *en*. Ap. 104. viii.
saints. Gr. *hagios*. See 9. 13, 32, 41. Only in these four places in Acts applied to God's people. Frequently in the epistles. Cp. Ps. 31. 23, 24.
shut up. Gr. *katakleiō*. Only here and Luke 3. 20.
authority. Gr. *exousia*. Ap. 172. 5.
from. Gr. *para*. Ap. 104. xii. 1.
chief priests. Gr. *archiereus*, as in 25. 15.
put to death. Gr. *anaireō*. See 2. 23.
gave = cast. Gr. *katapherō*. See 20. 9.
voice = vote. Gr. *psēphos*. The pebble used for voting. Only here and Rev. 2. 17.
11 I punished . . . and = punishing them . . ., I. See 22. 5.
in = throughout. Gr. *kata*. Ap. 104. x. 2.
synagogue. Ap. 120. I.
compelled = was compelling, or constraining, as in 28. 19. Gr. *anankazō*.
exceedingly. Gr. *perissōs*. Only here, Matt. 27. 23. Mark 10. 26.
mad against = maddened against. Gr. *emmainomai*. Only here. Cp. *v.* 24.
strange = foreign. Lit. the cities outside (Gr. *exō*).
12 Whereupon = In (Gr. *en*) which (circumstances).
went = was going.
to = unto. Gr. *eis*. Ap. 104. vi. **with.** Gr. *meta*. Ap. 104. xi. 1. **commission.** Gr. *epitropē*. Only here. Cp. the verb *epitrepō* (*v.* 1). **13 saw.** Gr. *eidon*. Ap. 133. I. 1. **in.** Gr. *kata*. Ap. 104. x. 2. **light.** Gr. *phōs*. Ap. 130. 1. **from heaven.** Gr. *ouranothen*. See 14. 17. **above.** Gr. *huper*. Ap. 104. xvii. 2. **brightness.** Gr. *lamprotēs*. Only here. Cp. the adj. *lampros* (10. 30). **shining round about.** Gr. *perilampō*. Only here and Luke 2. 9. **with.** Gr. *sun*. Ap. 104. xvi. **14 fallen** = fallen down. Gr. *katapiptō*. Only here and 28. 6. **earth.** Gr. *gē*. Ap. 129. 4. **speaking.** Gr. *laleō*. Ap. 121. 7, but the texts read "saying" (*legō*). **and saying.** The texts omit. **Hebrew.** See 21. 40. **tongue** = dialect. See 1. 19. **Saul, Saul.** Gr. *Saoul, Saoul*. See 9. 4. ***it is*, &c.** Fig. *Parœmia*. Ap. 6. **kick.** Gr. *laktizō*. Only here. **against.** Ap. 104. xv. 3. **pricks** = goads. Gr. *kentron*. Elsewhere, 1 Cor. 15. 55, 56. Rev. 9. 10. **15 Lord.** Gr. *kurios*. Ap. 98. VI. i. *β*. 2. B. **16 rise.** Gr. *anistēmi*. Ap. 178. I. 1. **stand.** Gr. *histēmi*. **upon.** Gr. *epi*. Ap. 104. ix. 3. **have appeared unto** = was seen by. Gr. *horaō*. Ap. 133. I. 8. **for.** Gr. *eis*. Ap. 104. vi. **make** = appoint. Gr. *procheirizomai*. See 22. 14. **minister.** Gr. *hupēretēs*. Ap. 190. I. 3. **witness.** See 1. 8; 22. 15. Fig. *Hendiadys*. Ap. 6. **appear.** Gr. *horaō*, as above. **17 Delivering.** Gr. *exaireō*. See 7. 10. **people.** Gr. *laos*. See 2. 47. **Gentiles.** Gr. *ethnos*. Contrast *v.* 4. **now.** Omit. **send.** Gr. *apostellō*. Ap. 174. 1. **18 *and* to turn** = that they may turn. **turn.** Gr. *epistrephō*. Cp. 3. 19. **from.** Gr. *apo*. Ap. 104. iv. Cp. Col. 1. 13. **power** = authority. Gr. *exousia*, as in *v.* 10. **unto.** Gr. *epi*. Ap. 104. ix. 3. **forgiveness.** Gr. *aphesis*. See 2. 38; 5. 31. **sins.** Gr. *hamartia*. Ap. 128. I. ii. 1. **inheritance** = a part. Gr. *klēros*. See 1. 17. **them which are, &c.** = the sanctified. Gr. *hagiazō*. Cp. 20. 32. John 17. 17, 19. **faith.** Gr. *pistis*. Ap. 150. II. 1. **in** = towards. Gr. *eis*. Ap. 104. vi. **19 not.** Ap. 105. I. **disobedient.** Gr. *apeithēs*. Cp. Ap. 150. I. 2. Occ. elsewhere Luke 1. 17. Rom. 1. 30. 2 Tim. 3. 2. Tit. 1. 16; 3. 3. "Not disobedient", which means emphatically "obedient", is the Fig. *Tapeinōsis*. Ap. 6. **unto** = to. **heavenly.** Gr. *ouranios*. Only here, Matt. 6. 14, 26, 32; 15. 13. Luke 2. 13. **vision.** Gr. *optasia*. Only here, Luke 1. 22; 24. 23. 2 Cor. 12. 1.

Fk 20 But shewed °first [19]unto them °of Damascus,

i and at Jerusalem, and °throughout all the coasts of Judæa, and *then* to the [17]Gentiles, that they should °repent and [18]turn °to [6]God, and do works °meet for °repentance.

G 21 For these causes the Jews °caught me [10]in the °temple, and °went about to °kill *me.*

H 22 Having therefore °obtained °help °of [6]God, I °continue °unto this day, °witnessing both to

J °small and great, saying °none other things than those which °the °prophets and °Moses °did say should come:

23 °That °Christ °should suffer, *and* °that He should be the first °that should rise from the dead, and

Km should °shew [13]light

l [19]unto the [17]people, and to the [17]Gentiles."

CL n 24 And as he thus °spake for himself, °Festus said with a loud voice, "Paul, thou art °beside thyself; much °learning doth °make thee °mad."

o 25 But he said, °"I am [19]not mad, °most noble Festus; but °speak forth the °words of truth and °soberness.

M 26 For the king °knoweth °of these things, °before whom °also I °speak °freely: for I °am persuaded that °none of these things °are hidden from him; for this thing was [19]not done [10]in a corner.

M 27 King Agrippa, °believest thou the prophets? I °know that thou °believest."

L n 28 Then Agrippa said [1]unto Paul, °"Almost thou [26]persuadest me to be a °Christian."

o 29 And Paul said, "I °would to [6]God, that [19]not only thou, but °also all that hear me this day, were both °almost, and °altogether such as I am, °except these bonds."

30 °And when he had thus spoken, the °king

20 first, &c. Read, "to them of Damascus first, and to them of Jerusalem".
of=in. Gr. *en.* Ap. 104. viii.
throughout. Gr. *eis.* Ap. 104. vi.
repent. Gr. *metanoeō.* Ap. 111. I. 1.
to. Gr. *epi.* Ap. 104. ix. 3.
meet=worthy of, or answering to. Cp. Matt. 3. 8.
repentance. Gr. *metanoia.* Ap. 111. II.

21 caught. Gr. *sullambanō.* See 1. 16.
temple. Gr. *hieron.* See Matt. 23. 16.
went about=were attempting. Gr. *peiraomai.* Only here.
kill. Gr. *diacheirizomai.* See 5. 30.

22 obtained. Gr. *tunchanō.* See 19. 11; 24. 2.
help. Gr. *epikouria.* Only here. A medical word.
of=from. Gr. *para.* Ap. 104. xii. 1, but the texts read *apo* (iv).
continue=stand. Gr. *histēmi.* Same as *v.* 16. See the Structure.
unto=until. Gr. *achri.*
witnessing. Same word as "testify" (*v.* 5).
small and great. Cp. 8. 10. Rev. 11. 18; 13. 16; 19. 5, 18; 20. 12.
none, &c.=nothing (Gr. *oudeis*) except the things which.
the prophets, &c. Usually "Moses and the prophets". See 28. 23. Luke 16. 29, 31. John 1. 45.
prophets. See Ex. 4. 16 and Ap. 82.
Moses. See 3. 22.
did say=spake. Gr. *laleō.* Ap. 121. 7.

23 That=If. Gr. *ei.* Ap. 118. 2. a. Cp. *v.* 8.
Christ=the Messiah. Ap. 98. IX.
should suffer=is liable or destined to suffer. Gr. *pathētos.* Only here. Justin Martyr puts the word into the mouth of Trypho the Jew, in his dialogue, Ch. xxxvi.
that should, &c.=by (Gr. *ek*) a resurrection (Gr. *anastasis.* Ap. 178. II. 1) of the dead (Gr. *nekrōn.* Ap. 139. 2).
shew=proclaim. Gr. *katangellō.* Ap. 121. 5.

26. 24-29 (*C*, p. 1650). CONCLUSION.
(*Introversion and Alternation.*)

C L | n | 24. Festus interposes.
 o | 25. Paul's reply.
 M | 26. Agrippa's knowledge challenged.
 M | 27. Agrippa's belief challenged.
 L | *n* | 28. Agrippa interposes.
 o | 29. Paul's reply.

24 spake for himself. Same as "answer for himself", *vv.* 1, 2.
Festus, &c. To Festus the resurrection of dead persons was as much beyond the range of possibility as it is to myriads to-day. "Modern views" have relegated the resurrection, as the hope of the believer, to the background. beside thyself=mad. Gr. *mainomai.* See 12. 15. learning. Lit. letters (Gr. *gramma*). As we say "a man of letters". Cp. John 7. 15. make=turn or pervert. Gr. *peritrepō.* Only here. A medical word. mad=to (Gr. *eis*) madness. Gr. *mania.* Only here. **25** I am ... mad. Gr. *mainomai,* as in *v.* 24. most noble. See 24. 3. Luke 1. 3. speak forth. Gr. *apophthengomai.* See 2. 4. words. Gr. *rhēma.* See Mark 9. 32. soberness. Gr. *sōphrosunē.* Here and 1 Tim. 2. 9, 15. **26** knoweth. Gr. *epistamai.* Ap. 132. I. v. of=concerning. Gr. *peri.* Ap. 104. xiii. 1. before. Gr. *pros.* Ap. 104. xv. 3. also I speak freely=I speak, using boldness also. speak. Gr. *laleō,* as in *vv.* 14, 22, 31. freely=speaking out, or without reserve. Gr. *parrhēsiazomai.* Occ. seven times in Acts. See 9. 27, 29; 13. 46; 14. 3; 18. 26; 19. 8. am persuaded. Gr. *peithō.* Ap. 150. I. 2. none. A double negative. Gr. *ou ouden.* are hidden, &c.=has escaped his notice. Gr. *lanthanō.* Only here, Mark 7. 24. Luke 8. 47. Heb. 13. 2. 2 Pet. 3. 5, 8. **27** believest. Gr. *pisteuō.* Ap. 150. I. 1. ii and i. know. Gr. *oida.* Ap. 132. I. i. **28** Almost. Gr. *En oligō.* In a little, i. e., briefly, or in short. Cp. Eph. 3. 3. Paul, carried away by his subject, ceases to be the advocate for the prisoner and has become the advocate for God. Agrippa perceives it, and intervenes with—"To put it briefly, thou art persuading me to become a Christian." There is no ground for supposing that Agrippa was "almost persuaded". Christian. See 11. 26. **29** would=could wish. Gr. *euchomai.* Ap. 134. I. 1. also all=all also. almost, and altogether. Lit. in (Gr. *en*) little and in (Gr. *en*) great. Fig. *Synœceiōsis.* Ap. 6. He takes up Agrippa's words with a higher meaning. except. Gr. *parektos.* Only here, Matt. 5. 32. 2 Cor. 11. 28. **30** And when, &c. All the texts omit. king. Paul's appeal had taken the case out of the hands of Festus; so this was not a court of justice, but an inquiry to please Agrippa, and to enable Festus to make his report to the Emperor. Agrippa was the chairman (*vv.* 1, 24, 26) and so gave the signal for closing the inquiry, probably afraid lest any more such searching questions should be put to him.

[16] rose up, and the °governor, and Bernice, and they that °sat with them:

31 And when they were °gone aside, they °talked °between themselves, saying, "This °man doeth °nothing worthy of death or of bonds."

32 Then said Agrippa [19] unto Festus, "This [31] man °might have been °set at liberty, °if he had °not °appealed unto Cæsar."

P N¹ O

27 And °when it was °determined that we should °sail °into Italy, they °delivered Paul and °certain °other °prisoners °unto °*one* named Julius, a °centurion of °Augustus' °band.

2 And °entering into a °ship of °Adramyttium, we °launched, °meaning to °sail °by the coasts of Asia; *one* °Aristarchus, a Macedonian of Thessalonica, being °with us.

3 And the °next *day* we °touched °at °Sidon. And Julius °courteously °entreated Paul, and °gave *him* liberty to go °unto his friends to °refresh himself.

P p¹

4 And when we had [2] launched from thence, we °sailed under Cyprus, °because the winds were contrary.

5 And when we had °sailed over the °sea of Cilicia and Pamphylia, we °came °to Myra, *a city* of Lycia.

6 And there the °centurion found a [2] ship of °Alexandria [2] sailing [1] into Italy; and he °put us °therein.

7 And °when we had sailed slowly °many days, and °scarce were come °over against

governor. Gr. *hēgemōn*. See 23. 24.
sat with them. Gr. *sunkathēmai*. Only here and Mark 14. 54.
31 gone aside. Gr. *anachōreō*. See 23. 19.
talked. Gr. *laleō*. Ap. 121. 7.
between themselves = to (Gr. *pros*. Ap. 104. xv. 3) one another.
man. Gr. *anthrōpos*. Ap. 123. 1.
nothing. Gr. *oudeis*, as 22, 26.
32 might have been = could have been, or was able to be.
set at liberty. Gr. *apoluō*. Ap. 174. 11.
if. Gr. *ei*, as in *v.* 8.
not. Gr. *mē*. Ap. 105. II.
appealed. Gr. *epikaleomai*. See 25. 11.

27. 1—28. 16 (*P*, p. 1639). JOURNEY TO ROME. (*Division*.)

P | N¹ | 27. 1-44. Cæsarea to Melita.
| N² | 28. 1-16. Melita to Rome.

27. 1-44 (N¹, above). CÆSAREA TO MELITA. (*Alternation*.)

N¹ | O | 1-3. Julius treats Paul kindly.
P | 4-41. Voyage and tempest.
O | 42, 43. Julius saves Paul.
P | 44. All escape to land.

1 when = as.
determined = decided. Gr. *krinō*. Ap. 122. 1.
sail. Gr. *apopleō*. See 13. 4.
into. Gr. *eis*. Ap. 104. vi.
delivered = were delivering. Gr. *paradidōmi*. See 3. 13.
certain. Gr. *tines*. Ap. 124. 4.
other. Gr. *heteros*. Ap. 124. 2.
prisoners. Gr. *desmōtēs*. Only here and *v.* 42. The usual word is *desmios*. See 25. 14.
unto = to.
one, &c. = a centurion of an Augustan cohort, by name Julius. **centurion.** Gr. *hekatontarchēs*. See 10. 1. **Augustus'.** Gr. *Sebastos*. Cp. 25. 21, 25. More than one legion is said to have borne the name. **band** = cohort. Gr. *speira*. See Matt. 27. 27. **2 entering into** = having embarked upon. Gr. *epibainō*. See 20. 18. **ship.** Gr. *ploion*. The usual word for "ship". **Adramyttium.** A city in Mysia, in the province of Asia, at the head of the gulf of that name. **launched.** Gr. *anagō*. See 13. 13. **meaning** = being about. According to the texts this does not refer to "we" but to the ship. It was on the return voyage to Adramyttium by the coasts of Asia. **sail.** Gr. *pleō*. See 21. 3. **by, &c.** = to the places against (Gr. *kata*) Asia. **Aristarchus.** See 19. 29; 20. 4. He and Luke could only have been allowed on board as Paul's servants. **with.** Gr. *sun*. Ap. 104. xvi. **3 next.** Gr. *heteros*, as in *v.* 1. **touched** = landed. Gr. *katagō*. See 21. 3. **at.** Gr. *eis*. Ap. 104. vi. **Sidon.** The great port of Phœnicia about 70 miles north of Cæsarea. The wind must therefore have been favourable, south-south-west. **courteously** = kindly. Gr. *philanthrōpōs*. Only here. Cp. Ap. 135. II. 2. **entreated . . . and** = using. Gr. *chraomai*. Elsewhere transl. "use". **gave . . . liberty.** Gr. *epitrepō*. See 26. 1. **unto.** Gr. *pros*. Ap. 104. xv. 3. **refresh himself** = obtain (Gr. *tunchanō*. See 26. 22) their care (Gr. *epimeleia*. Only here).

27. 4-41 (P, above). VOYAGE AND TEMPEST. (*Alternation*.)

P | p¹ | 4-8. Sidon to Fair Havens.
q¹ | 9, 10. Paul. Admonition.
p² | 11-20. To Clauda. Tempest-driven.
q² | 21-26. Paul. Encouragement.
p³ | 27-29. Drawing near to land.
q³ | 30, 31. Paul. Warning.
p⁴ | 32. The boat abandoned.
q⁴ | 33-38. Paul. Encouragement.
p⁵ | 39-41. The ship aground.

4 sailed under: i. e. under the lee (of Cyprus). Gr. *hupopleō*. Only here and *v.* 7. **because.** Gr. *dia*. Ap. 104. v. 2. **5 sailed over** = sailed across. Gr. *diapleō*. Only here. **sea of, &c.** = sea which is along (Gr. *kata*. Ap. 104. x. 2) Cilicia, &c. **came** = came down, or landed, as in 18. 22. **to** = unto. Gr. *eis*. Ap. 104. vi. **6 centurion.** Gr. *hekatontarchos*. See 21. 32. **Alexandria.** Egypt was the granary of the ancient world, and this was a corn ship, bound for Italy. See *v.* 38. **put us** = caused us to embark. Gr. *embibazō*. Only here. A medical word, used of setting a dislocated limb. **therein** = into (Gr. *eis*) it. **7 when, &c.** = sailing slowly. Gr. *braduploeō*. Only here. After leaving the lee of Cyprus, the wind, hitherto astern, would now be on their port bow, and as ancient ships had not the same facility in tacking as modern ones, they could not sail as "near to the wind", not nearer than seven points, it is believed. But illustrations on coins, &c., show that the ancients understood quite well to arrange their sails so as to "beat to windward". **many** = in (Gr. *en*) many (Gr. *hikanos*, as 14. 3, "long"). **scarce were come** = were come with difficulty. Gr. *molis*. Occ. *vv.* 8, 16; 14. 18. Rom. 5. 7, 1 Pet. 4. 18. **over against.** Gr. *kata*. Ap. 104. x. 2.

°Cnidus, the wind °not °suffering us, we sailed
under °Crete, °over against Salmone;
8 And, °hardly °passing it, came °unto a place
which is called °The fair havens; nigh whereunto was the city *of* Lasea.

q[1] 9 Now when much time was °spent, and when
°sailing was °now °dangerous, [4]because the
°fast was °now already past, Paul °admonished
them,
10 And said [1]unto them, °"Sirs, I °perceive
that this °voyage °will be °with °hurt and much
°damage, °not only of the °lading and [2]ship,
but °also of our °lives."

p[2] 11 °Nevertheless the °centurion °believed the
°master and the °owner of the ship, more than
those things which were °spoken °by Paul.
12 And because the haven was °not commodious °to winter in, the more part °advised
to °depart thence also, °if °by any means they
might °attain [5]to °Phenice, *and there* to
°winter; *which is* an haven of Crete, °and lieth
°toward the °south west and °north west.
13 And when the south wind °blew softly,
supposing that they had obtained *their* °pur-
pose, °loosing *thence,* they °sailed °close by
Crete.
14 °But [10]not long °after there °arose °against
it a °tempestuous wind, called °Euroclydon.
15 And when the [2]ship was °caught, and
could [7]not °bear up into the wind, °we let *her*
°drive.
16 And °running under a [1]certain °island
which is called °Clauda, °we had much work
to °come by the °boat:
17 Which when they had °taken up, they
°used °helps, °undergirding the [2]ship; and,
fearing °lest they should °fall [1]into the °quick-
sands, °strake °sail, and so were [15]driven.

Cnidus. An important city, situated at the extreme south-west of Asia Minor. Referred to in 1 Macc. 15. 23.
not. Gr. *mē.* Ap. 105. II.
suffering. Gr. *proseaō.* Only here. The simple verb *eaō* occ. several times. See *vv.* 32, 40; 28. 4.
Crete. Known also as Candia. Salmone was its eastern cape.
8 hardly. Gr. *molis,* as *v.* 7.
passing. Gr. *paralegomai.* Only here and *v.* 13. They had difficulty in weathering the point.
unto. Gr. *eis.* Ap. 104. vi.
The fair havens = Fair Havens. It bears the same name still.
9 spent = passed. Gr. *diaginomai.* See 25. 13.
sailing. Gr. *ploos.* See 21. 7.
now = already.
dangerous. Gr. *episphalēs.* Only here.
fast: i. e. the tenth day of the seventh month, the day of Atonement, about Oct. 1.
now already = already.
admonished = Gr. *paraineō.* Only here and *v.* 22.
10 Sirs. Gr. *anēr.* Ap. 123. 2. Cp. 7. 26; 14. 15; 19. 25.
perceive. Gr. *theōreō.* Ap. 133. I. 11.
voyage. Same as "sailing" in *v.* 9.
will = is about to.
with. Gr. *meta.* Ap. 104. xi. 1.
hurt. Gr. *hubris.* Only here, *v.* 21. 2 Cor. 12. 10.
damage = loss. Gr. *zēmia.* Only here, *v.* 21. Phil. 3. 7, 8.
not. Gr. *ou.* Ap. 105. I.
lading = cargo. Gr. *phortos.* Only here; but the texts read *phortion,* as in Matt. 11. 30; 23. 4. Luke 11. 46. Gal. 6. 5.
also of our lives = of our lives also.
lives. Gr. *psuchē.* Ap. 110. III. 1.
11 Nevertheless = But.
centurion. He was in authority, being on imperial service.
believed. Gr. *peithō.* Ap. 150. I. 2.
master. Lit. steersman. Gr. *kubernētēs.* Only here, and Rev. 18. 17.
owner, &c. = shipowner. Gr. *nauklēros.* Only here.
spoken = said. Gr. *legō.*
by. Gr. *hupo.* Ap. 104. xviii. 1.
12 not commodious = not well situated. Gr. *aneuthetos.* Only here.
to winter in = for (Gr. *pros*) wintering (Gr. *paracheimasia.* Only here). **advised** = gave their decision. Gr. *boulē.* Ap. 102. 4. **depart.** Same as "launch", *v.* 2. **if.** Gr. *ei.* Ap. 118. 2. b. **by any means** = at least. **attain.** Gr. *katantaō.* See 16. 1. **Phenice.** Now *Lutro.* At the western end of the island. **winter.** Gr. *paracheimazō.* Only here, 28. 11. 1 Cor. 16. 6. Tit. 3. 12. **and lieth** = looking. Gr. *blepō.* Ap. 133. I. 5. **toward** = down. Gr. *kata.* Ap. 104. x. 2. **south west** = south-west wind. Gr. *lips.* Only here. **north west** = north-west wind. Gr. *chōros.* Only here. The meaning is that the harbour looked in the same direction as that in which these winds blew, i. e. north-east and south-east, as in R.V. **13 blew softly.** Gr. *hupopneō.* Only here. **purpose.** See 11. 23. **loosing.** Gr. *airō,* to raise. Here it means to weigh anchor. **sailed . . . by.** Same as "pass", *v.* 8. **close.** Gr. *asson.* Comp. of *anchi,* near. Only here. **14 But not long after.** Lit. But after not much (time). **after.** Gr. *meta.* Ap 104. xi. 2. **arose against it** = beat down from it (i. e. Crete). **arose.** Gr. *ballō.* Ap. 174. 9. This verb is sometimes used intransitively. **against** = down. Gr. *kata.* Ap. 104. x. 1. **tempestuous** = typhonic. Gr. *tuphōnikos.* Only here. **Euroclydon.** The texts (not the Syriac) read *Eurakulōn,* which means north-north-east wind. But if so, it would hardly have been introduced by the words "which is called". It was evidently a hurricane, not uncommon in those waters, and called "Euroclydon" locally and by the sailors. **15 caught.** Gr. *sunarpazō.* See 6. 12. **bear up into** = face. Lit. look in the eye of. Gr. *antophthalmeō.* Only here. **we let *her* drive.** Lit. giving her up (Gr. *epididōmi*) we were driven (borne along, pass. of Gr. *pherō*). The A.V. rendering is the exact nautical expression. **16 running under** = having run under the lee of. Gr. *hupotrechō.* Only here. **island.** Gr. *nēsion,* a small island, dim. of *nēsos* (13. 6). Only here. **Clauda.** Clauda (some texts, Cauda) was due south of Phenice. **we had much work.** Lit. with difficulty (Gr. *molis, v.* 7) were we strong (Gr. *ischuō.* See 15. 10). **come by** = become masters of. Gr. *perikratēs.* Only here. **boat** = skiff. Gr. *skaphē.* Only here, *vv.* 30, 32. The verb *skaptō,* to dig, or hollow out, only in Luke 6. 48; 13. 8; 16. 3. **17 taken up.** Gr. *airō.* See *v.* 13. **used.** Gr. *chraomai.* See *v.* 3. **helps.** Gr. *boētheia.* Only here and Heb. 4. 16. **undergirding.** Gr. *hupozōnnumi.* Only here. The process of passing a cable or chain round a ship to prevent her going to pieces is called "frapping". **lest.** Gr. *mē.* Ap. 105. II. **fall.** Gr. *ekpiptō.* Occ. thirteen times; here, *vv.* 26, 29, 32; 12. 7. Mark 13. 25. Rom. 9. 6, &c. **quicksands.** Gr. *surtis.* Only here. There are two gulfs on the north coast of Africa, full of shoals and sandbanks, called Syrtis Major and Syrtis Minor. It may be the former of these, now Sidra, into which they were afraid of being driven. **strake sail.** Lit. having lowered the gear. **strake.** Gr *chalaō.* See Luke 5. 4. **sail.** Gr. *skeuos.* The great yard to which the sail was attached. Occ. twenty-three times. Always rendered "vessel", save here; Matt. 12. 29. Mark 3. 27 (goods). Luke 17. 31 (stuff).

18 And we being °exceedingly °tossed with a tempest, the °next *day* they °lightened the ship;
19 And the third *day* °we °cast out °with our own hands the °tackling of the [2]ship.
20 And when °neither sun °nor stars °in many days °appeared, and °no small °tempest °lay on *us*, all hope that we should be saved was then °taken away.
q[2] **21 But °after long °abstinence, Paul stood forth °in the midst of them, and said, [10]"Sirs, ye °should have °hearkened [1]unto me, and [7]not have °loosed °from Crete, and to have °gained this °harm and °loss.**
22 And °now I °exhort you to °be of good cheer: for there shall be °no °loss of °*any man's* [10]life °among you, °but of the [2]ship.
23 For there °stood by me this night °the angel of °God, Whose I am, and Whom I °serve,
24 Saying, 'Fear [7]not, Paul; thou °must °be brought before Cæsar; and, °lo, [23]God hath °given thee all them that [2]sail [10]with thee.'
25 Wherefore, [10]sirs, [22]be of good cheer: for I °believe [23]God, that it shall be °even as it was °told me.
26 °Howbeit we [24]must be °cast °upon a [1]certain °island."
p[3] **27 But when the fourteenth night was come, as we were °driven up and down [21]in °Adria, °about midnight the °shipmen °deemed that °they drew near to some country:**
28 And °sounded, °and found *it* twenty °fathoms: and °when they had gone a little further, they °sounded again, and found *it* fifteen °fathoms.
29 Then fearing °lest we should have [17]fallen °upon °rocks, they [19]cast four °anchors °out of the °stern, and °wished °for the day.
q[3] **30 And as the [27]shipmen were °about to flee [29]out of the [2]ship, °when they had let down the [16]boat [1]into the sea, °under colour as °though they would have °cast [29]anchors [29]out of the °foreship,**
31 Paul said to the [1]centurion and to the soldiers, °"Except these °abide [21]in the [2]ship, ye °cannot be saved."

18 exceedingly. Gr. *sphodrōs.* Only here. The usual word is *sphodra*, as in Matt. 2. 10.
tossed with a tempest. Gr. *cheimazomai.* Only here. Cp. *v.* 12.
next. Gr. *hexēs.* See 21. 1.
lightened the ship=they began to jettison the cargo. Lit. they were making a casting-out. Gr. *ekbolē.* Only here.
19 we. The texts read "they", which would mean the crew. But it would be superfluous to say of them, "with our own hands." Luke means that every one was pressed into the service, prisoners and all.
cast out. Gr. *rhiptō.* See Luke 4. 35.
with our own hands. Gr. *autocheir.* Only here. To emphasize the fact that all were called to help in this time of peril.
tackling. Gr. *skeuē.* The yard, sail, and all the ship's furnishings. Only here, but used in the Sept. Jonah 1. 5.
20 neither . . . nor. Gr. *mēte . . . mēte.*
in=for. Gr. *epi.* Ap. 104. ix. 3.
appeared=shone. Gr. *epiphainō.* Ap. 106. iii.
no. Gr. *ou.* Ap. 105. I.
tempest. Gr. *cheimōn.* Elsewhere transl. "winter", Matt. 24. 20. Mark 13. 18. John 10. 22. 2 Ti. 4. 21; except Matt. 16. 3 (foul weather). Cp. *v.* 18.
lay on *us*. Gr. *epikeimai.* See Luke 5. 1; 23. 23. 1 Cor. 9. 16. Heb. 9. 10.
taken away. Gr. *periaireō.* Only here, *v.* 40. 2 Cor. 3. 16. Heb. 10. 11.
21 after long abstinence. Lit. much fasting having taken place (Gr. *huparchō.* See Luke 9. 48).
abstinence. Gr. *asitia.* Only here. Cp. *v.* 33, and *v.* 38 (*sitos*).
in. Gr. *en.* Ap. 104. viii.
should=ought to.
hearkened. Gr. *peitharcheō.* See 5. 29.
loosed. Gr. *anagō.* See *vv.* 2, 4, 12.
from. Gr. *apo.* Ap. 104. iv.
gained=gotten, as R.V. Gr. *kerdainō.* Occ. sixteen times. Always transl. "gain", save Phil. 3. 8. 1 Pet. 3. 1 (win). Only here in Acts. First occ. Matt. 16. 26.
harm. Same as "hurt" (*v.* 10).
loss. Same as "damage" (*v.* 10).
22 now. See 4. 29.
exhort. Same as "admonish" (*v.* 9).
be of good cheer. Gr. *euthumeō.* Only here, *v.* 25, and Jas. 5. 13. **no.** Gr. *oudeis.*
loss=casting away. Gr. *apobolē.* Only here and Rom. 11. 15.
any man's **life**=a life.
among=out of. Gr. *ek.* Ap. 104. vii.
but=except. Gr. *plēn.*

23 stood by. Gr. *paristēmi.* Cp. 1. 10. **the**=an. **God.** Ap. 98. I. i. 1. **serve.** Gr. *latreuō.* Ap. 137. 4 and 190. III. 5. **24 must.** Same as "should", *v.* 21. **be brought**=stand. **lo.** Gr. *idou.* Ap. 133. I. 2. **given**=granted. Gr. *charizomai.* Ap. 184. II. 1. **25 believe.** Gr. *pisteuō.* Ap. 150. I. 1. ii. **even as.** Lit. thus according to (Gr. *kata.* Ap. 104. x. 2) the manner in which. **told**=spoken to. Gr. *laleō.* Ap. 121. 7. **26 Howbeit**=But. **cast.** Gr. *ekpiptō.* Same as "fall" (*v.* 17). **upon.** Gr. *eis.* Ap. 104. vi. **island.** Gr. *nēsos.* Elsewhere 13. 6; 28. 1, 7, 9, 11. Rev. 1. 9; 6. 14; 16. 20. **27 driven up and down.** Gr. *diapherō*=to carry hither and thither. Cp. 13. 49. Mark 11. 16. Then "to differ", as in the other occ. Matt. 6. 26; 10. 31; 12. 12. Luke 12. 7, 24. Rom. 2. 18. 1 Cor. 15. 41. Gal. 2. 6; 4. 1. Phil. 1. 10. **Adria**=the Adria. In Paul's day this term included the part of the Mediterranean lying south of Italy, east of Sicily, and west of Greece. Josephus was on board a ship which foundered in the Adriatic Sea and was picked up by a ship of Cyrene, which landed him at Puteoli (Life, § 3). **about.** Gr. *kata.* Ap. 104. x. 2. **shipmen**=seamen. Gr. *nautēs.* Only here, *v.* 30, and Rev. 18. 17. **deemed**=were supposing. See 13. 25. **they drew, &c.**=some country was drawing near to them. Gr. *prosagō.* See 16. 20. **28 sounded**=having sounded. Gr. *bolizō.* Only here. **and**=they. **fathoms.** Gr. *orguia.* See Ap. 51. III. 2. (2). **when, &c.**=having proceeded. Gr. *diistēmi*, to put, or stand, apart. Only here, and Luke 22. 59 (lit. one hour having intervened); 24. 51 (was parted). **29 lest**=lest perchance. **upon.** The texts read *kata.* Ap. 104. x. 2. **rocks**=rough (Gr. *trachus.* Only here and Luke 3. 5) places. **anchors.** Gr. *ankura.* Only here, *vv.* 30, 40. Heb. 6. 19. **out of.** Gr. *ek.* Ap. 104. vii. **stern.** Gr. *prumna.* Only here, *v.* 41, and Mark 4. 38. **wished**=were praying. Gr. *euchomai.* Ap. 134. I. 1. **for the day**=that the day would come. **30 about**=seeking. **when, &c.**=and had let down. Gr. *chalaō*, as in *v.* 17. **under colour**=by pretence. Gr. *prophasis.* Elsewhere, Matt. 23. 14. Mark 12. 40. Luke 20. 47. John 15. 22. Phil. 1. 18. 1 Thess. 2. 5. **though they would have**=being about to. **cast.** Gr. *ekteinō.* Elsewhere (fifteen times) transl. "stretch" or "put forth". **foreship**=bows or prow. Gr. *prōra.* Only here and *v.* 41. **31 Except**=If . . . not. Gr. *ean* (Ap. 118. I. b) *mē* (Ap. 105. II). **abide.** Gr. *menō.* See p. 1511. **cannot**=are not (Gr. *ou.* Ap. 105. I) able to.

p^4 **32** Then the soldiers cut off the °ropes of the
[16]boat, and let her [17]fall off.
q^4 **33** And while the day was coming on, Paul
°besought *them* all to °take °meat, saying,
°"This day is the fourteenth day that ye have
°tarried °and continued °fasting, having
°taken °nothing.
34 Wherefore I °pray you to [33-]take *some*
[33]meat, for this °is °for your °health: for °there
shall not an °hair °fall °from the head of any
of you."
35 And °when he had thus spoken, he took
bread, and °gave thanks to [23]God in presence
of them all: and when he had °broken *it*, he
began to eat.
36 Then were they all °of good cheer, and
they also [33-]took *some* [33]meat.
37 And we were °in all [21]in the [2]ship two
hundred threescore and sixteen °souls.
38 And °when they had eaten enough, they
°lightened the [2]ship, °and cast out the °wheat
[1]into the sea.
p^5 **39** And when it was day, they °knew [10]not
the °land: but they °discovered a [1]certain
°creek with a °shore, [1]into °the which they
°were minded, °if °it were possible, to °thrust
in the [2]ship.
40 And when they had °taken up the
[29]anchors, they °committed °*themselves* [8]unto
the sea, and °loosed the °rudder °bands, and
°hoised up the °mainsail to the °wind, and
°made °toward [39]shore.
41 °And °falling [1]into a place °where two
seas met, they °ran the °ship aground; and
the °forepart °stuck fast, and °remained
°unmoveable, but the °hinder part °was broken
°with the °violence of the °waves.
O **42** And the soldiers' °counsel was °to kill the
[1]prisoners, [17]lest °any °of them °should swim
out, and °escape.
43 But the [6]centurion, °willing to °save Paul,
°kept them from *their* °purpose; and commanded that they which °could °swim °should
cast *themselves* first *into the sea,* °and get °to
[39]land:

32 ropes. Gr. *schoinion.* Only here and John 2. 15 (cords).

33 besought=was entreating. Gr. *parakaleō.* Ap. 134. I. 6.

take. Gr. *metalambanō.* See 2. 46.

meat=food, or nourishment. Gr. *trophē.*

This day, &c. Lit. Tarrying (or waiting) to-day, the fourteenth day.

tarried. Gr. *prosdokaō.* Ap. 133. III. 3.

and continued=ye continue. Gr. *diateleō.* Only here.

fasting=without food. Gr. *asitos.* Only here. Cp. *v.* 21. Fig. *Synecdochē.* Ap. 6.

taken. Gr. *proslambanō.* See 17. 5.

nothing. Gr. *mēdeis.*

34 pray. Same as "besought", *v.* 33.

is. Gr. *huparchō.* See Luke 9. 48.

for. Gr. *pros.* Ap. 104. xv. 1.

health=salvation. Gr. *sōtēria.* The verb *sōzō* is frequently transl. "heal". Matt. 9. 21, 22. John 11. 12 (do well). Acts 4. 9; 14. 9.

there shall not, &c. Lit. a hair of no one (Gr. *oudeis*) of you shall fall from his head.

hair. Gr. *thrix.* Only occ. in Acts.

fall. The texts read "perish", as in Luke 21. 18. Fig. *Parœmia.* Ap. 6. Cp. 1 Sam. 14. 45. 2 Sam. 14. 11. 1 Kings 1. 52. Matt. 10. 30.

from. Gr. *apo,* with texts. Ap. 104. iv.

35 when, &c.=having said these things, and taken bread, he.

gave thanks. Gr. *eucharisteō.* Only here and 28. 15 in Acts. First occ. Matt. 15. 36.

broken. Gr. *klaō.* See 2. 46.

36 of good cheer. Gr. *euthumos.* Only here. The verb occ. *vv.* 22, 25.

37 in all . . . two hundred, &c. Lit. all the souls two hundred threescore and sixteen.

souls. Gr. *psuchē.* Ap. 110. II. Cp. *vv.* 10, 22. Josephus says in the ship in which he was wrecked there were 600, of whom only eighty were saved. Cp. *v.* 22.

38 when, &c. Having been satisfied (Gr. *korennumi.* Only here and 1 Cor. 4. 8) with food (Gr. *trophē,* as in *v.* 33).

lightened. Gr. *kouphizō.* Only here.

and cast out=casting out.

wheat. Gr. *sitos.*

39 knew=recognized. Gr. *epiginōskō.* Ap. 132. I. iii.

land. Gr. *gē.* Ap. 129. 4.

discovered=perceived. Ap. 133. II. 4.

creek. Gr. *kolpos,* bosom. Here, Luke 6. 38; 16. 22, 23. John 1. 18; 13. 23.

shore=beach. **the.** Omit.

were minded=took counsel or planned. Gr. *bouleuō.* **if.** Ap. 118. 2. b. **it were possible**=they might be able. **thrust in.** Gr. *exōtheō.* Only here and 7. 45. **40 taken up.** Gr. *periaireō.* Same as in *v.* 20. **committed.** Gr. *eaō.* Same as "let", *v.* 32. *themselves*=them, i.e. the anchors. They "slipped" the anchors. **loosed.** Gr. *aniēmi,* as in 16. 26. Eph. 6. 9. Heb. 13. 5. **rudder bands**=lashings of the rudders. **rudder.** Gr. *pēdalion.* Only here and Jas. 3. 4. There were two great paddles, one on either side, used for steering. **bands.** Gr. *zeuktēria.* The tackle by which the paddles were lashed to the hull when the ship was at anchor. Only here. **hoised**=hoisted. Gr. *epairō.* Generally take up, or lift up. 1. 9; 2. 14, &c. **mainsail**=foresail. Gr. *artemōn.* Only here. The mainsail had been thrown overboard (*v.* 19). **wind.** Lit. the blowing. Gr. *pneō.* Elsewhere, Matt. 7. 25, 27. Luke 12. 55. John 3. 8; 6. 18. Rev. 7. 1. **made**=were holding on. Gr. *katechō.* See 2 Thess. 2. 6. **toward**=for. Gr. *eis.* Ap. 104. vi. **41 And**=But. **falling.** Gr. *peripiptō.* Only here, Luke 10. 30. Jas. 1. 2. **where two seas met.** Gr. *dithalassos.* Only here. A sandbank formed by opposing currents. **ran . . . aground.** Gr. *epokellō,* but the texts read *epikellō,* meaning the same. Only here. **ship.** Gr. *naus.* Only here. Elsewhere the word for "ship" is *ploion.* It was no longer a ship, but a mere floating hulk. **forepart.** Same as "foreship", *v.* 30. Add "indeed". **stuck fast, and**=having stuck fast. Gr. *ereidō.* Only here. **remained.** Gr. *menō,* as in *v.* 31. **unmoveable.** Gr. *asaleutos.* Only here and Heb. 12. 28. **hinder part**=stern, *v.* 29. **was broken**=began to break up. Gr. *luō.* See 13. 43. **with**=by, as in *v.* 11. **violence.** Gr. *bia.* See 5. 26. **waves.** Gr. *kuma.* Only here, Matt. 8. 24; 14. 24. Mark 4. 37. Jude 13. **42 counsel.** Gr. *boulē.* Ap. 102. 4. See *v.* 12. **to kill**=in order that (Gr. *hina*) they might kill. **any**=any one. Ap. 123. 3. **of them.** Omit. **should swim out, and**=having swum out. Gr. *ekkolumbaō.* Only here. **escape**=make good his escape. Gr. *diapheugō.* Only here. **43 willing**=purposing. Gr. *boulomai.* Ap. 102. 3. **save.** Gr. *diasōzō.* See Matt. 14. 36. **kept**=hindered. **purpose.** Gr. *boulēma.* Ap. 102. 4. Only here and Rom. 9. 19. **could**=were able to. **swim.** Gr. *kolumbaō.* Only here. Cp. *v.* 42. **should, &c.**=having first cast (themselves) overboard. Gr. *aporrhiptō.* Only here. **and get.** Lit. should go forth. Gr. *exeimi.* See 13. 42. **to**=upon. Gr. *epi.* Ap. 104. ix. 3.

P 44 And °the rest, °some °on °boards, and
°some °on °*broken pieces* °of the [2]ship. And so
it came to pass, that they °escaped all safe [43] to
[39] land.

N² Q¹ R **28** And °when they were °escaped, then
°they °knew that the °island was called
°Melita.

S r¹ 2 And the °barbarous people shewed us °no
°little °kindness: for they °kindled a °fire, and
°received us every one, °because of the °present
rain, and °because of the °cold.

s¹ 3 And when Paul had °gathered a °bundle of
°sticks, and laid *them* °on the [2]fire, there came
a °viper °out of the °heat, and °fastened on his
hand.
4 And when the [2]barbarians °saw the *venomous* °beast °hang °on his hand, they said
°among themselves, "No doubt this °man is
a murderer, whom, °though he hath [1]escaped
°the sea, °yet °vengeance suffereth °not to
live."
5 °And he °shook off the [4]beast °into the fire,
and °felt °no °harm.
6 °Howbeit they °looked °when he °should
have °swollen, or °fallen down °dead °sudden-
ly: but after they had looked °a great while,
and °saw °no °harm come °to him, they
°changed their minds, and said that he was
a °god.

r² 7 °In the same quarters °were °possessions
of the °chief man of the [1]island, °whose name
was Publius; who °received us, and °lodged us
three days °courteously.

s² 8 And it came to pass, that the father of Publius lay °sick of °a fever and of a °bloody flux:
°to whom Paul entered in, and °prayed, and
laid his hands on him, and °healed him.
9 °So when this was done, °others also which

44 the rest. Gr. *loipos.* Ap. 124. 3.
some = some indeed.
on. Gr. *epi.* Ap. 104. ix. 2.
boards = planks. Gr. *sanis.* Only here.
on. Gr. *epi.* Ap. 104. ix. 1.
broken pieces: i. e. any kind of wreckage. Lit. some of the things.
of = from. Gr. *apo.* Ap. 104. iv.
escaped all safe = all escaped safe (same as "save", *v.* 43).

In this chapter there are over fifty words, mostly nautical, found nowhere else in the N.T.

28. 1-16 (N², p. 1653). **MELITA TO ROME.**
(*Division.*)

N² | Q¹ | 1-10. Sojourn at Melita.
   | Q² | 11-16. Journey to Rome.

28. 1-10 (Q¹, above). **SOJOURN AT MELITA.**
(*Introversion and Alternation.*)

Q¹ | R | 1. Arrival.
   | S | r¹ | 2. Hospitality.
   | | s¹ | 3-6. Miracle.
   | | r² | 7. Hospitality.
   | | s² | 8, 9. Miracles.
   | | r³ | 10-. Hospitality.
   | *R* | -10. Departure.

1 when they were = having.
escaped. Gr. *diasōzō.* Same as in 27. 43, 44. See Matt. 14. 36.
they. The texts read "we".
knew. Gr. *epiginōskō.* Ap. 132. I. iii.
island. Gr. *nēsos.* See 27. 26.
Melita = Malta. It was in the jurisdiction of the Prætor of Sicily. St. Paul's Bay, the traditional scene of the shipwreck, fulfils all the conditions.
2 barbarous people. Gr. *barbaros.* Elsewhere, *v.* 4. Rom. 1. 14. 1 Cor. 14. 11. Col. 3. 11. The Greeks called all people who did not speak Greek barbarians. The Maltese were Phœnicians.
no = not. Gr. *ou.* Ap. 105. I.
little = ordinary, as in 19. 11.
kindness. Gr. *philanthrōpia.* Ap. 135. II. 2
kindled = having kindled. Gr. *anaptō.* Only here, Luke 12. 49. Jas. 3. 5.
fire. Gr. *pura.* Only here, and in *v.* 3.
received. Gr. *proslambanō.* See 17. 5.
because of. Gr. *dia.* Ap. 104. v. 2.
present. Gr. *ephistēmi.* Lit. to come upon, as in Luke 2. 9. **cold.** Gr. *psuchos.* Only here, John 18. 18. 2 Cor. 11. 27. **3 gathered.** Gr. *sustrephō.* Only here. **bundle** = multitude. G. *plēthos.* **sticks.** Gr. *phruganon* Only here. **on.** Gr. *epi.* Ap. 104. ix. 3. **viper.** Gr. *echidna.* Only here, Matt. 3. 7; 12. 34; 23. 33. Luke 3. 7. **out of.** Gr. *ek.* Ap. 104. vii, but the texts read *apo* (Ap. 104. iv). **heat.** Gr. *thermē.* Only here. **fastened.** Gr. *kathaptō.* Only here. **4 saw.** Gr. *eidon.* Ap. 133. I. 1. **beast.** Gr. *thērion.* See 11. 6. **hang** = hanging. **on** = from. Gr. *ek.* Ap. 104. vii. **among themselves** = to (Gr. *pros.* Ap. 104. xv. 3) one another. **man.** Gr. *anthrōpos.* Ap. 123. 1. **though he hath.** Lit. having. **the sea** = out of (Gr. *ek*) the sea. **yet.** Omit. **vengeance.** Gr. *hē dikē.* Ap. 177. 4. The Greeks personified Justice, Vengeance, and other ideas; as we do when we speak of Nemesis. **not.** Gr. *ou.* Ap. 105. I. **5 And he** = He then indeed. **shook off.** Gr. *apotinassō.* Only here, and Luke 9. 5. **into.** Gr. *eis.* Ap. 104. vi. **felt** = suffered. **no** = nothing. Gr. *oudeis.* **harm** = evil. Gr. *kakos.* Ap. 128. III. 2. **6 Howbeit** = But. **looked** = were expecting, or watching in expectation. Gr. *prosdokaō.* Ap. 133. III. 3. **when** = that. **should have** = was about to. **swollen** = swell. Gr. *pimprēmi* Only here. **fallen down.** See 26. 14. **dead** = a corpse. Gr. *nekros.* Ap. 139. 2. **suddenly.** See 2. 2. **a great while** = for (Gr. *epi.* Ap. 104. ix. 3) much (time). **saw.** Gr. *theōreō.* Ap. 133. I. 11. **no** = nothing. Gr. *mēdeis.* **harm** = amiss. Gr. *atopos.* Only here, Luke 23. 41. 2 Thess. 3. 2. **to.** Gr. *eis.* Ap. 104. vi. **changed their minds.** Gr. *metaballomai.* Only here. **god.** Ap. 98. I. i. 5. **7 In, &c.** = Now in (Gr. *en*) the parts about (Gr. *peri.* Ap. 104. xiii. 2) that place. **were.** Gr. *huparchō.* See Luke 9. 48. **possessions** = lands. Gr. *chōrion.* See Matt. 26. 36. **chief man** = first. Gr. *prōtos.* This title has been found on an inscription. **whose name was** = by name. **received.** Gr. *anadechomai.* Only here and Heb. 11. 17. **lodged.** Gr. *xenizō.* See 10. 6; 21. 16. **courteously.** Gr. *philophronōs.* Only here. Cp. 27. 3, and 1 Pet. 3. 8. **8 sick of** = taken with. Gr. *sunechō.* See Luke 4. 38. **a fever** = fevers. Gr. *puretos.* Elsewhere Matt. 8. 15. Mark 1. 31. Luke 4. 38, 39. John 4. 52. Always in sing. But found in pl. in medical works. Perhaps to convey the idea of severity which is expressed by "great" in Luke 4 38, or of their recurrence **bloody flux.** Gr. *dusenteria.* Hence Engl. dysentery. Only here **to.** Gr. *pros.* Ap. 104. xv 3. **prayed.** Gr. *proseuchomai.* Ap. 134. I. 2. **healed.** Gr. *iaomai.* See Luke 6. 17. **9 So** = But. **others** = the rest. Ap. 124. 3.

had °diseases [7]in the [1]island came, and were °healed:

r^3 10 Who °also honoured us with many honours;

R and when we °departed, they °laded *us* with °such things as were necessary.

Q^2 t 11 And °after three months we [10]departed [7]in a °ship of Alexandria, which had °wintered [7]in the [1]isle, °whose °sign was °Castor and Pollux.

12 And °landing °at °Syracuse, we °tarried *there* three days.

13 And from thence we °fetched a compass, °and came [13]to °Rhegium: and [11]after one day °the south wind blew, and we came °the next day [6]to °Puteoli:

u 14 Where we found brethren, and were °desired to [12]tarry °with them seven days: and so we °went °toward Rome.

u 15 And from thence, when the brethren heard °of us, they came °to meet us as far as °Appii forum, and °The three °taverns: whom when Paul [4]saw, he °thanked °God, and took °courage.

t 16 And when we came °to °Rome, the °centurion °delivered the prisoners to the °captain of the guard: but °Paul was suffered to °dwell °by himself °with a soldier that °kept him.

O T^1 v 17 And it came to pass, that [11]after three days Paul called the °chief of the Jews together: and when they were come together, he said °unto them,

w °"Men *and* brethren, though **I** have committed °nothing against the °people, or °customs °of our fathers, yet was I [16]delivered °prisoner °from Jerusalem [5]into the hands of the Romans.

diseases. Gr. *astheneia*. See Matt. 8. 17. John 11. 4.
healed. Gr. *therapeuō*. See Luke 6. 18 and Ap. 137. 6.
10 also honoured, &c. = honoured us with many honours also.
departed = sailed. Gr. *anagō*. See "loosed" (13. 13).
laded *us* **with** = laid on us.
such things, &c. = the things for (Gr. *pros*. Ap. 104. xv. 3) the need (Gr. *chreia*). The texts read "needs". Cp. Phil. 4. 16.

28. 11-16 (Q^2, p. 1657). JOURNEY TO ROME. (*Introversion.*)

Q^2	t		11-13. Departure for Rome.
		u	14. Brethren. Puteoli.
		u	15. Brethren. Appii Forum.
	t		16. Arrival at Rome.

11 after. Gr. *meta*. Ap. 104. xi. 2.
ship of Alexandria. Another corn ship.
wintered. Gr. *paracheimazō*. See 27. 12.
whose sign, &c. = with sign the Dioscuri.
sign. Gr. *parasēmos*. Only here. Lit. signed or marked.
Castor and Pollux. Gr. *Dioskouroi*. Lit. sons of Zeus. These twin sons of Zeus and Leda were deified and their names given to the bright stars in the constellation Gemini. They were regarded as the patron deities of sailors. The "sign" was carried on the prow of the vessel, after the manner of our "figure-heads".
12 landing. Gr. *katagō*. See 21. 3.
at. Gr. *eis*. Ap. 104. vi.
Syracuse. An important town in Sicily (S.E.), still bearing the same name.
tarried. Gr. *epimenō*. See 10. 48.
13 fetched a compass = having tacked about. Gr. *perierchomai*. See 19. 13. Fig. *Idiōma*. Ap. 6.
and came = arrived. Gr. *katantaō*. See 16. 1.
Rhegium. Now Reggio, on the Straits of Messina.
the south wind blew, and = a south wind having sprung up. Gr. *epiginomai*. Only here.
the next day = the second day. Gr. *deuteraios*. Only here.

Puteoli. On the Bay of Naples. It was here Josephus and his shipwrecked companions were landed. Now *Pozzuoli*. **14 desired** = entreated. Gr. *parakaleō*. Ap. 134. I. 6. **with.** Gr. *epi*. Ap. 104. ix. 2, but the texts read *para* (xii. 2). **went** = came. **toward.** Gr. *eis*. Ap. 104. vi. Rome was used in a more extended sense here than in *v*. 16. **15 of us** = the things (i. e. the news) concerning (Gr. *peri*) us. **to meet us.** Lit. for (Gr. *eis*) meeting (Gr. *apantēsis*. See Matt. 25. 1) us. **Appii forum.** The market of Appius, a small town on the Appian Way, forty-three miles from Rome. **The three taverns.** About ten miles further on. **taverns.** Gr. *tabernē* transliterated from Lat. *taberna*. Only here. **thanked.** Gr. *eucharisteō*. See 27. 35. **God.** Ap. 98. I. i. 1. **courage.** Gr. *tharsos*. Only here. Cp. 23. 11. **16 Rome.** Cp. 19. 21; 23. 11. The purpose was fulfilled, but perhaps not in the way Paul expected. **centurion.** Gr. *hekatontarchos*. See 21. 32. Most texts omit this clause. **delivered.** Gr. *paradidōmi*. See 3. 13. **captain of the guard.** Gr. *stratopedarchēs*. Only here. Probably the Præfect of the Prætorians. **Paul was suffered.** Lit. it was permitted (Gr. *epitrepō*. See 26. 1) Paul. **dwell.** Gr. *menō*. See p. 1511. **by.** Gr. *kata*. Ap. 104. x. 2. **with.** Gr. *sun*. Ap. 104. xvi. **kept** = guarded. He was chained by the wrist to the prisoner. Paul speaks of this chain in *v*. 20. Eph. 6. 20. Phil. 1. 7, 13, 14, 16. Col. 4. 18. Philem. 10, 13.

28. 17-29 (*O*, p. 1639). PAUL AND THE JEWS IN ROME. TWO ADDRESSES. (*Division.*)

O	T^1	17-22. First meeting.
	T^2	23-29. Second meeting.

28. 17-22 (T^1, above). FIRST MEETING. (*Extended Alternation.*)

T^1	v				17-. Call.
		w			-17. Law and customs of Israel not violated.
			x		18. Romans find no capital charge.
				y	19. Jews speak against (*antilegō*) Paul's release.
	v				20-. Call.
		w			-20. Hope of Israel.
			x		21. Jews receive no complaints.
				y	22. The sect everywhere spoken against (*antilegō*).

17 chief = first, as in *v*. 7. **unto.** Gr. *pros*. Ap. 104. xv. 3. **Men, &c.** See 1. 16. **nothing.** Gr. *oudeis*. **people.** Gr. *laos*. See 2. 47. **customs of our fathers** = the ancestral customs. **customs.** Gr. *ethos*. See 6. 14. **of our fathers.** Gr. *patrōos*. See 22. 3. **prisoner.** See 25. 14. **from** = out of. Gr. *ek*. Ap. 104. vii.

x 18 Who, when they had °examined me,
°would have °let *me* go, [2]because there was
°no °cause of death [7]in me.

y 19 But when the Jews °spake against *it*, I
was °constrained to °appeal unto Cæsar; [4]not
that I had ought to °accuse my °nation of.

v 20 °For this [18]cause therefore have I °called
for you, to [4]see *you*, and to °speak with *you*:

w because that °for °the hope of Israel I am °bound
with this chain."

x 21 And they said [17]unto him, "We °neither
received °letters °out of Judæa °concerning
thee, °neither any of the brethren that came
°shewed or °spake °any harm [15]of thee.

y 22 But we °desire to hear °of thee what
thou thinkest: for °as [21]concerning this °sect,
°we know that every where it is [19]spoken a-
gainst."

T² U z 23 And when they had °appointed him a
day, there came many [8]to him [5]into *his* °lodg-
ing;

a to whom he °expounded and °testified the
°kingdom of [15]God, °persuading them [21]con-
cerning °Jesus, both [21]out of the law of °Moses,
and *out of* the °prophets, °from morning °till
°evening.

V 24 And some °believed the things which were
spoken, and some °believed not.
25 And °when they agreed not [4]among themselves, they °departed,

U a °after that Paul had spoken one °word,
°"Well [21]spake °the Holy Ghost °by °Esaias
the [23]prophet [17]unto °our fathers,
26 Saying, '**Go** [17]**unto this** [17]**people, and say,**
°**Hearing ye shall hear, and shall** °**not** °**understand; and** °**seeing ye shall** °**see, and** °**not** °**perceive:**
27 **For the heart of this** [17]**people** °**is waxed
gross, and** °**their ears are dull of hearing, and
their eyes have they** °**closed;** °**lest they should**
[4]**see with *their* eyes, and hear with *their* ears,
and** [26]**understand with *their* heart, and should**
°**be converted, and I should** [8]**heal them.**'
28 Be it [22]known therefore °unto you, that
the °salvation of [15]God °is sent °unto the °Gen-
tiles, and *that* they will hear it."

z 29 And when he had said these °words, the
Jews departed,

18 examined. Gr. *anakrinō.* Ap. 122. 2.
would have = were wishing to. Gr. *boulomai.* Ap. 102. 3.
let . . . go. Gr. *apoluō.* Ap. 174. 11.
no. Gr. *mēdeis.*
cause. Gr. *aitia,* as in 25. 27.
19 spake against. Gr. *antilegō.* See 13. 45.
constrained. Gr. *anankazō.* See 26. 11 (the only other occ. in Acts).
appeal unto. Gr. *epikaleomai.* See 25. 11.
accuse. Gr. *katēgoreō.* See 22. 30.
nation. Gr. *ethnos.*
20 For. Gr. *dia.* Ap. 104. v. 2.
called for. Gr. *parakaleō,* as in *v.* 14.
speak with. Gr. *proslaleō.* See 13. 43.
for. Gr. *heneken.* First occ. Matt. 5. 10 (for the sake of).
the hope of Israel = the Messiah whom Israel hoped for. Fig. *Metonymy.* Ap. 6.
bound with. Gr. *perikeimai.* Only here, Mark 9. 42. Luke 17. 2. Heb. 5. 2; 12. 1.
21 neither. Gr. *oute.*
letters. Gr. *gramma,* a letter of the alphabet. In pl. "writings". This and Gal. 6. 11 are the only places where it is used of an epistle, the usual word being *epistolē.*
out of = from. Gr. *apo.* Ap. 104. iv.
concerning. Gr. *peri.* Ap. 104. xiii. 1.
shewed = reported. Gr. *apangellō.* See 4. 23.
spake. Gr. *laleō.* Ap. 121. 7.
any harm = anything evil (Gr. *ponēros.* Ap. 128. III. 1).
22 desire = think it right. Gr. *axioō.* See 15. 38.
of = from. Gr. *para.* Ap. 104. xii. 1.
as, &c. = concerning this sect indeed.
sect. Gr. *hairesis.* See 5. 17.
we know = it is known (Gr. *gnōstos.* See 1. 19) to us.

28. 23–29 (T², p. 1658). SECOND MEETING.

T² | U | z | 23–. Jews assemble.
a | –23. Paul expounds.
V | 24 25–. Result. Disputation.
U | *a* | –25–28. Paul warns.
z | 29–. Jews depart.
V | –29. Result. Reasoning.

23 appointed = arranged. Gr. *tassō.* See 13. 48.
lodging. Gr. *xenia.* Only here and Philem. 22. Cp. 10. 6; 21. 16.
expounded. Gr. *ektithēmi.* See 7. 21.
testified. Gr. *diamarturomai.* See 2. 40. Ninth and last occ. in Acts.
kingdom of God. The Messianic kingdom was the subject. The mention of the Lord Jesus, and the law of Moses, and the prophets, establishes this. See Ap. 114.
persuading. Gr. *peithō.* Ap. 150. I. 2.
Jesus. Ap. 98. X.
Moses. Nineteenth occ. in Acts. See Matt. 8. 4.
prophets. Ap. 189.
from. Gr. *apo.* Ap. 104. iv.
till. Gr. *heōs.*
evening. Gr. *hespera.* See 4. 3.

24 believed = were persuaded of. Gr. *peithō,* as in *v.* 23. **believed not** = were disbelieving. Gr. *apisteō.* Elsewhere, Mark 16. 11, 16. Luke 24. 11, 41. Rom. 3. 3. 2 Tim. 2. 13. **25 when they agreed not** = being out of harmony. Gr. *asumphōnos.* Only here. See 5. 9; 15. 15. **departed.** Lit. were being sent away. Ap. 174. 11. The imperfect suggests that the chief men (*v.* 17) broke up the meeting and sent the rest away lest they should be convinced. **after that, &c.** = Paul having spoken. **word.** Gr. *rhēma.* See Mark 9. 32. **Well** = Rightly. **the Holy Ghost** = the Holy Spirit. Ap. 101. II. 3. **by** = through. Gr. *dia.* Ap. 104. v. 1. **Esaias** = Isaiah. See 8. 28, 30. The quotation is from 6. 9, 10. This is the third occasion of the quotation of these words. See Matt. 13. 14, 15. John 12. 40. **our.** The texts read "your". **26 Hearing** = In hearing. Gr. *akoē.* Cp. 17. 20. **not** = by no means. Gr. *ou mē.* Ap. 105. III. **understand.** Gr. *suniēmi.* Cp. Ap. 132. II. 3. **seeing . . . see.** Gr. *blepō.* Ap. 133. I. 5. **perceive.** Gr. *eidon.* Ap. 133. I. 1. Fig. *Polyptoton.* Ap. 6. **27 is waxed gross** = has become fat. Gr. *pachunomai.* Only here and Matt. 13. 15. **their ears, &c.** = with their ears they hear heavily. **closed.** Gr. *kammuō.* Only here and Matt. 13. 15. **lest** = lest at any time. Gr. *mēpote.* **be converted** = turn again. Gr. *epistrephō.* See 3. 19. **28 unto** = to. **salvation.** Gr. *sōtērion.* Elsewhere, Luke 2. 30 (which see); 3. 6. Eph. 6. 17. The more usual *sōtēria* occ. 13. 26, &c. **is sent** = was sent. Gr. *apostellō.* Ap. 174. 1. **Gentiles.** Gr. *ethnos.* **29 words** = things. The texts omit this verse.

V °and had great °reasoning °among themselves.
A 30 And Paul °dwelt °two whole years [7] in his own °hired house, and °received all that came in [17] unto him,
31 °Preaching the [23] kingdom of [15] God, and teaching those things °which concern °the Lord °Jesus Christ, °with all °confidence, °no man forbidding him.

and had = having.
reasoning = disputation. Gr. *suzētēsis*. See 15. 2.
among. Gr. *en*. Ap. 104. viii. 2.
30 dwelt. Gr. *menō*, as in *v.* 16, but texts read *emmenō* (continue) as in 14. 22.
two . . . years. Gr. *dietia*. See 24. 27. This was 61–63 A.D.
hired house. Gr. *misthōma*. Only here. Probably the means for this were provided by the Philippians (Phil. 4. 10–20) and other believers.
received = received freely. Gr. *apodechomai*. See 2. 41.
31 Preaching. Gr. *kērussō*. Ap. 121. 1.
which concern = concerning. Gr. *peri*. Ap. 104. xiii. 1.
the Lord. Ap. 98. VI. i. *β*. 2. A.
Jesus Christ. Ap. 98. XI.
with. Gr. *meta*. Ap. 104. xi. 1.
confidence = boldness. Gr. *parrhēsia*. See 4. 13.
no man, &c. = unhindered. Gr. *akōlutōs*. Only here.

THE INTER-RELATION OF THE SEVEN CHURCH EPISTLES AS SHOWN BY THE STRUCTURE AS A WHOLE.

(*Introversion.*)

A | **ROMANS.** "Doctrine and Instruction." The Gospel of God: never hidden, but "promised afore". God's justification of Jew and Gentile individually—dead and risen with Christ (1–8). Their relation dispensationally (9–11). The subjective foundation of the mystery (see page 1694).

B | **CORINTHIANS.** "Reproof." *Practical* failure to exhibit the teaching of Romans through not seeing their standing as having died and risen with Christ. "Leaven" in practice (1 Cor. 5. 6).

C | **GALATIANS.** "Correction." *Doctrinal* failure as to the teaching of Romans. Beginning with the truth of the new nature ("spirit"), they were "soon removed" (1. 6), and sought to be made perfect in the old nature ("flesh") (3. 3). "Leaven" in doctrine (5. 9).

A | **EPHESIANS.** "Doctrine and Instruction." The mystery of God, always hidden, never before revealed. Individual Jews and Gentiles gathered out and made "one new man" in Christ. Seated in the heavenlies with Christ.

B | **PHILIPPIANS.** "Reproof." *Practical* failure to exhibit the teaching of Ephesians in manifesting "the mind of Christ" as members of the one Body.

C | **COLOSSIANS.** "Correction." *Doctrinal* failure as to the teaching of Ephesians. Wrong doctrines which come from "not holding the Head" (2. 19) and not seeing their completeness and perfection in Christ (2. 8–10).

A | **THESSALONIANS.** "Doctrine and Instruction." Not only "dead and risen with Christ" (as in Romans); not only seated in the heavenlies with Christ (as in Ephesians); but "caught up to meet the Lord in the air, so to be for ever with the Lord". In Rom., justified in Christ; in Eph., sanctified in Christ; in Thess., glorified with Christ. No "reproof". No "correction". All praise and thanksgiving. A typical Church.

Thessalonians comes last, though written first (Ap. 180). There are no "Church" epistles beyond this, because there is no higher truth to be taught. The consummation is reached. This is the highest Form in the School of Grace, where the Holy Spirit is the great Divine Teacher. "All the truth" culminates here—the "all truth" into which He was to guide. The church of God is led from the depths of degradation (in Romans) to the heights of glory (in Thessalonians), caught up to be for ever with the Lord, and left there in eternal blessing "in" and "with" Christ.

The reader is further referred to Ap. 192. B.

ROMANS.

THE STRUCTURE OF THE EPISTLE AS A WHOLE.

(*Alternation and Introversion.*)

A | **C** | 1. 1-6. THE GOSPEL. PROMISED BEFORE BY THE PROPHETS, AND REVEALED BY THEM. NEVER HIDDEN.

D | **F** | 1. 7. SALUTATION.
G | 1. 8-10-. PRAYER CONCERNING PAUL'S VISIT TO THEM.
H | 1.-10-13. PAUL'S DESIRE TO VISIT THEM.
J | 1. 14-16-. HIS MINISTRY OF THE GOSPEL.

} EPISTOLARY.

E | **K** | 1.-16—8. 39. DOCTRINAL.
L | 9. 1—11. 35. DISPENSATIONAL.

B | 11. 36. THE ASCRIPTION. THE WISDOM OF GOD. AS TO THE DISPENSATIONS.

A | *E* | *K* | 12. 1—15. 7. PRACTICAL.
L | 15. 8-12. DISPENSATIONAL.

D | *J* | 15. 13-21. HIS MINISTRY OF THE GOSPEL.
H | 15. 22-29. PAUL'S DESIRE TO VISIT THEM.
G | 15. 30-33. PRAYER CONCERNING PAUL'S VISIT TO THEM.
F | 16. 1-24. SALUTATIONS.

} EPISTOLARY.

C | 16. 25, 26. THE MYSTERY. NEVER BEFORE PROMISED OR REVEALED, BUT KEPT SECRET THROUGH [ALL] THE AGE-TIMES.

B | 16. 27. THE ASCRIPTION. TO "GOD ONLY WISE." AS TO THE MYSTERY.

NOTES ON THE EPISTLE TO THE ROMANS.

1. ROMANS comes first in order of the three great doctrinal epistles (A[1], A[2], A[3]; Ap. 192). And rightly so, for it contains the A B C of the believer's education. Until its lesson is learned, we know and can know nothing. The Holy Spirit has placed it first in Canonical order because it lies at the threshold of all "church" teaching, and if we are wrong here we shall be wrong altogether.

The *design* and *scope* of the Epistle supply the key to a right interpretation, as is shown by the Structure of the Epistle as a whole.

The great subject is the revelation of God's wrath against sin, and of the ground upon which alone the sinner can stand in righteousness before Him. The fundamental text is "The just shall live by faith" (1. 17), and it shows Jew and Gentile alike short of the standard of God's glory (3. 23). All alike sinners, shut up under sin, and needing a Divine righteousness, the only difference being that to the Jew had been committed the oracles (utterances or revelations) of God.

2. The prominent feature of the Epistle is the long doctrinal portion from 1. 16 to 8. 39 (**K**). This shows that doctrine (instruction, 2 Tim. 3. 16) is the important part and dominates the whole. It reveals what God has done with "sins" and with "*sin*"; and how the saved sinner, taken out from the deepest degradation, is justified by faith, and united to Christ in His death, burial, and resurrection-life. It teaches him that though his "old Adam" nature continues with him till the end, in ever-present hostility to God, yet that for those *in Christ* there is no judgment and, consequently, no separation "from the love of God which is in Christ Jesus our Lord".

3. Chapters 9-11 are *dispensational* (**L**), and explain to us God's dealings with "Jew" and "Gentile". The Jew is for the time being set aside "until the fulness of the Gentiles be come in", and during this period "blindness (hardness) in part is happened to Israel" (11. 25).

4. The remainder of the Epistle is taken up with practical counsel as to the believer's life, and closes with the postscript concerning the "mystery" (16. 25, 26); for which see Ap. 193.

5. The Epistle was written from Corinth in the spring of A. D. 58, during the fourth year of Nero (see App. 180 and 192); probably during Paul's sojourn in Greece after the departure from Ephesus (Acts 20. 2, 3). It was sent by Phebe, "a servant of the church . . . at Cenchrea" (16. 1).

THE EPISTLE OF PAUL THE APOSTLE

TO THE

ROMANS.

A C **1** °PAUL, a °servant of °Jesus Christ, °called
to be an °apostle, °separated °unto °the
gospel of °God,
2 (Which He °had °promised afore °by His
°prophets °in the holy °scriptures,)
3 °Concerning His °Son °Jesus Christ our
°Lord, °Which was made °of the °seed of
°David °according to the °flesh,
4 And °declared *to be* the °Son of [1]God
°with °power, [3]according to the °spirit of
°holiness, °by the °resurrection °from the °dead:
5 [2]By Whom we have received °grace and
apostleship, °for °obedience to the °faith
°among all °nations, °for His °name:
6 [5]Among whom are ye also °the called of
[1]Jesus Christ:

D F 7 To °all that be [2]in Rome, °beloved of [1]God,
[1]called *to be* °saints: [5]Grace to you and peace
°from [1]God °our Father, and °the °Lord [1]Jesus
Christ.

G 8 First, I °thank my [1]God °through [1]Jesus
Christ °for you all, that your [5]faith is °spoken
of °throughout the whole °world.
9 For [1]God is my °witness, Whom I °serve
°with my °spirit [2]in °the gospel of His [3]Son,
that °without ceasing I °make mention of you
always °in my °prayers,
10 °Making request,

H °if by any means now at length I °might have

1. 1 Paul. Paul's name heads all his Epistles, except Hebrews.

servant. Gr. *doulos*. Ap. 190. I. 2. Cp. 2 Cor. 4. 5. Gal. 1. 10. Phil. 1. 1. Tit. 1. 1.

Jesus Christ. Ap. 98. XI.

called, &c. Lit. a called apostle; called at his conversion (Acts 26. 17, 18).

apostle. Ap. 189.

separated = set apart. Gr. *aphorizō*. Cp. Acts 13. 2; 19. 9. 2 Cor. 6. 17. Gal. 1. 15; 2. 12. Note the three stages in Paul's "separation" for God's purpose: birth (Gal. 1. 15, 16); conversion (Acts 9. 15); work (Acts 13. 2).

unto. Gr. *eis*. Ap. 104. vi.

the gospel of God: i.e. the "gospel of the grace of God" (Acts 20. 24. Cp. Acts 15. 7), not the "gospel of the kingdom". See Ap. 140. II and IV.

God. Ap. 98. I. i. 1.

2. had. Omit.

promised afore. Gr. *proepangellō*. Only here: *epangellō* occurs fifteen times; always rendered "promise", save 1 Tim. 2. 10; 6. 21 (professing).

by. Gr. *dia*. Ap. 104. v. 1.

prophets. Ap. 189.

in. Gr. *en*. Ap. 104. viii.

scriptures. Gr. *graphē*. Occ. fifty-one times (sing. and pl.). Fourteen times by Paul, but only here with adj. *hagios*, holy.

3. Concerning. Gr. *peri*. Ap. 104. xiii. 1.

Son. Gr. *huios*. Ap. 108. iii.

Jesus . . . Lord. In the Greek these words follow after "dead" in *v.* 4. Fig. *Hyperbaton*. Ap. 6.

Lord. Ap. 98. VI. i. β. 2. A.

Which was made = Who was born (Gal. 4. 4, R.V.).

of. Gr. *ek*. Ap. 104. vii.

seed: i.e. of David's line, but ending specifically in Mary, who was here the "seed" of David. Ap. 99. And Christ was "the Seed" of the woman (Gen. 3. 15. Isa. 7. 14. Matt. 1. 23). **David.** Cp. John 7. 42. 2 Tim. 2. 8. **according to.** Gr. *kata*. Ap. 104. x. 2. **flesh** = human nature. Gr. *sarx*. See 9. 3, 5. **4 declared** = marked out. Gr. *horizō*. See Acts 2. 23. Cp. Ps. 2. 7. **Son of God.** Ap. 98. XV. **with power** = in (Gr. *en*) power (Gr. *dunamis*. Ap. 172. 1); i.e. powerfully. Cp. Phil. 3. 10. **spirit.** Ap. 101. II. 13. **holiness.** Gr. *hagiōsunē*. Only here, 2 Cor. 7. 1. 1 Thess. 3. 13. Nowhere in Gr. literature. It is the Gen. of apposition (Ap. 17. 4). The expression is not to be confounded with *pneuma hagion* (Ap. 101. II. 14). His Divine spiritual nature in resurrection is here set in contrast with His human flesh as seed of David. **by.** Gr. *ek*. Ap. 104. vii. **resurrection.** Gr. *anastasis*. Ap. 178. II. 1. Cp. Acts 26. 23. **from** = of. **dead.** Ap. 139. 2. See Matt. 27. 52, 53. **5 grace and apostleship.** Some see here the fig. *Hendiadys* (Ap. 6), and read "apostolic grace". **grace.** Gr. *charis*. Ap. 184. I. 1. **apostleship.** See Acts 1. 25. **for.** Gr. *eis*. Ap. 104. vi. **obedience to the faith** = faith-obedience. **faith.** Ap. 150. II. 1. **among.** Gr. *en*. Ap. 104. viii. 2. **nations** = Gentiles. Gr. *ethnos*. Occ. in Rom. twenty-nine times; transl. "Gentiles" except here, 4. 17, 18; 10. 19; 16. 26. **for** = on behalf of. Gr. *huper*. Ap. 104. xvii. 1. **name.** See Acts 2. 21. **6 the called.** Cp. 1 Cor. 1. 24. **7 all, &c.**: i.e. all God's beloved ones in Rome. **beloved.** Gr. *agapētos*. Ap. 135. III. **saints.** See Acts 9. 13, and cp. Ps. 16. 3. **from.** Gr. *apo*. Ap. 104. iv. **our Father.** Cp. 8. 15; Gal. 4. 6; and see Ap. 98. III. **the** = our. **Lord.** Ap. 98. VI. i. β. 2. B. This salutation is found in all Paul's Epistles save Hebrews and the three Pastorals, where "mercy" is added. **8 thank.** See Acts 27. 35. **through.** Gr. *dia*. Ap. 104. v. 1. Cp. John 14. 6. **for.** Gr. *huper*, as in *v.* 5, but the texts read *peri*, concerning (Ap. 104. xiii. 1). **spoken of.** Gr. *katangellō*. Ap. 121. 5. **throughout.** Gr. *en*. Ap. 104. viii. **world.** Gr. *kosmos*. Ap. 129. 1. **9 witness.** Gr. *martus*; only here in Romans. Cp. 2 Cor. 1. 23. Phil. 1. 8. 1 Thess. 2. 5, 10. **serve.** Gr. *latreuō*. App. 137. 4; 190. III. 5. **with.** Gr. *en*. Ap. 104. viii. **spirit.** Ap. 101. II. 5. Cp. Phil. 3. 3. **the gospel of His Son.** This expression only here; elsewhere, the Apostle speaks of "the gospel of Christ", 1 Cor. 9. 12, 18. 2 Cor. 2. 12. Phil. 1. 27. Cp. 2 Cor. 4. 4. **without ceasing.** Gr. *adialeiptōs*. Only here and 1 Thess. 1. 3; 2. 13; 5. 17. **make mention.** Cp. Eph. 1. 16. Phil. 1. 3. 1 Thess. 1. 2; 3. 6. 2 Tim. 1. 3. Philem. 4. The same expression appears in a papyrus of second cent., from the Fayoum, in a letter from a Roman soldier to his sister. **in.** Gr. *epi*. Ap. 104. ix. 1. **prayers.** Gr. *proseuchē*. Ap. 134. II. 2. **10 Making request.** Gr. *deomai*. Ap. 134. I. 5. **if by any means.** Gr. *eipōs*. Ap. 118. 2. a. **might . . . journey.** Gr. *euodoumai*. Elsewhere, 1 Cor. 16. 2. 3 John 2.

a prosperous journey °by the °will of [1] God to
°come °unto you.
11 For I °long to °see you, °that I may °im-
part °unto you some °spiritual °gift, °to the
end ye may be °established;
12 °That is, that I may be °comforted together
[4] with you [2] by the °mutual [5] faith both of you
and me.
13 Now I °would °not °have you ignorant,
brethren, that oftentimes I °purposed to [10] come
[10] unto you, (but was °let hitherto,) [11] that I
might have some fruit [5] among you also, even
as [5] among °other Gentiles.

J 14 I am debtor both to °the °Greeks, and to
°the °Barbarians; both to °the °wise, and to
°the °unwise.
15 So, °as much as in me is, I am °ready to
°preach the gospel to °you that are °at Rome
also.
16 °For °I am [13] not °ashamed of the gospel
°of Christ:

K A[1] B a for it is the [4] power of [1] God [1] unto salvation
to every one that °believeth; to the Jew °first,
and also to the °Greek.

b 17 For °therein is °the °righteousness of
[1] God °revealed °from [5] faith

b °to [5] faith:

a as it is °written **"The °just shall °live [4] by
[5] faith."**

C 18 °For °the wrath of [1] God is [17] revealed

by. Gr. *en*. Ap. 104. viii.
will. Gr. *thelēma*. Ap. 102. 2.
come. Gr. *erchomai*. Ap. 106. I. vii.
unto. Gr. *pros*. Ap. 104. xv. 3.
11 long. Gr. *epipotheō*. Elsewhere, 2 Cor. 5. 2; 9. 14. Phil. 1. 8; 2. 26. 1 Thess. 3. 6. 2 Tim. 1. 4. Jas. 4. 5. 1 Pet. 2. 2.
see. Ap. 133. I. 1.
that = in order that. Gr. *hina*.
impart. Gr. *metadidōmi*. Elsewhere, 12. 8. Luke 3. 11. Eph. 4. 28. 1 Thess. 2. 8.
unto = to.
spiritual. Gr. *pneumatikos*. See 1 Cor. 12. 1.
gift. Gr. *charisma*. Ap. 184. I. 2. Cp. 12. 6. 1 Cor. 12. 4, &c.
to the end. Gr. *eis*. Ap. 104. vi.
established. Gr. *stērizō*. Elsewhere, 16. 25. Luke 9. 51; 16. 26; 22. 32. 1 Thess. 3. 2, 13. 2 Thess. 2. 17; 3. 3. Jas. 5. 8. 1 Pet. 5. 10. 2 Pet. 1. 12. Rev. 3. 2.
12 That is, &c. = But this (imparting some spiritual gift) is (or means) our being comforted by our mutual faith.
comforted together. Gr. *sumparakaleō*. Only here.
mutual = in (Gr. *en*) one another.
13 would, &c. First of six occ. Here; 11. 25. 1 Cor. 10. 1; 12. 1. 2 Cor. 1. 8. 1 Thess. 4. 13. See the positive form, 1 Cor. 11. 3. Col. 2. 1.
would. Gr. *thelō*. Ap. 102. 1.
not. Ap. 105. I.
have you, &c. = that you should be ignorant. Gr. *agnoeō*. Cp. Mark 9. 32. Luke 9. 45.
purposed. Gr. *protithēmi*; only here, 3. 25. Eph. 1. 9.
let = hindered. (Anglo-Saxon *lettan*, to delay.) Gr. *kōluō*; occ. twenty-three times (seventeen times "forbid").
other. Gr. *loipos*. Ap. 124. 3. Paul frequently uses the significant term, "the rest", to designate the unsaved. See 11. 7. Eph. 2. 3; 4. 17. 1 Thess. 4. 13; 5. 6. See also Rev. 20. 5.

14 the. Omit. **Greeks.** Gr. *Hellēn*. See John 7. 35 and 12. 20. **Barbarians.** See Acts 28. 2, 4. **wise.** Corresponds generally to "learned". **unwise.** Gr. *anoētos*, unintelligent. Such as the Pharisees despised (John 7. 49). Elsewhere, Luke 24. 25. Gal. 3. 1, 3. 1 Tim. 6. 9. Titus 3. 3. **15 as much as in me is** = as for (Gr. *kata*. Ap. 104. x. 2) me. **ready.** Gr. *prothumos*. Only here. Matt. 26. 41. Mark 14. 38. **preach the gospel.** Gr. *euangelizō*. Ap. 121. 4. **you, &c.** = you also that are at (Gr. *en*) Rome. **16 For.** This is Fig. *Ætiologia*. Ap. 6. **I am, &c.:** i.e. I count it my highest honour and glory to proclaim the gospel. Fig. *Tapeinosis*. Ap. 6. **ashamed.** Gr. *epaischunomai*. Here, 6. 21. Mark 8. 38. Luke 9. 26. 2 Tim. 1. 8, 12, 16. Heb. 2. 11; 11. 16. **of Christ.** All the texts omit.

1. -16—8. 39 (K, p. 1661). DOCTRINAL. (*Division.*)

K | A[1] | 1 -16—5. 11. Sins. The old nature. Its results.
  | A[2] | 5. 12—8. 39. Sin. The old nature. Itself.

1. -16—5. 11 (A[1], above). SINS. THE OLD NATURE. ITS RESULTS. (*Introversion.*)

A[1] | B | 1. -16, 17. The power of God revealing a righteousness from God.
  | C | 1. 18. The wrath of God revealed.
  | *C* | 1. 19—2. 11. The wrath of God revealed.
  | *B* | 2. 12—5. 11. The power of God revealing a righteousness from God.

1. -16, 17 (B, above). THE POWER OF GOD, &c. (*Introversion.*)

B | a | -16. Salvation by faith through God's power in providing righteousness.
  | b | 17-. A divine righteousness revealed by God on faith-principle (*ek pisteōs*), as regards Himself.
  | *b* | -17-. A divine righteousness revealed by God unto faith (*eis pistin*), as regards ourselves, i.e. exercised in us.
  | *a* | -17. Salvation by faith through God's power in imputing righteousness.

believeth. Ap. 150. I. 1. i. **first.** In point of national precedence and privilege. Cp. 2. 9, 10; 3. 1, 2. **Greek.** See *v.* 14. Representing all non-Jews. **17 therein** = in (Gr. *en*) it. **the.** Omit. **righteousness of God** = God's righteousness. **righteousness.** Gr. *dikaiosunē*. Ap. 191. 3. **revealed.** Gr. *apokaluptō*. Ap. 106. I. ix. **from.** Gr. *ek*. Ap. 104. vii. **to.** Gr. *eis*. Ap. 104. vi. God's righteousness is revealed on the ground of faith (faith-principle) (*ek pisteōs*), as the absolute condition of salvation, and is operative only for those who believe (*eis pistin*). For the use of *ek pisteōs*, cp. 3. 26, 30; 4. 16; 5. 1; 10. 6; 14. 23. Gal. 2. 16. **written.** See Matt. 2. 5 (first occ.). **just.** Gr. *dikaios*. Ap. 191. 1. **live.** Quoted from Hab. 2. 4. Cp. Gal. 3. 11. Heb. 10. 38. **18 For.** In the gospel not only is God's salvation revealed, but God's wrath also, and both are the revelation of God's righteousness. **the wrath of God.** This expression occ. only here, John 3. 36. Eph. 5. 6. Col. 3. 6. Cp. Rev. 19. 15. Referred to many times in N.T., e.g. 2. 5; 5. 9; 9. 22. Matt. 3. 7. Eph. 2. 3; 5. 6. Rev. 6. 16, 17.

[7] from °heaven °against all °ungodliness and
°unrighteousness of °men, who °hold °the
truth [2] in °unrighteousness;

C D F 19 Because that which may be °known of
[1] God is °manifest [2] in them; for [1] God °hath
°shewed *it* [11] unto them.
20 For the °invisible things of Him [7] from the
creation of the [8] world are °clearly seen, being
understood by the °things that are made, *even*
His °eternal [4] power and °Godhead; °so that
they are °without excuse:

G c 21 Because that when they °knew [1] God, they
°glorified *Him* [13] not as [1] God, neither were
[8] thankful;
d °but °became vain [2] in their °imaginations, and
their °foolish heart was darkened.

H e 22 °Professing themselves to be wise, they
°became fools,
23 And °changed the °glory of the °uncor-
ruptible [1] God °into an °image made like to
°corruptible [18] man, and to °birds, and °four-
footed beasts, and °creeping things.

f 24 Wherefore [1] God °also °gave them up [17] to
°uncleanness °through the °lusts of their own
hearts, °to dishonour their own bodies °between
themselves:

H e 25 °Who °changed °the [18] truth of [1] God [23] into
°a lie, and °worshipped and °served the °crea-
ture °more than the Creator, Who is °blessed
°for ever. °Amen.

f 26 °For this cause [1] God [24] gave them up [1] unto
°vile °affections: for even their women did
[25] change the °natural °use °into that which is
°against nature:

heaven. Sing. No article. See Matt. 6. 10.
against. Gr. *epi.* Ap. 104. ix. 3.
ungodliness. Gr. *asebeia.* Ap. 128. IV.
unrighteousness. Gr. *adikia.* Ap. 128. VII. 1.
men. Gr. *anthrōpos.* Ap. 123. 1.
hold = hold down, suppress. Cp. 2 Thess. 2. 6.
the truth. Gr. *alētheia,* p. 1511. Cp. Ap. 175. 1 and 2.

1. 19—2. 11 (*C*, p. 1663). THE WRATH OF GOD DESCRIBED AND SET FORTH. (*Alternation.*)

C | D | 1. 19—2. 1. Man's ungodliness deserves it.
  E | 2. 2. God's judgment just.
 D | 2. 3-5. Man's impenitence deserves it.
  E | 2. 6-11. God's judgment just.

1. 19—2. 1 (D, above). MAN'S UNGODLINESS PROVED AND SET FORTH. (*Introversion and Alternation.*)

D | F | 1. 19, 20. God's power known. Ungodliness, therefore, without excuse.
 G | c | 1. 21–. The glory of God rejected.
  d | 1. –21. Consequent mental corruption.
   H | e | 1. 22, 23. God's glory degraded.
    f | 1. 24. Consequent degradation of bodily acts.
   H | *e* | 1. 25. God's truth degraded.
    f | 1. 26, 27. Consequent degradation of bodily passions.
 G | *c* | 1. 28–. The knowledge of God rejected.
  d | 1. –28-31. Consequent mental corruption.
F | 1. 32—2. 1. God's judgment known. Ungodliness, therefore, inexcusable.

19 known. See Acts 1. 19.
manifest. Gr. *phaneros.* Ap. 106. I. viii.
hath. Omit.
shewed = manifested. Gr. *phaneroō.* Ap. 106. I. v.
20 invisible. Gr. *aoratos.* Here, Col. 1. 15, 16. 1 Tim. 1. 17. Heb. 11. 27.
clearly seen. Gr. *kathoraō.* Only here.
things that are made. Gr. *poiēma.* Only here and Eph. 2. 10.

eternal. Gr. *aidios.* Ap. 151. II. C. i. **Godhead.** Ap. 98. I. ii. 2. **so that, &c.** = to the end (Gr. *eis*) of their being. Cp. *v.* 11. **without excuse.** Gr. *anapologētos.* Only here and 2. 1. **21 knew.** Gr. *ginōskō.* Ap. 132. I. ii. **glorified.** See p. 1511. **but.** Emphatic. **became vain.** Gr. *mataioomai.* Only here. Cp. Acts 14. 15. **imaginations** = reasonings. See Matt. 15. 19. **foolish.** Gr. *asunetos,* as *v.* 31. **22 Professing, &c.** = saying that they were. Gr. *phaskō.* See Acts 24. 9. **became fools.** Lit. were fooled (i. e. by their perverted mind). Gr. *mōrainō.* Here, Matt. 5. 13. Luke 14. 34. 1 Cor. 1. 20. **23 changed.** Gr. *allassō*: see Acts 6. 14. **glory.** Gr. *doxa.* See p. 1511. **uncorruptible.** Gr. *aphthartos.* Here; 1 Cor. 9. 25; 15. 52. 1 Tim. 1. 17. 1 Pet. 1. 4, 23; 3. 4. **into.** Gr. *en.* Ap. 104. viii. **image, &c.** = likeness (Gr. *homoiōma.* Here, 5. 14; 6. 5; 8. 3. Phil. 2. 7. Rev. 9. 7) of an image of. **image.** Gr. *eikōn.* Occ. twenty-three times; always so rendered. This is the Fig. *Pleonasm.* Ap. 6. **corruptible.** Gr. *phthartos.* Here, 1 Cor. 9. 25; 15. 53, 54. 1 Pet. 1. 18, 23. **birds, &c.** In Egypt they worshipped the hawk and the ibis. **fourfooted beasts.** Gr. *tetrapous.* See Acts 10. 12. As the bull and the cow, held by the Egyptians sacred to *Apis* and *Hathor* (Venus); the dog to *Anubis*; &c. **creeping things.** Gr. *herpeton.* See Acts 10. 12. The asp, sacred to the gods of Egypt and found in every heathen pantheon; indeed, the worship of the serpent plays a prominent part in all forms of Paganism. The crocodile, tortoise, frog, and the well-known Scarabaeus beetle, sacred to the sun and to Pthah, and used as an emblem of the world (Wilkinson). **24 also.** Omit. **gave them up.** See John 19. 30. **uncleanness.** Gr. *akatharsia.* Occ. ten times, always so rendered. The cognate word *akathartēs* in Rev. 17. 4 only. Ceasing to know God (*v.* 21) results in idolatry, and idolatry ends in "filthiness of the flesh and spirit" (2 Cor. 7. 1). **through.** Ap. 104. viii. **lusts.** See John 8. 44. **to dishonour, &c.** = that their bodies should be dishonoured. Gr. *atimazō.* See Acts 5. 41. **between.** Gr. *en.* Ap. 104. viii. 2. **25 Who** = Since they. **changed.** Gr. *metallassō*; only here and *v.* 26. A stronger word than in *v.* 23. **the truth of God into a lie** = the truth of God for the lie. Man transferred his worship from God (the Truth) to the devil. Cp. John 8. 44. Eph. 4. 25. 2 Thess. 2. 9-11. **a lie** = the lie. Gr. *to pseudos.* Cp. 2 Thess. 2. 11. The lie is that Satan is man's benefactor and is to be worshipped. **worshipped.** Gr. *sebazomai.* Ap. 137. 3. Only here. **served.** Gr. *latreuō.* App. 137. 4 and 190. III. 5. **creature** = the things created; not only sun, moon, stars, men, the animate creation, but Satan himself, the arch-enemy, who by means of his "lie" (Gen. 3. 4, 5) transferred the worship of man from the Creator to himself, the creature. **more than.** Gr. *para.* Ap. 104. xii. 3. **blessed.** Gr. *eulogētos.* Cp. 9. 5. Mark 14. 61. (The) Blessed One. Not a statement of doctrine, but a well-known Hebraism of praise to God as Creator (Ap. 4. 1). **for ever.** Ap. 151. II. A. ii. 7. a. **Amen.** See Matt. 5. 18. John 1. 51, and p. 1511. **26 For this cause** = Because of (Ap. 104. v. 2) this. **vile affections** = passions of infamy (Gr. *atimia.* Here, 9. 21. 1 Cor. 11. 14; 15. 43. 2 Cor. 6. 8; 11. 21. 2 Tim. 2. 20). **affections** = passions, or lusts. Gr. *pathos.* Only here; Col. 3. 5. 1 Thess. 4. 5. **natural.** Gr. *phusikos.* Only here, *v.* 27. 2 Pet. 2. 12. **use.** Gr. *chrēsis.* Only here and *v.* 27. **into.** Ap. 104. vi. **against.** Gr. *para.* Ap. 104. xii. 3.

27 And likewise °also the °men, °leaving the
[26]natural [26]use of the woman,°burned [2]in their
°lust one °toward another; °men [4]with °men
°working °that which is unseemly, and °re-
ceiving [2]in themselves °that •recompence of
their °error which was meet.

G c 28 °And even as they °did [13]not like to retain
[1]God [2]in *their* °knowledge,

d [1]God [24]gave them over [17]to a °reprobate mind,
to do those things which are °not °convenient:
29 Being °filled with all [18]unrighteousness,
°fornication, °wickedness, covetousness, °mali-
ciousness; full of °envy, °murder, °debate,
°deceit, °malignity; °whisperers,
30 °Backbiters, °haters of God, °despiteful,
°proud, °boasters, °inventors of °evil things,
°disobedient to parents,
31 °Without understanding, °covenantbreak-
ers, °without natural affection, °implacable,
°unmerciful:

F 32 Who °knowing the °judgment of [1]God,
that they which °commit such things are
worthy of death, [13]not only do the same, but
°have pleasure in them that °do them.

2 °Therefore thou art °inexcusable, O °man,
°whosoever thou art that °judgest: for
°wherein thou °judgest °another, thou °con-
demnest thyself; for thou that °judgest °doest
the same things.

E 2 But [4]we °are sure that the °judgment of
°God is °according to °truth °against them
which °commit such things.

D 3 And °thinkest thou this, O [1]man, that
[1]judgest them which [1]do such things, and
doest the same, that thou shalt escape the
[2]judgment of [2]God?
4 Or despisest thou the °riches of His °good-
ness and °forbearance and longsuffering; °not
knowing that the °goodness of [2]God leadeth
thee °to °repentance?
5 But °after thy °hardness and °impenitent
heart °treasurest up °unto thyself wrath
°against °the day of wrath and °revelation of
the °righteous judgment of [2]God;

27 also the men = the men also. **men.** Ap. 123. 5. **leaving** = having forsaken. Ap. 174. 12. **burned** = were inflamed. Gr. *ekkaiomai.* Only here. **lust.** Gr. *orexis.* Only here. **toward.** Ap. 104. vi. **working.** Gr. *katergazomai.* Occ. eleven times in Romans, seven in 2 Corinthians. See also Jas. 1. 3, 20. 1 Pet. 4. 3. **that which is unseemly.** Gr. *aschēmosunē.* Only here and Rev. 16. 15. Cp. Gen. 19. 7. **receiving** = receiving back, or in full. Gr. *apolambanō.* **that** = the. **recompence.** Gr. *antimisthia,* retribution; only here and 2 Cor. 6. 13. **error.** Gr. *planē,* lit. a wandering = wrong action, wickedness. Here, Matt. 27. 64. Eph. 4. 14. 1 Thess. 2. 3. 2 Thess. 2. 11. Jas. 5. 20. 2 Pet. 2. 18; 3. 17. 1 John 4. 6. Jude 11.

28 And even . . . mind. There is a play upon two words here, not easily expressed in Eng. "As they rejected God, God rejected them." **did . . . like.** Gr. *dokimazō,* to accept after testing, to approve. Cp. 2. 18; 12. 2; 14. 22. 1 Cor. 9. 27. **knowledge.** Ap. 132. II. ii. **reprobate.** Gr. *adokimos.* The negative of *dokimos.* Cp. *dokimazō,* above. Here, 1 Cor. 9. 27. 2 Cor. 13. 5, 6, 7. 2 Tim. 3. 8. Tit. 1. 16. Heb. 6. 8. **not.** Gr. *mē.* Ap. 105. II. **convenient.** Gr. *kathēkon.* See Acts 22. 22. **29 filled.** Gr. *plēroō.* Ap. 125. 7. **fornication.** The texts omit. **wickedness** Gr. *ponēria.* Ap. 128. II. 1. **maliciousness.** Gr. *kakia.* Ap. 128. II. 2. **envy** = jealousy. Gr. *phthonos.* Cp. Matt. 27. 18. **murder.** Gr. *phonos.* Note the *Paronomasia, phthonos, phonos.* Ap. 6. See Acts 9. 1. **debate** = strife. **deceit.** Gr. *dolos.* See Acts 13. 10. **malignity.** Gr. *kakoētheia,* lit. disposition for mischief. Only here. **whisperers** = calumniators. Gr. *psithuristēs.* Only here. **30 Backbiters** = evil speakers (not necessarily behind the back). Gr. *katalalos.* Only here. Cp. 2 Cor. 12. 20. 1 Pet. 2. 1. **haters of God** = hateful to God. Gr. *theostugēs.* Only here. **despiteful** = insolent. Gr. *hubristēs.* Only here and 1 Tim. 1. 13. **proud.** Gr. *huperēphanos.* Here, Luke 1. 51. 2 Tim. 3. 2. Jas. 4. 6. 1 Pet. 5. 5. **boasters.** Gr. *alazōn.* Only here and 2 Tim. 3. 2. **inventors.** Gr. *epheuretēs.* Only here. **evil.** Gr. *kakos.* Ap. 128. III. 2. **disobedient.** See Acts 26. 19.

31 Without understanding. Gr. *asunetos.* See *v.* 21. Note the *Paronomasia* with next word. Ap. 6. **covenantbreakers.** Gr. *asunthetos.* Only here. **without natural affection.** Gr. *astorgos.* Only here and 2 Tim. 3. 3. **implacable.** The texts omit. **unmerciful** = pitiless. Gr. *aneleēmōn.* Only here. **32 knowing.** Gr. *epiginōskō.* Ap. 132. I. iii. **judgment** = righteous sentence. Gr. *dikaiōma.* App. 177. 3; 191. 4. **commit** = practise. **have pleasure in** = consent also to. See Acts 8. 1. **do.** Same as "commit", above. This list of heathen iniquities is the Fig. *Synathroesmos.* Ap. 6.

2. 1 Therefore. That is, on account of the decrees of God, 1. 32. **inexcusable.** Same word as 1. 20. **man.** Gr. *anthrōpos.* Ap. 123. 1. **whosoever,** &c. Lit. every one judging. **judgest.** Gr. *krinō.* Ap. 122. 1. **wherein** = in (Gr. *en.* Ap. 104. viii) which. **another** = the other. Gr. *heteros.* Ap. 124. 2. **condemnest.** Gr. *katakrinō.* Ap. 122. 7. The three occ. of *krinō* and one of *katakrinō* give the fig. *Paregmenon* (Ap. 6). **doest** = practisest. Same word as "commit", 1. 32. **2 are sure** = know. Gr. *oida.* Ap. 132. I. i. **judgment.** Gr. *krima.* Ap. 177. 6. **God.** Ap. 98. I. i. 1. **according to.** Gr. *kata.* Ap. 104. x. 2. **truth.** See 1. 18. **against.** Gr. *epi.* Ap. 104. ix. 3. **commit.** Same as "do", *v.* 1. **3 thinkest** = reckonest. Gr. *logizomai.* First of nineteen occ. in Romans of this important word; here, *v.* 26; 3. 28; 4. 3, 4, 5, 6, 8, 9, 10, 11, 22, 23, 24; 6. 11; 8. 18, 36; 9. 8; 14. 14. First occ. Mark 11. 31 (reasoned). **4 riches.** Cp. 9. 23; 11. 33. Eph. 1. 7, 18; 2. 7; 3. 8, 16. Phil. 4. 19. Col. 1. 27; 2. 2. **goodness.** Gr. *chrēstotēs.* Ap. 184. III. (*a*). **forbearance.** Gr. *anochē.* Only here and 3. 25. **not knowing.** Gr. *agnoeō.* See 1. 13. **goodness.** Gr. *chrēstos.* Ap. 184. III. Neut. adj. used as noun. **to.** Gr. *eis.* Ap. 104. vi. **repentance.** Gr. *metanoia.* Ap. 111. II. **5 after.** Gr. *kata.* Ap. 104. x. 2. **hardness.** Gr. *sklērotēs.* Only here. **impenitent.** Gr. *ametanoētos.* Only here. Cp. Ap. 111. **treasurest up.** Gr. *thēsaurizō.* Here, Matt. 6. 19, 20. Luke 12. 21. 1 Cor. 16. 2. 2 Cor. 12. 14. Jas. 5. 3. 2 Pet. 3. 7. **unto** = to. **against.** Gr. *en.* Ap. 104. viii. **the day of wrath.** Cp. Rev. 6. 17; 19. 15. Isa. 61. 2; 63. 4. **revelation.** Gr. *apokalupsis.* Ap. 106. II. 1. **righteous judgment.** Gr. *dikaiokrisia.* Only here. Cp. App. 191. 1 and 177. 7.

E 6 **Who will °render to °every man [2]according to his deeds:**
7 To them who °by °patient continuance °in well doing seek for °glory and honour and °immortality, °eternal °life:
8 But [5]unto them that are °contentious, and °do not obey the truth, but °obey °unrighteousness, indignation and [5]wrath,
9 °Tribulation and °anguish, °upon every °soul of [1]man that °doeth °evil, of the °Jew first, and °also of the °Gentile;
10 But [7]glory, honour, and peace, to every man that °worketh good, to the [9]Jew first, and [9]also to the [9]Gentile:
11 For there is °no °respect of persons °with [2]God.

B J1 12 For as many as °have °sinned °without law shall °also perish °without law: and as many as °have °sinned °in °the law shall be [1]judged °by °the law;

K1 13 (For °not the °hearers of °the law *are* °just °before [2]God, but the doers of °the law shall be °justified.
14 For when °the Gentiles, which have °not °the law, do °by nature the things °contained in the law, these, °having °not the law, are a law [5]unto themselves:
15 Which °shew the work of the law °written [12]in their hearts, their °conscience °also °bearing witness, and *their* °thoughts the mean while accusing or else °excusing one another;)
16 [12]In the [5]day when [2]God °shall [1]judge the °secrets of [1]men [12]by °Jesus Christ [2]according to my gospel.

J2 17 °Behold, thou art called a Jew, and °restest in °the law, and °makest thy boast °of [2]God.
18 And °knowest *His* °will, and °approvest the things that are °more excellent, °being instructed °out of the law;
19 And °art confident that thou thyself art a guide of the blind, a °light of them which are [12]in darkness,
20 An °instructor of the foolish, a °teacher of °babes, which hast the °form of °knowledge and of the truth [12]in the law.
21 Thou °therefore which teachest [1]another, teachest thou [13]not thyself? thou that °preachest °a man should [14]not steal, dost thou steal?
22 Thou that sayest °a man should [14]not commit adultery, dost thou commit adultery? thou that °abhorrest idols, dost thou °commit sacrilege?

6 render = recompense, as in 12. 17.
every man = each one. The two following *vv.*, giving details, form the Fig. *Merismos.* Ap. 6.
7 by = according to, as in *v.* 2.
patient continuance = patience.
in well doing. Lit. of a good work.
glory. See 1. 23.
immortality = incorruption. Gr. *aphtharsia.* Here, 1 Cor. 15. 42, 50, 53, 54. Eph. 6. 24. 2 Tim. 1. 10. Tit. 2. 7.
eternal. Ap. 151. II. B. i.
life. Gr. *zōē.* Ap. 170. 1.
8 contentious = of (Gr. *ek.* Ap. 104. vii) contention. Gr. *eritheia.* Here, 2 Cor. 12. 20. Gal. 5. 20. Phil. 1. 16; 2. 3. Jas. 3. 14, 16.
do not obey. Gr. *apeitheō.* See Acts 14. 2.
obey. Gr. *peithō.* Ap 150. I. 2.
unrighteousness. Gr. *adikia.* Ap. 128. VII. 1.
9 Tribulation. Gr. *thlipsis.* See Acts 7. 10.
anguish. Gr. *stenochōria.* Here, 8. 35. 2 Cor. 6. 4; 12. 10.
upon. Gr. *epi.* Ap. 104. ix. 3.
soul. Gr. *psuchē.* Ap. 110. II.
doeth = worketh. Gr. *katergazomai.* See 1. 27.
evil = the evil. Gr. *kakos.* Ap. 128. III. 2.
Jew . . . Gentile. Cp. 1. 16.
also. Omit. **Gentile** = Greek.
10 worketh. Gr. *ergazomai*, as 4. 1.
11 no. Ap. 105. I.
respect of persons = partiality. Gr. *prosōpolēpsia.* Only here, Eph. 6. 9. Col. 3. 25. Jas. 2. 1.
with. Gr. *para.* Ap. 104. xii. 2.

2. 12—5. 11 (*B*, p. 1663). THE POWER AND RIGHTEOUSNESS OF GOD REVEALED.
(*Repeated Alternation.*)

B | J1 | 2. 12. The case of Jew and Gentile.
  K1 | 2. 13–16. General reasons.
 J2 | 2 17–27. The case of the Jew.
  K2 | 2. 28, 29. General reflection.
 J3 | 3. 1–26. The case of the Jew.
  K3 | 3. 27–31. General conclusion.
 J4 | 4. 1–22. The case of Abraham.
  K4 | 4. 23—5. 11. General application.

12 have. Omit. The standpoint is the judgment time.
sinned. Gr. *hamartanō.* Ap. 128. I. i.
without law. Gr. *anomōs.* Only here.
also perish = perish also. The Mosaic Law will not be cited against non-Jews.
in. Gr. *en.* Ap. 104. viii.
the. Omit. **by.** Ap. 104. v. 1.
13 not. Gr. *ou.* Ap. 105. I.
hearers. Gr. *akroatēs.* Only here and Jas. 1. 22, 23, 25. Cp. Acts 25. 23.
the. The texts omit.
just. See 1. 17.
before. Gr. *para.* Ap. 104. xii. 2.
justified. Gr. *dikaioō.* Ap. 191. 2.

14 the. Omit. **not.** Gr. *mē.* Ap. 105. II. **by nature.** See 1. 26. **contained in** = of. **having,** &c. = not having law. **15 shew** = shew forth. Gr. *endeiknumi.* **written.** Gr. *graptos.* Only here. **conscience.** See Acts 23. 1. **also.** Omit. **bearing witness** = bearing witness therewith. Gr. *summartureō.* Here, 8. 16; 9. 1. Rev. 22. 18. **thoughts** = reckonings. Gr. *logismos.* Only here and 2 Cor. 10. 5. **excusing.** Gr. *apologeomai.* See Acts 19. 33. **16 shall** = will. **secrets.** Gr. *kruptos.* **Jesus Christ.** Ap. 98. XI. **17 Behold.** Gr. *ide.* Ap. 133. I. 3. The texts read "But if". **restest in** = restest upon. Gr. *epanapauomai.* Only here and Luke 10. 6. **the.** The texts omit. **makest,** &c. = gloriest, as 5. 3, and 1 Cor. 1. 29, 31. Gr. *kauchaomai.* Only in Paul's Epistles (thirty-six times) and in Jas. 1. 9; 4. 16. **of.** Gr. *en.* Ap. 104. viii. **18 knowest.** Gr. *ginōskō.* Ap. 132. I. ii. **will.** Gr. *thelēma.* Ap. 102. 2. **approvest.** Gr. *dokimazō.* See 1. 28. **more excellent.** Gr. *diapherō.* See Acts 27. 27. **being instructed.** Gr. *katēcheō.* See Acts 18. 25. **out of.** Gr. *ek.* Ap. 104. vii. **19 art confident.** Gr. *peithō.* Ap. 150. I. 2. **light.** Gr. *phōs.* Ap. 130. 1. **20 instructor** = preceptor. Gr. *paideutēs.* Only here and Heb. 12. 9. **teacher.** Ap. 98. XIV. v. 4. **babes.** Gr. *nēpios.* Ap. 108. vii. **form** = external form. Gr. *morphōsis.* Only here and 2 Tim. 3. 5. **knowledge.** Gr. *gnōsis.* Ap. 132. II. i. **21 therefore.** Ironical use of Gr. *oun.* **another.** As *v.* 1, but without article. **preachest.** Gr. *kērussō.* Ap. 121. 1. **a man,** &c. Lit. not to steal. **22 a man,** &c. Lit. not to commit. **abhorrest.** Gr. *bdelussomai.* Only here and Rev. 21. 8. **commit sacrilege** = rob temples. Gr. *hierosuleō.* Only here. Cp. Acts 19. 37.

23 Thou that [17]makest thy boast °of [12]the
law, °through °breaking the law °dishonourest
thou [2]God?
24 "**For the name of [2]God is °blasphemed**
°among the [14]Gentiles [23]through you," as °it is
written.
25 For circumcision verily profiteth, °if thou
°keep [12]the law: but °if thou be a °breaker of
[12]the law, thy circumcision °is made uncircumcision.
26 Therefore [25]if the uncircumcision keep
the °righteousness of the law, °shall °not his
uncircumcision be °counted °for circumcision?
27 And shall °not uncircumcision which is
°by [14]nature, if it fulfil the law, [1]judge thee,
who [12]by °the letter and circumcision °dost
transgress [12]the law?
K[2] 28 For he is [13]not a Jew, which is one °out-
wardly; °neither *is that* circumcision, °which is
outward [12]in the flesh:
29 But he *is* a Jew, which is one °inwardly;
and circumcision *is that* of the heart, [12]in °the
°spirit, *and* [13]not in °the [27]letter; whose praise
is [13]not °of [1]men, but °of [2]God.

J[3] 3 °What advantage then hath the Jew? or
what °profit *is there* of circumcision?
2 Much °every way: chiefly, because that
°unto them were °committed the °oracles of
°God.
3 For what °if °some °did not believe? °shall
their °unbelief °make the °faith of [2]God °with-
out effect?
4 °God forbid: yea, let [2]God be °true, but
every °man a °liar; as it is °written, "**That
Thou mightest be °justified °in Thy °sayings,
and mightest overcome °when Thou art
°judged.**"
5 But [3]if our °unrighteousness °commend the
°righteousness of [2]God, °what shall we say?
°*Is* [2]God unrighteous Who °taketh °vengeance?
(I speak °as a [4]man)
6 [4]God forbid: for then how shall [2]God [4]judge
the °world?
7 For [3]if the truth of [2]God °hath more
abounded °through my °lie °unto His °glory;
why yet am I also [4]judged as a °sinner?
8 And °not *rather*, (as we be °slanderously
reported, and as [3]some °affirm that we say,)
"Let us do °evil, °that °good may °come?"
whose °damnation is °just.
9 What then? °are we better *than they*? °No,
in no wise: for we have °before proved both

23 of. Gr. *en.* Ap. 104. viii.
through. Gr. *dia.* Ap. 104. v. 1.
breaking, &c. = the transgression (Gr. *parabasis.* Cp. Ap. 128. VI. 1, 3) of the law.
dishonourest. Gr. *atimazō.* See 1. 24.
24 blasphemed. Cp. Acts 13. 45.
among. Gr. *en.* Ap. 104. viii. 2.
it is written. Cp. Ezek. 36. 20, 23.
25 if. Gr. *ean.* Ap. 118. 1. b.
keep = practise, as in *v.* 1.
breaker. Gr. *parabatēs.* Ap. 128. VI. 3.
is made = has become.
26 righteousness = righteous requirements. Gr. *dikaiōma.* Ap. 191. 4
shall = will. **not.** Ap. 105. I (*a*).
counted. Same as "think", *v.* 3. I. e. in the day of *v.* 5.
for. Gr. *eis.* Ap. 104. vi.
27 not. Supplied from *v.* 26. **by.** Ap. 104. vii.
the letter = that which is written. Gr. *gramma,* i. e. *ta dikaiōmata* of *v.* 26.
dost transgress = art a transgressor. Gr. *parabatēs,* as *v.* 25.
28 outwardly . . . which is outward = in (Gr. *en*) outward (Gr. *phaneros.* Ap. 106. I. viii) guise.
neither. Gr. *oude.*
29 inwardly = in (Gr. *en*) secret. **the.** Omit.
spirit. Ap. 101. II. 7. **of.** Gr. *ek.* Ap. 104. vii.

3. 1 What, &c. = What then is the advantage of the Jew, or what is the, &c.
profit. Gr. *ōpheleia.* Only here and Jude 16.
2 every way = according to (Gr. *kata.* Ap. 104. x. 2) every way.
unto . . . committed = they were entrusted with. Gr. *pisteuō.* Ap. 150. I. 1. iv. Cp. 1 Thess. 2. 4.
oracles. Gr. *logion.* See Acts 7. 38.
God. Ap. 98. I. i. 1.
3 if. Gr. *ei.* Ap. 118. 2. a.
some. Gr. *tines.* Ap. 124. 4.
did not believe. Gr. *apisteō.* See Acts 28. 24.
shall. The question is introduced by *mē* (Ap. 105. II).
unbelief. Gr. *apistia.* Occ. twelve times; first Matt. 13. 58. In Rom., here, 4. 20; 11. 20, 23.
make . . . without effect = nullify. Gr. *katargeō.* See Luke 13. 7.
faith = faithfulness. Gr. *pistis.* Ap. 150. II. 1.
4 God forbid. Lit. Let it not be. Gr. *mē* (Ap. 105. II) *genoito.* This strong asseveration occ. fifteen times. Here, *vv.* 6, 31; 6. 2, 15; 7. 7, 13; 9. 14; 11. 1, 11. Luke 20. 16. 1 Cor. 6. 15. Gal. 2. 17; 3. 21; 6. 14.
true. Gr. *alēthēs.* Ap. 175. 1.
man. Gr. *anthrōpos.* Ap. 123. 1.
liar. Gr. *pseustēs.* In Paul's Epp. only here, 1 Tim. 1. 10. Tit. 1. 12.
written. Quoted from Ps. 51. 4 (Sept.).
justified. Gr. *dikaioō.* Ap. 191. 2. See 2. 13.
in. Gr. *en.* Ap. 104. viii.
sayings. Gr. *logos.* Ap. 121. 10.
when Thou art judged. Lit. in (Gr. *en*) Thy being judged (Gr. *krinō.* Ap. 122. 1).

5 unrighteousness. Gr. *adikia.* Ap. 128. VII. 1. **commend** = establish, set forth. Gr. *sunistēmi.* **righteousness.** Gr. *dikaiosunē.* Ap. 191. 3. Cp. 1. 17. **what shall we say?** Gr. *ti eroumen.* This expression occ. seven times; here, 4. 1; 6. 1; 7. 7; 8. 31; 9. 14, 30. ***Is,* &c.** See "shall", *v.* 3. **taketh** = inflicts. Gr. *epipherō.* Occ. Jude 9. **vengeance** = the wrath. See 1. 18. **as.** Gr. *kata.* Ap. 104. x. 2. Cp. 6. 19. This is the Fig. *Hypotimēsis.* Ap. 6. **6 world.** Ap. 129. 1. Cp. Gen. 18. 25. **7 hath more abounded** = abounded, as 5. 15; 15. 13. Gr. *perisseuō.* Lit. overflow. See 2 Cor. 8. 2, &c. **through.** Gr. *en.* Ap. 104. viii. **lie.** Gr. *pseusma.* Only here. **unto.** Gr. *eis.* Ap. 104. vi. **glory.** Gr. *doxa.* See 1. 23 and John 1. 14. **sinner.** Gr. *hamartōlos.* Cp. Ap. 128. I. i. ii. **8 not . . . come?** = (why) not (say), as we be slanderously reported, and as some affirm that we say, Let us do, &c. Fig. *Epitrechon* (Ap. 6). **not.** Gr. *mē.* Ap. 105. II. **slanderously reported.** Gr. *blasphēmeō.* Cp. 2. 24. Acts 13. 45. **affirm.** Gr. *phēmi.* Only here in Rom. Occ. fifty-eight times, always "say", except here. **evil.** Lit. the evil things. Gr. *kakos.* Ap. 128. III. 2. **that** = in order that. Gr. *hina.* **good.** Lit. the good things. **come.** Gr. *erchomai.* Ap. 106. I. 7. **damnation.** Gr. *krima.* Ap. 177. 6. **just.** Gr. *endikos.* Ap. 191. 1. **9 are . . . *they?*** = have we any advantage? or, have we any excuse to put forward? Gr. *proechō.* Only here; may be mid. or pass. voice. **No, in no wise** = Not (Gr. *ou.* Ap. 105. I) at all (Gr. *pantōs*). **before proved** = before convicted. Gr. *proaitiaomai.* Only here. Cp. 1. 21.

Jews and °Gentiles, °that they are °all °under
°sin;
10 As it is [4]written, "°**There is °none °right-**
eous, °no, [9]not one:
11 **There is °none that °understandeth, there**
is °none that °seeketh after [2]God.
12 °**They are all °gone out of the way, they**
are together °become unprofitable; there is
[11]**none that doeth °good, °no, not one.**
13 °**Their °throat *is* an °open °sepulchre;**
with °their °tongues they °have used deceit;
°**the °poison of °asps *is* [9]under their °lips:**
14 °**Whose mouth *is* °full of °cursing and**
°**bitterness:**
15 °**Their feet *are* °swift to °shed blood:**
16 °**Destruction and °misery *are* [4]in their**
ways:
17 **And the way of peace °have they °not**
°**known:**
18 **There is [9]no fear of [2]God °before their eyes."**
19 Now we °know that what things soever
the °law saith, it °saith to them who are °under
the °law: [18]that °every mouth may be °stopped,
and all the [6]world may become °guilty before
[2]God.
20 Therefore °by °the deeds of °the law there
shall [9]no flesh be [4]justified in His sight: for
°by °the law [5]*is* the °knowledge of [9]sin.
21 But °now the [5]righteousness of [2]God
°without the law °is manifested, being °wit-
nessed °by °the law and the °prophets;
22 °Even the [5]righteousness of [2]God *which*
is [-20]by [3]faith of °Jesus Christ [7]unto all °and
upon all them that °believe: for there is °no
°difference:
23 For all °have °sinned, and °come short of
the [7]glory of [2]God;
24 Being [4]justified °freely °by His °grace
°through the °redemption that is [4]in °Christ Jesus:
25 Whom [2]God °hath °set forth °to be a °pro-
pitiation [24]through [3]faith [4]in His blood, °to

Gentiles = Greeks. See 2. 9. **that they are** = to be. **all.** Emph. **under.** Gr. *hupo.* Ap. 104. xviii. 2. **sin.** Gr. *hamartia.* Ap. 128. I. ii. 1. Sin is the root, and "sins" are the fruit.

10 The quotation (10–18) is from several pass. of O.T. All refer to the same subject. Fig. *Gnome* (Ap. 6). *Vv.* 10–12 (general) are from Ecc. 7. 20. Ps. 14. 2, 3; 53. 2, 3 (3, 4); *vv.* 13–18 (particular) are from Ps. 5. 9 (10); 140. 3; 10. 7. Isa. 59. 7, 8. Ps. 36. 1 (2). Verification of these refs., from the standpoint of Paul's argument, throws much light upon the O.T. pass. in which they occur.

There . . . one. Lit. There is not (Gr. *ou*) a righteous (man), not even one.

righteous. Gr. *dikaios.* Ap. 191. 1. Cp. 1. 17.

no, not. Gr. *oude.*

11 none. Gr. *ou.* Ap. 105. I.

understandeth. Gr. *suniēmi.* Occ. twenty-six times. Always "understand", save Mark 6. 52 and 2 Cor. 10. 12. **seeketh after.** Gr. *ekzēteō.* See Acts 15. 17.

12 In Ps. 14 the Heb. stands as in A.V., but in the Sept. (Alex. MS.) additional matter appears, word for word as in these *vv.* 12–18. This is not found in Ps. 53, a practical repetition of Ps. 14.

They, &c. = All went.

gone . . . way. Gr. *ekklinō.* Only here, 16. 17. 1 Pet. 3. 11.

become unprofitable = are worthless. Gr. *achreioomai.* Only here.

good. Gr. *chrēstotēs.* Ap. 184. III (*a*).

no, not one = there is not as far as (Gr. *heōs*) one.

13 Their. Ps. 5. 9 shows that this refers to the boasters and workers of iniquity of *v.* 5. Cp. 1. 24–32; 2. 17, 23.

throat: i.e. speech; by Fig. *Metonymy.* Ap. 6. Gr. *larunx.* Only here.

open sepulchre = opened sepulchre; lit. a tomb that has been opened, emitting noisomeness.

sepulchre. Gr. *taphos.* Only here, Matt. 23. 27, 29; 27. 61, 64, 66; 28. 1. Applied to any place where dead bodies are deposited. *Mnēmeion*, rendered "sepulchre", is found only in Gospels and Acts 13. 29, and means a monumental tomb. Cp. Matt. 27. 60.

tongues. See Ps. 140. 11.

have used deceit = deceived. Gr. *dolioō*; only here. The kindred verb occ. 2 Cor. 4. 2.

the. Omit. **poison.** Gr. *ios.* Occ. here and Jas. 3. 8; 5. 3. **asps.** Rendered "adders" in Ps. 140. 3. Gr. *aspis.* Only here. Cp. Jas. 3. 5, 6, 8. Deut. 32. 33. **lips** = language. Fig. *Metonymy.* Ap. 6. **14 Whose mouth, &c.** Cp. Ps. 10. 7. **full.** Gr. *gemō.* Cp. Matt. 23. 25, 27. **cursing and bitterness** = bitter imprecations. Fig. *Hendiadys.* Ap. 6. **cursing.** Gr. *ara.* Only here. Properly a prayer, but commonly a prayer for evil, an imprecation. **bitterness.** Gr. *pikria.* See Acts 8. 23. **15 Their feet, &c.** See Prov. 1. 16. Isa. 59. 7. **swift** = sharp. Gr. *oxys.* Occ. only here and seven times in Rev., always "sharp". **shed.** Gr. *ekcheō.* Only here in Rom. Elsewhere seventeen times, generally "pour out". **16 Destruction.** Gr. *suntrimma.* Only here. Lit. a breaking, or bruising. Cp. 16. 20. John 19. 36. **misery** = distress. Gr. *talaipōria.* Here and Jas. 5. 1. Cp. 7. 24. Jas. 4. 9. **17 have they not known** = they knew not. **not.** Gr. *ou.* Ap. 105. I. **known.** Gr. *ginōskō.* Ap. 132. I. ii. **18** This is quoted from Ps. 36. 1. **before.** Gr. *apenanti.* See Acts 3. 16. **19 know.** Gr. *oida.* Ap. 132. I. i. **law.** See 2. 12. **saith.** Gr. *laleō.* Ap. 121. 7. **under.** Gr. Ap. 104. viii. **every mouth.** No partiality for the Jew. **stopped** = closed. Gr. *phrassō.* Here; 2 Cor. 11. 10. Heb. 11. 33. **guilty** = under penalty. Gr. *hupodikos.* Only here. **20 by.** Gr. *ek.* Ap. 104. vii. **the deeds of the law** = works of law. Cp. *v.* 27. **by.** Gr. *dia.* Ap. 104. v. 1. **the law** = law. See 2. 12. **knowledge.** Ap. 132. II. ii. **21 now** = at this present time. Gr. *nuni.* First of twenty-one occ. **without the law** = apart from (Gr. *chōris*) law. **is manifested.** Gr. *phaneroō.* Ap. 106. I. v. Cp. 1. 19. **witnessed.** Gr. *martureō.* Cp. 10. 2. 2 Tim. 2. 6. **by.** Gr *hupo.* Ap. 104. xviii. 1. **the law and the prophets.** An expression for the whole O.T. Cp. Matt. 7. 12. Luke 24. 44. **prophets.** Ap. 189. **22 Even** = And. **Jesus Christ.** Ap. 98. XI. **and upon all.** Most texts omit. **believe.** Ap. 150. I. 1. i. **no.** Gr. *ou.* **difference** = distinction. Gr. *diastolē.* Elsewhere, 10. 12. 1 Cor. 14. 7. **23 have.** Omit. **sinned.** Gr. *hamartanō.* Ap. 128. I. i. In the first Adam as the federal head of the old creation. **come short.** Gr. *hustereō.* Only here in Rom. Occ. sixteen times, always in the sense of failing, or lacking. Cp. Matt. 19. 20 (first occ.). Mark 10. 21. John 2. 3. Heb. 12. 15. **24 freely.** Gr. *dōrean.* See John 15. 25. **by.** Dative case. No prep. **grace.** Gr. *charis.* Ap. 184. I. 1. Cp. *v.* 28; 5. 1, 9. **through.** Gr. *dia.* Ap. 104. v. 1. **redemption.** Gr. *apolutrōsis.* Occ. ten times. Here; 8. 23. Luke 21. 28. 1 Cor. 1. 30. Eph. 1. 7, 14; 4. 30. Col. 1. 14. Heb. 9. 15; 11. 35. **Christ Jesus.** Ap. 98. XII. **25 hath.** Omit. **set forth** = foreordained (marg.). Gr. *protithēmi.* See 1. 13. **to be** = as. **propitiation.** Gr. *hilastērion.* Only here and Heb. 9. 5. The word comes to us from the Sept. In Ex. 25. 17 *kapporeth* (cover) is rendered *hilastērion epithema*, propitiatory cover, the cover of the ark on which the blood was sprinkled as the means of propitiation. **to, &c.** = for (Gr. *eis.* Ap. 104. vi) a declaration of (Gr. *endeixis.* Occ. also, *v.* 26. 2 Cor. 8. 24. Phil. 1. 28).

declare His [5]righteousness °for the °remission
of °sins that are °past, [7]through the °forbear-
ance of [2]God;
26 °To [25]declare, *I say,* °at this [2]time His
[5]righteousness: °that He might be °just, and
the [4]justifier of him °which believeth in
°Jesus.
K[3] 27 Where *is* °boasting then? It is °excluded.
-[20]By °what [19]law? of °works? °Nay: but
-[20]by °the [19]law of faith.
28 Therefore we °conclude that a [4]man is
[4]justified by [3]faith [21]without the [20]deeds of
°the law.
29 °*Is He* the [2]God of the Jews only? *is He*
°not °also of the °Gentiles? Yes, of the
°Gentiles also:
30 °Seeing °*it is* one [2]God, °Which shall
[4]justify the circumcision [20]-by faith, and uncircumcision [24]through [3]faith.
31 Do we then °make void the [19]law [24]through
[3]faith? [4]God forbid: °yea, we establish the
[19]law.

J[4] L **4** °What shall we say then that Abraham
our °father, °as pertaining to °the flesh,
hath found?
2 For °if Abraham were °justified °by works,
he hath *whereof* to °glory; but °not °before
°God.
3 For what saith °the Scripture? °"**Abraham**
°**believed** [2]**God, and it was** °**counted** °**unto him**
°**for** °**righteousness.**"
M g 4 Now to him that worketh, is the reward
[2]not °reckoned °of °grace, but °of °debt.
5 But to him that worketh °not, but °believeth
°on Him that [2]justifieth the °ungodly, his °faith
is [3]counted [3]for [3]righteousness.

h 6 Even as David also °describeth the °blessed-
ness of the °man, [3]unto whom [2]God °imputeth
[3]righteousness °without works,
7 *Saying,* "°**Blessed** ***are*** **they whose** °**iniquities are** °**forgiven, and whose** °**sins are**
°**covered.**
8 [7]**Blessed** ***is*** **the** °**man to whom the** °**LORD will**
°**not** [6]**impute** [7]**sin.**"
9 °*Cometh* this [6]blessedness then °upon the
circumcision *only,* or °upon the uncircumcision
also? for we say that [5]faith was [4]reckoned to
Abraham [3]for [3]righteousness.
10 How was it then [4]reckoned? when he
was °in circumcision, or °in uncircumcision?
[2]Not °in circumcision, but °in uncircumcision.
11 And he received the °sign of circumcision,
a seal of the [3]righteousness of the [5]faith which
he had yet °being uncircumcised: °that he

for = by reason of. Gr. *dia.* Ap. 104. v. 2.
remission. Lit. the passing over. Gr. ***paresis.*** Only here.
sins. Gr. *hamartēma.* Ap. 128. I. ii. 2.
past. Gr. *proginomai.* Only here. Cp. Acts 17. 30.
forbearance. Gr. *anochē.* See 2. 4.
26 To. Gr. *pros.* Ap. 104. xv. 3.
at this time = in (Gr. *en*) the present season (Ap. 195).
that, &c. = to (Gr. *eis*) His being.
just. Same as "righteous", *v.* 10.
which believeth, &c. Lit. the one out of (Ap. 104. vii) faith of Jesus; i.e. on the principle of faith in Jesus. Cp. 1. 17.
Jesus. Ap. 98. X.
27 boasting. I.e. of the Jew; 2. 17–23. Gr. *kauchēsis,* which means the act of boasting, while *kauchēma* (4. 2) refers to the subject of the boast.
excluded. Gr. *ekkleiō.* Only here and Gal. 4. 17.
what. Lit. what manner of. Cp. 1 Pet. 1. 11.
works. Same as "deeds", v. 20.
Nay. Gr. *ouchi.* Ap. 105. I. (a). the = a.
28 conclude = reckon. Gr. *logizomai.* See 2. 3.
the. Omit.
29 *Is . . . only?* Read, "What, is He, &c."? The question opens with the Gr. conjunction *ē,* translated "what" in 1 Cor. 6. 16. 19; 14. 36.
not. Same as "nay", *v.* 27.
also of the Gentiles = of Gentiles also.
Gentiles. See 1. 5.
30 Seeing = Since. Gr. *epeiper.* Only here.
it is one God = God is One, i.e. for both Jew and Gentile.
Which shall = Who will.
31 make void. Gr. *katargeo,* as *v.* 3.
Yea = Nay. Gr. *alla.*

4. 1–22 (J[4], p. 1666). **THE CASE OF ABRAHAM.**
(*Introversion and Alternation.*)

J[4] L | 1–3. Abraham's faith reckoned for righteousness.
  M | g | 4, 5. Not by works, but according to grace.
    h | 6–12. Blessing to all who have like faith.
  M | *g* | 13–16–. Not through law, but according to grace.
    h | –16–17. Blessing to all who have like faith.
L | 18–22. Abraham's faith reckoned for righteousness.

4. 1 What, &c. See 3. 5. Forcible form of Fig. *Erotēsis* (Ap. 6). Resuming from 3. 21.
father = forefather, as the texts read. Fig. *Synecdoche* of Species, Ap. 6.
as pertaining to. Gr. *kata.* Ap. 104. x. 2.
the flesh. All the Jews claimed Abraham as their father. See 9. 5. Luke 1. 73. John 8. 39 (cp. *v.* 56). Acts 7. 2.
2 if. Ap. 118. 2. a.
justified. Ap. 191. 2.
by. Gr. *ek.* Ap. 104. vii.
glory. Gr. *kauchēma.* See 3. 27 and 2 Cor. 9. 3.
not. Ap. 105. I.
before. Gr. *pros.* Ap. 104. xv. 3.
God. Ap. 98. I. i. 1.

3 the Scripture. Gen. 15. 6. **Abraham.** Read, "Now Abraham." **believed.** Ap. 150. I. 1. ii. **counted** = reckoned, imputed. Gr. *logizomai.* See 2. 3 (Paul quotes the Sept.). **unto** = to. **for.** Ap. 104. vi. **righteousness.** Ap. 191. 3. **4 reckoned.** Same as "counted", *v.* 3. **of.** Gr. *kata.* Ap. 104. x. 2. **grace.** Ap. 184. I. 1. **debt.** Gr. *opheilēma.* Only here and Matt. 6. 12. **5 not.** Ap. 105. II. **believeth.** Ap. 150. I. 1. v. (iii). 2. **on.** Ap. 104. ix. 3. **ungodly** = impious. Gr. *asebēs.* Here, 5. 6. 1 Tim. 1. 9. 1 Pet. 4. 18. 2 Pet. 2. 5; 3. 7. Jude 4, 15. Cp. Ap. 128. IV. **faith.** Ap. 150. II. 1. **6 describeth** = says of. **blessedness.** Gr. *makarismos.* Here, *v.* 9. Gal. 4. 15. **man.** Ap. 123. 1. **imputeth.** Same as "count", *v.* 3. **without** = apart from. See 3. 21. **7 Blessed.** Ap. 63. vi. **iniquities.** Ap. 128. III. 4. **forgiven.** Ap. 174. 12. **sins.** Ap. 128. I. ii. 1. **covered** = covered over. Gr. *epikaluptō.* Only here. **8 man.** Ap. 123. 2. **LORD.** Ap. 98. VI. i. *β.* 1. B. a. **not.** Ap. 105. III. Quoted from Ps. 32. 1, 2. Ap. 107. II. 3. C. **9** *Cometh,* &c. = This blessing, then, is it? **upon.** Gr. *epi.* Ap. 104. ix. 3. **10 in.** Gr. *en.* Ap. 104. viii. **11 sign.** Ap. 176. 3. **being uncircumcised** = in (Gr. *en*) uncircumcision. **that, &c.** = unto (Ap. 104. vi) his being.

might be the father of all °them that [5]believe,
°though they be not circumcised; °that [3]right-
eousness might be [6]imputed [3]unto them °also:
12 And the father of circumcision to them
who are [2]not °of the circumcision only, but
who also °walk in the °steps of that [5]faith of
our father Abraham, *which he had* [11]being *yet*
uncircumcised.
M g 13 °For the promise, that he should be the
°heir of the °world, *was* [2]not to Abraham, or
to his seed, °through the law, but °through the
[3]righteousness of [5]faith.
14 For [2]if they which are [12]of °the law *be*
heirs, [5]faith °is made void, and the promise
°made of none effect:
15 Because the law °worketh wrath: °for
where °no law is, *there is* °no °transgression.
16 °Therefore *it is* °of [5]faith, °that *it might
be* °by [4]grace;
h °to the end the promise °might be °sure to °all
the seed; [2]not to that only which is [12]of the
law, but to that also which is °of the [5]faith of
Abraham, who is the father of us all,
17 (As it is °written, "**I have °made thee
a father of many nations**") before Him Whom
he °believed, *even* [2]God, Who °quickeneth °the
dead, and °calleth those things which be [5]not,
as though they were.
L 18 Who °against hope °believed in hope,
[11]that he might become °the father of many
°nations, °according to that which was spoken,
°"**So shall thy seed be.**"
19 And °being [5]not weak in [5]faith, he °con-
sidered °not his own body °now °dead, °when
he was about °an hundred years old, °neither
yet the °deadness of Sarah's womb:
20 He °staggered [2]not °at the promise of [2]God
°through unbelief; but °was strong in [5]faith,
giving °glory to [2]God;
21 And being °fully persuaded that, what He
had promised, He was able °also to perform.
22 °And therefore **it was [6]imputed to him
[3]for [3]righteousness.**
K^4 *j* 23 Now it was [2]not written °for his sake
alone, that it was [6]imputed to him;
24 But °for us also, to whom it °shall be
[6]imputed, °if we [3]believe [5]on Him That °raised
up °Jesus our °Lord °from °the dead,
25 Who was °delivered [24]for our °offences, and
was [24]raised °again [24]for our °justification.

them, &c. Lit. of all the believing (ones). Ap. 150. I. 1. i.
though, &c. = through (Ap. 104. v. 1) uncircumcision.
also. Omit.
12 of. Ap. 104. vii.
walk. Gr. *stoicheō*. See Acts 21. 24.
steps. Gr. *ichnos*. Only here, 2 Cor. 12. 18. 1 Pet. 2. 21.
13 For, &c. The Greek reads, "For not through law was the promise." Cp. Gal. 3. 18.
heir. Cp. Gal. 3. 29 and Heb. 11. 8–10.
world. Ap. 129. 1.
through. Ap. 104. v. 1.
14 the. Omit.
is made void = Lit. has been emptied. Gr. *kenoō*. Elsewhere, 1 Cor. 1. 17; 9. 15. 2 Cor. 9. 3. Phil. 2. 7.
made of none effect. Gr. *katargeō*. See 3. 3.
15 worketh. See 1. 27.
for. The texts read "but".
no = not. Ap. 105. I.
no = neither. Gr. *oude*.
transgression. See 2. 23.
16 Therefore = On account of (Ap. 104. v. 2) this.
of faith. See 1. 17.
that = in order that. Gr. *hina*.
by. Gr. *kata*. Ap. 104. x. 2.
to the end. Gr. *eis*. Ap. 104. vi.
might = may.
sure. Gr. *bebaios*. Here, 2 Cor. 1. 7. Heb. 2. 2; 3. 6, 14; 6. 19; 9. 17. 2 Pet. 1. 10, 19.
all the seed. To every child of faithful Abraham, Jew and Gentile alike.
of the faith. See 1. 17.
17 written. Gen. 17. 5.
made = set, appointed. Gr. *tithēmi*.
believed. Ap. 150. I. 1. vi.
quickeneth = maketh alive. Gr. *zōopoieō*. Here, 8. 11. John 5. 21; 6. 63. 1 Cor. 15. 22, 36, 45. 2 Cor. 3. 6. Gal. 3. 21. 1 Tim. 6. 13. 1 Pet. 3. 18.
the dead. Ap. 139. 1.
calleth, &c. Primarily of Isaac. Cp. Gen. 15.
18 against. Ap. 104. xii. 3.
believed in. Ap. 150. I. 1. v. (iii). 1.
the. Omit.
nations. Gr. *ethnos*. See 1. 5.
according to. Gr. *kata*. Ap. 104. x. 2.
So, &c. Quoted from Gen. 15. 5.
19 being, &c. Fig. *Tapeinosis*. Ap. 6. See this Fig. in 5. 6 also.
considered. Ap. 133. II. 4.
not. The texts omit.
now = already.
dead. Gr. *nekroō*. See Col. 3. 5. Heb. 11. 12.
when he was = he being. Gr. *huparchō*. See Luke 9. 48.
an hundred years old. Gr. *hekatontaetēs*. Only here.
neither yet = and.
deadness. Gr. *nekrōsis*. Only here and 2 Cor. 4. 10.

20 staggered. Gr. *diakrinō*. Ap. 122. 4. Cp. Matt. 21. 21. at. Ap. 104. vi. through = by. was strong. Gr. *endunamoō*. See Acts 9. 22. glory. See 1. 23 and John 1. 14. **21** fully persuaded. Gr. *plērophoreō*. Occ. 14 5. Luke 1. 1. 2 Tim. 4. 5, 17. also, &c. = to perform also. **22** And therefore = Wherefore also.

4. 23—5. 11 (K^4, p. 1666). GENERAL APPLICATION. (*Introversion.*)

K^4 | j | 4. 23–25. Atonement made.
k | 5. 1, 2. Result: peace with God.
l | 5. 3–5. Not only so; glory also in tribulation.
m | 5. 6–8. Reason: the love of God in Christ.
l | 5. 9, 10. Much more then; saved from wrath by His life.
k | 11–. Result: joy in God.
j | –11. Atonement received.

23 for his sake = on account of (Ap. 104. v. 2) him. **24** for us = on account of (Ap. 104. v. 2) us. shall = is about to. if we believe = to (us) believing. Ap. 150. I. 1. v. (iii). 2. raised. Ap. 178 I. 4. First of ten occ. in Rom. Here; *v.* 25; 6. 4, 9; 7. 4; 8. 11, 11, 34; 10. 9; 13. 11. Jesus. Ap. 98. X. Lord. Ap. 98. VI. i. *β*. 2. A. from. Ap. 104. vii. the dead. Ap 139. 3. **25** delivered. See John 19. 30. offences. Ap. 128. I. ii. 3. again. Omit. justification = justifying. Ap. 191. 5.

k **5** Therefore being °justified °by °faith, °we
have peace °with °God °through our °Lord
°Jesus Christ:
2 °By Whom °also we °have °access °by [1]faith
°into this °grace °wherein we stand, and °re-
joice °in hope of the °glory of [1]God.
l 3 And °not only *so*, but we °glory °in °tribula-
tions also: °knowing that °tribulation °worketh
patience;
4 And patience, °experience; and °experience,
°hope:
5 And [2]hope °maketh [3]not ashamed; because
the °love of [1]God °is shed abroad [3]in our
hearts [2-]by the °Holy Ghost which °is given
°unto us.
m 6 For when we were yet °without strength,
°in °due time °Christ died °for the °ungodly.
7 For °scarcely [6]for a °righteous man will
°one die: °yet °peradventure [6]for a good man
°some would even °dare to die.
8 But [1]God °commendeth His [5]love °toward
us, °in that, while we were yet °sinners,
[6]Christ died [6]for us.
l 9 Much more then, being now [1]justified °by
His °blood, we shall be °saved °from °wrath
[1]through Him.
10 For °if, when we were °enemies, we were
°reconciled to [1]God [2-]by the death of His °Son,
much more, being reconciled, we shall be saved
[9]by His °life.
k 11 And [3]not only *so*, but we also °joy [3]in
[1]God [1]through our [1]Lord [1]Jesus Christ,
j [2-]by Whom we have now received the °atone-
ment.
A² N P n 12 °Wherefore, °as [2-]by one °man °sin entered

5. 1 justified. See 2. 13. Ap. 191. 2.
by. Ap. 104. vii.
faith. Ap. 150. II. 1., i. e. on faith-principle. See 1. 17.
we have peace. The R.V. "let us have peace" is not warranted. The apostle's teaching is plain. Having been justified, *therefore* we have peace with God.
with. Ap. 104. xv. 3.
God. Ap. 98. I. i. 1.
through. Ap. 104. v. 1.
Lord. Ap. 98. VI. i. β. 2. A.
Jesus Christ. Ap. 98. XI.
2 By. Ap. 104. v. 1.
also. Read after "access".
have = have had, have obtained.
access. Lit. the introduction. Gr. *prosagōgē.* Only here and Eph. 2. 18; 3. 12.
by. Dat. No prep.
into. Ap. 104. vi.
grace. See 1. 5.
wherein = in (Gr. *en*) which.
rejoice. Same as "boast", 2. 17.
in. Ap. 104. ix. 2.
glory. See 1. 23 and 4. 20.
3 not. Ap. 105. I.
glory . . . also = rejoice (as *v.* 2) also in &c.
in. Ap. 104. viii.
tribulations = the afflictions. Gr. *thlipsis.* See Acts 7. 10.
knowing. Ap. 132. I. i.
worketh. See 1. 27.
4 experience. Gr. *dokimē.* Here; 2 Cor. 2. 9; 8. 2; 9. 13; 13. 3. Phil. 2. 22.
hope. Cp. Tit. 2. 13. See 4. 18.
5 maketh . . . ashamed = causeth shame. Gr. *kataischunō.* Here, 9. 33; 10. 11. Luke 13. 17. 1 Cor. 1. 27; 11. 4, 5, 22. 2 Cor. 7. 14; 9. 4. 1 Pet. 2. 6; 3. 16.
love. Ap. 135. II. 1.
is shed abroad. Gr. *ekchunō.* See Acts 1. 18; 10. 45.
Holy Ghost. Ap. 101. II. 14.
is = was. **unto** = to.
6 without strength. Gr. *asthenēs.*
in. Ap. 104. x. 2. **due time** = season. Cp. Gal. 4. 4. **Christ.** Ap. 98. IX. **for.** Ap. 104. xvii. 1. **ungodly.** See 4. 5. **7 scarcely.** Gr. *molis.* See Acts 14. 18. **righteous.** Ap. 191. 1. **one.** Ap. 123. 3. **yet** = for. **peradventure.** Gr. *tacha.* Only here and Philem. 15. **some** = one. See above. **dare** = venture. **8 commendeth.** See 3. 5. In this verse the subject of the sentence comes last, and reads "commendeth His own love toward us—God", giving the Fig. *Hyperbaton* (Ap. 6), for emphasis. **toward.** Gr. *eis.* Ap. 104. vi. **in that** = because. **sinners.** Gr. *hamartōlos.* Cp. Ap. 128. I. i, ii. **9 by.** Gr. *en.* **blood.** Cp. *v.* 1 and 3. 24. **saved.** First of eight occ. in Romans. **from.** Gr. *apo.* Ap. 104. iv. **wrath.** See 1. 18. 1 Thess. 1. 10. **10 if.** Gr. *ei.* Ap. 118. 2. a. **enemies.** Note the fig. *Catabasis,* Ap. 6; without strength, sinners, enemies *vv.* 6, 8, 10. **reconciled.** Gr. *katallassō,* a more intensive word than *allassō* (1. 23). Elsewhere, 1 Cor. 7. 11. 2 Cor. 5. 18, 19, 20. **Son.** Ap. 108. iii. Cp. 6. 10. Gal. 2. 19, 20. **life.** Ap. 170. 1. **11 joy** = rejoice (*v.* 2). **atonement** = reconciliation, restoration to favour. Gr. *katallagē.* Here, 11. 15. 2 Cor. 5. 18, 19.

5. 12—8. 39 (A², p. 1663). SIN: THE OLD NATURE ITSELF. (*Introversion.*)

A² N | 5. 12–21. Condemnation to death of the first man; through the sin (*to paraptōma*) of one man: but, a justifying unto life through the righteous act (*to dikaiōma*) of one man, the Second Man.
  O | 6. 1—7. 6. We are not in sin, because we died with Christ.
  O | 7. 7–25. Sin is in us, though we have risen with Christ.
 N | 8. 1–39. No condemnation for the new man, to those who are alive unto God in Christ Jesus, and in whom is *pneuma Christou,* the new nature; because of condemnation of sin in the flesh (in Christ, the Second Man).

5. 12-21 (N, above). CONDEMNATION OF THE FIRST MAN. (*Introversion and Extended Alternation.*)

N | P | n | 5. 12. By one man's sin—death.
 o | 5. 13. Sin not imputed where no law.
  p | 5. 14–. The reign of death.
   q | 5. –14. The type, Adam.
    Q | 5. 15. Not as by one sin, so the gracious gift.
    Q | 5. 16, 17. Not as by one man, so the gracious gift.
P | *n* | 5. 18, 19. By One Man's righteous act many made righteous.
 o | 5. 20. Sin imputed when law came.
  p | 5. 21–. The reign of sin and death.
   q | 5. –21. The Antitype, Jesus Christ our Lord.

12 Wherefore = On account of (Ap. 104. v. 2) this. Having described the fruits of sin, the apostle now goes on to deal with the root. **as** = just as. **man.** Ap. 123. 1. Cp. 1 Cor. 15. 21. **sin.** Ap. 128. I. ii. 1.

[2]into the °world, and °death [2-]by °sin; and
so death °passed °upon all °men, °for that all
°have °sinned:

o 13 (For until the law [12]sin was [3]in the [12]world:
but [12]sin is [3]not °imputed °when there is °no
law.

p 14 Nevertheless death reigned [9]from Adam
°to °Moses, even °over them that had °not
[12]sinned °after the °similitude of Adam's
°transgression,

q who is °the °figure of °Him That was to come.

Q 15 But [3]not as the °offence, so also *is* the
°free gift. For [10]if °through the °offence of °one
°many °be dead, much more the [2]grace of
[1]God, and the °gift [9]by [2]grace, *which is* °by
°one [12]man, [1]Jesus Christ, °hath °abounded
°unto °many.

Q 16 °And [3]not as *it was* [2-]by one that [12]sinned,
so is the °gift: for the °judgment *was* [1]by one
°to °condemnation, but the [15]free gift *is* °of
many [15]offences [15]unto °justification.

17 °For [10]if °by one man's [15]offence death
reigned [2-]by one; much more they which receive °abundance of [2]grace and of the [15]gift of
°righteousness shall reign [8]in [10]life [2-]by One,
[1]Jesus Christ.)

P n 18 °Therefore as [2-]by the [15]offence of one
judgment came [12]upon all [12]men [16]to [16]condem-
nation; even so [2-]by the °righteousness of One
the free gift came [12]upon all [12]men [15]unto
°justification °of [10]life.

19 For as [2-]by [12]one [12]man's °disobedience
°many were °made [8]sinners, °so [2-]by the
°obedience of [12]One shall °many be °made
[7]righteous.

o 20 Moreover the law °entered, °that the
[15]offence might °abound. But where [12]sin
°abounded, [2]grace °did much more abound:

p 21 [20]That as [12]sin °hath reigned °unto death,
q °even [19]so might [2]grace reign [1]through [17]right-
eousness [15]unto °eternal [10]life [2-]by [1]Jesus
Christ our [1]Lord.

O R r **6** °What shall we say then? Shall we
°continue in °sin, °that °grace may
°abound?

world. Ap. 129. 1.
death, &c. = by means of sin, death.
passed = passed through.
upon = unto. Ap. 104. vi.
for that = because. Gr. *eph'* (Ap. 104. ix. 2) *hō*.
have. Omit.
sinned. I. e. in Adam, as representative. See 3. 23. Ap. 128. I. i.
13 imputed. Not the same word as in 4. 6, &c. Gr. *ellogeō*. Only here and Philem. 18.
when, &c. = there not (Gr. *mē*) being law.
no. Ap. 105. II.
14 to = until. Gr. *mechri*.
Moses. Occ. twenty-two times in the Epistles. Cp. Matt. 8. 4. over. Ap. 104. ix. 3.
not. Ap. 105. II. after. Ap. 104. ix. 2.
similitude = likeness. See 1. 23.
transgression. Gr. *parabasis*. See 2. 23.
the = a.
figure. Gr. *tupos*. See John 20. 25.
Him . . . come = The Coming One. A well-known Hebraism for the Messiah. See Matt. 11. 3. Adam was a type (Ap. 6) as the federal head of a new-created race.
15 offence. Ap. 128. I. ii. 3. See 4. 25.
free gift. Ap. 184. I. 2.
through = by. Dative. No prep.
one, many = the one, the many.
be dead = died.
gift. Gr. *dōrea*. See John 4. 10.
by = of. Gen. case.
hath. Omit. abounded. See 3. 7.
unto. Gr. *eis*. Ap. 104. vi.
16 And not, &c. Read, And not as by means of one having sinned is the free gift; for the judgment indeed of one (was) unto condemnation; but the free gift is of (or resulted from) many transgressions unto justification.
gift. Gr. *dōrēma*. Not the same word as *v.* 15. Occ. only here and Jas. 1. 17.
judgment. Gr. *krima*. Ap. 177. 6.
to. Ap. 104. vi.
condemnation. Gr. *katakrima*. Only here, *v.* 18; 8. 1. Cp. Ap. 122. 7; 177. 6. of. Ap. 104. vii.
justification. Gr. *dikaiōma*, a righteous acquittal. Ap. 191. 4.
17 For . . . one = For if by the trespass of the one, death reigned through the one.
by. Dative. No prep.
abundance = the abundance. Gr. *perisseia*. Here, 2 Cor. 8. 2; 10. 15. Jas. 1. 21.
righteousness. See 1. 17.
18 Therefore, &c. = So then as by means of one (act of) transgression (sentence came) upon all men unto condemnation, even so by means of one righteous act also (the free gift came) upon all men to justification of life. righteousness of one = one righteous act. Gr. *dikaiōma*. Ap. 191. 4, as *v.* 16. Add "also". justification. Gr. *dikaiōsis*. Ap. 191. 5. of = issuing in. Ap. 17. 5. **19** disobedience. Ap. 128. V. 2. many = the many. made = constituted. so = so also. obedience. The obedience unto death of Phil. 2. 8. This was the one righteous act of *v.* 18. **20** entered. Lit. came in beside. Gr. *pareiserchomai*. Only here and Gal. 2. 4. that = in order that. Gr. *hina*. abound = multiply. Gr. *pleonazō*. Here, 6. 1. 2 Cor. 4. 15; 8. 15. Phil. 4. 17. 1 Thess. 3. 12. 2 Thess. 1. 3. 2 Pet. 1. 8. did much more abound = superabounded. Gr. *huperperisseuō*. Only here and 2 Cor. 7. 4. **21** hath. Omit. unto. Ap. 104. viii. even so, &c. = so might grace also. eternal. Ap. 151. II. B. i.

6. 1–7. 6 (O, p. 1671). WE ARE NOT IN SIN BECAUSE WE DIED WITH CHRIST. (*Introversion.*)

O | R | 6. 1-11. Identification with Christ in death and life.
  S | 6. 12-14. Sin no longer has dominion, because we are dead to the law.
   T | 6. 15-19. The old, and the new, master and servant.
  S | 6. 20-23. Sin no longer has dominion, because we are alive in Christ.
 R | 7. 1-6. Identification with Christ in life and death.

6. 1-11 (R, above). IDENTIFICATION WITH CHRIST IN DEATH AND LIFE. (*Introversion.*)

R | r | 6. 1-3. Death to SIN cannot entail life in SINS.
  s | 6. 4-7. By identification with Christ in His death and *life*, there cannot be continuance in SIN.
  s | 6. 8-10. By identification with Christ in His death and *life*. there must be life with God.
 r | 6. 11. Death to SIN entails life with God.

6. 1 What, &c. See 3. 5. continue. Gr. *epimenō*. See Acts 10. 48. sin. Ap. 128. I. ii. 1. that = in order that. Gr. *hina*. grace. Ap. 184. I. 1. abound. See 5. 20.

2 °God forbid. How shall we, that °are dead
to [1]sin, live any longer °therein?
3 °Know ye not, that so many of us as were
°baptized °into °Jesus Christ were °baptized
°into His death?
s 4 Therefore we °are °buried with Him °by
°baptism [3]into death: [1]that like as °Christ was
°raised up °from the °dead °by the °glory of
the °Father, even so we also should walk °in
°newness of °life.
5 For °if we have °been °planted together °in
the °likeness of His death, °we shall be °also
in the likeness of *His* °resurrection:
6 °Knowing this, that our °old °man is °cru-
cified with *Him*, [1]that °the body of [1]sin might
be °destroyed, that °henceforth we should not
°serve [1]sin.
7 For he that °is dead °is freed °from [1]sin.
s 8 Now [5]if °we be dead °with [4]Christ, we
°believe that we shall °also °live with Him:
9 °Knowing that [4]Christ °being [4]raised
[4]from the [4]dead dieth °no more; death °hath
°no more dominion over Him.
10 For °in that He died, He died °unto [1]sin
°once: but in that He liveth, He liveth °unto
°God.
r 11 Likewise °reckon ye °also yourselves to be
[4]dead indeed [10]unto °sin, but alive [10]unto
[10]God °through [3]Jesus Christ °our Lord.
S t 12 Let °not [1]sin therefore reign [4]in your
°mortal body, °that ye should obey it [4]in the
lusts thereof.
u 13 °Neither °yield ye your members *as* °in-
struments of °unrighteousness [10]unto [1]sin:
u but °yield yourselves [10]unto [10]God, as those that
are [11]alive [4]from the [4]dead, and your members
as °instruments of °righteousness [10]unto [10]God.
t 14 For [1]sin shall °not [9]have dominion over
you: for ye are °not °under °the law, but °un-
der [1]grace.
T v 15 What then? °shall we °sin, because we
are [14]not [14]under the law, but [14]under [1]grace?
[2]God forbid.

2 God forbid. See 3. 4.
are dead = died.
therein = in (Ap. 104. viii) it.
3 Know ye not. Lit. Are ye ignorant. Gr. *agnoeō*. See 2. 4.
baptized. Ap. 115. I. iv.
into. Ap. 104. vi.
Jesus Christ = Christ Jesus. Ap. 98. XII. Cp. Matt. 20. 20–22.
4 are = were.
buried with. Gr. *sunthaptō*. Only here and Col. 2. 12.
by. Ap. 104. v. i.
baptism. Ap. 115. II. i. 1.
Christ. Ap. 98. IX.
raised up. Ap. 178. I. 4.
from. Ap. 104. vii.
dead. Ap. 139. 3.
glory. I. e. glorious power.
Father. Ap. 98. III.
in. Ap. 104. viii.
newness. Gr. *kainotēs*. Only here and 7. 6.
life. Ap. 170. 1.
5 if. Ap. 118. 2. a.
been = become.
planted together. I. e. with Him. Gr. *sumphutos*. Only here. Cp. John 12. 24. 1 Cor. 15. 36.
in. Dative case.
likeness. See 1. 23.
we . . . resurrection = yea, we shall be (in the likeness) of His resurrection also.
resurrection. Ap. 178. II. 1.
6 Knowing. Ap. 132. I. ii.
old man. The old Adam nature. Here, Eph. 4. 22. Col. 3. 9.
man. Ap. 123. 1.
crucified with. See John 19. 32.
the body of sin = the old nature which is the slave of sin. Cp. Col. 2. 11, 12.
destroyed = annulled. Gr. *katargeō*. See 3. 3 and Luke 13. 7.
henceforth. Gr. *mēketi*.
serve. Ap. 190. III. 2.
7 is dead = died (i. e. with Christ).
is freed = has been justified, cleared from the claims of sin. Ap. 191. 2.
from. Ap. 104. iv.
8 we be dead with = we died together with (Gr. *sun*. Ap. 104. xvi).
believe. Ap. 150. I. 1. iii.
also live with = live also with. Gr. *suzaō*; only here, 2 Cor. 7. 3. 2 Tim. 2. 11.
9 Knowing. Ap. 132. I. i.
being = having been.
no more. Gr. *ouketi*.
hath . . . dominion. Lit. "lords it over". Gr. *kurieuō*. Here, *v.* 14; 7. 1; 14. 9. Luke 22. 25. 2 Cor. 1. 24. 1 Tim. 6. 15. **10 in that He died** = (the death) He died. **unto** = to. Dat. case. **once** = once for all. Gr. *ephapax*. Only here, 1 Cor. 15. 6. Heb. 7. 27; 9. 12; 10. 10. **God.** Ap. 98. I. i. 1. **11 reckon.** See 4. 4. **also yourselves** = yourselves also. **through** = in. Ap. 104. viii. **our Lord.** The texts omit.

6. 12–14 (S, p. 1672). SIN (THE OLD MAN) NO LONGER HAS DOMINION. (*Introversion.*)

S | t | 12. Sin not to reign in the mortal body. (Dehortation.)
  | u | 13–. The members, therefore, not to be surrendered as instruments of unrighteousness. (Negative.)
  | *u* | –13. The members to be surrendered to God as instruments of righteousness. (Positive.)
  | *t* | 14. Sin not to lord it, because we are no longer under law but grace. (Reason for Dehortation in *v.* 12.)

12 not. Ap. 105. II. **mortal** = subject to death. Gr. *thnētos*. Here, 8. 11. 1 Cor. 15. 53, 54. 2 Cor. 4. 11; 5. 4. **that ye should obey** = for (Ap. 104. vi) obeying. The texts omit "it in" and read "obey its desires". **13 Neither.** Gr. *mēde*. **yield** = present. **instruments** = weapons. Gr. *hoplon*. Here, 13. 12. John 18. 3. 2 Cor. 6. 7; 10. 4. **unrighteousness.** Ap. 128. VII. 1. **righteousness.** Ap. 191. 3. **14 not.** Ap. 105. I. **under.** Ap. 104. xviii. 2. **the.** Omit.

6. 15–19 (T, p. 1672). THE OLD AND THE NEW MASTER. (*Introversion.*)

v | 15, 16. Acts of obedience indicate the master served.
  w | 17. Change in acts of obedience.
  w | 18. Change in commands of new master.
v | 19. The master served indicates the nature of obedience rendered.

15 shall we = are we to. **sin.** Cp. 2. 12. Ap. 128. I. i.

16 °Know ye [14]not, that to whom ye [13]yield
yourselves °servants °to obey, °his °servants
ye are to whom ye obey: °whether of [1]sin °un-
to death, or of obedience °unto [13]righteousness?

w 17 °But [10]God be thanked, that ye °were the
[16]servants of [1]sin, but ye have obeyed [4]from
the heart that °form of °doctrine °which was
delivered you.

w 18 °Being then made free [7]from [1]sin, ye °be-
came the servants of [13]righteousness.

r 19 I speak °after the manner of men °because
of the °infirmity of your °flesh: for as ye
have [13]yielded your members °servants to °un-
cleanness and to °iniquity °unto °iniquity; even
so now [13]yield your members °servants to
[13]righteousness °unto °holiness.

S U x 20 For when ye were the [16]servants of [1]sin,
y ye were free °from [13]righteousness.
V z 21 What °fruit had ye then in those things
°whereof ye are now ashamed?
a for the °end of those things *is* °death.
U y 22 But now [18]being made free [7]from [1]sin,
x and [18]become servants to [10]God,
V z ye have your fruit [16]unto holiness,
a and the [21]end °everlasting [4]life.
23 For the °wages of [1]sin *is* [21]death; but the
°gift of God *is* °eternal [4]life [11]through °Jesus
Christ [11]our Lord.

R b 7 °Know ye not, brethren, (for I °speak to
them that °know °the °law,) how that the
°law hath °dominion over °a °man °as long as
he liveth?

c d 2 For the woman °which hath an husband is
bound by [1]the law to *her* °husband °so long as
he liveth; but °if the °husband °be dead, she
is °loosed °from the law of °*her* °husband.

e 3 So then °if, while [2]*her* [2]husband liveth,
she °be married to °another °man, she shall °be
called an adulteress: but [2]if her [2]husband [2]be
dead, she is free [2]from °that law; so that she
is °no adulteress, though she °be married to
°another °man.

16 servants. Ap. 190. I. 2.
to obey = for (Ap. 104. vi) obedience.
his . . . obey = ye are servants to him whom ye obey.
whether. Gr. *ētoi*. An emphatic word. Only here.
unto. Ap. 104. vi.
17 But . . . thanked = But thanks (Gr. *charis*. Ap. 184. I. 1) to God. Cp. 1 Cor. 15. 57.
were. But that service is past.
form. Gr. *tupos*. See 5. 14.
doctrine = teaching. Gr. *didachē*. Only here and 16. 17 in Rom.
which . . . you = unto (Ap. 104. vi) which ye were delivered. See John 19. 30.
18 Being . . . free = Having, then, been set free. Gr. *eleutheroō*. Only here, *v.* 22; 8. 2, 21. John 8. 32, 36. Gal. 5. 1.
became the servants = were made bond-servants or enslaved. Ap. 193. III. 3.
19 after the manner, &c. Gr. *anthrōpinos*. Here, 1 Cor. 2. 4, 13; 4. 3; 10. 13. Jas. 3. 7. 1 Pet. 2. 13. Cp. 3. 5.
because of. Ap. 104. v. 2.
infirmity. Gr. *astheneia*. See John 11. 4.
flesh. See 1. 3.
servants. Gr. *doulon*. Only here. See Ap. 190. I. 2.
uncleanness. Gr. *akatharsia*. See 1. 24.
iniquity. Ap. 128. III. 4.
unto. Gr. *eis*. Ap. 104. vi. I. e. to work.
holiness. Gr. *hagiasmos*. Only here, *v.* 22. 1 Cor. 1. 30. 1 Thess. 4. 3, 4, 7. 2 Thess. 2. 13. 1 Tim. 2. 15. Heb. 12. 14. 1 Pet. 1. 2.

6. 20-23 (*S*, p. 1672). SIN NO LONGER HAS DOMINION. (*Alternation and Introversion.*)

S | U | x | 20-. Servants of sin.
      y | -20. Free men as to righteousness.
   V | z | 21-. The fruits, shame.
      a | -21. The end, death.
   U | *y* | 22-. Free from sin.
      x | -22-. Servants of God.
   V | *z* | -22-. The fruit, holiness.
      a | -22, 23. The end, eternal life.

20 from = with regard to.
21 fruit. Paul uses "fruit" of good results, never of evil ones. Cp. *v.* 22. Gal. 5. 22. Eph. 5. 9. Phil. 1. 11, 22; 4. 17. Heb. 12. 11.
whereof = in respect of (Gr. *epi*. Ap. 104. ix. 2) which.
end. Gr. *telos*. Antithesis to the *telos* of *v.* 22.
death. The second death. Cp. *v.* 23. Rev. 20. 6; 21. 8.
22 everlasting. Ap. 151. II. B. ii.
23 wages = rations. Gr. *opsōnion*. Only here, Luke 3. 14. 1 Cor. 9. 7. 2 Cor. 11. 8. In Luke 3. 14 the "wages" are the fish ration issued to Roman soldiers. Cp. *v.* 13.
gift. Ap. 184. I. 2.
eternal. Ap. 151. II. B. i.
Jesus Christ. The texts read "Christ Jesus". Ap. 98. XII.

7. 1-6 (*R*, p. 1672). IDENTIFICATION WITH CHRIST IN LIFE AND DEATH. (*Introversion and Alternation.*)

R | b | 1. Lordship of the law only during life.
   c | d | 2. Death releases from its claim.
      e | 3. Result—remarriage lawful.
   c | *d* | 4-. We are dead to the law, in Christ.
      e | -4, Result—the way open for union with Christ in resurrection.
   b | 5, 6. Lordship of the law by death.

7. 1 Know ye not. See 6. 3. **speak.** Ap. 121. 7. **know.** Ap. 132. I. ii. **the.** Omit. **law.** Gr. *nomos*. Occ. over 190 times, of which about two-thirds are in Paul's Epistles, the greater number being in Romans and 31 in Galatians. There are 23 in this chapter. **dominion over.** See 6. 9, 14. **a** = the. **man.** Gr. *anthrōpos*. Ap. 123. 1. The general term, meaning either man or woman. **as long** = for (Ap. 104. ix. 3) such time (Gr. *chronos*). **2 which hath, &c.** Gr. *hupandros*. Only here. **husband.** Ap. 123. 2. **so long, &c.** Lit. while living. **if.** Ap. 118. 1. b. **be dead** = should have died. **loosed** = free. Gr. *katargeō*. See 3. 3. **from.** Ap. 104. iv. *her* = the. **3 be married to.** Lit. become for. **another.** Ap. 124. 2. **man.** Ap. 123. 2. **be called.** Gr. *chrēmatizō*. See Luke 2. 26. **that** = the. **no** = not (Ap. 105. II) an. This is an illustration of the fact that death breaks all bonds; husband and wife, master and servant.

cd 4 Wherefore, my brethren, ye also °are become dead to °the law °by °the body of °Christ;
e °that ye should [3]be married to [3]another, *even* to Him who is °raised °from the dead, °that we °should bring forth fruit °unto °God.
b 5 For when we were °in °the flesh, the °motions of °sins, which °were [4]by °the law, did work °in our members °to bring forth fruit [4]unto death.
6 But now we are °delivered [2]from [5]the law, °that being dead °wherein we were held; °that we should °serve [5]in °newness of °spirit, and °not *in* the °oldness of the letter.
O W Y f 7 °What shall we say then? *Is* the law [5]sin? °God forbid. Nay, I had [6]not °known [5]sin, °but [4]by the law: for I had [6]not °known °lust, °except the law had said, "**Thou shalt [6]not °covet.**"
g 8 But [5]sin, taking °occasion [4]by the commandment, °wrought [5]in me all manner of °concupiscence. For °without the law [5]sin °*was* °dead.
Z h 9 For I was alive [8]without the law once: but when the commandment °came,
i [5]sin °revived,
k and I died.
Z h 10 And the commandment, which *was ordained* °to °life,
i °I found *to be*
k °unto death.
Y g 11 For [5]sin, taking [8]occasion [4]by the commandment, °deceived me, and [4]by it slew *me*.
f 12 Wherefore °the law *is* holy, and the commandment holy, and °just, and good.

4 are become dead = were put to death. Gr. *thanatoō*. See Matt. 10. 21. Mark 13. 12. 2 Cor. 6. 9. 1 Pet. 3. 18.
the law. Cp. 2. 12–14.
by. Ap. 104. v. 1.
the body: i. e. the crucified body, not the body of Christ mystical (Eph. 1. 23).
Christ. Ap. 98. IX.
that = to the end (Ap. 104. vi) that.
raised. Ap. 178. I. 4.
from the dead. Gr. *ek nekrōn*. Ap. 139. 3. Cp. 4. 24.
that = in order that. Gr. *hina*.
should = may.
unto = to.
God. Ap. 98. I. i. 1. No analogy here with the persons in the illustration. There the husband is dead. The law is not dead. But we have died to its claims. See 3. 19; 6. 14. Gal. 3. 23, 24.
5 in the flesh. Cp. 1. 3; 2. 28; 8. 8, 9.
in. Ap. 104. viii.
motions of sins = sinful passions (emphasis on "sinful"). Fig. *Antimereia*, Ap. 6.
motions. Gr. *pathēma*. Usually transl. sufferings, afflictions. See 8. 18. 2 Cor. 1. 5, 6, 7. Gal. 5. 24. Phil. 3. 10. Col. 1. 24. 2 Tim. 3. 11. Heb. 2. 9, 10; 10. 32. 1 Pet. 1. 11; 4. 13; 5. 1, 9.
sins. Ap. 128. I. ii. 1.
were = were (called out).
the law. I. e. the Mosaic Law.
to. Gr. *eis*. Ap. 104. vi.
6 delivered. Gr. *katargeō*. See *v.* 2.
that . . . held = having died (to that) in which we were held.
wherein = in (Ap. 104. viii) which.
that = so that.
serve. Ap. 190. III. 2. Cp. 6. 6.
newness. See 6. 4.
spirit. Ap. 101. II. 5.
not. Ap. 105. I.
oldness. Gr. *palaiotēs*. Only here. We now serve, not, as in our old nature, the letter of the Law, but, following the new nature, on a new and different principle. Cp. 2. 29. 2 Cor. 3. 6.

7. 7-25 (*O*, p. 1671). SIN IS IN US THOUGH WE HAVE RISEN WITH CHRIST. (*Introversion.*)

O | W | 7–12. The Law. Its conflict with the old nature.
  X | 13–16. Manifestation of the Law in the conscience. (The consent.)
  X | 17–20. Manifestation of the Law in the experience and the life. (The doing.
  W | 21–25. The Law. Its conflict with the new nature.

7. 7-12 (W, above). THE LAW. ITS CONFLICT WITH THE OLD NATURE.
(*Introversion and Extended Alternation.*)

W | Y | f | 7. The Law not sin. (Negative).
  g | 8. Sin using the commandment as a point of attack.
  Z | h | 9–. Alive without sin.
   i | –9–. Revival of sin.
   k | –9. Result—death.
  Z | *h* | 10–. Commandment ordained for life.
   i | –10–. Discovery on account of sin.
   k | –10. Result—death.
 Y | *g* | 11. Sin using the commandment as a point of attack.
  f | 12. The Law holy. (Positive.)

7 What, &c. See 3. 5. **God forbid.** See 3. 4. **known.** Ap. 132. I. ii. **but.** Lit. if (Ap. 118. 2) not (Ap. 105. II). **known** = recognized (it as). Ap. 132. I. i. **lust** = desire, i. e. of the old nature. See John 8. 44. **except.** Same as "but". **covet.** Gr. *epithumeō*. Quoted here and 13. 9 from the Sept. of Ex. 20. 17. The word is used of any strong desire, and applies to the desires of the new nature as well as to those of the old. Cp. Gal. 5. 17. **8 occasion** = opportunity. Gr. *aphormē*. Here, *v.* 11. 2 Cor. 5. 12; 11. 12. Gal. 5. 13. 1 Tim. 5. 14. **wrought** = worked out. Gr. *katergazomai*; see 1. 27. **concupiscence.** Same as "lust", *v.* 7. **without** = apart from. Gr. *chōris*. *was* = is. **dead.** Ap. 139. **9 came.** Ap. 106. vii. **revived.** Gr. *anazaō*. Here, 14. 9. Luke 15. 24, 32. Rev. 20. 5. **10 to, unto.** Ap. 104. vi. **life.** Ap. 170. 1. **I found** = was itself found by me. **11 deceived.** Gr. *exapataō*. Here, 16. 18. 1 Cor. 3. 18. 2 Cor. 11. 3. 2 Thess. 2. 3. **12 the law** = the law indeed (Gr. *men*. Omitted by A.V. and R.V.). **just** = righteous. Ap. 191. 1.

X A 13 °Was then that which is good made death [4]unto me? [7]God forbid. °But [5]sin,[-4] that it might °appear [5]sin, °working death in me [4]by that which is good; [-4]that [5]sin [4]by the commandment might become °exceeding °sinful.

B l 14 For we [-7]know that the law is °spiritual:

m but I am °carnal, sold °under [5]sin.

B l 15 For that which I °do I °allow [6]not:

m for °what I °would, °that °do I [6]not; but what I hate, °that °do I.

A 16 °If then I [-15]do that which I [15]would [6]not, I °consent [4]unto the law that *it is* good.

X n 17 °Now then it is °no more I that [15-]do it, but °sin that °dwelleth [5]in me.

o 18 For I [-7]know that [5]in me (that is, [5]in my °flesh,) [17]dwelleth °no good thing:

p for °to will °is present with me;

p but *how* to °perform that which is good, °I find [6]not.

o 19 For the good that I [15]would I [-15]do [6]not: but the °evil which I [15]would [6]not, that I °do.

n 20 °Now [16]if I [-15]do that I [15]would [6]not, °it is [17]no more I that [15-]do it, but [5]sin that [17]dwelleth [5]in me.

W C 21 I find then °a law, that, when I [15]would [-15]do good, evil [18]is present with me.

D q 22 For I °delight in the law of [4]God °after the °inward [1]man:

r 23 But I °see [3]another law [5]in my members, °warring against the law of my mind, and °bringing me into captivity to the °law of [5]sin which is [5]in my members.

D q 24 °O °wretched [1]man that I am!

r who shall °deliver me °from °the body of this death?

25 °I thank [4]God °through °Jesus Christ our °Lord.

7. 13-16 (X, p. 1675). MANIFESTATION OF LAW IN THE CONSCIENCE. (*Introversion and Alternation.*)

X | A | 13. Manifestation of the evil of sin to the conscience.
  B | l | 14-. The law spiritual.
      m | -14. The man sinful.
  B | *l* | 15-. The will like-minded with the law.
      m | -15. The will like-minded with the man.
  A | 16. Consent of the will to the good in the law.

13 Was . . . made. Did, then, that which is good become. **But**=Nay!
appear=be seen to be. Ap. 106. i.
working=working out. See 1. 27.
in. Dat. case. No prep.
exceeding. Gr. *kath'* (Ap. 104. x. 2) *huperbolēn.*
sinful. Gr. *hamartōlos.* So transl. in Mark 8. 38, Luke 5. 8; 24. 7. Elsewhere, "sinner". Cp. Ap. 128. I.
14 spiritual. See 1. 11.
carnal. Gr. *sarkikos,* according to the Received Text (Ap. 94. VI), but the Critical Texts read *sarkinos* (cp. 2 Cor. 3. 3).
under. Ap. 104. xviii. 2.
15 do. Same as work, *vv.* 8, 13.
allow=approve. The same as know", *vv.* 1, -7.
what, &c.=not what I wish, this I practise.
would. Ap. 102. 1. Note the use of *thelō,* on the right side, seven times in *vv.* 15-21.
that . . . not=this do I practise (Gr. *prassō.* See 1. 32. John 5. 29).
that do I=this I do (Gr. *poieō*). There are three Gk. words in this verse for "do". The first is *katergazomai,* work out, in *vv.* 8, 13, 15, 17, 18, 20. The second is *prassō,* practise, in *vv.* 15, 19, and the third *poieō,* do, in *vv.* 15, 16, 19, 20, 21.
16 If . . . not=But if what I do not wish, this I do.
If. Ap. 118. 2. c.
consent. Gr. *sumphēmi.* Only here.

7. 17-20 (*X*, p. 1675). MANIFESTATION OF THE LAW IN THE EXPERIENCE AND THE LIFE (*Introversion.*)

X | n | 17. No more I myself that do evil, but sin that dwelleth in me.
  o | 18-. No good in me as to my flesh.
    p | -18-. Will favours the good, but has no ability.
    p | -18. Will favours the good, but it is not performed.
  o | 19. Evil is what is performed as to my flesh.
  n | 20. No more I myself that do evil, but sin that dwelleth in me.

17 Now then=But now. **no more**=no longer. Gr. *ouketi.* **sin . . . me**=the indwelling sin (Ap. 128. I. ii. 1). **dwelleth.** Gr. *oikeō.* Here, *vv.* 18, 20; 8. 9, 11-. 1 Cor. 3. 16; 7. 12, 13. 1 Tim. 6. 16. **18 flesh.** I. e. old nature. **no**=not. Ap. 105. I. **to will.** Same as "would", *vv.* 15, 16, 19, 20, 21. **is present.** Gr. *parakeimai,* to be at hand. Only here and *v.* 21. **perform.** Same as "work", *v.* 13, and "do-", *v.* 15. **I find.** The texts read (is) "not" (present). **19 evil.** Ap. 128. III. 2. **do**=practise. Gr. *prassō.* As *v.* -15-. **20 Now, &c.**=But if what I do not myself wish, this I do. **it is, &c.**=no longer I myself (emph.).

7. 21-25 (*W*, p. 1675). THE LAW. ITS CONFLICT WITH THE NEW NATURE. (*Introversion and Alternation.*)

W | C | 21. Two opposing principles in the one man.
  D | q | 22. Delight in God's law.
      r | 23. Conflict.
  D | *q* | 24-. Distress at sin's law.
      r | -24, 25-. Deliverance.
  C | -25. Two opposing services continued in the one man.

21 a law, &c.=the law with me who wish. **22 delight.** Gr. *sunēdomai.* Only here. Cp. Ps. 1. 2; 112. 1; 119. 35 (Sept.). **after.** Ap. 104. x. 2. **inward.** Gr. *esō.* Adverb used as Adjective. Cp. 2 Cor. 4. 16. Eph. 3. 16. 1 Pet. 3. 4. **23 see.** Ap. 133. I. 5. **warring against.** Gr. *antistrateuomai.* Only here. **bringing . . . into captivity**=(seeking to) lead captive. Gr. *aichmalōtizō.* Only here. Luke 21. 24. 2 Cor. 10. 5. 2 Tim. 3. 6. The kindred verb, *aichmalōteuō,* only in Eph. 4. 8. **law of sin**: i. e. the old nature. **24 O.** Omit. This exclamation is an instance of Fig. *Ecphonēsis.* Ap. 6. **wretched.** Gr. *talaipōros.* Only here and Rev. 3. 17. Cp. *talaipōria,* misery, 3. 16. Jas. 5. 1; and the verb *talaipōreō,* only in Jas. 4. 9. **deliver**=rescue. See first occ. Matt. 6. 13. Gr. *rhuomai.* **from.** Gr. *ek.* Ap. 104. vii. **the body of this death.** The body of sin. Cp. *v.* 13; 6. 6; 8. 13. **25 I thank.** Gr. *eucharisteō.* See Acts 27. 35. The texts read "Thanks". Cp. 6. 17. Supply the *Ellipsis* (Ap. 6), He will deliver me. **through.** Ap. 104. v. 1. **Jesus Christ.** Ap. 98. XI. **Lord.** Ap. 98. VI. i. β. 2. A.

C So then with the °mind I myself [6]serve the law of [4]God; but with the flesh the law of [5]sin.

N E s **8** *There is* therefore now °no °condemnation to them which are °in °Christ Jesus, °who walk not after the flesh, but after the Spirit.

t 2 For °the law of the °Spirit of °life [1]in [1]Christ Jesus °hath made me free °from the law of °sin and death.

s 3 For °what the law could not do, [1]in that it was °weak °through the flesh, °God °sending His own °Son [1]in the °likeness of °sinful flesh, and °for [2]sin, °condemned [2]sin [1]in the °flesh:

t 4 °That the °righteousness of the law might be °fulfilled [1]in us, who walk °not °after the °flesh, but °after the [2]Spirit.

F u 5 For they that °are [4]after the [4]flesh °do mind the things of the [4]flesh; but they that °are [4]after the [2]Spirit the things of the [2]Spirit.

6 For °to be °carnally minded °*is* [2]death; but °to be spiritually minded °*is* [2]life and °peace.

7 Because the °carnal mind *is* °enmity °against [3]God: for °it is °not subject to the law of [3]God, °neither indeed can be.

v 8 °So then they that are [1]in the [4]flesh °cannot please [3]God.

w 9 But ye are [7]not [1]in the [4]flesh, but [1]in the [2]Spirit, °if so be that the [2]Spirit of [3]God °dwell [1]in you.

x °Now °if °any man have [7]not °the [2]Spirit of °Christ, he is °none of His.

x 10 °And [9]if [9]Christ *be* [1]in you, the °body *is* °dead °because of [2]sin; but the [2]Spirit *is* [2]life °because of °righteousness.

mind = mind (the new nature) indeed. This is the experience of every one who is the subject of the grace of God, and has received the gift of the new nature as the sign of God's justification. Not the experience of one man in two successive stages, but the co-existence of the two experiences in the one man at the same time. See *The Church Epistles*, by E. W. Bullinger, D.D., p. 64.

8. 1-39 (*N*, p. 1671). NO CONDEMNATION FOR THE NEW MAN. (*Introversion.*)

N | E | 1-4. "No condemnation" for those who are in Christ; and the reason.
F | 5-15. Spirit (the new nature) in us; now leading us.
F | 16-27. The Holy Spirit's witness with our "spirit", or new nature; leading it.
E | 28-39. "No separation" from Christ; secured for those who are in Christ; and the reason.

8. 1-4 (E, above). NO CONDEMNATION; AND THE REASON. (*Alternation.*)

E | s | 1. No condemnation to those in Christ.
t | 2. Reason. The law of the "spirit" (or new nature) sets us free from the claims of the law.
s | 3. Condemnation of sin in the flesh (or old nature) by God sending His Son in the likeness of sinful flesh.
t | 4. Result. The law of the "spirit" (or new nature) fulfils the righteous requirements of the law.

8. 1 no. Gr. *oudeis*. Emphatic, as it stands first in the Gr.
condemnation. Gr. *katakrima*. See 5. 16.
in. Ap. 104. viii.
Christ Jesus. Ap. 98. XII. Cp. 6. 23.
who ... Spirit. All the texts omit. Probably a gloss from *v.* 4.
2 the ... life = the spiritual law of life. Fig. *Antimereia*. Ap. 6.
Spirit. Ap. 101. II. 5.
life. Ap. 170. 1.
hath made me free = freed me. Gr. *eleutheroō*. See 6. 18.
from. Ap. 104. iv.
sin. Ap. 128. I. ii. 1.

3 what, &c. Lit. the impossible thing of the law. **weak** = impotent. Gr. *astheneō*. **through.** Ap. 104. v. 1. **God.** Ap. 98. I. i. 1. **sending** = having sent. Ap. 174. 4. Cp. John 17. 3. **Son.** Ap. 108. iii. **likeness.** See 1. 23; 6. 5. *Not sinful flesh*, for "in Him was no sin"; *nor the likeness of flesh*, because His was real flesh, but the *likeness of sin's flesh*. **sinful flesh** = flesh of sin (*v.* 3). , **for.** Ap. 104. xiii. 1. **condemned.** Ap. 122. 7. **flesh.** By the perfect humanity and perfect walk of the Incarnate Son, God exhibited a *living* condemnation of sinful flesh. **4 That** = In order that. Gr. *hina*. **righteousness** = righteous requirement. Ap. 191. 4. **fulfilled.** Ap. 125. 7. **not.** Ap. 105. II. **after.** Ap. 104. X. 2. **flesh** = the old nature.

8. 5-15 (F, above). THE SPIRIT OR NEW NATURE IN US. NOW LEADING US. (*Introversion.*)

F | u | 5-7. The carnal mind is death; the spiritual mind is life.
v | 8. Those who are in the flesh (old nature) cannot please God.
w | 9-. We are not in the flesh if Divine *pneuma* (the new nature) dwells in us.
x | -9. If *pneuma Christou* (the new nature) be not in us, we are not His.
x | 10. If Christ be thus in us, then, though the body is mortal,
w | 11. Our flesh is to be raised from the dead if Divine *pneuma* (the new nature) dwells in us.
v | 12. Those who are not debtors to the flesh (the old nature) can please God.
u | 13-15. The carnal to be reckoned as dead; then we live unto God, and are led by His Spirit as His sons.

5 are: i. e. live. **do mind** = set affection on. Gr. *phroneō*. Occ. ten times in Rom.; here, 12. 3, 3; 12. 16, 16; 14. 6, 6, 6, 6; 15. 5. Cp. Col. 3. 2. **6 to be, &c.** = the minding (Gr. *phronēma*. Only here and *v.* 7 27) of the flesh. ***is***: i. e. results in. **to be spiritually, &c.** = the minding of the spirit (Ap. 101. II. 5 as in *v.* 2). Cp. Phil. 4. 8, 9. Col. 3. 2. **peace.** Cp. 5. 1. **7 carnal mind** = minding of the flesh, as *v.* 6. **enmity.** Gr. *echthra*. Here, Luke 23. 12. Gal. 5. 20. Eph. 2. 15, 16. Jas. 4. 4. **against.** Ap. 104. vi. **it is not subject to** = does not submit itself to. Gr. *hupotassō*. See 10. 3. **not.** Ap. 105. I. **neither.** Gr. *oude*. **8 So, &c.** Cp. 7. 15-17. Gal. 5. 17. **cannot** = are not (*v.* 7) able to. **9 if so be.** Gr. *eiper*. **if.** Ap. 118. 2. a. **dwell.** See 7. 17. **Now** = But. **any man** = any one. Ap. 123. 3. **the.** Omit. **Christ.** Ap. 98. IX. See also Ap. 101. II. 5. **none** = not. Ap. 104. I. **10 And** = But. **body** = body indeed (Gr. *men*). **dead.** Gr. *nekros*. Ap. 139. See 6. 11. **because of.** Ap. 104. v. 2. **righteousness.** Ap. 191. 3.

w **11** But [9]if the [2]Spirit of Him That °raised up
°Jesus °from the dead [9]dwell [1]in you, He That
°raised up [9]Christ °from the dead shall °also
°quicken your °mortal bodies °by His [2]Spirit
That °dwelleth [1]in you.

v **12** °Therefore, brethren, we are °debtors, [7]not
to the [4]flesh, to live [4]after the [4]flesh.

u **13** For [9]if ye live [4]after the [4]flesh, ye °shall
die: but [9]if ye °through the [2]Spirit °do mortify the °deeds of the body, ye shall live.
14 For as many as are °led by °the [2]Spirit of
[3]God, they are the [3]sons of [3]God.
15 For ye °have [7]not received °the °spirit of
°bondage again °to fear; but ye °have received
°the °Spirit of °adoption, °whereby we cry,
°"Abba, Father."

F y **16** The °Spirit Itself °beareth witness with
our [2]spirit, that we are the °children of [3]God:
17 And [9]if [16]children, °then °heirs; °heirs of
[3]God, and °joint-heirs with [9]Christ; [9]if so be
that we °suffer with *Him*, [4]that we may be
°also glorified together.
18 For I °reckon that the °sufferings of °this
present time *are* [7]not worthy *to be compared*
°with the glory which [13]shall be °revealed °in
us.

z **19** For the °earnest expectation of the °creature °waiteth for the °manifestation of the
[3]sons of [3]God.
20 °For the [19]creature was made [7]subject to
°vanity, [7]not °willingly, but °by reason of Him
Who hath [7]subjected *the same* °in °hope,
21 Because the [19]creature itself also shall be
°delivered [2]from the [15]bondage of °corruption
°into the °glorious liberty of the [16]children of
[3]God.

z **22** For we °know that the whole [19]creation
°groaneth and °travaileth in pain together until now.
23 And [7]not only *they*, but ourselves also,
which have the °firstfruits of the [16]Spirit, even
we ourselves °groan °within ourselves, [19]waiting for the [15]adoption, *to wit*, [10]the °redemption of our body.
24 For we °are saved °by °hope: but °hope
that is °seen is [7]not °hope: for what °a man
°seeth, why doth he °yet hope for?

11 raised up. See 4. 24.
Jesus. Ap. 98. X.
from the dead. Gr. *ek nekrōn.* Ap. 139. 3.
also, &c. = quicken (Gr. *zōopoieō.* See 4. 17) your mortal (see 6. 12) bodies also.
by. Ap. 104. v. 1.
dwelleth = indwelleth. Gr. *enoikeō.* Cp. *v.* 7.
12 Therefore = So then.
debtors. Gr. *opheiletēs,* as 1. 14; 15. 27.
13 shall die. Lit. are about to die. R.V., must die.
through. Dat. case. No prep.
do mortify = are putting to death. Gr. *thanatoō.* See 7. 4.
deeds = practices. Gr. *praxis.* Occ. 12. 4. Matt. 16. 27. Luke 23. 51. Acts 19. 18. Col. 3. 9.
14 led. See 2. 4.
the Spirit. See Ap. 101. II. 5. In this chapter we have *pneuma Christou* and *pneuma Theou,* both referring to the new nature.
15 have. Omit. **the** = a.
spirit. Ap. 101. II. 7.
bondage. Ap. 190. II. 2.
to. Gr. *eis.* Ap. 104. vi.
adoption = sonship. Gr. *huiothesia.* Occ. here, *v.* 23; 9. 4. Gal. 4. 5. Eph. 1. 5. An "adopted" child may partake of all the privileges of the family, yet it is not begotten and born in the family. But the subjects of this verse are *begotten* of the Spirit (John 3. 6) and are, therefore, *sons of God* by spiritual generation. It is thus a real sonship-spirit that enables them to cry, "Abba, Father."
whereby = in (Ap. 104. viii) which.
Abba: i. e. Father. See Ap. 94. III. 3 (Heb. *'ab*). It is said that slaves were never allowed to use the word "Abba". Strictly, therefore, it can be employed only by those who have received the gift of the Divine nature.

8. 16-27 (*F*, p. 1677). THE HOLY SPIRIT'S WORK IN US: LEADING THE NEW NATURE.
(*Introversion.*)

F | y | 16-18. The Holy Spirit's witness with the new nature as to our *standing* as the sons of God.
 | z | 19-21. Creation waiting to share the coming glory of this manifestation of the liberty of the glory.
 | z | 22-25. Creation uniting its groaning with ours waiting for the manifestation of our resurrection glory.
 | y | 26, 27. The Holy Spirit Himself helping our infirmities owing to our *state*, by His intercessions.

16 Spirit Itself = Spirit Himself. Ap. 101. II. 3.
beareth witness. See 2. 15.
children. Ap. 108. i. See note 2, p. 1511.
17 then heirs = heirs also. **heirs.** See 4. 13.
heirs of God = heirs indeed of God.
joint-heirs. Gr. *sunklēronomos.* Here, Eph. 3. 6. Heb. 11. 9. 1 Pet. 3. 7. **suffer with.** Gr. *sumpaschō.* Only here and 1 Cor. 12. 26. The "suffering together with" (Him) here is that of 6. 3, 4, 6, 8, 11, and not the sufferings of this present time. **also . . . together** = glorified together with (Gr. *sundoxazomai.* Only here) (Him) also. **18 reckon.** See 4. 4. **sufferings.** Gr. *pathēma.* See 7. 5. **this present time.** Lit. the now time or season (Gr. *kairos*). **with.** Ap. 104. xv. 3. **revealed.** Ap. 106. I. ix. **in** = unto or with regard to. Ap. 104. vi. **19 earnest expectation** = anxious looking with outstretched head. Gr. *apokaradokia.* Only here and Phil. 1. 20. **creature** = creation. **waiteth for.** Gr. *apekdechomai.* Occ. here, *vv.* 23, 25. 1 Cor. 1. 7. Gal. 5. 5. Phil. 3. 20. Heb. 9. 28. **manifestation.** Ap. 106. II. 1. **20 For, &c.** This verse is in parenthesis, save the last two words. **vanity.** Gr. *mataiotēs.* Only here, Eph. 4. 17. 2 Pet. 2. 18. Here the meaning is disappointing misery, in which sense the word is frequently used by the Sept. for the Heb. *hebel,* e. g. Eccles. 1. 14; 2. 11, 17; 9. 9. **willingly.** Gr. *hekōn.* Only here and 1 Cor. 9. 17. **by reason of.** Gr. *dia.* Ap. 104. v. 2. **in hope.** Read, (waiteth, I say) in hope (see 4. 18). **in.** Ap. 104. ix. 2. **21 delivered** = set free, as in *v.* 2. **corruption.** Gr. *phthora.* Here, 1 Cor. 15. 42, 50. Gal. 6. 8. Col. 2. 22. 2 Pet. 1. 4; 2. 12, 19. **into.** Ap. 104. vi. **glorious liberty** = freedom of the glory. **22 know.** Ap. 132. I. i. **groaneth** = is groaning together. Gr. *sustenazō.* Only here. **travaileth . . . together** = travails together. Gr. *sunōdinō.* Only here. **23 firstfruits of the Spirit.** The gifts of the Holy Spirit as the foretaste and pledge of the eternal inheritance. Cp. Eph. 1. 14. Heb. 6. 5. See Ex. 23. 19. Lev. 23. 10, &c. **firstfruits.** Gr. *aparchē.* Occ. here, 11. 16; 16. 5. 1 Cor. 15. 20, 23; 16. 15. Jas. 1. 18. Rev. 14. 4. **groan.** Gr. *stenazō.* Here, Mark 7. 34. 2 Cor. 5. 2, 4. Heb. 13. 17. Jas. 5. 9. Cp. *v.* 21. **within.** Ap. 104. viii. **redemption.** See 3. 24. **24 are** = were. See 5. 9. **by.** Dat. case. No prep. **hope.** The creation also is waiting and hoping. **seen, seeth.** Ap. 133. I. 5. **a man** = any one, as *v.* 9. **yet hope for** = hope for also.

25 But °[9]if we hope for that we [24]see °[7]not, *then* do we °with °patience [19]wait for *it.*

y **26** Likewise the [16]Spirit also °helpeth our °infirmities: for we [22]know [7]not what we should °pray for as we ought: but the [16]Spirit Itself °maketh intercession °for us °with °groanings °which cannot be uttered.

27 °And °He That °searcheth the hearts [22]knoweth what *is* the °mind of the [16]Spirit, because He °maketh intercession °for the °saints °according to *the will of* [3]God.

E G¹ a **28** °And we [22]know that all things °work together °for good to them that °love [3]God, to them who are the called [27]according to *His* °purpose.

b **29** For whom He °did foreknow, He °also did °predestinate *to be* °conformed to the °image of His [3]Son, °that He might be °the firstborn °among many °brethren.

30 °Moreover whom He did [29]predestinate, them He °also called: and whom He called, them He °also justified: and whom He justified, them He °also glorified.

b **31** °What shall we then say °to these things? [9]If [3]God °*be* [27]for us, who °*can be* °against us?

32 He that °spared [7]not His own [3]Son, but °delivered Him up [27]for us all,

a how shall He °not °with Him also °freely give us all things?

G² c **33** Who shall °lay any thing °to the charge of [3]God's elect? °*It is* [3]God That [30]justifieth;

d **34** Who *is* he that [3]condemneth? *It is* [9]Christ That died, yea rather, That [11]is risen again, Who is °even °at the right hand of [3]God, Who °also [27]maketh intercession [27]for us.

d **35** Who shall °separate us [2]from the °love of [9]Christ? *shall* °tribulation, or °distress, or °persecution, or famine, or nakedness or °peril, or sword?

---

25 with=through. Ap. 104. v. 1.
patience. See 2. 7.
26 helpeth. Gr. *sunantilambanomai.* Only here and Luke 10. 40.
infirmities. The texts read infirmity. Gr. *astheneia.* See 6. 19. John 11. 4.
pray for. Gr. *proseuchomai.* See Ap. 134. I. 2.
maketh intercession. Gr. *huperentunchanō.* Only here.
for us. All the texts omit.
with. No prep.
groanings. Gr. *stenagmos.* Only here and Acts 7. 34.
which . . . uttered=unutterable. Gr. *alalētos.* Only here.
27 And=But.
He: i. e. the Holy Spirit.
searcheth. Gr. *ereunaō.* See John 5. 39 and 1 Cor. 2. 10.
mind. Gr. *phronēma*, as vv. 6, 7.
maketh intercession. Gr. *entunchanō.* See Acts 25. 24.
for. Ap. 104. xvii. 1.
saints. See 1. 7.
according to. Ap. 104. x. 2.

8. 28-39 (*E*, p. 1677). "NO SEPARATION" FROM CHRIST SECURED FOR THOSE WHO ARE IN CHRIST. THE REASON. (*Division.*)

E | G¹ | 28-32. Secured by God's *purpose*, as affecting our *standing.*
| G² | 33-39. Secured by God's *love*, as affecting our *state.*

8. 28-32 (G¹, above). SECURED BY GOD'S PURPOSE, AS AFFECTING OUR STANDING. (*Introversion.*)

G¹ | a | 28. God's purpose in *working* "all things" for good to His people.
| b | 29, 30. God's purpose in conforming us to His Son.
| *b* | 31, 32-. God's purpose in conforming His Son for us.
| *a* | -32. God's purpose in *giving* "all things" with His Son.

28 And=But.
work together. Gr. *sunergeō.* Only here, Mark 16. 20. 1 Cor. 16. 16. 2 Cor. 6. 1. Jas. 2. 22.
for. Ap. 104. vi.
love. Gr. *agapaō.* Ap. 135. I. 1.
purpose. Gr. *prothesis.* See Acts 11. 23.

29 did foreknow=foreknew. Gr. *proginōskō.* Ap. 132. I. iv. **also did predestinate**=foreordained (Gr. *proorizō.* See Acts 4. 28) also. **conformed.** Gr. *summorphos.* Only here and Phil. 3. 21. Cp. Phil. 3. 10. **image.** See 1. 23. **that He might be.** Lit. unto (Ap. 104. vi) His being. **the firstborn.** Gr. *prōtotokos.* Here, Matt. 1. 25. Luke 2. 7. Col. 1. 15, 18. Heb. 1. 6; 11. 28; 12. 23. Rev. 1. 5 (firstborn of the dead). Cp. Acts 13. 33. Col. 1. 18 **among.** Ap. 104. viii. 2. **brethren.** Cp. Heb. 2. 11, 12. **30 Moreover**=But. **also called**=called also. See 1 Cor. 1. 9. **also justified**=justified (Ap. 191. 2) also. Cp. 2. 13. **also glorified**=glorified (see 1. 21) also. In this beautiful *Climax* (Ap. 6), by another Fig. (*Heterosis* of Tenses, Ap. 6) the called ones are spoken of as already (in the Divine purpose) in Christ, justified, and glorified! **31 What, &c.** See 3. 5. **to.** Ap. 104. xv. 3. *be*=*is.* *can be*=*is.* **against.** Ap. 104. x. 1. **32 spared.** Gr. *pheidomai.* See Acts 20. 29. **delivered . . . up** See John 19. 30. **not.** Ap. 105. I. (*a*). **with.** Ap. 104. xvi. **freely give.** Ap. 184. II. 1.

8. 33-39 (G², above). SECURED BY GOD'S LOVE, AS AFFECTING OUR STATE. (*Introversion.*)

G² | c | 33. God's love in securing us against all who would *accuse.*
| d | 34. Christ's love (manifested in death and resurrection) securing us against all who would *condemn.*
| *d* | 35-37. Christ's love (thus manifested by Him that loved us) securing us against all separation arising from the *operations* of *things.*
| *c* | 38,.39. God's love in Christ in securing us against all separation from the *nature* of *things.*

33 lay any thing=bring charges, i. e. call to judicial account. Gr. *enkaleō.* See Acts 19. 38. **to the charge of.** Ap. 104. x. 1. *It* . . . **justifieth**=Shall God Who justifies (them)? **34** *It is*=*Shall.* **even**=also. **at.** Ap. 104. viii. **also, &c.**=intercedes also. **35 separate.** Gr. *chōrizō.* See Acts 18. 1. **love.** Ap. 135. II. 1. Cp. 5. 5. 2 Cor. 5. 14. **tribulation.** See 2. 9. **distress.** Rendered "anguish" in 2. 9. **persecution.** See Acts 8. 1. **peril.** Gr. *kindunos.* Only here and 2 Cor. 11. 26. These four questions and answers in *vv.* 33-35 form the Fig. *Anaphora.* *V.* 35 gives the Fig. *Paradiastolē.* See Ap. 6.

36 ° As it is ° written, ° "**For Thy sake we are killed all the day long; we are ° accounted as ° sheep ° for the slaughter.**"

37 Nay, [1]in all these things we are ° more than conquerors [3]through Him That [28]loved us.

38 For I am ° persuaded, that ° neither death, ° nor [2]life, ° nor angels, ° nor principalities, ° nor ° powers, ° nor things ° present, ° nor things to come,

39 [38]Nor ° height, [38]nor depth, [38]nor any other ° creature, shall be able to [35]separate us [2]from the [35]love of [3]God, which is [1]in [1]Christ Jesus our ° Lord.

L H e 9 I say the truth ° in ° Christ, I lie ° not, my conscience also ° bearing me witness ° in ° the Holy Ghost,

2 That I have great ° heaviness and ° continual ° sorrow in my heart.

3 For I ° could ° wish that myself were ° accursed ° from ° Christ ° for my brethren, my kinsmen ° according to the flesh:

f 4 Who are Israelites; ° to whom *pertaineth* the ° adoption, and the ° glory, and the ° covenants, and the ° giving of the law, and the ° service *of God*, and the promises;

f 5 Whose *are* the fathers,

e and ° of whom ° as concerning the flesh [3]Christ *came*, Who is ° over ° all, ° God ° blessed ° for ever. Amen.

L P 6 [1]Not as though the ° word of ° God hath ° taken none effect. For they *are* [1]not all Israel, which are [5]of Israel:

Q g 7 ° Neither, because they are the seed of Abraham, *are they* all ° children: but, [1]"**In Isaac shall thy seed be called.**"

8 That is, They which are the [7]children of the flesh, these *are* [1]not the [7]children of [6]God:

36 As=Even as. Ap. 6.
written. See 1. 17.
For Thy sake=On Thine account.
accounted. See 4. 5.
sheep, &c. Quoted from Ps. 44. 22.
for the=of.
37 more than conquerors. Gr. *hupernikaō*; only here.
38 persuaded. Cp. 2. 8 (obey). Ap. 150. I. 2.
neither, nor. Gr. *oute.*
principalities. Gr. *archē.* See Eph. 6. 12.
powers. Ap. 172. 1 and 176. 1.
present. Gr. *enistēmi.* Elsewhere, 1 Cor. 3. 22; 7. 26. Gal. 1. 4. 2 Thess. 2. 2. 2 Tim. 3. 1. Heb. 9. 9.
39 height. Gr. *hupsōma*; only here and 2 Cor. 10. 5.
creature=created thing. See *v.* 21.
Lord. Ap. 98. VI. i. β. 2. A. The question in *v.* 35, followed by the answer in *vv.* 38, 39, is a striking example of the Fig. *Paradiastolē.* Ap. 6. These *vv.* illustrate the importance also of the number 17, as there are seven things enumerated in *v.* 35, "tribulation", &c., and ten in *vv.* 38, 39, "neither death", &c. See Ap. 10. Cp. another illustration of the number 17 in Heb. 12. 18–24. See Ap. 10.

9. 1—11. 36 (*L*, p. 1661). DISPENSATIONAL.
(*Introversion and Division.*)

L | H | 9. 1-5. Paul's sorrow regarding Israel's failure.
  K | L | 9. 6-13. God's purpose had respect only to a portion.
    M | 9. 14-29. God's purpose regarded only a remnant.
      N | O[1] | 9. 30-33. Israel's failure in spite of the Prophets.
        O[2] | 10. 1-13. Israel's failure in spite of the Law.
        O[3] | 10. 14-21. Israel's failure in spite of the Gospel.
  K | *M* | 11. 1-10. God's purpose regarding the remnant accomplished.
    L | 11. 11-32. God's purpose will ultimately embrace the whole.
H | 11. 33-36. Paul's joy regarding God's purpose.

9. 1-5 (H, above). PAUL'S SORROW REGARDING ISRAEL'S FAILURE. (*Introversion.*)

H | e | 1-3. Paul's kinship to Israel according to flesh (*kata sarka*). His former wish to be accursed, and his present sorrow.
  f | 4. What belongs to Israel.
  f | 5-. Who belong to Israel.
e | -5. Christ's kinship to Israel according to flesh (*kata sarka*). His eternal existence as God over all, blessed for ever.

9. 1 in. Gr. *en.* Ap. 104. viii. **Christ.** Ap. 98. IX. **not.** Ap. 105. I. **bearing . . . witness.** See 2. 15. **the Holy Ghost.** Ap. 101. II. 14. **2 heaviness**=sorrow. **continual.** Gr. *adialeiptos.* Only here and 2 Tim. 1. 3. **sorrow**=pangs. Gr. *odunē.* Only here and 1 Tim. 6. 10. **3 could**=used to. Fig. *Anamnēsis.* Ap. 6. **wish.** Ap. 134. I. 1. **accursed.** See Acts 23. 14. **from.** Gr. *apo.* Ap. 104. iv. **Christ**=the Christ. See *v.* 1. The words in *v.* 3 "For I" to "Christ" are in a parenthesis. Fig. *Epitrechon.* Ap. 6. **for.** Gr. *huper.* Ap. 104. xvii. 1. **according to.** Gr. *kata.* Ap. 104. x. 2. The sorrow was on behalf of his brethren. **4 to whom, &c.**=whose are. **adoption.** See 8. 15. **glory.** See p. 1511. **covenants.** See Matt. 26. 28. **giving, &c.** Gr. *nomothesia.* Only here. **service.** Ap. 190. II. 3. **5 of.** Gr. *ek.* Ap. 104. vii. **as, &c.** Read "is the Christ as to the flesh". **as concerning.** Same as according to, *v.* 3. **over.** Gr. *epi.* Ap. 104. ix. 1. **all.** Cp. John 17. 2. 1 Cor. 15. 27, 28. Col. 1. 16–19; 2. 9. **God.** Ap. 98. I. i. 2. **blessed.** See 1. 25. **for ever.** Ap. 151. II. A. ii. 7. a. This is an example of the Fig. *Anamnēsis.* Ap. 6. Note the seven privileges of Paul's people in *v.* 4. Ap. 10. To account for various readings, the R.V. sometimes appeals in the margin to ancient authorities, meaning Greek MSS., &c., but here, and here only, *modern interpreters* are allowed to introduce, by varying punctuation, devices for destroying this emphatic testimony to the Deity of the Lord. See Ap. 94. V. i. 3.

9. 6-13 (L, above). GOD'S PURPOSE HAD RESPECT ONLY TO A PORTION.
(*Introversion and Alternation.*)

L | P | 6. The word of God not having failed.
  Q | g | 7, 8. Election of seed. Different mothers.
    h | 9. The promise.
  Q | *g* | 10, 11. Election of seed. Same mother.
    h | 12. The prophecy.
P | 13. The word of God confirmed.

6 word. Gr. *logos.* Ap. 121. 10. **God.** Ap. 98. I. i. 1. **taken, &c.** Lit. fallen out=failed. Cp. 1 Cor. 13. 8. **7 Neither.** Gr. *oude.* **children.** Gr. *teknon.* Ap. 108. i.

but the [7]children of the promise are °counted °for the seed.

h 9 For this *is* the [6]word of promise, °"**At this time will I come, and Sarah shall have a °son.**"

Q g 10 And [1]not only *this;* but when Rebecca also had conceived °by one, *even* °by our father Isaac;

11 (For *the children* being °not yet born, °neither having done any good or °evil, °that the °purpose of [6]God [3]according to election might °stand, [1]not [5]of works, but [5]of Him That calleth;)

h 12 It was said °unto her, "**The °elder shall °serve the °younger.**"

P 13 As it is written, "**Jacob °have I °loved, but Esau °have I hated.**"

M R i 14 °What shall we say then? *Is there* °unrighteousness °with [6]God? °God forbid.

15 For He saith to Moses, "**I will °have mercy on whom I °will °have mercy, and I will °have compassion on whom I °will °have compassion.**"

16 So then *it is* [1]not of him that °willeth, °nor of him that runneth, but of [6]God That sheweth [15]mercy.

k 17 For the Scripture saith [12]unto Pharaoh, "**Even [8]for this same °purpose have I °raised thee up, that I might °shew My °power [1]in thee, and that My name might be °declared °throughout all the °earth.**"

18 Therefore hath He [15]mercy on whom He [16]will *have mercy,* and whom He [16]will He °hardeneth.

S 19 Thou wilt say then [12]unto me, "Why doth He yet °find fault? For who hath resisted His °will?"

20 Nay but, O °man, who art thou that °repliest against [6]God? °"**Shall the °thing formed say to him that °formed *it* 'Why hast thou made me thus?'**"

21 Hath [1]not the potter °power °over the °clay, [5]of the same °lump to make one vessel °unto honour, and another °unto °dishonour?

S 22 *What* °if [6]God, [16]willing to [17]shew *His* wrath, and to make His °power known, endured °with much longsuffering °the vessels of wrath °fitted °to °destruction:

23 And [11]that He might make known the °riches of His [4]glory °on [22]the vessels of mercy, which He had °afore prepared [21]unto [4]glory,

24 °Even us, whom He hath called, [1]not [5]of the Jews only, but also [5]of the Gentiles?

R k 25 As He saith °also [1]in Osee, "**I will call them My °people, which were [1]not My °people; and her [13]beloved, which was [1]not [13]beloved.**

26 And it shall °come to pass, *that* [1]in the place where it was said [12]unto them, 'Ye *are* [1]not My [25]people;' there shall they be called the °children of the living [6]God."

8 counted. Gr. *logizomai.* See 2. 26.
for. Gr. *eis.* Ap. 104. vi.
9 At. Gr. *kata.* Ap. 104. x. 2.
son. Gr. *huios.* Ap. 108. iii. See Gen. 18. 14.
10 by. Gr. *ek.* Ap. 104. vii.
11 not. Gr. *mē.* Ap. 105. II.
neither. Gr. *mēde.*
evil. Gr. *kakos.* Ap. 128. III. 2.
that = in order that. Gr. *hina.*
purpose. Gr. *prothesis.* See Acts 11. 23.
stand = abide. Gr. *menō.* Only here transl. "stand". Cp. 1 Pet. 1. 23, 25.
12 unto = to. **elder** = greater.
serve. Gr. *douleuō.* Ap. 190. III. 2.
younger = less. See Gen. 25. 23.
13 have. Omit.
loved. Gr. *agapaō.* Ap. 135. I. 1. See Deut. 21. 15.

9. 14-29 (M, p. 1680). **GOD'S PURPOSE REGARDED ONLY A REMNANT.** (*Introversion.*)

M | R | i | 14–16. Divine election justified by Scripture.
k | 17, 18. Gentiles hardened for sake of Israel.
S | 19–21. Divine election not to be challenged.
S | 22–24. Divine election benevolent so far as man can apprehend.
R | *k* | 25, 26. Israel restored to supremacy over Gentiles.
i | 27–29. Divine election justified by Scripture.

14 What, &c. See 3. 5.
unrighteousness. Gr. *adikia.* Ap. 128. VII. 1.
with. Gr. *para.* Ap. 104. xii. 2.
God forbid. See Luke 20. 16.
15 have mercy = pity. **will.** Omit.
have compassion on = compassionate. Gr. *oikteirō.* Only here. Cp. 12. 1. See Ex. 33. 19.
16 willeth. Gr. *thelō.* Ap. 102. 1. Isaac willed, Esau ran.
nor. Gr. *oude.*
17 purpose. Lit. thing.
raised . . . up. Ap. 178. I. 6. The same word is used in the Sept. of 2 Sam. 12. 11.
shew. See 2. 15. **power.** Ap. 172. 1.
declared. See Luke 9. 60 (preach). Ap. 121. 6.
throughout. Ap. 104. viii.
earth. Ap. 129. 4. Quoted from Ex. 9. 16.
18 hardeneth. See Acts 19. 9. Cp. Ex. 4. 21.
19 find fault. Gr. *memphomai.* Only here, Mark 7. 2. Heb. 8. 8. **will.** Ap. 102. 4.
20 man. Ap. 123. 1.
repliest against. Gr. *antapokrinomai.* Only here and Luke 14. 6. Cp. Ap. 104. ii and 122. 3.
Shall. Question preceded by *me*, as *v.* 14.
thing formed. Gr. *plasma.* Only here.
formed. Gr. *plassō.* Only here and 1 Tim. 2. 13. Quoted from Isa. 45. 9.
21 power. Ap. 172. 5. **over** = of.
clay. See John 9. 6.
lump. Gr. *phurama.* Only here, 11. 16. 1 Cor. 5. 6, 7. Gal. 5. 9.
unto. Ap. 104. vi. Cp. Isa. 45. 9; 64. 8. Jer. 18. 1–6.
dishonour = not shame, but lack of honour.
22 if. Ap. 118. 2. a.
power. Gr. *to dunaton.*
with. Ap. 104. viii. **the.** Omit.
fitted = pieced up together, as a broken vessel. Ap. 125. 8.
to. Ap. 104. vi.
destruction = perdition, as in John 17. 12. From this is it not clear that in the resurrection the unjust come forth from the grave in the self-same bodies in which they entered it (John 5. 28, 29)?

23 riches. See 2. 4. **on.** Ap. 104. ix. 3. **afore prepared.** Gr. *proetoimazō.* Only here and Eph. 2. 10. **24 Even, &c.** = "Us whom He called . . . but of the Gentiles also?" **25 also, &c.** = in Hosea also. **people.** See Acts 2. 47. Quoted from Hos. 2. 23. Cp. 1 Pet. 2. 10. **26 come to pass** = be. **children.** Ap. 108. iii. Quoted from Hos. 1. 9, 10.

i 27 Esaias also crieth °concerning Israel,
°"**Though the number of the [26]children of**
Israel be as the sand of the sea, °**a** °**remnant**
shall be saved:
28 **For He will** °**finish the** °**work, and** °**cut *it***
short [1]**in** °**righteousness: because a short**
°**work will** °**the LORD make** °**upon the** [17]**earth.**"
29 And as Esaias said before, °"**Except** [28]**the**
LORD of °**Sabaoth had** °**left us a seed, we had**
been as Sodoma, and been made like unto
Gomorrha."

NO[1]l 30 [14]What shall we say then? That the
Gentiles, which followed °not after [28]right-
eousness, °have attained to [28]righteousness,
even the [28]righteousness which is [5]of °faith.

m 31 But Israel, which followed after °the law of
[28]righteousness, °hath [1]not °attained [22]to °the
law of [28]righteousness.
32 Wherefore? Because *they sought it* [1]not
[10]by [30]faith, but as it were [10]by the works °of
the law.

m For they °stumbled at that °stumblingstone;
33 As it is written, °"**Behold, I lay** [1]**in** °**Sion**
a [32]**stumblingstone and rock of** °**offence:**

l **and** °**whosoever** °**believeth on Him shall** [1]**not**
be °**ashamed.**"

O[2]n **10** Brethren, my heart's °desire and °prayer
°to °God °for °Israel is, °that they might
be saved.
2 For I °bear them record that they have
a zeal of [1]God, but °not °according to °know-
ledge.
3 For they being °ignorant of [1]God's °right-
eousness, and °going about to establish their
own °righteousness, have [2]not submitted themselves °unto the °righteousness of [1]God.

o 4 For °Christ *is* the end of the law °for
[3]righteousness to every one that °believeth.

n 5 For °Moses describeth the [3]righteousness
which is °of the law, that "**the** °**man which**
doeth those things shall live °**by them.**"
6 But the [3]righteousness which is [5]of °faith
speaketh on this wise, "**Say** °**not** °**in thine**
heart, 'Who shall °**ascend** °**into** °**heaven?'**"
(that is, to bring [4]Christ down *from above*:)
7 "**Or, 'Who shall descend** [6]**into the** °**deep?'**"
(that is, to bring up [4]Christ again °from the
dead.)
8 But what saith it? "**The** °**word is nigh thee,**
even [6]**in thy mouth, and** [6]**in thy heart:**" that
is, the °word of °faith, which we °preach;
9 That °if thou shalt confess °with thy
mouth °the °Lord °Jesus, and shalt °believe [6]in
thine heart that [1]God °hath °raised Him [7]from
the dead, thou shalt be saved.
10 For °with the heart °man [4]believeth °unto
[3]righteousness; and °with the mouth °con-
fession is made °unto salvation.

27 concerning = over. Ap. 104. xvii. 1.
Though. Ap. 118. 1. b. **a** = the.
remnant. Gr. *kataleimma.* Only here.
28 finish = close. Gr. *sunteleō.* See Acts 21. 27.
work = account. Gr. *logos.* Ap. 121. 10.
cut . . . short. Gr. *suntemnō.* Only here and next clause.
righteousness. Ap. 191. 3.
the Lord. Ap. 98. VI. i. *β.* 1. B. a.
upon. Ap. 104. ix. 1. Quoted almost verbatim from the Sept. of Isa. 10. 22, 23. Ap. 107. II. 3 (b).
29 Except = If (Ap. 118. 1. a) not (Ap. 105. II.)
Sabaoth = Hosts. Only here and Jas. 5. 4. First occ. 1 Sam. 1. 11. Quoted from Isa. 1. 9. Ap. 107. I. 3.
left. Gr. *enkataleipō.* See Acts 2. 27.

9. 30–33 (O[1], p. 1680). **ISRAEL'S FAILURE IN SPITE OF THE PROPHETS.** (*Introversion.*)

O[1] | l | 30. With the believer, no running or willing (*v.* 16).
m | 31, 32–. With the runner or willer, no believing.
m | –32, 33–. With the runner or willer, only stumbling.
l | –33. With the believer, no stumbling.

30 not. Ap. 105. II.
have attained to = obtained. Gr. *katalambanō.* See John 12. 35.
faith. Ap. 150. II. 1. That is, on faith-principle, as in 1. 17.
31 the = a. **hath** = omit.
attained. Gr. *phthanō.* Not the same word as in 30. See Luke 11. 20.
32 of the law. The texts omit.
stumbled. Gr. *proskoptō.* Here, 14. 21. 1 Pet. 2. 8, and five times in the Gospels.
stumblingstone. Gr. *proskomma.* Here, *v.* 33; 14. 13, 20. 1 Pet. 2. 8.
33 Behold. Ap. 133. I. 2. **Sion.** Ap. 68.
offence. See 1 Cor. 1. 23.
whosoever. The texts read "he who".
believeth. Ap. 150. I. v. (iii) 1.
ashamed = put to shame. See Rom. 5. 5.
Quoted from Isa. 28. 16. Ap. 107. II. 3 (b) and 4.

10. 1–13 (O[2], p. 1680). **ISRAEL'S FAILURE UNDER THE LAW.** (*Alternation.*)

O[2] | n | 1–3. The Righteousness of God. Israel's ignorance of it.
o | 4. Christ the end of the Law.
n | 5–10. The Righteousness of God. Teaching of the Law.
o | 11–13. Christ the end of the Law. Witness of the Prophets.

10. 1 desire. Gr. *eudokia.* See Luke 2. 14, and cp. Eph. 1. 5, 9. Phil. 1. 15; 2. 13. 2 Thess. 1. 11.
prayer. Ap. 134. II. 3.
to. Ap. 104. xv. 3. **God.** Ap. 98. I. i. 1.
for. Ap. 104. xvii. 1.
Israel. The texts read them.
that, &c. = for (Gr. *eis*) salvation.
2 bear . . . record. Gr. *martureō.* See 3. 21.
not. Ap. 105. I. **according to.** Ap. 104. x. 2.
knowledge. Ap. 132. II. ii.
3 ignorant. See 1. 13.
righteousness. Ap. 191. 3.
going about = seeking. **unto** = to.
4 Christ. Ap. 98. IX. **for.** Ap. 104. vi.
believeth. Ap. 150. I. i.

5 Moses. See 5. 14. **of.** Ap. 104. vii. **man.** Ap. 123. 1. **by.** Ap. 104. viii. Quoted from Lev. 18. 5. **6 faith.** Ap. 150. II. 1. Cp. 1. 17. **not.** Ap. 105. II. **in.** Gr. *en.* Ap. 104. viii. **ascend.** See John 3. 13. Acts 2. 34. **into.** Ap. 104. vi. **heaven** = the heaven. Matt. 6. 9, 10. **7 deep.** Gr. *abussos.* See Luke 8. 31. **from the dead.** Gr. *ek nekrōn.* Ap. 139. 3. **8 word.** Gr. *rhēma.* See Mark 9. 32. These quotations are from Deut. 30. 12–14. **faith** = the faith. Ap. 150. II. 1. **preach.** Ap. 121. 1. **9 if.** Ap. 118. 1. b. **with.** Gr. *en.* **the Lord Jesus** = Jesus as Lord. Cp. John 13. 13. 1 John 4. 15. **Lord.** Ap. 98. VI. i. *β.* 2. B. **Jesus.** Ap. 98. X. **believe.** Ap. 150. I. 1. iii. **hath.** Omit. **raised.** See 4. 24. **10 with.** No prep. Dat. case. **man believeth** = it is believed. **unto.** Ap. 104. vi. **confession, &c.** = it is confessed.

o 11 For the Scripture saith, "**Whosoever °believeth on Him shall [2]not be °ashamed.**"

12 For there is °no °difference between the Jew and the Greek: for the same [9]Lord °over all is rich [10]unto all that °call upon Him.

13 For "**whosoever shall [12]call upon the °name of the °LORD shall be saved.**"

O³ p 14 How then shall they [12]call °on Him in Whom they have [2]not °believed? and how shall they °believe in Him of Whom they have [2]not heard? and how shall they hear °without °a preacher?

15 And how shall they [14]preach, °except they be °sent? as it is written, "**How °beautiful are the feet of them that °preach the gospel of peace, and °bring glad tidings of good things!**"

q 16 But they have [2]not all obeyed the °gospel. For Esaias saith, [13]"**LORD, who °hath [4]believed °our report?**"

p 17 So then [6]faith *cometh* °by hearing, and hearing °by the [8]word of °God.

18 But I say, Have they [2]not heard? Yes verily, "**their °sound went [6]into all the °earth, and their [8]words [10]unto the °ends of the °world.**"

q 19 But I say, Did [2]not Israel °know? First [5]Moses saith, "**I will °provoke you to jealousy °by *them that are* [12]no °people, *and* °by a °foolish °nation I will °anger you.**"

20 But Esaias is °very bold, and saith, "**I was found of them that sought Me [6]not; I was made °manifest [3]unto them that °asked [6]not after Me.**"

21 But [1]to Israel He saith, "**All day long I have °stretched forth My hands °unto a °disobedient and °gainsaying °people.**"

K M r **11** I say then, °Hath °God °cast away His °people? °God forbid. For I °also am an Israelite, °of the seed of Abraham, *of* the tribe of Benjamin.

2 [1]God [1]hath °not [1]cast away His [1]people which He °foreknew. °Wot ye °not what the Scripture saith °of Elias? how he °maketh intercession to [1]God °against Israel, saying,

3 °"**LORD, they °have killed Thy prophets, and °digged down Thine altars; and I am °left alone, and they seek my °life.**"

s 4 But what saith the °answer of God °unto him? "**I have reserved to Myself seven thousand °men, who have [2]not bowed the knee to *the image of* Baal.**"

11 believeth. Ap. 150. I. 1. v. (iii). 1.
ashamed. See 9. 33. Quoted from Isa. 28. 16.
12 no. Gr. *ou.*
difference. See 3. 22.
over = of.
call upon. See Acts 2. 21.
13 name. See Acts 2. 38.
Lord. Ap. 98. VI. i. β. 1. B. a. Quoted from Joel 2. 32.

10. 14-21 (O³, p. 1680). ISRAEL'S FAILURE UNDER THE GOSPEL. (*Alternation.*)

O³ | p | 14, 15. Israel heard. God vindicated.
q | 16. Israel inexcusable.
p | 17, 18. Israel heard. God vindicated.
q | 19–21. Israel inexcusable.

14 on. Gr. *eis.*
believed. Ap. 150. I. 1. v. (i).
believe. Ap. 150. I. 1. vi.
without = apart from.
a preacher = one preaching (Ap. 121. 1).
15 except = if (Ap. 118. 1. b) not (Gr. *mē*).
sent. Ap. 174. 1.
beautiful. Gr. *hōraios.* Lit. happening in its time. Only here, Matt. 23. 27. Acts 3. 2, 10. Cp. Eccl. 3. 1, 11.
preach the gospel. Ap. 121. 4.
bring glad tidings. Same as above. Quoted from Isa. 52. 7 (Sept.).
16 gospel. See Ap. 140.
hath. Omit.
our report = the hearing of us. Quoted from Isa. 53. 1.
17 by. Ap. 104. vii.
by. Ap. 104. v. 1.
God. The texts read "Christ".
18 sound. Gr. *phthongos.* Only here and 1 Cor. 14. 7. Cp. Acts 4. 18.
earth. Ap. 129. 4.
ends. Gr. *peras.* Here, Matt. 12. 42. Luke 11. 31. Heb. 6. 16.
world. Ap. 129. 3. Quoted from Ps. 19. 4. This *v.* 18, by the Fig. *Prolepsis* (Ap. 6), anticipates the objection that they had not heard.
19 know. Ap. 132. I. ii.
provoke . . . to jealousy. Gr. *parazēloō.* Only here, 11. 11, 14. 1 Cor. 10. 22.
by. Ap. 104. ix. 2.
people. Gr. *ethnos.* foolish. See 1. 21.
nation = people, as above.
anger. Gr. *parorgizō.* Only here and Eph. 6. 4. Used frequently in the Sept. of provoking Jehovah to anger. Deut. 32. 21, &c.
20 very bold. Gr. *apotolmaō.* Only here.
manifest. Gr. *emphanēs.* Only here and Acts 10. 40.
asked. See Acts 5. 27. Quoted from Isa. 65. 1.
21 stretched forth. Gr. *ekpetannumi.* Only here. Used of a bird expanding its wings.
unto. Ap. 104. xv. 3.
disobedient. See 2. 8.
gainsaying. Gr. *antilegō.* See Acts 13. 45.
people. See Acts 2. 47. Quoted from Isa. 65. 2.

11. 1-10 (*M*, p. 1680). GOD'S PURPOSE REGARDING THE REMNANT ACCOMPLISHED. (*Introversion.*)

M | r | 1–3. The majority of Israel rejected God.
s | 4–6. A remnant reserved, according to God's election.
s | 7–. The remnant obtained what the nation lost.
r | –7–10. Fate of majority. God hardened them.

11. 1 Hath = Did. God. Ap. 98. I. i. 1. cast away = thrust aside. See Acts 7. 27. people. See 10. 21. God forbid. See 3. 4. also = indeed. of. Ap. 104. vii. **2** not. Ap. 105. I. foreknew. Ap. 132. I. iv. Wot = Know. Ap. 132. I. i. of Elias = in (Gr. *en*) Elijah: i. e. in the section which gives Elijah's history. Cp. Mark 12. 26. Luke 20. 37. maketh intercession. See 8. 27. against. Ap. 104. x. 1. **3** Lord. Ap. 98. VI. i. β. 1. B. a. have. Omit. digged down = overthrew. See Acts 15. 16. left. Gr. *hupoleipō.* Only here. life. Ap. 110. III. 1; Ap. 170. 3. **4** answer of God = Divine response. Gr. *chrēmatismos.* Only here. Cp. Acts 11. 26. unto = to. men. Ap. 123. 2. Quoted from 1 Kings 19. 10–18.

5 Even so then °at this present °time also there is a °remnant °according to the °election of °grace.
6 And °if by [5]grace, then *is it* °no more [1]of works: otherwise [5]grace is °no more [5]grace. But °if *it be* [1]of works, then is it °no more [5]grace: otherwise work is °no more work.

s 7 What then? Israel °hath [2]not °obtained that which he seeketh for; but the [5]election °hath °obtained it,

r and the °rest were °blinded
8 (According as it is written, [1]"**God °hath given them the °spirit of °slumber, eyes that they should °not °see, and ears that they should °not hear**";) unto this day.
9 And David saith, "**Let their °table be made °a snare, and °a trap, and °a °stumblingblock, and °a °recompence [4]unto them:**
10 **Let their eyes °be darkened, that they may [8]not [8]see, and °bow down their °back alway.**"

L T¹ t 11 I say then, °Have they stumbled °that they °should fall? [1]God forbid: but *rather* °through their °fall salvation *is come* [4]unto the Gentiles, °for to °provoke them to jealousy.

u 12 Now [6]if the [11]fall of them *be* the riches of the °world, and the °diminishing of them the riches of the Gentiles; how much more their °fulness?

t 13 For I speak to you Gentiles, inasmuch as I am the °apostle of the Gentiles, I °magnify mine °office:
14 [6]If by any means I may °provoke to emulation *them which are* my flesh, and might save °some [1]of them.

u 15 For [6]if the °casting away of them *be* the °reconciling of the [12]world, what *shall* the °receiving *of them be* °but °life °from the dead?
16 For [6]if the °firstfruit *be* holy, the °lump °*is* also *holy:* and [6]if the root *be* holy, °so *are* the branches.

T² v 17 And [6]if [14]some of the branches °be broken off, and thou, being a °wild olive tree, wert °graffed in °among them, and with them °partakest of the root and °fatness of the olive tree;
18 °Boast [8]not against the branches. But [6]if thou °boast, thou bearest [2]not the root, but the root thee.

5 at. Ap. 104. viii.
time. See 3. 26.
remnant. Gr. *leimma.* Only here. Cp. 9. 27.
according to. Ap. 104. x. 2.
election. See 9. 11.
grace. See 1. 5. Ap. 184. I. 1.
6 if. Ap. 118. 2. a.
no more = no longer. The texts omit last clause of the verse.
7 hath. Omit.
obtained. Gr. *epitunchanō.* Only here, Heb. 6. 15; 11. 33, Jas. 4. 2.
rest. See 1. 13. Ap. 124. 3.
blinded = hardened. Gr. *pōroō.* Here, 2 Cor. 3. 14, and three times in the Gospels. Cp. *v.* 25.
8 hath given = gave.
spirit. Ap. 101. II. 7.
slumber = stupor. Gr. *katanuxis.* Only here. Quoted from Isa. 29. 10.
not. Ap. 105. II.
see. Ap. 133. I. 5.
9 table. Put by Fig. *Metaphor* for material prosperity.
a = for (Gr. *eis*) a.
stumblingblock. See 9. 32.
recompence. Gr. *antapodoma.* Only here and Luke 14. 12.
10 be darkened. See Rom. 1. 21.
bow down. Gr. *sunkamptō.* Only here.
back. Gr. *nōtos.* Only here. Quoted from Ps. 69. 23. Cp. Deut. 28. 43.

11. 11-32 (*L*, p. 1680). **GOD'S PURPOSE WILL EMBRACE THE WHOLE.** (*Division.*)

L | T¹ | 11–16. Israel provoked to jealousy.
  | T² | 17–24. The wild olive graft.
  | T³ | 25–32. The hardening of Israel.

11. 11-16 (T¹, above). **ISRAEL PROVOKED TO JEALOUSY.** (*Alternation.*)

T¹ | t | 11. Salvation to Gentiles provokes Israel to jealousy.
   | u | 12. Benefit to world through Israel's fall. Greater benefit will come from their fulness.
   | *t* | 13, 14. Paul's apostleship provokes Israel to jealousy.
   | *u* | 15, 16. Benefit through Israel's rejection. Greater benefit will be through their restoration.

11 Have, &c. = Did they not (Gr. *mē*) stumble (Gr. *ptaiō.* Only here, Jas. 2. 10; 3. 2, 2 Pet. 1. 10)?
that = in order that. Gr. *hina.*
should = might.
through = by (Dat.).
fall. Ap. 128. I. ii. 3.
for. Ap. 104. vi.
provoke, &c. See 10. 19.
12 world. Ap. 129. 1.
diminishing. Gr. *hēttēma.* Only here and 1 Cor. 6. 7. Cp. 2 Cor. 12. 13.

fulness. Gr. *plērōma.* Cp. Ap. 125. 7. **13 apostle.** Ap. 189. **magnify** = glorify. See p. 1511. **office** = ministry. Ap. 190. II. 1. **14 provoke, &c.** See *v.* 11. **some.** Ap. 124. 4. **15 casting away.** See Acts 27. 22 (loss), and cp. Ex. 32. 11. **reconciling.** See 5. 11. **receiving.** Gr. *proslēpsis.* Only here. **but** = if not (Gr. *ei mē*). **life.** Ap. 170. 1. **from the dead.** Gr. *ek nekrōn.* Ap. 139. 3. **16 firstfruit.** See 8. 23. **lump.** See 9. 21. *is* **also** = also *is.* **so, &c.** = the branches also are.

11. 17-24 (T², above). **THE WILD OLIVE GRAFT.** (*Introversion.*)

T² | v | 17, 18. The wild olive graft, not to boast
   | w | 19, 20. The wild olive to fear.
   | *w* | 21, 22. Reason for fear.
   | *v* | 23, 24. The reason for not boasting.

17 be, &c. = were broken off. Gr. *ekklazō.* Only here and *vv.* 19, 20. **wild olive tree.** The oleaster which bears no fruit. Gr. *agrielaios.* Only here and *v.* 24. **graffed in.** Gr. *enkentrizō.* Only here and *vv.* 19, 23, 24. **among.** Ap. 104. viii. (2). **partakest** = art partaker (Gr. *sunkoinōnos.* Only here, 1 Cor. 9. 23. Phil. 1. 7. Rev. 1. 9). **fatness.** Gr. *piotēs.* Only here. **18 Boast.** Gr. *katakauchaomai.* Only here, Jas. 2. 13; 3. 14.

w 19 Thou wilt say then, °"The branches were
[17]broken off, [11]that I might be [17]graffed in."
20 Well; because of °unbelief they were
[17]broken off, and thou standest by °faith. Be
[8]not °highminded, but fear:

w 21 For [6]if [1]God spared [2]not the °natural
branches, *take heed* °lest He °also spare °not
thee.
22 °Behold therefore the °goodness and °se-
verity of [1]God: °on them which fell, °severity;
but °toward thee, °goodness, °if thou °continue
in *His* °goodness: otherwise thou also shalt be
cut off.

v 23 And they also, [22]if they °abide [8]not still in
[20]unbelief, shall be [17]graffed in: for [1]God is
able to [17]graff them in again.
24 For °if thou wert cut °out of the °olive tree
which is wild °by nature, and wert [17]graffed
°contrary to nature °into a °good olive tree:
how much more shall these, which be the
[21]natural *branches*, be [17]graffed into their own
olive tree?

[3]U W x 25 For °I would [2]not, brethren, that ye should
be ignorant of this °mystery, °lest ye should
be wise °in your own conceits; that °blindness
°in part is happened to Israel,

y until the °fulness of the Gentiles be come in.

X 26 And so all Israel shall be saved: as it is
written, **"There shall come [24]out of °Sion the
Deliverer, and shall turn away °ungodliness
°from Jacob:"**
27 **"For this is °My covenant 'unto them,
when I shall °take away their °sins."**

V 28 °As concerning the gospel, *they are* enemies °for your sakes:

V but °as touching the [5]election, *they are* °be-
loved °for the fathers' sakes.
29 For the °gifts and calling of [1]God *are*
°without repentance.

U W y 30 For as ye °in times past °have not believed
[1]God, yet have now °obtained mercy °through
their °unbelief:

x 31 Even so [30]have these also now [30]not believed, [11]that through your mercy they also
may [30]obtain mercy.

X 32 For [1]God °hath concluded them all °in
[30]unbelief, [11]that He might °have mercy upon
all.

H Y 33 O the depth of the °riches

19 The. Omit.
20 unbelief. See *v.* 30 and 3. 3.
faith. Ap. 150. II. 1.
highminded=arrogant. Gr. *hupsēlophroneō.* Only here and 1 Tim. 6. 17.
21 natural=according to (Ap. 104. x. 2) nature.
lest. The texts read "that".
also spare not=neither (Gr. *oude*) spare.
22 Behold. Ap. 133. I. 3.
goodness. See 2. 4.
severity=cutting off. Gr. *apotomia.* Only here.
on. Ap. 104. ix. 3.
toward=on, as above.
if. Ap. 118. 1. b. **continue.** See 6. 1.
23 abide=continue, as above.
24 if. Ap. 118. 2. c.
out of. Ap. 104. vii.
olive tree, &c. Read "wild olive tree which is so by (Ap. 104. x. 2) nature".
contrary to. Ap. 104. xii. 3.
into. Ap. 104. vi.
good olive tree. Gr. *kallielaios.* Only here. It is only in the kingdom of grace that such a process, thus contrary to nature, can be successful.

11. 25-32 (T[3], p. 1684). THE HARDENING OF ISRAEL. *(Introversion.)*

T[3] | U | W | x | 25–. Hardening to Israel.
 y | -25. The fulness of the Gentiles.
 X | 26, 27. The salvation of Israel, the end.
 V | 28–. The Gospel standpoint. Israel enemies.
 V | -28, 29. The election standpoint. Israel beloved.
 U | *W* | *y* | 30. Mercy to the nations. The result.
 x | 31. Disobedience of Israel, the means.
 X | 32. Mercy upon all, the end.

25 I would, &c. See 1. 13.
mystery=secret. Ap. 193.
lest=in order that . . . not. Gr. *hina mē.*
in your own conceits. Lit. with (Ap. 104. xii. 2) yourselves. Cp. Prov. 3. 7.
blindness=hardness. Gr. *pōrōsis.* See Mark 3. 5.
in part. Gr. *apo merous.*
fulness. Gr. *plērōma.* That is, the fulness of times when the full number of Acts 15. 17 is completed. Cp. Luke 21. 24. Isa. 59. 20.
26 Sion. Ap. 68.
ungodliness. Ap. 128. IV.
from. Ap. 104. iv.
27 My covenant=the covenant (see 9. 4) with (Ap. 104. xii. 1) Me.
take away. Gr. *aphaireō.* Cp. Heb. 10. 4. Rev. 22. 19.
sins. Ap. 128. I. ii. 1. This is a combined quotation from Isa. 59. 20, 21 and 27. 9. Ap. 107. II. 4.
28 As concerning. Ap. 104. x. 2.
for . . . sakes=on account of (Ap. 104. v. 2).
as touching=as concerning, as above.
beloved. Ap. 135. III.
29 gifts. Ap. 184. I.
without repentance=not to be repented of. Ap. 111. III. **30 in times past**=at one time (*pote*). **have not believed**=disobeyed. See 2. 8. **obtained mercy.** Lit. were pitied. **through.** No prep. **unbelief**=disobedience. Gr. *apeitheia.* Also *v.* 32. Eph. 2. 2; 5. 6. Col. 3. 6. Heb. 4. 6, 11. **32 hath concluded**=shut up. Gr. *sunkleiō.* Elsewhere, Luke 5. 6. Gal. 3. 22, 23. **in.** Gr. *eis.* **have mercy upon**=pity.

11. 33-35 (*H*, p. 1680). PAUL'S JOY REGARDING GOD'S PURPOSE. *(Introversion.)*

H | Y | 33–. The depth of the riches.
 Z | z | -33–. Wisdom.
 a | -33–. Knowledge.
 A | -33–. His judgments unsearchable.
 A | -33. His ways untraceable.
 Z | *a* | 34–. Knowledge.
 z | -34. His counsellor (wisdom).
 Y | 35. Who hath given Him His riches?

33 riches. See 2. 4. This *v.* is an example of the Fig. *Thaumasmos.* Ap. 6.

Z z both of the wisdom
a and °knowledge of [1]God!
A how °unsearchable *are* His °judgments, and
A His ways °past finding out!
Z a **34 For who °hath known the mind of the [2]LORD?**
z **or who °hath been His °counsellor?**
Y **35 Or who °hath first given to Him, and it shall be °recompensed [4]unto him again?**
B 36 For [1]of Him, and °through Him, and °to Him, *are* all things: to Whom *be* °glory °for ever. Amen.

A E K A[1] **12** I °beseech you °therefore, brethren, °by the °mercies of °God, °that ye °present your bodies a living sacrifice, holy, °acceptable °unto °God, *which is* your °reasonable °service.

2 And be °not °conformed to this °world: but be ye °transformed by the °renewing of °your mind, °that ye may prove what *is* °that good, and [1]acceptable, and °perfect, °will of [1]God.

A² B 3 For I say, °through the °grace given [1]unto me, to every °man that is °among you, [2]not to °think *of himself* more highly °than he ought to think; but to think °soberly, according as [1]God °hath dealt to °every °man the measure of °faith.

4 For as we have many °members °in one body, and all °members have °not the same °office:

5 So we, *being* many, are one body [4]in °Christ, and °every one [4]members one of another.

6 °Having then °gifts °differing °according to the [3]grace that is given to us, °whether prophecy, *let us prophesy* °according to the °proportion of °faith;

7 °Or °ministry, *let us wait* °on *our* ministering: °or he that teacheth, °on teaching;

8 [7]Or he that °exhorteth, [7]on °exhortation: he that °giveth, *let him do it* °with °simplicity; he that °ruleth, °with diligence; he that sheweth mercy, °with °cheerfulness.

knowledge. Ap. 132. II. 1.
unsearchable = inscrutable. Gr. *anexereunētos*. Only here.
judgments. Ap. 177. 6.
past finding out = untraceable. Gr. *anexichniastos*. Only here and Eph. 3. 8.
34 hath known = knew. Ap. 132. I. ii.
hath been = became.
counsellor = fellow-counsellor. Gr. *sumboulos*. Only here. Cp. Ap. 102. 4.
35 hath first given = gave first. Gr. *prodidōmi*. Only here.
recompensed... again = repaid. Gr. *antapodidōmi*. Here, 12. 19. Luke 14. 14. 1 Thess. 3. 9. 2 Thess. 1. 6. Heb. 10. 30. Cp. *v.* 9.
36 through. Ap. 104. v. 1.
to. Ap. 104. vi.
glory. See 1. 23.
for ever. Ap. 151. II. A. ii. 7. a. This *v.* is the Fig. *Polyptōton* (Ap. 6), the pronoun "Him" being introduced by three different prepositions, *ek*, *dia*, and *eis*.

12. 1—15. 7 (*E*, p. 1661). PRACTICAL. (*Division.*)

E | A¹ | 12. 1, 2. As regards God.
| A² | 12. 3—15. 7. As regards man.

12. 1 beseech. Ap. 134. I. 6.
therefore. This refers to 8. 39, chaps. 9–11 being a digression.
by. Ap. 104. v. 1.
mercies. Gr. *oiktirmos*. Only here, 2 Cor. 1. 3. Phil. 2. 1. Col. 3. 12. Heb. 10. 28. Cp. 9. 15, and Luke 6. 36. "Compassion" in the Sept. of Lam. 3. 22.
God. Ap. 98. I. i. 1.
that ye = to.
present. Same as "yield", 6. 13, 19. Cp. Luke 2. 22.
acceptable = well-pleasing. Gr. *euarestos*. Here, *v.* 2; 14. 18. 2 Cor. 5. 9. Eph. 5. 10. Phil. 4. 18. Col. 3. 20. Tit. 2. 9. Heb. 13. 21.
unto = to.
reasonable. Gr. *logikos*. Only here and 1 Pet. 2. 2.
service. Gr. *latreia*. Ap. 190. II. 3.
2 not. Gr. *mē*. Ap. 105. II.
conformed. Gr. *suschēmatizō*. Only here and 1 Pet. 1. 14. Cp. 1 Cor. 4. 6.
world. Gr. *aiōn*. Ap. 129. 2.
transformed. Gr. *metamorphoomai*. See Matt. 17. 2.
renewing. Gr. *anakainōsis*. Only here and Tit. 3. 5. Cp. Heb. 6. 6.
your = the.
that, &c. = to (Gr. *eis*) your proving.
that = the.
perfect. Gr. *teleios* Ap. 125. 1.
will. Gr. *thelēma*. Ap. 102. 2.

12. 3—15. 7 (A², above). AS REGARDS MAN. (*Introversion.*)

A² | B | 12. 3–8. The brethren.
| C | 12. 9–21. Social relationships.
| D | 13. 1–7. Civil relationships.
| *C* | 13. 8–14. Social relationships.
| *B* | 14. 1—15. 7. The brethren.

3 through. Gr. *dia*. Ap. 104. v. 1. grace. Gr. *charis* Ap. 184. I. 1. man = one. among. Gr. *en*. Ap. 104. viii. 2. think ... more highly = think overweeningly. Gr. *huperphroneō*. Only here. than = in comparison with (Gr. *para*. Ap. 104. xii. 3) what. soberly = unto (Gr. *eis*) the being sober. Gr. *sōphroneō*. Here, Mark 5. 15. Luke 8. 35. 2 Cor. 5. 13. Tit. 2. 6. 1 Pet. 4. 7. hath dealt = imparted. every = each. faith. Gr. *pistis*. Ap. 150. II. 1. **4** members = the members. in. Ap. 104. viii. not. Ap. 105. I. office. See 8. 13 (deeds). **5** Christ. Ap. 98. IX. every one = severally. Gr. *kath'* (Ap. 104. x) *heis*. **6** Having then = But having. gifts. Gr. *charisma*. Ap. 184. I. 2. differing. Gr. *diaphoros*. Only here; Heb. 1. 4; 8. 6; 9. 10. according to. Gr. *kata*. Ap. 104. x. 2. whether. Gr. *eite*. See Ap. 118. 2. a. proportion. Gr. *analogia*. Only here. faith = the faith (*v.* 3). **7** Or. Ap. 118. 2. a. ministry = ministering. Ap. 190. II. 1. on. Ap. 104. viii. **8** exhorteth. Ap. 134. I. 6. exhortation. Gr. *paraklēsis*. See Acts 4. 36. giveth. See 1. 11. with. Ap. 104. viii. simplicity. Gr. *haplotēs*. Elsewhere, 2 Cor. 1. 12; 8. 2; 9. 11, 13; 11. 3. Eph. 6. 5. Col. 3. 22. ruleth = presideth. Gr. *proistēmi*. Here; 1 Thess. 5. 12. 1 Tim. 3. 4, 5, 12; 5. 17. Tit. 3. 8, 14. cheerfulness. Gr. *hilarotēs*. Only here. The adj. in 2 Cor. 9. 7.

C 9 *Let* °love be °without dissimulation. °Abhor
°that which is evil; °cleave to °that which is
good.
10 *Be* °kindly affectioned one °to another
with °brotherly love; °in honour °preferring
one another;
11 [2]Not °slothful in °business; °fervent °in
°spirit; °serving the °Lord;
12 Rejoicing in °hope; °patient in tribulation;
continuing °instant in °prayer;
13 °Distributing to the necessity of °saints;
°given to °hospitality.
14 Bless them °which °persecute you: bless,
and curse [2]not.
15 °Rejoice °with them that do °rejoice, and
weep °with them that weep.
16 °*Be* of the same °mind one °toward another. °Mind [2]not °high things, but °con-
descend to °men of low estate. °**Be [2]not °wise
°in your own conceits.**
17 Recompense to °no man °evil °for evil.
°**Provide things °honest in the sight of all
°men.**
18 °If it be possible, °as much as lieth °in
you, °live peaceably [15]with all [17]men.
19 °Dearly °beloved, °avenge [2]not yourselves,
but °*rather* give place °unto °wrath: for it is
written, °**"Vengeance *is* Mine; I will °repay,
saith the °LORD."**
20 Therefore °**if thine enemy hunger,** °**feed
him;** °**if he thirst, give him** °**drink: for in so
doing thou shalt** °**heap coals of fire** °**on his
head.**
21 Be [2]not overcome °of [17]evil, but overcome
[17]evil [8]with good.

D **13** Let every °soul °be subject °unto the
°higher °powers. For there is °no
°power °but °of °God: the °powers that be are
°ordained °of °God.
2 Whosoever therefore °resisteth the [1]power,
°resisteth the °ordinance of [1]God: and they
that °resist shall receive to themselves °dam-
nation.
3 For °rulers are °not a terror to good works,
but to the °evil. °Wilt thou then °not be afraid
of the [1]power? °do that which is good, and
thou shalt have °praise °of the same:
4 For he is °the °minister of [1]God to thee °for
good. But °if thou do that which is [3]evil, be
afraid; for he °beareth [3]not the sword in vain:

9 love. Ap. 135. II. 1.
without dissimulation = unfeigned. Gr. *anupokritos.* Occ. 2 Cor. 6. 6. 1 Tim. 1. 5. 2 Tim. 1. 5. Jas. 3. 17. 1 Pet. 1. 22.
Abhor = abhorring. Gr. *apostugeō.* Only here.
that . . . evil = the evil. Ap. 128. III. 1.
cleave = cleaving. See Luke 15. 15.
that . . . good = the good.
10 kindly affectioned. Gr. *philostorgos.* Only here. Used of the affectionate regard of members of a family. **to.** Ap. 104. vi.
brotherly love = love for the brethren. Gr. *philadelphia.* Cp. 1 Pet. 1. 22.
in honour . . . another. I. e. in every honourable matter leading one another on.
preferring. Gr. *proēgeomai.* Lit. to lead before. Only here.
11 slothful. Gr. *oknēros.* Only here; Matt. 25. 26. Phil. 3. 1.
business. Gr. *spoudē,* as "diligence" in *v.* 8.
fervent. See Acts 18. 25.
in. Dat. case. No prep.
spirit = the spirit. Ap. 101. II. 7.
serving. Ap. 190. III. 2.
Lord. Ap. 98. VI. i. β. 2. A.
12 hope = the hope. Cp. 5. 2. Tit. 2. 13.
patient. Gr. *hupomenō.* Cp. Matt. 10. 22. 1 Cor. 13. 7.
instant = steadfastly. See Acts 1. 14.
prayer. Ap. 134. II. 2.
13 Distributing = Communicating. Gr. *koinōneō.* Sometimes transl. "partake".
saints. See 1. 7. **given to** = pursuing.
hospitality = kindness to strangers. Gr. *philoxenia.* Only here and Heb. 13. 2. The adj. in 1 Tim. 3. 2. Tit. 1. 8. 1 Pet. 4. 9.
14 which = that.
persecute. The same Gk. word as for "given to", *v.* 13.
15 Rejoice. Cp. 1 Cor. 12. 26.
with, with. Ap. 104. xi. 1.
16 *Be* . . . mind. I. e. Be in brotherly sympathy with.
mind. Gr. *phroneō.* See 8. 5.
toward. Ap. 104. vi.
high things. Cp. *v.* 3.
condescend = lit. be carried away with. Gr. *sunapagomai.* Only here, Gal. 2. 13. 2 Pet. 3. 17.
men . . . estate = the lowly (ones).
Be . . . conceits. Prov. 3. 7.
Be = Become.
wise = prudent. Gr. *phronimos.* Occ. 11. 25.
in. Ap. 104. xii. 2.
17 no man = no one. Gr. *mēdeis.*
evil. Ap. 128. III. 2.
for. Ap. 104. ii.
Provide = Take thought beforehand. Gr. *pronoeō.* Only here, 2 Cor. 8. 21. 1 Tim. 5. 8. See Prov. 3. 4 (Sept.).
honest = good or beautiful. Gr. *kalos.* Occ. 102 times, generally rendered "good". Cp. Luke 8. 15. 2 Cor. 8. 21; 13. 7. Jas. 2. 7. 1 Pet. 2. 12. **men.** Ap. 123. 1. **18 If.** Ap. 118. 2. a.
as . . . you = lit. as is of (Ap. 104. vii) you. **live peaceably** = be at peace. Gr. *eirēneuō.* Only here, Mark 9. 50. 2 Cor. 13. 11. 1 Thess. 5. 13. **19 Dearly.** Omit. **beloved.** Ap. 135. III. **avenge** = revenge. See Luke 18. 3. *rather.* Omit. **unto** = to. **wrath** = the wrath (i. e. of God). See 1. 18.
Vengeance. Gr. *ekdikēsis.* See Acts 7. 24. **repay** = recompense. Gr. *antapodidōmi.* See Deut. 32. 35.
Lord. Ap. 98. VI. i. β. 1. B. a. **20 if, if.** Ap. 118. 1. b. **feed.** Gr. *psōmizō.* Only here and 1 Cor. 13. 3. The noun only in John 13. 26, 27. **drink** = to drink. **heap.** Gr. *sōreuō.* Only here and 2 Tim. 3. 6. **on.** Ap. 104. ix. 3. Quoted from Prov. 25. 21, 22. **21 of.** Ap. 104. xviii. 1.

13. 1 soul. Ap. 110. II. **be subject.** See 8. 7. **unto** = to. **higher** = supreme. Gr. *huperechō.* Here, Phil. 2. 3; 3. 8; 4. 7. 1 Pet. 2. 13. **powers.** Ap. 172. 5. **no.** Ap. 105. I. **but** = if (Ap. 118. 2. a.) not (Ap. 105. II). **of.** Ap. 104. iv, but the texts read "under", Ap. 104. xviii. 1. **God.** Ap. 98. I. i. 1. **ordained.** See Acts 13. 48. **of.** Ap. 104. xviii. 1. **2 resisteth.** Gr. *antitassomai.* See Acts 18. 6. **resisteth, resist** = withstand. Gr. *anthistēmi.* See 9. 19. **ordinance.** See Acts 7. 53.
damnation. Ap. 177. 6. **3 rulers.** Ap. 172. 6. **not.** Ap. 105. I. **evil.** Ap. 128. III. 2.
Wilt . . . power? = desirest thou not then to fear the power? **Wilt.** Ap. 102. 1. **not.** Ap. 105. II.
do. Gr. *poieō.* **praise.** See 2. 29. **of.** Ap. 104. vii. **4 the** = a. **minister.** Ap. 190. I. 1.
for. Ap. 104. vi. **if.** Ap. 118. 1. b. **beareth** = weareth. Gr. *phoreō.* Elsewhere, Matt. 11. 8. John 19. 5. 1 Cor. 15. 49, 49. Jas. 2. 3.

for he is the °minister of [1]God, a °revenger °to
execute wrath °upon him that °doeth [3]evil.
5 Wherefore *ye* must needs be [1]subject, [3-]not
only °for °wrath, but also °for conscience
sake.
6 For °for this cause °pay you °tribute also:
for they are [1]God's °ministers, °attending continually °upon this very thing.
7 Render °therefore to all °their °dues: [6]tri-
bute to whom [6]tribute *is due;* °custom to
whom °custom; fear to whom fear; honour to
whom honour.

C 8 Owe °no man any thing, °but to °love one
°another: for he that °loveth °another hath
°fulfilled °the law.
9 For this, "**Thou shalt [3-]not commit adultery,
Thou shalt [3-]not kill, Thou shalt [3-]not steal,
Thou shalt [3-]not bear false witness, Thou shalt
[3-]not °covet;**" and °if *there be* °any °other
°commandment, it is °briefly comprehended
°in this °saying, °namely, "**Thou shalt [8]love
thy °neighbour as thyself.**"
10 °Love °worketh °no °ill to his [9]neigh-
bour: therefore °love *is* °the °fulfilling of °the
law.
11 And that, °knowing the °time, that now *it
is* °high time to °awake °out of sleep: for
now *is* our salvation nearer than when we
°believed.
12 The night is °far spent, the day is °at
hand: let us therefore °cast off the works of
°darkness, and let us put on the °armour of
°light.
13 Let us walk °honestly, as [9]in the day;
[-3]not in °rioting and drunkenness, [-3]not in
chambering and °wantonness, [-3]not in strife
and °envying.
14 But put ye on the °Lord Jesus Christ, and
make [-3]not °provision for °the flesh, °to *fulfil*
the lusts *thereof.*

B E[1] **14** Him that is weak in the °faith °receive
ye, °*but* °not °to °doubtful °disputa-
tions.

F[1] b 2 °For one °believeth that he may eat all
things: °another, who is weak, eateth herbs.

---

revenger = avenger. Gr. *ekdikos.* Only here and 1 Thess. 4. 6.
to *execute* = for. Ap. 104. vi.
upon him = to the one.
doeth = practiseth. Gr. *prassō.*
5 for. Ap. 104. v. 2.
wrath = the wrath.
for conscience sake = on account of (Ap. 104. v. 2) the conscience. See 2. 15; 9. 1. Acts 23. 1.
6 for this cause. Gr. *dia* (Ap. 104. v. 2) *touto.*
pay you = ye pay. Gr. *teleō.* As "fulfil" in 2. 27.
tribute. Gr. *phoros.* Tax as paid by those of another state or country. Only here; *v.* 7. Luke 20. 22; 23. 2.
ministers. Ap. 190. I. 4.
attending continually = persevering. Same Gr. word in 12. 12.
upon. Ap. 104. vi.
7 therefore. Omit.
their = the.
dues. Gr. *opheilē.* Only here and Matt. 18. 32.
custom. That which is paid for public ends. Gr. *telos.* Cp. Matt. 17. 25.
8 no man = no one. Gr. *mēdeis.*
but = if (Ap. 118. b) not (Ap. 105. II).
love. Ap. 135. I. 1.
another = the other. Ap. 124. 2.
fulfilled. See 1. 29. Ap. 125. 7. the. Omit.
9 covet. See 7. 7.
if . . . any. Gr. *ei* (Ap. 118. 2. a) *tis* (Ap. 123. 3).
other. Ap. 124. 2.
commandment. See 7. 8, 9.
briefly comprehended = summed up. Gr. *anakephalaioomai.* Only here and Eph. 1. 10.
in. Ap. 104. viii.
saying. Ap. 121. 10.
namely. Lit. in (Ap. 104. viii) the (saying).
neighbour. Gr. *plēsios.*
10 Love. Ap. 135. II. 1.
worketh. See 2. 10. no. Ap. 105. I.
ill. Gr. *kakos,* transl. "evil" in *vv.* 3, 4.
the, the. Omit.
fulfilling = fulfilment, or fulness. Gr. *plērōma.* See 11. 12, 25.
11 knowing. Ap. 132. I. 1.
time = season. Gr. *kairos.*
high time. Gr. *hōra.* See 1 John 2. 18 (hour).
awake = be awakened. Ap. 178. I. 4.
out of. Ap. 104. vii.
believed. See 1. 16. Ap. 150. I. 1. i.
12 far spent = advanced. See Luke 2. 52. Gal. 1. 14. 2 Tim. 2. 16; 3. 9, 13.
at hand = drawn nigh. Cp. Luke 21. 28.
cast off. See Acts 7. 58 (laid down).
darkness = the darkness. See 2. 19. Cp. Eph. 5. 11. Col. 1. 13. armour. See 6. 13. light = the light. Ap. 130. 1. See John 1. 4, and cp. 2 Cor. 6. 7.
13 honestly = decently. Gr. *euschēmonōs.* Only here, 1 Cor. 14. 40. 1 Thess. 4. 12. rioting = revelling. Gr. *kōmos.* Only here, Gal. 5. 21. 1 Pet. 4. 3. wantonness = lasciviousness. Here, Mark 7. 22. 2 Cor. 12. 21. Gal. 5. 19. Eph. 4. 19. 1 Pet. 4. 3. 2 Pet. 2. 7, 18. Jude 4. envying = jealousy. See Acts 5. 17. **14** Lord Jesus Christ. See 1. 7. provision. See Acts 24. 2. the flesh. I. e. the old nature. to . . . *thereof.* Lit. unto (Ap. 104. vi) lusts. See 1. 24.

14. 1–15. 7 (*B*, p. 1686). THE BRETHREN. (*Alternation.*)

B | E[1] | 14. 1. Reception of the weak.
  F[1] | 14. 2–23. Not to be judged. "For."
 E[2] | 15. 1. Their infirmities tolerated.
  F[2] | 15. 2–6. To be pleased. "For."
 E[3] | 15. 7. To be received.

14. 1 faith. Ap. 150. III. receive. See Acts 17. 5. *but.* Omit. not. Ap. 105. II. to. Ap. 104. vi. doubtful = criticizings. Gr. *diakrisis.* Only here; 1 Cor. 12. 10. Heb. 5. 14. disputations = of (his) thoughts. I. e. without presuming to judge his thoughts.

14. 2–23 (F[1], above). THE WEAK NOT TO BE JUDGED. (*Alternation.*)

F[1] | b | 2, 3. Weakness as to practice.
 c | 4. Not to be judged.
 b | 5–9. Weakness as to belief.
 c | 10–23. Not to be judged.

2 For one = The one indeed. believeth. Ap. 150. I. 1. iii. another = the (other).

3 Let [1]not him that eateth °despise him that
eateth [1]not; and let [1]not him which eateth
[1]not °judge him that eateth: for °God °hath
received him.

c 4 Who art thou that [3]judgest °another man's
°servant? to his own °master he standeth or
falleth. °Yea, he shall be °holden up: for °God
is able to make him stand.

b 5 °One man °esteemeth one day °above another: another esteemeth every day °*alike*.
Let °every man be °fully persuaded °in his
own mind.
6 He that °regardeth the day, °regardeth *it*
°unto the °Lord; °and he that regardeth not
the day, to the Lord he doth not regard *it*. He
that eateth, eateth to the °Lord, for he °giveth
[3]God thanks; and he that eateth [1]not, to the
°Lord he eateth °not, and °giveth [3]God thanks.
7 For °none of us °liveth to himself, and °no
man dieth to himself.
8 For °whether we [7]live, we [7]live [6]unto the
°Lord; and °whether we die, we die [6]unto
the °Lord: °whether we [7]live therefore, °or die,
we are the °Lord's.
9 For °to this end °Christ °both died, °and
rose, and °revived, °that He °might be Lord
both of the °dead and °living.

c 10 But why dost thou [3]judge thy brother?
or why dost thou °set at nought thy brother?
for we shall all °stand before the °judgment
seat of °Christ.
11 For it is written, "**As I [7]live, saith the
°LORD, every knee shall bow to Me, and every
tongue shall °confess to [3]God.**"
12 So then [5]every one of us shall give
°account °of himself to [3]God.
13 Let us °not therefore [3]judge one another
°any more: but [3]judge this rather, °that no
man put a °stumblingblock or an °occasion to
fall °in *his* brother's way.
14 I °know, and am °persuaded °by the °Lord
Jesus, that °*there is* nothing °unclean °of
itself: °but to him that °esteemeth any thing
to be °unclean, to °him *it is* °unclean.
15 °But °if thy brother °be grieved °with
°*thy* meat, °now walkest thou °not °charitably.
°Destroy [1]not °him °with thy meat, °for whom
[9]Christ died.
16 Let [1]not then your good be °evil spoken of:
17 For the °kingdom of [3]God is [6]not °meat
and °drink; but °righteousness, and peace, and
°joy [5]in the °Holy Ghost.
18 For he that [5]in °these things °serveth
[9]Christ *is* °acceptable to [3]God, and °approved
°of °men.
19 Let us therefore °follow after the °things
which make for peace, and °things wherewith
one may °edify another.

3 despise. Cp. Luke 18. 9; 23. 11.
judge. Ap. 122. 1.
God. Ap. 98. I. i. 1.
hath received = received.
4 another man's. Ap. 124. 6.
servant = household servant. See Luke 16. 13. Ap. 190. I. 6.
master. Gr. *kurios.* Ap. 98. VI. i.
Yea = But.
holden up = made to stand.
God. The texts read "the Lord".
5 One man = The one indeed.
esteemeth = judgeth. Gr. *krinō*, as *v.* 3.
above. Ap. 104. xii. 3.
alike. Omit.
every man = each.
fully persuaded = assured. See 4. 21.
in. Ap. 104. viii.
6 regardeth = observeth. See 8. 5.
unto = to.
Lord. Ap. 98. VI. i. β. 2. B.
and . . . *it.* The texts omit.
giveth . . . thanks. See Acts 27. 35.
not. Ap. 105. I.
7 none, no man. Gr. *oudeis.*
liveth. Gr. *zaō.* Ap. 170. 1.
8 whether (3), **or.** Ap. 118. 1. b.
Lord. Ap. 98. VI. i. β. 2. A.
9 to this end = unto (Ap. 104. vi) this (*touto*).
Christ. Ap. 98. IX.
both. Omit.
and rose. The texts omit.
revived = lived (again). Ap. 170. 1.
that = in order that. Gr. *hina.*
might be Lord. Gr. *kurieuō.* See 6. 9, 14.
dead. Ap. 139. 2.
living. Ap. 170. 1.
10 set at nought = "despise", as in *v.* 3.
stand before. See 6. 13 (yield).
judgment seat. See Acts 7. 5.
Christ = the Christ. Ap. 98. IX. The texts read "God".
11 LORD. Ap. 98. VI. β. 1. B. a.
confess. Gr. *exomologeomai.* Citation from Is. 45. 23. The Holy Spirit substitutes "As I live" for Heb., "By Myself have I sworn." See Ap. 107. I. 1.
12 account = an account. Ap. 121. 10.
of. Ap. 104. xiii. 1.
13 not . . . any more = no longer. Gr. *mēketi.* Ap. 105. II.
that . . . put = not (Ap. 105. II) to put.
stumblingblock. See 9. 32.
occasion to fall. Gr. *skandalon.* See 9. 33.
in, &c. Lit. to the brother.
14 know. Ap. 132. I. i.
persuaded. See 8. 38.
by. Ap. 104. viii.
Lord Jesus. See 10. 9.
***there is* nothing** = nothing (Gr. *oudeis*) is.
unclean. I. e. ceremonially unclean. See Acts 2. 44 (common).
of. Ap. 104. v. 1.
but = except. Lit. if (Ap. 118. 2) not (Ap. 105. II).
esteemeth = reckoneth. See 2. 3; 4. 3.
him = that same.
15 But. The texts read "For".
if. Ap. 118. 2. a.

be = is. **with.** Ap. 104. v. 2. ***thy.*** Omit. **now . . . not** = no longer. Gr. *ouketi.* Ap. 105. I. **charitably** = according to (Ap. 104. x. 2) love (Ap. 135. II. 1). **Destroy.** Lit. loose, or pull, away from; the opp. to build up. See *vv.* 19, 20; 2. 12. 1 Cor. 8. 11. **him** = that same. **with** = by. Dat. case. **for.** Ap. 104. xvii. 1. **16 evil spoken of** = blasphemed. See 2. 24. **17 kingdom of God.** Ap. 114. II. **not.** Ap. 105. I. **meat, drink** = eating, drinking. **righteousness.** See 1. 17. **joy.** Cp. Gal. 5. 22. **Holy Ghost.** Ap. 101. II. 5, 14. **18 these things** = this. **serveth.** See 6. 6. **acceptable** = well-pleasing. See 12. 1. **approved.** Gr. *dokimos.* First of seven occ., always "approved", save Jas 1. 12. **of** = by. **men.** Ap. 123. 1. **19 follow after** = pursue. See 9. 30. **things . . . peace.** Lit. the things of the peace. **things . . . another** = the things of mutual (Gr. *eis*, Ap. 104. vi, *allēlous*, others) edifying. **edify.** Gr. *oikodomē.* Cp. 15. 2. 1 Cor. 14. 3. Eph. 4. 12.

20 For meat °destroy [1]not the °work of [3]God.
All things indeed *are* °pure; but *it is* °evil for
that [18]man who eateth °with °offence.
21 *It is* good °neither to eat °flesh, °nor to
drink wine, °nor *any thing* °whereby thy brother °stumbleth, or is °offended, or is made
weak.
22 Hast thou [1]faith? have *it* °to thyself °before
[3]God. °Happy *is* he that °condemneth [1]not
himself [5]in that °thing which he °alloweth.
23 °And he that °doubteth is °damned °if he
eat, because *he eateth* [-6]not °of [1]faith: °for
°whatsoever *is* [-6]not °of [1]faith is °sin.

E[2] **15** °We then that are strong ought to
°bear the °infirmities of the °weak, and
°not to °please ourselves.

F[2] d 2 Let °every one of us [1]please °*his* neighbour
°for *his* good °to °edification.

e 3 For even °Christ [1]pleased °not Himself; but,
as it is written, "**The °reproaches of them that
°reproached Thee fell °on Me.**"
4 For whatsoever things were written aforetime were written [2]for our °learning, °that we
°through °patience and °comfort of the °Scrip-
tures °might have °hope.

d 5 Now the °God of [4]patience and °consolation
grant you to be °likeminded °one toward another

e °according to °Christ Jesus:
6 [4]That ye may °with one mind °*and* one
mouth glorify [5]God, even the °Father of our
°Lord Jesus Christ.

E[3] 7 Wherefore °receive ye one another, as
[3]Christ also °received us °to °the glory of
[5]God.

L 8 °Now I say that °Jesus [3]Christ °was a
°minister of °the °circumcision °for the °truth
of [5]God, °to °confirm the promises °*made* unto
the fathers:
9 And °that the Gentiles °might glorify [5]God
[8]for *His* °mercy; as it is written, °"**For this
cause I will °confess to Thee °among the Gentiles, and °sing °unto °Thy name.**"
10 And again He saith, °"**Rejoice, ye Gentiles, °with His people.**"

20 destroy. Lit. loosen down. Cp. *v.* 15, and see Acts 5. 38, 39.
work. Cp. Eph. 2. 10.
pure = clean. Gr. *katharos.* Only here in Rom. Cp. Tit. 1. 15. See Acts 18. 6.
evil. Ap. 128. III. 2.
with. Ap. 104. v. 1.
offence = stumblingblock, as *v.* 13.
21 neither = not. Ap. 105. II.
flesh. Cp. 1 Cor. 8. 13.
nor, nor. Gr. *mēde.* Ap. 105. II.
whereby = in (Ap. 104. viii) which.
stumbleth. See 9. 32.
offended. See John 16. 1.
22 to = as concerning. Ap. 104. x. 2. Cp. rendering of *kata* in Eph. 4. 22. Phil. 3. 6. Heb. 9. 9.
before = in the sight of. First occ. Luke 1. 6.
Happy. Gr. *makarios.* See 4. 7, 8.
condemneth = judgeth. As *v.* 3.
thing. Omit.
alloweth. Gr. *dokimazō.* See 1. 28.
23 And = But.
doubteth. See 4. 20.
damned = condemned. Ap. 122. 7.
if. Ap. 118. 1. b.
of, of. Ap. 104. vii.
for = and.
whatsoever . . . sin. I. e. whatever is done by the believer that does not proceed from the faith-principle by which he was saved, and is not in accordance therewith, is sin.
sin. Ap. 128. I. ii. 1. Here some MSS. insert 16. 25–27. See p. 1694.
15. 1 We then = And we.
bear. See 11. 18.
infirmities. Gr. *asthenēma.* Only here.
weak. See 8. 3.
not. Ap. 105. II.
please. See 8. 8.

15. 2-6 (F[2], p. 1688). **THE BRETHREN TO BE PLEASED. "FOR."** (*Alternation.*)

F[2] | d | 2. Each one to please his neighbour.
| e | 3, 4. Motive. The example of Christ, and the word of God.
| *d* | 5-. Each one to be likeminded.
| *e* | -5, 6. The example of Christ, and for the glory of God.

2 every = each.
his = the.
for *his* good. Lit. unto (Ap. 104. vi) the good.
to. Ap. 104. xv. 3.
edification. The same Gr. word as 14. 19.
3 Christ. Ap. 98. IX.
not. Ap. 105. I.
reproaches . . . reproached = revilings . . . reviled. Gr. *oneidismos, oneidizō.* The insulting with opprobrious language, when used against Christ and His people. The noun occ. here; 1 Tim. 3. 7. Heb. 10. 33; 11. 26; 13. 13. The verb here, Matt. 5. 11. Mark 15. 32. **on.** Ap. 104. ix. 3. Quoted from Ps. 69. 9. Ap. 107. I. 1. **4 learning** = teaching, as 12. 7. **that** = in order that. Gr. *hina.* **through.** Ap. 104. v. 1. **patience** = patient endurance. See 2. 7. **comfort** = the comfort. See Acts 4. 36. **Scriptures** = the Scriptures. See 1. 2. **might** = may. **hope** = the hope. Cp. 12. 12. This verse 4 is an example of *Parēchēsis* (Ap. 6), the two words of patience and hope in Hebrew (not in Gr.) having a similar sound. **5 God.** Ap. 98. I. i. 1. **consolation** = comfort, as *v.* 4. **likeminded.** See 12. 16. **one . . . another** = among (Ap. 104. viii. 2) yourselves. **according to.** Ap. 104. x. 2. **Christ Jesus.** See 8. 1. **6 with one mind** = with one accord. Twelfth and last occ. of *homothumadon.* See Acts 1. 14. ***and*** = with (Ap. 104. viii). **Father.** Ap. 98. III. **Lord Jesus Christ.** See 5. 1. **7 receive.** See Acts 17. 5. **to.** Ap. 104. vi. **the glory, &c.** I. e. their reception of others redounds unto God's glory. Cp. Eph. 1. 6. **8 Now.** The texts read "For". **Jesus.** Omit. **was** = has become. See Acts 1. 22. **minister.** Ap. 190. I. 1. **the.** Omit. **circumcision.** See 2. 25; 3. 30. Cp. Matt. 10. 5, 6. John 12. 36. **for.** Ap. 104. xvii. 1. **truth.** See 1. 25 and p. 1511. **to confirm** = for (Gr. *eis*) the confirming of. **confirm.** Gr. *bebaioō.* Here, Mark 16. 20. 1 Cor. 1. 6, 8. 2 Cor. 1. 21. Col. 2. 7. Heb. 2. 3; 13. 9. ***made* . . . fathers.** Lit. of the fathers. No prep. **9 that** = for. **might glorify** = to glorify. **mercy.** See 9. 23. **For this cause.** Gr. *dia* (Ap. 104. v. 2) *touto.* **confess.** See 14. 11. **among.** Ap. 104. viii. 2. **sing.** Gr. *psallō.* Only here; 1 Cor. 14. 15. Eph. 5. 19. Jas. 5. 13. **unto** = to. **Thy name.** See Acts 2. 21. Ps. 18. 49 (Sept.). **10 Rejoice.** Gr *euphrainō.* See Acts 2. 26. **with.** Ap. 104. xi. 1. See Deut. 32. 43 (Sept.).

11 And again, °"**Praise the °LORD, all ye Gentiles; and °laud Him, all ye °people.**"

12 And again, Esaias saith, "**There shall be °a Root of Jesse, and He That shall °rise to °reign over the Gentiles; °in Him shall the Gentiles °trust.**"

D J 13 Now the [5]God of °hope °fill you with all joy and peace °in °believing, °that ye may abound °in °hope, °through the °power of °the Holy Ghost.

14 And I myself also am °persuaded °of you, my brethren, that ye also are °full of °goodness, [13]filled with all °knowledge, able also to °admonish one another.

15 °Nevertheless, °brethren, I °have written the more °boldly °unto you °in some sort, as °putting you in mind, °because of the °grace that is given to me °of [5]God,

16 °That I should be °the °minister of °Jesus Christ [7]to the Gentiles, °ministering the °gospel of [5]God, [4]that the °offering up of the Gentiles might be °acceptable, being °sanctified °by the [13]Holy Ghost.

17 I have therefore whereof I may °glory [13]through [16]Jesus Christ in °those things °which pertain to [5]God.

18 For I will °not °dare to °speak of any of those things which [3]Christ hath °not °wrought °by me, °to make the Gentiles obedient, °by °word and °deed,

19 °Through mighty °signs and °wonders, [16]by the °power of °the Spirit of [5]God; so that °from Jerusalem, and round about °unto °Illyricum, I have °fully preached the °gospel of [3]Christ.

20 Yea, so °have I strived to °preach the gospel, [3]not where [3]Christ was °named, °lest I should build °upon °another man's foundation:

21 But as it is written, °"**To whom °He was [3]not °spoken of, they shall see: and they that have [3]not heard shall °understand.**"

H 22 For which cause also I have been much °hindered from coming [2]to you.

23 But now having °no more place [13]in these °parts, and having a °great desire °these many years to come °unto you;

24 °Whensoever I °take my journey °into Spain, I will come [2]to you: for I [12]trust to °see you °in my journey, and to be °brought on my way thitherward °by you, °if first I be °somewhat filled °with your *company*.

25 But now I °go °unto Jerusalem °to minister [15]unto the °saints.

11 Praise. See Acts 2. 47.
LORD. Ap. 98. VI. i. β. 1. A. a.
laud, &c. = let all the peoples praise Him.
laud = highly extol. Gr. *epaineō*. Here, Luke 16. 8. 1 Cor. 11. 2, 17, 22. See Ps. 117. 1.
people = peoples.
12 a = the.
rise. Ap. 178. I. 1.
reign over = rule. Gr. *archō*. Only here and Mark 10. 42.
in. Ap. 104. ix. 2.
trust = hope. See 8. 24. Isa. 11. 10.
13 hope, hope = the hope.
fill. Ap. 125. 7.
in, in. Ap. 104. viii.
believing. Ap. 150. I. 1. i.
that, &c. = unto (Ap. 104. vi) your abounding.
through. Ap. 104. viii.
power. Ap. 172. 1.
the Holy Ghost. Ap. 101. II. 14.
14 persuaded. See 8. 38.
of. Ap. 104. xiii. 1.
full. See 1. 29.
goodness. Gr. *agathōsunē*. Here, Gal. 5. 22. Eph. 5. 9. 2 Thess. 1. 11.
knowledge. Ap. 132. II. i.
admonish. See Acts 20. 31.
15 Nevertheless = But.
brethren. Omit.
have written = wrote.
boldly = freely.
unto = to.
in some sort = partly. Gr. *apo* (Ap. 104. iv) *merous*.
putting . . . mind = reminding. Gr. *epanamimnēskō*. Only here.
because of. Ap. 104. v. 2.
grace. Ap. 184. I. 1.
of. Ap. 104. xviii. 1. The texts give 104. iv.
16 That . . . be = For (Ap. 104. vi) me to be.
the = a.
minister. See 13. 6. Ap. 190. I. 4.
Jesus Christ = Christ Jesus. Ap. 98. XII.
ministering = to minister as a priest. Gr. *hierourgeō*. Only here.
gospel, &c. Ap. 140. III.
offering up. See Acts 21. 26.
acceptable = accepted, as *v.* 31.
sanctified. Gr. *hagiazō*. Only here in Rom.
by. Ap. 104. viii.
17 glory. See 3. 27.
those = the.
which pertain = pertaining to. Ap. 104. xv. 3.
18 not, not. Ap. 105. I.
dare. See 5. 7.
speak. Ap. 121. 7.
wrought. See 1. 27; 7. 8.
by, by. Ap. 104. v. 1.
to make . . . obedient = for (Ap. 104. vi) obedience of (the) Gentiles.
word. Ap. 121. 10.
deed = work.

19 Through mighty = By (Ap. 104. viii) the power (Ap. 172. 1). **signs.** Ap. 176. 3. **wonders.** Ap. 176. 2. **power.** Same Gr. word as for "mighty". **the Spirit of God.** Some texts read "the Holy Spirit" (Ap. 101. II. 3). **from.** Ap. 104. iv. **unto** = as far as. **Illyricum.** Not mentioned in Acts. It included Montenegro, Albania, Dalmatia, &c. **fully preached.** Gr. *plēroō*, rendered "fill", "filled", in *vv.* 13, 14. Cp. Acts 20. 24. Ap. 125. 7. **gospel.** See Ap. 140. **20 have I strived** = earnestly endeavouring. Gr. *philotimeomai*. Only here; 2 Cor. 5. 9. 1 Thess. 4. 11. **preach, &c.** See 1. 15. Ap. 121. 4. **named** = (already) named, as R.V. **lest . . . build** = in order that I should not (Ap. 105. II) build. **upon.** Ap. 104. ix. 3. **another man's** = another's (Ap. 124. 6). **21 To . . . see.** Lit. They shall see (Ap. 133. I. 8. (a)) to whom it was not (Ap. 105. I) reported. **He** = concerning (Ap. 104. xiii. 1) Him. **spoken.** Gr. *anangellō*. Cp. Acts 14. 27. 1 Pet. 1. 12. **understand.** See 3. 11. From Is. 52. 15. **22 hindered.** See Acts 24. 4. **23 no more** = no longer. Gr. *mēketi*. Ap. 105. II. **parts** = regions. 2 Cor. 11. 10. Gal. 1. 21. **great desire.** Gr. *epipothia*. Only here. **these** = from (Ap. 104. iv). **unto.** Ap. 104. xv. 3. **24 Whensoever.** Ap. 118. 1. b. **take . . . journey** = go, as *v.* 25. **into.** Ap. 104. vi. **to.** Ap. 104. xv. 3. **see.** Ap. 133. I. 12. **in . . . journey.** See Acts 16. 4. **brought.** See Acts 15. 3. **by.** Ap. 104. xviii. 1. **if.** Ap. 118. 1. b. **somewhat.** See *v.* 15. **with . . . company.** Lit. with you. Cp. 1. 12. **25 go.** See *v.* 24. **unto.** Ap. 104. vi. **to minister** = ministering. Gr. *diakoneō*. Ap. 190. III. 1. **saints.** See 1. 7.

26 For it °hath pleased °them of Macedonia
and Achaia to make a certain °contribution
[2]for the poor °saints which are °at Jerusalem.
27 It [26]hath pleased them verily; and their
debtors they are. For °if the Gentiles have
been made partakers of their °spiritual things,
their duty is also to °minister [15]unto them
[13]in °carnal things.
28 When therefore I have °performed this,
and have sealed to them this fruit, I °will
come [18]by you [24]into Spain.
29 And °I am sure that, when I come [23]unto
you, I shall come [13]in the fulness of the
°blessing °of the [19]gospel of [3]Christ.

G 30 Now I °beseech you, brethren, °for the
[6]Lord Jesus Christ's sake, and °for the °love of
the °Spirit, that ye °strive together with me
[13]in °*your* °prayers [2]to [5]God [8]for me;
31 [4]That I may be delivered [19]from them that
°do not believe [13]in Judæa; and that my °ser-
vice which *I have* [2]for Jerusalem may be
°accepted of the [25]saints;
32 [4]That I may come [23]unto you °with joy
[18]by the °will of [5]God, °and may with you be
°refreshed.
33 Now the [5]God of °peace *be* [10]with you all.
Amen.

F G^1 **16** I °commend °unto you °Phebe our sister,
°which is a °servant of the °church
which is °at °Cenchrea:
2 °That ye receive her °in the °Lord, °as
becometh °saints, and that ye °assist her °in
whatsoever °business she °hath need of you:
for **she** hath been a °succourer of many, and of
myself also.
3 °Greet °Priscilla and Aquila my °helpers [2]in
°Christ Jesus:
4 Who have °for my °life °laid down their
own °necks: [1]unto whom °not only **I** °give
thanks, but also all the [1]churches of the Gentiles.
5 Likewise *greet* the [1]church that is °in their
house. °Salute my °wellbeloved °Epænetus,
who is the °firstfruits of °Achaia °unto °Christ.
6 [3]Greet °Mary, °who °bestowed much labour °on °us.
7 [5]Salute °Andronicus and °Junia, my °kins-
men, and my °fellowprisoners, who are °of
note °among the °apostles, °who also were [2]in
[5]Christ °before me.
8 [3]Greet °Amplias my °beloved [2]in the [2]Lord.

26 hath pleased = pleased.
them of. Omit.
contribution. Gr. *koinōnia*. See Acts 2. 42.
saints = of the saints.
at. Ap. 104. viii.
27 if. Ap. 118. 2. a.
spiritual things. Gr. *pneumatikos*. See 1. 11.
minister. Gr. *leitourgeō*. See Acts 13. 2. Ap. 190. III. 6.
carnal things. See 7. 14.
28 performed = accomplished.
will come. See Acts 4. 15 (go aside).
29 I am sure. Ap. 132. I. i.
blessing. Gr. *eulogia*. First of sixteen occ.
of the gospel. The texts omit.
30 beseech. Ap. 134. I. 6.
for . . . sake, for. Ap. 104. v. 1.
love. Ap. 135. II. 1.
Spirit. Ap. 101. II. 3.
strive together with. Gr. *sunagōnizomai*. Only here.
your. Omit.
prayers. Ap. 134. II. 2.
31 do not believe = are disobedient. See 2. 8.
service = ministration. See 12. 7. Ap. 190. II. 1.
accepted of = acceptable to.
32 with. Ap. 104. viii.
will. Ap. 102. 2.
and . . . refreshed = together with you be refreshed. Gr. *sunanapauomai*. Only here.
33 peace = the peace. In *v.* 5 we have the God of the patience; in *v.* 13, the God of the hope; here, the God of the peace.

16. 1-24 (*F*, p. 1661). SALUTATIONS. (*Division*.)

F | G^1 | 1. -16-. From Paul himself.
| G^2 | -16-24. From others than Paul.

1 commend. See 3. 5. unto = to.
Phebe. Only here; "bright", or "pure", the fem. of Phœbus, otherwise Apollo, the sun-god. Her name indicates a convert from paganism. She was probably the bearer of the epistle to Rome. See Int. Notes, p. 1661.
which = who. servant. Ap. 190. I. 1.
church. Gr. *ekklēsia*. Ap. 186.
at. Ap. 104. viii.
Cenchrea. See Acts 18. 18.
2 That = In order that.
in. Ap. 104. viii.
Lord. Ap. 98. VI. i. *β*. 2. B.
as . . . saints. Lit. worthily of the saints. Gr. *axiōs tōn hagiōn*. Cp. Eph. 4. 1. Phil. 1. 27. Col. 1. 10. 1 Thess. 2. 12. 3 John 6.
assist = stand by. See 6. 13. Cp. Acts 27. 23.
business = thing. Gr. *pragma*. See Acts 5. 4.
hath = may have.
succourer. Gr. *prostatis*, protectress. Cp. Latin *patronus*, a defender of meaner persons. Athenian writers use the word of such as took care of strangers. Cp. 1 Tim. 5. 9, 10.
3 Greet = Salute. See Acts 18. 22.

Priscilla and Aquila. The texts read Prisca (dim.) as in 2 Tim. 4. 19. See Acts 18. 2, 18, 26. 1 Cor. 16. 19, for all we know of these helpers. Whether converts of Paul is not clear, but they were deeply taught in the Scriptures and the "Way" of God, as is shown in Acts 18. 26. helpers = fellow-labourers. Gr. *sunergos*. Cp. Phil. 4. 3. See 1 Cor. 3. 9. Christ Jesus. Ap. 98. XII. **4** for. Ap. 104. xvii. 1. life. App. 110 III. 1 and 170. 3. laid . . . necks = risked their own lives. A similar expression occ. in a roll from Herculaneum *c.* 160 B.C. necks = neck. not. Ap. 105. I. give thanks. See Acts 27. 35. The occasion is nowhere mentioned. **5** in their house. See 1 Cor. 16. 19. in. Ap. 104. x. 2. Salute. Same Gr. word as for "Greet", *v.* 3. wellbeloved. See Ap. 135. III. Epænetus. Only here. firstfruits. Cp. Acts 18. 27; 19. 21, 22. 1 Cor. 16. 15. Achaia. The texts read "Asia". unto. Ap. 104. vi. Christ. Ap. 98. IX. **6** Mary. Gr. *Mariam*. The only Heb. name in this list. who . . . us. On an inscription from a Roman cemetery, about the second century A. D., a wife records of her husband, "who laboured much for me". bestowed . . . labour = laboured. Gr. *kopiaō*. Cp. Luke 5. 5. John 4. 6. on. Ap. 104. vi. us. The texts read "you". **7** Andronicus. Gr. Only here. Junia. The Acc. case may indicate either masc. *Junias*, or fem. *Junia*. kinsmen. Gr. *sungenēs*. Literal here; in 9. 3 it is figurative. Benjamites and probably near relatives. Here, *v.* 11, and Acts 23. 16, are the only refs. to Paul's relatives. fellowprisoners. Gr. *sunaichmalōtos*; lit. a war-captive. Only here; Col. 4. 10. Philemon 23. of note = eminent. Gr. *episēmos*. Only here and Matt. 27. 16. among. Ap. 104. viii. 2. apostles. Ap. 189. who . . . me. Read "who before me also were in Christ". before. Ap. 104. xiv. **8** Amplias. Only here. beloved. As in *v.* 5.

9 [5]Salute °Urbane, our [3]helper [2]in [5]Christ,
and °Stachys my [8]beloved.
10 [5]Salute °Apelles °approved [2]in [5]Christ.
[5]Salute them which are °of °Aristobulus' °*house-*
hold.
11 [5]Salute °Herodion my [7]kinsman. [3]Greet
them that be [10]of the [10]*household* of °Narcis-
sus, °which are [2]in the [2]Lord.
12 [5]Salute °Tryphena and Tryphosa, who
°labour [2]in the [2]Lord. [5]Salute °the [5]beloved
°Persis, which °laboured much [2]in the [2]Lord.
13 [5]Salute °Rufus °chosen [2]in the [2]Lord, and
°his mother and mine.
14 [5]Salute °Asyncritus, Phlegon, °Hermas,
Patrobas, Hermes, and the brethren which
are °with them.
15 [5]Salute °Philologus, and Julia, °Nereus,
and his sister, and Olympas, and all the °saints
which are [14]with them.
16 [5]Salute one another °with °an °holy kiss.
G[2] °The [1]churches of [5]Christ [5]salute you.
17 Now I °beseech you, brethren, °mark them
which cause °divisions and °offences °contrary
to the °doctrine which ye °have learned; and
°avoid °them.
18 For they that are such °serve [4]not our
[2]Lord °Jesus Christ, but their own °belly; and
°by °good words and °fair speeches °deceive
the hearts of the °simple.
19 For your obedience is °come abroad [5]unto
all *men.* I °am glad therefore °on your behalf:
but °yet I °would have you °wise [5]unto
that which is °good, and °simple °concerning
°evil.
20 And °the °God of peace shall °bruise Satan
°under your feet °shortly. °The °grace of our
[18]Lord Jesus Christ *be* °with you. °Amen.
21 °Timotheus my °workfellow, and °Lucius,
and °Jason, and °Sosipater, my °kinsmen,
[5]salute you.
22 I °Tertius, who wrote *this* epistle, [5]salute
you [2]in the [2]Lord.
23 °Gaius mine host, and of the whole [1]church,
[5]saluteth you. °Erastus the °chamberlain of
the city [5]saluteth you, and °Quartus °a brother.

9 Urbane = Urban (masc.). A Latin name.
Stachys. Masc. Only here.
10 Apelles. Masc. Only here. A Greek name frequently adopted by Jews.
approved = the approved, a term pointing to one of tried excellence. See 14. 18.
of. Ap. 104. vii.
Aristobulus. Only here. A Greek name.
household. Lit. those from among the (ones) of Aristobulus. He himself may not have been a Christian, and those referred to may have been of his family, or slaves. Cp. Phil. 4. 22.
11 Herodion. Greek masc. name.
Narcissus. Only here. Common Greek name (masc.).
which = who.
12 Tryphena and Tryphosa. Only here. Gr. fem. names.
labour, laboured. As in *v.* 6.
the beloved. Not "my" as in 8, 9.
Persis. Greek fem. name.
13 Rufus. Common Latin name. Perhaps the Rufus of Mark 15. 21.
chosen = the elect (brother). See 8. 33. Cp. 1 Tim. 5. 21. 2 John 13. The term marks some special manifestation of grace, as in that of Apelles, *v.* 10.
his . . . mine. Implying tender relationship.
14 Asyncritus, &c. Five Greek masc. names. Only here. See Acts 14. 12.
Hermas. Not to be identified with the author of "The Shepherd of Hermas", written about 120 A.D.
with. Ap. 104. xvi.
15 Philologus, &c. These names occ. only here. "Nereus" was a sea-god of the Ægean, and this convert may have retained his original pagan name.
saints. Like the "brethren" of *v.* 14, known to God, but not to Paul by *name.*
16 with. Ap. 104. viii.
an = a.
holy kiss. Cp. 1 Cor. 16. 20. 2 Cor. 13. 12. 1 Thess. 5. 26. 1 Pet. 5. 14. The kiss was, and is, in the East a sign of respect and affection. Cp. the other two occ. of *philēma,* kiss, Luke 7. 45; 22. 48. See Acts 20. 37.
The. The texts read "All the"; i. e. those specifically mentioned or referred to above.
17 beseech. Ap. 134. I. 6. Cp. 12. 8.
mark = to mark. See Luke 11. 35.
divisions = factions. Gr. *dichostasia.* Only here; 1 Cor. 3. 3. Gal. 5. 20.
offences = stumbling-blocks, as in 11. 9
contrary to. Ap. 104. xii. 3.
doctrine. See 6. 17.
have learned = learned.
avoid = turn away. Cp. 3. 12. 1 Pet. 3. 11.
them = from (Ap. 104. iv) them. **18 serve.** Ap. 190. III. 2. **Jesus.** The texts omit. **belly.** See John 7. 38. **by.** Ap. 104. v. 1. **good . . . speeches** = their fine words and flatteries. **good words.** Gr. *chrēstologia.* Only here. **fair speeches.** Gr. *eulogia.* Occ. sixteen times (eleven transl. "blessing"). See 15. 29. **deceive** = deceive thoroughly. Gr. *exapataō.* Occ. 7. 11. 1 Cor. 3. 18. 2 Cor. 11. 3. 2 Thess. 2. 3. The usual word for "deceive" means "to lead astray" (Ap. 128. viii. 1). **simple** = guileless. Gr. *akakos.* Only here and Heb. 7. 26. **19 come abroad.** Gr. *aphikneomai.* Only here. **am glad** = rejoice. See 12. 12. **on . . . behalf.** Ap. 104. ix. 2. **yet . . . have** = I wish you indeed to be. **would.** Ap. 102. 1. **wise.** See 1. 14. **good** = the good. **simple** = harmless. Gr. *akeraios.* Only here; Matt. 10. 16. Phil. 2. 15. **concerning.** Ap. 104. vi. **evil** = the evil. **20 the God,** &c. See 15. 33. **God.** Ap. 98. I. i. 1. **bruise** = crush in pieces, or utterly. Gr. *suntribō.* Elsewhere, Matt. 12. 20. Mark 5. 4; 14. 3. Luke 4. 18; 9. 39. John 19. 36. Rev. 2. 27. **under.** Ap. 104. xviii. 2. **shortly** = with speed. Gr. *en* (Ap. 104. viii) *tachei.* **The grace,** &c. Each one of Paul's Epp. ends with a benedictory prayer that "grace" may be with churches and individuals alike. **grace.** Ap. 184. I. 1. **with.** Ap. 104. xi. 1. **Amen.** The texts, except B.E., omit.

THE FIRST POSTSCRIPT (TERTIUS).

21 Timotheus = Timothy. See Acts 16. 1. **workfellow** = fellow-labourer. See *v.* 3. **Lucius.** Probably referred to in Acts 13. 1. Not Luke. **Jason.** Only here, unless the Jason of Acts 17. 5, 7. **Sosipater.** May be the Berœan of Acts 20. 4. **kinsmen,** i. e. of amanuensis. See *v.* 7. **22 Tertius.** Prob. a Roman, writing to Romans. **23 Gaius.** Common Roman name. May be the same as in Acts 19. 29, or of Derbe, Acts 20. 4, but almost certainly Gaius of 1 Cor. 1. 14. The Gaius of 3 John 1, evidently a man of position, is probably another person. **Erastus.** Perhaps the same as in 2 Tim. 4. 20. The name, a Greek one, occ. Acts 19. 22. **chamberlain** = treasurer. Gr. *oikonomos.* Occ. ten times, rendered "steward" in eight. See Luke 12. 42. **Quartus.** Only here. Roman name. **a brother** = the brother (in Christ, *v.* 7).

24 °The [20] grace of our [20] Lord Jesus Christ *be*
[20] with you all. Amen.

C 25 Now to Him That is °of power to °stablish
you °according to my °gospel, and the °preach-
ing of °Jesus Christ, °according to °the °reve-
lation of °the °mystery, °which was kept
°secret °since the world began,
26 °But now is °made manifest, and [18] by
°the scriptures of the prophets, [25] according to
°the °commandment of the °everlasting [20] God,
°made known °to all °nations °for °the °obe-
dience of faith:

B 27 To [20] God only °wise, *be* °glory °through
[25] Jesus Christ °for ever. Amen.

24 The grace, &c. The amanuensis repeats the words which close the actual message of Paul, *v.* 20. Some ancient texts omit this second benediction, and the R. V. follows through not understanding the reason for the introduction of "the mystery", *vv.* 25, 26, and 27. There are clearly *two* postscripts, one after *v.* 20, the other after *v.* 24. The first closes the Ep. itself at the time of writing by Tertius in the spring of 58 A. D. The other was added by Paul himself during the first Roman imprisonment, and after Ephesians had been written. See longer Note below.

SECOND POSTSCRIPT (PAUL).

25 of power=able. Gr. *dunamai.* Cp. 8. 39. See Ap. 176. 1. **stablish.** See 1. 11. **according to.** Ap. 104. x. 2. **gospel.** Ap. 140. IV. **preaching.** Ap. 121. 3. **Jesus Christ.** Ap. 98. XI. **the**=a. **revelation.** Ap. 106. II. i. Cp. Eph. 3. 3. **mystery.** Gr. *musterion.* Ap. 193. **which . . . secret**=which (secret) has been kept in silence (Gr. *sigaō.* Cp. Acts 15. 12. 1 Cor. 14. 28, 30, 34). **since . . . began.** Ap. 151. II. B. iv. **26 But, &c.**=But *now* is manifested. **made manifest.** Ap. 106. I. v. **the . . . prophets**=prophetic writings. Gr. *graphē prophētikos.* The term *prophētikos* occ. only here and 2 Pet. 1. 19. Ap. 189. **the.** Omit. **commandment.** Gr. *epitagē.* Here; 1 Cor. 7. 6, 25. 2 Cor. 8. 8. 1 Tim. 1. 1. Tit. 1. 3; 2. 15. **everlasting.** Ap. 151. II. B. ii. **made known.** See 9. 22. **to.** Ap. 104. vi. **nations**=Gentiles, as *v.* 4. **for.** Ap. 104. vi. **obedience, &c.** See 1. 5. **27 wise.** See 1. 14. **glory**=the glory. **through.** Ap. 104. v. 1. **for ever.** See Ap. 151. II. A. ii. 7. a.

LONGER NOTE.

THE SECOND POSTSCRIPT (16. 25–27).

That the "doxology" is a postscript added by the apostle after he had arrived at, and was residing in, Rome (61–63 A. D.: see Ap. 180), and was writing *Ephesians*, seems clear for the following reasons:—

First, there is no question as to the genuineness or authenticity of these verses.

The question raised by their appearance not only after the close of the Epistle itself, but also after the postscript of the amanuensis, Tertius, is connected with the "mystery" "kept in silence from age-times but now manifested by means of prophetic writings". To find the subject-matter of *Ephesians* introduced suddenly, in such a position, and in the diction of this doxology, has been a difficulty for ancient transcribers and modern commentators alike.

The original MSS. prove this by the position the doxology occupies in many of them.

In over 190 it stands after 14. 23.

In two or three it is wanting.

In some it appears in both places (i. e. after 14. 23 and 16. 24).

In some, where the doxology stands as in the A.V. the second benediction (*v.* 24) is omitted.

This difficulty is shared by modern commentators. Some suppose the doxology was "the effusion of the fervent mind of the apostle on taking a general view of the Epistle".

Others say—"it needs only to read the doxology to see that its main purpose is nothing lower than thanksgiving for the Universal Gospel as a whole, and that its weighty grandeur of tone belongs to the close not of a section, but of the whole Epistle."

But the suggestion that this "postscript" was added later by the apostle removes all the difficulties, and shows that the minds of the ancient copyists were needlessly disturbed. The truth of the "mystery" had been lost *long before the date of our oldest MSS.* Hence the transcribers' excitement and perplexity. Had it been known, they would have at once understood that the doxology was subsequently added.[1] And the same remark applies to modern commentators.

Although Paul must have had the "secret" revealed to him beforehand, probably about 57 or 58 A. D., yet he was not permitted to publish the truths of the mystery *in writing* until after he was in Rome, and in prison. Consequently, when the Epistle was *sent first* to the Romans, it was closed by the second benediction (*v.* 24).

Although given to him before the expiry of the period of grace enjoyed by the pentecostal church, he was not allowed to divulge it. So long as the offer of the Kingdom (see App. 112–114) to earthly Israel was open, the "mystery" could not be made known.

But when the sentence of judicial blindness had been promulgated and the prophecy of Isa. 6 fulfilled (Acts 28. 26, 27), then the glorious truths for the later-born were allowed to be set forth by "prophetic writings", viz. the prison epistles.

Therefore the apostle was guided by the Holy Spirit to add the postscript to Romans; thus completing in beautiful perfection the Divine arrangement of the Epistle (see Structure, p. 1661) and striking the key-note in the doctrinal teaching which is taken up and developed at large in Ephesians.

[1] This suggestion was first made by Bishop Lightfoot in *Biblical Essays*, and adopted by others.

THE FIRST EPISTLE TO THE CORINTHIANS.

THE STRUCTURE OF THE BOOK AS A WHOLE.

(Introversion and Alternation.)

A | 1 1-9. INTRODUCTION.
  B | **D** | 1. 10—4. 16. MINISTERIAL. REPROOF AND EXPLANATIONS.
    E | **F** | 4. 17. MISSION OF TIMOTHY.
      G | 4. 18-21. VISIT OF PAUL.
        C | 5. 1—6. 20. THINGS HEARD BY PAUL.
        C | 7. 1—8. 13. THINGS WRITTEN TO PAUL.
  B | *D* | 9. 1—15. 58. MINISTERIAL. REPROOF AND EXPLANATIONS.
    E | *G* | 16. 1-9. VISIT OF PAUL.
      F | 16. 10-18. MISSION OF TIMOTHY.
A | 16. 19-24. CONCLUSION.

NOTES ON THE FIRST EPISTLE TO THE CORINTHIANS.

An account of Paul's labours in Corinth is given in Acts 18. 1-18. Some time after this Apollos, commended by the brethren at Ephesus, came to Corinth and produced a powerful impression by his eloquent presentation of the gospel (*vv.* 27, 28).

Two parties soon began to show themselves; one adhering to Paul and his simple preaching, the other to Apollos; to these was added a third, evidently the outcome of the visit of some Judaizers who claimed the authority of Peter, while a fourth, repudiating the other three, claimed that they only were the true followers of Christ. This was but one of the difficulties the apostle had to deal with in the infant church he had founded. Already he had written to them of the dangers due to their corrupt surroundings in such a city (1 Cor. 5. 9). He had moreover received a letter from them, asking advice on certain questions, but making no reference to their divisions. Of these he was informed by visitors to Ephesus (1. 11; 5. 1; 11. 18; 15. 12), who brought word also of the profanation of the Lord's Supper, of the toleration of the incestuous offender, and of the scepticism as to the resurrection. Paul had thus many matters to deal with. He begins by referring to their divisions, and vindicates his own ministry, appealing to them as his beloved sons. He then refers to the notorious offender of whom even the Gentiles would be ashamed, and whom he charges them to tolerate no longer, but to cut off from their assembly. He blames their litigious spirit, and charges them to settle their differences without the scandal of appealing to heathen courts. Next he takes up the question of marriage, which was one of the subjects of their letter, and the eating of food offered to idols, which was another, and again makes a defence of his apostolic authority. The rest of the Epistle deals with errors which affected the life of the assembly, the behaviour of women and their leaving the head uncovered, the disorder at the Lord's Supper, then spiritual gifts (especially speaking with tongues), and the scepticism as to the resurrection which evoked the noble fifteenth chapter.

In Paul's day Corinth was the chief city of the Roman province of Achaia. Situated on the Isthmus of the same name, and having a harbour on each side, it was notable for its commerce. And no less was it noted for the wealth and profligacy of its citizens. The great city has now become a mean village.

For the Chronology of the Acts period, see Ap. 180.
For the Church Epistles, see Ap. 192.

THE FIRST EPISTLE OF PAUL THE APOSTLE

TO THE

CORINTHIANS.

A A[1] 1 PAUL, °called *to be* an °apostle of °Jesus
Christ °through the °will of °God, and °Sos-
thenes °*our* brother,
2 °Unto the °church of [1]God which is °at
Corinth, to °them that are sanctified °in
°Christ Jesus, [1]called *to be* °saints, °with all
that °in every place °call upon °the name of
[1]Jesus Christ our °Lord, both theirs and ours:
3 °Grace *be* [2]unto you, and °peace, °from
[1]God our Father, and *from* the °Lord [1]Jesus
Christ.

A[2] 4 I °thank my [1]God always °on your behalf,
°for the [3]grace of [1]God which is given you
°by [1]Jesus Christ;
5 That [2]in every thing ye °are °enriched [4]by
Him, [2]in all °utterance, and *in* all °knowledge;
6 Even as the °testimony of °Christ was °con-
firmed [2]in you:
7 So that ye °come behind [2]in °no °gift;
°waiting for the °coming of our [2]Lord [1]Jesus
Christ:
8 Who shall °also [6]confirm you °unto the
°end, *that ye may be* °blameless [2]in the day of
our [2]Lord [1]Jesus Christ.
9 [1]God *is* °faithful, °by Whom ye were called
°unto the °fellowship of His °Son [1]Jesus
Christ our [2]Lord.

B D 10 °Now I °beseech you, brethren, [9]by [2]the
name of our [2]Lord [1]Jesus Christ, °that ye all
°speak the same thing, and *that* there be °no
°divisions °among you; but *that* ye be °per-
fectly joined together [2]in the same mind and
[2]in the same °judgment.

1. 1-9 (A, p. 1695). INTRODUCTION. (*Division.*)

A | A[1] | 1-3. Benediction.
  | A[2] | 4-9. Thanksgiving.

1. 1 called, &c. Lit. a called apostle. See Rom. 1. 1.
called. Gr. *klētos.* See Rom. 1. 1. No ellipsis of "to be", nor in *v.* 2.
apostle. Ap. 189.
Jesus Christ. Ap. 98. XI.
through. Ap. 104. v. 1.
will. Ap. 102. 2.
God. Ap. 98. I. i. 1.
Sosthenes. If he is the same as in Acts 18. 17, he had followed in the steps of Paul (Gal. 1. 23).
our=the.
2 Unto=to.
church of God. This expression occ. in 10. 32; 11. 22; 15. 9. Acts 20. 28. 2 Cor. 1. 1. Gal. 1. 13. 1 Tim. 3. 5, 15; and in the plural in 11. 16. 1 Thess. 2. 14. 2 Thess. 1. 4.
church. Ap. 186.
at=in. Ap. 104. viii.
them that are sanctified. Gr. *hagiazō.* See John 17. 17, 19.
in. Gr. *en*; as above.
Christ Jesus. Ap. 98. XII.
saints. Gr. *hagios.* See Acts 9. 13.
with. Ap. 104. xvi.
call upon. Gr. *epikaleō.* See Acts 2. 21. Same as "appeal to" (Acts 25. 11, &c.).
the name. See Acts 2. 38 and cp. *v.* 10.
Lord. Ap. 98. VI. i. β. 2. A.
3 Grace. Ap. 184. I. 1. See Rom. 1. 7.
peace. This has no reference to their divisions, as the same salutation is given in all Paul's epistles except those to Timothy and Titus.
from. Ap. 104. iv.
Lord. Ap. 98. VI. i. β. 2. B.
4 thank, &c. Gr. *eucharisteō.* See Acts 27. 35.
on your behalf=concerning (Ap. 104. xiii. 1) you.
for=upon. Ap. 104. ix. 2. **by**=in. Ap. 104. viii. Cp. Eph. 1. 3. **5 are**=were. **enriched.** Gr. *ploutizō.* Only here and 2 Cor. 6. 10; 9. 11. **utterance.** Ap. 121. 10. **knowledge.** Ap. 132. II. i. Cp. 2 Cor. 8. 7; 11. 6. **6 testimony.** Gr. *marturion.* Always rendered "testimony", save Matt. 24. 14. Acts 4. 33; 7. 44. Jas. 5. 3. In these "witness". **Christ.** Ap. 98. IX. **confirmed.** Gr. *bebaioō.* See Rom. 15. 8. **7 come behind**=are not (Ap. 105. II) lacking (Gr. *hustereō*). See Rom. 3. 23. **no.** Gr. *mēdeis.* A double negative. **gift.** Ap. 184. I. 2. **waiting for**=eagerly expecting. Gr. *apekdechomai.* See Rom. 8. 19. **coming**=revelation. Ap. 106. II. 1. There are two other words used with reference to the Lord's coming, *parousia* (see Matt. 24. 3), and *epiphaneia* (see 2 Thess. 2. 8). Cp. 2 Thess. 1. 7. 1 Pet. 1. 7, 13. **8 also, &c.**=confirm you also. **unto**=until. Gr. *heōs.* Cp. Phil. 1. 6. **end.** Gr. *telos.* See Matt. 10. 22. **blameless.** Gr. *anengklētos.* Here, Col. 1. 22. 1 Tim. 3. 10. Tit. 1. 6, 7. **9 faithful.** Ap. 150. III. Cp. 10. 13. 2 Cor. 1. 18. 1 Thess. 5. 24. 2 Thess. 3. 3. **by.** Ap. 104. v. 1. **unto.** Ap. 104. vi. **fellowship.** Gr. *koinōnia.* Cp. 2 Cor. 13. 14. 1 John 1. 3. **Son.** Ap. 108. iii. The title "Lord" is added to "Jesus Christ" six times in the first ten verses of this chapter.

1. 10—4. 16 (D, p. 1695). MINISTERIAL. REPROOF AND EXPLANATIONS.
(*Extended Alternation.*)

D | **B** | D | 1. 10-12. Reproof for their divisions.
  E | 1. 13. Questions. Is Christ divided? &c.
   F | 1. 14-16. Answer.
    C | 1. 17—3. 2. Paul's apostolic commission.
 D | 3. 3, 4. Reproof for their divisions.
  E | 3. 5. Questions. Who then is Paul? &c.
   F | 3. 6-8. Answer.
    C | 3. 9—4. 16. Paul's apostolic commission.

10 Now=But. **beseech**=exhort. Ap. 134. I. 6. **that**=in order that. Gr. *hina.* **speak**=say. **no**=not. Ap. 105. II. **divisions.** Gr. *schisma.* Elsewhere, 11. 18; 12. 25. Matt. 9. 16 (rent). Mark 2. 21 (rent). John 7. 43; 9. 16; 10. 19. Hence Engl. "schism". **among.** Ap. 104. viii. 2. **perfectly joined together**=fitted, or perfected. Fig. *Pleonasm.* Ap. 6. See Ap. 125. 8. **judgment**=opinion. Ap. 177. 2.

11 For it hath been °declared [2]unto me °of you, my brethren, °by them *which are of the house* of Chloe, that there are °contentions [10]among you.

12 [10]Now °this I say, that °every one of you saith, "I am of Paul"; and "I of °Apollos"; and "I of °Cephas"; and "I of [6]Christ".

E 13 °Is [6]Christ divided? °was Paul crucified °for you? or were ye °baptized °in the name of Paul?

F 14 I [4]thank [1]God that I °baptized °none of you, °but °Crispus and °Gaius;

15 °Lest °any should say that I °had [13]baptized [13]in mine own name.

16 And I [14]baptized °also the household of °Stephanas: °besides, I °know °not °whether I [14]baptized [15]any °other.

C G[1] 17 For [6]Christ °sent me [16]not to [14]baptize, but to °preach the gospel: [16]not °with wisdom of °words, [15]lest the cross of [6]Christ should be °made of none effect.

H[1]J 18 For the °preaching of the cross is to °them that perish °foolishness; but [2]unto °us which are °saved it is the °power of [1]God.

K 19 For it °is written, "**I will °destroy the wisdom of the wise, and will °bring to nothing the °understanding of the °prudent.**"

20 Where *is* the wise? where *is* the scribe? where *is* the °disputer of this °world? hath °not [1]God °made foolish the wisdom of °this °world?

21 For °after that [2]in the wisdom of [1]God the [20]world [9]by wisdom °knew [16]not [1]God,° it pleased [1]God [9]by the [18]foolishness of °preaching to save them that °believe.

22 For °the Jews °require a °sign, and °the Greeks °seek after wisdom:

11 declared = shown. Gr. *dēloō* = to make manifest. Elsewhere, 3. 13. Col. 1. 8. Heb. 9. 8; 12. 27. 1 Pet. 1. 11. In these three last, signify. 2 Pet. 1. 14 (show).

of = concerning; as in *v.* 4.

by. Ap. 104. xviii. 1.

contentions = strifes. Gr. *eris.* See Rom. 1. 29.

12 this I say = I mean this.

every, &c., i. e. each one is attached to some party.

Apollos. See Acts 18. 24.

Cephas. See John 1. 42.

13 Is Christ divided? The omission of *mē*, with the question, implies that the answer must be affirmative. "He is indeed." Cp. 12. 12–25. You are rending Him.

was Paul, &c.? The *mē* here requires a negative answer.

for = on behalf of. Ap. 104. xvii. 1.

baptized. Ap. 115. I. iv.

in = into. Ap. 104. vi.

14 baptized. Ap. 115. I. i.

none. Gr. *oudeis.*

but = except. Gr. *ei mē.*

Crispus. See Acts 18. 8.

Gaius. See Acts 19. 29. Rom. 16. 23.

15 Lest. Lit. in order that (Gr. *hina,* as in *v.* 10) not (Gr. *mē*).

any. Gr. *tis.* Ap. 123. 3.

had. Omit.

16 also, &c. = the household of Stephanas also.

Stephanas. Cp. 16. 15, 17.

besides = for the rest. Gr. *loipon.* Neut. of *loipos.* Ap. 124. 3.

know. Ap. 132. I. i.

not. Ap. 105 I.

whether = if. Ap. 118. 2. a.

other. Ap. 124. 1.

1. 17—3. 2 [For Structure see below].

17 sent. Ap. 174. 1.

preach the gospel = evangelize. Ap. 121. 4.

with = in. Ap. 104. viii.

words. Ap. 121. 10. This means either "eloquent language", or "clever reasoning". Perhaps both ideas were in the apostle's mind.

made of none effect. Gr. *kenoō.* See Rom. 4. 14.

1. 17—3. 2 (C, p. 1696). PAUL'S APOSTOLIC COMMISSION. (*Repeated Alternation.*)

C | G[1] | 1. 17. Personal. Commission given.
  H[1] | 1. 18–31. General. The subject. Christ and the Cross.
 G[2] | 2. 1–5. Personal. Commission carried out. Manner.
  H[2] | 2. 6–16. Special (in private). The wisdom of God to the initiated.
 G[3] | 3. 1. Personal. Commission carried out. Speaking.
  H[3] | 3. 2. General. Subject. The condition of the Corinthians.

1. 18–31 (H[1], above). GENERAL. SUBJECT. CHRIST AND THE CROSS. (*Alternation.*)

H[1] | J | 18. The Cross. Opposite effects.
  K | 19–22. Reason. "For."
 J | 23, 24. Christ. Opposite effects.
  K | 25–31. Reason. "Because."

18 preaching = word, or message. Gr. *logos,* as in *v.* 17. **them that perish** = those that are perishing. Gr. *apollumi.* Cp. 2 Cor. 2. 15; 4. 3. 2 Thess. 2. 10. See John 17. 12. **foolishness.** Gr. *mōria.* Only in this Epistle, *vv.* 21, 23; 2. 14; 3. 19. **us which are, &c.** = those who are being saved, (even) us. This is the order in the Greek. Salvation has more than one aspect. See Rom. 13. 11. Phil. 2. 12. 1 Thess. 5. 8, 9. 2 Tim. 1. 9; 3. 15; 4. 18. 1 Pet. 1. 5. **power.** Ap. 172. 1. Cp. Rom. 1. 16. **19 is** = has been. The reference is to Isa. 29. 14. Ap. 107. I. 3. **destroy.** Gr. *apollumi,* as in *v.* 18. **bring to nothing** = annul. Gr. *atheteō.* See John 12. 48. **understanding.** Gr. *sunesis.* First occ. Mark 12. 33. **prudent.** Gr. *sunetos.* Adj. akin to the above. See Acts 13. 7. This quotation agrees with the Sept., except that it reads "hide" (*kruptō*) instead of "bring to nought". In the Hebrew the form of the sentence is different. (See A.V.) **20 disputer.** Gr. *suzētētēs.* Only here. Cp. Acts 15. 2. **world** = age. Ap. 129. 2. It was an age of speculation. Acts 17. 21. **not.** Gr. *ouchi.* Ap. 105. I. (a). **made foolish.** Gr. *mōrainō.* See Rom. 1. 22. **this** = the. **world.** Gr. *kosmos.* Ap. 129. 1. The wisdom of the world is human wisdom generally. **21 after that** = since. **knew.** Ap. 132. I. ii. **it pleased God** = God was well pleased. Gr. *eudokeō.* Occ. twenty-one times. Generally transl. "pleased", "well pleased", "take pleasure". **preaching** = the thing proclaimed. Ap. 121. 3. **believe.** Ap. 150. I. 1. i. **22 the.** Omit. **require** = ask. Ap. 134. I. 4. **sign.** Ap. 176. 3. The texts read "signs". **seek after** = seek.

J 23 But we °preach [6]Christ °crucified, [2]unto °the Jews a °stumblingblock, and [2]unto °the °Greeks [18]foolishness;
24 But [2]unto °them which are [1]called, both Jews and Greeks, [6]Christ the [18]power of [1]God, and the wisdom of [1]God.

K 25 Because the °foolishness of [1]God is wiser than °men; and the °weakness of [1]God is stronger than °men.
26 For °ye °see your °calling, brethren, how that [16]not many wise men °after the flesh, [16]not many mighty, [16]not many °noble, *are called:*
27 But [1]God °hath chosen the [25]foolish things of the -[20]world °to °confound the wise; and [1]God °hath chosen the [25]weak things of the -[20]world °to °confound the things which are mighty;
28 And °base things of the -[20]world, and things which are °despised, [27]hath [1]God chosen, *yea,* and things which are °not, [27]to °bring to nought things that are:
29 That [10]no flesh should °glory in His presence.
30 But °of Him are ye [2]in [2]Christ Jesus, Who °of [1]God °is made [2]unto us wisdom, °and °righteousness, and °sanctification, °and °redemption:
31 [10]That, according as it °is written, "**He that [29]glorieth, let him [29]glory [2]in the °LORD.**"

G[2] L **2** And I, brethren, when I came °to you, came °not °with °excellency of °speech or of wisdom, °declaring °unto you the °testimony of °God.
2 For I °determined [1]not to °know any thing °among you, °save °Jesus Christ, and °Him crucified.

M 3 And I was °with you °in weakness, and °in fear, and °in much °trembling.

L 4 And my [1]speech and my °preaching *was* [1]not °with °enticing °words of °man's wisdom, but [3]in °demonstration °of the Spirit and of °power:

M 5 °That your °faith should °not °stand [3]in the wisdom of °men, but [3]in the [4]power of [1]God.

23 preach. Ap. 121. 1.
crucified. That is, a crucified Messiah.
the. Omit.
stumblingblock. Gr. *skandalon.* Occ. fifteen times. Nine times transl. "offence"; once "offend"; thrice "stumblingblock"; elsewhere "occasion to fall, or of stumbling". First occ. Matt. 13. 41. Instead of the signs of the kingdom promised by the prophets, the One who claimed to be their Messiah was crucified. This staggered them.
Greeks. The texts read "Gentiles" (*ethnos*).
24 them which are called = the called themselves.
25 foolishness. Lit. foolish thing. Gr. *mōros.*
men. Ap. 123. 1.
weakness. Lit. weak thing. Gr. *asthenēs.*
26 ye. Omit.
see. Ap. 133. I. 5.
calling. Gr. *klēsis.* See Rom. 11. 29. Here it means the way ye were called, i. e. the kind of persons whom God sent to call you. Hence instead of "are called" as in A.V. and R.V., the *ellipsis* should be supplied thus: "not many are wise", &c. Apollos was an eloquent man, but as to Paul, his speech was regarded as contemptible. See 2 Cor. 10. 10, and cp. Acts 17. 18.
after = according to. Ap. 104. x. 2.
noble. Gr. *eugenēs.* See Acts 17. 11.
27 hath chosen = chose. Gr. *eklegomai.* See Acts 1. 2.
to = in order to. Gr. *hina.*
confound = put to shame. Gr. *kataischunō.* See Rom. 5. 5.
28 base. Gr. *agenēs.* Lit. without family, or descent. Only here. The opp. of *eugenes, v.* 26.
despised. Gr. *exoutheneō.* Lit. counted as nothing. See Acts 4. 11.
not. Ap. 105. II.
bring to nought. Gr. *katargeō.* See Rom. 3. 3.
29 glory = boast. Gr. *kauchaomai.* See Rom. 2. 17.
30 of. Ap. 104. vii.
of = from. Ap. 104. iv. The Greek reads "became . . . wisdom from God".
is made = became. Gr. *ginomai.*
and = both.
righteousness. Ap. 191. 3.
sanctification = holiness. Gr. *hagiasmos.* See Rom. 6. 19.
and = even.
redemption. Gr. *apolutrōsis.* See Rom. 3. 24 and cp. Eph. 1. 7, 14; 4. 30.
31 is = has been. This is a summary of Jer. 9. 23.
LORD. Ap. 98. VI. i. *β.* 1. B. a.

2. 1-5 (G[2], p. 1697). PERSONAL. COMMISSION CARRIED OUT. MANNER. (*Alternation.*)

G[2] | L | 1, 2. His testimony.
  M | 3. His feelings.
  L | 4. His testimony.
  M | 5. The faith of the Corinthians.

2. 1 to = unto. Ap. 104. xv. 3. **not.** Ap. 105. I. **with** = according to. Ap. 104. x. 2. **excellency** = pre-eminence. Gr. *huperochē.* Only here and 1 Tim. 2. 2. **speech** = word. Ap. 121. 10. **declaring.** Ap. 121. 5. **unto** = to. **testimony.** Gr. *marturion,* as in 1. 6. **God.** Ap. 98. I. i. 1. **2 determined.** Ap. 122. 1. **know.** Ap. 132. I. i. **among** Ap. 104. viii. 2. **save** = except. Gr. *ei* (Ap. 118. 2. a) *mē* (Ap. 105. II). **Jesus Christ.** Ap. 98. XI. **Him** = This One. Emphatic. **3 with.** Ap. 104. xv. 3. **in.** Ap. 104. viii. **trembling.** Gr. *tromos.* Elsewhere, Mark 16. 8 (lit. trembling . . . seized them). 2 Cor. 7. 15. Eph. 6. 5. Phil. 2. 12. Fear is joined with trembling in all these passages save Mark 16. 8. His sense of weakness (cp. Gal. 4. 13) produced fear, and this resulted in trembling. Cp. 2 Cor. 4. 7. **4 preaching.** Gr. *kērugma,* as in 1. 21. **with** = in. Ap. 104. viii. **enticing** = persuasive. Gr. *peithos.* Only here. Cp. Ap. 150. I. 2. **words.** Gr. *logos,* as in *v.* 1. **man's** = human. Gr. *anthrōpinos.* See Rom. 6. 19. But the texts omit "man's". **demonstration.** Gr. *apodeixis.* Only here. Cp. 4. 9. **of the . . . power.** Here spirit = spiritual gift, in this case Divine wisdom. By Fig. *Hendiadys* (Ap. 6) = "the powerful gift". **power.** Ap. 172. 1. **5 That** = In order that. Gr. *hina.* **faith.** Ap. 150. II. 1. **not.** Ap. 105. II. **stand** = be. **men.** Ap. 123. 1.

H² N 6 °Howbeit we °speak wisdom [2]among °them
that are perfect:
O a yet [1]not the wisdom of this °world, °nor of the
°princes of this °world, that °come to nought:
b 7 But we [6]speak the wisdom of [1]God [3]in a
°mystery, *even* the °hidden *wisdom,* which
[1]God °ordained °before the °world °unto our
glory:
P c 8 Which °none of the [6]princes of this [6]world
°knew: for °had they °known *it,* they would
[1]not have crucified °the Lord °of glory.
d 9 But as it °is written, **"Eye °hath [1]not seen,
°nor ear heard, °neither have entered °into
the heart of [5]man, the things which [1]God
°hath prepared for them that °love Him."**
Q e 10 But [1]God °hath revealed *them* [1]unto us
°by °His °Spirit: for the °Spirit °searcheth
all things, yea, the deep things of [1]God.
f 11 For what [5]man [2]knoweth the things of a
[5]man, [2]save the °spirit of [5]man which is [3]in him?
g even so the °things of [1]God [2]knoweth °no
man, °but the [10]Spirit of [1]God.
12 Now we °have received, [1]not the [11-]spirit of
the °world, but the °spirit which is °of [1]God;
[5]that we might [2]know the things that are
°freely given to us °of [1]God.
N 13 Which things °also we [6]speak,
O a [1]not [3]in the [4]words °which [4]man's wisdom
teacheth,
b °but which the Holy Ghost teacheth; °comparing
°spiritual things °with °spiritual.
P c 14 But the °natural [5]man receiveth [1]not the
things of the [10]Spirit of [1]God:
d for they are °foolishness [1]unto him: [9]neither
can he [8]know *them,* because they are °spiritually
°discerned.
Q e 15 But he that is [13]spiritual °judgeth all
things, yet he himself is °judged [12]of [11]no man.
f 16 **For who °hath [8]known the mind of the
°LORD, °that he may °instruct Him?**
g But we have the mind of °Christ.

G ³ **3** And I, brethren, °could °not °speak °unto
you as °unto °spiritual, but as °unto °carnal,
even as °unto babes °in °Christ.
H ³ 2 I °have fed you with milk, and [1]not with
meat: for °hitherto ye were [1]not able *to bear
it,* °neither yet now are ye able.

2. 6-16 (H², p. 1697). THE WISDOM OF GOD (IN PRIVATE). (*Extended Alternation.*)

H² | N | 6-. Paul's speaking.
O | a | -6. Neg. Not the wisdom of this age.
b | 7. Pos. But the wisdom of God. } Subject.
P | c | 8. Neg. Ignorant of God's wisdom.
d | 9. Pos. Reason. Because of incapacity. } The rulers of this age.
Q | e | 10. Revelation needed.
f | 11-. Question.
g | -11, 12. Answer.
N | 13-. Paul's speaking.
O | *a* | -13-. Neg. Not the wisdom of man.
b | -13. Pos. But the power of God. } Subject.
P | *c* | 14-. Neg. Ignorant of revelation.
d | -14. Pos. Reason. Because of incapacity. } The natural man.
Q | *e* | 15. Spiritual judgment needed.
f | 16-. Question.
g | -16. Answer.

6 Howbeit=But. **speak.** Ap. 121. 7.
them, &c.=the perfect. Gr. *teleios.* Ap. 125. 1.
world=age. Ap. 129. 2. **nor.** Gr. *oude.*
princes=rulers.
come to nought=are being brought to nought. Gr. *katargeō.* See 1. 28. **7 mystery.** Ap. 193.
hidden. Same word as in Luke 10. 21. Eph. 3. 9. Col. 1. 26.
ordained=preordained. Gr. *proorizō.* See Acts 4. 28.
before. Ap. 104. xiv. Cp. Rom. 16. 25. Eph. 1. 4. 2 Tim. 1. 9.
world=ages, as in *v.* 6. **unto.** Ap. 104. vi.
8 none. Gr. *oudeis.* **knew.** Ap. 132. I. ii.
had they=if (Gr. *ei.* Ap. 118. 2. a) they had.
the Lord. Ap. 98. VI. i. *β.* 2. A.
of glory. Cp. Acts 7. 2. Eph. 1. 17. Col. 1. 27. Heb. 1. 3. Jas. 2. 1.
9 is=has been. The quotation is from Isa. 64. 4. Ap. 107. II. 2.
hath not seen=saw not. Ap. 133. I. 1.
nor ear heard=and ear heard not (Gr. *ou*).
neither have, &c.=and went not (Gr. *ou*) up.
into=upon. Ap. 104. ix. 3.
hath. Omit. **love.** Ap. 135. I. 1.
10 hath revealed=revealed. Ap. 106. ix.
by=through. Ap. 104. v. 1.
His. The texts read "the".
Spirit. Ap. 101. II. 3.
searcheth. Gr. *ereunaō.* See John 5. 39. Cp. Ps. 139. 1. Rev. 2. 23.
11 spirit. Ap. 101. II. 6. **things.** Add "also".
no man=no one. Gr. *oudeis.*
but=save, as *v.* 2. **12 have.** Omit.
world. Gr. *kosmos.* Ap. 129. 1.
spirit. Ap. 101. II. 5. **of**=by. Ap. 104. vii. **freely given.** Ap. 184. II. 1. **of**=by. Ap. 104. xviii. 1. **13 also we speak**=we speak also. **which man's, &c.**=taught (Gr. *didaktos.* Only here and John 6. 45) by man's wisdom. **but . . . teacheth.** Supply Ellipsis (Ap. 6), "but in (things) taught by the Spirit" (*v.* 10). The texts omit "Holy". **comparing**=interpreting. Gr. *sunkrinō.* Ap. 122. 8. Used in Sept. of interpreting dreams. Gen. 40. 8, 16, 22; 41. 12, 13, 15. Dan. 5. 16, 17. To interpret=to fit the meaning to the words. **spiritual.** I. e. spiritual (things) to spiritual (men). See 12. 1. **with.** No preposition. Dative case. **14 natural.** Gr. *psuchikos.* Elsewhere, 15. 44, 44, 46, and (transl. "sensual") Jas. 3. 15. Jude 19. Cp. *psuchē.* Ap. 110. **foolishness.** See 1. 18. **spiritually.** Gr. *pneumatikōs.* Only here and Rev. 11. 8. **discerned.** Ap. 122. 2. **15 judgeth**=discerneth. **judged.** As discerned, above. **16 hath known**=knew. **LORD.** Ap. 98. VI. i. *β.* 1. B. a. **that he may**=who shall. **instruct.** Gr. *sumbibazō.* See Acts 9. 22. Quoted from Is. 40. 14. **Christ.** Ap. 98. IX.
3. 1 could not=was not able to. **not.** Ap. 105. I. **speak.** Ap. 121. 7. **unto**=to. **spiritual.** Gr. *pneumatikos.* See 12. 1. **carnal.** Gr. *sarkikos,* as in Rom. 7. 14, but the texts read *sarkinos.* See 2 Cor. 3. 3. **in.** Ap. 104. viii. **Christ.** Ap. 98. IX. **2 have fed you with**=gave you . . . to drink (Gr. *potizō*). **hitherto, &c.**=ye were not as yet able to bear it. Instead of supplying the *ellipsis* with "to bear it", we might read "not as yet strong enough". **neither.** Gr. *oute* or *oude.*

D **3** For ye are yet °carnal: for whereas *there*
is °among you °envying, and °strife, and
°divisions, are ye °not °carnal, and walk °as
°men?
4 For °while one saith, "I am of Paul";
and °another, "I *am* of Apollos"; are ye [1]not
°carnal?
E **5** Who then is Paul, and who *is* Apollos, but
°ministers °by whom ye °believed, even as
°the Lord °gave to °every man?
F **6** I °have planted, Apollos °watered; but
°God °gave the increase.
7 So then °neither is he that planteth °any
thing, °neither he that watereth; but [6]God
That [6]giveth the increase.
8 Now he that [6]planteth and he that [6]watereth
are °one: and [5]every man shall receive °his
own reward °according to °his own labour.
C R h **9** For °we are °labourers together with [6]God:
k ye are [6]God's °husbandry, *ye are* [6]God's
°building.
h **10** [8]According to the °grace of [6]God which
is given [1]unto me, as a wise °masterbuilder, I
°have laid the °foundation, and °another °build-
eth thereon. But let [5]every man °take heed
how he °buildeth thereupon.
11 For [10]other [10]foundation can °no man lay
°than that is laid, which is °Jesus Christ.
12 °Now °if °any man [10]build °upon this
[10]foundation gold, silver, precious stones,
wood, °hay, °stubble;
13 [5]Every man's work shall °be made °mani-
fest: for °the day shall °declare it, because it
shall be °revealed °by fire; and the fire shall
°try [5]every man's work of what sort it is.
14 [12]If [12]any man's work °abide which he
hath [10]built thereupon, he shall receive a
reward.
15 [12]If [12]any man's work shall be °burned,
he shall °suffer loss: but he himself shall be
saved; yet so as [5]by fire.
k **16** °Know ye [1]not that ye are the °Temple
of [6]God, and *that* the °Spirit of [6]God dwelleth
°in you?

3 carnal. Gr. *sarkikos.* See *v.* 1. Rom. 7. 14.
among. Ap. 104. viii. 2.
envying. Gr. *zēlos.* See Acts 5. 17.
strife. Gr. *eris.* See 1. 11.
divisions. *dichostasia.* See Rom. 16. 17. But the texts omit "and divisions".
not. Ap. 105. I. (a).
as=according to. Ap. 104. x. 2.
men=a man. Ap. 123. 1.
4 while=whenever.
another. Ap. 124. 2.
carnal. Gr. *sarkikos,* as in *v.* 3; but the texts read "men" (*anthrōpoi*).
5 ministers=servants. Ap. 190. I. 1.
by=through. Ap. 104. v. 1.
believed. Ap. 150. I. 1. i.
the Lord. Ap. 98. VI. i. *β.* 2. A.
gave. See Eph. 4. 11.
every man=each (one).
6 have planted=planted. See Acts 18. 1–18.
watered. Gr. *potizō,* as in *v.* 2. See Acts 18. 27—19. 1.
God. Ap. 98. I. i. 1.
gave the increase=was causing it to grow. Imperf. because God's work was continuing, Paul's or any other's only temporary.
7 neither . . . neither. Gr. *oute . . . oute.*
any thing. Gr. neut. of *tis.* Ap. 123. 3. Cp. 2 Cor. 3. 5. Gal. 2. 6; 6. 3.
8 one=one thing. Both belong to the same company of servants, of whom God is the Master.
his own. Emph. Gr. *idios.*
according to. Ap. 104. x. 2.

3. 9—4. 16 (*C*, p. 1696). PAUL'S APOSTOLIC COMMISSION. (*Alternation.*)

C | R | 3. 9–17. Illustrations.
| S | 3. 18–23. Application.
| *R* | 4. 1–5. Illustration.
| *S* | 4. 6–16. Application.

3. 9–17 (R, above). ILLUSTRATIONS. "WE" AND "YE". (*Alternation.*)

R | h | 9–. "We." Paul and Sosthenes.
| k | -9. "Ye." God's husbandry, &c.
| *h* | 10–15. "We." Paul and others.
| *k* | 16, 17. "Ye." God's Temple.

9 we. I. e. Paul and Sosthenes. See 1. 1.
labourers together with God=God's fellow-workers. The word "God" is in the genitive of possession (Ap. 17), as in the two other clauses of the verse. It is the Fig. *Anaphora* (Ap. 6), and the verse should read:

"God's fellow-workers we are:
God's husbandry,
God's building, ye are."

Ministers are co-workers with one another, not with God, as though He were one of them. Were it so, "God" would be in the dative case. **labourers together with.** Gr. *sunergos.* Occ. thirteen times. Three times as here, used generally; in all other cases used of individuals, Timothy, Titus, Luke, &c. **husbandry**=tilled field. Gr. *geōrgion.* Only here. Cp. Num. 24. 6. Ps. 80. 15. **building.** Gr. *oikodomē.* Used in Matt. 24. 1. Mark 13. 1, 2. 2 Cor. 5. 1. Eph. 2. 21, of an edifice. Elsewhere twelve times of the act of building, and transl. "edifying", in a metaphorical sense. **10 grace.** Ap. 184. I. 1. **masterbuilder.** Gr. *architektōn.* Only here. **have.** The texts omit. **foundation.** Cp. Ap. 146. **another.** Ap. 124. 1. **buildeth thereon.** Gr. *epoikodomeō.* See Acts 20. 32. **take heed**=see. Ap. 133. I. 5. **11 no man**=no one. Gr. *oudeis.* **than**=beside. Ap. 104. xii. 3. **Jesus Christ.** Ap. 98. XI. **12 Now.** But. **if.** Ap. 118. 2. a. **any man**=any one. Gr. *tis.* Ap. 123. 3. **upon.** Ap. 104. ix. 3. **hay.** Gr. *chortos.* Transl. twelve times "grass", twice "blade", Matt. 13. 26. Mark 4. 28. Only here rendered "hay". Note the Fig. *Asyndeton* (Ap. 6). **stubble.** Gr. *kalamē.* Only here. All these six things are perishable (1 Pet. 1. 7). **13 be made**=become. **manifest.** Ap. 106. I. viii. **the day.** I. e. the day of the Lord. See Acts 2. 20. **declare.** Gr. *dēloō.* See 1. 11. **revealed.** Ap. 106. I. ix. **by**=in. Ap. 104. viii. **try**=test, or prove. Gr. *dokimazō.* **14 abide.** Gr. *menō.* See p. 1511. **15 burned**=burned up. Gr. *katakaiō.* Cp. Matt. 3. 12. Luke 3. 17. 2 Pet. 3. 10. **suffer loss.** Gr. *zēmioō.* Elsewhere, Matt. 16. 26. Mark 8. 36. Luke 9. 25. 2 Cor. 7. 9. Phil. 3. 8. He will lose his reward. Cp. 2 John 8. **16 Know ye not.** This expression occ. twelve times in Paul's epistles. Elsewhere, 5. 6; 6. 2, 3, 9, 15, 16, 19; 9. 13, 24. Rom. 6. 16; 11. 2. One other occ. is in Jas. 4. 4. It conveys a delicate reproach. **Know.** Ap. 133. I. 1. **Temple.** Gr. *naos.* See Matt. 23. 16. There is no art. because *naos* is the predicate. **Spirit.** The Holy Spirit. Ap. 101. II. 3. **in**=among. Ap. 104. viii. 2. The Spirit dwells in the shrine formed by the collective body of believers. Cp. Eph. 2. 22.

17 [12]If [12]any man °defile the [16]Temple of
[6]God, °him shall [6]God °destroy; for the [16]Temple
of [6]God is °holy, °which *temple* ye are.
S l 18 Let °no man °deceive himself. [12]If [12]any
man [3]among you seemeth to be wise [1]in this
°world, let him become a °fool, °that he may
°be wise.
m 19 For the wisdom of this °world is °foolish-
ness °with [6]God. For it °is written, "**He**
°**taketh the wise** [1]**in their own** °**craftiness.**"
20 And again, "°**The LORD** °**knoweth the**
°**thoughts of the wise, that they are** °**vain.**"
l 21 °Therefore let [18]no man °glory [1]in [3]men.
m For all things are yours;
22 Whether Paul, or Apollos, or Cephas, or
the [19]world, or °life, or death, or things
°present, or things °to come; all are yours;
23 And ye are [1]Christ's; and [1]Christ *is*
[6]God's.

R T **4** Let a °man °so °account of us, as of the
°ministers of °Christ,
U n and °stewards of the °mysteries of °God.
o 2 °Moreover it is °required °in [1]stewards,
°that °a man be found °faithful.
T 3 But °with me it is °a very small thing [2]that
I should be °judged °of you, or °of °man's
judgment: °yea, I °judge °not mine own self.
4 For I °know °nothing °by myself; yet am
I °not °hereby °justified: but He that [3]judgeth
me is °the Lord.
5 Therefore °judge °nothing °before the °time,
until °the Lord come,
U o Who both will °bring to light the hidden things
of darkness, and will °make manifest the
°counsels of the hearts:
n and then °shall every man have praise °of
[1]God.
S V 6 And these things, brethren, °I have in a
figure transferred °to myself and *to* Apollos
°for your sakes;

17 defile. Gr. *phtheirō.* Same word as "destroy" below. Occ. also in 15. 33. 2 Cor. 7. 2; 11. 3. Eph. 4. 22. Jude 10. Rev. 19. 2 (corrupt). The word "mar" will suit both clauses. **The man who mars God's Temple by introducing divisions, and the wisdom that is *not* from above (Jas. 3. 15), will himself be marred** (*v.* 15).
him = this one. Gr. *houtos.* Emphatic.
holy. Gr. *hagios.*
which = and such, i. e. holy, or separated. Omit "*temple*" in the last clause.

3. 18-23 (S, p. 1700). APPLICATION. (*Alternations.*)

S | l | 18. Dehortation. Let no man, &c.
  | m | 19, 20. Reason. For the Lord knoweth, &c.
  | *l* | 21-. Dehortation. Let no man glory, &c.
  | *m* | -21-23. Reason. All things are yours.

18 no man = no one. Gr. *mēdeis.*
deceive. Gr. *exapataō.* See Rom. 7. 11.
world. Ap. 129. 2.
fool. Gr. *mōros*, as in 1. 25, 27.
that = in order that. Gr. *hina.*
be = become.
19 world. Gr. *kosmos.* Ap. 129. 1.
foolishness. Gr. *mōria.* See 1. 18.
with. Ap. 104. xii. 2.
is = has been.
taketh. Gr. *drassomai.* Only here. Found in the Sept., but not in Job 5. 13, from which this is quoted.
craftiness. Gr. *panourgia.* See Luke 20. 23. This is the only time Job is quoted in the N.T.
20 The LORD. No art. Ap. 98. VI. i. *β.* 1. B. a.
knoweth. Ap. 132. I. ii.
thoughts = reasonings.
vain. Gr. *mataios.* See Acts **14. 15.** Quoted from Ps. 94. 11.
21 Therefore = So then.
glory = boast, as in 1. 29.
22 life. Gr. *zōē.* Ap. 170. 1.
present. Gr. *enistēmi.* See Rom. 8. 38.
to come = about to be. Gr. *mellō.*

4. 1-5 (*R*, p. 1700). ILLUSTRATION.
(*Alternation and Introversion.*)

R | T | 1-. Right judgment of us (Paul and Sosthenes).
  | U | n | -1. Stewards.
  | | o | 2. What is required defined.
  | *T* | 3-5-. Right judgment of me (Paul).
  | *U* | *o* | -5-. What is required discovered.
  | | *n* | -5. Stewards. Reward.

4. 1 man. Ap. 123. 1. **so.** This emphasizes the "as" which follows. **account** = reckon. Gr. *logizomai.* **ministers.** Ap. 190. I. 3. **Christ.** Ap. 98. IX. **stewards.** Gr. *oikonomos.* Occ. ten times. Always transl. "steward", except Rom. 16. 23 and Gal. 4. 2. See Luke 16. 1. **mysteries.** Gr. *mustērion.* Ap. 193. To Paul were committed various secrets. See 15. 51. Romans 11. 25. 2 Thess. 2. 7. 1 Tim. 3. 9, 16. **God.** Ap. 98. I. i. 1. **2 Moreover** = For the rest. Same as "besides" (1. 16). **required** = sought. **in** = among. Ap. 104. viii. 2. **that** = in order that. Gr. *hina.* **a man** = one. Ap. 123. 3. **faithful.** Ap. 150. III. **3 with** = for. **a very small** = the least. **judged** = examined. Ap. 122. 2. **of** = by. Ap. 104. xviii. 1. **man's judgment.** Lit. man's day. The day in which man is examining, and "judging", and God is silent. **man's.** Gr. *anthrōpinos*, as in 2 4, 13. **yea, &c.** = I do not even (Gr. *oude*) judge. **4 know** = am conscious of. Gr. *sunoida.* See Acts 5. 2. **nothing.** Gr. *oudeis.* **by** = against. No preposition. **not.** Ap. 105. I. **hereby** = in (Gr. *en*) this. **justified.** Ap. 191. 2. **the Lord.** Ap. 98. VI. i. *β.* 2. B. **5 judge.** Ap. 122. 1. **nothing** = not (Gr. *mē.* Ap. 105. II) anything (Gr. *tis*). **before.** Ap 104. xiv. **time** = season. **the Lord.** Ap. 98. VI. i. *β.* 2. A. **bring to light.** Gr. *phōtizō.* See Luke 11. 36. **make manifest.** Ap. 106. I. v. **counsels.** Gr. *boulē.* Ap. 102. 4. **shall every, &c.** Lit. praise shall be to each one. **of** = from. Ap. 104. iv.

4. 6-16 (*S*, p. 1700). APPLICATION. (*Introversion and Alternation.*)

S | V | 6-. Paul and Apollos
  | W | p | -6, 7. The Corinthians.
  | | q | 8. Their exaltation.
  | *W* | *p* | 9, 10. The apostles.
  | | *q* | 11-13. Their humiliation
  | *V* | 14-16. Paul.

6 I have in a figure transferred. Gr. *metaschēmatizō.* Elsewhere transl. "transform", 2 Cor. 11. 13, 14, 15; and "change", Phil. 3. 21. **to** = unto. Ap. 104. vi. **for your sakes** = on account of (Gr. *dia.* Ap. 104. v. 2) you.

W p [2]that ye might learn [2]in us °not to think *of*
men °above that which °is written, [2]that °no
one of you be °puffed up °for one °against
°another.
7 For who °maketh thee to differ *from*
another? and what hast thou that thou didst
[4]not receive? now °if thou didst receive *it,*
why dost thou °glory, °as if thou hadst °not
received *it?*

q 8 °Now ye °are full, °now ye are rich, ye have
reigned as kings °without us: and I °would to
[1]God ye did reign, [2]that we also might °reign
with you.

W p 9 For I think that [1]God °hath °set forth us
the °apostles °last, as it were °appointed to
death: for we are made a °spectacle °unto the
°world, °and to angels, and to [1]men.
10 We *are* °fools [6]for [1]Christ's sake, but ye *are*
wise [2]in [1]Christ; we *are* weak, but ye *are* strong;
ye *are* °honourable, but we *are* °despised.

q 11 °Even unto °this °present hour we both
hunger, and thirst, and °are naked, and °are
buffeted, and °have no certain dwellingplace;
12 And labour, °working with our own hands:
being °reviled, we bless; being persecuted, we
suffer it:
13 Being °defamed, we °intreat: we are made
as the °filth of the [9]world, *and are* the °off-
scouring of all things °unto this day.

V 14 °I write [4]not these things to °shame you,
but as my °beloved °sons I °warn *you.*
15 For °though ye °have ten thousand °in-
structers [2]in [1]Christ, yet *have ye* [4]not many
fathers: for [2]in °Christ Jesus I °have begotten
you °through the °gospel.
16 °Wherefore I °beseech you, °be ye °follow-
ers of me.

E F (p. 1695) 17 °For this cause have I °sent [9]unto you
°Timotheus, who is my [14]beloved [14]son, and
[2]faithful [2]in [4]the Lord, who shall °bring you
into remembrance of my ways °which be [2]in
[1]Christ, °as I teach every where [2]in every
°church.

G 18 Now °some are [6]puffed up, as though I
°would [6]not come °to you.
19 But I will come [18]to you °shortly, °if [5]the
Lord °will, and will °know, [4]not the °speech
of them which are [6]puffed up, but the °power.
20 For the °kingdom of God *is* [4]not [2]in °word,
but [2]in [19]power.
21 What [19]will ye? shall I come °unto you

not. Ap. 105. II.
above. Ap. 104. xvii. 2.
is = has been.
no one . . . one. Lit. ye be not (Gr. *mē*) puffed up, one on behalf of (Gr. *huper*. Ap. 104. xvii. 1) the one.
puffed up. Gr. *phusioō*. Elsewhere, *vv.* 18, 19; 5. 2; 8. 1; 13. 4. Col. 2. 18.
against. Ap. 104. x. 1.
another = the other. Ap. 124. 2.
7 maketh . . . to differ. Ap. 122. 4. Note the change from pl. in *v.* 6 to the sing. here.
if. Ap. 118. 2. a.
glory = boast, as in 1. 29.
as if thou hadst not = as not (Gr. *mē*) having.
8 Now = Already. Notice the Fig. *Amplificatio* (Ap. 6).
are full = have been filled. Gr. *korennumi*. See Acts 27. 38.
without = apart from. This is an instance of *Irony* (Ap. 6).
would to God. Gr. *ophelon*, from *opheilō*, to owe. Used to express a wish; also in 2 Cor. 11. 1. Gal. 5. 12. Rev. 3. 15.
reign with. Gr. *sumbasileuō*. Only here and 2 Tim. 2. 12.
9 hath. Omit.
set forth. Gr. *apodeiknumi*. See Acts 2. 22.
apostles. Ap. 189.
last. They were the successors of the prophets in this. Acts 7. 52.
appointed to death. Gr. *epithanatios*. Only here.
spectacle. Gr. *theatron*. In Acts 19. 29, 31, it means the place. It was also used for the actors, and the spectators.
unto = to.
world. Gr. *kosmos*. Ap. 129. 1.
and = both.
10 fools. Gr. *mōros*, as in 1. 25, 27.
honourable. Gr. *endoxos*. Elsewhere transl. "gorgeously", Luke 7. 25, and "glorious" in Luke 13. 17. Eph. 5. 27.
despised. Gr. *atimos*. Elsewhere, 12. 23. Matt. 13. 57. Mark 6. 4.
11 Even unto = Up to, or until. Gr. *achri*.
this = the. present. Gr. *arti* = now.
are naked = are scantily clothed. Gr. *gumnēteuō*. Only here.
are buffeted. Gr. *kolaphizō*. Here, Matt. 26. 67. Mark 14. 65. 2 Cor. 12. 7. 1 Pet. 2. 20.
have no certain dwellingplace. Gr. *astateō* = to be a wanderer. Only here.
12 working, &c. See Acts 18. 3; 20. 34. 1 Thess. 2. 9. 2 Thess. 3. 8.
reviled. Gr. *loidoreō*. See John 9. 28.
13 defamed. Gr. *blasphēmeō*. But some texts read *dusphēmeō*.
intreat. Ap. 134. I. 6.
filth = sweepings. Gr. *perikatharma*. Only here.
offscouring. Gr. *peripsēma*. Only here.
unto this day. Lit. until now. Gr. *heōs arti*.
14 I write, &c. Lit. Not as putting you to shame do I write these things. shame. Gr. *entrepō*. Occ. elsewhere, Matt. 21. 37. Mark 12. 6. Luke 18. 2, 4; 20. 13. 2 Thess. 3. 14. Tit. 2. 8. Heb. 12. 9, all in middle sense, meaning "to feel shame", and so "to reverence", as in the Gospels. beloved. Ap. 135. III. sons = children. Ap. 108. i. warn. Gr. *noutheteō*. See Acts 20. 31. **15** though = if. Ap. 118. 1. b. have = should have. instructers. Gr. *paidagōgos*. Only here and Gal. 3. 24, 25. Christ Jesus. Ap. 98. XII. have begotten = begat. Gr. *gennaō*. Cp. Philem. 10. through. Ap. 104. v. 1. gospel. Ap. 140. **16** Wherefore = On account of (Ap. 104. V. 2) this. beseech. Gr. *parakaleō*, as in *v.* 13. be = become. followers = imitators. Gr. *mimetēs*. Elsewhere, 11. 1. Eph. 5. 1. 1 Thess. 1. 6; 2. 14. Heb. 6. 12. 1 Pet. 3. 13. **17** For this cause = On account of (Gr. *dia*. Ap. 104. v. 2) this. sent. Ap. 174. 4. Timotheus. See 16. 10. bring you into remembrance = remind you. Gr. *anamimnēskō*. Elsewhere, Mark 11. 21; 14. 72. 2 Cor. 7. 15. 2 Tim. 1. 6. Heb. 10. 32. which be. Omit. as = even as. church. Ap. 186. **18** some. Ap. 124. 4. would not come = were not coming. to = unto. Ap. 104. xv. 3. **19** shortly = quickly. if. Ap. 118. 1. b. will. Gr. *thelō*. Ap. 102. 1. know. I. e. find out and expose. Ap. 132. I. ii. speech = word. Ap. 121. 10. power. Ap. 172. 1. **20** kingdom of God. Ap. 114. No verb in the sentence. Supply "is established". Fig. *Ellipsis*. Ap. 6. word. Gr. *logos*, as in *v.* 19. **21** unto. Gr. *pros*, as in *vv.* 18, 19. This *v.* is an example of Fig. *Anacœnōsis*. Ap. 6.

° with a ° rod, or [2] in ° love, and *in* the ° spirit of ° meekness?

X[1] Y[1] r[1] **5** It is ° reported ° commonly *that there is* fornication ° among you, and such fornication as is ° not so much as ° named ° among the ° Gentiles, that ° one should have his father's wife.

s[1] 2 And ye ° are ° puffed up, and ° have ° not rather mourned,

t[1] ° that he that ° hath done this deed might be ° taken away ° from among you.

Y[2] r[2] 3 For I ° verily, ° as absent ° in body, but present ° in ° spirit, have ° judged already, as though I were present, ° *concerning* him that hath ° so ° done this deed,

4 ° In ° the name of our ° Lord ° Jesus ° Christ, when ye are gathered together, and my [3] spirit, ° with the ° power of our ° Lord ° Jesus ° Christ,

5 ° To deliver such an one ° unto ° Satan ° for ° the ° destruction of the flesh, [2] that the ° spirit may be saved [4] in the ° day of the [4] Lord [4] Jesus.

s[2] 6 Your ° glorying *is* ° not good. ° Know ye ° not that a little ° leaven ° leaveneth the whole ° lump?

t[2] 7 ° Purge out therefore the old [6] leaven, [2] that ye may be a new [6] lump, as ye are unleavened. For even ° Christ our passover ° is sacrificed ° for us:

8 ° Therefore let us ° keep the feast, ° not ° with old [6] leaven, ° neither ° with the [6] leaven of ° malice and ° wickedness; but ° with the unleavened *bread* of ° sincerity and truth.

Y[3] r[3] 9 I wrote [5] unto you [4] in ° an epistle [8] not to ° company with fornicators:

10 Yet [6] not altogether with the fornicators of this ° world, or with the ° covetous, or ° extortioners, or with ° idolaters; for then ° must ye needs go ° out of the ° world.

11 But now I have written [5] unto you [8] not to ° keep company, ° if ° any man that is ° called a brother be a fornicator, or [10] covetous, or an

with = in. Gr. *en*, as in *v.* 2. Cp. Luke 22. 49, where *en* is transl. "with".
rod. Gr. *rabdos*. Transl. four times "staff", twice "sceptre" (Heb. 1. 8). Cp. Rev 2. 27; 12. 5; 19. 15. See also 2 Sam. 7. 14. Ps. 2. 9.
love. Ap. 135. II. 1. spirit. Ap. 101. II. 7.
meekness. Gr. *prautēs*. Cp. Ap. 127. 3. Occ. elsewhere, 2 Cor. 10. 1. Gal. 5. 23; 6. 1. Eph. 4. 2. Col. 3. 12. 1 Tim. 6. 11. 2 Tim. 2. 25. Tit. 3. 2. Jas. 1. 21; 3. 13. 1 Pet. 3. 15.

5. 1—6. 20 (C, p. 1695). THINGS HEARD BY PAUL. (*Division.*)

C | X[1] | 5. 1-13. Fornication. Declaration.
  | X[2] | 6. 1-11. Litigation.
  | X[3] | 6. 12-20. Fornication. Amplification.

5. 1-13 (X[1], above). FORNICATION. (*Extended and Repeated Alternation.*)

X[1] | Y[1] | r[1] | 1. Crimination.
  s[1] | 2-. Remonstrance.
  t[1] | -2. Purgation.
Y[2] | r[2] | 3-5. Judgment.
  s[2] | 6. Remonstrance.
  t[2] | 7, 8. Purgation.
Y[3] | r[3] | 9-11. Injunction.
  s[3] | 12, 13-. Remonstrance.
  t[3] | -13. Purgation.

5. 1 reported = heard. Cp. Matt. 2. 3; 4. 12. Gal. 1. 23.
commonly = altogether. Gr. *holōs*. Elsewhere, 6. 7; 15. 29. Matt. 5. 34.
among. Ap. 104. viii. 2.
not so much = not even. Gr. *oude*.
named. The texts omit. Supply the Ellipsis by "found". "Named" has been suggested by Eph. 5. 3.
Gentiles. Gr. *ethnos*.
one = a certain one. Ap. 123. 3.
2 are = have been.
puffed up. Gr. *phusioō*. See 4. 6.
have, &c. = did not rather mourn.
not. Gr. *ouchi*. Ap. 105. I. (a).
that = in order that. Gr. *hina*.
hath done = did.
taken away. Gr. *exairō*. Only here and *v.* 13. The texts read the commoner word *airō*. Had they mourned and humbled themselves for such a scandal in their midst they must have taken action (*v.* 13).
from among = out of (Gr. *ek*. Ap. 104. vii.) the midst of.
3 verily = indeed, or for my part.
as. The texts omit. in. No prep. Dat. case.
spirit. Ap. 101. II. 8. Absent bodily, he was present with them in thought and feeling. Cp. Col. 2. 5.
judged. Gr. *krinō*. Ap. 122. 1. *concerning*. Omit. so. I. e. so daringly. done this deed = wrought (Gr. *katergazomai*. See Rom. 1. 27) this. **4** In the name, &c. Read, "Having been gathered together in the name of our Lord Jesus, ye and my spirit." A Latin MS. of the seventh century in the British Museum reads "and the sanctifying Spirit Himself". In. Ap. 104. viii. the name. Cp. Acts 2. 38. Lord. Ap. 98. VI. i. *β*. 2. A. Jesus. Ap. 98. X. Christ. The texts omit. with. Ap. 104. xvi. power. Ap. 172. 1. Jesus Christ. Ap. 98. XI. **5** To deliver. I. e. That ye should deliver. Gr. *paradidōmi*. See John 19. 30. This clause depends on "judged" in *v.* 3. unto = to. Satan. Cp. 1 Tim. 1. 20. Satan is regarded as inflicting bodily suffering. See Luke 13. 16. 2 Cor. 12. 7. for. Ap. 104. vi. the. Omit. destruction. Gr. *olethros*. Elsewhere, 1 Thess. 5. 3. 2 Thess. 1. 9. 1 Tim. 6. 9. spirit. Ap. 101. II. 6. day. The day of resurrection, when the spirit which returns to God at death is restored. **6** glorying = boasting. Gr. *kauchēma*. See Rom. 4. 2. not. Ap. 105. I. Know. Ap. 132. I. i. See 3. 16. leaven. See Matt. 13. 33. leaveneth. See Matt. 13. 33. Fig. *Paroemia*. Ap. 6. Cp. Gal. 5. 9. lump. Gr. *phurama*. See Rom. 9. 21. **7** Purge out. Gr. *ekkathairō*. Only here and 2 Tim. 2. 21. Christ. Ap. 98. IX. is = was. for = on behalf of. Ap. 104. xvii. 1. But the texts omit "for us". **8** Therefore = So then. keep the feast. Gr. *heortazō*. Only here. He means, the Passover being past, we are living in the days of unleavened bread. Fig. *Allegory*. Ap. 6. not. Ap. 105. II. with. Gr. *en*, as in 4. 21. neither. Gr. *mēde*. malice . . . wickedness. Gr. *kakia* . . . *ponēria*. Ap. 128. II. 2 and 1. sincerity. Gr. *eilikrineia*. Elsewhere, 2 Cor. 1. 12; 2. 17. **9** an = the, i. e. the present one. company. Lit. mix together. Gr. *sunanamignumi*. Elsewhere, *v.* 11 and 2 Thess. 3. 14. **10** world. Gr. *kosmos*. Ap. 129. 1. covetous. Gr. *pleonektēs*. Elsewhere, *v.* 11; 6. 10. Eph. 5. 5. extortioners. Gr. *harpax*. Elsewhere, *v.* 11; 6. 10. Matt. 7. 15. Luke 18. 11. idolaters. Gr. *eidōlolatrēs*. Elsewhere, *v.* 11; 6. 9; 10. 7. Eph. 5. 5. Rev. 21. 8; 22. 15. must ye needs = ye ought to. out of. Ap. 104. vii. **11** keep company. Same as "company with" (*v.* 9). if. Ap. 118. 1. b. any man. Gr. *tis*, as in *v.* 1. called = named, i. e. bears the name of.

[10]idolater, or a °railer, or a °drunkard, or an
[10]extortioner; with such an one °no not to °eat.
s^3 12 For what °have I to do to [3]judge them also
that are without? do [2]not ye [3]judge them that
are within?
13 But them that are without °God [3]judgeth.
t^3 °Therefore °put away °from among yourselves
°that wicked person.

X^2 u **6** Dare °any of you, having a matter °against
°another, °go to law °before the °unjust,
and °not °before the °saints?
v 2 °Do ye °not °know that the [1]saints shall
°judge the °world? and °if the °world shall
be °judged °by you, are ye °unworthy °to
judge the smallest matters?
3 [2]Know ye [2]not that we shall [2]judge angels? °how much more °things that pertain
to this life?
4 °If then ye have °judgments of [3]things pertaining to this life, °set them to judge who are
°least esteemed °in the °church.
u 5 I speak °to your °shame. °Is it so, that
there is [2]not a wise man °among you? °no,
not one that shall be able to °judge °between
his °brethren?
6 But brother [1]goeth to law °with brother,
and that [1]before the °unbelievers?
7 Now therefore, there is °utterly a °fault
[5]among you, because ye °go to law °one [6]with
another.
v Why do ye [1]not rather °take wrong? why do
ye [1]not rather °*suffer yourselves to* °be defrauded?
8 °Nay, ye °do wrong, and [7]defraud, and that
your brethren.
9 [2]Know ye [2]not that the °unrighteous shall
[2]not inherit °the kingdom of God? Be °not
°deceived: °neither fornicators, °nor °idolaters, °nor adulterers, °nor °effeminate, °nor
°abusers of themselves with mankind,
10 [9]Nor °thieves, [9]nor °covetous, °nor drunkards, °nor revilers, °nor extortioners, shall
inherit [9]the kingdom of God.
11 And °such were °some of you: but ye are
°washed, but ye are °sanctified, but ye are
°justified [4]in the name of the °Lord °Jesus,
and [2]by the °Spirit of our °God.

railer. Gr. *loidoros*. Only here and 6. 10. Cp. 4. 12.
drunkard. Gr. *methusos*. Only here and 6. 10.
no not = not even. Gr. *mēde*, as in *v.* 8.
eat = eat with. Gr. *sunesthiō*. See Acts 10. 41.
12 have I to do. Lit. is it to me.
13 God. Ap. 98. I. i. 1.
Therefore. The texts omit. The injunction is more forcible without it.
put away. Gr. *exairō*, as in *v.* 2.
from among. Ap. 104. vii.
that, &c. = the wicked (one). Ap. 128. III. 1.
With this chapter should be compared the Lord's words in Matt. 18. 15-17, and Paul's injunctions in 2 Thess. 3. 6-15. The aim in every case was to bring the offender to repentance. Note also that this was a moral offence, and no sanction is given by these injunctions to the separation so common now on the ground of differing interpretations of Scripture statements.

6. 1-11 (X^2, p. 1703). LITIGATION. (*Alternation.*)

X^2 | u | 1. Litigation.
 v | 2-4. Remonstrance. "Know ye not?"
 u | 5-7-. Litigation.
 v | -7-11. Remonstrance. "Know ye not?"

6. 1 any. Ap. 123. 3.
against. Ap. 104. xv. 3.
another = the other. Ap. 124. 2.
go to law. Lit. be judged. Ap. 122. 1.
before. Ap. 104. ix. 1.
unjust. Gr. *adikos*. See Acts 24. 15 and cp. Ap. 128. VII. 1.
not. Gr. *ouchi*. Ap. 105. I (a).
saints. See Acts 26. 10.
2 Do ye not know = Know ye not. See 3. 16 and cp. *vv.* 3, 9, 15, 16, 19.
not. Ap. 105. I.
know. Ap. 132. I. i.
judge. Gr. *krinō*, as in *v.* 1.
world. Gr. *kosmos*. Ap. 129. 1.
if. Ap. 118. 2. a.
by. Gr. *en*. Ap. 104. viii.
unworthy. Gr. *anaxios*. Only here.
to judge, &c. Lit. of the least judgments (Ap. 177. 8).
3 how much more. Gr. *mēti ge*. Frequently used with a negative question, as a strong remonstrance. See Matt. 26. 22. John 18. 35. Acts 10. 47.
things, &c. Gr. *biōtikos*. Only here, *v.* 4, and Luke 21. 34 (which see).
4 If. Ap. 118. 1. b.
judgments. See *v.* 2.
set ... to judge. Lit. cause ... to sit. Gr. *kathizō*. Cp. Eph. 1. 20.
least esteemed = counted as nothing. Gr. *exoutheneō*. See Acts 4. 11.
in. Ap. 104. viii.
church. Ap. 186.

5 to. Ap. 104. xv. 3. **shame.** Gr. *entropē*. Only here and 15. 34. Cp. the verb in 4. 14. **Is it so.** Gr. *houtōs*. Emph. standing first in the sentence. It may be rendered "Has it come to this?" **among.** Ap. 104. viii. 2. **no, not one.** Gr. *oude* (not even) *heis* (one): but the texts read *oudeis*, no one. **judge.** Ap. 122. 4. **between** = in (Gr. *ana*. Ap. 104. i) the midst of. **brethren** = his brother. **6 with.** Ap. 104. xi. 1. **unbelievers.** Gr. *apistos*. See Ap. 150. III. **7 utterly** = altogether. See 5. 1. **fault.** Gr. *hēttēma*. Ap. 128. IX. Only here and Rom. 11. 12. **go to law.** Lit. have judgments (Gr. *krima*. Ap. 177. 6). **one with another.** Lit. with yourselves. **take wrong** = suffer unjustly. Gr. pass. of *adikeō*. See Acts 7. 24. *suffer*, &c. = be defrauded. Gr. *apostereō*. Elsewhere, *v.* 8; 7. 5. Mark 10. 19. 1 Tim. 6. 5. Jas. 5. 4. **8 Nay** = But. **do wrong** = act unjustly. Gr. *adikeō*, as above. **9 unrighteous.** Same as unjust (*v.* 1). **the kingdom of God.** See Ap. 114, and cp. 4. 20. **not.** Ap. 105. II. **deceived.** Gr. *planaō*. This caution occ. three times in Paul's epistles; here, 15. 33. Gal. 6. 7, and once in James (1. 16). **neither ... nor.** Gr. *oute*. **idolaters.** See 5. 10. **effeminate.** Gr. *malakos*. Elsewhere transl. "soft". Matt. 11. 8. Luke 7. 25. **abusers, &c.** Gr. *arsenokoitēs*. Only here and 1 Tim. 1. 10. Cp. Rom. 1. 27. **10 thieves.** Gr. *kleptēs*. See John 10. 1. **covetous, &c.** See 5. 10, 11. **nor.** The three last occ. are Gr. *ou*. **11 such.** Lit. these things. **some.** Ap. 123. 3. **washed.** Gr. *apolouō*. Ap. 136. iv. Only here and Acts 22. 16. Cp. John 13. 10. **sanctified.** Gr. *hagiazō*. See John 17. 17. **justified.** Ap. 191. 2. **Lord.** Ap. 98. VI. i. β. 2. A. **Jesus** = Jesus Christ. Ap. 98. XI. **Spirit.** Ap. 101. II. 3. **God.** Ap. 98. I. i. 1.

X[3] w[1] **12** All things are lawful ° unto me, but ° all
things are [2] not expedient: all things are lawful
° for me, but I will [2] not be ° brought under the
power ° of [1] any.
13 Meats for the belly, and the belly for meats:
but [11] God shall ° destroy both it and them.

x[1] Now the body *is* [2] not for fornication, but for
the [11] Lord; and the [11] Lord for the body.
14 And [11] God ° hath both ° raised up the [11] Lord,
and will also ° raise up us ° by His own ° power.

w[2] **15** [2] Know ye [2] not that your bodies are the
members of ° Christ? shall I then take the
members of ° Christ, and make *them* the members of an harlot? ° God forbid.
16 ° What? [2] know ye [2] not that he which is
° joined to an harlot is one body? ° **for two,**
saith He, shall be ° **one flesh.**
17 But he that is [16] joined [12] unto the [11] Lord is
one ° spirit.

x[2] **18** Flee fornication. ° Every ° sin that a ° man
doeth is ° without the body; but he that committeth fornication ° sinneth ° against his own
body.

w[3] **19** [16] What? [2] know ye [2] not that your body
is ° the ° Temple of the ° Holy Ghost *which is*
[4] in you, which ye have ° of [11] God, and ye are
[2] not your own?
20 For ye ° are ° bought with a price: therefore ° glorify [11] God [4] in your body, ° and [4] in
your spirit, which are [11] God's.

Z[1] A y **7** Now ° concerning ° the things whereof ° ye
wrote ° unto me: *It is* good for a ° man
° not to touch a woman.

z **2** ° Nevertheless, ° *to avoid* fornication,

a let ° every man have his own wife, and let
° every woman have her own ° husband.
3 Let the [2] husband render [1] unto the wife
due ° benevolence: and likewise ° also the wife
[1] unto the [2] husband.
4 The wife ° hath ° not power of her own
body, but the [2] husband: and likewise [3] also
the [2] husband ° hath ° not power of his own
body, but the wife.

6. 12-20 (X[3], p. 1703). FORNICATION. AMPLIFICATION. (*Repeated Alternation.*)

X[3] | w[1] | 12, 13-. General principles.
  x[1] | -13, 14. Application.
 w[2] | 15-17. Remonstrance. "Know ye not?"
  x[2] | 18. Purgation.
 w[3] | 19, 20. Remonstrance. "Know ye not?"

12 unto = to.
all things, &c. = not all things are profitable (Gr. *sumpherō*. Cp. John 11. 50; 16. 7. Acts 20. 20).
for = to.
brought under, &c. Gr. pass. of *exousiazō*, to have authority over. Elsewhere 7. 4. Luke 22. 25.
of = by. Ap. 104. xviii. 1.
13 destroy = bring to nought. Gr. *katargeō*. See Rom. 3. 3.
14 hath. Omit.
raised up. Gr. *egeirō*. Ap. 178. I. 4.
raise up. Gr. *exegeirō*. Ap. 178. I. 6. Cp. Rom. 9. 17.
by = through. Ap. 104. v. 1.
power. Gr. *dunamis*. Ap. 172. 1. Cp. 15. 43. 2 Cor. 13. 4. Eph. 1. 19, 21.
15 Christ. Ap. 98. IX.
God forbid. Gr. *mē genoito*. The eleventh occ. of this expression in Paul's epistles. See Rom. 3. 4.
16 What? = Or.
joined. Gr. *kollaō*. See Luke 15. 15.
for two, &c. The quotation is from Gen. 2. 24 (Sept.).
one = into (Gr. *eis*. Ap. 104. vi) one. Cp. Matt. 19. 5, where the same idiom occurs.
17 spirit. Ap. 101. II. 2. Cf. *v.* 15; 12. 13.
18 Every, i. e. every other.
sin. Ap. 128. I. ii. 2. man. Ap. 123. 1.
without. Gr. *ektos*. Occ. Matt. 23. 26 (outside). 2 Cor. 12. 2, 3 (out of).
sinneth. Ap. 128. I. i. against. Ap. 104. vi.
19 the = a. Temple. Gr. *naos*. See 3. 16.
Holy Ghost = Holy Spirit. Ap. 101. II. 3.
of = from. Ap. 104. iv.
20 are = were.
bought. Gr. *agorazō*. Occ. thirty-one times, always transl. "buy", save Rev. 5. 9; 14. 3, 4.
glorify. Gr. *doxazō*. See p. 1511.
and in your spirit, &c. All the texts omit.

7. 1—8. 13 **7. 1-9** [For Structures see below].

7. 1 concerning. Ap. 104. xiii. 1.
the things whereof = what things.
ye wrote. The Corinthians had written a letter, but carefully avoided any reference to the disorders among themselves. These had been reported by the members of Chloe's family (1. 11, 12), and the scandal referred to in ch. 5 was a common report, which was perhaps made known by Stephanas and others (16. 17).
unto = to. man. Ap. 123. 1. not. Ap. 105. II. But see Heb. 13. 4.

7. 1—8. 13 (*C*, p. 1695). THINGS WRITTEN TO PAUL. (*Division.*)

C | Z[1] | 7. 1-9. The unmarried.
 | Z[2] | 7. 10-17. The married and unmarried.
 | Z[3] | 7. 18-24. Circumcision and servitude.
 | Z[4] | 7. 25-40. Virgins.
 | Z[5] | 8. 1-13. Things offered to idols.

7. 1-9 (Z[1], above.) THE UNMARRIED. (*Extended Alternation.*)

Z[1] | A | y | 1. The benefit.
  z | 2-. The evil.
   a | -2-5. The remedy.
 | *A* | *y* | 6-8. The benefit.
  z | 9-. The evil.
   a | -9. The remedy.

2 Nevertheless = But. *to avoid* = on account of. Ap. 104. v. 2. every = each. husband. Ap. 123. 2. **3** benevolence. Gr. *eunoia*. Only here and Eph. 6. 7; but instead of "due benevolence", all the texts read "the debt", Gr. *opheilē*, which occ. elsewhere only in Matt. 18. 32. Rom. 13. 7. also the wife = the wife also. **4** hath . . . power. Gr. *exousiazō*. See 6. 12. not. Ap. 105. I.

5 ° Defraud ye [1]not ° one the other, ° except *it*
be ° with ° consent ° for a ° time, ° that ye may
° give yourselves to ° fasting and ° prayer; and
come ° together again, ° that Satan tempt you
[1]not ° for your ° incontinency.
A y 6 But I speak this ° by ° permission, *and* [4]not
° of ° commandment.
7 For I ° would that all [1]men were even as I
myself. But [2]every man hath his ° proper
° gift ° of ° God, one ° after this manner, and
another ° after that.
8 ° I say therefore to the ° unmarried and
widows, It is good for them ° if they ° abide
even as I.
z 9 But ° if they ° cannot contain,
a let them marry: for it is better to marry than
to ° burn.
Z² b 10 And [1]unto the married I ° command, ° *yet*
[4]not I, but the ° Lord,
c ° Let [1]not the wife ° depart ° from *her* [2]husband:
11 But and [8]if she [10]depart, let her ° remain
[8]unmarried, or be ° reconciled to *her* [2]husband:
and [10]let [1]not the [2]husband ° put away *his*
wife.
b 12 But to ° the rest speak I, [4]not the [10]Lord:
c [9]If ° any brother hath ° a wife that ° believeth
not, and she ° be pleased to ° dwell ° with him,
let him [1]not [11]put her away.
13 And the woman which hath ° an [2]husband
that [12]believeth not, and ° if he [12]be pleased to
[12]dwell [12]with her, let her [1]not ° leave ° him.
14 For the [12]unbelieving [2]husband is ° sanctified ° by the wife, and the [12]unbelieving wife is
° sanctified ° by the ° husband: ° else were your
° children ° unclean; but now are they ° holy.
15 But [9]if the [12]unbelieving [10]depart, let him
[10]depart. A brother or a sister ° is [4]not under
bondage ° in such *cases*: but [7]God hath called
us ° to peace.
16 For what ° knowest thou, O wife, ° whether
thou shalt save *thy* [2]husband? or how ° knowest thou, O ° man, ° whether thou shalt save
thy wife?
17 ° But as [7]God hath ° distributed to [2]every
man, as the [10]Lord hath called ° every one,
so let him walk. And so ° ordain I [15]in all
° churches.

5 Defraud. Gr. *apostereō*, as in 6. 7. Here, deprive
one the other = one another.
except. Gr. *ei mē*.
with = from. Ap. 104. vii.
consent. Gr. *sumphōnos*. Only here. Cp. Acts 5. 9.
for. Ap. 104. xv. 3.
time = season.
that = in order that. Gr. *hina*.
give yourselves to = have leisure for. Gr. *scholazō*. Only here and Matt. 12. 44. Cp. Acts 19. 9 (school).
fasting and. All the texts omit.
prayer. Ap. 134. II. 2.
together. Gr. *epi to auto*. See Acts 1. 15; 2. 1.
for = on account of. Ap. 104. v. 2.
incontinency. Gr. *akrasia*. Only here and Matt. 23. 25.
6 by = according to. Ap. 104. x. 2.
permission. Gr. *sungnōmē*. Only here.
of. Gr. *kata*, as above.
commandment. Gr. *epitagē*. See Rom. 16. 26.
7 would. Ap. 102. 1.
proper. Gr. *idios*. Same as "own" in *vv.* 2, 4, 37.
gift. Ap. 184. I. 2.
of = from. Ap. 104. vii.
God. Ap. 98. I. i. 1.
after this manner . . . after that. Gr. *houtōs . . . houtōs*.
8 I say therefore = But I say.
unmarried. Gr. *agamos*. Only here, *vv.* 11, 32, 34.
if. Ap. 118. 1. b.
abide = remain. Gr. *menō*. See p. 1511.
9 if. Ap. 118. 2. a.
cannot contain = have not (Gr. *ou*) self-control. Gr. *engkrateuomai*. Only here and 9. 25. Cp. Acts 24. 25. Tit. 1. 8. Occ. in Sept. Gen. 43. 31. 1 Sam. 13. 12 (forced).
burn. Gr. *puroomai*. Elsewhere, 2 Cor. 11. 29. Eph. 6. 16. 2 Pet. 3. 12. Rev. 1. 15; 3. 18.

7. 10-17 (Z², p. 1705). **THE MARRIED AND UNMARRIED.** (*Alternation.*)

Z² | b | 10–. The Lord.
 | c | –10, 11. His command.
 | *b* | 12–. The apostle.
 | *c* | –12–17. His appointment.

10 command. Gr. *parangellō*. See Acts 1. 4.
yet, &c. Fig. *Epanorthosis*. Ap. 6.
Lord. Ap. 98. VI. i. β. 2. A. Cp. Matt. 5. 32.
Let not the wife. Lit. That the wife should not.
depart = be separated. Gr. *chōrizō*. In Matt. 19. 6, put asunder.
from. Ap. 104. iv.
11 remain = abide, as in *v.* 8.
reconciled. Gr. *katallassō*. See Rom. 5. 10.
put away = send away. Gr. *aphiēmi*. Ap. 174. 12.
12 the rest. Ap. 124. 3.
any. Ap. 123. 3.
a wife, &c. = an unbelieving (Gr. *apistos*, as in 6. 6) wife. **be pleased.** Gr. *suneudokeō*. See Acts 8. 1. **dwell.** Gr. *oikeō*. See Rom. 7. 17. **with.** Gr. *meta*. Ap. 104. xi. 1. **13 an husband, &c.** = an unbelieving (as in *v.* 12) husband. **if.** Omit. **leave.** Gr. *aphiēmi*, as in *v.* 11. The same tense and voice, and should therefore be rendered "send away". The absolutely equal rights of husband and wife are insisted on throughout the chapter. See *vv.* 3, 4, 5, &c. **him.** All the texts read "her husband". **14 sanctified.** Gr. *hagiazō*. See John 17. 17, 19. **by** = in. Ap. 104. viii. **husband.** All the texts read "brother", i.e. believer, or Christian brother. **else** = since otherwise. **children.** Ap. 108. i. **unclean.** Cp. Peter's use of this word in Acts 10. 14, 28. **holy.** Gr. *hagios*. This, as contrasted with "unclean", must be in the same ceremonial sense, but there may be a thought of the dedication of the child to God by the believing parent, and the influence he or she would exercise upon it. **15 is not under bondage** = has not been enslaved (Ap. 190. III. 3). **in.** Ap. 104. viii. **to** = in, as above. Peace is the atmosphere of the Christian calling, and should decide all the problems of life. Cp. 14. 33. Rom. 12. 18. 2 Cor. 13. 11. Col. 3. 15. **16 knowest.** Ap. 132. I. i. **whether** = if. Ap. 118. 2. a. **man** = husband, as above. Here are the Figs. *Antimetathesis* and *Apostrophē*. Ap. 6. **17 But.** Gr. *ei mē*, as *v.* 5. **God . . . the Lord.** These should be transposed. Cp. 1. 9. Rom. 8. 30. Gal. 1. 15. Eph. 4. 4. 1 Thess. 2. 12. 2 Thess. 2. 13, 14. 2 Tim. 1. 9. **distributed** = divided, or imparted. Gr. *merizō*. Occ. fourteen times. Always transl. divided, save here, *v.* 34. Rom. 12. 3. 2 Cor. 10. 13. Heb. 7. 2. **every one.** Same as "every man". **ordain** = appoint. Gr. *diatassomai*. See Acts 7. 44. **churches.** Ap. 186.

Z^3 d 18 °Is °any man called °being circumcised? let him [1]not become uncircumcised. Is °any called [15]in uncircumcision? let him [1]not be circumcised.

19 Circumcision is °nothing, and uncircumcision is °nothing, but the °keeping of the commandments of [7]God.

e 20 Let [2]every man [8]abide [15]in the °same calling °wherein he was called.

d 21 °Art thou called *being* a °servant? °care [1]not for it: but [9]if thou °mayest °be made free, °use *it* rather.

22 For he that °is called [15]in the °Lord, *being* a [21]servant, is the °Lord's °freeman: likewise °also he that °is called, *being* free, is °Christ's [21]servant.

23 Ye °are °bought with a price; be [1]not ye the [21]servants of [1]men.

e 24 Brethren, let [2]every man, [20]wherein he [22]is called, °therein [3]abide °with [7]God.

Z^4 B 25 Now [1]concerning virgins I have °no [6]commandment of the [22]Lord: yet I give my °judgment, as one that hath °obtained mercy °of the [22]Lord to be °faithful.

26 I °suppose therefore that this °is good [5]for the °present °distress, *I say,* that *it is* good for a [1]man so to be.

C f 27 Art thou °bound [1]unto a wife? seek [1]not °to be loosed. Art thou °loosed [10]from a wife? seek [1]not a wife.

28 °But and [8]if thou marry, thou °hast [4]not °sinned; and [8]if a virgin marry, she °hath [4]not °sinned.

g Nevertheless such shall have °trouble in the flesh: but I °spare you.

f 29 But this I say, brethren, the °time *is* °short: °it remaineth, [5]that both they that have wives be as °though they had none;

30 And they that weep, as though they wept [1]not; and they that rejoice, as though they rejoiced [1]not; and they that buy, as though they °possessed [1]not;

31 And they that [21]use this °world, as [1]not °abusing *it;* for the °fashion of this °world °passeth away.

g 32 But I [7]would °have you °without carefulness. He that is [8]unmarried °careth for the things °that belong to the [10]Lord, how he may please the [10]Lord:

33 But he that is married [32]careth for the things °that are of the [31]world, how he may please *his* wife.

34 °There is difference *also* between a wife and a virgin. The [8]unmarried woman [32]careth for the things of the [10]Lord, [5]that she may be [14]holy both in °body and in °spirit: but she

---

7. 18-24 (Z^3, p. 1705). CIRCUMCISION AND SERVITUDE. (*Alternation.*)

Z^3 | d | 18, 19. Circumcision.
  e | 20. Abide in it.
 d | 21-23. Servitude.
  e | 24. Abide in it.

18 Is = Was.
any man, any = any (one). Gr. *tis.* Ap. 123. 3.
being = having been.
19 nothing. Gr. *oudeis.* Cp. Gal. 5. 6; 6. 15.
keeping = guarding. Gr. *tērēsis.* This is the Fig. *Ellipsis* (Ap. 6). Supply "is every thing", or "is alone important".
20 same. Omit.
wherein = in (Gr. *en*) which. The order in the Gr. is, "Each one in the calling in which he was called, in this let him remain".
21 Art = Wast.
servant = slave. Ap. 190. I. 2.
care, &c. = let it not be a care to thee.
mayest = canst.
be made = become.
use. Gr. *chraomai.* See Acts 27. 3.
22 is = was.
Lord. Ap. 98. VI. i. β. 2. B.
freeman = absolutely free. Gr. *apeleutheros,* a much stronger word than "free" in *v.* 21. Only here.
also. Omit.
Christ's. Ap. 98. IX.
23 are = were. **bought.** See 6. 20.
24 therein = in (Gr. *en*) this.
with. Gr. *para.* Ap. 104. xii. 2.

7. 25-40 (Z^4, p. 1705). VIRGINS. (*Alternations.*)

Z^4 | B | 25, 26. Paul's advice on his own account.
  C | f | 27, 28-. Marriage not sin.
   g | -28. Trouble.
   f | 29-31. To remain as they were.
   g | 32-34. Care.
 B | 35. Paul's advice for their profit.
  C | h | 36, 37. Permission to marry.
   k | 38. Preference not to do so.
   h | 39. Permission to marry again.
   k | 40. Preference not to do so.

25 no = not. Gr. *ou.* Ap. 105. I.
judgment = opinion. Ap. 177. 2.
obtained mercy. See 1 Tim. 1. 13, 16.
of = by. Ap. 104. xviii. 1.
faithful. Ap. 150. III and 175. 4.
26 suppose = reckon. Gr. *nomizō.* See Luke 3. 23. Acts 14. 19.
is. Gr. *huparchō.* See Luke 9. 48.
present. Gr. *enistēmi.* See Rom. 8. 38.
distress = need. Gr. *anangkē.* Cp. Luke 21. 23.
27 bound. Gr. *deō,* not *douloō,* as in *v.* 15.
to be loosed = release. Gr. *lusis.* Only here.
loosed. Gr. pass. of *luō.*
28 But and = Moreover.
hast not = wouldst not have.
sinned. Ap. 128. I. i.
hath not = would not have.
trouble = tribulation. Gr. *thlipsis.* See Acts 7. 10, and cp. Matt. 24. 19-21.
spare. Gr. *pheidomai.* See Acts 20. 29.
29 time = season.
short = shortened, or contracted. Gr. *sustellō.* Only here and Acts 5. 6. Cp. 1 John 2. 18.

---

it remaineth = as for the rest it is. See "besides" in 1. 16. **though they had none** = not (Gr. *mē*) having (any). **30 possessed.** Gr. *katechō,* to hold fast. Cp. 15. 2. **31 world.** Gr. *kosmos.* Ap. 129. 1. **abusing** = using to the full. Gr. *katachraomai.* Only here and 9. 18. The force of *kata* is intensive. Cp *katesthiō,* devour, eat up (2 Cor. 11. 20). See Col. 3. 2. 1 John 2. 15. **fashion.** Gr. *schēma.* Only here and Phil. 2. 8. Cp. Ps. 39. 6. **passeth away.** Gr. *paragō.* Cp. 1 John 2. 17, where the same word is used. **32 have you** = that you should be. **without carefulness** = free from anxiety. Gr. *amerimnos.* Only here and Matt. 28. 14. **careth.** Gr. *merimnaō.* Occ. twelve times in the Gospels transl. "take thought", save Luke 10. 41 (be careful); four times in this chapter; 12. 25. Phil. 2. 20; 4. 6. **that belong to** = of. Ap. 17. 3. **33 that are.** Omit. **34 There is, &c.** The texts vary here. See R.V. **There is difference between.** Gr. *merizō,* as in *v.* 17 (distributed). **body** = the body. **spirit** = the spirit. Ap. 101. II. 6.

that is married [32]careth for the things of the [31]world, how she may please *her* [2]husband.

B 35 And this I speak [5]for your own °profit; [4]not [5]that I may cast a °snare upon you, but [5]for °that which is comely, and °that ye may attend upon the [10]Lord °without distraction.

C h 36 But [9]if [18]any man °think that he °behaveth himself uncomely °toward his °virgin, [8]if she °pass the flower of *her* age, and °need so require, let him do what he [7]will, he [28]sinneth [4]not: let them marry.

37 Nevertheless he that standeth °stedfast [15]in his heart, °having °no °necessity, but hath °power °over his own °will, and hath so °decreed [15]in his heart that he will keep his [36]virgin, doeth well.

k 38 So then he that °giveth *her* in marriage doeth well; but he that °giveth *her* [1]not in marriage doeth better.

h 39 The wife is [27]bound °by the law °as long as her [2]husband liveth; but [8]if her [2]husband °be dead, she is °at liberty to be married to whom she [7]will; only [15]in the [22]Lord.

k 40 But she is happier [8]if she so [8]abide, °after my [25]judgment: and I think also that I have the °Spirit of [7]God.

Z[5] D[1] E **8** Now °as touching °things offered unto idols, we °know that we °all have °knowledge.

F °Knowledge °puffeth up, but charity °edifieth.
2 And °if °any man think that he [1]knoweth °any thing, he °knoweth °nothing yet as he ought to °know.

G 3 But [2]if [2]any man °love °God, °the same is [2]known °of Him.

H l 4 °As concerning therefore the °eating of °those °things that are offered in sacrifice unto idols, we [1]know that an idol *is* °nothing °in the °world,

m and that *there is* °none °other [3]God °but one.

H l 5 For though there be that are called °gods, whether [4]in °heaven or °in °earth, (as there be °gods many, and °lords many,)

m 6 But to us *there is but* one [3]God, the Father, °of Whom *are* all things, and we °in Him;

G and one °Lord °Jesus Christ, °by Whom *are* all things, and °we °by Him.

F 7 Howbeit *there is* °not [4]in °every man °that [1]knowledge:

35 profit. Gr. *sumpherō*. Same as "expedient" (6. 12).
snare. Gr. *brochos*. Only here. Something to hamper or fetter.
that which is comely = decorum or propriety. Gr. *euschēmōn*. See Acts 13. 50.
that ye may attend = for devoted attention. Gr. *euprosedros*. The texts read *euparedros*, with the same meaning. Only here.
without distraction. Gr. *aperispastōs*. Only here. The verb *perispaomai* is used in Luke 10. 40 (cumber).
36 think. Same as "suppose", *v.* 26.
behaveth, &c. = acts unseemly. Gr. *aschēmoneō*. Only here and 13. 5.
toward. Ap. 104. ix. 3.
virgin, i. e. virgin daughter.
pass, &c. = be of full age. Gr. *huperakmos*. Only here.
need so require = it ought to be so.
37 stedfast. Gr. *hedraios*. Elsewhere, 15 58. Col. 1. 23.
having no = not (Gr. *mē*, as *v.* 1) having.
necessity = constraint. Gr. *anangkē*, as in *v.* 26.
power = authority. Gr. *exousia*. Ap. 172 5.
over = concerning. Gr. *peri*, as in *v.* 1.
will. Ap. 102. 2.
decreed = decided, or judged. Ap. 122. 1.
38 giveth . . . in marriage. Gr. *ekgamizō*. Elsewhere, Matt. 22. 30; 24. 38. Luke 17. 27.
39 by the law. The texts omit.
as long as = for (Gr. *epi*. Ap. 104. ix. 3) such time as.
be dead. Ap. 171. 2.
at liberty = free, as in *vv.* 21, 22.
40 after = according to. Ap. 104. x. 2.
Spirit of God = Divine spirit. Ap. 101. II. 4.

8. 1-13 (Z[5], p. 1705). THINGS OFFERED TO IDOLS. (*Division.*)

Z[5] | D[1] | 1-8. Knowledge brings liberty to oneself.
D[2] | 9-13. Liberty may cause stumbling to others.

8. 1-8 (D[1], above). KNOWLEDGE BRINGS LIBERTY TO ONESELF.
(*Introversion and Alternation.*)

D[1] | E | 1-. Things offered to idols.
F | -1, 2. Knowledge.
G | 3. He who loves God, gets knowledge through Him.
H | l | 4-. The idol is nothing.
m | -4. There is only one God.
H | *l* | 5. There are idol gods so called.
m | 6-. There is only one God.
G | -6. Those who know God know Him through Christ.
F | 7-. Knowledge.
E | -7, 8. Things offered to idols.

8. 1 as touching = concerning. Ap. 104. xiii. 1.
things, &c. = the things offered to idols. Gr. *eidōlothutos*. See Acts 15. 29. This was another subject about which they had written.
know. Ap. 132. I. i.
all. I. e. the greater part. Fig. *Idiōma*. Ap. 6.
knowledge. Ap. 132. II. i.
puffeth up. Gr. *phusioō*. See 4. 6. This sentence and the next two verses form a parenthesis.
charity = love. Ap. 135. II. 1.
edifieth = buildeth up. Gr. *orkodomeō*. See Acts 9. 31. Contrast between a bubble and a building.

2 if. Ap. 118. 2. a. **any man . . . any thing.** Gr. *tis*. Ap. 123. 3. **knoweth.** Ap. 132. I. ii, with texts. **nothing yet** = not yet any thing. Gr. *oudepō oudeis*. A double negative. The texts read single negative. **3 love.** Ap. 135. I. 1. **God.** Ap. 98. I. i. 1. **the same** = this one. **of** = by. Ap. 104. xviii. 1. **4 As concerning.** Gr. *peri*, as in *v.* 1. **eating.** Gr. *brōsis*. **those** = the. **things . . . idols.** Same word as in *v.* 1, though it is transl. by a longer phrase. **nothing.** Gr. *oudeis*. **in.** Ap. 104. viii. **world.** Ap. 129. 1. **none** = no. Gr. *oudeis*. **other.** The texts omit. **but.** Gr. *ei mē*. **5 gods.** Ap. 98. I. i. 5 Cp. Ps. 82. 1, 6. **heaven.** No art. See Matt. 6. 9, 10. **in** = upon. Ap. 104. ix. 1. **earth.** Gr. *gē*. Ap. 129. 4. **lords.** Gr. *kurios*. Cp. Ap. 98. VI. i. and 4. B. **6 of.** Ap. 104. vii. **in** = unto. Ap. 104. vi. Cp. Rom. 11. 36. **Lord.** Ap. 98. VI. i. β. 2. B. **Jesus Christ.** Ap. 98. XI. **by** = by means of. Ap. 104. v. 1. Cp. John 1. 3. Col. 1. 16. Heb. 1. 2. **we by Him.** Cp. John 14. 6. Rom. 5. 1. Phil. 1. 11. **7 not.** Ap. 105. I. **every man** = all. **that** = the.

E for °some with °conscience of the idol °unto °this hour eat *it* as a [1]thing offered unto an idol; and their °conscience being weak is °defiled.

8 But meat °commendeth us [7]not to [3]God: for °neither, °if we eat, °are we the better; °neither, °if we eat °not, °are we the worse.

D² J 9 But °take heed °lest by any means this °liberty of yours become a °stumblingblock to °them that are weak.

K n 10 For [8]if [2]any man °see thee which hast [1]knowledge °sit at meat [4]in the °idol's temple,

o shall °not the °conscience of him °which is weak be °emboldened °to eat [4]those [1]things which are offered to idols?

K n 11 And °through thy [1]knowledge shall the weak brother °perish, °for whom °Christ died.

o 12 But when ye °sin so °against the brethren, and °wound °their weak [10]conscience, ye °sin °against [11]Christ.

J 13 °Wherefore, [2]if meat make my brother to °offend, I will °eat no °flesh °while the world standeth, °lest I make my brother to °offend.

D L M **9** Am I °not an °apostle? am I °not free? have I °not °seen °Jesus Christ our °Lord? are °not ye my work °in the °Lord?

2 °If I be [1-]not an [1]apostle °unto °others, yet °doubtless I am to you: for the °seal of mine °apostleship are ye [1]in the [-1]Lord.

N R¹ 3 Mine °answer to them that do °examine me is this;

4 Have we °not °power °to eat and to drink?

5 Have we [4]not [4]power to lead about °a sister a wife, as well as °other [1]apostles, and *as* the °brethren of the [1-]Lord, and Cephas?

some. Ap. 124. 4.
conscience. I. e. conviction. Gr. *suneidēsis*, but the texts read (first occ.) *sunētheia*, custom (see John 18. 39. 1 Cor. 11. 16). The meaning is much the same. Having been so long accustomed to believe the idol to have a real existence, they still regard the sacrifice as a real one.
unto = until. this hour = now.
defiled = polluted. Gr. *molunō*. Only here and Rev. 3. 4; 14. 4.
8 commendeth = presenteth. Gr. *paristēmi*. See Acts 1. 3, and cp. 2 Cor. 11. 2. Eph. 5. 27. Col. 1. 22, 28.
neither. Gr. *oute*.
if. Ap. 118. 1. b.
are we the better. Lit. do we exceed.
not. Ap. 105. II.
are we the worse. Lit. do we lack, or come short. Gr. *hustereō*. See Rom. 3. 23.

8. 9-13 (D², p. 1708). LIBERTY MAY CAUSE STUMBLING TO OTHERS. (*Introversion and Alternation.*)

D² | J | 9. Care lest liberty cause stumbling.
  K | n | 10-. Influence of one who has knowledge.
    o | -10. Effect of example on a weak brother.
  K | *n* | 11. Influence of one who has knowledge.
    o | 12. Effect of example on a weak brother.
J | 13. Care lest liberty cause stumbling.

9 take heed = see, or look to it. Ap. 133. I. 5.
lest by any means. Gr. *mēpōs*.
liberty = authority, or right. Ap. 172. 5.
stumblingblock. Gr. *proskomma*. See Rom. 9. 32.
them that are = the.
10 see. Ap. 133. I. 1.
sit at meat = sitting down.
idol's temple. Gr. *eidōleion*. Only here.
not. Ap. 105. I. (a).
conscience. Gr. *suneidēsis*.
which = since he.
emboldened. Lit. built up. Gr. *oikodomeō*, as in *v.* 1. There is *Irony* (Ap. 6) here. Instead of building up the weak brother, the edifice will come tottering down (*v.* 11).
to eat = for (Gr. *eis*) eating.
11 through = upon. Ap. 104. ix. 2. The texts read "in", Gr. *en*.

perish. Gr. *apollumi*. See 1. 18. **for** = on account of. Ap. 104. v. 2. **Christ.** Ap. 98. IX. This sentence is not a question. **12 sin.** Ap. 128. I. i. **against.** Ap. 104. vi. **wound** = strike. **their, &c.** = their conscience since it is weak. **13 Wherefore.** Gr. *dioper*. Here, 10. 14, and 14. 13. **offend** = stumble. Gr. *skandalizō*, to cast a snare before one. Occ. twenty-six times in the Gospels; here, Rom. 14. 21. 2 Cor. 11. 29. Cp. the noun, 1. 23. **eat no flesh** = by no means (Gr. *ou mē*. Ap. 105. III) eat flesh (Gr. *kreas*. Only here and Rom. 14. 21). **while the world standeth** = unto the age. Ap. 151. II. A. ii. 4. e. **lest I** = in order that (Gr. *hina*) I may not (Gr. *mē*. Ap. 105. II).

9. 1—15. 58 (*D*, p. 1695). MINISTERIAL REPROOF AND EXPLANATIONS. (*Introversion and Alternation.*)

D | L | M | 9. 1, 2. Apostleship asserted and claimed.
    N | 9. 3-27. Claim established by his practical teaching.
      O | P | 10. 1—11. 1. The Mosaic Dispensation typical.
        Q | 11. 2-16. The public use of spiritual gifts.
      O | *P* | 11. 17-34. The Gospel Dispensation antitypical.
        Q | 12. 1—14. 40. The public exercise of spiritual gifts.
  L | *M* | 15. 1-11. Apostleship asserted and claimed.
    N | 15. 12-58. Claim established by his doctrinal teaching.

9. 1 not. First two and fourth occ. Ap. 105. I. **apostle.** Ap. 189. The texts transpose the first two questions. **not.** Third occ. Ap. 105. I. (a). **seen.** Ap. 133. I. 8. **Jesus Christ** = Jesus. Ap. 98. X. **Lord.** Ap. 98. VI. i. *β*. 2. A. **in.** Gr. *en*. Ap. 104. viii. **Lord.** Ap. 98. VI. i. *β*. 2. B. **2 If.** Ap. 118. 2. a. **unto** = to. **others.** Ap. 124. 1. **doubtless** = at least. **seal.** Gr. *sphragis*. **apostleship.** Gr. *apostolē*. See Acts 1. 25.

9. 3-27 (N, above). CLAIM ESTABLISHED BY HIS PRACTICAL TEACHING. (*Repeated Alternation.*)

N | R¹ | 3-8. Claim to live of the Gospel equal to that of others.
  S¹ | 9-11. Teaching of the Law thereon.
R² | 12. Claim not advanced by Paul.
  S² | 13, 14. Teaching of the Sanctuary thereon.
R³ | 15-27. Claim not exercised by Paul.

3 answer = defence. Gr. *apologia*. See Acts 22. 1. **examine.** Ap. 122. 2. **4 not.** Gr. *mē ou*. The *mē* stands for the question. **power** = authority, or right. Gr. *exousia*. Ap. 172. 5. **to eat, &c.**, i. e. at the expense of the assembly. **5 a sister a wife.** I. e. a wife who is a believer, and so entitled to be provided for, as well as her husband. **other** = the rest of the. Ap. 124. 3. **brethren.** See Ap. 182.

6 Or I only and °Barnabas, have [1]-not we
[4]power °to forbear working?
7 Who °goeth a warfare any time at his own
°charges? who planteth a °vineyard, and eateth [1]-not °of the fruit thereof? or who feedeth
a flock, and eateth [1]-not °of the milk of the
flock?
8 °Say I these things °as a °man? or saith
°not the law °the same also?
S1 9 For it °is written [1]in the law of °Moses,
"**Thou shalt** [1]-**not** °**muzzle the mouth of the ox**
that °**treadeth out the corn.**" °Doth °God
take care for oxen?
10 Or saith He *it* altogether °for our sakes?
°For our sakes, no doubt, *this* °is written: that
he that °ploweth °should °plow °in hope; and
that he that °thresheth °in hope °should °be
partaker of his hope.
11 [2]If we have sown [2]unto you °spiritual things,
is it a great thing [2]if we shall reap your °carnal
things?
R2 12 [2]If [2]others [10]be partakers of *this* [4]power
over you, *are* [1]-not we rather? Nevertheless
we °have [1]-not used this [4]power; but °suffer
all things, °lest we should °hinder the °gospel
of °Christ.
S2 13 °Do ye [1]-not °know that they which °minis-
ter about °holy things °live *of the things* [7]of
the °temple? and they which °wait at the
altar °are partakers with the altar?
14 °Even so hath the [1]-Lord °ordained that
they which °preach the gospel should live [7]of
the [12]gospel.
R3 T 15 But I have [12]used °none of these things:
°neither have I written these things, °that it
should be so done °unto me:
U for *it were* °better for me to die, than that
°any man should °make my °glorying void.
16 For °though I °preach the gospel, I have
°nothing to glory of: for °necessity °is laid
upon me, °yea, woe is [2]unto me, °if I °preach
°not the gospel!
17 For [2]if I °do this thing °willingly, I have
a reward: but [2]if °against my will, °a °dispen-
sation *of the gospel* °is committed unto me.
V 18 What is my reward then?

6 Barnabas. It would appear then that Barnabas adopted the same method as Paul, of working for his living.
to forbear working=of not (Gr. *mē*) working.
7 goeth a warfare=serves as a soldier. Gr. *strateuomai*. Occ. elsewhere, Luke 3. 14 (which see). 2 Cor. 10. 3. 1 Tim. 1. 18. 2 Tim. 2. 4. Jas. 4. 1. 1 Pet. 2. 11.
charges. Gr. *opsōnion*. Lit. soldier's rations. Occ. elsewhere and transl. "wages", Luke 3. 14. Rom. 6. 23. 2 Cor. 11. 8.
vineyard. The only reference to a vineyard in N.T., besides our Lord's three parables.
of. Ap. 104. vii.
8 Say I, &c. The question is introduced by *mē* (*v.* 4), and there is an *Ellipsis* of "only".
as=according to. Gr. *kata*. Ap. 104. x. 2.
man. Gr. *anthrōpos* (Ap. 123. 1), i. e. according to the universal practice of men.
not. Gr. *ouchi*. Ap. 105. I. (a).
the same also=also these things.
9 is=has been.
Moses. Occ. twice in this Epistle, here and 10. 2. Cp. Matt. 8. 4.
muzzle. Gr. *phimoō*. See Luke 4. 35 (hold . . . peace).
treadeth out the corn=thresheth. Gr. *aloaō*. Only here, *v.* 10 and 1 Tim. 5. 18, where the same quotation from Deut. 25. 4 is found.
Doth, &c. The question begins with *mē*, as in *v.* 8, and expects the answer "No". But He does care. See Job 38. 41. Matt. 6. 26; 10. 29. So there is an *Ellipsis* of the word "only" after "oxen". Cp. *v.* 8.
God. Ap. 98. I. i. 1.
10 for our sakes=on account of (Gr. *dia*. Ap. 104. v. 2) us. **is**=was.
ploweth. Gr. *arotriaō*. Only here and Luke 17. 7.
should=ought to. **in**=upon. Ap. 104. ix. 2.
thresheth. See *v.* 9.
should be, &c. The texts read "(should do so) upon the hope of partaking (of the fruit)."
be partaker=share. Gr. *metechō*. Elsewhere, *v.* 12; 10. 17, 21, 30. Heb. 2. 14; 5. 13; 7. 13.
11 spiritual things=the spiritual (things). Gr. *pneumatikos*. See 12. 1.
carnal. Gr. *sarkikos*. See Rom. 7. 14.
12 have not used=did not use. Gr. *chraomai*. See Acts 27. 3.
suffer=bear. Gr. *stegō*, to cover. Elsewhere, 13. 7. 1 Thess. 3. 1, 5 (forbear).
lest, &c.=in order that (Gr. *hina*) we might not (Gr. *mē*. Ap. 105. II).
hinder. Lit. give any hindrance. Gr. *engkopē*. Only here. Cp. Acts 24. 4. **gospel.** Ap. 140.
Christ=the Christ. Ap. 98. IX.
13 Do ye not know=Know ye not. See 3. 16.

know. Ap. 132. I. i. **minister.** Same word as "work", *v.* 6. **holy things.** Gr. *hieros*. Only here and 2 Tim. 3. 15. **live**=eat. See Deut. 18. 1. **temple.** Gr. *hieron*, neut. of *hieros*. The temple generally. See Matt. 23. 16. **wait.** Gr. *prosedreuō*. Only here, but the texts read *paredreuō*, same meaning. **are partakers**=divide. Gr. *summerizomai*. Only here. **14 Even so, &c.**=So did the Lord also ordain. **ordained.** Gr. *diatassō*. See Acts 7. 44. **preach.** Ap. 121. 5.

9. 15-27 (R3, p. 1709). **CLAIM NOT EXERCISED BY PAUL.** (*Extended Alternation.*)

R3 | T | 15-. Forbearance.
  U | -15-17. Reason.
   V | 18-. Reward.
 T | -18-. Forbearance.
  U | -18-23. Reason.
   V | 24-27. Reward.

15 none. Gr. *oudeis*. **neither have I written**=and I wrote not (Gr. *ou*). **that**=in order that. Gr. *hina*. **unto**=in (Ap. 104. viii), i. e. in my case. **better, &c.**=well for me to die, rather. **any man.** Gr. *tis*. Ap. 123. 3. The texts read *oudeis*. **make . . . void.** Gr. *kenoō*. See Phil. 2. 7. **glorying**=boasting, as in 5. 6. **16 though**=if. Ap. 118. 1 b. **preach the gospel.** Ap. 121. 4. **nothing to glory of**=no (Gr. *ou*) (cause of) boasting (as in *v.* 15). **necessity.** Gr. *anankē*. Cp. 7. 37. **is laid**=lies. Gr. *epikeimai*. See Acts 27. 20. **yea.** The texts read "for". **if.** Ap. 118. 1. b. **not.** Ap. 105. II. **17 do**=practise. Gr. *prassō*. See John 3. 20. **willingly**=being willing. Gr. *hekōn*. Only here and Rom. 8. 20. **against my will**=being unwilling. Gr. *akōn*. Only here. **a dispensation, &c.**=I have been entrusted with (Gr. *pisteuō*. Ap. 150. I. 1. iv) a stewardship. I am therefore in duty bound to fulfil it. **dispensation**=stewardship, or administration, the work of an *oikonomos* (4. 1). Elsewhere, Luke 16. 2, 3, 4. Eph. 1. 10; 3. 2. Col. 1. 25. 1 Tim. 1. 4. **is committed.** Ap. 150. I. 1. iv.

T *Verily* [15]that, when I [16]preach the gospel, I may
make the [12]gospel °of [12]Christ °without charge,
U °that I °abuse [16]not my [4]power [1]in the gospel.
19 For though I be free °from °all *men*, yet
°have I °made myself servant [2]unto °all,
[15]that I might °gain the more.
20 And [2]unto the Jews I became as a Jew,
[15]that I might [19]gain the Jews; to them that
are °under °the law, as °under °the law, [15]that
I might [19]gain them that are °under °the law;
21 To them that are °without law, as °with-
out law, (being [16]not °without law to [9]God, but
°under the law to [12]Christ,) [15]that I might
[19]gain them that are °without law.
22 To the weak became I as weak, [15]that I
might [19]gain the weak: I am °made all things
to all *men*, [15]that I might by all means save
°some.
23 And this I do [10]for the [12]gospel's sake, [15]that
I °might be °partaker thereof with °*you*.
V p[1] 24 [13]Know ye [1-]not that they which run [1]in
a °race [1]run all, but one receiveth the °prize?
q[1] °So run, [15]that ye may °obtain.
p[2] 25 And every man that °striveth for the
mastery °is temperate in all things.
q[2] Now they *do it* °to obtain a °corruptible
°crown; but we an °incorruptible.
p[3] 26 I therefore [24]so run, [1-]not °as °uncertainly;
[23]so °fight I, [1-]not °as one that °beateth the air:
q[3] 27 But I °keep under my body, and °bring *it*
into subjection: °lest that by any means,
°when I have preached to [2]others, I myself
should °be °a °castaway.

O P W 10 °Moreover, brethren, I °would °not that
ye should °be ignorant, how that °all
our fathers were °under the cloud, and °all
passed °through the sea;
2 And were all °baptized °unto °Moses °in
the cloud and °in the sea;
3 And did all eat the same °spiritual °meat;
4 And did all drink the same [3]spiritual
°drink: °for they °drank °of that [3]spiritual

18 of Christ. The texts omit.
without charge = without cost or expense. Gr. *adapanos*. Only here. Cp. *dapanē*, cost (Luke 14. 28), and *dapanaō*, spend (Luke 15. 14).
that, &c. Lit. unto (Gr. *eis*) my not abusing.
abuse = use to the full. See 7. 31.
19 from. Ap. 104. vii.
all = all things, i.e. restrictions of meats, &c.
have. Omit.
made myself servant = enslaved myself. Ap. 190. III. 3.
gain. Gr. *kerdainō*. See Acts 27. 21.
20 under. Ap. 104. xviii. 2.
the law = law. The texts add, "Not as being myself under law".
21 without law. Gr. *anomos*. Ap. 128. III. 3. Here used in the sense of Rom. 2. 12, 14.
under the law. Gr. *ennomos*. See Acts 19. 39.
22 made = become.
some. Ap. 124. 4.
23 might be = may become.
partaker. Gr. *sunkoinōnos*. See Rom. 11. 17.
you = it, i.e. the gospel. Sharer in its triumphs.

9. 24-27 (*V*, p. 1710). **REWARD.**
(*Repeated Alternation.*)

V | p[1] | 24-. Running in a race.
  q[1] | -24. Application.
 p[2] | 25-. The training.
  q[2] | -25. Application.
 p[3] | 26. Running and boxing.
  q[3] | 27. Application.

24 race = race-course. Gr. *stadion*. Elsewhere transl. "furlong", the course being usually of this length.
prize. Gr. *brabeion*. Only here and Phil. 3. 14. Cp. the verb, Col. 3. 15. (rule).
So. I. e. as these runners do.
obtain = lay hold of. Gr. *katalambanō*. See Acts 4. 13.
25 striveth for the mastery. Gr. *agōnizomai*. See Luke 13. 24. The usual term for contending in the games.
is temperate = exercises self-control. Gr. *enkrateuomai*. See 7. 9. This refers to the severe training, extending over many months, before the contest.
to obtain = in order that (Gr. *hina*) they may receive. Same word as "receive" in *v.* 24.
corruptible. Gr. *phthartos*. See Rom. 1. 23.
crown. Gr. *stephanos*. See first occ. Matt. 27. 29. The crown was a chaplet of wild olive, parsley, &c.
incorruptible. Gr. *aphthartos*. See Rom. 1. 23. Cp. 1 Pet. 5. 4.
26 as. "As" should precede "not".
uncertainly. Gr. *adēlōs*. Only here. Cp. 14. 8. 1 Tim. 6. 17. He runs with clear understanding of the conditions and object. See "one thing", Phil. 3. 13.
fight = fight with the fist, box. Gr. *pukteuō*. Only here. The noun *pugmē*, fist, occ. Mark 7. 3. In these contests it was more than boxing. Instead of a padded glove the hand was covered with the *cestus*, which consisted of leather bands, studded with pieces of metal. as one, &c. Read "as one not beating the air". This was called *skiamachia*, shadow-fighting. **27** keep under. Gr. *hupōpiazō*. See Luke 18. 5. bring . . . into subjection = reduce to slavery. Gr. *doulagōgeō*. Only here. Cp. Ap. 190. III. 2, 3. lest that by any means. Gr. *mēpōs*. when, &c. = having preached. Gr. *kērussō*. Ap. 121. 1. There is an appropriateness in using here this verb, "to act as a herald". The herald summons the competitors. be = become, or prove to be. a castaway = disapproved, or rejected (for the prize). Gr. *adokimos*. See Rom. 1. 28, and cp. Heb. 6. 8.

10. 1—11. 1 (P, p. 1709). THE MOSAIC DISPENSATION TYPICAL. (*Alternation.*)

P | W | 10. 1-5. The Mosaic Dispensation.
  X | 10. 6-14. Application.
 W | 10. 15-20-. The Gospel (i. e. Kingdom) Dispensation.
  X | 10. -20—11. 1. Application.

10. 1 Moreover. The texts read, "For". It introduces an instance of some who were rejected. would not = do not desire. Gr. *thelō*. Ap. 102. 1. not. Ap. 105. I. be ignorant. Gr. *agnoeō*. See Rom. 1. 13. all. Notice the emphatic repetition of "all" in *vv.* 1-4. under. Ap. 104. xviii. 2. through. Ap. 104. v. 1. **2** baptized. Ap. 115. I. iii. 1. d. and iv. unto. Ap. 104. vi. Moses. See 9. 9. in. Ap. 104. viii. **3** spiritual. Gr. *pneumatikos*. See 12. 1. meat = food. Cp. Ps. 78. 24, 25. **4** drink. Gr. *poma*. Only here and Heb. 9. 10. for, &c. To the end of the verse is a parenthesis. drank = were drinking. Imperf. of. Ap. 104. vii.

Rock °that followed them: and that Rock was °Christ.

5 But °with °many of them °God was [1]not °well pleased: for they were °overthrown [2]in the wilderness.

X r 6 Now these things °were °our °examples, °to the intent we should °not °lust after °evil things, as they also °lusted.

7 °Neither be ye °idolaters, as *were* °some of them; as it °is written, "**The °people sat down to eat and drink, and °rose up to °play.**"

8 [7]Neither let us commit fornication, as [7]some of them committed, and fell [2]in one day °three and twenty thousand.

9 [7]Neither let us °tempt °Christ, as [7]some of them also °tempted, and °were destroyed °of serpents.

10 [7]Neither °murmur ye, as [7]some of them also °murmured, and [9]were destroyed [9]of the °destroyer.

s 11 Now all these things happened °unto them for °ensamples: and they °are written °for our °admonition, °upon whom the ends of the °world °are come.

12 °Wherefore let him that thinketh he standeth °take heed °lest he fall.

r 13 °There hath °no temptation taken you °but °such as is common to man: but [5]God *is* °faithful, Who will [1]not suffer you to be [-9]tempted °above that ye are able; but will °with the temptation °also make °a way to escape, that ye may be able to °bear *it*.

s 14 °Wherefore, my °dearly beloved, flee °from °idolatry.

W t 15 I speak as to wise men; °judge ye what I say.

16 The °cup of blessing °which we bless, is it °not the °communion of the blood of °Christ? The bread which we break, is it °not the °communion of the body of °Christ?

u 17 °For we *being* many are one °bread, *and* one body: for we °are all °partakers [4]of that one °bread.

that followed them. There is no word for "them". The meaning is, the miracle of the water from the Rock followed that of manna from heaven.

Christ. Ap. 98. IX. As the source of their supply, He is called the Rock. Fig. *Metaphor*. Ap. 6. Cp. Deut. 32. 4, 15, 18, 30, 31, 37. Ps. 19. 14; &c.

5 with. Ap. 104. viii.

many = the most.

God. Ap. 98. I. i. 1.

well pleased. Gr. *eudokeō*. See 1. 21.

overthrown. Gr. *katastrōnnumi*. Only here in N.T. But the word occ. twice in Sept., Num. 14. 16 (where the A.V. reads "slain") and Job 12. 23.

10. 6-14 (X, p. 1711). APPLICATION. (*Alternation.*)

X | r | 6-10. Types. Failures.
  s | 11, 12. Warning.
  r | 13. Temptations.
  s | 14. Warning.

6 were = became.

our. I.e. for us.

examples = types. Gr. *tupos*. Same word as "ensample" (*v.* 11). See first occ. John 20. 25.

to the intent. Gr. *eis*. Ap. 104. vi.

not. Ap. 105. II.

lust after. Lit. be desirers of. Gr. *epithumētēs*. Only here.

evil. Gr. *kakos*. Ap. 128. III. 2.

lusted. Gr. *epithumeō*, to desire. Occ. sixteen times, not always in a bad sense. Cp. Matt. 13. 17. Luke 17. 22; 22. 15. The reference is to Ex. 32. 6-25. Ap. 107. I. 3.

7 Neither. Gr. *mēde*.

idolaters. See 5. 10.

some. Ap. 124. 4.

is = has been.

people. Gr. *laos*. See Acts 2. 47.

rose up. Gr. *anistēmi*. Ap. 178. I. 1.

play. Gr. *paizō*. Only here in N.T. This quotation is word for word from the Sept. of Ex. 32. 6.

8 three and twenty thousand. See Num. 25. 1-9, where the number is given as 24,000, but this included the princes of the people of *v.* 4. See note there.

9 tempt = put thoroughly to the test. Gr. *ekpeirazō*. Only here and Matt. 4. 7. Luke 4. 12; 10. 25.

Christ. The texts read "the Lord".

tempted. Gr. *peirazō*, the word commonly used.

were destroyed. Gr. pass. of *apollumi*. See 1. 18.

of = by. Ap. 104. xviii. 1. See Num. 21. 5, 6.

10 murmur. Gr. *gonguzō*. Occ. here and six times in the Gospels.

destroyer. Gr. *olothreutēs*. Only here, but the verb is found in Heb. 11. 28, of the destroying angel, and also in Ex. 12. 23 and other places in the Sept. **11 unto** = to. **ensamples.** Gr. *tupos*, as in *v.* 6, but the texts read "typically". **are** = were. **for.** Ap. 104. xv. 3. **admonition** = warning. Gr. *nouthesia*. Elsewhere, Eph. 6. 4. Tit 3. 10. **upon.** Ap. 104. vi. **world** = ages. Ap. 129. 2. **are come.** Gr. *katantaō*. See Acts 16. 1. **12 Wherefore** = So then. **take heed** = look to it. Gr. *blepō*. Ap. 133. I. 5. **lest.** Ap. 105. II. This has passed into a proverb. Fig. *Parœmia*. Ap. 6. **13 There hath, &c.** Lit. Temptation hath not (Gr. *ou*). **but** = except. Gr. *ei mē*. **such, &c.** = a human (one). Gr. *anthrōpinos*. See 2. 4. **faithful.** Gr. *pistos*. Ap. 150. III and 175. 4. Cp. 1. 9. 1 Pet. 4. 19. 1 John 1. 9. **above.** Ap. 104. xvii. 2. **with.** Ap. 104. xvi. **also make, &c.** = make a way to escape also. **a way to escape.** Gr. *ekbasis* = a way out. Only here and Heb 13. 7. **bear** = endure. Gr. *hupopherō*. Only here, 2 Tim. 3. 11. 1 Pet. 2. 19. **14 Wherefore.** See 8 13. **dearly beloved.** Ap. 135. III. **from.** Ap. 104. iv. **idolatry.** Gr. *eidōlolatreia*. Only here, Gal. 5. 20. Col. 3. 5. 1 Pet. 4. 3. Cp. 2 Cor 6. 16. 1 John 5. 21.

10. 15-20- (*W*, p. 1711). THE GOSPEL (i.e. KINGDOM) DISPENSATION. (*Alternation.*)

W | t | 15, 16. Fellowship.
  u | 17. Reason.
  t | 18. Fellowship
  u | 19, 20-. Inference.

15 judge. Ap. 122. 1. This appeal is an instance of the Fig. *Anacœnosis*. Ap. 6. **16 cup, &c.** Four cups, one called the cup of blessing, were used at the Paschal Supper. **which we bless.** Cp. Matt. 26. 27 (gave thanks). **not.** Gr. *ouchi*. Ap. 105. I. (a). **communion.** Same as fellowship (1. 9). Fig. *Metaphor* (Ap. 6), and in the following verses. **Christ** = the Christ. Ap. 98. IX. **17 For, &c.** Lit. Because there is one loaf, we the many are one body. Cp. 12. 12. **bread.** Gr. *artos*. Always transl. "loaf" when the number is specified. See Matt. 14 17. Mark 8. 14, &c. **are . . . partakers** = partake. Gr. *metechō*. See 9. 10.

t 18 °Behold Israel °after the flesh: are [16]not
they which eat of the sacrifices °partakers of
the altar?

u 19 What say I then? that the idol is any
thing, or °that which is offered in sacrifice to
idols is any thing?
20 But *I say*, that the things which the
°Gentiles sacrifice, **they sacrifice to °devils, and**
[1]not to [5]God:

X v[1] and I [1]would [1]not that ye should °have fellowship with °devils.
21 Ye °cannot drink the cup of the °Lord,
and the cup of [20]devils: ye °cannot [17]be partakers of the °Lord's table, and of the table of
[20]devils.
22 Do we °provoke the °Lord to jealousy?
°are we stronger than He?
23 All things are lawful for me, but °all
things are [1]not expedient: all things are lawful for me, but °all things edify [1]not.

w[1] 24 Let °no man seek °his own, but °every
man °another's *wealth*.

v[2] 25 °Whatsoever is sold [2]in the °shambles,
that eat, °asking °no question °for °conscience
sake:

w[2] 26 **For the °earth *is* the °LORD'S, and the**
°fulness thereof.

v[3] 27 °If °any of °them that believe not °bid
you *to a feast*, and ye °be disposed to go,
[25]whatsoever is set before you, eat, [25]asking
[25]no question [25]for [25]conscience sake.
28 But °if °any man say [11]unto you, "This
is °offered in sacrifice unto idols", eat [6]not
[25]for his sake that °shewed it, and [25]for [25]con-
science sake:

w[3] **for the [26]earth *is* the [26]LORD'S, and the [26]fulness**
thereof:

4 29 [25]Conscience, I say, [16]not thine own, but
°of the [24]other: for why is my liberty [15]judged
[9]of °another *man's* [25]conscience?
30 For [27]if I by °grace [17]be a partaker, why
am I °evil spoken of °for that for which I
°give thanks?

w[4] 31 Whether therefore ye eat, or drink, or
whatsoever ye do, do all °to the glory of
[5]God.
32 °Give none offence, neither to the Jews,
nor to the °Gentiles, nor to the °church of
[5]God:
33 Even as I °please all *men* in all *things*,
[6]not seeking mine own °profit, but the *profit*
of °many, °that they may be saved.
11 °Be ye °followers of me, even as I also
am of °Christ.

Q x 2 Now I °praise you, brethren, that ye

18 Behold = See. Gr. *blepō*, as in *v.* 12.
after = according to. Ap. 104. x. 2.
partakers. Gr. *koinōnos.* Elsewhere, *v.* 20. Matt. 23. 30. Luke 5. 10. 2 Cor. 1. 7; 8. 23. Philem. 17. Heb. 10. 33. 1 Pet. 5. 1. 2 Pet. 1. 4.
19 that which, &c. Gr. *eidōlothutos.* See Acts 15. 29.
20 Gentiles. Gr. *ethnos.*
devils = demons. Gr. *daimonion.* See Acts 17. 18. Reference to Deut. 32. 17.

10. -20—11. 1 (*X*, p. 1711). APPLICATION.
(*Repeated Alternation.*)

X | v[1] | 10. -20-23. Distinctions in fellowships.
| w[1] | 10. 24. Inference.
| v[2] | 10. 25. Distinctions in knowledge.
| w[2] | 10. 26. Reason.
| v[3] | 10. 27, 28-. Distinction in meats.
| w[3] | 10. -28. Reason.
| v[4] | 10. 29, 30. Distinctions in conscience.
| w[4] | 10. 31—11. 1. Inference.

have fellowship = become partakers (*v.* 18).
21 cannot = are not (Gr. *ou*) able to.
Lord. Ap. 98. VI. i. *β*. 2. B.
22 provoke . . . to jealousy. Gr. *parazēloō.* See Rom. 10. 19.
Lord. Ap. 98. VI. i. *β*. 2. A.
are we, &c. This question is introduced by *mē*, expecting a negative answer. Notice the vividness given to the apostle's argument by the use of the Fig. *Erōtēsis* in *vv.* 16, 18, 19, 22.
23 all things, &c. = not all things are expedient, or profitable.
all things, &c. = not all things edify. Gr. *oikodomeō.* See Acts 9. 31.
24 no man = no one. Gr. *mēdeis.*
his own = his own things.
every man = each one, but the texts omit.
another's *wealth* = the things of the other (Gr. *heteros.* Ap. 124. 2). Cp. Phil. 2. 4.
25 Whatsoever = All which.
shambles. Gr. *makellon.* Only here.
asking no question = questioning nothing (Gr. *mēdeis*).
asking. Ap. 122. 2.
for . . . sake = on account of. Ap. 104. v. 2.
conscience. Gr. *suneidēsis.* Cp. 8. 7.
26 earth. Ap. 129. 4.
LORD'S. Ap. 98. VI. i. *β*. 1. A. *a.*
fulness. Gr. *plērōma.* See Ps. 24. 1.
27 If. Ap. 118. 2. a.
any. Ap. 123. 3.
them that believe not = the unbelievers. Gr. *apistos*, as in 7. 12.
bid = call.
be disposed = wish. Ap. 102. 1.
28 if. Ap. 118. 1. b.
any man = any one, as in *v.* 27.
offered, &c. Gr. *eidōlothutos*, as in *v.* 19, but the texts read *hierothutos*, "offered in sacrifice", as more appropriate language at a heathen feast.
shewed. Gr. *mēnuō.* See Luke 20. 37.
29 of the other = that of the other. This must be a weak believer, who wished to give warning: a heathen would have no "conscience" in the matter. Here, after the parenthesis of *vv.* 26-28, the word "conscience" is repeated from *v.* 25, giving the Fig. *Epanalepsis.* Ap. 6.
another. Ap. 124. 1.
30 grace. Ap. 184. I. 1.
evil spoken of. Gr. *blasphēmeō.* Same as "defamed" (4. 13). **for.** Ap. 104. xvii. 1. **give thanks.** Gr. *eucharisteō.* See Acts 27. 35. **31 to.** Ap. 104. vi. **32 Give none offence.** Lit. Become without offence. Gr. *aproskopos.* See Acts 24. 16. **Gentiles** = Greeks. Gr. *Hellēn.* **church.** Ap. 186. **33 please.** Gr. *areskō.* **profit.** Same as "expedient", *v.* 23. **many** = the many. **that** = in order that. Gr. *hina.*

11. 1 Be = Become. **followers** = imitators. Gr. *mimētēs.* See 4. 16. **Christ.** Ap. 98. IX.

11. 2-16 [For Structure see next page].

2 praise. Gr. *epaineō.* Elsewhere, *vv.* 17, 22. Luke 16. 8 (commend). Rom. 15. 11 (laud).

remember me in all things, and °keep the
°ordinances, as I °delivered *them* to you.
y 3 But I °would °have you °know, that the
head of every °man is [1]Christ; and the head
of the °woman *is* the °man; and the head of
[1]Christ *is* °God.
Y 4 Every [3]man °praying or °prophesying,
having °*his* head covered, °dishonoureth °his
head.
5 But every woman that [4]prayeth or [4]prophesieth with *her* head °uncovered [4]dishonoureth her head: for that is °even all one as if she
were °shaven.
6 For °if the woman be °not °covered, let her
°also be °shorn: but °if it be a shame for
a woman to be °shorn or [5]shaven, let her be
°covered.
Y z[1] 7 For a [3]man indeed ought [6]not to [6]cover *his*
head, °forasmuch as he is the °image and
glory of [3]God:
a[1] but the woman is the glory of the [3]man.
z[2] 8 For the [3]man is [6]not °of the woman;
a[2] but the woman °of the [3]man.
z[3] 9 °Neither was the [3]man created °for the
woman;
a[3] but the woman °for the [3]man.
10 °For this cause ought the woman to have
°power °on *her* head °because of °the angels.
z[4] 11 Nevertheless °neither is the [3]man °without
the [3]woman, °neither the woman °without the
[3]man, °in °the Lord.
a[4] 12 For as the woman *is* [8]of the [3]man, even so
is the [3]man also °by the woman; but °all
things [8]of [3]God.
y 13 °Judge [11]in yourselves: °is it comely that
a woman [4]pray unto [3]God [5]uncovered?
14 Doth °not even nature itself teach you,
that, °if a [3]man °have long hair, it is a °shame
unto him?
15 But [14]if a woman [14]have long °hair, it is
a glory to her: for *her* °hair °is given her °for
a °covering.
x 16 But [6]if °any man seem to be °contentious,
we have °no such °custom, °neither the °churches
of [3]God.
O P Z 17 Now °in this that I declare *unto you* I

11. 2-16 (Q, p. 1709). THE PUBLIC USE OF SPIRITUAL GIFTS. (*Introversion.*)

Q | x | 2. Praise of the obedient.
  y | 3. A revealed principle.
   Y | 4-6. Result.
   Y | 7-12. Reasons.
  y | 13-15. Nature's teachings.
 x | 16. Rejection of the contentious.

keep=hold fast. Gr. *katechō*, as in 1 Thess. 5. 21. Heb. 3. 6, 14; 10. 23.
ordinances. Gr. *paradosis.* Elsewhere, twelve times, always transl. "tradition".
delivered. Gr. *paradidōmi.* See John 19. 30.
3 would. Ap. 102. 1.
have you=that you should.
know. Ap. 132. 1. i. Cp. 10. 1. In the rest of the verse are the Figs. *Anaphora* and *Climax.* Ap. 6.
man. Ap. 123. 2.
woman. In this clause woman means wife, and man husband. Cp. Eph. 5. 23.
God. Ap. 98. I. i. 1.
4 praying. Ap. 134. I. 2.
prophesying. Ap. 189.
***his* head covered.** Lit. (something) upon (Ap. 104. x. 1) the head.
dishonoureth. Gr. *kataischunō.* See Rom. 5. 5.
his head. I. e. Christ in Whom he has access to God with unveiled face (2 Cor. 3. 18).
5 uncovered=unveiled. Gr. *akatakaluptos.* Only here and *v.* 13.
even all, &c.=one and the same with a shaven (one). If she discards the covering which is the symbol of her position, she may as well discard that which nature has given.
shaven. Gr. *xurađ.* See Acts 21. 24.
6 if. Ap. 118. 2. a.
not. Ap. 105. I.
covered. Gr. *katakaluptomai.* Only here and *v.* 7.
also be shorn=be shorn also.
shorn. See Acts 8. 32.

11. 7-12 (Y, above). REASONS.

Y | z[1] | 7-. Man. His glory.
  a[1] | -7. Woman. Her glory.
 z[2] | 8-. Man. His origin.
  a[2] | -8. Woman. Her origin.
 z[3] | 9-. Man. Purpose of his creation.
  a[3] | -9, 10. Woman. Purpose of her creation.
 z[4] | 11. Mutual dependence in the Lord.
  a[4] | 12. Mutual relationship by the ordinance of God.

7 forasmuch as he is=being originally. Gk. *huparchō.* See Luke 9. 48.
image. Gr. *eikōn.* See Rom. 1. 23. Cp. Gen. 1. 27; 9. 6.
8 of. Gr. *ek.* Ap. 104. vii.
9 Neither, &c. And truly the man was not (Gr. *ou*).
for=on account of. Ap. 104. v. 2.
10 For this cause=On account of (as above) this.
power=authority (Ap. 172. 5), i. e. the sign of authority, a veil, which betokened subjection to her husband. Cp. Gen. 24. 65. **on.** Ap. 104. ix. 1. **because of**=on account of, as above. **the angels.** Cp. Gen. 6. 2. 2 Peter 2. 4. Jude 6. Cannot refer to the bishop or other officer; for why should he be affected more than the other men in the congregation? **11 neither.** Gr. *oute.* **without**=apart from. Gr. *chōris.* **in.** Ap. 104. viii. **the Lord.** No art. Ap. 98. VI. i. β. 2. B. Cp. Gal. 3. 28. **12 by**=through. Ap. 104. v. 1. **all things.** Cp. 8. 6. 2 Cor. 5. 18. Eph. 3. 9. **13 Judge.** Ap. 122. 1. Fig. *Anacœnosis.* Ap. 6. **is it comely**=is it becoming. Gr. *prepei.* Elsewhere, Matt. 3. 15. Eph. 5. 3. 1 Tim. 2. 10. Tit. 2. 1. Heb. 2. 10; 7. 26. **14 not even.** Gr. *oude.* **if.** Ap. 118. 1. b. **have long hair**=let the hair grow. Gr. *komaō.* Only here and *v.* 15. **shame.** Gr. *atimia.* See Rom. 1. 26. **15 hair.** Gr. *komē.* Only here. **is**=has been. **for**=instead of. Ap. 104. ii. **covering.** Gr. *peribolaion.* Only here and Heb. 1. 12 (vesture). **16 any man**=any one. Ap. 123. 3. **contentious**=fond of strife. Gr. *philoneikos.* Only here. **no.** Ap. 105. I. **custom.** See John 18. 39. **neither.** Gr. *oude.* **churches.** Ap. 186.

11. 17-34 (P, p. 1709). THE GOSPEL DISPENSATION ANTITYPICAL. (*Alternation.*)

P | Z | 17. Censure.
  A | 18-22-. About coming together.
 Z | -22. Censure.
  A | 23-34. About the Lord's Supper.

17 in this, &c.=declaring this. Gr. *parangellō.* See Acts 1. 4.

[2]praise *you* [6]not, that ye °come together [6]not
°for the better, but °for the worse.

A 18 For first of all, when ye [17]come together
[11]in °the [16]church, I hear that there °be
°divisions °among you; and I °partly °believe it.

19 For there must be °also °heresies [18]among
you, °that they which are °approved may °be
made manifest [18]among you.

20 When ye [17]come together therefore °into
one place, *this* is [6]not to eat the °Lord's
Supper.

21 For [11]in eating °every one °taketh before
other his own supper: and one is hungry, and
another is drunken.

22 °What? have ye [6]not houses to eat and to
drink in? or despise ye the [16]church of [3]God,
and °shame them that have °not?

Z °What shall I say to you? shall I [2]praise you
[11]in this? I [2]praise *you* [6]not.

A B 23 For I °have received °of the °Lord that
which °also I [2]delivered °unto you, That the
°Lord °Jesus °the *same* night in which He was
°betrayed took bread:

24 And when He had °given thanks, He
brake *it,* and said, °"Take, eat, this °is My
body, which is °broken °for you: this do °in
°remembrance of Me."

25 °After the same manner °also *He took* the
cup, °when He had supped, saying, °"This cup
is the °new °testament [11]in My blood: this do
ye, °as oft as ye drink *it,* [24]in [24]remembrance
of Me.

C b^1 26 For [25]as often as ye eat this bread, and
drink this cup, ye do °shew the [23]Lord's death
till He come."

c^1 27 Wherefore whosoever shall eat this bread,
and drink *this* cup of the [23]Lord °unworthily,
shall be °guilty °of the body and blood of the
[23]Lord.

b^2 28 But let a °man °examine himself, and °so
let him eat [8]of *that* bread, and drink [8]of *that*
cup.

c^2 29 For he that eateth and drinketh °unworthily, eateth and drinketh °damnation to
himself, -22- not °discerning °the [23]Lord's body.

30 [10]For this cause many *are* weak and
sickly [18]among you, and °many °sleep.

b^3 31 For [6]if we °would °judge ourselves, we
should [6]not be [13]judged.

---

come together. Gr. *sunerchomai.* This was a voluntary assembling, not the authoritative "being gathered to His name" of Matt. 18. 20.
for = unto. Ap. 104. vi.
18 the. All the texts omit. "In church" means "in assembly". No buildings were set apart for Christian worship so early as this.
be. Gr. *huparchō.* See Luke 9. 48.
divisions. Gr. *schisma.* See 1. 10.
among. Ap. 104. viii. 2.
partly believe it = believe some part (of it), or believe it of some part of you.
believe. Ap. 150. I. 1. iii.
19 also heresies = heresies also.
heresies = sects. See Acts 5. 17.
that = in order that. Gr. *hina.*
approved. Gr. *dokimos.* See Rom. 14. 18.
be made = become. This is the reason why divisions are permitted, but is no justification of them. Cp. 1 John 2. 19.
20 into one place. Gr. *epi to auto.* See Acts 2. 1. These were the social meals of the early church, called love feasts (2 Pet. 2. 13. Jude 12), followed by the Lord's Supper. According to the Greek custom, each brought his own provisions, and while the rich fared sumptuously, the poor sometimes had little or nothing; for the spirit of division led to the exclusion by some of all who were not of their own party. Thus sectarianism invaded even the Lord's table.
Lord's. Gr. *kuriakos.* Only here and Rev. 1. 10. See note there.
21 every = each.
taketh before = first taketh. Gr. *prolambanō.* Only here, Mark 14. 8. Gal. 6. 1. Thus the over-indulgence of some unfitted them for the ordinance.
22 What? have ye not = For is it (Gr. *mē,* introducing the question) that ye have not (Gr. *ou*).
shame. Gr. *kataischunō.* Same as in *v.* 4.
not. Ap. 105. II.
What shall I say, &c. Fig. *Amphidiorthōsis.* Ap. 6.

11. 23-34 (*A*, p. 1714). ABOUT THE LORD'S SUPPER. (*Introversion and Alternation.*)

A | B | 23-25. Revelation received.
C | b^1 | 26. Worthy partaking.
c^1 | 27. Unworthy partaking.
b^2 | 28. Discerning oneself.
c^2 | 29, 30. Not discerning the body.
b^3 | 31. Self-judgment.
c^3 | 32. The Lord's chastening.
B | 33, 34. Counsel given.

23 have. Omit.
of = from. Ap. 104. iv.
Lord. Ap. 98. VI. i. β. 2. A.
also I delivered = I delivered also. Cp. 15. 3.
unto = to. **Jesus.** Ap. 98. X.
the *same* = in (Gr. *en*) the.
betrayed. Gr. *paradidōmi.* Same as "delivered", *v.* 2. See John 19. 30.
24 given thanks. Gr. *eucharisteō.* See Acts 27. 35.
Take, eat. The texts omit. **is.** See Matt. 26. 26.
broken. The texts omit. **for** = on behalf of. Ap. 104. xvii. 1. **in** = for. Ap. 104. vi. **remembrance of Me** = My memorial. Gr. *anamnēsis.* Only here, *v.* 25. Luke 22. 19. Heb. 10. 3. **25 After the same manner** = Likewise. **also** *He took,* &c. = He took the cup also. **when** = after. Ap. 104. xi. 2. **This cup, &c.** Fig. *Metaphor,* as in *v.* 24. Ap. 6. If, as Rome maintains, the wine is transubstantiated into the blood of Christ, can the cup be so too? **new.** Gr. *kainos.* See Matt. 9. 17. **testament** = covenant. See Luke 22. 20 and Heb. 9. 14-23. **as oft as.** Gr. *hosakis.* Only here, *v.* 26. Rev. 11. 6. **26 shew** = proclaim. Ap. 121. 5. **27 unworthily.** Gr. *anaxiōs.* Only here and *v.* 29 (which see). **guilty.** Gr. *enochos,* as Matt. 26. 66. **of** = in regard to. The Gen. of Relation. Ap. 17. 5. **28 man.** Ap. 123. 1. **examine** = test or try. Gr. *dokimazō.* Often transl. prove, or approve. Cp. *v.* 19 and 9. 27. **so.** I. e. after this self-testing. **29 unworthily.** The texts omit. In that case after "himself", read "since he does not discern", &c. **damnation** = condemnation, or judgment. Ap. 177. 6. **discerning.** Ap. 122. 4. **the Lord's body.** The texts read "the body". That is, he does not recognize the common membership of all the saints (10. 17). This was the sectarian and selfish spirit rebuked in *vv.* 19-22. Note the Fig. *Paregmenon.* Ap. 6. **30 many** = not a few, as R.V. **sleep.** Ap. 171. 2. This verse explains what the judgment of *v.* 29 was. Temporal suffering, and even death. Cp. 5. 5 and 1 John 5. 16, 17. **31 would** = were to. **judge.** Same as "discern", *v.* 29.

c[3] 32 But when we are [13]judged, we are °chastened °of the [23]Lord, [10]that we should [-22-]not be °condemned °with the °world.

B 33 Wherefore, my brethren, when ye [17]come together °to eat, °tarry one for another.
34 And [6]if [16]any man hunger, let him eat °at home; [19]that ye [17]come [-22-]not together °unto °condemnation. And the rest will I °set in order when I come.

Q D d **12** Now °concerning °spiritual *gifts*, brethren, °I would °not have you ignorant.
2 Ye °know that ye were °Gentiles, °carried away °unto °these °dumb idols, °even as ye were °led.
3 Wherefore I °give you to understand, that °no man °speaking °by the °Spirit of °God °calleth °Jesus °accursed: and *that* °no man can say °that °Jesus is the °Lord, °but °by the °Holy Ghost.

e 4 Now there are °diversities of °gifts, but the same °Spirit.
5 And there are °differences of °administrations, but the same [3]Lord.
6 And there are [4]diversities of °operations, but it is the same [3]God Which °worketh °all °in all.

f 7 But the °manifestation of the [4]Spirit is given to °every man °to profit withal.
8 For to one is given °by the [4]Spirit the °word of wisdom; to °another the °word of °knowledge, °by the same [4]Spirit;
9 To °another °faith, [3]by the same [4]Spirit; to [8]another the [4]gifts of °healing, [3]by the same [4]Spirit;
10 To [8]another the °working of °miracles; to [8]another prophecy; to [8]another °discerning of °spirits; to [8]another *divers* °kinds of tongues; to [8]another the °interpretation of tongues:
11 But all these [6]worketh that one and the °selfsame [4]Spirit, °dividing to [7]every man °severally as He °will.

g 12 For as the body is one, and hath many members, and all the members of °that one

32 chastened. Gr. *paideuō*. Cp. Heb. 12. 6, 7, 10. Rev. 3. 19.
of = by. Ap. 104. xviii. 1.
condemned. Ap. 122. 7.
with. Ap. 104. xvi.
world. Gr. *kosmos*. Ap. 129. 1. This shows that the judgment of *v.* 29 is not eternal judgment. In *vv.* 31, 32, the Fig. *Paregmenon* occ. again.
33 to eat = for (Gr. *eis*) eating.
tarry = wait. Cp. Acts 17. 16. Jas. 5. 7.
34 at home = in (Gr. *en*) the house.
unto. Ap. 104. vi.
condemnation. Same as "damnation", *v.* 29.
set in order. Gr. *diatassō*. See Acts 7. 44.

12. 1—14. 40 (*Q*, p. 1709). THE PUBLIC EXERCISE OF SPIRITUAL GIFTS. (*Introversion.*)

Q | D | 12. 1-31. Spiritual gifts.
E | 13. 1-13. Love more excellent than gifts.
D | 14. 1-40. Prophecy the best gift.

12. 1-31 (D, above). SPIRITUAL GIFTS. (*Introversion.*)

D | d | 1-3. Instruction as to spiritual gifts.
e | 4-6. Diversities of gifts.
f | 7-11. God's gifts to the saints.
g | 12-20. The many members of the body.
g | 21-27. Their mutual interdependence.
f | 28. God's provision for the church.
e | 29, 30. Diversities of gifts.
d | 31. Exhortation as to spiritual gifts.

12. 1 concerning. Ap. 104. xiii. 1.
spiritual. Gr. *pneumatikos*. It is the adj. of *pneuma* (Ap. 101), and is applied to things in the Divine sphere, as well as to those in Satan's realm (Eph. 6. 12). It is put in contrast with that which is natural, as in 3. 1; 15. 44. In 10. 3, 4 "supernatural" would express the meaning. It occ. twenty-six times and is always transl. "spiritual", and is the only word so rendered, except in 14. 12, which see. Supply *things* instead of *gifts*.
I would, &c. See Rom. 1. 13. This is the fifth occ. of this expression.
not. Ap. 105. I.
2 know. Ap. 132. I. i.
Gentiles. Gr. *ethnos*.
carried = led. Gr. *apagō*. First occ. Matt. 7. 13.
unto. Ap. 104. xv. 3. **these.** Omit.
dumb. Gr. *aphōnos*. See Acts 8. 32. Cp. Ps. 115. 5. Isa. 46. 7. Jer. 10. 5.
even as ye were = as ye chanced to be. The popularity of different gods waxed and waned. Cp. Deut. 32. 17. 2 Chron. 28. 23.
led. First occ. Matt. 10. 18 (brought).
3 give you to understand = make known to you. Gr. *gnōrizō*. **no man** = no one. Gr. *oudeis*. **speaking.** Ap. 121. 7. **by** = in. Ap. 104. viii. **Spirit of God.** Gr. *pneuma Theou*. The new nature. Ap. 101. II. 5. **God.** Ap. 98. I. i. 1. **calleth, &c.** = saith "accursed Jesus". This was probably a form of renunciation. **Jesus.** Ap. 98. X. **accursed.** Gr. *anathema*. See Acts 23. 14. **that Jesus is the Lord.** The texts read simply "Lord Jesus". **Lord.** Ap. 98. VI. i. *β*. 2. B. **but** = if not. Gr. *ei mē*. **Holy Ghost.** Ap. 101. II. 4. This means acknowledging Him as Lord and Master (Rom. 10. 9), not mere lip-service. **4 diversities.** Gr. *diairesis*. Only here and *vv.* 5, 6. Cp. *hairesis*, 11. 19. **gifts.** Ap. 184. I. 2. **Spirit.** Ap. 101. II. 3. In these *vv.* 4-6 we have the Spirit, the Son, and the Father working. **5 differences.** Same as "diversities", *v.* 4. **administrations** = services. Ap. 190. II. 1. **6 operations** = workings. Gr. *energēma*. Only here and *v.* 10. **worketh.** Gr. *energeō*. See Rom. 7. 5. **all in all.** I. e. all the gifts in all the members. Fig. *Ellipsis*. Ap. 6. **in.** Ap. 104. viii. Note the Fig. *Symplokē* in these three *vv.*, each beginning with "diversities", and ending the sentence with "the same". **7 manifestation.** Gr. *phanerōsis*. Only here and 2 Cor. 4. 2. Cp. Ap. 106. I. v. and viii. **every man** = each one. **to profit withal** = for (Gr. *pros*. Ap. 104. xv. 3) profiting, i. e. for the profit of others. **8 by** = through. Ap. 104. v. 1. **word.** Ap. 121. 10. **another.** Ap. 124. 1. **knowledge.** Ap. 132. II. i. **by** = according to. Ap. 104. x. 2. **9 another.** Ap. 124. 2. **faith.** Ap. 150. II. 1. Cp. Gal. 5. 22. Eph. 2. 8. **healing.** Gr. *iama*. Only here and *vv.* 28, 30. Cp. Luke 6. 17. **10 working.** See *v.* 6. **miracles.** Ap. 172. 1 and 176. 1. **discerning.** Gr. *diakrisis*. See Rom. 14. 1. Heb. 5. 14. Cp. Ap. 122. 4. **spirits.** Ap. 101. II. 11 or 12. **kinds.** Gr. *genos*, as in 14. 10. **interpretation.** Gr. *hermēneia*. Only here and 14. 26. **11 selfsame** = same. **dividing** = distributing. Gr. *diaireō*. Only here and Luke 15. 12. Cp. the noun *diairesis*, *vv.* 4-6. **severally** = in His own way. **will.** Ap. 102. 3. **12 that one.** The texts read "the".

body, being many, are one body: °so also *is*
°Christ.
13 For [3]by one [3]Spirit °are we all °baptized
°into one body, whether *we be* Jews or °Gen-
tiles, whether *we be* °bond or free; and °have
been all made to drink °into one [3]Spirit.
14 For the body is [1]not one member, but
many.
15 °If the foot shall say, "Because I am [1]not
°the hand, I am [1]not °of the body;" is it
°therefore [1]not °of the body?
16 And [15]if the ear shall say, "Because I am
[1]not [15]the eye, I am [1]not [15]of the body;" is it
[15]therefore [1]not [15]of the body?
17 °If the whole body *were* an eye, where
were the hearing? °If the whole *were* hearing,
where *were* the °smelling?
18 But now °hath [3]God °set the members
°every one of them [6]in the body, °as it hath
pleased Him.
19 And [17]if they were all one member, where
were the body?
20 But now *are they* many members, yet but
one body.

g 21 And the eye °cannot say °unto the hand,
"I have °no need of thee:" nor again the head
to the feet, "I have °no need of you."
22 °Nay, much more those members of the
body, which seem °to be more feeble, are
necessary:
23 And those *members* of the body, which
we think to be °less honourable, upon these
we °bestow more abundant honour; and our
°uncomely *parts* have more abundant °come-
liness.
24 For our °comely *parts* have [21]no need: but
[3]God °hath °tempered the body together, having given more abundant honour to that *part*
which °lacked:
25 °That there should be °no °schism [6]in the
body; but *that* the members °should have
the same care °one °for another.
26 And °whether one member suffer, all the
members °suffer with it; °or one member be
°honoured, all the members rejoice °with it.
27 Now ye are °the body of [12]Christ, and
members °in particular.

f 28 And [3]God [18]hath [18]set some [6]in the
°church, first °apostles, secondarily °prophets,
thirdly °teachers, °after that °miracles, then
[4]gifts of [9]healings, °helps, °governments,
°diversities of tongues.

e 29 °*Are* all [28]apostles? °*are* all [28]prophets?
°*are* all [28]teachers? °*are* all °workers of
[28]miracles?
30 [29]Have all the [4]gifts of [9]healing? [29]do all
[3]speak with tongues? [29]do all °interpret?

d 31 But °covet earnestly the °best [4]gifts: and
yet shew I [21]unto you a °more excellent way.

so also, &c. = so is Christ also.
Christ = the Christ. Ap. 98. IX.
13 are = were.
baptized. Ap. 115. I. iii. 1. b, and iv. It is the Lord who baptizes in *pneuma hagion*. See John 1. 33. Note that "by" is "in" (Gr. *en*) and "Spirit" has no art.
into. Ap. 104. vi.
Gentiles = Greeks.
bond = slaves. Ap. 190. I. 2.
have been = were.
into. Gr. *eis*, as above, but the texts omit, probably because of the difficulty of the expression; but *eis* may be rendered "at", as in Acts 8. 40; 18. 22; 20. 14-16, &c., the gifts of the Spirit being regarded as a fountain. Cp. John 4. 14.
15 If. Ap. 118. 1. b.
the = a.
of. Ap. 104. vii.
therefore = on account of (Gr. *para*. Ap. 104. xii. 3) this.
17 If. Ap. 118. 2. a.
smelling. Gr. *osphrēsis*. Only here.
18 hath. Omit.
set. Same word as "ordain" in John 15. 16.
every = each.
as it hath, &c. = as He pleased, or purposed. Ap. 102. 1. Cp. 15. 38.
21 cannot = is not (Gr. *ou*) able to.
unto = to.
no. Ap. 105. I.
22 Nay = But.
to be. I. e. naturally. Gr. *huparchō*. See Luke 9. 48.
23 less honourable. Gr. *atimos*. See 4. 10.
bestow. Lit. put around. Gr. *peritithēmi*. See first occ. Matt. 21. 33.
uncomely. Gr. *aschēmōn*. Only here.
comeliness. Gr. *euschēmosunē*. Only here.
24 comely. Gr. *euschēmōn*. See Acts 13. 50.
hath. Omit.
tempered . . . together = mingled together, or compounded. Gr. *sunkerannumi*. Only here and Heb. 4. 2.
lacked = came short. Gr. *hustereō*. See Rom. 3. 23.
25 That = In order that. Gr. *hina*.
no. Ap. 105. II.
schism. Gr. *schisma*. See 1. 10.
should have the same care = should care (Gr. *merimnaō*. See 7. 32) the same.
one for another = on behalf of (Gr. *huper*. Ap. 104. xvii. 1) one another.
26 whether = if at least. Gr. *eite*. Cp. Ap. 118. 2. a.
suffer with it = suffer together. Gr. *sumpaschō*. Only here and Rom. 8. 17.
or. Gr. *eite*, as above.
honoured = glorified. See 6. 20.
with it = together.
27 the body. There is no art. because *sōma* is the predicate. Cp. 3. 16.
in particular. Gr. *ek* (Ap. 104. vii.) *merous*. The meaning is "Each in his part", as R.V. m.
28 church. Ap. 186.
apostles . . . prophets. Ap. 189.
teachers. Gr. *didaskalos*. Ap. 98. XIV. v. 4.
after that. Gr. *epeita*.
miracles = powers. Gr. *dunamis*, as in *v.* 10. Here it means "workers of miracles".
helps. Gr. *antilēpsis*. Only here in N.T., but found in the Sept., Ps. 83. 8; &c., and in the Papyri (Ap. 94. IV).
governments. Gr. *kubernēsis*. Only here in N.T., but found in the Sept. The word means "guidance". Cp. Acts 27. 11. diversities = (different) kinds. Gr. *genos*. Not the same word as in *vv.* 4-6. **29 *Are*.** All these seven questions are introduced by *mē* (Ap. 105. II). workers of. There is no word for "workers". Fig. *Ellipsis*. Ap. 6. See *v.* 28. **30 interpret.** Gr. *diermēneuō*. See Acts 9. 36. **31 covet earnestly.** Gr. *zēloō*. See Acts 7. 9. best. The texts read "greater". more excellent. Lit. according to (Gr. *kata*. Ap. 104. x. 2) excellence. See Rom. 7. 13.

E h **13** °Though I °speak with the tongues of
°men and of angels, and have °not
°charity, I am become *as* °sounding °brass, or
a °tinkling °cymbal.
2 And [1]though I have *the gift of* prophecy,
and °understand all °mysteries and all °know-
ledge; and [1]though I have all °faith, so that
I could °remove mountains, and have [1]not
[1]charity, I am °nothing.
3 And [1]though I °bestow all my °goods to
feed *the poor,* and [1]though I °give my body
°to be burned, and have [1]not [1]charity, °it
profiteth me [2]nothing.

i 4 [1]Charity suffereth long, *and* °is kind;
[1]charity °envieth °not; [1]charity °vaunteth
°not itself, °is °not puffed up,
5 °Doth [4]not behave itself unseemly, seeketh
[4]not her own, °is [4]not easily °provoked, °think-
eth no °evil;
6 Rejoiceth [4]not °in °iniquity, but °rejoiceth
in the truth;
7 °Beareth all things, °believeth all things,
hopeth all things, endureth all things.
8 [1]Charity °never °faileth:

h but °whether *there be* prophecies, they shall
°fail; °whether *there be* tongues, they shall
cease; °whether *there be* [2]knowledge, it shall
°vanish away.
9 For we °know °in part, and we prophesy
°in part.
10 But when that which is °perfect is come,
then that which is [9]in part shall be °done
away.
11 When I was a °child, I [1]spake as a °child,
I understood as a °child, I °thought as a °child:
but when I became a °man, I °put away
°childish things.
12 For now we °see °through a °glass, °dark-
ly; but then face °to face: now I [9]know [9]in
part; but then shall I °know °even as also I
am °known.

i 13 And now °abideth [2]faith, hope, [1]charity,
these three; but the greatest of these *is*
[1]charity.

D F[1] G **14** Follow after °charity, and °desire °spirit-
ual *gifts,* but rather °that ye may pro-
phesy.

13. 1-13 (E, p. 1716). LOVE MORE EXCELLENT THAN GIFTS. (*Alternation.*)

E | h | 1-3. Love the pre-eminent grace.
  i | 4-8-. Its characteristics.
  h | -8-12. Gifts only transient.
  i | 13. Love abides and is supreme.

13. 1 Though = If. Ap. 118. 1. b.
speak. Ap. 121. 7.
men. Ap. 123. 1.
not. Ap. 105. II.
charity = love. Ap. 135. II. 1.
sounding. Gr. *ēcheō.* Only here and Luke 21. 25 (roaring).
brass. Gr. *chalkos.* See Matt. 10. 9. Rev. 18. 12. Elsewhere, Mark 6. 8; 12. 41; (money).
tinkling. Gr. *alalazō.* Only here and Mark 5. 38. An onomatopoeic word. Frequent in the Sept. of the battle shout; Josh. 6. 20. Judges 15. 14. 1 Sam. 17. 20, 52; &c.
cymbal. Gr. *kumbalon.* Only here, but frequent in the Sept.
2 understand = know. Ap. 132. I. i.
mysteries. Ap. 193.
knowledge. Ap. 132. II. i.
faith. Ap. 150. II. 1.
remove. Gr. *methistēmi.* See Acts 13. 22.
nothing. Gr. *oudeis.*
3 bestow = give away in doles. Gr. *psōmizō.* Only here and Rom. 12. 20. Cp. "sop", John 13. 26.
goods = the things belonging (*huparchō,* Luke 9. 48) to me.
give = deliver up. Gr. *paradidōmi.* See John 19. 30.
to be = in order that (Gr. *hina*) it may be.
it profiteth, &c. = I am nothing profited.
4 is kind. Gr. *chrēsteuomai.* Only here. Cp. Ap. 184. III. Note the Fig. *Asyndeton* in these *vv.* 4-8.
envieth. Gr. *zēloō.* See Acts 7. 9.
not. Ap. 105. I.
vaunteth. Gr. *perpereuomai.* Only here.
is . . . puffed up. See 4. 6.
5 Doth . . . behave, &c. Gr. *aschēmoneō.* Only here and 7. 36.
is . . . easily provoked = is . . . roused to anger. Gr. *paroxunomai.* Only here and Acts 17. 16. There is no word for "easily". The statement is absolute.
thinketh no evil = reckons not (Gr. *ou*) the evil (done to it).
evil. Ap. 128. III. 2.
6 in = upon, or at. Ap. 104. ix. 2.
iniquity = unrighteousness. Ap. 128. VII. 1.
rejoiceth in the truth = rejoiceth with (as in 12. 26) the truth, i. e. as it wins its way, truth being personified.
7 Beareth. Gr. *stegō.* See 9. 12. Here it means "is forbearing in all provocations".
believeth. Ap. 150. I. 1. iii.

8 never. Gr. *oudepote.* **faileth.** All the texts read "falleth". **whether.** Gr. *eite.* **fail** = be brought to nought. Gr. *katargeō.* See Rom. 3. 3. **vanish away.** Same as "fail". **9 know.** Ap. 132. I. ii. **in part.** Gr. *ek* (Ap. 104. vii) *merous.* **10 perfect.** Ap. 125. 1. **done away.** Same as "fail", *v.* 8. **11 child.** Ap. 108. vii. **thought** = reasoned. Gr. *logizomai.* **man.** Ap. 123. 2. **put away** = did away with. Gr. *katargeō,* as in *vv.* 8, 10. **childish things** = the things of a child. **12 see.** Ap. 133. I. 5. **through.** Ap. 104. v. 1. **glass** = mirror. Gr. *esoptron.* Only here and James 1. 23. **darkly.** Lit. in (Gr. *en*) a riddle. Gr. *ainigma.* Only here in N.T. In the Sept., Num. 12. 8. 1 Kings 10. 1. Prov. 1. 6, &c. **to.** Ap. 104. xv. 3. **know** = fully know. Ap. 132. I. iii. **even as, &c.** = even as I was fully known also. **13 abideth.** Gr. *menō.* See p. 1511.

14. 1-40 (*D,* p. 1716). PROPHECY THE BEST GIFT. (*Division.*)

D | F[1] | 1-20. Prophecy better than tongues.
  | F[2] | 21-40. Reasons and cautions.

14. 1-20 (F[1], above). PROPHECY BETTER THAN TONGUES.

F[1] | G | 1. Every gift to be desired.
  H | 2-4. But prophesying best.
  G | 5-. Tongues also to be desired.
  H | -5-20. But prophesying best.

14. 1 charity = love, as in 13. 1. **desire** = covet earnestly, as in 12. 31. **spiritual.** Gr. *pneumatikos.* See 12. 1. **that** = in order that. Gr. *hina.*

H **2** For he that °speaketh °in °an *unknown* tongue °speaketh °not °unto °men, but °unto °God: for °no man °understandeth *him*; °howbeit °in the °spirit he °speaketh °mysteries.

3 But he that prophesieth [2]speaketh [2]unto [2]men °*to* °edification, and °exhortation, and °comfort.

4 He that [2]speaketh in [2]an *unknown* tongue °edifieth himself; but he that prophesieth °edifieth the °church.

G **5** I °would that ye all [2]spake with tongues,
H k but rather [1]that ye prophesied: for greater *is* he that prophesieth than he that [2]speaketh with tongues, °except he °interpret, [1]that the [4]church may receive °edifying.

6 Now, brethren, °if I come °unto you [2]speaking with tongues, what shall I profit you, °except I shall [2]speak to you either °by °revelation, or °by °knowledge, or °by prophesying, or °by doctrine?

l **7** °And even things °without life giving °sound, °whether °pipe °or °harp, [6]except they give a °distinction in the °sounds, how shall it be °known what is °piped or °harped?

8 For [6]if the trumpet give an °uncertain [7]sound, who shall prepare himself °to the battle?

9 °So likewise ye, [6]except ye °utter °by the tongue °words °easy to be understood, how shall it be [7]known what is [2]spoken? for ye shall [2]speak °into the air.

10 There are, °it may be, so many kinds of °voices °in the °world, and °none of them *is* °without signification.

11 Therefore [6]if I °know °not the °meaning of the [10]voice, I shall be [2]unto him that [2]speaketh a °barbarian, and he that [2]speaketh *shall be* a °barbarian °unto me.

12 °Even so ye, forasmuch as ye are °zealous of °spiritual *gifts*, seek [1]that ye may °excel °to the [5]edifying of the [4]church.

k **13** °Wherefore let him that [2]speaketh in [2]an *unknown* tongue °pray [1]that he may [5]interpret.

l **14** For [6]if I [13]pray in [2]an *unknown* tongue, my °spirit [13]prayeth, but my °understanding is unfruitful.

15 What is it then? I will [13]pray with the [14]spirit, and I will [13]pray with the [14]understanding also: I will °sing with the [14]spirit, and I will °sing with the [14]understanding also.

16 Else °when thou shalt bless with the [14]spirit, how shall he that °occupieth the room of the °unlearned say °"Amen" °at thy °giving of thanks, °seeing he °understandeth [2]not what thou sayest?

2 speaketh. Gr. *laleō.* Ap. 121. 7.
in. No prep. Dat. case. **an** *unknown* = a.
not. Ap. 105. I.
unto = to.
men. Gr. *anthrōpos.* Ap. 123. 1.
God. Ap. 98. I. i. 1.
no man = no one. Gr. *oudeis.*
understandeth. Gr. *akouō.* Occ. over 420 times. Transl. hear, except in this and six or seven other passages. See Acts 9. 7.
howbeit = but.
spirit. Ap. 101. II. 4. There is no article.
mysteries. Ap. 193.
3 *to.* Supply the ellipsis by "for".
edification. Lit. building. Gr. *oikodomē.* See 3. 9. Here used metaphorically.
exhortation. Gr. *paraklēsis.* See Acts 4. 36 and 13. 15. Cp. Ap. 134. I. 6.
comfort. Gr. *paramuthia.* Only here. Cp. Phil. 2. 1, and the verb in John 11. 19.
4 edifieth. Gr. *oikodomeō.* See Acts 9. 31.
church. Ap. 186.
5 would = wish. Ap. 102. 1.

14. -5-20 (*H*, p. 1718). PROPHESYING BEST.
(*Alternation.*)

H | k | -5, 6. Interpretation needed.
l | 7-12. Otherwise gift of tongues useless.
k | 13. Interpretation needed.
l | 14-20. Otherwise gift of tongues useless.

except. A strong expression. Gr. *ektos ei mē.* Lit. without if not.
interpret. Gr. *diermēneuō.* See Acts 9. 36.
edifying. Same as "edification", *v.* 3.
6 if. Ap. 118. 1. b.
unto. Ap. 104. xv. 3.
except = unless. Gr. *ean* (Ap. 118. 1. b) *mē* (Ap. 105. II).
by = in. Gr. *en.* Ap. 104. viii.
revelation. Ap. 106. II. i.
knowledge. Ap. 132. II. i.
7 And even = Nevertheless. Gr. *homōs.* Only here, John 12. 42. Gal. 3. 15.
without life. Gr. *apsuchos.* Only here.
sound. Gr. *phōnē*, voice.
whether, or. Gr. *eite.*
pipe. Gr. *aulos.* Only here.
harp. Gr. *kithara.* Only here and Rev. 5. 8; 14. 2; 15. 2.
distinction. Gr. *diastolē.* See Rom. 3. 22.
sounds. Gr. *phthongos.* Only here and Rom. 10. 18. Not the same word as in the first part of the verse.
known. Ap. 132. I. ii.
piped. Gr. *auleō.* Only here, Matt. 11. 17. Luke 7. 32.
harped. Gr. *kitharizō.* Only here and Rev. 14. 2.
8 uncertain. Gr. *adēlos.* Only here and Luke 11. 44 (appear not).
to the battle = for (Gr. *eis.* Ap. 104. vi) war.
9 So likewise ye = So ye also.
utter = give.
by. Ap. 104. v. 1. **words.** Ap. 121. 10.
easy to be understood = intelligible. Gr. *eusēmos.* Only here.
into. Ap. 104. vi.

10 it may be = if (Ap. 118. 2. b) it may be. voices. Gr. *phonē.* See *v.* 7. in. Ap. 104. viii. world. Ap. 129. 1. none. Gr. *oudeis.* without, &c. = dumb. Gr. *aphōnos.* See Acts 8. 32. **11** know. Ap. 132. I. i. not. Ap. 105. II. meaning = force. Ap. 172. 1. **barbarian.** See Acts 28. 2. unto. Gr. *en.* Ap. 104. viii. I. e. in my regard. **12** Even so ye = So ye also. **zealous.** Gr. *zēlōtēs.* See Acts 21. 20. spiritual *gifts.* Lit. spirits. Here put for the operations of the Holy Spirit, as in *v.* 2. Ap. 101. II. 4. excel = abound. to. Gr. *pros.* Ap. 104. xv. 3. **13** Wherefore. See 8. 13. pray. Ap. 134. I. 2. **14** spirit. Ap. 101. II. 9. understanding. Gr. *nous.* Transl. seven times "understanding", seventeen times "mind". **15** sing. Gr. *psallō*, as Eph. 5. 15 (making melody). **16** when = if. Ap. 118. I. b. occupieth = fills up. Gr. *anaplēroō.* Here, 16. 17. Matt. 13. 14. Gal. 6. 2. Phil. 2. 30. 1 Thess. 2. 16. unlearned. See Acts 4. 13. Lit. "private" as opposed to "official". Amen = the amen. See p. 1511. at. Ap. 104. ix. 2. **giving of thanks.** Gr. *eucharistia.* See Acts 24. 3. seeing = since. understandeth = knoweth. Ap. 132. I. i.

17 For thou verily °givest thanks well, but the
°other is [2]not [4]edified.
18 I °thank my [2]God, °I [2]speak with tongues
more than ye all:
19 Yet [10]in the [4]church I °had rather [2]speak
five words °with my [14]understanding, [14]that *by*
my voice I °might teach °others also, than ten
thousand words [10]in [2]an *unknown* tongue.
20 Brethren, °be [11]not °children in °under-
standing: howbeit in °malice °be ye children,
but in °understanding °be °men.

F^2 m **21** [10]In °the law it is written, °"**With men**
of °other tongues °and [17]other lips will I
[2]speak [2]unto this °people; and °yet for all
that will they not °hear Me, saith the °LORD."
22 Wherefore tongues are °for a °sign, [2]not
to them that °believe, but to them that °believe
not: but prophesying °*serveth* [2]not for them
that °believe not, but for them which °believe.
23 [6]If therefore the whole [4]church be come
together °into one place, and all [2]speak with
tongues, and there come in *those that are*
[16]unlearned, or °unbelievers, will they [2]not
say that ye are °mad?
24 But [6]if all prophesy, and there come in
°one that [22]believeth not, or *one* [16]unlearned,
he is °convinced °of all, he is °judged °of all:
25 And thus °are the secrets of his heart
made °manifest; and so falling down °on *his*
face he will °worship [2]God, °and report that
[2]God is °in you °of a truth.

n **26** °How is it then, brethren? when ye come
together, °every one °of you hath a psalm, hath
a doctrine, hath a tongue, hath a [6]revelation,
hath an °interpretation.

o Let all things be done [6]unto [5]edifying.

m **27** °If °any man [2]speak in [2]an *unknown*
tongue, *let it be* °by two, or at the most *by*
three, and *that* °by course; and let one [5]inter-
pret.
28 But [6]if there be °no °interpreter, let him
keep silence [10]in the [4]church; and let him
[2]speak to himself, and to [2]God.
29 Let the °prophets [2]speak two or three,
and let °the [19]other °judge.
30 [6]If *any thing* be °revealed to [19]another
that sitteth by, let the first °hold his peace.
31 For ye °may all prophesy °one by one,
[1]that all may learn, and all may be °com-
forted.
32 And the °spirits of the [29]prophets are
°subject to the [29]prophets.
33 For [2]God is [2]not *the author* of °confusion,
but of peace, as [10]in all [4]churches of the
°saints.
34 Let your women keep silence [10]in the
[4]churches: for it is [2]not permitted [2]unto them

17 givest thanks. Gr. *eucharisteō*. See Acts 27. 35.
other. Gr. *heteros*. Ap. 124. 2.
18 thank. Same as "give thanks", *v.* 17.
I speak = speaking (as I do).
19 had rather = desire to. Ap. 102. 1.
with. Gr. *dia*, but the texts read "by" (Dat.)
might teach. Gr. *katēcheō*. See Acts 18. 25.
others. Ap. 124. 1.
20 be = become. children. Ap. 108. v.
understanding. Gr. *phrēn*. Only here.
malice. Ap. 128. II. 2.
be ye children = act as babes. Gr. *nēpiazō*. Cp. Ap. 108. vii.
men, i. e. of mature age and thought. Gr. *teleios*. See Ap. 123. 6, and 125. 1.

14. 21-40 (F^2, p. 1718). REASONS AND CAUTIONS.
(*Extended Alternation.*)

F^2 | m | 21-25. Divine prediction.
n | 26-. Remonstrance.
o | -26. Exhortation. Let, &c.
m | 27-35. Apostolic direction.
n | 36-39. Remonstrance.
o | 40. Exhortation. Let, &c.

21 the law. The Scriptures of the O.T. are called "the law", "the law and the Prophets", "the law, the Prophets, and the Psalms". Here the law includes Isaiah, just as in John 10. 34; 15. 25, it includes the Psalms.
With = In. Ap. 104. viii.
other tongues. Gr. *heteroglōssos* = other-tongued. Only here.
and other lips = and with lips of others.
people. Gr. *laos*. See Acts 2. 47.
yet for all that, &c. = not even (Gr. *oude*) so will they.
hear = hearken to. Gr. *eisakouō*. Elsewhere, Matt. 6. 7. Luke 1. 13. Acts 10. 31. Heb. 5 7; all of answered prayer. A stronger word than *akouō* which occ. over 400 times.
LORD. Ap. 98. VI. i. *β*. 1. B. a. The quotation is from Isa. 28. 11, 12. Ap. 107. II. 2.
22 for. Ap. 104. vi.
sign. Ap. 176. 3.
believe. Ap. 150. I. 1. i.
believe not = are unbelieving. Gr. *apistos*. See Ap. 150. III.
serveth = *is*.
23 into one place. See Acts 2. 1.
unbelievers. Gr. *apistos*, as in *vv.* 22, 24.
mad. Gr. *mainomai*. See Acts 12. 15.
24 one = any one. Ap. 123. 3.
convinced. Gr. *elenchō*. See John 8. 9. Occ. seventeen times; transl. four times "convince", once "convict", five times "rebuke", six times "reprove", and once "tell a fault" (Matt. 18. 15).
of = by. Ap. 104. xviii. 1.
judged = discerned. Ap. 122. 2.
25 are . . . made = become.
manifest. Ap. 106. viii.
on. Ap. 104. ix. 3.
worship. Ap. 137. 1.
and report = announcing, or declaring. Gr. *apangellō*. Cp. Ap. 121. 5, 6.
in = among. Gr. *en*. Ap. 104. viii. 2.
of a truth = indeed. Gr. *ontōs*. Cp. John 8. 36.
26 How. Gr. *ti*. Same as "What", *v.* 15.

every = each. of you. Omit. interpretation. See 12. 10. **27** If. Gr. *eite*. Ap. 118. 2. a. any man = any one, as in *v.* 24. by = according to. Ap. 104. x. 2. by course = in turn. Gr. *ana* (Ap. 104. i) *meros*. **28** no. Gr. *mē*, as in *v.* 11. interpreter. Gr. *diermēneutēs*. Only here. **29** prophets. Ap. 189. the other = the others. judge = discern, or discriminate. Ap. 122. 4. **30** revealed. Ap. 106. I. ix. hold his peace. Same as "keep silence" in *vv.* 28, 34. **31** may = can. one by one. Gr. *kath'* (Ap. 104. x. 2) *hena*. comforted. Ap. 134. I. 6. **32** spirits = spiritual gifts, as in *v.* 12. subject to. I. e. under the control of their possessors. So there was no warrant for the scenes of excitement sometimes exhibited in ancient, as well as in modern, days. **33** confusion = commotion. Gr. *akatastasia*. See Luke 21. 9. saints. Gr. *hagios*. See Acts 9. 13.

to [2]speak; but *they are commanded* to be °under obedience, °as also saith the law.
35 And °if they °will learn [27]any thing, let them ask °their °husbands °at home: for it is a shame for women to [2]speak [10]in the [4]church.

n 36 What? °came the °word of [2]God out °from you? or °came it °unto you only?
37 [35]If [27]any man think himself to be a [29]prophet, or [1]spiritual, let him °acknowledge that the things that I write [2]unto you are the commandments of °the °Lord.
38 But [35]if [27]any man °be ignorant, let him °be ignorant.
39 Wherefore, brethren, °covet to prophesy, and forbid [11]not to [2]speak with tongues.

o 40 Let all things be done °decently and °in °order.

L M p **15** °Moreover, brethren, I °declare °unto you the °gospel which I °preached °unto you,

q which °also ye have received, °and °wherein ye stand;
2 °By which °also ye are saved, °if ye °keep in memory °what I [1]preached [1]unto you, °unless ye °have °believed °in vain.

p 3 For I °delivered [1]unto you °first of all that

q which I °also received, how that °Christ died °for our °sins °according to the scriptures,
4 And that He was buried, and that He °rose again the third day [3]according to the °scriptures:
5 And that He was °seen °of °Cephas, then °of °the twelve:
6 °After that, He was [5]seen [5]of above five hundred brethren °at once, °of whom the greater part remain °unto this present, but °some °are fallen asleep.
7 [6]After that, He was [5]seen [5]of °James; then [5]of °all the °apostles.
8 And last of all He was [5]seen [5]of me also, °as of °one born out of due time.
9 For I am the °least of the [7]apostles, that am °not meet to be called an [7]apostle, because I persecuted the °church of °God.
10 But by the °grace of [9]God I am what I am: and His °grace °which *was bestowed* °upon me °was [9]not °in vain; but I laboured more abundantly than they all: yet [9]not I, but the °grace of [9]God which was °with me.
11 Therefore °whether *it were* I °or they, so we °preach, and so ye [2]believed.

N J 12 Now [2]if [3]Christ be [11]preached that He [4]rose °from the dead, how say [6]some °among

34 under obedience = subject, as in *v.* 32.
as also, &c. = as the law also saith. Reference is to Gen. 3. 16. Cp. 1 Tim. 2. 11-13.
35 if. Ap. 118. 2. a.
will = wish to. Ap. 102. 1.
their = their own.
husbands. Ap. 123. 2.
at home = in (Gr. *en*) the home.
36 came = went.
word. Ap. 121. 10.
from. Ap. 104. iv.
came. Gr. *katantaō*. See Acts 16. 1.
unto. Ap. 104. vi.
37 acknowledge. Ap. 132. I. iii.
the. All the texts omit.
Lord. Ap. 98. VI. i. *β*. 2. B.
38 be ignorant. Gr. *agnoeō*. See 10. 1.
39 covet. Same as desire, *v.* 1.
40 decently. Gr. *euschēmonōs*. Elsewhere (Rom. 13. 13. 1 Thess. 4. 12) transl. honestly. Cp. 7. 35; 12. 24.
in = according to. Gr. *kata*. Ap. 104. x. 2.
order. Gr. *taxis*. Elsewhere, Luke 1. 8. Col. 2. 5. Heb. 5. 6, 10; 6. 20; 7. 11, 17, 21.

15. 1-11 (*M*, p. 1709). APOSTLESHIP ASSERTED AND CLAIMED. (*Alternation*.)

M | p | 1-. Paul's gospel. Declared.
| q | -1, 2. Which *they* had received.
| *p* | 3-. Paul's gospel. Delivered.
| *q* | -3-11. Which *he* had received.

15. 1 Moreover = Now.
declare = make known. Gr. *gnōrizō*.
unto = to. gospel. Ap. 140.
preached. Ap. 121. 4.
also ye have received = ye received also.
and wherein, &c. = in (Gr. *en*. Ap. 104. viii) which ye stand also.
2 By = Through. Ap. 104. v. 1.
also, &c. = ye are saved also.
if. Ap. 118. 2. a.
keep in memory = hold fast. Gr. *katechō*. See 7. 30.
what = with what word. Gr. *logos*. Ap. 121. 10. He refers to the substance of his preaching, based as it was on the facts of the Lord's death and resurrection, which last was challenged by some false teachers (*v.* 12).
unless. See 14. 5 (except).
have. Omit.
believed. Ap. 150. I. 1. i.
in vain = to no purpose. Gr. *eikē*. See Rom. 13. 4.
3 delivered. Gr. *paradidōmi*. See John 19. 30. Cp. 11. 23.
first of all = among (Gr. *en*. Ap. 104. viii. 2) the first things.
also received = received also.
Christ. Ap. 98. IX.
for. Ap. 104. xvii. 1.
sins. Ap. 128. I. ii. 1.
according to. Ap. 104. x. 2.
4 rose again = has been raised. Ap. 178. I. 4.
scriptures. Ps. 16. 10. Isa. 53. 9-11. Jonah 1. 17. Cp. Matt. 12. 39. Luke 11. 29.

5 seen. Ap. 133. I. 8. In *vv.* 5-8 we have the Fig. *Protimēsis*. Ap. 6. of = by. Dat. case. Cephas. Luke 24. 34. the twelve. John 20. 19, 24. The term is used officially. **6** After that. Gr. *epeita*. at once. Gr. *ephapax*. See Rom. 6. 10. There is no mention of this in the Gospels, unless it be Matt. 28. 16-20, where "some doubted" may imply that others than the eleven were present. of. Ap. 104. vii. unto this present = until now. some. Gr. *tines*. Ap. 124. 4. are fallen asleep. Ap. 171. 2. **7** James. See Ap. 182. all, &c. Luke 24. 50-52. Acts 1. 6-9. apostles. Ap. 189. **8** as = as if (it were). Gr. *hōsperei*. Only here. one born, &c. = an abortion. Gr. *ektrōma*. Only here in N.T., but used in Sept. of Job 3. 16. Eccl. 6. 3. **9** least. Fig. *Meiōsis* (Ap. 6). not. Ap. 105. I. church. Ap. 186. God. Ap. 98. I. i. 1. **10** grace. Ap. 184. I. 1. which, &c. = Fig. *Ellipsis*. Ap. 6. upon. Ap. 104. vi. was not = did not become, i. e. prove to be. in vain. Gr. *kenos*, empty. Not the same word as in *vv.* 2, 17. with. Ap. 104. xvi. **11** whether, or. Ap. 118. 2. a. preach. Ap. 121. 1.

15. 12-58 [For Structure see next page].

12 from the dead. Gr. *ek nekrōn*. Ap. 139. 3. among. Ap. 104. viii. 2.

you that there is °no °resurrection of °the dead?

K r 13 But [2]if there be [12]no [12]resurrection of [12]the dead, °then is [3]Christ °not [4]risen:

s 14 And [2]if [3]Christ °be [9]not [4]risen, then *is* our °preaching [10]vain, and your °faith °*is* also [10]vain.

15 °Yea, and we are found °false witnesses of [9]God; because we °have °testified of [9]God that He [4]raised up [3]Christ: Whom He [4]raised [9]not up, °if so be that [12]the dead [4]rise [9]not.

r 16 For [2]if [12]the dead [4]rise [9]not, [13]then is °not [3]Christ [4]raised:

s 17 And [2]if [3]Christ [14]be [9]not [4]raised, your [14]faith *is* °vain; ye are yet °in your [3]sins.

18 Then they also which °are [6]fallen asleep [17]in [3]Christ °are °perished.

19 [2]If [17]in this °life only we °have hope [17]in [3]Christ, we are °of all °men most miserable.

L O t 20 But now °is [3]Christ [4]risen [12]from the dead, °*and* become the °firstfruits of °them that slept.

21 For since [2]by [19]man *came* death, [2]by [19]man °*came* also the [12]resurrection of [12]the dead.

22 For as [17]in °Adam °all die, °even so [17]in [3]Christ shall all be °made alive.

u 23 But °every man [17]in his own °order: [3]Christ the [20]firstfruits; °afterward they that are [3]Christ's, °at His °coming.

24 Then *cometh* the °end, when He °shall have [3]delivered up the °kingdom to [9]God, even the °Father; when He shall have °put down all °rule and all °authority and °power.

P 25 For He must reign, till He hath put all enemies °under His feet.

O t 26 °The last enemy *that* shall be °destroyed *is* death.

15. 12-58 (*N*, p. 1709). **CLAIM ESTABLISHED BY HIS DOCTRINAL TEACHING.**
(*Extended Alternation.*)

N | J | 12. Objection. What some say.
K | 13-19. Answer.
L | 20-28. Resurrection certain because Christ is raised.
M | 29-32. Present conflict to no purpose, if Christ be not raised.
N | 33, 34. Exhortation.
J | 35. Objections.
K | 36-41. Answer.
L | 42-49. Resurrection certain because Christ is raised.
M | 50-57. Victory worth all present conflicts.
N | 58. Exhortation.

no. Gr. *ou*, as in *v.* 9.
resurrection. Gr. *anastasis*. Ap. 178. II. 1.
the dead. No art. Ap. 139. 2.

15. 13-19 (K, above). **ANSWER.** (*Alternation.*)

K | r | 13. If no resurrection, Christ not risen.
s | 14, 15. Consequences. Our preaching vain. Your faith vain. We are false witnesses.
r | 16. If no resurrection, Christ not risen.
s | 17-19. Consequences. Your faith vain. The dead have perished. We most miserable.

13 then, &c. = not even (Gr. *oude*) has Christ been raised.
14 be not risen = has not been raised.
preaching. Ap. 121. 3.
faith. Ap. 150. II. 1.
***is* also** = also *is*.
15 Yea, and = Moreover.
false witnesses. Gr. *pseudomartur*. Only here and Matt. 26. 60.
have. Omit.
testified. Gr. *martureō*. See p. 1511.
of = against. Gr. *kata*. Ap. 104. x. 1.
if so be that = if (Ap. 118. 2. a) at least.
16 not. Gr. *oude*.
17 vain = to no purpose. Gr. *mataios*. See Acts 14. 15. Not the same word as in *vv.* 2, 10, 14, 58.
in. Ap. 104. viii.
18 are fallen = fell. **are.** Omit.
perished. Gr. *apollumi*. See 1. 18.

19 life. Gr. *zōē*. Ap. 170. 1. **have hope** = are having our hope. **of all men, &c.** = more to be pitied than all men. **men.** Gr. *anthrōpos*. Ap. 123. 1.

15. 20-28 (L, above). **RESURRECTION CERTAIN, BECAUSE CHRIST IS RAISED.**
(*Extended Alternation.*)

L | O | t | 20-22. Death counteracted.
u | 23, 24. Order. Firstfruits, &c.
P | 25. Reason.
O | *t* | 26, 27-. Death destroyed.
u | -27, 28-. Order. Father supreme.
P | -28. Purpose.

20 is, &c. = Christ has been raised. From *v.* 20 to *v.* 28 is a digression. Fig. *Parembolē*. Ap. 6. ***and* become.** All the texts omit. **firstfruits.** Gr. *aparchē*. See Rom. 8. 23, and cp. notes on John 20. 1, 17. **them, &c.** = those who have fallen asleep. See *v.* 6. **21** *came* **also** = also *came*. **22 Adam.** Lit. the Adam. **all die.** By virtue of their relationship to Adam. See Rom. 5. 12-19. **even so, &c.** = so in Christ also. Christ also has a relationship to the human race. It is that of Lordship (Rom. 14. 9). This is acknowledged by some now (John 13. 13; 20. 28), and brings salvation (Rom. 10. 9). It is the work of the Holy Spirit (12. 3). Hence Judas only said, "Master" (Matt. 26. 25, 49). The natural man rebels against such acknowledgment (Ex. 5. 2. Ps. 2. 2, 3; 12. 4. Luke 19. 14). But this Lordship shall one day be asserted and acknowledged by all, including the arch-rebel himself (Ps. 2. 6, 7. Phil. 2. 9-11. Rev. 19. 16). To this end all must be raised. **made alive.** Gr. *zōopoieō*. See Rom. 4. 17. Cp. John 5. 28, 29. **23 every man** = each one. **order.** Gr. *tagma*. Only here in N.T. It is used in the Sept. of a body of soldiers. Num. 2. 2, &c. (rank). 2 Sam. 23. 13 (army). **afterward.** Gr. *epeita*. Same as *vv.* 6, 7. **at** = in. Gr. *en*. Ap. 104. viii. **coming.** Gr. *parousia*. See Matt. 24. 3. **24 end.** Gr. *telos*. Not the same "end" as in 1. 8. Christ's coming brings that "end", but this is the end of the millennial age. **shall, &c.** The texts read, "delivers up". **kingdom.** App. 112-114. **Father.** Ap. 98. III. **put down** = brought to nought. Gr. *katargeō*. See Rom. 3. 3. **rule.** Gr. *archē*. Ap. 172. 6. **authority.** Ap. 172. 5. **power.** Ap. 172. 1. Cp. Eph. 1. 21. 1 Pet. 3. 22. **25 under.** Ap. 104. xviii. 2. It is God Who puts all enemies under Christ's feet. The fifth quotation of Ps. 110. 1. Cp. Matt. 22. 44. **26 The last enemy, &c.** Lit. Death, the last enemy, is destroyed. Fig. *Prolepsis* 1. Ap. 6. **destroyed.** Same word as "put down", *v.* 24.

27 For He °hath put all things [25]under His feet.
u But when He saith "**all things are °put under Him**", *it is* manifest that °He is excepted, Which did °put all things under Him.
28 And when all things shall be °subdued [1]unto Him, then shall the Son °also Himself be °subject [1]unto Him That [27]put all things under Him,
P °that [9]God may be °all [17]in all.
M 29 Else what shall they do which are °baptized [3]for °the dead, [2]if the [12]dead [4]rise [9]not at all? °why are they then °baptized [3]for °the dead?
30 And why °stand we in jeopardy every hour?
31 °I protest by your rejoicing which I have [17]in °Christ Jesus our °Lord, I die °daily.
32 [2]If °after the manner of [19]men I °have °fought with beasts [23]at Ephesus, °what advantageth it °me, [2]if the [12]dead [4]rise [9]not? °**let us eat and drink; for to morrow we die.**
N 33 Be °not °deceived: °evil °communications °corrupt °good °manners.
34 °Awake °to righteousness, and °sin [33]not; for [6]some °have not the knowledge of [9]God: I speak *this* °to your shame.
J 35 But °some *man* will say, "How are °the dead [4]raised up? and with °what body do they come?"
K 36 *Thou* °fool, that which thou sowest is [9]not °quickened, °except it die:
37 And that which thou sowest, thou sowest [9]not that body that shall be, but °bare grain, °it may chance of wheat, or °of some other *grain:*
38 But [9]God giveth it a body °as it hath pleased Him, and to °every seed °his own body.
39 °All flesh *is* [9]not the same flesh: but *there is* °one *kind of* flesh of [19]men, °another flesh of °beasts, °another of fishes, *and* °another of °birds.
40 *There are* also °celestial bodies, and bodies °terrestrial: but the glory of the °celestial *is* °one, and the *glory* of the °terrestrial *is* °another.
41 *There is* °one glory of the sun, and °another glory of the moon, and °another glory of the stars: for °*one* star differeth from °*another* star [17]in glory.

27 hath put = subjected. Gr. *hupotassō*. Contrast the first occ. Luke 2. 51.

put under *Him* = subjected. This quotation is from Ps. 8. 6.

He is excepted = it is with the exception of Him.

28 subdued = subjected, as above.

also Himself = Himself also.

subject = subjected. It is the Father Who puts all enemies as a footstool for the feet of the Son. See Matt. 22. 44. But when this is done, the Son rises up, takes His great power and reigns (Rev. 11. 17), and putting His feet on the footstool, treads down the nations His enemies, and continues to put down all that exalts itself against God throughout His millennial reign. See Pss. 18. 37–50; 60. 12; 101. 8 (R.V.); 145. 20. Isa. 63. 3, 6. Rev. 19. 15.

that = in order that. Gr. *hina*.

all in all. In *vv.* 27, 28, *panta* occ. six times, in five of them transl. "all things". It must be the same here. There is an ellipsis, and it should read "over all things in all (places)", i. e. everywhere supreme.

29 baptized, &c. See *v.* 20. This question follows on from *v.* 19. Ap. 115. I. vi.

baptized = being baptized.

the dead. Ap. 139. 4.

why are they, &c. Read, why are they baptized also? (It is) for the dead. It is to remain dead, as Christ remains, if there be no resurrection, *v.* 13. The argument is, What is the use of being baptized, if it is only to remain dead? No suggestion here of the vicarious baptism which sprang up later among the Marcionites and others.

30 stand . . . in jeopardy. See Acts 19. 27.

31 I protest, &c. = I affirm (a Greek particle used in affirmations) by the boasting concerning you. The pronoun "your" corresponds to the genitive, not of possession, but of relation. Ap. 17.

Christ Jesus. Ap. 98. XII.

Lord. Ap. 98. VI. i. *β*. 2. A. For this full title see Rom. 6. 23.

daily. Gr. *kath'* (Ap. 104. x. 2) *hēmeran*.

32 after the manner of men = according to (Ap. 104. x. 2) a man. **have.** Omit.

fought with beasts. Gr. *thēriomacheō*. Only here. Fig. *Metaphor*. Ap. 6. Referring to the riot (Acts 19. 28–31). Ignatius, in his epistle to the Romans, says, "From Syria even to Rome, I fight with beasts . . . being bound to ten leopards, I mean, a band of soldiers, who, even when they receive benefits, show themselves the worse". Clark's *Ante-Nicene Library*, vol. i, p. 213.

what, &c. = what is the profit? Gr. *ophelos*. Only here and James 2. 14, 16. **me** = to me.

let us eat, &c. Many similar expressions of Epicureanism are found in heathen writers. But this is probably cited from Isa. 22. 13. Cp. Wisdom 2. 5–9.

33 not. Ap. 105. II. **deceived.** See 6. 9.

evil. Ap. 128. III. 2.

communications = associations. Gr. *homilia*. Only here. Cp. the verb, Acts 20. 11.

corrupt. See 3. 17.

good. Ap. 184. III. **manners.** Gr. *ēthos*. Only here. In pl. = morals. A quotation from the *Thais* of Menander, an Athenian poet. Ap. 107. II. 5. **34 Awake.** Lit. Return to sobriety (of mind). Gr. *eknēphō*. Only here in N.T., but in Sept. Gen. 9. 24. 1 Sam. 25. 37; &c. **to righteousness** = righteously, i. e. as is right. Gr. *dikaiōs*, adv. of *dikaios*. Ap. 191. 1. **sin.** Ap. 128. I. i. **have not, &c.** Lit. have ignorance. Gr. *agnōsia*. Only here and 1 Pet. 2. 15. **to your shame.** See 6. 5. **35 some man** = some one. Ap. 123. 3. **the dead.** Ap. 139. 1. **what** = what kind of. **36 fool.** See Luke 11. 40. The fourth occ. **quickened.** Same as "made alive", *v.* 22. **except.** Gr. *ean* (Ap. 118. 1. b) *mē* (Ap. 105. II). **37 bare** = naked. Gr. *gumnos*. Always transl. "naked" elsewhere. **it may chance** = if (Ap. 118. 2. b) it should happen. **of some other** = of some one (Gr. *tis*) of the rest (Gr. *loipos*. Ap. 124. 3). **38 as it hath, &c.** = even as He purposed. Ap. 102. 1. Cp. 12. 18. **every seed** = each of the seeds. In *vv.* 36–38 the apostle shows that as we know not how *the seeds* come to life and grow up (Mark 4. 27), much less do we know how the *resurrection* change is effected. **his** = its. **39 All flesh, &c.** = Not all flesh *is* the same flesh. **one.** Ap. 124. 1. **another.** Same as "one". Gr. *allos*. **beasts.** See Acts 23. 24. **birds.** Gr. *ptēnon*. Only here. **40 celestial.** Gr. *epouranios*. Occ. twenty times. Transl. "heavenly" save in this verse, Eph. 6. 12. Phil. 2. 10. See John 3. 12. **terrestrial.** Gr. *epigeios*. Occ. seven times. Transl. "earthly" save here in this verse and Phil. 2. 10. The same contrast is seen in John 3. 12. Phil. 2. 10. **one . . . another.** Gr. *heteros*. Ap. 124. 2. For Longer Note on this verse see p. 1726. **41 one, another, another.** Gr. *allos*. Ap. 124. 1. *one, another.* Omit.

L 42 So °also *is* the [12] resurrection of [35] the dead. It is sown [17] in °corruption; it is [4] raised [17] in °incorruption:
43 It is sown [17] in dishonour; it is [4] raised [17] in glory: it is sown [17] in weakness; it is [4] raised [17] in °power:
44 It is sown a °natural body; it is [4] raised a °spiritual body. There is a °natural body, °and there is a °spiritual body.
45 °And so it is written, "**The first** [19] **man Adam** °**was made a living** °**soul;**" the last Adam *was made* °a [36] quickening °spirit.
46 °Howbeit that *was* [9] not first which is [44] spiritual, but that which is [44] natural; °and [23] afterward °that which is [44] spiritual.
47 The first [19] man *is* [6] of the °earth, °earthy: the second [19] man *is* °the Lord °from °heaven.
48 As *is* the [47] earthy, such *are* they also that are [47] earthy: and as *is* the °heavenly, such *are* they also that are °heavenly.
49 And as we have borne the °image of the [47] earthy, we shall °also bear the °image of the [48] heavenly.

M 50 Now this I say, brethren, that °flesh and blood °cannot inherit the °kingdom of [9] God; °neither doth [42] corruption inherit [42] incorruption.
51 °Behold, I °shew you a °mystery; We shall [9] not all °sleep, but we shall all °be changed,
52 [17] In a °moment, [17] in the °twinkling of an eye, [23] at the last trump: for the trumpet shall sound, and [35] the dead shall be [4] raised °incorruptible, and we shall [51] be changed.
53 For this °corruptible must put on [42] incorruption, and this °mortal *must* put on °immortality.
54 So when this [53] corruptible shall have put on [42] incorruption, and this [53] mortal shall have put on [53] immortality, then shall be brought to pass the °saying that is written, "**Death is** °**swallowed up** °**in** °**victory.**"
55 "**O death, where** *is* **thy** °**sting? O** °**grave, where** *is* **thy** [54] **victory?**"
56 The [55] sting of death *is* [3] sin; and the °strength of [3] sin *is* the law.
57 But °thanks *be* to [9] God, Which giveth us the [54] victory °through our [31] Lord °Jesus Christ.

N 58 °Therefore, my °beloved brethren, be ye °stedfast, °unmoveable, always abounding [17] in the work of the [31] Lord, °forasmuch as ye °know that your labour is [9] not [10] in vain [17] in the °Lord.

G (p. 1695) **16** Now °concerning the °collection °for the °saints, as I °have given order to the °churches of °Galatia, °even so do ye.
2 °Upon the °first *day* of the week let °every one of you lay °by him °in store, °as *God* hath

42 also, &c. = *is* the resurrection of the dead also, i. e. with a different body.
corruption. Gr. *phthora*. See Rom. 8. 21. The four contrasts in *vv.* 42–44 give the Fig. *Symplokē*. Ap. 6.
incorruption. Gr. *aphtharsia*. See Rom. 2. 7.
43 power. Ap. 172. 1.
44 natural. Gr. *psuchikos*. See 2. 14.
spiritual. Gr. *pneumatikos*. See 12. 1.
and there is = there is also.
45 And so, &c. = So it has been written also. We have the proofs from nature and analogy of the variety and resources in the Divine working, and the testimony of the Word besides.
was made. Lit. became into. Gr. *egeneto eis*. The exact expression used in Gen. 2. 7 (Sept.).
soul. Gr. *psuchē*. Ap. 110. II.
a quickening spirit = into (*eis*) a quickening spirit. See John 5. 21.
spirit. Ap. 101. II. 13.
46 Howbeit, &c. Read "But not first the spiritual, but the natural".
and. Omit. that which is = the.
47 earth. Ap. 129. 4.
earthy. Gr. *choikos*. Only here and in *vv.* 48, 49. The noun *chous*, dust, is found in the Sept. Gen. 2. 7. Ps. 22. 15; 104. 29. Ecc. 3. 20, &c.
the Lord. All the texts omit.
from. Ap. 104. vii. Same as "of", prev. line.
heaven. Sing. See Matt. 6. 10.
48 heavenly. Gr. *epouranios*. Same as "celestial", *v.* 40.
49 image. Gr. *eikōn*. See Rom. 1. 23.
also bear, &c. = bear the image also.
50 flesh and blood. See Matt. 16. 17.
cannot = are not (Gr. *ou*, as in *v.* 9) able to.
kingdom of God. Ap. 114.
neither. Gr. *oude*.
51 Behold. Ap. 133. I. 2.
shew = tell.
mystery = secret. Ap. 193.
sleep = be sleeping. Ap. 171. 2.
be changed. Gr. *allassō*. See Acts 6. 14.
52 moment. Gr. *atomos*, lit. that which cannot be cut or divided. Hence "atom". Only here.
twinkling. Gr. *ripē*. Only here.
incorruptible. Gr. *aphthartos*. See Rom. 1. 23.
53 corruptible. Gr. *phthartos*. See Rom. 1. 23.
mortal. Gr. *thnētos*. See Rom. 6. 12.
immortality. Gr. *athanasia*. Only here, *v.* 54, and 1 Tim. 6. 16. In Rom. 2. 7 and 2 Tim. 1. 10 *aphtharsia* is transl. immortality.
54 saying = word. Ap. 121. 10.
swallowed up. Gr. *katapinō*. Elsewhere Matt. 23. 24. 2 Cor. 2. 7; 5. 4. Heb. 11. 29. 1 Pet. 5. 8. Rev. 12. 16.
in = unto. Ap. 104. vi.
victory. Gr. *nikos*. Only here, *vv.* 55, 57: and Matt. 12. 20. The quotation is from Isa. 25. 8, and the following verse from Hos. 13. 14. Ap. 107. II. 4.
55 sting. Gr. *kentron*. See Acts 26. 14.
grave. Gr. *hadēs*. Ap. 131. II. The texts read "death" (Gr. *thanatos*).
56 strength = power, as in *vv.* 24, 43.
57 thanks. Ap. 184. I. 1.
through. Ap. 104. v. 1.
Jesus Christ. Ap. 98. XI.
58 Therefore = So then.
beloved. Ap. 135. III. stedfast. Gr. *hedraios*. See 7. 37. unmoveable. Gr. *ametakinētos*. Only here. forasmuch as ye know = knowing. Ap. 132. I. i. Lord. Ap. 98. VI. i. *β*. 2. B.

16. 1 concerning. Ap. 104. xiii. 1. collection. Gr. *logia*. Only here and *v.* 2, where it is transl. "gatherings". Found in the Papyri of tax-gathering. for. Ap. 104. vi. saints. Gr. *hagios*. See Acts 9. 13. have given order = commanded. Gr. *diatassō*. See Acts 7. 44. churches. Ap. 186. Galatia. Bengel says, "He proposes the Galatians as an example to the Corinthians, the Corinthians to the Macedonians (2 Cor. 9. 2), and the Corinthians and Macedonians to the Romans (Rom. 15. 26)". even so, &c. = so do ye also. **2** Upon. Ap. 104. x. 2. first, &c. See John 20. 1. Acts 20. 7. every = each. by. Ap. 104. xii. 2. in store = treasuring up. Gr. *thēsaurizō*. See Matt. 6. 19. as, &c. = whatever he may be prospered in. Gr. *euodoumai*.

prospered him, °that there be °no °gatherings
when I come.
3 And when I come, whomsoever ye shall
°approve °by *your* letters, °them will I °send
to °bring your °liberality °unto Jerusalem.
4 And °if it be meet that I go also, they shall
go °with me.
5 Now I will come °unto you, when I °shall
pass through Macedonia: for I °do pass through
Macedonia.
6 And it may be that I will °abide, yea, and
°winter °with you, [2]that ye may °bring me on
my journey whithersoever I go.
7 For I °will °not °see you now °by the way;
but I °trust to °tarry °a while [6]with you, [4]if
the °Lord permit.
8 But I will [7]tarry °at Ephesus until °Pente-
cost.
9 For a great °door and °effectual is opened
°unto me, and *there are* many adversaries.

F **10 Now [4]if Timotheus °come, °see [2]that he may**
be [6]with you °without fear: for he worketh
the work of the °Lord, as I also *do*.
11 °Let no man therefore °despise him: but
°conduct him forth °in peace, [2]that he may
come [5]unto me: for I °look for him °with the
brethren.
12 °As touching *our* brother Apollos, I greatly
°desired him °to come [5]unto you [11]with the
brethren: but his °will was [7]not at all °to come
°at this time; but he will come when he shall
°have convenient time.
13 °Watch ye, °stand fast [11]in the °faith,
°quit you like men, °be strong.
14 Let all your things be done °with °charity.
15 I °beseech you, brethren, (ye °know the
house of °Stephanas, that it is the °firstfruits
of Achaia, and *that* they °have °addicted them-
selves °to the °ministry °of the [1]saints,)
16 [2]That °ye °submit yourselves [9]unto such,
and to every one that °helpeth with *us*, and
laboureth.
17 I am glad °of the °coming of [15]Stephanas
and Fortunatus and Achaicus: for °that which
was lacking on your part they °have °sup-
plied.
18 For they °have refreshed my °spirit and
yours: therefore °acknowledge ye them that
are such.

that = in order that. Gr. *hina*.
no = not. Ap. 105. II.
gatherings. See *v.* 1.
3 approve. Gr. *dokimazō*. See 3. 13; 11. 28.
by (Ap. 104. v. 1), &c. Read, "them will I send with letters".
them = these.
send. Ap. 174. 4.
bring = carry away. Gr. *apopherō*. Elsewhere, Mark 15. 1. Luke 16. 22. Rev. 17. 3; 21. 10.
liberality = gift. Lit. grace. Gr. *charis*. Ap. 184. I. 1. Cp. 2 Cor. 8. 19.
unto. Ap. 104. vi.
4 if. Ap. 118. 1. b.
with. Ap. 104. xvi.
5 unto. Ap. 104. xv. 3.
shall pass = shall have passed.
do pass = am passing, i. e. purpose to pass.
6 abide. Gr. *paramenō*. Elsewhere, Heb. 7. 23. Jas. 1. 25.
winter. See Acts 27. 12.
with. Ap. 104. xv. 3.
bring me on my journey. Gr. *propempō*. See Acts 15. 3.
7 will. Ap. 102. 1.
not. Ap. 105. I.
see. Ap. 133. I. 1.
by the way = in (Gr. *en*. Ap. 104. viii) passing Gr. *parodos*. Only here.
trust = hope.
tarry. Gr. *epimenō*. See Acts 10. 48.
a while = some (Gr. *tis*) time (Gr. *chronos*).
Lord. Ap. 98. VI. i. *β*. 2. A.
8 at = in. Ap. 104. viii.
Pentecost. See Acts 2. 1.
9 door. Fig. *Metaphor*. Ap. 6. Cp. Acts 14. 27. 2 Cor. 2. 12. Col. 4. 3. Rev. 3. 8 See for the facts, Acts 19. 17–20.
effectual. Gr. *energēs*. Elsewhere, Philem. 6. Heb. 4. 12.
unto = to.
10 come = shall have come.
see. Gr. *blepō*. Ap. 133. I. 5.
without fear = fearlessly. Gr. *aphobōs*. Elsewhere, Luke 1. 74. Phil. 1. 14. Jude 12. Timothy was of a timid, shrinking disposition, and the apostle commends him to the support of the true believers at Corinth.
Lord. Ap. 98. VI. i. *β*. 2. B.
11 Let no man = Let not (Gr. *mē*. Ap. 105. II) any one (Gr. *tis*. Ap. 123. 3).
despise. Gr. *exoutheneō*. See Acts 4. 11. Cp. 1 Tim. 4. 12.
conduct . . . forth. Gr. *propempō*, as in *v.* 6.
in. Ap. 104. viii.
look for. Gr. *ekdechomai*. See 11. 33. Heb. 10. 13; 11. 10. 1 Pet. 3. 20. **with.** Ap. 104. xi. 1. It is clear from these verses (10, 11) that the letter was not sent by Timothy. He had already departed (4. 17), and as he was to travel by a circuitous route, he might not arrive till after the receipt of the letter. See Acts 19. 22. Paul was expecting him to be in time to return with the bearers of the letter, who were probably the three named in *v.* 17. **12 As touching** = Now concerning (Ap. 104. xiii. 1). **desired** = exhorted. Ap. 134. I. 6. **to** = in order that (Gr. *hina*) he should. **will.** Ap. 102. 2. **at this time** = now. **have convenient time** = have leisure. Gr. *eukaireō*. See Acts 17. 21. So far from being jealous of the popularity of Apollos (1. 12). Paul urges him to visit Corinth. To him God's glory was the one object to be sought (3. 5–7. Phil. 1. 18). **13 Watch.** Cp. Acts 20. 31. **stand fast.** Cp. Gal. 5. 1. Phil. 1. 27; 4. 1. 1 Thess. 3. 8. 2 Thess. 2. 15. **faith.** Ap. 150. II. 1. Cp. 15. 1. **quit you like men.** Gr. *andrizomai*. Only here. **be strong.** Gr. *krataioō*. Elsewhere, Luke 1. 80; 2. 40. Eph. 3. 16. **14 with** = in. Ap. 104. viii. **charity** = love. Gr. *agapē*. Ap. 135. II. 1. Cp. 14. 1. 1 Pet. 4. 8. **15 beseech.** Gr. *parakaleō*. See "desired", *v.* 12. **know.** Ap. 132. I. i. **Stephanas.** See 1. 16. **firstfruits.** Gr. *aparchē*. See Rom. 8. 23; 16. 5. **have.** Omit. **addicted** = set. Gr. *tassō*. See Acts 13. 48. **to** = for, as in *v.* 1. **ministry** = service. Ap. 190. II. 1. **of** = to. **16 ye** = ye also. **submit** = subject. Gr. *hupotassō*, as in 14. 32, &c. **helpeth with.** Gr. *sunergeō*, to work together with. Elsewhere, Mark 16. 20. Rom. 8. 28. 2 Cor. 6. 1. Jas. 2. 22. Cp. 3. 9. **17 of** = at. Ap. 104. ix. 2. **coming** = presence. Gr. *parousia*. See Matt. 24. 3. **that which was, &c.** = your lack. Gr. *husterēma*. Elsewhere, Luke 21. 4. 2 Cor. 8. 14; 9. 12; 11. 9. Phil. 2. 30. Col. 1. 24. 1 Thess. 3. 10. **have.** Omit. **supplied.** Gr. *anaplēroō*. See Phil. 2. 30. **18 have refreshed** = gave rest to. Same as in Matt. 11. 28. **spirit.** Ap. 101. II. 9. **acknowledge** = recognize. Ap. 132. I. iii.

A (p. 1695) 19 The [1] churches of Asia ° salute you. ° Aquila and Priscilla ° salute you much [11] in the [10] Lord, [4] with the [1] church that is ° in their house.
20 All the brethren ° greet you. ° Greet ye one another [14] with an holy ° kiss.
21 The ° salutation of *me* Paul with mine own hand.
22 ° If ° any man ° love [7] not the [7] Lord ° Jesus Christ, let him be ° Anathema ° Maran-atha.
23 The ° grace of ° our [7] Lord ° Jesus Christ *be* [11] with you.
24 My ° love *be* [11] with you all [11] in ° Christ Jesus. Amen.

19 salute. Gr. *aspazomai*. See Acts 20. 1.
Aquila. Cp. Acts 18. 2, 18, 26. Rom 16. 3. 2 Tim. 4 19
in. Gr. *kata*. Ap. 104. x. 2.
20 greet. Same as "salute", *v.* 19
kiss. Gr. *philēma*. See Rom. 16. 16; &c.
21 salutation, &c. Cp. Col. 4. 18. 2 Thess. 3. 17, and see Rom. 16. 22.
22 If. Ap. 118. 2. a.
any man = any one. Gr. *tis*. Ap. 123. 3.
love. Ap. 135. I. 2.
Jesus Christ. All the texts omit.
Anathema = accursed. Full stop after this word. See Acts 23. 14.
Maran-atha. Aramaic. Ap. 94. III. 3. 33
23 grace. Ap. 184. I. 1. **our** Read the **Jesus Christ.** Ap. 98. XI. Some texts omit "Christ". **24 love.** Same as "charity", *v.* 14. **Christ Jesus.** Ap. 98. XII.

LONGER NOTE ON 1 COR. 15. 40.

1. The subject of *vv.* 35–54 is the manner of the resurrection. And the basis is,—as the plant to the seed, so spiritual body to natural body, &c.: "thou sowest not the body *that shall be* (lit. come into existence), but a naked grain, as the case may be, of wheat (John 12. 24), or of some one of the rest" (*v.* 37).

2. But in *v.* 39 is set forth differentiation as to "flesh" of mundane organized beings; and in *v* 41 differentiation in glory (beauty) of the heavenly luminaries. Between these two is *v.* 40, where the differentiation is commonly regarded as merely between "the resurrection body" and the body that now is. But is the contrast not rather between

a. resurrection bodies fitted for life and activities "in the heavenlies", and

b. resurrection bodies fitted for life and activities on earth? (e g. Matt. 19. 28; cp. Ezek. 34. 23; 37. 24, &c)

3. The contrast (differentiation) in *v.* 39 concerns one thing only, i. e. "flesh". That in *v* 41 also concerns one thing only. Therefore, it is suggested, the contrast in *v.* 40 is between resurrection bodies *only*, and not between resurrection (flesh and bones) bodies and natural (flesh and blood) bodies. If the glory (*doxa*) spoken of here is to be applied to the body that now is, where, alas! is the evidence of it?

4. As the resurrection is still future, the ellipses may be supplied and the verse rendered, thus: "And heavenly bodies (there will be) and earthly bodies; but of one kind indeed (will be) the glory of the heavenly, and another kind that of the earthly."

THE SECOND EPISTLE TO THE CORINTHIANS.

THE STRUCTURE OF THE EPISTLE AS A WHOLE.

(Introversion and Alternation.)

A | 1. 1, 2. INTRODUCTION.

B | **C** | **E** | 1. 3-11. THANKSGIVING.

F | 1. 12. CHARACTER OF PAUL'S MINISTRY.

D | **G** | 1. 13, 14. THE PRESENT EPISTLE.

H | **K** | 1. 15, 16. PROPOSED VISIT.

L | 1. 17—2. 2. VINDICATION OF HIS ACTION.

J | **M** | **O** | 2. 3-11. FORMER EPISTLE. OBJECT.

P | 2. 12, 13-. NO REST IN SPIRIT.

N | 2. -13. MACEDONIA. JOURNEY.

B | *C* | *E* | 2. 14-17. THANKSGIVING.

F | 3. 1—7. 4. CHARACTER OF PAUL'S MINISTRY.

D | *J* | *M* | *P* | 7. 5-7. NO REST IN FLESH.

O | 7. 8-16. FORMER EPISTLE. EFFECT.

N | 8. 1—9. 15. MACEDONIA. ASSEMBLIES.

H | *L* | 10. 1—12. 13. VINDICATION OF HIS ACTION.

K | 12. 14—13. 1. PURPOSED VISIT.

G | 13. 2-10. THE PRESENT EPISTLE.

A | 13. 11-14. CONCLUSION.

THE SECOND EPISTLE TO THE CORINTHIANS.

INTRODUCTORY NOTES.

1. From various passages we learn that the apostle Paul wrote this Epistle under much pressure of spirit. The personal part of his first letter to the Corinthians had had its effect upon the obedient members of the church (see ch. 2 and 7), and he wrote a second time to comfort such, as well as to warn a disobedient element (13. 2, 10). It is plain that certain altogether denied his authority, and in ch. 10-13 he once more powerfully vindicates his apostleship, especially in connexion with false teachers, against whom he earnestly warned the Corinthians. The specific claim of authority as proceeding from his Lord and Master alone occupies a large part of the Epistle. Hence, also, the admonition that if he came he would enforce that authority. There is much to indicate Paul's anxiety for all the churches, while in the doctrinal portions occur some unsurpassed presentations of the Divine love in Christ.

2. Not only was this church burdened with internal trouble (ch. 1), but they had trials also from without (11. 13-15), just as the Lord Himself had foretold in Matt. 24. 9-12. In consolation, Paul held out before them (4. 14) the same hope of resurrection as he proclaimed in his first letter.

3. Timothy had been sent to Corinth (1 Cor. 4. 17) and had no doubt returned bearing news of the unhappy condition of the church. Titus delivered the first letter and, there being some delay in his return, Paul passed from Troas to Macedonia, where, later, Titus brought from Corinth (7. 7-16) such reports as only partially assured the apostle, and led him to send the Second Epistle by the same fellow worker.

4. Various explanations have been proposed with regard to the conditions under which the Epistle was written. Some think that, prior to its transmission, the apostle had sent by the hand of Timothy a severe letter which has been lost. Another suggestion is that Paul, hearing of the confusion in the church, made a hasty visit to Corinth from Ephesus, and, finding that he availed nothing but rather was set at naught, withdrew to another part of Achaia or to Macedonia, where he penned the Second Epistle. Still other views on similar lines are put forward, but all that can be said is that they are suppositions of which there is no hint in the Epistle. Connecting 1 Cor. 4. 19; 2 Cor. 1. 23, and 13. 2, the apostle had not been back on account of the disorders in the church, whatever may be meant by "the third time" in 13. 1. In 1. 15, 16 he is minded to come to them as a second benefit, and passing to Macedonia, to return to them, which would have been a third time.

5. Written from Macedonia not long after Paul's leaving Asia (1. 8), it would not be many months after the dispatch of the First Epistle. This was probably in A. D. 57 (winter) or spring of 58. See Ap. 180.

THE SECOND EPISTLE OF PAUL THE APOSTLE

TO THE

CORINTHIANS.

A 1 PAUL, an °apostle of °Jesus Christ °by the
°will of °God, and °Timothy °*our* brother,
°unto the °church of °God which is °at Corinth,
°with all the °saints which are °in all Achaia:
2 °Grace *be* to you and peace °from [1]God
our °Father, and *from* the °Lord [1]Jesus
Christ.

B C E 3 °Blessed *be* °God, °even the [2]Father of our
°Lord [1]Jesus Christ, the [2]Father of °mercies,
and °the [1]God of all °comfort;
4 Who °comforteth us °in all our °tribulation,
°that we may be able to °comfort them which
are [1]in °any °trouble, [1]by the [3]comfort wherewith we ourselves are °comforted °of [1]God.
5 For as the °sufferings of °Christ abound °in
us, so our °consolation also aboundeth [1]by
°Christ.
6 And °whether we be °afflicted, *it is* °for
your [5]consolation and salvation, which °is
effectual [1]in the °enduring of the same [5]suffer-
ings which **we** also suffer: or °whether we be
[4]comforted, *it is* °for your [5]consolation and
salvation.
7 And our hope °of you *is* °stedfast, °knowing,
that as ye are °partakers of the [5]sufferings, so
shall ye be °also of the [5]consolation.
8 For we °would °not, brethren, have you
°ignorant °of our [4]trouble which came °to us
[1]in Asia, that we were °pressed °out of measure,
°above °strength, °insomuch that we °despaired
even of °life:
9 But **we** had the °sentence of death [1]in ourselves, °that we should °not °trust [4]in ourselves,
but [4]in [1]God Which °raiseth °the dead:
10 Who °delivered us °from °so great a death,
and °doth °deliver: [5]in Whom we °trust that
He will °yet °deliver *us*;
11 Ye also °helping together °by °prayer [6]for

1. 1 apostle. Ap. 189. First occ. of this form of address Cp. Gal. 1. 1. Eph. 1. 1. Col. 1. 1. 1 Tim. 1. 1. 2 Tim. 1. 1.
Jesus Christ. Ap. 98. XI.
by=through. Gr. *dia.* Ap. 104. v. 1.
will. Gr. *thelēma.* Ap. 102. 2. Cp. 1 Cor. 1. 1.
God. Ap. 98. I. i. 1. Cp. Acts 9. 15.
Timothy. Timothy is associated with Paul in the address of the epistles to Philippians, Colossians; and with Paul and Silas in the two epistles to the Thessalonians.
our=the. **unto**=to.
church. Ap. 186. **at**=in. Ap. 104. viii.
with. Gr. *sun.* Ap. 104. xvi.
saints. Gr. *hagios.* See Acts 9. 13.
in. Ap. 104. viii.
2 Grace. Ap. 184. I. 1.
from. Gr. *apo.* Ap. 104. iv.
Father. Ap. 98. III.
Lord. Ap. 98. VI. i. *β*. 2. B.
3 Blessed. Gr. *eulogētos.* See Rom. 1. 25.
God=the God.
even=and, as in Eph. 1. 3. 1 Pet. 1. 3.
Lord. Ap. 98. VI. i. *β*. 2. A.
mercies. Gr. *oiktirmos.* See Rom. 12. 1.
the God of all comfort. Cp. Acts 7. 2.
comfort. Gr. *paraklēsis.* See Acts 4. 36. This word occ. eleven times in this Epistle, six times in this chapter. In *vv.* 5, 6, 7 transl. "consolation". Note the Fig. *Epanodos.* Ap. 6.
4 comforteth. Gr. *parakaleō.* Ap. 134. I. 6. Occ. eighteen times in this epistle.
in=upon. Gr. *epi.* Ap. 104. ix. 2.
tribulation. Gr. *thlipsis.* See Acts 7. 10.
that we may be=unto (Gr. *eis.* Ap. 104. vi) our being. **any**=every.
trouble. Same as "tribulation".
of=by. Gr. *hupo.* Ap. 104. xviii. 1.
5 sufferings. Gr. *pathēma.* See Rom. 8. 18.
Christ=the Christ. Ap. 98. IX.
in=towards. Gr. *eis*, as in *v.* 4.
consolation=comfort, as *v.* 3.
6 whether=if. Gr. *eite.* Ap. 118. 2. a.
afflicted. Gr. *thlibō.* Occ. here, 4. 8; 7. 5. Matt. 7. 14. Mark 3. 9. 1 Thess. 3. 4. 2 Thess. 1. 6, 7. 1 Tim. 5. 10. Heb. 11. 37. Cp. "tribulation", above. **for.** Gr. *huper.* Ap. 104. xvii. 1. **is effectual**=worketh. See Rom. 7. 5. **enduring.** Gr. *hupomonē.* Generally transl. "patience". **7 of**=on behalf of. Gr. *huper*, as in *v.* 6. **stedfast.** Gr. *bebaios.* See Heb. 2. 2. In some MSS. this clause stands at the beginning of *v.* 6, in others in the middle, after "suffer". **knowing.** Gr. *oida.* Ap. 132. I. i. **partakers.** Gr. *koinōnos.* See 1 Cor. 10. 18. **also, &c.**=of the consolation also. **8 would not**=do not wish (Gr. *thelō.* Ap. 102. 1) you to be. **not.** Gr. *ou.* Ap. 105. I. **ignorant.** Gr. *agnoeō.* See Rom. 1. 13. The sixth occ. of this expression. **of.** The texts read "concerning". Gr. *peri.* Ap. 104. xiii. 1. **to us.** The texts omit. **pressed**=weighed down. Gr. *bareō.* Elsewhere, 5. 4. Matt. 26. 43 (heavy). Mark 14. 40. Luke 9. 32. 1 Tim. 5. 16 (charged). **out of measure.** Lit. according to (Gr. *kata.* Ap. 104. x. 2) excellence (Gr. *huperbolē*) or excess. This phrase is used five times. See 4. 17. Rom. 7. 13. 1 Cor. 12. 31. Gal. 1. 13. **above.** Gr. *huper.* Ap. 104. xvii. 2. **strength**=power. Gr. *dunamis.* Ap. 172. 1. **insomuch**=so. **despaired.** Gr. *exaporeomai.* Only here and 4. 8. The reference may be to the riot at Ephesus (Acts 19. 28-34), where his life would have been in danger, but for the counsel of his friends (*v.* 31); but the following verses rather indicate some dangerous sickness. Both may have been in the apostle's mind. **life.** Gr. *zaō.* Cp. Ap. 170. 1. **9 sentence**=answer. Gr. *apokrima.* Only here. Cp. Ap. 122. 3. The only issue he could see from his troubles was "death". **that**=in order that. Gr. *hina.* **not.** Gr. *mē.* Ap. 105. II. **trust.** Gr. *peithō.* Ap. 150. I. 2. **raiseth.** Gr. *egeirō.* Ap. 178. I. 4. **the dead.** Ap. 139. 1. **10 delivered.** Gr. *ruomai.* Note the different tenses, giving the Fig. *Polyptōton.* Ap. 6. **from**=out of. Gr. *ek.* Ap. 104. vii. **so great.** Gr. *tēlikoutos.* Only here, Heb. 2. 3. Jas. 3. 4. Rev. 16. 18. **doth.** The texts read "will". **trust**=hope. **yet**=still also. **11 helping together**=co-operating. Gr. *sunupourgeō.* Only here. **by.** No Prep. Dat. case. **prayer.** Gr. *deēsis.* Ap. 134. II. 3.

us, [9]that for the °gift *bestowed* °upon us °by
the means of many persons, °thanks may be
given [1]by many °on our behalf.

F 12 For our °rejoicing is this, the °testimony
of our °conscience, that [1]in °simplicity and
°godly °sincerity, [8]not °with °fleshly wisdom,
but °by the [2]grace of [1]God, we °have had our
conversation [1]in the °world, and °more abundantly °to you-ward.

D G 13 For we write °none °other things [1]unto you,
than what ye read or °acknowledge; and I
[10]trust ye shall °acknowledge °even to the end;
14 As °also ye °have [13]acknowledged us °in
part, that we are your °rejoicing, even as ye
also *are* ours [1]in °the day of the [3]Lord °Jesus.

H K 15 And °in this °confidence I °was minded to
come °unto you °before, [9]that ye might have
a second °benefit;
16 And to pass [1]by you °into Macedonia, and
to come again °out of Macedonia [15]unto you,
and [4]of you to be °brought on my way °toward
Judæa.

L 17 When I therefore [15]was thus minded, °did
I use °lightness? or the things that I °purpose,
do I °purpose °according to the flesh, [9]that
°with me there should be °yea yea, and °nay
nay?
18 But *as* [1]God *is* °true, our °word °toward
you was [8]not [17]yea and [17]nay.
19 For the °Son of [1]God, [1]Jesus Christ, Who
was °preached °among you [1]by us, *even* [1]by
me and °Silvanus and Timotheus, was [8]not
[17]yea and [17]nay, but [1]in Him was [17]yea.
20 For °all the promises of [1]God [1]in Him *are*
[17]yea, °and [1]in Him °Amen, [15]unto the glory of
[1]God [1]by us.
21 Now He Which °stablisheth us [1]with you
[5]in [5]Christ, and °hath °anointed us, *is* [1]God;
22 Who °hath °also °sealed us, and °given
the °earnest of the °Spirit [1]in our hearts.
23 Moreover I °call [1]God for a °record °upon
my °soul, that to °spare you I came °not as yet
°unto Corinth.
24 [8]Not °for that we °have dominion over

gift. Gr. *charisma*. Ap. 184. I. 2.
upon. Gr. *eis*. Ap. 104. vi.
by the means of = from. Gr. *ek*. Ap. 104. vii.
thanks may be given. Lit. it may be thanked. Gr. *eucharisteō*. See Acts 27. 35.
on our behalf = on account of (Gr. *huper*. Same as "for", *v.* 6) us.

12 rejoicing = boasting. Gr. *kauchēsis*, the act of boasting. See Rom. 3. 27.
testimony. Gr. *marturion*. First occ. Matt. 8. 4.
conscience. See Acts 23. 1.
simplicity = guilelessness. Gr. *haplotēs*. Elsewhere 8. 2; 9. 11, 13; 11. 3. Rom. 12. 8. Eph. 6. 5. Col. 3. 22. The texts read *hagiotēs*, holiness; not the Syriac.
godly sincerity = sincerity of God.
sincerity. Gr. *eilikrineia*. See 1 Cor. 5. 8.
with = in. Gr. *en*. Ap. 104. viii.
fleshly. Gr. *sarkikos*. See Rom. 7. 14 and 1 Pet. 2. 11.
by = in, as above.
have had our conversation = behaved, or lived. Gr. *anastrephō*. Cp. Eph. 2. 3. 1 Tim. 3. 15. Heb. 10. 33; 13. 18. 1 Pet. 1. 17. 2 Pet. 2. 18.
world. Gr. *kosmos*. Ap. 129. 1.
more abundantly. Gr. *perissoterōs*. Out of thirteen occ. seven are in this Epistle. See 2. 4; 7. 13, 15; 11. 23, 23; 12. 15.
to you-ward = towards (Gr. *pros*. Ap. 104. xv. 3) you.

13 none = not (Gr. *ou*).
other. Gr. *allos*. Ap. 124. 1.
acknowledge. Gr. *epiginōskō*. Ap. 132. I. iii.
even. The texts omit.

14 also ye = ye also.
have. Omit.
in part. Gr. *apo merous*. A part of you, the faithful ones.
rejoicing = ground of boasting. Gr. *kauchēma*. See Rom. 4. 2.
the day, &c. See 1 Cor. 5. 5.
Jesus. Ap. 98. X.

15 in. No Prep. Dat. case.
confidence. Gr. *pepoithēsis*. Ap. 150. II. 2.
was minded = wished. Gr. *boulomai*. Ap. 102. 3.
unto. Gr. *pros*. Ap. 104. xv. 3.
before, i. e. before visiting Macedonia.
benefit. Gr. *charis*. Ap. 184. I. 1.

16 into. Gr. *eis*. Ap. 104. vi.
out of = from. Gr. *apo*. Ap. 104. iv.
brought on my way. Gr. *propempō*. See Acts 15. 3.
toward. Gr. *eis*, as above. This was the apostle's original intention, but was altered, because of his not finding Titus (2. 12, 13). See p. 1727. **17 did I, &c.** The question is introduced by *mēti*, expecting a negative answer. **lightness** = fickleness. Gr. *elaphria*. Only here. **purpose** = plan. Gr. *bouleuomai*. The "Received Text" reads *bouleuomai* at the beginning of the verse also. **according to.** Gr. *kata*. Ap. 104. x. 2. **with.** Gr. *para*. Ap. 104. xii. 2. **yea yea** = the yea yea. **nay nay** = the nay nay. Gr. *ou*. Ap. 105. I. That is, one thing to-day and another to-morrow. **18 true** = faithful. Gr. *pistos*. Ap. 150. III. **word.** Gr. *logos*. Ap. 121. 10. Cp. 1 Cor. 1. 18. **toward** = unto. Gr. *pros*, as in *vv.* 15, 16, 20. **19 Son.** Gr. *huios*. Ap. 108. iii. **preached.** Gr. *kērussō*. Ap. 121. 1. **among.** Gr. *en*. Ap. 104. viii. 2. **Silvanus** = Silas. Cp. 1 Thess. 1. 1. 2 Thess. 1. 1. 1 Pet. 5. 12. See Acts 18. 5. **20 all, &c.** = as many as are the promises of God, in Him they are. **and in Him.** The texts read "Wherefore also through (Ap. 104. v. 1) Him they are." **Amen.** This Hebrew word is transl. "verily" in the Gospels, except in Matt. 6. 13 at the end of the Lord's Prayer, and at the close of each Gospel. It does not occ. in the Acts. In the Epistles it comes at the close of benedictions and doxologies. In the Revelation occasionally at the beginning. There are three exceptions, here, 1 Cor. 14. 16, and Rev. 3. 14. In the last passage it is a title of the Lord. It means "truth", and He is the Truth (John 14. 6). Cp. Isa 65. 16, where "the God of truth" is "the God of Amen". **21 stablisheth** = confirms. Gr. *bebaioō*. See Rom. 15. 8. **hath.** Omit. **anointed.** Gr. *chriō*, the verb from which *Christos* is formed. Elsewhere, always of the Lord. Luke 4. 18. Acts 4. 27; 10. 38. Heb. 1. 9. **22 hath.** Omit. **also sealed us** = sealed us also. **sealed.** Gr. *sphragizō*. Cp. John 3. 33. **given** = gave. **earnest.** Gr. *arrabōn*. Only here, 5. 5. Eph. 1. 14. A foretaste or pledge of some future benefit. **Spirit.** Ap. 101. II. 4. The operation of the Spirit is the pledge of the fulfilment of the promises. **23 call God for a record** = invoke God as a witness. **call.** Gr. *epikaleomai*. See Acts 2. 21. Cp. Acts 25. 11, 12, 21, 25; &c. **record.** Gr. *martur*. Cp. Rom. 1. 9. **upon.** Gr. *epi*. Ap. 104. ix. 3. **soul.** Gr. *psuchē*. Ap. 110. IV. 1. **spare.** Gr. *pheidomai*. See Acts 20. 29. **not as yet.** Gr. *ouketi*. **unto.** Gr. *eis*. Ap. 104. vi. **24 for that** = because. **have dominion** = lord it. Gr. *kurieuō*. See Rom. 6. 9.

your ° faith, but are ° helpers of your joy: for by
° faith ye stand.

2 But I ° determined this with myself, ° that
I would ° not come again ° to you ° in
° heaviness.
2 For ° if I ° make you sorry, who is he then
that ° maketh me glad, ° but the same which is
° made sorry ° by me?
JMO 3 And I wrote this same ° unto you, ° lest,
when I came, I should have ° sorrow ° from
them of whom I ought to rejoice; ° having confidence ° in you all, that my joy is *the joy* of
you all.
4 For ° out of much ° affliction and ° anguish of
heart I wrote ° unto you ° with many tears;
° not ° that ye should be [2] grieved, but ° that ye
might ° know the ° love which I have ° more
abundantly ° unto you.
5 But [2] if ° any have [2] caused grief, he hath [4] not
[2] grieved me, but ° in part: [4] that I may [1] not
° overcharge you all.
6 Sufficient to such a ° man *is* this ° punishment, which *was inflicted* ° of ° many.
7 So that ° contrariwise ye *ought* rather to
° forgive *him*, and ° comfort *him*, ° lest perhaps
such a one should be ° swallowed up with
° overmuch [3] sorrow.
8 Wherefore I ° beseech you that ye would
° confirm *your* [4] love ° toward him.
9 For ° to this end ° also did I write, [4] that I
might [4] know the ° proof of you, ° whether ye be
° obedient ° in all things.
10 To whom ye [7] forgive any thing, ° I *forgive*
also: for [2] if I [7] forgave any thing, to whom I
[7] forgave *it*, ° for your sakes *forgave I it* [1] in the
° person of ° Christ;
11 [3] Lest ° Satan should get an advantage of
us: for we are [4] not ° ignorant of his ° devices.
P 12 ° Furthermore, when I came ° to ° Troas ° to
preach [10] Christ's gospel, and a ° door was
opened [4] unto me ° of the ° Lord,
13 I had ° no ° rest in my ° spirit, because I
found [1] not Titus my brother:
N but ° taking my leave of them, I ° went from
thence ° into Macedonia.
BCE 14 Now ° thanks *be* [4] unto ° God, Which always
° causeth us to triumph [1] in [10] Christ, and
° maketh manifest the ° savour of His ° knowledge ° by us [1] in every place.

faith. Gr. *pistis*. Ap. 150. II. 1.
helpers. Gr. *sunergos*. See 1 Cor. 3. 9.

2. 1 determined = judged, or decided. Gr. *krinō*. Ap. 122. 1.
that I would not = not to.
not. Gr. *mē*. Ap. 105. II.
to = unto. Gr. *pros*. Ap. 104. xv. 3.
in. Gr. *en*. Ap. 104. viii.
heaviness = sorrow or grief. Gr. *lupē*, transl. "sorrow" in *vv.* 3, 7.
2 if. Gr. *ei*. Ap. 118. 2. a.
make . . . sorry = grieve. Gr. *lupeō*, transl. "grieve", or "cause grief" in *vv.* 4, 5. Out of twenty-six occ. twelve are in this Epistle.
maketh . . . glad. Gr. *euphrainō*. See Acts 2. 26 (rejoice).
but = except. Gr. *ei mē*.
by. Gr. *ek*. Ap. 104. vii.
3 unto you. The texts omit.
lest = in order that (Gr. *hina*) not (Gr. *mē*).
sorrow. See *v.* 1.
from. Gr. *apo*. Ap. 104. iv.
having confidence = trusting. Gr. *peithō*. Ap. 150. I. 2.
in = upon. Gr. *epi*. Ap. 104. ix. 3.
4 out of. Gr. *ek*. Ap. 104. vii.
affliction. Gr. *thlipsis*, as in 1. 4.
anguish = straitening, or distress. Gr. *sunochē*. Only here and Luke 21. 25. Cp. the verb *sunechō*, 5. 14. Luke 12. 50. Acts 18. 5. Phil. 1. 23.
unto = to.
with = by, or through. Gr. *dia*. Ap. 104. v. 1.
not. Gr. *ou*. Ap. 105. I.
that = in order that. Gr. *hina*.
know. Gr. *ginōskō*. Ap. 132. I. ii.
love. Gr. *agapē*. Ap. 135. II. 1.
more abundantly. See 1. 12.
unto. Gr. *eis*. Ap. 104. vi.
5 any. Gr. *tis*. Ap. 123. 3.
in part. Gr. *apo merous*. The grief has come from a part of you who have been led away.
overcharge = lay a burden, or press heavily, upon. Gr. *epibareō*. Only here, 1 Thess. 2. 9. 2 Thess. 3. 8.
6 man = one, as *v.* 7.
punishment = censure. Gr. *epitimia*. Only here. Cp. the verb *epitimaō*. First occ. Matt. 8. 26. Fig. *Tapeinōsis*. Ap. 6.
of = by. Gr. *hupo*. Ap. 104. xviii. 1.
many = the more, i. e. the majority.
7 contrariwise = (on) the contrary. Gr. *tounantion*, for *to enantion*. Here, Gal. 2. 7. 1 Pet. 3. 9.
forgive. Gr. *charizomai*. Ap. 184. II. 1.
comfort. Gr. *parakaleō*. Ap. 134. I. 6.
lest = lest perhaps. Gr. *mēpōs*.
swallowed up. Gr. *katapinō*. See 1 Cor. 15. 54.
overmuch = more abundant.
8 beseech. Gr. *parakaleō*, as above.
confirm = ratify with authority. Gr. *kuroō*. Only here and Gal. 3. 15. Akin to *kurios*, lord.
toward. Gr. *eis*. Ap. 104. vi.

9 to this end = for (Gr. *eis*) this. also did I write = did I write also. proof. Gr. *dokimē*. See Rom. 5. 4 (experience). whether = if. Ap. 118. 2. a. obedient. Gr. *hupēkoos*. See Acts 7. 39. in. Gr. *eis*, as above. **10** I *forgive* also = I also *forgive*. for your sakes. Lit. on account of (Gr. *dia*. Ap. 104. v. 2) you. person = face, i. e. sight, or presence. Christ. Ap. 98. IX. **11** Satan, &c. Lit. we should be overreached (Gr. *pleonekteō*. Here, 7. 2; 12. 17, 18. 1 Thess. 4. 6) by (Gr. *hupo*, as in *v.* 6) Satan. ignorant. Gr. *agnoeō*. Cp. 1. 8. Fig. *Tapeinōsis*. Ap. 6. devices = thoughts. Gr. *noēma*. Elsewhere 3. 14; 4. 4; 10. 5; 11. 3. Phil. 4. 7. See 11. 3. Eph. 6. 11. Rev. 2. 24. **12** Furthermore = Now. to. Gr. *eis*. Ap. 104. vi. Troas. See Acts 16. 8. to *preach* Christ's gospel = for (Gr. *eis*) the gospel (Ap. 140) of the Messiah. door. See 1 Cor. 16. 9. of. Gr. *en*. Ap. 104. viii. Lord. Ap. 98. VI. i. *β*. 2. B. **13** no = not (Gr. *ou*). rest. Gr. *anesis*. See Acts 24. 23. spirit. Ap. 101. II. 9. taking . . . leave. Gr. *apotassomai*. See Acts 18. 18. went from thence = went forth. into. Gr. *eis*. Ap. 104. vi. **14** thanks. Gr. *charis*. Ap. 184. I. 1. God. Ap. 98. I. i. 1. causeth us to triumph = leadeth us in triumph (Gr. *thriambeuō*), or triumphs over us as in Col. 2. 15. Only in these two places. Paul was a captive won by grace. In a Roman triumph there were captives destined to be spared and captives destined to death. See *v.* 16. maketh manifest. Gr. *phaneroō*. Ap. 106. I. v. savour. Gr. *osmē*. Elsewhere, *v.* 16. John 12. 3 (odour). Eph. 5. 2. Phil. 4. 18 (odour). knowledge. Gr. *gnōsis*. Ap. 132. II. 1. by = by means of. Gr. *dia*. Ap. 104. v. 1. Paul gave evidence of the wisdom which dwelt in Him (Col. 2. 3) in his own conversion (1 Tim. 1. 16), as well as in his preaching.

15 For we are [4-]unto [14]God a °sweet savour of [10]Christ, [1]in them that are °saved, and [1]in them that °perish:
16 To the one *we are* the [14]savour of death [-4]unto death; and to the other the [14]savour of °life [-4]unto °life. And who *is* sufficient °for these things?
17 For we are [4]not as °many, which °corrupt the °word of [14]God: but as °of °sincerity, but as °of [14]God, °in the sight of [14]God °speak we [1]in [10]Christ.

F A C **3** °Do we begin °again to °commend ourselves? or need we, as °some *others*, °epistles of commendation °to you, or *letters* of commendation °from you?
2 Ye are our epistle °written °in our hearts, °known and °read °of all °men:
3 *Forasmuch as ye are* °manifestly declared to be the epistle of °Christ °ministered °by us, [2]written °not °with °ink, but °with the °Spirit of the living °God; °not [2]in °tables of stone, but [2]in °fleshy °tables of the heart.
D 4 And such °trust have we °through °Christ °to [3]God-ward:
5 [3]Not that we are sufficient °of ourselves to °think °any thing as °of ourselves; but our °sufficiency *is* °of [3]God;
E G 6 Who °also °hath made us able °ministers of °the °new °testament; [3]not of °the °letter, but of °the °spirit: for the °letter killeth, but the °spirit °giveth life.
H J[1] K[1] 7 But °if the °ministration of death, °written

15 sweet savour. Gr. *euōdia.* Elsewhere, Eph. 5. 2. Phil. 4. 18. saved = being saved. Cp. 1 Cor. 1. 18. perish = are perishing. Gr. *apollumi.* See 1 Cor. 1. 18.
16 life. Gr. *zōē.* Ap. 170. 1. for. Gr. *pros.* Ap. 104. xv. 3.
17 many. As in 2. 6. corrupt = adulterate. Gr. *kapēleuō.* Only here. The word *kapēlos*, which occ. once in the Sept., meant a huckster, tavern-keeper, and then the verb came to mean "adulterate". See Isa. 1. 22, where the Sept. reads, "thy wine-sellers mix the wine with water". word. Gr. *logos.* Ap. 121. 10. of. Gr. *ek.* Ap. 104. vii. sincerity. See 1 Cor. 5. 8. in the sight of = before. Gr. *katenōpion.* Elsewhere, 12. 19. Eph. 1. 4. Col. 1. 22. Jude 24. The texts read *katenanti*, over against. speak. Gr. *laleō.* Ap. 121. 7.

3. 1—7. 4 (*F*, p. 1727). CHARACTER OF PAUL'S MINISTRY. (*Alternation.*)

F | A | 3. 1—6. 10. Paul's services.
  B | 6. 11, 12. His interest in the Corinthians.
 A | 6. 13—7. 3. Paul's recompense.
  B | 7. 4. His joy in the Corinthians.

3. 1—6. 10 (A, above). PAUL'S SERVICES. (*Extended Alternation.*)

A | C | 3. 1-3. Commendation. Question.
  D | 3. 4, 5. Trust in, and sufficiency of, God.
   E | 3. 6-18. Ministry of the New Covenant.
    F | 4. 1—5. 11. Support under affliction.
 C | 5. 12, 13. Commendation. Negation.
  D | 5. 14—-18-. Love of Christ. All things of God.
   E | 5. -18—6. 2. Ministry of Reconciliation.
    F | 6. 3-10. Approval under affliction.

3. 1 Do we, &c. = Are we to begin. again. He had done so in 1 Cor. 9. commend. Gr. *sunistanō.* See on Rom. 3. 5. some. Gr. *tines.* Ap. 124. 4. epistles, &c. = commendatory (Gr. *sustatikos.* Only here) letters. Cp. Acts 18. 27. to. Gr. *pros.* Ap. 104. xv. 3. from. Gr. *ek.* Ap. 104. vii. Question preceded by *mē.*
2 written. Gr. *engraphō.* Only here and *v.* 3. in. Gr. *en.* Ap. 104. viii. known. Gr. *ginōskō.* Ap. 132. I. ii. read. Gr. *anaginōskō.* There is a *Paronomasia* here. Ap. 6. of = by. Gr. *hupo.* Ap. 104. xviii. 1. men. Ap. 123. 2. **3** manifestly declared = manifested. Gr. *phaneroō.* Ap. 106. I. v. Christ. Ap. 98. IX. ministered. Gr. *diakoneō.* Ap. 190. III. 1. by. Gr. *hupo*, as in *v.* 2. not. Gr. *ou.* Ap. 105. I. with. No Prep. Dat. case. ink. Gr. *melan.* Only here, 2 John 12. 3 John 13. Spirit. Ap. 101. II. 4. God. Ap. 98. I. i. 1. tables of stone = stone tables. tables. Gr. *plax.* Only here and Heb. 9. 4. fleshy. Gr. *sarkinos.* This word refers to the substance or material and carries no moral significance. Cp. Heb. 7. 16, where the texts read as here. **4** trust = confidence. Gr. *pepoithēsis.* Ap. 150. II. 2. through. Gr. *dia.* Ap. 104. v. 1. Christ = the Christ. to God-ward = toward (Gr. *pros.* Ap. 104. xv. 3) God. **5** of = from. Gr. *apo.* Ap. 104. iv. think = reckon. Gr. *logizomai.* See the frequent occ. in Rom. 4, count, reckon, &c. any thing. Gr. *tis.* Ap. 123. 3. of. Gr. *ek.* Ap. 104. vii. sufficiency. Gr. *hikanotēs.* Only here. of. Gr. *ek*, as above.

3. 6-18 (E, above). MINISTRY OF THE NEW COVENANT. (*Alternation.*)

E | G | 6. *Pneuma* necessary for life.
  H | 7-16. *Pneuma* changes the Old Covenant.
 G | 17. *Pneuma* necessary for liberty.
  H | 18. *Pneuma* changes us.

6 also. Read after "ministers". hath made us able = enabled us, or made us efficient as. Gr. *hikanoō.* Only here and Col. 1. 12. ministers. Gr. *diakonos.* Ap. 190. I. 1. the = a. new. Gr. *kainos.* See Matt. 9. 17. testament = covenant. Gr. *diathēkē.* See Matt. 26. 28. This is the covenant of Jer. 31. 31. Cp. Heb. 8. 6-13. the. Omit. letter. Gr. *gramma.* This is the Sinaitic covenant, called "the ministration of death" in *v.* 7. spirit. The old covenant could not give life. It was like a dead body, for lack of the spirit (James 2. 26). Cp. John 6. 63. Christ is the Spirit of the new covenant. See *v.* 17. giveth life = quickeneth. Gr. *zōopoieō.* See Rom. 8. 11 and 1 Cor. 15. 45.

3. 7-16 (H, above). PNEUMA CHANGES THE OLD COVENANT. (*Division.*)

H | J[1] | 3. 7-11. *Pneuma* gives life.
  | J[2] | 3. 12-16. *Pneuma* brings into liberty.

3. 7-11 (J[1], above). PNEUMA GIVES LIFE. (*Repeated Alternation.*)

J[1] | K[1] | 7. The Old Covenant came with glory, but Israel could not look upon it.
  L[1] | 8. The New Covenant also comes with glory.
 K[2] | 9-. The Old Covenant, which brought condemnation, came with glory.
  L[2] | -9. The New Covenant, which ministers righteousness, exceeds it in glory.
 K[3] | 10-. The Old Covenant had no glory in inflicting death.
  L[3] | -10. The New Covenant has surpassing glory in giving life.
 K[4] | 11-. The Old Covenant, which is annulled, was with glory.
  L[4] | -11. The New Covenant, which abides, will abide in glory.

7 if. Ap. 118. 2. a. ministration. Gr. *diakonia.* Ap. 190. II. 1. written = in (Gr. *en.* Ap. 104. viii) letters. See *v.* 6.

and °engraven [2]in stones, °was °glorious, so that the °children of Israel could °not °stedfastly behold the face of °Moses °for the glory of his countenance; which *glory* was °to be done away:

L1 8 How shall °not the [7]ministration of the [6]spirit be rather [7]glorious?

K2 9 For [7]if the [7]ministration of °condemnation *be* glory,

L2 much more doth the [7]ministration of °righteousness exceed [2]in glory.

K3 10 For even that which was °made glorious °had no glory [2]in this respect,

L3 by reason of the glory that °excelleth.

K4 11 For [7]if that which is [7]done away *was* °glorious,

L4 much more that which °remaineth *is* °glorious.

J2 M1 12 °Seeing then that we have such hope, we °use °great °plainness of speech:

N1 13 And [3]not as [7]Moses, *which* put a °vail °over his face, °that the [7]children of Israel could [7]not [7]stedfastly look °to the end of that which is °abolished:

14 But their °minds were °blinded: for until °this day [11]remaineth the same [13]vail °untaken away °in the °reading of the °old testament;

M2 °which *vail* is [7]done away [2]in [3]Christ.

N2 15 But even unto [14]this day, °when [7]Moses is read, the [13]vail °is °upon their heart.

M3 16 Nevertheless [15]when °it shall °turn [1]to the °Lord, the [13]vail shall be °taken away.

G 17 Now the °Lord is °that °Spirit: and where the °Spirit of the [16]Lord *is*, there *is* liberty.

H 18 But we all, with °open face °beholding as in a glass the glory of the [16]Lord, are °changed into the same °image °from glory [13]to glory, *even* as °by °the Spirit of the Lord.

F O **4** °Therefore °seeing we have this °ministry, as we °have °received mercy, we °faint °not;

engraven. Gr. *entupoō*. Only here.
was = came to be.
glorious = in (Gr. *en*) glory.
children = sons. Gr. *huios*. Ap. 108. iii.
not. Gr. *mē*. Ap. 105. II.
stedfastly behold = gaze upon. Gr. *atenizō*. Ap. 133. III. 6. Followed by the Gr. *eis* (Ap. 104. vi).
Moses. Occ. three times in this Epistle, here, *vv.* 13, 15.
for = on account of. Gr. *dia*. Ap. 104. v. 2.
to be done away = being done away. Gr. *katargeō*. See Rom. 3. 3.
8 not. Gr. *ouchi*. Ap. 105. I. (a).
9 condemnation. Gr. *katakrisis*. Only here and 7. 3. See Ap. 122. 7.
righteousness. Gr. *dikaiosunē*. Ap. 191. 3.
10 made glorious = glorified. Gr. *doxazō*. See p. 1511.
had no glory = was not glorified, as above.
excelleth. Gr. *huperballō*. Occ. here, 9. 14. Eph. 1. 19; 2. 7; 3. 19.
11 glorious = through (Gr. *dia*. Ap. 104. v. 1) glory.
remaineth. Gr. *menō*. See p. 1511.
glorious = in (Gr. *en*) glory.

3. 12-16 (J2, p. 1731). PNEUMA BRINGS INTO LIBERTY. (*Repeated Alternation.*)

J2 | M1 | 12. We speak plainly.
N1 | 13, 14-. Moses was veiled.
M2 | -14. Veil done away in Christ.
N2 | 15. Veil on the heart of Israel.
M3 | 16. Veil taken away.

12 Seeing . . . have = Having then.
use. Gr. *chraomai*. See Acts 27. 3.
great = much.
plainness of speech = outspokenness. Gr. *parrhēsia*. Often transl. boldly, or freely.
13 vail. Gr. *kalumma*. Only here and in *vv.* 14, 15, 16.
over = upon. Gr. *epi*. Ap. 104. ix. 3. See Ex. 34. 33.
that, &c. = with a view to (Gr. *pros*. Ap. 104. xv. 3) the children of Israel's not gazing to the end.
to. Gr. *eis*. Ap. 104. vi.
abolished = being done away, as in *v.* 7.
14 minds = thoughts. Gr. *noēma*. See 2. 11.
blinded = hardened. Gr. *pōroō*. See Rom. 11. 7, 25 (*pōrōsis*).
this day = to-day. Gr. *sēmeron*.
untaken away = not (Gr. *mē*. Ap. 105. II) unveiled, or revealed (Gr. *anakaluptō*, unveil, only here and *v.* 18). This should follow "old testament". It means, "it being not revealed that it is done away" (R.V. m.).
in. Gr. *epi*. Ap. 104. ix. 2.
reading. Gr. *anagnōsis*. See Acts 13. 15.
old testament = old covenant. The only place where the term is used. The usual designation is "the law", or "Moses" (*v.* 15).

which *vail* = that (Gr. *hoti*) it. **15** when. Gr. *hēnika*. Only here and *v.* 16. is = lieth. upon. Gr. *epi*. Ap. 104. ix. 3. **16** it. I. e. the heart of Israel. turn. Gr. *epistrephō*. Often trans. "return", or "be converted". See Matt. 13. 15. John 12. 40. Acts 3. 19; 28. 27. Lord. Ap. 98. VI. i. *β*. 2. B. taken away. Gr. *periaireō*. See Acts 27. 20. **17** Lord. Ap. 98. VI. i. *β*. 2. A. that = the. Spirit. Ap. 101. II. 2. Cp. *v.* 6. **18** open = unveiled. See *v.* 14. Here is the contrast. Moses alone beheld and reflected the Shekinah glory, we *all* behold and reflect the Lord's glory. beholding . . . glass = reflecting, as R.V. Gr. *katoptrizō*. Only here. changed = transformed. Gr. *metamorphoomai*. See Mark 9. 2. image. Gr. *eikōn*. Cp. Rom. 8. 29. Col. 3. 10. from. Gr. *apo*. Ap. 104. iv. by = from. Gr. *apo*. the Spirit of the Lord = the Lord the Spirit. The word "Spirit" is in the Gen. of Apposition. Ap. 17. 4. See *v.* 6.

4. 1—5. 11 (F, p. 1731). SUPPORT UNDER AFFLICTION. (*Extended Alternation.*)

O | 4. 1-6. Contrasts as to others.
P | 4. 7-14. Instrumentalities.
Q | 4. 15. Benefit to the Corinthians.
O | 4. 16—5. 5. Contrasts as to themselves.
P | 5. 6-10. Instrumentalities.
Q | 5. 11. Benefit to mankind.

4. 1 Therefore = On account of (Gr. *dia*. Ap. 104. v. 2) this. seeing we have = having. ministry. Gr. *diakonia*. Ap. 190. II. 1. have. Omit. received mercy. Cp. 1 Cor. 7. 25. faint. Gr. *ekkakeō*. Occ. *v.* 16, Luke 18. 1 (which see). Gal. 6. 9. Eph. 3. 13. 2 Thess. 3. 13. not. Gr. *ou*. Ap. 105. I.

2 But [1] have ° renounced ° the hidden things of ° dishonesty, ° not walking ° in ° craftiness, ° nor ° handling the ° word of ° God deceitfully; but by ° manifestation of the truth ° commending ourselves ° to ° every man's conscience in the sight of ° God.

3 But ° if our ° gospel be ° hid, it is ° hid ° to them that are ° lost:

4 [2] In whom the ° god of this ° world hath blinded the ° minds of ° them which believe not, ° lest the ° light of the ° glorious [3] gospel of ° Christ, Who is the ° image of [2] God, should ° shine ° unto them.

5 For we ° preach [1] not ourselves, but ° Christ Jesus ° the Lord; and ourselves your ° servants ° for Jesus' sake.

6 For [2] God, Who ° commanded the ° light to shine ° out of darkness, hath shined [2] in our hearts, [2] to ° *give* the light of the ° knowledge of the glory of [2] God [2] in the face of ° Jesus Christ.

P 7 But we have this treasure [2] in ° earthen vessels, ° that the ° excellency of the ° power may be of [2] God, and [2] not ° of us.

8 *We are* ° troubled ° on every side, yet [1] not ° distressed; *we are* ° perplexed, but [1] not ° in despair;

9 Persecuted, but [1] not ° forsaken; ° cast down, but [1] not ° destroyed;

10 ° Always ° bearing about [2] in the body the ° dying of the ° Lord [5] Jesus, [7] that the ° life also of [5] Jesus might be ° made manifest [2] in our body.

11 For we ° which live are ° alway ° delivered ° unto death [5] for [5] Jesus' sake, [7] that the [10] life also of [5] Jesus might be [10] made manifest [2] in our ° mortal flesh.

12 So then death ° worketh [2] in us, but [10] life [2] in you.

13 We having the same ° spirit of ° faith, ° according as it is written, "**I** ° **believed,** ° **and therefore** ° **have I spoken;**" we also ° believe, ° and therefore ° speak;

14 ° Knowing that He Which ° raised up the ° Lord [5] Jesus shall ° raise up us also ° by [5] Jesus, and shall present *us* ° with you.

2 renounced. Gr. *apeipon.* Only here.
the hidden, &c. = the shameful secret things. This is the Fig. *Antimereia.* Ap. 6.
dishonesty = shame. Gr. *aischunē.* Always transl. "shame", except here. Luke 14. 9. Phil. 3. 19. Heb. 12. 2. Jude 13. Rev. 3. 18.
not. Gr. *mē.* Ap. 105. II.
in. Gr. *en.* Ap. 104. viii.
craftiness. See Luke 20. 23.
nor. Gr. *mēde.*
handling . . . deceitfully. Gr. *doloō.* Only here.
word. Gr. *logos.* Ap. 121. 10.
God. Ap. 98. I. i. 1.
manifestation. Gr. *phanerōsis.* See 1 Cor. 12. 7.
commending. See 3. 1.
to. Gr. *pros.* Ap. 104. xv. 3.
every man's conscience. Lit. every conscience of men (Gr. *anthrōpos.* Ap. 123. 1).
3 if. Ap. 118. 2. a.
gospel. Cp. Ap. 140.
hid = hid (Gr. *kaluptō,* to cover or veil) also. Cp. Jas. 5. 20. 1 Pet. 4. 8, and see 3. 13-16.
hid. Same verb. **to** = in. Gr. *en.*
lost = perishing. Gr. *apollumi.* See 1 Cor. 1. 18.
4 god. Ap. 98. I. i. 4.
world = age. Gr. *aiōn.* Ap. 129. 2. Cp. John 12. 31; 14. 30; 16. 11; where, however, world is *kosmos* (Ap. 129. 1).
minds. Gr. *noēma.* See 2. 11.
them, &c. = the unbelieving. Gr. *apistos.* Cp. Ap. 150. III.
lest, &c. = to (Gr. *eis.* Ap. 104. vi) the end that the light . . . should not (Gr. *mē,* as in *v.* 2).
light = illumination. Gr. *phōtismos.* Ap. 130. 3.
glorious gospel = gospel (or good news) of the glory. Cp. 1 Tim. 1. 11. Tit. 2. 13. See Ap. 140.
Christ = the Christ. Ap. 98. IX.
image. See 3. 18. Col. 1. 15. Heb. 1. 3 (*charaktēr*).
shine. Gr. *augazō.* Only here. Cp. *apaugasma,* Heb. 1. 3.
unto them. The texts omit.
5 preach. Gr. *kērussō.* Ap. 121. 1.
Christ Jesus. Ap. 98. XII.
the Lord = as Lord. Ap. 98. VI. i. β. 2. B. Cp. Rom. 10. 9.
servants. Gr. *doulos.* Ap. 190. I. 2.
for, &c. = on account of (Gr. *dia.* Ap. 104. v. 2) Jesus (Ap. 98. X).
6 commanded. Lit. spoke. Cp. Gen. 1. 3.
light. Gr. *phōs.* Ap. 130. 1.
out of. Gr. *ek.* Ap. 104. vii.
***give* the light** = the illumination. Gr. *phōtismos,* as in *v.* 4.

knowledge. Gr. *gnōsis.* Ap. 132. II. i. **Jesus Christ.** Ap. 98. XI. The texts omit "Jesus". **7 earthen.** Gr. *ostrakinos.* Only here and 2 Tim. 2. 20. From *ostrakon,* a potsherd. Cp. Ap. 94. IV. Treasure in the East is often hidden in the earth and in a potter's vessel to protect from damp, &c. Cp. Jer. 32. 14. **that** = in order that. Gr. *hina.* **excellency.** Gr. *huperbolē.* Cp. 12. 7 (abundance). **power.** Gr. *dunamis.* Ap. 172. 1. **of** = out of. Gr. *ek.* Ap. 104. vii. It does not emanate from us. Above "of God" is the possessive case. The power not only emanates from God, but belongs to Him. He does not part with it. **8 troubled** = afflicted. Gr. *thlibō.* See 1. 6. **on every side** = in (Gr. *en*) every thing. **distressed.** Gr. *stenochōreomai.* Only here and 6. 12, where it is trans. "straitened". The Syriac reads "suffocated", referring probably to a wrestler who is compressed by his antagonist. **perplexed.** Gr. *aporeomai.* Not knowing which way to turn. See Acts 25. 20. **in despair.** Gr. *exaporeomai.* See 1. 8. **9 forsaken** = abandoned. Gr. *enkataleipō.* See Acts 2. 27. **cast down.** Gr. *kataballō.* Only here, Heb. 6. 1. Rev. 12. 10. **destroyed.** Gr. *apollumi,* as in *v.* 3. Notice the four "nots" in these two verses. Fig. *Mesodiplōsis.* Ap. 6. **10 Always.** Ap. 151. II. G. i. **bearing about.** Gr. *peripherō.* Mark 6. 55. Eph. 4. 14. Heb. 13. 9. Jude 12. **dying.** Gr. *nekrōsis.* Only here and Rom. 4. 19. It means the condition of a corpse. It was his constant experience. See next verse. **Lord.** The texts omit. **life.** Gr. *zōē.* Ap. 170. 1. **made manifest.** Gr. *phaneroō.* Ap. 106. I. v. **11 which live.** Lit. the living. Gr. *zaō.* Cp. Ap. 170. 1. **alway.** Ap. 151. II. F. ii. **delivered.** Gr. *paradidōmi.* See John 19. 30. **unto.** Gr. *eis.* Ap. 104. vi. **mortal.** Gr. *thnētos.* See Rom. 6. 12. **12 worketh.** Gr. *energeō.* See Rom. 7. 5. **13 spirit.** Ap. 101. II. 4. **faith.** Ap. 150. II. 1. It is the Gen. of Apposition (Ap. 17. 4) faith being the Spirit's gift. 1 Cor. 12. 9. **according as, &c.** = according to (Gr. *kata.* Ap. 104. x. 2) that which has been written. **believed.** Ap. 150. I. 1. i. **and.** Omit. **have I spoken** = I spoke. Gr. *laleō.* Ap. 121. 7. **and therefore speak** = therefore we also speak. **14 Knowing.** Gr. *oida.* Ap. 132. I. i. **raised up.** Gr. *egeirō.* Ap. 178. I. 4. **Lord.** Ap. 98. VI. i. β. 2. A. **by** = through. Gr. *dia,* but the texts read "with", Gr. *sun.* **with.** Gr. *sun.* Ap. 104. xvi.

Q 15 For all things *are* °for your sakes, [7]that the °abundant °grace might, °through the °thanksgiving of °many, °redound °to the glory of [2]God.

O 16 °For which cause we [1]faint [1]not; but °though our °outward °man °perish, yet the °inward *man* is °renewed day by day.

17 For °our °light °affliction, which is but °for a moment, °worketh for us a °far more exceeding *and* °eternal °weight of glory;

18 While we °look [2]not at the things which are °seen, but at the things which are [2]not °seen: for the things which are °seen *are* °temporal; but the things which are [2]not °seen *are* [17]eternal.

5 For we °know that °if our °earthly house of °*this* tabernacle were °dissolved, we have a °building °of °God, an house °not made with hands, °eternal °in the °heavens.

2 For [1]in this we °groan, earnestly desiring to be °clothed upon with our °house which is °from °heaven:

3 °If so be that °being clothed we shall °not be found naked.

4 For we that are [1]in [1]*this* tabernacle do [2]groan, being burdened: [3]not °for that we °would be °unclothed, but [2]clothed upon, °that °mortality might be °swallowed up °of °life.

5 Now He That hath °wrought us °for the selfsame thing *is* [1]God, Who °also hath given °unto us the °earnest of the °Spirit.

P 6 Therefore *we are* °always °confident, [1]knowing that, whilst we are °at home [1]in the body, we are °absent °from the °Lord:

7 (For we walk °by °faith, [3]not °by sight:)

8 We are [6]confident, *I say*, and °willing rather to be [6]absent [2]from the body, and to be °present °with the [6]Lord.

9 Wherefore we °labour, that, whether [8]present or [6]absent, we may be °accepted of Him.

10 For we must all °appear °before the °judgment seat of °Christ; [4]that °every one may receive the things *done* °in *his* body, °according to that he hath °done, whether *it be* good or °bad.

Q 11 [1]Knowing therefore the °terror of the [6]Lord, we °persuade °men; but we are °made manifest [5]unto [1]God; and I °trust °also are °made manifest [1]in your consciences.

C 12 For we °commend [3]not ourselves again

15 for your sakes = on account of (Gr. *dia*. Ap. 104. v. 2) you.
abundant = abounding. Gr. *pleonazō*. See Rom. 5. 20.
grace. Gr. *charis*. Ap. 184. I. 1.
through. Gr. *dia*. Ap. 104. v. 1.
thanksgiving. Gr. *eucharistia*. See Acts 24. 3. Cp. 1. 11.
many = the majority, as in 2. 6.
redound = overflow, or excel. Gr. *perisseuō*.
to. Gr. *eis*. Ap. 104. vi.
16 For which cause = Therefore.
though = even if. Ap. 118. 2. a.
outward (Gr. *exō*) man (Gr. *anthrōpos*. Ap. 123. 1). This expression occ. only here. It is one of the names of the old nature. Cp. Rom. 6. 6. 1 Cor. 2. 14. Eph. 4. 22. Col. 3. 9.
perish = is corrupted or destroyed. Gr. *diaphtheirō*. Occ. elsewhere, Luke 12. 33. 1 Tim. 6. 5. Rev. 8. 9; 11. 18.
inward. Gr. *esōthen*. In Rom. 7. 22. Eph. 3. 16, the word is *esō*.
renewed. Gr. *anakainoō*. Only here and Col. 3. 10.
17 our light, &c. Lit. the momentary lightness of our affliction.
light. Gr. *elaphros*. Only here and Matt. 11. 30. Cp. "lightness", 1. 17.
affliction. Gr. *thlipsis* as in 1. 4. Cp. the verb, *v.* 8.
for a moment. Gr. *parautika*. Only here.
worketh. Gr. *katergazomai*. To work out. See Rom. 7. 8.
far more exceeding. Lit. according to (Gr. *kata*. Ap. 104. x. 2) excess unto (Gr. *eis*. Ap. 104. vi) excess. The Gr. for "excess" is *huperbolē*, as in *v.* 7.
eternal. Gr. *aiōnios*. Ap. 151. II. B. i.
weight. Gr. *baros*. See Acts 15. 28.
18 look. Gr. *skopeō*. See Luke 11. 35.
seen. Gr. *blepō*. Ap. 133. I. 5.
temporal = temporary, for a season. Gr. *proskairos*. Only here, Matt. 13. 21. Mark 4. 17. Heb. 11. 25.

5. 1 know. Gr. *oida*. Ap. 132. I. i.
if. Ap. 118. 1. b.
earthly. Gr. *epigeios*. See John 3. 12.
this tabernacle = the tent. Gr. *skēnos*. Only here and *v.* 4. It is the Gen. of Apposition. Ap. 17. The earthly house is a tent. See 1 Cor. 4. 11.
dissolved. Gr. *kataluō*.
building. Gr. *oikodomē*. See 1 Cor. 3. 9.
of. Gr. *ek*. Ap. 104. vii. God. Ap. 98. I. i. 1.
not made with hands. Gr. *acheiropoiētos*. Only here, Mark 14. 58. Col. 2. 11.
eternal. Ap. 151. II. B. i.
in. Gr. *en*. Ap. 104. viii.
heavens (pl.). See Matt. 6. 9, 10.
2 groan. See Rom. 8. 23.
clothed upon. Gr. *ependuomai*. Here and *v.* 4. Cp. John 21. 7.
house. Gr. *oikētērion*. Only here and Jude 6.
from. Gr. *ek*. Ap. 104. vii.

heaven. Sing. See *v.* 1. **3** If. Ap. 118. 2. a. being clothed. Gr. *enduō*. Cp. 1 Cor. 15. 53, 54. Cp. Job 10. 11 (Sept.). not. Ap. 105. I. **4** for that. Gr. *eph'* (Ap. 104. ix. 2) *hō*. would = desire to. Ap. 102. 1. unclothed. Gr. *ekduō*, as Mk. 15. 20 (took off). that = in order that. Gr. *hina*. mortality = the mortal (thing). See Rom. 6. 12. swallowed up. See 1 Cor. 15. 54. of = by. Ap. 104. xviii. 1. life = the life. Ap. 170. 1. **5** wrought. See 4. 17. for. Gr. *eis*. Ap. 104. vi. also. Omit. unto = to. earnest. See 1. 22. The transliteration of the Heb. *'ērābon*. Spirit. Ap. 101. II. 4. **6** always. Ap. 151. II. G. i. confident. Gr. *tharreō*. Always in 2 Cor. save Heb. 13. 6. at home. Gr. *endēmeō*. Only here and *vv.* 8, 9 (present). absent. Gr. *ekdēmeō*. Only here and *vv.* 8, 9. The *dēmos* was the township to which an Athenian citizen belonged. Cp. Phil. 3. 20. from. Gr. *apo*. Ap. 104. iv. Lord. Ap. 98. VI. i. β. 2 A. **7** by. Gr. *dia*. Ap. 104. v. 1. faith. Ap. 150. II. 1. **8** willing = well pleased. See 1 Cor. 1. 21. present. As "at home", *v.* 6. with. Ap. 104. xv. 3. **9** labour = are ambitious. See Rom. 15. 20. Add "also". accepted = well pleasing. See Rom. 12. 1. **10** appear = be manifested. Ap. 106. I. v. before = in the presence of. See Matt. 5. 16. judgment seat. See Rom. 14. 10. Christ = the Christ. Ap. 98. IX. every = each. in = by means of. Ap. 104. v. 1. according to = with reference to. Ap. 104. xv. 3. done = practised. bad. Ap. 128. III. 2. The texts read *phaulos* as John 3. 20. **11** terror = fear, as in Acts 9. 31. persuade. Ap. 150. I. 2. men. Ap. 123. 1. made manifest. Same as "appear", *v.* 10. trust = hope. also. To follow "manifest". **12** commend. See Rom. 3. 5.

[5]unto you, but give you °occasion °to glory °on
our behalf, [4]that ye may have somewhat °to
answer them which °glory [1]in appearance,
and °not °in heart.
13 For °whether we be °beside ourselves, *it is*
to [1]God: °or whether we °be sober, *it is* for
°your cause.

D 14 For the °love of [10]Christ °constraineth us;
°because we thus °judge, that °if One died
°for all, then °were all dead:
15 And *that* He died [14]for all, [4]that °they
which °live should °not henceforth °live [5]unto
themselves, but [5]unto Him Which died [14]for
them, and °rose again.
16 Wherefore °henceforth [1]know **we** °no man
°after the flesh: °yea, °though we °have known
[10]Christ °after the flesh, yet now °henceforth
°know we *Him* °no more.
17 Therefore °if °any man *be* [1]in [10]Christ,
°*he is* °a °new °creature: °old things are passed
away; °behold, °all things are become °new.
18 And °all things *are* [1]of [1]God,

E R¹ a Who °hath °reconciled us to Himself [7]by
°Jesus [10]Christ,

b and °hath given to us the °ministry of °recon-
ciliation;

a 19 To wit, that [1]God was [1]in [10]Christ, [18]re-
conciling the °world [5]unto Himself, °not °im-
puting their °trespasses [5]unto them,

b and °hath committed °unto us the °word of
[18]reconciliation.

R² c 20 Now then we °are ambassadors [14]for
[10]Christ, as though [1]God °did beseech *you* [7]by
us:

d we °pray *you* °in [10]Christ's stead, be ye [18]re-
conciled to [1]God.

e 21 For °He hath made Him *to be* °sin [14]for
us, Who [16]knew °no °sin; [4]that we might °be
made °the °righteousness of [1]God [1]in Him.

c 6 We then, °*as* workers together °*with Him*,
d °beseech °*you* also that ye receive °not
the °grace of °God °in vain.

e 2 (For He saith, "I °have °heard thee in a time

occasion. See Rom. 7. 8.
to glory = of boasting. Rom. 4. 2.
on our behalf = on behalf of (Ap. 104. xvii. 1) us.
to *answer* = towards, or against. Ap. 104. xv. 3.
glory = boast. Rom. 2. 17.
in. No prep. Dat. case. The texts read *en*.
not. Gr. *ou*, but texts read *mē* (Ap. 105. II).
13 whether, or whether. Gr. *eite*. Ap. 118. 2. a.
beside ourselves. See Acts 2. 7 (amazed).
be sober = be of sound mind. Gr. *sōphroneō*. Here, Mark 5. 15. Luke 8. 35. Rom. 12. 3. Tit. 2. 6. 1 Pet. 4. 7.
your cause = you.
14 love. Ap. 135. II. 1. Cp. Rom. 8. 35.
constraineth. Gr. *sunechō*. See Luke 4. 38; 8. 45 (throng).
because, &c. = judging (Ap. 122. 1) this.
if. Texts omit.
for. Ap. 104. xvii. 1.
were, &c. = all died.
15 they which live = the living, as 4. 11.
live. See Ap. 170. 1.
not henceforth = no longer (*mēketi*).
rose. Ap. 178. I. 4.
16 henceforth = from (Gr. *apo*) now.
no man = no one.
after. Ap. 104. x. 2.
yea, though = even if (Ap. 118. 2. a).
have known, know. Ap. 132. I. ii.
henceforth . . . no more = no longer (*ouketi*).
17 if. Ap. 118. 2. a.
any man. Gr. *tis*. Ap. 123. 3.
he is. Supply the ellipsis by *there is*.
a new creature = a new creation.
new. Gr. *kainos*. See Matt. 9. 17.
old = the ancient.
behold. Ap. 133. I. 2.
all things. Texts read "they".
18 all things. Gr. *ta panta*. Cp. Acts 17. 25. Rom. 11. 36. 1 Cor. 8. 6.

5. -18—6. 2 (*E*, p. 1731). MINISTRY OF RECONCILIATION. (*Division.*)

E | R¹ | 5. -18, 19. Ministry.
  | R² | 5. 20—6. 2. Ministers.

5. -18, 19 (R¹, above). MINISTRY. (*Alternation.*)

R¹ | a | -18-. Reconciliation.
  | b | -18. Commission.
  | *a* | 19-. Reconciliation.
  | *b* | -19. Commission.

hath. Omit.
reconciled. See Rom. 5. 10.
Jesus. Omit.
hath given = gave.
ministry. Ap. 190. II. 1.
reconciliation = the reconciliation. See Rom. 5. 11.
19 world. Ap. 129. 1.
not. Ap. 105. II.
imputing. See Rom. 2. 3; 4. 6.
trespasses. Ap. 128. I. ii. 3.
hath committed unto = placed in (Gr. *en*). Cp. 4. 7.
word. Ap. 121. 10.

5. 20—6. 2 (R², above). MINISTERS. (*Extended Alternation.*)

R² | c | 5. 20-. Ambassadors.
  | d | 5. -20. Entreaty.
  | e | 5. 21. Enforcement.
  | c | 6. 1-. Fellow-labourers.
  | *d* | 6. -1. Entreaty.
  | *e* | 6. 2. Enforcement.

20 are ambassadors. Gr. *presbeuō*. Only here and Eph. 6. 20. did beseech = is beseeching. Ap. 134. I. 6. pray. Ap. 134. I. 5. in . . . stead = on behalf of. Gr. *huper*, as in *v.* 12. **21** For. Omit. He, &c. Read, Him Who knew not sin, for us He made sin. sin. Ap. 128. I. ii. 1. Only here and 11. 7, in this Epistle. The first occ. in this *v.* is by Fig. *Metonymy* (Ap. 6) put for sin-offering. Cp. Eph. 5. 2. The same Fig. appears in the same connexion in Gen. 4. 7. Exod. 29. 14; 30. 10. Lev. 4. 3; 6. 25. Num. 8. 8. Ps. 40. 6 (7); &c. no = not. Ap. 105. II. be made = become. the. Omit. righteousness. Ap. 191. 3.

6. 1 *as* workers together = working together. See Rom. 8. 28. *with Him*. Omit. See 1 Cor. 3. 9. beseech. Ap. 134. I. 6. *you*. Omit. not. Ap. 105. II. grace. See 1. 2. God. Ap. 98. I. i. 1. in vain. Lit. for (Gr. *eis*) that which is empty or of no effect. **2** have. Omit. heard = heard with favour. Gr. *epakouō*. Only here.

°**accepted, and** °**in the day of salvation** °**have I succoured thee:"** °behold, now *is* the °accepted time; °behold, now *is* the day of salvation.)

F 3 Giving °no °offence [2]in any thing, °that the °ministry be [1]not °blamed:
4 But [2]in all *things* °approving ourselves as the °ministers of [1]God, [2]in much patience, [2]in °afflictions, [2]in necessities, [2]in °distresses,
5 [2]In stripes, [2]in imprisonments, [2]in °tumults, [2]in labours, [2]in °watchings, [2]in fastings;
6 °By °pureness, °by °knowledge, °by long-suffering, °by °kindness, °by the °Holy Ghost, °by °love °unfeigned,
7 [6]By the °word of truth, [6]by the °power of [1]God, °by the °armour of °righteousness on the right hand and on the left,
8 [7]By °honour and °dishonour, [7]by °evil report and °good report: as °deceivers, and *yet* °true;
9 As °unknown, and *yet* °well known; as dying, and [2]behold, we live; as °chastened, and [1]not killed;
10 As °sorrowful, yet °alway rejoicing; as °poor, yet °making many rich; as having °nothing, and *yet* °possessing all things.

B 11 O *ye* Corinthians, °our mouth is open °unto you, our heart is °enlarged.
12 Ye are °not °straitened [2]in us, but ye are °straitened [2]in your own °bowels.

A S 13 Now for °a recompence in the same, (I speak as °unto *my* °children,) be ye also [11]enlarged.

T f[1] 14 °Be ye [1]not °unequally yoked °together with °unbelievers: for what °fellowship °hath [7]righteousness with °unrighteousness? and what communion °hath °light °with darkness?
15 And what °concord [14]hath °Christ [14]with °Belial? or what part [14]hath °he that believeth °with an °infidel?
16 And what °agreement [14]hath the °Temple of [1]God [15]with °idols?

accepted. Gr. *dektos.* Same Gk. verb. as "receive" in *v.* 1.
in. Gr. *en.* Ap. 104. viii
have I succoured = I helped. Quoted from Isa. 49. 8.
behold. Gr. *idou.* Ap. 133. I. 2.
accepted. Gr. *euprosdektos.* A stronger word than above. See Rom. 15. 16.
3 no . . . any thing. A double negative. Gr. *mēdeis . . . mēdeis.*
offence = cause of stumbling. Gr. *proskopē.* Only here. Cp. the verb *proskoptō,* Rom. 9. 32.
that = in order that. Gr. *hina.*
ministry. Gr. *diakonia.* Ap. 190. II. 1.
blamed. Gr. *mōmaomai.* Only here and 8. 20.
4 approving = commending. See 3. 1.
ministers. Gr. *diakonos.* Ap. 190. I. 1.
afflictions = tribulations. Gr. *thlipsis.* See 1. 4.
distresses. Gr. *stenochōria.* See Rom. 2. 9. Cp. *v.* 12.
5 tumults. Gr. *akatastasia.* See Luke 21. 9. Cp. Acts 14. 5, 19; 16. 22; 17. 5; 18. 12; 19. 29.
watchings = sleeplessness. Gr. *agrupnia.* Only here and 11. 27.
6 By = In. Gr. *en,* as in *v.* 2.
pureness. Gr. *hagnotēs.* Only here. Cp. the adj. *hagnos* in 7. 11.
knowledge. Gr. *gnōsis.* Ap. 132. II. i.
kindness. Ap. 184. III (a).
Holy Ghost. No arts. Ap. 101. II. 14.
love. Gr. *agapē.* Ap. 135. II. 1.
unfeigned. Gr. *anupokritos.* See Rom. 12. 9.
7 word. Ap. 121. 10. power. Ap. 172. 1.
by = through. Ap. 104. v. 1.
armour. Gr. *hoplon.* Either arms or armour. See Rom. 6. 13. The Greek soldier carried a sword or spear in his right hand and a shield in his left.
righteousness. Gr. *dikaiosunē.* Ap. 191. 3. Cp. Eph. 6. 14.
8 honour = glory. Gr. *doxa.* See p. 1511.
dishonour = shame. Gr. *atimia.* See Rom. 1. 26.
evil report. Gr. *dusphēmia.* Only here.
good report. Gr. *euphēmia.* Only here.
deceivers. Gr. *planos.* Occ. elsewhere, Matt. 27. 63. 1 Tim. 4. 1. 2 John 7. true. Ap. 175. 1.
9 unknown. Gr. *agnoeō.* See 1. 8.
well known. Gr. *epiginōskō.* Ap. 132. I. iii.
chastened. Gr. *paideuō.* See 1 Cor. 11. 32.
10 sorrowful = grieved. Gr. *lupeō.* See 2. 2.

alway. Ap. 151. II. F. ii. poor. Gr. *ptōchos.* Ap. 127. 1. making . . . rich. Gr. *ploutizō.* See 1 Cor. 1. 5. nothing. Gr. *mēdeis.* possessing. Gr. *katechō.* See 1 Cor. 7. 30. From "deceivers," *v.* 8, to end of *v.* 10 is an example of *Oxymōron* (Ap. 6). **11** our mouth, &c. A Hebraism for speaking with liberty. Cp. Judg. 11. 35. Ps. 78. 2; 109. 2. Prov. 8. 6; 31. 26. Ezek. 24. 27; 29. 21. Matt. 5. 2. Acts 8. 35. unto. Gr. *pros.* Ap. 104. xv. 3. enlarged. Gr. *platunō.* Only here, *v.* 13, and Matt. 23. 5. **12** not. Gr. *ou.* Ap. 105. I. straitened. Gr. *stenochōreomai.* See 4. 8. bowels. Gr. *splanchnon.* The inward parts. Metaphorically, of the affections, the seat of which we regard as the heart. Fig. *Catachrēsis.* Ap. 6. Occ. here, 7. 15. Luke 1. 78. Acts 1. 18. Phil. 1. 8; 2. 1. Col. 3. 12. Philem. 7, 12, 20. 1 John 3. 17. All metaph. save Acts 1. 18.

6. 13—7. 3 (*A*, p. 1731). PAUL'S RECOMPENCE. (*Introversion and Repeated Alternation.*)

A | S | 6. 13. Enlargement.
  T | f[1] | 6. 14–16–. Command. No unequal yoking.
    g[1] | 6. –16. Reason. Promise.
   f[2] | 6. 17–. Command. Separation.
    g[2] | 6. –17, 18. Reason. Promise.
   f[3] | 7. 1. Command. Cleansing.
 S | 7. 2, 3. Reception.

13 a recompence, &c. = the same recompence. Gr. *antimisthia.* Only here and Rom. 1. 27. unto = to. children. Gr. *teknon.* Ap. 108. i. **14** Be = Become. unequally yoked. Gr. *heterozugeō.* Only here. together with = to. unbelievers. Gr. *apistos.* See 4. 4. fellowship = partaking, or share. Gr. *metochē.* Only here. See 1 Cor. 9. 10. hath = is there to. unrighteousness = lawlessness. Gr. *anomia.* Ap. 128. III. 4. light. Gr. *phōs.* Ap. 130. 1. with = towards. Gr. *pros,* as in *v.* 11. **15** concord. Gr. *sumphōnēsis.* Cp. the verb in Acts 5. 9 and the adj. in 1 Cor. 7. 5. Christ. Ap. 98. IX. Belial. Only here in N.T. A Hebr. word, meaning worthlessness, occ. several times in O.T. he that believeth = the believer. Gr. *pistos.* Ap. 150. III. with. Gr. *meta.* Ap. 104. xi. 1. infidel. Same as "unbelievers", *v.* 14. **16** agreement. Gr. *sunkatathesis.* Only here. The verb is used in Luke 23. 51. Temple. Gr. *naos.* See Matt. 23. 16. idols. I. e. the temple of idols. Fig. *Ellipsis* of Repetition. Ap. 6.

g^1 for ye are the °Temple of the living [1]God; as
[1]God hath said, **"I will °dwell °in them, and**
°walk in *them*; and I will be their [1]God, and
they shall be My °people."

f^2 17 Wherefore **"come out °from among them,**
and be ye separate", saith the °LORD, **"and**
touch [1]not °the unclean *thing*;

g^2 **and I will °receive you,**
18 **And will be °a Father [13]unto you, and ye**
shall be °My sons and daughters," saith the
[17]LORD °Almighty.

f^3 7 Having therefore these promises, °dearly
beloved, let us cleanse ourselves °from all
°filthiness of the flesh and °spirit, °perfecting
°holiness °in the fear of °God.

S 2 °Receive us; we have °wronged °no man,
we have °corrupted °no man, we have °de-
frauded °no man.
3 I speak °not *this* °to condemn *you*: for I
have said before, that ye are [1]in our hearts °to
°die and °live with *you*.

B 4 Great *is* my °boldness of speech °toward
you, great *is* my °glorying °of you: I am °filled
with °comfort, I °am exceeding joyful °in all
our °tribulation.

DJMPa 5 For, when we were come °into °Macedonia,
our flesh had °no °rest, but we were °troubled
°on every side; without *were* °fightings, within
were fears.

b 6 Nevertheless [1]God, That °comforteth °those
that are cast down, °comforted us °by the
°coming of Titus;

b 7 And [3]not [6]by his [6]coming only, but [6]by
the °consolation wherewith he was [6]comforted
[4]in you, °when he told us your °earnest desire,
your °mourning, your °fervent mind °toward
me;

a so that I rejoiced the more.

O h 8 For °though I °made you sorry °with a
letter, I do [3]not °repent, °though I did °repent:

i for I °perceive that °the same epistle hath

dwell. Gr. *enoikeō*. See Rom. 8. 11.
in. Ap. 104. viii. 2.
walk. Gr. *emperipateō*. Only here.
people. Gr. *laos*. See Acts 2. 47. Quoted from Lev. 26. 12.
17 from among=out of (Gr. *ek*. Ap. 104. vii) the midst of.
LORD. Ap. 98. VI. i. *β*. I. B. a. Quoted from Isa. 52. 11.
the=an, i. e. any.
receive. Gr. *eisdechomai*. Only here.
18 a Father=for (Gr. *eis*. Ap. 104. vi) a Father. Ref. to 2 Sam. 7. 14.
My sons=to Me for (Gr. *eis*) sons (Gr. *huios*. Ap. 108. iii).
Almighty. Gr. *Pantokratōr*. In the N.T. only here, and nine times in the Revelation. See Ap. 4. VII.
7. 1 dearly beloved. Gr. *agapētos*. Ap. 135. III.
from. Gr. *apo*. Ap. 104. iv.
filthiness=pollution. Gr. *molusmos*. Only here. The verb occ. in 1 Cor. 8. 7.
spirit. Ap. 101. II. 9. Flesh and spirit being put for the whole person.
perfecting. Gr. *epiteleō*. Ap. 125. 3.
holiness. Gr. *hagiōsunē*. See Rom. 1. 4.
in. Gr. *en*. Ap. 104. viii.
God. Ap. 98. I. i. 1.
2 Receive=Make room for. Gr. *chōreō*. See John 21. 25. Cp. 6. 11, 13.
wronged. Gr. *adikeō*. See Acts 7. 24.
no man. Gr. *oudeis*.
corrupted. Gr. *phtheirō*. See 1 Cor. 3. 17.
defrauded. Gr. *pleonekteō*. See 2. 11. Fig. *Asyndeton* (Ap. 6) in this verse, also in *vv.* 4, -5, 7-.
3 not. Gr. *ou*. Ap. 105. I.
to condemn *you*=for (Gr. *pros*. Ap. 104. xv. 3) condemnation. Gr. *katakrisis*. See 3. 9.
to die, &c. Lit. unto (Gr. *eis*) the dying, &c.
die=die with. Gr. *sunapothnēskō*. Only here, Mark 14. 31. 2 Tim. 2. 11.
live with. Gr. *suzaō*. See Rom. 6. 8.
4 boldness of speech. Gr. *parrhēsia*. See 3. 12.
toward. Gr. *pros*. Ap. 104. xv. 3.
glorying. Gr. *kauchēsis*. See Rom. 3. 27.
of=on behalf of. Gr. *huper*. Ap. 104. xvii. 1.
filled. Gr. *plēroō*. Ap. 125. 7.
comfort=the comfort. Gr. *paraklēsis*. See 1. 3. Perhaps referring to *v.* 6.
am exceeding joyful. Lit. overabound (Gr. *huperperisseuō*. See Rom. 5. 20) with the joy.
in=upon. Gr. *epi*. Ap. 104. ix. 2. **tribulation.** Gr. *thlipsis*. See 1. 4.

7. 5-7 (*D J M P*, p. 1727). NO REST IN FLESH. (*Introversion*.)

a | 5. Troubled exceedingly.
 b | 6. God's comfort.
 b | 7-. His comfort by you.
a | -7. Rejoiced the more.

5 into. Gr. *eis*. Ap. 104. vi. **Macedonia.** This was after leaving Troas (2. 12, 13), where he was disappointed at not finding Titus. **no.** Gr. *oudeis*. **rest.** Gr. *anesis*. See 2. 13. **troubled.** Gr. *thlibō*. See 1. 6. **on.** Gr. *en*. Ap. 104. viii. See 4. 8. **fightings.** Gr. *machē*. Here, 2 Tim. 2. 23. Tit. 3. 9. Jas. 4. 1. **6 comforteth.** Gr. *parakaleō*. Ap. 134. I. 6. **those that are cast down**=the lowly. Gr. *tapeinos*. See Rom. 12. 16. **by.** Gr. *en*. Ap. 104. viii. **coming.** Gr. *parousia*. See Matt. 24. 3. **7 consolation.** Same as "comfort", *v.* 4. Add "also" after "consolation". **when, &c.**=telling us (as he did). Gr. *anangellō*. See Acts 14. 27. **earnest desire.** Gr. *epipothēsis*. Only here and *v.* 11. **mourning.** Gr. *odurmos*. Only here and Matt. 2. 18. **fervent mind**=zeal. Gr. *zēlos*. See *v.* 11. **toward**=on behalf of. Gr. *huper*. Ap. 104. xvii. 1.

7. 8-16 (*O*, p. 1727). FORMER EPISTLE. EFFECT. (*Extended Alternation*.)

O | h | 8-. Former Letter. Effect.
 i | -8-11-. Result. Godly sorrow. } The Corinthians.
 k | -11. Approving themselves.
 h | 12. Former Letter. Cause.
 i | 13-15. Result. Comfort. } Paul.
 k | 16. Confidence.

8 though. Gr. *ei*. Ap. 118. 2. a. **made . . . sorry**=grieved. Gr. *lupeō*. See 2. 2. **with**=by. Gr. *en*, as above. **repent.** Gr. *metamelomai*. Ap. 111. I. 2. The meaning is that Paul at first regretted he had written so severely, but afterwards changed his mind when he saw the salutary effect of his letter. **perceive**=see. Gr. *blepō*. Ap. 133. I. 5. **the same**=that.

°made you sorry, °though *it were* but °for a season.

9 Now I rejoice, [3]not that ye were [8]made sorry, but that ye °sorrowed °to °repentance: for ye were [8]made sorry °after a godly manner, °that ye might °receive damage °by us [1]in °nothing.

10 For °godly °sorrow °worketh [9]repentance [9]to salvation °not to be repented of: but the °sorrow of the °world °worketh death.

11 For °behold this selfsame thing, that ye [9]sorrowed [9]after a godly sort, what °carefulness it °wrought °in you, yea, *what* °clearing of yourselves, yea, *what* °indignation, yea, *what* fear, yea, *what* °vehement desire, yea, *what* °zeal, yea, *what* °revenge!

k [1]In all *things* ye have °approved yourselves to be °clear °in °this matter.

h 12 Wherefore, [8]though I wrote °unto you, *I did it* [3]not °for his cause that had °done the wrong, nor °for his cause that °suffered wrong, but that our °care °for you in the sight of [1]God might °appear °unto you.

i 13 °Therefore we were [6]comforted [4]in your [4]comfort: yea, and °exceedingly the more joyed we °for the joy of Titus, because his [1]spirit was °refreshed °by you all.

14 For °if I have °boasted any thing to him [4]of you, I am [3]not °ashamed; but as we °spake all things to you [1]in truth, °even so our °boasting, which *I made* °before Titus, is found a truth.

15 And his °inward affection is °more abundant °toward you, whilst he °remembereth the obedience of you all, how °with °fear and trembling ye received him.

k 16 I rejoice °therefore that I °have confidence [1]in you [1]in all *things*.

N U l **8** Moreover, brethren, we °do you to wit of the °grace of °God bestowed °on the °churches of Macedonia;

2 How that °in a great °trial of °affliction the abundance of their joy and their °deep poverty abounded °unto the riches of their °liberality.

though. Ap. 118. 1. a.
for. Gr. *pros.* Ap. 104. xv. 3.
9 sorrowed = were grieved.
to = unto. Gr. *eis,* as in *v.* 5.
repentance. Gr. *metănoia.* Ap. 111. II. Here is the difference between Paul's repentance and that of the Corinthians. The Corinthians were guilty of sin; Paul might have made an error of judgment.
after a godly manner = according to (Gr. *katá.* Ap. 104. x. 2) God, i. e. God's mind and will.
that = in order that. Gr. *hina.*
receive damage = suffer loss. Gr. *zēmioō.* See 1 Cor. 3. 15.
by = from. Gr. *ek.* Ap. 104. vii.
nothing. Gr. *mēdeis.*
10 godly sorrow = grief (Gr. *lupē.* See 2. 1) according to God, as in *v.* 9. Cp. Ps. 51. Matt. 26. 75.
worketh. Gr. *katergazomai,* as in 4. 17, but the texts read *ergazomai.*
not to be repented of. See Ap. 111. III.
world. Gr. *kosmos.* Ap. 129. 1. Cp. Saul (1 Sam. 15. 24, 30); Judas (Matt. 27. 3-5).
11 behold. Gr. *idou.* Ap. 133. I. 2.
carefulness = diligence. Gr. *spoudē.* See Rom. 12. 8.
wrought = worked. Gr. *katergazomai* as in *v.* 10.
in. No prep. Dat. case.
clearing of yourselves. Gr. *apologia.* See Acts 22. 1.
indignation. Gr. *aganaktēsis.* Only here.
vehement desire. Same as "earnest desire" in *v.* 7.
zeal. See *v.* 7.
revenge = vindication. Gr. *ekdikēsis.*
approved = commended. Gr. *sunistēmi.* See 3. 1.
clear. Gr. *hagnos* = pure. Occ. elsewhere, 11. 2. Phil. 4. 8. 1 Tim. 5. 22. Tit. 2. 5. Jas. 3. 17. 1 Pet. 3. 2. 1 John 3. 3.
this = the.
12 unto = to.
for . . . cause. Gr. *heineken.*
done the wrong. Gr. *adikeō,* as in *v.* 2.
suffered wrong = been wronged. Same verb.
care. Same as "carefulness", *v.* 11.
for = on behalf of. Gr. *huper,* as in *v.* 4. Some texts read, "your care for us".
appear = be manifested. Gr. *phaneroō.* Ap. 106. I. v.
unto = toward. Gr. *pros,* as in *v.* 4.
13 Therefore = On account of (Gr. *dia.* Ap. 104. v. 2) this.
exceedingly. See 1. 12.
for = upon. Gr. *epi,* as in *v.* 4.
refreshed. See 1 Cor. 16. 18.
by = from. Gr. *apo.* Ap. 104. iv.
14 if. Ap. 118. 2. a.
boasted = gloried. Gr. *kauchaomai.* See Rom. 2. 17.
ashamed. Gr. *kataischunō.* See Rom. 5. 5.
spake. Gr. *laleō.* Ap. 121. 7.
even so, &c. = so our glorying also. **boasting** = glorying, as in *v.* 4. **before.** Gr. *epi.* Ap. 104. ix. 1.
15 inward affection. Gr. *splanchnon.* See 6. 12. **more abundant.** Same as exceedingly, *v.* 13. **toward** = unto. Gr. *eis,* as in *v.* 9. **remembereth.** Gr. *anamimnēskō.* See 1 Cor. 4. 17. **with.** Gr. *meta.* Ap. 104. xi. 1. **fear and trembling.** See 1 Cor. 2. 3. **16 therefore.** Omit. **have confidence.** Gr. *tharreō.* See 5. 6.

8. 1—9. 15 (*N,* p. 1727). **MACEDONIA. ASSEMBLIES.** (*Alternation and Introversion.*)

N | U | l | 8. 1-5. Example of the Macedonians.
m | 8. 6. Mission of Titus.
V | n | 8. 7. Their graces.
o | 8. 8-12. Reasons for appeal.
p | 8. 13-15. Mutual beneficence.
U | *m* | 8. 16-23. Titus and others. Qualifications.
l | 8. 24. Appeal to Corinthians.
V | *n* | 9. 1, 2. Their zeal.
o | 9. 3-5. Reasons for appeal.
p | 9. 6-15. God's glory and munificence.

8. 1 do you to wit = make you to know. Gr. *gnōrizō.* Cp. 1 Cor. 12. 3. **grace.** Ap. 184. I. 1. **God.** Ap. 98. I. i. 1. **on.** Gr. *en.* Ap. 104. viii. **churches.** Ap. 186. **2 in.** Gr. *en,* as above. **trial.** Gr. *dokimē.* See Rom. 5. 4. **affliction.** Gr. *thlipsis.* See 1. 4. **deep poverty.** Lit. poverty according to (Gr. *kata.* Ap. 104. x. 1) depth. **unto.** Gr. *eis.* Ap. 104. vi. **liberality.** Gr. *haplotēs.* The adj. *haplous* means single-minded, not self-seeking.

3 For °to *their* °power, I °bear record, yea, and °beyond *their* °power, *they were* °willing of themselves;

4 °Praying us °with much °intreaty °that we would receive the °gift, and *take upon us* the fellowship of the °ministering °to the °saints.

5 And *this they did,* °not as we hoped, but first gave their own selves to the °Lord, and °unto us °by the °will of [1]God.

m **6** °Insomuch that we °desired Titus, °that as he had °begun, so he would °also °finish °in you °the same [1]grace also.

Vn **7** °Therefore, as ye abound [2]in every *thing, in* °faith, and °utterance, and °knowledge, and *in* all °diligence, and *in* °your °love to us, *see* [6]that ye abound [2]in this [1]grace also.

o **8** I speak [5]not °by °commandment, but °by occasion of the °forwardness of °others, and to prove the °sincerity of your [7]love.

9 For ye °know the [1]grace of our [5]Lord °Jesus Christ, that, though He was rich, yet °for your sakes He °became poor, [6]that ye through His poverty might be rich.

10 And °herein I give *my* °advice: for this is expedient for you, who have [6]begun before, [5]not only to do, but °also to °be forward °a year ago.

11 Now therefore °perform the °doing *of it;* that as *there was* a °readiness to °will, so *there may be* a °performance also °out of that which ye have.

12 For °if there °be first a °willing mind, *it is* °accepted according to °that a man hath, *and* [5]not according to that he hath [5]not.

p **13** For *I mean* [5]not [6]that °other men be eased, and °ye burdened:

14 But °by an °equality; *that* °now at this time your abundance *may be a supply* °for their °want, [6]that their abundance also may °be *a supply* °for your °want: that there may °be °equality:

15 As it °is written, "**He that *had gathered* much °had nothing over; and he that *had gathered* little °had no lack.**"

Um **16** But °thanks *be* to [1]God, Which put the same °earnest care °into the heart of Titus °for you.

17 For indeed he accepted the °exhortation;

3 to=according to. Gr. *kata.* Ap. 104. x. 2.
power. Gr. *dunamis.* Ap. 172. 1.
bear record=testify. Gr. *martureō.* See p. 1511.
beyond=above. Gr. *huper.* Ap. 104. xvii. 2. The texts read *para.*
willing of themselves. Lit. self-chosen. Gr. *authairetos.* Only here and *v.* 17.
4 Praying=Asking. Gr. *deomai.* Ap. 134. I. 5.
with. Gr. *meta.* Ap. 104. xi. 1.
intreaty = exhortation. Gr. *paraklēsis.* See Acts 4. 36, and 13. 15.
that we would receive. The texts omit, and read, "asking of us the gift and fellowship".
gift=grace. As in *v.* 1.
ministering = ministry. Gr. *diakonia.* Ap. 190. II. 1.
to=unto. Gr. *eis.* Ap. 104. vi.
saints. See Acts 9. 13.
5 not. Gr. *ou.* Ap. 105. I.
Lord. Ap. 98. VI. i. *β.* 2. A.
unto=to.
by=through. Gr. *dia.* Ap. 104. v. 1.
will. Gr. *thelēma.* Ap. 102. 2.
6 Insomuch, &c. Lit. Unto (Gr. *eis*) our exhorting (Gr. *parakaleō.* Ap. 134. I. 6).
that=in order that. Gr. *hina.*
begun = begun before. Gr. *proenarchomai.* Only here and *v.* 10.
also finish=finish also.
finish. Gr. *epiteleō.* Ap. 125. 3.
in=unto. Gr. *eis,* as above.
the same=this.
7 Therefore=But, or Moreover.
faith. Gr. *pistis.* Ap. 150. II. 1.
utterance=word. Gr. *logos.* Ap. 121. 10.
knowledge. Gr. *gnōsis.* Ap. 132. II. i.
diligence. Gr. *spoudē.* See 7. 11.
your love to us. Lit. the love from (Gr. *ek*) you in respect of (Gr. *en*) us.
love. Gr. *agapē.* Ap. 135. II. 1.
8 by. Gr. *kata.* Ap. 104. x. 2.
commandment. Gr. *epitagē.* See Rom. 16. 26.
by occasion of=through. Gr. *dia,* as in *v.* 5.
forwardness. Same as "diligence" in *v.* 7.
others. Gr. *heteros.* Ap. 124. 2.
sincerity=genuineness. Gr. *gnēsios.* Occ. elsewhere, Phil. 4. 3. 1 Tim. 1. 2. Tit. 1. 4.
9 know. Gr. *ginōskō.* Ap. 132. I. ii.
Jesus Christ. Ap. 98. XI.
for your sakes=on account of (Gr. *dia.* Ap. 104. v. 2) you.
became poor. Gr. *ptōcheuō.* Only here. Cp. Ap. 127. 1.
10 herein=in (Gr. *en*) this.
advice=judgment. Ap. 177. 2.
also, &c. to be forward also.
be forward=will. Gr. *thelō.* Ap. 102. 1.
a year ago=from (Gr. *apo.* Ap. 104. iv) a year ago. Gr. *perusi.* Only here and 9. 2. **11 perform.** Same word as "finish", *v.* 6. **doing**=doing also. **readiness.** Gr. *prothumia.* See Acts 17. 11. **will.** Gr. *thelō,* as *v.* 10. **performance**=performing, as above. **out of.** Gr. *ek.* Ap. 104. vii. **12 if.** Ap. 118. 2. a. **be first**=is set forth, or set before. Gr. *prokeimai.* Occ. elsewhere, Heb. 6. 18; 12. 1, 2. Jude 7. **willing mind.** Same as "readiness", *v.* 11. **accepted.** Gr. *euprosdektos.* See Rom. 15. 16. **that**=whatsoever. **13 other men be eased** =there should be ease or rest (Gr. *anesis.* See Acts 24. 23) to others (Gr. *allos.* Ap. 124. 1). **ye burdened**=to you affliction, as in *v.* 2. **14 by**=out of. Gr. *ek.* Ap. 104. vii. **equality.** Gr. *isotēs.* Only here and Col. 4. 1. **now at this time**=in (Gr. *en*) the present season. **for.** Gr. *eis.* Ap. 104. vi. **want.** Gr. *husterēma.* See 1 Cor. 16. 17. **be**=become. In this verse there is an *epanodos* (Ap. 6).

a | equality.
b | supply.
b | supply.
a | equality.

15 is=has been. **had nothing over**=did not (Ap. 105. I) abound. Gr. *pleonazō.* See 4. 15. **had no lack**=had not (Ap. 105. I) less (than enough). Gr. *elattoneō.* Only here. This is quoted almost word for word from the Sept. Ex. 16. 18. **16 thanks.** Gr. *charis.* Ap. 184. I. 1. **earnest care.** Same as "diligence", *v.* 7. **into**=in. Gr. *en.* Ap. 104. viii. **for.** Gr. *huper.* Ap. 104. xvii. 1. **17 exhortation.** Same as "intreaty", *v.* 4.

but °being °more forward, °of his own accord
he went °unto you.
18 And we have °sent [4] with him the brother,
whose praise *is* [2] in the °gospel °throughout all
the [1] churches;
19 And [5] not *that* only, but who was °also
°chosen °of the [1] churches °to travel with us
°with this [1] grace, which is °administered °by
us °to the °glory of the °same [5] Lord, and
°*declaration of* °your °ready mind:
20 °Avoiding this, °that no man should
°blame us [2] in this °abundance which is [19] administered [19] by us:
21 °Providing for °honest things, [5] not only
in the sight of the °Lord, but °also in the sight
of °men.
22 And we have [18] sent with them our brother,
whom we have oftentimes proved °diligent [2] in
many things, but now much more °diligent,
°upon the great °confidence which °*I have* [6] in
you.
23 Whether *any do enquire* °of Titus, *he is*
my °partner and °fellowhelper °concerning you:
or our brethren *be enquired of, they are* the
°messengers of the [1] churches, *and* the [19] glory
of °Christ.
l 24 Wherefore °shew ye [4] to them, and °before
the [1] churches, the °proof of your [7] love, and of
our °boasting °on your behalf.

V n **9** For as °touching the °ministering °to the
°saints, it is superfluous for me to write to
you:
2 For I °know °the forwardness of your mind,
for which I °boast °of you to °them of Macedonia, that °Achaia was ready °a year ago;
and your °zeal °hath °provoked °very many.
o 3 Yet °have I °sent the brethren, °lest our
°boasting [2] of you should be °in vain °in this
°behalf; °that, as I °said, ye may be ready:
4 °Lest haply °if [2] they of Macedonia come
°with me, and find you °unprepared, we ([3] that
we say °not, ye) should be °ashamed [3] in this
same °confident °boasting.
5 Therefore I thought it necessary to °exhort
the brethren, [3] that they would go before °unto
you, and °make up beforehand your °bounty,
°whereof ye had notice before, that the same
might be ready, as *a matter of* °bounty, and
[4] not as *of* covetousness.
p 6 But this *I say*, He which soweth °sparingly

being. Gr. *huparchō.* See Luke 9. 48.
more forward = more diligent. Gr. comp. of *spoudaios.* Only here and *v.* 22. Cp. *vv.* 7, 8, 16.
of his own accord. Gr. *authairetos.* See *v.* 3.
unto. Gr. *pros.* Ap. 104. xv. 3.
18 sent. Gr. *sumpempō.* Ap. 174. 8. Only here and *v.* 22. **gospel.** Ap. 140.
throughout. Gr. *dia.* Ap. 104. v. 1. The brother was probably Luke.
19 also chosen = chosen also.
chosen. Gr. *cheirotoneō.* See Acts 14. 23.
of = by. Gr. *hupo.* Ap. 104. xviii. 1.
to travel with us = as our fellow-traveller. Gr. *sunekdēmos.* See Acts 19. 29.
with. Gr. *sun.* Ap. 104. xvi. The texts read *en.*
administered. Gr. *diakoneō.* Ap. 190. III. 1.
by. Gr. *hupo,* as above.
to = with a view to. Gr. *pros.* Ap. 104. xv. 3. This depends on "chosen". The object of Paul's having a companion was to avert suspicions, which would tarnish the Lord's glory by bringing discredit on His servant, and also to remove Paul's reluctance. Cp. *v.* 20.
glory. See p. 1511.
same. The texts omit.
declaration of. Supply the *ellipsis* by "to show".
your. All the texts read "our".
ready mind. Same as "readiness", *v.* 11. Cp. *v.* 1[?].
20 Avoiding. Gr. *stellomai.* Only here and 2 Thess. 3. 6.
that no man = lest (Gr. *mē*) any one (Gr. *tis.* Ap. 123. 3).
blame. Gr. *mōmaomai.* See 6. 3.
abundance. Gr. *hadrotēs.* Only here.
21 Providing for. The texts read "For we provide". Gr. *pronoeō.* See Rom. 12. 17.
honest. See Rom. 12. 17.
Lord. Ap. 98. VI. i. *β.* 2. B.
also, &c. = in the sight of men also. This is a reply to the charge referred to in 12. 17.
men. Ap. 123. 1.
22 diligent. Same as "forward", *v.* 17.
upon = through. No preposition.
confidence. Gr. *pepoithēsis.* Ap. 150. II. 2.
I have. Supply the *ellipsis* by "*he has*". This was the reason of his diligence.
23 of = on behalf of. Gr. *huper.* Ap. 104. xvii. 1.
partner. Gr. *koinōnos.* See 1. 7.
fellowhelper. Gr. *sunergos.* See 1 Cor. 3. 9.
concerning = with reference to. Gr. *eis.* Ap. 104. vi.
messengers. Gr. *apostolos.* Ap. 189. Here and in Phil. 2. 25 used in the general sense.
Christ. Ap. 98. IX.
24 shew. Gr. *endeiknumi.* See Rom. 2. 15.
before. Lit. unto (Gr. *eis*) the face of.
proof, or evidence. Gr. *endeixis.* See Rom. 3. 25.
boasting. Gr. *kauchēsis.* See Rom. 3. 27.
on your behalf = on behalf of (Gr. *huper,* as above) you.

9. 1 touching = concerning. Gr. *peri.* Ap. 104. xiii. 1. **ministering.** Gr. *diakonia.* Ap. 190. II. 1. **to** = unto. Gr. *eis.* Ap. 104. vi. **saints.** See Acts 9. 13. **2 know.** Gr. *oida.* Ap. 132. I. i. **the forwardness of your mind** = your readiness. Gr. *prothumia.* See Acts 17. 11. **boast** = glory. Gr. *kauchaomai.* See Rom. 2. 17. **of** = on behalf of. Gr. *huper:* Ap. 104. xvii. 1. **them of, &c.** = the Macedonians. **Achaia** = Greece. **a year ago.** See 8. 10. **zeal.** Gr. *zēlos.* Cp. Acts 5. 17. **hath.** Omit. **provoked.** Gr. *erethizō.* Only here and Col. 3. 21. **very many** = the majority. **3 have.** Omit. **sent.** Gr. *pempō.* Ap. 174. 4. **lest** = in order that (Gr. *hina*) . . . not. Gr. *mē.* Ap. 105. II. **boasting** = glorying. Gr. *kauchēma.* See Rom. 4. 2. **in vain** = made void. Gr. *kenoō.* See Phil. 2. 7. **in.** Gr. *en.* Ap. 104. viii. **behalf** = part. Gr. *meros.* **that** = in order that. Gr. *hina.* **said** = was saying. **4 Lest haply** = Lest by any means. Gr. *mē pōs.* **if.** Ap. 118. 1. b. **with.** Gr. *sun.* Ap. 104. xvi. **unprepared.** Gr. *aparaskeuastos.* Only here. **not.** Gr. *mē.* Ap. 105. II. **ashamed.** Gr. *kataischunō.* See Rom. 5. 5. **confident** = confidence. Gr. *hupostasis.* Here, 11. 17. Heb. 1. 3; 3. 14; 11. 1. **boasting.** Gr. *kauchēsis.* See Rom. 3. 27. The texts omit. **5 exhort.** Gr. *parakaleō.* Ap. 134. I. 6. **unto.** Gr. *eis.* Ap. 104. vi. **make up beforehand.** Gr. *prokatartizō.* Only here. Cp. Ap. 125. 8. **bounty** = blessing. Gr. *eulogia.* Transl. "blessing" eleven times, "fair speech" Rom. 16. 18, and "bounty" here and *v.* 6. Cp. Joel 2. 14. Mal. 2. 2, where the same word is used in the Sept. **whereof ye had notice before** = before notified. Gr. *prokatangellō.* See Acts 3. 18. The texts read *proepangellō,* which occ. elsewhere only in Rom. 1. 2. **6 sparingly.** Gr. *pheidomenōs.* Only here. Compare *pheidomai,* 1. 23.

shall reap also °sparingly; and he which soweth °bountifully shall reap also °bountifully.
7 °Every man according as he °purposeth in
his heart, *so let him give;* [4]not °grudgingly, or
°of necessity: for °**God** °**loveth a** °**cheerful**
°**giver.**
8 And [7]God *is* °able to make °all °grace
abound °toward you; [3]that ye, °always having
°all °sufficiency [3]in °all *things,* may abound
[1]to °every good work,
9 (As it °is written, "**He hath** °**dispersed**
abroad; He hath given to the °**poor: His**° **right-**
eousness °**remaineth** °**for ever.**"
10 Now He That °ministereth seed to the
sower, both °minister bread °for *your* food, and
multiply your seed sown, and increase the
fruits of your [9]righteousness;)
11 °Being enriched [3]in every thing [1]to all
°bountifulness, which °causeth °through us
thanksgiving to [7]God.
12 For the °administration of this °service °not
only °supplieth the want of the [1]saints, but is
abundant also °by many thanksgivings °unto
[7]God;
13 Whiles [12]by the °experiment of this
°ministration they glorify [7]God °for °your professed °subjection [5]unto the °gospel of °Christ,
and for *your* °liberal °distribution [5]unto them,
and [5]unto all *men;*
14 And by their °prayer °for you, which long
after you °for the °exceeding [8]grace of [7]God °in
you.
15 °Thanks *be* [12]unto [7]God [13]for His °un-
speakable °gift.

L W[1] q **10** Now I Paul myself °beseech you °by
the °meekness and °gentleness of
°Christ, who °in presence *am* °base °among
you, but being absent °am bold °toward
you:
2 But I °beseech *you,* that I may °not [1]be

bountifully. Lit. upon (Gr. *epi.* Ap. 104. ix. 2) blessings, as above. Fig. *Symplokē.*

7 Every man = Each one.

purposeth. Gr. *proaireomai.* Only here. The texts read "hath purposed".

grudgingly. Lit. of (Gr. *ek.* Ap. 104. vii) grief.

of. Gr. *ek,* as above. **God.** Ap. 98. I. i. 1.

loveth. Gr. *agapaō.* Ap. 135. I. 1.

cheerful. Gr. *hilaros.* Only here. The noun in Rom. 12. 8. Cp. Eng. "hilarity".

giver. Gr. *dotēs.* Only here. Cp. Prov. 22. 9, where the Sept. reads, "God blesseth a cheerful giver". Fig. *Parœmia.*

8 able. Gr. *dunatos,* but the texts read the verb *dunateō,* which occ. elsewhere only in 13. 3.

all. Notice the four "alls" which, with "every", give the Fig. *Polyptōton.* Ap. 6.

grace. Gr. *charis.* Ap. 184. I. 1.

toward = unto. Gr. *eis,* as in *v.* 5.

always . . . *things.* Gr. *panti pantote pasan.* Fig. *Paronomasia.*

sufficiency. Gr. *autarkeia.* Only here and 1 Tim. 6. 6.

every. Gr. *pas.* Transl. "all" above.

9 is = has been, or standeth.

dispersed abroad = scattered. Gr. *skorpizō.* See John 16. 32.

poor. Gr. *penēs.* Ap. 127. 2. Only here.

righteousness. Gr. *dikaiosunē.* Ap. 191. 3.

remaineth. Gr. *menō.* See p. 1511.

for ever. Gr. *eis ton aiōna.* Ap. 151. II. A. ii. 4. a. Quoted from Ps. 112. 9.

10 ministereth. Gr. *epichorēgeō.* Occ. elsewhere, Gal. 3. 5. Col. 2. 19. 2 Pet. 1. 5, 11. The prefix *epi* suggests God's liberal supply. Cp. Isa. 55. 10.

minister. Gr. *chorēgeō.* Only here and 1 Pet. 4. 11. The *chorēgos* was the leader of a chorus, and then came to mean one who defrayed the cost of a chorus at the public festivals. The texts put these three verbs in the future, instead of the imperative.

for. Gr. *eis.* Ap. 104. vi.

11 Being enriched. Gr. *ploutizō.* See 1 Cor. 1. 5.

bountifulness. Gr. *haplotēs.* See 1. 12.

causeth = worketh. Gr. *katergazomai,* as 4. 17.

through. Gr. *dia.* Ap. 104. v. 1.

12 administration. Same as "ministering", *v.* 1.

service. Gr. *leitourgia.* Ap. 190. II. 4.

not. Gr. *ou.* Ap. 105. I.

supplieth = fully supplies. Gr. *prosanaplēroō.* Only here and 11. 9. by = through, as *v.* 11. unto = to. **13** experiment = proof. Gr. *dokimē.* See 2. 9. ministration. Same as "ministering", *v.* 1. for = upon. Gr. *epi.* Ap. 104. ix. 2. your professed subjection = the subjection of your confession, i.e. produced by your confession. confession. Gr. *homologia.* Occ. elsewhere, 1 Tim. 6. 12, 13. Heb. 3. 1; 4. 14; 10. 23. subjection. Gr. *hupotagē.* Occ. elsewhere Gal. 2. 5. 1 Tim. 2. 11; 3. 4. gospel. Ap. 140. Christ. Ap. 98. IX. liberal distribution = the bountifulness (Gr. *haplotēs,* as in *v.* 11) of your distribution. distribution = fellowship. Gr. *koinōnia.* **14** prayer. Gr. *deēsis.* Ap. 134. II. 3. for = on behalf of. Gr. *huper.* Ap. 104. xvii. 1. for = because of. Gr. *dia.* Ap. 104. v. 2. exceeding. Gr. *huperballō.* See 3. 10. in = upon. Gr. *epi.* Ap. 104. ix. 2. **15** Thanks. Gr. *charis,* as in *v.* 8. unspeakable = that cannot be fully declared. Gr. *anekdiēgētos.* Only here. gift. Gr. *dōrea.* See John 4. 10. It cannot be that Paul had in his mind anything less than God's supreme gift, the gift of His Son, of which he speaks in 8. 9. He frequently breaks out into thanksgiving in the midst of his epistles. Cp. Rom. 9. 5; 11. 33, 36. 1 Cor. 15. 57. Gal. 1. 5. Eph. 3. 20. 1 Tim. 1. 17.

10. 1–12. 13 (*L,* p. 1727). VINDICATION OF HIS ACTION. (*Division.*)

L | W[1] | 10. 1–18. Direct.
  | W[2] | 11. 1–12. 13. Indirect.

10. 1-18 (W[1], above). DIRECT. (*Alternation.*)

W[1] | q | 1, 2. Self-disparagement.
  | r | 3–6. Defence.
  | *q* | 7. Self-disparagement.
  | *r* | 8–18. Defence.

10. 1 beseech. Gr. *parakaleō.* Ap. 134. I. 6. by. Gr. *dia.* Ap. 104. v. 1. meekness. Gr. *praotēs.* See 1 Cor. 4. 21. gentleness. Gr. *epieikeia.* Only here and Acts 24. 4 (clemency). The adj. *epieikēs* occ. Phil. 4. 5 (moderation). Christ. Ap. 98. IX. in presence = according to (Gr. *kata.* Ap. 104. x. 2) outward appearance (*prosōpon*). base = lowly. Gr. *tapeinos.* See Rom. 12. 16. among. Gr. *en.* Ap. 104. viii. 2. am bold. Gr. *tharreō.* See 5. 6. toward. Gr. *eis.* Ap. 104. vi. This refers to what his opponents said of him (*v.* 10). **2** beseech = pray. Gr. *deomai.* Ap. 134. I. 5. not. Gr. *mē.* Ap. 105. II.

bold when I am present with °that °confidence, wherewith I °think to °be bold °against °some, which °think of us as if we walked °according to the flesh.

r 3 For though we walk °in the flesh, we do °not °war °after the flesh:

4 (For the °weapons of our °warfare *are* [3]not °carnal, but °mighty °through °God °to the °pulling down of °strong holds;)

5 Casting down °imaginations, and every °high thing that °exalteth itself °against the °knowledge of [4]God, and °bringing into captivity every °thought °to the obedience of [1]Christ;

6 And having [3]in a readiness to °revenge all °disobedience, when your obedience is °fulfilled.

q 7 Do ye °look on things [3]after the °outward appearance? °If °any man °trust to himself that he is [1]Christ's, let him °of himself [2]think this again, that, as he *is* [1]Christ's, °even so *are* we [1]Christ's.

r 8 For °though I should °boast somewhat more °of our °authority, (which the °Lord °hath given us °for °edification, and [3]not °for your [4]destruction,) I should [3]not °be ashamed:

9 °That I may [2]not seem as if I would °terrify you [1]by letters.

10 For *his* letters, say they, *are* °weighty and °powerful; but *his* bodily °presence *is* °weak, and *his* °speech °contemptible.

11 Let such an one [2]think this, that, such as we are °in °word [1]by letters when we are absent, such *will we be* also °in deed when we are present.

12 For we °dare [3]not °make ourselves of the number, or °compare ourselves with °some that °commend themselves: but they measuring themselves °by themselves, and °comparing themselves among themselves, °are [3]not wise.

13 But we will °not [8]boast °of °things without *our* measure, but [2]according to the measure of the °rule which [4]God hath °distributed to us, a measure to °reach °even unto you.

14 For we °stretch [3]not ourselves beyond *our measure,* as though we [13]reached [2]not °unto you: for we are come as far as to you also [3]in *preaching* the °gospel of [1]Christ:

15 [3]Not [8]boasting [13]of [13]things without *our* measure, *that is,* °of °other men's labours; but having hope, when your °faith is increased, that we shall be °enlarged °by you [2]according to our [13]rule °abundantly,

16 To °preach the gospel °in the *regions*

that = the.
confidence. Gr. *pepoithēsis.* Ap. 150. II. 2.
think = reckon.
be bold = dare, as in *v.* 12. Gr. *tolmaō. Tharreō* expresses "confidence", *tolmaō* carries the feeling into action.
against. Gr. *epi.* Ap. 104. ix. 3.
some. Gr. *tines.* Ap. 124. 4.
according to. Gr. *kata,* as in *v.* 1.
3 in. Gr. *en.* Ap. 104. viii.
not. Gr. *ou.* Ap. 105. I.
war. Gr. *strateuomai.* See 1 Cor. 9. 7.
after = according to, as above.
4 weapons. Gr. *hoplon.* See 6. 7.
warfare. Gr. *strateia.* Only here and 1 Tim. 1. 18.
carnal. Gr. *sarkikos.* See Rom. 7. 14 and 1 Pet. 2. 11.
mighty. Gr. *dunatos.* Same as "able", 9. 8.
through = by. No prep. Dat. case.
God. Ap. 98. I. i. 1.
to. Gr. *pros.* Ap. 104. xv. 3.
pulling down = destruction. Gr. *kathairesis.* Only here, *v.* 8, and 13. 10. The verb in *v.* 5.
strong holds. Gr. *ochurōma.* Only occ.
5 imaginations = thoughts, or reasonings. Gr. *logismos.* Only here and Rom. 2. 15.
high thing. Gr. *hupsōma.* Only here and Rom. 8. 39.
exalteth. Gr. *epairō.* See Acts 1. 9.
against. Gr. *kata.* Ap. 104. x. 1.
knowledge. Gr. *gnōsis.* Ap. 132. II. i.
bringing, &c. Gr. *aichmalōtizō.* See Rom. 7. 23.
thought. Gr. *noēma.* See 2. 11.
to. Gr. *eis.* Ap. 104. vi.
6 revenge = avenge. Gr. *ekdikeō.* See Luke 18. 3, and cp. 7. 11.
disobedience. Gr. *parakoē.* See Rom. 5. 19.
fulfilled. Gr. *plēroō.* Ap. 125. 7.
7 look on. Gr. *blepō.* Ap. 133. I. 5.
outward appearance. Gr. *prosōpon,* as in *v.* 1.
If. Ap. 118. 2. a.
any man = any one. Gr. *tis.* Ap. 123. 3.
trust. Gr. *peithō.* Ap. 150. I. 2.
of = from. Gr. *apo.* Ap. 104. iv. All texts save L give *epi* with gen. Ap. 104. ix. 1.
even so *are* we = so *are* we also.
8 though = if. Ap. 118. 1. b.
boast = glory. Gr. *kauchaomai.* See Rom. 2. 17.
of = concerning. Gr. *peri.* Ap. 104. xiii. 1.
authority. Gr. *exousia.* Ap. 172. 5.
Lord. Ap. 98. VI. i. *β*. 2. A.
hath given = gave.
for. Gr. *eis.* Ap. 104. vi.
edification. Gr. *oikodomē.* See 1 Cor. 3. 9.
be ashamed. Gr. *aischunomai.* Occ. elsewhere, Luke 16. 3. Phil. 1. 20. 1 Pet. 4. 16. 1 John 2. 28. The more frequent word in N.T. is *kataischunō.* See Rom. 5. 5.
9 That = In order that. Gr. *hina.*
terrify. Gr. *ekphobeō.* Only here.
10 weighty. Gr. *barus.* See Acts 20. 29.
powerful. Gr. *ischuros.* Cp. Ap. 172. 3.
presence. Gr. *parousia.* See Matt. 24. 3.
weak. As 1 Cor. 1. 27.

speech. Gr. *logos.* Ap. 121. 10. contemptible = of no account. Gr. *exoutheneō.* See Acts 4. 11. **11** in. No prep. Dat. case. word. Gr. *logos.* Same as "speech" above. **12** dare. Same as "be bold", *v.* 2. make . . . of the number. Gr. *enkrinō,* to judge or reckon among. Only here. Ap. 122. 5. compare. Gr. *sunkrinō.* Ap. 122. 8. some. Gr. *tines.* Ap. 124. 4. commend. Gr. *sunistanō.* See Rom. 3. 5. by = among. Gr. *en.* Ap. 104. viii. 2. are not wise = do not understand. First occ. Matt. 13. 13. **13** not. Gr. *ouchi.* Ap. 105. I. (a). of = with reference to. Gr. *eis.* Ap. 104. vi. things without our measure. Lit. the unmeasured (Gr. *ametros,* only here and *v.* 15) things. rule. Gr. *kanōn.* Occ. elsewhere, *vv.* 15, 16. Gal. 6. 16. Phil. 3. 16. Hence Engl. "canon". distributed. Gr. *merizō.* See 1 Cor. 7. 17. reach = arrive. Gr. *ephikneomai.* Only here and *v.* 14. even unto you = unto (Gr. *achri,* as far as) you also. **14** stretch . . . beyond. Gr. *huperekteinō,* stretch out over. Only here. unto. Gr. *eis.* Ap. 104. vi. gospel. Cp. Ap. 140. **15** of = in. Gr. *en.* Ap. 104. viii. other men's. Gr. *allotrios.* Ap. 124. 6. faith. Gr. *pistis.* Ap. 150. II. 1. enlarged = magnified. Gr. *megalunō.* See Acts 5. 13. by = in. Gr. *en.* Ap. 104. viii. abundantly = unto (Gr. *eis*) abundance. **16** preach the gospel. Gr. *euangelizō.* Ap. 121. 4. in = unto. Gr. *eis,* as above.

°beyond you, *and* [3]not to [8]boast [3]in °another man's °line [13]of things made ready to our hand.
17 But **he that °glorieth, let him °glory [3]in the °LORD.**
18 For [3]not he that [12]commendeth himself is °approved, but whom the [8]Lord [12]commendeth.

W[2] X Z **11** °Would to God ye could °bear with me a little in *my* °folly: and indeed °bear with me.
2 For I am °jealous over you with °godly °jealousy: for I °have °espoused you to one °husband, that I may present *you as* a °chaste virgin to °Christ.
3 But I fear, °lest by any means, as the serpent °beguiled Eve °through his °subtilty, so your °minds should be °corrupted °from the °simplicity that is °in [2]Christ.
4 For °if he that cometh °preacheth °another °Jesus, whom we have °not °preached, or *if* ye receive °another °spirit, which ye have °not received, or °another °gospel, which ye have °not accepted, °ye might well [1]bear with *him*.

A 5 For I °suppose I °was °not a whit behind the °very chiefest °apostles.
6 But °though *I be* °rude in °speech, yet [4]not in °knowledge; but we have been °throughly °made manifest °among you °in all things.

B s 7 Have I committed an °offence in °abasing myself °that ye might be °exalted, because I °have °preached to you the [4]gospel of °God °freely?
8 I °robbed °other °churches, taking °wages *of them,* °to do you service.
9 And when I was present °with you, and °wanted, I °was chargeable to °no man: for °that which was lacking to me the brethren °which came [3]from °Macedonia °supplied: and [6]in all *things* I have kept myself °from being burdensome °unto you, and *so* will I keep *myself.*
10 As the truth of [2]Christ is [6]in me, °no man shall stop me of this °boasting [6]in the °regions of Achaia.

t 11 Wherefore? because I °love you [4]not? [7]God °knoweth.

beyond. Gr. *huperekeina.* Only here.
another man's. Gr. *allotrios,* as in *v.* 15.
line. Same as "rule", *v.* 13.
17 glorieth. Same as boast, *v.* 8. The quotation is from Jer. 9. 24.
LORD. Ap. 98. VI. i. β. 1. B.
18 approved. Gr. *dokimos.* See Rom. 14. 18.

11. 1—12. 13 (W[2], p. 1741). VINDICATION. INDIRECT. (*Extended Alternation and Introversion.*)

W[2] | X | Z | 11. 1-4. Apology for boasting. Solicitude for them.
A | 11. 5, 6. Equality with other apostles. Not behind them in knowledge.
B | s | 11. 7-10. Gratuitous preaching.
t | 11. 11. Why? Because I love you not?
Y | 11. 12-15. False apostles.
X | Z | 11. 16-18. Apology for boasting. Solicitude for himself.
A | 11. 19—12. 11. Equality with other apostles. Not behind them in sufferings.
B | t | 12. 12, 13-. Why? Because I wronged you?
s | 12. -13. Gratuitous preaching.

11. 1 Would to God. See 1 Cor. 4. 8.
bear with. Gr. *anechomai.* See Luke 9. 41.
folly. Gr. *aphrosunē.* Only here, *vv.* 17, 21, and Mark 7. 22. Cp. *v.* 16.
bear = ye do bear.
2 jealous. Gr. *zēloō.* See Acts 7. 9.
godly = of God. Ap. 98. I. i. 1. It means a great jealousy. Cp. Acts 7. 20.
jealousy. Gr. *zēlos.* See Acts 5. 17.
have. Omit.
espoused. Gr. *harmozō.* Only here.
husband. Gr. *anēr.* Ap. 123. 2.
chaste. Gr. *hagnos.* See 7. 11.
Christ. Ap. 98. IX.
3 lest by any means. Gr. *mē pōs.*
beguiled = deceived. Gr. *exapataō.* See Rom. 7. 11.
through = in. Gr. *en.* Ap. 104. viii.
subtilty = craftiness. Gr. *panourgia.* See Luke 20. 23.
minds. Gr. *noēma.* See 2. 11; 3. 14.
corrupted. Gr. *phtheirō.* See 1 Cor. 3. 17.
from. Gr. *apo.* Ap. 104. iv.
simplicity. Gr. *haplotēs.* See 1. 12.
in = towards. Gr. *eis.* Ap. 104. vi.
4 if. Ap. 118. 2. a.
preacheth. Gr. *kērussō.* Ap. 121. 1.
another. Gr. *allos.* Ap. 124. 1.
Jesus. Ap. 98. X.
not. Gr. *ou.* Ap. 105. I.
another. Gr. *heteros.* Ap. 124. 2.

spirit. Ap. 101. II. 12. Cp. *vv.* 13-15. another. Gr. *heteros,* as above. Cp. Gal. 1. 6, 7. gospel. Cp. Ap. 140. ye might, &c. The meaning is, if the false teacher professed to bring a fresh gospel, there might be some excuse for their hearing what he had to say, but it is the same as Paul's message. **5** suppose = reckon. was . . . behind. Gr. *hustereō.* See 1 Cor. 1. 7. not a whit = in nothing. Gr. *mēdeis.* Whit is the O.E. *wiht* (wight), a person or thing. very chiefest. Gr. *huper* (Ap. 104. xvii) *lian* (exceeding). Farrar transl. "extra-super". apostles. Ap. 189. This is said ironically of the claims of those who decried him. **6** though = even if. Ap. 118. 2. a. rude. Gr. *idiōtēs.* See Acts 4. 13. speech. Gr. *logos.* Ap. 121. 10. knowledge. Gr. *gnōsis.* Ap. 132. II. i. throughly = in (Gr. *en*) every way. made manifest. Gr. *phaneroō.* Ap. 106. I. v. among. Gr. *eis.* Ap. 104. vi. in. Gr. *en.* Ap. 104. viii. **7** offence = sin. Gr. *hamartia.* Ap. 128. I. ii. 1. abasing. Gr. *tapeinoō.* Cp. *tapeinōsis,* Acts 8. 33. that = in order that. Gr. *hina.* exalted. Gr. *hupsoō.* See John 12. 32. have. Omit. preached. Gr. *euangelizō.* Ap. 121. 4. God. Ap. 98. I. i. 1. freely. Gr. *dōrean.* As a free gift. See Rom. 3. 24. **8** robbed. Gr. *sulaō.* Only here. Cp. Acts 19. 37. other. Gr. *allos,* as in *v.* 4. Cp. *v.* 9. churches. Ap. 186. wages. Gr. *opsōnion.* See Rom. 6. 23. to do you service. Lit. for (Gr. *pros.* Ap. 104. xv. 3) the service (Gr. *diakonia.* Ap. 190. II. 1) of you. **9** with. Gr. *pros,* as above. wanted = was in need. Gr. *hustereō,* as in *v.* 5. was chargeable = distressed. Gr. *katanarkaō.* Only here and 12. 13, 14. no man. A double negative here. Gr. *ou oudeis.* that which was lacking to me = my need. Gr. *husterēma.* See 1 Cor. 16. 17. which = when they. Macedonia. See Acts 18. 5. supplied. Gr. *prosanaplēroō.* See 9. 12. Cp. Phil. 4. 15, 16. from being, &c. Lit. unburdensome. Gr. *abarēs.* Only here. unto = to. **10** no man, &c. Lit. this glorying shall not (Gr. *ou*) be stopped (Gr. *phrassō.* See Rom. 3. 19) to (Gr. *eis*) me. boasting. Gr. *kauchēsis.* See Rom. 3. 27. regions. Gr. *klima.* See Rom. 15. 23. **11** love. Gr. *agapaō.* Ap. 135. I. 1. knoweth. Gr. *oida.* Ap. 132. I. i.

Y 12 But what I do, that I will do, [7]that I may
cut off °occasion from them which °desire
°occasion; [7]that °wherein they °glory, they
may be found even as we.
13 For such *are* °false apostles, °deceitful
workers, °transforming themselves °into °the
[5]apostles of [2]Christ.
14 And °no marvel; for Satan himself is
[13]transformed [13]into an angel of °light.
15 Therefore *it is* [14]no great thing [4]if his
°ministers also be [13]transformed as the
°ministers of °righteousness; whose end shall
be °according to their works.

X Z 16 I say again, Let °no °man think me a °fool;
[4]if °otherwise, yet as a °fool receive me, [7]that
I may °boast myself a little.
17 That which I °speak, I °speak *it* [4]not °after
the °Lord, but as it were °foolishly, [6]in this
°confidence of [10]boasting.
18 °Seeing that many [12]glory [17]after the flesh,
I will [12]glory also.

A C 19 For ye °suffer [16]fools °gladly, °seeing ye
yourselves are wise.
20 For ye [19]suffer, [4]if a [16]man °bring you into
bondage, [4]if a [16]man °devour *you*, [4]if a [16]man
take *of you*, [4]if a [16]man °exalt himself, [4]if
a [16]man smite you °on the face.

D 21 I speak °as concerning °reproach, as
°though we had been °weak. Howbeit °where-
insoever °any °is bold, (I speak [17]foolishly,) I
°am bold also.
22 °Are they Hebrews? so *am* I. Are they
Israelites? so *am* I. Are they the seed of
Abraham? so *am* I.

E 23 Are they [15]ministers of [2]Christ? (I [17]speak
°as a fool) I *am* °more; [6]in °labours °more
abundant, [6]in stripes °above measure, [6]in
prisons °more frequent, [6]in deaths oft.
24 °Of the Jews five times received I °forty
stripes °save one.
25 Thrice was I °beaten with rods, once was
I °stoned, thrice I °suffered shipwreck, °a night
and a day I have °been [6]in the °deep;
26 *In* °journeyings often, *in* °perils of waters,
in °perils of °robbers, *in* °perils °by *mine own*
°countrymen, *in* °perils °by the °heathen, *in*
°perils [6]in the city, *in* °perils [6]in the wilderness,
in °perils [6]in the sea, *in* °perils °among °false
brethren;
27 [6]In °weariness and °painfulness, [6]in

12 occasion. Gr. *aphormē*. See Rom. 7. 8.
desire. Gr. *thelō*. Ap. 102. 1.
wherein = in (Gr. *en*) what.
glory. Gr. *kauchaomai*. See Rom. 2. 17.
13 false apostles. Gr. *pseudapostolos*. Only here. Cp. *v.* 26 and 2 Pet. 2. 1.
deceitful. Gr. *dolios*. Only here. The verb in Rom. 3. 13.
transforming themselves. Gr. *metaschēmatizō*. See 1 Cor. 4. 6.
into. Gr. *eis*. Ap. 104. vi. **the.** Omit.
14 no. Gr. *ou*, as *v.* 4.
light. Gr. *phōs*. Ap. 130. 1. See 2. 11. Rev. 2. 24.
15 ministers. Gr. *diakonos*. Ap. 190. I. 1.
righteousness. Gr. *dikaiosunē*. Ap. 191. 3.
according to. Gr. *kata*. Ap. 104. x. 2.
16 no. Gr. *mē*. Ap. 105. II.
man = one. Gr. *tis*. Ap. 123. 3.
fool. Gr. *aphrōn*. See Luke 11. 40. The fifth, sixth, and seventh occ. in this *v.* and *v.* 19. Cp. *aphrosunē*, *v.* 1.
otherwise = not. Gr. *mē*, as above.
boast = glory, as in *v.* 12.
17 speak. Gr. *laleō*. Ap. 121. 7.
after = according to. Gr. *kata*, as in *v.* 15.
Lord. Ap. 98. VI. i. *β*. 2. B.
foolishly = in (Gr. *en*) folly (*v.* 1).
confidence. See 9. 4. Cp. Phil. 3. 4–6.
18 Seeing that = Since. I, &c. Read I also, &c.

11. 19—12. 11 (*A*, p. 1743). EQUALITY WITH OTHER APOSTLES. NOT BEHIND THEM IN SUFFERINGS. (*Introversion and Alternation.*)

A | C | 11. 19, 20. Fools suffered.
D | 11. 21, 22. Paul's position as a Jew.
E | 11. 23–29. Sufferings from men.
F | u^1 | 11. 30, 31. Glory wherein shown.
v^1 | 11. 32, 33. His humiliating escape.
u^2 | 12. 1–. Glory inexpedient.
v^2 | 12. -1–5. Visions and revelations.
u^3 | 12. 6. Grounds for glorying.
E | 12. 7, 8. Suffering from Satan.
D | 12. 9, 10. Paul's strength in Christ.
C | 12. 11. Paul a fool.

19 suffer. Same as "bear with", *v.* 1.
gladly. Gr. *hēdeōs*. Only here, 12. 9, 15. Mark 6. 20; 12. 37.
seeing, &c. Lit. being wise.
20 bring . . into bondage = enslave. Gr. *katadouloō*. Only here and Gal. 2. 4. Cp. Ap. 190. III. 3.
devour. Gr. *katesthiō*. Elsewhere, Matt. 23. 14. Mark 12. 40. Luke 20. 47. Gal. 5. 15. Rev. 11. 5.
exalt. Gr. *epairō*. See Acts 1. 9.
on = upon. Gr. *eis*. Ap. 104. vi.
21 as concerning = according to, or by way of. Gr. *kata*, as in *vv.* 15, 17.
reproach = shame. Gr. *atimia*. See Rom. 1. 26.
though = that.
weak. Supply the *Ellipsis* with "as they say".
whereinsoever = in (Gr. *en*) whatever.

any. Gr. *tis*, as in *v.* 16. is bold, am bold = dares, dare. See 10. 2. **22 Are they Hebrews?** &c. These questions are an example of the Fig. *Epiphoza*. Ap. 6. **23** as a fool = being beside myself. Gr. *paraphroneō*. Cp. 2 Pet. 2. 16 (madness). more. Gr. *huper* (Ap. 104. xvii. 2, here used adverbially). The *Ellipsis* of any object adds emphasis. labours. Gr. *kopos*. See *v.* 27. **more abundant.** See 1. 12. **above measure.** Gr. *huperballontōs*. Only here. Cp. 3. 10 (excel). See Acts 16. 23. **more frequent.** Same as "more abundant", above. **24** Of = By. Gr. *hupo*. Ap. 104. xviii. 1. **forty.** See Deut. 25. 3. save = beside. Gr. *para*. Ap. 104. xii. 3. **25** beaten, &c. Gr. *rhabdizō*. See Acts 16. 22. stoned. At Lystra, Acts 14. 19. **suffered shipwreck** = was shipwrecked. Gr. *nauageō*. Only here and 1 Tim. 1. 19. **a night and a day.** Gr. *nuchthēmeron*. Only here. **been.** Lit. made, i. e. spent. deep. Gr. *buthos*. Only here. Before this was written Paul made at least seven voyages. Acts 13. 4, 13; 14. 26; 16. 11; 18. 18, 19, 21. 2 Cor. 2. 12, 13; and possibly many more. **26 journeyings.** Gr. *hodoiporia*. Only here and John 4. 6. Cp. Acts 10. 9. **perils.** Gr. *kindunos*. Only in this verse and Rom. 8. 35. robbers = bandits. Gr. *lēstēs*. See John 18. 40. by = from. Gr. *ek*. Ap. 104. vii. countrymen = nation. Gr. *genos*. See Mark 7. 26. Gal. 1. 14. **heathen.** Gr. *ethnos*. Gen. transl. "nation", or "Gentile"; "heathen" here, Acts 4. 25. Gal. 1. 16; 2. 9; 3. 8. **among.** Gr. *en*. Ap. 104. viii. 2. **false brethren.** Gr. *pseudadelphos*. Only here and Gal. 2. 4. Cp. *v.* 13. **Only a few of these dangers and sufferings are described in Paul's history as recorded in Acts.** **27 weariness.** Same as "labours", *v.* 23. painfulness. Gr. *mochthos*. Only here, 1 Thess. 2. 9. 2 Thess. 3. 8.

°watchings often, [6]in hunger and °thirst, [6]in
fastings often, [6]in °cold and °nakedness.
28 °Beside °those things that are °without,
°that which cometh upon me °daily, the care of
all the [8]churches.
29 Who is weak, and I am [4]not weak? who
is °offended, and I °burn [4]not?
F u[1] 30 [4]If I must needs [12]glory, I will [12]glory of
the things °which concern mine infirmities.
31 The [7]God and °Father of our °Lord °Jesus
Christ, Which is °blessed °for evermore,
[11]knoweth that I lie [4]not.
v[1] 32 [6]In Damascus the °governor under °Aretas
the king °kept the city of the Damascenes with
a garrison, °desirous to °apprehend me:
33 And °through a °window [6]in a °basket
was I °let down °by the wall, and escaped his
hands.

u[2] **12** It is °not expedient for me doubtless to
°glory.
v[2] °I will come °to °visions and °revelations of
the °Lord.
2 I °knew a °man °in °Christ °above fourteen
years ago, (whether °in the body, I °cannot
tell; or whether °out of the body, I °cannot
tell: °God °knoweth;) such an one °caught up
°to the third °heaven.
3 And I [2]knew such a [2]man, (whether [2]in the
body, or [2]out of the body, I [2]cannot tell: [2]God
[2]knoweth;)
4 How that he was [2]caught up °into °paradise,
and heard °unspeakable °words, which it is
[1]not lawful for a [2]man to °utter.
5 °Of such an one will I [1]glory: yet °of
myself I will [1]not [1]glory, °but [2]in mine °in-
firmities.
u[3] 6 For °though I would °desire to [1]glory,
I shall [1]not be a °fool; for I will say the truth:
but *now* I °forbear, °lest °any man should
°think °of me °above that which he °seeth me
to be, or *that* he heareth °of me.
E 7 And °lest I should be °exalted above
measure °through the °abundance of the
[1]revelations, there was given to me a °thorn
in the flesh, °the °messenger of Satan °to °buffet
me, °lest I should be °exalted above measure.
8 °For this thing I °besought the °Lord thrice,
°that it might depart °from me.
D 9 And He said °unto me, "My °grace is
sufficient for thee: for °My °strength °is made

watchings. Gr. *agrupnia*. See 6. 5.
thirst. Gr. *dipsos*. Only here.
cold. Gr. *psuchos*. See Acts 28. 2.
nakedness. Gr. *gumnotēs*. See Rom. 8. 35, and cp. 1 Cor. 4. 11.

28 Beside = Apart from.
those . . . are = the things.
without. Gr. *parektos*. Cp. Acts 26. 29.
that which . . . me. Lit. my crowd. Gr. *episustasis*. Only here and Acts 24. 12.
daily. Gr. *kath'* (Ap. 104. x. 2) *hemeran*. The daily crowd of matters demanding his attention. Besides the letters which have come down to us, he must have written many others in answer to those from his converts. See 1 Cor. 5. 9; 7. 1.

29 offended. Gr. *skandalizō*. See 1 Cor. 8. 13.
burn. Gr. *puroomai*. See 1 Cor. 7. 9. Here it means, with zeal or indignation.

30 which concern = of.

31 Father. Ap. 98. III.
Lord. Ap. 98. VI. i. *β*. 2. A.
Jesus Christ. Ap. 98. XI, but the texts omit "Christ".
blessed. Gr. *eulogētos*. See 1. 3.
for evermore. Ap. 151. II. A. ii. 7. b.

32 governor. Gr. *ethnarchēs*. Only here. It means a prefect.
Aretas. The father-in-law of Herod Antipas. Ap. 109.
kept . . . with a garrison = guarded. Gr. *phroureō*. Only here, Gal. 3. 23. Phil. 4. 7. 1 Pet. 1. 5.
desirous = wishing. Gr. *thelō*. Ap. 102. 1, but the texts omit.
apprehend. Gr. *piazō*. See John 11. 57. No doubt to please the Jews in Damascus. Cp. Acts 12. 3; 24. 27; 25. 9.

33 through. Gr. *dia*. Ap. 104. v. 1.
window. Gr. *thuris*. See Acts 20. 9.
basket. Gr. *sarganē*. Only here. In Acts 9. 25 the word is *spuris*.
let down. Gr. *chalaō*. See Luke 5. 4.
by. Gr. *dia*, as above.

12. 1 not. Gr. *ou*. Ap. 105. I.
glory. Gr. *kauchaomai*. See Rom. 2. 17.
I will = But I will. to = unto. Gr. *eis*. Ap. 104. vi.
visions. Gr. *optasia*. See Acts 26. 19.
revelations. Gr. *apokalupsis*. Ap. 106. II. i.
Lord. Ap. 98. VI. i. *β*. 2. B.

2 knew. Gr. *oida*. Ap. 132. I. i. The 2nd Perf. with sense of the Present Tense.
man. Gr. *anthrōpos*. Ap. 123. 1.
in. Gr. *en*, Ap. 104. viii. Christ. Ap. 98. IX.
above, &c. Lit. before (Gr. *pro*. Ap. 104. xiv) fourteen years.
cannot tell = know (Gr. *oida*, as above) not (Gr. *ou*).
out of = without. Gr. *ektos*. See 1 Cor. 6. 18.
God. Ap. 98. I. i. 1.
caught up = caught away. Gr. *harpazō*. See John 10. 12.
to = as far as. Gr. *heōs*.
heaven. Sing. See Matt. 6. 9, 10.

4 into. Gr. *eis*. Ap. 104. vi.
paradise. See note on Ecc. 2. 5. unspeakable. Gr. *arrētos*. Only here. words. Gr. *rhēma*. See Mark 9. 32. utter. Gr. *laleō*. Ap. 121. 7. Paul was alive, and whether he was carried away bodily, as Philip was (Acts 8. 39), or not, he knew not, nor can we, only God knows. He may have been as Ezekiel was (Ezek. 8. 3), or John (Rev. 1. 10). **5** Of = On behalf of. Gr. *huper*. Ap. 104. xvii. 1. but = except. Gr. *ei mē*. infirmities = weaknesses. Same word in 9. 10. **6** though = if. Ap. 118. 1. b. desire. Gr. *thelō*. Ap. 102. 1. fool. Gr. *aphrōn*. See Luke 11. 40. This is the eighth occ. of the word, and the ninth is in *v.* 11. forbear = spare. Gr. *pheidomai*. See Acts 20. 29. lest. Gr. *mē*. Ap. 105. II. any man = any one. Gr. *tis*. Ap. 123. 3. think = reckon. of = with reference to. Gr. *eis*. Ap. 104. vi. above. Gr. *huper*. Ap. 104. xvii. 2. seeth. Gr. *blepō*. Ap. 133. I. 5. of. Gr. *ek*. Ap. 104. vii. **7** lest = in order that (Gr. *hina*) . . . not (Gr. *mē*, as above). exalted . . . measure = over-exalted. Gr. *huperairomai*. Only here and 2 Thess. 2. 4. through = by. No prep. Dat. case. abundance = excellence. Gr. *huperbolē*. thorn. Gr. *skolops*. Only here in N.T. Found in the Sept. Num. 33. 55. Ezek. 28. 24. Hos. 2. 6. Also in the Papyri. the = a. messenger. Gr. *angelos*. to = in order that (Gr. *hina*) he (or it) should. buffet. Gr. *kolaphizō*. See 1 Cor. 4. 11. **8** For = In behalf of. Gr. *huper*. Ap. 104. xvii. 1. besought. Gr. *parakaleō*. Ap. 134. I. 6. Lord. Ap. 98. VI. i. *β*. 2. A. that = in order that. Gr. *hina*. from. Gr. *apo*. Ap. 104. iv. **9** unto = to. grace. Ap. 184. I. 1. My. The texts omit. strength. Gr. *dunamis*. Ap. 172. 1. is made perfect. Gr. *teleioō*. Ap. 125. 2.

perfect [2]in [5]weakness." °Most gladly therefore
will I rather [1]glory [2]in my [5]infirmities, [8]that
the °power of [2]Christ may °rest °upon me.
10 Therefore I take pleasure [2]in [5]infirmities,
[2]in °reproaches, [2]in necessities, [2]in persecutions,
[2]in °distresses °for [2]Christ's sake: for when I
am weak, then am I strong.

C 11 I am become a [6]fool °in [1]glorying; ye have
compelled me: for I ought to have been
°commended °of you: for in °nothing °am I
behind the °very chiefest °apostles, °though I
be °nothing.

B t 12 Truly the °signs of an [11]apostle were
wrought °among you [2]in all patience, [2]in
°signs, and °wonders, and °mighty deeds.
13 For what is it wherein ye °were inferior °to
°other °churches,

s °except *it be* that I myself °was [1]not burdensome to you? °forgive me this °wrong

K G 14 °Behold, the °third time I am ready to
come °to you; and I will [1]not [13]be burdensome
°to you: for I seek [1]not yours, but you: for the
°children ought [1]not to °lay up for the parents,
but the parents for the °children.
15 And I will [9]very gladly °spend and °be
spent [8]for °you: [11]though the more abundantly
I °love you, the less I be °loved.
16 But be it so, I did [1]not °burden you:
nevertheless, °being °crafty, I caught you with
guile.
17 °Did I °make a gain of you °by °any of
them whom I °sent °unto you?
18 I °desired Titus, and °with *him* I sent
a brother. [17]Did Titus [17]make a gain of you?
walked we [1]not in the same °spirit? *walked*
we [1]not in the same °steps?

H 19 Again, think ye that we °excuse ourselves
[9]unto you? we °speak before [2]God [2]in [2]Christ:
but *we do* all things, °dearly beloved, [8]for your
°edifying.
20 For I fear, °lest, when I come, I shall [1]not
find you such as I °would, and *that* I shall be
found [9]unto you such as ye °would [1]not: °lest
there be °debates, °envyings, °wraths, °strifes,
°backbitings, °whisperings, °swellings, °tu-
mults:
21 *And* [6]lest, when I come again, my [2]God
will °humble me °among you, and *that* I shall
°bewail many °which have °sinned already,
and °have °not repented °of the uncleanness
and fornication and °lasciviousness which they
have committed.

Most gladly. Gr. *hēdista*. Neut. Pl. Superlative of *hēdus*; used adverbially.
power. Gr. *dunamis*, as above.
rest, i. e. as a tent is spread over one. Gr. *episkēnoō*. Only here. John uses *skēnoō* in 1. 14. See note there.
upon. Gr. *epi*. Ap. 104. ix. 3.
10 reproaches=insults. Gr. *hubris*. See Acts 27. 10.
distresses. Gr. *stenochōria*. See 6. 4.
for . . . sake. Gr. *huper*. Ap. 104. xvii. 1.
11 in glorying. The texts omit.
commended. Gr. *sunistēmi*. See 3. 1.
of=by. Gr. *hupo*. Ap. 104. xviii. 1.
nothing. Gr. *oudeis*.
am I behind. Gr. *hustereō*. See Rom. 3. 23, and cp. 11. 5 and 1 Cor. 1. 7.
very chiefest. See 11. 5. **apostles.** Ap. 189.
though=even if. Gr. *ei* (Ap. 118. 2. a) *kai*.
12 signs. Gr. *sēmeion*. Ap. 176. 3.
among. Ap. 104. viii. 2.
wonders. Gr. *teras*. Ap. 176. 2.
mighty deeds=powers. Gr. *dunamis*. Ap. 176. 1.
13 were inferior. Gr. *hēttaomai*. Only here and 2 Pet. 2. 19, 20. Lit. "were worsted".
to=beyond. Gr. *huper*. Ap. 104. xvii. 2.
other=the rest of. Ap. 124. 3. **churches.** Ap. 186.
except. Gr. *ei mē*. Same as "but", *v.* 5.
was . . . burdensome. Gr. *katanarkaō*. See 11. 9.
forgive. Gr. *charizomai*. Ap. 184. II. 1.
wrong. Gr. *adikia*. Ap. 128. VII. 1.

12. 14—13. 1 (*K*, p. 1727). **PURPOSED VISIT.**
(*Alternation.*)

K | G | 12. 14-18. The third time. Ready.
  H | 12. 19-21. Testing. His object.
G | 13. 1-. The third time. Coming.
  H | 13. -1. Testing. Its principle.

14 Behold. Gr. *idou*. Ap. 133. I. 2.
third time. See 13. 1 and Int. Notes.
to=unto. Gr. *pros*. Ap. 104. xv. 3.
to you. The texts omit.
children. Gr. *teknon*. Ap. 108. i.
lay up=treasure up. Gr. *thēsaurizō*. As 1 Cor. 16. 2 (in store).
15 spend. Gr. *dapanaō*. See Acts 21. 24.
be spent. Gr. *ekdapanaō*. Spend out, exhaust. Only here.
you=your souls (Ap. 110. IV. 4).
love. Gr. *agapaō*. Ap. 135. I. 1.
16 burden. Gr. *katabareō*. Only here.
being. Gr. *huparchō*. It means being essentially, from the beginning. See Luke 9. 48.
crafty. Gr. *panourgos*. Only here. Cp. Luke 20. 23. These words are spoken ironically, quoting what his opponents alleged.
17 Did I. The question, expecting a negative answer, is introduced by *mē*.
make a gain. Gr. *pleonekteō*. See 2. 11.
by. Gr. *dia*. Ap. 104. v. 1.
any. Gr. *tis*, as in *v.* 6.
sent. Gr. *apostellō*. Ap. 174. 1.
unto. Gr. *pros*, as in *v.* 14.
18 desired=besought, as in *v.* 8.

with, &c. Gr. *sunapostellō*. Ap. 174. 3. Only here. **a**=the. See 8. 18. **spirit.** Ap. 101. II. 8. Put by Fig. *Metonymy* for mind. The internal purpose, in contrast with the external walk. **steps.** Gr. *ichnos*. See Rom. 4. 12. **19 excuse ourselves**=are making an apology. Gr. *apologeomai*. See Acts 19. 33. **speak.** Gr. *laleō*, as in *v.* 4. **dearly beloved.** Gr. *agapētos*. Ap. 135. III. **edifying.** Gr. *oikodomē*. See 1 Cor. 3. 9. **20 lest**=lest in any way. Gr. *mē pōs*. **would**=wish. Gr. *thelō*. Ap. 102. 1. **debates.** Gr. *eris*, strife. See Rom. 1. 29. **envyings**=jealousies. Gr. *zēlos*. See Acts 5. 17. **wraths.** Gr. *thumos*. Occ. eighteen times. Transl. "wrath", except Rom. 2. 8 (indignation), and Rev. 16. 19; 19. 15 (fierceness). **strifes.** Gr. *eritheia*. Occ. seven times. Transl. "strife", except Rom. 2. 8. Phil. 1. 16 (contention). **backbitings.** Gr. *katalalia*, speaking against. Only here and 1 Pet. 2. 1. **whisperings.** Gr. *psithurismos*. Only here and Eccl. 10. 11 (enchantment, i. e. the muttering of the charmer). The verb occ. 2 Sam. 12. 19. Ps. 41. 7. See also Rom. 1. 29. **swellings.** Gr. *phusiōsis*. Only here. Cp. 1 Cor. 4. 6. **tumults.** Gr. *akatastasia*. See Luke 21. 9. **21 humble.** Gr. *tapeinoō*. See 11. 7. **among**=before. Gr. *pros*. Ap. 104. xv. 3. **bewail**=mourn for. **which**=of those who. **sinned already**=sinned before. Gr. *proamartanō*. Only here and 13. 2. Cp. Ap. 128. I. i. **have . . . repented**=repented. Gr. *metanoeō*. Ap. 111. I. 1. **not.** Gr. *mē*. Ap. 105. II. **of**=over. Gr. *epi*. Ap. 104. ix. 2. **lasciviousness.** Gr. *aselgeia*. First occ. Mark 7. 22.

G **13** This *is* the °third *time* I am coming °to
you.

H °**In the mouth of two or three °witnesses shall**
every °word °be established.

G J 2 I °told you before, and °foretell you, as °if
I were present the second time; and being
absent now °I write to them which °heretofore
have sinned, and to all °other, that, °if I come
°again, I will °not °spare:

K 3 Since ye seek a °proof of °Christ °speaking
°in me, °Which °to you-ward is [2]not weak, but
°is mighty °in you.
4 °For °though He was crucified °through
weakness, yet He °liveth °by the °power of
°God. For we also are weak [3]in Him, but we
shall °live °with Him °by the °power of °God
[3]toward you.

L 5 °Examine yourselves, °whether ye be [3]in
the °faith; prove your own selves. °Know ye
[2]not your own selves, how that °Jesus Christ
is [3]in you, °except ye be °reprobates?
6 But I °trust that ye shall °know that we are
[2]not [5]reprobates.

L 7 Now I °pray [1]to [4]God that ye °do °no °evil;
[2]not °that we should °appear °approved, but
°that ye should do that which is °honest, though
we be as [5]reprobates.
8 For we can do °nothing °against the truth,
but °for the truth.

K 9 For we are glad, when we are weak, and ye
are strong: and this °also we wish, *even* your
°perfection.

J 10 °Therefore I write these things being absent, °lest being present I should °use °sharp-
ness, °according to the °power which the °Lord
°hath given me °to °edification, and [2]not °to
°destruction.

A (p. 1727) 11 °Finally, brethren, farewell. °Be perfect,
°be of good comfort, °be of one mind, °live in
peace; and the [4]God of °love and peace shall
be °with you.
12 °Greet one another °with an holy kiss.
13 All the °saints °salute you.
14 The °grace of the [10]Lord [5]Jesus Christ,
and the [11]love of [4]God, and the °communion of
the Holy °Ghost, *be* [11]with you all. Amen.

13. 1 third. See 12. 14.
to = unto. Gr. *pros.* Ap. 104. xv. 3.
In. Gr. *epi.* Ap. 104. ix. 1.
witnesses. See p. 1511.
word. Gr. *rhēma.* See Mark 9. 32.
be established = stand. The reference is to Deut. 19. 15. Cp. Matt. 18. 16.

13. 2-10 (*G*, p. 1727). THE PRESENT EPISTLE.
(*Introversion.*)

G J | 2. Present and absent.
  K | 3, 4. Weakness and power.
   L | 5, 6. Exhortation to them.
   L | 7, 8. Prayer for them.
  K | 9. Weakness and strength.
J | 10. Absent and present.

2 told . . . before, foretell. Gr. *prolegō*, as Gal. 5. 21.
if I were = being. I write. The texts omit.
heretofore, &c. = have sinned before. See 12. 21.
other = the rest. Gr. *loipos.* Ap. 124. 3.
if. Ap. 118. 1. b.
again. Lit. for (Gr. *eis*) again.
not. Gr. *ou.* Ap. 105. I.
spare. Gr. *pheidomai.* See Acts 20. 29.
3 proof. Gr. *dokimē.* See 2. 9.
Christ. Ap. 98. IX.
speaking. Gr. *laleō.* Ap. 121. 7.
in. Gr. *en.* Ap. 104. viii. Which = Who.
to you-ward = unto (Gr. *eis.* Ap. 104. vi) you.
is mighty. Gr. *dunateō.* Only here. See 9. 8.
4 For = For indeed.
though. Most of the texts omit.
through = out of. Gr. *ek.* Ap. 104. vii.
liveth. Ap. 170. 1.
by = out of. Gr. *ek*, as above.
power. Gr. *dunamis.* Ap. 172. 1. Cp. Eph. 1. 19, 20.
God. Ap. 98. I. i. 1.
with. Gr. *sun.* Ap. 104. xvi.
5 Examine = Try. In John 6. 6, prove.
whether = if. Ap. 118. 2. a.
faith. Gr. *pistis.* Ap. 150. II. 1.
Know. Gr. *epiginōskō.* Ap. 132. I. iii.
Jesus Christ. Ap. 98. XI.
except = if (Gr. *ei.* Ap. 118. 2. a) . . . not (Gr. *mē.* Ap. 105. II) in some respect (Gr. *tis*).
reprobates. Gr. *adokimos.* See Rom. 1. 28.
6 trust = hope.
know. Gr. *ginōskō.* Ap. 132. I. ii.
7 pray. Gr. *euchomai.* Ap. 134. I. 1.
do no = should not (Gr. *mē*) do anything (Gr. *mēdeis*). A double negative.
evil. Gr. *kakos.* Ap. 128. III. 2.
that = in order that. Gr. *hina.*
appear. Gr. *phainō.* Ap. 106. I. i.
approved. Gr. *dokimos.* See Rom. 14. 18.
honest. See 8. 21.

8 nothing = not (Gr. *ou.* Ap. 105. I) any thing (Gr. *tis.* Ap. 123. 3). against. Gr. *kata.* Ap. 104. x. 1. for = on behalf of. Gr. *huper.* Ap. 104. xvii. 1. **9** also we wish = we pray for (Gr. *euchomai.* Ap. 134. I. 1) also. perfection. Gr. *katartisis.* Only here. Cp. *v.* 11 and Ap. 125. 8. **10** Therefore = On account of (Gr. *dia.* Ap. 104. v. 2) this. lest = in order that (Gr. *hina*) . . . not (Gr. *mē.* Ap. 105. II). use sharpness = act severely. use. Gr. *chraomai.* See Acts 27. 3. sharpness. Gr. *apotomōs.* Only here and Tit. 1. 13. Cp. Rom. 11. 22. according to. Gr. *kata.* Ap. 104. x. 2. power = authority. Gr. *exousia.* Ap. 172. 5. Lord. Ap. 98. VI. i. *β*. 2. A. hath given = gave. to = for. Gr. *eis.* Ap. 104. vi. edification. Gr. *oikodomē.* See 1 Cor. 3. 9. destruction. Gr. *kathairesis.* See 10. 4. **11** Finally = For the rest. Gr. *loipon.* See 1 Cor. 1. 16. Be perfect. Gr. *katartizō.* Ap. 125. 8. be of good comfort = be encouraged. Gr. *parakaleō.* Ap. 134. I. 6. be of one mind = mind (Gr. *phroneō*) the same thing. Cp. Rom. 12. 16; 15. 5. Phil. 2. 2; 3. 16; 4. 2. live in peace. Gr. *eirēneuō*, as Rom. 12. 18. love. Gr. *agapē.* Ap. 135. II. 1. with. Gr. *meta.* Ap. 104. xi. 1. **12** Greet = Salute. Gr. *aspazomai.* See Acts 20. 1. with. Gr. *en.* Ap. 104. viii. **13** saints. See Acts 9. 13. salute. Same as "greet", *v.* 12. **14** grace. Gr. *charis.* Ap. 184. I. 1. Cp. 8. 9. 2 Thess. 1. 12. 1 Tim. 1. 14. 2 Tim. 2. 1. communion = fellowship. Gr. *koinōnia*, as 1 Cor. 1. 9. Ghost = Spirit. Ap. 101. II. 3. Note the order in this benediction.

THE EPISTLE TO THE GALATIANS.

THE STRUCTURE OF THE BOOK AS A WHOLE.

(Introversion and Alternation.)

A | 1. 1-5. EPISTOLARY AND SALUTATION.

B[1] | C[1] | 1. 6—2. 14. SOLICITUDE.

D[1] | 2. 15—4. 11. DOCTRINAL CORRECTION.

B[2] | C[2] | 4. 12-20. SOLICITUDE.

D[2] | 4. 21—6. 10. DOCTRINAL CORRECTION.

B[3] | C[3] | 6. 11-14. SOLICITUDE.

D[3] | 6. 15. DOCTRINAL CORRECTION.

A | 6. 16-18. EPISTOLARY AND BENEDICTION.

THE EPISTLE TO THE GALATIANS.

INTRODUCTORY NOTES.

1. As with the Second Epistle to the Corinthians, a large part of this letter is taken up with proofs of the apostle's Divine authority. The major portion, however, is devoted to refuting the teaching of such as would lead back the Galatians to bondage, for many of them desired to be under the Law. And Paul declared to them that this was a removing unto a different gospel altogether, although, there being in reality no other gospel, it was a perverting of the gospel of Christ.

2. The likeness to Romans is noticeable, and although this Epistle was written before that to the Romans, Paul had taught the Galatians the same truth as he records in the later Epistle. *Galatians* has been happily likened to a sketch for the finished picture, *Romans.* In both is maintained the fundamental truth that there is no difference between Jew and Gentile before God. There would be many Jews among the churches of Galatia, for Paul ever went to the Jew first; yet the majority would be Gentiles, apparently too ready to yield to the persuasions of judaizers who taught the necessity of circumcision. Of profound interest to all believers is the record of the apostle's reception of the gospel which was preached by him. For he received it not from man, nor was he taught it, but it came to him through revelation of Jesus Christ.

3. There is difference of opinion as to where the churches of Galatia were situated. The province was a central one in Asia Minor, occupied in the northern parts by a mixed race in which the Keltic predominated; and some think that there were no churches at all in that portion of the province, but only in the southern parts, and that they probably included Antioch of Pisidia, Iconium, Derbe, and Lystra. It may be added that in Galatia proper, the people spoke the Keltic language until at least the time of Jerome, who records hearing the same tongue there as he heard in Treves.

4. DATE. Galatians was most probably written from Macedonia in the winter of A.D. 57, or the spring of A.D. 58. See Ap. 180.

THE EPISTLE OF PAUL THE APOSTLE

TO THE

GALATIANS.

A 1 PAUL, an °apostle, °(not °of °men, °neither
°by °man, but °by °Jesus Christ, and °God
the °Father, Who °raised Him °from °the
dead;)
2 And °all the brethren which are °with me,
°unto the °churches of °Galatia:
3 °Grace *be* to you and peace °from [1]God the
[1]Father, and *from* our °Lord [4]Jesus Christ,
4 Who gave Himself °for our °sins, °that He
might °deliver us [1]from °this present °evil
°world, °according to the °will °of [1]God and
our [1]Father:
5 To Whom *be* glory °for ever and ever. Amen.

C^1 A^1 a 6 I marvel that ye are so soon °removed
[3]from °Him that called you °into the [3]grace of
°Christ °unto °another °gospel:
7 Which is [1]not °another;

b °but there be °some that °trouble you, °and
would °pervert the [6]gospel of [6]Christ.

a 8 But °though *we*, or an angel [1]from °heaven,
°preach any other gospel [2]unto you °than
that which we °have °preached [2]unto you, let
him be °accursed.
9 As we said °before, °so say I now again, °If
°any *man* °preach any other gospel unto you
[8]than that ye [8]have received, let him be [8]accursed.

b 10 For °do I now °persuade [1]men, or [1]God?
or °do I seek to please [1]men? for [9]if I yet
°pleased [1]men, I should [1]not be the °servant of
[6]Christ.
11 But I °certify you, brethren, that the [6]gospel
which was [8]preached °of me is [1]not °after
[1]man.
12 For I °neither received it °of [1]man, °neither
was I taught *it*, but [1]by the °revelation of
[1]Jesus Christ.

1. 1 apostle. Ap. 189.
not. Gr. *ou.* Ap. 105. I.
of. Gr. *apo.* Ap. 104. iv.
men. Gr. *anthrōpos.* Ap. 123. 1.
neither = nor yet. Gk. *oude.* Cp. *vv.* 11, 12.
by. Gr. *dia.* Ap. 104. v. 1.
Jesus Christ. Ap. 98. XI.
God. Ap. 98. I. i. 1.
Father. Ap. 98. III.
raised. Gr. *egeirō.* Ap. 178. I. 4.
from. Gr. *ek.* Ap. 104. vii.
the dead. Ap. 139. 3.
2 all. Probably including Timothy.
with. Gr. *sun.* Ap. 104. xvi.
unto = to.
churches. Ap. 186. The only Epistle addressed to a group of churches. Cp. 1 Cor. 16. 1.
Galatia. See Int. Notes. In all his other epistles Paul adds some commendatory words, "Beloved of God", Rom. 1. 7; "of God", 1 Cor. 1. 2; "saints", &c, Eph. 1. 1; Phil. 1. 1; Col. 1. 2; "in God", 1 Thess. 1. 1. The omission shows how great was their apostasy.
3 Grace. Gr. *charis.* Ap. 184. I. 1.
from. Gr. *apo.* Ap. 104. iv.
Lord. Ap. 98. VI. i. β. 2. B. Cp. Rom. 1. 7.
4 for. Gr. *huper,* but the texts read *peri.* Ap. 104. xiii. 1.
sins. Gr. *hamartia.* Ap. 128. I. ii. 1.
that = so that.
deliver. Gr. *exaireō.* See Acts **7.** 10.
this = the.
evil. Gr. *ponēros.* Ap. 128. III. 1.
world. Gr. *aiōn.* Ap. 129. 2. Cp. Rom. 12. 2. 2 Cor. 4. 4. 1 John 5. 19 (*kosmos*).
according to. Gr. *kata.* Ap. 104. x. 2.
will. Gr. *thelēma.* Ap. 102. 2.
of God, &c. = of our God and Father.
5 for ever, &c. Ap. 151. II. A. ii. 9. a.

1. 6—2. 14 (C^1, p. 1748). SOLICITUDE. (*Division.*)

C^1 | A^1 | 1. 6-12. Declaration.
| A^2 | 1. 13—2. 14. Proof.

1. 6-12 (A^1, above). DECLARATION. (*Alternation.*)

A^1 | a | 6, 7-. Their defection.
| b | -7. The perverters.
| *a* | 8, 9. Their defection.
| *b* | 10-12. Himself who taught them.

6 removed. Read "removing". Gr. *metatithēmi.* The Mid. and Pass. with *apo,* mean "to desert". **Him.** I. e. God. Cp. Rom. 8. 30. 1 Thess. 2. 12. 2 Thess. 2. 14. **into.** Gr. *en.* Ap. 104. viii. **Christ.** Ap. 98. IX. **unto.** Gr. *eis.* Ap. 104. vi. **another.** Gr. *heteros.* Ap. 124. 2. **gospel.** See Ap. 140. **7 another.** Gr. *allos.* Ap. 124. 1. **but.** Gr. *ei mē.* **some.** Gr. *tines.* Ap. 124. 4. Cp. 2. 12. 1 Cor. 4. 18. 2 Cor. 3. 1; 10. 2. **trouble** = are troubling. Cp. 5. 10. Acts 15. 24. **and would** = wishing to. Gr. *thelō.* Ap. 102. 1. **pervert.** Gr. *metastrephō.* See Acts 2. 20. **8 though** = even if (Gr. *ean.* Ap. 118. 1. b). **heaven.** See Matt. 6. 9, 10. **preach, &c.** = preach a gospel (Gr. *euangelizō.* Ap. 121. 4) beside (Gr. *para.* Ap. 104. xii. 3), or than, that. **have.** Omit. **accursed.** Gr. *anathema.* See Acts 23. 14 and cp. 3. 10, 13. **9 before.** I. e. at his second visit (Acts 18. 23). **so** = and. **If.** Gr. *ei.* Ap. 118. 2. a. **any *man*** = any one. Ap. 123. 3. **preach, &c.** Same expression as *v.* 8. **10 do I, &c.** = am I persuading. Gr. *peithō.* Ap. 150. I. 2. **do I seek** = am I seeking. **pleased** = were pleasing. **servant.** Gr. *doulos.* Ap. 190. I. 2. **11 certify** = make known or declare to, as 1 Cor. 15. 1. Gr. *gnōrizō.* **of.** Gr. *hupo.* Ap. 104. xviii. 1. **after.** Same as "according to", *v.* 4. **12 neither.** Gr. *oude.* **of** = from. Gr. *para.* Ap. 104. xii. 1. **revelation.** Gr. *apokalupsis.* Ap. 106. II. i. Cp. Acts 9. 15; 26. 16-18.

A² B¹ **13** For ye [8]have heard of my °conversation °in time past °in °the Jews' religion, how that °beyond measure I °persecuted the [2]church of [1]God, and °wasted it:

14 And °profited [13]in [13]the Jews' religion °above many my °equals [13]in mine own °nation, °being more exceedingly °zealous of the traditions °of my fathers.

B² C **15** But when it pleased [1]God, Who °separated me [1]from my mother's °womb, and called *me* [1]by His [3]grace,

16 To °reveal His °Son [13]in me, °that I might [8]preach Him °among the °heathen; immediately I °conferred [1]not with °flesh and blood:

17 [12]Neither went I up °to Jerusalem °to them which were [1]apostles °before me; but I went °into °Arabia, and returned again [6]unto °Damascus.

D **18** Then °after three years I went up [17]to Jerusalem to °see °Peter, and °abode °with him fifteen days.

19 But °other of the [1]apostles °saw I °none, °save James °the Lord's brother.

20 Now the things which I write [2]unto you, °behold, before [1]God, I lie [1]not.

C **21** °Afterwards I came [17]into the °regions of °Syria and Cilicia;

22 And °was unknown by face [2]unto the [2]churches of Judæa which were [13]in [6]Christ:

23 But they °had heard only, that he which persecuted us [13]in times past, now [8]preacheth °the faith which once he °destroyed.

24 And they °glorified [1]God [13]in me.

D c **2** Then fourteen years °after, I went up again °to Jerusalem °with Barnabas, and °took Titus °with *me* °also.

2 And I went up °by °revelation, and °communicated °unto them °that °gospel which I °preach °among the Gentiles, but °privately to them °which were of reputation, °lest by any means I should run, or had run, °in vain.

3 But °neither Titus, who was °with me,

1. 13—2. 14 (A², p. 1749). PROOF. (*Division.*)

A² | B¹ | 1. 13, 14. Before his conversion.
   | B² | 1. 15—2. 14. After his conversion.

13 conversation = manner of life. Gr. *anastrophē*. Occ. thirteen times, always transl. conversation.
in time past. Lit. at one time. Gr. *pote*.
in. Gr. *en*. Ap. 104. viii.
the Jews' religion. Gr. *Ioudaismos*. Only here and *v.* 14. Cp. 2. 14. As the worship of the Father (Jehovah) at the time of Christ had degenerated into "the Jews' religion", so now the worship of Christ has become the "religion" of Christendom.
beyond measure = according to (Gr. *kata*) excess (Gr. *huperbolē*). See Rom. 7. 13.
persecuted = was persecuting.
wasted = was wasting. Gr. *portheō*. See Acts 9. 21.
14 profited. Gr. *prokoptō*. See Rom. 13. 12.
above. Gr. *huper*. Ap. 104. xvii. 2.
equals = of my own age. Gr. *sunēlikiōtēs*. Only here.
nation. Lit. race.
being. Gr. *huparchō*. See Luke 9. 48.
zealous. Gr. *zēlōtēs*. See Acts 21. 20.
of my fathers. Gr. *patrikos*. Only here.

1. 15—2. 14 (B², above). AFTER HIS CONVERSION. (*Alternations.*)

B² | C | 1. 15–17. Absence from Jerusalem. In Arabia and Damascus.
   | D | 1. 18–20. In Jerusalem. Three years after.
   | *C* | 1. 21–24. Absence from Jerusalem. In Syria and Cilicia.
   | *D* | 2. 1–14. In Jerusalem. Fourteen years after.

15 separated. Gr. *aphorizō*. Cp. Rom. 1. 1.
womb. Cp. Isa. 49. 1, 5. Jer. 1. 5. Note the steps: (1) Separation before birth; (2) calling, Acts 9; (3) setting apart for the ministry, Acts 13. 2, 3, in fulfilment of Acts 9. 15.
16 reveal. Gr. *apokaluptō*. Ap. 106. I. ix.
Son. Gr. *huios*. Ap. 108. iii.
that = in order that. Gr. *hina*.
among. Gr. *en*. Ap. 104. viii. 2.
heathen = Gentiles. Gr. *ethnos*.
conferred. Gr. *prosanatithēmi*. Only here and 2. 6.
flesh and blood. See on Matt. 16. 17.
17 to. Gr. *eis*. Ap. 104. vi.
to. Gr. *pros*. Ap. 104. xv. 3.
before. Gr. *pro*. Ap. 104. xiv.
into. Gr. *eis*. Ap. 104. vi.
Arabia. See Ap. 180 and 181.
Damascus. Whence he escaped as recorded in Acts 9. 25. 2 Cor. 11. 33.

18 after. Gr. *meta*. Ap. 104. xi. 2. This was three years from his conversion, viz. A. D. 37. See Ap. 180. **see.** Gr. *historeō*. Ap. 133. I. 13. **Peter.** The texts read *Kēphas*, also in 2. 11, 14. See John 1. 42. **abode.** Gr. *epimenō*. See Acts 10. 48. **with.** Gr. *pros*. Ap. 104. xv. 3. This first visit was cut short by the murder-plot of Acts 9. 29, and the command in the trance of Acts 22. 17–21. **19 other.** Gr. *heteros*, as in *v.* 6. **saw.** Gr. *eidon*. Ap. 133. I. 1. **none.** Gr. *ou*. **save** = except. Gr. *ei mē*. **the Lord's brother.** See Ap. 182. **20 behold.** Gr. *idou*. Ap. 133. I. 2. **21 Afterwards** = Then, as *v.* 18. **regions.** Gr. *klima*. See Rom. 15. 23. **Syria and Cilicia.** The only references to this journey and sojourn are found in Acts 9. 30; 11. 25. **22 was unknown** = continued unknown. Cp. 2 Cor. 6. 9. **23 had heard** = were hearing: i. e. kept hearing. These are strong Imperfects. **the faith.** Gr. *pistis*. Ap. 150. II. 1. **destroyed.** Same as "wasted", *v.* 13. **24 glorified, &c.** = were glorifying (Gr. *doxazō*. See p. 1511.) God in me, i. e. finding in Paul cause for glorifying God.

2. 1-14 (*D*, above). JERUSALEM. (*Alternation.*)

D | c | 1–3. Agreement.
   | d | 4, 5. Opposition.
   | *c* | 6–10. Agreement.
   | *d* | 11–14. Opposition.

2. 1 after. Gr. *dia*. Ap. 104. v. 1. I. e. after his conversion. See Ap. 180. Cp. Acts 15. 1, &c. **to.** Gr. *eis*. Ap. 104. vi. **with.** Gr. *meta*. Ap. 104. xi. 1. **took . . . with.** Gr. *sumparalambanō*. See Acts 12. 25. **also.** Read after Titus. Titus was one of the "certain other" of Acts 15. 2. This was the third visit, the second being that of Acts 11. 29, 30; 12. 25. **2 by** = according to. Gr. *kata*. Ap. 104 x. 2. **revelation.** Gr. *apokalupsis*. Ap. 106. II. i. The decision of Acts 15. 2 was Divinely guided. **communicated** Gr. *anatithēmi*. See Acts 25. 14 (declared). **unto** = to. **that** = the. **gospel.** See Ap. 140. **preach.** Gr. *kērussō*. Ap. 121. 1. **among.** Gr. *en*. Ap. 104. viii. 2. **privately.** See Acts 23. 19. **which were, &c.** Lit. who seemed. Gr. *dokeō*. See *vv.* 6, 9. **lest . . . means.** Gr. *mē pōs*. **in vain** = for (Gr. *eis*) no effect. Cp. 2 Cor. 6. 1. **3 neither** = not even. Gr. *oude*. **with.** Gr. *sun*. Ap. 104. xvi.

°being a Greek, was compelled to be circumcised:

d 4 And that °because of °false brethren °unawares brought in, who °came in privily to °spy out our liberty which we have °in °Christ Jesus, °that they might °bring us into bondage:

5 To whom we °gave place by °subjection, °no, not °for an hour; [4]that °the truth of the [2]gospel might °continue °with you.

c 6 But °of these who °seemed to be °somewhat, (whatsoever they °were, it °maketh no matter to me: °God accepteth °no °man's person:) °for they who °seemed *to be somewhat* °in conference added °nothing °to me:

7 But contrariwise, when they °saw that the [2]gospel of the uncircumcision °was committed unto me, °as *the gospel* of the circumcision *was* unto Peter;

8 (For He That °wrought effectually °in Peter [1]to the apostleship of the circumcision, the same °was mighty °in °me °toward the Gentiles:)

9 And when °James, °Cephas, and °John, who °seemed to be °pillars, °perceived the °grace that was given [2]unto me, they gave to me and Barnabas the right hands of fellowship, [4]that we *should go* °unto the °heathen, and they °unto the circumcision.

10 Only *they would*[4] that we should remember the °poor; the same which I °also °was forward to do.

d 11 But when °Peter °was come [1]to Antioch, I °withstood him °to the face, because he was to be °blamed.

12 For °before that °certain came °from James, he did °eat [1]with the Gentiles: but when they [11]were come, he °withdrew and separated himself, fearing them which were °of the circumcision.

13 And °the other Jews °dissembled °likewise with him; insomuch that Barnabas also was °carried away °with their °dissimulation.

14 But when I [7]saw that they °walked °not uprightly °according to the [5]truth of the [2]gospel, I said [2]unto [11]Peter before *them* all, °"If thou, °being a Jew, °livest °after the manner of Gentiles, and °not °as do the Jews, why compellest thou the Gentiles to °live as do the Jews?

being = (though) being.
4 because of. Gr. *dia.* Ap. 104. v. 2.
false brethren. Gr. *pseudadelphos.* See 2 Cor. 11. 26.
unawares, &c. = brought in stealthily. Gr. *pareisaktos.* Only here.
came in privily. Gr. *pareiserchomai.* See Rom. 5. 20.
spy out. Gr. *kataskopeō.* Only here.
in. Gr. *en.* Ap. 104. viii.
Christ Jesus. Ap. 98. XII.
that = in order that. Gr. *hina.*
bring, &c. Gr. *katadouloō.* See 2 Cor. 11. 20. Cp. Ap. 190. III. 3.
5 gave place = yielded. Gr. *eikō.* Only here.
subjection. Gr. *hupotagē.* See 2 Cor. 9. 13.
no, not = not even. Gr. *oude.* See *v.* 3. This emphatic statement is the Fig. *Negatio.* Ap. 6.
for. Gr. *pros.* Ap. 104. xv. 3.
the truth, &c. Cp. *v.* 14. Col. 1. 5, 6.
continue. Gr. *diamenō.* Elsewhere, Luke 1. 22; 22. 28. Heb. 1. 11. 2 Pet. 3. 4.
with. Gr. *pros,* as above.
6 of = from. Gr. *apo.* Ap. 104. iv.
seemed. Gr. *dokeō,* as in *v.* 2.
somewhat. Gr. *ti,* neut. of *tis.* Ap. 123. 3.
were = once were.
maketh, &c. = matters (Gr. *diapherō*) nothing (Gr. *ouden*). Cp. 4. 1. See Acts 27. 27.
God. Ap. 98. I. i. 1. **no.** Gr. *ou.* Ap. 105. I.
man's. Gr. *anthrōpos.* Ap. 123. 1. Here is the Fig. *Anacoluthon,* Ap. 6. He breaks off at "somewhat", and resumes with "for", changing the construction.
for = but.
in conference added. Same as "conferred", 1. 16.
nothing. Gr. *ouden,* as above.
to me. This is emph. and in the Gr. comes at the beginning of the sentence.
7 saw. Gr. *eidon.* Ap. 133. I. 1.
was committed, &c. = I have been entrusted with. Gr. *pisteuō.* Ap. 150. I. 1. iv.
as, &c. = even as Peter (with that) of the circumcision.
8 wrought, &c. Gr. *energeō.* See Rom. 7. 5, and cp. Ap. 172. 4.
in = by. No prep. Dat. case.
was mighty. Gr. *energeō,* as above.
me = me also.
toward. Gr. *eis.* Ap. 104. vi.
9 James. See 1. 19.
Cephas. Cp. 1. 18.
John. The only mention of him in Paul's epistles.
seemed. Cp. *vv.* 2, 6.
pillars. Gr. *stulos.* Elsewhere, 1 Tim. 3. 15. Rev. 3. 12; 10. 1. Applied by the Jews to teachers of the Law.
perceived. Gr. *ginōskō.* Ap. 132. I. ii.
grace. Gr. *charis.* Ap. 184. I. 1.
unto. Gr. *eis.* Ap. 104. vi.
heathen. Cp. 1. 16.
10 poor. Gr. *ptōchos.* Ap. 127. 1. The Lord's poor. See John 12. 8.
also, &c. = was forward also.

was forward = was zealous. Gr. *spoudazō.* Elsewhere, Eph. 4. 3. 1 Th. 2. 17. 2 Tim. 2. 15; 4. 9, 21. Tit. 3. 12. Heb. 4. 11. 2 Pet. 1. 10, 15; 3. 14. **11 Peter.** The texts read *Kēphas,* as in 1. 18. **was come** = came. This must have followed the council of Acts 15, and preceded the dispute of Acts 15. 36–40. **withstood.** Gr. *anthistēmi.* Occ. fourteen times, five times "withstand"; nine times "resist". **to** = against. Gr. *kata.* Ap. 104. x. 2. **blamed** = condemned. Gr. *kataginōskō.* Elsewhere, 1 John 3. 20, 21. **12 before.** Gr. *pro.* Ap. 104. xiv. **certain.** Gr. *tines.* Ap. 124. 4. **from.** Gr. *apo.* Ap. 104. iv. **eat with.** Gr. *sunesthiō.* See Acts 10. 41. **withdrew** = began to withdraw. Gr. *hupostellō.* See Acts 20. 20. **of.** Gr. *ek.* Ap. 104. vii. **13 the other** = the rest of. Gr. *loipos.* Ap. 124. 3. **dissembled . . . with.** Gr. *sunupokrinomai.* Only here. Cp. Ap. 122. 9. **likewise** = also. **carried away.** Gr. *sunapagomai.* See Rom. 12. 16. **with** = by. **dissimulation.** Gr. *hupokrisis.* **14 walked . . . uprightly.** Gr. *orthopodeō.* Only here. **not.** Gr. *ou.* Ap. 105. I. **according to.** Gr. *pros.* Ap. 104. xv. 3. **If.** Gr. *ei.* Ap. 118. 2. a. **being.** Gr. *huparchō.* See Luke 9. 48. **livest.** Gr. *zaō.* See Ap. 170. 1. The meaning here is,—if thou, a Jew, having become free from the Law, in Christ, 5. 1, how unreasonable to compel Gentiles to judaize (adopt the rites and customs of the Jews)? **after the manner, &c.** Gr. *ethnikōs.* Only here. Cp. the adj. in Matt. 6. 7; 18. 17. **as do the Jews.** Gr. *Ioudaikōs.* Only here. Cp. the adj. in Tit. 1. 14. **live, &c.** Gr. *Ioudaizō.* Only here. Cp. the noun in 1. 13, 14.

D¹ E G e 15 **We** *who are* Jews by nature, and [14]not °sinners [12]of the Gentiles,
16 °Knowing that a [6]man is [14]not °justified °by °the works of °the law, °but by °the °faith of °Jesus Christ, °even **we** °have °believed [2]in °Jesus Christ, [4]that we might be °justified °by the °faith of °Christ, and [14]not °by °the works of °the law: for °by °the works of °the law shall °no flesh be °justified.

f 17 But [14]if, while we seek to be [16]justified °by [16]Christ, we ourselves also are found [15]sinners, *is* therefore [16]Christ [16]the °minister of °sin? °God forbid."
18 For [14]if I build again the things which I destroyed, I °make myself a °transgressor.

e 19 For **I** °through [16]the law °am dead to [16]the law, [4]that I might [14]live [2]unto [6]God.
20 I °am °crucified with [16]Christ: nevertheless I [14]live; yet °not **I**, but [16]Christ [14]liveth [4]in me: and the °life which I now [14]live [4]in [16]the flesh I [14]live [17]by [16]the [16]faith of the °Son of [6]God, Who °loved me, and °gave Himself °for me.

f 21 I do [14]not °frustrate the [9]grace of [6]God: for [14]if °righteousness *come* °by [16]the law, then [16]Christ °is dead °in vain.

H **3** O °foolish Galatians, who °hath °bewitched you, °that ye should °not °obey the truth, °before whose eyes °Jesus Christ °hath been °evidently set forth, °crucified °among you?
2 This only °would I learn °of you, Received ye the °Spirit °by °the works of °the law, or °by °the hearing of °faith?
3 Are ye so [1]foolish? having °begun in [2]the [2]Spirit, are ye now °made perfect °by [2]the flesh?
4 Have ye suffered so many things °in vain? °if *it be* yet °in vain.
5 He therefore That °ministereth to you the [2]Spirit, and °worketh °miracles °among you, *doeth He it* [2]by [2]the works of [2]the law, or [2]by [2]the hearing of [2]faith?

F K 6 Even as **Abraham °believed °God, and it was °accounted to him °for °righteousness.**
7 °Know ye therefore that they which are °of [2]faith, °the same are [2]the °children of Abraham.

2. 15—4. 11 (**D¹**, p. 1748): **4. 21—6. 10** (**D²**, p. 1748). DOCTRINAL CORRECTION. (*Introversion and Alternation.*)

D¹ | E | G | 2. 15–21. Justification.
H | 3. 1–5. Expostulation.
F | 3. 6—4. 11. Illustration. Abraham and his seed.
D² | *F* | 4. 21–31. Illustration. The bond and the free.
E | *G* | 5. 1–6. Justification.
H | 5. 7—6. 10. Expostulation.

2. 15–21 (G, above). JUSTIFICATION. (*Alternation.*)

G | e | 15, 16. Justification by faith.
f | 17, 18. Inconsistency.
e | 19, 20. Life by faith.
f | 21. Consistency.

15 sinners. Gr. *hamartōlos.* Cp. Ap. 128. I, and Matt. 9. 10.
16 Knowing. Gr. *oida.* Ap. 132. I. i.
justified. Gr. *dikaioō.* Ap. 191. 2.
by. Gr. *ek.* Ap. 104. vii. **the.** Omit.
but by = except (Gr. *ean mē*) by (Gr. *dia.* Ap. 104. v. 1).
faith. Gr. *pistis.* Ap. 150. II. 1.
Jesus Christ. Ap. 98. XI.
even we = **we** also. **have.** Omit.
believed. Gr. *pisteuō.* Ap. 150. I. 1. v.
Christ. Ap. 98. IX.
no flesh. Lit. not (Gr. *ou*) all flesh. A Hebraism.
17 by = in. Gr. *en.* Ap. 104. viii.
minister. Gr. *diakonos.* Ap. 190. I. 1.
sin. Gr. *hamartia.* Ap. 128. I. ii. 1.
God forbid. See Luke 20. 16. Rom. 3. 4.
18 make = prove.
transgressor. Gr. *parabatēs.* Ap. 128. VI. 3. There is an ellipsis here. Read "to have been a transgressor", i. e. in destroying.
19 through. Gr. *dia.* Ap. 104. v. 1.
am dead = died.
20 am = have been.
crucified with. Gr. *sustauroō.* See John 19. 32 and Rom. 6. 6.
not = no longer. **life . . . flesh.** Cp. 1 Cor. 15. 45.
Son of God. Ap. 98. XV.
loved. Gr. *agapaō.* Ap. 135. I. 1.
gave = gave up, as John 19. 30.
for. Gr. *huper.* Ap. 104. xvii. 1.
21 frustrate. Gr. *atheteō.* See 3. 15 and John 12. 48.
righteousness. Gr. *dikaiosunē.* Ap. 191. 3.
by = through, as *v.* 19. **is dead** = died.
in vain. I.e. uselessly. Gr. *dōrean.* See John 15. 25.
3. 1 foolish = senseless. Gr. *anoētos.* See Rom. 1. 14.
hath. Omit.

bewitched. Gr. *baskainō.* Only here in N.T. In Sept. of Deut. 28. 54, 56. The noun *baskanos* in Prov. 23. 6; 28. 22. **that . . . truth.** The texts omit. **not.** Gr. *mē.* Ap. 105. II. **obey.** Gr. *peithō.* Ap. 150. I. 2. **before.** Gr. *kata.* Ap. 104. x. 2. **Jesus Christ.** Ap. 98. XI. **hath been** = was. **evidently set forth.** Gr. *prographō.* See Rom. 15. 4. **crucified** = as having been crucified. **among you.** The texts omit. **2 would.** Gr. *thelō.* Ap. 102. 1. **of.** Gr. *apo.* Ap. 104. iv. **Spirit.** Ap. 101. II. 5. **by.** Gr. *ek.* Ap. 104. vii. **the.** Omit. **faith.** Gr. *pistis.* Ap. 150. II. 1. Cp. Rom. 10. 16, 17. **3 begun.** Gr. *enarchomai.* Here and Phil. 1. 6. **made perfect** = being perfected. Gr. *epiteleō.* Ap. 125. 3. See 2 Cor. 7. 1. **by** = in. **4 in vain.** See Rom. 13. 4. **if.** Gr. *ei.* Ap. 118. 2. a. **5 ministereth.** Gr. *epichorēgeō.* See 2 Cor. 9. 10. **worketh.** See 2. 8. **miracles.** Gr. *dunamis.* Ap. 172. 1 and 176. 1. **among.** Gr. *en.* Ap. 104. viii. 2.

3. 6—4. 11 (F, above). ABRAHAM AND HIS SEED. (*Extended Alternation.*)

F | K | 3. 6–9. The promise was to Abraham's faith.
L | 3. 10–12. The curse of the Law.
M | 3. 13, 14. Redemption by Christ.
K | 3. 15–18. The promise was to Abraham's faith.
L | 3. 19–25. The use of the Law.
M | 3. 26—4. 11. Sonship in Christ.

6 believed. Gr. *pisteuō.* Ap. 150. I. 1. ii. **God.** Ap. 98. I. i. 1. **accounted.** Gr. *logizomai.* See Rom. 4. 3. **for.** Gr. *eis.* Ap. 104. vi. **righteousness.** Gr. *dikaiosunē.* Ap. 191. 3. Quoted from Gen. 15. 6. **7 Know.** Gr. *ginōskō.* Ap. 132. I. ii. **of.** Gr. *ek.* Ap. 104. vii. **the same** = these. **children.** Gr. *huios.* Ap. 108. iii.

8 And the Scripture, °foreseeing that [6]God
°would justify the °heathen °through [2]faith,
°preached before the gospel °unto Abraham, *saying,* °"**In thee shall all nations °be blessed.**"
9 So then they which be [7]of [2]faith are blessed
°with °faithful Abraham.

L 10 For as many as are [7]of [2]the works of [2]the
law are °under [2]the °curse: for it is written,
°"**Cursed *is* every one that °continueth °not
[8]in all things which are written [8]in the book
of the law to do them.**"
11 But that °no man is [8]justified °by [2]the
law °in the sight of [6]God, *it is* evident: for,
"**The °just shall °live [2]by [2]faith.**"
12 And the law is [10]not [7]of [2]faith: but, °"**The
man that doeth them shall [11]live [8]in them.**"

M 13 °Christ hath °redeemed us °from the
[10]curse of the law, °being made a [10]curse °for
us: for it is written, [10]"**Cursed *is* every one that
hangeth °on a tree:**"
14 °That the blessing of Abraham might come
°on the Gentiles °through [1]Jesus Christ;
°that we might receive the °promise of the
°Spirit °through °faith.

K 15 Brethren, I speak °after the manner of
[12]men; Though *it be* but a [12]man's °covenant,
yet °*if it be* °confirmed, [11]no man °disannul-
leth, or °addeth thereto.
16 Now to Abraham and his seed were the
[14]promises °made. He saith [10]not, "**And to
seeds,**" as °of many; but as °of one, "**And to
thy Seed,**" Which is [13]Christ.
17 And this I say, *that* the [15]covenant, that
was °confirmed before °of [6]God °in [13]Christ,
the law, which °was °four hundred and thirty
years °after, °cannot °disannul, °that it should
make the [14]promise of none effect.
18 For [4]if the inheritance *be* [7]of [2]the law, *it is*
°no more [7]of [14]promise: but [6]God °gave *it* to
Abraham °by [14]promise.

L N 19 Wherefore then *serveth* the law? It was
added because of °transgressions, till the seed
should come to whom °the promise was made;

O *and it was* ordained [18]by °angels [8]in the hand
of a °mediator.

O 20 Now a [19]mediator is [10]not *a mediator* of
one, but [6]God is one.

N g 21 *Is* the law then °against the [14]promises
of [6]God? °God forbid:

8 foreseeing. Gr. *proeidon.* Only here and Acts 2. 31.
would justify = justifieth. Gr. *dikaioō.* Ap. 191. 2.
heathen = nations. Same as Gentiles, *v.* 14.
through. Gr. *ek,* as *v.* 7; i.e. on the ground of, as Rom. 1. 17; 4. 16, &c.
preached before the gospel. Gr. *proeuangelizō.* Only here. Cp. Ap. 121. 4.
unto = to. In. Gr. *en.* Ap. 104. viii.
be blessed. Gr. *eneulogeomai.* Only here and Acts 3. 25. See Gen. 12. 3.
9 with. Gr. *sun.* Ap. 104. xvi.
faithful = the faithful. Gr. *pistos.* Ap. 150. III.
10 under. Gr. *hupo.* Ap. 104. xviii. 2.
curse. Gr. *katara.* Elsewhere, *v.* 13. Heb. 6. 8. Jas. 3. 10. 2 Pet. 2. 14.
Cursed. Gr. *epikataratos.* See John 7. 49.
continueth. Gr. *emmenō.* See Acts 14. 22.
not. Gr. *ou.* Ap. 105. I. Quoted from Deut. 27. 26.
11 no man = no one. Gr. *oudeis.*
by. Gr. *en.* Ap. 104. viii.
in the sight of = before. Gr. *para.* Ap. 104. xii. 2.
just. Gr. *dikaios.* Ap. 191. 1. Quoted from Hab. 2. 4. Cp. Rom. 1. 17. Heb. 10. 38.
live. Cp. Ap. 170. 1.
12 The man. Ap. 123. 1, but the texts read "He". This quotation is from Lev. 18. 5.
13 Christ. Ap. 98. IX.
redeemed. Gr. *exagorazō.* Elsewhere, 4. 5. Eph. 5. 16. Col. 4. 5.
from. Gr. *ek.* Ap. 104. vii.
being made = becoming. (Emph.)
for. Gr. *huper.* Ap. 104. xvii. 1.
on. Gr. *epi.* Ap. 104. ix. 1. Quoted from Deut. 21. 23.
14 That = In order that. Gr. *hina.*
on. Gr. *eis.* Ap. 104. vi.
through. Gr. *en.* Ap. 104. viii.
promise. See Luke 24. 49.
Spirit. Ap. 101. II. 3.
through. Gr. *dia.* Ap. 104. v. 1.
faith = the faith. Ap. 150. II. 1.
15 after the manner of. Gr. *kata.* Ap. 104. x. 2.
covenant. Gr. *diathēke.* See Matt. 26. 28.
if it be = when.
confirmed. Gr. *kuroō.* See 2 Cor. 2. 8.
disannulleth. Same as "frustrate", 2. 21.
addeth thereto. Gr. *epidiatassomai.* Only here.
16 made = spoken. See Gen. 21. 12.
of. Gr. *epi.* Ap. 104. ix. 1.
17 confirmed before. Gr. *prokuroō.* Only here.
of = by. Gr. *hupo.* Ap. 104. xviii. 1.
in Christ. The texts omit.
was. Lit. came to be.
four hundred, &c. See Exod. 12. 40. Ap. 50. III.
after. Gr. *meta.* Ap. 104. xi. 2.
cannot disannul = doth not (Gr. *ou*) disannul (Gr. *akuroō.* Only here, Matt. 15. 6. Mark 7. 13).
that it should = to. Gr. *eis.*
make . . . of none effect. Gr. *katargeō.* See Luke 13. 7. **18** no more. Gr. *ouketi,* no longer.
gave = has granted. Gr. *charizomai.* Ap. 184. II. 1. by. Gr. *dia.* Ap. 104. v. 1.

3. 19-25 (*L,* p. 1752). THE USE OF THE LAW. (*Introversion.*)

L | N | 19-. To reveal sin till the promised Seed should come.
  O | -19. A mediator manifests two parties. Shows the Law to be conditional.
  O | 20. No mediator; manifests one party. Shows the promise to be unconditional.
 N | 21-25. The Law given till Christ should come.

19 transgressions. Gr. *parabasis.* See Rom. 4. 15. Cp. Ap. 128. VI. 1. the . . . made. Lit. it has been promised. angels. Cp. Deut. 33. 2. Acts 7. 53. Heb. 2. 2. mediator. Gr. *mesitēs.* Here, *v.* 20. 1 Tim. 2. 5. Heb. 8. 6; 9. 15; 12. 24.

3. 21-25 (*N,* above). THE LAW GIVEN TILL CHRIST SHOULD COME. (*Alternation.*)

N | g | 21-. The promise not affected by the Law.
  h | -21. The incapacity of the Law.
  g | 22. The promise the original intention.
  h | 23-25. The purpose of the Law.

21 against. Gr. *kata.* Ap. 104. x. 1. God forbid. See 2. 17.

h for [14]if there had been a law given which could have °given life, verily [6]righteousness should have been [2]by [2]the law.

g 22 But the Scripture [1]hath °concluded all [10]under °sin, [14]that the [14]promise [2]by [2]faith of [1]Jesus Christ might be given to them that °believe.

h 23 But °before [2]faith came, we were °kept [10]under [2]the law, °shut up °unto the [2]faith which °should afterwards be °revealed.

24 Wherefore the law °was our °schoolmaster *to bring us* [23]unto [13]Christ, [14]that we might be [8]justified [2]by [2]faith.

25 But after that [2]faith is come, we are °no longer [10]under a [24]schoolmaster.

M P 26 For ye are all [2]the [7]children of [6]God [18]by [2]faith [8]in °Christ Jesus.

27 For as many of you as °have been °baptized °into [13]Christ °have put on [13]Christ.

28 There is °neither Jew °nor °Greek, there is °neither °bond °nor free, there is °neither °male °nor female: for ye are all one [8]in [26]Christ Jesus.

29 And [4]if ye *be* [13]Christ's, then are ye Abraham's seed, and °heirs °according to [2]the [14]promise.

Q R 4 Now I say, *That* the heir, °as long as he is a °child,

S differeth °nothing from a °servant, though he be °lord of all;

T 2 But is °under °tutors and °governors

U until the °time appointed

V of the father.

R 3 °Even so we, when we were [1]children,

S were °in bondage

T [2]under the °elements of the °world:

U 4 But when the °fulness of the time °was come,

V j °God °sent forth His °Son, °made °of a woman, °made [2]under °the law,

k 5 °To °redeem them that were [2]under [4]the law,

k °that we might °receive the °adoption of sons.

j 6 And because ye are °sons, [4]God °hath [4]sent forth the °Spirit of His [4]Son °into °your hearts, crying, °"Abba, °Father."

P 7 Wherefore thou art °no more a [1]servant,

given life. Gr. *zōopoieō*. See John 6. 63.
22 concluded. See Rom. 11. 32.
sin. Gr. *hamartia*. Ap. 128. I. ii. 1. Cp. Rom. 3. 10–18.
believe. Ap. 150. I. 1. i.
23 before. Gr. *pro*. Ap. 104. xiv.
kept = kept in custody.
shut up. Same as "concluded" above.
unto. Gr. *eis*. Ap. 104. vi.
should afterwards = was about to be.
revealed. Gr. *apokaluptō*. Ap. 106. I. ix.
24 was = has become.
schoolmaster. Gr. *paidagōgos*. This was a trustworthy slave who had the guardianship of the boys of a family. See 1 Cor. 4. 15.
25 no longer. See *v.* 18.

3. 26—4. 11 (*M*, p. 1752). SONSHIP IN CHRIST. (*Alternation.*)

M | P | 3. 26–29. Sons and heirs.
Q | 4. 1–6. Illustration.
P | 4. 7. Son and heir.
Q | 4. 8–11. Application.

26 Christ Jesus. Ap. 98. XII.
27 have been = were. baptized. Ap. 115. I. iv.
into. Gr. *eis*. Ap. 104. vi. have. Omit.
28 neither = not. Ap. 105. I.
nor. Gr. *oude*.
Greek. See Rom. 1. 14.
bond = bond slave. Gr. *doulos*. Ap. 190. I. 2.
male. Gr. *arsēn*. Ap. 123. 5. nor = and.
29 heirs. See Rom. 4. 13.
according to. Gr. *kata*, as *vv.* 1, 15.

4. 1–6 (Q, above). ILLUSTRATION AND INTERPRETATION. (*Extended Alternation.*)

Q | R | 1–. The child.
S | –1. The bond-servant.
T | 2–. Tutors, &c.
U | –2–. The appointed time.
V | –2. The father.
R | 3–. The children.
S | –3–. Bondage.
T | –3. The elements.
U | 4–. The appointed time.
V | –4–6. The Father (God).

4. 1 as long = for (Gr. *epi*. Ap. 104. ix. 3) such time.
child. Gr. *nēpios*. Ap. 108. vii.
nothing. Gr. *oudeis*.
servant. Gr. *doulos*. Ap. 190. I. 2.
lord = owner. Gr. *kurios*. Ap. 98. VI.
2 under. Gr. *hupo*. Ap. 104. xviii. 2.
tutors. Gr. *epitropos*. Elsewhere, Matt. 20. 8. Luke 8. 3 (steward).
governors. Gr. *oikonomos*. See Luke 16. 1 (steward).
time appointed. Gr. *prothesmios*. Only here. An adj. in fem. agreeing with "day" (understood).
3 Even so we = So ye also.
in bondage = enslaved. Gr. *douloō*. Ap. 190. III. 3.
elements = elementary rules. Gr. *stoicheion*. Here, *v.* 9. Col. 2. 8, 20. Heb. 5. 12. 2 Pet. 3. 10, 12. Cp. Rom. 2. 14, 15.

world. Gr. *kosmos*. Ap. 129. 1. 4 fulness. Gr. *plērōma*. First occ. Matt. 9. 16. was come = came.

4. –4–6 (*V*, above). THE FATHER. (*Introversion.*)

V | j | –4. The Son sent forth.
k | 5–. Redemption of the sons.
k | –5. Adoption of the sons.
j | 6. The Spirit sent forth.

God. Ap. 98. I. i. 1. sent forth. Gr. *exapostellō*. Ap. 174. 2. Son. Gr. *huios*. Ap. 108. iii. made. See John 1. 14. of. Gr. *ek*. Ap. 104. vii. the. Omit. 5 To = In order that (Gr. *hina*) He might. redeem. Gr. *exagorazō*. See 3. 13. that. Gr. *hina*, as above. receive = receive in full. Gr. *apolambanō*. See Rom. 1. 27. adoption of sons = sonship. Gr. *huiothesia*. See Rom. 8. 15. 6 sons. Ap. 108. iii. By begetting from above. Cp. James 1. 18. hath. Omit. Spirit. Ap. 101. II. 5. into. Gr. *eis*. Ap. 104. vi. your. The texts read "our". Abba. See Ap. 94. III. 3. 1. Father. Ap. 98. III. 7 no more = no longer. Gr. *ouketi*.

but a [4]son; and °if a [4]son, °then an heir °of [4]God °through Christ.

Q W 8 Howbeit then, when ye °knew °not [4]God,

X ye °did service °unto them which by nature are °no °gods.

W 9 But now, °after that ye have °known [4]God, or rather are °known °of [4]God,

X l how turn ye again °to the weak and °beggarly [3]elements,

m °whereunto ye °desire °again to °be in bondage?

l 10 Ye °observe days, and months, and times, and years.

m 11 I am afraid of you, °lest I have °bestowed °upon you labour °in vain.

C[2] n 12 Brethren, I °beseech you, °be as I *am;* °for I *am* as ye *are:* ye °have °not °injured me at all.

o 13 Ye [8]know how °through infirmity of the flesh I °preached the gospel [8]unto you °at the first.

14 And °my temptation which was °in my flesh ye °despised [8]not, °nor °rejected; but received me as an angel of [4]God, *even* as °Christ Jesus.

15 Where is then °the blessedness ye spake of? for I bear you record, that [7]if *it had been* possible, ye would have °plucked out your own eyes, and have given them to me.

16 Am I therefore become your enemy, °because I tell you the truth?

17 They °zealously affect you, *but* [8]not well; yea, they °would °exclude you, [5]that ye might °affect them.

18 But *it is* good to be [17]zealously affected always [14]in *a* good *thing,* and °not only °when I am present °with you.

n 19 My °little children, of whom I °travail in birth again until °Christ be °formed [14]in you,

o 20 I [9]desire to be present [18]with you now, and to °change my °voice; °for I °stand in doubt °of you.

. 1752) 21 Tell me, ye that [9]desire to be [2]under [4]the law, do ye [8]not hear the law?

22 For it is written, that Abraham had two [4]sons, [4]the one °by a °bondmaid, °the other °by a freewoman.

23 But he *who was* [4]of the [22]bondwoman was °born °after the flesh; but he [4]of the freewoman *was* °by °promise.

24 Which things are °an allegory: for °these °are [4]the two °covenants; °the one °from the

if. Ap. 118. 2. a. **then an heir** = an heir also.
of God through Christ. The texts read "through God". **through.** Gr. *dia.* Ap. 104. v. 1.

4. 8-11 (*Q*, p. 1754). THE APPLICATION. (*Alternation.*)

Q | W | 8-. Ignorance of God.
  X | -8. Unprofitable service.
 W | 9-. Knowledge of God.
  X | -9-11. Relapse to unprofitable service.

8 knew. Gr. *oida.* Ap. 132. I. i.
not. Gr. *ou.* Ap. 105. I.
did service. Gr. *douleuō.* Ap. 190. III. 2. Cp. *v.* 3.
unto = to. **no** = not. Gr. *mē.* Ap. 105. II.
gods. Ap. 98. I. i. 5.
9 after, &c. = having come to know.
known. Gr. *ginōskō.* Ap. 132. I. ii.
of. Gr. *hupo.* Ap. 104. xviii. 1.

4. -9-11 (*X*, above). RELAPSE TO UNPROFITABLE SERVICE. (*Alternation.*)

X | l | -9-. Elements of the world. General.
  m | -9. These are bondage.
 l | 10. Elements of the world. Particular.
  m | 11. Paul's labour in vain.

to. Gr. *epi.* Ap. 104. ix. 3.
beggarly. Gr. *ptōchos.* Ap. 127. 1.
whereunto = to which.
desire. Gr. *thelō.* Ap. 102. 1.
again. Gr. *palin anōthen.* This is emph. For *anōthen* see Luke 1. 3. The R.V. reads "over again".
be in bondage. Gr. *douleuō,* as *v.* 8.
10 observe. Gr. *paratēreō.* See Acts 9. 24. Cp. Col. 2. 16.
11 lest = lest by any means. Gr. *mē pōs.*
bestowed, &c. Cp. Rom. 16. 6.
upon. Gr. *eis.* Ap. 104. vi. **in vain.** See 3. 4.

4. 12-20 (C[2], p. 1748). SOLICITUDE. (*Alternation.*)

C[2] | n | 12. Conformity to him besought.
  o | 13-18. His former ministry.
 n | 19. Conformity to Christ desired.
  o | 20. His future ministry.

12 beseech. Gr. *deomai.* Ap. 134. I. 5.
be = become.
for I, &c. Read, for I (was) as ye (are).
have. Omit.
not . . . at all = (in) nothing. Gr. *oudeis*
injured = wronged. Gr. *adikeō.* See Acts 7. 24.
13 through = on account of. Gr. *dia.* Ap. 104. v. 2.
preached, &c. Gr. *euangelizō.* Ap. 121. 4.
at the first = before. Cp. 2 Cor. 12. 7.
14 my. The texts read "your". The malady (2 Cor. 12. 7) which led to his presence among them was a test to them, a temptation to reject him and his message.
in. Gr. *en.* Ap. 104. viii.
despised. Gr. *exoutheneō.* See Acts 4. 11.
nor. Gr. *oude.*
rejected. Lit. spat out. Gr. *ekptuō.* Only here.
Christ Jesus. Ap. 98. XII.
15 the blessedness, &c. = your blessedness. Gr. *makarismos.* See Rom. 4. 6.
plucked out. Lit. dug out. Gr. *exorussō.* Here and Mark 2. 4.
16 because, &c. = dealing truly with. Gr. *alētheuō.* Here and Eph. 4. 15. Cp. Ap. 175. 1.

17 zealously affect. Gr. *zēloō,* to be zealous, either for good or for bad. **would** = wish to. Ap. 102. 1. **exclude.** Gr. *ekkleiō.* See Rom. 3. 27. **affect.** Gr. *zēloō,* as above. **18 not.** Gr. *mē* Ap. 105. II. **when . . . present.** Lit. in (Gr. *en*) my being present. **with.** Gr. *pros.* Ap. 104. xv. 3. **19 little children.** Gr. *teknion.* Ap. 108. ii. Only occ. by Paul. Cp. 1 John 2. 1, &c. **travail,** &c. Gr. *ōdinō.* Here, *v.* 27. Rev. 12. 2. **Christ.** Ap. 98. IX. **formed.** Gr. *morphoomai.* Only here. **20 change.** Gr. *allassō.* See Acts 6. 14. **voice** = tone. **for** = because. **stand in doubt.** Gr. *aporeomai.* See Acts 25. 20. **of.** Gr. *en.* Ap. 104. viii. **22 by.** Gr. *ek.* Same as "of", *v.* 4. **bondmaid.** Gr. *paidiskē,* as *vv.* 23, 30, 31. Elsewhere transl. "maid" or "damsel". **the other** = and one. **23 born** = begotten. Gr. *gennaō.* **after** = according to. Gr. *kata.* Ap. 104. x. 2. **by.** Gr. *dia.* Ap. 104. v. 1. **promise.** See Luke 24. 49. **24 an allegory.** Lit. allegorized. Gr. *allēgoreō.* Only here. Cp. 1 Cor. 10. 11. **these.** Supply the *Ellipsis* by "two women". **are.** I. e. represent. Fig. *Metaphor.* Ap. 6. Cp. John 6. 35; 10. 9. **covenants.** Gr. *diathēkē.* See Matt. 26. 28. **the one** = one indeed. **from.** Gr. *apo.* Ap. 104 iv.

mount °Sinai, which °gendereth °to °bondage, which is °Agar.
25 For this [24]Agar °is mount [24]Sinai [14]in Arabia, and °answereth to Jerusalem which now is, and °is in bondage °with her °children.
26 But Jerusalem which is °above is free, which is the mother of us °all.
27 For it is written, "**Rejoice, *thou* barren that bearest [8]not; break forth and cry, thou that [19]travailest [8]not: for °the desolate hath many more [25]children than she which hath an °husband.**"
28 Now **we**, brethren, °as Isaac was, are [4]the [25]children of [23]promise.
29 But as then he that was [23]born [23]after [4]the flesh persecuted him *that was born* [23]after [4]the [6]Spirit, °even so *it is* now.
30 Nevertheless what saith the Scripture? °"**Cast out the [22]bondwoman and her [4]son: for the [4]son of the [22]bondwoman shall °not °be heir [25]with the [4]son of the freewoman.**"
31 °So then, brethren, we are [8]not [25]children of the [22]bondwoman, but of the free.

E G p **5** °Stand fast therefore in the °liberty wherewith °Christ °hath made us free, and be °not °entangled again with the yoke of °bondage.

q 2 °Behold, I Paul say °unto you, that °if ye °be circumcised, [1]Christ °shall profit you °nothing.
3 For I °testify again to every °man that [2]is circumcised, that he is a debtor to do the whole law.

p 4 °Christ is become of no effect unto you, whosoever of you are °justified °by °the law; ye are °fallen from °grace.

q 5 For **we** through the °Spirit °wait for the hope of °righteousness °by °faith.
6 For °in °Jesus Christ °neither circumcision °availeth any thing, °nor uncircumcision; but [5]faith °which worketh °by °love.

H Y r 7 Ye °did run well; who °did hinder you that ye should [1]not °obey °the truth?
8 °This °persuasion *cometh* °not °of °Him That calleth you.
9 °A little leaven leaveneth the whole °lump.
10 I °have confidence °in you °through the

Sinai. See Ex. 16. 1.
gendereth = beareth children. Gr. *gennaō*, as *v.* 23.
to. Gr *eis*, as *vv.* 6, 11.
bondage. Gr. *douleia*. Ap. 190. II. 2.
Agar = Hagar. In Arabic, Hagar (a stone) is a name for Mt. Sinai.
25 is. I. e. represents.
answereth to = stands in same rank with. Gr. *sustoicheō*. Only here. Cp. 5. 25.
is in bondage = serves. Gr. *douleuō*. Ap. 190. III. 2.
with. Gr. *meta*. Ap. 104. xi. 1.
children. Gr. *teknon*. Ap. 108. i.
26 above. Gr. *anō*. See John 8. 23.
all. The texts omit.
27 the desolate, &c. = many are the children of the desolate rather than of her that hath the husband. Quoted from Isa. 54. 1.
husband. Gr. *anēr*. Ap. 123. 2.
28 as Isaac was = according to (Gr. *kata*, as *v.* 23) Isaac, i. e. after the type of Isaac. Cp. Rom. 4. 19.
29 even so *it is* now = so *it is* now also.
30 Cast out. Gr. *ekballō*. Ap. 174. 10.
not = by no means. Gr. *ou mē*. Ap. 105. III.
be heir = inherit. Gr. *klēronomeō*. See 1 Cor. 6. 9. Quoted from Gen. 21. 10.
31 So then. The texts read, "Wherefore."

5. 1-6 (*G*, p. 1752). JUSTIFICATION. (*Alternation.*)

G | p | 1. Justification by faith. Exhortation based on 2. 15-21. (G.)
  q | 2, 3. Circumcision destructive of faith.
  p | 4. Justification by law makes Christ of no effect.
  q | 5, 6. Circumcision of no avail.

5. 1 Stand fast. See 1 Cor. 16. 13.
liberty. See 2. 4.
Christ. Ap. 98. IX.
hath. Omit.
not. Gr. *mē*. Ap. 105. II.
entangled. Gr. *enechō*. Here, Mark 6. 19 (quarrel against). Luke 11. 53 (urge).
bondage. See 4. 24.
2 Behold. Gr. *ide*. Ap. 133. I. 3.
unto = to. if. Gr. *ean*. Ap. 118. 1. b.
be circumcised = undergo circumcision.
shall = will.
nothing. Gr. *oudeis*.
3 testify. Gr. *marturomai*. See Acts 20. 26.
man. Gr. *anthrōpos*. Ap. 123. 1.
4 Christ is, &c. Lit. Ye were severed (Gr. *katargeō*. See Luke 13. 7) from (Gr. *apo*) Christ (*v.* 1).
justified. Gr. *dikaioō*. Ap. 191. 2.
by = in. Gr. *en*. Ap. 104. viii. the. Omit.
fallen = fallen off.
grace. Gr. *charis*. Ap. 184. I. 1.
5 Spirit. Ap. 101. II. 4.
wait for. Gr. *apekdechomai*. Cp. Rom. 8. 19, 23, 25. 1 Cor. 1. 7. Phil. 3. 20. Heb. 9. 28.

righteousness. Gr. *dikaiosunē*. Ap. 191. 3. by. Gr. *ek*. Ap. 104. vii. faith. Gr. *pistis*. Ap. 150. II. 1. **6** in. Gr. *en*. Ap. 104. viii. Jesus Christ = Christ Jesus. Ap. 98. XII. neither, nor. Gr. *oute*. availeth. Gr. *ischuō*. See Acts 6. 10. Cp. Ap. 172. 3. which worketh = working. Gr. *energeō*. See 2. 8. by = through. Gr. *dia*. Ap. 104. v. 1. love. Gr. *agapē*. Ap. 135. II. 1.

5. 7—6. 10 (*H*, p. 1752). EXPOSTULATION. (*Introversion and Alternation.*)

H | Y | r | 5. 7-10. Exhortation as to past failure.
      s | 5. 11, 12. Paul's teaching. Appeal.
   Z | t | 5. 13-15. Walking in the flesh.
      u | 5. 16-18. Walking in spirit.
      t | 5. 19-21. Works of the flesh.
      u | 5. 22-26. Fruit of the Spirit.
  Y | *r* | 6. 1-5. Exhortation as to future conduct.
      s | 6. 6-10. Paul's hearers. Appeal.

7 did run = were running. did hinder = impeded. Gr. *anakoptō*. Only here. But the texts read *enkoptō*. See Acts 24. 4. obey. Gr. *peithō*. Ap. 150. I. 2. the truth. I. e. Christ (John 14. 6). **8** This = The. persuasion = obedience. Gr. *peismonē*. Only here. not. Gr. *ou*. Ap. 105. I. of. Gk. *ek*. Ap. 104. vii. Him. God. See 1. 6, 15. **9** A little, &c. This proverb is quoted 1 Cor. 5. 6. lump. Gr. *phurama*. See Rom. 9. 21. **10** have confidence. Gr. *peithō*, as above. in = in regard to. Gr. *eis*. Ap. 104. vi. through. Gr. *en*. Ap. 104. viii.

°Lord, that ye will be °none °otherwise
°minded: but he that °troubleth you shall bear
his °judgment, whosoever he be.
s 11 And I, brethren, °if I yet °preach circumcision, why °do I yet suffer persecution? then
is the °offence of the cross °ceased.
12 I would they °were even cut off which
°trouble you.
Z t 13 For, brethren, ye have been called °unto
liberty; only *use* [1]not liberty °for an °occasion
to the flesh, but [6]by [6]love °serve one another.
14 For all the law is °fulfilled [6]in one °word,
even [6]in this; "**Thou shalt °love thy neighbour as thyself.**"
15 But [11]if ye °bite and °devour one another,
°take heed °that ye be [1]not °consumed one °of
another.
u 16 *This* I say then, Walk °in the °Spirit, and
ye shall °not °fulfil the lust of the °flesh.
17 For the flesh [16]lusteth °against the [16]Spirit,
and the [16]Spirit °against the [16]flesh: °and these
°are contrary the one to the other: °so that ye
°cannot do the things that ye °would.
18 But [11]if ye be led °of the [16]Spirit, ye are
[8]not °under [4]the law.
t 19 Now the °works of the flesh are °manifest,
°which are *these*; °Adultery, fornication, °un-
cleanness, °lasciviousness,
20 Idolatry, °witchcraft, °hatred, °variance,
°emulations, wrath, °strife, °seditions, °here-
sies,
21 °Envyings, murders, °drunkenness, °revel-
lings, and such like: of the which I tell you before, as I °have also told *you* in time past, that
they which °do such things shall [8]not °inherit
the °kingdom of °God.
u 22 But the fruit of the °Spirit is [6]love, joy,
peace, longsuffering, °gentleness, °goodness,
°faith,
23 °Meekness, °temperance: [17]against such
there is °no law.
24 And they that are °Christ's [21]have crucified the flesh °with the °affections and lusts.
25 [11]If we °live °in the [16]Spirit, °let us also
°walk °in the [16]Spirit.
26 Let us [1]not be °desirous of vain glory,
°provoking one another, °envying one another.

Y r **6** Brethren, °if a °man be °overtaken °in °a
°fault, ye which are °spiritual °restore
such an one °in the °spirit of °meekness, °con-
sidering thyself °lest thou also be tempted.

Lord. Ap. 98. VI. i. *β*. 2. B.
none=nothing. Gr. *oudeis.*
otherwise. Gr. *allos.* Ap. 124. 1.
minded. Gr. *phroneō.* See Rom. 8. 5.
troubleth. Gr. *tarassō*, as in 1. 7.
judgment. Gr. *krima.* Ap. 177. 6.
11 if. Gr. *ei.* Ap. 118. 2. a.
preach. Gr. *kērussō.* Ap. 121. 1.
do I, &c. = am I still persecuted.
offence. Gr. *skandalon.* See 1 Cor. 1. 23.
ceased. Gr. *katargeō.* See *v.* 4.
12 were, &c. = even dismembered themselves. Reference to the rite practised by the Phrygians in the worship of Cybele. Cp. Mark 9. 43. (R.V. would even cut themselves off.)
trouble. Gr. *anastatoō.* See Acts 17. 6.
13 unto=upon. Gr. *epi.* Ap. 104. ix. 2. Liberty is the foundation. **for.** Gr. *eis.* Ap. 104. vi.
occasion. Gr. *aphormē.* See Rom. 7. 8.
serve. Gr. *douleuō.* Ap. 190. III. 2.
14 fulfilled. Gr. *plēroō.* Ap. 125. 7
word. Gr. *logos.* Ap. 121. 10.
love. Gr. *agapaō.* Ap. 135. I. 1. Quoted from Lev. 19. 18.
15 bite. Gr. *daknō.* Only here.
devour. Gr. *katesthiō.* See 2 Cor. 11. 20.
take heed. Gr. *blepō.* Ap. 133. I. 5.
that . . . not=lest. Gr. *mē.* Ap. 105. II.
consumed. Gr. *analiskō.* Only here, Luke 9. 54. 2 Thess. 2. 8.
of=by. Gr. *hupo.* Ap. 104. xviii. 1.
16 in the Spirit=by spirit. Ap. 101. II. 5.
not. Gr. *ou mē.* Ap. 105. III.
fulfil. Gr. *teleō.* Cp. Ap. 125. 2.
flesh. See Rom. 6. 12, 19; 13. 14.
17 against. Gr. *kata.* Ap. 104. x. 1.
and. The texts read "for".
are contrary. Gr. *antikeimai.* See 1 Cor. 16. 9.
so that=in order that. Gr. *hina.*
cannot=may not (Gr. *mē*).
would. Gr *thelō.* Ap. 102. 1.
18 of=by. No prep.
under. Gr. *hupo.* Ap. 104. xviii. 2.
19 works. Contrast "fruit", *v.* 22.
manifest. Gr. *phaneros.* Ap. 106. I. viii.
which=such as. **Adultery.** The texts omit.
uncleanness. Gr. *akatharsia.* See Rom. 1. 24.
lasciviousness. Gr. *aselgeia.* See Rom. 13. 13.
20 witchcraft=sorcery. Gr. *pharmakeia.* Here and Rev. 9. 21; 18. 23. See also Rev. 21. 8; 22. 15. It means magical incantation by means of drugs (Gr. *pharmakon*).
hatred. Gr. *echthra.* See Rom. 8. 7.
variance. Gr. *eris.* See Rom. 1. 29.
emulations=jealousies. See Rom. 13. 13 (envying).
strife=factiousness. Gr. *eritheia.* See Rom. 2. 8.
seditions=divisions. Gr. *dichostasia.* See Rom. 16. 17.
heresies. See Acts 5. 17.
21 Envyings. See Rom. 1. 29.
drunkenness. See Luke 21. 34.
revellings. Lit. Comus banquets. Gr. *kōmos* (*Chemosh* of O.T.). See Rom. 13. 13. In this list two sins, idolatry and witchcraft, involve traffic with the powers of evil.

have, &c. = told you before also. **do**=practise. **inherit.** Gr. *klēronomeō.* Cp. 1 Cor. 6. 9. **kingdom.** See Ap. 114. II. **God.** Ap. 98. I. i. 1. **22 Spirit.** Ap. 101. II. 3. **gentleness.** Gr. *chrēstotēs.* Ap. 184. III. (a). **goodness.** Gr. *agathōsunē.* See Rom. 15. 14. **faith**=fidelity. Ap. 150. II. 1. Cp. Tit. 2. 10. **23 Meekness.** Gr. *praotēs.* See 1 Cor. 4. 21. **temperance**=self-control. Gr. *enkrateia.* See Acts 24. 25. **no.** Gr. *ou.* Ap. 105. I. **24 Christ's.** Most texts add "Jesus". **with.** Gr. *sun.* Ap. 104. xvi. **affections**=passions. See Rom. 7. 5. **25 live.** Cp. Ap. 170. 1. **in.** No prep. Dat. case. **let us, &c.** Read "we should walk also". **walk.** Gr. *stoicheō.* Cp. 4. 3, and see Acts 21. 24. Not the same word as in *v.* 16, which is *peripateō.* **26 desirous of vain glory.** Gr. *kenodoxos.* Only here. Cp. Phil. 2. 3. **provoking.** Gr. *prokaleomai.* Only here. **envying.** Gr. *phthoneō.* Only here.

6. 1 if. Gr. *ean.* Ap. 118. 1. b. **man.** Gr. *anthrōpos.* Ap. 123. 1. **overtaken**=found out or detected. Gr. *prolambanō.* Only here, Mark 14. 8. 1 Cor. 11. 21. Cp. 2 Cor. 2. 6–8. **in.** Gr. *en.* Ap. 104. viii. **a**=some. **fault.** Gr. *paraptōma.* Ap. 128. I. ii. 3. **spiritual.** Gr. *pneumatikos.* See 1 Cor. 12. 1. Cp. 5. 16. **restore.** Gr. *katartizō.* Ap. 125. 8. **spirit.** Ap. 101. II. 7. **meekness.** See 5. 23. **considering.** Gr. *skopeō.* See Luke 11. 35. **lest.** Gr. *mē.* Ap. 105. II. Cp. 1 Cor. 7. 5.

2 Bear ye one another's °burdens, and so °fulfil
the °law of °Christ.
3 For °if °a man think himself to be °something,
°when he is °nothing, he °deceiveth
himself.
4 But let °every man °prove his own work,
and then shall he have °rejoicing °in himself
alone, and °not °in °another.
5 For [4]every man shall bear his own °burden.
s 6 Let him that is °taught °in the °word °communicate
°unto him that °teacheth [1]in all
good things.
7 Be °not °deceived; °God is [4]not °mocked:
for whatsoever a [1]man soweth, that shall he
°also reap.
8 For he that soweth °to °his flesh shall °of
the flesh reap °corruption: but he that soweth
°to the °Spirit shall °of the °Spirit reap °life
°everlasting.
9 And let us [7]not be °weary in well doing:
for in °due season we shall reap, if we °faint
[7]not.
10 °As we have therefore °opportunity, let us
do good °unto all *men*, especially °unto them
who are °of the household of °faith.
C3 11 Ye °see °how large a letter I °have written
[6]unto you with mine own hand.
12 As many as °desire to °make a fair shew
[1]in the flesh, they °constrain you to be circumcised;
only °lest they should suffer persecution
for the cross of [2]Christ.
13 For °neither they themselves who are circumcised
°keep the law; but [12]desire °to have
you circumcised, °that they may °glory [1]in
your flesh.
14 °But °God forbid that I should [13]glory,
°save [1]in the cross of our °Lord °Jesus Christ,
°by °Whom the °world °is crucified [6]unto me,
and I [6]unto the °world.
D3 15 For [1]in °Christ Jesus °neither circumcision
°availeth any thing, °nor uncircumcision, but
a °new °creature.
A 16 And as many as °walk °according to this
°rule, peace *be* °on them, and mercy, and
°upon the °Israel of [7]God.
17 From henceforth let °no man trouble me:
for I bear [1]in my body the °marks of the
°Lord °Jesus.
18 Brethren, the °grace of our [14]Lord [14]Jesus
Christ *be* °with your °spirit. Amen.

2 burdens. Gr. *baros.* Cp. *v.* 5. *Baros* is the burden we can bear by help and sympathy.
fulfil. Gr. *anaplēroō.* See 1 Cor. 14. 16.
law. Cf. John 13. 34; 15. 12.
Christ. Ap. 98. IX.
3 if. Gr. *ei.* Ap. 118. 2. a.
a man. Gr. *tis.* Ap. 123. 3.
something. Gr. neut. of *tis.*
when he is = being.
nothing. Gr. neut. of *mēdeis.*
deceiveth. Gr. *phrenapataō.* Only here. Cp. Tit. 1. 10.
4 every man = each one.
prove = test. See 1 Thess. 2. 4 (allowed. R.V. approved).
rejoicing. Gr. *kauchēma.* See Rom. 4. 2.
in. Gr. *eis.* Ap. 104. vi.
not. Gr. *ou.* Ap. 105. I.
another = the other. Gr. *heteros.* Ap. 124. 2.
5 burden. Gr. *phortion.* Only here and Matt. 11. 30; 23. 4. Luke 11. 46 (cp. *v.* 2). This is the burden that cannot be shared.
6 taught. Gr. *katēcheō.* See Luke 1. 4.
in. Omit.
word. Gr. *logos.* Ap. 121. 10.
communicate = share with. Gr. *koinōneō.* Rom. 12. 13 (distributing).
unto = to.
7 not. Gr. *mē.* Ap. 105. II.
deceived. Gr. *planaō.* Ap. 128. VIII. 1.
God. Ap. 98. I. i. 1.
mocked. Gr. *muktērizomai.* Only here. It means to turn up the nose at. Cp. Luke 16. 14 and 23. 35, where the intensive form *ekmuktērizō* occ.
also reap = reap also.
8 to. Gr. *eis.* Ap. 104. vi.
his = his own.
of. Gr. *ek.* Ap. 104. vii.
corruption. Gr. *phthora.* See Rom. 8. 21.
Spirit. Ap. 101. II. 5.
Spirit. Ap. 101. II. 3.
life. Gr. *zōē.* Ap. 170. 1.
everlasting. Ap. 151. II. B. ii.
9 weary. Gr. *ekkakeō.* See Luke 18. 1. Cp. 2 Thess. 3. 13.
due = its own, or proper. Cp. Ecc. 3. 1. Cp. 1 Tim. 2. 6; 6. 15. Tit. 1. 3.
faint. Gr. *ekluō.* Here, Matt. 9. 36; 15. 32. Mark 8. 3. Heb. 12. 3, 5. Cp. Ap. 174. 11.
10 As . . . therefore = So then in proportion as.
opportunity. The same as season, *v.* 9.
unto. Gr. *pros.* Ap. 104. xv. 3.
of the household. Gr. *oikeios.* Only here, Eph. 2. 19. 1 Tim. 5. 8. It is used of the family. Cp. Acts 10. 7.
faith = the faith. Gr. *pistis.* Ap. 150. II. 1.
11 see. Gr. *eidon.* Ap. 133. I. 1.
how large, &c. = with how large letters. This refers to his handwriting.

have written = write. Epistolary aorist, as Philem. 19. 1 Pet. 5. 12. **12 desire.** Gr. *thelō.* Ap. 102. 1. **make a fair shew.** Gr. *euprosōpeō.* Only here; but the word is found in an Egyptian letter about 114 B.C. in the same sense. **constrain** = are compelling. Cp. 2. 3, 14. **lest, &c.** = in order (Gr. *hina*) they might not (Gr. *mē*) suffer persecution. **13 neither.** Gr. *oude.* **keep.** Cp. Rom. 2. 26. **to have you** = that you should be. **that.** Gr. *hina*, as in *v.* 12. **glory.** Gr. *kauchaomai.* See Rom. 2. 17. **14** The Gr. begins with "For me", making it emph. **God forbid.** See Rom. 3. 4. The fifteenth and last occ. of this expression. **save** = except. Gr. *ei mē.* **Lord.** Ap. 98. VI. i. β. 2. A. **Jesus Christ.** Ap. 98. XI. **by.** Gr. *dia.* Ap. 104. v. 1. **Whom.** Or which. **world.** Gr. *kosmos.* Ap. 129. 1. **is** = has been. **15 Christ Jesus.** Ap. 98. XII. **neither, nor.** Gr. *oute.* **availeth.** See 5. 6, but the texts read "is". Cp. 1 Cor. 7. 19. **new.** Gr. *kainos.* See Matt. 9. 17. **creature** = creation. Cp. John 3. 3, 5, 6. 2 Cor. 4. 16; 5. 17. Eph. 2. 10; 4. 24. Col. 3. 10. **16 walk** = shall walk. Gr. *stoicheō.* See 5. 25. **according to** = by. No prep. Dat. case. **rule.** Gr. *kanōn.* See 2 Cor. 10. 13. **on.** Gr. *epi.* Ap. 104. ix. 3. **upon.** Same as "on". **Israel of God.** The antithesis of Israel after the flesh (1 Cor. 10. 18). Cp. Rom. 9. 6. Phil. 3. 3. **17 no man** = no one. Gr. *mēdeis.* **marks.** Gr. *stigma.* Only here. Slaves were branded. So Paul, as the slave of the Lord, bore His marks. The initials of Mithra were branded, as Hindus mark themselves with the trident of Vishnu to-day. Cp. Note on 2 Chron. 36. 8. **Lord.** The texts omit. **Jesus.** Ap. 98. X. **18 grace.** Gr. *charis.* Ap. 184. I. 1. **with.** Gr. *meta.* Ap. 104. xi. 1. **spirit.** Ap. 101. II. 9.

THE EPISTLE TO THE EPHESIANS.

THE STRUCTURE OF THE EPISTLE AS A WHOLE.

(*Introversion.*)

A | 1. 1, 2. EPISTOLARY. SALUTATION.

B | 1. 3—3. 19. DOCTRINAL. AS TO OUR STANDING.

C | 3. 20, 21. DOXOLOGY.

B | 4. 1—6. 20. DOCTRINAL. AS TO OUR STATE.

A | 6. 21-24. EPISTOLARY. BENEDICTION.

1. EPHESIANS is the second (see Structure, p. 1660) of the great text-books of doctrinal instruction for believers in this Dispensation. In *Romans* is set forth all the truth concerning the standing of the sinner in Christ, as having died and risen with Him. Now we are taken a further stage and taught that the sinner not only died and rose again in Christ, but that he is now in God's sight and purpose *seated* with Christ in the heavenlies. *Romans* ends with a reference to the revelation of the Mystery (see Note on the second postscript, p. 1694); *Ephesians* takes up that subject and unfolds it to us. The doctrinal part of *Romans* ends with the eighth chapter, a chapter on which is built the foundation of the *Ephesians* truth.

2. The key-note is struck in the opening words, *v.* 3, which prove that its sphere is heavenly. In it is revealed the "great secret" of this Dispensation of grace, viz. that individual sinners among Jews and Gentiles are being "called out" and formed into "the church which is His body", in which there is neither Jew nor Gentile. And that this church should be "to the praise of the glory of His grace" throughout eternity (2. 7), and an object-lesson, so to speak, to supramundane rulers and authorities in the heavenlies (3. 10), of the glorious purpose (hitherto hidden in God) of Him in "heading up" in one all things in a Dispensation of fulness of times (1. 10), having Christ Personal as its glorified Head, and Christ Mystical, the glorified members together with Him of His Body.

This was the "secret" hid "from the ages and from the generations" (as Gr. of Col. 1. 26) which Paul was not permitted "to make known unto the sons of men" (3. 5) until the period of Israel's national probation was closed by the pronouncement of the decree in Acts 28. 25-28 (p. 1694). But that decree once declared, he is authorized to communicate by "prophetic writings" the secret which had been revealed to him by the Spirit. As truly said by Chrysostom (died A. D. 407);—"these lofty thoughts and doctrines which . . . things which he scarcely anywhere else utters, he here expounds."

3. The STRUCTURE of the Epistle as a whole (above) shows that the greater part is occupied with doctrine,—one-half as it concerns our standing, and the rest as it affects our state. Thus showing that sound doctrine is both the foundation and the source of right practice.

4. DATE. The Epistle was written from prison in Rome, probably about the end of A. D. 62, and, according to Bishop Lightfoot, *after* the Epistle to Philippians. See Int. Notes to latter, and Ap. 180.

5. The TITLE. To whom addressed? In some of the oldest MSS. the words "at Ephesus" (Gr. *en Ephesō*) are not found. And the writings of some of the early Christian apologists show that these words were not in their copies, e.g. Origen (fl. A. D. 230) and Basil (fl. A. D. 350). The explanation of the omission is probably that the Epistle was encyclical, and that the space now occupied in other of the MSS. by the words *en Ephesō* was originally blank, so that the names of the various churches to which it was sent could be filled in. From Col. 4. 16 we learn that Paul wrote a letter to the Laodiceans. There can be little doubt that this is the one, as was believed by Marcion, an early Christian writer (but one much tinged by Gnosticism). If *Ephesians* is not the letter, then an epistle has been lost, which is unthinkable. *Colossians* was apparently a similar letter to be sent round the other churches (Col. 4. 16). We conclude that (1) no epistle has been lost: (2) *Ephesians* was addressed not only to "saints at Ephesus", but to other churches also, and therefore in a very special manner to us; and that (3) it comes to us as the second great text-book of believers' doctrine in this Dispensation, and cannot be understood without our knowing the lessons taught by the Holy Spirit in *Romans*, for *Ephesians* is built on the foundation of the doctrinal portion of *Romans*, ending with the eighth chapter.

6. The CITY of Ephesus was one of the great commercial centres of Asia Minor, and was situated on the river Cayster, at no great distance from its mouth. Ephesus was chiefly noted, however, for the magnificent temple of Artemis (Diana), one of the wonders of the world (see Acts 19. 27). The site of the city is now covered with ruins, the only inhabited part being a small Turkish village.

THE EPISTLE OF PAUL THE APOSTLE

TO THE

EPHESIANS.

A **1** PAUL, an °apostle of °Jesus Christ °by the °will of °God, to the °saints which are °at °Ephesus, and to the °faithful °in °Christ Jesus:

2 °Grace *be* to you and peace, °from [1] God our °Father, and *from* the °Lord [1] Jesus Christ.

B A C a **3** °Blessed *be* the [1] God and [2] Father of our °Lord [1] Jesus Christ, Who °hath blessed us °with °all °spiritual °blessings [1] in °heavenly *places* [1] in °Christ:

b **4** °According as He °hath chosen us [1] in Him °before the °foundation of the °world, that we should be holy and °without blame °before Him [1] in °love:

c **5** Having °predestinated us °unto the °adoption of children by [1] Jesus Christ °to Himself,

d °according to the °good pleasure of His [1] will,

6 [5] To the °praise of the °glory of His [2] grace, °wherein He hath °made us accepted [1] in the °Beloved:

e **7** [1] In Whom °we have °redemption °through °His blood, the forgiveness of °sins,

f [5] according to the °riches of His [2] grace,

g **8** Wherein He °hath abounded °toward us [1] in all wisdom and °prudence;

9 °Having made known °unto us the °mystery of His [1] will,

h [5] according to His [5] good pleasure which He °hath purposed [1] in Himself;

10 °That in the °dispensation of the °fulness of times °He might gather together in one all

1. 1 apostle. Ap. 189.
Jesus Christ. The texts read Christ Jesus (Ap. 98. XII).
by. Ap. 104. v. 1.
will. Ap. 102. 2.
God. Ap. 98. I. i. 1.
saints. See Acts 9. 13. 1 Cor. 1. 2.
at. Ap. 104. viii.
Ephesus. See Introductory Notes.
faithful. Ap. 150. III.
in. Same as at, above.
Christ Jesus. As above.
2 Grace. Ap. 184. I. 1. Occ. twelve times in Eph.
from. Ap. 104. iv.
Father. Ap. 98. III.
Lord. Ap. 98. VI. i. *β*. 2. B.

1. 3—3. 19 (**B**, p. 1759). DOCTRINAL, AS TO OUR STANDING. (*Introversion and Alternation.*)

B | A | C | 1. 3-14. The purpose of God in Himself concerning Christ Personal.
  D | 1. 15-23. Prayer to the God of our Lord Jesus Christ.
 B | 2. 1-22. Ourselves, the objects of these purposes.
 A | *C* | 3. 1-13. The purpose of God concerning Christ mystical.
  D | 3. 14-21. Prayer to the Father of our Lord Jesus Christ.

1. 3-14 (C, above). THE PURPOSE OF GOD, &c. (*Continued Alternation.*)

C | a | 3. All spiritual blessings.
 b | 4. Measure.
 c | 5-. Sonship.
 d | -5, 6. Measure.
 e | 7-. Redemption.
 f | -7. Measure.
 g | 8, 9-. Blessing. The Mystery.
 h | -9, 10. Measure.
 i | 11-. Inheritance.
 k | -11-14. Measure.

3 Blessed, &c. Cp. 2 Cor. 1. 3. 1 Pet. 1. 3. Always applied to God. Lord. Ap. 98. VI. i. *β*. 2. A. hath = having. Note the use and importance of aorist participles throughout this section. with. Ap. 104. viii. all = every. spiritual. See 1 Cor. 12. 1. blessings = blessing (sing.). Gr. *eulogia*. See Rom. 15. 29. heavenly *places* = the heavenlies, i.e. heavenly spheres. Gr. *epouranios*. Cp. *v.* 20; 2. 6; 3. 10; 6. 12. Christ. Ap. 98. IX. **4** According = Even. hath chosen = chose out. Gr. *eklegomai*. Cp. Acts 1. 2. before. Ap. 104. xiv. foundation. Ap. 146. world. Ap. 129. 1. Cp. 2 Tim. 1. 9. without blame. Gr. *amōmos*. Here; 5. 27. Col. 1. 22. Heb. 9. 14. 1 Pet. 1. 19. Jude 24. Rev. 14. 5. before Him = in His sight. See 2 Cor. 2. 17. love. Ap. 135. II. 1. Some insert "in love" after "predestinated us" in *v.* 5. **5** predestinated = foreordained. Gr. *proorizō*. See Acts 4. 28. Rom. 8. 29. unto, to. Gr. *eis*. Ap. 104. vi. adoption of children. Gr. *huiothesia*. See Rom. 8. 15. Cp. Ap. 108. iii. according to. Gr. *kata*. Ap. 104. x. 2. good pleasure. Gr. *eudokia*. See Rom. 10. 1. **6** praise. See Rom. 2. 29. glory. Gr. *doxa*. See p. 1511. wherein. The texts read which. made . . . accepted = lit. en-graced. Ap. 184. II. 2. Cp. Luke 1. 28. Beloved. Ap. 135. I. 1. Cp. Matt. 3. 17; 17. 5; &c. and see Ap. 99. **7** we have. Cp. Rom. 5. 1. redemption = the redemption. See Rom. 3. 24; 5. 1. through. Gr. *dia*. Ap. 104. v. 1. His blood. The price of the redemption. Cp. Acts 20. 28. 1 Cor. 6. 20. 1 Pet. 1. 18, 19; &c. sins = transgressions. Ap. 128. I. ii. 3. riches, &c. Cp. *v.* 18; 2. 7; 3. 8, 16. Rom. 9. 23. Col. 1. 27. **8** hath. Omit. toward. Gr. *eis*. Ap. 104. vi. prudence. Gr. *phronēsis*. Only here and Luke 1. 17. **9** Having made known. Gr. *gnōrizō*. As in 3. 3. Phil. 1. 22 (wot). Cp. Ap. 132. II. 1. unto = to. mystery. See Ap. 193. hath. Omit. purposed. Gr. *protithēmi*. See Rom. 1. 13. **10** That in. Gr. *eis*. Ap. 104. vi. dispensation. Gr. *oikonomia*. See 1 Cor. 9. 17. fulness. Gr. *plērōma*. First occ. Matt. 9. 16. He might gather together in one = to sum up (lit.: "head up"). Gr. *anakephalaioomai*. See Rom. 13. 9. The verb in this place being in Mid. Voice is reflexive, implying "for Himself" (cp. *vv.* 5, 9).

things [1]in [3]Christ, °both which are °in °heaven,
and which are °on earth; °*even* [1]in Him:
i 11 [1]In Whom also we °have °obtained an inheritance, °being [5]predestinated
k [5]according to the °purpose of Him Who °work-
eth all things °after the °counsel of His own
[1]will:
12 °That we should be [5]to the [6]praise of His
[6]glory, who °first trusted [1]in [3]Christ.
13 °In Whom ye also *trusted,* °after that ye
heard the °word of °truth, the °gospel of your
°salvation: °in Whom also after that ye °be-
lieved, ye were °sealed °with °that holy Spirit
of °promise,
14 °Which is °the earnest of our °inheritance
°until the [7]redemption of the °purchased possession, [5]unto [6]the praise of His [6]glory.
D E[1] 15 °Wherefore I also, °after I heard of °your
°faith [1]in °the Lord Jesus, and °love [5]unto all
the [1]saints,
16 Cease °not to °give thanks °for you,
°making mention of you °in my °prayers;
17 °That the [1]God of our [3]Lord [1]Jesus Christ,
the °Father of [6]glory, may give °unto you
°the spirit of wisdom and °revelation [1]in the
°knowledge of Him:
E[2] L[1] 18 The eyes of your °understanding °being
enlightened, °that ye may °know what is °the
hope of His calling,
L[2] and what the riches of the [6]glory of °His inheritance [1]in the [1]saints,
L[3] 19 And what *is* the °exceeding °greatness of
His °power [8]to us-ward who °believe, °accord-
ing to the °working of °His mighty power,

both. Omit.
in. The texts read *epi*, as below.
heaven = the heavens (pl.). See Matt. 6. 9, 10.
on. Gr. *epi.* Ap. 104. ix. 2.
earth. Ap. 129. 4. **even.** Omit.
11 have. Omit.
obtained an inheritance. Gr. *klēroomai.* Only here.
being = having been.
purpose. Gr. *prothesis.* See Rom. 8. 28.
worketh. Gr. *energeō.* See 1 Cor. 12. 6.
after. Gr. *kata.* Ap. 104. x. 2.
counsel. Ap. 102. 4.
12 That = To the end that. Gr. *eis.* Ap. 104. vi.
first trusted = have before hoped. Gr. *proelpizō.* Only here. The "we" being the saved members of the Pentecostal church closed by the judgment pronouncement of Acts 28. 25, 28 (see Longer Note, p. 1694).
13 In Whom, &c. The Ellipsis (Ap. 6) should be supplied from the subject of *v.* 11. In (Gr. *en*) Whom ye were made an inheritance also; or, allotted as God's own inheritance.
after, &c. = having heard. See *v.* 5.
word of truth. The Word always the instrument of the new begetting. Cp. John 17. 17. Jas. 1. 18. 1 Pet. 1. 23.
word. Ap. 121. 10. **truth** = the truth.
gospel. Ap. 140.
salvation. Only occ. of the word in Eph.
in Whom, &c. = in (Gr. *en*) Whom ye also on believing were sealed. **believed.** Ap. 150. I. 1. v (ii).
sealed. Cp. 4. 30. Matt. 27. 66. John 3. 33. 2 Cor. 1. 22. Rev. 7. 3; &c. A seal affixed implies possession, or security, as well as being a distinctive mark.
with. No prep. Dat. case.
that = the (Emph.).
holy Spirit. Although both articles occur (see Ap. 101. II. 14), yet it is clear from the "earnest" (*v.* 14) that it is the *gift*, not the *Giver*.
promise = the promise. See John 16. 13, and cp. Acts 1. 4, which latter refers to the beginning of the fulfilment of the promise in John 16. 13.
14 Which . . . possession. In parenthesis.
the earnest = a pledge. See 2 Cor. 1. 22. The gift of the new nature (spirit) is a pledge of God's future gifts *in the same kind*, thus differing from any ordinary pledge. Cp. 1 Pet. 1. 4. **inheritance.** Gr. *klēronomia.* See Acts 20. 32. Cp. *our* inheritance here, and *His* inheritance, *v.* 18. **until** = unto. Gr. *eis.* Ap. 104. vi. **purchased possession.** Gr. *peripoiēsis.* Here; 1 Thess. 5. 9. 2 Thess. 2. 14. Heb. 10. 39. 1 Pet. 2. 9. Cp. Acts 20. 28.

1. 15-23 (D, p. 1760). PRAYER TO THE GOD AND FATHER. (*Division.*)

D | E[1] | 15-17. The cause (their faith and love) and the sum (the knowledge of Him) of the prayer.
| E[2] | 18-23. The effect (their enlightenment) and the elements forming the sum of the prayer.

15 Wherefore = on account of this. Gr. *dia* (Ap. 104. v. 2) *touto.* **after I** = having. **your** = among (Gr. *kata*, Ap. 104. x. 2) you. **faith.** Ap. 150. II. 1. **the Lord Jesus.** I.e. Jesus (Ap. 98. X.) as Lord (Ap. 98. VI. i. β. 2. A). See Rom. 10. 9. **love.** Ap. 135. II. 1. **16 not.** Gr. *ou.* Ap. 105. I. **give thanks.** Gr. *eucharisteō.* First occ. Matt. 15. 36. With its noun and adj. occ. fifty-five times (thirty-eight in Paul's Epp.). See Ap. 10. **for.** Gr. *huper.* Ap. 104. xvii. 1. **making mention, &c.** See Rom. 1. 9. In a papyrus of second century A. D. the mention of assurance of intercession for a sister in the same words is found in a letter from a soldier. **in.** Gr. *epi.* Ap. 104. ix. 1. **prayers.** Ap. 134. II. 2. **17 That** = In order that. Gr. *hina.* **Father of glory.** Cp. 1 Cor. 2. 8. **Father.** See Ap. 98. III. **unto** = to. **the spirit** = a spirit. Ap. 101. II. 4. **revelation.** Ap. 106. II. i. **knowledge.** Ap. 132. II. ii.

1. 18-23 (E[2], above). THE EFFECT AND THE ELEMENTS OF THE PRAYER. (*Division.*)

E[2] | L[1] | 18-. Knowledge of the hope of His calling.
| L[2] | -18. Knowledge of the riches of His glory.
| L[3] | 19-23. Knowledge of the greatness of His power.

18 understanding = mind. Cp. Matt. 22. 37; &c. Gr. *dianoia*, but the texts read *kardia*, heart. **being** = having been. **that.** Gr. *eis.* See *v.* 12. **know.** Ap. 132. I. 1. **the hope of His calling.** I. e. to the *sonship*, *vv.* 4, 5; our acceptance as sons in the "Beloved" (Son). Cp. Gal. 4. 5-7. **His inheritance in the saints.** Cp. 2. 7. Tit. 2. 14; &c. Israel will be God's inheritance ("peculiar treasure", Ex. 19. 5) on earth. The church which is His body will be His inheritance in heaven. In Tit. 2. 14 the Greek *periousion* (peculiar treasure) is used by the Sept. for *s^egullāh*, Ex. 19. 5. Deut. 7. 6; 14. 2; 26. 18. Cp. Mal. 3. 17. A cognate word is used in Ps. 135. 4. **19 exceeding** = surpassing. See 2 Cor. 3. 10; 9. 14. **greatness.** Gr. *megethos.* Only here. **power.** Ap. 172. 1. **believe.** Ap. 150. I 1. i. **according to . . . all in all.** Parenthetic (Fig. *Parembole.* Ap. 6), the main argument being continued in 2. 1, which should read, "Even you", &c. **according to.** Same as *v.* 5. **working.** Ap. 172. 4. Occ. 3. 7; 4. 16. Phil. 3. 21. Col. 1. 29; 2. 12. 2 Thess. 2. 9, 11. **His mighty power.** Lit. the strength (Ap. 172. 2) of His might (Ap. 172. 3).

20 Which He ° wrought [1]in [3]Christ, °when He
raised Him °from the dead, and °set *Him* °at
His own right hand [1]in the [3]heavenly *places*,
21 °Far above °all °principality, and °power,
and °might, and °dominion, and every name
that is named, [16]not only [1]in this °world, but
°also [1]in that which is to come:
22 And °**hath** °**put all *things*** °**under His feet,**
and gave Him *to be* °the Head °over all *things*
to the °church,
23 Which is °His body, the °fulness of Him
That °filleth all [1]in all.

B F **2** °And you °*hath He quickened,* who were
°dead °in °trespasses and °sins;
2 °Wherein °in time past ye walked °accord-
ing to °the °course of this °world, °according
to the °prince of the °power of the air, the
°spirit that now °worketh °in the °children of
°disobedience:
3 °Among whom °also **we** all had our °con-
versation [2]in times past [2]in the °lusts of our
°flesh, °fulfilling the °desires of the °flesh and
of the °mind; and were °by nature °the °chil-
dren of °wrath, °even as °others.

G 4 But °God, °Who is rich [2]in °mercy, °for
His great °love wherewith He °loved us,
5 Even when we were dead [1]in °sins, °hath
°quickened us together with °Christ, (°by °grace
ye °are saved;)
6 And °hath raised *us* up together, and °made
us sit together [2]in °heavenly *places* [2]in °Christ
Jesus:
7 °That [2]in the °ages to come He might
shew the °exceeding riches of His [5]grace [2]in
His °kindness °toward us °through [6]Christ
Jesus.
8 For [5]by grace [5]are ye saved °through °faith;
and that °not °of yourselves: *it is* the gift of
[4]God:
9 [8]Not [8]of works, °lest °any man should
°boast.
10 For we are **His** °workmanship, °created
[2]in [6]Christ Jesus °unto good works, which

20 wrought. Gr. *energeō*, as in *v.* 11.
when He raised=having raised. Ap. 178. I. 4.
from the dead. Ap. 139. 3.
set=sat. Cp. Mark. 16. 19.
at. Gr. *en.* Ap. 104. viii.
21 Far above. Gr. *huperanō*. Here; 4. 10. Heb. 9. 5.
all=every.
principality. Gr. *archē*. See Rom. 8. 38, and Ap. 172. 6.
power. Ap. 172. 5.
might=power. Gr. *dunamis*, *v* 19.
dominion. Gr. *kuriotēs*. Here, Col. 1. 16. 2 Pet. 2. 10. Jude 8.
world. Ap. 129. 2.
also, &c.=the coming one also.
22 hath. Omit.
put, &c. Cp. 1 Cor. 15. 27.
under. Ap. 104. xviii. 2.
the. Omit.
over. Ap. 104. xvii. 2.
church. Ap. 186. Here, the "church" of the Mystery. In these *vv.* note the sevenfold (Ap. 10) Headship of the Lord,—above (1) all principality, (2) power, (3) might, (4) dominion, (5) every name, (6) all things, (7) the church.
23 His body. Cp. 3. 5, 6.
fulness. See *v.* 10. His members "fill up" the body of Christ, and the body of Christ fills up and completes "the dispensation of the fulness of the times". The apostle adopts the term used by the Gnostics, *plērōma* (Col. 2. 9, 10). See note on 2. 2 (prince).
filleth all in all. He fills up all the members with all spiritual gifts and graces.

2. 1-22 (B, p. 1760). **THE OBJECTS OF PAUL'S MINISTRY.** (*Alternation.*)

B | F | 1-3. Past condition by nature.
  G | 4-10. Present condition by grace.
  F | 11, 12. Past condition by birth.
  G | 13-22. Present condition by superabounding grace.

1 And you=Even you. Resuming from 1. 19. *hath He quickened.* Omit. The Ellipsis in A.V. and R.V. supplied from *v.* 5.
dead. Ap. 139.
in=by. No prep. Dat. case.
trespasses. Ap. 128. I. ii. 3. The texts prefix "your".
sins. Ap. 128. I. ii. 1.
2 Wherein=In (Gr. *en*) which.
in time past=once.
according to. Ap. 104. x. 2.
the course (*aiōn*) **of this world**=the age of this world (Ap. 129. 1).
course. Gr. *aiōn.* Ap. 129. 2.

prince=ruler, i. e. Satan. Cp. 2 Cor. 4. 4. Gr. *archōn.* In this Epistle Paul uses the very terminology of the Gnostic teaching that the universe was ruled by AEONS, emanations of Deity. The *archōn* here being the one who had dominion over the air, and the whole body of AEONS forming the *plērōma* (fulness) of the spiritual world, in contrast with the emptiness (*kenōna*) or unsubstantial character of the material world (*kosmos*). **power.** Ap. 172. 5. **spirit.** Ap. 101. II. 12. **worketh**=is working. See 1. 11. **in.** Ap. 104. viii. **children of disobedience.** Hebraism: *not* disobedient children, but sons (Ap. 108. iii) of Satan in a special manner, being those in whom he works, and on whom the wrath of God comes (5. 6). **disobedience**=the disobedience. See Rom. 11. 30. **3 Among.** Gr. *en.* Ap. 104. viii. 2. **also we... past**=**we** also all once lived. **conversation.** See 2 Cor. 1. 12. **lusts.** Gr. *epithumia*, strong desire. See Luke 22. 15. Not necessarily evil desire, as see the verb in 1 Tim. 3. 1. **flesh.** Old nature. See Rom. 7. 5. **fulfilling**=doing. Gr. *poieō.* **desires.** Ap. 102. 2. **flesh.** The coarse lusts of the body. **mind.** Gr. *dianoia*, thought. The refined lusts of the mind. **by nature.** See Rom. 2. 27. **the.** Omit. **children.** Ap. 108. i. **wrath.** See Rom. 1. 18. **even as.** Add "also". **others.** Ap. 124. 3. **4 God.** Ap. 98. I. i. 1. **Who is**=being. **mercy.** Cp. Rom. 9. 23. **for**=on account of. Ap. 104. v. 2. **love, loved.** Ap. 135. II. 1; I. 1. **5 sins.** As trespasses in *v.* 1. **hath.** Omit. **quickened... together**=made... alive with. Gr. *suzōopoieō.* Only here and Col. 2. 13. **Christ.** Ap. 98. IX. **by.** No prep. Dat. case. **grace.** Ap. 184. I. 1. **are**=were. **6 hath raised, &c.**=raised... together (with Him). Gr. *sunegeirō.* Only here. Col. 2. 12; 3. 1. **made *us*, &c.**=made us to sit down together. Gr. *sunkathizō.* Only here and Luke 22. 55. **heavenly *places*.** As in 1. 3. **Christ Jesus.** See 1. 1. **7 That**=In order that. Gr. *hina.* **ages.** See Ap. 129. 2. **exceeding.** See 1. 19. **kindness.** See Rom. 2. 4. Ap. 184. III. (a). **toward.** Gr. *epi.* Ap. 104. ix. 3. **through.** Gr. *en.* Ap. 104. viii. **8 through.** Gr. *dia.* Ap. 104. v. 1. **faith.** Ap. 150 II. 1. We are saved by grace, not by faith, which is the channel through (*dia*) which flows to us the Divine stream of saving grace. Both alike God's gifts. **not.** Ap. 105. I. **of.** Gr. *ek.* Ap. 104. vii. **9 lest any man**=in order that (Gr. *hina*) no (Gr. *mē.* Ap. 105. II) one (Gr. *tis.* Ap. 123. 3). **boast.** See Rom. 2. 17. **10 workmanship**=handiwork. Gr. *poiēma.* Only here and Rom. 1. 20. Refers to the new creation of *vv.* 5, 6. **created**=having been created. Gr *ktizō.* See Rom. 1. 25. **unto.** Gr. *epi.* Ap. 104. ix. 2.

[4]God °hath before ordained °that we should
walk [2]in them.
F 11 Wherefore remember, that ye *being* [2]in time
past Gentiles [2]in °the [3]flesh, who are called
°Uncircumcision °by that which is called °the
Circumcision [2]in °the [3]flesh °made by hands;
12 That at that time ye were °without [5]Christ,
°being aliens from the °commonwealth of
°Israel, and °strangers from the covenants of
°promise, having °no hope, and °without God
[2]in the [2]world.
G 13 But °now [2]in [6]Christ Jesus ye who °some-
times were far off °are made nigh °by °the
blood of [5]Christ.
14 For He is our °peace, Who °hath made
°both one, and °hath broken down the °middle
wall of °partition °*between us;*
15 Having °abolished [2]in °His flesh the °en-
mity, *even* °the law of commandments *contained* [2]in °ordinances; °for to make [2]in Himself of °twain °one new °man, *so* making
[14]peace;
16 And that He might °reconcile both °unto
[4]God [2]in one body °by °the cross, having slain
°the enmity °thereby:
17 And °came °and °preached [14]peace to you
which were afar off, °and to them that were
nigh.
18 For [8]through Him we both have °access
[13]by one °Spirit °unto the °Father.
19 °Now therefore ye are °no more [12]strangers
and °foreigners, but °fellowcitizens with the
saints, and of the °household of [4]God;
20 °And are built °upon °the °foundation of
the °apostles and prophets, °Jesus Christ Himself being °the °chief corner *stone;*
21 [2]In Whom °all the °building °fitly framed
together °groweth °unto an holy °Temple [2]in
°the Lord:
22 [2]In Whom ye also are °builded together
°for an °habitation of [4]God [7]through the °Spirit.

C M °**3** °For this cause I Paul, the prisoner of
°Jesus Christ °for you °Gentiles,

hath before ordained = afore prepared. Gr. *proetoimazō.* See Rom. 9. 23, the only other occ.
that = in order that. Gr. *hina.*
11 Uncircumcision. See Rom. 2. 25.
by. Ap. 104. xviii. 1. **the.** Omit.
made by hands. Gr. *cheiropoiētos.* In the Epp. only here and Heb. 9. 11, 24. Made Jews by *rite.* Cp. Rom. 2. 28, 29.
12 without = apart from.
being aliens = having been estranged from. Gr. *apallotrioō.* Only here; 4. 18. Col. 1. 21.
commonwealth = polity. Gr. *politeia.* Only here and Acts 22. 28.
Israel. In the Prison Epp. only here and Phil. 3. 5.
strangers. Gr. *xenos.* See Acts 17. 21.
promise = the promise
no. Ap. 105. II.
without God. Gr. *atheos.* Only here.
13 now. Emph.
sometimes = once. **are** = were.
by. Gr. *en.* Ap. 104. viii.
the blood. I. e. His death, not His life. Cp. 1. 7 Rom. 5. 9. Phil. 2. 8. Col. 1. 14, 20.
14 peace. Peace itself, objectively, and its Author (1 Thess. 5. 23. 2 Thess. 3. 16), to us and in us. Cp. Isa. 9. 6; 52. 7; 53. 5; 57. 19. Mic. 5. 5. Hag. 2. 9. Zech. 9. 10. Luke 2. 14. John 14. 27; 20. 19, 21, 26.
hath = having. **both.** Jews and Gentiles.
hath broken down = having destroyed. See 1 John 3. 8.
middle wall. Gr. *mesotoichon.* Only here. The type is seen in the stone palisade, about three cubits high, which separated the Court of the Gentiles from that of the Jews, to pass which was death to any Gentile. A notice, of which Josephus speaks, was found in 1871.
partition = the partition. Only here; Matt. 21. 33. Mark 12. 1. Luke 14. 23 (hedge).
between us. Omit.
15 abolished = done away with. Gr. *katargeō.* See Rom. 3. 3. **His flesh.** I. e. His death.
enmity. See Rom. 8. 7.
the law . . . in ordinances = the law of the dogmatic commandments. Cp. Rom. 8. 4.
ordinances. Gr. *dogma.* See Col. 2. 14.
for to make = in order that (Gr. *hina*) He might create (as *v.* 10).
twain = the two, Jew and Gentile.
one new man = into (Gr. *eis*) one new (Gr. *kainos.* See Matt. 9. 17) man.

man. Ap. 123. 1. **16 reconcile** = bring together again. Gr. *apokatallassō.* Only here and Col. 1. 20, 21. The intensive form, *katallassō* with prefix *apo* (Ap. 104. iv), implies reinstatement. Here it refers to the bringing together again of the two, so that "in one body" they may be united to God, *in Christ.* See Ap. 196. **unto** = to. **by.** Ap. 104. v. 1. **the cross.** Cp. 1 Cor. 1. 17. Gal. 6. 12, 14. **the enmity.** I. e. of the law of dogmatic commandments (*v.* 15) which was against us (see Col. 2. 14), and which we could not keep. **thereby** = by (Gr. *en*) it, i. e. the cross. **17 came** = having come (Aor.). **and preached peace** = He preached the good news (Ap. 121. 4) peace. **and.** The texts add "peace". **18 access** = the access. Gr. *prosagōgē.* Occ. 3. 12. See Rom. 5. 2. **Spirit.** Ap. 101. II. 3. **unto.** Gr. *pros.* Ap. 104. xv. 3. **Father.** Ap. 98. III. **19 Now therefore** = So then. **no more** = no longer. Gr. *ouketi.* **foreigners** = sojourners. Gr. *paroikos.* See Acts 7. 6. **fellowcitizens.** Gr. *sumpolitēs.* Only here. Whose seat of government (*politeuma*) is in heaven. See Phil. 3. 20. **household.** Lit. the domestics. Gr. *oikeios.* Only here; Gal. 6. 10. 1 Tim. 5. 8. **20 And are** = Having been. Cp. Acts 20. 32. **upon.** Ap. 104. ix. 2. **the foundation . . . prophets.** The foundation *laid* by the apostles and prophets (cp. Heb. 2. 3, 4; 6. 1, 2), or (2) the foundation of the apostles and prophets themselves, laid by God. **foundation.** Gr. *themelios.* See Ap. 146. **apostles and prophets.** Ap. 189. **Jesus Christ.** The texts read "Christ Jesus". Ap. 98. XII. **the.** Omit. **chief corner** *stone* = foundation corner-stone. Gr. *akrogōniaios.* Only here and 1 Pet. 2. 6. See Sept. of Isa. 28. 16. Christ is both foundation corner-stone, and head of the corner. Cp. Ps. 118. 22. See Acts 4. 11. **21 all the building** = Every building (Gr. *oikodomē*). The texts omit "the". Cp. 1 Cor. 3. 9. **fitly framed together** = harmoniously fitted together. Gr. *sunarmologeō.* Only here and 4. 16. **groweth** = is growing, increasing. **unto.** Ap. 104. vi. **Temple** = Sanctuary. Gr. *naos.* See Matt. 23. 16. **the Lord.** Ap. 98. VI. i. *β.* 2 B. **22 builded together** = being built in together. Gr. *sunoikodomeō.* Only here. **for.** Ap. 104. vi. **habitation.** Gr. *katoikētērion.* Only here and Rev. 18 2. **Spirit.** Ap. 101. II. 3.

3. 1-13 [For Structure see next page].

3. This chapter is parenthetical, and within it is another parenthesis, *vv.* 2-13. Both must be carefully noted. **1 For this cause** = On this account. **Jesus Christ** = Christ Jesus. Ap. 98. XII. **for.** Ap. 104. xvii. 1. **Gentiles.** Cp. Acts 22. 21; 26. 23.

N p 2 °If ye °have heard of the °dispensation of
°the °grace of °God which °is given me °to
you-ward:
3 How that °by °revelation °He made known
°unto me the °mystery; (°as I °wrote afore °in
°few words,
4 °Whereby, when ye read, ye °may understand my °knowledge [3]in °the mystery of
°Christ)

q 5 Which °in °other ages was °not made known
°unto the °sons of °men,

r as it °is °now °revealed °unto His °holy
°apostles and prophets °by °the Spirit;
6 °That the Gentiles should be °fellowheirs,
and °of the same body, and °partakers of °His
promise [3]in °Christ °by the °gospel:

N p 7 °Whereof I was made °a minister, °accord-
ing to the °gift of the [2]grace of [2]God given
°unto me °by the °effectual working of His
°power.
8 °Unto me, °who am less than the least of all
°saints, °is this [2]grace given, that I should
°preach °among the Gentiles the °unsearchable
°riches of [4]Christ;
9 °And to °make all *men* see what *is* the
°fellowship of the [3]mystery,

q which °from the beginning of the world hath
been °hid [3]in [2]God, Who °created all things
°by Jesus Christ:

r 10 °To the intent that now °unto the °princi-
palities and °powers [3]in °heavenly *places*
°might be known [6]by the °church the °mani-
fold °wisdom of [2]God,
11 [7]According to the °eternal purpose °which
He °purposed [3]in °Christ Jesus our °Lord:
12 [3]In Whom we have boldness and °access
°with °confidence [6]by the °faith of Him.

M 13 Wherefore I °desire that ye °faint °not °at
my tribulations [1]for you, which is your glory.

3. 1-13 (*C*, p. 1760). **THE PURPOSE OF GOD IN CHRIST.** (*Introversion and Extended Alternation.*)

- *C* | M | 1. Paul. Imprisonment for their sake.
  - N | p | 2-4. The SECRET revealed and committed to Paul's stewardship (*oikonomia*).
    - q | 5-. The SECRET hidden before.
    - r | -5, 6. The SECRET now revealed to the church through the apostles and prophets by the Spirit.
  - *N* | *p* | 7-9-. The SECRET made known by Paul according to the stewardship (*oikonomia*) committed to him.
    - *q* | -9. The SECRET hidden before.
    - *r* | 10-12. The SECRET made known through the church to heavenly beings by God.
- *M* | 13. Paul. Tribulations for their sake.

2 If=If indeed. Gr. *eige*. See Ap. 118. 2. a.
have. Omit.
dispensation=stewardship. Gr. *oikonomia.* See 1. 10.
the=that.
grace. Ap. 184. I. 1.
God. Ap. 98. I. i. 1.
is=was.
to . . . -ward. Gr. *eis.* Ap. 104. vi. The grace of God which concerned them and us. Not the grace of God as to "the kingdom", or "the heavenly calling" (see Ap. 193), but the gospel of God's grace as to the church which is the body of Christ.
3 by. Ap. 104. x. 2.
revelation. Ap. 106. II. 1.
He. All the texts read "was".
unto=to.
mystery. See 5. 32. 1 Tim. 3. 16. Ap. 193.
as=even as.
wrote afore. See Rom. 15. 4.
in (Ap. 104. viii) **few words**=briefly. See Rom. 16. 25, 26.
4 whereby=according to (Ap. 104. xv. 3) which.
may=can.
knowledge. Ap. 132. II. iii.
the mystery. I. e. the great secret (5. 32). See Ap. 193.
Christ. Ap. 98. IX.
5 in other ages=to (no prep., Dat. case) other generations.
not. Ap. 105. I.
unto, unto=to, to. **sons.** Ap. 108. iii. **men.** Ap. 123. 1. **is**=was. **now.** Emph. This present time. **revealed.** Gr. *apokaluptō.* Ap. 106. I. ix. **holy apostles and prophets.** See 2. 20, and cp. "prophetic writings" (Rom. 16. 26). Ap. 189. **by.** Gr. *en.* Ap. 104. viii. **the Spirit.** Ap. 101. II. 3. **6 That, &c.** The subject of the revelation. **fellowheirs**=joint-heirs. Gr. *sunklēronomos.* See Rom. 8. 17. Occ. elsewhere, Heb. 11. 9. 1 Pet. 3. 7. **of the same body**=members-of-a-joint-body. Gr. *sussōmos.* Only here. Not joined on to an existing Jewish body, but a new body "of the twain". **partakers**=joint-partakers. Gr. *summetochos.* Only here and 5. 7. **His**=the, as all the texts. **Christ.** The texts read Christ Jesus. See 1. 1. **by.** Ap. 104. v. 1. **gospel.** See Ap. 140. **7 Whereof**=of which. **a minister**=minister (Ap. 190. I. 1). I. e. of the good news concerning the "secret". **according to.** Ap. 104. x. 2. **gift.** Gr. *dōrea.* **unto**=to. **by.** Same as "according to", above. **effectual working**=working. Ap. 172. 4. **power.** Ap. 172. 1; 176. 1. **8 Unto**=To. **who . . . least**=to the less than the least. Gr. *elachistoteros.* Only here. That is what Paul *was.* What he became, see 1 Cor. 15. 10 (laboured more abundantly, &c.). **saints.** In *v.* 5, "holy". See Acts 9. 13. **is**=was. **preach.** Ap. 121. 4. **among**=to. **unsearchable**=untraceable. Only here and Rom. 11. 33, which see. **riches.** See 1. 7. **9 And . . . God**=And to enlighten all as to what is the stewardship (committed to me) of the mystery (Ap. 193) that hath been hidden from the ages in God. **make . . . see**=enlighten. See 1. 18. **fellowship.** The texts read *oikonomia* (*v.* 2), instead of *koinōnia.* **from . . . world**=from the ages. Ap. 151. II. A. ii. 2. **hid.** Gr. *apokruptō.* See 1 Cor. 2. 7. **created.** See 2. 10. **by Jesus Christ.** The texts omit. **10 To the intent that**=In order that. Gr. *hina.* **unto**=to. **principalities**=rulers. Gr. *archē.* Ap. 172. 6. **powers**=authorities. Gr. *exousia.* Ap. 172. 5. See 1. 21. **heavenly** *places*=the heavenlies. See 1. 3. **might be known**=may be made known. **church.** Ap. 186. **manifold.** Gr. *polupoikilos.* Only here. Implies "infinitely diversified". **wisdom.** See 1. 8. **11 eternal purpose**=purpose (Gr. *prothesis.* See 1. 11) of the ages (Ap. 151. II. A. 4). **which.** I. e. which (purpose). **purposed**=made. Gr. *poieō.* **Christ Jesus our Lord.** Ap. 98. XII, and VI. i. β. 2. A. **12 access.** See 2. 18. **with.** Gr. *en.* Ap. 104. viii. **confidence**=confident assurance. See 2 Cor. 1. 15. **faith.** Ap. 150. II. 1. **13 desire**=beg. Ap. 134. I. 4. **faint not**=not (Gr. *mē*) to be cast down. **at.** Gr. *en.* Ap. 104. viii. The parenthesis ending with *v.* 13, the teaching is continued from *v.* 1, "For this cause", &c.

D °14 For this cause I bow my knees °unto the
°Father °of our Lord Jesus Christ,
15 °Of Whom °the whole °family [3]in °heaven
and °earth is °named,
16 °That He °would grant °you, [7]according
to the [8]riches of His glory, °to be strengthened
with °might [6]by His °Spirit °in the °inner °man;
17 That °Christ may °dwell [3]in your hearts
[6]by [12]faith; [16]that ye, being °rooted and
°grounded [3]in °love,
18 May be °able to comprehend °with all
°saints °what *is* the breadth, and length, and
depth, and height;
19 °And to °know the [17]love of [4]Christ, which
passeth °knowledge, [16]that ye °might be
°filled °with all the °fulness of [2]God.

C 20 Now [3]unto Him °That is able to do °exceed-
ing abundantly °above °all that we ask or
think, [7]according to the °power that °worketh
[3]in us,
21 °Unto Him *be* °glory [3]in the [10]church °by
[11]Christ Jesus °throughout all ages, world without end. Amen.

B O s **4** °I therefore, the °prisoner °of the °Lord,
°beseech you that ye walk worthy of
the °vocation wherewith ye °are called,
2 °With all °lowliness and °meekness, °with
long-suffering, °forbearing one another °in
°love;
3 °Endeavouring to keep the °unity of the
°Spirit [2]in the °bond of °peace.

t 4 °*There is* one °body, and one °Spirit, even
as ye °are called [2]in one hope of your calling;
5 One °Lord, one °faith, one °baptism,
6 One °God and °Father of all, Who *is* °above
all, and °through all, and [2]in °you °all.

t 7 But °unto °every one of us °is given °grace
°according to the °measure of the °gift of
°Christ.

14 This verse going back to the subject of *v.* 1 is Fig. *Anachorēsis*. Ap. 6.
unto. Ap. 104. xv. 3. **Father.** Ap. 98. III.
of . . . Christ. The texts omit.
15 Of. Gr. *ek*. Ap. 104. vii.
the whole family=every (Gr. *pasa*) family. No article.
family. Gr. *patria*. Only here; Luke 2. 4. Acts 3. 25. See Longer Note, p. 1771.
heaven=the heavens. See Matt. 6. 9, 10.
earth=upon (Gr. *epi*) earth (Gr. *gē*. Ap. 129. 4). See 1. 10.
named. See 1. 21.
16 That=In order that. Gr. *hina*.
would grant=may give. **you**=to you.
to be strengthened. See 1 Cor. 16. 13.
might. Ap. 172. 1.
Spirit. Ap. 101. II. 3.
in. Gr. *eis*. Ap. 104. vi.
inner. See Rom. 7. 22. **man.** Ap. 123. 1.
17 Christ, &c. See Rom. 8. 9.
dwell. See Acts 2. 5.
rooted. Gr. *rhizoomai*. Only here and Col. 2. 7.
grounded=founded. Gr. *themelioō*. See Ap. 146 and Matt. 7. 25.
love. See 2. 4. Ap. 135. II. 1.
18 able=fully able. Gr. *exischuō*. Only here. Cp. Ap. 172. 3.
with. Ap. 104. xvi.
saints=the saints. See *v.* 8.
what . . . height. Omit "is". After "height" read "of love is", i.e. God's love in Christ. In breadth, *boundless*: in length, *endless*: in depth, *fathomless*, *exhaustless*: in height, *measureless*.
19 And=Even.
know. Ap. 132. I. ii.
knowledge. Ap. 132. II. i. **might**=may.
filled. See 1. 23. Ap. 125. 7.
with. Gr. *eis*. Ap. 104. vi.
fulness. Gr. *plērōma*. See 1. 23.
20 That=Who.
exceeding abundantly. Lit. beyond (Gr. *huper*) of (Gr. *ek*) abundance=infinitely.
above. Gr. *huper*. Ap. 104. xvii. 2.
all=all things.
power. Same as "might" *v.* 16.
worketh. See 1. 11.
21 Unto=To.
glory=the glory. See p. 1511. **by.** Gr. *en*. **throughout . . . end.** Ap. 151. II. A. ii. 10.

4. 1–6. 20 (*B*, p. 1759). DOCTRINAL. THEIR WALK. (*Alternation.*)

B | O | 4. 1-16. Among themselves; as worthy of their calling, being members of the one Body. Ecclesiastical.
  P | 4. 17—5. 21. Among others. Spiritual.
O | 5. 22—6. 9. Among themselves. Domestic.
  P | 6. 10-20. Among others. Spiritual.

4. 1-16 (O, above). THEIR WALK: AMONG THEMSELVES. ECCLESIASTICAL. (*Introversion.*)

O | s | 1-3. Exhortation.
  t | 4-6. Unity of the Body.
  t | 7-13. Gifts to the Body.
s | 14-16. Exhortation.

4. 1 I therefore. Resuming his teaching after the parenthesis of 3. 1-21. **prisoner.** See 3. 1. **of.** Gr. *en*. **Lord.** Ap. 98. VI. i. *β*. 2. B. **beseech.** Gr. *parakaleō*. Ap. 134. 6. Cp. 1 Thess. 4. 1. 1 Tim. 2. 1; &c. **vocation**=calling, as 1. 18. **are**=were. **2 With.** Ap. 104. xi. 1. **lowliness**=humility of mind. See Acts 20. 19. **meekness.** See 1 Cor. 4. 21. **forbearing**=bearing with. See 2 Cor. 11. 1. **in.** Ap. 104. viii. **love.** Ap. 135. II. 1. **3 Endeavouring.** Cp. 2 Tim. 2. 15 (studying). **unity.** Lit. oneness. Gr. *henotēs*. Only here and *v.* 13. **Spirit.** Ap. 101. II. 3. **bond.** See Acts 8. 23. **peace**=the peace. **4** *There is*. Supply the Ellipsis by "*Ye are*". **body.** See 2. 15, 16. **Spirit.** Ap. 101. II. 5. **are called**=were called also. **5 Lord.** Ap. 98. VI. i. *β*. 2. B. **faith.** I. e. doctrine; by Metonymy, Ap. 6. See Ap. 150. II. 1. **baptism.** Gr. *baptisma*. Ap. 115. II. i. 1. The baptism of the Spirit by Whom we are baptized into the one body. (See *How to Enjoy the Bible*, by the late Dr. E. W. Bullinger, p. 128.) **6 God.** Ap. 98. I. i. 1. **Father.** Ap. 98. III. Note the seven occ. of "one"; body, Spirit, hope, Lord, faith, baptism, God and Father; three on either side of the Lord Jesus Christ. **above.** Ap. 104. ix. 1. **through.** Ap. 104. v. 1. **you.** The texts omit. **all.** The indwelling of God in the members of the body by *pneuma theou*. See Rom. 8. 9. **7 unto**=to. **every**=each. **is**=was. **grace**=the grace. Ap. 184. I. 1. **according to.** Ap. 104. x. 2. **measure.** Gr. *metron*. See Rom. 12. 3. **gift.** Gr. *dōrea*. See 3. 7. **Christ.** Ap. 98. IX.

8 Wherefore He saith, °"**When He ascended °up °on °high, He °led °captivity captive, and °gave °gifts °unto °men.**"
9 (°Now that He ascended, °what is it °but that He °also descended first °into the °lower parts of the °earth?
10 He That descended is the same °also That ascended [8]up °far above all °heavens, °that He might °fill all things.)
11 And He gave °some, °apostles; and some, °prophets; and some, evangelists; and some, °pastors and °teachers;
12 °For the °perfecting of the °saints, °for the work of the °ministry, °for the °edifying of °the body of [7]Christ:
13 Till we all °come °in the [3]unity of the [5]faith, °and of the °knowledge of the °Son of God, °unto a °perfect °man, °unto the [7]measure of the °stature of the °fulness of [7]Christ:

s 14 [10]That we *henceforth* °be °no more °children, °tossed to and fro, and °carried about with every °wind of °doctrine, °by the °sleight of [8]men, °*and* cunning craftiness, °whereby they lie in wait to deceive;
15 But °speaking the truth [2]in [2]love, °may grow up [9]into Him in all things, °Which is the °Head, *even* [7]Christ:
16 °From Whom the whole body °fitly joined together and °compacted °by that which every °joint °supplieth, [7]according to °the °effectual working [2]in the measure of °every part, maketh °increase of the body [13]unto the [12]edifying of itself [2]in [2]love.

P Q 17 This I say therefore, and °testify [2]in the [1]Lord, that ye °henceforth walk not as °other °Gentiles walk, [2]in the °vanity of their °mind,
18 °Having °the understanding darkened, °being °alienated from °the °life of [6]God °through the °ignorance that is [2]in them, °because of the °blindness of their heart:

8 When, &c. From Ps. 68. 18. See Ap. 107. I. 1.
up. Omit.
on. Ap. 104. vi.
high. See Luke 1. 78. Rendered "height" in 3. 18. Rev. 21. 16.
led . . . captive. Gr. *aichmalōteuō.* Only here and 2 Tim. 3. 6. In Luke 21. 24. Rom. 7. 23. 2 Cor. 10. 5, the word is *aichmalōtizō.*
captivity=a body of captives. See Matt. 27. 52. Rom. 1. 4.
gave. Having *received* according to Ps. 68. 18, He *gave.*
gifts. Gr. *doma.* Here; Matt. 7. 11. Luke 11. 13. Phil. 4. 17.
unto=to.
men. Ap. 123. 1.
9 (Now . . . ascended=(Now this fact), He ascended.
what is it=what does it imply.
but=except. Gr. *ei* (Ap. 118. 2) *mē* (Ap. 105. II).
also descended=descended also.
into. Gr. *eis.* Ap. 104. vi.
lower parts. I. e. Hades. Ap. 131. II.
earth. Ap. 129. 4.
10 also That ascended=That ascended also.
far above. Gr. *huperanō.* See 1. 21.
heavens=the heavens. Matt. 6. 9, 10.
that=in order that. Gr. *hina.*
fill. See 1. 23.
11 some. Add "indeed" (Gr. *men*).
apostles, prophets. Ap. 189.
pastors=(as) shepherds. So every other occ. (seventeen in all).
teachers. Gr. *didaskalos.*
12 For. Ap. 104. xv. 3.
perfecting. Gr. *katartismos.* Only here. For the verb, see Ap. 125. 8. Cp. Rom. 9. 22.
saints. See Acts 9. 13.
for. Ap. 104. vi.
ministry. Ap. 190. II. 1. **edifying.** As in 2. 21.
the body of Christ. See 1. 23.
13 come=attain. Gr. *katantaō.* Cp. Phil. 3. 11.
in. Ap. 104. vi.
and=even.
knowledge=full, or perfect, knowledge. Ap. 132. II. ii.
Son of God. See 2 Cor. 1. 19. Ap. 98. XV.
unto, unto. Ap. 104. vi.

perfect=complete, full grown. Ap. 123. 6; 125. 1. **man.** Ap. 123. 2. **stature.** See Matt. 6. 27. **fulness.** Gr. *plērōma.* Cp. 3. 19; 1. 23. **14 be**=may be. **no more**=no longer. Gr. *mēketi.* **children.** Ap. 108. vii. **tossed to and fro.** Lit. "surging about (as waves)". Only here. **carried about**=borne hither and thither. See 2 Cor. 4. 10. **wind.** Gr. *anemos.* **doctrine**=the teaching. Gr. *didaskalia.* The evil teaching of the ruler of the power of the air and of demons. Cp. 1 Tim. 4. 1. **by**=(or) by. Gr. *en.* Ap. 104. viii. **sleight.** Gr. *kubeia*; hence our "cube". Only here. ***and* cunning craftiness**=with (Gr. *en*) subtilty. Gr. *panourgia.* Cp. 2 Cor. 11. 3. **whereby . . . deceive**=with a view to (Gr. *pros.* Ap. 104. xv. 3) the wile, or stratagem (Gr. *methodeia*: only here and 6. 11), of the error (Gr. *planē*). The association of *methodeia* with Satan (in 6. 11) shows that, here, *planē*=*planos*; i. e. the method or scheme is that of the devil himself, and not merely error. **15 speaking the truth.** Lit. truthing it. Gr. *alētheuō.* Only here and Gal. 4. 16. See Ap. 175. 1, 2. **may grow up.** See 2. 21. **Which**=Who. **Head.** See 1. 22. **16 From.** Ap. 104. vii. **fitly joined together**=being perfectly fitted together. Only here and 2. 21. **compacted**=knit together. Gr. *sumbibazō.* See Acts 9. 22. Occ. Col. 2. 2. **by.** Ap. 104. v. 1. **joint**=ligament. Gr. *haphē*; only here and Col. 2. 19. Here the ligament is "the *bond* of peace" (*v.* 3). **supplieth**=of the supply, i. e. from the Head. Gr. *epichorēgia*; only here and Phil. 1. 19. Gen. of relation. Ap. 17. 5. **the**=an. **effectual working.** Gr. *energeia.* See 1. 19. **every**=each several. **increase.** Gr. *auxēsis.* Only here and Col. 2. 19.

4. 17—5. 21 (P, p. 1765). SPIRITUAL WALK AMONG OTHERS. (*Division.*)

P | Q | 4. 17-19. The others.
  | R | 4. 20-32. Themselves. Negative and positive.
  | *R* | 5. 1-4. Themselves. Positive and negative.
  | *Q* | 5. 5-21. The others.

17 testify. Gr. *marturomai.* See Acts 20. 26. **henceforth . . . not**=no longer. Gr. *mēketi.* **other.** Omit. **Gentiles**=the Gentiles. They *were* Gentiles, but now are members of the church His body. Cp. 1 Cor. 10. 32. **vanity.** See Rom. 8. 20. **mind.** Cp. Rom. 1. 21. **18 Having . . . darkened**=Having been darkened. Gr. *skotizō.* See Rom. 1. 21. 2 Cor. 4. 4. **the understanding**=in the understanding. See 1. 18. **being**=having been. **alienated.** Gr. *apallotrioomai.* See 2. 12. **the life of God.** Only occurrence. **life.** Gr. *zoē.* Only here in Eph. Ap. 170. 1. **through.** Ap. 104. v. 2. **ignorance.** See Acts 3. 17. **because of.** Ap. 104. v. 2. **blindness**=hardness. Gr. *pōrōsis.* Cp. Rom. 11. 25.

19 Who being °past feeling °have given themselves over °unto °lasciviousness, °to °work
all °uncleanness °with °greediness.
R 20 But ye °have °not so learned [7] Christ;
21 °If so be that ye °have heard Him, and
°have been taught [14] by Him, °as °the °truth is
[2] in °Jesus:
22 That ye °put off °concerning the °former
°conversation °the old °man, which is °corrupt
[7] according to °the deceitful lusts;
23 And be °renewed in the °spirit of your
mind;
24 And that ye °put on °the new man, °which
°after [6] God °is °created [2] in °righteousness and
°true °holiness.
25 Wherefore °putting away °lying, °**speak
every man truth [2] with his neighbour**: °for we
are °members one of another.
26 Be ye °angry, °and °sin °not: let °not the
sun °go down °upon your °wrath:
27 °Neither give °place to the °devil.
28 Let him that stole steal [14] no more: but
rather let him °labour, working with *his* hands
°the thing which is good, [10] that he may have
to °give to him that needeth.
29 Let °no °corrupt °communication proceed
°out of your mouth, but that which is good °to
°the use of [12] edifying, [10] that it may °minister
[7] grace °unto the hearers.
30 And °grieve [26] not °the holy Spirit of [6] God,
°whereby ye °are °sealed [13] unto °the day of
°redemption.
31 Let all °bitterness, °and °wrath, °and
°anger, °and °clamour, °and °evil speaking, be
put away °from you, °with all °malice:
32 And be ye °kind one °to another, °tender-
hearted, °forgiving °one another, even as [6] God
°for Christ's sake °hath °forgiven you.

R 5 Be ye therefore °followers of °God, as
°dear °children;
2 And walk °in °love, as °Christ also °hath
loved °us, and °hath given Himself °for us an
offering and a sacrifice to [1] God °for a °sweet-
smelling °savour.

19 past feeling. Lit., hardened. Gr. *apalgeō*. Only here.
have given . . . over=gave up.
unto=to.
lasciviousness. See Mark 7. 22.
to work=unto (Gr. *eis*) the working.
work. Gr. *ergasia*, a word implying regular occupation, craft for gain. Cp. Acts 16. 16; 19. 24, 25.
uncleanness. Cp. Rom. 1. 24.
with. Gr. *en*. Ap. 104. viii.
greediness=covetousness. Gr. *pleonexia*. Always "covetousness", save here and 2 Pet. 2. 14.
20 have . . . learned=did . . . learn.
not. Ap. 105. I.
21 If so be. Ap. 118. 2. a.
have. Omit.
have been taught=were instructed.
as the truth is in Jesus. Frequently misquoted. No article. See John 14. 6. **the.** Omit.
as=even as.
Jesus. Ap. 98. X.
22 put off=put away. See Rom. 13. 12.
concerning. Ap. 104. x. 2.
former. Gr. *proteros*. Only here as adj.
conversation. Gr. *anastrophē*. Cp. Gal. 1. 13.
the old man. The old (Adam) nature. See Rom. 6. 6.
man. Ap. 123. 1.
corrupt=being corrupted. Gr. *phtheirō*. Cp. 1. Cor. 15. 33.
the deceitful lusts=the desires of the deceit (Gr. *apatē*). Here, the desires of the deceiver, as in *v.* 14 "the error" is used for the cause of it, the devil. Cp. Rev. 12. 9; 20. 3, 8, 10.
23 renewed. Gr. *ananeoō*. Only here. Occ. frequently in Apocrypha. Implies that the whole course of life now flows in a different direction. See 2 Cor. 4. 16; 5. 17.
spirit. Ap. 101. II. 7, 8, 9.
24 put on. Gr. *enduō*. See Rom. 13. 12, 14. Gal. 3. 27.
the new man. The new nature.
which=that which.
after. Ap. 104. x. 2. **is**=was (Aor.).
created. Gr. *ktizō*. See 2. 10.
righteousness . . . holiness=true holiness and righteousness. Contrast Adam, Gen. 1. 27.
righteousness. Ap. 191. 3.
true. Lit. of the truth. Gr. *alētheia*, as *v.* 21.
holiness. Gr. *hosiotēs*. Only here, and Luke 1. 75.
25 putting=having put. Gr. *apotithēmi*. As *v.* 22.
lying = the lie. Gr. *to pseudos*. Cp. John 8. 44. Rom. 1. 25. 2 Thess. 2. 11. **speak, &c.** From Zech. 8. 16. **for**=because. **members.** Cp. 5. 30. **26 angry.** Gr. *orgizō*, imperative. Positive command, the context showing that "righteous indignation" is referred to. **and**=yet. **sin not.** Lit. be not sinning. Cp. 1 John 2. 1. Gr. *hamartanō*. Ap. 128. I. i. The anger is to be transitory. The quotation is from Ps. 4. 4 (Sept.), where Heb. reads, "tremble, and sin not", the meaning of which is shown by the use here, for it is as easy to tremble from anger as from other powerful emotions. **not.** Ap. 105. II. **go down.** Gr. *epiduō*. Only here. **upon.** Ap. 104. ix. 2. **wrath.** Gr. *parorgismos*. Only here. The verb occ. 6. 4, and cp. Rom. 10. 19, the only other occ. **27 Neither.** Gr. *mēde*. **place**=opportunity. **devil.** The ruler of the darkness, cp. 6. 12; the deceiver of *vv.* 14, 22; the "lie" of *v.* 25. Now revealed as the devil. See Rev. 12. 9. **28 labour.** As Acts 20. 35. **the thing**=that. **give.** See Rom. 12. 8. **29 no.** Ap. 105. II. **corrupt.** Lit. putrid. **communication**=word. Ap. 121. 10. **out of.** Ap. 104. vii. **to.** Ap. 104. xv. 3. **the . . . edifying.** See R.V. marg. Some ancient texts, including the Vulgate, read "of the faith", instead of "to the use". **minister**=give. **grace.** Ap. 184. I. 1. **unto**=to. **30 grieve.** Gr. *lupeō*. Occ. frequently; cp. Rom. 14. 15. **the holy Spirit.** Ap. 101. II. 3. **whereby** =by (Gr. *en*) Whom. The Giver here is the Sealer. **are**=were. **sealed.** Cp. 1. 13, where the sealing is the gift. **the**=a. **redemption.** Final deliverance; *now* we have the earnest. See 1. 14. **31 bitterness.** Gr. *pikria*. See Rom. 3. 14. **and.** Fig. *Polysyndeton*. Ap. 6. **wrath.** Luke 4. 28. **anger.** Gr. *orgē*. **clamour**=uproar. See Acts 23. 9. **evil speaking**=railing. Gr. *blasphēmia*. See 1 Tim. 6. 4. **from.** Ap. 104. iv. **with.** Ap. 104. xvi. **malice.** As Rom. 1. 29. Ap. 128. II. 2. **32 kind**=gracious. Gr. *chrēstos*. Ap. 184. III. **to.** Ap. 104. vi. **tenderhearted**=tenderly compassionate. Gr. *eusplanchnos*. Only here and 1 Pet. 3. 8. **forgiving, forgiven.** Ap. 184. II. 1. **one another**=each other. **for Christ's sake**=also in (Gr. *en*) Christ (Ap. 98. IX). **hath forgiven**=forgave.
5. 1 followers=imitators. Gr. *mimētēs*. See 1 Cor. 4. 16. **God.** Ap. 98. I. i. 1. **dear**=beloved. Ap. 135. III. **children.** Ap. 108. i. **2 in.** Ap. 104. viii. **love.** Ap. 135. II. 1. **Christ.** Ap. 98. IX. **hath loved**=loved. Ap. 135. I. 1. **us.** The texts read "you". **hath given**=gave up. Cp. Rom. 4. 25. John 19. 30. **for.** Ap. 104. xvii. 1. **for.** Ap. 104. vi. **sweetsmelling savour**=an odour of a sweet smell. **sweetsmelling.** Gr. *euodia*. See 2 Cor. 2. 15. **savour.** Gr. *osmē*. Cp. John 12. 3.

3 But fornication, and all °uncleanness, or
covetousness, let it °not be once named °among
you, as becometh °saints;
4 °Neither °filthiness, nor °foolish talking,
°nor °jesting, which are °not °convenient: but
rather °giving of thanks.

Q 5 For this ye °know, that °no °whoremonger,
nor unclean person, nor °covetous man, °who
is an °idolater, hath any °inheritance [2]in the
°kingdom of [2]Christ and °of [1]God.
6 Let °no man °deceive you with °vain °words:
for °because of these things cometh °the wrath
of [1]God °upon the °children of °disobedience.
7 °Be °not ye therefore °partakers with
them.
8 For ye were °sometimes °darkness, but now
are ye °light [2]in the °Lord: walk as °children
of °light,
9 (For the fruit of the °Spirit *is* [2]in all °good-
ness and °righteousness and °truth;)
10 Proving what is °acceptable °unto the
°Lord:
11 And have °no °fellowship with the °unfruit-
ful works of °darkness, but rather °reprove
them.
12 For it is a °shame even to speak of those
things which are °done °of them °in secret.
13 But all things that are [11]reproved are
°made manifest °by the [8]light: for whatsoever
doth °make manifest is [8]light.
14 Wherefore He saith, °"**Awake thou that**
°**sleepest, and** °**arise** °**from the dead, and**
[2]**Christ** °**shall give thee light.**"
15 °See then that ye walk °circumspectly, [7]not
as °fools, but as °wise,
16 °Redeeming the °time, because the days
are °evil.
17 °Wherefore [7]be ye [7]not °unwise, but °un-
derstanding what the °will of the [10]Lord
is.
18 And °be [7]not drunk with wine, °wherein
is °excess; but be °filled °with the °Spirit;
19 Speaking to yourselves °in °psalms and
°hymns and °spiritual °songs, singing and
°making melody °in your heart to the
[10]Lord;
20 °Giving thanks °always [2]for all things
[10]unto [1]God °and the °Father [2]in °the name of
our °Lord Jesus Christ;
21 °Submitting yourselves one to another [2]in
the fear of °God.

3 uncleanness. As in Rom. 1. 24.
not . . . once = not even. Gr. *mēde.*
among. Ap. 104. viii. 2.
saints. See Acts 9. 13.
4 Neither = Nor.
filthiness. Gr. *aischrotēs.* Only here.
foolish talking. Gr. *mōrologia.* Only here.
nor = or.
jesting = ribaldry. Occ. only here.
not. Ap. 105 I.
convenient = befitting. Gr. *anēkō.* Only here; Col. 3. 18. Philemon 8.
giving of thanks. Gr. *eucharistia.* The verb in *v.* 20.
5 know. Ap. 132. I. ii.
no. Ap. 105. I.
whoremonger = fornicator.
covetous = avaricious. Gr. *pleonektēs.* See 1 Cor. 5. 10, 11; 6. 10.
who = which.
idolater. Cp. 1 Cor. 5. 10.
inheritance. As in 1. 14.
kingdom of Christ = kingdom of the Messiah. Ap. 114. I.
of God. See Ap. 114. II.
6 no man. Gr. *mēdeis.*
deceive. Gr. *apataō.* Occ. only here; 1 Tim. 2. 14. Jas. 1. 26.
vain = hollow. See Col. 2. 8. First occ. Mark 12. 3 (empty).
words. Ap. 121. 10.
because of. Ap. 104. v. 2.
the wrath of God. See Rom. 1. 18.
upon. Ap. 104. ix. 3.
children = sons. Ap. 108. iii.
disobedience = the disobedience. See 2. 2.
7 Be = Become.
not. Ap. 105. II.
partakers = partners. See 3. 6.
8 sometimes = once.
darkness. The darkness of blindness. Cp. 4. 18.
light. Not *in* the light, but having received the Light, *are* light. Ap. 130. 1.
Lord. Ap. 98. VI. i. *β*. 2. B.
children. Ap. 108. i.
9 Spirit. Ap. 101. II. 3, but the texts read "light".
goodness. Cp. Rom. 15. 14.
righteousness. Ap. 191. 3.
truth. See 4. 21.
10 acceptable. As in Rom. 12. 1.
unto = to.
Lord. Ap. 98. VI. i. *β*. 2. A.
11 no. Ap. 105. II.
have . . . fellowship = have partnership. Gr. *sunkoinōneō.* Only here; Phil. 4. 14. Rev. 18. 4.
unfruitful works. Cp. dead works, Heb. 6. 1; wicked works, Col. 1. 21; all works of the darkness, Rom. 13. 12. Consequently, the works of the devil, 1 John 3. 8. Cp. John 8. 44, and contrast 2. 10.
darkness = the darkness. **reprove** = convict. See Luke 3. 19. **12 shame.** See 1 Cor. 11. 6. **done** = being done. **of.** Ap. 104. xviii. 1. **in secret.** Gr. *kruphē.* Only here. **13 made manifest.** Gr. *phaneroō.* Ap. 106. I. v. **by.** Ap. 104. xviii. 1. **14 Awake.** Ap. 178. I. 4. **sleepest** = art sleeping. Gr. *katheudō.* Ap. 171. 1. **arise.** Ap. 178. I. 1. **from the dead.** Ap. 139. 4. **shall . . . light** = will shine upon thee. Gr. *epiphauō*; occ. only here. A paraphrase of Isa. 60. 1, 2. Ap. 107. I. 2. **15 See.** Ap. 133. I. 5. **circumspectly.** Ap. 125. 4. **fools** = unwise. Gr. *asophos*; only here. **wise.** Gr. *sophos.* First occ. Matt. 11. 25. **16 Redeeming.** Gr. *exagorazō*; lit. to buy out. See Gal. 3. 13. **time.** Gr. *kairos.* Cp. Ap. 195. Here, the opportunity. **evil.** Gr. *ponēros.* Cp. 6. 13. Ap. 128. III. 1. **17 Wherefore** = On account of (Ap. 104 v. 2) this. **unwise.** See Luke 11. 40. **understanding.** The texts read "understand ye". Cp. Rom. 3. 11. **will.** Ap. 102. 2. **18 be . . . drunk.** Gr. *methuskomai.* Only here; Luke 12. 45. 1 Thess. 5. 7. **wherein** = by (Gr. *en*) which. **excess** = debauchery. Gr. *asōtia.* Only here; Tit. 1. 6. 1 Peter 4. 4. The adverb only in Luke 15. 13. **filled.** See 3. 19. **with** = by (Gr. *en*). **Spirit.** See Ap. 101. II. 3, and Note at end of Ap. **19 in** = with. No prep. **psalms.** Gr. *psalmos.* See 1 Cor. 14. 26. **hymns.** Gr. *humnos*; only here and Col. 3. 16. **spiritual songs.** As sung by spiritual persons. **spiritual.** Gr. *pneumatikos.* See 1 Cor. 12. 1. **songs.** Gr. *ōdē*, a song of thanksgiving. Here; Col. 3. 16. Rev. 5. 9; 14. 3, 3; 15. 3, 3. **making melody.** Gr. *psallō.* See Rom. 15. 9. **in** = with. No prep. **20 Giving thanks.** See *v.* 4; 1. 16. **always.** Ap. 151. II. G. i **and** = even. **Father.** Ap. 98. III. **the name.** See Acts 2. 38. **Lord Jesus Christ.** See 1. 17 and Ap. 98. XI. **21 Submitting.** Same as "subject", *v.* 24. **God.** The texts read "Christ".

O u1 22 Wives, submit yourselves [10]unto your own
°husbands, as [10]unto the Lord.
23 For °the [22]husband is the head of the wife,
°even as [2]Christ is the Head of the °church:
°and He is °the Saviour of °the body.
24 °Therefore as the [23]church is °subject
[10]unto [2]Christ, so *let* the wives *be* to their own
[22]husbands [2]in every thing.
v1 25 [22]Husbands, °love your wives, even as
[2]Christ also °loved the [23]church, and °gave
Himself [2]for °it;
26 °That He might °sanctify °and cleanse it
°with the washing of water °by °the word,
27 [26]That He might °present °it to Himself
a °glorious [23]church, [7]not having °spot, or
°wrinkle, or any such thing; but [26]that it
°should be holy and °without blemish.
28 So ought °men to [25]love their °wives as
their own bodies. He that [25]loveth his °wife
[25]loveth himself.
29 For °no man ever °yet hated his own flesh;
but °nourisheth and °cherisheth it, even as
°the Lord the [23]church:
30 For we are °members °of His body, °of
His flesh, and of His bones.
31 °**For this °cause shall a °man leave his
father and mother, and °shall be °joined °unto
his wife, and °they two °shall be °one flesh.**
32 This is °a great °mystery: but I speak
°concerning [2]Christ °and the [23]church.
33 Nevertheless let °every one of you °in particular so [25]love his wife even as himself; and
the wife *see* [26]that she °reverence *her* [22]husband.

u2 **6** °Children, obey your parents °in the
°Lord: for this is °right.
2 °**Honour thy father and mother;** (which is
the first commandment °with promise),
3 °**That it may be well with thee, and thou
mayest live long °on the °earth.**
v2 4 And, °*ye* fathers, °provoke °not your
[1]children to wrath: but °bring them up °in the
°nurture and °admonition of the [1]Lord.
u3 5 °Servants, be obedient to them that are *your*
°masters °according to the flesh, °with °fear
and trembling, [1]in °singleness of your heart,
as °unto °Christ;
6 [4]Not °with °eyeservice, as °menpleasers;
but as °the [5]servants of [5]Christ, doing the °will
of °God °from the °heart;

5. 22—6. 9 (*O*, p. 1765). WALK AMONG THEMSELVES. DOMESTIC. (*Division.*)

O u1 | 5. 22-24. Wives.
 v1 | 5. 25-33. Husbands.
 u2 | 6. 1-3. Children.
 v2 | 6. 4. Fathers.
 u3 | 6. 5-8. Servants.
 v3 | 6. 9. Masters.

22 husbands. Ap. 123. 2.
23 the=a.
even as Christ=as Christ also.
church. Ap. 186.
and He is=He Himself (being).
the saviour=Saviour. Gr. *sōtēr*; only here in Eph.: not in Rom., Cor., Gal.
the body. See 1. 23.
24 Therefore=But.
subject. The same as "submit" in *v.* 21.
25 love, loved. Ap. 135. I. 1.
gave=gave up. See *v.* 2.
it=her (fem. pronoun).
26 That=In order that. Gr. *hina.*
sanctify. Gr. *hagiazō.* See 1 Cor. 1. 2.
and cleanse=having cleansed. Gr. *katharizō.*
with the washing=by (no prep.: dat. case) the laver. Gr. *loutron*; only here and Tit. 3. 5 (*q.v.*) Fig. *Anthropopatheia* (Ap. 6), the laver being put for Christ's death and its results. Cp. Num. 19, especially *vv.* 9, 17. Has nothing to do with baptism.
by. Gr. *en.*
the word. Gr. *rhēma.* First occ. Matt. 4. 4. See Mark 9. 32.
27 present. Gr. *paristēmi.* See Rom. 12. 1.
it. The texts read Gr. *autos*=Himself.
glorious. Gr. *endoxos.* Elsewhere, Luke 7. 25; 13. 17. 1 Cor. 4. 10.
spot=blemish. Gr. *spilos*; only here and 2 Pet. 2. 13.
wrinkle. Only here. **should**=may.
without blemish=faultless. Gr. *amōmos.* See 1. 4.
28 men. Same as "husbands", above.
wives=own wives. Cp. "own husbands", *v.* 22.
wife=own wife.
29 no man=no one. Gr. *oudeis.* **yet.** Omit.
nourisheth. Gr. *ektrephō.* Only here and 6. 4.
cherisheth. Gr. *thalpō.* Only here and 1 Thess. 2. 7.
the Lord. The texts read "Christ also".
30 members. See 4. 25. Cp. Rom. 12. 4, 5. 1 Cor. 6. 15; 12. 27.
of His body. Being part of the Bridegroom, the church which is His body is not the "bride", as is so commonly taught.
of. Ap. 104. vii.
of . . . bones. The texts omit.
31 For, &c. From Gen. 2. 24. See Ap. 107. I. 2.
For. Ap. 104. ii.
cause. Omit. **man.** Ap. 123. 1.
shall be=shall.
joined=cleave. Gr. *proskollaomai.* Occ. elsewhere, Matt. 19. 5. Mark 10. 7. Acts 5. 36. **unto.** Ap. 104. xv. 3. **they**=the. **shall be one flesh.** Men and their wives being "one flesh", a man ought to love his wife, inasmuch as she is himself, *as* Christ loves His own body, the church. The apostle does not once hint that Christ is the husband, or that the church is the wife, but uses the "great mystery" of *v.* 32 in regard to the reciprocal obligations of husband and wife. **one**=for (Gr. *eis.* Ap. 104. vi) one. Does this suggest *one*, in the offspring? **32 a**=the. **mystery.** See Rom. 16. 25, 26 and Ap. 193. **concerning.** Gr. *eis.* Ap. 104. vi. **and**=and concerning. The Gr. *eis* is omitted by A.V. **33 every one**=each. **in particular.** Gr. *kath'* (Ap. 104. x. 2) *hena.* **reverence**=fear (as her "head"). Gr. *phobeō.* Occ. ninety-three times; always rendered "fear" or "be afraid", save here.

6. 1 Children. Ap. 108. i. Cp. Col. 3. 20. **in.** Ap. 104. viii. **Lord.** Ap. 98. VI. i. *β.* 2. B. **right.** Ap. 191. 1. **2 Honour, &c.** From Exod. 20. 12. **with.** Gr. *en.* Ap. 104. viii. **3 That**=In order that. Gr. *hina.* **on.** Ap. 104. ix. 1. **earth.** Ap. 129. 4. **4 *ye***=the. **provoke . . . to wrath.** See Rom. 10. 19. **not.** Ap. 105. II. **bring . . . up**=nurture. As in 5. 29. Cp. 2 Tim. 3. 15. **in the nurture**=with (Gr. *en*) discipline. Gr. *paideia.* Only here; 2 Tim. 3. 16. Heb. 12. 5, 7, 8, 11. **admonition.** Gr. *nouthesia.* Only here; 1 Cor. 10. 11. Tit. 3. 10. **5 Servants.** Ap. 190. I. 2. **masters.** Gr. *kurios.* See Ap. 98. VI. i. **according to.** Ap. 104. x. 2. **with.** Ap. 104. xi. 1. **fear and trembling.** Cp. 1 Cor. 2. 3, the same phrase. **singleness.** Gr. *haplotēs.* See Rom. 12. 8. **unto**=to. **Christ.** Ap. 98. IX. **6 with**=according to. Ap. 104. x. 2. **eyeservice.** Only here and Col. 3. 22. **menpleasers.** Only here and Col. 3. 22. **the.** Omit. **will.** Ap. 102. 2. **God.** Ap. 98. I. i. 1. **from.** Ap. 104. vii. **heart**=soul. Ap. 110. V. 2.

7 [5] With ° good will ° doing service, as to the
° Lord, and ° not to ° men:
° 8 ° Knowing that whatsoever good thing ° any
man doeth, the same shall he ° receive ° of the
[1] Lord, whether *he be* ° bond or free.

v^3 9 ° And, ye [5] masters, do the same things ° unto
them, ° forbearing threatening: [8] knowing
that ° your ° Master also is [1] in ° heaven; ° neither
is there ° respect of persons ° with Him.

P S 10 ° Finally, ° my brethren, ° be strong [1] in the
[1] Lord, and [1] in the ° power of His ° might.

T U^1 11 ° Put on the ° whole armour of [6] God,

V ° that ye may be able to stand ° against the
° wiles of the devil.
12 For ° we wrestle [7] not ° against ° flesh and
blood, but ° against ° principalities, ° against
° powers, ° against the ° rulers of ° the ° darkness
° of this world, ° against ° spiritual wickedness
[1] in ° high *places*.

U^2 13 ° Wherefore ° take unto you the [11] whole
armour of [6] God,

V [3] that ye may be able to ° withstand [1] in ° the
evil day, and having ° done all, to ° stand.

U^3 14 ° Stand therefore, ° having your loins girt
about ° with ° truth, and ° having on the ° breastplate of ° righteousness;
15 And your feet ° shod [14] with the ° preparation
of the ° gospel of ° peace;
16 ° Above all, [13] taking the ° shield of ° faith,
° wherewith ye shall be able to ° quench all the
fiery ° darts of the ° wicked.
17 And ° take the ° helmet of ° salvation, and
the sword of the ° Spirit, which is the ° word of
[6] God:

S 18 ° Praying ° always ° with all ° prayer and
° supplication [1] in the [17] Spirit, and ° watching
° thereunto [2] with all ° perseverance and ° supplication ° for all ° saints,
19 And ° for me, [3] that ° utterance may be given

7 good will. Gr. *eunoia*. See 1 Cor. 7. 3, the only other occ.
doing service. Ap. 190. III. 2.
Lord. Ap. 98. VI. i. β. 2. A.
not. Ap. 105. I.
men. Ap. 123. 1.
8 This *v.* contains an example of Fig. *Tmēsis*. Ap. 6.
Knowing. Ap. 132. I. i.
any man = each one.
receive. Cp. 2 Cor. 5. 10.
of. Ap. 104. xii. 1.
bond. Ap. 190. I. 2.
9 And, ye masters = The masters also.
unto. Ap. 104. xv. 3.
forbearing = refraining from. See Acts 16. 26 (loosed).
your Master. The texts read, "both their Master and yours".
Master. Ap. 98. VI. i. β. 2. A.
heaven = heavens. See Matt. 6. 9, 10.
neither is there = and there is not (Gr. *ou*).
respect of persons. As in Rom. 2. 11.
with. Gr. *para*. Ap. 104. xii. 2.

6. 10-20 (*P*, p. 1765). THEIR WALK. AMONG OTHERS. SPIRITUAL.

(*Introversion and Alternation.*)

P | S | 6. 10. Exhortation: be strong in the Lord.
T | U^1 | 11-. The armour, or panoply, of God.
V | -11, 12. The purpose: that ye may be able to stand (Gr. *stēnai*).
U^2 | 13-. The armour, or panoply, of God.
V | -13. The purpose: that ye may be able to withstand (Gr. *anistēnai*), and stand (Gr. *stēnai*).
U^3 | 14-17. The armour: defined and explained.
S | 18-20. Exhortation to prayer for all the saints and for himself.

10 Finally = From henceforth. The texts read *tou loipou*, as Gal. 6. 17.
my brethren. The texts omit.
be strong = be empowered; pass. of Gr. *endunamoō*. Cp. Acts 9. 22.
power. Ap. 172. 2.
might. Ap. 172. 3.
11 Put on. See 4. 24.
whole armour = panoply. Gr. *panoplia*; only here, *v.* 13, and Luke 11. 22. Freq. in Apocrypha.
that, against. The same Gr. word, *pros*. Ap. 104. xv. 3.
wiles. See 4. 14. **12 we wrestle** = to us the wrestling (Gr. *palē*; only here) is. **against.** Gr. *pros*, as *v.* 11. **flesh and blood** = blood and flesh; i. e. human beings, contrasted with the wicked spirits mentioned below. **principalities.** Ap. 172. 6. **powers.** Ap. 172. 5. **rulers** = world-rulers. Gr. *kosmokratōr*; only here. **the** = this. **darkness.** The present order of things. **of . . . world.** The texts omit. **spiritual wickedness.** Lit. spiritual (hosts) of the wickedness (Gr. *ponēria*. Ap. 128. II. 1). These are the wicked spirits of the evil one (Gr. *ponēros*, see 1 John 2. 13, and Ap. 128. III. 1. **high** *places* = the heavenlies. See 1. 3. **13 Wherefore** = On account of (Gr. *dia*) this. **take unto you** = take up. **withstand.** Gr. *anthistēmi*. See Rom. 9. 19. **the evil day.** Perpetually, because the days are evil; 5. 16. Cp. Gal. 1. 4. **done.** Gr. *katergazomai*. See Rom. 1. 27. **stand** = stand (fast). Gr. *histēmi*. Cp. 2 Thess. 2. 15. **14 Stand,** &c. Here are defined the *panoplia* of God. These are seven (Ap. 10); three for enduement,—girdle, breastplate, shoes; two are weapons of defence, shield and helmet; two for offence,—sword and spear. **having your loins girt about** = having girded your loins. **with.** Gr. *en*. Ap. 104. viii. **truth.** Gr. *alētheia*. See Ap. 175. 1. **having on** = having put on, as in *v.* 11. **breastplate of righteousness.** Cp. Messiah's panoply, Isa. 11. 5; 59. 17. **righteousness.** Ap. 191 3. **15 shod** = having shod. Occ. Mark 6. 9. Acts 12. 8. **preparation.** Gr. *hetoimasia*; only here. The verb occ. first in Matt. 3. 3. **gospel.** Ap. 140. **peace** = the peace. **16 Above.** Gr. *en*. Ap. 104. viii. **shield.** Gr. *thureos*. The shield is Christ Himself. Cp. Gen. 15. 1. **faith** = the faith. Ap. 150. II. 1. **wherewith.** Gr. *en* (Ap. 104. viii) *hō*. **quench.** Cp. 1 Thess. 5. 19. **darts.** Gr. *belos*, anything thrown. Occ. only here. Satanic temptations. **wicked** = wicked one. See *v.* 12. **17 take** = receive. Gr. *dechomai*. Occ. fifty-nine times (fifty-two "receive"). We *receive*, we do not *take*, salvation. **helmet.** Only here, and 1 Thess. 5. 8. Cp. Isa. 59. 17. **salvation.** Gr. *sōtērion*. See Luke 2. 30; 3. 6. Acts 28. 28. **Spirit.** Ap. 101. II. 3; Ap. 17. 3. **word** = utterance. Gr. *rhēma*. The written word. See Mark 9. 32, and cp. Isa. 8. 20. Matt. 4. 4, 6, 7. **18 Praying.** Ap. 134. I. 2. **always** = on (Gr. *en*) every occasion. **with.** Gr. *dia*. Ap. 104. v. 1. **prayer.** Ap. 134. II. 2. **supplication.** Ap. 134. II. 3. **watching.** Lit. lying sleepless. See Mark 13. 33. Luke 21. 36. Heb. 13. 17. **thereunto** = unto (Gr. *eis*) this. **perseverance.** Only here; the verb in Rom. 12. 12. **for** = concerning. Ap. 104. xiii. 1. **saints** = the saints. See Acts 9. 13. **19 for.** Ap. 104. xvii. 1. **utterance.** Ap. 121. 10.

[5]unto me, [3]that °I may open my mouth °boldly,
to °make known the °mystery of the [15] gospel,
20 [19]For which °I am an ambassador [1]in
°bonds; [3]that °therein I may °speak boldly, as
I ought to speak.

A 21 But [3]that ye also may [8]know °my affairs,
and how I °do, °Tychicus, °a °beloved brother
and °faithful °minister [1]in the [1]Lord, °shall
[19]make known to you all things:
22 Whom I °have sent [9]unto you °for °the
same purpose, [3]that ye °might °know °our
affairs, and *that* he °might °comfort your hearts.
23 °Peace *be* to the brethren, and °love [5]with
°faith, °from [6]God the °Father and °the Lord
Jesus Christ.
24 °Grace *be* [5]with all them that °love our
[23]Lord Jesus Christ [1]in °sincerity. °Amen.

I . . . mouth. Lit. in (Gr. *en*) opening (Gr. *anoixis*, only here) of my mouth.
boldly=with (Gr. *en*) boldness.
make known. As Phil. 1. 22.
mystery. Ap. 193.
20 I am an ambassador. Gr. *presbeuō*; only here and 2 Cor. 5. 20. Ancient inscriptions show that *presbeuō* and *presbutēs* (ambassador) were the terms employed in the Greek East to indicate the Emperor's Legate.
bonds=a chain. See Acts 28. 20. 2 Tim. 1. 16. Cp. Mark 5. 3. An ambassador in a chain!
therein=in (Gr. *en*) it; i. e. the mystery.
speak boldly=speak freely, as in Acts 26. 26.
21 my affairs=the things concerning (Ap. 104. x. 2) me. **do**=fare. Gr. *prassō*. Cp. Acts 15. 29.
Tychicus. See Acts 20. 4. Col. 4. 7. 2 Tim. 4. 12. Tit. 3. 12. Named in association with Trophimus (Acts 20. 4), he also was probably an Ephesian. Cp. Acts 21. 29.
a=the. **beloved.** Ap. 135. III.
faithful. Ap. 150. III.
minister. Ap. 190. I. 1. **shall**=will. **22 have sent**=sent. Ap. 174. 4. **for.** Ap. 104. vi. **the same**=this very. **might**=may. **know.** Ap. 132. I. ii. **our affairs**=the things concerning (Ap. 104. xiii. 1) us. **comfort.** Gr. *parakaleō*. Ap. 134. I. 6. **23 Peace.** See 1. 2. The seventh and last occ. in the Ep. of grace and peace. **love.** Ap. 135. II. 1. Tenth and last occ. in Eph. **faith.** As *v.* 16, but without article. **from.** Ap. 104. iv. **Father.** Ap. 98. III. **the Lord Jesus Christ.** See 1. 3. **24 Grace**=The grace. Ap. 184. I. 1. **love.** Ap. 135. I. 1. **sincerity.** Lit. uncorruptness. Gr. *aphtharsia*. See Rom. 2. 7. 1 Cor. 15. 42. **Amen.** Omit, with all the texts.

LONGER NOTE ON 3. 15.

"The whole family in heaven and earth."

1. The word "family" is an unfortunate rendering of the Gr. *patria*. Our English word takes its derivation from the lowest in the household, *famulus*, the servant, or slave. The Latin *familia* was sometimes used of the household of servants, and sometimes of all the members of a family under the power of a *paterfamilias*. But the idea of *patria* is Hebrew, a group or class of families all claiming descent from one *pater* (father), e. g. the twelve tribes of Israel. "Joseph was of the house and lineage (family, Gr. *patria*) of David" (Luke 2. 4). The word occurs only in Luke 2. 4. Acts 3. 25. Eph. 3. 15, and denotes a clan all descended from a common stock.

2. To apply this:—God has many families in heaven and earth, both in this age and in that which is to come. But with selfish disregard of this fact we see only one family, and that of course must be the "church", for that is the family to which we belong. Thus we claim everything for ourselves, especially if blessing, mercy, or glory is attached, and so we completely ignore the fact that many of these families of God are named in Scripture. In 1. 21 we have "principality", "power", "might", "dominion"; the first two being again mentioned in 3. 10, the principalities and powers in the heavenlies to whom God is even now manifesting His manifold wisdom by means of the church (His body) as an object-lesson. Others are mentioned in Col. 1. 16. 1 Peter 3. 22. What these heavenly families may be we do not know. The Greek words reveal to us no more than the English do, because they pertain to the unseen world of which we know nothing.

To limit this verse to the "church" as many do, and to interpret it in wholly unscriptural terms of the "church militant" and the "church triumphant", and in hymn-book diction to sing

One family we dwell in Him,
One church, above, beneath;
Though now divided by the stream,
The narrow stream of death":

is not only to lose the revelation of a great truth of God, but to put error in its place. Rightly divided, the families of God named in the N. T. are:—in heaven, principalities, powers, might, dominions, thrones, angels, and archangels. Among the families on earth are Israel, the Israel of God (Gal. 6. 16), and the church of God (1 Cor. 10. 32).

THE EPISTLE TO THE PHILIPPIANS.

THE STRUCTURE AS A WHOLE.

(*Introversion.*)

A | **1. 1, 2.** Epistolary, and Salutation. "Grace" to Them.

B | **1. 3-26.** Paul's Solicitude for the Philippians.

C | **1. 27—2. 18.** Exhortation, and Example of CHRIST.

D | **2. 19-24.** The Example of TIMOTHY.

D | **2. 25-30.** The Example of EPAPHRODITUS.

C | **3. 1—4. 9.** Exhortation and Example of PAUL.

B | **4. 10-20.** The Philippians' Solicitude for PAUL.

A | **4. 21-23.** Epistolary, and Doxology. "Grace" to Them.

THE EPISTLE TO THE PHILIPPIANS.

INTRODUCTORY NOTES.

1. The apostle's first visit to the city of Philippi, probably about A. D. 52-53 (Ap. 180), is recorded in Acts 16. He had as companions Silas and Timothy, and the use of the first personal pronoun, in *v.* 10 of that chapter, indicates that a fourth worker was with him. Probably Luke, the "beloved physician". Although we have no particulars of later visits, yet Paul almost certainly was twice at Philippi subsequently (Acts 20. 1 and 6).

2. We infer that but few Jews would be at Philippi, there being no intimation of obstruction from them, and there was no synagogue there, unless, indeed, the "place of prayer" by the river-side refers to one. The believers had retained the fervency of their first love, and had sent once and again unto his need. The apostle's gratitude is shown repeatedly, and he greatly honours his Philippian "brethren, dearly beloved and longed for", by designating them "my joy and crown".

3. No one of Paul's Epistles is more elevated in character or more animating to believers. Nor, it may be added, one of better-defined frame, as will be seen from the complete Structure (above). Written from Rome towards the end of his imprisonment, probably in A. D. 62, the apostle's position was then one of waiting, for he was now close to the day for his cause to be heard before the tribunal to which he had appealed. And most likely this necessitated a more rigid condition of imprisonment than when he dwelt, as at first, in his own hired house. But this, instead of hindering, had even furthered the preaching of Christ. Hence one cause for the tone of rejoicing throughout the Epistle. Like golden threads, "joy" and its kindred words run throughout Philippians, as "grace" does in Ephesians.

4. The city of Philippi, a Roman colony, was situated about eight miles inland from its port, Neapolis, the modern Kavalla. Not being a commercial centre, this may explain the paucity of Jews among the inhabitants. Philippi no longer exists, for although the nearest Turkish hamlet bears the ancient name in a corrupted form, it is not on the site of the old city.

THE EPISTLE OF PAUL THE APOSTLE

TO THE

PHILIPPIANS.

A 1 PAUL and °Timotheus, the °servants of
°Jesus Christ, to all the °saints °in °Christ
Jesus which are °at Philippi, °with the °bishops
and °deacons:
2 °Grace *be* °unto you, and peace, °from °God
our °Father, and *from* the °Lord [1] Jesus Christ.

B A 3 I °thank my [2] God °upon every remembrance
of you,
4 Always [1] in every °prayer of mine °for you
all making °request °with joy,
5 °For your fellowship °in the °gospel [2] from
the first day until now;

B 6 °Being confident of this very thing, that
He Which hath °begun a good work [1] in you
will °perform *it* until the day of [1] Jesus Christ:
7 Even as it is °meet for °me to think this °of
you all, °because I have you [1] in my heart,
inasmuch as both [1] in my bonds, and [1] in the
°defence and °confirmation of the [5] gospel, ye
all are °partakers of my °grace.

A 8 For [2] God is my °record, how °greatly I long
after you all [1] in the °bowels of °Jesus Christ.
9 And this I °pray, °that your °love may
abound yet more and more [1] in °knowledge and
in all °judgment;
10 °That ye may approve things that °are
excellent; [9] that ye may be °sincere and °with-
out offence °till the °day of °Christ;
11 °Being filled with the fruits of °righteous-
ness, which are °by [1] Jesus Christ, °unto the
°glory and praise of [2] God.

B a 12 But I °would ye should °understand, brethren, that the °things *which happened* unto
me have °fallen out rather [11] unto the °further-
ance of the [5] gospel;

1. 1 Timotheus. See 2 Cor. 1. 1.
servants. Ap. 190. I. 2.
Jesus Christ. Ap. 98. XI.
saints. See Acts 9. 13.
in. Ap. 104. viii.
Christ Jesus. Ap. 98. XII.
at. Ap. 104. viii. **with.** Ap. 104. xvi.
bishops. Gr. *episkopos.* See Acts 20. 28.
deacons. Ap. 190. I. 1. The only place where these officers are mentioned together.
2 Grace. Ap. 184. I. 1.
unto=to. **from.** Ap. 104. iv.
God. Ap. 98. I. i. 1.
Father. Ap. 98. III.
Lord. Ap. 98. VI. i. β. 2. B.

1. 3-26 (B, p. 1772). PAUL'S CONCERN FOR THE PHILIPPIANS. (*Alternation.*)

B | A | 3-5. Thanksgiving.
  B | 6, 7. Confidence with reference to the Philippians.
A | 8-11. Prayer.
  B | 12-26. Confidence with reference to himself.

3 thank. See Acts 27. 35.
upon. Ap. 104. ix. 2.
4 prayer. Ap. 134. II. 3.
for. Ap. 104. xvii. 1.
request. Same as "prayer", above.
with. Ap. 104. xi. 1.
5 For. Ap. 104. ix. 2.
in. Gr. *eis.* Ap. 104. vi.
gospel. Ap. 140.
6 Being confident. Lit. Trusting. Ap. 150. I. 2.
begun. Gr. *enarchomai.* Only here and Gal. 3. 3.
perform=complete. Gr. *epiteleō.* Ap. 125. 3. See Luke 13. 32.
7 meet=just, or right. Ap. 191. 1.
me. Emph.
of. Ap. 104. xvii. 1.
because. Ap. 104. v. 2.
defence. Gr. *apologia.* See Acts 22. 1.
confirmation. Gr. *bebaiōsis.* Only here and Heb. 6. 16. A legal term for a guarantee. So used in the Papyri. **partakers, &c.**=fellow-partakers with me of grace. **partakers.** Gr. *sunkoinōnos.* See Rom. 11. 17. **grace.** Ap. 184. I. 1. A bond which unites all who receive it. **8 record**=witness. Cp. Rom. 1. 9. **greatly . . . long.** Gr. *epipotheō.* See Rom. 1. 11. **bowels.** Gr. *splanchna.* See 2 Cor. 6. 12. **Jesus Christ.** The texts read Christ Jesus. **9 pray.** Ap. 134. I. 2. **that.** Gr. *hina.* Generally denoting a purpose, but here only the subject of the prayer. **love.** Ap. 135. II. 1. **knowledge.** Ap. 132. II. ii. **judgment.** Ap. 177. 1. **10 That ye may, &c.**=To (Ap. 104. vi) your proving, or trying. **are excellent**=differ. We are to test the things, and having found them to differ, must not join them together, but rightly divide them (2 Tim. 2. 15). **sincere.** Gr. *eilikrinēs.* Only here and 2 Pet. 3. 1. Cp. 1 Cor. 5. 8. **without offence.** Gr. *aproskopos.* See Acts 24. 16. **till.** Ap. 104. vi. **day of Christ.** The same expression in 2. 16. Cp. *v.* 6 and 1 Cor. 1. 8; 5. 5. 2 Cor. 1. 14. 2 Thess. 2. 2, where see note. **Christ.** Ap. 98. IX. **11 Being filled**=Having been filled. Ap. 125. 7. **righteousness.** Ap. 191. 3. **by.** Ap. 104. v. 1 **unto.** Ap. 104. vi. **glory.** See p. 1511.

1. 12-26 (*B*, above). **CONFIDENCE WITH REFERENCE TO HIMSELF.**

B | a | 12, 13. What Paul would have them know.
  b | 14-18-. Christ preached.
   c | -18. Paul's rejoicing.
a | 19. What Paul knew.
  b | 20-25. Christ magnified.
   c | 26. Their rejoicing.

12 would, &c.=wish (Ap. 102. 3) you. **understand.** Ap. 132. I. ii. **things, &c.**=things with reference to (Ap. 104. x. 2) me. **fallen out.** Lit. come. **furtherance.** Gr. *prokopē.* Here, *v.* 25, and 1 Tim. 4. 15. Cp. Rom. 13. 12.

13 So that °my bonds [1]in [10]Christ °are °manifest [1]in all the °palace, and °in all other *places;*

b 14 And °many of the brethren [1]in the [2]Lord, °waxing [6]confident by my bonds, are much more bold to °speak the °word °without fear.
15 °Some indeed °preach [10]Christ even °of envy and strife; and °some °also °of °good will:
16 The one °preach [10]Christ °of °contention, °not °sincerely, °supposing to °add °affliction to my bonds:
17 But the other [16]of [9]love, °knowing that I am set °for the [7]defence of the [5]gospel.
18 What then? °notwithstanding, every way, whether in °pretence, or in truth, [10]Christ is [16]preached;
c and I °therein do rejoice, yea, and will rejoice.

a 19 For I [17]know that this shall °turn °to my salvation °through your [4]prayer, and the °supply of the °Spirit of [1]Jesus Christ,

b 20 °According to my °earnest expectation and *my* hope, that [1]in °nothing I shall be °ashamed, but *that* °with all °boldness, as always, *so* now also [10]Christ shall be magnified [1]in my body, whether *it be* [11]by °life, or [11]by death.
21 For to °me to °live *is* [10]Christ, and to die *is* °gain.
22 But °if °I live [1]in the flesh, °this *is* the °fruit of my labour: yet what I shall choose I °wot [16]not.
23 For I °am in a strait °betwixt °two, having °a desire °to °depart, and to be [1]with [10]Christ; which is °far better:
24 Nevertheless to °abide [1]in the flesh *is* more needful °for you.
25 And °having this confidence, I [17]know that I shall °abide and °continue with you all, [17]for your [12]furtherance and °joy of °faith;

c 26 [9]That your °rejoicing may be more abundant [1]in [8]Jesus Christ °for me [11]by my coming °to you again.

13 my bonds, &c. = "my bonds in relation to Christ"; i. e. that my being a prisoner is not on account of any crime, but solely for preaching the gospel.
are = have become.
manifest. See Ap. 106. I. viii.
palace. Gr. *praitōrion.* Cp. Matt. 27. 27, but Bishop Lightfoot gives good reasons why it could not at Rome be used of the palace, but must refer to the Prætorian guard. This accords with Acts 28. 30.
in all, &c. = to all the rest (Ap. 124. 3), i. e. to the civilian population.
14 many = the majority.
waxing confident = having become confident. See *v.* 6; "in the Lord" belongs to "confident", not to "brethren". Cp. 2. 24. Rom. 14. 14. Gal. 5. 10. 2 Thess. 3. 4.
speak. Ap. 121. 7.
word. Ap. 121. 10. The texts add "of God".
without fear. See 1 Cor. 16. 10.
15 Some. Ap. 124. 4. **preach.** Ap. 121. 1.
of = through. Ap. 104. v. 2.
also, &c. = of good will also.
good will. Gr. *eudokia.* See Rom. 10. 1.
16 preach. Ap. 121. 5.
of. Ap. 104. vii.
contention. Gr. *eritheia.* See Rom. 2. 8.
not. Ap. 105. I.
sincerely = of pure motive. Gr. *hagnōs.* Only here.
supposing = thinking. Only here, and Jas. 1. 7.
add . . . to. Gr. *epipherō.* See Acts 19. 12, but the texts read "raise" (Ap. 178. II. 4).
affliction. Gr. *thlipsis.* See Acts 7. 10.
17 knowing. Ap. 132. I. i.
for. Ap. 104. vi.
18 notwithstanding = except. Gr. *plēn.* There is an ellipsis here. "What shall we say then? Nothing, except that." See Ap. 6, *Affirmation.*
pretence. See John 15. 22.
therein = in (Ap. 104. viii) this. No personal consideration prevented his rejoicing.
19 turn = turn out. See Luke 21. 13.
to my = to me for (Ap. 104. vi).
through. Ap. 104. v. 1.
supply. Gr. *epichorēgia.* See Eph. 4. 16.
Spirit. Ap. 101. II. 5. Cp. Rom. 8. 9. It was this that enabled Paul to suffer no personal considerations to weigh with him. He had the mind of Christ. Cp. 2. 5. 1 Cor. 2. 16.
20 According to. Ap. 104. x. 2.
earnest expectation. See Rom. 8. 19.
nothing. Gr. *oudeis.*
ashamed. See 2 Cor. 10. 8.

with. Ap. 104. viii. **boldness.** Gr. *parrhēsia.* See John 7. 4. **life.** Ap. 170. 1. **21 me.** Emph. **live.** Cp. Ap. 170. 1. **gain.** Gr. *kerdos.* Here, 3. 7. Tit. 1. 11. Not to Paul, but to Christ, as is clear from *v.* 20. To Paul, life and death were of no account so long as the cause of Christ was advanced. His bonds had furthered the gospel, what might not his death do? Cp. 2. 17. 2 Cor. 7. 3. **22 if.** Ap. 118. 2. a. **I live.** Lit. to live (is my lot). **this.** I.e. gain to Christ. **fruit, &c.** I.e. the result of my work. **wot** = declare. Gr. *gnōrizō.* Occ. twenty-four times. In classical Gr. to know or to make known, but in N.T. elsewhere transl. make known, certify, declare, &c. See 4. 6. His will was surrendered to God, so he made no choice as to life or death for himself, but there *was* something he earnestly desired, which he states in the next verse. **23 am in a strait** = am being pressed. Gr. *sunechō.* See Acts 7. 57. 18. 5. **betwixt** = out of. Ap. 104. vii. While *ek* occ. 857 times, it is only transl. "betwixt" here, and "between" in John 3. 25, where the meaning is that the question arose *from* John's disciples. In all other places *ek* is transl. "of", "out of", "from", &c., but in every case the context shows the idea conveyed is one of these two latter. Cp. notes on Matt. 27. 7. John 12. 3. Acts 19. 25. **two** = the two, i. e. living and dying. **a desire** = the desire. Gr. *epithumia.* Transl. "lust" thirty-one times; "concupiscence" thrice, and "desire", thrice. Cp. Luke 22. 15. 1 Thess. 2. 17. **to depart** = for (Ap. 104. vi) the return (Gr. *analuō.* Verb only here and Luke 12. 36; the noun 2 Tim. 4. 6. The verb freq. transl. "return" in Apocrypha; also in class. Gr. = to unloose, as of a ship weighing anchor). **far better.** All the texts read "for it is very far better". Than what? Clearly, than either of the two above. Therefore it cannot mean "death": but some event by which alone Paul could be with Christ, either the calling on high (see on 3. 11) or the resurrection from the dead, or being caught up alive of 1 Thess. 4. 16, 17. **24 abide.** Gr. *epimenō.* See Acts 10. 48. **for** = on account of. Ap. 104. v. 2. **25 having this confidence** = being confident of this, as in *v.* 6. **abide.** Gr. *menō.* See p. 1511. **continue with.** Gr. *sumparamenō.* Only here, but the texts read *paramenō.* See 1 Cor. 16. 6. Fig. *Hendiadys.* Ap. 6. **joy.** Cp. Rom. 15. 13. **faith** = the faith. Ap. 150. II. 1. **26 rejoicing.** Gr. *kauchēma.* See Rom. 4. 2. **for** = in. Ap. 104. viii. **to.** Ap. 104. xv. 3.

C C 27 Only °let your conversation be °as it
becometh the [5]gospel of [10]Christ: [9]that whether
I come and °see you, or else be absent, I may
hear °of °your affairs, that ye °stand fast [1]in
one °spirit, with one °mind °striving together
for °the [5]faith of the [5]gospel;
28 And [1]in °nothing °terrified °by your adversaries:
which is to them an °evident token of
°perdition, but to you of °salvation, and that
°of [2]God.
29 For [2]unto you it °is given °in the behalf of
[10]Christ, [16]not only to °believe on Him, but
°also to suffer °for His sake;
30 Having the same °conflict which °ye [27]saw
[1]in me, and now hear *to be* [1]in me.

2 °If *there be* therefore any °consolation °in
°Christ, °if any °comfort of °love, °if any
fellowship of the °Spirit, °if any °bowels and
°mercies,
2 °Fulfil ye my joy, °that ye °be likeminded,
having the same [1]love, *being* °of one accord,
°of one mind.
3 *Let* °nothing *be done* °through °strife or
°vainglory; but °in °lowliness of mind °let
each esteem other °better than themselves.
4 °Look °not °every man on his own things,
but °every man °also on the things of °others.
D 5 °Let this mind be [1]in °you, which was
°also [1]in °Christ Jesus:
6 Who, °being [1]in the °form of °God, °thought
it °not °robbery °to be equal with °God:
7 But °made Himself of no reputation, °and
took upon Him the [6]form of a °servant, and
°was made [1]in the °likeness of °men:
8 And being found in °fashion as a [7]man, He
°humbled Himself, °and became °obedient
°unto death, even the death of the °cross.

1. 27—2. 18 (C, p. 1772). EXHORTATION AND EXAMPLE OF CHRIST. (*Introversion.*)

C | C | 1. 27—2. 4. Exhortation.
  D | 2. 5-8. Christ's Humiliation.
  D | 2. 9-11. Christ's Exaltation.
  C | 2. 12-18. Exhortation.

27 let, &c. = exercise your citizenship, or behave as citizens. Gr. *politeuomai.* Elsewhere only in Acts 23. 1. See also 2 Macc. 6. 1; 11. 25. In all cases it means to live according to certain rules and obligations, e. g. as a Jew, "according to the law and customs". Here, those of heavenly citizenship (cp. 3. 20).
as it becometh = worthily of. **see.** Ap. 133. I. 1.
of your affairs = the things concerning (Ap. 104. xiii. 1) you.
stand fast. Gr. *stēkō.* See 1 Cor. 16. 13.
spirit. Ap. 101. II. 8.
mind. Ap. 110. V. 3.
striving together. Gr. *sunathleō.* Only here and 4. 3. Cp. 2 Tim. 2. 5.
the faith, i. e. the substance of things believed.
28 nothing. A double negative. Gr. *mē mēdeis.* Ap. 105. II.
terrified. Gr. *pturomai.* Only here.
by. Ap. 104. xviii. 1.
evident token. Gr. *endeixis.* See Rom. 3. 25.
perdition = destruction. See John 17. 12.
salvation. See *v.* 19. Cp. Heb. 11. 7.
of. Ap. 104. iv.
29 is given = was granted. Ap. 184. II. 1.
in the behalf of. Ap. 104. xvii. 1.
believe on. Ap. 150. I. 1. v. (i).
also, &c. = to suffer for (Ap. 104. xvii. 1) His sake also. Cp. Acts 9. 16.
30 conflict. Gr. *agōn.* Here, Col. 2. 1. 1 Thess. 2. 2. 1 Tim. 6. 12. 2 Tim. 4. 7. Heb. 12. 1.
ye saw. See Acts 16. 19-24. 1 Thess. 2. 2.

2. 1 If. Ap. 118. 2. a.
consolation. Gr. *paraklēsis.* See Luke 6. 24. See Ap. 134. I. 6.
in. Ap. 104. viii.
Christ. Ap. 98. IX.
comfort. Or, stimulating force, incentive. Gr. *paramuthion.* Only here. Cp. 1 Cor. 14. 3. John 11. 19. **love.** Ap. 135. II. 1. **Spirit.** Ap. 101. II. 8. There is no article, and the whole context is an exhortation to being of one mind. Cp. 1. 27. **bowels.** See 1. 8. **mercies.** Gr. *oiktirmos.* See Rom. 12. 1. **2 Fulfil** = Complete. Ap. 125. 7. **that** = in order that. Gr. *hina.* **be likeminded** = mind, or think the same thing. Gr. *phroneō.* **of one accord.** Gr. *sumpsuchos.* Only here. **of one mind** = minding (Gr. *phroneō,* as above) the one thing. **3 nothing.** Gr. *mēdeis.* **through** = according to. Ap. 104. x. 2. **strife.** Gr. *eritheia.* See 1. 16. **vainglory.** Gr. *kenodoxia.* Only here. **in** = by. No prep. Dat. case. **lowliness of mind.** Gr. *tapeinophrosunē.* See Acts 20. 19. **let each, &c.** = reckoning one another. **better.** Gr. *huperechō.* See Rom. 13. 1. **4 Look.** Gr. *skopeō.* See Luke 11. 35. **not.** Ap. 105. II. **every man** = each one. **also, &c.** = on the things of others also. **others.** Ap. 124. 2. **5 Let, &c.** Lit. Mind, or think, this. Gr. *phroneō,* as in *v.* 2. **you** = yourselves, i. e. your hearts. **also, &c.** = in Christ Jesus also. **Christ Jesus.** Ap. 98. XII. **6 being** = subsisting, or being essentially. Gr. *huparchō.* See Luke 9. 48. **form** = the essential form, including all the qualities which can be made visible to the eye. Gr. *morphē.* Only here, *v.* 7, and Mark 16. 12. **God.** Ap. 98. I. i. 1. **thought** = reckoned. Same word as "esteem", *v.* 3. **not.** Ap. 105. I. **robbery** = an act of robbery, or a usurpation. **to be equal** = the being on an equality. **7 made Himself of no reputation** = emptied Himself. Gr. *kenoō.* See Rom. 4. 14. Of what He divested Himself is not stated, but Geo. Herbert's words, "He laid His glory by", i. e. the outward attributes of Deity, well suggest the meaning here. It is assumed by some that when taking the form of a bondservant, He not only divested Himself of His Divine powers, but became as His fellows, and limited Himself (or *was limited*) to the knowledge and "mental status" of the age in which He lived. In support of this Luke 2. 52 and Mark 13. 32 are adduced, but neither affords any warrant whatever for such assumption. The Lord's wisdom and knowledge were astonishing to the Rabbis (Luke 2. 47). He came only to accomplish the work the Father gave Him to do (John 17. 4), so He only spoke the words the Father gave Him (John 3. 34; 7. 16; 8. 28; 12. 49, 50; 14. 10, 24; 17. 8, 14). His perfect obedience (as far as death, *v.* 8) was shown in that He did and said only what was appointed Him to do and say, not His own will, but the will of Him that sent Him (Heb. 10. 5-7) **and took, &c.** = having taken. **servant.** Ap. 190. I. 2. **was made.** Lit. becoming. **likeness** Gr. *homoiōma.* See Rom. 1. 23. **men.** Ap. 123. 1. **8 fashion.** Gr. *schēma.* Only here and 1 Cor. 7. 31. The noun *morphē* occ. thrice and is used only of the Lord; here (*vv.* 6, 7), and Mark 16. 12: *schēma* occ. only here and 1 Cor. 7. 31, as above. For their compounds see the Notes. **humbled.** Gr. *tapeinoō.* See 2 Cor. 11. 7. **and became.** Lit. becoming. **obedient.** Gr. *hupēkoos.* See Acts 7. 39. **unto** = as far as. **cross.** That death, the shame of which made it such a stumbling-block to the Jews. Cp. Heb. 12. 2. The seven successive steps of the Lord's humiliation illustrate the Fig. *Catabasis.* Ap. 6. The seven steps upward in His glorification are given in *vv.* 9-11.

D 9 Wherefore [6]God also °hath °highly exalted
Him, and °given Him °a name which is °above
every name:
10 [2]That °at the name of °Jesus every knee
should °bow, of *things* °in heaven, and *things*
°in earth, and *things* °under the earth;
11 And *that* every tongue should confess that
°Jesus Christ *is* °Lord, °to the glory of [6]God
the °Father.

C 12 Wherefore, my °beloved, as ye have always
obeyed, [4]not as [1]in my °presence only, but now
much more [1]in my °absence, work out your
own salvation °with °fear and trembling.
13 For it is [6]God Which °worketh [1]in you
both to °will and to °do, °of *His* °good pleasure.
14 Do all things without °murmurings and
disputings:
15 [2]That ye may °be °blameless and °harmless,
the °sons of [6]God, °without rebuke, [1]in the
midst of a °crooked and °perverse °nation,
°among whom ye °shine as °lights [1]in the
°world;
16 °Holding forth the °word of °life; °that I
may rejoice °in the day of [1]Christ, that I have
[6]not run °in vain, neither laboured °in vain.
17 Yea, °and if I be °offered °upon the sacrifice
and °service of your °faith, I joy, and rejoice
with you all.
18 °For the same cause also do ye joy, and
rejoice with me.

D E 19 But I °trust [1]in the [11]Lord [10]Jesus to °send
Timotheus °shortly °unto you, [2]that I also
may °be of good comfort, when I °know °your
state.

F 20 For I have °no man °likeminded, who will
°naturally care for [19]your state.
21 For all seek their own, [6]not the things
which are [11]Jesus Christ's.

F 22 But ye [19]know the °proof of him, that, as
a [15]son with the father, he °hath °served °with
me [16]in the °gospel.
23 Him therefore I °hope to [19]send °presently,
so soon as I shall °see °how it will go with me.

E 24 But I °trust [1]in the [11]Lord that I also
myself shall come [19]shortly.

D G 25 Yet I °supposed it necessary to [19]send °to

9 hath. Omit.
highly exalted. Gr. *huperupsoō*. Only here. Cp. John 12. 32.
given = gave. Ap. 184. II. 1. a. The texts read the.
above. Ap. 104. xvii. 2.
10 at = in. Ap. 104. viii.
Jesus. Ap. 98. X.
bow. Gr. *kamptō*. See Rom. 11. 4. Cp. Isa. 45. 23. Rom. 14. 11.
in heaven. Gr. *epouranios*. See Eph. 3. 10.
in earth. Gr. *epigeios*. See 1 Cor. 15. 40 (terrestrial).
under the earth. Gr. *katachthonios*. Only here. Cp. Prov. 15. 24. These are the dead who shall yet be raised to give glory to Him. Cp. Rev. 5. 13; and the angels and demons of the abyss. Luke 8. 31. Rev. 9. 11. And see Ps. 148.
11 Jesus Christ. Ap. 98. XI.
Lord. Ap. 98. VI. i. β. 2. B.
to. Ap. 104. vi.
Father. Ap. 98. III.
12 beloved. Ap. 135. III.
presence. Gr. *parousia*. This and 1. 26 (coming) are the only occ. of *parousia* in the epistles written from Paul's prison at Rome. See Matt. 24. 3.
absence. Gr. *apousia*. Only here.
with. Ap. 104. xi. 1.
fear and trembling. See 1 Cor. 2. 3.
13 worketh. Gr. *energeō*. Not the same as "work out" (*v*. 12), *katergazomai* (see Eph. 6. 13).
will. Ap. 102. 1.
do = work. Gr. *energeō*.
of. Ap. 104. xvii. 1.
good pleasure. Gr. *eudokia*. See Rom. 10. 1.
14 murmurings. Gr. *gongusmos*. See Acts 6. 1.
15 be. Lit. become.
blameless. Gr. *amemptos*. Only here; 3. 6. Luke 1. 6. 1 Thess. 3. 13. Heb. 8. 7.
harmless. Gr. *akeraios*. See Rom. 16. 19.
sons. Ap. 108. i.
without rebuke. Gr. *amōmētos*. Only here and 2 Pet. 3. 14, but the texts read *amōmos* (as Eph. 1. 4). Both words are akin to *amemptos*.
crooked. Gr. *skolios*. See Acts 2. 40.
perverse. See Acts 13. 8.
nation = generation.
among. Ap. 104. viii. 2.
shine = appear. Ap. 106. I. i.
lights. Ap. 130. 2.
world. Ap. 129. 1. Cp. Matt. 5. 14.
16 Holding forth. Gr. *epechō*. See Acts 3. 5.
word. Ap. 121. 10.
life. Ap. 170. 1.
that I may, &c. = for (Ap. 104. vi) rejoicing to me. Cp. 1 Thess. 2. 19, 20.
in. Ap. 104. vi.
in vain. Gr. *eis kenon*. See Gal. 4. 11.
17 and if = even if (Ap. 118. 2. a).
offered = poured out (as a drink offering). Gr. *spendomai*. Only here and 2 Tim. 4. 6.
upon. Ap. 104. ix. 2.
service. Ap. 190. II. 4.
faith. Ap. 150. II. 1.
18 For the same, &c. = In respect to the same thing do ye also joy.

2. 19-24 (D, p. 1772). THE EXAMPLE OF TIMOTHY. (*Introversion*.)

D | E | 19. Paul's hope to send Timothy.
  | F | 20, 21. Reason. None like him.
  | *F* | 22, 23. Proof from experience.
  | *E* | 24. Paul's trust to come himself.

19 trust = hope. Gr. *elpizō*. **send.** Ap. 174. 4. **shortly** = quickly. **unto** = to. **be, &c.** Gr. *eupsucheō*. Only here. **know.** Ap. 132. I. ii. **your state** = the things concerning (Ap. 104. xiii. 1) you. **20 no man** = no one. Gr. *oudeis*. **likeminded** = of equal mind. Gr. *isopsuchos*. Only here. **naturally.** Gr. *gnēsiōs*. Only here. Cp. 4. 3. 1 Tim. 1. 2. **22 proof.** Gr. *dokimē*. See Rom. 5. 4. **hath.** Omit. **served.** Ap. 190. III. 2. **with.** Ap. 104. xvi. **gospel.** Ap. 140. **23 hope.** As trust, *v*. 19. **presently** = forthwith. **see.** Gr. *apeidon*, used as aorist of *aphoraō*. Ap. 133. I. 9. **how . . . me** = the things concerning me, as *vv*. 19, 20. **24 trust.** Ap. 150. I. 2.

2. 25-30 (*D*, p. 1772). THE EXAMPLE OF EPAPHRODITUS. (*Alternation*.)

D | G | 25. His character.
  | H | 26, 27. His desire to see them.
  | *G* | 28, 29. His mission.
  | *H* | 30. Commendation of him.

25 supposed. Same word in *v*. 3 (esteem) and *v*. 6 (thought). **to.** Ap. 104. xv. 3.

you °Epaphroditus, my brother, and °com-
panion in labour, and °fellowsoldier, but your
°messenger, and °he that ministered to my
°wants.
H 26 For he °longed after you all, and was
°full of heaviness, because that ye had heard
that he had been sick.
27 For indeed he was sick °nigh °unto death:
but [6]God had mercy on him; and [6]not on him
only, but on me also, °lest I should have sorrow
°upon sorrow.
G 28 I [19]sent him therefore the more °carefully,
[2]that, when ye °see him again, ye may rejoice,
and that I may be the °less sorrowful.
29 Receive him therefore [1]in the [11]Lord [12]with
all gladness; and hold such °in reputation:
H 30 Because °for the work of [1]Christ he °was
nigh unto death, °not regarding his °life, °to
°supply your lack of °service °toward me.

CJ[1] **3** Finally, my brethren, rejoice °in the °Lord.
To write the same things to you, to me
indeed *is* °not °grievous, but for you *it is* °safe.
2 °Beware of dogs, °beware of °evil workers,
°beware of the °concision.
3 For we are °the circumcision, which °wor-
ship °God in the °spirit, °and rejoice [1]in °Christ
Jesus, and °have no confidence [1]in the flesh.
K[1] 4 Though °I might also have confidence [1]in
the flesh. °If °any °other man thinketh °that
he hath whereof he might °trust [1]in the flesh,
I more:
5 °Circumcised the eighth day, °of the °stock
of Israel, *of* the tribe of Benjamin, an Hebrew
°of °the Hebrews; °as touching the law,
a °Pharisee;
6 °Concerning zeal, persecuting the °church;
°touching the °righteousness which is [1]in the
law, °blameless.
7 But what things were °gain to me, those I
°counted °loss °for °Christ.
8 Yea doubtless, and I [7]count all things *but*
[7]loss [7]for the °excellency of the °knowledge of
[3]Christ Jesus my °Lord: [7]for Whom I have
°suffered the loss of all things, and do [7]count
them °*but* dung, °that I may °win [7]Christ,
9 And be found [1]in Him, °not having °mine
own [6]righteousness, which is [5]of the law, but
that which is °through °the °faith of [7]Christ,
the [6]righteousness which is [5]of [3]God °by °faith:

Epaphroditus. See 4. 18.
companion in labour. Gr. *sunergos*, fellowlabourer, as 4. 3; &c.
fellowsoldier. Gr. *sustratiōtēs.* Only here and Philem. 2.
messenger=apostle. Ap. 189.
he that ministered=minister. Ap. 190. I. 4.
wants. See 4. 16 (necessity), 19 (need).
26 longed=was longing. Gr. *epipotheō*, as 1. 8.
full of heaviness. Gr. *adēmoneō.* Only here; Matt. 26. 37. Mark 14. 33.
27 nigh. Gr. *paraplēsion.* Only here.
unto=to.
lest=in order that (Gr. *hina*) not (Ap. 105. II).
upon. Ap. 104. ix. 3.
28 carefully=diligently.
see. Ap. 133. I. 1.
less sorrowful=more free from grief. Gr. *alupoteros.* Only here.
29 in reputation=as honourable, or esteemed. Gr. *entimos.* Here, Luke 7. 2; 14. 8. 1 Pet. 2. 4, 6.
30 for. Ap. 104. v. 2.
was=drew.
not regarding=disregarding. Gr. *parabouleuomai.* The texts read *paraboleuomai*, to expose to danger.
life. Ap. 110. III. 1.
to=that (Gr. *hina*) he might.
supply=fill up. Gr. *anaplēroō.* See 1 Cor. 14. 16. Cp. Ap. 125. 7.
service. Ap. 190. II. 4.
toward. Ap. 104. xv. 3. Paul's joy at their kind ministration lacked one thing, their personal presence. This Epaphroditus, their messenger, supplied.

3. 1—4. 9 (*C*, p. 1772). THE EXAMPLE OF PAUL.
(*Repeated Alternation.*)

C | J[1] | 3. 1-3. The present and true circumcision: in Christ.
  K[1] | 3. 4-14. Paul's example.
 J[2] | 3. 15, 16. The present and perfect standard: completeness in Christ.
  K[2] | 3. 17-21. Paul's example.
 J[3] | 4. 1-8. The present walk and effect (Gr. *en*, *v.* 7): in Christ.
  K[3] | 4. 9. Paul's example.

3. 1 in. Ap. 104. viii.
Lord. Ap. 98. VI. i. *β*. 2. B.
not. Ap. 105. I.
grievous=irksome. Gr. *oknēros.* See Rom. 12. 11.
safe. Gr. *asphalēs.* See Acts 21. 34.
2 Beware. Ap. 133. I. 5.
evil. Ap. 128. III. 2.
concision. Gr. *katatomē.* Only here. The verb *katatemnō* occ. in the Sept. of heathen mutilations. Lev. 21. 5. 1 Kings 18. 28. Paul regards the circumcision of the Judaizers as a mere ordinance, no better than a heathen one. Cp. Rom. 2. 25-29. 1 Cor. 7. 19. Gal. 5. 6; 6. 15.

3 the circumcision. I. e. the true circumcision. Gr. *peritomē.* Note the *Paronomasia* (Ap. 6), *katatomē*, *peritomē.* **worship.** Ap. 137. 4, and 190. III. 5. **God.** Ap. 98. I. i. 1. All the texts have *Theou*, instead of *Theō*, making it dependent upon *pneumati*, and reading, "worship by the spirit of God", i. e. the new nature. Ap. 101. II. 5. Cp. Rom. 8. 9. **and rejoice**=rejoicing, or glorying. **Christ Jesus.** Ap. 98. XII. **have, &c.**=not (Ap. 105. I) trusting (Ap. 150. I. 2). **4 I might, &c.**=having myself confidence (Ap. 150. II. 2) in the flesh also. Here Paul takes the Judaizers on their own ground. **If.** Ap. 118. 2. a. **any other man**=any (Ap. 123. 3) other (Ap. 124. 1). **that . . . trust.** Lit. to have confidence. **trust.** Ap. 150. I. 2. **5 Circumcised**=In circumcision, as in *v.* 3. **of.** Ap. 104. vii. **stock.** Gr. *genos.* 1 Cor. 12. 10 (kind). Gal. 1. 14 (nation). **the Hebrews.** Omit "the". He refers to his parents, both Hebrews. **as touching**=according to. Ap. 104. x. 2. **Pharisee.** Ap. 120. II. **6 Concerning, touching.** Ap. 104. x. 2. **church.** Ap. 186. **righteousness.** Ap. 191. 3. **blameless**=found blameless, i. e. before men. Cp. Acts 24. 20. **7 gain.** Gr. *kerdos.* See 1. 21. Note the seven gains in *vv.* 5, 6. **counted.** Same as "esteem", 2. 3. **loss.** Gr. *zēmia.* See Acts 27. 10. **for.** Ap. 104. v. 2. **Christ.** Ap. 98. IX. **8 excellency**=excelling. Gr. *huperechō.* See 2. 3. **knowledge.** Ap. 132. II. i. **Lord.** Ap. 98. VI. i. *β*. 2. A. **suffered, &c.** Gr. *zēmioō.* See 1 Cor. 3. 15. ***but* dung**=to be dung. Gr. *skubalon.* Only here. **that**=in order that. Gr. *hina.* **win**=gain. *kerdainō.* Occ. sixteen times, transl. gain except here, and 1 Pet. 3. 1. First occ. Matt. 16. 26. **9 not.** Ap. 105. II. **mine own, &c.**=any . . . of mine. **through.** Ap. 104. v. 1. **the faith of Christ**=Christ's faith. See Heb. 12. 2. **faith.** Ap. 150. II. 1. **by.** Ap. 104. ix. 2.

10 That I may °know Him, and the °power of His °resurrection, and the fellowship of His °sufferings, °being made conformable °unto His death;
11 °If °by any means I might °attain °unto the °resurrection °of the dead.
12 [1]Not °as though I °had already °attained, either were already °perfect: but I °follow after, [11]if that I may °apprehend that °for which °also I °am °apprehended °of [3]Christ Jesus.
13 Brethren, I count °not myself to have [12]apprehended: but *this* one thing *I do*, forgetting those things which are behind, and °reaching forth unto those things which are before,
14 I °press °toward the °mark °for the °prize of the °high calling of [3]God [1]in [3]Christ Jesus.
J2 15 Let us therefore, as many as *be* °perfect, °be thus minded: and [4]if in any thing ye °be °otherwise minded, [3]God shall °reveal °even this [10]unto you.
16 Nevertheless, °whereto we have already °attained, let us walk by the same °rule, let us mind the same thing.
K2 17 Brethren, °be °followers together of me, and °mark them which walk so as ye have us for an °ensample.
°18 (For many walk, of whom I have told you often, and now tell you even weeping, *that they are* the enemies of the cross of [7]Christ:
19 Whose °end *is* °destruction, whose °god *is their* °belly, and *whose* glory *is* [1]in their shame, who mind °earthly things.)
20 For our °conversation °is [1]in °heaven; °from °whence °also we °look for the Saviour, the [1]Lord °Jesus Christ:
21 Who shall °change our °vile body, °that it may be °fashioned like [10]unto °His glorious body, °according to the °working °whereby He is able even to °subdue all things [10]unto Himself.

J3 **4** Therefore, my brethren °dearly beloved and °longed for, °my joy and crown, so °stand fast °in the °Lord, *my* °dearly beloved.
2 I °beseech °Euodias, and °beseech Syntyche, that they °be of the same mind [1]in the [1]Lord.

10 know. Ap. 132. I. ii. **power.** Ap. 172. 1. **resurrection.** Ap. 178. II. 1. **sufferings.** Cp. 2 Cor. 1. 5–7. 1 Pet. 4. 13. **being made conformable.** Gr. *summorphoomai.* Only here. See *v.* 21. **unto**=to.
11 If. Ap. 118. 2. c. **by any means.** As Acts 27. 12. **attain.** Gr. *katantaō.* See Acts 16. 1. **unto.** Ap. 104. vi. **resurrection**=out-resurrection. Ap. 178. II. 2. Only here. **of the dead.** All the texts read, "the one from (Gr. *ek*) the dead", making the expression emphatic. Ap. 139. 3. The term resurrection of the dead (*anastasis nekrōn*) is of frequent occurrence (Matt. 22. 31. Acts 17. 32; 23. 6. 1 Cor. 15, 12, 13, 21, 42. Heb. 6. 2, &c.), and includes the resurrection to life, of the just, and the resurrection to judgment, of the unjust (John 5. 29. Acts 24. 15. Dan. 12. 2). Resurrection *from* the dead (*ek nekrōn*) implies the resurrection of *some*, the former of these two classes, the others being left behind. See Luke 20. 35. Acts 4. 2. Paul had no doubt of attaining to this, as may be seen from 1 Thess. 4. 15–17, written some ten years before. The *exanastasis* must therefore mean a further selection of some before the *anastasis* of 1 Thess. 4. 14, and Paul was not yet sure of attaining to this. Perhaps he had the assurance when he wrote 2 Tim. 4. 7. It is noteworthy that there is no reference to any living ones being caught up, or any *parousia* of the Lord here, as in 1 Thess. 4. 15, 16.
12 as though=that. **had.** Omit. **attained**=received. **perfect**=perfected. Ap. 125. 2. **follow after.** Same as *v.* 6 (persecuting), and *v.* 14 (press). **apprehend.** Gr. *katalambanō.* See John 1. 5. Eph. 3. 18. The Gr. adds "also". **for.** Ap. 104. ix. 2. **also.** Read after "apprehended". **am**=was. **of**=by. Ap. 104. xviii. 1.
13 not. Many texts read "not yet". **reaching forth.** Gr. *epekteinomai.* Only here.
14 press. Same as "follow after", *v.* 12. **toward.** Ap. 104. x. 2. **mark.** Gr. *skopos.* Only here. **for.** Ap. 104. ix. 3, but the texts read *eis* (Ap. 104. vi). **prize.** Gr. *brabeion.* Only here and 1 Cor. 9. 24. **high calling**=the calling above, or on high (Gr. *anō*, see John 8. 23). No shout, or voice of archangel or trumpet here, as in 1 Thess. 4. 16.
15 perfect. Ap. 125. 1. **be thus minded**=have this in mind. Gr. *phroneō*, as in *vv.* 16, 19. **be . . . minded.** Same word. **otherwise.** Gr. *heterōs.* Only used thus here. Cp. Ap. 124. 2. **reveal.** Ap. 106. I. ix. **even**=also. **16 whereto**=to (Ap. 104. vi) which (point). **attained**=come, as Matt. 12. 28. **rule.** Gr. *kanōn.* See 2 Cor. 10. 13, but the texts omit "rule", &c. **17 be.** Lit. become. **followers together.** Lit. fellow-imitators. Gr. *summimētēs.* Only here. **mark.** Gr. *skopeō.* See Luke 11. 35. **ensample.** Gr. *tupos*, pattern. **18, 19.** These verses form a *Parembole*, Ap. 6. **19 end.** Cp. Rom. 6. 21. 2 Cor. 11. 15. Heb. 6. 8. **destruction.** Same as "perdition", 1. 28. **god.** Ap. 98. I. i. 5. **belly.** Cp. Rom. 16. 18. **earthly.** See 2. 10. **20 conversation.** Gr. *politeuma.* Only here in N.T. It occ. in the Sept. and in 2 Macc. 12. 7. The seat of the government of which we are citizens (Gr. *politēs*), and of which we have both rights and responsibilities. Cp. the verb, 1. 27. **is**=exists even now. Gr. *huparchō.* See Luke 9. 48. **heaven**=heavens. See Matt. 6. 9, 10. **from.** Ap. 104. vii. **whence**=which, sing., referring to *politeuma.* **also.** To follow "Saviour". **look for**=eagerly wait for. Gr. *apekdechomai.* See Rom. 8. 19. **Jesus Christ.** Ap. 98. XI. **21 change**=transform, or change the fashion of. Gr. *metaschēmatizō.* See 1 Cor. 4. 6. **vile body**=body of humiliation (Gr. *tapeinōsis.* See Acts 8. 33). **that it may be.** The texts omit. **fashioned like**=(to be) conformed. Gr. *summorphos.* See Rom. 8. 29. Cp. *v.* 10, above. Notice the use of and contrast between *schēma*, fashion, in *metaschēmatizō*, and *morphē*, form, in *summorphos*, and cp. 2. 8. **His glorious body**=the body of His glory. **according to.** Ap. 104. x. 2. **working.** Gr. *energeia.* See Eph. 1. 19. **whereby He is able**=of His ability. **subdue**=subject. Cp. 1 Cor. 15. 27, 28.

4. 1 dearly beloved. Ap. 135. III. **longed for.** Gr. *epipothētos.* Only here. Cp. 1. 8. Rom. 1. 11. **my joy and crown.** Cp. 1 Thess. 2. 19, 20. **stand fast.** Cp. 1. 27. **in.** Ap. 104. viii. **Lord.** Ap. 98. VI. i. β. 2. B. **2 beseech.** Ap. 134. I. 6. **Euodias.** This should be Euodia (fem.). **be of the same mind.** Lit. mind (Gr. *phroneō*, as in 2. 2) the same thing.

3 And I °entreat thee also, °true °yokefellow,
help those women °which °laboured with me
[1]in the °gospel, °with Clement also, and *with*
°other my °fellowlabourers, whose names *are*
[1]in the °book of °life.
4 Rejoice [1]in the [1]Lord alway: *and* again I
say, Rejoice.
5 Let your °moderation be °known °unto all
°men. The °Lord *is* at hand.
6 Be °careful for °nothing; but [1]in every thing
by °prayer and °supplication [3]with thanksgiving let your °requests be °made known
°unto °God.
7 And the peace of [6]God, °which passeth °all
understanding, shall °keep your hearts and
°minds °through °Christ Jesus.
8 Finally, brethren, whatsoever things are
°true, whatsoever things *are* °honest, whatsoever things *are* °just, whatsoever things *are*
°pure, whatsoever things *are* °lovely, whatsoever things *are* °of good report; °if *there be*
°any °virtue, and °if *there be* °any praise,
°think on these things.

K^3 9 Those things which ye °have both learned,
and received, and heard, and °seen [1]in me, do:
and the [6]God of peace shall be [3]with you.

B L^1 10 °But I rejoiced [1]in the [1]Lord °greatly, that
now at the last your °care °of me °hath
flourished again; °wherein ye were °also careful, but ye °lacked opportunity.

M^1 11 °Not that I speak °in respect of °want: for
I °have learned, [1]in whatsoever state I am,
therewith to be °content.
12 I °know both how to °be abased, and I
°know how to abound: °every where and [1]in
all things I °am instructed both to be full and to
be hungry, both to abound and to suffer need.
13 I °can do all things [7]through °Christ
Which °strengtheneth me.

L^2 14 Notwithstanding ye have well done, °that
ye did communicate with my °affliction.

M^2 15 Now °ye Philippians [12]know also, that [1]in
the beginning of the gospel, when I departed
°from Macedonia, °no °church °communicated
with me °as concerning °giving and °receiving,
°but ye only.
16 For °even [1]in Thessalonica ye °sent once
and °again °unto my necessity.
17 [11]Not °because I °desire °a gift: but I
°desire °fruit °that may abound °to your
°account.

3 entreat = ask. Ap. 134. I. 3.
true. Gr. *gnēsios.* See 2 Cor. 8. 8.
yokefellow. Gr. *suzugos.* Only here. It is unknown who was intended.
which = since they.
laboured with. Gr. *sunathleō.* See 1. 27.
gospel. Ap. 140. **with.** Ap. 104. xi. 1.
other = the rest of. Ap. 124. 3. This may refer to Euodia and Syntychē.
fellowlabourers. Gr. *sunergos.* See 1 Cor. 3. 9.
book of life. See Rev. 3. 5; 13. 8; 20. 15; 22. 19, and cp. 21. 27. **life.** Ap. 170. 1.
5 moderation = forbearance. Gr. *epieikēs*: adj. only here; 1 Tim. 3. 3. Tit. 3. 2. Jas. 3. 17. 1 Pet. 2. 18.
known. Ap. 132. I. ii.
unto = to.
men. Ap. 123. 1.
Lord. Ap. 98. VI. i. β. 2. A.
6 careful = anxious. First occ. Matt. 6. 25.
nothing. Gr. *mēdeis.*
prayer . . . supplication. Ap 134. II. 2, 3.
requests. Ap. 134. II. 5.
made known. G. *gnōrizō.* See 1. 22.
unto. Ap. 104. xv. 3.
God. Ap. 98 I. i. 1.
7 which passeth = surpassing. Gr. *huperechō.* Cp. 3. 8. See Rom. 13. 1. Cp. Eph. 3. 20.
all understanding = every mind, or thought (Gr. *nous*).
keep = garrison. Gr. *phroureō.* See on 2 Cor. 11. 32. Occ. Gal. 3. 23. 1 Pet. 1. 5.
minds = thoughts. Gr. *noēma.* See 2 Cor. 2. 11.
through = in. Ap. 104. viii.
Christ Jesus. Ap. 98. XII.
8 true. Ap. 175. 1.
honest = honourable, venerable, grave. Gr. *semnos.* Here, 1 Tim. 3. 8, 11. Tit. 2. 2.
just. Ap. 191. 1.
pure. Gr. *hagnos.* See 2 Cor. 7. 11.
lovely. Gr. *prosphilēs.* Only here.
of good report. Gr. *euphēmos.* Only here.
if. Ap. 118. 2. a. **any.** Ap. 123. 3.
virtue. Gr. *aretē.* Only here, 1 Pet. 2. 9. 2 Pet. 1. 3, 5.
think on = take account of. Gr. *logizomai,* as Rom. 4. 3, &c.
9 have. Omit.
seen = saw. Ap. 133. I. 1.

4. 10-20 (*B*, p. 1772). THE PHILIPPIANS' SOLICITUDE FOR PAUL. (*Repeated Alternation*)

B | L^1 | 10. Their past lack.
  M^1 | 11-13. Paul's own content.
 L^2 | 14. Their well-doing.
  M^2 | 15-18. Paul's gratitude.
 L^3 | 19. Their need will be supplied.
  M^3 | 20. Paul's ascription.

10 This *v.* illustrates the Fig. *Epitherapeia* (Qualification), Ap. 6.
greatly. Gr. *megalōs.* Only here.
care = thinking. Gr. *phroneō,* as in *v.* 2.
of = on behalf of. Ap. 104. xvii. 1. **hath flourished again.** Lit. ye revived (Gr. *anathallō.* Only here). **wherein** = on (Ap. 104. ix. 2) which. **also careful** = mindful (Gr. *phroneō,* as above) also. **lacked opportunity.** Gr. *akaireomai.* Only here. **11 Not.** Ap. 105. I. **in respect of.** Ap. 104. x. 2. **want.** Gr. *husterēsis.* Only here and Mark 12. 44. **have.** Omit. **content.** Gr. *autarkēs.* Only here. Cp. 1 Tim. 6. 6. **12 know.** Ap. 132. I. i. **be abased.** See 2. 8, and 2 Cor. 11. 7. **every where** = in (Ap. 104. viii) every (place). **am instructed.** Lit. have been initiated into the secret. Gr. *mueō,* to initiate, whence is derived *musterion.* **13 can do** = am strong for. Gr. *ischuō.* Cp. Ap. 172. 3. **Christ.** Ap. 98. IX, but the texts read "Him". **strengtheneth.** Gr. *endunamoō.* See Acts 9. 22. **14 that ye did communicate with** = having had fellowship with. Gr. *sunkoinōneō.* See Eph. 5. 11. **affliction.** See 1. 16. **15 ye,** &c. = ye also, O Philippians, know. **from.** Ap. 104. iv. **no.** Gr. *oudeis.* **church.** Ap. 186. **communicated.** Gr. *koinōneō.* See Rom. 12. 13. **as concerning** = for (Ap. 104. vi) taking account (Ap. 121. 10). **giving.** Gr. *dosis.* Only here, and Jas. 1. 17. **receiving.** Gr. *lēpsis.* Only here. **but** = except. Gr. *ei mē.* **16 even,** &c. = in Thessalonica also. **sent.** Ap. 174. 4. **again.** Lit. twice. Gr. *dis.* Cp. 1 Thess. 2. 18. **unto.** Ap. 104. vi. **17 because** = that. **desire** = seek. Gr. *epizēteō.* First occ. Matt. 6. 32. **a** = the. **fruit** = the fruit. **that may abound** = increasing. **to.** Ap. 104. vi. **account.** Gr. *logos.* Ap. 121. 10.

18 But I °have all, and abound: I °am full, having received °of Epaphroditus the things *which were sent* °from you, an °odour of a °sweet smell, a sacrifice acceptable, °wellpleasing to [6] God.

L[3] 19 But my [6] God shall °supply all your need °according to His riches [1] in glory °by [7] Christ Jesus.

M[3] 20 Now [5] unto [6] God and our °Father *be* glory °for ever and ever. Amen.

A 21 Salute every °saint [1] in [7] Christ Jesus. The brethren which are °with me °greet you.
22 All the [21] saints salute you, °chiefly they that are °of Cæsar's °household.
23 The °grace of our [5] Lord °Jesus Christ *be* [3] with °you all. °Amen.

18 have. Gr. *apechō.* See Matt. 6. 2.
am full=have been filled. Ap. 125. 7.
of. Ap. 104. xii. 1.
from. Same as "of", above.
odour. Gr. *osmē.* See 2 Cor. 2. 14.
sweet smell. Gr. *euōdia.* See 2 Cor. 2. 15.
wellpleasing. Gr. *euarestos.* See Rom. 12. 1.
19 supply. Ap. 125. 7, as in *v.* 18.
according to. Ap. 104. x. 2. by=in (Gr. *en*).
20 Father. Ap. 98. III.
for ever and ever. Ap. 151. II. A. ii. 9. a.
21 saint. See Acts 9. 13.
with. Ap. 104. xvi. greet=salute.
22 chiefly=specially. of. Ap. 104. vii.
household. Lit. house. Gr. *oikia.*
23 grace. Ap. 184. I. 1.
Jesus Christ. Ap. 98. XI.
you all. All the texts read "your spirit". Ap. 101. II. 9, as in Gal. 6. 18.
Amen. Most texts omit.

THE EPISTLE TO THE COLOSSIANS.

THE STRUCTURE AS A WHOLE.

(Introversion.)

A | 1. 1, 2. EPISTOLARY AND SALUTATION.
B | 1. 3-8. REPORTS AND MESSAGES BY EPAPHRAS.
C | 1. 9—2. 7. PAUL'S SOLICITUDE FOR THE COLOSSIANS, AND PRAYER THAT THEY MIGHT ACKNOWLEDGE THE MYSTERY.
D | 2. 8-23. DOCTRINAL CORRECTION FOR FAILURE AS TO EPHESIAN TRUTH. HAVING DIED WITH CHRIST.
D | 3. 1—4. 1. DOCTRINAL CORRECTION FOR FAILURE AS TO EPHESIAN TRUTH. HAVING RISEN WITH CHRIST.
C | 4. 2-6. PAUL'S SOLICITUDE FOR THEM, AND THEIR PRAYERS ASKED CONCERNING HIS PREACHING THE MYSTERY.
B | 4. 7-9. REPORTS AND MESSAGES BY TYCHICUS AND ONESIMUS.
A | 4. 10-18. EPISTOLARY AND SALUTATION.

INTRODUCTORY NOTES.

1. Doctrine has more place than practice in the Epistle to the Colossians. There is a marked resemblance between it and the letter to the Ephesians, a prominent element of both, as well as of Philippians, being the apostle's insistence upon the reality of our union with Christ, as having died and risen again in Him, and the necessity for "holding fast the Head" (2. 19).

2. Subject. Colossians, like Galatians, proclaims our freedom from the "elements", or "rudiments", of the world. What those elements are, is sufficiently explained by the term "ceremonialism", the rites and ceremonies of religion as distinct from Christianity. Hence Paul's earnest admonition against a return to such, Jewish or other, inasmuch as this is to deny our completeness and perfection in Christ. Practically, it is to say that He is not sufficient, that something more is needed to be added to Him, some ordinance is wanted to make us quite complete. But, as the apostle unfolds to us, we died with Christ, and, consequently, ordinances are of no use to dead persons. In this Epistle all practical holiness is shown to spring from the holding of true doctrine, i. e. our life is the outcome of our belief. Then, our standing being complete and perfect in Christ, we cannot *grow* in this *standing*, but we may grow in the knowledge, experience, and enjoyment of it.

3. The statement in 2. 1 indicates that, at the time of writing the Epistle, Paul had not yet visited Colossæ, although commentators are divided on this point. Some believe that the apostle could not have missed out the city in one or other of his missionary journeys, although no mention is made in Acts. Others, referring to 1. 7, hold that Epaphras had been Paul's deputy to bear the good news to his fellow-citizens, for he was a Colossian (4. 12).

4. Date. The Epistle was written towards the end of the apostle's first imprisonment in Rome, about A.D. 62 (Ap. 180).

5. The Phrygian city of Colossæ was only a few miles from Laodicea, the importance of which gradually increased as the other city declined. Both so entirely disappeared that only in recent times were the sites discovered, and various ruins traced, by modern explorers.

THE EPISTLE OF PAUL THE APOSTLE

TO THE

COLOSSIANS.

A **1** PAUL, an apostle of ° Jesus Christ ° by the
° will of ° God, and Timotheus *our* brother,
2 To the ° saints and ° faithful brethren ° in
° Christ which are ° at Colosse: ° Grace *be*
° unto you, and peace, ° from [1] God our ° Father
° and the Lord Jesus Christ.

B 3 We ° give thanks to [1] God ° and ° the [2] Father
of our ° Lord ° Jesus Christ, ° praying always
° for you,
4 ° Since we heard of your ° faith [2] in ° Christ
Jesus, and of the ° love *which ye have* ° to all
the [2] saints,
5 ° For the hope which is ° laid up for you [2] in
° heaven, whereof ye ° heard before [2] in the
° word of the truth of the ° gospel;
6 Which ° is come ° unto you, as *it is* [2] in all
the ° world; and ° bringeth forth fruit, as *it
doth* ° also [2] in you, ° since the day ye heard *of
it*, and ° knew the [2] grace of [1] God [2] in truth:
7 As ye ° also learned ° of ° Epaphras our
° dear ° fellowservant, who is ° for you a [2] faithful ° minister of [2] Christ;
8 Who ° also ° declared [2] unto us your [4] love
[2] in the ° spirit.

C A^1 9 ° For this cause we also, [6] since the day we
heard *it*, do ° not cease to [3] pray [7] for you, and
to ° desire ° that ye might be ° filled with the
° knowledge of His [1] will [2] in all wisdom and
° spiritual ° understanding;
10 ° That ye might walk ° worthy of the [3] Lord
[6] unto all ° pleasing, ° being fruitful [2] in every
good work, and increasing ° in the [9] knowledge
of [1] God;
11 ° Strengthened ° with all ° might, ° according
to ° His glorious power, [6] unto all patience and
longsuffering ° with joyfulness;

B^1 C 12 [3] Giving thanks [2] unto the [2] Father, Which
° hath ° made us meet ° to be partakers of the
° inheritance of the [2] saints [2] in ° light:

1. 1 apostle. Ap. 189. Cp. 2 Cor. 1. 1.
Jesus Christ. The texts read Christ Jesus. Ap. 98. XII.
by. Ap. 104. v. 1.
will. Ap. 102. 2.
God. Ap. 98. I. i. 1.
2 saints. See Acts 9. 13.
faithful. Ap. 150. III. **in.** Ap. 104. viii.
Christ. Ap. 98. IX.
at = in, as above.
Grace. Ap. 184. I. 1. **unto** = to.
from. Ap. 104. iv.
Father. Ap. 98. III.
and, &c. Omit, with most of the texts.
3 give thanks. See Acts 27. 35.
and. The texts omit.
the Father. See John 1. 14.
Lord. Ap. 98. VI. i. β. 2. A.
Jesus Christ. Ap. 98. XI.
praying. Ap. 134. I. 2.
for. Ap. 104. xiii. 1.
4 Since we = Having.
faith. Ap. 150. II. 1.
Christ Jesus. Ap. 98. XII.
love. Ap. 135. II. 1. **to.** Ap. 104. vi.
5 For. Ap. 104. v. 2.
laid up = stored away. Gr. *apokeimai.* Only here, Luke 19. 20. 2 Tim. 4. 8. Heb. 9. 27.
heaven = the heavens. See Matt. 6. 9, 10.
heard before. Gr. *proakouō.* Only here.
word. Ap. 121. 10. **gospel.** Ap. 140.
6 is come. Gr. *pareimi,* whence *parousia.*
unto. Ap. 104. vi.
world. Ap. 129. 1.
bringeth forth fruit. See Rom. 7. 4. The texts add "and increasing".
also in you = in you also.
since = from. Ap. 104. iv.
knew. Ap. 132. I. iii.
7 also. Omit.
of. Ap. 104. iv.
Epaphras. See 4. 12. Philem. 23.
dear. Ap. 135. III.
fellowservant = fellow-slave. Gr. *sundoulos.* Occ. here, 4. 7: five times in Matt., and thrice in Rev. See Ap. 190. I. 2.
for. Ap. 104. xvii. 1. **minister.** Ap. 190. I. 1. **8 also, &c.** = declared also. **declared.** See 1 Cor. 1. 11. **spirit.** I. e. the product of the new nature. Ap. 101. II. 5.

1. 9—2. 7 (**C**, p. 1780). PAUL'S SOLICITUDE. (*Repeated Alternation.*)

C | A^1 | 1. 9–11. Solicitude as to their faith and walk.
  B^1 | 1. 12–22. Christ the Head of the body.
 A^2 | 1. 23–25. Solicitude as to continuing in the faith.
  B^2 | 1. 26, 27. The faith stated. The Mystery declared.
 A^3 | 1. 28—2. 2–. Solicitude as to their growth and assurance.
  B^3 | 2. –2, 3. The Mystery acknowledged.
 A^4 | 2. 4–7. Solicitude as to their stablishment in the faith.

9 For this cause = On account of (Ap. 104. v. 2) this (i. e. their faith and love). **not.** Ap. 105. I. **desire.** Ap. 134. I. 4. **that** = in order that. Gr. *hina.* **filled.** Ap. 125. 7. **knowledge.** Ap. 132. II. ii. **spiritual.** See 1 Cor. 12. 1. **understanding.** See 1 Cor. 1. 19. Ap. 132. II. iii. **10 That ye might** = To. **worthy** = worthily. **pleasing.** Gr. *areskeia.* Only here. **being fruitful** = fruit-bearing (*v.* 6). **in.** Ap. 104. vi. The texts read "by" (dative). **11 Strengthened.** Gr. *dunamoō.* Only here. Cp. Ap. 172. 1. **with.** Ap. 104. viii. **might.** Ap. 172. 1. **according to.** Ap. 104. x. 2. **His glorious power.** Lit. the might (Ap. 172. 2) of His glory. See Eph. 1. 19. **with.** Ap. 104. xi. 1.

1. 12–22 [For Structure see next page].

12 hath. Omit. **made, &c.** See 2 Cor. 3. 6. **to be partakers** = for (Ap. 104. vi) the share. **inheritance** = lot. Gr. *klēros.* **light** = the light. Ap. 130. 1.

13 Who °hath °delivered us °from the °power
of °darkness, and °hath °translated *us* °into
the °kingdom of °His dear Son;
14 [2]In Whom we have °redemption °through
His blood, *even* the °forgiveness of °sins:

D a 15 Who is the °image of the °invisible [1]God,
the °Firstborn of °every creature:

b 16 °For °by Him were all things created, that
are [2]in [5]heaven, and that are °in °earth,
°visible and [15]invisible, whether *they be*
thrones, or °dominions, or principalities, or
[13]powers: all things were created [1]by Him,
and °for Him:

E 17 And He °is °before all things, and [16-]by
Him all things °consist.

E 18 And He [17]is the °Head of the body, the
°church: Who is the °beginning, the [15]First-
born °from the dead;

D a [9]that [2]in all *things* He might °have the pre-
eminence.

b 19 [16]For it pleased °*the Father* that [2]in Him
should °all fulness °dwell;
20 And, °having made peace °through the
blood of His cross, [1]by Him to °reconcile all
things [6]unto Himself; [1]by Him, *I say*, whether
they be things [-16]in [16]earth, or things [2]in
[5]heaven.

C 21 And you, that were sometime °alienated and
enemies in *your* mind [16-]by °wicked works,
yet now °hath He [20]reconciled
22 [2]In the body of His flesh [20]through death,
to °present you holy and °unblameable and
°unreproveable in His sight:

A[2] 23 °If ye °continue in the [4]faith °grounded
and °settled, and *be* °not °moved away [2]from
the °hope of the °gospel, which ye °have
heard, *and* which was °preached °to [15]every
creature which is °under °heaven; whereof
I Paul °am made a [7]minister;
24 Who now rejoice [2]in my °sufferings [7]for
you, and °fill up °that which is behind of the
°afflictions of °Christ [2]in my flesh °for His
body's sake, which is the [18]church:
25 Whereof I [23]am made a [7]minister, [11]ac-
cording to the °dispensation of [1]God which °is
given to me [16]for you, to °fulfil the °word of
[1]God;

B[2] 26 *Even* the °mystery which hath been °hid
[2]from °ages and [2]from generations, but now is
°made manifest to His [2]saints,
27 To whom [1]God °would make known what
is the °riches of °the glory of this [26]mystery
°among the Gentiles, which is [24]Christ °in you,
the hope of °glory:

A[3] 28 Whom we °preach, °warning every °man,
and teaching every °man [2]in all wisdom;

1. 12-22 (B[1], p. 1781). CHRIST THE HEAD OF THE BODY. (*Introversion and Alternation.*)

B[1] | C | 12-14. Gentiles made meet.
  D | a | 15. Christ's essential glory.
    b | 16. Reason. Creation of all things.
      E | 17. Upholds all things.
      E | 18-. The Head of the body.
  D | *a* | -18. Christ's acquired glory.
    b | 19, 20. Reason. Reconciliation of all things.
C | 21, 22. Gentiles reconciled and presented perfect.

13 hath. Omit.
delivered = rescued. See Matt. 6. 13. Rom. 7. 24.
from. Ap. 104. vii. **power.** Ap. 172. 5.
darkness = the darkness. See Luke 22. 53. Eph. 6. 12.
translated. See Acts 13. 22.
into. Ap. 104. vi. **kingdom.** Ap. 112. 5.
His dear Son = the Son (Ap. 108. iii) of His love (Ap. 135. II. 1).
14 redemption. See Rom. 3. 24.
through His blood. All the texts omit.
forgiveness. Cp. Eph. 1. 7.
sins. Ap. 128. I. ii. 1.
15 image. Cp. Rom. 8. 29.
invisible. See Rom. 1. 20.
Firstborn. See Rom. 1. 23; 8. 29.
every creature = all creation.
16 For = Because.
by. Ap. 104. viii. **in.** Ap. 104. ix. 1.
earth. Ap. 129. 4.
visible. Gr. *horatos.* Only here.
dominions, &c. See Eph. 1. 21.
for. Ap. 104. vi.
17 is. Emph. **before.** Ap. 104. xiv.
consist = cohere, or hold together. Cp. Heb. 1. 3.
18 Head. See Eph. 1. 22, 23. **church.** Ap. 186.
beginning. See Prov. 8. 22-30.
from the dead. Ap. 139. 4.
have, &c. = become the pre-eminent One. Gr. *prōteuō.* Only here.
19 Instead of "*the Father*" supply the ellipsis with "*God*".
all fulness = all the fulness. Gr. *plērōma.* See Eph. 1. 23; 3. 19. **dwell.** See Acts 2. 5.
20 having made peace. Gr. *eirēnopoieō.* Only here. The noun Matt. 5. 9.
through. Ap. 104. v. 1.
reconcile. See Eph. 2. 16, and Ap. 196. 3. d.
21 alienated. See Eph. 2. 12.
wicked. Ap. 128. III. 1. **hath.** Omit.
22 present. See 1 Cor. 8. 8.
unblameable. See Eph. 1. 4.
unreproveable = unimpeachable. See 1 Cor. 1. 8.
23 If = If (Ap. 118. 2. a) at least.
continue. See Acts 10. 48.
grounded. See Eph. 3. 17.
settled. Gr. *hedraios.* See 1 Cor. 7. 37.
not. Ap. 105. II.
moved away. Gr. *metakineō.* Only here.
hope of the gospel. I. e. the return of the Lord. Cp. Tit. 2. 13.
gospel. Ap. 140. **have.** Omit.
preached. Ap. 121. 1. **to.** Ap. 104. viii.
under. Ap. 104. xviii. 2.
heaven = the heaven. See Matt. 6. 9, 10.
am made. Lit. became. Cp. "ordained" (same Gr. word) Acts 1. 22.

24 sufferings. Cp. Rom. 8. 18. 2 Cor. 1. 5. **fill up.** Gr. *antanaplēroō.* Only here. **that, &c.** = that which is lacking. Cp. 1 Cor. 16. 17. **afflictions.** See Acts 7. 10. **Christ:** i. e. the tribulations of the members of the body of which He is the Head. **for . . . sake** = for, as *v.* 7. **25 dispensation.** See 1 Cor. 9. 17 and cp. Eph. 3. 2. **is** = was. **fulfil.** Same as "fill", *v.* 9. **word.** Ap. 121. 10. **26 mystery.** Ap. 193, and cp. Rom. 16. 25. **hid.** See 1 Cor. 2. 7, and cp. Eph. 3. 9. **ages.** App. 129. 2 and 151. II. A. i. 1. **made manifest.** Ap. 106. I. v. **27 would** = desired to. Ap. 102. 1. **riches.** See Eph. 1. 7. **the glory.** See p. 1511. **among.** Ap. 104. viii. 2. **in** = among, as above. **glory** = the glory. **28 preach.** Ap. 121. 5. **warning** = admonishing. Gr. *noutheteō.* Cp. 3. 16. **man.** Ap. 123. 1.

[9]that we may [22]present every °man °perfect
[2]in [2]Christ °Jesus:
29 °Whereunto °I also labour, °striving
[11]according to His °working, which °worketh
[2]in me °mightily.

2 For I °would that ye °knew what great
°conflict I have °for you, and *for* them
°at Laodicea, and *for* as many as have °not
°seen my face °in the flesh;
2 °That their hearts might be °comforted,
being °knit together [1]in °love, and °unto all
°riches of the °full assurance of °understanding,
B[3] °to the °acknowledgement of the °mystery of
°God, °and of the Father, and of °Christ,
3 [1]In Whom are °hid all the treasures of
wisdom and °knowledge.
A[4] **4** And this I say, °lest any man should
°beguile you °with °enticing words.
5 For °though I be absent in the flesh, yet am
I °with you in the °spirit, joying and °behold-
ing your °order, and the °stedfastness of your
°faith °in [2]Christ.
6 As ye have therefore received °Christ Jesus
the °Lord, *so* walk ye [1]in Him;
7 °Rooted and °built up [1]in Him, and °stab-
lished °in the [5]faith, as ye have been taught,
abounding °therein [4]with thanksgiving.
D c **8** °Beware °lest °any man °spoil you °through
°philosophy and vain deceit, °after the tradition
of °men, °after the °rudiments of the °world,
and [1]not °after [2]Christ:
d **9** °For [1]in Him °dwelleth all the °fulness of
the °Godhead °bodily.
10 And ye are °complete [1]in Him, °Which is
the head of all °principality and °power:
e **11** [1]In Whom °also ye °are circumcised with
the circumcision °made without hands, [1]in
°putting off the body °of the sins of the flesh,
°by the circumcision of [2]Christ:
12 °Buried with Him [1]in °baptism, °wherein
°also ye are risen with *Him* [8]through the [5]faith
of the °operation of [2]God Who °hath °raised
Him °from the dead.
13 And you, °being dead [1]in your °sins and
the uncircumcision of your flesh, hath He
°quickened together [5]with °Him, having °for-
given you all °trespasses;

man. Ap. 123. 1.
perfect. Ap. 125. 1.
Jesus. The texts omit.
29 Whereunto=Unto (Ap. 104. vi) which.
I also labour=I labour also.
striving. See Luke 13. 24.
working. See Eph. 1. 19.
worketh. See Eph. 1. 11.
mightily=by (Gr. *en*) might (Ap. 172. 1).

2. 1 would=desire. Ap. 102. 1.
knew. Ap. 132. I. i.
conflict. See Phil. 1. 30.
for. Ap. 104. xiii. 1, but the texts read xvii. 1.
at. Ap. 104. viii.
not. Ap. 105. I. **seen.** Ap. 133. I. 8.
in. Ap. 104. viii.
2 That. Gr. *hina*, in order that.
comforted. Ap. 134. I. 6.
knit together. See Acts 9. 22.
love. Ap. 135. II. 1.
unto. Ap. 104. vi.
riches. See 1. 27.
full assurance. Gr. *plērophoria.* Here, 1 Thess. 1. 5. Heb. 6. 11; 10. 22.
understanding. Ap. 132. II. iii.
to=unto, as above; or, with a view to.
acknowledgement. Ap. 132. II. ii.
mystery. Ap. 193.
God. Ap. 98. I. i. 1.
and, &c. The texts read "*even* Christ".
Christ. Ap. 98. IX.
3 hid. Gr. *apokruphos.* Only here, Mark 4. 22. Luke 8. 17.
knowledge. Ap. 132. II. i.
4 lest, &c.=in order that (Gr. *hina*) no one (Gr. *mēdeis*).
beguile=deceive. Gr. *paralogizomai.* Here and Jas. 1. 22.
with. Ap. 104. viii.
enticing words. Gr. *pithanologia.* Only here.
5 though=even if (Ap. 118. 2. a).
with. Ap. 104. xvi.
spirit. Ap. 101. II. 8.
beholding. Ap. 133. I. 5.
order. See 1 Cor. 14. 40.
stedfastness. Gr. *stereōma.* Only here.
faith. Ap. 150. II. 1.
in=unto. Ap. 104. vi.
6 Christ Jesus. Ap. 98. XII.
Lord. Ap. 98. VI. i. β. 2 A. For this full title see Rom. 6. 23.
7 Rooted. See Eph. 3. 17.
built up. See Acts 20. 32, and cp. Eph. 2. 20.
stablished. See Rom. 15. 8 (confirm).
in=by.
therein=in (Ap. 104. viii) it.

2. 8–23 (**D**, p. 1780). DOCTRINAL CORRECTION. (*Extended Alternation.*)

D | c | 2. 8. Caution. Let no man deceive you.
d | 2. 9, 10. Christ the Head, and the body complete in Him.
e | 2. 11–15. Ordinances therefore done away in Christ.
c | 2. 16–18. Caution. Let no man judge you.
d | 2. 19. Christ the Head, and the body nourished by Him.
e | 2. 20–23. Ordinances therefore done away in Christ.

8 Beware=See (Ap. 133. I. 5) to it. **lest.** Ap. 105. II. **any man.** Ap. 123. 3. **spoil.** Gr. *sulagōgeō.* Only here. **through.** Ap. 104. v. 1. **philosophy.** Gr. *philosophia.* Only here. **after.** Ap. 104. x. 2. **men.** Ap. 123. 1. **rudiments.** See Gal. 4. 3. **world.** Ap. 129. 1. **9 For**=Because. **dwelleth.** See 1. 19. **fulness.** See 1. 19. **Godhead.** Ap. 98. I. ii. 1. **bodily.** Gr. *sōmatikōs.* Only here. The adj. in Luke 3. 22. 1 Tim. 4. 8. **10 complete.** See 1. 9. **Which**=Who. **principality.** Ap. 172. 6. **power.** Ap. 172. 5. **11 also.** Should follow "circumcised". **are**=were. **made without hands.** See 2 Cor. 5. 1. **putting off.** Gr. *apekdusis.* Only here. **of the sins.** Omit. **by.** Ap. 104. viii. **12 Buried with.** See Rom. 6. 4. **baptism.** Ap. 115. II. i. 1. I. e. His baptism unto death. **wherein**=in (Ap. 104. viii) Whom. **also, &c.**=ye were raised (Ap. 178. I. 8) also, and cp. 3. 1 and Eph. 2. 6. **operation.** Ap. 172. 4. **hath.** Omit. **raised.** Ap. 178. I. 4. **from, &c.** Ap. 139. 4. **13 being.** I. e. at that time. **sins.** Ap. 128. I. ii. 3. **quickened together**=made alive together. See Eph. 2. 5. **Him.** Texts add, "even you". **forgiven**=graciously forgiven. Ap. 184. II. 1. **trespasses.** Same as "sins", above.

14 °Blotting out the °handwriting of °ordinances that was °against us, which was
°contrary to us, and took it °out of the °way,
°nailing it to °His cross;
15 *And* having °spoiled [10] principalities and
[10] powers, He °made a shew of them °openly,
°triumphing over them [1] in °it.

c 16 Let °no °man therefore °judge you [1] in
°meat, or [1] in drink, or [1] in °respect of an °holyday, or of the °new moon, or of the °sabbath
days:
17 Which are a shadow of things to come;
but the body *is* of [2] Christ.
18 Let °no man °beguile you of your reward
°in a voluntary °humility and °worshipping of
angels, °intruding into those things which he
hath °not °seen, vainly °puffed up °by °his
fleshly mind,

d 19 And [1] not °holding the Head, °from °Which
all the body °by °joints and °bands °having
nourishment ministered, and [2] knit together,
increaseth with the °increase of [2] God.

e 20 Wherefore °if ye °be dead [5] with [2] Christ
°from the [8] rudiments of the [8] world, why, as
though living [1] in the [8] world, are ye °subject
to ordinances,
21 (Touch [16] not; taste °not; °handle °not;
22 Which all are °to perish with the °using;)
[8] after the °commandments and °doctrines of
[8] men?
23 °Which things °have indeed a °shew of
wisdom [1] in °will worship and [18] humility, and
°neglecting of the body; [1] not [1] in any °honour
°to the °satisfying of the flesh.

D f **3** °If ye then °be risen with °Christ, seek
those °things which are above, where
°Christ sitteth °on the right hand of °God.
2 °Set your affection °on [1] things above, °not
on things °on the °earth.
3 For ye °are dead, and your °life °is °hid
°with [1] Christ °in [1] God.
4 When [1] Christ, *Who is* our [3] life, shall
°appear, then shall ye also °appear [3] with Him
[3] in °glory.
5 °Mortify therefore your members which are
°upon the [2] earth; fornication, uncleanness,

14 Blotting out=Having blotted out. See Acts 3. 19.
handwriting. Gr. *cheirographon.* Only here.
ordinances. See Acts 16. 4.
against. Ap. 104. x. 1.
contrary. Gr. *hupenantios.* Only here and Heb. 10. 27.
out of. Ap. 104. vii. **way**=midst.
nailing=having nailed. Gr. *prosēloō.* Only here.
His. Read "the".
15 spoiled=put off. Gr. *apekduomai.* Only here and 3. 9.
made a shew of. Gr. *deigmatizō.* Only here. The verb *paradeigmatizō*, to expose to public infamy, occ. Matt. 1. 19 and Heb. 6. 6.
openly. See Mark 8. 32.
triumphing over. Cp. 2 Cor. 2. 14.
it. I. e. the cross.
16 no. Ap. 105. II. **man.** Ap. 123. 1.
judge. Ap. 122. 1.
meat, &c.=eating and drinking.
respect. Lit. part, i. e. taking part.
holyday=feast. See Lev. 23.
new moon. See 1 Chron. 23. 31.
sabbath *days*=sabbaths. See Lev. 23. 3, 7, 8, 21, 24, 27–32, 35, 36, 38, 39. John 20. 1.
18 no man. Gr. *mēdeis.*
beguile you of your reward=defraud you of your prize. Gr. *katabrabeuō.* Only here.
in, &c. Lit. willing (Ap. 102. 1) in (Ap. 104. viii), i. e. being a devotee to.
humility. See Acts 20. 19.
worshipping. See Acts 26. 5 (religion).
intruding into=investigating. Gr. *embateuō.* Only here.
not. Most texts omit.
seen. Ap. 133. I. 8.
puffed up. See 1 Cor. 4. 6.
by. Ap. 104. xviii. 1.
his fleshly mind=the mind of his flesh, i. e. the old Adam nature.
19 holding=holding fast. The central theme of the Epistle is the necessity of holding fast to the Head.
from. Ap. 104. vii.
Which=Whom.
by. Ap. 104. v. 1.
joints. See Eph. 4. 16.
bands. See Acts 8. 23 (bond).
having nourishment ministered. See 2 Cor. 9. 10.
increase. See Eph. 4. 16.
20 if. Ap. 118. 2. a.
be dead=died.
from. Ap. 104. iv.
subject, &c. Mid. of Gr. *dogmatizō*, which means to impose dogmas upon one. Supply *Ellipsis* with "*such as*".

21 not. Gr. *mēde.* **handle.** Gr. *thinganō.* Only here, Heb. 11. 28; 12. 20. **22 to perish**=for (Ap. 104. vi) corruption. See Rom. 8. 21. **using.** Gr. *apochrēsis.* Only here. **commandments.** Gr. *entalma.* Only here, Matt. 15. 9. Mark 7. 7. **doctrines.** The doctrines of men and demons are various, and therefore plural. See Matt. 15. 9. Mark 7. 7. 1 Tim. 4. 1; but the Divine teaching is one—1 Tim. 1. 10; 4. 6, 13, 16, &c. **23 Which**=Which order of. **have**=is having. **shew**=reputation. Ap. 121. 10. **will worship.** Gr. *ethelothrēskeia*, i. e. self-imposed worship. Only here. **neglecting**=not sparing. Gr. *apheidia.* Only here. **honour**=value. **to.** Ap. 104. xv. 3. **satisfying.** Gr. *plēsmonē.* Only here. Ascetic observances are of no value as remedies against the old nature.

3. 1–4. 1 (*D*, p. 1780). DOCTRINAL CORRECTION, AS HAVING RISEN WITH CHRIST.

(*Extended Alternation.*)

D | f | 3. 1–9. Our calling, as risen with Christ; the rule of the old man put off.
  g | 3. 10, 11. The new man put on.
   h | 3. 12–14. The effects seen in the exercise of love, the bond of perfectness.
 f | 3. 15. Our calling in the one body; the rule of God's peace begun.
  g | 3. 16. The word of Christ dwelling within.
   h | 3. 17—4. 1. The effects seen in the exercise of love, as the bond of all domestic relations.

3. 1 If. Ap. 118. 2. a. **be risen with**=were raised with. Ap. 178. I. 8. **Christ.** Ap. 98. IX. **things . . . above.** See Phil. 3. 13, 14. **on.** Ap. 104. viii. **God.** Ap. 98. I. i. 1. **2 Set your affection on**=Mind. Gr. *phroneō.* See Rom. 8. 5. **not.** Ap. 105. II. **on.** Ap. 104. ix. 1. **earth.** Ap. 129. 4. **3 are dead**=died. **life.** Ap. 170. 1. **is**=has been. **hid.** I. e. laid up (in store). Cp. Matt. 13. 44. **with.** Ap. 104. xvi. **in.** Ap. 104. viii. **4 appear**=be manifested. Ap. 106. I. v. **glory.** See p. 1511. **5 Mortify**=Put to death. See Rom. 4. 19; 6. 6–11. **upon.** Ap. 104. ix. 1.

°inordinate affection, °evil °concupiscence, and
°covetousness, which is idolatry:
6 °For which things' sake the °wrath of [1]God
cometh °on the °children of disobedience;
7 [3]In the which ye also walked some time,
when ye °lived [3]in them.
8 But now ye also °put off all these; °anger,
°wrath, °malice, blasphemy, °filthy communication °out of your mouth.
9 Lie [2]not °one °to another, °seeing that ye
have °put off °the old °man [3]with his °deeds;
g 10 And °have °put on the °new *man*, which
is °renewed °in °knowledge °after the °image
of Him That created him:
11 Where there is °neither Greek nor °Jew,
circumcision nor uncircumcision, °Barbarian,
°Scythian, °bond *nor* free: but [1]Christ *is* °all,
and [3]in all.
h 12 [10]Put on therefore, as the elect of [1]God,
holy and °beloved, bowels of °mercies, °kind-
ness, °humbleness of mind, °meekness, longsuffering;
13 °Forbearing one another, and °forgiving one
another, °if °any man have a °quarrel °against
°any; even as °Christ °forgave you, so °also
do ye.
14 And °above all these things *put on* °charity,
which is °the °bond of °perfectness.
f 15 And let the peace of °God °rule [3]in your
hearts, [9]to the which °also ye are called [3]in
one body; and be ye °thankful.
g 16 Let the °word of [1]Christ °dwell [3]in you
°richly [3]in all wisdom; teaching and °ad-
monishing one another in psalms and °hymns
and °spiritual °songs, °singing °with °grace
[3]in your hearts to °the Lord.
h 17 And whatsoever ye do [3]in [16]word or °deed,
do all [3]in the °name of the °Lord °Jesus,
°giving thanks to [1]God °and the °Father °by
Him.
18 Wives, °submit yourselves unto your own
°husbands, as it is °fit [3]in the [17]Lord.
19 [18]Husbands, [12]love *your* wives, and °be
[2]not bitter [13]against them.
20 °Children, obey *your* parents °in all things,
for this is °well pleasing °unto the [17]Lord.
21 Fathers, °provoke [2]not your [20]children *to*
anger, °lest they °be discouraged.
22 °Servants, obey [20]in all things *your*
°masters °according to the flesh; [2]not [16]with
°eyeservice, as menpleasers; but [3]in °single-
ness of heart, fearing °God:
23 And whatsoever ye do, do *it* °heartily, as
to the °Lord, and °not [20]unto [9]men;
24 °Knowing that °of the [17]Lord ye shall
receive the °reward of the °inheritance: for ye
°serve the [17]Lord [1]Christ.

inordinate affection = passion, or lust. See Rom. 1. 26.
evil. Ap. 128. III. 2.
concupiscence = desire. See John 8. 44.
covetousness. See Rom. 1. 29, and Eph. 5. 5.
6 For . . . sake. Ap. 104. v. 2.
wrath. See Rom. 1. 18.
on. Ap. 104. ix. 3.
children. Ap. 108. iii. See Eph. 2. 2.
7 lived. See Ap. 170. 1.
8 put off. See Eph. 4. 22.
anger. Same as "wrath", *v.* 6.
wrath. Gr. *thumos.* See Rom. 2. 8.
malice. Ap. 128. II. 2.
filthy communication. Gr. *aischrologia.* Only here.
out of. Ap. 104. vii.
9 one to another = to (Ap. 104. vi) one another.
seeing, &c. = having. **put off.** See 2. 15.
the old, &c. See Rom. 6. 6.
man. Ap. 123. 1.
deeds = practices. Cp. Rom. 8. 13.
10 have = having.
put on. See Rom. 13. 12, 14.
new. Gr. *neos.* See Matt. 9. 17.
renewed. See 2 Cor. 4. 16. **in.** Ap. 104. vi.
knowledge. Ap. 132. II. ii.
after. Ap. 104. x. 2.
image = pattern. See 1. 15.
11 neither. Ap. 105. I.
Jew, &c. Cp. Gal. 3. 28.
Barbarian. See Acts 28. 2.
Scythian. Regarded by the ancients as the lowest type of barbarians.
bond. Ap. 190. I. 2.
all, &c. See Eph. 1. 23.
12 beloved. Ap. 135. I. 1.
mercies. See Rom. 12. 1.
kindness. Ap. 184. III. a.
humbleness, &c. See 2. 18.
meekness. See Eph. 4. 2.
13 Forbearing. See Eph. 4. 2.
forgiving. See 2. 13.
if. Ap. 118. 1. b.
any man, any. Ap. 123. 3.
quarrel = grievance. Gr. *momphē.* Only here.
against. Ap. 104. xv. 3.
Christ. Most texts read "the Lord".
also *do* ye = do ye also.
14 above. Ap. 104. ix. 2.
charity = the love. Ap. 135. II. 1.
the = a. **bond.** See 2. 19.
perfectness. Gr. *teleiotēs.* Only here and Heb. 6. 1. See Ap. 125. 1.
15 God. The texts read "Christ".
rule. Lit. be umpire. Gr. *brabeuō.* Only here. Cp. 2. 18.
also, &c. = ye were called also.
thankful. Gr. *eucharistos.* Only here.
16 word. Ap. 121. 10.
dwell. See Rom. 8. 11.
richly. Gr. *plousiōs.* Only here, 1 Tim. 6. 17. Tit. 3. 6. 2 Pet. 1. 11.
admonishing. See 1. 28, and Acts 20. 31.
hymns. See Eph. 5. 19.
spiritual. See 1 Cor. 12. 1.
songs. See Eph. 5. 19.
singing. See Eph. 5. 19. **with.** Ap. 104. viii.

grace. See 1. 2. Ap. 184. I. 1. **the Lord.** The texts read "God". **17 deed** = in (Gr. *en*) work. **name.** See Acts 2. 21. **Lord.** Ap. 98. VI. i. *β.* 2. B. **Jesus.** Ap. 98. X. **giving thanks.** See Acts 27. 35. **and.** Omit. **Father.** Ap. 98. III. **by.** Ap. 104. v. 1. **18 submit.** See Eph. 5. 22. **husbands.** Ap. 123. 2. **fit.** See Eph. 5. 4. **19 be . . . bitter.** Gr. *pikrainō.* Only here, Rev. 8. 11; 10. 9, 10. **20 Children.** Ap. 108. i. **in** = according to. Ap. 104. x. 2. **well pleasing.** See Rom. 12. 1. **unto** = to, but the texts read "in" (Gr. *en*). **21 provoke.** See 2 Cor. 9. 2. **lest** = in order that (Gr. *hina*) . . . not (Ap. 105. II). **be discouraged** = have their spirit broken. Gr. *athumeō.* Only here. **22 Servants.** Ap. 190. I. 2. **masters.** Ap. 98. VI. i. *a.* 4. A. **according to.** Ap. 104. x. 2. **eyeservice . . . menpleasers.** See Eph. 6. 6. **singleness.** See Eph. 6. 5. **God.** The texts read "the Lord". **23 heartily.** Gr. *ek psuchēs.* See Ap. 110. V. 4. **Lord.** Ap. 98. VI. i. *β.* 2. A. **not** Ap. 105. I. **24 Knowing.** Ap. 132. I. i. **of.** Ap. 104. iv. **reward** = recompense. Gr. *antapodosis.* Only here. **inheritance.** See Eph. 1. 14. **serve.** Ap. 190. III. 2.

25 But he that doeth wrong shall receive °for the wrong which he hath done: and there is °no °respect of persons.

4 °Masters, give °unto *your* °servants that which is °just and equal; °knowing that ye also have a °Master °in °heaven.

C 2 °Continue in °prayer, and watch [1]in °the same °with °thanksgiving;
3 Withal °praying °also °for us, °that °God would open °unto us a °door of °utterance, to °speak the °mystery of °Christ, °for which I °am also in bonds;
4 [3]That I may °make it °manifest, as I ought to [3]speak.
5 Walk [1]in wisdom °toward them that are °without, °redeeming the time.
6 Let your °speech *be* alway [2]with °grace, °seasoned °with salt, that ye may [1]know how ye ought to °answer every man.

B 7 °All my state shall Tychicus °declare [1]unto you, °*who is* a °beloved brother, and °a °faithful °minister and fellowservant [1]in the °Lord:
8 Whom I °have °sent °unto you °for the same purpose, °that he might °know °your estate, and °comfort your hearts;
9 °With Onesimus, °a [7]faithful and [7]beloved brother, who is *one* °of you. They shall °make known [1]unto you all things °which *are done* here.

A 10 °Aristarchus my fellowprisoner saluteth you, and °Marcus, °sister's son to °Barnabas, (°touching whom ye received commandments: °if he come [8]unto you, receive him;)
11 And °Jesus, which is called °Justus, who are [9]of the circumcision. These only *are my* °fellowworkers °unto the °kingdom of [3]God, which have °been a °comfort [1]unto me.
12 °Epaphras, who is *one* [9]of you, a °servant of °Christ, saluteth you, always °labouring fervently °for you [1]in °prayers, [3]that ye may stand °perfect and °complete [1]in all the °will of [3]God.
13 For I °bear him record, that he hath a great °zeal [12]for you, and them *that are* [1]in Laodicea, and them [1]in Hierapolis.
14 Luke, the [7]beloved physician, and °Demas, greet you.
15 Salute the brethren which are [1]in Laodicea, and °Nymphas, and the °church which is °in his house.
16 And when this epistle is read °among you, cause [3]that it be read also [1]in the [15]church of the Laodiceans; and [3]that ye likewise read the *epistle* °from Laodicea.
17 And say to Archippus, °"Take heed to the °ministry which thou hast received [1]in the [7]Lord, [3]that thou °fulfil it."
18 The salutation by °the hand of me Paul. Remember my °bonds. [6]Grace *be* °with you. °Amen.

25 for the wrong, &c.=the wrong that he wronged. See Gal. 6. 7. no. Ap. 105. I. respect, &c. See Rom. 2. 11.

4. 1 Masters. See 3. 22. unto=to. servants. See 3. 22. just. Ap. 191. 1. knowing. Ap. 132. I. i. in. Ap. 104. viii. heaven. See Matt. 6. 9, 10.
2 Continue. See Rom. 12. 12. prayer. Ap. 134. II. 2. the same=it. with. Ap. 104. viii. thanksgiving. See 2. 7.
3 praying. Ap. 134. I. 2. also for us=for us also. for. Ap. 104. xiii. 1. that=in order that. Gr. *hina*. God. Ap. 98. I. i. 1. unto=to. door. See 1 Cor. 16. 9. utterance. Ap. 121. 10. speak. Ap. 121. 7. mystery. Ap. 193. Christ. Ap. 98. IX. for. Ap. 104. v. 2. am also, &c.=have been bound also. Cp. Acts 22. 21, 22.
4 make . . . manifest. Ap. 106. I. v. Cp. Eph. 6. 20.
5 toward. Ap. 104. xv. 3. without. See 1 Cor. 5. 12. redeeming. See Eph. 5. 16.
6 speech. Gr. *logos*. Ap. 121. 10. grace. Ap. 184. I. 1. seasoned. Gr. *artuō*. Only here, Mark 9. 50. Luke 14. 34. with. No prep. Dat. case. answer. Gr. *apokrinomai*. Ap. 122. 3.
7 All my state. Lit. all things according to (Gr. *kata*. Ap. 104. x. 2) me. declare=make known. Gr. *gnōrizō*. See Phil. 1. 22. *who is* a=the. beloved. Gr. *agapētos*. Ap. 135. III. a. Omit. faithful. Gr. *pistos*. Ap. 150. III. minister. Gr. *diakonos*. Ap. 190. I. 1. Lord. Ap. 98. VI. i. β. 2. B.
8 have. Omit. sent. Gr. *pempō*. Ap. 174. 4. unto. Gr. *pros*. Ap. 104. xv. 3. for. Gr. *eis*. Ap. 104. vi. that . . . your. The texts read "that ye may know our". that=in order that. Gr. *hina*. know. Gr. *ginōskō*. Ap. 132. I. ii. your estate. Lit. the things concerning (Gr. *peri*. Ap. 104. xiii. 1) you. Cp. *v.* 7. comfort. Gr. *parakaleō*. Ap. 134. I. 6.
9 With. Ap. 104. xvi. a=the. of. Ap. 104. vii. make known. Same as "declare", *v.* 7. which *are done*. Omit.
10 Aristarchus. See Acts 19. 29. Marcus. See Acts 12. 12. sister's son=cousin. Gr. *anepsios*. Only here. Barnabas. See Acts 4. 36. touching. Ap. 104. xiii. 1. if. Gr. *ean*. Ap. 118. 1. b.
11 Jesus. Cp. Acts 7. 45. Justus. See Acts 18. 7. fellowworkers. Gr. *sunergos*. See 1 Cor. 3. 9. unto. Gr. *eis*. Ap. 104. vi. kingdom. See Ap. 112. 2. been=become. comfort. Gr. *parēgoria*. Only here.

12 Epaphras. See 1. 7. servant. Gr. *doulos*. Ap. 190. I. 2. Christ. The texts add "Jesus". labouring fervently=striving, 1. 29. for. Gr. *huper*. Ap. 104. xvii. 1. prayers. Gr. *proseuchē*. Ap. 134. II. 2. perfect. Gr. *teleios*. Ap. 125. 1. complete. Gr. *plēroō*. Ap. 125. 7. The texts read "*plērophoreō*", as in Rom. 4. 21. will. Gr. *thelēma*. Ap. 102. 2. **13** bear . . . record. See 2 Cor. 8. 3. zeal. Gr. *zēlos*, but the texts read "*ponos*", labour. Cp. *v.* 12. **14** Demas. See 2 Tim. 4. 10. Philem. 24. **15** Nymphas. Not mentioned elsewhere. church. Ap. 186. in. Gr. *kata*. Ap. 104. x. 2. **16** among. Gr. *para*. Ap. 104. xii. 2. from. Gr. *ek*. Ap. 104. vii. **17** Take heed. Gr. *blepō*. Ap. 133. I. 5. ministry. Gr. *diakonia*. Ap. 190. II. 1. fulfil. Ap. 125. 7. **18** the hand, &c.=my hand of Paul. bonds. Cp. *v.* 3. with. Gr. *meta*. Ap. 104. xi. 1. Amen. Omit.

THE FIRST EPISTLE TO THE THESSALONIANS.

THE STRUCTURE OF THE EPISTLE AS A WHOLE.

(*Introversion and Alternation.*)

A | 1. 1. EPISTOLARY. INTRODUCTION.

B | A | 1. 2—3. 10. THANKSGIVING. NARRATION. APPEAL.

B | B | 3. 11-13. PRAYER.

B | *A* | 4. 1—5. 22. EXHORTATION. INSTRUCTION.

B | *B* | 5. 23-25. PRAYER.

A | 5. 26-28. EPISTOLARY. CONCLUSION.

THE FIRST EPISTLE TO THE THESSALONIANS.

INTRODUCTORY NOTES.

1. The church of the Thessalonians was planted by Paul, in association with Silas and Timothy (Acts 17. 1-9). Although some of the Jews believed, it was composed mainly of Gentiles, and their joyful reception of the message as the word of God was the prelude to active missionary operations in all Achaia and Macedonia (1. 8), a territory about as large as Great Britain. In this respect especially they were a model church. From them sounded forth "the word of the Lord", and they became examples to believers, showing the power of that word in their lives. The apostle writes in a joyful spirit, for he had just received from Timothy glad tidings of their faith and love (3. 6).

2. A large part of the Epistle is occupied with the doctrine of the Lord's coming, that coming which He Himself announced, Matt. 24. 36; 25. 31; 26. 64; *et al.*, the same coming of which He spoke in Acts 1. 7, "it is not for you to know the times and the seasons, which the Father hath put in His own power". The similarity of Paul's language, concerning "the times and the seasons" (5. 1), bears instruction for us. Indeed throughout the Epistle the nearness of that coming is emphasized (1. 10; 2. 12, 19; 3. 13; 4. 13-18; 5. 1-11, 23). But, as has been well observed, that which draws near may withdraw also, and such we know to be the case, for owing to His people's rejection of the King and kingdom, the latter is in abeyance till the "times of the Gentiles" are ended. 1 and 2 Thessalonians are unique in many respects; e.g. *chronologically*, as well as *canonically* (see App. 180, 192); the use of special terms in relation to the coming (*parousia* and *epiphaneia*) of our Lord; for these see Notes. And they are the only Epistles addressed to a church specifically.

3. This Epistle is the earliest of the writings of Paul, having been sent out from Corinth about the end of 52 or the beginning of 53 A.D. Some hold that, of all the books of the New Testament, it was the first written.

4. Thessalonica, now Salonica, on the bay of the same name, has always been one of the busiest ports of the Ægean. It was the chief city of a division of Macedonia, and is said to have had a population of 200,000 at the beginning of our era. Much smaller now, the city has always had a large proportion of Jews among its inhabitants.

THE FIRST EPISTLE OF PAUL THE APOSTLE

TO THE

THESSALONIANS.

A 1 °PAUL, and °Silvanus, and °Timotheus,
°unto the °church of the °Thessalonians
which is °in °God the °Father and *in* the
°Lord °Jesus Christ: °Grace *be* °unto you,
and peace, °from °God our °Father, and the
°Lord °Jesus Christ.

B A C a 2 We °give thanks to [1]God °always °for
you all, °making mention of you °in our
°prayers;
3 Remembering °without ceasing your work
°of °faith, and labour °of °love, and patience
°of hope °in our °Lord [1]Jesus Christ, in the
sight of [1]God °and our [1]Father;
4 °Knowing, brethren °beloved, your °election
°of [1]God.

b 5 For our °gospel came °not °unto you [1]in
°word only, but °also [1]in °power, and [1]in the
°Holy Ghost, and [1]in much °assurance; as ye
[4]know what manner of men we °were °among
you °for your sake.

c 6 And ye became °followers of us, and of the
[3]Lord, having received the [5]word [1]in much
°affliction, °with joy of the [5]Holy Ghost:
7 So that ye [5]were °ensamples to all that
°believe [1]in Macedonia and Achaia.
8 For [1]from you °sounded out the [5]word of
the [3]Lord [5]not only [1]in Macedonia and Achaia,
but °also [1]in every place your [3]faith °to [1]God-ward
°is spread abroad; so that we need °not
to °speak any thing.
9 For they themselves °shew °of us what

1. 1 Paul. In all his other Epistles, save Philippians, 2 Thessalonians, and Philemon, *apostolos* is added. He was held in terms of tender regard and affection by the converts at Philippi and Thessalonica, and there was no need to assert his authority.

Silvanus. Same as Silas. A leader of the church at Jerusalem (Acts 15. 22), and a prophet (*v.* 32), he accompanied Paul on his second missionary journey, and took part in the founding of the churches of Macedonia. Acts 15. 40–18. 18.

Timotheus. See 2 Cor. 1. 1.

unto=to.

church. Ap. 186.

Thessalonians. This and the Second Epistle are the only ones addressed in this form. Romans, Ephesians, Philippians and Colossians are addressed to "saints". The two Epistles to the Corinthians to "the church of God at Corinth", and Galatians to the "churches of Galatia".

in. Ap. 104. viii.

God. Ap. 98. I. i. 1.

Father. Ap. 98. III.

Lord. Ap. 98. VI. i. *β*. 2. B.

Jesus Christ. Ap. 98. XI.

Grace. Ap. 184. I. 1. Cp. Rom. 1. 7.

from. Ap. 104. iv. This last clause is omitted in most texts.

1. 2—3. 10 [For Structure see below].

2 give thanks. Gr. *eucharisteō*. See Acts 27. 35.

always. Ap. 151. II. G. i.

for. Ap. 104. xiii. 1.

making mention. See Rom. 1. 9.

in. Ap. 104. ix. 1.

prayers. Ap. 134. II. 2.

1. 2—3. 10 (A, p. 1787). THANKSGIVING. NARRATION. APPEAL. (*Extended Alternation.*)

B A | C | a | 1. 2–4. Thanksgiving.
b | 1. 5. Reason. The Gospel received not in word but power.
c | 1. 6–9. Its effect.
d | 1. 10–. Believers wait for God's Son.
e | 1. –10. Deliverance *from* the wrath to come.
D | 2. 1–12. Paul and the brethren. Their teaching while present.
C | *a* | 2. 13–. Thanksgiving.
b | 2. –13. Reason. The Gospel received as the word of God.
c | 2. 14. Its effect.
d | 2. 15, 16–. Unbelieving Jews killed God's Son.
e | 2. –16. Delivered *to* the wrath to come.
D | 2. 17—3. 10. Paul and the brethren. Their feelings while absent.

3 without ceasing. Gr. *adialeiptōs*. Only here, 2. 13; 5. 17. Rom. 1. 9. **of**=proceeding from. Gen. of origin. Ap. 17. 2; or, it may be Gen. of character. Ap. 17. 1, and would read "faithful work, loving labour, and hopeful patience". **faith.** Ap. 150. II. 1. **love.** Ap. 135. II. 1. Cp. 5. 8. Col. 1. 4, 8. Rev. 2. 4. **in**=of. Ap. 17. 5. **Lord.** Ap. 98. VI. i. *β*. 2. A. **and**=even. **4 Knowing.** Ap. 132. I. i. **beloved.** Ap. 135. I. 1. **election.** Gr. *eklogē*. See Acts 9. 15. **of.** Ap. 104. xviii. 1. **5 gospel.** Ap. 140. **not.** Ap. 105. I. **unto.** Ap. 104. vi. **word.** Ap. 121. 10. **also, &c.**=in power also. **power.** Ap. 172. 1. **Holy Ghost**=Divine power. Ap. 101. II. 14. **assurance.** Gr. *plērophoria*. See Col. 2. 2. **were**=became. **among.** Ap. 104. viii. 2. **for your sake**=on account of (Ap. 104. v. 2) you. **6 followers**=imitators. Gr. *mimētēs*. See 1 Cor. 4. 16. **affliction.** Gr. *thlipsis*. See Acts 7. 10. **with.** Ap. 104. xi. 1. **7 ensamples.** Gr. *tupos*. See Phil. 3. 17, and cp. 1 Tim. 4. 12. Tit. 2. 7. 1 Pet. 5. 3. **believe.** Ap. 150. I. 1. i. **8 sounded out.** Gr. *exēcheomai*. Only here. Cp. Luke 4. 37, and 1 Cor. 13. 1. **also.** The texts omit. **to God-ward**=towards (Ap. 104. xv. 3) God. **is spread abroad**=has gone forth. **not.** Ap. 105. II. **speak.** Ap. 121. 7. **9 shew**=report. **of.** Ap. 104. xiii. 1.

manner of °entering in we had °unto you, and
how ye turned °to [1]God [1]from °idols to °serve
°the living and °true [1]God;
d 10 And to °wait for His °Son °from °heaven,
Whom He °raised °from the dead, *even* °Jesus,
e Which °delivered °us °from the °wrath to
come.

D f **2** For yourselves, brethren, °know our °en-
trance in °unto you, that it was °not °in
vain:
2 But even °after that we had °suffered before,
and °were shamefully entreated, as ye [1]know,
°at Philippi, we °were bold °in our °God to
°speak [1]unto you the °gospel of °God °with
much °contention.
g 3 For our °exhortation *was* [1]not °of deceit,
°nor °of uncleanness, °nor [2]in °guile:
h 4 But as we were °allowed °of [2]God to °be
put in trust with the [2]gospel, even so we [2]speak;
[1]not as °pleasing °men,
i but [2]God, Which trieth our hearts.
5 For °neither at any time °used we °flattering
°words, as ye [1]know, °nor a °cloke of covetousness, [1]God *is* witness:
6 °Nor [3]of [4]men °sought we °glory, [5]neither
°of you, °nor *yet* °of °others, °when we might
have been °burdensome, as the °apostles of
°Christ.
k 7 But we were °gentle °among you, even as
a °nurse °cherisheth °her °children:
f 8 So being °affectionately desirous of you, we
were °willing to have imparted °unto you, [1]not
the [2]gospel of [2]God only, but °also our own
souls, because ye were °dear unto us.
g 9 For ye remember, brethren, our labour and
°travail: for labouring night and day, °because
h we would °not be chargeable unto °any of you,
we °preached °unto you the [2]gospel of [2]God.
i 10 Ye *are* witnesses, and [2]God *also*, how
°holily and °justly and °unblameably we
°behaved ourselves °among you that °believe:
k 11 As ye [1]know how we °exhorted and °com-
forted and °charged °every one of you, as
a father *doth* his [7]children,
12 °That ye would walk worthy of [2]God,
Who °hath °called you [9]unto °His °kingdom
and [6]glory.

entering in. Gr. *eisodos.* See Acts 13. 24.
unto. Ap. 104. xv. 3.
to. Same as "unto", above.
idols. This shows that these converts were mainly Gentiles. The Jews were bitterly hostile. Acts 17. 4-6, 13.
serve. Ap. 190. III. 2. **the** = a.
true. Ap. 175. 2.
10 wait for. Gr. *anamenō.* Only here in N.T. In Sept. of Job 7. 2. Isa. 59. 11. A much stronger word than *menō*, p. 1511.
Son. Ap. 108. iii. **from.** Ap. 104. vii.
heaven = the heavens. See Matt. 6. 9, 10.
raised. Ap. 178. I. 4.
from the dead. Ap. 139. 3, but with the texts, 139. 4.
Jesus. Ap. 98. X.
delivered = rescueth.
us. Paul and the brethren are intended, being Jews. See *v.* 9.
from. Ap. 104. iv, but texts read 104. vii.
wrath, &c. = the coming wrath. See 2. 16.

2. 1-12 (D, p. 1788). PAUL AND THE BRETHREN. THEIR TEACHING WHILE PRESENT.
(*Extended Alternation.*)

D | f | 1, 2. The Gospel of God imparted.
g | 3. Their exhortation; not of deceit.
h | 4-. Their preaching.
i | -4-6. God their witness.
k | 7. Comparison; as a nursing mother.
f | 8. The Gospel of God imparted.
g | 9-. Their labour; not to be chargeable.
h | -9. Their preaching.
i | 10. God their witness.
k | 11, 12. Comparison; as a father.

2. 1 know. Ap. 132. I. i.
entrance in. See 1. 9.
unto. Ap. 104. xv. 3.
not. Ap. 105. I. **in vain.** See 3. 5.
2 after that we had = having.
suffered before. Gr. *propaschō.* Only here.
were, &c. = having been treated with contumely. Gr. *hubrizō.* See Acts 14. 5. Referring to their being scourged, though Romans (Acts 16. 37, 38).
at. Ap. 104. viii.
were bold. Gr. *parrhēsiazomai.* See Acts 9. 27.
in. Ap. 104. viii.
God. Ap. 98. I. i. 1.
speak. Ap. 121. 7. **gospel.** Ap. 140.
with. Ap. 104. viii. In this one verse the preposition *en* is transl. "at", "in", "with".
contention. Gr. *agōn.* See Phil. 1. 30.
3 exhortation. Gr. *paraklēsis.* See Acts 4. 36, and Ap. 134. I. 6.
of. Ap. 104. vii. **nor.** Gr. *oude.*
guile. Gr. *dolos.* See Acts 13. 10.
4 allowed = tested, and so approved. Gr. *dokimazō.* Same as "trieth", and as "prove" (5. 21).

of. Ap. 104. xviii. 1. **be put in trust with.** Ap. 150. I. 1. iv. **pleasing men.** Cp. Gal. 1. 10. **men.** Ap. 123. 1. **5 neither, nor.** Gr. *oute.* **used we.** Lit. were (became) we in (Gr. *en*). **flattering words.** Lit. a word (Ap. 121. 10) of flattery. **cloke** = pretence. Gr. *prophasis.* See Acts 27. 30. **6 Nor.** Gr. *oute.* **sought we** = seeking. **glory.** See p. 1511. **of.** Ap. 104. iv. **others.** Ap. 124. 1. **when, &c.** = though able to be. **burdensome.** Lit. in (Gr. *en*) a burden, i. e. for a burden. Gr. *baros.* See Acts 15. 28. Cp. *v.* 9. **apostles.** Ap. 189. **Christ.** Ap. 98. IX. **7 gentle.** Gr. *ēpios.* Only here and 2 Tim. 2. 24. **among** = in (Gr. *en*) the midst of. **nurse.** Gr. *trophos.* Only here. **cherisheth.** Gr. *thalpō.* See Eph. 5. 29. **her** = her own. This shows that a mother is meant. The image expresses the intensity of the apostle's love for them. **children.** Ap. 108. i. **8 affectionately desirous.** Gr. *himeiromai*, or *homeiromai.* Only here. **willing** = well pleased. **unto** = to. **also, &c.** = our own lives (Ap. 110. III. 2) also. **dear unto.** Ap. 135. III. **9 travail** = toil. Gr. *mochthos.* See 2 Cor. 11. 27. **because, &c.** = with a view to (Ap. 104. xv. 3) our not (Ap. 105. II) being chargeable unto. Gr. *epibareō.* See 2 Cor. 2. 5. **any.** Ap. 123. 3. **preached.** Ap. 121. 1. **unto.** Ap. 104. vi. **10 holily.** Gr. *hosiōs.* Only here. Cp. the adj. Acts 2. 27. **justly.** Gr. *dikaiōs.* See 1 Cor. 15. 34, and cp. Ap. 191. 1. **unblameably.** Gr. *amemptōs.* Only here and 5. 23. Cp. 3. 13. **behaved ourselves.** Lit. became. **among** = towards. No prep. **believe.** Ap. 150. I. 1. i. **11 exhorted.** Ap. 134. I. 6. **comforted.** Gr. *paramutheomai.* See John 11. 19. **charged** = testified to. Gr. *marturomai*, with texts. See Gal. 5. 3. **every** = each. **12 That, &c.** = With a view to (Ap. 104. vi) your walking. **hath.** Omit. **called.** Some texts read "calleth". **His** = His own. **kingdom.** See App. 112, 114.

C a 13 °For this cause °also thank we [2]God °without ceasing, because,

b when ye received the [5]word of [2]God °which ye heard °of us, ye received *it* [1]not *as* the [5]word of [4]men, but as it is °in truth, the [5]word of [2]God, which °effectually worketh also [2]in you that [10]believe.

c 14 For ye, brethren, became °followers of the °churches of [2]God which [2]in Judæa are [2]in °Christ Jesus: for ye also °have suffered °like things [4]of your own °countrymen, even as °they *have* [4]of the Jews;

d 15 Who both killed the °Lord °Jesus, and °their own °prophets, and °have persecuted us; and they please [9]not [2]God, and are contrary to all [4]men;

16 Forbidding us to [2]speak to the Gentiles °that they might be saved, °to fill up their °sins °alway:

e for °the wrath °is come °upon them °to the °uttermost.

D E l 17 But we, brethren, °being taken °from you °for °a short time in °presence, [1]not in heart, °endeavoured the more abundantly to °see your °face [2]with great desire.

18 Wherefore we °would have come [1]unto you, even I Paul, °once and again; but Satan °hindered us.

m 19 For what *is* our hope, or joy, or °crown of °rejoicing? *Are* °not even ye in the presence of our [15]Lord °Jesus Christ [2]at His °coming?

20 For ye are our [6]glory and joy.

F n **3** Wherefore °when we could °no longer °forbear, we °thought it good to be left °at °Athens alone;

o 2 And °sent Timotheus, our brother, and °minister of °God, and our °fellowlabourer °in the °gospel of °Christ, °to establish you, and to °comfort you °concerning your °faith:

3 That °no man should be °moved °by these °afflictions: for yourselves °know that we °are appointed °thereunto.

4 For verily, when we were °with you, we °told you before that we °should °suffer tribulation; even as it °came to pass, and ye [3]know.

F n 5 °For this cause, [1]when I could [1]no longer [1]forbear,

o I [2]sent [2]to °know your [2]faith, °lest by some means the tempter °have tempted you, and our labour be °in vain.

13 For this cause = On account of (Ap. 104. v. 2) this.
also thank we = we also thank. See 1. 2.
without ceasing. See 1. 3.
which ye heard. Lit. of hearing. Gr. *akoē*, as in Gal. 3. 2, 5.
of. Ap. 104. xii. 1.
in truth = truly.
effectually worketh = is made energetic. See Ap. 172. 4.

14 followers. See 1. 6.
churches. Ap. 186.
Christ Jesus. Ap. 98. XII. have. Omit.
like = the same.
countrymen. Gr. *sumphuletēs*. Only here.
they = they also.

15 Lord. Ap. 98. VI. i. β. 2. A.
Jesus = even Jesus. Ap. 98. X.
their own = the.
prophets. Ap. 189.
have persecuted us = chased us out. Gr. *ekdiōkō*. Only here and Luke 11. 49.

16 that = in order that. Gr. *hina*.
to, &c. = with a view to (Ap. 104. vi) their filling up (Gr. *anaplēroō*). See 1 Cor. 14. 16.
sins. Ap. 128. I. ii. 1.
alway. Ap. 151. II. G. i.
the wrath: the appointed wrath. See Lev. 26. Deut. 28 and 32.
is come. Gr. *phthanō*. See Luke 11. 20.
upon. Ap. 104. ix. 3.
to. Ap. 104. vi.
uttermost = end. Gr. *telos*.

2. 17—3. 10 (*D*, p. 1788). PAUL AND THE BRETHREN. THEIR FEELINGS WHILE ABSENT. (*Introversion and Alternation.*)

D | E | l | 2. 17, 18. Their departure.
m | 2. 19, 20. Joy in the Thessalonians.
F | n | 3. 1. Their solicitude.
o | 3. 2–4. Mission of Timothy.
F | *n* | 3. 5-. Their solicitude.
o | 3. -5. Mission of Timothy.
E | *l* | 3. 6. Timothy's return.
m | 3. 7–10. Joy in the Thessalonians.

17 being taken = having been bereaved. Gr. *aporphanizomai*. Only here. Cp. John 14. 18.
from. Ap. 104. iv. for. Ap. 104. xv. 3.
a short time. Lit. a season of an hour.
presence, face. Cp. 1 Cor. 5. 3. Col. 2. 5.
endeavoured = were diligent.
see. Ap. 133. I. 1.

18 would have = wished to. Ap. 102. 1.
once and again. Cp. Phil. 4. 16.
hindered. Gr. *enkoptō*. See Acts 24. 4.

19 crown. Cp. Phil. 4. 1.
rejoicing. Gr. *kauchēsis*. See Rom. 3. 27.
not. Ap. 105. I (a).
Jesus Christ. Ap. 98. XI, but the texts omit "Christ".
coming. Gr. *parousia*. See Matt. 24. 3. The first of seven occ. in these two Epistles. See 3. 13; 4. 15; 5. 23. 2 Thess. 2. 1, 8, 9.

3. 1 when, &c. = no longer bearing it, i. e. able to bear it. thought it good = were well pleased. no longer. Gr. *mēketi*. forbear = bear. See 1 Cor. 9. 12. Same as "were willing" (2. 8). at. Ap. 104. viii. Athens. See Acts 17. 15, 16. When Silas and Timothy joined Paul, he and Silas must have agreed to dispatch Timothy to Thessalonica, and then Silas must have departed on some other mission. See in *v.* 5 the change from "we" to "I". **2** sent. Ap. 174. 4. minister. Ap. 190. I. 1. God. Ap. 98. I. i. 1. fellowlabourer. Gr. *sunergos*. See 1 Cor. 3. 9. The texts vary here. in. Ap. 104. viii. gospel. Ap. 140. Christ. Ap. 98. IX. to, &c. = with a view to (Gr. *eis*) establishing. comfort: or, exhort. Ap. 134. I. 6 concerning. Ap. 104. xiii. 1, but the texts read *huper* (Ap. 104. xvii. 1). faith. Ap. 150. II. 1. **3** no man. Gr. *mēdeis*. moved: or, agitated. Gr. *sainō*. Only here. by. Ap. 104. viii. afflictions. Gr. *thlipsis*. See 1. 6. know. Ap. 132. I. i. are appointed. Lit. lie. Gr. *keimai*. Cp. Luke 2. 34. Phil. 1. 17. thereunto = unto (Ap. 104. vi) this. **4** with. Ap. 104. xv. 3. told . . . before = foretold. Gr. *prolegō*. See 2 Cor. 13. 2. should = were about to. suffer, &c. = be afflicted. Gr. *thlibō*. came to pass. Add "also". **5** For this cause = On account of (Ap. 104. v. 2) this. know. Ap. 132. I. ii. lest, &c. Gr. *mē pōs*. have. Omit. in vain. See 2. 1, and cp. 2 Cor. 6. 1. Gal. 2. 2. Phil. 2. 16.

E *l* 6 But now when Timotheus came °from you
°unto us, and °brought us good tidings of your
[2]faith and °charity, and that ye have good
remembrance of us °always, °desiring greatly
to °see us, as we also *to see* you:

m 7 °Therefore, brethren, we were [2]comforted
°over you °in all our [3]affliction and °distress
°by your [2]faith:
8 For now we °live, °if ye °stand fast [2]in the
°Lord.
9 For what thanks can we render to [2]God
again °for you, °for all the joy wherewith we
joy °for your sakes before our [2]God;
10 Night and day °praying °exceedingly °that
we might [6]see your face, and might °perfect
°that which is lacking °in your [2]faith?

B 11 Now [2]God Himself and our °Father, and
our °Lord °Jesus Christ, °direct our way
[6]unto you.
12 And the [11]Lord make you to °increase and
abound in °love one °toward another, and
°toward all *men*, even as °we *do* °toward you:
13 °To the end He may °stablish your hearts
°unblameable [2]in °holiness °before [2]God, even
our [11]Father, [1]at the °coming of our [11]Lord
[11]Jesus Christ °with all His °saints.

B A G J **4** Furthermore then we °beseech you,
brethren, and °exhort *you* °by the °Lord
°Jesus, °that as ye have received °of us how
ye ought to walk and to please °God, *so* ye
would abound °more and more.

K 2 For ye °know what °commandments we
gave you °by the °Lord [1]Jesus.

L p 3 For this is the °will of [1]God, *even* your
°sanctification, that ye should °abstain °from
fornication:
4 That °every one of you should [2]know how
to °possess °his °vessel °in [3]sanctification and
honour;
5 °Not [4]in the °lust of °concupiscence, even as
the °Gentiles which [2]know °not [1]God:
q 6 That °no *man* °go beyond and °defraud his
brother [4]in °*any* matter: because that the
[1]Lord *is* the °avenger °of all °such, as we °also
have forewarned you and °testified.

6 from. Ap. 104. iv.
unto. Ap. 104. xv. 3.
brought . . . good tidings. Ap. 121. 4. The only place, save Luke 1. 19, where *euangelizō* does not refer to the gospel.
charity = love. Ap. 135. II. 1.
always. Ap. 151. II. G. i.
desiring greatly. Gr. *epipotheō*. See Rom. 1. 11.
see. Ap. 133. I. 1.
7 Therefore. Same as "For this cause", *v.* 5.
over. Ap. 104. ix. 2. in. Same as "over".
distress = necessity, as 1 Cor. 7. 26.
by. Ap. 104. v. 1.
8 live. See Ap. 170. 1. if. Ap. 118. 1. b.
stand fast. Gr. *stēkō*. See Phil. 4. 1.
Lord. Ap. 98. VI. i. *β*. 2. B.
9 for. Ap. 104. xiii. 1. for. Ap. 104. ix. 2.
for your sakes = on account of (Ap. 104. v. 2) you.
10 praying. Ap. 134. I. 5.
exceedingly. Gr. *huper* (Ap. 104. xvii. 1) *ek* (Ap. 104. vii) *perissou*. Most of the texts read as one word. See Eph. 3. 20.
that we might. Lit. for (Ap. 104. vi) the seeing (Ap. 133. I. 1). perfect. Ap. 125. 8.
that, &c. = the shortcomings. Gr. *husterēma*. See 1 Cor. 16. 17. in = of.
11 Father. Ap. 98. III.
Lord. Ap. 98. VI. i. *β*. 2. A.
Jesus Christ. Ap. 98. XI, but the texts omit "Christ" here and *v.* 13.
direct. Gr. *kateuthunō*. Here; 2 Thess. 3. 5. Luke 1. 79. Cp. *euthunō* in John 1. 23 and Jas. 3. 4.
12 increase. Gr. *pleonazō*. See Rom. 5. 20.
love. Same as "charity", *v.* 6.
toward. Ap. 104. vi. we = we also.
13 To the end. Ap. 104. vi.
stablish. Gr. *stērizō*. See Rom. 1. 11.
unblameable. Gr. *amemptos*. See Phil. 2. 15.
holiness. Gr. *hagiōsunē*. See Rom. 1. 4.
before. See John 12. 37.
coming. Gr. *parousia*. Cp. 2. 19.
with. Ap. 104. xi. 1. saints. See Acts 9. 13.

4. 1—5. 22 [For Structures see below].

4. 1 beseech. Ap. 134. I. 3.
exhort. Ap. 134. I. 6. by. Ap. 104. viii.
Lord. Ap. 98. VI. i. *β*. 2. B.
Jesus. Ap. 98. X.
that = in order that. Gr. *hina*.
of. Ap. 104. xii. 1. God. Ap. 98. I. i. 1.
more and more = the more.
2 know. Ap. 132. I. i.
commandments. Gr. *parangelia*. Cp. 1 Tim. 1. 18 (charge).

4. 1—5. 22 (*A*, p. 1787). EXHORTATION AND INSTRUCTION. (*Introversion.*)

A | G | 4. 1-12. Exhortation.
  H | 4. 13—5. 11. Instruction.
G | 5. 12-22. Exhortation.

4. 1-12 (G, above). EXHORTATION. (*Introversion and Alternation.*)

G | J | 1. Walk, as before God.
  K | 2. Commandments.
    L | p | 3-5. God's will: sanctification (positive and negative).
      q | 6. Brethren: not to be defrauded (negative).
    L | *p* | 7, 8. God's call: sanctification (negative and positive).
      q | 9, 10. Brethren: to be loved (positive).
  K | 11. Commandments.
J | 12. Walk, as regards men.

by. Ap. 104. v. 1. Lord. Ap. 98. VI. i. *β*. 2. A. **3** will. Ap. 102. 2. sanctification. Gr. *hagiasmos*. See Rom. 6. 19. abstain. Gr. *apechomai*. See Acts 15. 20. from. Ap. 104. iv. **4** every = each. possess. Gr. *ktaomai*. See Luke 21. 19. his = his own. vessel. Gr. *skeuos*. Cp. 1 Pet. 3. 7. in. Ap. 104. viii. **5** Not. Ap. 105. II. lust. Gr. *pathos*. See Rom. 1. 26. The R.V renders it "passion". concupiscence = lust, or desire. Gentiles = Gentiles also. **6** no *man* = that he (should) not (Ap. 105. II). go beyond. Gr. *huperbainō*. Only here. defraud. Gr. *pleonekteō*. See 2 Cor. 2. 11. *any* = the. avenger. Gr. *ekdikos*. Only here and Rom. 13. 4. of = concerning. Ap. 104. xiii. 1. such = such (sins). also have forewarned = forewarned also. Gr. *proeipō*. Only here; Acts 1. 16. Gal. 5. 21. testified. Gr. *diamarturomai*. See Acts 2. 40.

Lp 7 For [1]God °hath °not called us °unto uncleanness, but °unto °holiness.

8 He therefore that °despiseth, °despiseth [7]not °man, but [1]God, Who °hath also given °unto °us His °holy Spirit.

q 9 But °as touching °brotherly love ye need [7]not that I write °unto you: for ye yourselves are °taught of God °to °love one another.

10 And indeed ye do it °toward all the brethren which are [4]in all Macedonia: but we °beseech you, brethren, that ye °increase [1]more and more;

K 11 And that ye °study to °be quiet, and to °do your own business, and to work with your own hands, as we °commanded you;

J 12 [1]That ye may walk °honestly °toward °them that are without, and *that* ye may have lack of °nothing.

H r 13 But °I °would [7]not °have you to be ignorant, brethren, °concerning them which are °asleep, [1]that ye sorrow [5]not, even as °others which have °no hope.

s 14 °For °if we °believe that [1]Jesus died and °rose again, °even so them also which °sleep °in [1]Jesus will [1]God bring °with Him.

t 15 [14]For this we say [9]unto you [1]by °the °word of the [1]Lord, that we which are alive *and* °remain [8]unto the °coming of the [2]Lord, shall °not °prevent them which are °asleep.

u 16 °For the [2]Lord Himself shall descend [3]from °heaven °with a °shout, °with the voice of the °archangel, and °with the °trump of [1]God: and °the dead [4]in °Christ shall [14]rise first:

17 °Then we which are alive, *and* [15]remain, shall be °caught up °together [14]with them [4]in °the clouds, [9]to °meet the [2]Lord °in the air: and °so shall we °ever be [14]with the [1]Lord.

v 18 °Wherefore °comfort one another [16]with these [15]words.

7 hath. Omit. **not.** Ap. 105. I. **unto.** Ap. 104. ix. 2. **unto.** Ap. 104. viii. **holiness.** Same as "sanctification", *v.* 3.
8 despiseth. Gr. *atheteō.* See John 12. 48. **man.** Ap. 123. 1. **hath also given.** The texts read "giveth". **unto.** Ap. 104. vi. **us.** The texts read "you". **holy Spirit.** Though there are two articles, the reference is to the gifts of Acts 2. 4, the Spirit being always the Giver. Ap. 101. II. 14.
9 as touching. Ap. 104. xiii. 1. **brotherly love.** Gr. *philadelphia.* See Rom. 12. 10. **unto**=to. **taught of God.** Gr. *theodidaktos.* Only here. **to.** Ap. 104. vi. **love.** Ap. 135. I. 1.
10 toward. Ap. 104. vi. **beseech.** Same as "exhort", *v.* 1. **increase.** Same as "abound", *v.* 1.
11 study. Gr. *philotimeomai.* See Rom. 15. 20. **be quiet.** Gr. *hēsuchazō.* See Luke 23. 56. **do, &c.**=attend to your own affairs. Cp. 2 Thess. 3. 11. **commanded.** Gr. *parangellō.* See Acts 1. 4.
12 honestly. Gr. *euschēmonōs.* See Rom. 13. 13. **toward.** Ap. 104. xv. 3. **them that are without.** Cp. 1 Cor. 5. 12, 13. Col. 4. 5. **nothing.** Gr. *mēdeis.*

4. 13—5. 11 (H, p. 1791). INSTRUCTION.
(*Extended Alternation.*)

H | r | 4. 13. Instruction necessary as to those who are asleep.
  s | 4. 14. First reason. For (*gar*) God will bring them from the dead.
    t | 4. 15. Second reason. For (*gar*) those who are alive shall not precede them.
      u | 4. 16, 17. Third reason. Because (*hoti*) both shall be caught up together (*hama*).
        v | 4. 18. Wherefore comfort one another.
  r | 5. 1. Instruction not necessary as to times and seasons.
  s | 5. 2–6. First reason. For (*gar*) they knew already the character of the day of the Lord.
    t | 5. 7, 8. Second reason. For (*gar*) they that sleep sleep in the night.
      u | 5. 9, 10. Third reason. Because (*hoti*) we are appointed to live together (*hama*) with Him.
        v | 5. 11. Wherefore comfort one another.

13 I. Texts read "we". **would.** Ap. 102. 1. **have you, &c.** See Rom. 1. 13. **concerning.** Ap. 104. xiii. 1. **asleep**=falling asleep. Ap. 171. 2. **others**=the rest. Ap. 124. 3. Add "also". **no**=not, as *v.* 5. **14 For.** Gr. *gar.* **if.** Ap. 118. 2. a. **believe.** Ap. 150. I. 1. iii. **rose again.** Ap. 178. I. 1. **even so them also.** Read "so (*we believe*) also that them". **sleep**=are fallen asleep. **in Jesus**=through (Ap. 104. v. 1) Jesus. This stands in the Gr. between the words "sleep" and "bring". To which does it belong? "Sleep in Jesus" is an expression not found elsewhere. In *v.* 16 the "dead in Christ" are spoken of, with which may be compared 1 Cor. 15. 18. And the proper meaning of *dia* with the Genitive is "through", though it is wrongly transl. "in" Matt. 26. 61. Mark 14. 58. 1 Tim. 2. 15. Heb. 7. 9; 13. 22, and "among" 2 Tim. 2. 2. The context will show that "through" is the meaning, as the R.V. renders it in margin. "Through" the Lord Jesus Christ we have peace, reconciliation, sonship, the Holy Spirit's gifts, victory, and many other blessings; Rom. 5. 1, 10; Rom. 8. 37. 1 Cor. 15. 57. 2 Cor. 5. 18. Eph. 1. 5. Col. 1. 20. Tit. 3. 6. Death is not a blessing, but an enemy. Inflicted by the Lord (Rev. 2. 23; 19. 21), and permitted by Him, it is the work of the devil (Heb. 2. 14. Rev. 2. 10), whose works He came to destroy. It is better, therefore, to take the words "through Jesus" with "bring", and read, "God will through Jesus bring with Him", in harmony with John 5. 25; 11. 25. Phil. 3. 21. **with.** Ap. 104. xvi. **15 the.** Omit. **word.** Ap. 121. 10. **remain.** Gr. *perileipomai.* Only here and *v.* 17. Is this subsequent to Phil. 3. 11? **coming.** Cp. 2. 19. **not.** Ap. 105. III. **prevent**=anticipate. Gr. *phthanō.* See Rom. 9. 31. "Prevent" meant "go or come before". Now it only means "stand in the way of". **asleep**=fallen asleep. **16 For**=Because. Gr. *hoti.* **heaven.** Sing. See Matt. 6. 9, 10. **with.** Ap. 104. viii. **shout**=word of command. Gr. *keleusma.* Only here in N.T. In the Sept. in Prov. 30. 27, the rendering of which is, The locust has no king, yet it marches orderly at one word of command. **archangel.** Only here and in Jude 9, where he is called Michael, which connects this event with Dan. 12. 1. **trump.** Cp. Matt. 24. 31 and 1 Cor. 15. 52. **the dead.** Ap. 139. 1. **Christ.** Ap. 98. IX. **17 Then.** Gr. *epeita,* thereupon, thereafter. **caught up.** Gr. *harpazō.* See Acts 8. 39. 2 Cor. 12. 2, 4. Rev. 12. 5. **together.** Gr. *hama.* **the.** Omit. **meet.** Gr. *apantēsis.* See Matt. 25. 1. **in.** Ap. 104. vi. **so.** I. e. by resurrection, or translation. **ever.** Ap. 151. II. G. ii. **18 Wherefore**=So then. **comfort.** Same as "beseech", *v.* 10.

r 5 But °of the °times and the °seasons, brethren, ye have °no need that I write °unto
you.
s 2 °For yourselves °know °perfectly that the
day of the °Lord so cometh as a thief °in the
night.
3 °For when they °shall say, "Peace and
safety;" then °sudden °destruction cometh
upon them, as °travail upon a woman with
child; and they shall °not escape.
4 But ye, brethren, are [1]not [2]in darkness, °that
that day should °overtake you as a thief.
5 Ye are all the °children of °light, and the
°children of the day: we are [1]not of the night,
°nor of darkness.
6 Therefore let us °not °sleep, as *do* °others;
but let us °watch and °be sober.
t 7 [2]For they that [6]sleep [6]sleep in the night;
and they that be drunken are drunken in the
night.
8 But let us, who are of the day, [6]be sober,
putting on the °breastplate of °faith and °love;
and for an °helmet, the hope of salvation.
u 9 °For °God °hath [1]not appointed us °to
°wrath, but °to °obtain salvation °by our °Lord
°Jesus Christ,
10 Who died °for us, [4]that, whether we °wake
or [6]sleep, we should live °together °with Him.
v 11 Wherefore °comfort yourselves together,
and edify one another, even as °also ye do.
G 12 And we °beseech you, brethren, to [2]know
them which labour °among you, and °are over
you [2]in the [2]Lord, and admonish you;
13 And to °esteem them °very highly [2]in
[8]love °for their work's sake. *And* °be at
peace [12]among yourselves.
14 Now we °exhort you, brethren, °warn
them that are °unruly, °comfort the °feeble-
minded, °support the weak, be patient °toward
all *men*.
15 °See °that none render °evil °for °evil
[1]unto °any *man;* but °ever follow that which
is good, both °among yourselves, and °to all
men.
16 Rejoice °evermore;
17 °Pray °without ceasing;
18 [2]In every thing °give thanks: for this is
the °will of [9]God [2]in °Christ Jesus °concerning
you.
19 Quench [6]not the °Spirit;
20 °Despise [6]not °prophesyings;
21 °Prove all things; °hold fast that which is
good.
22 °Abstain °from °all °appearance of °evil.
B 23 And °the very [9]God of peace °sanctify you
°wholly; and *I pray God* your °whole °spirit

5. 1 of. Ap. 104. xiii. 1.
times, seasons. See Ap. 195.
no = not. Ap. 105. I. unto = to.
2 For. Gr. *gar.*
know. Ap. 132. I. i.
perfectly. Gr. *akribōs.* See Acts 18. 25.
Lord. Ap. 98. VI. i. β. 2. B.
in. Ap. 104. viii.
3 For. The texts omit.
shall. Omit.
sudden. Gr. *aiphnidios.* Only here and Luke 21. 34.
destruction. Gr. *olethros.* See 1 Cor. 5. 5.
travail. Gr. *ōdin.* See Acts 2. 24.
not. Ap. 105. III.
4 that = in order that. Gr. *hina.*
overtake. Gr. *katalambanō.* See John 1. 5.
5 children. Ap. 108. iii.
light. Ap. 130. 1. nor. Gr. *oude.*
6 not. Ap. 105. II.
sleep. Ap. 171. 1.
others. Ap. 124. 3.
watch. See Matt. 24. 42.
be sober. Gr. *nēphō.* Here, *v.* 8. 2 Tim. 4. 5. 1 Pet. 1. 13; 4. 7; 5. 8.
8 breastplate. Gr. *thōrax.* See Eph. 6. 14.
faith. Ap. 150. II. 1.
love. Ap. 135. II. 1.
helmet. Gr. *perikephalaia.* See Eph. 6. 17.
9 For = Because. Gr. *hoti.*
God. Ap. 98. I. i. 1. hath. Omit.
to. Ap. 104. vi. wrath. Cp. 1. 10.
obtain = obtaining. Gr. *peripoiēsis.* See Eph. 1. 14.
by. Ap. 104. v. 1.
Lord. Ap. 98. VI. i. β. 2. A.
Jesus Christ. Ap. 98. XI.
10 for. Ap. 104. xvii. 1. wake = watch.
together. Gr. *hama,* as in 4. 17.
with. Ap. 104. xvi.
11 comfort. Ap. 134. I. 6. Same as in 4. 18.
also ye do = ye are doing also.
12 beseech. Ap. 134. I. 3. Not the same as 4. 10.
among. Ap. 104. viii. 2.
are over. Gr. *proistēmi.* See Rom. 12. 8.
13 esteem = reckon.
very highly. Gr. *huperekperissōs.* See 3. 10 and Eph. 3. 20.
for their work's sake = on account of (Ap. 104. v. 2) their work.
be at peace. Gr. *eirēneuō.* See Rom. 12. 18.
14 exhort. Ap. 134. I. 6.
warn. Same as "admonish", *v.* 12.
unruly. Gr. *ataktos.* Only here. Cp. 2 Thess. 3. 6, 11 (the adv. transl. "disorderly").
comfort. Gr. *paramutheomai.* See 2. 11.
feebleminded = fainthearted. Gr. *oligopsuchos.* Only here.
support. Gr. *antechomai.* Here; Matt. 6. 24. Luke 16. 13. Tit. 1. 9.
toward. Ap. 104. xv. 3.
15 See. Ap. 133. I. 8.
that none = lest (Ap. 105. II) any (Ap. 123. 3).
evil. Ap. 128. III. 2.
for. Gr. *anti.* Ap. 104. ii.
any *man.* Gr. *tis.* Ap. 123. 3.
ever. Ap. 151. II. G. ii.
among yourselves = towards (*eis*) one another.

to. Gr. *eis.* Ap. 104. vi. **16 evermore.** Ap. 151. II. G. iii. **17 Pray.** Gr. *proseuchomai.* Ap. 134. I. 2. without ceasing. See 1. 3. **18 give thanks.** Gr. *eucharisteō.* See 1. 2. will. Ap. 102. 2. Christ Jesus. Ap. 98. XII. concerning = in regard to. Gr. *eis.* Ap. 104. vi. **19 Spirit.** Ap. 101. II. 4. **20 Despise.** Gr. *exoutheneō.* See Acts 4. 11. prophesyings. Cp. 1 Cor. 12. 10; 13. 2, 8; 14. 6, 22. The reference to these gifts explains *v.* 19. **21 Prove.** Gr. *dokimazō.* See Rom. 12. 2. Eph. 5. 10. 1 John 4. 1. hold fast. Gr. *katechō.* See Matt. 21. 38. **22 Abstain.** See 4. 3. from. Gr. *apo.* Ap. 104. iv. all = every. appearance = form. Gr. *eidos.* See John 5. 37. evil. Ap. 128. III. 1. **23 the very, &c.** = may the God of peace Himself. Cp. Acts 7. 2. Heb. 13. 20. sanctify. See John 17. 17. wholly. Gr. *holotelēs.* Only here. whole, &c. Read, "your spirit and soul and body be kept entire". whole. Gr. *holoklēros.* Only here and Jas. 1. 4. The noun in Acts 3. 16. spirit. Ap. 101. II. 6.

and °soul and body be preserved °blameless
°unto the °coming of our [9]Lord [9]Jesus Christ.
24 °Faithful *is* He That calleth you, Who
°also will do *it*.
25 Brethren, [17]pray °for us.

A
26 Greet all the brethren °with an °holy kiss.
27 I °charge you by the [9]Lord that °this
epistle be read [1]unto all the °holy brethren.
28 The °grace of our [9]Lord [9]Jesus Christ *be*
°with you. °Amen.

soul. Ap. 110. III. 2.
blameless. See 2. 10.
unto = at. Gr. *en*. Ap. 104. viii.
coming. See 2. 19. Notice how in every chapter of this Epistle the coming of the Lord is presented, and in a different aspect: 1. 10; 2. 19; 3. 13; 4. 14–17; 5. 23. In this verse there is a beautiful correspondence.

H | The work of the God of peace. Sanctification: complete.
J | w | The whole person.
  x | One part of it (the *pneuma*).
J | *w* | The whole person (the living soul).
  x | The other part of it (the body).
H | The coming of the Lord Jesus Christ. Preservation: without blemish.

24 Faithful. Gr. *pistos*. Ap. 150. III. Cp. 1 Cor. 1. 9; 10. 13. 2 Thess. 3. 3. 2 Tim. 2. 13. Heb. 10. 23; 11. 11. 1 Pet. 4. 19. Rev. 3. 14; 19. 11. **also, &c.** = will do it also. **25 for.** Gr. *peri*. Ap. 104. xiii. 1. **26 with.** Gr. *en*. Ap. 104. viii. **holy kiss.** See Rom. 16. 16. **27 charge.** Gr. *orkizō*. See Acts 19. 13, but the texts read *enorkizō*, which occ. only here. **this** = the. **holy.** Most texts omit. **28 grace.** Gr. *charis*. Ap. 184. I. 1. **with.** Gr. *meta*. Ap. 104. xi. 1. **Amen.** Omit, with texts.

THE SECOND EPISTLE TO THE THESSALONIANS.

THE STRUCTURE OF THE EPISTLE AS A WHOLE.

(*Introversion and Extended Alternation.*)

A | 1. 1, 2. EPISTOLARY. INTRODUCTION. GRACE AND PEACE.
B | A | D | 1. 3–. THANKSGIVING.
  E | 1. –3–5. REASON. THEIR FAITH AND LOVE AND PATIENCE.
  F | 1. 6–10. THE OBTAINING OF REST AND GLORY.
  B | G | 1. 11. PRAYER FOR THEM.
   H | 1. 12–. THAT THE NAME OF THE LORD MAY BE GLORIFIED.
   J | 1. –12. AND THEY GLORIFIED IN HIM.
  C | 2. 1–12. ADMONITION.
B | *A* | *D* | 2. 13–. THANKSGIVING.
  E | 2.–13. REASON. THEIR SALVATION.
  F | 2. 14, 15. THE OBTAINING OF GLORY.
  B | *G* | 2. 16—3. 1–. PRAYER FOR PAUL.
   H | 3. –1–4. THAT THE WORD MAY BE GLORIFIED.
   J | 3. 5. AND THEIR HEARTS MAY BE DIRECTED INTO GOD'S LOVE
  C | 3. 6–15. ADMONITION.
A | 3. 16–18. EPISTOLARY. CONCLUSION. PEACE AND GRACE.

THE SECOND EPISTLE TO THE THESSALONIANS.

INTRODUCTORY NOTES.

1. The Second Epistle to the Church of the Thessalonians was, like the First, written from Corinth, and at no long interval after the earlier letter, both Silas and Timothy being still with the apostle. Apparently it was called forth, and sent, in order to repair for its recipients, and for us too, the mischief caused by false teachers. And the new revelation made here by the Holy Spirit through Paul concerning "things to come", as promised in John 16. 13, gives important details connected with the coming of our Lord and "the day of the Lord". Paul reminded the Thessalonians (2. 5) that he had told them these things, yet some part at least had taken up the belief that that day had already "set in" (2. 2 and Note). Hence the ap stle's warning that that day would not come unless the falling away came first, a warning much needed in these days when it is widely taught that the day of the Lord will not come until the world is converted to Christ!

2. The important prophecy regarding the "man of sin" ("lawlessness") has been the subject of many divergent interpretations. With regard to its main features, no interpretation is needed, for we have here a careful statement in plain terms of events that were then in the future, and which, not having yet taken place, are future still. The prophecy is given in such language that the simplest reader may understand. There is yet to appear an individual who will be the very incarnation of all evil, of whom past opposers of God and of His Christ were but faint types. Him will the Lord "destroy with the brightness of His coming". It may be added that all the "early fathers" believed that this great opposer would be an individual.

THE SECOND EPISTLE OF PAUL THE APOSTLE

TO THE

THESSALONIANS.

A 1 °PAUL, and Silvanus, and Timotheus,° unto
the °church of the Thessalonians °in °God
our °Father and the °Lord °Jesus Christ:
2 °Grace [1] unto you, and peace, °from [1] God
our [1] Father and the [1] Lord [1] Jesus Christ.

B A D 3 We are bound to °thank [1] God °always °for
you, brethren, as it is meet,
E because that your °faith °groweth exceedingly,
and the °charity of °every one of you all
°toward °each other °aboundeth;
4 So that we ourselves °glory [1] in you [1] in the
[1] churches of [1] God °for your patience and [3] faith
[1] in all your persecutions and °tribulations that
ye endure:
5 *Which is* a °manifest token of the °righteous
°judgment of [1] God, °that ye may be °counted
worthy of the °kingdom of [1] God, [4] for which ye
°also suffer:
F K 6 °Seeing *it is* a [5] righteous thing °with [1] God to
recompense [4] tribulation to them that °trouble
you;
L a 7 And to you who are [6] troubled °rest °with
us,
b °when the °Lord °Jesus shall be revealed
[2] from °heaven °with °His mighty angels,

1. 1 Paul, &c. The opening words of this Epistle are the same as those of the First Epistle as far as "peace" (*v.* 2). **unto**=to.
church. Ap. 186.
in. Ap. 104. viii.
God. Ap. 98. I. i. 1.
Father. Ap. 98. III.
Lord. Ap. 98. VI. i. β. 2. B.
Jesus Christ. Ap. 98. XI.
2 Grace. Ap. 184. I. 1.
from. Ap. 104. iv.
3 thank. See 1 Thess. 1. 2.
always. Ap. 151. II. G. i.
for. Ap. 104. xiii. 1.
faith. Ap. 150. II. 1.
groweth exceedingly. Gr. *huperauxanō.* Only here.
charity=love. Ap. 135. II. 1. No reference to hope as in 1 Thess. 1. 3.
every=each.
toward. Ap. 104. vi.
each other=one another.
aboundeth. Same as increase, 1 Thess. 3. 12.
4 glory. Gr. *kauchaomai.* See Rom. 2. 17. The texts read *enkauchaomai.* Nowhere else in N.T.
for. Ap. 104. xvii. 1.
tribulations. Gr. *thlipsis.* See Acts 7. 10.
5 manifest token. Gr. *endeigma.* Only here.
righteous. Ap. 191. 1.
judgment. Ap. 177. 7. Cp. Phil. 1. 28.
that ye may be=to (Gr. *eis*) your being.
also suffer=suffer also.
counted worthy. See Acts 5. 41. **kingdom.** App. 112, 114.

1. 6-10 (F, p. 1794). THE OBTAINING OF REST AND GLORY. (*Alternation and Introversion.*)

F | K | 6. Tribulation to the troublers.
  L | a | 7-. Rest to the troubled.
    b | -7. When the Lord shall be revealed.
K | 8, 9. Vengeance to the enemies.
  L | *b* | 10-. When He shall come.
    a | -10. To be glorified in the saints.

6 Seeing=If so be. Gr. *eiper.* **with.** Ap. 104. xii. 2. **trouble.** Gr. *thlibō*, afflict. The noun in *v.* 7. **7 rest.** Gr. *anesis.* See Acts 24. 23. **with.** Ap. 104. xi. 1. **when, &c.**=in (Gr. *en*) the revelation (Ap. 106. II. i) of. **Lord.** Ap. 98. VI. i. β. 2. A. **Jesus.** Ap. 98. X. **heaven.** Sing. See Matt. 6. 9, 10. **His, &c.**=the angels of His power (Ap. 172. 1).

K 8 [1]In °flaming fire, °taking °vengeance on
them that °know °not [1]God, and that obey
°not the °gospel of our [7]Lord [1]Jesus °Christ:
9 Who shall °be punished with °everlasting
°destruction [2]from the presence of the [7]Lord,
and [2]from the °glory of His °power;
Lb 10 When He °shall come
a to be °glorified [1]in His °saints, and to be
admired [1]in all them that °believe (because our
testimony °among you was °believed) [1]in that
day.
B G 11 °Wherefore °also we pray [3]always [3]for you,
°that our [1]God would °count you worthy of
this calling, and °fulfil all the °good pleasure
of *His* °goodness, and the work of [3]faith °with
°power:
H 12 That the name of our [7]Lord [1]Jesus [8]Christ
may be [10]glorified [1]in you,
J and ye [1]in Him, °according to the [2]grace of our
[1]God and the [1]Lord [1]Jesus Christ.

C M **2** Now we °beseech you, brethren, °by the
°coming of our °Lord °Jesus Christ, and
by our °gathering together °unto Him,
2 °That ye be °not °soon shaken °in mind,
°or °be troubled, °neither °by °spirit, °nor °by
°word, °nor °by letter, as °from us, as that the
day of °Christ is °at hand.
3 Let °no man °deceive you °by any means:
N c °for *that day shall not come*, °except there
come °a °falling away first,
d and °that °man of °sin °be revealed, the °son
of °perdition,
e 4 Who °opposeth and °exalteth himself °above
all that is called °God, or that is °worshipped;
so that he °as God sitteth °in the °Temple of
°God, °shewing himself that he is °God.
M 5 Remember ye °not, that, when I was yet
°with you, I told you these things?
6 And now ye °know what °withholdeth [2]that
he might [3]be [3]revealed °in °his time.
N c 7 For the °mystery of °iniquity doth already
°work: only he who now °letteth *will let*, until
he be taken °out of the way.
d 8 And then shall °that wicked [3]be revealed,

8 flaming fire=fire of flame (Gr. *phlox*. Here; Luke 16. 24. Acts 7. 30. Heb. 1. 7. Rev. 1. 14; 2. 18; 19. 12).
taking . . . on=giving . . . to.
vengeance. Gr. *ekdikēsis.* See Luke 18. 8.
know. Ap. 132. I. i.
not. Ap. 105. II. **gospel.** Ap. 140.
Christ. The texts omit.
9 be punished with=pay (Gr. *tinō.* Only here) the penalty (Ap. 177. 4), (*even*).
everlasting. Ap. 151. II. B. ii.
destruction. Gr. *olethros.* See 1 Cor. 5. 5.
glory. See p. 1511. **power.** Ap. 172. 3.
10 shall=shall have.
glorified. Gr. *endoxazomai.* Only here and *v.* 12.
saints. See Acts 9. 13.
believe, believed. Ap. 150. I. 1. i.
among. Ap. 104. ix. 3.
11 Wherefore=With a view to (Gr. *eis*) which.
also we pray=we pray (Ap. 134. I. 2) also.
that=in order that. Gr. *hina.*
count . . . worthy. Gr. *axioō.* See Acts 15. 38.
fulfil. Ap. 125. 7.
good pleasure. Gr. *eudokia.* See Rom. 10. 1.
goodness. Gr. *agathōsunē.* See Rom. 15. 14.
with. Ap. 104. viii.
power. Ap. 172. 1, as *v.* 7.
12 according to. Ap. 104. x. 2.

2. 1-12 (C, p. 1794). ADMONITION. (*Alternation.*)

C | M | 1-3-. Exhortation: negative.
  N | c | -3-. The apostasy: open.
    d | -3. The man of sin.
      e | 4. The character of his acts.
  M | 5, 6. Exhortation: positive.
  N | *c* | 7. The mystery: secret.
    d | 8. The lawless one.
      e | 9-12. The character of his acts.

2. 1 beseech. Ap. 134. I. 3.
by=on behalf of. Ap. 104. xvii. 1.
coming. See 1 Thess. 2. 19.
Lord. Ap. 98. VI. i. β. 2. A.
Jesus Christ. Ap. 98. XI.
gathering together. Gr. *episunagōgē.* Only here and Heb. 10. 25. Cp. the verb in Matt. 23. 37; 24. 31.
unto. Ap. 104. ix. 3.
2 That=To the end that. Ap. 104. vi.
not. Ap. 105. II.
soon=quickly.
in=from. Ap. 104. iv.
or=nor. Gr. *mēte.* Same as **neither** and **nor,** below.
be troubled. Gr. *throeomai.* Elsewhere, Matt. 24. 6. Mark 13. 7.

by. Ap. 104. v. 1. **spirit**=spirit-communication. Ap. 101. II. 12. **word.** Ap. 121. 10. **from.** Ap. 104. v. 1. **Christ**=the Lord, as the texts. The day of Christ is the day of *v.* 1. Cp. Phil. 1. 10; 2. 16. The day of the Lord is the day of O.T. prophecy. See Isa. 2. 12. **at hand**=present. Gr. *enistēmi.* See Rom. 8. 38. **3 no man**=not (Ap. 105. II) any one (Ap. 123. 3). **deceive.** Gr. *exapataō.* See Rom. 7. 11. **by any means.** Lit. according to (Ap. 104. x. 2) no (Gr. *mēdeis*) way. A double negative for emphasis. **for**=because. **except**=if (Ap. 118. i. b.) . . . not (Ap. 105. II). **a**=the. **falling away**=apostasy. Gr. *apostasia.* Only here and Acts 21. 21. **that**=the. **man.** Ap. 123. 1. **sin.** Ap. 128. I. ii. 1. Some texts read III. 4, as *v.* 7. **be revealed.** Ap. 106. I. ix. **son.** Ap. 108. iii. **perdition.** See John 17. 12. Rev. 17. 8, 11. **4 opposeth.** Gr. *antikeimai.* Gen. transl. be an adversary to. **exalteth himself.** Gr. *huperairomai.* See 2 Cor. 12. 7. **above.** Ap. 104. ix. 3. **God.** Ap. 98. I. i. 1. **worshipped**=an object of worship. Gr. *sebasma.* See Acts 17. 23. **as God.** The texts omit. **in.** Ap. 104. vi. **Temple.** Gr. *naos.* See Matt. 23. 16. **shewing.** Gr. *apodeiknumi.* See Acts 2. 22. **5 not.** Ap. 105. I. **with.** Ap. 104. xv. 3. **6 know.** Ap. 132. I. i. **withholdeth**=holds fast. Gr. *katechō.* See the other occ. of this word, *v.* 7; Matt. 21. 38. Luke 4. 42; 8. 15; 14. 9. John 5. 4. Acts 27. 40. Rom. 1. 18; 7. 6. 1 Cor. 7. 30; 11. 2; 15. 2. 2 Cor. 6. 10. 1 Thess. 5. 21. Philem. 13. Heb. 3. 6, 14; 10. 23. **in.** Ap. 104. viii. **his time**=his own season. That which holds him fast is neuter. It is a place, the pit of the abyss (Rev. 9. 1; 11. 7; 13. 1). **7 mystery.** Ap. 193. **iniquity**=lawlessness. Ap. 128. III. 4. **work**=work actively, as 1 Thess. 2. 13. **letteth**=holds fast. Gr. *katechō*, as *v.* 6. Supply the Ellipsis by "*there is* one who holds fast", instead of by repeating the verb "*will let*". But *katechō* is a transitive verb, and an object must be supplied too. See all the occ. *v.* 6. If the subject be Satan, the object must be his position in the heavenlies (Eph. 6. 12), from which he will be ejected by Michael (Rev. 12. 7-9). **out of the way**=out of (Gr. *ek*) the midst. Cp. the same expression in Acts 17. 33; 23. 10. 1 Cor. 5. 2. 2 Cor. 6. 17. Col. 2. 14. **8 that wicked**=the lawless one. Ap. 128. III. 3.

whom the [1]Lord shall °consume with the
°spirit of His mouth, and shall °destroy with
the °brightness of His [1]coming:
e 9 *Even him*, whose [1]coming is °after the
°working of Satan °with all °power and °signs
and °lying °wonders,
10 And [9]with °all °deceivableness of °un-
righteousness °in °them that perish; °because
they received [5]not the °love of the truth, [2]that
they might be saved.
11 And °for this cause [4]God shall °send them
°strong delusion, [2]that they should °believe
[3]a lie:
12 °That they all might be °damned who
[11]believed [2]not the truth, but °had pleasure [6]in
[10]unrighteousness.
B A D 13 But **we** are °bound to give thanks °alway to
[4]God °for you, brethren °beloved °of the °Lord,
E because [4]God °hath °from the beginning °chosen
you °to salvation °through °sanctification of
the °Spirit and °belief of the truth:
F 14 °Whereunto He called you [2]by our °gospel,
[13]to the °obtaining of the °glory of our [1]Lord
[1]Jesus Christ.
15 Therefore, brethren, °stand fast, and °hold
the °traditions which ye have been taught,
whether [2]by [2]word, or °our epistle.
B G 16 Now our [1]Lord [1]Jesus Christ Himself, and
[4]God °even our °Father, Which °hath [13]loved
us, and °hath given *us* °everlasting °con-
solation and good hope [13]through °grace,
17 °Comfort your hearts, and °stablish you
[6]in every good [2]word and work.
3 Finally, brethren, °pray °for us,
H °that the °word of the °Lord may °have
free course, and be glorified, even as *it is* °with
°you:
2 And [1]that we may be °delivered °from °un-
reasonable and °wicked °men: for all *men* have
°not °faith.
3 But the [1]Lord is °faithful, Who shall °stab-
lish you, and °keep *you* [2]from °evil.
4 And we °have confidence °in the °Lord
°touching you, that ye both do and will do the
°things which we °command you.
J 5 And the [1]Lord °direct your hearts °into the
°love of °God, and °into the °patient waiting
°for Christ.
C f^1 6 Now we [4]command you, brethren, [4]in the

consume. Gr. *analiskō*. See Gal. 5. 15.
spirit = breath. Ap. 101. II. 8. Cp. Isa. 11. 4; 30. 27, 30, 33.
destroy = bring to nought. Gr. *katargeō*. See Rom. 3. 3.
brightness. Ap. 106. II. ii.
9 after. Ap. 104. x. 2.
working. Gr. *energeia*. See *v.* 7. Ap. 172. 4.
with. Ap. 104. viii.
power . . . signs . . . wonders. Ap. 176. 1. 3. 2.
lying. Lit. of a lie. Gr. *pseudos*. See John 8. 44. Rom. 1. 25.
10 all = every.
deceivableness = (form of) deceit.
unrighteousness. Ap. 128. VII. 1.
in. The texts omit. Dat. case.
them that perish = the perishing. See same phrase, 1 Cor. 1. 18. 2 Cor. 2. 15; 4. 3.
because. Gr. *anth' ōn*, indicating exchange. Cp. Rom. 1. 25 (R.V.).
love. Ap. 135. II. 1.
11 for this cause = because of (Ap. 104. v. 2) this.
send. Ap. 174. 4.
strong delusion = a working (*v.* 9) of error (Gr. *planē*, as Rom. 1. 27).
believe. Ap. 150. I. 1. ii.
12 That = In order that. Gr. *hina*.
damned = condemned, or judged. Ap. 122. 1.
had pleasure = were well pleased. See Matt. 3. 17.
13 bound, &c. Cp. 1. 3.
alway. Ap. 151. II. G. i.
for. Ap. 104. xiii. 1.
beloved. Ap. 135. I. 1.
of. Ap. 104. xviii. 1.
Lord. Ap. 98. VI. i. *β*. 2. B. hath. Omit.
from the beginning. Gr. *ap' archēs*. See John 8. 44.
chosen = chose. Gr. *haireomai*. See Phil. 1. 22.
to. Ap. 104. vi.
through. Ap. 104. viii.
sanctification. Gr. *hagiasmos*. See Rom. 6. 19.
Spirit. The Sanctifier. Ap. 101. II. 3. Cp. 1 Pet. 1. 2.
belief. Gr. *pistis*. Ap. 150. II. 1.
14 Whereunto = Unto (Gr. *eis*) which.
gospel. Ap. 140.
obtaining. Gr. *peripoiēsis*. See Eph. 1. 14.
glory. See p. 1511.
15 stand fast. See 1 Thess. 3. 8.
hold = lay hold on, hold fast.
traditions. Gr. *paradosis*, as in 3. 6.
our. Should come after "by".
16 even. Omit.
Father. Ap. 98. III.
hath. Omit. hath given = gave.
everlasting. Ap. 151. II. B. ii.
consolation. Gr. *paraklēsis*. See Luke 6. 24. Acts 4. 36. Cp. Ap. 134. I. 6.
grace. Ap. 184. I. 1 **17** Comfort. Ap. 134. I. 6. stablish. Gr. *stērizō*. See Rom. 1. 11.

3. 1 pray. Ap. 134. I. 2. Paul is the only N.T. writer who asks the prayers of those to whom he writes. See Rom. 15. 30. 2 Cor. 1. 11. Eph. 6. 19. Phil. 1. 19. Col. 4. 3. Philem. 22. Heb. 13. 18. for. Ap. 104. xiii. 1. that = in order that. Gr. *hina*. word. Ap. 121. 10. Lord. Ap. 98. VI. i. *β*. 2. A. have, &c. = run and be glorified. By Fig. *Hendiadys* (Ap. 6) = triumph gloriously. with. Ap. 104. xv. 3. Cp. Acts 13. 48. you. Add "also". **2** delivered. Gr. *rhuomai*, as in Rom. 15. 31. from. Ap. 104. iv. unreasonable. Gr. *atopos*. See Acts 28. 6. wicked. Ap. 128. III. 1. men. Ap. 123. 1. not. Ap. 105. I. faith. Ap. 150. II. 1. **3** faithful. Ap. 150. III. Cp. 1 Cor. 1. 9. stablish. See 2. 17. keep = guard. evil = the wicked one. Ap. 128. III. 1. Cp. 1 John 5. 18. **4** have confidence. Ap. 150. I. 2. in. Ap. 104. viii. Lord. Ap. 98. VI. i. *β*. 2. B. touching. Ap. 104. ix. 3. things. I. e. in *vv.* 6–14. Cp. 1 Thess. 4. 11. command = charge. Gr. *parangellō*. See Acts 1. 4. **5** direct. Gr. *kateuthunō*. See 1 Thess. 3. 11. into. Ap. 104. vi. love. Ap. 135. II. 1. God. Ap. 98. I. i. 1. patient waiting = patience, as 1. 4. for Christ = of Christ (Ap. 98. IX).

3. 6–15 (*C*, p. 1794). ADMONITION. (*Repeated Alternation.*)

C f^1 | 6. Charge to the orderly.
g^1 | 7–9. The example of Paul and the brethren.
f^2 | 10. Charge to the non-workers.
g^2 | 11. Instance of such.
f^3 | 12, 13. Charge to the disorderly.
g^3 | 14, 15. The disobedient to be admonished.

name of our [1]Lord °Jesus Christ, that ye
°withdraw yourselves [2]from every brother
that walketh °disorderly, and °not °after the
°tradition which he received °of us.

g1 7 For yourselves °know how ye ought to
°follow us: for we °behaved [2]not ourselves
disorderly °among you;
8 °Neither did we eat °any man's bread °for
nought; but °wrought °with labour and
°travail night and day, °that we might [6]not be
°chargeable to °any of you:
9 [2]Not because we have [2]not °power, but °to
make ourselves an °ensample °unto you °to
[7]follow us.

f2 10 For even when we were [1]with you, this we
[4]commanded you, that °if [8]any °would [2]not
work, °neither should he eat.

g2 11 For we hear that there are °some which
walk [7]among you [6]disorderly, working [6]not
at all, but °are busybodies.

f3 12 Now them that are such we [4]command
and °exhort °by our [4]Lord [6]Jesus Christ,
[1]that °with °quietness they work, and eat their
own bread.
13 But **ye**, brethren, °be [6]not weary °in well
doing.

g3 14 And [10]if [8]any man obey [2]not our [1]word
°by this epistle, °note °**that** man, and °have °no
company with him, [1]that he may °be ashamed.
15 Yet °count *him* [6]not as an enemy, but
admonish *him* as a brother.

A 16 Now the [1]Lord °of peace Himself give you
peace °always °by all means. The [1]Lord *be*
[12]with you all.
17 The °salutation of Paul with mine own
hand, which is the °token [4]in every epistle: so
I write.
18 The °grace of our [1]Lord [6]Jesus Christ *be*
[12]with you all. °Amen.

6 Jesus Christ. Ap. 98. XI.
withdraw yourselves. Gr *stellomai.* See 2 Cor. 8. 20.
disorderly. Gr. *ataktōs.* Only here and *v.* 11.
not. Ap. 105. II.
after. Ap. 104. x. 2.
tradition. See 2. 15.
of. Ap. 104. xii. 1.
7 know. Ap. 132. I. i.
follow = imitate. Gr. *mimeomai.* Occ. also *v.* 9. Heb. 13. 7. 3 John 11. Cp. 1 Cor. 4. 16.
behaved . . . disorderly. Gr. *atakteō.* Cp. *vv.* 6, 11. 1 Thess. 5. 14.
among. Ap. 104. viii. 2.
8 Neither. Gr. *oude.*
any man's bread = bread from (Gr. *para,* Ap. 104. xii. 1) any one (Ap. 123. 3).
for nought. Gr. *dōrean.* See John 15. 25.
wrought = working.
with. Ap. 104. viii.
travail. Gr. *mochthos.* See 2 Cor. 11. 27.
that we, &c. = with a view to (Ap. 104. xv. 3) our not being.
chargeable to. Gr. *epibareō.* See 2 Cor. 2. 5. 1 Thess. 2. 9.
any. Ap. 123. 3.
9 power. Ap. 172. 5.
to = in order that (as *v.* 1) we may.
ensample. Gr. *tupos.* Cp. Phil. 3. 17. 1 Thess. 1. 7. 1 Tim. 4. 12.
unto = to.
to. Gr. *eis.* Ap. 104. vi.
10 if. Ap. 118. 2. a.
would = is . . . willing. Ap. 102. 1.
neither. Gr. *mēde.*
11 some. Ap. 124. 4.
not at all = (in) nothing. Gr. *mēdeis.*
are busybodies. Gr. *periergazomai,* to be busy about useless matters.
12 exhort. Ap. 134. I. 6.
by. Ap. 104. v. 1, but the texts read *en.*
with. Ap. 104. xi. 1.
quietness. Gr. *hēsuchia.* See Acts 22. 2.
13 be . . . weary = faint. Gr. *ekkakeō.* See 2 Cor. 4. 1.
in well doing. Gr. *kalopoieō.* Only here. Cp. Gal. 6. 9.
14 by. Ap. 104. v. 1.
note. Gr. *sēmeioomai.* Only here.
that man = this one. have . . . company. Gr. *sunanamignumi.* See 1 Cor. 5. 9, 11. no = not, *v.* 6.
be ashamed. Gr. *entrepomai.* See 1 Cor. 4. 14. **15** count = reckon. Gr. *hēgeomai.* See Phil. 2. 6.
16 of peace. Note the eight statements as to God in Note on Acts 7. 2, and cp. 1 Cor. 1. 3. always = through (Ap. 104. v. 1) everything. by all means = in (Gr. *en*) every way. **17** salutation, &c Cp. 1 Cor. 16. 21. Col. 4. 18. Read, "by the hand of me Paul". token = sign. Gr. *sēmeion.* Ap. 176. 3.
18 grace. Ap. 184. I. 1. Amen. Omit.

STRUCTURE OF THE PERSONAL EPISTLES. (CANONICAL ORDER.)

COVERING THE PERIOD OF BOTH THE EARLIER AND THE LATER EPISTLES TO ASSEMBLIES (Ap. 186).

(*Alternation.*)

A | **I. TIMOTHY.** Earlier period. Timothy at Ephesus. Organized assemblies. Instruction as to officers and their duties. Assemblies seen in their order and rule.

B | **II. TIMOTHY.** Later period. Organization ignored. Orderly rule succeeded by ruin. Officers superseded by "faithful men". Individual.

A | **TITUS.** Earlier period. Organized assemblies as in 1 Timothy.

B | **PHILEMON.** Later period. Practical exhibition of individual walk in the truth of the later Epistles.

THE FIRST EPISTLE TO TIMOTHY.

THE STRUCTURE OF THE BOOK AS A WHOLE.

(*Introversion.*)

A | 1. 1, 2. BENEDICTION.
B | 1. 3-20. ADMONITION. PRACTICAL.
C | 2. 1—3. 13. INSTRUCTION AND DISCIPLINE.
D | 3. 14, 15. INTENDED VISIT AND INTERVAL.
E | 3. 16. THE MYSTERY OF GODLINESS.
E | 4. 1-12. THE MYSTERY OF INIQUITY.
D | 4. 13-16. INTENDED VISIT AND INTERVAL.
C | 5. 1—6. 2. INSTRUCTION AND DISCIPLINE.
B | 6. 3-21-. ADMONITION. PRACTICAL.
A | 6. -21. BENEDICTION.

THE FIRST EPISTLE TO TIMOTHY.

INTRODUCTORY NOTES.

1. The son of a Gentile father and of a Jewish mother, Timothy was born either at Derbe or Lystra, probably the latter. He is already a "disciple" when first mentioned (Acts 16. 1). His father is nowhere named, but his mother, Eunice, and his grandmother, Lois, have secured honourable mention wherever the Scriptures are read (2 Tim. 1. 5; 3. 14). Most likely Timothy had been brought to the light during the apostle's first visit to Lystra, and thereafter the two were much in association. Paul refers to him in affectionate terms as his own son in the faith, his dearly beloved son, his son Timothy, and while undergoing his second imprisonment at Rome he earnestly begged that his fellow-worker should come to him. See also Phil. 2. 19-22.

2. This, the earliest of the three Pastoral Epistles, as they are termed, was written probably in A. D. 67 (Ap. 180), but it is not known where the apostle was at the time, although some think he was at Troas, others in Macedonia (Ap. 180).

3. To Timothy were given the earliest instructions for orderly arrangement in the church, these instructions being of the simplest nature, and, as Dean Alford well observes with regard to the Pastoral Epistles as a whole, the directions given "are altogether of an ethical, not of an hierarchical, kind". These directions afford no warrant whatever for the widespread organizations of the "churches" as carried on to-day.

4. Even in the earliest period the increasing heresies are much in evidence. Some there were who had swerved and turned aside altogether; others denied vital truth and thus overthrew "the faith of some". Hence Paul's constant warnings against such, and instructions to enlighten the opposers, "if God peradventure will give them repentance to the acknowledging of the truth". How the leaven spread is only too plainly shown in Paul's Second Epistle, which has been aptly termed a picture of the ruin of the church through departure from the apostolic doctrine.

THE FIRST EPISTLE OF PAUL THE APOSTLE

TO

TIMOTHY.

A 1 PAUL, an °apostle of °Jesus Christ °by the
°commandment of °God our °Saviour, and
°Lord °Jesus Christ, °*which is* our °hope;
2 °Unto Timothy, *my* °own °son °in the
°faith: °Grace, mercy, *and* peace, °from [1] God
our °Father and °Jesus Christ our °Lord.

B A a 3 As I °besought thee to °abide still °at
Ephesus, when I went °into Macedonia, °that
thou mightest °charge °some °that they teach
°no other doctrine,
4 °Neither give heed to °fables and °endless
°genealogies, which minister °questions, rather
than °godly edifying which is [2] in [2] faith:
so do.

b 5 Now the end of the °commandment is
°charity °out of a pure heart, and *of* a °good
conscience, and *of* [2] faith °unfeigned:

c 6 From which [3] some °having swerved °have
°turned aside °unto °vain jangling;
7 °Desiring to be °teachers of the law, °under-
standing °neither what they say, °nor °where-
of they °affirm.
8 But we °know that the law *is* good, °if °a
man use it °lawfully;
9 [8] Knowing this, that the law is °not °made
for a °righteous man, but for the °lawless and
°disobedient, for the °ungodly and for °sinners,
for °unholy and °profane, for °murderers of
fathers and murderers of mothers, for °man-
slayers,
10 For whoremongers, for °them that defile
themselves with mankind, for °menstealers,
for liars, for °perjured persons, and °if °there
be any °other thing °that is contrary to °sound
doctrine;

1. 1 apostle. Ap. 189. See Phil. 1. 1.
Jesus Christ. Ap. 98. XI. Most texts read "Christ Jesus".
by. Ap. 104. x. 2.
commandment. Gr. *epitagē.* See Rom. 16. 26.
God. Ap. 98. I. i. 1.
Saviour. God is called "Saviour", here, 2. 3. Luke 1. 47. Tit. 1. 3; 2. 10; 3. 4. Jude 25. Elsewhere the title is used of the Lord Jesus Christ.
Lord. The texts omit.
Jesus Christ. The texts read "Christ Jesus". Ap. 98. XII. *which is.* Read "Who is".
hope. Cp. Col. 1. 5, 23, 27. Tit. 2. 13.
2 Unto=To.
own. Gr. *gnēsios.* See 2 Cor. 8. 8.
son. Ap. 108. i. **in.** Ap. 104. viii.
faith. Ap. 150. II. 1.
Grace, mercy, *and* peace. This salutation is peculiar to the Epistles to Timothy and Titus.
Grace. Ap. 184. I. 1. **from.** Ap. 104. iv.
Father. Ap. 98. III.
Jesus Christ. Read "Christ Jesus".
Lord. Ap. 98. VI. i. β. 2. A.

1. 3-20 (B, p. 1799). ADMONITION. (*Introversion*)

B | A | a | 3, 4. The charge. Personal.
b | 5. Faith and a good conscience defined.
c | 6-10. Some who have turned aside.
B | 11. The blessed God.
C | 12. Paul, the trusted minister.
D | 13. The chief of sinners unsaved.
E | 14-. The Lord's abounding grace.
E | -14. Faith and love which is in Christ Jesus.
D | 15. The chief of sinners saved.
C | 16. Paul, the pattern of sinners saved.
B | 17. The only God.
A | *a* | 18. The charge. Personal.
b | 19-. Faith and a good conscience to be held fast.
c | -19, 20. Some who have made shipwreck.

3 besought. Ap. 134. I. 6. **abide.** Gr. *prosmenō.* See Acts 11. 23. **at.** Ap. 104. viii. **into.** Ap. 104. vi. **that**=in order that. Gr. *hina.* **charge.** Gr. *parangellō.* See Acts 1. 4. **some,** Ap. 124. 4. **that they, &c.**=not (Ap. 105. II) to teach otherwise (Gr. *heterodidaskaleō.* Only here and 6. 3). **4 Neither.** Gr. *mēde.* **fables.** Gr. *muthos.* Occ. also 4. 7. 2 Tim. 4. 4. Tit. 1. 14. 2 Pet. 1. 16. **endless.** Gr. *aperantos.* Ap. 151. II. E. **genealogies.** Gr. *genealogia.* Only here and Tit. 3. 9. Referring to the list of emanations of AEONS according to the Gnostics. **questions.** Gr. *zētēsis.* See Acts 25. 20. All the occ. of the word show what questions occupy the natural mind. **godly edifying**=dispensation (Gr. *oikonomia,* 1 Cor. 9. 17) of God (*v.* 1). A few texts read *oikodomē,* as 1 Cor. 14. 3, 5, 12. **5 commandment.** Gr. *parangelia.* See Acts 5. 28. **charity.** Ap. 135. II. 1. **out of.** Ap. 104. vii. **good conscience.** See Acts 23. 1. **unfeigned.** Gr. *anupokritos.* See Rom. 12. 9. **6 having swerved.** Gr. *astocheō.* Elsewhere, 6. 21. 2 Tim. 2. 18. **have.** Omit. **turned aside.** Gr. *ektrepomai.* Elsewhere, 5. 15; 6. 20. 2 Tim 4. 4. Heb. 12. 13. **unto.** Ap. 104. vi. **vain jangling.** Gr. *mataiologia.* Only here. Cp. Tit. 1. 10 **7 Desiring.** Ap. 102. 1. **teachers of the law.** Gr. *nomodidaskalos.* See Luke 5. 17. **understanding, &c.** There are double negatives in this phrase, *mē* at the beginning, and *mēte, mēte,* neither, nor. **whereof**=concerning (Ap. 104. xiii. 1) what. **affirm.** Gr. *diabebaioomai.* Only here and Tit. 3. 8. **8 know.** Ap. 132. I. i. **if.** Ap. 118. 1. b. **a man.** Gr. *tis.* Ap. 123. 3. **lawfully.** Gr *nomimōs.* Only here and 2 Tim. 2. 5. **9 not.** Ap. 105. I. **made**=appointed. **righteous.** Ap. 191. 1. **lawless.** Ap. 128. III. 3. **disobedient**=not under subjection, undisciplined. Gr. *anupotaktos.* Here; Tit. 1. 6, 10. Heb. 2. 8. **ungodly.** Gr. *asebēs* See Rom. 4. 5. **sinners.** Gr. *hamartōlos.* Cp. Ap. 128. I i. **unholy.** Gr. *anosios.* Here and 2 Tim. 3. 2. Contrast Acts 2. 27. **profane.** Gr. *bebēlos.* Here, 4. 7; 6. 20. 2 Tim. 2. 16. Heb. 12. 16. **murderers, &c.** Gr. *patralōas . . . mētralōas.* Only here. **manslayers.** Gr. *androphonos.* Only here. **10 them that, &c.** Gr. *arsenokoitēs.* See 1 Cor. 6. 9. **menstealers.** Gr. *andrapodistēs.* Only here. **perjured persons.** Gr. *epiorkos.* Only here **if.** Ap. 118. 2. a. **there be.** Omit. **other.** Ap. 124 2. **that.** Omit. **sound.** Gr. *hugiainō.* See Luke 5. 31.

B 11 °According to the °glorious °gospel of the °blessed [1]God, °which was committed to my trust.

C 12 °And I °thank °Christ Jesus our [2]Lord, Who °hath °enabled me, for that He counted me °faithful, putting me [3]into the °ministry;

D 13 Who was before a blasphemer, and a °persecutor, and °injurious: but I °obtained mercy, because I did *it* °ignorantly [2]in unbelief.

E 14 And the [2]grace of our [2]Lord °was exceeding abundant

E °with [2]faith and °love which is [2]in [12]Christ Jesus.

D 15 This *is* a [12]faithful °saying, and worthy of all °acceptation, that [12]Christ Jesus came [3]into the °world to save [9]sinners; of whom I am °chief.

C 16 Howbeit °for this cause I [13]obtained mercy, [3]that [2]in me °first [1]Jesus Christ might shew forth all longsuffering, °for a °pattern °to them which °should hereafter °believe on Him °to °life °everlasting.

B 17 Now [2]unto the °King eternal, °immortal, °invisible, the only °wise [1]God, *be* °honour and °glory °for ever and ever. Amen.

A a 18 This °charge I °commit [2]unto thee, [2]son Timothy, [11]according to the prophecies °which went before °on thee, [3]that thou °by them mightest °war °a good °warfare;

b 19 Holding [2]faith, and a [5]good conscience;

c which [3]some having °put away, °concerning °faith °have °made shipwreck:

20 Of whom is °Hymenæus and °Alexander; whom I °have °delivered [2]unto °Satan, [3]that they may learn °not to blaspheme.

C F **2** I °exhort therefore, that first of all, °supplications, °prayers, °intercessions, *and* °giving of thanks, be made °for all °men;

2 [1]For kings, and *for* all that are °in °authority; °that we may °lead a °quiet and °peaceable °life °in all °godliness and °honesty.

3 For this *is* good and °acceptable in the sight of °God our °Saviour;

11 According to. Ap. 104. x. 2.
glorious gospel = gospel (Ap. 140) of the glory (p. 1511). Cp. 2 Cor. 4. 4.
blessed. Only in this epistle is "blessed" (or happy), Gr. *makarios*, applied to God, here and 6. 15.
which, &c. = with which I was entrusted. Ap. 150. I. 1. iv.
12 And. Omit.
thank. Lit. I have thanks (Ap. 184. I. 1) to.
Christ Jesus. Ap. 98. XII. **hath.** Omit.
enabled. Gr. *endunamoō*. See Acts 9. 22.
faithful. Ap. 150. III.
ministry. Ap. 190. II. 1.
13 persecutor. Gr. *diōktēs*. Only here.
injurious = an insulter. Gr. *hubristēs*. Only here and Rom. 1. 30.
obtained mercy. Cp. 1 Cor. 7. 25. 2 Cor. 4. 1.
ignorantly = not knowing. Cp. Luke 23. 34. Acts 3. 17.
14 was exceeding, &c. = abounded over all. Gr. *huperpleonazō*. Only here. Cp. Rom. 5. 20.
with. Ap. 104. xi. 1.
love. Same as "charity", *v.* 5.
15 saying. Ap. 121. 10. This is the first of five "faithful sayings" in the Pastoral Epistles. Cp. 3. 1; 4. 9. 2 Tim. 2. 11. Tit. 3. 8. Cp. Rev. 21. 5; 22. 6.
acceptation. Gr. *apodochē*. Only here and 4. 9.
world. Ap. 129. 1.
chief. Gr. *prōtos*. Here "foremost", i.e. first in position.
16 for this cause = on account of (Ap. 104. v. 2) this.
first. See "chief", *v.* 15.
for. Ap. 104. xv. 3.
pattern. Gr. *hupotupōsis*. Only here and 2 Tim. 1. 13.
to = of.
should hereafter = are about to.
believe on. Ap. 150. I. 1. v. (iii) 1.
to. Ap. 104. vi. **life.** Ap. 170. 1.
everlasting. Ap. 151. II. B. ii. Paul was converted through the visible appearance of the Lord from heaven. Others will be (Zech. 12. 10).
17 King eternal = King of the ages (Ap. 151. II. A. i. 4). The same expression occ. in the Greek text of Tobit 13. 6, 10, and the "God of the ages", *Theos tōn aiōnōn*, in Ecclus. 36. 17. Cp. Isa. 9. 6. Jer. 10. 10.
immortal. Gr. *aphthartos*. See Rom. 1. 23. Cp. 6. 16.
invisible. Gr. *aoratos*. See Rom. 1. 20. Cp. 6. 16. Ex. 33. 20. John 1. 18. Col. 1. 15. Heb. 11. 27.
wise. The texts omit, the word having crept in from Rom. 16. 27.
honour and glory. These words are coupled together in Heb. 2. 7, 9. 2 Pet. 1. 17. Rev. 4. 9, 11; 5. 12, 13; 19. 1, in describing Divine glory, and in reference to man in Rom. 2. 7, 10. Rev. 21. 24, 26.
glory. See p. 1511.
for ever and ever. Ap. 151. II. A. ii. 9. a.

18 charge. Same as "commandment", *v.* 5. **commit.** Gr. *paratithēmi*. See Acts 17. 3. **which went before** = going before. Cp. 4. 14. **on.** Ap. 104. ix. 3. **by.** Ap. 104. viii. **war.** Gr. *strateuomai*. See 1 Cor. 9. 7. **a** = the. **warfare.** Gr. *strateia*. Only here and 2 Cor. 10. 4. This clause exhibits the Figs. *Paronomasia* and *Polyptōton*, Ap. 6. Gr. *strateuē strateian*. **19 put away** = thrust away. Gr. *apōtheomai*. See Acts 7. 27. **concerning.** Ap. 104. xiii. 2. **faith** = the faith (*v.* 2). **have.** Omit. **made shipwreck.** Gr. *nauageō*. Only here and 2 Cor. 11. 25. **20 Hymenæus.** Cp. 2 Tim. 2. 17, 18. **Alexander.** Cp. 2 Tim. 4. 14, 15. **have.** Omit. **delivered.** Gr. *paradidōmi*. See John 19. 30. **Satan.** Cp. 1 Cor. 5. 5. **not.** Ap. 105. II, as in *v.* 7.

2. 1—3. 13 (**C**, p. 1799). INSTRUCTION AND DISCIPLINE. (*Introversion.*)

C | F | 2. 1–8. Men. Kings and others.
  G | 2. 9–15. Women.
F | 3. 1–13. Men. Overseers and ministers.

2. 1 exhort. Ap. 134. I. 6. **supplications.** Ap. 134. II. 3. **prayers.** Ap. 134. II. 2. **intercessions.** Ap. 134. II. 4. **giving of thanks.** Gr. *eucharistia*. See Acts 24. 3. **for.** Ap. 104. xvii. 1. **men.** Ap. 123. 1. **2 in.** Ap. 104. viii. **authority.** Gr. *huperochē*. See 1 Cor. 2. 1. **that** = in order that. Gr. *hina*. **lead.** Gr. *diagō*. Only here and Tit. 3. 3. **quiet.** Gr. *ēremos*. Only here. **peaceable.** Gr. *hēsuchios*. Only here and 1 Pet. 3. 4. **life.** Ap. 170. 2. **godliness.** Gr. *eusebeia*. See Acts 3. 12. **honesty** = gravity. Gr. *semnotēs*. Only here, 3. 4, and Tit. 2. 7. Cp. 3. 8. **3 acceptable.** Gr. *apodektos*. Only here and 5. 4. **God.** Ap. 98. I. i. 1. **Saviour.** See 1. 1.

4 Who °will °have all [1]men to be saved, and
°to come °unto the °knowledge of the truth.
5 For *there is* one [3]God, and one °Mediator
°between [3]God and [1]men, the [1]Man °Christ
Jesus,
6 Who gave Himself a °ransom [1]for all, °to be
testified in °due time.
7 °Whereunto I am °ordained a °preacher,
and an °apostle, (I speak the truth [2]in °Christ,
and lie °not;) a teacher of the Gentiles [2]in
°faith and °verity.
8 I °will therefore that °men °pray °every
where, lifting up °holy hands, without wrath
and °doubting.
G 9 °In like manner °also, that °women °adorn
themselves [2]in °modest °apparel, °with °shame-
facedness and °sobriety; °not °with °broided
hair, or gold, or pearls, or °costly array;
10 But (which becometh [9]women professing
°godliness) °with good works.
11 Let the [9]woman learn [2]in silence -[9]with all
°subjection.
12 But I suffer [7]not a [9]woman to teach, °nor
to °usurp authority over the [8]man, but to be
[2]in silence.
13 For Adam was first °formed, then Eve;
14 And Adam was [7]not °deceived, but the
[9]woman °being deceived °was [2]in the °trans-
gression:
15 °Notwithstanding she shall be saved °in
°childbearing, °if they °continue [2]in [7]faith
and °charity and °holiness [9]-with [9]sobriety.

F **3** This *is* a °true °saying, °"If a man °desire
°the office of a bishop, he °desireth a good
work."
2 A °bishop then must be °blameless, the
°husband of one wife, °vigilant, °sober, °of
good behaviour, °given to hospitality, °apt to
teach;
3 °Not °given to wine, °no striker, °not
greedy of filthy lucre; but °patient, °not a
brawler, °not covetous;
4 One that °ruleth well his own house, having
his °children °in °subjection °with all °gra-
vity;
5 (For [1]if a man °know °not how to [4]rule his
own house, how shall he °take care of the
°church of °God?)
6 [3]Not a °novice, °lest being °lifted up with

4 will = wills. Ap. 102. 1.
have . . . to be = that . . . should be.
to. Omit.
unto. Ap. 104. vi.
knowledge. Ap. 132. II. ii.
5 Mediator. Gr. *mesitēs.* See Gal. 3. 19.
between = of.
Christ Jesus. Ap. 98. XII.
6 ransom. Gr. *antilutron.* Only here. Cp. Matt 20. 28. Mark 10. 45 (*lutron*). Tit. 2. 14. Heb. 9. 12.
to be testified = the testimony.
due time = its own seasons (Ap. 195). Cp. Gal. 4. 4.
7 Whereunto = For (Gr. *eis*) which.
ordained = appointed. Same word in 1. 12 (putting).
preacher. Ap. 121. 2.
apostle. Ap. 189.
Christ. Ap. 98. IX, but the texts omit "in Christ".
not. Ap. 105. I. Cp. Rom. 9. 1. 2 Cor. 11. 31. Gal. 1. 20.
faith. Ap. 150. II. 1. **verity** = truth.
8 will. Ap. 102. 3.
men = the men, i. e. husbands. Ap. 123. 2.
pray. Ap. 134. I. 2.
every where = in (Gr. *en*) every place.
holy. Gr. *hosios.* See Acts 2. 27.
doubting = reasoning or disputing.
9 In like manner = Likewise.
also. The texts omit.
women. The whole context shows that wives are in the apostle's mind. See *vv.* 12–15.
adorn. Gr. *kosmeō.* Five times in the Gospels. Tit. 2. 10. 1 Pet. 3. 5. Rev. 21. 2, 19.
modest = becoming, orderly. Gr. *kosmios.* Only here and 3. 2.
apparel. Gr. *katastolē.* Only here. Cp. Mark 12. 38.
with. Ap. 104. xi. 1.
shamefacedness = shamefastness, as originally in A.V. 1611. Gr. *aidōs.* Only here and Heb. 12. 28.
sobriety. Gr. *sōphrosunē.* See Acts 26. 25. Cp. 2 Tim. 1. 7. Tit. 2. 4, 12.
not. Ap. 105. II. **with.** Ap. 104. viii.
broided hair = plaits, or braids. Gr. *plegma.* Only here. Cp. 1 Pet. 3. 3.
costly. Gr. *polutelēs.* Elsewhere, Mark 14. 3. 1 Pet. 3. 4.
10 godliness. Gr. *theosebeia.* Only here.
with. Ap. 104. v. 1.
11 subjection. Gr. *hupotagē.* See 1 Cor. 14. 34. 2 Cor. 9. 13.
12 nor. Gr. *oude.*
usurp authority. Gr. *authenteō.* Only here.
13 formed. Gr. *plassō.* Only here and Rom. 9. 20.
14 deceived. Gr. *apataō.* See Eph. 5. 6.
being deceived. Gr. *apataō,* but the texts read *exapataō,* as in 2 Cor. 11. 3 (thoroughly deceived, or as we say, "taken in").
was = came to be. **transgression.** Gr. *parabasis.* Cp. Ap. 128. VI. 1, 3. **15 Notwithstanding** = But. **in** = through. Ap. 104. v. 1. **childbearing** = the childbearing. Gr. *teknogonia.* Only here. **if.** Ap. 118. 1. b. **continue.** Gr. *menō.* See p. 1511. **charity** = love, as in 1. 5. **holiness.** Gr. *hagiasmos.* See Rom. 6. 19.

3. 1 true = faithful. Ap. 150. III. See 1. 15. **saying.** Ap. 121. 10. **If a man** = If (Ap. 118. 2. a) any one (Ap. 123. 3). **desire.** Gr. *oregomai.* Here, 6. 10. Heb. 11. 16. **the office,** &c. Gr. *episkopē.* See Acts 1. 20. **desireth.** Gr. *epithumeō,* as Heb. 6. 11. **2 bishop.** Gr. *episkopos.* See Acts 20. 28. **blameless.** Gr. *anepilēptos.* Only here, 5. 7; 6. 14. **husband.** Ap. 123. 2. **vigilant** = sober. Gr. *nēphaleos.* Here, *v.* 11. Tit. 2. 2. **sober.** Gr. *sōphrōn.* Here, Tit. 1. 8; 2. 2, 5. Cp. 2. 9, 15. 2 Tim. 1. 7. Tit. 2. 4, 6, 12. **of good behaviour.** Gr. *kosmios.* See 2. 9. **given to hospitality.** Gr. *philoxenos.* Here; Tit. 1. 8. 1 Pet. 4. 9. Cp. Rom. 12. 13. **apt to teach.** Gr. *didaktikos.* Here and 2 Tim. 2. 24. **3 Not.** Ap. 105. II. **given to wine.** Gr. *paroinos.* Here and Tit. 1. 7. **no striker** = not (Gr. *mē*) a striker (Gr. *plēktēs.* Here and Tit. 1. 7). **not greedy,** &c. The texts omit, the idea being expressed at the end of the verse. **patient.** Gr. *epieikēs.* See Phil. 4. 5. **not a brawler** = not contentious. Gr. *amachos.* Here and Tit. 3. 2. **not covetous** = not loving money. Gr. *aphilarguros.* Here and Heb. 13. 5. **4 ruleth.** Gr. *proistēmi.* See Rom. 12. 8. **children.** Ap. 108. i. **in.** Gr. *en.* Ap. 104. viii. **subjection.** See 2. 11. **with.** Ap. 104. xi. 1. **gravity.** See "honesty", 2. 2. **5 know.** Ap. 132. I. i. **not.** Ap. 105. I. **take care of.** Gr. *epimeleomai.* Only here and Luke 10. 34, 35. **church.** Ap. 186. **God.** Ap. 98. I. i. 1. **6 novice.** Gr. *neophutos.* Only here. **lest** = in order that (Gr. *hina*) . . . not (Gr. *mē*). **lifted up,** &c. = puffed up. Gr. *tuphoomai.* Here, 6. 4. 2 Tim. 3. 4. The noun *tuphos* means smoke. Cp. Matt. 12. 20.

pride he fall °into the °condemnation of the
devil.
7 °Moreover he must have a good °report
°of them which are without; [6]lest he fall [6]into
°reproach and the °snare of the devil.
8 Likewise *must* the °deacons *be* °grave,
[3]not °doubletongued, [3]not given to much wine,
[3]not °greedy of filthy lucre;
9 Holding the °mystery of the °faith [4]in a
pure conscience.
10 And let these also first be °proved; then let
them °use the office of a deacon, being *found*
°blameless.
11 Even so *must their* wives *be* [8]grave, [3]not
°slanderers, °sober, °faithful [4]in all things.
12 Let the [8]deacons be the [2]husbands of one
wife, [4]ruling their [4]children and their own
houses well.
13 For they that °have [10]used the office of a
deacon well °purchase to themselves a good
°degree, and great °boldness [4]in the [9]faith
which is [4]in °Christ Jesus.
D 14 These things write I °unto thee, hoping to
(p. 1799) come °unto thee shortly:
15 But °if I °tarry long, °that thou mayest
[5]know how thou oughtest to °behave thyself
[4]in the house of [5]God, which is the [5]church of
the living [5]God, the °pillar and °ground of the
truth.
E 16 And °without controversy °great is the
[9]mystery of °godliness: °God °was manifest
[4]in °the flesh, °justified [4]in °the °Spirit, °seen
of angels, °preached °unto the Gentiles, °be-
lieved on [4]in the °world, °received up °into
°glory.

E H[1] d **4** Now the °Spirit °speaketh °expressly, that
°in the °latter °times °some shall °depart
from the °faith, giving heed to °seducing °spi-
rits, and °doctrines of °devils;
e 2 °Speaking lies [1]in hypocrisy; °having
their conscience °seared with a hot iron;
e 3 °Forbidding to marry, *and commanding* to
°abstain from °meats, which °God °hath
created °to be received °with °thanksgiving
°of them which believe and °know the truth.

into. Ap. 104. vi. **condemnation.** Ap. 177. 6.
7 Moreover = But.
report = testimony. Add "Also".
of. Ap. 104. iv.
reproach. Gr. *oneidismos.* See Rom. 15. 3.
snare. Gr. *pagis.* Here, 6. 19. Luke 21. 35. Rom. 11. 9. 2 Tim. 2. 6.
8 deacons. Ap. 190. I. 1.
grave. Gr. *semnos.* See Phil. 4. 8.
doubletongued. Gr. *dilogos.* Only here.
greedy, &c. Gr. *aischrokerdēs.* Here and Tit. 1. 7. Cp. 1 Pet. 5. 2.
9 mystery. Ap. 193. **faith.** Ap. 150. II. 1.
10 proved = tested.
use, &c. = serve. Ap. 190. III. 1.
blameless. Gr. *anenklētos.* See 1 Cor. 1. 8.
11 slanderers. Gr. *diabolos,* adj.
sober. Same as "vigilant", *v.* 2.
faithful. Same as "true", *v.* 1.
13 have. Omit.
purchase. Gr. *peripoieomai.* See Acts 20. 28.
degree. Gr. *bathmos.* Only here.
boldness. Gr. *parrhēsia.* Transl. "freely", in Acts 2. 29. **Christ Jesus.** Ap. 98. XII.
14 unto = to. **unto.** Ap. 104. xv. 3.
15 if. Ap. 118. 1. b.
tarry long = delay. Gr. *bradunō.* Here and 2 Pet. 3. 9.
that = in order that. Gr. *hina.*
behave thyself. Gr. *anastrephō.* See 2 Cor. 1. 12. An alternative reading, as R.V., "how men ought to behave themselves".
pillar. Gr. *stulos.* See Gal. 2. 9.
ground. Gr. *hedraiōma.* Only here.
16 without controversy = confessedly. Gr. *homologoumenōs.* Only here.
great. Emph. **godliness.** See 2. 2.
God. The R.V. prints "He Who", and adds in margin, "*Theos* (God) rests on no sufficient evidence". The probability is that the original reading was *ho* (which), with the Syriac and all the Latin Versions, to agree with *mustērion* (neut.). The Gr. uncial being O, some scribe added the letter s, making OC (He Who), which he thought made better sense. Later another put a mark in this O, making the word ΘC, the contraction for ΘEOC, God. This mark in Codex A, in the British Museum, is said by some to be in different ink.
was manifest. Ap. 106. I. v. **the.** Omit.
justified. Ap. 191. 2. **Spirit.** Ap. 101. II. 4.
seen. Ap. 106. I. vi.
preached. Ap. 121. 1.
unto = among. Gr. *en.* Ap. 104. viii. 2.
believed on. Ap. 150. I. 1. i.
world. Ap. 129. 1.
received up. Same word as Mark 16. 19. Acts 1. 2, 11, 22. **into** = in. Gr. *en.* **glory.** See p. 1511.

4. 1-12 (*E*, p. 1799). THE MYSTERY OF INIQUITY. (*Division.*)

E | H[1] | 1-5. Its characteristics.
 | H[2] | 6-12. What is needed to meet it.

4. 1-5 (H[1], above). ITS CHARACTERISTICS. (*Introversion.*)

H[1] | d | 1. Teachings of demons.
 | e | 2. Lies.
 | *e* | 3. Prohibitions.
 | *d* | 4, 5. Teaching of truth.

4. 1 Spirit. Ap. 101. II. 3. **expressly** = in express words. Gr. *rhētōs.* Only here. **in.** Ap. 104. viii. **latter.** Gr. *husteros.* Only here as adj. **times** = seasons. See Gen. 49. 1. See Ap. 195. **some.** Ap. 124. 4. **depart** = apostatize. Gr. *aphistēmi.* **faith.** Ap. 150. II. 1. **seducing.** Gr. *planos.* See 2 Cor. 6. 8. **spirits.** Ap. 101. II. 12. **doctrines** = teachings. **devils** = demons. **2 Speaking, &c.** = By (Gr. *en*) the hypocrisy of liars (Gr. *pseudologos.* Only here). **having, &c.** = having been seared with a hot iron as to their own conscience. **seared, &c.** Gr. *kautēriazomai.* Only here. **3 Forbidding to marry.** This has been taken as indicating the Church of Rome, but that church only enjoins the celibacy of priests and monks and nuns. Spiritism, or the teaching of demons, enjoins being united only to the "spiritual affinity" and has wrecked many homes. **abstain.** Gr. *apechomai.* See Acts 15. 20. **meats** = foods. Spiritist teaching is that animal food is unfavourable to the development of mediumistic power. The permission of Gen. 9. 3 is significant, coming immediately after the outbreak of Gen. 6. 1-4. **God.** Ap. 98. I. i. 1. **hath.** Omit. **to be received** = for (Gr. *eis*) reception. Gr. *metalēpsis.* Only here. **with.** Ap. 104. xi. 1. **thanksgiving.** See 2. 1. **of, &c.** = by believers. Ap. 150. III. **know** = have (fully) known. Ap. 132. I. iii.

d 4 For every °creature of [3]God *is* good, and
°nothing °to be refused, °if it be received [3]with
[3]thanksgiving:
5 For it is sanctified °by the °word of [3]God
and °prayer.
H² J f 6 °If thou put the brethren in remembrance
of these things, thou shalt be a good °minister
of °Jesus Christ,
g °nourished up in the [5]words of [1]faith, and of
good doctrine, °whereunto thou hast °attained.
K h 7 But °refuse °profane and °old wives'
°fables,
i and °exercise thyself *rather* °unto °godliness.
K h 8 For bodily °exercise °profiteth °little,
i but [7]godliness °is profitable [7]unto all things,
having promise of the °life that now is, and of
that which is to come.
9 This *is* a °faithful saying °and worthy of all
°acceptation.
10 For °therefore we both labour and °suffer
reproach, because we °trust °in the °living
[3]God, Who is the °Saviour of °all °men,
°specially of °those that believe.
J f 11 These things °command and teach.
g 12 Let °no man despise thy °youth; but °be
thou an °example of the °believers, [1]in [5]word,
[1]in °conversation, [1]in °charity, °in spirit, [1]in
[1]faith, [1]in °purity.
D 13 Till I come, °give attendance to °reading,
to °exhortation, to °doctrine.
14 °Neglect °not the °gift that is [1]in thee,
which was given thee [5]by °prophecy, [3]with
the laying on of the hands of the °presbytery.
15 °Meditate upon these things; °give thyself wholly °to them; °that thy °profiting
may °appear to all.
16 °Take heed °unto thyself, and °unto the
doctrine; °continue in them: for °in doing
this thou shalt °both save thyself, and them
that hear thee.

C L **5** °Rebuke °not an °elder, but °intreat *him*
as a father, *and* the younger men as
brethren;
M j 2 The °elder women as mothers;
k the younger as sisters, °with all °purity.

4 creature. Gr. *ktisma.* Here; Jas. 1. 18. Rev. 5. 13; 8. 9.
nothing. Gr. *oudeis.*
to be refused. Gr. *apoblētos.* Only here. Cp. Heb. 10. 35.
if it be = being.
5 by. Ap. 104. v. 1.
word. Ap. 121. 10.
prayer. Ap. 134. II. 4.

4. 6-12 (H², p. 1803). ITS REQUIREMENTS.
(*Introversion and Alternation.*)

H² | J | f | 6-. Good ministers.
| | g | -6. Their duty.
| K | h | 7-. Negative } instruction.
| | i | -7. Positive }
| *K* | *h* | 8-. Negative } instruction.
| | *i* | -8-10. Positive }
| *J* | *f* | 11. Good ministers.
| | *g* | 12. Their example.

6 If thou put, &c. Lit. Putting . . . in remembrance. Gr. *hupotithēmi.* Only here and Rom. 16. 4.
minister. Ap. 190. I. 1.
Jesus Christ. Ap. 98. XI. The texts read "Christ Jesus" (XII).
nourished up. Gr. *entrephomai.* Only here.
whereunto = to which.
attained. Lit. followed up. Gr. *parakoloutheō.* Here; Mark 16. 17. Luke 1. 3. 2 Tim. 3. 10.
7 refuse. Gr. *paraiteomai.* See Acts 25. 11.
profane = the profane. Referring to 1. 4. See 1. 9.
old wives'. Gr. *graōdēs.* Only here.
fables. See 1. 4.
exercise. Gr. *gumnazō.* Here; Heb. 5. 14; 12. 11. 2 Pet. 2. 14.
unto. Ap. 104. xv. 3.
godliness. See 2. 2.
8 exercise. Gr. *gumnasia.* Only here.
profiteth, is profitable. Gr. *ōphelimos.* Here; 2 Tim. 3. 16. Tit. 3. 8.
little = unto (as *v.* 7) a little (matter).
life. Ap. 170. 1.
9 faithful, &c. See 1. 15.
and. Omit.
acceptation. See 1. 15.
10 therefore = for (Gr. *eis*) this.
suffer reproach = are reviled. The texts read "strive", as in 1 Cor. 9. 25.
trust = have hoped.
in. Ap. 104. ix. 2.
living God. See Acts 14. 15.
Saviour. See 1. 1.
all men. When our first parents incurred the penalty of immediate judicial death, the race would have been extinguished, had not God interposed, before dealing with the culprits, with the promise of the Redeemer, and so suspending the execution of the sentence denounced.
men. Ap. 123. 1.
specially. Occ. N. T. twelve times. Rendered "specially", "especially" (nine); "most of all" (Acts 20. 38); "chiefly" (Phil. 4. 22. 2 Pet. 2. 10).
those that believe = the believing. Ap. 150. III.
11 command. See Acts 1. 4. Cp. 1. 3.
12 no man. Gr. *mēdeis.*
youth. See Acts 26. 4.
be = become.
example. Gr. *tupos.* See John 20. 25.
believers. Same as "those that believe", *v.* 10.
conversation. Gr. *anastrophē.* See Gal. 1. 13.
charity. See 1. 5.
in spirit. The texts omit.
purity. Gr. *hagneia.* Only here and 5. 2.
13 give attendance = take heed, as *v.* 1 (giving heed).
reading. See Acts 13. 15.
exhortation. Gr. *paraklēsis.* See Acts 4. 36.
doctrine = teaching.
14 Neglect. Gr. *ameleō.* Here; Matt. 22. 5. Heb. 2. 3; 8. 9. 2 Pet. 1. 12.
not. Ap. 105. II.
gift. Ap. 184. I. 2.
prophecy. Cp. 1. 18.
presbytery. See Acts 22. 5.
15 Meditate upon. Gr. *meletaō.* See Acts 4. 25.
give, &c. Lit. be in them, i. e. occupied in them.
to. Ap. 104. viii.
that = in order that. Gr. *hina.*
profiting. Gr. *prokopē.* See Phil. 1. 12.
appear = be manifest. Ap. 106. I. viii.
16 Take heed. Gr. *epechō.* See Acts 3. 5.
unto = to.
continue. Gr. *epimenō.* See Acts 10. 48.
in. Omit.
both save = save both.

5. 1—6. 2 (*C*, p. 1799). INSTRUCTION AND DISCIPLINE. (*Introversion.*)

C | L | 5. 1. Men.
| M | 5. 2-16. Women.
| *L* | 5. 17—6. 2. Men.

5. 1 Rebuke. Gr. *epiplēssō.* Only here.
not. Ap. 105. II.
elder. Ap. 189.
intreat. Same as "exhort", 2. 1 and 6. 2.

5. 2-16 [For Structure see next page].

2 elder women. Fem. of "elder", *v.* 1.
with. Ap. 104. viii.
purity. See 4. 12.

j 3 Honour widows that are widows °indeed.
4 But °if °any widow have °children or °nephews, let them learn first to °shew piety at home, and to °requite their °parents: for that is good and °acceptable °before °God.
5 Now she that is a widow [3]indeed, and °desolate, °trusteth °in [4]God, and °continueth in °supplications and °prayers night and day.
6 But she that °liveth in pleasure is dead while she °liveth.
7 And these things °give in charge, °that they may be °blameless.
8 But [4]if [4]any °provide [c]not for his own, and specially for °those of his °own house, he hath denied the °faith, and is worse than an °infidel.
9 Let [1]not a widow be °taken into the number °under threescore years old, having been the wife of one °man,
10 °Well reported of °for good works; [4]if she have °brought up children, [4]if she have °lodged strangers, [4]if she have washed the °saints' feet, [4]if she have °relieved the °afflicted, [4]if she have °diligently followed every good work.

k 11 But the younger widows °refuse: for when they have °begun to wax wanton against °Christ, they °will marry;
12 Having °damnation, because they have °cast off their first [8]faith.
13 And withal they learn *to be* °idle, °wandering about from house to house; and [8]not only °idle, but °tattlers also and °busybodies, °speaking things which they ought [1]not.
14 I °will therefore that the younger women marry, °bear children, °guide the house, give °none °occasion to the adversary °to speak reproachfully.
15 For °some are already °turned aside after Satan.
16 [4]If [4]any °man or woman that believeth have widows, let them [10]relieve them, and let [1]not the °church be °charged; [7]that it may [10]relieve them that are widows [3]indeed.

L l 17 Let the [1]elders that °rule well °be counted worthy of °double honour, especially they who labour °in the °word and doctrine.
18 For the Scripture saith, "**Thou shalt [8]not °muzzle the ox that °treadeth out the corn.**" And, "The labourer *is* worthy of his °reward."

5. 2-16 (M, p. 1804). WOMEN. (*Alternation.*)

M | j | 2-. Elder. } In respect of age.
  | k | -2. Younger. }
  | *j* | 3-10. Elder. } Widows.
  | *k* | 11-16. Younger. }

3 indeed. See John 8. 36.
4 if. Ap. 118. 2. a. **any.** Ap. 123. 3.
children. Ap. 108. i.
nephews = grandchildren or other descendants. Gr. *ekgonos.* Only here. Shakespeare in *Othello* uses the word nephews for grandchildren.
shew piety at home = treat reverently (Gr. *eusebeō.* Only here and Acts 17. 23) their own household.
requite = return recompenses (Gr. *amoibē.* Only here) to.
parents. Gr. *progonos.* Only here and 2 Tim. 1. 3.
acceptable. Gr. *apodektos.* Only here and 2. 3.
before = in the sight of.
God. Ap. 98. I. i. 1.
5 desolate. Gr. *monoomai.* Only here.
trusteth = has hoped. Implying continued hoping.
in. Ap. 104. ix. 3.
continueth. Gr. *prosmenō.* See 1. 3.
supplications. Ap. 134. II. 3.
prayers. Ap. 134. II. 2.
6 liveth in pleasure. Gr. *spatalaō.* Only here and Jas. 5. 5. **liveth.** See Ap. 170. 1.
7 give in charge. Gr. *parangellō.* See Acts 1. 4. Cp. 1. 3; 4. 11; 6. 13, 17.
that = in order that. Gr. *hina.*
blameless. See 3. 2.
8 provide. Gr. *pronoeō.* See Rom. 12. 17.
not. Ap. 105. I.
those, &c. Gr. *oikeios.* See Gal. 6. 10.
own. Omit. **faith.** Ap. 150. II. 1.
infidel = unbeliever. Gr. *apistos.* See 1 Cor. 6. 6; 7. 12.
9 taken, &c. = enrolled. Gr. *katalegomai.* Only here.
under = less than. Gr. *elassōn.* See Rom. 9. 12.
man. Ap. 123. 2.
10 Well reported of = Borne witness to.
for. Ap. 104. viii.
brought up, &c. Gr. *teknotropheō.* Only here.
lodged strangers. Gr. *xenodocheō.* Only here.
saints'. See Acts 9. 13.
relieved. Gr. *eparkeō.* Only here and *v.* 16.
afflicted. Gr. *thlibō.* See 2 Cor. 1. 6.
diligently followed. Gr. *epakoloutheō.* Here, *v.* 24. Mark 16. 20. 1 Pet. 2. 21.
11 refuse. See 4. 7.
begun to wax wanton = grown wanton. Gr. *katastrēniazō.* Only here.
Christ. Ap. 98. IX.
will. Ap. 102. 1.
12 damnation = judgment. Ap. 177. 6.
cast off. Gr. *atheteō.* See John 12. 48.
13 idle. Gr. *argos.* See Matt. 12. 36. Cp. the verb *katargeō.* Luke 13. 7. Add "also".
wandering about. Gr. *perierchomai.* See Acts 19. 13. **tattlers.** Gr. *phluaros.* Only here. The verb 3 John 10. **busybodies.** Gr. *periergos.* See Acts 19. 19 **speaking.** Ap. 121. 7. **14 will.** Ap. 102. 3. **bear children.** Gr. *teknogoneō.* Only here. Cp. 2. 15. **guide the house.** Gr. *oikodespoteō.* Only here. **none.** Gr. *mēdeis.* **occasion.** Gr. *aphormē.* See Rom. 7. 8. **to speak reproachfully.** Lit. for the sake of (Gr. *charin,* acc. case of *charis,* used as a preposition) reviling (Gr. *loidoria.* Here and 1 Pet. 3. 9. Cp. John 9. 28. Acts 23. 4. 1 Cor. 4. 12. 1 Pet. 2. 23). **15 some.** Ap. 124. 4. **turned aside.** See 1. 6. **16 man or woman that believeth, &c.** The texts read "believing (*woman*) . . . let her:" "believing" being fem. of Ap. 150. III. **church.** Ap. 186. **charged** = burdened. Gr. *bareō.* See 2 Cor. 1. 8.

5. 17—6. 2 (*L,* p. 1804). MEN. (*Alternation.*)

L | l | 5. 17-20. Elders.
  | m | 5. 21-25. Charge.
  | *l* | 6. 1, 2-. Bond-servants.
  | *m* | 6. -2. Charge.

17 rule. See 3. 4. **be counted worthy.** Gr. *axioō.* See Acts 15. 38. **double.** Gr. *diplous.* Only here; Matt. 23. 15 (compar.). Rev. 18. 6. **in.** Ap. 104. viii. **word.** Ap. 121. 10. **18 muzzle.** Gr. *phimōo.* See Luke 4. 35. **treadeth out, &c.** See 1 Cor. 9. 9, where the same quotation occurs. The latter part of the verse is from Matt. 10. 10, &c. **reward** = pay. Gr. *misthos.*

19 °Against an [1]elder °receive [1]not an °accusation, °but °before °two or three witnesses.
20 Them that °sin °rebuke [4]before all, [7]that °others also may °fear.

m 21 I °charge *thee* [4]before [4]God, and the °Lord °Jesus Christ, and the elect angels, [7]that thou °observe these things °without °preferring one before another, doing °nothing °by °partiality.
22 Lay hands °suddenly on °no man, °neither be partaker of °other men's °sins: keep thyself °pure.
23 °Drink °no longer water, but use a little wine °for thy °stomach's sake and thine °often infirmities.
24 [15]Some °men's [22]sins are °open beforehand, °going before °to °judgment; and [15]some *men* they [10]follow after.
25 Likewise °also the good works *of some* are °manifest beforehand; and they that are °otherwise °cannot be hid.

l **6** Let as many °servants as are °under the yoke count their own °masters worthy of all honour, °that the name of °God and *His* doctrine be °not blasphemed.
2 And they that have °believing [1]masters, let them [1]not despise *them*, because they are brethren;

m but rather °do *them* service, because they are °faithful and °beloved, °partakers of the °benefit. These things teach and °exhort.

B N 3 °If °any man °teach otherwise, and consent [1]not to °wholesome °words, °*even* the words of our °Lord °Jesus Christ, and to the doctrine which is °according to °godliness;
4 He is °proud, °knowing °nothing, but °doting °about °questions and °strifes of words, °whereof cometh envy, strife, railings, evil °surmisings,
5 °Perverse disputings of °men °of corrupt minds, and °destitute of the truth, supposing that °gain is [3]godliness: °from such °withdraw thyself.
6 But [3]godliness °with °contentment is great [5]gain.

19 Against. Ap. 104. x. 1.
receive. Gr. *paradechomai.* See Acts 16. 21.
accusation. Gr. *katēgoria.* Here; Luke 6. 7. John 18. 29. Tit. 1. 6.
but. See 1 Cor. 14. 5 (except).
before. Ap. 104. ix. 1.
two, &c. Cp. Deut. 19. 15. Matt. 18. 16. 2 Cor. 13. 1.
20 sin. Ap. 128. I. i.
rebuke. Gr. *elenchō.* See 1 Cor. 14. 24.
others. Ap. 124. 3. **fear** = have fear.
21 charge. Gr. *diamarturomai.* See Acts 2. 40.
Lord. The texts omit.
Jesus Christ. The texts read "Christ Jesus". Ap. 98. XII.
observe = guard. **without** = apart from.
preferring . . . another = prejudgment, prejudice. Gr. *prokrima.* Only here.
nothing. Gr. *mēdeis,* as in *vv.* 14, 22.
by. Ap. 104. x. 2.
partiality. Lit. inclining towards. Gr. *prosklisis.* Only here.
22 suddenly = hastily, i.e. without sufficient testing.
no man = no one. Gr. *mēdeis.* See *v.* 21.
neither. Gr. *mēde.* **other men's.** Ap. 124. 6.
sins. Ap. 128. I. ii. 1.
pure. Gr. *hagnos.* See 2 Cor. 7. 11. Not as the word is used to-day, but as clear from aiding in sending unfit men into the ministry, from which all the churches are suffering at this hour. Cp. Jude 11.
23 Drink . . . water. Gr. *hudropoteō.* Only here.
no longer. Gr. *mēketi.*
for . . . sake. Ap. 104. v. 2.
stomach's. Gr. *stomachos.* Only here.
often = frequent. Gr. *puknos.* See Luke 5. 33.
24 men's. Ap. 123. 1.
open beforehand. Gr. *prodēlos.* Only here, *v.* 25, and Heb. 7. 14.
going before. See 1. 18.
to. Ap. 104. vi.
judgment. Ap. 177. 7. Some are notoriously unfit; the unfitness of others is not manifest till they are tested.
25 also. Should follow works.
manifest beforehand. Same as "open beforehand", *v.* 24.
otherwise. Gr. *allōs.* Only here.
cannot = are not (Ap. 105. I) able to.
6. 1 servants. Ap. 190. I. 2.
under. Ap. 104. xviii. 2.
masters. Ap. 98. XIV. ii.
that = in order that. Gr. *hina.*
God. Ap. 98. I. i. 1.
not. Ap. 105. II.

2 believing. Ap. 150. III. **do . . . service.** Ap. 190. III. 2. **faithful.** Same as "believing". **beloved.** Ap. 135. III. **partakers** = those who are partaking. Gr. *antilambanomai.* See Acts 20. 35. **benefit** = good work. Gr. *euergesia.* See Acts 4. 9. **exhort.** Ap. 134. I. 6.

6. 3-21- (*B*, p. 1799). ADMONITION. (*Introversion and Alternation.*)

B | N | 3–6. False teachers.
  O | n | 7–10. Riches. Danger.
      o | 11–14. Charge.
    P | 15, 16. Ascription and Doxology.
  O | n | 17–19. Riches. Duty.
      o | 20. Charge.
N | 21–. False teachers.

3 If. Ap. 118. 2. a. **any man** = any one. Ap. 123. 3. **teach otherwise.** See 1. 3. **wholesome.** Same as "sound", 1. 10. **words.** Ap. 121. 10. *even* **the words** = those. **Lord.** Ap. 98. VI. i. β. 2. A. **Jesus Christ.** Ap. 98. XI. **according to.** Ap. 104. x. 2. **godliness.** See 2. 2. **4 proud** = puffed up. See 3. 6. **knowing.** Ap. 132. I. v. **nothing.** Gr. *mēdeis.* **doting** = sick, or diseased. Gr. *noseō.* Only here. Cp. Matt. 4. 24. **about.** Ap. 104. xiii. 2. **questions.** See 1. 4. **strifes, &c.** Gr. *logomachia.* Only here. The verb in 2 Tim. 2. 14. **whereof** = out of (Ap. 104. vii) which. **surmisings.** Gr. *huponoia.* Only here. **5 Perverse disputings.** Gr. *paradiatribē.* Only here. The texts read *diaparatribē.* **men.** Ap. 123. 1. **of corrupt minds** = corrupted (Gr. *diaphtheirō.* See 2 Cor. 4. 16) as to their mind. **destitute** = deprived. Gr. *apostereō.* See 1 Cor. 6. 7. **gain, &c.** Read "godliness is *a way of* gain". **gain.** Gr. *porismos.* Here and *v.* 6. **from.** Ap. 104. iv. **withdraw thyself.** Same as "depart", 4. 1, but the texts omit "from such", &c. **6 with.** Gr. *meta.* Ap. 104. xi. 1. **contentment.** Gr. *autarkeia.* See 2 Cor. 9. 8. Cp. Phil. 4. 11.

O n 7 For we brought °nothing °into *this* °world,
°*and it is* certain we can carry °nothing
out.
8 And having °food and °raiment let us be
therewith °content.
9 But they that °will be rich °fall [7]into temptation and a °snare, and *into* many °foolish
and °hurtful lusts, which °drown [5]men °in
°destruction and °perdition.
10 For the °love of money is °the root of °all
°evil: which while °some °coveted after, they
°have erred [5]from the °faith, and °pierced
themselves through °with many °sorrows.

o 11 But thou, O [5]man of [1]God, flee these things;
and follow after °righteousness, [3]godliness,
[10]faith, °love, patience, °meekness.
12 °Fight the good °fight of [10]faith, lay hold
on °eternal °life, °whereunto thou art also
called, and °hast °professed °a good °profes-
sion °before many witnesses.
13 I °give thee charge °in the sight of [1]God,
Who °quickeneth all things, and *before* °Christ
Jesus, Who °before Pontius Pilate witnessed
[12]a good °confession;
14 That thou keep *this* commandment °with-
out spot, °unrebukeable, until the °appearing
of our [3]Lord [3]Jesus Christ:

P 15 °Which in °His °times He shall shew,
°*Who is* the °blessed and only °Potentate, the
King of kings, and Lord of °lords;
16 Who only hath °immortality, °dwelling in
°the °light °which °no [5]man can approach
unto; Whom °no [5]man hath °seen, °nor can
°see: to Whom *be* honour and °power °ever-
lasting. Amen.

O n 17 [13]Charge them that are rich °in °this
°world, that they be [1]not °highminded, °nor
°trust °in °uncertain riches, but °in °the living
[1]God, Who °giveth us °richly all things °to
enjoy;
18 That they °do good, that they be rich [17]in
good works, °ready to distribute, °willing to
communicate;
19 °Laying up in store for themselves a good
foundation °against the time to come, [1]that
they may °lay hold on °eternal [12]life.

o 20 O Timothy, °keep °that which is committed to thy trust, °avoiding °profane °*and*

7 nothing. Gr. *oudeis.*
into. Ap. 104. vi.
world. Ap. 129. 1.
***and it is* certain.** Read "neither" (Gr. *oude*). This makes with the second *ouden* a double negative.
certain. The texts omit.
8 food=nourishment. Gr. *diatrophē.* Only here.
raiment=covering, perhaps including shelter. Gr. *skepasma.* Only here.
content. Same word as 2 Cor. 12. 9 (sufficient). Heb. 13. 5.
9 will. Ap. 102. 3.
fall, &c. Cp. 3. 6, 7.
snare. See 3. 7.
foolish. Gr. *anoētos.* See Rom. 1. 14.
hurtful. Gr. *blaberos.* Only here.
drown. Gr. *buthizō.* Only here and Luke 5. 7.
in. Ap. 104. vi.
destruction. Gr. *olethros.* See 1 Cor. 5. 5.
perdition. See John 17. 12.
10 love of money. Gr. *philarguria.* Only here. Cp. 2 Tim. 3. 2. **the**=a.
all, &c.=all the evils.
evil. Ap. 128. III. 2. **some.** Ap. 124. 4.
coveted after. See 3. 1.
have erred=were seduced. Gr. *apoplanaō.* Only here and Mark 13. 22.
faith. Ap. 150. II. 1.
pierced . . . through. Gr. *peripeirō.* Only here.
with=by. Dat. case.
sorrows=pangs. Gr. *odunē.* Only here and Rom. 9. 2.
11 righteousness. Ap. 191. 3.
love. Ap. 135. II. 1.
meekness. See 1 Cor. 4. 21.
12 Fight. Gr. *agōnizomai.* See Luke 13. 24.
fight. Gr. *agōn.* See Phil. 1. 30. Fig. *Paronomasia.* Ap. 6.
eternal. Ap. 151. II. B. i.
life. Ap. 170. 1.
whereunto=unto (Ap. 104. vi) which.
hast. Omit.
professed=confessed. Gr. *homologeō.* Occ. twenty-three times; seventeen times "confess", three times "profess"; "make confession", "promise", "give thanks", once each.
a=the.
profession=confession. Gr. *homologia.* See 2 Cor. 9. 13. Fig. *Hyperbaton.* Ap. 6.
before=in the sight of.
13 give . . . charge. See 1. 3.
in the sight of="before", as above.
quickeneth. See Rom. 4. 17. The texts read *zoōgoneō*, preserve alive.
Christ Jesus. Ap. 98. XII.
before. Ap. 104. ix. 1.
confession. Same as "profession", *v.* 12. **14 without spot**=unspotted. Gr. *aspilos.* Here; Jas. 1. 27. 1 Pet. 1. 19. 2 Pet. 3. 14. **unrebukeable.** Same as "blameless", 3. 2; 5. 7. **appearing.** Ap. 106. II. ii. **15 Which.** Refers to "appearing". **His**=His own. **times**=seasons. Cp. Acts 1. 7. See Ap. 195. ***Who is.*** Omit. **blessed.** See 1. 11. **Potentate.** Ap. 98. V. **lords.** Gr. *kurieuō.* See Luke 22. 25. **16 immortality**=deathlessness. Gr. *athanasia.* Only here and 1 Cor. 15. 53, 54. **dwelling in**=inhabiting. Gr. *oikeō.* **the.** Omit. **light.** Ap. 130. 1. **which, &c.**=unapproachable. Gr. *aprositos.* Only here. **no man**=no one (Gr. *oudeis*) of men (Ap. 123. 1). **seen, see.** Ap. 133. I. 1. **nor.** Gr. *oude.* **power.** Ap. 172. 2. **everlasting.** Ap. 151. II. B. ii. Cp. *v.* 12. **17 in.** Ap. 104. viii. **this**=the present. **world.** Ap. 129. 2. **highminded.** Gr. *hupsēlophroneō.* Only here and Rom. 11. 20. **nor.** Gr. *mēde.* **trust**=set their hope. **in**=upon. Ap. 104. ix. 1. **uncertain**=the uncertainty of. Gr. *adēlotēs.* Only here. **in.** The texts read Ap. 104. ix. 2. **the living.** The texts omit. **giveth**=provideth. See 1. 4 (minister). **richly.** See Col. 3. 16. **to enjoy**=for (Ap. 104. vi) enjoyment. Gr. *apolausis.* Here and Heb. 11. 25. **18 do good.** Gr. *agathoergeō.* Only here. **ready to distribute.** Gr. *eumetadotos.* Only here. **willing to communicate.** Gr. *koinōnikos.* Only here. "Sociable" (A.V. m.). **19 Laying up, &c.** Gr. *apothēsaurizō.* Only here. **against.** Ap. 104. vi. **lay hold, &c.** Cp. *v.* 12. **eternal life.** The texts read, "the life that is life indeed": for *aiōnios* reading *ontōs.* Cp. 5. 3. **20 keep**=guard, as in 5. 21 (observe). Cp. 2 Tim. 1. 12, 14. **that . . . trust.** Gr. *parakatathēkē.* Only here and 2 Tim. 1. 14. But the texts read *parathēkē* in both places, thus agreeing with 2 Tim. 1. 14. Both words mean "deposit". The deposit entrusted to Timothy was the teaching regarding the Mystery (3. 16). **avoiding**=turning aside from. See 1. 6; 5. 15. **profane.** Gr. *bebēlos.* See 1. 9. ***and.*** Omit.

° vain babblings, and ° oppositions of ° science
° falsely so called:
N 21 Which [10] some professing ° have ° erred
° concerning the [10] faith.
A ° Grace *be* [6] with ° thee. ° Amen.

vain babblings. Gr. *kenophōnia*. Only here and 2 Tim. 2. 16.
oppositions. Gr. *antithesis*. Only here.
science. Ap. 132. II. i.
falsely so called. Gr. *pseudōnumos*. Only here. There is much science (knowledge) which does not deserve the name, being only speculation.
concerning. Ap. 104. xiii. 2. Grace. Ap. 184. I. 1.

21 have. Omit. erred. See 1. 6 (swerved). thee. The texts read "you". Amen. Omit.

THE SECOND EPISTLE TO TIMOTHY.

THE STRUCTURE OF THE BOOK AS A WHOLE.

(*Introversion.*)

A | 1. 1, 2. GREETING AND BENEDICTION.

B | 1. 3-18. EPISTOLARY. PRIVATE AND PERSONAL.

C | 2. 1-26. CHARGES CONNECTED WITH THE GOSPEL.

C | 3. 1—4. 8. CHARGES CONNECTED WITH THE APOSTASY.

B | 4. 9-21-. EPISTOLARY. PRIVATE AND PERSONAL.

A | 4. -21-22. GREETINGS. BENEDICTION.

THE SECOND EPISTLE TO TIMOTHY.

INTRODUCTORY NOTES.

1. The Second Epistle to Timothy is the latest of all Paul's writings. It was written during his second imprisonment at Rome, within a short time of his martyrdom (4. 6), probably at the end of A. D. 67 or early 68. It is thought that at this time Timothy was at Ephesus. The apostle's regard for his "dearly beloved son" is seen in 1. 4, and it is affecting to observe the pathetic desire to see Timothy once more before death, 4. 9, 11, 21. No further mention is made of Timothy. The tradition that he suffered martyrdom about the end of the first century is only tradition.

2. The prominent feature of this Epistle is the "church's" departure from the truth (see 1. 15; 2. 17; 3. 8; 4. 4). When "all they which are in Asia (cp. Acts 19. 10) be turned away from" Paul, he exhorts Timothy, his "son", *therefore* to "be strong in the grace that is in Christ Jesus". No more is there heard, as in the First Epistle and in that to Titus, the apostolic guidance for church rule or administration of any kind. Only two things are possible now, "Preach the word" (4. 2), and "The things that thou hast heard of me among many witnesses, the same commit thou to faithful men, who shall be able to teach others also" (2. 2). And, as in the First Epistle, the Holy Spirit through Paul tells of even worse days to come, perilous, or grievous, times "in the last days" (3. 1; 4. 3), the only charge in connexion with which is "Continue thou in the things which thou hast learned and hast been assured of" (3. 14).

THE SECOND EPISTLE OF PAUL THE APOSTLE

TO

TIMOTHY.

A 1 PAUL, an °apostle of °Jesus Christ °by the
°will of °God, °according to the promise of
°life which is °in °Christ Jesus,
2 To Timothy, *my* °dearly beloved °son:
°Grace, mercy, *and* peace, °from [1]God the
°Father and [1]Christ Jesus our °Lord.

B A 3 I °thank [1]God, Whom I °serve [2]from *my*
°forefathers °with pure conscience, that °with-
out ceasing I have °remembrance °of thee [1]in
my °prayers night and day,
4 °Greatly desiring to °see thee, °being mindful of thy tears, °that I may be °filled with
joy;
5 °When I call to °remembrance the °un-
feigned °faith °that is [1]in thee, which °dwelt
first [1]in thy °grandmother Lois, and thy
mother Eunice; and I am °persuaded that [1]in
thee also.

B a 6 °Wherefore I °put thee in remembrance
that thou °stir up the °gift of [1]God, which is
[1]in thee [1]by the putting on of my hands.
7 For [1]God °hath °not given us °the °spirit
of °fear; but of °power, and of °love, and of
a °sound mind.
8 Be °not thou therefore ashamed of the
testimony °of our [2]Lord, °nor of me His
prisoner: but be thou °partaker of the afflictions °of the °gospel [1]according to the [7]power
of [1]God;
9 Who °hath °saved us, and °called *us* with
an holy calling, [7]not [1]according to our works,
but [1]according to His own °purpose and
[2]grace, which was given us [1]in [1]Christ Jesus
°before the world began,
10 But is now °made manifest [1]by the °ap-
pearing of our Saviour [1]Jesus Christ, °Who
°hath °abolished death, and °hath °brought
[1]life and °immortality to light °through the
[8]gospel:
11 °Whereunto I °am appointed a °preacher,
and an [1]apostle, and a teacher of the °Gen-
tiles.

b 12 °For the which cause I °also suffer these
things: nevertheless I am [7]not ashamed; for
I °know Whom I have °believed, and am

1. 1 apostle. Ap. 189.
Jesus Christ. Ap. 98. XI.
by. Ap. 104. v. 1. **will.** Ap. 102. 2.
God. Ap. 98. I. i. 1.
according to. Ap. 104. x. 2.
life. Ap. 170. 1.
in. Ap. 104. viii.
Christ Jesus. Ap. 98. XII.
2 dearly beloved. Ap. 135. III.
son. Ap. 108. i.
Grace. Ap. 184. I. 1.
from. Ap. 104. iv.
Father. Ap. 98. III.
Lord. Ap. 98. VI. i. β. 2. A. Cp. Phil. 1. 2. 1 Thess. 1. 1. 1 Tim. 1. 1, 2.

1. 3-18 (B, p. 1808). EPISTOLARY. PRIVATE AND PERSONAL. (*Introversion and Alternation.*)

B | A | 3-5. Thanksgiving for Timothy.
  B | a | 6-11. Exhortation.
    b | 12. Paul's sufferings.
  B | *a* | 13, 14. Exhortation.
    b | 15. Desertion of Paul.
A | 16-18. Prayer for Onesiphorus's household.

3 thank. See 1 Tim. 1. 12.
serve. Ap. 190. III. 5.
forefathers. Gr. *progonos.* See 1 Tim. 5. 4.
with = in. Gr. *en.*
without ceasing. Gr. *adialeiptos.* See Rom. 9. 2. Cp. Rom. 1. 9.
remembrance. Gr. *mneia.* See Rom. 1. 9.
of. Ap. 104. xiii. 1.
prayers. Ap. 134. II. 3.
4 Greatly desiring. Gr. *epipotheō.* See Rom. 1. 11.
see. Ap. 133. I. 1.
being mindful = having remembered.
that = in order that. Gr. *hina.*
filled. Ap. 125. 7.
5 When I call, &c. Lit. Having received remembrance (Gr. *hupomnēsis.* Here and 2 Pet. 1. 13; 3. 1).
unfeigned. See 1 Tim. 1. 5.
faith. Ap. 150. II. 1.
that is. Omit.
dwelt = indwelt. Gr. *enoikeō.* See Rom. 8. 11.
grandmother. Gr. *mammē.* Only here.
persuaded. Ap. 150. I. 2.
6 Wherefore = on account of (Ap. 104. v. 2) which cause.
put . . . in remembrance. Gr. *anamimnēskō.* See 1 Cor. 4. 17.
stir up. Lit. stir into flame. Gr. *anazōpureō.* Only here.
gift. Ap. 184. I. 2.

7 hath . . . given = gave. **not.** Ap. 105. I. **the** = a. **spirit.** Ap. 101. II. 7. **fear** = cowardice. Gr. *deilia.* Only here. **power.** Ap. 172. 1. **love.** Ap. 135. II. 1. **sound mind.** Gr. *sōphronismos.* Only here. Cp. 1 Tim. 2. 9; 3. 2. Tit. 2. 4, 6, 12. **8 not.** Ap. 105. II. **of.** Gen. of relation, concerning. **nor.** Gr. *mēde.* **partaker of the afflictions** = suffer evil with (me). Gr. *sunkakopatheō.* Only here. **of** = for. **gospel.** Ap. 140. **9 hath.** Omit. **saved.** Cp. 1 Tim. 1. 1. **called.** Cp. 1 Tim. 6. 12. **purpose.** See Acts 11. 23. **before, &c.** Ap. 151. II. B. iv. **10 made manifest.** Ap. 106. I. v. **appearing.** Ap. 106. II. ii. **Who** = in that He. **hath.** Omit. **abolished.** Gr. *katargeō.* See Luke 13. 7. **brought . . . to light** = shed light on. Gr. *phōtizō.* See Luke 11. 36. **immortality** = incorruption. Gr. *aphtharsia.* See Rom. 2. 7. The Lord did this in His own person, when He rose from the dead, alive for evermore. Acts 13. 34. Rom. 6. 9. Rev. 1. 18. **through.** Ap. 104. v. 1. **11 Whereunto** = Unto (Gr. *eis*) which. **am** = was. **preacher.** Ap. 121. 2. **Gentiles.** Gr. *ethnos.* Cp. Acts 22. 21; 28. 28. Rom. 11. 13; 15. 16. Gal. 1. 16; 2. 2. Eph. 3. 1, 8. 1 Tim. 2. 7. **12 For the which cause.** Same as "wherefore", *v.* 6. **also, &c.** = I suffer these things also. **know.** Ap. 132. I. i. **believed.** Ap. 150. I. 1. ii.

[5]persuaded that He is able to °keep °that which I have committed unto Him °against °that day.

B a 13 Hold °fast the °form of °sound °words, which thou hast heard °of me, [1]in [5]faith and [7]love which is [1]in [1]Christ Jesus.

14 °That good thing which was committed unto thee [12]keep [1]by the °Holy Ghost Which [5]dwelleth [1]in us.

b 15 This thou [12]knowest, that all they which are [1]in Asia °be turned away from me; of whom are °Phygellus and °Hermogenes.

A 16 The [2]Lord give mercy °unto the °house of Onesiphorus; for he oft °refreshed me, and was [7]not ashamed of my °chain,

17 But, when he was [1]in Rome, he sought me out very diligently, and found *me*.

18 The [2]Lord grant [16]unto him that he may find mercy [13]of the °Lord [1]in [12]that day: and in how many things he °ministered °unto me °at Ephesus, thou °knowest °very well.

C C E **2** Thou therefore, my °son, °be strong °in the °grace that is °in °Christ Jesus.

2 And the things that thou hast heard °of me °among many witnesses, °the same commit thou to °faithful °men, °who shall be °able to teach °others also.

F c 3 Thou therefore °endure hardness, as a good soldier of °Jesus Christ.

d 4 °No man that °warreth °entangleth himself with the °affairs of *this* °life; °that he may please him who °hath chosen him to be a soldier.

e 5 And °if °a man °also °strive for masteries,

f *yet* is he °not °crowned, °except he °strive °lawfully.

g 6 The husbandman

h that laboureth must be °first partaker of the fruits.

E 7 Consider what I say; and the °Lord °give thee understanding [1]in all things.

D j 8 Remember °that °Jesus Christ °of the seed of °David, °was °raised °from the dead °according to my °gospel:

---

keep = guard, as in 1 Tim. 6. 20.
that which I have committed unto Him = my deposit. Gr. *parathēkē*. See 1 Tim. 6. 20.
against = unto. Gr. *eis*.
that day. The day of His appearing. Cp. 4. 8.
13 fast. Omit.
form. Gr. *hupotupōsis*. See 1 Tim. 1. 16.
sound. See 1 Tim. 1. 10 and 6. 3.
words. Ap. 121. 10.
of = from. Gr. *para*. Ap. 104. xii. 1.
14 That good . . . thee = The good deposit. Gr. *parathēkē*, as in *v.* 12.
Holy Ghost. Ap. 101. II. 14.
15 be turned = turned.
Phygellus, &c. Nothing is known of these two.
16 unto = to.
house = household. Onesiphorus must have recently died.
refreshed. Gr. *anapsuchō*. Only here. Cp. Acts 3. 19.
chain. Cp. Acts 28. 20. Eph. 6. 20.
18 Lord. Ap. 98. VI. i. *β*. 2. B.
ministered. Ap. 190. III. 1.
unto me. Omit. **at** = in. Ap. 104. viii.
knowest. Ap. 132. I. ii.
very well. Gr. *beltion*. Only here.

2. 1-26 (**C**, p. 1808). CHARGES CONNECTED WITH THE GOSPEL. (*Introversion.*)

C | C | 1-7. Charge.
  D | 8-13. The Gospel.
 C | 14-26. Charge.

2. 1-7 (C, above). CHARGE. (*Introversion and Alternation.*)

C | E | 1, 2. Grace.
  F | c | 3. The soldier.
   d | 4. Conditions of approval.
   e | 5-. The athlete.
   f | -5. Conditions of being crowned.
   g | 6-. The husbandman.
   h | -6. Conditions of partaking of fruits.
 E | 7. Wisdom.

2. 1 son. Ap. 108. i.
be strong. Gr. *endunamoō*. See Acts 9. 22, and cp. Eph. 6. 10.
in. Ap. 104. viii.
grace. Ap. 184. I. 1.
Christ Jesus. Ap. 98. XII.
2 of. Ap. 104. xii. 1.
among = by means of. Ap. 104. v. 1.
the same = these.
faithful. Ap. 150. III.
men. Ap. 123. 1.
who = such as.
able = competent. See 2 Cor. 2. 16 (sufficient).
others. Ap. 124. 2. No reference to bishops and ecclesiastical organizations. All these have failed. **3 endure hardness.** Gr. *kakopatheō*. Lit. suffer evil. Here, *v.* 9; 4. 5. Jas. 5. 13. **Jesus Christ.** The texts read "Christ Jesus", as *v.* 1. **4 No man** = No one. Gr. *oudeis*. **warreth.** Cp. 1 Tim. 1. 18. **entangleth.** Gr. *emplekō*. Only here and 2 Pet. 2. 20. **affairs.** Gr. *pragmateia*. Only here. **life.** Ap. 170. 2. **that** = in order that. Gr. *hina*. **hath chosen, &c.** = chose, &c. Gr. *stratologeō*. Only here. The Master's "Well done" is the reward. **5 if.** Ap. 118. 1. b. **a man** = any one. Ap. 123. 3. **also strive** = strive also. **strive for masteries** = contend in the games. Gr. *athleō*. Only here. **not.** Ap. 105. I. **crowned.** Gr. *stephanoō*. Only here and Heb. 2. 7, 9. The crown was of wild olive or laurel leaves. **except** = if (*ean*) . . . not (*mē*). **lawfully.** See 1 Tim. 1. 8. **6 first, &c.** = the first to partake. **7 Lord.** Ap. 98. VI. i. *β*. 2. A. **give.** The texts read "shall give".

2. 8-13 (D, above). THE GOSPEL. (*Alternation.*)

D | j | 8. Christ's death and resurrection.
  k | 9, 10. Paul faithful unto bonds.
  j | 11, 12. Death with Christ, life with Him.
  k | 13. Christ faithful, though we be unfaithful.

8 that. Omit. **Jesus Christ.** Ap. 98. XI. The thoughts of Timothy are directed to the person of Jesus Christ, as well as to His work. Cp. Heb. 3. 1; 12. 3; 13. 7, 8. **of.** Ap. 104. vii. **David.** Cp. Rom. 1. 3. **was.** Omit. **raised.** Ap. 178. I. 4. **from the dead.** Ap. 139. 3. **according to.** Ap. 104. x. 2. **gospel.** Ap. 140.

k 9 °Wherein I °suffer trouble, as an °evil
doer, *even* °unto bonds; but the °word of
°God is [5]not bound.
10 °Therefore I endure all things °for the
elect's sakes, [4]that they °may also obtain the
salvation which is [1]in [1]Christ Jesus °with
°eternal °glory.

j 11 °*It is* a [2]faithful °saying: "For °if we °be
dead with *Him,* we shall °also live with *Him:*
12 [11]If we °suffer, we shall °also reign with
Him: [11]if we deny *Him,* He also will deny us:

k 13 [11]If we °believe not, *yet* He °abideth [2]faith-
ful: He °cannot deny Himself."

C l 14 Of these things °put *them* in remembrance,
°charging *them* before °the [7]Lord that they
°strive °not about words °to °no profit, *but*
°to the °subverting of the hearers.

m 15 °Study to °shew thyself °approved °unto
[9]God, a °workman °that needeth not to be
ashamed, °rightly dividing the [9]word of truth.

n 16 But °shun °profane *and* °vain babblings:
for they will °increase °unto more °ungodli-
ness.

o 17 And their [9]word will °eat as doth a °can-
ker: of whom is °Hymenæus and °Philetus;
18 °Who °concerning the truth °have °erred,
saying that the °resurrection °is past already,

p and °overthrow the °faith of °some.

p 19 Nevertheless °the foundation of [9]God
standeth °sure, having this seal, **The °Lord
°knoweth them that are His. And, Let every
one that nameth the name of °Christ depart
°from °iniquity.**

o 20 But [1]in a great house there are [5]not only
vessels of gold and of silver, but °also °of
wood and °of earth; and some °to honour,
and some °to dishonour.
21 [5]If [5]a man therefore °purge himself [19]from
these, he shall be a vessel °unto honour, sanctified, and °meet for the °Master's use, *and*
prepared °unto every good work.

n 22 Flee also °youthful lusts: but follow
°righteousness, [18]faith, °charity, peace, [10]with
them that call on the [7]Lord °out of a pure
heart.
23 But °foolish and °unlearned °questions
°avoid, °knowing that they do °gender °strifes.

9 Wherein = In (Gr. *en*) which.
suffer trouble. Gr. *kakopatheō,* as in *v.* 3.
evil doer. Gr. *kakourgos.* Only here and Luke 23. 32, 33, 39 (of the malefactors crucified with the Lord). For the other word for evil doer, *kakopoios,* see John 18. 30.
unto = as far as. Gr. *mechri.*
word. Ap. 121. 10. **God.** Ap. 98. I. i. 1.
10 Therefore = On account of (Ap. 104. v. 2) this.
for . . . sakes. Ap. 104. v. 2.
may also = also may. **with.** Ap. 104. xi. 1.
eternal. Ap. 151. II. B. i.
glory. See p. 1511.
11 *It is,* &c. = Faithful is the saying. The fourth occ. See 1 Tim. 1. 15.
saying = word. Ap. 121. 10. **if.** Ap. 118. 2. a.
be dead with = died with (Gr. *sunapothnēskō*) *Him.* See 2 Cor. 7. 3.
also live, &c. = live together also with (Gr. *suzaō*) *Him.* See Rom. 6. 8.
12 suffer. Same as "endure", *v.* 10.
also reign, &c. = reign together also, &c. Gr. *sumbasileuō.* Only here and 1 Cor. 4. 8.
13 believe not = are unbelieving. Gr. *apisteō.* Acts 28. 24. **abideth.** See p. 1511.
He. The texts prefix "For".
cannot = is not (Ap. 105. I) able to.

2. 14-26 (*C,* p. 1810). **CHARGE.** (*Introversion.*)

C | l | 14. The aim of the enemy. Subversion.
m | 15. The workman.
n | 16. Exhortation. "Shun."
o | 17, 18-. Illustration. A canker.
p | -18. Effect of error.
p | 19. Effect of truth.
o | 20, 21. Illustration. Vessels.
n | 22, 23. Exhortation. "Flee, avoid."
m | 24, 25-. The bondservant.
l | -25, 26. The aim of the enemy. Ensnaring.

14 put, &c. Gr. *hupomimnēskō.* See John 14. 26.
charging = earnestly testifying to. Gr. *diamarturomai.* See Acts 2. 40.
the Lord. Some texts read "God".
strive . . . about words. Gr. *logomacheō.* Only here. The noun in 1 Tim. 6. 4.
not. Ap. 105. II.
to. Ap. 104. vi, but the texts read ix. 3.
no profit = nothing (Gr. *oudeis*) profitable (Gr. *chrēsimos.* Only here).
to. Ap. 104. ix. 2.
subverting. Gr. *katastrophē.* Only here and 2 Pet. 2. 6.
15 Study = Be diligent. Gr. *spoudazō.* See Gal. 2. 10.
shew = present, as Col. 1. 22, 28.
approved. Gr. *dokimos.* See Rom. 14. 18.
unto = to. Dat. case.
workman. Gr. *ergatēs.* This word is transl. "labourer", ten times; "worker", or "workman", six times.
that, &c. = without cause for shame. Gr. *anepaischuntos.* Only here.

rightly dividing. Gr. *orthotomeō.* Only here. **16 shun.** Gr. *periistēmi.* See Acts 25. 7. **profane.** See 1 Tim. 1. 9. **vain babblings.** See 1 Tim. 6. 20. **increase** = advance. Gr. *prokoptō.* See Rom. 13. 12. **unto.** Ap. 104. ix. 3. **ungodliness.** Ap. 128. IV. **17 eat.** Lit. have pasture (Gr. *nomē.* Only here and John 10. 9). **canker** = gangrene. Gr. *gangraina.* Only here. **Hymenæus.** Cp. 1 Tim. 1. 20 **Philetus.** Nothing is known of him. **18 Who** = For they. **concerning.** Ap. 104. xiii. 2. **have.** Omit. **erred.** See 1 Tim. 1. 6. **resurrection.** Ap. 178. II. 1. **is past** = has taken place. **overthrow** = overturn. Gr. *anatrepō.* Only here and Tit. 1. 11. **faith.** Ap. 150. II. 1. **some.** Ap. 124. 4. **19 the foundation, &c.** = God's firm foundation. **sure** = firm. Gr. *stereos.* Here; Heb. 5. 12, 14. 1 Pet. 5. 9. Cp. Acts 16. 5. Col. 2. 5. **Lord.** Ap. 98. VI. i. β. 2. B. **knoweth** = knew. Ap. 132. I. ii. A reference here to Num. 16. 5. **Christ.** The texts read "the Lord", as above. **from.** Ap. 104. iv. **iniquity.** Ap. 128. VII. 1. May allude to Num. 16. 26. **20 also, &c.** = wooden also. **of wood** = wooden. Gr. *xulinos.* Only here and Rev. 9. 20. **of earth.** Gr. *ostrakinos.* See 2 Cor. 4. 7. **to.** Ap. 104. vi. **21 purge** = thoroughly purge. Gr. *ekkathairō.* See 1 Cor. 5. 7. **unto.** Ap. 104. vi. **meet** = useful or profitable. Gr. *euchrēstos.* Only here, 4. 11. Philemon 11. **Master's.** Ap. 98. XIV. ii. **22 youthful** = the youthful. Gr. *neōterikos.* Only here. **righteousness.** Ap. 191. 3. **charity.** Ap. 135. II. 1. **out of.** Ap. 104. vii. **23 foolish** = the foolish. Gr. *mōros.* See 1 Cor. 1. 25. **unlearned** = uninstructed, and so, trifling. Gr. *apaideutos.* Only here in N.T., but occ. in the Sept. several times transl. "fools". **questions.** Gr. *zētēsis.* See Acts 25. 30. **avoid** = reject, or refuse. See 1 Tim. 4. 7. **knowing.** Ap. 132. I. i. **gender** = beget. **strifes.** Gr. *machē.* See 2 Cor. 7. 5.

m 24 And the °servant of the [19]Lord must [5]not
°strive; but be °gentle °unto all *men*, °apt to
teach, °patient,
25 [1]In °meekness °instructing °those that
oppose themselves;
l °if [9]God peradventure °will give them °re-
pentance [20]to the °acknowledging of the
truth;
26 And *that* they may °recover themselves
[22]out of the °snare of the devil, who are °taken
captive °by him °at His °will.

C G **3** This °know also, that °in the °last days
°perilous °times shall come.
2 For °men shall be °lovers of their own
selves, °covetous, °boasters, °proud, blasphemers, °disobedient to parents, °unthank-
ful, °unholy,
3 °Without natural affection, °trucebreakers,
°false accusers, °incontinent, °fierce, °de-
spisers of those that are good,
4 °Traitors, °heady, °highminded, °lovers of
pleasures more than °lovers of God;
5 Having a °form of °godliness, but denying the °power thereof: °from such °turn
away.
6 For °of °this sort are they which °creep
°into °houses, and °lead captive °silly women
°laden with °sins, led away with divers lusts,
7 °Ever learning, and °never able to come
°to the °knowledge of the truth.
8 Now °as Jannes and Jambres °withstood
°Moses, so do these also °resist the truth:
[2]men °of corrupt minds, °reprobate °concern-
ing the °faith.
9 But they shall °proceed no °further: for
their °folly shall be °manifest °unto all *men*, as
theirs also was.
H K 10 But thou °hast fully known my doctrine,
°manner of life, °purpose, [8]faith, longsuffering,
°charity, patience,
11 Persecutions, °afflictions, which came
[9]unto me °at °Antioch, °at Iconium, °at Lystra; what persecutions I °endured: but °out
of *them* all the °Lord °delivered me.

24 servant. Ap. 190. 1. 2.
strive. Gr. *machomai.* See Acts 7. 26.
gentle. See 1 Thess. 2. 7.
unto. Ap. 104. xv. 3.
apt to teach. See 1 Tim. 3. 2.
patient. Lit. enduring evil. Gr. *anexikakos* Only here.
25 meekness. See 1 Cor. 4. 21.
instructing. Gr. *paideuō*, which means to train a child, and so to chastise, chasten. Cp. Acts 22. 3. 2 Cor. 6. 9. Heb. 12. 6.
those that, &c. = the opposers. Gr. *antidiatithēmi.* Only here.
if . . . peradventure = lest at any time. Gr. *mēpote.*
will = should.
repentance. Ap. 111. II.
acknowledging. Ap. 132. II. ii.
26 recover themselves. Lit. become sober again. Gr. *ananēphō.* Cp. 4. 5.
snare. See 1 Tim. 3. 7.
taken captive. Gr. *zōgreō.* See Luke 5. 10.
by. Ap. 104. xviii. 1.
at = unto. Ap. 104. vi.
will. Ap. 102. 2. The pronouns "him" and "His" have not the same ref. The first refers to the servant, the second to God, and the meaning of the passage is, the devil stirs up those he has ensnared to oppose, *lest* God should give them repentance, and lest, having been taken captive by God's servant, they should escape the snare, to do the will of God.

3. 1—4. 8 (*C*, p. 1808). **CHARGES CONNECTED WITH THE APOSTASY.**
(*Alternation and Introversion.*)

C | G | 3. 1-9. The last days Their character.
  | H | K | 3. 10-13. Paul's sufferings.
  | | L | 3. 14—4. 2. Timothy. Ministry.
  | *G* | 4. 3, 4. The last days. Their character.
  | *H* | *L* | 4. 5. Timothy. Ministry.
  | | *K* | 4. 6-8. Paul's reward.

3. 1 know. Ap. 132. I. ii.
in. Gr. *en.* Ap. 104. viii.
last days. See Acts 2. 17.
perilous = hard, difficult, grievous. Gr. *chalepos.* Only here and Matt. 8. 28.
times = seasons. Ap. 195.
2 men. Ap. 123. 1.
lovers, &c. Gr. *philautēs.* Only here.
covetous = lovers of money. Gr. *philarguros.* Only here and Luke 16. 14.
boasters. Gr. *alazōn.* See Rom. 1. 30.
proud. Gr. *huperēphanos.* See Rom. 1. 30.
disobedient, &c. See Rom. 1. 30. **unthankful.** Gr. *acharistos.* Only here and Luke 6. 35. **unholy.** See 1 Tim. 1. 9. **3 Without, &c.** See Rom. 1. 31. **trucebreakers.** Gr. *aspondos.* See Rom. 1. 31, where it is rendered "implacable". **false accusers** = slanderers. Gr. *diabolos.* **incontinent.** Gr. *akratēs.* Only here. Cp. 1 Cor. 7. 5. **fierce.** Gr. *anēmeros.* Only here. **despisers, &c.** Lit. not lovers of the good. Gr. *aphilagathos.* Only here. **4 Traitors.** Gr. *prodotēs.* Only here; Luke 6. 16. Acts 7. 52. **heady** = headstrong. See Acts 19. 36. **highminded** = puffed up. See 1 Tim. 3. 6. **lovers, &c.** Gr. *philēdonos.* Only here. **lovers of God.** Gr. *philotheos.* Only here. **5 form.** Gr. *morphōsis.* Only here and Rom. 2. 20. **godliness.** See 1 Tim. 2. 2. **power.** Ap. 172. 1. **from such** = and from these. **turn away.** Gr. *apotrepomai.* Only here. **6 of.** Ap. 104. vii. **this sort** = these. **creep.** Gr. *endunō.* Only here. Akin to *enduō*, to clothe, to put on. **into.** Ap. 104. vi. **houses** = the houses. **lead captive.** See Eph. 4. 8. **silly women.** Gr. *gunaikarion*, neut. A diminutive form of *gunē*, used as a term of contempt. Only here. **laden.** Gr. *sōreuō.* See Rom. 12. 20. **sins.** Ap. 128. I. ii. 1. **7 Ever** = Always. Ap 151. II. G. ii. **never** = not at any time. Gr. *mēdepote.* Only here **to.** Ap. 104. vi. **knowledge.** Ap. 132. II. ii. **8 as.** Lit. in the manner in which. **Jannes and Jambres.** The names of the magicians of Ex. 7. 11. Found in the Targum of Jonathan. **withstood.** Gr. *anthistēmi.* Transl. nine times "resist", five times "withstand". **Moses.** The tenth occ. of the name in the Epistles. See Rom. 5. 14. **resist.** Same as "withstood". **of corrupt minds** = utterly corrupted (Gr. *kataphtheirō.* Only here and 2 Pet. 2. 12) as to their mind. **reprobate.** See Rom. 1. 28. **concerning.** Ap. 104. xiii. 2. **faith.** Ap. 150. II. 1. **9 proceed no** = not (Ap. 105. I) proceed. Gr. *prokoptō*, as in Rom. 13. 12. **further.** Lit. to (Ap. 104. ix. 3) more. The magicians were allowed to imitate Moses up to a certain point, and then God stopped them. Ex. 7. 11, 12, 22; 8. 7, 18, 19. **folly.** Gr. *anoia.* Only here and Luke 6. 11. **manifest** = thoroughly manifest. Gr. *ekdēlos.* Only here. **unto** = to. **10 hast, &c.** = didst follow up. See 1 Tim. 4. 6. **manner of life.** Gr. *agōgē.* Only here. **purpose.** See 1. 9. **charity.** See 2. 22. **11 afflictions.** Gr. *pathēma.* Generally transl. suffering. See Rom. 7. 5. **at.** Ap. 104. viii. **Antioch, &c.** See Acts 13. 50; 14. 5, 19. **endured.** See 1 Cor. 10. 13. **out of.** Ap. 104. vii. **Lord.** Ap. 98. VI. i. β. 2. A. **delivered.** Cp. 2 Cor. 1. 10.

12 Yea, and all that °will °live °godly [1]in °Christ Jesus shall °suffer persecution.
13 But °evil [2]men and °seducers shall °wax °worse and worse, deceiving, and being deceived.

L M 14 But °continue thou [1]in the things which thou °hast learned and °hast been assured of, °knowing °of °whom thou hast learned *them;*
15 And that °from a °child thou hast [14]known the °holy °Scriptures, which are able to °make thee wise °unto salvation °through [8]faith which is [1]in [12]Christ Jesus.

N q 16 °All Scripture *is* °given by inspiration of God,

r and *is* °profitable °for doctrine,

s °for °reproof,

s °for °correction,

r °for °instruction [1]in °righteousness:

q 17 °That °the [2]man of °God may be °perfect, °throughly furnished °unto °all good works.

M **4** I °charge *thee* therefore °before °God, and °the Lord Jesus Christ, Who °shall °judge °the °quick and °the °dead °at His °appearing and His °kingdom;

N 2 °Preach the °word; be instant °in season, °out of season; °reprove, °rebuke, °exhort °with all longsuffering and °doctrine.

G 3 For the °time will °come when they will °not endure °sound °doctrine; but °after their own lusts shall they °heap to themselves teachers, °having °itching ears;
4 And they shall turn away *their* °ears °from the truth, and shall be °turned °unto °fables.

H L 5 But °watch thou °in all things, °endure afflictions, do the work of an °evangelist, °make full proof of thy °ministry.

---

12 will. Ap. 102. 1. live. Ap. 170. 1. godly. Gr. *eusebōs.* Only here and Tit. 2. 12. Christ Jesus. Ap. 98. XII. suffer persecution = be persecuted.
13 evil. Ap. 128. III. 1. seducers. Gr. *goēs.* Only here. wax. Same as "proceed", *v.* 9. worse, &c. = to (Ap. 104. ix. 3) the worse.

3. 14—4. 2 (L, p. 1812). TIMOTHY. MINISTRY. (*Alternation.*)

L | M | 3. 14, 15. Exhortation.
  N | 3. 16, 17. All Scripture inspired. Statement.
  M | 4. 1. Exhortation.
  N | 4. 2. All Scripture inspired. Consequence.

14 continue = abide. Gr. *menō.* See p. 1511. hast learned = didst learn. hast been, &c. = wast assured of. Gr. *pistoomai.* Only here. knowing. Ap. 132. I. i. of = from. Ap. 104. xii. 1. whom. Ap. 124. 4.
15 from. Ap. 104. iv. child. Ap. 108. viii. holy. Gr. *hieros.* Only here and 1 Cor. 9. 13. Scriptures. Gr. pl. of *gramma.* See John 7. 15. The usual word for the "Scriptures" is *graphē, v.* 16. make . . . wise. Gr. *sophizō.* Only here and 2 Pet. 1. 16. unto. Ap. 104. vi. through. Ap. 104. v. 1.

3. 16, 17 (N, above). ALL SCRIPTURE INSPIRED. STATEMENT.

N | q | 16–. God's Divinely inspired Word.
  r | –16–. For doctrine. Teaching what is true. } Faith. } Its profitableness.
  s | –16–. For reproof. Convicting of what is false. } Faith.
  s | –16–. For correction of what is wrong. } Works.
  r | –16. For instruction in what is right. } Works.
  q | 17. God's Divinely fitted man.

16 All Scripture. Gr. *pasa graphē* (sing.) given by inspiration of God = God-inbreathed. Gr. *theopneustos.* Only here. profitable. See 1 Tim. 4. 8. for. Ap. 104. xv. 3. reproof. Gr. *elenchos.* It means "proof" and so "conviction". Only here and Heb. 11. 1. The texts read *elegmos.* correction. Gr. *epanorthōsis.* Only here. instruction. Gr. *paideia.* See Eph. 6. 4. righteousness. Ap. 191. 3. It will be noticed that in the earlier part of the verse the word "*is*" appears in italics, showing that there is no word for it in the Greek and it has therefore to be supplied. The R.V. omits "*is*" in the first case and reads, "Every Scripture inspired of God *is* also profitable", thus suggesting that some Scriptures are not inspired. There are eight other passages which present exactly the same construction, and not one of these has been altered by the Revisers. Had they done so in the same manner as they have done in this case, the result would have been as follows:—Rom. 7. 12. The holy commandment is also just. 1 Cor. 11. 30. Many weak are also sickly. 2 Cor. 10. 10. His weighty letters are also powerful. Similarly with the other passages, which are 1 Tim. 1. 15; 2. 3; 4. 4, 9. Heb. 4. 13. It is true the A.V. rendering is given in the margin of the R.V., but it is difficult to see why that should be disturbed.
17 That = In order that. Gr. *hina.* the man of God. See Ap. 49. God. Ap. 98. I. i. 1. perfect = fitted. Gr. *artios.* Only here. Ap. 125. 6. throughly furnished = equipped. See Acts 21. 5. Ap. 125. 9. unto. Ap. 104 xv. 3. all . . . works = every work.

4. 1 charge. Gr. *diamarturomai.* See 2. 14. before = in the sight of. God. Ap. 98. I. i. 1. the Lord Jesus Christ. The texts read "Christ Jesus". Ap. 98. XII. shall = is about to. judge. Ap. 122. 1 the. Omit. quick = living. dead. Ap. 139. 2. at. Ap. 104. x. 2. The texts read "and by". appearing. Ap. 106. II. ii. kingdom. See Ap. 112.
2 Preach. Ap. 121. 1. word. Ap. 121. 10. in season. Gr. *eukairōs.* Only here and Mark 14. 11. out of season. Gr. *akairōs.* Only here. reprove. Gr. *elenchō.* See John 8. 9. 1 Tim. 5. 20. rebuke. Gr. *epitimaō.* Occ. twenty-nine times, twenty-four times "rebuke", five times "charge". All in Gospels, save here and Jude 9. The difference between these two Gr. words is that the former means to bring to conviction, as used in John 8. 46; 16. 8; while the latter can be used of unjust or ineffectual rebuke, as in Matt. 16. 22. Luke 23. 40. exhort. Ap. 134. I. 6. with. Ap. 104. viii. doctrine = teaching. Gr. *didachē.*
3 time = season. come = be. not. Ap. 105. I. sound = the sound. See 1 Tim. 1. 10. doctrine. Gr. *didaskalia,* as 1 Tim. 4. 6. after. Ap. 104. x. 2. heap. Gr. *episōreuō.* Only here. having itching ears = itching in regard to hearing. itching. Gr. *knēthō.* Only here.
4 ears = hearing, as in *v.* 3. from. Ap. 104. iv. turned. See 1 Tim. 1. 6. unto. Ap. 104. ix. 3. fables = myths. See 1 Tim. 1. 4.
5 watch. Gr. *nēphō.* See 1 Thess. 5. 6. in. Ap. 104. viii. endure afflictions = suffer evil. Gr. *kakopatheō.* See 2. 3. evangelist. Cp. Ap. 121. 4. make full proof of = fully accomplish. Gr. *plērophoreō.* See Rom. 4. 21. ministry. Ap. 190. II. 1.

K 6 For I am ° now ready to be offered, and the
[3] time of my ° departure is ° at hand.
7 I have ° fought ° a good ° fight, I have
° finished ° *my* ° course, I have kept the ° faith:
8 Henceforth there is ° laid up for me ° a
crown of ° righteousness, which the ° Lord, the
° righteous ° Judge, shall ° give me ° at that day:
and [3] not to me only, but ° unto all them also
that ° love His [1] appearing.

B t 9 ° Do thy diligence to come ° shortly ° unto
me:

u 10 For ° Demas ° hath forsaken me, having
[8] loved ° this present ° world, and is departed
° unto Thessalonica; ° Crescens ° to Galatia,
Titus ° unto Dalmatia.

v 11 Only ° Luke is ° with me. ° Take ° Mark,
and bring him ° with thee: for he is ° profitable
to me ° for ° the ministry.
12 And ° Tychicus ° have I ° sent [10] to Ephesus.
13 The ° cloke that I left [8] at Troas ° with
Carpus, when thou comest, bring *with thee,*
and the books, *but* especially the ° parchments.

v 14 ° Alexander the ° coppersmith ° did me
° much evil: the [8] Lord ° reward him ° according to his works:
15 Of whom be thou ° ware also; for he hath
greatly ° withstood our [2] words.

u 16 [8] At my first ° answer ° no man ° stood with
me, but all *men* [10] forsook me: ° *I pray God*
that it may ° not be ° laid to their charge.
17 ° Notwithstanding the [8] Lord stood with
me, and ° strengthened me; ° that ° by me the
° preaching might be ° fully known, and *that*
all the Gentiles might hear: and I was ° delivered ° out of the mouth of the ° lion.
18 And the [8] Lord shall [17] deliver me [4] from
every ° evil work, and will ° preserve *me* [10] unto
His ° heavenly [1] kingdom: to Whom *be* glory
° for ever and ever. Amen.
19 Salute ° Prisca and Aquila, and the ° household of ° Onesiphorus.
20 ° Erastus abode [8] at Corinth: but ° Trophimus have I left [8] at Miletum ° sick.

t 21 Do thy diligence to come ° before winter.

A Eubulus greeteth thee, and ° Pudens, and
° Linus, and ° Claudia, and all the brethren.
22 The [8] Lord ° Jesus Christ *be* [11] with thy
° spirit. ° Grace *be* [11] with you. ° Amen.

6 now ready, &c. = already being poured out. Gr. *spendomai.* See Phil. 2. 17.
departure. Gr. *analusis.* Only here. Cp. Phil. 1. 23.
at hand. Same as "instant", *v.* 2.
7 fought. Gr. *agōnizomai.* See Luke 13. 24.
a = the.
fight. Gr. *agōn.* See Phil. 1. 30 and cp. 1 Tim. 6. 12.
finished. Gr. *teleō.* Cp. Ap. 125. 1, 2.
my = the.
course. Gr. *dromos.* See Acts 13. 25.
faith. Ap. 150. II. 1.
8 laid up. Gr. *apokeimai.* See Col. 1. 5.
a = the.
righteousness. Ap. 191. 3.
Lord. Ap. 98. VI. i. *β*. 2. A.
righteous. Ap. 191. 1.
Judge. Cp. *v.* 1. Acts 17. 31.
give = repay or recompense. Gr. *apodidōmi.* See *v.* 14.
at. Ap. 104. viii.
unto = to.
love. Ap. 135. I. 1. Perf. tense, "have loved".

4. 9-21- (*B*, p. 1808). EPISTOLARY. PRIVATE AND PERSONAL. (*Introversion.*)

B t | 9. Charge to come speedily.
u | 10. Desertion and absences.
v | 11-13. Helpers.
v | 14, 15. Opponents.
u | 16-20. Salutations.
t | 21-. Charge to come before winter.

9 Do, &c. = Hasten.
shortly = speedily.
unto. Gr. *pros.* Ap. 104. xv. 3.
10 Demas. See Col. 4. 14. Philem. 24.
hath forsaken = forsook. Gr. *enkataleipō.* See Acts 2. 27.
this, &c. = the age that is now.
world. Ap. 129. 2. **unto.** Ap. 104. vi.
Crescens. He is not mentioned elsewhere, and perhaps had gone to Galatia at his own instance and with the apostle's consent. The same may be said of Titus. There is no condemnation of them, as of Demas, but they are not said to have been sent, as Tychicus was.
to. Same as "unto".
11 Luke. This faithful and devoted companion, sharer of Paul's labours and afflictions for so many years, always modestly keeping himself in the background, must have been a comfort indeed.
with. Ap. 104. xi. 1.
Take = Take up, i. e. on the way. Cp. Acts 20. 13, 14.
Mark. See Acts 12. 25; 13. 5, 13; 15. 37-39. Col. 4. 10. Philem. 24.
profitable. See "meet", 2. 21.
for. Ap. 104. vi.
the ministry = ministering. Ap. 190. II. 1.
12 Tychicus. See Acts 20. 4. Eph. 6. 21. Col. 4. 7. Tit. 3. 12.

have. Omit. **sent.** Ap. 174. 1. **13 cloke.** Gr. *phailonēs.* Only here. **with.** Ap. 104. xii. 2. **parchments.** Gr. *membrana.* Only here. **14 Alexander.** The addition of "coppersmith" suggests his identity with the Ephesian Jew of Acts 19. 33, 34. **coppersmith.** Gr. *chalkeus.* Only here. **did.** Lit. showed forth. **much evil** = many evil (Ap. 128. III. 2) things. **reward.** See *v.* 8. **according to.** Ap. 104. x. 2. **15 ware also** = also ware. **withstood.** See 3. 8. **16 answer** = defence. See Acts 22. 1. **no man** = no one. Gr. *oudeis.* **stood with.** Gr. *sumparaginomai.* Only here and Luke 23. 48. ***I pray,*** &c. = may it not. **not.** Ap. 105. II. **laid to their charge** = reckoned to them. **17 Notwithstanding** = But. **strengthened.** See Acts 9. 22. **that** = in order that. Gr. *hina.* **by.** Ap. 104. v. 1. **preaching.** Ap. 121. 3. **fully known.** See *v.* 5. **delivered.** Gr. *rhuomai.* See 3. 11. **out of.** Gr. *ek.* Ap. 104. vii. **lion.** This may mean that Paul established his claim, as a Roman citizen, not to meet his death in the amphitheatre; or it may be a metaphor for Nero. **18 evil.** Ap. 128. III. 1. **preserve** = save. **heavenly.** Gr. *epouranios,* as in Eph. 1. 3, &c. **for ever,** &c. Ap. 151. II. A. ii. 9. a. **19 Prisca.** Elsewhere called Priscilla. Acts 18. 2, 18, 26. Rom. 16. 3. 1 Cor. 16. 19. **household.** As 1. 16. **Onēsiphorus.** Cp. 1. 16. **20 Erastus.** See Acts 19. 22. Rom. 16. 23. **Trophimus.** Acts 20. 4; 21. 29. **sick.** Paul's authority to heal had ceased. Cp. Phil. 2. 25-27. 1 Tim. 5. 23. **21 before.** Ap. 104. xiv. **Pudens.** Pudens and Claudia are supposed by some to be man and wife, and have been identified with Titus Claudius and Claudia Quinctilia, whose inscription over a child they lost has been discovered near Rome. **Linus.** Probably a bishop of Rome. **22 Jesus Christ.** The texts omit. **spirit.** Ap. 101. II. 9. **Grace.** Ap. 184. I. 1. **Amen** Omit.

THE EPISTLE TO TITUS.

THE STRUCTURE OF THE EPISTLE AS A WHOLE.

(*Introversions.*)

A | 1. 1-4. EPISTOLARY. SALUTATION. BENEDICTION.

B | 1. 5-9. ASSEMBLIES. THEIR ORDER.

C | 1. 10-16. CONTENTIOUS CRETANS. CENSURED.

D | 2. 1-10. THE WALK AND WORKS BECOMING BELIEVERS (SOCIALLY). TITUS TO BE A PATTERN OF GOOD WORKS.

E | A | 2. 11. REASON. THE GRACE OF GOD HATH APPEARED TO ALL.

B | 2. 12-14. WHAT WE SHOULD BE IN CONSEQUENCE OF THE TEACHINGS OF GRACE.

C | 2. 15. CHARGE TO TITUS TO SPEAK, REBUKE, AND EXHORT.

E | *C* | 3. 1, 2. CHARGE TO TITUS TO PUT IN MIND (CIVIL DUTIES).

B | 3. 3. REASON. WHAT WE WERE BEFORE GRACE'S TEACHINGS.

A | 3. 4-7. REASON. THE KINDNESS OF GOD APPEARED.

D | 3. 8. THE WALK AND WORKS BECOMING BELIEVERS. TITUS TO EXHORT TO GOOD WORKS.

C | 3. 9. CONTENTIOUS CRETANS. CONDEMNED.

B | 3. 10, 11. ASSEMBLIES. THEIR DISCIPLINE.

A | 3. 12-15. EPISTOLARY. SALUTATION. BENEDICTION.

THE EPISTLE TO TITUS.

INTRODUCTORY NOTES.

The apostle Paul had no more highly esteemed fellowlabourer than Titus, yet his name is not mentioned in the Acts. It has been suggested that this is owing to his being the authority to whom Luke is indebted for various portions of the book. A Gentile (Gal. 2. 3), and possibly a native of Crete, the words "Titus, mine own son after the common faith" (Tit. 1. 4) indicate that he was led to the truth by Paul himself. The two were companions in Antioch prior to the Council assembled at Jerusalem as recorded in Acts 15, for to this Council he accompanied the apostle (Gal. 2. 1). Titus is repeatedly referred to in the two Epistles to the Corinthians, to which church he was apparently sent on two occasions: see 2 Cor. 8. 6, and chapters 2 and 7. From this Epistle we learn that after Paul's release from the Roman prison, the two journeyed together and preached in Crete (1. 5, 11, 13), where the apostle left him to "set in order the things that are wanting, and ordain elders in every city". Later, he was instructed to join Paul at Nicopolis (3. 12), and it is probable that from there he went to Dalmatia (2 Tim. 4. 10). The apostle's affectionate regard for him is shown in 2 Cor. 2. 13; 8. 23.

The Epistle was one of the latest written by Paul, probably in the end of A. D. 67.

THE EPISTLE OF PAUL TO

TITUS.

A A B 1 PAUL, a °servant of °God, and an °apos-
C tle of °Jesus Christ, °according to the
°faith of °God's elect, and the °acknowledg-
B² ing of the °truth which is °after °godliness;

C² D E 2 °In °hope of °eternal °life, which [1]God,
F °that cannot lie, °promised °before the world
began;

C² F E 3 But °hath °in due °times °manifested His
D °word °through °preaching, which °is °com-
B² mitted unto me [1]according to the °command-
ment of [1]God our °Saviour;

A B C 4 To Titus, °*mine* °own °son [1]after the
°common [1]faith: °Grace, mercy, *and* peace,
°from [1]God the °Father and the °Lord °Jesus
Christ our [3]Saviour.

B 5 °For this cause °left I thee °in °Crete, °that
thou shouldest °set in order °the things that
are wanting, and °ordain °elders °in every
city, as I had °appointed thee:
6 °If °any be °blameless, the °husband of one
wife, having °faithful °children °not °accused
of riot or °unruly.
7 For °a °bishop must be [6]blameless, as the
°steward of [1]God; [6]not °selfwilled, [6]not °soon
angry, [6]not °given to wine, °no °striker, [6]not
°given to filthy lucre;
8 But a °lover of hospitality, a °lover of good
men, °sober, °just, °holy, °temperate;
9 °Holding fast the [6]faithful [3]word °as he
hath been °taught, [5]that he may be °able °by

1. 1-4 (A, p. 1815). EPISTOLARY. SALUTATION. BENEDICTION. (*Alternation. Introversion.*)

A | A | 1-. Paul.
B | -1-. A servant of God and an apostle of Jesus Christ.
C | -1-. According to the faith of God's elect, and the acknowledging of the truth.
B² | -1. According to godliness.
C² D | 2-. In hope of eternal life.
E | -2-. Promised by God Who cannot lie.
F | -2. Before the world began.
C² | *F* | 3-. But hath manifested in its own seasons.
E | -3-. His Word through preaching.
D | -3-. Committed unto me.
B² | -3. According to the commandment of God our Saviour.
A | 4-. Titus.
B | -4-. Mine own son.
C | -4-. According to the common faith.

1 servant of God. Nowhere else does Paul so designate himself.
servant. Ap. 190. I. 2.
God. Ap. 98. I. i. 1. **apostle.** Ap. 189.
Jesus Christ. Ap. 98. XI.
according to. Ap. 104. x. 2.
faith. Ap. 150. II. 1.
acknowledging=full knowledge. Ap. 132. II. ii.
truth. Gr. *alētheia.* Cp. Ap. 175. 1.
after. Same as according to.
godliness. Gr. *eusebeia.* Cp. Ap. 137. 5.
2 In. Gr. *epi.* Ap. 104. ix. 2.
hope. See 3. 7. Cp. Col. 3. 4. 1 Tim. 1. 1.
eternal. Ap. 151. II. B. i.
life. Ap. 170. 1.
that cannot lie. Lit., the unlying. Gr. *apseudēs.* Only here.
promised. Gr. *epangellomai.* Cp. Ap. 121. 5, 6.

before . . . began. Ap. 151. II. B. iv. **3 hath.** Omit. **in.** No prep. **times.** Gr. *kairos,* the fit season. Fig. *Heterōsis* of number. Ap. 6. See Ap. 195. **manifested.** Ap. 106. v. **word.** Ap. 121. 10. **through.** Gr. *en.* Ap. 104. viii. **preaching.** Ap. 121. 3. **is**=was. **committed.** Ap. 150. I. 1. iv. **commandment.** Gr. *epitagē.* Occ. 2. 15. Rom. 16. 26. 1 Cor. 7. 6, 25. 2 Cor. 8. 8. 1 Tim. 1. 1. **Saviour.** Gr. *sōtēr.* Six times in this short Ep. Here, *v.* 4; 2. 10, 13; 3. 4, 6. **4 *mine* own son.** See 1 Tim. 1. 2. ***mine* own.** Ap. 175. 3. **son**=child. Ap. 108. i. **common.** Gr. *koinos.* Cp. Acts 2. 44. Jude 3. **Grace, &c.** See 1 Tim. 1. 2. Fig. *Synonymia.* Ap. 6. **from.** Ap. 104. iv. **Father.** Ap. 98. III. **Lord.** The texts omit. **Jesus Christ.** The texts read "Christ Jesus". **5 For . . . cause.** Gr. *charin.* Occ. *v.* 11. See Eph. 3. 1, 14. **left.** Gr. *kataleipō.* The texts read *apoleipō,* as 2 Tim. 4. 20. **in.** Ap. 104. viii. **Crete.** The island lying in the Aegean Sea still bears the ancient name. It is about 140 miles long by about 30 wide. **that**=in order that. Gr. *hina.* **set in order.** Gr. *epidiorthoō.* Only here. **the . . . wanting.** Lit. the left things. Cp. 3. 13. **ordain**=appoint. Gr. *kathistēmi.* First occ. Matt. 24. 45. **elders.** See Acts 20. 17. Cp. 1 Tim. 5. 17. Ap. 189. **in every city**=city by city. Gr. *kata* (Ap. 104. x. 2) *polin.* **appointed.** Gr. *diatassō.* Occ. sixteen times, generally "command". **6 If.** Ap. 118. 2. a. **any.** Ap. 123. 3. **blameless.** Gr. *anenklētos.* Elsewhere, *v.* 7. 1 Cor. 1. 8. Col. 1. 22. 1 Tim. 3. 10. Cp. 1 Tim. 3. 2. **husband.** Ap. 123. 2. **faithful.** Ap. 150. III. **children.** Ap. 108. i. **not.** Ap. 105. II. **accused.** Gr. *en* (Ap. 104. viii) *katēgoria.* See John 18. 29. **unruly.** Gr. *anupotaktos.* Occ. *v.* 10, and elsewhere, 1 Tim. 1. 9. Heb. 2. 8. **7 a**=the. **bishop.** Ap. 189. **steward.** Gr. *oikonomos.* Occ. ten times; "steward", except Rom. 16. 23. Gal. 4. 2. **self-willed.** Gr. *authadēs.* Only here and 2 Pet. 2. 10. **soon angry.** Gr. *orgilos.* Only here. **given to wine.** Gr. *paroinos.* Only here and 1 Tim. 3. 3. **no.** Ap. 105. II. **striker.** Gr. *plēktēs.* Only here and 1 Tim. 3. 3. **given . . . lucre.** Gr. *aischrokerdēs.* Occ. 1 Tim. 3. 3, 8, and the adverb in 1 Pet. 5. 2. See also *v.* 11. **8 lover of hospitality.** Gr. *philoxenos.* Occ. 1 Tim. 3. 2. 1 Pet. 4. 9. The noun in Rom. 12. 13, and Heb. 13. 2. **lover of good men**=lover of the good (thing). Gr. *philagathos.* Only here. **sober**=right-minded. Gr. *sōphrōn.* Occ. 2. 2, 5. 1 Tim. 3. 2. Cp. Mark 5. 15. **just.** Ap. 191. 1. **holy.** Gr. *hosios.* See on Acts 2. 27. **temperate.** Gr. *enkratēs.* Only here. See on Acts 24. 25. **9 Holding fast.** Gr. *antechomai.* Elsewhere, Matt. 6. 24. Luke 16. 13. 1 Thess. 5. 14. **as . . . taught**= according to (Ap. 104. x. 2) the teaching (*didachē,* occ. thirty times, always "doctrine" save here). **able.** Gr. *dunatos.* Cp Ap. 172. 1. **by.** Gr. *en.* Ap. 104. viii.

°sound °doctrine both to °exhort, and to °con-
vince the °gainsayers.

C D 10 For there are many [6]unruly, °and °vain
talkers and °deceivers, specially they °of the
°circumcision:

E 11 Whose °mouths must be stopped, who
°subvert whole °houses, teaching things which
they ought [6]not, °for °filthy °lucre's sake.

F 12 °One [10]of themselves, *even* a °prophet of
their own, said, °"The Cretians *are* °alway
liars, °evil °beasts, °slow °bellies."

F 13 This °witness is °true.

E °Wherefore °rebuke them °sharply, [5]that
they may be [9]sound [5]in the °faith;
14 [6]Not °giving heed to °Jewish fables, and
°commandments of °men that °turn from the
[1]truth.

D 15 °Unto the °pure °all things *are* °pure:
but °unto them that are °defiled and °un-
believing *is* °nothing °pure; but even their
°mind and °conscience is °defiled.
16 They °profess that they °know [1]God; but
°in works they °deny *Him*, being °abomina-
ble, and °disobedient, and °unto every °good
work °reprobate.

D G **2** But °speak thou the things which °become
°sound doctrine:

H J a 2 °That the °aged men be °sober, °grave,
°temperate, [1]sound in °faith, in °charity, in
°patience.

b 3 The °aged women likewise, that *they* be
°in °behaviour °as becometh holiness, °not

sound doctrine. See 1 Tim. 1. 10, and cp. 2 Tim. 1. 13.
doctrine. Gr. *didaskalia.* Occ. twenty-one times, always doctrine, save Rom. 12. 7 (teaching); 15. 4 (learning).
exhort. Ap. 134. I. 6. Read, "exhort (*the believers*)".
convince = convict. Gr. *elenchō.* See *v.* 13, and first occ., Matt. 18. 15.
gainsayers = the contradicters. Occ. ten times. See first occ., Luke 2. 34.

1. 10-16 (C, p. 1815). CONTENTIOUS CRETANS. CENSURED. (*Introversion.*)

C | D | 10. Impostors.
  E | 11. Rebuke.
   F | 12. Witness against them by a prophet of their own.
   F | 13-. Witness confirmed by Paul.
  E | -13, 14. Rebuke.
 D | 15, 16. Impostors.

10 and. Omit.
vain talkers. Gr. *mataiologos.* Only here. Cp. 1 Tim. 1. 6.
deceivers. Gr. *phrenapatēs.* Only here. Not peculiar to N.T. The verb occ. Gal. 6. 3. **of.** Ap. 104. vii.
circumcision. Those here referred to were Jewish Christians.
11 mouths . . . stopped. Gr. *epistomizō.* Only here.
subvert = overthrow. Gr. *anatrepō.* Only here and 2 Tim. 2. 18.
houses = households. Gr. *oikos.* Fig. *Metonymy* (of Subject). Ap. 6.
for . . . sake. Gr. *charin,* as in *v.* 5.
filthy. Gr. *aischros.* Only here. See *v.* 7.
lucre's = gain's. Only here; Phil. 1. 21; 3. 7.
12 One. Ap. 123. 3.
prophet. Ap. 189. Fig. *Metonymy* (of Adjunct). Ap. 6. To Paul, a prophet by *repute* only. It is supposed that the reference is to Epimenides.
The . . . bellies. Fig. *Gnome.* Ap. 6 (8).
alway. Ap. 151. II. F. i. (ii).
evil. Ap. 128. III. 2. **beasts** = wild beasts.
slow. Gr. *argos.* Occ. eight times, generally "idle".
bellies = persons. Fig. *Synecdoche* (of Part). Ap. 6.
13 witness = testimony. **true.** Ap. 175. 1.
Wherefore = on account of (Gr. *dia.* Ap. 104. v. 2) which. **rebuke.** Gr. *elenchō.* See *v.* 9. Occ. also 2. 15. **sharply.** Gr. *apotomōs.* Elsewhere only 2 Cor. 13. 10; the noun in Rom. 11. 22. **faith.** See *v.* 1. Here, doctrine of the gospel. Fig. *Metonymy* (of Adjunct). Ap. 6. **14 giving heed.** Gr. *prosechō.* Cp. 1 Tim. 1. 4. **Jewish fables.** Cp. Col. 2. 16-22. 1 Tim. 1. 4. **commandments.** Gr. *entolē.* **men.** Ap. 123. 1. **turn from.** Gr. *apostrephō.* Cp. 2 Tim. 4. 4. **15 Unto . . . *are* pure.** Fig. *Parœmia.* Ap. 6. **Unto** = To. **pure.** Gr. *katharos.* First occ. Matt. 5. 8. **all, &c.** The use of all things, i. e. meats. Cp. Rom. 14. 14, 20. ***are.*** Fig. *Ellipsis* (Absolute). Ap. 6. **defiled.** Gr. *miainō.* Elsewhere, John 18. 28. Heb. 12. 15. Jude 8. Cp. the adj. in 2 Peter 2. 10, and noun 2 Peter 2. 20. **unbelieving.** Gr. *apistos.* Cp. Ap. 150. III. **nothing.** Gr. *oudeis.* **mind** = understanding (Gr. *nous*), as in first occ. Luke 24. 45. **conscience.** Gr. *suneidēsis.* First occ. John 8. 9. See Acts 23. 1. **16 profess.** Gr. *homologeō.* Cp. Rom. 10. 9, 10. **know.** Ap. 132. I. i. **in** = by. No prep. **deny.** Gr. *arneomai.* See 2. 12. Cp. 2 Tim. 2. 12; 3. 5. **abominable.** Gr. *bdeluktos.* Only here. The noun in Matt. 24. 15; &c. **disobedient.** Cp. Ap. 128. V. 1. **unto.** Ap. 104. xv. 3. **good work.** See 2. 7; 3. 1, 8, 14. **reprobate.** Gr. *adokimos.* See Rom. 1. 28.

2. 1-10 (D, p. 1815). WALK AND WORKS. (*Alternation.*)

D | G | 1. Titus the instructor.
  H | 2-6. Those exhorted.
 G | 7, 8. Titus the pattern.
  H | 9, 10. Those exhorted.

2. 1 speak. Ap. 121. 7. **become.** Gr. *prepei.* Occ. seven times. First occ. Matt. 3. 15. **sound doctrine.** See 1. 9.

2. 2-6 (H, above). THOSE EXHORTED. (*Introversion.*)

H | J | a | 2. Men. } Aged.
    b | 3. Women. } Aged.
  J | *b* | 4, 5. Women. } Young.
    a | 6. Men. } Young.

2 That = (*Exhort*) that. Fig. *Ellipsis* (of Repetition). Ap. 6. **aged men.** Gr. *presbutēs.* Elsewhere, Luke 1. 18. Philem. 9. **sober.** Gr. *nēphalios.* Elsewhere, 1 Tim. 3. 2, 11. **grave.** Gr. *semnos.* Occ. Phil. 4. 8. 1 Tim. 3. 8, 11. The noun in *v.* 7. 1 Tim. 2. 2; 3. 4. **temperate.** Gr. *sōphrōn.* See 1. 8. **faith** = the faith. See Ap. 150. II. 1. **charity** = the love. Ap. 135. II. 1. **patience** = the patience. Gr. *hupomonē.* Occ. about thirty times, first in Luke 8. 15. **3 aged women.** Gr. *presbutis.* Only here. **in.** Ap. 104. viii. **behaviour.** Gr. *katastēma.* Only here. **as . . . holiness.** Gr. *hieroprepēs.* Only here. **not.** Ap. 105. II.

°false accusers, °not °given to much wine,
°teachers of good things;

J b 4 °That they may °teach the °young women
to be sober, to °love their husbands, to °love
their children,
5 *To be* °discreet, °chaste, °keepers at home,
good, °obedient to their own °husbands, [4]that
the °word of °God be °not °blasphemed.

a 6 °Young men likewise °exhort to be °sober
minded.

G 7 °In all things °shewing thyself a °pattern
of °good works: [3]in °doctrine *shewing* °un-
corruptness, °gravity, °sincerity,
8 °Sound °speech, °that cannot be condemned; [4]that he that is °of the °contrary
part may be °ashamed, having °no °evil thing
to °say °of you.

H 9 *Exhort* °servants to be [5]obedient °unto
their own °masters, *and* to °please *them* well
[3]in all *things;* [5]not °answering again;
10 [5]Not °purloining, but °shewing all good
°fidelity; [4]that they may °adorn the [1]doctrine
of [5]God our °Saviour [3]in all things.

E A 11 For the °grace of [5]God °that bringeth
salvation °hath °appeared to all °men,

B 12 °Teaching us [4]that, °denying °ungodli-
ness and °worldly °lusts, we should °live
°soberly, °righteously, and °godly, [3]in °this
present °world;
13 °Looking for °that °blessed °hope, and
the °glorious appearing of the °great [5]God
and our [10]Saviour °Jesus Christ;
14 Who gave Himself °for us, [4]that He might
°redeem us °from all °iniquity, and purify
[9]unto Himself a °peculiar people, °zealous °of
[7]good works.

C 15 These things [1]speak, and [6]exhort, and
°rebuke °with all °authority. Let °no man
°despise thee.

E C **3** °Put them in mind to be °subject to °prin-
cipalities and °powers, to °obey magistrates, to be ready °to every °good work,

false accusers. Fig. *Idiōma.* Ap. 6. Gr. *diabolos.* Occ. thirty-eight times, always "devil", save here, 1 Tim. 3. 11. 2 Tim. 3. 3.
not. The texts read "nor", Gr. *mēde.*
given. Gr. *douloō.* Ap. 190. III. 3.
teachers, &c. Gr. *kalodidaskalos.* Only here.
4 That = In order that. Gr. *hina.*
teach . . . to be sober. Gr. *sōphronizō.* Only here. Cp. 2. 6, 12. 1 Tim. 2. 9.
young women. Fem. of Gr. *neos.* See John 21. 18.
love . . . husbands. Gr. *philandros.* Only here.
love . . . children. Gr. *philoteknos.* Only here.
5 discreet. Gr. *sōphrōn.* Cp. *vv.* 2, 4; 1. 8.
chaste. Gr. *hagnos.* Elsewhere, 2 Cor. 7. 11; 11. 2. Phil. 4. 8. 1 Tim. 5. 22. Jas. 3. 17. 1 Pet. 3. 2. 1 John 3. 3.
keepers at home. Gr. *oikouros.* Only here.
obedient. Gr. *hupotassō,* as in *v.* 9; 3. 1.
husbands. Ap. 123. 2. word. Ap. 121. 10.
God. Ap. 98. I. i. 1. not. Ap. 105. II.
blasphemed. Gr. *blasphēmeō.* Occ. 3. 2.
6 Young men = The younger. Gr. *neōteros,* as in 1 Tim. 5. 1.
exhort. Ap. 134. I. 6.
sober minded. Gr. *sōphroneō.* Cp. *vv.* 4, 5, 12, and see Rom. 12. 3.
7 In. Ap. 104. xiii. 2.
shewing. Gr. *parechō.* Elsewhere, offer, give, minister, &c.
pattern. Gr. *tupos.* See John 20. 25.
good works. See 1. 16.
doctrine. See 1. 9.
uncorruptness. Gr. *adiaphthoria.* The texts read *aphthoria.* Only here.
gravity. Gr. *semnotēs.* Elsewhere, 1 Tim. 2. 2; 3. 4. The adj. in *v.* 2.
sincerity. The texts omit.
8 Sound. Gr. *hugiēs.* Occ. fourteen times, always "whole", save here. Cp. *vv.* 1. 2; 1. 9. 13.
speech. Ap. 121. 10.
that . . . condemned. Gr. *akatagnōstos.* Only here.
of. Ap. 104. vii.
contrary part. Gr. *enantios.* Occ. eight times, first in Matt. 14. 24.
ashamed. Gr. *entrepō.* See 2 Thess. 3. 14.
no. Gr. *mēdeis.*
evil. Gr. *phaulos.* Only here; John 3. 20; 5. 29. Jas. 3. 16.
say. Gr. *legō.* Cp. Ap. 121. 10.
of. Ap. 104. xiii. 1.
9 servants. Ap. 190. I. 2. unto = to.
masters. Ap. 98. XIV. ii.
please . . . well. Gr. *euarestos.* See Rom. 12. 1.

answering again. Gr. *antilegō.* Cp. 1. 9. **10** purloining. Gr. *nosphizomai.* Only here; Acts 5. 2, 3. shewing. Gr. *endeiknumi.* Occ. 3. 2. fidelity. Ap. 150. II. 1. adorn. Gr. *kosmeō.* Occ. ten times, first in Matt. 12. 44. Saviour. See 1. 3. **11** grace. Gr. *charis.* Ap. 184. I. 1. that bringeth salvation. Gr. *sōtērios.* Only here. hath. Omit. appeared. Ap. 106. I. iii. men. Ap. 123. 1.
12 Teaching. Gr. *paideuō.* Elsewhere, twelve times, gen. "chasten", "chastise". denying. Gr. *arneomai.* Occ. thirty-one times, always "deny", save Acts 7. 35. Heb. 11. 24. See 1. 16. ungodliness. Ap. 128. IV. worldly. Gr. *kosmikos.* Only here and Heb. 9. 1. Cp. Ap. 129. 1. lusts. See Eph. 2. 3. Phil. 1. 23 (desire). live. Gr. *zaō.* Cp. Ap. 170. 1. soberly. Gr. *sōphronōs.* See *vv.* 2, 4, 5, 6. righteously. See Ap. 191. godly. See Ap. 137. 5. this present. Lit. the now (Gr. *nun*). world. Ap. 129. 2, and Ap. 151. II. A. i. 3. **13** Looking for. See Luke 12. 36. that = the. blessed. See 1 Tim. 1. 11. hope . . . appearing. Fig. *Hendiadys.* Ap. 6. hope. Cp. 1. 2; 3. 7. "Blessed object of hope." Fig. *Metonymy* (of Adjunct). Ap. 6. glorious appearing = appearing (Ap. 106. II. ii) of the glory (see p. 1511). Fig. *Antimereia* (of Noun). Ap. 6. Cp. 2 Cor. 4. 4. great, &c. = our great Saviour God. Jesus Christ. Ap. 98. XI. **14** for. Ap. 104. xvii. 1. redeem. Gr. *lutroō.* Only here; Luke 24. 21. 1 Pet. 1. 18. from. Ap. 104. iv. iniquity. Ap. 128. III. 4. peculiar people = a people as an acquisition. Gr. *periousios.* Only here. Cp. 1 Pet. 2. 9. Occ. in Sept. Ex. 19. 5. Deut. 7. 6; 14. 2; 26. 18; and in kindred forms, 1 Chron. 29. 3. Ps. 135. 4. Ecc. 2. 8. Mal. 3. 17. zealous. Gr. *zēlōtēs.* Elsewhere, Acts 21. 20; 22. 3. 1 Cor. 14. 12. Gal. 1. 14. of. Genitive of relation; "with respect to". Ap. 17. 5.
15 rebuke. See 1. 9, 13. with. Ap. 104. xi. 1. authority. The same Gr. word in 1. 3 is translated "commandment". no man = no one. Gr. *mēdeis.* despise. Gr. *periphroneō.* Only here.

3. 1-3 Put, &c. Fig. *Association.* Ap. 6. **1** Put . . . in mind. Gr. *hupomimnēskō.* Elsewhere, Luke 22. 61. John 14. 26. 2 Tim. 2. 14. 2 Pet. 1. 12. 3 John 10. Jude 5. subject. See 2. 5, 9. principalities, powers. See Ap. 172. 6 and 5. obey magistrates. Gr. *peitharcheō.* Elsewhere, Acts 5. 29, 32; 27. 21. to. Ap. 104. xv. 3. good work. See 1. 16 and 2. 7.

2 To °speak evil of °no man, to be °no brawlers, *but* °gentle, °shewing all °meekness °unto all °men.

B 3 For we ourselves also were °sometimes °foolish, °disobedient, deceived, °serving divers °lusts and °pleasures, °living °in °malice and °envy, °hateful, *and* hating one another.

A 4 But °after that the °kindness and °love of °God our °Saviour toward man °appeared,

5 °Not °by works °of °righteousness which we °have done, but °according to His mercy He saved us, °by °the °washing of °regeneration, and °renewing °of the °Holy Ghost,

6 Which He °shed °on us °abundantly, °through °Jesus Christ our [4] Saviour;

7 °That being °justified by His °grace, we should °be made heirs [5] according to the °hope of °eternal °life.

D 8 °*This is* a °faithful °saying, °and these things I °will that thou °affirm constantly, [7] that they which have °believed °in [4] God might be °careful to °maintain °good works. These things are good and °profitable °unto °men.

C 9 But °avoid °foolish questions, and °genealogies, and °contentions, and °strivings °about the law; for they are °unprofitable and °vain.

B 10 A °man that is an °heretick, °after °the first and second °admonition reject;

11 °Knowing that he that is such is °subverted, and °sinneth, being °condemned of himself.

A 12 When I shall °send °Artemas [2] unto thee, or °Tychicus, be °diligent to come [2] unto me °to °Nicopolis: for I have °determined there to °winter.

13 °Bring °Zenas the lawyer and °Apollos on their journey °diligently, [7] that °nothing be °wanting [8] unto them.

14 And let °ours also learn to [8] maintain [8] good works °for °necessary °uses, [7] that they be °not °unfruitful.

15 All that are °with me °salute thee. °Greet them that °love us [3] in °the °faith. °Grace *be* °with you all. °Amen.

2 speak evil. See 2. 5.
no man=no one. Gr. *mēdeis.*
no brawlers. Gr. *amachos.* Only here and 1 Tim. 3. 3.
gentle. Gr. *epieikēs.* See Phil. 4. 5. Elsewhere, 1 Tim. 3. 3. Jas. 3. 17. 1 Pet. 2. 18.
shewing. See 2. 10.
meekness. Gr. *praotēs.* Cp. 2 Cor. 10. 1.
unto. Gr. *pros.* Ap. 104. xv. 3.
men. Ap. 123. 1.
3 sometimes=at one time.
foolish. Gr. *anoētos.* See Rom. 1. 14.
disobedient. See 1. 16.
serving. Gr. *douleuō*; the condition of being a slave. Cp. 2. 3. Ap. 190. III. 2. **lusts.** See 2. 12.
pleasures. Gr. *hēdonē.* Elsewhere, Luke 8. 14. Jas. 4. 1, 3. 2 Pet. 2. 13.
living. Gr. *diagō.* Only here and 1 Tim. 2. 2.
in. Ap. 104. viii.
malice, envy. See Rom. 1. 29.
hateful. Gr. *stugētos.* Only here.
4 after that=when.
kindness. Ap. 184. III. (a).
love . . . toward man. Gr. *philanthrōpia.* Only here and Acts 28. 2. The adv. in Acts 27. 3.
God. See Ap. 98. I. i. 1. **Saviour.** See 1. 3.
appeared. See Ap. 106. I. iii.
5 Not. Ap. 105. I. **by.** Gr. *ek.* Ap. 104. vii.
of. Gr. *en.* Ap. 104. viii.
righteousness. Ap. 191. 3. **have done**=did.
according to. Ap. 104. x. 2, with texts.
by. Ap. 104. v. 1.
the washing . . . Ghost. Fig. *Hendiadys.* Ap. 6. Two things mentioned but only one thing meant. A reference here to the gifts abundantly bestowed "on us" before the truth was announced regarding the believer's completeness in Christ, apart from ordinances.
washing. Gr. *loutron.* Only here and Eph. 5. 26. The word means, primarily, a vessel for bathing.
regeneration. Gen. of Apposition. Ap. 17. 4. Gr. *palingenesia.* The reference is to the new man. Only here and Matt. 19. 28.
renewing. Gr. *anakainōsis.* Only here and Rom. 12. 2. The verb in Col. 3. 10.
of=by. **Holy Ghost.** Ap. 101. II. 3.
6 shed. Gr. *ekcheō.* See Acts 2. 17, 18, 33. Fig. *Anthrōpopatheia.* Ap. 6. "Pouring out" attributed to God, and the Spirit spoken of as if water.
on. Ap. 104. ix. 3.
abundantly. Gr. *plousiōs.* Elsewhere, Col. 3. 16. 1 Tim. 6. 17. 2 Pet. 1. 11. **through.** Ap. 104. v. 1.

Jesus Christ. Ap. 98. XI. **7 That**=In order that. Gr. *hina.* **justified.** Ap. 191. 2. **grace.** See 2. 11. Ap. 184. I. 1. **be made**=become. **hope.** See 1. 2. **eternal.** Ap. 151. II. B. i. **life.** Ap. 170. 1. **8** *This,* &c.=Faithful the saying. Fig. *Ellipsis* (of Repetition). Ap. 6. See 1 Tim. 1. 15. Fig. *Hyperbaton.* Ap. 6. **faithful.** Ap. 150. III. **saying.** Ap. 121. 10. **and**=and concerning (Ap. 104. xiii. 1). **will.** Ap. 102. 3. **affirm constantly**=affirm strongly. Gr. *diabebaioomai.* Only here and 1 Tim. 1. 7. **believed.** Ap. 150. I. 1. ii. **in.** Omit. **careful.** Gr. *phrontizō.* Only here. **maintain.** Gr. *proïstēmi.* Occ. *v.* 14. Rom. 12. 8. 1 Thess. 5. 12. 1 Tim. 3. 4, 5, 12; 5. 17. **good works.** See 1. 16. **profitable.** Gr. *ōphelimos.* Elsewhere, 1 Tim. 4. 8. 2 Tim. 3. 16. **unto**=to. **men.** Ap. 123. 1. **9 avoid.** Gr. *periistēmi.* Elsewhere, John 11. 42. Acts 25. 7. 2 Tim. 2. 16. **foolish questions.** Cp. 2 Tim. 2. 23. **genealogies.** Gr. *genealogia.* Only here and 1 Tim. 1. 4. **contentions.** Gr. *eris.* See Rom. 1. 29. **strivings.** Gr. *machē.* Elsewhere, 2 Cor. 7. 5. 2 Tim. 2. 23. Jas. 4. 1. **about the law.** Gr. *nomikos.* Elsewhere (eight times) transl. "lawyer". **unprofitable.** Gr. *anōphelēs.* Only here and Heb. 7. 18. **vain.** Gr. *mataios.* See 1. 10. **10 man.** Ap. 123. 1. **heretick.** Gr. *hairetikos.* Only here. See Acts 5. 17. **after.** Ap. 104. xi. 2. **the**=a. **admonition.** Gr. *nouthesia.* Elsewhere, 1 Cor. 10. 11. Eph. 6. 4. **11 Knowing.** Ap. 132. I. i. **subverted.** Gr. *ekstrephomai.* Only here. **sinneth.** Ap. 128. I. i. **condemned,** &c. Gr. *autokatakritos.* Only here. **12 send.** Ap. 174. 4. **Artemas.** Not mentioned elsewhere. **Tychicus.** See Acts 20. 4. Eph. 6. 21. Col. 4. 7. 2 Tim. 4. 12. **diligent.** Gr. *spoudazō.* Cp. *v.* 13. **to.** Ap. 104. vi. **Nicopolis.** It is uncertain which of the cities bearing this name is here referred to. **determined.** Ap. 122. 1. **winter.** Gr. *paracheimazō.* Elsewhere, Acts 27. 12; 28. 11. 1 Cor. 16. 6. **13 Bring . . . journey.** Gr. *propempō.* See Acts 15. 3. Cp. Ap. 174. 4. **Zenas.** Not referred to elsewhere. **Apollos.** Mentioned Acts 18. 24; 19. 1, and seven times in 1 Cor. **diligently.** Cp. *v.* 12. **nothing.** Gr. *mēdeis.* **wanting.** See 1. 5. **14 ours**=our people. **for.** Ap. 104. vi. **necessary.** Gr. *anankaios.* As in Acts 13. 46. **uses.** Lit. needs. Gr. *chreia.* **not.** Ap. 105. II. **unfruitful.** Gr. *akarpos.* Elsewhere, Matt. 13. 22. Mark 4. 19. 1 Cor. 14. 14. Eph. 5. 11. 2 Pet. 1. 8. Jude 12. **15 with.** Ap. 104. xi. 1. **salute, Greet.** Gr. *aspazomai.* **love.** Ap. 135. I. 2. **the.** Omit. **faith.** Ap. 150. II. 1. **Grace**=The grace. Gr. *charis.* Ap. 184. I. 1. **Amen.** Omit.

THE EPISTLE TO PHILEMON.

THE STRUCTURE OF THE EPISTLE AS A WHOLE.

(*Introversion*)

A | A | 1, 2. EPISTOLARY SALUTATIONS.
B | 3. BENEDICTION.

B | C | 4-6. PAUL'S PRAYER FOR PHILEMON.
D | a | 7-. PAUL'S JOY IN PHILEMON: CONFESSED.
b | -7. BOWELS OF SAINTS REFRESHED.
} PAUL AND PHILEMON.

C | G | 8. I MIGHT ENJOIN (BUT I DO NOT).
H | 9. PAUL THE AGED.
J | c | 10, 11. ONESIMUS PROFITABLE (*ONESIMOS*) TO THEE AND ME.
d | 12. RECEIVE HIM AS MYSELF.
K | 13. ONESIMUS MINISTERED IN THY STEAD.
K | 14. THY BENEFIT.

C | *J* | *c* | 15, 16. BELOVED TO ME AND THEE.
d | 17. RECEIVE HIM AS MYSELF.
H | 18, 19-. PAUL THE DEBTOR.
G | -19. I DO NOT SAY (BUT I MIGHT).
} ONESIMUS.

B | *D* | *a* | 20-. PAUL'S JOY IN PHILEMON: BESOUGHT.
b | -20. "REFRESH MY BOWELS."
C | 21, 22. PHILEMON'S PRAYER FOR PAUL.
} PAUL AND PHILEMON.

A | *A* | 23, 24. EPISTOLARY.
B | 25. BENEDICTION

NOTES ON THE EPISTLE TO PHILEMON.

1. All that we know of Philemon is to be gathered from the Epistle bearing his name. He seems to have been a believer at Colosse, from the references to certain in the church there (see Notes below), and must have been possessed of means (*v.* 22). Paul's words indicate that he held his friend in high esteem.

2. Onesimus is the Latinized form of the Greek *Onēsimos*, which means "useful", or "profitable". He was a slave (*v.* 16), and, fleeing from his master, found his way to Rome, where he was, under Paul, led to become the Lord's freeman, and "called being a servant (slave)", he cared not for it, but was willing to return to his master's service, whether to continue as slave or as "brother beloved" (*v.* 16). Paul sends the letter by Onesimus.

3. From Col. 4. 9. we learn that Paul had sent unto the church at Colosse Tychicus "with Onesimus, a faithful and beloved brother, who is one of you". For other references, see Notes.

4. The Epistle was written during Paul's first imprisonment at Rome, probably in A. D. 62. In no one of his Epistles is more clearly shown the great heart of the apostle in his care for every member of the church. See 2 Cor. 11. 28, 29.

THE EPISTLE OF PAUL TO

PHILEMON.

A A 1 PAUL, a °prisoner of °Jesus Christ, and Timothy °*our* brother, °unto Philemon our °dearly beloved, and °fellowlabourer,

2 And to [1]*our* °beloved °Apphia, and °Archippus our °fellowsoldier, and to the °church °in thy house:

B 3 °Grace to you, and peace, °from °God our °Father and the °Lord °Jesus Christ.

B C 4 I °thank my [3]God, making °mention of thee always °in my °prayers,

5 Hearing of thy °love and °faith, which thou hast °toward the °Lord °Jesus, and °toward all °saints;

6 °That the °communication of thy [5]faith may become °effectual °by the °acknowledging of every good thing which is °in °you °in °Christ °Jesus.

D a 7 For °we have great joy and °consolation °in thy [5]love,

b because the °bowels of the [5]saints °are °refreshed °by thee, [1]brother.

C G 8 Wherefore, °though I might be much bold [6]– in [6]Christ to °enjoin thee that which is °convenient,

H 9 °Yet °for [5]love's sake I rather °beseech *thee*, being such an one as Paul the °aged, and now °also a prisoner of [1]Jesus Christ.

J c 10 I [9]beseech thee °for my °son Onesimus, whom I °have begotten [6]– in my bonds;

11 Which in time past was to thee °unprofitable, but now °profitable to thee and to me:

d 12 Whom I °have °sent again: °thou therefore receive him, that is, °mine own bowels:

K 13 Whom I °would have retained °with me, °that °in thy stead he °might have ministered [1]unto me [6]– in the bonds of the °gospel:

K 14 But °without thy °mind °would I do °nothing; [13]that °thy benefit should °not be as °it were °of necessity, but °willingly.

C J c 15 For °perhaps he °therefore °departed °for a °season, [13]that thou shouldest °receive him °for ever;

1 prisoner. Cp. Eph. 3. 1; 4. 1. 2 Tim. 1. 8.
Jesus Christ = Christ Jesus. Ap. 98. XII.
our = the.
unto = to.
dearly beloved. Gr. *agapētos.* Ap. 135. III.
fellowlabourer. Gr. *sunergos.* See 1 Cor. 3. 9.
2 beloved. The texts read "sister".
Apphia. Tradition says she was the wife of Philemon.
Archippus. See Col. 4. 17.
fellowsoldier. Only here and Phil. 2. 25, which see.
church. Ap. 186.
in. Gr. *kata.* Ap. 104. x. 2.
3 Grace. Gr. *charis.* Ap. 184. I. 1.
from. Ap. 104. iv.
God. Ap. 98. I. i. 1.
Father. Ap. 98. III.
Lord. Ap. 98. VI. i. *β.* 2. B.
Jesus Christ. Ap. 98. XI.
4 thank. Gr. *eucharisteō.* See Acts 27. 35.
mention. Gr. *mneia.* See Rom. 1. 9. Eph. 1. 16. 1 Thess. 1. 2.
always. Ap. 151. II. G. i.
in. Gr. *epi.* Ap. 104. ix. 1.
prayers. Gr. *proseuchē.* Ap. 134. II. 2.
5 love = the love. Ap. 135. II. 1.
faith = the faith. Ap. 150. II. 1.
toward. Gr. *pros.* Ap. 104. xv. 3.
Lord. Ap. 98. VI. i. *β.* 2. A.
Jesus. Ap. 98. X.
toward. Gr. *eis.* Ap. 104. vi.
saints = the saints. See Acts 9. 13.
6 That. Supply the ellipsis by "(Praying) that".
communication = fellowship. Gr. *koinōnia.* See Acts 2. 42.
effectual. Gr. *energēs.* See 1 Cor. 16. 9. Elsewhere, Heb. 4. 12. See Ap. 172. 4.
by. Ap. 104. viii.
acknowledging. Ap. 132. II. ii.
in. Ap. 104. viii.
you. The texts read "us".
in. Gr. *eis.* Ap. 104. vi.
Christ. Ap. 98. IX.
Jesus. The texts omit.
7 we have. The texts read "I had".
consolation. See Acts 4. 36.
in. Ap. 104. ix. 2.
bowels. See 2 Cor. 6. 12.
are = have been.
refreshed. See 1 Cor. 16. 18.
by. Ap. 104. v. 1.
8 though . . . bold. Lit. having much boldness (Gr. *parrhēsia,* freedom of speech). Cp. Acts 2. 29. **enjoin** = command. Gr. *epitassō.* **convenient.** Gr. *anēkō.* See Eph. 5. 4. **9 Yet.** Omit. **for . . . sake.** Ap. 104. v. 2. **beseech.** Ap. 134. I. 6. Cp. *v.* 7. **aged.** Gr. *presbutēs.* See Tit. 2. 2. Elsewhere, Luke 1. 18. **also, &c.** = a prisoner also. **10 for.** Ap. 104. xiii. 1. **son.** Ap. 108. i. **have begotten** = begat. Cp. Phil. 1. 12, 13. **11 unprofitable** = not useful. Gr. *achrēstos.* Only here. Fig. *Meiosis.* Ap. 6. **profitable.** Gr. *euchrēstos.* See 2 Tim. 2. 21. **12 have.** Omit. **sent again** = sent back. Ap. 174. 5. **thou therefore receive.** The texts omit, and read "sent again to thee". **mine own bowels** = as mine own self. Fig. *Synecdochē.* Ap. 6. **13 would, &c.** = was minded (Ap. 102. 3) to retain. **with.** Ap. 104. xv. 3. **that** = in order that. Gr. *hina.* **in . . . stead.** Ap. 104. xvii. 1. **might have, &c.** = may minister. Ap. 190. III. 1. **gospel.** See Ap. 140. **14 without** = apart from. Gr. *chōris.* **mind.** Ap. 177. 2. **would.** Lit. was willing to. Ap. 102. 1. **nothing.** Gr. *ouden.* **thy benefit.** Lit. the good thing of thee. **not.** Ap. 105. II. **it were.** Omit. **of.** Ap. 104. x. 2. **willingly** = according to (Ap. 104. x. 2) free-will. Gr. *hekousios.* Only here. The adverb in Heb. 10. 26. 1 Pet. 5. 2. **15 perhaps.** Gr. *tacha.* Only here and Rom. 5. 7. **therefore** = because of (Ap. 104. v. 2) this. **departed** = was separated. Gr. *chōrizō.* First occ. Matt. 19. 6. **for.** Ap. 104. xv. 3. **season.** Lit. hour. Gr. *hōra.* **receive.** Gr. *apechō.* See Matt. 6. 2. **for ever.** Ap. 151. II. B. iii.

16 °Not now as a °servant, but °above a °servant, a [1]brother [2]beloved, specially to me, but how much more [1]unto thee, both [6]-in the flesh, and [6]-in the [3]Lord?

d 17 °If thou °count me therefore a °partner, °receive him as myself.

H 18 [17]If he °hath wronged thee, or oweth *thee* ought, °put that on mine account;
19 I Paul °have written *it* with mine own hand, I will °repay *it;*

G °albeit I do [14]not say to thee °how thou °owest [1]unto me even thine own self besides.

B D a 20 Yea, [1]brother, °let me have joy of thee [6]-in the [3]Lord:

b [7]refresh my [7]bowels [6]-in °the Lord.

C 21 °Having confidence in thy obedience I [19]wrote [1]unto thee, °knowing that thou wilt °also do °more than I say.
22 But °withal prepare °me also a °lodging: for I °trust that °through your [4]prayers I shall be °given [1]unto you.

A A 23 There °salute thee °Epaphras, my °fellowprisoner [6]-in °Christ Jesus;
24 °Marcus, °Aristarchus, °Demas, °Lucas, my [1]fellowlabourers.

B 25 °The [3]grace of our [5]Lord [3]Jesus Christ *be* °with your °spirit. Amen.

16 Not now = No longer. Gr. *ouketi.*
servant. Ap. 190. I. 2.
above. Ap. 104. xvii. 2.
17 If. Ap. 118. 2. a.
count. Lit. have. Gr. *echō.*
partner = partaker. Gr. *koinōnos.* See 1 Cor. 10. 18.
receive. Gr. *proslambanō.* "You have received me; receive him in addition, as myself." Cp. Rom. 15. 7.
18 hath. Omit.
put . . . on . . . account. Gr. *ellogeō.* Only here and Rom. 5. 13 (imputed).
19 have written = wrote.
repay. Gr. *apotinō.* Only here.
albeit = that. Gr. *hina.*
how = that.
owest . . . besides. Gr. *prosopheilō.* Only here.
20 let me have joy = may I profit. Gr. *oninēmi,* the root-word from which comes *onēsimos.* "Let me have profit from thee, seeing I am sending back Onesimus (profitable) to thee."
the Lord. The texts read "Christ". Ap. 98. IX.
21 Having confidence. Ap. 150. I. 2.
knowing. Ap. 132. I. i.
also do more = do more also.
more than = above (Ap. 104. xvii. 2) that which.
22 withal. Gr. *hama.* See Col. 4. 3. 1 Tim. 5. 13.
me also = also for me.
lodging. Gr. *xenia.* Only here and Acts 28. 23.
trust = hope. Gr. *elpizō.*
through. Ap. 104. v. 1.
given = granted as a favour. Gr. *charizomai.* Ap. 184. II. 1.
23 salute = greet. Gr. *aspazomai.* Cp. Col. 4. 12.
Epaphras. See Col. 1. 7.
fellowprisoner. Gr. *sunaichmalōtos.* See Rom. 16. 7.
Christ Jesus. Ap. 98. XII. **24 Marcus.** See Acts 12. 12, 25; 15. 37, 39. Col. 4. 10. 2 Tim. 4. 11. 1 Pet. 5. 13. **Aristarchus.** See Acts 19. 29; 20. 4; 27. 2. Col. 4. 10. **Demas.** See Col. 4. 14. 2 Tim. 4. 10. **Lucas.** See Col. 4. 14. 2 Tim. 4. 11; also Int. Notes to Luke's Gospel, especially the foot-note. **25 The grace, &c.** Paul's constant benediction. **with.** Ap. 104. xi. 1. **spirit.** Ap. 101. II. 9.

THE EPISTLE TO THE HEBREWS.

THE STRUCTURE OF THE EPISTLE AS A WHOLE.

(*Introversion and Alternation.*)

A | 1. 1—2. 18. DOCTRINAL INTRODUCTION.

B | C | 3. 1—4. 13. THE MISSION OF CHRIST.

D | 4. 14-16. GENERAL APPLICATION. "HAVING THEREFORE."

B | C | 5. 1—10. 18. THE PRIESTHOOD OF CHRIST.

D | 10. 19—12. 29. PARTICULAR APPLICATION. "HAVING THEREFORE."

A | 13. 1-25. PRACTICAL CONCLUSION.

THE EPISTLE TO THE HEBREWS.

INTRODUCTORY NOTES.

The general subject of the Epistle is that the Messiah of the Old Testament Scriptures must suffer as *Man* (i.e. as Incarnate Man), and that Jesus is the Messiah.

ADDRESSED. "To the Hebrews": to the nation under its earliest name, Palestinian Jews and the *Diaspora* (John 7. 35) alike. Outwardly for believers (cp. 3. 1; 6. 9; 10. 34), it is aimed at waverers (cp. 4. 14; 10. 23, 32) and opposers (cp. 6. 8; 12. 15, 16; 13. 10).

AUTHORSHIP. The arguments in favour of the Pauline authorship are much more weighty than those in favour of all other candidates put together, and may be stated thus:—

1. The thoughts and reasonings are Paul's, whatever the style and language may be. All his other epistles were written to churches mainly composed of Gentiles. In addressing such an epistle to *Hebrews*, he would naturally write as an instructed scribe, one brought up "at the feet of Gamaliel, and taught according to the perfect manner of the law of the fathers" (Acts 22. 3). It is therefore futile to argue that if Paul were really the author, the language and style would have been in exact accord with those of the other epistles. Had this been so, it would be an argument *against*, and not in favour of, Paul's authorship.

2. There is a certain amount of external testimony that Paul was the writer, but none as to any other.

3. The testimony of 2 Pet. 3. 15, 16, strictly interpreted, proves that Paul wrote an epistle to the *Hebrews*, and if this is not the epistle, where is it? No trace or indication of any other has ever been found.

4. Its anonymity is eminently in favour of Pauline authorship. The suspicion with which the Jews regarded Paul, and their furious hatred of him (cp. Acts 21. 21; 2 Cor. 11. 24; Phil. 3. 2; 1 Thess. 2. 15, &c.), would be ample reason why, in addressing so important a letter to his own race, he should withhold his name. If it was necessary at the time of its publication to send out such an epistle, equally necessary was it that it should not be handicapped with a name regarded generally by the Jews as that of an infamous renegade. The argument of the value of an unsigned article in any important journal applies with great force in the case of *Hebrews*.

5. DATE of writing and publication. Owing to the fixed idea in the minds of most commentators that the reference to Timothy in 13. 23 (see note there) *must* have been connected with the Neronian persecution, the date is usually assigned to a period shortly before the destruction of the Temple, which took place late in A.D. 69 (Ap. 50. VI). The very latest "guess" is that "it may have been written at any time between A. D. 65 and 85". This is vague and unconvincing. In Ap. 180 the chronological position of *Hebrews* is shown, A. D. 53-54. Modern tradition places it after 2 Tim., *circa* A. D. 68. That the former is correct seems clear for the following reasons:—

(*a*) If *Hebrews* was written in or about the year 68, Paul's ministry had existed for twenty-two years (since his and Barnabas's "separation" for the work, in 46, Acts 13. 2) without the aid of a written statement of such paramount importance as this. What was the immediate object of publishing *then*, only a year or two before the destruction of the Temple, and very shortly before his own death (2 Tim. 4. 6), so weighty an argument that Jesus was both Messiah and true Man, and as Man must have suffered? That the Old Covenant was ended and its place taken by a New (Heb. 8. 13)? It is incredible that the apostle who was inspired to write and publish *Romans* at a comparatively early date should not have been allowed to put forth *Hebrews* till the very end of his ministry. "To the Jew first" is verily applicable in this connexion.

(*b*) Paul was at Jerusalem for the Council meeting (51) when the very subjects of *Hebrews* had evidently been bitterly discussed (Acts 15. 5-7). Shortly thereafter he writes *Thess.* 1 and 2, both of which contain poignant references to "shameful treatment" at the hands of his own people.

(*c*) Some authoritative statement must be placed in the hands of even an earthly ambassador in regard to new and altered relationships between his supreme head and those to whom he is commissioned and sent. The 1919 Treaty of Versailles may be used as illustration. No representative there reported ultimately by word of mouth to his country, but by presentation of a copy of the entire Treaty. So with this treatise-epistle. Paul, as God's ambassador to the *Diaspora* and Gentiles, *must* have had some documentary argument, proof, and testimony, in support of his (and of Timothy's and others') oral teaching and instruction, for circulation among the "many thousands" of Jews who *believed* at and after Pentecost, yet all of whom were "zealous of the Law" (Acts 2. 41; 4. 4; 6. 7; 21. 20), and with whom Paul and his fellow-workers must have come into contact. To have attached his own name to this would have defeated his purpose, as above mentioned.

(*d*) The approximate time therefore for writing and publishing such a body of doctrine must have been shortly after the beginning of his ministry, and, consequently, *Hebrews* was in all probability written during the eighteen months of Paul's sojourn at Corinth, during which he was "teaching among them the word of God" (Acts 18. 11).

(*e*) Lastly, weighty support is given to these conclusions by the position *Hebrews* occupies in the four most important MSS., ℵ, A, B, C, and in others. In some MSS. *Hebrews* is found in different positions with regard to the other books of the New Testament. In certain it appears as it stands in our Bibles, but in these four, ℵ (*Codex Sinaiticus*), A (*Codex Alexandrinus*), B (*Codex Vaticanus*), and C (*Codex Ephraemi*), it is placed after 2 *Thessalonians*. This testimony to the foregoing is significant, and is not to be lightly set aside.

THE EPISTLE OF PAUL THE APOSTLE

TO THE

HEBREWS.

A A **1** °GOD, Who °at sundry times and °in
divers manners °spake °in time past °unto
the fathers °by the °prophets,
2 °Hath °in these last days [1]spoken [1]unto
us [1]by *His* °Son,
B a Whom He °hath appointed Heir of all things,
°by Whom °also He °made the °worlds;
3 Who being the °brightness of *His* °glory,
and the °express image of His °person, and
upholding all things by the °word of His
°power, °when He had °by Himself purged
°our °sins, sat down °on the right hand of the
°Majesty °on °high;
b 4 °Being made so much better than the angels,
as He °hath by inheritance obtained a °more
excellent °name °than they.
5 °For [1]unto which of the angels said He at
any time, "**Thou art My [2]Son, this day have I**
°begotten Thee"? And again, "**I will be to**
Him °a °Father, and He shall be to Me °a
[2]Son"?
6 °And again, when He bringeth in the °First-
begotten °into the °world, He saith, "**And let**
all the angels of [1]God °worship Him."
7 And °of the angels He saith, "**Who maketh**
His angels °spirits, and His °ministers a flame
of fire."
a 8 But °unto the [2]Son *He saith,* "**Thy throne,**
O °God, *is* °for ever and ever: °a °sceptre of
°righteousness *is* the sceptre of Thy kingdom.
9 Thou °hast loved °righteousness, and °hated
°iniquity; °therefore [1]God, *even* Thy [1]God,
°hath °anointed Thee with the oil of gladness
°above Thy °fellows."
10 And, "**Thou, °LORD, °in the beginning**
°hast laid the foundation of the °earth; and
the °heavens are the works of Thine hands:

TITLE, The. Most texts read "To Hebrews". Cp. Matt. Title, and *v.* 1.

1. 1—2. 18 (A, p. 1822). DOCTRINAL INTRODUCTION. (*Alternation.*)

A | A | 1. 1, 2-. God speaking.
  B | -2-14. Son of God. Better than angels.
 A | 2. 1-4. God speaking.
  B | 2. 5-18. Son of Man. Lower than angels.

1 God. Ap. 98. I. i. 1.
at sundry times = in many portions. Gr. *polumerōs.* Only here.
in divers manners = in many ways. Gr. *polutropōs.* Only here.
spake. Gr. *laleō.* Ap. 121. 7.
in time past = of old. Gr. *palai.* Elsewhere, Matt. 11. 21. Mark 15. 44. Luke 10. 13. 2 Pet. 1. 9. Jude 4.
unto = to.
by = in. Gr. *en.* Ap. 104. viii.
prophets. Ap. 189.
2 Hath . . . spoken = Spake.
in . . . days = at the end of these days. I.e. at the period closed by the ministry of John.
in. Gr. *epi.* Ap. 104. ix. 1.
Son. Gr. *huios.* Ap. 108. iii. No article, but its absence only "more emphatically and definitely expresses the exclusive character of His Sonship". See 5. 8.

1. -2-14 (B, above). SON OF GOD. BETTER THAN ANGELS. (*Alternation.*)

B | a | -2, 3. Glory of His Person and work.
  b | 4-7. Superiority over angels.
 a | 8-12. Glory of His character and eternal being.
  b | 13, 14. Superiority over angels.

hath. Omit. **by.** Gr. *dia.* Ap. 104. v. 1.
also. Read after "worlds".
made. Or, prepared.
worlds. Gr. *aiōn.* Ap. 129. 2 and 151. II. A. i. Cp. 11. 3.
3 brightness = effulgence. Gr. *apaugasma.* Only here. Cp. Wisdom 7. 26. **glory.** See p. 1511.
express image. Gr. *charaktēr.* Only here. The word means the exact impression as when metal is pressed into a die, or as a seal upon wax. **person** = substance. Gr. *hupostasis.* See 2 Cor. 9. 4. **word** Gr. *rhēma.* See Mark 9. 32. **power.** Gr. *dunamis.* Ap. 172. 1. **when, &c.** = having made purification of. **by Himself.** The texts omit. **our.** The texts omit. **sins.** Gr. *hamartia.* Ap. 128. I. ii. 1. **on.** Gr. *en.* Ap. 104. viii. **Majesty.** Gr. *megalōsunē.* Only here, 8. 1. Jude 25. **high.** Cp. Ps. 93. 4; 113. 4. **4 Being made** = Having become. **hath . . . obtained** = hath inherited. **more excellent.** Gr. *diaphoros.* See Rom. 12. 6. **name.** Cp. Acts 2. 21; 3. 16. Isa. 9. 6. **than.** Gr. *para.* Ap. 104. xii. 3. **5 For . . . Thee?** Fig. *Erotēsis.* Ap. 6. **begotten, &c.** = brought Thee to the birth. I.e. at resurrection, when the Son became the glorified federal Head of a new order of beings. Cp. 5. 5; Acts 13. 33. Rom. 1. 4, with 1 Cor. 15. 45, &c., and Ps. 2. 7 (Sept.). **a** = for (Gr. *eis*) a. Quoted from Ps. 2. 7, which, with Acts 13. 33, tells us that this day was the day of His resurrection. **Father.** Ap. 98. III. **6 And, &c.** Read, "But when He again shall have brought in". Cp. 1 Thess. 4. 14. **Firstbegotten.** Gr. *prōtotokos.* See Rom. 8. 29. Col. 1. 15. **into.** Gr. *eis.* Ap. 104. vi. **world.** Gr. *oikoumenē.* Ap. 129. 3. **worship** Gr. *proskuneō.* Ap. 137. 1. Quoted from Deut. 32. 43, which in the Sept. reads, "Rejoice, ye heavens, together with Him, and let all the angels of God worship Him. Rejoice, ye nations, with His people, &c." **7 of** = with reference to. Gr. *pros.* Ap. 104. xv. 3. **spirits.** Ap. 101 II. 11. **ministers.** Gr. *leitourgos.* Ap. 190. I. 4. This verse is from the Sept. of Ps. 104. 4. **8 unto.** Gr. *pros,* as *v.* 7. **God.** Ap. 98. I. i. 2. **for ever, &c.** Ap. 151. II. A. ii. 6. **a** = the. **sceptre.** Cp. Ps. 2. 9. Rev. 2. 27. **righteousness** = rightness. Gr. *euthutēs.* See Ap. 191. 3. **9 hast loved** = lovedst. Gr. *agapaō.* Ap. 135. I. 1. **righteousness.** Gr. *dikaiosunē.* Ap. 191. 3. **hated** = hatedst. **iniquity.** Gr. *anomia.* Ap. 128. III. 4. **therefore** = because of (Ap. 104. v. 2) this. **hath.** Omit. **anointed.** Cp. Luke 4. 18. Acts 4. 27; 10. 38. 2 Cor. 1. 21. **above.** Gr. *para,* as *v.* 4. **fellows.** Gr. *metochos.* Here, 3. 1, 14; 6. 4; 12. 8, and Luke 5. 7. Quoted from Ps. 45. 6, 7. Of no other could this be said. **10 LORD.** Ap. 98. VI. i. *β.* 1. B. a. **in the beginning.** Gr. *kat' archas.* See John 1. 1. **hast . . . foundation.** Lit. didst found. Gr. *themelioō.* Ap. 146. **earth.** Gr. *gē.* Ap. 129. 4. **heavens.** See Matt. 6. 9, 10.

11 They shall perish; but Thou °remainest; and they all shall °wax old as doth a garment;
12 And as a °vesture shalt Thou °fold them up, and they shall be °changed: but Thou art the same, and Thy years shall °not °fail."

b 13 But °to which of the angels said He at any time, "**Sit °on My right hand, until I make Thine enemies °Thy footstool**"?

14 Are they °not all °ministering [7]spirits, °sent forth °to minister °for them who °shall be heirs of salvation?

A **2** °Therefore we ought to °give the more earnest heed to the things which we have heard, °lest °at any time we should let *them* slip.

2 For °if the °word °spoken °by angels was °stedfast, and every °transgression and °disobedience received a °just °recompence of reward;

3 How shall we escape, °if we neglect so great salvation, °which at the first began to be [2]spoken [2]by the °Lord, °and was °confirmed °unto us °by them that heard *Him;*

4 °God also °bearing *them* witness, both with °signs and °wonders, and with divers °miracles, and °gifts of the °Holy Ghost, °according to His own °will?

B C 5 °For °unto the angels hath He °not put in subjection the °world to come, °whereof we [2]speak.

6 But °one in a certain place °testified, saying, "**What is °man, that Thou °art mindful of him? or the °Son of °Man, that Thou °visitest Him?**

D **7 Thou °madest Him °a little lower °than °the angels; Thou °crownedst Him with °glory and honour, and didst set Him °over the works of Thy hands:**

8 Thou hast [5]put all things in subjection under His feet." For °in that He [5]put all in subjection under Him, He left °nothing *that is* °not put under Him.

E But °now we °see °not yet all things °put under Him.

C 9 But we °see °Jesus, Who was [7]made [7]a little lower [7]than [7]the angels, °for the suffering of death, [7]crowned with [7]glory and honour,

---

11 remainest. Gr. *diamenō*. See Gal. 2. 5.
wax old. Gr. *palaioō*. Only here, 8. 13. Luke 12. 33.
12 vesture. Gr. *peribolaion*. Only here and 1 Cor. 11. 15.
fold . . . up = roll . . . up. Gr. *helissō*. Only here. But see Rev. 6. 14.
changed. Gr. *allassō*. See Acts 6. 14.
not. Gr. *ou*. Ap. 105. I.
fail. Gr. *ekleipō*. Only here, and Luke 16. 9; 22. 32.
Verses 10–12 are from Ps. 102. 25–27.
13 to. Gr. *pros*. Ap. 104. xv. 3.
on. Gr. *ek*. Ap. 104. vii.
Thy footstool = a footstool (Gr. *hupopodion*) of Thy feet. See Matt. 22. 44. Cited from Ps. 110. 1.
14 not. Ap. 105. I (a).
ministering. Gr. *leitourgikos*. Only here. Cp. 1. 7 and Ap. 191. II. 4.
sent forth. Gr. *apostellō*. Ap. 174. 1.
to minister = for (Gr. *eis*) ministry (Gr. *diakonia*. Ap. 190. II. 1).
for = on account of. Gr. *dia*. Ap. 104. v. 2.
shall be heirs = are about to inherit; cp. *v.* 4.

2. 1 Therefore = On account of (Gr. *dia*. Ap. 104. v. 2) this.
give, &c. Lit. give heed more abundantly.
lest. Gr. *mē*. Ap. 105. II.
lest . . . slip = lest . . . we should let glide away. Gr. *pararreō*. Lit. flow beside. Only here.
at any time = haply.
2 if. Gr. *ei*. Ap. 118. 2. a.
word. Gr. *logos*. Ap. 121. 10.
spoken. Gr. *laleō*. Ap. 121. 7.
by. Gr. *dia*. Ap. 104. v. 1.
stedfast. Gr. *bebaios*. See Rom. 4. 16. Cp. *v.* 3.
transgression. Gr. *parabasis*. See Rom. 2. 23. Cp. Ap. 128. VI. 1.
disobedience. Gr. *parakoē*. Ap. 128. V. 2.
just. Gr. *endikos*. See Ap. 191. 1.
recompence, &c. Gr. *misthapodosia*. Only here, 10. 35; 11. 26. Cp. 11. 6.
3 if we neglect = neglecting. Gr. *ameleō*. See 1 Tim. 4. 14.
which, &c. Lit. receiving a beginning.
Lord. Ap. 98. VI. i. β. 2. A. and. Omit.
confirmed. Gr. *bebaioō*. See Rom. 15. 8.
unto. Gr. *eis*. Ap. 104. vi.
by. Gr. *hupo*. Ap. 104. xviii. 1.
4 God. Ap. 98. I. i. 1.
bearing . . . witness = bearing witness with. Gr. *sunepimartureō*. Only here.
signs, wonders, miracles. See Ap. 176, 3, 2, 1.
gifts = distributions. Gr. *merismos*. Only here and 4. 12. Holy Ghost. Ap. 101. II. 14.
according to. Gr. *kata*. Ap. 104. x. 2.
will. Gr. *thelēsis*. Only here. Cp. Ap. 102. 2.

2. 5–18 [For Structure see below].

5 For, &c. Read, "For not (Ap. 105. I) to angels did He subject". unto = to.
world. Gr. *oikoumenē*. Ap. 129. 3. Cp. 1. 6.

2. 5–18 (*B*, p. 1824). SON OF MAN. LOWER THAN ANGELS. (*Alternation.*)

B | C | 5, 6. God's purpose. Not angels, but man, to have dominion.
  D | 7, 8–. Man's equipment for dominion.
   E | –8. First Adam's failure.
 C | 9–. Purpose fulfilled in the Lord Jesus.
  D | –9–18. His fitness for dominion.

whereof = concerning (Gr. *peri*. Ap. 104. xiii. i) which. **6** one. Ap. 123. 3. testified. Gr. *diamarturomai*. See Acts 2. 40. man. Gr. *anthrōpos*. Ap. 123. 1. art mindful. Gr. *mimnēskomai*. Cp. 13. 3. Son of Man. See Ap. 98. XVI. No article. visitest. Gr. *episkeptomai*. Ap. 133. III. 5. **7** madest . . . lower. Gr. *elattoō*. Only here, *v.* 9, and John 3. 30 (decrease). a little = for a little while. than. Gr. *para*. See 1. 4. the. Omit. crownedst. Gr. *stephanoō*. See 2 Tim. 2. 5. glory. See p. 1511. over. Gr. *epi*. Ap. 104. ix. 3. Cited from Ps. 8. 4–6. **8** in. Gr. *en*. Ap. 104. viii. nothing. Gr. *oudeis*. not, &c. Gr. *anupotaktos*. See 1 Tim. 1. 9. This is said by Fig. *Prolēpsis*, or Anticipation. Ap. 6. now. Emph. see. Gr. *horaō*. Ap. 133. I. 8. not yet. Gr. *oupō*. put under = subjected to. **9** see. Gr. *blepō*. Ap. 133. I. 5. Read, "see Him Who was made . . . angels, even Jesus". Jesus. Ap. 98. X. for . . . honour. Parenthesis (Ap. 6) inserted. Omit the comma after "death". for = because of. Gr. *dia*. Ap. 104. v. 2.

D c that He by the °grace of [4]God should taste death °for every man.

d **10** For it became Him, [9-] for Whom *are* °all things, and [2]by Whom *are* °all things, in bringing many °sons [3]unto glory, to °make the °Captain of their salvation perfect °through sufferings.

11 For both He That sanctifieth and they who are sanctified *are* all °of °One: [9-]for which cause He is [5]not ashamed to call them °brethren,

12 Saying, "**I will °declare Thy Name [5]unto My brethren, [8]in the midst of the °church will I °sing praise unto Thee.**"

13 And again, "**I will °put my trust °in Him.**" And again, °"**Behold, I and the °children which [4]God °hath given Me.**"

c **14** Forasmuch then as the [13]children are partakers of °flesh and blood, °He also Himself °likewise °took part of °the same; °that [10]through death He might °destroy him °that had the °power of death, that is, the devil;

15 And °deliver them who °through fear of death were °all their lifetime °subject to °bondage.

16 For °verily He °took [5]not on *Him the nature of* angels; but He °took on *Him* the seed of Abraham.

d **17** Wherefore °in all things it behoved Him to be made like [5]unto *His* brethren, [14]that He might °be a merciful and °faithful °High Priest in things °*pertaining* to [4]God, °to °make reconciliation for the °sins of the °people.

18 For °in that He Himself hath suffered being °tempted, He is able to °succour them that are °tempted.

B C F e **3** Wherefore, °holy °brethren, °partakers of the °heavenly °calling, °consider the °Apostle and High Priest of our °profession, °Christ °Jesus;

f **2** Who was °faithful to Him That appointed Him, as °also Moses *was faithful* °in all His house.

g **3** For °this *Man* was °counted worthy of more °glory °than [2]Moses, inasmuch as he who

---

2. -9-18 (*D*, p. 1825). FITNESS FOR DOMINION. (*Alternation.*)

D | c | -9. Vicarious death.
  d | 10-13. Perfected by experience of suffering.
  c | 14-16. Victorious death.
  d | 17, 18. Qualified by experience of trials.

grace. Gr. *charis.* Ap. 184. I. 1.
for. Gr. *huper.* Ap. 104. xvii. 1.
10 all things. Cp. Rom. 11. 36. Eph. 3. 9. Col. 1. 17.
sons. Gr. *huios.* Ap. 108. iii.
make . . . perfect. Gr. *teleioō.* Ap. 125. 2.
Captain. Gr. *archēgos.* See Acts 3. 15.
through. Gr. *dia.* Ap. 104. v. 1.
11 of. Gr. *ek.* Ap. 104. vii.
One. I. e. God.
brethren. The Lord's condescension does not justify the irreverence of calling Him our "elder Brother".
12 declare. Gr. *apangellō.* See Acts 4. 23.
church. Gr. *ekklēsia.* Ap. 186.
sing praise unto. Gr. *humneō.* See Acts 16. 25. Cited from Ps. 22. 22. The Fig. *Pleonasm* (Ap. 6).
13 put my trust. Gr. *peithō.* Ap. 150. I. 2.
in = upon. Gr. *epi.* Ap. 104. ix. 2. Cited from 2 Sam. 22. 3.
Behold. Gr. *idou.* Ap. 133. I. 2.
children. Gr. *paidion.* Ap. 108. v.
hath given = gave. Cited from Isa. 8. 18.
14 flesh and blood. The texts read "blood and flesh". In *Hebrews* flesh is never used in the moral sense of Rom. 7. 18, but always of natural body.
He, &c. = Himself also.
likewise. Gr. *paraplēsiōs.* Only here. Cp. Phil. 2. 27.
took part. Gr. *metechō.* See 1 Cor. 9. 10.
the same. The same (things), i. e. flesh and blood, not the same flesh and blood, which had become corrupted by Adam's sin. "This same Jesus" was a direct creation of God. Cp. Luke 1. 35.
that = in order that. Gr. *hina.*
destroy. Gr. *katargeō.* See Luke 13. 7.
that had = holding.
power. Gr. *kratos.* Ap. 172. 2.
15 deliver. Gr. *apallassō.* See Acts 19. 12.
through. No prep. Dat. case.
all = through (Gr. *dia*) all.
subject to. Gr. *enochos.* See Matt. 26. 66.
bondage. Gr. *douleia.* Ap. 190. II. 2.
16 verily = certainly. Gr. *dēpou.* Only here.
took, &c. = taketh not (Ap. 105. I) hold of angels.
took. Gr. *epilambanomai.* First occ. Matt. 14. 31. Cp. Acts 9. 27.
17 in = according to, as in *v.* 4. **be** = become.
faithful. Gr. *pistos.* Ap. 150. III.
High Priest. Occ. very frequently in Gospels and Acts; seventeen times in Hebrews; and nowhere else after Acts. A significant silence.

pertaining **to.** Gr. *pros.* Ap. 104. xv. 3. **to.** Gr. *eis*, as *v.* 3. **make reconciliation.** Gr. *hilaskomai.* See Luke 18. 13 and Ap. 196. **sins.** Gr. *hamartia.* Ap. 128. I. ii. 1. **people.** Gr. *laos.* See Acts 2. 47. **18 in that** = wherein. **tempted** = tried or tested. Cp. Matt. 4. 1 and Luke 22. 23. **succour.** Cp. 2 Cor. 6. 2.

3. 1—4. 13 (**B C**, p. 1822). THE MISSION OF CHRIST. (*Introversion.*)

B C | F | 3. 1-6-. The Apostle and High Priest.
  G | 3. -6-19. Warning.
  F | 4. 1-13. The Rest-giver.

3. 1-6- (F, above). THE APOSTLE, &c. (*Introversion.*)

F | e | 1. Christ.
  f | 2. His faithfulness.
  g | 3. Greater than Moses.
  g | 4. Reason.
  f | 5. Moses' faithfulness.
  e | 6-. The Son.

3. 1 holy. See Acts 9. 13. **brethren.** I. e. of one another. **partakers.** Gr. *metochos.* See 1. 9. **heavenly.** Gr. *epouranios.* See John 3. 12. **calling.** Cp. 12. 25. **consider.** Ap. 133. II. 4. **Apostle.** Only here applied to the Lord. Ap. 189. **profession.** Gr. *homologia.* See 2 Cor. 9. 13. **Christ.** The texts omit. **Jesus.** Ap. 98. X. **2 faithful.** Gr. *pistos.* Ap. 150. III. **also Moses** = Moses also. See Rom. 5. 14. The name occ. eleven times in Hebrews. **in.** Gr. *en.* Ap. 104. viii. **3 this** *Man* = He. **counted worthy.** Gr. *axioō.* See Acts 15. 38. **glory.** See p. 1511. **than.** Gr. *para.* See 1. 4.

°hath builded the house hath more honour than the house.

g 4 For every house is builded [3]by °some *man;* but He That built all things *is* °God.

f 5 And [2]Moses verily *was* [2]faithful [2]in all His house, as a °servant, °for a testimony of those things which were °to be spoken after;

e 6 But °Christ as °a Son °over His °own house;

G h Whose house are **we**, °if we °hold fast the °confidence and the °rejoicing of the hope °firm unto the end.

i 7 Wherefore (as the °Holy Ghost saith, **"To day [6]if ye °will hear His voice,**

8 °Harden °not your hearts, as [2]in the °provocation, °in the day of temptation [2]in the wilderness:

k **9 When your fathers tempted Me, °proved Me, and °saw My works forty years.**

l **10 Wherefore I was °grieved with °that °generation, and said, They do °alway err in *their* heart; and they °have °not known My ways.**

m **11 So I sware [2]in My wrath, °They shall not enter °into My °rest.")**

n 12 °Take heed, brethren, °lest there be [2]in °any of you an °evil heart of unbelief, [2]in °departing °from the °living [4]God.

13 But °exhort one another °daily, while it is called To day; °lest [12]any °of you be [8]hardened through the °deceitfulness of °sin.

h 14 For we °are made [1]partakers of [6]Christ, [6]if we [6]hold the °beginning of our °confidence °stedfast unto the end;

i 15 °While it is said, **"To day [6]if ye will hear His voice, [8]harden [8]not your hearts, as [2]in the [8]provocation."**

k 16 For °some, °when they had heard, did °provoke: howbeit [10]not all that came °out of Egypt °by [2]Moses.

l 17 But with whom was He [10]grieved forty years? *was it* °not with them that °had °sinned, whose °carcases fell [2]in the wilderness?

m 18 And to whom sware He that they should [8]not enter [11]into His [11]rest, °but to them that °believed not?

n 19 °So we °see that they could [10]not enter in °because of unbelief.

F H L **4** Let us therefore fear, °lest, a promise being left *us* of entering °into His °rest, °any °of you should seem to °come short of it.

hath builded = built. Gr. *kataskeuazō.* Occ. eleven times. Six in Heb., four in Gospels ("prepare"). See Matt. 11. 10; &c.

4 by. Gr. *hupo.* Ap. 104. xviii. 1.

some *man* = some one. Gr. *tis.* Ap. 123. 3.

God. Ap. 98. I. i. 1.

5 servant. Gr. *therapōn.* Ap. 190. I. 8. Used of Moses. Ex. 14. 31 (Sept.). **for.** Gr. *eis.* Ap. 104. vi.

to be spoken after = about to be spoken. Gr. *laleō.* Ap. 121. 7. **6 Christ.** Ap. 98. IX.

a Son = Son. Ap. 108. iii, and see 1. 2.

over. Gr. *epi.* Ap. 104. ix. 3. **own.** Omit.

3. -6-19 (G, p. 1826). **WARNING.**

(Extended Alternation.)

G | h | -6. Condition of belonging to the Lord's house.
  i | 7, 8. "Harden not."
   k | 9. Provocation.
    l | 10. God grieved.
     m | 11. God's oath.
      n | 12, 13. Unbelief.
 h | 14. Condition of being partakers of Christ.
  i | 15. "Harden not."
   k | 16. Provocation.
    l | 17. God grieved.
     m | 18. God's oath.
      n | 19. Unbelief.

if. Gr. *ean.* Ap. 118. 1. b.

hold fast. Gr. *katechō.* See 2 Thess. 2. 6.

confidence. Gr. *parrhēsia.* See Acts 4. 13; 28. 31.

rejoicing. Gr. *kauchēma.* See Rom. 4. 2.

firm. Same as "stedfast", *v.* 14.

7 Holy Ghost. Ap. 101. II. 3. **will** = should.

8 Harden. Gr. *sklērunō.* See Acts 19. 9.

not. Ap. 105. II.

provocation. Gr. *parapikrasmos.* Only here and *v.* 15. Used in the Sept. in Ps. 95. 8, from which this is quoted. Cp. *v.* 16. **in** = according to. Gr. *kata.* Ap. 104. x. 2.

9 proved. Gr. *dokimazō,* to put to the test, but the texts read *en dokimasia,* in, or by, a testing.

saw. Gr. *eidon.* Ap. 133. I. 1.

10 grieved. Gr. *prosochthizō.* Only here and *v.* 17. Many times in the Sept., including Ps. 95. 10, whence this is quoted. **that.** The texts read "this".

generation. Gr. *genea,* nation, or race. Primarily of those in wilderness, prophetically of whole race.

alway. Ap. 151. II. F. ii.

have . . . known = knew. Gr. *ginōskō.* Ap. 132. I. ii.

not. Gr. *ou.* Ap. 105. I.

11 They, &c. Lit. If (Ap. 118. 2. a) they shall.

into. Gr. *eis.* Ap. 104. vi.

rest. Gr. *katapausis.* See Acts 7. 49.

12 Take heed. Gr. *blepō.* Ap. 133. I. 5.

lest. Gr. *mē.* Ap. 105. II.

any = any one. Gr. *tis.* Ap. 123. 3.

evil. Gr. *ponēros.* Ap. 128. III. 1.

departing = falling away. Cp. Luke 8. 13. 1 Tim. 4. 1.

from. Gr. *apo.* Ap. 104. iv.

living God. See 9. 14; 10. 31; 12. 32. Acts 14. 15. Cp. Deut. 5. 26.

13 exhort. Gr. *parakaleō.* Ap. 134. I. 6.

daily. Lit. according to (Gr. *kata,* as *v.* 8) each day.

lest = in order that (Gr. *hina*) not (Gr. *mē*).

of. Ap. 104. vii.

deceitfulness. Gr. *apatē.* See Eph. 4. 22.

sin. Gr. *hamartia.* Ap. 128. I. ii. 1.

14 are made = have become. **beginning.** Gr. *archē.* See Ap. 172. 6. **confidence.** Gr. *hupostasis.* See 1. 3. **stedfast.** See *v.* 6 and 2. 2. **15 While, &c.** Lit. In (Gr. *en*) its being said. I. e. the exhortation of *v.* 13 is to them. Cp. *vv.* 7, 8. **16 some.** Gr. *tines.* Ap. 124. 4. **when . . . heard** = having heard. **provoke.** Gr. *parapikrainō.* Only here. Often in the Sept. **out of.** Gr. *ek.* Ap. 104. vii. **by.** Gr. *dia.* Ap. 104. v. 1. **17 not.** Gr. *ouchi.* Ap. 105. I (a). **had.** Omit. **sinned.** Gr. *hamartanō.* Ap. 128. I. i. **carcases.** Gr. *kōlon.* Only here. See Num. 14. 29 (Sept.). **18 but** = if not. Gr. *ei mē.* **believed not** = disbelieved or disobeyed. Gr. *apeitheō.* Cp. Ap. 128. V. 1, and Rom. 2. 8; 10. 21. **19 So** = And. **see.** Gr. *blepō,* as in *v.* 12. **because of.** Gr. *dia.* Ap. 104. v. 2.

4. 1-13 [For Structure see next page].

4. 1 lest = lest haply. Gr. *mēpote.* **into.** Gr. *eis.* Ap. 104. vi. **rest.** Gr. *katapausis.* See Acts 7. 49. **any.** Gr. *tis.* Ap. 123. 3. **of.** Gr. *ek.* Ap. 104. vii. **come short** = have failed. Gr. *hustereō.* See Rom. 3. 23.

M 2 For °unto us was the gospel preached, °as
well as unto them: but the °word °preached
did °not profit them, °not being °mixed with
°faith in them that heard *it*.

J o 3 For we which °have °believed do enter
[1]into [1]rest, as He said, **"As I have sworn °in**
My wrath, °if they shall enter [1]into My [1]rest:"
although the works were finished °from the
°foundation of the °world.

4 For He °spake in a certain place °of the
seventh *day* on this wise, **"And °God did °rest**
°the seventh day [3]from all His works."

5 And [3]in this *place* again, [3]**"If they shall**
enter [1]into My [1]rest."

p 6 Seeing therefore it remaineth that °some
must enter °therein, and they °to whom it was
first preached entered [2-]not in °because of
°unbelief:

7 °Again, He °limiteth a certain day, saying
[3]in °David, **"To day,"** °after so long a time;
as it is said, **"To day °if ye will hear His voice,**
°harden [-2]not your hearts."

8 For [3]if °Jesus °had given them rest, then
would He [2-]not °afterward have °spoken [4]of
°another day.

o 9 There remaineth therefore a °rest to the
°people of [4]God.

10 For he that is entered [1]into his [1]rest, he
also hath °ceased [3]from his °own works, as
[4]God *did* [3]from °His.

H L 11 Let us °labour therefore to enter [1]into that
[1]rest, °lest [1]any man fall °after the same
°example of [6]unbelief.

M q 12 For the [2]word of [4]God

r *is* °quick, and °powerful, and °sharper °than
any °twoedged °sword,

s °piercing even to the °dividing asunder of
°soul and °spirit, and of the °joints and °marrow, and

r *is* a °discerner of the °thoughts and °intents
of the heart.

4. 1-13 (*F*, p. 1826). THE REST-GIVER.
(*Alternation and Introversion.*)

F | H | L | 1. Exhortation. "Let us fear, lest."
M | 2. Reason. The Word of God.
J | o | 3, 4, 5. God's rest and its character.
p | 6, 7, 8. Perfect rest future.
o | 9, 10. Rest for God's people, and its character.
H | *L* | 11. Exhortation. "Let us labour, lest."
M | 12, 13. Reason. God and His Word.

2 unto us, &c. = we also were evangelized. Gr. *euangelizō*. Ap. 121. 4. **as, &c.** = as they also (were).
word. Gr. *logos*. Ap. 121. 10.
preached = of hearing. Gr. *akoē*. Ap. 121. 9.
not. Gr. *ou*. Ap. 105. I.
not. Gr. *mē*. Ap. 105. II.
mixed. Gr. *sunkerannumi*. Only here and 1 Cor. 12. 24. The texts prefer the acc. pl. of this word, agreeing with "them", rather than the nom. sing. agreeing with "word". There is the addition of one letter in the Gr. Read "them, since they were not united by faith to those that heard".
faith. Gr. *pistis*. Ap. 150. II. 1. Occ. thirty-two times in Heb. See Ap. 10.
3 have. Omit.
believed. Gr. *pisteuō*. Ap. 150. I. 1. i.
in. Gr. *en*. Ap. 104. viii. **if, &c.** See 3. 11.
from. Gr. *apo*. Ap. 104. iv.
foundation. See Ap. 146.
world. Gr. *kosmos*. Ap. 129. 1.
4 spake = hath said.
of. Gr. *peri*. Ap. 104. xiii. 1. **God.** Ap. 98. I. i. 1.
rest. Gr. *katapauō*. See Acts 14. 18. Quoted from Gen. 2. 2. **the seventh, &c.** = on (Gr. *en*) the seventh, &c.
6 some. Gr. *tines*. Ap. 124. 4.
therein = into (Gr. *eis*) it.
to whom, &c. = who were first evangelized. See *v.* 2.
because of. Gr. *dia*. Ap. 104. v. 2. Cp. 3. 19.
unbelief = disobedience. Gr. *apeitheia*. See Rom. 11. 30. Eph. 2. 2; &c.
7 Again, &c. Read Again (seeing), &c. Fig. *Ellipsis*. Ap. 6.
limiteth = defineth. Gr. *horizō*. See Acts 2. 23.
David. In Ps. 95. 7, 8. Pss. 92-99 (with the exception of 94) are used on "the Inauguration of the Sabbath".
after, &c. = so long after.
after. Gr. *meta*. Ap. 104. xi. 2.
if. Gr. *ean*. Ap. 118. 1. b.

harden. See 3. 8. **8 Jesus** = Joshua. Cp. Acts 7. 45. **had given . . . rest** = caused . . . to rest. Gr. *katapauō*, as *v.* 4. **afterward** = after (Gr. *meta*) these things. **spoken.** Gr. *laleō*. Ap. 121. 7. **another.** Ap. 124. 1. **9 rest** = a Rest Day. I. e. the great day of "rest" under the rule of the great "Priest (King) upon His throne". See Zech. 6. 13. Gr. *sabbatismos*. Only here. The verb *sabbatizō*, to keep sabbath, occ. several times in the Sept. **people.** Gr. *laos*. See Acts 2. 47, and cp. Gal. 6. 16. **10 ceased** = rested, as *v.* 4. **own.** Omit. **His.** Add "own". **11 labour.** Gr. *spoudazō*. See Gal. 2. 10. **lest.** Gr. *hina mē*, as 3. 13. **after** = in. Gr. *en*. Ap. 104. viii. **example.** Gr. *hupodeigma*. See John 13. 15.

4. 12, 13 (*M*, above). REASON. GOD AND HIS WORD. (*Introversion.*)

M | q | 12-. God Whose Word is wonderful.
r | -12-. What His Word is. Living, powerful, a sharp sword.
s | -12-. What His Word does. Pierces, divides asunder.
r | -12. What His Word is. A critic of the heart.
q | 13. God Whose eye sees all.

12 quick = living. Gr. *zaō*. Cp. Ap. 170. 1. **powerful.** Gr. *energēs*. See 1 Cor. 16. 9, and cp. Ap. 172. 4. **sharper.** Gr. *tomōteros*. Only here. **than** = above. Gr. *huper*. Ap. 104. xvii. 2. **twoedged.** Gr. *distomos*. Only here and Rev. 1. 16; 2. 12. **sword.** Gr. *machaira*. Same word Eph. 6. 17, but not Luke 2. 35. Rev. 1. 16; &c. **piercing.** Gr. *diikneomai*. Only here. **dividing asunder.** Gr. *merismos*. See 2. 4. **soul.** Ap. 110. III. 2. and 170. 3. **spirit.** Ap. 101. II. 6. **joints.** Gr. *harmos*. Only here. **marrow.** Gr. *muelos*. Only here. **discerner.** Gr. *kritikos*. Only here. **thoughts.** Gr. *enthumēsis*. See Acts 17. 29. **intents.** Gr. *ennoia*. Only here and 1 Pet. 4. 1. The *written* Word *is* a sword (cp. Eph. 6. 17), and the *living* Word *has* a sword (Rev. 1. 16; 19. 15). Once, and once only, has God used the word *kritikos*; thus confining it to His own Word as a "critic". That Word is to be man's Judge (John 12. 48. Cp. Ap. 122 and 177). Yet man claims the word "critic" and dares to sit in judgment on that very Word which is to judge him, in what he terms "higher criticism", which is only human reasoning based on the deceit of his own heart (Jer. 23. 26). "In the last day" man will be criticized (judged) by the same Word on which he now sits in judgment. "Dividing asunder of soul and spirit" means not only differentiating between that which is begotten of the flesh and that which is begotten of the Spirit (John 3. 6) in the individual; but also between the natural (Gr. *psuchikos*) man and the spiritual (Gr. *pneumatikos*) man. See 1 Cor. 2. 13-15.

q 13 °Neither is there any creature °that is not manifest °in His sight: but all things *are* naked and °opened °unto the eyes of Him °with Whom °we have to do.

D t 14 °Seeing then that we have a great °High Priest, That is °passed into the °heavens, °Jesus the °Son of [4]God,

u let us hold fast *our* °profession.

t 15 For we have [2-]not an [14]high priest °which cannot °be touched with the feeling of our °infirmities; but was °in all points °tempted °like as *we are, yet* °without °sin.

u 16 Let us therefore °come °boldly [13]unto the throne of °grace, °that we may °obtain °mercy, and find °grace °to help in time of need.

B C N v **5** For every high priest taken °from among °men is ordained °for °men in things °*pertaining* to °God,

w °that he may °offer both gifts and sacrifices °for °sins:

x 2 °Who can °have compassion on the °ignorant, and on °them that are out of the way;

x for that he himself also is °compassed with °infirmity.

w 3 And °by reason hereof he ought, as °for the °people, so °also °for himself, to [1]offer °for [1]sins.

v 4 And °no man taketh this honour °unto himself, but °he that is °called °of [1]God, °as *was* Aaron.

13 Neither, &c. = And there is not (Gr. *ou*) a created thing. See Rom. 8. 39.
that, &c. Lit. not manifested. Gr. *aphanēs.* Only here. Cp. Ap. 106. I. i.
in His sight = before His eyes. The Divine X-rays allow nothing to be hidden. Fig. *Anthrōpopatheia.* Ap. 6.
opened. Gr. *trachēlizomai.* Only here. This word in classical Gr. is used of bending back the neck (*trachēlos*) of animals to be sacrificed, and may refer to the separating of the victim into its parts. See Lev. 1. 6–9; &c.
unto = to.
with. Gr. *pros.* Ap. 104. xv. 3.
we have to do. Lit. is our account (Gr. *logos,* as v. 2).

4. 14-16 (**D**, p. 1822). GENERAL APPLICATION. (*Alternation.*)

D | t | 14-. Our great High Priest. The Son of God.
u | -14. Exhortation based upon it.
t | 15. Our great High Priest. The Son of Man.
u | 16. Exhortation based upon it.

14 Seeing . . . have = Having therefore.
High Priest. See 2. 17.
passed into = passed through. Same word as in 1 Cor. 10. 1; 16. 5. Cp. 7. 26. Eph. 4. 10.
heavens. See Matt. 6. 9, 10.
Jesus. Ap. 98. X.
Son of God. Ap. 98. XV.
profession. See 3. 1.
15 which cannot = not (Gr. *mē*) able to.
be touched . . . of = sympathize with. Gr. *sumpatheō.* Only here and 10. 34. Cp. 1 Pet. 3. 8.
infirmities. See John 11. 4, same Gr. word.
in all points. According to (Gr. *kata,* Ap. 104. x. 2) all things.
tempted. Gr. *peirazō.* See 2. 18.
like, &c. Lit. according to (Gr. *kata,* as above) our likeness. Gr. *homoiotēs.* Only here and 7. 15.
without = apart from. Gr. *chōris.*
sin. Gr. *hamartia.* Ap. 128. I. ii. 1.
16 come = draw near. Gr. *proserchomai.* A key-word; occ. seven times in Heb.: here, 7. 25; 10. 1, 22; 11. 6; 12. 18, 22. **boldly** = with (Gr. *meta.* Ap. 104. xi. 1) boldness (Gr. *parrhēsia.* See 3. 6). **grace.** Gr. *charis.* Ap. 184. I. 1. **that** = in order that. Gr. *hina.* **obtain** = receive. **mercy.** Gr. *eleos.* Occ. twenty-eight times, twenty-three times associated with God. Cp. Exod. 34. 6, 7. God's own character of Himself, which the O.T. saints delight to quote. Deut. 4. 31. 2 Chron. 30. 9. Neh. 9. 17. Ps. 86. 15; 103. 17; 111. 4; 130. 7; 145. 8. Joel 2. 13. Micah 7. 18, &c. **to help,** &c. = for (Gr. *eis*) seasonable (Gr. *eukairos.* Only here and Mark 6. 21) help (Gr. *boētheia.* Only here and Acts 27. 17).

5. 1—10. 18 (*C*, p. 1822). THE PRIESTHOOD OF CHRIST. (*Introversion and Alternation.*)

C | N | 5. 1-4. Priesthood in general. "For every" (*Pas gar*).
O | P | 5. 5-10. Christ called of God after the order of Melchisedec.
Q | 5. 11—6. 20. Digression before considering Melchisedec as a type.
O | *P* | 7. 1-28. Christ called by God after the order of Melchisedec.
Q | 8. 1, 2. Summation. Christ the Antitype.
N | 8. 3—10. 18. The efficacy of Christ's priesthood in particular. "For every" (*Pas gar*).

5. 1-4 (N, above). PRIESTHOOD IN GENERAL. (*Introversion.*)

N | v | 1-. The ordination of the High Priest.
w | -1. His offering for sins.
x | 2-. His compassion for others' infirmities.
x | -2. The reason; his own infirmities.
w | 3. His offering for sins.
v | 4. The ordination of the High Priest.

1 from among. Gr. *ek.* Ap. 104. vii. **men.** Gr. *anthrōpos.* Ap. 123. 1. **for.** Gr. *huper.* Ap. 104. xvii. 1. *pertaining* **to.** Gr. *pros.* Ap. 104. xv. 3. **God.** Ap. 98. I. i. 1. **that** = in order that. Gr. *hina.* **offer.** Gr. *prospherō.* Occ. twenty times in Hebrews in relation to blood and bloodless "offerings". Elsewhere, only in Gospels and Acts. In the Sept. over a hundred times, eighty times in the Pentateuch. **sins.** Gr. *hamartia.* Ap. 128. I. ii. 1. **2 Who can** = Being able (to). **have compassion on.** Gr. *metriopatheō.* Only here. **ignorant.** Gr. *agnoeō.* Sinners through ignorance. Lev. 4. 2, 22, 27. Num. 15. 28. **them,** &c. = erring (Lev. 5. 1-6, 7). Cp. Ap. 128. VIII. 1. **compassed with.** Gr. *perikeimai.* Here, 12. 1. Mark 9. 42. Luke 17. 2. Acts 28. 20. **infirmity.** See 4. 15. **3 by reason hereof** = on account of (Gr. *dia.* Ap. 104. v. 2) it. See Lev. 4. 3-12. **for** = concerning. Gr. *peri.* Ap. 104. xiii. 1. **people.** See Acts 2. 47. **also,** &c. = for himself also. **for.** The texts read Ap. 104. xiii. 1. **4 no man** = not (Gr. *ou*) any (Gr. *tis*) one. **unto** = to. **he that is.** The texts omit. **called** = when called. **of.** Gr. *hupo.* Ap. 104. xviii. 1. **as,** &c. = even as Aaron also was. Cp. Ex. 28. 1. Num. 3. 10; and contrast Num. 16. 1-40.

P y 5 So °also Christ °glorified °not Himself to
be made °an °High Priest; but He That °said
°unto Him, °"**Thou art My Son, to day have I**
begotten Thee."
6 As He saith °also °in °another *place*,
"**Thou** *art* **a °Priest °for ever °after the °order**
of °Melchisedec."

z 7 Who [6] in the days of His flesh, °when He
had [1] offered up °prayers and °supplications
°with strong °crying and tears [5] unto Him
That was able to save Him [1] from °death, and
was heard °in that He feared;
8 Though He were °a °Son, yet learned He
°obedience °by the things which He suffered;

z 9 And °being made perfect, He became the
°Author of °eternal salvation [4] unto all them
that obey Him;

y 10 °Called [4] of [1] God an High Priest [6] after the
[6] order of [6] Melchisedec.

Q R a 11 °Of Whom we have °many things to say,
and °hard to be uttered, °seeing ye °are °dull
of hearing.

b 12 For when °for the time ye ought to be
teachers, ye have need that °one teach you
again which *be* the °first principles of the
°oracles of [1] God;

c and are become such as have need of °milk,
and [5] not of °strong meat.

c 13 For every one that °useth [12] milk *is* °un-
skilful in the °word of °righteousness: for he
is a °babe.
14 But [12] strong meat belongeth to them
that are °of full age, *even* those who [3] by
reason of °use have their °senses °exercised
°to discern both good and °evil.

b **6** Therefore °leaving the °principles of the
doctrine of °Christ, let us °go on °unto
°perfection; °not °laying again the °founda-

5. 5–10 (P, p. 1829). CHRIST CALLED OF GOD AFTER THE ORDER OF MELCHISEDEC. (*Introversion.*)

P | y | 5, 6. Christ a High Priest.
 z | 7, 8. His salvation and obedience.
 z | 9. His people's salvation and obedience.
 y | 10. Christ a High Priest.

5 also, &c. = Christ (Ap. 98. IX) also.
glorified. See p. 1511. **not.** Ap. 105. I.
an. Omit. **High Priest.** See 2. 17.
said. Gr. *laleō.* Ap. 121. 7.
unto. Gr. *pros.* Ap. 104. xv. 3. **Thou, &c.** See 1. 5.
6 also, &c. = in another *place* also.
in. Gr. *en.* Ap. 104. viii.
another. Gr. *heteros.* Ap. 124. 2.
Priest. Gr. *hiereus.*
for ever. Ap. 151. II. A. ii. 4. a. I.e. for the (coming) age, the Messianic reign. The priesthood ends when He delivers up the kingdom. See 1 Cor. 15. 24. Cp. Rev. 21. 22. In the "day of God" succeeding, there will be no Temple (Rev. 21. 22), therefore neither "priest" nor "offerings".
after = according to. Gr. *kata.* Ap. 104. x. 2.
order. Gr. *taxis.* Here, *v.* 10; 6. 20; 7. 11, 17, 21. Luke 1. 8. 1 Cor. 14. 40. Col. 2. 5.
Melchisedec. See 7. 1. Cited from Ps. 110. 4.
7 when He had = having.
prayers = both prayers. Gr. *deēsis.* Ap. 134. II. 3.
supplications. Gr. *hiketēria.* Only here. In classical Greek the olive branch in the hand of a suppliant, implying *need* and *claim.*
with. Gr. *meta.* Ap. 104. xi. 1.
crying. Gr. *kraugē.* See Acts 23. 9.
death. Not *from* death, for the Gr. word is *ek*, not *apo.* He went down *into* death, but was saved *out of* (Gr. *ek*) it by resurrection.
in that, &c. = for (Gr. *apo.* Cp. Acts 12. 14) His piety, or godly fear (Gr. *eulabeia.* Here and 12. 28). This verse is a Divine supplement to the Gospel records.
8 a. Omit. **Son.** Gr. *huios.* Ap. 108. iii. See 1. 2.
obedience. See Rom. 5. 19.
by = from. Gr. *apo.* Ap. 104. iv.
9 being, &c. = having been perfected. Gr. *teleioō.* Ap. 125. 2.
Author = Causer. Gr. *aitios.* Only here.
eternal. Ap. 151. II. B. i.
10 Called . . . an = Having been designated. Gr. *prosagoreuomai.* Only here.

5. 11—6. 20 (Q, p. 1829). DIGRESSION. (*Introversion.*)

Q | R | 5. 11—6. 3. Exhortation.
 S | 6. 4–6. Peril of apostasy.
 R | 6. 7–20. Exhortation.

5. 11—6. 3 (R, above). EXHORTATION. (*Introversion.*)

R | a | 5. 11. Personal.
 b | 5. 12–. First principles.
 c | 5. –12. Milk and strong meat.
 c | 5. 13, 14. Milk and strong meat.
 b | 6. 1, 2. First principles.
 a | 6. 3. Personal.

11 Of = Concerning. Gr. *peri.* Ap. 104. xiii. 1. **many things.** Lit. much word (Gr. *logos.* Ap. 121. 10). **hard to be uttered** = difficult to explain. Gr. *dusermēneutos.* Only here. **seeing** = since. **are** = have become. **dull.** Same as "slothful" (6. 12). Gr. *nōthros.* Only in these two verses. Cp. Matt. 13. 14, 15. Acts 28. 27. **12 for** = by reason of. Gr. *dia.* Ap. 104. v. 2. **one.** Ap. 123. 3. **first principles** = rudiments (Gr. *stoicheion.* See Gal. 4. 3) of the beginning (Gr. *archē.* Ap. 172. 6). **oracles.** Gr. *logion.* See Acts 7. 38. Rom. 3. 2. **milk.** Cp. 1 Cor. 3. 2. 1 Pet. 2. 2. **strong meat** = solid food. **13 useth** = partaketh of. Gr. *metechō.* See 2. 14; 7. 13 (pertaineth to) and 1 Cor. 9. 10. **unskilful** = inexperienced of. Gr. *apeiros.* Only here. **word.** Gr. *logos*, as *v.* 11. **righteousness.** Gr. *dikaiosunē.* Ap. 191. 3. **babe.** Gr. *nēpios.* Ap. 108. vii. **14 of full age.** Gr. *teleios.* Ap. 123. 6. **use.** Gr. *hexis.* Ap. 125. 10. Only here. **senses.** Gr. *aisthētērion.* Cp. Phil. 1. 9. **exercised** = trained. Gr. *gumnazō.* See 1 Tim. 4. 7. **to discern** = for (Gr. *pros*, as *v.* 5) the discrimination (Gr. *diakrisis.* See Rom. 14. 1) of. Cp. Ap. 122. **evil.** Gr. *kakos.* Ap. 128. III. 2.

6. 1 leaving = having left. **principles of the doctrine** = word (Gr. *logos.* Ap. 121. 10) of the beginning (Gr. *archē.* Cp. 5. 12). **Christ** = the Messiah. Ap. 98. IX. **go on** = be borne along; the Instructor being the Holy Spirit. Cp. 2 Pet. 1. 21. **unto.** Gr. *epi.* Ap. 104. ix. 3. **perfection.** Gr. *teleiotēs.* See Col. 3. 14. **not** Gr. *mē.* Ap. 105. II. **laying.** Gr. *kataballō.* See 2 Cor. 4. 9. **foundation.** Ap. 146.

tion °of °repentance °from °dead works, and
of °faith °toward °God,
2 Of the °doctrine of °baptisms, and of °lay-
ing on of hands, and of °resurrection of the
°dead, and of °eternal °judgment.
a 3 And this will we do, °if [1] God permit.
S 4 For *it is* impossible for those who were
°once °enlightened, and °have tasted of the
°heavenly °gift, and °were made °partakers
of the °Holy Ghost,
5 And [4] have tasted the good °word of [1] God,
and the °powers of °the °world to come,
6 °If they shall fall away, to °renew them
again °unto [1] repentance; °seeing they crucify
to themselves the °Son of [1] God afresh, and °put
Him to an open shame.
R d 7 For the °earth which drinketh in the rain
that cometh oft °upon it, and bringeth forth
°herbs °meet for them °by whom it is °dressed,
receiveth blessing [1] from [1] God:
8 But that which beareth thorns and °briers
is °rejected, and *is* nigh unto °cursing; whose
end *is* °to be burned.
9 But, °beloved, we are °persuaded better
things °of you, and things °that accompany
salvation, °though we thus °speak.
10 For [1] God *is* °not °unrighteous to forget
your work and °labour of °love, which ye
°have °shewed °toward His Name, °in that
ye have °ministered to the °saints, and °do
minister.
11 And we °desire that °every one of you do
[10] shew the same diligence °to the °full assurance of hope °unto the end:
e 12 °That ye be [1] not °slothful, but °followers
of them who °through [1] faith and °patience °in-
herit the °promises.
13 For when [1] God made promise to Abraham,
because He could swear °by °no greater, He
sware °by Himself,
14 Saying, °"**Surely °blessing I will bless
thee, and multiplying I will multiply thee.**"
15 And so, °after he had patiently endured,
he °obtained the °promise.

of. Gen. of Apposition. Ap. 17. 4.
repentance. Gr. *metanoia*. Ap. 111. II. 1.
from. Gr. *apo*. Ap. 104. iv.
dead works. Works of the old nature. Cp. 9. 14.
dead. Gr. *nekros*. Cp. Ap. 139.
faith. Gr. *pistis*. Ap. 150. II. 1.
toward. Gr. *epi*. Ap. 104. ix. 3.
God. Ap. 98. I. i. 1.
2 doctrine = teaching.
baptisms = washings. Ap. 115. II. ii. 2.
laying on, &c. See Acts 8. 18; &c.
resurrection. Gr. *anastasis*. Ap. 178. II. 1.
dead. Ap. 139. 2.
eternal. Gr. *aiōnios*. Ap. 151. II. B. i.
judgment. Gr. *krima*. Ap. 177. 6. Of the six things enumerated, two are *esoteric* experiences, two *exoteric* rites, two *eschatological* facts, and all have to do with the dispensation of the kingdom. Cp. App. 70 and 140.
3 if = if, that is. Gr. *eanper*. Ap. 118. 1. b.
4 once. Gr. *hapax*. Here, 9. 7, 26, 27, 28; 10. 2; 12. 26, 27. 2 Cor. 11. 25. Phil. 4. 16. 1 Thess. 2. 18. 1 Pet. 3. 18, 20. Jude 3, 5. Cp. 7. 27.
enlightened. Gr. *phōtizō*. See Luke 11. 36. Cp. Ap. 130. 3.
have. Omit.
heavenly. See 3. 1.
gift. Gr. *dōrea*. See John 4. 10.
were made = became.
partakers. Gr. *metochos*. See 1. 9.
Holy Ghost. Ap. 101. II. 14.
5 word. Gr. *rhēma*. See Mark 9. 32.
powers. Gr. *dunamis*. Ap. 172. 1; 176. 1.
the . . . come = a coming age.
world. Gr. *aiōn*. Ap. 129. 2.
6 If, &c. = And fall away. Gr. *parapiptō*. Only here.
renew. Gr. *anakainizō*. Only here.
unto. Gr. *eis*. Ap. 104. vi.
seeing, &c. = crucifying (*as they do*), &c. Gr. *anastauroō*. Only here.
Son of God. Ap. 98. XV.
put, &c. = putting (as they do) Him to an open shame. Gr. *paradeigmatizō*. Only here and Matt. 1. 19 (where the texts read *deigmatizō*). Cp. Col. 2. 15. The warning is that if, after accepting Jesus the Nazarene as Messiah and Lord, they go back to Judaism, they cut themselves off (see Gal. 5. 4), as there is no other Messiah to be looked for, and by rejecting Him they put Him to open shame. Though the interpretation is for apostates who go back to Judaism, the application remains a solemn warning to all who profess to "believe".

6. 7-20 (*R*, p. 1830). EXHORTATION. (*Introversion.*)

R | d | 7-11. Hope based on illustration of earth, and rain upon it.
e | 12-15. The promises and the oath.
e | 16, 17. The oath and the promises.
d | 18-20. Hope based on illustration of heaven, and Jesus having entered therein.

7 earth. Gr. *gē*. Ap. 129. 4. upon. Gr. *epi*. Ap. 104. ix. 1. herbs. Gr *botanē*. Only here. meet = fit. Gr. *euthetos*. Only here and Luke 9. 62 and 14. 35. by = on account of. Gr. *dia* Ap. 104. v. 2. dressed = tilled. Gr. *geōrgeomai*. Only here. Add "also". **8** briers. Gr. *tribolos* Only here and Matt. 7. 16. rejected. Gr. *adokimos*. See Rom. 1. 28. cursing = a curse. Cp. Ps. 37. 22. to be burned = for (Gr. *eis*) burning Gr. *kausis*. Only here **9** beloved. Gr. *agapētos*. Ap. 135. III. persuaded Gr *peithō*. Ap. 150. I. 2. of = concerning Gr *peri*. Ap. 104. xiii. 1. that accompany = nigh to. Antithesis to "nigh unto cursing" above. Gr. *echomai*. The mid. of *echō* is to hold on to, depend on, be close to. See Mark 1. 38. Acts 20 15; 21. 26. though = even if. Gr. *ei*. Ap. 118. 2. a. speak. Gr *laleō*. Ap. 121. 7. **10** not. Gr. *ou*. Ap. 105. I. unrighteous. Gr. *adikos*. See Rom. 3. 5. labour of. The texts omit. love. Gr. *agapē*. Ap. 135. II. 1. have. Omit. shewed = exhibited Gr. *endeiknumi*. See Rom. 2. 15. toward. Gr *eis*. Ap. 104. vi. in that ye have = having. ministered. Gr. *diakoneō*. Ap. 190. III. 1. saints. See Acts 9. 13. do, &c. = ministering. **11** desire. As 1 Tim. 3. 1. every = each. to. Gr. *pros*. Ap. 104. xv. 3. full assurance. Gr. *plērophoria*. See Col. 2. 2. unto = until. **12** That = In order that. Gr. *hina*. slothful. Gr. *nōthros*. See 5. 11. followers. Gr. *mimētēs*. See 1 Cor. 4. 16. through. Gr. *dia*. Ap. 104. v. 1. patience = longsuffering or patient endurance. See Rom. 2. 4. Cp. the verb in *v.* 15. inherit = are inheritors of. promises. Cp. Luke 24. 49. Acts 1. 4. Gal. 3. 14; &c. **13** by = according to. Gr. *kata*. Ap. 104. x. 1. no = no one. Gr. *oudeis*. **14** Surely. Gr. *ē* (the texts read *ei*) *mēn*. Only here. blessing, &c. Quoted from the Sept of Gen. 22. 17. **15** after he had = having. obtained. Gr. *epitunchanō*. See Rom. 11. 7. promise. I. e. Isaac (the Land is still future); Gen. 18. 10, 14; 21. 3. Gal. 4. 23.

e 16 For °men °verily swear [13] by the greater:
and °an oath °for °confirmation *is* to them an
°end of all °strife.
17 °Wherein [1] God, °willing more abundantly
to shew °unto the heirs of °promise the °im-
mutability of His °counsel, °confirmed *it* by an
oath:

d 18 [12] That °by °two [17] immutable things, °in
which *it* °*was* impossible for [1] God to lie, we
°might have a strong °consolation, who °have
°fled for refuge to lay hold upon the hope °set
before us:
19 Which *hope* we have as an °anchor of the
°soul, both °sure and °stedfast, and °which
entereth °into that °within the °veil;
20 Whither °the °Forerunner is °for us entered, *even* °Jesus, °made °an High Priest °for
ever °after the °order of Melchisedec.

P f **7** For this °Melchisedec, king of °Salem,
priest of the °Most High °God, who °met
Abraham returning °from the °slaughter of
the kings, and blessed him;
2 To whom °also Abraham °gave a °tenth
part °of all: first being by °interpretation king
of °righteousness, and after that °also king of
[1] Salem, which is, King of peace;
3 °Without father, without mother, without
descent, having °neither beginning of days,
°nor end of °life;

g but °made like °unto °the Son of [1] God; °abid-
eth a priest °continually.

h 4 Now °consider how great this °man *was*,
[3] unto whom even the patriarch Abraham gave
the [2] tenth °of the °spoils.
5 And °verily they that are [4] of the °sons of
Levi, who receive the °office of the priesthood,
have a commandment to °take tithes of the
people °according to the law, that is, of their
brethren, though they come °out of the loins
of Abraham:
6 But he whose °descent is °not counted
°from them °received tithes of Abraham, and
blessed him that had the promises.

16 men. Gr. *anthrōpos.* Ap. 123. 1.
verily. Omit. **an** = the.
for. Gr. *eis.* Ap. 104. vi.
confirmation. Gr. *bebaiōsis.* See Phil. 1. 7.
end. Gr. *peras.* See Rom. 10. 18.
strife. Gr. *antilogia.* Here, 7. 7; 12. 3. Jude 11.
17 Wherein = In (Gr. *en*) which.
willing. Gr. *boulomai.* Ap. 102. 3.
unto = to.
promise = the promise. See Gal. 3. 22, 29.
immutability = unchangeableness. Gr. *to ametatheton.* The neut. of the adj. used as a noun. Here and in *v.* 18. Fig. *Antimereia.* Ap. 6 (3).
counsel. Gr. *boulē.* Ap. 102. 4.
confirmed it = intervened. Gr. *mesiteuō.* Only here. Cp. Gal. 3. 19.
18 by. Gr. *dia.* Ap. 104. v. 1.
two, &c. I. e. God's promise and God's oath.
in Gr. *en.* Ap. 104. viii.
was = is. **might** = may.
consolation. Gr. *paraklēsis.* See Acts 4. 36 and Ap. 134. I. 6. **have.** Omit.
fled, &c. Gr. *katapheugō.* Only here and Acts 14. 6.
set before. Gr. *prokeimai.* See 2 Cor. 8. 12.
19 anchor . . . soul = our anchor.
soul. Ap. 110. III. 2.
sure. Gr. *asphalēs.* See Acts 21. 34.
stedfast. See 2. 2. **which entereth** = entering.
into. Gr. *eis.* Ap. 104. vi.
within. Gr. *esōteros.* See Acts 16. 24.
veil. See Matt. 27. 51.
20 the = as.
Forerunner. Gr. *prodromos.* Only here.
for. Gr. *huper.* Ap. 104. xvii. 1.
Jesus. Ap. 98. X.
made = having become. **an.** Omit.
for ever. Ap. 151. II. A. ii. 4. a.
after. Gr. *kata.* Ap. 104. x. 2.
order. See 5. 6. This order is unique, being that of a high priest without altar, offering, sacrifice, or successor.

7. 1-28 [For Structure see below].

1 Melchisedec. See Gen. 14. 18-20.
Salem. Only here and *v.* 2 in N.T.
Most High. See Acts 7. 48.
God. Ap. 98. I. i. 1.
met. Gr. *sunantaō.* See Acts 10. 25.
from. Gr. *apo.* Ap. 104 iv.
slaughter = defeat, or smiting. Gr. *kopē.* Only here. Used Gen. 14. 17 (Sept.).

7. 1-28 (*P*, p. 1829). PRIESTHOOD OF THE SON (MESSIAH); AFTER THE ORDER OF MELCHISEDEC. (*Introversion*)

P | f | 1-3-. Melchisedec's greatness. Greater than Levitical priests.
g | -3. His priesthood not transmissible.
h | 4-10. Greater than Abraham, and therefore than Levi.
i | 11-14. Change of priesthood. Change of law.
i | 15-19 Change of priesthood. Disannulling of commandment.
h | 20-23. The Lord's greatness God's oath.
g | 24. His Priesthood intransmissible.
f | 25-28. The Lord's greatness. Greater than Levitical priests.

2 also. Read after "part". **gave** = apportioned. **tenth.** Cp. Gen. 28. 20-2, and Ap. 15. **of.** Gr. *apo.* Ap. 104. iv. **interpretation.** See John 1. 38. **righteousness.** Gr. *dikaiosunē.* Ap. 191. 3. **also King** = King also. **3 Without father, &c.** Gr. *apatōr, amētōr, agenealogētos.* Therefore without recorded pedigree. These three words found only here **neither, nor.** Gr. *mēte.* **life.** Gr. *zōē.* Ap. 170. 1. **made like.** Gr. *aphomoioō.* Only here **unto** = to. **the Son of God.** Ap. 98. XV. **abideth.** See p. 1511. **continually.** See Ap. 151. II. H. i. Melchisedec is presented to us without reference to any human qualifications for office. His genealogy is not recorded, so essential in the case of Aaron's sons (Neh. 7. 64). Ordinary priests began their service at thirty, and ended at fifty, years of age (Num. 4. 47). The high priest succeeded on the day of his predecessor's decease. Melchisedec has no such dates recorded; he had neither beginning of days nor end of life. We only know that he *lived*, and thus he is a fitting type of One Who lives continually. **4 consider.** Gr. *theōreō.* Ap. 133. I. 11. **man** = one. I. e. priest (*v.* 3). **of.** Gr. *ek* Ap. 104 vii **spoils.** Gr. *akrothinion* Only here. **5 verily they** = they indeed **sons** Gr. *huios* Ap. 108. iii. **office, &c** Gr. *hierateia.* Only here and Luke 1. 9. **take tithes of** Gr. *apodekatoō* See Luke 11. 42 **according to.** Gr. *kata.* Ap. 104 x. 2 **out of.** Gr. *ek*, as above **6 descent is . . . counted** Gr. *genealogeomai.* Only here. **not** Gr. *mē.* Ap. 105. II. **from** = out of. Gr. *ek*, as above. **received tithes** Gr. *dekatoō.* Only here and *v.* 9.

7 And ° without all ° contradiction the less is
blessed ° of the better.
8 And ° here ° men that die receive ° tithes; but
there ° he ° *receiveth them,* of whom it is ° witnessed that he ° liveth.
9 And as I may so say, Levi also, who receiveth [8] tithes, ° payed tithes ° in Abraham.
10 For he was yet ° in the loins of his ° father,
when [1] Melchisedec [1] met him.

i 11 ° If therefore ° perfection were ° by the ° Levitical ° priesthood, (for ° ° under it the people
° received the law,) what further need *was there*
that ° another priest should ° rise ° after the
° order of [1] Melchisedec, and ° not be called
° after the ° order of Aaron?
12 For the [11] priesthood being ° changed, there
is made [4] of necessity a ° change ° also of the
law.
13 For He ° of Whom these things are spoken
° pertaineth to [11] another tribe, [2] of which ° no
man gave attendance at the altar.
14 For *it is* ° evident that our ° Lord ° sprang
[5] out of Juda; ° of which tribe ° Moses ° spake
° nothing ° concerning ° priesthood.

i 15 And it is yet far more ° evident: ° for that
[11] after the ° similitude of [1] Melchisedec there
° ariseth [11] another Priest,
16 Who ° is made, [11] not [11] after the law of a
° carnal commandment, but [11] after the ° power
of an ° endless [3] life.
17 For He ° testifieth, "**Thou *art* a Priest ° for
ever [11] after the [11] order of [1] Melchisedec.**"
18 For there is ° verily a ° disannulling of the
commandment going before ° for ° the weakness and ° unprofitableness ° thereof.
19 For the law ° made [14] nothing perfect, but
the ° bringing in of ° a better hope *did;* [11] by
the which we draw nigh [3] unto [1] God.

h 20 And ° inasmuch as [11] not [7] without an
° oath *He was made Priest;*
21 (For those priests were made [7] without an
[20] oath; but This ° with an [20] oath [11] by Him
That said ° unto Him, "**The ° LORD sware and
will [11] not ° repent, Thou *art* a Priest [17] for ever
[11] after the [11] order of [1] Melchisedec:**")
22 ° By so much ° was ° Jesus made a ° surety
of a better ° testament.
23 And they truly were many priests, ° because ° they were not suffered to ° continue ° by
reason of death:

g 24 But ° this *Man,* [23] because He ° continueth
° ever, hath an ° unchangeable [11] priesthood.

f 25 Wherefore He is able ° also to save them
° to the uttermost that come [3] unto [1] God [11] by

7 without. Gr. *chōris*, apart from.
contradiction. See 6. 16 (strife).
of = by. Gr. *hupo*. Ap. 104. xviii. 1. Both these adjectives, "the less" and "the better", are by Fig. *Heterōsis* (of Gender, Ap. 6. 7) in the neuter gender though referring to persons.
8 here. Add "indeed".
men. Ap. 123. 1.
tithes. Same as "tenth", *v.* 2.
he. Read *one*. *receiveth them.* Omit.
witnessed. Gr. *martureō*. See p. 1511.
liveth. I. e. as there is no mention of his death Melchisedec in the Scripture record is an illustration of perpetuity of life, a type of Him Who liveth for ever.
9 payed tithes. Gr. Pass. of *dekatoō*, as *v.* 6.
in = through. Gr. *dia*. Ap. 104. v. 1.
10 in. Gr. *en*. Ap. 104. viii.
father. I. e. ancestral father.
11 If. Ap. 118. 2. a.
perfection Gr. *teleiōsis*. Only here and Luke 1. 45 (performance). Cp. Ap. 125. 2.
by. Gr. *dia* Ap. 104. v. 1.
Levitical. Only here.
priesthood. Gr. *hierōsunē*. Only here and *vv.* 12, 14, 24.
under = upon (as a basis). Gr *epi* Ap. 104 ix. 2, but the texts read ix. 1.
received the law = were furnished with law. Gr *nomotheteō*. Only here and 8 6 (established).
another. Gr. *heteros* Ap. 124. 2.
rise. Gr. *anistēmi*. Ap. 178. I. 1.
after. Gr. *kata*. Ap. 104. x. 2.
order. See 5. 6. **not.** Gr. *ou* Ap. 105. I.
12 changed. Gr. *metatithēmi*. See Acts 7. 16.
change. Gr. *metathesis*. Only here, 11. 5; 12. 27.
also, &c. = of the law also.
13 of = on. Gr. *epi*. Ap. 104. ix. 3.
pertaineth. Gr. *metechō*. See 2. 14.
no man = no one. Gr. *oudeis*.
14 evident. Gr. *prodēlos*. See 1 Tim. 5. 24.
Lord. Ap. 98. VI. i *β*. 2. A.
sprang = hath risen. Gr. *anatellō*. Generally used of the sun rising.
of = with regard to. Gr. *eis*. Ap. 104. vi.
Moses. See 3. 2. **spake.** Gr. *laleō*. Ap. 121. 7.
nothing. Gr. *oudeis*.
concerning. Gr. *peri*. Ap. 104. xiii. 1.
priesthood. The texts read "priests".
15 evident. Gr. *katadēlos*. Only here. Cp. *v.* 14.
for = if. Gr. *ei*. Ap. 118. 2. a.
similitude. Gr. *homoiotēs*. See 4. 15.
ariseth. Same as "rise", *v.* 11.
16 is made = hath become.
carnal. Gr. *sarkikos*, but texts read *sarkinos*. See 2 Cor. 3. 3.
power. Gr. *dunamis*. Ap. 172. 1; 176. 1.
endless. Ap. 151. II. D.
17 testifieth. Same as "witnessed", *v.* 8.
for ever. See 6. 20. Quoted from Ps 110. 4.
18 verily = indeed.
disannulling. Gr. *athetēsis*. Only here and 9. 26. Cp. Gal. 3. 15.
for = on account of. Gr. *dia*. Ap. 104. v. 2.
the weakness. See Rom. 5. 6.
unprofitableness. Gr. *anōphelēs*. Only here and Tit. 3. 9. **thereof.** Omit. **19 made . . . perfect.** Gr. *teleioō*. Ap. 125. 2. **bringing in** = superinduction. Gr. *epeisagōgē*. Only here. **a better hope.** Note that there are also a better covenant (*v.* 22); better promises (8. 6); better sacrifices (9. 23); a better substance (10. 34); a better country (11. 16); a better resurrection (11. 35); a better thing (11. 40). In chap. 1, Christ is shown to be better than angels; in 3, better than Moses; in 4, better than Joshua; in 7, better than Aaron; in 10, better than the Law. **20 inasmuch as.** Gr. *kath'* (Ap. 104. x. 2) *hoson*. **oath.** Gr. *horkōmosia*. Only here and *vv.* 21, 28. Cp. 6. 16, 17. **21 with.** Gr. *meta*. Ap. 104. xi. 1. **unto.** Gr. *pros*. Ap. 104. xv. 3. **LORD.** Ap. 98. VI. i. *β*. 1. B. a. **repent.** Gr. *metamelomai*. Ap. 111. I. 2. **22 By.** Gr. *kata*, as in *v.* 20. **was . . . made** = hath become. **Jesus.** Ap. 98. X. **surety.** Gr. *enguos*. Only here. **testament** = covenant. Gr. *diathēkē*. See Matt. 26. 28. First of *seventeen* occs. in Heb. (Ap. 10). **23 because.** Gr. *dia*. Ap. 104. v. 2. **they were not, &c.** = of their being hindered from continuing. **continue.** Gr. *paramenō*. See 1 Cor. 16. 6. **by reason of** = by. Ap. 104. v. 2. **24 this.** Supply "*Priest*", in place of "*Man*". **continueth.** Same as "abideth", *v.* 3. **ever.** See *vv.* 17, 21. **unchangeable.** Gr. *aparabatos*. Lit. not passing over to another. Only here. **25 also to save** = to save also. **to the uttermost.** Gr. *eis to panteles*. See Luke 13. 11.

Him, °seeing He °ever liveth °to °make intercession °for them.
26 For such an High Priest became us, *Who is*
°holy, °harmless, °undefiled, °separate [1] from
sinners, and °made higher than °the heavens;
27 Who needeth [11] not °daily, as °those high
priests, to °offer up sacrifice, first [25] for His
own °sins, and then for the people's: for this
He did °once, when He °offered up Himself.
28 For the law °maketh [8] men high priests
which have infirmity; but the °word of the
[20] oath, which was °since the law, °*maketh* the
°Son, Who is °consecrated °for evermore.

Q (p. 1829) **8** Now °of the things which we have spoken *this is* the °sum: We have °such an
High Priest, Who °is set °on the right hand
of the throne of the °Majesty °in °the heavens;
2 A °Minister of the °sanctuary, and of the
°true °tabernacle, which the °LORD °pitched,
°and °not °man.
N U 3 For every high priest is ordained °to °offer
gifts and sacrifices: wherefore *it is* of necessity
that °this Man have somewhat also to °offer.
4 For °if He were °on °earth, He °should
°not be a priest, seeing that there are °priests
that offer gifts °according to °the law:
5 Who °serve °unto the °example and shadow
of °heavenly things, as °Moses was °admon-
ished of God when he was about to °make the
[2] tabernacle: for, °"**See**," saith He, °"***that*** **thou**
make all things [4] **according to the** °**pattern**
shewed to thee [1] **in the mount.**"
6 But now hath He obtained a °more excellent °ministry, by how much °also He is the
°Mediator of a better °covenant, which was
°established °upon better promises.
V Y 7 For [4] if that first *covenant* had been °fault-
less, then °should °no place have been sought
for the second.

seeing He ever liveth = ever living, *as He is*.
ever. Ap. 151. II. G. ii.
to. Gr. *eis*. Ap. 104. vi.
make intercession. Gr. *entunchanō*. See Acts 25. 24.
for. Gr. *huper*. Ap. 104. xvii. 1.
26 holy. Gr. *hosios*. See Acts 2. 27.
harmless. Gr. *akakos*. See Rom. 16. 18.
undefiled. Gr. *amiantos*. Here, 13. 4. Jas. 1. 27. 1 Pet. 1. 4.
separate. Gr. *chōrizō*. See Acts 1. 4. Cp. Gen. 49. 26. Deut. 33. 16. made, &c. Cp. 4. 14.
the heavens. See Matt. 6. 9, 10. I. e. than those who dwell in them, by Fig. *Metonymy* (Adjunct). Ap. 6 (4).
27 daily. Gr. *kath'* (Ap. 104. x. 2) *hēmeran*.
those = the.
offer up. Gr. *anapherō*. Here, 9. 28; 13. 15. Matt. 17. 1. Mark 9. 2. Luke 24. 51. Jas. 2. 21. 1 Pet. 2. 5, 24.
sins. Gr. *hamartia*. Ap. 128. I. ii. 1.
once = once for all. Gr. *ephapax*. See Rom. 6. 10.
28 maketh = appointeth.
word. Gr. *logos*. Ap. 121. 10.
since = after. Gr. *meta*. Ap. 104. xi. 2. Cp. Ps. 110. 4.
Son. Cp. *v*. 3.
consecrated = perfected, as *v*. 19.
for evermore. Ap. 151. II. A. ii. 4. d.

8. 1 of = upon. Gr. *epi*. Ap. 104. ix. 2.
sum = main point. Gr. *kephalaion*. See Acts 22. 28.
such. Emphatic.
is set = sat down. See 1. 3.
on. Gr. *en*. Ap. 104. viii.
Majesty. Gr. *megalōsunē*. See 1. 3.
in. Gr. *en*.
the heavens. See Matt. 6. 9, 10.
2 Minister. Gr. *leitourgos*. Ap. 190. I. 4.
sanctuary. Lit. the Holies, i. e. the Holy of Holies. Cp. 9. 3. Gr. *hagion*. Neut. used ten times in Heb.: here, 9. 1, 2, 3, 8, 12, 24, 25; 10. 19; 13. 11.
true. Gr. *alēthinos*. Ap. 175. 2.
tabernacle = tent. Gr. *skēnē*.
LORD. Ap. 98. VI. i. β. 1. A. b.
pitched. Gr. *pēgnumi*. Only here.
and. Omit. not. Gr. *ou*. Ap. 105. I.
man. Gr. *anthrōpos*. Ap. 123. 1.

8. 3—10. 18 (*N*, p. 1829). THE EFFICACY OF CHRIST'S PRIESTHOOD. (*Extended Alternation.*)

N | U | 8. 3-6. A more excellent ministry. A better Covenant on better promises.
  V | 8. 7-13. The Old and New Covenants compared and contrasted.
    W | 9. 1-5. The earthly sanctuary a copy of the heavenly pattern.
      X | 9. 6-10. The offerings.
| *U* | 9. 11-14. A greater and more perfect tabernacle. His own blood.
  V | 9. 15-23. The Old and New Covenants compared and contrasted.
    W | 9. 24. The heavenly sanctuary the pattern of the earthly copy.
      X | 9. 25—10. 18. The offerings.

3 to. Gr. *eis*. Ap. 104. vi. offer. See 5. 1. this Man . . . also. Read "this *High Priest* also". **4** if. Gr. *ei*. Ap. 118. 2. a. on. Gr. *epi*. Ap. 104. ix. 1. earth. Gr. *gē*. Ap. 129. 4. should not be = would not even be. not. Gr. *oude*. See Ap. 105. I. priests. The texts omit. Read "those who offer". according to. Gr. *kata*. Ap. 104. x. 2. the. Omit. **5** serve. Gr. *latreuō*. Ap. 190. III. 5. unto = for. example. Gr. *hupodeigma*, rendered "pattern", 9. 23. See John 13. 15. heavenly. See 3. 1. Moses. See 3. 2. admonished of God. Gr. *chrēmatizō*. See Luke 2. 26. make. Gr. *epiteleō*. Ap. 125. 3. See. Gr. *horaō*. Ap. 133. I. 8. *that*, &c. The texts read, "thou shalt make". pattern. Gr. *tupos*. See John 20. 25. Here it means "model". See Ex. 25. 9. The Sept. uses this word for *tab'nîth* in Ex. 25. 40, whence this is quoted, but in *v*. 9 of the same chapter uses for the same Heb. word *paradeigma*, which does not occur in the N.T. Cp. the verb in 6. 6. **6** more excellent. See 1. 4. ministry. Gr. *leitourgia*. Ap. 190. II. 4. also. Read after "covenant". Mediator. Gr. *mesitēs*. See Gal. 3. 19. covenant. Gr. *diathēkē*. See 7. 22. established. Gr. *nomotheteō*. See 7. 11. upon. Gr. *epi*. Ap. 104. ix. 2.

8. 7-13 (V, above). THE OLD AND NEW COVENANTS COMPARED AND CONTRASTED.
(*Introversion and Alternation.*)

V | Y | 7, 8. The First Covenant faulty.
  Z | k | 9. The New Covenant. Not the same in the persons taking part (Neg.).
      l | 10. The New Covenant spiritual (Pos.).
  Z | *k* | 11. The New Covenant. Not the same in result (Neg.).
      l | 12. The New Covenant spiritual (Pos.).
| *Y* | 13. The First Covenant evanescent.

7 faultless. Gr. *amemptos*. See Phil. 2. 15. should = would. no. Gr. *ou*. Ap. 105. I.

8 For °finding fault with them, He saith, °**"Behold, the days come, saith the °LORD, when I will °make a °new [6]covenant °with the house of Israel and °with the house of Judah:**

Z k **9 [2]Not [4]according to the [6]covenant that I made with their fathers [1]in the day °when I took them by °the hand to lead them °out of the °land of Egypt; because they °continued [2]not [1]in My [6]covenant, and I °regarded them not, saith the [8]LORD.**

l **10 For this *is* the [6]covenant that I will °make with the house of Israel °after those days, saith the [8]LORD; °I will put My laws °into their mind, and °write them °in their hearts: and I will be to them °a °God, and they shall be to Me °a °people:**

Z k **11 And they shall °not teach °every man his °neighbour, and °every man his brother, saying, °Know the [2]LORD: for all shall °know Me, °from the °least to the greatest.**

l **12 For I will be °merciful to their °unrighteousness, and their °sins and their °iniquities will I remember °no more."**

Y 13 [1]In that He saith, "A [8]new *covenant*," He hath °made the first old. Now that which °decayeth and °waxeth old *is* °ready to °vanish away.

W **9** °Then verily the first °*covenant* had also °ordinances of °divine service, and a °worldly °sanctuary.

2 For there was a °tabernacle °made; the first, °wherein *was* the °candlestick, and the °table, and the °shewbread; which is called the [1]sanctuary.

3 And °after the second °veil, the [2]tabernacle which is called the °Holiest of all;

4 Which had the golden °censer, and the °ark of the °covenant overlaid round about with gold, [2]wherein *was* the golden °pot that had manna, and Aaron's rod that °budded, and the °tables of the °covenant;

5 And over it the °cherubims of °glory °shadowing the °mercyseat; °of which °we cannot now speak °particularly.

X 6 Now °when these things were thus ordained, the priests °went °always °into the first [2]tabernacle, °accomplishing the °service °*of God*.

7 But [6]into the °second *went* the high priest alone °once °every year, °not °without blood, which he offered °for himself and *for* the °errors of the °people:

8 The °Holy Ghost this °signifying, that the °way into the °Holiest °of all was °not yet °made manifest, °while as the first [2]tabernacle was yet standing:

9 Which °*was* a °figure °for the °time °then

8 finding fault. Gr. *memphomai.* See Rom. 9. 19.
Behold. Gr. *idou.* Ap. 133. I. 2.
LORD. Ap. 98. VI. i. *β.* 1. B. a.
make = consummate, or complete.
new. Gr. *kainos.* See Matt. 9. 17.
with. Gr. *epi.* Ap. 104. ix. 3.
9 when, &c. Lit. of My taking hold of. Gr. *epilambanomai.* See 2. 16. **the** = My.
out of. Gr. *ek.* Ap. 104. vii.
land. Gr. *gē*, as *v.* 4.
continued. Gr. *emmenō.* See Acts 14. 22.
and I regarded . . . not = I also disregarded. Gr. *ameleō.* See 1 Tim. 4. 14.
10 make. Gr. *diatithēmi.* See Acts 3. 25.
after. Gr. *meta.* Ap. 104. xi. 2.
I will put. Lit. "giving". Same Gr. word in 2 Cor. 8. 16; &c. **into.** Gr. *eis.* Ap. 104. vi.
write. Gr. *epigraphō.* See Mark 15. 26.
in = upon. Gr. *epi.* Ap. 104. ix. 3. **a** = for (Gr. *eis*).
God. Ap. 98. I. i. 1. **people.** See Acts 2. 47.
11 not. Gr. *ou mē.* Ap. 105. III.
every man = each one.
neighbour. The texts read *politēs* (*fellow*)-citizen, instead of *plēsios.*
Know. Gr. *ginōskō.* Ap. 132. I. ii.
know. Gr. *oida.* Ap. 132. I. i.
from. Gr. *apo.* Ap. 104. iv.
least, &c. Lit. little to great.
12 merciful. Gr. *hileōs.* See Matt. 16. 22.
unrighteousness. Gr. *adikia* (pl.). Ap. 128. VII. 1.
sins. Gr. *hamartia.* Ap. 128. I. ii. 1.
iniquities. Gr. *anomia.* Ap. 128. III. 4.
no. Gr. *ou mē*, as *v.* 11. The quotation is from Jer. 31. 31–34. **13 made . . . old.** Gr. *palaioō.* See 1. 11.
decayeth. Same as "made old".
waxeth old. Gr. *gēraskō.* Only here and John 21. 18. **ready** = near.
vanish away = vanishing. Gr. *aphanismos.* Only here. Cp. Acts 13. 41.

9. 1 Then verily . . . also = Now even.
covenant. No Gr. word. The ellipsis is rightly supplied by "*covenant*".
ordinances. Gr. *dikaiōma.* Ap. 191. 4.
divine service. Gr. *latreia.* Ap. 190. II. 3.
worldly = earthly. Gr. *kosmikos.* See Tit. 2. 12.
sanctuary. See 8. 2. Read "the sanctuary, an earthly one".
2 tabernacle. Gr. *skēnē*, tent, which is used by the Sept. to render the Hebrew *mishkān* (the structure) and *'ohel* (the tent which covered it). Cp. Ex. 17. 19, 21.
made = prepared.
wherein = in (Gr. *en.* Ap. 104. viii) which.
candlestick = lampstand. Ex. 25. 31–40. According to Josephus, only one in Herod's Temple. Ten in Solomon's; see 1 Kings 7. 49. **table.** Ex. 25. 23–30.
shewbread. Lit. the setting forth of the loaves. Ex. 25. 30. **3 after** = behind. Gr. *meta.* Ap. 104. xi. 2.
veil. See 6. 19. **Holiest of all** = Holy of Holies.
4 censer. Gr. *thumiatērion.* Only here.
ark. See Ex. 25. 10–22.
covenant. See 8. 6. Exod. 25. 10–22.
pot. Gr. *stamnos.* Only here. See Ex. 16. 32–34.
budded. Gr. *blastanō.* Here; Matt. 13. 26. Mark 4. 27. Jas. 5. 18. See Num. 17. 8.

tables. Gr. *plax.* Only here and 2 Cor. 3. 3. See Ex. 25. 16. **5 cherubims** = cherubim. Only here in N.T., but see Rev. 4. 6. **glory.** See p. 1511. **shadowing** = overshadowing. Gr. *kataskiazō.* Only here. **mercyseat.** Gr. *hilastērion.* See Rom. 3. 25 and Ex. 25. 17. **of** = concerning. Gr. *peri.* Ap. 104. xiii. 1. **we . . . speak.** Lit. it is not (Ap. 105. I) now to speak. **particularly** = in detail. Gr. *kata* (Ap. 104. x. 2) *meros* (part). **6 when, &c.** = these things having been thus prepared. **went** = go. **always.** Gr. *diapantos.* **into.** Gr. *eis.* Ap. 104. vi. **accomplishing.** Gr. *epiteleō.* Ap. 125. 3. **service.** As *v.* 1. *of God.* Omit. **7 second.** I. e. the Holy of Holies. **once.** Gr. *hapax.* See 6. 4. **every.** Lit. "of the". **not.** Gr. *ou.* Ap. 105. I. **without** = apart from. Gr. *chōris.* **for.** Gr. *huper.* Ap. 104. xvii. 1. **errors** = ignorances. Gr. *agnoēma.* Only here. See Lev. 4. 2. **people.** Gr. *laos.* See Acts 2. 47. **8 Holy Ghost.** Ap. 101. II. 3. **signifying.** Gr. *dēloō.* See 1 Cor. 1. 11. **way, &c.** Lit. "the way of the Holy (*places*)". **Holiest.** Lit. "holies". **of all.** Omit. **not yet.** Gr. *mēpō.* **made manifest.** Gr. *phaneroō.* Ap. 106. I. v. **while as, &c.** Read "while the first tabernacle is as yet standing". **9 *was* = *is*.** **figure.** Gr. *parabolē.* Here and 11. 19 transl. "figure". Elsewhere in the Gospels always "parable", save Mark 4. 30. Luke 4. 23. **for.** Gr. *eis.* Ap. 104. vi. **time.** See Ap. 195. **then.** Omit.

present, °in which °were offered both gifts and sacrifices, that could °not °make him that °did the service perfect, °as pertaining to °the °conscience;

10 *Which stood* only °in meats and drinks, and divers °washings, and °carnal [1]ordinances, °imposed *on them* until the time of °reformation.

U 11 But °Christ °being come °an High Priest of °good things to come, °by °a greater and more °perfect [2]tabernacle, [7]not °made with hands, that is to say, [7]not of this °building;

12 °Neither [11]by the blood of goats and calves, but [11]by His own blood He entered in °once [6]into the [8]holy place, having °obtained °eternal °redemption *for us.*

13 For °if the blood of °bulls and of goats, and the °ashes of an heifer °sprinkling the unclean, sanctifieth °to the °purifying of the flesh:

14 How much more shall the blood of [11]Christ, Who °through the [12]eternal °Spirit °offered Himself °without spot to °God, purge your conscience °from °dead works °to °serve the living °God?

V A 15 And °for this cause He is the °Mediator of °the °new °testament, that °by means of death, [9]for the °redemption of the °transgressions *that were* °under the first °testament, they which are called might receive the °promise of [12]eternal °inheritance.

B m 16 For where a [15]testament *is,* °there must also of necessity be the death of the °testator.

n 17 For a [15]testament *is* °of force °after men are dead: otherwise it is of °no °strength at all while the [16]testator liveth.

B m 18 °Whereupon [12]neither the first *testament* was °dedicated [7]without blood.

n 19 For °when Moses had spoken every precept to all the [7]people °according to °the law, he took the blood of calves and of goats, °with water, and °scarlet °wool, and °hyssop, and [13]sprinkled both the °book, and all the [7]people,

20 Saying, °"**This is the blood of the [15]testament which [14]God hath °enjoined °unto you.**"

21 Moreover he [13]sprinkled with blood both the [2]tabernacle, and all the vessels of the °ministry.

22 And °almost all things are °by the law purged °with blood; and [7]without °shedding of blood °is °no remission.

in = according to. Gr. *kata.* Ap. 104. x. 2.
were = are. The Temple ritual still continuing.
not. Gr. *mē.* Ap. 105. II.
make . . . perfect. Gr. *teleioō.* Ap. 125. 2.
did the service = serves. Gr. *latreuō.* See 8. 5.
as pertaining to. Gr. *kata,* as above.
the. Omit. conscience. See Acts 23. 1.
10 in = upon. Gr. *epi.* Ap. 104. ix. 2.
washings. Gr. *baptismos.* Ap. 115. II. ii. 1.
carnal, &c. I. e. rites and ceremonies. Cp. Acts 15. 10.
imposed *on.* Gr. *epikeimai.* See Luke 23. 23.
reformation. Gr. *diorthōsis.* Only here. In this *v.* is the Fig. *Antimereia* (Ap. 6).
11 Christ. Ap. 98. IX. being = having.
an. Omit. good = the good.
by. Gr. *dia.* Ap. 104. v. 1. a = the.
perfect. Gr. *teleios.* Ap. 125. 1.
made, &c. Gr. *cheiropoiētos.* See Acts 7. 48.
building = creation.
12 Neither. Gr. *oude.*
once. Gr. *ephapax.* See 7. 27.
obtained = found, as in 4. 16 (find).
eternal. Ap. 151. II. B. i.
redemption. Gr. *lutrōsis.* Only here and Luke 1. 68; 2. 38.
13 if. Gr. *ei.* Ap. 118. 2. a.
bulls, &c. See Lev. 16.
ashes, &c. See Num. 19. 2-20.
sprinkling. Gr. *rhantizō.* See Ap. 136. ix.
to. Gr. *pros.* Ap. 104. xv. 3.
purifying. Gr. *katharotēs.* Only here.
14 through. Gr. *dia.* Ap. 104. v. 1.
Spirit. Same as *v.* 8.
offered. Observe,—not sacrificed.
without spot. Gr. *amōmos.* See Eph. 1. 4.
God. Ap. 98. I. i. 1.
from. Gr. *apo.* Ap. 104. iv.
dead works. See 6. 1.
to. Gr. *eis.* Ap. 104. vi.
serve. See *v.* 9 (did the service).

9. 15-23 (*V,* p. 1834) THE OLD AND NEW COVENANTS COMPARED AND CONTRASTED.
(*Introversion and Alternation*)

V | A | 15. The Old Covenant related to the promise of the eternal inheritance.
  B | m | 16. Death necessary for its making.
    n | 17. Reason.
  B | *m* | 18. Blood necessary for its consecration.
    n | 19-23-. Reason.
  A | -23. The New Covenant related to the heavenly things themselves.

15 for this cause = on account of (Gr. *dia*) this.
Mediator. See 8. 6. the = a.
new. See 8. 8.
testament = covenant, as in *v.* 4.
by means, &c. Lit. death having taken place.
redemption. Gr. *apolutrōsis.* See Rom. 3. 24. Cp. *v.* 12.
transgressions. Gr. *parabasis.* See 2. 2. Cp. Ap. 128. VI. 1.
under = upon (based upon). Gr. *epi.* Ap. 104. ix. 2.

promise, &c. = the promised eternal inheritance. Fig. *Hypallagē.* Ap. 6. inheritance. Cp. 1 Pet. 1. 4. **16** there must, &c. = it is necessary that the death . . . be brought in. testator = appointed (victim). Gr. *diatithēmi.* See 8. 10. **17** of force = sure. Gr. *bebaios.* See 6. 19. after, &c. = over (Gr. *epi*) the dead (victims). See Gen. 15. 9-18. Jer. 34. 18. no . . . at all. Gr. *mē pote.* strength. Gr. *ischuō.* Cp. Ap. 172. 3. The two covenants referred to above show the necessity of a victim being slain for the validity of a covenant, and the ceremony of passing between the parts thereof. To the unconditional covenant with Abraham, Jehovah was the only party (Gen. 15. 17, 18); in the other, note *vv.* 18, 19. The passage here has nothing to do with a "will" or "will-making". **18** Whereupon, &c. = Wherefore not even. dedicated = inaugurated. Gr. *enkainizō.* Only here and 10. 20. Cp. John 10. 22. **19** when, &c. Lit. every command having been spoken (Gr. *laleō.* Ap. 121. 7) by (Gr. *hupo*) Moses. See 3. 2. according to. Gr. *kata.* Ap. 104. x. 2. the = Omit. with. Gr. *meta.* Ap. 104. xi. 1. scarlet. Gr. *kokkinos* Only here; Matt. 27. 28. Rev. 17. 3, 4; 18. 12, 16. wool. Gr. *erion.* Only here and Rev. 1. 14. hyssop. Gr. *hussōpos.* Only here and John 19. 29. book. See Ex. 24. 7. **20** This, &c. Quoted from Ex. 24. 8. enjoined = commanded. unto. Gr. *pros.* Ap. 104. xv. 3. **21** ministry. Gr. *leitourgia.* See 8. 6. **22** almost. Gr. *schedon.* See Acts 13. 44. by = according to. Gr. *kata.* Ap. 104. x. 2. with = in. Gr. *en.* Ap. 104. viii. shedding, &c. Gr. *haimatekchusia.* Only here. is. Gr. *ginomai,* to become. no = not. Ap. 105. I.

23 *It was* therefore necessary that the °pat-
terns of things °in °the heavens should be
purified with these;
A but the °heavenly things themselves with
°better sacrifices °than these.
W 24 For [11]Christ is [7]not entered [6]into the [8]holy
places [11]made with hands, *which are* the °figures
of the °true; but [6]into [23]heaven itself, now to
°appear in the presence of [14]God [7]for us:
X o1 25 °Nor yet °that He should offer Himself
often, as the high priest entereth [6]into the
[8]holy place °every year [22]with blood °of others;
p1 26 For then must He often have suffered
°since the °foundation of the world: but now
[7]once [10]in the °end of the °world hath He
°appeared °to put away °sin [11]by the sacrifice of Himself.
27 And °as it is °appointed °unto men [7]once
to die, but [3]after this the °judgment:
28 So [11]Christ was [7]once offered [14]to °bear
the [26]sins of many; and [27]unto them that °look
for Him shall He °appear the second time
[7]without [26]sin, °unto salvation.

o2 **10** For the law having a shadow of good
things to come, *and* °not the very
°image of the things, can °never with those
sacrifices which they offered °year by year
°continually, °make the comers thereunto °per-
fect.
2 For then would they [1]not have ceased to be
offered, °because that the °worshippers °once
purged °should have °had °no more °con-
science of °sins?
3 But °in those *sacrifices there is* a °remem-
brance again *made* of [2]sins °every year.
4 For *it is* not possible that the blood of bulls
and of goats should °take away [2]sins.
p2 5 Wherefore when He cometh °into the
°world, He saith, "**Sacrifice and °offering
Thou °wouldest not, but a °body hast Thou
°prepared °Me:**
6 **In °burnt offerings and *sacrifices* °for [2]sin
Thou °hast had [1]no pleasure.**
7 **Then said I, °Lo, I °come ([3]in the °volume of
the book it is written °of Me) to do Thy °will,
O °God."**
8 Above when He said, °"**Sacrifice and °offer-
ing and [6]burnt offerings and *offering* [6]for [2]sin
Thou [5]wouldest [1]not, °neither [6]hadst pleasure
therein;"** which are offered °by the law;
9 Then said He, [7]"**Lo, I come to do Thy [7]will,
°O God."** He taketh away the first, °that He
may establish the second.
10 °By the which [7]will we °are sanctified
°through the [5]offering of the body of °Jesus
Christ °once *for all.*
o3 11 And every priest standeth °daily °minis-

23 patterns. Here = copies; "example" in 8. 5.
in. Gr. *en.* Ap. 104. viii.
the heavens. See Matt. 6. 9, 10.
heavenly. See 3. 1.
better sacrifices. I.e. one greater and better sacrifice. Fig. *Heterōsis.* Ap. 6. Cp. Ps. 51. 17.
than. Gr. *para.* Ap. 104. xii. 3.
24 figures. Gr. *antitupon.* Only here and 1 Pet. 3. 21.
true. Gr. *alēthinos.* See 8. 2.
appear. Gr. *emphanizō.* Ap. 106. I. iv.

9. 25—10. 18 (*X*, p. 1834). THE OFFERINGS. (*Alternation.*)

X o1 | 9. 25. Yearly sacrifices ineffectual. Because offered oftentimes.
p1 | 9. 26–28. Christ's sacrifice effectual. Once (*hapax*).
o2 | 10. 1–4. Yearly sacrifices ineffectual. Offered continually.
p2 | 10. 5–10. Christ's sacrifice effectual. Once for all (*ephapax*).
o3 | 10. 11. Daily sacrifices ineffectual. Offered oftentimes.
p3 | 10. 12–18. Christ's sacrifice effectual. Having offered One, He sat down for a continuance.

25 Nor yet. Gr. *oude.*
that = in order that. Gr. *hina.*
every year. Gr. *kat'* (Ap. 104. x. 2) *eniauton.* On the Day of Atonement.
of others. Ap. 124. 6.
26 since = from. Gr. *apo.* Ap. 104. iv.
foundation, &c. See 4. 3.
end. Gr. *sunteleia.* See Matt. 13. 39.
world = ages. Pl. of Gr. *aiōn.* Ap. 129. 2.
appeared. Same as "made manifest", *v.* 8.
to put away = for (Gr. *eis*) putting away (Gr. *athetēsis.* See 7. 18).
sin. Ap. 128. I. ii. 1.
27 as = inasmuch as. Gr. *kath'* (Ap. 104. x. 2) *hoson.*
appointed. Gr. *apokeimai.* See Col. 1. 5.
unto = to.
men. Ap. 123. 1.
judgment. Gr. *krisis.* Ap. 177. 7.
28 bear. Gr. *anapherō.* See 7. 27.
look. Gr. *apekdechomai.* See Rom. 8. 19.
appear. Gr. *horaō.* Ap. 133. I. 8.
unto. Gr. *eis.* Ap. 104. vi.

10. 1 not, &c. = not itself (emph.).
not. Gr. *ou.* Ap. 105. I.
image. Gr. *eikōn.* See Rom. 1. 23.
never. Gr. *oudepote.* See *v.* 11.
year, &c. Gr. *kat' eniauton,* as 9. 25.
continually. Gr. *eis to diēnekes.* Ap. 151. II. H. i.
make . . . perfect. Gr. *teleioō.* Ap. 125. 2.
2 because. Gr. *dia.* Ap. 104. v. 2.
worshippers. Ap. 190. III. 5.
once. See 6. 4.
should = would.
had. Omit.
no. Gr. *mēdeis.* Lit. not (Ap. 105. II) one.
conscience of sins. I. e. of unpardoned sins.
conscience. See 9. 14.
sins. Gr. *hamartia.* Ap. 128. I. ii. 1.
3 in. Gr. *en.* Ap. 104. viii.
remembrance again. Gr. *anamnēsis.* See 1 Cor. 11. 24.
every year. Same as "year by year", *v.* 1.
4 take away. See Rom. 11. 27.
5 into. Gr. *eis.* Ap. 104. vi.

world. Gr. *kosmos.* Ap. 129. 1. offering. Gr. *prosphora.* See Acts 21. 26. wouldest. Gr. *thelō.* Ap. 102. 1. The Heb. is "demandedst". body, &c. See Ps. 40. 6, 7. prepared. Gr. *katartizō.* Ap. 125. 8. Me = for Me. **6** burnt offerings = whole burnt offerings. Gr. *holokautōma.* Here, *v.* 8, and Mark 12. 33. for = concerning. Gr. *peri.* Ap. 104. xiii. 1. hast, &c. = didst not take pleasure. **7** Lo = Behold. Gr. *idou.* Ap. 133. I. 2. come = am come. volume. Gr. *kephalis.* Only here. Used in the Sept. of a roll. Ps. 40. 7. Ezra 6. 2; &c. From the head (Gr. *kephalē*) of the wooden roller on which the scroll was rolled. of = concerning. Gr. *peri,* as above. will. Gr. *thelēma.* Ap. 102. 2. God. Ap. 98. I. i. 1. This quotation is from Ps. 40. **8** Sacrifice, offering. The Gr. words are in pl. neither. Gr. *oude.* by. See 9. 19. **9** O God. The texts omit. that = in order that. Gr. *hina.* **10** By = In, as *v.* 3. are = have been. through. Gr. *dia.* Ap. 104. v. 1. Jesus Christ. Ap. 98. XI. once *for all.* Gr. *ephapax.* See 7. 27. **11** daily. Gr. *kath'* (Ap. 104. x. 2) *hēmeran.* ministering. Gr. *leitourgeō.* Ap. 190. III. 6.

tering and offering oftentimes the same sacrifices, which can [1] never °take away [2] sins:

p[3] 12 But this °Man, °after He had offered one sacrifice °for [2] sins °for ever, sat down °on the right hand of [7] God;
13 From henceforth °expecting till His enemies be made °His footstool.
14 For by one [5] offering He hath [1] perfected [12] for ever them that are sanctified.
15 *Whereof* the °Holy Ghost also °is a witness to us: for °after °that He had said before,
16 "This *is* the °covenant that I will °make °with them [15] after those days, saith the °LORD; °I will put My laws °into their hearts, and °in their minds will I °write them;
17 And their [2] sins and °iniquities will I remember °no more."
18 Now where remission of these *is, there is* °no more [5] offering [6] for [2] sin.

D C E 19 Having therefore, brethren, °boldness °to enter into °the holiest [10] by the blood of °Jesus,
20 By a °new °and °living way which He °hath °consecrated for us, [10] through the °veil, that is to say, His flesh;
21 And *having* °an High Priest °over the °house of [7] God;
22 Let us draw near °with a °true heart [3] in °full assurance of °faith, °having our hearts sprinkled °from an °evil [2] conscience, and °our bodies washed with pure water.
23 Let us °hold fast the °profession of °*our* faith °without wavering; (for He *is* °faithful That promised;)

F 24 And let us °consider one another °to provoke °unto love and to good works:
25 °Not °forsaking the °assembling of ourselves together, as the manner of °some *is;* but °exhorting *one another:* and so much the more, as ye °see the °day °approaching.

G 26 For °if we sin °wilfully [15] after °that we have received the °knowledge of the truth, there °remaineth °no more sacrifice [6] for [2] sins,
27 But a °certain °fearful °looking for of °judgment, and °fiery indignation °which shall devour the °adversaries.

take away. Gr. *periaireō*. See Acts 27. 20.
12 Man = Priest. **after He had** = having.
for. Gr. *huper*. Ap. 104. xvii. 1.
for ever = continually. Ap. 151. II. H. ii. Cp. *v.* 1. In A.V. from 1611 to 1630 the comma was placed after "ever". But in 1638 it was removed to after "sins", thus going back to the punctuation of the Bishops' Bible of 1568. The Gr. expression is not the usual one, *eis ton aiōna*, but as *vv.* 1, 14, and 7. 3—*eis to diēnekes* (Ap. 151. II. H), and means "continually", in distinction from "interruptedly". It is not concerned with the offering of sacrifice, but with His having sat down. So that it does not contradict 9. 28.
on. Gr. *en*. Ap. 104. viii.
13 expecting. Gr. *ekdechomai*. See Acts 17. 16. Cp. 9. 28.
His footstool = footstool of His feet. The seventh reference to Ps. 110. 1 in the N.T. See 1. 13.
15 Holy Ghost. Ap. 101. II. 3.
is, &c. = beareth witness. Gr. *martureō*. See p. 1511.
after. Gr. *meta*. Ap. 104. xi. 2.
that He had = having.
16 covenant. See 8. 6.
make. Gr. *diatithēmi*. See 8. 10.
with. Gr. *pros*. Ap. 104. xv. 3.
LORD. Ap. 98. VI. i. β. 1. B. a.
I will put = giving.
into = upon. Gr. *epi*. Ap. 104. ix. 3.
in = upon, as above. **write.** See 8. 10.
17 iniquities. Gr. *anomia*. Ap. 128. III. 4.
no more = by no means (Gr. *ou mē*. Ap. 105. III) any more (Gr. *eti*).
18 no more = no longer. Gr. *ouketi*. The argument of the Priesthood of Christ, begun in 5. 1, here triumphantly concluded.

10. 19—12. 29 (*D*, p. 1822). PARTICULAR APPLICATION. (*Extended Alternation.*)

D | C | E | 10. 19-23. Exhortation to draw near in view of Christ being accessible and faithful.
        F | 10. 24, 25. Duty to accept exhortation.
        G | 10. 26-31. Warning in view of God's being the living God.
    D | H | 10. 32-37. Patience in view of the promise.
        I | 10. 38, 39. Living by faith.
    D | *I* | 11. 1-40. Examples of faith.
        H | 12. 1. Patience in view of the examples.
    C | *E* | 12. 2-4. Exhortation to look away from examples to the supreme Example.
        F | 12. 5-24. Duty to endure chastening.
        G | 12. 25-29. Warning in view of God's being a consuming fire.

19 boldness. Gr. *parrhēsia*. See 3. 6. **to enter** = for (Gr. *eis*) the entering (Gr. *eisodos*. Acts 13. 24) of. **the holiest.** See 8. 2. The Heavenly Holiest. **Jesus.** Ap. 98. X. **20 new** = newly slain. Gr. *prosphatos*. Only here. The adv. Acts 18. 2 (lately). **and** = and yet. **living way.** Fig. *Idiōma*. Ap. 6. **hath.** Omit. **consecrated.** Gr. *enkainizō*. See 9. 18. **veil.** See 6. 19. **21 an High** = a Great. **over.** Gr. *epi*. Ap. 104. ix. 3. **house.** See 3. 6. **22 with.** Gr. *meta*. Ap. 104. xi. 1. **true.** Gr. *alēthinos*. Ap. 175. 2. **full assurance.** See 6. 11. **faith.** Gr. *pistis*. Ap. 150. II. 1. **having, &c.** = sprinkled (9. 13) as to the hearts. **from.** Gr. *apo*. Ap. 104. iv. **evil.** Gr. *ponēros*. Ap. 128. III. 1. **our bodies, &c.** = bathed (Gr. *louō*. Ap. 136. iii) as to the body. **23 hold fast.** Gr. *katechō*. See 3. 6, 14. **profession** = confession. Gr. *homologia*. See 2 Cor. 9. 13. *our* **faith** = the hope. Gr. *elpis*. **without wavering** = unwavering. Gr. *aklinēs*. Only here. This agrees with "confession". **faithful.** Gr. *pistos*. Ap. 150. III. **24 consider.** Ap. 133. II. 4. **to provoke** = for (Gr. *eis*) provoking. Gr. *paroxusmos*. See Acts 15. 39. Cp. Acts 17. 16. **unto love** = of love. Ap. 135. II. 1. **25 Not.** Gr. *mē*. Ap. 105. II. **forsaking.** Gr. *enkataleipō*. See Acts 2. 27. **assembling . . . together.** Gr. *episunagōgē*. See 2 Thess. 2. 1. **some.** Gr. *tines*. Ap. 124. 4. **exhorting.** Gr. *parakaleō*. Ap. 134. I. 6. **see.** Gr. *blepō*. Ap. 133. I. 5. **day.** See notes on Isa. 2. 12. **approaching** = drawing nigh, as Jas. 5. 8. **26 if, &c.** = we sinning. Gr. *hamartanō*. Ap. 128. I. i. **wilfully.** Gr. *hekousiōs*. Only here and 1 Pet. 5. 2 (willingly). The adj. only in Philem. 14. The sin here is the deliberate turning back to Judaism. Cp. 6. 4-6. **that we have** = having. **knowledge.** Gr. *epignōsis*. Ap. 132. II. ii. **remaineth.** See 4. 6. **no more** = no longer. Gr. *ouketi*. **27 certain.** Gr. *tis*. Ap. 123. 3. **fearful.** Gr. *phoberos*. Only here, *v.* 31, and 12. 21. **looking for.** Gr. *ekdochē*. Only here. Cp. *v.* 13. **judgment.** See 9. 27. **fiery indignation** = jealousy, or fervour of fire. A Hebraism. See Ps. 79. 5. Ezek. 36. 5; 38. 19. Zeph. 1. 18; 3. 8. Cp. Deut. 29. 20. **which shall** = about to. **adversaries.** Gr. *hupenantios*. Only here and Col. 2. 14.

28 °He that °despised °Moses' law °died °with-
out °mercy °under two or three °witnesses:
29 Of how much °sorer °punishment, suppose ye, shall he be °thought worthy, who hath
°trodden under foot the °Son of [7]God, and
hath °counted the blood of the [16]covenant,
°wherewith He was sanctified, an °unholy
thing, and hath °done despite unto the [15]Spirit
of °grace?
30 For we °know Him that °hath said,
°"**Vengeance *belongeth* °unto Me, I will
recompense, saith the [16]LORD.**" And again,
"**The [16]LORD shall °judge His people.**"
31 *It is* a [27]fearful thing to fall [5]into the
hands of the °living [7]God.
D H 32 But °call to remembrance the former days,
[3]in which, °after ye were °illuminated, ye °en-
dured a great °fight of °afflictions;
33 °Partly, °whilst ye were °made a gazingstock both by °reproaches and °afflictions;
and partly, whilst ye became °companions of
them that °were so used.
34 For ye °had compassion °of me in my
bonds, and took °joyfully the °spoiling of your
goods, °knowing °in yourselves that ye have
°in heaven a better and an °enduring °sub-
stance.
35 °Cast [25]not away therefore your °confi-
dence, which hath great °recompence of reward.
36 For ye have need of °patience, [9]that, °after
ye have done the [7]will of [7]God, ye °might
receive the °promise.
37 For yet °a little while, and °**He That shall
come will come, and will [1]not °tarry.**
I 38 **Now the °just shall live °by [22]faith: but
°if *any man* °draw back, My °soul shall have
[6]no pleasure [3]in him.**
39 But we are [1]not of °them who draw back
°unto °perdition; but of °them that believe
[19]to the °saving of the °soul.

I K M O **11** Now °faith is the °substance of things
hoped for, the °evidence of things °not
°seen.

28 He, &c. = Any one (Gr. *tis*) despising (Gr. *atheteō*, set at nought. See John 12. 48). **Moses'.** See 3. 2. **died** = dieth. **without.** See 9. 7. **mercy.** Gr. *oiktirmos.* See Rom. 12. 1. The word is in the plural, "mercies", for emphasis. Fig. *Heterōsis* (of number), Ap. 6. **under** = upon (the testimony of). Gr. *epi.* Ap. 104. ix. 2. **witnesses.** Gr. *martus.* See John 1. 7 & cp. p. 1511. Reference to Deut. 17. 2–6.

29 sorer = worse, as elsewhere. Gr. *cheirōn.* **punishment.** Gr. *timōria.* Only here. **thought worthy.** Gr. *axioō.* See 3. 3. **trodden** = trampled. Same as Matt. 7. 6. **Son of God.** Ap. 98. XV. **counted.** Gr. *hēgeomai.* See Acts 26. 2. **wherewith** = with (Gr. *en.* Ap. 104. viii) which. **unholy** = "unclean", or "valueless". Cp. Mark 7. 2. Acts 11. 8; &c. **done, &c.** = insulted. Gr. *enubrizō.* Only here. Cp. Acts 14. 5. **grace.** Gr. *charis.* Ap. 184. I. 1. This expression only here.

30 know. Gr. *oida.* Ap. 132. I. i. **hath.** Omit. **Vengeance.** Gr. *ekdikēsis.* See Acts 7. 24. **unto** = to. **judge.** Gr. *krinō.* Ap. 122. 1 These quotations are from Deut. 32. 35, 36. Cp. Rom. 12. 19.

31 living God. See 3. 12.

32 call to remembrance = keep ever in mind. Gr. *anamimnēskō.* See 1 Cor. 4. 17. **after ye were** = having been. **illuminated.** Gr. *phōtizō.* See 6. 4 and cp. Ap. 130. 3. **endured.** Gr. *hupomenō.* Same word in 12. 2, 3, 7. **fight.** Gr. *athlēsis.* Only here. **afflictions.** Gr. *pathēma,* as Rom. 8. 18.

33 Partly. Add "indeed". **whilst, &c.** = being. **made a gazingstock.** Gr. *theatrizomai.* Only here. Cp. 1 Cor. 4. 9 and Ap. 133. I. 11. **reproaches.** Gr. *oneidismos.* See Rom. 15. 3. **afflictions.** Gr. *thlipsis.* See Acts 14. 22. **companions.** Gr. *koinōnos.* See 2 Cor. 1. 7. **were . . . used** = were thus living. Gr. *anastrephō.* See 2 Cor. 1. 12.

34 had compassion of = sympathized with. Gr. *sumpatheō.* See 4. 15. **of me, &c.** The texts read "of prisoners". Gr. *desmios* instead of *desmos.* **joyfully** = with (Gr. *meta.* Ap. 104. xi. 1) joy. **spoiling.** Gr. *harpagē.* Only here, Matt. 23. 25 (extortion). Luke 11. 39 (ravening). **knowing.** Gr. *ginōskō.* Ap. 132. I. ii. **in.** Omit. **in heaven.** The texts omit. **enduring.** Gr. *menō.* See p. 1511. **substance.** Gr. *huparxis.* See Acts 2. 45. This *v.* contains an example of Fig. *Paregmenon* (Ap. 6).

35 Cast . . . away. Gr. *apoballō.* Only here and Mark 10. 50. **confidence.** Same as "boldness", *v.* 19. **recompence, &c.** Gr. *misthapodosia.* See 2. 2.

36 patience. See Luke 8. 15. **after ye have** = having. **might** = may. **promise.** See 4. 1.

37 a little while. Gr. *mikron hoson hoson* = a very, very little while. See Isa. 26. 20 (Sept.). **He That shall come** = the Coming One. Cp. Dan. 7. 13, 14. Matt. 11. 3. Luke 7. 19. **tarry.** Gr. *chronizō.* Only here and Matt. 24. 48; 25. 5. Luke 1. 21; 12. 45.

38 just. Gr. *dikaios.* Ap. 191. 1. The third time of quoting Hab. 2. 4. See Rom. 1. 17. **by.** Gr. *ek.* Ap. 104. vii. **if.** Gr. *ean.* Ap. 118. 1. b. **draw back.** Gr. *hupostellō.* See Gal. 2. 12. **soul.** Ap. 110. IV. 1.

39 them who draw back = the drawing back. Gr. *hupostolē.* Only here. **unto.** Gr. *eis.* Ap. 104. vi. **perdition.** Gr. *apōleia.* See John 17. 12. **them that believe** = of faith, *v.* 38. **saving.** Gr. *peripoiēsis.* See Eph. 1. 14. **soul.** Ap. 110. III. 2.

11. 1–40 (*I*, p. 1838). EXAMPLES OF FAITH. (*Alternation and Introversion.*)

D | *I* | K | M | O | 1–7. A group of three. Abel, Enoch, Noah.
P | 8–12. Abraham and Sarah.
N | 13–19. General reflections.
L | Q | 20, 21. Isaac and Jacob.
R | 22. Joseph.
Q | 23–28. Moses' parents and Moses.
K | *M* | *P* | 29–31. Israel and Rahab.
O | 32–38. Two groups. Faith conquering through God; faith suffering for God.
N | 39, 40. General reflections.

11. 1 faith. Gr. *pistis.* Ap. 150. II. 1. **substance.** Gr. *hupostasis.* See 1. 3 and 2 Cor. 9. 4. Used of title-deeds in the Papyri. **evidence** = proof. Gr. *elenchos.* Only here and 2 Tim. 3. 16. Cp. Rom. 10. 17. **not.** Gr. *ou.* Ap. 105. I. **seen.** Gr. *blepō.* Ap. 133. I. 5.

2 For °by it the °elders °obtained a good report.

3 Through [1]faith we understand that the °worlds were °framed by the °word of °God, °so that things which are [1]seen °were °not made °of things which do °appear.

4 By [1]faith °Abel offered °unto [3]God a more excellent sacrifice °than Cain, °by which he °obtained witness that he was °righteous, [3]God °testifying °of his gifts: and °by it he being dead yet °speaketh.

5 By [1]faith °Enoch was °translated that he should [3]not °see death; and was [1]not found, because [3]God had °translated him: for °before his °translation he °had this testimony, that he °pleased [3]God.

6 But °without [1]faith *it is* impossible to [5]please *Him:* for he that cometh to [3]God must °believe that He °is, and *that* He °is a °rewarder of them that °diligently seek Him.

7 By [1]faith °Noah, °being warned of God °of things °not [1]seen as yet, °moved with fear, prepared an ark °to the °saving of his house; [4]by the which he °condemned the °world, and became heir of the °righteousness which is °by [1]faith.

P 8 By [1]faith °Abraham, when he was called to go out °into a place which he °should after receive °for an inheritance, obeyed; and he went out, [3]not °knowing whither he went.

9 By [1]faith he °sojourned° in the °land of promise, as *in* a °strange *country*, dwelling °in °tabernacles °with Isaac and Jacob, the °heirs with him of the same promise:

10 For he °looked for °a city which hath °foundations, whose °builder and °maker *is* [3]God.

11 Through [1]faith °also Sara herself °received °strength °to °conceive seed, and °was delivered of a child when she was °past °age, because she °judged Him °faithful Who had promised.

12 Therefore °sprang there even °of one, and °him as good as dead, *so many* **as the °stars of the °sky in multitude, and as the °sand which is °by the sea shore °innumerable.**

2 by. Gr. *en.* Ap. 104. viii.
elders. See Acts 2. 17: equivalent to "fathers" of 1. 1.
obtained, &c. = were borne witness to. Gr. *martureō.* See p. 1511.
3 worlds = ages. Gr. *aiōn.* Ap. 129. 2.
framed = prepared, as 10. 5. Gr. *katartizō.* Ap. 125. 8.
word. Gr. *rhēma.* See Mark 9. 32.
God. Ap. 98. I. i. 1.
so = to (Gr. *eis*) the end.
were . . . made = came into being. Gr. *ginomai,* to become.
not. Gr. *mē.* Ap. 105. II.
of. Gr. *ek.* Ap. 104. vii.
appear. Gr. *phainō.* Ap. 106. I. 1. The reference is not to creation, but to the ordering by God of the dispensations, each of which succeeded but did not spring from its predecessor as a plant does from its seed. By rendering *aiōnas* as "worlds" here; *katērtisthai* as "framed", instead of "prepared"; and *gegonenai* as "made", instead of "came into being", or "came to pass", the meaning of this important statement is lost.
4 Abel. Abel illustrates faith's *worship.*
unto = to. **than.** Gr. *para.* Ap. 104. xii. 3.
by. Gr. *dia.* Ap. 104. v. 1.
obtained witness. Gr. *martureō,* as in *v.* 2.
righteous. Gr. *dikaios.* Ap. 191. 1.
testifying. Gr. *martureō,* as above.
of = upon. Gr. *epi.* Ap. 104. ix. 2.
speaketh. Gr. *laleō.* Ap. 121. 7.
5 Enoch. In Enoch we see faith's *walk.*
translated. Gr. *metatithēmi.* See Acts 7. 16.
see. Gr. *eidon.* Ap. 133. I. 1.
before. Gr. *pro.* Ap. 104. xiv.
translation. Gr. *metathesis.* See 7. 12.
had this testimony = was borne witness to, as *v.* 2.
pleased. Gr. *euaresteō.* Only here, *v.* 6, and 13. 16.
6 without. Gr. *chōris.* See 4. 15.
believe. Gr. *pisteuō.* Ap. 150. I. 1. iii.
is. Gr. *esti.* The verb substantive.
is. Gr. *ginomai,* to become.
rewarder. Gr. *misthapodotēs.* Only here. Cp. *v.* 26, and 10. 35.
diligently seek. Gr. *ekzēteō.* See Acts 15. 17.
7 Noah. Noah is an example of faith's *witness.* Cp. 2 Pet. 2. 5.
being warned of God. Gr. *chrēmatizō.* See Luke 2. 26.
of. Gr. *peri.* Ap. 104. xiii. 1.
not . . . as yet. Gr. *mēdepō.* Only here.
moved with fear. Gr. *eulabeomai.* See Acts 23. 10.
to = for. Gr. *eis.* Ap. 104. vi.

saving = salvation. **condemned.** Gr. *katakrinō.* Ap. 122. 7. **world.** Gr. *kosmos.* Ap. 129. 1. **righteousness.** Gr. *dikaiosunē.* Ap. 191. 3. **by** = according to. Gr. *kata.* Ap. 104. x. 2. **8 Abraham.** In Abraham we see the obedience of faith (cp. Rom. 4. 3-22), and in Sarah faith's reckoning, or judging. **into.** Gr. *eis.* Ap. 104. vi. **should after** = was about to. **for.** Gr. *eis.* **knowing.** Gr. *epistamai.* Ap. 132. I. v. See Ap. 50. III, Part I, pp. 51, 52. **9 sojourned.** Gr. *paroikeō.* Only here and Luke 24. 18. **in.** Gr. *eis.* Ap. 104. vi. **land.** Gr. *gē.* Ap. 129. 4. **strange.** Gr. *allotrios.* Ap. 124. 6. **in.** Gr. *en.* Ap. 104. viii. **tabernacles** = tents. **with.** Gr. *meta.* Ap. 104. xi. 1. **heirs with him.** Gr. *sunklēronomos.* See Rom. 8. 17. **10 looked.** Gr. *ekdechomai.* See 10. 13. **a** = the. **foundations** = the foundations. Gr. *themelios.* Rev. 21. 14-20. See Ap. 146. **builder.** Gr. *technitēs* = Architect or Designer. See Acts 19. 24. From the same root we have *tektōn,* rendered "carpenter", Matt. 13. 55. Mark 6. 3, meaning builder or constructor. The word used in contempt of our Lord's earthly occupation (as being apart from Rabbinical connexion and teaching) is profoundly significant. Does it not suggest the reason why He elected for the period of His Incarnation to become a *carpenter,* rather than, e.g., a *shepherd,* as the Antitype of David? He, the great Architect, Designer, and Fabricator of "all things visible", including "the city which hath the foundations"! He, the Preparer, Arranger, and Constitutor of the ages or dispensations (*aiōns, v.* 3 and 1. 2), condescended to follow during "the days of His flesh" a trade involving the planning, calculation, and manual skill of a craftsman! **maker.** Gr. *dēmiourgos.* Only here. A word used by the Gnostics; and by Plato and Xenophon for the Creator of the world. **11 also** = even. **received.** It was given from above. **strength.** Gr. *dunamis.* Ap. 172. 1. **to conceive.** Lit. for (Gr. *eis*) casting down (Gr. *katabolē.* See Ap. 146). Cp. 2 Kings 19. 3. The strength was Divinely supplied not only to conceive, but to bring to the birth. **was delivered of** = brought forth. **past.** Gr. *para.* Ap. 104. xii. 3. **age** = season. Gr. *kairos.* Gen. 18. 11. **judged.** Same as "counted", 10. 29. **faithful.** Gr. *pistos.* Ap. 150. III. **12 sprang** = were begotten. **of.** Gr. *apo.* Ap. 104. iv. **him, &c.** = and that too, one having become dead. Gr. *nekroō.* See Rom. 4. 19. **stars, sand.** Gen. 15. 5; 22. 17; 26. 4. Ex. 32. 13. Isa. 48. 19. **sky** = heaven. See Matt. 6. 9, 10. **by.** Gr. *para.* Ap. 104. xii. 3. **innumerable.** Gr. *anarithmētos.* Only here.

N 13 These all died °in [1] faith, [3] not having
received the °promises, but having [5] seen them
°afar off, °and were persuaded of *them,* and
°embraced *them,* and confessed that they were
°**strangers and °pilgrims °on the °earth.**
14 For they that say such things °declare
plainly that they seek a °country.
15 And °truly °if they had been mindful of
that *country* °from whence they came out,
they might have had opportunity to have °re-
turned.
16 But °now they °desire a better *country,*
that is, an °heavenly: wherefore [3] God is [1] not
°ashamed to be °called their [3] God: for He
°hath prepared for them a °city.
17 By [1] faith Abraham, when he was °tried,
°offered up Isaac: and he that had °received
the promises °offered up his °only begotten
son,
18 °Of whom it was [4] said, That [-9] "**In Isaac**
°**shall thy seed be called:**"
19 °Accounting that [3] God *was* able to °raise
him up, even °from the dead; from whence
°also he received him [-9] in a °figure.

L Q 20 By [1] faith °Isaac blessed Jacob and Esau
°concerning things to come.
21 By [1] faith °Jacob, when he was a dying,
blessed °both the °sons of Joseph; and °wor-
shipped, *leaning* °upon the top of his staff.

R 22 By [1] faith Joseph, when °he died, made
mention [7] of the °departing of the °children of
Israel; and °gave commandment [20] concerning his bones.

Q 23 By [1] faith °Moses, when he was born, was
hid °three months °of his parents, because they
[5] saw *he was* a °proper °child; and they were
[1] not afraid of the king's °commandment.
24 By [1] faith [23] Moses, °when he was come to
years, °refused to be called the [21] son of Pharaoh's daughter;
25 °Choosing rather to °suffer affliction with
the °people of [3] God, than to °enjoy the pleasures of °sin °for a season;
26 °Esteeming the °reproach of °Christ
greater riches than the treasures °in Egypt:
for he °had respect °unto the °recompence of
the reward.
27 By [1] faith he forsook Egypt, [3] not fearing
the °wrath of the king: for he °endured, as
°seeing Him Who is °invisible.

13 in=according to. Gr. *kata.* Ap. 104. x. 2. Cp. *v.* 7.
promises. I. e. the things promised. Fig. *Metonymy* (of Adjunct). Ap. 6.
afar off=from afar. Gr. *porrōthen.* Only here and Luke 17. 12.
and were persuaded of. The texts omit.
embraced. Gr. *aspazomai.* Same as "salute", 13. 24.
strangers. Gr. *xenos.* See Acts 17. 18.
pilgrims. Gr. *parepidēmos.* Only here, 1 Pet. 1. 1; 2. 11. We must be strangers to the world ere we can become pilgrims in it. See Gen. 23. 4. 1 Chron. 29. 15. Ps. 39. 12.
on. Gr. *epi.* Ap. 104. ix. 1.
earth. Gr. *gē,* as *v.* 9.
14 declare plainly. Gr. *emphanizō.* See 9. 24. Ap. 106. I. iv.
country=a (true) home. Gr. *patris.* Only here and seven times in the Gospels.
15 truly if=if indeed.
if. Gr. *ei.* Ap. 118. 2. a.
from. Gr. *apo.* Ap. 104. iv.
returned. Gr. *anakamptō.* See Acts 18. 21.
16 now=as a matter of fact.
desire. Gr. *oregomai.* Only here, 1 Tim. 3. 1; 6. 10.
heavenly. See 3. 1.
ashamed. See 2. 11. Add "of them". Fig. *Tapeinōsis.* Ap. 6.
called. Gr. *epikaleomai.* See Acts 2. 21.
hath. Omit.
city. See *v.* 10.
17 tried=tested.
offered=hath offered.
received. Gr. *anadechomai.* See Acts 28. 7.
offered=was offering.
only begotten. Gr. *monogenēs.* See John 1. 14.
18 Of=With reference to. Gr. *pros.* Ap. 104. xv. 3.
shall, &c. Lit. shall a seed be called for thee. This is quoted from Gen. 21. 12.
19 Accounting=Reckoning. Gr. *logizomai.* See Rom. 4. 4.
raise up. Gr. *egeirō.* Ap. 178. I. 4.
from the dead. Gr. *ek nekrōn.* Ap. 139. 3.
also, &c.=he did even in a figure receive (Gr. *komizō,* as Matt. 25. 27) him back.
figure. Gr. *parabolē.* See 9. 9. Isaac was, as far as Abraham was concerned, to all intents and purposes, dead, and so became a type of Christ in resurrection.
20 Isaac. Isaac shows us faith overcoming the will of the flesh, in that he blessed Jacob instead of Esau.
concerning. Gr. *peri.* Ap. 104. xiii. 1.
21 Jacob. Jacob's faith was manifested by his blessing each of Joseph's sons, putting Ephraim first according to God's will. See Gen. 48. 5-20.
both=each of.
sons. Gr. *huios.* Ap. 108. iii.
worshipped. Gr. *proskuneō.* Ap. 137. 1.
upon. Gr. *epi.* Ap. 104. ix. 3. Jacob's worship was because he had just secured Joseph's promise that he would not bury him in Egypt but in Machpelah, thus enabling him to express his confidence in God's promises. This is recorded in Gen. 47. 31, before the blessing of Joseph's sons. **22 he died**=was ending (life). **departing.** Gr. *exodos.* Only here, Luke 9. 31, and 2 Pet. 1. 15. **children**=sons, as in *v.* 21. **gave commandment.** Gr. *entellomai.* First occ. Matt. 4. 6. The faith of Joseph was shown in his confidence that God would fulfil the promise to Abraham, Isaac, and Jacob. Gen. 50. 24, 25. Cp. Gen. 48. 21. **23 Moses.** See 3. 2. **three months.** Gr. *trimēnon.* Only here. **of**=by. Gr. *hupo.* Ap. 104. xviii. 1. **proper.** Gr. *asteios.* See Acts 7. 20. **child.** Gr. *paidion.* Ap. 108. v. **commandment.** Gr. *diatagma.* Only here. Cp. Rom. 13. 2. Moses' parents must have had some revelation from God, on which their faith could act. **24 when he was, &c.** Lit. having become great, i. e. grown up. **refused.** Gr. *arneomai.* Gen. transl. "deny". **25 Choosing**=Having chosen. Gr. *haireomai.* See Phil. 1. 22. **suffer affliction with.** Gr. *sunkakoucheomai.* Only here. **people.** Gr. *laos.* See Acts 2. 47. **enjoy the pleasures**=have enjoyment (Gr. *apolausis.* See 1 Tim. 6. 17). **sin.** Gr. *hamartia.* Ap. 128. I. ii. 1. **for a season.** Gr. *proskairos.* See 2 Cor. 4. 18. **26 Esteeming.** Same as judged, *v.* 11. **reproach.** Gr. *oneidismos.* See 10. 33. **Christ.** I. e. the Messiah. Ap. 98. IX. Gen. of Relation. Ap. 17. 5. Moses, as well as Abraham, looked forward to His day. John 8. 56. **in.** The texts read "of". **had respect.** Gr. *apoblepō,* lit. look away. Only here. **unto.** Gr. *eis.* Ap. 104. vi. **recompence, &c.** Gr. *misthapodosia.* See 2. 2. **27 wrath.** See Ex. 10. 28, 29; 11. 4-8. **endured.** Gr. *kartereō.* Only here. Cp. Acts 1. 14. **seeing.** Gr. *horaō.* Ap. 133. I. 8. **invisible.** Gr. *aoratos.* See Rom. 1. 20. He feared not the visible king, because he had seen the Invisible. Cp. Elijah (1 Kings 17. 1; 18. 15), and Elisha (2 Kings 3. 14; 5. 16).

28 °Through [1]faith he kept the °passover,
and the °sprinkling of blood, °lest he that
°destroyed the °firstborn should °touch them.
M P 29 By [1]faith they °passed through the Red
sea as [4]by dry *land:* which the Egyptians
°assaying to do were °drowned.
30 By [1]faith the walls of Jericho fell down,
after they were °compassed about °seven
days.
31 By [1]faith the harlot Rahab °perished [1]not
with them that °believed not, when she had
received the °spies °with peace.
O 32 And what shall I more say? for the time
would °fail me °to tell [7]of Gedeon, and *of* Barak,
and *of* Samson, and *of* Jephthae; *of*
David also, and Samuel, and *of* the prophets:
33 Who °through [1]faith °subdued °kingdoms,
wrought [7]righteousness, °obtained promises,
°stopped the mouths of lions,
34 Quenched the °violence of fire, escaped the
°edge of the sword, °out of weakness were
°made strong, °waxed valiant [-9]in fight, °turned
to flight the armies of the °aliens.
35 Women received their [19]dead °raised to
life again: and °others were °tortured, [1]not
accepting °deliverance; °that they might obtain
a better °resurrection:
36 And °others had °trial of *cruel* °mockings
and scourgings, yea, moreover of bonds and
°imprisonment:
37 They were °stoned, they were °sawn
asunder, were tempted, °were slain °with the
sword: they °wandered about [-9]in °sheepskins
°and °goatskins; being °destitute, °afflicted,
°tormented;
38 (Of whom the [7]world was [1]not worthy:)
they wandered °in deserts, and *in* mountains,
and *in* °dens and °caves of the [13]earth.
N 39 And these all, having [2]obtained a good
report [33]through [1]faith, °received [1]not the
promise,
40 [3]God having °provided some better thing
°for us, [35]that they [6]without us should [3]not be
°made perfect.
H **12** °Wherefore °seeing we also are °compassed
about with so great a °cloud of
°witnesses, °let us lay aside every °weight,

28 Through. In *vv.* 3, 11, 28, the dative case is rendered "Through", in fourteen other *vv.* it is rendered "By".

passover. Gr. *pascha.* After the Gospels only here, Acts 12. 4 (Easter). 1 Cor. 5. 7.

sprinkling. Gr. *proschusis.* Only here.

lest=in order that (Gr. *hina*) not (Gr. *mē*).

destroyed. Gr. *olothreuō.* Only here.

firstborn. Gr. *prōtotokos.* See Rom. 8. 29. This adj. is neuter plural. Cp. 12. 23.

touch. Gr. *thinganō.* See 12. 20. Col. 2. 21.

29 passed through. Gr. *diabainō.* See Acts 16. 9.

assaying=endeavouring or attempting (Gr. *peira*; here and *v.* 36).

drowned=swallowed up. Gr. *katapinō*, as 1 Cor. 15. 54.

30 compassed about=encircled. Gr. *kukloō.* See Acts 14. 20.

seven days=for (Gr. *epi.* Ap. 104. ix. 3) seven days.

31 perished . . . with. Gr. *sunapollumi.* Only here.

believed not=were disobedient. See 3. 18.

spies. Gr. *kataskopos.* Only here. The verb. in Gal. 2. 4.

with. Gr. *meta.* Ap. 104. xi. 1.

32 fail. Gr. *epileipō.* Only here.

to tell=in narrating. Gr. *diēgeomai.* See Acts 8. 33. By Fig. *Paraleipsis* (Ap. 6), the writer briefly alludes to many worthies, of whom time fails to speak in detail. Also Fig. *Epitrochasmos*, or *Summarising.* In the summary are four judges, two prophets, and a group in which all other prophets are included.

The four judges form an introversion.

α | Gedeon. Judg. 6 and 7.
β | Barak. Judg. 4 and 5.
β | Samson. Judg. 13-16.
α | Jephthae. Judg. 11 and 12.

Gedeon and Jephthae stand out together as higher examples of faith, Barak and Samson as associated with women, the former in his rise, the latter in his fall. The other three form another introversion.

γ | David.
δ | Samuel.
γ | The prophets.

33 through. Gr. *dia.* Ap. 104. v. 1.

subdued. Gr. *katagōnizomai.* Only here. Cp. Luke 13. 24.

kingdoms. See Deut. 4. 46, 47. Josh. 5-14.

obtained, &c. See 6. 15.

stopped. Gr. *phrassō.* See Rom. 3. 19. Judg. 14. 5, 6. 1 Sam. 17. 34-37. Dan. 6. 22, 23.

34 violence=strength, *v.* 11. See Dan. 3. 27.

edge=mouth. A Hebraism; occ. over thirty times in the O.T. Cp. Luke 21. 24. See Josh. 6. 21. 2 Kings 10. 25; &c.

out of. Gr. *apo.* Ap. 104. iv.

made strong. Gr. *endunamoō.* Cp. Ex. 4. 10-16. Isaiah, ch. 6. Jer. 1. 6-10.

waxed, &c.=became mighty in battle. **turned . . . armies**=overturned the camps. **aliens.** Same as strange, *v.* 9. **35 raised, &c.**=from (Gr. *ek*) resurrection (Ap. 178. II. 1). **others.** Gr. *allos.* Ap. 124. 1. **tortured**=bastinadoed to death. Gr. *tumpanizomai.* Only here. **deliverance.** Same as "redemption", 9. 15. See 2 Macc. 6. 19-30; 7. 1-42. **that**=in order that. Gr. *hina.* **resurrection.** Gr. *anastasis*, as above. **36 others.** Gr. *heteros.* Ap. 124. 2. **trial.** See *v.* 29. **mockings.** Gr. *empaigmos.* Only here. **imprisonment**=prison. See Gen. 39. 20 (Joseph). 1 Kings 22. 26, 27 (Micaiah). **37 stoned.** 1 Kings 21. 13 (Naboth). 2 Chron. 24. 20, 21 (Zechariah). Jeremiah after the scene in Pathros (ch. 44), according to the Gemara. **sawn asunder.** Gr. *prizō.* Only here. This was the death of Isaiah during the Manassean persecution (cp. 2 Kings 21. 16), according to the Gemara. **were slain**=died. **with the sword.** Lit. in (Gr. *en*) the slaughter of the sword. **wandered about.** Gr. *perierchomai.* See Acts 19. 13. **sheepskins.** Gr. *mēlōtē.* Only here. **and.** Read "in" (Gr. *en*). **goatskins.** Gr. *aigeios (derma).* Only here. **destitute.** Gr. *hustereō*, to lack. See Luke 15. 14. **afflicted.** Gr. *thlibō.* See 2 Cor. 1. 6. **tormented**=vilely treated. Gr. *kakoucheō.* Cp. *v.* 25; 13. 3 (suffer adversity). See 1 Thess. 2. 2. **38 in.** The texts read *epi.* Ap. 104. ix. 2. **dens.** Gr. *spēlaion.* See Luke 19. 46. **caves.** Gr. *opē.* Only here and James 3. 11 (place). **39 received.** Same Gr. word as in 19. See Note there. **40 provided.** G. *problepō.* Only here. **for**=concerning. Gr. *peri.* Ap. 104. xiii. 1. **made perfect**=perfected. Gr. *teleioō.* Ap. 125. 2. Cp. 2. 10.

12. 1 Wherefore. Gr. *toigaroun*, a very emph. word of inference; occ. only here and 1 Thess. 4. 8. Resume from 10. 39. **seeing, &c.**=we also having so great a cloud of witnesses surrounding us. **compassed about**=surrounding. Gr. *perikeimai.* See Acts 28. 20. **cloud**=throng. Gr. *nephos.* Only here. The usual word for "cloud" is *nephelē.* **witnesses.** Gr. *martus.* See John 1. 7. Whose lives witness to the power of faith. Not "spectators", for then the word would be *autoptēs* (Luke 1. 2) or *epoptēs* (2 Pet. 1. 16). **let us lay aside**=laying aside. See Rom. 13. 12. **weight.** Gr. *onkos.* Only here.

and the °sin which °doth so easily beset *us*,
and let us run °with °patience the °race that
is °set before us,
C E **2** °Looking °unto °Jesus the °Author and
°Finisher of °*our* °faith, Who °for the joy that
was [1]set before Him °endured °the cross, despising °the shame, and °is set down °at the
right hand of the throne of °God.
3 For °consider Him °That [2]endured such
°contradiction °of sinners °against Himself,
°lest ye °be wearied °and faint in your °minds.
4 Ye have °not yet °resisted °unto blood,
°striving °against °sin.

F S¹ q¹ **5** And ye have °forgotten the °exhortation
which °speaketh °unto you as °unto °children,
**"My °son, °despise °not thou the °chastening
of the °LORD, °nor [3]faint when thou art °re-
buked [3]of Him:**

r¹ **6 For whom the [5]LORD °loveth He °chasten-
eth, and °scourgeth every [5]son whom He receiveth."**

q² **7** °If ye [2]endure [5]chastening, [2]God °dealeth
with you as with [5]sons; for what [5]son is he
whom °the father [6]chasteneth °not?

r² **8** But °if ye be °without °chastisement,
whereof all °are °partakers, then are ye °bas-
tards, and [7]not [5]sons.

q³ **9** °Furthermore, we °have had fathers of our
flesh °which corrected *us*, and we °gave °*them*
reverence:

r³ shall we [7]not much rather °be in subjection
[5]unto the °Father of °spirits, and °live?

q⁴ **10** For they verily °for a few days [6]chas-
tened *us* °after their own pleasure;

sin. Ap. 128. I. ii. 1.
doth so easily beset. Gr. *euperistatos*. Only here.
with = through. Gr. *dia*. Ap. 104. v. 1.
patience = patient continuance. See Rom. 2. 7.
race. Gr. *agōn*. See Phil. 1. 30. Always transl. fight, conflict, &c., save here. The word means the place of assembly, and then the games witnessed, and then any contest, a lawsuit, &c.
set before. Gr. *prokeimai*. Cp. 6. 18.
2 Looking = Looking away from (these witnesses). Gr. *aphoraō*. Ap. 133. 9. Cp. Phil. 2. 23.
unto. Gr. *eis*. Ap. 104. vi.
Jesus. Ap. 98. X.
Author. See 2. 10 and Acts 3. 15.
Finisher = Perfecter. Gr. *teleiōtēs*. Only here. Cp. Ap. 125. 1, 2.
faith. Gr. *pistis*. Ap. 150. II. 1. He stands at the head of the train of faith's heroes, and alone brought faith to perfection. Omit *our*.
for. Gr. *anti*. Ap. 104. ii.
endured = patiently endured. See 10. 32.
the = a. **the shame** = shame.
is set. All the texts read, "hath sat".
at = on. Gr. *en*. Ap. 104. viii.
God. Ap. 98. I. i. 1. The charge is to look away from the witnesses of the past to Him Who is the faithful and true Witness (Rev. 3. 14).
3 consider. Gr. *analogizomai*. Only here.
That = That hath.
contradiction. Gr. *antilogia*. See 6. 16. Cp. Luke 2. 34, where the verb *antilegō* occurs.
of = by. Gr. *hupo*. Ap. 104. xviii. 1.
against. Gr. *eis*. Ap. 104. vi.
lest = in order that (Gr. *hina*) not (Gr. *mē*).
be wearied. Gr. *kamnō*. Only here, Jas. 5. 15. Rev. 2. 3.
and faint = fainting. Gr. *ekluō*. See Gal. 6. 9.
minds = souls. Ap. 110. IV. 2.
4 not yet. Gr. *oupō*.
resisted. Gr. *antikathistēmi*. Only here.
unto. Gr. *mechris*. Cp. Phil. 2. 8.
striving. Gr. *antagōnizomai*. Only here.
against. Gr. *pros*. Ap. 104. xv. 3. sin. Ap. 128. I. ii. 1. The Lord's example is set before them. Hitherto they had to endure spoliation and shameful treatment, but not martyrdom. This is in favour of the early date of the Epistle (Ap. 180). The words "not yet" suggest a time before the persecution under Nero, which began A. D. 65 and lasted till his death A. D. 68.

12. 5-24 (*F*, p. 1838). CHASTISEMENT. (*Division.*)

F | S¹ | 5-11. Duty to endure chastening.
  | S² | 12-24. Counsels and encouragements.

12. 5-11 (S¹, above). DUTY TO ENDURE CHASTENING. (*Extended alternation.*)

S¹ | q¹ | 5. Chastening not to be despised.
   | r¹ | 6. Proof of love.
   | q² | 7. A mark of sonship. Positive.
   | r² | 8. The lack of it. Negative.
   | q³ | 9-. Submission to earthly fathers.
   | r³ | -9. Much more to Father of spirits.
   | q⁴ | 10-. The earthly fathers as they thought well.
   | r⁴ | -10. The Heavenly Father for our profit.
   | q⁵ | 11-. Chastening for the present grievous.
   | r⁵ | -11. The fruits afterwards.

5 forgotten. Gr. *eklanthanomai*. Only here. **exhortation.** Gr. *paraklēsis*. See Rom. 12. 8 and Ap. 134. I. 6. **speaketh.** Gr. *dialegomai*. See Acts 17. 2. **unto** = to. **children, son.** Gr. *huios*. Ap. 108. iii. **despise.** Gr. *oligōreō*. Only here. See Prov. 3. 11, 12. **not.** Gr. *mē*. Ap. 105. II. **chastening.** Gr. *paideia*. See Eph. 6. 4. **LORD.** Ap. 98. VI. i. β. 1. B. a. **nor.** Gr. *mēde*. **rebuked.** Gr. *elenchō*. See Eph. 5. 11. **6 loveth.** Gr. *agapaō*. Ap. 135. I. 1. See Rev. 3. 19. **chasteneth.** Gr. *paideuō*. See 1 Cor. 11. 32. **scourgeth.** Gr. *mastigoō*. See John 19. 1. **7 If.** Gr. *ei*, but the texts read *eis*, i. e. Ye are suffering patiently for (*eis*) discipline. **dealeth.** Gr. *prospherō*. Occ. in Heb. twenty times; transl. "offer", save here. In this verse it is passive and means to do business with, deal with. **the** = a. **not.** Ap. 105. I. **8 if.** Gr. *ei*. Ap. 118. 2. a. **without.** Gr. *chōris*. See 4. 15. **chastisement** = chastening, as *vv.* 5, 7, 11. **are** = have become. **partakers.** Gr. *metochos*. See 1. 9. **bastards.** I. e. fictitious. Gr. *nothos*. Only here. **9 Furthermore** = Moreover. **have.** Omit. **which, &c.** = as correctors. Gr. *paideutēs*. Only here and Rom. 2. 20. **gave . . . reverence.** Gr. *entrepomai*. See 1 Cor. 4. 14. *them*. Omit. **be in subjection.** Gr. *hupotassō*. See 2. 5. **Father.** Ap. 98. III. **spirits.** Ap. 101. II. 5. Cp. Num. 16. 22. Job 33. 4. Eccl. 12. 7. Isa. 42. 5. Zech. 12. 1. Here not "angels" as some interpret, but the new-created spirits of His "sons". **live.** Ap. 170. 1. **10 for.** Gr. *pros*. Ap. 104. xv. 3. **after their own pleasure** = according as (Gr. *kata*) it seemed good to them.

r4 but He °for °*our* profit, °that *we* might °be partakers of His °holiness.

q5 11 Now °no [5]chastening [10]for the present seemeth to be °joyous, but °grievous:

r5 nevertheless afterward it yieldeth the °peaceable fruit of °righteousness [5]unto them which are °exercised °thereby.

S2 s1 12 Wherefore °**lift up the hands which °hang down, and the °feeble knees;**

13 And make °straight °paths for your feet, [8]lest that which is lame °be turned out of the way, but let it rather be °healed.

t1 14 °Follow peace °with all *men*,

s2 and °holiness [8]without which °no man °shall see °the LORD:

t2 15 °Looking diligently °lest °any °man °fail °of the °grace of [2]God; °lest °any root of °bitterness °springing up °trouble *you*,

s3 and °thereby many °be defiled;

t3 16 [15]Lest there *be* [15]any fornicator, or °profane person, as Esau, who °for one °morsel of meat °sold °his °birthright.

17 For ye °know how that °afterward, °when he would have °inherited the blessing, he was °rejected: for he found [11]no place of °repentance, °though he sought it carefully [14]with tears.

s4 18 For ye are [7]not come [5]unto the °mount °that might be touched, °and that burned with fire, °nor [5]unto °blackness, and °darkness, and °tempest,

19 And the °sound of a trumpet, and the voice of °words; which *voice* they that heard °intreated that the °word should [5]not be °spoken to them any more:

t4 20 (For they could [7]not endure that which was commanded, And °**if so much as a °beast °touch the mountain, it shall be stoned, °or thrust through with a dart:**

21 And so °terrible was the °sight, *that* °Moses said, "**I °exceedingly fear and quake:**")

s5 22 But ye are come [5]unto mount Sion, and

for. Gr. *epi*. Ap. 104. ix. 3.
our profit = that which is profitable.
that = to the end (Gr. *eis*) that.
be partakers. Gr. *metalambanō*. See 6. 7.
holiness. Gr. *hagiotēs*. Only here. Not the word in *v.* 14.
11 no chastening. Lit. all chastening seemeth not (Gr. *ou*).
joyous = of joy. Ap. 17. 1.
grievous = of grief.
peaceable. Gr. *eirēnikos*. Only here and Jas. 3. 17.
righteousness. Gr. *dikaiosunē*. Ap. 191. 3.
exercised. See 5. 14.
thereby = by (Gr. *dia*. Ap. 104. v. 1) it.

12. 12-24 (S2, p. 1843). COUNSELS AND ENCOURAGEMENTS. (*Extended Alternation.*)

S2 s1 | 12, 13. The weak to be helped.
t1 | 14-. Peace with all.
s2 | -14. Holiness essential.
t2 | 15-. Watching against failure.
s3 | -15. The defiling defect of bitterness.
t3 | 16, 17. The warning of Esau's disappointment.
s4 | 18, 19. The terribleness of Sinai.
t4 | 20, 21. Its threatening of death.
s5 | 22, 23. The blessedness of the heavenly Jerusalem.
t5 | 24. Its promise of life.

12 lift up. Gr. *anorthoō*. See Luke 13. 13. Elsewhere Acts 15. 16.
hang down. Gr. *pariemai*. Only here.
feeble = palsied. Gr. *paraluomai*. See Luke 5. 18.
13 straight. Gr. *orthos*. Only here and Acts 14. 10.
paths. Gr. *trochia*. Only here.
be turned out of the way. Gr. *ektrepomai*. See 1 Tim. 1. 6.
healed. Gr. *iaomai*. See Luke 6. 17.
14 Follow = Pursue. The force of the Gr. *diōkō* is seen in Phil. 3. 14 (press toward).
with. Gr. *meta*. Ap. 104. xi. 1.
holiness. Gr. *hagiasmos*. See Rom. 6. 19.
no man = no one. Gr. *oudeis*.
shall see. Gr. *opsomai*. Ap. 133. I. 8 (a.).
the Lord. Ap. 98. VI. i. β. 1. A. b.
15 Looking diligently. Gr. *episkopeō*. Only here and 1 Pet. 5. 2.
lest. Gr. *mē*. Ap. 105. II.
any. Gr. *tis*. Ap. 123. 3.
man = one.
fail. Gr. *hustereō*. Cp. 4. 1; 11. 37.
of = from. Gr. *apo*. Ap. 104. iv.
grace. Ap. 184. I. 1.

bitterness. Gr. *pikria*. See Acts 8. 23. springing = germinating. Gr. *phuō*. Only here and Luke 8. 6, 8. trouble. Gr. *enochleō*. Only here. See Acts 15. 19. thereby. Gr. *dia tautēs*. Some texts read *di' autēs*, the same as *v.* 11. be defiled. Gr. *miainō*. See John 18. 28. **16 profane.** Gr. *bebēlos*. See 1 Tim. 1. 9. for. Gr. *anti*. Ap. 104. ii. morsel of meat. Gr. *brōsis*. See Rom. 14. 17. sold. Gr. *apodidōmi*. Same as "yield", *v.* 11. his. The texts read "his own". birthright. Gr. *prōtotokia*. Only here. **17 know.** Gr. *oida*. Ap. 132. I. i. afterward. Gr. *metepeita*. Only here. Add "also". when he would have = wishing to. Gr. *thelō*. Ap. 102. 1. inherited. Gr. *klēronomeō*. See 1. 4. rejected. Gr. *apodokimazō*. Only here and 1 Pet. 2. 4, 7, after the Gospels. Cp. *dokimazō*, 3. 9. repentance. Gr. *metanoia*. Ap. 111. II. Repentance means a change of mind, and Esau sought to change his (father's) mind. though he sought . . . carefully = having sought carefully. Gr. *ekzēteō*. See 11. 6. **18 mount.** The texts omit. that might, &c. = that was touched. Gr. *psēlaphaō*. The ref. is to Ex. 19. 16-19. and. This and other five "ands" in *vv.* 18, 19 exemplify the Fig. *Polysyndeton* (Ap. 6). nor = and. blackness = a thick cloud. Gr. *gnophos*. Only here. darkness. Gr. *skotos*, but the texts read *zophos*. See 2 Pet. 2. 4, 17. Jude 6, 13. tempest. Gr. *thuella*. Only here. **19 sound.** Gr. *ēchos*. See Acts 2. 2. words. Gr. *rhēma*. See Mark 9. 32. intreated. Gr. *paraiteomai*. Same as "refuse" in *v.* 25. See Luke 14. 18 (make excuse). word. Gr. *logos*. Ap. 121. 10. spoken = added. **20 if.** Gr. *ean*. Ap. 118. 1. b. beast. Gr. *thērion*, not *zōon*. touch. See 11. 28. or thrust through, &c. All the texts omit. No doubt this is because of the complex Ellipsis. In Ex. 19. 13 we read, "There shall not a hand touch it, but he shall surely be stoned or shot through; whether it be beast or man, it shall not live". The work on "Figures of Speech" makes it clear thus:—"And if so much as [a man, or] a beast touch the mountain—[if a man] he shall be stoned or [if a beast] thrust through with a dart". **21 terrible.** Gr. *phoberos*. See 10. 27, 31. sight = spectacle. Gr. *phantazō*. Only here. See Acts 25. 23. Moses. See 3. 2. exceedingly fear and quake = am fearful (Gr. *ekphobos*. Cp. Mark 9. 6) and quaking (Gr. *entromos*. See Acts 7. 32).

[5]unto the city of °the living [2]God, the °heaven-
ly °Jerusalem, and to an °innumerable company of angels,
23 To the °general assembly and °church of
the °firstborn which are °written °in °heaven,
and to [2]God the °Judge of all, and to the
°spirits of °just men °made perfect,
t [5] 24 And to [2]Jesus the °Mediator of °the new
°covenant, and to the °blood of sprinkling that
°speaketh better things °than *that of* Abel.
G (p. 1838) 25 °See that ye °refuse [5]not Him That
[24]speaketh. For [8]if they escaped [7]not who °re-
fused Him That °spake °on °earth, much more
shall not we *escape*, °if we °turn away °from
Him That *speaketh* °from [23]heaven:
26 Whose voice then °shook the [25]earth: but
now He hath promised, saying, "**Yet °once more**
I °shake [7]not the [25]earth only, but °also
°heaven."
27 And this *word*, "Yet [26]once more," °signi-
fieth the °removing of those things that are
[26-]shaken, as of things that are made, °that
those things which °cannot be [26-]shaken may
°remain.
28 Wherefore we receiving a kingdom °which
cannot be moved, let us have [15]grace, °where-
by we may °serve [2]God °acceptably [14]with
°reverence and °godly fear:
29 For our [2]God *is* a °consuming fire.
A T **13** Let °brotherly love °continue.
2 °Be °not °forgetful °to entertain
strangers: for °thereby °some have °enter-
tained angels °unawares.
3 °Remember °them that are in bonds, as
°bound with them; *and* °them which suffer
adversity, as being yourselves also °in the
body.
4 °Marriage *is* honourable [3]in all, and the bed
°undefiled: but °whoremongers and adulterers
°God will °judge.
5 *Let your* °conversation *be* °without covetousness; *and* °*be* content with °such things as
ye have: for °He hath said, "**I will °never °leave**
thee, °nor °forsake thee."

22 the living God. See 3. 12.
heavenly. Gr. *epouranios.* Cp. 3. 1.
Jerusalem. Cp. Gal. 4. 26. Rev. 3. 12; 21. 2, 10.
innumerable company = myriads.
23 general assembly. Gr. *panēguris.* Only here.
church. Ap. 186.
firstborn = firstborn ones. Gr. *prōtotokos.* See 11. 28.
written. Gr. *apographō.* Only here and Luke 2. 1, 3, 5.
in. Gr. *en.* Ap. 104. viii.
heaven. Pl. See Matt. 6. 9, 10.
Judge. Gr. *kritēs.* Cp. Ap. 122. 1.
spirits. Ap. 101. II. 5.
just men. Gr. *dikaios.* Ap. 191. 1.
made perfect = perfected. See 11. 40. Ap. 125. 2. The standpoint is from "the glory" as in Rom. 8. 30.
24 Mediator. Gr. *mesitēs.* See 9. 15.
the = a.
covenant. See Matt. 26. 28.
blood of sprinkling (Gr. *rhantismos*). The phrase only here and 1 Pet. 1. 2 (sprinkling of blood).
speaketh. Gr. *laleō.* Ap. 121. 7.
than. Gr. *para.* Ap. 104. xii. 3. Cp. 1. 4. In verses 18–24 *seven* statements are set forth as to the Old Covenant dispensation, followed by *ten* of the New. Together *seventeen* (see Ap. 10).
25 See. Gr. *blepō.* Ap. 133. I. 5.
refuse. Same word as "intreat", *v.* 19.
spake. Gr. *chrēmatizō.* See 8. 5; 11. 7.
on. Gr. *epi.* Ap. 104. ix. 1.
earth. Gr. *gē.* Ap. 129. 4. **if we** = who.
turn away. Gr. *apostrephō*, as Acts 3. 26.
from. Gr. *apo.* Ap. 104. iv.
26 shook. Gr. *saleuō.* As Matt. 24. 29.
once. See 6. 4.
shake. Gr. *seiō.* See Hag. 2. 6, 7. Occ. Matt. 27. 51; 28. 2; &c. Cp. *seismos*, earthquake.
also heaven = the heaven (sing. Matt. 6. 9, 10) also.
27 signifieth. Gr. *dēloō.* See 1 Cor. 1. 11.
removing. Gr. *metathesis.* Cp. 7. 12; 11. 5.
that = in order that. Gr. *hina.*
cannot be = are not (Gr. *mē*) to be.
remain. Gr. *menō.* See p. 1511.
28 which cannot be moved = immovable. Gr. *asaleutos.* Only here and Acts 27. 41.
whereby = by (Gr. *dia.* Ap. 104. v. 1) which.
serve. Gr. *latreuō.* Ap. 190. III. 5.
acceptably. Gr. *euarestōs.* Only here. The adj. in 13. 21.
reverence. Gr. *aidōs.* Only here and 1 Tim. 2. 9. The texts read *deos*, awe.
godly fear. Gr. *eulabeia.* See 5. 7, the only other occ. **29 consuming fire.** From Deut. 4. 24. Cp. Exod. 24. 17. Ps. 50. 3; 97. 3. 2 Thess. 1. 8; &c. **consuming.** Gr. *katanaliskō.* Only here. Intensive of *analiskō* (Luke 9. 54. Gal. 5. 15. 2 Thess. 2. 8).

13. 1–25 (*A*, 1822). PRACTICAL CONCLUSION. (*Introversion.*)

T | 1–6. Exhortation.
  U | 7–9. Their teachers. Strange teachings unprofitable.
    V | 10, 11. The servers of the tabernacle.
    V | 12–16. The sanctified people.
  U | 17. Their teachers. Disobedience unprofitable.
T | 18–25. Closing requests and doxology.

13. 1 brotherly love. Gr. *philadelphia.* See Rom. 12. 10. **continue.** Gr. *menō.* See p. 1511. **2 Be not forgetful** = Forget not. **Be . . . forgetful.** Gr. *epilanthanomai.* See 6. 10. **not.** Gr. *mē.* Ap. 105. II. **to entertain, &c.** = hospitality. Gr. *philoxenia.* Only here and Rom. 12. 13. **thereby** = by (Gr. *dia.* Ap. 104. v. 1) this. **some.** Gr. *tines.* Ap. 124. 4. **entertained.** Gr. *xenizō.* See Acts 10. 6. The word only in Acts, here, and 1 Pet. 4. 4, 12. As Abraham, Lot, Manoah, Gideon; and cp. Matt. 25. 35. **unawares.** Gr. *lanthanō.* See Acts 26. 26. **3 Remember.** Gr. *mimnēskomai.* Cp. 2. 6. **them, &c.** = the bound ones. Gr. *desmios.* **bound, &c.** Gr. *sundeomai.* Only here. **them which, &c.** Gr. *kakoucheomai.* See 11. 37. Pagan writers notice the kindness of "Christians" to their brethren in affliction. **in.** Gr. *en.* Ap. 104. viii. **4 Marriage.** This is not a statement of fact, but an exhortation, "Let marriage be", &c. **undefiled.** Gr. *amiantos.* See 7. 26. **whoremongers** = fornicators, as 12. 16. **God.** Ap. 98. I. i. 1. **judge.** Gr. *krinō.* Ap. 122. 1. I. e. punish (Fig. *Metonymy* of cause. Ap. 6). **5 conversation** = bent, manner (of life). Gr. *tropos.* See Acts 1. 11. **without, &c.** Gr. *aphilarguros*, lit. without love of money. Only here and 1 Tim. 3. 3. ***be* content.** Gr. *arkeō.* See 2 Cor. 12. 9. 1 Tim. 6. 8. **such things, &c.** = the things that are present. **He** = Himself. **never** = by no means. Gr. *ou mē.* Ap. 105. III. **leave** = let . . . go. Gr. *aniēmi* See Acts 16. 26. **nor.** Lit. nor by no means. Gr. *oud' ou mē.* The strongest negative possible. **forsake.** Gr. *enkataleipō.* See Acts 2. 27.

6 So that we may boldly say, "**The °Lord is**
my °Helper, and I will °not fear what °man
shall do °unto me."

U 7 °Remember °them which have the rule over
you, °who °have spoken [6]unto you the °word
of [4]God; whose °faith °follow, °considering
the °end of *their* °conversation.
8 °Jesus Christ °the same yesterday, and to
day, and °for ever.
9 Be [2]not °carried about with °divers and
°strange doctrines. For *it is* a good thing that
the heart be °established °with °grace; [6]not
°with °meats, °which have [6]not profited them
that have been occupied therein.

V 10 We have an °altar, °whereof they have
°no °right to eat which °serve the tabernacle.
11 For the bodies of those °beasts, whose blood
is brought °into °the sanctuary °by the high
priest °for °sin, are burned °without the camp.

V 12 Wherefore °Jesus also, °that He might
sanctify the °people °with His own blood, suffered [11]without the gate.
13 Let us go forth therefore °unto Him [11]with-
out the °camp, bearing His °reproach.
14 For here have we [10]no [1]continuing city, but
we °seek °one to come.
15 [11]By Him therefore let us offer the sacrifice of °praise to [4]God °continually, that is, °the
fruit of *our* lips °giving thanks to His °name.
16 But °to do good and °to communicate [2]for-
get [2]not: for with such sacrifices [4]God °is well
pleased.

U 17 °Obey [7]them that have the rule over you,
and °submit °yourselves: for they °watch °for
your °souls, as °they that must give °account;
[12]that they may do it °with joy, and [2]not °with
grief: for that *is* °unprofitable for you.

T 18 °Pray [11]for us: for we °trust we have a
good °conscience, [3]in all things °willing to
°live honestly.
19 But I °beseech *you* °the rather to do this,
[12]that I may be °restored to you the sooner.
20 Now the [4]God of °peace, That °brought
again °from the dead our °Lord [12]Jesus, °that
great °Shepherd of the sheep, °through the
blood of the °everlasting °covenant,
21 °Make you perfect [3]in every good °work
°to do His °will, °working [3]in you that which

6 Lord. Ap. 98. VI. i. *β*. 1. B. a.
Helper = Succourer. Gr. *boēthos*. Only here; cp. Ps. 10. 14; 22. 11, &c.
not. Gr. *ou*. Ap. 105. I.
man. Gr. *anthrōpos*. Ap. 123. 1.
unto = to. The quotation is from Ps. 118. 6.
7 Remember. See 11. 15.
them, &c. = your leaders (Gr. *hēgeomai*, as *vv.* 17, 24).
who = such as.
have spoken = spoke. Gr. *laleō*. Ap. 121. 7.
word. Ap. 121. 10.
faith. Ap. 150. II. 1.
follow = imitate. Gr. *mimeomai*. See 2 Thess. 3. 7.
considering. Ap. 133. II. 3.
end. Gr. *ekbasis*. Only here and 1 Cor. 10. 13.
conversation = (manner of) life. Gr. *anastrophē*. See Gal. 1. 13.
8 Jesus Christ. Ap. 98. XI.
the same. Gr. *ho autos*. This is the transl. in the Sept. of the Heb. *'attāh hū*, a Divine title. See Ps. 102. 27. Cp. Mal. 3. 6.
for ever. Ap. 151. II. A. ii. 7. a.
9 carried about. Gr. *peripherō*. See Eph. 4. 14. The texts read "carried away".
divers. Gr. *poikilos*. See 2. 4.
strange. Gr. *xenos*. See Acts 17. 18.
established. Same as "confirm", 2. 3.
with = by. No prep.: dat. case.
grace. Ap. 184. I. 1.
meats. By Fig. *Synecdochē* of species (Ap. 6) = for various and "strange doctrines" of no profit to those who practise them.
which, &c. = in (Gr. *en*) which they who walked have not been profited. See 4. 2.
10 altar. The reference is to the sin-offering, which was wholly burnt outside the camp. Lev. 4. 1-21; 16. 27.
whereof = of (Gr. *ek*) which.
no. Gr. *ou* Ap. 105. I.
right. Gr. *exousia*. Ap. 172. 5.
serve. Gr. *latreuō*. Ap. 190. III. 5.
11 beasts. Gr. *zōon*. Cp. 12. 20.
into. Gr. *eis*. Ap. 104. vi.
the sanctuary. The Holy of Holies. See 8. 2.
by. Ap. 104. v. 1.
for = concerning. Gr. *peri*. Ap. 104. xiii. 1.
sin. Gr. *hamartia*. Ap. 128. I. ii. 1.
without = outside. Gr. *exō*.
12 Jesus. Ap. 98. X.
that = in order that. Gr. *hina*.
people. Gr. *laos*. See Acts 2. 47.
with = by, as *v.* 11.
13 unto. Gr. *pros*. Ap. 104. xv. 3.
camp. I.e. Apostate Judaism. Hebrew believers would understand the reference to Exod. 33. 7, after the apostasy of the "calf".
reproach. See 11. 26.
14 seek. Same word in 11. 14.

one to come = the coming one. **15 praise.** Gr. *ainesis*. Only here. Cp. Acts 2. 47. **continually.** See 9. 6 (always). the fruit of *our* lips. This is a reference to Hos. 14. 2, where the Sept. renders the Heb. *pārīm sᵉphāthēynu* by "bullocks of our lips". Cp. Isa. 57. 19. **giving thanks** = confessing. Gr. *homologeō*. See 11. 13. Fig. *Catachrēsis*. Ap. 6. **name.** See Acts 2. 38. **16 to do good.** Lit. the doing well. Gr. *eupoiia*. Only here. **to communicate** = fellowship Gr. *koinōnia*. Cp. 1 Tim. 6. 18. **is well pleased.** See 11. 5, 6. **17 Obey.** Gr. *peithō*. Ap. 150. I. 2. **submit** = be submissive. Gr. *hupeikō*. Only here. Cp. *eikō* (Gal. 2. 5). **yourselves.** Omit. **watch.** Gr. *agrupneō*. See Eph. 6. 18. **for.** Gr. *huper*. Ap. 104. xvii. 1. **souls.** Ap. 110. III. 2. **they that must give** = those about to give. Gr. *apodidomi*. **account.** Gr. *logos*. Ap. 121. 10. **with.** Gr. *meta*. Ap. 104. xi. 1. **with grief** = groaning. Gr. *stenazō*, as Mark 7. 34. **unprofitable.** Gr. *alusitelēs*. Only here. Fig. *Meiōsis*. Ap. 6. **18 Pray.** Gr. *proseuchomai*. Ap. 134. I. 2. **trust.** Gr. *peithō*. Ap. 150. 1. 2. **conscience.** See Acts 23. 1. **willing.** Gr. *thelō*. Ap. 102. 1. **live.** Gr. *anastrephō*. See 10. 33. The noun in *v.* 7. **19 beseech.** Gr. *parakaleō*. Ap. 134. I. 6. **the rather** = more abundantly. Gr. *perissoterōs*. Occ. 2. 1. **restored.** Gr. *apokathistēmi*. See Acts 1. 6. **20 peace** = the peace. Cp. Rom. 15. 33; 16. 20. 1 Thess. 5. 23. 2 Thess. 3. 16. **brought again** = brought up. Cp. Rom. 10. 7. **from the dead.** Gr. *ek nekrōn*. Ap. 139. 3. **Lord.** Ap. 98. VI. i. *β*. 2. A. **that** = the. **Shepherd.** Fig. *Anthrōpopatheia* (Ap. 6). Cp. John 10. 11. 1 Pet. 5. 4, and Sept. of Isa. 63. 11. **through.** Gr. *en*. Ap. 104. viii. **everlasting.** Ap. 151. II. B. ii. **covenant.** Gr. *diathēkē*. See Matt. 26. 28. Cp. Gen. 9. 16. **21 Make . . . perfect.** Gr. *katartizō*. Same word 1 Pet. 5. 10. Ap. 125. 8. **work.** Some texts read "thing". **to.** Gr. *eis*. Ap. 104. vi. **will.** Gr. *thelēma*. Ap. 102. 2. **working** = doing. Same Gr. verb in *vv.* 6, 17, 19.

is °wellpleasing °in His sight, °through [8] Jesus Christ; to Whom *be* glory °for ever and ever. Amen.
22 And I [19] beseech you, brethren, °suffer the [7] word of °exhortation: for I °have written a letter [6] unto you °in few words.
23 °Know ye that *our* brother Timothy °is set at liberty; [17] with whom, °if he come shortly, I will °see you.
24 °Salute all [7] them that have the rule over you, and all the °saints. °They °of Italy °salute you.
25 [9] Grace *be* [17] with you all. Amen.

wellpleasing. Gr. *euarestos*. See Rom. 12. 1.
in His sight = before Him.
through. Gr. *dia*. Ap. 104. v. 1.
for ever and ever. Ap. 151. II. A. ii. 9. a.
22 suffer. Gr. *anechomai*. See Luke 9. 41.
exhortation. See 12. 5.
have written a letter = wrote.
in. Gr. *dia*. Ap. 104. v. 1.
23 Know ye. May be imperative, or indicative, present tense. Gr. *ginōskō*. Ap. 132. I. ii.
is set at liberty = has been released, dismissed: or sent away on some special mission (as in 1 Cor. 4. 17). Gr. *apoluō*. Ap. 174. 11. Cp. Acts 13. 3; 15. 30, 33; 19. 41; 23. 22; 28. 25 (departed), &c. See Introductory Notes (5) and Ap. 180.
if. Gr. *ean*. Ap. 118. 1. b. **see.** Ap. 133. I. 8 (a). **24 Salute.** Gr. *aspazomai*. See 3 John 14.
saints. See Acts 9. 13. **They of Italy.** Latins dwelling in the place whence *Hebrews* was dispatched. No clue here to the locality or to whom the Epistle was originally sent. **of.** Gr. *apo*. Ap. 104. iv.

THE EPISTLE OF JAMES.

THE STRUCTURE AS A WHOLE.

(*Introversion and Alternation.*)

A | A | 1. 1-4. PATIENCE.
  B | 1. 5-8. PRAYER.
B | C | 1. 9, 10-. THE LOW EXALTED. THE RICH MADE LOW.
  D | 1. -10, 11-. LIFE LIKENED TO GRASS.
  E | 1. -11. END OF THE RICH.
C | 1. 12-16. LUST.
D | 1. 17. GOOD GIFTS FROM ABOVE.
E | 1. 18-27. GOD'S WORD AND ITS EFFECTS.
F | 2. 1-7. THE FAITH. WITHOUT PARTIALITY.
G | 2. 8. THE ROYAL LAW.
H | 2. 9, 10. MOSES' LAW. ONE OFFENCE BREAKS IT.
H | 2. 11. MOSES' LAW. ONE OFFENCE BREAKS IT.
G | 2. 12, 13. THE LAW OF LIBERTY.
F | 2. 14-26. FAITH. WITHOUT WORKS.
E | 3. 1-14. MAN'S WORD AND ITS EFFECTS.
D | 3. 15-18. THE WISDOM FROM ABOVE.
C | 4. 1-5. LUSTS.
B | *C* | 4. 6-10. THE PROUD RESISTED. THE HUMBLE EXALTED.
  D | 4. 11-17. LIFE LIKENED TO A VAPOUR.
  E | 5. 1-6. END OF THE RICH
A | *A* | 5. 7-12. PATIENCE.
  B | 5. 13-20. PRAYER.

NOTES ON THE EPISTLE OF JAMES.

1. The Epistle of James has been the subject of controversy both as regards the identity of the writer, and as to the time of writing. There is little doubt, however, that the writer was James, "the Lord's brother" (Gal. 1. 19), he who was one of the "pillars" (Gal. 2. 9), he who gave the "judgment" of the apostles and elders of the church at Jerusalem (Acts 15. 13, 19).

2. The distinctly Jewish character of the teaching marks off the epistle as having been written at an early period of the *Acts* history, and it is noticeable that the doctrinal tone closely follows the precepts of "the Sermon on the Mount" (Matt. 5-7). The Jews still assembled in synagogues (2. 2); the "poor" (John 12. 8) were heirs of the kingdom (2. 5); they were reproved according to the law (2. 8, &c.); they had Abraham to their father (2. 21), and were, in harmony with Acts 3. 19-21, looking for the coming *(parousia)* of the Lord which was "at hand" (5. 7, 8). If we distinguish the dispensations, *James* affords instruction for all believers, but is plainly addressed "to the twelve tribes "which are scattered abroad", lit. "in the dispersion". The dispersion, Gr. *diaspora*, which is referred to in 1 Pet. 1. 1 also, and is before our eyes even now. In days not far off the epistle will appeal to Israel when to them the gospel of the Kingdom (see Ap. 140. II) is once more announced. To the preachers will again be committed the "powers" of Pentecostal days, to be exercised as exemplified in 5. 14, 15.

3. Some commentators rightly place the time of writing before the Jerusalem Council of about A. D. 45. (According to tradition, James was martyred in 62 or 68.) One well qualified to value fairly the evidence says, "And a careful study of the chronological question has convinced me that they are right who hold the Epistle of James to be perhaps the earliest of the New Testament writings. It belongs to that period of the Pentecostal dispensation when the whole Church was Jewish, and when their meeting-places still bore the Jewish designation of 'synagogues' (chap. 2. 2)." See Ap. 180.

THE EPISTLE OF
JAMES.

A A 1 JAMES, a °servant of °God and of the
°Lord °Jesus Christ, to the °twelve tribes
which are °scattered abroad, °greeting.
2 My brethren, count it all joy when ye °fall
into divers °temptations;
3 °Knowing *this*, that the °trying of your
°faith worketh °patience.
4 But let [3] patience have *her* °perfect work,
°that ye may be °perfect and °entire, °want-
ing °nothing.

B 5 °If °any of you °lack wisdom, let him °ask
°of [1] God, That giveth to all *men* °liberally,
and upbraideth °not; and it shall be given
him.
6 But let him [5] ask °in [3] faith, °nothing
°wavering. For he that °wavereth °is like
a °wave of the sea °driven with the wind and
°tossed.
7 For let [5] not that °man °think that he shall
receive °any thing [5] of the °Lord.
8 A °double minded °man *is* °unstable [6] in all
his ways.

B C 9 Let °the brother of low degree °rejoice [6] in
°that he is exalted:
10 But the rich, [6] in °that he is made low:

D because as the °flower of the grass he shall
pass away.
11 For the sun °is no sooner risen °with °a
°burning heat, °but it withereth the grass,
and the [10] flower thereof °falleth, and the °grace
of the °fashion of it °perisheth:

E so °also shall the rich man °fade away [6] in his
°ways.

C 12 °Blessed *is* the [8] man that endureth [2] temptation: for when he °is °tried, he shall receive
the crown of °life, which the [7] Lord hath promised to them that °love Him.
13 Let °no man say when he is tempted, I am
tempted °of [1] God: for [1] God °cannot be tempted
with °evil, °neither tempteth He any man:
14 But °every man is tempted, °when he is
drawn away °of his own °lust, and °enticed.
15 Then °when [14] lust hath conceived, it bringeth forth °sin: and °sin, when it is °finished,
°bringeth forth °death.
16 °Do [5] not err, my °beloved brethren.

1. 1 servant. Ap. 190. I. 2.
God. Ap. 98. I. i. 1.
Lord. Ap. 98. VI. i. *β*. 2. B.
Jesus Christ. Ap. 98. XI. Only here and 2. 1 in this epistle.
twelve. No suggestion of the separate houses of Judah and Israel. Note the complete number.
scattered abroad = in (Gr. *en*) the dispersion (Gr. *diaspora*. See John 7. 35).
greeting. Gr. *chairō*. Used in this sense in Acts 15. 23; 23. 26. Gen. "rejoice".
2 fall. Gr. *peripiptō*. See Acts 27. 41.
temptations = trials. Cp. Luke 22. 28. Acts 20. 19. 1 Pet. 1. 6; 4. 12.
3 Knowing. Ap. 132. I. ii.
trying = testing. Gr *dokimion*. Only here and 1 Pet. 1. 7.
faith. Ap. 150. II. 1. Read, "your tested faith".
patience. Cp. Rom. 5. 3.
4 perfect. Ap. 125. 1.
that = in order that. Gr. *hina*.
entire. Gr. *holoklēros*. Only here and 1 Thess. 5. 23.
wanting = lacking. Gr. *leipō*. See 2. 15.
nothing = in (Gr. *en*) nothing (Gr. *mēdeis*).
5 If = But if. Ap. 118. 2. a.
any. Ap. 123. 3. **lack.** Gr. *leipō*, as *v.* 4.
ask. Ap. 134. I. 4. **of** = from. Ap. 104. xii. 1.
liberally. Gr. *haplōs*. Only here. The noun in 2 Cor. 9. 11, 13. **not.** Ap. 105. II.
6 in. Ap. 104. viii.
nothing. Gr. *medeis*, as *v.* 4.
wavering. Ap. 122. 4. Cp. Matt. 7. 7, 8.
is like. Gr. *eoika*. Only here and *v.* 23. The root (obs.) is *eikō*; cp. *eikōn*, image.
wave. See Luke 8. 24.
driven. Gr. *anemizomai*. Only here.
tossed. Gr. *rhipizomai*. Only here.
7 man. Ap. 123. 1.
think. Only here and Phil. 1. 16. See John 21. 25.
any thing. Neut. of *tis*. Ap. 123. 3.
Lord. Ap. 98. VI. i. *β*. 2. A.
8 double minded. Gr. *dipsuchos*. Only here and 4. 8. There is no verb, but "double minded" and "unstable" qualify "that man". Cp. Ps. 119. 113.
man. Ap. 123. 2.
unstable. Gr. *akatastatos*. Only here and 3. 8. The noun, Luke 21. 9.
9 the brother, &c. = the lowly (Gr. *tapeinos*. See Rom. 12. 16) brother. **rejoice.** See Rom. 2. 17.
that he is exalted = his exaltation. Gr. *hupsos*. See Luke 1. 78.
10 that he is made low = his humbling (Gr. *tapeinōsis*. See Acts 8. 33).
flower. Gr. *anthos*. Only here; *v.* 11. 1 Pet. 1. 24.
11 is no sooner risen. Lit. rose.
with. Ap. 104. xvi. **a** = the.
burning heat. Gr. *kausōn*. Only here; Matt. 20. 12. Luke 12. 55. **but, &c.** = and withered. **falleth** = fell. Same word in Rom. 9. 6. **grace.** Ap. 184. I. 3. **fashion.** Lit. presence or face (*v.* 23). **perisheth** = perished. Gr. *apollumi*. See Rom. 14. 15. **also shall, &c.** = shall the rich man also. **fade away.** Gr. *marainō*. Only here. **ways.** Gr *poreia*. Only here and Luke 13. 22. Not the same word as in *v.* 8.
12 Blessed. Gr. *makarios*, as in Matt. 5. 3, &c. **is** = hath become. **tried** = tested. Gr. *dokimos*. Elsewhere trans. "approved". See Rom. 14. 18. **life.** Ap. 170. 1. **love.** Ap. 135. I. 1. Cp. Heb. 12. 5, 6.
13 no man = no one. Gr. *mēdeis*. **of** = from. Ap. 104. iv. **cannot be, &c.** = is incapable of being tempted. Gr. *apeirastos*. Only here. **evil.** Ap. 128. III. 2. **neither tempteth He any man** = and He Himself tempteth no one (Gr. *oudeis*). **14 every man** = each one. **when, &c.** = being drawn away. Gr. *exelkomai*. Only here. **of.** Ap. 104. xviii. 1. **lust.** See John 8. 44, and cp. Rom. 7. 7. **enticed.** Gr. *deleazō*. Only here and 2 Pet. 2. 14, 18. **15 when lust, &c.** = lust, having conceived. **sin.** Ap. 128. I. ii. 1. **finished** = completely finished. Gr. *apoteleō*. Only here. **bringeth forth.** Gr. *apokueō*. Only here and *v.* 18. **death.** See Rom. 6. 21. **16 Do not err** = Be not deceived. **beloved.** Ap. 135. III.

D 17 Every good °gift and every [4] perfect °gift
is °from above, °and cometh down °from the
°Father of °lights, °with Whom °is °no
°variableness, °neither °shadow °of °turning.
E F 18 °Of His own will °begat He us with the
°word of truth, °that we should be °a kind of
firstfruits of His °creatures.
G a 19 Wherefore, my [16] beloved brethren, let
every [7] man be °swift °to hear, slow °to °speak,
slow °to wrath:
b 20 For the wrath of [8] man worketh °not the
°righteousness of [1] God.
G a 21 Wherefore lay apart all °filthiness and
°superfluity of °naughtiness, and receive °with
°meekness the °engrafted [18] word, which is
able to save your °souls.
22 But °be ye doers of the [18] word, and [5] not
°hearers only, °deceiving your own selves.
b 23 For [5] if [5] any be a [22] hearer of the [18] word,
and [20] not a doer, he [6] is like °unto a [8] man °be-
holding °his natural face [6] in a °glass:
24 For he °beholdeth himself, and °goeth his
way, and straightway °forgetteth what manner of °man he was.
25 But °whoso °looketh °into °the °perfect
law of liberty, and °continueth *therein*, °he
[22] being [20] not a °forgetful [22] hearer, but a doer of
°the work, °this man shall be [12] blessed [6] in his
°deed.
F 26 [5] If [5] any °man °among you °seem to be
°religious, and °bridleth [5] not his tongue, but
°deceiveth his own heart, this °man's °religion
is °vain.
27 Pure [26] religion and °undefiled °before
[1] God and the [17] Father is this, to °visit the
°fatherless and widows [6] in their °affliction,
and to keep himself °unspotted [17] from the
°world.

F **2** My brethren, °have °not the °faith of our
°Lord °Jesus Christ, *the Lord* of °glory,
°with °respect of persons.
2 For °if there come °unto your °assembly
a °man °with a gold ring, °in °goody °ap-
parel, and there come in °also a °poor man °in
°vile °raiment;

17 gift. Gr. *dosis*. Only here and Phil. 4. 15.
gift. Gr. *dōrēma*. Only here and Rom. 5. 16.
from above. Gr. *anōthen*. See John 3. 3.
and cometh = coming.
from. Ap. 104. iv.
Father. Ap. 98. III.
lights. Ap. 130. 1.
with. Ap. 104. xii. 2.
is no. Lit. there is not (Ap. 105. I) present (Gr. *eneimi*).
variableness. Gr. *parallagē*. Only here.
neither = or.
shadow. Gr. *aposkiasma*. Only here.
of. I.e. cast by, or due to.
turning. Gr. *tropē*. Only here.

1. 18-27 (E, p. 1847). GOD'S WORD AND ITS EFFECTS. (*Introversion and Alternation.*)

E | F | 18. Statement.
| G | a | 19. Exhortation.
| | b | 20. Reason.
| *G* | *a* | 21, 22. Exhortation.
| | *b* | 23-25. Reason.
| *F* | 26, 27. Statement.

18 Of His own will = Having willed. Ap. 102. 3.
begat. Gr. *apokueō*. See *v.* 15.
word. Ap. 121. 10. Cp. 1 Pet. 1. 23.
that = to the end that. Gr. *eis*. Ap. 104. vi.
a kind of firstfruits = a certain (Gr. *tis*) firstfruit (Gr. *aparchē*). See Rom. 8. 23. Cp. Rom. 11. 16.
creatures. See 1 Tim. 4. 4.
19 swift. Gr. *tachus*. Only here, but the adv. occ. frequently.
to. Ap. 104. vi. **speak.** Ap. 121. 7.
20 not. Ap. 105. I. **righteousness.** Ap. 191. 3.
21 filthiness. Gr. *rhuparia*. Only here. Cp. 2. 2. 1 Pet. 3. 21. Rev. 22. 11.
superfluity = abundance. Gr. *perisseia*. See Rom. 5. 17.
naughtiness. Ap. 128. II. 2. "Naughty" and "naughtiness" had a much more forcible meaning in King James's day than now. Cp. Prov. 6. 12; 11. 6; 17. 4. Jer. 24. 2. **with.** Ap. 104. viii.
meekness. Gr. *praütēs*. Only here; 3. 13. 1 Pet. 3. 15. Cp. Ap. 127. 3.
engrafted = implanted. Gr. *emphutos*. Only here. Not the word in Rom. 11. 17-24.
souls. Ap. 110. III. 2.
22 be = become.
hearers. Gr. *akroatēs*. Only here, *vv.* 23, 25. Rom. 2. 13.
deceiving. Gr. *paralogizomai*, to deceive by false reasoning. Only here and Col. 2. 4.

23 unto = to. **beholding.** Gr. *katanoeō*. Gen. rendered "consider." Ap. 133. II. 4. **his natural face.** Lit. the face (*v.* 11) of his birth (Gr. *genesis*. Only here, 3. 6, and Matt. 1. 1). **glass** = mirror. Gr. *esoptron*. Only here and 1 Cor. 13. 12. **24 beholdeth** = beheld. See *v.* 23. **goeth, &c.** = departed. **forgetteth** = forgot. **man** = *man*. **25 whoso** = he that. **looketh.** Lit. stooped down (to look). Gr. *parakuptō*. Ap. 133. III. 2. See John 20. 5. **into.** Ap. 104. vi. **the perfect, &c.** = the perfect law, that of liberty. **perfect.** Ap. 125. 1. **continueth** = continued. Gr. *paramenō*. See 1 Cor. 16. 6. **he.** The texts omit. **forgetful hearer** = hearer of forgetfulness. Ap. 17. 1. **forgetful.** Gr. *epilēsmonē*. Only here. **the.** Omit. **this man** = this one. **deed** = doing. Gr. *poiēsis*. Only here. **26 man** = one. **among you.** The texts omit. **seem** = thinks himself. Cp. 4. 5. **religious.** Gr. *thrēskos*. Only here in N.T., and nowhere found in Classical Greek. It means a careful follower of the observances connected with his belief. **bridleth.** Gr. *chalinagōgeō*. Only here and 3. 2. **deceiveth.** Gr. *apataō*. See Eph. 5. 6. **religion.** Gr. *thrēskeia*. See Acts 26. 5. **vain.** Gr. *mataios*. See Acts 14. 15. **27 undefiled.** Gr. *amiantos*. See Heb. 7. 26. **before.** Ap. 104. xii. 2. **visit.** Ap. 133. III. 5. Cp. Matt. 25. 36, 43. Personal interest and sympathy are enjoined. Cp. Mic. 6. 8. **fatherless.** Gr. *orphanos*. Only here and John 14. 18. **affliction.** See Acts 7. 10. **unspotted.** Gr. *aspilos*. See 1 Tim. 6. 14. **world.** Ap. 129. 1.

2. 1 have = hold. **not.** Ap. 105. II. **faith.** Ap. 150. II. 1. **Lord.** Ap. 98. VI. i. *β*. 2. A. **Jesus Christ.** Ap. 98. XI. **glory.** Cp. 1 Cor. 2. 8. See p. 1511. **with.** Ap. 104. viii. **respect of persons.** Gr. *prosōpolēpsia*. See Rom. 2. 11. **2 if.** Ap. 118. 1. b. **unto.** Ap. 104. vi. **assembly** = synagogue. Gr. *sunagōgē*. Ap. 120. I. **man.** Ap. 123. 2. **with a gold ring.** Lit. gold-ringed. Gr. *chrusodaktulios*. Only here. **in.** Ap. 104. viii. **goodly** = bright, or shining. Gr. *lampros*. Here, *v.* 3 (gay). Luke 23. 11. Acts 10. 30. Rev. 15. 6; 18. 14; 19. 8; 22. 1, 16. **apparel.** Gr. *esthēs*. In this and in the next verse transl. by three different words, "apparel", "raiment", "clothing". Cp. Luke 23. 11. Acts 1. 10; 10. 30; 12. 21. **also, &c.** = a poor *man* also. **poor.** Ap. 127. 1. **vile.** Gr. *rhuparos*. Only here. Cp. 1. 21.

3 And ye °have respect °to him that weareth
the [2]gay [2]clothing, and say °unto him, "Sit
thou here °in a good place;" and say to the
[2]poor, "Stand thou there, or sit here °under my
footstool:"
4 °Are ye °not then partial [2]in yourselves,
and are become judges °of °evil °thoughts?
5 Hearken, my °beloved brethren, °Hath [4]not
°God chosen the [2]poor of °this °world rich [2]in
[1]faith, and heirs of the °kingdom which He
°hath promised to them that °love Him?
6 But ye °have °despised the °poor. Do [4]not
rich men °oppress you, and °draw you °before
the °judgment seats?
7 Do [4]not they blaspheme °that °worthy °name
°by the which ye are °called?
G 8 °If ye fulfil the °royal law °according to the
°Scripture, "**Thou shalt [5]love thy neighbour
as thyself,**" ye do well:
H 9 But [8]if ye °have respect to persons, ye commit
°sin, °and are convinced °of the law as
°transgressors.
10 For whosoever shall keep the whole law,
and yet °offend [2]in one *point*, he °is °guilty
of all.
H 11 For He That said, "**Do [1]not commit adultery,**"
°said also, "**Do [1]not kill.**" Now [8]if
thou commit °no adultery, yet if thou kill,
thou art become a [9]transgressor of the law.
G 12 So °speak ye, and so do, as they that
°shall be °judged °by the law of °liberty.
13 For °he shall have °judgment °without
mercy, that hath shewed °no mercy; and
mercy °rejoiceth against °judgment.
F 14 °What *doth it* °profit, my brethren,
°though °a man say he hath [1]faith, and have
[1]not °works? °can [1]faith save him?
15 [2]If a brother or sister °be naked, and °destitute
of °daily food,
16 And °one °of you say [3]unto them, "Depart
[2]in peace, be *ye* warmed and filled;" notwithstanding
ye give them [1]not those things
which are °needful to the body; [14]what *doth it*
[14]profit?
17 Even so [1]faith, [2]if it hath [1]not [14]works, is
°dead, being °alone.
18 Yea, [14]a man may say, "Thou hast [1]faith,
and I have [14]works: shew me thy [1]faith °without
thy [14]works, and I will shew thee my [1]faith
°by my [14]works."
19 Thou °believest that there is one [5]God;
thou doest well: the °devils also °believe, and
°tremble.
20 But °wilt thou °know, O vain °man, that
[1]faith [18]without [14]works is °dead?
21 Was [4]not Abraham our father °justified
[18]by [14]works, when he had offered Isaac his
°son °upon the altar?
22 °Seest thou how [1]faith °wrought with
his [14]works, and [18]by [14]works was [1]faith °made
perfect?
23 And the [8]Scripture was °fulfilled which
saith, "**Abraham °believed [5]God, and it was**

3 have respect. Ap. 133. III. 4.
to. Ap. 104. ix. 3. **unto**=**to.**
in a good place. Lit. well. Gr. *kalōs.*
under. Ap. 104. xviii. 2.
4 Are . . . partial. Ap. 122. 4.
not. Ap. 105. I.
of. Gen. of quality or character. Ap. 17. 1.
evil. Ap. 128. III. 1.
thoughts=reasonings. See Matt. 15. 19.
5 beloved. Ap. 135. III.
Hath . . . chosen=Did . . . choose.
God. Ap. 98. I. i. 1. **this**=the.
world. Ap. 129. 1.
kingdom. See App. 112–114.
hath. Omit.
love. Ap. 135. I. 1.
6 have. Omit.
despised=shamed. Gr. *atimazō.* See Acts 5. 41.
poor. Sing., as *v.* 2.
oppress. See Acts 10. 38.
draw=themselves drag. Gr. *helkō.* See Acts 21. 30.
before=to. Ap. 104. vi.
judgment seats. Ap. 177. 8.
7 that=the.
worthy=honourable. Gr. *kalos.* See Rom. 12. 17.
name. See Acts 2. 38; 15. 26.
by the which, &c.=which is called upon (Ap. 104. ix. 3) you.
called. See Acts 2. 21.
8 If. Ap. 118. 2. a.
royal. Gr. *basilikos.* See John 4. 46.
according to. Ap. 104. x. 2.
Scripture. Gr. *graphē.* The quotation is from Lev. 19. 18.
9 have respect, &c. Gr. *prosōpolēpteō.* Only here. Cp. *v.* 1 and Acts 10. 34. See Lev. 19. 15.
sin. Ap. 128. I. ii. 1.
and are, &c.=being convicted. Gr. *elenchō.* See 1 Cor. 14. 24 (convince).
of. Ap. 104. xviii. 1.
transgressors. Ap. 128. VI. 3.
10 offend=stumble. Gr. *ptaiō.* See Rom. 11. 11.
is=has been.
guilty. See Deut. 27. 26. Matt. 26. 66. Gal. 3. 10.
11 said also, &c. See Ex. 20. 14, 13.
no=not, *v.* 4.
12 speak. Ap. 121. 7. **shall**=are about to.
judged. Ap. 122. 1. **by.** Ap. 104. v. 1.
liberty. Cp. 1. 25.
13 he . . . judgment=(there shall be) judgment to him.
judgment. Ap. 177. 7.
without mercy. Gr. *anileōs.* Only here.
no=not, as *v.* 1.
rejoiceth against=boasteth over. Gr. *katakauchaomai.* See 3. 14 and Rom. 11. 18.
14 What *doth*, &c.=What *is* the profit (Gr. *ophelos*)? See 1 Cor. 15. 32.
though=if, as in *v.* 2.
a man=one. Ap. 123. 3.
works. Cp. Mat. 5. 16.
can, &c. Question preceded by *mē*, assuming a neg. answer.
15 be. Gr. *huparchō.* See Luke 9. 48.
destitute=lacking. Gr. *leipō*, as in 1. 4, 5.
daily. Gr. *ephēmeros.* Only here.
16 one. Ap. 123. 3, as in *v.* 14. **of.** Ap. 104. vii.
needful. Gr. *epitēdeios.* Only here.
17 dead. Gr. *nekros.* Cp. Ap. 139.
alone=by (Ap. 104. x. 2) itself.
18 without=apart from. Gr. *chōris.*
by. Gr. *ek.* Ap. 104. vii.
19 believest. Ap. 150. I. 1. iii.
devils=demons. See Ap. 101. II. 12.
believe. Ap. 150. I. 1. i. **tremble**=shudder. Gr. *phrissō.* Only here. **20 wilt.** Ap. 102. 1. **know.** Ap. 132. I. ii. **man.** Ap. 123. 1. **dead.** In the *Textus Receptus* the same as *v.* 17, but the texts read *argos*, idle or barren. See Matt. 12. 36 and 2 Pet. 1. 8. **21 justified.** Ap. 191. 2. **son.** Ap. 108. iii. **upon.** Ap. 104. ix. 3. **22 Seest.** Ap. 133. I. 5. **wrought with.** Gr. *sunergeō.* See Rom. 8. 28. **made perfect.** Ap. 125. 2. **23 fulfilled.** Ap. 125. 7. **believed.** Ap. 150. I. 1. ii.

°**imputed** [3]**unto him** °**for** °**righteousness:"**
and he was called **the** °**friend of** [5]**God.**
24 Ye °see then how that [18]by works a [20]man
is [21]justified, and [4]not [18]by [1]faith only.
25 Likewise °also was [4]not Rahab the harlot
[21]justified [18]by works, when she had received
the messengers, and had °sent *them* out °an-
other way?
26 For as the body [18]without °the °spirit is
[17]dead, °so [1]faith [18]without works is [17]dead
also.

E H **3** My brethren, be °not many °masters,
°knowing that we shall receive the greater
°condemnation.
2 For in many things we °offend all. °If
°any man °offend °not °in °word, the same *is*
a °perfect °man, *and* able °also to °bridle the
whole body.
J c^1 3 °Behold, we put °bits °in the horses' mouths,
°that they may °obey us, and we °turn about
their whole body.
4 °Behold °also the ships, which though *they*
be so great, and *are* driven °of °fierce winds,
yet are they [3]turned about °with a very small
°helm, whithersoever °the °governor listeth.
d^1 5 Even so the tongue is a little member, and
°boasteth great things. [4]Behold, how °great
a matter °a little fire °kindleth!
6 And the tongue *is* a fire, °a °world of °ini-
quity: so °is the tongue °among our members,
°that it defileth the whole body, °and °setteth
on fire the °course of °nature; and °it is °set
on fire [4]of °hell.
c^2 7 For every °kind of °beasts, and of birds, and
of serpents, and of °things in the sea, is °tamed,
and hath been °tamed °of °mankind:
d^2 8 But the tongue can °no man [7]tame; *it is*
an °unruly °evil, full of °deadly °poison.
9 °Therewith bless we °God, even the °Father;
and °therewith curse we [8]men, which are made
°after the °similitude of °God.
10 °Out of the same mouth proceedeth blessing
and cursing. My brethren, °these things ought
[2]not so to be.
c^3 11 Doth a fountain °send forth °at the same
°place sweet *water* and °bitter?
12 °Can the fig tree, my brethren, bear °olive
berries? either a vine, figs? °so *can* no fountain both yield salt water and fresh.
H 13 Who *is* a wise man and °endued with

imputed = reckoned. Gr. *logizomai*. See Rom. 2. 3 (thinkest).
for. Ap. 104. vi.
righteousness. Ap. 191. 3. Quoted from Gen. 15. 6, but it received a further fulfilment after 22. 10, which obtained the testimony of *vv.* 15–18.
friend of God. See 2 Chron. 20. 7. Isa. 41. 8.
24 see. Ap. 133. I. 8.
25 also. Should follow "harlot".
sent . . . out. Ap. 174. 10.
another. Ap. 124. 2.
26 the. Omit.
spirit. Ap. 101. II. 6. See A.V. m., and cp. Gen. 2. 7.
so, &c. = so faith also.

3. 1–14 (*E*, p. 1847). **MAN'S WORD AND ITS EFFECTS.** (*Introversion and Alternation.*)

E | H | 1, 2. Deprecation. The tongue.
J | c^1 | 3, 4. Comparisons.
d^1 | 5, 6. The tongue.
c^2 | 7. Comparisons.
d^2 | 8–10. The tongue.
c^3 | 11, 12. Comparisons.
H | 13, 14. Exhortation. Behaviour.

3. 1 not. Ap. 105. II.
masters = teachers. Ap. 98. XIV. v. 4.
knowing. Ap. 132. I. i.
condemnation. Ap. 177. 6.
2 offend all = all stumble. See 2. 10.
If. Ap. 118. 2. a.
any man = any one. Ap. 123. 3.
not. Ap. 105. I. in. Ap. 104. viii.
word. Ap. 121. 10.
perfect. Ap. 125. 1. man. Ap. 123. 2.
also. Should come after "body".
bridle. See 1. 26.
3 Behold. Ap. 133. I. 2; but the texts read *ei* (Ap. 118. 2. a) *de*, "But if".
bits. Gr. *chalinos*. Here and Rev. 14. 20.
in. Ap. 104. vi.
that = to the end that (Ap. 104. xv. 3), but the texts read *eis* (vi).
obey. Ap. 150. I. 2.
turn about. Gr. *metagō*. Only here and *v.* 4.
4 Behold. Ap. 133. I. 2.
also the ships = the ships also.
of. Ap. 104. xviii. 1.
fierce. Gr. *sklēros*. Elsewhere transl. "hard".
with. Same as "of", above.
helm. Gr. *pēdalion*. Only here and Acts 27. 40.
the governor listeth = the impulse (Gr. *hormē*. Only here and Acts 14. 5) of the governor wishes (Ap. 102. 3).
governor = helmsman, the one who directs, or makes straight (Gr. *euthunō*). Only here and John 1. 23.
5 boasteth. Gr. *auchеō*. Only here.
great, &c. = much wood. Gr. *hulē*. Only here.
a little = how little a.

kindleth. See Acts 28. 2. **6** a = the. world. Ap. 129. 1. Used here in the sense of aggregate. iniquity. Ap. 128. VII. 1. is = is constituted or takes its place. Gr. *kathistēmi*, as in 4. 4. among. Ap. 104. viii. 2. that it defileth = the one defiling. Gr. *spiloō*. Only here and Jude 23. and setteth, &c. = setting on fire. Gr. *phlogizō*. Only in this verse. Cp. 2 Thess. 1. 8. course. Gr. *trochos*. Only here. nature. Gr. *genesis*. See 1. 23. it is = being. hell. Ap. 131. I. **7** kind = nature. Gr. *phusis*. See Rom. 1. 26. beasts = wild beasts. things in the sea. Gr. *enalios*. Only here. tamed. Gr. *damazō*. Only here, *v.* 8, and Mark 5. 4. of = by. No prep. Dat. case. mankind = human (Gr. *anthrōpinos*. See Rom. 6. 19) nature (Gr. *phusis*, above). **8** no man = no one (Gr. *oudeis*) of men (Ap. 123. 1). unruly. Gr. *akataschetos*. Only here, but the texts read *akatastatos*, unstable, restless, as in 1. 8. evil. Ap. 128. III. 2. deadly. Gr. *thanatēphoros*. Only here. poison. Gr. *ios*. See Rom. 3. 13. **9** Therewith = With (Ap. 104. viii) it. God. Ap. 98. I. i. 1, but the texts read "the Lord" (Ap. 98. VI. i. 1. A. b). Father. Ap. 98. III. after. Ap. 104. x. 2. similitude. Gr. *homoiōsis*. Only here. In the Sept. in Gen. 1. 26. Ezek. 1. 10. Dan. 10. 16; &c. God. Ap. 98. I. i. 1. **10** Out of. Ap. 104. vii. these things, &c. = it is not fitting (Gr. *chrē*. Only here) that these things should so be. **11** send forth. Gr. *bruō*. Only here. at = out of. Ap. 104. vii. place = hole. Gr. *opē*. See Heb. 11. 38 (caves). bitter. Gr. *pikros*. Only here and *v.* 14. **12** Can, &c. Question preceded by *mē*. olive berries = olives. so, &c. The texts read "neither (Gr. *oute*) can salt water bring forth, or produce, sweet". **13** endued with knowledge. Gr. *epistēmōn*. Only here. Cp. Ap. 132. I. v. See Deut. 1. 13, 15; 4. 6. Isa. 5. 21; where the same word is used in the Sept.

knowledge [6]among you? let him shew [10]out
of °a good °conversation his works °with
°meekness of wisdom.
14 But °if ye have [11] bitter °envying and
°strife [2]in your hearts, °glory [1]not, and lie
°not °against the truth.
D 15 This wisdom °descendeth [2]not °from
above, but *is* °earthly, °sensual, °devilish.
16 For where [14]envying and [14]strife *is*, there
is °confusion and every °evil work.
17 But the wisdom that is [15]from above is
first °pure, then °peaceable, °gentle, *and* °easy
to be intreated, full of mercy and good fruits,
°without partiality, and °without hypocrisy.
18 And the fruit of °righteousness is sown [2]in
peace °of them that make peace.

C **4** From whence *come* °wars °and °fightings
°among you? *come they* °not hence, *even*
°of your °lusts that °war °in your members?
2 Ye lust, and have [1]not: ye kill, and °desire
to have, and °cannot °obtain: ye °fight and
°war, yet ye have [1]not, °because ye °ask °not.
3 Ye [2]ask, and receive [1]not, because ye [2]ask
°amiss, °that ye may °consume *it* °upon your
[1]lusts.
4 °Ye adulterers and °adulteresses, °know
ye [1]not that the °friendship of the °world is
°enmity with °God? whosoever therefore
°will be a friend of the °world °is the enemy
of °God.
5 °Do ye think that the Scripture saith °in
vain, The °spirit that dwelleth [1]in us lusteth
[1]to envy?
B C 6 But He giveth °more °grace. Wherefore
He saith, [4]"**God °resisteth the °proud, but
giveth °grace °unto the °humble.**"
7 Submit yourselves therefore to [4]God. Resist the devil, and he will flee °from you.
8 Draw nigh to [4]God, and He will draw nigh
to you. Cleanse *your* hands, *ye* sinners; and
°purify *your* hearts, *ye* °double minded.
9 °Be afflicted, and mourn, and weep: let
your °laughter °be turned °to mourning, and
your joy °to °heaviness.
10 °Humble yourselves in the sight of the
°LORD, and He shall °lift you up.
D 11 °Speak [2]not evil °one of another, brethren.
He that °speaketh evil of *his* brother, and
°judgeth his brother, °speaketh evil of the
law, and °judgeth the law: but °if thou °judge
the law, thou art [1]not a doer of the law, but a
judge.
12 There is one °Lawgiver, Who is able to

a = his.
conversation = behaviour. See Gal. 1. 13.
with. Ap. 104. viii, as in *v.* 9.
meekness. See 1. 21.
14 if. Ap. 118. 2. a.
envying. Gr. *zēlos.* See Acts 5. 17.
strife. Gr. *eritheia.* See Rom. 2. 8.
glory = boast. Gr. *katakauchaomai.* See Rom. 11. 18.
not. Does not appear in Gr. text.
against. Ap. 104. x. 1.
15 descendeth = is coming down.
from above. Gr. *anōthen.* See 1. 17. Cp. 1. 5.
earthly. Gr. *epigeios.* See 1 Cor. 15. 40.
sensual. Gr. *psuchikos.* See 1 Cor. 2. 14.
devilish = demoniacal. Gr. *daimoniōdēs.* Only here.
16 confusion = commotion, or unrest. Gr. *akatastasia.* See Luke 21. 9. Cp. *v.* 8.
evil. Gr. *phaulos.* See John 3. 20.
17 pure. Gr. *hagnos.* See 2 Cor. 7. 11.
peaceable. Gr. *eirēnikos.* Only here and Heb. 12. 11. Peace must not be sought at the expense of truth.
gentle. Gr. *epieikēs.* See Phil. 4. 5.
easy, &c. Gr. *eupeithēs.* Only here.
without partiality. Gr. *adiakritos.* Only here. Cp. Ap. 122. 4.
without hypocrisy. Gr. *anupokritos.* See Rom. 12. 9. Cp. Ap. 122. 9.
18 righteousness. Ap. 191. 3.
of = by, or for. No prep. Dat. case.

4. 1 wars. Gr. *polemos.* See Matt. 24. 6.
and. The texts add "whence".
fightings. Gr. *machē.* See 2 Cor. 7. 5.
among. Ap. 104. viii. 2.
not. Ap. 105. I. of. Ap. 104. vii.
lusts = pleasures. Gr. *hēdonē.* See Tit. 3. 3.
war. Gr. *strateuomai.* See 1 Cor. 9. 7.
in. Ap. 104. viii.
2 desire to have = covet earnestly. Gr. *zēloō.* See Acts 7. 9.
cannot = are not (Ap. 105. I) able to.
obtain. See Rom. 11. 7.
fight. Gr. *machomai.* See Acts 7. 26.
war. Gr. *polemeō.* Only here and Rev. 2. 16; 12. 7; 13. 4; 17. 14; 19. 11. Note the different words for war in these two verses.
because, &c. = on account of (Ap. 104. v. 2) your not asking.
ask. Ap. 134. I. 4. not. Ap. 105. II.
3 amiss = with evil intent. Gr. *kakōs.* Cp. Ap. 128. III. 2.
that = in order that. Gr. *hina.*
consume = spend. See Luke 15. 14.
upon = in (gratifying). Ap. 104. viii.
4 Ye adulterers and. The texts omit.
adulteresses. Cp. Matt. 12. 39. Jer. 3. 9. Ezek. 16; 23. Hos. 2; &c.
know. Ap. 132. I. i.
friendship. Gr. *philia.* Only here.
world. Ap. 129. 1.
enmity. Gr. *echthra.* See Rom. 8. 7.
God. Ap. 98. I. i. 1. will. Ap. 102. 3.
is = is constituted, or constitutes himself, as in 3. 6.
5 Do ye = Or do ye.

in vain. Gr. *kenōs.* Only here. The adj. occ. frequently. spirit. Ap. 101. II. 6. to. Ap. 104. xv. 3. This can only refer to the general testimony of Scripture that the natural man is prone to selfish desires, leading to envy of others who possess the things desired. Cp. Gen. 6. 5; 8. 21. **6** more = greater. grace. Ap. 184. I. 1. This has reference to the new nature. Cp. 1 Cor. 2. 12. resisteth. Gr. *antitassomai.* See Acts 18. 6. proud. See Rom. 1. 30. unto = to. humble = lowly. Cp. 1. 9. Matt. 11. 29. Quoted from Prov. 3. 34. **7** from. Ap. 104. iv. **8** purify. Gr. *hagnizō.* See Acts 21. 24. Used of Levitical purifying four times. Used here, 1 Pet. 1. 22. 1 John 3. 3, in a spiritual sense. double minded. See 1. 8. **9** Be afflicted. Gr. *talaiporeō.* Only here. Cp. 5. 1. Rom. 7. 24. laughter. Gr. *gelōs.* Only here. be turned. See Acts 2. 20. to. Ap. 104. vi. heaviness. Gr. *katēpheia.* Only here. It means casting down the eyes. Cp. Luke 18. 13. **10** Humble yourselves. Gr. *tapeinoō.* See 2 Cor. 11. 7. LORD. Ap. 98. VI. i. β. 2. A (B acc. to texts). lift . . . up. Gr. *hupsoō.* See John 12. 32. **11** Speak . . . evil = Speak against, or backbite. Gr. *katalaleō.* Only here and 1 Pet. 2. 12; 3. 16. Cp. Rom. 1. 30. 2 Cor. 12. 20. one of another = one another. judgeth. Ap. 122. 1. if. Gr. *ei.* Ap. 118. 2. a. **12** Lawgiver. Gr. *nomothetēs.* Only here. Cp. Rom. 9. 4. Heb. 7. 11.

save and to °destroy: who art thou that
[11]judgest °another?
13 °Go to now, ye that say, "To day or to
morrow we will go °into °such a city, °and
°continue there a year, °and °buy and sell,
°and get gain:"
14 °Whereas ye °know [1]not what *shall be*
on the morrow. For what *is* your °life? °It
is even a °vapour, that °appeareth °for a little
time, and then °vanisheth away.
15 °For that ye *ought* to say, °"If the °Lord
°will, we shall live, and do this, or that."
16 But now ye °rejoice [1]in your °boastings:
all such °rejoicing is °evil.
17 Therefore to him that [4]knoweth to do
good, and doeth *it* [2]not, to him it is °sin.

E 5 °Go to now, *ye* rich men, weep and °howl
°for your °miseries that °shall come upon
you.
2 Your °riches are °corrupted, and your garments °are °motheaten.
3 Your gold and silver is °cankered; and the
°rust of them shall be °a witness against you,
and shall eat your flesh as it were fire. Ye
°have heaped treasure together °for the °last
days.
4 °Behold, the °hire of the labourers who
°have °reaped down your fields, which is °of
you °kept back by fraud, crieth: and the °cries
of them which °have °reaped are entered °into
the ears of the °LORD of Sabaoth.
5 Ye °have °lived in pleasure °on the °earth,
and °been wanton; ye have nourished your
hearts, as °in a day of °slaughter.
6 Ye have condemned *and* killed the °just;
and he doth °not resist you.
A A 7 Be patient therefore, brethren, °unto the
°coming of the °Lord. [4]Behold, the husbandman waiteth for the precious fruit of the [5]earth,
and °hath long patience [1]for it, °until he receive the °early and °latter rain.
8 Be ye also patient; °stablish your hearts:
for the [7]coming of the [7]Lord °draweth nigh.
9 °Grudge °not °one against another, brethren, °lest ye be °condemned: [4]behold, the
Judge standeth °before the door.
10 Take, my brethren, °the prophets, who
°have spoken °in the name of the [4]LORD, °for
an °example of °suffering affliction, and of
°patience.
11 [4]Behold, we °count them happy which
endure. Ye °have heard of the °patience of
Job, and °have °seen the °end of the [4]LORD;
that the °LORD is °very pitiful, and °of tender
mercy.

destroy. Cp. 1. 11 (perish).
another = the other. Ap. 124. 2. The texts read "neighbour", as in 2. 8.
13 Go to = Come. Gr. *age*. Imp. of *agō*, used as an adverb. Here and 5. 1.
into. Ap. 104. vi. **such a** = this.
and. Note the Fig. *Polysyndeton*. Ap. 6.
continue. Lit. make, or do. Cp. Acts 20. 3. Fig. *Synecdochē*. Ap. 6.
buy and sell = trade. Gr. *emporeuomai*. Only here and 2 Pet. 2. 3. Cp. Matt. 22. 5. John 2. 16. This eagerness to travel for trade purposes is a prominent characteristic of the Jew of to-day.
14 Whereas ye = Such as ye are.
know. Ap. 132. I. v. **life.** Ap. 170. 1.
It is even = For it is. The texts read "For ye are".
vapour. Gr. *atmis*. See Acts 2. 19.
appeareth. Ap. 106. I. i.
for. Ap. 104. xv. 3.
vanisheth away. See Acts 13. 41.
15 For that, &c. = Instead of (Ap. 104. ii) your saying.
If. Ap. 118. 1. b.
Lord. Ap. 98. VI. i. *β*. 2. A.
will. Ap. 102. 1.
16 rejoice = boast. Gr. *kauchaomai*. See Rom. 2. 17; 5. 2.
boastings. Gr. *alazoneia*. Only here and 1 John 2. 16. Cp. Rom. 1. 30.
rejoicing = boasting. Gr. *kauchēsis*. See Rom. 3. 27.
evil. Ap. 128. III. 1.
17 sin. Ap. 128. I. ii. 1.

5. 1 Go to. See 4. 13.
howl. Gr. *ololuzō*. Only here. An onomatopoeic word.
for. Ap. 104. ix. 2.
miseries. Gr. *talaipōria*. See Rom. 3. 16. Cp. 4. 9.
shall come = are coming.
2 riches = wealth. The Gk. word *ploutos* conveys the idea of abundance. Cp. Luke 12. 19.
corrupted. Gr. *sēpō*. Only here.
are = have become.
motheaten. Gr. *sētobrōtos*. Only here.
3 cankered = rusted. Gr. *katioō*. Only here.
rust. Gr. *ios*. See 3. 8. **a** = for (Ap. 104. vi) a.
have, &c. = treasured up. See Rom. 2. 5. 1 Cor. 16. 2.
for. Ap. 104. viii. **last days.** See 2 Tim. 3. 1.
4 Behold. Ap. 133. I. 2.
hire = pay. Gr. *misthos*, gen. transl. "reward".
have. Omit.
reaped down. Gr. *amaō*. Only here in N.T. Occ. five times in Sept. Cp. Mic. 6. 15.
of = on the part of, arising from. Ap. 104. iv.
kept back by fraud. Gr. *apostereō*. See 1 Cor. 6. 7.
cries. Gr. *boē*. Only here.
reaped. Gr. *therizō*. Of freq. occ. in N.T.
into. Gr. *eis*. Ap. 104. vi.
LORD of Sabaoth. This O.T. expression (= LORD of hosts) is used only here by a N.T. writer. In Rom. 9. 29 it is quoted from Isaiah.
LORD. Ap. 98. VI. i. *β*. 1. B. b.
5 have. Omit. **lived in pleasure.** Gr. *truphaō*. Only here. Cp. 2 Pet. 2. 13 (riot). **on.** Ap. 104. ix. 1. **earth.** Ap. 129. 4. **been wanton.** See 1 Tim. 5. 6. **in.** Ap. 104. viii. **slaughter.** See Acts 8. 32. Cp. Isa. 30. 25; 34. 6. Jer. 12. 3. **6 just.** Ap. 191. 1. Cp. Matt. 12. 7; 27. 19. Acts 3. 14. **not.** Ap. 105. I. This is the Fig. *Asyndeton*. Ap. 6. The two *ands* should be omitted. **7 unto, until.** Same Gr. word, *heōs*. **coming.** Gr. *parousia*. First occ. Matt. 24. 3. **Lord.** Ap. 98. VI. i. *β*. 2. A. **hath long patience** = being patient. **early.** Gr. *prōimos*. Only here. **latter.** Gr. *opsimos*. Only here. Cp. Joel 2. 23. **8 stablish.** See Rom. 1. 11. **draweth nigh** = hath drawn near. See Matt. 3. 2. **9 Grudge** = Groan, or Murmur. See Heb. 13. 17. **not.** Ap. 105. II. **one against another** = against (Ap. 104. x. 1) one another. **lest** = in order that (Gr. *hina*) not (Gr. *mē*). **condemned.** The texts read "judged". Ap. 122 1. **before.** Ap. 104. xiv. **10 the prophets.** I. e. the O.T. prophets. Ap. 189. **have spoken** = spoke. Ap. 121. 7. **in.** Ap. 104. viii. as the texts. **for** = as. **example.** See John 13. 15. **suffering affliction.** Gr. *kakopatheia*. Only here. Cp. *v*. 13. **patience.** As in Heb. 6. 12. **11 count . . . happy.** Gr. *makarizō*. Only here and Luke 1. 48 (call blessed). **have.** Omit. **patience.** As in Tit. 2. 2. **seen** = saw. Ap 133. I. 1. **end.** Cp. Job 42. 6. **LORD.** Ap. 98. VI. i. *β*. 1. A. b. **very pitiful.** Gr *polusplanchnos*. Only here. **of tender mercy.** Gr. *oiktirmōn*. Only here and Luke 6. 36.

12 But °above all things, my brethren, swear
[9]not, °neither by °heaven, °neither by the
[5]earth, °neither by °any °other oath: but let
your yea be yea; and *your* °nay, °nay; [9]lest
ye fall °into °condemnation.

B 13 Is [12]any °among you °afflicted? let him
°pray. Is [12]any °merry? let him °sing
psalms.
14 Is [12]any sick [13]among you? let him call
for the °elders of the °church; and let them
[13]pray °over him, °anointing him with oil [5]in
the name of the [7]Lord:
15 And the °prayer of °faith shall save the
°sick, and the [7]Lord shall °raise him up; °and
if he have committed °sins, they shall be forgiven him.
16 Confess *your* °faults [9]one to another, and
°pray [9]one °for another, that ye may be °healed.
The °effectual fervent °prayer of a °righteous
man °availeth much.
17 Elias was a °man °subject to like passions
as we are, and he [13]prayed °earnestly that it
might [9]not °rain: and it °rained [6]not [5]on the
[5]earth °by the space of three years and six
months.
18 And he [13]prayed again, and the [12]heaven
gave rain, and the [5]earth °brought forth her
fruit.
19 Brethren, °if any °of you do err °from the
truth, and °one convert him;
20 Let him °know, that he which converteth
°the sinner °from the error of his way shall
save a °soul °from death, and shall °hide a
multitude of [15]sins.

12 above = before. Ap. 104. xiv.
neither. Gr. *mēte*.
heaven = the heaven. See Matt. 6. 9, 10.
any. Ap. 123. 3. other. Ap. 124. 1.
nay. Ap. 105. I.
into. The texts read "under". Ap. 104. xviii. 2.
condemnation. Ap. 177. 7.
13 among. Ap. 104. viii. 2.
afflicted. Gr. *kakopatheō*. See 2 Tim. 2. 3 and cp. *v.* 10, above.
pray. Ap. 134. I. 2.
merry. See Acts 27. 22.
sing psalms. Gr. *psallō*. See Rom. 15. 9.
14 elders. Ap. 189.
church. Ap. 186. Here the church must mean the assembly which worshipped in the synagogue of 2. 2.
over. Ap. 104. ix. 3.
anointing = having anointed. Gr. *aleiphō*. Occ. here and eight times in the Gospels. Cp. Mark 6. 13.
15 prayer. Ap. 134. II. 1.
faith. Ap. 150. II. 1.
sick. Gr. *kamnō*. See Heb. 12. 3. Not the same word as *v.* 14.
raise . . . up. Ap. 178. I. 4.
and if. Gr. *kan* (*kai*, with Ap. 118. 1. b).
sins. Ap. 128. I. ii. 1.
16 faults. Ap. 128. I. ii. 3, but the texts read "sins", as above.
pray. Ap. 134. I. 1.
for. Ap. 104. xvii. 1.
healed. Gr. *iaomai*. See Luke 6. 17. This makes it clear that the circumstances in view are those of 1 Cor. 11. 30. The offenders were those who had wronged their brethren, or had shown an unbrotherly spirit, and so had brought chastisement upon themselves.
effectual fervent = inwrought, or energized. Gr. *energeō*. Cp. 172. 4.
prayer. Ap. 134. II. 3.
righteous = just, *v.* 6. Ap. 191. 1. Read, "a prayer of a just *man* inwrought"; i. e. by the Spirit.
availeth much. Lit. is strong (Gr. *ischuō*. Cp. Ap. 172. 3) for much. **17 man.** Ap. 123. 1. subject, &c. = of like feelings. Gr. *homoiopathēs*. Only here and Acts 14. 15. earnestly = with prayer. Ap. 134. II. 2. This is a Hebraism. Fig. *Polyptōton*. Ap. 6. rain. Ap. 136. viii. by the space of. Omit. **18 brought forth.** Gr. *blastanō*. See Heb. 9. 4. Cp. 1 Kings 17. 1; 18. 1, 41-45. Elijah's praying for drought is first revealed in this passage. **19 if.** Ap. 118. 1. a. of = among. Ap. 104. viii. 2. from. Ap. 104. iv. one = any one, as *v.* 12. **20 know.** Ap. 132. I. ii. the = a. from. Gr. *ek* Ap. 104. vii. soul. Ap. 110. II. hide = cover. Cp. 1 Pet. 4. 8. This refers to Prov. 10. 12.

THE FIRST EPISTLE OF PETER.

THE STRUCTURE OF THE EPISTLE AS A WHOLE.

(*Introversion and Alternation.*)

A | 1. 1, 2. EPISTOLARY.
B | 1. 3-12. INTRODUCTION. THANKSGIVING; FORESHADOWING THE SUBJECT OF THE EPISTLE.
C | D | 1. 13—2. 10. EXHORTATIONS (GENERAL) IN VIEW OF THE END.
E | 2. 11—4. 6. EXHORTATIONS (PARTICULAR) AS TO SUFFERINGS AND GLORY.
C | *D* | 4. 7-19. EXHORTATIONS (GENERAL) IN VIEW OF THE END.
E | 5. 1-9. EXHORTATIONS (PARTICULAR) AS TO SUFFERINGS AND GLORY.
B | 5. 10, 11. CONCLUSION. PRAYER; EMBODYING THE OBJECT OF THE EPISTLE.
A | 5. 12-14. EPISTOLARY.

NOTES ON THE FIRST EPISTLE OF PETER.

1. The writer is unquestionably the apostle whose name the Epistle bears. "Simon, son of Jona" (Ap. 94. III. 3), was one of the earliest disciples, of whom all that we know is furnished by the Gospels and Acts, apart from the incidents recorded in Gal. 1 and 2. His surname (*Cephas*) occurs four times in the First Epistle to the Corinthians. The apostle "of the circumcision" (Gal. 2. 7); yet through him "at the first" (Acts 15. 14) the door was opened to the Gentiles. Nothing certain is known of him after the Council of the apostles at Jerusalem (Acts 15), and there is not the least proof that he ever visited Rome, much less that he was "bishop" there. We know that he was imprisoned in Jerusalem (Acts 12), A. D. 44; in 51 he was at the Council of Acts 15; in 52 he joined Paul at Antioch (Gal. 2); in 58 Paul, writing to Romans, makes no mention of Peter, although he greets many others; in 61 Paul was sent a prisoner to Rome, and at the meetings with brethren and others Peter's name is not once mentioned; at Rome were written by the apostle of the Gentiles the letters to Ephesians, Philippians, Colossians, Philemon, yet Peter is never referred to; finally, Paul's latest letter was written from Rome, and in it we read, "Only Luke is with me" (2 Tim. 4. 11). We have no record of Peter's death, but our Lord's words (John 21. 18, 19) plainly indicate death by martyrdom. It is noteworthy that never in the least degree does Peter claim pre-eminence over the other apostles, but writes as a *fellow-worker*, e. g. 1 Pet. 5. 1.

2. Written to (lit.) "the elect sojourners of the dispersion (see John 7. 35. Jas. 1. 1) of Pontus, Galatia, Cappadocia, Asia, and Bithynia". These were Christian Jews of the dispersion.

3. Teaching. The practical character of the Epistle is marked, and is illustrated by reference to the Divine dealings recorded in the Old Testament. Admonition, exhortation, and encouragement, for all circumstances, show how faithfully the apostle obeyed his Lord's command to feed the flock of God. In 5. 12 he refers to his brief epistle as "exhorting and testifying that this is the true grace of God wherein ye stand" (lit. "in which stand ye"). So far as is known, he had never seen those to whom he wrote, nor does he make reference to a single one of those "strangers" who had doubtless been taught by Paul and his fellow-workers in their "journeyings often". Thus the teaching delivered to them by "our beloved brother Paul" is that to which Peter refers as "the true grace of God wherein ye stand" (cp. 1 Cor. 15. 1).

4. The time of writing was probably about A. D. 60 (see Ap. 180), and the Epistle was written from Babylon (5. 13).

THE FIRST EPISTLE OF
PETER.

A 1 PETER, an °apostle of °Jesus Christ, to the
°strangers °scattered °throughout °Pontus,
°Galatia, °Cappadocia, °Asia, and °Bithynia,
2 °Elect, °according to the °foreknowledge of
°God the °Father, °through °sanctification of the
°Spirit, °unto obedience and °sprinkling of the
°blood of [1]Jesus Christ: °Grace °unto you, and
peace, be multiplied.
B 3 °Blessed *be* the [2]God and [2]Father of our
°Lord [1]Jesus Christ, Which [2]according to His
abundant mercy °hath begotten us again [2]-unto
a °lively hope °by the °resurrection of [1]Jesus
Christ °from the dead,
4 °To an inheritance °incorruptible, and °undefiled, and °that fadeth not away, reserved °in
°heaven °for you,
5 Who are °kept °by the °power of [2]God
°through °faith [2]-unto °salvation ready °to be
revealed [4]in the °last time.
6 °Wherein ye °greatly rejoice, though now
for a season, °if need be, ye are °in heaviness
[2]through °manifold temptations,
7 °That °the trial of your [5]faith, being much
more precious than of gold that °perisheth,
though it be tried °with fire, might be found
[2]-unto praise and honour and °glory °at the
°appearing of [1]Jesus Christ:

1. 1 apostle. Ap. 189.
Jesus Christ. Ap. 98. XI.
strangers. Gr. *parepidēmos.* See 2. 11 and Heb. 11. 13. The word "elect" from *v.* 2 must be read here—"elect strangers"; cp. R.V.
scattered = of the dispersion. See John 7. 35. Jas. 1. 1.
throughout = of.
Pontus . . . Cappadocia, Asia. See Acts 2. 9.
Galatia. See Acts 16. 6; 18. 23. Gal. 1. 2.
Bithynia. See Acts 16. 7.
2 Elect. Read before "strangers". See *v.* 1.
according to. Ap. 104. x. 2.
foreknowledge. See Acts 2. 23.
God. Ap. 98. I. i. 1.
Father. Ap. 98. III.
through. Ap. 104. viii.
sanctification, &c. See 2 Thess. 2. 13.
Spirit. Ap. 101. II. 3.
unto. Ap. 104. vi.
sprinkling. See Heb. 12. 24.
blood. Fig. *Metalepsis.* Ap. 6. Blood put for death, and death for the redemption it brings.
Grace. Ap. 184. I. 1. unto = to.
3 Blessed, &c. See 2 Cor. 1. 3. Eph. 1. 3.
Lord. Ap. 98. VI. i. *β*. 2. A.
hath begotten . . . again = begat . . . again. Gr. *anagennaō.* Only here and *v.* 23.
lively = living. The hope of living again, because it is by His resurrection.
by. Ap. 104. v. 1.
resurrection. Ap. 178. II. 1. from the dead. Ap. 139. 3. **4** To. Ap. 104. vi. incorruptible. See Rom. 1. 23. undefiled. See Heb. 7. 26. that fadeth, &c. = unfading. Gr. *amarantos.* Only here. Cp. 5. 4. in. Ap. 104. viii. heaven = the heavens. See Matt. 6. 9, 10. for. Ap. 104. vi. **5** kept. See 2 Cor. 11. 32. by. Ap. 104. viii. power. Ap. 172. 1. through. Ap. 104. v. 1. faith. Ap. 150. II. 1. salvation. Cp. 1 Thess. 5. 9, 10. to be revealed. Ap. 106. I. ix. last time. Cp. Acts 2. 17. **6** Wherein = In (Ap. 104. viii) which (salvation). greatly rejoice. See Matt. 5. 12. if. Ap. 118. 2. a. in heaviness = grieved. manifold, &c. See Jas. 1. 2. **7** That = In order that. Gr. *hina.* the trial of your faith = your tested faith, as in Jas. 1. 3. perisheth. Gr. *apollumi.* See first occ. Matt. 2. 13. with. Ap. 104. v. 1. glory. See p. 1511. at. Ap. 104. viii. appearing. Ap. 106. II. i.

8 Whom having °not °seen, ye °love; °in
Whom, though now ye °see *Him* °not, yet
°believing, ye [6]rejoice with joy °unspeakable
and °full of glory:
9 Receiving the end of your [5]faith, *even* the
[5]salvation of *your* °souls.
10 °Of which [5]salvation the °prophets °have
°enquired and °searched diligently, who prophesied °of the [2]grace *that should come* [2-] unto
you:
11 °Searching °what, or what manner of time
the °Spirit °of °Christ which was [4]in them
did °signify, when it °testified beforehand the
sufferings °of °Christ, and the [7]glory °that
should follow.
12 °Unto whom it was [5]revealed, that [8-]not
°unto themselves, but °unto °us, they did
°minister the things, which are now °reported
°unto you [3]by them that °have preached the
gospel °unto you °with the °Holy Ghost °sent
down °from °heaven; °which things the angels
desire to °look into.

C D A 13 Wherefore °gird up the loins of your mind,
°be sober, and hope °to the end °for the [2]grace
that is °to be brought [12]unto you [7]at the °reve-
lation of [1]Jesus Christ;

B 14 As °obedient children, [-8]not °fashioning
yourselves according to the former lusts [4]in
your ignorance:
15 But °as He Which hath called you is
holy, °so be ye holy [4]in °all manner of °con-
versation;
16 Because it is written, °"**Be ye holy; for I am holy.**"
17 And [6]if ye call on the [2]Father, Who °with-
out respect of persons °judgeth [2]according to
°every man's work, pass the time of your °so-
journing *here* [4]in fear:

C 18 °Forasmuch as ye know that ye were
[8-]not °redeemed °with °corruptible things, *as*
silver and gold, °from your vain [15]conversa-
tion °*received* by tradition from your fathers;
19 But [18]with the precious blood of [11]Christ,
as of a °Lamb °without blemish and °without
spot:
20 °Who verily was foreordained °before the
°foundation of the °world, but was °manifest
°in °these last °times °for you,
21 Who [3]by Him do [8]believe [8]in [2]God, That
°raised Him up [3]from the dead, and gave Him
[7]glory; that your [5]faith and hope might be [8]in
[2]God.

D 22 °Seeing ye have °purified your °souls [4]in
°obeying the truth °through the Spirit [2-]unto

8 not. Ap. 105. I.
seen. Ap. 133. I. 1.
love. Ap. 135. I. 1.
in. Ap. 104. vi.
see. Ap. 133. I. 8.
not. Ap. 105. II.
believing. Ap. 150. I. 1. v (i).
unspeakable. Gr. *aneklalētos*. Only here.
full of glory. Lit. glorified.
9 souls. Ap. 110. III. 2.
10 Of. Ap. 104. xiii. 1.
prophets. See Jas. 5. 10.
have. Omit.
enquired. Gr. *ekzēteō*. See Acts 15. 17.
searched diligently. Gr. *exereunaō*. Only here.
of. Ap. 104. xiii. 1.
11 Searching. Gr. *ereunaō*. See John 5. 39.
what = unto (Ap. 104. vi) what.
Spirit. Ap. 101. II. 3.
of. Gen. of Relation. Ap. 17.
Christ. Ap. 98. IX. These words "of Christ" should come after "signify".
signify = point. Gr. *dēloō*. See 1 Cor. 1. 11.
testified beforehand. Gr. *promarturomai*. Only here.
of = with reference to. Ap. 104. vi.
that should follow = after (Ap. 104. xi. 2) these things.
12 Unto = To.
us. The texts read "you".
minister. Ap. 190. III. 1.
reported. Same as "shew" in Acts 20. 20.
have preached . . . you. Lit. evangelized (Ap. 121. 4) you.
with. Ap. 104. viii.
Holy Ghost. No art. Ap. 101. II. 14.
sent down. Ap. 174. 1.
from. Ap. 104. iv.
heaven. Sing. See Matt. 6. 9, 10.
which . . . into = into (Ap. 104. vi) which.
look = stoop down (to look). Gr. *parakuptō*. See John 20. 5.

1. 13—2. 10 (D, p. 1854). EXHORTATIONS (GENERAL), &c. (*Extended Alternation.*)

C D | A | 1. 13. Exhortation to sobriety. (Positive.)
B | 1. 14-17. Comparison, "obedient children".
C | 1. 18-21. Reason. God's people, and redeemed by the blood of Christ (the Lamb).
D | 1. 22-25. Result.
A | 2. 1. Exhortation against malice. (Negative.)
B | 2. 2, 3. Comparison, "newborn babes".
C | 2. 4-8. Reason. God's people, and built as "living stones" on Christ (the Stone).
D | 2. 9, 10. Result.

13 gird up. Gr. *anazōnnumi*. Only here.
be sober, and = being sober. Gr. *nēphō*. See 1 Thess. 5. 6.
to the end = perfectly. Gr. *teleiōs*. Only here. See Ap. 125. 1.
for. Ap. 104. ix. 3. to be = being.
revelation. Same as "appearing", *v.* 7.

14 obedient children = children (Ap. 108. i) of (Ap. 17. 1) obedience. fashioning, &c. See Rom. 12. 2. **15** as, &c. Lit. according to (Ap. 104. x. 2) the (One) having called you (is) holy. so, &c. = become ye yourselves also. all manner of = all. conversation = behaviour. Gr. *anastrophē*. See Gal. 1. 13. **16** Be ye holy, &c. Quoted from Lev. 11. 44. See also Lev. 19. 2; 20. 7. **17** without respect, &c. Gr. *aprosōpolēptōs*. Only here. judgeth. Ap. 122. 1. every man's = each one's. sojourning. See Acts 13. 17. **18** Forasmuch, &c. = Knowing. Ap. 132. 1. i. redeemed. See Tit. 2. 14. with = by. No prep. corruptible. See Rom. 1. 23. from. Ap. 104. vii. *received*, &c. = handed down from your fathers. Gr. *patroparadotos*. Only here. **19** Lamb. See John 1. 29. without blemish. Gr. *amōmos*. See Eph. 1. 4 (without blame). Cp. Ex. 12. 5. without spot. See 1 Tim. 6. 14. **20** Who verily, &c. = Foreknown indeed. Ap. 132. I. iv. before. Ap. 104. xiv. foundation, &c. Ap. 146. world. Ap. 129. 1. manifest = manifested. Ap. 106. I. v. in. Ap. 104. ix. 1. these last. Read "the last of the". times. See Ap. 195. for. Ap. 104. v. 2. **21** raised . . . up, Ap. 178. I. 4. **22** Seeing ye have = Having. purified. Gr. *hagnizō*. See Acts 21. 24. souls. Ap. 110. IV. 1. obeying = the obedience of. through the Spirit. All the texts omit.

°unfeigned °love of the brethren, *see that ye*
[8]love one another °with a °pure heart °fer-
vently:
23 °Being °born again, [8-]not °of [18]corruptible
°seed, but of [4]incorruptible, [3]by the °word of
[2]God, °which liveth and abideth °for ever.
**24 For all flesh *is* as °grass, and all the [7]glory
of °man as the flower of °grass. The °grass
°withereth, and the flower thereof falleth
away:**
**25 But the °word of the °LORD °endureth °for
ever.** And this is the °word °which by the
gospel is preached [2-] unto you.

A **2** Wherefore °laying aside all °malice, and
all °guile, and hypocrisies, and envies, and
all °evil speakings,
B 2 As °newborn °babes, °desire the °sincere
°milk °of the word, °that ye may grow °there-
by:
3 °If so be ye °have °tasted that the °Lord *is*
°gracious.
C 4 °To Whom coming,° *as unto* a °living stone,
°disallowed indeed °of °men, but chosen °of
°God, *and* °precious,
5 Ye also, as °lively stones, are built up a
°spiritual house, an holy °priesthood, to °offer
up °spiritual sacrifices, °acceptable to [4]God °by
°Jesus Christ.
6 °Wherefore also it is °contained °in the
Scripture, °**"Behold, I lay °in Sion a °chief
corner stone, elect, [4]precious: and he that
°believeth on Him shall °not be °confounded."**
7 °Unto you therefore which °believe °*He is*
precious: but °unto them which be °disobedient,
**the Stone Which the builders [4]disallowed, the
same °is made °the head of the corner,**
**8 And a Stone of °stumbling, and a Rock of
°offence,** *even to them* which °stumble °at the
°word, being [7]disobedient: °whereunto °also
they were °appointed.
D 9 But ye *are* a chosen °generation, a °royal
[5]priesthood, an holy °nation, °a peculiar °peo-
ple, that ye should °shew forth the °praises
of Him Who [3]hath called you °out of darkness
°into His marvellous °light:
10 Which °in time past *were* °not a [9]people,
but *are* now the [9]people of [4]God: which had
°not °obtained mercy, but now have °obtained
mercy.

unfeigned. Gr. *anupokritos*. See Rom. 12. 9 (without dissimulation).
love, &c. Gr. *philadelphia*. See Rom. 12. 10.
with. Ap. 104. vii.
pure. The texts omit. Read "from the heart".
fervently = intently. Gr. *ektenōs*. Only here. See the adj. in 4. 8. Acts 12. 5, and the comparative in Luke 22. 44.
23 Being = Having been.
born. Same as "begotten", *v.* 3.
of. Ap. 104. vii.
seed. Gr. *spora*. Only here.
word. Ap. 121. 10.
which liveth, &c. = living (Ap. 170. 1) and abiding (see p. 1511). for ever. All the texts omit.
24 grass. Cp. Jas. 1. 10, 11.
man. The texts read "it", referring to "flesh".
withereth = withered. Cp. Jas. 1. 11, where the verbs are in the past tense, as here.
25 word. Gr. *rhēma*. See Mark 9. 32.
LORD. Ap. 98. VI. i. *β*. 1. B. a.
endureth. Gr. *menō*. Same as "abide", *v.* 23.
for ever. Ap. 151. II. A. ii. 4. a. The above is quoted from Isa. 40. 6–8. Ap. 107. II. 2.
which . . . preached. Lit. evangelized, as *v.* 12.

2. 1 laying aside = having put away. Gr. *apotithēmi*. See Rom. 13. 12.
malice. Ap. 128. II. 2. guile. See Acts 13. 10.
evil speakings. Gr. *katalalia*. See 2 Cor. 12. 20.
2 newborn. Gr. *artigennētos*. Only here.
babes. Ap. 108. viii.
desire = earnestly desire. Gr. *epipotheō*. See Rom. 1. 11. Cp. Prov. 2. 1–6.
sincere. Gr. *adolos* = without guile. Only here.
milk. Cp. 1 Cor. 3. 2.
of the word. Gr. *logikos*. Only here and Rom. 12. 1, where it is rendered "reasonable". The milk to be found in the Word of God is in the highest sense "reasonable". See 3. 15.
that = in order that. Gr. *hina*.
thereby = in (Ap. 104. viii) it. Cp. 2 Pet. 3. 18. The texts add "unto (Ap. 104. vi) salvation".
3 If so be = If. Ap. 118. 2. a.
have. Omit. tasted. Cp. Heb. 6. 4, 5.
Lord. Ap. 98. VI. i. *β*. 2. A.
gracious. Ap. 184. III.
4 To. Ap. 104. xv. 3. *as unto*. Omit.
living. Ap. 170. 1.
disallowed = having been rejected. Gr. *apodokimazō*, as Matt. 21. 42; &c.
of. Ap. 104. xviii. 1. men. Ap. 123. 1.
of = in the sight of. Ap. 104. xii. 2.
God. Ap. 98. I. i. 1.
precious. Gr. *entimos*. See Phil. 2. 29.
5 lively = living. Ap. 170. 1.
spiritual. See 1 Cor. 12. 1.
priesthood. Gr. *hierateuma*. Only here and *v.* 9.

offer up. Gr. *anapherō*. See Heb. 7. 27. acceptable. Gr. *euprosdektos*. See Rom. 15. 16. by. Ap. 104. v. 1. Jesus Christ. Ap. 98. XI. **6** Wherefore also. The texts read "Because", as 1. 16. contained. Gr. *periechō*. Only here; Luke 5. 9. Acts 23. 25. in. Ap. 104. viii. Behold. Ap. 133. I. 2. chief corner. See Eph. 2. 20. believeth on. Ap. 150. I. 1. v (iii). 1. not. Ap. 105. III. confounded = put to shame. Gr. *kataischunō*. See Rom. 5. 5. Quoted from Isa. 28. 16. Ap. 107. I. 1. **7** Unto = To. believe. Ap. 150. I. 1. i. *He is* precious. Gr. *timē* = the honour, or preciousness. The verb to be supplied is "belongs", or "attaches". The preciousness in Christ is reckoned unto you that believe. Cp. 1 Cor. 1. 30. disobedient. Gr. *apeitheō*. See Acts 14. 2. The texts read *apisteō*, as Rom. 3. 3. is made = became. the head = for (Ap. 104. vi) the head. **8** stumbling. Gr. *proskomma*. See Rom. 9. 32. offence. Gr. *skandalon*. See 1 Cor. 1. 23, and cp. Rom. 9. 33. This is a composite quotation from Ps. 118. 22 and Isa. 8. 14. Ap. 107. II. 4. stumble. Gr. *proskoptō*. See Rom. 9. 32. at the word, &c. = being disobedient to the word. word. Ap. 121. 10. whereunto = unto (Ap. 104. vi) which. also, &c. = they were appointed also. appointed. Gr. *tithēmi*. Occ. ninety-six times and transl. "appoint", here; Matt. 24. 51. Luke 12. 46. 1 Thess. 5. 9. 2 Tim. 1. 11. Heb. 1. 2. **9** generation = race. Gr. *genos*. See 1 Cor. 12. 10 (kind). royal. Gr. *basileios*. Only here. Cp. Jas. 2. 8. Rev. 1. 6; 5. 10. nation. Gr. *ethnos*. Pl., usually transl. "Gentiles", in Pl. a peculiar people = a people (Gr. *laos*. See Acts 2. 47) for (Ap. 104. vi) possession, or acquisition. Gr. *peripoiēsis*. See Eph. 1. 14. shew forth. Gr. *exangellō*. Only here. praises = virtues. See Phil. 4. 8. out of. Ap. 104. vii. into. Ap. 104. vi. light. Ap. 130. 1. **10** in time past = once, at one time. Gr. *pote*. not. Ap. 105. I. obtained mercy. As Rom. 11. 31. Cp. Hos. 2. 23.

E E 11 °Dearly beloved, I °beseech *you* as °stran-
gers and °pilgrims, °abstain from °fleshly lusts,
which °war °against the °soul;

F 12 Having your °conversation °honest °among
the Gentiles: [2]that, °whereas they °speak
against you as °evildoers, they may °by *your*
°good works, °which they shall behold, glorify
[4]God [6]in the day of °visitation.

G H a 13 °Submit yourselves to every °ordinance
°of man °for the [3]Lord's sake: whether it be
to the king, as °supreme;
14 Or [7]unto °governors, as [7]unto them that
are °sent [5]by him °for the °punishment of
[12]evildoers and for the praise of °them that
do well.

b 15 For so is the °will of [4]God, that with °well
doing ye may °put to silence the °ignorance of
°foolish [4]men:
16 As free, and °not °using *your* liberty for
a °cloke of [1]maliciousness, but as the °servants
of [4]God.
17 Honour all *men*. °Love the °brotherhood.
Fear [4]God. Honour the king.

J c 18 °Servants, °*be* subject to *your* °masters
°with all fear; [10]not only to the good and
°gentle, but °also to the °froward.

d 19 For this *is* °thankworthy, [3]if °a man °for
°conscience °toward [4]God °endure grief, suffering °wrongfully.
20 For what °glory *is it*, [3]if, °when ye be
°buffeted for your faults, ye shall take it
patiently? but [3]if, when ye [15]do well, and
suffer *for it*, ye take it patiently, this *is* °ac-
ceptable °with [4]God.

K 21 For °even hereunto were ye called; because °Christ also suffered °for °us, °leaving
°us an °example, [2]that ye should °follow His
°steps:
**22 Who did °no °sin, °neither was [1]guile
found [6]in His mouth:**
23 Who, when He was °reviled, °reviled [10]not
again; when He suffered, He °threatened [10]not;
but °committed *Himself* to Him That °judgeth
°righteously:
24 Who °His own self °bare our [22]sins [6]in
His °own body °on the °tree, [2]that we, °being
dead to [22]sins, should °live [7]unto °righteous-
ness: **by Whose °stripes ye were °healed.**

2. 11—4. 6 (E, p. 1854). EXHORTATION (PARTICULAR) AS TO SUFFERINGS AND GLORY.
(*Extended Alternation.*)

E | E | 2. 11. Exhortation. Personal.
  F | 2. 12. Calumnies.
    G | 2. 13—3. 7. Submission. The will of God (2. 15). Example of Christ (2. 21-25).
  E | 3. 8-15. Exhortation. General.
    F | 3. 16. Calumnies.
      G | 3. 17—4. 6. Submission. The will of God (3. 17). Example of Christ (3. 18-22).

11 Dearly beloved. Ap. 135. III.
beseech. Ap. 134. I. 6.
strangers. Gr. *paroikos.* See Acts 7. 6. Cp. 1. 17.
pilgrims. Same as "strangers", 1. 1.
abstain. See Acts 15. 20.
fleshly. Gr. *sarkikos.* See Rom. 7. 14.
war. Gr. *strateuomai.* See 1 Cor. 9. 7.
against. Ap. 104. x. 1.
soul. Ap. 110. III. 2.
12 conversation. See 1. 15, 18 and Gal. 1. 13.
honest. See Rom. 12. 17.
among. Ap. 104. viii. 2.
whereas = wherein, or, in (Ap. 104. viii) what.
speak against. Gr. *katalaleō.* See Jas. 4. 11.
evildoers. See John 18. 30.
by = from. Ap. 104. vii.
good. Same as "honest", above.
which, &c. = beholding (them). Ap. 133. II. 2.
visitation. Gr. *episkopē.* See Acts 1. 20.

2. 13—3. 7 (G, above). SUBMISSION.
(*Introversion and Alternation.*)

G | H | a | 2. 13, 14. All to rulers.
        b | 2. 15-17. Reason.
    J | c | 2. 18. Servants to masters.
        d | 2. 19, 20. Reason.
      K | 2. 21-25. The example of Christ.
    J | *c* | 3. 1-4. Wives to husbands.
          d | 3. 5, 6. Reason.
  H | *a* | 3. 7-. Husbands to be considerate to their wives.
        b | 3. -7. Reason.

13 Submit. Same word in *v.* 18 (subject).
ordinance. Gr. *ktisis.* Always transl. "creature" or "creation", except Heb. 9. 11 and here.
of man = human. Gr. *anthrōpinos.* See Rom. 6. 19.
for, &c. = on account of (Ap. 104. v. 2) the Lord.
supreme. Same as "higher", Rom. 13. 1.
14 governors. Gr. *hēgemōn.* Elsewhere, only in the Gospels and Acts. The title of Pilate, Felix, and Festus.
sent. Ap. 174. 4. **for.** Ap. 104. vi.
punishment of = vengeance on. Gr. *ekdikēsis.* See Acts 7. 24.
them, &c. Gr. *agathopoios.* Only here. Cp. 4. 19.

15 will. Ap. 102. 2. **well doing.** Gr. *agathopoieō.* See Acts 14. 17. **put to silence.** Same as "muzzle", 1 Cor. 9. 9. **ignorance.** Gr. *agnōsia.* See 1 Cor. 15. 34. **foolish.** See Luke 11. 40. **16 not.** Ap. 105. II. **using** = having. **cloke.** Gr. *epikalumma.* Only here. The word *kalumma* only in 2 Cor. 3. 13-16. **servants.** Ap. 190. I. 2. **17 Love.** Ap. 135. I. 1. **brotherhood.** Gr. *adelphotēs.* Only here and 5. 9. **18 Servants.** Ap. 190. I. 6. *be* **subject** = submit, *v.* 13. **masters.** Ap. 98. XIV. ii. **with** = in. Ap. 104. viii. **gentle.** Gr. *epieikēs.* See Phil. 4. 5. **also, &c.** = to the froward also. **froward.** Gr. *skolios.* See Acts 2. 40. **19 thankworthy.** Ap. 184. I. 1. **a man.** Ap. 123. 3. **for.** Ap. 104. v. 2. **conscience.** See Acts 23. 1. **toward** = of. **endure.** See 2 Tim. 3. 11. **wrongfully.** Gr. *adikōs.* Only here. **20 glory.** Gr. *kleos.* Only here. **when, &c.** = sinning (Ap. 128. I. i) and being buffeted (see 1 Cor. 4. 11). **acceptable.** Ap. 184. I. 1. **with.** Ap. 104. xii. 2. **21 even hereunto** = unto (Ap. 104. vi) this. **Christ.** Ap. 98. IX. **for.** Ap. 104. xvii. 1. **us.** All the texts read "you". **leaving.** Gr. *hupolimpanō.* Only here. **example.** Gr. *hupogrammos.* Only here. **follow** = diligently follow. See 1 Tim. 5. 10. **steps.** See Rom. 4. 12. **22 no.** Ap. 105. I. **sin.** Ap. 128. I. ii. 1. Cp. John 8. 46. 2 Cor. 5. 21. 1 John 3. 5. **neither.** Gr. *oude.* Verse quoted from Isa. 53. 9. **23 reviled.** Gr. *loidoreō.* See John 9. 28. **reviled . . . again.** Gr. *antiloidoreō.* Only here. **threatened.** See Acts 4. 17. **committed.** See John 19. 30. **judgeth.** Ap. 122. 1. **righteously.** Gr. *dikaiōs.* See 1 Cor. 15. 34. **24 His own self** = Himself. **bare.** Same as "offer up", *v.* 5. **own.** Omit. **on.** Ap. 104. ix. 3. **tree.** Cp. Acts 5. 30; 10. 39; 13. 29. Gal. 3. 13. **being dead.** Gr. *apoginomai,* to be away from, to die. Only here. **live.** Ap. 170. 1. **righteousness.** Ap. 191. 3. **stripes** = bruise. Gr. *mōlōps.* Only here, but in the Sept. in several places, one of which is Isa. 53. 5. **healed.** Gr. *iaomai.* See Luke 6. 17.

25 °**For ye were as sheep going astray; but
are now returned °unto the Shepherd and
° Bishop of your [11]souls.**

J c **3** Likewise, ye wives, °*be* in subjection to
your own °husbands; °that, °if °any °obey
not the °word, they °also may without the
°word be °won °by the °conversation of the
wives;
2 °While they behold your °chaste [1]conversa-
tion °*coupled* with °fear.
3 Whose °adorning let it °not be °that outward *adorning* of °plaiting the hair, and of
°wearing of °gold, or of °putting on of apparel;
4 But *let it be* the hidden °man of the heart,
°in °that which is not corruptible, *even the
ornament* of a °meek and °quiet °spirit, which
is in the sight of °God °of great price.
d 5 For °after this manner in the old time the
holy women also, who °trusted °in [4]God,
°adorned themselves, [1]being in subjection °un-
to their own [1]husbands:
6 °Even as Sara obeyed Abraham, calling
him °lord: whose °daughters ye °are, as long
as ye °do well, and are °not afraid with °any
°amazement.
H a 7 Likewise, ye [1]husbands, °dwell with *them*
°according to °knowledge, °giving °honour
[5]unto the °wife, as [5]unto °the weaker vessel,
and as being °heirs together of the °grace of
°life;
b °that your °prayers be [6]not °hindered.
E 8 Finally, *be ye* all °of one mind, °having
compassion one of another, °love as brethren,
be °pitiful, *be* °courteous:
9 [6]Not rendering °evil °for °evil, or °railing
°for °railing; but °contrariwise blessing; °know-
ing that ye °are °thereunto called, [1]that ye
should inherit a blessing.
10 **For he that °will °love [7]life, and °see good
days, let him °refrain his tongue °from [9]evil,
and his lips °that they speak no °guile:**
11 **Let him °eschew [9]evil, and do good; let
him seek peace, and °ensue it.**
12 **For the eyes of the °LORD *are* °over the
°righteous, and His ears *are open* °unto their
°prayers: but the face of the °LORD *is* °against
them that do [9]evil.**
13 And who *is* he that will °harm you, °if ye
°be °followers of that which is good?

25 For, &c. This clause and that which precedes are quoted from Isa. 53. 5, 6.
unto. Ap. 104. ix. 3.
Bishop. See Phil. 1. 1. A Latin manuscript in the British Museum adds, after "souls", "the Lord Jesus Christ".

3. 1 *be* **in subjection**=submit, as 2. 13.
husbands. Ap. 123. 2.
that=in order that. Gr. *hina.*
if. Ap. 118. 2. a.
any. Pl. of *tis.* Ap. 123. 3.
obey not=are disobedient to. Gr. *apeitheō.* See 2. 7.
word. Ap. 121. 10.
also. Read as "even", before "if", "even if".
won=gained. Gr. *kerdainō.* See Acts 27. 21. Cp. Matt. 18. 15. 1 Cor. 9. 19.
by=through. Ap. 104. v. 1.
conversation. See 1. 15.
2 While, &c.=Having beheld. Ap. 133. II. 2.
chaste. Gr. *hagnos.* See 2 Cor. 7. 11.
coupled **with**=in. Ap. 104. viii.
fear. Here used in the sense of reverence. Cp. Eph. 5. 33, where the verb is used.
3 adorning. Gr. *kosmos.* Elsewhere transl. "world". See Ap. 129. 1.
not. Ap. 105. I.
that, &c.=the outward one.
plaiting. Gr. *emplokē.* Only here.
wearing=putting around. Gr. *perithesis.* Only here. Referring to putting coronets, bracelets, &c., round the head, arms, &c.
gold=gold (ornaments).
putting on. Gr. *endusis.* Only here.
4 man. Ap. 123. 1. "The hidden man" means "the inward man" of Rom. 7. 22. 2 Cor. 4. 16. Eph. 3. 16.
in. Ap. 104. viii.
that which, &c.=the incorruptible (Gr. *aphthartos.* See Rom. 1. 23). Supply "ornament" again here.
meek. Ap. 127. 3. **quiet.** See 1 Tim. 2. 2.
spirit. Ap. 101. II. 7.
God. Ap. 98. I. i. 1.
of great price. See 1 Tim. 2. 9.
5 after this, &c.=thus in the old time=thus once.
trusted=hoped.
in. Ap. 104. ix. 3, but the texts read Ap. 104. vi.
adorned=used to adorn (Imperfect). Gr. *kosmeō.* See 1 Tim. 2. 9. **unto**=to.
6 Even. Omit.
lord. Gr. *kurios.* Cp. Ap. 98. VI (cp. i. *a.* 4. B).
daughters=children. Ap. 108. I.
are=are become.
do well. See 2. 15.
not. Ap. 105. II.
any=no. Gr. *mēdeis.* A double negative here.
amazement=terror. Gr. *ptoēsis.* Only here. The verb *ptoeomai* occ. Luke 21. 9; 24. 37.
7 dwell with. Gr. *sunoikeō.* Only here.
according to. Ap. 104. x. 2. **knowledge.** Ap. 132. II. i. **giving**=dispensing. Gr. *aponemō.* Only here. In the Sept. in Deut. 4. 19 (divided). The word *nemō* is not found in N.T., but is frequent in the Sept. of feeding cattle and sheep. **honour.** This is part of the wife's daily portion. **wife.** Gr. *gunaikeios.* Only here. An adjective. **the, &c.** Read "the female vessel as weaker". **heirs together.** See Rom. 8. 17. **grace.** Ap. 184. I. 1. **life.** Ap. 170. 1. **that**=to the end that. Ap. 104. vi. **prayers.** Ap. 134. II. 2. **hindered.** Gr. *enkoptō.* See Acts 24. 4. **8 of one mind.** Gr. *homophrōn.* Only here. Cp. Rom. 12. 16; 15. 5. 2 Cor. 13. 11. Phil. 2. 2; 3. 16; 4. 2. **having . . . another**=sympathetic. Gr. *sumpathēs.* Only here. The verb *sumpatheō* occ. Heb. 4. 15; 10. 34. **love, &c.**=loving as brethren. Gr. *philadelphos.* Only here. Cp. 1. 22. **pitiful.** Gr. *eusplanchnos.* Only here and Eph. 4. 32. **courteous.** Gr. *philophrōn.* Only here. Cp. Acts 28. 7. But the texts read "humble-minded". Gr. *tapeinophrōn*, nowhere else in N.T. Cp. 5. 5. **9 evil.** Ap. 128. III. 2. **for.** Ap. 104. ii. **railing.** Gr. *loidoria.* See 1 Tim. 5. 14. Cp. 2. 23. 1 Cor. 5. 11. **contrariwise.** See 2 Cor. 2. 7. **knowing.** Ap. 132. I. i. The texts omit and read "for ye", &c. **are**=were. **thereunto**=unto (Ap. 104. vi) this. **10 will.** Ap. 102. 1. **love.** Ap. 135. I. 1. **see.** Ap. 133. I. 1. **refrain**=cause to cease. Gr. *pauomai.* **from.** Ap. 104. iv. **that, &c.**=not (Ap. 105. II) to speak (Ap. 121. 7). **guile.** See 2. 1, 22. **11 eschew**=turn away (Gr. *ekklinō.* See Rom. 3. 12) from (*v.* 10). **ensue**=pursue. **12 LORD.** Ap. 98. VI. i. β. 1. B. a. **over.** Ap. 104. ix. 3. **righteous.** Ap. 191. 1. **unto.** Ap. 104. vi. **prayers.** Ap. 134. II. 3. **against.** Ap. 104. ix. 3. The reference in *vv.* 10–12 is to Ps. 34. 12–16. **13 harm**=ill-treat. Gr. *kakoō.* Acts 7. 6. **if.** Ap. 118. 1. b. **be**=become. **followers**=imitators. Gr. *mimētēs.* See 1 Cor. 4. 16, but the texts read *zēlōtēs*, as in Acts 21. 20.

14 But and °if ye suffer °for righteousness' sake, °happy *are ye:* and **be** [6] **not afraid of their terror, °neither be troubled;**

15 But °sanctify °the [12] **LORD** [4] **God** [4] **in your hearts:** and *be* ready °always °to *give* an °answer to every man that °asketh you °a reason °of the hope that is [4] in you, °with °meekness and fear:

F 16 Having °a good conscience; [1] that, °whereas they °speak evil of you, as of °evildoers, they may °be ashamed that °falsely accuse your good [1] conversation [4] in °Christ.

G L e 17 For *it is* better, [14] if the °will of [4] God °be so, that ye suffer °for well doing than °for [16] evil doing.

f 18 For [16] Christ also °hath once °suffered °for °sins, the °Just °for the unjust, [1] that He might °bring us to [4] God, being put to death °in the flesh,

M N g but °quickened °by the Spirit:

h 19 °By which °also He went and °preached [5] unto the °spirits [4] in prison,

k 20 Which sometime were [1] disobedient, when once the longsuffering of [4] God waited [4] in the days of Noah, while the ark was a preparing,

O °wherein few, that is, eight °souls °were saved [1] by water.

O 21 °The like figure whereunto *even* °baptism doth °also now save us ([3] not the °putting away of the °filth of the flesh, but the °answer of a good °conscience °toward [4] God),

N g [1] by the °resurrection of °Jesus Christ:

h 22 Who °is gone °into °heaven, °and is °on the right hand of [4] God;

k angels and °authorities and °powers being made [1] subject [5] unto Him.

L f **4** Forasmuch then as °Christ hath suffered °for us °in the flesh, °arm yourselves °likewise with the same °mind;

14 if. Ap. 118. 2. b.
for, &c. = on account of (Ap. 104. v. 2) righteousness (Ap. 191. 3).
happy. Gr. *makarios.* Gen. transl. "blessed".
neither. Gr. *mēde.*
15 sanctify. I. e. separate. Give Him His right place.
the LORD God. The texts read "the Christ as Lord". There is no art. before Lord, which shows that it is the predicate. Cp. Rom. 10. 9. Phil. 2. 6. The quotation is from Isa. 8. 12, 13.
always. Ap. 151. II. F.
to *give* = for. Ap. 104. xv. 3.
answer. Gr. *apologia.* See Acts 22. 1.
asketh. Ap. 134. I. 4.
a reason = an account. Ap. 121. 10.
of = concerning. Ap. 104. xiii. 1.
with. Ap. 104. xi. 1.
meekness. Gr. *praütēs.* See Jas. 1. 21. Cp. *v.* 4.
16 a good conscience. See Acts 23. 1.
whereas = in (Ap. 104. viii) what.
speak evil. Gr. *katalaleō.* See Jas. 4. 11.
evildoers. See 2. 12. be ashamed. See 2. 6.
falsely accuse = calumniate. Gr. *epēreazō.* Also in Matt. 5. 44. Luke 6. 28. Christ. Ap. 98. IX.

3. 17—4. 6 (*G*, p. 1858). SUBMISSION.
(*Alternation and Introversion.*)

G | L | e | 3. 17. Suffering according to the will of God.
    f | 3. 18-. Christ's sufferings as to the flesh.
   M | 3. -18-22. Christ's triumph.
 L | *f* | 4. 1-. Christ's sufferings as to the flesh.
    e | 4. -1. The saints' sufferings as to the flesh.
   M | 4. 2-6. The saints' new life.

17 will. Ap. 102. 2.
be so = should will. Ap. 102. 1.
for, &c. = as well doers (*v.* 6).
for, &c. = as evildoers. Gr. *kakopoieō.* See Mark 3. 4.
18 hath. Omit.
suffered. The texts (but not R.V.) read "died".
for = concerning. Ap. 104. xiii. 1.
sins. Ap. 128. I. ii. 1. Just. Ap. 191. 1.
for. Ap. 104. xvii. 1. bring. See Acts 16. 20.
in the flesh = in flesh. No art. or prep. Dat. case.
3. -18-22 [For Structures see below].
quickened. See Rom. 4. 17.
by the Spirit = in spirit. No prep. (Dat. case), and though the A.V. has the art. it is rejected by all the texts. Ap. 101. II. 13. The reference is to the resurrection body, and the contrast is between His condition when He was put to death and when He rose from the dead.

3. -18-22 (M, above). CHRIST'S TRIUMPH. (*Introversion and Alternation.*)

M | N | g | -18. The Resurrection of Christ.
   h | 19. His going to Tartarus.
    k | 20-. The insubjection of spirits in Noah's day.
     O | -20. Noah saved then.
     O | 21-. We saved now.
  N | *g* | -21. The Resurrection of Christ.
   h | 22-. His going into heaven.
    k | -22. The subjection of angels.

19 By which = In (Gr. *en*) which (condition). also, &c. = having gone, He even preached. preached = heralded. Ap. 121. 1. Not the Gospel, which would be Ap. 121. 4. He announced His triumph. spirits. Ap. 101. II. 11. These were the angels of Gen. 6. 2, 4. See Ap. 23, where 2 Pet. 2. 4 and Jude 6 are considered together with this verse. **20** wherein = into (Ap. 104. vi) which. souls. Ap. 110. II. were saved = (entered and) were saved. Fig. *Ellipsis.* Ap. 6. **21 The like figure, &c.** Lit. Which (i. e. water; the relative, being neuter, can only refer to the word "water") being antitypical (Gr. *antitupos*, here and Heb. 9. 24). baptism. Ap. 115. II. i. 1. also, &c. = now save you (all the texts read "you") also. putting away. Gr. *apothesis.* Only here and 2 Pet. 1. 14. filth. Gr. *rupos.* Only here. Cp. Jas. 1. 21. answer = inquiry, or seeking. Gr. *eperōtēma.* Only here. The verb *erōtaō* (Ap. 134. I. 3) and *eperōtaō* (Acts 1. 6) always mean "to ask". conscience. See Acts 23. 1. toward. Ap. 104. vi. resurrection. Ap. 178. II. 1. Jesus Christ. Ap. 98. XI. **22** is = having. into. Ap. 104. vi. heaven. Sing. See Matt. 6. 9, 10. and. Omit. on. Ap. 104. viii. authorities. Ap. 172. 5. Cp. Eph. 1. 21; 3. 10; 6. 12. Col. 2. 10, 15. Tit. 3. 1. powers. Ap. 172. 1. Cp. Matt. 24. 29. Rom. 8. 38. 1 Cor. 15. 24. 2 Thess. 1. 7. 2 Pet. 2. 11.

4. 1 Christ. Ap. 98. IX. for us. The texts omit. in the flesh. Gr. *sarki*, as 3. 18. arm yourselves . . . with = put on as armour. Gr. *hoplizomai.* Only here. Cp. Rom. 6. 13. likewise = also. mind. Gr. *ennoia.* See Heb. 4. 12.

e for he that hath suffered °in the flesh hath ceased from °sin;

M1 2 °That he °no longer should °live the °rest of *his* time °in the flesh to the lusts of °men, but to the °will of °God.

m 3 For the time past °of *our* life °may suffice °us to have wrought the °will of the °Gentiles, when we walked [2]in °lasciviousness, lusts, °excess of wine, °revellings, °banquetings, and °abominable °idolatries:

n 4 °Wherein they °think it strange that ye run °not with *them* °to the same °excess of °riot, °speaking evil of *you:*

n 5 Who shall °give °account to Him That °is ready to °judge the °quick and the °dead.

m 6 For °for this cause °was the gospel preached °also to them that are [5]dead, °that °they might be [5]judged °according to [2]men [1-]in the flesh,

but live °according to [2]God in the °spirit.

CD P1 7 But the end of all things °is at hand:

Q1 °be ye therefore sober, and °watch °unto °prayer.

8 And °above all things °have °fervent °charity °among yourselves; °for °**charity shall cover the multitude of [1]sins.**

9 °Use hospitality °one [4]to another without °grudging.

10 As °every man °hath received the °gift, *even so* °minister °the same °one [4]to another, as good °stewards of the °manifold °grace of [2]God.

11 °If °any man °speak, *let him speak* °as the °oracles of [2]God; °if °any man [10]minister, *let him do it* as °of the °ability which [2]God °giveth: [6]that [2]God [2]in all things may be glorified °through °Jesus Christ, to Whom °be °praise and °dominion °for ever and ever. Amen.

P2 12 °Beloved, [4]think it [4]not strange °concerning °the °fiery °trial which is to try you, as

in the flesh. The Received text (Ap. 94. VI) has *en*, but the texts omit.
sin. Ap. 128. I. ii. 1. Cp. Rom. 6. 7.

4. 2-6 (*M*, p. 1860). THE SAINTS' NEW LIFE. (*Introversion.*)

M | l | 2. New life in the spirit.
  m | 3. Time past. Insubjection of the flesh.
   n | 4. Men's judgment.
   n | 5. God's judgment.
  m | 6-. Time past. Death as to flesh.
 l | -6. Life as to the spirit.

2 That=To (Ap. 104. vi) the end that.
no longer. Gr. *mēketi.*
live. Gr. *bioō.* Only here. Cp. Ap. 170. 2.
rest of *his*=remaining. Gr. *epiloipos.* Only here. Cp. Ap. 124. 3.
in. Ap. 104. viii.
men. Ap. 123. 1.
will. Ap. 102. 2.
God. Ap. 98. I. i. 1.
3 of *our* **life.** The texts omit.
may suffice=is sufficient (Gr. *arketos.* Only here and Matt. 6. 34; 10. 25).
us. The texts omit.
will. Ap. 102. 2, as above, but the texts read Ap. 102. 4.
Gentiles. Gr. *ethnos.*
lasciviousness. See Rom. 13. 13.
excess of wine. Gr. *oinophlugia.* Only here.
revellings. Gr. *kōmos.* See Rom. 13. 13.
banquetings. Gr. *potos.* Only here.
abominable=unlawful. See Acts 10. 28.
idolatries. See 1 Cor. 10. 14.
4 Wherein=In (Ap. 104. viii) which.
think, &c. See Acts 17. 20.
not. Ap. 105. II.
to. Ap. 104. vi.
excess. Gr. *anachusis.* Only here.
riot. Gr. *asōtia.* See Eph. 5. 18.
speaking evil of. Gr. *blasphēmeō.*
5 give=render. As in Heb. 13. 17.
account. Ap. 121. 10.
is ready. See Acts 21. 13.
judge. Ap. 122. 1.
quick=living. Ap. 170. 1.
dead. Ap. 139. 2.
6 for this cause=unto (Ap. 104. vi) this (end).
was the gospel preached. Ap. 121. 4.
also, &c.=to the dead also. **that**=in order that. Gr. *hina.* **they might**=though they might. The particle *men*, marking the contrast, is ignored in the A.V. and R.V. **according to.** Ap. 104. x. 2. Supply "the will of". **live.** Ap. 170. 1. **spirit.** No art. or prep. Ap. 101. II. 13. Cp. 3. 18. This is man's day (1 Cor. 4. 3), when he is judging and condemning. God's day is to come. (See also Ap. 139. 5.)

4. 7-19 (*D*, p. 1854). EXHORTATIONS IN VIEW OF THE END. (*Extended Alternation.*)

CD | P1 | 7-. The end of all things.
  Q1 | -7-11. Exhortation. In well doing to glorify God in all things.
 P2 | 12. The fiery trial.
  Q2 | 13-16. Exhortation. In well doing to glorify God in suffering.
 P3 | 17, 18. The beginning of judgment.
  Q3 | 19. Exhortation. In well doing to commit themselves to God.

7 is at hand=has drawn near. Cp. Matt. 3. 2. **be . . . sober.** See Rom. 12. 3. **watch.** See 2 Tim. 4. 5. **unto.** Ap. 104. vi. **prayer.** Ap. 134. II. 2. **8 above**=before. Ap. 104. xiv. **have, &c.**=having your love toward (Gr. *eis*) one another intense. **fervent.** Gr. *ektenēs.* Only here and Acts 12. 5. Cp. 1. 22. **charity.** Ap. 135. II. 1. **among.** Ap. 104. vi. **for, &c.** Cp. Prov. 10. 12. Jas. 5. 20. See 1 Cor. 13. 5-7. **9 Use hospitality**=Be hospitable. See 1 Tim. 3. 2 and cp. Rom. 12. 13. **one, &c.**=to one another. **grudging**=murmuring. See Acts 6. 1. **10 every man**=each one. **hath.** Omit. **gift.** Ap. 184. I. 2. See 1 Cor. 7. 7. **minister.** Ap. 190. III. 1. **the same**=it. **one to another**=among yourselves (*v.* 8). **stewards.** See 1 Cor. 4. 1. **manifold.** See 1. 6. **grace.** Ap. 184. I. 1. **11 If.** Ap. 118. 2. a. **any man.** Ap. 123. 3. **speak.** Ap. 121. 7. **as.** I. e. in harmony with, according. **oracles.** See Acts 7. 38. **of.** Ap. 104. vii. **ability.** Ap. 172. 3. **giveth.** See 2 Cor. 9. 10. Cp. 2 Pet. 1. 5. **through.** Ap. 104. v. 1. **Jesus Christ.** Ap. 98. XI. **be**=is. **praise**=the glory. Gr. *doxa.* See p. 1511. **dominion**=the dominion. Ap. 172. 2. **for ever, &c.** Ap. 151. II. A. ii. 9. a. A summary of the Divine operations in their finality. **12 Beloved.** Ap. 135. III. **concerning**=as to. **the fiery trial, &c.** Lit. the fire (of persecution) which is among (Ap. 104. viii. 2) you, coming to you for (Ap. 104. xv. 3) trial. Not coming in the future, but a present condition. **fiery.** Gr. *purōsis.* Here and Rev. 18. 9, 18. **trial.** Gr. *peirasmos.* See 1. 6 and 2 Pet. 2. 9.

though °some °strange thing happened °unto
you:
Q[2] 13 But rejoice, inasmuch as ye are partakers
of [1]Christ's sufferings; [6]that, °when His °glory
shall be °revealed, ye may be glad also °with
exceeding joy.
14 [11]If ye be °reproached °for the name of
[1]Christ, °happy *are ye;* for the °Spirit of [13]glory
and of [2]God resteth °upon you: °on their part
He is [4]evil spoken of, but on your part He is
glorified.
15 °But let °none of you suffer as a murderer,
or *as* a thief, or *as* an °evildoer, or as a °busy-
body in other men's matters.
16 Yet [11]if *any man suffer* as a °Christian, let
him [4]not be ashamed; but let him glorify [2]God
°on this °behalf.
P[3] 17 For °the time *is come* °that judgment
must begin °at the °house of [2]God: and [11]if *it*
first *begin* °at us, what shall the end *be* of them
that °obey not the °gospel of [2]God?
18 And [11]if the °righteous °scarcely be saved,
where shall the °ungodly and the sinner °ap-
pear?
Q[3] 19 Wherefore let °them that suffer [6]according
to the [2]will of [2]God °commit the keeping of
their °souls *to Him* [2]in °well doing, °as °unto
a °faithful °Creator.

E 5 The °elders which are °among you I °ex-
hort, °who am also an elder, and a witness
of the sufferings of °Christ, and also °a °par-
taker of the °glory °that shall be °revealed:
2 °Feed the °flock of °God which is [1]among
you, °taking the oversight *thereof,* °not °by
constraint, but °willingly; °not °for filthy lucre,
but °of a ready mind;
3 °Neither as °being lords over *God's* °heri-
tage, but being °ensamples to the [2]flock.
4 And when the °chief Shepherd shall °appear,
ye shall °receive °a °crown of [1]glory °that
fadeth not away.
5 Likewise, ye younger, °submit yourselves
°unto the [1]elder. Yea, all *of you* °be subject
°one to another, and °be clothed with °humility:
for [2]**God °resisteth the °proud, and giveth
°grace to the °humble.**
6 °Humble yourselves therefore °under the
°mighty hand of [2]God, °that He may °exalt
you °in °due time:
7 °Casting all your °care °upon Him; for He
careth °for you.
8 °Be sober, °be vigilant; because your adver-

some = a.
strange. Gr. *xenos.* See Acts 17. 18.
unto = to.
13 when, &c. = in (Ap. 104. viii) the revelation (Ap. 106. II. 1) also of His glory (see p. 1511).
revealed. See 1. 5, 7, 13.
with exceeding joy. Lit. rejoicing greatly. See 1. 6, 8.
14 reproached. Gr. *oneidizō.* See Rom. 15. 3.
for = in. Ap. 104. viii. **happy.** See 3. 14.
Spirit, &c. Fig. *Hendiadys* (Ap. 6). The glorious Spirit of God. Ap. 101. II. 3.
upon. Ap. 104. ix. 3.
on their part . . . glorified. This clause is omitted by all the texts.
15 But = For.
none = not (Gr. *mē*) any one (Ap. 123. 3).
evildoer. See 2. 12.
busybody in, &c. Gr. *allotrioepiskopos.* Only here. An overseer in things concerning another. See Ap. 124. 6. Cp. 1 Thess. 4. 11. 2 Thess. 3. 11. 1 Tim. 5. 13, and see Luke 12. 13. John 21. 22.
16 Christian. See Acts 11. 26.
on. Ap. 104. viii.
behalf = respect, lit. part, but the texts read "name".
17 the time, &c. = (*it is*) the season.
that judgment, &c. Lit. of judgment (Ap. 177. 6) beginning.
at = from. Ap. 104. iv.
house. Cp. 2. 5. 1 Tim. 3. 15. Heb. 3. 6; 10. 21.
obey not = are disobedient to. See 2. 7.
gospel of God. Ap. 140. III.
18 righteous. Ap. 191. 1.
scarcely. See Acts 14. 18.
ungodly. Gr. *asebēs.* Cp. Ap. 128. IV.
appear. Ap. 106. I. 1. Cp. Prov. 11. 31 (Sept.).
19 them. Add "also".
commit the keeping of. Gr. *paratithēmi.* See Acts 17. 3.
souls. Ap. 110. III. 2.
well doing. Gr. *agathopoiia.* Only here. Cp. 2. 14.
as. The texts omit.
unto = to. **faithful.** Ap. 150. III.
Creator. Gr. *ktistēs.* Only here.
5. 1 elders. Ap. 189.
among. Ap. 104. viii. 2.
exhort. Ap. 134. I. 6.
who, &c. = the fellow-elder. Gr. *sumpresbuteros.* Only here.
Christ. Ap. 98. IX. **a** = the.
partaker. See 1 Cor. 10. 18. **glory.** See p. 1511.
that shall = about to.
revealed. Ap. 106. I. ix. Cp. 4. 13.
2 Feed. Gr. *poimainō.* Cp. John 21. 16. Acts 20. 28.
flock. Gr. *poimnion.* See Acts 20. 28.
God. Ap. 98. I. i. 1.
taking, &c. Gr. *episkopeō.* Only here and Heb. 12. 15. Cp. Ap. 189. **not.** Ap. 105. II.
by constraint. Gr. *anankostōs.* Only here.
willingly. Cp. *hekousiōs.* See Heb. 10. 26, and cp. Philem. 14. **not** = neither. Gr. *mēde.* **for filthy lucre.** Gr. *aischrokerdōs.* Only here. Cp. 1 Tim. 3. 3. **of, &c.** = readily. Gr. *prothumōs.* Only here. Cp. Acts 17. 11. Rom. 1. 15. **3 Neither.** Gr. *mede,* as above. **being, &c.** See Acts 19. 16. **heritage** = the heritages. Gr. *klēros,* pl. Cp. Acts 1. 17, 25. "*God's*" is supplied from *v.* 2. Cp. Deut. 4. 20. Ps. 28. 9; 33. 12, &c. **ensamples.** Gr. *tupos.* See Phil. 3. 17. 2 Thess. 3. 9. 1 Tim. 4. 12. Tit. 2. 7. **4 chief Shepherd.** Gr. *archipoimēn.* Only here. See John 10. 11. **appear.** Ap. 106. I. v. **receive.** See 1. 9. **a** = the. **crown.** Gr. *stephanos.* The victor's crown. Cp. Rev. 12. 3 (*diadēma*). **that fadeth not away.** Gr. *amarantinos.* Only here. Cp. 1. 4. 1 Cor. 9. 25. **5 submit.** As 2. 13, &c. **unto** = to. **be subject . . . and** = submitting. The texts omit. **one to, &c.** = to one another. **be clothed with** = gird yourselves with. Gr. *enkomboomai.* Only here. **humility.** See Acts 20. 19. **resisteth.** See Acts 18. 6. **proud.** See Rom. 1. 30. **grace.** Ap. 184. I. 1. **humble.** Gr. *tapeinos.* See Matt. 11. 29. Quoted from Prov. 3. 34. Cp. Jas. 4. 6. **6 Humble yourselves.** See 2 Cor. 11. 7. **under.** Ap. 104. xviii. 2. **mighty.** Gr. *krataios.* Only here. Cp. 1 Cor. 16. 13 and Ap. 172. 2. **that** = in order that. Gr. *hina.* **exalt.** See John 12. 32. **in.** Ap. 104. viii. **due time** = season. **7 Casting . . . upon.** Gr. *epirriptō.* Only here and Luke 19. 35. **care** = anxiety. Cp. Phil. 4. 6. **upon.** Gr. *epi.* Ap. 104. ix. 3. The same prep. as is seen in the verb. **for.** Ap. 104. xiii. 1. **8 Be sober.** See 1. 13. **be vigilant.** Gr. *grēgoreō.* Transl. "watch", save here and 1 Thess. 5. 10 (wake).

sary the devil, as a °roaring lion, walketh
about, seeking whom he may °devour:
9 Whom resist °stedfast in the °faith, °know-
ing that the same °afflictions are °accomplished
in your °brethren that are [6]in the °world.
B 10 But the [2]God of all °grace, Who °hath called
°us °unto His °eternal [1]glory °by °Christ Jesus,
°after that ye have suffered °a while, °make
you °perfect, °stablish, °strengthen, °settle *you*.
11 To Him *be* °glory and °dominion °for ever
and ever. Amen.
A 12 °By °Silvanus, a °faithful brother [5]unto
you, as I °suppose, I have written °briefly,
[1]exhorting, and °testifying that this is the
°true [5]grace of [2]God °wherein °ye stand.
13 The °*church that is* °at °Babylon, °elected
together with *you*, saluteth you; and *so doth*
°Marcus my °son.
14 °Greet ye one another °with a °kiss of
°charity. Peace *be* °with you all that are [6]in
[10]Christ °Jesus. °Amen.

roaring. Gr. *ōruomai.* Only here. Cp. 2 Cor. 11. 3, 14.
devour = swallow up. See 1 Cor. 15. 54.
9 stedfast. Gr. *stereos.* See 2 Tim. 2. 19.
faith. Ap. 150. II. 1. **knowing.** Ap. 132. I. i.
afflictions. Same as "sufferings", *v.* 1.
accomplished. Ap. 125. 3.
brethren = brotherhood. See 2. 17.
world. Ap. 129. 1.
10 grace. Ap. 184. I. 1. Cp. Acts 7. 2.
hath. Omit. **us.** The texts read "you".
unto. Ap. 104. vi.
eternal. Ap. 151. II. B. i.
by. Ap. 104. viii.
Christ Jesus. Ap. 98. XII, but the texts omit "Jesus".
after that ye have = having.
a while = a little (time). The contrast is between the affliction now and the glory hereafter. Cp. 2 Cor. 4. 17.
make you, &c. The texts read "shall Himself perfect *you*", &c.
perfect. Cp. Heb. 13. 21. See Ap. 125. 8.
stablish. See Rom. 1. 11.
strengthen. Gr. *sthenoō.* Only here.
settle = ground, as on a foundation. Gr. *themelioō.* Cp. Eph. 3. 17. Col. 1. 23, and Ap. 146. These four verbs describe God's working, not *after*, but *during* the sufferings. **11 glory and.** The texts omit. **dominion.** Ap. 172. 2. **for ever, &c.** Ap. 151. II. A. ii. 9. a. **12 By.** Ap. 104. v. 1. **Silvanus.** See 2 Cor. 1. 19. **faithful.** Ap. 150. III. **suppose** = reckon. Gr. *logizomai,* as Rom. 4. 3, &c. **briefly.** Lit. by means of (Ap. 104. v. 1) few (words). **testifying** = earnestly testifying. Gr. *epimartureō.* Only here. **true.** Ap. 175. 1. **wherein** = in (Ap. 104. vi) which. **ye stand.** All the texts read the imp. "stand ye". Cp. Phil. 4. 1. **13 church.** The adj. "elected together with" is fem. sing., and the ellipsis must be supplied by some noun of that gender. Hence, some have thought that the reference is to Peter's wife (1 Cor. 9. 5). This would accord with the inclusion of an individual (Marcus) in the same salutation, and would agree with Paul's custom of sending salutations from individuals; but he also sends salutations from churches (Rom. 16. 16, 23. 1 Cor. 16. 19), and from all the saints, or brethren, i. e. in the place where he was writing (2 Cor. 13. 13. Gal. 1. 2. Phil. 4. 22. 2 Tim. 4. 21. Tit. 3. 15). So Peter may be uniting all the brethren with him here, and the ellipsis should be supplied, not with *ekklēsia,* which occ. nowhere in either of his epistles, but with *diaspora,* the dispersion, whom he addresses as elect (1. 1). Those in Babylon were elect with them. **at** = in. Ap. 104. viii. **Babylon.** A great many sojourners of the dispersion were in Babylon. See Josephus, *Ant.*, XV. ii. 2. **elected together with.** Gr. *suneklektos.* Only here. **Marcus** = Mark. See Acts 12. 12. **son.** Ap. 108. iii. This must be in the same sense as in 1 Tim. 1. 2. Tit. 1. 4, where Paul uses *gnēsios.* If Mark be the same as in Acts 12. 12, he could not be Peter's literal son. **14 Greet.** Same as "salute", *v.* 13. **with.** Ap. 104. viii. **kiss.** See Rom. 16. 16. **charity** = love. Ap. 135. II. 1. In Paul's epistles the epithet "holy" (*hagios*) is used. **with** = to. **Jesus.** The texts omit. **Amen.** Omit.

THE SECOND EPISTLE OF PETER.

THE STRUCTURE OF THE EPISTLE AS A WHOLE.

(*Introversion and Extended Alternation.*)

A | 1. 1-4. INTRODUCTION. BENEDICTION.
  B | 1. 5-11. EXHORTATION.
    C | A | 1. 12-15. PETER.
        B | 1. 16-21. APOSTLES AND PROPHETS.
          C | 2. 1-22. THE WICKED.
    C | *A* | 3. 1. PETER.
        B | 3. 2. PROPHETS AND APOSTLES.
          C | 3. 3-13. THE WICKED.
  B | 3. 14-18-. EXHORTATION.
A | 3. -18. CONCLUSION. BENEDICTION.

NOTES ON THE SECOND EPISTLE OF PETER.

1. **Authorship.** In spite of much divergence of opinion, we conclude that the apostle who wrote the First Epistle wrote this one also. While there is some difference between the tone of the two, this difference has been exaggerated by those who deny that Peter wrote the second letter. And a comparison of the language used shows close resemblance between the two epistles.

2. **Written** to the same readers as was the First Epistle (see 3. 1).

3. **Subject.** The apostle continues the practical teaching of the earlier letter, exhorts, and warns, illustrating again from the Old Testament history, while himself foretelling the conditions of "the last days", "the day of judgment", "the day of the Lord", and "the day of God". The similarity to the teaching in *Jude* should be noticed.

4. **Time of writing.** This is generally placed between 61 and 65 A. D., but the year is conjectural, although it may reasonably be presumed that this epistle was written within a comparatively short period after the First.

THE SECOND EPISTLE OF
PETER.

A **1** °SIMON Peter, a °servant and an °apostle of °Jesus Christ, to them that °have °obtained °like precious °faith with us °through the °righteousness °of °God and our Saviour °Jesus Christ:

2 °Grace and peace be °multiplied °unto you [1]through the °knowledge of [1]God, and of °Jesus our °Lord,

3 According as His °divine °power hath °given [2]unto us °all things °that *pertain* unto °life and °godliness, °through the [2]knowledge of Him That °hath called us °to °glory and °virtue;

4 °Whereby are [3]given [2]unto us °exceeding great and precious °promises; °that °by these ye might °be °partakers of the [3]divine nature, having °escaped the °corruption that is °in the °world [1]through lust.

B a 5 °And °beside this, giving all °diligence, °add °to your [1]faith [3]virtue; and °to [3]virtue °knowledge;

6 And [5]to [5]knowledge °temperance; and [5]to °temperance patience; and [5]to patience [3]godliness;

7 And [5]to [3]godliness °brotherly kindness; and [5]to °brotherly kindness °charity.

b 8 For °if these things be in you and abound, they °make *you that ye shall* °neither *be* °barren °nor unfruitful °in the [2]knowledge of our [2]Lord [1]Jesus Christ.

9 But he °that lacketh these things is blind, °and cannot see afar off, °and hath forgotten °that he was purged from his °old °sins.

a 10 Wherefore the rather, brethren, °give diligence to make your °calling and °election °sure:

b for °if ye do these things, ye shall °never °fall:

11 For so an °entrance shall be °ministered [2]unto you °abundantly °into the °everlasting °kingdom of our [2]Lord and Saviour [1]Jesus Christ.

C A 12 Wherefore I will °not be °negligent to °put you always in remembrance °of these things, though ye °know *them*, and be °established [4]in °the present truth.

1. 1 Simon. Gr. *Sumeōn*, as in Acts 15. 14.
servant. Ap. 190. I. 2.
apostle. Ap. 189.
Jesus Christ. Ap. 98. XI.
have. Omit.
obtained. Gr. *lanchanō*. See Acts 1. 17.
like precious. Gr. *isotimos*. Only here.
faith. Ap. 150. II. 1.
through. Ap. 104. viii.
righteousness. Ap. 191. 3.
of, &c. = of our God and, &c.
God. Ap. 98. I. i. 1.
2 Grace. Ap. 184. I. 1.
multiplied. Cp. 1 Pet. 1. 2 and Jude 2.
unto = to.
knowledge. Ap. 132. II. ii.
Jesus. Ap. 98. X.
Lord. Ap. 98. VI. i. *β*. 2. A.
3 divine. Gr. *theios*. See Acts 17. 29.
power. Ap. 172. 1.
given = been given. It is the same perfect passive transl. "are given" in *v.* 4. Gr. *dōreō*. See Mark 15. 45.
all = (as to) all.
that *pertain* unto = for. Ap. 104. xv. 3.
life. Ap. 170. 1.
godliness. See 1 Tim. 2. 2.
through. Ap. 104. v. 1.
hath. Omit. **to** = to His own, as the texts.
glory. See p. 1511.
virtue. See Phil. 4. 8.
4 Whereby = By (Ap. 104. v. 1) which.
exceeding = the exceeding.
promises. Gr. *epangelma*. Only here and 3. 13.
that = in order that. Gr. *hina*.
by. Ap. 104. v. 1.
be = become.
partakers. See 1 Cor. 10. 18.
escaped. Gr. *apopheugō*. Only here and 2. 18, 20.
corruption. Gr. *phthora*. See Rom. 8. 21.
in. Ap. 104. viii. **world.** Ap. 129. 1.

1. 5-11 (**B**, p. 1863). **EXHORTATION.** (*Alternation*.)

B | a | 5-7. Exhortation. Diligence.
b | 8, 9. Reasons. Positive and Negative.
a | 10-. Exhortation. Diligence.
b | -10, 11. Reasons. Negative and Positive.

5 And. Note the Fig. *Polysyndeton*. Seven "ands" in *vv.* 5-7.
beside this, giving. Lit. bringing in by the side of (Gr. *pareispherō*. Only here) this very thing.
diligence. Gr. *spoudē*, as Jude 3.
add = minister, or supply. Gr. *epichorēgeō*. See 2 Cor. 9. 10.
to = in. Ap. 104. viii. **knowledge.** Ap. 132. II. i. **6 temperance** = self-control. Gr. *enkrateia*. See Acts 24. 25. **7 brotherly kindness.** See Rom. 12. 10. **charity** = love. Ap. 135. II. 1. **8 if, &c.** = these things existing (Gr. *huparchō*. See Luke 9. 48) in you, and abounding. **make** = render. Gr. *kathistēmi*. First occ. Matt. 24. 45. **neither** = not. Ap. 105. I. **barren** = useless. Gr. *argos*. See Matt. 12. 36. **nor.** Gr. *oude*. **in.** Ap. 104. vi. **9 that lacketh, &c.** = to whom these things are not (Ap. 105. II) present. **and cannot, &c.** = being short-sighted. Gr. *muōpazō*. Only here. **and hath, &c.** = having received forgetfulness (Gr. *lēthē*. Only here). **that he was purged from** = of the cleansing (Gr. *katharismos*. See Heb. 1. 3) of. **old sins** = sins of long ago (Gr. *palai*). **sins.** Ap. 128. I. ii. 1. **10 give diligence** = be diligent. Gr. *spoudazō*. See noun in *v.* 5. **calling.** See Rom 11. 29. **election.** See Acts 9. 15. **sure.** Gr. *bebaios*. See Rom. 4. 16. **if ye do** = doing. **never** = by no means (Ap. 105. III) at any time. **fall** = stumble. Gr. *ptaiō*. See Rom. 11. 11. **11 entrance.** Same word in Heb. 10. 19. **ministered.** Same as "add", *v.* 5. **abundantly.** Gr. *plousiōs*. See Col. 3. 16. **into.** Ap. 104. vi. **everlasting.** Ap. 151. II. B. ii. **kingdom.** Ap. 112. 6. **12 not.** Ap. 105. I. **negligent.** Gr. *ameleō*. See 1 Tim. 4. 14. **put . . . in remembrance.** Gr. *hupomimnēskō*. See John 14. 26. **of.** Ap. 104. xiii. 1. **know.** Ap. 132. I. i. **established.** Cp. 1. Pet. 5. 10. **the present truth** = the truth which is present (cp. *v.* 9), i. e. which is your possession.

13 Yea, I think it °meet, °as long as I am [4]in this °tabernacle, to °stir you up °by putting *you* [4]in °remembrance;
14 [12]Knowing that °shortly °I must put off *this* my [13]tabernacle, even as our [2]Lord [1]Jesus Christ °hath °shewed me.
15 Moreover I will °endeavour that ye may be able °after my °decease °to have these things °always in °remembrance.

B D c 16 For we °have [12]not °followed °cunningly devised °fables,

d when we made known [2]unto you the [3]power and °coming of our [2]Lord [1]Jesus Christ, but °were °eyewitnesses of His majesty.

E 17 For He received °from [1]God the °Father honour and [3]glory, when there °came °such a voice to Him °from the °excellent [3]glory, "This is My °beloved °Son, [8]in Whom I am °well pleased."
18 And this voice which [17]came °from °heaven we heard, when we were °with Him [4]in the °holy mount.

D d 19 We have also °a more [10]sure word of prophecy; °whereunto ye do well °that ye take heed, as [2]unto a °light that °shineth [4]in a °dark place, until the day °dawn, and the °day star °arise [4]in your hearts:

c 20 °Knowing this first, that °no prophecy of the Scripture °is of °any private °interpretation.

E 21 For the prophecy [17]came [12]not °in old time °by the °will of °man: but °holy men °of [1]God °spake *as they were* °moved °by °the Holy Ghost.

C F **2** But there °were °false prophets also °among the °people, °even as there shall be °false teachers °among you, °who °privily shall bring in °damnable heresies, °even denying the °Lord That °bought them,

G °and bring upon themselves °swift °destruction.

13 meet = just. Ap. 191. 1.
as long as = for (Ap. 104. ix. 3) such (time) as.
tabernacle. Gr. *skēnōma.* See Acts **7.** 46.
stir . . . up. Ap. 178. I. 5.
by putting *you* **in** = in.
remembrance. Gr. *hupomnēsis.* See 2 Tim. **1.** 5.
14 shortly. Gr. *tachinos.* Only here and 2. 1 (swift).
I must put off = is the putting off of. Gr. *apothesis.* See 1 Pet. **3.** 21.
hath. Omit, and supply "also".
shewed = declared. Gr. *dēloō.* See 1 Cor. **1.** 11. Cp. John **21.** 18, 19.
15 endeavour. Same as "give diligence", *v.* 10.
after. Ap. 104. xi. 2.
decease. Gr. *exodos.* See Luke **9.** 31.
to have, &c. = to make remembrance (Gr. *mnēmē.* Only here) of these things.
always = at every time. Gr. *hekastote.* Only here.

1. 16-21 (B, p. 1863). **APOSTLES AND PROPHETS.**
(*Alternation and Introversion.*)

B | D | c | 16-. What the apostolic witness was not. A myth.
d | -16. What it was. A vision of the coming of Christ.
E | 17, 18. How it came. Voice borne from heaven.
D | *d* | 19. What the Prophetic Word is. A light till Christ's coming.
c | 20. What it is not. Not of its own revealing.
E | 21. How it came. Brought by power from on high.

16 have not followed = did not follow.
followed. Gr. *exakoloutheō.* Only here and 2. 2, 15.
cunningly, &c. Gr. *sophizō.* See 2 Tim. **3.** 15.
fables. See 1 Tim. **1.** 4.
coming. See Matt. **24.** 3 (first occ.).
were = became.
eyewitnesses. Gr. *epoptēs.* Only here. The verb in 1 Pet. **2.** 12; **3.** 2. Cp. Luke **1.** 2.
majesty. Gr. *megaleiotēs.* See Acts **19.** 27.
17 from. Ap. 104. xii. 1.
Father. Ap. 98. III.
came = was borne. Gr. *pherō,* as in 1 Pet. **1.** 13 (brought).
such. Gr. *toiosde.* Only here. Implying emphasis. The usual word is *toioutos,* which occ. 61 times.
from = by. Ap. 104. xviii. 1.
excellent. Gr. *megaloprepēs.* Only here. Cp. *v.* 16.
beloved. Ap. 135. III. **Son.** Ap. 108. iii.
well pleased. See Matt. **3.** 17; **12.** 18; **17.** 5.

18 from. Ap. 104. vii. **heaven.** Sing. See Matt. **6.** 9, 10. **with.** Ap. 104. xvi. **holy.** Because, and while, the Lord was there. **19 a more sure, &c.** = the prophetic (Gr. *prophētikos.* See Rom. **16.** 26) word (Ap. 121. 10) more sure. **whereunto** = to which. **that ye take heed** = taking heed; "in your hearts" should follow here. **light.** Ap. 130. 4. **shineth.** Ap. 106. I. i. **dark.** Gr. *auchmēros.* Only here. **dawn.** Gr. *diaugazō.* Only here. **day star.** Gr. *phōsphoros.* Only here. **arise.** It will be a fulfilment of Num. **24.** 17. Mal. **4.** 2. Not a spiritual experience. **20 Knowing.** Ap. 132. I. ii. **no.** Ap. 105. I. **is** = comes. **any private** = its own. Gr. *idios.* **interpretation.** Gr. *epilusis.* Only here. The verb *epiluō* is found in Mark **4.** 34 (expounded), and Acts **19.** 39 (determined). This shows that the meaning is that prophecy is not self-originated by the speaker. **21 in old time** = at any time. Gr. *pote.* **by.** No prep. Dat. case. **will.** Ap. 102. 2. **man.** Ap. 123. 1. **holy.** Omit. **of.** The texts read *apo,* from. **spake.** Ap. 121. 7. **moved** = borne along. Gr. *pherō,* as in *v.* 17. **by.** Ap. 104. xviii. 1. **the Holy Ghost** = Divine power. No art. Ap. 101. II. 14.

2. 1-22 (C, p. 1863). **THE WICKED.** (*Extended Alternation.*)

C | F | 1-. Character.
G | -1. Judgment.
H | 2. Followers.
F | 3-. Character.
G | -3-17. Judgment.
H | 18-22. Followers.

2. 1 were = arose. **false prophets.** Gr. *pseudoprophētēs.* Cp. Matt. **24.** 11, 24. Luke **6.** 26. Acts **13.** 6. 1 John **4.** 1. **among.** Ap. 104. viii. 2. **people.** See Acts **2.** 47. **even as, &c.** Read, as among you also, &c. **false teachers.** Gr. *pseudodidaskalos.* Only here. **who** = such as. **privily . . . in.** Gr. *pareisagō.* Only here. Cp. Rom. **5.** 20 and Gal. **2.** 4. **damnable heresies** = heresies (Acts **5.** 17) of destruction, or perdition (Gr. *apōleia*). See John **17.** 12. **even denying** = denying even. **Lord.** Ap. 98. VI. ii. 2. **bought.** See Matt. **13.** 44, 46. **and bring upon** = bringing upon. Gr. *epagō.* See Acts **5.** 28. **swift.** See 1. 14. **destruction.** See "damnable", above.

H 2 And many shall °follow their °pernicious ways; °by reason of whom the way of truth shall be °evil spoken of.

F 3 And °through °covetousness shall they with °feigned °words °make merchandise of you:

G J L whose °judgment °now of a long time °lingereth °not, and their °damnation °slumbereth °not.

M e1 4 For °if °God °spared [3]not °the angels °that °sinned,

f1 but °cast *them* down to hell, and °delivered *them* into °chains of °darkness, °to be reserved °unto °judgment;

e2 5 °And [4]spared [3]not the °old °world, but °saved Noah °the eighth *person*, a °preacher of °righteousness,

f2 [1]bringing in the flood upon the °world of the °ungodly;

e3 6 [5]And °turning the cities of Sodom and Gomorrha into ashes

f3 °condemned *them* with an °overthrow, °making *them* an °ensample °unto those °that after should °live ungodly;

7 [5]And °delivered °just °Lot, °vexed °with the °filthy °conversation of the °wicked:

8 (For °that righteous man °dwelling [1]among them, in °seeing and hearing, °vexed *his* °righteous °soul °from day to day with *their* °unlawful deeds;)

J K 9 The °Lord °knoweth how to [7]deliver the °godly °out of °temptations,

L and to reserve the unjust [4]unto °the day of [4]judgment to be °punished:

M g 10 But chiefly them that walk after the flesh °in the lust of °uncleanness, and despise °government. °Presumptuous *are they,* °selfwilled, they °are [3]not afraid to °speak evil of °dignities.

2 follow. See 1. 16.
pernicious ways. Gr. *apōleia*, as *v.* 1, but the texts read "lasciviousnesses". Gr. *aselgeia.* See Rom. 13. 13.
by reason of. Ap. 104. v. 2.
evil spoken of = blasphemed, as 1 Pet. 4. 4.
3 through. Ap. 104. viii.
covetousness. Gr. *pleonexia.* First occ. Mark 7. 22.
feigned = formed, i. e. fabricated. Gr. *plastos.* Only here.
words. Ap. 121. 10.
make merchandise of. Gr. *emporeuomai.* See Jas. 4. 13.

2. -3-17 (*G*, p. 1865). JUDGMENT.
(*Introversion and Alternation.*)

G | J | L | -3. Judgment.
  M | 4-8. Ungodly of old times.
   K | 9-. Deliverance of godly.
 J | *L* | -9. Judgment.
  M | 10-17. Ungodly of later times.

judgment. Ap. 177. 6.
now, &c. = from (Ap. 104. vii) of old (as in 3. 5).
lingereth. Gr. *argeō.* Only here. Cp. 1. 8.
not. Ap. 105. I.
damnation. Same as "destruction", *v.* 1.
slumbereth. Gr. *nustazō.* Only here and Matt. 25. 5.

2. 4-8 (M, above). UNGODLY OF OLD TIME.
(*Repeated Alternation.*)

M | e1 | 4-. Angels.
 f1 | -4. Cast down to Tartarus.
 e2 | 5-. The old world.
 f2 | -5. The flood.
 e3 | 6-. Sodom and Gomorrha.
 f3 | -6-8. Overthrown.

4 if. Ap. 118. 2. a.
God. Ap. 98. I. i. 1.
spared. See Acts 20. 29.
the. Omit.
that = when they.
sinned. Ap. 128. I. i.
cast . . . down to hell, and = having thrust down to Tartarus. Ap. 131. 3.
delivered. See John 19. 30.
chains. Gr. *seira,* a cord. Only here. The texts read "pits". Gr. *seiros.*
darkness. Gr. *zophos.* Only here, *v.* 17, and Jude 6, 13.
to be. Omit. **unto.** Ap. 104. vi.

judgment. Ap. 177. 7. **5 And.** Note the Fig. *Polysyndeton* (Ap. 6) in *vv.* 5-7. **old** = ancient. See Matt. 5. 21. **world.** Ap. 129. 1. **saved** = preserved. Same word John 17. 12. **the eighth.** A Gr. idiom for himself and seven others. **preacher.** Ap. 121. 2. **righteousness.** Ap. 191. 3. **ungodly.** Gr. *asebēs.* See Ap. 128. IV. **6 turning . . . into ashes.** Gr. *tephroō.* Only here. **condemned.** Ap. 122. 7. **overthrow.** Gr. *katastrophē.* See 2 Tim. 2. 14. **making** = having made. **ensample.** Gr. *hupodeigma.* See John 13. 15. **unto** = of. **that after should.** Lit. about to. **live ungodly.** Gr. *asebeō.* Only here and Jude 15. Cp. *v.* 5. **7 delivered** = rescued. As in 2 Cor. 1. 10. **just.** Ap. 191. 1. **Lot.** As believing Jehovah, Lot was justified. We do not know all his life, and we do not know all implied by the rest of this verse and by *v.* 8. **vexed** = oppressed. See Acts 7. 24. **with** = by. Ap. 104. xviii. 1. **filthy conversation** = behaviour (see Gal. 1. 13) in (Gr. *en*) lasciviousness (Gr. *aselgeia.* See 1 Pet. 4. 3). **wicked** = lawless. Gr. *athesmos.* Only here and 3. 17. **8 that righteous man** = the just one. Cp. *v.* 7. **dwelling.** Gr. *enkatoikeō.* Only here. **seeing.** Gr. *blemma.* Only here. **vexed.** Gr. *basanizō.* Transl. "torment", except Matt. 14. 24. Mark 6. 48 (where see note). Rev. 12. 2. **righteous.** Same as "just", above. **soul.** Ap. 110. IV. 1. **from.** Ap. 104. vii. **unlawful.** Ap. 128. III. 3. **9 Lord.** Ap. 98. VI. i. β. 1. B. b. **knoweth.** Ap. 132. I. i. **godly.** Gr. *eusebēs.* See Acts 10. 2. **out of.** Ap. 104. vii. **temptations** = temptation. See 1 Pet. 1. 6. **the** = a. **punished.** Cp. Job 21. 30.

2. 10-17 (*M*, above). UNGODLY OF LATER TIME. (*Extended Alternation.*)

M | g | 10. Description. Fleshly lusts and presumption.
 h | 11. Contrast. Angels.
  i | 12, 13-. End.
 g | -13, 14. Description. Lusts and covetousness.
 h | 15, 16. Comparison. Balaam.
  i | 17. End.

10 in. Ap. 104. viii. **uncleanness.** Gr. *miasmos.* Only here. Cp. *v.* 20. **government** = dominion. Gr. *kuriotēs.* See Eph. 1. 21. Jude 8. **Presumptuous** = Daring. Gr. *tolmētēs.* Only here. **selfwilled.** Gr. *authadēs.* See Tit. 1. 7. **are not afraid** = do not tremble. **speak evil of** = blaspheme, as *v.* 2. **dignities.** Lit. glories. Gr. *doxa.* See p. 1511. Only here and Jude 8 used as a title.

h 11 Whereas angels, °which are greater in °power and °might, bring [3]not °railing °accusation °against them °before the [9]LORD.

i 12 But these, as °natural °brute °beasts made °to be taken and °destroyed, [10]speak evil °of the things that they °understand not, and shall °utterly perish [10]in their own °corruption;
13 And shall receive the °reward of °unrighteousness,

g °*as* they that count it pleasure °to riot [10]in °the day time. °Spots *they are* and °blemishes, °sporting themselves °with their own °deceivings while they °feast with you;
14 Having eyes full of °adultery, and °that cannot cease from °sin; °beguiling °unstable °souls; °an heart they have °exercised with °covetous practices; °cursed °children;

h 15 Which have forsaken the right way, and are gone astray, [2]following the way of °Balaam *the son* of °Bosor, who °loved the °wages of [13]unrighteousness;
16 But °was rebuked for °his °iniquity: the °dumb °ass °speaking [13]with °man's voice °forbad the °madness of the °prophet.

i 17 These are °wells °without water, °clouds that are °carried [7]with a °tempest; to whom the °mist of darkness is reserved °for ever.

H j 18 For when they [16]speak °great swelling *words* of °vanity, they °allure [3]through the lusts of the flesh, °*through much* wantonness,

k those that were °clean °escaped from them who °live [10]in error.

j 19 While they promise them liberty, they themselves °are the °servants of [12]corruption: for of whom °a man is °overcome, of the same is he °brought in bondage.

k 20 For [4]if after they have [18]escaped the °pollutions of the [5]world [3]through the °knowledge of the °Lord and Saviour °Jesus Christ, they are again °entangled therein and [19]overcome, the °latter end °is worse with them than the °beginning.

11 which are=though being.
power. Ap. 172. 3.
might. Ap. 172. 1. Cp. Ps. 103. 20. 2 Thess. 1. 7.
railing. Gr. *blasphēmos*, as 1 Tim. 1. 13.
accusation. Ap. 177. 7.
against. Ap. 104. x. 1.
before. Ap. 104. xii. 2. Cp. Jude 9. Zech. 3. 1, 2.
12 natural. Gr. *phusikos.* See Rom. 1. 26.
brute. Gr. *alogos.* See Acts 25. 27.
beasts=living creatures. Gr. *zōon.* Same as Heb. 13. 11.
to be taken, &c.=for (Ap. 104. vi) capture (Gr. *halōsis.* Only here) and destruction (Gr. *phthora.* See Rom. 8. 21).
of=in. Ap. 104. viii.
understand not=are ignorant of. Gr. *agnoeō.*
utterly perish. Gr. *kataphtheirō.* See 2 Tim. 3. 8. The texts read "even perish" (*kai phtheirō*).
corruption. Gr. *phthora*, as above.
13 reward=wages. Gr. *misthos.*
unrighteousness. Ap. 128. VII. 1. Cp. *v.* 15 and Acts 1. 18.
as **they, &c.**=reckoning it (as they do).
to riot=living delicately. Gr. *truphē.* Only here and Luke 7. 25. Cp. Jas. 5. 5.
the day time. Lit. a day.
Spots. Gr. *spilos.* Here and Eph. 5. 27.
blemishes. Gr. *mōmos.* Only here. Cp. 2 Cor. 6. 3 (blamed).
sporting themselves=living delicately. Gr. *entruphaō.* Only here. Cp. *truphē*, above.
with=in. Ap. 104. viii.
deceivings. Gr. *apatē.* See Eph. 4. 22. Some texts read "love feasts". Gr. *agapē*, as in Jude 12. Cp. 1 Cor. 11. 21.
feast with. Gr. *suneuōcheomai.* Only here and Jude 12.
14 adultery=an adulteress.
that cannot cease. Gr. *akatapaustos.* Only here.
sin. Ap. 128. I. ii. 1.
beguiling. See Jas. 1. 14.
unstable. Gr. *astēriktos.* Only here and 3. 16.
souls. Ap. 110. II.
an heart, &c.=having a heart.
exercised. See 1 Tim. 4. 7.
covetous practices=covetousness.
cursed children=children (Ap. 108. i) of (the) curse.
15 Balaam. See Num. 22.
Bosor. See Num. 22. 5 (note). Some texts read "Beor".
loved. Ap. 135. I. 1.
wages. Same as reward, *v.* 13.
16 was rebuked=had rebuke (Gr. *elenxis.* Only here). **his**=his own. **iniquity.** Ap. 128. VII. 3. Only here. **dumb.** See Acts 8. 32. **ass.** Gr. *hupozugion.* Only here and Matt. 21. 5. **speaking.** See Acts 4. 18. **man's.** Ap. 123. 1. **forbad**=hindered. **madness.** Gr. *paraphronia.* Only here. Cp. 2 Cor. 11. 23. **prophet.** Ap. 189. Balaam delivered Jehovah's messages (Num. 23. 5, 16; 24. 4, 13), however unwillingly. He afterwards became a minister of Satan, in the counsel he gave Balak (Num. 31. 8, 16). **17 wells.** Gr. *pēgē.* Always transl. "fountain", save here and John 4. 6, 14. **without water.** Gr. *anudros.* Only here; Matt. 12. 43 (dry). Luke 11. 24 (dry), and Jude 12. **clouds.** The texts read "mists" (Gr. *homichlē.* Only here) **carried**=driven. **tempest.** Gr. *lailaps.* Here and Mark 4. 37. Luke 8. 23. **mist.** Same as "darkness", *v.* 4. **for ever.** Ap. 151. II. A. ii. 4. a. But the texts omit.

2. 18-22 (*H*, p. 1865). **FOLLOWERS.** (*Alternation.*)

H | j | 18-. Seducers. Their methods.
  k | -18. The seduced. Their past escape.
j | 19. Seducers. Their promise.
  k | 20-22. The seduced. Their apostasy.

18 great swelling. Gr. *huperonkos.* Only here and Jude 16. **vanity.** Gr. *mataiotēs.* See Rom. 8. 20. **allure.** Same as "beguile", *v.* 14. *through*, **&c.** Lit. by (dat. case) lasciviousnesses. See "filthy", *v.* 7. **clean**=indeed. Gr. *ontōs.* See 1 Cor. 14. 25. **escaped.** See 1. 4. The texts read "scarcely" or "but just (Gr. *oligōs*) escaping". **live.** Gr. *anastrephō.* See 1 Pet. 1. 17. **19 are**=being. Gr. *huparchō.* See Luke 9. 48. **servants.** Ap. 190. I. 2. **a man.** Ap. 123. 3. **overcome.** Gr. *hēttaomai.* See 2 Cor. 12. 13. **brought in bondage**=enslaved. Ap. 190. III. 3. Add "also". **20 pollutions.** Gr. *miasma.* Only here. Cp. *v.* 10. **knowledge.** See 1. 2, 3, 8. **Lord.** Ap. 98. VI. i. *β.* 2. A. **Jesus Christ.** Ap. 98. XI. Cp. 3. 18. **entangled.** Gr. *emplekō.* See 2 Tim. 2. 4. **latter end.** Lit. last things. **is**=is become. **beginning**=first.

21 For it had been better for them °not to have °known the way of [5] righteousness, than, after they have °known *it*, to °turn °from the holy commandment [4] delivered °unto them.

22 But °it is happened [21] unto them °according to the °true °proverb, "**The dog** *is* °**turned** °**to his own** °**vomit** °**again**"; and the °sow that was °washed °to her °wallowing in the °mire.

C A **3** This °second epistle, °beloved, I now write °unto you; °in *both* °which I °stir up your °pure °minds °by way of °remembrance;

B **2** °That ye may °be mindful of the °words which were spoken before °by the holy °prophets, and of the commandment of °us the °apostles of the °Lord and Saviour:

C N **3** °Knowing this first, that there shall come °in the °last days °scoffers, °walking °after their own lusts,

4 And saying, "Where is the promise of His °coming?

O for °since the fathers °fell asleep, all things °continue as *they were* °from the beginning of the creation."

P l **5** For °this they willingly are ignorant of,

m that by the °word of °God the °heavens were °of old, and the °earth °standing °out of °the water and °in °the water:

6 °Whereby °the world that then was, being °overflowed with water, °perished:

7 But the [5] heavens and the [5] earth which are now, by the same [5] word are °kept in store, reserved °unto fire °against °the day of °judgment and °perdition of °ungodly °men.

l **8** But, [1] beloved, °be °not ignorant of this one thing,

m that one day *is* °with the °LORD as a thousand years, and a thousand years as one day.

N **9** The [8] LORD °is °not slack °concerning His promise, as °some men °count °slackness;

O but is longsuffering °to us-ward, [8] not °willing that °any should [6] perish, but that all should come °to °repentance.

21 not. Ap. 105. II.
known. Ap. 132. I. iii.
turn = turn back.
from. Ap. 104. vii.
unto = to.
22 it is = there hath.
according to = the (fulfilment) of.
true. Ap. 175. 1.
proverb. Gr. *paroimia*. See John 10. 6.
turned = turned back.
to. Ap. 104. ix. 3.
vomit. Gr. *exerama*. Only here.
again. Omit. Quoted from Prov. 26. 11.
sow. Gr. *hus*. Only here.
washed. Ap. 136. iii.
to. Ap. 104. vi.
wallowing. Gr. *kulisma*. Only here. Cp. Mark 9. 20.
mire. Gr. *borboros*. Only here.

3. 1. second. This shows that the epistle is addressed to the same readers as is the first.
beloved. Ap. 135. III.
unto = to.
in. Ap. 104. viii.
which. Pl. Hence the insertion of *both*.
stir up. Ap. 178. I. 5. See 1. 13.
pure. See Phil. 1. 10 (sincere).
minds = mind.
by way of = in, as above.
remembrance. See 1. 13.
2 That ye may = To.
be mindful. See 2 Tim. 1. 4.
words. Gr. *rhēma*. See Mark 9. 32.
by. Ap. 104. xviii. 1.
prophets. Ap. 189.
us the. The texts read "your".
apostles. Ap. 189.
Lord. Ap. 98. VI. i. *β*. 2. A.

3. 3-13 (*C*, p. 1863). THE WICKED.
(*Extended Alternation.*)

C | N | 3, 4-. The Coming. Scoffed at.
O | -4. Reason.
P | 5-8. Day of judgment.
N | 9-. The Coming. Delayed.
O | -9. Reason.
P | 10-13. Day of the Lord.

3 Knowing. Ap. 132. I. ii.
in. Ap. 104. ix. 1.
last days. See Acts 2. 17. 2 Tim. 3. 1.
scoffers = mockers. Gr. *empaiktēs*. Only here and Jude 18.
walking. All the texts add after walking, "in (Ap. 104. viii) mockery". Gr. *empaigmonē*. Only here. Cp. Heb. 11. 36.

after. Ap. 104. x. 2. **4** coming. See Matt. 24. 3. since = from (Ap. 104. iv) the (day). fell asleep. Ap. 171. 2. continue. Gr. *diamenō*. See Gal. 2. 5. from. Ap. 104. iv.

3. 5-8 (P, above). DAY OF JUDGMENT. (*Alternation.*)

P | l | 5-. Wilful ignorance.
m | -5-7. Past and future judgment.
l | 8-. Warning against ignorance.
m | -8. Divine periods.

5 this, &c. Lit. this is hid from (Gr. *lanthanō*. See Acts 26. 26) them willing (Ap. 102. 1) it. word. Ap. 121. 10. God. Ap. 98. I. i. 1. heavens. Pl. See Matt. 6. 9, 10. of old. Gr. *ekpalai*. See 2. 3. earth. Ap. 129. 4. standing = consisting. Gr. *sunistēmi*. See Col. 1. 17. out of = of. Ap. 104. vii. the. Omit. in = through. Ap. 104. v. 1. The reference is to Pss. 24. 2; 136. 5, 6. Cp. Gen. 1. 6, 7. **6** Whereby = By (Ap. 104. v. 1) which (means). the world, &c. Lit. the then world (Ap. 129. 1). overflowed. Gr. *katakluzō*. Only here. Cp. 2. 5. perished. See John 17. 12. **7** kept in store = treasured up. unto = for. against = unto. Ap. 104. vi. the = a. judgment. Ap. 177. 7. perdition. See John 17. 12. ungodly. See 1 Pet. 4. 18. men. Ap. 123. 1. **8** be not, &c. Lit. let not this one thing be hidden (as *v.* 5) from you. not. Ap. 105. II. with. Ap. 104. xii. 2. LORD. Ap. 98. VI. i. *β*. 1. B. b. **9** is not slack = does not delay. See 1 Tim. 3. 15. not. Ap. 105. I. concerning. Ap. 17. 5. some men. Ap. 124. 4. count = reckon. Same word "account", *v.* 15. slackness. Gr. *bradutēs*. Only here. to us-ward = toward (Ap. 104. vi) us, but the texts read "you" willing. Ap. 102. 3. any. Ap. 123. 3. to. Ap. 104. vi. repentance. Ap. 111. II.

P n 10 But the day of the [8]LORD will come as a thief °in the night;

o [1]in the which the [5]heavens shall pass away °with a great noise, and the °elements shall °melt °with fervent heat, the [5]earth also and the works that are °therein shall be °burned up.

p 11 *Seeing* then *that* all these things shall be °dissolved,

q what manner *of persons* ought ye to °be [1]in *all* holy °conversation and °godliness,

n 12 °Looking for and °hasting unto the [4]coming of the day of [5]God,

o °wherein the [5]heavens °being on fire shall be [11]dissolved, and the [10]elements shall °melt [10]with fervent heat?

p 13 Nevertheless we, °according to His °promise, [12]look for °**new** [5]**heavens and a new** [5]**earth,**

q °wherein °dwelleth °righteousness.

B Q r 14 Wherefore, [1]beloved,

s seeing that ye [12]look for °such things,

t °be diligent that ye may be found °of Him [1]in peace, °without spot, and °blameless.

u 15 And [9]account *that* the longsuffering of our [2]Lord *is* salvation;

R even as our [1]beloved brother Paul also, [13]according to the wisdom given [1]unto him, °hath written [1]unto you;

16 As °also [1]in all *his* epistles, °speaking [1]in them °of these things; [1]in which are °some things °hard to be understood, which they that are °unlearned and °unstable °wrest, as *they do* °also the other Scriptures, °unto their own °destruction.

Q r 17 Ye therefore, [1]beloved,

s seeing ye °know *these things* before,

t °beware °lest ye also, being °led away with the error of the °wicked, °fall from your own °stedfastness.

u 18 But grow [1]in °grace, and *in* the °knowledge of our [2]Lord and Saviour °Jesus Christ.

A To Him *be* °glory both now and °for ever. Amen.

3. 10-13 (*P*, p. 1868). THE DAY OF THE LORD.
(*Extended Alternation.*)

P | n | 10-. The Day certain though unexpected.
  o | -10. Heavens and earth destroyed.
    p | 11-. Dissolved.
      q | -11. Holiness.
n | 12-. The Day desired.
  o | -12. Heavens and earth destroyed.
    p | 13-. Re-Creation.
      q | -13. Righteousness.

10 in the night. The texts omit. Cp. 1 Thess. 5. 2, 4.

with a great noise=with a rushing sound. Gr. *rhoizēdon.* Only here.

elements. See Gal. 4. 3.

melt=be dissolved. Gr. *luō*, to loose. Cp. Ap. 174. 11.

with fervent heat=being burnt up. Gr. *kausoō.* Only here and *v.* 12.

therein=in (Ap. 104. viii) it.

burned up. See 1 Cor. 3. 15.

11 dissolved. See "melt", *v.* 10.

be. See Luke 9. 48.

conversation. See 1 Pet. 1. 15.

godliness. See 1 Tim. 2. 2.

12 Looking for. Ap. 133. III. 3. See Luke 3. 15 (be in expectation).

hasting unto=hastening. Gr. *speudō.* Elsewhere intransitive. Luke 19. 5. Acts 22. 18; &c. Man can neither hinder nor advance the kingdom of God. But here the meaning is "Looking for, yes and earnestly looking for, the coming of the day of God".

wherein=on account of (Ap. 104. v. 2) which (pl.).

being on fire. See Eph. 6. 16 (fiery).

melt. Gr. *tēkomai.* Only here.

13 according to. Ap. 104. x. 2.

promise. See 1. 4. Is. 65. 17; 66. 22.

new. Gr. *kainos.* See Matt. 9. 17.

wherein=in (Ap. 104. viii) which.

dwelleth. See Acts 2. 5.

righteousness. Ap. 191. 3.

3. 14-18 (*B*, p. 1863). EXHORTATION.
(*Introversion and Extended Alternation.*)

B | Q | r | 14-. Address.
      s | -14-. Reason.
        t | -14. Warning as to conduct.
          u | 15-. The Lord's longsuffering.
    R | -15, 16. Confirmation by Paul.
  Q | r | 17-. Address.
      s | -17-. Reason.
        t | -17. Warning as to falling away.
          u | 18-. Knowledge of the Lord.

14 such=these.

be diligent. See 1. 10.

of. Dat. case. No prep. **without spot.** See 1 Tim. 6. 14. **blameless.** Gr. *amōmētos.* See Phil. 2. 15. **15 hath written**=wrote. Some think this refers to the Epistle to the Hebrews. **16 also, &c.**=in all *his* epistles also. **speaking.** Ap. 121. 7. **of.** Ap. 104. xiii, 1. **some.** Ap. 124. 4 (neut.). **hard, &c.** Gr. *dusnoētos.* Only here. **unlearned.** Gr. *amathēs.* Only here. Cp. Acts 4. 13. 1 Cor. 14. 16. 2 Tim. 2. 23. **unstable.** See 2. 14. **wrest.** Gr. *streblŏō.* Only here and in Sept. of 2 Sam. 22. 27 (m. wrestle). It means to strain or twist, and so to torture. Occ. in Apocrypha. **also, &c.**=the other (Ap. 124. 3) Scriptures also. Note that St. Paul's epistles are called "Scripture". **unto.** Ap. 104. xv. 3. **destruction.** Same as "perdition", *v.* 7. **17 know . . . before.** Gr. *proginōskō.* Ap. 132. I. iv. **beware**=be on your guard. **lest**=in order that (Gr. *hina*) not (Gr. *mē*, as in *v.* 8). **led away.** Gr. *sunapagomai.* See Rom. 12. 16. Gal. 2. 13. **wicked.** See 2. 7. **fall.** Gr. *ekpiptō.* Occ. Gal. 5. 4. **stedfastness.** Gr. *stērigmos.* Only here. The verb in 1. 12. **18 grace.** Ap. 184. I. 1. **knowledge.** Ap. 132. II. i. **Jesus Christ.** Ap. 98. XI. **glory.** See p. 1511. **for ever.** Ap. 151. II. A. ii. 5.

THE FIRST EPISTLE OF JOHN.

THE STRUCTURE OF THE EPISTLE AS A WHOLE.

(*Introversion and Alternation.*)

A | 1. 1–2. 17. CHRIST.

  B | **C** | 2. 18–29. ANTICHRIST.

      D | 3. 1–24. LOVE.

  B | ***C*** | 4. 1–6. ANTICHRIST.

      D | 4. 7–21. LOVE.

A | 5. 1–21. CHRIST.

NOTES.

1. Written by the apostle John, as is proved no less by its character than by external testimony. The similarity in tone and language to the Fourth Gospel shows both to be the work of that disciple whom Jesus loved (John 21. 7).

2. Written, as generally understood, to the "circle of Asiatic churches". But it is suggested that this First Epistle of John may be reckoned among the *Diaspora* and earlier epistles, for the following reasons :—

(*a*) The occurrence of the word *parousia* (2. 28). See Matt. 24. 3; 1 Thess. 2. 19, &c.

(*b*) The significance of the possessive pronoun *hēmeteros* (1. 3; 2. 2 : see Notes), and

(*c*) Paul's statement that John was one of the "pillars", i. e. teachers of the Law, and therefore a minister of the circumcision (see Gal. 2. 9).

The *position* that the epistle occupies canonically among the *Diaspora* writings strengthens the argument that it also is to be reckoned among them.

3. The contents are practical teaching in the light of the love of God. God is Life, is Light, is Truth, is Righteous, is Love, and we have fellowship with Him through the Lord Jesus Christ by the Holy Spirit. "We know that He abideth in us by the spirit which He hath given us" (3. 24). The apostle sets in vivid contrast the death, darkness, falsehood, hate, which are the characteristics of the devil who "sinneth from the beginning" (3. 8), and of those who are led by the spirit of error (4. 6), with the work of the Holy Spirit in believers. But the dominant conception running throughout the epistle is that of the love which constraineth, as it constrained Paul (2 Cor. 5. 14).

4. Written from Ephesus according to tradition, but no definite statement can be made as to either place or time of writing. The character of the contents indicates a much earlier date than is usually supposed (see Ap. 180).

THE FIRST EPISTLE OF
JOHN.

A a[1] 1 THAT which was °from the beginning,
which we have heard, which we have
°seen with our eyes, which we °have °looked
upon, and our hands °have °handled, °of the
°Word of °life;
2 °(For the [1]life was °manifested, and we have
[1]seen *it*, and °bear witness, and °shew °unto
you that °eternal [1]life, which was °with the
°Father, and was °manifested °unto us;)
3 That which we have [1]seen and heard °de-
clare we [2]unto you, °that ye also may have
°fellowship °with us: and truly our °fellow-
ship *is* °with the [2]Father, and °with His °Son
°Jesus Christ.
4 And these things write we [2]unto you, [3]that
your joy may be °full.
5 °This then is the °message which we have
heard °of Him, and °declare [2]unto you, that
°God is °light, and °in Him is °no darkness
at all.
b[1] 6 °If we say that we have [3]fellowship [3]with
Him, and walk [5]in darkness, we lie, and do
°not the °truth:
7 But [6]if we walk [5]in the [5]light, °as He is [5]in
the [5]light, we have [3]fellowship °one [3]with
another, and the blood of °Jesus Christ His
[3]Son cleanseth us [1]from all °sin.
8 [6]If we say that we have °no [7]sin, we deceive ourselves, and the [6]truth is [6]not [5]in us.
9 [6]If we confess our [7]sins, He is °faithful and
°just °to °forgive us *our* [7]sins, and to cleanse
us [1]from all °unrighteousness.
10 [6]If we say that we have [6]not °sinned, we
make Him a °liar, and His °word is [6]not
[5]in us.

a[2] 2 My °little children, these things write
I °unto you, °that ye °sin °not. And
°if °any man °sin, we have an °advocate
°with the °Father, °Jesus Christ the °righteous:
2 And He is the °propitiation °for our °sins:
and °not °for °ours only, but °also °for *the*
sins of the whole °world.
b[2] 3 And °hereby we do °know that we °know
Him, [1]if we keep His commandments.
4 He that saith "I [3]know Him," and keepeth
[1]not His commandments, is a liar, and the
°truth is [2]not °in him.
5 But whoso keepeth His °word, [4]in him
verily is the °love of °God °perfected: [3]hereby
[3]know we that we are [4]in Him.

1. 1—2. 17 (**A**, p. 1870). CONCERNING CHRIST.
(*Repeated Alternation.*)

A | a[1] | 1. 1-5. Cause of writing.
  b[1] | 1. 6-10. Test of fellowship.
 a[2] | 2. 1, 2. Cause of writing.
  b[2] | 2. 3-6. Test of knowing God.
 a[3] | 2. 7, 8. Cause of writing.
  b[3] | 2. 9-11. Test of being in the Light.
 a[4] | 2. 12-14. Cause of writing.
  b[4] | 2. 15-17. Test of loving God.

1. 1 from the beginning. Gr. *ap'* (Ap. 104. iv) *archēs.* See John 8. 44. Occ. nine times in this epistle.
seen. Ap. 133. I. 8. **have.** Omit.
looked upon. Ap. 133. I. 12.
handled. Gr. *psēlaphaō.* See Acts 17. 27.
of. Ap. 104. xiii. 1.
Word. Ap. 121. 10. Fig. *Anabasis.* Ap. 6.
life. Ap. 170. 1. Cp. John 1. 4.
2 For = And.
manifested. Ap. 106. I. v.
bear witness. See John 1. 7, and p. 1511.
shew = report. Gr. *apangellō.* See Acts 4. 23.
unto = to.
eternal. Ap. 151. II. B. i. "Eternal life" occ. in this epistle six times.
with. Ap. 104. xv. 3. **Father.** Ap. 98. III.
3 declare. Same as "shew", *v.* 2.
that = in order that. Gr. *hina.*
fellowship. See 1 Cor. 1. 9.
with. Ap. 104. xi. 1. **Son.** Ap. 108. iii.
Jesus Christ. Ap. 98. XI.
4 full = fulfilled or filled full. Ap. 125. 7. Cp. John 15. 11; 16. 24; 17. 13.
5 This then = And this.
message. Gr. *angelia.* Only here and 3. 11.
of = from. Ap. 104. iv, as *v.* 1.
declare. Gr. *anangellō.* See Acts 20. 27.
God. Ap. 98. I. i. 1. **light.** Ap. 130. 1.
in. Ap. 104. viii.
no . . . at all. Gr. *ou oudeis.* A double negative. This is the Fig. *Pleonasm* (Ap. 6), as in *v.* 8.
6 If. Ap. 118. 1. b. **not.** Ap. 105. I.
truth. See p. 1511 and Ap. 175. 1.
7 as He. This refers to the Father. Cp. 2. 6.
one with another = with one another. Not with fellow-believers, but with the Father and the Son.
Jesus Christ. The texts read "Jesus".
sin. Ap. 128. I. ii. 1. Here is the Fig. *Metalepsis.* Ap. 6.
8 no = not (*v.* 6).
9 faithful. Ap. 150. III.
just. Ap. 191. 1.
to. Gr. *hina*, as in *v.* 3. Lit. in order that He might forgive.
forgive. Ap. 174. 12.
unrighteousness. Ap. 128. VII. 1.
10 sinned. Ap. 128. I. i.
liar. See 5. 10. John 8. 44. **word.** Ap. 121. 10.

2. 1 little children. Ap. 108. ii. Seven times in this epistle. Elsewhere only in John 13. 33. Gal. 4. 19. In *vv.* 13, 18 a different word is used. **unto** = to. **that ye . . . sin.** Note carefully the telic force of the Gr. *hina* here;—"to the end that ye may not (commit) sin (habitually)." **that.** Gr. *hina.* **sin not** = may not sin. **sin.** Ap. 128. I. i. **not.** Ap. 105. II. **if . . . sin** = should any man sin, i. e. commit an act of sin **if.** Ap. 118. 1. b. **any man.** Ap. 123. 3. **advocate.** Gr. *paraklētos.* See John 14. 16. Cp. Rom. 8. 34. **with.** Ap. 104. xv. 3. **Father.** Ap. 98. III. **Jesus Christ.** Ap. 98. XI. **righteous.** Ap. 191. 1. **2 propitiation.** Gr. *hilasmos.* Only here and 4. 10. Several times in the Sept. Lev. 25. 9. Num. 5. 8, &c. Cp. Rom. 3. 25. **for.** Ap. 104. xiii. 1. **sins.** Ap. 128. I. ii. 1. **not.** Ap. 105. I. **ours.** Gr. *hēmeteros.* Emphatic. **also.** This should follow "world". **world.** Ap. 129. 1. Cp. John 3. 16. Rom. 5. 18, 19. 2 Cor. 5. 15. **3 hereby** = in (Ap. 104. viii) this. **know.** Ap. 132. I. ii. The second "know" is in perf. tense, as in *v.* 4 also. **4 truth.** See 1. 6. **in.** Ap. 104. viii. **5 word.** Ap. 121. 10. **love.** Ap. 135. II. 1. **God.** Ap. 98. I. i. 1. **perfected.** Ap. 125. 2.

6 He that saith he °abideth [4]in Him ought himself also so to walk, °even as He walked.

a[3] 7 Brethren, I write °no °new commandment [1]unto you, but an old commandment which ye had °from the beginning. The old commandment is the [5]word which ye °have heard °from the beginning.

8 Again, a [7]new commandment I write [1]unto you, which thing is °true [4]in Him and [4]in you: because the darkness °is past, and the °true °light °now °shineth.

b[3] 9 He that saith he is [4]in the [8]light, and hateth his brother, is [4]in darkness °even until °now.

10 He that °loveth his brother [6]abideth [4]in the [8]light, and there is [7]none °occasion of stumbling [4]in him.

11 But he that hateth his brother is [4]in darkness, and walketh [4]in darkness, and °knoweth [2]not whither he °goeth, because that darkness °hath °blinded his eyes.

a[4] 12 I write [1]unto you, [1]little children, because your [2]sins °are forgiven you °for His name's sake.

13 I write [1]unto you, fathers, because ye have [3]known Him *That is* [7]from the beginning. I write [1]unto you, °young men, because ye have °overcome the °wicked one. I °write [1]unto you, °little children, because ye have [3]known the [1]Father.

14 I °have written [1]unto you, fathers, because ye have [3]known Him *That is* [7]from the beginning. I °have written [1]unto you, [13]young men, because ye are strong, and the [5]word of [5]God [6]abideth [4]in you, and ye have [13]overcome the [13]wicked one.

b[4] 15 [10]Love [1]not the [2]world, °neither the things *that are* [4]in the [2]world. [1]If [1]any man [10]love the [2]world, the [5]love of the [1]Father is [2]not [4]in him.

16 For all that *is* [4]in the [2]world, the lust of the flesh, and the lust of the eyes, and the °pride of °life, is [2]not °of the [1]Father, but is °of the [2]world.

17 And the [2]world [8]passeth away, and the lust thereof: but he that doeth the °will of [5]God [6]abideth °for ever.

B C A[1] c 18 [13]Little children, it is the °last time: and as ye °have heard that °antichrist °shall come, even now °are there many °antichrists; °whereby we [3]know that it is the °last time.

d 19 They went out °from us, but they were [2]not [16]of us; for °if they had been [16]of us, they would *no doubt* have °continued °with us: but *they went out,* [1]that they might be °made manifest that they were [2]not all [16]of us.

e 20 °But ye have an °unction [7]from the Holy One, and ye [11]know all things.

d 21 I [14]have [2]not written [1]unto you because ye [11]know [2]not the [4]truth, but because ye [11]know it, and that [7]no lie is [16]of the [4]truth.

c 22 Who is °a liar °but he that °denieth that °Jesus °is the °Christ? He is [18]antichrist, that °denieth the [1]Father and the °Son.

23 Whosoever [22]denieth the [22]Son, °the same hath °not the [1]Father: [*but*] °*he that* °*acknowledgeth the* [22]*Son hath the* [1]*Father also.*

6 abideth. See p. 1511.
even as. Gr. *kathōs*. The expression "as He", referring to the Son, occ. six times in this epistle. See 3. 2, 3, 7, 23; 4. 17, and cp. 1. 7.
7 no = not, as *v.* 2.
new. Gr. *kainos*. See Matt. 9. 17.
from the beginning. Gr. *ap'* (Ap. 104. iv) *archēs*. See 1. 1.
have. Omit.
from, &c. The texts omit.
8 true. Ap. 175. 1.
is past = passes away. Gr. *paragō*, as *v.* 17.
true. Ap. 175. 2.
light. Ap. 130. 1.
now = already. Gr. *ēdē*.
shineth. Ap. 106. I. i.
9 even until. Gr. *heōs*.
now. Gr. *arti*.
10 loveth. Ap. 135. I. 1.
occasion, &c. Gr. *skandalon*. See Rom. 9. 33.
11 knoweth. Ap. 132. I. i.
goeth. Cp. John 12. 35.
hath. Omit.
blinded. Gr. *tuphloō*. See 2 Cor. 4. 4.
12 are forgiven. Ap. 174. 12.
for, &c. = on account of (Ap. 104. v. 2) His name.
13 young men. Ap. 108. x.
overcome. See John 16. 33.
wicked. Ap. 128. III. 1.
write. The texts read "wrote".
little children. Here and in *v.* 18 the word *paidion* (Ap. 108. v) is used.
14 have written = wrote.
15 neither. Gr. *mēde*.
16 pride. Gr. *alazoneia*. Only here and Jas. 4. 16 (boastings).
life. Ap. 170. 2.
of. Ap. 104. vii.
17 will. Ap. 102. 2.
for ever. Ap. 151. II. A. ii. 4. a.

2. 18-29 (**C**, p. 1870). ANTICHRIST. (*Division*.)

C	A[1]	18-23.	Antichrist. Definition.
	A[2]	24-29.	Antichrist. Protection against.

2. 18-23 (A[1], above). ANTICHRIST. DEFINITION. (*Introversion*.)

A[1]	c	18.	Antichrist.
	d	19.	Rejection of the truth.
	e	20.	Unction.
	d	21.	Rejection of the lie.
	c	22, 23.	Antichrist.

18 last time = last hour. Cp. Acts 2. 17.
have. Omit.
antichrist. Cp. John 5. 43. 2 Thess. 2. 3-9.
shall come = cometh. are there = have arisen.
whereby = whence.
19 from. Ap. 104. vii.
if. Ap. 118. 2. a.
continued. Same as "abide", *v.* 6.
with. Gr. *meta*. Ap. 104. xi. 1.
made manifest. Ap. 106. I. v.
20 But = And.
unction. Gr. *chrisma*. Only here and *v.* 27. For the verb *chriō* see 2 Cor. 1. 21.
22 a = the. Cp. John 8. 44. 2 Thess. 2. 11 (*the* lie).
but = except. Gr. *ei mē*.
denieth. Gr. *arneomai*. Always "deny" save Acts 7. 35; Heb. 11. 24 (both "refused").
Jesus. Ap. 98. X.
is = is not (Ap. 105. I). A negative sometimes follows such verbs as *arneomai*. Cp. the French usage.
Christ. Ap. 98. IX.
Son. Ap. 108. iii.
23 the same = he. not. Gr. *oude*.
he that, &c. This clause is added by all the texts.
acknowledgeth = confesseth, as Matt. 10. 32, &c.

A² f¹ **24** Let that therefore °abide [6] in you, which
ye [18] have heard [7] from the beginning. [1] If that
which ye [18] have heard [7] from the beginning
shall °remain [4] in you, ye also shall [19] continue
[4] in the [22] Son, and [4] in the [1] Father.

g¹ **25** And this is the °promise that He °hath
promised us, *even* °eternal °life.

f² **26** These *things* [14] have I written [1] unto you
°concerning them that °seduce you.
27 [20] But the °anointing which ye [18] have received °of Him [6] abideth [4] in you, and ye need
[2] not [1] that [1] any man teach you:

g² but as the same °anointing teacheth you °of
all things, and is °truth, and is °no lie, and
even as it [18] hath taught you, °ye shall [6] abide
[4] in °Him.

f³ **28** And now, [1] little children, [6] abide [4] in Him;
[1] that, °when He shall °appear, we may have
°confidence,
and [1] not be °ashamed °before Him °at His
°coming.

g³ **29** [1] If ye [11] know that He is °righteous, ye
[3] know that every one that °doeth °righteous-
ness is °born [16] of Him.

D B **3** °Behold what manner of °love the °Father
hath °bestowed upon us, °that we should
be called the °sons of °God: °therefore the
°world °knoweth us °not, because it °knew
Him °not.
2 °Beloved, now are we °the [1] sons of [1] God,
and it doth °not yet °appear what we shall
be: °but we °know that, °when He shall °ap-
pear, we shall be like Him; for we shall °see
Him °as He is.

C D¹ E h **3** And every *man* that hath this hope °in Him
°purifieth himself, °even as He is °pure.

i **4** °Whosoever °committeth °sin °transgress-
eth also the law: °for °sin is °the transgression of the law.

k **5** And ye [2] know that He °was manifested °to
°take away °our [4] sins; and °in Him °is °no
[4] sin.

2. 24-29 (A², p. 1872). ANTICHRIST. PROTECTION AGAINST. (*Alternation.*)

A² | f¹ | 24. The word heard: abiding in them.
  g¹ | 25. His promise: eternal life.
 f² | 26, 27-. The anointing: abiding in them.
  g² | -27. His teaching: truth.
 f³ | 28. Confidence through abiding in Him.
  g³ | 29. His righteousness: they born of Him.

24 remain. Same as "abide", *v.* 6.
25 promise. Gr. *epangelia*, the only occ. in John's writings.
hath. Omit. eternal. Ap. 151. II. B. i.
life. Ap. 170. 1. See 1. 2.
26 concerning. Ap. 104. xiii. 1.
seduce = lead astray, or cause to err.
27 anointing. Same as "unction", *v.* 20.
of. Ap. 104. iv.
of = concerning, as *v.* 26.
truth = true. Ap. 175. 1.
no lie = not (Ap. 105. I) a lie.
ye shall. Omit. Him. Or, it.
28 when. The texts read "if" (Ap. 118. 1. b).
appear. Same as "made manifest", *v.* 19.
confidence. Gr. *parrhēsia*. See Acts 28. 31.
ashamed. Gr. *aischunō*. See 2 Cor. 10. 8.
before = from. Ap. 104. iv.
at = in. Ap. 104. viii.
coming. See Matt. 24. 3.
29 righteous. Ap. 191. 1.
doeth = practiseth. Gr. *poieō*, as 3. 7, 10.
righteousness. Ap. 191. 3.
born = begotten. A Latin MS., the Fleury Palimpsest, instead of "ashamed, &c.", reads "confounded by Him. If in His presence ye have known Him that is faithful, know that every one that doeth the truth hath been born of Him." E. S. Buchanan's transl. in *The Records Unrolled*.

3. 1-24 (**D**, p. 1870). LOVE. (*Alternation.*)

D | B | 1, 2. The Father's love to us.
 C | 3-15. Effect upon us.
 B | 16-. The Son's love to us.
 C | -16-24. Effect upon us.

3. 1 Behold. Ap. 133. I. 3. Plural.
love. Ap. 135. II. 1. Father. Ap. 98. III.
bestowed upon = given to.
that = in order that. Gr. *hina*.
sons = children. Ap. 108. i.
God. Ap. 98. I. i. 1. All the texts add, "and we are (so)".
therefore = on account of (Ap. 104. v. 2) this.
world. Ap. 129. 1.
knoweth. Ap. 132. I. ii. not. Ap. 105. I.
2 Beloved. Ap. 135. III.
the. Omit. not yet. Gr. *oupō*. appear. Ap. 106. I. v. but. The texts omit. know. Ap. 132. I. i. when. Ap. 118. 1. b. see. Ap. 133. I. 8 (a). as = even as. Cp. 2. 6.

3. 3-15 (C, above). EFFECT UPON US. (*Division.*)

C | D¹ | 3-9. Inward purity.
 | D² | 10-15. Outward manifestation.

3. 3-9 (D¹, above). INWARD PURITY. (*Introversion and Extended Alternation.*)

D¹ | E | h | 3. Purity.
  i | 4. Sin's character. Lawless.
  k | 5. Christ manifested. Reason.
  l | 6. Test of abiding.
 F | 7-. Warning against deceivers.
 E | *h* | -7. Righteousness.
  i | 8-. Sin's origin. The devil.
  k | -8. Christ manifested. Reason.
  l | 9. Test of being begotten of God.

3 in = upon (Ap. 104. ix. 2), i. e. set, or fixed on. purifieth. Gr. *hagnizō*. See Acts 21. 24. even as. See 2. 6. pure. Gr. *hagnos*. See 2 Cor. 7. 11. **4** Whosoever = Every one who. committeth = doeth, i. e. practiseth. See 2. 29. sin. Ap. 128. I. ii. 1. transgresseth, &c. = doeth lawlessness (Gr. *anomia*. Ap. 128. III. 4) also. for = and. the transgression, &c. Gr. *anomia*, as above. **5** was manifested. Same as "appear", *v.* 2. to = in order that (Gr. *hina*) He might. take away Gr. *airō*. Cp. John 1. 29. Col. 2. 14. our. The texts omit. in. Ap. 104. viii. is no = there is not (Ap. 105. I).

l 6 [4]Whosoever °abideth [5]in Him °sinneth
[1]not: whosoever °sinneth hath [1]not °seen
Him, °neither [1]known Him.

F 7 °Little children, let °no man °deceive you:

E h he that °doeth °righteousness is °righteous,
[3]even as He is °righteous.

i 8 He that [4]committeth [4]sin is °of the devil;
for the devil [6]sinneth °from the beginning.

k °For this purpose the °Son of [1]God [5]was manifested, [1]that He might °destroy the works of
the devil.

l 9 [4]Whosoever is °born [8]of [1]God doth [1]not
[4]commit [4]sin; for His seed °remaineth [5]in
him: and he °cannot [6]sin, because he is °born
[8]of [1]God.

D² G m 10 [5]In this the °children of [1]God are °manifest,
and the °children of the devil: [4]whosoever
[7]doeth °not [7]righteousness is [1]not [8]of [1]God,
°neither he that °loveth °not his brother.
11 For this is the °message that ye heard
[8]from the beginning, [1]that we should [10]love
one another.

n 12 [1]Not as Cain, *who* was [8]of °that °wicked
one, and °slew his brother. And °wherefore
°slew he him? Because his °own works were
°evil, and his brother's [7]righteous.

H 13 Marvel [10]not, my brethren, °if the [1]world
hate you.

G m 14 We [2]know that we have °passed °from
death °unto °life, because we [10]love the brethren.
He that [10]loveth [10]not °*his* brother [6]abideth
[5]in death.

n 15 [4]Whosoever hateth his brother is a °murderer: and ye [2]know that °no °murderer hath
°eternal [14]life [6]abiding [5]in him.

B 16 °Hereby °perceive we the [1]love *of God*,
because He laid down His °life °for us:

C o and we ought to lay down *our* °lives °for the
brethren.
17 But °whoso hath this [1]world's °good, and
°seeth his brother have need, and shutteth up
his °bowels *of compassion* °from him, how
°dwelleth the [1]love of [1]God [5]in him?
18 My [7]little children, let us [10]not [10]love °in
°word, °neither °in tongue; but °in deed and in
°truth.

p 19 And [16]hereby we [1]know that we are [8]of
the [18]truth, and shall °assure our hearts before
Him.
20 For °if our heart °condemn us, [1]God is
greater than our heart, and [1]knoweth °all
things.
21 [2]Beloved, [20]if our heart [20]condemn us [10]not,
then have we °confidence °toward [1]God;
22 And whatsoever we °ask, we receive °of
Him, because we °keep His commandments,
and do those things that are °pleasing in His
sight.

o 23 And this is His commandment, [1]That we

6 abideth. Gr. *menō.* See p. 1511.
sinneth. Ap. 128. I. i.
seen. Ap. 133. I. 8.
neither. Gr. *oude.*
7 Little children. Ap. 108. ii.
no man = no one. Gr. *mēdeis.*
deceive. See 2. 26 (seduce).
doeth. See 2. 29.
righteousness. Ap. 191. 3.
righteous. Ap. 191. 1. Cp. 2. 29.
8 of. Ap. 104. vii.
from the beginning. See 1. 1 and John 8. 44.
For, &c. = For (Ap. 104. vi) this.
Son of God. Ap. 98. XV.
destroy. Gr. *luō.* Cp. John 2. 19.
9 born = begotten.
remaineth. The same as "abideth", *v.* 6.
cannot = is not (Ap. 105. I) able to.

3. 10-15 (D², p. 1873). **OUTWARD MANIFESTATION.** (*Introversion and Alternation.*)

D² | G | m | 10, 11. Character of the two classes.
| | n | 12. The origin of Cain.
| H | 13. The world's choice.
| *G* | *m* | 14. Test of the two states.
| | *n* | 15. Cain's followers.

10 children. Ap. 108. i. See *vv.* 1, 2.
manifest. Ap. 106. I. viii.
not. Ap. 105. II.
neither = and.
loveth. Ap. 135. I. 1.
11 message. Gr. *angelia.* Only here and 1. 5.
12 that = the.
wicked. Ap. 128. III. 1. See John 8. 44.
slew. Gr. *sphazō.* Only here and Rev. 5. 6, 9, 12; 6. 4, 9; 13. 3, 8; 18. 24.
wherefore = for the sake (Gr. *charin*) of what. The acc. case of *charis* (Ap. 184. I. 1) is used as a preposition.
own. Omit.
evil. Same as "wicked", above.
13 if. Ap. 118. 2. a.
14 passed. Gr. *metabainō.* Cp. John 5. 24 (same word).
from. Ap. 104. vii.
unto. Ap. 104. vi.
life. Ap. 170. 1.
his **brother.** The texts omit.
15 murderer. Gr. *anthrōpoktonos*, manslayer. Only here and John 8. 44.
no = not (*v.* 1) any.
eternal. Ap. 151. II. B. i.
16 Hereby = In (Ap. 104. viii) this.
perceive we = we know, as in *v.* 1.
life. Ap. 110. III. 1. See John 10. 15.
for. Ap. 104. xvii. 1.

3. -16-24 (*C*, p. 1873). **EFFECT UPON US.** (*Alternation.*)

C | o | -16-18. Love manifested to the brethren.
| p | 19-22. Proof of our state before God.
| *o* | 23. Commandment of God.
| *p* | 24. Proof of His abiding in us.

17 whoso = whoever.
good = goods, or living. Ap. 170. 2. Cp. Luke 15. 12, 30.
seeth. Ap. 133. I. 11.
bowels. Gr. *splanchna.* See Philem. 7, 12, 20.
from. Ap. 104. iv.
dwelleth. Same as "abide", *v.* 6.
18 in, in. No prep. Dat. case.
word. Ap. 121. 10.
neither. Gr. *mēde.* **in.** Gr. *en*, with texts.
truth. See 1. 6. **19 assure.** Ap. 150. I. 2. **20 if.** Ap. 118. 1. b. **condemn.** Gr. *kataginōskō.* See Gal. 2. 11 (blamed). **all things.** Cp. Peter's answer, John 21. 17. **21 confidence.** See 2. 28. **toward.** Ap. 104. xv. 3. **22 ask.** Ap. 134. I. 4. **of.** Ap. 104. xii. 1, but the texts read *apo* (Ap. 104. iv). **keep.** See Matt. 19. 17. **pleasing.** Gr. *arestos.* See Acts 6. 2 (reason).

should °believe on the name of His [8]Son °Jesus
Christ, and [10]love one another, as He gave us
commandment.

p 24 And he that [22]keepeth His commandments
[17]dwelleth [5]in Him, and He [5]in him. And
[16]hereby we [1]know that He [6]abideth [5]in us,
°by the °Spirit which He °hath given us.

B C J **4** °Beloved, °believe °not every °spirit, but
°try the °spirits, °whether they are °of
°God: because many °false prophets are gone
out °into the °world.

K 2 °Hereby °know ye the °Spirit of [1]God:
every °spirit that confesseth °that °Jesus Christ
°is come °in °the flesh is [1]of [1]God:
3 And every °spirit that confesseth [1]not °that
[2]Jesus Christ is come in the flesh is °not
[1]of [1]God: and this is °that *spirit* of °antichrist,
whereof ye have heard that it °should come;
and even now already is it [2]in the [1]world.

J 4 Ye are [1]of [1]God, °little children, and have
overcome them: because greater is He That is
[2]in you, than he that is [2]in the [1]world.
5 They are [1]of the [1]world: °therefore °speak
they [1]of the [1]world, and the [1]world heareth
them.

K 6 We are [1]of [1]God: he that [2]knoweth [1]God
heareth us; he that is [3]not [1]of [1]God heareth
[3]not us. °Hereby [2]know we the °spirit °of
truth, and the °spirit °of error.

D q 7 [1]Beloved, let us °love one another: for °love
is [1]of [1]God; and every one that °loveth is °born
[1]of [1]God, and [2]knoweth [1]God.
8 He that [7]loveth [1]not [2]knoweth [3]not [1]God;
for [1]God is [7]love.

r 9 [2]In this was °manifested the [7]love of [1]God
°toward us, because that [1]God °sent His °only
begotten °Son into the [1]world, °that we might
°live °through Him.

s 10 °Herein is [7]love, [3]not that we [7]loved [1]God,
but that He [7]loved us, and [9]sent His [9]Son *to be*
the °propitiation °for our °sins.

t 11 [1]Beloved, °if [1]God so [7]loved us, we °ought
also to [7]love one another.
12 °No man hath °seen [1]God at any time.
°If we [7]love one another, [1]God °dwelleth [2]in
us, and His [7]love is °perfected [2]in us.

u 13 [2]Hereby [2]know we that we [12]dwell [2]in
Him, and He [2]in us, because He hath given us
[1]of His °Spirit.
14 And we have [12]seen and do °testify that
the °Father [9]sent the [9]Son *to be* the Saviour
of the [1]world.

v 15 Whosoever shall °confess that °Jesus is
the [9]Son of [1]God, [1]God [12]dwelleth [2]in him,
and he [2]in [1]God.

23 believe. Ap. 150. I. 1. ii.
Jesus Christ. Ap. 98. XI.
24 by. Ap. 104. vii.
Spirit = spirit, i. e. the new nature, not the Giver Himself. Ap. 101. II. 5.
hath given = gave.

4. 1-6 (*C*, p. 1870). ANTICHRIST. (*Alternation.*)

C | J | 1. Discrimination of spirits.
  K | 2, 3. Test of spirits.
 J | 4, 5. Discrimination of professors.
  K | 6. Test of professors.

4. 1 Beloved. Ap. 135. III.
believe. Ap. 150. I. 1. ii.
not. Ap. 105. II.
spirit. Ap. 101. II. 11.
try = test, prove. By the Word of God. Gr. *dokimazō*. See Rom. 1. 28 and 12. 2.
whether = if. Ap. 118. 2. a.
of. Ap. 104. vii.
God. Ap. 98. I. i. 1.
false prophets. Gr. *pseudoprophētēs*. First occ. Matt. 7. 15.
into. Ap. 104. vi.
world. Ap. 129. 1.
2 Hereby. See 3. 16.
know. Ap. 132. I. ii.
Spirit. Ap. 101. II. 3.
spirit. Ap. 101. II. 11. that. Omit.
Jesus Christ. Ap. 98. XI.
is come = to have come.
in. Ap. 104. viii.
the. Omit.
3 spirit. Ap. 101. II. 12.
that Jesus . . . flesh. The texts read "Jesus".
not. Ap. 105. I. that = the.
antichrist = the Antichrist. See 2. 18.
should come = cometh.
4 little children. Ap. 108. ii.
5 therefore = on account of (Ap. 104. v. 2) this.
speak. Ap. 121. 7.
6 Hereby = From (Ap. 104. vii) this.
spirit. Ap. 101. II. 11.
of truth. Gen. of character, or relation. Ap. 17. 1, or 5.
truth. See 1. 6.
spirit. Ap. 101. II. 12.
of error. Gen. of character, as above.

4. 7-21 (*D*, p. 1870). LOVE. (*Introversion.*)

D | q | 7, 8. Call to love of the brethren.
  r | 9. Proof of God's love to us.
   s | 10. God's love first.
    t | 11, 12. Love perfected.
     u | 13, 14. Hereby (*en touto*) . . . because.
      v | 15. God's indwelling.
      v | 16. Dwelling in God.
     u | 17. Herein (*en touto*) . . . because.
    t | 18. Perfected in love.
   s | 19. God's love first.
  r | 20. Proof of our love to God.
 q | 21. Command to love the brethren.

7 love. Ap. 135. I. 1.
love. Ap. 135. II. 1.
born = begotten.
9 manifested. Ap. 106. I. v.
toward = in. Ap. 104. viii. The sphere in which the manifestation takes place.
sent = hath sent. Ap. 174. 1. See note on John 17. 3.

only begotten. See John 1. 14. Son. Ap. 108. iii. that = in order that. Gr. *hina*. live. Cp. Ap. 170. 1. through. Ap. 104. v. 1. **10** Herein = In (Ap. 104. viii) this. propitiation. Gr. *hilasmos*. Only here and 2. 2. Cp. Rom. 3. 25. for = concerning. Ap. 104. xiii. 1. sins. Ap. 128. I. ii. 1. **11** if. Ap. 118. 2. a. ought also = also ought. **12** No man = No one. Gr. *oudeis*. seen = beheld. Ap. 133. I. 12. If. Ap. 118. 1. b. dwelleth. Gr. *menō*. See p. 1511. perfected = made perfect. Ap. 125. 2. **13** Spirit. I. e. the gifts. Ap. 101. II. 4. **14** testify = bear witness. Gr. *martureō*. See p. 1511. Father. Ap. 98. III. **15** confess, &c. See Matt. 16. 16. Jesus. Ap. 98. X.

v 16 And we have [2]known and °believed the [7]love that [1]God hath °to us. [1]God is [7]love; and he that [12]dwelleth [2]in [7]love [12]dwelleth [2]in [1]God, and [1]God [2]in him.

u 17 [10]Herein is °our [7]love °made perfect, [9]that we may have °boldness [2]in the day of °judgment: because °as He is, so are we [2]in this [1]world.

t 18 There is °no fear [2]in [7]love; but °perfect [7]love casteth out fear: because fear hath °torment. He that feareth is [-3]not [17]made perfect [2]in [7]love.

s 19 We [7]love °Him, because He first [7]loved us.

r 20 [12]If °a man say, "I [7]love [1]God," and hateth his brother, he is a liar: for he that [7]loveth [1]not his brother whom he hath °seen, how can he [7]love [1]God Whom he hath [-3]not °seen?

q 21 And this commandment have we °from Him, [9]that he who [7]loveth [1]God [7]love his brother also.

A L **5** °Whosoever °believeth that °Jesus is the °Christ is °born °of °God: and every one that °loveth Him That °begat °loveth him also that is °begotten °of Him.

2 °By this we °know that we [1]love the °children of [1]God, when we [1]love [1]God, and °keep His commandments.

3 For this is the °love of [1]God, °that we °keep His commandments: and His commandments are °not °grievous.

4 °For whatsoever is [1]born [1]of [1]God overcometh the °world: and this is the victory that overcometh the °world, *even* our °faith.

5 Who is he that overcometh the [4]world, °but he that [1]believeth that [1]Jesus is the °Son of [1]God?

M 6 This is He That came °by °water and blood, *even* °Jesus Christ; [3]not [2]by °water only, but [2]by °water and °blood. And it is the °Spirit That °beareth witness, because the °Spirit is °truth.

7 For there are three that °bear record °in heaven, the Father, the Word, and the Holy Ghost: and these three are one.

8 And there are three that bear witness in earth, the [6]Spirit, and the [6]water, and the blood: and these three agree °in one.

9 °If we receive the °witness of °men, the °witness of [1]God is greater: for this is the °witness of [1]God which He hath °testified °of His [5]Son.

10 He that °believeth on the [5]Son of [1]God hath the [9]witness °in himself: he that °believeth °not [1]God hath made Him a °liar; because he °believeth [3]not the °record that [1]God °gave [9]of His [5]Son.

11 And this is the [10]record, that [1]God °hath given to us °eternal °life, and this °life is [10]in His [5]Son.

12 He that hath the [5]Son hath °life; *and* he that hath [10]not the [5]Son of [1]God hath [3]not °life.

L 13 These things °have I written °unto you °that believe on the name of the Son of

16 believed = have believed. Ap. 150. I. 1. iii.
to = in. Ap. 104. viii. Cp. *v.* 9.
17 our love = love with (Ap. 104. xi. 1) us.
made perfect. Ap. 125. 2.
boldness. Gr. *parrhēsia.* See 2. 28.
judgment. Ap. 177. 7.
as He is. See 2. 6.
18 no = not, *v.* -3. perfect. Ap. 125. 1.
torment = punishment. Gr. *kolasis.* See Matt. 25. 46.
19 Him. The texts omit.
20 a man = any one. Ap. 123. 3.
seen. Ap. 133. I. 8.
21 from. Ap. 104. iv. Cp. 3. 11, 23. John 13. 34; 15. 12.

5. 1-21 (*A*, p. 1870). CHRIST. (*Alternation.*)

A | L | 1-5. Belief in Christ.
  M | 6-12. Witnesses to us that He has come.
 L | 13-19. Belief in Christ.
  M | 20, 21. Witnesses in us that He has come.

5. 1 Whosoever = Every one who.
believeth. Ap. 150. I. 1. iii.
Jesus. Ap. 98. X. Christ. Ap. 98. IX.
born = begotten.
of. Ap. 104. vii. God. Ap. 98. I. i. 1.
loveth. Ap. 135. I. 1.
begat, begotten. Same word as "born", above.
2 By = In. Ap. 104. viii.
know. Ap. 132. I. ii.
children. Ap. 108. i.
keep. The texts read "do".
3 love. Ap. 135. II. 1.
that. Gr. *hina.* Keeping His commandments is a result of His love being shed abroad in our hearts (Rom. 5. 5). Cp. Ps. 119. 97, 119, 163, &c.
keep. See Matt. 19. 17.
not. Ap. 105. I.
grievous = burdensome. Gr. *barus.* See Acts 20. 29.
4 For = Because.
world. Ap. 129. 1. faith. Ap. 150. II. 1.
5 but = except. Gr. *ei mē.*
Son of God. Ap. 98. XV.
6 by. Ap. 104. v. 1.
water. Referring to His baptism, when witness was given to Him by the voice from heaven and the descent of the Spirit.
Jesus Christ. Ap. 98. XI.
blood. The texts read "in (Gr. *en*) the blood".
Spirit. Ap. 101. II. 3.
beareth witness. See 1. 2.
truth. See 1. 6.
7 bear record = bear witness, as in *v.* 6.
in heaven, &c. The texts read, "the Spirit, and the water", &c., omitting all the words from "in heaven" to "in earth" (*v.* 8) inclusive. The words are not found in any Gr. MS. before the sixteenth century. They were first seen in the margin of some Latin copies. Thence they have crept into the text.
8 in. Ap. 104. vi.
9 If. Ap. 118. 2. a.
witness. Gr. *marturia.* See p. 1511.
men. Ap. 123. 1.
testified. Same as "bear witness", *v.* 6.
of = concerning. Ap. 104. xiii. 1.
10 believeth on. Ap. 150. I. 1. v. (i).
in. Ap. 104. viii.
believeth. Ap. 150. I. 1. ii.
not. Ap. 105. II. liar. Cp. 1. 10.
believeth = believeth on, as above.
record. Same as "witness", *v.* 9.
gave. Lit. hath witnessed.
11 hath given = gave. See Rom. 6. 23.
eternal. Ap. 151. II. B. i. life. Ap. 170. 1.
12 life = the life (*v.* 11).
13 have I written = I wrote.
unto = to.
that believe, &c. This clause is omitted by all the texts and by the Syriac.

God; [3]that ye may °know that ye have
[11]eternal [11]life, °and that ye may [10-]believe
on the name of the [5]Son of [1]God.
14 And this is the °confidence that we have
°in Him, that °if we °ask any thing °according
to His °will, He heareth us:
15 And °if we [13]know that He hear us whatsoever we [14]ask, we [13]know that we have the
°petitions that we °desired °of Him.
16 [14]If °any man °see his brother °sin a °sin
which is [10]not °unto death, he shall [14]ask, and
He shall give him [11]life for them that °sin [10]not
°unto death. There is °a °sin °unto death: I
do [3]not say [3]that he shall °pray °for °it.
17 All °unrighteousness is [16]sin: and there is
[16]a [16]sin [3]not [16]unto death.
18 We [13]know that [1]whosoever is [1]born [1]of
[1]God °sinneth [3]not; but °He that is [1]begotten
[1]of [1]God [3]keepeth °himself, and that °wicked
one °toucheth him [3]not.
19 *And* we [13]know that we are [1]of [1]God, and
the whole [4]world lieth [10]in °wickedness.
M 20 And we [13]know that the [5]Son of [1]God °is
come, and hath given us an °understanding,
[3]that we may [2]know Him That is °true, and
we are [10]in Him That is °true, *even* [10]in His
[5]Son [6]Jesus Christ. °This is the °true [1]God,
and [11]eternal [11]life.
21 °Little children, °keep yourselves °from
°idols. °Amen.

know. Ap. 132. I. i.
and . . . may. The texts read "even unto you that".
14 confidence. See 2. 28.
in = toward. Ap. 104. xv. 3.
if. Ap. 118. 1. b.
ask. Ap. 134. I. 4.
according to. Ap. 104. x. 2.
will. Ap. 102. 2.
15 if. Ap. 118. 1. a.
petitions. Ap. 134. II. 5. Cp. Matt. 7. 7. John 14. 13; 15. 7.
desired = have desired. Same as "ask", *v.* 14.
of. Ap. 104. xii. 1.
16 any man = any one. Ap. 123. 3.
see. Ap. 133. I. 1.
sin = sinning. Ap. 128. I. i.
sin. Ap. 128. I. ii. 1.
unto. Ap. 104. xv. 3. **a.** Omit.
pray. Ap. 134. I. 3.
for = concerning. Ap. 104. xiii. 1.
it = that. The sin unto death was one that might result in the brother being cut off. Cp 1 Cor. 11. 30, where many had sinned unto death—"many sleep". See also Jas. 5. 14, 16, where there is the same recognition of sickness being due to some special sins, as in 1 Cor. 11. 30, and of intercessory prayer as here. It is not a single act, but a continued habit.
17 unrighteousness. Ap. 128. VII. 1. Cp. 3. 4.
18 sinneth not. I. e. does not practise, or continue in, sin. Cp. 3. 6, 9. Rom. 6. 1-12. Ap. 128. I. i.
He that, &c. This refers to the Lord. As the Jehovah of the O.T. He was the keeper of Israel (Ps. 121. 4, 5, &c.). See also John 17. 12. 2 Thess. 3. 3. Rev. 3. 10.
himself. Most texts read "him".

wicked one. Ap. 128. III. 1. Cp. 2. 13, 14; 3. 12. toucheth. Gr. *haptomai.* In John's writings only here and in John 20. 17. Thirty-one times in the three other Gospels, generally in connexion with the Lord's miracles. Elsewhere, 1 Cor. 7. 1. 2 Cor. 6. 17. Col. 2. 21. **19 wickedness** = the wicked one, as *v.* 18. He is the prince of this world (John 14. 30, &c.), and the god of this age (2 Cor. 4. 4). **20 is come.** Not the word used in 4. 2, 3; 5. 6 (*erchomai*), but *hēkō*, to be present. Cp. John 8. 42. Heb. 10. 7, 9, 37. In the last ref. the two verbs are seen: "shall come" (*erchomai*); "will come" (*hēkō*). **understanding.** Gr. *dianoia.* Transl. nine times "mind", once "imagination" (Luke 1. 51), and "understanding" here, Eph. 1. 18; 4. 18. true. Ap. 175. 2. This refers to the Father. Cp. 2. 5, 24; 3. 24; 4. 12-16. **This, &c.** Also referring to the Father, the source of life (John 5. 26), which life was manifested in His Son (1. 2), and is given to us through, and in, Him (*vv.* 11, 12 above, and Rom. 6. 23). **21 Little children.** Ap. 108. ii. keep = guard, as Jude 24. from. Ap. 104. iv. idols. As in 1 Cor. 8. 4. An idol may not be a material one, but may consist in whatever a man looks to for help, apart from the Living God. See Eph. 5. 5. Col. 3. 5. Amen. The texts omit.

THE SECOND EPISTLE OF JOHN.

THE STRUCTURE OF THE EPISTLE AS A WHOLE.

(*Introversion.*)

A | 1-3. ELECT LADY AND CHILDREN: BENEDICTION.

B | 4-6. CHILDREN WALKING ACCORDING TO THE FATHER'S COMMANDMENT.

C | 7-8. WARNING AGAINST DECEIVERS.

B | 9-11. TRANSGRESSORS REJECTING CHRIST'S TEACHING.

A | 12, 13. JOY FULFILLED: CHILDREN OF ELECT SISTER. SALUTATION.

THE SECOND AND THIRD EPISTLES OF JOHN.

NOTES.

The likeness of these two epistles indicates that both were by one writer, and in each case the internal evidence supports the traditional belief that both were written by the apostle John. Several of the early "fathers" quote the Second Epistle, certain passages of which so closely resemble parts of the First Epistle as to confirm the view of its being by the same writer.

The Second Epistle is addressed "unto the elect lady and her children", and some have understood a certain church and its members. Alford, however, gives good grounds for believing that an individual is meant. The Third Epistle is to "Gaius the beloved", a notable believer. The name was a common one, and the bearer may not be of those mentioned in *Acts*, &c.

The probability is that both epistles were written from Ephesus and about the same time, but nothing is known definitely as to either place or time of writing.

The reader will readily see the Structure of these two short epistles. Each takes the form of an *Introversion*, the intermediate members marking exhortation and warning. The Third Epistle contains a personal element, commendation of Gaius and Demetrius, and condemnation of Diotrephes.

THE SECOND EPISTLE OF JOHN.

A 1 THE °elder °unto the °elect °lady and her
°children, whom I °love °in °the °truth;
and °not I only, but °also all they that have
°known the °truth;
2 °For the [1]truth's sake, which °dwelleth [1]in
us, and shall be °with us °for ever.
3 °Grace °be [2]with you, °mercy, *and* peace,
°from °God the °Father, and °from the °Lord
°Jesus Christ, the °Son of the °Father, [1]in
[1]truth and °love.

B 4 I °rejoiced °greatly that I found °of thy
[1]children walking [1]in [1]truth, as we °have received a commandment [3]from the [3]Father.
5 And now I °beseech thee, [1]lady, [1]not as
though I wrote a °new commandment [1]unto
thee, but that which we had °from the beginning, °that we [1]love one another.
6 And this is [3]love, [5]that we walk °after His
commandments. This is the commandment,
[5]that, as ye °have heard [5]from the beginning,
ye should walk [1]in it.

C 7 For many °deceivers are entered °into the
°world, who confess °not °that [3]Jesus Christ
is come [1]in the flesh. This is °a °deceiver
and °an °antichrist.
8 °Look to yourselves, [5]that °we °lose [7]not
those things which we °have wrought, but that
°we receive a full °reward.

B 9 Whosoever °transgresseth and °abideth
[7]not [1]in the doctrine of °Christ, hath [1]not
[3]God. He that °abideth [1]in the doctrine °of
Christ, he hath both the [3]Father and the
[3]Son.

1 elder. Ap. 189. Here not an official title, but referring to the apostle's age. Cp. Philem. 9.
unto = to.
elect. Cp. 1 Pet. 1. 2. But perhaps used in the sense of "excellent".
lady. Gr. *kuria*, fem. of *kurios*. In all probability a proper name, "Kyria".
children. Ap. 108. i.
love. Ap. 135. I. 1.
in. Ap. 104. viii.
the. Omit.
truth. See p. 1511. The element or sphere in which the love was seen. Cp. Eph. 4. 15.
not. Ap. 105. I.
also, &c. = all they also.
known. Ap. 132. I. ii.
2 For, &c. = On account of (Ap. 104. v. 2) the truth.
dwelleth = abideth. Gr. *menō*. See p. 1511.
with. Ap. 104. xi. 1.
for ever. Ap. 151. II. A. ii. 4. a.
3 Grace. Only here, and three times in the Gospel, and twice in Rev., in John's writings. Ap. 184. I. 1. Cp. 1 Tim. 1. 2.
be = shall be.
mercy. Only here in John.
from. Ap. 104. xii. 1.
God. Ap. 98. I. i. 1.
Father. Ap. 98. III.
Lord. The texts omit.
Jesus Christ. Ap. 98. XI.
Son. Ap. 108. iii. The expression "The Son of the Father", is found here only. Cp. John 1. 18. 1 John 1. 3.
love. Ap. 135. II. 1.
4 rejoiced. Cp. 3 John 3. Several of Paul's epistles open with thanksgiving.
greatly. Gr. *lian*. Only here and 3 John 3 in John's writings.

of. Ap. 104. vii. Not implying that there were others who did not so walk, but referring to such as he had met. **have.** Omit. **5 beseech** = ask. Ap. 134. I. 3. **new.** Gr. *kainos*. See Matt. 9. 17. **from the beginning.** Gr. *ap' archēs*. See 1 John 1. 1. **that** = in order that. Gr. *hina*. **6 after.** Ap. 104. x. 2. **have.** Omit. In this verse is the Fig. *Antimetabolē*, "walk . . . commandments—commandment . . . walk". **7 deceivers.** Gr. *planos*. See 2 Cor. 6. 8. Cp. 1 John 4. 1. **into.** Ap. 104. vi. **world.** Ap. 129. 1. **not.** Ap. 105. II. **that, &c.** Lit. Jesus Christ coming in the flesh. The present participle is used, as in Rev. 1. 4. In 1 John 4. 2, 3, the perfect is used, referring to His first coming. This refers to His second coming. Cp. Acts 1. 11. **a, an** = the. **antichrist.** See 1 John 2. 18. **8 Look to.** Ap. 133. I. 5. **we.** The texts read "ye" in both occ. **lose.** Gr. *apollumi*. See John 17. 12. **have wrought.** I. e. the truth and love resulting from John's teaching. **reward.** Gr. *misthos*. In John's writings only here, John 4. 36 (wages), and Rev. 11. 18; 22. 12. **9 transgresseth.** Ap. 128. VI. 1. The texts read "goeth before", Gr. *proagō*. See 1 Tim. 1. 18; 5. 24. Heb. 7. 18. This refers to false teachers who claimed to bring some higher teaching, beyond the apostle's doctrine. Cp. 1 Tim. 6. 3. 2 Tim. 1. 13; 3. 14. **abideth.** See "dwelleth", *v.* 2. **Christ.** Ap. 98. IX. **of Christ.** The texts omit.

10 °If °there come °any °unto you, and bring
[1]not this doctrine, receive him [7]not [7]into *your*
house, °neither °bid him God speed:
11 For he that [10]biddeth him God speed °is
partaker of his °evil deeds.

A 12 Having many things to write [1]unto you,
I °would [1]not *write* °with °paper and °ink: but
I °trust to come [10]unto you, and °speak °face to
face, [5]that °our °joy may be °full.
13 The [1]children of thy [1]elect sister °greet
thee. °Amen.

10 If. Ap. 118. 2. a.
there . . . any = any one (Ap. 123. 3) cometh.
unto. Ap. 104. xv. 3.
neither, &c. = and . . . not (Ap. 105. II).
bid . . . God speed. Lit., say, Hail! (Gr. *chairein,* to rejoice. See Matt. 26. 49).
11 is partaker = partaketh. Gr. *koinōneō.* See Rom. 15. 27. 1 Tim. 5. 22.
evil. Ap. 128. III. 1.
12 would. Ap. 102. 3.
with = by means of. Ap. 104. v. 1.
paper. Gr. *chartēs.* Only here.
ink. See 2 Cor. 3. 3.
trust = hope.
speak. Ap. 121. 7. **face,** &c. Lit. mouth to (Ap. 104. xv. 3) mouth. **our.** The texts read "your". **joy.** See 1 John 1. 4. **full.** See 1 John 1. 4. **13 greet** = salute. **Amen.** The texts omit.

THE THIRD EPISTLE OF
JOHN.

THE STRUCTURE OF THE EPISTLE AS A WHOLE.

(*Introversion.*)

A | 1, 2. SALUTATION.
  B | 3, 4. WITNESS AS TO WALK IN THE TRUTH.
    C | 5–8. COMMENDATION: LOVE TO STRANGERS.
      D | 9, 10. MALICE OF DIOTREPHES.
    C | 11. EXHORTATION: FOLLOW GOOD.
  B | 12. WITNESS AS TO WALK IN THE TRUTH.
A | 13, 14. SALUTATION.

A 1 °THE elder °unto the °wellbeloved °Gaius,
whom I °love °in °the °truth.
2 [1]Beloved, I °wish °above all things that thou
mayest °prosper and °be in health, even as thy
°soul °prospereth.

B 3 For I °rejoiced greatly, when °the brethren
came and °testified of °the [1]truth that is in thee,
even as thou walkest [1]in [1]the [1]truth.
4 I have °no greater °joy, °than to hear that
°my °children °walk [1]in °truth.

C 5 [1]Beloved, thou doest °faithfully whatsoever thou °doest °to the brethren, and °to
strangers;
6 Which °have borne witness of thy °charity
°before the °church: whom °if thou bring forward on their journey °after a godly sort, thou
shalt do well:
7 °Because that °for °His name's sake they
went forth, °taking °nothing °of the °Gentiles.
8 We therefore ought to receive such, °that we
°might °be °fellowhelpers to the [1]truth.

D 9 I °wrote [1]unto the [6]church: but °Diotrephes,
°who loveth to have the preeminence °among
them, °receiveth us [4]not.

1 The elder. See 2 John 1.
unto = to.
wellbeloved. Ap. 135. III. Same as "beloved", *v.* 2, &c.
Gaius. It is impossible to say whether this was the same as any one of the others of the same name mentioned Acts 19. 29; 20. 4. Rom. 16. 23. 1 Cor. 1. 14.
love. Ap. 135. I. 1.
in. Ap. 104. viii. **the.** Omit.
truth. See p. 1511.
2 wish = pray. Ap. 134. I. 1.
above = concerning. Ap. 104. xiii. 1.
prosper. Gr. *euodoumai.* See Rom. 1. 10.
be in health. Gr. *hugiainō.* See Luke 5. 31.
soul. Ap. 110. V. 1. As Gaius had a sound mind, John desires for him a sound body also.
3 rejoiced greatly. See 2 John 4.
the. Omit.
testified. Gr. *martureō.* See p. 1511.
the truth, &c. Lit. thy truth.
4 no = not. Ap. 105. I.
joy. See 1 John 1. 4.
than, &c. Lit. than these things, that (Gr. *hina*) I may hear of.
my = mine own.
children. Ap. 108. i.
walk = walking.
truth = the truth.
5 faithfully = as a faithful (deed). Ap. 150. III.
doest = workest. **to.** Ap. 104. vi. **to.** The texts read "that to". The brethren referred to were strangers. Cp. Heb. 13. 2. **6 have borne witness** = bare witness. Same as "testify", *v.* 3. **charity** = love. Ap. 135. II. 1. **before** = in the sight of. **church.** Ap. 186. **if . . . journey.** Lit. having sent forward. Gr. *propempō.* See Acts 15. 3. Cp. Ap. 174. 4. **after a godly sort** = worthily of God (Ap. 98. I. i. 1). **7 Because that** = For. **for,** &c. = on behalf of (Ap. 104. xvii. 1) His name. **His.** The texts read "the". **taking** = receiving. **nothing.** Gr. *mēdeis.* **of.** Ap. 104. iv. **Gentiles.** Gr. *ethnos.* **8 that** = in order that. Gr. *hina.* **might** = may. **be** = become. **fellowhelpers.** Gr. *sunergos.* See 1 Cor. 3. 9. **9 wrote** = wrote something, as the texts. **Diotrephes.** Nothing is known of him. **who loveth,** &c. Gr. *philoprōteuō,* love to be first. **among** = of. **receiveth.** Gr. *epidechomai.* Only here and *v.* 10.

10 ° Wherefore, ° if I come, I will ° remember
his deeds which he doeth, ° prating against us
with ° malicious ° words: and ° not content
° therewith, ° neither doth he himself [9] receive
the brethren, and ° forbiddeth ° them that would,
and ° casteth *them* ° out of the [6] church.

C 11 [1] Beloved, ° follow [10] not that which is ° evil,
but that which is good. He that ° doeth good
is ° of ° God: but he that ° doeth evil hath [4] not
° seen ° God.

B 12 Demetrius ° hath good report ° of all *men*,
and ° of the [1] truth itself: yea, and we *also* ° bear
record; and ° ye know that our ° record is
° true.

A 13 I had many things to write, but I ° will [4] not
° with ° ink and ° pen write [1] unto thee:
14 But I ° trust ° I shall ° shortly see thee, and
we shall ° speak ° face to face. Peace *be* to thee.
Our friends ° salute thee. ° Greet the friends
° by name.

10 Wherefore = On account of (Ap. 104. v. 2) this. if. Ap. 118. 1. b. **remember.** See John 14. 26. prating. Gr. *phluareō.* Only here. Cp. 1 Tim. 5. 13. malicious. Ap. 128. III. 1. words. Ap. 121. 10. not. Ap. 105. II. therewith = upon (Ap. 104. ix. 2) these (things). neither. Gr. *oute.* forbiddeth = hindereth, as Luke 11. 52. them that would. Lit. the willing (ones). Ap. 102. 3. casteth. Gr. *ekballō.* Cp. John 9. 34. out of. Ap. 104. vii. **11** follow. See 2 Thess. 3. 7. evil. Ap. 128. III. 2. doeth good. Gr. *agathopoieō.* See Acts 14. 17. of. Ap. 104. vii. God. Ap. 98. I. i. 1 doeth evil. Gr. *kakopoieō.* See Mark 3. 4. seen. Ap. 133. I. 8. **12** hath good report = is borne witness to. See *v.* 6. of = by. Ap. 104. xviii. 1. bear record = testify, *v.* 3. ye know. The texts read, "thou knowest". Ap. 132. I. i. record = testimony. See p. 1511. true. Ap. 175. 1. **13** will. Ap. 102. 1. with = by means of. Ap. 104. v. 1. ink. See 2 Cor. 3. 3. pen. Gr. *kalamos.* Elsewhere transl. "reed". **14** trust = hope. I shall, &c. = to see (Ap. 133. I. 1) thee, &c. shortly. Gr. *eutheōs.* Generally transl. "immediately", or "straightway". speak. Ap. 121. 7. face, &c. See 2 John 12. salute. Gr. *aspazomai.* See Acts 18. 22. Greet = Salute. Here, as in the close of so many epistles, the word *aspazomai* is transl. by two different English words in successive verses or even in the same verse. Cp. Rom. 16. 3–23. 1 Cor. 16. 19, 20. 2 Cor. 13. 12, 13. Phil. 4. 21. Col. 4. 10, 12, 14. 2 Tim. 4. 19, 21. Tit. 3. 15. 1 Pet. 5. 13, 14. by. Ap. 104. x. 2.

THE EPISTLE OF JUDE.

THE STRUCTURE OF THE EPISTLE AS A WHOLE.

(Introversion.)

A | 1, 2. SALUTATION.
 B | 3. EXHORTATION.
  C | 4. UNGODLY. DENYING.
   D | 5-. REMEMBRANCE.
    E | -5–16. RETRIBUTION.
   D | 17. REMEMBRANCE.
  C | 18, 19. UNGODLY. SEPARATING.
 B | 20–23. EXHORTATION.
A | 24, 25. DOXOLOGY.

NOTES.

1. Written by "Judas, a servant of Jesus Christ, and brother of James". This is how he describes himself, and we know nothing more of him, save that in Matt. 13. 55 and Mark 6. 3 "Judas" is mentioned as one of the Lord's brethren (see Ap. 182). A very early tradition assigns the authorship to Jude. The James to whom he was brother was doubtless the writer of the Epistle of James, the pillar of the church at Jerusalem (see Acts 15. 13; Gal. 2. 9).

2. Written probably from Palestine to Hebrew Christians both of the "Dispersion" and those living in Palestine, if we may decide from the Jewish character of the epistle.

3. The contents in part bear a strong resemblance to portions of 2 Peter, but of the originality of both no one need doubt. The tone is one of stern reproof in regard to certain serious evils brought in by men who had professed to receive the grace of God, and he warns of the certainty of the Divine judgment, illustrating from the Old Testament history.

4. The date can be gauged only approximately, but it is thought to have been very early, perhaps A. D. 41–46. See Ap. 180.

THE EPISTLE OF
JUDE.

A 1 °JUDE, °the °servant of °Jesus Christ, and
brother of °James, to them that are °sanctified
°by °God the °Father, and °preserved in °Jesus
Christ, *and* called:
2 Mercy °unto you, and peace, and °love, be
°multiplied.
B 3 °Beloved, °when I gave all diligence to
write [2]unto you °of °the °common salvation,
°it was needful for me to write [2]unto you,
°and exhort *you* °that ye should °earnestly
contend for the °faith which was °once °de-
livered [2]unto the °saints.
C 4 For °there are °certain °men °crept in unawares, who were °before of old ordained °to
this °condemnation, °ungodly men, °turning
the °grace of our [1]God °into °lasciviousness,
and °denying the only °Lord °God, and our
°Lord [1]Jesus Christ.
D 5 I °will therefore °put you in remembrance,
though ye [3]once °knew this, how that the
°LORD, having saved the °People °out of the
°land of Egypt,
E A °afterward °destroyed them that °believed
°not.
6 And the angels which °kept [5]not °their
first estate, but left their own °habitation, He
hath °reserved in °everlasting °chains °under
°darkness °unto the °judgment of the great °day.
7 Even as Sodom and Gomorrha, and the
cities °about them, in like °manner °giving
themselves over to fornication, and going after
°strange flesh, °are set forth for an °example,
°suffering the °vengeance of °eternal fire.
B 8 Likewise °also these *filthy* °dreamers °defile
the flesh, °despise °dominion, and °speak evil
of °dignities.

1 Jude. See Introductory Notes. **the**=a.
servant. Ap. 190. I. 2.
Jesus Christ. Ap. 98. XI.
James. See Jas. 1. 1.
sanctified. All the texts and the Syriac read "beloved" (Ap. 135. I. 1).
by=in. Ap. 104. viii.
God. Ap. 98. I. i. 1. **Father.** Ap. 98. III.
preserved=kept. Gr. *tēreō.* Occ. five times in the epistle, *vv.* 1, 6, 6, 13, 21. The word *phulassō* is used in *v.* 24.
2 unto=to.
love. Ap. 135. II. 1. The only salutation where "love" is mentioned.
multiplied. Cp. 1 Pet. 1. 2. 2 Pet. 1. 2.
3 Beloved. Ap. 135. III.
when I gave=making.
of. Ap. 104. xiii. 1. **the.** The texts read "our".
common. Cp. Tit. 1. 4.
it was needful for me=I had need.
and exhort=exhorting. Ap. 134. I. 6.
that ye should=to.
earnestly contend. Gr. *epagōnizomai.* Only here. Cp. *agōnizomai.* Luke 13. 24.
faith. Ap. 150. II. 1. **once**=once for all.
delivered. Gr. *paradidōmi.* See John 19. 30.
saints. See Acts 9. 13.
4 there are. Omit.
certain. Ap. 124. 4. **men.** Ap. 123. 1.
crept in unawares. Gr. *pareisduō.* Only here. Cp. Gal. 2. 4. 2 Pet. 2. 1.
before . . . ordained=before written. Gr. *prographō.* See Rom. 15. 4. **to.** Ap. 104. vi.
condemnation. Ap. 177. 6.
ungodly men=impious. Gr. *asebēs.* See Rom. 4. 5, and cp. Ap. 128. IV.
turning=changing. Gr. *metatithēmi.* See Acts 7. 16.
grace. Ap. 184. I. 1. **into.** Ap. 104. vi.=
lasciviousness. Gr. *aselgeia.* See Rom. 13. 13.
denying. See 2 Pet. 2. 1. **Lord.** Ap. 98. VI. ii. 2.
God. The texts omit.
Lord. Ap. 98. VI. i. *β.* 2. B.

5 will. Ap. 102. 3. **put . . . in remembrance.** Gr. *hupomimnēskō.* See John 14. 26. **knew.** Ap. 132. I. i. **LORD.** Ap. 98. VI. i. *β.* 1. A. b. Some texts (not the Syriac) read "Jesus". Cp. 1 Cor. 10. 4. **People.** Gr. *laos.* See Acts 2. 47. **out of.** Ap. 104. vii. **land.** Ap. 129. 4.

-5-16 (**E**, p. 1880). RETRIBUTION. (*Extended Alternation.*)

E | A | -5-7. Three classes of apostates: Israelites. Fallen angels. Sodomites.
  B | 8. Lawlessness.
    C | 9. Judgment denounced. Michael.
      D | 10. Corruption.
| *A* | 11. Three individual apostates: Cain. Balaam (the soothsayer). Korah.
  B | 12, 13. Spots in love-feasts.
    C | 14, 15. Judgment predicted. Enoch.
      D | 16. Walking after lusts.

afterward. Lit. the second time, or in the second place. **destroyed.** Gr. *apollumi.* See John 17. 12. **believed.** Ap. 150. I. 1. i. **not.** Ap. 105. II. **6 kept.** Same as "preserved", *v.* 1. **their first estate**= their own principality (Ap. 172. 6). Cp. Eph. 1. 21; 3. 10; 6. 12. Col. 1. 16; 2. 10, 15. **habitation.** Gr. *oikētērion.* Only here and 2 Cor. 5. 2. **reserved.** Same as "kept", above. **everlasting.** Ap. 151. II. C. ii. **chains.** Gr. *desmos.* Not same word as Rev. 20. 1. **under.** Ap. 104. xviii. 2. **darkness.** See 2 Pet. 2. 4. **unto.** Ap. 104. vi. **judgment.** Ap. 177. 7. **day.** See Matt. 25. 41. Rev. 20. 10, 11. **7 about.** Ap. 104. xiii. 2. **manner.** Add "to these", i. e. the angels of *v.* 6. The sin of Sodom and Gomorrha, like that of the angels of Gen. 6 (Ap. 23, 25), was an unnatural one, breaking through the bounds which God had set. **giving, &c.** Gr. *ekporneuō.* Only here. An intensive form of *porneuō,* which occ. 1 Cor. 6. 18, &c. **strange**=other. Ap. 124. 2. **are set forth.** Gr. *prokeimai.* See 2 Cor. 8. 12. **example.** Gr. *deigma.* Only here. **suffering**=undergoing. Gr. *hupechō.* Only here. **vengeance.** Ap. 177. 4. **eternal.** Ap. 151. II. B. i. **8 also these**=these also. **dreamers**= in their dreamings. Gr. *enupniazomai.* See Acts 2. 17. **defile.** See John 18. 28. **despise.** Gr. *atheteō.* See John 12. 48 (rejecteth). **dominion**=lordship. See Eph. 1. 21. 2 Pet. 2. 10 (government). **speak evil of**=blaspheme. **dignities.** Lit. glories. Cp. 2 Pet. 2. 10.

C **9** Yet °Michael the °archangel, when °contending with the devil he °disputed °about the body of °Moses, durst °not °bring against him a °railing accusation, but said, "The °LORD rebuke thee."

D **10** But these [8]speak evil of those things which they [5]know [9]not: but what they °know °naturally, as °brute beasts, °in those things they °corrupt themselves.

A **11** Woe [2]unto them! for they °have gone in the way of °Cain, and °ran greedily after the error of Balaam for °reward, and °perished in the °gainsaying of °Core.

B **12** These are °spots [10]in your °feasts of charity, °when they feast with you, °feeding °themselves without fear; clouds *they are* without water, carried about °of winds; trees °whose fruit withereth, °without fruit, twice dead, plucked up by the roots;

13 °Raging waves of the sea, °foaming out their own shame; °wandering stars, to whom °is [6]reserved the °blackness of darkness °for ever.

C **14** °And Enoch also, the seventh °from Adam, prophesied of these, saying, °"Behold, the [9]LORD cometh °with ten thousands of His °saints,

15 To execute [6]judgment °upon all, and to °convince all °that are [4]ungodly °among them [3]of all °their °ungodly deeds which they °have °ungodly committed, and [3]of all their hard *speeches* which [4]ungodly sinners °have spoken °against Him."

D **16** These are °murmurers, °complainers, walking °after their own lusts; and their mouth [15]speaketh °great swelling *words,* °having men's persons in admiration °because of °advantage.

D **17** But, [3]beloved, remember ye the °words which °were spoken before [12]of the °apostles of our °Lord [1]Jesus Christ;

C **18** How that they °told you there °should be °mockers °in the last time, °who should walk [16]after their own °ungodly lusts.

19 These be they who °separate themselves, °sensual, having [5]not the °Spirit.

B **20** But ye, [3]beloved, °building up yourselves on your most holy °faith, °praying [10]in the °Holy Ghost,

21 [6]Keep yourselves [10]in °the [2]love of [1]God, °looking for the mercy of our [17]Lord [1]Jesus Christ [6]unto [7]eternal °life.

---

9 Michael. See Dan. 10. 13.

archangel. See 1 Thess. 4. 16. No other angel bears this title.

contending. Ap. 122. 4.

disputed. Gr. *dialegomai.* See Acts 17. 2.

about. Ap. 104. xiii. 1.

Moses. The seventy-ninth occ. of the name. See Matt. 8. 4. This dispute must have taken place after the death of Moses and his burial by Jehovah, for "death reigned from Adam to (until) Moses" (Rom. 5. 14). The devil claimed Moses for the death-state, but God raised him as representative of those hereafter to be raised, as Elijah of those to be caught up without dying.

not. Ap. 105. I.

bring against. Gr. *epipherō.* See Acts 19. 12.

railing accusation. Lit. judgment (Ap. 177. 7) of railing (Gr. *blasphēmia*).

LORD. Ap. 98. VI. i. β. 1. B. b.

10 know. Ap. 132. I. v.

naturally. Gr. *phusikōs.* Only here. Cp. 2 Pet. 2. 12.

brute. See 2 Pet. 2. 12.

in. Ap. 104. viii.

corrupt themselves = are destroyed. Gr. *phtheirō.* See 1 Cor. 3. 17.

11 have gone = went.

Cain. His way was that of natural religion, not the way God had appointed.

ran greedily = rushed. Lit. were poured out. Gr. *ekchunō.* Often transl. "shed".

reward. Same word as in 2 Pet. 2. 13, 15.

perished. Gr. *apollumi.* See John 17. 12.

gainsaying. Gr. *antilogia.* See Heb. 6. 16; 12. 3. In five places where the Heb. has "Meribah", the Sept. transl. it by *antilogia.* Num. 20. 13; 27. 14. Deut. 32. 51; 33. 8. Ps. 81. 7.

Core. Korah, as the two others, resisted the declared will of God.

12 spots = hidden rocks, as the texts. Gr. *spilas.* Only here. The word in Eph. 5. 27 and 2 Pet. 2. 13 is *spilos.*

feasts of charity. Lit. loves, i. e. love-feasts. Ap. 135. II. 1.

when they feast = feasting. See 2 Pet. 2. 13.

feeding. Lit. pasturing, as a shepherd does his flock.

themselves. Making the love-feast an occasion of gratifying the appetite, instead of promoting spiritual edification. Cp. Ezek. 34. 2.

of. Ap. 104. xviii. 1.

whose fruit withereth = in autumnal decay. Gr. *phthinopōrinos.* Only here.

without fruit. Gr. *akarpos.* Elsewhere transl. "unfruitful".

13 Raging = Wild. Gr. *agrios.* Occ. Matt. 3. 4. Mark 1. 6.

foaming out. Gr. *epaphrizō.* Only here.

wandering. Gr. *planētēs.* Only here.

is = hath been.

blackness. Same as "darkness", *v.* 6.

for ever. Ap. 151. II. A. ii. 4. a.

14 And, &c. Read, "And to these also Enoch".

from. Ap. 104. iv.

Behold. Ap. 133. I. 2.

cometh. Lit. came.

with = among. Ap. 104. viii. 2.

saints = holy ones, i. e. angels. Cp. Deut. 33. 2, R.V. Matt. 25. 31. Mark 8. 38.

15 upon = against. Ap. 104. x. 1. **convince** = convict. Gr. *exelenchō.* Only here, but the texts read *elenchō,* as John 8. 9. **that are** = the. **among** = of. The texts omit. **their** = the. **ungodly deeds** = works of impiety (Ap. 128. IV). **have.** Omit. **ungodly committed.** See 2 Pet. 2. 6. **have spoken** = spake. Ap. 121. 7. **against.** Ap. 104. x. 1. **16 murmurers.** Gr. *gongustēs.* Only here. Cp. John 6. 41. Acts 6. 1. **complainers.** Gr. *mempsimoiros.* Only here. **after.** Ap. 104. x. 2. **great swelling.** See 2 Pet. 2. 18. **having, &c.** = admiring persons. **because of.** Gr. *charin.* See 1 John 3. 12. **advantage** = profit. See Rom. 3. 1. **17 words.** Gr. *rhēma.* See Mark 9. 32. **were** = have been. **apostles.** Ap. 189. **Lord.** Ap. 98. VI. i. β. 2. A. **18 told** = said to. **should** = shall. **mockers** = scoffers. See 2 Pet. 3. 3. **in.** The texts read Ap. 104. ix. 1. **who, &c.** = walking. **ungodly lusts** = lusts of impieties (Ap. 128. IV). **19 separate themselves** = are separating. Gr. *apodiorizō.* Only here. **sensual.** Gr. *psuchikos.* See 1 Cor. 2. 14. Jas. 3. 15. **Spirit.** Here "spirit". Ap. 101. II. 5. **20 building up.** See Acts 20. 32. **faith.** Ap. 150. II. 1; i. e. the object of faith. Cp. 1 Cor. 3. 11. **praying.** Ap. 134. I. 2. **Holy Ghost** = holy spirit. Ap. 101. II. 14. **21 the love of God** = God's love to you, i. e. the assurance of it, based on His Word. **looking for.** Gr. *prosdechomai.* See Acts 23. 21. **life.** Ap. 170. 1.

22 And of some °have compassion, °making
a difference:
23 And others save °with fear, pulling *them*
[5]out of the fire; hating even the garment
°spotted °by the flesh.
A 24 Now [2]unto Him That is able to °keep you
°from falling, and to °present *you* °faultless
°before the presence of His °glory [23]with °exceeding joy,
25 To the only °wise [1]God our Saviour, *be*
[24]glory and °majesty, °dominion and °power,
°now and °ever. Amen.

22 have compassion. Some texts read *elenchō*, "convict".
making, &c. Ap. 122. 4, but several texts read "when they contend".
23 with. The texts read *en*. Ap. 104. viii.
spotted. Gr. *spiloō*. See Jas. 3. 6, and cp. Rev. 3. 4.
by. Ap. 104. iv.
24 keep = guard. Gr. *phulassō*. Cp. John 17. 12.
from falling = without falling. Gr. *aptaistos*. Only here. Cp. Rom. 11. 11 (stumble).
present = set, or make stand. See Acts 22. 30.
faultless = blameless. Gr. *amōmos*. See Eph. 1. 4. Col. 1. 22.
before the presence of. Gr. *katenōpion*. See 2 Cor. 2. 17.
glory. See p. 1511.
exceeding joy = exultation. Gr. *agalliasis*. See Acts 2. 46.
25 wise. All the texts omit. Cp. 1 Tim. 1. 17.
majesty. Gr. *megalōsunē*. See Heb. 1. 3.
dominion. Ap. 172. 2.
power. Ap. 172. 5.
now, &c. The texts read "before every age and now and unto all the ages".
ever. Ap. 151. II. A. ii. 8.

THE REVELATION.

THE STRUCTURE OF THE BOOK AS A WHOLE.

A | 1. INTRODUCTION.
 B | 2, 3. THE PEOPLE ON THE EARTH.
  X i. H[1] | 4. 5. IN HEAVEN. (The Throne, the Book, and the Lamb.)
     E[1] | 6. 1—7. 8. ON EARTH. (The Six Seals and 144,000.)
   ii. H[2] | 7. 9—8. 6. IN HEAVEN. (The Great Multitude and the Seventh Seal.)
     E[2] | 8. 7—11. 14. ON EARTH. (The Six Trumpets.)
   iii. H[3] | 11. 15-19-. IN HEAVEN. (The Seventh Trumpet.)
     E[3] | 11. -19. ON EARTH. (The Earthquake, &c.)
   iv. H[4] | 12. 1-12. IN HEAVEN. (Woman, Child, and Dragon.)
     E[4] | 12. 13—13. 18. ON EARTH. (The Dragon and Two Beasts.)
   v. H[5] | 14. 1-5. IN HEAVEN. (The Lamb and 144,000.)
     E[5] | 14. 6-20. ON EARTH. (The Six Angels.)
   vi. H[6] | 15. 1-8. IN HEAVEN. (The Seven Vial Angels.)
     E[6] | 16. 1—18. 24. ON EARTH. (The Seven Vials.)
   vii. H[7] | 19. 1-16. IN HEAVEN. (The Marriage of the Lamb, &c.)
     E[7] | 19. 17—20. 15. ON EARTH. (The Final Five Judgments.)
 B | 21. 1—22. 5. THE PEOPLE ON THE NEW EARTH.
A | 22. 6-21. CONCLUSION.

(*Note*. The Structures in the Notes are taken from Dr. E. W. Bullinger's comprehensive work, *The Apocalypse*, but as not all in that volume are here given, the lettering is not consecutive throughout. This, however, does not interfere with the study of the Structures presented.)

INTRODUCTORY NOTES.

1. Title of the Book. Man calls it "The Revelation of St. John the Divine". But its God-given title is in the first verse, "The Revelation of Jesus Christ", that is, the Unveiling, Revealing, and Presentation to earth and heaven of the Lord Jesus Christ (Messiah) as "KING of Kings and LORD of Lords".

It is spoken of as:

(*a*) "The word of God" (1. 2), in the sense in which the term occurs in the Old Testament (cp. 1 Chron. 17. 3. Jer. 1. 4, 13. Ezek. 1. 3. Joel 1. 1; &c):

(*b*) "This prophecy" (1. 3): therefore a *prophetic* message. The "blessing" here promised makes it clear that from this verse (and not 4. 1, as many suppose) to the end the book concerns things yet future:

(*c*) "The testimony of Jesus Christ" (1. 2, 9). Either as testimony to Him as the Coming One (Genitive of the Object): or, the testimony He bore on earth (Gen. of the Subject; Ap. 17); probably both.

2. Authorship. The testimony of *Melito*, bishop of Sardis (c. 170), quoted by Eusebius; *Irenæus* (c. 180); the *Muratorian Canon* fragment (c. 200); *Clement* of Alexandria (c. 200); *Tertullian* (c. 220); *Origen* (c. 233); *Hippolytus*, bishop of Pontus (c. 240); &c., may fairly be accepted as to the writer being John the "beloved disciple" and apostle, as against the claims of a supposed John, "an Elder (cp. Peter's eldership, 1 Pet. 5. 1) resident in Asia", who is hailed by "the majority of modern critics" as being the author of the Johannine letters (see Introductory Notes to 1 John) and The Revelation (Ap. 197).

3. Date of Writing. This by almost unanimous consent of the early Church writers is ascribed to the close of the reign of the Emperor Domitian, about A. D. 96. At the time of the so-called "Second General Persecution" of the "Christians".

4. To Whom it was originally sent is unknown. We have no clue, and therefore all speculations on the subject are valueless.

(For Characteristics, Scope, Symbolism, &c., of *Revelation*, see Ap. 197.)

THE REVELATION.

A 1 °THE Revelation of °Jesus Christ, which
°God gave °unto Him, to °shew °unto His
°servants °things which must °shortly come
to pass; and He °sent and signified *it* °by
His angel °unto His °servant John,
2 Who bare °record of °the °word of [1]God,
and of the °testimony of [1]Jesus Christ, °and of
°all things that he °saw.
3 °Blessed *is* he that readeth, and they that
hear the [2]words of °this °prophecy, and °keep
°those things which are written °therein: for
the °time *is* at hand.

4 JOHN to the °seven °churches which are °in
°Asia: °Grace *be* [1]unto you, and peace, °from
°Him °Which is, and °Which was, and °Which
is to come; and °from the °seven °Spirits
which are before His throne;
5 And [4]from [1]Jesus Christ, *Who is* the °faith-
ful °Witness, *and* the °First Begotten °of the
dead, and the °Prince of the °kings of the
°earth. [1]Unto Him That °loved us, and
°washed us °from our °sins °in His own blood,
6 And °hath made us °kings and priests [1]unto
[1]God and His °Father; to Him *be* °glory and
°dominion °for ever and ever. °Amen.
7 °Behold, He cometh °with °clouds; and
every °eye shall °see Him, and °they *also*
which °pierced Him: and all °kindreds of the
[5]earth shall wail °because of Him. °Even so,
[6]Amen.
8 "I am °Alpha and Omega, °the beginning
and the ending," saith the °LORD, "Which is,
and Which was, and Which is to come, the
°Almighty."
9 I John, °who also am your brother, and
°companion [4]in °tribulation, and °in the °king-
dom and °patience °of °Jesus °Christ, °was [4]in
the isle that is called °Patmos, °for the [2]word of
[1]God and °for the [2]testimony of °Jesus °Christ.

1. 1 The . . . Christ. The Divine title of the Book.
The Revelation = Revelation. Gr. *apokalupsis*, whence our "Apocalypse". Ap. 106. II. i and Ap. 197.
Jesus Christ. Ap. 98. XI.
God. Ap. 98. I. i. 1. **unto** = to.
shew = point out. First occ. Matt. 4. 8. Cp. 22. 6.
servants, servant. Ap. 190. I. 2. The word is peculiarly appropriated to Israel throughout O. T., and in this Book is used (fourteen times) as the proper title of those who are its subjects. Contrast "servants" and "sons", Rom. 8. 14-17. Gal. 4. 1-7. 1 John 3. 1.
things, &c. = what things must needs come to pass. See Dan. 2. 29 (Sept.).
shortly = with (Gr. *en*) speed.
sent = having sent. Ap. 174. 1.
by. Ap. 104. v. 1.
2 record = witness. See p. 1511. The verb occ. only here and 22. 16, 20 in Rev.
the word of God. Thus a direct prophetic communication, as 1 Sam. 9. 27. 1 Kings 12. 22. 1 Chron. 17. 3. Yet cp. *v.* 9; 6. 9; 19. 13; 20. 4.
word. Ap. 121. 10.
testimony = witness. See John 1. 7 and p. 1511.
and, &c. Not merely "heard" but saw in vision.
all things that = whatsoever things.
saw. Ap. 133. I. 1.
3 Blessed = Happy. Gr. *makarios*, by which the Sept. renders the Heb. *'ashrēy*. See Ap. 63. VI. First of seven occ. in Rev. (fifty in N. T.). **this** = the.
prophecy. Occ. seven times (Ap. 10) in Rev.
keep. See Luke 2. 19, 51. Occ. eleven times in Rev.
those = the.
therein = in (Gr. *en*) it.
time. Gr. *kairos*. Cp. Ap. 195.
4 seven. See App. 10 and 197. 6.
churches. Gr. *ekklēsia*. App. 120. I and 186.
in. Ap. 104. viii.
Asia. Not Europe, and consequently not Christendom.
Grace. Ap. 184. I. 1.
from. Ap. 104. iv.
Him . . . come. Gk. paraphrase of "Jehovah". See Ap. 4. II.
Which = Who, and so throughout Rev.
Spirits. Ap. 101. II. 11.

5 faithful. Ap. 150. III; 175. 4. Cp. Is. 55. 4. **Witness.** Gr. *martus*. See 3. 14 and p. 1511. **First Begotten.** See Rom. 8. 29. Heb. 1. 6. Cp. Ps. 2. 7. Acts. 13. 33. 1 Cor. 15. 20. Col. 1. 18. **of the dead.** Ap. 139. 1. The texts omit *ek*. **Prince** = Ruler. See John 12. 31. **kings, &c.** See 6. 15 and Ps. 89. 27, 37. **earth.** Ap. 129. 4. **loved.** The texts read "loveth". Ap. 135. I. 1. **washed.** The texts read "loosed". Ap. 95. I. 1; note 2, p 138. **from.** Gr. *ek*. Ap. 104. vii. **sins.** Ap. 128. I. ii. 1. Elsewhere in Rev. 18. 4, 5. **in** = by. Gr. *en*. Ap. 104. viii. **6 hath.** Omit. **kings and priests** = (to be) a kingdom (so all texts) and (to be) priests. See 5. 10; 20. 6. Ex. 19. 6 (Sept. "a royal priesthood"). No priesthood on earth in this Dispensation. **Father.** See Ap. 98. III. **glory** = the glory. See p. 1511. **dominion** = the dominion. Ap. 172. 2. **for ever, &c.** Ap. 151. II. A. ii. 9. a. First of fourteen occ. (including 14. 11). **Amen** = even (the) Amen; see 3. 14. **7 Behold.** Ap. 133. I. 2. **with.** Ap. 104. xi. 1. **clouds** = the clouds. **eye.** Fig. *Synecdochē* (Ap. 6), for person. **see.** Ap. 133. I. 8 (a). **they, &c.** Allusion to Zech. 12. 10. **pierced.** Cp. John 19. 34. **kindreds** = tribes, as Matt. 19. 28; 24. 30; &c. Gr. *phulē*. **because of.** Gr. *epi*. Ap. 104. ix. 3. See Zech. 12. 10. **Even so** = Yea. **8 Alpha and Omega** = The Alpha and the Omega. See *v.* 17; 22. 13. **the . . . ending.** The texts omit. **LORD.** The texts read "LORD God" (see Ap. 4. I, II, X). **LORD.** Ap. 98. VI. i. *β*. 1. B. b. **Almighty.** Ap. 98. IV. The Gr. word occ. nine (Ap. 10) times in Rev. Only once elsewhere (2 Cor. 6. 18) in N. T. **9 who also am.** Omit. **companion** = partaker, as Rom. 11. 17. Phil. 1. 7; &c. **tribulation** = the tribulation. Here; 2. 9, 10, 22; 7. 14. **in the.** The texts omit. **kingdom and patience.** With this "kingdom" the "tribulation" is specially connected. Fig. *Hendiatris* (Ap. 6). See Acts 14. 22. **patience.** Occ. seven times in Rev. Cp. Luke 21. 19. 2 Thess. 3. 5. **of.** The texts read "in" (Gr. *en*). **Jesus.** Ap. 98. X. **Christ.** The texts omit. **was** = came to be. **Patmos.** An island (mod. *Patino*) in the Ægean, about thirty miles south-west of Samos. **for.** Ap. 104. v. 2. Nothing to indicate that John had been "banished". **for.** The texts omit. **Christ.** The texts omit.

10 I [9]was [4]in the °Spirit °on °the Lord's
day, and heard behind me a great voice, as of
a °trumpet,
11 Saying, "°I am Alpha and Omega, the
first and the last: and what thou °seest, write °in
a °book, and °send *it* [1]unto the [4]seven [4]churches
°which are in Asia; °unto Ephesus, and °unto
Smyrna, and °unto Pergamos, and °unto Thyatira,
and °unto Sardis, and °unto Philadelphia,
and °unto Laodicea."
12 And I turned to [11]see the °voice that °spake
[7]with me. And °being turned, I [2]saw [4]seven
golden °candlesticks;
13 And [4]in the midst of the [4]seven [12]candlesticks
one like [1]unto °the °Son of Man, clothed
with a garment down to the foot, and girt
°about the °paps with a golden girdle.
14 °His head and *His* hairs *were* white °like
wool, as white as snow; and His eyes *were* as
a flame of fire;
15 And His feet like [1]unto °fine brass, °as if
they burned [4]in a °furnace; and His °voice as
the sound of many waters.
16 And °He had [4]in His right hand [4]seven
°stars: and °out of His mouth went a sharp
°twoedged °sword: and His °countenance *was*
as the sun °shineth [4]in his °strength.
17 And when I [2]saw Him, I °fell °at His feet
as °dead. And He laid His right hand °upon
me, saying °unto me, "Fear °not; °I am the
First and the Last:
18 °*I am* He That °liveth, °and °was °dead; and
[7]behold, °I am °alive °for evermore, °Amen;
and have the keys of °hell and of death.
19 °Write the things which thou °hast seen,
and °the things which are, °and the things
which °shall be °hereafter;
20 The °mystery of the seven °stars which
thou [2]sawest °in My [16]right hand, and the
seven golden [12]candlesticks. The seven °stars
°are °the °angels of the seven [4]churches: and
the seven [12]candlesticks °which thou sawest
are °the seven [4]churches.

B X **2** °Unto the °angel of the °church °of °Ephesus
write; 'These things saith He That
°holdeth the °seven stars °in His right hand,

10 Spirit. Ap. 101. II. 3. See 4. 2; 17. 3; 21. 10.
on = in (Gr. *en*).
the Lord's day = the day of the Lord (Isa. 2. 12, &c.), the Heb. terms for which are equivalent to the Greek *hē kuriakē hēmera*, the Lord's day. Occ. 1 Thess. 5. 2. 2 Thess. 2. 2 (with texts). 2 Pet. 3. 10. Not our Sunday. See Ap. 197.
trumpet. In O. T. connected with war and the day of the Lord. See Zeph. 1. 14–16; &c.
11 I am . . last: and. The texts omit.
seest. Ap. 133. I. 5. **in.** Gr. *eis.* Ap. 104. vi.
book = roll, or scroll, as 6. 14. **send.** Ap. 174. 4.
which . . . Asia. The texts omit.
unto. Gr. *eis*, as above.
12 voice. The Speaker (Figs. *Metonymy of Effect*, and *Catachrēsis.* Ap. 6). See *v.* 10.
spake = was speaking. **being** = having.
candlesticks = lampstands. Occ. seven times in Rev.
13 the. Omit.
Son of Man. App. 98. XVI and 99.
about. Gr. *pros.* Ap. 104. xv. 2. **paps** = breasts.
14 His head. Read "And His head".
like. The texts read "as". Cp. this and the following *vv.* with Ezek. 1. 7. Dan. 7. 9; 10. 6.
15 fine brass. Only here and 2. 18.
as . . . burned = as glowing.
furnace. Only here; 9. 2. Matt. 13. 42, 50.
voice . . . waters. See *v.* 10; 14. 2; 19. 6. Ezek. 1. 24; 43. 2.
voice. Same word as "sound". Gr. *phōnē.*
16 He had = having. **stars.** See *v.* 20.
out . . . sword. For the Figure cp. Ps. 55. 21; 57. 4; 59. 7. The significance is seen in Isa. 11. 4; 49. 2. 2 Thess. 2. 8. See also 2. 12, 16; 19. 15, 21. Luke 19. 27. **out of.** Ap. 104. vii.
twoedged. Cp. Heb. 4. 12.
sword. Gr. *rhomphaia.* Occ. only in Rev. (six times) and Luke 2. 35.
countenance. Gr. *opsis.* Only here; John 7. 24; 11. 44. **shineth.** Ap. 106. I. i.
strength. App. 172. 1; 176. 1.
17 fell. Gr. *piptō.* See 7. 16 (light).
at. Gr. *pros.* Ap. 104. xv. 3.
dead = one dead. Ap. 139. 2.
upon. Ap. 104. ix. 3.
unto me. The texts omit. **not.** Ap. 105. II.
I am . . . Last. Cp. Isa. 41. 4; 43. 10; 44. 6; 48. 11, 12.
18 I . . . liveth = And the Living One.
liveth, alive. Ap. 170. 1.
and. Read "and yet". **was** = became.
dead. See Ap. 139. 2.
I am alive = Living (emph.) am I.
for evermore. Ap. 151. II. A. ii. 9. b. **Amen.** Omit. **hell . . death.** The texts read "death and of hell". **hell** = grave. Ap. 131. II. See 20. 13 (marg.). 1 Cor. 15. 55. R. V. transliterates the Gr. word *hadēs.* **19 Write.** The texts add "therefore". **hast seen** = sawest, as *v.* 2. **the . . . are** = what they are, i. e. what they signify. **and** = even. **shall be** = are about to happen. **hereafter.** Lit. after (Gr. *meta.* Ap. 104. xi. 2) these things (Gr. *tauta*). Heb. idiom; cp. Gen. 22. 1. First of ten occ. in Rev. **20 mystery** = secret symbol. See Ap. 193. **stars.** Gr. *astēr.* Occ. fourteen (Ap. 10) times in Rev. **in.** Gr. *epi.* Ap. 104. ix. 1. **are** = represent, or signify. **the.** Omit. **angels.** Ap. 120. I. 1, 2. **which . . . sawest.** The texts omit. **the.** Omit.

B 2 and 3. STRUCTURE OF THE SEVEN EPISTLES TO THE CHURCHES, AS A WHOLE.
(*Introversion and Alternation.*)

Correspondent to Israel in the Wilderness.

B | X | 1 | EPHESUS. Israel's espousals.
| | 2 | SMYRNA. Israel's testing.
| | 3 | PERGAMOS. Israel's failure.

In the Land.

| Y | 4 | THYATIRA. The day of Israel's kings.
| | 5 | SARDIS. Israel's removal.
| | 6 | PHILADELPHIA. The day of Judah's kings.
| | 7 | LAODICEA. Judah's removal.

2. 1 Unto = To. **angel.** See 1. 20. **church.** Ap. 186. **of.** Gr. *en.* Ap. 104. viii. **Ephesus.** Not for those addressed in *Ephesians*, on whom all blessing is bestowed by grace. Here blessing is promised to overcomers only. **holdeth.** Occ. eight times in Rev. Cp. Ap. 172. 2. See Col. 2. 19. Heb. 4. 14; &c. **seven stars.** See 1. 16, 20. **in.** Ap. 104. viii.

Who walketh °in the midst of the seven golden
°candlesticks;
2 I °know thy °works, and °thy °labour and
thy °patience, and how thou canst °not °bear
them which are °evil, and thou °hast tried
them which °say they are °apostles, and are
°not, and °hast found them °liars:
3 And °hast [2]borne, and hast [2]patience, and
°for My °name's sake hast laboured, and hast
[2]not °fainted.
4 Nevertheless I have *somewhat* °against
thee, because thou °hast left °thy first °love.
5 Remember therefore °from whence thou
°art fallen, and °repent, and do the first
[2]works; or °else I °will come [1]unto thee
°quickly, and will °remove thy candlestick
°out of his place, °except thou °repent.
6 But this thou hast, that thou hatest the
°deeds of the °Nicolaitanes, which I also hate.
7 °He that hath an ear, let him hear what
the °Spirit °saith [1]unto the [1]churches; To
him that °overcometh will I give to eat °of
°the °tree of °life, which is [1]in the midst of the
°Paradise of °God.'
8 And [1]unto the [1]angel of the [1]church in
°Smyrna write; 'These things saith the
°First and the Last, Which °was °dead, and
°is alive;
9 I [2]know thy °works, and tribulation, and
°poverty (but thou art rich), and *I know* the
blasphemy of them which say they are °Jews,
and are [2]not, but *are* the °synagogue of °Satan.
10 Fear °none of those things which thou
°shalt suffer: °behold, the °devil °shall cast
some [7]of you °into prison, °that ye may be
°tried; and ye shall have tribulation ten
°days: °be thou °faithful °unto °death, and
I will give thee °a °crown of [7]life.
11 [7]He that hath an ear, let him hear what
the [7]Spirit saith [1]unto the [1]churches; He that
[7]overcometh shall °not be °hurt [7]of the °second
death.'
12 And to the [1]angel of the [1]church [1]in
°Pergamos write; 'These things saith °He
Which hath the sharp sword with two edges;
13 I [2]know °thy [2]works, and where thou
°dwellest, *even* where [9]Satan's °seat *is*: and
thou °holdest fast My [3]name, and °hast [2]not
°denied °My °faith, even [1]in those days
°wherein °Antipas *was* My °faithful °martyr,
who was slain °among you, where [9]Satan
°dwelleth.
14 But I have a few things [4]against thee, because thou hast there them that [1]hold the doc-

candlesticks. See 1. 12, 13, and cp. Lev. 26. 12. Deut. 23. 14, &c. 2 Cor. 6. 16.

2 know. Ap. 132. I. i.

works. The Lord deals according to works in "the day of the Lord". See Is. 66. 18.

thy. Omit.

labour = toil. The verb in *v.* 3 and Matt. 6. 28.

patience. As in *v.* 3 and 1. 9. See Rom. 2. 7.

not. Ap. 105. I.

bear. Gr. *bastazō*. In Rev. here, *v.* 3; 17. 7 (carrieth).

evil. Ap. 128. III. 2.

hast tried = didst try.

say they. The texts read "call themselves".

apostles. Ap. 189.

hast found = didst find.

liars. Gr. *pseudēs*. Only here; 21. 8. Acts 6. 13.

3 hast, &c. The texts read "and hast patient endurance and didst bear (*v.* 2) for", &c.

for ... sake. Ap. 104. v. 2.

name's. See Acts 5. 41.

fainted = wearied. Gr. *kamnō*. Only here; Heb. 12. 3. Jas. 5. 15 (sick).

4 against. Ap. 104. x. 1.

hast left = didst leave.

thy, &c. Cp. Deut. 7. 7–9. Jer. 2. 1, 2. Ezek. 16. 8–10.

love. Ap. 135. II. 1. Only here and *v.* 19 in Rev.

5 from. Omit.

art fallen = hast fallen.

repent. Cp. Lev. 26. 40–42. Deut. 30. 1–3. Dan. 9. 3, 4. Matt. 4. 17. Acts 2. 38; &c. Contrast Eph. 1. 3. Ap. 111. I. 1.

else = if (Ap. 118. 2. a) not (Ap. 105. II).

will. Omit. quickly. The texts omit.

remove = move, as 6. 14. out of. Ap. 104. vii.

except. If (Ap. 118. 1. b) not (Ap. 105. II).

6 deeds = works, as *v.* 5.

Nicolaitanes. History has no record of these. Tradition says much. They will appear "in that day". All we do know is that they are hateful to God.

7 He, &c. A formula used by the Lord alone. See Ap. 142.

Spirit. Ap. 101. II. 3.

saith = is saying.

overcometh. See John 16. 33. The verb *nikaō*, to conquer or overcome, occ. seventeen times in Rev.

of. Gr. *ek*. Ap. 104. vii.

the tree, &c. = *the* tree of *the* life. Promise fulfilled 22. 14, where also the articles differentiate from Ezek. 47. 12.

tree. Lit. wood. Gr. *xulon*, as used frequently in Sept., e. g. Exod. 7. 25.

life. Ap. 170. 1.

Paradise of God. See ref. in Ap. 173. Paradise is always used in Scripture for a definite place; is *described* in Gen. 2; *lost* in Gen. 3; its *restoration* spoken of by the Lord in Luke 23. 43; *seen in vision* by Paul, 2 Cor. 12. 2, 4; *promised* here, Rev. 2. 7; *restored*, Rev. 22. 1–5, 14–17.

God. Ap. 98. I. i. 1.

8 Smyrna. About fifty miles north-west of Ephesus. A great centre now of Levantine trade. **First . . . Last.** See 1. 17. **was** = became. **dead.** Ap. 139. 2. **is alive** = lived (again). See Ap. 170. 1. **9 works, and.** The texts omit. **poverty.** See Ap. 127. 1. **Jews.** Only here, and 3. 9 in Rev. **the** = a. **synagogue.** Ap. 120. I. **Satan.** See Ap. 19. **10 none of** = not. Ap. 105. II. **shalt** = art about to. **behold.** Ap. 133. I. 2. **devil.** See 12. 9. **shall** = is about to. **into.** Ap. 104. vi. **that** = in order that. Gr. *hina*. **tried** = tested. Cp. Matt. 10. 22; 24. 9, 10; &c. **days.** Not "periods". Cp. Gen. 7. 4, 10. Num. 14. 33; &c. **be** = become. **faithful.** Ap. 150. III. **unto** = until. Gr. *achri*. **death.** See 12. 11. **a** = the. **crown.** Gr. *stephanos*. See 1 Pet. 5. 4. **11 not.** Ap. 105. III. **hurt.** See 22. 11. **second death.** See 20. 6, 14; 21. 8. **12 Pergamos.** A city of Mysia famous for the worship of Æsculapius, to whom the title of *sōtēr* (saviour) was given and whose emblem was the serpent. Identified with Apollo; cp. Acts 16. 16. Some trace the Babylonian pagan priesthood as removing to Pergamos. **He Which hath, &c.** See 1. 16. **13 thy works, and.** The texts omit. **dwellest, dwelleth.** Gr. *katoikeō*, to take up abode. See Acts 2. 5. **seat** = throne. Cp. 13. 2; 16. 10. **holdest fast.** Same as hold, *v.* 1. **hast . . . denied** = didst . . . deny. **denied.** Gr. *arneomai*. First occ. Matt. 10. 33. **My faith.** See 14. 12. **faith.** See Ap. 150. II. 1. **wherein.** Most texts omit. **Antipas.** A witness in future who will be faithful unto death. Mentioned proleptically. **faithful.** Ap. 150. III. **martyr** = witness. See 1. 5. **among.** Gr. *para*. Ap. 104. xii. 2.

trine of °Balaam, who taught Balac to °cast a
°stumblingblock before the °children of Israel,
to eat °things sacrificed unto idols, and to commit fornication.
15 So hast thou also them that [1]hold the
doctrine of the [6]Nicolaitanes, °which thing I
hate.
16 [5]Repent; or [5]else I °will come [1]unto thee
quickly, and will °fight °against them° with
the [12]sword of My mouth.
17 [7]He that hath an ear, let him hear what
the Spirit saith [1]unto the [1]churches. To him
that [7]overcometh will I give °to eat of the
°hidden °manna, and will give him a white
°stone, and °in the °stone a °new name
written, which °no man °knoweth °saving he
that °receiveth *it*.'
Y 18 And [1]unto the [1]angel of the [1]church [1]in
°Thyatira write; 'These things saith the
°Son of God, Who hath His eyes like unto
a flame of fire, and His °feet *are* like fine
brass;
19 I [2]know thy [2]works, °and °charity,
°and °service, °and °faith, °and thy [2]patience,
°and thy [2]works; °and the last *to be* more
than the first.
20 Notwithstanding, I have °a few things
[4]against thee, because thou sufferest °that
woman °Jezebel, which calleth herself a °pro-
phetess, °to teach and to °seduce My °ser-
vants to commit [14]fornication, and to eat [14]things
sacrificed unto idols.
21 And I gave her °space °to [5]repent [7]of her
fornication; °and she [5]repented [2]not.
22 [10]Behold, I °will cast her [10]into a bed, and
them that commit adultery °with her [10]into
great °tribulation, [5]except they [5]repent [7]of
°their [6]deeds.
23 And I will kill her °children [16]with °death;
and all the [1]churches shall °know that I am
He Which °searcheth the reins and hearts:
and I will give [1]unto °every one of you °accord-
ing to your [2]works.
24 But [1]unto you I say, °and [1]unto the °rest
[1]in Thyatira, as many as have [2]not this doctrine, and which have [2]not [23]known the °depths
of [9]Satan, as they speak; °I will put °upon you
°none °other burden.
25 But that which ye have °*already*, [13]hold
fast till I °come.
26 And he that [7]overcometh, and °keepeth
My [2]works unto the °end, **to him will I give**
°power °over the °nations:
27 **And he shall °rule them [16]with a °rod of**
iron; °as the vessels of a potter shall they be
broken to shivers: °even as I °received °of
My °Father.
28 And I will give him the °morning star.
29 [7]He that hath an ear, let him hear what
the Spirit saith [1]unto the churches.'

3 And °unto the °angel of the °church °in
°Sardis write; 'These things saith He
That hath the °seven Spirits of °God, and the

14 Balaam. See Num. 22–25. Josh. 13. 22.
cast, &c. See Num. 25. 1, &c.; 31. 16, &c. 2 Pet. 2. 15. Jude 11.
stumblingblock. Gr. *skandalon*. See Num. 25 (Sept.).
children. Ap. 108. iii.
things . . . idols. Gr. *eidōlothuton*. First occ. Acts 15. 29.
15 which . . . hate. The texts omit, and read "in like manner".
16 will. Omit.
fight = make war. Gr. *polemeō*. Occ. only in Rev. and James. A threat which is not addressed to the church of this age.
against. Gr. *meta*. Ap. 104. xi. 1.
with. Gr. *en*. Ap. 104. viii.
17 to eat of. The texts omit.
hidden. Gr. *kruptō*, as in Col. 3. 3.
manna. See John 6. 58. Cp. Ex. 16. 14, 32–34. Ps. 78. 24, 25.
stone. Gr. *psēphos*. See Acts 26. 10. A white stone was known to the ancients as a "victory" stone.
in. Gr. *epi*. Ap. 104. ix. 3.
new name. Cp. 3. 12. See Isa. 62. 2; 65. 15, and cp. Acts 15. 17. **new.** See Matt. 9. 17.
no man = no one. Gr. *oudeis*.
knoweth. Ap. 132. I. i, as the texts.
saving. Same as else, *v.* 5.
receiveth. As in John 3. 27.
18 Thyatira. A town lying between Pergamos and Sardis. See Acts 16. 14. Another centre of Apollo and Artemis worship.
Son of God. Ap. 98. XV.
feet . . . brass. Prepared for treading down in judgment. See 1. 15. Mal. 4. 3, and fulfilment in 19. 13–15.
19 and. These "ands" form the Fig. *Polysyndeton*. Ap. 6. **charity** = love, as *v.* 4.
service. Ap. 190. II. 1. **faith.** Ap. 150. II. 1.
20 a few things. Omit. **that** = the.
Jezebel. See 1 Kings 16. 30–34; 21. 25. This patroness of Baal-worship will have her sinister antitype in the future.
prophetess. Only here and Luke 2. 36 (Anna) in N.T.
to teach, &c. The texts read "and she teacheth and seduceth".
seduce. Ap. 128. viii. 1.
servants. Ap. 190. I. 2.
21 space = time. Gr. *chronos*. See 6. 11; 20. 3, and Ap. 195. I. 1.
to repent = in order that (Gr. *hina*) she might repent.
and she, &c. The texts read, "and she is not willing to repent of her fornication".
22 will = do. **with.** Ap. 104. xi. 1.
tribulation. Cp. Rom. 2. 8, 9, 16.
their = her, according to some texts.
23 children. Ap. 108. i.
death. I. e. pestilence, as 6. 8; 18. 8.
know. Ap. 132. I. ii.
searcheth, &c. Cp. 1 Kings 8. 39. Jer. 11. 20; 17. 10; 20. 12. **every** = each.
according to. Ap. 104. x. 2.
24 and. Omit.
rest. Ap. 124. 3. **depths.** Cp. 2 Cor. 2. 11.
I will put . . . none. Read "I lay not" (Ap. 105. I).
upon. Ap. 104. ix. 3.
other. See Ap. 124. 1.
25 *already*. Omit. **come** = shall have come.
26 keepeth. See 1. 3.
end. See Matt. 24. 13. Cp. Ap. 125. 1.
power. Ap. 172. 5. **over.** Ap. 104. ix. 1.
nations. Gr *ethnos*. Gen. transl. Gentiles.
27 rule. Lit. "shepherd", as Matt. 2. 6. See Ps. 2. 7–9.
rod = sceptre, as Heb. 1. 8. Gr. *rhabdos*.
as the, &c. See Ps. 2. 9. **even as I** = as I also. **received** = have received. **of.** Gr. *para*. Ap. 104. xii. 1. **Father.** Ap. 98. III. **28 morning star.** Fulfilled 22. 16. See Num. 24. 17, connecting the "star" with Israel and the day of the Lord's judgment.

3. 1 unto = to. **angel . . . church.** See 1. 20. **in.** Ap. 104. viii. **Sardis.** The ancient capital of Lydia. Its commercial activity attracted merchants from all parts of Asia. The remains of a vast temple to Cybele (the "mother of the gods") still exist. **seven Spirits.** See 1. 4. **God.** Ap. 98. I. i. 1.

°seven °stars; I °know thy works, that thou
hast °a name that thou °livest, and art °dead.
2 °Be °watchful, and strengthen °the things
which remain, that °are ready to die: for I
have °not found thy works °perfect before
[1]God.
3 Remember therefore how thou hast received
and heard, and °hold fast, and °repent. °If
therefore thou shalt °not watch, I will come
°on thee °as a thief, and thou shalt °not °know
what hour I will come °upon thee.
4 °Thou hast a few names °even [1]in Sardis
which °have [2]not °defiled their °garments;
and they shall walk °with Me [1]in white: for
they are °worthy.
5 He that °overcometh, °the same shall be
clothed [1]in white raiment; and I will °not
°blot out his name °out of the °book of °life,
°but I will °confess his name before My °Father,
and before His angels.
6 °He that hath an ear, let him hear what the
Spirit saith [1]unto the churches.'
7 And to the [1]angel of the [1]church [1]in °Phila-
delphia write; 'These things saith He That is
°Holy, He That is °True, He That hath the °key
of David, He That openeth, and °no man
shutteth, and shutteth, and °no man openeth;
8 I [1]know thy works: °behold, I have °set
before thee an open door, and [7]no man can
shut it: for thou hast a little °strength, and
°hast kept My °word, and °hast [2]not denied
°My name.
9 [8]Behold, I °will make them °of the °syna-
gogue of °Satan, which say they are °Jews,
and are [2]not, but do lie; [8]behold, I will °make
them to come and °worship before thy feet,
and to [3]know that I °have °loved thee.
10 Because thou hast [8]kept the [8]word of My
patience, I also will [8]keep thee °from the hour
of °temptation, which °shall come °upon all
the °world, to °try them that dwell °upon the
°earth.
11 °Behold, I come quickly: °hold that fast
which thou hast, °that °no man take thy
crown.
12 Him that [5]overcometh will I make a pillar
[1]in the °Temple of My [1]God, and he shall go
°no more out: and I will write °upon him the
name of My [1]God, and the name of the city of
My [1]God, *which is* °new Jerusalem, which
cometh down [5]out of °heaven °from My [1]God:
and *I will write upon him* My °new name.
13 [6]He that hath an ear, let him hear what
the Spirit saith [1]unto the churches.'
14 And [1]unto the [1]angel of the [1]church °of
the Laodiceans write; 'These things saith
°the Amen, the °faithful and [7]true °Witness,
the °beginning of the creation of [1]God;
15 I [1]know thy works, that thou art neither
cold nor hot: I would thou wert cold or hot.

seven, &c. See 1. 20. **stars.** See 1. 16.
know. Ap. 132. I. i.
a name, &c. Not suited for this dispensation of grace, for Christ's people now live "in Him". We who were dead are now alive in Christ.
livest. See Ap. 170. 1. **dead.** Ap. 139. 2.
2 Be=Become. **watchful.** See Matt. 24. 42.
the . . . remain=the remaining (things). Ap. 124. 3.
are=were, with the texts. **not.** Ap. 105. I.
perfect. Ap. 125. 7. Only here and 6. 11 in Rev.
3 hold fast. Gr. *tēreō.* Same as "keep" in 1. 3.
repent. See 2. 5. **If.** Ap. 118. 1. b.
not. Ap. 105. II. **on thee.** The texts omit.
as, &c. See 16. 15. 1 Thess. 5. 2. 2 Pet. 3. 10.
not. Ap. 105. III.
know. Ap. 132. I. ii. These words are not addressed to the members of the "church which is His body" (Eph. 1. 22, 23). See 2 Thess. 2. 1. 1 Tim. 3. 16. We do not "watch" for the "thief", but "wait" for the Lord. **upon.** Ap. 104. ix. 3.
4 Thou. The texts read "But thou".
even. The texts omit. **have, &c.**=defiled not.
defiled. Gr. *molunō.* Only here; 14. 4. 1 Cor. 8. 7. The noun occ. only in 2 Cor. 7. 1.
garments. Gr. *himation.* First of seven occ. (see Ap. 197) in Rev.
with. Ap. 104. xi. 1. **worthy.** See Ap. 197. 6.
5 overcometh. See 2. 7.
the same. The texts read "thus".
not. Ap. 105. III.
blot out. Occ. 7. 17; 21. 4 (wipe away). Acts 3. 19. Col. 2. 14.
out of. Ap. 104. vii. **book, &c.** See Phil. 4. 3.
life. Ap. 170. 1. **but**=and.
confess, &c. See Matt. 10. 32.
Father. Ap. 98. III.
6 He, &c. See 2. 7.
7 Philadelphia. About thirty miles south-east of Sardis. Very little known of it beyond a few references in Pliny, but the Greek name indicates a Macedonian population.
Holy=The Holy One. See 4. 8. Cp. Hos. 11. 9, &c. The Gr. *hagios* occ. twenty-six times in Rev. See Ap. 197. 6. **True.** Ap. 175. 2.
key of David. See Isa. 22. 22.
no man=no one. Gr. *oudeis.*
8 behold. Ap. 133. I. 2. **set**=given.
strength. App. 172. 1; 176. 1.
hast kept=didst keep. Same word as "hold fast", *v.* 3. **word.** Ap. 121. 10.
hast not denied=didst not deny.
My name. In opposition to confessing (see 2. 13) the name of the beast, 13. 17; 14. 9, 11, 12.
9 will make=give. **of.** Gr. *ek.* Ap. 104. vii.
synagogue, &c. See 2. 9.
Satan. Ap. 19, and see 2. 9. **Jews.** See 2. 9.
make, i. e. compel.
worship. Gr. *proskuneō.* Ap. 137. 1. Occ. twenty-four times (Ap. 10) in Rev. Twelve times connected with worship of God, eleven times with worship of Satan and the beast, and here. See Ap. 197. 6.
have. Omit. **loved.** Ap. 135. I. 1.
10 from. Gr. *ek.* Ap. 104. vii.
temptation=trial. Gr. *peirasmos.* Only occurrence in Rev. **shall**=is about to.
upon. Ap. 104. ix. 1. **world.** Ap. 129. 3.
try=test. Gr. *peirazō.* Here, and 2. 2, 10.

upon. Ap. 104. ix. 1. **earth.** Ap. 129. 4. Cp. Zeph. 1. 14–18. **11 Behold.** Omit. **hold . . . fast.** Same Gr. word as 2. 1, 13, 14, 15, 25, not as *v.* 3. **that**=in order that. Gr. *hina.* **no man**=no one. Gr. *mēdeis.* These words do not relate to such as through grace are perfect "in Him". See Rom. 8. 38, 39.
12 Temple=sanctuary. Gr. *naos.* See Matt. 23. 16 and Ap. 88. 1. **no.** Ap. 105. III. **upon.** Ap. 104. ix. 3. **new Jerusalem.** See 21. 2, 3, 10. Cp. Ps. 48. 1, 2, 8, 9. Ezek. 48. 35. See Ap. 88 and Ap. 197. 4. **new, new.** Gr. *kainos.* See Matt. 9. 17. **heaven.** See Matt. 6. 9. Occ. fifty-two times in Rev., always in sing. save 12. 12. **from.** Ap. 104. iv. **new name.** See 14. 1; 22. 4. Isa. 62. 2; 65. 15. Contrast the name *branded* on the worshippers of the beast, 13. 16; 14. 11; 19. 20; 20. 4. **14 of, &c.**=in (Gr. *en*) Laodicea (an important city of Phrygia, a few miles west of Colosse. Rebuilt by Antiochus II, and named after his wife, Laodice). **the Amen.** A Hebrew word transliterated. See 2 Cor. 1. 20 and p. 1511. **faithful.** Ap. 150. III. **Witness.** See p. 1511. **beginning.** Ap. 172. 6. Cp. Prov. 8. 22–31. Col. 1. 15–19.

16 So then because thou art °lukewarm, and
neither cold nor hot, I °will °spue thee [5]out of
My mouth.
17 Because thou sayest, "I am rich, and
increased with goods, and have need of
°nothing;" and °knowest [2]not that thou art
°wretched, and miserable, and °poor, and
blind, and naked:
18 I counsel thee to °buy °of Me gold tried
°in °the °fire, [11]that thou mayest be rich; and
white raiment, [11]that thou mayest °be clothed,
and *that* the shame of thy nakedness °do not
appear; and anoint thine eyes with eyesalve,
[11]that thou mayest °see.
19 As many as I °love, I °rebuke and chasten:
be zealous therefore, and [3]repent.
20 [8]Behold, I °stand °at the door, and °knock:
°if °any man hear My voice, and open the
door, I will come in °to him, and will °sup
[4]with him, and he [4]with Me.
21 To him that [5]overcometh will I grant to
sit [4]with Me [1]in My throne, even as I also
[5]overcame, and °am set down [4]with My
[5]Father [1]in His throne.
22 [6]He that hath an ear, let him hear what
the Spirit saith [1]unto the churches.'"

i 𝔐¹ A
4 °After °this I °looked, and °behold, a door
°*was* opened °in °heaven: and the °first
voice which I heard *was* as °it were of a
trumpet °talking °with me, which said,
"Come up hither, and I will shew thee °things
°which must °be °hereafter."
2 And immediately I was °in the °Spirit:
and [1]behold, a throne was set [1]in [1]heaven,
and *One* °sat °on the throne.
3 And He That sat was to °look upon like a
°jasper and a °sardine stone: and *there was* a
°rainbow round about the throne, °in sight like
°unto an °emerald.
4 And round about the throne *were* °four and
twenty °seats: and °upon the °seats °I saw
°four and twenty °elders sitting, clothed [1]in
white raiment; and °they had °on their heads
°crowns of gold.
5 And °out of the throne °proceeded lightnings and thunderings and voices: and *there*
were °seven °lamps of fire °burning before the
throne, which are the seven °Spirits of °God.
6 And before the throne °*there was* a sea of
glass like °unto crystal: and [1]in the midst of
the throne, and °round about the throne,
°*were* four °beasts full of °eyes before and behind.

16 lukewarm. Gr. *chliaros.* Only here.
will = am about to.
spue. Gr. *emeō.* Only here. Occ. Isa. 19. 14 (Sept.).
17 nothing. Gr. *oudeis.*
knowest. Ap. 132. I. i.
wretched = the wretched one. See Rom. 7. 24, and cp. Hos. 2. 11; 5. 15.
poor. Ap. 127. 1.
18 buy. The members of the church of this dispensation have nothing to buy and nothing to pay with; our salvation is the free-grace gift of God.
of. Gr. *para.* Ap. 104. xii. 1.
in. Gr. *ek.* Ap. 104. vii. **the.** Omit.
fire. Cp. Hag. 2. 8. Zech. 13. 9. Mal. 3. 3.
be clothed = clothe thyself.
do not appear = be not (Ap. 105. II) made manifest (Ap. 106. I. v). Cp. 16. 15.
see. Ap. 133. I. 5.
19 love. Ap. 135. I. 2. This is preceded by Gr. *ean* (Ap. 118. 1. a). Cp. Isa. 43. 4; &c.
rebuke = convict. Gr. *elenchō.* See John 16. 8.
20 stand. Lit. have taken my station.
at. Gr. *epi.* Ap. 104. ix. 3.
knock. The call to the wedding feast (19. 9), to which the parables pointed, e.g. Luke 12. 35-38—"when He cometh and knocketh". The popular belief that the Lord is ever knocking at the hearts of sinners is a distortion of Scripture akin to blasphemy.
if. Ap. 118. 1. b.
any man. Ap. 123. 3. **to.** Ap. 104. xv. 3.
sup, &c. A gracious promise to His servants (see 1. 1), not to the church of this dispensation. See Luke 12. 37.
21 am set down = sat down. See Acts 2. 33, 34. Eph. 1. 20, 21. Heb. 1. 3; 8. 1. The Lord now stands (ch. 1), and is about to come down in judgment.

𝔐¹ (p. 1883). **4. 1—5. 14. THE FIRST VISION IN HEAVEN.** (*Alternation.*)

𝔐¹ | A | 4. 1-8-. The throne, the elders, and the *zōa.*
| B | -8-11. The utterances of the *zōa* and the elders. Theme: *creation.*
| *A* | 5. 1-7. The throne and the book: the Lion and the Lamb.
| *B* | 8-14. The newsong of the *zōa* and the elders. Other heavenly utterances. Theme: *redemption.*

4. 1 After. Ap. 104. xi. 2.
this = these things, as 1. 19.
looked. Ap. 133. I. 1.
behold. Ap. 133. I. 2.
***was* opened.** I.e. already opened.
in. Ap. 104. viii. **heaven.** See 3. 12.
first. Or "former". See 1. 10. **it were.** Omit.
talking. Ap. 121. 7.
with. Gr. *meta.* Ap. 104. xi. 1.
things = what things. **which.** Omit.
be = come to pass.
hereafter = after (Gr. *meta,* above) these things.
2 was = became, came to be. See 1. 9, 10.
in the Spirit. I.e. in or by the power of the Spirit, as 1. 10.

Spirit. Ap. 101. II. 3. **sat** = sitting. **on.** Ap. 104. ix. 3. **3 look upon.** Cp. Ap. 133. I. 8. **jasper** = jasper stone. According to Pliny, this stone was translucent. **sardine stone** = sardius stone. A precious stone from Sardis, red in colour. **rainbow.** Gr. *iris.* Only here and 10. 1. In Gen. 9. 13; Ezek. 1. 28, &c., the Sept. uses *toxon,* bow, for the Heb. *ḳesheth.* **in sight.** Same words as "to look upon", above. **unto** = to. **emerald.** Only here. A kindred word in 21. 19, and in Exod. 28. 18 and 39. 8 (Sept.). **4 four and twenty.** See Ap. 10 and Ap. 197. 6. **seats** = thrones, as *v.* 2. See 1. 4. **upon, on.** Ap. 104. ix. 3. **I saw.** The texts omit. **elders.** Gr. *presbuteros.* These are evidently heavenly beings, "a pattern" after which David arranged his twenty-four courses of the sons of Aaron (1 Chron. 24. 3-5). **they had.** The texts omit. **crowns of gold.** The only other wearer is the Son of Man (14. 14), a fact which proves the exalted station of these "elders". **5 out of.** Ap. 104. vii. **proceeded** = proceed. **seven.** See Ap. 197. **lamps.** Ap. 130. 6. See John 18. 3. **burning.** Gr. *kaiō.* See John 5. 35. **Spirits.** Ap. 101. II. 11. **God.** Ap. 98. I. i. 1. **6 *there was* . . . glass.** The texts read "as it were a glassy sea". **unto** = to. **round about.** Gr. *kuklō.* In Rev. only here and 7. 11. Occ. Mark 3. 34. ***were.*** Omit. **beasts** = living ones, or living creatures (as Heb. 13. 11, first occ.). Gr. *zōon.* Occ. twenty times (Ap. 10). Not the word in chs. 13 and 17. These *zōa* are the cherubim of Gen. 3. 24. Ezek. 1. 5-14. Cp. Ezek. 10. 20. They are distinguished from angels (5. 8, 11). These *zōa* speak of creation and of redemption also. **eyes.** See Ezek. 1. 8; 10. 12.

7 And the first [6]beast *was* like a lion, and the second [6]beast like a calf, and the third [6]beast °had a face as a °man, and the fourth [6]beast *was* like a flying eagle.

8 And the four [6]beasts had each of them °six wings about *him;* °and *they were* full of [6]eyes within: and they rest °not day and night, saying,

B °"Holy, holy, holy, °LORD [5]God °Almighty, Which was, and is, and is to come."

9 And when °those [6]beasts °give °glory and honour and thanks to Him °That sat °on the throne, Who °liveth °for ever and ever,

10 The four and twenty [4]elders °fall down before Him That [9]sat [9]on the throne, and °worship Him That [9]liveth [9]for ever and ever, and °cast their crowns before the throne, saying,

11 "Thou art worthy, °O LORD, to receive °glory and °honour and °power: for Thou °hast created all things, and °for Thy °pleasure they °are and were created."

A **5** And I °saw °in the right hand of Him That °sat °on the throne a °book written within and on the °backside, °sealed with °seven seals.

2 And I [1]saw a °strong angel °proclaiming °with a °loud voice, "Who is °worthy to open the [1]book, and to °loose the seals thereof?"

3 And °no man °in °heaven, °nor °in °earth, °neither °under the °earth, was able to open the [1]book, °neither to °look thereon.

4 And I °wept much, because [3]no man was found [2]worthy to open °and to read the book, [-3]neither to [3]look thereon.

5 And one °of the °elders saith °unto me, [4]"Weep °not: °behold, the °Lion °of the °tribe of Juda, the Root of David, °hath °prevailed to open the [1]book, and °to loose the [1]seven seals thereof."

6 And I °beheld, °and lo, [3-]in the midst of the throne and of the four °beasts, and [3-]in the midst of the [5]elders, °stood a °Lamb as °it had been slain, having [1]seven °horns and [1]seven eyes, which are the [1]seven Spirits of °God °sent forth °into all the [3]earth.

7 And He came and °took °the book °out of the right hand of Him That [1]sat °upon the throne.

B 8 And when He °had taken the [1]book, the four [6]beasts and four *and* twenty [5]elders fell down before the [6]Lamb, having °every one of them °harps, and golden °vials full of °odours, which °are the °prayers of °saints.

9 And they sung a °new song, saying, "Thou art [2]worthy to take the [1]book, and to open the seals thereof: for Thou wast slain, and °hast °redeemed °us to [6]God °by Thy blood [7]out of every °kindred, and tongue, and people, and nation;

10 And °hast made °us °unto our [6]God

7 had = having, as the texts.
man. Ap. 123. 1.
8 six. See Ap. 197. 6. and *they were* = are.
not. Ap. 105. I.
Holy, &c. The first of the seventeen (Ap. 10) heavenly utterances in Rev. Here, 4. 8; 4. 11; 5. 9, 10; 5. 12; 5. 13; 5. -14- (Amen); 7. 10; 7. 12; 11. 15; 11. 17; 12. 10-12; 14. 13; 15. -3; 19. -1-3; 19. -4; 19. 5; 19. -6, 7.
Holy . . . holy. God's holiness proclaimed, prior to judgment. See Pss. 93; 97; 99, and Isa. 6. 3. Cp. Num. 6. 24-26.
LORD. Ap. 98. VI. i. *β*. 1. B. b.
Almighty. See 1. 8.
9 those = the. give = shall give.
glory. See p. 1511 and Ap. 197. 6.
That sat = the *One* sitting.
on. Ap. 104. ix. 1. liveth. Ap. 170. 1.
for ever, &c. Ap. 151. II. A. ii. 9. a. See 1. 6.
10 fall = shall fall.
worship = shall worship. Ap. 137. 1.
cast = shall cast.
11 O LORD. The texts read "our LORD (Ap. 98. VI. *β*. 1. A. b) and our God" (Ap. 98. I. i. 1).
glory, honour, power. The texts place article "the" before each.
glory, as *v.* 9. power. App. 172. 1; 176. 1.
hast created = didst create. Gr. *ktizō*. In Rev. only here and 10. 6.
for. Ap. 104. v. 2. pleasure. Ap. 102. 2.
are. The texts read "were".

5. 1 saw. Ap. 133. I. 1.
in = upon. Gr. *epi*. Ap. 104. ix. 3.
sat. See 4. 2.
on. Gr. *epi*. Ap. 104. ix. 1. book. See 1. 11.
backside = back. Like a papyrus sheet.
sealed = having been sealed up. Gr. *katasphragizō*, intensive of *sphragizō*, to affix a seal. Only here. Occ. Job 9. 7; 37. 7 (Sept.).
seven. See App. 10 and 197. 6.
2 strong = mighty. Gr. *ischuros*. Cp. Ap. 172. 3.
proclaiming. Ap. 121. 1.
with. Gr. *en*. Ap. 104. viii. loud = great.
worthy. See Ap. 197. 6.
loose. See *v.* 5; 9. 14, 15; 20. 3. 7.
3 no man = no one. Gr. *oudeis*. in. Ap. 104. viii.
heaven = the heaven. See 3. 12.
in. Ap. 104. ix. 1.
nor, neither. Gr. *oude*. earth. Ap. 129. 4.
under. Gr. *hupokatō*. Occ. nine times (four in Rev.).
neither. Gr. *oute*. look. Ap. 133. I. 5.
4 wept = was weeping.
and to read. Texts omit.
5 of. Ap. 104. vii.
elders. See 4. 4. unto = to.
not. Ap. 105. II.
behold. Ap. 133. I. 2. Lion. See Gen. 49. 8-10.
of = which is of (Ap. 104. vii).
tribe. Gr. *phulē*. Same as "kindred", *v.* 9.
hath. Omit.
prevailed. I.e. at Calvary. Same word as "overcome" in chs. 2 and 3.
to loose. The texts omit.
6 beheld. Same word as "saw", *vv.* 1, 2.
and lo. Omit. beasts. The *zōa* of 4. 6.
stood . . . Lamb = a Lamb standing.
Lamb = little Lamb. Gr. *arnion*. See John 21. 15 and Ap. 197. 6. it had = having.
horns. A symbol indicating His power. Cp. 2 Sam. 22. 3; &c. Spirits. See 1. 4. God. Ap. 98. I. i. 1. sent forth. Ap. 174. 1. into. Ap. 104. vi.
7 took = hath taken. the book. The texts read "it". out of. Ap. 104. vii. upon. Ap. 104. ix. 1.
8 had taken = took. every . . . them = each one. harps. The texts read "a harp". Gr. *kithara*. vials = bowls. Gr. *phialē*. Word characteristic of Rev. Occ. twelve times (Ap. 10). odours = incense. Gr. *thumiama*. are. I. e. symbolize. prayers. Ap. 134. II. 2. saints = the saints. Gr. *hagios*. See Acts 9. 13. **9** new song. See 14. 3. new. See Matt. 9. 17. hast redeemed = didst purchase. redeemed. Gr. *agorazō*. Always "buy", save here and 14. 3, 4 (redeem). us. Most texts omit "us", and find object in *v.* 10, "them". by. Gr. *en*. Ap. 104. viii. kindred = tribe, *v.* 5. **10** hast made = madest. us. See *v.* 9. unto = to, or for.

°kings and °priests, and °we shall reign [1]on
the [3]earth."
11 And I [6]beheld, and I heard the voice of
many angels round about the throne and the
[6]beasts and the [5]elders; and the number of
them was °ten thousand times ten thousand,
and thousands of thousands;
12 Saying with a °loud voice, "Worthy is
the [6]Lamb That was slain to receive °power,
°and riches, °and wisdom, °and °strength, °and
honour, °and °glory, °and blessing."
13 And every °creature which is [3]in [3]heaven,
and °on the [3]earth, and [3]under the [3]earth, and
°such as are °in the sea, and all that are [3]in
them, heard I saying, °"Blessing, and honour,
and [12]glory, and °power, *be* [5]unto Him That
sitteth [7]upon the throne, and [5]unto the [6]Lamb
°for ever and ever."
14 And the four [6]beasts said, "Amen."
And the °four *and* twenty [5]elders fell down
and °worshipped °Him That liveth for ever
and ever.

i. E[1] A[1] 6 And I °saw when the °Lamb opened one
°of the °seals, and I heard, °as it were the
noise of thunder, one °of the four °beasts saying, "Come °and see."
2 And I [1]saw, and °behold, a white horse:
and °he that sat °on him had a °bow; and a
°crown was °given °unto him: and he °went
forth °conquering, and to °conquer.
B[1] 3 And when He °had opened the second seal,
I heard the second [1]beast °say, "Come [1]and
see."
4 And there °went out °another horse *that
was* red: and °*power* was given to him that
sat °thereon to take °peace °from the °earth,
and °that they should kill one another: and
there was given [2]unto him a great sword.
5 And when He had opened the third seal,
I heard the third [1]beast [3]say, "Come [1]and
see." And I °beheld, and °lo, a °black horse;
and he that sat [2]on him had a °pair of balances
°in his hand.
6 And I °heard a °voice [5]in the midst of the
four [1]beasts [3]say, "A °measure of wheat for
a °penny, and three °measures of barley for
a °penny; and °*see* thou hurt °not the °oil and
the wine."
7 And when He had opened the fourth seal,
I heard the [6]voice of the fourth [1]beast [3]say,
"Come [1]and see."
8 And I °looked, and [2]behold, a °pale horse:
°and his name that sat °on him was °Death,
and °Hell followed °with him. And °power
was given [2]unto them °over the °fourth part
of the [4]earth, to kill °with sword, and °with

kings = a kingdom, with all the texts.
priests. I. e. a priestly kingdom. See 1. 6 and Heb. 12. 28.
we. All texts read "they".
11 ten . . . thousand = myriads of myriads. Hebraism for countless numbers. See Dan. 7. 10.
12 loud = great.
power = the power. Ap. 172. 1.
and. The repeated "ands" in *vv.* 12, 13 form a remarkable *Polysyndeton* (Ap. 6). In *v.* 12 the sevenfold (Ap. 10) ascription is noticed. Cp. 4. 11.
strength. Ap. 172. 3. **glory.** See p. 1511.
13 creature = created thing. Gr. *ktisma*. Only here; 8. 9. 1 Tim. 4. 4. Jas. 1. 18. **on.** Ap. 104. ix. 1.
such as are. Omit.
in. The texts read "on" (Ap. 104. ix. 1).
Blessing, &c. The fourfold (Ap. 10) ascription by the whole creation. Prefix the def. art. to each term.
power. Ap. 172. 2.
for . . . ever. As 1. 6.
14 four *and* twenty. The texts omit.
worshipped. See 3. 9.
Him . . . ever. The texts omit.

E[1] (p. 1883). **6. 1–7. 8.** THE SIX SEALS AND THE SEALING. (*Alternation.*)

E[1] A[1] | 6. 1, 2. The false Christ going forth to make war on the saints. (1st seal.) Matt. 24. 4, 5.
B[1] | 6. 3–8. Judgments on him and his followers. (2nd, 3rd, and 4th seals.) Matt. 24. 6, 7.
A[2] | 6. 9–11. The effects of the war with the saints. Their martyrdom. (5th seal.) Matt. 24. 8–28.
B[2] | 6. 12–17. Judgments on him and his followers. (6th seal.) Matt. 24. 29, 30. Question, "Who shall be able to stand?"
A[3] | 7. 1–8. Answer to question, by the sealing of 144,000, enabling them to stand in the judgment. Matt. 24. 31.

6. 1 saw. Ap. 133. I. 1. **Lamb.** See 5. 6.
of. Ap. 104. vii.
seals. Read "seven seals", with texts.
as . . . saying. Read, "one of the four *zōa* saying as with a voice of thunder". **beasts.** See 4. 6.
and see. All the texts omit.
2 behold. Ap. 133. I. 2.
he that sat, &c. Not to be identified with the white horse and rider of 19. 11, for here is the beginning of the series of terrible judgments. See *v.* 12 and the order of events in Matt. 24. 4–28.
on him = thereon. Gr. *epi* (Ap. 104. ix. 3) *auton*.
bow. Gr. *toxon*. Only here in N. T. Cp. 4. 3.
crown. See Ap. 197. 6.
given. The giver not mentioned. See 13. 5, 7. Luke 4. 6. 2 Thess. 2. 3–9.
unto = to.
went. Or "came", see *v.* 1.
conquering, &c. Lit. conquering and in order that (Gr. *hina*) he may conquer. The verb is the same as "overcame" in 2. 7, &c.
3 had. Omit. **say** = saying, *v.* 1.
4 went out. Or "came forth".
another. Ap. 124. 1.
***power*.** Read "it".
thereon = on him, as *v.* 2.

peace = the peace. **from.** Gr. *ek*. Ap. 104. vii. **earth.** Ap. 129. 4. **that** = in order that. Gr. *hina*. **5 beheld** = saw, *v.* 1. **lo** = behold, *v.* 2. **black.** Signifying famine. See Lam. 4. 4–8, &c. **pair, &c.** = balance. **in.** Ap. 104. viii. **6 heard.** The texts add "as it were". **voice.** Same as noise, *v.* 1. **measure.** Gr. *choenix*. Ap. 51. III. 3 (11), (10). **penny.** Ap. 51. I. 4. Bread by weight means scarcity (cp. Ezek. 4. 10, 16, 17). A *denarius* was a day's wage (Matt. 20. 2), and a *choenix* of corn was a slave's daily ration, an amount usually purchaseable for one-eighth of a *denarius*. ***see*.** Omit, and read the clause "and hurt thou not" (Ap. 105. II). **oil . . . wine.** By Fig. *Metalēpsis* this may point to special protection of the elect in famine times. See 12. 14. Zech. 13. 8. Rom. 3. 1, 2; 9. 4, 5. **8 looked** = saw, as *v.* 1. **pale** = livid. Gr. *chlōros*; in 8. 7; 9. 4. Mark 6. 39, rendered "green". **and . . . Death.** Lit. and the one sitting on (Gr. *epanō*, first occ. Matt. 2. 9, "over") him, the name to him (is) Death. **Death.** By *Metonymy* (*of Effect*) (Ap. 6) = pestilence. Famine is invariably followed by pestilence. Here, Death and *Hadēs* are personified. Cp. 9. 11. **Hell.** Ap. 131. II. **with.** Ap. 104. xi. 1. **power.** Ap. 172. 5. **over.** Ap. 104. ix. 3. **fourth.** See Ap. 10. **with.** Gr. *en*. Ap. 104. viii.

hunger, and °with death, and °with the °beasts
of the [4]earth.

A[2] 9 And when He [3]had opened the fifth seal, I
[1]saw under the °altar the °souls of them that
°were slain °for the °word of °God, and °for
the °testimony which they held:
10 And they cried with a °loud °voice, saying,
"How long, O °Lord, °holy and °true, dost
Thou °not °judge and °avenge our blood °on
them that dwell °on the [4]earth?"
11 And °white robes °were given [2]unto °every
one of them; and it was said [2]unto them, [4]that
they should rest °yet for a little season, until
their °fellowservants also and their brethren,
°that should be killed °as they *were*, should be
°fulfilled.

B[2] 12 And I [5]beheld when He had opened the
°sixth seal, and, °lo, there °was a great
°earthquake; and the sun became black as
sackcloth of hair, and the °moon became °as
blood;
13 And the °stars of °heaven fell °unto the
[4]earth, even as a fig tree casteth her untimely
figs, when she is shaken °of a °mighty wind.
14 And the [13]heaven °departed as a °scroll
°when it is rolled together; and every mountain
and island were °moved °out of their
places.
15 And °the kings of the [4]earth, and the
°great °men, and the rich °men, and the chief
captains, and the °mighty °men, and every
°bondman, and °every free °man, hid themselves
°in the dens and °in the rocks of the
mountains;
16 And °said to the mountains and rocks,
°"Fall °on us, and hide us °from the °face of
Him That sitteth °on the throne, and °from
the °wrath of the °Lamb:
17 For the °great day of His [16]wrath is come;
and °who °shall be able to stand?"

A[3] **7** °And °after °these things I °saw four
angels standing °on the four corners of
the °earth, °holding the °four winds of the
°earth, °that the wind should °not blow °on
the °earth, °nor °on the sea, °nor °on °any
°tree.
2 And I [1]saw °another angel ascending °from
the °east, having °the seal of the °living
°God: and he cried with a °loud voice to the

with, fourth occ. Gr. *hupo*. Ap. 104. xviii. 1.
beasts = wild beasts. Gr. *thērion*. Occ. thirty-eight times in Rev., thirty-seven of "the beast". And here it may indicate the nations supporting "the beast". See Dan. 7 for the Divine description of "the powers" as "wild beasts".
9 altar. Gr. *thusiastērion*. First of eight occ.
souls. App. 110. II; 170. 3. Cp. Ap. 13.
were = had been.
for. Ap. 104. v. 2. word. Ap. 121. 10.
God. Ap. 98. I. i. 1.
testimony. See John 1. 7.
10 loud = great.
voice. As Abel's blood was said to cry (Gen. 4. 10).
Lord. Ap. 98. XIV. ii.
holy = the Holy.
true = the True. Ap. 175. 2.
not. Ap. 105. I. judge. Ap. 122. 1.
avenge. See Deut. 32. 43. Luke 18. 3. A call consistent with the day of judgment, not with the present day of grace.
on. *apo*. Ap. 104. iv, but the texts read *ek*.
on. Ap. 104. ix. 1.
11 white robes = a white robe. See 7. 9 and Mark 12. 38.
were = was. every one = each one.
yet for, &c. = yet a little time (Gr. *chronos*. Ap. 195).
fellowservants. Gr. *sundoulos*. Occ. only in Matt., Col., and Rev. See Ap. 190. I. 2.
that should be = that are about to be.
as they *were* = even as they also (*had been*).
fulfilled. Ap. 125. 7.
12 sixth seal. The signs immediately preceding the Advent of ch. 19. Matt. 24 covers exactly the period of the six seals, thus:—

MATT. 24.	THE SEALS.	REV. 6.
4, 5.	1st. The false Messiah.	1, 2.
6, 7–.	2nd. Wars.	3, 4.
–7–.	3rd. Famines.	5, 6.
–7.	4th. Pestilences.	7, 8.
8–28.	5th. Martyrdoms.	9–11.
29, 30.	6th. Signs in heaven of Advent.	12–17.

lo. Omit. was = came to be.
earthquake. Gr. *seismos*. See Hag. 2. 6, 7, 21, 22. Zech. 14. 5. Matt. 8. 24. Heb. 12. 26. Cp. Ps. 46.
moon. The texts add "whole", i. e. the full moon.
as blood. I. e. as to colour.
13 stars, &c. See 9. 1 and cp. Dan. 8. 10, &c.
heaven. See 3. 12. unto. Gr. *eis*. Ap. 104. vi.
of. Ap. 104. xviii. 1.
mighty = great, as *vv*. 4, 10, 17.
14 departed = parted asunder. See Acts 15. 39.
scroll. See 1. 11.

when, &c. = rolling itself up. moved = removed, as 2. 5. out of. Ap. 104. vii. **15** the kings of the earth. See Ap. 197. 6. As regards the social fabric, the present conditions will exist when the Lord comes. great men. Gr. *megistanes*. Only here; 18. 23. Mk. 6. 21. men, man = ones, one. mighty. Gr. *ischuros* (with the texts). As in 19. 18. Cp. Ap. 172. 3. bondman. Ap. 190. I. 2. every. Omit. in. Gr. *eis*. Ap. 104. vi. **16** said = they say. Fall, &c. See Hos. 10. 8, and cp. Luke 23. 30. on. Gr. *epi*. Ap. 104. ix. 3. from. Ap. 104. iv. face. Gr. *prosōpon*. Same word "presence" in 2 Thess. 1. 9. on. Gr. *epi*. Ap. 104. ix. 1. wrath. Gr. *orgē*. Only once in N. T. is "wrath" attributed to the Lord; see Mark 3. 5. Elsewhere it pertains to God. "Wrath of the Lamb"! Divine love spurned and rejected turning to judicial "wrath" and destruction. Lamb. In 5. 5 the Lamb-Lion; here, the Lion-Lamb. **17** great day. All preceding judgments lead up to this. See Joel 2. 11, 31. Zeph. 1. 14. Cp. Jude 6. who, &c. This solemn question now to be answered by the sealing of 144,000 specially protected and blessed ones. shall be = is.

7. 1 And. Some texts omit. after. Ap. 104. xi. 2. these things. The texts read "this". saw. Ap. 133. I. 1. on (first and fourth occ.). Gr. *epi*. Ap. 104. ix. 3. earth. Ap. 129. 4. holding = holding fast. Gr. *krateō*. Cp. Ap. 172. 2. four winds. See Jer. 49. 36. Dan. 7. 2; 8. 8; 11. 4. Zech. 2. 6; 6. 5. that = in order that. Gr. *hina*. not. Ap. 105. II. on (second and third occ.). Gr. *epi*. Ap. 104. ix. 1. nor, nor. Gr. *mēte*. See Ap. 105. II. any. Ap. 123. 3. tree. Gr. *dendron*. Not as in 2. 7. **2** another. Ap. 124. 1. from. Ap. 104. iv. east. Lit. sunrising. the = a. living. Ap. 170. 1. God. Ap. 98. I. i. 1. loud = great.

four angels, to whom it was given to °hurt the [1]earth and the sea,

3 Saying, [2]"Hurt [1]not the [1]earth, °neither the sea, [1]nor the [1]trees, till we °have °sealed the °servants of our [2]God °in their foreheads."

4 And I heard the number of °them which were [3]sealed: *and there were* [3]sealed °an hundred *and* forty *and* four thousand °of all the tribes of the °children of Israel.

5 [4]Of the tribe of Juda °*were* sealed °twelve thousand. [4]Of the tribe of Reuben °*were* sealed twelve thousand. [4]Of the tribe of Gad °*were* sealed twelve thousand.

6 [4]Of the tribe of Aser [5]*were* sealed twelve thousand. [4]Of the tribe of Nepthalim [5]*were* sealed twelve thousand. [4]Of the tribe of Manasses [5]*were* sealed twelve thousand.

7 [4]Of the tribe of Simeon [5]*were* sealed twelve thousand. [4]Of the tribe of Levi [5]*were* sealed twelve thousand. [4]Of the tribe of Issachar [5]*were* sealed twelve thousand.

8 [4]Of the tribe of Zabulon [5]*were* sealed twelve thousand. [4]Of the tribe of Joseph [5]*were* sealed twelve thousand. [4]Of the tribe of Benjamin *were* sealed twelve thousand.

ii. 𝔥² A 9 °After this I °beheld, and, °lo, a great °multitude, which °no man could number, [4]of all nations, and °kindreds, and °people, and tongues, °stood before the throne, and before the Lamb, clothed with white robes, and °palms °in their hands;

10 And °cried with a [2]loud voice, saying, °"Salvation to our [2]God Which sitteth °upon the throne, and °unto the Lamb."

11 And all the angels °stood round about the throne, and *about* the elders and the four beasts, and fell before the throne °on their faces, and °worshipped [2]God,

12 Saying, °"Amen: °Blessing, and glory, and wisdom, and thanksgiving, and honour, and power, and might, *be* [10]unto our [2]God °for ever and ever. °Amen."

B 13 And one [4]of the elders °answered, saying [10]unto me, °"What are these which are arrayed in white robes? and whence came they?"

14 And I said [10]unto him, °"Sir, thou °knowest." And he said to me, "These are they °which came °out of °great tribulation, and °have °washed their robes, and made them white °in the blood of the Lamb.

B 15 °Therefore are they before the throne of [2]God, and °serve Him °day and night [9]in His °Temple: and He That sitteth °on the throne shall °dwell °among them.

16 **They shall hunger °no more, °neither thirst any more; °neither shall the sun °light [11]on them, °nor any °heat.**

17 **For the Lamb Which is °in the midst of the throne °shall °feed them, and °shall lead them °unto °living fountains of waters: and [2]God °shall wipe away all tears °from their eyes."**

---

hurt. Gr. *adikeō*, as 2. 11.

3 neither. Same as nor, *v.* 1. **have** = shall have.

sealed. See Ap. 197. 6. Cp. 9. 4; 14. 1; 22. 4, and see 13. 16; 14. 9. This sealing is visible and protects the elect (Matt. 24. 31) of Israel during the tribulation, marking them off as worshippers of the true God.

servants. Ap. 190. I. 2.

in = upon. Ap. 104. ix. 1.

4 them which were = the.

an hundred, &c. See Ap. 197. 6.

of. Ap. 104. vii. **children.** Ap. 108. iii.

5 *were* sealed. Omit. **twelve.** See Ap. 197. 6.

5–8. These *vv.* foretell a literal sealing of a literal number of people taken from these tribes of Israel. No Jew now knows for certain his tribe, but the Divine sealers know. 144,000 (Ap. 10) are set apart for God's purposes. Dan and Ephraim are omitted, Levi and Joseph taking their places. For the reason, see Lev. 24. 10–16. Deut. 29. 18–21. Judg. 18. 2–31. 1 Kings 12. 26–33. Hos. 4. 17. Their restoration to earthly inheritance is shown (Ezek. 48), the reason being given in Rom. 11. 29.

𝔥² (p. 1883). **7. 9—8. 6.** THE SECOND VISION IN HEAVEN. (*Introversion.*)

𝔥² | A | 7. 9–12. The heavenly voices and utterances.
 B | 13, 14. The great multitude. Whence they came.
 B | 15–17. The great multitude. Where they are.
 A | 8. 1–6. The heavenly silence and activities (seventh seal).

9 After this. As 1. 19.

beheld. As *v.* 1 (saw). **lo.** Ap. 133. I. 2.

multitude. These are converts during the great tribulation. **no man** = no one. Gr. *oudeis.*

kindreds. As *v.* 4 (tribes). **people** = peoples.

stood = were standing.

palms. Gr. *phoinix.* Only here and John 12. 13. Cp. the "great hosanna" of the Jews on the last day of "Tabernacles". **in.** Ap. 104. viii.

10 cried = they cry.

Salvation. Gr. *sōtēria.* In Rev. only here, 12. 10; 19. 1.

upon. Ap. 104. ix. 1. **unto** = to.

11 stood = were standing.

on. Ap. 104. ix. 3. **worshipped.** Ap. 137. 1.

12 Amen. See 1. 6.

Blessing, &c. A sevenfold (Ap. 10) ascription. Cp. 5. 12, where it is to the Lamb, while here it is to God. Prefix the def. art. to each term.

for . . . ever. See 1. 6.

13 answered = asked. Fig. *Idiōma.* Ap. 6.

What = Who.

14 Sir. Most texts read "My lord" (Ap. 98. VI. i. α. 4. B.)

knowest. See Ap. 132. I. i.

which came = who come. **out of.** Ap. 104. vii.

great, &c. = the great, &c. Cp. Matt. 24. 21. See Jer. 30. 5–7. Dan. 12. 1. Nothing to do with Christ's sufferings and death on the cross. **have.** Omit.

washed. Gr. *plunō.* Only here. Ap. 136. v. Sept. uses in Ps. 51. 2, 7 for Heb. *kābaṣ.* These wash "their own robes"—the standing of *works*, not of *grace.* For latter see 1 Cor. 6. 11.

in = by. I.e. by virtue of, the *en* being here the efficient cause. Ap. 104. viii. See 1. 5; 5. 9, and Ap. 95 (p. 138), note 2, "washing in blood".

15 Therefore = For this cause, or On this account. Gr. *dia touto.*

serve. App. 137. 4; 190. III. 5. **day and night.** Hebraism for "continually". **Temple.** See 3. 12. **on.** Ap. 104. ix. 1. **dwell.** Gr. *skēnoō.* Here; 12. 12; 13. 6; 21. 3. See John 1. 14 and cp. Isa. 4. 5, 6. **among** = over. Gr. *epi.* Ap. 104. ix. 3. **16 no.** Ap. 105. I. **neither, neither, nor.** Gr. *oude*, the second occ. followed by *mē* (Ap. 105. II). **light.** Gr. *piptō.* Occ. twenty-three times in Rev., always "fall" save here. See 16. 8. Cp. Isa. 30. 26. **heat** = scorching heat. Gr. *kauma.* Only here and 16. 9. **17 in.** Gr. *ana.* Ap. 104. i. **shall** = will. **feed** = tend, or shepherd. See 2. 27. Mic. 5. 4. **unto.** Gr. *epi.* Ap. 104. ix. 3. **living, &c.** The texts read "fountains of waters of life" (Ap. 170. 1). See 21. 4. **from.** Gr. *ek.* Ap. 104. vii. These two *vv.* refer to Isa. 49. 8–10; 25. 8. Jer. 31. 9, 10–25. Ezek. 47. 1, 12.

A **8** And when He °had opened the seventh seal, there °was °silence °in °heaven about °the space of half an hour.

2 And I °saw the seven angels which °stood before °God; and to them were given seven °trumpets.

3 And °another angel came and [2]stood °at the altar, having a golden °censer; and there was given °unto him much °incense, °that he should °offer *it* with the °prayers of all °saints °upon the °golden altar which was before the throne.

4 And the °smoke of the incense, *which came* with the [3]prayers of the [3]saints, ascended up before [2]God °out of the angel's hand.

5 °And the angel took the [3]censer, °and °filled it °with fire of the altar, °and cast *it* °into the °earth: °and there [1]were voices, °and thunderings, °and lightnings, °and an °earthquake.

6 And the seven angels which had the seven trumpets prepared themselves °to sound.

ℨii. 𝔈²ABa **7** The first °angel [6]sounded,

b and there °followed hail and fire mingled with blood, and they were cast °upon the °earth:

c and the °third part of °trees was °burnt up, and all °green grass was °burnt up.

C d **8** And the second angel [6]sounded,

e and as it were a great mountain burning with fire was cast [5]into the sea:

f and the [7]third part of the sea became blood;

g **9** And the [7]third part of the °creatures which were [1]in the sea, °and had °life, died; and the [7]third part of the ships were °destroyed.

C d **10** And the third angel [6]sounded,

e and there fell a great star °from [1]heaven, burning as it were a °lamp, and it fell [3]upon the [7]third part of the rivers, and [3]upon the fountains of °waters;

8. 1 had. Omit. was = came to be. silence. Gr. *sigē*. Only here and Acts 21. 40. in. Ap. 104. viii. heaven = the heaven. See 3. 12. the space of. Omit.

2 saw. Ap. 133. I. 1. stood = stand. God. Ap. 98. I. i. 1. trumpets. Cp. Num. 10. 9, &c.

3 another. Ap. 124. 1. at. Gr. *epi*. Ap. 104. ix. 1. censer. Gr. *libanōton*. Only here and *v.* 5. Fig. *Metonymy of Adjunct*. Ap. 6. See 1 Chron. 9. 29 (Sept.). unto = to. incense. See 5. 8. that = in order that. Gr. *hina*. offer *it* with. Or, add (lit. give) *it* to. prayers. Ap. 134. II. 2. saints = the saints. See Acts 9. 13. upon. Ap. 104. ix. 3. golden altar, &c. Glorious realities in heaven. The small golden altar of the Tabernacle and the larger one of Solomon's Temple were but copies in miniature. See Heb. 8. 5; 9. 23, 24.

4 smoke. Gr. *kapnos*. Occ. thirteen times, all in Rev., except Acts 2. 19. Save here, always associated with "judgment" or the "pit". out of. Ap. 104. vii.

5 And. The seven "ands" give an instance of Fig. *Polysyndeton*. Ap. 6. filled. Gr. *gemizō*. Here and 15. 8. with. Gr. *ek*. Ap. 104. vii. into. Ap. 104. vi. earth. Ap. 129. 4. earthquake. See 6. 12. Here apparently a convulsion of earth alone.

Chs. 6 and 7 present the six seals, the sixth carrying on to the end. The *seventh* seal contains a new series of judgments under the seven trumpets (8. 7—11. 14) and the seven vials (16. 1—18. 24). The seventh seal thus embraces the period of both trumpets and vials (8. 7—18. 24), and is immediately followed by the Apocalypse (Unveiling of "The Word of God": see Ap. 197), the Son of Adam (Ap. 99). The first six trumpets relate to the earth, the seventh to heaven (11. 15). The seven are divided into four and three, the last three being *woe* trumpets. The judgments and woes now to be set forth are just as real, as literal, as the judgments predicted and fulfilled in the past history of Israel; Ex. 34. 10. Deut. 28. 10. Isa. 11. 15, 16. Mic. 7. 13-15.

6 to sound = in order that (Gr. *hina*) they might sound (Gr. *salpizō*. First of ten occ.).

𝔈² (p. 1883). **8. 7—11. 14.** THE SECOND VISION ON EARTH. (*Alternation.*)

The first six trumpets.

𝔈² | A | B | a | 8. 7-. The FIRST trumpet.
    b | 8. -7-. The *earth* smitten (hail and fire, &c.).
    c | 8. -7. The third part of trees.
  C | d | 8. 8-. The SECOND trumpet.
    e | 8. -8-. The *sea* smitten (burning mountain, &c.).
    f | 8. -8. Third part of sea blood.
    g | 8. 9. Death of living creatures in sea.
  C | *d* | 8. 10-. The THIRD trumpet.
    e | 8. -10, 11-. The *waters* smitten (star falling, &c.).
    f | 8. -11-. Third part of waters wormwood.
    g | 8. -11. Death of men.
  B | *a* | 8 12-. The FOURTH trumpet.
    b | 8. -12-. The *heaven* smitten (sun, moon, and stars).
    c | 8. -12. Third part darkened.

} The four trumpets.

A | D | 8. 13. Three woes yet to come.
  E | h | 9. 1-11. The FIFTH trumpet. (The *first* WOE)
    i | 9. 12. The termination of first woe ("The first woe is past").
  E | *h* | 9. 13—11. 13. The SIXTH trumpet. (The *second* WOE.)
    i | 11. 14-. The termination of second woe ("The second woe is past").
  D | 11. -14. "The third woe cometh quickly."

} The first two woe trumpets.

7 angel. Omit. followed = came to be, as *v.* 1. upon. Gr. *eis*. Ap. 104. vi. earth. Add, with all texts, "and the third part (see Ap. 197. 6) of the earth (Ap. 129. 4) was burnt up". third part. See Ap. 197. 6. trees. As in 7. 1, 3; 9. 4. burnt up. As 17. 16; 18. 8. green. Gr. *chlōros*. Occ. 6. 8 (pale); 9. 4. Mark 6. 39. **9** creatures. See 5. 13. and = which. life. App. 110. I. 1 and 170. 3. Not only "living souls" (Gen. 2. 19) *in* the waters of the sea, but the "living souls" (Gen. 2. 7) *on* it. See Ap. 13. destroyed. The word occ. elsewhere, 11. 18. Luke 12. 33. 2 Cor. 4. 16. 1 Tim. 6. 5. The noun only in Acts 2. 27, 31; 13. 34-37. **10** from. Ap. 104. vii. lamp. Gr. *lampas*. Elsewhere 4. 5. Matt. 25. 1-8. John 18. 3 (torch). Acts 20. 8 (light). waters. The texts read "the waters".

11 And the name of the star is called °Wormwood:

f and the [7]third part of the [10]waters became °wormwood;

g and many °men died °of the [10]waters, because they were made bitter.

B a 12 And the fourth angel [6]sounded,

b and the [7]third part of the °sun was smitten, and the [7]third part of the °moon, and the [7]third part of the °stars;

c °so as the [7]third part of them °was darkened, and the day °shone °not for a [7]third part of it, and the night likewise.

A D 13 And I °beheld, and heard °an °angel flying °through °the midst of heaven, saying with a °loud voice, "Woe, woe, woe, °to the inhabiters of the [5]earth °by reason of the °other voices of the trumpet of the three angels, which are °yet to [6]sound!"

E h **9** And the fifth angel sounded, and I °saw a °star °fall °from °heaven °unto the °earth: and to him was given the key of °the °bottomless °pit.

2 And he opened the [1]bottomless [1]pit; and there arose a smoke °out of the [1]pit, as the smoke of a great °furnace; and the sun and the air were darkened °by reason of the smoke of the [1]pit.

3 And there came [2]out of the smoke °locusts °upon the [1]earth; and °unto them was given °power, as the °scorpions of the [1]earth have °power.

4 And it was °commanded them °that they should °not hurt the grass of the [1]earth, °neither any green thing, °neither any tree; °but °only those °men which have °not the seal of °God °in their foreheads.

5 And to them it was given °that they should °not kill them, but [4]that they should be °tormented °five months: and their °torment *was* as the °torment of a [3]scorpion, when °he striketh a [4]man.

6 And °in those days shall [4]men °seek death, and shall °not find it; and shall desire to die, and death °shall flee °from them.

7 And the °shapes of the [3]locusts *were* like [3]unto °horses prepared [1]unto battle; and °on their heads °*were* as it were °crowns like gold, and their faces *were* as the faces of [4]men.

8 And they had hair as the hair of women, and their teeth were as *the teeth* of lions.

9 And they had breastplates, as it were breastplates of iron; and the °sound of their wings *was* as the °sound of chariots of many horses running °to battle.

11 Wormwood. Gr. *apsinthos.* Only occ.
men. Ap. 123. 1. The second occ. is preceded by "the".
of. Gr. *ek.* Ap. 104. vii.
12 sun, moon, stars. The Lord Himself foretold these signs. See Matt. 24. 29. Mark 13. 24. Luke 21. 25, and cp. Isa. 5. 30. Jer. 4. 28. Ezek. 32. 7, 8. Joel 2. 10, 30, 31; 3. 15. Amos 5. 20; 8. 9. Zeph. 1. 14-16.
so as=in order that. Gr. *hina.*
was=should be.
shone not=should not shine (Ap. 106. I. i).
not. Ap. 105. II.
13 beheld=saw, as *v.* 2. **an**=one.
angel. The texts read "eagle". Gr. *aetos.* Elsewhere, 4. 7; 12. 14. Matt. 24. 28. Luke 17. 37. Cp. Deut. 28. 49. 2 Sam. 1. 23. Isa. 40. 31. Hos. 8. 1. Hab. 1. 8.
through=in. Gr. *en.* Ap. 104. viii.
the . . . heaven. Gr. *mesouranēma.* Elsewhere, 14. 6; 19. 17. **loud**=great.
to . . . earth=to them dwelling (see Acts 2. 5) on (Ap. 104. ix. 1) earth.
by reason of. Gr. *ek.* Ap. 104. vii.
other. Ap. 124. 3.
yet=about.

9. 1 saw. Ap. 133. I. 1.
star. The symbol of him who had already become "fallen" before John "saw". Cp. Luke 10. 18. Isa. 14. 12.
fall=fallen.
from. Ap. 104. vii.
heaven. See 3. 12.
unto. Ap. 104. vi.
earth. Ap. 129. 4.
the . . . pit=the pit (Gr. *phrear.* Here, *v.* 2. Luke 14. 5. John 4. 11, 12, "well") of the abyss (Gr. *abussos.* Here, *vv.* 2, 11; 11. 7; 17. 8; 20. 1, 3. Luke 8. 31. Rom. 10. 7). See Ap. 197. 6.
2 out of. Ap. 104. vii.
furnace. Cp. 1. 15. Indicating a place of fire, but not to be confused with *Hadēs* (Sheol) or with Tartarus. Cp. Jer. 4. 23-28, where the judgments are against Judah and the Land. Here, John sees them extended to the whole earth.
by reason of. Gr. *ek.* Ap. 104. vii.
3 locusts. Gr. *akris.* Here; *v.* 7. Matt. 3. 4. Mark 1. 6.
upon. Gr. *eis.* Ap. 104. vi. **unto**=to.
power. Ap. 172. 5.
scorpions. Gr. *skorpios.* Here; *vv.* 5, 10. Luke 10. 19; 11. 12. As in Ex. 10. 14, these are no ordinary locusts, which "have no king" (Prov. 30. 27). See *v.* 11 and cp. Joel 2. 25. Here "men" are the objects of their power to inflict hurt.
4 commanded=said.
that . . . not=in order that (Gr. *hina*) . . . not (Ap. 105. II). **neither.** Gr. *oude.*
but. Gr. *ei* (Ap. 118. 2. a) *mē* (Ap. 105. II).
only. The texts omit.
men. Ap. 123. 1.
not. Ap. 105. I.
God. Ap. 98. I. i. 1.
in=upon. Gr. *epi.* Ap. 104. ix. 1.
5 that . . not. As in *v.* 4.
tormented. Gr. *basanizō,* lit. to test (metals) by the touchstone, then to torture. Occ. 11. 10; 12. 2 (pained); 14. 10; 20. 10. See Matt. 8. 29. Mark 5. 7. Luke 8. 28. "Torment" is specially connected with demons.
five months. Cp. the fixed periods of Num. 11. 19, 20. 2 Sam. 24. 13; where the term is taken literally, as it should be here also. The period of locusts is five months: May-September. See Gen. 7. 24. **torment.** Gr. *basanismos.* Here; 14. 11; 18. 7, 10, 15. See Ap. 197. 6. The verb, above. **he**=it. **6 in.** Ap. 104. viii. **seek.** As in Rom. 2. 7. **not.** The texts read "in no wise", the strong negative. Ap. 105. III. **shall flee**=fleeth. **from.** Ap. 104. iv. **7 shapes**=likenesses. See Rom. 1. 23. **horses.** See Joel 2 for similar creatures which (Joel 2. 8) it is impossible to wound or kill. **on.** Ap. 104. ix. 3. ***were.*** Omit. **crowns.** Gr. *stephanos.* Occ. eight times in Rev., always connected with heavenly purposes save here. **9 sound.** Locusts in flight give out a great sound. These supernatural creatures will appal by the sound of their wings. **to.** Ap. 104. vi.

10 And they °had tails like [3]unto [3]scorpions,
and there were stings [6]in their tails: and
their [3]power *was* to [4]hurt [4]men [5]five months.
11 °And they [10]had a king °over them, *which*
is the angel of the [1]bottomless [1]pit, whose
name °in the Hebrew tongue *is* °Abaddon, but
[6]in the Greek tongue hath °*his* name °Apol-
lyon.
i 12 °One woe is past; °*and* °behold, there
come two woes °more °hereafter.
E h 13 And the sixth angel sounded, and I heard
°a voice [1]from the °four horns of the golden
°altar which is before [4]God,
14 Saying to the sixth angel which [10]had the
trumpet, "Loose the four angels which are
bound °in the great river °Euphrates."
15 And the four angels were loosed, which
°were prepared °for °an °hour, and a °day,
and a °month, and a °year, °for to slay the
°third part of [4]men.
16 And the number of the °army of the horsemen *were* °two hundred thousand thousand:
°and I heard the number of them.
17 And thus I [1]saw the horses [6]in the °vision,
and them that sat °on them, having breastplates °of fire, and of jacinth, and °brimstone:
and the heads of the horses *were* as the heads
of [8]lions; and [2]out of their mouths issued fire
and smoke and °brimstone.
18 °By these °three was the [15]third part of
[5]men killed, °by the fire, and °by the smoke,
and °by the [17]brimstone, which issued [2]out of
their mouths.
19 For °their [3]power is [6]in their mouth, and
[6]in their tails: for their tails *were* like [3]unto
°serpents, and had heads; and °with them
they do hurt.
20 And the °rest of the [4]men which were -[4]not
killed °by these °plagues, yet °repented -[4]not
°of the works of their hands, °that they should
[4]- not °worship °devils, and °idols of gold, and
silver, and brass, and stone, and of wood:
which °neither can °see, °nor hear, °nor walk:
21 °Neither [20]repented they [20]of their murders,
[20]nor [20]of their °sorceries, [20]nor [20]of their fornication, [20]nor [20]of their thefts.

10 And I °saw °another °mighty angel
°come down °from °heaven, clothed
with a °cloud: and °a °rainbow °*was* °upon
his head, and his face *was* as it were the sun,
and his feet as pillars of fire:
2 And °he had °in his hand °a little book
open: and he °set his right foot °upon the sea,
and *his* left *foot* °on the °earth,
3 And cried with a °loud voice, as *when* a lion
roareth: and when he °had cried, °seven
°thunders °uttered their voices.
4 And when the [3]seven [3]thunders [3]had
[3]uttered °their voices, I was about to write:
and I heard a voice [1]from [1]heaven saying
°unto me, °"Seal up °those things which the
[3]seven [3]thunders [3]uttered, and write them
°not."

10 had = have.
11 And. The texts omit.
over. Ap. 104. ix. 1.
in . . . tongue. Gr. *Hebraïsti.*
Abaddon. Heb. word. The "destruction" of Job 26. 6; 28. 22; 31. 12. Ps. 88. 11. Prov. 15. 11; 27. 20. Here personified as *Abaddōn* and *Apollyōn*, the "Destroyer". Cp. Isa. 16. 4. Jer. 4. 7; 6. 26. Dan. 8. 24, 25; 9. 26; 11. 44. **his** = **a.**
12 One. I. e. the first woe.
and. Omit.
behold. Ap. 133. I. 2.
more = yet.
hereafter. Gr. *meta tauta.*
13 a = one (8. 13). **four.** Omit.
altar. See 6. 9.
14 in. Gr. *epi.* Ap. 104. ix. 2.
Euphrates. Connected with the judgments of the great day. See Jer. 46. 4–10.
15 were = had been.
for. Gr. *eis.* Ap. 104. vi. **an** = the
hour, day, month, year. A fixed point of time, not a period of duration. The four notes of time being under one article and one preposition show that the occasion is one particular moment appointed by God.
for = in order. Gr. *hina.*
third part. See 8. 7.
16 army = armies.
two . . . thousand. Lit. two myriads of myriads, a literal number which John heard and recorded. Cp. 7. 4. See Ap. 197. 6. **and.** Omit.
17 vision. Gr. *horasis.* Occ. 4. 3 and Acts 2. 17. Cp. Ap. 133. I. 8. **on.** Ap. 104. ix. 1.
of fire. Gr. *purinos.* Only here.
brimstone. Gr. *theiōdēs.* Only here.
brimstone. Gr. *theion,* six times in Rev., and in Luke 17. 29. See Ap. 197. 6.
18 By. Gr. *apo.* Ap. 104. iv, as the texts.
three. The texts add "plagues". See Ap. 197. 6.
by. Gr. *ek.* Ap. 104. vii. The texts omit the last two occ. of *ek* (by).
19 their power. The texts read "the power of the horses".
serpents. Gr. *ophis,* as in 12. 9, 14, 15; 20. 2. See Jer. 8. 17.
with. Gr. *en.* Ap. 104. viii.
20 rest. Ap. 124. 3.
by. Ap. 104. viii.
plagues. See note, *v.* 18.
repented. Ap. 111. I. 1.
of. Gr. *ek.* Ap. 104. vii.
that . . . not. See *v.* 5.
worship. Ap. 137. 1.
devils = demons. A worship which is widespread over the world at this hour, despite the Divine warnings. Distinguished from worship of idols.
idols = the idols. Gr. *eidōlon.* Only occ. in Rev. Not found in the Gospels.
neither, nor. Gr. *oute.*
see. Ap. 133. I. 5. Cp. Ps. 115. 4–8.
21 Neither = And . . . not (Ap. 105. I).
sorceries. Gr. *pharmakeia.* Occ. 18. 23. See Gal. 5. 20 (witchcraft).

10. 1 saw. Ap. 133. I. 1.
another. Ap. 124. 1. The term shows him to be not one of the "seven". **mighty.** See 5. 2.
come = coming.
from. Ap. 104. vii. **heaven.** See 3. 12.
cloud. Cp. 1. 7. Ps. 18. 11; 104. 3. Isa. 19. 1. Matt. 24. 30. 1 Thess. 4. 17. **a** = the.

rainbow. See 4. 3. *was.* Omit. upon. Ap. 104. ix. 3. **2 he had** = having. **in.** Ap. 104. viii. **a little book.** Gr. *biblaridion.* Only here and *vv.* 9, 10. Cp. 1. 11 and 5. 1, &c., where the scroll was sealed. Here it is opened. **set.** Gr. *ithēmi.* As in Acts 1. 7 (put); 2. 35 (make). **upon,** on. Ap. 104. ix. 1. **earth.** Ap. 129. 4. **3 loud** = great. **had.** Omit. **seven** = the seven (1. 4). **thunders.** Cp. the "seven thunders" (voice of the Lord) in Ps. 29. **uttered.** Lit. spake. Ap. 121. 7. **4 their voices.** The texts omit. **unto me.** The texts omit. **Seal.** See 7. 3. **those** = the. **not.** Ap. 105. II.

5 And the angel which I [1]saw stand [2]upon the
sea and [2]upon the [2]earth lifted up his °hand
°to [1]heaven,
6 And sware °by Him That °liveth for ever
and ever, Who °created [1]heaven, and the
things that °therein are, and the [2]earth, and
the things that °therein are, and the sea, and
the things which are °therein, °that there
°should be °time °no longer:
7 But [2]in the days of the voice of the seventh
angel, when he °shall begin to sound, the
°mystery of °God °should be °finished, as °He
hath declared to °His °servants the °prophets.
8 And the voice which I heard [1]from [1]hea-
ven °spake °unto me again, °and said, "Go
and take the °little book which is open [2]in the
hand of the angel which standeth [2]upon the
sea and [2]upon the [2]earth."
9 And I went °unto the angel, °and °said °unto
him, "Give me the [2]little book." And he °said
°unto me, "Take *it*, and °eat it up; and it
shall make thy belly bitter, but it shall be [2]in
thy mouth sweet as honey."
10 And I took the [2]little book °out of the
angel's hand, and [9]ate it up; and it was [2]in
my mouth sweet as honey: and as soon as I
had eaten it, my belly was bitter.
11 And °he said °unto me, "Thou must
°prophesy again °before many peoples, and
nations, and tongues, and kings."

11 And there was given me a °reed like
°unto a °rod: °and the angel stood,
°saying, °"Rise, and measure the °Temple of
°God, and the °altar, °and them that °worship
°therein.
2 But the court which is °without the [1]Temple
°leave °out, and measure it °not; for it °is
given [1]unto the °Gentiles: and the °holy city
shall they °tread under foot °forty *and* two
months.
3 And I will °give *power* [1]unto °My two
witnesses, and they shall °prophesy a °thou-
sand two hundred *and* threescore days, clothed
in sackcloth."
4 These °are the °two olive trees and the
two candlesticks, °standing before the °God °of
the °earth.
5 And °if °any man °will hurt them, °fire
proceedeth °out of their mouth, and devoureth
their enemies; and °if °any man °will hurt
them, he must in this manner be killed.
6 These have °power to shut °heaven, °that it
rain °not °in the days of their °prophecy: and
have °power °over °waters to turn them °to
blood, and °to smite the [4]earth °with all
°plagues, as often as they °will.

5 hand. The texts read "right hand". See 1. 16; 5. 1, &c.
to. Gr. *eis*. Ap. 104. vi.
6 by. Ap. 104. viii. **liveth, &c.** As 4. 9.
created. Cp. 4. 11.
therein = in (Ap. 104. viii) it.
that . . . longer. Lit. that time shall be no longer, I. e. no more delay in executing final vengeance. See 6. 10, 11. **should** = shall.
time. Gr. *chronos*. See Ap. 195.
no longer. Gr. *ouketi*.
7 shall begin = is about.
mystery. See 1. 20; 17. 5, 7. Ap. 193.
God. Ap. 98. I. i. 1.
should be = shall have been.
finished. (Add "also".) Gr. *teleō*. In Rev. here; 11. 7; 15. 1, 8; 17. 17; 20. 3, 5, 7. Cp. Ap. 125. 1.
He . . . declared. Ap. 121. 4. **His** = His own.
servants. Ap. 190. I. 2.
prophets. See Ap. 189.
8 spake. Read, "(I heard) speaking". Same as "uttered" in *v.* 3.
unto = with. Gr. *meta*. Ap. 104. xi. 1.
said = saying.
little book = book. Gr. *biblion*.
9 unto. Ap. 104. xv. 3. **and.** Omit.
said = saying.
unto = to. **said** = saith.
eat . . . up. Hebraism for receiving knowledge.
10 out of. Ap. 104. vii.
11 he said. The texts read "they say".
unto = to.
prophesy. In Rev. only here and 11. 3. Cp. Ap. 189.
before = over, or concerning. Gr. *epi*. Ap. 104. ix. 2.

11. 1 reed. Gr. *kalamos*. Elsewhere (in Rev.) 21. 15, 16. See Ap. 88, first note.
unto = to.
rod = sceptre, as elsewhere in Rev. See 2. 27; 12. 5; 19. 15. This measuring reed is like a sceptre, and measures for destruction, not for building. See Lam. 2. 8.
and . . . stood. The texts omit.
saying. I. e. (the giver) saying.
Rise. Ap. 178. I. 4. Only here in Rev.
Temple. Gr. *naos*. See 3. 12. Matt. 23. 16.
God. Ap. 98. I. i. 1.
altar. See 8. 3, &c.
and them. Read "and (record) them". Fig. *Ellipsis*. Ap. 6.
worship. Ap. 137. 1. **therein** = in (Gr. *en*) it.
2 without, out. Gr. *exōthen*, meaning outside.
leave = cast out. Gr. *ekballō*, a strong term.
not. Ap. 105. II. **is** = was.
Gentiles. Gr. *ethnos*. Occ. twenty-three times in Rev., invariably transl. "nations", save here. See Ap. 197. 6.
holy city. See Matt. 4. 5.
tread . . . foot. Gr. *pateō*. Only here; 14. 20; 19. 15. Luke 10. 19; 21. 24, where see note. All these particulars refer to an actual Temple. The church of God knows nothing of an altar here, of a *naos*, of a court of the Gentiles. All point to the Temple yet to be built in the holy city, i. e. Jerusalem. This Temple will be on earth (see Structure E[2], p. 1894).

forty *and* two months = 1,260 days = 3 years and a half. A specific period stated in literal language. Cp. *v.* 3; 12. 6, 14; 13. 5. Dan. 7. 25; 12. 7. Luke 4. 25. Jas. 5. 17. **3 give.** Add "*power*". Fig. *Ellipsis*. Ap. 6. **My two witnesses.** God has not specified their names. We know that two men are to be raised up "in that day", endowed with wondrous powers to execute a special mission. They are called emphatically "MY two witnesses" (see 1. 5). **prophesy.** See 10. 11 and Ap. 189. **a thousand . . . days** = forty-two months, *v.* 2. The periods are probably synchronous. **thousand.** See 14. 20 and Ap. 197. 6. **4 are.** I. e. represent. **two olive trees.** Cp. Zech. 4. 3, 11, 14, where by the same Fig. (*Metaphor*) two persons are represented. **standing.** The texts read "which stand". **God.** The texts read "Lord". Ap. 98. VI. i. *β*. 2. A. **of the earth.** Ap. 129. 4. See Josh. 3. 11, 13. Zech. 6. 5, and cp. Ps. 115. 16. **5 if.** Ap. 118. 2. a, with the texts. **any man** = any one. Ap. 123. 3. **will.** Ap. 102. 1. **fire.** Cp. Jer. 5. 14. **out of.** Ap. 104. vii. **if.** Ap. 118. 2. c. **6 power.** Ap. 172. 5. **heaven.** See 3. 12. **that** = in order that. Gr. *hina*. **not.** Ap. 105. II. **in.** Gr. *en*, but the texts omit. **prophecy.** See Ap. 189. **over.** Ap. 104. ix. 1. **waters** = the waters. **to** = into. Ap. 104. vi. **with.** The texts read Gr. *en*. **plagues.** See Ap. 197. 6. **will** = shall desire. Ap. 102. 1.

7 And when they shall have °finished their °testimony, the °beast that ascendeth [5]out of the °bottomless pit shall make war °against them, and shall °overcome them, and °kill them.
8 And their °dead bodies °*shall lie* °in the °street of °the great city, which °spiritually is called °Sodom and Egypt, where also °our °Lord was °crucified.
9 And they °of the °people and °kindreds and tongues and nations °shall see their [8]dead bodies °three days and an half, and °shall °not suffer their [8]dead bodies to be put °in °graves.
10 And they that dwell °upon the [4]earth °shall rejoice °over them, and make merry, and shall °send gifts one to another; because these two °prophets °tormented them that dwelt °on the [4]earth.
11 And °after °three days and an half the °spirit of life °from [1]God entered °into them, and they stood °upon their feet; and great fear °fell °upon them which °saw them.
12 And they heard a great voice [11]from [6]heaven saying [1]unto them, "Come up hither." And they ascended up °to [6]heaven °in °a °cloud; and their enemies °beheld them.
13 And °the same hour °was there a great earthquake, and the °tenth part of the city fell, and [12]in the earthquake were slain °of °men °seven thousand: and the °remnant °were affrighted, and gave °glory to the [1]God of [6]heaven.
i 14 The °second woe is past;
D °*and* °behold, the third woe °cometh quickly.
Ƶ iii. 𝔥[3] A 15 And the °seventh angel sounded;
B a and there °were great voices [12]in [6]heaven,
b saying, "The °kingdoms of this °world °are become *the kingdoms* of our °LORD, and of His °Christ; and °**He shall reign** °**for ever and ever.**"
B a 16 And the four and twenty elders, which °sat before [1]God °on their °seats, °fell [11]upon their faces, and [1]worshipped [1]God,
b 17 Saying, "We give thee thanks, O °LORD [1]God °Almighty, Which art, and wast, °and art to come; because Thou hast taken °to Thee Thy great °power, and °hast reigned.
18 And the nations were angry, and Thy wrath °is come, and the °time of the °dead

7 finished. See 10. 7.
testimony. As in 1. 2, &c. Their testimony ended, they are at the mercy of their enemies.
beast = wild beast, see 6. 8. First mention of this terrible being, whose rise is depicted in ch. 13.
bottomless pit. See 9. 1.
against. Gr. *meta.* Ap. 104. xi. 1.
overcome. As in chs. 2 and 3. See Ap. 197. 6.
kill. The two witnesses are on earth during ch. 13, and the beast is on earth in ch. 11.
8 dead bodies = corpse (sing., with all texts). Gr. *ptōma.* Only here, *v.* 9 (pl.). Matt. 24. 28. Mark. 6. 29.
shall lie. Read "*lie*".
in. Gr. *epi.* Ap. 104. ix. 1.
street. Gr. *plateia*, a broad place or way, rather than "street". See 21. 21; 22. 2.
the great city. See Jer. 22. 8. Jerusalem will have been rebuilt only to be again destroyed. See Isa. 25. 2-9.
spiritually. See 1 Cor. 2. 14.
Sodom and Egypt. Cp. Isa. 1. 9, 10. Ezek. 16. 46, 53; 23. 3, 8, 19, 27. See Ps. 9. 9; 10. 1, and 79.
our. The texts read "their". The Holy Spirit thus points to the city in the plainest way.
Lord. Ap. 98. VI. i. *β*. 2. A.
crucified. Only here in Rev.
9 of. Ap. 104. vii. **people** = peoples.
kindreds = tribes. As 1. 7.
shall see = see, with texts. Ap. 133. I. 5.
shall. Omit.
three days and an half. A literal period.
shall not suffer = suffer not.
not. Ap. 105. I. **in.** Ap. 104. vi.
graves = a tomb, a word destructive of interpretations of the two witnesses as the O. T. and N. T.
10 upon, on. Ap. 104. ix. 1. **shall.** Omit.
over. Gr. *epi.* Ap. 104. ix. 2.
send. Ap. 174. 4. **prophets.** Ap. 189.
tormented. See 9. 5.
11 after. Ap. 104. xi. 2.
three = the three.
spirit of life = breath of life. Gr. *pneuma* (cp. Ap. 101. II. 6) *zoēs* (Ap. 170. 1). Cp. Sept. of Gen. 6. 17; 7. 15. See also Gen. 2. 7; 7. 22 (*pnoē*).
from. Gr. *ek.* Ap. 104. vii.
into. Gr. *en.* Ap. 104. viii.
upon. Ap. 104. ix. 3.
fell. Gr. *piptō.* The texts read the strong word *epipiptō*, indicating a paralysing fear.
saw. Ap. 133. I. 11.
12 to heaven = into (Gr. *eis*) the heaven (see 3. 12).
in. Ap. 104. viii. **a** = the.
cloud. See Acts 1. 9.
beheld. Same as "saw", *v.* 11.
13 the same = in (Gr. *en*) that.
was there = there came to be.
tenth part = tenth (App. 10 and 197. 6).
of men. Lit. names of men (Ap. 123. 1).
seven thousand. See Ap. 197. 6.
remnant. Ap. 124. 3.
were = became. **glory.** See p. 1511 and Ap. 197. 6. **14 second.** One of the three in 8. 13. ***and.*** Omit. **behold.** Ap. 133. I. 2. **cometh** = is coming.

𝔥[3] (p. 1883). **11. 15-19-.** THE THIRD VISION IN HEAVEN. (*Alternation.*)

𝔥[3] | A | 11. 15-. The sounding of the seventh trumpet in heaven.
B | a | -15-. Great voices in heaven.
b | -15. Their utterance.
B | *a* | 16. The twenty-four elders.
b | 17, 18. Their utterance.
A | 19-. The opening of God's Temple in heaven.

15 seventh angel. This seventh trumpet embraces the seven vials, or last seven plagues, which make up the third woe, and reaches on to 18. 24, if not 20. 15. **were.** Lit. came to be. **kingdoms.** The texts read "kingdom", i. e. sovereignty. **world.** Ap. 129. 1. **are** = is. **LORD.** Ap. 98. VI. *β*. I. A. b. **Christ.** Ap. 98. IX. **He . . . ever.** See Ex. 15. 18. Ps. 146. 10. **for . . . ever.** See 1. 6.
16 sat = sit. **on.** Ap. 104. ix. 3. **seats** = thrones. **fell, &c.** See 4. 10. **17 LORD.** Ap. 98. VI. i. *β*. 1. B. b. **Almighty** = the Almighty. See 1. 8. **and . . . come.** The texts omit. Now, here, He *has* come. See 1. 4. **to Thee.** Omit. **power.** App. 172. 1; 176. 1. **hast reigned** = reignedst.
18 is come = came. See Isa. 26. 20, 21. **time.** Gr. *kairos.* See Ap. 195. **dead.** Ap. 139. 1.

that they should be °judged, and °that Thou shouldest give °reward [1]unto Thy °servants the °prophets, and to the °saints, and them that fear Thy name, °small and great; and °shouldest destroy them which °destroy the [4]earth."

A 19 And the [1]Temple of [1]God °was opened [12]in [6]heaven, and there was °seen [12]in His [1]Temple the ark of His °testament:

iii. E[3] and [13]there were lightnings, and voices, and thunderings, and an earthquake, and °great hail.

iv. H[4] 12 °And there °appeared a great °wonder °in °heaven; a °woman clothed with the sun, and the moon under her feet, and °upon her head a crown of °twelve stars:

2 And she being with child °cried, °travailing in birth, and °pained to be delivered.

3 And there [1]appeared °another [1]wonder [1]in [1]heaven; and °behold, a great red °dragon, having °seven heads and ten horns, and seven °crowns °upon his heads.

4 °And his tail °drew the third part of the stars of [1]heaven, and °did cast them °to the °earth: and the [3]dragon °stood before the [1]woman which °was ready to be delivered, °for to °devour her °child as soon as it was born.

5 And she brought forth a °man child, who °was **to rule all °nations °with a °rod of iron**: and her [4]child was caught °up °unto °God, and °*to* His throne.

6 And the [1]woman fled °into the °wilderness, where she hath a place prepared °of [5]God, °that they should feed her there a thousand two hundred *and* threescore days.

7 And there °was war [1]in °heaven: °Michael and his angels °fought °against the [3]dragon; and the [3]dragon fought and his angels,

8 And °prevailed °not, °neither was their place found any °more [1]in [1]heaven.

9 And the great [3]dragon was °cast out, °that °old °serpent, called the °Devil and °Satan, °which deceiveth the whole °world: he was °cast out [6]into the [4]earth, and his angels were °cast out °with him.

10 And I heard a °loud voice saying [1]in [1]heaven, "Now is come °salvation, and °strength, and the °kingdom of our [5]God, and the °power of His °Christ: for the °accuser of our brethren °is °cast down, which °accused them before our [5]God day and night.

11 And they overcame him °by the blood of the Lamb, and °by the °word of their °testimony; and they °loved [8]not their °lives unto °the death.

judged. Ap. 122. 1. See 20. 12–15. John 5. 24. Rom. 8. 1.
that Thou shouldest = to.
reward = the reward. **servants.** Ap. 190. I. 2.
prophets. Ap. 189. See Heb. 11. 32.
saints. See 13. 7, 10; 14. 12; 16. 6. This special term for O. T. saints is found in Dan. 7. 18, &c. See Acts 9. 13.
small . . . great = the small . . . the great.
shouldest = to.
destroy = are destroying. *They* are found in chs. 18, 19, 20.
19 was . . . heaven. The texts read "which is in heaven was opened".
seen. Ap. 133. I. 8.
testament = covenant. Gr. *diathēkē*. Only occ. in Rev.
great hail. Corresponds with 16. 21.

12. 1 And . . . heaven = And a great sign was seen in heaven.
appeared = was seen. Ap. 133. I. 8.
wonder. Ap. 176. 3. What follows is a *sign*.
in. Ap. 104. viii. **heaven.** See 3. 12.
woman. I. e. Israel. See John 16. 21.
upon. Ap. 104. ix. 1.
twelve stars. Probably the zodiacal signs, representing the *Israel* nation in embryo. See Ap. 12.
2 cried = crieth out.
travailing, &c. Gr. *ōdinō*. Only here and Gal. 4. 19, 27. See Mic. 5. 3.
pained. Lit. tormented. See 9. 5.
3 another. Ap. 124. 1. **behold.** Ap. 133. I. 2.
dragon. Gr. *drakōn*. First of thirteen (App. 10 and 197. 6) occ., in Rev. only. See *v.* 9.
seven heads . . . heads. "Signs" of universality of earthly power. See App. 10 and 197. 6.
crowns. Gr. *diadēma*. Only here, 13. 1; 19. 12.
upon. Ap. 104. ix. 3.
4 And his, &c. Refers to Satan's first rebellion and to those who followed him.
drew = draggeth. See John 21. 8.
did. Read "he". **to.** Ap. 104. vi.
earth. Ap. 129. 4.
stood = is standing. Perf. tense, indicating abiding action.
was . . . delivered = is about to bring forth.
for = in order. Gr. *hina*.
devour. Same word as 10. 9, 10 (eat up); 20. 9. From Gen. 3. 15 till now Satan stands ready to devour the promised "seed". **child.** Ap. 108. i.
5 man child = a son (Ap. 108. iii) a male (as Luke 2. 23).
was = is about.
nations = the nations. Cp. Ps. 2. 9.
with. Gr. *en*. Ap. 104. viii. **rod.** See 2. 27.
up = away.
unto. Ap. 104. xv. 3. **God.** Ap. 98. I. i. 1.
to. The texts add *pros*, as above.
An interval of years occ. after this *v.*
6 Anticipatory, the flight being consequent on the war in heaven (*v.* 14). **into.** Ap. 104. vi.
wilderness. Cp. Ezek. 20. 33–38.
of. Gr. *apo*. Ap. 104. iv.
that. Gr. *hina*, as *v.* 4.

7 was = came to be. **heaven** = the heaven. See 3. 12. A particular sphere above earth which is dwelt in by, or accessible to, the dragon and his evil powers. Cp. Job 1 and 2. Zech. 3. 6. See Luke 10. 18. **Michael.** See Dan. 10. 13, 21; 12. 1. Jude 9, and Ap. 179. II. 2. **fought against.** The texts read "(going forth) to war with". **against.** Gr. *meta*. Ap. 104. xi. 1. **8 prevailed.** Gr. *ischuō*, as Acts 19. 16, 20. Only here in Rev. Cp. Ap. 172. 3. **not.** Ap. 105. I. **neither.** Gr. *oude*. **more.** First occ. Matt. 5. 13 (thenceforth). **9 cast out** = cast down, as *v.* 10. **that** = the. **old** = ancient. **serpent.** See 20. 2. Gen. 3. 1, and Ap. 19. **Devil.** Lit. slanderer. See *v.* 10 and Matt. 4. 1. **Satan** = Adversary. Cp. Matt. 4. 10. See Ap. 19. **which deceiveth.** Lit. the one deceiving. Ap. 128. viii. 1. See 20. 3. **world.** Ap. 129. 3. **with.** Ap. 104. xi. 1. **10** The central verse in *Revelation*. **loud** = great. **salvation** = the salvation. **strength** = the power. App 172. 1; 176. 1. **kingdom.** See Ap. 114. **power.** Ap. 172. 5. **Christ.** Ap. 98. IX. **accuser.** Gr. *katēgoros*. Only here in Rev. **is** = was. **cast down.** As "cast out", *v.* 9, with the texts. **accused** = accuseth. First occ. Matt. 12. 10; last, here. **11 by.** Ap. 104. v. 2. **word.** Ap. 121. 10. **testimony.** See 1. 2. **loved.** Ap. 135. I. 1. **lives** = life. App. 110. III. 1; 170. 3. **the.** Omit.

12 °Therefore rejoice, *ye* °heavens, and ye
that °dwell [1]in them. °Woe to °the inhabiters
of the [4]earth and of the sea! for the [9]devil is
°come down [5]unto you, having great °wrath,
°because he °knoweth that he hath but a short
°time."

Fiv. E^4 W 13 And when the [3]dragon °saw that he was
°cast °unto the [4]earth, he persecuted the
[1]woman which brought forth the °man *child*.
14 And to the [1]woman were given °two
wings of °a °great eagle, [6]that she °might
°fly [6]into the [6]wilderness [6]into her place,
where she is nourished for a °time, and times,
and half a time, °from the face of the [9]serpent.
15 And the [9]serpent cast °out of his mouth
water as a °flood after the [1]woman, [6]that he
might cause her to be °carried away of the
flood.
16 And the [4]earth helped the [1]woman, and
the [4]earth °opened her mouth, and °swallowed
up the [15]flood which the [3]dragon cast [15]out of
his mouth.
17 And the [3]dragon was wroth °with the
woman, and °went to make war [9]with the
°remnant of her °seed, which keep the commandments of [5]God, °and have the [11]testimony
of °Jesus °Christ.

X **13** °And I stood °upon the sand of the sea,
°and °saw a °beast °rise up °out of the
sea, °having seven heads and ten horns, and
°upon his horns ten °crowns, and °upon his
heads °the name of blasphemy.
2 And the [1]beast which I [1]saw was like
°unto a °leopard, and his feet were as *the feet*
of a bear, and his mouth as the mouth of
a °lion: and the °dragon gave °him his °power,
and his °seat, and great °authority.
3 And °I saw °one of his heads as it were
°wounded °to death; and his °deadly °wound
was °healed: and all the °world wondered
°after the [1]beast.
4 And they °worshipped the [2]dragon °which
gave °power [2]unto the [1]beast: and they
°worshipped the [1]beast, saying, "Who *is* like
[2]unto the [1]beast? °who is able to °make war
°with him?"
5 And there was given [2]unto him a mouth
°speaking great things and blasphemies; and
[4]power was given [2]unto him to °continue forty
and two months.
6 And he opened his mouth °in °blasphemy
°against °God, to blaspheme °His name, and
His °tabernacle, °and °them °that dwell °in
°heaven.

12 Therefore = For (Ap. 104. v. 2) this cause.
heavens. In Rev. only here in plural, while fifty-one occ. in sing. See 3. 12 and Matt. 6. 10.
dwell. Lit. tabernacle. See 7. 15 and 13. 6.
Woe. Third and most terrible of the three woes (8. 13).
the . . . of. The texts omit. **come** = gone.
wrath. Gr. *thumos.* First of ten occ. in Rev.
because . . . that = knowing (Ap. 132. I. i) that.
time. Gr. *kairos.* Ap. 195.

E^4 (p. 1883). **12. 13—13. 18.** THE FOURTH VISION "ON EARTH". (*Division.*)

E^4 | W | 12. 13–17. The effect as regards Israel.
  | X | 13. 1–18. The effect as regards the earth.

13 saw. Ap. 133. I. 1.
cast = cast down, *v.* 9. **unto.** Ap. 104. vi.
man *child* = male. See *v.* 5.
14 two = the two. **a** = the.
great eagle. Great is emph. Cp. Deut. 32. 11, 12.
might = may.
fly. Gr. *petomai.* See *v.* 6. Cp. Ex. 14. 5. Ps. 35. 1–5. Isa. 11. 16. Ezek. 20. 33–38. Hos. 2. 14, 5. Zeph. 2. 3. Matt. 24. 15–28. Mark 13. 14–23.
time, &c. See 11. 2 and Ap. 195.
from, &c. See Sept. of Judges 9. 21 for same Fig. *Idioma* (Ap. 6).
from. Ap. 104. iv.
15 out of. Ap. 104. vii.
flood = river.
carried . . . flood. Gr. *potamophorētos.* Only here.
16 opened, &c. See Num. 16. 30.
swallowed up. Gr. *katapinō.* Occ. seven times in N.T. See 1 Cor. 15. 54. Cp. Isa. 59. 19.
17 with. Gr. *epi.* Ap. 104. ix. 2.
went = went away, as in John 11. 46.
remnant. Ap. 124. 3.
seed. Believers, Jew and Gentile, who are seen 7. 9.
and have = holding.
Jesus. Ap. 98. X.
Christ. The texts omit. They add here the first clause of 13. 1, altering to "he stood".

13. 1-8. Note the Fig. *Polysyndeton.* Ap. 6.
And . . . sea. See 12. 17.
upon. Ap. 104. ix. 3.
and saw = and I saw (Ap. 133. I. 1).
beast = wild beast. See 6. 8.
rise up = coming up, as 7. 2 (ascending).
out of. Ap. 104. vii.
having, &c. The texts read "having ten horns and seven heads". Cp. 12. 3 and 17. 7–12.
upon. Ap. 104. ix. 1. **crowns.** See 12. 3.
upon. Ap. 104. ix. 3.
the name. Read "names". See 17. 3.
2 unto = to.
leopard. Gr. *pardalis.* Only here. In Sept. it occ. Jer. 5. 6; 13. 23. Hos. 13. 7. Hab. 1. 8.
lion. See Dan. 7. 4, 5, 6, and esp. *v.* 7 and Note.
dragon. See 12. 3.
him. The being from the abyss (17. 8); the "another" of John 5. 43, and see Luke 4. 6.

power. App. 172. 1; 176. 1. Cp. Dan. 8. 24. 2 Thess. 2. 9. **seat** = throne. **authority.** Ap. 172. 5. Its source will not be recognized by the peoples at the outset. **3 I saw.** Texts omit. **one of** = one from among (Gr. *ek*). **wounded** = slain. Same word in 5. 6. **to.** Gr. *eis.* Ap. 104. vi. **deadly wound** = death-stroke. **wound.** Gr. *plēgē.* See 9. 20. **healed.** Gr. *therapeuō.* Only here, and *v.* 12, in Rev. **world.** Ap. 129. 4. **after.** Read, "(and followed) after". **4 worshipped.** Ap. 137. 1. **which.** The texts read "because he". **power** = the power. Ap. 172. 5; "authority" in *v.* 2. **who.** The texts read "and who". **make war.** The same word in 17. 14. This being will stop wars and be acclaimed by the peoples on that account. **with.** Gr. *meta.* Ap. 104. xi. 1. **5 speaking.** Ap. 121. 7. **continue.** Lit. do, or act. 2 Thess. 2. 3 records the coming of "the man of sin (lawlessness)", who is this beast from the sea. In 2 Thess. 2. 8 "that wicked" = "the lawless one", who is the beast from the earth, *vv.* 11–18. **6 in.** Gr. *eis.* Ap. 104. vi. **blasphemy.** The texts read "blasphemies". **against.** Gr. *pros.* Ap. 104. xv. 3. **God.** Ap. 98. I. i. 1. **His name** = His Name, i. e. the Christ of God. See Acts 2. 21 and cp. Ex. 23. 21. **tabernacle.** Gr. *skēnē.* In Rev. here; 15. 5; 21. 3. **and.** Omit, and supply ellipsis with "that is". **them** = those. **that dwell.** Lit. tabernacling. **in.** Ap. 104. viii. **heaven.** See 3. 12.

7 And it was given [2] unto him to °make war
[4] with the °saints, and to overcome them: and
[4]power was given him °over °all kindreds,
and °tongues, and °nations.
8 And all that dwell [-1-]upon the °earth shall
[4] worship °him, whose °names °are °not
written [-6] in the book of °life of the Lamb slain
°from the °foundation of the world.
9 °If °any man have an ear, let him hear.
10 °He that leadeth into captivity shall go
°into captivity: °he that killeth °with the
sword must be killed °with the sword. Here is
the patience and the °faith of the [7] saints.
11 And I °beheld °another °beast coming up
[1] out of the [8] earth; and he had two °horns
like a lamb, and he °spake as a [2] dragon.
12 And he exerciseth all the [4] power of the
first [1] beast before him, and °causeth the [8] earth
and them which dwell °therein °to [4] worship
the first [1] beast, whose [3] deadly wound was
[3] healed.
13 And he doeth great °wonders, °so that he
maketh °fire come down °from [6] heaven °on
the [8] earth °in the sight of °men,
14 And °deceiveth them that dwell °on
the [8] earth °by *the means of* those °miracles
°which he had power to do [13] in the sight of
the [1] beast; saying to them that dwell °on
the [8] earth, that they should make an °image
to the [1] beast, which had the [3] wound °by
a sword, and °did live.
15 And °he had power to give °life [2] unto the
[14] image of the [1] beast, °that the [14] image of the
[1] beast should both °speak, and cause °that
as many as would °not [4] worship the [14] image
of the [1] beast should be killed.
16 And °he causeth all, °both °small and
great, rich and poor, free and °bond, °to
receive a °mark °in their right hand, or °in
their °foreheads:
17 And [15] that °no °man °might °buy or sell,
°save he that °had the [16] mark, °or the name
of the [1] beast, or the number of his name.
18 °Here is °wisdom. °Let him that hath
°understanding °count the number of the
[1] beast: for it is the number of a °man; and his
number *is* °Six hundred threescore *and* six.

𝔛 v. 𝔥[5] **14** And I °looked, and °lo, °a Lamb °stood
°on the °mount Sion, and °with Him an
°hundred forty *and* four thousand, having
°His Father's name written °in their foreheads.

7 make war. Not the term in *v.* 4 (*polemeō*), but indicating a special attack upon "the saints". See 11. 7. Dan. 7. 21; 8. 12, 24; 11. 31.
saints. See 5. 8 and 11. 18.
over. Ap. 104. ix. 3.
all kindreds=every tribe. The texts add "and people".
tongues, nations. Sing. number.
8 earth. Same as "world", *v.* 3.
him. The ellipsis follows, (every one).
names. All the texts read "name".
are not=hath not (Ap. 105. I) been.
life=the life. Ap. 170. 1. **from.** Ap. 104. iv.
foundation, &c. See Ap. 146.
9 If, &c. See 2. 7. Eighth and last occ. Here to *individuals*, no longer to corporate churches. Note Fig. *Polyptōton*. Ap. 6.
If. Ap. 118. 2. a. **any man.** Ap. 123. 3.
10 He that, &c.=If any one is for captivity, into captivity he goeth; if any one is to be killed with the sword, with the sword he is killed. Heb. idioms for destiny. See Jer. 15. 2; 43. 11. Ezek. 5. 2, 12. Zech. 11. 9. None will escape the beast.
He that. Read, If (Ap. 118. 2. a) any one (Ap. 123. 3).
into. Ap. 104. vi.
with. Gr. *en.* Ap. 104. viii.
faith. Ap. 150. II. 1.
11 beheld=saw, as *v.* 1. **another.** Ap. 124. 1.
beast=wild beast, but distinguished from that of *v.* 1. See *vv.* 12, 14, 15, &c. The beast of *v.* 1 is political, this beast is religious.
horns. Gr. *keras*, horn, occ. ten times in Rev. (first in 5. 6) and once Luke 1. 69. Nowhere else in N. T.
spake=was speaking. Ap. 121. 7.
12 before him=in his sight.
causeth. Occ. eight times in connection with this "false prophet". See Ap. 197. 6.
therein=in (Gr. *en*) it.
to worship=in order that (Gr. *hina*) they shall worship (Ap. 137. 1). The texts read future tense.
13 wonders. Ap. 176. 3.
so that. Gr. *hina.* **fire.** Add "also".
from. Gr. *ek.* Ap. 104. vii.
on. Gr. *eis.* Ap. 104. vi.
in the sight of=before, as *v.* 12.
men. Ap. 123. 1.
14 deceiveth=he deceiveth. Cp. 2 Thess. 2. 9–11. 1 Tim. 4. 1–3. For miracles of themselves are no proof of a Divine mission. The Lord's miracles were "signs" for His People to ponder. The miracles here are to impress credulous unbelievers. **on.** Ap. 104. ix. 1.
by *the means of*. Ap. 104. v. 2.
miracles. Same as "wonders", *v.* 13.
which . . . power=which it was given him.
image. Gr. *eikōn.* First of ten occ. in Rev. See Matt. 22. 20. See Ap. 197. 6.
by=of. Gen. case. No prep.
did live=lived (again). See Ap. 170. 1.

15 he had power=it was given him. **life.** Gr. *pneuma.* Ap. 101. II. 12. **that**=in order that. Gr. *hina.* **speak.** Ap. 121. 7. **not.** Ap. 105. II. **16 he.** I. e. the second beast. **both.** Omit, and read "and" before "the rich" and "the free". **small, &c.**=the little, &c. (Note Fig. *Polysyndeton.* Ap. 6.) **bond.** Ap. 190. I. 2. **to receive.** Lit. in order that (Gr. *hina*) they may be given (the texts read plural). **mark.** Gr. *charagma.* First of eight occ. in Rev. See Acts 17. 29. **in**=upon. Ap. 104. ix. 1. **in**=upon. Ap. 104. ix. 3, with texts. **foreheads.** Texts read sing. **17 no.** Ap. 105. II. **man.** Ap. 123. 3. **might**=should be able to. **buy or sell.** The great boycott of the future. **save**=except. Gr. *ei* (Ap. 118. 2) *mē* (Ap. 105. II). **had**=hath. **or.** Omit. **18 Here, &c.** See 17. 9. **wisdom.** Cp. Ap. 132. II. iii. **Let him that**=He that. **understanding.** Gr. *nous.* See 1 Cor. 14. 14. **count**=calculate. See Luke 14. 28. **man.** Ap. 123. 1. **Six hundred, &c.** The Gr. for this number is χξϛ: three letters which by gematria (Ap. 10)=600, 60, 6=666. It is the number of a *name.* When the *name* of the "beast" (antichrist) is known, it will doubtless be recognized by both computation (see above) and gematria. The three letters SSS (=666) formed the symbol of *Isis* and the secret symbol of the old "Mysteries". That ancient "mysteries" and modern "beliefs" are becoming closely allied, witness the rapid growth and spread of Spiritism, Theosophy, and Occultism of every kind. (Some ancient authorities read 616, used by the Jews of the worship of the Emperor.)

14. 1 looked=saw. Ap. 133. I. i. **lo.** Ap. 133. I. 2. **a**=the, as all the texts. **stood**=standing. **on.** Ap. 104. ix. 3. **mount Sion.** Cp. Heb. 12. 22. **with.** Ap. 104. xi. 1. **hundred, &c.** See 7. 3–8. **His . . . name.** The texts read "His name and His Father's name". **in**=upon. Ap. 104. ix. 1.

2 And I heard a voice ° from ° heaven, as ° the
voice of ° many waters, and as ° the voice of
° a great thunder: and ° I heard the voice of
° harpers harping ° with their harps:
3 And they ° sung as it were a ° new song
before the throne, and before the four beasts,
and the elders: and ° no man could learn ° that
song ° but the hundred *and* forty *and* four
thousand, which ° were ° redeemed ° from the
° earth.

C 4 These are they which were ° not defiled
[1] with women; for they are ° virgins. These
are they which follow the Lamb whithersoever He goeth. These were [3] redeemed ° from
among ° men, ° *being* the ° firstfruits ° unto ° God
and to the Lamb.
5 And ° in their mouth ° was found ° no guile:
for they are ° without fault ° before the throne
of God.

𝔛 v. $\mathfrak{E}^5$ A i. a^1 6 And I ° saw ° another angel ° fly [5] in ° the
° midst of heaven, having ° the ° everlasting
° gospel to ° preach [4] unto them that dwell [1] on
the [3] earth, and ° to every nation, and kindred,
and tongue, and people;

b^1 7 Saying [2] with a ° loud voice, "Fear [4] God, and
give ° glory to Him; for ° the hour of His
° judgment is come: and ° worship Him That
made [2] heaven, and [3] earth, and ° the sea, and
° the fountains of waters."

ii. a^2 8 And ° there followed [6] another angel, saying,
b^2 ° "Babylon is fallen, is fallen, that great ° city,
° because she made all nations drink ° of the
wine of the wrath of her fornication."

iii. a^3 9 And ° the third angel followed them, saying
[2] with a [7] loud voice,

b^3 ° "If ° any man [7] worship the beast and his
image, and receive *his* mark [1] in his forehead,
or ° in his hand,
10 ° The same shall drink [8] of the wine of ° the
wrath of [4] God, which is poured out ° without
mixture ° into the cup of His indignation; and
he shall be ° tormented [2] with fire and ° brimstone
in the presence of the ° holy angels, and in the
presence of the Lamb:
11 And the ° smoke of their ° torment ascendeth
up ° for ever and ever: and they have [5] no rest
day nor night, who [7] worship the beast and
his image, and ° whosoever receiveth the
mark of his name."
12 Here is the patience of the ° saints: ° here
are they that keep the ° commandments of
[4] God, and ° the faith of ° Jesus.

2 from = out of. Ap. 104. vii.
heaven. See 3. 12. **the** = a.
many waters. See 1. 15; 19. 6. **a.** Omit.
I heard, &c. The texts read "the voice which I heard (was that) of harpers", &c.
harpers, &c. Accompanying the voice.
with. Ap. 104. viii.
3 sung = sing. **new song.** See 5. 9.
new. See Matt. 9. 17. **no man.** Gr. *oudeis.*
that song = the song. Only instance where the words of the song are not given. A *new* song, by a *new* company, with a *new* theme.
but. Lit. if (Ap. 118. 2. a) not (Ap. 105. II).
were = had been.
redeemed = purchased. Rendered "buy" in 13. 17, &c. See Matt. 13. 44. 1 Cor. 6. 20.
from. Ap. 104. iv. **earth.** Ap. 129. 4.
4 not. Ap. 105. I.
virgins. The reference is to the pollutions connected with the great religious system under antichrist in the coming days.
from among. Ap. 104. iv. **men.** Ap. 123. 1.
being. Read "*to be*".
firstfruits. See Rom. 8. 23. **unto** = to.
God. Ap. 98. I. i. 1.
5 in. Ap. 104. viii.
was . . . guile = was not found (*the*) lie, as the texts.
no. Ap. 105. I. **without fault.** See Eph. 1. 4.
before . . . God. The texts omit.

$\mathfrak{E}^5$ (p. 1883). **14. 6–20.** THE FIFTH VISION "ON EARTH". (*Alternation.*)

The Six Angels and the Son of Man.

$\mathfrak{E}^5$ | A | i. | a^1 | 6. The *first* angel.
b^1 | 7. His proclamation.
ii. | a^2 | 8–. The *second* angel.
b^2 | –8. His declaration.
iii. | a^3 | 9–. The *third* angel.
b^3 | –9–13. His denunciation (–9–11). His consolation (12, 13).
A | B | iv. | a^4 | 14–. THE SON OF MAN.
b^4 | –14. What He had. A sharp sickle.
v. | a^5 | 15–. The *fourth* angel.
b^5 | –15, 16. His command to the Son of Man (–15). Its execution (16). } The harvest.
B | vi. | a^6 | 17–. The *fifth* angel.
b^6 | –17. What he had. A sharp sickle.
vii. | a^7 | 18–. The *sixth* angel.
b^7 | –18–20. His command to the fifth angel (–18). Its execution (19, 20). } The vintage.

6 saw. As "looked", *v.* 1.
another. Ap. 124. 1. **fly** = flying.
the. Omit. **midst of heaven.** See 8. 13.
the = an. **everlasting.** Ap. 151. II. B. ii. 3.
gospel. Gr. *euangelion.* Only here in Rev. Cp. App. 121. 4 and 140. I. **preach.** Ap. 121. 4.
to. The texts read *epi* (Ap. 104. ix. 3).
7 loud = great. **glory.** See p. 1511.
the hour, &c. Cp. Isa. 61. 2 and the point where our Lord stopped in His reading (Luke 4. 19). **judgment.** Ap. 177. 7. Here; 16. 7; 18. 10; 19. 2. **worship.** Ap. 137. 1. **the.** Omit. **8 there,** &c. Read "another (*v.* 6), a second angel, followed". **Babylon . . . city** = Fallen, fallen (*is*) Babylon the great. Cp. 18. 2 and Isa. 21. 9. **city.** The texts omit. **because she.** The texts read "which". **of.** Ap. 104. vii. **9 the third,** &c. Read "another (*v.* 6), a third". **If.** Ap. 118. 2. a. **any man.** Ap. 123. 3. **in.** Ap. 104. ix. 3. **10 The same,** &c. = He also (emph.) shall drink. **the . . . God** = God's (Ap. 98. I. i. 1) fury. **without mixture** = undiluted. **into.** Gr. *en.* Ap. 104. viii. **tormented.** See 9. 5. **brimstone.** Gr. *theion.* See 9. –17. **holy.** Gr. *hagios.* See Acts 9. 13. **11 smoke . . . torment.** Cp. Isa. 34. 10. **torment.** See 9. 5. **for . . . ever** = unto ages of ages. Gr. *eis* (Ap. 104. vi) *aiōnas aiōnōn.* No art., only occ. in this form. Cp. Ap. 151. II. A. ii. 9. a and Ap. 129. 2. **whosoever** = if (Ap. 118. 2. a) any one (Ap. 123. 3). Fig. *Synecdochē* (of Genus). Ap. 6. **12 saints.** Same as "holy", *v.* 10. See 11. 18. **here** *are.* Omit. **commandments.** Gr. *entolē.* In Rev. only here; 12. 17; 22. 14. **the faith,** &c. I. e. the faith (Ap. 150. II. 1) which Jesus gives. Genitive of Relation (Subjective or Objective). Ap. 17. **Jesus.** Ap. 98. X. The first of five occ. in Rev. of the name without the title "Lord" or "Christ".

13 And I heard a voice [2]from [2]heaven saying °unto me, "Write, °'Blessed *are* °the dead which die [5]in the °Lord [3]from °henceforth: Yea, saith the °Spirit, °that they may °rest [2]from their °labours; °and their °works do °follow them.'"

B iv. a[4] 14 And I °looked, and °behold, a white cloud, and °upon the cloud *One* °sat like °unto the °Son of Man, having °on His head a golden °crown,

b[4] and [5]in His hand a sharp sickle.

v. a[5] 15 And [6]another angel came °out of the °Temple, crying [2]with a [7]loud voice to °Him That sat [14]on the cloud,

b[5] °"Thrust in Thy sickle, and reap: for the °time is come °for Thee to reap; for the harvest of the [3]earth is °ripe."

16 And He That sat [14]on the cloud °thrust in His sickle [1]on the [3]earth; and the [3]earth was reaped.

B vi. a[6] 17 And [6]another angel came [15]out of the [15]Temple which is [5]in [2]heaven,

b[6] He also having a sharp sickle.

vii. a[7] 18 And [6]another angel came °out from the °altar, °which had °power °over °fire;

b[7] and °cried with a [7]loud cry to him that had the sharp sickle, saying, [15]"Thrust in thy sharp sickle, and gather the clusters of the °vine of the [3]earth; for her grapes °are fully ripe."

19 And the angel [16]thrust in his sickle °into the [3]earth, and gathered the [18]vine of the [3]earth, and °cast *it* °into the great winepress of the wrath of [4]God.

20 And the winepress was trodden without the city, and blood came [15]out of the winepress, even unto the horse bridles, °by the space of a °thousand *and* °six hundred °furlongs.

vi. **D**[6] A **15** And I °saw °another °sign °in °heaven, great and marvellous, °seven angels having the °seven last °plagues; for °in them is °filled up the wrath of °God.

B 2 And I [1]saw as it were a °sea of glass mingled with fire: and them that had gotten the °victory °over the beast, and °over his image, and °over his mark, °*and* °over the number of his name, °stand °on the °sea of glass, having °the harps of [1]God.

3 And they sing the °song of Moses the °servant of [1]God, °and the °song of the Lamb, saying, "**Great and marvellous** *are* **Thy works,** °LORD [1]God °Almighty; °**just and** °**true** *are* **Thy ways,** Thou King of °saints.

4 Who shall °not fear °Thee, O [3]LORD, and °glorify Thy name? **for** ***Thou*** **only** ***art*** °**holy:** for all °nations shall come and °worship before Thee, for Thy °judgments °are °made manifest."

A 5 And °after that I °looked, and °behold, the °Temple of the tabernacle of the °testimony [1]in [1]heaven was opened:

13 unto me. Omit. Blessed. See 1. 3.
the dead. Ap. 139.
Lord. Ap. 98. VI. i. *β*. 2. B.
henceforth. Observe the period referred to.
Spirit. Ap. 101. II. 3.
that = in order that. Gr. *hina*.
rest. Cp. 6. 11. labours = toilsome labours. See 2. 2.
and. The texts read "for".
works = rewards. Fig. *Metonymy* (of Cause). Ap. 6.
follow. Add "with" (Ap. 104. xi. 1).
14 looked = saw, as *v.* 1. behold. As "lo", *v.* 1.
upon. Ap. 104. ix. 3.
sat = sitting. unto = to.
Son of Man. Last occ. of this title. See Matt. 8. 20 and Ap. 98. XVI. See Ps. 8. 4. Ezek. 2. 1. Dan. 7. 13.
on. Ap. 104. ix. 1.
crown. See 2. 10 and Ap. 197. 6.
15 out of. Ap. 104. vii.
Temple. Gr. *naos*. See 3. 12 and Matt. 23. 16.
Him That sat. Lit. The One sitting.
Thrust in. Ap. 174. 4. time = hour.
for Thee. Omit. ripe. Lit. dried up.
16 thrust in = cast. Gr. *ballō*. Not the word in *v.* 15.
18 out from. Ap. 104. vii. altar. See 6. 9.
which had = the (one) having.
power. Ap. 172. 5. over. Ap. 104. ix. 1.
fire = the fire. I.e. the altar fire.
cried = he called. Gr. *phōneō*. Only occ. in Rev.
vine. The vine is the vine of the earth (Deut. 32. 32, 33). Cp. Isa. 34. 1–8. Joel 3. 12–15. Zeph. 3. 8. See 19. 15 and cp. Isa. 63. 1–4.
are fully ripe. Gr. *akmazō*. Only here.
19 into. Ap. 104. vi. cast. As "thrust", *v.* 16.
20 by the space of = as far as. Gr. *apo*. Ap. 104. iv.
thousand. Gr. *chilioi*. As 11. 3; 12. 6, and in ch. 20.
six hundred. See 13. 18.
furlongs. See Ap. 51. III. 1 (2).

D[6] (p. 1883). **15. 1–8.** THE SIXTH VISION "IN HEAVEN". (*Alternation.*)

D[6] A | 15. 1. The seven angels.
  B | 2–4. Worship offered.
 A | 5–7. The seven angels.
  B | 8. Worship no longer possible.

15. 1 saw. Ap. 133. I. 1. another. Ap. 124. 1.
sign. Ap. 176. 3. See 12. 1.
in. Ap. 104. viii. heaven. See 3. 12.
seven angels. Occ. *seven* times; here, *vv.* 6, 7, 8; 16. 1; 17. 1; 21. 9. See 197. 6.
seven. See App. 10 and 197.
plagues. See 9. 20 and Ap. 197. 6.
filled up. Cp. Ap. 125. 2. God. Ap. 98. I. i. 1.
2 sea of glass = glassy sea. See 4. 6.
victory. See 2. 7 and Ap. 197. 6.
over. Gr. *ek*. Ap. 104. vii.
over . . . mark. The texts omit.
and. Omit. stand = standing.
on. Ap. 104. ix. 3. the. Omit.
3 song of Moses. See Ex. 15. 1–19. Deut. 32. 1–43.
song. Gr. *ōdē*. See 5. 9.
servant. Ap. 190. I. 2.
and the song, &c. Two songs are specified in this *v.* In connection with this "song of the Lamb" cp. Ps. 86. 9–12. Isa. 66. 15, 16, 23. Zeph. 2. 11. Zech. 14. 16, 17, &c. "Great . . . made manifest" (*vv.* 3, 4). These are the words of the song of the Lamb; distinct from, but the complement of, the song of Moses.
LORD = O LORD. Ap. 98. VI. i. *β*. 1. B. b.
Almighty = the Almighty. Ap. 98. IV.
just. Ap. 191. 1.
true. Ap. 175. 2. See p. 1511.
saints. The texts read "nations".
4 not. Ap. 105. III. Thee. The texts omit.
glorify. Gr. *doxazō*. Only here and 18. 7 in Rev. See p. 1511. holy. See Acts 2. 27. nations = the nations. worship. Ap. 137. 1. judgments = righteous sentence. App. 177. 3 and 191. 4. are = were. made manifest. Ap. 106. I. v. **5** after that. See 1. 19. looked. As "saw", *v.* 1. behold. The texts omit. Temple. See Matt. 23. 16. testimony. Gr. *marturion*. Only here in Rev.; *marturia* in nine other places. See p. 1511.

6 And the [1]seven angels came °out of the
[5]Temple, having the [1]seven [1]plagues, clothed
°in pure and white linen, and °having their
breasts girded with golden girdles.
7 And one °of the four °beasts gave °unto the
[1]seven angels [1]seven golden °vials full of the
wrath of [1]God, Who °liveth °for ever and ever.
B 8 And the [5]Temple was filled with smoke
°from the °glory of [1]God, and °from His
°power; and °no man was able to enter °into
the [5]Temple, till the [1]seven [1]plagues of the
[1]seven angels °were fulfilled.

ℨ vi. E6 **16** And I heard a great voice °out of the
°Temple saying to the °seven angels,
°"Go your ways, and pour out the °vials of the
wrath of °God °upon the °earth."
2 And the first °went, and poured out his
[1]vial °upon the [1]earth; and there °fell a
°noisome and °grievous °sore °upon the °men
which had the °mark of the °beast, and °*upon*
them °which worshipped his image.
3 And the second °angel poured out his [1]vial
[1]upon the sea; and it became as the blood of
a °dead *man:* and every °living °soul died °in
the sea.
4 And the third [3]angel poured out his [1]vial
[1]upon the rivers and fountains of waters;
and they became blood.
5 And I heard the angel of the waters say,
"Thou art °righteous, °O Lord, Which art, and
wast, °and shalt be, because Thou hast °judged
thus.
6 For they °have shed the blood of °saints
and °prophets, and Thou hast given them blood
to drink; °for they are worthy."
7 And I heard °another out of the altar say,
"Even so, °LORD [1]God °Almighty, °true and
[5]righteous *are* Thy °judgments."
8 And the fourth [3]angel poured out his [1]vial
°upon the sun; and °power was given °unto
him to scorch [2]men °with fire.
9 And [2]men were scorched with great heat,
and blasphemed the name of [1]God, Which hath
°power °over these plagues: and they °re-
pented °not to give Him °glory.
10 And the fifth [3]angel poured out his [1]vial
[8]upon the °seat of the [2]beast; and his kingdom
°was full of darkness; and they gnawed their
tongues °for pain,
11 °And blasphemed °the [1]God of °heaven
°because of their pains °and their [2]sores,
and [9]repented [9]not °of their deeds.
12 And the sixth [3]angel poured out his [1]vial
[8]upon the great river Euphrates; and the
water thereof was dried up, °that the way of
the °kings °of °the east might be prepared.
13 And I °saw three unclean °spirits °like
frogs *come* [1]out of the mouth of the °dragon,
and [1]out of the mouth of the [2]beast, and [1]out of
the mouth of the °false prophet.
14 For they are °the [13]spirits of °devils,
working °miracles, *which* go forth °unto the
kings °of the earth and of the whole °world,
to gather them °to the battle of °that great
day of [1]God °Almighty.

6 out of. Ap. 104. vii.
in . . . linen. The texts read "with *precious* stone pure and bright".
having, &c.=girt about (Gr. *peri.* Ap. 104. xiii. 2) the breasts.
7 of. Ap. 104. vii.
beasts. See 4. 6. **unto**=to.
vials. See 5. 8 and Ap. 197. 6.
liveth, &c. See 1. 18. **liveth.** Ap. 170. 1.
for . . . ever. Ap. 151. II. A. ii. 9. a.
8 from. Ap. 104. vii. **glory.** See p. 1511.
power. Ap. 172. 1.
no man=no one. Gr. *oudeis.*
into. Ap. 104. vi.
were fulfilled. Cp. Ap. 125. 2.

16. 1 out of. Ap. 104. vii.
Temple. See Matt. 23. 16.
seven angels. See 15. 1.
Go . . . ways=Go forth. Gr. *hupagō.*
vials. See 15. 7. **God.** Ap. 98. I. i. 1.
upon=into. Gr. *eis.* Ap. vi.
earth. Ap. 129. 4.
2 went=went forth. Gr. *aperchomai.*
upon. Gr. *epi,* but the texts read *eis* as *v.* 1.
fell. Lit. came or became.
noisome. Ap. 128. III. 2.
grievous. Ap. 128. III. 1.
sore=ulcer. Gr. *helkos.* Only here, *v.* 11. Luke 16. 21.
upon. Gr. *eis,* but the texts read *epi* (Ap. 104. ix. 3).
men. Ap. 123. 1. **mark.** See 13. 16.
beast. See 12. 1. ***upon* them.** Omit.
which worshipped = those worshipping (Ap. 137. 1).
3 angel. Omit.
dead *man.* Ap. 139.
living soul. Lit. soul of life. Cp. Ap. 13.
living. Ap. 170. 1.
soul=creature. Ap. 110. I. 2. **in.** Ap. 104. viii.
5 righteous. Ap. 191. 1.
O Lord. The texts omit.
and shalt be. The texts read "Thou Holy One".
judged. Ap. 122. 1.
6 have. Omit. **saints.** See Acts 9. 13.
prophets. Ap. 189.
for. The texts omit.
7 another out of. The texts omit. Supply the ellipsis with "the angel of"; cp. angel of the waters, *v.* 5.
LORD=O LORD. Ap. 98. VI. i. *β.* 1. B. b.
Almighty. Ap. 98. IV.
true. Ap. 175. 2. See p. 1511.
judgments. Ap. 177. 7.
8 upon. Ap. 104. ix. 3.
power, &c. = it was given. **unto**=to.
with. Gr. *en.* Ap. 104. viii.
9 power. The texts add "the". Ap. 172. 5.
over. Ap. 104. ix. 3.
repented. Ap. 111. I. 1.
not. Ap. 105. I. **glory.** See p. 1511.
10 seat=throne.
was, &c.=became darkened. Cp. 8. 12; 9. 2.
for. Gr. *ek.* Ap. 104. vii.
11 And. Add "they".
the God of heaven. See 11. 13.
heaven. See 3. 12.
because of, of. Gr. *ek.* Ap. 104. vii.
and. Add "because of" (*ek,* as above).
12 that=in order that. Gr. *hina.*
kings. Supply "*that come*".
of. Gr. *apo.* Ap. 104. iv.
the east. Lit. the rising of the sun.
13 saw. Ap. 133. I. 1.
spirits. Ap. 101. II. 12.
like=as it were, with texts. **dragon.** See 12. 3.
false prophet. Gr. *pseudoprophētēs.* In Rev. here; 19. 20; 20. 10. See 13. 11-17.

14 the. Omit. **devils**=demons. **miracles.** Ap. 176. 3. **unto.** Gr. *epi.* Ap. 104. ix. 3. **of the earth and.** The texts omit. **world.** Ap. 129. 3. **to.** Gr. *eis.* Ap. 104. vi. **that**=the. **Almighty.** Add "the". See *v.* 7.

15 °Behold, I °come as a thief. °Blessed *is* he
that watcheth, and keepeth his garments,
°lest he walk naked, and they °see his °shame.
16 And he gathered them together °into
°a place called in °the Hebrew °tongue °Arma-
geddon.
17 And the seventh [3]angel poured out his
[1]vial °into the air; and there came a great
voice °out of the [1]Temple °of heaven, °from the
throne, saying, "It is done."
18 And there °were °voices, and thunders,
and lightnings; and there °was a great °earth-
quake, such as °was [9]not since [2]men °were
°upon the [1]earth, so mighty an °earthquake,
°*and* so great.
19 And the great city °was divided [16]into
three parts, and the cities of the nations fell:
and °great Babylon °came in remembrance
before [1]God, to give [8]unto her the cup of the
wine of the °fierceness of His °wrath.
20 And every island fled away, and the mountains were [9]not found.
21 And there fell [8]upon [2]men a great hail
[1]out of [11]heaven, *every stone* about the weight
of a °talent: and [2]men blasphemed [1]God [11]be-
cause of the plague of the hail; for the plague
thereof °was exceeding great.

17 And there came one °of the °seven angels
which had the seven vials, and °talked
°with me, saying °unto me, "Come hither; I
will shew °unto thee the °judgment of the
great whore that sitteth °upon many °waters:
2 [1]With whom the kings of the °earth °have
committed fornication, and °the inhabiters of
the °earth have been made drunk °with the
wine of her fornication."
3 °So he carried me away °in the °Spirit °into
°the wilderness: and I °saw °a woman °sit
°upon a scarlet coloured beast, full of names
of blasphemy, having seven °heads and ten
horns.
4 And the woman was arrayed in purple and
scarlet colour, and °decked with gold and precious °stones and pearls, having a °golden cup
[3]in her hand full of °abominations °and filthiness of her fornication:
5 And [3]upon her forehead *was* a name
written, °MYSTERY, BABYLON THE
GREAT, THE MOTHER OF °HARLOTS
AND [4]ABOMINATIONS °OF THE [2]EARTH.
6 And I [3]saw the [3]woman drunken [2]with the
blood of the °saints, and [2]with the blood of the
°martyrs of °Jesus: and when I [3]saw her, I
wondered with great °admiration.
7 And the angel said unto me, "Wherefore
didst thou °marvel? I will tell thee the
[5]mystery of the [3]woman, and of the beast
that carrieth her, which hath the seven [3]heads
and ten horns.
8 The beast that thou [3]sawest °was, and is
°not; and °shall ascend °out of the bottomless
pit, and go [3]into °perdition: and they that
dwell °on the [2]earth shall [6]wonder, whose
°names °were °not written °in the °book of
°life °from the °foundation of the world, when

15 This *v.* forms a parenthesis. **Behold.** Ap. 133. I. 2.
come, &c. See 1 Thess. 5. 2. **Blessed.** See 1. 3.
lest = in order that (Gr. *hina*) not (Ap. 105. II).
see. Ap. 133. I. 5.
shame. The Gr. word only here and Rom. 1. 27 (unseemly). **16 into.** Ap. 104. vi.
a = the. **the.** Omit. **tongue.** Omit.
Armageddon. Gr. *harmagedōn*, as most texts. The word = mount of Megiddo. Therefore in Palestine, not Europe. See Judges 5. 19, &c. In Isa. 10. 28 the Sept. reads "*Maggedō*", for Migron.
17 into. Gr. *eis* as in *v.* 16; but the texts read *epi* (Ap. 104. ix. 3).
out of. Gr. *apo.* The texts read *ek* (as *v.* 1).
of heaven. The texts omit. **from.** Ap. 104. iv.
18 were, was. Lit. came to be.
voices, &c. The texts read "lightnings, and voices, and thunders". See 4. 5.
earthquake. Occ. seven times in Rev. See 6. 12.
upon. Ap. 104. ix. 1. ***and.*** Read "*or*".
19 was divided. Lit. became.
great Babylon. Cp. Dan. 4. 30.
came, &c. Lit. was remembered.
fierceness. Gr. *thumos* (wrath, in *v.* 1).
wrath. Gr. *orgē.* Fig. *Pleonasm.* Ap. 6.
21 talent. See Ap. 51. II. 6. (2). **was** = is.
17. 1 of. Gr. *ek.* Ap. 104. vii.
seven angels . . . vials. See 15. 7.
talked. Ap. 121. 7. **with.** Ap. 104. xi. 1.
unto me. The texts omit. **unto** = to.
judgment. Ap. 177. 6.
upon. Ap. 104. ix. 1. **waters.** See *v.* 15.
2 earth. Ap. 129. 4. **have.** Omit.
the inhabiters, &c. The texts read "they that inhabit the earth were made drunken", &c.
with. Gr. *ek.* Ap. 104. vii.
3 So = And. **in.** Ap. 104. viii.
Spirit. Ap. 101. II. 3. See 1. 10. **into.** Ap. 104. vi.
the. No art., but this is often omitted after a prep.
saw. Ap. 133. I. 1.
a woman. I. e. "that great city" of *v.* 18.
sit = sitting; as supported by that being described in *vv.* 8–11. **upon.** Ap. 104. ix. 3.
heads. These are the kings of *v.* 10.
4 decked. Lit. "gilded". **stones** = stone.
golden cup. Cp. Jer. 51. 7.
abominations. Gr. *bdelugma*, used in Sept. of *an idol* (2 Kings 23. 13, &c.); in plural, of *idolatry* (Deut. 18. 9, &c.). Called "abominations" because of the uncleanness practised in the worship.
and filthiness = and having the unclean things; as the texts.
5 MYSTERY. See Ap. 193, and 1. 20. The verse should be read, "And upon her forehead (she had) a name written, a secret symbol (*mustērion*), BABYLON THE GREAT, the mother of the harlots and of the abominations of the earth". The name of the woman is therefore a secret sign or symbol of "that great city" which she personifies (*v.* 18).
HARLOTS = the harlots.
OF THE EARTH. Babylon is the fountain-head of all idolatry and systems of false worship This is the "mystery of iniquity" (2 Thess. 2. 7) seen in all the great "religions" of the world. All alike substitute another god for the God of the Bible; a god made either with the hands or with the imagination, but equally *made*; a religion consisting of human merit and endeavour. The "Reunion of the Churches" of Christendom and the "League of Nations" are two of the most arresting signs of the times.
6 saints. See Acts 9. 13. **martyrs.** See p. 1511.
Jesus. Ap. 98. X.
admiration = wonder. In this phrase is the Fig. *Polyptōton.* Ap. 6.

7 marvel. As "wonder", *vv.* 6, 8. **8 was, &c.** Implying a time between chs. 12 and 13. **not.** Ap. 105. I. **shall** = is about to. **out of.** Ap. 104. vii. **perdition.** See John 17. 12. **on.** Ap. 104. ix. 1. **names.** The texts read "name". **were not** = hath not been. **not.** Ap. 105. I. **in.** Gr. *epi.* Ap. 104. ix. 3. **book, &c.** See Phil. 4. 3. **life.** Ap. 170. 1. **from.** Ap. 104. iv. **foundation, &c.** See Ap. 146.

they °behold the beast °that was, and is °not, °and yet is.

9 °And here *is* the °mind which hath °wisdom. °The seven [3]heads °are seven mountains, °on which the [3] woman sitteth.

10 And °there [9]are seven kings: five °are fallen, °and °one °is, °*and* the °other is °not yet come; and when he °cometh, he must °continue a short space.

11 And the beast that [8]was, and [8]is [8]not, even °𝔥𝔢 is °the eighth, and °is [1]of the seven, and goeth [3] into [8] perdition.

12 And the ten horns which thou [3]sawest [9]are ten kings, which have received °no kingdom as yet; but receive °power as kings °one hour [1] with the beast.

13 These have one °mind, and °shall give their °power and °strength [1] unto the beast.

14 These shall make war [1] with the Lamb, and the Lamb shall °overcome them: for He is °Lord of °lords, and King of kings: and they that are [1] with Him *are* °called, and °chosen, and °faithful."

15 And he saith [1] unto me, "The waters which thou [3]sawest, where the whore sitteth, [9]are peoples, and multitudes, and nations, and tongues.

16 And the ten horns which thou [3]sawest °upon the beast, these °shall hate the whore, and °shall make °her desolate and naked, and °shall eat her flesh, and burn °her °with fire.

17 For °God °hath put °in their hearts to °fulfil His °will, and to °agree, and give their °kingdom [1] unto the beast, until the °words of °God shall be °fulfilled.

18 And the [3]woman which thou [3]sawest is °that great city, which °reigneth °over the °kings of the [2]earth."

E⁶ F¹ m¹ **18** °And °after these things I °saw °another angel °come down °from °heaven, having great °power; and the °earth was °lightened °with his °glory.

2 And he cried °mightily °with a strong °voice, saying, °"Babylon the great is fallen, is fallen, and is become °the °habitation of °devils, and the °hold of every °foul °spirit, and a °cage of every °unclean and hateful bird.

n¹ 3 For all °nations have drunk °of the °wine of the wrath of her fornication, and the kings

behold. Ap. 133. I. 5.
that. The texts read "because it".
and yet is = and shall be present; as the texts.
9 And. Omit.
mind. Same as "understanding" in 13. 18.
wisdom. Cp. Ap. 132. II. iii.
The . . . sitteth. This belongs to *v.* 10.
are. I. e. represent.
on. Ap. 104. ix. 1.
10 there. Or, they. **are fallen** = fell.
and. Omit. **one** = the one.
is. I. e. at this stage of the vision.
and. Omit.
other. The seventh. Ap. 124. 1.
not yet. Gr. *oupō.*
cometh = shall have come.
continue. See p. 1511 (abide).
11 𝔥𝔢 = he himself (emph.). **the** = an.
is. Omit. This being is described as an eighth *head,* not *king.*
12 no . . . as yet. As "not yet" above.
power. Ap. 172. 5.
one hour, i. e. at one and the same hour. Confusion results from substituting "kingdoms" for "kings" in the connection. The Holy Spirit says *kings*; who and what they are will be known at the time of their association with the beast.
13 mind. Ap. 177. 2.
shall give. The texts read "they give", i. e. of their own free will.
power. App. 172. 1 and 176. 1.
strength. Ap. 172. 5.
14 overcome. As in chs. 2 and 3. See Ap. 197. 6.
Lord. Ap. 98. VI. i. *β.* 2. B.
lords. Ap. 98. VI. i.
called. Gr. *klētos.* Only here in Rev. First occ. Matt. 20. 16.
chosen. Gr. *eklektos.* Only here in Rev. See Matt. 20. 16 (first occ.).
faithful. App. 150. III and 175. 4.
16 upon. Gr. *epi*; but the texts read "and".
shall = will.
her. I. e. the city. Cp. Jer. 50. 32.
with. Gr. *en.* Ap. 104. viii.
17 God. Ap. 98. I. i. 1.
hath put = put. Lit. "gave".
in. Ap. 104. vi.
fulfil. Lit. "do".
will. Ap. 177. 2.
agree = carry out (lit. "do") one purpose (Ap. 177. 2).
kingdom. Sing. Cp. *v.* 12.
words. Gr. *rhema,* but the texts read Ap. 121. 10.
fulfilled. Cp. Ap. 125. 2.
18 that = the.
reigneth. Lit. having a kingdom, or sovereignty.
over. Ap. 104. ix. 1.
kings . . . earth. Those who are so called in 16. 14. See also *v.* 2.

See E⁶ (p. 1883). **18. 1–24. THE JUDGMENT OF THE GREAT CITY.** (*Alternation.*)

E⁶ | F¹ | m¹ | 1, 2. Babylon's judgment. Announcement of it.
n¹ | 3. Babylon's associates. Their sin.
G¹ | 4. God's people. Call to "Come out of her".
F² | m² | 5–8. Babylon's judgment. Reasons for it.
n² | 9–19. Babylon's inhabitants. Their lamentation.
G² | 20. God's people. Call to "Rejoice over her".
F³ | m³ | 21. Babylon's judgment. Manner of it.
n³ | 22, 23. Babylon's inhabitants. Their silence.
G³ | 24. God's people. Their blood "found in her".

18. 1 And. Omit. **after, &c.** See 1. 19. **saw.** Ap. 133. I. 1. **another.** Ap. 124. 1. Not the speaker of ch. 17, but one invested with great authority and glory. **come** = coming. **from.** Ap. 104. vii. **heaven.** See 3. 12. **power.** Ap. 172. 5. **earth.** Ap. 129. 4. **lightened.** Gr. *phōtizō.* Cp. Ap. 130. 3. **with.** Same as "from", above. **glory.** See p. 1511. **2 mightily.** The texts read "with (Gr. *en*) a mighty (cp. Ap. 172. 3) voice (Gr. *phōnē*)". **Babylon . . . fallen.** See 14. 8. Isa. 21. 9. Jer. 51. 8. **the** = a. **habitation.** Gr. *katoikētērion.* Only here and Eph. 2. 22, which see. **devils** = demons. See Ap. 101. II. 12. **hold** = prison, or cage, as below. See 2. 10; 20. 7. **foul** = unclean, as below. **spirit.** Ap. 101. II. 12. **cage.** See "hold" above. **unclean.** See "foul" above. **3 nations** = the nations. **of.** Ap. 104. vii. **wine . . . wrath** = furious wine. Fig. *Antimereia* (of Noun). Ap. 6.

of the [1]earth °have committed fornication
°with her, and the merchants of the [1]earth
°are waxed rich °through the °abundance of
her °delicacies."
G[1] 4 And I heard °another [2]voice [1]from [1]heaven,
saying, °"Come °out of her, °My People, °that
ye be °not partakers of her °sins, and °that ye
receive °not [3]of her °plagues.
F[2] m[2] 5 For her [4]sins °have °reached °unto [1]heaven, and °God °hath remembered her °iniquities.
6 °Reward her even as she °rewarded °you,
and °double °unto her double °according to
her works: °in the cup which she °hath filled
°fill to her double.
7 How much she °hath °glorified herself, and
°lived deliciously, so much °torment and sorrow give her: for she saith [6]in her heart,
°'I sit a °queen, and am °no widow, and shall
°see °no sorrow.'
8 °Therefore shall her [4]plagues °come [6]in
one day, death, and mourning, and famine;
and she shall be utterly burned °with fire:
for °strong *is* the °LORD [5]God Who °judgeth
her.
n[2] 9 And the kings of the [1]earth, who °have
committed fornication and [7]lived deliciously
[3]with her, shall bewail her, and lament °for
her, when they °shall °see the smoke of her
°burning,
10 Standing afar °off °for the fear of her
[7]torment, saying, [16]'Alas, alas, °that great city
Babylon, °that °mighty city! for [6]in one hour
is thy °judgment come.'
11 And the merchants of the [1]earth °shall
weep and mourn °over her; for °no man
°buyeth their merchandise °any °more:
12 The merchandise of gold, and silver, and
°precious stones, and of pearls, and fine linen,
and purple, and silk, and scarlet, and all thyine
wood, and all manner vessels of ivory, and all
manner vessels[3] of °most precious wood, and of
brass, and iron, and marble,
13 And cinnamon, and odours, and ointments,
and frankincense, and wine, and oil, and fine
flour, and wheat, and °beasts, and sheep, and
horses, and °chariots, and °slaves, and °souls of
°men.
14 And the fruits °that thy soul lusted after
are departed °from thee, and all things which
were dainty and goodly are °departed °from
thee, and °thou shalt find them °no more
at all.
15 The merchants of these things, which
were made rich °by her, shall stand afar [10]off
[10]for the fear of her [7]torment, weeping and
wailing,

have. Omit.
with. Ap. 104. xi. 1. **are.** Omit.
through=by. Gr. *ek.* Ap. 104. vii.
abundance. App. 172. 1; 176. 1.
delicacies=luxury. Gr. *strēnos.* Only here in N.T.; its verb only in *vv.* 7, 9. This identifies the city with that of ch. 17. In addition, it is here implied that Babylon will become the head-quarters of Spiritism, the habitation of demons, and the hold of every unclean spirit. Jer. 50 and 51 should be carefully studied in connection with these two ch., as many of the things predicted there await fulfilment in the coming evil days.
4 another. Ap. 124. 1.
Come = Come forth.
out of. Ap. 104. vii.
My People. See Jer. 50. 4-9, and cp. Isa. 10. 20, 24.
that=in order that. Gr. *hina.*
not. Ap. 105. II. **sins.** Ap. 128. I. ii. 1.
plagues. Gr. *plēgē.* See 13. 3 (wound) and Ap. 197. 6.
5 have, hath. Omit.
reached. The texts read "joined" or "built together". **unto**=up to.
God. Ap. 98. I. i. 1. **iniquities.** Ap. 128. vii. 2.
6 Reward=Render. Cp. Mark 12. 17 and Jer. 51. 24.
rewarded=rendered. Same word.
you. Omit, and supply "others".
double. This word is put for full compensation. Fig. *Metonymy.* Ap. 6.
unto her. Omit.
according to. Ap. 104. x. 2.
in. Ap. 104. viii.
hath filled, fill=mixed, mix.
7 hath. Omit.
glorified. See p. 1511.
lived deliciously. See *v.* 3 above.
torment. Gr. *basanismos.* Here; *vv.* 10, 15. See 9. 5.
I sit, &c. See Isa. 47. 8.
queen. A queen who is not a widow, implies a king-consort. Or, "no widow" may be Fig. *Tapeinosis.* Ap. 6.
no. Ap. 105. I. **see.** Ap. 133. I. 1.
no. Ap. 105. III.
8 Therefore=For this cause. Gr. *dia* (Ap. 104. v. 2) *touto.*
come. I. e. suddenly. Same word in 2 Pet. 3. 10.
with. Ap. 104. viii.
strong=mighty, as *vv.* 10, 21. See *v.* 2.
LORD. Ap. 98. VI. i. *β.* 1. B. b.
judgeth. The texts read "judged". Ap. 122. 1. The suddenness and completeness of Babylon's judgment and disappearance from the face of the earth is the prominent feature of this prophecy, proving that that judgment *has not yet taken place.* Isa. 13. 20. Jer. 50. 13, 39, 40; 51. 29, 37, 43; &c., await fulfilment.
9 have. Omit.
for=over. Ap. 104. ix. 3.
shall. Omit.
see. Ap. 133. I. 5.
burning. Gr. *purōsis.* Only here, *v.* 18, and 1 Pet. 4. 12.
10 off. Gr. *apo.* Ap. 104. iv.
for. Ap. 104. v. 2. **that**=the.
mighty. See *v.* 8.
judgment. Ap. 177. 7. These "kings of the earth" are those of 17. 2. The ten kings are never seen by John apart from the beast, and the "kings of the earth" are always seen in connection with Babylon. **11 shall.** Omit. **over.** Ap. 104. ix. 3. **no man**=no one. Gr. *oudeis.* **buyeth.** Gr. *agorazō,* rend. "redeemed" in 5. 9; 14. 3, 4; elsewhere always "buy". First occ. Matt. 13. 44. **any**=no. Ap. 105. I. **more**=longer. The texts read here *ouketi.* **12 precious.** Gr. *timios.* The noun in *v.* 19. **most precious.** Superl. of Gr. *timios* above. **13 beasts**=cattle. **chariots.** Gr. *rheda.* Only here. Gallic word for a four-wheeled coach or vehicle, a sign of luxury. **slaves.** Lit. bodies. Gr. *sōma.* By Fig. *Metonymy* (Ap. 6) for "slaves". See Gen. 36. 6 (Sept.). **souls of men** = men. A Hebraism for "persons of men", or simply "men". See (Sept.) Num. 31. 35. 1 Chron. 5. 21. Ezek. 27. 13. **souls.** App. 110. II. and 170. 3. **men.** Ap. 123. 1. Fig. *Polysyndeton* in *vv.* 12, 13. **14 that . . . after.** Lit. of thy soul's (Ap. 110) desire (Gr. *epithumia.* See 1 John 2. 16, 17). **from.** Ap. 104. iv. **departed.** Most texts read "perished". **thou, &c.** Most of the texts read "and they (men) shall never more at all (Gr. *ouketi ou mē.* Ap. 105. III. 6) find them". The list consists entirely of luxuries (see *v.* 3). **15 by.** Gr. *apo.* Ap. 104. iv.

16 °And saying, ° 'Alas, alas, °that great city,
that was clothed in fine linen, and purple,
and scarlet, and decked with gold, and precious
°stones, and pearls!
17 For °in one hour so great riches is °come
to nought.' And every shipmaster, and °all
the company in ships, and sailors, and as many
as °trade by sea, stood afar [10]off,
18 And cried °when they saw the smoke of
her [9]burning, saying, 'What *city is* like °unto
°this great city!'
19 And they cast dust °on their heads, and
cried, weeping and wailing, saying, [16]'Alas,
alas, °that great city, °wherein were [3]made
rich all that had °ships [6]in the sea °by reason
of her costliness! for [6]in °one hour °is she
°made desolate.'
G2 20 Rejoice °over her, *thou* [1]heaven, and *ye*
°holy °apostles and °prophets; for [5]God °hath
avenged you °on her."
F3 m3 21 And a mighty angel took up a stone °like
a great millstone, and cast *it* °into the sea,
saying, "Thus with °violence shall °that
great city Babylon be thrown down, and shall
be found °no more °at all.
n3 22 And the voice of harpers, and musicians,
and of pipers, and trumpeters, shall be heard
[21]no more at all [6]in thee; and no craftsman,
of whatsoever craft *he be*, shall be found
°any more [6]in thee; and the sound of a millstone shall be heard [21]no more at all [6]in thee;
23 And the °light of a °candle shall °shine
[21]no more at all [6]in thee; and the [2]voice of
°the bridegroom and of °the bride shall be
heard [21]no more at all [6]in thee: for thy [3]mer-
chants were the great men of the [1]earth;
for °by thy °sorceries were all °nations °de-
ceived."
G3 24 And [6]in her was found the blood of
°prophets, and of °saints, and of all that were
slain °upon the [11]earth.

𝔛 vii. 𝔥7 P A a **19** °And °after these things I °heard a
great voice of much people °in °heaven,
saying,
b d °"Alleluia; °Salvation, and °glory, °and honour, and °power, °unto the °LORD our °God:
e 2 For °true and °righteous *are* His °judg-
ments: for He °hath °judged the great whore,
which did corrupt the °earth °with her fornication, and °hath avenged the blood of His
°servants °at her hand."

16 And. Omit.
Alas, alas, = Woe! woe! as *vv.* 10 and 19.
that = the.
stones = stone.
17 in one hour. See *v.* 19.
come, &c. As "made desolate", *v.* 19.
all . . . ships. The texts read "every one that saileth any whither", indicating travellers of all kinds.
trade . . . sea. Lit. work the sea, i.e. for a living.
18 when, &c. = as they looked upon (the texts read Ap. 133. I. 5).
unto. Omit. **this** = the.
19 on. Ap. 104. ix. 3.
that = the.
wherein = in (Ap. 104. viii) which.
ships = the ships.
by reason of. Gr. *ek.* Ap. 104. vii.
one hour. See *v.* 10 and cp. Isa. 47. 11; *v.* 17 and Jer. 50. 26: *v.* 19 and Jer. 51. 8. Ancient Babylon, after its capture by Cyrus, *gradually* diminished.
is = was.
made desolate. See "come to nought", *v.* 17.
20 over. Ap. 104. ix. 2, with texts.
holy = saints (see Acts 9. 13) and.
apostles, prophets. Ap. 189.
hath avenged. Lit. judged your judgment (App. 122. 1 and 177. 6); i.e. hath fully avenged you. Fig. *Polyptōton.* Ap. 6.
on. Gr. *ek.* Ap. 104. vii. Now has come the time of the avenging—Luke 18. 7, 8.
21 like = as it were.
into. Ap. 104. vi.
violence = furious rush. Gr. *hormēma.* Only here. R. V. reads "mighty fall". Cp. Acts 14. 5 (assault. Gr. *hormē*). **that** = the.
no more at all. Six times here. Ap. 105. III. 6.
at all. Cp. Jer. 51. 64. Ezek. 26. 21.
22 any more = no more, as above.
23 light. Ap. 130. 1. **candle** = lamp.
shine. See Ap. 106. I. i. **the, the.** Omit.
by. Gr. *en.* Ap. 104. viii.
sorceries = sorcery. See 9. 21.
nations = the nations.
deceived. Ap. 128. VIII. 1. Cp. Isa. 47. 9.
24 prophets. Ap. 189. **saints.** See *v.* 20 (holy).
upon. Ap. 104. ix. i.

19. 1-10 [For Structure see below].

19. 1 And. Omit. **after, &c.** See 4. 1.
heard. The texts add "as it were".
in. Ap. 104. viii.
heaven. See 3. 12.
Alleluia. See Ps. 104. 35.
Salvation = The salvation.
glory = the glory. See p. 1511.
and honour. The texts omit.
power = the power. App. 172. 1 and 176. 1.
unto, &c. The texts read "of our God".
LORD. Ap. 98. VI. i. *β.* 1. B. b.
God. Ap. 98. I. i. 1.

𝔥7 (p. 1883). **19. 1-10.** THE FINAL HEAVENLY UTTERANCES. (*Alternation.*)

𝔥7 | P | A | a | 19. 1-. The voice of the great multitude.
  b | d | -1. Hallelujah. } (1st utterance).
  e | 2, 3-. Reason. }
 B | -3. The smoke and destruction of the harlot.
  C | f | 4. Prostration of the elders (2nd utterance).
  g | 5. Exhortation from the throne (3rd utterance) to the servants of God (Pos.).
 A | a | 19. 6-. The voice of the great multitude.
  b | d | -6-7-. Hallelujah. } 4th utterance).
  e | -7. Reason. }
 B | 8, 9-. The array and blessedness of the wife.
  C | f | -9, 10-. Prostration of John.
  g | -10. Exhortation of angel to John, his fellow servant (Neg.).

2 true. Ap. 175. 2. **righteous.** Ap. 191. 1. **judgments.** Ap. 177. 7. **hath.** Omit. **judged.** Ap. 122. 1. **earth.** Ap. 129. 4. **with.** Gr. *en.* Ap. 104. viii. **servants.** Ap. 190. I. 2. **at.** Gr. *ek.* Ap. 104. vii.

3 And again they °said, [1]"Alleluia."
B And her smoke °rose up °for ever and ever.
C f 4 And the four and twenty °elders and the four °beasts fell down and °worshipped [1]God °That sat °on the throne, saying, °"Amen; [1]Alleluia."
g 5 And a voice came °out of the throne, saying, "Praise our [1]God, all ye His °servants,° and ye that fear Him, °both small and great."
A a 6 And I heard as it were the voice of a great multitude, and as the voice of many waters, and as the voice of °mighty thunderings, saying,
b d [1]"Alleluia: for the [1]LORD °God °Omnipotent reigneth.
7 Let us be glad and °rejoice, and give °honour to Him:
e for the °marriage of the Lamb is come, and His °wife hath made herself ready."
B 8 And to her was granted °that she should be arrayed in fine linen, °clean and white: for the fine linen is the °righteousness of °saints.
9 And he saith °unto me, "Write, °'Blessed *are* they which are °called °unto the [7]marriage °supper of the Lamb.'"
C f And he saith °unto me, "These are the °true °sayings of [1]God."
10 And I fell °at his feet to °worship him.
g And he °said °unto me, °"See *thou do it* °not: I am thy °fellowservant, and °of thy brethren that °have the °testimony of °Jesus: °worship [1]God: for the °testimony of °Jesus is the °spirit of °prophecy."
11 And I °saw °heaven opened, and °behold, a °white horse; and °He That sat °upon him *was* called °Faithful and °True, and [1]in °righteousness He doth °judge and make war.
12 °His eyes °*were* as a flame of fire, and °on His head *were* many °crowns; and He °had a name written, that °no man °knew, °but He Himself.
13 And He *was* clothed with a vesture °dipped °in blood: and His name is °called The °Word of [1]God.
14 And the armies *which* °*were* [1]in [1]heaven followed Him °upon white horses, clothed in fine linen, [8]white and [8]clean.
15 And °out of His mouth goeth a sharp sword, [8]that [2]with it He should smite the nations: and He shall °rule them [2]with a °rod of iron: and He treadeth the winepress of the fierceness °and wrath of [6]Almighty [1]God.
16 And He hath [12]on *His* vesture and [12]on His thigh a name written, °KING OF KINGS, AND LORD OF LORDS.

3 said = have said. Notice Fig. *Epanadiplōsis*. Ap. 6.
rose = goeth.
for, &c. See 1. 6 and Ap. 151. II. A. ii. 9. a.
4 elders. See 4. 4.
beasts. Gr. *zōa*, as 4. 6. Elders and beasts mentioned here for the last time.
worshipped. Ap. 137. 1.
That sat. Lit. the (*One*) sitting.
on. Ap. 104. ix. 2, with texts.
Amen. See 3. 14 and p. 1511 (Verily).
5 out of = from. Gr. *ek*, but the texts read *apo*. Ap. 104. iv.
servants. Ap. 190. I. 2. See Ps. 134. 1.
and, both. Omit.
6 mighty. Cp. Ap. 172. 3.
God. Ap. 98. I. i. 1. Most of the texts read "our God".
Omnipotent = The Omnipotent. Ap. 98. IV. "Almighty" in *v.* 15.
7 rejoice = be exceeding glad. Only here in Rev. First occ. Matt. 5. 12.
honour = the glory. See *v.* 1.
marriage = marriage-feast. Gr. *gamos*. See Matt. 22. 2, &c.; 25. 10; and (Sept.) Gen. 29. 22. Esther 1. 5; 2. 18; 9. 22. In *v.* 9 "supper". See Ap. 140. II. 2 and Ap. 197. 4.
wife. Gr. *gunē*. Here and 21. 9 "wife". Elsewhere in Rev. "woman".
8 that = in order that. Gr. *hina*.
clean and white. The texts read "bright *and* pure". See 15. 6.
righteousness. Ap. 191. 4. Plural.
saints = the saints. See Acts 9. 13.
9 unto = to.
Blessed. Gr. *makarios*. The fourth of the seven occ. of "Blessed" in Rev., and the forty-seventh in N.T. See Matt. 5. 3.
called . . . Lamb. See Ps. 45. 14 for some of the "called" there indicated. **unto.** Ap. 104. vi.
supper. Gr. *deipnon*. First occ. Matt. 23. 6. Here equiv. to the marriage feast of *v.* 7. **unto** = to.
true. Ap. 175. 2. **sayings.** Ap. 121. 10.
10 at = before. Gr. *emprosthen*.
worship. Ap. 137. 1. **said.** Lit. saith.
unto = to. **See.** Ap. 133. I. 8.
not. Ap. 105. II. Cp. 22. 9.
fellowservant. Gr. *sundoulos*. Here, 6. 11; 22. 9, in Rev. Cp. Ap. 190. I. 2. **of** = with.
have = hold.
testimony. See 1. 2.
Jesus. Ap. 98. X. **spirit.** Ap. 101. II. 7.
prophecy. Gr. *prophēteia*. Occ. seven times in Rev. See 1. 3. This testimony may be as concerning Jesus, or as sent or borne by Him, as in 1. 1
11 saw. Ap. 133. I. 1.
heaven = the heaven. See 3. 12.
behold. Ap. 133. I. 2.
white horse. Contrast that and its rider of 6. 2.
He That sat, &c. The prophecy in Zech. 9. 9 as to the Lord entering Jerusalem riding on an ass was fulfilled literally (Matt. 21. 4–11); why then stumble, as do some, at the prediction here of "this same Jesus" riding on a "white horse"? Zech. 9. 9, 10 takes in both comings. See also Ps. 45.
upon him = thereon. **upon.** Ap. 104. ix. 3.
Faithful. App. 150. III and 175. 4. **True.** Ap. 175. 2. **righteousness.** Ap. 191. 3. **judge.** Ap. 122. 1. **12 His.** Read "And His". *were* **as** = *are*. The texts omit "as". **on.** Same as "upon", *v.* 11. **crowns** = diadems. See 12. 3; 13. 1. **had** = hath. **no man** = no one. Gr. *oudeis*. **knew.** Ap. 132. I. i. **but** = if (Ap. 118. 2. a) not (Ap. 105. II). **13 dipped** = dyed, or stained. Gr. *baptō*, as Luke 16. 24. John 13. 26. Some texts read "sprinkled", Gr. *rhantizō*. See the word in Heb. 9. 13. **in** = with. No prep. Cp. Isa. 9. 5; 63. 1–6. **called.** If the comma is after "called", as in some Bibles, it would mean "announced" or "called", with inverts: if omitted, it is descriptive without inverts. **Word.** Ap. 121. 10. **14** *were* = *are*. **upon.** As "on", *v.* 4. **15** This *v.* contains refs. to Ps. 2. 9. Isa. 11. 4; 49. 2; 63. 3. **out of.** Ap. 104. vii. **rule.** Lit. "shepherd". Gr. *poimainō*. See 2. 27; 7. 17; 12. 5. **rod** = sceptre. See Ps. 2. 9. **and.** The texts read here "of the Almighty" (*v.* 6). **16 KING . . . LORDS.** See 17. 14. Here at length we have the final fulfilment of Ps. 2.

X vii. E[7] A[1] 17 And I °saw °an angel standing [1]in the
sun; and he cried with a loud voice, saying to
all the fowls that fly [1]in °the midst of heaven,
"Come and °gather yourselves together [9]unto
°the supper of the great [1]God;
18 [8]That ye may eat °the flesh of kings, and
°the flesh of captains, and °the flesh of
°mighty °men, and °the flesh of horses, and of
them that sit [12]on them, and °the flesh of all
°*men, both* °free and °bond, both small and
great."
19 And I [11]saw the beast, and the kings of
the [2]earth, and their armies, °gathered together to make °war °against Him °That sat
°on the horse, and °against His army.
20 And the beast was °taken, and °with him
the °false prophet that °wrought °miracles
before him, [2]with which he °deceived them
that had received the mark of the beast, and
them that °worshipped his image. These both
were °cast alive °into °a lake of fire burning
[2]with °brimstone.
21 And °the remnant were slain [2]with the
sword of Him [19]That sat °upon the horse,
which *sword* °proceeded [15]out of His mouth:
and all the fowls were filled °with their flesh.

B[1] **20** And I °saw an angel °come down °from
°heaven, having the key of the bottomless pit and a great chain °in his hand.
2 And he °laid hold °on the °dragon, °that old
serpent, which is the Devil, and °Satan, and
bound him a °thousand years,
3 And cast him °into the bottomless pit, and
shut °him up, and °set a seal upon him, °that
he °should °deceive the nations °no °more,
till the [2]thousand years should be °fulfilled:
°and °after that he must be loosed a little
°season.

A[2] 4 And I [1]saw thrones, and °they sat °upon
them, and °judgment °was given °unto °them;
°and °*I saw* the °souls of them that °were beheaded °for the °witness of °Jesus, and °for the
°word of °God, and °which °had °not worshipped the beast, °neither his image, °neither
had received °*his* mark °upon their foreheads,
°or [1]in their °hands; and they °lived and
reigned °with °Christ a [2]thousand years.
5 °But °the rest of °the dead [4]lived [4]not
again until the [2]thousand years °were °finished.
This °*is* the first °resurrection.
6 °Blessed and holy *is* he that hath part °in
the first [5]resurrection: °on such the second

E[7] (p. 1883). **19. 17—20. 15.** THE SEVENTH (AND LAST) VISION "ON EARTH". (*Alternation and Introversion.*)

E[7] A[1] | 19. 17–21. *Men.* The judgment of the beast and the false prophet.
B[1] | 20. 1–3. *Satan.* The judgment of Satan (before the millennium).
A[2] | 20. 4–6. *Men.* The judgment of the overcomers. The "rest of the dead" left for judgment.
B[2] | 20. 7–10. *Satan.* The judgment of Satan (after the millennium).
A[3] | 20. 11–15. *Men.* The judgment of the great white throne.

17 saw. Ap. 133. I. 1. **an** = one.
the midst of heaven = mid-heaven, as 14. 6.
gather . . . together. The texts read "be gathered together".
the supper . . . God. The texts read "the great supper of God".
18 the. Omit. **mighty.** Cp. Ap. 172. 3.
men, *men*. Omit. **free.** See 6. 15.
bond. Ap. 190. I. 2. See *vv.* 2, 5. Cp. Ezek. 39. 17–22 concerning this, or a subsequent, period. The invitation of "beasts" to the feast in Ezek. not mentioned here.
19 gathered together. Gr. *sunagō*, as *v.* 17.
war. The texts add "the". See 16. 14.
against = with. Gr. *meta.* Ap. 104. xi. 1.
That sat = Who sitteth. **on.** Ap. 104. ix. 1.
20 taken = arrested. In Acts 12. 4 and 2 Cor. 11. 32, "apprehend". See the use of the verb in John 7. 30; 10. 39. **with.** Ap. 104. xi. 1.
false prophet. See 16. 13 and 20. 10.
wrought = did. Gr. *poieō.* Same as "**make**", *v.* 19.
miracles = the signs. Ap. 176. 3.
deceived. Ap. 128. VIII. 1.
worshipped. Ap. 137. 1.
cast, &c. Cp. Dan. 7. 11.
into. Ap. 104. vi. **a** = the.
brimstone. Gr. *theion.* See 9. 17.
21 the remnant = the rest. Ap. 124. 3.
upon. Same as "on", *v.* 19.
proceeded. The texts read "came forth".
with Ap. 104. vii.

20. 1 saw. Ap. 133. I. 1.
come = coming. **from.** Ap. 104. vii.
heaven. See 3. 12.
in = upon. Gr. *epi.* Ap. 104. ix. 3.
2 laid hold on. Gr. *krateō.* Cp. Ap. 172. 2.
on = of. **dragon.** See 12. 3.
that = the.
Satan. The texts add "the". See Ap. 19.
thousand years. I. e. the millennium.
3 into. Ap. 104. vi. **him.** Or "it" (the pit).
set, &c. Lit. sealed *it* over him.
that = in order that. Gr. *hina.*
should, &c. = should not (Ap. 105. II) deceive (Ap. 128. VIII. 1).
more = longer. **fulfilled.** Cp. Ap. 125. 2.

and. Omit. **after that.** Gr. *meta tauta*, as 1. 19 (hereafter). **season** = time. Gr. *chronos.* Ap. 195. Satan is literal; the angel who binds him is literal; the abyss into which he is cast is literal; and the chain, whatever it may be composed of, is literal too. **4 they.** I. e. the Father and Christ (3. 21), and the heavenly beings associated with them as assessors (1. 4; and cp. Matt. 25. 31. 1 Tim. 5. 21). **upon.** Ap. 104. ix. 3. **judgment.** Ap. 177. 6. **was given.** I. e. not judging or ruling authority, but sentence, or pronouncement, or award in their favour. **unto** = for. No prep. Dat. case. **them.** I. e. those who had been beheaded. **and** = even. ***I saw.*** Omit. **souls.** App. 110. II. Fig. *Synecdochē* (of Part). Ap. 6. **were** = had been. **for.** Ap. 104. v. 2. **witness** = testimony. See 19. 10 and p. 1511. **Jesus.** Ap. 98. X. **word.** Ap. 121. 10. **God.** Ap. 98. I. i. 1. **which** = whosoever. Gr. *hoitines*, as Matt. 5. 39, 41. **had, &c.** = did not (Ap. 105. I) worship (Ap. 137. 1). **neither.** Gr. *oude.* **neither . . . received** = and received (see 13. 16) not (Ap. 105. I). ***his*** = the. **or in** = and upon (as above). **hands** = hand. **lived.** I. e. lived again. Ap. 170. 1. **with.** Ap. 104. xi. 1. **Christ.** Ap. 98. IX. The resurrection of these not mentioned but necessarily implied. **5 But.** The texts omit. **the rest, &c.** The texts read "the rest of the dead lived not until (i. e. again until)", which presumes that "the rest of the dead" are not living during the thousand years. **the rest.** Ap. 124. 3. Occ. Rom. 11. 7. 1 Cor. 15. 37 (other). 1 Thess. 4. 13 (others); &c. **the dead.** Ap. 139. 1. **were** = should be. **finished.** See "fulfilled", *v.* 3. ***is.*** No verb. **resurrection.** Ap. 178. II. 1. **6 Blessed.** Gr. *makarios.* Forty-eighth occ. in N. T. **in.** Ap. 104. viii. **on such** = over (Ap. 104. ix. 1) these.

death hath °no °power, but they shall be
°priests of [4] God and of [4] Christ, and shall reign
[4] with Him °a [2] thousand years.
B[3] 7 And when the [2] thousand years are °expired,
[2] Satan shall be loosed °out of his prison,
8 And shall go out to [3] deceive the nations
which are [6] in the four °quarters of the °earth,
°Gog and Magog, to gather them together °to
°battle: the °number of whom *is* °as the sand
of the sea.
9 And they went up °on the breadth of the
°earth, and compassed the camp of the °saints
about, and the °beloved city: and fire came
down °from [4] God [7] out of [1] heaven, and °de-
voured them.
10 And the [2] devil that [3] deceived them was
cast [3] into the °lake of fire and brimstone,
°where the °beast and the °false prophet °*are*,
°and shall be °tormented day and night °for
ever and ever.
A[3] 11 And I [1] saw a °great °white throne, and
Him That sat [6] on it, [9] from Whose face the
[8] earth and the [1] heaven fled away; and there
was found [6] no place for them.
12 And I [1] saw °the dead, °small and great,
°stand before °God; and °the books were
opened: and °another book was opened, which
is *the book* of °life: and °the dead were °judged
[7] out of °those things which were written [6] in
the books, °according to their works.
13 And the sea gave up [12] the dead which
were [6] in it; and death and °hell delivered up
[12] the dead which were [6] in them: and they
were [12] judged °every man [12] according to their
works.
14 And death and [13] hell were cast [3] into the
[10] lake of fire. This is the second °death.
15 And °whosoever was [4] not found written
[6] in the book of [12] life was cast [3] into the [10] lake
of fire.

ℌ A **21** And I °saw a °new °heaven and a °new
°earth: for the °first °heaven and the
°first °earth were passed away; and °there
was no more sea.
2 And I °John [1] saw the holy city, °new
Jerusalem, coming down °from °God °out of
[1] heaven, prepared as a °bride adorned for her
°husband.
B 3 And I heard a great °voice [2] out of [1] heaven
saying, °"Behold, the tabernacle of [2] God *is*
°with °men, and He will °dwell °with them, and
they shall be His °people, and [2] God Himself
shall be °with them, *and be* their [2] God.
4 **And [2] God shall wipe away all tears** °**from
their eyes**; and °there shall be no more
death, °neither sorrow, °nor crying, °neither
shall there be °any more pain: °for the
°former things are passed away."

no. Ap. 105. I.
power. Ap. 172. 5. **priests.** See 1. 6.
a. Some texts read "the". The "first resurrection" is the *former* of the two resurrections referred to in this passage. It is the antithesis of the resurrection implied though not specifically mentioned in *v.* 12. This is the resurrection which was both the subject of revelation and the hope of Israel. Cp. the antithesis in Dan. 12. 2. John 5. 29. Acts 24. 15. This "first resurrection" should not be confused with 1 Thess. 4. 13–17 (see notes there and on Phil. 3. 11).

7 expired. See "fulfilled", *v.* 3.
out of. Ap. 104. vii.
8 quarters. As 7. 1 (corners). **earth.** Ap. 129. 4.
Gog and Magog. Here, apparently an inclusive term for *all* the Gentile nations; East (Gog) and West (Magog). The destruction of Gog and Magog, Ezek. 39, is pre-millennial. See Ezek. 39. 25.
to. Ap. 104. vi.
battle = the war. The texts add the article. Ref. to *the* war predicted and determined.
number. Gr. *arithmos.* One of the ten (Ap. 10 and Ap. 197. 6) occ. words in Rev.
as the sand, &c. Fig. *Parœmia.* Ap. 6. Cp. Heb. 11. 12.
9 on. Ap. 104. ix. 3.
earth. Ap. 129. 4. Cp. Isa. 8. 8 and Hab. 1. 6.
saints. See Dan. 7. 18, 27. Acts 9. 13.
beloved. Ap. 135. I. 1.
from. Ap. 104. iv.
devoured. As 12. 4.
10 lake, &c. See 19. 20.
where. The texts add "also".
beast, false prophet. See 19. 20.
are. No verb. Read "were", or "were cast".
and. Add "they".
tormented. Last of five occ. in Rev. Cp. 9. 5.
for ever, &c. Ap. 151. II. ii. A. 9. a.
11 great. That in 4. 2–6 was seen by John in heaven; this on earth.
white. Indicating holiness and righteousness. No adjuncts mentioned. Only one throne and one Judge.
12 the dead. Those of *v.* 5. See Ap. 139.
small, &c. Read "the great and the small".
stand = standing.
God. The texts read "the throne". **the.** Omit.
another. Ap. 124. 1. **life.** Ap. 170. 1.
judged. Ap. 122. 1. **those** = the.
according to. Ap. 104. x. 2.
13 hell = the grave. See 1. 18; 6. 8, and Ap. 131. II. 2.
every man = each one.
14 death. The texts add "the lake of fire".
15 whosoever = if (Ap. 118. 2. a) any one (Ap. 123. 3). Note the Fig. *Polysyndeton* (Ap. 6) *vv.* 9–15.

ℌ (p. 1883). **21. 1—22. 5.** THE PEOPLE ON THE NEW EARTH. (*Introversion.*)

ℌ | A | 21. 1, 2. Visions (heavens and earth, &c.).
  B | 21. 3–8. Voices.
 A | 21. 9—22. 5. Visions (the bride).

21. 1 saw. Ap. 133. I. 1.
new heaven, &c. See Isa. 51. 16 (plant, &c.); 65. 17; 66. 22. 2 Pet. 3. 7, 13. **new.** See Matt. 9. 17.
heaven. See 3. 12. **earth.** Ap. 129. 4.
first. Or, former, as *v.* 4.
there . . . sea = the sea is no (Ap. 105. I) more (longer). A proof that this belongs to the post-millennial period. See Ps. 72. 8. Zech. 9. 10. **2 John.** The texts omit. **new Jerusalem.** See 3. 12. The city "above" (Gal. 4. 26); "which hath the foundations" (Heb. 11. 10); "the heavenly Jerusalem" (Heb. 12. 22). **from.** Ap. 104. iv. **God.** Ap. 98. I. i. 1. **out of.** Ap. 104. vii. **bride.** Gr. *numphē.* See *v.* 9; 22. 17, and Ap. 197. 4. **husband.** Ap. 123. 2.
3 heaven. The texts read "the throne". **Behold.** Ap. 133. I. 2. **with.** Ap. 104. xi. 1. **men.** Ap. 123. 1. **dwell** = tabernacle. Gr. *skēnoō.* See John 1. 14. **with them.** Cp. Exod. 29. 46, &c., for God's promise to dwell among His People in the Land. For the promise to dwell among His People, restored Israel, in the millennial Land, see Zech. 2. 10, 11; 8. 3, &c. Here we have the final and glorious fulfilment of the promise in Isa. 7. 14 and Matt. 1. 23—IMMANUEL, God with us. **people** = peoples. Gr. *laos.* Whereas it *was* people, Israel, it is now peoples, called "the nations" in *v.* 24. **4 from.** The texts read Gr. *ek.* Ap. 104. vii. **there shall, &c.** Read "death shall be no (Ap. 105. I) more" (longer). **neither, nor.** Gr. *oute.* **any more** = no more, as above. **for.** The texts omit. **former things.** Cp. Isa. 25. 7, 8; 35. 10. Jer. 31. 16.

5 And He That °sat °upon the throne said,
[3]"Behold, I make all things [1]new." And He
°said °unto me, "Write: for these °words are
°true and °faithful."
6 And He said °unto me, °"It is done. I am
°Alpha and Omega, the °Beginning and the
°End. I will give °unto him that is athirst
°of the fountain of the water of °life °freely.
7 He that °overcometh shall °inherit °all
things; and I will be His [2]God, and he shall be
My °son.
8 But the °fearful, and °unbelieving, and the
°abominable, and murderers, and whoremongers, and °sorcerers, and idolaters, and °all
liars, shall have their part °in the lake which
burneth with fire and brimstone; which is the
second death."

A 9 And there came °unto me one [6]of the
°seven angels which had the seven vials
full of the seven last plagues, and °talked
[3]with me, saying, "Come hither, I will shew
thee the °bride, the Lamb's °wife."
10 And he carried me away [8]in the °spirit
°to a great and high mountain, and shewed
me °that great city, the holy Jerusalem, descending [2]out of [1]heaven [2]from [2]God,
11 Having the °glory of [2]God: °and °her
°light *was* like [6]unto a stone most precious,
even like a jasper stone, clear as crystal;
12 °And °had a wall great and high, *and*
°had °twelve gates, and °at the gates twelve
angels, and names written thereon, which are
the names of the twelve tribes of the °children
of Israel:
13 °On the east three gates; °on the north
three gates; °on the south three gates; and
°on the west three gates.
14 And the wall of the city had twelve °foun-
dations, and °in them the names of the twelve
°apostles of the Lamb.
15 And he that [9]talked [3]with me had a
°golden reed °to °measure the city, and the
gates thereof, and the wall thereof.
16 And the city lieth foursquare, and the
length is as large as the breadth: and he
[15]measured the city with the [15]reed, twelve
thousand °furlongs. The °length and the
breadth and the height of it are equal.
17 And he [15]measured the wall thereof, an
°hundred *and* forty *and* four cubits, °*according to* the [15]measure of a °man, that is, of °the
angel.
18 And the °building of the wall of it was *of*
jasper: and the city *was* °pure gold, like [6]unto
°clear glass.
19 °And the [14]foundations of the wall of the
city *were* garnished with all manner of precious
stones. The first [14]foundation *was* °jasper;
the second, sapphire; the third, a chalce-
dony; the fourth, an emerald;
20 The fifth, sardonyx; the sixth, sardius;
the seventh, chrysolyte; the eighth, beryl;
the ninth, a topaz; the tenth, a chrysopra-
sus; the eleventh, a jacinth; the twelfth, an
amethyst.

5 sat=sitteth. Lit. the (*One*) sitting.
upon. Ap. 104. ix. 2, with texts. **said**=saith.
unto me. The texts omit. **words.** Ap. 121. 10.
true, &c. The texts read "faithful and true". Cp. 19. 11. **true.** Ap. 175. 2.
faithful. App. 150. III and 175. 4.
6 unto=to.
It is done. The texts read "They are come to pass". Cp. 16. 17. **Alpha, &c.** See 1. 8.
Beginning. Ap. 172. 6.
End. Cp. Ap. 125. 1.
of. Ap. 104. vii. **life.** Ap. 170. 1.
freely. See John 15. 25.
7 overcometh. Last of seventeen occ. in Rev. See 2. 7 and Ap. 197. 6.
inherit. Gr. *klēronomeō.* Only here in Rev.
all. The texts read "these".
son. Ap. 108. iii.
8 fearful. Gr. *deilos.* Only here; Matt. 8. 26, and Mark 4. 40. In Sept. Deut. 20. 8. Judg. 7. 3, 10.
unbelieving. Gr. *apistos.* First occ. Matt. 17. 17 (faithless).
abominable. Gr. *bdelussomai.* Only here and Rom. 2. 22. Freq. in Sept. See the noun in 17. 4.
sorcerers. Gr. *pharmakeus.* Only here and 22. 15 (*pharmakos*). See 9. 21; 18. 23 and Gal. 5. 20 (witchcraft). Those who have commerce with evil spirits, as modern "Spiritists". Occ. in Sept.
all liars=all the false (Gr. *pseudēs*). Here; 2. 2. Acts 6. 13 (false).
in. Ap. 104. viii. *V.* 8 contains the Fig. *Polysyndeton.* Ap. 6.
9 unto me. The texts omit.
seven . . . plagues. See 15. 1. **talked.** Ap. 121. 7.
bride. Gr. *numphē.* See *v.* 2. Matt. 10. 35. Luke 12. 53. John 3. 29. Rev. 18. 23; **22. 17.** The "wife" and the "bride" here must not be confused with "the wife" of 19. 7. The wife of 19. 7 is Israel, called out from all the nations for blessing in the Land, the earthly consort of "the great King" (cp. Ps. 45. Jer. 3. 14). The "bride, the Lamb's wife" here is still of Israel, but that Israel of the "heavenly calling" (Heb. 3. 1); all those connected with the "heavenly" country and "the city which hath the foundations", for which "they looked" (Heb. 11. 13–16). See Ap. 197. 4.
wife. Gr. *gunē*, always rend. "wife", or "woman". The wife of 19. 7 is not called *numphē.* Here she is both *numphē* and *gunē* (first occ. Matt. 1. 20). See Ap. 197. 4.
10 spirit. Ap. 101. II. 3, or 5. **to.** Ap. 104. ix. 1.
that great. The texts omit, and read "the holy city Jerusalem".
11 glory. See p. 1511. **and.** Omit.
light. Ap. 130. 2.
12 And. Omit. **had**=having.
twelve gates. Cp. Ezek. 48. 31–34. Both John and Ezekiel wrote as they were moved by the Holy Spirit, and their specific descriptions refer to different cities. See *v.* 9. **at.** Gr. *epi.* Ap. 104. ix. 2.
children. Ap. 108. iii.
13 On. Gr. *apo.* Ap. 104. iv.
14 foundations. Gr. *themelios.* See Ap. 146.
in. The texts read Ap. 104. ix. 1.
apostles. The twelfth will be Matthias, not Judas. See App. 174. 1 and 189. Twelve is the basic number of the measurements of the city. See Ap. 197. 6 and Ap. 10.
15 golden reed, &c. The texts add *metron* here, as *v.* 17, and read "for a measure".
to=in order that. Gr. *hina.*
measure=he might measure.
16 furlongs. Gr. *stadion.* See 14. 20 and Ap. 51. III. 1 (2).
length . . . equal. The "holy city" is presented to us as a perfect cube of 12,000 furlongs. In Solomon's Temple "the Holy of Holies" was a perfect cube of twenty cubits. **17 hundred . . . cubits.** About 300 feet. See Ezek. 43. 13 and Ap. 88. 4 (foot-note). *according to.* Omit. **man.** Ap. 123. 1. **the**=an.
18 building=fabric, or material. Gr. *endomēsis.* Only here. **pure, clear.** Same word. **19 And.** Omit. **jasper.** Cp. this and the other stones here with those in Aaron's breastplate (Exod. 28. 17–21).

21 And the twelve gates *were* twelve pearls;
every several gate was [6]of one pearl: and
the °street of the city *was* [18]pure gold, °as it
were transparent glass.
22 And I [1]saw °no °Temple °therein: for the
°LORD [2]God °Almighty and the Lamb are the
°Temple of it.
23 And the city °had [22]no °need of the sun,
°neither of the moon, °to °shine °in it: for the
[11]glory of [2]God did °lighten it, and the Lamb
is the °light thereof.
24 And the nations °of them which are
saved shall walk °in the °light of °it: and the
°kings of the [1]earth °do bring their [11]glory
°and honour °into °it.
25 And the gates of it shall °not be shut
at all by day: for there shall be [22]no night
there.
26 And they shall bring the [11]glory and
°honour of °the nations [24]into it.
27 And there shall °in no wise enter [24]into
it any thing °that defileth, °neither *whatsoever*
°worketh abomination, °or *maketh* a lie:
°but they which are written [8]in the °Lamb's
book of [6]life.

22 And he shewed me a °pure river of
°water of °life, clear as crystal, proceeding
°out of the °throne of °God and of the
Lamb.
2 °In the midst of the street of it, and on
either side of the river, *was there* the °tree
of [1]life, °which bare twelve *manner of* fruits,
°*and* yielded her fruit °every month: and the
leaves of the °tree *were* °for the °healing of the
nations.
3 And there shall be °no more° curse: °but
the [1]throne of [1]God and of the Lamb shall
be [2]in it; and His °servants shall °serve
Him;
4 And they shall °see His face; and His name
shall be °in their foreheads.
5 And there shall be °no night °there; and
they need °no °candle, °neither °light of °the
sun; for the °LORD [1]God giveth them light:
and they °shall reign °for ever and ever.
A 6 And °he said °unto me, "These °sayings
are °faithful and °true: and °the LORD °God
°of the holy prophets °sent His angel to shew
°unto His [3]servants the things which must
°shortly be done.
7 °Behold, I come °quickly: °blessed *is* he
that °keepeth the [6]sayings of the prophecy
of this book."

21 street. Gr. *plateia*. See 22. 2 and cp. 11. 8. Fig. *Heterōsis* (of Number). Ap. 6.
as it were. Not that it is glass, but gold of a kind unknown to us.
22 no. Ap. 105. I.
Temple. Last occ. of the word.
therein=in (Gr. *en*) it.
LORD. Ap. 98. VI. i. β. 1. A. b.
Almighty. Ap. 98. IV.
Temple of it. This shows clearly that the wonders and glories revealed here belong to post-millennial times and ages. Therefore, the city of the great King during the thousand years, with "the sanctuary" of Ezek. 45. 2, *et al.*, and its palace-temple, will have "passed away". There cannot be two Jerusalems on the earth at one and the same time. The *new* Jerusalem comes down on the *new* earth, thus taking the place of the former city. See Ap. 197. 4.
23 had=hath.
need, &c. Cp. Isa. 60. 19, 20 for the privileges of the millennial reign, foreshadowing the extended ones set forth here.
neither. Gr. *oude*. **to**=in order to. Gr. *hina*.
shine. Ap. 106. I. i.
in it. The texts omit "in", reading "on (dat. case) her".
lighten. Same as 18. 1. **light.** Ap. 130. 4.
24 of . . . saved. The texts omit.
in. Ap. 104. viii, but the texts read Ap. 104. v. 1.
light. Ap. 130. 1.
it. Or "her", as above. So also *vv.* 25, 27.
kings, &c. Notice the order in *that* day.
do. Omit. **and honour.** The texts omit.
into. Ap. 104. vi.
25 not . . . at all. Ap. 105. III.
26 honour=the honour.
the nations. These are the "sheep" nations of His right hand during the millennial reign. See Matt. 25. 31-46.
27 in no wise. Ap. 105. III.
that defileth=unclean. Gr. *koinoō*, as the texts.
neither *whatsoever*. Read "or he that".
worketh . . . lie=worketh (or maketh) a lying abomination, i. e. an idol (Gr. *bdelugma*. See 17. 5).
or=and. **but**=only. Gr. *ei mē*.
Lamb's book of life. See 13. 8. Note the Fig. *Polysyndeton* (Ap. 6) in *vv.* 22-27.
22. 1 pure. The texts omit.
water of life. I. e. living water.
life. Ap. 170. 1. **out of.** Ap. 104. vii.
throne. The throne of the great Priest-King (Zech. 6. 13) of the "thousand years" now gives place to the glorious "throne of God and of the Lamb", for God is now "all in all". Contrast Ezek. 47. 1-11, where the river proceeds from the "house" associated with the altar; here, from the throne.
God. Ap. 98. I. i. 1.
2 In. Ap. 104. viii.
tree. Gr. *xulon*. Here, *vv.* 14, 19; 2. 7, and Luke 23. 31, the only occs. of the word as used of *living* wood.
which bare=bearing. ***and* yielded**=yielding.
every month. Lit. according to (Ap. 104. x. 2) each month. **for.** Ap. 104. vi. **healing.** In Ezek. 47. 12 is the Divine provision for preserving and restoring *health*. Here, the fruits are for the enjoyment of the citizens of the new Jerusalem, and the "leaves" for the healing (health and "haleness") of *the nations*. For the former things having "passed away", there will be no sickness there (21. 4). **3 no more**=no (Ap. 105. I) longer. **curse.** Gr. *katanathema*, or with the texts, *katathema*, an accursed thing. Cp. Zech. 14. 11 (Sept. *anathema*). **but**=and. **servants.** Ap. 190. I. 2. **serve.** App. 137. 4 and 190. III. 5. **4 see.** Ap. 106. I. vi. **in**=upon. Gr. *epi*. Ap. 104. ix. 1. **5 no.** Ap. 105. I. **there.** The texts read "longer". **candle.** Ap. 130. 4. **neither.** Lit. and. **light.** Ap. 130. 1. **the.** Omit. **LORD.** Ap. 98. VI. i. β. 1. B. b. **shall reign, &c.** Cp. the reign of the saints with Messiah for 1,000 years and the reign here with God "for ever and ever". **for ever and ever.** Ap. 151. II. A. ii. 9. a. The last of the twenty-one (Ap. 10) occ. in N. T. (fourteen in Rev.) of the full phrase. **6 he.** I. e. the angel of 1. 1. **unto**=to. **sayings**=words. Ap. 121. 10. **faithful.** Ap. 150. III. **true.** Ap. 175. 2. **the LORD God.** As *v.* 5. **God**=the God. **of . . . prophets.** The texts read "of the spirits (Ap. 101. II. 4) of the prophets" (Ap. 189). **sent.** Ap. 174. 1. **shortly.** As 1. 1. Note Fig. *Polysyndeton* (Ap. 6) in *vv.* 1-6. **7 Behold.** The texts read "And behold" (Ap. 133. I. 2). **quickly.** Gr. *tachu*. The words of the angel pass into the words of Christ; see *vv.* 12, 20; 3. 11. Cp. 1. 7 and *v.* 16 below. **blessed.** The forty-ninth occ. of *makarios* in N.T. **keepeth.** See John 17. 6.

8 And ℑ John °saw these things, and heard
them. And when I °had heard and °seen,
I fell down to °worship before the feet of the
angel which shewed me these things.
9 °Then saith he [6]unto me, °"See *thou do it*
°not: °for I am thy °fellowservant, and of thy
brethren the °prophets, and of them which
[7]keep the [6]sayings of this book: [8]worship
[1]God."
10 And he saith [6]unto me, "Seal [9]not the
[6]sayings of the prophecy of this book; for the
°time is at hand.
11 He that is °unjust, °let him be unjust
still: and he which is °filthy, let him be °filthy
still: and he that is °righteous, let him °be
°righteous still: and he that is holy, let him
°be holy still.
12 °And [7]behold, I come [7]quickly; and My
reward *is* °with Me, to give °every man °ac-
cording as his work °shall be.
13 ℑ am °Alpha and Omega, the Beginning
and the End, the First and the Last.
14 °Blessed *are* they that °do His commandments, °that they may have °right °to the
[2]tree of [1]life, and may enter in °through the
gates °into the city.
15 °For without *are* °dogs, and sorcerers,
and whoremongers, and murderers, and
idolaters, and whosoever °loveth and maketh
a °lie."
16 °"ℑ °Jesus °have sent Mine angel to
°testify [6]unto you these things °in the
°churches. ℑ am the Root and the °Off-
spring of °David, °*and* the bright °and °morn-
ing °Star."
17 And the °Spirit and the °bride say, Come.
And let him that heareth say, Come. And
let him that is athirst come. °And °who-
soever °will, let him take the [1]water of [1]life
°freely.
18 °For °I °testify [6]unto °every man that
heareth the °words of the prophecy of this
book, °If °any man shall add °unto °these
things, [1]God shall add °unto him the plagues
that are written [2]in this book:
19 And [18]if [18]any man shall °take away
°from the [18]words of the book of this prophecy, [1]God shall °take away his part °out
of the °book of [1]life, and [1]out of the holy city,
°and *from* the things which are written [2]in
this book."
20 He Which [16]testifieth these things saith,
"Surely I come °quickly." °Amen. °Even so,
come, °Lord [16]Jesus.
21 The °grace of °our °Lord [16]Jesus °Christ
be [12]with °you all. [20]Amen.

8 saw, &c. The texts read "am he that heard and saw these things". **saw.** Ap. 133. I. 5. **had.** Omit. **seen** = saw, as above. **worship.** Ap. 137. 1.

9 Then = And. **See, &c.** Cp. 19. 10. **not.** Ap. 105. II. **for.** The texts omit. **fellowservant.** As 6. 11; 19. 10. Cp. Ap. 190. I. 2. **prophets.** Ap. 189.

10 time. Gr. *kairos.* See 1. 3 and Ap. 195.

11 unjust = unrighteous. Pres. part. of Gr. *adikeō*: everywhere in Rev. save here rend. "hurt". See 2. 11 and cp. Ap. 128. VII. 1.
let . . . unjust = let him act unrighteously. Aor. tense.
filthy = morally defiled. Gr. *rhupoō.* Only here. Cp. James 1. 21 (*rhuparia*) and 1 Pet. 3. 21 (*rhupos*). The texts, however, read here *rhuparos rhupanthētō.*
righteous. Ap. 191. 1.
be righteous. The texts read "do (or work) righteousness" (Ap. 191. 2).
be holy. Gr. *hagiazō.* Only occ. of the verb in Rev. In N.T. almost invariably "sanctify". Note Fig. *Epistrophē* (Ap. 6) in this *v.*

12 And. The texts omit. **with.** Ap. 104. xi. 1. **every man** = each one. **according.** Omit. **shall be.** The texts read "is".

13 Alpha, &c. See 1. 8.

14 Blessed. Gr. *makarios.* Fiftieth (Ap. 10) and last occ. in N. T. Cp. the forty-two occs. of the Heb. equivalent, *'ashrey,* the first in Deut. 33. 29 (Happy).
do His commandments. The texts read "wash their robes", but it is probable that the reading of the Received Text is correct. It is a question of *reading* in the original MSS., and not of *translation.*
that = in order that. Gr. *hina.*
right. Ap. 172. 5.
to = over. Ap. 104. ix. 3.
through = by. No prep. **into.** Ap. 104. vi.

15 Fig. *Synecdochē* of Species (Ap. 6) in this *v.*
For. The texts omit.
dogs. The word "dog" appears in Phœnician remains, as applied to a class of servants attached to a temple of Ashtoreth in Cyprus.
loveth. Ap. 135. I. 2. **lie.** Cp. 21. 27.

16 ℑ. The Lord Himself speaks.
Jesus. Ap. 98. X.
have sent = sent. Ap. 174. 4.
testify. See p. 1511. **in.** Gr. *epi.* Ap. 104. ix. 2.
churches. See 1. 4 and Ap. 186. The "assemblies" of chs. 2 and 3 specifically, during the fulfilment of "the prophecy of this book".
Offspring. Fig. *Synecdochē* (of Species). Ap. 6. See Acts 17. 28.
David. See 3. 7; 5. 5. ***and,* and.** Omit.
morning = the morning. Gr. *orthrinos,* only here. The texts read *ho prōïnos,* as 2. 28.
Star. Gr. *astēr.* Fourteenth and last occ. in Rev. See Ap. 197. 6. Cp. Num. 24. 17.

17 This *v.* illustrates the Fig. *Polysyndeton.* Ap. 6.
Spirit. Ap. 101. II. 3.
bride. Gr. *numphē.* See 21. 9.
And. The texts omit.
whosoever will. Lit. the one willing.
will. Ap. 102. 1. **freely.** See 21. 6.

18 For. Omit. **I.** The texts read ℑ (emphatic). **testify.** As *v.* 16, with the texts. **every man** = every one. **words.** Ap. 121. 10. **If.** Ap. 118. 1. b. **any man** = any one. Ap. 123. 3. **unto.** The texts read *epi* (Ap. 104. ix. 3). **these things.** The texts read "them". **unto.** Gr. *epi,* as above.

19 take away. Gr. *aphaireō.* Only here in Rev. Cp. Heb. 10. 4. **from.** Ap. 104. iv. **out of.** Same as "from" above. **book of life.** The texts read "tree of life". With the last two *vv.* cp. Deut. 4. 2; 12. 32. Prov. 30. 5, 6. Gal. 1. 8. **and . . . things.** The texts omit.

20 quickly. Gr. *tachu,* as *vv.* 7, 12. The seventh and last solemn warning by the Lord Himself, in Rev., of His coming. It is the one great subject of the whole book, which is all prophecy. **Amen.** See 3. 14 and 2 Cor. 1. 20. **Even so.** The texts omit; and link "Amen" with John's response, as R.V. **Lord.** Ap. 98. VI. i. β. 2. B. The use of the word "Lord" shows the utterance to be John's. None of His people, when He was on earth, were ever so irreverent as to *address* Him as "Jesus".

21 grace, &c. See 1. 4. **our.** The texts read "the". **Lord.** Ap. 98. VI. i. β. 2. A. **Christ.** Most texts omit. **you all.** Many texts read "all the saints".

APPENDIXES
TO
THE COMPANION BIBLE.

NUMERICAL INDEX.

APPENDIXES TO THE COMPANION BIBLE.

APPENDIXES TO THE COMPANION BIBLE.

APPENDIXES TO THE COMPANION BIBLE.

APPENDIXES.

1 THE STRUCTURE OF THE BOOKS OF THE OLD TESTAMENT ACCORDING TO THE HEBREW CANON.

I.—THE LAW (*Tōrāh*).

A | GENESIS. The beginning. All produced by the Word of God (Gen. 1. 3). Israel as a "family" (Gen. 15. 1).

B | EXODUS. History. Israel emerging from Families and Tribes to a Nation. Called "Hebrews" according to their "tongue."

C | LEVITICUS. Worship. Jehovah in the midst. He, Israel's God; and they, His People.

B | NUMBERS. History. Israel, now a "Nation," numbered, and blessed, as such (23, 24).

A | DEUTERONOMY. The end. All depending on the Word of Jehovah. Israel regarded as in the "Land."

II.—THE PROPHETS (*Nebī'īm*).

A | JOSHUA. "The Lord of all the earth" giving possession of the Land. Government under Priests.

B | JUDGES. Israel forsaking and returning to God; losing and regaining their position in the Land. "No king." Bethlehem. Failure under Priests.

C | SAMUEL. Man's king "rejected"; God's king (David) "established."

D | KINGS. Decline and Fall under the kings.

The former Prophets (Zech. 7. 7).

D | ISAIAH. Final blessing under God's King.

C | JEREMIAH. Human kings "rejected." David's "righteous Branch" "raised up."

B | EZEKIEL. God forsaking Israel, and returning in glory, to say for ever of His Land and city "Jehovah-Shammah."

A | MINOR PROPHETS. "The Lord of all the earth" giving restored possession of the Land, and foretelling final and unending possession.

The latter Prophets.

III.—THE PSALMS (*Kethūbīm*, Writings).

A | PSALMS. *Tehillim.* "Praises." God's purposes and counsels as to His doings in the future.

B | PROVERBS, i.e. Rules: Words which govern or rule man's life. God's moral government set forth.

C | JOB. "The end of the Lord" shown in Satan's defeat, and the saint's deliverance from tribulation.

D | CANTICLES. Virtue rewarded. Read by the Jews at the Passover: the Feast which commemorates the deliverance from Pharaoh, the Jews' oppressor.

E | RUTH. The stranger gathered in to hear of, and share in, God's goodness in Redemption. Read at Pentecost, which commemorates God's goodness in the Land.

F | LAMENTATIONS. "Alas!" The record of Israel's woes. Read at the *Fast* of the ninth of Abib.

E | ECCLESIASTES. "The Preacher." The People collected to hear of man's vanity. Read at the Feast of Tabernacles, which commemorates God's goodness in the wilderness.

D | ESTHER. Virtue rewarded. Read at the Feast of Purim, which commemorates the deliverance from Haman, "the Jews' enemy."

The five *Megillōth.*

C | DANIEL. "God's judgment." Here are shown the final defeat of Antichrist, and the deliverance out of "the Great Tribulation."

B | EZRA-NEHEMIAH. Men who governed and ruled God's People in their resettlement in the Land.

A | CHRONICLES. *Dibrae hayyāmīm.* "Words of the Days"; or, God's purposes and counsels as to Israel's doings in the past, and until the time of the end.

2 GENESIS: THE FOUNDATION OF DIVINE REVELATION.

Genesis is the seed-plot of the whole Bible. It is essential to the true understanding of its every part. It is the foundation on which Divine Revelation rests; and on which it is built up. It is not only the foundation of all Truth, but it enters into, and forms part of, all subsequent inspiration; and is at once the warp and woof of Holy Writ.

Genesis is quoted or referred to *sixty* times in the New Testament; and Divine authority is set like a seal on its historical facts. See Matt. 19. 4-6; 24. 37-39. Mark 7. 4, 10; 10. 3-8. Luke 11. 49-51; 17. 26-29, 32. John 1. 51; 7. 21-23; 8. 44-56.

It, and the Book of the Law, of which it forms part, are ascribed to Moses. See Deut. 31. 9, 10, 24-26. Josh. 1. 7; 8. 32, 35; 23. 6. 1 Kin. 2. 3; 2 Kin. 14. 6; 23. 25; 2 Chron. 23. 18; 30. 16; 34. 14. Ezra 3. 2; 7. 6. Neh. 8. 1. Dan. 9. 11, 13. Mal. 4. 4. Mark 12. 26. Luke 2. 22. John 7. 23. Acts 13. 39; 15. 5; 28. 23. 1 Cor. 9. 9. Heb. 10. 28.

3 GENESIS FINDS ITS COMPLEMENT IN THE APOCALYPSE.

GENESIS.	APOCALYPSE.
1. Genesis, the book of the beginning.	1. Apocalypse, the book of the end.
2. The Earth created (1. 1).	2. The Earth passed away (21. 1).
3. Satan's first rebellion.	3. Satan's final rebellion (20. 3, 7-10).
4. Sun, moon and stars for Earth's government (1. 14-16).	4. Sun, moon, and stars, connected with Earth's judgment (6. 13; 8. 12; 16. 8).
5. Sun to govern the day (1. 16).	5. No need of the sun (21. 23).
6. Darkness called night (1. 5).	6. "No night there" (22. 5).
7. Waters called seas (1. 10).	7. "No more sea" (21. 1).
8. A river for Earth's blessing (2. 10-14).	8. A river for the New Earth (22. 1, 2).
9. Man in God's image (1. 26).	9. Man headed by one in Satan's image (13).
10. Entrance of sin (3).	10. Development and end of sin (21, 22).
11. Curse pronounced (3. 14, 17).	11. "No more curse" (22. 3).

12. Death entered (3. 19).
13. Cherubim, first mentioned in connection with man (3. 24).
14. Man driven out from Eden (3. 24).
15. Tree of life guarded (3. 24).
16. Sorrow and suffering enter (3. 17).
17. Man's religion, art, and science, resorted to for enjoyment, apart from God (4).
18. Nimrod, a great rebel and king, and *hidden* anti-God, the founder of Babylon (10. 8, 9).
19. A flood from God to destroy an evil generation (6-9).
20. The Bow, the token of God's covenant with the Earth (9. 13).
21. Sodom and Egypt, the place of corruption and temptation (13, 19).
22. A confederacy against Abraham's people overthrown (14).
23. Marriage of first Adam (2. 18-23).
24. A bride sought for Abraham's son (Isaac) and found (24).
25. Two angels acting for God on behalf of His people (19).
26. A promised seed to possess the gate of his enemies (22. 17).
27. Man's dominion ceased and Satan's begun (3. 24).
28. The old serpent causing sin, suffering, and death (3. 1).
29. The doom of the old serpent pronounced (3. 15).
30. Sun, moon, and stars, associated with Israel (37. 9).

12. "No more death" (21. 4).
13. Cherubim, finally mentioned in connection with man (4. 6).
14. Man restored (22).
15. "Right to the Tree of Life" (22. 14).
16. No more sorrow (21. 4).
17. Man's religion, luxury, art, and science, in their full glory, judged and destroyed by God (18).
18. The Beast, the great rebel, a king, and *manifested* anti-God, the reviver of Babylon (13-18).
19. A flood from Satan to destroy an elect generation (12).
20. The Bow, betokening God's remembrance of His covenant with the Earth (4. 3; 10. 1).
21. Sodom and Egypt again: (spiritually representing Jerusalem) (11. 8).
22. A confederacy against Abraham's seed overthrown (12).
23. Marriage of last Adam (19).
24. A Bride made ready and brought to Abraham's Son (19. 9). See Matt. 1. 1.
25. Two witnesses acting for God on behalf of His People (11).
26. The promised seed coming into possession (11. 18).
27. Satan's dominion ended, and man's restored (22).
28. The old serpent bound for 1,000 years (20. 1-3).
29. The doom on the old serpent executed (20. 10).
30. Sun, moon, and stars, associated again with Israel (12).

4 THE DIVINE NAMES AND TITLES.

I. ELOHIM occurs 2,700 times. Its first occurrence connects it with *creation*, and gives it its essential meaning as *the Creator*. It indicates His relation to mankind as His *creatures* (see note on 2 Chron. 18. 31, where it stands in contrast with Jehovah as indicating *covenant relationship*). *'Elohim* is God the Son, the living "WORD" with creature form *to create* (John 1. 1. Col. 1. 15-17. Rev. 3. 14); and later, with *human* form to redeem (John 1. 14). "Begotten of His Father before all worlds; born of His mother, in the world." In this creature form He appeared to the Patriarchs, a form not temporarily assumed. *'Elohim* is indicated (as in A.V.) by ordinary small type, "God". See table on page 7.

II. JEHOVAH. While Elohim is God as the *Creator* of all things, Jehovah is the same God in *covenant relation* to those whom He has created (Cp. 2 Chron. 18. 31). Jehovah means *the Eternal*, the Immutable One, He Who WAS, and IS, and IS TO COME. The Divine definition is given in Gen. 21. 33. He is especially, therefore, the God of Israel; and the God of those who are redeemed, and are thus now "in Christ". We can say "My God," but not "My Jehovah", for Jehovah is "MY God."

Jehovah is indicated (as in A.V.) by small capital letters, "LORD"; and by "GOD" when it occurs in combination with Adonai, in which case Lord GOD = Adonai Jehovah.

The name Jehovah is combined with ten other words, which form what are known as "the Jehovah Titles."

They are as follows in the order in which they occur in the Hebrew Canon (Ap. 1). All are noted in the margin, in all their occurrences:—

1. JEHOVAH-JIREH = Jehovah will see, or provide. Gen. 22. 14.
2. JEHOVAH-ROPHEKA = Jehovah that healeth thee. Ex. 15. 26.
3. JEHOVAH-NISSĪ = Jehovah my banner. Ex. 17. 15.
4. JEHOVAH-MEKADDISHKEM = Jehovah that doth sanctify you. Ex. 31. 13. Lev. 20. 8; 21. 8; 22. 32. Ezek. 20. 12.
5. JEHOVAH-SHĀLŌM = Jehovah [send] peace. Judg. 6. 24.
6. JEHOVAH-ZEBĀ'ŌTH = Jehovah of hosts. 1 Sam. 1. 3, and frequently.
7. JEHOVAH-ZIDKĒNŪ = Jehovah our righteousness. Jer. 23. 6; 33. 16.
8. JEHOVAH-SHĀMMĀH = Jehovah is there. Ezek. 48. 35.
9. JEHOVAH-'ELYŌN = Jehovah most high. Ps. 7. 17; 47. 2; 97. 9.
10. JEHOVAH-RO'Ī = Jehovah my Shepherd. Ps. 23. 1.

We have *seven* of these, experimentally referred to, in Ps. 23, inasmuch as Jehovah, as the "Good," "Great," and "Chief Shepherd," is engaged, in all the perfection of His attributes, on behalf of His sheep:—

In verse 1, we have No. 1 above.
" 2, we have No. 5.
" 3, we have Nos. 2 and 7.
" 4, we have No. 8.
" 5, we have Nos. 3 and 4.

III. JAH is Jehovah in a special sense and relation. Jehovah as having BECOME our Salvation (first occ. Ex. 15. 2), He Who IS, and WAS, and IS TO COME. It occurs 49 times (7 × 7. See Ap. 10). *Jah* is indicated by type thus: 𝔏𝔬𝔯𝔡.

IV. EL is essentially *the Almighty*, though the word is never so rendered (see below, "Shaddai"). EL is Elohim in all His strength and power. It is rendered "God" as Elohim is, but *El* is God the Omnipotent. *Elohim* is God the *Creator* putting His omnipotence into operation. Eloah (see below) is God Who wills and orders all, and Who is to be the one object of the worship of His people. *El* is the God Who *knows* all (first occ. Gen. 14. 18-22) and sees all (Gen. 16. 13) and that *performeth* all things for His people (Ps. 57 2); and in Whom all the Divine attributes are concentrated.

El is indicated in this edition by type in large capital letters, thus: "GOD." It is sometimes transliterated in proper names Immanu-*'el*, Beth-*'el*, &c., where it is translated, as explained in the margin.

V. ELOAH is Elohim, Who is to be worshipped. Eloah is God in connection with His *Will* rather than His power. The first occurrence associates this name with worship (Deut. 32. 15, 17). Hence it is the title used whenever the contrast (latent or expressed) is with false gods or idols. Eloah is essentially "the living God" in contrast to inanimate idols.

Eloah is rendered "God", but we have indicated it by type thus: GOD.

VI. ELYŌN first occurs in Gen. 14. 18 with *El*, and is rendered "the most high (God)". It is El and Elohim, not as the powerful Creator, but as "the possessor of heaven and earth." Hence the name is associated with Christ as the Son of "the Highest" (Luke 1. 35).

It is *Elyōn*, as possessor of the earth, Who divides the nations "their inheritance". In Ps. 83. 18, He is "over all the earth". The title occurs 36 times (6×6, or 6^2. See Ap. 10).

Elyōn is the Dispenser of God's blessings in the earth; the blessings proceeding from a Priest Who is a King upon His throne (cp. Gen. 14. 18-22 with Zech. 6. 13; 14. 9).

VII. SHADDAI is in every instance translated "Almighty", and is indicated by small capital letters ("ALMIGHTY"). It is God (*El*), not as the source of strength, but of *grace*; not as Creator, but as the *Giver*. Shaddai is the All-bountiful. This title does not refer to His *creative* power, but to His power to *supply* all the needs of His people. Its first occurrence is in Gen. 17. 1, and is used to show Abraham that He Who called him out to walk alone before Him could supply all his need. Even so it is the title used in 2 Cor. 6. 18, where we are called to "come out" in separation from the world. It is always used in connection with *El* (see above).

VIII. ADON is one of three titles (ADON, ADONAI, and ADONIM), all generally rendered "Lord"; but each has its own peculiar usage and association. They all denote *headship* in various aspects. They have to do with God as "over-lord."

(1) ADON is the Lord as Ruler *in* the earth. We have indicated this in type by printing the preceding article or pronouns in small capitals, not because either are to be emphasised, but to distinguish the word "Lord" from *Adonai*, which is always so printed in the A.V.

(2) ADONAI is the Lord in His relation *to* the earth; and as carrying out His purposes of blessing in the earth. With this limitation it is almost equivalent to Jehovah. Indeed, it was from an early date so used, by associating the vowel points of the word *Jehovah* with *Adon*, thus converting *Adon* into *Adonai*. A list of 134 passages where this was deliberately done is preserved and given in the Massorah (§§ 107-115). (See Ap. 32.) We have indicated these by printing the word like Jehovah, putting an asterisk, thus: LORD*.

(3) ADONIM is the plural of *Adon*, never used of man. *Adonim* carries with it all that *Adon* does, but in a greater and higher degree; and more especially as *owner* and *proprietor*. An *Adon* may rule others who do not belong to him. Hence (without the article) it is often used of men. But *Adonim* is the Lord Who *rules* His own. We have indicated it by type, thus: LORD.

The three may be thus briefly distinguished:—
Adon is the Lord as overlord or *ruler*.
Adonim is the Lord as *owner*.
Adonai is the Lord as *blesser*.

IX. The TYPES used to indicate the above titles, in the text, are as follows:—

God = *Elohim*.
GOD = *Jehovah* (in combination with *Adonai*, "Lord").
GOD* = Jehovah in the Primitive Texts, altered by *Sōpherim* to *Elohim* as in the Printed Text. (See Ap. 32.)
GOD = *El*.
GOD = *Eloah*.
LORD = *Jehovah*.
THE LORD = *Jah*.
LORD* = Jehovah in the Primitive Text, altered by *Sōpherim* to *Adonai* as in the Printed Text. (See Ap. 32.)
Lord = *Adonai*.
LORD = *Adonim*.
ALMIGHTY = *Shaddai*.
MOST HIGH = *Elyōn*.

X. THE COMBINATIONS are indicated as follows:—
Adonai Jehovah = Lord GOD.
Jehovah Elohim = LORD God.
Elyōn El = MOST HIGH GOD.
El Shaddai = GOD ALMIGHTY.

5 CREATION *VERSUS* EVOLUTION.

The Introduction to Genesis (and to the whole Bible) Gen. 1. 1—2. 3, ascribes everything to the living God, creating, making, acting, moving, and speaking. There is no room for evolution without a flat denial of Divine revelation. One must be true, the other false. All God's works were pronounced "good" seven times (see Ap. 10), viz. Gen. 1. 4, 10, 12, 18, 21, 25, 31. They are "great," Ps. 111. 2. Rev. 15. 3. They are "wondrous," Job 37. 14. They are "perfect," Deut. 32. 4.

Man starts from nothing. He begins in helplessness, ignorance, and inexperience. All his works, therefore, proceed on the principle of *evolution*. This principle is seen *only in human* affairs: from the hut to the palace; from the canoe to the ocean liner; from the spade and ploughshare to machines for drilling, reaping, and binding, &c. But the birds build their nests to-day as at the beginning. The moment we pass the boundary line, and enter the Divine sphere, no trace or vestige of evolution is seen. There is growth and development *within*, but no passing, change, or evolution out from one into another. On the other hand, *all* God's works are *perfect*.

In the Introduction to Genesis (ch. 1. 1—2. 3) forty-six times everything is ascribed to direct acts and volitions on the part of God as the Creator (see Ap. 4. I.):—

God (or He) created	6 times	(1. 1, 21, 27, 27, 27; 2. 3).
God moved	1 once	(1. 2).
God said	10 times	(1. 3, 6, 9, 11, 14, 20, 24, 26, 28, 29).
God saw	7 times	(1. 4, 10, 12, 18, 21, 25, 31).
God divided	2 twice	(1. 4, 7).
God (or He) called	5 times	(1. 5, 5, 8, 10, 10).
Brought forward.	31	
God (or He) made	7 times	(1. 7, 16, 25, 31; 2. 2, 2, 3).
God set	1 once	(1. 17).
God blessed	3 times	(1. 22, 28; 2. 3).
God ended	1 once	(2. 2).
He rested	2 twice	(2. 2, 3).
He sanctified	1 once	(2. 3).
	—	
	46	

It will be noted that the word "God" (Elohim, see Ap. 4. I.) occurs in this Introduction thirty-five times (7×5), the *product* of 7 and 5, the numbers of spiritual perfection, and grace. (See Ap. 10.)

There are also *ten* words connected with the word "God"; this is the number of ordinal perfection (Ap. 10).

There is only one verb used alone with the pronoun "He", instead of "God", and that is the verb "rested". This makes eleven in all; for the significance of which see Ap. 10.

The word "and" is repeated 102 times: thus, by the figure *Polysyndeton* (Ap. 6), marking and emphasising each separate act as being equally independent and important.

Evolution is only one of several theories invented to explain the phenomena of created things. It is admitted by all scientists that no one of these theories covers all the ground; and the greatest claim made for Evolution, or Darwinism, is that "it covers more ground than any of the others."

The Word of God claims *to cover all the ground*: and the only way in which this claim is met, is by

a denial of the inspiration of the Scriptures, in order to weaken it. This is the special work undertaken by the so-called "Higher Criticism", which bases its conclusions on human assumptions and reasoning, instead of on the documentary evidence of manuscripts, as Textual Criticism does.

6 (Acc.) FIGURES OF SPEECH. (Ant.)

It is most important to notice these. It is absolutely necessary for true interpretation. God's Word is made up of "words which the Holy Ghost teacheth" (1 Cor. 2. 13. 1 Thess. 2. 13. 2 Tim. 3. 16. 2 Pet. 1. 21, &c.).

A "Figure of speech" relates to the *form* in which the words are used. It consists in the fact that a word or words are used out of their ordinary sense, or place, or manner, for the purpose of attracting our attention to what is thus said. A Figure of speech is a designed and legitimate departure from the laws of language, in order to emphasise what is said. Hence in such Figures we have the Holy Spirit's own marking, so to speak, of His own words.

This peculiar form or unusual manner may not be true, or so true, to the *literal* meaning of the words; but it is more true to their *real* sense, and truer to truth.

Figures are never used but for the sake of emphasis. They can never, therefore, be ignored. Ignorance of Figures of speech has led to the grossest errors, which have been caused either from taking literally what is figurative, or from taking figuratively what is literal.

The Greeks and Romans named some hundreds of such figures. The only work on Biblical *Figures of speech* in the English language is by Dr. Bullinger[1], from which we have taken the whole of the information given here as well as in the marginal notes. He has classified some 217 separate figures (some of them with many varieties or subdivisions), and has given over 8,000 illustrations.

In Gen. 3. 14, 15 we have some of the earliest examples. By interpreting these figures literally as meaning "belly", "dust", "heel", "head", we lose the volumes of precious and mysterious truth which they convey and intensify. It is the *truth* which is literal, while the *words* employed are figurative. (See under Ap. 19.)

In the marginal notes will be found the names of most of these figures; and we append a list with their pronunciation and English definitions (giving one or more references as examples:—

Ac-cis′-mus; or, **Apparent Refusal** (Matt. 15. 22-26). So named because it is an apparent or assumed refusal.

Ac-ro′-stichion; or, **Acrostic** (Ps. 119). Repetition of the same or successive letters at the beginnings of words or clauses.

Æ-nig′-ma; or, **Dark Saying** (Gen. 49. 10. Judg. 14. 14). A truth expressed in obscure language.

Æ′-ti-o-log′-ia; or, **Cause Shown** (Rom. 1. 16). Rendering a reason for what is said or done.

Affirmatio; or, **Affirmation** (Phil. 1. 18). Emphasising words to affirm what no one has disputed.

Ag′-an-ac-te′-sis; or, **Indignation** (Gen. 3. 13. Acts 13. 10). An expression of feeling by way of indignation.

Al′-le-go-ry; or, **Continued Comparison by Representation (Metaphor)** (Gen. 49. 9. Gal. 4. 22, 24), **and Implication (Hypocatastasis)** (Matt. 7. 3-5). Teaching a truth about one thing by substituting another for it which is unlike it.

Am-œ-bae′-on; or, **Refrain** (Ps. 136). The repetition of the same phrase at the end of successive paragraphs.

Am-phi-bo-log′-ia; or, **Double Meaning** (Ezek. 12. 13). A word or phrase susceptible of two interpretations, both absolutely true.

Am′-phi-di-or-thō′-sis; or, **Double Correction** (1 Cor. 11. 22). A correction setting right both hearer and speaker.

[1] Published by Eyre and Spottiswoode, London, 1898.

Am′-pli-a′-tio; or, **Adjournment** (Gen. 2. 23. 1 Sam. 30. 5). A retaining of an old name after the reason for it has passed away.

An-ăb′-a-sĭs; or, **Gradual Ascent** (Ps. 18. 37, 38). An increase of emphasis or sense in successive sentences.

An-a-cho′-rē-sis; or, **Regression** (Eph. 3. 14). A return to the original subject after a digression.

An′-a-cœ-nō-sis; or, **Common Cause** (1 Cor. 4. 21) An appeal to others as having interests in common.

An′-a-co-lū′-thon; or, **Non-Sequence** (Gen. 35. 3. Mark 11. 32). A breaking off the sequence of thought.

An′-a-di-plo′-sis; or, **Like Sentence Endings and Beginnings** (Gen. 1. 1, 2. Ps. 121. 1, 2). The word or words concluding one sentence are repeated at the beginning of another.

An′-a-mnē′-sis; or, **Recalling** (Rom. 9. 3). An expression of feeling by way of recalling to mind.

An-a′-pho-ra; or, **Like Sentence Beginnings** (Deut. 28. 3-6). The repetition of the same word at the beginning of successive sentences.

An-a′-stro-phe; or, **Arraignment** (Acts 7. 48). The position of one word changed, so as to be out of its proper or usual place in a sentence.

An′-ĕ-sis; or, **Abating** (2 Kings 5. 1). The addition of a concluding sentence which diminishes the effect of what has been said.

Ant-eis′-a-gō-ge; or, **Counter Question** (Matt. 21. 23-25). The answering of one question by asking another.

An-thrōp′-o-path-ei′-a; or, **Condescension** (Gen. 1. 2; 8. 21. Ps. 74. 11. Jer. 2. 13. Hos. 11. 10). Ascribing to God what belongs to human and rational beings, irrational creatures, or inanimate things.

Ant-i-cat′-ē-gor′-ia; or, **Tu Quoque** (Ezek. 18. 25). Retorting upon another the very insinuation or accusation he has made against us.

Ant′-i-me′-rei-a; or, **Exchange of Parts of Speech.**

1. Of the Verb. The Verb used instead of some other part of speech (Gen. 32. 24. Luke 7. 21).
2. Of the Adverb. The Adverb used instead of some other part of speech (Gen. 30. 33. Luke 10. 29).
3. Of the Adjective. The Adjective used instead of some other part of speech (Gen. 1. 9. Heb. 6. 17).
4. Of the Noun. The Noun used instead of some other part of speech (Gen. 23. 6. Jas. 1. 25).

Ant-i-me-tab′-o-le; or, **Counterchange** (Gen. 4. 4, 5. Isa. 5. 20). A word or words repeated in a reverse order, with the object of opposing them to one another.

Ant-i-met-a-the′-sis; or, **Dialogue** (1 Cor. 7. 16). A transference of speakers; as when the reader is addressed as if actually present.

Ant-i′-phras-is; or, **Permutation** (Gen. 3. 22). The use of a word or phrase in a sense opposite to its original signification.

Ant′-i-pros-o′-po-pœ-i-a; or, **Anti-Personification** (2 Sam. 16. 9). Persons represented as inanimate things.

Ant′-i-ptōs′-is; or, **Exchange of Cases** (Ex. 19. 6, cp. 1 Pet. 2. 9). One Case is put for another Case, the governing Noun being used as the Adjective instead of the Noun *in regimen.*

Ant-i′-strŏ-phe; or, **Retort** (Matt. 15. 26, 27). Turning the words of a speaker against himself.

Ant-i′-thĕs-is; or, **Contrast** (Prov. 15. 17). A setting of one phrase in contrast with another.

Ant′-o-no-mă′-si-a; or, **Name Change** (Gen. 31. 21).

The putting of a proper name for an Appellative or common Noun, or the reverse.

Aph-aer′-e-sis; or, **Front Cut** (Jer. 22. 24). The cutting off of a letter or syllable from the beginning of a word.

Ap′-o-di-ōx′-is; or, **Detestation** (Matt. 16. 23). An expression of feeling by way of detestation.

Ap-o′-phas-is; or, **Insinuation** (Philem. 19). When, professing to suppress certain matters, the writer adds the insinuation negatively.

A-pō′-ria; or, **Doubt** (Luke 16. 3). An expression of feeling by way of doubt.

Ap-o-si-o-pes′-is; or, **Sudden Silence.** It may be associated with:—

1. Some great promise (Ex. 32. 32).
2. Anger and threatening (Gen. 3. 22).
3. Grief and complaint (Gen. 25. 22. Ps. 6. 3).
4. Inquiry and deprecation (John 6. 62).

Ap-o′-stro-phe; or, **Apostrophe.** When the speaker turns away from the real auditory whom he is addressing to speak to another, who may be—

1. God (Neh. 6. 9).
2. Men (2 Sam. 1. 24, 25).
3. Animals (Joel 2. 22).
4. Inanimate things (Jer. 47. 6).

Association; or, **Inclusion** (Acts 17. 27). When the speaker associates himself with those whom he addresses, or of whom he speaks.

As′-ter-is′-mos; or, **Indicating** (Ps. 133. 1). Employing some word which directs special attention to some particular point or subject.

A-syn′-de-ton; or, **No-Ands** (Mark 7. 21–23. Luke 14. 13). The usual conjunction is omitted, so that the point to be emphasised may be quickly reached and ended with an emphatic climax (cp. **Polysyndeton**, and Luke 14. 21).

Bat-to-log′-i-a; or, **Vain Repetition** (1 Kings 18. 26). Not used by the Holy Spirit: only by man.

Ben′-e-dic′-ti-o; or, **Blessing** (Gen. 1. 22, 28. Matt. 5. 3–11). An expression of feeling by way of benediction or blessing.

Bra-chy′-lo-gi-a; or, **Brachyology.** A special form of Ellipsis (Gen. 25. 32). See **Ellipsis** I. 3.

Cat-a′-bas-is; or, **Gradual Descent** (Phil. 2. 6–8). The opposite of Anabasis. Used to emphasise humiliation, sorrow, &c.

Cat′-a-chres-is; or, **Incongruity.** One word used for another, contrary to the ordinary usage and meaning of it.

1. Of two words, where the meanings are remotely akin (Lev. 26. 30).
2. Of two words, where the meanings are different (Ex. 5. 21).
3. Of one word, where the Greek receives its real meaning by permutation from another language (Gen. 1. 5. Matt. 8. 6).

Cat′-a-ploc′-e; or, **Sudden Exclamation** (Ezek. 16. 23). This name is given to a parenthesis when it takes the form of a sudden exclamation.

Chleu-as′-mos; or, **Mocking** (Ps. 2. 4). An expression of feeling by mocking and jeering.

Chron′-o-graph′-i-a; or, **Description of Time** (John 10. 22). The teaching of something important by mentioning the time of an occurrence.

Climax; or, **Gradation** (2 Pet. 1. 5–7). Anadiplosis repeated in successive sentences (see "Anadiplosis", above).

Cœ′-nō-tes; or, **Combined Repetition** (Ps. 118. 8, 9). The repetition of two different phrases, one at the beginning, and the other at the end of successive paragraphs.

Correspondence. This term is applied to the repetition of a subject or subjects, which reappear in varying order, thus determining the "Structure" of any portion of the Sacred Text. This Correspondence is found in the following forms:—

1. Alternate. Where the subjects of the alternate members correspond with each other, either by way of similarity or contrast.
   - (a) Extended. Where there are two series, but each consisting of several members (Ps. 72. 2–17. Ps. 132).
   - (b) Repeated. Where there are more than two series of subjects, either consisting of two members each (Ps. 26. Ps. 145), or consisting of more than two members each (Ps. 24).
2. Introverted. Where the first subject of the one series of members corresponds with the last subject of the second (Gen. 43. 3–5. Lev. 14. 51, 52).
3. Complex or Combined. Where both Alternation and Introversion are combined together in various ways (Ex. 20. 8–11. Ps. 105).

Cy-clo-id′-es; or, **Circular Repetition** (Ps. 80. 3, 7. 19). The repetition of the same phrase at regular intervals.

De′-i-sis; or, **Adjuration** (Deut. 4. 26). An expression of feeling by oath or asseveration.

Dep-re-ca′-ti-o; or, **Deprecation** (Ex. 32. 32). An expression of feeling by way of deprecation.

Di′-a-log-is-mos; or, **Dialogue** (Isa. 63. 1–6). When one or more persons are represented as speaking about a thing, instead of saying it oneself.

Di′-a-syrm-os; or, **Raillery** (Matt. 26. 50). Tearing away disguise, and showing up a matter as it really is.

Di-ex′-od-os; or, **Expansion** (Jude 12, 13). A lengthening out by copious exposition of facts.

Ec′-phō-nē′-sis; or, **Exclamation** (Rom. 7. 24). An outburst of words, prompted by emotion.

Ei′-ron-ei-a; or, **Irony.** The expression of thought in a form that naturally conveys its opposite.

1. Divine Irony. Where the speaker is Divine (Gen. 3. 22. Judg. 10. 14).
2. Human Irony. Where the speaker is a human being (Job 12. 2).
3. Peirastic Irony. By way of trying or testing (Gen. 22. 2).
4. Simulated Irony. Where the words are used by man in dissimulation (Gen. 37. 19. Matt. 27. 40).
5. Deceptive Irony. Where words are clearly false as well as hypocritical (Gen. 3. 4, 5. Matt. 2. 8).

E-jac′-u-la′-ti-o; or, **Ejaculation** (Hos. 9. 14). A parenthesis which consists of a short wish or prayer.

El-eu′-ther-i′-a; or, **Candour** (Luke 13. 32). The speaker, without intending offence, speaks with perfect freedom and boldness.

El-lips′-is; or, **Omission.** When a gap is purposely left in a sentence through the omission of some word or words.

I. Absolute Ellipsis. Where the omitted word or words are to be supplied from the nature of the subject.

1. Nouns and Pronouns (Gen. 14. 19, 20. Ps. 21. 12).
2. Verbs and participles (Gen. 26. 7. Ps. 4. 2).
3. Certain connected words in the same member of a passage (Gen. 25. 32. Matt. 25. 9). Called **Brachyology.**
4. A whole clause in a connected passage (Gen. 30. 27. 1 Tim. 1. 3, 4).

II. Relative Ellipsis.

1. Where the omitted word is to be supplied from a cognate word in the context (Ps. 76. 11).
2. Where the omitted word is to be supplied from a related or contrary word (Gen. 33. 10. Ps. 7. 11).

3. Where the omitted word is to be supplied from analogous or related words (Gen. 50. 23. Isa. 38. 12).
4. Where the omitted word is contained in another word, the one word comprising the two significations (Gen. 43. 33).

III. Ellipsis of Repetition.

1. Simple; where the Ellipsis is to be supplied from a preceding or a succeeding clause (Gen. 1. 30. 2 Cor. 6. 16).
2. Complex; where the two clauses are mutually involved, and the Ellipsis in the former clause is to be supplied from the latter; and, at the same time, an Ellipsis in the latter clause is to be supplied from the former (Heb. 12. 20).

E-nan-ti-ō'-sis; or, Contraries (Luke 7. 44-46). Affirmation or negation by contraries.

En'-thy-mē-ma; or, Omission of Premiss (Matt. 27. 19). Where the conclusion is stated, and one or both of the premisses are omitted.

Ep-i-dip'-lo-sis; or, Double Encircling (Ps. 47. 6). Repeated Epanadiplosis (see below).

Ep'-an-a-di-plō'-sis; or, Encircling (Gen. 9. 3. Ps. 27. 14). The repetition of the same word or words at the beginning and end of a sentence.

Ep'-an-a-leps'-is; or, Resumption (1 Cor. 10. 29. Phil. 1. 24). The repetition of the same word after a break or parenthesis.

Ep-an'-od-os; or, Inversion (Gen. 10. 1-31. Isa. 6. 10). The repetition of the same word or words in an inverse order, the sense being unchanged.

Ep'-an-or-thō-sis; or, Correction (John 16. 32). A recalling of what has been said in order to substitute something stronger in its place.

Ep-i'-bo-le; or, Overlaid Repetition (Ps. 29. 3, 4, 5, 7, 8, 9). The repetition of the same phrase at irregular intervals.

Ep'-i-cri'-sis; or, Judgment (John 12. 33). A short sentence added at the end by way of an additional conclusion.

Ep'-i-mo-ne; or, Lingering (John 21. 15-17). Repetition in order to dwell upon, for the sake of impressing.

Ep'-i-phō-nē'-ma; or, Exclamation (Ps. 135. 21). An exclamation at the conclusion of a sentence.

Ep-i'-pho-za; or, Epistrophe in Argument (2 Cor. 11. 22). The repetition of the same word or words at the end of successive sentences used in argument.

Ep-i'-stro-phe; or, Like Sentence-Endings (Gen. 13. 6. Ps. 24. 10). The repetition of the same word or words at the end of successive sentences.

Ep-i'-ta-sis; or, Amplification (Ex. 3. 19). Where a concluding sentence is added by way of increasing the emphasis.

Ep'-i-ther-a-pei'-a; or, Qualification (Phil. 4. 10). A sentence added at the end to heal, soften, mitigate, or modify what has been before said.

Ep-i'-the-ton; or, Epithet (Gen. 21. 16. Luke 22. 41). The naming of a thing by describing it.

Ep'-i-ti-mē'-sis; or, Reprimand (Luke 24. 25). An expression of feeling by way of censure, reproof, or reproach.

Ep'-i-tre-chon; or, Running Along (Gen. 15. 13. John 2. 9). A sentence, not complete in itself, thrown in as an explanatory remark. A form of Parenthesis (see below).

Ep'-i-troch-as'-mos; or, Summarising (Heb. 11. 32). A running lightly over by way of summary.

Ep-i'-trop-e; or, Admission (Ecc. 11. 9). Admission of wrong, in order to gain what is right.

Ep'-i-zeux'-is; or, Duplication (Gen. 22. 11. Ps. 77. 16). The repetition of the same word in the same sense.

Er'-o-tē-sis; or, Interrogating (Gen. 13. 9. Ps. 35. 10). The asking of questions, not for information, or for an answer. Such questions may be asked (1) in positive affirmation, (2) in negative affirmation, (3) in affirmative negation, (4) in demonstration, (5) in wonder and admiration, (6) in rapture, (7) in wishes, (8) in refusals and denials, (9) in doubts, (10) in admonition, (11) in expostulation, (12) in prohibition or dissuasion, (13) in pity and commiseration, (14) in disparagement, (15) in reproaches, (16) in lamentation, (17) in indignation, (18) in absurdities and impossibilities, (19) double questions.

Eth'-o-pœ'-i-a; or, Description of Manners (Isa. 3. 16). A description of a person's peculiarities as to manners, caprices, habits, &c.

Eu'-che; or, Prayer (Isa. 64. 1, 2). An expression of feeling by way of prayer, curse, or imprecation.

Eu'-phēm-is'-mos; or, Euphemy (Gen. 15. 15). Where a pleasing expression is used for one that is unpleasant.

Exemplum; or, Example (Luke 17. 32). Concluding a sentence by employing an example.

Ex-er-gas'-i-a; or, Working Out (Zech. 6. 12, 13). A repetition so as to work out or illustrate what has already been said.

Ex'-ou-then-is'-mos; or, Contempt (2 Sam. 6. 20). An expression of feeling by way of contempt.

Gnō'-mē; or, Quotation. The citation of a well-known saying without quoting the author's name.

1. Where the sense originally intended is preserved, though the words may vary (Matt. 26. 31).
2. Where the original sense is modified in the quotation or reference (Matt. 12. 40).
3. Where the sense is quite different from that which was first intended (Matt. 2. 15).
4. Where the words are from the Hebrew or from the Septuagint (Luke 4. 18).
5. Where the words are varied by omission, addition, or transposition (1 Cor. 2. 9).
6. Where the words are changed by a reading, or an inference, or in number, person, mood, or tense (Matt. 4. 7).
7. Where two or more citations are amalgamated (Matt. 21. 13).
8. Where quotations are from books other than the Bible (Acts 17. 28).

Hen-dī'-a-dy̆s; or, Two for One (Gen. 2. 9. Eph. 6. 18). Two words used, but one thing meant.

Hen-dī'-a-tris; or, Three for One (Dan. 3. 7). Three words used, but one thing meant.

Her-men'-ei-a; or, Interpretation (John 7. 39). An explanation immediately following a statement to make it more clear.

Het'-er-ō'-sis; or, Exchange of Accidence. Exchange of one voice, mood, tense, person, number, degree, or gender for another.

1. Of forms and voices (1 Pet. 2. 6).
2. Of moods (Gen. 20. 7. Ex. 20. 8).
3. Of tenses (Gen. 23. 11. Matt. 3. 10).
4. Of persons (Gen. 29. 27. Dan. 2. 36).
5. Of adjectives (degree) and adverbs (2 Tim. 1. 18).
6. Of nouns (number), adjectives, and pronouns (Gen. 3. 8. Heb. 10. 28).
7. Of gender (Gen. 2. 18. Heb. 7. 7).

Ho-mœ-o'-pto-ton; or, Like Inflections (2 Tim. 3. 2, 3). Similar endings arising from the same inflections of verbs, nouns, &c. This figure belongs peculiarly to the original languages.

Ho-mœ-o-pro'-pher-on; or, Alliteration (Judg. 5). The repetition of the same letter or syllable at the commencement of successive words.

Hō'-mœ-o-tel-eu'-ton; or, Like Endings (Mark 12. 30). The repetition of the same letters or syllables at the end of successive words. Used also of an omission in the text caused by such-like endings: the scribe's eye going back to the latter of such similar words, instead of the former. See Josh. 2. 1.

Hyp-al'-la-ge; or, Interchange (Gen. 10. 9. 1 Kings 17. 14). A word logically belonging to one connection is grammatically united with another.

Hyp-er'-bat-on; or, Transposition (Rom. 5. 8). The placing of a word out of its usual order in a sentence.

Hy-per'-bo-le; or, **Exaggeration** (Gen. 41. 47. Deut. 1. 28). When more is said than is literally meant.

Hy'-po-cat-as'-ta-sis; or, **Implication** (Matt. 15. 13; 16. 6). An implied resemblance or representation.

Hy-po-ti-mē'-sis; or, **Under Estimating** (Rom. 3. 5). Parenthetic addition by way of apology or excuse.

Hy'-po-ty-po'-sis; or, **Word Picture** (Isa. 5. 26-30). Representation of objects or actions by words.

Hys'-ter-ē-sis; or, **Subsequent Narration** (Gen. 31. 7, 8. Ps. 105. 18). When a later record gives supplemental or new particulars, not inserted in the historical record.

Hys'-ter-o-log'-ia; or, **The First Last** (Gen. 10 and 11. 2 Sam. 24). A prior mention of a subsequent event.

Id-i-ō'-ma; or, **Idiom**. The peculiar usage of words and phrases, as illustrated in the language peculiar to one nation or tribe, as opposed to other languages or dialects.

1. Idiomatic usage of verbs (Gen. 42. 38. 1 John 1. 10).
2. Special idiomatic usages of nouns and verbs (Gen. 33. 11. Jer. 15. 16).
3. Idiomatic degrees of comparison (Luke 22. 15).
4. Idiomatic use of prepositions (Luke 22. 49).
5. Idiomatic use of numerals (Ps. 103. 2).
6. Idiomatic forms of quotations (Ps. 109. 5).
7. Idiomatic forms of question (Luke 22. 49).
8. Idiomatic phrases (Gen. 6. 2, 4. Matt. 11. 25).
9. Idioms arising from other figures of speech (see notes in margin).
10. Changes of usage of words in the Greek language (Gen. 43. 18. Matt. 5. 25).
11. Changes of usage of words in the English language (Gen. 24. 21. 2 Kings 3. 9).

In'-ter-jec'-ti-o; or, **Interjection** (Ps. 42. 2). Parenthetic addition by way of feeling.

Mal'-e-dic'-ti-o; or, **Imprecation** (Isa. 3. 11). Expression of feeling by way of malediction and execration.

Mei-ō'-sis; or, **a Belittleing** (Gen. 18. 27. Num. 13. 33). A belittleing of one thing to magnify another.

Mĕ-ris'-mos; or, **Distribution** (Rom. 2. 6-8). An enumeration of the parts of a whole which has been just previously mentioned.

Mes-ar-chi'-a; or, **Beginning and Middle Repetition** (Ecc. 1. 2). The repetition of the same word or words at the beginning and middle of successive sentences.

Mes-o-di-plo'-sis; or, **Middle Repetition** (2 Cor. 4. 8, 9). The repetition of the same word or words in the middle of successive sentences.

Mes-o-tel-eu'-ton; or, **Middle and End Repetition** (2 Kings 19. 7). The repetition of the same word or words in the middle and at the end of successive sentences.

Met-a'-bas-is; or, **Transition** (1 Cor. 12. 31). A passing from one subject to another.

Met'-a-lep'-sis; or, **Double Metonymy** (Gen. 19. 8. Ecc. 12. 6. Hos. 14. 2). Two metonymies, one contained in the other, but only one expressed.

Met-al'-la-ge; or, **a Changing Over** (Hos. 4. 18). A different subject of thought substituted for the original subject.

Met'-a-phor; or, **Representation** (Matt. 26. 26). A declaration that one thing is (or *represents*) another: while **Simile** *resembles* it, and **Hypocatastasis** *implies* it.

Met-a-sta-sis; or, **Counter-Blame** (1 Kings 18. 17, 18). A transferring of the blame from one's self to another.

Met-o'-ny-my; or, **Change of Noun**. When one name or noun is used instead of another, to which it stands in a certain relation.

1. Of the Cause. When the cause is put for the effect (Gen. 23. 8. Luke 16. 29).
2. Of the Effect. When the effect is put for the cause producing it (Gen. 25. 23. Acts 1. 18).
3. Of the Subject. When the subject is put for something pertaining to it (Gen. 41. 13. Deut. 28. 5).
4. Of the Adjunct. When something pertaining to the subject is put for the subject itself (Gen. 28. 22. Job 32. 7).

Mi-mē-sis; or, **Description of Sayings** (Ex. 15. 9). Used when the sayings, &c., of another are described or imitated by way of emphasis.

Neg-a'-ti-o; or, **Negation** (Gal. 2. 5). A denial of that which has not been affirmed.

Œ'-ōn-is'-mos; or, **Wishing** (Ps. 55. 6). An expression of feeling by way of wishing or hoping for a thing.

Ox'-y-mōr-on; or, **Wise-Folly** (1 Tim. 5. 6). A wise saying that seems foolish.

Pae-an'-is'-mos; or, **Exultation** (Zeph. 3. 14). Calling on others to rejoice over something.

Pal'-in-ōd'-i-a; or, **Retracting** (Rev. 2. 6). Approval of one thing after reproving for another thing.

Par-a-bol-a; or, **Parable, i.e., Continued Simile** (Luke 14. 16-24). Comparison by continued resemblance.

Par'-a-di-a'-stol-e; or, **Neithers and Nors** (Ex. 20. 10. Rom. 8. 35, 38, 39). The repetition of the disjunctives neither and nor, or, either and or.

Par'-ae-net'-ic-on; or, **Exhortation** (1 Tim. 2). An expression of feeling by way of exhortation.

Par-a-leips'-is; or, **a Passing By** (Heb. 11. 32). When a wish is expressed to pass by a subject, which is, notwithstanding, briefly alluded to subsequently.

Parallelism; or, **Parallel Lines**. The repetition of similar, synonymous, or opposite thoughts or words in parallel or successive lines. Cp. "Correspondence".

1. Simple *synonymous*, or *gradational*. When the lines are parallel in thought, and in the use of synonymous words (Gen. 4. 23, 24. Ps. 1. 1).
2. Simple *antithetic*, or opposite. When the words are contrasted in the two or more lines, being opposed in sense the one to the other (Prov. 10. 1).
3. Simple *synthetic*, or constructive. When the parallelism consists only in the similar form of construction (Ps. 19. 7-9).
4. Complex *alternate*. When the lines are placed alternately (Gen. 19. 25. Prov. 24. 19, 20).
5. Complex *repeated alternation*. The repetition of the two parallel subjects in several lines (Isa. 65. 21, 22).
6. Complex *extended alternation*. Alternation extended so as to consist of three or more lines (Judg. 10. 17).
7. Complex *introversion*. When the parallel lines are so placed that the first corresponds with the last, the second with the last but one, &c. (Gen. 3. 19. 2 Chron. 32. 7, 8).

Par-ec'-bas-is; or, **Digression** (Gen. 2. 8-15). A temporary turning aside from one subject to another.

Par-ē-che'-sis; or, **Foreign Paronomasia** (Rom. 15. 4). The repetition of words similar in sound, but different in language.

Par-eg'-men-on; or, **Derivation** (Matt. 16. 18). The repetition of words derived from the same root.

Par-em'-bol'-e; or, **Insertion** (Phil. 3. 18, 19). Insertion of a sentence between others which is independent and complete in itself.

Par-en'-the-sis; or, **Parenthesis** (2 Pet. 1. 19). Insertion of a word or sentence, parenthetically, which is necessary to explain the context.

Par-œ'-mi-a; or, **Proverb** (Gen. 10. 9. 1 Sam. 10. 12). A wayside-saying in common use.

Par'-o-mœ-o'-sis; or, **Like-Sounding Inflections** (Matt. 11. 17). The repetition of inflections similar in sound.

Par-o-no-ma'-si-a; or, **Rhyming Words** (Gen. 18. 27). The repetition of words similar in sound, but not necessarily in sense.

Path'-o-pœ'-i-a; or, **Pathos** (Luke 19. 41, 42). The expression of feeling or emotion.

Per-i'-phras-is; or, **Circumlocution** (Gen. 20. 16. Judg. 5. 10). When a description is used instead of the name.

Per-i'-stas-is; or, **Description of Circumstances** (John 4. 6).

Ple'-ŏn-asm; or, **Redundancy.** Where what is said is, immediately after, put in another or opposite way to make it impossible for the sense to be missed.

The Figure may affect (1) words (Gen. 16. 8); or (2) sentences (Gen. 1. 20. Deut. 32. 6).

Plok'-e; or, **Word-Folding** (Jer. 34. 17). The repetition of the same word in a different sense, implying more than the first use of it.

Po-ly-o-ny'-mi-a; or, **Many Names** (Gen. 26. 34, 35. 2 Kings 23. 13). Persons or places mentioned under different names.

Po-ly-ptō'-ton; or, **Many Inflections.** The repetition of the same part of speech in different inflections.

1. Verbs (Gen. 50. 24. 2 Kings 21. 13).
2. Nouns and pronouns (Gen. 9. 25. Rom. 11. 36).
3. Adjectives (2 Cor. 9. 8).

Po'-ly-syn'-de-ton; or, **Many Ands** (Gen. 22. 9, 11. Josh. 7. 24. Luke 14. 21). The repetition of the word "and" at the beginning of successive clauses, each independent, important, and emphatic, with no climax at the end (Compare **Asyndeton** and Luke 14. 13).

Prag'-mato-graph-i-a; or, **Description of Actions** (Joel 2. 1–11).

Pro-ec'-thĕ-sis; or, **Justification** (Matt. 12. 12). A sentence added at the end by way of justification.

Pro-lēp's-is (Ampliatio); or, **Anticipation** (Heb. 2. 8). Anticipating what is going to be, and speaking of future things as present.

Pro-lēp's-is (Occupatio); or, **Anticipation.** Answering an argument by anticipating it before it is used.

1. Open. When the anticipated objection is both answered and stated (Matt. 3. 9).
2. Closed. When the anticipated objection is either not plainly stated or not answered (Rom. 10. 18).

Pros-a-po'-do-sis; or, **Detailing** (John 16. 8–11). A return to previous words or subjects for purposes of definition or explanation.

Pros'-ō-po-graph'-i-a; or, **Description of Persons** (Matt. 3. 4). A vivid description of a person by detailed delineation.

Pros'-ō-po-pœ'-i-a; or, **Personification.** Things represented as persons.

1. The members of the human body (Gen. 48. 14. Ps. 35. 10).
2. Animals (Gen. 9. 5. Job 12. 7).
3. The products of the earth (Nah. 1. 4).
4. Inanimate things (Gen. 4. 10).
5. Kingdoms, countries, and states (Ps. 45. 12).
6. Human actions, &c., attributed to things, &c. (Gen. 18. 20. Ps. 85. 10).

Pro'-ther-a-pei'-a; or, **Conciliation** (Matt. 19. 16). Conciliating others, by way of precaution, because of something we are about to say.

Pro'-ti-mē-sis; or, **Description of Order** (1 Cor. 15. 5–8). The enumeration of things according to their places of honour or importance.

Repeated Negation; or, **Many Noes** (John 10. 28). The repetition of divers negatives.

Repetitio; or, **Repetition** (2 Chron. 20. 35–37. John 14. 1–4). Repetition of the same word or words irregularly in the same passage.

Sim'-i-le; or, **Resemblance** (Gen. 25. 25. Matt. 7. 24–27). A declaration that one thing resembles another. (Cp. **Metaphor,** above.)

Sim'-ul-ta'-ne-um; or, **Insertion** (Rev. 16. 13–16). A kind of historical parenthesis, an event being put out of its historical place between two others which are simultaneous.

Syl-leps'-is; or, **Combination** (2 Chron. 31. 8). The repetition of the sense without the repetition of the word.

Syl-leps'-is; or, **Change in Concord** (John 21. 12). A change in the grammatical concord in favour of a logical concord.

Syl'-lo-gis'-mus; or, **Omission of the Conclusion** (1 Sam. 17. 4–7). The conclusion, though implied, is unexpressed, in order to add emphasis to it.

Symbol (Isa. 22. 22). A material object substituted for a moral or spiritual truth.

Sym'-per-as'-ma; or, **Concluding Summary** (Matt. 1. 17). When what has been said is briefly summed up.

Sym'-plo-ke'; or, **Intertwining** (1 Cor. 15. 42–44). The repetition of different words in successive sentences in the same order and the same sense.

Syn'-ath-rœs'-mos; or, **Enumeration** (1 Tim. 4. 1–3). The enumeration of the parts of a whole which has not been mentioned.

Syn'-chō-rē'-sis; or, **Concession** (Hab. 1. 13). Making a concession of one point in order to gain another.

Syn'-cri-sis; or, **Repeated Simile** (Isa. 32. 2). Repetition of a number of resemblances.

Syn-ec'-do-che; or, **Transfer.** The exchange of one idea for another associated idea.

1. Of the Genus. When the genus is put for the species, or universals for particulars (Gen. 6. 12. Matt. 3. 5).
2. Of the Species. When the species is put for the genus, or particulars for universals (Gen. 3. 19. Matt. 6. 11).
3. Of the Whole. When the whole is put for a part (Gen. 6. 12).
4. Of the Part. When a part is put for the whole (Gen. 3. 19. Matt. 27. 4).

Syn'-œ-cei-o'-sis; or, **Cohabitation** (Matt. 19. 16, 17). The repetition of the same word in the same sentence with an extended meaning.

Syn-o-ny-mi-a; or, **Synonymous Words** (Prov. 4. 14, 15). The repetition of words similar in sense, but different in sound and origin.

Syn'-the-ton; or, **Combination** (Gen. 18. 27). A placing together of two words by usage.

Ta-pei-nō'-sis; or, **Demeaning** (Gen. 27. 44. Rom. 4. 19). The lessening of a thing in order to increase and intensify that same thing. (Cp. **Meiosis.**)

Thau-mas'-mos; or, **Wondering** (Rom. 11. 33). An expression of feeling by way of wonder.

Tmē'-sis; or, **Mid-Cut** (Eph. 6. 8). A change by which one word is cut in two, and another word put in between.

Top'-o-graph'-i-a; or, **Description of Place** (Isa. 10. 28–32). Throwing light on the subject dealt with by alluding to locality.

Type (Rom. 5. 14). A figure or ensample of something future, and more or less prophetic, called the Antitype.

Zeug'-ma; or, **Unequal Yoke.** When one verb is yoked on to two subjects, while grammatically a second verb is required.

1. Proto-zeugma, or, Ante-yoke or Fore-yoke (Gen. 4. 20. 1 Tim. 4. 3).
2. Meso-zeugma, or, Middle yoke (Luke 1. 64).
3. Hypo-zeugma, or, End yoke (Acts 4. 27, 28).
4. Syne-zeugmenon, or, Joint yoke (Ex. 20. 18).

7 ITALIC TYPE IN THE REVISED VERSION.

The Revisers ill-advisedly decided that "all such words, now printed in italics, as are plainly implied in the Hebrew, and necessary in English, be printed in common type."

One of the consequences of this decision is that the verb "to be" is not distinguished from the verb "to become", so that the lessons conveyed by the A.V. "was" and "*was*" in Gen. 1. 2; 3 and 4; 9 and 10; 11 and 12, are lost. See the notes on Gen. 1. 2.

For the general uses of various types in the English Bible see Ap. 48.

8 THE SO-CALLED "CREATION TABLETS."

The Cosmogony of Genesis is in flat contradiction to that of the so-called "Creation Tablets," preserved in an epic poem in honour of Merodach, the patron god of Babylon. If Genesis looks back to Creation, it is to put on record the profound contrast between them, and to give, instead of the corruption of primitive truth, which had been handed down by tradition, the Divine account by Him Who created all things, by the hand and pen of Moses.

The word "without form" (Heb. *tohū*) is used of a subsequent event which, we know not how long after the Creation, befell the primitive creation of Gen. 1. 1. It occurs in Gen. 1. 2. Deut. 32. 10. 1 Sam. 12. 21 (twice). Job 6. 18; 12. 24; 26. 7. Ps. 107. 40. Isa. 24. 10; 29. 21; 34. 11; 40. 17, 23; 41. 29; 44. 9; 45. 18, 19; 49. 4; 59. 4. Jer. 4. 23.

The Heb. *bohū*, rendered "void", means *desolate*, and occurs in Gen. 1. 2. Isa. 34. 11. Jer. 4. 23.

The two words together occur in Gen. 1. 2. Isa. 34. 11. Jer. 4. 23.

1. The Tablets begin with chaos.
   The Bible with perfection (Gen. 1. 1).
2. The Tablets make the heavenly bodies to be gods.
   Genesis makes them created matter.
3. The Tablets are all polytheistic mythology.
   Genesis is monotheistic truth.
4. The Tablets make all the work of a craftsman.
   In Genesis, God speaks, and it is done.
5. In the Tablets we meet everywhere with the puerilities of a grotesque superstition.
   In Genesis we find the grand and solemn realities of righteousness and holiness.

9 THE USAGE OF *RŪACH, SPIRIT.*

The word *rūach* occurs 389 times in the Hebrew O.T.

In the A.V. it is rendered *spirit* in 237 passages (and no other word is rendered spirit except *neshāmāh*, "breath", in Job 26. 4 and Prov. 20. 27. See Ap. 16). In the remaining 152 places it is translated in 22 different ways, which are to be carefully distinguished.

[In the R.V. *rūach* is rendered spirit 224 times, and in the remaining 165 passages is rendered in many different ways.]

The meaning of the word is to be deduced only from its *usage*. The one root idea running through all the passages is *invisible force*. As this force may be exerted in varying forms, and may be manifested in divers ways, so various renderings are necessitated, corresponding thereto.

Rūach, in whatever sense it is used, always represents that which is *invisible* except by its manifestations. These are seen both externally to man, as well as internally within man.

As coming from God, it is the invisible *origin of life*. All apart from this is death. It comes from God, and returns to God (Ecc. 3. 19, 20). Hence, *rūach* is used of

I.—GOD, as being invisible. "The Spirit of Jehovah" is Jehovah Himself, in His manifestation of invisible power.

2 Sam. 23. 2. Ps. 139. 7 (=Thee). Is. 40. 13.

II.—THE HOLY SPIRIT: the Third Person of the Trinity.

2 Sam. 23. 2. 1 Kings 18. 12; 22. 24. 2 Kings 2. 16. 2 Chron. 18. 23. Neh. 9. 20, 30. Job 26. 13; 33. 4. Isa. 40. 13; 48. 16; 59. 19, 21; 61. 1; 63. 10, 1-4. Ezek. 3. 12, 14 (1st); 8. 3; 11. 1, 24; 37. 1; 43. 5. Mic. 2. 7; 3. 8. Zech. 4. 6; 6. 8; 7. 12. Mal. 2. 15.

III.—INVISIBLE DIVINE POWER MANIFESTING ITSELF

In creation. Gen. 1. 2.
In giving life. Ezek. 37. 14.
In executing judgment—
"blast." Ex. 15. 8. Isa. 37. 7.
"breath." 2 Sam. 22. 16. 2 Kings 19. 7. Job 4. 9; 15. 30. Ps. 18. 15; 33. 6. Isa. 11. 4; 30. 28.
"spirit." Isa. 4. 4; 28. 6; 34. 16; 40. 7.

IV.—INVISIBLE "POWER FROM ON HIGH", MANIFESTING ITSELF AS DIVINE POWER in *giving spiritual gifts*. Spoken of as coming upon, clothing, falling on, and being poured out. Rendered "Spirit", but should be "spirit".

Gen. 41. 38. Ex. 28. 3; 31. 3; 35. 31. Num. 11. 17, 25, 25, 26, 29; 24. 2; 27. 8. Deut. 34. 9. Judg. 3. 10; 6. 34; 11. 29; 13. 25; 14. 6, 19; 15. 14. 1 Sam. 10. 6, 10; 11. 6; 16. 13, 14; 19. 20, 23. 2 Kings 2. 9, 15. 1 Chron. 12. 18; 28. 12. 2 Chron. 15. 1; 20. 14; 24. 20. Ps. 51. 11, 12; 143. 10. Prov. 1. 23. Isa. 11. 2, 2, 2, 2; 30. 1; 32. 15; 42. 1, 5; 44. 3; 59. 21; 61. 1; 63. 11. Ezek. 2. 2; 3. 24; 11. 5, 19; 36. 27; 39. 29. Dan. 4. 8, 9, 18; 5. 11, 12, 14. Joel 2. 28, 29. Hag. 2. 5. Zech. 12. 10.

V.—THE INVISIBLE PART OF MAN (Psychological). Given by God at man's formation at birth, and returning to God at his death.

"Breath." Gen. 6. 17; 7. 15, 22. Job 9. 18; 12. 10; 17. 1. Ps. 104. 29; 135. 17; 146. 4. Ecc. 3. 19. Jer. 10. 14; 51. 17. Lam. 4. 20. Ezek. 37. 5, 6, 8, 9, 10. Hab. 2. 19. Zech. 12. 1.

"spirit." Gen. 6. 3. Num. 16. 22; 27. 16. Job 27. 3; 34. 14. Ps. 31. 5; 104. 30. Ecc. 3. 21, 21; 8. 8, 8; 11. 5; 12. 7. Isa. 42. 5.

"Wind." Ezek. 37. 9, 9.

VI.—THE INVISIBLE CHARACTERISTICS OF MAN; manifesting themselves in states of mind and feeling (by the Fig. *Metonymy*. See Ap. 6, p. 11).

"Mind." Gen. 26. 35. Prov. 29. 11. Ezek. 11. 5; 20. 32. Dan. 5. 20. Hab. 1. 11.
"Breath." Job 19. 17 (=manner).
"Courage." Josh. 2. 11.
"Anger." Judg. 8. 3.
"Blast." Isa. 25. 4.
"Spirit." Gen. 41. 8; 45. 27. Ex. 6. 9; 35. 21. Num. 5. 14, 14, 30; 14. 24. Josh. 5. 1. Judg. 15. 19. 1 Sam. 1. 15; 30. 12. 1 Kings 10. 5; 21. 5. 1 Chron. 5. 26, 26. 2 Chron. 9. 4; 21. 16; 36. 22. Ezra 1. 1, 5. Job 6. 4; 7. 11; 10. 12; 15. 13; 20. 3; 21. 4; 32. 8, 18. Ps. 32. 2; 34. 18; 51. 10, 11, 12, 17; 76. 12; 78. 8; 142. 3; 143. 4, 7. Prov. 11. 13; 14. 29; 15. 4, 13; 16. 2, 18, 19, 32; 17. 22, 27; 18. 14, 14; 25. 28; 29. 23. Ecc. 1. 14, 17; 2. 11, 17, 26; 4. 4, 6, 16; 6. 9; 7. 8, 8, 9; 10. 4. Isa. 19. 3, 14; 26. 9; 29. 10, 24; 33. 11; 38. 16; 54. 6; 57. 15, 15, 16; 61. 3; 65. 14; 66. 2. Jer. 51. 11. Ezek. 13. 3. Dan. 7. 15. Hos. 4. 12; 5. 4. Mic. 2. 11 (by *Hendiadys* (Ap. 6), for a false or lying spirit).

VII.—Put by the Fig. *Synecdoche* for THE WHOLE PERSON (see Ap. 6).

Ps. 77. 3, 6; 106. 33. Ezek. 21. 7. Dan. 2. 1, 3. Mal. 2. 15, 16.

VIII.—INVISIBLE SPIRIT-BEINGS.

"Angels." Ps. 104. 4.
"Cherubim." Ezek. 1. 12, 20, 20, 20, 21; 10. 17.

Neutral spirit-beings. Job 4. 15. Isa. 31. 3.

Evil angels. Judg. 9. 23. 1 Sam. 16. 14, 15, 16, 23, 23; 18. 10; 19. 9. 1 Kings 22. 21, 22, 23. 2 Chron. 18. 20, 21, 22. Zech. 13. 2.

IX.—THE INVISIBLE MANIFESTATIONS OF THE ATMOSPHERE.

Temperature. Gen. 3. 8 ("cool").

Air.

"Wind" or "winds" in every place where the words "wind" or "winds" occur.

"Whirlwind." Ezek. 1. 4.

"Windy." Ps. 55. 8.

"Spirits." Zech. 6. 5.

"Air." Job 41. 16.

"Tempest." Ps. 11. 6.

"Blast." Ex. 15. 8. 2 Kings 19. 7. Isa. 25. 4; 37. 7.

"Quarters" (of the four winds). 1 Chron. 9. 24.

"Side" or "sides" (of the four winds). Jer. 52. 23. Ezek. 42. 16, 17, 18, 19, 20.

10 THE SPIRITUAL SIGNIFICANCE OF NUMBERS.

Numbers are used in Scripture, not merely as in Nature, with *supernatural design*, but with *spiritual significance*, which may be summarised as follows[1]:—

ONE. Denotes *unity, and commencement.* The first occurrences of words or utterances denote their essential significance, in interpretation. Words that occur only once, in the originals, are emphatic and important. First day, Light. The first occurrences of all important words and expressions are noted in the margin.

Two. Denotes *difference.* If two different persons *agree* in testimony it is conclusive. Otherwise two implies *opposition, enmity,* and *division,* as was the work of the Second day. Compare the use of the word "double" applied to "heart", "tongue", "mind", &c.

THREE. Denotes *completeness,* as three lines complete a plane figure. Hence, three is significant of Divine perfection and completeness. The third day completes the fundamentals of creation-work. The fourth, fifth, and sixth days are the counterpart and repetition of the first, second, and third, and correspond respectively. (See the structure of Gen. 1, p. 3.) The number, three, includes *resurrection* also; for on the third day the earth *rose up* out of the deep, and fruit rose up out of the earth.

FOUR. Denotes *creative works* (3 + 1), and always has reference to the material creation, as pertaining to the *earth,* and things "under the sun", and things terrestrial.

FIVE. Denotes Divine *grace.* It is 4 + 1. It is God adding His gifts and blessing to the works of His hands. The Heb. *Ha'aretz* (the earth), by "Gematria" (i.e. the addition of the numerical value of the letters together) is a multiple of four, while *Hashamayim* (the heavens) is a multiple of five. The Gematria of **Χάρις** (*charis*), the Greek for *Grace,* is also a multiple of five. It is the leading factor in the Tabernacle measurements.

SIX. Denotes the *human number.* Man was created on the *sixth* day; and this first occurrence of the number makes it (and all multiples of it) the hall-mark of all connected with man. He works six days. The hours of his day are a multiple of six. Athaliah usurped the throne of Judah six years. The great men who have stood out in defiance of God (Goliath and Nebuchadnezzar and Antichrist) are all emphatically marked by this number.

SEVEN. Denotes *spiritual perfection.* It is the number or hall-mark of the Holy Spirit's work. He is the Author of God's Word, and seven is stamped on it as the water-mark is seen in the manufacture of paper. He is the Author and Giver of *life*; and seven is the number which regulates every period of Incubation and Gestation, in insects, birds, animals, and man.

EIGHT. Denotes *resurrection, regeneration*; a new beginning or commencement. The eighth is a new first. Hence the octave in music, colour, days of the week, &c. It is the number which has to do with the LORD, Who rose on the eighth, or new "first-day". This is, therefore, the *Dominical* number. By Gematria (see above), **Ἰησοῦς** (*Jesus*) makes the numbers 888. It, or its multiple is impressed on all that has to do with the Lord's Names, the Lord's People, the Lord's works.

NINE. Denotes *Finality* of *judgment.* It is 3 × 3, the *product* of Divine completeness. The number nine, or its factors or multiples, is seen in all cases when *judgment* is the subject.

TEN. Denotes *Ordinal perfection.* Another new first; after the ninth digit, when numeration commences anew.

ELEVEN. Denotes *disorder, disorganization,* because it is one short of the number twelve (see below).

TWELVE. Denotes *Governmental perfection.* It is the number or factor of all numbers connected with government: whether by Tribes or Apostles, or in measurements of time, or in things which have to do with government in the heavens and the earth.

THIRTEEN. Denotes *rebellion, apostasy, defection, disintegration, revolution,* &c. The first occurrence fixes this (Gen. 14. 4); and the second confirms it (Gen. 17. 25). It, and its multiples, are seen in all numbers, and in the Gematria (see above) of all names and passages that are associated with rebellion, &c.

SEVENTEEN. Denotes a combination of *spirit* and *order* (10+7). It is the seventh prime number (as 13 is the sixth prime number).

Other numbers follow the laws which govern the smaller numbers, as being their factors, sums, products or multiples: e.g. 24 is 12×2, a higher form of 12.

$25 = 5^2$. Grace intensified.

$27 = 3^3$. Divinity intensified.

$28 = 7 \times 4$. Spiritual perfection in connection with the earth.

$29 = 3^3$. Intensifying of Divine judgement.

$30 = 3 \times 10$. Divine perfection, applied to order.

$40 = 10 \times 4$. Divine order applied to earthly things. Hence, the number of *probation.*

The four *perfect numbers,* 3, 7, 10, and 12, have for their product the remarkable number 2,520. It is the Least Common Multiple of the ten digits governing all numeration; and can, therefore, be divided by each of the nine digits, without a remainder. It is the number of chronological perfection (7×360).

[1] The whole subject may be studied in Dr. Bullinger's work on *Number in Scripture* (London: Eyre and Spottiswoode).

11 THE WORD "DAY" IN GENESIS 1.

The word "day", when used without any limiting words, may refer to a long or prolonged period: as, the "day of grace", the "day of visitation", the "day of salvation", the "day of judgment", the "day of the Lord", "man's day", &c. But when the word "day" is used *with a numeral* (cardinal or ordinal), as one, two, three, &c., or first, second, third, &c., "evening and morning" (Gen. 1), or the "seventh day" (Ex. 20. 9, 11, &c.), it is defined, limited, and restricted to an ordinary day of twenty-four hours.

The word "day" is never used for a year. Sometimes a corresponding number of days is used for a corresponding number of years, but in that case it is always expressly stated to be so used; as in Num. 14. 33, 34. But, even in these cases, the word "day" means a day, and the word "year" means a year. It is not said that a day *means* a year; but the number of the forty years is said to be "after the number of the days in which ye searched the land, even forty days".

It is the same in Ezek. 4. 5, where the years of Israel's

iniquity were laid on Ezekiel "according to the number of the days". In this case also, the word "days" means days, and the word "years" means years.

There is no Scriptural warrant for arbitrarily assuming this to be a general principle in the absence of any statement to that effect.

12 "THE STARS ALSO."

In the first mention of the heavenly bodies, the purpose of the Creator is clearly stated. Gen. 1. 14–19 reveals the fact that they were created, not only "to divide the day from the night, and to give light upon the earth"; but, they were set "for SIGNS, and for SEASONS, and for days and years".

The figure *Polysyndeton* (see Ap. 6) emphasises these four purposes, and bids us single them out and consider them separately and independently.

They are "for SIGNS".

Heb. *'ōth*, from *'āthah, to come.* Signs, therefore, of something or some One *to come.* Those who understand them are enlightened by them. Those who do not may well be "dismayed" (Jer. 10. 2).

The stars are numbered and named. There are twelve signs of the Zodiac, called "the stars" in Gen. 37. 9 (eleven of which bowed down to Joseph's, the twelfth). The word *Zodiac* means the *degrees* or *steps*, which mark the stages of the sun's path through the heavens, corresponding with the twelve months.

The stars were all named by God (Ps. 147. 4). Most of these names have been lost; but over 100 are preserved through the Arabic and Hebrew, and are used by astronomers to-day, though their meaning is unknown to them. Many of them are used in Scripture as being well known, though the translations are somewhat speculative: e.g. Job 9. 9. Heb. *'āsh* (Arcturus, R. V. the Bear), *kesīl* (A. V. Orion), *kīmāh* (Pleiades). Job 38. 31, 32, *mazzārōth* (margin, and R. V., the twelve signs; margin, the signs of the *Zodiac*). Cp. 2 Kings 23. 5, *'āsh* (Arcturus with her sons, R. V. the Bear with her train, both versions being incorrect as to the names). See also Isa. 13. 10. Amos 5. 8.

These names and the twelve "signs" go back to the foundation of the world. Jewish tradition, preserved by Josephus, assures us that this Bible astronomy was invented by Adam, Seth, and Enoch.

We see evidence of it as early as Gen. 11. 4, where we read of the Tower of Babel having "his top with the heavens". There is nothing about the wrongly supplied italics "may reach unto". The words, doubtless, refer to the signs of the Zodiac, pictured at the top of the Tower, like the Zodiacs in the Temples of Denderah, and Esnéh in Egypt.

The Babylonian "Creation Tablets" refer to them, though their primitive meaning had been either corrupted or lost. It is the same with the Greek mythology, which is a corruption of primitive truth which had been lost and perverted.

We have to remember that our *written* Scriptures began with Moses, say in 1490 B.C.: and thus, for more than 2,500 years, the revelation of the hope which God gave in Gen. 3. 15 was preserved in the *naming* of the stars and their *grouping* in Signs and Constellations.

These groupings are quite arbitrary. There is nothing in the positions of the stars to suggest the pictures originally drawn around them. The Signs and Constellations were first designed and named; then, the pictures were drawn around them respectively. Thus the truth was enshrined and written in the heavens, where no human hand could touch it. In later years, when Israel came into the possession of the written "Scriptures of truth", there was no longer any need for the more ancient writing in the heavens. Hence, the original teaching gradually faded away, and the heathen, out of the smattering they had heard by tradition, evolved their cosmogonies and mythologies.

Ps. 19 contains a vivid reference to these two Books of revelation. That is why there is the very sudden change of subject at verse 7; a change which still perplexes and baffles all the skill of commentators.

The teaching is preserved in the structure of the Psalm, where we have

A | 1-4-. The Heavens.
  B | -4-6. "In them, the sun".
A | 7-10. The Scriptures.
  B | 11-14. "In them[1], Thy servant".

In this structure every line emphasises the elaboration of the design: for, while, in the first half, all the terms are *literary*, in the latter half they are all *astronomical*, thus welding the two portions of the Psalm into one harmonious whole.

For the meaning of the words, reference must be made to the Psalm itself. We can only note here that the first part does not refer to the *wonders* of creation, but to the *eloquence of its teaching* and *revelation*: they "declare", tell, or narrate (Gen. 24. 66. Ps. 71. 15), they "utter speech", but without words (omit "where" in *v.* 3); Heb. = they "show forth", exhibit (Gen. 3. 11. Ps. 97. 6; 111. 6); they prophesy "day by day", "night by night". The question is: What do they prophesy? What knowledge do they show forth? What glory do they tell of?

The answer is—Gen. 3. 15. The one great central truth of all prophecy—the coming of One, Who, though He should suffer, should in the end crush the head of the old serpent, the Devil.

But, where are we to open this book? Where are we to break into this circle of the Zodiacal signs?

Through the "precession of the Equinoxes" the sun gradually shifts its position a little each year, till in about every 2,000 years it begins the year in a different sign. This was foreseen; and it was also foreseen that succeeding generations would not know when and where the sun began its course, and where the teaching of this Heavenly Book commenced, and where we were to open its first page. Hence the "Sphinx" was invented as a memorial. It had the head of a woman and the body and tail of a lion, to tell us that this Book, written in the Heavens, began with the sign "Virgo", and will end with the sign "Leo". The word "sphinx" is from the Greek *sphingo, to join*; because it binds together the two ends of this circle of the heavens.

The number of the Signs is twelve, the number of governmental perfection or "rule": cp. Gen. 1. 18 (Ap. 10). They are divided into three books of four chapters (or signs) each: twelve being the product of 3×4, i. e. of Divine truth working in the heavens and in the earth (see Ap. 10).

Each book, therefore, consists of four signs; and these are all arranged, by structure, in exactly the same way. Each is an introversion. Thus we have the three books:

First Book. **The Redeemer.**

(His first coming).

A | VIRGO. The prophecy of the promised seed.
  B | LIBRA. The Redeemer's work (grace).
  B | SCORPIO. The Redeemer's conflict.
A | SAGITTARIUS. The prophecy fulfilled.

Second Book. **The Redeemed.**

(His work and its results).

C | CAPRICORNUS. The prophecy of deliverance.
  D | AQUARIUS. Results of work bestowed.
  D | PISCES. Results of work enjoyed.
C | ARIES. The prophesied deliverance fulfilled.

[1] The same Heb. as in *v.* 4.

Third Book. The Redeemer.

(His Second Coming.)

E | TAURUS. The prophecy of coming judgment.
F | GEMINI. The Redeemer's reign in glory.
F | CANCER. The Redeemer's possession safe.
E | LEO. The prophecy of triumph fulfilled.

Each of the four chapters in each of these three Books consists of three sections; and each section is represented by a Constellation. There are thus thirty-six (3×12) Constellations, which, with the twelve Signs, make forty-eight (4×12) in all.

They may thus be set forth:

The First Book The Redeemer.

"The sufferings of Christ."

I. VIRGO (A).

The prophecy of the promised seed.

1. COMA (=The desired). The woman and child the desired of all nations (in the most ancient Zodiacs).
2. CENTAURUS (with two natures). The despised sin-offering.
3. BOÖTES. The coming One with branch.

II. LIBRA (B).

The Redeemer's atoning work.

1. CRUX. The Cross endured.
2. LUPUS. The Victim slain.
3. CORONA. The Crown bestowed.

III. SCORPIO (*B*).

The Redeemer's conflict.

1. SERPENS. Assaulting the man's heel.
2. OPHIUCHUS. The man grasping the serpent.
3. HERCULES. The mighty man victorious.

IV. SAGITTARIUS (*A*).

The Redeemer's triumph.

1. LYRA. Praise prepared for the Conqueror.
2. ARA. Fire prepared for His enemies.
3. DRACO. The dragon cast down.

The Second Book. The Redeemed.

I. CAPRICORNUS (C).

The result of the Redeemer's sufferings.

1. SAGITTA. The arrow of God sent forth.
2. AQUILA. The smitten One falling.
3. DELPHINUS. The dead One rising again.

II. AQUARIUS (D).

The Blessings assured.

1. PISCIS AUSTRALIS. The blessings bestowed.
2. PEGASUS. The blessings quickly coming.
3. CYGNUS. The Blesser surely returning.

III. PISCES (*D*).

The Blessings in abeyance.

1. THE BAND. The great enemy, "*Cetus*."
2. ANDROMEDA. The redeemed in bondage.
3. CEPHEUS. The Deliverer coming to loosen.

IV. ARIES (*C*).

The Blessings consummated.

1. CASSIOPEIA. The captive delivered.
2. CETUS. The great enemy bound.
3. PERSEUS. The "Breaker" delivering.

The Third Book. The Redeemer.

"The glory that should follow."

I. TAURUS. (E).

Messiah coming to rule.

1. ORION. The Redeemer breaking forth as Light.
2. ERIDANUS. Wrath breaking forth as a flood.
3. AURIGA. Safety for His redeemed in the day of wrath.

II. GEMINI (F).

Messiah as Prince of princes.

1. LEPUS. The enemy trodden under foot.
2. CANIS MAJOR. The coming glorious Prince.
3. CANIS MINOR. The exalted Redeemer.

III. CANCER (*F*).

Messiah's redeemed possessions.

1. URSA MINOR. The lesser sheepfold.
2. URSA MAJOR. The fold and the flock.
3. ARGO. The pilgrim's arrival at home.

IV. LEO (*E*).

Messiah's consummated triumph.

1. HYDRA. The old serpent destroyed.
2. CRATER. The cup of wrath poured out.
3. CORVUS. The birds of prey devouring.

It will be noted that the modern names are used, but only for the purposes of readier identification. Some of these names were given in ignorance, by those who had lost the primitive signification of the twelve Signs and of the thirty-six Constellations.

The Hebrew and Arabic names of these, and of the principal stars contained in them, are full of truth, and eloquent in their teaching. Thus:

VIRGO (the Virgin). Here we have the star *Al Zimach*. Heb. *Ẓemach*, the branch. Isa. 4. 2. Jer. 23. 5, 6. Zech. 3. 8; 6. 12. All the other stars have cognate meanings.

COMA. The Desired (Hag. 2. 7). Num. 24. 17. (Egyptian *Shes-nu*=the desired son.)

CENṬAURUS, *Al Beze*, the despised (Isa. 53. 3).

BOÖTES (Heb. *bō', to come*), Ps. 96. 13. Heb. *Arcturus* (Job 9. 9=He cometh). Egyptian=*Smat*, one who rules.

LIBRA was anciently *the Altar* (Accadian=*Tulki*). The two bright stars are to-day called in Arabic *Zuben al Genubi*=the price which is deficient, and *Zuben al Chemali*=the price which covers.

CRUX. Heb. *kārath, cut off* (Dan. 9. 26).

LUPUS. Greek name *Thera*, a beast. Lat. *Victima*. Heb. *zābaḥ*, slain. In the Zodiac of Denderah=*Sura*, a lamb.

CORONA. Heb. *'ăṭārāh*, a royal crown. Arab. *Al iclil*, a jewel. Its brightest star=*Al phena*, the shining one.

SCORPIO. Heb. *'aḳrab* (Ps. 91. 13). Coptic name =*Isidis*=the attack of the enemy. Arabic=*Al aterah*, the wounding of the coming One. The brightest star is *Antares* (Arab.=wounding). Heb. *Lᵉzuth*, perverseness.

SERPENS. The brightest star is called (Heb.) *'ānaḳ* = encompassing. Heb. *ḳᵉlālāh* = the accursed. Arab. *Al hay*, the reptile.

OPHIUCHUS is from Arab. *Afeichus*=the serpent held. The brightest star is *Ras al hagus* = the head of him who holds. Other names are *Megeras* = contending. In the Zodiac of Denderah he is *Api-bau* = the chief who cometh. Other stars are *Triophas*=treading under foot; *Saiph* = bruised; *Carnebas* = bruised.

HERCULES. In the Zodiac of Denderah called *Bau*=who cometh. Arab. *Al giscale*, the strong one. The brightest star, *Ras al Gethi* = the head of him who bruises.

SAGITTARIUS. Heb. *kesheth* (an archer) (Gen. 21. 20). The brightest star, Heb. *channūn* = the gracious one (Ps. 45. 2). Accadian, *Nun-ki*=Prince of the earth. In Zodiac of Denderah, *Pi-maere*=graciousness, and *Knem*, He conquers.

LYRA. (Ps. 65. 1.) The brightest star *Vega*=He shall be exalted. In Zodiac of Denderah= *Fent-kar*=the serpent ruled. Originally an eagle, from confusion between Heb. *nesher*, and *shīr* (song, or music).

ARA, an altar upside down, pointing to Tartarus (Isa. 63. 4, 5). Arab. *Al mugamra*=the completing or finishing (Ps. 21. 9-12).

DRACO. Ends the first book. The dragon cast down. CETUS ends the second book. Leviathan bound. HYDRA ends the third book. The old serpent destroyed. Draco=trodden on. (Ps. 91. 13; 74. 12-14. Isa. 27. 1). In Zodiac of Denderah it is a serpent under the fore-feet of Sagittarius and called *Her-fent*=the serpent accursed. The brightest star called *Thuban*=the subtil.

CAPRICORNUS = the goat of atonement. In Zodiac of Denderah and Esneh, *Hu-penius*=the place of the sacrifice. Heb. *Gᵉdī*, the kid, or *Gād'a*, cut off. The brightest star is *Al-gedi* = the kid. The next is *Deneb al gedi*=the sacrifice of the kid.

SAGITTA, the arrow. (Ps. 38. 2. Isa. 53. 4, 5.) Heb. *Shamad*, or *shamᵉm*=destroying.

AQUILA, the eagle, pierced and wounded and falling. The brightest star, *Al tair*=wounding. All the others are similar.

DELPHINUS. Always a fish full of life, the head upwards. Heb. *Dālaph* = the pouring out of water. Arab. *Dalaph*=coming quickly.

AQUARIUS. In the Zodiac of Denderah he has two urns. The fish seems to have come out of one of them. Heb. name *Dāli* = water-urn or bucket (Num. 24. 7). Brightest star *Sa'ad al Melik*=the record of the pouring forth. The next *Sa'ad al Sund*=who goeth and returneth (cp. Isa. 32. 1, 2; 35. 1, 6; 41. 18; 44. 2-6; 51. 3).

PISCIS AUSTRALIS. The southern fish. Arab. *Fom al haut*=the mouth of the fish. Zodiac of Denderah=*Aar*, a stream.

PEGASUS. The winged horse. Zodiac of Denderah Pe and ka = *Peka*, or *pega*. Heb. *pehāh* =the chief, and *sūs*, a horse; name thus come down. The brightest is *Markab*, Heb. *merhak* =returning from afar.

CYGNUS. In the Zodiac of Denderah, *Tes-ark* =this from afar. A mighty bird, not falling dead like Aquila. Brightest star *Deneb*=the Judge; called also *Adige*=flying swiftly. The second, *Al Bireo*=flying quickly. Two others: *Azel* = who goes and returns quickly, and *Fafage*=gloriously shining forth.

PISCES. Egyptian name in the Zodiac of Denderah=*Pi-cot Orion* or *Pisces Hori*=the fishes (i. e. swarms or multitudes) of Him Who cometh. Heb. *Dāgīm*, the fishes (Gen. 48. 16). Syr. name, *Nuno* =lengthened out (i. e. in posterity). Cp. Isa. 53. 10. Ps. 33. 12; 37. 22; 115. 14, 15. Isa. 61. 9; 65. 23; 26. 15; 9. 3. Jer. 30. 19. Ezek. 36. 10, 11; 37. 26. Note the two fishes =the earthly and heavenly callings (one fish horizontal, the other looking upward). 113 stars much of the same magnitude. The brightest star is *Okda*=the united. The next (Arabic) *Al samaca*=the upheld. (Isa. 41. 8-10.)

THE BAND. Egyptian name *U-or*=He cometh binding them together (Hos. 11. 4); and breaking the band which binds them to their old enemy *Cetus*.

ANDROMEDA. Name in the Zodiac of Denderah is *Set*, which means seated as a queen. Also, *Sirco*=the chained. The brightest star is *Al Phiratz*=the broken down. The next, *Mirach* =the weak. The next, *Al amok* (Arab)=struck down. (Isa. 54. 11-14; 51. 21—52. 3. Jer. 14. 17.)

CEPHUS. The king. In the Zodiac of Denderah *Pe-ku-hor*=this one cometh to rule. *Cepheus* is Greek from the Heb. *zemah* = the Branch. Ethiopian name, *Hyh*=a king. The brightest star is *Al Deramin*=coming quickly. The next is *Al Phirk*=the Redeemer. The next, *Al Rai'* =who bruises or breaks. (Jer. 31. 1.)

ARIES. The ram or lamb full of vigour. Not falling in death like *Capricornus*. The name in the Zodiac of Denderah *Tametouris Ammon*=the reign or rule of Ammon. Heb. name *Tāleh*=the lamb. Arab. *Al Hamel*=the sheep. Syr. *Amroo*, as in John 1. 29. The Accadian name was *Bar-Ziggar*=the altar making right=the sacrifice of righteousness. The brightest star is *El nath*, or *El natik*=wounded, or slain. The next, *Al Sharatan*=the bruised, or wounded. Cp. Rev. 5. 9-12.

CASSIOPEIA. The enthroned woman. Arabic name *El seder*=the freed. In the Zodiac of Denderah *Set*=seated as queen. Arabic *Ruchba* =the enthroned. The brightest star is *Schedir* =the freed. The next, *Kaph* (Heb.) = the branch. (Isa. 54. 5-8; 62. 3-5. Jer. 31. 3-12. Ps. 45. 9-17. Isa. 61. 10, 11.)

CETUS. The sea monster. The great enemy bound (Rev. 20. 10; cp. 20. 1-3). The name in the Zodiac of Denderah is *Knem* = subdued. The brightest star is *Menkar*=the enemy chained. The next is *Diphda*, or *Deneb Kaitos*=overthrown, or thrust down. Another is *Mira*=the rebel. (Job 41. 1-10. Isa. 51. 22, 23; 26. 21—27. 1. Ps. 74. 12-14.)

PERSEUS. The Breaker. Heb. *Perez*. Greek, *Perses*, or *Perseus* (Rom. 16. 12. Mic. 2. 12, 13). Name in the Zodiac of Denderah is *Kar Knem*= he who fights and subdues. The brightest star is *Mirfak*=who helps. The next, *Al Genib*=who carries away. The next is *Athik*=who breaks.

TAURUS Messiah coming in judgment. Chald. *Tōr*. Hence, Arabic *Al Thaur*; Greek, Tauros; Lat. Taurus. The common Heb. name is *Shūr*=coming and ruling, and *Rᵉ'ēm*=pre-eminence. The brightest star is *Al Debaran*= the Leader or Governor. The next is *El nath*=wounded or slain. The group Pleiades is *Kīmah*=heap or accumulation. (Job 9. 9; 38. 31, 32. Amos 5. 8.) A bright star is *Al Cyone*=the centre. Heb. and Syr. name is *Succoth*=booths. Another group, *Hyades*=the congregated. (Deut. 33. 17. Ps. 44. 5. Isa. 13. 11-15; 34. 2-8; 26. 21.)

ORION. The coming Prince. Light breaking forth, through the Redeemer. In the Zodiac of Denderah it is *Ha-ga-t*=this is He Who triumphs *Oarion* = Heb. *'Or*, light; or coming forth as light (cp. Job 9. 9; 38. 31. Amos 5. 8). Heb. *Kᵉsīl* = a strong one (translated "Orion" in Job 9. 9; 38. 31. Amos 5. 8). The brightest star is *Betelgeuz*=the coming of the Branch (Mal. 3. 2). The next is *Rigel* or *Rigol*=the foot of him that crusheth. The next is *Bellatrix*=swiftly destroying. Another is *Al Nitak*=the wounded One. Many others with names of cumulative meanings. (See Isa. 42. 13, 14; 60. 1-3.)

ERIDANUS. The river of judgment. In the Zodiac of Denderah it is *Peh-ta-t*=the mouth of the river. The brightest star is *Achernar*= the after part of the river. So with the other names, going forth, flowing on (to the lower regions of the south). Dan. 7. 9-11. Ps. 97. 3-5; 50. 3. Hab. 3. 5. Isa. 30. 27-33. Nah. 1. 5, 6. Isa. 66. 15, 16. 2 Thess. 1. 7, 8.

AURIGA. The Shepherd. (Isa. 40. 10, 11. Ezek. 34. 22). Auriga=Charioteer. The brightest star is *Alioth*=a she-goat. Modern Lat. name is *Capella*, same meaning. The next is *Menkilinon*=the band of the goats; bound, never to be again lost. (John 10. 11.) In the Zodiac of Denderah, the shepherd carries a sceptre (*Trun*), the top with a goat, and bottom with a cross. (Mal. 4. 1-3. Ps. 37. 38-40).

GEMINI. The Twins. Name in the Zodiac of Denderah is *Clusus*, or *Claustrum Hori*=the place of Him Who cometh. The old Coptic name was *Pi-Mahi* =the united. Heb. *Thaumim* (from *tā'am*)=double. The root used in Ex. 26. 24 (twinned together). The brightest star is *Apollo* = ruler or judge. The next is *Hercules*=who cometh to labour and suffer. Another

is *Al Henah* = hurt, wounded. (Isa. 4. 2; 32. 1, 2. Jer. 23. 5, 6; 33. 14, 15.)

LEPUS (the enemy trodden under foot). In the Zodiac of Denderah the name is *Bashti-beki* =falling confounded. Aratus says "chased eternally". The brightest star is *Arnebo*=the enemy of Him Who cometh. Other stars are *Nibal*=the mad; *Rakis*, the bound; *Sugia*, the deceiver. (Isa. 63. 3, 4.)

CANIS MAJOR. *Sirius*, the Prince. In Zodiac of Denderah it is *Apes*=the head. In Persian Planisphere=a wolf (Heb. *Ze'ēb*). The brightest star is *Sirius*=the Prince. In Persian *Tistrya* or *Tistar*=the chieftain. The next is *Mirzam* =the prince. Another is *Wesen*=the shining, and another *Adhara*=the glorious. Many other cognate names. (Isa. 9. 6; 55. 4. Dan. 8. 23, 25.)

CANIS MINOR. The second Dog. In the Zodiac of Denderah it is *Sebak*=conquering, victorious. The brightest star is *Procyon*=Redeemer. The next is *Gomeisa* (Arabic)=the burdened, bearing for others. Many other cognate names. (Isa. 49. 24-26; 59. 19, 20; 53. 12).

CANCER. The Crab. Messiah's possessions held fast. In the Zodiac of Denderah and Esneh it is a sacred beetle. Its name there given is *Klaria* =cattle-folds. Arabic name is *Al Sarta'n*=He Who holds or binds together (Gen. 49. 11). The Greek name is *Karkinos*=encircling; the same as the Lat. *Cancer*, from Arabic *Khan* an Inn, and *Ker*, or *Cer*=encircling. The ancient Accadian is *Su-kul-na* = the seizer, or possessor of seed. A bright cluster is called *Praesepe* =a multitude or offspring. The brightest star is *Tegmine*=holding. Another is *Acubene*=the sheltering or hiding-place. Another, *Ma'alaph*=assembled thousands. North and south of *Praesepe* are two bright stars, *Assellus* North and *Assellus* South: their sign is ♋, and called the two asses, thus connecting it with Cancer, which is the sign of Issachar (cp. Gen. 49. 14. Num. 2. 5).

URSA MINOR. The little Bear = the lesser sheep-fold. The brightest star of Ursa Minor is *Dubheh*=a herd. Arabic *Dubah* means cattle. Heb. *Dober*=a fold, from *dobe'*=rest or security, rendered "strength" in Deut. 33. 25. See R. V. marg. All points to this (cp. Judg. 5. 16). The Heb. *Dōb*=a bear. So Arabic *Dub*, and Persian *Deeb* or *Dob*. Hence the mistake. The brightest star is *Al riccaba*=the turned or ridden on, denoting it as the Polar star. The Greeks called it *Kunosoura*=Cynosure, but this word is Accadian. *An-nas-sur-ra*=high in rising; or high in heavenly position. The next bright star is *Kochab*=waiting Him Who cometh.

URSA MAJOR. The great Bear = the Fold and the Flock (Obad. 17-19). In Job 9. 9 and 38. 31, 32, it is called *'Ash* and her offspring. A. V.= Arcturus and her sons. R. V.=Bear and his train (marg., sons). Arabs still call it *Al Naish* or *Annaish*=the assembled together as in a fold. The brightest star is *Dubhe*=a flock, which gives its name to the two constellations. The next is *Merach*=the flock (Arabic =purchased). The next is *Phaeda* or *Pharda* =numbered or guarded (Ps. 147. 4). Another is called *Benet Naish*=daughters of the assembly. Another, *Al Kaid* = the assembled. Many other cognate names. (Cp. Ezek. 34. 12-16.)

ARGO. The Ship = the Pilgrims, safe at home. In the Egyptian Planisphere there are two ships (like the two folds). They occupy one-half of the south meridians. The brightest star is *Canopus*=the possession of Him Who cometh. Other names are *Sephina*=the multitude. *Tureis* = the possession. *Asmidiska* =the released who travel, &c. (See Jer. 30. 10, 11. Isa. 60. 4-9.)

LEO. The Lion. Messiah's consummated triumph. In the Zodiac of Denderah it is *Pi Mentikeon*=the pouring out (of Divine wrath). The three constellations crystallize the truth:

1. Hydra=the old serpent destroyed.
2. Crater=the cup of wrath poured out on him.
3. Corvus=the bird of prey devouring him.

The Denderah picture exhibits all four in one. The Syr. name is *Aryo*=the rending lion. Arab. *Al Asad* = the lion leaping forth as a flame. The brightest star is *Regulus*=treading under foot (as pictured). The next is *Denebola*=the Judge or Lord Who cometh. The next is *Al Giebha* = the exaltation. Another is *Zosma* = shining forth. All the others are cognate. (Gen. 49. 8, 9. Num. 24. 8, 9. Amos 3. 4, 8. Isa. 42. 13.)

HYDRA. The Old Serpent. *Hydra*=he is abhorred. The brightest star is *Cor Hydra*=the heart of Hydra. Its ancient name is *Al phard*=the put away. Another is *Al Drian*=the abhorred. Another is *Minchar al Sugia*=the piercing of the deceiver.

CRATER. The Cup [of wrath poured out]. (Ps. 75. 8; 11. 6. Rev. 14. 10; 16. 19.) The constellation has thirteen stars, (cp. Ap. 10).

CORVUS. The Raven. The birds of prey devouring. The name in the Zodiac of Denderah, *Her-na* = the enemy breaking up. There are nine stars (see Ap. 10). The brightest star is *Chiba* (Num. 23. 8) = accursed. Another is *Minchar al Gorab*=the raven tearing to pieces.

Thus end the Scriptures of the Heavens. This is the story they tell forth. This is the "speech" they "utter". This is the "knowledge" they "shew forth". There is no articulate speech or voice; and no words are heard; but, their sayings have gone out into all the world (Ps. 19. 1-6).

They are "for SEASONS".

Not only are the stars made for signs (*'othoth*, from the root *'āthāh*=to come), but for Seasons. These are not the four seasons of the year, but Cycles of time. The figure *Polysyndeton* (see Ap. 6) in Gen. 1. 14 emphasises this: "and for seasons, and for days, and years". The word means *appointed times*. (Cp. Gen. 17. 21; 18. 14; 21. 2.) Thus the sun, moon and stars are for "signs" (things to come), and for "seasons" (appointed times).

There are no less than ten of these cycles, all of them different; not concentric, but yet all of them coinciding at creation, but never since: like a number of hoops of different sizes hanging from a nail. This shows that they must have had a given simultaneous start.

1. The cycle of 24 hours for the day, an evening and morning.
2. The revolution of the Moon round the earth.
3. The lunar cycle, which began at the same moment as the solar cycle.
4. The daily revolution of the Sun, which places him on the meridian at noon each day.
5. The Solar Cycle, coinciding with the first of the seven years of lunar motion and repeating itself every 365 days.
6. The beginning of a Week of seven days on the first day of the week, of the first month of the first year of the first solar cycle.
7. The first Eclipse of a cycle of eighteen years and eleven days, to which the ancient astronomers gave the name of *Saros*; each Saros containing an average of seventy eclipses, divided into two portions of 594 years and 666 years, making together 1,260 years.
8. Beside these, there is the period of the Heliacal risings of Sirius, in a cycle of 162 years.
9. The Transits of Venus,
10. And the grand cycle known as the Precession of the Equinoxes.

All these combine and unite in showing that the chronology of Archbishop Usher was substantially correct. And this proves that the inflated chronology of modern historians and theologians is entirely unscientific, being the hypothesis of men who dabbled in things outside their own sphere, and of which they were incompetent to form a correct judgment.

13 THE USE OF *NEPHESH* IN THE OLD TESTAMENT.

The word *nephesh* occurs 754 times in the Hebrew Old Testament. Each occurrence is noted in the margin, but it will be useful for the Bible student to have a complete list.

In the A.V. and R.V. it is translated "*soul*" 472 times, while in the other 282 places it is represented by forty-four different words or phrases. In fifty-three of these places there is a marginal rendering which calls attention to the fact that the word is "*nephesh*", while in 229 passages the English reader has hitherto been left in ignorance of the fact. The English word "soul" is in every occurrence the rendering of the Hebrew *nephesh*, except in Job 30. 15 and Isa. 57. 16. See the notes. The time has come to "open the book", and let it speak for itself. Henceforth, every one who uses *The Companion Bible* will have complete information as to the facts, and can use it in determining his definitions, making his own classifications, and formulating his doctrines as to the Biblical use of the word.

Though, with these two exceptions, the English word "soul" always represents the Hebrew *nephesh*, *nephesh* is not always translated "soul".

This Appendix will exhibit all the varieties of translation; and, while it is not intended to teach either Theology or Psychology, it will give such information as will enable every Bible reader to form his own views and come to his own conclusions on an important subject, about which there is such great controversy.

This can be done only by giving every occurrence of the Hebrew word *nephesh*.

Each occurrence is noted in the margin of *The Companion Bible*; but it is well to present a complete, separate, and classified list of the recognized Lexical usages of the word; and the reader will be left to form his own judgment as to how far the following classification is correct.

The usage of the word *nephesh* by the Holy Spirit in the Word of God is the only guide to the true understanding of it.

It will be seen that the word "soul", in its theological sense, does not cover all the ground, or properly represent the Hebrew word "*nephesh*". The English word "soul" is from the Latin *solus* = *alone* or *sole*, because the maintenance of man as a *living organism*, and all that affects his health and well-being, is the one *sole* or main thing in common with every living thing which the LORD God has made. The correct Latin word for the theological term "soul" (or *nephesh*) is *anima*; and this is from the Greek *anemos* = air or breath, because it is this which keeps the whole in life and in being.

[The usage of the corresponding New Testament word *psuchē* will be presented in a later Appendix.]

The *first* occurrence of *nephesh* is in Gen. 1. 20, "the moving creature that hath life (*nephesh*)".[1]

The following are twelve classifications of *nephesh*:

I. *Nephesh* is used of the *lower animals* only, in twenty-two passages, and is rendered in nine different ways:—

1. "creature". Gen. 1. 21, 24; 2. 19; 9. 10, 12. Lev. 11. 46, 46. — 7
2. "thing". Lev. 11. 10. Ezek. 47. 9. — 2
3. "life". Gen. 1. 20, 30. — 2
4. "the life". Gen. 9. 4. Deut. 12. 23, 23. Prov. 12. 10. — 4
5. "beast". Lev. 24. 18, 18, 18. (See margin). — 3
6. "the soul". Job 12. 10. (See margin). — 1
7. "breath". Job 41. 21. — 1

— 20

Brought forward — 20

8. "fish". Isa. 19. 10. (See margin). — 1
9. "her". Jer. 2. 24. — 1

— 22

II. *Nephesh* is used of the Lower Animals and Man in seven passages, and rendered in three different ways:—

1. "creature". Gen. 9. 15, 16. — 2
2. "the life". Lev. 17. 11, 14, 14, 14. — 4
3. "soul". Num. 31. 28. — 1

— 7

III. *Nephesh* is used of *Man*, as an individual person, in 53 passages, and is rendered in six different ways:—

1. "soul". Gen. 2. 7; 12. 5; 46. 15, 18, 22, 25, 26, 26, 27, 27. Ex. 1. 5, 5; 12. 4. Lev. 22. 11. Ps. 25. 20. Prov. 10. 3; 11. 25, 30; 14. 25; 19. 15; 22. 23 (R.V. life); 25. 25; 27. 7, 7. Jer. 38. 16. Lam. 3. 25. Ezek. 13. 18, 18, 20, 20, 20; 18. 4, 4, 4. — 34
2. "person". Gen. 14. 21; 36. 6 (R.V. souls). Ex. 16. 16. Lev. 27. 2. Num. 31. 40, 40, 46. Deut. 10. 22. Jer. 43. 6; 52. 29, 30, 30. Ezek. 16. 5; 27. 13. — 14
3. "persons". Num. 31. 35. — 1
4. "any". Deut. 24. 7. — 1
5. "man". 2 Kings 12. 4. — 1
6. "and". 1 Chron. 5. 21. — 1

Not rendered (Num 31. 35*). — 1

— 53

IV. *Nephesh* is used of Man, as exercising certain powers, or performing certain acts (may be often well rendered by emphatic pronouns), in ninety-six passages, and with eleven different renderings:—

1. "soul". Gen. 27. 4, 19, 25, 31. Lev. 4. 2; 5. 1, 2, 4, 15, 17; 6. 2; 7. 18, 20, 21, 27; 16. 29, 31; 17. 12, 15; 20. 6, 25; 22. 6; 23. 27, 30, 32. Num. 15. 27, 28, 30; 19. 22; 29. 7; 30. 2, 4, 4, 5, 6, 7, 8, 9, 10, 11, 12, 13. Deut. 13. 6. Judg. 5. 21. 1 Sam. 1. 26; 17. 55; 18. 3; 20. 3, 17; 25. 26. 2 Sam. 11. 11; 14. 19. 2 Kings 2. 2, 4, 6; 4. 30. Job 16. 4, 4; 31. 30 (R.V. life). Ps. 35. 13; 120. 6. Prov. 6. 32; 8. 36; 11. 17; 13. 2; 15. 32; 16. 17; 19. 8, 16; 20. 2 (R.V. life); 21. 23; 22. 5; 29. 24. Ecc. 4. 8; 6. 2. Isa. 51. 23; 58. 3, 5. Jer. 4. 19. Ezek. 4. 14. Mic. 6. 7. — 81
2. "man". Ex. 12. 16. — 1
3. "any". Lev. 2. 1. — 1
4. "one". Lev. 4. 27. — 1
5. "yourselves". Lev. 11. 43, 44. Jer. 17. 21. — 3
6. "person". Num. 5. 6. — 1
7. "themselves". Est. 9. 31. Isa. 46. 2. — 2
8. "himself". Job 18. 4 (R.V. thyself); 32. 2. — 2
9. "he". Ps. 105. 18. — 1
10. "herself". Jer. 3. 11. — 1
11. "Himself". Jer. 51. 14. Amos 6. 8 (used of Jehovah). — 2

— 96

V. *Nephesh* is used of Man, as possessing *animal* appetites and desires, in twenty-two passages, rendered in five different ways:—

1. "soul". Num. 11. 6 (dried away). Deut. 12. 15 (lusteth), 20 (longeth to eat flesh), 20 (lusteth after), 21 (lusteth); 14. 26 (lusteth), 26 (desireth); 21. 5 (loatheth). 1 Sam. 2. 16 (desireth). Job 6. 7 (refused); 33. 20 (abhorreth). Ps. 107. 18 (abhorreth). Prov. 6. 30 (hunger); 13. 25 (satisfying). Isa. 29. 8 (empty), 8 (hath appetite). Mic. 7. 1 (desired ... figs). — 17

[1] It is used of the lower animals four times before it is used of man; and out of the first thirteen times in Genesis, it is used ten times of the lower animals.

* Lit. "and *the soul* of man ... were 32,000 *souls*."

Brought forward 17

2. "pleasure". Deut. 23. 24. 1

3. "lust". Ps. 78. 18. 1

4. "appetite". Prov. 23. 2. Ecc. 6. 7. 2

5. "greedy". Isa. 56. 11. 1

22

VI. *Nephesh* is used of Man, as exercising *mental* faculties, and manifesting certain feelings and affections and passions, in 231 passages, and rendered in twenty different ways:—

1. "soul". Gen. 34. 3 (clave), 8 (longeth); 42. 21 (anguish); 49. 6 (come not). Lev. 26. 11 (not abhor), 15 (abhor), 30 (abhor), 43 (abhor). Num. 21. 4 (discouraged). Deut. 4. 9 (keep), 29 (seek); 6. 5 (love); 10. 12 (serve); 11. 13 (love), 18 (lay up in); 13. 3 (love); 26. 16 (keep); 30. 2 (return), 6 (love), 10 (turn). Josh. 22. 5 (serve); 23. 14 (know). Judg. 10. 16* (grieved); 16. 16 (vexed). 1 Sam. 1. 10 (bitterness of), 15 (poured out); 18. 1 (knit with), 1 (loved as); 20. 4 (desireth); 23. 20 (desire); 30. 6 (grieved). 2 Sam. 5. 8 (hated). 1 Kings 2. 4 (walk); 8. 48 (return); 11. 37 (desired). 2 Kings 4. 27 (vexed); 23. 3 (keep), 25 (turned). 1 Chron. 22. 19 (seek). 2 Chron. 6. 38 (return); 15. 12 (seek); 34. 31 (keep). Job 3. 20 (bitter); 7. 11 (bitterness); 9. 21 (know) (R.V. myself); 10. 1 (weary), 1 (bitterness); 14. 22 (mourn); 19. 2 (vex); 21. 25 (bitterness); 23. 13* (desireth); 24. 12 (wounded); 27. 2 (vexed); 30. 16 (poured out), 25 (grieved). Ps. 6. 3 (sore vexed); 11. 5* (hateth); 13. 2 (take counsel); 19. 7 (converting); 24. 4 (not lifted up); 25. 1 (lifted up), 13 (dwell at ease); 31. 7 (in adversities), 9 (consumed with grief); 33. 20 (waiteth); 34. 2 (boast); 35. 9 (be joyful); 42. 1 (panteth), 2 (thirsteth), 4 (pour out), 5 (cast down), 6 (cast down), 11 (cast down); 43. 5 (cast down); 44. 25 (bowed down); 49. 18 (blessed); 57. 1 (trusteth), 6 (bowed down); 62. 1 (waiteth), 5 (wait); 63. 1 (thirsteth), 5 (satisfied), 8 (followeth hard); 69. 10 (chastened); 77. 2 (refused comfort); 84. 2 (longeth); 86. 4 (rejoiced), 4 (lift up); 88. 3 (full of troubles); 94. 19 (delight); 103. 1, 2, 22; 104. 1, 35 (bless); 107. 5 (fainted), 9 (satisfied), 9 (filled with goodness), 26 (melted); 116. 7 (return to rest); 119. 20 (longing), 25 (cleaveth unto the dust), 28 (melteth for heaviness), 81 (fainteth), 129 (keep), 167 (kept); 123. 4 (filled with scorning); 130. 5 (wait), 6 (waiteth); 131. 2 (quieted); 138. 3 (strengthened); 139. 14 (knoweth); 143. 6 (thirsteth), 8 (lifted up), 11 (bring out of trouble), 12 (afflict); 146. 1 (praise). Prov. 2. 10 (knowledge pleasant); 3. 22 (be life to); 13. 4 (desireth), 4 (made fat), 19; 16. 24 (sweet to); 19. 2 (without knowledge), 18 (spare) (R.V. heart); 21. 10 (desireth); 22. 25 (get a snare to); 24. 14 (wisdom unto); 25. 13 (refresheth); 29. 17 (give delight). Ecc. 2. 24 (enjoy good); 6. 3 (not filled); 7. 28 (seeketh). Song 1. 7; 3. 1, 2, 3, 4 (loveth); 5. 6 (failed); 6. 12* (made me like chariots). Isa. 1. 14 (hateth); 26. 8 (desire), 9 (desire); 32. 6 (made empty); 38. 15 (bitterness of); 42. 1*; 55. 2 (delight); 58. 10 (drawn out), 10 (afflicted), 11 (satisfied); 61. 10 (joyful); 66. 3 (delighteth). Jer. 4. 31 (wearied); 5. 9, 29 (avenged); 6. 8 (depart), 16 (find rest); 9. 9* (avenged); 12. 7 (dearly beloved of); 13. 17 (shall weep); 14. 19 (lothed); 31. 12 (watered), 14, 25 (satiated), 25 (sorrowful); 32. 41* (whole); 50. 19 (satisfied). Lam. 3. 17 (removed), 20 (humbled), 24 (saith). Ezek. 7. 19 (satisfied); 24 21 (pitieth). Jonah 2. 7 (fainted). Hab. 2. 4 (not upright). Zech. 11. 8 (lothed), 8 (abhorred). 176

* Used of God.

Brought forward 176

2. "mind". Gen. 23. 8 (your). Deut. 18. 6 (desire); 28. 65 (sorrow). 1 Sam. 2. 35.* 2 Sam. 17. 8 (chafed). 2 Kings 9. 15. 1 Chron. 28. 9 (willing). Jer. 15. 1.* Ezek. 23. 17 (R.V. soul), 18* (R.V. soul), 18* (R.V. soul), 22 (R.V. soul), 28 (R.V. soul) (alienated); 24. 25 (R.V. heart) (set); 36. 5 (R.V. soul) (despiteful). 15

3. "heart". Ex. 23. 9. Lev. 26. 16. Deut. 24. 15. 1 Sam. 2. 33 (grieve). 2 Sam. 3. 21 (desireth). Ps. 10. 3 (desire). Prov. 23. 7 (R.V. himself); 28. 25 (proud heart. R.V. greedy spirit); 31. 6 (heavy heart. R.V. bitter in soul). Jer. 42. 20 (dissembled. R.V. souls). Lam. 3. 51 (affected. R.V. soul). Ezek. 25. 6 (rejoiced. R.V. soul), 15 (despiteful. R.V. soul); 27. 31 (bitterness). Hos. 4. 8 (set). 15

4. "hearty". Prov. 27. 9 (counsel). 1

5. "will". Deut. 21. 14 (she will). Ps. 27. 12; 41. 2. Ezek. 16. 27. 4

6. "desire". Ecc. 6. 9. Jer. 22. 27; 44. 14. Mic. 7. 3 (R.V. soul). Hab. 2. 5. 5

7. "pleasure". Ps. 105. 22. Jer. 34. 16. 2

8. "lust". Ex. 15. 9. 1

9. "angry". Judg. 18. 25. 1

10. "discontented" 1 Sam. 22. 2. 1

11. "thyself". Est. 4. 13. 1

12. "myself". Ps. 131. 2. 1

13. "he". Prov. 16. 26 (R.V. appetite). 1

14. "his own". Prov. 14. 10 (R.V. its own). 1

15. "Him". Prov. 6. 16.* 1

16. "himself". Jon. 4. 8. 1

17. "herself". Isa. 5. 14 (R.V. her desire). 1

18. "yourselves". Jer. 37. 9. 1

19. "man". Isa. 49. 7. 1

20. "so would we have it". Ps. 35. 25. 1

231

VII. *Nephesh* is used of Man, (a) as being "cut off" by God; (b) and as being slain or killed by man, in fifty-four passages: and is rendered in eight different ways:—

(a) *Soul cut off* by God, in twenty-two passages, and rendered "soul". Gen. 17. 14. Ex. 12. 15, 19; 31. 14. Lev. 7. 20, 21, 25, 27; 17. 10; 18. 29; 19. 8; 20. 6; 22. 3; 23. 29, 30. Num. 9. 13; 15. 30, 31; 19. 13, 20. Ezek. 18. 4, 20. 22

(b) Slain or killed by man, in thirty-two passages, rendered in eight different ways:—

1. "soul". Josh. 10. 28, 30, 32, 35, 37, 37, 39; 11. 11. Jer. 2. 34. Ezek. 13. 19; 22. 25, 27. 12

2. "person". Deut. 27. 25. Josh. 20. 3, 9. 1 Sam. 22. 22. Prov. 28. 17. Ezek. 17. 17; 33. 6. 7

3. "any". Lev. 24. 17. 1

4. "any person". Num. 31. 19; 35. 11, 15, 30, 30. 5

5. "him". Gen. 37. 21. Deut. 19. 6; 22. 26. 3

6. "mortally". Deut. 19. 11. 1

7. "life". 2 Sam. 14. 7. 1

8. "thee". Jer. 40. 14, 15. 2

54

VIII. *Nephesh* is used of Man as being mortal, subject to death of various kinds, from which it can be saved and delivered and life prolonged, in 243 passages, rendered in eleven different ways:—

1. "soul". Gen. 12. 13; 19. 20. Ex. 30. 12, 15, 16. Lev. 17. 11, 11 (R.V. life). Num. 16. 38 (R.V. lives); 31. 50. 1 Sam. 24. 11; 25. 29, 29, 29; 26. 21 (R.V. life). 2 Sam. 4. 9. 1 Kings 1. 29; 17. 21, 22. Job 7. 15; 27. 8. Ps. 3. 2; 6. 4; 7. 2, 5; 11. 1; 17. 13; 22. 20, 29; 23. 3; 25. 20; 26. 9; 33. 19; 34. 22; 35. 3, 4, 12, 17; 40. 14; 41. 4; 49. 8, 15; 54. 3, 4; 55. 18; 56. 6, 13; 57. 4; 59. 3; 63. 9; 66. 9, 16; 69. 1, 18; 70. 2; 71. 10,

* Used of God.

Brought forward 55
13, 23; 72. 13, 14; 74. 19; 78. 50; 86. 2, 14; 88. 14; 94. 21; 97. 10; 106. 15; 109. 20, 31; 116. 4, 8; 119. 109, 175; 120. 2; 121. 7; 124. 4, 5, 7; 141. 8; 142. 4, 7; 143. 3. Prov. 18. 7; 24. 12; 29. 10. Isa. 3. 9; 10. 18; 44. 20; 53. 10, 11, 12; 55. 3. Jer. 4. 10; 20. 13; 26. 19; 38. 17, 20; 44. 7; 51. 6 (R.V. life), 45 (R.V. yourselves). Lam. 1. 11, 16, 19; 2. 12; 3. 58. Ezek. 3. 19, 21; 13. 18, 19; 14. 14, 20; 18. 27; 33. 5, 9. Hos. 9. 4 (R.V. appetite). Jon. 2. 5. Hab. 2. 10. 117

2. "life, lives". Gen. 9. 5, 5; 19. 17, 19; 32. 30; 35. 18; 44. 30, 30. Ex. 4. 19; 21. 23, 23, 30. Num. 35, 31. Deut. 19. 21, 21; 24. 6. Josh. 2. 13, 14; 9. 24. Judg. 5. 18; 9. 17; 12. 3; 18. 25, 25. Ruth 4. 15. 1 Sam. 19. 5, 11; 20. 1; 22. 23, 23; 23. 15; 26. 24, 24; 28. 9, 21; 2 Sam. 1. 9; 4. 8; 16. 11; 18. 13; 19. 5, 5, 5, 5; 23. 17. 1 Kings 1. 12, 12; 2. 23; 3. 11; 19. 2, 2, 3, 4, 10, 14; 20. 31, 39, 39, 42, 42. 2 Kings 1. 13, 13, 14; 7. 7; 10. 24, 24. 1 Chron. 11. 19, 19. 2 Chron. 1. 11. Est. 7. 3, 7; 8. 11; 9. 16. Job 2. 4, 6; 6. 11 (R.V. be patient); 13. 14; 31. 39. Ps. 31. 13; 38. 12. Prov. 1. 18, 19; 6. 26; 7. 23; 13. 3, 8. Isa. 15. 4 (R.V. soul); 43. 4. Jer. 4. 30; 11. 21; 19. 7, 9; 21. 7, 9; 22. 25; 34. 20, 21; 38. 2, 16; 39. 18; 44. 30, 30; 45. 5; 46. 26; 48. 6; 49. 37. Lam. 2. 19; 5. 9. Ezek. 32. 10. Jon. 1. 14; 4. 3. 110
3. "ghost". Job 11. 20. Jer. 15. 9. 2
4. "person". 2 Sam. 14. 14 (R.V. life). 1
5. "tablets". Isa. 3. 20 (R.V. perfume boxes). Heb. "houses of the soul" = boxes of scent for the *nose*. 1
6. "deadly". Ps. 17. 9 (Heb. "enemies against my *nephesh*"). 1
7. "himself". 1 Kings 19. 4. Amos 2. 14, 15. 3
8. "me". Num. 23. 10. Judg. 16. 30. 1 Kings 20. 32. 3
9. "they". Job 36. 14. 1
10. "themselves". Isa. 47. 14. 1
11. "yourselves". Deut. 4. 15. Josh. 23. 11. 2

243

IX. *Nephesh* is used of man, as actually dead, in thirteen passages, and is rendered in three different ways:—

1. "the dead". Lev. 19. 28; 21. 1; 22. 4. Num. 5. 2; 6. 11. 5
2. "dead body". Num. 9. 6, 7, 10. 3
3. "body". Lev. 21. 11. Num. 6. 6; 19. 11, 13. Hag. 2. 13. 5

13

X. *Nephesh*, in thirteen passages (all rendered "soul"), is spoken of as going to a place described by four different words, rendered as shown below:—

i. "sh^e^ōl" = THE grave (as distinct from *ḳeber, A grave*), gravedom (or the dominion of death), in five passages, rendered in this connection in two different ways:—

1. "grave". Ps. 30. 3 (R.V. "Sheol"); 89. 48 (R.V. "Sheol", marg. *grave*). (Cp. Ps. 49. 15). 2
2. "hell". Ps. 16. 10 (R.V. "Sheol"); 86. 13 (marg. *grave*. R.V. "pit", marg. *lowest Sheol*). Prov. 23. 14 (R.V. "Sheol", marg. *the grave*). 3

ii. "shachath" = a pit (for taking wild beasts); hence, *a grave*. The Septuagint and New Testament take it in the sense of *corruption*; but, if so, not implying putridity, but *destruction*. Occurs in six passages, and is rendered in two different ways:—

1. "pit". Job 33. 18, 28, 30. Ps. 35. 7. Isa. 38. 17. 5
2. "grave". Job 33. 22 (R.V. "pit"). 1

iii. "shūchāh" = a deep pit (cp. all the occurrences, Prov. 22. 14; 23. 27. Jer. 2. 6; 18. 20, 22). In one passage only:—

1. *Pit*. Jer. 18. 20. 1

iv. "dūmāh" = silence. Ps. 94. 17. 1

13

Total 754

14 THE SYNONYMOUS WORDS USED FOR "MAN".

There are four principal Hebrew words rendered "man", and these must be carefully discriminated. Every occurrence is noted in the margin of *The Companion Bible*. They represent him from four different points of view:—

1. *'Ādām*, denotes his *origin*, as being made from the "dust of the *Adamah*" ground (Lat. *homo*).
2. *'Ish*, has regard to sex, a male (Lat. *vir*).
3. *'Enōsh*, has regard to his infirmities, as physically *mortal*, and as to character, *incurable*.
4. *Geber*, has respect to his *strength*, a *mighty man*.

I. *'Ādām*, *without* the article, denotes man or mankind in general (Gen. 1. 26; 2. 5; 5. 1, followed by plural pronoun). *With* the article, it denotes *the man, Adam*, though rendered "man" in Gen. 1. 27; 2. 7 (twice), 8, 15, 16, 19 (marg.), 22 (twice); 3. 12, 22, 24; 5. 1; 6. 1 (rendered "men"), 2, 3, 4. After this, the Hebrew *'Ādām*=man or men, is used of the descendants of Adam. Hence, Christ is called "the son of Adam", not a son of Enosh.

With the particle את (*'eth*) in addition to the article it is very emphatic, and means *self, very, this same, this very*. See Gen. 2. 7 (first occurrence), 8, 15.

Rendered in the Septuagint ἄνθρωπος (*anthrōpos*) 411 times; ἀνήρ (*anēr*) eighteen times (fifteen in Proverbs); once θνητός (*thnetos*), Prov. 20. 24=dying; four times βροτός (*brotos*), *mortal* (all in Job); once γηγενής (*gegenēs*), *earth-born*, Jer. 32. 20.

II. *'Īsh*. First occurrence in feminine, Gen. 2. 23, *'ishah*, =*woman*. Therefore, *'ish*=male, or husband; a man, in contrast with a woman. A great man in contrast with ordinary men (Ps. 49. 2, where "low" are called the children of *Adam*, and the "high" = children of *'ish*. So Ps. 62. 9 and Isa. 2. 9; 5. 15; 31. 8). When God is spoken of as man, it is *'ish* (Ex. 15. 3. So Josh. 5. 13. Dan. 9. 21; 10. 5; 12. 6, 7. Zech. 1. 8, &c.). Also, in such expressions as "man of God", "man of understanding", &c. In the early chapters of Genesis we have it in chapters 3. 22, 24 and 4. 1.

Translated in Septuagint 1,083 times by ἀνήρ (*anēr*), Latin *vir*, and only 450 by ἄνθρωπος (*anthrōpos*), Latin *homo*.

It is rendered "husband" sixty-nine times, "person" twelve times, and once or twice each in thirty-nine different ways.

III. *'Enōsh*. First occurrence Gen. 6. 4, *men of name*. Always in a bad sense (Isa. 5. 22; 45. 14. Judg. 18. 25). Morally=*depraved*, and physically=*frail, weak*. It is from *'ānash, to be sick, wretched, weak*, and denotes *inability*, for strength, physically; and for good, morally (cp. 2 Sam. 12. 15. Job 34. 6. Jer. 15. 18; 17. 9; 30. 12, 15. Mic. 1. 9). Note the contrasts, Isa. 2. 11 and 17, "The lofty looks of man (*'Ādām*) shall be humbled, and the haughtiness of men (*'Enōsh*) shall be bowed down" (Cp. Isa. 13. 12. Job 25. 6. Ps. 8. 4; 90. 3; 144. 3. Job 4. 17; 10. 5; 7. 17. Dan. 4. 16). Other instructive

passages are Isa. 8. 1; 66. 24. Ezek. 24. 17 (afflicted, or mourners. Cp. Jer. 17. 16, "day of man"). In 1 Sam. 4. 9 it is probably plural of *'Ish* (so probably Gen. 18 and 19, where the indefinite plural must be interpreted by the context, because *'Ādām* would have denoted *human*, and *'Ish*, males).

It is rendered "man" 518 times, "certain" eleven times, and once or twice each in twenty-four other and different ways.

IV. *Geber*. First occurrence in Gen. 6. 4[1], *mighty men*, and denotes man in respect of his physical strength, as *'Ĕnōsh* does in respect of the depravity of his nature. It is rendered "man" sixty-seven times, "mighty" twice, "man-child" once, "every one" once. In the Septuagint rendered fourteen times ἄνθρωπος (*anthrōpos*) and the rest by ἀνήρ (*anēr*).

For illustrative passages see Ex. 10. 11; 12. 37. 1 Sam. 16. 18. 2 Sam. 23. 1. Num. 24. 3, 15. 1 Chron. 26. 12; 28. 1. 2 Chron. 13. 3. Ezra 4. 21; 5. 4, 10; 6. 8.

V. *M^ethīm* (plural) = adults as distinguished from children, and males as distinguished from females. Occurs Gen. 34. 30. Deut. 2. 34; 3. 6; 4. 27; 26. 5; 28. 62; 33. 6. 1 Chron. 16. 19. Job 11. 3, 11; 19. 19; 22. 15; 24. 12; 31. 31. Ps. 17. 14; 26. 4; 105. 12. Isa. 3. 25; 5. 13; 41. 14. Jer. 44. 28.

[1] In Gen. 6. 4, we have three out of the above four words: "daughters of men" (=daughters of [the man] 'Adam); "mighty men" = (*geber*); "men of renown" = Heb. men (*'Ĕnōsh*) of name, i. e. renowned for their moral depravity.

15 LAWS BEFORE SINAI.

The existence of Laws in the book of Genesis and Exodus is evident, though there is no formal record of their delivery. Cp. Ex. 18. 16.

Doubtless some were made known to mankind, as such, by God, e.g. (1) the Law of the Sabbath (Gen. 2. 3). (2) The days noted in connection with the flood are all *sabbaths* except one, Gen. 8. 5, Tuesday. See note on Gen. 8. 10, 12, 14. (3) The law of the place to worship (Gen. 4. 3, 4, 16). (4) The law of offerings (Gen. 4. 4), &c.

But, side by side with these special Divine communications, the Babylonian laws were codified in the age of Abraham.

In A.D. 1901, the Code of Amraphel (Khammurabi), Gen. 14. 1, was discovered in Susa by M. J. de Morgan. The latest date for this code is 2139 B.C.

Eight hundred years before Moses, these laws governed the peoples from the Persian Gulf to the Caspian Sea, and from Persia to the Mediterranean, and were in force throughout Canaan.

This discovery overthrew the two main pillars of the "higher critics", one of which was that such writing was unknown before Moses; the other, that a legal code was impossible before the Jewish kings.

Hence, we have now before us both codes; and are in a position to answer Jehovah's question in Deut. 4. 8, "What nation is there so great, that hath statutes and judgments so righteous as all this law, which I set before you this day?"

Khammurabi calls his laws the "judgments of righteousness", but some of them, at least, are both unrighteous and unequal, as the following brief contrast shows at a glance:—

Offence.	*Punishment by Jehovah's Law.*	*Punishment by Khammurabi's Law.*
Stealing.	Restoring double (Ex. 22. 9).	Death (§ 4).
Burglary.	Restoring double (Ex. 22. 7).	Death (§ 21).
Harbouring a fugitive slave.	No offence (Deut. 23. 15).	Death (§ 16).
Injuring a slave.	Freedom given to slave.	Master compensated (§ 199).
Injuring a rich man.	Same injury inflicted on injurer.	Same injury inflicted on injurer (§§ 196, 197).
Injuring a poor man.	Same injury inflicted (Ex. 21. 23–25).	Fine of one *mina* of silver (§ 198).
Injury followed by death to a rich man's daughter.	Each case judged on its own merits.	Death of injurer's daughter (§ 209).
Injury followed by death to a poor man's daughter.	Each case judged on its own merits.	Fine of 5 shekels of silver (§§ 211, 213).

We see the laws of Khammurabi operating in Genesis in the following instances:

1. The law of adoption made Eliezer Abram's heir (Gen. 15). § 191.

2. The giving of Hagar to Abraham (Gen. 16); and of Bilhah (Gen. 30. 4) and Zilpah (Gen. 30. 9) to Jacob, accorded with this code. § 146.

3. The purchase of Machpelah by Abraham (Gen. 23) was conducted in strict conformity with its commercial enactments. § 7.

4. The taking of life for stealing, proposed by Jacob to Laban (Gen. 31. 32), was enacted by this code, which punished sacrilege with death. § 6.

5. The taking of life by burning, with which Judah threatened his daughter-in-law Tamar (Gen. 38. 24), is also according to the Babylonian code. § 110.

6. The proposal of Joseph's steward, that the one with whom the cup was found should die (Gen. 44. 9), harmonized with the law punishing with death any theft from a palace. § 6.

7. The giving of a special portion by Jacob to his favourite son Joseph (Gen. 48. 22) was provided for by this code. § 165.

8. The cutting off of Reuben from his birthright (Gen. 49. 4) was the prescribed way of punishing his offence according to Khammurabi's law. § 158.

9. The inability of Abram to sell Hagar (Gen. 16. 6). § 119.

The following is a list of thirty-four laws seen in force in Genesis, given by Jehovah, and subsequently confirmed in the Mosaic code:—

The law of the sabbath (Gen. 2. 3). Ex. 16. 23; 20. 10; 31. 13–17. Deut. 5. 14.

The law of the place to worship (Gen. 3. 24; 4. 3, 4, 16; 9. 26, 27). Ex. 25. 8. Deut. 12. 5–7. Lev. 17. 3, 4.

The law of the acceptance of sacrifice by fire from heaven (Gen. 4. 4, 5). Cp. strange fire, Ex. 30. 9. Lev. 6. 9; 10. 1.

The law of sacrifices (Gen. 4. 4; 15. 9; 22. 2, 3, 13). Ex. 29. 36. Lev. 1. 2–5.

The law of clean and unclean (Gen. 7. 2; 8. 20). Lev. 11. Deut. 14. 3–20.

The law of the altar (Gen. 8. 20; 12. 7, 8; 13. 4, 18; 22. 9; 26. 25). Ex. 20. 24.

The law of eating flesh (Gen. 9. 3). Deut. 12. 20.

The law against eating blood (Gen. 9. 4). Lev. 7. 26; 17. 10–14.

The law against murder (Gen. 9. 5, 6). Ex. 20. 13. Deut. 5. 17.

The law of parental authority (Gen. 9. 25; 18. 19; 22; 37. 13). Ex. 20. 12. Lev. 19. 3. Deut. 5. 16.

The law of monogamy (Gen. 12. 18; 16. 1). Deut. 24. 1, 2.
The law against adultery (Gen. 12. 18; 20. 3, 9; 26. 10, 11; 38; 39. 9; 49. 4). Lev. 20. 10.
The law as to (1) priesthood (Gen. 14. 18). Ex. 28. 1. (2) priestly garments (Gen. 27. 15; 37. 3). Ex. 28. 4.
The law of tithes (Gen. 14. 20; 28. 22). Lev. 27. 30-32.
The law as to covenant-making (Gen. 15. 10, 18; 21. 27, 32). Ex. 34. 27; 19. 5.
The law of intercession (Gen. 17; 18; 20. 17; 24).
The law of righteousness (Gen. 17. 1). Deut. 18. 13.
The law of circumcision (Gen. 17. 9, 10). Lev. 12. 3.
The law of hospitality (Gen. 18). Lev. 19. 33, 34. Deut. 10. 18, 19.
The law against licentiousness (Gen. 18. 20). Lev. 18.
The law against fornication (Gen. 34. 7).
The law as to oaths (Gen. 21. 23; 24. 41; 26. 28). Ex. 22. 11. Num. 5. 19.
The law of binding sacrifices (Gen. 22. 9). Ps. 118. 27.
The law of the birthright (Gen. 25. 33). Deut. 21. 16, 17.
The law of anointing with oil (Gen. 28. 18; 31. 13). Ex. 40. 15.
The obligation of vows (Gen. 28. 20-22; 31. 13). Deut. 23. 21. Num. 30. 2.
The law against idolatry (implied in the word "dominion", Gen. 1. 26; 31. 32, 35). Ex. 20. 3-6. Deut. 5. 7-10.
The law of uncleanness (Gen. 31. 35). Lev. 15.
The law against marriage between circumcised and uncircumcised (Gen. 34. 14). Deut. 7. 3.
The law of ceremonial cleansing for worship (Gen. 35. 2). Ex. 19. 10.
The law of drink offerings (Gen. 35. 14). Ex. 29. 40. Lev. 23. 18.
The law of marrying the brother's widow (Gen. 38. 8). Deut. 25. 5-10.
The law of preaching (2 Pet. 2. 5). Lev. 10. 11. Deut. 33. 10.
The law of dowry (Gen. 34. 12). Ex. 22. 16.

16 THE OCCURRENCES OF נְשָׁמָה (*N^eshāmāh*), "BREATH".

Gen. 2. 7; 7. 22. Deut. 20. 16. Josh. 10. 40; 11. 11, 14. 2 Sam. 22. 16. 1 Kings 15. 29; 17. 17. Job 4. 9; 26. 4; 27. 3; 32. 8; 33. 4; 34. 14; 37. 10. Ps. 18. 15; 150. 6. Prov. 20. 27. Isa. 2. 22; 30. 33; 42. 5; 57. 16. Dan. 5. 23; 10. 17.

17 THE GENITIVE CASE.

"Of" is usually the sign of the Genitive Case, though it is used also to represent fourteen different Greek words, viz., *from, around, away, under, beside, upon, over, in, into, down, through, towards, with, before.* Where, however, it represents the Genitive Case of a noun, the Holy Spirit uses it in a variety of different senses, the recognition of which is necessary to an intelligent appreciation of the passage.

These several usages may be conveniently grouped in the following nine classes, it being borne in mind that sometimes a Genitive may belong to more than one class; and also, that a study of the *context* will prove the surest way of determining to which class a particular Genitive belongs, where, at first sight, it seems difficult to classify.

1. The Genitive of Character. Here the emphasis is always on the adjectival particle, which appears in the original as a noun in the Genitive Case. Ps. 2. 6, Heb. "the hill of My holiness"="My **holy** hill". Eph. 2. 2, "Children of disobedience" = "**disobedient** children. 2 Thess. 1. 7, Greek "angels of His might" "His **mighty** angels".

2. The Genitive of Origin. This marks the source from which anything has its origin. Ezek. 1. 1, "Visions of God"=Visions proceeding from God. Rom. 4. 11, 13, "Righteousness of faith" = Righteousness coming through faith. 2 Cor. 11. 26, "Perils of waters" =Perils occasioned by waters.

3. The Genitive of Possession. This is, perhaps, the most frequent, and is generally unmistakable; though some occurrences are difficult to identify. It may be said to answer the question "Whose?" Luke 2. 49, Greek "The business of My Father" = My Father's business. Rev. 14. 12, "The patience of the saints"= the patience possessed by the saints. Eph. 6. 16, "The shield of faith" = faith's shield, which is the living Word, Christ, Gen. 15. 1. Eph. 6. 17, "The sword of the Spirit"=the Spirit's sword, which is the written Word, the Scriptures.

4. The Genitive of Apposition. Here the "of" is equivalent to "that is to say", or, "consisting of". Gen. 2. 7, "The breath of life"= the breath, that is to say, life. John 2. 21, "The temple of His body"= the temple, that is to say, His body. Rom. 4. 11, "The sign of circumcision"= the sign, that is to say, circumcision. 2 Cor. 5. 1, "The house of our tabernacle"= the house, that is to say, our tabernacle. 2 Cor. 3. 17, 18, "The spirit of the Lord"=the spirit, that is to say, the Lord (Christ) Who is the *life* of the old covenant, as the body without the spirit is dead (Jas. 2. 26). 1 Pet. 1. 1, "Sojourners of the Dispersion"=sojourners, that is to say, the Dispersion.

5. The Genitive of Relation. This is, perhaps, the most interesting of all; and the manner of expressing the particular relation must be gathered from the context. Frequently the "of" is equivalent to "pertaining to". It may be objective, subjective, or both, e.g. 2 Cor. 5. 14, "The love of Christ", which may be the love Christ bears to us (subjective); the love we bear to Christ (objective); or both may be true, and the truth. Gen. 2. 9, "The tree of life" i.e. the tree which preserved life. Isa. 55. 3. Acts 13. 34, "The sure mercies of David"= pertaining, or made, to David. Matt. 6. 28, "Lilies of the field"=which grow in the field. Rom. 8. 36, "Sheep of slaughter" = sheep destined for slaughter. Heb. 11. 26, "Reproach of Christ"= reproach for Christ's sake.

6. The Genitive of Material. Denoting that of which anything is made, hence the "of" here is equivalent to "made of". Gen. 6. 14, "An ark of gopher wood". Ps. 2. 9, "A rod of iron". Dan. 2. 38, "This head of gold".

7. The Genitive of the Contents. Denoting that with which anything is filled, or which it contains, hence the "of" is equivalent to "filled with", or "containing". 1 Sam. 16. 20, "A bottle of wine". Matt. 10. 42, "A cup of cold water". Matt. 26. 7, "An alabaster box of very precious ointment". The Genitive of the contents always follows the verb "to fill", while the vessel filled takes the Accusative case, and the filler is put in the Dative case, e.g. Rom. 15. 13, "Now the God of hope fill you (Accusative case) with all joy and peace (Genitive case) in (or by) believing (Dative case)". Eph. 5. 18, "Filled with the Spirit" is the Dative case, and therefore="by the Spirit"—the Filler. Therefore, not "with", which would have required the Genitive case.

8. The Genitive of Partition. Separation, where this denotes a part taken from the whole; the "of" being equivalent to such expressions as "share in", "part of", or "from among". Luke 20. 35, Greek "To attain of that world"=to attain a place in that world. 1 Cor. 15. 9, "The least of the Apostles"=the least among the Apostles.

9. Two Genitives depending on one another. Acts 5. 32, "We are witnesses of (Genitive of possession) Him of (i.e. in relation to, Genitive of relation) these things". Acts 20. 24, "The Gospel of (i.e. concerning, Genitive of relation) the grace of (Genitive of origin or possession) God".

18 "IN THE DAY". (Gen. 2. 17.)

B^eyōm=when. It is the figure *Synecdoche*, by which a part is put for the whole, or the whole for a part (see Ap. 6). What that "part" is must be determined by the context in each particular case.

In Gen. 2. 4, it is put for the whole six days.

In Num. 7. 84, it is put for the whole twelve days of the dedication of the altar.

In Lev. 13. 14, it is rendered "when". R.V. whensoever. Num. 28. 26, see notes.

In Lev. 14. 57, it is rendered "when", both in A.V. and R.V. Cp. Deut. 21. 16. 1 Sam. 20. 19. 2 Sam. 21. 12.

In 1 Kings 2. 37, it is rendered "on the day", but *v.* 41 shows that Shimei had been to Gath and back before Solomon executed the sentence (*vv.* 37, 42).

In Ps. 18. 18, it is rendered "in the day", but evidently means *at the time when.*

In Isa. 11. 16, it includes the whole period of the Exodus.

In Jer. 11. 4, 7, it includes the Exodus and the whole time of giving the law at Sinai. Cp. ch. 7. 22; 31. 32; 34. 13.

In Ezek. 20. 5, 6[1], it includes the whole time of God's choice of Israel.

In Ezek. 36. 33, it includes the whole time of rebuilding the waste places of Israel in the future restoration. Cp. ch. 38. 18[2]. A.V.=at the same time. R.V.=in that day.

[1] In verse 6 it has the definite article (*bāyōm*), and denotes the specific day when Jehovah delivered them, in contrast with the indefinite past time of His choice.

[2] Here the definite article is used to mark a specific occasion. See A. V.

19 THE SERPENT OF GENESIS 3.

In Genesis 3 we have neither allegory, myth, legend, nor fable, but literal historical facts set forth, and emphasised by the use of certain Figures of speech (see Ap. 6).

All the confusion of thought and conflicting exegesis have arisen from taking literally what is expressed by Figures, or from taking figuratively what is literal. A Figure of speech is never used except for the purpose of calling attention to, emphasising, and intensifying, *the reality of the literal sense*, and the truth of the historical facts; so that, while the words employed may not be so strictly true to the letter, they are all the more *true to the truth conveyed by them*, and to the historical events connected with them.

But for the figurative language of verses 14 and 15 no one would have thought of referring the third chapter of Genesis to a snake: no more than he does when reading the third chapter from the end of Revelation (ch. 20. 2). Indeed, the explanation added there, that the "*old* serpent" is the Devil and Satan, would immediately lead one to connect the word "old" with the *earlier* and former mention of the serpent in Gen. 3: and the fact that it was Satan himself who tempted "the second man", "the last Adam", would force the conclusion that no other than the personal Satan could have been the tempter of "the first man, Adam".

The Hebrew word rendered "serpent" in Gen. 3. 1 is *Nāchāsh* (from the root *Nāchāsh, to shine*), and means *a shining one.* Hence, in Chaldee it means *brass* or *copper*, because of its *shining*. Hence also, the word *Nehushtān*, a piece of brass, in 2 Kings 18. 4.

In the same way *Sārāph*, in Isa. 6. 2, 6, means *a burning one*, and, because the serpents mentioned in Num. 21 were burning, in the poison of their bite, they were called *Saraphim*, or *Seraphs.*

But when the LORD said unto Moses, "Make thee a fiery serpent" (Num. 21. 8), He said, "Make thee a *Sārāph*", and, in obeying this command, we read in *v.* 9, "Moses made a *Nāchāsh* of brass". *Nāchāsh* is thus used as being interchangeable with *Sārāph.*

Now, if *Sārāph* is used of a serpent because its bite was *burning*, and is also used of a celestial or spirit-being (a burning one), why should not *Nāchāsh* be used of a serpent because its appearance was *shining*, and be also used of a celestial or spirit-being (a shining one)?

Indeed, a reference to the structure of Gen. 3 (on p. 7) will show that the *Cherubim* (which are similar celestial or spirit-beings) of the last verse (Gen. 3. 24) require a similar spirit-being to correspond with them in the first verse (for the structure of the whole chapter is a great Introversion). The *Nāchāsh*, or serpent, who beguiled Eve (2 Cor. 11. 3) is spoken of as "an angel of light" in *v.* 14. Have we not, in this, a clear intimation that it was not a snake, but a glorious shining being, apparently an angel, to whom Eve paid such great deference, acknowledging him as one who seemed to possess superior knowledge, and who was evidently a being of a superior (not of an inferior) order? Moreover, in the description of Satan as "the king of Tyre"[1] it is distinctly implied that the latter being was of a supernatural order when he is called "a cherub" (Ezek. 28. 14, 16, read from *vv.* 11–19). His presence "in Eden, the garden of *'Elohim*" (*v.* 13), is also clearly stated, as well as his being "perfect in beauty" (*v.* 12), his being "perfect in his ways from the day he was created till iniquity was found in him" (*v.* 15), and as being "lifted up because of his beauty" (*v.* 17).

These all compel the belief that Satan was *the shining one* (*Nāchāsh*) in Gen. 3, and especially because the following words could be addressed to him:—"Thine heart was lifted up because of thy beauty, thou hast corrupted thy wisdom by reason of thy brightness: I will cast thee to the ground, I will lay thee before kings, that they may behold thee" (*v.* 17).

Even supposing that these things were spoken to, and of, an exalted human being in later days (in Ezek. 28), still "the king of Tyre" is not compared to a being who was non-existent; and facts and circumstances which never happened are not introduced into the comparison.

There is more about "the king of Tyre" in Ezek. 28. 11–19 than was literally true of "the prince of Tyre" (*vv.* 1–10). The words can be understood only of the mightiest and most exalted supernatural being that God ever created; and this for the purpose of showing how great would be his fall. The *history* must be true to make the *prophecy* of any weight.

Again, the word rendered "subtle" in Gen. 3. 1 (see note) means *wise*, in a good sense as well as in a bad sense. In Ezek. 28. 12 we have the good sense, "Thou sealest up the sum, full of wisdom"; and the bad sense in *v.* 17, "thou hast corrupted thy wisdom" (referring, of course, to his fall). So the word rendered "subtle" is rendered "prudent" in Prov. 1. 4; 8. 12; 12. 23; 14. 8; and in a bad sense in Job 15. 5. 1 Sam. 23. 22. Ps. 83. 3.

The word "beast" also, in Gen. 3. 1, *chay*, denotes *a living being*, and it is as wrong to translate *zōa* "beasts" in Rev. 4, as it is to translate *chay* "beast" in Gen. 3. Both mean *living creature.* Satan is thus spoken of as being "more wise than any other *living creature* which Jehovah Elohim had made". Even if the word "beast" be retained, it does not say that either a serpent or Satan *was* a "beast", but only that he was "more wise" than any other living being.

We cannot conceive Eve as holding converse with

[1] Ezek. 28. 11–19, who is quite a different being from "the Prince of Tyre", in *vv.* 1–10, who is purely human.

a snake, but we can understand her being fascinated[1] by one, apparently "an angel of light" (i.e. a glorious angel), possessing superior and supernatural knowledge.

When Satan is spoken of as a "serpent", it is the figure *Hypocatastasis* (see Ap. 6) or *Implication*; it no more means a snake than it does when Dan is so called in Gen. 49. 17; or an animal when Nero is called a "lion" (2 Tim. 4. 17), or when Herod is called a "fox" (Luke 13. 32); or when Judah is called "a lion's whelp". It is the same figure when "doctrine" is called "leaven" (Matt. 16. 6). It shows that something much more real and truer to truth is intended. If a Figure of speech is thus employed, it is for the purpose of expressing the truth more impressively; and is intended to be a figure of something much *more real* than the letter of the word.

Other Figures of speech are used in *vv.* 14, 15, but only for the same purpose of emphasising the truth and the reality of what is said.

When it is said in *v.* 15, "thou shalt bruise His heel", it cannot mean His literal heel of flesh and blood, but suffering, more temporary in character. When it is said (*v.* 15), "He shall crush thy head", it means something more than a skull of bone, and brain, and hair. It means that all Satan's plans and plots, policy and purposes, will one day be finally crushed and ended, never more to mar or to hinder the purposes of God. This will be effected when Satan shall be bruised under our feet (Rom. 16. 20). This, again, will not be our literal feet, but something much more real.

The bruising of Christ's heel is the most eloquent and impressive way of foretelling the most solemn events; and to point out that the effort made by Satan to evade his doom, then threatened, would become the very means of insuring its accomplishment; for it was through the death of Christ that he who had the power of death would be destroyed; and all Satan's power and policy brought to an end, and all his works destroyed (Heb. 2. 14. 1 John 3. 8. Rev. 20. 1-3, 10). What literal words could portray these literal facts so wonderfully as these expressive Figures of speech?

It is the same with the other Figures used in *v.* 14, "On thy belly shalt thou go". This Figure means infinitely more than the literal belly of flesh and blood; just as the words "heel" and "head" do in *v.* 15. It paints for the eyes of our mind the picture of Satan's ultimate *humiliation*; for prostration was ever the most eloquent sign of subjection. When it is said "our belly cleaveth unto the ground" (Ps. 44. 25), it denotes such a prolonged prostration and such a depth of submission as could never be conveyed or expressed in literal words.

So with the other prophecy, "Dust shalt thou eat". This is not true to the letter, or to fact, but it is all the more *true to truth.* It tells of constant, continuous disappointment, failure, and mortification; as when deceitful ways are spoken of as feeding on deceitful food, which is "sweet to a man, but afterward his mouth shall be filled with gravel" (Prov. 20. 17). This does not mean literal "gravel", but something far more disagreeable. It means *disappointment* so great that it would gladly be exchanged for the literal "gravel". So when Christians are rebuked for "biting and devouring one another" (Gal. 3. 14, 15), something more heart-breaking is meant than the literal words used in the Figure.

When "His enemies shall lick the dust" (Ps. 72. 9) they will not do it on their knees with their literal tongues; but they will be so prostrated and so utterly defeated, that no words could literally depict their overthrow and subjugation.

If a serpent was afterward called a *nāchash*, it was because it was more *shining* than any other creature; and if it became known as "wise", it was not because of its own innate positive knowledge, but of its wisdom in hiding away from all observation; and because of its association with one of the names of Satan (that old serpent) who "beguiled Eve" (2 Cor. 11. 3, 14).

It is wonderful how a snake could ever be supposed to speak without the organs of speech, or that Satan should be supposed able to accomplish so great a miracle[1].

It only shows the power of tradition, which has, from the infancy of each one of us, put before our eyes and written on our minds the picture of a "snake" and an "apple": the former based on a wrong interpretation, and the latter being a pure invention, about which there is not one word said in Holy Scripture.

Never was Satan's wisdom so craftily used as when he secured universal acceptance of this traditional belief: for it has succeeded in fixing the attention of mankind on the *letter* and the *means*, and thus blinding the eyes to the solemn fact that the Fall of man had to do solely with the Word of God, and is centred in the sin of believing Satan's lie instead of Jehovah's truth.

The temptation of "the first man Adam" began with the question "Hath God said?" The temptation of "the second man, the Lord from heaven" began with the similar question "If Thou be the Son of God", when the voice of the Father had scarcely died away, which said "This IS My beloved Son".

All turned on the truth of what Jehovah had said.

The Word of God being questioned, led Eve, in her reply, (1) to *omit* the word "freely" (3. 2, cp. 2. 16); then (2) to *add* the words "neither shalt thou touch it" (3. 3, cp. 2. 17); and finally (3) to *alter* a certainty into a contingency by changing "thou SHALT SURELY die" (2. 17) into "LEST ye die" (3. 3).

It is not without significance that the first Ministerial words of "the second Man" were "It is written", three times repeated; and that His last Ministerial words contained a similar threefold reference to the written Word of God (John 17. 8, 14, 17).

The former temptation succeeded because the Word of God was three times misrepresented; the latter temptation was successfully defeated because the same Word was faithfully repeated.

The history of Gen. 3 is intended to teach us the fact that Satan's sphere of activities is in the *religious* sphere, and not the spheres of crime or immorality; that his battlefield is not the sins arising from human depravity, but the *unbelief* of the human heart. We are not to look for Satan's activities to-day in the newspaper press, or the police courts; but in the pulpit, and in professors' chairs. Wherever the Word of God is called in question, there we see the trail of "that old serpent, which is the Devil, and Satan". This is why anything against the true interests of the Word of God (as being such) finds a ready admission into the newspapers of the world, and is treated as "general literature". This is why anything in favour of its inspiration and Divine origin and its spiritual truth is rigidly excluded as being "controversial".

This is why Satan is quite content that the *letter* of Scripture should be accepted in Gen. 3, as he himself accepted the letter of Ps. 91. 11. He himself could say "It is written" (Matt. 4. 6) so long as the *letter* of what is "written" could be put instead of the *truth* that is conveyed by it; and so long as it is misquoted or misapplied.

This is his object in perpetuating the traditions of the "snake" and the "apple", because it ministers to the acceptance of his lie, the hiding of God's truth, the support of tradition, the jeers of the infidel, the opposition of the critics, and the stumbling of the weak in faith.

[1] It is remarkable that the verb *nāchash* always means to enchant, fascinate, bewitch; or of one having and using occult knowledge. See Gen. 30. 27; 44. 5, 15. Lev. 19. 26. Deut. 18. 10. 1 Kings 20. 33. 2 Kings 17. 17; 21. 6. 2 Chron. 33. 6. So also is the noun used in Num. 23. 23; 24. 1.

[1] Greater than that wrought by God Himself, who opened the mouth of Balaam's ass.

20 THE POSTERITY OF CAIN.

It is important to note that the posterity of Cain comes in the First *Tōl^edōth*, viz., that of "the generations of the heavens and the earth"; and not in "the book of the generations of Adam."

The posterity of Seth commences with "the generations of Adam": showing that the two accounts are distinct, and deal with two different subjects. See the Structures on pp. 3 and 5 (Gen. 2. 4—4. 26; 5. 1—6. 8).

The generations of the heavens and the earth (2. 4—4. 26).

J¹ | 2. 4-25. Before the Fall.
J² | 3. 1-34. The Fall.
J³ | 4. 1-26. After the Fall.

The expansion of J³. "After the Fall" (4. 1-26), p. 8.

J³ | L | 1-16. Adam's sons: Cain and Abel.
M | 17-24. Cain's son: Enoch.
L | 25. Adam's son: Seth.
M | 26. Seth's son: Enos.

There were 130 years before Seth was born and substituted for Abel in the line of the promised seed.

In those 130 years after Cain, Adam must have begotten "sons and daughters", as in the 800 years after Seth.

If Abel died in A.M. 125, and Abel and Cain had children before that year, even supposing they had no descendants till they reached the age of sixty-five, Adam could have had 130 children. And if each of these could have a child at sixty-five years of age, one in each successive year, there would have been 1,219 in A.M. 130. If we suppose Adam's earlier sons and daughters to have had children at the age of twenty-one instead of at sixty-five, there would have been over half a million in the 130 years, without reckoning the old or young, and this at a very moderate rate of increase.

It is generally assumed that Adam and Eve had no children *beyond those named*. But, as in the line of Seth, it is clear from Gen. 5. 4 that they had, we may well conclude that the same was the case in the line of Cain. It is a gratuitous assumption that Abel had no posterity.

It is manifest that the history assumes a considerable population; and the fact that there is no attempt to explain it, proves its genuineness, and shows that we are left to explain it for ourselves in the only natural way by which it can be explained.

21 ENOS. (GEN. 4. 26.) "CALLING ON THE NAME OF THE LORD."

"Then began men to call upon the name of Jehovah." If this refers to Divine worship it is not true: for Abel and Cain both began, and their descendants doubtless followed their example.

What was really begun was *the profanation of the Name of Jehovah*. They began to call *something* by the Name of Jehovah. The A.V. suggests "themselves", in the margin. But the majority of the ancient Jewish commentators supply the Ellipsis by the words "their gods"; suggesting that they called the stars and idols their gods, and worshipped them.

The Targum of Onkelos explains it: "then in his days the sons of men desisted from praying in the Name of the Lord."

The Targum of Jonathan says: "That was the generation in whose days they began to err, and to make themselves idols, and surnamed their idols by the Name of the Word of the Lord."

Kimchi, Rashi, and other ancient Jewish commentators agree with this. Rashi says: "Then was there profanation in calling on the Name of the Lord."

Jerome says that this was the opinion of many Jews in his days.

Maimonides, in his *Commentary on the Mishna* (a constituent part of the Talmud), A.D. 1168, in a long treatise on idolatry, gives the most probable account of the origin of idolatry in the days of Enos.

The name Enos agrees with this, for his name means *frail, weak, sickly, incurable*. The sons of men, as "Enōsh", are so called for a similar reason (Job 7. 17; 15. 14. Ps. 9. 20; 103. 15. Dan. 2. 43). See Ap. 14.

If Jonathan, the grandson of Moses, became the first idolatrous priest in Israel (see notes on Judg. 18. 30), what wonder that Enos, the grandson of Adam, introduced idolatry among mankind.

Moreover, what "ungodliness" did Enoch, "the seventh from Adam" have to prophesy about in Jude 14, 15, if purity of worship was begun in the days of Enos, instead of profanation in calling on the Name of the Lord?

Surely this is sufficient evidence that this profanation of the Name of the Lord was the reason why Enoch was raised up to prophesy against it.

22 THE ANTEDILUVIAN PATRIARCHS, AND THE FLOOD-DATE.

(Gen. 5.)

				A.M.	B.C.
Gen. 1. 27.	Adam	formed in Creation year		0 =	0 = 3996
5. 3.	Seth	born when Adam	was	130 =	130 = 3866
6.	Enos	,, ,,	Seth	105 =	235 = 3761
9.	Cainan	,, ,,	Enos	90 =	325 = 3671
12.	Mehalaleel	,, ,,	Cainan	70 =	395 = 3601
15.	Jared	,, ,,	Mehalaleel	65 =	460 = 3536
18.	Enoch	,, ,,	Jared	162 =	622 = 3374
21.	Methuselah	,, ,,	Enoch	65 =	687 = 3309
25.	Lamech	,, ,,	Methuselah	187 =	874 = 3122
28.	Noah	,, ,,	Lamech	182 =	1056 = 2940
7. 11.	Flood year	,, ,,	Noah	600 =	1656 = 2340

23 "THE SONS OF GOD" IN GEN. 6. 2, 4.

It is only by the Divine specific act of creation that any created being can be called "a son of God". For that which is "born of the flesh is flesh". God is spirit, and that which is "born of the Spirit is spirit" (John 3. 6). Hence Adam is called a "son of God" in Luke 3. 38. Those "in Christ" having "the new nature" which is by the direct creation of God (2 Cor. 5. 17. Eph. 2. 10) can be, and are called "sons of God" (John 1. 13. Rom. 8. 14, 15. 1 John 3. 1).[1]

[1] The word "offspring" in Acts 17. 28 is quite different. It is γένος (*genos*), which means merely *kin* or *kind*, our *genus* as being originated by God.

This is why angels are called "sons of God" in every other place where the expression is used in the Old Testament. Job 1. 6; 2. 1; 38. 7. Ps. 29. 1; 89. 6. Dan. 3. 25 (no art.).[1] We have no authority or right to take the expression in Gen. 6. 2, 4 in any other sense. Moreover, in Gen. 6. 2 the Sept. renders it "angels".

Angels are called "spirits" (Ps. 104. 4. Heb. 1. 7, 14), for spirits are created by God.

That there was a fall of the angels is certain from Jude 6.

The nature of their fall is clearly stated in the same verse. They left their own οἰκητήριον (*oikētērion*). This word occurs only in 2 Cor. 5. 2 and Jude 6, where it is used of the spiritual (or resurrection) body.

The nature of their sin is stated to be "in like manner" to that of the subsequent sins of Sodom and Gomorrha, Jude 7.

The time of their fall is given as having taken place "in the days of Noah" (1 Pet. 3. 20. 2 Pet. 2. 7), though there may have been a prior fall which caused the end of "the world that then was" (Gen. 1. 1, 2. 2 Pet. 3. 6).

For this sin they are "reserved unto judgment", 2 Pet. 2. 4, and are "in prison", 1 Pet. 3. 19.

Their progeny, called *Nephīlim* (translated "giants"), were monsters of iniquity; and, being superhuman in size and character, had to be destroyed (see Ap. 25). This was the one and only object of the Flood.

Only Noah and his family had preserved their pedigree pure from Adam (Gen. 6. 9, see note). All the rest had become "corrupt" (*shāchath*) *destroyed* [as Adamites]. The only remedy was *to destroy it* (*de facto*), as it had become *destroyed* (*de jure*). (It is the same word in *v.* 17 as in *vv.* 11, 12.) See further under Ap. 25 on the *Nephīlim*.

This irruption of fallen angels was Satan's first attempt to prevent the coming of the Seed of the woman foretold in Gen. 3. 15. If this could be accomplished, God's Word would have failed, and his own doom would be averted.

As soon as it was made known that the Seed of the woman was to come through ABRAHAM, there must have been another irruption, as recorded in Gen. 6. 4, "and also *after that*" (i.e. after the days of Noah, more than 500 years after the first irruption). The aim of the enemy was to occupy Canaan in advance of Abraham, and so to contest its occupation by his seed. For, when Abraham entered Canaan, we read (Gen. 12. 6) "the Canaanite was then (i.e. already) in the land."

In the same chapter (Gen. 12. 10-20) we see Satan's next attempt to interfere with Abraham's seed, and frustrate the purpose of God that it should be in "Isaac". This attempt was repeated in 20. 1-18.

This great conflict may be seen throughout the Bible, and it forms a great and important subject of Biblical study. In each case the human instrument had his own personal interest to serve, while Satan had his own great object in view. Hence God had, in each case, to interfere and avert the evil and the danger, of which His servants and people were wholly ignorant. The following assaults of the great Enemy stand out prominently:—

The destruction of the chosen family by famine, Gen. 50. 20.

The destruction of the male line in Israel, Ex. 1. 10, 15, &c. Cp. Ex. 2. 5. Heb. 11. 23.

The destruction of the whole nation in Pharaoh's pursuit, Ex. 14.

After David's line was singled out (2 Sam. 7), that was the next selected for assault. Satan's first assault was in the union of Jehoram and Athaliah by Jehoshaphat, notwithstanding 2 Chron. 17. 1. Jehoram killed off all his brothers (2 Chron. 21. 4).

The Arabians slew all his children, except Ahaziah (2 Chron. 21. 17; 22. 1).

When Ahaziah died, Athaliah killed "all the seed royal" (2 Chron. 22. 10). The babe Joash alone was rescued; and, for six years, the faithfulness of Jehovah's word was at stake (2 Chron. 23. 3).

Hezekiah was childless, when a double assault was made by the King of Assyria and the King of Terrors (Isa. 36. 1; 38. 1). God's faithfulness was appealed to and relied on (Ps. 136).

In Captivity, Haman was used to attempt the destruction of the whole nation (Est. 3. 6, 12, 13. Cp. 6. 1).

Joseph's fear was worked on (Matt. 1. 18-20). Notwithstanding the fact that he was "a just man", and kept the Law, he did not wish to have Mary stoned to death (Deut. 24. 1); hence Joseph determined to divorce her. But God intervened: "Fear not".

Herod sought the young Child's life (Matt. 2).

At the Temptation, "Cast Thyself down" was Satan's temptation.

At Nazareth, again (Luke 4), there was another attempt to cast Him down and destroy Him.

The two storms on the Lake were other attempts.

At length the cross was reached, and the sepulchre closed; the watch set; and the stone sealed. But "God raised Him from the dead." And now, like another Joash, He is *seated* and *expecting* (Heb. 10. 12, 13), hidden in the house of God on high; and the members of "the one body" are hidden there "in Him" (Col. 3. 1-3), like another Jehoshaba; and going forth to witness of His coming, like another Jehoiada (2 Chron. 23. 3).

The irruption of "the fallen angels" ("sons of God") was the first attempt; and was directed against the whole human race.

When Abraham was called, then he and his seed were attacked.

When David was enthroned, then the royal line was assailed.

And when "the Seed of the woman" Himself came, then the storm burst upon Him.

[1] In Hos. 1. 10, it is not *beni-hā-Elohim*, as here, but *beni-el-chai*.

24 THE "HUNDRED AND TWENTY YEARS" OF GENESIS 6. 3.

These are generally taken as meaning 120 years before the Flood. But this mistake has been made by not observing that the word for "men" in Gen. 6. 1, 2 is in the singular number with the definite article, as in *v.* 3 "man", and means THE MAN ADAM. The word "also" clearly refers to him. It has no meaning if "men" be read, in the plural. It means, and can mean, only that Adam himself, "*also*", *as well as the rest of mankind*, had "corrupted his way".[1] If "men" be the meaning, then it may be well asked, who are the others indicated by the word "also"?

In Gen. 2. 17, the Lord God had declared that Adam should die. Here, in Gen. 6, it was made more clear that though he had lived 810 years he should surely die; and that his breath, or the spirit of life from God, should not for ever remain in him. See the notes on Gen. 6.

This fixes the chronology of *v.* 3, and shows that long before that time, A.M. 810, and even before Enoch, this irruption of fallen angels had taken place. This was the cause of all the "ungodliness" against which the prophecy of Enoch was directed in Jude 14, and which ultimately brought on the fulfilment of his prophecy in the Judgment of the Flood. See Ap. 23 and 25.

[1] (*b'shaggam*) *because that also* is so pointed in the Codex Hilleli. This makes it the Inf. Kal. of *shāgag, to transgress, go astray*, and means, "because that in their going astray, he (Adam) also is flesh".

25 THE *NEPHILIM*, OR "GIANTS" OF GEN. 6, &c.

The progeny of the fallen angels with the daughters of Adam (see notes on Gen. 6, and Ap. 23) are called in Gen. 6, *Ne-phil'-im*, which means *fallen ones* (from *nāphal, to fall*). What these beings were can be gathered only from Scripture. They were evidently great in size, as well as great in wickedness. They were superhuman, abnormal beings; and their destruction was necessary for the preservation of the human race, and for the faithfulness of Jehovah's Word (Gen. 3. 15).

This was why the Flood was brought "upon the world of the ungodly" (2 Pet. 2. 5) as prophesied by Enoch (Jude 14).

But we read of the *Nephīlīm* again in Num. 13. 33: "there we saw the *Nephīlīm*, the sons of Anak, which come of the *Nephīlīm*". How, it may be asked, could this be, if they were all destroyed in the Flood? The answer is contained in Gen. 6. 4, where we read: "There were *Nephīlīm* in the earth in those days (i.e. in the days of Noah); and also AFTER THAT, when the sons of God came in unto the daughters of men, and they bare children to them, the same became [the] mighty men (Heb. *gibbōr*, the heroes) which were of old, men of renown" (lit. *men of the name*, i.e. who got a name and were renowned for their ungodliness).

So that "after that", i.e. after the Flood, there was a *second* irruption of these fallen angels, evidently smaller in number and more limited in area, for they were for the most part confined to Canaan, and were in fact known as "the nations of Canaan". It was for the destruction of these, that the sword of Israel was necessary, as the Flood had been before.

As to the date of this second irruption, it was evidently soon after it became known that the seed was to come through Abraham; for, when he came out from Haran (Gen. 12. 6) and entered Canaan, the significant fact is stated: "The Canaanite was then (i.e. *already*) in the land." And in Gen. 14. 5 they were already known as "Rephaim" and "Emim", and had established themselves at Ashteroth Karnaim and Shaveh Kiriathaim.

In ch. 15. 18–21 they are enumerated and named among Canaanite Peoples: "Kenites, and the Kenizzites, and the Kadmonites, and the Hittites, and the Perizzites, and the Rephaims, and the Amorites, and the Girgashites, and the Jebusites" (Gen. 15. 19–21; cp. Ex. 3. 8, 17; 23. 23. Deut. 7; 20. 17. Josh. 12. 8).

These were to be cut off, and driven out, and utterly destroyed (Deut. 20. 17. Josh. 3. 10). But Israel failed in this (Josh. 13. 13; 15. 63; 16. 10; 17. 18. Judg. 1. 19. 20, 28, 29, 30–36; 2. 1–5; 3. 1–7); and we know not how many got away to other countries to escape the general destruction. If this were recognised it would go far to solve many problems connected with Anthropology.

As to their other names, they were called *Anakim*, from one Anak which came of the *Nephīlīm* (Num. 13. 23), and *Rephaim*, from Rapha, another notable one among them.

From Deut. 2. 10, they were known by some as *Emim*, and *Horim*, and *Zamzummim* (v. 20, 21) and *Avim*, &c.

As *Rephaim* they were well known, and are often mentioned: but, unfortunately, instead of this, their proper name, being preserved, it is variously translated as "dead," "deceased", or "giants". These *Rephaim* are to have no resurrection. This fact is stated in Isa. 26. 14 (where the proper name is rendered "deceased," and *v.* 19, where it is rendered "the dead").

It is rendered "dead" seven times (Job 26. 5. Ps. 88. 10. Prov. 2. 18; 9. 18; 21. 16. Isa. 14. 8; 26. 19).

It is rendered "deceased" in Isa. 26. 14.

It is retained as a proper name "Rephaim" ten times (two being in the margin). Gen. 14. 5; 15. 20. Josh. 12. 15 (marg.). 2 Sam. 5. 18, 22; 23. 13. 1 Chron. 11. 15; 14. 9; 20. 4 (marg.). Isa. 17. 5.

In all other places it is rendered "giants", Gen. 6. 4, Num. 23. 33, where it is *Nephīlīm*; and Job 16. 14, where it is *gibbōr* (Ap. 14. iv).

By reading all these passages the Bible student may know all that can be known about these beings.

It is certain that the second irruption took place before Gen. 14, for there the *Rephaim* were mixed up with the five nations or peoples, which included Sodom and Gomorrha, and were defeated by the four kings under Chedorlaomer. Their principal locality was evidently "Ashtaroth Karnaim"; while the *Emim* were in the plain of Kiriathaim (Gen. 14. 5).

Anak was a noted descendant of the *Nephīlīm*; and *Rapha* was another, giving their names respectively to different clans. Anak's father was *Arba*, the original builder of Hebron (Gen. 35. 27. Josh. 15. 13; 21. 11); and this Palestine branch of the *Anakim* was not called *Arbahim* after him, but *Anakim* after Anak. They were great, mighty, and tall (Deut. 2. 10, 11, 21, 22, 23; 9. 2), evidently inspiring the ten spies with great fear (Num. 13. 33). Og king of Bashan is described in Deut. 3. 11.

Their strength is seen in "the giant cities of Bashan" to-day; and we know not how far they may have been utilized by Egypt in the construction of buildings, which is still an unsolved problem.

Arba was rebuilt by the *Khabiri* or confederates seven years before Zoan was built by the Egyptian Pharoahs of the nineteenth dynasty. See note on Num. 13. 22.

If these *Nephīlīm*, and their branch of *Rephaim*, were associated with Egypt, we have an explanation of the problem which has for ages perplexed all engineers, as to how those huge stones and monuments were brought together. Why not in Egypt as well as in "the giant cities of Bashan" which exist, as such, to this day?

Moreover, we have in these mighty men, the "men of renown," the explanation of the origin of the Greek mythology. That mythology was no mere *invention* of the human brain, but it grew out of the traditions, and memories, and legends of the doings of that mighty race of beings; and was gradually evolved out of the "heroes" of Gen. 6. 4. The fact that they were supernatural in their origin formed an easy step to their being regarded as the demi-gods of the Greeks.

Thus the Babylonian "Creation Tablets", the Egyptian "Book of the dead", the Greek mythology, and heathen Cosmogonies, which by some are set on an equality with Scripture, or by others adduced in support of it, are all the corruption and perversion of primitive truths, distorted in proportion as their origin was forgotten, and their memories faded away.

26 NOAH "PERFECT". (GEN. 6. 9).

The Heb. word *tāmīm* means *without blemish*, and is the technical word for bodily and physical perfection, and *not moral*. Hence it is used of animals of *sacrificial purity*. It is rendered *without blemish* in Ex. 12. 5; 29. 1. Lev. 1. 3, 10; 3. 1, 6; 4. 3, 23, 28, 32; 5. 15, 18; 6. 6; 9. 2, 3; 14. 10; 22. 19; 23. 12, 18. Num. 6. 14; 28. 19, 31; 29. 2, 8, 13, 20, 23, 29, 32, 36. Ezek. 43. 22, 23, 25; 45. 18, 23; 46. 4, 6, 13.

Without spot. Num. 19. 2; 28. 3, 9, 11; 29. 17, 26.

Undefiled. Ps. 119. 1.

This shows that Gen. 6. 9 does not speak of Noah's moral perfection, but tells us that he and his family alone had preserved their pedigree and kept it pure, in spite of the prevailing corruption brought about by the fallen angels. See Ap. 23 and 25.

27 WINE.

There are *eight* Hebrew words translated wine. A careful observation of their use will tell us all that there is to be known on the subject.

I. *Yayin*, from the root *yāyan*, to *ferment*, used of every sort of wine. The word occurs 142 times, and includes fermented wine of all kinds.

The first occurrence is:

Gen. 9. 21. "Noah planted a vineyard and drank *yayin* and was drunken."

Gen. 14. 18. "Melchizedek . . . brought forth bread and wine."

1 Sam. 25. 36, 37. Nabal drank *yayin* and "was very drunken."

Isa. 28. 1. "The drunkards of Ephraim . . . are overcome (i.e. knocked down) with *yayin*."

Jer. 23. 9. "I am like a drunken man, and like a man whom *yayin* hath overcome".

It is perfectly certain, therefore, from these passages, that *yayin* was fermented, and was intoxicating.

Yayin was also used for sacred purposes and for blessing:

Gen. 49. 12. "His (Judah's) eyes shall be red with *yayin*, and his teeth white with milk."

Amos 9. 13. "I will bring again the captivity of my people, and they shall plant vineyards and drink the *yayin* thereof." (*v.* 14 is No. V.)

Ecc. 9. 7. "Drink thy *yayin* with a merry heart, for God now accepteth thy works."

The Nazarite, at the expiration of his vow, drank *yayin*. See Num. 6. 13-20. It was used at the Feasts of Jehovah (Deut. 14. 24-26), and was poured out as a drink-offering to Jehovah (Ex. 29. 40. Lev. 23. 13. Num. 15. 5).

II. *Tīrōsh*, from *yārash*, *to possess* = must, or new wine, so called because it gets possession of the brain. It occurs thirty-four times in the Old Testament.

Hos. 4. 11. "Whoredom and *yayin* and *tīrōsh* take away the heart" (i.e. they blunt the feelings, derange the intellect).

Some say that *tīrōsh* means *grapes*, and is used as *solid* food, because in Gen. 37. 28 we read of "*tīrōsh* and corn". We might as well say that when we speak of "bread and water", that water is also a solid, because bread is a solid. On the contrary, "*tīrōsh* and corn" mean *liquids and solids*, by the figure of *Synecdoche* (of Genus), Ap. 6.

Prov. 3. 10. "Thy presses shall burst out with *tīrōsh*."

Isa. 62. 8. "The sons of the stranger shall not drink thy *tīrōsh*."

Joel 2. 24. "The fats (vats) shall overflow with *tīrōsh* and oil."

Mic. 6. 15. "Thou shalt tread . . . *tīrōsh*, but shalt not drink *yayin*."

III. *Chemer*, from *chamar*, *to ripen*. Hence used of strong *red wine*. It occurs eight times.

Deut. 32. 14. 'The pure *chemer* of the grape."

Is. 27. 2, 3. "A vineyard of *chemer*. I the Lord do keep it".

Ezra 6. 9. Cyrus and Artaxerxes commanded that *chemer* should be given to the people of Israel for the service of the God of Heaven.

The Rabbins called it *neat wine*, because, unmixed with water, it disturbs the head and brain.

IV. *Shēkār*=strong drink (from *shākar*, *to get drunk*), a very intoxicating drink made from barley, honey, or dates.

Num. 28. 7. "In the holy place shalt thou cause the *shēkar* (strong wine) to be poured unto the Lord for a drink offering."

Deut. 14. -25, 26. "Thou . . . shalt go unto the place which the Lord thy God shall choose: and thou shalt bestow that money for whatsoever thy soul lusteth after, for oxen, or for sheep, or for *yayin* (wine), or for *shēkar* (strong drink), or for whatsoever thy soul desireth: and thou shalt eat there before the Lord thy God, and thou shalt rejoice, thou, and thine household".

V. *'Āṣīṣ* (from *'āṣaṣ*, *to tread*) *new or sweet wine* of the vintage year.

Isa. 49. 26. "They shall be drunken with their own blood, as with *'āṣīṣ* (sweet wine)".

The drinking of this was held out by God as a blessing conferred by Him. Joel 3. 17, 18. Amos 9. 13.

VI. *Sob'e*, any kind of strong intoxicating drink: from *sāb'ā*, *to drink to excess*, *become drunk*: occurs twice.

Isa. 1. 22. "Thy silver is become dross, thy *ṣob'e* (wine) mixed with water".

Hos. 4. 18. "Their *ṣob'e* (*drinking bout* or *carouse*) is over" (A.V. their drink is sour (marg. *gone*). R.V. marg. *their carouse is over*).

VII. *Mimṣāk*, *mixed* or *spiced wine*.

Prov. 23. 30. "They that tarry long at the *yayin*; they that go to seek *mimṣāk* (mixed wine)."

Isa. 65. 11. "That prepare a table for Fortune, and that fill up mingled wine (*mimṣāk*) unto Destiny" (R.V.).

VIII. *Shemārīm*, from *shāmar*, *to keep*, *preserve*, *lay up*; hence, *old wine*, purified from the lees and racked off.

Ps. 75. 8. "But the *shemārīm* (dregs), all the wicked of the earth shall wring them out, and drink them."

Isa. 25. 6. "Wines on the lees."

Zeph. 1. 12. "I will . . . punish the men that are settled on their *shemārīm* (lees)".

Jer. 48. 11. "Moab . . . hath settled on his lees."

N.B. The word translated "flagons of wine" is *'ăshīshāh*, from *'āshash*, to press; hence a hardened syrup made of grapes, a sweet cake of dried grapes or pressed raisins. It occurs in 2 Sam. 6. 19. 1 Chron. 16. 3. Song 2. 5. Hos. 3. 1.

With these *data* it will be seen that the modern expression, "unfermented wine", is a *contradiction of terms*. If it is wine, it must have fermented. If it has not been fermented, it is not wine, but a syrup.

Leaven is sour dough, and not wine. It is that which *causes* the fermentation. There can be no leaven after the process of fermentation has ceased.

28 NIMROD. GEN. 10. 8, 9. 1 CHRON. 1. 10.

Josephus (*Ant. Jud.* i. c. 4. 2) says: "Nimrod persuaded mankind not to ascribe their happiness to God, but to think that his own excellency was the source of it. And he soon changed things into a tyranny, thinking there was no other way to wean men from the fear of God, than by making them rely upon his own power."

The Targum of Jonathan says: "From the foundation of the world none was ever found like Nimrod, powerful in hunting, and in rebellions against the Lord."

The Jerusalem Targum says: "He was powerful in hunting and in wickedness before the Lord, for he was a hunter of the sons of men, and he said to them, 'Depart from the judgment of the Lord, and adhere to the judgment of Nimrod!' Therefore is it said: 'As Nimrod [is] the strong one, strong in hunting, and in wickedness before the Lord.'"

The Chaldee paraphrase of 1 Chron. 1. 10 says: "Cush begat Nimrod, who began to prevail in wickedness, for he shed innocent blood, and rebelled against Jehovah."

Nimrod was the founder of Babylon, which partook of his character as being the great antagonist of God's Truth and God's People.

We cannot fail to see, in Nimrod, Satan's first attempt to raise up a human universal ruler of men. There have been many subsequent attempts, such as Nebuchadnezzar, Alexander, Napoleon, and others. He will finally succeed in the person of the Antichrist.

29 THE GENERATIONS OF TERAH, ISAAC, AND JACOB.

The generations of ABRAHAM are not given separately, but are included in Terah's.

- **Terah** (Gen. 11. 25—25. 11.)
  - **Haran**
    - Lot
      - *Moab*
      - *Ammon*
    - Milcah
    - Iscah
  - **Nahor, m. Milcah his niece**
    - 7 sons and Bethuel
      - Laban
        - Leah
        - Rachel
      - Rebekah m. Isaac
  - **Abraham**
    - By Hagar: *Ishmael*
    - (By Sarah his half-sister): **Isaac** Gen. 25. 19—25. 31, m. Rebekah
      - *Esau* or *Edom*
        - *Amalek*
      - **Jacob** (Gen. 37. 1—50. 26)
        - By Leah:
          - Reuben (4 sons)
          - Simeon (6 sons)
          - **Levi**
            - Gershom
            - Kohath
              - Amram (m. his aunt Jochebed)
                - Miriam
                - Aaron
                  - Nadab
                  - Abihu
                  - Eleazar
                    - Phineas
                  - Ithamar
                - Moses
                  - Gershom
                    - Jonathan (Judg. 18. 30).
                  - Eliezer
            - Merari
            - Jochebed (born in Egypt, Num. 26. 59)
          - **Judah** (By Thamar)
            - Pharez
              - Esrom
                - Aram
                  - Amminadab
                    - Elisheba
                    - Naashon
                      - Salmon (Nephew of Aaron, m. Rahab)
                        - Boaz (m. Ruth)
                          - Obed
                            - Jesse
                              - David
            - Zarah
          - Issachar (4 sons)
          - Zebulun (3 sons)
          - Dinah
        - By Rachel:
          - Joseph (2 sons)
          - Benjamin (10 sons)
        - By Bilhah:
          - Dan (1 son)
          - Naphtali (4 sons)
        - By Zilpah:
          - Gad (7 sons)
          - Asher (4 sons)
    - By Keturah: *Midian*
  - By another wife.
    - Sarai

NOTE.

It will be seen from page 17, Gen. 11. 20—25. 1, that "THE GENERATIONS OF TERAH" are arranged in a *Repeated Alternation*, and that the Alternation there given is only so far as ABRAHAM is concerned. The *Histories* are divided up, and alternated with a brief summary of certain *Posterities*.

But the same principle of structure runs through not only the history of Terah, but also that of Abraham, Isaac, and Jacob. The sevenfold alternations may be presented as follows:—

A1 | 11. 27—22. 19. History of Abraham. I.		Abraham.
B1 | 22. 20-24. Posterity of Nahor.		
A2 | 23. 24. History of Abraham. II.		
B2 | 25. 1-4. Posterity of Keturah.		
A3 | 25. 5-11. History of Abraham. III.		
B3 | 25. 12-18. Posterity of Ishmael.		
A4 | 25. 19—35. 22. History of Isaac (Life). I.		Isaac.
B4 | 35. 22-26. Posterity of Jacob (Land).		
A5 | 35. 27-29. History of Isaac (Death). II.		
B5 | 36. Posterity of Esau.		
A6 | 37. 1—46. 7. History of Jacob. I.		Jacob.
B6 | 46. 8-27. Posterity of Jacob (Land).		
A7 | 46. 28—50. 26. History of Jacob. II.		
B7 | Ex. 1. 1-6. Posterity of Jacob (Egypt).		

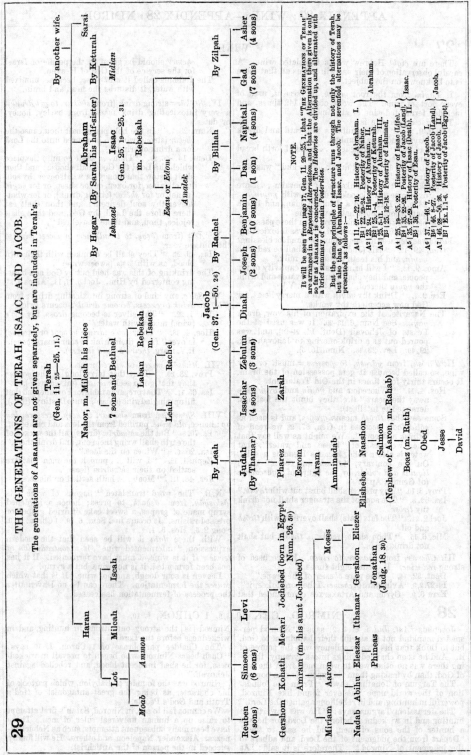

30 THE *MASSŌRAH.*

All the oldest and best manuscripts of the Hebrew Bible contain on every page, beside the Text (which is arranged in two or more columns), a varying number of lines of smaller writing, distributed between the upper and lower margins. This smaller writing is called the *Massōrah Magna* or Great *Massōrah,* while that in the side margins and between the columns is called the *Massōrah Parva* or Small *Massōrah.*

The illustration given on p. 32 is a reduced facsimile of a Hebrew MS. (16¼ inches × 12⅜), written in a German hand, about the year A.D. 1120.

The small writing in the margins in this particular MS. is seen to occupy seven lines in the lower margin, and four lines in the upper; while in the outer margins and between the three columns is *the Massōrah Parva.*

The word *Massōrah* is from the root *māsar, to deliver something into the hand of another,* so as to commit it to his trust. Hence the name is given to the small writing referred to, because it contains information necessary to those into whose trust the Sacred Text was committed, so that they might transcribe it, and hand it down correctly.

The Text itself had been fixed before the *Massorites* were put in charge of it. This had been the work of the *Sōpherīm* (from *ṣāphar,* to *count,* or *number*). Their work, under Ezra and Nehemiah, was to set the Text in order after the return from Babylon; and we read of it in Neh. 8. 8 [1] (cp. Ezra 7. 6, 11). The men of "the Great Synagogue" completed the work. This work lasted about 110 years, from Nehemiah to Simon the first, 410–300 B.C.

The *Sōpherīm* were the authorised revisers of the Sacred Text; and, their work being completed, the *Massorites* were the authorised custodians of it. Their work was to preserve it. The *Massōrah* is called "A Fence to the Scriptures," because it locked all words and letters in their places. It does not contain notes or comments as such, but facts and phenomena. It records the number of times the several letters occur in the various books of the Bible; the number of words, and the middle word; the number of verses, and the middle verse; the number of expressions and combinations of words, &c. All this, not from a perverted ingenuity, but for the set purpose of safeguarding the Sacred Text, and preventing the loss or misplacement of a single letter or word.

This *Massōrah* is not contained in the margins of any one MS. No MS. contains the whole, or even the same part. It is spread over many MSS., and Dr. C. D. Ginsburg has been the first and only scholar who has set himself to collect and collate the whole, copying it from every available MS. in the libraries of many countries. He has published it in three large folio volumes, and only a small number of copies has been printed. These are obtainable only by the original subscribers.

When the Hebrew Text was printed, only the large type in the columns was regarded, and the small type of the *Massōrah* was left, unheeded, in the MSS. from which the Text was taken.

When translators came to the printed Hebrew Text, they were necessarily destitute of the information contained in the *Massōrah*; so that the Revisers as well as the Translators of the Authorised Version carried out their work without any idea of the treasures contained in the *Massōrah*; and therefore, without giving a hint of it to their readers.

This is the first time that an edition of the A.V. has been given containing any of these treasures of the *Massōrah,* that affect so seriously the understanding of the Text. A vast number of the Massoretic notes concern only the orthography, and matters that pertain to the Concordance. But many of those which affect the sense, or throw any additional light on the Sacred Text, are noted in the margin of *The Companion Bible.*

Some of the important lists of words which are contained in the *Massōrah* are also given, viz. those that have the "extraordinary points" (Ap. 31); the "eighteen emendations" of the *Sōpherīm* (see Ap. 33); the 134 passages where they substituted *Adonai* for Jehovah (see Ap. 32); and the Various Readings called *Severin* (see Ap. 34). These are given in separate Appendixes; but other words of any importance are preserved in our marginal notes.

Readers of *The Companion Bible* are put in possession of information denied to former generations of translators, commentators, critics, and general Bible students.

For further information on the *Massōrah* see Dr. Ginsburg's *Introduction to the Hebrew Bible,* of which only a limited edition was printed; also a small pamphlet on *The Massōrah* published by the King's Printers.

[1] The Talmud explains that "the book" meant the original text; "distinctly" means explaining it by giving the Chaldee paraphrase; "gave the sense" means the division of words, &c. according to the sense; and "caused them to understand the reading" means to give the traditional pronunciation of the words (which were then without vowel points).

31 THE FIFTEEN EXTRAORDINARY POINTS OF THE *SŌPHERĪM.*

There are fifteen words which present an abnormal appearance in the printed Hebrew Bibles. These are of the utmost importance, as they represent the most ancient result of Textual Criticism on the part of the *Sōpherīm.*

Ten of these words are in the Pentateuch, and five occur in the Prophets and Hagiographa.

Some are without effect as to translation or interpretation; others are more important, and will be noted in the passages where they occur. The following is the list. (For further information see Dr. Ginsburg's *Introduction to the Hebrew Bible,* pp. 318–34):

Gen. 16. 5.	Num. 3. 39.	2 Sam. 19. 29.
„ 18. 9.	„ 9. 10.	Isa. 44. 9.
„ 19. 33, 35.	„ 21. 30.	Ezek. 41. 20.
„ 33. 4.	„ 29. 15.	„ 46. 22.
„ 37. 12.	Deut. 29. 29.	Ps. 27. 13.

32 THE 134 PASSAGES WHERE THE *SŌPHERĪM* ALTERED "JEHOVAH" TO "ADONAI".

Out of extreme (but mistaken) reverence for the Ineffable Name "Jehovah", the ancient custodians of the Sacred Text substituted in many places "Adonai" (see Ap. 4. viii. 2). These, in the A.V. and R.V., are all printed "Lord". In all these places we have printed it "LORD*", marking the word with an asterisk in addition to the note in the margin, to inform the reader of the fact.

The official list given in the *Massōrah* (§§ 107–15, Ginsburg's edition) contains the 134.

Gen. 18. 3, 27, 30, 32; 19. 18; 20. 4.

Ex. 4. 10, 13; 5. 22; 15. 17; 34. 9, 9.

Num. 14. 17.

Josh. 7. 8.

Judg. 6. 15; 13. 8.

1 Kings 3. 10, 15; 22. 6.

2 Kings 7. 6; 19. 23.

Isa. 3. 17, 18; 4. 4; 6. 1, 8, 11; 7. 14, 20; 8. 7; 9. 8, 17; 10. 12; 11. 11; 21. 6, 8, 16; 28. 2; 29. 13; 30. 20; 37. 24; 38. 14, 16; 49. 14.

Ezek. 18. 25, 29; 21. 13; 33. 17, 29.

Amos 5. 16; 7. 7, 8; 9. 1.

Zech. 9. 4.

Mic. 1. 2.

Mal. 1. 12, 14.

Ps. 2. 4; 16. 2; 22. 19, 30; 30. 8; 35. 3, 17, 22; 37. 12;

REDUCED FACSIMILE OF MS. IN THE BRITISH MUSEUM LIBRARY

(ARUNDEL ORIENTAL 16, FOL. 372 A), CONTAINING DAN. 9. 17–10. 6 (SEE P. 31).

38. 9, 15, 22; 39. 7; 40. 17; 44. 23; 51. 15; 54. 4; 55. 9; 57. 9; 59. 11; 62. 12; 66. 18; 68. 11, 17, 19, 22, 26, 32; 73. 20; 77. 2, 7; 78. 65; 79. 12; 86. 3, 4, 5, 8, 9, 12, 15; 89. 49, 50; 90. 1, 17; 110. 5; 130. 2, 3, 6.

Dan. 1. 2; 9. 3, 4, 7, 9, 15, 16, 17, 19, 19, 19.
Lam. 1. 14, 15, 15; 2. 1, 2, 5, 7, 18, 19, 20; 3. 31, 36, 37, 58.
Ezra 10. 3.
Neh. 1. 11; 4. 14.
Job 28. 28.

(See Ginsburg's ed. of *The Massōrah*, §§ 107-115.)

To these may be added the following, where "Elohim" was treated in the same way:—

2 Sam. 5. 19-25 }
„ 6. 9-17 } Where the A.V. has "LORD."

1 Chron. 13. 12 }
„ 14. 10, 11, 14, 16 }
„ 16. 1 }
Ps. 14. 1, 2, 5 }
„ 53. 1, 2, 4, 5 } Where in A.V. and R.V. it still appears as "God". It is printed "GOD*" in the *Companion Bible.*

33 THE "EIGHTEEN EMENDATIONS" OF THE *SŌPHERĪM.*

The *Massōrah* (Ap. 30), i.e. the small writing in the margins of the standard Hebrew codices, as shown in the plate on p. 32, consists of a concordance of words and phrases, &c., safeguarding the Sacred Text.

A note in the *Massōrah* against several passages in the manuscripts of the Hebrew Bible states: "*This is one of the Eighteen Emendations of the Sopherim,*" or words to that effect.

Complete lists of these emendations are found in the *Massōrah* of most of the model or standard codices of the Hebrew Bible, and these are not always identical; so that the total number exceeds eighteen: from which it would appear that these examples are simply typical.

The *Siphri*[1] adduces seven passages; the *Yalkut*,[2] ten; the *Mechiltha*,[3] eleven; the *Tanchuma*,[4] seventeen; while the St. Petersburg Codex gives two passages not included in any other list (Mal. 1. 12; 3. 9; see below).

These emendations were made at a period long before Christ, before the Hebrew text had obtained its present settled form, and these emendations affect the Figure called *Anthropopatheia.* See Ap. 6.

The following is a list of the eighteen "Emendations," together with eight others not included in the official lists. Particulars will be found on consulting the notes on the respective passages.

Gen.	18. 22.	2 Chron.	10. 16.	Ecc.	3. 21.
Num.	11. 15.	Job	1. 5.	Jer.	2. 11.
„	12. 12.	„	1. 11.	Lam.	3. 20.
1 Sam.	3. 13.	„	2. 5.	Ezek.	8. 17.
2 Sam.	12. 14.	„	2. 9.	Hos.	4. 7.
„	16. 12.	„	7. 20.	Hab.	1. 12.
1 Kings	12. 16.	„	32. 3.	Zech.	2. 8 (12).
„	21. 10.	Ps.	10. 3.	Mal.	1. 13.
„	21. 13.	„	106. 20.	„	3. 9.

[1] An ancient commentary on Leviticus (*circa* A.D. 219-47).

[2] A *catena* of the whole Hebrew Scriptures, composed in the eleventh century, from ancient sources by Rabbi Simeon.

[3] An ancient commentary on Exodus, compiled about A.D. 90 by Rabbi Ishmael ben Elisa.

[4] A commentary on the Pentateuch, compiled from ancient sources by Rabbi Tanchuma ben Abba, about A.D. 380.

34 THE READINGS CALLED *SEVERĪN.*

Josephus tells us (*Life*, § 75) that Titus brought away with him from Jerusalem the *codices* (or manuscripts) that were in the Temple. These were among the spoils he took to Rome, and were deposited in the royal palace, about A.D. 70.

About A.D. 220 the Emperor Severus, who built a synagogue in Rome which was called after his name, handed over the codex of the Pentateuch to the Jewish community.

Both codex and synagogue have perished, but a list of thirty-two passages is preserved in the *Massōrah*, wherein this codex differed in letters and words from other codices. There are two lists extant: one (prior to A.D. 1280) in the possession of the Jewish community of Prague, and the other in the Paris National Library (no. 31, folio 399 a). But there are other *Severin* preserved, which are noted in the margin of this edition.

The following is the complete list. Those that affect the sense and furnish instruction are referred to in the margin, in notes on the passages affected. Some of them relate only to spelling, and have no instruction in them.[1]

1.	Gen.	1. 31.	12.	Gen.	45. 8*.	23.	Num.	30. 12.
2.	„	3. 21*.	13.	„	46. 8.	24.	„	31. 12.
3.	„	18. 21*.	14.	„	48. 7.	25.	„	36. 1.
4.	„	24. 7*.	15.	Ex.	12. 37.	26.	Deut.	1. 26.
5.	„	25. 33*.	16.	„	19. 3.	27.	„	1. 27.
6.	„	27. 2.	17.	„	26. 27.	28.	„	3. 20.
7.	„	27. 7.	18.	Lev.	4. 34.	29.	„	22. 6.
8.	„	36. 5.	19.	„	14. 10.	30.	„	29. 22.
9.	„	36. 10.	20.	„	15. 8.	31.	„	29. 22.
10.	„	36. 14.	21.	Num.	4. 3.	32.	„	32. 26
11.	„	43. 15.	22.	„	15. 21.			

[1] For further information see Ginsburg's *Introduction to the Hebrew Bible*, pp. 409-20.

35 "SHEŌL". HEBREW, *SHEŌL.*

The first occurrence of this word is in Gen. 37. 35, where it is rendered "grave". It occurs sixty-five times in the Hebrew of the Old Testament; and only by studying each passage by itself can the student hope to gather the *Biblical usage* of the word. All heathen or traditional usages are not only worthless, but mischievous. The following are all the passages where the word "Sheol" occurs, with the rendering in each passage indicated thus: 1=grave, 2=pit, 3=hell.

1. Gen. 37. 35.	3. Job 11. 8.	3. Ps. 16. 10.
1. „ 42. 38.	1. „ 14. 13.	3. „ 18. 5.
1. „ 44. 29, 31.	1. „ 17. 13.	1. „ 30. 3.
2. Num. 16. 30, 33.	2. „ 17. 16.	1. „ 31. 17.
3. Deut. 32. 22.	1. „ 21. 13.	1. „ 49. 14, 14, 15.
1. 1 Sam. 2. 6.	1. „ 24. 19.	3. „ 55. 15
3. 2 Sam. 22. 6.	3. „ 26. 6.	(marg. *grave*).
1. 1 Kings 2. 6, 9.	1. Ps. 6. 5.	
1. Job 7. 9.	3. „ 9. 17.	

3. Ps. 86. 13	3. Prov. 23. 14.	1. Isa. 38. 18.
(marg. *grave*).	3. „ 27. 20.	3. „ 57. 9.
1. „ 88. 3.	1. „ 30. 16.	1. Ezek. 31. 15.
1. „ 89. 48.	1. Ecc. 9. 10.	3. „ 31. 16, 17.
3. „ 116. 3.	1. Song 8. 6.	3. „ 32. 21, 27.
3. „ 139. 8.	3. Isa. 5. 14.	1. Hos. 13. 14, 14.
1. „ 141. 7.	3. „ 14. 9	3. Amos 9. 2.
1. Prov. 1. 12.	(marg. *grave*).	3. Jonah 2. 2
3. „ 5. 5.	1. „ 14. 11.	(marg. *grave*).
3. „ 7. 27.	3. „ 14. 15.	3. Hab. 2. 5.
3. „ 9. 18.	3. „ 28. 15, 18.	
3. „ 15. 11, 24.	1. „ 38. 10.	

As meaning "THE grave," it is to be distinguished from *ķeber*, *A grave*, or, *burying-place* (from *ķābar*, to bury, first occurrence Gen. 23. 4): and *bōr*, a *pit*, generally *hewn* in the rock, hence used of a cistern (Gen. 37. 20) or a dungeon, &c., when dry. (See note on the word "well" in Gen. 21. 19.)

36 "THY SALVATION". GEN. 49. 18.

"I have waited for Thy salvation, O Jehovah."

These words are repeated three times (and in three different ways) by every pious Jew, morning and evening.

In the note on Gen. 49. 18 it is pointed out that by the Fig. *Metonymy* (of Effect), see Ap. 6, "salvation" is put for Him Who brings it. The meaning is beautifully put, thus, in the Jerusalem Targum:—

"Not to the salvation wrought by Gideon, the son of Joash, does my soul look, for it is temporal. Not to the salvation wrought by Samson, the son of Manoah, is my longing directed, for it is transient: but to the salvation, the completion of which Thou hast promised, by Thy everlasting Word, to bring to Thy people the descendants of Israel.

"To Thy salvation, O Jehovah, to the salvation of Messiah the son of David, Who will one day redeem Israel and bring her back from the dispersion, to that salvation my soul looks forward; for Thy salvation is an everlasting salvation."

37 THE PHARAOHS OF GENESIS AND EXODUS.

It was intended to include a list of the Pharaohs mentioned in Genesis and Exodus, and an elaborate table had been drawn up. But, as the data are still incomplete, and scholars and explorers are not fully agreed, it is felt to be wiser to postpone a subject which is still a subject of controversy.

The title "Pharaoh," being an appellative, leaves the dynasties and individuals referred to open to question and doubt.

Of only one thing we are assured; that, when all the real facts have been discovered, they will be confirmed and attested by "the scriptures of truth."

38 "LEAVEN."

Its first occurrence in Ex. 12. 15 significantly marks it as something to be "put away." There is no dispute as to the meaning of the word, which is *sour* or *fermenting dough*. The difference lies in its interpretation. This can be gathered only from its usage by the Holy Spirit.

1. It is used of its work in permeating *the whole* of that with which it is mixed (Matt. 13. 33. Luke 13. 21. 1 Cor. 5. 6. Gal. 5. 9. Hos. 7. 4).

2. It is used of the *bread* which is made from the meal so permeated (Ex. 12. 15, 19, 20, 34, 39; 13. 7).

3. It is used in connection with sacrifices, as *never to be offered* to God with any offering made by fire (Lev. 2. 11; 6. 17; 10. 12).

4. It is used by *Metaphor* (see Ap. 6) for doctrine (Matt. 16. 12. Mark 8. 15. Luke 12. 1. Gal. 5. 9).

5. It is used of the effects of evildoers (1 Cor. 5. 6–8; 15. 33).

6. In Lev. 23. 17 it is used in that which symbolizes mankind, and in a proper sense of being corrupted. The sin-offering associated with the leaven in the two wave-loaves corresponds with this.

7. In Amos 4. 4, 5 it is either the language or Figure of *Irony* (see Ap. 6); or, it shows that the "thanksgiving with leaven" is symbolical of the sin which is ever present even in the worshippers of God.

Thus in every instance it is associated with, and symbolical of, only that which is evil.

39 THE DECALOGUE. EXODUS 20. 2–17.

The Ten Commandments have been divided in various ways. The table below exhibits the principal differences.

Commands.	English (Reformed).	Jewish (Talmud).	Massoretic.	Greek (Origen).	Roman and Lutheran.
I.	*v.* 2, 3	2	3–6	3	3–6
II.	*v.* 4–6	3–6	7	4–6	7
III.	*v.* 7	7	8–11	7	8–11
IV.	*v.* 8–11	8–11	12	8–11	12
V.	*v.* 12	12	13	12	13
VI.	*v.* 13	13	14	13	14
VII.	*v.* 14	14	15	14	15
VIII.	*v.* 15	15	16	15	16
IX.	*v.* 16	16	17–	16	17–
X.	*v.* 17	17	–17	17	–17

The difference between the Roman Catholic and Lutheran is this: that the Roman Catholic makes Commandment IX protect the *wife*, while the Lutheran makes it protect the *house*. The Massoretic divisions agree with the Roman Catholic. The English Reformed division agrees with the Jewish and Talmudical division in including *v.* 2, but differs in including *v.* 3 in Commandment I instead of in Commandment II. The Structure proves this to be correct.

It is interesting to note here, that Christ put His seal upon each one of the ten, in the following passages:— I. Matt. 22. 37. II. John 4. 24. III. Matt. 5. 34. IV. Mark 2. 27. Luke 13. 14–16. V. Matt. 15. 4–6; 19. 19. Mark 7. 10. VI. Matt. 5. 21. VII. Matt. 5. 28; 19. 9, 18. VIII. Matt. 15. 19. IX. Matt. 12. 34–37. X. Matt. 5. 28.

In Matt. 19. 18, the Lord omitted Commandment X in order to convict His questioner, who said, "ALL these have I kept." Upon which the Lord's command in *v.* 21 convicted him of its breach, as shown by the man's sorrow in *v.* 22.

40 THE NAMES OF THE TABERNACLE.

It is important to distinguish the different words used by the Holy Spirit to describe the Tabernacle, and to express His design. They are variously translated in the A.V. They are distinguished severally in the notes; and are here brought together, so that the different shades of meaning may be compared and understood. It is called:

1. The House (*Beth*).
2. The Tabernacle (*Mishkān*)=dwelling-place, from *shākan, to dwell*: or, habitation, indicating it as containing the *presence* of Jehovah in the Light, called *Shechinah*, cp. Ex. 25. 8.
3. The Tent (*'Ohel*). Erected as a special place of worship before the Tabernacle was set up. Hence to be always distinguished from the Tabernacle proper. Its full title was
4. *'Ohel Moh'ed* = Tent of assembly, or of the congregation.
5. The Tabernacle of witness, *'ohel ha-eduth.*=The Tent as containing the tables of the Law, which were an abiding *witness* to their covenant with Jehovah. (See Ex. 16. 32–34; 25. 21.)
6. Sanctuary. Heb. *kodesh*, or holy place.

In this connection it is well to notice that congregation is *'edah*, which is general; while assembly is *kahal*, which is more local and partial.

41 THE *CHERUBIM.*

It is hopeless to arrive at the meaning of the *Cherubim* from etymology. Only by the *usage* of the whole of Scripture can we form an approximately true idea.

Their description is twice given (Ezek. 1. 5-14; 10. 20; and Rev. 4. 6-9).

By a process of elimination we arrive at the fact that they are a celestial order of spirit-beings, and we can form no more notion of them than we can of other heavenly orders which are named, but not explained, and for the want of better words are called "Thrones," "Dominions," "Principalities," "Powers," &c.

They are to be distinguished from the symbolic figures of them, which were made to represent them.

Negatively, we may note:

1. That they cannot be the Godhead, or Divine in their nature, for (1) likeness of any kind was strictly forbidden (Deut. 4. 15, 16, &c.); and (2) the Godhead is distinguished from them by being mentioned at the same time.

2. Though heavenly, or celestial and spiritual in their nature and character, they are distinguished from the *angels* (who, as their name implies, were spirits used as *messengers*). Compare Rev. 5. 8, 11 and 7. 11, where, first the *cherubim* offer worship, and then the angels. They must therefore be real spirit-beings, for they could hardly be represented emblematically and really in the same verse. Moreover, they are never dismissed on errands as angels are, and are never seen apart from the Throne.

3. They cannot be *merely* symbols, for, though symbolic and emblematic representations of them were allowed to be made, they themselves are not symbolic, or we should have symbolic symbols of symbols, and no reality at all.

4. They cannot be a symbol of the "Church" or any portion of redeemed humanity, for they are distinguished from them in Rev. 5. 9, 10, according to the best readings of the most ancient MSS. and critical Greek texts, where the "us" of *v.* 9 should be omitted, and the "us" and "we" of *v.* 10 should be "them" and "they." Compare also Rev. 7. 9-11.

5. For the same reason they cannot be symbols of "the four gospels" or books of any kind, for the cherubim are ministers associated with wrath; and call for the judgment plagues. See Rev. 6. and 15. 7. Moreover, there is no connection between these and the presence of the cherubim in Eden, in the Tabernacle, in the Temple, and the Throne of God.

Positively, we may note:

1. That the three root letters of *k^{e}rūb*, כ=k, ר=r, and ב=b, are the root letters of the word KaRaB, which reappear in our GRiP, GRaB, GRiPe, GRasP. In a passive sense the notion would be that of *holding* something in safe keeping: and, as a matter of fact, the symbolic representation of them were held fast to the mercy-seat, being made out of the same piece of gold (Ex. 25. 18, 23).

2. In Gen. 3. 24 they were placed to KEEP (or guard) the way to the tree of life, and *preserve* the hope of re-genesis for a ruined creation (cp. Gen. 2. 15, where we have the word "keep" in this sense).

3. Their presence on the mercy-seat binds this hope with atonement, and with Israel.

4. On the vail the hope is bound up with the coming of the Christ in incarnation and redemption.

5. They are four in number, and four is the number of Creation (see Ap. 10).

6. They are represented by the symbolic heads of the four great divisions of animate creation: the lion (of wild beasts), the ox (of tame beasts), the eagle (of birds), man (of humanity).

7. They are *beneath* the Throne, for the earth is Jehovah's footstool.

8. Their song, when they speak, is of *creation* (Rev. 4. 11), and is in connection with *the earth.*

Redemption is a "new song" for them, relating to others.

9. We conclude therefore, that the *cherubim* are celestial or real spirit-beings, associated in some way with the embodiment of *creation's hope* as expressed in Rom. 8. 19-23. The emblematic representations made of them connect that hope with "the hope of Israel" and associate it with the blood-sprinkled mercy-seat, and the rent vail (Heb. 10. 10, 20).

42 THE *'ASHĒRAH.*

The word *'Ashērah* is from the root *'āshar, to be straight, erect,* or *upright.* From this comes the meaning, in a moral sense, *to be upright*, hence, *to prosper* or *be happy.* The *'Ashērah* was so called because it was something set *upright* or *erect* in the ground, and worshipped. The word occurs forty times, and only a careful study of each passage will give a correct view.

Compared with this, all that men may think or say about the *'Ashērah* is of little value. The word is always rendered *grove* or *groves* in the A.V.; and always left as a proper name in the R.V.

From a conspectus of the passages, we learn that it was either a living tree with the top cut off, and the stump or trunk fashioned into a certain shape (Deut. 16. 21); or it was artificially fashioned and set erect in the ground (Isa. 17. 8. 1 Kings 14. 15; 16. 33). It was made of wood (Judg. 6. 26) or stone. What the shape was is indicated in 1 Kings 15. 13, and 2 Chron. 15. 16, where the A.V. "an idol in a grove", should be (as in the R.V.) "an abominable image for an Ashērah". It could be "cut down" (Ex. 34. 13, the first occurrence of the word); "plucked up" (Mic. 5. 14); "burnt" (Deut. 12. 3); or "broken in pieces" (2 Chron. 34. 4).

It is often coupled with *mazzevoth*, or stone "pillars" (R.V.) (and rendered images in A.V.), connected with Baal-worship.

That it could not have been a "grove" is clear from 2 Kings 17. 10, where it is forbidden to set one up "under any green tree".

While it is distinguished from *Ashtoreth* the goddess, it is yet associated with that goddess, *Ashtoreth* being representative of the *productive* (or passive) principle of life; and *Baal* being representative of the *generative* (or active) principle.

The image which represents the Phoenician *Ashtoreth* of Paphos, as the sole object of worship in her temple, was an *upright block of stone*, anointed with oil, and covered with an embroidered cloth.

Such stones are to be met with all over the Semitic world; especially in Babylonia, in Syria, Palestine and Arabia. Even the Mahommedan sacred stone (*kaaba*) at Mecca remains an object of reverence.

The place Beth-el was so called because of its anointed stone. There was another Beth-el in Northern Israel.

Two columns of stone stood before every Phoenician temple. Those at Tyre are described by Herodotus (ii. 44); and the "pillars of the sun" are mentioned in 2 Chron. 34. 4. Isa. 17. 8, &c.

Like every form of "religion," it had to do with the "flesh;" and hence, by the law of evolution (which is seen operating only in human affairs) it soon became corrupted. Evolution is seen in the progress of man's works, because he begins from ignorance, and goes on learning by his mistakes and failures. From the

moment he ends his works devolution at once sets in and deterioration begins. This is specially true in the "religious" sphere. All religions have become corrupt.

So with the *'Ashērah*. Originally a tree, symbolical of the "tree of life," it was an object of reverence and veneration. Then came the perversion of the earlier idea which simply honoured the origin of life; and it was corrupted and debased into the organ of procreation, which was symbolized by the form and shape given to the *'Ashērah*. It was the *Phallus* image of Isa. 57. 8, and the "image of the male", Ezek. 16. 17.

These symbols, in turn, became the incentive to all forms of impurity which were part of its libidinous worship, with the swarms of "devotees" involved in its obscene orgies.

The serpent was accepted as the symbol of the nexus, and was thus associated with the "pillar" and the "tree". Hence, it too became an object of worship.

The principal factor in this form of Canaanite idolatry is that it was not a primitive conception of a religious rite, but *the corruption of an earlier idea* which began with honouring the origin of life.

All the ancient systems of idolatry, connected with Astrology and Mythology, &c., were, in the same way, not original inventions of what was new; but the corruption of what was old, and the perversion of primitive truth.

There can be no doubt about its being, in its essence, *Phallic* worship pure and simple, whatever may have been its origin. This abomination was common to all the ancient nations; and relics of it are found to-day in various forms, in India and elsewhere. The *menhirs* of the Celtic religion are the true descendants of the *'Ashērim*.

At first it was centred in the Canaanitish nations; and from them it spread to the others. It was the great abomination of Canaan, and that is one reason why the Canaanites, as the descendants of the *N^ephīlīm*, had to be destroyed by the sword of Israel. The other reason was the origin of those nations themselves (see Ap. 23 and 25), with which it was closely connected. The first mention of the *'Ashērah* stamps it as being the special object of Jehovah's hatred. It is given to explain His name as "jealous"; for that is the name He takes in denouncing it. Compare His threats in 1 Kings 14. 15; 15. 13; 16. 32, 33; 2 Chron. 36. 14, &c.

It led to Israel's banishment from the land; and subsequently to that of Judah's.

It is still preserved in veiled language in secret fraternities, Freemasonry, Theosophy[1], and in the Roman Church; language so conceals it that probably those who use it to-day have little idea of what they are perpetuating; while the ancient symbols I O proclaim "sex as the true God of Hosts," as the *Kabbala* declares.

A recrudescence of this is more than hinted at; and it will be better understood when "the abomination" of Antichrist shall stand once again[2] in the Temple at Jerusalem (Matt. 24. 15).

The following passages will show further the nature of this form of idolatry:—Jer. 5. 7; 7. 30, 31; 19. 4, 5; 37. 34-35. Hos. 4. 12-14. Amos 2. 7-9.

The word *'Ashērah* is noted in the margin of each passage where it occurs in *The Companion Bible*, but the following complete list is given to put the student in possession of the whole of the data; and thus to enable him to form his own conclusions.

Exod.	34. 13.	2 Kings	23. 4, 6, 7, 14, 15.
Deut.	7. 5.	2 Chron.	14. 3.
	12. 3.		15. 16.
	16. 21.		17. 6.
Judg.	3. 7.		19. 3.
	6. 25, 26, 28, 30.		24. 18.
1 Kings	14. 15, 23.		31. 1.
	15. 13.		33. 3, 19.
	16. 33.		34. 3, 4, 7.
	18. 19 (sing).		
2 Kings	13. 6.	Isa.	17. 8.
	17. 10, 16.		27. 9.
	18. 4.	Jer.	17. 2.
	21. 3, 7.	Mic.	5. 14.

[1] See *The Perfect Way*, p. 2, and *The Computation of* 666, pp. 105-9.

[2] Matt. 24. 15; cp. Dan. 9. 27; 12. 11.

43 "OFFER" AND "OFFERINGS".

There are some twenty-four Hebrew words, more or less synonymous, which are translated "offer" and "offering" in the Hebrew Old Testament. These Hebrew words are also translated in other ways, so that it is important for the truth-seeker to know, in every passage, which word is used.

The various words are noted in the margin, except when they are clearly translated by their distinctive meanings, such as burnt-offering, peace-offering, heave-offering, &c.

I. The VERB "to offer".

i. **Ḳārab** means *to draw near*, but in the Hiphil conjugation, *to make to approach*, or *draw near*: hence, *to bring near*. See *Ḳorban*, No. 1 below.

ii. **Nāgash** = *to come near*, after having been so brought, i.e., to enjoy the presence which the *Korban* (see below II. i.) has secured. Cp. Jer. 30. 21 where we have both words. Hence used of *coming near* with offerings. Cp. Greek *engizō*, Heb. 7. 19, and *prospherō*, Matt. 2. 11; 5. 23; 8. 4. Mark 1. 44. Luke 5. 14. John 16. 2. In the Epistle to the Hebrews it is used twenty times in a sacrificial sense, except Heb. 12. 7, "God brings you near as sons". See also Heb 9. 14, 28. Used also of the sinner's approach to God by offering, Heb. 4. 16; 7. 25; 10. 1, 22; 11. 6.

iii. **'Āsāh**, *to make ready* or *prepare* a victim for sacrifice; to make a victim a specific offering. Hence, *to offer*. First occurrence in Ex. 10. 25 (sacrifice). Then Ex. 29. 36, 38, 39 (offer), &c.

iv **Zābăch**, *to slay* [and offer up]; hence *to offer what has been slain*; *to sacrifice*. Hence No. xii. below.

v. **Shaḥaṭ**, *to kill* or slay (as a butcher); used of men as well as of animals. Judg. 12. 6. 1 Kings 18. 40. First occurrence Gen. 22. 10; 37. 31. Then Ex. 12. 6.

vi. **'Ālāh** = *to offer up*, especially a burnt offering, from its name in II. ii. below.

vii. **Ḳāṭar** = *to burn* or *turn into vapour*. Used of the incense which = *Kethoreth*, but also of the *'Olah* (II. ii.) and parts of the *Minchah* (II. iii.) and the Zebach (II. xii.) because these ascended to Jehovah.

viii. **Sāraph** is used of *burning up* (or rather, down) the sin-offering, because nothing ascended up to God in that offering.

ix. **Rūm**, to offer up as a heave-offering.

II. The NOUN "offering".

i. **Ḳorban** = *a gift*, or *an admittance-offering*: from I. i. above. It is the present brought, to this day in the East, in order to secure an audience, or to see the face of the superior, and find access to his presence. Hence called to-day, "the *face*-offering". When the admittance has

been secured and entrance has been obtained, then the real offering or present has to be given. Hence *Korban* is essentially an *admittance-offering*; securing the entrée. Cp. the verb, Judg. 3. 18. Cp. its use in New Testament, Matt. 5. 23; 8. 4; 23. 18. Mark 7. 11. Heb. 5. 1.

ii. **'Olāh** = *the burnt offering*: so called from the Hiphil of the verb *'ālāh, to cause to ascend* [as the flame and smoke ascend by burning]. In Greek *holocausta*, which conveys its meaning as being *wholly* burnt.

iii. **Minchah** = *the Meal offering* = a present, as such. Hence a gift-offering, not necessarily to secure admittance, but to secure favour. It might be sacrifice by blood, or more generally and later, without blood. It is used of the offerings of Cain and Abel (Gen. 4. 3, 4, 5), of Jacob's present to Esau (Gen. 32. 13-21), &c. In Exodus and Leviticus it acquires a special limitation, and is the only word rendered "meat", or better (with R.V.), "meal offering" (though it has a wider signification than literal "meal").

iv. **Shelem** = *the Peace offering*, from the root *Shālam*, which conveys the idea of peace on the ground of perfection of compensation or recompense. Hence connected with the thought of rendering payment of vows or praises because of peace enjoyed. Sometimes combined with *Zebach* (No. xii, below). It is eucharistic rather than propitiatory.

v. **Chattāth** = *the Sin offering*, from *chaṭ'a*, to sin by *coming short of*, by missing the mark in sins of commission. In the *Piel* it means to purge from such sin (Ps. 51. 7). In the *'Olah* (II. ii) the blood went *upward*, in the *chattath* it went *downward and outward* "without the camp". The former was *burnt up* on the altar, the latter *went down* on the ground.

vi. **'Asām** = *the Trespass offering*. Relates to sins of *omission*, while *chattath* relates to sins of *commission* = sin in general; *'Āshām* sin in relation to Mosaic Law; sins of error arising from ignorance or negligence.

vii. **Nedābāh** = *Free-will or Voluntary offerings*. See Lev. 22. 18, &c. It refers not to the *nature* or *mode* of the offering, but to the *motive*. Not the same as Lev. 1. 4, "voluntary will", which = "for his acceptance".

viii. **Terūmāh** = *the Heave offering*. So called because it was *lifted* up on high in presentation to Jehovah for Himself alone. See I. ix. above and Ex. 29. 27.

ix. **Tenūphāh** = *the Wave offering*, because it was waved to and fro (not up and down like No. viii), and presented for the four quarters of the earth.

x. **Nesek** = *the Drink offering*. From *naṣak*, to pour out. Cp. Ps. 2. 6 (set). Phil. 2. 17. 2 Tim. 4. 6.

xi. **'Ishsheh** = any offering made by fire (cp. Ex. 29. 18. Lev. 24. 7, 9).

xii. **Zebach** = *any offering slain* (from No. II. iv, above). The proper word for a victim, *slain* and offered. The Hebrew name for altar (*mizbeaḥ*) is derived from the same root, and denotes *the place of slaughter*. Cp. Gen. 22.

44 SIN, TRESPASS, INIQUITY, &c.

There are many synonymous words to represent the outworking of man's fallen nature. As these are not always translated by the same English word, it is necessary that we should distinguish them. The student, by reference to the following list, will be able to do so:—

i. **chāṭ'ā**, *to sin*; to miss the mark (as in Judg. 20. 16). Also of the feet, *to stumble* and *fall* (Prov. 19. 2). Hence, morally, *a coming short*, blameworthiness—not necessarily wilful. An act of thought, word, or deed, not a condition. Usually (but by no means always) rendered *sin*, and other words also so rendered.

ii. **'āshām**, *trespass*, to sin through error or ignorance. Cp. Lev. 4. 13; 5. 2, 3. Num. 5. 6, 7. Judg. 21. 22. 1 Chron. 21. 3. 2 Chron. 19. 10; 28. 10, 13. *'Ashām* is a breach of commandment, done in ignorance, but, when the guilt is proved, requiring atonement.

iii. **'āven**, iniquity, specially connected with idolatry. Used because an idol is nothing and vanity (cp. Hos. 4. 15; 5. 8; 10. 5, 8. Amos 5. 5, marg.). Hence, *'avĕn* comes to mean *vanity* (cp. Job 15. 35. Ps. 10. 7. Prov. 22. 8, &c.). The word has many renderings, which are pointed out in the passages when it occurs. *'Avĕn* is rather a course of bad conduct flowing from the evil desires of fallen nature, than breaches of the law as such.

iv. **'āvāh,** *perverseness*, from the root *to be bent*, or *crooked*. English *wrong*, i.e. wrung out of course, expresses it (cp. 1 Sam. 20. 30. 2 Sam. 19. 19. 1 Kings 8. 47. Job 33. 37, &c.).

v. **'āmāl**, *trouble, labour, toil*. Sin viewed in the light of the trouble it causes; and of its *burden*; and its *grievousness* (Isa. 10. 1. Hab. 1. 3). Often rendered *perverseness* (Num. 23. 21), also *mischief* (Job 15. 35).

vi. **'āval**, *unjust*, unfairness, sin in its nature as *deceitful*, dishonesty, that which is not equal and right, unfairness in dealings. Rendered *unjust* (Ps. 43. 1; 82. 2. Prov. 29. 27. Isa. 26. 10), *unrighteous* (Lev. 19. 15, 35).

vii. **'ābar,** to pass beyond, transgress. Hence, *transgression* (Ps. 17. 3. Hos. 6. 7; 8. 1).

viii. **rā'a',** *wicked, injurious*. From its root, which indicates its nature as *breaking up* all that is good or desirable; injurious to all others. In Greek *ponēros, evil*, or *kakos, bad*. Hence especially of moral depravity and corruption, and lewdness. English "good-for-nothing" (1 Sam. 17. 28), *naughty* (2 Kings 2. 19. Prov. 20. 14. Jer. 24. 2).

ix. **pash'a,** *revolt, rebellion.* Sin against lawful authority. Often rendered *transgression* (Ps. 51. 13. Prov. 28. 21. Isa. 43. 27). In Prov. 10. 12 the action of love or mercy shown stands in strong contrast to this character of the sin.

x. **rāshā',** *wickedness*, in the sense of the restless activity of fallen nature (Job 3. 17. Isa. 53. 9; 57. 20, 21); where it refers to the activity of the impious and ungodly, or robbers.

xi. **mā'al,** *treachery, unfaithfulness, breach of trust*, often rendered trespass and transgression. It is used of Achan (Josh. 7. 1; 22. 20). Cp. Josh. 22. 16. 2 Chron. 26. 18; 28. 22; 33. 19. Ezra 9. 2, 4. Neh. 13. 27, &c.

xii. **shāgag,** erring from imprudence, rashness, being deceived, not wilfully; and **shāgāh,** erring wilfully through passion or wine, hence, *to go astray*. As sin it is to be distinguished from presumptuous or high-handed sin. Cp. Lev. 4. 13. Num. 15. 22, &c., with Num. 15. 30. Ps. 119. 21.

xiii. **zimmah,** *meditated wickedness*, plotted, planned, and designed; wicked, or lewd purpose, especially of sins of unchastity.

xiv. **chasad** = shameful. A *Homonym*, meaning (1) Here, and Job 37. 13 (where it is rendered "mercy" in A.V. and R.V.). But "lightning" is not "mercy", but chastisement. (2) The other meaning is *mercy, lovingkindness*, or *grace*. See note on Lev. 20. 14.

xv. **shal,** *fault*, committed inadvertently through negligence.

45 THE ORDER AND GROUPING OF THE TWELVE TRIBES.

There are twenty different lists given of the Twelve Tribes. These vary according to the different objects with which they are given, and the different connections in which they stand, according to birth: mothers, encampment, numeration, blessing, geographical relation, &c. All are worthy of attention and study[1]. They may be thus presented:—

	GENESIS.			EX.	NUMBERS.						DEUT.		JOSH.	JUDGES.	I CHRONICLES.				EZEK.	REV.
	29, 35	46	49	1	1. 1-15	1. 20-43	2. 7, 10	13	26	34	27	33	13, &c.	5	2. 1-	2. 3-8	12	27	48	7
1	Reuben				Reuben	Reuben	Judah	Reuben	Reuben	‡	Simeon	Reuben	Reuben	Ephraim	Reuben	Judah	Judah	Reuben	Dan	Judah
2	Simeon				Simeon	Simeon	Issachar	Simeon	Simeon	Judah	Levi	Judah	Gad	Benjamin	Simeon	Simeon	Simeon	Simeon	Asher	Reuben
3	Levi				Judah	Gad	Zebulun	Judah	Gad		Judah	Levi	Man. E.	Machir = Man.	Levi	Reuben	Levi	Levi	Naphtali	Gad
4	Judah				Issachar	Judah	Reuben	Issachar	Judah	Simeon	Issachar	Benj.	Judah		Judah	Gad	Benj.	Aaron = Levi	Man.	Asher
5	Dan	Issachar	Zebulun	Issachar	Zebulun	Issachar	Simeon	Ephraim	Issachar	Benj.	Joseph	Joseph	Ephraim	Zebulun	Issachar	Man. E.	Ephraim	Judah	Ephraim	Naphtal.
6	Naphtali	Zebulun	Issachar	Zebulun	Ephraim	Zebulun	Gad	Benj.	Zebulun	Dan	Benj.	Zebulun	Man. W.	Issachar	Zebulun	Levi	Man. E.	Issachar	Reuben	Man.
7	Gad		Dan	Benj.	Man.	Ephraim	Ephraim	Zebulun	Man.	Man.	Reuben	Issachar	Benj.	Reuben	Dan	Issachar	Issachar	Zebulun	Judah	Simeon
8	Asher		Gad	Dan	Benj.	Man.	Man.	Man.	Ephraim	Ephraim	Gad	Gad	Simeon		Joseph	Benj.	Zebulun	Naphtali	Levi	Levi
9	Issachar	Joseph	Asher	Naphtali	Dan	Benj.	Benj.	Dan	Benj.	Zebulun	Asher	Dan	Zebulun	Gilead = Gad	Benj.	Naphtali	Naphtali	Ephraim	Benj.	Issachar
10	Zebulun	Benj.	Naphtali	Gad	Asher	Dan	Dan	Asher	Dan	Issachar	Zebulun	Naphtali	Issachar	Dan	Naphtali	Man. W.	Dan	Man. W.	Simeon	Zebulun
11	Joseph	Dan	Joseph	Asher	Gad	Asher	Asher	Naphtali	Asher	Asher	Dan	Asher	Asher	Asher	Gad	Ephraim	Asher	Man. E.	Issachar	Joseph
12	Benj.	Naphtali	Benj.	*	Naphtali	Naphtali	Naphtali	Gad	Naphtali	Naphtali	Naphtali		Naphtali	Zebulun	Asher	Asher	Reuben	Benjamin	Zebulun	Benj.
13					†	†	‡	†	†	‖		§	Dan	Naphtali			Gad	Dan	Gad	
14													§§	¶		**	Man. W.	††		‡‡

* Joseph omitted, he being in Egypt.
† Levi omitted.
‡ This is the only order which occurs three times. Levi mentioned in ch. 2. 17 after Gad. The order is that of importance.
‖ Eastern Tribes omitted.

§ Simeon omitted. Benjamin before Joseph, because the order is geographical.
§§ Here the Tribes are in the four groups which are to furnish cities for the four classes of Priests.
¶ Judah and Simeon omitted.

** Zebulun and Dan omitted, unless Dan is read in 7. 12.
†† Gad and Asher omitted.
‡‡ Dan omitted.

[1] Two orders mentioned but not detailed. (1) The order "according to *birth*", on the two stones on the High Priest's shoulders (the place of strength). (2) The order on the twelve stones of the High Priest's breastplate (the place of love). This was according to their *tribes*, as chosen by Jehovah's love.

46 DEUTERONOMY.

References to Deuteronomy in the New Testament, quoted by Jesus Christ in His conflict with Satan. Deut. 6. 13, 16; 8. 3; 10. 20. Cp. Matt. 4. 4, 7, 10.

The following important passages are referred to:—

Deut. 1. 31. See Acts 13. 18 (R.V. margin).
4. 24. „ Heb. 12. 29.
4. 35. „ Mark 12. 32.
6. 4, 5. „ Matt. 22. 37, 38. Luke 10. 27.
10. 17. „ Acts 10. 34. Rom. 2. 11. Gal. 2. 6. Eph. 6. 9. Col. 3. 25. 1 Pet. 1. 17.
17. 6. „ Matt. 18. 16. 2 Cor. 13. 1. Heb. 10. 28.
Deut. 18. 15. See Acts 3. 22; 7. 37.
19. 15. „ Deut. 17. 6, above.
21. 23. „ Gal. 3. 13.
24. 1. „ Matt. 5. 31; 19. 7.
25. 4 „ 1 Cor. 9. 9. 1 Tim. 5. 18.
27. 26. „ Gal. 3. 10.
29. 4. „ Rom. 11. 8.
29. 18. „ Heb. 12. 15.
30. 4. „ Matt. 24. 31.
30. 11–14. „ Rom. 10. 6–8.
31. 6–8. „ Heb. 13. 5 (cp. Josh. 1. 5).
32 and 33. 1–29. „ Rev. 15. 3.
32. 17. „ 1 Cor. 10. 20.
32. 21. „ Rom. 10. 19. 1 Cor. 10. 22.
Deut. 32. 35, 36. See Heb. 10. 30.
32. 43 (Sept.). „ Heb. 1. 6. Rom. 15. 10.

Any variations in the laws, as compared with those given nearly forty years before, are explained (1) either by reference to different events (cp. 1. 13, 18 with Ex. 18 and Num. 11); (2) or, repeated with a different object, and from a different point of view (cp. 1. 22 with Num. 13. 1–3); (3) or, because wilderness laws were not suitable for the Land (cp. 12. 15 with Lev. 17. 3, 4): (4) or, modified for the same reason (cp. 1, 12, and 16 with Lev. 23 and Num. 28 and 29). Other variations are complementary (1. 45; 3. 4; 25. 17, 18).

47 "THE BOOK OF THE LAW."

It is an allegation of the "Higher" Criticism (which dispenses with documentary or MS. evidence, and therefore differs altogether from "Textual" Criticism) that the five books known as the Pentateuch were not written by, or during the time of Moses, but in the time of king Manasseh, or even as late as Ezra.

But a definite "book" is spoken of throughout the Old Testament as being constantly written in, with directions how it was to be added to and kept up by the prophets raised up from time to time for that purpose, among others.

The first occurrence is in Ex. 17. 14. To this, in the margin, all the others are referred back. They are given below, so that the chain may be examined link by link and its completeness and perfection seen.

1. Ex. 17. 14. Written by Jehovah's command (cp. Deut. 25. 19). Heb. "the book" (*bassēpher*).
2. Ex. 24. 4, 7. Written by Moses, and "the book of the covenant sprinkled", with the people.
3. Ex. 34. 27. Jehovah's command, "Write thou".
4. Num. 33. 1, 2. Written by Moses "by the commandment of Jehovah". From the first three months of first year to last quarter of fortieth year (cp. Deut. 1. 2, 3 with 2. 14).
5. Deut. 1. 5. The word "declare" = *set forth plainly*, and implies *writing* (the word occurs only in Deut. 27. 8 and Hab. 2. 2), and includes from Deut. 1. 6 to 33. 29.
6. Deut. 4. 8 includes more than this book of Deuteronomy, and 4. 2 must refer to what was then written (cp. 26. 16; 29. 21).
7. Deut. 17. 18. The book kept "before the priests the Levites", and to be copied by the king. This was the standard copy (ch. 31. 9, 25, 26); to be read at the Feast of Tabernacles in the Sabbatic years (ch. 31. 10-13).
8. Deut. 31. 19, 22, 24. "The song of Moses" to be written (cp. the reason, *vv.* 16-18). Ascribed to Jehovah.
9. Josh. 1. 8. "This book of the law" came into the custody of Joshua (cp. 1-8) as distinct from the book of Joshua, and containing, not Deuteronomy merely, but the whole "book of the law" as thus traced above (cp. Ps. 1. 2. Luke 24. 44).
10. Josh. 8. 30-35. A copy of the law made from "the book" on the rocks in mount Ebal.
11. Josh. 23. 6, 7 again referred to.
12. Josh. 24. 26. Joshua himself "wrote in the book", and doubtlessly added Deut. 34.
13. 1 Sam. 10. 25. Samuel continued the writing in "the book". (So the Hebrew.)
14. 1 Kings 2. 1-4. David charges Solomon with regard to this "written" law of Moses.
15. 2 Chron. 17. 7-9. Jehoshaphat sent the princes, Levites, and priests, and they "taught in Judah, and had the book of the law of Jehovah with them".
16. 2 Chron. 23. 11 (2 Kings 11. 12). It was given to Joash according to Deut. 17. 18.
17. 2 Chron. 25. 4 (2 Kings 14. 6). Amaziah spared the children of his father's murderers according to "that which was written in the book of the law of Moses" (cp. Deut. 24. 4).
18. 2 Chron. 30. 2, 5, 18. Hezekiah's passover kept in second month as "it was written". This was written in Num. 9. 6-14.
19. 2 Chron. 35. 12. Josiah's passover kept "as it is written in the book of Moses".
20. 2 Kings 17. 37. "The law . . . which He wrote for you", i.e., Jehovah (cp. *v.* 35).
21. 2 Kings 22. 8. "Hilkiah, the high priest . . . found the book of the law in the house of the Lord". In *v.* 10, "Shaphan read it before the king" (Josiah). Huldah the prophetess confirms this reference (*vv.* 14-20). In 2 Chron. 34. 14 it is described as "the book of the law of Jehovah *by* the hand of Moses".
22. Jeremiah refers to this event when he speaks, as in ch. 15. 16.
23. Isaiah refers to this book as, in his day, a "sealed" book (ch. 29. 11-13). The Lord Jesus refers to this as opposed to the "precepts of man" (Matt. 15. 1-9. Mark 7. 1-13).
24. Ezra ascribes the law to Moses. Cp. 3. 2 (Num. 28, 29); 6. 18; 7. 6, 10, 14, 21, 25. And all is to be done according to it (cp. 10. 3 with 9. 11, 12. Lev. 18. 24-30, and Deut. 23. 3-6).
25. In Esther 3. 8, the laws were extant, and known as "diverse from all people".
26. Nehemiah (1. 7-9) speaks to Jehovah of the "statutes and judgments He gave by Moses".
27. Neh. 8. 8. The book is read according to its requirements.
28. Neh. 8. 14, 17. The Feast of Tabernacles was kept according to Lev. 23. 39-43.
29. Neh. 10. 28, 29. A solemn covenant was made "to walk in God's law, which was given by Moses the servant of God".
30. Neh. 13. 1. "They read in the book of Moses" concerning the law as written in Deut. 23. 3, 4.
31. Daniel in his prayer (ch. 9. 11) refers to the curse fulfilled on the nation as "written in the law of Moses the servant of God".
32. Mal. 4. 4 completes the cycle, and refers all to Horeb where the people received the law (as distinct from Sinai, where Moses received it), and to Moses by whom it was given (not to Ezra or to some "Redactors" of a later day).

48 THE USE OF VARIOUS TYPES IN THE ENGLISH BIBLE.

The practice of indicating, by different types, words and phrases which were not in the Original Text, was, it is believed, first introduced by Sebastian Münster, of Basle, in a Latin version of the Old Testament published in 1534.

The English New Testament (published at Geneva, 1557) and the Geneva Bible (1560) "put in that word which, lacking, made the sentence obscure, but set it in such letters as may easily be discerned from the common text." The example was followed and extended in the Bishops' Bible (1568, 1572), and the *roman* and *italic*[1] types of these Bibles (as distinguished from the *black letter* and *roman* type of previous Bibles) were introduced into the A.V. (1611).

[1] The word *italic* means relating to Italy, and is used of a kind of type dedicated to the States of Italy, by Aldus Manutius, about the year 1500.

The following seem to have been the principles guiding the translators of the A.V.:—

1. To supply the omissions under the Figure *Ellipsis*, or what they considered to be *Ellipsis*.
2. To supply the words necessary to give the sense, when the Figure *Zeugma* is employed.
3. Once, at least, to indicate a word or words of doubtful MS. authority, 1 John 2. 23 (first introduced in Cranmer's Bible—doubtless from the Vulgate). Perhaps also Judg. 16. 2 and 20. 9.
4. Where the English idiom differs from that of the Originals, and requires essential words to be added, which are not necessary in the Hebrew or Greek.

For the use of italic type in the R.V. see Ap. 7.

The use of large capital letters for certain words and phrases originated with the A.V. None of the previous or "former translations" have them.

The revisers abandoned this practice, but have not been consistent in the plan they substituted for it. In most of the cases they have used small capital letters instead of the large capitals; but in three cases (Jer. 23. 6. Zech. 3. 8; 6. 12) they have used ordinary roman type.

The use of the large capitals by the translators of the A.V. is destitute of any authority, and merely indicates the importance which they attached to such words and phrases thus indicated.

The following is a complete list:—

Large capitals in A.V. Small capitals in R.V.

Ex. 3. 14. "I am that I am."
Ex. 3. 14. "I am."
Ex. 6. 3. "Jehovah."
Ex. 28. 36; 39. 30. "Holiness (R.V. "Holy") to the Lord."
Deut. 28. 58. "The Lord thy God."
Ps. 68. 4. "Jah."
Ps. 83. 18. "Jehovah."
Isa. 26. 4. "Jehovah."
Dan. 5. 25–28. "Mene, Mene, Tekel, Upharsin." (*v.* 28, "Peres".)
Zech. 14. 20. "Holiness (R.V. "Holy") unto the Lord."
Matt. 1. 21. "Jesus."
Matt. 1. 25. "Jesus."
Matt. 27. 37. The inscriptions on the Cross. Also Mark 15. 26. Luke 23. 38. John 19. 19.
Luke 1. 31; 2. 21. "Jesus."
Acts 17. 23. "To the (R.V. "an") unknown God."
Rev. 17. 5. "Mystery, Babylon the Great, the Mother of (R.V. "the") Harlots and (R.V. "the") Abominations of the Earth."
Rev. 19. 16. "King of Kings, and Lord of Lords."

Large capitals in A.V. Small roman letters in R.V.

Jer. 23. 6. "The Lord our Righteousness."
Zech. 3. 8. "Branch."
Zech. 6. 12. "Branch."

49 "THE MAN OF GOD."

The first occurrence of this expression is in Deut. 33. 1, and is used of Moses.

Its use in connection with Moses (Ps. 90, title), who was, *par excellence*, the prophet, like unto whom Christ was to be "raised up" (Deut. 18. 15–19), shows that it is to be understood of what Moses was, viz., "the prophet".

He was so called, not because he foretold, but because he spoke FOR God. This is the meaning of the word "prophet" as taught by its first occurrence in Gen. 20. 7. The prophet was God's "spokesman" (Ex. 4. 16. Cp. Ex. 7. 1).

God's spokesman could know what to speak for Him only (1) from His Spirit (Neh. 9. 30. Cp. Hos. 9. 7, margin, and see Num. 11. 16, 17, 25–29); (2) from Jehovah making Himself known (Num. 12. 6. Ezek. 3. 17. Jer. 15. 19. Cp. 2 Chron. 36. 12); and (3) from God's written word. This is why Timothy is the only one called a "man of God" in the New Testament (1 Tim. 6. 11), and why, to-day, one, and only one who knows "all scripture", which is so profitable, can be called a "man of God" (2 Tim. 3. 17).

All such are God's spokesmen because they alone know what He wishes to be spoken. They are His witnesses (Acts 1. 8; 22. 15). Christ was THE prophet because He spoke only those things which were given Him to speak (see note on Deut. 18. 18), and He alone is "the faithful Witness" (Rev. 1. 5).

It was for the above reasons that the expression "the man of God" (i.e. God's man) became the general name for a *prophet* among the common people.

See all the occurrences:—

Deut. 23. 1.
Josh. 14. 6.
Judg. 13. 6, 8.
1 Sam. 2. 27.
„ 9. 6, 7, 8, 10.
1 Kings 12. 22.
„ 13. 1, 4, 5, 6, 6, 7, 8, 11, 12, 14, 14, 21, 26, 29, 31.
„ 17. 18, 24.
„ 20. 28.
2 Kings 1. 9, 10, 11, 12, 13.
„ 4. 7, 9, 16, 21, 22, 25, 25, 27, 27, 40, 42.
„ 5. 8, 14, 15, 20.
„ 6. 6, 9, 10, 15.
„ 7. 2, 17, 18, 19.
„ 8. 2, 4, 7, 8, 11.
„ 13. 19.
„ 23. 16, 17.
1 Chron. 23. 14.
2 Chron. 8. 14.
„ 11. 2.
„ 25. 7, 9, 9.
„ 30. 16.
Ezek. 3. 2, 2.
Neh. 12. 24, 36.
Ps. 90, title.
Jer. 35. 4.

Number of occurrences:—

Pentateuch	1
Prophets	65
Other books	12
	—
	78 = 6 × 13 (see Ap. 10).
New Testament	2
	—
	80 = 8 × 10 (see Ap. 10).

50 CHRONOLOGICAL CHARTS, AND TABLES.

INTRODUCTION.

1. Systematic tabulation being the only satisfactory method, to eye and understanding alike, of presenting Biblical, or any other numbers, this course has been adopted in the following charts.

To ensure accuracy, "Section" paper has been used throughout.

The importance of this is, that, for the first time, (it is believed) Bible readers will have placed in their hands a series of Chronological Tables of the main dated events in the Old Testament, which they can test and check for themselves.

As a rule, the Chronological Charts already available are set before the reader, either on a scale so minute that they must be received or rejected as a whole, or else so encumbered with extraneous matter relating to Babylon, Egypt, Greece, Rome, &c., as to be hopelessly bewildering to the ordinary Bible reader.

2. The problems of Biblical Chronology cannot be solved by mere computation, after the manner of some.

Neither must they be dealt with by arbitrarily adopting a particular date, and reckoning from that onward to Christ, and back to Adam. This is a position that cannot be maintained; as the charts will show.

3. Again, the use of "Sothic cycles", eclipses, and other astronomical methods for "settling" Biblical dates, has not been sought. On the contrary, any

appeals for aid from such sources have been carefully avoided.

If the record of the Scripture as to its own times and numbers is not self-contained, then it must be hopeless to *supplement* it by guesses and "explanations" as to the movements of the heavenly bodies, used mainly in support of human arguments and assumptions.

4. The position occupied in *The Companion Bible* is that *all* Scripture is "given by inspiration of God," θεόπνευστος (*theopneustos*) = *God breathed.* Therefore, the record of the dates and periods stated in the Bible are as much inspired as any other portion of it; and are as much to be relied on for accuracy as those statements upon which we rest in hope of eternal salvation. They must be as unreservedly received and believed as any other statements contained in its pages.

5. When it is stated that a certain king began to reign in such or such a year of the reign of another king, and that he reigned for so many years, it is accepted, and charted down accordingly.

6. One of the greatest difficulties which chronologers have to face is, and always has been, the *apparent* conflict between the record in 1 Kings 6. 1, that Solomon's temple was commenced "in the four hundred and eightieth year after the children of Israel were come out of the land of Egypt"; while in Acts 13. 17–22 the same period amounts to 573 years; a difference of ninety-three years.

In the majority of cases 1 Kings 6. 1 has been adopted by chronologists as being correct, St. Paul's reckoning being left to take care of itself; or, they say he was "misinformed", or "only speaking generally."

The simple fact is *both are right.*

The solution of the difficulty is that St. Paul's statement is according to *Anno Mundi* years (573)—the other on the principle of what we may call *Anno Dei* reckoning (480). (See the "*Lo-Ammi*" periods chart, 50. vii. 11).

The charts show that, on the plain and straightforward statements of the Scriptures themselves, the actual *Anno Mundi* period from the Exodus to the commencement of Solomon's temple was exactly 573 years, thus agreeing with St. Paul, and absolutely verifying the reckoning in Acts 13. 17–22.

But the four hundred and eightieth year of 1 Kings 6 is also as absolutely correct, only it is reckoned from the Exodus on a different principle—viz. *according to God's reckoning.*

The difference in years between the two statements is, as already said, the ninety-three years of the servitudes.

Now, to ignore ninety-three years in *the lifetime of the world* cannot be done without upsetting all other dates.

Yet this is precisely what is generally done.

Understanding the "four hundred and eightieth year" as being on *Anno Mundi* reckoning instead of according to *Anno Dei* reckoning, chronologers are compelled, in order to make things "agree", to handle and compress the figures and facts of the *Judges* period in the most arbitrary manner.

St. Paul's testimony is that "God gave (them) Judges about 450 years *until* Samuel the prophet". (Acts 13. 20.)

The adverb of time here translated *until* (ἕως, *heōs, until, as long as*), marks the completion of an action up to the time of the commencement of another. Here, it denotes the *fulfilment* of the times of the Judges, ending with the close of Samuel's forty years, and the commencement of the kingdom. (Cp. the use of ἕως —*heōs*—in Matt. 1. 25, "*until* she had brought forth her firstborn son.")

The chart 50. iv. exactly coincides with St. Paul's statement. The *Judgeship* period ends, and the kingdom time begins with Saul in 1000 B.C.

7. The advantage of the SECTIONAL LINES in the charts will be apparent to all students of the Word of God.

The difficulty experienced in making the two lines of the kings of Judah and Israel "agree" is overcome quite simply by setting the Davidian dynasty, and those of the kings of Israel, on what may be termed an *interlocking* system, by the use of the parallel horizontal section lines.

When, for instance, it is stated in 2 Kings 8. 16, "In the fifth year of Joram the son of Ahab king of Israel (Jehoshaphat *being* then king of Judah), Jehoram the son of Jehoshaphat king of Judah began to reign": Chart 50. vii shows this; and, while vindicating the accuracy of the statement in the text—followed in the A.V. and R.V. (with a doubtful note in the latter) as to Jehoshaphat being *at that time* king of Judah—it shows further that Jehoshaphat had joined his son with him in associate-kingship in the third year before his death.

The extreme value to the student of this principle will be seen in this and other instances, especially in the Ezra–Nehemiah period. See Chart 50. vii. 5.

8. In Chart 50, vii. 7, 8, 9, 10, are given a few of the significant periods of 430, 450, 490, and 1,000 years.

The Tables will enable others to follow up these figures on the same lines; and doubtless many other important periods will be noted by those who delight in searching into the wonders of the Word of Life.

This, by means of the Section lines, can be done accurately.

9. In the Charts themselves the *terminus a quo* is the creation of Adam; while the *terminus ad quem* is the Crucifixion (although the charting is continued on to the destruction of Jerusalem by Titus).

The *unit of measurement* is the number of years given as the lifetime of Adam: viz. 930. (Gen. 5. 5.)

Commencing with this, and taking each link as it follows, the chain is seen to extend in perfect sequence until it ends with the "cutting off of the Messiah" at the *close* of the sixty-ninth of the seventy sevens of Dan. 9. 25, 26—in A.D. 29. That is, 4,033 from the Creation.

It shows also that the period from Adam to the Nativity was eighty jubilees (on *Anno Mundi* reckoning, but see note on p. 70) or 4,000 years.

Each shaded column stands for 100 years (same in the detail charts) consisting of 10 sections of 10 years each.

Every year, therefore, from beginning to end is shown, and nothing is left, in this respect, to chance or guesswork.

The figures to the left of this shaded column are B.C. dates: that is, they are reckoned from the common era of A.D. 0. But, all are agreed that the birth of Christ took place four years earlier:—therefore, for any date required from the *Nativity itself*, these four years must be deducted in each case.

On so small a scale it is almost humanly impossible to avoid some slight *overlappings* in connection with the periods of the kings, owing to the use of the cardinal and ordinal numbers, and the absence in most cases of hints as to the time of year at which some of the reigns began or ended. But the "charting" has been done with the most careful and anxious exactitude, and the "interlocking" system, above referred to, has reduced such minutiæ to (it is believed) the narrowest limits.

10. The principle employed in the Scriptures of this interlocking, or cross-checking, is of great significance and importance.

On the charts these are set down exactly as they are given.

No attempt is made to manipulate the figures, e.g.—

(*a*) When the record says "in the *thirty and eighth* year of Asa king of Judah began Ahab the son of Omri to reign over Israel, and Ahab . . . reigned over Israel in Samaria *twenty and two* years" (1 Kings 16. 29), it is charted accordingly, and this shows that Ahaziah was joined in

co-regency with his father Ahab two years before the death of the latter, in the *seventeenth* year of Jehoshaphat (1 Kings 22. 51).

(*b*) In 2 Kings 14. 23 it is stated—"in the *fifteenth* year of Amaziah, the son of Joash king of Judah Jeroboam (II) the son of Joash king of Israel began to reign in Samaria, (and reigned) *forty and one* years."

Now, Amaziah's twenty-nine years of reigning in Jerusalem (2 Kings 14. 2) end, as the chart shows, in the *fourteenth* year of Jeroboam; and, as Uzziah, Amaziah's son, began his reign in the *twenty-seventh* year of Jeroboam (2 Kings 15. 1), it follows that a *gap of thirteen years* intervenes in the line of Judah between Amaziah and Uzziah.

No attempt is made to bridge this gap, much less to curtail or ignore it.

The Scriptures are silent as to the *reason* for this break. The interval stands there, a plainly recorded fact, and is charted down accordingly.

In the same way there is an interval of twenty-four years on the Israel side between Jeroboam II and his son Zechariah's accession. But Scripture gives no detail as to how the intervening space was occupied.

In the case of the Davidian dynasty, *the periods omitted* (shown in black) were not to be included in the *Anno Dei* reckoning.

11. The "Lo-Ammi" periods. It will be noticed at once that, in many instances, from shortly after the entry into the Land and onwards, there are wide differences between the chart dates and the "received dates" for certain events.

For instance, Jehoiakim's fourth and Nebuchadnezzar's first years (Jer. 25. 1) are charted as 496 B.C., whereas the generally "received" date is 606 B.C. (according to some, 605 or 604).

This means a discrepancy of 108–110 years; and shortens the period between the year in which Judah became tributary to Babylon, and the Gentile supremacy over the land of Jerusalem began, and the time of Christ, by those 108–110 years.

At once, it may be said, "Here is manifest error! We are told that leading chronologers are 'agreed' that the point of contact between sacred and profane chronology, and therefore the first certain date in Biblical history, is the accession of Nebuchadnezzar to the throne of Babylon in B.C. 625."

But the chart of the "Lo-Ammi" periods (50. VII. 11) shows that chronologists have mixed up *Anno Mundi* reckoning with the *Anno Dei* reckoning.

The *black* portions of the columns in the charts show the times when the children of Israel were in servitude or under usurped authority (as in Athaliah, &c.), and therefore such periods were not to be reckoned, while Israel was *Lo-Ammi*, "Not My People!"

Take, for example, from the Exodus to Jehoiachin's Captivity. On "received" dates this period is 1491–599=892 years. According to the charts this period is 1491–489=1003 years.

A difference of 110 years.

The explanation is in the charts, and shows that the *Anno Mundi* years include the ninety-three of servitude in the *Judges*, and the three intervals in the Kings (together twenty years), totalling 113 years.

Deducting this 113 from 1002, or adding it to 892, we have 889 and 1005 respectively.

Allowing for the portions of years at beginning and end of this period, and the overlapping at the intervals, it will be seen that these figures are practically identical.

The same *Anno Dei* reckoning removes the difficulty presented by "the four hundred and eightieth year," and shows that every date from the time of Eli to the usurpation of Athaliah is ninety-three years out of place in the *ordinary* reckoning; from Joash to the end of Amaziah every date is ninety-nine years wrong; and from Uzziah's death to the Captivity every date is 113 years wrong.

This is not inference but fact, as those who use the charts can test for themselves.

This one date in 1 Kings 6. 1, having been accepted by almost all the "leading chronologers" as representing literal *Anno Mundi* years, has become the pivot upon which *all* chronology, "sacred" and secular, has been made to turn, and all the "received" dates gathered from "monumental" or other sources, as well as by "computation", have been forced to "fit in" accordingly.

12. This also applies to the Jubilee Years. On *Anno Mundi* reckoning, from the entry into the Land till the Nativity, there are exactly twenty-nine jubilees; but on *Anno Dei* reckoning there are only twenty-five jubilees (the number of grace again, 5×5, i.e., 5^2. See Ap. 10): and the Sabbatic years accordingly, as shown on the charts.

13. The Scales of the *detailed* charts explain themselves.

14. The Ezra-Nehemiah period (50. vi. and vii. 5).

According to "received" dates, the building of the second Temple was begun in 536 B.C., and finished in 516–515 B.C., and the walls of Jerusalem were built by Nehemiah in 444 B.C., that is seventy-two years later, and ninety-one years from the going forth of the decree to build *Jerusalem*.

Now, in the second year of Darius Hystaspes (Hag. 1. 1) the LORD'S HOUSE *was not built*. Hence the word of Jehovah: "Is it time for you to dwell in your ceiled houses, and *this house lie waste?*" (1. 4). "Go up and BUILD the House" (*v.* 8).

If this be so, we may ask—When was Jerusalem rebuilt?

On "received" dates we are asked to believe that this was completed by Nehemiah in 444, i.e. seventy-two years later. According to this dating the Temple was finished and dedicated in 516 B.C., *seventy-two years before the houses and walls of Jerusalem were built!*

The key to this period—indeed, to the whole of Scripture chronology—is in Dan. 9. 25, "From the going forth" of the decree to BUILD JERUSALEM. Not a word is said about the Temple in this important passage; whereas the decree of Cyrus is entirely concerned with the Temple, "the House of the Lord God of Israel ... which is in Jerusalem." Ezra 1. 3.

The charts show that the going forth of the decree to build JERUSALEM was issued in the twentieth year of Artaxerxes (ASTEIAGES="Darius the Median,"—the father of Cyrus), and in the forty-second year of Nebuchadnezzar's reign. This was just at the close of the great king's seven years of "madness." (See the Structures of Ezra–Nehemiah, and Ap. 58.)

This decree to build Jerusalem was in 454 B.C.; and the decree of Cyrus to build the Temple was issued in 426 B.C.; *twenty-eight years later*.

An illustration from the Book of Exodus may help to illustrate the *principle* on which the books of Ezra–Nehemiah are placed in the Jewish (and our own) Bible.

The specification of the Tabernacle, its materials and furniture, is placed first (canonically), beginning with the ARK. Then the construction itself follows. The order is reversed in actual building; and the chronological order comes first.

It is the same here. The building of the House of God being paramount, the decree, &c., concerning it comes first (canonically), on the same Divine principle. Afterwards we have the detail of the *setting* for the gem, so to speak—the building of Jerusalem. Just as the Tabernacle was (chronologically) built first (Ex. 36) to contain the ark, so here, the city was built *first* to contain, guard, and protect the "House of Jehovah."

Finally, the best explanation of the charts will be found in the charts themselves. They are presented in the order set forth on p. 3 of the Appendixes.

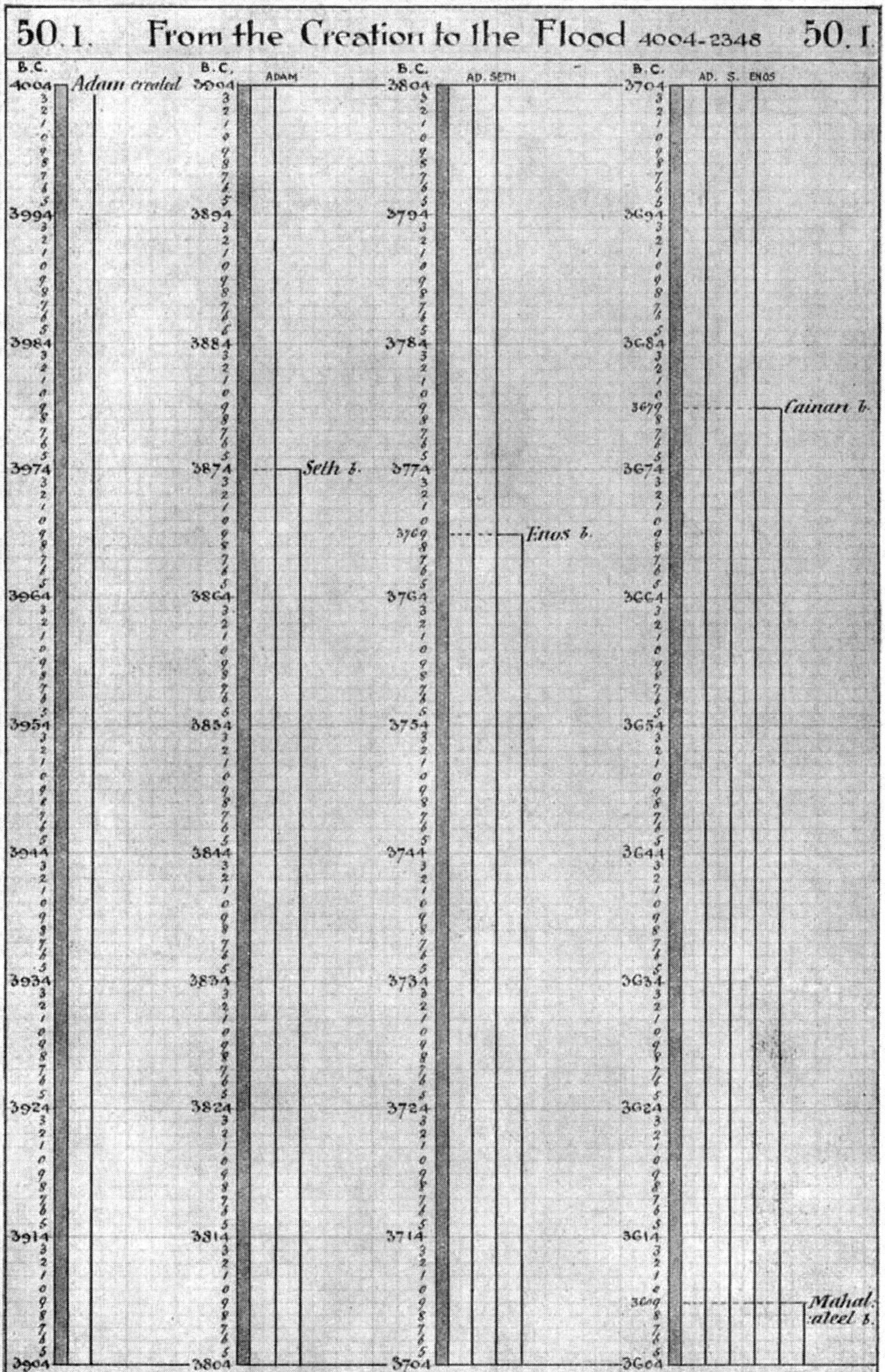

50. I. From the Creation to the Flood 4004-2348 50. I.
B.C.
4004 Adam created
3994
3984
3974
3964
3954
3944
3934
3924
3914
3904
B.C.
ADAM
3894
3884
3874 Seth b.
3864
3854
3844
3834
3824
3814
3804
B.C.
AD. SETH
3804
3794
3784
3774
3769 Enos b.
3764
3754
3744
3734
3724
3714
3704
B.C.
AD. S. ENOS
3704
3694
3684
3679 Cainan b.
3674
3664
3654
3644
3634
3624
3614
3609 Mahal-aleel b.
3604

50.1. From the Creation to the Flood 4004-2348 50.1.

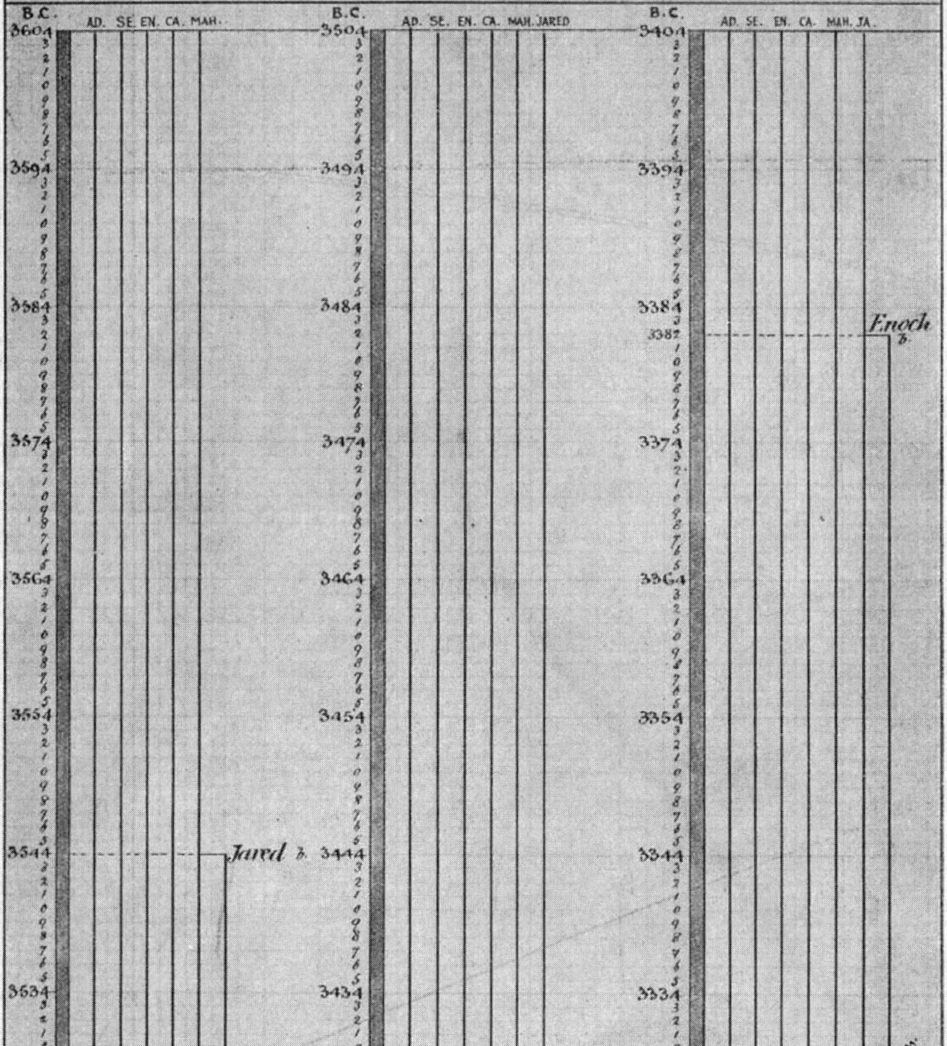

50.I. From the Creation to the Flood 4004-2348 50.I.

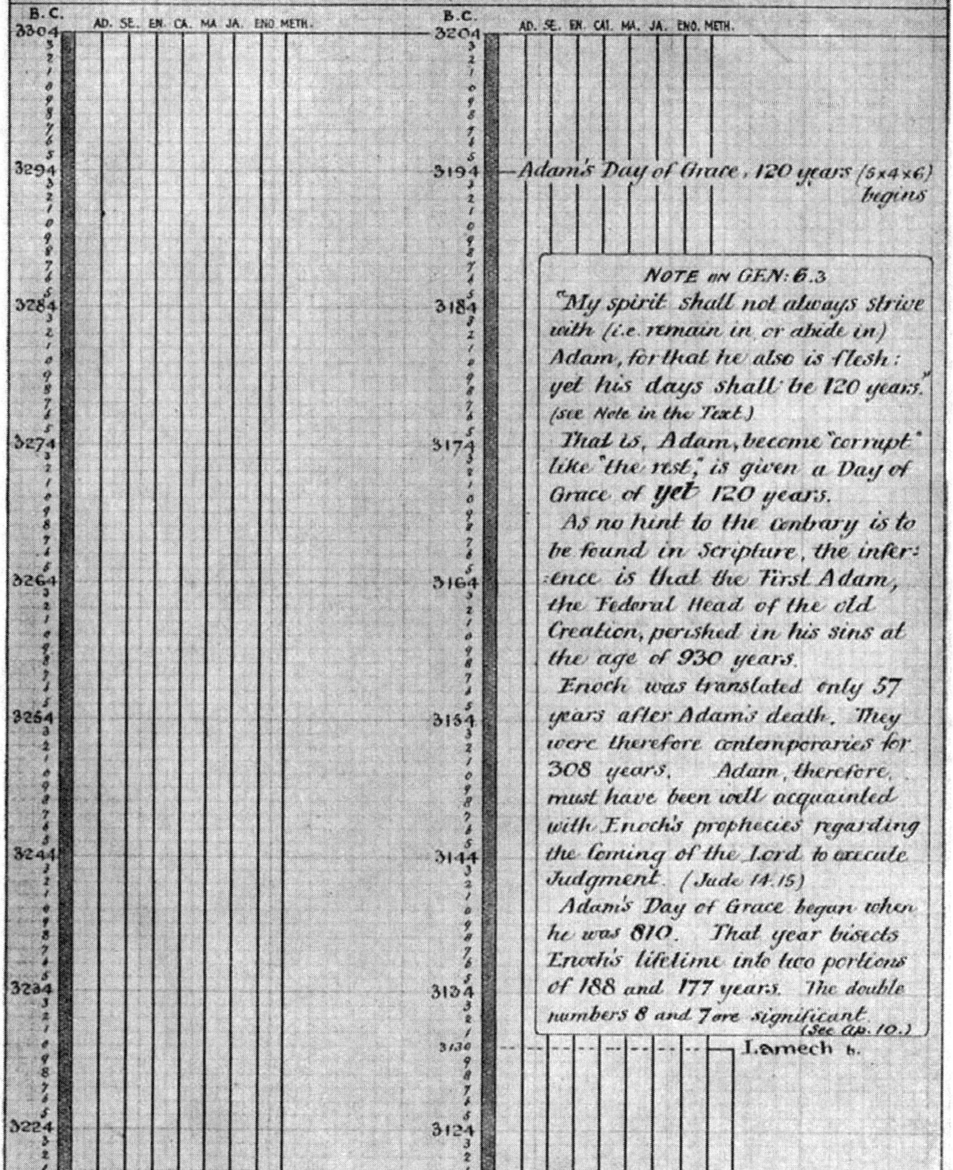
B.C.
AD. SE. EN. CA. MA. JA. ENO. METH.
3304
3294
3284
3274
3264
3254
3244
3234
3224
3214
3204
B.C.
AD. SE. EN. CAI. MA. JA. ENO. METH.
3204
3194
3184
3174
3164
3154
3144
3134
3130
3124
3114
3104
Adam's Day of Grace, 120 years (5×4×6) begins
NOTE on GEN: 6.3
"My spirit shall not always strive with (i.e. remain in, or abide in) Adam, for that he also is flesh: yet his days shall be 120 years."
(see Note in the Text.)
That is, Adam, become "corrupt" like "the rest," is given a Day of Grace of yet 120 years.
As no hint to the contrary is to be found in Scripture, the inference is that the First Adam, the Federal Head of the old Creation, perished in his sins at the age of 930 years.
Enoch was translated only 57 years after Adam's death. They were therefore contemporaries for 308 years. Adam, therefore, must have been well acquainted with Enoch's prophecies regarding the Coming of the Lord to execute Judgment. (Jude 14.15)
Adam's Day of Grace began when he was 810. That year bisects Enoch's lifetime into two portions of 188 and 177 years. The double numbers 8 and 7 are significant.
(See Ap. 10.)
Lamech b.

50.1. From the Creation to the Flood 4004-2348 50.1.

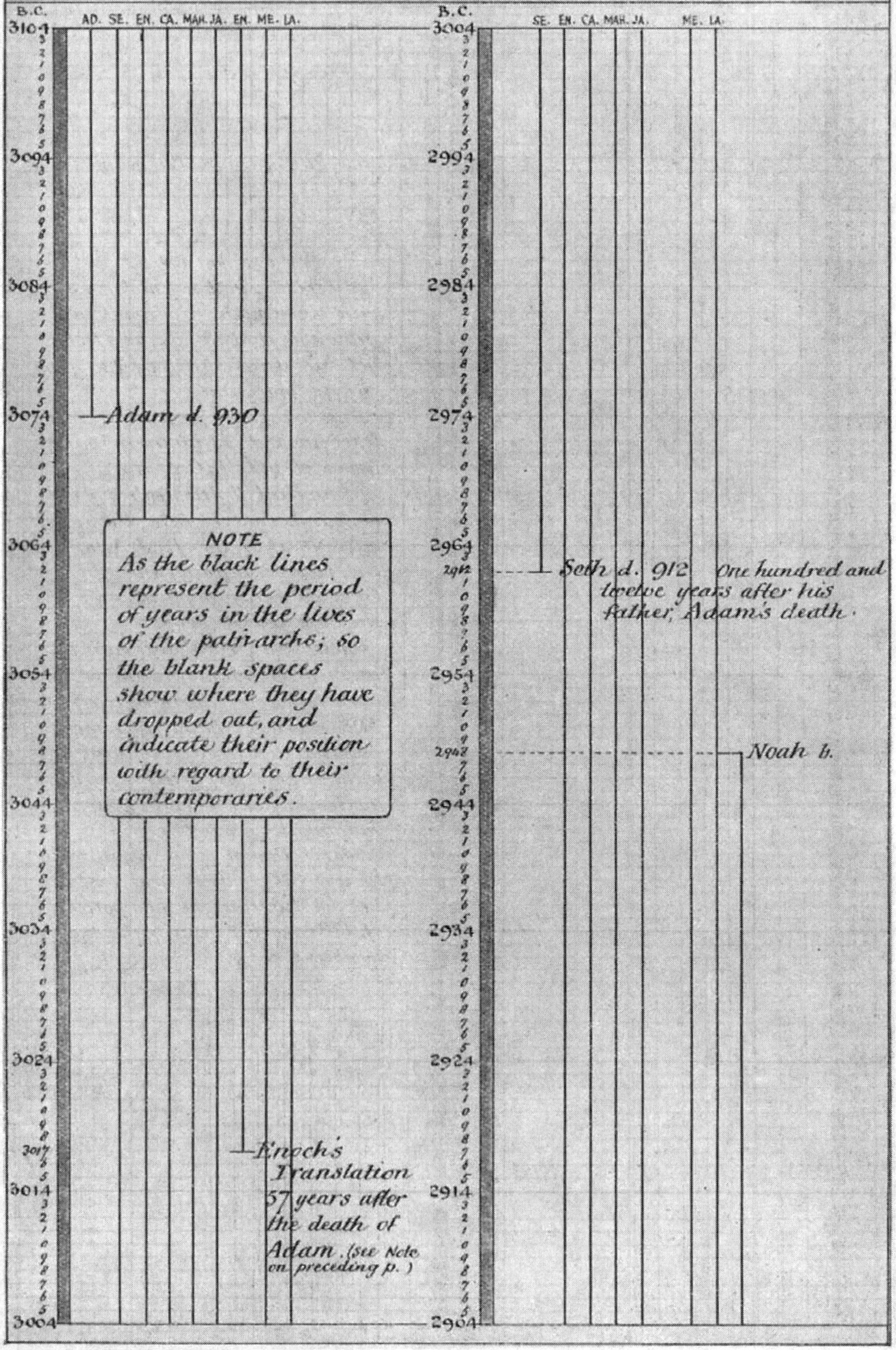

B.C.
AD. SE. EN. CA. MAH. JA. EN. ME. LA.
3104
3094
3084
3074
Adam d. 930
NOTE
As the black lines represent the period of years in the lives of the patriarchs; so the blank spaces show where they have dropped out, and indicate their position with regard to their contemporaries.
3064
3054
3044
3034
3024
3017
Enoch's Translation 57 years after the death of Adam (see Note on preceding p.)
3014
3004
B.C.
SE. EN. CA. MAH. JA. ME. LA.
3004
2994
2984
2974
2964
2962
Seth d. 912 One hundred and twelve years after his father, Adam's death.
2954
2948
Noah b.
2944
2934
2924
2914
2904

50.I. From the Creation to the Flood 4004-2348 50.I.

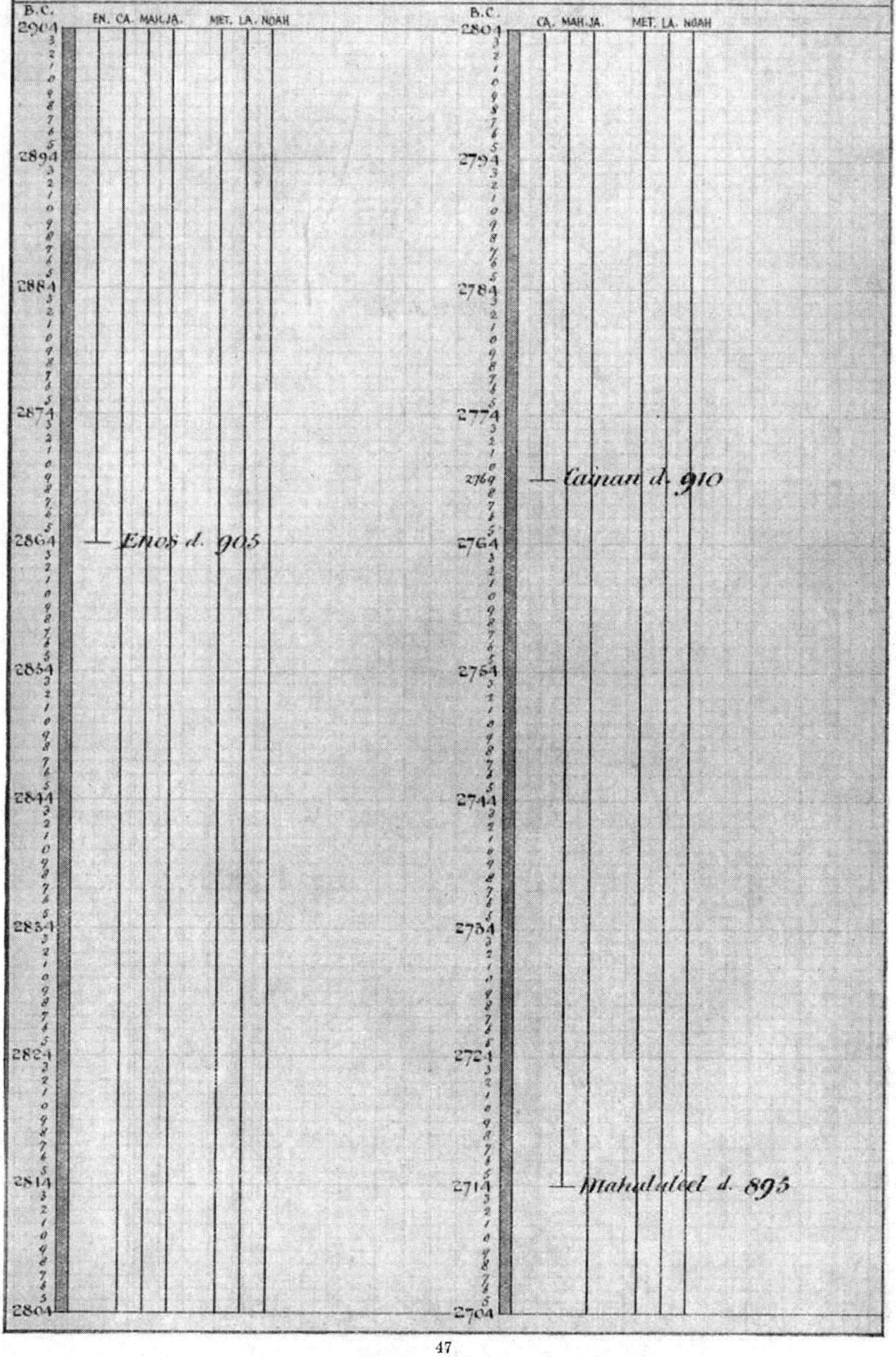

50.I. From the Creation to the Flood 4004-2348 50.I.

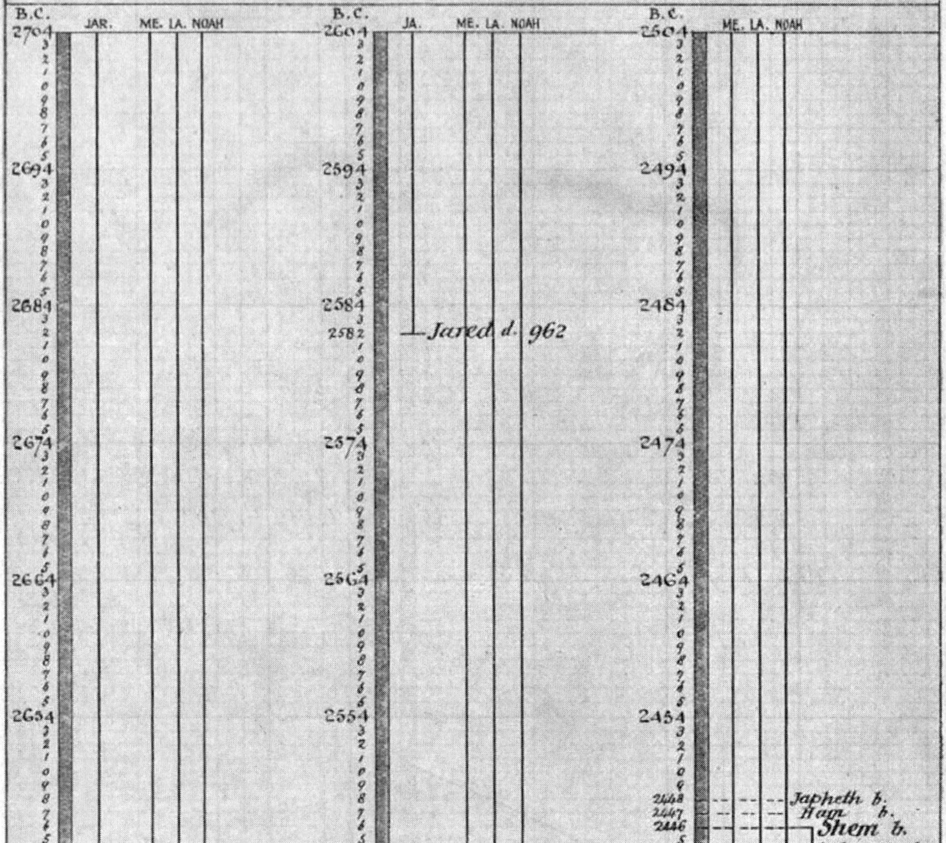

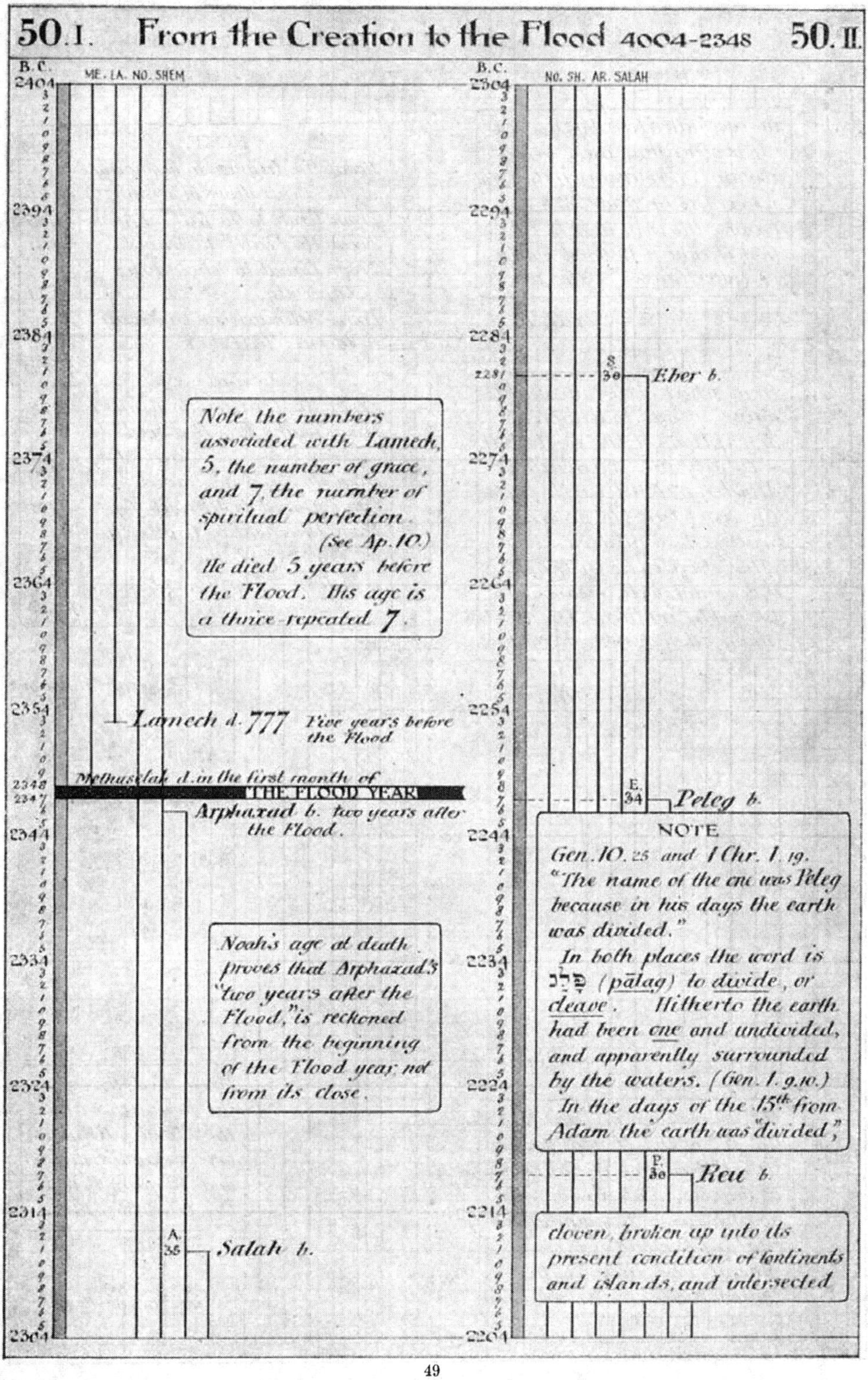
50.I. From the Creation to the Flood 4004-2348 50.II.
B.C.
ME. LA. NO. SHEM
NO. SH. AR. SALAH
Note the numbers associated with Lamech, 5, the number of grace, and 7, the number of spiritual perfection. (See Ap. 10.) He died 5 years before the Flood. His age is a thrice-repeated 7.
Lamech d. 777 Five years before the Flood
Methuselah d. in the first month of THE FLOOD YEAR
Arphaxad b. two years after the Flood.
Noah's age at death proves that Arphaxad's "two years after the Flood," is reckoned from the beginning of the Flood year; not from its close.
A. 35 Salah b.
S. 30 Eber b.
E. 34 Peleg b.
NOTE
Gen. 10. 25 and 1 Chr. 1. 19. "The name of the one was Peleg because in his days the earth was divided."
In both places the word is פָּלַג (pālag) to divide, or cleave. Hitherto the earth had been one and undivided, and apparently surrounded by the waters. (Gen. 1. 9, 10.) In the days of the 15th from Adam the earth was "divided,"
P. 30 Reu b.
cloven, broken up into its present condition of continents and islands, and intersected

50.II. From the Flood to Abraham 2348-1996 50.II.

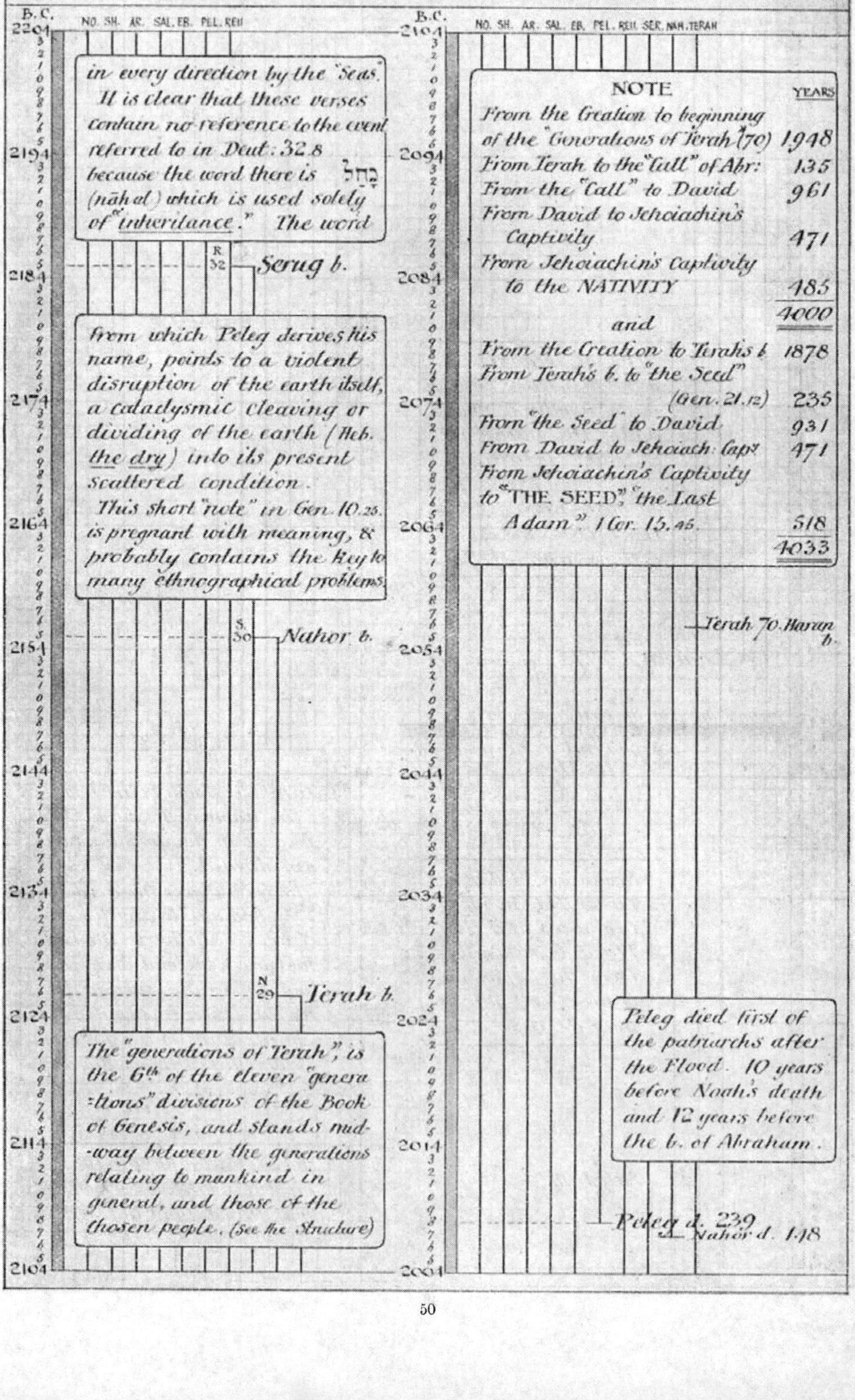
B.C.
2204
2194
2184
2174
2164
2154
2144
2134
2124
2114
2104
NO. SH. AR. SAL. EB. PEL. REU
in every direction by the "Seas". It is clear that these verses contain no reference to the event referred to in Deut: 32.8 because the word there is נָחַל (nāhal) which is used solely of "inheritance." The word
R 32
Serug b.
from which Peleg derives his name, points to a violent disruption of the earth itself, a cataclysmic cleaving or dividing of the earth (Heb. the dry) into its present scattered condition.
This short "note" in Gen. 10.25. is pregnant with meaning, & probably contains the key to many "ethnographical problems.
S. 30
Nahor b.
N 29
Terah b.
The "generations of Terah", is the 6th of the eleven "generations" divisions of the Book of Genesis, and stands mid-way between the generations relating to mankind in general, and those of the chosen people. (See the Structure)
B.C.
2104
2094
2084
2074
2064
2054
2044
2034
2024
2014
2004
NO. SH. AR. SAL. EB. PEL. REU. SER. NAH. TERAH
NOTE
YEARS
From the Creation to beginning of the "Generations of Terah"(70) 1948
From Terah to the "Call" of Abr: 135
From the "Call" to David 961
From David to Jehoiachin's Captivity 471
From Jehoiachin's Captivity to the NATIVITY 485
4000
and
From the Creation to Terah's b. 1878
From Terah's b. to "the Seed" (Gen. 21.12) 235
From "the Seed" to David 931
From David to Jehoiach: Capt. 471
From Jehoiachin's Captivity to "THE SEED", "the Last Adam". 1 Cor. 15.45. 518
4033
Terah 70. Haran b.
Peleg died first of the patriarchs after the Flood. 10 years before Noah's death and 12 years before the b. of Abraham.
Peleg d. 239
Nahor d. 148

50.III. From Abraham to the Exodus 1996-1491 50.III

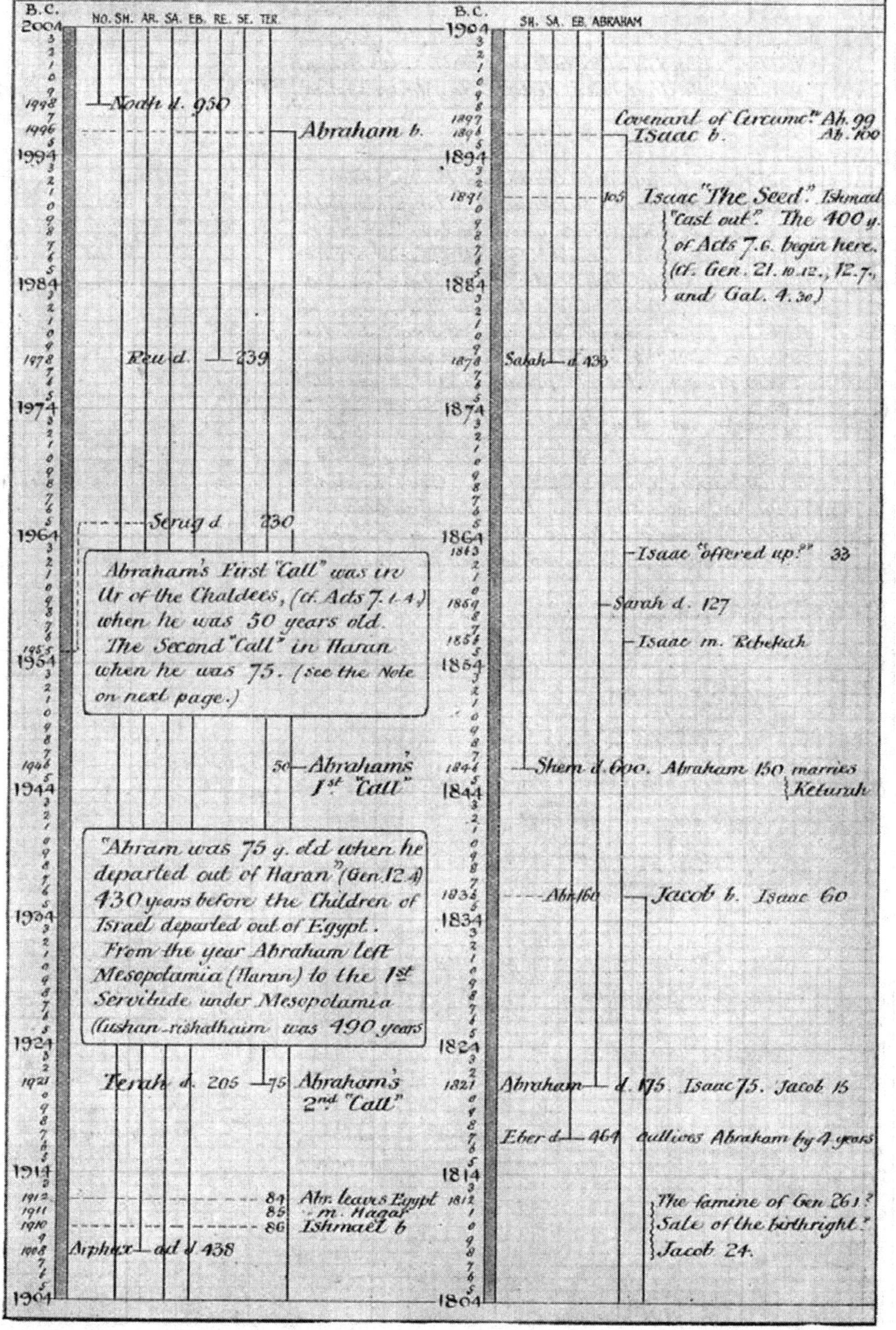

B.C.
NO. SH. AR. SA. EB. RE. SE. TER.
Noah d. 950
Abraham b.
Reu d. 239
Serug d. 230
Abraham's First "Call" was in Ur of the Chaldees, (cf. Acts 7. 2-4.) when he was 50 years old. The Second "Call" in Haran when he was 75. (see the Note on next page.)
50 Abraham's 1st "Call"
"Abram was 75 y. old when he departed out of Haran" (Gen. 12.4) 430 years before the Children of Israel departed out of Egypt. From the year Abraham left Mesopotamia (Haran) to the 1st Servitude under Mesopotamia (Cushan-rishathaim was 490 years
Terah d. 205
75 Abraham's 2nd "Call"
84 Abr. leaves Egypt
85 m. Hagar
86 Ishmael b
Arphax-ad d 438
SH. SA. EB. ABRAHAM
Covenant of Circumc.n Ab. 99
Isaac b. Ab. 100
105 Isaac "The Seed." Ishmael "cast out". The 400 y. of Acts 7.6. begin here. (cf. Gen. 21. 10.12., 12.7., and Gal. 4.30)
Salah d. 433
Isaac "offered up" 33
Sarah d. 127
Isaac m. Rebekah
Shem d. 600. Abraham 150 marries Keturah
Ab. 160 Jacob b. Isaac 60
Abraham d. 175 Isaac 75. Jacob 15
Eber d. 464 outlives Abraham by 4 years
The famine of Gen 26.1? Sale of the birthright? Jacob 24.

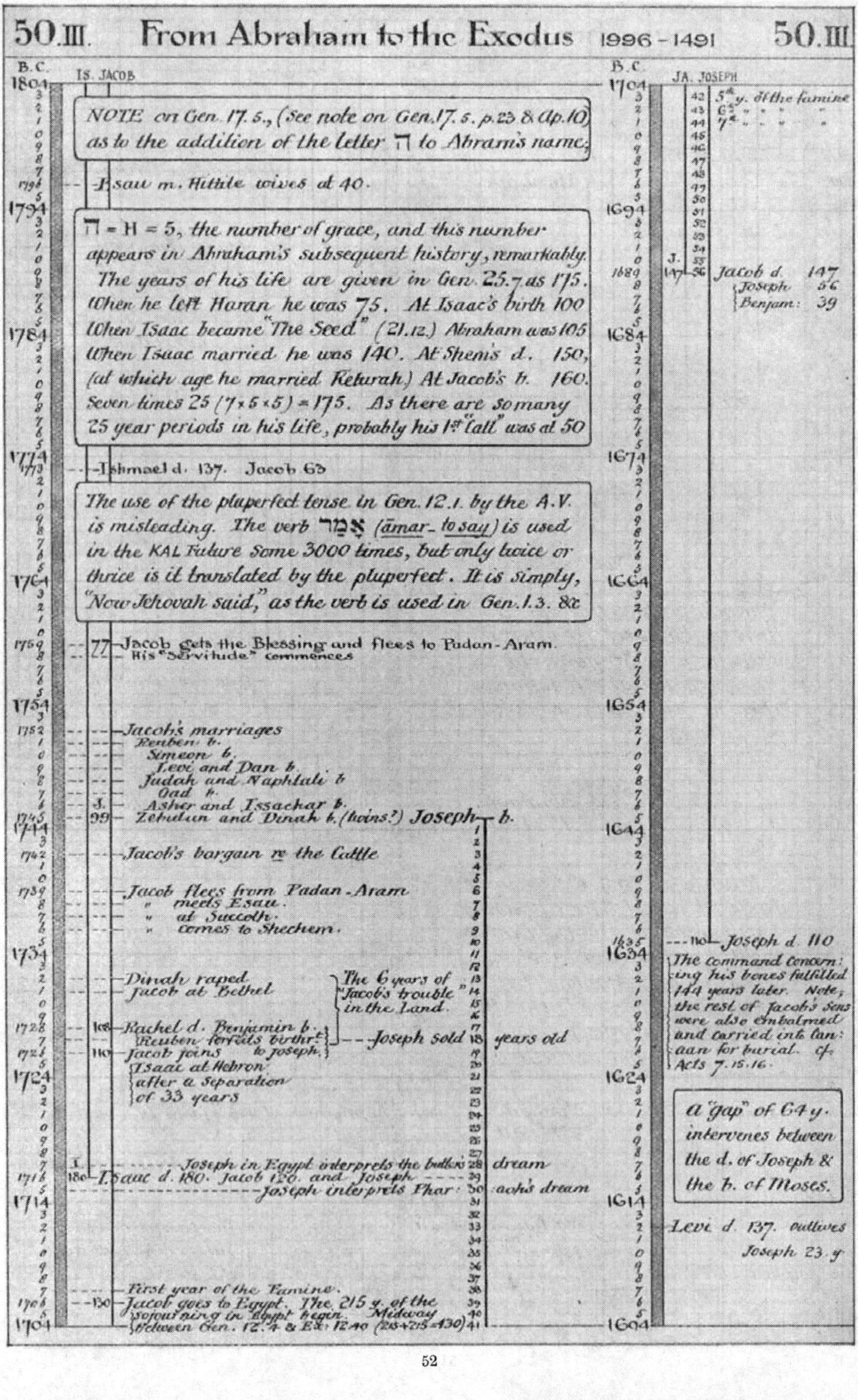
50.III. From Abraham to the Exodus 1996 - 1491 50.III.
B.C.
IS. JACOB
B.C.
JA. JOSEPH
1804
1794
1784
1774
1764
1754
1744
1734
1724
1714
1704
1694
1684
1674
1664
1654
1644
1634
1624
1614
1604
NOTE on Gen. 17.5., (See note on Gen. 17.5. p.23 & Ap. 10) as to the addition of the letter ה to Abram's name.
1796 Esau m. Hittite wives at 40.
ה = H = 5, the number of grace, and this number appears in Abraham's subsequent history, remarkably. The years of his life are given in Gen. 25.7 as 175. When he left Haran he was 75. At Isaac's birth 100 When Isaac became "The Seed" (21.12.) Abraham was 105 When Isaac married he was 140. At Shem's d. 150, (at which age he married Keturah) At Jacob's b. 160. Seven times 25 (7×5×5) = 175. As there are so many 25 year periods in his life, probably his 1st "call" was at 50
1773 Ishmael d. 137. Jacob 63
The use of the pluperfect tense in Gen. 12.1. by the A.V. is misleading. The verb אָמַר (āmar - to say) is used in the KAL Future some 3000 times, but only twice or thrice is it translated by the pluperfect. It is simply, "Now Jehovah said," as the verb is used in Gen. 1.3. &c
1759 77 Jacob gets the Blessing and flees to Padan-Aram. His "Servitude" commences
1752 Jacob's marriages
Reuben b.
Simeon b.
Levi and Dan b.
Judah and Naphtali b.
Gad b.
J. Asher and Issachar b.
1745 99 Zebulun and Dinah b. (twins?) Joseph b.
1742 Jacob's bargain re the Cattle
1739 Jacob flees from Padan-Aram
" meets Esau.
" at Succoth.
" comes to Shechem.
Dinah raped
Jacob at Bethel
The 6 years of "Jacob's trouble" in the Land.
1728 108 Rachel d. Benjamin b. Reuben forfeits birthright to Joseph.
1726 110 Jacob joins Isaac at Hebron after a separation of 33 years
Joseph sold 18 years old
I. Joseph in Egypt interprets the butler's 28 dream
1716 180 Isaac d. 180. Jacob 120. and Joseph 29
Joseph interprets Phar 30 aoh's dream
First year of the Famine.
1706 130 Jacob goes to Egypt. The 215 y. of the sojourning in Egypt begin. Midway between Gen. 12.4 & Ex. 12.40 (215+215=430)
42 5th y. of the famine
43 6th " " "
44 7th " " "
J. 1689 147 56 Jacob d. 147
Joseph 56
Benjam: 39
1635 110 Joseph d. 110
The command concerning his bones fulfilled 144 years later. Note, the rest of Jacob's Sons were also embalmed and carried into Canaan for burial. cf. Acts 7.15.16.
A "gap" of 64 y. intervenes between the d. of Joseph & the b. of Moses.
Levi d. 137. outlives Joseph 23 y.

50.III Abraham to the Exodus. Exodus to the Kingdom 50.IV

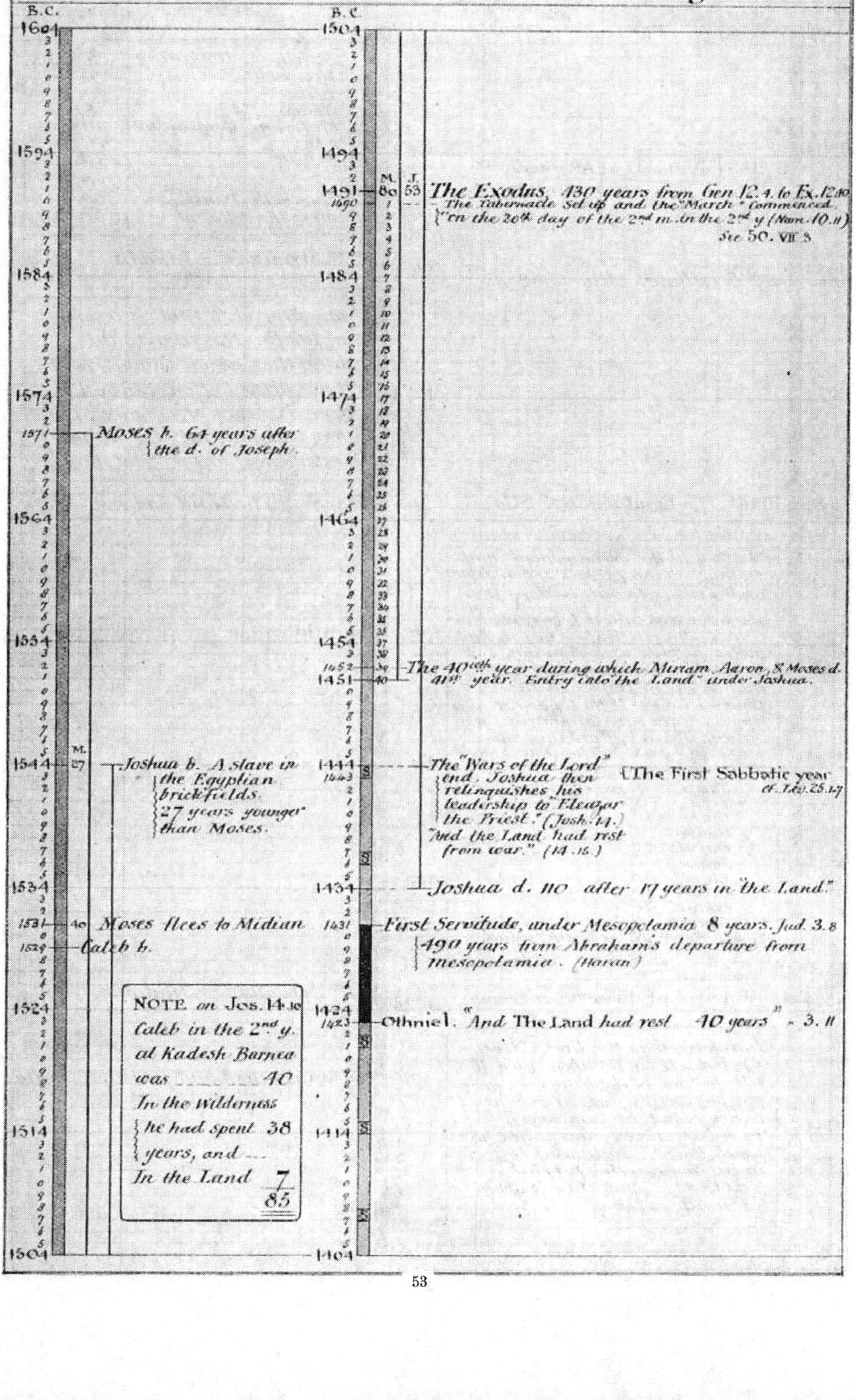

50. IV. From the Exodus to the Kingdom 1491–1000 50. IV.

B.C.

1404

1394

1393 FIRST JUBILEE YEAR (*Anno Dei reckoning*)

1384

1383 2nd Servitude. Moab 18 y.

1374

1365 Ehud. "The Land had rest" 80 y.

1364

The key to the arrangement and sequence of the periods of "Servitude" and "Rest", is found in Judg. 11. 26.

Jephtha was called to be "Captain" in Gilead (11. 6) in 1151. In the diplomatic dispute with Ammon and Moab, Jephtha's argument is one that would be advanced now in a Court of Law;– "If the lands are yours why have you not claimed possession during the 300 years they have been held by us?" The 300 is made up as follows;– viz.

Jair's	4 years	(see Note on Jair)
Tola	23	
Gideon	40	
Midian	7	
Barak	40	
Jabin	20	
Ehud	80	
Moab	18	
Othniel	40	
Cushan	8	
To the Entry into the Land	20	
	300	

1354

1344

1334

1325 Jubilee Year. (*Anno Dei reckoning*)

1324

Therefore, from the time "Israel first dwelt in Heshbon", (Jud. 11. 26) till the end of Jephtha's 1st year (the pourparlers with Ammon would occupy about twelve months);– we have – first, this – 300 years, which leaves a balance of 150 "until Samuel the prophet". (Acts 13. 20.) And this is apportioned as follows;– viz.–

1314

1304

Jephtha's remaining	5 years
Ibzan	7
Elon	10
Abdon	8
Philistine domination	40
Eli	40
Samuel	40
	150
This with Jephtha's	300
gives the total of	450 years

1294

1285 3rd Servitude. Canaan 20 y.

1284

according to St. Paul's reckoning in Acts 13. This removes the "difficulties" about Samuel, as it shows, not only that Eli had a clear 40 years of "judging"; but that Samuel had also 40 years of Judgship, until Saul begins.

1274

1265 Barak. "The Land had rest" 40 y.

1264

1254 Jubilee Year

1244

1234

1225 4th Servitude. Midian 7 y.

1224

1218 Gideon. "The Land had rest" 40 y.

1214

1204

50.IV. From the Exodus to the Kingdom 1491-1000 50.IV.

1204

1198 Jubilee Year

1194

1184

1178 Tola *judged Israel* 23 y. *(Jud. 10. 2.)*

1174

Note. *As the Philistines & Ammon "vexed" and "oppressed" the Children of Israel "on the other side Jordan" (Judg: 10. 8.) for 18 years out of Jair's 22, this obviously leaves him only 4 clear y. of "Judging"*

1164

1155 Jair *judged Israel* 4 y. *(Judg. 10. 3. 8. & see Note.)*

1154

1151 Jephtha *judged Israel* 6 y. *(12. 7. and see Note under "Ehud.")*

1148 Jubilee Year

1146 *Eli born*

1145 Ibzan *judged Israel* 7 y. *(12. 9.)*

1144

1138 Elon *judged Israel* 10 y. *(12. 11.)*

1134

1128 Abdon *judged Israel* 8 y. *(12. 14.)*

1124

1120 *5th Servitude. Philistine.* 40 y.

1114

1104

1104

Note *That the "Servitudes" are marked by the number of grace, 5. And these periods of grace shewn by punishment, are only 93 out of 450 years in the times of the Judges. The "Servitudes" being only about 1/5th of the "Rest" periods.*

1094

1084

1080 Eli *judged Israel* 40 y. *(1 Sam. 4. 18.)*

1074

Periods of the 5 Servitudes, from the Entry into the Land, until Samuel the prophet;–

Mesopotamia	8 years
Moab	18
Canaan	20
Midian	7
Philistine	40
	93

(Cf. the Note under "Saul", and Table 50. VII. 11.)

1064

1058 Jubilee Year

1054

1044

1040 Samuel *"judged Israel all the days of his life" (1 Sam. 7. 15.)* 40 y. *(See Note, and cf. Acts 13. 20.)*

1034

1024

1020 *The Reformation (1 Sam. 7.) Recovery of The Ark and its Contents. (430 years after the Entry into the Land.)*

1014

1008 Jubilee Year

1004

50.V. From the Kingdom to the Captivities 1000-426 50.V.

B.C.

1004

1000 Saul. 40 years. The Kingdom begins. With the anointing of Saul the 450 years of Acts 13. 20. end, completing the time of Samuel the prophet. (see NOTE below.)

Saul's accession took place 490 years after the Tabernacle was "set up" for Jehovah to dwell among, and reign over the children of Israel. cf. Exod. 25. 8 & 1 Sam. 8. 7.

994

990 David b.

984

NOTE. The chronology in Acts 13. 18-23, gives us the following;–
"Forty years .... in the wilderness,"–
(then follows verse 19 in parenthesis and the record continues with v. 20).
"After that He gave (unto them) Judges about the space of 450 years until (ἕως – heōs = completing the time of) Samuel the prophet."

The wilderness years	40
The Judges period	450
Saul	40
David	40
Solomon's first three	3
	573

(See Table 50 VII. II.)

974 David's first "anointing". 1 Sam. 16
1000 years before the anointing of the "Man after God's own heart" at his baptism in Jordan.
(cf 1 Sam. 16. 12. "This is he," and Matthew. 3. 17. "This is my Beloved Son)"

964

960 David 40 years (Second anointing) 1 K. 2. 11

I. Jubilee

954

953 David's reign "over all Israel and Judah" begins. (2 Sam. 5. 5) (Third anointing.)

944

934

924

920 Solomon 40 years 1 K. 4. 1

917 The Temple was begun in the 2nd m. of Solomon's 4th y (1 K. 6. 1.)
According to Anno Mundi reckoning this was 573 y. from the Exodus, but on Anno Dei reckoning, the Temple was begun in the 480th year.
(see Table 50. VII. II.)

914

910 The Temple "finished" in Solomon's 11th year (1 K. 6. 38.)
433 years before its destruction in the 19th year of Nebuchadnezzar; and 505 years before the dedication of the Second Temple.

II. Jubilee

904

50.V. From the Kingdom to the Captivities 1000-426 50.V.

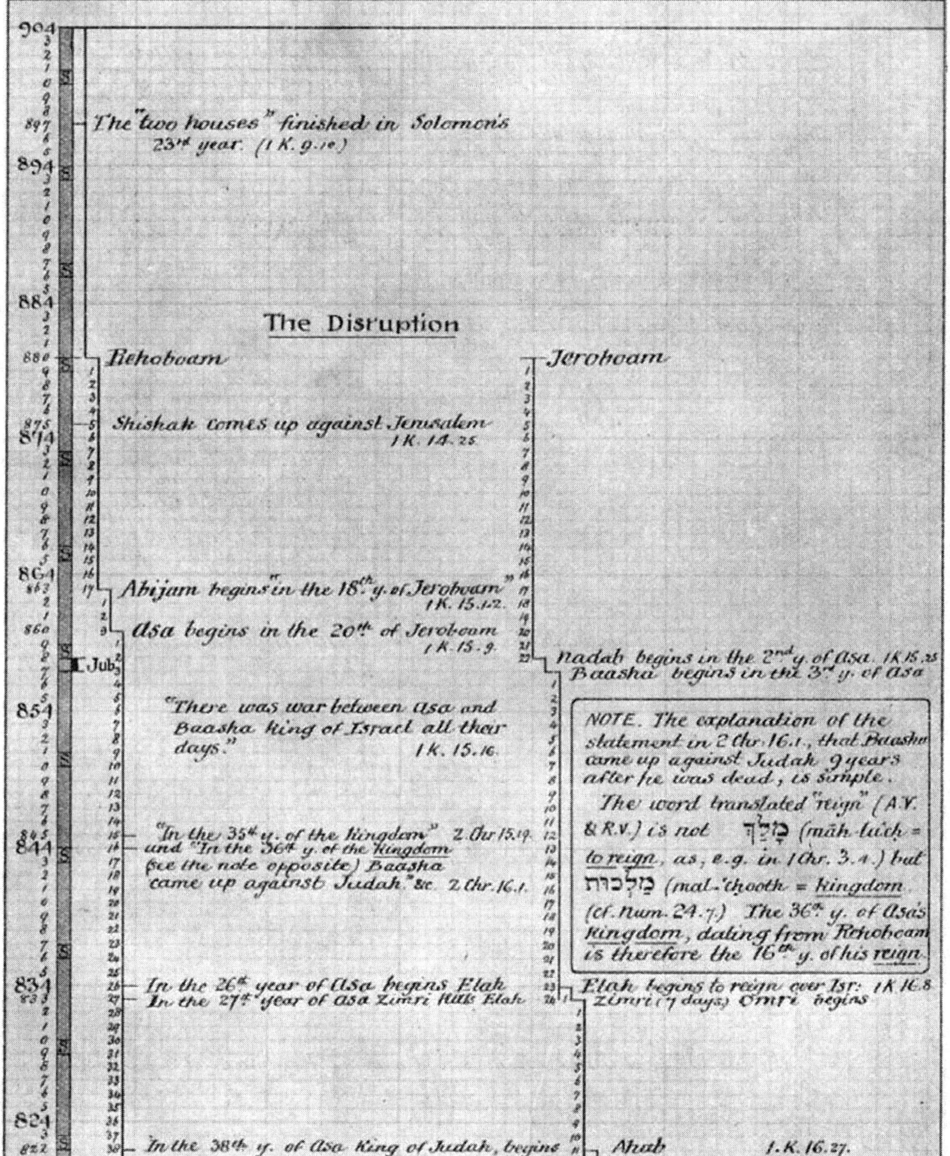

The "two houses" finished in Solomon's 23rd year. (1 K. 9.10.)
The Disruption
Rehoboam
Jeroboam
Shishak comes up against Jerusalem 1 K. 14.25
Abijam begins "in the 18th y. of Jeroboam" 1 K. 15.1-2.
Asa begins in the 20th of Jeroboam 1 K. 15.9.
Nadab begins in the 2nd y. of Asa. 1 K. 15.25
Baasha begins in the 3rd y. of Asa
Jub.
"There was war between Asa and Baasha king of Israel all their days." 1 K. 15.16.
NOTE. The explanation of the statement in 2 Chr. 16.1., that Baasha came up against Judah 9 years after he was dead, is simple.
The word translated "reign" (A.V. & R.V.) is not מָלַךְ (māh-lach = to reign, as, e.g. in 1 Chr. 3.4.) but מַלְכוּת (mal-'chooth = kingdom. (cf. Num. 24.7.) The 36th y. of Asa's Kingdom, dating from Rehoboam is therefore the 16th y. of his reign.
"In the 35th y. of the kingdom" 2 Chr. 15.19. and "In the 36th y. of the kingdom (see the note opposite) Baasha came up against Judah." &c. 2 Chr. 16.1.
In the 26th year of Asa begins Elah
In the 27th year of Asa Zimri kills Elah
Elah begins to reign over Isr: 1 K. 16.8
Zimri (7 days) Omri begins
In the 38th y. of Asa King of Judah, begins Ahab 1 K. 16.27.
Jehoshaphat begins in the 4th of Ahab 1 K. 22.41
"In the 3rd y. of his reign" Jehoshaphat sends princes and Levites to teach the Law of Jehovah throughout all the cities of Judah. 2 Chr. 17.7-9.
Jub.
904
897
894
884
880
875
874
864
863
860
854
845
844
834
833
824
822
819
816
814
804

50.V. From the Kingdom to the Captivities 1000-426 50.V.

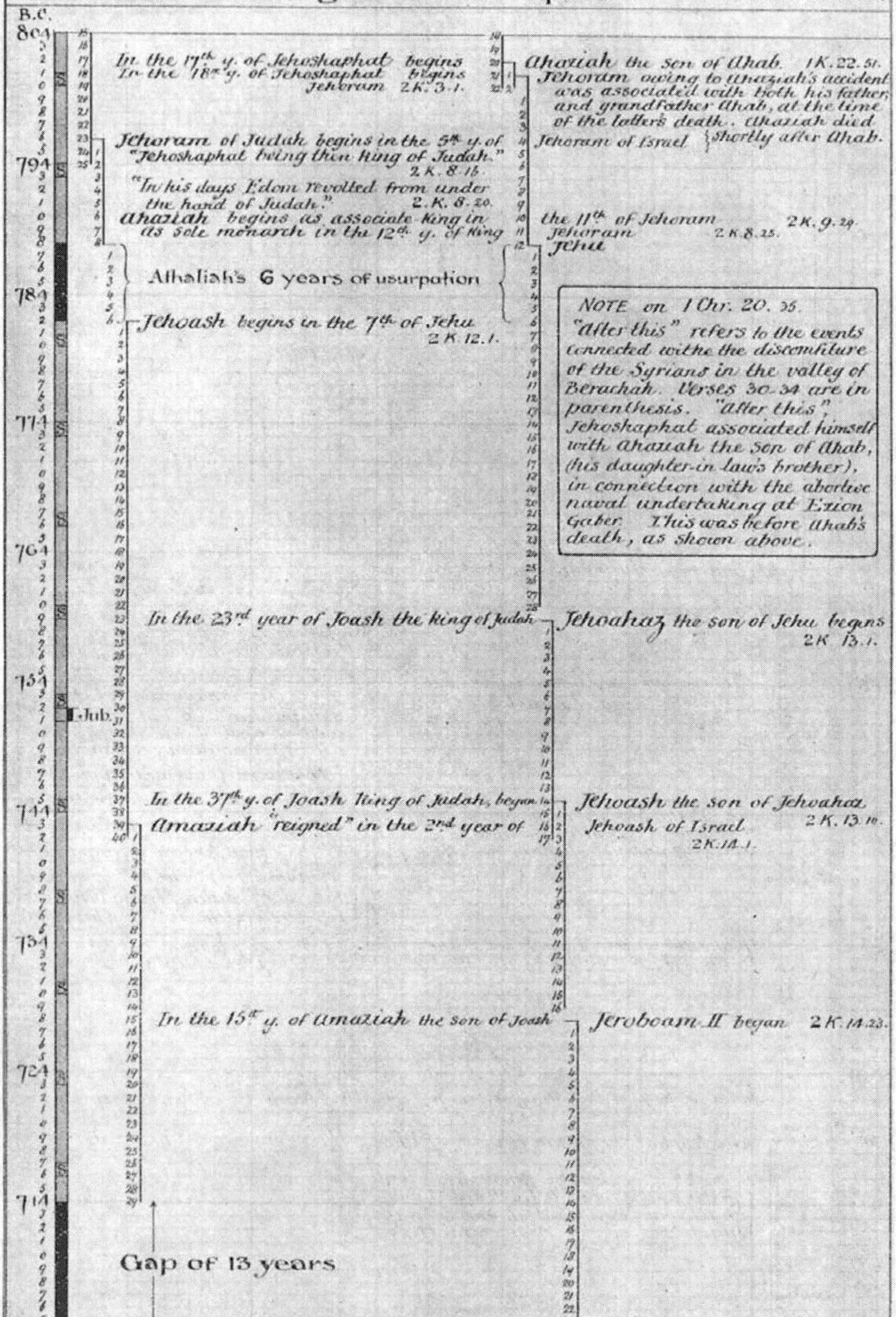
B.C.
804
794
784
774
764
754
744
734
724
714
704
Jub.
In the 17th y. of Jehoshaphat begins
In the 18th y. of Jehoshaphat begins
Jehoram 2K. 3. 1.
Ahaziah the son of Ahab. 1K. 22. 51.
Jehoram owing to Ahaziah's accident was associated with both his father, and grandfather Ahab, at the time of the latter's death. Ahaziah died shortly after Ahab.
Jehoram of Israel
Jehoram of Judah begins in the 5th y. of "Jehoshaphat being then king of Judah." 2 K. 8. 16.
"In his days Edom revolted from under the hand of Judah." 2. K. 8. 20.
Ahaziah begins as associate king in the 11th of Jehoram 2K. 9. 29.
as sole monarch in the 12th y. of king Jehoram 2. K. 8. 25.
Jehu
Athaliah's 6 years of usurpation
Jehoash begins in the 7th of Jehu 2 K. 12. 1.
NOTE on 1 Chr. 20. 35.
"After this" refers to the events connected with the discomfiture of the Syrians in the valley of Berachah. Verses 30-34 are in parenthesis. "After this", Jehoshaphat associated himself with Ahaziah the Son of Ahab, (his daughter-in-law's brother), in connection with the abortive naval undertaking at Ezion Gaber. This was before Ahab's death, as shown above.
In the 23rd year of Joash the king of Judah
Jehoahaz the son of Jehu begins 2K. 13. 1.
In the 37th y. of Joash king of Judah, began
Jehoash the son of Jehoahaz 2 K. 13. 10.
Amaziah "reigned" in the 2nd year of
Jehoash of Israel 2K. 14. 1.
In the 15th y. of Amaziah the son of Joash
Jeroboam II began 2 K. 14. 23.
Gap of 13 years

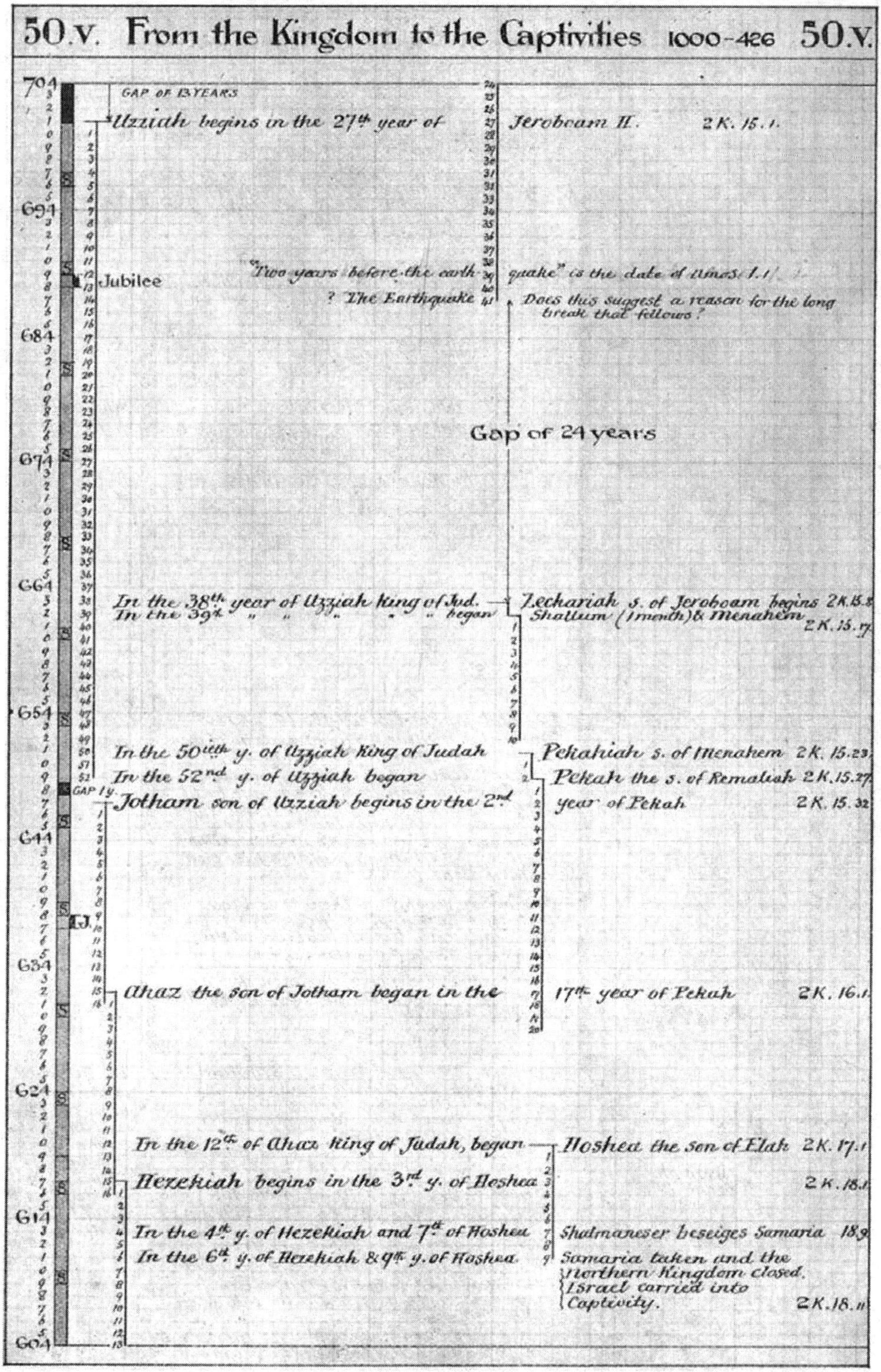
50.V. From the Kingdom to the Captivities 1000-426 50.V.
GAP OF 13 YEARS
Uzziah begins in the 27th year of Jeroboam II. 2 K. 15. 1.
"Two years before the earthquake" is the date of Amos (1.1)
Jubilee
? The Earthquake
Does this suggest a reason for the long break that follows?
Gap of 24 years
In the 38th year of Uzziah King of Jud. → Zechariah s. of Jeroboam begins 2 K. 15. 8
In the 39th " " " " began Shallum (1 month) & Menahem 2 K. 15. 17
In the 50th y. of Uzziah King of Judah Pekahiah s. of Menahem 2 K. 15. 23
In the 52nd y. of Uzziah began Pekah the s. of Remaliah 2 K. 15. 27
GAP 1 y.
Jotham son of Uzziah begins in the 2nd year of Pekah 2 K. 15. 32
Ahaz the son of Jotham began in the 17th year of Pekah 2 K. 16. 1
In the 12th of Ahaz King of Judah, began Hoshea the son of Elah 2 K. 17. 1
Hezekiah begins in the 3rd y. of Hoshea 2 K. 18. 1
In the 4th y. of Hezekiah and 7th of Hoshea Shalmaneser beseiges Samaria 18. 9
In the 6th y. of Hezekiah & 9th y. of Hoshea Samaria taken and the Northern Kingdom closed. Israel carried into Captivity. 2 K. 18. 11
704
694
684
674
664
654
644
634
624
614
604

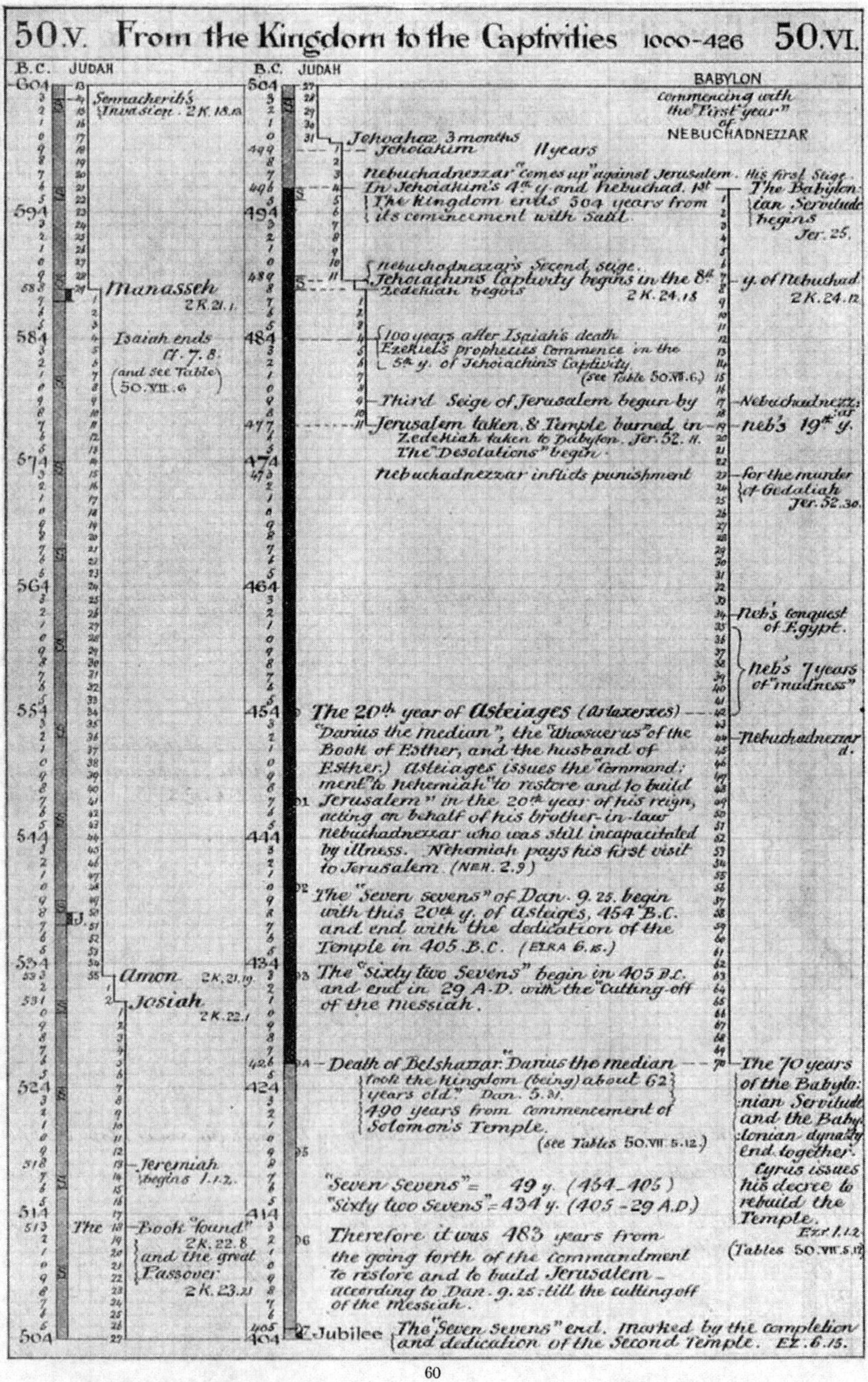
50.V. From the Kingdom to the Captivities 1000-426 50.VI.
B.C. JUDAH
B.C. JUDAH
BABYLON
Commencing with the "First year" of NEBUCHADNEZZAR
Sennacherib's Invasion. 2 K. 18.13
Manasseh 2 K. 21. 1.
Isaiah ends ch. 7. 8. (and see Table 50. VII. 6)
Amon 2 K. 21. 19.
Josiah 2 K. 22. 1
Jeremiah begins 1. 1. 2.
The "Book found" 2 K. 22. 8 and the great Passover 2 K. 23. 21
Jehoahaz 3 months
Jehoiakim 11 years
Nebuchadnezzar "comes up" against Jerusalem. His first Siege.
In Jehoiakim's 4th y. and Nebuchad. 1st
The Kingdom ends 504 years from its commencement with Saul.
The Babylonian Servitude begins Jer. 25.
Nebuchadnezzar's Second siege.
Jehoiachin's Captivity begins in the 8th y. of Nebuchad. 2 K. 24. 12
Zedekiah begins 2 K. 24. 18
100 years after Isaiah's death
Ezekiel's prophecies commence in the 5th y. of Jehoiachin's Captivity (see Table 50. VII. 6.)
Third Seige of Jerusalem begun by Nebuchadnezzar
Jerusalem taken & Temple burned in Neb's 19th y.
Zedekiah taken to Babylon. Jer. 52. 11.
The "Desolations" begin.
Nebuchadnezzar inflicts punishment for the murder of Gedaliah Jer. 52. 30.
Neb's conquest of Egypt.
Neb's 7 years of "madness"
The 20th year of Asteiages (Artaxerxes)
"Darius the Median", the "Ahasuerus" of the Book of Esther, and the husband of Esther.) Asteiages issues the "Commandment" to Nehemiah "to restore and to build Jerusalem" in the 20th year of his reign, acting on behalf of his brother-in-law Nebuchadnezzar who was still incapacitated by illness. Nehemiah pays his first visit to Jerusalem (NEH. 2. 9)
Nebuchadnezzar d.
The "Seven sevens" of Dan. 9. 25. begin with this 20th y. of Asteiages, 454 B.C. and end with the dedication of the Temple in 405 B.C. (EZRA 6. 15.)
The "Sixty two Sevens" begin in 405 B.C. and end in 29 A.D. with the "Cutting-off of the Messiah.
Death of Belshazzar: "Darius the Median took the Kingdom (being) about 62 years old." Dan. 5. 31.
490 years from commencement of Solomon's Temple. (see Tables 50. VII. 5. 12.)
The 70 years of the Babylonian Servitude and the Babylonian dynasty end together.
Cyrus issues his decree to rebuild the Temple. Ezr. 1. 1. 2. (Tables 50. VII. 5. 12)
"Seven Sevens" = 49 y. (454-405)
"Sixty two Sevens" = 434 y. (405 - 29 A.D)
Therefore it was 483 years from the going forth of the commandment to restore and to build Jerusalem - according to Dan. 9. 25: till the cutting off of the Messiah.
Jubilee
The "Seven sevens" end. Marked by the completion and dedication of the Second Temple. EZ. 6. 15.

50.VI From Ezra-Nehemiah to the destruction of Jerusalem 50.VI.

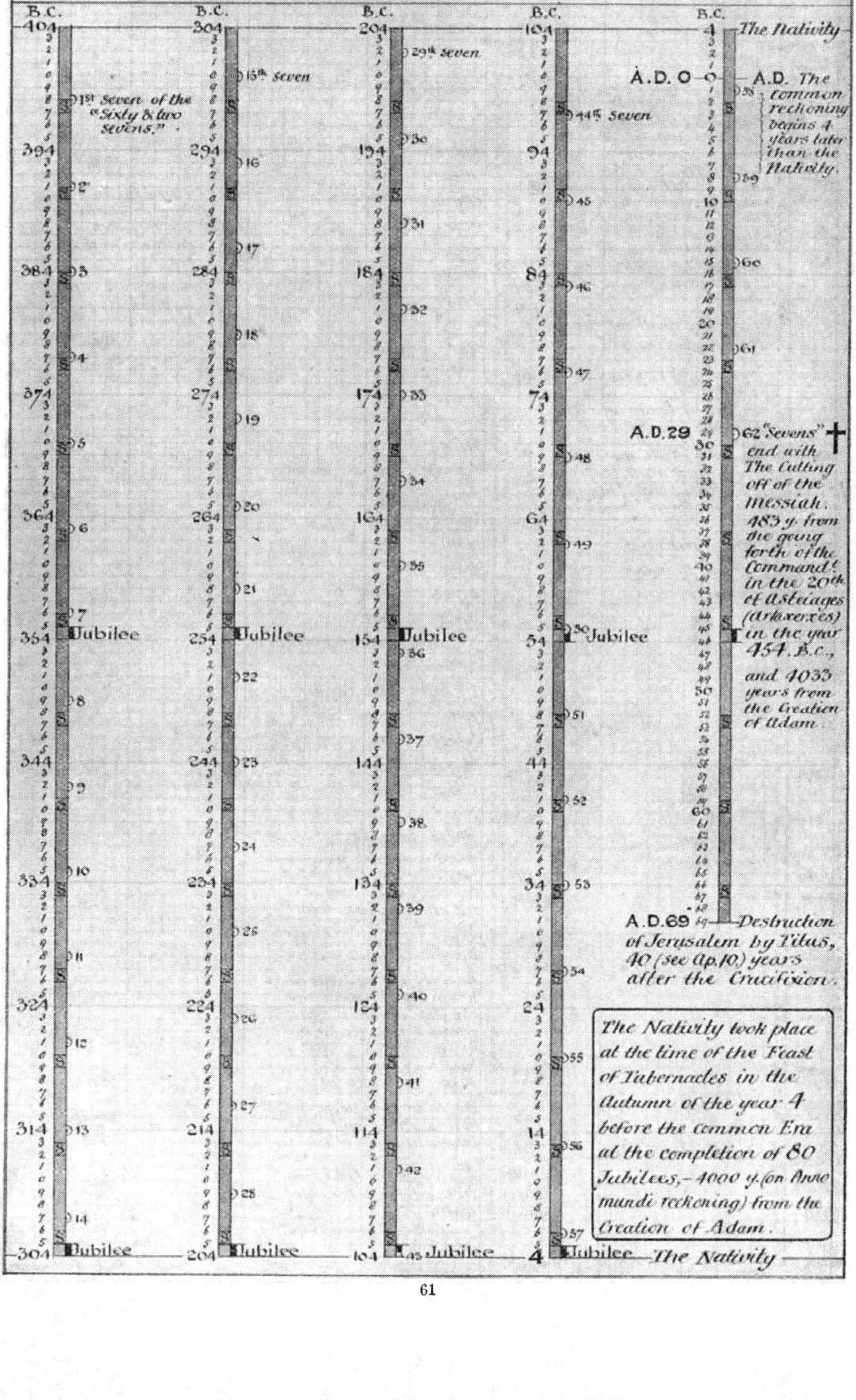

50.VII.(1) Details of the Exodus Week in 1491 B.C. 50.VII.(1)

ABIB 1491

14th — PASSOVER DAY (Midnight – Noon – Midnight)

End of the 3 days Darkness. Pharaoh's permission to "go" given & withdrawn. 10. 24-27.
Moses receives message of the last Plague in Pharaoh's presence; delivers it & goes out in a great anger. 11. 1-9
(Moses gives command re the Passover lamb during the morning.) 12. 6.
Passover lamb killed "in the evening." 12. 28.
"And they shall eat the flesh in that night."
"At midnight there was a great cry." 12. 29-30.

15th — 1st day of the week. An Holy Convocation.

On the morning after the Passover they "went out with an high hand in the sight of all the Egyptians, and while the Egyptians were burying their firstborn." Num. 33. 4
They "removed from Rameses and pitched in Succoth." Num. 33. 5.

16th — 2nd day of the week

"They took their Journey from Succoth" Ex. 13. 20.

17th — 3rd day of the week

on the way to Etham

ABIB 1491

18th — 4th day of the week

and "encamped in Etham in the edge of the Wilderness." Ex. 13. 20.
"It was told the King of Egypt that the People fled." (LXX says, πέφευγεν = had fled) .... and he made ready his chariot, ... & pursued after the Children of Israel." 14. 5, 8. (Pursuit begun.)

19th — 5th day of the week

They remove from Etham and turn again unto
Pharaoh's "Expeditionary Force" in hot pursuit.
"And he pursued." 14. 8.

20th — 6th day of the week

"Pihahiroth, between Migdol & the Sea."
The Pursuit continues. "And the Egyptians pursued after them." 14. 9
Speak unto the Child: of Isr: that they encamp before Pihahiroth". 14. 2. They pitched before Migdol." Num. 33. 7. till after the close of the next day, of "an Holy Convocation." No work, so no travelling.

21st — 7th day. An Holy Convocation

Last day of unleavened bread. "An Holy Convocation."
Pharaoh overtakes Israel encamped beside the Sea at Pihahiroth. 14. 9.
Israel sees Phar: drawing nigh, & cries unto Jehovah.
The Pillar of Cloud goes behind Israel "and stood behind them." 14. 9-20.
The Exodus takes place in the "First" & "Middle" watches 9 p.m. of the 21st till 3 a.m. of the 22nd. [14. 21, 22.
First Watch

ABIB 1491

22nd — 1st day of the 2nd week

Middle Watch. The Exodus ends.
"In the Morning Watch Jehovah troubled the Egyptians" 14. 24.
"When the morning appeared, the Lord overthrew the Egyptians in the midst of the Sea." 14. 27.
"And Israel saw the Egyptians dead upon the sea shore." 14. 30.
Moses' & the Childrens' Song of Praise

The "Watches", see Ap. 51. iv.

50.VII.(2) General Plan of the "Forty years." 50.VII.(2)

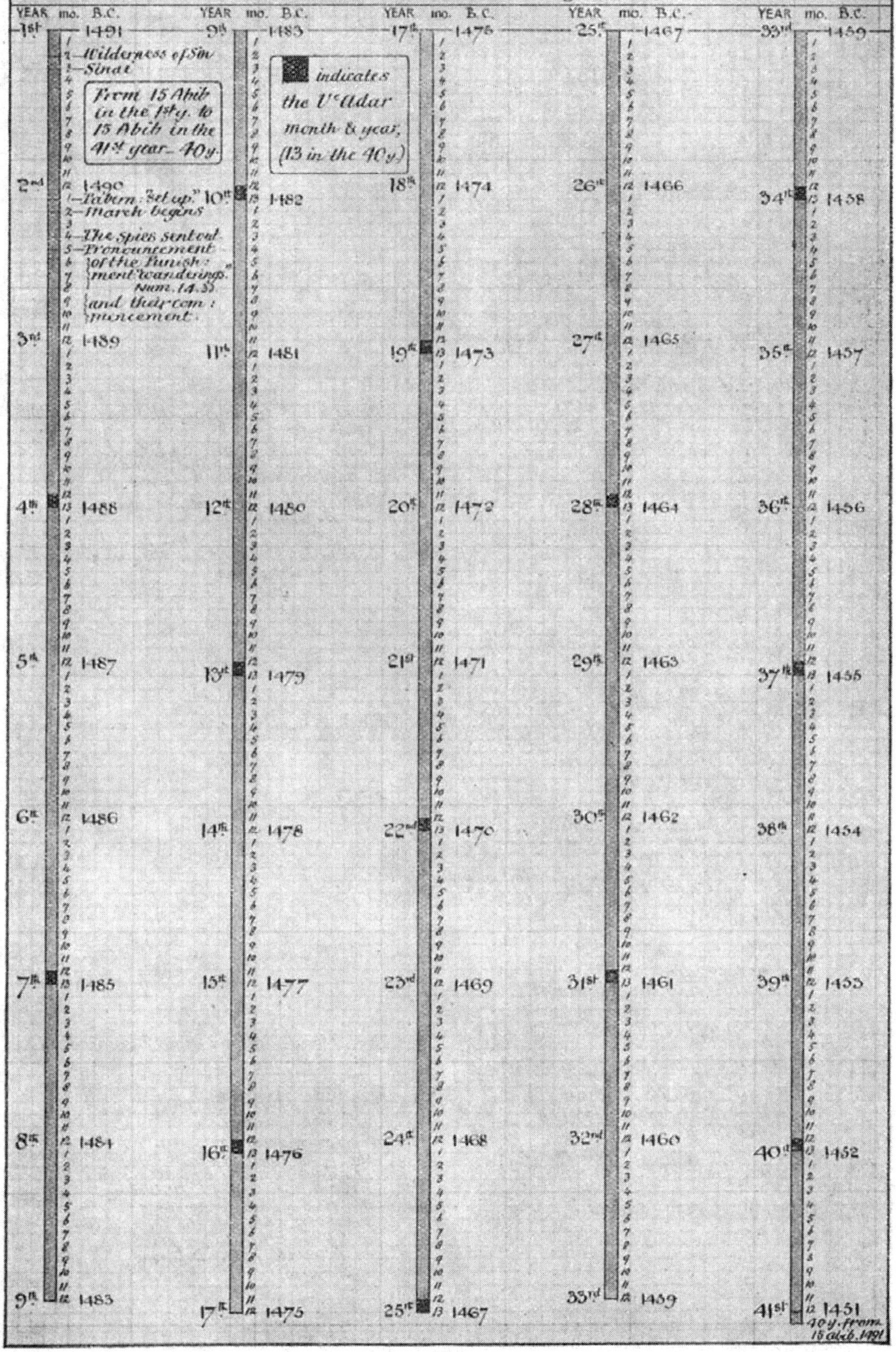

Details of the First two years 1491-1490

50. VII. (3)

1491 | 1491

"S" shows the Sabbaths

Month

- **1st** — 1. Abib. 30 d. (Exod. 13.4.) (called Nisan in Esther 3.7.)
- 10 — The Lamb "taken".
- 14 — The Passover instituted.
- S 15 — The Exodus begins; 430 y. from Genesis 12.4. cf. Exod: 12.40.
- 21 — They pass through the Red Sea. Bondage ends
- S 22 — and Resurrection life begins. Ex. 14 & 15.
- 25 — Marah. cf. Numb. 33. 8.
- 27 — Elim, where they dug 12 wells 15. 27. (and see note in loc.)
- S 29
- **2nd** — 30 — Zif. 29 d. (1 K. 6.1.)
- S 6
- S 13
- 15 — Wilderness of Sin. Quails at even 16. 1.
- 16 — The manna in the morning after 16. 13.
- 19 — On the 6th day they gathered double. 16.22.
- S 20 — "So the People rested on the 7th d." 16.30.
- 21 — "And they took their journey out of the wilderness of Sin & encamped in Dophkah." Num. 33.12.
- And they departed from Dophkah and encamped in Alush. 33.13.
- S 27
- 28 — And they departed from Alush & pitched in Rephidim, where was no water for the People to drink. 33.14.
- **3rd** — 29 — Sivan. 30 d. (Est. 8.9.)
- 4 — Water given in Horeb. Ex. 17.6.
- S 5 — Then came Amalek & fought with Israel. 17.8.
- And they departed from Rephidim and pitched in the Wilderness of Sinai — Ex. 19.1. Num. 33.15.
- S 12
- 16 — Moses begins his 6 "ascents" Ex. 19. 3.
- 17 — Sanctifies the People 19. 14.
- S 19 — "On the 3rd day" the LAW given 20. 1-17.
- 20–24 — "Six days" and the "Seventh", the "Glory of the Lord abode upon Mount Sinai." 24. 16.
- S 26 — Moses' First "40 days in the Mount" begins (ends on 6th AB.) 24. 18.
- **4th** — 30 — Thammuz. 29 d. (Ezekiel 8. 14.)
- S 3

Month

- S 10
- S 17
- S 24
- **5th** — 29 — Ab. 30 d.
- S 2
- 6 — Moses First "40 days in the Mount" ends 32.15
- 7 — The "Calf." 32. 1-28.
- S 9 — Moses "returned unto the Lord." 32. 31.
- 10–11 — Comes down again and pitches The "Tent" without the camp. 33. 7.
- 12–15 — The "cloudy Pillar" at the door of The "Tent". 33.7–34.3.
- S 16 — Moses "went up" and the Second "40 days in the Mount" begins (ends on 25th Elul.) 34.4.
- S 23
- **6th** — 30 — Elul. 29 d. (Neh: 6.15.)
- S 7
- S 14
- S 21
- 25 — The Second "40 days in the Mount" ends 34.29.
- S 28
- **7th** — 29 — Ethanim. 30 d. (1 K. 8.2.)
- 1 — The Tabernacle commenced. "Then wrought Bezaleel." 36. 1.
- The Tabernacle was set up on the 1st of Abib in the 2nd year. 177 days, exactly 6 months, from its commencement. Deducting the 25 Sabbaths, the time actually spent on the Construction until the day it was "reared up" on 1st Abib, 1490 B.C., was 152 days. 40. 17.
- S 5
- S 12

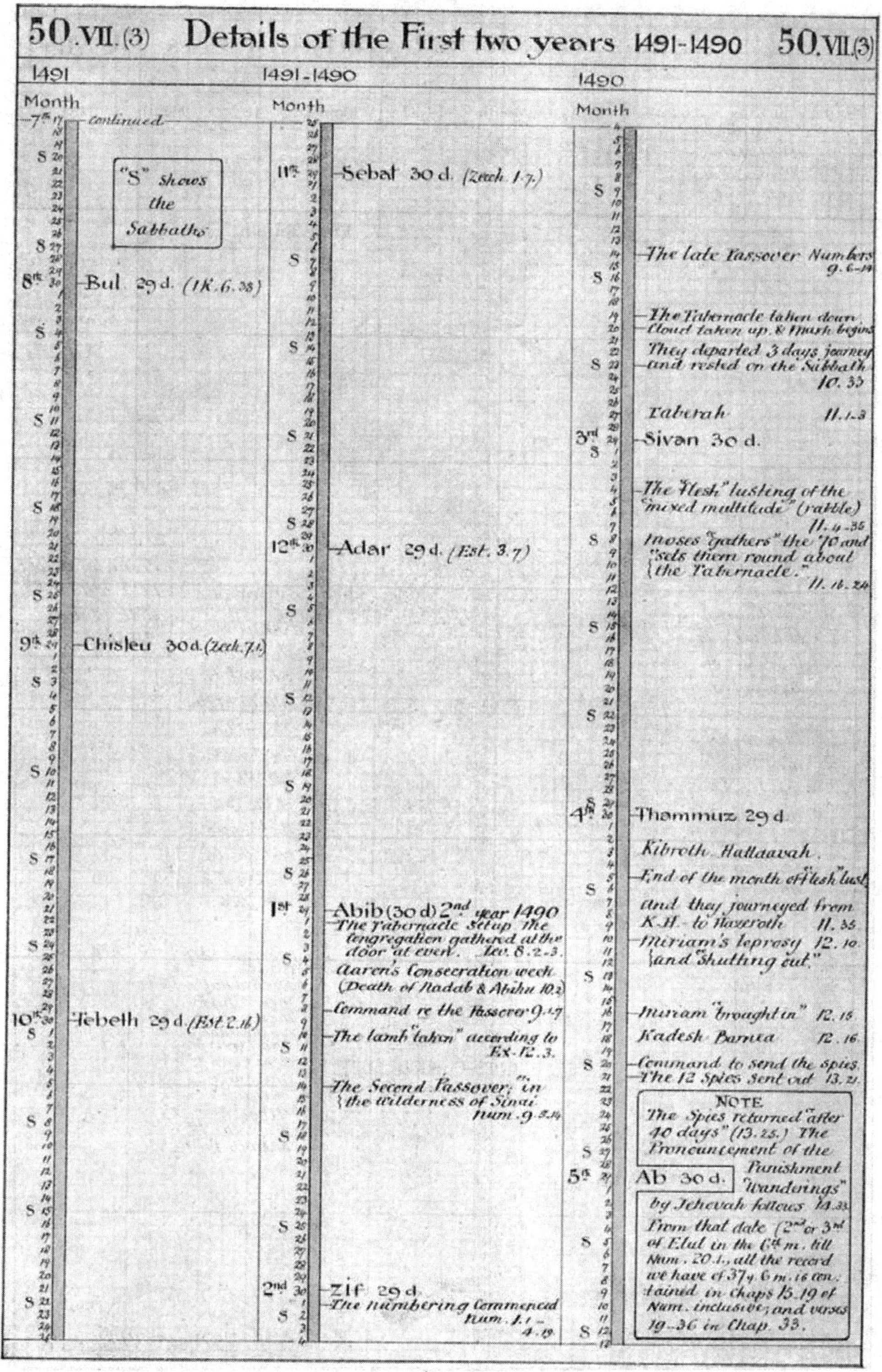
50. VII. (3) Details of the First two years 1491-1490 50. VII. (3)
1491
1491-1490
1490
Month
7th 17 continued
"S" shews the Sabbaths
8th 30 Bul 29 d. (1 K. 6. 38)
9th 29 Chisleu 30 d. (Zech. 7. 1)
10th 30 Tebeth 29 d. (Est. 2. 16)
11th 29 Sebat 30 d. (Zech. 1. 7)
12th 30 Adar 29 d. (Est. 3. 7)
1st 29 Abib (30 d) 2nd year 1490
The Tabernacle setup the congregation gathered at the door at even. Lev. 8. 2-3.
Aaron's Consecration week (Death of Nadab & Abihu 10. 2)
Command re the Passover 9. 1-7
The lamb "taken" according to Ex. 12. 3.
The Second Passover; "in the wilderness of Sinai." Num. 9. 5. 14
2nd 30 Zif 29 d.
The numbering commenced Num. 1. 1-4. 19
The late Passover Numbers 9. 6-14
The Tabernacle taken down Cloud taken up, & March begins
They departed 3 days journey and rested on the Sabbath 10. 33
Taberah 11. 1-3
3rd 29 Sivan 30 d.
The "Flesh" lusting of the "mixed multitude" (rabble) 11. 4-35
Moses "gathers" the "70 and "sets them round about the Tabernacle." 11. 16. 24
4th 30 Thammuz 29 d.
Kibroth Hattaavah.
End of the month of "Flesh" lust
And they journeyed from K.H. to Hazeroth 11. 35
Miriam's leprosy 12. 10 and "Shutting out."
Miriam "brought in" 12. 15
Kadesh Barnea 12. 16
Command to send the spies
The 12 Spies sent out 13. 21
NOTE The Spies returned "after 40 days" (13. 25.) The Pronouncement of the Punishment "wanderings" by Jehovah follows 14. 33. From that date (2nd or 3rd of Elul in the 6th m. till Num. 20. 1., all the record we have of 37 y. 6 m. 16 con: tained in chaps 15-19 of Num. inclusive; and verses 19-36 in Chap. 33.
5th 29 Ab 30 d.

50. VII. (4) Details of the Fortieth & Forty-first years 50. VII. (4)

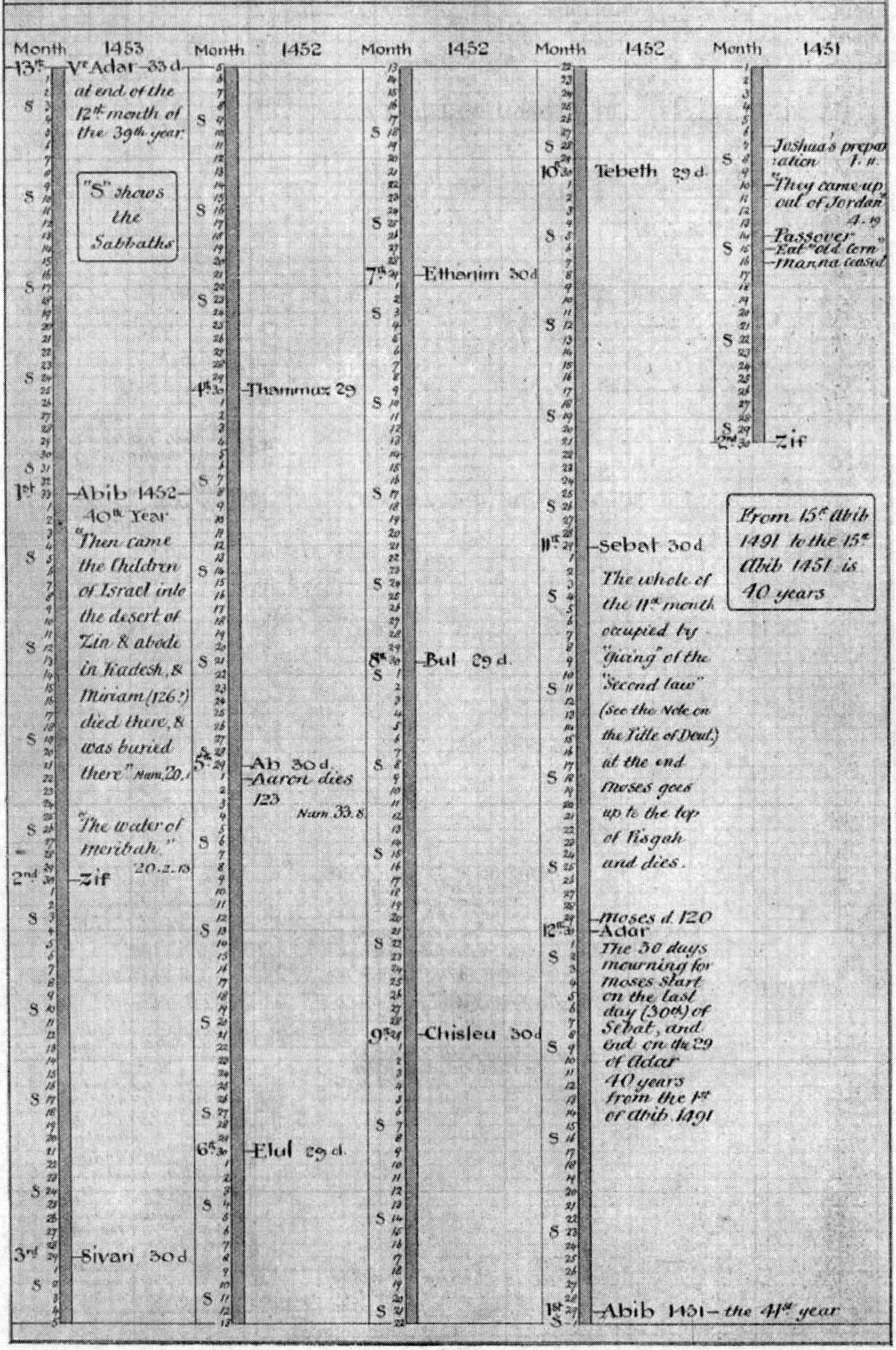

50 VII. (5) Details of the Ezra-Nehemiah Period. 50 VII. (5)

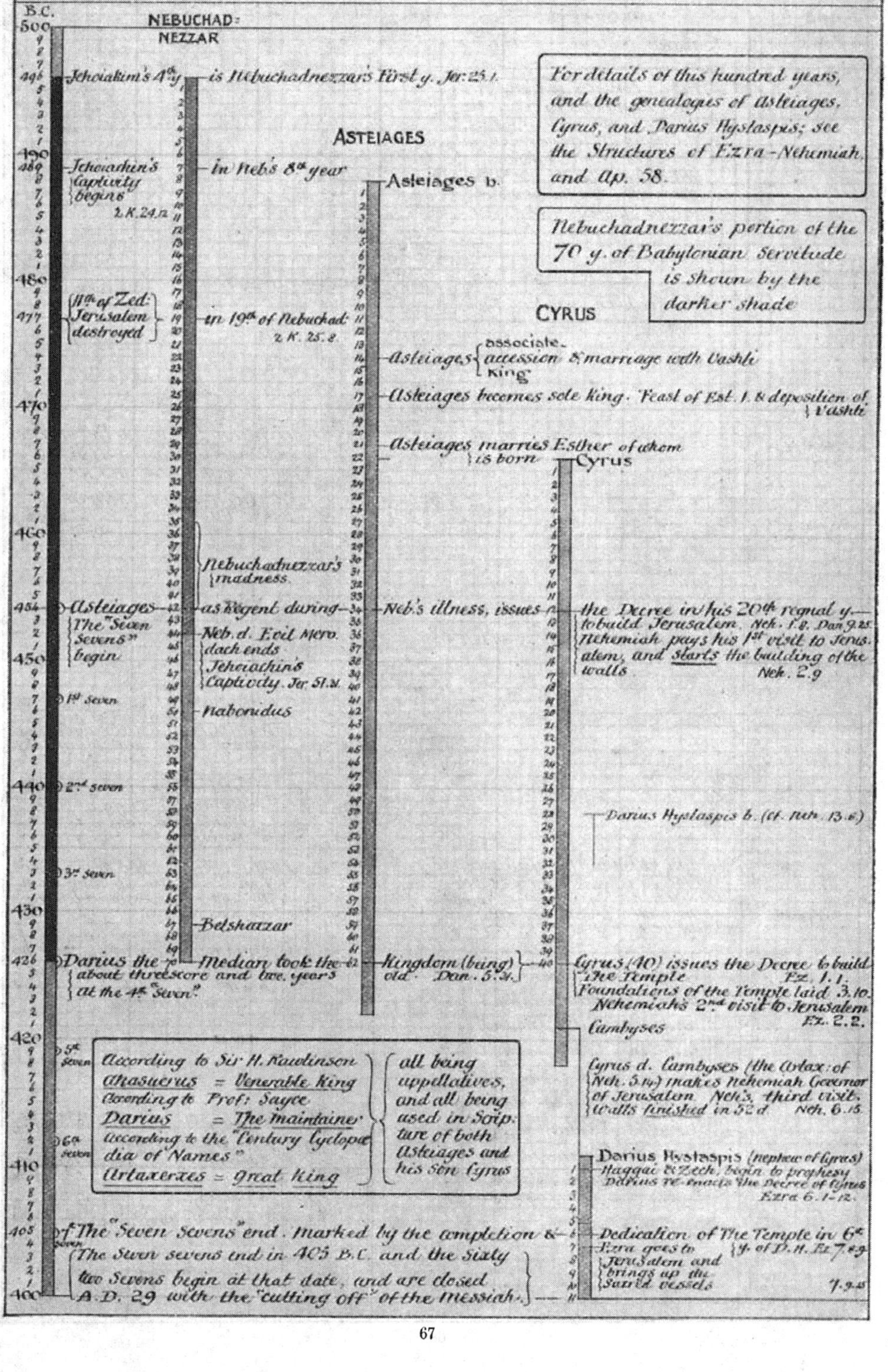
B.C.
NEBUCHAD-NEZZAR
ASTEIAGES
CYRUS
For details of this hundred years, and the genealogies of Asteiages, Cyrus, and Darius Hystaspis; see the Structures of Ezra-Nehemiah, and Ap. 58.
Nebuchadnezzar's portion of the 70 y. of Babylonian Servitude is shown by the darker shade
Jehoiakim's 4th y. — is Nebuchadnezzar's First y. Jer. 25.1.
Jehoiachin's Captivity begins 2 K. 24.12 — in Neb's 8th year
Asteiages b.
11th of Zed: Jerusalem destroyed — in 19th of Nebuchad: 2 K. 25.8.
Asteiages associate. accession King & marriage with Vashti
Asteiages becomes sole King. Feast of Est. 1. & deposition of Vashti
Asteiages marries Esther of whom is born Cyrus
Nebuchadnezzar's madness.
Asteiages The "Seven Sevens" begin — as Regent during — Neb's illness, issues — the Decree in his 20th regnal y. to build Jerusalem. Neh. 1.8. Dan 9.25. Nehemiah pays his 1st visit to Jerusalem, and starts the building of the walls Neh. 2.9
Neb. d. Evil Merodach ends Jehoiachin's Captivity. Jer. 51.31.
Nabonidus
1st Seven
2nd seven
Darius Hystaspis b. (cf. Neh. 13.6.)
3rd Seven
Belshazzar
Darius the Median took the Kingdom (being) about threescore and two years old Dan. 5.31. at the 4th "Seven".
Cyrus (40) issues the Decree to build The Temple Ez. 1.1. Foundations of the Temple laid 3.10. Nehemiah's 2nd visit to Jerusalem Ez. 2.2.
Cambyses
5th Seven
According to Sir H. Rawlinson Ahasuerus = Venerable King
According to Prof: Sayce Darius = The maintainer
according to the "Century Cyclopedia of Names" Artaxerxes = Great King
all being appellatives, and all being used in Scripture of both Asteiages and his Son Cyrus
Cyrus d. Cambyses (the Artax: of Neh. 5.14) makes Nehemiah Governor of Jerusalem. Neh's. third visit. Walls finished in 52 d. Neh. 6.15.
6th seven
Darius Hystaspis (nephew of Cyrus) Haggai & Zech. begin to prophesy Darius re-enacts the Decree of Cyrus Ezra 6.1-12.
of The "Seven Sevens" end. marked by the completion & Dedication of The Temple in 6th y. of D. H. Ez. 7.8,9.
Ezra goes to Jerusalem and brings up the Sacred vessels 7.9.15
The Seven sevens end in 405 B.C. and the Sixty two Sevens begin at that date, and are closed A.D. 29 with the "cutting off" of the Messiah.

50. VII. (6) Details of the Prophets and Kings 50. VII. (6)

KINGS	B.C.	PROPHETS
	650	
Uzziah d.	649	Isaiah's vision — Isa. 6. 1
Jotham 2 K. 15. 32	647	
	640	Hosea covers a longer period than any other prophet, viz. 73–77 years. He begins in the days of Jeroboam II. in 688 or 687 and continues till at least the 2nd or 3rd y. of Hezekiah. The language of Hos. 14 suggests the close of the Northern kingdom (611.)
	632	Micah begins?
Ahaz 2 K. 16. 1	631	
	630	
	620	
Hezekiah 2 K. 18. 1	617	
	615	Hosea ends?
Israel ends 2 K. 18. 11	611	
	610	
Sennacherib invades Judah in Hezekiah's 14th year 2 K. 18. 13	603	Micah ends? After 30 years as contemporary of Isaih and 18 with Hosea?
	600	
	590	
Manasseh 2 K. 21. 1.	588	
	584	Isaiah killed in the Manassean persecution (according to Jewish tradition) 65 years after the date of the vision "in the year that King Uzziah died." cf. Isa. 7. 8.
	580	
	570	A gap of 66 years intervenes between Isaiah and Jeremiah's Commencement in 518 B.C., in the 13th of Josiah: a period that is broken only one dated prophet Zephaniah, who comes in the early years of Josiah's reign.
	560	
	550	

KINGS	B.C.	PROPHETS
	550	
	540	
Amon 2 K. 21. 19		
Josiah 2 K. 22. 1	530	Zephaniah
	520	
	518	Jeremiah begins in 13th of Josiah and covers a period of 41 years ending with Zedekiah's 11th year.
Passover in Josiah's 18th year.		The Book "found" by Jeremiah's father Hilkiah (2 K. 22. 8 and cf. Jer. 15. 16.)
	510	
Jehoahaz	500	
Jehoiakim	499	
	497	Nebuchadnezzar takes Jerusalem &
	496	Daniel is taken to Babylon
Jehoiakim burns the Roll	495	Daniel begins, Nebuchadnezzar's dream of the "Great Image. 2. 1.
	490	Jeremiah had been prophesying for 23 years before Daniel was taken to Babylon.
Jehoiachin	489	
Zedekiah	488	
	484	Ezekiel begins. 100 years after Isaiah's d. and 30 years from Josiah's Passover, in which y. he was born.
	480	
	477	Jeremiah's prophecies end with the destruction of Jerusalem in the 11th y. of Zedekiah & the 19th of Nebuchadnezzar.
	470	
	464	25th y. Ezekiel's vision of the Millenial Temple 40-48
	462	27th y. Ezekiel's last date "the twenty-seventh year" of the captivity 29. 17.
	460	Ezekiel's prophecies cover 22 years, of which the first seven were contemporaneous with Jeremiah in Jerusalem, and Daniel in Babylon.
Astyages 20th year	454	
Neb. d.	452	
	450	

50.VII.(6) The Prophets and Kings (cont^d) 50.VII.(6)

KINGS	B.C.	PROPHETS
	450	
	9	
	8	
	7	
Nabonidus	446	
	5	
	4	
	3	
	2	
	1	
	440	
	9	
	8	
	7	
	6	
	5	
	4	
	3	
	2	
	1	
	430	
Belshazzar	429	Daniel's vision of the Four beasts.
	8	
	7	
Darius the Median Dan. 5.31.	426	"In the 3rd of Belshazzar" the Ulai vision; & "In the 1st of Darius" (i.e. Cyrus, see 50.VII.(5)) Daniel "understood by books" the 70 years of the Desolations, & receives the revelation of the "Seventy Sevens." Dan. 9. 1-27.
	5	
	424	In the 3rd of Cyrus the Hiddekel vision. Daniel's last date. 10.1.
	3	
	2	
Cambyses	421	
	420	
	9	
	8	
	7	
	6	
	5	
	4	
	3	
	2	
Darius Hystaspis	411	
	410	Haggai (1.1.) & Zechariah (1.1.) begin their prophecies.
	9	Darius Hyst: re-enacts the Decree of Cyrus Ezr. 6. 1-12.
	8	Zechariah's last date (7.1.)
	7	
	6	
	405	The Temple finished & dedicated in the 6th of Darius Hystaspis. Ez. 6.15.
	404	The Seven Sevens end and the Sixty & two Sevens begin, & end A.D. 29. — 404. Ezra goes up to Jerusalem with the Sacred vessels handed over to Nehemiah by Cyrus in 426. B.C. Ez. 1. 7-8.
	3	
	2	
	1	
	400	

Daniel's prophecies commence with the interpretation of Nebuchadnezzar's dream "in the 2nd y. of his reign" (in 495 B.C.) His last vision (Hiddekel) is dated, "in the 3rd y. of Cyrus." (i.e. in 424. B.C.) He therefore "continued" for 71 years, or 72 years from his deportation to Babylon.

The **Undated** prophets are not shown on the Charts.
Joel probably belongs to the close of Zedekiah's reign, & not to the period to which he is usually assigned, viz; Manasseh's time.
Amos is fixed by the earthquake which took place in Uzziah's reign.
Obadiah 11-14 suggests the destruction of Jerusalem. cf. Ps. 137.
Jonah & **Nahum** concern the Gentiles.
Habakkuk Just before the Captivity.
Malachi after the Restoration (cf. Neh. 13).

50.VII. (7. 8. 9. 10.) Examples of the Important Periods of 430, 450, 490, & 1000 50.VII. (7. 8. 9. 10.)

Years. (On Anno Mundi reckoning.)

(7) 430 years

	Years
1. From Abraham's "Call" to the Exodus,	430
2. From the 1st y. after the Entry into the Land till the "Reformation" (Sam)	430
3. From the 1st Servitude till the Kingdom (under Saul),	430
4. From Solomon's accession to the last year of Jehoiakim,	430
5. From the dedication of the Second Temple till the beginning of "the Ministry" of CHRIST,	430

(8) 450 years

1. From the 1st y. after the Entry into the Land till the close of the time of Samuel the prophet, and beginning of the Kingdom,	450
2. From the Decree of Asteiages (454) appointing Nehemiah "Tirshatha" (Ruler or Governor) till He came ...."Who is to be Ruler in Israel" (Mic 5.2.)	450

(9) 490 years

1. From Abraham's leaving Mesopotamia till the 1st Servitude (Mesopotamia),	490
2. From the "Tabernacle" to the Kingdom,	490
3. From the Kingdom to the beginning of Jehoiachin's Captivity year,	490
4. From Solomon's 4th year to the end of the Babylonian Servitude,	490
5. From the going forth of the "Command" in the 20th of Astiages till the end of the "70 Sevens",	490

(10) 1000 years

1. From Abraham's 2nd "Call" (in Haran) to Solomon's accession,	1000
2. From the y. the People should have entered the Land, until they went out of it in Jehoiachin's Captivity,	1000
3. From David's 1st anointing to the "Anointing" (at Baptism) of CHRIST,	1000

50.VII.(11) The "LO-AMMI" Periods. 50.VII.(11)

"Call his name LO-AMMI, for ye are not MY People." Hosea 1.9.

When Israel was regarded by Jehovah as "Lo-ammi," i.e. Not My People (cf. Hos 1.8, 21) then, Jehovah dealt with them on a different principle in recording time. During these periods their national history years are omitted from the years of the world's lifetime.

When they were Lo-ammi, the events recorded in the Scriptures, were recorded according to a reckoning we have termed Anno Dei (in GOD'S year) and not according to Anno mundi (in the year of the world) reckoning.

Herein is the key to a right understanding of Biblical Chronology; and it will be found, when rightly applied, to unlock many "difficulties" and to remove many supposed "discrepancies" between certain passages in Scripture.

1) *Between the year of the Entry into the Land, (1451. B.C.) & the end of Samuel's Judgeship — and the beginning of the Kingdom, — there are 5 Lo-ammi periods, during which Jehovah "sold" His People into the hand of their enemies. These periods are as follows, (See also 50.IV) Mesopotamia 8 years, Moab 18, Canaan 20, Midian 7, Philistine 40 =* **93 years.**

2) *In the Kingdom time, from Saul (1000 B.C) to Jehoiakim's 4th (496) (when the Kingdom had been "given" to Nebuchadnezzar in the beginning of Jehoiakim's reign, cf. Jer. 27.1-6.) there are 3 Lo-ammi periods viz:— Athaliah's 6 years of usurpation. The "gap" of 13 y. between Amaziah & Uzziah, and the "gap" of 1 year, shown by the "interlocking" regnal years [between Uzziah and Jotham* } **20 years**

113 "

3) *The Lo-ammi Babylonian Servitude Period. This is from the 4th of Jehoiakim = 1st of Neb.r, till the decree of Cyrus (426) =* **70 "**

To this must be added the years between the decree of Cyrus, and the dedication of the Temple, (405 B.C.) and the the restoration of the Temple worship at the Passover in the 7th y. of Darius Hyst. in 404. (Ezr. 6.15-19), viz: **21 "** } But — note Ezekiel 11.16.

204 years

Through taking the 480th y. of 1 K. 6.1., as an Anno Mundi date, instead of — as it is — on Anno Dei reckoning, — confusion has resulted all down the line, and many interesting and important facts escape notice in consequence. For instance, David's First anointing took place c. 1067 B.C., on supposed Anno Mundi reckoning; but the real Anno Mundi date is given in Chart 50 V. viz: 974. B.C., when David was 16 y. old, 917 years after Isaac became "The Seed" of Abraham, through whom was to come "THE SEED," and 1000 years from the "anointing" of Christ at the Jordan. A.D. 26. By noting the "LO-AMMI" periods, many other important details will come to light.

50 VII (12) "The going forth of the Commandment" Dan. 9.25. 50.VII.(12)

On "received" dates this commandment is generally assumed to be the decree of Cyrus, & its date 536. B.C. The date in Charts 50.VI. & VII.5., is 454. B.C., for the following reasons:—

1) *It falls in the last year of Nebuchadnezzar's "madness". Asteiages, his brother-in-law, (see Ap. 58) acting on his behalf; at the instance of Nehemiah, (Chaps 1 & 2) issues the decree to build JERUSALEM. (Asteiages = the Ahasuerus of Esther = the Artaxerxes of Neh. 1. = Darius the Median of Dan. 5.31 = the Ahasuerus of Dan 9.1. (See the Note on 50 VII. 5.)*

2) *The year 454 marks the close of 42 (7×6) years of the 70 of the Babylonian Servitude leaving 28 (7×4) years still to run. The Babylonian dynasty and the "Servitude" end together in 426 B.C., & the date is marked by the decree of Cyrus, the son of Asteiages & Esther, to rebuild the TEMPLE, in the same year that "Darius the Median (his father Asteiages) took the kingdom (being) about threescore & two years old." (Dan 5.31)*

3) *The "Seven Sevens," it will be seen (Charts 50.VI. & VII. 5.), begin with the "going forth of the Commandment" of Asteiages (to Nehemiah) in 454. B.C., and end with the dedication of the Second Temple in 405 B.C., in the 6th y. of Darius Hystaspis.*

The "Sixty two Sevens" then commence & close with the "cutting off of the Messiah" in A.D. 29. It will be noted that the Babylonian "Servitude" ends at the 4th "Seven."

50. VIII. SUMMARY OF PRINCIPAL EVENTS.

B.C.[1]

4004 Adam created.

3874 Seth b. "Adam begat a son in his own likeness" (Gen. 5. 3).

3769 Enos b.

3679 Cainan b.

3609 Mahalaleel b.

3544 Jared b.

3382 Enoch b. "seventh from Adam" (Jude 14).

3317 Methuselah b.

3194 Adam's "day of grace" begins when he is 810 (Gen. 6. 3).

3130 Lamech b.

3074 Adam d. (930).

3017 Enoch translated, fifty-seven years after Adam's d.

2962 Seth d. (912).

2948 Noah b.

2864 Enos d. (905).

2769 Cainan d. (910).

2714 Mahalaleel d. (895).

2582 Jared d. (962).

2448 Japheth b.

2447 Ham b.

2446 Shem b. (Noah 502).

2353 Lamech d. (777).

2348 Methuselah d. (969) in the first month of the Flood year.

2348 } 2347 } The Flood year. (Noah's 600th year. Gen. 7. 6, 11.)

2346 Arphaxad b. "two years after the Flood".

2311 Salah b.

2281 Eber b.

2247 Peleg b. "In his days the earth was divided" (Gen. 10. 25). See note on 50. II.

2217 Reu b.

2185 Serug b.

2155 Nahor b.

2126 Terah b.

2056 Terah's "generations" begin with the b. of Haran.

2008 Peleg d. (239).

2007 Nahor d. (148).

1998 Noah d. (950).

1996 Abraham b. (1,992 years from the Nativity).

1978 Reu d. (239).

1955 Serug d. (230).

1946? Abraham's First "Call", in Ur of the Chaldees (Acts 7. 2–4).

1921 Terah d. (205). Abraham's Second "Call" (Haran). The 430 years of the sojourning begin. (See note on Gen. 12. 1, and Ap. 50. III)

1920 to 1912 { Abraham goes down into Egypt. Attempted destruction of the Seed (see note on Gen. 12. 10, and Ap. 23).
Abraham returns from Egypt.

1911 Abraham (85) marries Hagar (Gen. 16. 3).

1910 Ishmael b. (Abraham 86).

1897 Covenant of Circumcision. (Abraham 99).

1896 Isaac b. (Abraham 100).

1891 Isaac becomes "the Seed" (Gen. 21, 10; 12. 7). Ishmael "cast out". The 400 years of Acts 7. 6 begin.

1878 Salah d. (433).

1863? Isaac (33) offered up.

1859 Sarah d. (127). The only woman whose age is given in Scripture. For significance of this, cp. Gal. 4. In Sarah's age we have, allegorically, the period of duration of the Old Covenant.

1856 Isaac (40) marries Rebekah.

1846 Shem (Melchizedek?) d. (600). Abraham (150) marries Keturah?

B.C.

1836 Jacob b. (Isaac 60).

1821 Abraham d. (Isaac 75. Jacob 15).

1817 Eber d. (464), outlives Abraham by four years.

1812? The famine of Gen. 26. 1. The cause of sale of the birthright?

1796 Esau (40) marries Hittite wives.

1773 Ishmael d. (137. Jacob 63).

1759 Jacob (77) gets the Blessing, and flees to Padan-aram.

1758 His "servitude" begins.

1752 His marriages.

1751 Reuben b.

1750 Simeon b.

1749 Levi and Dan b.

1748 Judah and Naphtali b.

1747 Gad b.

1746 Asher and Issachar b.

1745 Zebulun and Dinah (twins?) and Joseph b.

1742 Jacob's bargain about the cattle.

1739 Jacob flees from Padan-aram.

1738 " meets Esau.

1737 " at Succoth.

1736 " comes to Shechem.

1732 Dinah raped. Another attempt to destroy the "Seed", by raising the country against the "tribe". (Cp. Gen. 34. 30; 35. 5; and see Ap. 23.)

1731 Jacob at Beth-el.

1728 Rachel d. Benjamin b. Reuben forfeits the birthright to Joseph (17), to whom it rightly belonged. (Cp. 1 Chron. 5. 1, 2.)

} The six years of "Jacob's trouble" in the Land.

1727 Joseph sold (18).

1726 Jacob (110) joins his father Isaac (170) at Hebron (after a separation of thirty-three years).

1717 Joseph (28) in Egypt. Interprets butler's dream.

1716 Isaac d. (180. Jacob 120. Joseph 29).

1715 Joseph (30) interprets Pharaoh's dream.

1707 First year of the famine.

1706 Second year of the famine. Jacob (130) goes down into Egypt. The 215 years of the sojourning in Egypt begin. (Half of the 430 years from Gen. 12. 4.)

1705 Third year of the famine.

1704 Fourth year of the famine.

1703 Fifth year of the famine.

1702 Sixth year of the famine.

1701 Seventh year of the famine.

1689 Jacob d. (147), after seventeen years in Egypt. (Joseph 56. Benjamin 39.)

1635 Joseph d. (110).

1612 Levi d. (137).

1635 } 1571 } Gap of sixty-four years from d. of Joseph to b. of Moses.

1571 Moses b.

1544 Joshua b. (Moses 27).

1529 Caleb b.

1491 The Exodus. 430 years from Gen. 12. 4, and 400 years from Gen. 21. 10.

1490 The Tabernacle set up. This year the people *should* have entered the Land.

1452 Miriam, Aaron, and Moses d.

1451 Entry into the Land.

1444 The "Wars of the Lord" end (Josh. 14. 15). Caleb 85. Joshua hands over the leadership to Eleazar.

1444 } 1443 } First Sabbatic year.

1434 Joshua d. (110).

[1] That is, from the Common Era A.D.

B.C.			Years	Years
1431	First servitude	Mesopotamia		8
1423	Othniel		40	
1393 } 1392 }	First Jubilee year (*Anno Dei* reckoning).			
1383	Second servitude	Moab . .		18
1365	Ehud		80	
1285	Third servitude	Canaan		20
1265	Barak		40	
1225	Fourth servitude	Midian		7
1218	Gideon		40	
1178	Tola		23	
1155	Jair		4	
1151	Jephthah		6[1]	
1145	Ibzan		7	
1138	Elon		10	
1128	Abdon		8	
1120	Fifth servitude	Philistine .		40
			258	93

1080 Eli, 40 years.
1040 Samuel, 40 years.
1020 The "Reformation". 1 Sam. 7.
1000 Ends the 450 years of Acts 13. 20, and 490 years from the year they should have entered into the Land.
1000 THE KINGDOM. Saul, 40 years.
990 David b.
974 David's first anointing (16).
960 David, 40 years. Second anointing (30).
953 David's third anointing (37).
920 Solomon, 40 years.
917 The Temple begun. 573 years after the Exodus. (Cp. Acts 13. 20–23).
910 The Temple finished.
897 At the end of twenty years, the "two houses" finished (1 Kings 9. 10).
880 The Disruption. Rehoboam, 17 years.
863 Abijam, 3 years.
860 Asa, 41 years.
819 Jehoshaphat, 25 years.
796 Jehoram's accession.
794 Jehoshaphat d.
789 Ahaziah's accession.
788 Ahaziah slain by Jehu.
788 } 782 } Gap, 6 years. Athaliah's usurpation.
782 Jehoash, 41 years.
743 Amaziah, 29 years.
714 Amaziah ends.
714 } 701 } Gap, 13 years.
701 Uzziah, 52 years.
687 *Hosea's* prophecies begin.?
649 { Uzziah d. *Isaiah's* vision in chap. 6. Gap. One year between Uzziah's death and Jotham's accession.
647 Jotham, 16 years.
634 *Micah's* prophecies begin?
632 Ahaz, 16 years.
617 Hezekiah's accession.
616 Ahaz d.
615 *Hosea* ends?
613 Siege of Samaria begun.
611 Samaria taken and Israel ends.
603 Sennacherib invades Judah in the fourteenth year of Hezekiah (2 Kings 18. 13).

1 (300 years from the entry into the Land. See note on chart 50. IV.)

B.C.
588 Manasseh, 55 years.
584 Isaiah killed? (Cp. Isa. 7. 6).
533 Amon, 2 years.
531 Josiah, 31 years.
530 *Zephaniah*?
518 *Jeremiah's* prophecies begin in Josiah's thirteenth year.
513 The Book "found" and the Passover in Josiah's eighteenth year.
500 Jehoahaz, 3 months.
499 Jehoiakim, 11 years.
497 Nebuchadnezzar's first siege of Jerusalem.
496 Jehoiakim's fourth year, Nebuchadnezzar's first. *Daniel* taken to Babylon.
495 Jehoiakim burns the roll.
494 Nebuchadnezzar's second year. His dream of the Great Image. *Daniel* interprets.
489 Jehoiachin, 3 months. Captivity begins in Nebuchadnezzar's eighth year (second siege).
488 Zedekiah, 11 years.
484 *Ezekiel's* prophecies begin.
478 Nebuchadnezzar's third siege of Jerusalem begins.
477 { Jerusalem taken and Temple destroyed in Nebuchadnezzar's nineteenth year. *Jeremiah* ends.
473 Punishment for the murder of Gedaliah (Jer. 52. 30).
462 *Ezekiel's* last dated prophecy.
461 } 454 } Nebuchadnezzar's seven years of "madness".
454 Twentieth year of Asteiages (Artaxerxes). The commandment to rebuild Jerusalem. (See 50. VI, VII. 5, 12.) Nehemiah's first visit to Jerusalem.
452 Nebuchadnezzar d. after forty-four years' reign.
452 Evil-Merodach. Jehoiachin's captivity ends.
446 Nabonidus.
429 Belshazzar, 3 years.
426 { Belshazzar slain. "Darius the Median" (Asteiages) takes the kingdom. Cyrus (Asteiages' son) issues the Decree to rebuild the Temple. *Daniel's* vision of the "seventy sevens". The "seven sevens" begin. Foundations of the Temple laid. Nehemiah's second visit to Jerusalem.
421 Cyrus ends.
418 Cambyses makes Nehemiah governor. Nehemiah's third visit to Jerusalem.
411 Darius Hystaspis re-enacts the decree of Cyrus.
410 *Haggai* and *Zechariah* begin. The Temple superstructure commenced and carried on to completion, from the second to the sixth year of Darius.
408 *Zechariah's* last date.
405 The Temple finished and dedicated. The "seven sevens" end, and the "sixty-two sevens" commence.
404 The Passover.
403 *Ezra's* last date: 1st of Nisan.
375? Darius Hystaspis d. (according to Herodotus, 63 years old).
4 The Nativity.

A.D.
0 The Common Era of A.D.
29 The "sixty-nine sevens" end with the "cutting off of the Messiah", 483 years from the "going forth of the commandment to build Jerusalem" in 454 B.C.
69 Destruction of Jerusalem by Titus.

51 MONEY AND COINS, WEIGHTS AND MEASURES.

I. MONEY AND COINS.

1. **Dram** (Old Testament).
   (1.) 'Adarkōn (Heb.). (1 Chron. 29. 7. Ezra 8. 27.)
   (2.) Dark^emōn (the Persian Daric). (Ezra 2. 69. Neh. 7. 70, 71, 72.) A gold coin, value £1 2*s.* 0*d.*, or $5.28.

2. **Farthing** (New Testament).
   (1.) Kodrantes (Matt. 5. 26. Mark 12. 42). A bronze coin, value ¾ of a farthing, or ⅜ of a cent.
   (2.) Assarion (Matt. 10. 29. Luke 12. 6). A bronze coin, value about 3 farthings, or 1·5 cents.

3. **Mite** (New Testament). (Mark 12. 42. Luke 12. 59; 21. 2.) Lepton, a copper coin, value ⅜ of a farthing, or 3/16 of a cent.

4. **Penny** (New Testament), so rendered in fourteen of the sixteen occurrences of *Dēnarion.* A silver coin, value 8½*d.*, or 17 cents. Generally plural, is twice rendered "pennyworth." (Mark 6. 37. John 6. 7.)

5. **Piece of Money** (Matt. 17. 27). Gr. Stater, a silver coin, value 2*s.* 8*d.*, or 64 cents.

6. **Piece of Silver.** In Old Testament usually = a shekel of silver (see Weights), or may mean uncoined silver in 1 Sam. 2. 36. Ps. 68. 30. Josh. 24. 32. Job 42. 11.
   In New Testament:—
   (1.) Argurion (Matt. 26. 15; 27. 3, 5, 9. Acts 19. 19). Value 2*s.* 8*d.*, or 64 cents.
   (2.) Drachmē (Luke 15. 8, 9). Cp. IV, above. Value 8½*d.*, or 17 cents.

7. **Silver Piece.** Gr. Argurion (Matt. 27. 6). See VI. 1, above.

8. **Tribute Money.** (New Testament.) (Matt. 17. 24.)
   (1.) Didrachmon, a double Drachmē, see VI. 2, above. A silver coin, value 1*s.* 4*d.*, or 32 cents.
   (2.) Kēnsos (Matt. 22. 19). Latin *census* = a poll-tax.

II. WEIGHTS.

1. **Bekah.** Heb. *beḳ'a* (Ex. 38. 26) = half a shekel (see V, below). Weight about 5 drams, Avoirdupois.

2. **Gerah.** Heb. *gērāh* (Ex. 30. 13. Lev. 27. 25. Num. 3. 47). Weight 1/20 of a shekel, or about ½ a dram, Avoirdupois.

3. **Maneh.** Heb. *māneh* (Ezek. 45. 12). See "Pound" (IV, 1), below.

4. **Pound.**
   (1.) Maneh. Heb. *māneh* (1 Kings 10. 17. Ezra 2. 69. Neh. 7. 71, 72). Weight = 100 shekels (cp. 1 Kings 10. 17 with 2 Chron. 9. 16).
   (2.) Mna. Gr. Lat. *mina* (Luke 19. 13, 16, 16, 18, 18, 20, 24, 24, 25). Weight about 16 ozs., Avoirdupois.
   (3.) Litra. Gr. Lat. *libra* (John 12. 3; 19. 39). Weight about 12 ozs., Avoirdupois.

5. **Shekel.** Heb. *shekel* (Ex. 30. 13, and frequently). Weight about 10 drams, Avoirdupois.
   There is the shekel of the sanctuary (Ex. 30. 13), and the shekel of the king (2 Sam. 14. 26). Their precise relative weights unknown.

6. **Talent** (Ex. 25. 39, and frequently).
   (1.) Heb. *kikkar.* Weight = 3,000 shekels of the sanctuary (Ex. 38. 25, 26).
   Talent of the king = 158 lb. Troy.
   Talent of gold = 131 lb. Troy. About £6,150; $290,85.
   Talent of silver = 117 lb. Troy.
   (2.) Gr. *talantos* (in N. T.). About 114 lb. Avoirdupois.

III. MEASURES.

1. DISTANCE.
   (1.) **Day's journey.** About 30 English miles.
   (2.) **Furlong.** Gr. *stadios* (Luke 24. 13. John. 6. 19; 11. 18. Rev. 14. 20; 21. 16). About 202 English yards.
   (3.) **Mile.** Gr. *mileon* (Matt. 5. 41). About 1,616 English yards.
   (4.) **Pace.** Heb. *ẓa'ad* (2 Sam. 6. 13). Rather more than an English yard.
   (5.) **Sabbath day's journey.** About 2,000 English yards.

2. LENGTH.
   (1.) **Cubit.** Length still in dispute.
   (a) Heb. *'ammāh.* Ranging between 21 and 25 inches.
   (b) Heb. *yomed* (only in Judg. 3. 16).
   (2.) **Fathom.** Gr. *orguia.* The length of the arms outstretched = about six feet (Acts 27. 28).
   (3.) **Reed.** Heb. *ḳāneh* (Ezek. 40 and 41). About 6 cubits, or about 3½ English yards.
   (4.) **Span.** Heb. *zereth* (Ex. 28. 16; 39. 9. 1 Sam. 17. 4. Isa. 40. 12. Ezek. 43. 13). About half a cubit, or about 10½ inches.

3. CAPACITY.
   (1.) **Bath.** Heb. *bāth* (1 Kings 7. 26, 38. 2 Chron. 2. 10; 4. 5. Ezra 7. 22. Isa. 5. 10. Ezek. 45. 10, 11, 14). About 6 English gallons (liquid).
   (2.) **Bushel.** Gr. *modios* (Matt. 5. 15. Mark 4. 21. Luke 11. 33). About 1 peck, English.
   (3.) **Cab.** Heb. *ḳab* (2 Kings 6. 25). About 1 quart, English dry measure.
   (4.) **Cor.** Heb. *kor* (Ezek. 45. 14). About 8 bushels.
   (5.) **Ephah.** Heb. *'ephāh* (Ex. 16. 36. Lev. 5. 11; 6. 20; 19. 36. Num. 5. 15; 28. 5. Judg. 6. 19. Ruth 2. 17. 1 Sam. 1. 24; 17. 17. Isa. 5. 10. Ezek. 45. 10, 11, 13, 24; 46. 5, 7, 11, 14. Amos 8. 5. Zech. 5. 6, 8). About 3 pecks, English.
   (6.) **Firkin.** Gr. *metrētēs* (John 2. 6). About 9 gallons, English liquid measure.
   (7.) **Half homer.** Heb. *letheḥ* (Hos. 3. 2). About 4 bushels.
   (8.) **Hin.** Heb. *hīn* (Ex. 29. 40; 30. 24. Lev. 19. 36; 23. 13. Num. 15. 4, 5, 6, 7, 9, 10; 28. 5, 7, 14. Ezek. 4. 11; 45. 24; 46. 5, 7, 11, 14). About 1 gallon, liquid measure.
   (9.) **Homer.** Heb. *chomer* (Lev. 27. 16. Num. 11. 32. Isa. 5. 10. Ezek. 45. 11, 11, 11, 13, 13, 14, 14. Hos. 3. 2) = 10 ephahs. Cp. No. 12. See No. 5, above. About 8 bushels, English.
   (10.) **Log.** Heb. *log* (Lev. 14. 10, 12, 15, 21, 21). About ⅔ of a pint, liquid measure.
   (11.) **Measure.** The rendering of six Hebrew and four Greek words:
   (1) *'ēyphah* (Deut. 25. 14, 15. Prov. 20. 10. Micah 6. 10), measure. See No. 5, above.
   (2) *Cor.* Heb. *kor* (1 Kings 4. 22; 5. 11. 2 Chron. 2. 10; 27. 5. Ezra 7. 22). See No. 4, above).
   (3) *Mādad.* Used of any hollow measure: of capacity as well as of length = to mete out.
   (4) *Mesūrah* (Lev. 19. 35. 1 Chron. 23. 29. Ezek. 4. 11, 16). A measure of liquids.
   (5) *Se'āh* (Gen. 18. 6. 1 Sam. 25. 18. 1 Kings 18. 32. 2 Kings 7. 1, 16, 18. Isa. 27. 8). About 1 peck.
   (6) *Shālīsh* (Ps. 80. 5. Isa. 40. 12) = a third. Probably the third part of an ephah. See No. 5, above.
   (7) *Batos* (Gr.), same as Heb. *bāth* (Luke 16. 6). About 6 gallons (liquid).

(8) *Koros* (Gr.), same as Heb. *cor* (Luke 16. 7). See No. 4, above.

(9) *Saton* (Gr.), same as Heb. *sᵉ'āh*. (Matt. 13. 33. Luke 13. 21.) See No. 7, above.

(10) *Chœnix* (Gr.) (Rev. 6. 6). An Attic dry measure: the daily allowance of corn for a slave, about 1 quart (dry).

(12.) **Omer.** Heb. *'omer* (Ex. 16. 16, 18, 22, 32, 33, 36). The 1/10 of ephah. Cp. Ezek. 45. 11.

(13.) **Tenth deal.** Heb. *'isārōn* (Ex. 16. 36; 29. 40. Lev. 14. 10, 21; 23. 13, 17; 24. 5. Num. 15. 4, 6, 9; 28. 9, 13, 20, 28; 29. 3, 4, 9, 10, 14, 15). About ½ a gallon (dry).

4. TIME.

(1.) **Beginning of the Watches** (Lam. 2. 19). About 9 p.m.

(2.) **Cock-crowing** (Mark 13. 35). There were two: one after midnight, and one before dawn. Both are mentioned in Mark 14. 30. The latter was "THE" cock-crowing.

(3.) **Cool of the Day** (Gen. 3. 8). From about 2 to about 6 p.m.

(4.) **Day.** Reckoned from sunset to sunset.

(5.) **Eleventh Hour** (Matt. 20. 6, 9). About 5 p.m.

(6.) **Fourth Watch** (Matt. 14. 25). From about 3 a.m. till about 6 a.m.

(7.) **Heat of the Day** (Gen. 18. 1). From about 10 a.m. till 2 p.m.

(8.) **Middle Watch** (Judg. 7. 19). From about midnight till about 3 a.m.

(9.) **Morning Watch** (Ex. 14. 24). From about 3 a.m. till 6 a.m.

(10.) **Night.** The natural night was from sunset to sunrise.

(11.) **Ninth hour** (Matt. 20. 5; 27. 45, 46. Mark 15. 33, 34. Luke 23. 44. Acts 3. 1; 10. 3. 30). About 3 p.m.

(12.) **Second Watch** (Luke 12. 38). About 9 to 12 p.m.

(13.) **Seventh hour** (John 4. 52). About 1 p.m.

(14.) **Sixth hour** (Matt. 20. 5; 27. 45. Mark 15. 33. Luke 1. 26, 36; 23. 44. John 4. 6; 19. 14. Acts 10. 9). About 12 midday.

(15.) **Tenth hour** (John 1. 39). About 4 p.m.

(16.) **Third hour** (Matt. 20. 3. Mark 15. 25. Acts 2. 15; 23. 23). About 9 a.m.

(17.) **Third Watch** (Luke 12. 38). From about midnight till about 3 a.m.

(18.) **Watch.** Three hours.

Old Testament.

First Watch, 9 p.m. till midnight.
Middle Watch, midnight till 3 a.m.
Morning Watch, 3 a.m. till 6 a.m.

New Testament.

First Watch, 6 p.m. to 9 p.m.
Second Watch, 9 p.m. to midnight.
Third Watch, midnight to 3 a.m.
Fourth Watch, 3 a.m. to 6 a.m.

5. THE JEWISH MONTHS.

N.B. The Civil months are six months later than the Sacred months.

SACRED MONTH.	NAME OF MONTH.	CORRESPONDING ENGLISH MONTH.		FESTIVAL OF MONTH.
I.	Abib, or Nisan.	April.	14th day.	The Passover.
			16th day.	Firstfruits of Barley Harvest presented.
II.	Zif.	May.	14th day.	Second Passover, for those who could not keep the first.
III.	Sivan.	June.	6th day.	Pentecost, or Feast of Weeks.
				Firstfruits of Wheat harvest, and Firstfruits of all the ground.
IV.	Thammuz.	July.		
V.	Ab.	August.		
VI.	Elul.	September.		
VII.	Tisri, or Ethanim.	October.	1st day.	Feast of Trumpets.
			10th day.	Day of Atonement.
			15th day.	Feast of Tabernacles.
				Firstfruits of Wine and Oil.
VIII.	Bul.	November.		
IX.	Chisleu.	December.	25th day.	Feast of Dedication.
X.	Tebeth.	January.		
XI.	Shebat.	February.		
XII.	Adar.	March.	14th and 15th days.	Feast of Purim.

52

PROPER NAMES.

A great latitude has to be allowed in any attempt to indicate the correct pronunciation of the Proper Names in the Bible.

Our knowledge of their original pronunciation is imperfect; and names have undergone changes in becoming transliterated from one language into another.

Custom also has in many cases sanctioned a pronunciation which, while incorrect according to the original languages, is yet so universal that any interference with it would be pedantic, not to say intolerable.

Again, we sometimes meet with a varying pronunciation of the same name in different English-speaking countries. Thus, an exhaustive list of Biblical names, with a perfect and final system of syllabification and pronunciation, is not practicable.

There are, however, a certain number of names too uncommon for custom to have fixed their pronunciation, and hence, generally acknowledged to present difficulties to the general reader.

Some 250 of these are here gathered together, and presented in alphabetical order, with such division of syllables and accentuation as approximate to the original tongues, and will serve as a guide to their more or less correct pronunciation.

The hyphen (-) marks the division of syllables, and the accent (′) the syllable to be emphasised.

It has been thought better to present them in an Appendix, and in one list, than to burden the text with an innumerable variety of hyphens and accents, which, while attempting to remove one difficulty, would introduce a greater.

A-bed′ne-gó.
A′bel-beth-ma′a-cha.
Ab-i-al′bon.
A-bi-le′ne.
Ab-i-sha′lom.
A-cel′da-ma.
A-chai′a.
A-cha′i-cus.
Ada′dah.
A-da′iah.
Ad-i-tha′īm.
A-do′ni-be′zek.
A-do′ni-ze′dek.
Ad′ram-me′lech.
Ad-ra-myt′ti-um.
A-gee′.
A-has-u-e′rus.
A-hi-e′zer.
A-hi-sa′mach.
A-hi-sha′har.
A-hi-tho′phel.
A′holi-ba′mah.
A′iah.
A′lam-me′lech.
Al′mon-dib-la-tha′īm.
Am-mi-shad′dai.
Am-mi-za′bad.
A-na′har′ath.
A′nam-me′lech.
An-dro-ni′cus.
A-pel′les.
A-phar′sa-chites.
A-phar-sath′chites.
Ap′phi-a.
Aq′ui-la.
Ar-che-la′us.
Ar′che-vites.
A-re-o-pa′gus.
Ar-is-to-bu′lus.
Ar-tax-er′xes.
A-sar-e′lah.
As-nap′per.
A-syn′cri-tus.

Ba′al-sha-li′sha.
Ba-ase′iah.
Bak′bu-kiah.
Ba′rach-el.
Be-el-ia′da.
Be′er-la-hai′-ro′i.
Bel-te-shaz′zar.
Ber-ni′ce.
Be-ro′dach-ba′la-dan.
Be-so′de-iah.
Beth-bi′re-i.
Beth-dib-la-tha′īm.
Beth-hac-ce′rem.
Be-zal′e-el.
Biz-joth′jah.
Bo′che-ru.

Can-da′ce.
Cap-pa-do′ci-a.
Car′che-mish.
Ca-siph′i-a.
Cas-lu′hīm.
Cen′chre-a.
Cha-ra′shīm.
Char′che-mish.
Che-dor′la-o′mer.
Che-ma′rīm.
Che-na′a-nah.
Che-nan′iah.
Che′phar-ha-am-mo′nai.
Chu′shan-rish-a-tha′īm.
Col-ho′zeh.
Co-nan′iah.

Dab-ba′sheth.
Dal-ma-nu′tha.
Di-o-nys′i-us.
Di-ot′re-phes.

Eb-i-a′saph.
El-ea′-leh′.
El-ea′sah′.
Ele-a′zar′.
E-li-e′nai.
El-iho-e-na′-i.
E-li-ho′reph.
El-io-e′nai.
E-li-pha′let.
E-li′-phe-leh′.
E-li-phe′let.
E-li-sha′phat.
En-eg-la′īm.
E-pæ′ne-tus.
Ep′a-phras.
E-paph-ro-di′tus.
E-phes-dam′mīm.
Eu-bu′lus.
Eu-ni′ce.
Eu-o′di-as.
Eu-roc′ly-don.
Eu′ty-chus.

Ge-de-ro-tha′īm.
Ge-mar′iah.
Gen-nes′a-ret.
Ger′ge-senes′.
Gi-la′lai.
Ha-a-hash-ta′ri.
Ham-me-da′tha.
Ham-mo-le′keth.
Ha-nam′e-el.
Ha-nan′e-el.
Ha-ru′maph.
Ha-se-nu′ah.
Hash-ba-da′na.
Has-sen-a′ah.
Ha-ze-lel′-po-ni.
Her-mog′e-nes.
Hi-e-rap′o-lis.
Ho-dav′iah.
Hor-ha-gid′gad.
Ho-ro-na′īm.

Ib′ne-iah.
I′ge-al.
I′je-aba′rīm.
Il-ly′ri-cum.
Iph′e-de-iah.
Ish′bi-be-nob′.
Ish′bo-sheth.
Ish-ma′iah.
Iz-e-ha′rites.

Ja-a-ko′bah.
Ja′a-re-o′re-gīm.
Ja-a-zan′iah.
Ja-i′rus.
Ja-sho′be-am.
Ja-shu′bi-le′hem.
Ja′son.
Je-ber-e-chi′ah.
Je-di′a-el.
Jed-i-di′ah.
Je′gar-sa-ha-du′tha.
Je′hal′e-lel.
Je-ho-ia′rib.
Je-hu-di′jah.
Je′rub-be′sheth.
Je-shar-e′lah.
Je-sheb′e-ab.
Je-sho-ha′iah.
Jo-ia′rib.
Jo′nath-e′lem-recho′kīm.
Josh-be-ka′shah.
Ju′shab-he′sed.

Kar′ka-a.
Ke-he-la′thah.
Kib-roth′-hat-ta′-a-vah′.
Kir-ha-re′seth.
Kir-ia-tha′īm.

La-hai'roi.
La-o-di-ce'a.
Lyc-a-o'ni-a.

Ma-a-cha'thi.
Ma'a-leh-ac-rab'bim.
Ma-a-se'iah.
Ma-as'i-ai.
Mach-nad'e-bai.
Ma-hal-al'e-el.
Ma'her-sha'lal-hash'baz.
Ma-le'le-el.
Me-che'ra-thite.
Me-he-tab'e-el.
Me-he-ta'-bel'.
Mel-chiz'e-dek.
Me-o-no'thai.
Me-phib'o-sheth.
Me-she'lem-iah'.
Me-she-zab'eel.
Mik-ne'iah.
Mi-le'tus.
Min-ia'min.
Mis're-photh-ma'im.
Mo-re'sheth-gath.

Na-ha'li-el.
Na-ha-ma'ni.
Ne-bu-chad-nez'zar.
Ne-bu-chad-rez'zar.
Ne-bu-shas'ban.
Ne-bu-zar'-a-dan.
Ne-phi'she-sim.
Ne'reus.

Ner'gal-sha-re'zer.
Nic-o-la'i-tanes.

Olym'pas.
On-e-siph'o-rus.

Pa-gi'el.
Par-shan-da'tha.
Pat'ro-bas.
Pe-thah'iah.
Phe-ni'ce.
Phi-lol'o-gus.
Phle'gon.
Pi'ha-hi'roth.
Po-che'reth.
Proch'o-rus.
Pto-le-ma'is.
Pu-te'o-li.

Rab'sa-ris.
Rab'sha-keh.
Re-a'ia.
Re-a'iah.
Re-e-la'iah.

Sa-la'thi-el.
Sa-mo-thra'ci-a.
Sar'se-chim.
Se-ca'cah.
Se'la-ham-mah'le-koth.
Se-na'ah.
Sen-na-che'rib.
Seph-ar-va'im.
Sha-a-lab'bim.
Sha-a-ra'im.
Sha-ash'gaz.
Sha'ge.
Sha-ha-ra'im.
Sha-ha-zi'mah.
She-de'ur.
She-phu'phan.
Shu'thal'hites.
So'pa-ter.
So-sip'a-ter.
Sta'chys.
Steph'a-nas.
Syn'ty-che.

Ta'a-nach.
Ta-hap'a-nes.
Tah-pan'hes.
Te-haph'ne-hes.
Tah'tim-hod'shi.
Thim-na'thah.
Tig'lath-pil-e'ser.
Til'gath-pil-ne'-ser.
Tir-ha'-kah.
Tir-sha'tha.
Tych'i-cus.

Ur'bane.

Va-je-za'tha.

Zaph'nath-pa-a-ne'ah.
Ze-lo'phe-had.
Ze-lo'tes.
Zu'ri-shad'dai.

53 THE SIEGES OF JERUSALEM.

The first occurrence of the name "Jerusalem", *as a city*[1], is in Judg. 1. 8, and confirms the fact that the first occurrence contains an epitome of its subsequent history.

The history of the city has been a record of its sieges. No fewer than twenty-seven go to complete the list.

This number is striking in the light of Appendix No. 10; being composed of 3×9, the factors being those of Divine completeness (3), and judgment (9) respectively (= 3^3).

A cycle of ordinal completeness is marked by the 10th and 20th (2×10) sieges. These were the two characterised by the destruction of the Temple by fire, which is in accord with the number 10, being that of *ordinal perfection*. (See Ap. 10.) Both also were foretold: the former by Jer. and Ezek.; the latter by our Lord.

Seven is the number of spiritual perfection, and it is worthy of note that the 7th, 14th (2×7), and 21st (3×7) sieges were each the subject of *Divine prophecy*. Further, a 28th (4×7) siege, yet future, is foretold in Zech. 14, &c.

While 14 (2×7) of the sieges are recorded in Holy Scripture, 13 are recorded in profane history.

The following is a complete list of the sieges:

1. By the tribe of Judah against the Jebusites, about 1443 B.C. This was some 700 years before Rome was founded. It was only partial, for in David's reign we still find the Jebusites occupying the citadel (the future Zion). The solemn words in Judg. 1. 8, describing this first siege, vividly portray the after history of the city.
2. By David against the Jebusites (2 Sam. 5. 6–10; 1 Chron. 11. 4–7), about 960 B.C.
3. By Shishak king of Egypt, against Rehoboam (1 Kings 14. 25, 26. 2 Chron. 12. 2–12), about 875 B.C. To this there was only a feeble resistance; and the Temple was plundered.
4. By the Philistines, Arabians, and Ethiopians, against Jehoram (2 Chron. 21. 16, 17), about 794 B.C. In this siege the royal palace was sacked, and the Temple again plundered.
5. By Jehoash king of Israel, against Amaziah king of Judah (2 Kings 14. 13, 14), about 739 B.C. The wall was partially broken down, and the city and Temple pillaged.
6. By Rezin king of Syria, and Pekah king of Israel, against Ahaz (2 Chron. 28), about 630 B.C. The city held out, but Ahaz sought the aid of Tiglath-Pileser king of Assyria, for whom he stripped the Temple.
7. By Sennacherib king of Assyria, against Hezekiah (2 Kings 24. 10–16), about 603 B.C. In this case the siege was raised by a Divine interposition, as foretold by Isaiah the prophet.
8. By Nebuchadnezzar king of Babylon, against Jehoiakim (2 Chron. 36. 6, 7), about 496 B.C., when the Temple was partly pillaged.
9. By Nebuchadnezzar again, against Jehoiachin (2 Chron. 36. 10), about 489 B.C., when the pillage of the Temple was carried further, and 10,000 people carried away.
10. By Nebuchadnezzar, against Zedekiah (2 Chron. 36. 17–20), 478–477 B.C. In this case the Temple was burnt with fire, and the city and Temple lay desolate for fifty years.
11. By Ptolemy Soter king of Egypt, against the Jews, 320 B.C. More than 100,000 captives were taken to Egypt.
12. By Antiochus the Great, about 203 B.C.
13. By Scopus, a general of Alexander, about 199 B.C., who left a garrison.

[1] The *king* of Jerusalem had been mentioned in Josh. 10. 1, &c., but not the city as such.

14. By Antiochus IV, surnamed Epiphanes, 168 B.C. This was the worst siege since the 10th. The whole city was pillaged; 10,000 captives taken; the walls destroyed; the altar defiled; ancient manuscripts perished; the finest buildings were burned; and the Jews were forbidden to worship there. Foretold Dan. 11.
15. By Antiochus V, surnamed Eupator, against Judas Maccabæus, about 162 B.C. This time honourable terms were made, and certain privileges were secured.
16. By Antiochus VII, surnamed Sidetes king of Syria, against John Hyrcanus, about 135 B.C.
17. By Hyrcanus (son of Alex. Jannæus) and the priest Aristobulus. The siege was raised by Scaurus, one of Pompey's lieutenants, about 65 B.C.
18. By Pompey against Aristobulus, about 63 B.C. The machines were moved on the Sabbath, when the Jews made no resistance. Only thus was it then reduced; 12,000 Jews were slain. [Antigonus, son of Aristobulus, with a Parthian army, took the city in 40 B.C.; but there was no siege, the city was taken by a sudden surprise.]
19. Herod with a Roman army besieged the city in 39 B.C. for five months.
20. By Titus, A.D. 69 (See Ap. 50. VI, p. 61). The second Temple (Herod's) was burnt, and for fifty years the city disappeared from history, as after the 10th siege (Jer. 20. 5).
21. The Romans had again to besiege the city in A.D. 135 against the false Messiah, Bar-Cochebas, who had acquired possession of the ruins. The city was obliterated, and renamed Ælia Capitolina, and a temple was erected to Jupiter. For 200 years the city passed out of history, no Jews being permitted to approach it. This siege was foretold in Luke 19. 43, 44; 21. 20-24.
22. After 400 years of so-called Christian colonization, Chosroes the Persian (about A.D. 559) swept through the country; thousands were massacred, and the Church of the Holy Sepulchre was destroyed. The Emperor Heraclius afterwards defeated him, and restored the city and the church.
23. The Caliph Omar, in A.D. 636-7, besieged the city against Heraclius. It was followed by capitulation on favourable terms, and the city passed into the hands of the Turks, in whose hands it remains to the present day.
24. Afdal, the Vizier of the Caliph of Egypt, besieged the two rival factions of Moslems, and pillaged the city in 1098.
25. In 1099 it was besieged by the army of the first Crusade.
26. In 1187 it was besieged by Saladin for seven weeks.
27. The wild Kharezmian Tartar hordes, in 1244, captured and plundered the city, slaughtering the monks and priests.

There will be a 28th according to Zech. 14, which will be raised by Messiah, even as the 7th was by Jehovah.

54 THE MOABITE STONE.

This ancient monument was discovered by the Rev. F. Klein in 1868 at *Dîbân* (the Dibon of the O.T.) in Moab.

The inscription consists of thirty-four lines (the last two being undecipherable), and was written by Mesha king of Moab to commemorate his successful revolt from the yoke of Israel, recorded in 2 Kings 1. 1 and chapter 3; and to honour his god Chemosh, to whom he ascribed his successes.

The writing is in the ancient Hebrew characters, which continued in use down to quite 140, 139 B.C., but was gradually replaced by the modern square Hebrew characters which are in use to-day.

The inscription is proved to be genuine by the Bible account, the two throwing light on each other. See the notes on 2 Kings 3.

The following translation, by Dr. Neubauer, is taken from *Records of the Past* (New Series), Vol. II, pp. 200, &c.:

1. "I, Mesha son of Chemosh-Melech king of Moab, the Di-
2. bonite. My father reigned over Moab thirty years and I reign-
3. ed after my father. I made this monument to Chemosh at Korkhah. A monument of sal-
4. vation, for he saved me from all invaders, and let me see my desire upon all my enemies. Om-
5. ri [was] king of Israel, and he oppressed Moab many days, for Chemosh was angry with his
6. land. His son followed him, and he also said: I will oppress Moab. In my days Che[mosh] said;
7. I will see my desire on him and his house. And Israel surely perished for ever. Omri took the land of
8. Medeba[1] and [Israel] dwelt in it during his days and half the days of his son[2], altogether forty years. But there dwelt in it
9. Chemosh in my days. I built Baal-Meon[3] and made therein the ditches; I built
10. Kirjathaim[4]. The men of Gad dwelt in the land of Ataroth[5] from of old, and built there the king of
11. Israel Ataroth; and I made war against the town and seized it. And I slew all the [people of]
12. the town, for the pleasure of Chemosh and Moab: I captured from thence the Arel[6] of Dodah and tore
13. him before Chemosh in Kerioth[7]: And I placed therein the men of Sh(a)r(o)n, and the men
14. of M(e)kh(e)rth. And Chemosh said to me: Go, seize Nebo[8] upon Israel; and
15. I went in the night and fought against it from the break of dawn till noon: and I took
16. it, and slew all, 7,000 men, [boys ?], women, [girls ?]
17. and female slaves, for to Ashtar-Chemosh I devoted them. And I took from it the Arels[6] of Yahveh, and tore them before Chemosh. And the king of Israel built
18 Jahaz[9], and dwelt in it, while he waged war against me; Chemosh drove him out before me. And

[1] Num. 21. 30; Isa. 15. 2. [2] "son" = successor. [3] Now, *Tell M'aīn*, Num. 32. 38. Josh. 13. 17. [4] Num. 32. 37. Josh. 13. 19. [5] Num. 32. 3. Josh. 16. 2. [6] Arel, two lions, or, lion-like men (?) Cp. 2 Sam. 23. 20. [7] Now, *Khan el Kureitin* (?) Jer. 48. 24. Amos 2. 2. [8] Num. 32. 3, 38. Isa. 15. 2. [9] Isa. 15. 4.

19. I took from Moab 200 men, all chiefs, and transported them to Jahaz, which I took,
20. to add to it Dibon. I built Korkhah, the wall of the forests and the wall
21. of the citadel: I built its gates, and I built its towers. And
22. I built the house of Moloch, and I made sluices of the water-ditches in the middle
23. of the town. And there was no cistern in the middle of the town of Korkhah, and I said to all the people, Make for
24. yourselves every man a cistern in his house. And I dug the canals for Korkhah by means of the prisoners
25. of Israel. I built Aroer[1], and I made the road in [the province of] the Arnon. [And]
26. I built Beth-Bamoth[2], for it was destroyed. I built Bezer[3], for in ruins
27. [it was. And all the chiefs] of Dibon were 50, for all Dibon is subject; and I placed
28. one hundred [chiefs] in the towns which I added to the land: I built
29. Beth-Medeba and Beth-diblathaim[4] and Beth-Baal-Meon[5], and transported thereto the [shepherds]? . . .
30. and the pastors] of the flocks of the land. And at Horonaim[6] dwelt there
31. . . . And Chemosh said to me, Go down, make war upon Horonaim. I went down [and made war]
32. . . . And Chemosh dwelt in it during my days. I went up from thence . . ."

[1] Now, *'Ar'air*, Deut. 2. 36; 3. 12; 4. 48. [2] Num. 21. 19. Isa. 15. 2. (A.V. "high places"), cp. Josh. 13. 17. [3] Deut. 4. 43.
[4] Jer. 48. 22. [5] Josh. 13. 17. Jer. 48. 23. [6] Isa. 15. 5. Jer. 48. 3, 5, 34.

55 THE DYNASTY OF OMRI.

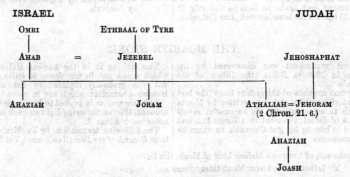

ISRAEL | **JUDAH**

OMRI — ETHBAAL OF TYRE

AHAB = JEZEBEL — JEHOSHAPHAT

AHAZIAH — JORAM — ATHALIAH = JEHORAM (2 Chron. 21. 6.)

AHAZIAH

JOASH

Athaliah was thus the granddaughter of Omri, king of Israel (2 Chron. 22. 2), and daughter of Jezebel.

The marriage between Jehoram and Athaliah was part of Satan's design to introduce idolatry into Judah, so that Athaliah might do for Judah what her mother Jezebel had done for Israel, and thus secure the same result.

Jehoshaphat began by strengthening himself against Israel (2 Chron. 17. 1), but married his son to the daughter (an idolatress) of Ahab, the worst of Israel's kings.

The leaven worked, morally and politically; and was then used by Satan for the destruction of the line by which "the seed of the woman" was to come into the world. See Ap. 23 and 25.

Jehoram, king of Judah, began by killing off all his brethren (2 Chron. 21. 4).

The Arabians came and slew all his sons, save the youngest, Ahaziah (2 Chron. 22. 1), called also Joash, Jehoahaz (2 Chron. 21. 17), and Azariah (2 Chron. 22. 6).

Athaliah slew all the sons of Ahaziah on his death (2 Kings 11. 1. 2 Chron. 22. 10), or thought she did; but the infant Joash was rescued.

Joash (called also Jehoash) was hid for six years, while the faithfulness of Jehovah's word hung upon the Divine preservation of that infant's life. Hence Jehoiada's text (2 Chron. 23. 3). See, on the whole subject, Ap. 23. And, note the parallel in the history of England, by James I marrying his son Charles to (an idolatress) Henrietta of France, with similar political results.

56 PARALLEL PASSAGES OF THE HISTORICAL BOOKS.

The following table, showing one hundred and eleven parallel passages between the books of Samuel and Kings on the one hand, and the books of Chronicles on the other, will be useful.

1. It will show the *mutual relation* of the sections, and will enable the reader to find at a glance the corresponding portions, and thus serve the purpose of ordinary and ready reference.

2. It will help to exhibit the special design of the two great principles governing the whole of these books.

In the former (Samuel and Kings) we have the history from the *exoteric* point of view; in the latter (Chronicles) we have, for the most part, the same history, but from the *esoteric* point of view.

In the former we have the events viewed from the human standpoint, as they would be seen by the natural

eye; in the latter we have the same events viewed from the Divine standpoint, and as seen and understood by the spiritual mind.

Consequently, while in the former we have the event in its historical aspect; in the latter we have it in its moral aspect. In the former we have the historic record; in the latter we have the Divine reason for it, or the Divine "words" and judgment on it. (Cp. Saul's death, 1 Sam. 31. 6, and 1 Chron. 10. 13, 14).

It is this principle which determines the amount of literary space accorded to the same historic event. For example: in the former books we have three *chapters* (or 88 verses) given to the *secular* events of Hezekiah's reign (2 Kings 18, 19, and 20), and only three *verses* (2 Kings 18. 4–6) given to his great *religious* reformation. In Chronicles this is exactly reversed. *Three* chapters (or 84 verses) are devoted to his reformation (2 Chron. 29–31), while *one* chapter (or 32 verses) suffices for the secular events of his reign.

In the same way Jehoshaphat's three alliances with Ahab can be spiritually and morally understood only from 2 Chron. 17, of which there is not a word in Kings.

3. This principle determines also the *order* in which the events are treated. In the books of Kings the events are recorded in *chronological* order; while in Chronicles this order is sometimes ignored, in order to bring the *moral* causes or consequences of the two events together, for the purposes of comparison or contrast. (Cp. the list of David's mighty men; David's numbering the People, and the account of the plague).

4. The object of these two great principles is further seen in the fact that the design of the former is to give the whole history of *Israel's* kingdom complete; while the design of the latter is to give only that which pertains to the house of David and the tribe of *Judah*, as being founded on Jehovah's covenant in 2 Sam. 7 and 1 Chron. 17.

5. The conclusion is that the book of Chronicles is entirely independent of the books of Samuel and Kings; and that the differences between them are independent and designed. The critics *create* their own difficulties by first *assuming* that the books *ought to be alike;* and then, because they are not what they are assumed to be, treating the variations as "discrepancies," or "corruptions of the text", instead of as being full of Divine instruction "written for our learning".

The following is the table:

1 Sam. 27	1 Chron. 12. 1–7.
29. 1–3	,, 12. 19–22.
31	,, 10.
2 Sam. 5. 1–5........	,, 11. 1–3.
5. 6–10	,, 11. 4–9.
5. 11–16...........	,, 14. 1–7.
5. 17–25...........	,, 14. 8–17.
6. 1–11	,, 13.
6. 12–23	,, 15 & 16.
7	,, 17.
8	,, 18.
10	,, 19.
11. 1–27	,, 20. 1.
12. 29–31...........	,, 20. 1–3.
23. 8–39	,, 11. 10–47.
24. 1–9	,, 21. 1–6.
,,	,, 27. 23, 24.
24. 10–17...........	,, 21. 7–17.
24. 18–24...........	,, 21. 18–22. 1.
1 Kings 2. 1	,, 23. 1.
2. 1–4	,, 28. 20, 21.
2. 10–12...........	,, 29. 23–30.
2. 46	2 Chron. 1. 1.
3. 4–15	,, 1. 2–13.
5	,, 2.
6	,, 3. 1–14; 4. 9.
7. 15–21...........	,, 3. 15–17.
7. 23–26...........	,, 4. 2–5.
7. 38–46...........	,, 4. 6, 10, 17.
7. 47–50	,, 4. 18–22.
7. 51	,, 5. 1.
8	,, 5. 2–7. 10.
9. 1–9	,, 7. 11–22.
9. 10–28...........	,, 8.
10. 1–13	,, 9. 1–12.
10. 14–25	,, 9. 13–24.
10. 26–29...........	,, 9. 25–28; 1. 14–17.
11. 41–43	,, 9. 29–31.

1 Kings 12. 1–19 ...	2 Chron. 10.
12. 21–24...........	,, 11. 1–4.
12. 25	,, 11. 5–12.
12. 26–31...........	,, 11. 13–17.
14. 22–24	,, 12. 1.
14. 25–28...........	,, 12. 2–12.
14. 21, 29–31	,, 12. 13–16.
15. 1	,, 13. 1, 2.
15. 6	,, 13. 2–21.
15. 7, 8	,, 13. 22; 14. 1.
15. 11, 12......... ..	,, 14. 1–5.
15. 13–15...........	,, 15. 16–18.
15. 16–22...........	,, 16. 1–6.
15. 23, 24	,, 16. 11–14.
22. 1–40, 44	,, 18.
22. 41–43	,, 17. 1; 20. 31–33.
22. 45	,, 20. 34.
22. 47–49...........	,, 20. 35–37.
22. 50	,, 21. 1.
2 Kings 1. 1; 3. 4, 5.	,, 20. 1–3.
8. 16–19...........	,, 21. 2–7.
8. 20–22	,, 21. 8–15.
8. 23, 24	,, 21. 18–20.
8. 25–27	,, 22. 1–4.
8. 28, 29; 9. 1–28	,, 22. 5–7, 9.
10. 11–14...........	,, 22. 8.
11. 1–3	,, 22. 10–12.
11. 4–20	,, 23.
11. 21; 12. 1–3 ...	,, 24. 1–3.
12. 6–16	,, 24. 4–14.
12. 17, 18...........	,, 24. 23, 24.
12. 19–21...........	,, 24. 25–27.
14. 1–6	,, 25. 1–4.
14. 7	,, 25. 11–16.
14. 8–14	,, 25. 17–24.
14. 17–20	,, 25. 25–28.
14. 21, 22; 15. 1–4	,, 26. 1–15.
15. 6, 7, 27, 28 ...	,, 26. 22, 23.
15. 32–35	,, 27. 1–8.

2 Kings 15. 38	2 Chron. 27. 9.
16. 1, 2.	,, 28. 1, 2.
16. 3, 4, 6	,, 28. 3–8.
16. 7	,, 28. 16–19.
15. 29	,, 28. 20.
16. 8–18	,, 28. 21–25.
16. 19, 20	,, 28. 26, 27.
18. 1–3	,, 29. 1, 2.
18. 13...............	Isa. 36. 1.
18. 14–16...........	2 Chron. 32. 2–8.
20. 1–11	{ 2 Chron. 32. 24; Isa. 38.
20. 12–19...........	Isa. 39. 1–8.
18. 17–37.........	{ 2 Chron. 32. 9–19. Isa. 36. 2–22.
19. 1–5	{ 2 Chron. 32. 20. Isa. 37. 1–4.
19. 6, 7...............	,, 37. 6, 7.
19. 8–19	{ 2 Chron. 32. 17. Isa. 37. 8–20.
19. 20–37.........	{ 2 Chron. 32. 21. Isa. 37. 21–38.
20. 20, 21...........	2 Chron. 32. 32, 33.
21. 1–16	,, 33. 1–9.
21. 17, 18...........	,, 33. 18–20.
21. 19–26...........	,, 33. 21–25.
22. 1, 2	,, 34. 1–7.
22. 3–20	,, 34. 8–28.
23. 1–3	,, 34. 29–32.
23. 21–23...........	,, 35. 1–19.
23. 24–26...........	,, 34. 33.
23. 28–30...........	,, 35. 20–27.
23. 30–33...........	,, 36. 1–3.
23. 34–37...........	,, 36. 4, 5.
24. 8, 9	,, 36. 9.
24. 15–17...........	,, 36. 10.
24. 18, 19...........	,, 36. 11, 12.
24. 20	,, 36. 13–16.
25. 8–21	,, 36. 18–21.

57 THE GENEALOGY OF THE PERSIAN KINGS.

The main sources of information on this subject are Herodotus, Xenophon, Ctesias, Nicolas of Damascus (all B.C.); and Arrian (cent. 2 A.D.)

The writers of a former generation were occupied in unravelling and piecing together the varying accounts of these ancient historians without the knowledge of the still more ancient Inscriptions recently discovered, which were caused to be written by the persons concerned in the events recorded.

In 1846 Major (afterward Sir Henry) Rawlinson published a complete translation of the trilingual Persian text on the isolated *rock of Behistūn*, (or more

correctly *Bahistūn*) which rises 1,700 feet out of the Plain, on the high road from Babylonia to the East; in which DARIUS HYSTASPIS gives his own genealogy.

This famous rock (of which a view is given on page 82 by the kind permission of Messrs. Longmans & Co., the publishers of Canon Rawlinson's *Memoir of Major-General Sir H. C. Rawlinson*) derives its name from the village of *Bisitūn* or *Bisutūn*, near its foot. It is on the high road from Baghdad to Teheran, about sixty-five miles from Hamadan (on the site of the ancient Ecbatana).

On this rock, on a prepared surface about 500 feet from the level of the plain, and most difficult of access, DARIUS HYSTASPIS caused to be carved the principal events of his reign; and he commences with an account of his genealogy.

The following is the translation of the Persian text[1]:—

§ I. "I am Darius, the great king, the king of kings, the king of Persia, the king of the provinces, the son of Hystaspes, the grandson of Arsames the Achæmenian.

§ II. (Thus) saith Darius the king: My father is Hystaspes; the father of Hystaspes was Arsames; the father of Arsames was Ariyaramnes; the father of Ariyaramnes was [Teispes]; the father of Teispes was Achæmenes.

§ III. (Thus) saith Darius the king: On that account are we called Achæmenians; from antiquity are we descended; from antiquity hath our race been kings.

§ IV. (Thus) saith Darius the king: Eight of my race were kings before (me); I am the ninth[2]. In two lines[3] have we been kings", &c.

It must be noted that the confusion which has hitherto been experienced arises from the fact that appellatives have been mistaken for proper names; to say nothing of the confusion arising from their transliteration or translation into other languages.

These appellatives are, like Pharaoh and Abimelech, the general titles of a line of kings, such as the modern Czar, Sultan, Shah, &c. Hence

AHASUERUS means "the Mighty", and "is the name, or rather the title, of four Median and Persian monarchs" (Kitto, *Bib. Encycl.* I, p. 91). "In every case the identification of the person named is a matter of controversy". See *The Encycl. Brit.*, 11th (Cambridge) edn., vol. i, p. 429.

ARTAXERXES means *Great King*, or *Kingdom*, and is synonymous with *Artachshast* (*Arta*=Great, and *Kshatza*=Kingdom, preserved in the modern "Shah"). According to Prideaux he is identified with the Ahasuerus of Est. 1. 1 (vol. i, p. 306).

DARIUS means *the Restrainer* (Her. VI. 98); or, according to Professor Sayce, *the Maintainer*. DARIUS "appears to be originally an appellative meaning 'king', 'ruler'", (Herbelot, *Biblioth. Orient.*, Article 'Dara'); Herodotus (VI. 98) renders it *Erxeiēs*=Coercer. "It was assumed as his throne-name by Ochus (=Darius Nothus), son and successor of Artaxerxes Longimanus (Ctesias, *de Reb. Pers.*, 48, 57, Müller)". See Kitto, *Bib. Cycl.*, vol. i, p. 625. XERXES, in his inscription at Persepolis, actually calls himself "DARIUS"; one paragraph beginning "XERXES the great king," and the next beginning "DARIUS the king."

This is why DARIUS HYSTASPIS is thus called, to denote him as DARIUS the son of HYSTASPES; and to distinguish him from "Darius the Mede", who was ASTYAGES his grandfather.

[1] For full particulars see the handsome volume published by the Trustees of the British Museum, *The Sculptures and Inscription of Darius the Great on the Rock of Behistūn, in Persia.* London, 1907. (Price 21*s.*)

[2] We have indicated this enumeration by placing the figures against the names on p. 81.

[3] The "two lines" are the Lydian and the Medo-Persian, as shown in the Table on p. 81.

ASTYAGES

is the Persian monarch with which this Appendix is concerned. According to Herodotus, ASTYAGES was the son of CYAXARES, who was the son of PHRAORTES (II), who was the son of DEIOKES (Bk. I. 73), who, again, was the son of PHRAORTES (I). (Bk. I. 96.)

In the genealogy given by CYRUS on the Cuneiform Cylinder, he calls his great-grandfather TEISPES (see below).

This TEISPES is to be identified with TEISPES the son of ACHÆMENES in the Behistūn Rock genealogy of DARIUS HYSTASPIS.

The ACHÆMENES of DARIUS, identified with the DEIOKES of Herodotus (I. 96), was the real founder of the Achæmenian dynasty of which Darius speaks, although his father (PHRAORTES I) was the first of the line. Herodotus describes him (DEIOKES) as a man "famous for wisdom", of great ambition, "aiming at the aggrandisement of the Medes and his own absolute power" (I. 96).

PHRAORTES I. would therefore be the first of the *eight* kings before DARIUS HYSTASPIS, who speaks of himself as the *ninth*. See translation given above.

ARSAMES.

As the grandfather of DARIUS HYSTASPIS, he is (according to the *Behistūn* Inscription) to be identified with the ASTYAGES of Herodotus.

At the close of the Lydio-Median War "Syannesis the Cilician and Labynetus (or Nabonnedus) the Babylonian (identified by Prideaux, vol. i, p. 82 note, and pp. 135, 136, 19th edn., with Nebuchadnezzar) persuaded ALYATTES to give his daughter ARYENIS in marriage to ASTYAGES, son of KYAXARES" (Her. I. 74). Of this marriage came HYSTASPES and DARIUS his son.

CYRUS.

In the Cuneiform Cylinder account of the capture of Babylon, CYRUS states:—

> "I am CYRUS the king . . . the great king, the mighty king, king of Tintir (Babylon), king of Sumir, and Akkad, king of the regions of the earth, the son of CAMBYSES the great king, king of the city of Anzan, grandson of CYRUS, the great king, king of the city of Anzan, great-grandson of TEISPES, the great king of the city of Anzan, of the ancient seed of royalty, whose dominion (reign, i.e. of Cyrus himself) Bel and Nebo had exalted according to the beneficence of their hearts" (E. Wallis Budge, *Babylonian Life and History*, p. 87).

Here we have the statement of Cyrus that his father was known as CAMBYSES, his grandfather as CYRUS, and his great-grandfather under the name (or title), common to the *Behistūn* Inscription and the Cylinder alike, of TEISPES.

TEISPES.

If TEISPES' grandson was ARSAMES (according to the *Behistūn* Inscription), and this TEISPES and the TEISPES of Cyrus's Cylinder are one and the same,—then, it follows that the CAMBYSES of the Cylinder and the ARSAMES of the Inscription must be one and the same person, well known under different names, titles, or appellatives.[1]

Moreover, if the TEISPES of the *Behistūn* Inscription and the one of the Cylinder of Cyrus are to be identified with the PHRAORTES (II) of Herodotus (I. 73), then the grandson of this PHRAORTES (II) must be ASTYAGES.

[1] "Dareios the son of Hystaspês, who traces his descent through Arsamês and Ariarannês to Teispês the son of Akhæmenês, probably refers to the same Teispês" (Sayce, *Ancient Empires of the East*, p. 243).

Consequently we have, under these three names, titles, or appellatives, from Greek, Median, and Persian sources, *three persons*, called by Herodotus ASTYAGES, by Darius ARSAMES, and by Cyrus CAMBYSES [1], who are in reality one and the same.

But, if the father of CYRUS was CAMBYSES, by Esther (see the Table of the Genealogy, below), then it follows that not only does CAMBYSES=ARSAMES=ASTYAGES, but =also the AHASUERUS of the book of Esther (Prideaux i, p. 306).

1 "The names *Kyros* and *Kambysês* seem to be of Elamite derivation. Strabo, indeed, says that *Kyros* was originally called *Agradates*, and took the name of *Kurus* or *Kyros* from the river that flows past Pasargadœ" (Sayce, id. p. 248).
Cyrus and *Cambyses* both seem to be territorial titles rather than names.

Therefore in the presence of all these identifications from independent sources and authorities, we have:—

ASTYAGES, ARSAMES, CAMBYSES } = { the AHASUERUS of Est. 1. 1, &c.; ,, ARTAXERXES of Ezra 6. 14; Neh. 2. 1.; ,, "DARIUS the Median" of Dan. 5 31.

all one and the same person.

We now give the Genealogy, according to the Inscription of DARIUS HYSTASPIS on the *Behistūn* rock, referred to above.

The names in large capitals are the Greek names given by HERODOTUS. Those in small capitals are the corresponding Persian names as given by DARIUS HYSTASPIS on the *Behistūn* rock, and by CYRUS on his Cylinder; while the names in ordinary small type are the appellatives.

THE LINE OF THE PERSIAN KINGS

ACCORDING TO

HERODOTUS (Lydian Line).	HERODOTUS, THE *BEHISTŪN* ROCK, AND THE CYLINDER OF CYRUS (Medo-Persian Line), COMBINED.		INSCRIPTION ON THE *BEHISTŪN* ROCK.		THE CYLINDER OF CYRUS.
ATYS (I. 7)	(1) **PHRAORTES I** [1] (Her. I. 96)				
LYDUS (I. 7)					
CANDAULES (I. 7)[1]	(2) **DEIOKES** (Her. I. 94)	=	(2) ACHÆMENES		
GYGES (I. 8)	(3) **PHRAORTES II** (Her. I. 73)	=	(3) TEISPES	=	(3) TEISPES
ARDYS (I. 16)					
SADYATTES (I. 16)	(4) **CYAXARES** (Her. I. 73)	=	(4) ARIYARAMNES	=	(4) CYRUS I
ALYATTES (I. 74)					
ARYENIS=VASHTI, m. (I. 74) (Est. 1. 9)	(5) **ASTYAGES** (m. ESTHER) [2] (Her. I. 73) (Est. 2. 17) Ahasuerus (Est. 1. 1) Artaxerxes (Ezra 6. 14. Neh. 2. 1) "Darius the Median" (Dan. 5. 31)	=	(5) ARSAMES	=	(5) CAMBYSES
	(6) **CYRUS** [3] "The Persian" (Isa. 45. 1. Ezra 6. 14)				(6) CYRUS II
	(7) **CAMBYSES II** [3]				(7) CAMBYSES II
(8) HYSTASPES —	(8) **HYSTASPES**	—	(8) HYSTASPES		
(9) DARIUS (HYST.)	(9) **DARIUS HYSTASPIS** [1] Artaxerxes (Ezra 7. 1)		(9) DARIUS (HYST.)[4]		

1 Herodotus says the ancestors of Candaules reigned for twenty-two generations, covering a period of 505 years (I. 7).
2 This marriage resulted in the birth of Cyrus, in fulfilment of Isa. 44. 28—45. 4. And the part taken by Esther and Mordecai in his training, explains all that we read of Cyrus in Ezra and Nehemiah.
3 Darius, in giving his own *direct* line, omits the *names* of Phraortes I, Cyrus, and Cambyses II, but he *includes* them in the *numbering* of his *eight* predecessors.
There was a still later "Cyrus" (the Cyrus of Xenophon). See Her. VII. 11.
4 When Darius (Hyst.) says "in two lines we have been kings", he must refer to the Lydian and Medo-Persian lines.

THE ROCK OF BEHISTŪN, IN PERSIA, SHOWING THE INSCRIPTION OF DARIUS HYSTASPIS (see pages 79–81).
(*By the kind permission of Messrs. Longmans & Co.*)

58 A HARMONY OF THE EZRA-NEHEMIAH HISTORY.

REFS.	EZRA.	B.C.	NEHEMIAH.	REFS.
		455 454	Hanani's report in month of Chisleu leads to the "going forth of the commandment to rebuild Jerusalem" (Dan. 9. 25) by Artaxerxes (i.e. ASTYAGES) in his twentieth year.	1. 1–2. 8.
			NEHEMIAH'S JOURNEY. He visits the Governors, and presents Credentials.	2. 9.
			SANBALLAT'S RECEPTION.	2. 10.
			NEHEMIAH'S NIGHT SURVEY OF RUINS.	2. 12–15.
			HIS REPORT TO THE JEWS.	2. 16–18.
			OPPOSITION THREATENED (Moab, Ammon, and Ishmael) on charge of rebellion against the Suzerain King (i.e. of Babylon) Nebuchadnezzar.	2. 19.
			NEHEMIAH'S ANSWER. Foundation work of Wall begun. Wall itself finished to half its height.	2. 20—4. 6.
			ATTEMPTED OPPOSITION BY FORCE.	4. 7, 8.
			NEHEMIAH'S COURSE. PRAYER AND WATCH.	4. 9.
			COMPLAINT OF JUDAH. Used by Adversaries.	4. 10–14.
			RESULT.	4. 15.
			WALL COMPLETED (second half) in fifty-two days.	4. 16.—6. 15.

Refs.	EZRA.	B.C.	NEHEMIAH.	Refs.
			Effect on Enemies.	6. 16.
			Reference to Hindrance during the Building.	6. 17-19.
			Condition of the City.	
			Wall Built.	7. 1.
			Hanani appointed Governor.	7. 2, 3.
			City Open. People Few. Houses not Builded. (Cp. Hag. 1. 4.)	7. 4.
1. 1-4.	Emancipation Act of Cyrus.	426	(Interval of twenty-eight years.)	
1. 5—2. 2.	Return under Zerubbabel. [N.B. Cyrus's specification for building the Temple recorded in 6. 3-5, falls into its proper place here between 2. 1 and 2.]			
2. 1-70.	**Genealogies of those who Returned.**		**Genealogies of those who Returned.**	7. 5-73-.
	The Seventh Month.		**The Seventh Month.**	7. -73.
3. 1-3.	The Altar of Burnt Offering set up.			
			The First Day.	8. 1-12.
			The Second Day. Instruction.	8. 13-15.
3. 4-6-.	**Feast of Tabernacles Kept.**	426	**Feast of Tabernacles Kept.**	8. 16-18.
3. -6.	"But the Foundation of Temple not yet laid."			
3. 7.	Six Months' Preparation for the Building.			
3. 8-13.	Second Year of Return. Second Month. Temple Foundation laid.	425		
	Fifteen Years of Opposition. From second year of Return to second year of Darius Hystaspis.	419	Nehemiah Goes Back for twelve years (cp. 13. 6).	(5. 14.)
	[N.B. Chapters 4. 1-6. 22 are a retrospective reference to the Wall-building of Neh. 2. 20—6. 15.]	410		
	Second Year of Darius Hystaspis. Sixth month: "This People say, 'The time is *not come*, the time that the Lord's house should be built.'" Hag. 1. 2.			
	Command: "Is it time for you, O ye, to dwell in your cieled houses, and this House lie waste?" Hag. 1. 4. "Go up . . . and Build." Hag. 1. 8.			
	Sixth Month. Twenty-fourth Day. The Work Begun. Hag. 1. 14-15.			
	Seventh Month (7th day of Feast of Tabernacles). The word to Zerubbabel (Hag. 2. 1-9).			
	Eighth Month. The Word to Zechariah. Zech. 1. 1.			
	Ninth Month. Twenty-fourth Day. The Word to the Priests. Hag. 2. 10-19.			
	Ninth Month. Twenty-fourth Day. The Final Word to Zerubbabel. Hag. 2. 20-23.			
	Eleventh Month. Twenty-fourth Day. The Word to Zechariah. Zech. 1. 7.			
	Fourth Year of Darius Hystaspis. Ninth Month. Fourth Day. The Word to Zechariah. (N.B. His last date.) Zech. 7. 1.	407	Nehemiah Obtains Leave of Absence, and Returns to be present at	(13. 6.)
6. 15.	Sixth Year, Twelfth Month of Darius Hystaspis. Temple Finished.			

REFS.	EZRA.	B.C.	NEHEMIAH.	REFS.
6. 16–18.	**The Dedication of the Temple.** Twenty years after laying the Foundation, 3. 8–13 (in 425): and five years and six months from beginning the House itself (Hag. 1. 14, 15). Ending the "Seven Sevens" from "the going forth of the commandment" of Dan. 9. 25 in 454 B.C.		**The Dedication of the Temple.**	
6. 19–22.	THE FIRST PASSOVER.	404		
7. 1—8. 36.	EZRA "WENT UP FROM BABYLON" as TIRSHATHA. Appointed by the Persian Council of State. Four months' journey, from 1st of NISAN, and arrival at Jerusalem 1st of AB.			
9. 1, 2.	**Separation of the People.** Report of the Princes *re* the NON-SEPARATION of the Princes, Priests and Levites.	404	**Separation of the People.**	9. 1, 2.
9. 3, 4.	THE "ASSEMBLY" of all that were troubled at the words of the God of Israel.		THE "ASSEMBLY," and reading of the Law of Jehovah, on the twenty-fourth day of the seventh month. (The second day of the Feast of Tabernacles.)	9. 3.
9. 5–15.	EZRA'S PRAYER.		THE LEVITES' PRAYER.	9. 4–37.
10. 1–17.	**"Strange Wives" and the Covenant.**		**"Strange Wives" and the Covenant.**	9. 38—10. 39
10. 18–44.	NAMES OF THE PRIESTS, Levites, and others who had married strange wives.		NAMES OF THOSE WHO "SEALED" THE COVENANT.	10. 1–39.
10. 17.	EZRA'S LATEST DATE: 1st of NISAN, in eighth year of DARIUS HYSTASPIS.	403		
			RESIDENTS IN JERUSALEM.	11. 1–36.
			LIST OF PRIESTS WHO RETURNED with ZERUBBABEL and EZRA for the Dedication of the WALL.	12. 1–26.
			THE DEDICATION OF THE WALL.	12. 27–47.
			THE REFORMATION OF THE PEOPLE.	13. 1–31.
	The Whole Period covered by EZRA twenty-three years (426–403 B.C.).		The Whole Period covered by NEHEMIAH fifty-two years (455–403 B.C.).	

59 THE TWELVE GATES OF JERUSALEM (Nehemiah, chs. 3 and 12).[1]

1. The Valley Gate (2. 13; 3. 13). Cp. 2 Chron. 26. 9.
2. The Gate of the Fountain (2. 14; 3. 15; 12. 37), on Ophel at the Gihon spring (that mentioned in 2 Kings 25. 4. Jer. 39. 4).
3. The Sheep Gate (3. 1; 12. 39). North of the Temple.
4. The Fish Gate (3. 3; 12. 39). Cp. 2 Chron. 33. 14. Zeph. 1. 10.
5. The Old Gate (3. 6; 12. 39). Cp. 2 Chron. 33. 14, and 2 Kings 22. 14, "college". Called also the "First Gate" (Zech. 14. 10).
6. The Dung Gate (2. 14; 3. 14; 12. 31). Probably same as Ḥarsith Gate (Jer. 19. 2); sometimes rendered the Gate of Potsherds, from *ḥeres*, a potter's vessel. Leading to Hinnom. N.B. Better = Pottery Gate.
7. The Water Gate (3. 25, 26).
8. The Horse Gate (3. 28). Cp. 2 Kings 11. 16. 2 Chron. 23. 15. Jer. 31. 40. South-east of the Temple, and close to the city and house of David.
9. The East Gate (3. 29). East of the Temple, and connected with it.
10. The Gate of Miphkad (3. 31). Probably north-east of Temple. (= The Registry Gate.)
11. The Gate of Ephraim (8. 16; 12. 39). Cp. 2 Chron. 25. 23.
12. The Prison Gate (12. 39), or Gate of the Guard (2 Kings 11. 6, 19).

[1] In Neh. 3. the first sixteen verses refer to Jerusalem, and the latter sixteen verses to Zion (or the city of David), south of Moriah. A study of these, and a comparison with ch. 12, will explain most of the difficulties connected with the topography of the city. See also the Plan of Zion, and Solomon's buildings. Ap. 68.

60 THE NAME OF JEHOVAH IN THE BOOK OF ESTHER.

It has been observed by many that no Divine Name or Title is found in the book of Esther.

This is the more remarkable, since, in this short book of only 167 verses, the Median King is mentioned 192 times, his kingdom is referred to 26 times, and his name[1] "Ahasuerus" is given 29 times.

Jehovah had declared (Deut. 31. 16–18)[2], that if His People forsook Him, He would hide His face from them. Here this threatening was fulfilled. But, though He was hidden from them, He was working for them. Though the book reveals Him as overruling all, His Name is hidden. It is there for His People to see, not for His enemies to see or hear.

Satan was at work, using Haman to blot out the Nation, as once before he had used Pharaoh for the same purpose (see Ap. 23 and 25). Jehovah's counsel must stand. His promise of Messiah, the coming "Seed" of the woman (Gen. 3. 15), must not fail. Therefore He must overrule all for the preservation of His People, and of the line by which that "Seed" was to come into the world.

His working was secret and hidden: hence, the name of "JEHOVAH" is hidden secretly four times in this book, and the name "EHYEH" (I am that I am) once. The *Massōrah* (Ap. 30) has a rubric calling attention to the former fact; and (at least)[3] three ancient manuscripts are known in which the Acrostic[4] letters in all five cases are written *Majuscular* (or, larger than the others) so that they stand out boldly and prominently, showing the four consonant letters of the name J e H o V a H. In Hebrew י, ה, ו, ה, or, as written in Hebrew from right to left, ה, ו, ה, י. In English, L, O, R, D. Also the five letters of the fifth Acrostic, "E H Y H."

THE FOUR ACROSTICS.

The following phenomena are noticed in examining the four Acrostics which form the name "Jehovah":

1. In each case the four words forming the Acrostic are consecutive.
2. In each case (except the first) they form a sentence complete in itself.
3. There are no other such Acrostics in the whole book, except the fifth Acrostic at the end; though there is one other, forming another Divine Title, in Ps. 96. 11. (See note there.)
4. In their construction there are not two alike, but each one is arranged in a manner quite different from the other three.
5. Each is uttered by a different speaker. The first by Memucan (1. 20); the second by Esther (5. 4); the third by Haman (5. 13); the fourth by the inspired writer (7. 7).
6. The first two Acrostics are a pair, having the name formed by the *Initial* letters of the four words.
7. The last two are a pair, having the name formed by the *Final* letters of the four words.
8. The first and third Acrostics are a pair, having the name spelt *backward*.
9. The second and fourth are a pair, having the name spelt *forward*. They thus form an *alternation*:

A | Backward.
  B | Forward.
A | Backward.
  B | Forward.

10. The first and third (in which the name is formed backward) are a pair, being spoken by *Gentiles*.
11. The second and fourth (in which the name is spelt forward) are a pair, being spoken by *Israelites*. They thus form an *Alternation*:—

C | Spoken by a Gentile (Memucan).
  D | Spoken by an Israelite (Esther).
C | Spoken by a Gentile (Haman).
  D | Spoken by an Israelite (the inspired writer).

12. The first and second form a pair, being connected with *Queens and Banquets*.
13. The third and fourth are a pair, being connected with *Haman*.
14. The first and fourth are a pair, being spoken *concerning* the Queen (Vashti) and Haman respectively.
15. The second and third are a pair, being spoken *by* the Queen (Esther) and Haman respectively. They thus form an Introversion:—

E | Words concerning a Queen.
  F | Words spoken by a Queen.
  F | Words spoken by Haman.
E | Words concerning Haman.

16. It is remarkable also that, in the two cases where the name is formed by the *initial* letters, the facts recorded are *initial also*, and are spoken of an event in which Jehovah's overruling was initiated; while in the two cases where the name is formed by the *final* letters, the events are *final also*, and lead rapidly up to the end toward which Jehovah was working.

Thus in the two cases where the name is spelt *backward*[1], Jehovah is seen *overruling* the counsels of Gentiles for the accomplishment of His own; and where the name is spelt *forward*[1], He is *ruling* directly in the interests of His own People unknown to themselves.

THE FIRST ACROSTIC (1. 20)

is formed by the *initial* letters, for the event was initial; and the name is spelt *backward* because Jehovah was *turning back* and *overruling* the counsels of man. The whole clause reads as follows; the words forming the Acrostic being put in italic type:—

"And when the king's decree which he shall make, shall be published throughout all his empire, (for it is great,) *all the wives shall give* to their husbands honour, both to great and small." The four words we give, 1st, in the Hebrew type (with the Majuscular letters at the beginning of each word); 2nd, with the Transliteration; and 3rd, in English paraphrase, reproducing the sentence in the word LORD with the initial letters backward:—

4 3 2 1

הִיא וְכָל־הַנָּשִׁים יִתְּנוּ

1 2 3 4

Hi' Vekāl Hannāshīm Yittenū.

1	2	3	4
it	and-all	the-wives	shall-give

"Due Respect Our Ladies

shall give to their husbands, both to great and small."

---

1 In the note on Est. 1. 1 this Ahasuerus is identified with Astyages, who is the same as Darius the Mede. See notes on p. 618, and Ap. 57.

2 The Talmud (*Kelim* 139) says "Where do we get Esther in the Law?" And the answer is "Deut. 31. 18, 'and I will surely hide my face'". So here, the outward form of the revelation takes on the form of its inward and spiritual meaning. For the same reason we have the Divine Title "the God of heaven" as characterising the book Ezra-Nehemiah. See note on 2 Chron. 36. 23.

3 How many more there may be will be ascertained only when all the special scrolls of Esther shall be examined.

4 For other examples of Acrostics in the Hebrew text, see Ap. 63. vii.

1 In the use of these terms, "backward" and "forward" the English reader must bear in mind that Hebrew is read from right to left both in the spelling and wording.

THE SECOND ACROSTIC (5. 4)

is formed, as before, by the *initial* letters, for Jehovah is initiating His action; but the name is spelt *forward* because He is *ruling* and causing Esther to act; and take the first step, which was to lead up to so great an end.

The four words are:

4 3 2 1

יָבוֹא הַמֶּלֶךְ וְהָמָן הַיּוֹם

1 2 3 4

Yābō' Hammelek VeHāmān Hayyōm

1 2 3 4

let-come the-king and-Haman this-day

"Let Our Royal Dinner
this day be graced by the king and Haman."

The name of Jehovah is read in the invitation, intimating that there would be *a fourth* at that banquet."

THE THIRD ACROSTIC (5. 13)

is the beginning of the end; for Haman had gone forth from that banquet "joyful and with a glad heart" (5. 9) "that day." Yet it was to be his last. Hence the third Acrostic is formed with the *final* letters, for the *end* was approaching; and the name is spelt *backward*, for Jehovah was *overruling* Haman's gladness, and turning back Haman's counsel.

The four words are:

4 3 2 1

זֶה אֵינֶנּוּ שֹׁוֶה לִי

1 2 3 4

zeH-'ēynennV shoveH leY

1 3 2 4

this availeth nothing to-me

The English may be freely rendered "Yet am I
saD; foR, nO avaiL
is all this to me."

THE FOURTH ACROSTIC (7. 7)

is formed, like the third, by the *final* letters, for Haman's end had come. But it is spelt *forward* like the first, for Jehovah was *ruling* and bringing about the end He had determined. Haman saw there was cause for fear. A *fourth* is there—Jehovah Himself! And when Esther pleads for her life (7. 3), the king asks "Who is he and where is he?" which brings in Jehovah's own ineffable name—the Acrostic of the five final letters spelling in Hebrew "*I am*" (see the fifth Acrostic below). Esther replies: "The adversary and enemy is this wicked Haman." The king, filled with wrath, rises, and goes forth into the palace garden. Haman, filled with fear, rises, "to make request for his life to Esther the queen, for he saw

that evil was determined against him

by the king."

This was the climax, the end had come. Hence the name is spelt by the final letters:

4 3 2 1

כִּי כָלְתָה אֵלָיו הָרָעָה

1 2 3 4

kY kālethāH 'ēlāyV hārā'āH

1 4 2 3

that evil was-determined against-him

Translated, as before, the Acrostic appears in English thus: "For he saw that there was

eviL tO feaR determineD

against him by the king."

THE FIFTH ACROSTIC (7. 5)

in this book does not form the name "Jehovah," but the remarkable name E H Y H which means

"I AM."

It is noted in some manuscripts by Majuscular letters, which have *Massoretic* authority (see Ap. 30).

The Acrostic is formed by the final letters, and the name is spelt backward.

The king asks "*Who is he, and where is he*, that durst presume in his heart to do so?": i. e. to sell for destruction Queen Esther and her People. In saying this he unconsciously gives the name of Him who came down to deliver His People out of the hand of Pharaoh, and had then come down to deliver them again out of the hand of Haman, "the Jews' enemy", who, like Pharaoh, sought to destroy the whole nation (cp. Exodus 2. 23-25 with 3. 14, 15). The great enemy of the Messiah—the living Word—was seeking to destroy all hope of His promised coming (Gen. 3. 15), and make void the repeated promise of Jehovah.

Ahasuerus only pointed to human agency, but his words point us to the Satanic agency which was behind it. The Acrostic is in the final letters of his question "Who is he, and where is he?" Only the great "I am that I am" could know that, and could answer that question. Esther and Mordecai knew the human instrument, but none could know who was directing him but the One Who sees the end from the beginning.

The words forming the Acrostic are

4 3 2 1

הוּא זֶה וְאֵי זֶה

1 2 3 4

hū'E zeH ve'eY zeH

2 3 4

[who is] he this [man] and where [is] this [man]

"who durst presume in his heart to do so": i. e. to conspire against the life of the Queen and her People.

We may English it thus:

"WherE dwelletH the-enemY that-daretH
presume in his heart to do this thing?"

Thus was the name of the great "I AM" of Exodus 3. 14 presented to the eye, to reveal the fact that He who said of E H Y H "this is My Name for ever, and this is My Memorial unto all generations" (*v.* 15), was there to remember His People. Here was a "generation" in Persia who experienced the truth and the power of this Name, as a former "generation" had done in Egypt.

The same "I AM" had indeed come down to deliver them from Haman; as He had from Pharaoh, and from the great "enmity" (of Gen. 3. 15) which instigated both to accomplish the Satanic design of exterminating the Nation of Israel.

In these five Acrostics we have something far beyond a mere coincidence; we have design. When we read the denunciation in Deut. 31. 16-18, and see it carried out in Persia, we learn that though God was not *among* His people there, He was *for* them. Though He was not acting as Jehovah, "that dwelleth between the Cherubim," He was "the God of Heaven," ruling and over-ruling all in the Heaven above and in the Earth beneath" for the fulfilment of His purposes, and in the deliverance of His People. Hence, though His name, as well as His presence, is HIDDEN, yet, it is there, in the Word; and so wonderfully interwoven that no enemy will ever know how to put it out.

61 QUOTATIONS FROM THE BOOK OF JOB IN THE OTHER BOOKS OF THE BIBLE.

The quotations from, and references to, the book of Job in the other books of the Bible show that it was well known and read in the days of David and Solomon and the Prophets, and cannot be referred to as late a period as the 7th—4th centuries B.C., as most of the "higher" critics do.

The following table will enable the reader to judge for himself. There are 65 passages referred to: 37 in the Psalms; 18 in Proverbs; 9 in the Prophets; and 1 in the N.T.

JOB.	Quoted or referred to in other books.	JOB.	Quoted or referred to in other books.	JOB.	Quoted or referred to in other books.
3. 3–11	Jer. 20. 14, 15, 18.	9. 34	Ps. 39. 10.	23. 10	Ps. 66. 10.
3. 16	Ps. 58. 8.	10. 3	Ps. 138. 8.	23. 11	Ps. 44. 18.
3. 21	Prov. 2. 4.	10. 8	Ps. 119. 73.	24. 14, 15	Pss. 10. 8, 11; 11. 4.
4. 3, 4	Isa. 35. 3.	10. 10, 11	Ps. 139. 14–16.	24. 23	Prov. 15. 3.
4. 8	Prov. 22. 8. Hos. 10. 13.	10. 20, 21	Ps. 39. 5, 13.	26. 8	Prov. 30. 4.
5. 3	Ps. 37. 35, 36.	11. 17	Ps. 37. 6.	28. 13, &c.	Prov. 3. 13, &c.
5. 10	Ps. 65. 9.	11. 18, 19	Isa. 17. 2. Ezek. 34. 28. Mic. 4. 4. Zeph. 3. 13.	28. 15	Prov. 3. 14, 15.
5. 13	1 Cor. 3. 19.	13. 21, 28	Ps. 39. 10, 11.	28. 28	Prov. 1. 7; 9. 10. Ps. 111. 10.
5. 14	Isa. 59. 10.	14. 1, 2	Ps. 90. 3, 5, 6.	29. 18	Ps. 30. 6.
5. 15	Ps. 35. 10.	15. 35	Ps. 7. 14. Isa. 59. 4.	30. 9	Ps. 69. 12.
5. 17	Ps. 94. 12. Prov. 3. 11.	16. 10	Ps. 22. 13. Mic. 5. 1.	30. 16	Ps. 42. 4.
5. 20	Pss. 33. 19; 37. 19. Heb. 12. 5.	17. 7	Pss. 6. 7; 31. 9.	31. 7	Ps. 44. 18, 21.
5. 21	Ps. 31. 20.	18. 5	Prov. 13. 9; 24. 20.	32. 8	Prov. 2. 6.
5. 25	Pss. 72. 16; 112. 2.	19. 5–9, 13	Pss. 38. 16; 88. 8; 89. 44.	32. 21	Prov. 24. 23.
6. 4	Ps. 38. 2.	19. 13, 14	Ps. 88. 8, 18.	34. 11	Prov. 24. 12.
7. 7	Ps. 78. 39.	19. 26	Ps. 17. 15.	35. 12	Prov. 1. 28.
7. 10	Ps. 103. 16.	19. 29	Ps. 58. 10, 11.	36. 19	Prov. 11. 4.
7. 17	Pss. 8. 4; 144. 3.	21. 30	Prov. 16. 4. Zeph. 1. 15–18. 2 Pet. 2. 9.	36. 26, 27, 32	Pss. 90. 2; 147. 8.
8. 13	Prov. 10. 28.			40. 4, 5	Ps. 51. 4.
8. 22	Pss. 35. 26; 109. 29.				

62 THE SEPTUAGINT ENDING OF THE BOOK OF JOB.

In the Septuagint translation of the Old Testament into Greek, there is a long subscription. A similar subscription is found in the Arabic Version. It professes to be taken out of "the Syriac book"; but there is nothing to be found of it in the Syriac Version as published in Walton's Polyglot.

It was doubtless written B.C. It is interesting, especially when compared with the notes on p. 666, but what authority there is for it is not stated.

The last verse of Job (42. 17), "And Job died, an old man, and full of days," reads on as follows:

"And it is written that he will rise again with those whom the Lord raises up.

"This man is described in the Syriac book as dwelling in the land of Ausis, on the borders of Idumea and Arabia; and his name before was Jobab; and having taken an Arabian wife, he begat a son whose name was Ennōn. He himself was the son of his father Zara, a son of the sons of Esau, and of his mother Bosorrha, so that he was the fifth[1] from Abraham. And these were the kings who reigned in Edom, which country he also ruled over. First Balak the son of Beor,[2] and the name of his city was Dennaba. After Balak, Jobab, who is called Job: and after him, Asōm, who was governor out of the country of Thæman; and after him Adad, the son of Barad, that destroyed Madiam in the plain of Moab; and the name of his city was Gethaim. And the friends that came to him were Eliphaz of the sons of Esau, king of the Thæmanites, Baldad sovereign of the Sauchæans, Sōphar, king of the Minæans".

[1] Fifth. If he was the son of Issachar this corresponds with what is said in the notes on p. 666.

[2] So the Sinaitic MS. The Alexandrian MS. reads "Semphor," which is probably the same as "Zippor".

63 THE BOOK OF PSALMS. MISCELLANEOUS PHENOMENA.

I. THE TITLE OF THE BOOK.

The name given to the Book of Psalms as a whole by the Jews is *Tᵉhillīm*; but it is not recognised by this name in the Book itself.

Our English name "Psalms" is a transliteration of the Greek Title of the Septuagint, "*Psalmoi*",[1] which means "songs"; while the word "Psalter" is from the Greek *Psaltērion*, a harp, or other stringed instrument.

There is no correspondence between the Greek and the Hebrew in these cases. Only once does a Psalm bear this word in its title, and that is Ps. 145 (sing. *Tᵉhillah*).

Tᵉhillīm is invariably rendered "praises". It is a verbal noun from the root *hālal*, to make a jubilant sound.

To make *ellell* means to rejoice. Cp. German *hallen* and English halloo, yell.

Tᵉhillīm has, therefore, a wide meaning, and includes all that is worthy of praise or celebration; and, especially the works and ways of Jehovah.

Hence, in this book, we have these works and ways set forth as they relate to the Divine counsels of God, (1) as to *Man*, (2) as to *Israel*, (3) as to the *Sanctuary*, (4) as to the *Earth*, and (5) as to *the Word of Jehovah*. See the Structure of the separate Books of the Psalms, p. 720. In those Structures light is thrown upon the "ways" of God. The need for this instruction is seen from the other meaning of *hālal*, which in the Hithpael and Hithpolel means to praise or boast of one's self, hence *to be foolish*. Cp. 1 Kings 20. 11; Job 12. 17; Isa. 44. 25 (mad); Prov. 20. 14[1]. This instruction is given concerning God's ways and works exhibited in the Word of God from the beginning to the end.

[1] The word occurs *seven* times in the N. T. (Luke 20. 42; 24. 44. Acts 1. 20; 13. 33. 1 Cor. 14. 26. Eph. 5. 19. Col. 3. 16), four referring to the Book of Psalms, and the last *three* to Psalms in general.

[1] As it is foolish to glory in any object except in Jehovah (Jer. 4. 2; 9. 23, 24), so to boast of oneself is *to be foolish* in this case (Ps. 49. 6. Prov. 27. 1. See Pss. 5. 5; 73. 3; 75. 4; and cp. 44. 8).

II. THE QUOTATIONS FROM THE PSALMS IN THE NEW TESTAMENT.

(i) The Formulas used in direct Quotations.

"As it is written"; or "It is written": Matt. 4. 6[1] (91. 11). John 2. 17 (69. 9); 6. 31 (78. 24, 25). Acts 13. 33 (2. 7). Rom. 3. 4 (51. 4). 2 Cor. 4. 13 (116. 10).

"David", or "in David"[2]: Matt. 21. 43 (110. 1). Acts 2. 25 (16. 8), 34 (110. 1). Rom. 4. 6 (32. 1, 2); 11. 9, 10 (69. 22, 23). Heb. 4. 7 (95. 7).

"He (God) saith", "said", or "spake": Acts 13. 35 (16. 10). Eph. 4. 8 (68. 18). Heb. 1. 10-12 (102. 25-27); 4. 3 (95. 11); 5. 5 (2. 4); 5. 6 (110. 4).

"He (God) limiteth": Heb. 4. 7 (95. 7).

"He (God) testifieth": Heb. 7. 17 (110. 4).

"In the Scriptures": Matt. 21. 42 (118. 2, 3).

[1] This (with Ps. 91. 13) was Satan's quotation, mutilated by a significant suppression and omission.

[2] In David. The Fig. *Ellipsis* (Ap. 6), i. e. "in [the Psalm] of David"; or, "in [the person] of David".

"In their law"[1]: John 15. 25 (35. 19; 69. 4).

"In your law"[1]: John 10. 34 (82. 6).

"One in a certain place testified": Heb. 2. 6 (8. 4; 144. 3).

"Spoken by (or through) the prophet": Matt. 13. 35 (78. 2).

"The Book of Psalms": Acts 1. 20 (69. 25).

"The mouth of David"[2]: Acts 1. 16 (41. 9); 4. 25, 26 (2. 1, 2).

"The scripture": John 7. 42 (132. 11); 13. 18 (41. 9); 19. 24 (22. 18), 28 (69. 21), 36 (34. 20), 37 (22. 16, 17).

"The second Psalm": Acts 13. 33 (2. 7).

[1] "Law" is used by Fig. *Metonymy* (of the Part) for the whole of the O. T.

[2] David's "mouth", but not David's *words*.

(ii) The Adaptation of Words of the Psalms, without a Specific Quotation, or Reference to Fulfilment.

2. 7 (Heb. 1. 5).
2. 9 (Rev. 2. 27).
4. 4 (Eph. 4. 26).
6. 8 (Matt. 7. 23).
8. 2 (Matt. 21. 16).
8. 6 (1 Cor. 15. 25, 27. Eph. 1. 20, 22).
9. 8 (Acts 17. 31).
19. 4 (Rom. 10. 18).
22. 1 (Matt. 27. 46. Mark 15. 34).
22. 8 (Matt. 27. 43). The chief priests.
22. 21 (2 Tim. 4. 17).
24. 1 (1 Cor. 10. 26, 28).
27. 1 (Heb. 13. 6). See 118. 6, below.
34. 8 (1 Pet. 2. 3).
40. 6-8 (Heb. 10. 5-7).
41. 9 (Mark 14. 18).[1]
48. 2 (Matt. 5. 35).
50. 14 (Heb. 13. 15).
55. 22 (1 Pet. 5. 7).
56. 4, 11 (Heb. 13. 6).
69. 9 (John 2. 17).
69. 21, 27 (Matt. 27. 34, 38. Mark 15. 36).
74. 2 (Acts 20. 28).
78. 24, 25 (John 6. 31).
79. 6 (2 Thess. 1. 8).
89. 27, 37 (Rev. 1. 5; 3. 14).
91. 13 (Luke 10. 19).
102. 25-27 (Heb. 1. 10-12).
106. 20 (Rom. 1. 23).
110. 1 (Mark 16. 19. 1 Cor. 15. 25, 27. Col. 3. 1. Eph. 1. 20, 22).
110. 4 (Heb. 5. 10).
116. 10 (2 Cor. 4. 13).
116. 11 (Rom. 3. 4).
118. 6 (Heb. 13. 6). See 27. 1, above.
118. 22 (Acts 4. 11. Matt. 21. 42. 1 Pet. 2. 4, 7).
118. 26 (Matt. 21. 9).
125. 5 (Gal. 6. 16).
143. 2 (Gal. 2. 16).
146. 6 (Acts 14. 15).

[1] John (13. 18; 19. 28, 29) uses the formula "that it might be fulfilled" because of the object of his Gospel (20. 31).

III. QUOTATIONS AS BEING THE DIRECT FULFILMENT OF PROPHECIES IN THE PSALMS.

22. 18 (John 19. 23, 24).
34. 20 (John 19. 36).
35. 19 (John 15. 25).
41. 9 (John 13. 18. Acts 1. 16).
69. 4 (John 15. 25).
78. 2 (Matt. 13. 35).
97. 7 (Heb. 1. 6).
109. 3, 119. 161 (John 15. 25).

IV. QUOTATIONS AS BEING THE DIRECT UTTERANCES OF THE FATHER, THE SON, AND THE HOLY SPIRIT, RESPECTIVELY.

The Father.

2. 7 (Heb. 1. 5, 6. Acts 13. 33).
45. 6, 7 (Heb. 1. 8, 9).
89. 26, 27 (Heb. 1. 5).
97. 7 (Heb. 1. 6).
102. 25-27 (Heb. 1. 10-12).
104. 4 (Heb. 1. 7).
110. 1 (Heb. 1. 13).

The Son.

18. 2 (Heb. 2. 13).
22. 1 (Matt. 27. 46. Mark 15. 34).
22. 22, 25 (Heb. 2. 12).
40. 6-8 (Heb. 10. 5-7, 8, 9).
45. 6 (Heb. 1. 8).

The Holy Spirit.

41. 9 (Acts 1. 16).
95. 7-11 (Heb. 3. 7-11).

V. DIVINE TITLES APPLIED DIRECTLY TO CHRIST IN THE NEW TESTAMENT.

9. 8, 96. 13, 98. 9 (Acts 17. 31).
34. 8 (1 Pet. 2. 3.).
45. 6 (Heb. 1. 8).
62. 12 (Matt. 16. 27).
74. 2 (1 Pet. 1. 19).
97. 7 (Heb. 1. 6).
102. 25-27 (Heb. 1. 10-12).
104. 4 (Heb. 1. 7).

VI. THE BEATITUDES IN THE PSALMS.

The word rendered "blessed" in the "Beatitudes" is not always "*bārak*," to bless; but *'ashrēy*, happinesses. Its first occurrence is Deut. 33. 29. It is the plural of majesty or accumulation, and means "O the happinesses", or, "O the great happiness", or, "O How happy".

'Ashrēy occurs twenty-six times in the book of Psalms. It is translated "blessed" nineteen times, and "happy" seven times. In the list below, these latter are marked with an asterisk (*).

The following is the complete list:

Pss. 1. 1; 2. 12; 32. 1, 2; 33. 12; 34. 8; 40. 4; 41. 1; 65. 4; 84. 4, 5, 12; 89. 15; 94. 12; 106. 3; 112. 1; 119. 1, 2; 127. 5*; 128. 1, 2*; 137. 8*, 9*; 144. 15*, 15*; 146. 5*.

The word is distributed in the five books of the Psalms as follows: Book I, eight times; Book II, once; Book III, four times; Book IV, twice; Book V, eleven times; making twenty-six in all.

APPENDIX 63: THE PSALMS. MISCELLANEOUS PHENOMENA (*cont.*).

VII. THE ACROSTIC PSALMS.

There are nine examples of Acrostics in the Book of Psalms, while eleven other Acrostic Scriptures are found in the Old Testament[1].

i. Psalms 9 and 10 are linked together by an Acrostic which, like "the times of trouble" (the great tribulation), of which the two Psalms treat, is purposely broken, and is irregular and out of joint. This Acrostic tells us that the subject of the two Psalms is one, and that they are to be connected together. See notes there on the many expressions common to both.

ii. Psalm 25. Here, again, the Acrostic is designedly incomplete, a proof of its genuineness instead of its "corruption". No writer would or could omit a letter from carelessness. The Psalm has the same phenomena as Psalm 34, where the same letter ו (*Vau*=V) is omitted, and the same letter פ (*Pe*=P) is duplicated, in the word *Pādah*, "redeem". The last verse is thus, in each case, made to stand out prominently by itself.

iii. Psalm 34. See under ii, above.

iv. Psalm 37. In this Psalm the series is perfect and complete. Every letter has two verses of two lines each, except three: *vv.* 7 (ד, *Daleth*=D), 20 (כ, *Kaph* =K), and 34 (ק, *Ḳoph*=Ḳ).

v. Psalm 111. In this Psalm the series is complete. The Psalm has twenty-two lines, each line commencing with the successive letters of the alphabet.

vi. Psalm 112 is formed on the model of Psalm 111, the two Psalms forming a pair[2]; Psalm 111 being occupied with Jehovah, and Psalm 112 with the man that revereth Jehovah. See the notes there.

vii. Psalm 119. This Psalm consists of twenty-two groups, consisting of eight verses each. The eight verses in each group begin with the same letter. For example: the first eight verses begin with א (*Aleph*=A), the eight verses of the second group with ב (*Beth*=B), and so through the whole Psalm of 176 verses (8 × 22. See Ap. 10).

It is impossible to reproduce this (or any of the other alphabetical Acrostics), seeing that the Hebrew and English alphabets do not correspond, either in equivalents, order, or number of the letters.

It so happens that in the group beginning with T (*vv.* 65–72), each verse in the A.V. does begin with T, except *vv.* 67 and 71. These can be readily conformed by changing "Before" to "Till" in *v.* 67; and "It is" to "'Tis" in *v.* 71.

[1] There are five in the Book of Esther, each giving the Divine names in the form of an Acrostic. (See Ap. 60.)
One other Divine name in Ps. 96. 11. See note there.
One perfect Acrostic in Prov. 31. 10–31. See note there.
In the Book of Lamentations, each of the first four chapters is characterised by an Acrostic. See notes there.

[2] With the further peculiarity that the first three verses in each Psalm consist of two portions: the last two, of three portions.

The first two letters being the same in both alphabets, can be thus presented:

Ah! the happinesses of the perfect in the way,
  Such as walk by the Law of Jehovah.
Ah! the happinesses of the keepers of His testimonies,
  Who seek Him with their whole heart.
Assuredly they have not worked iniquity:
  In His ways they have ever walked.
As to Thy commandments—Thou hast commanded us,
  That we should diligently keep them.
Ah Lord, that my ways were prepared
  To keep Thy statutes;
Ashamed, then, should I never be,
  While I have respect unto all Thy commandments.
All my heart shall praise Thee in uprightness,
  While I learn the judgments of Thy righteousness.
All Thy statutes also I will keep:
  Leave me not utterly.

By what means shall a young man cleanse his way?
  By taking heed thereto according to Thy word.
By every means my heart hath sought Thee:
  Let me not err from Thy commandments.
Besides, I have laid up Thy Word in my heart,
  That I might not sin against Thee.
Blessed art Thou, O Jehovah:
  Teach me Thy statutes.
By my lips have I recounted
  All the judgments of Thy mouth.
By walking in Thy mandates' way,
  I found joy beyond all wealth.
By Thy precepts shall I guide my musings,
  And shall pore over Thy paths.
By Thy statutes shall I be delighted:
  Thy Word I shall not forget.

viii. Psalm 145. In this Psalm the Acrostic is perfect, with the exception of the letter נ (*Nun*=N), which should come between *vv.* 13 and 14. See note there.

Through the infirmity of some transcriber, the verse was probably omitted by him. It must have been in the more ancient manuscripts, because it is preserved in the ancient Versions: viz. the Sept., Syr., Arabic, Ethiopic, and Vulgate. One Heb. Codex is known which contains it, as follows:

"The LORD is faithful in all His words,
  And holy in all His works."

Moreover, the Structure of the Psalm shows that it originally had its proper place in the Psalm. See the notes on Ps. 145. 13, 14.

ix. For the other Acrostic in the Psalms, see the note on Ps. 96 11.

VIII. THE AUTHORS NAMED IN THE PSALMS.

1. The Psalms bearing the name of "DAVID" are seventy-three in all: thirty-seven in Book I (3, 4, 5, 6, 7, 8, 9, 11, 12, 13, 14, 15, 16, 17, 18, 19, 20, 21, 22, 23, 24, 25, 26, 27, 28, 29, 30, 31, 32, 34, 35, 36, 37, 38, 39, 40, 41); eighteen Psalms in Book II (51, 52, 53, 54, 55, 56, 57, 58, 59, 60, 61, 62, 63, 64, 65, 68, 69, 70); one in Book III (Ps. 86); two in Book IV (101 and 103); and fifteen in Book V (108, 109, 110, 122, 124, 131, 133, 138, 139, 140, 141, 142, 143, 144, 145).

2. By "Asaph", twelve Psalms: one being in Book II (Ps. 50), and eleven in Book III (73, 74, 75, 76, 77. 78, 79, 80, 81, 82, 83).

3. By "the sons of Korah", eleven Psalms: seven being in Book II (42, 44, 45, 46, 47, 48, 49); and four in Book III (84, 85, 87, 88), as set out in *The Companion Bible*. In Pss. 46 and 88 it is repeated as the *sub*-scription of Pss. 45 and 87, and is not the *super*-scription of 46 and 88 as in all the Versions.

4. For, or of "Solomon", two Psalms: one in Book II (Ps. 72), and one in Book V (Ps. 127).

5. "By Heman the Ezrahite", one in Book III (Ps. 88).

6. By "Ethan the Ezrahite", one in Book III (Ps. 89).

7. By "Moses the man of God", one in Book IV (Ps. 90).

IX. THE DISPENSATIONAL CHARACTER OF THE PSALMS.

In reading the Book of Psalms, we must constantly bear in mind the character of the Dispensation to which they belong. The word "Dispensation" means "administration": and God's principles of administration varied according as man was in a Dispensation of innocence, or mankind was "without Law", or Israel was "under Law", or as we are under grace in this present Dispensation.

God's principles of administration have varied with each of these: and in the future they will vary yet more: in the coming Dispensation of judgment, and in the Dispensation of millennial glory by which it will be followed.

If we read what pertains to one Dispensation into another which is administered on different lines, we shall have only confusion. Unless they be rightly divided, we shall not find "the truth" (2 Tim. 2. 15).

Much of what we read in the Psalms is truth *for all time*: but, some things are *peculiar* to that Dispensation of Law, and are neither suitable nor appropriate for the present Dispensation of grace. That is why many readers stumble when they judge "the imprecatory Psalms" from the standpoint of grace. Those Psalms were appropriate for the past Dispensation of works, as they will be for the coming Dispensation of judgment; but they are not appropriate for the present Dispensation, in which God's administration is on the principles of grace (according to Matt. 5. 44-48). It was true, in the former Dispensation of Law, that "when the wicked man turneth away from his wickedness, and doeth that which is lawful and right, he shall save his soul alive" (Ezek. 18. 27). But that is not the way of salvation now. The Scriptures for this present Dispensation are written and contained in the Pauline Epistles (fulfilling the promise of the Lord in John 16. 13); and these declare with one voice that we are not saved by works, but by grace (Rom. 3. 23, 24; 11. 6. Eph. 2. 3-9. Titus 3. 5-8).

Even so with the "imprecatory Psalms", and similar expressions in other Psalms: they were *true* and appropriate for that Dispensation, but are equally inappropriate for this.

X. THE DISTRIBUTION OF THE DIVINE TITLES IN THE FIVE BOOKS.

It may conduce to the completeness of the study of the usage of the Divine Titles, in relation to the Dispensational character of the five Books of the Psalms, if we give a connected list. They are given under the Structure of each Book separately.

A comparison of these numbers will show that they correspond with the subject of each Book as exhibited in the Structure prefixed to each Book. When "God" is used, the thought is of the Creator and His creatures. When "Jehovah" is used, it speaks of a Covenant God, in covenant relation with His own People.

i. The Genesis Book. (Psalms 1-41), p. 720.

Jehovah occurs 279 times, Elohim only forty-eight (nine of them connected with Jehovah).

ii. The Exodus Book. (Psalms 42-72), p. 720.

Jehovah occurs only thirty-seven times, Elohim occurs 262 times (twice in connection with Jehovah). El occurs fourteen times, and Jah once.

iii. The Leviticus Book. (Psalms 73-89), p. 720.

In the *First* Section (A^1) Jehovah occurs only fifteen times, while Elohim occurs sixty-five times (twice with Jehovah).

In the *Second* Section (A^2) Jehovah occurs fifty times, while Elohim occurs only 28 times (four of which are connected with Jehovah). El occurs five times.

iv. The Numbers Book. (Psalms 90-106), p. 720.

Jehovah occurs 126 times, and Elohim only thirty-one times (in ten of which it is combined with Jehovah). El occurs six times.

v. The Deuteronomy Book. (Psalms 107-150), p. 720.

Jehovah occurs 293 times, while Elohim occurs only forty-one times (in four of which it is combined with Jehovah). Jah occurs thirteen times. El occurs ten times. Eloah twice.

XI. THE PRAYER BOOK VERSION OF THE PSALMS.

The Authorised Version of the Bible of 1611 was preceded by several other Versions made into the English tongue.

1. The earliest was that by John Wycliffe, about A.D. 1380. This existed only in MS. until 1831, when the N.T. was printed for the first time, followed by the O.T. in 1848. The complete Bible was not published till 1850.

2. Tyndale's Version. The N.T. was published in 1525, and the Pentateuch in 1530.

3. Coverdale's Version followed in 1535, and was the first complete printed English Bible.

4. Matthew's Bible (largely based on Tyndale) was published under this assumed name in 1537 by John Rogers.

5. The Great Bible followed in 1539. It was Coverdale's Version revised by himself, and was in large folio, which gave it its name. In 1540 Cranmer wrote a preface; and hence this and subsequent editions[1] became known as "Cranmer's Bible". It was from this Version that the Psalms and other portions of Scripture were taken, and used in the Prayer Book, from the edition of 1552 to the last revision in 1662.

When the A.V. was published in 1611, it was "authorised (or appointed) to be read in churches" (hence its name), instead of the Versions which had preceded it, and which were thenceforth superseded. Extracts from it, such as the opening sentences, and the Epistles and Gospels, were at the same time substituted for those previously in use[2].

But it was found that, from the use of the Psalms in Public Worship, people had become so accustomed to the older Version (many being able to sing or say them from memory), that when the last revision of the Prayer Book was made in 1662 the Psalter was retained, it being deemed unwise to make a change which would be so revolutionary.

This is why the Prayer Book Version differs from the Bible Version.

This is also the reason why a change in "the names and order" of the Books of the Bible to the order of the Hebrew Canon is likewise now impossible. The translators of the Septuagint arbitrarily adopted a different order, and gave the books different names. This was followed by the Vulgate and all subsequent Versions[1]. No change in these respects would now be tolerated.

In comparing the two Versions, regard must be had:

(1) To the NUMBERS OF THE VERSES, as these are not the same in each, and differ sometimes in the numeration. For example, Ps. 19. 14 in A.V. is 19. 14, 15, in the Prayer Book Version; and Ps. 18. 1, 2 in A.V. is 18. 1 in the Prayer Book Version. The reference to the Psalms in *The Companion Bible* and its Appendixes is always to the A.V., not to the Prayer Book Version.

(2) As to OBSOLETE WORDS in the Prayer Book Version, the following is a list of the more important, which will show the extent of the changes made in 1611:

Abjects, worthless persons, 35. 15.
after (*prep.*), according to, 90. 15.
apace, swiftly, 58. 6.
at large, loose, without restraint, 118. 5.
brawn, muscle, boar's flesh, 119. 70.
cast their heads, consult, conspire, 83. 5.
certify, to make certain, 39. 5 (*v.* 4 in A.V.); to show knowledge, 19. 2.
comfortable, consoling, 54. 6.
conversation, mode of life, 50. 23.
darling, favourite, A.S. *dear-ling*, 22. 20; 35. 17.
discovereth, strippeth of leaves, 29. 8 (*v.* 9 in A.V.).
dragons, serpents, 74. 14 (*v.* 13 in A.V.).
due, appointed, 9. 9.
ensue, pursue, 34. 14.
eschew, avoid, shun, 34. 14.
fain, glad, 71. 21 (*v.* 23. in A.V.).
fie, Lat. *phy*, an expression of disgust, 35. 21; 40. 18.

[1] The other Versions published between this and the A. V. were *The Geneva Bible* in 1557-60; and Archbishop Parker's in 1568, known as the *Bishops' Bible*; the *Rhemish N.T.* in 1582; and the *Douai Bible* in 1610, both the latter being of Roman Catholic origin.
[2] Except the "comfortable words" in the Communion Service, which appear to be original translations and not wholly from any preceding Version, and have never been changed.

flittings, wanderings, 56. 8.
froward, perverse, 18. 26; 58. 3; 64. 2.
glory, tongue (which gives glory), 16. 10.
graven, dig, digged, 7. 16.
ground, bottom, 68. 26.
harnessed, armed, root=made of *iron*, 78. 10.
health, salvation, 51. 14; 67. 2; 119. 123.
hell, grave, 49. 14, 15.
hold of, hold to, 31. 7.
holpen, helped, 22. 5; 86. 17.
horn, head, 75. 5, 6, 12; 89. 18.
inditing, dictating, 45. 1.
inquisition, search, inquiry, 9. 12.
knappeth, snappeth, 46. 9.
laud (Lat.), praise, 135. 1.
lay to, apply, 119. 126.
learn, teach, 25. 4, 8; 119. 66.
leasing, falsehood, 4. 2; 5. 6.
lien, lain, 68. 13.
lighten, enlighten, 13. 3; 34. 5.
make thou all his bed, nurse, 41. 3.
minished, lessened, 12. 1; 107. 39.
mistake, take wrongly, 56. 5.
nethermost, lowest, 86. 13.
noisome, noxious, 91. 3.
ordereth, arrangeth, 40. 6.
pate, crown of the head, 7. 17.
pit, grave, 6. 5; 9. 15; 69. 16.
poor, oppressed, 34. 6; 69. 30.
ports, gates, 9. 14.
potsherd, broken pottery, 22. 15.
prevent, precede, anticipate, 18. 18; 21. 3; 119. 148, &c.
quick, living, alive, 55. 16.
quicken, make alive, 119. 25, &c.
refrain, restrain, 76. 12.
reins, kidneys, 7. 10, &c.
require, ask, 27. 4; 38. 16.
room, place, 18. 36; 31. 9.
runagates, rebels, 68. 6.
set by, esteem highly, 15. 4.
set in, put in the way of, 38. 17.
shawms, wind instruments, 98. 7.
simple, undesigning, artless, 72. 4, 13.
simpleness, artlessness, guilelessness, 69. 5.
still, silent, 62. 1.
stomach, pride, 101. 7.
stool, seat, 94. 20.
strange, foreign, 18. 45; 114. 1.
tell, count, 22. 17; 56. 8.
thereafter, according, 90. 11.
thievish, given to theft, 10. 8.
treadings, footsteps, 73. 2.
tush, an expression of impatience, like pish, or tut, 10. 6, &c.
unto, in comparison with, 16. 2.
vengeance, vindication or avengement, 79. 11.
water-pipes, cataracts or torrents, 42. 9.
weights (upon the), scales; i.e. when weighed, 62. 9.
whet, sharpen, 7. 13.
wholesome, saving, 20. 6; 28. 9
within, within doors, 45. 14.
wont, accustomed, 119. 156.
worship, worthy of honour, 3. 3.

64 "TO THE CHIEF MUSICIAN."

The key to the interpretation of these words has been lost for over twenty-two centuries.

Commentators and critics have confessed that they can make only conjectures as to the primitive meaning and use of the word (for it is only one word in Hebrew) *lamᵉnazzēaḥ*.

The Ancient Versions attempt a rendering. The Sept. has *eis to telos*=unto, for, or, with a view to the end. The Arabic, Ethiopic, and Vulgate render it "at the end". The Chald. renders it (Ps. 45) "to the praise". The Talmudists hold that it related to Him Who is to come; while Aquila (one of the Sept. Revisers, A.D. 130) renders it "*tō Nikopoiō*"=to the giver of victory.

It is clear that a Person was intended by these various renderings; but they appear to be interpretations rather than translations. Regarded as the former, they may be useful in showing us how the Psalms point to Christ; for He is the end. It is He Who giveth victory; it is He Who is the Coming One: and, while the book is called *Sepher Tᵉhillīm*, the Book of Praises, it is He Who "inhabiteth the praises of Israel" (Ps. 22. 3).

All ancient Hebrew manuscripts, with the early and best later printed editions, show no break whatever between the lines of one Psalm and another.

The Septuagint translators had been many years in Babylon, and the oldest among them must have been very young when carried away thither.

There were none who had full knowledge and experience of the ancient usages of the Temple worship.

Consequently, when they came to their task some 197 years after the latest carrying away to Babylon, there was nothing to show them where one Psalm ended and where the next Psalm began.

Hence, when they came to the word *lamᵉnazzēaḥ*, "To the chief Musician", they took it as being the *first* line of a Psalm, instead of the *last* line of the preceding Psalm which they had just translated. All subsequent Versions, in all languages, have followed them in this mistake. For mistake it was, as we may see from the only two examples of independent Psalms given us in the Scriptures: viz. Isa. 38. 9–20, and Hab. 3.

In each of these isolated Psalms we have the true models on which all other Psalms are based.

In each case we have

1. The *Super*-scription, or Title proper.
2. The body of the Psalm itself.
3. The *Sub*-scription.

In each of these two cases the word *lamᵉnazzēaḥ* forms the *sub*-scription, and appears at the end of the Psalm.

This is the key thus discovered by Dr. J. W. Thirtle[1] which had been lost for so many centuries; and *The Companion Bible* is the first edition of the Bible in which the Psalms are thus correctly presented in harmony with the two Psalm-models, Isa. 38. 9–20, and Hab. 3.

The unspeakable importance of Dr. Thirtle's discovery is at once seen. For it shows two things:

1. That, whatever the interpretation or application of the words may be, a Psalm which had this word in the *sub*-scription had a use beyond its local, temporary, or original purpose; and, being considered appropriate for public use, or for special occasions, was handed over to the Director of the Temple worship with any instructions which might be necessary for its use.

2. That such word or words of instruction, which today stand in the Septuagint and all subsequent Versions of the Bible as the *super*-scription, belong, not to that Psalm, but to the *sub*-scription of the Psalm preceding it.

This, at one stroke, removes the great difficulty, and solves the heretofore insoluble problem and impossible task which all Commentators have experienced, when they struggled in the attempt to find in one Psalm the explanation of words which belong to another.

Few problems so difficult and baffling have been removed by a solution so simple and self-explanatory.

This one feature, which, by Dr. Thirtle's kind permission, has been taken over into *The Companion Bible*, must greatly enhance its value and usefulness, making it unique among all existing editions of the Bible.

[1] See foot-note on p. 92 (col. 1).

65 THE PSALM-TITLES, AND WORDS EMPLOYED IN THEM.

From what is written in the preceding Appendix (64), it will be seen that, though the words "Psalm-Titles" are used here in this Appendix in their ordinary traditional sense, our understanding of them must be seriously modified; all the words used in them, and explained below, occur in the *sub*-scription of the preceding Psalm, and belong to that Psalm. It is there we have placed them in *The Companion Bible*, and it is in those Psalms that we have to look for their elucidation and find the key to the meaning of the words.[1]

Commentators who revered the Word of God have struggled to find some logical, spiritual, or mystical meaning in these "titles"; while modern critics do not seem able to rise beyond musical instruments and terminology, or "catch-words" of popular songs or tunes.

The *Teaching*, which is deep and grand beyond all conception, they fritter down to some commonplace reference; while the *Text*, which is clear, they mystify with their puerile guesses and vain imaginations.

We look for something more worthy of this work of the Holy Spirit of God; something more worthy indeed of the Bible, regarding it merely as a literary production. We look for something more dignified than a "tom-tom" or a "catch-word", and we shall find it.

The words used in these *sub*-scriptions (which no commentator of any repute regards as other than integral parts of Holy Writ, being numbered, and forming as they do the first verse of each Psalm in the Hebrew text, and actually quoted as Scripture in the N.T.) refer to momentous truths, and not to musical terms; to teaching, and not to tunes; to instruction, and not to instruments; to sense, and not to sound. They are for those who have a heart for music, and not merely an ear for music; they are for Enochs who walk with God, and not for Tubal-Cains who handle the harp and the organ. They pertain to the things of the Spirit, and not to "things made with hands".

We shall present these words and expressions in the spelling, and in the order in which the Bible reader will look for them in this Appendix, viz. in alphabetical order.

We may first note here that thirty-four Psalms have no title at all, and are without *super*-scription or *sub*-scription: viz. Psalms 1, 2, 10, 33, 43, 71, 91, 93, 94, 95, 96, 97, 99, 104, 105, 106, 107, 111, 112, 113, 114, 115, 116, 117, 118, 119, 135, 136, 137, 146, 147, 148, 149, 150.

The words in the *super*-scriptions and *sub*-scriptions are as follows, and are given in the spelling of the A.V. to which English readers are accustomed.

I. AIJELETH-SHAHAR (The Day-Dawn).

This title, which in the versions has stood in the *super*-scription of Ps. 22, now finds its proper place and stands (in *The Companion Bible*) as the *sub*-scription to Ps. 21.

The meaning given both in A.V. and R.V. is "the hind of the morning".

The Jewish commentators, Rashī (A.D. 1040–1145, Troyes) and Kimchi (A.D. 1160–1232, Narbonne) render it "a hind fair as the morning". Luther rendered it "the hind early chased". The Targum has it "the morning sacrifice".

The moment we regard it in the light of Psalm 21 instead of Psalm 22, a new field of inquiry presents itself.

The expression is a Figure of speech common in the East, and frequently met with in Arabian poetry.

It is used of *the Day-Dawn*, in which the beams of light from the rising sun are seen shooting up (like horns) above the horizon before the sun actually appears. It is used in Psalm 21 of the rays of Messiah's coming glory, and tells of the dawn of His approaching coronation which is the one great subject of Psalm 21. See the Structure and notes.

It is the same DAY-DAWN that forms the theme of David's "last words". See the notes on 2 Sam. 23. 1–5 and Ps. 72, with the Structures and notes there; and compare 2 Pet. 1. 19.

II. AL ALAMOTH (relating to maidens).

There is no dispute or question as to the meaning of these words: *'Al*=relating to, or concerning, or connected with. *'Al* has a wide range of meaning, and we may select the one which lends itself best to the context. As to *'Alamōth* (fem. pl.), there is a consensus of opinion that it can mean only *damsels* or *maidens*. *'Almah* occurs (in sing. and pl.) seven times in the Heb. O.T., and is rendered "*virgin*" in Gen. 24. 43. Song 1. 3; 6. 8. Isa. 7. 14; "*maid*" in Ex. 2. 8. Prov. 30. 19; and "*damsel*" in Ps. 68. 25. The proper word for virgin is *b^{e}thūlāh* (Gen. 24. 16, &c.), while *'almāh* denotes a young woman of marriageable age, still under the care of others. Every *b^{e}thūlāh* is an *'almāh*, but not every *'almāh* is, necessarily, a *b^{e}thūlāh*.[1]

In the plural, therefore, *'alamōth* can mean only *maidens*. There is no need to think about music, or to restrict the use of the word here to "a maidens' choir", standing, as it now must stand, as the *sub*-scription to Ps. 45, and not as the *super*-scription of Ps. 46. There is no connection between "maidens" and Ps. 46, but there are many points in the subject-matter of Ps. 45 which link it on to that Psalm. There are references to the "king's daughter", and "honourable women" (*v.* 9). It is a "daughter" that is addressed as the bride (*v.* 10). There is the "daughter of Tyre" (*v.* 12); "the king's daughter" (*v.* 13); and "the virgins her companions" (*v.* 14).

There are special reasons, therefore, in the subject-matter of Ps. 45, which connect it with that Psalm; and make it very appropriate that, even if the Psalms were intended to be sung by *maidens*, such singing need not be connected with the Temple or its services. There was *processional* singing in the open air. And in 1 Chron. 15 we have just the occasion for the use of the word in this connection. In the procession in which the Ark was carried up from the house of Obed-edom to Zion three bodies of singers are mentioned: (1) the Levites (*vv.* 16–19), (2) *the maidens* (*v.* 20); and (3) the *Sh^{e}mīnith* or men-singers (see No. XIX, p. 95) who brought up the rear of the procession (*v.* 21). This is the very order which is mentioned in Ps. 68: (1) the singers going before (1 Chron. 15. 16–19); (2) the players on instruments following after (*v.* 22); in the midst, "the damsels (the *'Alamōth*) playing with timbrels" (*v.* 20). Ps. 68 begins with the words of Num. 10. 35, which prescribes the formula for the setting forth of the Ark. The "goings" of Ps. 68. 24 refer to the great going up of the Ark to Zion. The company of those who published the word of Jehovah (*v.* 11) is fem. plural, and the reference is not to Ex. 15. 20 or 1 Sam. 18. 6, but to 1 Chron. 15. 20. From all this it is clear that this Psalm (68) must be carried back to as early a date as 951–950 B.C., instead of being assigned to the later dates of 537 B.C. or 167 B.C. as demanded by modern criticism.

III. AL-TASCHITH=Destroy not.

There are four Psalms which have this *sub*-scription, viz. 56, 57, 58, and 74 (*not* Psalms 57, 58, 59, and 75, which in all the versions have it as the *super*-scription).

The first three are David's, the fourth is by Asaph.

Two by David (56 and 57) are each connected with a crisis in his life, while the third belongs to a peculiar time of trouble.

There is no dispute as to the meaning of the word.

It is rendered by A.V. and R.V. as "Destroy not". It is a cry of distress, a *cry at a crisis*. But this cry is found, in the Psalms to which we have placed it, as a

[1] These facts have been discovered, and admirably set forth by Dr. J. W. Thirtle, in his two works on this subject, viz. *The Titles of the Psalms: their Nature and Meaning explained* (1904), and *Old Testament Problems* (1907). Both published by Henry Frowde, Oxford Bible Warehouse, London.

[1] The Greek word *parthenos*, in Matt. 1. 23, shows that the *'almāh* of Isa. 7. 14 must have been a virgin. The Septuagint also renders *'almah* by *parthenos* in Isa. 7. 14.

sub-scription, and not in the others where it has formerly stood as a *super*-scription.

Such a cry had been made by Moses at a great crisis (Ex. 32. 11-14, cp. Deut. 9. 25), and by David (2 Sam. 24. 16, 17) where we have the same Heb. word (*shāḥath*). David acted on the injunction of Deut. 4. 30, 31; the reason being "for Jehovah thy God is a MERCIFUL God, He will not forsake thee, neither DESTROY thee". This is why Pss. 56 and 57 begin "Be merciful".

For further references to this *sub*-scription, compare Pss. 56. 1, 9, 10, 11; 57. 1-3, 6, 7; 58. 3, 6, 7, 11, and 74. 1-3, 10, 11, 18-20, 22, 23. Ps. 74 is prophetic of the latter days (spoken of in Deut. 4. 30) when "Destroy not" will be an appeal suited to "the day of Jacob's trouble".

David was a prophet (Acts 2. 30), and spake of things yet future; why should not some Psalms speak prophetically and proleptically of Zion before it was built, and of the Exile before it took place, instead of being styled "post-Exilic" by the modern critics?

IV. GITTITH=Winepresses (relating to the Autumn Feast of Tabernacles).

There are three Psalms which have this word in the *sub*-scription. They are 7, 80, and 83 (not 8, 81, and 84, over which they have hitherto stood as the *super*-scription).

There is no doubt about Gittith meaning *winepresses*; from *Gath* (Judg. 6. 11. Neh. 13. 15. Isa. 63. 2. Lam. 1. 15), not the "vat" which receives the juice from the 'press" (which is *yeḳeb*, Num. 18. 27, 30. Deut. 15. 14, &c.). The word speaks of the autumn, just as *Shoshannim*, No. XX below (lilies), speaks of the spring. Hence *Shoshannim* (flowers) is associated with the *Spring* Festival (the Passover), as *Gittōth* (fruit) is associated with the *Autumn* Festival (Tabernacles). The Passover told of Jehovah's goodness in Divine *redemption*; the Feast of Tabernacles told of Jehovah's goodness in Divine *keeping*. A study of the three Gittith Psalms (7, 80, and 83) in this connection will yield instruction and profit, and remove all the perplexity involved in associating the word with the subject-matter of Pss. 8, 81, and 84, with which it has no connection.

There will be no longer need to be troubled with such guesses as "Gittite instruments", or "Gittite guards", or "Levites of Gath-rimmon", which are as meaningless as they are irrelevant. See further under *Shoshannim* (No. XX, below).

V. HIGGAION.

As this word occurs in the Text, see Ap. 66. I (p. 96).

VI. JEDUTHUN.

JEDUTHUN was one of the three directors (or the "chief Musicians") of the Temple worship (1 Chron. 16. 41, 42; 25. 1-6; 2 Chron. 5. 12; 35. 15). The three sons of Aaron were thus represented by the three men whose names occur in this category. JEDUTHUN was a descendant of MERARI (1 Chron. 26. 10); while ASAPH was a descendant of GERSHOM; and HEMAN of KOHATH.

JEDUTHUN seems to have had another name, "ETHAN" (1 Chron. 15. 17, 19, compared with 16. 41, 42; 25. 1, 3, 6, and 2 Chron. 35. 15). That there was an "Ethan", a Merarite, is seen from 1 Chron. 6. 44; 15. 17.

Since he is associated with those two men, it is going out of one's way to create a difficulty by supposing Jeduthun to be "a musical instrument", or the "name of a tune" (R.V. marg.) or of a "measure".

In 2 Chron. 35. 15 he is called "the king's seer"; and in 1 Chron. 25. 1 it was the duty of these three men "to prophesy" and "to confess, and to praise Jehovah" (*v.* 3). This was according to the king's order (*v.* 6).

There are three Psalms connected with JEDUTHUN (38, 61, and 76), and they will be found to fulfil these conditions.

By comparing these Psalms as set out in *The Companion Bible*, the confusion, caused by two of these Psalms appearing to have the names of two different authors, vanishes. The *sub*-scription of each Psalm now stands "To the chief Musician—Jeduthun."

VII. JONATH-ELEM-RECHOKIM=The Dove in the distant Terebinths.

There is only one Psalm with this *sub*-scription, i. e. Ps. 55 (not Ps. 56, over which it has hitherto stood in other Bibles and Versions as the *super*-scription or title).

There is a general agreement that this Title means "*Relating to the dove in the distant terebinths* (*or oaks*)".

David is the "dove". He is far away in the distant woods, moaning over the trouble that has come upon him through the rebellion of Absalom, recorded in 2 Sam. 15-19.

There is no reference to a dove in Ps. 56, but there is in Ps. 55. 6. In *v.* 2 he says, "I mourn in my complaint, and moan" (R.V.). In Isa. 38. 14, Hezekiah, in trouble equally great, says, "I did moan as a dove" (the same word as in Ps. 55. 17 (R.V.). Cp. Ezek. 7. 16, where we have it again). David speaks further concerning this moaning in Ps. 55. 4-8; also in *vv.* 16, 17. The desertion of Ahithophel at this crisis is alluded to in *vv.* 12-14. All Psalms of, or "relating to David", refer to the true David; so we may compare David's desertion with Christ's betrayal, and the end of Ahithophel (2 Sam. 17. 23) with the end of Judas Iscariot (Matt. 27. 5-8. Acts 1. 18, 19).

VIII. LEANNOTH.

See No. X, below.

IX. MAHALATH (The great Dancing).

This word stands in *The Companion Bible* as the *sub*-scription of Ps. 52, and not in the *super*-scription or title of Ps. 53, as in all other Bibles and Versions.

The Septuagint translators could make nothing of the words (there being no vowel points); so they simply transliterated the word, spelling it *maeleth*, which has no meaning whatever. AQUILA, a reviser of the Sept. (about A.D. 160), supplied different vowels, and read the Hebrew as though it meant *choreia*, dancing. He must have taken the Hebrew *M^ecḥolōth* to mean *dancing* (or, by the plural of majesty, *the great dancing*). SYMMACHUS, another reviser of the Sept. (about A.D. 193-211), follows AQUILA.

This rendering, which takes the Hebrew as being *M^ecḥolōth* (instead of *Maḥalath*), at once connects Ps. 52 with 1 Sam. 18. 6, 7, the occasion being celebrated and known afterwards as "the great dancing". Twice, later in David's life, this event is referred to as a landmark in David's history (1 Sam. 21. 11; 29. 5). If we read Ps. 52, we shall note the references to Doeg's mischievous tongue (in *vv.* 1-4); to David's assertion (1 Sam. 17. 37) in *v.* 5; to David's words, "all this assembly shall know" (1 Sam. 17. 47); in *vv.* 6, 7 "the righteous also shall see and fear". The victory is ascribed to God in *v.* 9, as it is in 1 Sam. 17. 37. When we read these remarkable references, we shall not heed the modern critics' talk about "catchwords of an *older* song", or the "name of a tune called 'Sickness'", or "the name of a choir at Abel-meholah".

X. MAHALATH LEANNOTH (The great Dancing and Shouting).

These words are found as the *sub*-scription to Ps. 87 in *The Companion Bible* (not as the *super*-scription or title to Ps. 88 over which it stands in all other Bibles and Versions).

As *M^ecḥolōth* means dancing (see No. IX above), so all are agreed that *Leannoth* means *shoutings* (and, with the pl. of majesty, the great shouting). (Cp. Ex. 15. 20, 21; 32. 17, 18. Num. 21. 17. 1 Sam. 18. 6, 7. Ezra 3. 11). So that the combined words "The Great Shouting and Dancing" give us the subject-matter of Ps. 87.

We have only to read the Psalm in the light of 1 Sam. 6. 14, 15 to see the obvious connection with David's bringing the Ark to Zion. In *v.* 2 there is a distinct allusion to the other places where the Ark had found a temporary dwelling, Shiloh (1 Sam. 1. 3; 2. 14; 3. 21. Ps. 78. 60); Beth-shemesh (1 Sam. 6. 13); Kirjath-jearim (1 Sam. 7. 1); Gibeah (2 Sam. 6. 3, 4); the

house of Obed-edom (*vv.* 10–12). But none of these was the dwelling-place Jehovah had chosen. Hence, Zion is celebrated as "the Mount Zion which He loved".

XI. MASCHIL. Understanding or Instruction. (Public.)

This word is found in the *super*-scription proper of thirteen Psalms (32, 42, 44, 45, 52, 53, 54, 55, 74, 78, 88, 89, 142).

Unlike the "Michtam" Psalms (which are all by David, see No. XII below), these are by various authors.

Six are by David (32, 52, 53, 54, 55, and 142).
Three are by the sons of Korah (42, 44, and 45).
Two are by Asaph (74 and 78).
One is by Heman the Ezrahite (88).
One is by Ethan the Ezrahite (89).

Maschīl is from *sākal*, to look at, scrutinise, to look well into anything (1 Sam. 18. 30); hence the noun will mean *understanding* arising from deep consideration (Prov. 13. 15. Neh. 8. 8). The Sept. rendering is *suneseōs* = *understanding* and *eis sunesin* = for understanding. It is the O.E. verb *to skill*.

The first of these Psalms (32) gives the basis of all true instruction and understanding. In *v.* 8 it is given:

"I will instruct thee
And teach thee in the way thou shouldest go . . .
Be not as the horse, or as the mule, which have no understanding".

Or Ps. 44. 1, "We have heard", &c.; or 45. 10, "Hearken, O daughter, and incline thine ear", &c.

The idea "to play skilfully" seems trivial in comparison with such "*instruction*" as this.

XII. MICHTAM (Engraven).

This word is found (in all Versions of the Bible) in the *super*-scription of six Psalms (16, 56, 57, 58, 59, 60). All are by David. The last five form a group by themselves.

See the Structure of "the Exodus Book" (or the Second Book) of the Psalms (p. 759), where, in Group F^1–F^5, God's People speak to Him as Israel's Redeemer; and His work as telling of His death and resurrection.

The word *Michtam* is from *Kātam*, to cut in, or engrave, as in Jer. 2. 22, "thine iniquity is *graven* before me" (not "marked", as in A.V. and R.V.).

The Sept. renders it *stēlographia* = a sculptured writing. Hence, *stēlē* = a *sepulchral monument*, on account of the inscription graven on it.

The word, therefore, points to a *graven* and therefore a permanent writing; *graven* on account of its importance (cp. Job 19. 24). What that importance is can be gathered only from the *Michtam* Psalms themselves.

The A.V. and R.V. derive the word from *Kethem* gold, either from its being precious, or hidden away.

This meaning is not far out; but it lacks the *raison d'être* for this importance, which the other derivation gives in connecting it with *death* and *resurrection*.

The *Michtam* Psalms are all pervaded by the common characteristic of being Personal, Direct, and more or less Private.

The reference is to David's Son and David's Lord; and especially to His death and resurrection; or to a deliverance from imminent danger, or death, or even from the grave itself. See Pss. 16. 10, 11; 56. 13; 57. 3; 58. 10, 11; 59. 16; 60. 5, 12. It is David who, "being a prophet" (Acts 2. 25–31), knew that God "would raise up Messiah to sit on his throne". Hence this is the truth *engraven* in the first of these *Michtam* Psalms (16).

XIII. MUTH-LABBEN (The Death of the Champion).

This, in *The Companion Bible*, stands now as the *sub*-scription of Ps. 8, and not as the *super*-scription or title of Ps. 9, as in other Bibles and Versions. All are agreed that *mūth* can mean only *death*. As to the other word *labbēn*, the matter is not so simple. For *bēn* means *son*, but there is nothing about a "son" in either Psalm (8 or 9): and, as it must relate (like the other Titles) to *subject-matter*, and not to the name of a "song", or a "tune", or a "musical instrument", there must be another explanation of *bēn*. Now *bēn* may be *beyn*, written what is called "defective", i.e. without the full sign for its vowel (which is very often found in Hebrew). In that case it would mean *the separator*, and thus be related to *bayin* = "between" which is the dual form of this word in the designation of Goliath in 1 Sam. 17. 4, 23, "the man between [the two hosts" of Israel and the Philistines], or "the duellist". Hence, *labbēn* ("for the son") may be read *labbēyn*, "for the duellist" or "the champion", or "the one standing between". Indeed, this is exactly how the words are given in the ancient Jewish commentary called the Targum: "To praise; relating to the death of the man who went between the camps". That is to say, the champion, as he is called in 1 Sam. 17. 4, 23.[1]

Read in this light, Psalm 8 stands out with quite a new signification, seeing it relates to "the death of the champion", Goliath of Gath.

We may compare with this Ps. 144, which in the Sept. version has this remarkable title, "by David, concerning Goliath": in *v.* 3 of which Psalm we have the very words of Ps. 8. 4. And in *v.* 10 the words, "Who delivereth David His servant from the hateful sword": i.e. of Goliath.

XIV. NEGINAH.

See "Neginoth", No. XV below, of which it is the singular.

XV. NEGINOTH (Smitings).

This word, in *The Companion Bible*, stands in the *sub*-scriptions of eight Psalms, i.e. 3, 5, 53, 54, 60 (sing.), 66, 75, and Hab. 3. (Not in the *super*-scriptions of Pss. 4, 6, 54, 55, 61 (sing. with *'al* instead of *Beth*), 67, and 76).

"Neginoth" is from *nāgan*, to strike, or smite. Hence it has hitherto been associated with the striking of the strings of some musical instrument! But why should the striking be connected with strings? Is there no other kind of *smiting* known? Why may it not refer to the *stroke* of affliction, or the *smiting* with words? Indeed, it is so associated in Lam. 3. 63: "I am he whom they smite [with their words]". In all these *Neginoth* Psalms there is the note of deliverance from personal smitings. See 3. 2; 5. 6; 53. 1; 54. 3; 60. 3, 5, 11; 66. 10–12; 75. 4, 5. We have the verb again in 77. 7, "I call to remembrance my song", or my stroke of affliction. So in Isa. 38. 20, "We will sing, or make songs", or, we will make songs concerning my stroke, or afflictions. In Hab. 3. 19 we may, in the same way, understand it as "relating to my smitings", i.e. those referred to in *v.* 16.

XVI. NEHILOTH (Inheritances, or The Great Inheritance).

This word is found in *The Companion Bible* in the *sub*-scription to Ps. 4 (not in the *super*-scription of Ps. 5 as in other Bibles and Versions).

The word is *Neḥīlōth*, which has been taken from *ḥālal, to bore*; but, even then, human imagination does not seem able to rise higher than the *boring* of holes to make a flute!

The Sept. has "concerning her that inherits". AQUILA in his revision (A.D. 160) has "Division of Inheritances". SYMMACHUS (A.D. 193–211) has "Allotments"; while the Latin Versions have similar renderings. This shows that they must have had before them the consonants N, Ḥ, L, TH, with the vowel-points *Neḥa-LōTH* which gives the intelligible meaning, *inheritances*, or *the great inheritance*. In Ps. 4 this reference is quite clear. Jehovah was the inheritance of His People (Ps. 16. 5; cp. 73. 26; 119. 57; 142. 5. Jer. 10. 16. Lam. 3. 24). Hence, in Ps. 4. 6, the question is asked, "Who will show us [what] good [is]"? And the answer which follows is "Thou". For, joy in Jehovah is greater than joy in harvest.

The same truth is seen in Ps. 144. See notes on *vv.* 11–15–, with the true answer in *v.* -15.

[1] The word "champion" in verse 51 is not the same word, but is *gibbōr*. See Ap. 14. IV.

XVII. PSALM (Heb. *Mizmōr*).

This word is used in the super-scriptions forty-four times in all (Pss. 3, 4, 5, 6, 8, 9, 12, 13, 15, 19, 20, 21, 22, 23, 24, 29, 31, 38, 39, 40, 41, 47, 49, 50, 51, 62, 63, 64, 73, 77, 79, 80, 82, 84, 85, 98, 100, 101, 109, 110, 139, 140, 141, 143. Of these, twenty-one are in Book I, seven in Book II, seven in Book III, three in Book IV, and six in Book V.

Mizmōr means, and is invariably rendered, "a Psalm", and occurs nowhere but in the Psalm-Titles. It differs from *Shīr* (see below), which is "a Song": i.e. for singing, whereas *Mizmōr* may be for meditation, &c.

Mizmōr is joined with *Shīr* in thirteen Psalms (30, 65, 67, 68, 75, 76, 87, 92, preceding it; and 48, 66, 83, 88, 108, following it).

XVIII. SELAH. See Ap. 66. II.

XIX. SHEMINITH. (The Eighth Division.)

This word occurs in the sub-scription of two Psalms (5 and 11 in *The Companion Bible*); not in the super-scription of Psalms 6 and 12, as in other Bibles and Versions.

There is a general agreement that it means "the eighth", and in its thirty-one occurrences it is always so rendered, except in 1 Chron. 15. 21 and in these two sub-scriptions (Pss. 5 and 11), where it is transliterated "Sheminith".

The A.V. puts "the eighth" in the margin in all three cases. The R.V. puts "the eighth" only in the case of the two Psalms.

Though it is agreed that the word means "eighth", it is not agreed as to what "the eighth" refers to. It varies between "the eighth mode", "the eighth (or octave) below" (i.e. the bass), "the eighth day", or year, or "an instrument with eight strings".

The latter is out of the question, because, in 1 Chron. 15. 21, those with harps are set "over the *Shemīnīth*" (as others are set "over the *'Alamōth*"), and we cannot speak of certain "instruments" being "set" over others. Moreover, the *Shemīnīth* are additional to *Neginoth* in the sub-scription to Ps. 5.

1 Chron. 15. 21 helps us to the solution. The *'Alamōth* being maidens (*v.* 20), it would seem obvious that the *Shemīnīth* must be men (*v.* 21).

But what class of men? The Talmud[1] suggests *a class of true Israelites*, i.e. those circumcised on *the eighth day*, and thus distinguished from all other Jews or Gentiles; for other nations who practise circumcision always do so on a later day[2], *never on the eighth day*.

As all others in the procession were, in this sense, *Shemīnīth*, and the *Shemīnīth* are distinguished from these as well as the *'Alamōth*, Dr. Thirtle concludes that it must refer, as well, to a *division* in that procession. Everything points to divisional order in such processions (cp. Ex. 25. 14. Num. 4. 15; 7. 9. So also in 1 Chron. 24. 1; 26. 1, 12). The definite article seems conclusive. In 1 Chron. 15. 21 *the Shemīnīth* were to lead (R.V.), not "to excel" (as in A.V.). This is its general meaning (see 1 Chron. 23. 4. 2 Chron. 34. 12. Ezra 3. 8, 9), where it is rendered "set forward".

An examination of Pss. 5 and 11 show us that there is special emphasis on "righteous worshippers" as distinct from others. Cp. 5. 7, 11 with 11. 1 and 7, and see the Structures of those Psalms.

XX. SHIGGAION (A crying aloud).

This word occurs only in the super-scription of Ps. 7, and in the super-scription of the prayer in Hab. 3. 1, where it is in its right place. The scope of the Psalm guides Dr. Thirtle to the choice of *sha'ag*, to cry aloud, in trouble, danger, or pain, and to discard *shāgah*, which means to wander, or go astray. There is nothing in the Psalm to agree with the latter, and everything that points to *the loud cry* of David when he was in danger of being torn in pieces, and to the loud cries (pl.) of Habakkuk: of pain in *v.* 16 and of praise in *v.* 18.

[1] *Yebamoth* 43b, cp. 53b. *Yebamoth* is the first of seven treatises in the third book (*Nashim*) which treats of the distinctive rights of men and women.

[2] Josephus, *Ant.* 1. 12.

XXI. SHOSHANNIM (Lilies, or, The Spring Festival, Passover).

This word is found in the sub-scription of two Pss. i.e. 44 and 68, not in the super-scription of Pss. 45 and 69, as it stands in other Bibles and Versions.

We have already seen under "GITTITH" (No. IV above) that, as the spring and autumn were appropriately represented by flowers and fruit respectively, so lilies and winepresses were singled out from each.

The Passover and Feast of Tabernacles divided the year into two fairly equal parts; the former being the spring festival and the latter the autumn.

Israel is symbolized again and again by the vine[1], and Dr. Thirtle refers us to 2 Esdras 5. 23-28 (R.V.) for the use of the lily. It is the prayer of Esdras: "O Lord That bearest rule of all the woods of the earth, and of all the trees thereof, Thou hast chosen Thy ONE VINE; and of all the lands of the world Thou hast chosen the ONE COUNTRY; and of all the flowers of the world, ONE LILY . . .; and among all its peoples Thou hast gotten the ONE PEOPLE . . .: now, O Lord, why hast Thou given this ONE PEOPLE over unto many", &c.

Lilies and pomegranates (spring flowers and autumn fruits) were everywhere seen in the Temple (1 Kings 7. 20-22), and the knops (or knobs) of flowers of Ex. 25. 31-34 were doubtless the same globe-like pomegranates and lilies. The Sept. has "globes" and lilies. Cp. Ex. 28. 33, 34; 39. 25, 26, where the "bell"-like flower is doubtless meant.

In the Jewish Prayer Book, at the Feast of Purim, Israel is spoken of as "the lily of Jacob"; and at the Feast of Dedication (*Chanucha*) God is praised for delivering "the standard of the lilies" (i.e. of Israel).

The Hebrew shekel had, on one side, sometimes a lamb (Passover), and, on the other side, a wine-bowl (Tabernacles).

The half-shekel had a triple lily and a wine-bowl:

SILVER SHEKEL OF SIMON MACCABÆUS.

In old Jewish cemeteries, tombs are seen with the seven-branched candlestick with its knops and flowers, and sometimes with a triple lily and pomegranate.

Interpreters who are guided by tradition see in these lilies only "poppy heads", betokening eternal sleep! and "a round fruit" or husk from which the kernel (or spirit) has fled! Thus Babylonian and Egyptian heathenism is forced to interpret and replace Divine Biblical symbols. But we may ask in this case: "Does not the *lily* say, 'Here lies one of Jehovah's redeemed'? and the pomegranate, 'Here lies one safe in Jehovah's keeping'"?

Read, now, the two *Shoshannim* Psalms (44 and 68), and the Passover story will be seen in all its fulness and beauty.

[1] Ps. 80. 8. Isa. 5. 1-7; 27. 2-6. Jer. 2. 21; 12. 10. Hos. 10. 1, &c.

XXII. SHUSHAN, AND SHOSHANNIM EDUTH.

(Instruction as to the Spring Festival, or the Second Passover.)

This title is found in the *sub*-scription of Ps. 79 in *The Companion Bible* (not the *super*-scription of Ps. 80, as in other Bibles and Versions), while SHUSHAN (sing.) EDUTH is found in the *sub*-scription of Ps. 59 in *The Companion Bible* (not the *super*-scription of Ps. 60, as in other Bibles and Versions).

The first of these two words refers to the Spring Festival (see under No. XXI above), the latter refers to some testimony concerning it. There is no dispute as to the *'Edūth* meaning "testimony". It is one of "the ten words" found twenty-three times in Ps. 119 (see Ap. 73). But what is the "testimony" to which these two Psalms refer? It must be concerning something connected with the Spring Festival (Passover), and Dr. Thirtle sees in it the Law and the "Testimony" respecting the keeping of the Passover in the *second* month, when, under special circumstances, it could not be kept in the *first* month (see Num. 9. 10, 11, and cp. 2 Chron. 30. 1-3). Psalms 59 and 79 treat of enemies being then in the land, which might well have created a difficulty in keeping the Passover in the *first* month.

In any case, this interpretation is more reasonable, and more worthy of the dignity of the Sacred Text than the unsupported guesses as to its being the name of "a popular song", or "the name of a tune", or a choir whose President lived at Shushan.

XXIII. SONG.

Is always the rendering of *Shīr*, and denotes words that are to be *sung*, as distinct from *Mizmōr* (see No. XVII above). It is joined with *Mizmōr* thirteen times (see above). It is used by itself fifteen times (in the Songs of the degrees); and in Pss. 18 (*shīrāh*), 45 (with *Maschil*), and 46.

66 HEBREW WORDS IN THE TEXT OF THE PSALMS.

Certain Hebrew words are retained *in the body of the text* of the Psalms, being transliterated instead of translated. Not forming any part of the title, superscription, or sub-scription, they are considered here in a separate Appendix.

They are two in number, i.e. HIGGAION and SELAH, and we preserve the spelling of the A.V. for the sake of convenience.

I. HIGGAION=SOLILOQUY.

The word is found in three Psalms: viz. 9. 16; 19. 14, and 92. 3.

In 9. 16 it is transliterated "Higgaion".

In 19. 14 it is translated "meditation"; and

In 92. 3 it is rendered "solemn sound".

The word occurs also in Lam. 3. 62, where it is rendered in the A.V. "device", and in the R.V. "imagination".

It is derived from *hāgāh*, and means to *soliloquize, to speak to one's self*; hence, *to meditate* (Josh. 1. 8. So Pss. 77. 12 and 143. 5).

As a noun, it would mean a *meditation*, or a speaking in premeditated words; and therefore worthy of memory or repetition.

If the three Psalms be read in the light of this word, we shall note the subjects which are so worthy of our meditation, and not think about music.

In Ps. 9. 16 it is the judgment of Jehovah.

In Ps. 19. 14 it is the words and the work of Jehovah.

In Ps. 92. 2, 3 it is the lovingkindness and faithfulness of Jehovah.

II. SELAH.

This word may be from one of two roots; from *ṣālāh*=to pause; or from *ṣālal*=to lift up.

There is no need to descend to the guesses as to musical terms. A reference to Ap. 65 (p. 92, Int. Col. 1) will lead us to connect it with *subject-matter*, not with music; and with *truth*, not with tunes.

Some say it occurs always at the beginning of a strophe; others, always at the end. But this is a question of fact, and not of argument.

The outstanding fact is that in four cases it comes in *the middle of a verse*, i.e. Ps. 55. 19; 57. 3; and Hab. 3. 3, 9.

This is fatal to both theories, but yet it helps us to, and agrees with, the right conclusion, that both are the two halves of one truth. *Selah* does connect the end of one strophe with the beginning of the next; and, indeed, in four cases it connects the end of one Psalm with the beginning of the next, thus uniting the two Psalms (see Pss. 3 with 4; 9 with 10; 24 with 25, and 46 with 47).

Selah, therefore, neither ends nor begins a passage, but it CONNECTS the two passages between which it is placed.

An examination of each occurrence will show what this connection is. It is neither the pausing on one subject; nor the passing on from one subject to another: but it is the connecting of the two subjects together.

Sometimes it is the Structures which are connected.

Sometimes it is synthetic, and adds a development of thought by connecting a prayer with that which forms the basis of it.

Sometimes it is antithetic, and adds a contrast.

Or it connects a cause with an effect, or an effect with a cause.

It is a *thought-link*, which bids us look *back* at what has been said, and mark its connection with what is *to follow*; or to some additional consequent teaching.

Thus, if it be derived from *ṣālāh*, to pause, it is not the instruments of music which are to pause while the voices continue to sing; but it is our hearts which are to pause and to note the connection of precious truths.

If it be derived from *ṣālal*, to lift up, then, it is not the instruments which are to lift up their sound in a louder degree, but our hearts which are to be lifted up to consider more solemnly the two truths which are about to be connected.

These connections, showing the importance and object of each "Selah", are given in the notes on each occurrence of the word.

The phenomena connected with "Selah" may be thus stated:

The word occurs seventy-four times in the Bible, and all are in the Old Testament.

Of these, seventy-one are in the Book of Psalms, and three are in the model Psalm, "the prayer of Habakkuk", ch. 3.

The use of the word is confined to thirty-nine Psalms out of the 150. In sixteen of these thirty-nine it occurs once (7, 20, 21, 44, 47, 48, 50, 54, 60, 61, 75, 81, 82, 83, 85, and 143): of these thirty-nine Psalms, thirty-one are in Psalms handed over to "the chief Musician". (See Ap. 64.)

In fifteen Psalms it occurs *twice* (4, 9, 24, 39, 49, 52, 55, 57, 59, 62, 67, 76, 84, 87, and 88).

In seven Psalms it occurs *thrice* (3, 32, 46, 66, 68, 77, and 140).

In one Psalm it occurs *four* times, viz. Ps. 89.

It is distributed over the five Books of the Psalms (see p. 720) as follows:

Book I (1—41), seventeen times in nine Psalms.
Book II (42—72), thirty times in seventeen Psalms.
Book III (73—89), twenty times in eleven Psalms.
Book IV (90—150), four times in two Psalms.

67 THE SONGS OF THE DEGREES.

There is no difference of opinion as to the meaning of the word "degrees". It means "steps", but interpretations of the use of the word in this connection manifest a great difference and discordance.

Some think these Psalms were so called because they were sung on the fifteen steps of the Temple. But there is no evidence that there were fifteen steps. In Ezekiel's Temple (Ezek. 40. 22, 31) there are to be two flights; one of *seven* steps in the *outer* court, and another of *eight* steps in the *inner* court. But that Temple is the subject of prophecy, and is still future.

Others suggest "a Song of the higher choir", "on the stairs of some high place"; others, "in a higher key". Others interpret them of "the going up of the Ark" to Zion; others, of "the going up of the tribes" to the feasts; others, "a Song of high degree". Others refer them to "a synthetic arrangement of the parallel lines"; others, that they refer to "the going up from Babylon", which makes them all "post-exilic". Others regard them as referring to the yet future return of Israel from their long dispersion; while yet others spiritualize all the expressions, and interpret them of the experiences of the Church of God at all times, and in the present day.

One thing is clear, i.e. that *all* these interpretations cannot be correct. So we still look for one which shall be worthy of the dignity of the Word of God as "written for our learning"; and one which shall produce and combine intellectual enjoyment with experimental satisfaction.

Dr. Thirtle[1] has called attention to the use of the definite article. The Hebrew reads "A Song of THE Degrees" (*Shīr hamma'ălōth*). In this simple fact lies the key to the solution of the problem, which is as simple in its nature as it is grand in its results.

Once we note the use of the definite article, "THE Degrees", we naturally ask *what* Degrees? The answer comes from the Word of God itself, and not from the guesses and imaginations of men. The only "degrees" of which we read in the Bible are "the degrees" on the sundial of Ahaz, by which the shadow of the sun went backward in the days of his son Hezekiah, as a sign from Jehovah that he should recover from his sickness, while Jerusalem was surrounded by the armies of the king of Assyria, and Hezekiah was under sentence of death from the King of Terrors (see 2 Kings 20. 8–11, and the Structure of the chapters in Isa. 36—39). Scripture knows of no other steps or "degrees" that can be connected with the shadow of the sun.

On recovery from his sickness, Hezekiah said (Isa. 38. 20):

"Jehovah was ready to save me:
Therefore we will sing MY SONGS[2] to the stringed instruments
All the days of our life
In the house of Jehovah."[3]

More than 250 years ago (1602–75) this interpretation was suggested in a passing remark by Dr. John Lightfoot in his work on *Old Testament Chronology*: but so far as Dr. Thirtle is concerned, it was his own independent discovery.

The number of these Psalms (fifteen) adds its testimony to the certainty of this interpretation. It corresponds with the number of the years (fifteen), which were added to Hezekiah's life: while the number written by himself (ten) corresponds with the number of "the degrees" by which "the shadow of the sun went backward".

Hezekiah called them "MY songs". There was no need to put his own name to them, but he put the names to the other five. The one by Solomon is in the centre, with two by David on either side. In each of the seven Psalms (on either side of the central Psalm) the name "Jehovah" occurs twenty-four times, and "Jah" twice (once in the third Psalm of each seven). In the central Psalm, "Jehovah" occurs three times.

There are five groups consisting of three Psalms each. The first of each group has *Distress* for its subject; the second has *Trust in Jehovah*; while the third has *Blessing and peace in Zion.*

In the notes on these Psalms, the passages in the Kings, Chronicles, and Isaiah, to which they refer, are carefully supplied: the passages in the historical books also are referred to in these Psalms.

Here we give, in order, the facts of Hezekiah's history which are referred to in these Psalms. These fifteen points of contact can be used in connection both with the Psalms and the historical books.

We have noted *fifteen* events in the life of Hezekiah which find their counterpart, and are celebrated, in these fifteen Psalms. Space forbids our giving here more than the bare references. Further details will be found in the notes in the historical books, the prophet Isaiah, and the Psalms in question.

(i) RAB-SHAKEH'S BLASPHEMOUS TONGUE,

Which is mentioned in Isa. 37. 4, and 2 Kings 19. 16, is referred to in Pss. 120. 2, 3, and 123. 3, 4.

(ii) SENNACHERIB'S REPROACHES,

Which we find in 2 Kings 19. 25, 26, and Isa. 37. 26, 27, are repeated and practically quoted in Ps. 129. 5–7.

(iii) SENNACHERIB'S SHAME,

In 2 Chron. 32. 21. This is referred to in Ps. 129. 4, 5.

(iv) HEZEKIAH'S EARNEST PRAYER.

Isa. 38. 3, 10–20. 2 Chron. 32. 20, and 2 Kings 19. 2, 4, 15–19; 20. 2, 3, finds more than its echo in Pss. 120. 1; 123. 1–3; 130. 1, 2.

(v) GOD, "THE MAKER OF HEAVEN AND EARTH",

Was He to Whom Hezekiah addressed his prayer. This was in retort to idolatrous railings of Rab-shakeh in 2 Chron. 32. 19. See notes on Pss. 121. 1, 2, 6; 123. 1 (cp. 2 Kings 19. 15. Isa. 37. 16); 124. 8; 134. 3.

(vi) HEZEKIAH'S DESIRE FOR PEACE

Is seen in Isa. 38. 17; and in Ps. 120. 6, 7 we see the expression of it; for in 2 Chron. 32. 1–3 Sennacherib's "face was for war": hence, when Hezekiah says "I am for peace", who can doubt the reference to 2 Kings 18. 19, &c. and Isa. 36. 5, &c. See further Ps. 122. 6, 7, 125. 5, and 128. 6, and his own last desire for peace in 2 Kings 20. 19.

(vii) JEHOVAH'S PROMISED HELP.

In 2 Kings 19. 32–34; 20. 6, we have Jehovah's own answer to Sennacherib's challenge (2 Chron. 32. 10, 15, 17. Isa. 36. 20; 37. 11). Notice how Hezekiah treasured up this Divine pledge: Ps. 121. 2–8; 124. 1–3, 6; 125. 2; 126. 2, 3; 127. 1.

(viii) "FOR MY SERVANT DAVID'S SAKE".

This was the ground of Jehovah's promise (2 Kings 19. 34) in answer to Hezekiah's prayer in *v.* 14. See also 2 Kings 20. 5, 6. Observe how these words are taken up in 132. 1–10.

(ix) JEHOVAH'S SIGN TO HEZEKIAH.

In 2 Kings 19. 29, and Isa. 37. 30 this sign is given; and we see it referred to in Ps. 126. 5, 6; 128. 2. The continued perseverance of the sowers under great disappointment gives a picture of peaceful agriculturists at work at home, and not of exiles in a foreign land, or on their way home from Babylon.

(x) HEZEKIAH'S TRUST IN JEHOVAH.

This is the first thing recorded of Hezekiah (2 Kings 18. 5). It was the taunt of Rab-shakeh (2 Kings 18. 28–31), and is mentioned again and again (Isa. 36. 18; 37. 10). Now compare Ps. 121. 2; 125. 1–3; 127. 1; 130. 5–8.

[1] *Old Testament Problems.* London: Henry Frowde, 1907.

[2] In the Psalms the word is *shīr* (see Ap. 65. xxiii), while in Isa. 38. 20 it is *n^egīnah* (see Ap. 65. xiv). But the latter word, by the Fig. *Metonomy* (of the Subject), refers to the *words*, as *shīr* does (Ps. 69. 12; 77. 6. Lam. 3. 14, and in *v.* 63) to the "musick"; and the two words are used synonymously in the *super*-scriptions and *sub*-scriptions of Pss. 66 and 75.

[3] Note the Fig. *Epanadiplōsis* (Ap. 6), by which this statement is marked off, and its completeness emphasised by beginning and ending with the same word, "Jehovah".

(xi) Hezekiah like a Bird in a Cage.

This is not mentioned in Scripture; but Sennacherib has written it down for us, and it may be read to-day in the British Museum in London, on a hexagonal cylinder of this very Sennacherib, King of Assyria (607–583 B.C.).[1]

By the kind permission of the Oxford University Press, we are privileged to give a reproduction of a photograph of this cylinder.

It is "one of the finest and most perfect objects of its class and kind ever discovered, and its importance as an historical document can hardly be overrated. It contains four hundred and eighty-seven lines of closely written but legible cuneiform text, inscribed in the Eponymy of Belimuranni, prefect of Karkemish".

The text records eight expeditions of Sennacherib. Among them is his description of this very siege of Jerusalem in the reign of Hezekiah.

By the same kind permission we are enabled to give a photographic facsimile of that portion of the cylinder, beginning with the eleventh line of the central column, which is shown in the illustration below.

SENNACHERIB'S CYLINDER, 607–583[1] B.C. (RECORDING HIS CAMPAIGNS) NOW IN THE BRITISH MUSEUM (55-10-3. 1).

LINES 11-24 OF THE CENTRAL COLUMN OF THE CYLINDER.

The words we wish to refer to are in the eleventh to the twenty-first lines. Sennacherib says:

11. "I fixed upon him. And of Hezekiah [king of the]
12. Jews, who had not submitted to my yoke,
13. forty-six of his fenced cities, and the strongholds, and the smaller cities
14. which were round about them and which were without number,
15. by the battering of rams, and by the attack of engines
16. and by the assaults of foot soldiers, and . . . .[2]
17. I besieged, I captured, 200,150 people, small and great, male and female,
18. horses, and mules, and asses, and camels, and men,
19. and sheep innumerable from their midst I brought out, and
20. I reckoned [them] as spoil. **[Hezekiah] himself like a caged bird within Jerusalem,**
21. **his royal city, I shut in, &c.**

---

[1] According to "received" dating this is usually given as 705–681 B.C. Sennacherib's siege of Jerusalem took place in the 14th year of Hezekiah (603 B.C. Ap. 50. V). According to Professor Sayce, "Bible and Monuments" (*Variorum Aids*, p. 80), this invasion took place four years after his accession; and, as he is supposed to have reigned twenty years afterward (twenty-four years in all), his true regnal period would be, according to *The Companion Bible* dating (Ap. 50. V), 607–583 B.C. and not 705–681 B.C.

[2] The three words at the end of this line are the proper names of military engines.

Now read the words of Hezekiah in Ps. 124. 7:

"Our soul is escaped as a bird out of the snare of the fowlers:
The snare is broken, and we are delivered".

This takes the Psalm right back to the very days of Hezekiah and Sennacherib.

Indeed, it takes us back beyond the days of Hezekiah and Sennacherib: for *it is a Psalm of David.*

Some 360 years before Hezekiah (964-603 B.C.), David had found himself in similar trouble. He was hunted like a partridge in the mountains, pursued as a dog, and sought as a flea, by Saul. He had been shut up in his hiding places[1]. At such a time it was that David penned this Psalm (124). At such a similar time of Hezekiah's need, when he was shut up in his house by sickness, and besieged in Jerusalem by Sennacherib, he was indeed "like a caged bird". What Psalm could more suitably express the sense of his need, and his praise for Divine deliverance?

He had no need himself to write another "Song". Here was one ready to his hand. Indeed, David's reference to his escape "as a bird out of the snare of the fowlers" would be seized on by Hezekiah as exactly suited to express his deliverance from the "snare", as well as from the siege of Sennacherib.

It makes the history live again before our eyes.

We can see the vain boasting of his enemies; and hear his own praise, as he exclaims:

"Blessed be Jehovah, Who hath not given us as a prey to their teeth" (Ps. 124. 6).

(xii) THE CAPTIVITY OF ZION.

The foregoing statement of Sennacherib (see xi, p. 98), that he had taken away 200,150 captives from all the tribes of Israel, enables us to understand Hezekiah's prayer "for the remnant that are left". There is no need to forcibly introduce the captivity in Babylon. The "turning of captivity" was an idiomatic expression (by the Fig. *Paronomasia*[2], Ap. 6), used to emphasise the return of good fortune: not necessarily deliverance from a literal captivity or bondage. Jehovah "turned the captivity of Job" (Job 42. 10) by delivering him out of his troubles and giving him twice as much as he had before.

Ps. 126. 1-3 refers to the deliverance of Hezekiah and Zion, as well as to the captives mentioned on the cylinder of Sennacherib (see p. 98).

(xiii) HEZEKIAH'S ZEAL FOR "THE HOUSE OF JEHOVAH".

This was one of the most prominent features of Hezekiah's character. It occupied his thoughts and filled his heart. The first act of his reign was to "open the doors of the house of Jehovah" (2 Chron. 29. 3) which Ahaz his father had "shut up" (2 Chron. 28. 24). This was "in the first year of his reign, in the first month". See also Isa. 37. 1, 14. 2 Kings 20. 8. Isa. 38. 20, 22. Now read Pss. 122. 1, 9 and 134. 1, 2.

(xiv) HEZEKIAH CHILDLESS.

While the king of Assyria was besieging the gates of Zion, and the King of Terrors was besieging Hezekiah who was on his bed of sickness, Hezekiah at that moment had no heir to his throne; and the promise of Jehovah to David (2 Sam. 7. 12) seemed about to fail. Like Abraham when he had "no seed" (Gen. 15), Hezekiah must have been anxious at such a crisis.

He trusted in Jehovah for victory over his enemies; and he trusted in Jehovah for His faithfulness as to His promise to David. This is shown in Ps. 132. 11. In this crisis Jehovah sent Isaiah to Hezekiah with the promise of a son (2 Kings 20. 18. Isa. 39. 7). Not until three of the fifteen added years had passed was the promise fulfilled, in the birth of Manasseh. This it is which accounts for Hezekiah's anxiety.

There is nothing in the return from Babylon that can have any connection whatever with Psalms 127 and 128. Rejoicing in the multiplication of children in those sad days would be quite out of place. But in the case of Hezekiah, they stand out in all their full significance, and furnish an undesigned coincidence of the greatest importance. Read 127. 3-5, and the whole of Ps. 128, the last verse of which reflects Hezekiah's words (Isa. 39. 8).

(xv) THE PASSOVER FOR "ALL ISRAEL".

The proper time for keeping the Passover was already past, but rather than wait eleven months, Hezekiah resolved to keep it in the *second* month, according to the provision made for such an occasion in Num. 9. 1-11 (2 Chron. 30. 1-3).

Moreover, Hezekiah would have it for "all Israel" (2 Chron. 30. 5, 6). So the tribes from the North came down and united with the tribes of the South (2 Chron. 30. 11, 18). The hand of God was with them to give them "ONE HEART" (2 Chron. 30. 12). Then we read in 2 Chron. 30. 25, 26 of the happiness of it all.

Psalm 133 celebrates this great event of Hezekiah's reign; but it is a Psalm of David. Yes, but it celebrates another occasion precisely similar, when David's message "bowed the heart of all the men of Judah, even as the heart of ONE MAN" (2 Sam. 19. 14; cp. *v.* 9). It was exactly suited, therefore, to Hezekiah's circumstances. Hezekiah's purpose was to unite the tribes of the Northern Kingdom with the tribes of the South. Hermon's dew was one with the dew on Zion. The same cloud of the *night mist* united Israel and Judah; and we are invited to "Behold how good and pleasant it was for brethren to dwell together AT ONE".

These fifteen points put these "Songs of THE degrees" back into their historic setting, more than 600 years before Christ; and rescues them from the hands of those who would bring them down to about 150 B.C. and force them to have some connection with times and events for which no historical basis whatever can be found.

[1] Read 1 Sam. 23. 1-13, 19-24, 12, 14; 26. 1-20.

[2] *v^eshabtī, eth-sh^ebūth.* Cp. 2 Chron. 28. 11. Neh. 8. 17. Job 42. 10. Pss. 14. 7; 53. 6; 85. 1; 126. 1, 4. Jer. 30. 3, 18; 31. 23; 32. 44; 33. 7, 11, 26; 48. 47; 49. 6, 39. Lam. 2. 14. Ezek. 16. 53; 29. 14; 39. 25. Amos 9. 14. Zeph. 2. 7; 3. 20.

68 ZION.

I. OPHEL, OR "THE CITY OF DAVID".
II. THE JEBUSITE WATER-SUPPLY.
III. HEZEKIAH'S CONDUIT AND POOL.
IV. THE "SILOAM INSCRIPTION"
V. THE TEMPLE OF SOLOMON ON MOUNT MORIAH.
VI. SOLOMON'S ROYAL BUILDINGS ON MORIAH.
VII. SOLOMON'S ASCENT.
VIII. THE "DUNG GATE" OF NEHEMIAH.

I. OPHEL, OR "THE CITY OF DAVID".

THAT Zion (Heb.) or Sion (Greek) was "the city of David" is clear from 2 Sam. 5. 7. That Ophel and Zion are equivalent names applied to the highest point or mound of the hill ridge running due south from Mount Moriah is now generally conceded.

That Zion was the name of the original Jebusite fortress on this summit, almost directly above Gihon (now known as "the Virgin's Fount"), is also accepted by the majority of the authorities on the topography of Jerusalem.

It therefore becomes necessary to readjust some of the place-names which have been given to a Zion on the west side of Jerusalem on traditionary accounts (which, from the time of Josephus onwards, have located Zion on the south-western hill of the city), and to transfer them to a Zion south of Mount Moriah.

This readjustment will transfer the name to the true site and satisfy the requirements of fulfilled prophecy, which declares that "Zion shall be ploughed as a field" (Jer. 26. 18. Micah 3. 12). This is true of the site now claimed for it; but is not wholly true of the traditional

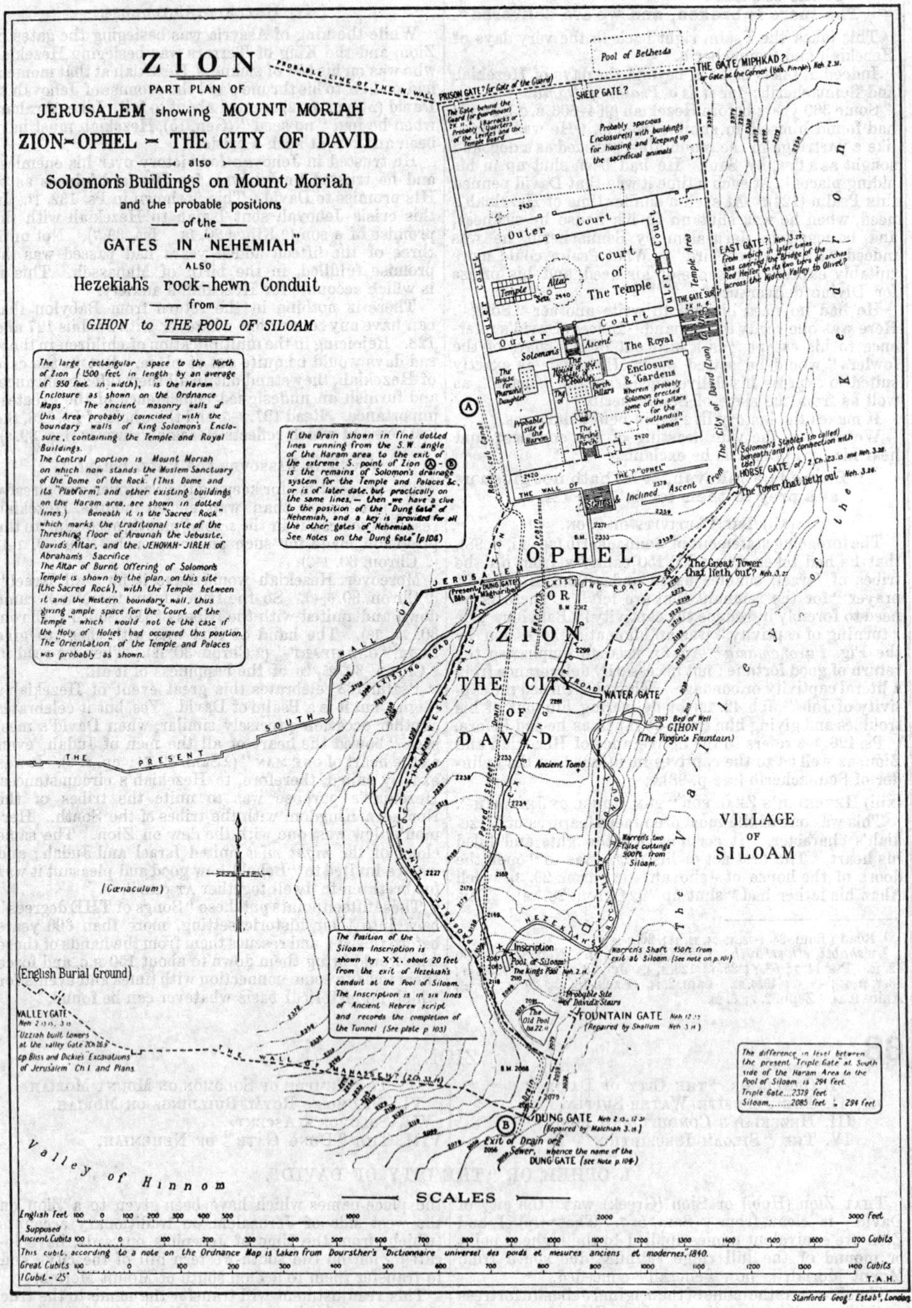
ZION
PART PLAN OF
JERUSALEM showing MOUNT MORIAH
ZION-OPHEL — THE CITY OF DAVID
also
Solomon's Buildings on Mount Moriah
and the probable positions
of the
GATES IN NEHEMIAH
ALSO
Hezekiah's rock-hewn Conduit
from
GIHON to THE POOL OF SILOAM
The large rectangular space to the North of Zion (1500 feet in length by an average of 950 feet in width), is the Haram Enclosure as shown on the Ordnance Maps. The ancient masonry walls of this Area probably coincided with the boundary walls of King Solomon's Enclosure, containing the Temple and Royal Buildings.
The Central portion is Mount Moriah on which now stands the Moslem Sanctuary of the "Dome of the Rock." (This Dome and its "Platform" and other existing buildings on the Haram area, are shown in dotted lines.) Beneath it is the "Sacred Rock" which marks the traditional site of the Threshing floor of Araunah the Jebusite, David's Altar, and the JEHOVAH-JIREH of Abraham's Sacrifice
The Altar of Burnt Offering of Solomon's Temple is shown by the plan, on this site (the Sacred Rock), with the Temple between it and the Western boundary wall, thus giving ample space for the "Court of the Temple" which would not be the case if the Holy of Holies had occupied this position. The "Orientation" of the Temple and Palaces was probably as shown.
If the Drain shown in fine dotted lines running from the S.W. angle of the Haram area to the exit of the extreme S. point of Zion (A) - (B) is the remains of Solomon's drainage system for the Temple and Palaces &c, or is of later date, but practically on the same lines, — then we have a clue to the position of the "Dung Gate" of Nehemiah, and a key is provided for all the other gates of Nehemiah.
See Notes on the "Dung Gate" (p 104)
PROBABLE LINE OF THE N. WALL
PRISON GATE? (or Gate of the Guard)
SHEEP GATE?
Pool of Bethesda
THE GATE MIPHKAD?
Probably spacious Enclosure(s) with buildings for housing and keeping up the sacrificial animals
Outer Court
Court of The Temple
Temple
Altar
The Royal Enclosure & Gardens
Solomon's Ascent
EAST GATE? Neh 3.29
HORSE GATE Neh 3.28
The Tower that lieth out Neh 3.26
OPHEL
OR
ZION
THE CITY OF DAVID
The Great Tower that lieth out? Neh 3.27
WATER GATE
GIHON (The Virgin's Fountain)
Ancient Tomb
Warren's Shaft
VILLAGE OF SILOAM
The Valley of Kedron
THE PRESENT SOUTH WALL
JERUSALEM
(Cœnaculum)
English Burial Ground
The Position of the Siloam Inscription is shown by X X, about 20 feet from the exit of Hezekiah's conduit at the Pool of Siloam. The Inscription is in six lines of Ancient Hebrew script and records the completion of the Tunnel (See plate p 103)
Inscription
Pool of Siloam
The King's Pool Neh 2.14
Probable Site of David's Stairs
The Old Pool Isa 22.11
FOUNTAIN GATE Neh 12.37 (Repaired by Shallum Neh 3.15)
VALLEY GATE Neh 2.13,15, 3.13
Uzziah built towers at the valley Gate 2Ch 26.9
cp Bliss and Dickie's "Excavations of Jerusalem" Ch I and Plans
THE WALL OF MANASSEH? (2Ch 33.14)
DUNG GATE Neh 2.13, 12.31 (Repaired by Malchiah 3.14)
Exit of Drain or Sewer, whence the name of the DUNG GATE (see Note p. 104)
Valley of Hinnom
The difference in level between the present "Triple Gate" at South side of the Haram Area to the Pool of Siloam is 294 feet.
Triple Gate...2379 feet
Siloam......2085 feet ∴ 294 feet
SCALES
English Feet
Supposed Ancient Cubits
This cubit, according to a note on the Ordnance Map is taken from Doursther's "Dictionnaire universel des poids et mesures anciens et modernes," 1840.
Great Cubits 1 Cubit = 25"
T.A.H.
Stanford's Geogl Estabt, London

site on the south-west side of Jerusalem, which still has buildings upon it.

The general plan on p. 100 is from the Ordnance Map of Jerusalem, from the survey by Sir Charles Wilson, and shows Moriah now occupied by the *Haram ash Sharif*, i. e. "*The noble Sanctuary*", which stands on its rectangular "platform" about the centre of what is known as "the Haram area". This and the other more or less ancient and modern buildings on this area are shown in dotted lines on the plans.

Immediately to the south lies the ridged hill on the summit or "swelling" of which stood the Jebusite fortress or citadel of Zion (or Ophel), from which the whole area immediately adjoining took its name, when captured by David, as "the city of David". Both name and title became in later times ascribed to the whole area of the city of Jerusalem.

The key to a right understanding of the whole question concerning the correct location of Zion is undoubtedly the spring known in the O.T. as Gihon (the modern name being "the Virgin's Fount"), with its underground rock-hewn conduit constructed by Hezekiah to convey the waters of the Fount to the Pool of Siloam *within* the enclosing wall of the city (see plan, p. 100).

Starting from the SE. angle of the "Haram area", this enclosing wall ran southward on the steep slope of the Zion or Ophel Hill, till it reached a point south of "the Old Pool" (Isa. 22. 11). Thence, turning sharply almost due N., the wall was carried round the bottom of the western slope of the Zion Hill, and ran NE. till it reached the south-westerly end of Moriah, at the corner of the present "Haram area"; and thence due E. till it completed the circuit at the SE. corner of the Haram. The line of this wall is indicated on the plan (p. 100) by the thick dotted line[1] thus - - - -.

[1] On the plan (p. 100) a point is, marked at the south end of the conduit, as "Warren's Shaft". In his "Recovery of Jerusalem", Sir Charles Warren tells us that "at 450 feet from the Siloam end . . . we found a shaft leading upwards apparently to the open air." This is of great importance, as it alters considerably the conjectured line of wall that is shown on the P.E.F. plans as running due N. up the east slope of Ophel, from the great masonry dam below the Old Pool. This shaft *must* have been within the city wall. Therefore, as 450 feet from the exit at Siloam locates it as being beyond the first bend in the serpentine course of the conduit, the city wall must necessarily have been carried up at least 100 feet nearer to the east, and probably in the position it is shown in on the plan on p. 100.

N.B.—All the plans on these pages have been specially made for *The Companion Bible*.

II. THE JEBUSITE WATER-SUPPLY.

The rock-hewn conduit from Gihon (or the Virgin's Fount) is shown with remarkable accuracy on the Ordnance Survey maps. If, as it is confidently asserted, Gihon (or the well-spring or Fount of the Virgin) is the only *spring* in the immediate vicinity of Jerusalem, then Melchizedek, King of Salem, and, later, the Jebusites, would be in possession of the only unfailing water-supply of the district. That the Jebusites had access to this well or spring from *within* their wall and fortress is clear: but, in the end, it proved their undoing, for David's men obtained possession of Jebus by means of the *tzinnōr* (A.V. "gutter"), i. e. the channel and shaft leading from the well into their citadel. (See notes on 2 Sam. 5. 6-8 and 1 Chron. 11. 6; also the Section on p. 102).[1]

The spring is intermittent, overflowing periodically, thus pointing to the existence of either a natural chasm or reservoir, or a *made* reservoir, whose site is at present unknown. Possibly it is under Mount Moriah itself. Tradition has much to say as to a deep well with an unfailing water-supply beneath the Temple area. (Cp. also Ps. 46. 4.)[1]

The fortress or citadel of Zion was immediately above this well-spring, and its defenders could thus command their water-supply from within, and also the security of the source without.

Before the time of Hezekiah, "the city of David" was dependent upon *this source* for its water-supply in times of danger threatened from without, in the same manner that the Jebusites were, viz. they descended from Ophel by means of rock-hewn passages, with steps and slopes (still in existence) till they reached the top of Warren's Shaft (see Section of David's *tzinnōr* or "gutter", p. 102), and by means of buckets drew their water from the unfailing well-spring some 40 to 50 feet below. At the top of this shaft is still to be seen the iron ring employed for this purpose.

[1] This Section, by Sir Charles Warren's kind permission, is presented W. to E. (and facing north), like the other plans on pp. 100 and 105, so as not to confuse the reader. In the Section, as shown on p. 102, it must be understood that the opening to the canal running south is thus shown by way of accommodation.

[1] The Heb. word *nāchar* here is used of a constant flow of water in contrast with *nāhal*, which means a *wady* or *summer* stream dependent on rains.

III. HEZEKIAH'S CONDUIT AND POOL.

The rock-hewn tunnel or conduit discovered by Sir Charles Warren in 1867, and first mentioned by him, conveyed the overflow water[1] from this spring to the Pool of Siloam.

That this conduit and pool were made by Hezekiah is now considered certain from the inscription found in the tunnel itself (see the plan on p. 100). Hezekiah, before the Assyrian invasion, in 603 B.C. (see Ap. 50. V, p. 60), constructed this tunnel and brought the water from Gihon to a new pool (*above* "the Old Pool" of Isa. 22. 11) that he had made for the purpose (2 Kings 20. 20). This pool henceforth became known as "the King's Pool" (Neh. 2. 14). When the Assyrian army approached, Hezekiah "stopped the waters of the fountains which were without the city" (2 Chron. 32. 3-5), i. e. he concealed their extramural approaches and outlets.

The Siloam Inscription, discovered in 1880, on a stone on the right wall of the tunnel about 20 feet from its exit into the Pool of Siloam, is undoubtedly the work of Hezekiah (see plate, p. 103). An interesting fact with regard to this inscription is that it gives the length of the conduit in *cubits*, which, being compared with modern measurements in English feet, shows that the cubit used was 17·5 inches or thereabouts.

If we knew for certain that the exact points from which Hezekiah measured exactly corresponded with those of the moderns, then we should be able to settle the vexed question as to the length of the cubit used, at all events in secular matters, by King Hezekiah. We do not, of course, know this, but it is of great interest to note the fact that the Inscription's 1,200 cubits, and the latest measurement of (about) 1,750 English feet yield a cubit of 17·5 inches[1].

[1] Before Hezekiah's time the overflow water must have escaped from the Virgin's Fount at a lower level than is now possible, and flowed out and down the lower end of the Kidron valley, past the king's garden, probably being the feeder for *Joab's* well (En-rogel ?)

[1] In a recent letter, Sir Charles Warren writes on this subject: "Stress must not be laid on the exactness of measurements made under conditions so difficult to obtain absolute accuracy." He adds, "it is impossible that any of the plans of the aqueduct can be rigidly correct, because the roof is so low that your head is horizontal in looking at the compass, so that you can only squint at it". It is necessary to remember this warning, coming from such a source. Nevertheless the figures, as above shown, are highly interesting.

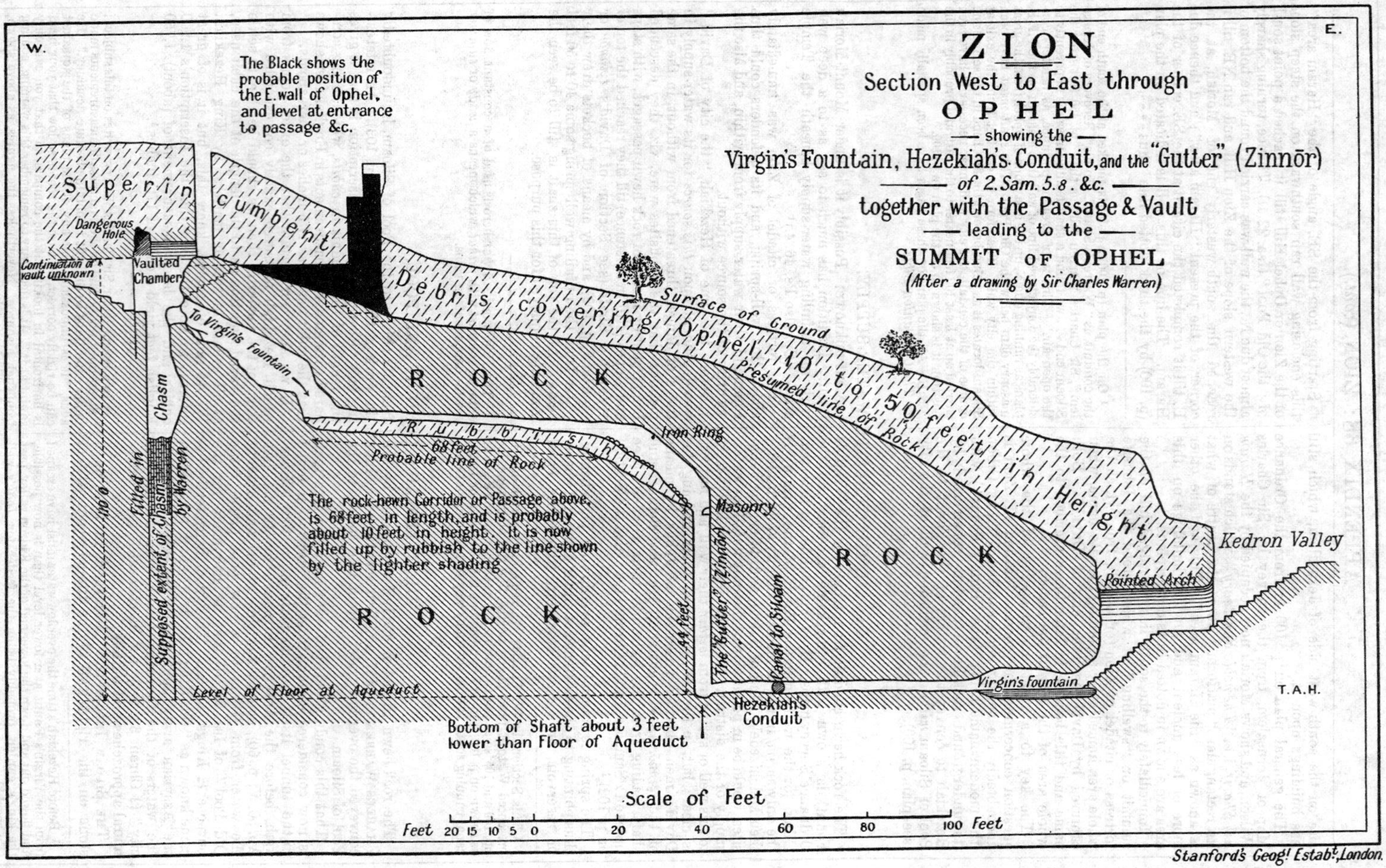

Stanford's Geog! Estab.t, London.

IV. THE SILOAM INSCRIPTION.

According to *The Companion Bible* Chronology (see Ap. 50 and 86) the date of this Inscription (see § III, pp. 101, 102) is given as 608–7 B.C. for the following reasons.

The fall of Samaria was in 611 B.C. Hezekiah, foreseeing that Judah's turn would follow, started the work of making the "Pool" and the "conduit" of 2 Kings 20. 20. This difficult undertaking would probably occupy two or three years.

When the siege of Jerusalem by Sennacherib was begun in Hezekiah's fourteenth year, this water-supply was complete and in working order, as Hezekiah had stopped the extra-mural outlets (2 Chron. 32. 2-4).

Therefore, the rock-hewn conduit from Gihon (now known as "the Virgin's Fountain") to Siloam must have been constructed between Hezekiah's sixth and fourteenth years (611–603 B.C.).

If we assume that it was begun soon after the fall of Samaria and occupied three years in construction, and that the Inscription was made on completion, as the record itself indicates, this gives us the date (above) 608–7 B.C.

It is graven in ancient Hebrew characters, similar to those of the Moabite Stone (see Ap. 54); and occupies six lines; the translation of which is given below.

TRANSLATION OF THE SILOAM INSCRIPTION.

Line 1. [Behold] the excavation. Now this is the history of the breaking through. While the workmen were still lifting up
„ 2. The pickaxe, each toward his neighbour, and while three cubits still remained to [cut through, each heard] the voice of the other calling
„ 3. to his neighbour, for there was an excess (or cleft) in the rock on the right . . . And on the day of the
„ 4. breaking through, the excavators struck, each to meet the other, pickaxe against pickaxe; and there flowed
„ 5. the waters from the spring to the pool over [a space of] one thousand and two hundred cubits. And . . .
„ 6. of a cubit was the height of the rock above the heads of the excavators.

V. THE TEMPLE OF SOLOMON ON MOUNT MORIAH.

The Plan on p. 105 shows the various buildings on the Temple area on the Moriah site to a larger scale. No attempt is made either to "design afresh" or, with the ready and often disastrous zeal of the modern iconoclast, to "restore" Solomon's Temple in this plan. The efforts put forth in the majority of cases by those who, with the best intentions, set forth their "ideas", result in melancholy exhibitions, from the crudely unhappy delineations of the earnest student, who works in entire ignorance of scales of measurement or the simplest requirements of the builder's art, to the redundantly fanciful productions of the professional designer, who, by his very acquaintance with the requirements of architecture, is often led to try and set before us what he imagines the Temple of Solomon, &c., ought to be. Accordingly, we have on the one hand bald representations of a Temple of practical impossibility, or, on the other, the most elaborate architectural confections from all sorts of sources—Phœnician, Egyptian, Grecian, Roman, and even Gothic.

Not content with these "styles" of architecture for Solomon's Temple, it is not unusual for illustrators of this subject to import into their designs all the details they can possibly assimilate from the specification of the *Millennial Temple* given by Ezekiel, and to add these on to the meagre details given of the Temple of Solomon!

One moment's serious attention to David's solemn statement in 1 Chron. 28. 12, 19, that he had received direct instruction from Jehovah for "the *pattern* of all that he had by the Spirit", and "in *writing*"—in other words, both *model* and *specification* from on High—ought to preserve us from such mistakes. The Temple was built from a heavenly plan and specification, and there is an entire absence of every detail that would enable us to "restore" such a building. Just as, in the case of the Tabernacle, the *essential* details are omitted, so that men may not copy the *Mishkān* (or habitation) of Jehovah, so, in the case of Solomon's Temple, we are placed in the same position.

The plan therefore given on p. 105 deals mainly with the figures given in the sacred records in bulk, merely arranging the various buildings in accordance with the position of the altar of burnt offering and the Temple in relation thereto.

The Altar of Burnt Offering is shown on the site of the "Sacred Stone", which is exactly under the centre of the present Moslem Sanctuary over it, known as "the *Dome of the Rock*".[1] This is the traditional site of David's altar on "the threshingfloor of Araunah the Jebusite". The Temple with its porch, the twin pillars *Jachin* and *Boaz*, and the molten sea, are shown to the west of the altar, and the wide open space, the Court of the Temple, is left blank—for the best of all reasons: we have no revelation as to how the space was occupied. Josephus and the Jewish rabbinical writings are alike useless for the purpose of informing us about Solomon's Temple. The simple fact is that we know next to nothing, and beyond the statements of "block" measurements, so to speak, we have no guide as to details. That there was an inner and outer court to the Temple is most probable, although there is no mention of *courts* until a later date.

[1] This and the other main buildings on the Haram area are shown on the plans by dotted lines.

VI. SOLOMON'S ROYAL BUILDINGS ON MOUNT MORIAH.

With regard to these the case is different. We are not told that David or Solomon received a Divine plan and specification for "the house of the forest of Lebanon", &c. Therefore it is permissible to try and arrange these buildings, according to the very slight details given, and according to the dictates of common sense.

It seems to be forgotten by some modern "Restorers" of Solomon's house, and other buildings, that the great king had received specially the gift of "*wisdom*". He was a man with "a *wise* and understanding heart", so that there was none like him before and after. Therefore he would not have fallen into the mistakes of palace building with which he is credited by some writers.[1]

Solomon's house was built of wood from the "forest of Lebanon", or, as we should say, "of Lebanon wood". It was 100 cubits long, 50 cubits broad, and 30 cubits in height. Although the number of cedar pillars is given, it is impossible to do more than indicate them on the plan by number. No details as to arrangement are given. The same remark applies to the Porch of Pillars, which apparently was a magnificent portico, to the house itself, and also to the statements concerning the *Porch of Judgment*. The gross dimensions are given of "*the Porch of Pillars*" (50 cubits by 30 cubits) and that is all; and we are told that "the house of Pharaoh's daughter" was like unto this porch. This probably means 50 cubits by 30 cubits, as shown on the plan. Apart from this, all is left *un*specified and vague.

[1] e.g. Prof. STADE in his *Geschichte des Volkes Israel*, gives an elaborate plan, which has been reproduced in one of the latest and most important works on Jerusalem. It is, however, completely at variance with the Scripture record. This plan makes havoc of the Bible statements as to the royal buildings, for it shows (1) The King's House, (2) The House of the Forest of Lebanon, (3) Hall of Pillars, (4) The Throne Hall, (5) House of Pharaoh's Daughter—whereas the Hebrew text of 1 Kings 7. 1-8 plainly records the fact that *Solomon's House* and the *House of the Forest of Lebanon* were one. This house had a "Porch of Pillars", probably to the south, and also, probably, south again, lay the *Porch of Judgment*, where Solomon sat to administer justice. This, as shown on p. 105, was situated in a position easy of access from "the city of David"—for the people's sake—and at a *sufficient distance* from the royal residence for the monarch s own sake. Solomon was a gentleman as well as a king, and it is incredible that he would have allowed the populace admission to the Judgment Hall through his own private grounds. The *House for Pharaoh's daughter* completes the buildings *specified*, although an extensive Harem must have been added later on.

VII. SOLOMON'S ASCENT.

This ascent, by which Solomon went up to the house of Jehovah, would be between the house and the outer court of the Temple, and would probably comprise two or three flights of steps or "stairs", protected by another covered portico or "porch", with pillars in accordance with the other buildings. The Temple area level would probably be some 15 or 20 feet above that of the king's house, and this difference in level would admit of the construction of an "ascent" that must have possessed features of unusual interest and magnificence from the account given of the visit of the Queen of Sheba (2 Kings 10. 1-10; 2 Chron. 9. 1-12).

To reach the level of the present Haram area at the south side from "the city of David", some means of easy ascent must have been employed. This is shown on the plan, p. 105, as being by a series of steps—forming an important stairway, giving direct means of approach to a spacious plateau on to which opened out the south end of the Judgment Hall or Porch. This would afford direct access to the people to the Hall for Judgment concerning their disputes, &c.

In addition to this great stairway for the people, there must also have been an easy way of "going up" from "the city of David" to the Temple area. This would probably be by means of an inclined ascent, such as that indicated on the plan (p. 105). It must be remembered that this would also be requisite for a roadway for the king's chariots, &c. The evidence is abundant that Solomon had a number of horses and chariots. These would hardly have been installed on the Haram area level, in juxtaposition with the royal buildings. The fact that beneath the SE. corner of the Haram is still to be seen the great underground series of pillars and arches known as "Solomon's stables", gives strength to the suggestion that the originals of these and the "Horse Gate" were in very close proximity. (See plan, p. 100.)

VIII. THE "DUNG GATE" OF NEHEMIAH.

On the plan (p. 100) is shown in dotted lines a large drain, running round the SW. angle of the Haram, to its exit at the extreme S. point of "the city of David" (Zion). This drain is of very great importance with regard to the question of locating the "Dung Gate" of Nehemiah.

In all probability this drain indicates the position of the "main-drainage system" of the Temple area, and the adjacent royal buildings, from the time of Solomon and onwards. Ample provision must have been made in buildings of the character and extent of the Temple and palace for the disposal of the blood of the sacrificial animals and the water of the ceremonial cleansings, in addition to the sewage from the Levitical quarters, and the huge court entourage of Solomon[1] and possibly some of the later kings. For this purpose a great drain must have been employed to convey all this sewage matter to the lower levels and outside the city.

The fact that the remains of such a large drain or sewer are still in existence in much the position necessitated by the buildings on the Temple area, &c., suggests that this was either the one constructed by Solomon, or else one laid down on about the same lines at a later date[2].

As shown by the latest Palestine Exploration Fund plan of Jerusalem, this drain runs S. down the slope of the Tyropœon valley, past the Pool of Siloam (the King's Pool, Neh. 2. 14), and passes out under an ancient gateway, recently discovered, to the south of "the Old Pool" (Isa. 22. 11).

In all likelihood this gateway marks the position (there or thereabouts) of Nehemiah's "DUNG GATE". It would be so named from its close association with—as we should say now—the sewage outfall, as the drain (still existing here) passed out beneath it, to discharge itself a little lower down into the gully formed by the junction of the Kidron and Hinnom Valleys, and not far distant from the ridge site identified by some as *Aceldama*.

[1] The occupants of the *Harem*, and their attendants alone, would probably number at least 2,000.

[2] Another large drain is shown on the latest maps in this neighbourhood. This is known as "Warren's Drain". It starts from the Haram area, a little to the left of, and nearly parallel with, the one just referred to. This drain runs due south for some 700 feet, and then ends, apparently, abruptly. (See plan, p. 100.)

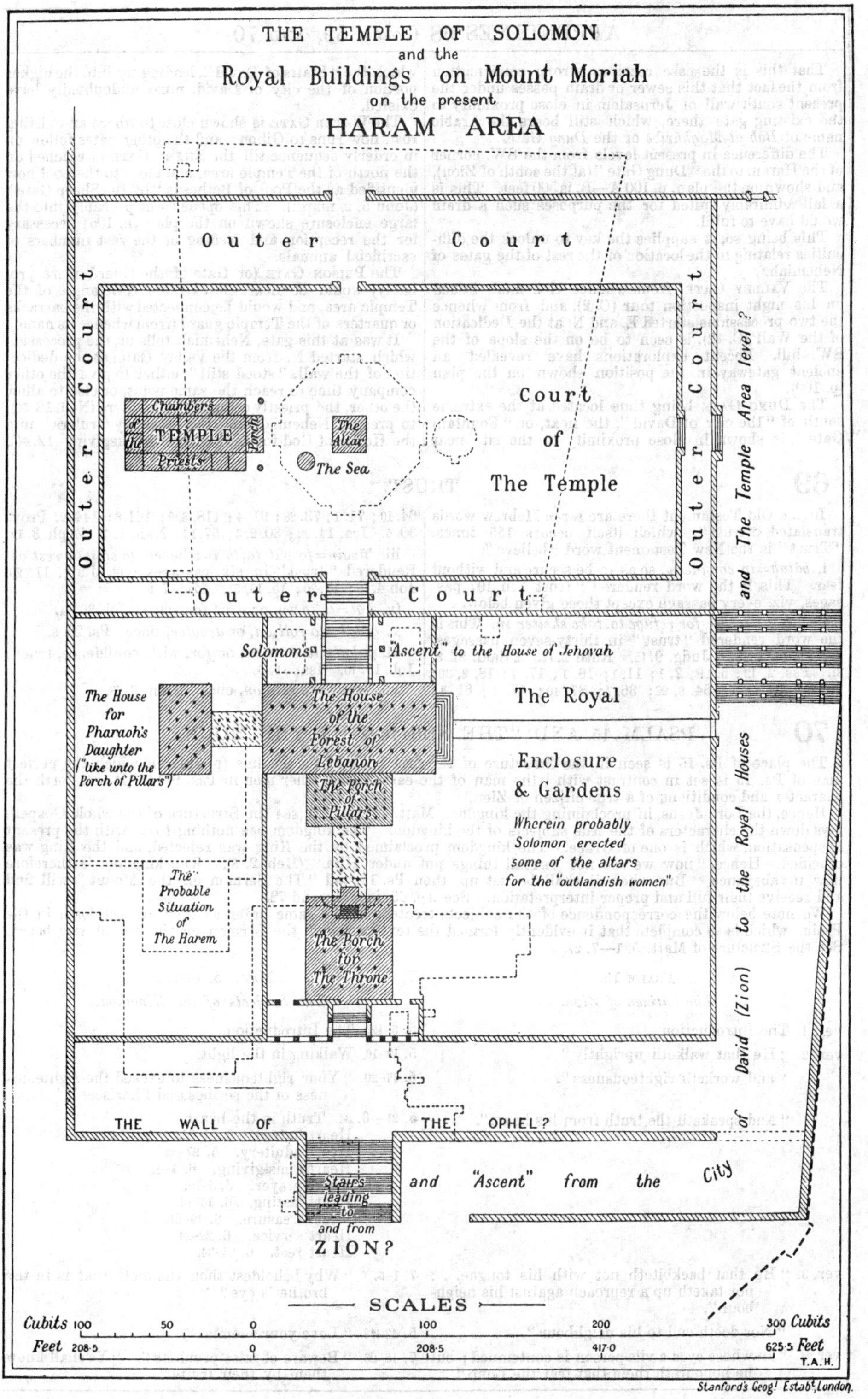
THE TEMPLE OF SOLOMON
and the
Royal Buildings on Mount Moriah
on the present
HARAM AREA
Outer Court
Outer Court
Outer Court
Outer Court
Court of The Temple
Chambers of the Priests
TEMPLE
Porch
The Altar
The Sea
and The Temple Area level?
Solomon's "Ascent" to the House of Jehovah
The House for Pharaoh's Daughter ("like unto the Porch of Pillars")
The House of the Forest of Lebanon
The Porch of Pillars
The Royal Enclosure & Gardens
Wherein probably Solomon erected some of the altars for the "outlandish women"
The Probable Situation of The Harem
The Porch for The Throne
the Royal Houses
THE WALL OF THE OPHEL?
Stairs leading to and from ZION?
and "Ascent" from the City of David (Zion) to the Royal Houses
SCALES
Cubits 100 50 0 100 200 300 Cubits
Feet 208·5 0 208·5 417·0 625·5 Feet
T.A.H.
Stanford's Geog! Estabt, London.

That this is the case receives strong confirmation from the fact that this sewer or drain passes under the present south wall of Jerusalem in close proximity to the existing gate there, which still bears the Arabic name of *Bâb al Maghâribè* or the *Dung* Gate.

The difference in present levels from the SW. corner of the Haram to the "Dung Gate" (at the south of Zion), and shown on the plan, p. 100 A—B, is 300 feet. This is a fall admirably suited for the purposes such a drain would have to fulfil.

This being so, it supplies the key to unlock the difficulties relating to the location of the rest of the gates of Nehemiah.

The VALLEY GATE, from whence Nehemiah issued on his night inspection tour (C. 2), and from whence the two processions started E. and N. at the Dedication of the Wall (C. 12), is seen to be on the slope of the SW. hill. Recent explorations have revealed an ancient gateway in the position shown on the plan (p. 100).

The DUNG GATE being thus located at the extreme south of "the city of David", the next, or "Fountain Gate", is shown in close proximity to the site near which the "Stairs of David", leading up into the higher portion of the city of David, must undoubtedly have existed.

The WATER GATE is shown close to where an existing road now runs to Gihon; and the other gates follow on in orderly sequence till the SHEEP GATE is reached on the north of the Temple area, and close to the pool now identified as the Pool of Bethesda "by the Sheep Gate" (John 5. 2, marg.). This opened out probably into the large enclosure shown on the plan (p. 105) necessary for the reception and feeding of the vast numbers of sacrificial animals.

The PRISON GATE (or Gate of the Guard more probably) would be near the extreme NW. angle of the Temple area, and would be connected with the barracks or quarters of the Temple guard (from whence its name).

It was at this gate, Nehemiah tells us, the procession which started N. from the Valley Gate, at the dedication of the wall, "stood still", either to give the other company time to reach the same point, or else to allow the other, the priestly company under Ezra (Neh. 12. 36), to precede Nehemiah and the other lay "rulers" into the House of God for the general thanksgiving (12. 40).

69 TRUST.

In the Old Testament there are *seven* Hebrew words translated "trust", which itself occurs 155 times. "Trust" is the New Testament word "believe".

i. *bāṭaḥ=to confide in*, so as to be secure and without fear. This is the word rendered "trust" in 107 passages, viz. every passage except those given below.

ii. *ḥāṣāh=to flee for refuge to, take shelter in.* This is the word rendered "trust" in thirty-seven passages, viz. Deut. 32. 37. Judg. 9. 15. Ruth 2. 12. 2 Sam. 22. 3, 31. Pss. 2. 12; 5. 11; 7. 1; 11. 1; 16. 1; 17. 7; 18. 2, 30; 25. 20; 31. 1, 19; 34. 8, 22; 36. 7; 37. 40; 57. 1; 61. 4; 64. 10; 71. 1; 73. 28; 91. 4; 118. 8, 9; 141. 8; 144. 2. Prov. 30. 5. Isa. 14. 32; 30. 2, 3; 57. 13. Nah. 1. 7. Zeph. 3. 12.

iii. *'āman=to put faith in*; hence, *to stay* or *rest on.* Rendered "trust" in six passages, viz. Judg. 11. 20. Job 4. 18; 12. 20; 15. 15, 31. Mic. 7. 5.

iv. *ḥūl=to tarry*, or *wait for*, once: Job 35. 14.

v. *gālal=to roll on*, or *devolve*, once: Ps. 22. 8.

vi. *yaḥal=to wait on*, or *for*, with confidence, twice: Job 13. 15. Isa. 51. 5.

vii. *reḥaẓ=to rely on*, once. Dan. 3. 28.

70 PSALM 15 AND "THE SERMON ON THE MOUNT".

The place of Ps. 15 is seen in the Structure of the first book of the Psalms (p. 721), in which the perfect man of Ps. 15 is set in contrast with "the man of the earth" and other men in Pss. 9–14. It sets forth the character and conditions of a true citizen of Zion.

Hence, the Lord Jesus, in proclaiming the kingdom, Matt. 4. 17—7. 29 (see the Structure of the whole Gospel), lays down the characters of the true subjects of the kingdom. The kingdom has nothing to do with the present Dispensation, which is one of Grace. The kingdom proclaimed by the King was rejected, and the King was crucified. Hence, "now we see NOT YET all things put under Him" (Heb. 2. 8). The kingdom is therefore now in abeyance. But when it shall be set up, then Ps. 15 and "The Sermon on the Mount" will find and receive their full and proper interpretation. See Ap. 63. ix; 71; and 72.

We note below the correspondence of the subjects treated, in the same order as they are set forth in the Psalm, which is so complete that it evidently formed the text on which the Sermon on the Mount was based. See the Structure of Matt. 5. 1—7. 27.

PSALM 15. *The Citizen of Zion.*		MATT. 5. 1—7. 29 *The Subjects of the Kingdom.*	
ver. 1.	The Introduction.	5. 3-12.	The Introduction.
ver. 2.	"He that walketh uprightly"	5. 13-16.	Walking in the light.
	"and worketh righteousness".	5. 17-20.	"Your righteousness to exceed the righteousness of the scribes and Pharisees".
	"And speaketh the truth from his heart".	5. 21—6. 34.	Truth in the heart. Heart hatred. 5. 21-26. Heart adultery. 5. 27-32. Heart alms-giving. 6. 1-4. Heart prayer. 6. 5-15. Heart fasting. 6. 16-18. Heart treasure. 6. 19-21. Heart service. 6. 22-24. Heart rest. 6. 25-34.
ver. 3.	"He that backbiteth not with his tongue. . . nor taketh up a reproach against his neighbour".	7. 1-5.	"Why beholdest thou the mote that is in thy brother's eye?"
	"Nor doeth evil to his neighbour".	5. 43-48.	"Love your enemies".
ver. 4.	"In whose eyes a vile person is contemned; but he honoureth them that fear the LORD".	7. 15-23.	"Beware of false prophets". "Ye shall know them by their fruits".

The Citizen of Zion (cont.).

"He that sweareth to his own hurt, and changeth not".

ver. 5. "He that putteth not out his money to usury, nor taketh reward against the innocent".

"He that doeth these things shall never be moved".

The Subjects of the Kingdom (cont.).

5. 33-37. "Let your communication be, Yea, yea; Nay, nay".

5. 38-42. "Give to him that asketh thee, and from him that would borrow of thee, turn not thou away".

7. 24-27. "Therefore whosoever heareth these sayings of mine, and doeth them, I will liken him unto a wise man, which built his house upon a rock. ... it fell not".

71 "THE SUFFERINGS, AND THE GLORY".

We are told, in 1 Peter 1. 10-12, that the prophets of old searched "what, or what manner of time the Spirit of Christ which was in them did signify, when it testified beforehand the sufferings of Christ, and the glory that should follow. Unto whom it was revealed, that not unto themselves, but unto us they did minister the things, which are now reported unto you ... with the Holy Ghost sent down from heaven".

They wrote of the sufferings, and they wrote of the glory that should follow; but there was nothing to tell them about the times or seasons. Whether the glory was to follow immediately on the sufferings, or whether there was to be an interval, and whether that interval was to be short or long, no hint was given. Hence, they searched as to "what manner of time was signified".

This "time" refers to the "unsearchable riches of Christ". They could not then be traced. Even angels desire to look into these things (1 Pet. 1. 12).

"Now," all is revealed. It is ministered unto us, in the Scriptures of truth, on earth; and God is making known, by means of the Church, something of His manifold wisdom to the principalities and powers in the heavenly places (Eph. 3. 9, 10).

Angels and prophets saw the "sufferings" like the tops of a distant mountain range—while beyond it a farther range was seen in a distant haze of glory. But what lay between they could neither see nor know. But now it is revealed. The sufferings are past, and we are in the valley between these two mountain ranges. The glory is beyond. The secret "hid in God" has been made known; and we can understand, a little, the answer to the question of Christ to the two disciples: "Ought not Christ to have suffered these things, and to enter into His glory?" (Luke 24. 26).

They are linked together inseparably, especially in the first epistle of Peter. See 1 Pet. 1. 11; 3. 18; 4. 13; 5. 1.

In the Old Testament they are each frequently dwelt upon together: but, we find that, while the *glory* is often mentioned and enlarged upon by itself, without any reference to the sufferings, we never find the sufferings mentioned without the glory being referred to immediately after. Sometimes the change is quite sudden. In Ps. 22, note the change from *v.* 21 to *vv.* 22-end. In Ps. 102, note the change from *v.* 11 to *vv.* 12-end. In Isa. 53 note the change in the middle of *v.* 10. (See Ap. 72.)

It seems that when the sufferings are mentioned, we are not left to think that all is to end there. The glory may be mentioned alone, because there is to be no end to it. But to the sufferings there was to be an end, and that end was to be revealed in glory.

That is why, when the Lord makes the first mention of His sufferings, in Matt. 16. 21, He at once proceeded to speak of the time when He "shall come in the glory of His Father" (*v.* 27), and to add that some of those who were standing there should see it. And then, after six days, three of them saw the *power and coming* of our Lord Jesus Christ, and were eye-witnesses of His majesty, when they were with Him in the holy mount (2 Pet. 1. 16-18. Cp. John 1. 14).

Having heard of the sufferings, the disciples were not left to conclude that all was to end there: hence they were at once given the most wonderful exhibition of the glory which was to follow.

This is why the Transfiguration scene occurs in the third part of the Lord's ministry, which had to do with His sufferings. See notes on the Scriptures referred to above, and compare Ap. 72.

72 THE PARENTHESIS OF THE PRESENT DISPENSATION.

From what has been said in Ap. 63. ix and Ap. 71, it will be seen that there are different Dispensations, or different characters of Divine administration, suited to the different times in which such administrations are exercised.

The object of this appendix is to show that, in the Old Testament, while this present Dispensation was kept secret (cp. Matt. 13. 34, 35. Rom. 11. 25. Eph. 3. 5, 9, &c), there are remarkable breaks which can be explained only after we have the key put into our hands.

There are certain scriptures which we cannot understand unless we use this key. Like the angels and prophets (1 Pet. 1. 11, 12) we may search in vain, while others may refuse to search and "look into" these things, and profanely speak of it as the "gap theory".

Whether it be a "theory", let Scripture decide, and the Saviour Himself teach.

In the synagogue at Nazareth "He found the place where it was written:

The Spirit of the Lord is upon Me,
Because He hath anointed Me to preach the gospel
to the poor;
He hath sent Me to heal the brokenhearted,
To preach deliverance to the captives,
And recovering of sight to the blind,
To set at liberty them that are bruised,
To preach the acceptable year of the Lord.

* * * * * * *

And He CLOSED THE BOOK, and He gave it again to the minister, and sat down" (Luke 4. 18-20). Why this mysterious action? Why not continue the reading? Because He could not; for the words which immediately follow refer to the end of this present Dispensation of Grace, and speak of the coming Dispensation of Judgment. Had he continued to read Isa. 61. 1, 2, the next line would have been

"And the day of vengeance of our God".

But this part of the prophecy was not then to be fulfilled

As far as He had read, He could truly say, "This day is this Scripture fulfilled in your ears." But He could not have said "This day is this Scripture fulfilled", had He not "closed the book", but gone on to read the next line.

And yet, in the A.V. and all other versions, there is only a comma between the two lines, while there is a period of nearly 2,000 years between the two statements. (In the MSS. there is no mark of punctuation at all.)

This will show the importance of "searching" and "looking into" the "manner of time" of which the prophets wrote.

Other examples may be found in

Gen. 1, between verses 1 and 2.
Ps. 22, between verses 21 and 22.
Ps. 118, in the middle of verse 22.
Isa. 9. 6, after the first clause.
Isa. 53, in the middle of verse 10.
Isa. 61, in the middle of verse 2 (see above).
Lam. 4, between verses 21 and 22.
Dan. 9, between verses 26 and 27.
Dan. 11, between verses 20 and 21.
Hos. 2, between verses 13 and 14.
Hos. 3, between verses 4 and 5.
Amos 9, between verses 10 and 11.
Micah 5, between verses 2 and 3.
Hab. 2, between verses 13 and 14.
Zeph. 3, between verses 7 and 8.
Zech. 9, between verses 9 and 10.
Matt. 10, in the middle of verse 23.
Matt. 12, in the middle of verse 20.
Luke 1, between verses 31 and 32.
Luke 21, in the middle of verse 24.
John 1, between verses 5 and 6.
1 Pet. 1, in the middle of verse 11.
Rev. 12, between verses 5 and 6.

73 THE TEN WORDS OF PSALM 119.

The number of the words which are frequently repeated in Ps. 119 has been variously given and enumerated by expositors and commentators. It will be better to give them here on the authority of the *Massōrah* (Ap. 30).

The rubric on verse 122 is as follows: "Throughout the whole of the Great Alphabet [i.e. the Alphabetic Psalm, 119] there is in every verse one of the following ten expressions: DEREK (=Way), 'ĒDŪTH (=Testimony), PIKKŪDĪM (=Precepts), MIZVĀH (=Commandment), 'IMRĀH (=Saying), TŌRĀH (=Law), MISHPĀṬ (=Judgment), ZEDEK, ZᵉDĀKĀH, and ZADDĪK (=Righteousness), HOK, and HUKKĀH (=Statutes), DĀBĀR (=Word), which correspond to the Ten Commandments; except one verse, in which there is none of these: viz. verse 122." (*Massōrah*, Ginsburg's Edition, Vol. II.)

The following list includes all the "Ten Words" given above, with every occurrence in the Psalm, together with the first occurrence of each word.

(i) WAY (*derek*) is from *dārak, to tread with the feet*, and denotes *the act of walking*. Hence it is used of *a going*, or *way*, or *journeying*. The first occurrence is Gen. 3. 24. It occurs in this Psalm thirteen times: *vv.* 1, 3, 5, 14, 26, 27, 29, 30, 32, 33, 37, 59, 168.

(ii) TESTIMONIES (*'ēdūth*) is from *'ūd, to turn back again, to go over again, to reiterate*, hence, *to testify*. The first occurrence is Gen. 21. 30 (*ēdah*). It occurs in this Psalm twenty-three times; nine times (*'ēdūth*), *vv.* 14, 31, 36, 88, 99, 111, 129, 144, 157; fourteen times (*'ēdāh*, fem. sing.), *vv.* 2, 22, 24, 46, 59, 79, 95, 119, 125, 138, 146, 152, 167, 168.

(iii) PRECEPTS (*pikkūdīm*) is from *pākad, to take oversight or charge*: hence, *mandates enjoined on others*. It occurs only in the Book of Psalms (see 19. 8; 103. 18; 111. 7). In Ps. 119 twenty-one times: *vv.* 4, 15, 27, 40, 45, 56, 63, 69, 78, 87, 93, 94, 100, 104, 110, 128, 134, 141, 159, 168, 173.

(iv) COMMANDMENTS (*mizvāh*) is from *zāvāh, to set up, constitute*. Hence, *constitutional commands*. First occurrence Gen. 26. 5. In Ps. 119 it occurs twenty-two times: *vv.* 6, 10, 19, 21, 32, 35, 47, 48, 60, 66, 73, 86, 96 (sing.), 98, 115, 127, 131, 143, 151, 166, 172, 176.

(v) WORD (*'imrāh*) is from *'āmar, to bring forth to light*; hence, *to say*. The verb is very regularly followed by the words used; hence *'imrah* means an utterance and the purport of it. Not the same as *dābār* (No. x below), which refers to the articulate utterance of it. The first occurrence is in Gen. 4. 23, and is rendered "speech". In plural only once, Ps. 12. 6 (the only place where the plural is found). In Ps. 119 it occurs nineteen times: viz. 11, 38, 41, 50, 58, 67, 76, 82, 103, 116, 123, 133, 140, 148, 154, 158, 162, 170, 172. With *dābār* the two occur forty-two times.

(vi) LAW (*tōrāh*) is from *yārāh, to project, issue*: hence, *to point out, to show* (Prov. 6. 13). Then, *to instruct, teach*. The Tōrāh contains Jehovah's *Instructions* to His People, pointing out to them His will. First occurrence is in Gen. 26. 5 (pl.). In Ps. 119 it occurs twenty-five times: always in the singular: viz. *vv.* 1, 18, 29, 34, 44, 51, 53, 55, 61, 70, 72, 77, 85, 92, 97, 109, 113, 126, 136, 142, 150, 153, 163, 165, 174.

(vii) JUDGMENT (*mishpāt*) is from *shāphat, to set upright, erect* (cp. Eng. *right*, and German *richten* and *recht*); hence, *to judge*. *Mishpāt* means judgment. Its first occurrence is in Gen. 18. 19 (in Jehovah's mouth). In Ps. 119 it occurs twenty-three times (always in plural, except four times), viz.: *vv.* 7, 13, 20, 30, 39, 43, 52, 62, 75, 84, 91 (ordinances), 102, 106, 108, 120, 121, 132 (as thou usest to do, see note), 137, 149, 156, 160, 164, 175.

(viii) RIGHTEOUSNESS, RIGHT, &c. (*zedek*, masc.), is from *zādak, to be right, upright, just, righteous*. Hence the noun means *rightness*. By comparing the first occurrence (Lev. 19. 15) with the second (Lev. 19. 36) we get the idea that the word has special reference to *equal balancing*. *Zedek* (masc.) occurs twelve times, and is rendered "righteousness": *vv.* 123, 142 (second), 144, 172; "right", *v.* 75 (marg. righteousness); "righteous", *vv.* 7, 62, 106, 138, 160, 164; "justice", *v.* 121. *Zᵉdākāh* (fem.), first occurrence, Gen. 15. 6. In Ps. 119, "righteousness", *vv.* 40, 142 (first). *Zaddīk* (adj.), spoken of a king (2 Sam. 23. 3), once, in *v.* 137. The three words fifteen times in all.

(ix) STATUTE (*hok* and *hukka*) is from *hākak, to hew, cut in, engrave, inscribe*; hence, *to decree*, or *ordain*. The noun=a decree or ordinance. First occurrence, Gen. 26. 5 (*hūkkāh* fem.). In Ps. 119 it occurs twenty-two times: viz.: *vv.* 5, 8, 12, 16 (*hūkkāh*, fem.), 23, 26, 33, 48, 54, 64, 68, 71, 80, 83, 112, 117, 118, 124, 135, 145, 155, 171.

(x) WORD, WORDS (*dābār*), is from *dābar, to arrange in a row*; hence, *to set forth in speech*. It refers to the articulate form of what is said, whether spoken or written (cp. v above); to the mode or manner by which the *ipsissima verba* are imparted. The first occurrence is in Gen. 11. 1 ("speech"). In Ps. 119 it occurs twenty-four times, three of them in pl., viz.: *vv.* 9, 16, 17, 25, 28, 42 (twice), 43, 49, 57 (pl.), 65, 74, 81, 89, 101, 105, 107, 114, 130 (pl.), 139 (pl.), 147, 160, 161, 169.

74 THE BOOK OF PROVERBS: INTRODUCTION AND ANALYSIS.[1]

The Book of Proverbs is generally described as belonging to a branch of Hebrew literature which has for its subject Wisdom, or, as we should say, Philosophy. This view has some truth in it; but it does not express the whole truth, as will appear from an analysis of the book, and a careful examination of its constituent parts.

The book makes no claim to unity of authorship; it is avowedly a collection, and includes the work of others besides Solomon the king. Hence, though in some sections there may be wisdom of a general order, in others one may find cautions and counsels which were intended for a particular individual, and not for "all sorts and conditions of men"; and which, therefore, are not abstract Wisdom in the sense implied by most expositors of the book.

The conviction that this is the case will grow upon those who discriminate the material of which the book is composed, noting the varying motives of the writers, and the outstanding characteristics of their proverbs, or sayings.

On the surface one distinguishes four divisions—The Proverbs of Solomon, the Words of the Wise, the Words of Agur, and the Words of Lemuel. As these several writings may be easily distinguished, there is no reason why we should summarily conclude that all the sections are of the "Wisdom" order.

Taken as a whole, the material rightly answers to the description of "Proverbs" (ch. 1, *v.* 1), or sententious sayings, generally completed in the distich, or verse of two lines; but, as the authorship is complex, so also there may be diversity of motive and object in the writings.

The present contention is that, while the Proverbs of Solomon may consist of teaching for all and sundry—dealing with prudence, discretion, and the conduct of life—the sections which contain "the Words of the Wise" were intended as instruction for a prince, and therefore designed to teach elementary lessons in policy and statecraft, even to show a young ruler how he might "cleanse his way", as the representative of Jehovah upon the throne of Israel. These parts of the book have hitherto been treated as if designed to emphasize certain commands of the Decalogue: whereas, in reality, they demand closer attention, as dealing with dangers and temptations such as would inevitably beset a king on the throne of Israel.

Hence, in a word, we find in the first twenty-nine chapters of the book several series of Proverbs which were FOR Solomon, and again several series which were BY Solomon.[2] Between the two classes there is a wide difference. Of those that were FOR the king, being, in fact, "Words of the Wise" (men, or teachers), given for the instruction of the young man, it may be said that, having a relation to the principles which were fundamental in the Divinely ordained constitution of Israel, they stand apart from the class of Proverbs which, enunciated by Solomon himself, were more or less generally concerned with the life and behaviour of the individual Israelite of the time.

The following is an analysis of the book from the point of view thus propounded:—

A. GENERAL INTRODUCTION—TITLE
(ch. 1. *vv.* 1-6).

Misapprehension on the part of the Massorites or their predecessors in the editing of the text, led to inclusion in the title of the line which, as heading, opens Section I. "The Words of the Wise and their dark sayings", or sententious utterances.

1. "Words of the Wise" (men, or teachers)—addresses by a father to a son, or rather by a teacher to a pupil, the distinctive terms being the same (*v.* 6-). The addresses are fifteen in number, and all of them introduced by the formula "My son" (1. 7—7. 27). The general subject of this section is embodied in the words "The fear of the LORD is the beginning of knowledge; but fools despise wisdom and instruction" (*v.* 7). The "son" is addressed directly, "thou" and "thee", "thy" being also used; and again and again he is warned, in the most solemn terms, against "the strange woman," i. e. the foreign or alien woman—such women having from time to time led astray any Israelites that consorted with them. Recall the allurements of the daughters of Moab; and the cases of Samson and Ahab. In other sections "my son" is warned against "sinners" and "the wicked",—that is, the heathen who knew not the true God, but who were haters of righteousness, lovers of war, and given to oppression. He is, in particular, counselled not to "strike hands" with such—i. e. not to enter into alliance or covenant with any such.

2. Two addresses, in the former of which (ch. 8, E[5]) Wisdom makes her claim upon the devotion of one who is urged to esteem her as better than gold or silver, and is reminded that by Wisdom alone can kings reign and princes decree justice; while in the latter (ch. 9), Wisdom and Folly are contrasted, the fear of Jehovah (or piety, as we know it to have been esteemed in Israel) is magnified, and a warning is uttered against the foolish woman, already introduced as "the strange woman", with whom no Israelite should have any association—assuredly no king in Israel should seek her company. In this section the address is sometimes to "ye", "them", "they" (that is, in the *plural*); at other times to "thee", "thou" (i. e. in the *singular* number). So far, after the title of the book, we have met with no mention of Solomon; and none of his work. Hitherto, we have had proverbs which Solomon *was taught*.

3. A collection of Proverbs by Solomon, being so described in the opening verse (10. 1, **C**). If the contents of sections 1 and 2 (**A** 1. -6—9. 18, p. 864), already described, had been by Solomon, there would have been no need in this place for the introductory line "The Proverbs of Solomon." The mode of address is quite unlike that of section 1, with its *second person* of the pronoun; the proverbs are not spoken to "my son", but they mention "he" and "him", using generally the *third person* of the pronoun. Apparently, they continue to ch. 19. 26, or thereabouts. They were for *men* in general to learn, and not for a prince or distinguished individual (as "my son").

4. Another section of addresses to "my son" begins with 19. 20 (**D**, p. 864) or thereabouts; and continues to the end of ch. 24. Here we have further lessons upon the ways of a king—like those of the earlier sections of the book, but quite unmatched by anything in "The Proverbs of Solomon" (see 19. 27, "My son"; and "the king" 20. 2, 8, 26, 28; 21. 1; 22. 11). These are "Words of the Wise" (men, or teachers): this is twice affirmed (22. 17; 24. 23 R.V.); and the occurrences of the formula "my son" are six in number (19. 27; 23. 15, 19, 26; 24. 13, 21). The counsels, like those of sections 1 and 2, are such as would eminently befit a prince in Israel: "my son" is instructed to regard the fear of the LORD as more desirable than riches (22. 1, 4). Apparently the words are addressed to one who is to sit among rulers (23. 1); one whose duty it is, for the present, to fear the king as well as God (24. 21); but one who is learning the duties of judicial administration (20. 8, 26, 28; 21. 3; 22. 11). There is nothing commonplace in warnings against "having respect of persons" in judgment: such counsel is for a ruler (24. 23, 24). In this section again the foreign woman is denounced (22. 14; 23. 27, 33); and riches are shown to be of no account in comparison with wisdom and righteousness (20. 15; 21. 6; 23. 4). In the earlier portion of this division the pronouns are mostly in the third person, "he" and "him"; afterwards in the second person, "thou", "thy", and "thee". The

[1] Contributed by Dr. J. W. Thirtle.

[2] See the Structure on p. 864, which corresponds with this analysis.

counsels are manifestly such as King Solomon should have taken to heart.

5. A second collection of Proverbs by Solomon—chapters 25 and 26 (see opening verse of chapter 25, **C**, p. 864). The book having been brought into its present shape in the reign of King Hezekiah, this section was "copied out" by the scribes of that time. They would find in the royal library at Jerusalem many writings for the good of the nation, and among them some of the best utterances of Solomon, as well as of his father David, who was likewise a great patron of literature. The things said about kings are what might well be expected from one who was himself the occupant of a throne (25. 2-7).

6. Without special introduction, ch. 27 (**D**) begins another series of "Words of the Wise". The indication is found in the substance of the proverbs, which are so obviously designed as instruction for a prince, and also in the occurrence of the formula "my son" (27. 11). The general applicability of these words to the case of a ruler in Israel is obvious (see 28. 2, 6-8, 16; 29. 4, 12, 14, 26).

7. The words of Agur, the son of Jakeh (ch. 30, **A**, p. 864).

8. The words of King Lemuel, the prophecy that his mother taught him (31. 1-9), leading to the poem on

9. The virtuous woman (31. 10-31).

In order to a proper understanding of "the Words of the Wise", it is needful to bear in mind the following facts:—

(1) The word "father" is used for a teacher—2 Kings 2. 12; 6. 21; 13. 14 (cp. Judg. 17. 10; 18. 19); and thus came to be the common designation of the Jewish Rabbins.

(2) The word "son" is used for a pupil—1 Sam. 3. 6, 16; 1 Kings 20. 35; 2 Kings 2. 3, 5, 7, 15, and elsewhere; for the Israelitish prophets, in some cases, conducted schools for young men, and received from them the obedience which was due to parents, in whose place they stood for the time being. In this connection, note the words of remorse, suggested as used by "my son" in the event of disobedience: I "have not obeyed the voice of MY TEACHERS, nor inclined mine ear to THEM THAT INSTRUCTED ME" (ch. 5. 13).

Again (3): The expressions "sinners", "wicked", "fools", and "hypocrites" were applied in Israel to the heathen, and those who followed their ways (Isa. 13. 11; 14. 5: cp. Ps. 9. 5; 26. 5; Prov. 3. 33; 28. 4, 28; 29. 2). Though, as suggested, dealing with politics, the "Words of the Wise" are in the language of the school; and the prince to whom the wise men address themselves is led to view the surrounding nations and their ways from the standpoint of those who find the beginning and end of knowledge in "the fear of the LORD".

(4) The "strange woman", whether answering to the Hebrew word *zarah* or *nokriah*, was not an erring Israelite, but an ALIEN woman, to traffic with whom would inevitably lead to declension from the Lord. Both Hebrew words are found in ch. 5. 20; and in ch. 6 (22 ff.) the subject is extended, and associated with adultery, in order that personal purity may be properly emphasized. As the Divine intention was that Israel should be separate from the nations of the earth (Deut. 7. 6, and refs.: cp. Ezek. 20. 32 ff.), it follows that the consorting with "strange women" implied contempt of the covenant purpose of God in regard to the elect family of Abraham. There were, moreover, other consequences. In the event of the transgressor being of the seed royal, such acts would bring confusion, and would imperil the dynasty of David, the king of Jehovah's choice; while all such offenders in Israel were thereby liable to be led into idolatry (Ex. 34. 16).

Through misinterpretation of ch. 2. 17, some have held that the "strange woman" was an adulteress of the house of Israel, and this has excluded from view the aspect which has thus far been presented. Careful examination of the passage, however, finds in the word "god", as here employed, no reference to Jehovah, but rather to the national "god", or gods, of the "alien woman". In this verse the teacher would emphasize the audacity of the flatterer: "she forsaketh the guide of her youth, and forgetteth the covenant of her god". That is, leaving her own people in Philistia, Edom, Moab, or Egypt, she has assumed the part of an adventuress, and come among a community of whose God she knows nothing.

It was quite in order, on the one hand, to speak of nations as the people of their god (Num. 21. 29: cp. 2 Kings 11. 17; Ps. 47. 9); and likewise, on the other hand, to speak of gods as the gods of distinctive peoples. (Judg. 11. 24; Jer. 43. 12; 48. 7: cp. Josh. 7. 13; Judg. 5. 3, 5; Isa. 8. 19; 40. 1). The usage thus indicated was sanctified in relation to the faithful in many passages of Holy Scripture: see the divergent courses of Orpah and Ruth (Ruth 1. 15, 16), and compare the gracious words of Jehovah: "I will be YOUR God, and ye shall be MY People" (Lev. 26. 12: cp. Ex. 6. 7; Jer. 7. 23; 11. 4; 24. 7; 30. 22; Ezek. 11. 20; 14. 11; 36. 28; 37. 27; Zech. 13. 9).

Another ground for the contention that the "strange woman" merely means an Israelite of evil reputation has been found by some in ch. 7. 19, 20—"the goodman is not at home, he is gone a long journey", &c. This, however, proves nothing against the position taken up in the analysis now presented. In fact, it may be assumed that, in the days of Solomon (as ever since) female corrupters of men, alien or otherwise, included some who had the protection of husbands, or men who sustained such a relation.

Thus we find "the Words of the Wise" to have been addressed by teachers to Solomon the prince, teachers whose desire it was to instruct him in the ways of his father's God: in fact, both parents are mentioned (1. 8; 6. 20). Accordingly, these sections of the book deal with the domestic politics of Israel. After the opening verse there is no mention of the nation in specific terms; but the fear of the Lord, the pious service of Jehovah, is inculcated as fundamental. The "Words" or "Sayings", as the title of the book intimates, treat of "discretion" and "wise dealing", as these are shown to relate to "the fear of the LORD". Moreover, the "Words" range themselves in classes that were distinctly anticipated in the Pentateuch as proper subjects for the consideration of rulers in Israel. This fact has an important bearing upon the age of the book, and also upon the age of other portions of the Old Testament.

For instance: in Deut. 17. 14-20 it is stipulated that, if, on settlement in the Land of Canaan, the People should desire a king, then in such matter they should have regard to the Divine choice, which would be, not to put responsibility upon a foreigner, but upon "one from among thy brethren". The stipulations are continued thus: (1) He shall not multiply horses, after the manner of the Egyptians; (2) he shall not multiply wives, who might "turn away his heart" from God; (3) he shall not greatly multiply to himself silver and gold; (4) he shall make a copy of the Law, and read therein daily, that he may learn to fear the Lord; (5) all this is to be to the end that he may prolong his days in his kingdom, and never lack successors on the throne. Moreover, in Deut. 7. 2-5 (cp. Ex. 34. 12 ff., and Josh. 23. 12, 13) it is laid down that the Israelites should destroy the Canaanites and their symbols of worship; should make no covenant with them, and should guard against intermarriage with them; the last-named prohibition being supported by the warning that it would lead to apostasy from Jehovah: "They will turn away thy son from following Me, that they may serve other gods."

To the thoughtful reader of the Book of Proverbs it is clear that the sanctions and prohibitions of these passages of the Pentateuch form the warp and woof of the teaching of the wise men to whose care the son of David was committed. The Proverbs of Solomon, strictly so called, as found in sections 3 and 5 of the book, are quite distinct from "The Words of the Wise", as given in sections 1, 2, 4 and 6, and addressed to "my son". The prince was, in these latter, diligently fortified against practices that would bring about religious apostasy, and eventuate in dynastic disaster. Hence,

in these divisions of the book, we find instruction which answers with precision to the stipulations given in the Pentateuch, thus:—(1) Horses are treated as of no account, for "victory is of the Lord" (21. 31). (2) The taking of foreign wives is condemned with unceasing energy (2. 16 ff.; 6. 24 ff.; 7. 5 ff.). (3) Gold and silver, riches, are declared to be inferior to the fear of the Lord; in fact, to be at the disposal of wisdom, and therefore not to be desired apart therefrom (3. 16; 8. 18, 19; 22. 1–4; 23. 4, 5; 27. 24; 28. 6–8). (4) The majesty of the Law is affirmed, and to keep it is a mark of wisdom; while the man who turns away from hearing (and heeding) the Law cannot offer acceptable worship to God (6. 20–23; 28. 4–9; 29. 18). (5) Obedience is commended, and shown to bring prolongation of life (3. 2, 16; 4. 10; 9. 11; cp. 10. 27).

These several points agree with the stipulations of Deut. 17, as we have indicated them in the light of Deut. 7. Further, as the ruler was not to make covenant with the nations, so also we find denunciations of alliance with "sinners" and "strangers", as distinct from women (1. 10–15), "come with us . . . one purse" (6. 1; cp. 20. 26); also counsels against following the ways of the nations in regard to war (1. 10–18; 3. 30, 31; 4. 14–17). The lessons were of the utmost gravity; but, as we know, they were not, in their entirety, taken to heart by the young prince.

When, at length, Solomon was called upon to make his life-choice, he rightly prayed for wisdom rather than wealth; and, as we know, was given "a wise and understanding heart", also, in addition, that which he did not request, "both riches and honour" (1 Kings 3. 9–13). Hence, in his own Proverbs, Solomon spoke in praise of wisdom (13. 1; 14. 1), and accorded a secondary place to riches (11. 28; 13. 7, 8; 14. 24; 15. 6, 16; 16. 16; 18. 11). That teaching, however, which was of the greatest moment, he did not receive and hold fast. Accordingly, we peruse his Proverbs in vain for any warnings against the "strange woman". Clearly this lesson was not learnt. Hence, in the record of his life (1 Kings 11) we read:—

> King Solomon loved many strange women (the plural of the word *nokriah*), together with the daughter of Pharaoh, women of the Moabites, Ammonites, Edomites, Zidonians, and Hittites; of the nations concerning which the LORD said unto the children of Israel, Ye shall not go in to them, neither shall they come in unto you: for surely they will turn away your heart after their gods: Solomon clave unto these in love (1, 2).

The words "concerning which the LORD said unto the children of Israel" take us back to Ex. 34. 16, and Deut. 7. 3, 4. The thing that was apprehended took place. We further read:—

> It came to pass, when Solomon was old, that his wives turned away his heart after other gods: and his heart was not perfect with the LORD his God, as was the heart of David his father. For Solomon went after Ashtoreth the goddess of the Zidonians, and after Milcom the abomination of the Ammonites. And Solomon did evil in the sight of the LORD, and went not fully after the LORD, as did David his father. Then did Solomon build an high place for Chemosh, the abomination of Moab, in the hill that is before Jerusalem, and for Molech, the abomination of the children of Ammon. And likewise did he for all his strange wives, which burnt incense and sacrificed unto their gods (4–8).

In further contempt of the will of the Lord for his kingdom, Solomon introduced horses from Egypt (1 Kings 10. 26–29; cp. ch. 9. 19). The result was terrible. The kingdom was divided, in execution of the purpose set forth in 1 Kings 11. 11–13, and the ten tribes taken from under Rehoboam, the son of Solomon, of whom we read the significant (and repeated) words: "His mother's name was Naamah THE AMMONITESS" (1 Kings 14. 21, 31). And primarily this evil came from the folly of the king in consorting with foreign women, in defiance of the instructions of teachers whose words have come down to us in "the Words of the Wise". Such conduct was a breach of the Divine covenant. The serious view which was taken of all such proceedings by the pious Israelite may be gathered from the words and deeds of Ezra the Scribe, at the time of the Return (Ezra 9, 10 *passim*; cp. Neh. 13. 23 ff. See also Josephus *Antiq.* VIII. vii. 5).

Having thus discriminated the Proverbs, and seen that, while some were written BY Solomon, others were written FOR him, we suggest that the instruction which was given to the young prince shows an intimate acquaintance with Israelitish policy, as Divinely ordained, and set out in the Book of Deuteronomy. That is to say, in the tenth century B.C., the cautions and warnings given in Deut. 7 and 17 were developed in detail by those who were charged with the education of him who was to succeed King David on the throne of Israel.

Yet the theory has been advanced, and is by many maintained, that the Book of Deuteronomy had no existence in the age of Solomon! Indeed, it has been boldly declared that Deuteronomy was written in the reign of Manasseh, some time near 650 B.C. And, naturally, scholars, who have not been able to distinguish allusions to the book in the early Prophets, have not been careful to look for any reflection of its teaching in the Book of Proverbs, which, so readily, has been placed in its entirety in the class of Wisdom Literature. Now, however, with due place and significance given to "the Words of the Wise", we see that the Fifth Book of the Pentateuch is demanded in the history of Israel over three hundred years before the time of its presumed "discovery" in the days of Manasseh, and still longer before its suggested fabrication in the days of Josiah.

If that is so, then the facts before us furnish another reason for profound distrust in regard to a system of criticism which exhibits tendency to hurry conclusions, while as yet the essential facts are not gathered, much less understood with thoroughness.

Thus we find that a study of the Book of Proverbs, with due attention to the divisions (most of them expressly indicated in the text), not only reflects light upon a great chapter of Israelitish history, but also has an important bearing upon critical questions, with which, hitherto, it has not been thought to have any intimate connection.

75 SPECIAL PASSAGES IN THE BOOK OF PROVERBS ACQUIRING NEW LIGHT.

In the Companion notes to the Book of Proverbs, it will be observed that certain words are carefully discriminated: such as the words for "fool", "poor"; the singular and plural of the wicked, the righteous, &c., are noted. But certain proverbs also are presented in a new light altogether. Among these are the following:

1. 7. "The fear of the LORD".
1. 17. "In vain the net is spread in the sight of any bird".
2. 7. "He layeth up sound wisdom for the righteous".
3. 2, 16. "Length of days" supposed to be given by "wisdom". See also 4. 10; 9. 11; 10. 27.
5. 2. "That thy lips may keep knowledge".
5. 14. "Almost in all evil".
16. 1. "The preparations of the heart in man . . . is from the LORD".
21. 1. "The king's heart is in the hand of the LORD as the rivers of water".
21. 4. "An high look, and a proud heart . . . is sin".

76 SUPPOSED "LATER" HEBREW WORDS IN ECCLESIASTES.

It is alleged by some modern critics that the Book of Ecclesiastes belongs to a much later date, and was written by a later hand, because certain words are alleged to belong to a later period of Hebrew literature. Several of these words are noted in the margin, but it may be useful to the student to find them together in one list.

i. *kānaṣ*, "gathered", ch. 2. 8. But it occurs in Pss. 33. 7; 147. 2. Ezek. 22. 21; 39. 28.

ii. *m*^{e}*dinah*, "provinces", ch. 2. 8; 5. 8. But it is found in 1 Kings 20. 14, 15, 17, 19. Lam. 1. 1. Ezek. 19. 8.

iii. *mikreh*, "event", or happening, ch. 2. 14, 15; 3. 19 (that which befalleth), and 9. 2, 3. But it is found in Ruth 2. 3; and 1 Sam. 6. 9; 20. 26.

iv. *shalaṭ*, "have rule", ch. 2. 19. But the word is found in Ps. 119. 133, and a derivative of it even in Gen. 42. 6.

v. *ḥēphēẓ*, "purpose", ch. 3. 1, 17; 5. 4, 8; 8. 6; 12. 1, 10. But it is found in 1 Sam. 15. 22, where it is rendered "delight"; also 18. 25. 2 Sam. 22. 20 (the verb). 1 Kings 5. 8, 9, 10; 9. 11; 10. 13; where it is rendered "desire". Even in Job 21. 21; 22. 3; where it is rendered "pleasure". In Isa. 53. 10 "pleasure" evidently means what Jehovah has been pleased to purpose. Cp. Isa. 44. 28; 46. 10.

vi. *sôph*, "the end", ch. 3. 11; 7. 2; 12. 13 (conclusion). This is found in 2 Chron. 20. 16. Joel 2. 20, where it is rendered "hinder part". The verb is found in Num. 22. 30, 30, and repeatedly in Job.

vii. *taḳaph*, "prevail", ch. 4. 12; but the only two other places where it occurs are Job 14. 20 and 15. 24.

viii. *miṡkēn*, "poor", ch. 4. 13; 9. 15, 15, 16; but the derivative of it is found in Deut. 8. 9.

ix. *n*^{e}*kāṣîm*, "wealth", ch. 5. 19; 6. 2. This is found as early as Josh. 22. 8. 2 Chron. 1. 11, 12.

x. *'āmad*, "stand" "appear", ch. 8. 3. This occurs in Gen. 18. 8, 22; 19. 27; 24. 30; 41. 1, 17; 43. 15. Ex. 9. 10; 14. 19; 18. 13; 20. 18, 21, &c.; Lev. 19. 16.

xi. *kāshēr*, "prosper", ch. 10. 10 (profitable); 11. 6 (prosper). But it is found in Ps. 68. 6, where "with chains" should perhaps be rendered "into prosperity".

xii. *zūa'*, "tremble", ch. 12. 3. But we find it in Hab. 2. 7 ("vex"), and its derivative *z*^{e}*va'āh*, Isa. 28. 19. Jer. 15. 4; 24. 9.

These examples will be sufficient to show how slender is the argument on which an objection so grave, and a conclusion so premature, is based. Some of the references given above may be later, of course, than the true date of Ecclesiastes; nevertheless, they are all much earlier than the alleged date, which is about 200 B.C. or less.

77 THE CHRONOLOGICAL ORDER OF THE PROPHETS.

1. That the *Canonical* order of the books of the prophets is not their *Chronological* order is well known.

But the dates usually to be found at the head or in the margin of our Bibles—as well as in many of the "Tables" supplied in "Aids" to students—involve the subject in hopeless confusion.

The four prophets commonly styled "Greater" (or Longer), viz. ISAIAH, JEREMIAH, EZEKIEL, and DANIEL, are all dated.

Of the other twelve, called "Minor" (or Shorter), *six* are dated and *six* are *un*dated. (See the Structure on p. 1206.)

The dated books are HOSEA, AMOS, MICAH, ZEPHANIAH, HAGGAI, and ZECHARIAH.

The *un*dated books are JOEL, OBADIAH, JONAH, NAHUM, HABAKKUK, and MALACHI.

Of the whole sixteen, therefore, we have *ten* dated and *six* undated. (See Ap. 10.)

From the particulars given in the dated books themselves, we are enabled to lay down with precision the years and periods covered by the respective prophecies.

With regard to the undated books the case is different; and we have to rely upon the guidance of their internal evidence. But this in almost every case is so clear, that there is no great difficulty in assigning each of the prophetical books to its respective chronological position (*Obadiah* being perhaps the only exception).

The Chart on p. 113 has been prepared accordingly.

It must be premised that the periods indicated by the thick black lines are the duration of the periods in which the Divine Message continued to "come" to and through the particular prophet named: e.g. ISAIAH is shown on the Chart as 649–588 B.C., thus comprising a period of *sixty-one* years. This does not represent the years of the prophet's *life*, which in all probability extended to some 81 or 83 years. (See notes on p. 930.)

2. It is a Jewish belief that JEREMIAH and ZECHARIAH were contemporaries. This is quite possible. We are not told when, or how, or where Jeremiah died. When Jerusalem was destroyed finally by Nebuchadnezzar (477 B.C.) Jeremiah would be about 57 years old. He may easily have lived another thirty or forty, or even more, years after that event.[1]

If we suppose he outlived the destruction of Jerusalem by *forty* years, then the year of his death would be 437 B.C., eleven years before the end of the Babylonian Captivity, in 426 B.C.

ZECHARIAH began his *seven* years of prophetic ministry twenty-seven years later, in 410 B.C.

But we are not told anything about him in Scripture, save that his *grandfather* was a prophet; neither have we any clue to his age, as we have e.g. in the cases of JEREMIAH and DANIEL. ZECHARIAH may very well have been at least thirty or forty years of age in 410 B.C., when he gives us his first date (1. 1). Consequently, he would have been contemporary with the great Benjamite priest for from *three* to *thirteen* years!

3. It is further necessary to state, and important to be observed, that the dates given in the Chart on p. 113 have been charted down from the dating given (or suggested by internal evidence) in the prophetic books themselves, and NOT *vice versâ*. So the student may understand that the remarkable and significant groupings of the prophets as therein depicted are in no wise "manipulated" or "fitted in" to suit any preconceived ideas or theories. They are charted down simply from the dates and the data afforded by the sacred records themselves, and tell clearly their own story.

4. Turning now to the Chart itself (p. 113), it must be further premised that "section-paper" has been used, as in Ap. 50. This is highly important; as only thus can the exact *relative proportions* of the length of each prophetical ministry be presented accurately to the *eye*. The thick black lines represent the period

[1] The belief of some that Heb. 11. 37 refers to Jeremiah is based on the Jewish tradition that the prophet was "stoned" to death in Egypt. But of this we have no proof.

APPENDIX 77: THE CHRONOLOGICAL ORDER OF THE PROPHETS (*cont.*).

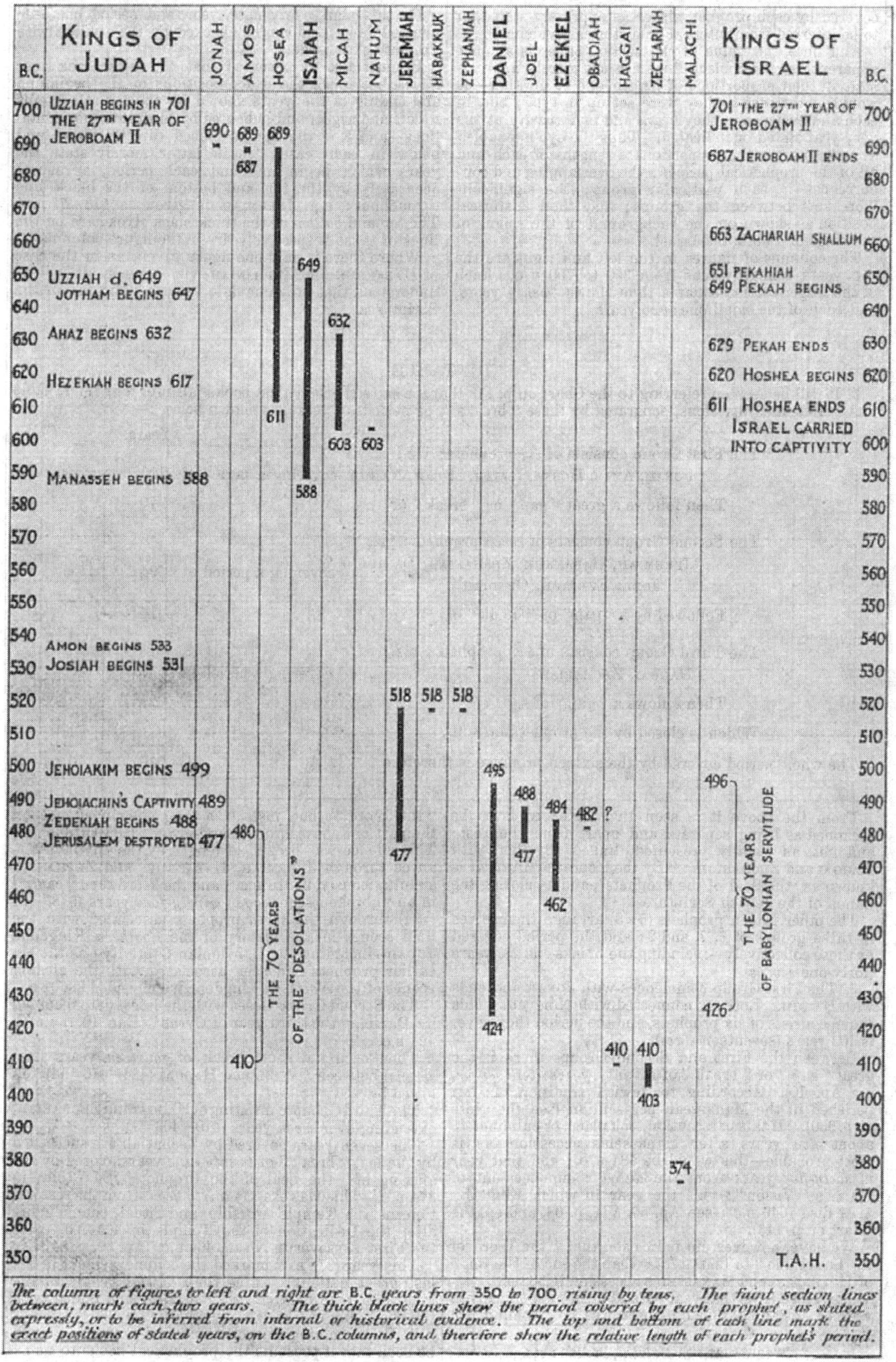

The column of figures to left and right are B.C. *years from* 350 *to* 700 *rising by tens. The faint section lines between, mark each two years. The thick black lines shew the period covered by each prophet, as stated expressly, or to be inferred from internal or historical evidence. The top and bottom of each line mark the exact positions of stated years, on the* B.C. *columns, and therefore shew the relative length of each prophet's period.*

covered by each prophet, either as expressly stated, or to be inferred from internal or historical evidence.

And here, the value of the Section-paper is at once apparent: as these black lines are not merely *approximate* in their proportions of length one to another—as would be the case if they were set up in type; but, in each and every case, they begin and end *exactly* at the very year stated or indicated. Thus the eye is enabled at once to grasp the proportionate lengths of each and all of the prophetical periods; the overlapping and concurrences in each particular group; the significant "breaks" between the groups; and their historical position as shown on the background of the reigns of the kings of Judah and Israel.

The columns of figures to the left and right are the B.C. years, rising by tens from 350 to 700 B.C. Each of the larger section-squares thus shows *twenty* years, and each of the small ones *two* years.

On this plan, every date, year, and period has been charted down, and can be checked by the student with absolute exactitude.

It must also be observed that the thick black lines *themselves* mark the exact positions of the beginning and ending of the years shown on the figure-columns to left and right, and indicated by the fainter horizontal lines—and NOT the figures placed directly above and below in each case. These latter merely state the years which begin and end each period, as shown accurately by the top and bottom of the black line throughout: e.g. JEREMIAH is given as 518-477 B.C. The *top* and *bottom* of the thick black stroke are on the lines of these respective years in the figure-columns.

Where there is only one figure given, as in the case of HABAKKUK and ZEPHANIAH, viz. 518 B.C., it will be understood that only one date year is indicated in the Scriptures.

THE TABLE.

5. It will be seen on referring to the Chart on p. 113 that the sixteen prophetical books fall into four remarkable and well-defined divisions, separated by three "breaks", or periods of years, as shown below:—

	Years.
The First Group consists of *six* prophets: viz.:	
JONAH, AMOS, HOSEA, ISAIAH, MICAH, NAHUM, covering a period of	102
Then follows a great "gap" or "break" of	70
The Second Group consists of *seven* prophets: viz.	
JEREMIAH, HABAKKUK, ZEPHANIAH, DANIEL, JOEL, EZEKIEL, OBADIAH } covering a period of	94
Followed by a "gap" or "break" of	14
The Third Group consists of *two* prophets: viz.:	
HAGGAI, ZECHARIAH . . . . . . covering a period of	7
Then follows a "gap" of	29
Which is closed by the prophet MALACHI.	
The whole period covered by the sixteen prophets is therefore	316

From the above it is seen that MALACHI is to be reckoned as being separate and apart from the rest; and not, as usually presented, linked together with HAGGAI and ZECHARIAH. "By the Hebrews, *Malachi* is known as 'the Seal of the Prophets', and as closing the Canon of the Jewish Scriptures."[1]

The other fifteen prophets (5×3) arrange themselves in three groups of 6, 7, and 2; and the period covered by these collectively—including the breaks—is 287 years (forty-one *sevens*).

6. The First Group commences with JONAH and ends with NAHUM. Both are connected with Nineveh. This group consists of six prophets, and the period they cover is 102 years (seventeen *sixes*).

Between the First and Second Groups there is the great "gap" or "break" of seventy years (ten *sevens*, see Ap. 10). According to Jewish tradition, ISAIAH perished in the Manassean persecution (see the Note on p. 930). If this persecution took place, or culminated, about *five* years after Manasseh's accession—as is most probable—this would be 584 B.C.; and that year is *sixty-five* years from the *dated* commencement of Isaiah's "Vision": viz., the year in which King UZZIAH died (649 B.C.: see Ap. 50. VII, p. 68, and cp. the Chart on p. 113).

We have, however, no indication that "the Word of the Lord came" to ISAIAH *later* than the end of the reign of HEZEKIAH, and MANASSEH'S accession in 588 B.C.

Therefore, from that year on, and until "the thirteenth year of Josiah" (518 B.C.), there was no "coming" of "the Word"; but, instead, a long solemn silence on the part of Jehovah for *seventy years!* (588 − 518 = 70.) This silence was broken at length by the Divine utterances through JEREMIAH, HABAKKUK, and ZEPHANIAH simultaneously, in 518 B.C.; and the Word then "came" in an unbroken sequence of *ninety-four* years (518 − 424 = 94) through the *seven* prophets associated with the final scenes in the history of the *Southern* Kingdom, JUDAH—including the Babylonian Captivity—as the *six* earlier prophets had been associated with the closing scenes of the *Northern* Kingdom, which ended in 601 B.C.

The Second Group closes with the latest date recorded by Daniel, "the third year of Cyrus" (Dan. 10. 1), i.e. in 424 B.C.

Then occurs a short break of *fourteen* years (two *sevens*) between DANIEL and HAGGAI (424 − 410 = 14), followed by

The Third Group, consisting of HAGGAI and ZECHARIAH, extending over *seven* years (410 − 403 = 7).

The seven years covered by Zechariah are succeeded by the last "break" of *twenty-nine* years, closed by the affixing of "the Seal of the Prophets", MALACHI, in 374 B.C. This was exactly *thirty years* from the restoration of the Temple worship and ritual, commencing after the Dedication of the Temple in 405 B.C., with the First Passover in Nisan, 404 B.C. (Ap. 58, p. 84).

This year (374 B.C.) marked the commencement of the last great national testing time of the People in the land: viz. *four hundred years* (40 × 10), and ended with the beginning of Christ's ministry in A.D. 26.

7. On examining this chronological grouping, it will be seen that it presents the prophetical books to us *as*

[1] WORDSWORTH on *Malachi*, Prelim. note.

a whole; and thus, in a manner is at variance with the usual classification into "Four Prophets the Greater (or Longer), and Twelve Prophets the Minor or (Shorter)."

Although it is, of course, manifestly true that ISAIAH, JEREMIAH, EZEKIEL, and DANIEL are "greater", in the sense that they are messages of ampler dimensions, and far wider scope than the majority of the others, yet—according to their chronological positions in the Scriptures, as shown in the Chart (p. 113)—it would appear that they are grouped together by the Divine Spirit, with the so-called "Minor" (or Shorter) prophets, as being *units* only in a particular "coming" of the Word of Jehovah, during certain clearly defined periods of time connected with the close of the national history of Israel's sons as possessors of the land.

It is interesting to note the close association of the figures "6" and "7" with these periods.

(*a*) The three groups together cover a period of 203 years, during which "the Word of the Lord came" through the prophets (102 × 94 × 7 = 203); and 203 is twenty-nine *sevens*.

(*b*) The prophecies of the First Group, linked together by the number of Man "6" (Ap. 10), are seen to be closely connected with the last hundred years or so of the Northern Kingdom.

The prophecies of the Second Group, linked together by the special number of Spiritual Perfection "7" (Ap. 10), are as closely connected with the destruction and punishment of JUDAH and JERUSALEM.

(*c*) In the First Group, HOSEA, ISAIAH, and MICAH were contemporary for twenty-one years (three *sevens*); viz. from 632 to 611 B.C.

In the Second Group, JEREMIAH, DANIEL, JOEL, and EZEKIEL are contemporaries for seven years (one *seven*); viz. from 484 to 477 B.C.

If OBADIAH's date is 482 B.C., then we have five prophets all contemporaries during this period. And five is the number associated with Divine Grace (Ap. 10).

After the "break" of fourteen years (two *sevens*) between the Second and Third Groups, we have ZECHARIAH, the last of the *fifteen* prophets of the three groups, continuing from 410 to 403 B.C. (one *seven*); HAGGAI being contemporary with him in 410.

The *fifteen* prophets represent the number of Grace thrice repeated (5 × 3).

8. MALACHI's date is 374 B.C. As stated above, this is exactly thirty years after the Restoration, and the resumption of the Temple worship and ritual, beginning with the Passover in 404 B.C. (Ezra 6. 19). The "Seal of the Prophets" was therefore affixed thirty years from that important start-point, and *twenty-nine* clear years from Ezra's last date: viz., 1st of Nisan 403 B.C. (Ezra 10. 17), the year that witnessed the Dedication of the Wall (Neh. 12. 27-47) and the Reformation of the People under Nehemiah (Neh. 13. 1-31).

9. It may also be noted that the Book of JONAH—the prophet quoted by our Lord as the "Sign" of His own Resurrection—*commences* the grouped fifteen, while ZECHARIAH *ends* them with the glorious and detailed statements of the Return of the King to reign as "the Lord of all the earth".

Again: as the "break" of twenty-nine years follows after ZECHARIAH, before the "Seal", MALACHI, is affixed in 374 B.C., this points to a fact of great importance: viz., that *the O.T. is really closed by the Book of Zechariah and not Malachi, as usually understood.* Malachi marks the commencement of the great final probationary period of 400 years, which ended with the coming of "My Messenger" (John the Baptist) followed by the Advent of "the Messenger of the Covenant" (Messiah Himself).

MALACHI is thus seen to be linked on to John the Baptist (cp. Mal. 4. 5, 6, and Matt. 11. 10-15), and "seals" together the last page of the O.T., and the beginning of "The Book of the Generation of Jesus the Messiah."

78 THE INTER-RELATION OF THE PROPHETICAL BOOKS.

In the Hebrew Canon (Ap. 1) we have

The *five* books of the "Law". This is the number of *Grace.*

(2) The *eight* books of the "Prophets"—this is the *Dominical* number.

(3) The *eleven* books of the Hagiographa—this is the remarkable number (the fifth *prime*) which plays so important a part in the works of God. (See Ap. 10.)

In the Law, the grace of God was shown to Israel (Deut. 4. 31-37, &c.); but *true* grace came by Jesus Christ. (See note on John 1. 16, 17.)

In the Prophets, we have Jehovah's special dealing with Israel. In the "former prophets" we see the law-principle; and in the latter prophets we see faith-principle; the two together presenting us with a wonderful picture of the failure of man on the one hand, and the faithfulness of Jehovah on the other.

THE BOOKS OF THE PROPHETS.

Through the changing of the order of the books of the prophets, by the Translators of the Septuagint, the Church has lost sight of the one grand illustration of the great principle of Old Testament teaching, which is currently supposed to be taught only in the New; viz. that law-principle brings in "the curse", whereas faith-principle brings in "the blessing".

The non-recognition of the fact that this is *Old* Testament teaching has obscured the specific doctrine of the *New*: viz., that over and above belief on the Lord Jesus Christ, a "mystery" or "secret", which had been hid in God "from the beginning of the world" (Eph. 3. 9), was made manifest *after* Pentecost, and after the Dispensation covered by the Acts of the Apostles, to the apostle Paul. See notes on Eph. 1. 9; 3; and 5. 32.

There is another Structure, differing from that given in Ap. 1, but equally true, viz.:—

THE FORMER PROPHETS.

LAW-PRINCIPLE.

A | JOSHUA. Israel *brought into the Land.* God keeps His covenant. Israel under priests.

B | JUDGES. Israel *in the Land.* Man breaks the covenant. Failure of the priesthood.

B | SAMUEL. Israel *in the Land.* God shows mercy in appointing prophets, and a king whose throne shall be established for ever.

A | KINGS. Israel *ejected from the Land.* Man breaks the covenant as before; the ten tribes and the kings break the one made with David.

Here, in the "former" prophets (Zech. 7. 7), we see, arranged in an *Introversion*, the whole of Israel's failure in the Land, set forth by the Lord.

Now we are shown in the "latter" prophets how God's faithfulness was going to secure His own purposes, and Israel's blessing.

THE LATTER PROPHETS.

FAITH-PRINCIPLE.

Priests and kings were anointed: but *God* would now send an anointed One, i.e. Messiah; and, if they would believe on Him they would be established. For He would be also a Prophet. *Corporate* testimony had failed: therefore there would be a division among *individuals* of the nation on account of Him; so that in times of crisis those whose sins had not been *expiated* by His *priestly* work would be excluded from the Nation for not hearkening to Him as Prophet (Deut. 18. 18, 19), and *extirpated* by His work as *King* (Isa. 6. 9-13, 7. 9; John 7. 40-43; Acts 3. 19-26; 13. 38-52; Matt. 13. 36-43). In *Him*, then, the righteous Servant of Jehovah, the future of Israel is seen in the latter prophets (Isa. 49).

He is both rejected and accepted. The Nation went back to the land to try that question under Divine auspices (Dan. 9. 24–27). When they rejected Him, they were not established, but again scattered. But when they accept Him they will be regathered, and never again rooted out.

They can come back only through David (from whom their second breach of covenant referred to was a departure), before the first breach of covenant can be healed up; for the character and form of the Structure (here, as elsewhere) corresponds with the subject-matter; and, in this, the *Introversion* of the Structure is the same as the principle on which God works: viz., by introversion. The *Law* must go forth from *Zion*.

We find then that the following is the Structure, showing

THE INTER-RELATION OF THE PROPHETIC BOOKS.

C | ISAIAH. Restoration of the throne of David through the priestly work of Messiah, from the standpoint of the two tribes.

D | JEREMIAH. Political disruption, and final restoration of Judah and Ephraim (the twelve tribes) by a new Covenant.

D | EZEKIEL. Ecclesiastical disruption, God ceasing to rule the Land in demonstration; and final restoration of the same, re-establishing all the twelve tribes.

C | THE TWELVE MINOR PROPHETS. Restoration of the throne of David through the priestly work of Messiah, from the standpoint of the ten tribes. (See the Structure of these, preceding HOSEA.)

The New Covenant of Jeremiah 31. 31–34 has indeed been made (Matt. 26. 28); and can never be made again: for His "blood of the Covenant" has been shed, once for all. Had the nation repented on the proclamation of Peter (Acts 2. 38; 3. 19–26), all would have been fulfilled; in the same way as John the Baptist would have been taken for Elijah the prophet (Mal. 3. 1; 4. 5, 6. Cp. Matt. 11. 10–15) had the nation, through its rulers, repented at his proclamation (Matt. 3. 1, 2) and that of Messiah (Matt. 4. 17, &c.). But, seeing that these great calls to "repent" were not obeyed, both fulfilments stand in abeyance, until this one great condition of national restoration and blessing shall have taken place. The modern doctrine, in certain circles, that that New Covenant holds good with Gentiles now, or with the present-day "house of Israel", would bestow justification on unbelievers. This is not the teaching of Heb. 8 and 10. This does not affect the position of those who are "in Christ" in this Dispensation of the "Mystery". They have all, and more than all, in that "New Covenant" which will yet bring back blessing to Restored Israel.

When that national repentance does take place, the time will come for the travailing woman to bring forth (Isa. 66. 8; John 16. 19–22). But that is still future. What is true, is the declaration of Jehovah by Micah: "Therefore will He give them up, until the time that she which travaileth hath brought forth; then the remnant of his brethren shall return unto the children of Israel" (Mic. 5. 3).

79 ISAIAH: THE EVIDENCES FOR ONE AUTHORSHIP.

The hypothesis of modern critics is that Isaiah is not the sole author of the prophecy bearing his name, but that he only wrote chapters 1–39 (called by them "the former portion"), and that an unknown author or authors (for there are now alleged to have been three, or more, Isaiahs) are responsible for chapters 40 to the end (called by them "the latter portion").

Thus, they would treat this prophecy much as Isaiah himself is said to have been treated, who, as tradition tells us, was "sawn asunder".

This "latter portion" also modern critics would relegate to a later date: viz., toward the close of the seventy years' exile.

This is a very modern theory; for, the one authorship of this prophecy has been held without question by both Jews and Christians for over 2,000 years.

I. THE USE OF HIS NAME IN THE NEW TESTAMENT.

A sufficient and conclusive answer to this matter is afforded by Holy Scripture itself, in the fact that Isaiah is twenty-one times mentioned by name in the New Testament as the author of this prophecy.

Eleven of these passages attribute to him words occurring in the *latter* portion of the book, and ten of them words occurring in the *former* portion.

A complete list is appended, divided as follows:—

(i) THE TEN PASSAGES NAMING ISAIAH AS THE AUTHOR OF THE "FORMER" PORTION.

1.	Matt. 4. 14.	Isa.	9. 1, 2.
2.	,, 13. 14.	,,	6. 9.
3.	,, 15. 7.	,,	29. 13.
4.	Mark 7. 6.	,,	29. 13.
5.	John 12. 39.	,,	6. 9.
6.	,, 12. 41.	,,	6. 9.
7.	Acts 28. 25.	,,	6. 9.
8.	Rom. 9. 27.	,,	10. 22, 23.
9.	,, 9. 29.	,,	1. 9.
10.	,, 15. 12.	,,	11. 10.

(ii) THE ELEVEN PASSAGES NAMING ISAIAH AS THE AUTHOR OF THE "LATTER" PORTION.

1.	Matt. 3. 3.	Isa.	40. 3.
2.	,, 8. 17.	,,	53. 4.
3.	,, 12. 17.	,,	42. 1–3.
4.	Luke 3. 4.	,,	40. 3–5.
5.	,, 4. 17.	,,	61. 1, 2.
6.	John 1. 23.	,,	40. 3.
7.	,, 12. 38.	,,	53. 1.
8.	Acts 8. 28.	,,	53. 7, 8.
9.	,, 8. 30.	,,	53. 7, 8.
10.	Rom. 10. 16.	,,	53. 1.
11.	,, 10. 20.	,,	65. 1, 2.

(iii) The above twenty-one passages are distributed over *six* books of the New Test.: viz., Matt. (six times); Mark (once); Luke (twice); John (four times); Acts (three times); Romans (five times).

(iv) And the prophet is named by *seven* different speakers or writers in the New Testament:

Four times by Christ Himself; *three* being from the *former* portion of Isaiah (Matt. 13. 14; 15. 7. Mark 7. 6), and *one* from the *latter* (Matt. 12. 17).

Twice by Matthew: *once* from the former portion (Matt. 4. 14), and *once* from the latter portion (Matt. 8. 17).

Four times by Luke: all from the *latter* portion of Isaiah (Luke 3. 4; 4. 17. Acts 8. 28; 8. 30).

Three times by John the Evangelist: *twice* from the *former* portion (John 12. 39, 41), and *once* from the *latter* portion (John 12. 38).

Twice by John the Baptist: both from the *latter* portion (Matt. 3. 3. John 1. 23).

Six times by Paul the Apostle: *four* from the *former* portion (Acts 28. 25. Rom. 9. 27, 29; 15. 12), and *twice* from the *latter* portion (Rom. 10. 16, 20).

II. THE EMPLOYMENT OF CERTAIN WORDS.

A further evidence of the unity of Isaiah is furnished by the Structure of the book: which, as the student of *The Companion Bible* will readily perceive, does not lend itself in any degree to the arbitrary ending suggested, at chapter 39.

A "pillar" of this "theory" is found in the supposed occurrence of certain words in the "former" portion of the prophecy which are not found in the "latter" portion, and vice versa. An examination of a few such words which are cited by modern critics will show the palpable inaccuracy characterizing their assertions.

It is asserted that the following are found only in the "latter" portion of Isaiah (chapters 40 to the end):—

1. The titles Creator, Redeemer, Saviour. But the facts of creating, redeeming, and saving are referred to in 1. 27; 12. 1, 2; 14. 1; 17. 10; 25. 9; 27. 11; 29. 22; 30. 18; 33. 22; 35. 10.
2. The thought of Jehovah as "Father". But the relation is stated in 1. 2.
3. The word *bachar* (to choose). But see 1. 29; 7. 15, 16; 14. 1.
4. The word *halal* (to praise). But see 13. 10; 38. 18.
5. The word *paēr* (to glorify). But see 10. 15.
6. The word *patsach* (to break forth into joy). But see 14. 7.
7. The word *tsemach* (to spring forth). But see 4. 2.
8. The word *zerō'* (the arm [of Jehovah]). But see 9. 20; 17. 5; 30. 30; 33. 2.

There are more than 300 words and expressions which are common to both the alleged "former" and "latter" portions of Isaiah's prophecy; and which do not occur at all in the later prophecies of Daniel, Haggai, Zechariah, and Malachi.

A sufficient number of these, to illustrate this fact amply, will be found given in the notes under their occurrences.

80 ISAIAH. QUOTATIONS AND ALLUSIONS IN THE NEW TESTAMENT.

The prophet Isaiah is quoted or referred to some eighty-five times in the New Testament. But several passages are cited or alluded to more than once; so that sixty-one separate passages are referred to in these eighty-five New Testament citations.

Of these sixty-one passages in Isaiah, it will be noticed that twenty-three are from the alleged "former" part of Isaiah (chs. 1-39), and are cited thirty-two times; while thirty-eight (the larger number) are cited from the alleged "latter" part (chs. 40-66) which is most called in question by modern critics. These sixty-one passages are cited eighty-five times.

The following table exhibits the whole; and the evidence hereby afforded, as to the unity of the authorship of Isaiah, may be added to that already given in Ap. 79:—

(The alleged "former" part)

	Isaiah.		New Test.		Isaiah.		New Test.		Isaiah.		New Test.
1	1. 9.	1	Rom. 9. 29.	8	9. 1, 2.	12	Matt. 4. 14-16.	17	28. 16.	23	Rom. 9. 33.
2	6. 1-3.	2	John 12. 41.	9	10. 22, 23.	13	Rom. 9. 27, 28.			24	,, 10. 11.
3	,, 9, 10.	3	Matt. 13. 14.	10	11. 4.	14	2 Thess. 2. 8.			25	1 Pet. 2. 6.
		4	Mark 4. 12.	11	,, 10.	15	Rom. 15. 12.	18	29. 10.	26	Rom. 11. 8.
		5	Luke 8. 10.	12	21. 9.	16	Rev. 14. 8.	19	,, 13.	27	Matt. 15. 8, 9.
		6	John 12. 40.			17	,, 18. 2.			28	Mark 7. 6, 7.
		7	Acts 28. 26, 27.	13	22. 13.	18	1 Cor. 15. 32.	20	,, 14.	29	1 Cor. 1. 19.
4	7. 14.	8	Matt. 1. 23.	14	,, 22.	19	Rev. 3. 7.	21	,, 16.	30	Rom. 9. 20.
5	8. 12, 13.	9	1 Pet. 3. 14, 15.	15	25. 8.	20	1 Cor. 15. 54.	22	34. 4, 10.	31	Rev. 6. 13, 14.
6	,, 14.	10	Rom. 9. 32, 33.			21	Rev. 7. 17.	23	35. 3.	32	Heb. 12. 12.
7	,, 18.	11	Heb. 2. 13.	16	28. 11, 12.	22	1 Cor. 14. 21.				

(The alleged "latter" part)

	Isaiah.		New Test.		Isaiah.		New Test.		Isaiah.		New Test.
1	40. 3-6.	1	Matt. 3. 3.	10	49. 8.	19	2 Cor. 6. 2.			37	Mark 11. 17.
		2	Mark 1. 2, 3.	11	,, 10.	20	Rev. 7. 16.			38	Luke 19. 46.
		3	Luke 3. 4-6.	12	52. 5.	21	Rom. 2. 24.	27	57. 19.	39	Eph. 2. 17.
		4	John 1. 23.	13	,, 7.	22	,, 10. 15.			40	Rom. 3. 15.
2	,, 6-8.	5	1 Pet. 1. 24, 25.	14	,, 11.	23	2 Cor. 6. 17.	28	59. 7, 8.	41	Eph. 6. 14-17.
		6	Jas. 1. 10, 11.	15	,, 15.	24	Rom. 15. 21.	29	,, 17.	42	1 Thess. 5. 3.
3	,, 13.	7	Rom. 11. 34.	16	53. 1.	25	John 12. 38.	30	,, 20, 21.	43	Rom. 11. 26, 27.
		8	1 Cor. 2. 16.			26	Rom. 10. 16.	31	60. 3, 10, 11.	44	Rev. 21. 24-26.
4	41. 4.	9	Rev. 1. 8, 11, 17.	17	,, 4.	27	Matt. 8. 17.	32	61. 1, 2.	45	Luke 4. 17-19.
		10	,, 21. 6.	18	,, 5.	28	1 Pet. 2. 24, 25.	33	63. 2, 3.	46	Rev. 19. 13-15.
		11	,, 22. 13.	19	,, 7, 8.	29	Acts 8. 32, 33.	34	64. 4.	47	1 Cor. 2. 9.
5	42. 1-4.	12	Matt. 12. 17-21.	20	,, 9.	30	1 Pet. 2. 22.	35	65. 1, 2.	48	Rom. 10. 20, 21.
6	43. 18, 19.	13	2 Cor. 5. 17.	21	,, 12.	31	Mark 15. 28.	36	,, 17.	49	2 Pet. 3. 13.
7	45. 9.	14	Rom. 9. 20.	22	54. 1.	32	Gal. 4. 27.			50	Rev. 21. 1.
8	,, 23.	15	,, 14. 11.	23	,, 13.	33	John 6. 45.	37	66. 1, 2.	51	Acts 7. 49, 50.
		16	Phil. 2. 10, 11.	24	55. 3.	34	Acts 13. 34.			52	Matt. 5. 34, 35.
9	49. 6.	17	Luke 2. 32.	25	,, 10.	35	2 Cor. 9. 10.	38	,, 24.	53	Mark 9. 44.
		18	Acts 13. 47.	26	56. 7.	36	Matt. 21. 13.				

The eighty-five citations or allusions are distributed as follows: In Matt. there are nine; Mark, six; Luke five; John, five; Acts, five; Rom., eighteen (eight from the "former" part, and ten from the "latter"); 1 Cor., six; 2 Cor., four; Gal., one; Eph., two; Phil., one; 1 Thess., one; 2 Thess., one; Heb., two; James one; 1 Pet., five; 2 Pet., one; Rev., twelve (five from the "former" part, and seven from the "latter").

Twelve books give six direct quotations.

Eighteen books contain eighty-five allusions to Isaiah.

Only seven books out of twenty-seven have none.

The greater part of the New Testament is concerned with establishing the genuineness and authority of the book of the prophet Isaiah, and its one authorship. (See Ap. 79.)

81 THE "ALTAR TO JEHOVAH IN THE LAND OF EGYPT" (Isa. 19. 19).

The fulfilment of this prophecy took place in 1 B.C., and is recorded by Josephus (*Ant.* xiii. 3. 1-3; 6; *Wars* 7. 10, 3; and *Against Apion*, 2. 5):—

In consequence of wars between the Jews and Syrians, ONIAS IV, the High Priest, fled to Alexandria; where, on account of his active sympathy with the cause of Egypt against Syria, he was welcomed by PTOLEMY PHILOMETOR, and rewarded by being made prince over the Jews in Egypt,[1] with the title of Ethnarch and Alabarch. Josephus says:—

"Onias asked permission from Ptolemy and Cleopatra to build a temple in Egypt like that at Jerusalem, and to appoint for it priests and Levites of his own Nation. This he devised, relying chiefly on the prophet Isaiah, who, 600 years before, predicted that a temple must be builded in Egypt by a Jew to the supreme God. He therefore wrote to Ptolemy and Cleopatra the following epistle:—

'Having come with the Jews to Leontopolis of the Heliopolite district, and other abodes of my Nation, and finding that many had sacred rites, not as was due, and were thus hostile to each other, which has befallen the Egyptians also through the vanity of their religions, and disagreeing in their services, I found a most convenient place in the fore-mentioned stronghold, abounding with wood and sacred animals. I ask leave, then, clearing away an idol temple, that has fallen down, to build a temple to the supreme God, that the Jews dwelling in Egypt, harmoniously coming together, may minister to thy benefit. For Isaiah the prophet has predicted thus: "There shall be an altar in Egypt to the LORD God"; and he prophesied many other such things concerning the place.'

"The King and Queen replied: 'We have read thy request asking leave to clear away the fallen temple in Leontopolis of the Heliopolite nome. We are surprised that a temple should be pleasing to God, settled in an impure place, and one full of sacred animals. But since thou sayest that Isaiah the prophet so long ago foretold it, we grant thee leave, if, according to the Law, we may not seem to have offended against God.'" (*Ant.* xiii. 6.)

The place of this temple was the identical spot where, many centuries before, Israel had light in their dwellings while the rest of Egypt was suffering from a plague of darkness. Here again was light in the darkness, which continued for more than 200 years (about 160 B.C. to A.D. 71), when it was closed by Vespasian.

The Jerusalem Jews were opposed to, and jealous of, this rival temple; and, by changing two letters almost identical in form (ח = Ḥ (or CH) to ה = H) turned "the city of the sun" (*cheres*) into "the city of destruction" (*heres*). But the former reading is found in many codices, two early printed editions, and some ancient versions, as well as in the margins of the A.V. and R.V. The Septuagint reading shows that the Hebrew MSS. from which that version was made, read *'ir-ha-ẓedek* = "the city of righteousness."

The "five cities" of Isa. 19. 18 were probably Heliopolis (the city of the sun, where this temple was built), Leontopolis, Daphne, Migdol, and Memphis.

[1] See longer note in the Text on p. 1096.

82 THE *FORMULÆ* OF PROPHETIC UTTERANCE.

It is clear that there was an appropriate and recognised style of prophetic address, and of the introduction to special prophetic utterances.

By attending to this we shall read the prophetic books to an advantage that cannot be realised by submitting, without thought, to the superficial guidance of chapter-beginning and chapter-ending. These will be found of little use in helping us to distinguish separate and distinct prophecies.

In JEREMIAH, the formulæ are generally "The word of the LORD came", "Thus saith the LORD", or "The word that came".

In EZEKIEL, the call is to the prophet as "son of man",[1] and the formula is "the word of the LORD came", many times repeated.

In the Minor (or Shorter) Prophets, it is "The word of the LORD by", "Hear the word that the LORD hath spoken", or "The burden of the word of the LORD".

In ISAIAH, the prophetic utterances have two distinct forms. As to Israel, the chosen People, they open with exclamations, commands, or appeals, such as "Hear", "Listen", "Awake", "Ho", "Arise, shine", "Behold"; while in the case of surrounding nations it was a series of "Burdens" or "Woes"; as well as to Ephraim (28), and to the rebellious sons who go down to Egypt, to the "Assyrian", &c. See the Structures on pp. 930, 1015, and 1104.

An illustrative example of the usefulness of noting these *formulæ* is furnished by Isa. 34 and 35. Most Commentators make chapter 35 commence a new prophecy, and thus entirely obscure the great issue of the prophecy, which begins in ch. 34. 1 with the Call:— "COME NEAR, YE NATIONS, to hear; and HEARKEN, ye peoples: let the earth HEAR", &c.

The Call is to witness Jehovah's JUDGMENT ON EDOM (in ch. 34), which issues in the salvation of ISRAEL (in ch. 35).

Thus the prophecy is seen to have no break, but forms one complete and comprehensive whole, embracing these two great parts of one subject.

In ch. 34 we have the desolation of Edom: wild beasts celebrate the discomfiture of its inhabitants: then, in ch. 35, the wilderness and solitary place are seen to be glad; and, as it were, in sympathy with Divine judgment, the desert rejoices and blossoms as the rose (35. 1, 2).

In the result, ch. 35 shows that the People of Jehovah enjoy the inheritance of the Edomites. Not only are their enemies gone, but so are the wild beasts which were at once the evidences and tokens of their judgment. It will have become the way of holiness; the unclean shall not pass over it; no lion shall be there, but the redeemed shall walk there (35. 8, 9).

But all the beauty of this wonderful transition is lost, when chapter 35 is made the beginning of a new and distinct prophecy; and, more than this, the difficulty is created by the Hebrew suffix "for them", in 35. 1. Not knowing what to do with it, the Revisers solve the difficulty by simply omitting these two words "for them"; and this in the absence of any manuscript authority, and without giving in the margin even the slightest hint that they have entirely ignored the Hebrew suffix in the verb *susūm* (i.e. the final "m").

The two chapters (34 and 35) form a comprehensive message, a matter of world concern: for it combined an implied vindication of the righteousness of God, and a confirmation of His promise to save His People Israel with an everlasting salvation.

A failure to recognise the *formula* of Isaiah's prophetic utterances led, first, to a misapplication of the chapter, and then to an unjustifiable disregard of the pronominal suffix.

This typical case of confusion, resulting primarily from an unfortunate arrangement in chapter-division, suggests the great importance of care being exercised in a correct individualizing of the prophecies of Holy Scripture.

[1] Without the article. For the expression "THE Son of Man" belongs only to Him Who was "the second man", "the last Adam", the successor or superseder of "the first man Adam" to Whom dominion in the earth is now committed. Cp. Gen. 1. 26, Ps. 8. 1, 9; and *vv.* 4-6, Heb. 2. 8 "not yet". See Ap. 98.

83 JEREMIAH 83

THE CHRONOLOGICAL ORDER OF HIS PROPHECIES

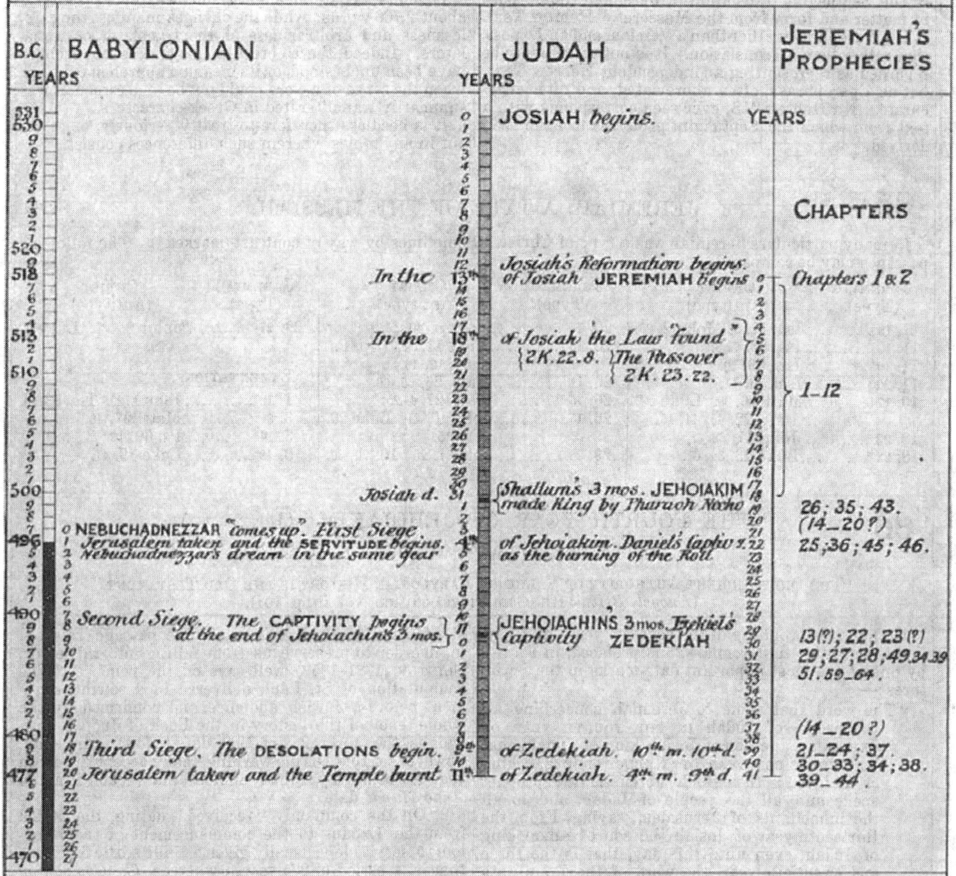

SUMMARY

B.C.		B.C.	
519	*In the twelfth year of his reign JOSIAH begins his Reformation* in	519	2 Ch. 34.3
518	*In the thirteenth year JEREMIAH begins his prophecies* "	518	Jer. 1.2; 25.3.
513	*In the eighteenth year the Law is "found" (to which Jeremiah refers in chapter 15.16., after Josiah's death) and the Passover held.*	513	2K. 22.8. 2 Ch. 34.14 2 Ch. 35.19.
500_499	*JOSIAH dies. Shallum's 3 mos. JEHOIAKIM made king by Ph: Necho*	500_499	2K. 23.34
497	*In the third y. of Jehoiakim (Dan 1.1) NEBUCHADNEZZAR "comes up" against Jerusalem, besieges, and takes the City in the year*	497	2K. 24.1_8 Dan 1.1
496	*following, which is the Fourth of Jehoiakim and First of Nebu: chadnezzar. In this year Daniel is taken to Babylon (Dan: 1.3) & The Roll is written (Jer. 36.1.4) in the 23rd y. from the 13th of Josiah.*	496	2K. 24.1_7 Dan 1.2
495	*In the succeeding year Nebuchadnezzar's second y.—he has his Dream, and in the 9th month of the same year Jehoiakim burns the Roll.*	495	Dan: 2.1-49 Jer: 36.23.

NOTE *"The Roll" was __written__ in the year of the capture of Jerusalem by Nebuchadnezzar* (496) *and it was __burned__ in the year of his Dream* (495). *The Word of JEHOVAH written and for the last time presented officially to Judah, is followed by its official rejection. Hence the announcement in vision to Neb: of Gentile supremacy until "the Times of the Gentiles be fulfilled."* (Lk. 21.24.)

T.A.H.

84 THE SEPTUAGINT VERSION OF JEREMIAH.

The Septuagint translation of Jeremiah differs both in matter and form from the Massoretic Hebrew Text. It is a Paraphrase rather than a Version, and an Exposition rather than a Translation. It is not therefore to be regarded as representing an independent Hebrew Text, but as a paraphrase, often abbreviated, and often inaccurate. No Hebrew MS. ever seen corresponds with a text from which the Septuagint professes to have been derived.

It omits about one-eighth of the Hebrew text, or about 2,700 words; while the changes manifest the carelessness and arbitrariness of the translator or translators. Indeed, the Hebrew language does not seem to have been understood, or its meaning apprehended; for, when the sense of a word could not be understood, it was summarily transliterated in Greek characters.

It is needless therefore to treat it seriously, or to set out in any tables wherein such differences consist.

85 JEREMIAH, A TYPE OF THE MESSIAH.

In many particulars Jeremiah was a type of Christ. Sometimes by way of contrast (marked *). The following passages may be compared:—

JEREMIAH (Type).	CHRIST (Antitype).	JEREMIAH (Type).	CHRIST (Antitype).	JEREMIAH (Type).	CHRIST (Antitype).
11. 18	Isa. 11. 2. John 2. 25.	20. 7	Mark 5. 40.	29. 27	John 8. 53. Luke 7. 39.
11. 19	Isa. 53. 7, 8.	20. 10	Luke 11. 54. (Cp. Ps. 55. 12, 13.)		
11. 19*	Isa. 53. 10.			LAMENTATIONS.	
11. 20*	Isa. 53. 11.	26. 11	Matt. 26. 65, 66.	1. 12	John 1. 29. Isa. 53. 10.
13. 17	Matt. 26. 38. Luke 19. 41; 22. 41, 44, 45.	26. 15	Matt. 27. 4–25.	3. 8	Matt. 27. 46.
18. 23	John 11. 53.	26. 15, 16	John 10. 21. Luke 23. 13-15.	3. 14	Ps. 69. 12.
18. 23*	Luke 23. 34, 61.	29. 26	John 7. 20; 10. 20, 39.	3. 48	Luke 19. 41.

86 "THE FOURTH YEAR OF JEHOIAKIM" (Jer. 25. 1-3)
(Being supplemental to Appendix 50, p. 42).

"THE ONLY ANCIENT AUTHORITY OF VALUE ON BABYLONIAN HISTORY IS THE OLD TESTAMENT"
(*Encycl. Brit.*, 11th (Cambridge) edition, vol. iii, p. 101).

1. The great prophecy of the seventy years of Babylonian servitude in Jeremiah 25 is prefaced, in *vv.* 1-3, by one of the most important date-marks in the Scriptures:—

> "The word that came to Jeremiah concerning all the people of Judah IN THE FOURTH YEAR OF JEHOIAKIM the son of Josiah king of Judah, that was THE FIRST YEAR OF NEBUCHADREZZAR king of Babylon; the which Jeremiah the prophet spake unto all the people of Judah, and to all the inhabitants of Jerusalem, saying, From the thirteenth year of Josiah the son of Amon king of Judah, even unto this day, that is the three and twentieth year, the word of the LORD hath come unto me."

On what is called "received" dating, the fourth year of Jehoiakim (being the first year of Nebuchadnezzar) is usually given as 606 B.C.; whereas in *The Companion Bible*, both in the margin, and in Ap. 50. V, p. 60, and VII, p. 67, it is shown as 496 B.C.—a difference of 110 years. This is a serious matter, but the reason is simple, and is as follows:—

In the majority of the systems of dating extant, chronologers have ignored, and omitted from their sequence of *Anno Mundi* years, the ninety-three years included in St. PAUL's reckoning in Acts 13. 19-22; and also, in the majority of cases, the *interregnum* and "gaps" in the later kings of Judah, amounting together to 110-113 years[1]; and, further, by accepting the 480th year of 1 Kings 6. 1 as being a cardinal, instead of an ordinal number; and as being an *Anno Mundi* date, instead of one to be understood according to *Anno Dei* reckoning (see Ap. 50, Introduction, § 6).

The Holy Spirit, we may believe, expressly made use of St. Paul, in the statement in the passage referred to, in order to preserve us from falling into this error. CLINTON (1781-1852) well says on the point[1]: "The computation of St. Paul, delivered in a solemn argument before a Jewish audience, and confirmed by the whole tenor of the history in the Book of Judges, outweighs the authority of that date" (480). In spite, however, of this Divine warning, many accept the 480th year as being a cardinal number, and reckon it as an *Anno Mundi* date.

2. On the commonly "received" dating, the period from the Exodus to the commencement of the Babylonian servitude is usually given as 1491 B.C. to 606 B.C.; that is, a period of 885 years; whereas *The Companion Bible* dates are 1491 B.C. to 496 B.C. = 995 years.

But, if ST. PAUL is correct in adding ninety-three years to the period between the Exodus and the Temple (making thus 573 instead of 479); and if the interregnum between Amaziah and Uzziah, and the "gaps" clearly indicated in the sacred record and shown on the Charts in Ap. 50 are recognized, then it is perfectly clear that the majority of the chronologers are 110 to 113 years out of the true *Anno Mundi* reckoning, and, instead of the Babylonian servitude commencing in the year 606 B.C. (the fourth of Jehoiakim and first of Nebuchadnezzar), the real *Anno Mundi* year for that most important event is 496 B.C., as shown in Ap. 50.

3. This, no doubt, will be startling to some who may be inclined to suppose that certain dates and periods of time in the Scriptures have been irrevocably "fixed".

On the authority of certain well-known names, we are asked to believe that "profane history", and the annals of ancient nations, supply us with *infallible* proofs and checks, whereby we can test and correct the chronological statements of Holy Scripture.

But we need to be reminded that this is very far from being true.

Chronologists of all ages are, as a rule, very much

[1] The uncertainty of the three years here is "necessitated", as Professor SAYCE says in another connection, by the absolute impossibility of avoiding overlapping owing to the use of both cardinal and ordinal numbers throughout in the successions of the kings.

[1] *Fasti Hellenici*, Scripture Chronology, I, p. 313.

like sheep—they follow a leader: and, once the idea became current that the "correct" (supposed) dates of certain epochs and periods in Greek (and other) history could be brought to bear upon and override certain Biblical chronological statements, which presented "difficulties" to these modern chronologers, then it soon became almost a matter of course to *make* the figures of Divine revelation submit and conform to "profane" figures, derived from parchment or clay, instead of vice versa.[1]

4. FYNES CLINTON, in his learned work *Fasti Hellenici* (Vol. I, pp. 283-285) has such an appropriate and weighty statement that bears on this subject, in the Introduction to his *Scripture Chronology*, that it is well to quote the testimony of one who is regarded as among the ablest of chronologers. He remarks:—

"The history contained in the Hebrew Scriptures presents a remarkable and pleasing contrast to the early accounts of the Greeks. In the latter, we trace with difficulty a few obscure facts preserved to us by the poets, who transmitted, with all the embellishments of poetry and fable, what they had received from oral tradition. In the annals of the Hebrew nation we have authentic narratives, written by contemporaries, and these writing under the guidance of inspiration. What they have delivered to us comes, accordingly, under a double sanction. They were aided by Divine inspiration in recording facts upon which, as mere human witnesses, their evidence would be valid. But, as the narrative comes with an authority which no other writing can possess, so, in the matters related, it has a character of its own. The history of the Israelites is the history of miraculous interpositions. Their passage out of Egypt was miraculous. Their entrance into the promised land was miraculous. Their prosperous and their adverse fortunes in that land, their servitudes and their deliverances, their conquests and their captivities, were all miraculous. Their entire history, from the call of *Abraham* to the building of the sacred Temple, was a series of miracles. It is so much the object of the sacred historians to describe these, that little else is recorded. The ordinary events and transactions, what constitutes the civil history of other States, are either very briefly told, or omitted altogether; the incidental mention of these facts being always subordinate to the main design of registering the extraordinary manifestations of Divine power. For these reasons, the history of the Hebrews cannot be treated like the history of any other nation; and he who would attempt to write their history, divesting it of its miraculous character, would find himself without materials. Conformably with this spirit, there are no historians in the sacred volume of the period in which miraculous intervention was withdrawn. After the declaration by the mouth of *Malachi* that *a messenger should be sent to prepare the way*, the next event recorded by any inspired writer is the birth of that messenger. But of the interval of 400[2] years between the promise and the completion no account is given."

And then CLINTON significantly remarks:—

"And this period of more than 400[2] years between *Malachi* and the Baptist is properly the only portion in the whole long series of ages, from the birth of Abraham to the Christian era, which is capable of being treated like the history of any other nation.

"From this spirit of the Scripture history, the writers not designing to give a full account of all transactions, but only to dwell on that portion in which the Divine character was marked, many things which we might desire to know are omitted; and on many occasions a mere outline of the history is preserved. It is mortifying to our curiosity that a precise date of many remarkable facts cannot be obtained.

"The destruction of the Temple is determined by concurrent sacred and profane testimony to July, 587 B.C. From this point *we ascend to the birth of Abraham*. But between these two epochs, the birth of *Abraham* and the destruction of the temple, two breaks occur in the series of Scripture dates; which *make it impossible to fix the actual year* of the birth of *Abraham*; and this date being unknown, and assigned only upon conjecture, *all the preceding epochs are necessarily unknown also*."

This important statement deserves the most serious consideration; for CLINTON himself frequently transgresses its spirit in his *Scripture Chronology*: e.g. he "determines" the "captivity of Zedekiah to June, 587 B.C." And this he accomplishes by "bringing", as he says, Scripture and profane accounts to "a still nearer coincidence by comparing the history of ZEDEKIAH and JEHOIACHIN with *the dates assigned to the Babylonian kings by the Astronomical Canon*" (*Fasti Hellenici*, I, p. 319). In other words, this means that he "squares" the scriptural records of events, some 200 *years before the commencement of the period* which he has before stated is alone "capable of being treated like the history of any other nation", by means of the Astronomical Canon of Ptolemy.

PTOLEMY'S Canon (cent. 2 A.D.) is to CLINTON and his disciples what the monuments are to PROFESSOR SAYCE and his followers. Both "necessitate" the accommodation of Biblical chronology to suit their respective "Foundations of Belief" in dating.

5. But it is on the principle so excellently enunciated

---

[1] e.g. in *The Variorum Aids to Bible Students* we are told by Professor SAYCE, in a special head-note to his article *The Bible and the Monuments*, that the dates he gives throughout are *necessitated* by the Assyrian Canon (p. 78).

[2] CLINTON, apparently in these two passages, speaks of the 400 years as being a *round* number; meaning that it was *about* 400 years from MALACHI to the birth of JOHN THE BAPTIST, and therefore the Incarnation.

A reference to Ap. 50. VII, p. 67, VII (6), p. 69, and Ap. 58, p. 84, will show that the 400 years he speaks of are not a *round* number, but the actual number of years that elapsed between the prediction of MALACHI—"the seal of the prophets"—and the coming of "My messenger" (John the Baptist) followed by "the Messenger of the Covenant", 3. 1 (Jesus Christ). From its internal evidence it is perfectly clear that the prophecy of Malachi—"the burden of Jehovah"—must be dated several years after the Restoration, and the Dedication of the Temple of Zerubbabel.

From the first Passover in Nisan 404 B.C.—following immediately after the Dedication—to the birth of John the Baptist in the spring of the year 4 B.C. was *four hundred* years (10×40), the Incarnation being six months later in the same year.

But the ministries of both the Baptist and Christ began *thirty years* later; i.e. in 26 A.D.

Four hundred years back from this date gives us 374 B.C., and 374 B.C. is of course *thirty* years after the recommencement of the Mosaic ritual dating from the Passover in Nisan 404 B.C.

It is therefore a fair inference that the "seal of the prophets" should have been affixed thirty years after the Restoration of the Temple services, and exactly *four hundred* years before the fulfilment (Matt. 3. 1-3. Mk. 1. 2, 3. Lk. 3. 2-6. John 1. 6-23) of Malachi's prediction in 3. 1.

The language used by Malachi describes a condition of things that could not well have been reached under *twenty* or *thirty* years.

On the other hand the period could not have been longer. See Ap. 77, p. 113, and the notes on Malachi.

Another illustration of the *principle* of *Anno DEI* reckoning should be noted here.

The fourth year of JEHOIAKIM and first of NEBUCHADNEZZAR is dated 496 B.C.: that is, 492 years from the Nativity.

The Babylonian servitude, seventy years, and the succeeding twenty-two years, from the decree of Cyrus (426 B.C.) to the First Passover after the Dedication of the Temple (404 B.C.), are together ninety-two years. If this, the *Great Lo-Ammi* period (corresponding to the ninety-three *Lo-Ammi* years in *Judges*), is deducted we get again 400 years (496 - 92 - 4 = 400). Thus we have the scriptural *Great* number of probation (10×40=400) significantly connected with this fourth year of JEHOIAKIM. Cp. also Gen. 21. 10. Acts 7. 6; and see Ap. 50, pp. 51-53. There are other examples in the Scriptures.

by CLINTON, and quoted above, that the dating of *The Companion Bible* is set forth: viz., that "the history of the Hebrews cannot be treated like the history of any other nation". If this is granted, the same argument *must* necessarily apply to the *chronology* of such a people. And it may be carried a step farther. The chronology of the history of the Chosen People is unlike that of any other nation, in that it has a system of reckoning by *durations*, and not, like other nations, by *dates*; and a system of registering events and periods of time by what it may be permitted to call "double entry". This is to say, not only do we find in the Bible a regular *sequence* of years, commencing with Adam and ending with Christ, and consequently a true and perfect record of *Anno Mundi* years in the *lifetime of mankind* during that period; but also, concurrently with this, we find another system of dealing with dates and periods concerning the Hebrew race alone. This system is used and referred to in *The Companion Bible* as being according to *Anno Dei* reckoning. (See Introduction to Ap. 50, pp. 40-42.)

And it may be strongly urged that failure on the part of the majority of chronologers, and partial failure on the part of others to recognize this, so to speak, *double entry* system of Bible dating has "necessitated", as we are told, the *adjustment* of the Biblical figures to suit the *requirements* of Astronomical Canons and ancient monuments.

6. But, to the candid mind it is incredible that the inspired Scriptures should be found so faulty in their chronological records and statements as many would have us suppose; or that it is "necessitated" that they should be "determined" from profane sources and uninspired canons, whether on parchment or stone![1]

CLINTON's Calendar of Greek dates, it must be borne in mind, only commences with the *traditional* date of the first Olympiad[2] (776 B.C.). From that year on and backwards, everything in his Scripture Chronology is assumed to be capable of being arranged, and made to harmonize with that date.

But, it must also be remembered that grave suspicions have been entertained as to the correctness of this view.

SIR ISAAC NEWTON (1642-1727), for instance, in his *Chronology of Ancient Kingdoms Amended*, charges the Greek chroniclers with having made the antiquities of Greece 300 or 400 years older than the truth. The whole passage reads thus (*Works*, vol. v, p. 4 of the Introduction):—

"A little while after the death of ALEXANDER THE GREAT, they began to set down the generations, reigns, and successions, in numbers of years; and, by putting reigns and successions equipollent (equivalent) to generations; and three generations to an hundred or an hundred and twenty years, as appears by their chronology, they have made the antiquities of Greece 300 or 400 years older than the truth. And this was the original of the technical chronology of the Greeks. ERATOSTHENES wrote about an hundred years after the death of ALEXANDER THE GREAT; he was followed by APOLLODORUS; and these two have been followed ever since by chronologers."

NEWTON then goes on to quote the attack on HERODOTUS by PLUTARCH (born about 46 A.D.), for chronological nebulosity[1], in support of his contention as to the uncertainty and doubtfulness of the chronology of the Greeks. He further adds:—

"As for the chronology of the Latins, that is still more uncertain. . . . The old records of the Latins were burnt by the Gauls, sixty-four years before the death of ALEXANDER THE GREAT: and QUINTIUS FABIUS PICTOR (cent. 3 B.C.), the oldest historian of the Latins, lived an hundred years later than that king."

7. If NEWTON was right, then it follows that the Canon of PTOLEMY, upon which the faith of modern chronologers is so implicitly—almost pathetically—pinned, must have been built upon unreliable foundations. Grecian chronology is the basis of "PTOLEMY's Canon"; and, if his foundations are "suspect", and this is certainly the case, then the elaborate superstructure reared upon them must necessarily be regarded with suspicion likewise.

EUSEBIUS, the Church historian and bishop of Cæsarea (A.D. 264-349), is mainly responsible for the modern system of dating which results in squaring scriptural chronology with the Greek Olympiad years, and it is upon EUSEBIUS's reckonings and quotations that CLINTON also mainly relies.

In his *Chronicle of Universal History*, the first book, entitled *Chronography*, contains sketches of the various nations and states of the old world from the Creation to his own day.

The second book of this work consists of synchronical tables with the names of the contemporary rulers of the various nations, and the principal events in the history of each from ABRAHAM to his own time. EUSEBIUS gets his information from various sources. He makes use of JOSEPHUS (A.D. 37-95), AFRICANUS (cent. 3 A.D.), BEROSUS (cent. 3 B.C.), POLYHISTOR (cent. 1 B.C.), ABYDENUS (about 200 B.C.), CEPHALION (cent. 1 A.D.), MANETHO (cent. 3 B.C.), and other lost writers—equally "profane".

In his turn, he is largely used by moderns to "determine" scriptural dates; and it is mainly through his instrumentality that many of the so-called "received" datings of the O. T., from Abraham to the Christian era, have been "fixed".

In addition to these and other ancient records, and "systems" of chronology, we have notably the *Canon of Ptolemy* referred to above. PTOLEMY, an astronomer of the second century A.D., gives a list of Babylonian, Persian, Greek, Egyptian, and Roman rulers, "from about 750 B.C. to his own time."

The *Seder Olam* is a Jewish chronological work of about the same date (cent. 2 A.D.).

Now, to-day, we have what is called "the Witness of the Monuments", of which it may be remarked that frequently their testimony is accepted in preference to the scriptural record, and is often used to impugn the statements and chronology of the Bible. The result of recent modern explorations in Assyria, Babylonia, and Egypt, has been that we have almost every date in the O. T. redated, because we are told by some (as PROFESSOR SAYCE, quoted above) that this is "*necessitated*" by the Assyrian Canon.

The Assyrian Eponym Canon is a list, compiled from several imperfect copies[2] on clay tablets of lists of public officials (called "Eponyms") who held office, one for each year. This list contains some 270 names, and is *supposed* to cover the period from soon after the close of Solomon's reign to the reign of Josiah. It is spoken of as showing "some slight discrepancies,[3] but on the whole is held to be highly valuable". This is the *Assyrian Canon* which, according to PROFESSOR SAYCE, "necessitates" the redating of the Biblical events and periods!

[1] See note on 2 Kings 15. 27.

[2] His authority for this date is given in the following sentences:—

"The first Olympiad is placed by CENSORINUS (c. 21) in the 1014th year before the consulship of ULPIUS and PONTIANUS in A.D. 238=776 B.C.... If the 207th games were celebrated in July, A.D. 49, 206 Olympiads, or 824 years had elapsed, and the first games were celebrated in July, 776 B.C." That is to say, a date is taken, supposed to be A.D. 49 (*Fasti Hellenici*, Vol. I, Tables, p. 150), on testimony quoted from another ancient writer (SOLINUS, cent. 3, A.D.), that in that year the 207th Olympic games were held; and, as 206 Olympiads = 824 years, therefore the first games were celebrated in 776 B.C. This year 776 B.C. therefore has become the pivot upon which *all* chronology has been made to depend, and Scripture events to "fit" in!

[1] HERODOTUS was in the same boat with CENSORINUS and PTOLEMY. See p. 123.

[2] No complete list is yet known.

[3] See note on 2 Kings 15. 27.

The Babylonian and Egyptian Monumental Records also contribute their quota towards the "fixing" of scriptural chronology; but these are, it is acknowledged, more or less incomplete, and therefore, more or less untrustworthy.

So far as supplying interesting sidelight details of the *periods with which they deal*, and that impinge upon sacred history, these sources are all more or less useful. But, so far as affording absolutely trustworthy material from which a *complete chronological compendium* can be formed from the Creation to Christ, is concerned, they are all more or less useless, for the simplest of all reasons, viz. that they have no *datum line* or start-point in common. They possess, so to speak, no "common denominator".

8. It must be remembered that the ancients, excepting of course the "Church" historians, *had not the Hebrew Scriptures of Truth to guide them.* They knew not at what period in the duration of the world they were living! The only knowledge they had of the *origin* of the world, and man's beginning, was derived from myth and fable. Had they possessed such knowledge as we possess in the Word of God, they would undoubtedly have used it; and, instead of finding, as we do, their chronological systems, commencing (and ending) with *floating periods*, concerning which they had more or less reliable information, they would have extended their chronological hawsers backward, and anchored their systems firmly at "the beginning".

CENSORINUS (quoted in the note on p. 122) may be taken to voice the whole body of ancient chronologers when, in writing on chronological subjects, he says:—

"If the origin of the world had been known unto man, I would thence have taken my beginning ... Whether time had a beginning, or whether it always was, the certain number of years cannot be comprehended."

And PTOLEMY, the author of the famous "Canon", says:—

"To find observation upon the passages of the whole world, or such an immense crowd of times *I think much out of their way that desire to learn and know the truth.*"

He means, it was a hopeless matter to fix upon the *original start-point* for chronology!

9. An illustration may be permitted from the fundamental principles governing the engineering world.. Suppose a line of railway to be projected, say, for the sake of argument, 4,000 miles more or less in length [1]. The line is to run through countries of varied physical character, from flat plains to lofty hill districts. Preparatory to constructing the line, it is essential that an accurate survey of *the whole length* of territory through which it has to pass be made.

For this purpose two things are absolutely necessary to the engineer: viz. a "*bench-mark*" (or marks) and a "*datum line*".

The "bench-mark" is a mark cut in stone or some durable material in a *fixed position*, and forms the *terminus a quo*, *from which every measurement of distance on the whole length of line is measured off.*

The *datum line* is a supposed *perfectly horizontal* line extending beneath the whole distance between the proposed *termini*; and from which all the levels are to be calculated. The *first bench-mark* is the starting-point in a line of levels for the determination of altitudes over the whole distance; or one of a number of similar marks, made at suitable carefully measured distances, as the survey proceeds, in order that the exact distances between each, and ultimately between the *terminus a quo* and the *terminus ad quem* may be ascertained *before the work is carried out.*

10. To apply this to our subject:—

All are agreed that the FOURTH YEAR OF JEHOIAKIM, and the FIRST YEAR OF NEBUCHADREZZAR form a point of contact between sacred and profane history of the utmost importance.

From this point of contact it is claimed that a "complete scheme of dates may be derived", as some put it; or, according to others, "from this date we reckon on to Christ and back to Adam."

The year of the point of contact is generally said to be 606 B.C. or 604 B.C.

It is perfectly justifiable to occupy this position; but, only if the *dating* of the point of contact can be demonstrated and maintained.

It is quite easy to *say* that this year of contact between sacred and profane history is 606 B.C. or 604 B.C., and from this we can reckon "back to Adam and on to Christ".

But a question of paramount importance at once suggests itself, viz. What is the *datum*, or *foundation*, or *bench-mark* date from which the year, say 606 B.C., is obtained?

The answer usually received is "we determine it from (the date of) the captivity of Zedekiah" (CLINTON). Or, "the agreement of leading chronologers is a sufficient guarantee that David began to reign in 1056–1055 B.C., and, therefore, that all dates subsequent to that event can be definitely fixed." Or else we are told that the Assyrian Canon (and the "Monuments" generally) "necessitate" the date of this year of contact as being 604 B.C. (PROFESSOR SAYCE).

11. But all this is only begging the question. The argument—if mere *ipse dixit* assertions based on *floating dates* and periods, as acknowledged by CENSORINUS and PTOLEMY, can be truly called an argument—when examined, is found to be quite unreliable; and, in the engineering world would be described as "fudging the levels!"

This exactly describes the present case, because this *date*-level (i.e. 606 or 604 B.C.), so to speak, makes its appearance in the *middle* of the supposed line (or, to be more accurate, towards the *end* of it) *without being referred back to datum*, that one definite "fixed" departure point or *bench-mark* at the *terminus a quo* from which the years can alone be accurately reckoned.

12. It is as though the engineer took a map showing the district through which it was intended to construct the last 600 or 700 miles of his line, and the proposed terminus, but without any *absolute certainty* as to where the actual position of that terminus should be; and should then say to himself, "from information received", and from the general appearance and apparent scale of this map, I "determine" the highest point of my line to be 606 miles from where I "conjecture" my *terminus ad quem* ought to be! From this point therefore, 606 miles from our *supposed* terminus, we will measure back 450 miles, and "fix" an important station (David); and then, another 569 miles back from *David*, we "determine" another important station (Exodus), and so on.

13. This system of "*measuring on the flat*", to use a technical engineering term, for fixing stations and important positions for his railway, would be charmingly simple for the engineer—*on paper*. But "The Standing Orders" of the joint Committee of both Houses of Parliament would shut out those said plans from receiving one moment's consideration.

It would be impossible to find an engineer who would be guilty of such folly. He would accurately measure his distances from a fixed point at the *terminus a quo*, referring *everything* back to that, and using his datum line to check his levels, otherwise he might easily find himself 100 miles or more out.

14. To apply this:—

In the chronology of the Bible we have given to us one primal fixed point (or bench-mark) and *one only*, from which every distance-point on the line of time, so to speak, *must* be measured, and to which everything must be *referred back* as *datum*!

That datum-point, or bench-mark, is *the creation of Adam*, and is represented by the datum-mark 0 (nought) or *zero*. And as the unit of measurement, in the

[1] And for comparison with the 4,000 years in question.

illustration suggested above, is one mile[1], so the unit of measurement in the chronology of the Bible is *one year* (whether sidereal or lunar matters not for the sake of the argument).

15. Working therefore from our *datum-point* or first *bench-mark* 0 (*zero*), which represents the creation of Adam, we measure off 130 years on our line and reach the first station, so to speak, SETH. This gives us a second bench-mark from which to measure on to ENOS. Thus, by measuring onward, but always checking by referring back to *datum*, which is the primal station, we are able to mark off and locate exactly the various stations and junctions (junctures) all down the line, from the *terminus a quo* until we reach a point which some of the *later stations themselves* will indicate as being the exact position for the *terminus ad quem*. This may be either the Incarnation or the Crucifixion and Resurrection of our Lord.

If Holy Scripture had definitely stated the exact period in years between the creation of "the First Man Adam", and "the Last Adam", or had given us the exact date of the Incarnation or Resurrection of Christ, we should then have been justified in *reckoning back* from this fixed date as from the known and authoritative *terminus ad quem*.

But this is not the case, although we believe the period is clearly inferred and indicated, as the Charts in Ap. 50 show, which thus agree with USSHER'S *conclusions*, although not reaching them by USSHER'S *methods*, or figures.[1]

We have therefore no alternative. We *must* make our measurements, i.e. reckon our years, from the only *terminus* we possess, viz. the start-point or *bench-mark* laid down for us in "the Scriptures of truth", that is, the creation of Adam.

16. This is the principle adopted in the chronology of *The Companion Bible*: and, on this principle alone all the important "stations" on the chronological line have been laid down, or "determined" (to borrow CLINTON'S word), not by Astronomical or Assyrian Canons, but on the authority of the Biblical Canon alone.

Acting on this principle we recognise the fact that ST. PAUL'S period, from the Exodus to the Temple, is the real period of 573 *Anno Mundi* years; while the 479 (480th) years of 1 Kings 6. 1 are to be taken as according to *Anno DEI* reckoning. Thus, by accepting this, and admitting, instead of omitting, the "gaps" so clearly indicated in the line of the later kings of Judah, it will appear that the important chronological contact-point between sacred and secular history, which Scripture calls "THE FOURTH YEAR OF JEHOIAKIM and THE FIRST YEAR OF NEBUCHADNEZZAR", is to be dated 496 B.C., instead of the usually "received" date of 606 B.C., or thereabout.

[1] Of course, the real unit is one inch; but, for convenience, the mile is considered as the unit in such a case.

[1] See his *Annales Veteris et Novi Testamenti* (1650-1654).

87 "PHARAOH'S HOUSE IN TAHPANHES" (Jer. 43. 9).

In the year 1886 W. M. Flinders Petrie was exploring at *Tell Defenneh*, in Egypt; he was told that the name of one of the mounds was *Kasr Bint el Jehudi*, which means "the palace of the Jew's daughter". This name recalled to his mind the passage in Jeremiah 43. 6, 7, and at once connected *Defenneh* with "Tahpanhes", where in *vv.* 8-11 Jeremiah received this order:

"Take great stones in thine hand, and hide them in the clay in the brickkiln, which is at the entry of Pharaoh's house in Tahpanhes, in the sight of the men of Judah; and say unto them, Thus saith the LORD of hosts, the God of Israel; Behold, I will send and take Nebuchadrezzar the king of Babylon, My servant, and will set his throne upon these stones that I have hid; and he shall spread his royal pavilion over them", &c. Jer. 43. 8-10.

In the notes on 2 Sam. 12. 31, Jer. 43. 9, and Nah. 3. 14, we have shown that the Heb. *malben* cannot mean a "brickkiln" as rendered in the A.V. and in R.V. (2 Sam. 12. 31, and Nah. 3. 14 (marg. *brickmould*)), but *brickwork* of any kind. In 2 Sam. 12. 31, and Jer. 43. 9, a pavement of brickwork; and in Nah. 3. 14, fortresses built of brick.

That this is so is fully proved by Jer. 43. 9, as the prophecy could not be fulfilled by Nebuchadrezzar's spreading his pavilion over the stones hidden in a "brickkiln", to say nothing of a brickkiln being situated "at the entry of Pharaoh's house". Neither would a brickkiln require to be fortified.

But it was left to Professor Flinders Petrie to discover the solution of the difficulty on clearing around the fort:

"The entrance was in the side of a block of buildings projecting from the fort; and in front of it, on the opposite side of the roadway, similarly projecting from the fort, was a large platform of brickwork suitable for out-door business, . . . just what is now called a *mastaba*. . . . Jer. 43. 9 is the exact description of the *mastaba* which I found." See the illustration below, which we give by permission.

Restoration of the Fort among the ruins of *Defenneh* (now *Daphnae*), in Egypt, showing the large platform before the entry of Pharaoh's palace at *Tahpanhes*.

88 THE MILLENNIAL "SANCTUARY" AND "OBLATION" OF EZEKIEL 40-48.

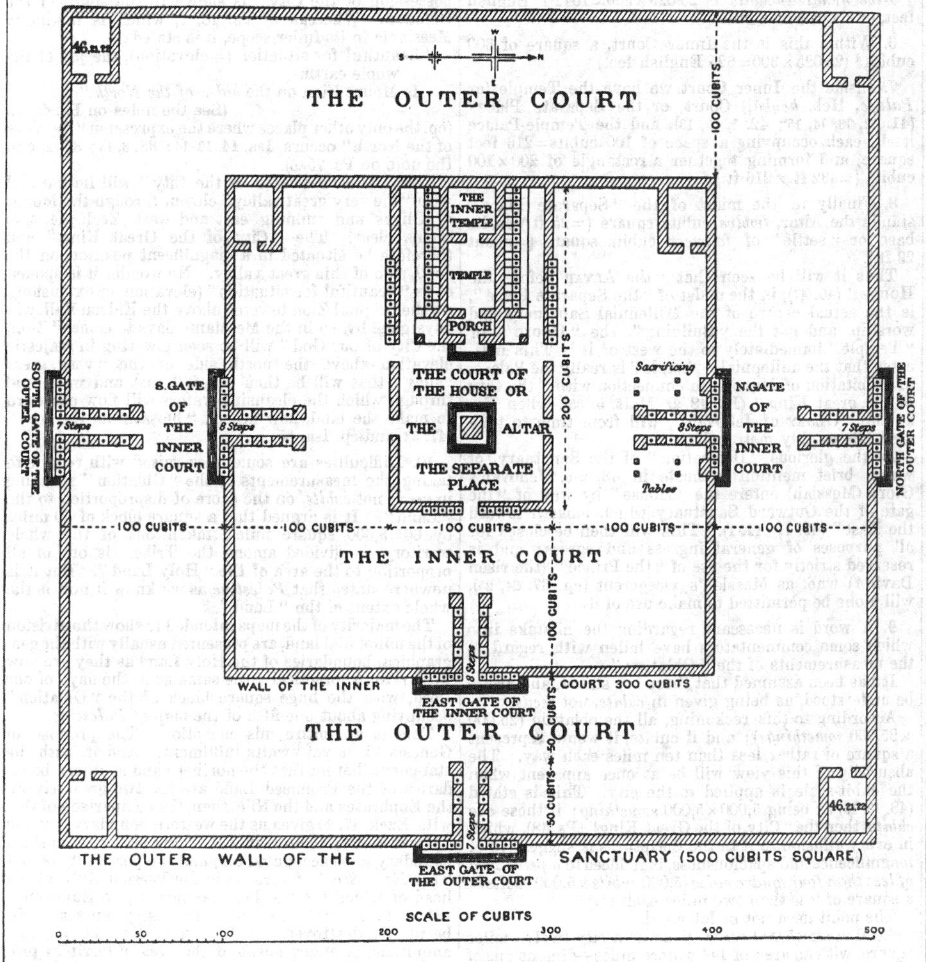

NOTES ON THE "SANCTUARY" OF EZEKIEL.

1. It is a mistake to speak of the wonderful series of courts and buildings, described in the closing chapters of Ezekiel, *collectively* as the Temple. The proper term is "The Sanctuary", as it is set forth in 45. 1-4 (see plan above).

2. The governing figure of the dimensions given throughout the last eight chapters—not only in connection with the Sanctuary, but also in the measurements of the holy "Oblation unto Jehovah", of the Land—is the number "5" (Ap. 10).

3. The Sanctuary is in the midst of the central portion of the middle (the Priests') portion of the "Oblation" (see block plan, p. 127). The *Altar* which occupies the *exact centre* of the Sanctuary (*not the Temple* proper, see below), is thus twelve miles from the north gate of the city, twelve miles from the southern boundary of the Levites' portion, and thirty miles from the eastern and western boundaries of the "Oblation" respectively.

4. The Sanctuary is comprised in a great square (42. 15-20) enclosed with a wall measuring 500 *reeds* each way.

If the "measuring reed" = 12 ft. 6 in., then 500 reeds will be equivalent to about *nine* English furlongs, or a little more than one mile square.[1]

5. In the centre of this great square we have next

[1] The "measuring reed" is given as being "of six cubits (long) by the cubit and an handbreadth" (40. 5; 43. 13); and in 41. 8 we have the specified *standard* length of the reed as "a full reed of *six great* cubits". This "great cubit" is therefore *one* cubit + *one* handbreadth. *Six* handbreadths are reckoned to the ordinary cubit. In this case there is one extra. So that the "great cubit" employed in the measurements of the Sanctuary and the Land is equal to *seven* handbreadths (Ap. 10). It follows therefore that "*six* great cubits" = 42 (6×7) handbreadths. If the handbreadth is taken as being 3·575 in., or a little more than $3\frac{1}{2}$ in., which is most probably about the exact figure, then the "great cubit" is 3·575×7 = 25·025 in.; and "the full reed" will therefore be 25·025 × 6 = 150·150 in. This = 12·5125 English feet, or in round numbers 12 feet 6 inches.

the boundary wall enclosing the OUTER COURT. This wall is 12 ft. 6 in. high by 12 ft. 6 in. broad, and forms a square of 500 cubits[1] (external measurements).

Five hundred cubits is 25·025 × 500 = 1042·7 English feet, or about ⅕ of a mile.

6. Within this is the Inner Court, a square of 300 cubits[1] (25·025 × 300 = 625 English feet).

7. Inside the Inner Court we have the Temple (or *Palace*, Heb. *heykāl*) Court, or the Separate Place[2] (41. 12, 13, 14, 15; 42. 1, 10, 13), and the Temple-Palace itself, each occupying a space of 100 cubits = 216 feet square, and forming together a rectangle of 200 × 100 cubits (= 432 ft. × 216 ft.).

8. Finally in the midst of the "Separate Place" stands the Altar, *twelve* cubits square (= 25 ft.) on its base or "settle" of *fourteen* cubits square (= about 29 ft.).

Thus it will be seen that "the ALTAR before the HOUSE" (40. 47), in the midst of "the Separate Place", is the actual centre of the Millennial Sanctuary and worship, and *not* the "Building", the "House", or "Temple" immediately to the west of it.[3] This indicates that the millennial "*Temple*" is really the Palace, or Habitation of Messiah in connection with "the City of the great King" (Ps. 48. 2. Matt. 5. 35), when He, as the "GLORY of Jehovah", will from time to time visit His earthly metropolis.

At the glorious "Dedication" of the Sanctuary, of which brief mention is made in 43. 2-6, Jehovah's Glory (Messiah) enters the "House" by way of "the gate of the Outward Sanctuary which looketh toward the East" (43. 4; 44. 1). This will then be closed for all purposes of general ingress and egress; and is reserved strictly for the use of "the Prince" (the risen David?) who, as Messiah's vicegerent (cp. 37. 24, 25), will alone be permitted to make use of it.

9. A word is necessary regarding the mistake into which some commentators have fallen with regard to the measurements of the "Oblation".

It has been assumed that these are stated, and are to be understood, as being given in *cubits*, not *reeds*.

According to this reckoning, all the oblation (25,000 × 25,000 *somethings*); and if cubits, it would represent a square of rather less than ten miles each way. The absurdity of this view will be at once apparent when the cubit-scale is applied to the city. This is stated (48. 15, 16) as being 5,000 × 5,000 *something*; if these are *cubits*, then the "City of the Great King" (Ps. 48), which in every allusion to it in the Scriptures is suggestive of magnificence and spaciousness, is reduced to *a petty area of less than four square miles* (5,000 *cubits* × 5,000 *cubits* = a square of less than two miles each way).

The point need not be laboured.

5,000 *reeds* × 5,000 *reeds* gives us a city twelve miles square, with an area of 144 square miles—dimensions of dignity and importance befitting the metropolis of the world.

In measuring or "setting out" buildings and distances, *rods* and *tapes* or *chains* are used now of recognised standardised lengths.

This is precisely what we have in 40. 3; where the angelic measurer or surveyor is presented to us "with a line of flax" (= tape) in his hand, and "a measuring reed" (= a rod). Cf. 47. 3.

In the block plan (p. 127) it will be seen that "the possession of the City" is shown to the south of the Oblation. Whereas in Ps. 48. 2, which is distinctly Messianic in its fuller scope, it is stated:

'Beautiful for situation (= elevation), the joy of the whole earth,
Is Mount Zion on the *sides of the North*."
(See the notes on Ps. 48. 2.)

(cp. the only other places where the expression "the sides of the North" occurs, Isa. 14. 12-14; 38. 6, 15; 39. 2, and the note on Ps. 75. 6).

That "the Possession of the City" will lie parallel with "the very great valley" cloven through the Mount of Olives and running east and west (Zech. 14. 4, 5) seems clear. The "City of the Great King" will therefore be situated in a magnificent position on the *north* side of this great valley. No wonder it is spoken of as "beautiful for situation" (elevation, or extension). As the original Zion towered above the Kidron Valley in days gone by, so in the Messianic days to come, "Zion, the City of our God" will be seen towering in majestic elevation above the north side of the "very great valley" that will be then "cleft" east and west, and through which the cleansing waters will flow eastward to make the land, now desert, "blossom as the rose" (47. 8: and cp. Isa. 35).

10. Difficulties are sometimes raised with regard to taking the measurements of the "Oblation" as being in *reeds* not *cubits*, on the score of disproportion to the "Land". It is argued that a square block of 60 miles by 60 = 3,600 square miles, taken out of the whole territory as divided among the Tribes, is out of all proportion to the area of the "Holy Land". But it is nowhere stated that *Palestine* as we know it now is the whole extent of the "Land".

The majority of the maps intended to show the division of the millennial land, are presented usually with the geographical boundaries of the Holy Land as they are now known to us, practically the same as in the days of our Lord, with the huge square block of the "Oblation" occupying about one-fifth of the *map of Palestine*.

This is an entire misconception. The promise in Genesis 15. 18 yet awaits fulfilment. And if, with the statement therein that the northern and southern boundaries of the Promised Land are the two great rivers, the Euphrates and the Nile, then, the comparison of this with Ezek. 47. 20 gives us the western boundary, viz. the "Great Sea" (Mediterranean). This leaves the eastern boundary to be accounted for; and the possibility is that "*the East Sea*" of verse 18 is the Persian Gulf, at the head of which the northern boundary (the Euphrates) will end. As "the tongue of the Egyptian sea" will be utterly destroyed "in that day" (Isa. 11. 15), this amplitude, or enlargement of the area of territory promised to Abraham on the south gives strength for the suggestion of a corresponding extension to the east. If this is so, then the whole of the Promised Land will be a magnificent territory, bounded on the north by the Euphrates, on the east by the Indian Ocean (the east sea), on the south by the Nile, and on the west by the Mediterranean. This will include not only the Arabian peninsula, but the great Arabian and Syrian deserts, and the plains of Babylonia. A glorious patrimony truly, and worthy of occupation by the "strong nation" of Mic. 4. 7, the People through whom all the nations of the earth are yet to be blessed! See Gen. 12. 3; and especially 28. 14. It may be that the Twelve Tribes may be allotted special strips or "lots" of the land on either side of the Oblation as usually shown; but that an enormously increased territory N., E., and S., will become "in that Day" the realisation of the Promised Land is certain.

---

[1] The main dimensions given supply us with these figures, although they are not specifically stated as in the case of the 500 reeds of 42. 16-20.

[2] The Separate Place has in its centre the ALTAR and seems to be the court for worship of "separated ones".

[3] In the "Specification", it is a remarkable fact that the *Altar* is the item numbered 27. The whole number of "items" specified from 40. 1—48. 35 is 53. This gives 26 *items on either side of* 27—thus placing the Altar exactly in the midst of the angelic specification—as it is placed in the centre of the Sanctuary.

BLOCK PLAN, SHOWING "ALL THE OBLATION" (48. 20).

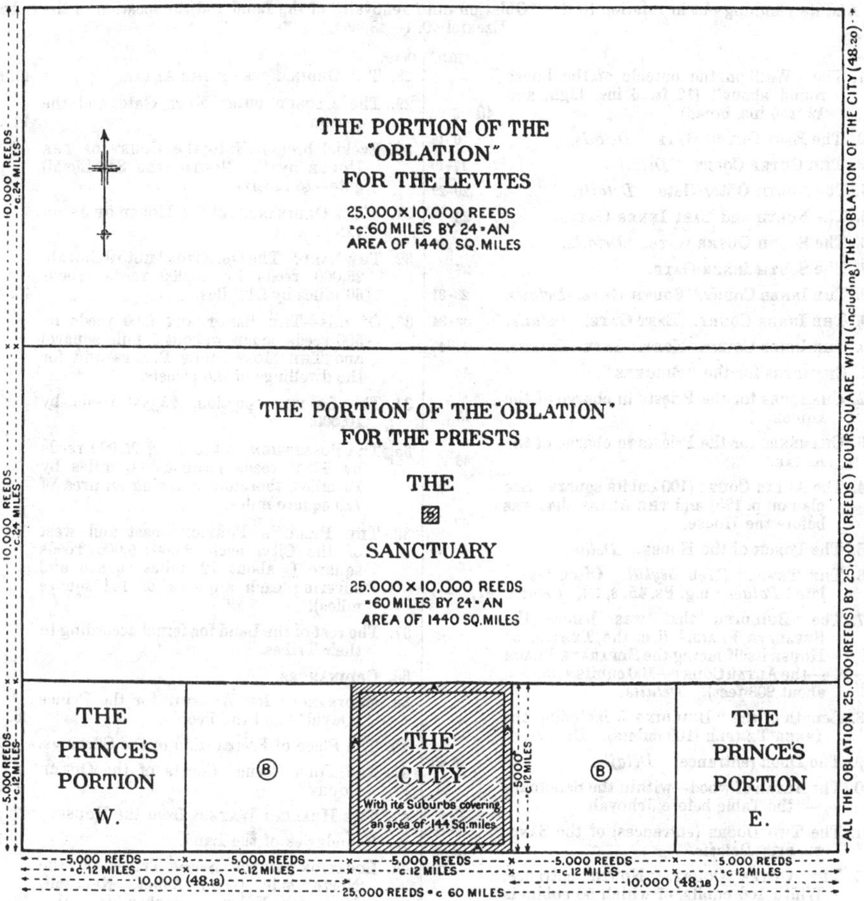

THE "POSSESSION OF THE CITY" LIES PARALLEL WITH THE "VERY GREAT VALLEY" of Zech. 14. 4, 5; which valley probably will form the Southern boundary of the City (see note on p. 126, par. 9).

The whole size of the "OBLATION" is 25,000×25,000 REEDS (48. 20), and equals about 60 ENGLISH MILES square. Divided into three main Portions:

(1) The Portion for the Priests, containing in the centre the Sanctuary, The Holy Portion of the Land, 25,000×10,000 Reeds (45. 1-4)=60 miles by 24.

(2) The Portion for the Levites, 25,000×10,000 (45. 5)=60 miles by 24.

(3) The "Possession of the City", 25,000×5,000 (45. 6)=60 miles by 12, including the Two "Portions" for the Prince, one on the W., the other on the E. of the City (see block plan above).

The CITY is set in the midst of the "Possession of the City", and its dimensions are given (48. 15) as 5,000×5,000 reeds=about 12 miles square; thus covering an area of 144 square miles (English). Of this, 250 reeds all round are marked off as "suburbs", thus reducing the actual size of the "City" itself to about 11 miles square, covering an area of 121 square miles (48. 15-17). Verse 18 gives the length of the "possession", to E. and W., as being 10,000 reeds each way. This manifestly includes the "Prince's Portions" at either end. Between these portions and the suburbs of the City lies on either side (B B) the remainder of "the residue in length over against (i.e. alongside) the oblation of the holy (portion)", which is evidently the "garden" portion of the City, as "the increase (Heb. *tebû'âh*, 48. 18) thereof shall be for food for them that serve the City".

The "City Portion" is therefore seen to be divided into 5 (Ap. 10) portions, each 5,000 reeds square, or into 5 blocks of 144 English square miles each. The total area covered being 144×5=720 square miles.

The "Priests' Portion" is one large block containing a superficial area exactly double, viz. 1,440 square miles.

The "Levites' Portion" is of equal size. The total area of "All the Oblation" is therefore, in English miles, 1,440+1,440+720=3,600 square miles.

The above figures will enable the student to grasp fully a fact that is often lost sight of: viz. that everything in connection with the whole of the Oblation to Jehovah, including the City, will be planned, as shown by these dimensions, on a "magnifical" scale. To give one instance of the scale on which the Oblation will be "laid out"—the nearest point from which the outside wall of the Sanctuary, in the midst of the Priests' portion, can be reached from the Northern Gate of the City is 11½ miles. There will be no overcrowding or jerry-building in "that day". It is not possible for us now to do more than faintly imagine to ourselves what the City will be like; 12 miles square, perfectly planned, with "garden" spaces on either hand occupying like areas, and these again bounded by the Prince's "private gardens", so to speak, and abode, of similar size.

APPENDIX 88: THE MILLENNIAL "SANCTUARY" AND "OBLATION" (*cont.*).

SPECIFICATION OF "THE SANCTUARY"

And its planning out in relation to the "Oblation unto Jehovah" of the Land and the location of the tribes.
Ezekiel 40. 1—48. 35.

Order.	Refs.
1. The "Wall on the outside of the house round about" (12 ft. 6 ins. high, and 12 ft. 6 ins. broad).	40 5
2. The EAST OUTER GATE. *Details.*	6–16
3. THE OUTER COURT. *Details.*	17–19
4. The NORTH Outer Gate. *Details.*	20–22
5. The NORTH and EAST INNER GATES.	23
6. The SOUTH OUTER GATE. *Details.*	24–26
7. The SOUTH INNER GATE.	27
8. THE INNER COURT. SOUTH GATE. *Details.*	28–31
9. THE INNER COURT. EAST GATE. *Details.*	32–34
10. THE INNER COURT. NORTH GATE. *Details.*	35–43
11. CHAMBERS for the "SINGERS".	44
12. CHAMBERS for the Priests in charge of the HOUSE.	45
13. CHAMBERS for the Priests in charge of the ALTAR.	46
14. The ALTAR COURT (100 cubits square. See plan on p. 125) and THE ALTAR that was before the House.	47
15. The PORCH of the HOUSE. *Details.*	48, 49
16. THE TEMPLE (Heb. *hēykāl*. Often translated *Palace*: e.g. Ps. 45. 8, 15). *Details.*	41. 1–11
17. The BUILDING that was before the SEPARATE PLACE [1] (i.e. the TEMPLE or HOUSE itself facing the SEPARATE PLACE —the ALTAR COURT—100 cubits square= about 208 feet). *Details.*	12–14
18. Length of the "BUILDING", including the INNER TEMPLE (100 cubits). *Details.*	15
19. The DOOR (entrance). *Details.*	16–21
20. The ALTAR of wood—within the Sanctuary —"the Table before Jehovah".	22
21. The Two DOORS (entrances) of the SANCTUARY. *Details.*	23–26
22. THE OUTER COURT. NORTH entrance. Width 100 cubits, of which 50 cubits is occupied by the porch of the outer gate. *Details.*	42. 1–8
23. THE OUTER COURT. EAST entrance. *Details.* Concerning the Priests.	9–12
24. Measurements of the space separating between the Sanctuary and the profane place: i.e. the great outer "surround" of 500 reeds square (=a little more than a mile square) enclosed within a wall of unspecified dimensions.	15–20
25. The OUTER EAST GATE—and the Vision of the Triumphal First Entry of the Messiah KING into the HOUSE (when Ps. 24. 7–10 will be fulfilled).	43. 1–5
26. JEHOVAH'S Command from "the HOUSE" giving "the LAW OF THE HOUSE".	6–12
27. THE ALTAR. 12 cubits square (=25 ft.× 25 ft.) on its base (settle) of 14 cubits square (=about 29 ft.×29 ft.).	13–17

[1] The Separate Place. Only used here *seven* times (41. 12, 13, 14, 15; 42. 1, 10, 13), and in Lam. 4. 7 where the word is rendered *polishing*.

Order.	Refs.
28. THE ORDINANCES OF THE ALTAR.	43. 18–27
29. The CLOSED outer EAST Gate and the reason.	44. 1–3
30. Ezekiel brought into the COURT OF THE HOUSE by the NORTH (the Sacrificial) gate—to receive	4
31. "THE ORDINANCES of the HOUSE OF JEHOVAH".	5–31
32. THE LAND. The OBLATION [1] unto Jehovah, 25,000 reeds by 10,000 reeds (about 60 miles by 24 miles).	45. 1
33. Of this—THE SANCTUARY (500 reeds by 500 reeds square=about 1 mile square) and THE MOST HOLY PLACE—and for the dwellings of the priests.	2–4
34. The LEVITES' portion, 25,000 reeds by 10,000.	5
35. The POSSESSION of the CITY, 25,000 reeds by 5,000 reeds (=about 60 miles by 12 miles, therefore covering an area of 720 square miles.	6
36. THE PRINCE'S PORTIONS east and west of the City, each 5,000×5,000 reeds square (=about 12 miles square and covering each an area of 144 square miles).	7
37. The rest of the Land for Israel according to their Tribes.	8
38. ORDINANCES.	9–25
39. ORDINANCES for WORSHIP for the Prince (David?) and the People.	46. 1–18
40. The Place of Preparation of the Offerings.	19, 20
41. The FOUR Corner Courts of the OUTER COURT.	21–24
42. THE HEALING WATERS from the HOUSE.	47. 1–12
43. Boundaries of the Land.	13–23
44. LOCATION of the *Seven* Tribes on the North side (Dan, Asher, Naphtali, Manasseh, Ephraim, Reuben, JUDAH).	48. 1–7
45. JEHOVAH'S OBLATION for THE SANCTUARY and the Priests, 25,000×10,000 reeds.	8–12
46. The PORTION for the LEVITES.	13, 14
47. The PORTION for THE CITY.[1]	15–19
48. "ALL THE OBLATION", 25,000 reeds by 25,000 reeds=60×60 square miles=an area of about 3,600 square miles.	20
49. The PRINCE'S portions east and west of the City (see block plan on p. 127).	21, 22
50. LOCATION of the remaining Five Tribes—BENJAMIN, Simeon, Issachar, Zebulun, Gad.	23–28
51. SUMMARY.	29
52. "Goings out of the City" (exits) and its Gates.	30–35–
53. THE NAME OF THE CITY, "JEHOVAH-SHAMMAH" (JEHOVAH [is] THERE).	–35

[1] See the Plan (to scale), and Notes on p. 127.

89 THE VISIONS OF DANIEL (chs. 7-12), SYNCHRONOUS.

The visions recorded in these chapters are synchronous, and all relate to "the time of the end" (i.e. the last seven years of the seventy sevens of chapter 9. 24-27, see Ap. 91). This will be seen from the similar expressions exhibited in the following table:—

Daniel 7.	Daniel 8.	Daniel 9.	Daniel 11.	Daniel 12.	Matthew 24.
A little horn (*vv.* 8, 20, 21, 24-26).	The little horn (*vv.* 9-12, 23-25).		A vile person (*vv.* 21-30).		
	The daily sacrifice taken away (*vv.* 11, 12, 13).	The daily sacrifice taken away (*v.* 27).	The daily sacrifice taken away (*v.* 31).	The daily sacrifice taken away (*v.* 11)	
	Abomination of desolation set up (*v.* 13).	Abomination of desolation set up (*v.* 27).	Abomination of desolation set up (*v.* 31).	Abomination of desolation set up (*v.* 11).	Abomination of desolation set up (*v.* 15).
Time: The midst of the week (1,260 days) *v.* 25.	Time: The 2,300 days (*v.* 14).	Time: The midst of the week (1,260 days), *v.* 27.		Time: The midst of the week (the 1,260, 1,290, and 1,335 days), *vv.* 7, 11, 12.	
	The Sanctuary cleansed (*v.* 14).	The anointing of the Holy of Holies (*v.* 24).			
The end (*v.* 26).	The time of the end (*vv.* 17, 19).	The end (*v.* 26).	The time of the end (*v.* 40).	The time of the end (*vv.* 4, 9, 13).	The end (*v.* 14).

90 THE "TIMES", AND NUMBERED "DAYS" OF DANIEL 7. 25; 8. 14; 12. 7, 11, 12.

There are five[1] specific periods of "time" and "days" mentioned in the Book of Daniel (7. 25; 8. 14; 12. 7, 11, 12).

In addition to these five, we have the great period of the "seventy sevens" (or *weeks*) of years in chapter 9.

Sixty-nine of these were completed at the "cutting off" of the Messiah; the last or "seventieth seven" is yet to come (see Ap. 91). All the other five periods of time in the book are to be referred to, and are *standardized*, so to speak, by this last "seven".

The "seventy weeks" (*sevens*) are confessedly to be reckoned as *years*. Therefore, on the basis of a Jewish year of 360 days, one "seven" is 360×7=2,520 days.

The *terminus a quo* of **1**, **4**, **5**, **6** (see diagram) is manifestly determined by the term "in the midst of the week" (the last "seven" of years), of the *standard* (col. **3**): that is, 1,260 days, or 3½ years from either end of the column.

"The prince that shall come" (Antichrist) "will make *a*[2] covenant with many for one week" (i.e. *seven* years) (9. 27).

After 3½ years, on grounds not stated, he breaks this covenant (or "*league*", 11. 23), the daily sacrifice is "taken away", the "abomination" set up, and "Jacob's trouble" (Jer. 30. 7) commences and continues for the remainder of the "seven": viz.: for the 1,260 days or 3½ years.

It is this "midst of the week" that determines both the *a quo* and the *ad quem* of these Numbered Days.

In 8. 14 it is stated, "then shall the Sanctuary be cleansed"[3]. With regard to this "cleansing", all the periods, **1**, **2**, **3**, **4**, **5**, **6** (see diagram) synchronise at the end (see Ap. 89); while the last two columns (**5** and **6**) are *extended* and prolonged beyond the close of the 1,260 days by two significant periods of days, viz. 30 days and 75 days, respectively.

The first of these, 1,290 days is 1,260+30. And the 30 days here may be taken as a "Ve-Adar" or intercalary month of 30 days of "cleansing" following directly after the destruction of the false Messiah, and the break up of his confederacy. These *thirty* days may possibly be the period allotted for the construction of the new and glorious "Sanctuary" of Ezekiel 40-43, which is to be erected *after* the destruction and removal of the Jewish temple which will have been built by the sons of Israel some time previously to its profanation by the Antichrist—as the antitype of Antiochus Epiphanes.

With regard to the 1,335 days of 12. 12: This is 1,260 days with an excess of 75 days. This again being an excess of 45 days beyond the 1,290 of 12. 11. 1,335 is, therefore, 1,260+30+45.

If the 30 days are occupied with the "cleansing", i.e. with the "justifying" or "making righteous" a new and glorious "Sanctuary", then it may be that the further 45 days, over and above the 1,290, will cover the preparation time for the fulfilment of the forty-fifth psalm (such preparation including, the resurrection to life of those concerned in 12. 2), in order that the nuptials of the king may be celebrated as described in such wonderful and minute detail in that psalm.[1]

In connection with this period (1,335 days) we have the only Beatitude in the book! "Blessed (ashrēy) is he that waiteth (=is steadfast) and cometh to the thousand three hundred and five and thirty days" (12. 12). A blessed "lot" indeed for those who will have passed *through* "the Trouble" and are counted

[1] See last paragraph on p. 130.
[2] No definite art. in the Heb.
[3] Heb. *ẓadak*=justified or made righteous. Not the word used of ceremonial or moral cleansing (Heb. *ṭāh-hēēr*); and it may be noted that the word is here employed in the Niphal-Præterite form—and is therefore equal to—*the Sanctuary was justified or made, or appointed righteous.*

[1] Further, it is interesting to note in connection with the numbers 30 and 45, that Ps. 30 was sung "at the dedication of the house of David"—its subject being praise for deliverance in "The Day of (the) Trouble" (Ps. 20. 1)—which is prophetically this very 1,260 days of "Jacob's trouble" in *Daniel* and *Revelation*. And 45 is the *number* of the Psalm which, as the Great King's Nuptial Ode—sets before us the glory and triumph of the Messiah at His marriage with the elect remnant of Israel—the "*wife*" of such passages as Isa. 54. 5-8; 62. 4, 5. Jer. 3. 14, &c. Moreover, the No. 75 is that of the Psalm which sets before us "God's anointed" in the Sanctuary, and emphatically declares (*v.* 7) "God is Judge" (or Ruler).

APPENDIX 90: THE "TIMES" AND NUMBERED DAYS (*cont.*).

THE SPECIFIED PERIODS OF TIME IN THE BOOK OF DANIEL IN RELATION TO THE SEVENTIETH "SEVEN", OR THE LAST WEEK OF DANIEL 9. 27.

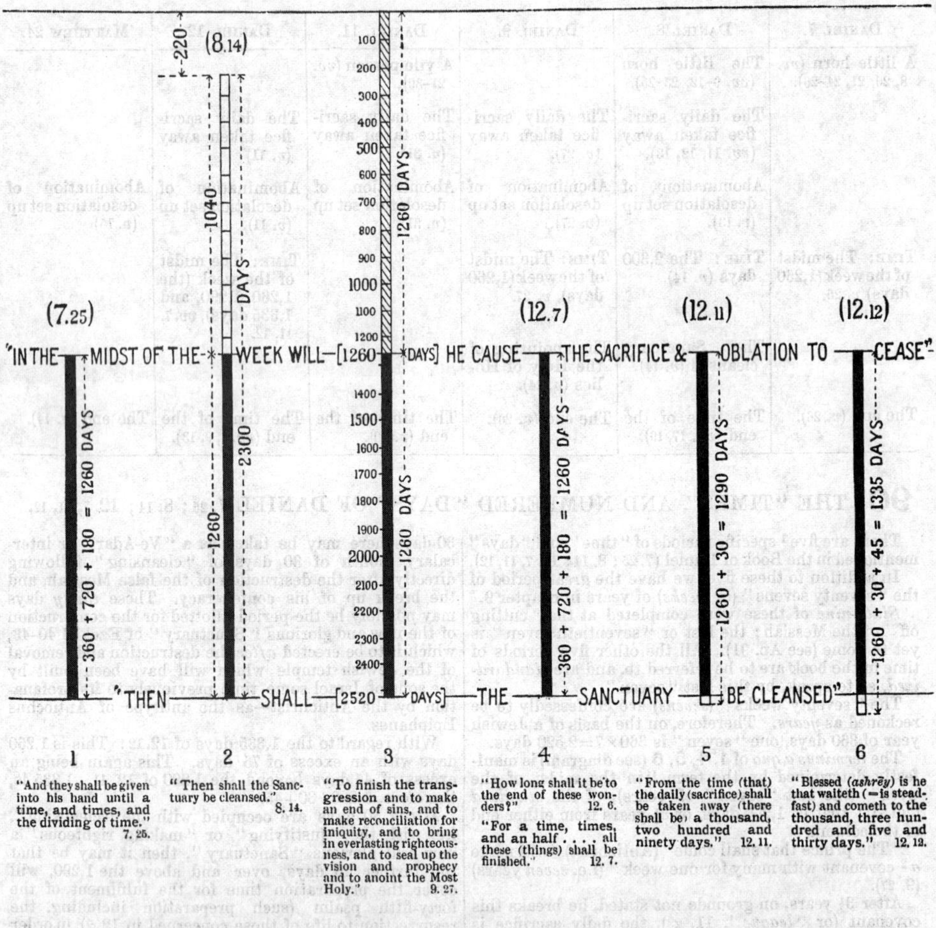

1 "And they shall be given into his hand until a time, and times, and the dividing of time." 7. 25.

2 "Then shall the Sanctuary be cleansed." 8. 14.

3 "To finish the transgression and to make an end of sins, and to make reconciliation for iniquity, and to bring in everlasting righteousness, and to seal up the vision and prophecy and to anoint the Most Holy." 9. 27.

4 "How long shall it be to the end of these wonders?" 12. 6. "For a time, times, and an half . . . . all these (things) shall be finished." 12. 7.

5 "From the time (that) the daily (sacrifice) shall be taken away (there shall be) a thousand, two hundred and ninety days." 12. 11.

6 "Blessed (*ashrēy*) is he that waiteth (= is steadfast) and cometh to the thousand, three hundred and five and thirty days." 12. 12.

worthy to be participators in the scenes of glory and triumph of the King when He is united to restored Israel in that Day, as pourtrayed in the forty-fifth psalm!

In examining the diagram and the references in the book, it will be seen (1) that the only one of these five periods of "time" and "days" that presents any serious difficulty is that of the 2,300 days. (2) That its *terminus ad quem* is the same as the others, viz. the *end* of the seventieth *seven* is clear from 8. 14, which gives it as being marked by the "cleansing of the Sanctuary". Reckoning backwards, therefore, the *terminus a quo* of this period is seen to be 220 days short of the commencement of the seventieth "*seven*".

It is not clearly revealed what event or events will mark the *commencement* of these 2,300 days, but it will be probably some political crisis connected with the confederated kingdoms under the sway of the Antichrist. The key is possibly to be found in chapter 8, *typified* by the contention between the ram and he-goat representing Medo-Persia and Greece. But, though the *terminus a quo* of *this* period is not given to us in plain language (like e.g. the "midst of the week" of 9. 27), yet it will be known to, and understood by, the people of God, who pass through "the Trouble" time of the seventieth "*seven*", for "the wise (in that day) shall understand" (12. 10).

If the "time of trouble" of Dan. 12. 1 is a "time" like the "time" of 7. 25; 12. 7 (Nos. 1 and 4, above), i.e. one year, then there are *six* specific periods of time in the book of Daniel, in addition to the seventieth, or last "seven". If so, the "time" of Dan. 12. 1 suggests that "Jacob's trouble" will be closed by a "time" (or year) of acutest "tribulation". Does this correspond with "the acceptable year" of Isa. 61. 2, immediately preceding the "Vengeance"?

The Diagram will illustrate the above remarks.

APPENDIX 91.

91 THE "SEVENTY WEEKS" OF DAN. 9. 24-27.

For the meaning of this passage, reference must be made to the notes, and especially to the Structures, which are always the best commentary and the surest guide to interpretation.

We may set out the three divisions of the whole period on the diagram (not exact to scale):—

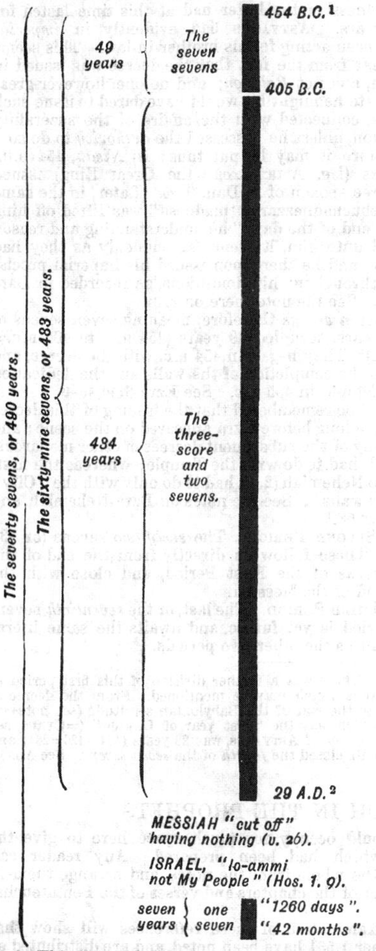

I. THE FIRST PERIOD is simple, being the "seven sevens", or 49 years.

II. THE SECOND PERIOD. The "threescore and two sevens", or 434 years, from 405 B.C. to A.D. 29=the year of the "cutting off" of Messiah (see Ap. 50, pp. 60, 61). This was 483 years from the issuing of the decree in 454 B.C. (i.e. 49+434=483 years).

The "cutting off" of Messiah is stated as being "after" the "threescore and two weeks". The word "after", here, evidently means, and is intended to be understood as indicating, the *completion* of the period named; i.e. on the expiration of the sixty-two sevens will "Messiah be cut off". Beyond this exactness it is hardly necessary for us to go.

III. THE THIRD PERIOD. This is the *one seven*, i.e. the seventieth (or "last"), seven which has still to be accounted for. That it must be yet future seems certain, from the agreement of its events with those of the visions of chapters 7-12 (Ap. 89), and the numbered "days" of chs. 8. 14 and 12. 7, 11, 12 (Ap. 90); also from the fact that none of the six definite events (of 9. 24), which mark its end has as yet taken place.[1] These belong to the whole seventy sevens, and are thus connected with the seventieth or last seven, being the object and end of the whole prophecy. The following three, among other reasons, may be added:-

1. If the seventieth, or "one seven", is to be reckoned from the *cutting off* of Messiah in direct, continuous, and historic sequence, then it leads us nowhere—certainly not to any of the six events of *v.* 24, which are all categorically stated to relate to Daniel's People, "all Israel" (*v.* 7), and to the holy City "Jerusalem".

No interpretation which transfers these six events to Gentiles or to Gentile times, is admissible.

If they are continuous, then there is no point or crisis in the Acts of the Apostles which marks their end. If they coincided with any events of importance, such as the end of Peter's ministry or the beginning of that of Paul, or Acts 12 and 13, that would be something. But there is nothing.

2. Messiah was to "have nothing" that was His, "after" His cutting off. This clearly points to the crucifixion of Messiah, and the rejection of His Messianic kingdom. For nearly 2,000 years Messiah has "had nothing" of all the many "glorious things" which have been spoken of Him, in connection with Himself or with His People Israel.

3. This last, or "one seven" of years, is divided into two distinct equal parts (see Ap. 90), and the division takes place in connection with an event which has no connection whatever with any event which has yet taken place. Messiah did not "make a (not *the*) covenant" of any kind, either with Israel or with any one else, at the end of, or "after" the sixty-ninth week; nor did He "break" any covenant three and a half years later. Man may "make" and "break" covenants, but Divine Covenants are *never* broken.

On the other hand: of "the prince that shall come" it is distinctly stated that he shall do both these very things (*vv.* 26, 27); and, in Ap. 89 and 90 both are connected with "the time of the end".

Hence, we are forced to the conclusion that this last seven of years still awaits its fulfilment; and this fulfilment must be as literal and complete as that of all the other parts of this vision and prophecy; for the end must be the glorious consummation for Israel of *v.* 24, the complete destruction of "the coming prince" (the false Messiah or Antichrist), and the setting up of Messiah's kingdom.

[1] Archbishop Ussher s Chronology was first added to the A.V. by Bishop Lloyd in the edition of 1701. But, in Neh. 2. 1, Bishop Lloyd put *his own* date, "445 B.C.", to suit his own theory. Archbishop Ussher's date for the commencement of the reign of Artaxerxes was A.M. 3531, which, in his *Collatio Annorum*, corresponds to 474 B.C. "The twentieth year of Artaxerxes" would, therefore, be 454 B.C. as given above.

[2] The era called "*Anno Domini*" was first fixed by a monk (*Denys le Petit*, commonly known by his Latin name, *Dionysius Exiguus*), about A.D. 532. It did not come into general use for some centuries. Charles III of Germany was the first who used the expression, "*in the year of our Lord*", in 879. It was found afterward that a mistake had been made by fixing the era *four years* too late! This explains the marginal notes in Matt. 2. 1, and Luke 2. 20, "The fourth year before the Common Account called Anno Domini." (In some editions of the A.V. we have seen "the fifth year", Luke 2. 1, also "the sixth year", Luke 1. 6.) Hence, the year *called* A.D. 33 was *really* the year A.D. 29. This, with 454, makes exactly 483 years, or 69 weeks of years.

Nothing less will satisfy all the requirements of Daniel's vision of "the seventy weeks".

The Hebrew word rendered "week" is *shābūa'*, and means, simply, a "septad", a "hebdomad", or *a seven*, hence *a week*, because it is a seven (of days). But in this passage it is confessedly used of *a seven* of years; and this of necessity, for no other seven of any other portion of time will satisfy the prophecy and fall within its *terminus a quo*, and the *terminus ad quem*.

Seventy of these sevens of years (or 490 years) are the one subject of this prophecy. We are told exactly *when* they would commence, and *how* they were to end. They sum up, within their bounds, all the then counsels of God as to His future dealings with His People Israel; for they are "determined" (the angel said to Daniel) "upon thy People, and upon thy Holy City" (*v.* 24). These words cannot have any other interpretation than "all Israel" (*v.* 7), and Jerusalem, and the Holy Sanctuary; for that had been the subject of Daniel's prayer, to which this prophecy was sent as the specific answer. (See *vv.* 2, 7, 16, 17, 18, 19, and especially *v.* 24.)

These "seventy sevens [of years]" are divided into three distinct and separate periods:—

I. The seven sevens, or 49 years.	483 years	490 years.
II. The sixty-two sevens, or 434 years.		
III. The one seven, or 7 years.		

The *terminus a quo* of the whole period is *the issuing of a decree* "to restore and to build (or rather, rebuild) Jerusalem."

The *terminus ad quem* of the whole period is *the cleansing of the Sanctuary*. This is also the end of all the visions of Daniel in chaps. 7–12 (Ap. 89); and all the numbered "days" of 7. 25; 8. 14; and 12. 7, 11, 12, have this *cleansing* as their object and end.

As to the *whole* period, Daniel is bidden by the angelic *Hierophant* to "understand . . . and consider" (*v.* 23); while, as to its three separate *divisions*, Daniel is to "know therefore and understand" (*v.* 25). See the Structures of these passages, pp. 1196, 1198, 1199.

THE FIRST PERIOD. The *seven sevens* (or 49 years). These commence with "the going forth of the commandment to restore and to build Jerusalem".

This was in the first month, *Nisan*, 454 B.C. (see Ap. 50, pp. 60, 67, and 70). Hanani's report to Nehemiah was made in the *ninth* month *Chisleu*, in 455 B.C., three months before; both months being in the "twentieth year of Artaxerxes". See notes on Neh. 1. 1 and 2. 1; also on pp. 615–18; and Ap. 57.

The ARTAXERXES (or Great King) of Neh. 1. 1; 2. 1, who issues this decree, is identified with the great king ASTYAGES. (See Ap. 57.)

ASTYAGES was brother-in-law to Nebuchadnezzar. The madness of the latter had at this time lasted for seven years. ASTYAGES had evidently in *imperial* matters been acting for his brother-in-law. This seems to be clear from the fact that the decree was issued in Shushan, and not *Babylon*; and no one, however great a potentate he might be, would have dared to issue such a decree, connected with the affairs of the suzerainty of Babylon, unless he possessed the *authority* to do so.

Therefore it may be put thus: In *Nisan*, 454 B.C., ASTYAGES (i.e. Artaxerxes = the Great King) issued the decree spoken of in Dan. 9. 25. Later, in the same year, Nebuchadnezzar's "madness" was lifted off him. "At the end of the days" his understanding and reason *returned* unto him, it seems, as suddenly as they had left him; and he thereupon issued his imperial proclamation throughout his dominions, as recorded in Dan. 4. 34–37. See the note there on *v.* 34.

The *seven sevens* therefore, meaning seven sevens of literal years, occupied 49 years (454 B.C. to 405 B.C.= 49 years). They began in 454 B.C. with the decree, and end with the completion of the walls and the dedication of the Temple in 405 B.C. See Ezra 6. 10, 15–19.

It must be remembered that the issuing of this decree took place long before Ezra appeared on the scene; and before any of the subsequent decrees of other monarchs, which all had to do with the Temple; whereas the first, issued to Nehemiah (2. 1), had to do only with the "City" and its "walls". See the notes on Ezra-Nehemiah, and Appendix 58.[1]

THE SECOND PERIOD. The *sixty-two* sevens (or 434 years). These follow on directly from the end of the *seven sevens* of the First Period, and close with the cutting off of the Messiah.

THE THIRD PERIOD. The last, or the *seventieth* seven. This period is yet future, and awaits the same literal fulfilment as the other two periods.

[1] N.B. There was a further division of this first period of seven sevens which may be mentioned. From the decree of Neh. 2. 1 to the end of the Babylonian servitude (see notes on p. 615), which was the "first year of DARIUS" (=CYRUS, see Ap. 57) the son of ASTYAGES, was 28 years (454 – 426 = 28); and those events closed the *fourth* of the *seven sevens*. See Ap. 50, p. 60.

92 REFERENCES TO THE PENTATEUCH IN THE PROPHETS.

It is alleged by modern critics that, while Deuteronomy was the work of some anonymous writer in the reigns of Josiah and Manasseh, the ritual portions of Exodus, Leviticus, and Numbers were the work of Ezra and the priests in Babylon. Thus, practically, the greater part of the Pentateuch is assumed to be post-exilic, and therefore not written by Moses; and this in spite of the fact that the claims of the whole Bible necessitate the Mosaic authorship.

On the other hand, it is admitted by the same modern critics that the prophets lived and wrote in the reigns of those kings with whose reigns they are respectively associated.

But the Pentateuch is full of technical terms and legal phraseology; and has its own peculiar vocabulary. The constant reference to these by all the prophets proves conclusively that the Pentateuch as a whole must have had a prior existence; and must have been well known by the prophets, and understood by those who heard the prophetic utterances and read the prophetic writings.

Throughout all the books of the prophets such references to the Pentateuch have been noted in the margin of *The Companion Bible* with the brief indication "Ref. to Pent.", followed by the passages referred to. It is not claimed that none have been overlooked: so that the number will be greater rather than less.

It would occupy too much space here to give the table which had been prepared. Any reader can collect the whole from the notes, and arrange them in the order of the chapters and verses of the Pentateuchal books.

An examination of these references will show that altogether 1,531 have been noted, and are distributed as follows: GENESIS is referred to 149 times; EXODUS, 312; LEVITICUS, 285; NUMBERS, 168; while DEUTERONOMY is referred to 617 times.

Thus DEUTERONOMY, of which the modern critics have made the greatest havoc, is referred to more often than any of the other four books: 468 times more often than Genesis; 305 times more often than Exodus; 332 times more often than Leviticus; and 449 times more often than Numbers. That is to say, more often than any two of the other books put together.

It is also remarkable that the references to technical, legal, and ritual terms are more numerous than to those relating to historical events. The latter would necessarily be better known and remembered; but the former could not have been thus referred to unless the ritual itself (less easily remembered) had existed in writing, and thus been generally known and understood. It is evident that it would have been perfectly useless for the prophets to write and quote aught but what was well known, or could be easily referred to and verified.

Regard must also be had to the fact that the canonical order of the prophetic books is not the same as their chronological order; for Malachi (the latest prophet) refers (Mal. 1. 2) to an earlier passage of Deuteronomy (Deut. 7. 8) than Isaiah (one of the earliest prophets), who refers, in Isa. 1. 2, to a later passage (Deut. 32. 1).

93 THE ALLEGED "CORRUPTION" OF THE HEBREW TEXT.

In modern commentaries we very frequently meet with the objectionable word "corruption" used of the Hebrew text of the Old Testament.

As specimens of this feature of modernism, the following are taken at random from one of the latest commentaries:—

1. This "probably signifies not only a new paragraph but a later hand."
2. This "leads to the conclusion that there is some original corruption of the Hebrew text."
3. "The text in this verse is extremely difficult to interpret; and no satisfactory translation can be given of it."
4. "The Hebrew of this verse seems to be so corrupt that there is no satisfactory meaning to be obtained from it."
5. "It is certain that the original text must be corrupt."
6. "It is better to regard it as being in some way a corrupted text . . . but is now unintelligible."
7. "These three verses are extremely corrupt, and it is probably impossible to restore the text with any certainty."

Such remarks abound; and very few pages are free from them. There is a continual running confession of inability to understand the Hebrew text. Like the schoolboy who always thinks "the book is wrong", modern critics never seem to suspect that the difficulty lies with themselves and not with "the Book". We must accept their confession, whatever the explanation may be.

The object of this Appendix is to show that those who are so ready to speak about "corruption" can have little or no knowledge of the *Massōrah*, or of its object.

We have explained its character somewhat in Ap. 30. We now propose to point out that its one great special aim and end was to make such "corruption" impossible.

Well knowing the frailties and infirmities of human nature, those who had charge of the Sacred Text hedged it round on all sides with regulations and information called the *Massōrah*, because it was meant to be "a fence to the Scripture", and because it should be, thus, next to impossible for a scribe to make a mistake in copying it.

Some general facts are given in Ap. 30 (which should here be consulted); but further particular features are now added from Dr. C. D. Ginsburg's four large folio volumes, which contain the *Massōrah* so far as he has been able to collect, arrange, and transcribe the writing in smaller characters at the top and bottom of every page of most of the accessible manuscripts containing it.

I. All the letters of the Hebrew text were counted: not as a piece of mere curiosity, but that the number of each letter in each book being thus known to the scribe he might easily check his work, and ascertain whether one letter had escaped or got over "the fence". He was informed how many *Alephs* (א=A) there should be, how many *Beths* (ב=B), &c., in each book respectively.

II. There are five consonants, which when they occur at the beginning of a word *must* have a dot within them, called a *Dagesh*. This dot in no way affects the meaning of the word.

In certain positions, other than at the beginning of a word, these five letters may, or may not, require this *Dagesh*. Now, each of these dots was safeguarded; for one might so easily be omitted or misplaced: hence, the scribe was assisted by an instruction that, in cases where any of these five letters should not have a *Dagesh*, he must make a small mark over it, called a *Raphē*. This again in no way affected either the sound or the sense; but it reminded the scribe that in these cases he had to do one thing or the other. He must write it (if the letter were, say, a Beth (ב=B) either בּ or בֿ.

III. Again: certain letters have come down with the text, from the most ancient times, having a small ornament or flourish on the top: for example, we find

Aleph (=A) with 7 *Taagin* 

Beth (=B) with 3 *Taagin* 

Gimel (=G) with 4 *Taagin* 

Daleth (=D) with 3 *Taagin* 

These ornamented letters were quite exceptional, and implied no added meaning of any kind: but, so jealously was the sacred text safeguarded, that the scribe was informed how many of each of the letters had these little ornaments: i.e. how many *Alephs* (א=A), and how many *Beths* (ב=B), &c., had one, two, three, or more.

These ornaments were called *Tā'āgīm* (or *Tāgin*), meaning *little crowns*. The Greek-speaking Jews called them *little horns* (Heb. *keranōth*) because they looked like "horns". The A.V. and R.V. rendering of *keraia* (Gr.= *horn*) is "tittle", which is the diminutive of "title" and denotes a small mark forming such *title*.

Modern commentators, and even the most recent *Dictionaries of the Bible*, still cling to the traditional explanation that this "tittle" is the small projection or corner by which the letter *Beth* (ב=B) differs from *Kaph* (כ=K); or *Daleth* (ד=D) differs from *Resh* (ר=R), &c.

But the *Massōrah* informs us that *this is not the case*, and thus, tradition is quite wrong. We give a few examples showing how even these little ornaments were safeguarded:—

Rubric א, § 2 (Ginsburg's *Massōrah*, vol. ii, pp. 680-701) says: "Aleph with one *Tāg*: there are two instances in the Pentateuch (Ex. 13. 5, א in *'asher* (=which), and *v.* 15[1], א in *'ādām* (=man).

Rubric א, § 3, says: "There are seven *Alephs* (א=A) in the Pentateuch which respectively have seven *Tāāgin*".

Rubric ב, § 2, notes *Beth* (ב=B) with one *Tāg*, as occurring only once (Ex. 13. 11, *yebi'ăkā* = brings thee).

Rubric ב, § 3, notes *Beth* (ב=B), as occurring in four instances with two *Tāāgin*: viz. Gen. 27. 29 (*ya'abdūkā* =may serve thee); Gen. 28. 16 (*bammākōm*=place); Ex. 7. 14 (*kābēd*=is hardened); Ex. 23. 23 (*vehāyebūsī*=and the Jebusites).

Rubric ב, § 4, gives four instances where *Beth* (ב=B) has three *Tāāgin*: and so on, through all the alphabet, noting and enumerating each letter that has any *Tāgin*: thus safeguarding the sacred text, so that not one of these little ornaments might be lost.

It was to these *Tāāgin* the Lord referred in Matt. 5. 18, and Luke 16. 17; when He said that not only the smallest letter (י= *Yod*= Y), but that not even the merest mark or ornament (*Tāg*) should pass away from the Law until all things should come to pass. So that our Lord Him-

[1] Ginsburg gives *v.* 13; but vol. ii shows that it is *v.* 15.

self recognized these *Tāāgin*, which must have been in His Bible from which He quoted.

IV. In cases of spelling, where a word occurs a certain number of times, but in one or two cases with a slightly different spelling (where, for example, one was with a short vowel and another with a long or full vowel), these are noted, numbered, and thus safeguarded.

The scribe is not left to imagine that some of these are incorrect, and so be tempted to correct the smaller number by making them conform with the larger number of cases in which the word is spelt differently. It is needless to give examples of such instances.

V. Where a certain word or expression occurs more or less frequently in varying forms, these are all noted, numbered, and distinguished. For example, the word *bayith* (=house); its occurrences with different vowels and accents are all safeguarded.

So with its occurrences with certain prefixes and suffixes: e.g. "in the house", six occurrences, where the letter *Beth* has a *Sheva* (בְ) are safeguarded against thirty-two where it has a *Pathach* (בַ) instead.

So with its combinations with other words: two are noted as being "in this house which is called" (ב, § 244); nineteen as being "into the house" (ב, § 245); twice "and within the house" (ב, § 246); four times "and the house of", and "and into the house of" (ב, § 247); twice "the house of her husband" (ב, § 249); "house of Elohim" five times without the Article: these five exceptional cases being thus safeguarded against the forty-eight occurrences where Elohim has the Article (ב, § 251).

In nine instances "House of Elohim" is followed by the demonstrative pronoun "this": but, in five cases this pronoun is the Chald. *dēk* (Ezra 5. 17; 6. 7, 7, 8, 12), and in four cases it is *ēdenāh*. These latter are thus safeguarded.

The occurrences of the expression "the house of Israel" are noted separately in the Pentateuch and the Prophets (ב, §§ 254, 255); and in ב, § 256, these are further distinguished from the expression "the sons of Israel" (the words *bēyth*, "house of", and *beney*, "sons of", being much alike in Hebrew).

"Shearing house" is noted as occurring twice (ב, § 258), and "house of restraint" as occurring three times (ב, § 257).

"*Jehovah Adonai*" is noted as occurring 291 times; but the fewer occurrences of "*Adonai Jehovah*" are safeguarded against the more usual form (י, § 178).

Jehovah our Adonay is safeguarded against the more usual form "Jehovah our Elohim" (י, § 179).

In the same way, the following exceptional phrases are distinguished: "Jehovah the Elohim", "Jehovah Elohim of", "Jehovah Elohim *Zeba'ōth*", "Jehovah Elohim of heaven", "Jehovah my Elohim", &c., &c.

The expression "the sins of Jeroboam", which occurs fifteen times, is in ten instances followed by "the son of Nebat". The shorter phrase is thus exceptional; and the scribe is warned not to make any of the five like the other ten by adding "the son of Nebat".

These examples might be enumerated by hundreds from Dr. Ginsburg's *Massōrah*; but enough are here given to show how the Massorah was indeed "a fence to the Scriptures".

In the face of these facts one might smile (if the case were not so serious) at the readiness of modern critics to use the word "corruption" whenever they have to admit that they cannot understand the text as it stands. We have no reason to doubt the truth of their confessions; but it is better, and easier, and happier, and safer to believe God.

94 THE GREEK TEXT OF THE NEW TESTAMENT.

I. INTRODUCTION. While modern critics are occupied with the problem as to the origin of the Four Gospels, and with their so-called "discrepancies", we believe that MATTHEW, MARK, and JOHN got their respective Gospels where Luke got his, viz. *anōthen*="from above" (Luke 1. 3, see note there); and that the "discrepancies", so called, are the creation of the Commentators and Harmonists themselves. The latter particularly; for when they see two *similar* events, they immediately assume they are *identical*; and when they read similar discourses of our Lord, they at once assume that they are discordant accounts of the same, instead of seeing that they are *repetitions*, made at different times, under different circumstances, with different antecedents and consequents, which necessitate the employment of words and expressions so as to accord with the several occasions. These differences thus become proofs of accuracy and perfection.

The Bible claims to be the Word of God, coming from Himself as His revelation to man. If these claims be not true, then the Bible cannot be even "a good book". In this respect "the living Word" is like the written Word; for, if the claims of the Lord Jesus to be God were not true, He could not be even "a good man". As to those claims, man can believe them, or leave them. In the former case, he goes to the Word of God, and is overwhelmed with evidences of its truth; in the latter case, he abandons Divine revelation for man's imagination.

II. INSPIRATION. In Divine revelation "holy men spake from God as they were moved (or borne along) by the Holy Spirit" (2 Pet. 1. 21). The wind, as it is borne along among the trees, causes each tree to give forth its own peculiar sound, so that the experienced ear of a woodman could tell, even in the dark, the name of the tree under which he might be standing, and distinguish the creaking elm from the rustling aspen. Even so, while each "holy man of God" is "moved" by One Spirit, the individuality of the inspired writers is preserved. Thus we may explain the medical words of "Luke the beloved physician" used in his Gospel and in the Acts of the Apostles (Col. 4. 14).

As to Inspiration itself, we have no need to resort to human theories, or definitions, as we have a Divine definition in Acts 1. 16 which is all-sufficient. "This scripture must needs have been fulfilled, which the Holy Ghost, by the mouth of David, spake before concerning Judas." The reference is to Ps. 41. 9.

It is "by the mouth" and "by the hand" of holy men that God has spoken to us. Hence it was David's voice and David's pen, but the words were not David's words.

Nothing more is required to settle the faith of all believers; but it requires Divine operation to convince unbelievers; hence, it is vain to depend on human arguments.

III. THE LANGUAGE. With regard to this, it is generally assumed that, because it comes to us in Greek, the N.T. ought to be in *classical* Greek, and is then condemned because it is not! Classical Greek was at its prime some centuries before; and in the time of our Lord there were several reasons why the N.T. was not written in classical Greek.

1. The writers were Hebrews; and thus, while the language is Greek, the thoughts and idioms are Hebrew. These idioms or Hebraisms are generally pointed out in the notes of *The Companion Bible*. If the Greek of the N.T. be regarded as an inspired translation from Hebrew or Aramaic originals, most of the various readings would be accounted for and understood.

2. Then we have to remember that in the time of our Lord there were no less than four languages in use in Palestine, and their mixture formed the "Yiddish" of those days.

(*a*) There was HEBREW, spoken by Hebrews;

(*b*) There was GREEK, which was spoken in Palestine by the educated classes generally;

(*c*) There was LATIN, the language of the Romans, who then held possession of the land;

(*d*) And there was ARAMAIC, the language of the common people.

Doubtless our Lord spoke all these (for we never read of His using an interpreter). In the synagogue He would necessarily use Hebrew; to Pilate He would naturally answer in Latin; while to the common people He would doubtless speak in Aramaic.

3. ARAMAIC was Hebrew, as it was developed during and after the Captivity in Babylon [1].

There were two branches, known roughly as Eastern (which is Chaldee), and Western (Mesopotamian, or Palestinian).

This latter was known also as Syriac; and the Greeks used "Syrian" as an abbreviation for Assyrian. This was perpetuated by the early Christians. Syriac flourished till the seventh century A.D. In the eighth and ninth it was overtaken by the Arabic; and by the thirteenth century it had disappeared. We have already noted that certain parts of the O.T. are written in Chaldee (or Eastern Aramaic): viz. Ezra 4. 8—6. 18; 7. 12-26; Dan. 2. 4—7. 28. Cp. also 2 Kings 18. 26.

Aramaic is of three kinds:—1. Jerusalem. 2. Samaritan. 3. Galilean.

Of these, Jerusalem might be compared with High German, and the other two with Low German.

There are many Aramaic words preserved in the Greek of the N.T., and most of the commentators call attention to a few of them; but, from the books cited below, we are able to present a more or less complete list of the examples to which attention is called in the notes of *The Companion Bible* [2].

1. *Abba* [3]. Mark 14. 36. Rom. 8. 15. Gal. 4. 6.
2. *Ainias*. Acts 9. 33, 34.
3. *Akeldama*. Acts 1. 19. *Akeldamach* (L A). *Acheldamach* (T Tr.). *Hacheldamach* (WH). See Ap. 161. I. Aram. *Ḥăḳal dᵉmā'*, or *Ḥăḳal dᵉmaḥ*.
4. *Alphaios*. Matt. 10. 3. Mark 2. 14; 3. 18. Luke 6. 15. Acts 1. 13.
5. *Annas*. Luke 3. 2. John 18. 13, 24. Acts 4. 6.
6. *Bar-abbas*. Matt. 27. 16, 17, 20, 21, 26. Mark 15. 7, 11, 15. Luke 23. 18. John 18. 40, 40.
7. *Bartholomaios*. Matt. 10. 3. Mark 3. 18. Luke 6. 14. Acts 1. 13.
8. *Bar-iēsous*. Acts 13. 6.
9. *Bar-iōna*. Matt. 16. 17. See No. 27, below.
10. *Bar-nabas*. Acts 4. 36, &c. 1 Cor. 9. 6. Gal. 2. 1, 9, 13. Col. 4. 10.
11. *Bar-sabas*. Acts 1. 23; 15. 22 (*Barsabbas* all the texts).
12. *Bar-timaios*. Mark 10. 46.
13. *Beël-zeboul*. Matt. 10. 25; 12. 24, 27. Mark 3. 22. Luke 11. 15, 18, 19.
14. *Bēthesda*. John 5. 2. (*Bēthzatha*, T WH; *Bēthsaïda*, or *Bēthzather*, L WH Rm.)
15. *Bēthsaïda*. Matt. 11. 21. Mark 6. 45; 8. 22. Luke 9. 10; 10. 13. John 1. 44; 12. 21.
16. *Bēthphagē*. Matt. 21. 1. Mark 11. 1. Luke 19. 29.
17. *Boanerges*. Mark 3. 17. (*Boanērges*, L T Tr. A WH.)
18. *Gethsēmanei*. Matt. 26. 36. Mark 14. 32.
19. *Golgotha*. Matt. 27. 33. Mark 15. 22. John 19. 17.
20. *Elōï*. Mark 15. 34.
21. *Ephphatha*. Mark 7. 34.
22. *Zakchaios*. Luke 19. 2, 5, 8.
23. *Zebedaios*. Matt. 4. 21, 21; 10. 2; 20. 20; 26. 37; 27. 56. Mark 1. 19, 20; 3. 17; 10. 35. Luke 5. 10. John 21. 2.
24. *Ēli*. Matt. 27. 46. (*Ēlei* (voc.), T WH m.; *Eloi*, WH.)
25. *Thaddaios*. Matt. 10. 3. Mark 3. 18.
26. *Thōmās*. Matt. 10. 3. Mark 3. 18. Luke 6. 15. John 11. 16; 14. 5; 20. 24, 26, 27, 28, 29; 21. 2. Acts 1. 13.
27. *Iōannēs*. John 1. 42; 21. 15, 16, 17. (*Iōānēs*, Tr. WH.) See *Bar-iōna*. (*Iōna* being a contraction of *Iōana*.
28. *Kēphās*. John 1. 42. 1 Cor. 1. 12; 3. 22; 9. 5; 15. 5. Gal. 2. 9.
29. *Kleopas*. Luke 24. 18.
30. *Klōpās*. John 19. 25.
31. *Lama*. Matt. 27. 46. Mark 15. 34. (*Lēma*, L. *Lema*, T Tr. A WH).
32. *Mammōnas*. Matt. 6. 24. Luke 16. 9, 11, 13. (*Mamōnas*, L T Tr. A WH.)
33. *Maran-atha*. 1 Cor. 16. 22 (=Our Lord, come!). Aram. *Māranā' thā'*.
34. *Martha*. Luke 10. 38, 40, 41. John 11. 1, &c.
35. *Matthaios*. Matt. 9. 9; 10. 3. Mark 3. 18. Luke 6. 15. Acts 1. 13, 26. (All the critics spell it *Maththaios*.)
36. *Nazareth* (-*et*). Matt. 2. 23; 4. 13 (*Nazara*, T Tr. A WH); 21. 11. Mark 1. 9. Luke 1. 26; 2. 4, 39, 51; 4. 16 (*Nazara*. Omit the Art. L T Tr. A WH and R.) John 1. 45, 46. Acts 10. 38.
37. *Pascha*. Matt. 26. 2, 17, 18, 19. Mark 14. 1, 12, 12, 14, 16. Luke 2. 41; 22. 1, 7, 8, 11, 13, 15. John 2. 13, 23; 6. 4; 11. 55, 55; 12. 1; 13. 1; 18. 28, 39; 19. 14. Acts 12. 4. 1 Cor. 5. 7. Heb. 11. 28. The Hebrew is *pesaḥ*.
38. *Rabboni*, *Rabbouni* (*Rabbonei*, WH). Mark 10. 51. John 20. 16.
39. *Raka*. Matt. 5. 22. (*Rēyḳā'* is an abbreviation of *Rēyḳān*.)
40. *Sabachthani*. Matt. 27. 46. Mark 15. 34. (*Sabachthanei*, T Tr. WH.)
41. *Sabbata* (Aram. *sabbāta'*). Heb. *shabbāth*. Matt. 12. 1, 5, 10, 11, 12, &c.
42. *Tabitha*. Acts 9. 36, 40.
43. *Talītha ḳūmi*. Mark 5. 41. (In Galilæan Aramaic it was *ṭalitha' ḳūmī*.)
44. *Hōsanna* (in Aram. = Save us; in Heb. = Help us). Matt. 21. 9, 9, 15. Mark 11. 9, 10. John 12. 13.

IV. THE *PAPYRI* and *OSTRACA*. Besides the Greek text mention ought to be made of these, although it concerns the interpretation of the text rather than the text itself.

We have only to think of the changes which have taken place in our own English language during the last 300 years, to understand the inexpressible usefulness of documents written on the material called *papyrus*, and on pieces of broken pottery called *ostraca*, recently discovered in Egypt and elsewhere. They are found in the ruins of ancient temples and houses, and in the rubbish heaps of towns and villages, and are of great importance.

They consist of business-letters, love-letters, contracts, estimates, certificates, agreements, accounts, bills-of-sale, mortgages, school-exercises, receipts, bribes,

[1] It is so called because it was the language of *Aram*, or *Mesopotamia*, which is Greek for *Aram Naharaim*=Aram between the two rivers (Gen. 24. 10. Deut. 23. 4. Judg. 3. 8. Ps. 60, title). It is still called "The Island". There were other Arams beside this: (2) *Aram Dammāsek* (north-east of Palestine), or simply Aram, because best known to Israel (2 Sam. 8. 5. Isa. 7. 8; 17. 3. Amos 1. 5); (3) *Aram Zobah* (not far from Damascus and Hamath), under Saul and David (1 Sam. 14. 47. 2 Sam. 8. 3); (4) *Aram Beth-rehob* (N. Galilee, Ap. 169), 2 Sam. 10. 6; (5) *Aram Maachah* (1 Chron. 19. 6, 7); (6) *Aram Geshur* (2 Sam. 15. 8).

[2] Further information may be found in the following works:—

AD. NEUBAUER: On the dialects spoken in Palestine in the time of Christ, in *Studia Biblica* . . . by members of the University of Oxford. Vol. I, pp. 39-74. Oxford, 1885.

F. W. J. DILLOO: *De moedertaal vanonzen heere Jesus Christus en van zyne Apostelen*, p. 70. Amsterdam, 1886.

ARNOLD MEYER: *Jesu Mutter-Sprache*. Leipzig, 1896.

G. DALMAN: *Die Worte Jesu, mit Berücksichtigung des nathkanonischen jüdischen Schrifttums und der aram. Sprache erörtert*. Vol. I. Leipzig, 1898. Also *Grammatik des jüdisch-palästinischen Aramäisch*. 2. Auflage. Leipzig, 1905. In the Index of Greek words.

[3] The order of the words is that of the Greek alphabet.

pawn-tickets, charms, litanies, tales, magical literature, and every sort of literary production.

These are of inestimable value in enabling us to arrive at the true meaning of many words (used in the time of Christ) which were heretofore inexplicable. Examples may be seen in the notes on "scrip" (Matt. 10. 10. Mark 6. 8. Luke 9. 3); "have" (Matt. 6. 2, 5, 16. Luke 6. 24. Philem. 15); "officer" (Luke 12. 58); "presseth" (Luke 16. 16); "suffereth violence" (Matt. 11. 12), &c.[1]

V. THE MANUSCRIPTS of the Greek New Testament dating from the fourth century A.D. are more in number than those of any Greek or Roman author, for these latter are rare, and none are really ancient; while those of the N.T. have been set down by Dr. Scrivener at not less than 3,600, a few containing the whole, and the rest various parts, of the N.T.

The study of these from a literary point of view has been called "Textual Criticism", and it necessarily proceeds altogether on documentary evidence; while "Modern Criticism" introduces the element of human opinion and hypothesis.

Man has never made a proper use of God's gifts. God gave men the sun, moon, and stars for signs and for seasons, to govern the day, and the night, and the years. But no one to-day can tell us what year (*Anno Mundi*) we are actually living in! In like manner God gave us His Word, but man, compassed with infirmity, has failed to preserve and transmit it faithfully.

The worst part of this is that man charges God with the result, and throws the blame on Him for all the confusion due to his own want of care!

The Old Testament had from very early times official custodians of the Hebrew text. Its Guilds of Scribes, *Nakdanīm*, *Sopherīm*, and *Massorites* elaborated plans by which the original text has been preserved with the greatest possible care (see Ap. 93).[2] But though, in this respect, it had advantages which the Greek text of the N.T. never had, it nevertheless shows many signs of human failure and infirmity. Man has only to touch anything to leave his mark upon it.

Hence the MSS. of the Greek Testament are to be studied to-day with the utmost care. The materials are:—

i. The MSS. themselves in whole or in part.

ii. Ancient versions made from them in other languages[3].

iii. Citations made from them by early Christian writers long before the oldest MSS. we possess (see Ap. 168).

i. As to the MSS. themselves we must leave all palæographical matters aside (such as have to do with paper, ink, and caligraphy), and confine ourselves to what is material.

1. These MSS. consist of two great classes: (*a*) Those written in *Uncial* (or capital) letters; and (*b*) those written in "running hand", called *Cursives*.

The former are considered to be the more ancient, although it is obvious and undeniable that some cursives may be transcripts of uncial MSS. more ancient than any existing uncial MS.

This will show that we cannot depend altogether upon textual criticism.

2. It is more to our point to note that what are called "breathings" (soft or hard) and accents are not found in any MSS. before the seventh century (unless they have been added by a later hand).

3. *Punctuation* also, as we have it to-day, is *entirely absent*. The earliest two MSS. (known as B, the MS. in the Vatican and א the Sinaitic MS., now at St. Petersburg) have only an occasional dot, and this on a level with the top of the letters.

The text reads on without any divisions between letters or words until MSS. of the ninth century, when (in Cod. Augiensis, now in Cambridge) there is seen for the first time a single point which separates each word. This dot is placed in the middle of the line, but is often omitted.

None of our modern marks of punctuation are found until the ninth century, and then only in Latin versions and some cursives.

From this it will be seen that the punctuation of all modern editions of the Greek text, and of all versions made from it, rests entirely *on human authority*, and has no weight whatever in determining or even influencing the interpretation of a single passage. This refers also to the employment of capital letters, and to all the modern literary refinements of the present day[1].

4. Chapters also were alike unknown. The Vatican MS. makes a new section where there is an evident break in the sense. These are called *titloi*, or *kephalaia*[2].

There are none in א (Sinaitic), see above. They are not found till the fifth century in Codex A (British Museum), Codex C (Ephraemi, Paris), and in Codex R (Nitriensis, British Museum) of the sixth century.

They are quite foreign to the original texts. For a long time they were attributed to HUGUES DE ST. CHER (Huego de Sancto Caro), Provincial to the Dominicans in France, and afterwards a Cardinal in Spain, who died in 1263. But it is now generally believed that they were made by STEPHEN LANGTON, Archbishop of Canterbury, who died in 1227.

It follows therefore that our modern chapter divisions also are destitute of MS. authority.

5. As to verses. In the Hebrew O.T. these were fixed and counted for each book by the Massorites; but they are unknown in any MSS. of the Greek N.T. There are none in the first printed text in *The Complutensian Polyglot* (1437–1517), or in the first printed Greek text (Erasmus, in 1516), or in R. Stephens's first edition in 1550.

Verses were first introduced in Stephens's smaller (16mo) edition, published in 1551 at Geneva. These also are therefore destitute of any authority.

VI. THE PRINTED EDITIONS OF THE GREEK TEXT. Many printed editions followed the first efforts of ERASMUS. Omitting the Complutensian Polyglot mentioned above, the following is a list of all those of any importance:—

1.	Erasmus (1st Edition)	1516
2.	Stephens	1546–9
3.	Beza	1624
4.	Elzevir	1624
5.	Griesbach	1774–5
6.	Scholz	1830–6
7.	Lachmann	1831–50
8.	Tischendorf	1841–72
9.	Tregelles	1856–72
10.	Alford	1862–71
11.	Wordsworth	1870

[1] The examples given in the notes are from Deissmann's *Light from the Ancient East*, 1910; *New Light on the New Testament*, 1901; *Bible Studies*, 1901. Milligan's *Selections from the Greek Papyri*, &c. Cambridge Press, 1910.

[2] Ancient copies of the Septuagint reveal two other orders: that of *Diorthōtēs* (or Corrector) and the *Antiballōn* (or Comparer). But these attended chiefly to "clerical" and not textual errors.

[3] Of these, the Aramaic (or Syriac), i. e. the *Peshitto*, is the most important, ranking as superior in authority to the oldest Greek manuscripts, and dating from as early as A. D. 170.

Though the Syrian Church was divided by the Third and Fourth General Councils in the fifth century, into three, and eventually into yet more, hostile communions, which have lasted for 1,400 years with all their bitter controversies, yet the same version is read to-day in the rival churches. Their manuscripts have flowed into the libraries of the West, "*yet they all exhibit a text in every important respect the same.*" *Peshitto* means a version simple and plain, without the addition of allegorical or mystical glosses.

Hence we have given this authority, where needed throughout our notes, as being of more value than the modern critical Greek texts; and have noted (for the most part) only those "various readings" with which the Syriac agrees. See § VII, below.

[1] Such as are set forth in the *Rules for Compositors and Readers* at the University Press, Oxford.

[2] There are sixty-eight in Matthew; forty-eight in Mark; eighty-three in Luke; and eighteen in John.

12. Revisers' Text 1881
13. Westcott and Hort 1881-1903
14. Scrivener 1886
15. Weymouth 1886
16. Nestlé 1904

All the above are "Critical Texts", and each editor has striven to produce a text more accurate than that of his predecessors.

Beza (No. 3 above) and the Elzevir (No. 4) may be considered as being the so-called "Received Text" which the translators of the Authorized Version used in 1611.

VII. THE MODERN CRITICAL TEXTS. In the notes of *The Companion Bible* we have not troubled the general English reader with the names or distinctive characters or value of the several MANUSCRIPTS. We have thought it more practical and useful to give the combined judgment of six of the above editors; viz. Lachmann, Tischendorf, Tregelles, Alford, Westcott and Hort, and the Greek Text as adopted by the Revisers of the English N.T., 1881, noting the agreement or disagreement of the Syriac Version therewith. (See note 3, p. 136.)

A vast number of various readings are merely different spellings of words, or a varying order of two or more words. These are not noticed in *The Companion Bible*, as they do not affect the sense.

There are many more, consisting of cases of nouns and inflexions of verbs, &c., but these are noticed only when they are material to the interpretation. All are noted in cases where it really matters, but these are not numerous. A few are the subject of separate Appendixes. The number of these Appendixes may be found under the respective passages, such as Matt. 16. 18. Mark 16. 9-20. Acts 7. 17. Rom. 16. 25. 1 Pet. 3. 19. Rev. 1. 10.

The six critical Greek texts are indicated in the notes by their initial letters (see below). Where the reading is placed within brackets by the respective editors, the initial letter itself is also placed within brackets, and it is followed by "m" where the reading is placed in the margin.

It will thus be seen which of the above editors retain, insert, or omit a particular reading; and which of these expresses his doubts by placing it within brackets or in the margin.

To enable the reader to form his own judgment as to the value of any particular reading, it remains only to give a brief statement of the principles on which the respective editors [1] framed their texts.

GRIESBACH [1] based his text on the theory of Three Recensions of the Greek manuscripts, regarding the collective witness of each Recension as one; so that a Reading having the authority of all three was regarded by him as genuine. It is only a theory, but it has a foundation of truth, and will always retain a value peculiarly its own.

LACHMANN (L.), disregarding these Recensions, professed to give the text based only on the evidence of witnesses up to the end of the fourth century. All were taken into account up to that date; and all were discarded after it, whether uncial MSS., or cursives, or other documentary evidence. He even adopted Readings which were palpably errors, on the simple ground that they were the best attested Readings up to the fourth century.

TISCHENDORF (T.) followed more or less the principles laid down by Lachmann, but not to the neglect of other evidence as furnished by Ancient Versions and Fathers. In his eighth edition, however, he approaches nearer to Lachmann's principles.

TREGELLES (Tr.) produced his text on principles which were substantially the same as Lachmann, but he admits the evidence of uncial manuscripts down to the seventh century, and includes a careful testing of a wide circle of other authorities.

The chief value of his text lies not only in this, but in its scrupulous fidelity and accuracy; and it is probably the best and most exact presentation of the original text ever published.

ALFORD (A.) constructed his text, he says, "by following, in all ordinary cases, the united or preponderating evidence of the most ancient authorities."

When these disagree he takes later evidence into account, and to a very large extent.

Where this evidence is divided he endeavours to discover the cause of the variation, and gives great weight to *internal probability*; and, in some cases, relies on his own independent judgment.

At any rate he is fearlessly honest. He says, "that Reading has been adopted which, on the whole, seemed most likely to have stood in the original text. Such judgments are, of course, open to be questioned."

This necessarily deprives his text of much of its weight; though where he is in agreement with the other editors, it adds to the weight of the evidence as a whole.

WESTCOTT AND HORT (WH). In this text, the classification of MSS. into "families" is revived, with greater elaboration than that of Griesbach. It is prepared with the greatest care, and at present holds a place equal in estimation to that of Tregelles.

Where all these authorities agree, and are supported by the Syriac Version, the text may be regarded as fairly settled, until further MS. evidence is forthcoming.

But it must always be remembered that some *cursive* MSS. may be copies of uncial MSS. more ancient than any at present known. This fact will always lessen the value of the printed critical editions.

The Revisers of the N.T. of 1881 "did not deem it within their province to construct a continuous and complete Greek text." They adopted, however, a large number of readings which deviated from the text presumed to underlie the Authorized Version. In 1896 an edition known as the Parallel N. T. Greek and English, was published by the Clarendon Press for both Universities. In the Cambridge edition the *Textus Receptus* is given, with the Revisers' alternative readings, in the margin. In the Oxford edition, the Revisers give their Greek with the readings of the *Textus Receptus* in the margin.

[1] We include *Griesbach's* principles, though his edition is not included in the notes of *The Companion Bible.*

95 THE NEW TESTAMENT AND THE ORDER OF ITS BOOKS.

I. THE NEW TESTAMENT IN RELATION TO THE BIBLE AS A WHOLE.

The word "Testament", as a translation of the Greek word *diathēkē* (which means *covenant*), has been nothing less than a great calamity; for, by its use, truth has been effectually veiled all through the centuries; causing a wrong turning to be taken as to the purpose and character of this present Dispensation, by which the errors of tradition have usurped the place of important truth.

The word "Testament" as a name for a collection of books is unknown to Scripture. It comes to us through the Latin Vulgate. This was the rendering in the older Latin Versions before JEROME's time; but JEROME, while using *foedus* or *pactum* for the Heb. *b^erīth* in the O.T., unfortunately reverted to *testamentum* in his revision of his N.T. translation (A.D. 382–405). Some of the Latin Fathers preferred *instrumentum*, much in the sense of our legal use of the word [1]. RUFINUS uses the expression *novum et vetus instrumentum* [2], and AUGUSTINE uses both words *instrumentum* and *testamentum* [3].

[1] Tertullian (A.D. 150-200), *Adv. Marc.* iv. 1. In iv. 2, he uses it of a single gospel (Luke).
[2] *Expos. Symb. Apostol.*
[3] *De Civ. Dei*, xx. 4.

From the Vulgate, the word testament passed both into the English Bibles and the German. The Greek word is *diathēkē*, which means "covenant", and the R.V. substitutes this meaning in every place except two (Heb. 9. 16, 17, on which see the notes). But even this word was never used as the title for the collection of books which make up the New Testament so called.

When these books were placed beside the books of the Hebrew Canon it became desirable, if not necessary, to distinguish them; and, as the then two Dispensations were already spoken of in Scripture as "old" and "new" (2 Cor. 3. 6. Heb. 8. 6-13), so the books, which were connected with them, came to be called by the same names also.

In Ex. 24. 7 and 2 Kings 23. 2, 21, we read of "the book of the covenant"[1], and this distinction of the two covenants was already confirmed by 2 Cor. 3. 6, 14, where the Apostle speaks of "the reading of the old covenant".

The term "New Covenant" is indeed a Scriptural expression, but it is not used of a collection of books. It is used of the great prophecy and promise of Jer. 31. 31—32. 40 and Ezek. 37. 26 (which is referred to in Heb. 8. 8-12; 9. 15-21; 10. 15-18).

The time for the making of this "New Covenant" with the House of Israel and the House of Judah was drawing near. The last prophet, MALACHI, had spoken of the coming of the "Angel of the Covenant", and of the "Messenger" who was to prepare His way before Him (Mal. 3. 1). He announces also the sending of ELIJAH the prophet to prepare the way of MESSIAH, and connects his name with that of MOSES (Mal. 4. 4, 5).

In due time JOHN THE BAPTIST was sent "in the spirit and power of ELIJAH" (Luke 1. 17); and, had the people "received" him and obeyed his call to national repentance, he would have been counted for Elijah the prophet (Matt. 11. 14; 17. 11-13). In like manner we may well conclude that the act and word of MESSIAH at the last supper was the making of the New Covenant itself; for the Lord said of the cup "this is [i.e. represents] My blood of the New Covenant" (Matt. 26. 28. Mark 14. 24. Luke 22. 20), thus fulfilling the prophecy of Jer. 31. 31-34, as testified by Heb. 8. 8-12; 9. 15-21; 10. 15-18.

The use of blood was confined to two purposes:—

(1) Atonement for sin (Lev. 17. 11. Heb. 9. 22),[2] and (2) the making of a covenant (Ex. 24. 6-8. Heb. 9. 16-22).

The use of the Greek word *diathēkē* (covenant) in relation to a collection of books is appropriate only so far as these books are regarded as belonging to the "new covenant" foretold by Jeremiah, and as being distinct from "the book of the (old) covenant", made in Ex. 24. 6-8.

The one great fact, which stands out in connection with the whole of the books which we call the Bible, is that they form the "Word of God", and are made up of the "words" of God (Jer. 15. 16. John 17. 8, 14, 17).

This is the claim that is made by the book itself, and it is ours to receive it as such. We, therefore, neither set out to discuss it, nor to prove it. "God hath spoken"; and this, for our learning, and not for our reasoning; for our faith, and not for our questioning; still less for our criticism: for the Word which He hath spoken is to be our judge in that day (John 12. 48, Deut. 18. 19, 20, and Heb. 4. 12, where it is declared to be "able to judge" (A.V. "a discerner", Gr. *kritikos*; hence our "critic")). See further, Ap. 94.

Thousands of infidels to-day believe and teach that the Council of Nice, held in A.D. 325, separated the "spurious" scriptures from the genuine ones, by some vote, or trick, when the sacred books were placed under a communion table, and, after prayer, the inspired books jumped upon the table, while the false books remained beneath.

This story originated with one "John Pappus", and infidels make a great mistake in identifying him with "Papias", or "Pappius", one of the earliest Fathers, called by Eusebius (iii. 36) a "Bishop" of Hierapolis, who wrote about A.D. 115. The *Encycl. Brit.*, 11th (Camb.) ed., vol. xx, p. 737, suggests about A.D. 60-135 as the period of his life.

But John Pappus, who gave currency to the above story, was a German theologian born in 1549. In 1601 he published the text of an *Anonymous* Greek MS. This MS. cannot be older than A.D. 870, because it mentions events occurring in 869. Now the Council of Nice was held 544 years before, and all its members had been dead and buried for some five centuries. The Council of Nice was not called to decide the Canon. Nothing relating to the Canon of Scripture can be found in any of its canons or acts. And, even if it were otherwise, the votes of Councils could no more settle the Canon of the New Testament than a Town Council could settle the laws of a nation.

The great outstanding fact is that

"JEHOVAH HATH SPOKEN",

and that the Bible as a whole claims to give us His words; for speaking or writing cannot be without *words*. Moreover, He tells us (Heb. 1. 1) that He has spoken

"AT SUNDRY TIMES AND IN DIVERS MANNERS",

or, according to the Greek, in many parts (or portions) and by many ways (or methods).

If we rightly divide these (according to 2 Tim. 2. 15) we have

THE CONTENTS OF THE BIBLE AS A WHOLE,

which may be exhibited as follows[1]:—

A1 | DIVINE. By the FATHER Himself. The "times" being from Gen. 2. 16 to Ex. 3. 10. The "manner" being to individuals from Adam onward.

B1 | HUMAN AGENCY. "By the Prophets.". The "time" being from the call and mission of Moses (Ex. 3. 10) to that of John the Baptist, "greater than them all" (Matt. 11. 11). The "manner" was by human agency.

A2 | DIVINE. "By HIS SON" (Heb. 1. 1, 2. Cp. Deut. 18. 18, 19). The "time" being from the beginning of His ministry (Matt. 4. 12) to the end of it (Matt. 26. 46). See Ap. 119.

B2 | HUMAN AGENCY. "By them that heard HIM", ("the Son", Heb. 2. 3, 4). The "time" from Acts 1—28. The "manner" was by apostolic testimony and writings, contained in the General Epistles; and in the earlier Pauline Epistles written during that "time".

A3 | DIVINE. By "THE SPIRIT OF TRUTH" (as promised in John 16. 12-15). The "time" from the end of the Dispensation covered by the Acts of the Apostles, when He revealed "the things concerning Christ"; which could not be spoken by Him until the events had taken place, which were the foundation of the doctrines revealed in the later Pauline Epistles (Eph., Phil., Col.). See esp. Eph. 2. 4-7.[2] In these Epistles the Holy Spirit "guided" into all the truth, and thus fulfilled the promise of the Lord, in John 16. 12-15.

B3 | HUMAN AND ANGELIC AGENCY. By "HIS SERVANT JOHN", who bare record of the Word of God, and of all things that he saw (Rev. 1. 1, 2). The "time" was that covered by the giving the Book of the Revelation in Patmos. The "manner" was that it was "sent and signified (showed by signs) by His angel[3]."

---

[1] See also 1 Macc. 1. 57 and Ecclus. 24. 23.

[2] "*Washing* in blood" would defile, not cleanse. *Sprinkling* with blood, and *washing* in water, alone known to the O.T. (save in Ps. 58. 10). As to Rev. 1. 5 and 7. 14, see notes there.

[1] While the divisions shown in the Structure are true as a whole, it is not denied that there may be exceptions to the general rule; but these only go to establish the truth of the rule itself.

[2] The other later Epistles of Paul were written to *individuals*, and to a special class of Hebrew believers.

[3] Not by "the Spirit of Truth". His mission, in A3, was to guide into the truth, while, in the Acts of the Apostles (B2), it was to bear witness by miracles to the *confirmation* of them that heard the Son. In the Apocalypse it was not Divine speaking by "the Spirit of Truth", but the showing by an Hierophant.

Since this written Word—"the Scripture of Truth"—was thus complete, God has not spoken directly or indirectly to mankind, either by Himself or by human agency. "The Silence of God" during this Dispensation is a solemn reality.

But He is going to speak again when this Dispensation comes to a close, and in Psalm 50 we are told what He is going to say when the silence is broken.

According to the division of the "times" exhibited above (p. 138), it will be seen that they are *six* in number (the number of "man", Ap. 10). And it will be noted that the order of the Divine three is FATHER (A^1), SON (A^2), and HOLY SPIRIT (A^3).

When the "time" comes for Him to speak "once again", it will be apart from human agency. This will make these "times and manners" *seven* in all (the number of spiritual perfection, Ap. 10).

Until, therefore, God shall speak once more, we have God's word—written. To this we are now shut up; to this we do well "to take heed in our hearts" (2 Pet. 1. 19). We may not add to or take away from it (Rev. 22. 18, 19). We may not receive any other writing purporting to have come from God. There are many such in the present day; some of the authors being bold impostors and deceivers[1], others being deceived by "automatic" writings through demons and evil spirits (1 Tim. 4. 1-3).

To all such we are to say "Anathema", and to treat them as accursed things (Gal. 1. 6-9).

II. THE ORDER OF THE BOOKS OF THE NEW "TESTAMENT".

Our English Bibles follow the order as given in the Latin Vulgate. This order, therefore, depends on the arbitrary judgment of one man, Jerome (A.D. 382-405). All theories based on this order rest on human authority, and are thus without any true foundation.

The original Greek manuscripts do not agree among themselves as to any particular order of the separate books, and a few of them have most remarkable differences.

We are, however, on safe ground in stating that the books are generally divided into

FIVE WELL-DEFINED GROUPS.

For the most part these groups are in the following order:—

1. The Four Gospels.
2. The Acts of the Apostles.
3. The General Epistles[2].
4. The Pauline Epistles[3].
5. The Apocalypse.

Even the order of these five groups varies in very few cases.[4] But these are so exceptional as not to affect the general order as given above; indeed, they help to confirm it.

While the order of these five groups may be regarded as fairly established, yet, within each, the order of the separate books is by no means uniform, except in the fourth, which never varies[4]. (See notes on the chronological and canonical orders of the Pauline Epistles, preliminary to the Structure of ROMANS, as a whole.)

Even in the first group, while the Four Gospels are almost always the same as we have them in the A.V. and R.V., yet in the *Codex Bezae* (Cent. 6) John follows Matthew; and in another, precedes it.

When we divide the Pauline Epistles (Group 4 above), and re-combine them in their chronological and historical order, we find that they re-arrange themselves so as to be distributed between the fourth and sixth of the six groups shown above on p. 138.[5]

The five groups of the New Testament order of books (shown above) thus fall into four chronological groups, being the same as the last four of the whole Bible, corresponding with A^2, B^2, A^3, and B^3 (p. 138):—

C | THE FOUR GOSPELS: where the SON is the Divine Speaker, according to Heb. 1. 2-.

D | THE ACTS OF THE APOSTLES, THE GENERAL EPISTLES, THE EARLIER PAULINE EPISTLES: } Where human agency is employed in "them that heard" the Son (Heb. 2. 3, 4), and Paul also, who both heard and saw Him.

C | THE LATER PAULINE EPISTLES:— EPHESIANS, PHILIPPIANS, COLOSSIANS: } Where "the Spirit of Truth" is the Divine Speaker, Teacher, and Guide, according to John 16. 12-15.

D | THE APOCALYPSE: where human agency is again employed in the person of John the Apostle and Evangelist, instructed by angelic agency.

From these four groups we may gather the one great scope of the New Testament books as a whole.

Corresponding with the above we may set them out as follows:—

C | The KING and the KINGDOM. Proclaimed to the Nation in the LAND. The Kingdom rejected and the King crucified in JERUSALEM, the capital.

D | The re-offer of both (Acts 2. 38; 3. 19-26) to the Dispersion among the Gentiles; and their final rejection in ROME, the capital of the Dispersion (Acts 28. 16-28).

C | The KING exalted, and made the Head over all things for the Church, which is His Body (Eph. 1. 20-23. Phil. 2. 9-11. Col. 1. 13-19), in the Kingdom of His beloved Son (Col. 1. 13). The mystery revealed (Eph. 3. 1-12. Col. 1. 24-29). The Kingdom on earth in abeyance. "Not yet" (Heb. 2. 8).

D | The KINGDOM set up in judgment, power, and glory. The King enthroned. Set forth as the great subject of the Apocalypse.

[1] Such as Swedenborg, Joanna Southcote, Joe Smith (of Mormonite fame), the author of "The Flying Roll", Mrs. Eddy, Dowie, and others.
[2] James usually coming first, following next after the Acts of the Apostles.
[3] Invariably in their present canonical order, as given in the A.V.
[4] For example: the fourth follows the second; the second and fourth are followed by the first; and in one case the fifth comes between the second and third.
[5] Except that, in the best and oldest Codices, Hebrews follows 2 Thess. (instead of Philemon); while in one (that from which Cod. B was taken) Hebrews follows Galatians.

96 THE DIVERSITY OF THE FOUR GOSPELS.

We have already seen from the Structure on p. 1304, and notes there, that each of the Four Gospels has its own special character and design.

These are not to be determined by human ingenuity or on modern lines, but to be gathered from the Structure.

This shows that they may be regarded as being the completion of the Old Testament, rather than the beginning of the New. In any case they have nothing whatever to do with the founding of "the Church", or with the beginning of "Christianity" (see Ap. 113, notes on the Structure of the Acts as a whole, and Rom. 15. 8).

They are four distinct presentations of the Messiah, and together form one perfect whole.

The twofold subject of the Lord's fourfold ministry (Ap. 119) shows this very clearly; and excludes all modern hypotheses.

This being so, only those events, miracles, and discourses of our Lord are selected which are needed for the presentation of our Lord and His ministry, and which bear upon, illustrate, and thus emphasize the special object of each Gospel.

This is why certain words and works are peculiar to one Gospel, and are omitted from another; and why certain utterances of the Lord are *repeated* on other occasions, and with varying words. Also why we have "the kingdom of heaven" only in Matthew, and "the kingdom of God" in the other Gospels (see Ap. 114).

It has been too generally assumed that events and discourses which are *similar* are *identical* also. But this is not the case, as may be seen from Ap. 116, 152, 153, 155, 156, 157, 158, 163, 164.

By failing to distinguish or to "try the things that differ" (Phil. 1. 10), and to rightly divide "the word of truth" (2 Tim. 2. 15) as to its *times*, events separated by great landmarks of time are brought together and treated as though they were one and the same, whereby difficulties are created which baffle all the attempts of those who would fain remove them.

The special object of each of the Four Gospels may be seen from the Structure on p. 1304.

97 THE UNITY OF THE FOUR GOSPELS.

In the notes on pp. 1304 and 1305, and in Ap. 96, we have shown that there is a Diversity in the Four Gospels. But there is a Unity also, as is shown by the fact that all Four Gospels follow the same general Structure. This runs through them all alike, showing that, after all, the presentation of the Lord is one[1].

While it was not in God's purpose to give us one Gospel, yet amid all the diversity of the parts there is a continuity of the whole.

The parts are distributed according as they are appropriate to the special design and character of each Gospel, and this in perfect order and accuracy.

After what has been said in Ap. 96, and in the notes to the Structure on p. 1304, it would be out of place to attempt to present anything like a complete "Harmony"; but, in order to show how needless it is to dislocate certain passages in order to bring together *similar* events and discourses (supposed to be *identical*, as though nothing the Lord said or did was ever repeated), a condensed outline is presented.

It will be noted that there are great events which were *never repeated*: such as the Mission of the Twelve, the Transfiguration, the Dividing of the Garments, &c. These help us in determining the order and place of other events which, though *similar*, are *not identical*.

From the outline given below it will be easy to see how the several accounts of similar events and discourses are distributed in the several Gospels, without violently altering the sequence of verses and chapters, as is done in most so-called "Harmonies".

	MATTHEW.	MARK.	LUKE.	JOHN.
PRE-MINISTERIAL ...	...	...	...	1. 1-5.
	...	...	...	1. 6-14.
	...	...	1. 1—2. 7.	
	1. 1-25.			
	2. 1.			
	...	...	2. 8-20.	
	...	...	2. 21.	
	...	...	2. 22-39.	
	2. 2-23	...	2. 40.	
	...	...	2. 41-52.	
THE FORERUNNER...	3. 1-12 ...	1. 2-8	3. 1-20	1. 15-28.
THE BAPTISM ...	3. 13-17 ...	1. 9-11	3. 21, 22 ...	1. 29-34.
			3. 23-38.	
THE TEMPTATION ...	4. 1, 2 ...	1. 12, 13-	4. 1, 2.	
			4. 3-13.	
	4. 3-11-			
	4. -11 ...	1. -13.		
THE MINISTRY (FIRST PERIOD)				1. 35-51.
	4. 12-17 ...	1. 14, 15.		
	...	...	4. 14, 15.	
	...	...	4. 16-32.	
	4. 18-22 ...	1. 16-20.		
	...	...	...	2. 1—4. 54.
	4. 23—7. 29.			

[1] But note that in the Structure of John there is no "Temptation" and no "Agony".

	MATTHEW.	MARK.	LUKE.	JOHN.
THE MINISTRY (SECOND PERIOD) ...	8.1.			
	... ...	1.21-.		
	8.2-13.			
	... ...	1.-21-28	4.33-37.	
	8.14-17	1.29-34	4.38-41.	
	... ...	1.35-39	4.42-44.	
	... ...	... ...	5.1-11.	
	... ...	1.40-45	5.12-16.	
	8.18—9.1.			
	9.2-26	2.1-12	5.17-26.	
	9.27—11.30.			
	... ...	... ...	... ...	5.1-47 ("after this").
	12.1-21 ("at that time") ...	2.23—3.6 ...	6.1-11.	
	... ...	3.7-21.		
	... ...	... ...	6.12—8.18.	
	12.22-45 ...	3.22-30.		
	12.46-50 ...	3.31-35 ...	8.19-21.	
	13.1-52 ...	4.1-34.		
	... ...	4.35—5.20 ...	8.22-39.	
	... ...	5.21-43 ...	8.40-56.	
	13.53-58 ...	6.1-6.		
	... ...	6.7-13 ...	9.1-6.	
	14.1-14 ("at that time") ...	6.14-29 ...	9.7-9. ...	6.1, 2.
	14.15-22 ...	6.30-46 ...	9.10-17 ...	6.3-15.
	14.23-36 ...	6.47-56 ...	... ...	6.16-21.
	... ...	... ...	... ...	6.22-71.
	15.1—16.12 ...	7.1—8.21.		
	... ...	8.22-26.		
	16.13-20 ...	8.27-30 ...	9.18-21.	
THE MINISTRY (THIRD PERIOD) ...	16.21—18.9 ...	8.31—9.50 ...	9.22-50.	
	18.10-35.			
	19.1- ...	10.1- ...	9.51-56 ...	7.1-10.
	19.-1, 2 ...	10.-1 ...	9.57-62.	
	... ...	... ...	10.1-42.	
	... ...	... ...	... ...	7.11-13.
	... ...	... ...	... ...	7.14—10.21.
	... ...	... ...	11.1-28.	
	19.3-12 ...	10.2-12 ...	11.29—13.22.	
	... ...	... ...	... ...	10.22-42.
	... ...	... ...	13.23-30.	
	... ...	... ...	13.31-35.	
	... ...	... ...	14.1-24.	
	... ...	... ...	14.25-35.	
	... ...	... ...	15.1—18.14.	
	... ...	... ...	... ...	11.1-16 ("then").
	... ...	... ...	... ...	11.17-54 ("after that").
	19.13-20 ...	10.13-34 ...	18.15-34.	
	20.20-28 ...	10.35-45.		
	... ...	... ...	18.35-43.	
	... ...	10.46-52.		
	20.29-34.			
	... ...	... ...	19.1-28.	

[For the Fourth Period of the Lord's Ministry and subsequent events, see Appendix 156.
For the sequence of events after the resurrection of the Lord, see Appendix 166.]

98 THE DIVINE NAMES AND TITLES IN THE NEW TESTAMENT.

All names and titles used of one Person represent the different *relationships* which are sustained by Him.

In the New Testament these are more varied, and not less important than those in the Old Testament; and Ap. 4 should be compared with this Appendix.

The following exhibition of them practically embraces all that is necessary to enable the English reader to understand them, and to grasp something of the perfection with which each is used.

The list of the Names, &c., is given according to the common English rendering of the A.V., as being more easy for reference. It does not include "Spirit" or "Holy Spirit": for which see the separate Appendix, No. 101.

Reference is made, in the notes, to the following divisions and subdivisions :—

I. GOD.

GOD. Gr. *Theos*. The Greek language, being of human origin, utterly fails (and naturally so) to exhibit the wonderful precision of the Hebrew, inasmuch as the language necessarily reflects, and cannot go beyond the knowledge, or rather the lack of knowledge, of the Divine Being apart from revelation.

i. ***Theos*** corresponds, generally, with *'Elohīm* of the O.T., denoting the Creator (see Ap. 4. I); but it corresponds also with *Ēl* (Ap. 4. IV), and *Eloah* (Ap. 4. V). Sometimes it corresponds with *Jehovah* (who is *'Elohīm* in Covenant relation), in which case it is printed GOD, as in the Old Testament (both A.V. and R.V.).

1. *Theos* is used in the N.T. of the Father, as the revealed God (see John 1. 1. Acts 17. 24, &c.).
2. It is used of the Son (Matt. 1. 23. John 1. 1; 20. 28, &c. Rom. 9. 5. 2 Pet. 1. 1. 1 John 5. 20). Cp. Col. 2. 9 and 2 Pet. 1. 3, 4.
3. It is used of the Holy Spirit (Acts 5 *v.* 3, compared with *v.* 4).
4. It is used generically, as in John 10. 34. Acts 12. 22. 2 Cor. 4. 4. Phil. 3. 19, &c.
5. It is used of false gods, as in Acts 7. 43, &c.; and is printed "god" as in the O.T.

ii. Cognate with *Theos*, there are three other words to be noted:

1. *Theotēs*, rendered "Deity", and used of Christ. Occurs only in Col. 2. 9, and has relation to the Godhead *personally*; while
2. *Theiotēs*, rendered "Deity" also, is Deity in the *abstract*. Occurs only in Rom. 1. 20.
3. *Theios*, rendered "Divine", and is used of Christ. Occurs only in 2 Pet. 1. 3, 4; and, with the Article, in Acts 17. 29, where it is rendered "Godhead". Gr.=that which [is] Divine.

II. I AM.

Used by Christ of Himself, in John 8. 58. See note on Ex. 3. 14.

III. FATHER.

FATHER. Gr. *Patēr*. Expresses relationship, the correlative of which is "son". When used of man it not only denotes parentage, but it sometimes has the wider meaning of "ancestor", "founder", or a "senior" (as in 1 John 2. 13, 14); also the author or source of anything (John 8. 44. Heb. 12. 9); and expresses a spiritual relationship, as in 1 Cor. 4. 15.

When used of God it denotes His relationship to His "beloved Son"; and to those ("sons") who have been *begotten* (not "born", see note on Matt. 1. 1) into a new creation.

It implies "sons", not "offspring", as in Acts 17. 28, 29. These were "offspring", and were existing (Gr. *huparchō*), as such, according to nature, on the ground of *creation*; not "sons" as being "begotten" into a new creation.

IV. ALMIGHTY.

ALMIGHTY. Gr. *Pantokratōr*. This title belongs to the same God, as Creator, but expresses His relationship to all He has created, by the exercise of His power over "all the works of His hands". It occurs only in 2 Cor. 6. 18. Rev. 1. 8; 4. 8; 11. 17; 15. 3; 16. 7, 14; 19. 6, 15; 21. 22.

V. POTENTATE.

POTENTATE. Gr. *Dunastēs* = a mighty Prince, or Ruler (cp. Engl. "dynasty"). Used of God, only in 1 Tim. 6. 15. Elsewhere used, only twice, of earthly rulers, in Luke 1. 52 (generally), and of the Ethiopian eunuch in Acts 8. 27.

VI. LORD.

This is the rendering of two Greek words: i. *Kurios*, and ii. *Despotēs*; and one Aramaic, iii. *Rabboni*.

i. ***Kurios***. Kurios means "owner" (and is so translated in Luke 19. 33). It expresses the authority and lordship arising from and pertaining to *ownership*. Hence, while it is used of each Person of the Trinity, it is similarly used of the lower and human relationship of "master". Cp. Luke 19. 33 and see below *a*. 4.

So much depends on the presence or absence of the Greek Article, when used of the Divine relationship, that these are carefully distinguished in the subdivisions below.

For obvious reasons the four Gospels have been treated, below, apart from the other books of the N.T.

a. In the Four Gospels.

1. Used of Jehovah (Ap. 4. II), and printed "LORD" throughout.

A. With the Article (*ho Kurios*).

a. In quotations from the O.T. it occurs four[1] times: in Matt. 1. 22; 2. 15; 5. 33; 22. 44-.

b. In other connexions it occurs fourteen times: once in Matt. (9. 38); once in Mark (5. 19); twelve times in Luke (1. 6, 9, 15, 25, 28, 46; 2. 15, 22, -23, 38; 10. 2; 20. 42-).

B. Without the Article (*Kurios*).

a. In quotations from the O.T. it occurs twenty-nine times: eight times in Matt. (3. 3; 4. 7, 10; 21. 9, 42; 22. 37; 23. 39; 27. 10); eight times in Mark (1. 3; 11. 9, 10; 12. 11, 29, 29, 30, 36-); nine times in Luke (3. 4; 4. 8, 12, 18, 19; 10. 27; 13. 35; 19. 38; 20. 37); four times in John (1. 23; 12. 13, 38, 38).

b. In other connexions twenty-four times: six times in Matt. (1. 20, 24; 2. 13, 19; 11. 25; 28. 2); once in Mark (13. 20); seventeen times in Luke (1. 11, 16, 17, 32, 38, 45, 48, 66, 68, 76; 2. 9, 23-, 24, 26, 39; 5. 17; 10. 21).

2. Used by Christ of Himself.

A. With the Article (*ho Kurios*).

a. In direct reference: six times (Matt. 21. 3; 24. 42; Mark 11. 3; Luke 19. 31; John 13. 13, 14).

b. In indirect reference: twice (Matt. 22. -44; Luke 20. -42).

B. Without the Article (*Kurios*).

a. In direct reference: eleven times (Matt. 7. 21, 21, 22, 22; 12. 8; 25. 37, 44; Mark 2. 28; Luke 6. 5, 46, 46).

b. In indirect reference: four times (Matt. 22. 43, 45; Mark 12. 37; Luke 20. 44).

3. Used of Christ by others.

A. By His disciples: fifty-nine times (Matt. 8. 21, 25; 13. 51; 14. 28, 30; 16. 22; 17. 4; 18. 21; 26. 22; [not one in Mark[2]] Luke 1. 43; 5. 8; 9. 54, 57, 59, 61; 10. 17, 40; 11. 1; 12. 41; 13. 23; 17. 37; 19. 8, 34; 22. 31, 33, 38, 49; 23. 42; 24. 34; John 6. 68; 9. 36, 38; 11. 3, 12, 21, 27, 32, 34, 39; 13. 6, 9, 25, 36, 37; 14. 5, 8, 22; 20. 2, 13, 18, 20, 25, 28; 21. 7, 15, 16, 17, 20, 21).

B. By others than His disciples.

a. Rendered "Lord" eighteen times: twelve in Matt. (8. 2, 6, 8; 9. 28; 15. 22, 25, 27-; 17. 15; 20. 30, 31, 33; 28. 6); only twice in Mark[3] (7. 28; 9. 24); four times in Luke (2. 11; 5. 12; 7. 6; 18. 41); twice in John (6. 34; 8. 11).

b. Rendered "Sir" six times: John 4. 11, 15, 19, 49; 5. 7; 20. 15 (Mary, addressing the supposed gardener).

c. By the Holy Spirit frequently in the narratives of the Evangelists.

---

[1] These numbers refer to the Received Greek Text. In some cases there are various readings, but in most of them the difference consists in the omission of the article. Any important variations are referred to in the notes.

[2] Because, in Mark, the presentation of the Lord is as "Jehovah's Servant"; and a servant is not usually addressed as Lord. See notes on p. 1381. This is not a *peculiarity* of Mark, but shows the *accuracy* and *perfection* of this presentation by the Holy Spirit.

[3] Once by a Gentile, the other being omitted by the Critical texts (though not by the Syr.).

4. Used of others than Christ.

A. With the Article (*ho Kurios*), emphasizing ownership. Occurs forty-two times: twenty-one times in Matt. (10. 24, 25; 15. -27; 18. 25, 27, 31, 32, 34; 20. 8; 21. 40; 24. 45, 46, 48, 50; 25. 18, 19, 21, 21, 23, 23, 26); twice in Mark (12. 9; 13. 35); sixteen times in Luke (12. 36, 37, -42, 43, 45, 46, 47; 14. 21, 23; 16. 3, 5, 5, 8; 19. 33; 20. 13, 15); three times in John (13. 16; 15. 15, 20).

B. Without the Article (*Kurios*). Generally in courtesy, emphasizing superior relationship. Occ. nineteen times. Rendered "Lord" fourteen times (Matt. 18. 26; 25. 11, 11, 20, 22, 24. Luke 13. 8, 25, 25; 14. 22; 19. 16, 18, 20, 25); "Master" twice (Matt. 6. 24. Luke 16. 13); "Sir" four times (Matt. 13. 27; 21. 30; 27. 63. John 12. 21).

β. In the other books of the New Testament.

1. Used of Jehovah (Ap. 4. II), and printed "LORD" throughout; as in the O.T.

A. With the Article (*ho Kurios*).

a. In quotations from the O.T. Occurs ten times (Acts 2. 25, 34; 4. 26; 7. 33; 13. 47; 15. 17. Rom. 15. 11. 1 Cor. 10. 26, 28. Heb. 8. 11).

b. In other connexions: Acts 2. 47. 2 Cor. 10. 18. Heb. 8. 2; 12. 14. James 5. -11. 2 Pet. 3. 9, 15. Jude 5. Rev. 11. 15, 21, 22.

B. Without the Article (*Kurios*).

a. In quotations from, or references to, the O.T.: Acts 2. 20, 21; 3. 22; 7. 30, 31, 37, 49. Rom. 4. 8; 9. 28, 29; 10. 13, 16; 11. 3, 34; 12. 19; 14. 11. 1 Cor. 1. 31; 2. 16; 3. 20; 14. 21. 2 Cor. 6. 17, 18; 10. 17. Heb. 1. 10; 7. 21; 8. 8, 9, 10; 10. 16, 30, 30; 12. 5, 6; 13. 6. 1 Pet. 1. 25; 3. 12, 12.

b. In other connexions: Acts 1. 24; 2. 39; 5. 9, 19; 17. 24. 2 Cor. 3. 16. James 5. 4, 10, 11-. 2 Pet. 2. 9, 11; 3. 8, 10. Jude 9, 14. Rev. 4. 8; 11. 17; 15. 3, 4; 16. 5, 7; 18. 8; 19. 1, 6; 22. 5, 6.

2. Used of Christ.

A. With the Article, as in Acts 2. -34. 2 Cor. 3. 17-, &c.

B. Without the Article, as in 1 Cor. 8. 6, &c.

ii. ***Despotēs.*** Like *Kurios* (i, above) it denotes owner; but it includes (when used of God) the exercise of more absolute, unlimited and despotic authority and power in heaven and on earth. It is derived from *deō* = to bind, and *pous* = the foot. It occurs ten times in the New Testament, and is rendered five times "Lord"; and five times "Master" (see No. XIV. 2, below).

1. Used of Jehovah (Ap. 4. II) three times (Luke 2. 29. Acts 4. 24. Rev. 6. 10).

2. Used of Christ, twice (2 Pet. 2. 1. Jude 4).

iii. ***Rabboni.*** Aramaic for the Heb. Rabbi = my Master, or Teacher. See Ap. 94. III. 3. Occurs twice, once translated "Lord" (Mark 10. 51); and once transliterated "Rabboni" (John 20. 16).

VII. EMMANUEL.

EMMANUEL. Heb. *'Immānūēl* = God (*Ēl*) with us (Isa. 7. 14; 8. 8). Used of Christ, Matt. 1. 23, being another proof of His Deity (see No. VI. i. *a*. 2. A. a. b.).

VIII. MESSIAH.

This is the Greek transliteration of the Heb. *Māshīaḥ*, with the same meaning, Anointed. Used twice of Christ (John 1. 41; 4. 25).

IX. CHRIST.

This is the Greek translation of the Heb. *Māshīaḥ*. See No. VIII. *Christos* has the same meaning, from *chriō*, to anoint. Hence, the Noun is used of and for the Messiah, and in the Gospels should always be translated "Messiah", as well as in the Acts, and sometimes in the later books of the New Testament.

X. JESUS.

Iēsous is the same as the Heb. Jehoshua, or the abbreviated form Joshua (cp. Heb. 4. 8), and means [the] Salvation of Jehovah, or Jehovah [the] Saviour.

The name "Jesus" expresses the *relation* of Jehovah to Him in Incarnation, by which "He humbled Himself, and became obedient unto death, even the death of the cross" (Phil. 2. 8); Who, being God, did not deem His glory a thing not to be thus relinquished (see note on "robbery", Phil. 2. 6). The name "Jesus" is the name associated with "the shame" which He endured in order to "save His People from their sins" (Matt. 1. 21). His People therefore never addressed Him as "Jesus", but always as "Master" (No. XIV. v) or "Lord" (VI. i. *a*. 3). (John 13. 13, 14. Luke 6. 46), and so should all His people to-day; not following the example of demons (Matt. 8. 29), or of His enemies, who irreverently called Him "Jesus".

XI. JESUS CHRIST.

In the combination of these two names, the former is emphatic by its position, the second being subsidiary and explanatory. In the Gospels it means "Jesus the Messiah". In the Epistles it means Jesus Who humbled Himself but is now exalted and glorified as Christ. Care should be taken to note the various readings.

XII. CHRIST JESUS.

This is the converse of "Jesus Christ" (XI) and denotes the now exalted One, Who once humbled Himself.

XIII. CHRIST THE LORD.

This is the Heb. *Māshīaḥ Jehovah* = Jehovah's Anointed, as in 1 Sam. 24. 6. Occ. only in Luke 2. 11; and with the Article = the Anointed of Jehovah, Luke 2. 26.

XIV. MASTER.

This title is the translation of eight distinct Greek words, which are all carefully distinguished in the notes.

i. ***Kurios*** (the same as No. VI. i. *a*. 2, 3, above). Is used of the Lord in Mark 13. 35. Eph. 6. 9, and Col. 4. 1. Used of others (Matt. 6. 24. Luke 16. 13). See VI. i. *a*. 4. B., above.

ii. ***Despotēs***, see No. VI. ii, above. It occurs ten times, and is rendered five times "Lord" (see VI. ii); and five times "Master", once of the Divine Master (2 Tim. 2. 21); and four times of human masters.

iii. ***Oikodespotēs*** = master of a house; house-master. It occurs twelve times, and is used in Parables by the Lord of Himself seven times, and of others thrice: it is rendered four times "householder"; five times "goodman of the house"; and three times "master" (Matt. 10. 25. Luke 13. 25; 14. 21). Twice it is used of others than Christ (Mark 14. 14. Luke 22. 11).

iv. ***Epistatēs*** = Commander. Occurs five times as addressed to the Lord (Luke 5. 5; 8. 24, 24, 45; 9. 33, 49; 17. 13).

v. ***Didaskalos*** = Teacher. or as we should say "Doctor". Occurs fifty-eight times, and is twice explained as meaning "Rabbi". See No. vii, p. 144.

1. The Lord was addressed as *Didaskalos* (= Teacher), rendered "Master" thirty-one times; six times in

Matthew (8. 19; 12. 38; 19. 16; 22. 16, 24, 36); ten times in Mark (4. 38; 9. 17, 38; 10. 17, 20, 35; 12. 14, 19, 32; 13. 1); twelve times in Luke (3. 12; 7. 40; 9. 38; 10. 25; 11. 45; 12. 13; 18. 18; 19. 39; 20. 21, 28, 39; 21. 7); three times in John (1. 39; 8. 4; 20. 16).

2. The Lord spoken of as "Master" by Himself eight times: three times in Matthew (10. 24, 25; 26. 18); once in Mark (14. 14); thrice in Luke (6. 40, 40; 22. 11); once in John (13. 14).

3. The Lord spoken of as "Master" by others than Himself six times: twice in Matthew (9. 11; 17. 24); once in Mark (5. 35); once in Luke (8. 49); twice in John (11. 28; 13. 13).

4. Spoken of others than the Lord twice, and rendered "master" in John 3. 10. Jas. 3. 1. In other renderings once "doctor" (Luke 2. 46), and ten times "teacher", once of the Lord (John 3. 2), and nine times of human teachers (Acts 13. 1. Rom. 2. 20. 1 Cor. 12. 28, 29. Eph. 4. 11. 1 Tim. 2. 7. 2 Tim. 1. 11; 4. 3. Heb. 5. 12).

vi. ***Kathegētes***=A Guide or Leader. Used of the Lord by Himself three times (Matt. 23. 8, 10, 10).

vii. ***Rabbi.*** The Hebrew term for "my Teacher", transliterated into Greek. Twice explained as meaning the same as the Gr. *Didaskalos* (see XIV. v, p. 143). Occurs seventeen times, and used as follows:

1. The Lord addressed as "Rabbi" five times (John 1. 39, 49; 3. 2, 26; 6. 25). Rendered "Master" nine times (Matt. 26. 25, 49. Mark 9. 5; 11. 21; 14. 45, 45. John 4. 31; 9. 2; 11. 8).

2. Used of others than the Lord four times (Matt. 23. 7, 7, 8. John 3. 26).

viii. ***Rabboni.*** Aramaic for Rabbi (see Ap. 94. III. 38). Occurs twice, once transliterated (John 20. 16); and once translated "Lord" (Mark 10. 51).

XV. THE SON OF GOD.

This title expresses the relation of the Son to the Father (Matt. 1. 20. Luke 1. 31, 35); and of all those who are begotten of God (see note on Matt. 1. 1. 1 John 3. 1).

It differs therefore from the relationship expressed by "the Son of man", which relates to "dominion" in the earth (see XVI, below).

As the Son of God, Christ is "the heir of all things" (Heb. 1. 2), and is invested with "all power", and is "the Resurrection and the Life" (John 11. 25), having power to raise the dead (John 5. 25). As "the Son of man", all judgment is committed to Him (John 5. 27) in the earth. See on No. XVI, below.

XVI. THE SON OF MAN.

This title, when used of Christ, always has the Article; and the word for man is *anthrōpos* (see Ap. 123. I).

When used of a human being, as in Ezekiel, it never has the Article (see notes on Ps. 8. 4, and Ezek. 2. 1).

To the "first man, Adam" was given dominion over the works of the Creator (Gen. 1. 26). Through the Fall (Gen. 3), this dominion was forfeited, and lost, and is now in abeyance; no one son of Adam having any right to universal dominion. Hence, all the chaos, "unrest", and conflicts between men and nations, which must continue until He shall come Whose right it is to rule in the earth (Ezek. 21. 27). The great enemy, who wrought all the mischief at the Fall, has tried, from time to time, to exercise this authority by setting up some human head. He tried Nebuchadnezzar, Alexander the Great, and others, and in later days Napoleon; but he will finally succeed for a brief period with the Antichrist, until "the second man", "the last Adam" (1 Cor. 15. 45), "the Son of Man", to Whom all dominion in the earth has, in the counsels of God, been given, shall take unto Him His great power and reign.

All this and more is contained in His title as "the Son of man". Its first occurrence is in Psalm 8, where in verses 1 and 8 His connection with the "earth" is proclaimed; and "dominion" over it is given to Him. It denotes Him Who is "the heir of all things", in virtue of which all things shall one day be put under His feet. "But now we see not yet all things put under Him. But we see Jesus, Who was made a little lower than the angels", humbling Himself unto death, even the death of the Cross (cp. Heb. 2. 8, 9).

In support of this, the occurrences and distribution of this title in the N.T. are full of significance and instruction.

(1) As to the *occurrences*. We find the expression eighty-eight times: Matt. 8. 20; 9. 6; 10. 23; 11. 19; 12. 8, 32, 40; 13. 37, 41; 16. 13, 27, 28; 17. 9, 12, 22; 18. 11; 19. 28; 20. 18, 28; 24. 27, 30, 30, 37, 39, 44; 25. 13, 31; 26. 2, 24, 24, 45, 64. Mark 2. 10, 28; 8. 31, 38; 9. 9, 12, 31; 10. 33, 45; 13. 26; 14. 21, 21, 41, 62. Luke 5. 24; 6. 5, 22; 7. 34; 9. 22, 26, 44, 56, 58; 11. 30; 12. 8, 10, 40; 17. 22, 24, 26, 30; 18. 8, 31; 19. 10; 21. 27, 36; 22. 22, 48, 69; 24. 7. John 1. 51; 3. 13, 14; 5. 27; 6. 27, 53, 62; 8. 28; 12. 23, 34, 34; 13. 31. Acts 7. 56. Heb. 2. 6.[1] Rev. 1. 13; 14. 14. On John 9. 35 see note there.

The *first* is in Matt. 8. 20, where the first thing stated of, and by, the One Who humbled Himself is that in this same earth "the Son of man had not where to lay His head."

The *second*, in like manner, is connected with *the earth*, and shows that He was God, as well as Man, having "authority *on earth* to forgive sins" (Matt. 9. 6); and so the order of the occurrences may be carried out.

Note, in this connection, the contrast between the relationship to mankind of the Lord, as "the Son of God", and as "the Son of man" in John 5. 25–27. Cp. Acts 10. 40–42; 17. 31.

(2) As to the *distribution* of this title: out of the whole number (88), no less than 84 are in the Four Gospels, which contain the record of His coming for this special purpose; and of His rejection. They are all used by the Lord of Himself.

After these 84 occurrences, we have *one* in the Acts (7. 56) where Stephen sees Him "standing" as though not yet "set down", and waiting to be "sent" according to the promise of Jehovah by Peter in Acts 3. 20 (cp. Heb. 10. 13); and *two* in the Apocalypse (Rev. 1. 13 and 14. 14), where He comes to eject the usurper, and reign in righteousness over a restored earth. Heb. 2. 6[1] is a quotation from Ps. 8, which can only be realized by Him.

This distribution of the title shows us that it has nothing whatever to do with "the Church of God"; and that those who belong to it have no relation to the Lord Jesus as "the Son of man". They stand related to Him as "the Son of God".

The distribution between the four separate Gospels is equally significant. In Matthew it occurs 32 times. Matt. 8. 20 is the first occurrence in the New Testament, and it is interesting to contrast it with the last occurrence (Rev. 14. 14). In the first He had "not where to lay His head", but in the last that head has on it "a golden crown", and in His hands is seen "a sharp sickle". With this He reaps in judgment the harvest of the earth, for the time to reap it will then have come. This is emphasized by the word "earth" being 6 times repeated in the verses 15, 16, 18, 19.

In Mark it occurs 14 times, which is twice seven; the two of testimony, and the seven of spiritual perfection of Jehovah's Servant.

In Luke it occurs 26 times.

In John it occurs 12 times, the number which stands associated with Divine governmental perfection. (See Ap. 10.)

(*continued on* p. 146)

[1] The reference in Heb. 2. 6 is a quotation from Ps. 8. 4, and refers to "the first man", Adam; and only by application to the Lord.

"THE BOOK OF THE GENERATION OF JESUS CHRIST" (THE MESSIAH)

ACCORDING TO MATTHEW	ACCORDING TO LUKE
THE REGAL LEGAL LINE ("The Throne of His father David")	**THE NATURAL LEGAL LINE** ("The seed of the Woman")
	GOD
	1 ADAM
	2 Seth
	3 Enos
	4 Cainan
	5 Maleleel
	6 Jared
	7 Enoch
	8 Mathusala
	9 Lamech
	10 Noe
	11 Sem
	12 Arphaxad
	[Cainan]*
	13 Sala
	14 Heber
	15 Phalec
	16 Ragau
	17 Saruch
	18 Nachor
	19 Thara
THE FOURTEEN LAY GENERATIONS	
1 ABRAHAM	20 ABRAHAM
2 Isaac	21 Isaac
3 Jacob	22 Jacob
4 Judas	23 Judas
5 Phares	24 Phares
6 Esrom	25 Esrom
7 Aram	26 Aram
8 Aminadab	27 Aminadab
9 Naasson	28 Naasson
10 Salmon	29 Salmon
11 Booz	30 Booz
12 Obed	31 Obed
13 Jesse	32 Jesse
14 DAVID the king (in Hebron, 2 Sam. 2. 4, 11)	33 DAVID
THE REGAL FOURTEEN GENERATIONS	
1 DAVID (THE KING "over all Israel", 2 Sam. 5. 4, 5)	
2 SOLOMON (eldest *surviving* son of Bathsheba)	34 NATHAN second (*surviving*) son of Bathsheba
3 ROBOAM	35 Mattatha
4 ABIA	36 Menan
5 ASA	37 Melea
6 JOSAPHAT	38 Eliakim
7 JORAM the son-in-law of Ahab "died of sore diseases", 2 Chron. 21. 19	39 Jonan
AHAZIAH his son (called "son-in-law of the House of Ahab", 2 Kings 8. 27) and	40 Joseph
JOASH his grandson, and	41 Juda
AMAZIAH his great-grandson—all died violent deaths.	42 Simeon
8 OZIAS	43 Levi
9 JOATHAM	44 Matthat
	45 Jorim
10 ACHAZ	46 Eliezer
11 EZEKIAS	47 Jose
12 MANASSES	48 Er
13 AMON	49 Elmodam
14 JOSIAS	50 Cosam
JEHOIAKIM	51 Addi
JECHONIAH	52 Melchi
THE FOURTEEN LAY GENERATIONS	
1 Jechonias	53 Neri
2 Salathiel	54 SALATHIEL
3 Zorobabel	55 Zorobabel
	56 Rhesa *
4 Abiud	57 Joanna
	58 Juda
5 Eliakim	59 Joseph
	60 Semei
	61 Mattathias
6 Azor	62 Maath
	63 Nagge
7 Sadoc	64 Esli
	65 Naum
8 Achim	66 Amos
	67 Mattathias
9 Eliud	68 Joseph
	69 Janna
10 Eleazar	70 Melchi
	71 Levi
11 Matthan	72 Matthat
12 Jacob	73 Heli
13 JOSEPH { SON reckoned "*according to Law*" (*hōs enomizeto*, Luke 3. 23) of Heli by betrothal to Heli's daughter: therefore {also "according to Law" cp. Matt. 1. 20. Luke 2. 5 with Deut. 22. 23, 24} HUSBAND of	74 (MARY) of whom was born
14	14 JESUS 75

Ahaziah was slain by Jehu (2 K. 9. 27).
Joash ,, ,, his servants (2 K. 12. 20).
Amaziah ,, ,, the people of Jerusalem (2 K. 14. 19).
Thus GOD'S "visiting" for idolatry was fulfilled literally "to the THIRD and FOURTH generation" (Exod. 20. 4, 5). Their names were therefore "blotted out" *according to Law* (Deut. 29. 20).

Both Jehoiakim and his son Jechoniah are alike omitted from the *regal* fourteen generations for, first, the paramount reason that the kingdom as an independent kingdom *ended* with the death of Josiah at Megiddo when Judah passed under the power of Egypt, and ultimately Babylon; and secondly, in the case of Jehoiakim for "that which was found *on* him" (2 Chron. 36. 8, note), and in that of Jechoniah for the reasons given in Jer. 22. 24-30. Their names are thus also blotted out *according to Law*.

* Undoubtedly an interpolation in certain copies of the Septuagint towards the close of the Fourth Cent. A.D. "The evidence against his existence is to the utmost possible degree, clear, full, and positive, and not liable to any mistake or perversion. On the contrary, the evidence for his existence . . . is inferential, obscure, or open to the suspicion of falsification".—LORD A. HERVEY, *The Genealogies of Our Lord*, ch. viii, p. 195.

* It is held by some that *Rhesa* is not a proper name, but a title applying to Zorobabel. But the case is "not proven".

WHO IS CALLED "MESSIAH"

"THE SON OF ADAM

(בֶּן־הָאָדָם=ho huios tou anthrōpou)

WHO WAS THE SON OF

GOD"

Similarly significant are the first and last occurrences in the Four Gospels respectively: the first being in connection with the humiliation of "the Son of man", and the last with His glorification. Cp. Matt. 8. 20 with 26. 64; Mark 2. 10 with 14. 62; Luke 5. 24 with 24. 7; and John 3. 13, 14 with 13. 31.

Thus, while as "the Son of God" He is "the Heir of all things" (Heb. 1. 2), as "the Son of man" He is the Heir to that dominion in the earth which was entrusted to the first man, and forfeited by him.

XVII. THE SON OF ABRAHAM (Matt. 1. 1).

Expresses the relation of the Son of man, as being heir to the land given to Abraham (Gen. 15. 18-21).

XVIII. THE SON OF DAVID (Matt. 1. 1. Luke 1. 32, &c.).

Expresses His relationship, as being the Heir to David's throne (2 Sam. 7. 12-16. Isa. 11. 1. Acts 2. 29-32; 13. 33-37. Rev. 5. 5; 22. 16).

100 THE SIX MARYS.

The name "Mary", when used of the Lord's mother, is always in Greek *Mariam*=the Heb. *Miriam*, as in Ex. 15. 20.

The other five are usually "*Maria*".

1. Mary the mother of our Lord (Matt. 1. 16, &c.). The context never leaves room for any doubt as to her identity.
2. Mary the mother of James the less and Joses (Matt. 27. 56. Mark 15. 40; 16. 1. Luke 24. 10). She is called "the other Mary" (Matt. 27. 61; 28. 1), and the wife of Cleopas (John 19. 25).
3. Mary the sister of Martha, who anointed the Lord's feet (John 12. 3), see Ap. 156 and 158. She is mentioned by name only in Luke 10. 39, 42 and John 11. 1, 2, 19, 20, 28, 31, 32, 45; and 12. 3.
4. Mary Magdalene, of Magdala (Matt. 15. 39). She is always to be identified by this designation (Matt. 27. 56. Mark 16. 1, 9. Luke 8. 2. John 20. 18, &c.); there is no authority whatever for identifying her with the unnamed woman of Luke 7. 37-50.
5. Mary the mother of John Mark (Acts 12. 12).
6. Mary, one of Paul's helpers (Rom. 16. 6).

101 THE USAGE OF *PNEUMA* IN THE NEW TESTAMENT.

Pneuma= Spirit, is the Greek word corresponding with the Heb. *rūach* in the Old Testament.

The usage of the latter will be found in Ap. 9, and should be compared with this Appendix.

As to the Greek word (*pneuma*): we must consider I. the occurrences, and II. the usage :—

I. *Pneuma* occurs in the Received Greek Text 385 times. Of these, all the Critical Texts (see Ap. 94. vii) agree in omitting nine[1] (or in substituting another reading) and in adding three.[2]

The occurrences are thus distributed :—

	Received Text.	To be omitted.[1]	To be added.[2]	Net result.
In the Gospels . . .	105	2	—	103
In the Acts	69	1	1	69
In the earlier Pauline	21	2	—	19
In the later Pauline .	140	2	1	139
In the Apostolic Epp.	27	2	—	25
In the Apocalypse .	23	—	1	24
	385	9	3	379

The above 385 occurrences in the Received Text are thus rendered in the A.V. :—

"Spirit", 133; "spirit", 153; "spiritual", 1; "ghost", 2; "life", 1; and "wind", 1 . =291
In the Genitive Case, "spiritually", 1 . . = 1
With "*hagion*" (=holy)="Holy Spirit", 4; "Holy Ghost", 89 . . . . . = 93
385

In the margin :—
"Breath" is given twice as an alternative for "spirit", and once for "life".
"Of the spirit" is given as an alternative for "spiritually"; and
"spirit" is given as an alternative for "spiritual".

II. The usages of *pneuma*. The following have been noted in *The Companion Bible*. It is used for

1. GOD. "God is *pneuma*" (John 4. 24-). Not "a" spirit, for there is no indefinite Article in the Greek.
2. CHRIST, as in 1 Cor. 6. 17; 15. 45; and especially 2 Cor. 3. 17, 18 (=the *pneuma* of *v.* 6-, &c.).
3. THE HOLY SPIRIT, generally with the Article, denoting the *Giver*, as distinct from His *gifts*. See No. 14, p. 147. After a Preposition the Article is sometimes to be understood, as being latent.
4. THE OPERATIONS OF THE HOLY SPIRIT, in the bestowal of spiritual gifts, as in 1 Cor. 12. 4-11.
5. THE NEW NATURE in the child of God, because "begotten" in us by God, as in John 3. 3-7. 1 John 5. 1, 4. See note on Matt. 1. 1. This is more especially the Pauline usage: *spirit* as opposed to what is of the *flesh* (John 3. 6. Rom. 8. 4). Hence called "*pneuma Theou*" (=Divine *pneuma* (Rom. 8. 9. 1 Cor. 7. 40; 12. 3-), and *pneuma Christou* (=*Christ pneuma*) in Rom. 8. 9.
6. MAN (*psychologically*), *pneuma* being imparted to man, making him "a living *psuchē*" (="a living soul", or being, as in Gen. 2. 7. Ps. 104 29, 30. Ecc. 12. 7). When taken back to and by God, man, without *pneuma*, becomes and is called "a dead soul" in each of the thirteen occurrences rendered in A.V. "dead body", &c. See Ap. 13. ix, p. 21.
7. CHARACTER, as being in itself invisible, and manifested only in one's actions, &c. Rom. 8. 15. (2 Tim. 1. 7, &c.).
8. OTHER INVISIBLE CHARACTERISTICS (by Fig. *Metonymy*, Ap. 6): such as feelings or desires (Matt. 26. 41, &c.); or that which is supernatural.
9. MAN (*physiologically*), *pneuma* being put by Fig. *Synecdoche* (Ap. 6) for the whole person; a part for the whole (as in Luke 1. 47, "my spirit"=I myself.) See Ap. 9. VII.
10. ADVERBIALLY. But this is only once, in the A.V., where it is translated "spiritually" in Rom. 8. 6. Cp. the R.V. rendering.
11. ANGELS, OR SPIRIT-BEINGS. As in Acts 8. 29. Heb. 1. 7, 14. 1 Pet. 3. 19. Rev. 1. 4.
12. DEMONS, or evil spirit-beings, as in Mark 7. 25, 26. Luke 10. 17, 20, &c.
13. THE RESURRECTION BODY, as in 1 Cor. 15. 45. 1 Pet. 3. 18; 4. 6.
14. *Pneuma hagion*=holy spirit, and is so printed in *The Companion Bible*. This usage (without Articles) occurs 52 times in the N.T., and is

[1] Luke 2. 40; 9. 55. Acts 18. 5. Rom. 8. 1. 1 Cor. 6. 20. Eph. 5. 9. 1 Tim. 4. 12. 1 Pet. 1. 22. 1 John 5. 7.
[2] Acts 4. 25. Phil. 4. 23. Rev. 22. 6.

always wrongly rendered "the Holy Spirit" (with the definite Article, and capital letters). Consequently there is no stronger rendering available when there are two Articles present in the Greek (*to pneuma to hagion*), which means "the Spirit the Holy [Spirit]". Hence, the English reader can never tell which of the two very different Greek expressions he is reading.

Pneuma hagion (without Articles) is never used of the Giver (the Holy Spirit), but only and always of His gift. What this gift is may be seen by comparing Acts 1.4, 5 with Luke 24. 49, where "the promise of the Father" is called (in the former passage) *pneuma hagion*, and in the latter is called "power from on high". This "power from on high" includes whatever *gifts* the Holy Spirit may bestow "according to His own will". What particular gift is meant is sometimes stated, e.g. "faith", "power", &c. This will be found to be the case in every one of the 52 occurrences. See Acts 2.4 (the first occurrence subsequent to Acts 1.4, 5), where we read "they were all filled[1] with *pneuma hagion*, and began to speak with other tongues, as THE Spirit gave". Here the *Giver* and His *gift* are strictly distinguished.

The following are the 52 occurrences of *pneuma hagion*. Those marked * are the subject of a various reading, and *h.p.* denotes *hagion pneuma*: Matt. 1.18, 20; 3. 11. Mark 1. 8. Luke 1. 15, 35, 41, 67; 2. 25; 3. 16; 4. 1-; 11. 13. John 1. -33; 7. -39; 20. 22. Acts 1. 2, 5; 2. 4-; 4. 8, 31*; 6. 3, 5; 7. 55; 8. 15, 17, 19; 9. 17; 10. 38; 11. 16, 24; 13. 9, 52; 19. 2, 2. Rom. 5. 5; 9. 1; 14. 17; 15. 13, 16. 1 Cor. 2. 13*; 6. 19 *h.p.*; 12. -3. 2 Cor. 6. 6. 1 Thess. 1. 5, 6. 2 Tim. 1. 14. Titus 3. 5. Heb. 2. 4; 6. 4. 1 Pet. 1. 12. 2 Pet. 1. 21. Jude 20.

The above 14 usages of *pneuma*, and the 52 occurrences of *pneuma hagion*, are all indicated in the notes of *The Companion Bible*.

[1] The Verb *to fill* takes three Cases after it. In the Active, the Accusative of the *vessel*, or whatever is filled; and the Genitive, of what it is filled with. In the Passive, the Dative, of the *filler*; and the Genitive, of what the vessel is *filled with*. In Eph. 5. 18 it is the Dative, strengthened by the Preposition (*en pneumati*), denoting the Holy Spirit Himself as being the one Who fills with other gifts than "wine".

102 THE SYNONYMOUS WORDS FOR "WILL" AND "WISH".

The difference between these two words is important; and, in the occurrences of each, this Appendix is referred to.

1. ***thelō*** means *to wish or desire*, and is the emotional element which leads to the consequent action. It is therefore stronger than *boulomai*, because the natural impulse is stronger than the reasoned resolve.

2. The Noun ***thelēma*** must also be noted, with the same distinction from *boulēma*, as denoting the desire rather than the resolve.

3. ***boulomai***, though it sometimes means much more, yet has reference to the result of *thelō*; viz. the deliberate determination, whether in accordance with, or contrary to, the original wish or impulse.

4. In like manner the Noun ***boulēma*** is to be distinguished from *thelēma* (No. 2) as denoting resolve, counsel, or determination, rather than the wish or desire. *Boulēma* occurs only twice, Acts 27. 43. Rom. 9. 19. The Noun, *boulē*, with a similar meaning, occurs twelve times.

For illustrations of the differences see Matt. 1. 19. Mark 15. 9, 12, 15. Rom. 7. 15, &c.

103 THE FIRST FULFILMENT OF PROPHECY IN THE N.T. (Matt. 1. 22, 23. Isa. 7. 14).

I. Prophecy is the word of Jehovah (2 Pet. 1. 21); and, as Jehovah is He Who was, and is, and is to come, prophecy must partake of, and relate to, the past, present, and future also; and must have this threefold interpretation or application. The prophecy first quoted by the Holy Spirit in the New Testament will show us how He uses the prophecy which He had Himself inspired; and therefore will furnish us with the principles on which we are to interpret other prophecies.

It will be seen that a prophecy may have (1) a reference to the time and occasion on which it was first spoken; (2) a reference to a later event or circumstance (when it is quoted as having been "spoken", or "written"); and (3) a reference to a yet later or future or final event, which exhausts it (when it is quoted as being "fulfilled;" i.e. filled full).

Hence, instead of speaking of "præterists" and "futurists", we must sometimes take a larger view, and be prepared to see both a *past*, *present*, and *future* interpretation.

II. The subject of this first quoted prophecy (Isa. 7. 14) is Messiah, Christ the Lord; for "the testimony concerning Jesus is the spirit of prophecy" (Rev. 19. 10).

III. Prophecy is always associated with man's failure, from Gen. 3 onward. There was no place for prophecy until man had failed; or for prophets, until the priests became absorbed in their ritual, and ceased to be God's spokesmen, and the teachers of His word. Hence, God's true prophets and teachers of His word have always been opposed to the pretensions of priests.

IV. This prophecy was originally uttered when AHAZ, king of Judah, in a great crisis, had failed to ask the sign which Jehovah had proffered; and which He Himself afterward gave to Ahaz. It therefore of necessity had reference to the then present circumstances. There was evidently a certain damsel, spoken of as "the" well-known damsel (see the note on "virgin", Isa. 7. 14), in connection with whom this prophecy should find a then speedy accomplishment. And it evidently did so, or it would have been no "sign" to Ahaz, as nothing would have been signified by it.

But it is equally true that that did not exhaust it, for only a part of the whole prophecy was then fulfilled.

The prophecy begins at Isa. 7. 10, and runs on to Isa. 9. 7. It is clearly wrong, therefore, to take a *part*, and put it for the *whole*; for it reaches on to future Millennial times, and is connected with the glorious coming of Messiah.

The *whole* prophecy, therefore, is Messianic; and, although the first part had a partial and preliminary fulfilment at the time it was spoken, it cannot be separated from the last part, which takes in the fact that the "children" are used as symbolical "signs." For it ends by declaring that they "are for signs and for wonders in Israel from the Lord of hosts, which dwelleth in Mount Zion" (Isa. 8. 18). The two parts are connected and linked together by the use of the word "Immanuel" (7. 14 and 8. 8, 10, R.V. marg.).

1.—THE PAST.

As to the *past*: it is clear from the prophecy that Ahaz, greatly moved at the confederacy of Ephraim (put by *Metonymy*, Ap. 6, for Israel) with Syria, was tempted to make a counter-confederacy with the king of Assyria. A sign was given to him that he need not yield to the temptation, for the danger would pass away. That "sign" must have had a signification for Ahaz that would convince him of the truth of the prophet's words. The sign was that a man-child would be born to some certain and well-known maiden (for it is *Ha-'Almah*—"*the* maiden"), which man-child would be called Immanuel; and, before that child would know how to distinguish between good and evil, the kings of Ephraim and Syria would both be removed. No record of this birth is given; but it must have taken place; as Jehovah gave the sign for that very purpose.

In chap. 8 another "sign" was given to Ahaz. Another child would be born, this time to the prophetess. He, too, would have a fore-determined name—*Maher-shalal-hash-baz*; and, before he should be able to say "father" or "mother", both Syria and Ephraim should be spoiled by the king of Assyria.

2.—THE FUTURE.

In chap. 9. 6 there is a third sign, and again it is a child. It is a sign connected with the *future*; or rather one that connects the first sign with this and with the future.

"Unto us a child is born,
Unto us a son is given."

This child is also forenamed, and the name is "Wonderful, Counsellor, The Mighty God, The Everlasting Father, The Prince of Peace". And the prophecy closes by declaring that His kingdom shall have no end; and shall be associated with the throne of David.

There were, altogether, four "children" who were set "for signs and for wonders in Israel by the LORD of hosts" (8. 18). Two were only "signs", but two were "wonders", and they are given, and placed, in alternate correspondence.

A | SHEAR-JASHUB, 7. 3 (The son of the Prophet), a "sign".
B | IMMANUEL, 7. 14, a "wonder".
A | MAHER-SHALAL-HASH-BAZ, 8. 1-3 (The son of the Prophet), a "sign".
B | "WONDERFUL", &c., 9. 6, 7, a "wonder".

Does not this point to the fact that the child of chap. 7. 14 is to be associated with the child of chap. 9. 6? and, though it was a "sign" of events then transpiring, those events did not and could not *exhaust* it or the "wonders" to which it pointed.

The names also of these "children" are signs. The meaning of the name Isaiah was itself a sign of that *salvation of Jehovah* of which he prophesied.

i. SHEAR-JASHUB (7. 3) meant *the remnant shall return*, i.e. repent, and stay upon Jehovah, and wait for Him.

ii. IMMANUEL (7. 14) told of the fact that salvation would come to Israel only when *God with us* should be true as a blessed and glorious reality.

iii. MAHER-SHALAL-HASH-BAZ (8. 1-3) tells of the Assyrian *hasting to make a prey and spoil* of the nation, and reveals the need of the salvation of Jehovah. That, too, was only partially fulfilled. For there is another who is called "the Assyrian", and in Dan. 9. 26 is called "the prince that shall come" (cp. Isa. 14. 25). He will *hasten to make a prey* of the nation; but there is yet another—Emmanuel, the Prince of the Covenant—Who will destroy him, and bring in, for Israel, final and eternal salvation. His name is called,

iv. "WONDERFUL"—"THE PRINCE OF PEACE."

3.—THE PRESENT.

But what is happening now—as a *present* application of this great prophecy? What else is signified by these "signs"? Jehovah has been hiding His face from the house of Jacob (8. 17). What is this "stone of stumbling"? What is this "rock of offence to both the houses of Israel" which causeth the Lord to hide His face? Is it not the rejection of Messiah as the Immanuel of Isa. 7. 14? And is He not the "Child born" of chap. 9. 6, 7?

Thus, (1) in this first use of His own prophecy (Isa. 7. 14) in Matt. 1. 22, 23, the Holy Spirit takes the words out of their original combinations to which their first utterance refers.

(2) The prophecy is then resolved into its elements, and by the same Spirit Who gave it, the elements are re-combined in accordance with the Divine purpose.

(3) He takes up the threads of the whole prophecy (Isa. 7. 10; 9. 7), and shows that the original circumstances did not allow of the complete fulfilment at the time the words were spoken and written; and finally,

(4) He connects the names and meanings with prophetic truth, and shows that even these looked forward to times and scenes far beyond their original use; so that even the IMMANUEL of 7. 14 which was fulfilled in Matt. 1. 22, 23 did not exhaust the IMMANUEL of Isa. 8. 10, which is yet future according to Luke 1. 31, 33.

104 PREPOSITIONS.

For the true understanding of the New Testament a knowledge of the Greek Prepositions is indispensable.

They might be exhibited in groups, or according to the Cases[1] of the Noun which they govern, or according to their geometrical relations to a line, a superficies, and a solid, or according to the relative frequency of their occurrences.[2] But we have given them below in their *alphabetical* order, so that they may be more readily found by the reader.

They are eighteen in number, and may thus be defined:—

i. ***ana*** governs only one case (the Accusative), and denotes *up, upon*, formed from *anō* (as *kata* is from *katō*, with which *ana* stands in direct antithesis). In relation to vertical lines it denotes *the top*. With numerals it is used as a distributive (Matt. 20. 9, 10. Luke 9. 3. John 2. 6); also adverbially (Rev. 21. 21).

ii. ***anti*** governs only one case (the Genitive), and denotes *over against*, or opposite. Hence it is used as instead of or in the place of (e.g. Matt. 2. 22. Luke 11. 11); and denotes *equivalence* (e.g. Matt. 20. 28. Heb. 12. 16. 1 Pet. 3. 9), while *huper* (No. xvii, below) denotes in the interest of, or on behalf of (Luke 6. 28. John 17. 19).

iii. ***amphi*** is used only in composition in the N.T. and is rare in Classical Greek. It denotes *about*, or *around*. Used of a solid, it denotes *both sides*.

iv. ***apo*** governs only one case (the Genitive), and denotes motion from the surface of an object, as a line drawn from the circumference; it thus stands in contrast with *ek* (No. vii, below), which denotes a line drawn from the centre; while *para* denotes a line drawn as a tangent, thus—

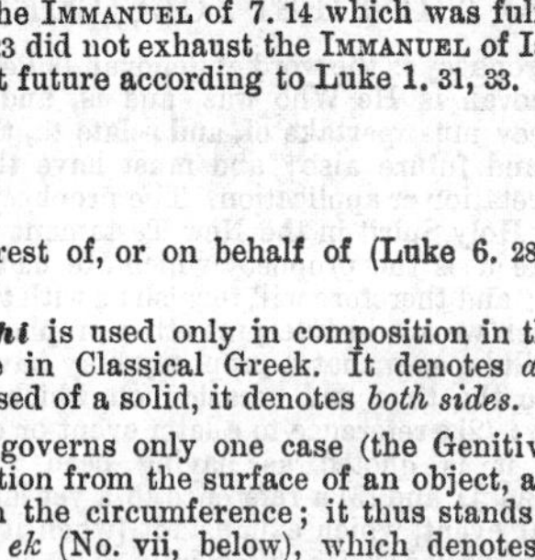

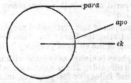

Hence, it is used of *motion away from* a place (e.g. Matt. 3. 16; 8. 1. Acts 15. 38); marking the distance which separates the two places, or the interval of time between two events (e.g. Matt. 19. 4. Acts 20. 18). It also marks the origin or source whence anything comes, such as birth, descent, residence (e.g. Matt. 2. 1; 15. 1; 21. 11. Acts 10. 23; 17. 13), or of information (e.g. Matt. 7. 16).

Apo may consequently be used of deliverance or passing *away from* any state or condition (e.g. Matt. 1. 21; 14. 2. Mark 5. 34. Acts 13. 8; 14. 15. Heb. 6. 1).

[1] The Cases governed by the Prepositions stand in the following *proportion*: Genitive, 17; Accusative, 19; and Dative, 15, according to Helbing (Schanz's *Beiträge*, No. 16 (1904), p. 11.

[2] On p. 98 of his *Grammar of N.T. Greek*, Professor J. H. Moulton gives a list as follows:—If *en* represents unity, the order of the frequency of the other Prepositions work out thus: *eis*, ·64; *ek*, ·34; *epi*, ·32; *pros*, ·25; *dia*, ·24; *apo*, ·24; *kata*, ·17; *meta*, ·17; *peri*, ·12; *hupo*, ·08; *para*, ·07; *huper*, ·054; *sun*, ·048; *pro*, ·018; *anti*, ·008; and *ana*, ·0045.

It would thus differ from *hupo* (No. xviii, below), which would imply a cause immediate and active, while *apo* would imply a cause virtually passive, and more remote.

v. ***dia*** governs two cases (the Genitive and Accusative).

1. With the Genitive it has the general sense of *through*, as though dividing a surface into two by an intersecting line. It includes the idea of *proceeding from* and *passing out* (e.g. Mark 11. 16. 1 Cor. 3. 15. 1 Tim. 2. 15. 1 Pet. 3. 20). Cp. diameter.

In a temporal sense; after an interval (Matt. 26. 61. Mark 2. 1. Gal. 2. 1).

From the ideas of space and time *dia* (with the Gen.) denotes any cause *by means of* which an action passes to its accomplishment (e.g. Matt. 1. 22. John 1. 3. Acts 3. 18. 1 Cor. 16. 3. 2 Cor. 9. 13); hence, it denotes the passing through whatever is interposed between the beginning and the end of such action.

2. With the Accusative it has the sense of *on account of*, or *because of* (e.g. Matt. 27. 18. Mark 2. 27. Rev. 4. 11), indicating both the exciting cause (Acts 12. 20. Rom. 4. 25. 1 Cor. 11. 10), the impulsive cause (e.g. John 12. 9. Rom. 4. 23; 15. 15. Heb. 2. 9), or the prospective cause (Rom. 6. 19; 8. 11; 14. 15. Heb. 5. 3).

vi. ***eis*** governs only one case (the Accusative). Euclid uses *eis* when a line is drawn to meet another line, at a certain point. Hence, it denotes motion *to* or *unto* an object, with the purpose of reaching or touching it (e.g. Matt. 2. 11; 3. 10. Luke 8. 14. Acts 16. 10).

From this comes the idea of the object toward which such motion is directed (e.g. Matt. 18. 20, 30. 1 Cor. 12. 13. Gal. 3. 27); and *for*, or *with respect to* which such action or movement is made.

In contrast with *eis*, *pros* (No. xv, below) may mark one object as the means of reaching an ulterior object which is denoted by *eis* (e.g. John 6. 35. Rom. 5. 1. Eph. 4. 12). It is the opposite of *ek* (No. vii), below.

vii. ***ek*** governs only one case (the Genitive), and denotes motion from the interior. See under *apo* (No. iv, above, and diagram there). It is used of time, place, and origin. It means *out from*, as distinguished from *apo* (No. iv, above), which means *off*, or *away from*. *Ek* marks the more immediate origin, while *apo* marks the more remote origin; *of* expressing the intermediate meanings.

viii. ***en*** governs only one case (the Dative), and denotes being or remaining *within*, with the primary idea of rest and continuance. It has regard to place and space (e.g. Matt. 10. 16. Luke 5. 16), or sphere of action (e.g. Matt. 14. 2. Rom. 1. 5, 8; 6. 4).

It is also used for the efficient cause as emanating from within, and hence has sometimes the force of *by*, denoting the instrument, *with*, passing on to union and fellowship; *en* denoting *inclusion*, and *sun* (No. xvi, below) denoting *conjunction*. *En* denotes also continuance in *time* (Matt. 2. 1; 27. 40. John 11. 10).

2. with plural = among.

ix. ***epi*** governs three cases (the Genitive, Dative, and Accusative), and denotes *superposition*.

1. With the Genitive it denotes *upon*, as proceeding or springing from, and answers to the question "Where?" (e.g. Matt. 9. 2; 10. 27. Mark 8. 4. Luke 22. 30. John 6. 21).

With the idea of *locality* it conveys the sense, *in the presence of* (e.g. Matt. 28. 14. Mark 13. 9. Acts 24. 19. 1 Cor. 6. 1).

With the idea of *time*, it looks backward and upward, e.g. "in the days of" (Matt. 1. 11. Heb. 1. 2).

With the idea of *place*, it denotes dignity and power (e.g. Matt. 23. 2. Acts 12. 21. Rom. 9. 5. Rev. 2. 26).

2. With the Dative it implies *actual superposition*, as one thing resting upon another, as upon a foundation or basis which may be actual (e.g. Mark 6. 25, 28, 39), or moral (e.g. Matt. 18. 13. Mark 3. 5). Both senses occur in 1 Thess. 3. 7.

Hence it is used of the moving principle or motive suggesting the purpose or object (e.g. Eph. 2. 10), and sometimes including the result (e.g. 2 Tim. 2. 14).

3. With the Accusative it implies the downward pressure on that upon which a thing rests; active motion being suggested (e. g. 2 Cor. 3. 15. 1 Tim. 5. 5).

Hence, it denotes any extended motion downward (Matt. 13. 2; 18. 12; 19. 28; 27. 45) from heaven to earth (Mark 4. 20. Acts 11. 15. 2 Cor. 12. 9).

Compared with *pros* (No. xv, below), *pros* marks the motion, the direction to be taken, while *epi* (with Acc.) marks the point to be reached.

This downward pressure may be that of the mind, or feeling (e.g. Matt. 25. 21; 27. 43. Heb. 6. 1. 1 Pet. 1. 13).

For the difference between *eis* (No. vi, above) and *epi* (with the Acc.) see Rom. 9. 21, "one vessel unto (*eis*) honour", and *v.* 23, "riches of glory on (*epi*) the vessels of mercy".

x. ***kata*** governs two cases (the Genitive and Accusative), and denotes two motions, vertical and horizontal.

1. With the Genitive it denotes vertical motion, the opposite of *ana* (No. i, above), descent, or detraction from a higher place or plane (e.g. Matt. 8. 32. Mark 5. 13); and direction to, or against (e. g. Mark 9. 40. John 18. 29. Acts 25. 27. 2 Cor. 13. 8).

2. With the Accusative it denotes horizontal motion, *along* which the action proceeds (e. g. Luke 8. 39; 10. 33. Acts 5. 15; 8. 26. Phil. 3. 14). Sometimes it includes the purpose or intention (e. g. 2 Tim. 1. 1; 4. 3. Tit. 1. 1). In this connection *eis* (No. vi, above. 2 Tim. 4. 14) marks the more immediate purpose, *pros* (No. xv. 3. Eph. 4. 12. Philem. 5) the ultimate purpose; and *kata* (No. x. 2) the destination to be reached. It has regard to the duration of the motion (e.g. Matt. 27. 15. Heb. 3. 8) and the accordance, conformity or proportion of the two things which such motion thus connects (e. g. Matt. 16. 27; 23. 3; 25. 15. Luke 2. 22).

xi. ***meta*** governs two cases (the Genitive and the Accusative), and denotes *association and companionship with*. It thus differs from *sun* (No. xvi, below), which denotes *proximity to*, and hence *conjunction* or *coherence*.

Compare Eph. 6. 23 (*meta*) with Eph. 4. 31 (*sun*); and 1 Thess. 3. 13 (*meta*) with Col. 3. 3 (*sun*).

1. Hence *meta*, with the Genitive, denotes *among*, *amid* (e.g. Matt. 26. 58. Mark 1. 13. Rev. 21. 3), or *in company with* (e.g. Matt. 9. 15. John 11. 31. 2 Thess. 1. 7. Rev. 14. 13).

It refers specially to the mental disposition with which an action is performed (e.g. Matt. 12. 30. Mark 3. 5. Luke 1. 39; 9. 49. John 8. 28. 2 Cor. 7. 15).

2. With the Accusative it means *after*, always in connection with time (e. g. Matt. 17. 1; 26. 32. John 13. 7. Heb. 4. 7; 7. 28).

xii. ***para*** governs three cases (Gen., Dat., and Acc.), and the uniform meaning is *beside*, or *alongside of*. See *apo*, No. iv, above, and cp. diagram there.

1. With the Genitive it denotes *from beside*, implying the source from which anything proceeds (e.g. Matt. 2. 4; 21. 42. Luke 2. 1; 6. 19. Acts 26. 10. Phil. 4. 18).

As distinguished from *hupo* (No. xviii, below) it denotes the *general* sense of motion, while *hupo* marks the *special* sense or efficient cause of such motion.

As distinguished from *apo* (No. iv, above) it marks the motion from a person (e. g. Matt. 2. 16), while *apo* may imply motion from a place (e. g. Matt. 2. 1).

2. With the Dative it denotes rest *beside and at* a person, place, or thing, expressing rest and position there (e. g. John 19. 25. Acts 9. 43); laid up with, or in store with (e. g. Matt. 6. 1. Luke 1. 30), or proximity to (e. g. Matt. 22. 25. Col. 4. 16).

Hence it implies in the power of (Matt. 19. 26. Luke 1. 37); in the judgment of (e.g. Rom. 2. 12. 2 Pet. 2. 11).

3. With the Accusative it denotes motion to a place, so as to be alongside it (e.g. Matt. 15. 29. Mark 4. 1).

Hence, *beside* and *beyond*, and so *against* (e.g. Acts 18. 13. Rom. 1. 25, 26; 4. 18. 1 Cor. 3. 11. Gal. 1. 8); and *beside*, i. e. *more* or *less than* (e.g. Luke 3. 13; 13. 2. Rom. 14. 5. 2 Cor. 11. 24). Compare *pros*, No. xv, below.

xiii. ***peri*** governs two cases (Genitive and Accusative), and denotes *around*, or *about*, like a completed circle. Hence *concerning*. It marks the object about which the action of the verb takes place.

1. With the Genitive it means *as concerning*, or, *as regards*, but always with the primary idea, and marking the central point of the activity (e.g. Matt. 4. 6. Luke 24. 19, 27, 44).

2. With the Accusative it denotes the extension of such activity, hence, *around* (e.g. Mark 9. 42. Luke 13. 8. Acts 28. 7. Phil. 2. 23).

xiv. ***pro*** governs only one case (the Genitive), and denotes the position as being *in sight*, or, *before* one, in *place* (e.g. Luke 7. 27; 9. 52; James 5. 9); *time* (e.g. Matt. 5. 12. John 17. 24. Acts 21. 38); or *superiority* (e.g. Jas. 5. 12. 1 Pet. 4. 8).

xv. ***pros*** governs three cases (the Genitive, Dative, and Accusative), and denotes *to*, or, *toward*, implying motion *onward*. Its general meaning with the three cases is the *motive*—as *in consideration of* (with the Genitive); *in addition to* anything—as an act (with the Dative); *with a view to* anything—as an end (with the Accusative).

Compared with *para* (No. xii, above), *pros* denotes only direction and tendency, whereas *para* denotes both motion and change of place of some object.

1. With the Genitive the only occurrence is Acts 27. 34.

2. With the Dative it occurs five times: Luke 19. 37. John 18. 16; 20. 12, 12. Rev. 1. 13.

3. With the Accusative, see e.g. Matt. 2. 12; 3. 10; 21. 34; 26. 57. Mark 5. 11; 11. 1; 14. 54. Luke 7. 7. Acts 6. 1. 1 Thess. 3. 6.

xvi. ***sun*** governs only one case (the Dative). See under *meta* (No. xi, above) (e.g. Luke 23. 11. Rom. 6. 8).

xvii. ***huper*** governs two cases (the Genitive and Accusative), and denotes *above*, or *over*, with respect to the upper plane of a solid. Latin, *super*.

1. With the Genitive it is used in its relative rather than its absolute sense. *In the place of* (e.g. John 11. 50; 18. 14. Rom. 5. 6. 1 Tim. 2. 6. Philem. 13. 1 Pet. 3. 18).

In the interests of (e.g. 2 Thess. 2. 1).

In behalf of (e.g. Matt. 5. 44. Acts 9. 16).

For the purpose of (e.g. John 11. 4. Rom. 15. 8. 2 Cor. 12. 19. Phil. 2. 13).

With the Genitive *huper* is connected with *peri*, being the apex of the triangle, or the fixed point of the compass, whereas *peri* (see No. xiii, above) is the circle described around it. Hence *huper* has regard to feeling, and implies the pleading a case on behalf of another, whereas *peri* implies the mere description of the circumstances of the case (e.g. 1 Pet. 3. 18. Jude 9).

2. With the Accusative it denotes *beyond*, in *excess* of measure, honour, number, or time (e.g. Matt. 10. 24. 2 Cor. 1. -8. Eph. 1. 22. Phil. 2. 9. Philem. 16).

xviii. ***hupo*** governs two cases (the Genitive and Accusative), denotes the *under side* of a solid, and is thus the opposite of *huper* (see No. xvii, above).

With the Genitive it describes motion from beneath; with Dative (not used in the N.T.), position beneath; and with the Accusative, motion or extension underneath.

1. With the Genitive, *hupo* is used to mark the efficient or instrumental agent, *from under* whose hand or power the action of the verb proceeds (e.g. Matt. 1. 22; 2. 16. Luke 14. 8).

2. With the Accusative, it denotes the place whither such action extends (e.g. Matt. 8. 8. Mark 4. 32. Jas. 2. 3).

Hence it implies moral or legal subjection (e.g. Matt. 8. 9. Rom. 6. 14; 7. 14; 16. 20. 1 Tim. 6. 1).

105 THE USAGE OF NEGATIVES IN THE NEW TESTAMENT.

There are two principal negatives used in the New Testament, all others being combinations of one or other of these with other particles.

I. ***ou*** (before a vowel *ouk*; before an aspirated vowel *ouch*)=no, not; expressing full and direct negation, independently and absolutely; not depending on any condition expressed or implied.

(*a*) *ouchi*, a strengthened form, often used in questions.

II. ***mē***=no, not; expressing conditional negation, depending on *feeling*, or on some idea, conception, or hypothesis.

Hence, *ou* is objective.
mē is subjective.

ou denies a matter of fact.
mē denies a matter of feeling.

ou denies absolutely.
mē denies conditionally.

ou negatives an affirmation.
mē negatives a supposition, and prohibits or forbids.

ou is generally used with the Indicative Mood.
mē with the other moods of the verb.

For the difference, see John 3. 18: "He that believeth on Him is not (*ou*) condemned: but he that believeth not (*mē*, supposing such a case) is condemned already, because he hath not (*mē*) believed (according to the supposition made).

See also Matt. 22. 29: "Ye do err, *not* knowing the Scriptures". Had the negative here been "*ou*" it would imply the *fact* that they did not know, because of not possessing them. But it is "*mē*", implying the *feeling*; they did not wish to know.

The same distinctions apply to all the compounds of *ou* and *mē* respectively.

III. ***ou mē***. The two negatives when combined lose their distinctive meanings, and form the strongest and most emphatic asseveration; but, solemn and strong as it is, whenever it was used by a human being the result always belied it, and the speaker never made it good:—

Matt. 16. 22. Peter said, "This shall *not* be unto Thee". (But it was.)
" 26. 35. Peter said, "I will *not* deny Thee." (But he did.)
John 11. 56. Some said, "What think ye, that He will *not* come to the feast?" (But He did.)
" 13. 8. Peter said, "Thou shalt *never* wash my feet". (But He did.)
" 20. 25. Thomas said, "Except I shall see . . . I will *not* believe". (But he did.)

2. On the other hand, when the Lord used this solemn asseveration it was always absolutely true, and was, or will yet be, made good. It is variously rendered, as a simple negative (as above): no, not, by no means, in no wise, or in no case, &c.

This expression was used by our Lord on forty-six

separate occasions (omitting the parallel passages, which are placed within brackets), adding three (Matt. 25. 9. Luke 8. -17, and John 16. 7), and omitting two (Matt. 24. -2 and Luke 22. 34), with the critical texts. They are as follows, and are all worthy of the closest attention (see Matt. 5. 18; 16. 28; 24. 34. John 6. 37, &c.).

Matt. 5. 18, 20, 26; **10.** 23, 42; **13.** 14, 14; **15.** 6; **16.** 28 (Mark 9. 1; Luke 9. 27); **18.** 3 (Luke 18. 17); **23.** 39; **24.** 2, 2 (omitted by all, but retained in Mark 13. 2), 21, 34 (Mark 13. 30. Luke 21. 32), 35 (Mark 13. 31. Luke 21. 33); **25.** 9 (added by all); **26.** 29 (Mark 14. 25. Luke 22. 18).

Mark 9. 41; **13.** 2, 2 (omitted in Matt. 24. -2, retained here); **16.** 18.

Luke 6. 37, 37; **8.** -17 (added by most); **10.** 19; **12.** 59; **13.** 35; **18.** 7, 30; **21.** 18; **22.** 16, 34 (omitted by all, retained in John 13. 38), 67, 68.

John 4. 14, 48; **6.** 35, 35, 37; **8.** 12, 51, 52; **10.** 5, 28; **11.** 26; **13.** 38 (omitted in Luke 22. 34, but retained here); **16.** 7 (added by some).

3. The expression *ou mē* is used once by an angel (Luke 1. 15).

4. Fourteen times by Paul: three in Acts (13. 41; 28. 26, 26), and eleven times in his Epistles (Rom. 4. 8. 1 Cor. 8. 13. Gal. 4. 30; 5. 16. 1 Thess. 4. 15; 5. 3. Heb. 8. 11, 12; 10. 17; 13. 5, 5).

5. Twice by Peter (1 Pet. 2. 6. 2 Pet. 1. 10).

6. Sixteen times in the Apocalypse (one being added in all the critical texts, 9. 6): Rev. 2. 11; 3. 3, 5, 12; 9. 6; 15. 4; 18. 7, 14, 21, 22, 22, 22, 23, 23; 21. 25, 27.

The occurrences are thus eighty-four in all (twelve sevens). See Ap. 10.

106 THE SYNONYMOUS WORDS FOR "APPEAR", "APPEARING", ETC.

I. Appear (the Verb).

There are eight words (or expressions) rendered appear, &c., in the A.V., which are to be distinguished as follows:—

i. ***phainō***=to shine forth so as to be seen: having reference to the manner in which a matter presents or shows itself, independently of any observer. Hence the word *phenomenon*.

ii. ***anaphainomai.*** Passive of No. i, with *ana* prefixed=to be shown forth, come to light, come into sight.

iii. ***epiphainō***=to shine, shew light upon. No. i with *epi* (Ap. 104. ix).

iv. ***emphanizō***=to cause to be manifested or shown plainly and clearly; used of causing that to be seen (or known) which would not otherwise have been cognizable by the unaided eye (or mind). It occurs ten times: Matt. 27. 53. John 14. 21, 22. Acts 23. 15, 22; 24. 1; 25. 2, 15. Heb. 9. 24; 11. 14. Cp. the Sept. use for Heb. *hōdiaʿ* (Ex. 33. 13); and for *'āmar* (Est. 2. 22).

v. ***phaneroō***=to bring to light, make manifest. Cp. *phaneros*=manifest in No. viii below.

vi. ***optomai***=to see with the eye, referring to the thing seen (objectively); thus differing from *blepō* (see Ap. 133. I. 5), which denotes the act of seeing or of using the eye.

vii. ***erchomai***=to come. Rendered "appear" only in Acts 22. 30, where all the critical texts (see Ap. 94) read *sunerchomai*="come together".

viii. ***eimi phaneros***=to be visible, manifest, or open to sight (*phaneros*, adj. of No. v, above, with *eimi*=to be). So rendered only in 1 Tim. 4. 15.

ix. ***apokaluptō***=to unveil so as to be visible to the eye.

II. Appearing (the Noun).

i. ***apokalupsis***=unveiling, revelation, manifestation. Hence Eng. "Apocalypse". From *apo*=from (Ap. 104. iv), and *kaluptō*, to cover=uncovering, or unveiling. When used of a person it always denotes that he is visible. Occurs Luke 2. 32. Rom. 2. 5; 8. 19; 16. 25. 1 Cor. 1. 7; 14. 6, 26. 2 Cor. 12. 1, 7. Gal. 1. 12; 2. 2. Eph. 1. 17; 3. 3. 2 Thess. 1. 7. 1 Pet. 1. 7, 13; 4. 13. Rev. 1. 1.

ii. ***epiphaneia,*** a shining forth upon. Hence, Eng. epiphany. From No. iii, above.

107 THE PRINCIPLE UNDERLYING THE QUOTATIONS FROM THE OLD TESTAMENT IN THE NEW.

It is a fact that in quotations from the Old Testament the Greek text sometimes differs from the Hebrew.

The difficulties found in connection with this subject arise from our thinking and speaking only of the human agent as the writer, instead of having regard to the fact that the Word of God is the record of the words which He Himself employed when He spoke "at sundry times and in divers manners" (Heb. 1. 1, see Ap. 95); and from not remembering (or believing) that "holy men of God spake as they were moved by the Holy Ghost" (2 Pet. 1. 21, and cp. Matt. 15. 4. Mark 12. 36. Acts 1. 16; 3. 18; 28. 25. Heb. 3. 7; 9. 8; 10. 15).

If we believe that throughout the Scriptures we have the words of God, and not of man, all difficulties vanish. The difficulties are created by first assuming that we are dealing with merely human documents, and then denying the Divine Speaker and Author the right that is claimed by every human writer for himself.

It thus seems that man may take any liberty he chooses in quoting, adapting, or repeating in a varied form his own previously written words; but that he denies the Divine Author of Holy Scripture the right to deal in the same manner with His own words. This is the cause of all the so-called "discrepancies" and "difficulties" arising from man's ignorance.

The Holy Spirit, in referring to words which He has before caused to be written in connection with the special circumstances of each particular case, frequently refers to them again in relation to different circumstances and other cases. He could have employed other words had He chosen to do so; but it has pleased Him to repeat His own words, introducing them in different connections, with other applications, and in new senses.

All these things are done, and words are even sometimes changed, in order to bring out some new truth for our learning. This is lost upon us when we charge upon God our own ignorance, and the supposed infirmities of human agencies.

One great source of such difficulties is our failure to note the difference between what is said to be "spoken", and what is said to be "written". If we introduce the latter assumption when the former is definitely stated, we at once create our own "discrepancy". True, by a figure of speech we can say that an author has *said* a certain thing when he has *written* it; but we may not say that he *spoke* it when he distinctly says that he *wrote* it, or *vice versa*. Some prophecies were spoken and not written; some were written but not spoken; while others were both spoken and written.

There is, surely, all the difference in the world between *to rhēthen*=that which was spoken, and *ho gegraptai*=that which standeth written. If we deliberately substitute the one for the other, of course there is a discrepancy; but it is of our own creating. This at

once disposes of two of the greatest and most serious of so-called discrepancies, Matt. 2. 23, and 27. 9 (see Ap. 161).

One other consideration will help us when the quotations are prophecies. Prophecies are the utterances of Jehovah; and Jehovah is He Who was, and is, and is to come—the Eternal. His words therefore partake of His attributes, and may often have a past and present as well as a future reference and fulfilment (see Ap. 103); and (1) a prophecy may refer to the then present circumstance under which it was spoken; (2) it may have a further and subsequent reference to some great crisis, which does not exhaust it; and (3) it may require a final reference, which shall be the consummation, and which shall fill it full, and thus be said to fulfil it.

Certain prophecies may therefore have a preterite reference, as well as a future fulfilment; but these are too often separated, and *the part* is put for *the whole*, one truth being used to upset another truth, to the contempt of Divine utterance, and to the destruction of brotherly love.

The principles underlying the New Testament quotations were fully set out by Solomon Glassius (A.D. 1623) in his great work (written in Latin) entitled, *Philologia Sacra*, chapter on "Gnomes"; and, as this has never been improved upon, we follow it here.

The notes on the N.T. passages must be consulted for further information, e.g. Luke 4. 18 (II. 1, below).

I. As to their Internal form: i.e. the *sense*, as distinct from the *words*:—

1. *Where the sense originally intended by the Holy Spirit is preserved, though the words may vary.*

Matt. 1. 23 (Isa. 7. 13, 14), "spoken", see above. Matt. 2. 6 (Mic. 5. 2); 3. 3 (Isa. 40. 3); 11. 10[1] (Mal. 3. 1); 12. 17 (Isa. 42. 1-4); 13. 14, 15[s] (Isa. 6. 9, 10); 21. 16[s] (Ps. 8. 2); 21. 42[s] (Ps. 118. 22, 23); 22. 44[s] (Ps. 110. 1); 26. 31 (Zech. 13. 7); 27. 35[s] (Ps. 22. 18); Mark 15. 28 (Isa. 53. 12). Luke 4. 18, 21 (Isa. 61. 1, 2). John 19. 37 (Zech. 12. 10); Acts 3. 22, 23[s] (Deut. 18. 15–19); 13. 33[s] (Ps. 2. 7); 15. 16, 17 (Amos 9. 11, 12). Rom. 14. 11 (Isa. 45. 23); 15. 3[s] (Ps. 69. 9); 15. 12[s] (Isa. 11. 1, 10). Eph. 4. 8 (Ps. 68. 18). Heb. 1. 8, 9[s] (Ps. 45. 6, 7); 1. 10–13[s] (Ps. 102. 25); 5. 6 and 7. 17, 21 (Ps. 110. 4); 10. 5, 6[s] (Ps. 40. 6–9. See below, II. 3. a). 1 Pet. 2. 6[s] (Isa. 28. 16).

2. *Where the original sense is modified, and used with a new and different application.*

Matt. 12. 40 (Jonah 1. 17). John 3. 14, 15 (Num. 21. 8, 9); 19. 36 (Ex. 12. 46). Eph. 5. 31, 32 (Gen. 2. 23, 24).

3. *Where the sense is* Accommodated, *being different from its first use, and is adapted to quite a different event or circumstance.*

Matt. 2. 15[H] (Hos. 11. 1); 2. 17, 18 (Jer. 31. 15); 8. 17[H] (Isa. 53. 4); 13. 35, "spoken" (Ps. 78. 2); 15. 8, 9 (Isa. 29. 13); 27. 9, 10.[2] Acts 13. 40, 41[s] (Hab. 1. 5). Rom. 9. 27, 28[s*] (Isa. 10. 22, 23); 9. 29[s] (Isa. 1. 9); 10. 6[s], 7, 8[s] (Deut. 30. 12–14). 1 Cor. 1. 19, 20 (Isa. 29. 14; 33. 18); 10. 6 (Exod. 32. 6–25). Rev. 1. 7 (Zech. 12. 10); 1. 17 (Isa. 41. 4); 11. 4 (Zech. 4. 3, 11, 14).

II. As to their External form: i.e. the *words*, as distinct from the *sense*.

1. *Where the words are from the Hebrew text or Septuagint Version.*

Matt. 12. 7 (Hos. 6. 6); 22. 32[H] (Ex. 3. 6); Mark 12. 26[H] (Ex. 3. 6); 11. 17[H] (Isa. 56. 17. Jer. 7. 11). Luke 4. 18. (Isa. 61. 1, 2-).

2. *Where the words are varied by omission, addition, or transposition.*

Matt. 4. 10 (Deut. 6. 13; 10. 20); 4. 15, 16 (Isa. 9. 1, 2); 5. 31 (Deut. 24. 1); 5. 38 (Ex. 21. 24. Lev. 24. 20); 12. 18–21 (Isa. 42. 1–4); 19. 5[s] (Gen. 2. 24); 22. 24 (Deut. 25. 5, 6). Rom. 11. 3, 4 (1 Kings 19. 10, 14, 18). 1 Cor. 2. 9 (Isa. 64. 4); 14. 21 (Isa. 28. 11, 12). 1 Pet. 1. 24, 25 (Isa. 40. 6–8).

3. *Where the words are changed, by a various reading, or by an inference, or in Number, Person, Mood, or Tense.*

The necessity for this is constantly experienced today in adapting a quotation for any special purpose beyond its original intention. It is no less authoritative as Scripture, nor does it alter the Word of God.

(a) *By a different reading.*

Heb. 10. 5[s] (Ps. 40. 6; see the notes in both passages).

(b) *By an inference.*

Matt. 2. 6 (Micah 5. 2). See notes. Acts 7. 43 (Amos 5. 25–27). Rom. 9. 27[s] (Isa. 10. 22); 9. 29 (Isa. 1. 9); 9. 33 (Isa. 28. 16); Eph. 4. 8 (Ps. 68. 18).

(c) *In Number.*

Matt. 4. 7 (Deut. 6. 16), Rom. 4. 7 (Ps. 32. 1); Rom. 10. 15 (Isa. 52. 7).

4. *Where two or more citations are combined. Composite quotations.*

This is a common practice in all literature.

Plato (429–347 B.C.), *Ion*, p. 538, connects two lines from Homer (about 850 B.C.), one from *Iliad*, xi. l. 638, and the other from l. 630.

Xenophon (430–357 B.C.) *Memorabilia*, Bk. I, ch. 2, § 58, gives as one quotation two passages from Homer (*Iliad*, ii. 188, &c., and 198, &c.).

Lucian (A.D. 160), in his *Charon*, § 22, combines five lines together from Homer from different passages (*Iliad*, ix. 319, 320; and *Odyssey*, x. 521, and xi. 539).

Plutarch (about A.D. 46), in his *Progress in Virtue*, combines in one sentence Homer (*Odyssey*, vi. 187, and xxiv. 402).

Cicero (106–43 B.C.), *De Oratore*, Bk. II, § 80, combines in two lines parts of Terence's lines (*Andria*, 115, 116, Parry's Edn.).

Philo (20 B.C.–A.D. 40), in *Who is the Heir of Divine Things* (§ 5), quotes, as one address of Moses, parts of two others (Num. 11. 13 and 22). In the same treatise (§ 46) he combines parts of Gen. 17. 19 and 18. 14.

Illustrations could be given from English authors.

Man may make a mistake in doing this, but not so the Holy Spirit.

In Matt. 21. 5, Isa. 62. 11 is combined with Zech. 9. 9.
In Matt. 21. 13, Isa. 56. 7 is combined with Jer. 7. 11.
In Mark 1. 2, 3, Mal. 3. 1 is combined with Isa. 40. 3.
In Luke 1. 16, 17, Mal. 4. 5, 6 is combined with 3. 1.
In Luke 3. 4, 5, Mal. 3. 1 is combined with Isa. 40. 3.
In Acts 1. 20, Ps. 69. 25 is combined with 109. 8.
In Rom. 3. 10–12, Eccles. 7. 20 is combined with Ps. 14. 2, 3 and 53. 2, 3.
In Rom. 3. 13–18, Ps. 5. 9 is combined with Isa. 59. 7, 8 and Ps. 36. 1.
In Rom. 9. 33, Is. 28. 16 is combined with 8. 14.
In Rom. 11. 26, 27[s], Isa. 59. 20, 21 is combined with 27. 9.
In 1 Cor. 15. 54–56, Isa. 25. 8 is combined with Hos. 13. 14.
In 2 Cor. 6. 16, Lev. 26. 11, 12 is combined with Ezek. 37. 27.
In Gal. 3. 8, Gen. 12. 3 is combined with 18. 18.
In 1 Pet. 2. 7, 8, Ps. 118. 22 is combined with Isa. 8. 14.

5. *Where quotations are made from secular writers.*

See the notes on Acts 17. 22, 23, and 28. 1 Cor. 15. 33. Col. 2. 21. Tit. 1. 12.

---

[1] And the parallel passages in the other Gospels, which can be easily found.

[s] This denotes that it agrees with the Septuagint Version in these cases, and not with the Hebrew. With (*[s]) it denotes that it is nearly, but not exactly, the same.

[H] This denotes that it agrees with the Hebrew, but not with the Septuagint Version.

[2] This was "spoken", not written, and is therefore not a quotation. See Ap. 161.

108 THE SYNONYMOUS WORDS FOR "CHILD", "CHILDREN", ETC.

There are seven Greek words translated "child" in the N.T., which are to be distinguished as follows:—

i. ***teknon***=that which is borne or born (from *tiktō*, to bring forth). Anglo-Saxon=bearn, from *beran*, to bear. Hence, Scottish *bairn*. Used of a child by natural descent, whether boy or girl.

ii. ***teknion.*** Diminutive of *teknon* (No. i, above); a term of endearment.

iii. ***huios***=a son, or male, having reference to *origin* and nature, including that of relationship to the father.

iv. ***pais***=a child, whether son or daughter (in relation to law); a boy or girl (in relation to age); a servant, or maid (in relation to condition), like the French *garçon*.

v. ***paidion.*** Diminutive of *pais* (No. iv, above); hence, a young or little child, an infant; also a term of endearment.

vi. ***paidarion.*** Another diminutive of *pais* (No. iv, above), a lad; a little boy or girl.

vii. ***nēpios.*** Not old enough to speak (from *nē*, negative, and *epō*, to speak).

viii. ***brephos.*** An *embryo*, or newly-born babe.

ix. ***korasion***=a young girl, or maiden. Diminutive of *korē*, a girl; like *paidion*, used as a term of endearment.

x. ***neaniskos***=a young man (always so translated), from the age of twenty to forty.

109 THE HERODS OF THE NEW TESTAMENT.

HEROD THE GREAT (Matt. 2. 1. Luke 1. 5)

- married MARIAMNE I.
  - ARISTOBULUS
    - HEROD (King of Chalcis) m. his niece BERENICE (Acts 25. 13)
    - HEROD AGRIPPA I. (Acts 12. 1-23)
      - AGRIPPA II. (Acts 25. 13)
      - BERENICE (Acts 25. 13)
      - DRUSILLA married FELIX (Acts 24. 24)
    - HERODIAS (Matt. 14. 3. Mark 6. 17. Luke 3. 19)
- married MARIAMNE II.
  - HEROD PHILIP I married HERODIAS (Matt. 14. 3. Mark 6. 17. Luke 3. 19)
- married MALTHACE
  - ARCHELAUS (Matt. 2. 22)
  - HEROD ANTIPAS married HERODIAS (Luke 3. 1–, 19; 9. 7; 13. 31; 23. 7. Matt. 14. 1, 3. Mark 6. 14)
- married CLEOPATRA
  - HEROD PHILIP II (Luke 3. –1)

110 THE USE OF *PSUCHĒ* IN THE NEW TESTAMENT.

psuchē is the only word translated "soul" in the N.T. It occurs 105 times, and is rendered "soul" 58 times, "life" 40 times, "mind" 3 times, and "heart", "heartily", "us", and "you" once each.

To ascertain its meaning, it is useless to go to heathen authors. The Greek philosophers were at variance among themselves. ARNOBIUS, a Christian writer of the latter part of the third century, in his work *Adversus Gentes*, speaking of the speculations of the heathen of his day, says: "In exactly the same way (as the creation and the gods) is the condition of souls discussed. For this one thinks they are both immortal, and survive the end of our earthly life; that one believes that they do not survive, but perish with the bodies themselves; the opinion of another, however, is that they suffer nothing immediately, but that, after the [form of] man has been laid aside, they are allowed to live a little longer, and then come under the power of death."[1]

We must, therefore, let Scripture be its own interpreter. *Psuchē* exactly corresponds to the Hebrew *Nephesh* (Ap. 13), as will be seen from the following passages: Mark 12. 29, 30, compared with Deut. 6. 4, 5; Acts 2. 27 with Ps. 16. 10; Rom. 11. 3 with 1 Kings 19. 10; 1 Cor. 15. 45 with Gen. 2. 7. In all these places, *psuchē* in the New Testament represents *nephesh* in the Old.

[1] Clark's *Ante-Nicene Christian Library*, vol. xix, p. 125.

The following are the occurrences of the word:—

I. ***psuchē***, used of the lower animals twice, is rendered

1. "life": Rev. 8. 9. 1
2. "soul": Rev. 16. 3. 1

2

II. ***psuchē***, used of man as an individual (just as we speak of a ship going down with every soul on board, or of so many lives being lost in a railway accident), occurs 14 times, and is rendered

"soul": Acts 2. 41, 43; 3. 23; 7. 14; 27. 37. Rom. 2. 9; 13. 1. 1 Cor. 15. 45. James 5. 20. 1 Pet. 3. 20. 2 Pet. 2. 14. Rev. 6. 9; 18. 13; 20. 4. 14

III. ***psuchē***, used of the life of man, which can be lost, destroyed, saved, laid down, &c., occurs 58 times, and is rendered

1. "life": Matt. 2. 20; 6. 25, 25; 10. 39, 39; 16. 25, 25; 20. 28. Mark 3. 4; 8. 35, 35; 10. 45. Luke 6. 9; 9. 24, 24, 56; 12. 22, 23; 14. 26; 17. 33[2]. John 10. 11, 15, 17; 12. 25, 25; 13. 37, 38; 15. 13. Acts 15. 26; 20. 10, 24; 27. 10, 22. Rom. 11. 3; 16. 4. Phil. 2. 30. 1 John 3. 16, 16. Rev. 12. 11. 39
2. "soul": Matt. 10. 28, 28; 16. 26, 26. Mark 8. 36, 37. Luke 12. 20; 21. 19. 1 Thess. 2. 8; 5. 23. Heb. 4. 12; 6. 19; 10. 39; 13. 17. James 1. 21. 1 Pet. 1. 9; 2. 11, 25; 4. 19. 19

58

[2] In this verse "life" occurs twice in the English, but *psuchē* only once in the Greek.

IV. ***psuchē***, used to emphasize the pronoun, as we use "self" (e.g. "my soul" = "myself"), occurs 21 times, and is rendered

1. "soul": Matt. 11. 29; 12. 18; 26. 38. Mark 14. 34. Luke 1. 46; 12. 19, 19. John 12. 27. Acts 2. 27, 31; 14. 22; 15. 24. 2 Cor. 1. 23. Heb. 10. 38. 1 Pet. 1. 22. 2 Pet. 2. 8. Rev. 18. 14.	17
2. "mind": Acts 14. 2. Heb. 12. 3.	2
3. "us": John 10. 24.	1
4. "you": 2 Cor. 12. 15 (see margin).	1
	21

V. ***psuchē***, used with intensive force, to express all the powers of one's being, occurs 10 times, and is rendered

1. "soul": Matt. 22. 37. Mark 12. 30, 33. Luke 2. 35; 10. 27. Acts 4. 32. 3 John 2.	7
2. "heart": Eph. 6. 6.	1
3. "mind": Phil. 1. 27.	1
4. "heartily": Col. 3. 23.	1
	10
Total	105

111 THE SYNONYMOUS WORDS FOR "REPENT", "REPENTANCE".

I. The Verb.

1. ***metanoeō*** = to change one's mind, always for the better, and morally. Because of this it is often used in the Imperative (Matt. 3. 2; 4. 17. Acts 2. 38; 3. 19). Not merely to forsake sin, but to change one's apprehension regarding it. It occurs thirty-four times. It answers to the Latin *resipisco* = to recover one's senses, to come to one's self.

2. ***metamelomai*** = to regret; to have after-care or annoyance at the *consequences* of an act of sin rather than a deep regret at the *cause* from want of not knowing better. Hence it is never used in the Imperative. It occurs *six* times, and in each case (except Matt. 21. 29, 32) never in the real Biblical sense of "repentance toward God". It is from *meta* = after, and *melo* = to be an object of care. See notes on 2 Cor. 7. 8 and 10. It is used of Judas Iscariot (Matt. 27. 3); negatively of Paul's regret (2 Cor. 7. 8); and of God (Heb. 7. 21).

The Noun, *metameleia*, is not used in the N.T.

II. The Noun.

metanoia = a real change of mind and attitude toward sin itself, and the *cause* of it (not merely the *consequences* of it), which affects the whole life and not merely a single act. It has been defined as a change in our principle of action (Gr. *nous*) from what is by nature the exact opposite. It occurs twenty-four times, and except Heb. 12. 17 is a real "repentance toward God". It is associated with the work of the Holy Spirit, and is connected with the remission of sins and the promises of salvation.

III. The Negative Adjective, *ametamelētos*, is used twice, viz. Rom. 11. 29, and 2 Cor. 7. 10.

112 THE SYNONYMOUS EXPRESSIONS FOR "KINGDOM".

For a true understanding of the New Testament, it is essential that the "Word of Truth" should be "rightly divided" (2 Tim. 2. 15) as to the various usages of the word "kingdom" in all the different combinations and contexts in which we find it.

Each has its own peculiar and particular sense, which must not be confused with another.

As to the word *basileia*, it denotes *sovereignty*, which requires the actual *presence* of a sovereign, or king. There can be no kingdom apart from a king. We all know of countries which were once "kingdoms" but are now "republics", for the simple but sufficient reason that they have no "king", but are governed by the "public", which is sovereign.

The countries remain the same, have the same peoples, the same cities, the same mountains and rivers, but they are no longer *kingdoms*.

The common practice of taking the Kingdom as meaning the Church (see Ap. 113), has been the source of incalculable misunderstanding; and not "trying the things that differ" (Phil. 1. 10, see note there) has led to great confusion in the interpretation of the whole of the New Testament.

The following definitions may help towards a clearer view of many important passages:—

1. **"The Kingdom of Heaven".** The word "heaven" is generally in this connection in the plural, "of (or from) the heavens". For the difference between the use of the singular and plural of this word, see the notes on Matt. 6. 9, 10. This expression is used only in the Gospel of Matthew, as being specially in harmony with the purpose of that Gospel. See notes on pp. 1304–5, and Ap. 114.

It is the *dispensational* term; and is used sometimes of Messiah's Kingdom *on* earth, and sometimes of the heavenly sovereignty *over* the earth. It is not from or out of (Gr. *ek*, Ap. 104. vii) "this world" (Gr. *kosmos*, Ap. 129. 1). This sovereignty comes from heaven, because the King is to come from thence (John 18. 36). It was to this end He was born, and this was the first subject of His ministry (see Ap. 119). That Kingdom (Matt. 4. 17, &c.) was rejected, as was also the further proclamation of it in Acts 3. 19–26 (according to the prophetic parable of Matt. 22. 2–7). Thenceforth the *earthly* realization of this Kingdom was postponed, and is now in abeyance until the King shall be sent from heaven (Acts 3. 20). The "secrets" of this Kingdom (Matt. 13. 11) pertained to the postponement of its earthly realization, on account of its being rejected.

2. **"The Kingdom of God"** is the sovereignty of God, which is moral and universal. It existed from the beginning, and will know no end. It is over all, and embraces all. See Ap. 114.

3. **"The Kingdom of the Father"** (Matt. 13. 43) is not universal, but has regard to *relationship*, and to "a heavenly calling" (Heb. 3. 1), and to the heavenly sphere of the Kingdom, in its relation to the earthly. It is sovereignty exercised toward obedient sons, when the Son of man shall have gathered out of His Kingdom "all things that offend" (Matt. 13. 41). Cp. Dan. 7. 25–27. Matt. 25. 31–46. Luke 20. 34–36. The way of entrance into this may be seen in John 3. 3. It is going on now concurrently with No. 5.

4. **"The Kingdom of the Son of man"** (Matt. 16. 28). This aspect of "the Kingdom of heaven" has regard to *Israel on earth* (cp. Dan. 7. 13, 14, 18, 21, 22), as distinct from the "sons" who, as partakers of "a heavenly calling" (Heb. 3. 1), will possess the heavenly sphere as sons of the resurrection (Luke 20. 34–36. Cp. 1 Cor. 15. 23. Rev. 20. 4–6). These two spheres are distinct, though they are one. No. 3 concerns "the saints of the most high [places]" (Dan. 7. 18, 24). No. 4 concerns "*the people* of the saints of the most high". These have their portion in "the Kingdom *under* the whole heaven", which has regard to earthly sovereignty, in which "all dominions shall serve and obey Him" (Dan. 7. 27).

These two would have had their realization even then, had Israel repented at the summons of the Lord, and of "them that heard Him" in Acts 3. 19–26. In that case the later revelation of the "Mystery" (or the great secret) which, with its *exanastasis* and its "heavenward Call" (Phil. 3. 11, 14), was *hidden* in God, would have remained in the keeping of the Father's Divine sovereignty.

5. **"The Kingdom of His dear Son".** Gr. the Kingdom of the Son of His love, or of His beloved Son (Col. 1. 13), has regard to quite another sphere, above all heavens, and refers to the sovereignty of God's beloved Son as made the

"Head over all things to His *ekklēsia*, which is His body, the fulness of Him that filleth all in all" (Eph. 1. 10, 20–23). See also Eph. 5. 5.

This sovereignty had been "kept secret" (Rom. 16. 25), "hid in God" (Eph. 3. 9), "hid from ages and from generations" (Col. 1. 26); but after the Kingdom (No. 4) proclaimed by the Lord and by "them that heard Him" (Heb. 2. 4) had been postponed, it was revealed and "made known" (Eph. 3) for the "obedience of faith" (Rom. 16. 26). The subjects of this Divine sovereignty, on their believing this subsequent revelation, are "sealed" (or designated) for their inheritance, which is to be enjoyed with Christ (Eph. 1. 13).

This relates to the *position* of those who come under that sovereignty.

6. **"The Everlasting Kingdom of our Lord and Saviour Jesus Christ"** (2 Pet. 1. 11). This has regard to No. 5, but was then future (not having been revealed when Peter wrote); but it relates to the *outward display* of His sovereignty in millennial glory; while No. 5 relates to the *inward position* and experimental enjoyment of it in present grace.

7. **"The Kingdom of our Lord and of His Christ"** (or Messiah). (Rev. 11. 15). This has regard to the end of the present time of abeyance of Nos. 3 and 4, and the millennial manifestation of both by Divine power, and in glory. See also Rev. 12. 10.

At the end of the thousand years, No. 1, and perhaps others of them will cease, and be absorbed in the Kingdom of God (No. 2).

113 THE "KINGDOM" AND THE "CHURCH".

From Appendixes 112 and 114 it will be seen that, if each use of the term "kingdom" has its own special and particular meaning and must not be confused with others that differ, there must be still greater confusion if any one of them is identified with "the Church", as is very commonly done: though which of the Kingdoms and which of the Churches is never definitely pointed out.

The following reasons may be given which will show that "the Kingdom" and "the Church" cannot thus be identified:—

1. The subjects of the former are spoken of as "inheriting", or as being "heirs of the Kingdom"; but we cannot speak of *inheriting* or being *heirs* of "the Church".

2. We read of the possibility of "receiving the Kingdom", but in no sense can *any Church* be spoken of as being received.

3. We read of "the elders of the Churches", messengers or servants of the Churches, but never of the *elders*, &c., of the Kingdom.

4. The word *basileia*, translated "kingdom", occurs 162 times, and in the plural only in Matt. 4. 8. Luke 4. 5. Heb. 11. 33. Rev. 11. 15. On the other hand, the word *ekklēsia* occurs 115 times, and of these 36 are in the plural and 79 in the singular, all rendered "church" except Acts 19. 32, 39, 41, "assembly".

5. We read of "the children (or sons) of the Kingdom", but the Bible knows nothing of the *sons* of "the Church".

6. The characteristics of each are distinct.

7. The names and appellatives of "the Church" are never used of the Kingdom (Eph. 1. 23; 2. 21; 4. 4, 16; 5. 30. Col. 1. 24. 1 Tim. 3. 15).

8. The privilege of "that Church" which consists of the partakers of "a heavenly calling", Heb. 3. 1 (see Ap. 112. 4, 5); Rev. 20. 4–6, will be to reign with Christ *over* the earthly Kingdom, whereas that Kingdom will be "*under* the whole heaven" (Dan. 7. 27).

9. "The Church" of the Prison Epistles (Eph., Phil., Col.) is here and now, *in the world*, and is waiting for its *exanastasis*, and its "heavenward call" (Phil. 3. 11, 14); whereas the Kingdom is not here, because the King is *not here* (Heb. 2. 8).

10. The Kingdom is the one great subject of prophecy; whereas the Church (of the Prison Epistles) is not the subject of prophecy, but, on the contrary, was kept secret, and hidden in God, until the time came for the secret to be revealed. (See Ap. 112. 5.)

It must be understood that this "secret" (Gr. *mustērion*, see Ap. 182) did not and could not refer to Jews and Gentiles in future blessing, because this was *never a secret*, but was part of the original promise made to Abraham in Gen. 12. 3, and was repeatedly spoken of throughout the Psalms and the Prophets. See Deut. 32. 43. Ps. 18. 49; 117. 1. Isa. 11. 1, 10, &c. Cp. Rom. 15. 8–12, and the quotations there given.

114 THE "KINGDOM OF HEAVEN" AND THE "KINGDOM OF GOD".

We have seen in Ap. 112 that the word "kingdom", like the Greek *basileia*, has regard to *sovereignty* rather than *territory*, and to the *sphere* of its exercise rather than to its *extent*.

Using the word "kingdom" in this sense, and in that which is conveyed in its English termination "dom", which is short for dominion, we note that the former expression, "the Kingdom of heaven", occurs only in Matthew, where we find it thirty-two times.[1]

But in the parallel passages in the other Gospels we find, instead, the expression "the Kingdom of God" (e.g. cp. Matt. 11. 11 with Luke 7. 28).

The explanation of this seeming difference is that the Lord spoke in Aramaic; certainly not in the Greek of the Gospel documents. See Ap. 94. III.

Now "heaven" is frequently used by the Figure *Metonymy* (of the Subject), Ap. 6, for God Himself, Whose dwelling is there. See Ps. 73. 9. Dan. 4. 26, 29. 2 Chron. 32. 20. Matt. 21. 25. Luke 15. 21 ("I have sinned against heaven" is thus contrasted with the words "and in thy sight"). John 3. 27.

[1] The Kingdom of God occurs only five times in Matt. (6. 33; 12. 28; 19. 24; 21. 31, 43).

Our suggestion is that in all the passages where the respective expressions occur, identical words were spoken by the Lord, "the Kingdom of heaven"; but when it came to putting them into *Greek*, Matthew was Divinely guided to retain the figure of speech *literally* ("heaven"), so as to be in keeping with the special character, design, and scope of his Gospel (see Ap. 96); while, in the other Gospels, *the figure was translated* as being what it also meant, "the Kingdom of God".

Thus, while the same in a general sense, the two expressions are to be distinguished in their meaning and in their interpretation, as follows:—

I. The Kingdom (or Sovereignty) of HEAVEN

1. Has *Messiah* for its King;
2. It is *from heaven*; and *under* the heavens *upon* the earth;
3. It is *limited* in its scope;
4. It is *political* in its sphere;
5. It is *Jewish and exclusive* in its character;
6. It is *national* in its aspect;
7. It is the *special subject* of *Old Testament prophecy*;
8. And it is *dispensational* in its duration.

II. The Kingdom (or Sovereignty) of GOD
1. Has *God* for its Ruler;
2. It is *in heaven, over* the earth;
3. It is *unlimited* in its scope;
4. It is *moral* and *spiritual* in its sphere;
5. It is *inclusive* in its character (embracing the natural and spiritual seeds of Abraham, "the heavenly calling", and the "Church" of the Mystery). Hence,
6. It is *universal* in its aspect;
7. It is (in its *wider* aspect) the subject of *New Testament revelation*;
8. And will be *eternal* in its duration.

115 BAPTIZE", "BAPTISM", ETC.

It will be useful for the student to have a complete and classified list of the various usages of these words in the N.T.; the following *conspectus* has been prepared, so that the reader may be in a position to draw his own conclusions.

I. The VERB *baptizō* occurs *eighty*[1] times, as follows:

i. In its absolute form, or followed by a noun in the accusative case. See Matt. 3. 16; 20. 22, 22, 23, 23. Mark 6. 14; 10. 38, 38, 39, 39; 16. 16. Luke 3. 12, 21, 21; 7. 29; 12. 50. John 1. 25, 28; 3. 22, 23, 26; 4. 1, 2; 10. 40. Acts 2. 41; 8. 12, 13, 36, 38; 9. 18; 10. 47; 16. 15, 33; 18. 8; 19. 4; 22. 16. 1 Cor. 1. 14, 16, 16, 17 40

ii. With the Dative case (implying the element): Luke 3. 16. Acts 1. 5; 11. 16. . . . 3

iii. With *en* (Ap. 104. viii), denoting
1. The element, described as being
a. Water. Matt. 3. 11. Mark 1. 8. John 1. 26, 31, 33 5
b. *Pneuma hagion.* (See Ap. 101. II. 14.) Matt. 3. 11. Mark 1. 8. Luke 3. 16. John 1. 33. Acts 1. 5; 11. 16. 1 Cor. 12. 13*. 7
c. The name of the Lord. Acts 10. 48 1
d. The cloud and sea. 1 Cor. 10. 2* . . 1
14
2. The locality. Matt. 3. 6*. Mark 1. 4, 5*. John 3. 23. 4

iv. with *eis* (Ap. 104. vi). Matt. 28. 19. Mark 1. 9*. Acts 8. 16; 19. 3, 5. Rom. 6. 3, 3. 1 Cor. 1. 13, 15; 10. 2*; 12. 13*. Gal. 3. 27 . . . 12

v. with *epi* (Ap. 104. ix). Acts 2. 38 (with Dative) 1

vi. with *huper* (Ap. 104. xvii). 1 Cor. 15. 29, 29. 2

vii. with *hupo* (Ap. 104. xviii). Matt. 3. 6*, 13, 14. Mark 1. 5*, 9*. Luke 3. 7; 7. 30 . . . 7

viii. Translated "wash". Mark 7. 4. Luke 11. 38 2
85

II. The NOUNS.

i. *Baptisma.* Occurs twenty-two times, as follows:
1. General. Matt. 20. 22, 23. Mark 10. 38, 39. Luke 12. 50. Rom. 6. 4. Eph. 4. 5. Col. 2. 12. 1 Pet. 3. 21 9
2. John's baptism. Matt. 3. 7; 21. 25. Mark 1. 4; 11. 30. Luke 3. 3; 7. 29; 20. 4. Acts 1. 22; 10. 37; 13. 24; 18. 25; 19. 3, 4. . 13
22

ii. *Baptismos.* Occurs four times:
1. Translated "washing". Mark 7. 4, 8. Heb. 9. 10 3
2. Translated "baptisms". Heb. 6. 2 . . . 1
4

[1] In the five passages thus marked (*), the verb is followed by two phrases, and therefore appears under two heads. They are: Matt. 3. 6. Mark 1. 5, 9. 1 Cor. 10. 2; 12. 13.

116 THE TEMPTATIONS OF OUR LORD.

It is well known that the order of the temptations in Matthew is not the same as in Luke. Commentators and Harmonizers assume that one is right and the other is wrong; and proceed to change the order of one in order to make it agree with the other. See Ap. 96.

But an examination of the combined accounts, giving due weight to the words and expressions used, will explain all the differences, and show that both Gospels are absolutely correct; while the differences are caused by the three temptations being repeated by the devil in a different order, thus making six instead of three.

Mark and Luke agree in stating that the temptations continued all the forty days (Mark 1. 13. Luke 4. 2); they are described as follows:—

I. (Luke 4. 3, 4.) "The devil (*ho diabolos*) said to Him, 'Speak to this stone (*tō lithō toutō*) that it become a loaf (*artos*).'" This appears to be the first temptation: and there is no reason whatever why it should not have been repeated in another form; for it is nowhere stated that there were three, and only three temptations[1].

II. (Luke 4. 5–8.) "And the devil, conducting (*anagōn*) Him, shewed to Him all the kingdoms of the habitable world, or land (Gr. *oikoumenē*, Ap. 129. 3), in a moment of time." Nothing is said about "an exceeding high mountain". Lachmann brackets the words "into an high mountain", and Tischendorff, Tregelles, Alford, WH, and R.V. omit them.

The devil claims to possess the right to the kingdoms of the world, and the Lord does not dispute it. Satan says: "To Thee will I give this authority (*exousia*) and all their glory, for to me it has been delivered, and to whomsoever I wish I give it. Therefore, if Thou wilt worship before me, all shall be Thine".

Nothing is said here about "*falling down*", as in Matthew. Here, only "authority" is offered; for all the critical Greek texts read "*pasa*" (not "*panta*") fem. to agree with *exousia*.

The Lord did not say, "Get thee hence" (as in Matt. 4. 10), but "Get thee behind Me", which was a very different thing. Satan did not depart then, any more than Peter did when the same was said to him (Matt. 16. 23).

III. (Luke 4. 9–12.) "And he conducted (*ēgagen*) Him to Jerusalem, and set Him upon the wing (or battlement, Dan. 9. 27 m.) of the temple, and said to Him, 'If Thou art the Son of God, cast Thyself down hence, for it is written, that to His angels He will give charge concerning Thee, to keep Thee (*tou diaphulaxai se*)'", &c.

There is nothing said about this "*keeping thee*" in

[1] This is like other traditional expressions; for where do we read of "three" wise men? We see them only in mediæval paintings. Where do we read of angels being women? Yet as such they are always painted. Where do we find in Scripture other common sayings, such as "the talent hid in a *napkin*"? It was hidden "in the earth". Where do we ever see a picture of the crucifixion with the mark of the spear on the *left* side?

Matthew; moreover, it is stated that having finished every form of temptation, "he departed from Him for a season". Note that the devil departed (*apestē*) of his own accord in Luke 4. 13, while in Matthew the Lord summarily dismissed him, and commanded him to be gone (Matt. 4. 10).

IV. (Matt. 4. 3, 4.) After the "season" (referred to in Luke 4. 13), and on another occasion therefore, "he who was tempting Him (*ho peirazōn*), having come (*proselthōn*), said, "If Thou art the Son of God, say that these stones become loaves (*artoi*)". Not "this stone", or "a loaf" (*artos*), as in Luke 4. 3. Moreover he is not plainly called "the devil", as in Luke 4. 3, but is spoken of as the one who had already been named as tempting Him (*ho peirazōn*); and as "having come" (*proselthōn*): not as simply speaking as being then present.

V. (Matt. 4. 5-7.) "Then (*tote*)"—in strict succession to the preceding temptation of the "stones" and the "loaves"—"Then the devil taketh (*paralambanei*) Him unto the holy city, and setteth Him upon the wing (or battlement) of the temple", &c. Nothing is said here about the angels being charged to "keep" Him (as in Luke 4. 10); nor is there any reason why any of these three forms of temptation should not have been repeated, under other circumstances and conditions.

VI. (Matt. 4. 8-10.) Here it is plainly stated that the second temptation (Luke 4. 5-8) was repeated: for "Again the devil taketh Him unto an exceedingly high mountain, and sheweth to Him all the kingdoms of the world, *kosmos* (Ap. 129. 1), not *oikoumenē* (Ap. 129. 3), as in Luke 4. 5, and their glory, and said to Him: "All these things, not "all this authority", as in Luke 4. 6, will I give to Thee if, *falling down*, Thou wilt worship me". Here, in this last temptation, the climax is reached. It was direct worship. Nothing is said in Luke about *falling down*. Here it is boldly and plainly said, "Worship me". This was the crisis. There was no departing of Satan's own accord here. The moment had come to end all these temptations by the Lord Himself. "Go! said the Lord (*hupage*), Get thee hence, Satan . . . Then the devil leaveth (*aphiēsin*) Him, and, behold, angels came and ministered to Him".

This angelic ministry marked the end. There is no such ministry mentioned at the end of the third temptation in Luke 4. 3-12; for then Satan "departed" of his own accord, returning (in Matt. 4. 3) after "a season" (Luke 4. 13).

True, the Lord had said "Get thee behind Me, Satan" (Luke 4. 8); but He did not, then, summarily dismiss him, nor did Satan depart: he continued with his third temptation, not departing till after the third had been completed.

We thus conclude that, while there were temptations continuous during the whole of the forty days (Mark 1. 13. Luke 4. 2), they culminated in six direct assaults on the Son of man, in three different forms; each form being repeated on two separate occasions, and under different circumstances, *but not in the same order*.

This accords with all the variations of the words used, explains the different order of events in the two Gospels, and satisfies all the conditions demanded by the sacred text.

The two different orders in Matthew and Luke do not arise from a "mistake" in one or the other, so that one may be considered correct and the other incorrect; they arise from the punctilious accuracy of the Divine record in describing the true and correct order in which Satan varied the six temptations; for which variation, he alone, and neither of the Evangelists, is responsible.

117 THE LORD'S KNOWLEDGE

I. OF THE PAST: IN THE WRITTEN WORD OF GOD IN THE OLD TESTAMENT.

(Allusions are indicated by an asterisk.)

New Test.	Old Test.
Matt 4. 4	Deut. 8. 3.
„ 4. 7	„ 6. 16.
„ 4. 10	„ 6. 13.
„ 5. 17, 18*	
„ 5. 21	Ex. 20. 13.
„ 5. 27	„ 20. 14.
„ 5. 31	Deut. 24. 1.
„ 5. 33-...	Lev. 19. 12.
	Num. 30. 2.
„ 5. -33......	Deut. 23. 21.
„ 5. 38	Ex. 21. 24.
„ 5. 43	Lev. 19. 18.
„ 8. 4*	
„ 9. 13	Hos. 6. 6.
„ 10. 35, 36...	Mic. 7. 6.
„ 11. 10	Mal. 3. 1.
„ 12. 3, 4 ...	1 Sam. 21. 1-6.
„ 12. 7	Hos. 6. 6.
„ 12. 40	Jonah 1. 17.
„ 13. 14, 15...	Isa. 6. 9, 10.
„ 15. 4	Ex. 20. 12; 21. 17.
„ 15. 8, 9 ...	Isa. 29. 13.
„ 16. 4*	
„ 17. 11*	
„ 19. 4	Gen. 1. 27.
„ 19. 5	„ 2. 24.
„ 19. 8	Deut. 24. 1.
„ 19. 18 ...	Ex. 20. 12-16.
	Deut. 5. 16-20.
Matt. 19. 19	Lev. 19. 18.
„ 21. 13	Isa. 56. 7. Jer. 7. 11.
„ 21. 16	Ps. 8. 2.
„ 21. 42	„ 118. 22, 23.
„ 22. 29*	
„ 22. 32	Ex. 3. 6.
„ 22. 37	Deut. 6. 5.
„ 22. 39	Lev. 19. 18.
„ 22. 44	Ps. 110. 1.
„ 23. 39	„ 118. 26.
„ 24. 7	Isa. 19. 2.
„ 24. 10	„ 8. 15.
„ 24. 15.	Dan. 9. 27.
„ 24. 21	„ 12. 1.
„ 24. 29	Isa. 13. 10; 34. 4.
„ 24. 30	Zech. 12. 12.
„ 24. 31 ...	Isa. 27. 13.
	Deut. 30. 4.
„ 24. 37* ...	Gen. 7.
„ 26. 24*	
„ 26. 31	Zech. 13. 7
„ 26. 54*	
„ 26. 64 ...	Ps. 110. 1.
	Dan. 7. 13.
„ 27. 46	Ps. 22. 1.
Mark 8. 18	Jer. 5. 21.
„ 9. 48	Isa. 66. 24.
„ 10. 3*	
„ 13. 12	Mic. 7. 6.
Mark 14. 49*	
Luke 4. 18, 19 ...	Isa. 61. 1, 2.
„ 10. 27	Deut. 6. 5; 10. 12.
„ 11. 51	Gen. 4. 8-10.
„ 16. 31*	
„ 17. 26, 27...	Gen. 6.
„ 17. 28, 29...	Gen. 19.
„ 18. 31*	
„ 20. 18	Dan. 2. 45.
„ 21. 22	Hos. 9. 7.
„ 21. 26	Isa. 34. 4.
„ 21. 35	Isa. 24. 17.
„ 22. 37	Isa. 53. 12.
„ 23. 30 ...	Isa. 2. 19.
	Hos. 10. 8.
„ 23. 46	Ps. 31. 5.
„ 24. 27 ...	
„ 24. 44-47*	
John 3. 14	Num. 21. 9.
„ 5. 39*	
„ 5. 46, 47*	
„ 6. 32	Ex. 16. 15.
„ 6. 45	Isa. 54. 13.
„ 7. 38*	
„ 8. 17	Deut. 19. 15.
„ 10. 34	Ps. 82. 6.
„ 13. 18	„ 41. 9.
„ 15. 25	„ 35. 19; 69. 4; 119. 78.
„ 19. 28	„ 69. 21.

II. OF THE FUTURE: IN HIS OWN PROPHETIC WORDS.

Matt. 4.17,19.	**Matt. 22.30.**	**Luke 8.48,50.**	**John 7.34,37–39.**
„ 5.3–12,17,18,20–22.	**„ 23.36–39.**	**„ 12.32.**	**„ 8.12,28,51.**
„ 6.2,4,16,18.	**„ 24.**	**„ 13.25.**	**„ 9.5.**
„ 7.7,22.	**„ 25.**	**„ 14.14.**	**„ 10.15,28.**
„ 8.11,12.	**„ 26.23,29,32,34,64.**	**„ 15.10.**	**„ 11.25,26,40,43.**
„ 9.6,15.	**Mark 4.12.**	**„ 17.34–36.**	**„ 12.23,32,48.**
„ 10.15,32.	**„ 7.29.**	**„ 19.9,43.**	**„ 13.19,20.**
„ 11.11,22–24,29.	**„ 8.35,38.**	**„ 22.19–21,29,31,37.**	**„ 14.2,6,9,16,19,23.**
„ 12.6,31,36,41,42,45.	**„ 9,1,9,31,41,48.**	**„ 23.28,30,43.**	**„ 15.1–7.**
„ 13.40–50.	**„ 10.45.**	**„ 24.26,47,49.**	**„ 16.4,7–13.**
„ 15.13.	**„ 11.2,3,14,26.**	**John 1.51.**	**„ 17.1.**
„ 16.25,27.	**„ 12.34,40.**	**„ 2.19,24,25.**	**„ 18.36,37.**
„ 17.12,22,23.	**„ 13.2.**	**„ 3.13,14.**	**„ 20.17,21,23.**
„ 18.14,35.	**„ 14.8,13.**	**„ 4.10,14,21–23,50.**	**„ 21.6,18,19,22.**
„ 19.28–30.	**Luke 2.49.**	**„ 5.8,17,19.**	
„ 20.18,23.	**4.21.**	**„ 6.27,33,35,37,39,40, 44,47,51,64,70.**	
„ 21.2,43,44.	**„ 7.47,48.**		

118 "IF": THE VARIOUS CONDITIONS CONVEYED BY ITS USE.

1. *ean*=if haply, if so be that, from *ei* (No. 2) and *an*, haply, perchance. The exact condition is shown by the *Mood* of the verb with which it is used:

a. Followed by the *Indicative Mood* (with the Present Tense), it expresses the condition simply; without any reference to its being decisive by experience, or by the event, as in 1 John 5.15, elsewhere, and in the *Papyri*.

b. Followed by the *Subjunctive Mood*, it expresses a hypothetical but possible condition, contingent on circumstances which the future will show (John 7.17).

2. *ei*=if. Putting the condition simply.

a. Followed by the *Indicative Mood*, the hypothesis is assumed as an actual fact, the condition being unfulfilled, but no doubt being thrown upon the supposition (1 Cor. 15.16).

b. Followed by the *Optative Mood*, it expresses an entire uncertainty; a mere assumption or conjecture of a supposed case (Acts 17.27. 1 Pet. 3.14).

c. Followed by the *Subjunctive Mood*, like No. 1. b; except that this puts the condition with more certainty, and as being more dependent on the event (1 Cor. 14.5).

For two illustrations, see Acts 5.38, 39. "If this counsel or this work be of men (1. b, a result which remains to be seen) . . . but if it is of God (1. a which I assume to be the case)", &c.

John 13.17. "If ye know these things (2. a, which I assume to be the fact) happy are ye if ye do them (1. b, a result which remains to be seen)".

Note four "ifs" in Colossians, "if ye died with Christ" (2.20); and "if ye were raised with Christ" (3.1), both of which are No. 2. a (assuming the fact to be true); "if any man have a quarrel" (3.13); "if he come to you" (4.10), both of which are No. 1. b, being uncertainties.

One other "if" in Colossians is 1.23: "If ye continue in the faith" (*eige*=if indeed, a form of 2. a), which ye will assuredly do.

119 THE FOURFOLD MINISTRY OF OUR LORD.

In the Four Gospels the Ministry of our Lord is divided, not into "years", but by *subjects*, which are of far greater importance than time. The "years" are mainly conjectural, but the subjects are Divinely recorded facts.

The subjects are two in number: the Kingdom and the King; and, since these are repeated in the form of *Introversion*, it brings the Person of the Lord into the Structure of the Gospel as the one great *central* subject of each, for all four Gospels are similarly constructed. See pages 1305, 1381, 1427, and 1510.

As, however, the index-letters are not the same in each Gospel, we set them out in their order:—

The Four Subjects.

**The First is THE KINGDOM.
The Second is THE KING.** } **Their Proclamation.**

**The Third is THE KING.
The Fourth is THE KINGDOM.** } **Their Rejection.**

These Subjects begin and end respectively in the Four Gospels as follows:—

MATTHEW.	MARK.	LUKE.	JOHN.
1st. 4.12—7.29 (125 verses).	**1st. 1.14–20. (7 verses).**	**1st. 4.14—5.11 (42 verses).**	**1st. 1.35—4.54 (132 verses).**
2nd. 8.1—16.20 (347 verses).	**2nd. 1.21—8.30 (295 verses).**	**2nd. 5.12—9.21 (204 verses).**	**2nd. 5.1—6.71 (118 verses).**
3rd. 16.21—20.34 (134 verses).	**3rd. 8.31—10.52 (110 verses).**	**3rd. 9.22—18.43 (409 verses).**	**3rd. 7.1—11.53 (248 verses).**
4th. 21.1—26.35 (263 verses).	**4th. 11.1—14.25 (139 verses).**	**4th. 19.1—22.38 (171 verses).**	**4th. 11.54—17.26 (209 verses).**

From the above it will be seen that, including all the Four Gospels,

The First Subject (the Proclamation of the Kingdom) occupies in all 306 verses.

The Second Subject (the Proclamation of the King) occupies in all 964 verses.

The Third Subject (the Rejection of the King) occupies in all 901 verses.

The Fourth Subject (the Rejection of the Kingdom), occupies in all 782 verses.

Thus, the Subject that occupies the greatest number of verses is the KING: viz. 1865 verses in all (964 concerning the proclamation, and 901 concerning His rejection).

The Subject of the KINGDOM occupies 1088 verses in all (306 verses concerning its proclamation, and 782 concerning its rejection).

The Gospel which has most to say about the First Subject (the Proclamation of the Kingdom) is JOHN, having 132 verses; while MARK has the least, having only 7 verses on this Subject.

The Gospel which has most to say about the Second Subject (the Proclamation of the King) is MATTHEW, having 347 verses; while JOHN (strange to say) has the least, 118 verses; the reason being that in Matthew, the Lord is presented in His human relationship as King; whereas in John He is presented as God manifest in the flesh.

The Gospel which has most to say on the Third Subject (the Rejection of the King) is LUKE, having 409 verses; while MARK has the least, only 110 verses.

The Gospel which has most to say about the Fourth Subject (the Rejection of the Kingdom) is MATTHEW, having 263 verses; while Mark again has the least, 139 verses.

These particulars, when compared with the interrelation of the four Gospels as set forth in their respective Structures, are full of interest, and help to determine more specifically the great design of each Gospel.

Taking the Gospel of Matthew as an example, we find:—

The first subject is marked by the beginning and ending being both noted (4. 17 and 7. 28). All between these verses referred to the Kingdom which had drawn near in the Person of the King, but which, owing to His rejection, and the rejection of the "other servants" (22. 4) in the Acts of the Apostles, was postponed, and is now in abeyance (Heb. 2. 8, "not yet").

The commencement of the Second Subject is noted by the ending of the First Subject (7. 28). In ch. 8. 2, 6, 8 the Lord is immediately addressed as "Lord"; and, in *v.* 20 He gives His other title, "the Son of man".[1] The great miracles manifesting His Divine and Human perfections are recorded in this section, which ends with His question focussing the whole Subject: "Who do men say that I, the Son of man, am?" and Peter's answer: "Thou art the Messiah, the Son of the living God" (16. 13-16).

The Third Subject is marked in 16. 21: "From that time forth began Jesus to shew unto His disciples how He must go unto Jerusalem, and suffer many things", &c.

Thus there was a moment at which He introduced the Subject of His rejection, of which He had never before given even a hint. When once He had begun, He repeated it four times (in each Gospel), each time adding fresh details. See 16. 21; 17. 22; 20. 18; 20. 28.

The Fourth Subject (the Rejection of the Kingdom) begins at 21. 1 and continues down to 26. 35, when He goes forth from the Upper Room to Gethsemane.

In this section comes the second series[2] of Parables which deals with the Rejection and Postponement of the Kingdom, which was to be henceforth in abeyance. The approaching end of this period is marked off in 26. 1, closing with the last Supper at 26. 26-29.

The same four subjects may be traced in like manner in the other Gospels.

[1] Its first occurrence in the N.T., the last being in Rev. 14. 14. It is the title connected with dominion in the earth. See Ap. 98. XVI.

[2] The first series being recorded in Matt. 13 (see Ap. 145); the second series, beginning with Matt. 21. 28, being specially marked by the word "again" in Matt. 22. 1.

120 THE SYNAGOGUE; AND JEWISH SECTS.

I. THE SYNAGOGUE.

Synagogues are mentioned as existing in Old Testament times, Ps. 74. 4, 8. The Heb. here is *mo'ēd*, and in *v.* 8 it is rendered "synagogues" in the A.V. and R.V. (margin, "places of assembly"). AQUILA also, a reviser of the Septuagint (about A. D. 130), renders it *sunagōgē*.

Synagogues were in use from the earliest times, and Dr. John Lightfoot (*Works*, vol. v, p. 112) identifies them with "the 'high places' so often mentioned in Scripture in a commendable sense, as 1 Sam. 9. 19; 10. 5. 1 Kings 3. 4, &c." These are to be distinguished from the "high places" connected with idolatry and false worship (as 1 Kings 11. 7 and 12. 31. Jer. 7. 31 and 19. 5, &c.). How else could the "holy convocations" be held in accordance with Lev. 23. 3, 4, &c.?

On the return from the captivity, laws were made to regulate their erection, constitution, and use.

The days of assembly were three: the Sabbath, the second day of the week (our Sunday sunset to Monday sunset), and the fifth day (our Wednesday sunset, &c.). The expression in Acts 13. 42, which in the Greek=the Sabbath between, may therefore refer to one of these intervening days.

The officers of the Synagogue were:—

1. The *Archisunagōgos*=the ruler of the Synagogue, having charge of its affairs, regulating the service, &c.

2. The *Sheliach* (or *mal'ak*) *hazzibbōr*=the angel of the *ekklēsia*, who was the constant minister of the Synagogue, to pray, preach, have charge of the law and appoint its readers. Hence he was called *episkopos*, or overseer. See notes on 1 Cor. 11. 10. Rev. 1. 20.

II. THE PHARISEES AND SADDUCEES.

1. The word PHARISEE is the Hebrew for one who was *separated* by special beliefs and practices, which were very strict as to tithing and eating, &c. (see Matt. 23. 23. Luke 18. 12). It was for this reason that the Lord was upbraided by the Pharisees (Matt. 9. 9-11; 11. 19. Mark 2. 16. Luke 5. 30; 7. 34).

Doctrinally, they held that the *oral* law was necessary to complete and explain the *written* law; hence, the strong denunciations of the Lord. Moreover, they held the natural immortality of man; and, JOSEPHUS says, the transmigration of souls.

[The ESSENES cultivated an intensified form of Pharisaism.]

2. The word SADDUCEE is the Greek form of the Heb. *zaddūkīm*, which is derived from one *Zadōk*, said to be the founder of the sect, who was a disciple of ANTIGONUS of SOCOH (200-170 B.C.). They were the aristocratic and conservative party politically; and, doctrinally (generally speaking) they negatived the teaching of the Pharisees, even denying the doctrine of the resurrection.

Neither of these sects had any existence, as such, till the return from Babylon.

121 THE SYNONYMOUS WORDS FOR "PREACH", ETC.

1. ***kērussō***=to proclaim (as a herald), from *kērux*, a herald; without reference to the *matter* proclaimed (which is contained in No. 4); and without including the idea of *teaching*.

2. ***kērux***=a herald.

3. ***kērugma***=that which is proclaimed.

4. ***euangelizō***=to announce a joyful message; having regard to the *matter* announced (not the manner, which is contained in No. 1).

5. ***katangellō***=to bring word down to any one, bring it home by setting it forth.

6. ***diangellō***=to make known (through an intervening space), report further (by spreading it far and wide).

7. ***laleō***=to talk or to use the voice, without reference to the words spoken (see Mark 2. 2).

8. ***dialegomai***=to speak to and fro (alternately), converse, discuss (see Acts 20. 7, 9). Hence Eng. dialogue.

9. ***akoē***=hearing. Put by Fig. *Metonymy* (of Subject) for what is heard.

10. ***logos***=the word (spoken, as a means or instrument, not as a product); the expression (both of sayings and of longer speeches); hence, an account, as in Matt. 12. 36; 18. 23. Luke 16. 2. Acts 19. 40. Rom. 9. 28 (m.); 14. 12. Phil. 4. 17. Heb. 13. 17. 1 Pet. 4. 5. For the difference between *logos* and *rhēma*, see note on Mark 9. 32.

122 THE SYNONYMOUS WORDS FOR "JUDGE", "CONDEMN", ETC.

1. ***krinō***=to judge, used of a legal or other decision; generally translated "judge", sometimes "determine", "conclude", &c.

2. ***anakrinō.*** No. 1 with *ana* (Ap. 104. i) prefixed= to examine; translated, with a negative, "ask no question" in 1 Cor. 10. 25, 27.

3. ***apokrinomai.*** Middle of No. 1 with *apo* (Ap. 104. iv) prefixed=to give forth a decision for oneself; hence to answer. According to Hebrew idiom, which prevails in both Testaments, it is often combined with the word "said" in the expression "answered and said", and receives its meaning from the context. See note on Deut. 1. 41. It thus frequently occurs when no question had been asked: e.g. in Matt. 11. 25, "answered and said" means "prayed and said"; 22. 1, "taught"; in Mark 9. 5, "exclaimed"; 12. 35, "asked"; Luke 13. 14, "burst forth"; John 1. 49, "confessed"; 5. 19, "declared". The word occurs so frequently (more than 240 times), always translated "answer", that it has not been deemed necessary to call attention to it in the notes.

4. ***diakrinō.*** No. 1 with *dia* (Ap. 104. v) prefixed= to discriminate, make a difference; hence to doubt. It is translated "stagger at" in Rom. 4. 20.

5. ***enkrinō.*** No. 1 with *en* (Ap. 104. viii) prefixed= to adjudge to a particular position. Occurs only in 2 Cor. 10. 12, translated "make of the number".

6. ***epikrinō.*** No. 1 with *epi* (Ap. 104. ix) prefixed= to pronounce sentence upon. Occurs only in Luke 23. 24.

7. ***katakrinō.*** No. 1 with *kata* (Ap. 104. x) prefixed= to give sentence against, to condemn. Occurs 19 times, translated "condemn", except in Mark 16. 16 and Rom. 14. 23.

8. ***sunkrinō.*** No. 1 with *sun* (Ap. 104. xvi) prefixed= to put together, in order to judge; hence to compare. Occurs only in 1 Cor. 2. 13. 2 Cor. 10. 12.

9. ***hupokrinomai.*** Middle of No. 1 with *hupo* (Ap. 104. xviii) prefixed=to answer (like No. 3), and so to act on the stage; hence to feign. Occurs only in Luke 20. 20. The nouns *hupokrisis* and *hupokritēs*, which we have anglicized into "hypocrisy" and "hypocrite", are always so translated, save in Gal. 2. 13, and James 5. 12.

123 THE SYNONYMOUS WORDS FOR "MAN", "MEN".

Sometimes the word "man" is added in translating the Masc. Gender of Adjectives or Nouns, in which case it is not one of the words given below.

1. ***anthrōpos***=an individual of the Genus *Homo*; a human being as distinct from animals. See Ap. 98. XVI, for "the Son of man".

2. ***anēr***=an adult male person. Lat. *vir*, an honourable title (as distinct from a mere "man", No. 1); hence, used of a husband.

3. ***tis***=some one, a certain one.

4. ***arrēn***=a male; of the male sex.

5. ***arsēn.*** The same as No. 4; being the old *Ionic* form, as No. 4 is the later *Attic* form.

6. ***teleios***=one who has reached maturity as to age or qualification, or by initiation. Rendered "man" in 1 Cor. 14. 20. See note there; also Ap. 125. 1, and cp. 1 Cor. 2. 6.

124 THE SYNONYMOUS WORDS FOR "OTHER", "ANOTHER".

1. ***allos***=another of the same kind (denoting *numerical* distinction). The second of two where there may be more: e.g. Matt. 10. 23; 25. 16, 17, 20; 27. 42, 61; 28. 1. John 18. 15, 16; 20. 2-4. Rev. 17. 10. See note on John 19. 18.

2. ***heteros***=another of a different kind (usually denoting *generic* distinction). The "other" of two, where there are only two: e.g. Matt. 6. 24; 11. 3. Luke 5. 7; 7. 41; 14. 31; 16. 13, 18; 17. 34, 35; 18. 10; 23. 40.

3. ***loipos***=the remaining one. Pl.=those who are left.

4. ***tines***=certain ones. 2 Cor. 3. 1.

5. ***kakeinos***=and that one there. Contraction of *kai ekeinos*, only translated "other" in Matt. 23. 23 and Luke 11. 42.

6. ***allotrios***=not one's own, belonging to another, or others (Heb. 9. 25). Hence, a foreigner. See Luke 16. 12.

125 THE SYNONYMOUS WORDS FOR "PERFECT" (Adj. and Verb).

1. ***teleios***=that which has reached its end. From *telos*, end. Lat. *finis*, nothing beyond; hence perfect, in the sense of initiated. See 1 Cor. 2. 6. Phil. 3. 15.

2. ***teleioō***=to make a full end, consummate.

3. ***epiteleō***=to finish, or bring through to an end.

4. ***akribōs***=accurately, precisely, exactly, assiduously.

5. ***akribeia***=accuracy, preciseness, exactness.

6. ***artios***=fitting like a joint=perfect adaptation for given uses. Occ. only in 2 Tim. 3. 17.

7. ***plēroō***=to fulfil, accomplish.

8. ***katartizō***=to arrange or set in order, adjust, &c. It occurs thirteen times, and is rendered "mend" (Matt. 4. 21. Mark 1. 19); "prepare" (Heb. 10. 5); "frame" (Heb. 11. 3); "restore" (Gal. 6. 1); "make perfect" (Heb. 13. 21. 1 Pet. 5. 10. All the texts read "will perfect"); "perfected" (Matt. 21. 16. 1 Thess. 3. 10); "fit" (Rom. 9. 22). *Passive* "be perfect" (Luke 6. 40. 2 Cor. 13. 11); "be perfectly joined together" (1 Cor. 1. 10).

9. ***exartizō***=to equip, fit out (as a vessel for sea); i.e. ready for every emergency (occ. only in Acts 21. 5 and 2 Tim. 3. 17).

10. ***hexis***=habitude (as the result of long practice or habit). Occ. only in Heb. 5. 14.

126 THE EIGHT BEATITUDES OF MATT. 5, AND THE EIGHT WOES OF MATT. 23.

The eight Beatitudes of Matt. 5. 3-12 are best understood and interpreted by the eight contrasts, or "Woes" of 23. 13-33. The comparison shows that 5. 10-12 form *one* (the eighth) Beatitude, having one subject (persecution) corresponding with the eighth "Woe" of 23. 29-33.

They may be thus set out:—

"THE BEATITUDES" (5. 3-12).	"THE WOES" (23. 13-33).
1. The kingdom opened to the poor (*v.* 3).	1. The kingdom shut (*v.* 13).
2. Comfort for mourners (*v.* 4).	2. Mourners distressed (*v.* 14).
3. The meek inheriting the earth (*v.* 5).	3. Fanatics compassing the earth (*v.* 15).
4. True righteousness sought by true desire (*v.* 6).	4. False righteousness sought by casuistry (*vv.* 16-22).
5. The merciful obtaining mercy (*v.* 7).	5. Mercy "omitted" and "left undone" (*vv.* 23, 24).
6. Purity within, and the vision of God hereafter (*v.* 8).	6. Purity without, uncleanness within. "Blindness" (*vv.* 25, 26).
7. Peacemakers, the sons of God (*v.* 9).	7. Hypocrites, and lawless (*vv.* 27, 28).
8. The persecuted (*vv.* 10-12).	8. The persecutors (*vv.* 29-33).

Beside these eight contrasts there is an internal correspondence of the principal thoughts, suggested by the combined series, and forming the Structure given in the note on Matt. 5. 3, 4.

It may be further noted that these Beatitudes rest on special passages in the Psalms: Matt. 5. 3 (Ps. 40. 17); 5. 4 (Ps. 119. 136); 5. 5 (Ps. 37. 11); 5. 6 (Ps. 42. 1, 2); 5. 7 (Ps. 41. 1); 5. 8 (Ps. 24. 4; 73. 1); 5. 9 (Ps. 133. 1); 5. 10 (Pss. 37; 39; 40).

127 THE SYNONYMOUS WORDS FOR "POOR", ETC.

1. ***ptōchos***=destitute, and in want: always rendered "poor": except Luke 16. 20, 22 (beggar); Gal. 4. 9 (beggarly); Jas. 2. 2 (poor man).

2. ***penēs***=poor, as opposed to rich. Occurs only in 2 Cor. 9. 9.

3. ***praüs***=meek, as distinguished from passionate. Occ. only in Matt. 5. 5; 21. 5; 1 Pet. 3. 4.

These words are used in the Septuagint interchangeably for the same Hebrew word; but the contexts show that they are all used for the same class, viz., the *fellahin*, or poor of an oppressed country, living quiet lives under tyrannical and oppressive rulers; and suffering deprivation from tax-gatherers and lawless neighbours.

128 THE SYNONYMOUS WORDS USED FOR "SIN", "WICKEDNESS", "EVIL", "UNGODLINESS", "DISOBEDIENCE", "TRANSGRESSION", ETC.

I. SIN.

i. The Verb.

hamartanō=to miss the mark or aim; then, to miss or wander from the right path; to go, or do, wrong.

ii. The Noun.

1. ***hamartia***=a failing to hit the mark; aberration from prescribed law (connected with and resulting from the above). In N.T. always in a moral sense=a sin, whether by omission or commission, in thought, word, or deed. Also used in connection with the sin-offering (Heb. 10. 6, 8, 18; 13. 11, as in Ps. 40. 6, cp. Lev. 5. 8).

2. ***hamartēma***=the actual sin. The evil principle in action; the sinful act or deed.

3. ***paraptōma***=a falling aside, when one should have stood upright. Hence (morally) a fall, a falling aside from truth and equity; a fault, or trespass.

In Romans 5. 12, No. 1 entered the world. The disobedience of Adam (*vv.* 15, 17, 18) was No. 3, and the law entered that No. 3 which before was error, might become criminal in the knowledge of the sinner. After this, where No. 1 abounded, grace did much more abound.

II. WICKEDNESS.

1. ***ponēria***=depravity; iniquity, the wicked acting of the evil nature. See No. III. 1 below.

2. ***kakia***=depravity, the vicious disposition and desires, rather than the active exercise of them, which is No. 1 (*ponēria*).

III. EVIL (Adj. and Noun).

1. ***ponēros***=full of labours and pains in working mischief; evil intent (Matt. 12. 39. Luke 11. 29); grudging, in connection with the idea expressed in the "evil eye" (Matt. 6. 23; 20. 15. See the context, and cp. Luke 11. 13).

2. ***kakos***=depraved, bad in nature. Cp. No. II. 2.

3. ***anomos***=lawless, contempt of law.

4. ***anomia***=lawlessness.

5. ***athesmos***=breaking through all restraints of ordinances or institutes, divine or human, to gratify one's lusts. Occurs only in 2 Pet. 2. 7; 3. 17.

IV. UNGODLINESS.

asebeia=impiety, absence of "the fear of God", having no reverence for sacred things; irreligious. Sept. for *pāsha'*. Ap. 44. ix.

V. DISOBEDIENCE, ETC.

1. ***apeitheia***=unwillingness to be persuaded, leading to obstinacy.

2. ***parakoē***=unwillingness to hear, disobedient.

VI. TRANSGRESS, TRANSGRESSOR.

1. ***parabainō***=to step on one side, overstep, go aside from, violate, transgress.

2. ***parerchomai***=to go past, pass by, neglect.

3. ***parabatēs***, one who steps aside, or oversteps.

VII. INIQUITY.

1. ***adikia***=unrighteousness, wrongdoing.

2. ***adikēma***=a wrong done.

3. ***paranomia***=acting contrary to law or custom. Occ. only in 2 Pet. 2. 16.

VIII. ERR, ERROR.

1. ***planaō***=to cause to wander or go astray; used of doctrinal error and religious deceit. Cp. *planos* (1 Tim. 4. 1, "seducing").

2. ***apoplanaō***. No. 1 with *apo*=away from, prefixed (Ap. 104. iv). In Pass., to go astray from, swerve. Occ. only in Mark 13. 22 and 1 Tim. 6. 10.

3. ***astocheō***=to deviate from. Occ. only in 1 Tim. 1. 6; 6. 21. 2 Tim. 2. 18.

IX. FAULT.

hēttēma=a diminishing of that which should have been rendered in full measure; diminution, decrease. Occ. in Rom. 11. 12 and 1 Cor. 6. 7.

129 THE SYNONYMOUS WORDS FOR "WORLD", "EARTH", ETC.

There are four Greek words which are thus translated; and it is most important that they should be, in each occurrence, carefully distinguished. They are as follows:—

1. ***kosmos***=the world as created, ordered, and arranged. Hence it is used in the LXX for the Heb. word rendered "ornament". See Ex. 33. 5, 6. Isa. 49. 18. Jer. 4. 30. Ezek. 7. 20, &c. It denotes the opposite of what man has called "chaos", which God never created. See notes on Isa. 45. 18 and Gen. 1. 2: for the Heb. *bāra'* means not only to create, but that what was created was beautiful. The root, meaning to carve, plane, polish, implies both order and beauty. Cp. Ap. 146.

2. ***aiōn***=an age, or age-time, the duration of which is indefinite, and may be limited or extended as the context of each occurrence may demand.

The root meaning of *aiōn* is expressed by the Heb. *'olām* (see Ap. 151. I. A and II. A) which denotes indefinite, unknown or concealed duration: just as we speak of "the patriarchal age", or "the golden age", &c. Hence, it has come to denote any given period of time, characterized by a special form of Divine administration or dispensation.

In the plural we have the Heb. *'olāmīm* and Gr. *'aiōnes* used of ages, or of a succession of age-times, and of an abiding from age to age. From this comes the adjective *aiōnios* (Ap. 151. II. B), used of an unrestricted duration, as distinct from a particular or limited age-time. These age-times must be distinct or they could not be added to, or multiplied, as in the expression *aiōns* of *aiōns*.

These ages or age-times were all prepared and arranged by God (see Heb. 1. 2; 11. 3); and there is a constant distinction in the New Testament between "this age", and the "coming age" (see Matt. 12. 32. Heb. 1. 2. Eph. 1. 21).

"This age" is characterized by such passages as Matt. 13. 24–30, 36–43. Mark 4. 19; 10. 30. Rom. 12. 2. 1 Cor. 2. 8. 2 Cor. 4. 4. Gal. 1. 4. Eph. 2. 2 (transl. "course"). 2 Tim. 4. 10. Tit. 2. 12.

The "coming age" is characterized in such passages as Matt. 13. 39, 40, 49; 24. 3; 28. 20. Mark 10. 30. Luke 18. 30; 20. 35. 1 Cor. 15. 23. Tit. 2. 13.

The conjunction of these ages is spoken of as the *sunteleia*, marking the end of one age and the beginning of another.

Other indefinite durations are mentioned, but they always refer to some unknown and prolonged continuance, the end of which cannot be seen; such as the end of life (Ex. 21. 6). Hence the Hebrew Priesthood was so characterized because its end could not be foreseen (see Ex. 40. 15. 1 Sam. 1. 22. Heb. 7. 12). It is used in the same way in other connections (see Matt. 21. 19. John 8. 35). For further information see Ap. 151. II. A.

3. ***oikoumenē***=the world as inhabited. It is from the verb *oikeō*=to dwell. It is used of the habitable world, as distinct from the *kosmos* (No. 1 above, which=the world as *created*). Hence, it is used in a more limited and special sense of the Roman Empire, which was then predominant. See Luke 2. 1; 4. 5; 21. 26. It is sometimes put by the Fig. *Metonymy* (of the *Adjunct*), Ap. 6, for the inhabitants (Acts 17. 6, 31. Heb. 2. 5, &c.).

4. ***gē***=land, as distinct from water; or earth as distinct from heaven; or region or territory, used of one special land, or country, as distinct from other countries, in which peoples dwell, each on its own soil.

130 THE SYNONYMOUS WORDS FOR "LIGHT", ETC.

1. ***phōs***=light (underived and absolute); the opp. of darkness. Used therefore specially of God (John 1. 4, 5; 8. 12. 1 John 1. 5, &c.).

2. ***phōstēr***=a light, or light-giver, used of star light, and light holders or bearers (cp. Gen. 1. 14, 16).

3. ***phōtismos***=a lighting, illumination, shining.

4. ***luchnos***=a portable hand-lamp fed by oil, burning for a time and then going out. See John 5. 35, where *luchnos* is used of John the Baptist in contrast with No. 1 (*phōs*), which is used of Christ (John 8. 12, &c.).

5. ***luchnia***=a lampstand.

6. ***lampas***=a torch (Judg. 7. 16, 20) fed with oil from a small vessel (the *angeion* of Matt. 25. 4) constructed for the purpose.

7. ***phengos***=light (No. 1) in its effulgence, used of moonlight, except in Luke 11. 33 where it is used of lamp-light. Occurs elsewhere only in Matt. 24. 29 and Mark 13. 24.

131 THE SYNONYMOUS WORDS FOR "HELL", ETC.

"Hell" is the English rendering of *two* different Greek words in the N.T.

The English word is from the Anglo-Saxon *hel*, Genitive Case *helle*=a hidden place, from the Anglo-Saxon *helan*=to hide.

It is in the N.T. used as the translation of two Greek words:—

I. ***Gehenna.*** Gr. *geenna.* This is the transliteration of the Heb. *Gai' Hinnōm*, i.e. the Valley of Hinnōm or "the Valley" of [the sons of] Hinnōm, where were the *fires* through which children were passed in the worship of Moloch.

In the O.T. *Tophet* was the Heb. word used, because it was a place in this valley.

In our Lord's day the idolatry had ceased, but the *fires* were still continually burning there for the destruction of the refuse of Jerusalem. Hence, *geenna* was used for the fires of destruction associated with the judgment of God. Sometimes, "*geenna* of fire". See 2 Kings 23. 10. Isa. 30. 33. Jer. 7. 31, 32; 19. 11–14.

Geenna occurs 12 times, and is always rendered "hell", viz. Matt. 5. 22, 29. 30; 10. 28; 18. 9; 23. 15, 33. Mark 9. 43, 45, 47. Luke 12. 5. Jas. 3. 6.

II. ***Hadēs.*** Gr. *hadēs*, from *a* (privative) and *idein*, to see (Ap. 133. I. i); used by the Greeks for *the unseen* world.

The meaning which the Greeks put upon it does not concern us; nor have we anything to do with the imaginations of the heathen, or the traditions of Jews or Romanists, or the teachings of demons or evil spirits, or of any who still cling to them.

The Holy Spirit has used it as one of the "words pertaining to the earth", and in so doing has "purified" it, "as silver tried in a furnace" (see notes on Ps. 12. 6). From this we learn that His own words "are pure", but words belonging to this earth have to be "purified"

The Old Testament is the fountain-head of the Hebrew language. It has no literature behind it. But the case is entirely different with the Greek language. The Hebrew *Sh^eōl* is a word Divine in its origin and usage. The Greek *Hades* is human in its origin and comes down to us laden with centuries of development, in which it has acquired new senses, meanings, and usages.

Seeing that the Holy Spirit has used it in Acts 2. 27, 31 as His own equivalent of *Sh^eōl* in Psalm 16. 10, He has settled, once for all, the sense in which we are to understand it. The meaning He has given to *Sh^eōl* in Ps. 16. 10

is the one meaning *we* are to give it wherever it occurs in the N.T., whether we transliterate it or translate it. We have no liberty to do otherwise, and must discard everything outside the Word of God.

The word occurs eleven times (Matt. 11. 23; 16. 18. Luke 10. 15; 16. 23. Acts 2. 27, 31. 1 Cor. 15. 55. Rev. 1. 18; 6. 8; 20. 13, 14); and is rendered "hell" in every passage except one, where it is rendered "grave" (1 Cor. 15. 55, marg. "hell").

In the R.V. the word is always transliterated "Hades", except in 1 Cor. 15. 55 (where "death" is substituted because of the reading, in all the texts, of *thanate* for *hadē*), and in the American R.V. also.

As *Hades* is the Divine Scriptural equivalent of *Sh^eōl*, further light may be gained from Ap. 35, and a reference to the 65 passages there given. It may be well to note that while "Hades" is rendered "hell" in the N.T. (except once, where the rendering "the grave" could not be avoided), *Sh^eōl*, its Hebrew equivalent, occurs 65 times, and is rendered "the grave" 31 times (or 54 %); "hell" 31 times (4 times with margin "the grave", reducing it to 41·5 %); and "pit" only 3 times (or 4·5 %).

"The grave", therefore, is obviously the best rendering, meaning *the state of death* (Germ. *sterbend*, for which we have no English equivalent); not the *act* of dying, as an examination of all the occurrences of both words will show.

1. The rendering "pit" so evidently means "the grave" that it may at once be substituted for it (Num. 16. 30, 33. Job 17. 16).

2. The rendering "the grave" (not "a grave", which is Hebrew *ḳeber*, or *bōr*) exactly expresses the meaning of both *Sh^eōl* and *Hades*. For, as to *direction*, it is always down: as to *place*, it is in the earth: as to *relation*, it is always in contrast with the state of the living (Deut. 32. 22–25 and 1 Sam. 2. 6–8); as to *association*, it is connected with mourning (Gen. 37. 34, 35), sorrow (Gen. 42. 38. 2 Sam. 22. 6. Ps. 18. 5; 116. 3), fright and terror (Num. 16. 27, 34), mourning (Isa. 38. 3, 10, 17, 18), silence (Ps. 6. 5; 31. 17. Ecc. 9. 10), no knowledge (Ecc. 9. 5, 6, 10), punishment (Num. 16. 29, 34. 1 Kings 2. 6, 9. Job 24. 19. Ps. 9. 17 (R.V.=*re*-turned)), corruption (Ps. 16. 10. Acts 2. 27, 31); as to *duration*, resurrection is the only exit from it (Ps. 16. 11. Acts 2. 27, 31; 13. 33–37. 1 Cor. 15. 55. Rev. 1. 18; 20. 5, 13, 14).

III. ***Tartaroō*** (occurs only in 2 Pet. 2. 4)=to thrust down to Tartarus, *Tartarus* being a Greek word, not used elsewhere, or at all in the Sept. Homer describes it as subterranean (cp. Deut. 32. 22, which may refer to this). The Homeric *Tartarus* is the prison of the Titans, or giants (cp. Heb. *Rephaim*, Ap. 25), who rebelled against *Zeus*.

132 THE SYNONYMOUS WORDS FOR "KNOW", "KNOWLEDGE", ETC.

I. The Verb.

i. ***oida***=to know (intuitively) without effort, to understand. No. i is subjective, while No. ii is objective.

ii. ***ginōskō***=to know (by experience, or effort); to acquire knowledge, become acquainted with; hence, to come or get to know, learn, perceive. See John 1. 48. 1 John 5. 20. Eph. 5. 5.

iii. ***epi-ginōskō.*** No. ii with *epi*=upon (Ap. 104. ix); to know thereupon, to become thoroughly acquainted with; to know thoroughly and accurately, recognize. See 1 Cor. 13. 12.

iv. ***pro-ginōskō.*** No. ii with *pro* (Ap. 104. xiv)=to get to know beforehand, to foreknow.

v. ***epistamai***=to obtain, and thus have a knowledge of anything by proximity to it, or as the result of prolonged attention; in contrast with the process of getting to know it, or with a mere casual, *dilettante* acquaintance with it. See Acts 15. 7; 18. 25; and see note on 19. 15.

II. The Noun.

i. ***gnōsis***=knowledge acquired by learning, effort, or experience. The result of No. ii, above.

ii. ***epignōsis***=precise or further knowledge, thorough acquaintance with; true knowledge.

iii. ***sunesis***=native insight, understanding, capacity to apprehend; used of reflective thought, while *sophia* (wisdom) is used of productive thought.

133 THE SYNONYMOUS WORDS FOR "SEE", "LOOK", "BEHOLD", ETC.

The following twenty-three words are to be thus distinguished and understood:—

I. SEE.

1. ***eidon***=to see: implying not the mere act of looking, but the actual perception of the object; thus differing from *blepō* (No. 5, below).

2. ***idou*** is the Imperative Aorist Middle of *eidon* (see No. 1, above)=See! Behold! calling attention to something external to one's self.

3. ***ide*** is the Imperative Active of the Second Aorist *eidon* (No. 1, above), as calling attention to something *present*.

4. ***oida***=to know intuitively, without effort or experience; to have perceived or apprehended. Cp. the verb *ginōskō*, which means *to get to know*, by effort, experience, or revelation. See the two verbs in the same verse (John 8. 55; 13. 7. 1 John 5. 20), and Ap. 132. I. 1.

5. ***blepō***=to have the power of seeing, to use the eyes, to look at; used of the act of looking, even though nothing be seen. Hence, to observe accurately and with desire; used of mental vision, and implying more contemplation than *horaō* (see No. 8, below).

6. ***anablepō.*** This is *blepō* (No. 5, above), with the Preposition *ana* prefixed (see Ap. 104. i)=to look up (e.g. Mark 8. 24), to look again; hence, to recover sight (e.g. Matt. 11. 5).

7. ***emblepō***=to look in or into, fix the eyes upon, or look intently. It is *blepō* (No. 5, above) with the Preposition *en* (Ap. 104. viii) prefixed, and denotes a looking or regarding fixedly. Hence, to know by inspection (e.g. Matt. 19. 26. Mark 8. 25. Acts 22. 11).

8. ***horaō***=to perceive with the eyes. It is used of bodily sight, and with special reference to the thought as to the object looked at. It thus differs from No. 5, above, in the same way as No. 1 does, and from No. 1 in that it has regard to the *object*, while No. 1 refers to the *subject*.

(a) ***opsomai*** is used as the Future of *horaō* (No. 8, above), and has regard to the object presented to the eye, and to the subject which perceives, at the same time. It denotes, not so much the act of seeing (like Nos. 5 and 8, above), but the state and condition of the one to whose eye the object is presented. Hence, to truly comprehend.

9. ***aphoraō***=to look away from others at one who is regarded earnestly (e.g. Heb. 12. 2, where alone it occurs). It is No. 8, with *apo* (Ap. 104. iv) prefixed.

10. ***optanomai*** = to behold, and in Passive, to appear or be seen. It is a rare form of the Present, formed from No. 8, as above. Occurs only in Acts 1. 3.

11. ***theōreō***=to be a spectator of, to gaze at, or on, as a spectacle. Our. Eng. word "theatre" is from the same root. Hence, it is used of bodily sight, and assumes the actual presence of the object on which the gaze is fixed, and that it is a continued and prolonged gaze. It differs from No. 8, above, as that may be only the act of an instant.

12. ***theaomai*** is, in meaning, like No. 11, above, but differing from it in that No. 11 has regard to the *object* gazed upon, while this has regard to the *subject* who gazes. Hence, it is used of gazing with a purpose; to see with desire, or regard with admiration.

13. ***historeō***=to inquire: i.e. to have an interview with a person with a view to becoming personally acquainted through conversation. Occ. only in Gal. 1. 18.

II. BEHOLD.

1. ***epeidon.*** This is No. I. 1, with *epi*=upon (Ap. 104. ix) prefixed; to look upon. It is the second Aorist of *ephoraō* (No. I. 8), with *epi*=upon (Ap. 104. ix) prefixed. It occurs only in Luke 1. 25 and Acts 4. 29.

2. ***epopteuō***=to look over, overlook, watch, and thus be an eyewitness of. Occ. only in 1 Pet. 2. 12; 3. 2. It is derived from No. I. 8, above, with *epi* (Ap. 104. ix) prefixed.

3. ***anatheōreō.*** It is No. I. 11, with *ana* (Ap. 104. i) prefixed. Hence it=to gaze on with purpose and attention. Occ. only in Acts 17. 23; and Heb. 13. 7.

4. ***katanoeō***=to perceive with the senses, referring to the *object* of observation rather than to the act of getting to know (as with *ginōskō*, Ap. 132. I. ii). It has regard to the conscious action of the mind in getting to see or understand.

III. LOOK.

1. ***anablepō.*** See No. I. 6, above.

2. ***parakuptō***=to stoop down beside (*para.* Ap. 104. xii) anything in order to look at it more closely.

3. ***prosdokaō***=to watch for (*pros.* Ap. 104. xv) anything, expect and thus look or wait for.

4. ***epiblepō.*** This is No. I. 5, above, with *epi*=upon (Ap. 104. ix) prefixed.

5. ***episkeptomai***=to look upon (Ap. 104. ix), as though to select; to look out, so as to select.

6. ***atenizō***=to fix the eyes intently upon.

134 THE SYNONYMOUS WORDS FOR "PRAY" AND "PRAYER".

I. The Verb.

1. ***euchomai***=to speak out, utter aloud. Hence, to wish or vow (Acts 26. 29. 2 Cor. 13. 7. Jas. 5. 16).

2. ***proseuchomai.*** No. 1 with *pros* (Ap. 104. xv) prefixed=to pray to. It is restricted to prayer to God in N.T. First occ. in Matt. 5. 44.

3. ***erōtaō***=to ask or request a *person* to do (rarely to give) something: thus differing from No. 4 below.

4. ***aiteō***=to ask for something to be given (not done, as No. 3). Commonly used of an inferior addressing a superior.

5. ***deomai***=to want, lack, or need; then, to make known one's need; hence, to supplicate, beseech.

6. ***parakaleō***=to call aside, appeal to (by way of exhortation, entreaty, comfort, or instruction).

II. The Noun.

1. ***euchē***=a prayer (to God); also, a vow made to God.

2. ***proseuchē***=No. 1 with *pros* (Ap. 104. xv, prefixed). The word is quite common in the *Papyri*, though in the N.T. it is restricted to prayer offered to God, having regard to the power of Him Who is invoked and giving prominence to *personal devotion.* Also used of a place of prayer (Acts 16. 13).

3. ***deēsis***=a petition for a special object, having regard to our necessity rather than to God's sufficiency to supply it: giving prominence to *personal need.* In Byzantine Greek it was used of a *written* petition (as in Eng.).

4. ***enteuxis***=confiding access to God, giving prominence to childlike confidence in prayer. Occ. only in 1 Tim. 2. 1; 4. 5.

5. ***aitēma***=a specific petition for a particular thing, cp. No. I. 4. Occurs only in Luke 23. 24. Phil. 4. 6. 1 John 5. 15.

135 THE SYNONYMOUS WORDS FOR "LOVE".

I. The Verb.

1. ***agapaō***=to regard with favour, to make much of a thing or person, on principle. The cause or ground of No. 2.

2. ***phileō***=to kiss, to be fond of, having regard to *feeling* as distinct from principle. The demonstration of No. 1. Hence No. 2 is never used of man's love to God: this is always No. 1. Both words are used of God's love to man. No. 2 is used of the Lord's love for Lazarus (John 11. 3, 36), but not in *v.* 5, where the sisters are included. See the notes on John 21. 15–17; and on John 12. 25.

II. The Noun.

1. ***agapē.*** No. 2, below, was the common word used by the Greeks, for love; and even this is far lower than the N.T. *philadelphia* (=love of the brethren). *Agapē* is spontaneous love, irrespective of "rights". The word was supposed to be peculiar to the N.T., but it is found in the *Papyri.*

2. ***philanthrōpia***=philanthropy, or love of man, which did not go beyond giving man his "rights", among the Greeks. It is used in a far higher sense in Tit. 3. 4; occurs elsewhere only in Acts 28. 2. Cp. the Adverb *philanthrōpōs* (Acts 27. 3, "courteously").

III. The Adjective.

agapētos=beloved. The word used of the Lord Jesus by the Father. See Matt. 3. 17; 12. 18; 17. 5. Mark 1. 11; 9. 7. Luke 3. 22; 9. 35; and in Mark 12. 6. Luke 20. 13, by Himself. A special epithet of the Saints in the Epistles.

136 THE SYNONYMOUS WORDS FOR "WASH".

The following nine Greek words are rendered "wash" in the English N.T.:—

i. ***niptō***=to wash some part of the body (as the face, hands, or feet).

ii. ***aponiptō.*** No.1 with *apo*=away from (Ap.104.iv); to wash off from (a *part* of the body) and for one's self.

iii. ***louō***=to bathe (the whole body).

iv. ***apolouō.*** No.3 with *apo*=away from (Ap.104.iv); to wash off from the whole body by bathing. Occ. only in Acts 22.16, and 1 Cor. 6.11.

v. ***plunō***=to wash (inanimate things, such as clothes). Occ. only in Rev. 7.14.

vi. ***apoplunō.*** No.5 with *apo*=away from (Ap.104.iv); to wash inanimate things thoroughly. Used only of nets (Luke 5.2).

vii. ***baptizō.*** Rendered "wash" only in Mark 7.4, and Luke 11.38. See Ap. 115.

viii. ***brechō***=to wet (on the surface, like rain), moisten.

These words must be carefully distinguished. See notes on John 13.10: "He that is washed (No. 3) needeth not save to wash (No. 1) his feet".

In the Septuagint of Lev. 15.11, the three principal words are used in one verse: "And whomsoever he toucheth that hath the issue, and hath not rinsed (No. 1) his hands in water, he shall wash (No. 5) his clothes, and bathe himself (No. 3) in water", &c.

ix. ***rhantizō***=to sprinkle (ceremonially), and thus cleanse or purify. Occ. only in Heb. 9.13, 19, 21; 10.22.

137 THE SYNONYMOUS WORDS FOR "WORSHIP".

The following six Greek words are rendered "worship" in the A.V.:—

1. ***proskuneō***=to prostrate one's self (in reverence), do homage. Used, therefore, of the *act* of worship.

2. ***sebomai***=to revere, to feel awe. Used, therefore, of the *inward feelings* (as No. 1 is of the outward act).

3. ***sebazomai***=to be shy, or timid at *doing anything*. Occurs only in Rom. 1.25.

4. ***latreuō***=to serve in official service (for hire, or reward). Used of serving God in the externals of His worship.

5. ***eusebeō***=to be pious or devout towards any one; to act with reverence, respect, and honour.

6. ***therapeuō***=to wait upon, minister to (as a doctor does); hence=to heal; to render voluntary service and attendance. Thus differing from No. 4.

138 THE DOUBLE MIRACLES OF MATT. 9.18; MARK 5.22; AND LUKE 8.41.

Discrepancies, so-called, are manufactured when similar miracles are regarded as identical. One such example is seen in the case of the two demoniacs of Matt. 8.28 and the one demoniac of Mark 5.1–20. (See note on Matt. 8.28).

Another is that of the two storms on the lake of Matt. 8.24 (Mark 4.37–41) and Luke 8.22–25.

Another is that of the lepers of Matt. 8.2 (Mark 1.40) and Luke 5.12. See the notes, and cp. Ap. 152.

Why should not words be repeated at different times and under other circumstances? And as there were many people suffering in various places from similar diseases, why should we not expect to find similar miracles?

Why assume that two miracles, which are apparently alike in general character, are identical, and then talk about the two accounts being contradictory?

Two examples are furnished, not only in the case of two separate miracles, but in the case of *pairs* of double miracles.

1. There were two females raised from the dead.

The first (Matt. 9.18) was *to korasion* (a little girl), whose father was probably a civil magistrate (*archōn*). She died before her father started to see the Lord, and so no messengers were dispatched with the news.

The second (Mark 5.22. Luke 8.41) was *to paidion*, a girl of about twelve years (see Ap. 108.v), whose father was one of the rulers of the Synagogue (*archisunagōgos*), by name Jairus. She was not dead. No mourning had commenced, but as the Lord approaches news of her death was brought.

Other antecedents and consequents of time and place and circumstances are all different.

2. There were two women suffering from the same disease. And why not? It is not surprising that there were two, but surprising there were not more—as probably there were among the many unrecorded (Matt. 14.36. Mark 3.10; 6.56. Luke 6.19).

The first (Matt. 9.20) was evidently watching her opportunity, and had probably heard the report of the Lord's "touch". She came behind Him; and there is no mention of a crowd as in the case of the other woman.

The first spoke "within herself" of what she would do; the second had spoken to her friends.

The Lord saw the first woman, and spoke before the healing was effected. He did not see the second, and inquired after the healing was accomplished.

In the first the disciples said nothing, but in the second they reasoned with the Lord as to the crowds.

In the first there is no mention of physicians or of spiritual blessing received. In the second case both are mentioned.

It appears, therefore, that in these cases we have two pairs of double miracles, with differences so great that they cannot be combined and treated as being identical.

139 "DEAD" AND "THE DEAD".

The word *nekros* (Noun and Adjective) has different meanings, according as it is used in different connections:—

1. With the Article (*hoi nekroi*) it denotes *dead bodies*, or corpses or carcasses in the grave, apart from the personality they once had. This is the O.T. idiom also. See Sept., Gen. 23.3, 4, 6, 8. Deut. 18.11; 28.26. Jer. 7.33; 9.22; 19.7. Ezek. 37.9. See notes on Matt. 22.31. 1 Cor. 15.35.

2. Without the Article (*nekroi*) it denotes the persons who were once alive, but who are now alive no longer: i.e. dead persons as distinct from dead bodies. Cp. Deut. 14.1. Judg. 4.22. Lam. 3.6. And see notes on Matt. 22.32. Acts 26.23. 1 Cor. 15.12, 12, 13, 15, 16. Heb. 13.20, &c.

3. With a Preposition, but *without* the Article, which may be latent in the Preposition (*ek nekrōn*), it denotes out from among dead people. See notes on

Mark 9. 9, 10. Luke 16. 30, 31. John 20. 9. Acts 10. 41. Rom. 6. 13; 10. 7, 9; 11. 15. 1 Cor. 15. 12–, 20. Heb. 11. 19.

4. With a Preposition, and *with* the Article; e.g. '*ek tōn nekrōn*, it denotes emphatically out from among the dead bodies, or corpses. Cp. Eph. 5. 14. Col. 1. 18; 2. 12.

5. The bearing of this on 1 Pet. 4. 6 will be better seen if we note that we have *nekroi* (See No. 2, above), meaning people who were then dead, but who had had the Gospel preached (Ap. 121. 4) to them while they were alive; and this is confirmed by the Gr. Particle, *men* (=although) in the next clause, which is ignored both by the A.V. and R.V. The verse reads thus: "For to this end to those who are (now) dead was the Gospel preached, that though they might be judged in the flesh, according to [the will of] men[1], yet they might live [again, in resurrection], according to [the will of] God, as regards [the] spirit"; i.e. in spiritual bodies, spoken of in 1 Cor. 15. 44, 45.

To this end—to give those to whom the apostle wrote this hope—the Gospel was preached to them, as described in 1 Pet. 1. 12, 25. The hope of glory was thus set over against their sufferings (1 Pet. 1. 11; 4. 13).

[1] That this is the meaning may be seen from the use of *kata* (Ap. 104. x. 2). Rom. 8. 27; 15. 5. 1 Cor. 12. 8; 15. 32; 2 Cor. 11. 17. Gal. 1. 4, 11. Eph. 1. 5, 9, 11, 19; 2. 2. Col. 2. 8. 1 Pet. 4. 14, 19. 1 John 5. 14.

140 "THE GOSPEL OF THE KINGDOM" AND OTHER "GOSPELS".

About the meaning of the word rendered "Gospel" there is no question or doubt; and the origin and exact meaning of the English word does not matter.

The Greek word *euangelion* means *good news*, glad tidings; and these good tidings, which may be concerning various and different subjects, must be distinguished. See Phil. 1. 10, note. There is, first:—

I. "THE EVERLASTING GOSPEL" (or GOOD NEWS).

This was proclaimed from the first, i.e. after the Fall, and it was proclaimed to men as men, by God, the Creator, to His creatures. Its message was that the Creator was alone to be feared and worshipped, and men were to have no other gods beside Him. He was the holy and righteous One, and He was, and is, and will be the only and final Judge of men. God proclaimed this from the first, and among its heralds were ENOCH, "the seventh from Adam", who proclaimed His coming for this judgment of the ungodly (Jude 14, 15); and NOAH, a herald of righteousness and of coming righteous judgment (Heb. 11. 7 and 2 Pet. 2. 5).

When the "calling on high" shall have been given (Phil. 3. 14), and when "transgressors are come to the full" (Dan. 8. 23), and before the Kingdom is set up in glory, this Gospel (or good news) will again be proclaimed (Rev. 14. 6). It is "everlasting", and men, as such, will be called upon to "Fear God, and give glory to Him; for the hour of His judgment is come: and worship Him that made heaven, and earth", &c. (Rev. 14. 7).

This is the Gospel proclaimed by the Creator to His sinful creatures after the Fall; and it will be proclaimed again at the end. Hence its name "everlasting". Then followed:—

II. THE GOSPEL (or GOOD NEWS) OF THE KINGDOM.

To Abraham and his seed was the good news proclaimed, and the promise given that God would make of him a nation in whom all the families of the earth should be blessed (Gen. 12. 1–3). This good news was gradually expanded and developed.

In Gen. 15. 4 the heir was announced, and this heir was to be the Messiah (Gal. 3. 16).

In Gen. 15. 8–21 the inheritance was secured by an unconditional promise (not by a covenant between two parties, one of whom might break it, Gal. 3. 18–20). That inheritance was (and is yet to be) "the Holy Land", "Immanuel's Land" (Isa. 8. 8), Immanuel Himself being the Governor (Isa. 9. 6, 7), and "the zeal of the LORD of hosts" its security.

In 2 Sam. 7 the throne was secured to David and his seed by another unconditional promise, and in due time Messiah came unto His own (John 1. 11).

This "good news" was first heralded by angels sent specially from heaven; and the exact terms of the proclamation are recorded. The angel of Jehovah spoke from the glory of Jehovah, and said:—

> "Behold, I bring you good tidings of great joy, which shall be to all people. For unto you is born this day, in the city of David, a SAVIOUR, which is CHRIST, THE LORD."

Thus the *good news* concerned a Person, Who would "save His People from their sins" (Matt. 1. 21): the Saviour Whom God had anointed (Messiah), appointed, given, and sent. [At this point see and note the object and subject of Christ's ministry as set forth in Appendix 119.]

In the proclamation of this Kingdom the Lord taught in parables; for there were "mysteries" (i.e. *secrets*) which concerned the rejection, and consequent postponement and abeyance of the Kingdom, which could not openly be made known, but only in private ("in the house", Matt. 13. 36).

It had been foreseen, and therefore foretold, that His People would not receive Him, and would reject Him (Isa. 53, &c.) and put Him to death. This would not affect the fulfilment of all the promised glories connected with the Kingdom. See Luke 24. 26: "Ought not Christ to have suffered these things, and to enter into His glory?" Cp. Acts 3. 18; 17. 3.

True, Christ had been put to death; but God had sworn to David, that of the fruit of his loins, according to the flesh, He would raise up Christ to sit on his throne (Acts 2. 30). This was now fulfilled: therefore the proclamation of the Kingdom and the King (for there cannot be the one without the other) was at once formally made by Peter in Acts 3. 18–26.

This proclamation was made by Peter and the Twelve in the capital of the Land (according to Matt. 22. 1–7), and by Paul throughout the synagogues of the Dispersion, until it was all brought to a crisis in Rome (the capital of the Dispersion). Paul and those who heard the Lord thus "confirmed what at the first began to be spoken by the Lord". They did not go beyond it by altering its terms; and God bare them "witness by signs and wonders, and divers miracles, and spiritual gifts" (Heb. 2. 1–4).

In Acts 28 this was brought to a conclusion by a formal rejection on the part of "the chief of the Jews" (Acts 28. 17–29), and of these, not a few, but "many" (*v.* 23); and, after a discussion, which lasted throughout the whole day, the proclamation was finally rejected; and, after the prophecy of Israel's blindness (Isa. 6. 9, 10) had been quoted for the third and last time[1], the dispensation of the proclamation of "the Gospel (or good news) of the Kingdom" ceased, and is now, therefore, in abeyance, for "NOW, we see NOT YET all things put under Him" (Heb. 2. 8).

All these "mysteries" (or *secrets*) concerning the postponement and abeyance of the Kingdom were spoken "in parables", "because (the Lord said), it is given unto you (unto the disciples) to know the secrets of the kingdom of heaven, but to them (to the People) it is not given" (Matt. 13. 11); going on to explain His action by quoting (for the first time) the prophecy of Israel's blindness (Isa. 6. 9, 10)[1].

There was nothing in Old Testament prophecy that told of what the Lord reveals in these Parables of the Kingdom: how it would be rejected, and to what lengths the People would go in the rejection of the King; what would happen in consequence; how a second offer would be proclaimed, and how that too would be rejected; and what new revelation would be made in consequence.

[1] The *second* time being in John 12. 37–41.

All this was hidden in the parables spoken by the Lord, yet revealed to the disciples, and written for our learning (Matt. 13. 16, 36, 51, 52. Luke 24. 26, 27, 44–46. Acts 1. 3, 6, 7). Any interpretation which proceeds on other lines can only end in a blindness equal to that which fell on the Jewish nation. This *interpretation* will in no wise detract from, or lessen, the value of such *application* as we may make for ourselves, so long as such application does not ignore the definite revelation made subsequently in the Prison Epistles in fulfilment of the Lord's promise in John 16. 12–15.

The following parables set forth the proclamation of the Gospel of the Kingdom, from various points of view:—

1. The Parable of the Sower (Matt. 13. 3–23).

This, the first parable, covers the whole ground.

The "seed" was "the word of (or concerning) the Kingdom". When repeated later (Luke 8. 5–15), the sphere is extended and widened, and is less local and exclusive. This is by way of application.

The First Sowing was "by" the wayside. This must have been the proclamation by John the Baptist (Matt. 3. Mark 1. 1–8. Luke 3. 1–18. John 1. 6–36). This was "by the wayside", and the opposition of the evil one is shown in the birds of evil omen (as in the case of the mustard tree, *vv.* 31, 32). Hence the seed was "devoured" and the word was "not understood" (*vv.* 4, 19).

The Second Sowing was by Christ Himself (Matt. 4. 17), the Twelve (Matt. 10. 7), and the Seventy (Luke 10. 1–20). This sowing was on the stony ground, and was received "with joy" (Matt. 13. 20; see Mark 6. 20, and 12. 37. Luke 4. 22). This was unfruitful (Mark 4. 16, 17).

The Third Sowing was by Peter and the Twelve, and "by them that heard Him" (the Son, Heb. 2. 3) during the Dispensation of the Acts. It was "among the thorns". Peter proclaimed the Kingdom (Acts 3. 18–26), and repeated the call to national repentance, which was the one abiding condition of national blessing. But the seed was choked. The "thousands of Jews" who at first "received the word", continued "all zealous of the law" (Acts 21. 20. Gal. 3. 1–5, 10–13; 4. 9; 5. 1–4). This sowing came to a crisis in Acts 28, when the Kingdom was rejected, and has since been in abeyance. See Ap. 112, 113, and 114.

The Fourth Sowing is in the future. It will be the final proclamation of "the Gospel of the Kingdom", immediately preceding and during the Tribulation (Matt. 24. 14). Blindness has "happened to Israel", but it is only "in part" (Rom. 11. 25). The "how long" of Isa. 6. 11 will ere long be seen. This sowing will be of short duration only, as were the other three, and numbered by "days" (Dan. 12. 13. Matt. 24. 22. Luke 17. 26). There will be a special manifestation of the presence and power of the Lord (Matt. 28. 20), at the end (*sunteleia*) of this age; and, when this sowing is over, the end (*telos*) will come (Matt. 24. 13, 14), concerning which the disciples had enquired in *v.* 3.

2. The Parable of the Marriage Feast. (Matt. 22. 1–14).

The servants first sent forth were John the Baptist, the Twelve, and the Seventy, and these were sent to those who had been previously bidden. But "they would not come".

The "other servants" who were next sent were Peter, the Twelve, and "them that heard Him" (Heb. 2. 3, 4) during the dispensation of the Acts, as foreshown in *v.* 4.

They proclaimed that "all things were ready". Nothing now was wanting. The "sufferings" had been fulfilled and the glory was ready to be revealed (Luke 24. 26, 46. Acts 3. 18. 1 Pet. 1. 5). Therefore, "Repent ye", &c." (Acts 2. 38, 39; 3. 19).

But instead of repenting they "took His servants, and entreated them spitefully, and slew them" (Matt. 22. 5, 6). Some they imprisoned (Acts 4. 3; 5. 18; 8. 3; 9. 1, 13, 21); one they stoned (Acts 7. 59); another they "killed with the sword" (Acts 12. 2). This shows that that dispensation could not have ended with the stoning of Stephen in Acts 7, for James was slain after that; and other persecutions were continued up to the end (Acts 28. 17).

"But the King was wroth, and sent His armies, and destroyed those murderers, and burned up their city" (Matt. 22. 7). The Temple was burned, and the nation was dispersed.

The last servants sent will go "into the highways" of the world. Here we have, again, a reference to the yet future proclamation of "the Gospel of the Kingdom".

Now, this marriage-feast is postponed; and all invitations to it are in abeyance. Its future fulfilment is yet to take place. This is referred to in Matt. 24. 14, and is proved by Rev. 19. 6–9, where we have the same word in *v.* 9 as in Matt. 22. 2.

3. "The Great Supper" (Luke 14. 15–24).

This was spoken in immediate connection with the blessedness of eating bread in the Kingdom of God.

Again we have the Four Ministries, as in the above parables.

The supper was made by "a certain man", and many were bidden. This bidding was the ministry of John the Baptist. It is set forth as a simple statement of a past and accomplished fact. This was the First Ministry (*v.* 16).

The *Second* Invitation was sent to those who had been already bidden by John. It was sent by "His Servant", Who was none other than the Lord Jesus Himself. His Ministry is expressed in one sentence: "Come; for all things are now ready" (*v.* 17). He was sent "at supper-time", according to Eastern custom. But they all with one consent began to make excuse (*vv.* 18–20).

The *Third* Invitation was sent, not to those who had been already bidden, but to another class altogether. It was sent by "The Master of the House", Who has perfect right and authority to invite whom He will. He sent "quickly": i. e. very soon after the return of the second servant; and "into the streets and lanes of the city". This was the ministry of Peter, the Twelve, and Paul.

The *Fourth* Invitation is yet future, as shown above in the other parables. It will be sent forth by "the Lord" (*v.* 23), by Him Who has all power in heaven and earth (Matt. 28. 18–20). This will be a ministry of compulsion, carried out in the "highways and hedges" of the wide world; and it will be effectual like the last in the preceding cases. All, in turn, receive the call, but it is the last who "hear and understand" (Matt. 13. 23); who "hear and receive" (Mark 4. 20); who "hear and keep" (Luke 8. 15); and who "bring forth fruit". For this, special wisdom and understanding is needed, as foretold in Dan. 11. 33; 12. 3, 10.

Thus the present dispensation (since the destruction of Jerusalem and dispersion of Israel, which took place shortly after Acts 28, has nothing to do with the Kingdom, and the proclamation of the good news connected with it is postponed and in abeyance. Meanwhile, and during this dispensation, we have:—

III. "THE GOSPEL (or Good News) OF GOD".

This is the Gospel unto which Paul the Apostle was separated (Rom. 1. 1), and is supplementary to "the Gospel of the Kingdom", of which it was another aspect.

"The Gospel of the Kingdom" was first proclaimed by John the Baptist and the Lord. But both were rejected and put to death.

The Lord, however, was raised from the dead, and the Gospel of God has to do with a risen Messiah. It characterizes the ministry of the Acts rather than that of the Gospels; especially Paul's share in it.

The Gospel of a risen Messiah, re-proclaimed as about to come and restore all things, was the burden of the apostolic proclamation during the dispensation of the Acts. See Acts 2. 23–36; 3. 12–18; 4. 2, 10–12.

"With *great power* gave the Apostles witness of the resurrection of the Lord Jesus; and *great grace* was upon them all" (4. 33). Also 5. 29–32; 10. 34–43; 13. 23–39.

This, too, was the burden of Paul's proclamation, as we may see from Acts 17. 1–3, 7. He proclaimed "Jesus, and the resurrection" (*vv.* 18, 31, 32). True, it was

the proclamation of the Kingdom, and, in its wider aspect, "the kingdom of God" (14. 22; 19. 8); because it was He Who had raised Christ from the dead, and the proclamation was being sent out by God Himself. It was His own special good news. It was of His own motion and will. And it was all of grace. If "His own" would even now receive Messiah, He would "send Jesus Christ" (Acts 3. 20).

In spite of all their sins, and their heinous crime in murdering His beloved Son, He would blot out all their sins and fulfil all His promises. Truly, this was in very deed:—

IV. "THE GOSPEL (or GOOD NEWS) OF THE GRACE OF GOD".

This is why, in the canonical order of the books of the New Testament, God's overruling is seen in the fact that the first writing which comes to us following on the *double* rejection of His Son (in the Gospels and the Acts) is the word and good news of His grace in Rom. 1. 1. In spite of all that we should consider the unpardonable nature of Israel's crime, the first written words which meet our eyes are these:—

"Paul, a servant of Jesus Christ, a called Apostle (or, an Apostle by Divine calling), separated to God's Gospel (or glad tidings), which He before promised by means of His prophets in sacred writings concerning His Son, Who came of the seed of David according to the flesh, Who was demonstrated [to be] God's Son, in power, with respect to [His] holy spirit [body, 1 Cor. 15. 45], by resurrection of the dead—even Jesus Christ our Lord, by Whom we received GRACE—yea, apostolic grace, with a view to the obedience of faith among all the nations, on behalf of His Name (or for His glory), among whom yourselves also are [the] called of Jesus Christ" (Rom. 1. 1-6).

Here we have the sum and the substance of the good news of the grace of God.

It was not new. It was promised before and written down by His prophets. The sufferings, death and resurrection and glory, were all foretold. But now "those things, which God before had showed by the mouth of all His prophets that Christ should suffer, He hath so fulfilled. THEREFORE, Repent ye, and turn again that your sins may be blotted out, so that [haply] may come seasons of refreshing from the presence (or face) of the LORD, and [that] He may send Him Who was before proclaimed (or, according to all the critical texts, "was foreordained") for you—even Jesus Christ" (Acts 3. 18-20).

Thus "God's Gospel" was based on the prophecies of the Old Testament, and was the logical development of them.

It is in this that it is distinguished from that which had not been before revealed by the prophets in the concluding verses of Romans. That epistle begins with what had been written in the Scriptures; it ends with what had never been written till "now", when the SECRET which had been kept in silence from times eternal, or during [the] times of [the] ages was then at length made manifest (Rom. 16. 25, 26. Eph. 3. 1-12. Col. 1. 26-28). (See Ap. 192.)

The time had come for this secret to be revealed, and to be committed to prophetic writings. This revelation is contained in the three Epistles written by Paul from his prison in Rome, to the Ephesians, Philippians, and Colossians.

Thus "the Gospel of the Kingdom" was the proclamation by and concerning the Messiah made by John the Baptist and Himself, and is the subject of the Four Gospels.

"The Gospel of God" is the proclamation concerning the same Messiah, made by the Twelve, the apostle Paul, and "them that heard" the Lord, during the dispensation of the Acts of the Apostles, and is the subject of their testimony and of their writings and the earlier Epistles of Paul. Seeing it was good news sent after the resurrection of Christ, it is all of pure grace and favour, and hence is "the Gospel of the Grace of God".

V. THE GOSPEL (or GOOD NEWS) OF THE GLORY OF CHRIST (2 Cor. 4. 4).

This is connected with Christ's exaltation as Head over all things to His Church, which is His body, which is developed and revealed more fully in the Prison Epistles (Eph. 1. 21-23. Phil. 2. 9-11. Col. 1. 14-19). It not only involves the present glory of Messiah, but includes the final defeat of Satan, the crushing of his head, and the subjugation of all spiritual beings, be they powers, principalities, authorities, dominions, or thrones, &c.

Hence, it is Satan's great aim now, at this present time, to blind the eyes of them that believe not, so that they may not learn of his coming defeat, as foretold in Gen. 3. 15, and seen fulfilled in Rev. 20 (see 2 Cor. 4. 4).

Knowing his object, and being "not ignorant of his devices", we know also what should be our own object: viz. the making known this good news which he would seek to hide; and proclaiming "the Gospel of the glory of Christ".

141 THE TWELVE APOSTLES.

There are four lists of the names of the Twelve Apostles: three in the Gospels and one in the Acts. In each list the order of the names varies, but with this remarkable agreement that they are always given in three groups, the first of each group being the same (Peter, Philip, and James the son of Alphæus), while the other three, though they vary in order within the group, are never given in a different group.

They may be presented thus:—

	Matt. 10. 2-4.	Mark 3. 16-19.	Luke 6. 14-16.	Acts 1. 13, 26.
1	... ...	... ... PETER		
2	and Andrew;	and James,	and Andrew,	and James,
3	James,	and John;	James	and John,
4	and John;	and Andrew,	and John,	and Andrew,
5	... ...	... ... PHILIP		
6	and Bartholomew[1];	and Bartholomew[1],	and Bartholomew[1],	and Thomas,
7	Thomas,	and Matthew,	Matthew	Bartholomew[1],
8	and Matthew;	and Thomas,	and Thomas,	and Matthew,
9	... ...	... ... JAMES (son of Alphæus)		
10	and Lebbæus[2];	and Thaddæus[2],	and Simon[3] (Zelōtēs),	and Simon[3] (Zelōtēs),
11	Simon[3] (Can.),	and Simon[3] (Can.),	and Judas[2] (of James),	and Judas[2] (of James).
12	and Judas Iscariot.	and Judas Iscariot.	and Judas Iscariot.	[Matthias (*v.* 26)].

[1] A patronymic for NATHANAEL (John 1. 44-46). where he is joined with Philip, and in John 21. 2 with Thomas.

[2] JUDAS the brother of James, to distinguish him from Judas Iscariot. He was called Lebbæus or Thaddæus, which words have a similar meaning, the latter being Aramaic. See Ap. 94. III. 3.

[3] SIMON, the Canaanite or Cananean. Not meaning a Gentile, but an Aramaic word meaning the same as *Zēlotēs*.

Further detailed particulars may be given as follows :—

1. Simon (Matt. 10. 2. Mark 3. 16. Luke 6. 14. John 1. 42). Peter (Acts 1. 13), so surnamed (Matt. 10. 2) by Christ (Mark 3. 16. Luke 6. 14), who also called him Cephas (John 1. 42). He was the son of Jona[1] (John 1. 42) and a native of Bethsaida[1] (John 1. 44).

2. Andrew (Matt. 10. 2. Mark 3. 18. Luke 6. 14. Acts 1. 13), of Bethsaida[1] (John 1. 44), and Peter's brother (Matt. 10. 2. Luke 6. 14).

3. James (Matt. 10. 2. Mark 3. 17. Luke 6. 14. Acts 1. 13), the son of Zebedee[1] (Matt. 10. 2. Mark 3. 17), surnamed by Christ, with John, Boanerges[1] (Mark 3. 17).

4. John (Matt. 10. 2. Mark 3. 17. Luke 6. 14. Acts 1. 13), the brother of James (Matt. 10. 2. Mark 3. 17), surnamed by Christ, with James, Boanerges[1] (Mark 3. 17).

5. Philip (Matt. 10. 3. Mark 3. 18. Luke 6. 14. Acts 1. 13), of Bethsaida[1] (John 1. 44).

6. Bartholomew[1] (Matt. 10. 3. Mark 3. 18. Luke 6. 14. Acts 1. 13).

7. Thomas[1] (Matt. 10. 3. Mark 3. 18. Luke 6. 15. Acts 1. 13), called Didymus (John 11. 16; 21. 2).

8. Matthew[1] (Matt. 10. 3. Mark 3. 18. Luke 6. 15. Acts 1. 13), the Publican (Matt. 10. 3. Luke 5. 27); called also Levi (Mark 2. 14. Luke 5. 27), the son of Alphæus (Mark 2. 14).

9. James (Matt. 10. 3. Mark 3. 18. Luke 6. 15. Acts 1. 13), the son of Alphæus[1] (Matt. 10. 3. Mark 3. 18. Luke 6. 15. Acts 1. 13).

10. Lebbæus (Matt. 10. 3), whose surname (Matt. 10. 3) was Thaddæus[1] (Matt. 10. 3. Mark 3. 18); called also Judas, brother of James (Luke 6. 16. Acts 1. 13), and "Judas (not Iscariot)" (John 14. 22).

11. Simon (Matt. 10. 4. Mark 3. 18. Luke 6. 15. Acts 1. 13), the Canaanite (Matt. 10. 4. Mark 3. 18); called Zēlōtēs (Luke 6. 15. Acts 1. 13).

12. Judas (Matt. 10. 4. Mark 3. 19. Luke 6. 16) Iscariot (Matt. 10. 4. Mark 3. 19. Luke 6. 16), the traitor (Luke 6. 16) who betrayed Him (Matt. 10. 4. Mark 3. 19. John 6. 71; 12. 4; 13. 2), the son of Simon (John 6. 71; 12. 4; 13. 2, 26).

[1] These are *Aramaic* words. See Ap. 94. III. 3

142 "HE THAT HATH EARS TO HEAR, LET HIM HEAR."

These words were never used by mortal man. They were heard only from the lips of Him Who spoke with Divine authority (Matt. 7. 29); and on earth only on *seven* distinct occasions, in order to emphasize and call attention to the utterance He had just made.

This is an important example of the Figure *Polyptōton* (Ap. 6), the repetition of the same verb in a different inflection, by which great emphasis is put upon the injunction here given. See Ap. 6, and notes on Gen. 2. 17 and 26. 28.

The *seven* (Ap. 10) occasions are thus marked out for our special attention, as being what was said to ears which God had opened.

1. The first is in Luke 8. 8, at the close of the first giving of the Parable of the Sower, *before* the formal calling and mission of the Twelve Apostles, which took place and is recorded in ch. 9. 1–6. This parable was *repeated* on a later occasion, when it was needed to complete the setting of the eight parables which are grouped together in Matt. 13 (see Ap. 145).

In this case it refers to the sowing of the good seed of the Kingdom: i.e. its proclamation by Jehovah's servants, John the Baptist and the Lord (as further explained in the Parable of the Marriage Feast in Matt. 22. 1–7). See Ap. 140. II.

2. The second occasion is recorded in Matt. 11. 15, *after* the calling and mission of the Twelve, when we are bidden to give earnest heed to the important mission of John the Baptist, and to understand that had the people repented at his proclamation he would have been reckoned as Elijah the prophet (Mal. 4. 5), in whose "spirit and power" he was to come. This was declared before his birth, in Luke 1. 17.

When the Lord's disciples asked Him "Why then say the scribes that Elijah must first come?" Jesus answered and said unto them, "Elijah truly (Gr. *men*, i.e. on the one hand) shall first come, and restore all things. But (Gr. *de*, i.e. on the other hand) I say unto you, That Elijah is come already, and they knew him not, but have done unto him whatsoever they listed. Likewise shall the Son of man also suffer of them. Then the disciples understood that He spake unto them of John the Baptist" (Matt. 17. 10–13). To "understand" this, it required the opened ear. Hence (Matt. 11. 14) the Lord's words, "If ye will receive (him), this is Elijah who was about to come"

Had the nation repented, the real Elijah would indeed have come and effected "the *restoration* of all things, which God had spoken by the mouth of all His holy prophets from of old" (Acts 3. 21). The nation did not repent; therefore Mal. 4. 5 still awaits its literal fulfilment, and they "who have ears to hear" will understand.

3. The third occasion of the utterance of this solemn exhortation was when the Lord, *after* the Mission of the Twelve, repeated the Parable of the Sower (Matt. 13. 9), which He had spoken by itself *before* the Mission of the Twelve (Luke 8. 8) but which He then united with seven others, to make one complete whole, revealing the coming change of dispensation. In this setting the Lord twice declared "He that hath ears to hear, let him hear": once at the end of the Parable of the Sower (see Ap. 145);

4. And again (the fourth occasion) in *v.* 43, at the end of the interpretation of the Parable of the Tares. Both these parables required and still require the opened ear in order to understand their dispensational teaching.

5. The fifth occasion is recorded in Mark 4. 23, after the *application* of the illustration of the Lamp put under a measure, when the utterance is repeated to emphasize the fact that the Lord was revealing things which had been hitherto hidden, concerning the secrets of the Kingdom of heaven.

6. The sixth occasion is in Mark also (7. 16), and here it is used in another connection, but with the same solemn emphasis, in order to call attention to the important truth, prefaced by the words preceding it, "Hearken unto Me every one of you, and understand: There is nothing from without a man, that entering into him can defile him: but the things which come out of him, those are they that defile the man. If any man have ears to hear, let him hear" (Mark 7. 14–16).

7. The seventh occasion is recorded in Luke 14. 35, and is connected with true discipleship, and counting its cost. Great multitudes were following Him (*v.* 25), and publicans and sinners were drawing near to hear Him. But not all received what they heard. These the Lord likened unto salt which had lost its savour, which was neither fit for the land nor yet for the dunghill; but men cast it out. "He that hath ears to hear, let him hear" (Luke 14. 34, 35).

This was the last occasion on earth. For the eight occasions after His ascension, see Rev. 2. 7, 11, 17, 29; 3. 6, 13, 22; 13. 9.

143 "HAVE YE NOT READ?" (Matt. 12. 3, &c.).

This question was asked by our Lord on six different occasions. Six books of the O.T. were referred to, and *seven* separate passages thus received the *imprimatur* of Him Who spoke, not His own words, but only the words given to Him to speak by the Father (John 7. 16; 8. 28, 46, 47; 12. 49; 14. 10, 24; 17. 8). Cp. Deut. 18. 18, 19.

1. Matt. 12. 3 (Mark 2. 25. Luke 6. 3). "What David did", covering 1 Sam. 21. 6: "the Shewbread" (*v.* 4) covering Lev. 24. 6-9: "not lawful for him to eat . . . but only for the priests", covering Lev. 24. 9.

2. Matt. 12. 5. "In the temple the priests profane the sabbath", covering Num. 28. 9, 10 (cp. John 7. 22, 23).

3. Matt. 19. 4. Creation. "At the beginning He made them male and female", covering Gen. 1. 27 (cp. 5. 2), and thus effectually shutting out the modern idea of "evolution".

4. Matt. 21. 16. "Out of the mouth of babes and sucklings", &c., covering Psalm 8. 2.

5. Matt. 21. 42 (Mark 12. 10. Luke 20. 17). "The stone which the builders refused", &c., covering Psalm 118 22. (Cp. Isa. 28. 16. Acts 4. 11. 1 Pet. 2. 6, 7.)

6. Matt. 22. 31, 32 (Mark 12. 26. Luke 20. 37). Resurrection, covering Ex. 3. 6.

The six books of the O.T. covered by the Lord's question are four books of the Pentateuch (Genesis, Exodus, Leviticus, and Numbers), with 1 Samuel and the Psalms.

The seven distinct passages referred to are as follows, omitting the parallel passages in the other Gospels, viz.:—

1. Gen.	1. 27.	Matt.	19. 4.
2. Ex.	3. 6.	"	22. 31, 32
3. Lev.	24. 6-9.	"	12. 3.
4. Num.	28. 9, 10.	"	12. 5.
5. 1 Sam.	21. 6.	"	12. 3.
6. Ps.	8. 2.	"	21. 16.
7. "	118. 22.	"	21. 42.

144 THE "THREE DAYS" AND "THREE NIGHTS" OF MATT. 12. 40.

The fact that "three days" is used by Hebrew idiom for any part of three days and three nights is not disputed; because that was the common way of reckoning, just as it was when used of years. Three or any number of years was used inclusively of any part of those years, as may be seen in the reckoning of the reigns of any of the kings of Israel and Judah.

But, when the number of "nights" is stated as well as the number of "days", then the expression ceases to be an idiom, and becomes a literal statement of fact.

Moreover, as the Hebrew day began at sunset the day was reckoned from one sunset to another, the "twelve hours in the day" (John 11. 9) being reckoned from sunrise, and the twelve hours of the night from sunset. An evening-morning was thus used for a whole day of twenty-four hours, as in the first chapter of Genesis. Hence the expression "a night and a day" in 2 Cor. 11. 25 denotes a complete day (Gr. *nuchthēmeron*).

When Esther says (Est. 4. 16) "fast ye for me, and neither eat nor drink three days", she defines her meaning as being three complete days, because she adds (being a Jewess) "night or day". And when it is written that the fast ended on "the third day" (5. 1), "the third day" must have succeeded and included the third night.

In like manner the sacred record states that the young man (in 1 Sam. 30. 12) "had eaten no bread, nor drunk any water, three days and three nights". Hence, when the young man explains the reason, he says, "because three days agone I fell sick". He means therefore three complete days and nights, because, being an *Egyptian* (*vv.* 11, 13) he naturally reckoned his day as beginning at sunrise according to the Egyptian manner (see *Encycl. Brit.*, 11th (Cambridge) ed., vol. xi, p. 77). His "three days agone" refers to the beginning of his sickness, and includes the whole period, giving the reason for his having gone without food during the whole period stated.

Hence, when it says that "Jonah was in the belly of the fish three days and three nights" (Jonah 1. 17) it means exactly what it says, and that this can be the only meaning of the expression in Matt. 12. 40; 16. 4. Luke 11. 30, is shown in Ap. 156.

In the expression, "the heart of the earth" (Matt. 12. 40), the meaning is the same as "the heart of the sea", "heart" being put by the Fig. *Metonymy* (of the Subject), Ap. 6, for "the midst", and is frequently so translated. See Ps. 46. 2. Jer. 51. 1. Ezek. 27. 4, 25, 26, 27; 28. 2. It is used of ships when sailing "in the heart of the seas", i.e. in, or on the sea. See Ezek. 27. 25, 26; 28. 8; also of people dwelling in the heart of the seas, i. e. on islands (Ezek. 28. 2). Jonah uses the Heb. *beten* (= womb) in the same way (2. 2).

145 THE EIGHT PARABLES OF THE KINGDOM OF HEAVEN IN MATT. 13.

There are eight Parables in Matt. 13, and not seven, as is usually held.

For the Structure of the whole chapter, see page 1336.

The Parables themselves, apart from their respective contexts, may be thus exhibited:—

Matt. 13. 3-52.	A	B | 3-9. The Sower. The seed sown broadcast, in public.	To the multitudes "out of the house".
		C | 24-30. The Tares. Good and bad together. Separated at the end of the age.	
		D | 31, 32. The Mustard Seed. One tree.	
		E | 33. The Leaven. Hid in the meal.	
	A	*E* | 44. The Treasure. Hid in a field.	To the Disciples within the house.
		D | 45, 46. The Goodly Pearls. One pearl.	
		C | 47-50. The Drag-net. Good and bad together. Separated at the end of the age.	
		B | 52. The Scribe. The treasures shown to those in the house in private.	

The above Structure exhibits the *eight* Parables as a whole. But without disturbing these correspondences, the *four* spoken outside the house and the *four* spoken "within the house" have their own separate Structures (*Introversions*, like the Structure of the whole), corresponding one with the other:—

The first four, outside the house. (Apparent failure.)

A	F | The Sower. Three kinds of bad ground.	
	G | The Tares. Grow till harvest	in the earth.
	G | The Mustard Seed. When it is grown	in the earth.
	F | The Leaven. Three leavened measures.	

The last four, within the house. (Hidden purpose.)

A | H | The Treasure in the field.
J | The Goodly Pearls } in the sea.
J | The Good and Bad Fish } in the sea.
H | The Treasure in the house.

The Four Parables outside the house, spoken to the multitudes, seem therefore to call for an *exoteric* interpretation; while the four spoken within the house call for an *esoteric* interpretation.

In this case, the first four would find their interpretation in the three proclamations of John the Baptist, the Lord Jesus, and "them that heard Him" (see Ap. 95); the Leaven and the Tares showing the secret cause of the failure which led to the postponement of the Kingdom, while the Mustard Tree would exhibit the external consequences.

The latter four would find their interpretation in "the secrets of the kingdom of the heavens" (Ap. 114), showing that notwithstanding the apparent (outward) failure, God, all the while, has His hidden purpose concerning the Remnant, His peculiar treasure hidden: the earthly calling, in the field (which is the world), and "the heavenly calling", "in the house"; and the end of the age would exhibit the one "pearl of great price": the Remnant, according to the Election of Grace, on the one hand, and the "good and bad" receiving their awards, on the other.

146 "THE FOUNDATION OF THE WORLD."

To arrive at the true meaning of this expression, we must note that there are two words translated "foundation" in the New Testament: (1) *themelios*, and (2) *katabolē*.

The Noun, *themelios*, occurs in Luke 6. 48, 49; 14. 29; Acts 16. 26. Rom. 15. 20. 1 Cor. 3. 10, 11, 12. Eph. 2. 20. 1 Tim. 6. 19. 2 Tim. 2. 19. Heb. 6. 1; 11. 10. Rev. 21. 14, 19, 19. It is never used of the world (*kosmos*) or the earth (*gē*). The corresponding Verb (*themelioō*) occurs in Matt. 7. 25. Luke 6. 48. Eph. 3. 17. Col. 1. 23. Heb. 1. 10 and 1 Pet. 5. 10. The verb is only once used of the earth (*gē*). Heb. 1. 10.

A comparison of all these passages will show that these are proper and regular terms for the English words "to found", and "foundation".

The Noun, *katabolē*, occurs in Matt. 13. 35; 25. 34. Luke 11. 50. John 17. 24. Eph. 1. 4. Heb. 4. 3; 9. 26; 11. 11. 1 Pet. 1. 20. Rev. 13. 8; 17. 8; and the corresponding Verb (*kataballō*) occurs in 2 Cor. 4. 9. Heb. 6. 1; and Rev. 12. 10.

A comparison of all these passages (especially 2 Cor. 4. 9, and Rev. 12. 10) will show that *kataballō* and *katabolē* are not the proper terms for founding and foundation, but the correct meaning is *casting down*, or *overthrow*.

Consistency, therefore, calls for the same translation in Heb. 6. 1, where, instead of "not laying again", the rendering should be "not casting down". That is to say, the foundation already laid, of repentance, &c., was not to be cast down or overthrown, but was to be *left*—and progress made unto the perfection.

Accordingly, the Noun *katabolē*, derived from, and cognate with the Verb, ought to be translated "disruption", or "ruin".

The remarkable thing is that in all occurrences (except Heb. 11. 11) the word is connected with "the world" (Gr. *kosmos*. Ap. 129. 1), and therefore the expression should be rendered "the disruption (or ruin) of the world", clearly referring to the condition indicated in Gen. 1. 2, and described in 2 Pet. 3. 5, 6. For the earth was not *created tohū* (Isa. 45. 18), but *became* so, as stated in the Hebrew of Gen. 1. 2 and confirmed by 2 Pet. 3. 6, where "the world that then was by the word of God" (Gen. 1. 1), perished, and "the heavens and the earth which are now, by the same word" were created (Gen. 2. 4), and are "kept in store, reserved unto fire against the day of judgment" (2 Pet. 3. 7) which shall usher in the "new heavens and the new earth" of 2 Pet. 3. 13.

"The disruption of the world" is an event forming a great dividing line in the dispensations of the ages. In Gen. 1. 1 we have the *founding* of the world (Heb. 1. 10 = *themelioō*), but in Gen. 1. 2 we have its *overthrow*.

This is confirmed by a further remarkable fact, that the phrase, which occurs ten times, is associated with the Preposition *apo* = from (Ap. 104. iv) seven times, and with *pro* = before (Ap. 104. xiv) three times. The former refers to the *kingdom*, and is connected with the "counsels" of God; the latter refers to the Mystery (or Secret. See Ap. 192) and is connected with the "purpose" of God (see John 17. 24. Eph. 1. 4. 1 Pet. 1. 20).

Ample New Testament testimony is thus given to the profoundly significant fact recorded in Gen. 1. 2, that "the earth became *tohū* and *bohū* (i.e. waste and desolate); and darkness was on the face of the deep", before the creation of "the heavens and the earth which are now" (2 Pet. 3. 7).

147 "THOU ART PETER" (Matt. 16. 18).

As explained in the notes, the two Greek words *petros* and *petra* are quite distinct, the former being masculine gender, and the latter feminine. The latter denotes a rock or cliff, *in situ*, firm and immovable. The former denotes a fragment of it, which one traveller may move with his foot in one direction and another may throw in another. This former word *petros* is the Greek translation of *kēphās*, a stone, which was Peter's name in Aramaic, as was his appellative "Bar-jona" (John 1. 42). See Ap. 94. III. 3.

It is remarkable that there is only one other instance (Luke 22. 34) in which our Lord addressed him as "Peter"; but, in all other cases, by his fore-name "Simon", reminding him of what he was before his call, and of the characteristics of his human nature. In that other instance it is used in connection with the coming exhibition of his weakness, in the prediction of his denial of his Lord.

There is thus a special significance in the use of the word "Peter" in Matt. 16. 18. It was the name connected with his commission and apostleship; another commission being about to be committed to him.

It was not Peter, the man, who would be the foundation, for, as we have said, *petra* is feminine, and must refer to a feminine noun expressed or implied. That noun could hardly be any other than *homologia*, which means a *confession*; and it was Peter's confession that was the one subject of the Father's revelation and the Son's confirmation.

Moreover, in 1 Cor. 3. 11 it has once for all been declared by the Holy Spirit that "OTHER foundation can no man lay than that IS LAID, which is JESUS CHRIST."

The earliest known reference to Matt. 16. 18 is found in ORIGEN'S *Commentary* (A.D. 186–253), which is older than any extant Greek manuscript. He says:

"If we also say the same as Peter, 'Thou art the Christ, the Son of the living God', not by the instruction of flesh and blood, but by the illumination

of the heavenly Father in our hearts, we ourselves become the same thing as Peter.

"If you should think that the whole Church was built by God only on that one, Peter, what will you say of John, . . . or each of the apostles?"[1]

This is conclusive as to the interpretation. But there are other and later references to these words by AUGUSTINE (A.D. 378), and JEROME (A.D. 305), alike older than any Greek MSS. now extant.

JEROME wrote thus in his exposition (Benedictine ed.):

"And I tell thee, that thou hast said to Me, 'Thou art the Christ', &c., and I tell thee that thou art Peter, and on this rock, &c."[2]

AUGUSTINE wrote in his *Retractationes* (Benedictine ed., vol. i, p. 33):

"I have somewhere said, concerning the apostle Peter, that the Church was founded on him, as a *petra*, or rock; but I know that I have since very often explained what our Lord said to signify on Him Whom Peter confessed; but between these two opinions, let the reader choose that which is the more probable."[3]

In AUGUSTINE'S Sermon *In die Pentecostis* (Benedictine ed., tom. v. p. 1097; also Pusey's Translation, *Sermons on the New Testament*, vol. i. p. 215), he explains the reason for this retractation in a paraphrastic citation of the whole context:—

"When our Lord had asked His disciples who men said that He was, and when, in reporting the opinions of others, they had said that some said He was John, some Elijah, others Jeremiah or one of the prophets, He said to them: 'But ye, Who do ye say that I am?' Peter (one alone for the rest, one for all) answered, 'Thou art the Christ, the Son of the living God.' This, most excellently, most truly spoken, was deservedly rewarded with this reply: 'Blessed art thou, Simon Bar-Jonah, because flesh and blood revealed not this to thee, but My Father Who is in heaven; and I tell thee that thou hast said': (hast said, observe, hast made confession unto Me: receive therefore the benediction): 'and I tell thee that thou art Peter; and on this rock I will build My church.'"[4]

Some have conjectured from these words "tu dixisti" (thou hast said it) that AUGUSTINE and JEROME must have had in the MSS. from which they translated six lettters, which they divided into two words "SU EIPS"[5], taking EIPS as an abbreviation of EIPAS (=thou hast said).

There must have been another division of the same six letters into three words, which was current even then, for both these Fathers add "SU EI PETROS"=thou art Peter; taking the same "PS" as an abbreviation of PETROS.

It is evident, however, that these Fathers give only a *paraphrase*; and do not profess to be giving an exact *quotation*.

One thing, however, is certain, and that is our only point in this Appendix, viz. that the earliest references made to this passage disclaim all idea of its having any reference to the apostle Peter, but only to HIM Who was the subject of Peter's confession.

---

[1] *ei de epi ton hena ekeinon Petron nomizeis hupo tou Theou oikodomeisthai tēn pasan ekklēsian monon, ti oun phēsais peri Iōannou, tou tēs brontēs, e hekastou tōn apostolōn.*

[2] "Quid est quod ait? Et ego dico tibi tu mihi dixisti (tu es Christus filius Dei vivi); *et ego dico tibi quia* TU *mihi dixisti* (tu es Christus filius Dei vivi); et *ego dico tibi* (non sermone casso et nullum habenti opus, sed dico tibi, quia meum dixisse, fecisse est) *quia tu es Petrus*; et super hanc petram aedificabo ecclesiam meam."

[3] "Dixi in quodam loco de apostolo Petro, quod in *illo*, quasi in *petra*, fundata sit ecclesia; sed scio me postea saepissime sic exposuisse *quod a Domino dictum est*, ut super *hunc* intelligetur *quem confessus est Petrus*: horum autem duarum sententiarum *quae sit probabilior*, eligat lector." (Italics, ours.)

[4] "Cum interrogasset ipse Dominus discipulos suos, quis ab hominibus diceretur, et aliorum opiniones recolendo dixissent; quod alii eum dicerent Ioannem, alii Eliam, alii Ieremiam, aut unum ex prophetis, ait illis, '*Vos autem quem Me esse dicitis?*' Et Petrus, unus pro ceteris, unus pro omnibus, 'Tu es, inquit, Christus filius Dei vivi.' Hoc, optime, veracissime, merito tale responsum accipere meruit: 'Beatus es, Simon Bar Ionae, quia non tibi revelavit caro et sanguis, sed Pater Meus qui in coelis est: et Ego dico tibi, quia *tu dixisti*': Mihi dixisti, audi; dedisti confessionem. Recipe benedictionem ergo: 'Et dico tibi, Tu es Petrus—et super hanc petram aedificabo ecclesiam Meam'".

[5] It will be seen from Ap. 94. V. i. 3 that in the Greek manuscripts there was no division between the letters or words until the ninth century.

148 "THE THIRD DAY."

In the first mention of His sufferings (Matt. 16. 21) the Lord mentions the fact that He would be "raised again the third day". In John 2. 19 He had already mentioned "three days" as the time after which He would raise up "the Temple of His body".

The expression occurs eleven times with reference to His resurrection (Matt. 16. 21; 17. 23; 20. 19. Mark 9. 31; 10. 34. Luke 9. 22; 18. 33; 24. 7, 46. Acts 10. 40. 1 Cor. 15. 4).

We have the expression "after three days" in Mark 8. 31, used of the same event.

This shows that the expression "three days and three nights" of Matt. 12. 40 must include "three days" and the three preceding "nights". While it is true that a "third day" may be a part of three days, including two nights, yet "after three days", and "three nights and three days" cannot possibly be so reckoned.

This full period admits of the Lord's resurrection on the third of the three days, each being preceded by a night, as shown in Ap. 144 and 156.

But, why this particular period? Why not two, or four, or any other number of days? Why "three" and no more nor less?

1. We notice that the man who contracted defilement through contact with a dead body was to purify himself on the third day (Num. 19. 11, 12).

2. The flesh of the peace offering was not to be kept beyond the third day, but was then to be burnt (Lev. 7. 17, 18) as unfit for food.

3. John Lightfoot (1602–75) quotes a Talmudic tradition that the mourning for the dead culminated on "the third day", because the spirit was not supposed to have finally departed till then (*Works*, Pitman's ed., vol. xii. pp. 351–353).

4. Herodotus testifies that embalmment did not take place until after three days (Herod. ii. 86–89).

5. The Jews did not accept evidence as to the identification of a dead body after three days.

This period seems, therefore, to have been chosen by the Lord (i. e. Jehovah, in the type of Jonah) to associate the fact of resurrection with the certainty of death, so as to preclude all doubt that death had actually taken place, and shut out all suggestion that it might have been a trance, or a mere case of resuscitation. The fact that Lazarus had been dead "four days already" was urged by Martha as a proof that Lazarus was dead, for "by this time he stinketh" (John 11. 17, 39).

We have to remember that corruption takes place very quickly in the East, so that "the third day" was the proverbial evidence as to the certainty that death had taken place, leaving no hope.

149 THE TRANSFIGURATION (Matt. 17. 1-8. Mark 9. 2-8. Luke 9. 28-36).

It has been said that "to most ordinary men the Transfiguration seemed to promise much and yield little"; but, by a careful comparison of Scripture with Scripture we shall find some of what it promises so much, and receive much of what it seems to yield so little.

1. The event is recorded in three out of the four Gospels. It is therefore of great importance.

2. It is dated in all three accounts, and is therefore of particular importance. It took place "*about* six days" (exclusive reckoning), or "*about* eight days" (Luke 9. 28, inclusive reckoning) from the Lord's prediction.

3. The event from which it is dated, in all three Gospels, is the Lord's first mention of His sufferings, and rejection (Matt. 16. 21. Mark 8. 31. Luke 9. 22). It must therefore have some close connexion with this[1].

4. What this connection is may be seen from the fact that, in the O.T., while the "glory" is often mentioned without the "sufferings" (Isa. 11; 32; 35; 40; 60, &c.), the "sufferings" are never mentioned apart from the "glory". (See Ap. 71.)

5. It is so here; for in each account the Lord goes on to mention His future coming "in the glory of His Father"; and this is followed by an exhibition of that "glory", and a typical foreshadowing of that "coming" (2 Pet. 1. 16–18) on "the holy mount".

6. The Transfiguration took place "as He prayed"; and there are only two subjects recorded concerning which He prayed: the *sufferings* (Matt. 26. 39, 42, 44) and the *glory* (John 17. 1, 5, 24).

7. It was on "the holy mount" that He "received from God the Father *honour and glory*" (*timē kai doxa*, 2 Pet. 1. 17), and was "crowned with *glory and honour*, for the suffering of death" (Gr. *doxa kai timē*, Heb. 2. 9). In these passages the reference is to Exodus 28. 2, where the High Priest at his consecration for the office of high priest was clothed with garments, specially made under Divine direction, and these were "for glory and for beauty". In the Greek of the Sept. we have the same two words (*timē kai doxa*).

8. These garments were made by those who were "wise hearted", whom Jehovah said He had "filled with the spirit of wisdom that they may make Aaron's garments *to consecrate him, that he may minister unto Me in the priest's office*" (Ex. 28. 3). These latter words are repeated in *v.* 4, in order to emphasize the Divine object. This tells us assuredly that the Transfiguration was the consecration of our Lord for His special office of High Priest and for His priestly work, of which Aaron was the type.

9. This is confirmed by what appears to be the special Divine *formula* of consecration: (1) In Matt. 3. 17, &c. "This is My beloved Son", at His Baptism, for His office of Prophet (at the commencement of His Ministry): (2) In Matt. 17. 5 "This is My beloved Son" at His Transfiguration, for His office of High Priest (Heb. 5. 5–10): and (3) at His Resurrection, "Thou art My Son; this day have I begotten Thee", i.e. brought Thee to the birth. Gr. *gegennēka*, as in Acts 13. 33 and Ps. 2. 7 (Sept.).

10. At His resurrection His *sufferings* were over; and nothing further was needed before He should "enter into His glory" according to Luke 24. 26. There was nothing to hinder that glory which He had then "received" from being "beheld" by those whom He had loved (John 17. 24). The *sufferings* had first to be accomplished; but, this having been done, the glory of His kingdom and His glorious reign would have followed the proclamation of that kingdom by Peter in Acts 3. 18–26. It was, as we know, rejected: in Jerusalem, the capital of the land (Acts 6. 9—7. 60), and afterward in Rome, the capital of the dispersion (Acts 28. 17–28). Hence, He must come again, and when He again bringeth the First-begotten into the world, the Father will say "Thou art My Son", and, "let all the angels of God worship Him" (Heb. 1. 5, 6).

[1] This is doubtless the reason why it finds no place in John's Gospel; for, like the Temptation, and the Agony, it is not needed in that Gospel for the presentation of the Lord Jesus as God.

150 "BELIEVE": THE USE OF THE WORD IN VARIOUS CONNECTIONS, ETC.

There are two Verbs, two Nouns, and one Adjective to be considered in connection with this subject.

I. VERBS.

1. ***pisteuo*** = to have faith (*pistis*) in; hence to believe. Translated "believe", except in eight instances, see below (iv).

i. Used absolutely: Matt. 8. 13; 21. 22; 24. 23, 26. Mark 5. 36; 9. 23, 23, 24; 13. 21; 15. 32; 16. 16, 17. Luke 1. 45; 8. 12, 13, 50; 22. 67. John 1. 7, 50; 3. 12, 12, -18-; 4. 41, 42, 48, 53; 5. 44; 6. 36, 64, 64; 9. 38; 10. 25, 26; 11. 15, 40; 12. 39, 47; 14. 29; 16. 31; 19. 35; 20. 8, 25, 29, 29, -31. Acts 2. 44; 4. 4, 32; 5. 14; 8. 13, 37-; 11. 21; 13. 12, 39, 48; 14. 1; 15. 5, 7; 17. 12, 34; 18. -8, 27; 19. 2, 18; 21. 20, 25; 26. -27. Rom. 1. 16; 3. 22; 4. 11; 10. 4, 10; 13. 11; 15. 13. 1 Cor. 1. 21; 3. 5; 14. 22, 22; 15. 2, 11. 2 Cor. 4. 13, 13. Gal. 3. 22. Eph. 1. 19. 1 Thess. 1. 7; 2. 10, 13. 2 Thess. 1. 10, 10. 1 Tim. 3. 16. Heb. 4. 3. James 2. -19. 1 Pet. 2. 7. Jude 5. 94

ii. With dative of person or thing believed: Matt. 21. 25, 32, 32, 32; 27. 42. Mark 11. 31; 16. 13, 14. Luke 1. 20; 20. 5. John 2. 22; 4. 21, 50; 5. 24, 38, 46, 46, 47, 47; 6. 30; 8. 31, 45, 46; 10. 37, 38, 38; 12. 38; 14. 11, 11. Acts 8. 12; 13. 41; 16. 34; 18. 8-; 24. 14; 26. 27-; 27. 25. Rom. 4. 3; 10. 16. Gal. 3. 6. 2 Thess. 2. 11, 12. 2 Tim. 1. 12. Titus 3. 8. James 2. 23. 1 John 3. 23; 4. 1; 5. -10-. 47

iii. With direct object of the fact believed, either a Noun in the Acc. Case, or a sentence: Matt. 9. 28. Mark 11. 23, 24. John 4. 21; 6. 69; 8. 24; 9. 18; 10. -38; 11. -26, 27, 42; 13. 19; 14. 10, 11-; 16. 27, 30; 17. 8, 21; 20. 31-. Acts 8. -37; 9. 26; 15. 11. Rom. 6. 8; 10. 9; 14. 2. 1 Cor. 11. 18; 13. 7. 1 Thess. 4. 14. Heb. 11. 6. James 2. 19-. 1 John 4. 16; 5. 1, 5. 33

iv. Translated "commit": Luke 16. 11. John 2. 24 (both followed by Dative and Accusative); "committed to", or "put in trust with" (Passive): Rom. 3. 2. 1 Cor. 9. 17. Gal. 2. 7. 1 Thess. 2. 4. 1 Tim. 1. 11. Ti. 1. 3. 8

v. With Prepositions.

(i) *eis* (Ap. 104. vi): Matt. 18. 6. Mark 9. 42. John 1. 12; 2. 11, 23; 3. 15, 16, 18-, -18, 36; 4. 39; 6. 29, 35, 40, 47; 7. 5, 31, 38, 39, 48; 8. 30; 9. 35, 36; 10. 42; 11. 25, 26-, 45, 48; 12. 11, 36, 37, 42, 44, 44, 46; 14. 1, 1, 12; 16. 9; 17. 20. Acts 10. 43; 14. 23; 19. 4. Rom. 10. 14-. Gal. 2. 16. Phil. 1. 29. 1 Pet. 1. 8, 21. 1 John 5. 10-, -10, 13, 13. 52

(ii) *en* (Ap. 104. viii): Mark 1. 15. Eph. 1. 13. 2

(iii) *epi* (Ap. 104. ix).

1. With Dative: Luke 24. 25. Rom. 4. 18; 9. 33; 10. 11. 1 Tim. 1. 16. 1 Pet. 2. 6. 6

2. With Acc.: Acts 9. 42; 11. 17; 16. 31; 22. 19. Rom. 4. 5, 24. 6

vi. In two instances, through the object being a Relative Pronoun, and attracted to the case of its antecedent, the Verb is followed by a Genitive: Rom. 4. 17; 10. -14. 2

250

There are only 248 occurrences of the Verb *pisteuō* (of which 99 are found in John's Gospel), but in two cases, besides those noted in iv, it is followed by a direct object of the thing believed, as well as a Dative of the person. These are John 4. 21; 14. 11–, and are therefore noted under both ii and iii.

2. ***peitho***, which is found 55 times, means to "persuade", and is so translated in Matt. 27. 20; 28. 14. Luke 16. 31; 20. 6. Acts 13. 43; 14. 19; 18. 4; 19. 8, 26; 21. 14; 26. 26, 28; 28. 23. Rom. 8. 38; 14. 14; 15. 14. 2 Cor. 5. 11. Gal. 1. 10. 2 Tim. 1. 5, 12. Heb. 6. 9; 11. 13. 22

The Passive, "to be persuaded" or the Middle, "to persuade oneself", is translated "believe" in Acts 17. 4; 27. 11; 28. 24. 3

"Obey" in Acts 5. 36, 37. Rom. 2. 8. Gal. 3. 1; 5. 7. Heb. 13. 17. James 3. 3; "agreed" in Acts 5. 40; and "yield" in Acts 23. 21. 9

In Acts 12. 20, the active is rendered "made ... friend", and in 1 John 3. 19 "assure". 2

peithō has a Middle Perfect, *pepoitha*, with a reflexive sense, "I have persuaded myself": i.e. "I trust". This is rendered "trust", "have confidence", &c., in Matt. 27. 43. Mark 10. 24. Luke 11. 22; 18. 9. Rom. 2. 19. 2 Cor. 1. 9; 2. 3; 10. 7. Gal. 5. 10. Phil. 1. 6, 14, 25; 2. 24; 3. 3, 4. 2 Thess. 3. 4. Philem. 21. Heb. 2. 13; 13. 18. 19

55

II. NOUNS.

1. ***pistis***[1] = faith. The living, Divinely implanted principle. It connects itself with the second Aorist of *peithō* (I. 2, above), Gr. *epithon*, occurs 242 times, and is always translated "faith", except in Acts 17. 31, "assurance"; Titus 2. 10, "fidelity"; and Rom. 3. 26, and Heb. 10. 39, where "of faith" is rendered "him which believeth", and "them that believe".

2. ***pepoithesis*** = confidence. It is derived from the Middle Perfect of *peithō* (I. 2, above), which is always to be distinguished from the Passive Perfect (*pepeismai*). The latter refers to persuasion *wrought from without*; the former refers to a *persuasion realised from within*, and this is what *pepoithēsis* seems always to mean. *Pistis* (No. 1) refers rather to the *principle*, and *pepoithēsis* refers more to the *feeling*. It occurs 6 times, and is rendered "confidence" in 2 Cor. 1. 15; 8. 22; 10. 2. Eph. 3. 12. Phil. 3. 4; and "trust" in 2 Cor. 3. 4.

III. ADJECTIVE.

pistos occurs 67 times, and is rendered "faithful" 54 times. It is unnecessary to give the references, as it is the only word so translated. It is translated "sure" in Acts 13. 34, "true" in 2 Cor. 1. 18. 1 Tim. 3. 1, and 10 times "believer", "he that believeth", &c.: viz. John 20. 27. Acts 10. 45; 16. 1. 2 Cor. 6. 15. 1 Tim. 4. 3, 10, 12; 5. 16, 16; 6. 2.

[1] The English word "faith" is always the translation of *pistis*, except in Heb. 10. 23, where the Greek word is *elpis*, everywhere else rendered "hope".

151 "EVERLASTING", "ETERNAL", "FOR EVER", ETC.

I. In the Old Testament there are several words and expressions thus translated, the principal of which is

A. ***'ōlām***. This word is derived from *'ālam* (to hide), and means the *hidden* time or age, like *aiōn* (see below, II. A), by which word, or its Adjective *aiōnios*, it is generally rendered in the Sept. In Ezra 4, and Dan. 2–7, the Chaldee form *'ālam* is used. There are 448 passages where the word occurs.

i. It is doubled, "from *'ōlām* to *'ōlām*", in 11 places, and is translated :—

1. "for ever and ever" in 1 Chron. 16. 36; 29. 10. Neh. 9. 5. Jer. 7. 7; 25. 5. Dan. 2. 20; 7. -18. 7

2. "from everlasting to everlasting" in Ps. 41. 13; 90. 2; 103. 17; 106. 48. 4

11

ii. It is used in the plural 11 times, and translated:—

1. "for ever" in 1 Kings 8. 13. 2 Chron. 6. 2. Ps. 61. 4; 77. 7. 4

2. "everlasting" in Ps. 145. 13 (see marg.). Isa. 26. 4 (see marg.); 45. 17-. Dan. 9. 24. 4

3. "of ancient times or old time" in Ps. 77. 5. Ecc. 1. 10. 2

4. "of old" in Isa. 51. 9. 1

11

iii. It is rendered "for ever" in Gen. 3. 22; 13. 15. Ex. 3. 15; 12. 14, 17, 24; 14. 13; 19. 9; 21. 6; 27. 21; 28. 43; 29. 28; 30. 21; 31. 17; 32. 13. Lev. 6. 18, 22; 7. 34, 36; 10. 9, 15; 16. 29. 31; 17. 7; 23. 14, 21, 31, 41; 24. 3; 25. 46. Num. 10. 8; 15. 15; 18. 8, 11, 19, 19, 23; 19. 10. Deut. 5. 29; 12. 28; 13. 16; 15. 17; 23. 3, 6; 28. 46; 29. 29; 32. 40. Josh. 4. 7; 8. 28; 14. 9. 1 Sam. 1. 22; 2. 30; 3. 13, 14; 13. 13; 20. 15, 23, 42; 27. 12. 2 Sam. 3. 28; 7. 13, 16, 16, 24, 25, 26, 29, 29. 1 Kings 1. 31; 2. 33, 33, 45; 9. 3. 5; 10. 9. 2 Kings 5. 27; 21. 7. 1 Chron. 15. 2; 16. 34, 41; 17. 12, 14, 22, 23, 24, 27, 27; 22. 10; 23. 13, 13, 25; 28. 4, 7, 8; 29. 18. 2 Chron. 2. 4; 5. 13; 7. 3, 6, 16; 9. 8; 13. 5; 20. 7, 21; 30. 8; 33. 4, 7. Ezra 3. 11; 9. 12, 12. Neh. 2. 3; 13. 1. Job 41. 4. Ps. 9. 7; 12. 7; 28. 9; 29. 10; 30. 12; 33. 11; 37. 18, 28; 41. 12; 44. 8; 45. 2; 48. 8; 49. 8, 11; 52. 9; 61. 7; 66. 7; 72. 17, 19; 73. 26; 75. 9; 78. 69; 79. 13; 81. 15; 85. 5; 89. 1, 2, 4, 36, 37; 102. 12; 103. 9; 104. 31; 105. 8; 106. 1; 107. 1; 110. 4; 111. 9; 112. 6; 117. 2; 118. 1, 2, 3, 4, 29; 119. 89, 111, 152, 160; 125. 1, 2; 131. 3; 135. 13; 136. 1–26; 138. 8; 146. 6, 10. Prov. 27. 24. Ecc. 1. 4; 2. 16; 3. 14; 9. 6. Isa. 9. 7; 32. 14, 17; 34. 10, 17; 40. 8; 47. 7; 51. 6, 8; 57. 16; 59. 21; 60. 21. Jer. 3. 5, 12; 17. 4, 25; 31. 40; 33. 11; 35. 6; 49. 33; 51. 26, 62. Lam. 3. 31; 5. 19. Ezek. 37. 25, 25; 43. 7, 9. Dan. 2. 4, 44; 3. 9; 4. 34; 5. 10; 6. 6, 21, 26; 7. 18–; 12. 7. Hos. 2. 19. Joel 3. 20. Obad. 10. Jonah 2. 6. Mic. 2. 9; 4. 7. Zech. 1. 5. Mal. 1. 4. 246

iv. In conjunction with *'ad* (see below, B) it is rendered :—

1. "for ever and ever" in Ex. 15. 18. Ps. 9. 5; 10. 16; 21. 4; 45. 6, 17; 48. 14; 52. 8; 111. 8; 119. 44; 145. 1, 2, 21; 148. 6. Isa. 30. 8. Dan. 12. 3. Mic. 4. 5. 17

2. "for ever" in Ps. 104. 5. 1

3. "world without end" in Isa. 45. -17.[1] 1

19

v. With a negative it is rendered "never" in Judg. 2. 1. 2 Sam. 12. 10. Ps. 15. 5; 30. 6; 31. 1; 55. 22; 71. 1; 119. 93. Prov. 10. 30. Isa. 14. 20; 25. 2; 63. 19. Ezek. 26. 21. Dan. 2. 44. Joel 2. 26, 27. 16

[1] *'ōlām* is plural here, as well as in No. ii.

vi. Rendered "everlasting" in Gen. 9. 16; 17. 7, 8, 13, 19; 21. 33; 48. 4; 49. 26. Ex. 40. 15. Lev. 16. 34; 24. 8. Num. 25. 13. Deut. 33. 27. 2 Sam. 23. 5. 1 Chron. 16. 17. Ps. 24. 7, 9; 93. 2; 100. 5; 105. 10; 112. 6; 119. 142, 144; 139. 24. Prov. 8. 23; 10. 25. Isa. 24. 5; 33. 14; 35. 10; 40. 28; 51. 11; 54. 8; 55. 3, 13; 56. 5; 60. 19, 20; 61. 7, 8; 63. 12, 16. Jer. 10. 10; 20. 11; 23. 40; 31. 3; 32. 40; Ezek. 16. 60; 37. 26. Dan. 4. 3, 34; 7. 14, 27; 12. 2, 2. Mic. 5. 2. Hab. 3. 6. 56

vii. Rendered "perpetual" in Gen. 9. 12. Ex. 29. 9; 31. 16. Lev. 3. 17; 24. 9; 25. 34. Num. 19. 21. Ps. 78. 66. Jer. 5. 22; 18. 16; 23. 40; 25. 9, 12; 49. 13; 50. 5; 51. 39, 57. Ezek. 35. 5, 9; 46. 14. Hab. 3. 6. Zeph. 2. 9. 22

viii. Rendered "for evermore" in 2 Sam. 22. 51. 1 Chron. 17. 14. Ps. 18. 50; 37. 27; 86. 12; 89. 28, 52; 92. 8; 106. 31; 113. 2; 115. 18; 121. 8; 133. 3. Ezek. 37. 26, 28. 15

ix. Rendered "of old" or "ever of old" in Gen. 6. 4. Deut. 32. 7. 1 Sam. 27. 8. Ps. 25. 6; 119. 52. Isa. 46. 9; 57. 11; 63. 9, 11. Jer. 28. 8. Lam. 3. 6 Ezek. 26. 20. Amos 9. 11. Mic. 7. 14. Mal. 3. 4. 15

x. Rendered "old" or "ancient" in Ezra 4. 15, 19. Job 22. 15. Prov. 22. 28; 23. 10. Isa. 44. 7; 58. 12; 61. 4. Jer. 5. 15; 6. 16; 18. 15. Ezek. 25. 15; 36. 2. 13

xi. Rendered "of" or "in old time" in Josh. 24. 2. Jer. 2. 20. Ezek. 26. 20. 3

xii. Rendered "alway" or "always" in Gen. 6. 3. 1 Chron. 16. 15. Job 7. 16. Ps. 119. 112. Jer. 20. 17. 5

xiii. Rendered "ever" in Ps. 5. 11; 111. 5; 119. 98. Joel 2. 2. 4

xiv. Rendered "any more" in Ezek. 27. 36; 28. 19; "long" in Ps. 143. 3. Ecc. 12. 5; "world" in Ps. 73. 12. Ecc. 3. 11; "continuance" in Isa. 64. 5; "eternal" in Isa. 60. 15; "lasting" in Deut. 33. 15; "long time" in Isa. 42. 14; "at any time" in Lev. 25. 32; and "since the beginning of the world" in Isa. 64. 4. 12

Total 448

B. **'ad** from the verb *'ādāh* (to pass on), as a Noun is used of time past or future. It is also a Preposition or Conjunction, meaning "until" (see *Oxford Gesenius*, pp. 723, 4). The noun occurs 49 times, 19 of which occurrences are given above (A iv). The remaining 30 are rendered:

i. "for ever" in Num. 24. 20, 24. 1 Chron. 28. 9. Job 19. 24. Ps. 9. 18; 19. 9; 21. 6; 22. 26; 37. 29; 61. 8; 83. 17; 89. 29; 92. 7; 111. 3, 10; 112. 3. 9; 132. 14. Prov. 12. 19; 29. 14. Isa. 26. 4; 64. 9; 65. 18. Mic. 7. 18. 24

ii. "everlasting" in Isa. 9. 6. Hab. 3. 6. 2

iii. "eternity" in Isa. 57. 15; "evermore" in Ps. 132. 12; "of old" in Job 20. 4; and "perpetually" in Amos 1. 11. 4

30

Other words are:—

C. **nēẓach,** which means "excellence" or "completeness", and is the word used in the subscription of 55 Psalms for "chief" in "chief Musician". It is rendered:—

i. "for ever" in 2 Sam. 2. 26. Job 4. 20; 14. 20; 20. 7; 23. 7; 36. 7. Ps. 13. 1; 44. 23; 49. 9; 52. 5; 68. 16; 74. 1, 10, 19; 77. 8; 79. 5; 89. 46. Jer. 50. 39. Lam. 5. 20. Amos 1. 11. 20

ii. "never" (with a negative) in Ps. 10. 11; 49. 19. Isa. 13. 20; Amos 8. 7. Hab. 1. 4. 5

iii. alway(s) in Ps. 9. 18; 103. 9. Isa. 57. 16. 3

iv. "perpetual" in Ps. 9. 6; 74. 3. Jer. 15. 18. 3

v. "ever" in Isa. 28. 28; 33. 20; "Strength" in 1 Sam. 15. 29. Lam. 3. 18; "the end" in Job 34. 36. Jer. 3. 5; "victory" in 1 Chron. 29. 11. Isa. 25. 8. "evermore" in Ps. 16. 11; "constantly" in Prov. 21. 28, and "for ever and ever" in Isa. 34. 10. In this last passage it is doubled, *lenēẓach neẓāḥim*=to completeness of completenesses. 11

42

D. **ḳedem,** from the verb *ḳādam*, to precede or prevent (2 Sam. 22. 6, &c.), means that which is before, of time or place; hence often translated the east (Gen. 3. 24, &c.). It is always used of the past, and is rendered "ever" in Prov. 8. 23; "eternal" in Deut. 33. 27; "everlasting" in Hab. 1. 12; "old" or "ancient" in Deut. 33. 15. 2 Kings 19. 25. Neh. 12. 46. Ps. 44. 1; 55. 19; 68. 33; 74. 2, 12; 77. 5, 11; 78. 2; 119. 152; 143. 5. Isa. 19. 11; 23. 7; 37. 26; 45. 21; 46. 10; 51. 9. Jer. 46. 26. Lam. 1. 7; 2. 17; 5. 21. Mic. 5. 2; 7. 20; and "past" in Job 29. 2.

E. **ẓemīthūth,** from *ẓāmath* (to cut), means "for cutting off". It occurs only in Lev. 25. 23 (see marg.), 30, and is rendered "for ever".

F. **tāmīd**=always, is rendered:—

"ever" in Lev. 6. 13. Ps. 25. 15; 51. 3; "evermore" in Ps. 105. 4, and (with a negative) "never" in Isa. 62. 6.

G. **dōr**=generation, is translated (with a negative) "never" in Ps. 10. 6, and "for evermore" in Ps. 77. 8, where the margin in both cases gives "to generation and generation".

H. **yōm**=day, occurs nearly 2,500 times. The expression *orek yāmīm*, "length of days", is translated "for ever" in Ps. 23. 6; 93. 5. In both cases the margin gives "to length of days". *Kāl yāmīm*, or *kāl hayyāmīm*, "all days" or "all the days", is translated "for ever" in Gen. 43. 9; 44. 32. Deut. 4. 40; 18. 5. Josh. 4. 24. 1 Sam. 2. 32, 35; 28. 2. 1 Kings 11. 39; 12. 7. 2 Chron. 10. 7; 21. 7. Jer. 31. 36; 32. 39; 35. 19; "ever" in Deut. 19. 9. 1 Kings 5. 1. Ps. 37. 26; and "evermore" in Deut. 28. 29. 2 Kings 17. 37.

II. In the N.T. the words rendered "for ever", &c., are the Noun *aiōn*, the Adjectives *aiōnios*, *aidios*, *akatalutos*, and *aperantos*; the Adverbs *aei* and *pantote*, and the adverbial phrase *eis to diēnekes*.

A. **aiōn,** which means "age" (Ap. 129. 2), is found 128 times in 105 passages, in 23 of which it is doubled (see below, ii. 6, 9, 10). It occurs in its simple form 37 times, and with Prepositions 68 times.

i. In its simple form it is rendered:—

1. "age". Eph. 2. 7 (pl.). Col. 1. 26 (pl.). 2

2. "course". Eph. 2. 2. 1

3. "world". Matt. 12. 32; 13. 22, 39, 40, 49; 24. 3; 28. 20. Mark 4. 19; 10. 30. Luke 16. 8; 18. 30; 20. 34, 35. Rom. 12. 2. 1 Cor. 1. 20; 2. 6, 6, 7 (pl.), 8; 3. 18; 10. 11 (pl.). 2 Cor. 4. 4. Gal. 1. 4. Eph. 1. 21; 6. 12. 1 Tim. 6. 17. 2 Tim. 4. 10. Tit. 2. 12. Heb. 1. 2 (pl.); 6. 5; 9. 26 (pl.); 11. 3 (pl.). 32

4. "eternal". Eph. 3. 11. 1 Tim. 1. 17 (lit. "of the ages"). 2

37

ii. In prepositional phrases:—

1. *ap' aiōnos* [from (Ap. 104. iv) an (the) age], rendered "since the world began" in Luke 1. 70. Acts 3. 21; and "from the beginning of the world" in Acts 15. 18. 3

2. *apo tōn aiōnōn* [from (Ap. 104. iv) the ages], rendered "from the beginning of the world" in Eph. 3. 9. 1

3. *ek tou aiōnos* [out of (Ap. 104. vii) the age], rendered "since the world began" in John 9. 32. 1

4. *eis ton aiōna* [to (Ap. 104. vi) the age], rendered:—
   a. "for ever" in Matt. 21. 19. Mark 11. 14. Luke 1. 55. John 6. 51, 58; 8. 35, 35; 12. 34; 14. 16. 2 Cor. 9. 9. Heb. 5. 6; 6. 20; 7. 17, 21. 1 Pet. 1. 23, 25. 2 Pet. 2. 17 (no Art.). 1 John 2. 17. 2 John 2. Jude 13. 20
   b. "never" (with a negative) in Mark 3. 29. John 4. 14; 8. 51, 52; 10. 28; 11. 26. 13. 8. 7
   c. "ever" in Heb. 7. 24. 1
   d. "for evermore" in Heb. 7. 28. 1
   e. "while the world standeth" in 1 Cor. 8. 13. 1

5. *eis hēmeran aiōnos* [to (Ap. 104. vi) day of an age], rendered "for ever" in 2 Pet. 3. 18. 1

6. *eis ton aiōna tou aiōnos* [to (Ap. 104. vi) the age of the age], rendered "for ever and ever" in Heb. 1. 8. 1

7. *eis tōus aiōnas* [to (Ap. 104. vi) the ages], rendered:—
   a. "for ever" in Matt. 6. 13. Luke 1. 33. Rom. 1. 25; 9. 5; 11. 36; 16. 27. Heb. 13. 8. 7
   b. "for evermore" in 2 Cor. 11. 31. 1

8. *eis pantas tous aiōnas* [to (Ap. 104. vi) all the ages], rendered "ever" in Jude 25.

9. *eis tous aiōnas tōn aiōnōn* [to (Ap. 104. vi) to the ages of the ages], rendered:—
   a. "for ever and ever" in Gal. 1. 5. Phil. 4. 20. 1 Tim. 1. 17. 2 Tim. 4. 18. Heb. 13. 21. 1 Pet. 4. 11; 5. 11. Rev. 1. 6; 4. 9, 10; 5. 13, 14; 7. 12; 10. 6; 11. 15; 14. 11 (no Arts.); 15. 7; 19. 3; 20. 10; 22. 5. 20
   b. "for evermore" in Rev. 1. 18. 1

10. *eis pasas tas geneas tou aiōnos tōn aiōnōn* [to (Ap. 104. vi) all the generations of the age of the ages], rendered "throughout all ages, world without end" in Eph. 3. 21. 1

68

Total 105

B. ***aiōnios***, of or belonging to an age, occurs 71 times, and is rendered:—

i. "eternal" in Matt. 19. 16; 25. 46. Mark 3. 29; 10. 17, 30. Luke 10. 25; 18. 18. John 3. 15; 4. 36; 5. 39; 6. 54, 68; 10. 28; 12. 25; 17. 2, 3. Acts 13. 48. Rom. 2. 7; 5. 21; 6. 23. 2 Cor. 4. 17, 18; 5. 1. 1 Tim. 6. 12, 19. 2 Tim. 2. 10. Tit. 1. 2; 3. 7. Heb. 5. 9; 6. 2; 9. 12, 14, 15. 1 Pet. 5. 10. 1 John 1. 2; 2. 25; 3. 15; 5. 11, 13, 20. Jude 7, 21. 42

ii. "everlasting" in Matt. 18. 8; 19. 29; 25. 41, 46. Luke 16. 9; 18. 30. John 3. 16, 36; 4. 14; 5. 24; 6. 27, 40, 47; 12. 50. Acts 13. 46. Rom. 6. 22; 16. 26. Gal. 6. 8. 2 Thess. 1. 9; 2. 16. 1 Tim. 1. 16; 6. 16. Heb. 13. 20. 2 Pet. 1. 11. Rev. 14. 6. 25

iii. "for ever" in Philem. 15. 1

iv. "Before or since the world began", in the phrases, *chronois aiōniois*, or *pro chronōn aiōniōn* (in, or before age-times), strangely rendered in the R.V. "through, or before times eternal", in Rom. 16. 25. 2 Tim. 1. 9. Tit. 1. 2. 3

71

C. ***aidios***, said to be from *aei* (see F below), but perhaps from *a* not and *idein* to see, = unseen or hidden, occurs twice, and is rendered:—

i. "eternal" in Rom. 1. 20. 1

ii. "everlasting" in Jude 6. 1

2

D. ***akatalutos*** (indissoluble) occurs once, and is rendered "endless" in Heb. 7. 16. 1

E. ***aperantos*** (interminable) occurs once, and is rendered "endless" in 1 Tim. 1. 4. 1

F. ***aei*** (always) occurs 8 times, and is rendered:—

i. "ever" in Mark 15. 8. 1

ii. "alway" or "always" in Acts 7. 51. 2 Cor. 4. 11; 6. 10. Tit. 1. 12. Heb. 3. 10. 1 Pet. 3. 15. 2 Pet. 1. 12. 7

8

G. ***pantote*** (always) occurs 42 times, and is rendered:—

i. "alway" or "always" in Matt. 26. 11, 11. Mark 14. 7, 7. Luke 18. 1. John 7. 6; 8. 29; 11. 42; 12. 8, 8; 18. 20. Rom. 1. 9. 1 Cor. 1. 4; 15. 58. 2 Cor. 2. 14; 4. 10; 5. 6; 9. 8. Gal. 4. 18. Eph. 5. 20. Phil. 1. 4, 20; 2. 12; 4. 4. Col. 1. 3; 4. 6, 12. 1 Thess. 1. 2; 2. 16; 3. 6. 2 Thess. 1. 3, 11; 2. 13. Philem. 4. 34

ii. "ever" in Luke 15. 31. John 18. 20. 1 Thess. 4. 17; 5. 15. 2 Tim. 3. 7. Heb. 7. 25. 6

iii. "evermore" in John 6. 34. 1 Thess. 5. 16. 2

42

H. ***eis to diēnekes*** [to (Ap. 104. vi) that which is continuous] occurs 4 times, rendered:—

i. "continually" in Heb. 7. 3; 10. 1. 2

ii. "for ever" in Heb. 10. 12, 14. 2

4

152 THE HEALING OF THE BLIND MEN AT JERICHO.

(Luke 18. 35-43. Mark 10. 46-52. Matt. 20. 29-34.)

Commentators and harmonizers agree in treating these three accounts as recording one single miracle. As in other cases, they assume *similar* discourses, sayings, and miracles to be identical, as though the Lord never repeated a single word or work. (See App. 116, 138, 153, 155, 157, 158, 160, 163.)

The same may be seen in dealing with the healing of the blind men at Jericho.

From a comparison of the three Gospels it will be readily seen that four blind men were healed, and that there were three separate miracles on the Lord's visit to Jericho.

The following particulars may be noted and considered:—

I. The Occasion.

1. In the first miracle the Lord was "come nigh unto Jericho".
2. The second was "as He went out of Jericho".
3. The third took place "as they departed from", and had evidently left Jericho.

II. The Blind Men.

1. In the first there was one, unnamed.
2. In the second there was one, named (Bartimæus).
3. In the third there were two men.

III. The Circumstances.

1. The one man was begging.
2. The second likewise.
3. The two men were not begging, and apparently were simply waiting for the Lord's passing by.

IV. Their Knowledge.

1. The first man did not know what the crowd meant, and asked.
2. The second (Bartimæus) heard, but seems to have made no inquiry and at once cried out.
3. The two men also heard, and cried out at once.

V. Their Cry.

1. The first man cried "Jesus, thou Son of David".
2. The second man cried "Son of David".
3. The two men cried "O Lord, Son of David".

VI. The Lord's Action.

1. The Lord "commanded (the first man) to be brought".
2. He "commanded (the second man) to be called".
3. He called the two men Himself.

VII. Their Healing.

1. The first desired that he might be able to see (*anablepō*).
2. The second in like manner.
3. The two men asked that "their eyes might be opened" (*anoigō*).

VIII. The Lord's Reply.

In the first case, the Lord said: "Receive thy sight, thy faith hath saved thee."

2. In the second case, the Lord said: "Go thy way, thy faith hath saved thee."
3. In the third case, the Lord "had compassion on them, and touched their eyes", saying nothing.

IX. The Result.

1. The first man "followed Him, glorifying God, and all the people gave praise to God".
2. Bartimæus "followed Jesus in the way", apparently in silence.
3. The two men "followed Him", in silence also.

We thus gather that the first two men were beggars who sat daily at either gate of Jericho: Jericho having at that time some 100,000 people, and doubtless many blind men.

In face of this and of the above details, all that a recent commentator has to say is:—

"The variation is undeniable, and the accounts cannot be harmonized at this point. But of course it is quite immaterial.... According to Matthew there were two blind men. Calvin therefore suggests that Bartimæus met Jesus on His entrance to the city, and then went for the other blind man, and that both were healed as Jesus was leaving the city. This is very artificial dealing with the plain narratives. It is better to accept them as varying accounts of one single incident."

True, we cannot harmonize "one man" and "two men" without abandoning all idea of inspiration. We submit therefore that "it is better" to take all the details as being evidences of the minutest perfection, and avoid both artificial and superficial dealing with the Divine narratives.

153 THE TWO ENTRIES INTO JERUSALEM.

Most "Harmonies" assume that because each Gospel records an entry of the Lord into Jerusalem the four accounts must be *identical* because they are similar: and therefore conclude that because they differ in certain particulars there are "discrepancies".

Whereas, if we treat them in their chronological sequences, and have regard to the antecedent and consequent circumstances, the supposed discrepancies will disappear, and the similar, but diverse, expressions will be seen to be necessary to the different events.

In this present case, one entry (Matt. 21. 1-9) takes place before the other, which is recorded in Mark 11. 1-10, Luke 19. 30-34, and John 12. 12-15).

1. In Matthew the Lord *had actually arrived at* Bethphage. In Luke He "*was come nigh*" (*ēngisen*); in Mark "they were *approaching*" (*engizousin*).

2. In Matthew the village lay just *off* the road (*apenanti*); in Luke and Mark it was *below* them, and opposite (*katenanti*).

3. In the former, *two* animals were sent for and used; in the latter, only *one*.

4. In the former, the prophecy of Zech. 9. 9, which required the *two* animals, is said to have been *fulfilled*; in the latter, the prophecy was not said to be fulfilled, and only so much of it is quoted (John 12. 15) as agrees with it.

5. The former seems to have been *unexpected*, for "all the city was moved, saying, 'Who is this?'" (Matt. 21. 10, 11), while, if there was only one entry, the two accounts are inexplicable, seeing that the later and subsequent entry was *prepared for*: much people in the city "heard that He was coming", and "went forth to meet Him" (John 12. 12. 13).

The latter, therefore, was the great formal entry of the Lord, called "the Triumphal Entry", which took place on what is called "Palm Sunday".

The significance of the *two* animals, and the *one*, seems to be this:—

The first had special reference to the whole work of His mission. He came on the ass with its unbroken colt, the clothes being put some on one and some on the other, and the Lord sitting on "them"—*the clothes* (not on both beasts). He came to cleanse the Temple, and make His final presentation of the King and the Kingdom.

But when He came on the one—an ass's colt—it was in judgment, to pronounce the doom on the city; and on the nation.

When He appears again it will be to a nation which will then say (as the result of Zech. 12. 10): "Blessed is He that cometh in the name of the Lord" (Matt. 23. 39).

For the events of the "six days before the Passover", see Ap. 156; and the notes on the various passages.

154 "WHAT THINK YE OF CHRIST?" (Matt. 22. 42).

DIVERS THOUGHTS CONCERNING HIM.

"King of the Jews" (wise men from the east. Matt. 2. 2).
"Mightier than I" (John Baptist. Matt. 3. 11).
"Son of God" (demons. Matt. 8. 29).
"A blasphemer" (certain Scribes. Matt. 9. 3).
"Son of David" (two blind men. Matt. 9. 27).
" " (a woman of Canaan. Matt. 15. 22).
"The carpenter's son" (His fellow countrymen. Matt. 13. 55).
"John the Baptist" (Herod and others. Matt. 14. 2; 16. 14).
"The Son of God" (they that were in the ship. Matt. 14. 33).
"Elijah" (some. Matt. 16. 14).
"Jeremiah" (others. Matt. 16. 14).
"One of the prophets" (some men. Matt. 16. 14).
"The Christ, the Son of the living God" (Peter. Matt. 16. 16).
"The Christ, the Son of God" (Martha. John 11. 27).
"My beloved Son" (God the Father. Matt. 17. 5).
"Good Master" (a certain ruler. Matt. 19. 16).
"The prophet of Nazareth" (the multitude. Matt. 21. 11).
"The carpenter, the son of Mary" (many hearing Him. Mark 6. 3).
"Thy salvation . . . a light . . . the glory" (Simeon. Luke 2. 30, 32).
"Joseph's son" (all in the synagogue. Luke 4. 22).
"A great prophet" (all witnessing the raising of the widow's son. Luke 7. 16).
"A righteous man" (the Roman centurion. Luke 23. 47).
"A prophet mighty in deed and word" (the two going to Emmaus. Luke 24. 19).
"The Lamb of God" (John the Baptist. John 1. 29).
"The Messias" (Andrew. John 1. 41).
"The Son of God, . . . the King of Israel" (Nathanael. John 1. 49).
"A teacher come from God" (Nicodemus. John 3. 2).
"A prophet" (a woman of Samaria. John 4. 19).
"Jesus the son of Joseph" (the Jews. John 6. 42).
"A Samaritan" and having a demon (the Jews. John 8. 48).
"A prophet" (the blind man. John 9. 17).
"The King of Israel" (much people. John 12. 13).

155 THE TWO GREAT PROPHECIES OF "THE END OF THE AGE"

(Luke 21 and Matt. 24. Mark 13).

The great prophecy recorded in Luke 21 is different both in *time*, *place*, and *subject* from that recorded in Matt. 24 and Mark 13.

The one recorded in Luke was spoken "on one of those days, as He taught the people *in the Temple*" (Luke 20. 1). For one note of time is in 21. 1, "and He looked up and saw the rich men casting their gifts *into the Treasury*." So that He was still "in the Temple" when He uttered the prophecy recorded in Luke 21, for the whole conversation with the disciples follows without a break the Lord's commendation of the widow.

But with regard to the prophecy recorded in Matt. 24, we distinctly read (*v.* 1) "and Jesus went out and departed *from the Temple* . . . and *as He sat upon the Mount of Olives*, the disciples came to Him privately" (*v.* 3). So, in Mark 13. 1, "He *went out of the Temple* . . . and *as He sat upon the Mount of Olives, over against the Temple*, Peter and James and John and Andrew asked Him privately" (*v.* 3).

So that we have *two* great prophecies. One (Luke) spoken in the Temple, the other (Matthew and Mark) spoken *later* upon the Mount of Olives. As parts of the first are repeated on the second occasion, we will give the leading points of the three in parallel columns, so that the object of each, and the difference between them, may be clearly seen.

They both open with a summary of events which might have taken place in the lifetime and experience of those who heard the words :—

FROM THE CROSS ONWARDS.

LUKE 21. 8-9.	MATT. 24. 4-6.	MARK 13. 5-7.
'Take heed that ye be not deceived: for many shall come in My name, saying, I am Christ; and the time draweth near: go ye not therefore after them. But when ye shall hear of wars and commotions, be not terrified: for these things must first come to pass; **but the end is not by and by** (i.e. immediately; so R.V.)."	"Take heed that no man deceive you. For many shall come in My name, saying, I am Christ; and shall deceive many. And ye shall hear of wars and rumours of wars: see that ye be not troubled: for all these things must come to pass, **but the end is not yet.**"	"Take heed lest any man deceive you. For many shall come in My name, saying, I am Christ; and shall deceive many. And when ye shall hear of wars and rumours of wars, be ye not troubled: for such things must needs be; **but the end shall not be yet.**"

John refers to this first sign in his First Epistle (2. 18); but had the nation repented at the proclamation by Peter in Acts 3. 18-26, by the Twelve in the Land, by "them that heard Him" (Heb. 2. 3), and by Paul in the Synagogues of the Dispersion, "all that the prophets had written" would have been fulfilled.

LUKE 21. 10, 11.	MATT. 24. 7, 8.	MARK 13. 8.
"Nation shall rise against nation, and kingdom against kingdom: and great earthquakes shall be in divers places, and famines, and pestilences, and fearful sights and great signs shall there be from heaven."	"Nation shall rise against nation, and kingdom against kingdom: and there shall be famines, and pestilences, and earthquakes, in divers places. **All these are the beginning of sorrows.**"	"Nation shall rise against nation, and kingdom against kingdom: and there shall be earthquakes in divers places, and there shall be famines, and troubles: **these are the beginnings of sorrows.**"

Now, it will be observed in the Lord's discourse as recorded in Luke, that, instead of saying "these are the beginning of sorrows", and going on with the account of them, He stops short; He goes back; He introduces a parenthesis detailing and describing events that would take place "BEFORE ALL THESE" beginnings of sorrows. He describes in *v.* 12,

THE DESTRUCTION OF JERUSALEM.

12. **But before all these,**

that is to say "BEFORE" the great Tribulation, all that is recorded concerning Jerusalem in *vv.* 12-24 would take place. These are the closing words:—

24. "And they shall fall by the edge of the sword, and shall be led away captive into all nations: and Jerusalem shall be trodden down of the Gentiles, until the times of the Gentiles be fulfilled."

Now, in the discourse recorded in Matt. 24, instead of going back to speak of the condition of Jerusalem before and until the beginning of the great Tribulation; having said "All these are the beginning of sorrows", He *goes on to describe* the sorrows, or birth-pangs of the Tribulation (Matt. 24. 9-28. Mark 13. 9-23), and He continues the prophecy concerning these sorrows up to the moment of His appearing in the clouds of heaven.

While, in the discourse recorded in Luke 21, having gone back, and described what should take place "before all these" beginnings of sorrows, the Lord does not speak further of the great Tribulation, but takes it up at the end, and, as in Matthew and Mark, speaks concerning

HIS COMING IN THE CLOUDS OF HEAVEN

(of course, in Luke the words are slightly different from those in Matthew and Mark):—

LUKE 21. 25-27.

"And there shall be signs in the sun, and in the moon, and in the stars; and upon the earth distress of nations, with perplexity; the sea and the waves roaring; men's hearts failing them for fear, and for looking after those things which are coming on the earth; for the powers of the heavens shall be shaken. And then shall they see the Son of man coming in a cloud with power and great glory."

MATT. 24. 29, 30.

"IMMEDIATELY after the tribulation of those days[1] shall the sun be darkened, and the moon shall not give her light, and the stars shall fall from heaven, and the powers of the heavens shall be shaken: and then shall appear the sign of the Son of man in heaven: and then shall all the tribes of the earth mourn, and they shall see the Son of man coming in the clouds of heaven with power and great glory."

MARK 13. 24-26.

"But in those days, after that tribulation[1], the sun shall be darkened, and the moon shall not give her light, and the stars of heaven shall fall, and the powers that are in heaven shall be shaken, and then shall they see the Son of man coming in the clouds with great power and glory."

The *first* prophecy, in the Temple (Luke 21), was uttered in answer to *two* general questions: (1) "When shall these things be?" and (2) "What sign shall there be when these things shall come to pass?" The answer to (1) is given in *vv.* 8-24, and the answer to (2) in *vv.* 25-28.

The *second* prophecy, on the Mount of Olives (Matt. 24 and Mark 13), was uttered in answer to *three* distinct questions: (1) "When shall these things be?" (2) "What shall be the sign of Thy coming?" and (3) "And [what shall be the sign] of the end of the age?" The answer to (1) was given in Matt. 24. 4-14. Mark 13. 5-13. The answer to (2) was given in Matt. 24. 15-27. Mark 13. 14-23; and to (3) in Matt. 24. 29-31 and Mark 13. 24-27 (and in Luke 21. 25-28).

And then both prophecies conclude with the Parable of the Fig-tree, and the final solemn assurance:—

"Verily I say unto you, This generation shall by no means (see Ap. 105. III) pass, till all these things may be fulfilled"[2] (Matt. 24. 34. Mark13. 30. Luke 21. 32).

This latter is the last of four equally impressive statements: Matt. 10. 23; 16. 28; 23. 39; 24. 34.

Each of these consists of two clauses, the former of which contains the strongest negative that could possibly have been used (see Ap. 105. III); and should be rendered "by no means", or "in no wise", as it is often rendered elsewhere; while in the latter clause the verb is in the subjunctive mood with or without the Greek Particle "*an*", which (though it cannot be represented in translation) makes the clause hypothetical and dependent on some condition expressed or implied. This condition was, in each of these four passages, the repentance of the nation, in response to the appeal of "the other servants" of Matt. 22. 4, as recorded in Acts 3. 18-26 and elsewhere, culminating in Acts 28. 17-29.

The conclusion of both prophecies thus consists of an assured *certainty*, with a definite contingency, or *uncertainty*, which was not fulfilled.

Had the nation repented, then Jesus Christ would have been "sent", and "the restoration of all things which God had spoken by all His holy prophets since the world began" would have taken place, in accordance with God's Divine assurance given by Peter in Acts 3. 18-26; but the condition of national repentance (Lev. 26. 40-42; Hos. 14. 1-4, &c.) was not fulfilled; hence that generation passed away, and both prophecies (with all the others) are now *postponed*. The first sign of all did (and will again) take place—the rising of the "many Antichrists", whereby John could say they knew that it was "the last hour" before "the end of that age" (1 John 2. 18).

[1] Leaving no space, therefore, for a millennium of peace between the great Tribulation and the appearance of the Lord in glory; proving that the second coming must be pre-millennial.

[2] In all three passages the verb is *genētai* = may arise, or may have come to pass: not *plēroō* = be entirely fulfilled or finished, as in Luke 21. 24. This was so in both cases.

156 "SIX DAYS BEFORE THE PASSOVER" (John 12. 1).

We are furnished by Scripture with certain facts and fixed points which, taken together, enable us (1) to determine the events which filled up the days of "the last week" of our Lord's life on earth; (2) to fix the day of His crucifixion; and (3) to ascertain the duration of the time He remained in the tomb.

The difficulties connected with these three have arisen (1) from not having noted these fixed points; (2) from the fact of Gentiles' not having been conversant with the law concerning the three great feasts of the LORD; and (3) from not having reckoned the days as commencing (some six hours before our own) and running from sunset to sunset, instead of from midnight to midnight.

To remove these difficulties, we must note:—

I. That the first day of each of the three feasts.

Passover, Pentecost, and Tabernacles, was "a holy convocation", a "sabbath" on which no servile work was to be done. See Lev. 23. 7, 24, 35. Cp. Ex. 12. 16.

"That sabbath" and the "high day" of John 19. 31, was the "holy convocation", the first day of the feast, which quite overshadowed the ordinary weekly sabbath.

It was called by the Jews *Yōm tōv* (=Good day), and this is the greeting on that day throughout Jewry down to the present time.

This *great* sabbath, having been mistaken from the earliest times for the *weekly* sabbath, has led to all the confusion.

II. This has naturally caused the further difficulty as to the Lord's statement that "even as Jonah was in the belly of the fish three days and three nights, so shall the Son of man be in the heart of the earth three days and three nights" (Matt. 12. 40). Now, while it is quite correct to speak according to Hebrew idiom of "three days" or "three years", while they are only parts of three days or three years, yet that idiom does not apply in a case like this, where "three nights" are mentioned *in addition to* "three days". It will be noted that the Lord not only definitely states this, but repeats the full phraseology, so that we may not mistake it. See the subject fully discussed in Ap. 144.

III. We have therefore the following facts furnished for our sure guidance:

1. The "high day" of John 19. 31 was the first day of the feast.
2. The "first day of the feast" was on the 15th day of Nisan.
3. The 15th day of Nisan, commenced at sunset on what we should call the 14th.
4. "Six days before the passover" (John 12. 1) takes us back to the 9th day of Nisan.
5. "After two days is the passover" (Matt. 26. 2. Mark 14. 1) takes us to the 13th day of Nisan.
6. "The first day of the week", the day of the resurrection (Matt. 28. 1, &c.), was from our Saturday sunset to our Sunday sunset. This fixes the days of *the week*, just as the above fix the days of *the month*, for:
7. Reckoning back from this, "three days and three nights" (Matt. 12. 40), we arrive at the day of the burial, which must have been before sunset, on the 14th of Nisan; i.e. before our Wednesday sunset.
8. This makes the sixth day before the passover (the 9th day of Nisan) to be our Thursday sunset to Friday sunset.

Therefore Wednesday, Nisan 14th (commencing on the Tuesday at sunset), was "the preparation day", on which the crucifixion took place: for all four Gospels definitely say that this was the day on which the Lord was buried (before our Wednesday sunset), "because it was the preparation [day]" the bodies should not remain upon the cross on the sabbath day, "for that sabbath day was a high day", and, therefore, not the ordinary seventh day, or weekly sabbath. See John 19. 31.

IV. It follows, therefore, that the Lord being crucified on "the preparation day" could not have eaten of the Passover lamb, which was not slain until the evening of the 14th of Nisan (i.e. afternoon). On that day the daily sacrifice was killed at the 6th hour (noon) and offered about the 7th hour (1 p.m.). The killing of the Passover lambs began directly afterwards. Thus it is clear, that if the killing of the Passover lambs did not *commence* until about four hours after our Lord had been hanging upon the Cross, and would not have been concluded at the *ninth* hour (3 p.m.) when "He gave up the ghost;"—no "Passover lamb" could have been eaten at the "last supper" on the previous evening.

V. With these facts before us, we are now in a position to fill in the several days of the Lord's last week with the events recorded in the Gospels. By noting that the Lord returned to Bethany (or to the Mount of Olives) each night of that week, we are able to determine both the several days and the events that took place in them.

THE SIXTH DAY BEFORE THE PASSOVER, THE 9th DAY OF NISAN.

(*Our Thursday sunset to Friday sunset.*)

	MATTHEW.	MARK.	LUKE.	JOHN.
The Lord approaches Jerusalem from Jericho			19. 1-10	
He passes our Thursday night at the house of Zacchæus (Luke 19. 5.)				
And delivers the Parable of the Pounds			19. 11-27	
He proceeds toward Jerusalem			19. 28	
He sends two disciples (*apenanti*) for an "ass" and a "colt" (two animals)	21. 1-7			
And makes His first entry from Bethphage (not Bethany) (Ap. 153)	21. 8, 9			
He is unexpected, and they ask "Who is this?"	21. 10, 11			
He cleanses the Temple	21. 12-16			
HE RETURNS TO BETHANY	21. 17			12. 1

THE FIFTH DAY BEFORE THE PASSOVER, THE 10th DAY OF NISAN.

(*Our Friday sunset to Saturday sunset.*)

The Lord passes the Sabbath at Bethany; and after sunset (on our Saturday), the first of three suppers was made, probably at the house of Lazarus, in Bethany (Ap. 157)				12. 2
At this supper the first of two anointings took place (Ap. 158)				12. 3-11

THE FOURTH DAY BEFORE THE PASSOVER, THE 11th DAY OF NISAN.

(*Our Saturday sunset to Sunday sunset*), the Gentile "Palm Sunday".

The second, or triumphal entry into Jerusalem. He sends two disciples (*katenanti*) for a colt (one animal). See Ap. 153		11. 1-7	19. 29-35	12. 12-
The Lord starts from Bethany (not Bethphage) and is met by multitudes from Jerusalem (Ap. 153)		11. 8-10	19. 36-40	12. -12-19
He weeps over the city			19. 41-44	
He enters the Temple, looks around		11. 11-		
And RETURNS TO BETHANY		11. -11		

APPENDIX 156: "SIX DAYS BEFORE THE PASSOVER" (*cont.*)

THE THIRD DAY BEFORE THE PASSOVER, THE 12th DAY OF NISAN

(*Our Sunday sunset to Monday sunset*).

	MATTHEW.	MARK.	LUKE.	JOHN.
In the morning (our Monday a.m.) the Lord returns to Jerusalem	21. 18	11. 12		
The Fig-tree cursed	21. 19-22	11. 13, 14		
The Temple. Further cleansing		11. 15-17	19. 45, 46	
In the Temple. Further teaching. "Certain Greeks"			19. 47-	12. 20-50
Opposition of Rulers		11. 18	19. -47, 48	
He goes out of the city (probably to Bethany; see Luke 21. 37, 38, below)		11. 19		

THE SECOND DAY BEFORE THE PASSOVER, THE 13th DAY OF NISAN.

(*Our Monday sunset to Tuesday sunset.*)

	MATTHEW.	MARK.	LUKE.	JOHN.
In the morning (our Tuesday a.m.) on the way to Jerusalem, the question of the disciples about the Fig Tree		11. 20-26		
In Jerusalem again: and in the Temple	21. 23-27	11. 27-33	20. 1-8	
In Jerusalem teaching in Parables; and questions	21. 28—23. 39	12. 1-44	20. 9—21. 4	
The first great prophecy, in the Temple (Ap. 155)			21. 5-36	
(Parenthetical statement as to the Lord's custom during this last week)			21. 37, 38	
The second great prophecy, on the Mount of Olives	24. 1-51	13. 1-37		
The second great prophecy, continued (see Ap. 155)	25. 1-46			
"After two days is the Passover"	26. 1-5	14. 1, 2		
HE RETURNS TO BETHANY, and is present at the second supper in the house of Simon the leper. The second Anointing. See Ap. 157 and 158	26. 6-13	14. 3-9		

THE DAY BEFORE THE PASSOVER—THE 14th DAY OF NISAN—"THE PREPARATION DAY"—THE DAY OF THE CRUCIFIXION.

(*Our Tuesday sunset to Wednesday sunset.*)

	MATTHEW.	MARK.	LUKE.	JOHN.
The plot of Judas Iscariot to betray the Lord	26. 14-16	14. 10, 11	22. 1-6	
The "preparation" for the last supper[1]	26. 17-19	14. 12[1]-16	22. 7[1]-13	
"The even was come" (our Tuesday after sunset) when the plot for the betrayal was ripe for execution	26. 20	14. 17		
The last supper, commencing with the washing of the feet				13. 1-20
The announcement of the betrayal, &c.	26. 21-25	14. 18-21		13. 21-30
The supper eaten, the "New Covenant" made (Jer. 31. 31). The lamb abolished, bread and wine substituted	26. 26-29	14. 22-25	22. 14-23	
The first prophecy of Peter's denials (Ap. 160)				13. 31-38
The strife; who should be the greatest, &c.			22. 24-30	
The second prophecy of Peter's denials (Ap. 160)			22. 31-34	
The final appeal to His first commission (Luke 9. 3)			22. 35-38	
The last discourse to the eleven, followed by His prayer				14. 1—17. 26
They go to Gethsemane	26. 30-35	14. 26-29	22. 39	18. 1
The third prophecy of Peter's denials (Ap. 160)		14. 30, 31		
The agony in the garden	26. 36-46	14. 32-42	22. 40-46	
The apprehension of the Lord (Ap. 165)	26. 47-56	14. 43-50	22. 47-54	18. 2-11
The escape of Lazarus (see notes on Mark 14. 51, 52)		14. 51, 52		
The trials: continued throughout our Tuesday night	26. 57—27. 31	14. 53—15. 19	22. 54—23. 25	18. 12—19. 13
About the sixth hour (our Tuesday midnight) Pilate said "Behold your King"				19. 14, 15
Led away to be crucified	27. 31-34	15. 20-23	23. 26-31	19. 16, 17
And "led with Him" two "malefactors" (*kakourgoi*) (Ap. 164)			23. 32, 33	19. 18
Discussion with Pilate about the Inscriptions (Ap. 163)				19. 19-22
The dividing of the garments	27. 35-37	15. 24	23. 34	19. 23, 24
"It was the third hour, and they crucified Him" (our 9 a.m. Wednesday)		15. 25, 26		
"Then were there two robbers" (*lēstai*) crucified with Him" (Ap. 164)	27. 38	15. 27, 28		
The revilings of the rulers, both "robbers", and one "malefactor"	27. 39-44	15. 29-32	23. 35-43	
The Lord's mother and John				19. 25 27
"The sixth hour" (our Wednesday noon) and the darkness (Ap. 165)	27. 45-49	15. 33	23. 44, 45	
"The ninth hour" (our Wednesday 3 p.m.) and the expiring cry (Ap. 165)	27. 50	15. 34-37	23. 46	19. 28-30
Subsequent events	27. 51-56	15. 38-41	23. 47-49	19. 31-37
Buried in haste before sunset (our Wednesday about 6 p.m.), before the "high day" (the first day of the Feast began), our Wednesday sunset	27. 57-66	15. 42-47	23. 50-56	19. 38-42

[1] The words in Mark 14. 12 and Luke 22. 7 refer to "the first day of unleavened bread", which was the 14th day of Nisan, and therefore "the preparation day". That is why the Lord goes on to tell the two disciples to go and *make preparation for the Passover*.

"THE FIRST DAY OF THE FEAST"—"THE HIGH DAY" (*Yōm tōv*)—THE 15TH DAY OF NISAN.

(*Our Wednesday sunset to Thursday sunset.*)

THE FIRST NIGHT AND FIRST DAY IN THE TOMB.

THE SECOND DAY OF THE FEAST—THE 16TH DAY OF NISAN.

(*Our Thursday sunset to Friday sunset.*)

THE SECOND NIGHT AND SECOND DAY IN THE TOMB.

THE THIRD DAY OF THE FEAST—"THE (WEEKLY) SABBATH"—THE 17TH DAY OF NISAN.

(*Our Friday sunset to Saturday sunset.*)

THE THIRD NIGHT AND THIRD DAY IN THE TOMB.

"THE FIRST DAY OF THE WEEK"—THE 18TH DAY OF NISAN.

(*Our Saturday sunset*: "the third day" of Matt. 16. 21, &c.; not the third day of the Feast).

	MATTHEW.	MARK.	LUKE.	JOHN.
Thus, the Resurrection of the Lord took place at our Saturday sunset, or thereabouts, on "the third day"; cp. "after three days" (Matt. 27. 63. Mark 8. 31)	28. 1-10	16. 1-18	24. 1-49	20. 1-23

[For the sequence of events connected with and following the Resurrection, see Ap. 166.]

It will be seen from the above that we have neither power nor authority to alter or shift any day or date; or to change the order or position of any of the events recorded in Holy Writ.

Each day is marked by a return to Bethany during the last week (up to the Preparation Day); and each day is filled with the recorded events.

It follows, therefore, that the Lord was crucified on our Wednesday; was buried on that day before sunset; and remained "three days and three nights" in the tomb, as foretold by Him in Matt. 12. 40; rising from the dead on "the third day", "the first day of the week".

The fixed days and dates, at either end, hold the whole period as in a vice, and place the whole subject on a ure foundation.

157 THE THREE SUPPERS.

That there were three suppers, and not only two, at the close of our Lord's ministry will be clear from a careful comparison of the three Scriptures.

1. There was the supper recorded in John 12. 1-9. This was probably in the house of Lazarus [1], and, being "six days before the Passover", must have taken place on the Friday evening, on the Lord's return from His first entry into Jerusalem from Bethphage (see Ap. 153).

Having slept there on the Friday night and spent the last Sabbath in retirement there, this first supper was made after the Sabbath had ended at 6 p.m. At this supper there was an anointing of the Lord by Mary (see Ap. 158)

[1] For all the family were present; and "Martha served" (cp. Luke 10. 40-42).

2. The second supper, recorded in Matt. 26. 6-13, took place "two days before the Passover" at the house of Simon the leper, which was also in Bethany. See Mark 14. 1-9. At this supper there was also an anointing by a woman unknown (see Ap. 158).

3. The supper recorded in John 13. 1-20 is the same as that recorded in Matt. 26. 20, Mark 14. 17, and Luke 22. 14. It was "the last supper", "the hour was come", and when supper was begun, or going on (not "ended"; see note on John 13. 2), the Lord first washed the disciples' feet; and, later, the events took place as recorded in all four Gospels. John's Gospel adds some antecedents; but gives the same consequents.

The rendering of *genomenou* in John 13. 2, by "ended" instead of by "taking place", or "beginning", has been the cause of much confusion.

158 THE TWO ANOINTINGS.

There can be no doubt that, during the last week, the Lord was anointed on two separate occasions.

1. The former is recorded in John 12. 3-8, "six days before the Passover", in the house of Lazarus, at Bethany. (See Ap. 157, and note above.)

The latter is recorded in Matt. 26. 7-13, and Mark 14. 3-9, "two days before the Passover", in the house of Simon the leper, also in Bethany.

Thus the times and places are distinct.

2. In the former case it was "a pound of ointment" that was used (John 12. 3).

In the latter case it was an alabaster vessel (Matt. 26. 7).

3. In the former case it was "the feet" of the Lord that were anointed (John 12. 3).

In the latter case it was His "head" (Matt. 26. 7).

4. In the former case the term used is "anointed" (John 12. 3).

In the latter case the term is "poured" (Matt. 26. 7. Mark 14. 3).

5. In the former case it was Judas who asked the question why it was not sold, &c., as there was plenty of time to do so during the six days (John 12. 4).

In the latter it was the disciples who "had indignation" (Matt. 26. 8) "among themselves" (Mark 14. 4); and their words (not necessarily spoken aloud to all) seem to refer to what Judas had said before.

6. In the former the Lord directs the ointment to be reserved for His burial; and not sold (John 12. 7).

In the latter He declared that it had been kept for that purpose (Matt. 26. 12. Mark 14. 8).

7. In the former case the Lord said, "Let her alone," in order that she may keep it (John 12. 7).

In the latter He declared that she had well used it (Matt. 26. 10–13).

8. In the former case the woman is named "Mary" (John 12. 3).

In the latter case the woman is unnamed.

9. Thus, on each occasion both the antecedents and consequents are different.

Instead of wondering that there should be two anointings the wonder should be that there were *only* two, seeing that examples are so easily followed.

159 "THIS IS MY BODY" (Matt. 26. 26).

A figure of speech consists of a word or words used out of the ordinary sense, or order; just as we call a person dressed out of the ordinary manner or fashion a "figure": both attract our attention; and, in the case of words, the one and only object is in order to call the reader's attention to what is thus emphasized. For examples see the notes on Matt. 16. 6: where, had the Lord said "the doctrine of the Pharisees is *like* leaven", that would have been the Fig. *Simile* (Ap. 6). Had He said "the doctrine of the Pharisees *is* leaven", the Fig. in this case would have been *Metaphor* (Ap. 6); by which, instead of saying one thing is *like* another, it is carried over (as the word *Metaphor* means), and states that the one thing *is* the other. But in Matt. 16. 6, the Lord used another Figure altogether, viz. *Hypocatastasis* (from *hupo*=under (Ap. 104. xviii), *kata*=down (Ap. 104. x), and *stasis*=a stationing), which means putting one of the *two* words (which are necessary in the case of *Simile* and *Metaphor*) down underneath, i.e. out of sight, and thus *implying* it. He said, "beware of the leaven", thus implying the word "doctrine", which He really meant; and, by thus attracting the disciples' attention to His words, thereby emphasized them.

In these three Figures we have a Positive, Comparative, and Superlative emphasis. The essence of *Simile* is *resemblance*; the essence of *Metaphor* is *representation* (as in the case of a portrait, which is representative of some person); the essence of *Hypocatastasis* is *implication*, where only one word is mentioned and another is *implied*.

Through non-acquaintance with Figures of Speech every Figure is to-day called a "Metaphor". But this is not the case. A *Metaphor* is a special Figure different and distinct from all others.

"This is My body" is the Figure *Metaphor*: and the Figure lies in the Verb "IS", which, as in this case, always means "*represents*", and must always be so expressed. It can *never mean* "*is changed into*". Hence in the Figure *Metaphor*, the Verb "represents" can always be substituted for "is". For example:

"The field is (or represents) the world" (Matt. 13. 38).

"The good seed are (represent) the sons of the kingdom" (Matt. 13. 38).

"The reapers are (represent) angels" (Matt. 13. 39).

"The odours are (represent) the prayers of the saints" (Rev. 5. 8).

"The seven heads are (represent) seven mountains" (Rev. 17. 9).

"This cup is (represents) the new covenant" (1 Cor. 11. 25).

"The cup of blessing which we bless, is it not (does it not represent) the blood of Christ?" (1 Cor 10. 16).

Furthermore, it is a fundamental law in Greek grammar, without exception, that the Article, Pronoun, and Adjective *must* agree in gender with the Noun to which they refer. For example, in Matt. 16. 18, the Pronoun "this" is Feminine, and thus agrees with *petra*, which is also Feminine, and not with *petros* (Peter), which is Masculine. See note, and Ap. 147.

So here: the Pronoun "this" is Neuter, and cannot agree with *artos* (=bread) because *artos* is Masculine. It must refer to what is Neuter; and this could only be the whole act of *breaking* the bread, which would be Neuter also; or to *klasma*, the broken piece (which is also Neuter).

In like manner, when He said (in *v.* 28) "this is my blood of the New Covenant"; "this", being Neuter, refers to *potērion* (= cup) [1] and not to *oinos* (=wine), which is Masculine, and means:—"This [cup] represents My blood of the New Covenant, which is poured out for many, for remission of sins".

For, what was the Lord doing? He was making the New Covenant foretold in Jer. 31. 31—34. If it were not made then, it can never be made at all (see Ap. 95), for no more has He blood to shed (Luke 24. 39).

Now, "blood" was shed, and sacrificially used, only in connection with *two* things, the making of a *covenant*, and the making of *atonement*. In the former, the victim which made or ratified the covenant was slain and the body divided in two, the parties to the covenant passing between (see notes on Gen. 15. 9–18. Jer. 34. 18. Gal. 3. 20, and Ap. 95). As long as the victim (the covenant-maker) was alive the covenant could have no force. See notes on Heb. 9. 16–22.

At the last supper this New Covenant was made; and Peter's proclamation in Acts 2. 38; 3. 19–26; 5. 31; and Paul's in 13. 38; 17. 30; 20. 21; 26. 20; were based upon it. Messiah had to be "cut off", that the Scriptures might be fulfilled (Acts 3. 18). But that having been accomplished, and the *sufferings* having been endured, nothing stood in the way of the *glory* which should follow. "Repent ye THEREFORE and turn [to the Lord] *that your sins may be blotted out*", &c. The New Covenant which had been made had provided for that, as the Lord had said in Matt. 26. 28, "for the remission of sins".

In that last supper the Lord was not *instituting* anything with a view to the Secret (the "Mystery" to be yet revealed in the Prison Epistles); but was *substituting* bread and wine for the Paschal Lamb (the type being exhausted in the Antitype), because of the new meaning which the Passover should henceforth convey. It was to be the *Memorial*, not of the Exodus from Egypt, but of the *Exodus* which the Lord afterward accomplished in Jerusalem (Luke 9. 31), according to the New Covenant made by His death.

[1] *Potērion* being put by *Metonymy* (of Adjunct), Ap. 6, for the contents, for the "cup" itself could not be swallowed.

160 THE DENIALS OF PETER.

There are several facts that have to be noticed before we can arrive at a clear understanding of all the denials recorded of Peter by the four evangelists:—

I. We have to note that the fact that Peter would deny His Lord was foretold in *three distinct prophecies* uttered on three separate occasions, and differing both as to the occasion and as to particulars.

1. The *first* was in the upper chamber, recorded in John 13. 38. It was absolute as to the *fact*, general as to the *day*, but particular as to the *number* of denials: "a cock shall by no means crow [from this time forth] until thou hast denied Me thrice" (see Ap. 156).

2. The *second* was in the upper chamber, recorded by Luke 22. 34. It was after the "strife", and immediately before leaving the room. It was absolute as to the *fact*, but particular as to the *day* and the *number* of the denials: "a cock shall not crow this day, before thou wilt thrice deny that thou knowest Me" (see Ap. 156).

3. The *third* was after the Lord had left the city and immediately before entering the garden of Gethsemane. It is recorded in Mark 14. 30, and was particular *in every detail*: "Verily I say unto thee that (*hoti*) thou (added by all the texts) this day, in this night, before a cock crow twice, thrice thou wilt deny Me". Cp. the fulfilment, and see Ap. 156.

This last prophecy furnishes the key to the whole problem. For, note:—

(*a*) that a cock was to crow twice, and

(*b*) that Peter would deny thrice;

i.e. before each of the two cockcrowings Peter would thrice deny His Lord. This is confirmed by the repetition in the fulfilment (Mark 14. 72).

Thus, there would be *six* denials in all; three before each cockcrowing.

Note that the word "cock" has no Article in any of the four records: in each case it is not "the", but "a cockcrowing".

II. Consonant with these data, we have the remarkable fact that Matthew, Luke, and John each record three denials, and one concluding cockcrowing. Mark also records three denials, but mentions the *two* cockcrowings.

Consequently, in the *four* Gospels there are no less than twelve denials mentioned. And the questions are, which of these are duplicates, and which are the resulting *six* required by the Lord's third prophecy in Mark 14. 30?

III. If we note accurately the marks of *time* in each Gospel, the *place*, and the *persons* addressing Peter, every condition required by each of the Greek words employed is fully and perfectly satisfied, without a shadow or suggestion of "discrepancy".

i. The First Series of Three.

1. The First Denial, John 18. 17. *Place*: the door (*thura*) without. *Time*: entering. *The questioner*: the porteress (Gr. *thurōros*).
2. The Second Denial, Matt. 26. 70 (Mark 14. 68). *Place*: the hall (*aulē*). *Time*: sitting. *Questioner*: a certain maid. Luke 22. 56–58 combines the same place and time, with the same maid, and another (*heteros*, masc.).
3. The Third Denial, Matt. 26. 71. *Place*: the gateway, or porch (*pulōn*). *Time*: an interval of an hour. John 18. 25, 26 combines the same place and time, with another maid and bystanders, one of them being a relative of Malchus.

A COCK CREW.

(Mark 14. 68. John 18. 27.)

ii. The Second Series of Three.

1. The First Denial, Mark 14. 69. *Place*: "beneath in the hall". *Time*: shortly after. *Questioner*: the maid again.
2. The Second Denial, Matt. 26. 73 (Mark 14. 70). *Place*: the gate (*pulōn*). *Time*: shortly after. *Questioners*: the bystanders.
3. The Third Denial (Luke 22. 59, 60). *Place*: the midst of the hall (*aulē*, *v.* 55). *Time*: "an hour after" (*v.* 59). *Questioner*: a certain one (masc.).

A COCK CREW.

(Matt. 26. 74. Mark 14. 72. Luke 22. 61.)

IV. We thus have a combined record in which there remains no difficulty, while each word retains its own true grammatical sense.

161 THE PURCHASE OF "THE POTTER'S FIELD" (Matt. 27. 6-8, and Acts 1. 18, 19) AND THE FULFILMENT OF THE PROPHECY (Matt. 27. 9, 10).

There are two difficulties connected with these scriptures:

I. The two purchases recorded in Matt. 27. 6–8, and Acts 1. 18, 19, respectively; and

II. The fulfilment of the prophecy connected with the former purchase (Matt. 27. 9, 10.

I. THE TWO PURCHASES.

For there were two. One by "the chief priests", recorded in Matt. 27. 6; and the other by Judas Iscariot, recorded in Acts 1. 18. The proofs are as follows:—

1. The purchase of Judas was made some time *before* that of the chief priests; for there would have been no time to arrange and carry this out between the betrayal and the condemnation.

The purchase of the chief priests was made *after* Judas had returned the money.

2. What the chief priests bought was "a field" (Gr. *agros*).

What Judas had acquired (see 3, below) was what in English we call a "Place" (Gr. *chōrion*=a farm, or small property).

The two are quite distinct, and the difference is preserved both in the Greek text and in the Syriac version. (See note 3, p. 136.)

3. The verbs also are different. In Matt. 27. 7 the verb is *agorazō*=to buy in the open market (from *agora*=a market-place); while, in Acts 1. 18, the verb is *ktaomai*=to acquire possession of (see Luke 18. 12; 21. 19; Acts 22. 28), and is rendered "provide" in Matt. 10. 9. Its noun, *ktēma*=a possession (occ. Matt. 19. 22. Mark 10. 22. Acts 2. 45; 5. 1).

4. How and when Judas had become possessed of this "place" we are not told in so many words; but we are left in no doubt, from the plain statement in John 12. 6 that "he was a thief, and had the bag". The "place" was bought with this stolen money, "the reward (or wages) of iniquity". This is a Hebrew idiom (like our Eng. "money ill-got"), used for money obtained by unrighteousness (Ap. 128. VII. 1; cp. Num. 22. 7. 2 Pet. 2. 15). This stolen money is wrongly assumed to be the same as the "thirty pieces of silver".

5. The two places had different names. The "field" purchased by the chief priests was originally known as "the potter's field", but was afterward called "*agros haimatos*"=the field of blood; i.e. a field bought with the price of blood ("blood" being put by the Fig. *Metonymy* (of the Subject), Ap. 6, for murder, or blood-guiltiness).

The "possession" which Judas had acquired bore an Aramaic name, "*Ḥakāl dᵉmā'*" (see Ap. 94 (III.) 3, p. 135), which is transliterated *Akeldama*, or according to some *Akeldamach*, or *Hacheldamach*= "place (Gr. *chōrion*) of blood": a similar meaning but from a different reason: viz. Judas's suicide. It is thus shown that there is no discrepancy between Matt. 27. 6–8 and Acts 1. 18, 19.

II. THE FULFILMENT OF THE PROPHECY.

(Matt. 27. 9, 10.)

Many solutions have been proposed to meet the two difficulties connected with Matt. 27. 9, 10.

i. As to the first difficulty, the words quoted from Jeremiah are not found in his written prophecy: and it has been suggested

1. That "Matthew quoted from memory" (Augustine and others).
2. That the passage was originally in Jeremiah, but

the Jews cut it out (Eusebius and others); though no evidence for this is produced.

3. That it was contained in another writing by Jeremiah, which is now lost (Origen and others).
4. That Jeremiah is put for the whole body of the prophets (Bishop Lightfoot and others), though no such words can be found in the other prophets.
5. That it was "a slip of the pen" on the part of Matthew (Dean Alford).
6. That the mistake was allowed by the Holy Spirit on purpose that we may not trouble ourselves as to who the writers were, but receive all prophecy as direct from God, Who spake by them (Bishop Wordsworth).
7. That some annotator wrote "Jeremiah" in the margin and it "crept" into the text (Smith's *Bible Dictionary*).

These suggestions only create difficulties much more grave than the one which they attempt to remove. But all of them are met and answered by the simple fact that Matthew does not say it was *written* by Jeremiah, but that it was "*spoken*" by him.

This makes all the difference: for some prophecies were spoken (and not written), some were written (and not spoken), while others were both spoken and written.

Of course, by the Fig. *Metonymy* (of Cause, Ap. 6), one may be said to "say" what he has written; but we need not go out of our way to use this figure, if by so doing we *create* the very difficulty we are seeking to solve. There is all the difference in the world between *to rhēthen* (=that which was spoken), and *ho gegraptai* (=that which stands written).

ii. As to the second difficulty: that the prophecy attributed to Jeremiah is really written in Zechariah 11. 10-13, it is created by the suggestion contained in the margin of the Authorized Version.

That this cannot be the solution may be shown from the following reasons:—

1. Zech. 11. 10-13 contains no reference either to a "field" or to its *purchase*. Indeed, the word "field" (*shādāh*) does not occur in the whole of Zechariah except in 10. 1, which has nothing to do with the subject at all.
2. As to the "thirty pieces of silver", Zechariah speaks of them with approval, while in Matthew they are not so spoken of. "A goodly price' (*'eder hayeḳār*) denotes *amplitude, sufficiency*, while the Verb *yāḳār* means *to be priced, prized, precious*; and there is not the slightest evidence that Zechariah spoke of the amount as being paltry, or that the offer of it was, in any sense, an insult. But this latter is the sense in Matt. 27. 9, 10.
3. The *givers* were "the poor of the flock". This enhanced the value. "The worth of the price" was accepted as "goodly" on that account, as in Mark 12. 43, 44. 2 Cor. 8. 12.
4. The *waiting* of the "poor of the flock" was not hostile. but friendly, as in Prov. 27. 18. Out of above 450 occurrences of the Heb. *shāmar*, less than fourteen are in a hostile sense.
5. In the disposal of the silver, the sense of the Verb "cast" is to be determined by the context (not by the Verb itself). In Zech. 11, the context shows it to be in a good sense, as in Ex. 15. 25. 1 Kings 19. 19. 2 Kings 2. 21; 4. 41; 6. 6. 2 Chron. 24. 10, 11.
6. The "potter" is the fashioner, and his work was not necessarily confined to fashioning "clay", but it extended to *metals*. Cp. Gen. 2. 7, 8. Ps. 33. 15; 94. 9. Isa. 43. 1, 6, 10, 21; 44. 2, 9-12, 21, 24; 45. 6, 7; 54. 16, 17. Out of the sixty-two occurrences of the Verb (*yāẓar*), more than three-fourths have nothing whatever to do with the work of a "potter".
7. A "potter" in connection with the Temple, or its service, is unknown to fact, or to Scripture.
8. The *material*, "silver," would be useless to a "potter", but necessary to a fashioner of metallic vessels, or for the payment of artizans who wrought them (2 Kings 12. 11-16; 22. 4-7. 2 Chron. 24. 11-13). One might as well cast *clay* to a silversmith as *silver* to a potter.
9. The prophecy of Zechariah is rich in reference to metals; and only the books of Numbers (31. 22) and Ezekiel name as many. In Zechariah we find *six* named: Gold, six times (4. 2, 12, 12; 6. 11; 13. 9; 14. 14). Fine gold, once (9. 3). Silver, six times, (6. 11; 9. 3; 11. 12, 13; 13. 9; 14. 14). Brass, once (6. 1, marg.). Lead, twice (5. 7, 8). Tin, once (4. 10, marg.). Seventeen references in all.
10. Zechariah is full of refs. to what the prophet *saw* and *said*; but there are only *two* refs. to what he *did*; and both of these have reference to "silver" (6. 11; 11. 13).
11. The Septuagint, and its revision by Symmachus, read "cast them (i.e. the thirty pieces of silver) *into the furnace*" (Gr. *eis to chōneutērion*), showing that, before Matthew was written, *yōtẓēr* was interpreted as referring not to a "potter" but to a fashioner of metals.
12. The *persons*, also, are different. In Matthew we have "they took", "they gave", "the price of him"; in Zechariah we read "I took", "I cast", "I was valued".
13. In Matthew the money was given "for the field", and in Zechariah it was cast "unto the fashioner".
14. Matthew names *three* parties as being concerned in the transaction; Zechariah names only *one*.
15. Matthew not only quotes Jeremiah's *spoken* words, but names him as the speaker. This is in keeping with Matt. 2. 17, 18. Jeremiah is likewise named in Matt. 16. 14; but nowhere else in all the New Test.

iii. The conclusion. From all this we gather that the passage in Matthew (27. 9, 10) cannot have any reference to Zech. 11. 10-13.

(1) If Jeremiah's *spoken* words have anything to do with what is recorded in Jer. 32. 6-9, 43, 44, then in the reference to them other words are interjected by way of parenthetical explanation. These are not to be confused with *the quoted words*. They may be combined thus:—

"Then was fulfilled that which was SPOKEN by Jeremiah the prophet, saying: 'And they took the thirty pieces of silver [**the price of him who was priced, whom they of the sons of Israel did price**], and they gave them for the potter's field, as the LORD appointed me.'"

Thus Matthew quotes that which was "SPOKEN" by Jeremiah the prophet, and *combines with the actual quotation* a parenthetical reference to the price at which the prophet Zechariah had been priced.

(2) Had the sum of money been twenty pieces of silver instead of thirty, a similar remark might well have been interjected thus:—

"Then was fulfilled that which was SPOKEN by Jeremiah the prophet, saying: 'And they took the twenty pieces of silver [**the price of him whom his brethren sold into Egypt**], and they gave them for the potter's field'", &c.

(3) Or, had the reference been to the compensation for an injury done to another man's servant, as in Ex. 21. 32, a similar parenthetical remark might have been introduced thus:—

"Then was fulfilled that which was SPOKEN by Jeremiah the prophet, saying: 'And they took the thirty pieces of silver [**the price given in Israel to**

the master whose servant had been injured by an ox], and they gave them for the potter's field' ", &c.

A designed parenthetical insertion by the inspired Evangelist of a *reference* to Zechariah, in a direct quotation from the prophet Jeremiah, is very different from a "mistake", or "a slip of the pen", "a lapse of memory", or a "corruption of the text", which need an apology.

The quotation itself, as well as the parenthetical reference, are both similarly exact.

162 THE CROSS AND CRUCIFIXION.

In the Greek N.T. two words are used for "the cross", on which the Lord was put to death.

1. The word *stauros*; which denotes an upright pale or stake, to which the criminals were nailed for execution.

2. The word *xulon*, which generally denotes a piece of a dead log of wood, or timber, for fuel or for any other purpose. It is not like *dendron*, which is used of a living, or green tree, as in Matt. 21. 8; Rev. 7. 1, 3; 8. 7; 9. 4, &c.

As this latter word *xulon* is used for the former *stauros*, it shows us that the meaning of each is exactly the same. The verb *stauroō* means to drive stakes.[1]

Our English word "cross" is the translation of the Latin *crux*; but the Greek *stauros* no more means a *crux* than the word "stick" means a "crutch".

Homer uses the word *stauros* of an ordinary pole or stake, or a single piece of timber.[2] And this is the meaning and usage of the word throughout the Greek classics.[3]

It never means *two* pieces of timber placed across one another at any angle, but always of one piece alone. Hence the use of the word *xulon* (No. 2, above) in connection with the manner of our Lord's death, and rendered "tree" in Acts 5. 30; 10. 39; 13. 29. Gal. 3. 13. 1 Pet. 2. 24. This is preserved in our old Eng. name *rood*, or *rod*. See the *Encycl. Brit.*, 11th (Camb.) ed., vol. 7, p. 505 d.

There is nothing in the Greek of the N.T. even to imply two pieces of timber.

The letter *chi*, Χ, the initial of the word Christ (Χριστος), was originally used for His Name; or Χρ. This was superseded by the symbols ☧ and ⳨, and even the first of these had four *equal* arms.

These crosses were used as symbols of the Babylonian sun-god, ⊕, and are first seen on a coin of Julius Cæsar, 100–44 B.C., and then on a coin struck by Cæsar's heir (Augustus), 20 B.C.[4]

On the coins of Constantine the most frequent symbol is ☧; but the same symbol is used without the surrounding circle, and with the four equal arms vertical and horizontal; and this was the symbol specially venerated as the "Solar Wheel". It should be stated that Constantine was a sun-god worshipper, and would not enter the "Church" till some quarter of a century after the legend of his having seen such a cross in the heavens (EUSEBIUS, *Vit. Const.* I. 37).

The evidence is the same as to the pre-Christian (phallic) symbol in Asia, Africa, and Egypt, whether we consult *Nineveh* by Sir A. H. LAYARD (ii. 213), or *Manners and Customs of the Ancient Egyptians*, by Sir J. GARDNER WILKINSON, iii. pp. 24, 26, 43, 44, 46, 52, 82, 136.

Dr. SCHLIEMANN gives the same evidence in his *Ilios* (1880), recording his discoveries on the site of prehistoric Troy. See pp. 337, 350, 353, 521, 523.

Dr. MAX OHNEFALSCH-RICHTER gives the same evidence from Cyprus; and these are "the oldest extant Phœnician inscriptions"; see his *Kypros, the Bible, and Homer: Oriental Civilisation, Art, and Religion in Ancient Times*, Plates XIX, XXV, XXVI, XXX, XXXI, XXXII, XL, LVIII, LXIX, &c.

The Catacombs in Rome bear the same testimony: "Christ" is never represented there as "hanging on a cross", and the cross itself is only pourtrayed in a veiled and hesitating manner. In the Egyptian churches the cross was a pagan symbol of life, borrowed by the Christians, and interpreted in the pagan manner. See the *Encycl. Brit.*, 11th (Camb.) ed., vol. 14, p. 273.

In his *Letters from Rome* Dean Burgon says: "I question whether a cross occurs on any Christian monument of the first four centuries".

In Mrs. Jameson's famous *History of our Lord as Exemplified in Works of Art*, she says (vol. ii, p. 315): "It must be owned that ancient objects of art, as far as hitherto known, afford no corroboration of the use of the cross in the simple transverse form familiar to us, at any period preceding, or even closely succeeding, the time of Chrysostom"; and Chrysostom wrote half a century after Constantine!

"The Invention of the Cross" by Helena the mother of Constantine (in 326), though it means her *finding* of the cross, may or may not be true; but the "invention" of it in pre-Christian times, and the "invention" of its use in later times, are truths of which we need to be reminded in the present day. The evidence is thus complete, that the Lord was put to death upon an upright stake, and not on two pieces of timber placed at any angle.

[1] There are two compounds of it used: *sustauroō*=to put any one thus to death with another (Matt. 27. 44. Mark 15. 32. John 19. 32. Rom. 6. 6. Gal. 2. 20); and *anastauroō*=to raise up and fix upon the stake again (Heb. 6. 6). Another word used is equally significant: *prospēgnumi*=to fix or fasten anything (Acts 2. 23).

[2] *Iliad* xxiv. 453. *Odyssey* xiv. 11.

[3] e.g. Thucydides iv. 90. Xenophon, *Anabasis* v. 2. 21.

[4] Other coins with this symbol were struck by Augustus, also by Hadrian and other Roman emperors. See *Early Christian Numismatics*, by C. W. King, M.A.

163 THE INSCRIPTIONS ON THE CROSS.

Each of the four Gospels gives a different wording of these inscriptions:—

1. Matt. 27. 37: "This is Jesus, the King of the Jews."
2. Mark 15. 26: "The King of the Jews."
3. Luke 23. 38: "This is the King of the Jews."
4. John 19. 19: "Jesus of Nazareth, the King of the Jews."

Here again the difficulty is created by assuming that these *similar* but differing records are *identical*, without noticing the exact words which are written. It is universally assumed that there was only *one*, and then follow the efforts to explain the alleged "discrepancies" between the different versions of it.

If we note carefully what is actually said all will be clear.

I. Mark 15. 26 can be dismissed; for he does not say anything about a "title" (Gr. *titlos*, John 19. 19) being put on the cross or anywhere else, which any one had seen. It is a question of the Lord's "accusation" or "indictment", or the ground or cause of His condemnation as claiming to be "the King of the Jews".

II. John 19. 19 speaks of a "*title*" written by Pilate, *before it left Pilate's presence*; for no one suggests that Pilate went to the scene of the execution and wrote anything there.

In Pilate's writing the three languages were in this

order: (1) Hebrew, (2) Greek, and (3) Latin (cp. IV. below). And it was read *after the cross had been set up*.

This was the one which gave rise to the argument between the Chief Priests and Pilate (John 19. 21, 22); and this argument took place before the parting of the garments (*vv.* 23, 24).

III. The inscription in Matt. 27. 37 was the result of that discussion; for another "title" was brought and was "set up over his head", *after they had "parted His garments,"* and having sat down, they watched Him there (*vv.* 35, 36).

As there could hardly have been two titles at the same time, the former must have been then taken down and the other substituted.

We are not told how long the argument lasted or when it ceased, or what was the final result of it.

IV. A further result is seen in Luke 23. 38; for another was brought much later, close upon "the sixth hour" (*v.* 44), when the darkness fell. It was written with the languages in a different order: (1) Greek, (2) Latin, and (3) Hebrew (*v.* 38).[1] It was put up "over Him" (Gr *ep' autō*, *v.* 38), "*after the revilings of the People*" (cp. *vv.* 35-37, with *v.* 38); whereas Matthew's (No. III) was set up *before the revilings* (cp. Matt. 27. 37 with *v.* 39).

[1] But see the texts.

The result is that:—

1. Mark's was only His *indictment*.
2. John's was the *first*, written by Pilate himself (or by his order, in (1) Hebrew, (2) Greek, and (3) Latin, and was put on the cross *before it left Pilate's presence*.
3. Matthew's was the *second*, substituted for the first, in consequence of the arguments which took place, and was set up "over His head" *after* the garments had been divided, and *before* the revilings.
4. Luke's was the *third* (and last), put up "over Him", *after* the revilings (Luke 23. 35), and was seen just before the darkness of the "sixth hour" (*v.* 44). This was written in three languages, but in a different order:[1] (1) Greek, (2) Latin, and (3) Hebrew (*v.* 38). Not in Hebrew, and Greek, and Latin, as No. II in John 19. 19.

Thus, such differences as these are marks of Divine accuracy; and, instead of being sources of difficulties, become, when rightly divided, the means of their removal.

164 THE "OTHERS" CRUCIFIED WITH THE LORD (Matt. 27. 38 and Luke 23. 32).

Misled by tradition and the ignorance of Scripture on the part of mediæval painters, it is the general belief that *only two* were crucified with the Lord.

But Scripture does not say so. It states that there were two "thieves" (Gr. *lēstai*=robbers, Matt. 27. 38. Mark 15. 27); and that there were two "malefactors" (Gr. *kakourgoi*, Luke 23. 32).

It is also recorded that *both* the robbers reviled Him (Matt. 27. 44. Mark 15. 32); while in Luke 23. 39 only *one* of the malefactors "railed on Him", and "the other rebuked him" for so doing (*v.* 40). If there were only *two*, this is a *real* discrepancy; and there is another, for the two malefactors were "led with Him to be put to death" (Luke 23. 32), and when they were come to Calvary, "they" then and there "crucified Him and the malefactors, one on the right hand and the other on the left" (*v.* 33).

But the other discrepancy is, according to Matthew, that *after* the parting of the garments, and *after* "sitting down they watched Him there", that "THEN were there two *robbers* crucified with Him, one on the right hand and the other on the left" (Matt. 27. 38. Mark 15. 27). The two malefactors had already been "led with Him" and were therefore crucified "with Him", *before* the dividing of the garments, and *before* the two robbers were brought.

The first two (malefactors) who were "led with Him" were placed one on either side. When the other two (robbers) were brought, much later, they were also similarly placed; so that there were two (one of each) on either side, and the Lord in the midst. The malefactors were therefore the nearer, and being on the inside they could speak to each other better, and the one with the Lord, as recorded (Luke 23. 39-43).

John's record confirms this for he speaks only of *place*, and *not of time*. He speaks, generally of the *fact*: "where they crucified Him, and with Him others, two on this side, and that side, and Jesus in the midst" (John 19. 8). In Rev. 22. 2 we have the same expression in the Greek (*enteuthen kai enteuthen*), which is accurately rendered "on either side". So it should be rendered here: "and with Him others, on either side."

But John further states (19. 32, 33): "then came the soldiers and brake the legs of the first, and of the other which was crucified with Him. But when they came (Gr.=having come) to Jesus, and saw that He was dead already, they brake not His legs." Had there been only two (one on either side) the soldiers would not have *come* to the Lord, but would have passed Him, and then turned back again. But they came to Him after they had broken the legs of the first two.

There are two words used of the "other" and "others" in John 19. 32 and Luke 23. 32 (see Ap. 124. 1). In the former passage we read, "they brake the legs of the first and of *the other*." Here the Greek is *allos*, which is the other (the second) of two *when there are more* (see Matt. 10. 23; 25. 16, 17, 20; 27. 61; 28. 1. John 18. 15, 16; 20. 2, 4, 8, and Rev. 17 10).

THE FIVE CROSSES AT
PLOUBÉZÉRÉ, NEAR LANNION,
Côtes-du-Nord, Brittany.

In the latter passage (Luke 23. 32) the word is *heteros*

=different (see Ap. 124. 2): "and others also, two, were being led with Him." These were different [1] from Him with Whom they were led, not different from one another; for they were "in the same condemnation", and "justly", while He had "done nothing amiss" (*vv.* 40, 41).

From this evidence, therefore, it is clear that there were four "others" crucified with the Lord; and thus, on the one hand, there are no "discrepancies", as alleged; while, on the other hand, every word and every expression, in the Greek, gets (and gives) its own exact value, and its full significance.

[1] Cp. Matt. 6. 21, 24; 8. 21; 11. 3. Luke 5. 7; 6. 6; 7. 41; 9. 56; 14. 31; 16. 13, 18; 17. 34, 35; 18. 10; 23. 40.

To show that we are not without evidence, even from tradition, we may state that there is a "Calvary" to be seen at Ploubézéré near Lannion, in the Côtes-du-Nord, Brittany, known as *Les Cinq Croix* ("The Five Crosses"). There is a high cross in the centre, with four lower ones, two on either side. There may be other instances of which we have not heard.

"In the Roman Catholic church . . . the altar-slab or 'table' alone is consecrated, and in sign of this are cut in its upper surface five Greek crosses, one in the centre and one in each corner . . . but the history of the origin and development of this practice is not fully worked out" (*Encycl. Brit.*, 11th (Cambridge) ed., vol. i, pp. 762, 763). This practice may possibly be explained by the subject of this Appendix.

165 THE HOURS OF THE LORD'S LAST DAY.

The Diagram below shows the 24 hours of the "Preparation Day", i.e. the day before the Passover (John 19. 14, &c.). The Four Gospels agree in stating that the Lord was *laid in the Sepulchre on the Preparation Day*, which was Nisan 14th, immediately before "the High Sabbath", Nisan 15th (Matt. 27. 62. Mark 15. 42. Luke 23. 54. John 19. 31, 42). Therefore He must have been crucified on Wednesday, 14th of Nisan (see Ap. 144, 156, 166).

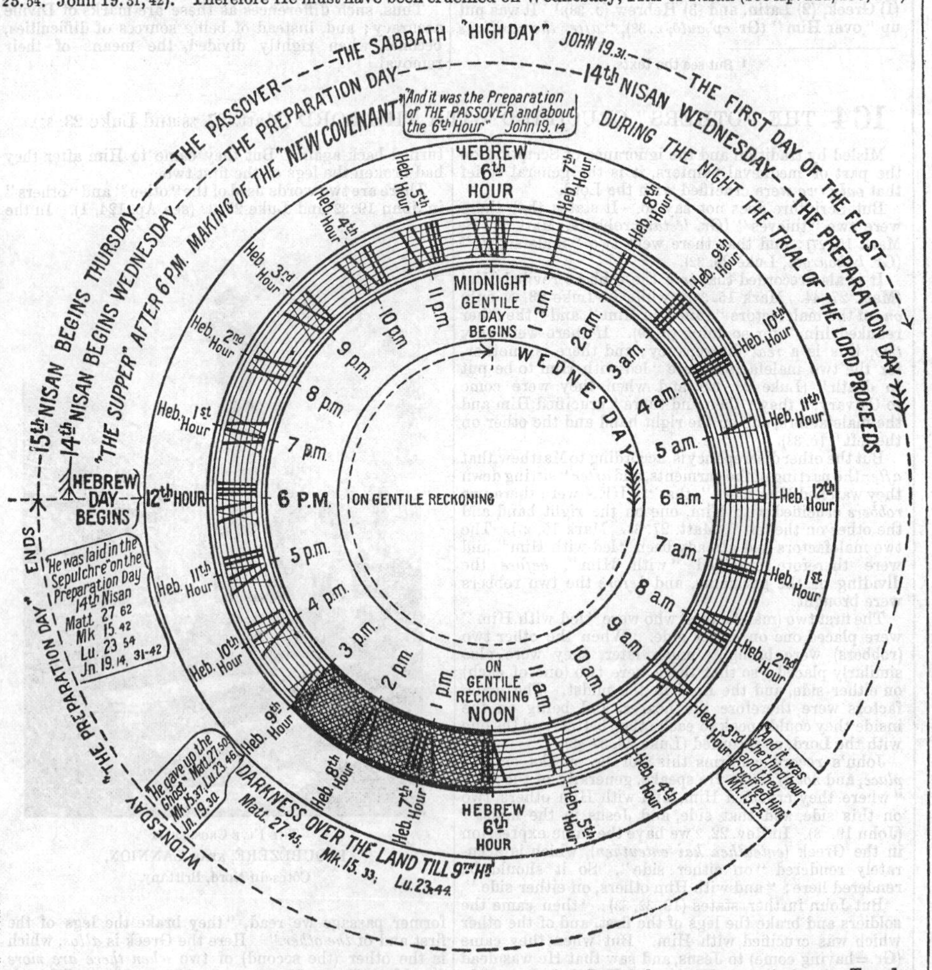

As shown above, the 14th of Nisan, which was the "Preparation Day", began at sunset on our Tuesday (Gentile reckoning). "The sixth hour" of John 19. 14 is the sixth hour of the night, and therefore corresponds to *midnight*, at which, according to Gentile reckoning, Wednesday began.

The Roman numerals on the dial-plate show the 24 hours of the complete Gentile day. And on either side of the dial are shown the Hebrew "hours" corresponding to the Gentile hours a.m. and p.m.

The twenty-four hours were divided into the twelve hours of the *night* (reckoned from sunset), and "twelve hours in the *day*" (reckoned from sunrise. See John 11. 9). Hence "the sixth hour" of John 19. 14 was our midnight; "the third hour" of Mark 15. 25 was our 9 a.m.; "the sixth hour" of Matt. 27. 45; Mark 15. 33; Luke 23. 44; was our *noon*; and "the ninth hour" of Matt. 27. 45, 46; Mark 15. 33, 34; Luke 23. 44; was our 3 p.m.

166 THE SEQUENCE OF EVENTS FOLLOWING THE LORD'S RESURRECTION.

The order of these events in the Four Gospels is partly independent and partly supplementary, taking up the narrative at different points of time. They may be set out as follows:—

	MATTHEW.	MARK.	LUKE.	JOHN.
The observation of the women where and how the body was laid	27. 61	15. 47	23. 55	
The preparation of the spices by the women from Galilee on the eve of the *High* Sabbath			23. 56-	
Their rest according to the Commandment (Lev. 23. 7). See Ap. 156			23. -56	
The visit of the women at the close of the *weekly* Sabbath, on "the first day of the week"	28. 1	16. 1, 2	24. 1	20. 1-
"Who shall roll us away the stone?"		16. 3		
The stone already rolled away	28. 2-4			
They find the stone rolled away		16. 4, 5	24. 2	20. -1
Address of the angel to the women	28. 5-7	16. 6, 7	24. 3-7	
Departure of the women	28. 8	16. 8	24. 8, 9	
They meet with the Lord	28. 9, 10			
And tell His disciples, and Peter		16. 9-11	24. 10, 11	20. 2 (*oun*)
The report of the watch	28. 11-15			
The visit of Peter and John			24. 12	20. 3-10 (*oun*)
Mary's visit to the sepulchre				20. 11-18
The appearing to the two going to Emmaus		16. 12 (*meta tauta*)	24. 13-32	
Their return to the eleven		16. 13	24. 33-35	
The first appearance of the Lord to the eleven			24. 36-44	20. 19-23
The FIRST COMMISSION			24. 45-49	
The second appearance to the eleven (and Thomas)		16. 14 (*husteron*)		20. 24-29
The SECOND COMMISSION		16. 15-18		
[Parenthetic statement by the Evangelist]				20. [30, 31]
Departure of the eleven into Galilee	28. 16-18			
The THIRD COMMISSION	28. 19, 20			
The appearance to the seven in Galilee				21. 1-23 (*meta tauta*)
The Ascension and after		16. 19, 20	24. 50-53.	
[Closing statement of the Evangelist]				21. [24, 25]

167 THE THREE COMMISSIONS.

It will be seen from Ap. 166 that there were three separate Commissions given to the Eleven Apostles, at different times, on distinctly specified occasions and in varying words.

The first is recorded in Luke 24. 47. This was given *in Jerusalem* on the evening of the day of the resurrection. It was given, not to the Eleven only, but also to "them that were with them" (*v.* 33). The commission was the continuation of His own ministry and that of John the Baptist (Matt. 22. 1-10). They were all to proclaim "repentance and remission of sins". The New Covenant had been made, in virtue of which this message of pardon could be declared (Matt. 26. 26-29. Mark 14. 22-25. Luke 22. 14-23. Acts 3. 19), first in Jerusalem, and then to all nations. This was done by Peter (Acts 2. 38; 3. 19, &c.).

The second is recorded in Mark 16. 15-18, and was given when the Lord appeared to the Eleven *as they sat at meat*; and it was carried out by "them that heard Him", as foretold in Matt. 22. 4-7, and fulfilled in Mark 16. 20, as confirmed in Heb. 2. 3, 4. The Acts of the Apostles is the inspired history of the fulfilment of this commission, so far as it is necessary for our instruction. It was given for the personal ministry of the Apostles, to be fulfilled by them before the destruction of the Temple and of Jerusalem.

The third is recorded in Matt. 28. 19, 20, and was given *on a mountain in Galilee* (Ap. 169). It was the proclamation of the King, Who had left Jerusalem, according to the Parable (Luke 19. 12), until He returns in power to set up His kingdom (26. 64). It is the summons to the Gentile nations to submit to the Lord Jesus, as the king of Israel, according to Ps. 2. 10-12. It is the proclamation of "the Gospel of the Kingdom" (Ap. 140. II) for a witness to all nations, immediately before the end of the age (Matt. 24. 14. Rev. 14. 6). It is still wholly future in its application, and proclaims the judgment on the Gentiles for the final deliverance of Israel, according to Ps. 2. 9, when verse 6 shall be fulfilled.

168 THE LAST TWELVE VERSES OF MARK'S GOSPEL.

Most modern critics are agreed that the last twelve verses of Mark 16 are not an integral part of his Gospel. They are omitted by T [A]; not by the Syr. Ap. 94.V. ii.

The question is entirely one of evidence.

From Ap. 94. V. we have seen that this evidence comes from three sources: (1) manuscripts, (2) versions, and (3) the early Christian writers, known as "the Fathers". This evidence has been exhaustively analysed by the late Dean Burgon, whose work is epitomized in Nos. I-III, below.

I. As to MANUSCRIPTS, there are none older than the fourth century, and the oldest two uncial MSS. (B and ℵ, see Ap. 94. V.) are without those twelve verses. Of all the others (consisting of some eighteen uncials and some six hundred cursive MSS. which contain the Gospel of Mark) there is *not one* which leaves out these twelve verses.

II. As to the Versions:—

1. The SYRIAC. The oldest is the Syriac in its various forms: the "Peshitto" (cent. 2), and the "Curetonian Syriac" (cent. 3). Both are older than any Greek MS. in existence, and both contain these twelve verses. So with the "Philoxenian" (cent. 5) and the "Jerusalem" (cent. 5). See note [3] on page 136.

2. The LATIN Versions. JEROME (A. D. 382), who had access to Greek MSS. older than any now extant, includes these twelve verses; but this Version (known as the Vulgate) was only a revision of the VETUS ITALA, which is believed to belong to cent. 2, and contains these verses.

3. The GOTHIC Version (A. D. 350) contains them.

4. The EGYPTIAN Versions: the Memphitic (or Lower Egyptian, less properly called "COPTIC"), belonging to cent. 4 or 5, contains them; as does the "THEBAIC" (or Upper Egyptian, less properly called the "SAHIDIC"), belonging to cent. 3.

5. The ARMENIAN (cent. 5), the ETHIOPIC (cent. 4–7), and the GEORGIAN (cent. 6) also bear witness to the genuineness of these verses.

III. The FATHERS. Whatever may be their value (or otherwise) as to doctrine and interpretation yet, in determining actual *words*, or their *form*, or *sequence*, their evidence, even by an allusion, as to whether a verse or verses existed or not in their day, is more valuable than even manuscripts or Versions.

There are nearly a hundred ecclesiastical writers older than the oldest of our Greek codices; while between A.D. 300 and A.D. 600 there are about two hundred more, and they all refer to these twelve verses.

PAPIAS (about A. D. 100) refers to *v.* 18 (as stated by Eusebius, *Hist. Ecc.* iii. 39).

JUSTIN MARTYR (A.D. 151) quotes *v.* 20 (*Apol.* I. c. 45).

IRENÆUS (A. D. 180) quotes and remarks on *v.* 19 (*Adv. Hær.* lib. iii. c. x.).

HIPPOLYTUS (A. D. 190–227) quotes *vv.* 17–19 (Lagarde's ed., 1858, p. 74).

VINCENTIUS (A. D. 256) quoted two verses at the seventh Council of Carthage, held under CYPRIAN.

The ACTA PILATI (cent. 2) quotes *vv.* 15, 16, 17, 18 (Tischendorf's ed., 1853, pp. 243, 351).

The APOSTOLICAL CONSTITUTIONS (cent. 3 or 4) quotes *vv.* 16, 17, 18.

EUSEBIUS (A. D. 325) discusses these verses, as quoted by MARINUS from a lost part of his History.

APHRAARTES (A. D. 337), a Syrian bishop, quoted *vv.* 16–18 in his first Homily (Dr. Wright's ed., 1869, i., p. 21).

AMBROSE (A. D. 374–97), Archbishop of Milan, freely quotes *vv.* 15 (four times), 16, 17, 18 (three times), and *v.* 20 (once).

CHRYSOSTOM (A. D. 400) refers to *v.* 9; and states that *vv.* 19, 20 are "the end of the Gospel".

JEROME (b. 331, d. 420) includes these twelve verses in his Latin translation, besides quoting *vv.* 9 and 14 in his other writings.

AUGUSTINE (fl. A.D. 395–430) more than quotes them. He discusses them as being the work of the Evangelist MARK, and says that they were publicly read in the churches.

NESTORIUS (cent. 5) quotes *v.* 20, and

CYRIL OF ALEXANDRIA (A. D. 430) accepts the quotation.

VICTOR OF ANTIOCH (A. D. 425) confutes the opinion of Eusebius, by referring to very many MSS. which he had seen, and so had satisfied himself that the last twelve verses were recorded in them.

IV. We should like to add our own judgment as to the root cause of the doubts which have gathered round these verses.

They contain the promise of the Lord, of which we read the fulfilment in Heb. 2. 4. The testimony of "them that heard Him" was to be the *confirmation* of His own teaching when on earth: "God also bearing them witness, both with signs and wonders, and divers miracles, and gifts of *pneuma hagion* (i.e. spiritual gifts. See Ap. 101. II. 14), according to His own will".

The Acts of the Apostles records the fulfilment of the Lord's promise in Mark 16. 17, 18; and in the last chapter we find a culminating exhibition of "the Lord's working with them" (*vv.* 3, 5, 8, 9). But already, in 1 Cor. 13. 8–13, it was revealed that a time was then approaching when all these spiritual gifts should be "done away". That time coincided with the close of that dispensation, by the destruction of Jerusalem; when they that heard the Lord could no longer add their confirmation to the Lord's teaching, and there was nothing for God to bear witness to. For nearly a hundred years [1] after the destruction of Jerusalem there is a complete blank in ecclesiastical history, and a complete silence of Christian speakers and writers [2]. So far from the Churches of the present day being the *continuation* of Apostolic times, "organized religion", as we see it to-day, was the work of a subsequent and quite an independent generation.

When later transcribers of the Greek manuscripts came to the last twelve verses of Mark, and saw no trace of such spiritual gifts in existence, they concluded that there must be something doubtful about the genuineness of these verses. Hence, some may have marked them as doubtful, some as spurious, while others omitted them altogether.

A phenomenon of quite an opposite kind is witnessed in the present day.

Some (believers in these twelve verses), earnest in their desire to serve the Lord, but not "rightly dividing the Word of truth" as to the dispensations, look around, and, not seeing these spiritual gifts in operation, determine to have them (!) and are led into all sorts of more than doubtful means in their desire to obtain them. The resulting "confusion" shows that God is "not the author" of such a movement (see 1 Cor. 14. 31–33).

[1] See Col. 1, opposite.

[2] Except the *Didachē*, or *Teaching of the Twelve*, which is supposed to be about the middle of the second century, but which shows how soon the corruption of New Testament "Christianity" had set in.

169 GALILEE.

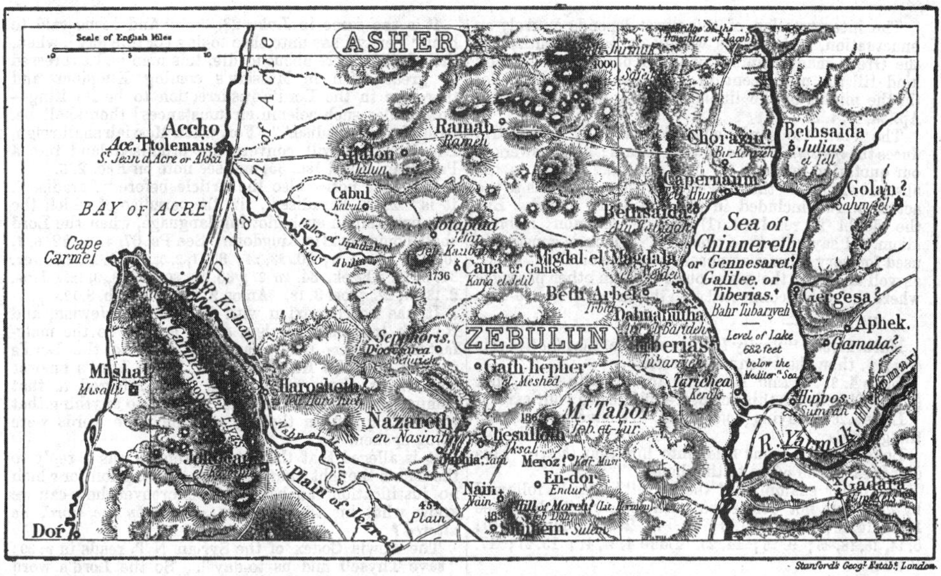

Stanford's Geogl. Estabt. London.

170 THE SYNONYMOUS WORDS FOR "LIFE".

There are three principal words translated "LIFE". Their shades of meaning are to be distinguished as follows:—

1. ***zōē***=life in all its manifestations; from the life of God down to the lowest vegetable. It is life in activity, and thus especially is the opposite of death. It involves resurrection life and eternal life; and hence, as such, is the "gift of God" (Rom. 6. 23. 1 John 5. 12). For the same reason its verb *zaō* is frequently used of, and put for, resurrection life (Matt. 9. 18. Mark 16. 11. Luke 24. 5, 23. John 11. 25, 26. Acts 1. 3; 9. 41; 25. 19. Rom. 6. 10; 14. 9. 2 Cor. 13. 4. Rev. 1. 18; 2. 8; 13. 14; 20. 4, 5).

2. ***bios***=life, as lived, manner of life; life as led, &c.; *zōē* being life as one experiences it; *bios* as others see it. This is used therefore, only of mankind, who not only live but lead lives. Hence the difference between ZO-ology and BIO-graphy. *Zōē* is life in its principle; *bios* is life in its manifestations (Luke 8. 14). *Bios* is also put by Fig. *Metonymy* (of Adjunct), Ap. 6, for livelihood, or that which supports animal life (Luke 8. 43). It occurs eleven times (Mark 12. 44. Luke 8. 14, 43; 15. 12, 30; 21. 4. 1 Tim. 2. 2. 2 Tim. 2. 4. 1 Pet. 4. 3. 1 John 2. 16; 3. 17).

3. ***psuchē***=the breath of animal life; one of the manifestations of *zōē*, common to all living animals. In one passage (Isa. 10. 18, the Heb. *nephesh* (Ap. 13), Gr. *psuchē*) is applied to vegetable life. It is used of the living individual as such. For its various renderings and usages, see Ap. 110.

171 THE SYNONYMOUS WORDS FOR "SLEEP".

There are two words rendered "Sleep":—

1. ***katheudō***=to compose one's self for sleep. Occurs twenty-two times; never used of death.

2. ***koimaomai***=to fall asleep (unintentionally). Hence this latter is used of death, as it is involuntary, while *katheudō* is voluntary. See this difference illustrated in 1 Thess. 4. 14 (where it is *koimaomai*), and 5. 6, 7, 10 (where it is *katheudō*). Occurs eighteen times; always of death, save Matt. 28. 13. Luke 22. 45. John 11. 12. Acts 12. 6.

172 THE SYNONYMOUS WORDS FOR "POWER", ETC.

1. ***dunamis***=inherent power; the power of reproducing itself: from which we have Eng. dynamics, dynamo, &c. See Acts 1. 8.

2. ***kratos***=strength (as exerted); power put forth with effect, and in government: from which we have the Eng. theocracy, government by God; aristocracy, government by the best; democracy, government by the people. The Greek *enkrateia*=mastery over one's self =self-control, or having one's self reined in (from *krateia*, a rein). This (i.e. *enkrateia*) is the only word rendered "temperance", and occurs only in Acts 24. 25. Gal. 5. 23. 2 Pet. 1. 6, 6.

3. ***ischus***=strength (as an endowment), physical strength possessed. See, e.g., Mark 12. 30.

4. ***energeia***=energy; strength (No. 3 above) put forth from within in effectual operation. See, e.g., 2 Thess. 2. 9.

5. ***exousia***=authority, or, delegated power; the liberty and right to put forth power. See, e.g., John 1. 12.

6. ***archē***=beginning; then, the chief rule or ruler. See Luke 12. 11 (magistrates).

173 "TO-DAY" (Luke 23. 43).

The interpretation of this verse depends entirely on punctuation, which rests wholly on *human* authority, the Greek manuscripts having no punctuation of any kind till the ninth century, and then it is only a dot (in the middle of the line) separating each word. See Ap. 94, V. i. 3.

The Verb "to say", when followed by *hoti*, introduces the *ipsissima verba* of what is said; and answers to our quotation marks. So here (in Luke 23. 43), in the absence of *hoti* = "that", there may be a doubt as to the actual words included in the dependent clause. But the doubt is resolved (1) by the common Hebrew idiom, "I say unto thee this day", which is constantly used for very solemn emphasis (see note on Deut. 4. 26); as well as (2) by the usage observable in other passages where the verb is connected with the Gr. *sēmeron* = to-day.

1. With *hoti* :—

Mark 14. 30: "Verily I say unto thee, that (*hoti*) 'this day . . . thou shalt deny me thrice.'"

Luke 4. 21: "And He began to say unto them, that (*hoti*) 'This day is this scripture fulfilled in your ears.'"

Luke 5. 26: "Saying (*hoti* = that), 'We have seen strange things to-day.'"

Luke 19. 9: "Jesus said unto him that (*hoti*), 'This day is salvation come to this house.'"

For other examples of the verb "to say", followed by *hoti*, but not connected with *sēmeron* (to-day), see Matt. 14. 26; 16. 18; 21. 3; 26. 34; 27. 47. Mark 1. 40; 6. 14, 15, 18, 35; 9. 26; 14. 25. Luke 4. 24, 41; 15. 27; 17. 10; 19. 7.

2. Without *hoti* :—

On the other hand, in the absence of *hoti* (=that), the relation of the word "to-day" must be determined by the context.

Luke 22. 34: "And He said, 'I tell thee, Peter, in no wise shall a cock crow to-day before thou shalt thrice deny that thou knowest Me.'" Here the word "to-day" is connected with the verb "crow", because the context requires it. Compare Heb. 4. 7.

It is the same in Luke 23. 43: "And Jesus said to him, 'Verily I say unto thee to-day [or this day[1], when, though they were about to die, this man had expressed so great faith in Messiah's coming Kingdom, and therefore in the Lord's resurrection to be its King—now, under such solemn circumstances] thou shalt be, with Me, in Paradise.'" For, when Messiah shall reign, His Kingdom will convert the promised land into a Paradise. Read Isa. 35, and see note on Ecc. 2. 5.

We must notice also the Article before "Paradise". It is "THE Paradise", viz. the paradise of which the prophets tell in such glowing language, when the Lord shall come in His Kingdom. See Ps. 67. 4, 6; 72. 6, 7, 16, 17. Isa. 4. 2; 30. 23, 24; 35. 1, 2, 5, 6; 41. 18, 20. Jer. 31. 5, 12. Ezek. 34. 25–27; 36. 29, 30; 47. 8, 9, 12. Hos. 2. 18, 21, 22. Joel 3. 18. Amos 9. 13–15. Zech. 8. 12.

It has no connexion with Babylonian, Jewish, and Romish tradition, but is a *direct* answer to the malefactor's prayer. His prayer referred to the Lord's coming and His Kingdom; and, if the Lord's answer was direct, the promise must have referred to that coming and to that Kingdom, and not to anything that was to happen on the day on which the words were being spoken.

It is alleged that the Lord's promise was a reply to the man's thought; but this is an assumption for which no justification can be found. Moreover, how can we know what his thought was, *except by the words he uttered?*

The Lewis Codex of the Syrian N.T. reads in *v.* 39: "save Thyself and us to-day". So the Lord's word "to-day" may have reference to the revilings of the one, as well as to the request of the other.

[1] It is rendered "to-day" eighteen times in the Gospels, Hebrews and James; but "this day" twenty-three times (five times in Matthew; once in Mark; four times in Luke; nine times in Acts; once in Romans; twice in 2 Corinthians; and once in Hebrews).

174 THE SYNONYMOUS WORDS FOR "SEND", "SENT", ETC.

1. ***apostellō*** = to send forth, or off, or away from (as a messenger, or with a commission), the sender remaining behind[1]; implying authority on the part of the sender. Hence used of prophets; and the Noun, "apostle", denotes one thus sent.

2. ***exapostellō*** = to send off, or away out of (the place where one is); implying the same mission and authority. No. 1, with the Prep. *ek* prefixed. See Ap. 104. vii.

3. ***sunapostellō*** = to send off together (or in conjunction) with another. No. 1, with *sun* (Ap. 104. xvi) prefixed. Occurs only in 2 Cor. 12. 18.

4. ***pempō*** = to send (esp. with an escort), the sender accompanying those sent[2]. See Luke 7. 3 (where No. 1, above, is used), and *v.* 6 (where *pempō* is used).

5. ***anapempō*** = to send up (as to a judge for trial); or to send back, remit (as in Luke 23. 11); or to send again.

6. ***ekpempō*** = to send out from, send out. No. 4, with *ek* (Ap. 104. vii) prefixed. Occ. only in Acts 13. 4; 17. 10.

[1] See John 20. 22: "as the Father hath sent (No. 1) Me, even so send I (No. 4) you."

[2] See note above, where *pempō* is thus emphasized.

7. ***metapempō*** = to send for, so as to be *with* one's self. No. 4, with *meta* (Ap. 104. xi) prefixed. Occurs only (except once) in Middle Voice. Acts 10. 5, 5, 22, -29; 11. 13; 24. 24, 26; 25. 3. See Passive Voice, Acts 10. 29-.

8. ***sumpempō*** = to send in company with. No. 4, with *sun* (Ap. 104. xvi) prefixed. Occ. only in 2 Cor. 8. 18, 22.

9. ***ballō*** = to throw, to cast (the context determining the nature or degree of force exercised). Cp. Matt. 10. 34.

10. ***ekballō*** = to throw or cast out of, or from. No. 9, with *ek* (Ap. 104. vii) prefixed. Cp. Matt. 12. 20.

11. ***apoluō*** = to loosen off from, let loose from, release, let go away. Cp. Matt. 15. 23.

12. ***aphiēmi*** = to send off, or away from one's self (in any manner); hence, to dismiss. Cp. Matt. 13. 36.

13. ***apotassomai*** = to withdraw from by taking formal leave of; to bid farewell or say "adieu" to: as Elisha did from Elijah (Josephus, *Ant.* viii. 13. 7). Cf. Mark 6. 46. Luke 9. 61; 14. 33. Acts 18. 18, 21. 2 Cor. 2. 13.

14. ***bruō*** = to emit, or send forth abundantly (as a fountain). Occurs only in James 3. 11.

175 THE SYNONYMOUS WORDS FOR "TRUE".

1. ***alēthēs***=true[1] (as contrasted with what is *false*). Hence, used of God (John 3. 33) in that He cannot lie (see also John 5. 31; 8. 13). The opposite of a lie. Gr. *apseudēs*. Tit. 1. 2. Cp. John 4. 18. 1 John 2. 27.

2. ***alēthinos***=very[1]. Fr. *véritable*: i.e. genuine, real, substantial, as contrasted with that which is fictitious, unreal, shadowy, or symbolical. Hence, *alēthinos* is that which has truth for its base and is all that it claims to be (John 6. 32; 15. 1). See 1 Thess. 1. 9. Heb. 8. 2; 9. 24.

3. ***gnēsios***=legitimate. Spoken of children. Occ. only in Phil. 4. 3. 1 Tim. 1. 2. Tit. 1. 4. With Art.=sincerity (2 Cor. 8. 8). The Adverb *gnēsiōs*=naturally, occ. only in Phil. 2. 20.

4. ***pistos***=faithful. A verbal Adj., from *peithō*=to persuade, and Pass. to be persuaded and convinced. Hence, believing, faithful, trustworthy. Transl "true" in 2 Cor. 1. 18. 1 Tim. 3. 1. See Ap. 150. III.

[1] See notes on the Structure of the Gospel of John.

176 THE EIGHT "SIGNS" IN JOHN'S GOSPEL.

Miracles are spoken of in the New Testament under three names:—

1. ***dunamis***=power. In the singular, power in the abstract; but in the plural it=mighty works, i. e. the manifestations of power. (See Ap. 172. 1.) The word occurs 38 times in three of the four Gospels: 13 times in Matthew, and is rendered "power", or "powers" 5 times; "mighty works" 6 times; "wonderful works" once (7. 22), and once "ability" (25. 15). It occurs ten times in Mark; and is rendered "virtue" once (5. 30); "mighty works" 3 times; "power", or "powers", 5 times; and "miracle" once (9. 39). In Luke it occurs 15 times, and is rendered "power", or "powers", 11 times; "virtue" twice; "mighty works", twice. In John it does not occur at all.

2. ***teras***=a wonder. This word has regard to the *effect produced* on those who witnessed the mighty work. It is always translated "wonder", and occurs three times in three of the Gospels: viz. Matt. 24. 24. Mark 13. 22. John 4. 48. Outside the Gospels it occurs in Acts 2. 19, 22, 43; 4. 30; 5. 12; 6. 8; 7. 36; 14. 3; 15. 12. Rom. 15. 19. 2 Cor. 12. 12. 2 Thess. 2. 9. Heb. 2. 4. It does not occur in Luke's Gospel; and only once in Matthew, Mark, and John. The rendering "miracle" should be confined to this word, *teras*.

3. ***sēmeion***=a sign. This word has regard to the *significance* of the work wrought, whether in itself, or in the reason, object, design, and teaching intended to be conveyed by it. It occurs in the Gospels 48 times, viz.: 13 times in Matt.; 7 times in Mark; 11 times in Luke; and is rendered "miracle" only once (23. 8).

In John it occurs 17 times, and is quite wrongly rendered "miracle" 13 times, and "sign" only 4 times. No other word is used for a "miracle" in John, except in 4. 48 (see 2 above).

The English word "miracle" is from the Latin word *miraculum*, which means "a wonder", and should therefore be confined to the rendering of *teras* (No. 2) above, and not used for either *dunamis* (No. 1), or *sēmeion* (No. 3).

All three of the above words occur in one verse (Heb. 2. 4): "God also bearing [them] witness by signs (*sēmeion*), both with wonders (*teras*), and various mighty works (*dunamis*), and distributions of *pneuma hagion* (see Ap. 101. II. 14), according to His own will".

John does not use the first of these words (*dunamis*) at all. He uses the second (*teras*) only once (4. 48). In all the other passages he uses the third (*sēmeion*), and this 17 times. It is rendered "miracle" in all but four passages (2. 18; 4. 48; 6. 30; 20. 30, where it is correctly rendered "sign"). It should, of course, have been rendered "sign" throughout, because it has regard to that which is signified by the work wrought.

Out of all the miracles wrought by our Lord, John records only *eight*; and these are all "signs", not "wonders" or "mighty works".

The number (eight) is Divinely ordered. Of the first we read, "This beginning of the signs" (2. 11); and of the second, "This is again a second sign" (4. 54). We are thus invited to continue and carry out this important enumeration to the completion of the eighth.

Hence these eight[1] must have been Divinely selected only on account of their special *signification*.

It is ours to study them with the view of finding out what it is that is signified by them. For this purpose they are set out on page 194, according to their Structure; for, like all the other words and works of God, their *order* is perfect as well as all else connected with them.

They are at once seen to be arranged as an *Introversion*. This tells us that the *historical* order in which they were wrought must have had regard also to the *literary* order in which they are recorded.

The *Introversion* shows that the *first* corresponds with the *eighth*; the *second* corresponds with the *seventh*; the *third* with the *sixth*; and the *fourth* with the *fifth*.

Thus there are four pairs; the latter sign and signification in each pair is always an advance on the former: so that, while the former deals with what is preliminary and partial, it leads up to the latter corresponding sign, which is permanent and final.

[1] For the significance of the enumeration of the eight signs as a whole, see the Conclusion, page 195.

[For Structure see next page.]

THE SIGNIFICATION.

We are now in a position to examine these eight "signs" more minutely; and are able, at once, to see that the points which correspond are intended to emphasize the signification of each.

Two things stand out most clearly: they all manifest ISRAEL's need, and condition of helplessness and death; and MESSIAH's glory, and His ability to meet that need and restore Israel's lost condition.

We need not go outside these to learn the *signification* of these "signs". All else must be by way of *application* and not *interpretation*. Messiah was baptized and anointed by the Holy Ghost "that He might be manifested unto Israel" (John 1. 31). The first sign is called "the beginning", and the next is called the "second", to intimate to us that we are to continue the enumeration, and thus be led on to emphasize the signification of each. It "manifested forth His glory". This is the signification of the whole eight.

THE FIRST (A) AND THE EIGHTH (*A*).

The Marriage in Cana (2. 1–11), and the Draught of Fishes (21. 1–14).

The signification is the same in each case, as to Messiah. In the first He "manifested forth His glory" (2. 11); in the eighth He "manifested Himself" (21. 14, note the same word in each): as to Israel, it was to manifest the depth of the nation's destitution. He alone could supply that need by becoming "the glory of His

[*continued on* p. 195

THE EIGHT "SIGNS".

A | **2. 1-11. THE MARRIAGE IN CANA.**
a | The background. Nathanael's faith (1. 49-51).
b | The Place. Galilee (*v.* 1).
c | "The third day" (*v.* 1).
d | Wine provided (*vv.* 8, 9).
e | "Jesus was called, and His disciples" (*v.* 2).
f | Failure confessed. "They have no wine" (*v.* 3).
g | Numbers. Six waterpots, holding two or three firkins apiece (*v.* 6).
h | Command. "Fill the waterpots with water" (*v.* 7-).
i | Obedience. "They filled them" (*v.* -7-).
k | Waterpots filled to the last drop. "Up to the brim" (*v.* -7).
l | The servants bare (*ēnenkan, v.* 8).
m | Glory manifested (*ephanerōse, v.* 11-).
n | His disciples' faith (*v.* -11).

B | **4. 46-50. THE RULER'S SON.**
o | The background. Rejection (*vv.* 43, 44).
p | Time. "After two days" (*v.* 43).
q | His son. "Sick" (*ēsthenei, v.* 46).
r | Parenthetic explanation *re* the place (Cana) (*v.* 46).
s | "At the point of death" (*v.* 47). "Death" only here, and in "B". below.
t | "Ye will not believe" (*v.* 48).
u | "Ere my child die" (*v.* 49).
v | The servants "met him" (*v.* 51).
w | "Thy son liveth" (*v.* 51).
x | "The fever left him" (*aphēken, v.* 52).

C | **5. 1-47. THE IMPOTENT MAN.**
a | The Place. Jerusalem (*v.* 1).
b | The Pool. Bethesda (*v.* 2).
c | The longstanding case, "thirty-eight years" (*v.* 5).
d | "Jesus saw him" (*v.* 6).
e | The Lord takes the initiative (*v.* 6).
f | "The same day was the Sabbath" (*v.* 9).
g | "Afterward Jesus findeth him" (*v.* 14).
h | "Sin no more" (*v.* 14). Sin, only here and in "*C*", below.
i | "My Father worketh hitherto, and I work" (*v.* 17).
k | A double reference to "Moses" (*vv.* 45, 46).

D | **6. 1-14. THE FEEDING OF THE FIVE THOUSAND.**
l | The only "sign" (with *D*) recorded in the other Gospels (Matt. 14. 15. Mark 6. 35. Luke 9. 10).
m | "Jesus went up into the mountain" (*v.* 3).
n | Followed by a discourse (*vv.* 26-65). Signification.
o | "Many disciples went back" (*v.* 66).
p | The testimony of Peter (*vv.* 68, 69).

D | **6. 15-21. THE WALKING ON THE SEA.**
l | The only "sign" (with D) recorded in the other Gospels (Matt. 14. 23. Mark 6. 47).
m | "Jesus departed again into the mountain" (*v.* 15).
n | Followed by a discourse (ch. 7). Signification
o | "Many of the people believed" (7. 31).
p | The testimony of Nicodemus (7. 50).

C | **9. 1-41. THE MAN BORN BLIND.**
a | The Place. Jerusalem (8. 59; 9. 1).
b | The Pool. Siloam (*vv.* 7, 11).
c | The longstanding case, "from birth" (*v.* 1).
d | "Jesus saw" him (*v.* 1).
e | The Lord takes the initiative (*v.* 6).
f | "It was the Sabbath day" (*v.* 14).
g | "When He had found him" (*v.* 35).
h | "Who did sin?" (*v.* 2. Cp. *vv.* 24, 25, 31, 34). Sin, only here, and in "C", above.
i | "I must work the works of Him that sent Me" (*v.* 4).
k | A double reference to "Moses" (*vv.* 28, 29).

B | **11. 1-44. THE SISTERS' BROTHER.**
o | The background. Rejection (10. 31, 39; 11. 8).
p | Time. "Jesus abode two days where He was" (*v.* 6).
q | "Lazarus was sick" (*ēsthenei, v.* 2).
r | Parenthetic explanation *re* the person (Mary) (*v.* 2).
s | "Lazarus is dead" (*v.* 14). "Death" only here, and in "B", above.
t | "That ye may believe" (*v.* 15).
u | "Our brother had not died" (*v.* 21, 32).
v | Martha "met Him" (*vv.* 20, 30).
w | "Lazarus, come forth" (*v.* 43).
x | "Let him go" (*aphete, v.* 44).

A | **21. 1-14. THE DRAUGHT OF FISHES.**
a | The background. Thomas's unbelief (20. 24-29).
b | The Place. Galilee (*v.* 1).
c | "The third time" (*v.* 14).
d | A meal provided (*v.* 9).
e | The Lord was the Caller of His disciples (*vv.* 5, 12).
f | Failure confessed. They had "caught nothing" (*v.* 3). Had "no meat" (*v.* 5).
g | Numbers: 200 cubits (*v.* 8); 153 fishes (*v.* 11).
h | Command. "Cast the net into the water" (*v.* 6).
i | Obedience. "They cast therefore" (*v.* 6).
k | Net full, to the last fish (*vv.* 8, 11).
l | "Bring of the fish" (*enenkate, v.* 10).
m | The Lord manifested (*ephanerōthē, v.* 14).
n | His disciples' love (*vv.* 15-17).

People Israel" (Luke 2. 32). Apart from Messiah, Israel could have no joy, no supplies, no blessing, no glory.

The first sign signified that need: "they have no wine" (2. 3), while the last signified that with all their toil they had "caught nothing", and had "no meat"; but it signified also that Messiah could supply both the one and the other—sustenance and joy.

Religion with all its punctilious observances could not supply either. Religion grossly corrupted (cp. Isa. 1. 22), was in full evidence: the "waterpots" and "the purifying of the Jews" only manifested the truth of the inspired indictment of Isa. 1. 10–23; while the next recorded event (John 2. 13–16) manifested that they were destitute of all idea of true worship of Jehovah.

The discourses which followed carried the signification further, and showed that this spiritual destitution could be remedied only by the Divine gifts; yea, in spiritual regeneration and resurrection.

Nicodemus, who was attracted by the signs (3. 2), sought their signification, and was taught the need of spiritual birth from Ezek. 36. 24–32. The word "must" of 3. 7 and 3. 14 enforced and explained it; while the gift of God (*v.* 16) was the only answer to his question "How?"

From Jerusalem and a ruler He goes to Samaria (4. 4), like Peter in a later day (Acts 8. 14–25); and again shows, to a Samaritan woman, the need of spiritual worship, enforcing it by the same "must" (4. 24); and answering her question "How?" by the same "gift of God" (4. 10).

When Messiah gives joy to the nation, it will be filled "up to the brim" (2. 7. Cp. Isa. 9. 2–7. John 21. 11); and when He fills the Land with restored Israel in resurrection, it will be to the last one (Ezek. 37. 12–14). For in the eighth sign Messiah was the Caller, signifying that He will be the Gatherer (Jer. 31. 10); while the *seven* disciples (John 21. 2, Ap. 10) signify the spiritual perfection with which Israel will be gathered, yea, "one by one" (Isa. 27. 12) to the last one ("153"). For "though Israel be sifted among the nations, as corn is sifted in a sieve, yet shall not the least grain fall upon the earth" (Amos 9. 9).

THE SECOND (B) AND THE SEVENTH (*B*).

The Ruler's Son (4. 46–50), **and the Sisters' Brother** (11. 1–44).

If in the first and eighth the signification was national destitution of all *good*, in the second and seventh it is destitution of national *life*. The "sign" in each case was connected with *death*; and, as in all the other pairs, the latter is an advance upon the former: so here, the son being on the point of death (4. 47) in the death chamber, the brother is actually dead and in the tomb. The signification being that in the former, which took place during the first period of our Lord's ministry, which was the proclamation of the kingdom, the nation was at the point of death, though not actually dead (see Ap. 119): but in the latter case the "sign" was given in the third period when the King had been already rejected (10. 39; 11. 8, 53; 12. 10), and national life was in God's sight practically dead.

The nation's only hope was in Messiah, the great Lifegiver. He would raise it again from the dead, according to Ezek. 37. There is a reference here to Hos. 13. 14. Can there be a reference also in the "two days" (4. 43 and 11. 6) to Hos. 6. 1–3?

THE THIRD (C) AND THE SIXTH (*C*).

The Impotent Man (5. 1–47), **and the Man born Blind** (9. 1–41).

In both these two "signs" the condition of Israel is "manifested" in another phase, as being of long standing and hopeless (5. 5; 9. 1); and Messiah is manifested in His grace as the only Helper and Healer.

In both cases Messiah is the Seeker (5. 6; 9. 1), and takes the initiative; while in both the preceding pairs He was the One Who was sought.

Both "signs" were manifested in Jerusalem (5. 1 and 8. 59 with 9. 1), and thus have special reference to Government and its seat.

Both are associated with a pool (5. 2 and 9. 7, 11), and may signify that Pool of spiritual cleansing which in a future day is yet to be "opened to the house of David and to the inhabitants of Jerusalem for sin and for uncleanness" (Zech. 13. 1). In connection with this it is significant that these two "signs" are the only two out of all the eight that have any reference to *sin* (5. 14 and 9. 2, 24, 25, 34), as the second and seventh are the only two connected with *death*.

Sin had been the cause, in the case of Israel, both of the *impotence* and the *blindness*.[1]

It was the cause of Israel's thirty-eight years' typical and helpless wandering (see Ap. 50. VII; cp. 2 and 3) before the nation entered into rest; as it was the cause of the suffering of this impotent man, before he met with the great and only Giver of Rest.

This rest is emphasized by the reference to a "Sabbath-day" (5. 9 and 9. 14) and by the "sign" that Messiah (the true Joshua) can alone lead them into that true rest and sabbath-keeping that yet remains for Jehovah's People (Heb. 4. 4–10).

Messiah is Himself not only the Seeker (5. 6; and 9. 1), but He is also the Finder (5. 14 and 9. 35).

The double reference to Moses' *words* (5. 45, 46 and 9. 28, 29), and to the Father's *works* (5. 17 and 9. 4), are both "signs" also, full of the utmost significance as deepening the sin of Israel, and enhancing the grace of God Who had raised up Messiah as the Prophet, like unto Moses (Deut. 18. 15–19), and sent His Son to seek and to find and to save that which was lost (Luke 19. 9, 10).

THE FOURTH (D) AND THE FIFTH (*D*).

The Feeding of the Five Thousand (6. 1–14), **and the Walking on the Sea** (6. 15–21).

These are the two central "signs", and are emphasized by being the only "signs" which are recorded in the other three Gospels; thus implying that all four Gospels are needed in order to give us their full signification.

Both "signs" are followed by the Lord's own signification in the discourses which manifested the special glory of His Deity.

The two "signs" are connected together by the parenthesis of 6. 23, which shows that the signification is one, manifesting Messiah as Divine; in the former, as the Creator and the only Supplier of all His People's needs; temporal as in 6. 6–13, and spiritual as in 6. 32–51; in the latter, as the Creator and Lord of the elements.

The discourse which follows is to signify the enormity of the sin of His rejection, as shown in 7. 1, 11, 12, 25, 30, 32, 43, 44, 45; as the second and seventh are the only two connected with death.

Thus, these two central "signs" manifest the two central truths which are common to all the four Gospels: viz., the glory of the Messiah, and His rejection by the nation.

They were connected by His departing from them, and going up into a mountain (6. 3 and 6. 15), signifying that He was about to depart from them, until His return from heaven on the repentance of the nation.

CONCLUSION.

As to the eight "signs" as a whole, they are divided into seven and one; the seven taking place during the ministry of our Lord; and the one (the eighth) after His resurrection; the number eight being symbolical of that fact, the Resurrection having taken place on the eighth day (see Ap. 10).

The seven are divided into two, three, and two; the first two occurred in the *first* period of His ministry, which was the proclamation of the Kingdom (see Ap. 119).

[1] See *v.* 2, which shows that they believed the Babylonian "tradition" of reincarnation.

The next three (the third, fourth, and fifth) during the *second* period of His ministry, which was the manifestation of His Person as *Jehovah-Ropheka*, the Healer of His People; *Jehovah-Ro'i*, and *Jehovah-Jireh*, the Supplier of all His People's needs; and Jehovah the Creator of heaven and earth, the sea and all that in them is.

The next two (the sixth and seventh) occurred during the *third* period of His ministry, the period of His rejection; manifesting the enormity of their sin, in the rejection of Him Who is the Restorer of His People's sight, and the Lord and Giver of life. Both were parabolic and prophetic with reference to His rejection.

The eighth stands out alone, in this connection; occurring as it does in the Post-resurrection period, and referring to the future gathering of Israel by the rejected Messiah, Who is seen as the Seeker, the Finder, and the Gatherer of His scattered People, Israel.

177 THE SYNONYMOUS WORDS FOR "JUDGMENT".

1. ***aisthēsis***=perception. Occurs only in Phil. 1. 9, where A.V. reads "sense" in the margin and R.V. reads "discernment".

2. ***gnomē***, from *ginōskō* (Ap. 132. ii)=opinion, the result of knowledge. Occurs nine times: translated "purposed" in Acts 20. 3; "judgment" in 1 Cor. 1. 10; 7. 25, 40; "advice" in 2 Cor. 8. 10; "mind" in Philem. 14; Rev. 17. 13; "will" in Rev. 17. 17; and (with a verb) "agree" in Rev. 17. 17.

3. ***dikaiōma***=that which is deemed right or just (*dikaios*). Occurs ten times: translated "judgment" in Rom. 1. 32; Rev. 15. 4; elsewhere "ordinance", righteousness", and once "justification" (Rom. 5. 16).

4. ***dikē***=right, as established custom or usage, hence a suit at law, penalty, vengeance. Occurs four times: translated "judgment" in Acts 25. 15; "vengeance" in Acts 28. 4; Jude 7; and "punished" in 2 Thess. 1. 9 (see R.V.)

5. ***hēmera***=day, rendered "judgment" in 1 Cor. 4. 3 (see A.V. marg.).

6. ***krima***. This and the two following words are akin to the verb *krinō* (Ap. 122. 1). *Krima* occurs twenty-eight times, and is rendered "judgment", "damnation", or "condemnation", save in Luke 24. 20; 1 Cor. 6. 7; and Rev. 18. 20, where see notes.

7. ***krisis***=a separating, a judgment, especially of judicial proceedings. Our English word "crisis" means a turning-point. The word occurs forty-eight times: translated "damnation" (Matt. 23. 33; Mark 3. 29; John 5. 29), "condemnation" (John 3. 19; 5. 24), "accusation" (2 Pet. 2 11; Jude 9), and everywhere else "judgment".

8. ***kritērion***=the place, or means of judgment. It occurs three times (1 Cor. 6. 2, 4; James 2. 6). This word we have also adopted into the English language as a "standard" for judging.

178 THE SYNONYMOUS WORDS FOR "RAISE", "RESURRECTION", ETC.

There are eight verbs and three nouns to be noticed in this connection.

I. VERBS.

1. ***anistēmi*** (*ana*, Ap. 104. i, *histēmi*) is either transitive or intransitive, according to the tense, &c., and means to make to stand up, i.e. to raise up, or to rise up, arise, rise again. It occurs 111 times, thirty-five of which refer to resurrection. See (e.g.) Matt. 17. 9; 20. 19. John 6. 39, 40, 44, 54.

2. ***exanistēmi***. No. 1 with *ek* (Ap. 104. vii) prefixed. Not used of resurrection. Occurs only in Mark 12. 19. Luke 20. 28. Acts 15. 5.

3. ***epanistamai*** is middle voice of No. 1 with *epi* (Ap. 104. ix) prefixed. Not used of resurrection. Occurs only in Matt. 10. 21. Mark 13. 12.

4. ***egeirō***=to rouse up from sleep. Pass., to awake. Occurs 141 times, of which seventy refer to resurrection. See (e.g.) Matt. 10. 8; 27. 63, 64. Luke 20. 37; 24. 6, 34. John 12. 1, 9, 17. Eph. 1. 20; 5. 14, &c.

5. ***diegeirō***. No. 4, with *dia* (Ap. 104. v) prefixed= to rouse thoroughly. Not used of resurrection. Occurs only in Matt. 1. 24. Mark 4. 38, 39. Luke 8. 24. John 6. 18. 2 Pet. 1. 13; 3. 1 (stir up).

6. ***exegeirō***. No. 4, with *ek* (Ap. 104. vii) prefixed. Occurs only in Rom. 9. 17. 1 Cor. 6. 14.

7. ***epegeirō***. No. 4, with *epi* (Ap. 104. ix) prefixed. Not used of resurrection. Occurs only in Acts 13. 50; 14. 2.

8. ***sunegeirō***. No. 4, with *sun* (Ap. 104. xvi) prefixed. Occurs only in Eph. 2. 6. Col. 2. 12; 3. 1.

II. NOUNS.

1. ***anastasis***. Cp. I. 1. Occurs forty-two times. Always transl. resurrection, except Luke 2. 34.

2. ***exanastasis***. No. 1, with *ek* prefixed. Occurs only in Phil. 3. 11.

3. ***egersis***. Cp. I. 4. Occurs only in Matt. 27. 53.

179

I. PARALLEL DATINGS OF THE TIMES OF OUR LORD.
II. DATES OF "THE BEGETTING" AND THE NATIVITY, ETC.
III. "THE COURSE OF ABIA".

A.M.=*Anno Mundi*; i.e. in the year of the world. B.C.=*Before Christ.* Reckoned as from 4004 A.M.
A.C.=*Anno Christi*; i.e. in the year of Christ. Reckoned from the Nativity, in 4000 A.M. and 749-750 A.U.C.
A.U.C.=*Anno Urbis Conditæ*; i.e. the year in which the City (Rome) was founded.

I.

PARALLEL DATINGS OF THE TIMES OF OUR LORD.

A.M.		B.C.—A.D.		A.C.		A.U.C.					
3960		44				9					
1		43				710					
2		42				11					
3		41				12					
4		40				13					
5		39				14	Herod declared king by the Romans, according to Josephus				
6		38				15	(*Ant.* xvii. 8 § 1), who states that his death took place thirty-				
7		37				16	seven years later, and as he always reckoned his years from				
8		36				17	Nisan to Nisan (including initial and terminal fractions of Nisan				
9		35				18	as complete years), the death of Herod would be in 749-750 A.U.C.,				
3970		34				19	or 4-3 B.C.				
1		33				720			YEARS OF THE REIGN OF		
2		32				21			AUGUSTUS (OCTAVIUS).		
3	Battle of Actium	31				722		1st year of Octavius.			
4		30	Decree of Senate of Rome			23		2			
5		29				24		3			
6		28				25		4			
7		27				26		5	AUGUSTUS (Octavius) IMPERATOR.		
8		26				27		6			
9		25				28		7			
3980		24				29		8			
1		23				730		9			
2		22				31		10			
3		21				32		11			
4		20				33		12			
5		19				34		13			
6		18				35		14			
7		17				36		15			
8		16				37		16			
9		15				38		17			
3990		14				39		18			
1		13				740		19			
2		12				41		20			
3		11				42		21			
4		10				43		22			
5		9				44		23			
6		8				45		24			
7		7				46		25			
8		6		YEARS OF THE		47		26			
9		5		AGE OF THE LORD		48		27			
(See Ap. 50) 4000	THE NATIVITY	4		0		749	Herod d.*c.* end	28	Our Lord b. 15th Tisri=29th Sept. 4 B.C.		
1 {	1st taxing or Census }	3	{ Quirinus' First	1	}	750	of Jan. 3 B.C.	29			
2 {	Luke 2. 2 }	2	Governorship.	2	}	51		30			
3		1		3		52		31			
4004		0	A.D.	4		753		32	A.D. reckoning begins, owing to the mistake of		
5		1		5		54		33	*Dionysius Exiguus*, in arranging the Calendar		
6		2		6		55		34	of the Christian Era in A.D. 532.		
7		3		7		56		35			
8		4		8		57		36			
9		5		9		58		37			
4010		6		10		59		38			
1		7		11		760		39			
2		8	Christ in	12	the Temple	61		40			
3		9		13		62		41			
4	2nd Census (?)	10		14		63		42		YEARS OF THE REIGN	
5		11		15		64		43		OF TIBERIUS.	
6		12		16		65		44	1st yr. of Tiberius'	1	joint reign with Augustus.
7		13		17		66		45		2	
8		14		18		67	19th August	46	Augustus dies.	3	Tiberius alone.
9		15		19		68				4	
4020		16		20		69				5	
1		17		21		770				6	
2		18		22		71				7	
3		19		23		72				8	
4		20		24		73				9	
5		21		25		74				10	
6		22		26		75				11	
7		23		27		76				12	
8	3rd Census (?)	24		28		77				13	3rd Census this year (?).
9		25		29		78				14	
4030	The Ministry	26	of our	30	Lord	779	begins (Luke 3. 23) in the			15th	year of Tiberius.
1		27		31		780				16	
2		28		32		81				17	
ANNO MUNDI 4033	THE CRUCIFIXION	29	A.D. THE LORD	33	YEARS OF AGE.	782	A.U.C. ROMAN RECKONING.			THE 18th	,, ,,

1. ZUMPT fixes Quirinus' (Cyrenius') *First* Governorship as 4 B.C. to 1 B.C. Justin Martyr thrice says that our Lord was born under Quirinus (*Apol.* 1. XXXIV, p. 37; XLVI, p. 46; *Dial.* LXXVIII, p. 195. Clark's ed.).

2. According to some, Augustus died August 19, A.D. 14. Therefore if Tiberius' co-regnancy was for two years before Augustus' death his *first* year was 765 A.U.C.=12 A.D. His fifteenth year consequently was A.U.C. 779=26 A.D.=4030 A.M. and A.C. 30, for our Lord was thirty years of age when He begun His Ministry (Luke 3. 23). Clement of Alexandria gives the years of Augustus' reign as being 43-46, according to different reckonings in his day.

3. According to Clement of Alexandria (*c.* A.D. 190-220) "Our Lord was born in the twenty-eighth year when *first* the census was ordered to be taken in the reign of Augustus" (*Stromata*, Book i, see Clark's ed. i, pp. 444-445). If that is correct, and it is true that a Census was taken every *fourteen* years, then the next would fall in A.D. 10, and the succeeding one would have been due A.D. 24.

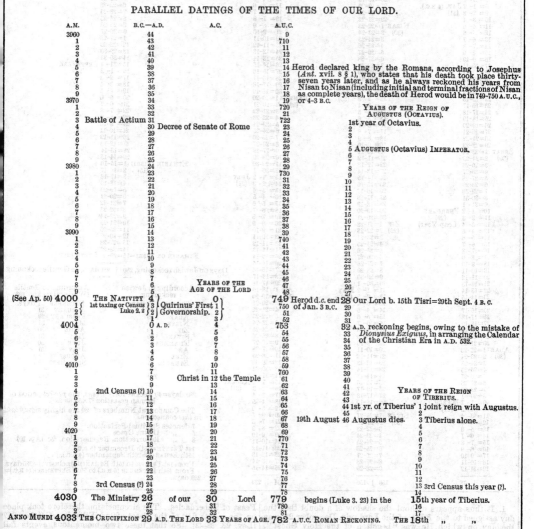

II.

DATES OF "THE BEGETTING" (*hē gennēsis*, Matt. 1. 18, 20 (see R.V. marg.). John 1. 14-) OF OUR LORD AND HIS BIRTH. (Luke 2. 7. John 1. -14.)

TEBETH	1=25-26	DEC. (5 B.C.).
(29)	2=26-27	(7)
	3=27-28	
	4=28-29	
	5=29-30	
	6=30-31	
	7=31- 1	
	8= 1- 2	JAN. (4 B.C.).
	9= 2- 3	(31)
	10= 3- 4	
	11= 4- 5	
	12= 5- 6	
	13= 6- 7	
	14= 7- 8	
	15= 8- 9	
	16= 9-10	
	17=10-11	
	18=11-12	
	19=12-13	
	20=13-14	
	21=14-15	
	22=15-16	
	23=16-17	
	24=17-18	
	25=18-19	
	26=19-20	
	27=20-21	
	28=21-22	
	29=22-23	
SEBAT	1=23-24	
(30)	2=24-25	
	3=25-26	
	4=26-27	
	5=27-28	
	6=28-29	
	7=29-30	
	8=30-31	
	9=31- 1	
	10= 1- 2	FEBRUARY
	11= 2- 3	(29)
	12= 3- 4	(Leap Year)
	13= 4- 5	
	14= 5- 6	
	15= 6- 7	
	16= 7- 8	
	17= 8- 9	
	18= 9-10	
	19=10-11	
	20=11-12	
	21=12-13	
	22=13-14	
	23=14-15	
	24=15-16	
	25=16-17	
	26=17-18	
	27=18-19	
	28=19-20	
	29=20-21	
	30=21-22	
ADAR	1=22-23	
(29)	2=23-24	
	3=24-25	
	4=25-26	
	5=26-27	
	6=27-28	
	7=28-29	
	8=29- 1	
	9= 1- 2	MARCH
	10= 2- 3	(31)
	11= 3- 4	
	12= 4- 5	
	13= 5- 6	
	14= 6- 7	
	15= 7- 8	
	16= 8- 9	
	17= 9-10	
	18=10-11	
	19=11-12	
	78 | 78	

	78 | 78	
	20=12-13	
	21=13-14	
	22=14-15	
	23=15-16	
	24=16-17	
	25=17-18	
	26=18-19	
	27=19-20	
	28=20-21	
	29=21-22	
NISAN	1=22-23	
(30)	2=23-24	
	3=24-25	
	4=25-26	
	5=26-27	
	6=27-28	
	7=28-29	
	8=29-30	
	9=30-31	
	10=31- 1	
	11= 1- 2	APRIL
	12= 2- 3	(30)
	13= 3- 4	
	14= 4- 5	
	15= 5- 6	
	16= 6- 7	
	17= 7- 8	
	18= 8- 9	
	19= 9-10	
	20=10-11	
	21=11-12	
	22=12-13	
	23=13-14	
	24=14-15	
	25=15-16	
	26=16-17	
	27=17-18	
	28=18-19	
	29=19-20	
	30=20-21	
ZIF	1=21-22	
(29)	2=22-23	
	3=23-24	
	4=24-25	
	5=25-26	
	6=26-27	
	7=27-28	
	8=28-29	
	9=29-30	
	10=30- 1	
	11= 1- 2	MAY
	12= 2- 3	(31)
	13= 3- 4	
	14= 4- 5	
	15= 5- 6	
	16= 6- 7	
	17= 7- 8	
	18= 8- 9	
	19= 9-10	
	20=10-11	
	21=11-12	
	22=12-13	
	23=13-14	
	24=14-15	
	25=15-16	
	26=16-17	
	27=17-18	
	28=18-19	
	29=19-20	
SIVAN	1=20-21	
(30)	2=21-22	
	3=22-23	
	4=23-24	
	5=24-25	
	6=25-26	
	7=26-27	
	8=27-28	
	9=28-29	
	156 | 156	

	156 | 156	
	10=29-30	
	11=30-31	
	12=31- 1	
	13= 1- 2	JUNE
	14= 2- 3	(30)
	15= 3- 4	
	16= 4- 5	
	17= 5- 6	
	18= 6- 7	
	19= 7- 8	
	20= 8- 9	
	21= 9-10	
	22=10-11	
	23=11-12	
	24=12-13	
	25=13-14	
	26=14-15	
	27=15-16	
	28=16-17	
	29=17-18	
	30=18-19	
THAMMUZ	1=19-20	
(29)	2=20-21	
	3=21-22	
	4=22-23	
	5=23-24	
	6=24-25	
	7=25-26	
	8=26-27	
	9=27-28	
	10=28-29	
	11=29-30	
	12=30- 1	
	13= 1- 2	JULY
	14= 2- 3	(31)
	15= 3- 4	
	16= 4- 5	
	17= 5- 6	
	18= 6- 7	
	19= 7- 8	
	20= 8- 9	
	21= 9-10	
	22=10-11	
	23=11-12	
	24=12-13	
	25=13-14	
	26=14-15	
	27=15-16	
	28=16-17	
	29=17-18	
AB	1=18-19	
(30)	2=19-20	
	3=20-21	
	4=21-22	
	5=22-23	
	6=23-24	
	7=24-25	
	8=25-26	
	9=26-27	
	10=27-28	
	11=28-29	
	12=29-30	
	13=30-31	
	14=31- 1	
	15= 1- 2	AUGUST
	16= 2- 3	(31)
	17= 3- 4	
	18= 4- 5	
	19= 5- 6	
	20= 6- 7	
	21= 7- 8	
	22= 8- 9	
	23= 9-10	
	24=10-11	
	25=11-12	
	26=12-13	
	27=13-14	
	28=14-15	
	234 | 234	

	234 | 234	
	29=15-16	
	30=16-17	
ELUL	1=17-18	
(29)	2=18-19	
	3=19-20	
	4=20-21	
	5=21-22	
	6=22-23	
	7=23-24	
	8=24-25	
	9=25-26	
	0=26-27	
	1=27-28	
	12=28-29	
	13=29-30	
	14=30-31	
	15=31- 1	SEPTEMBER
	16= 1- 2	(29)
	17= 2- 3	
	18= 3- 4	
	19= 4- 5	
	20= 5- 6	
	21= 6- 7	
	22= 7- 8	
	23= 8- 9	
	24= 9-10	
	25=10-11	
	26=11-12	
	27=12-13	
	28=13-14	
	29=14-15	
ETHANIM (TISRI)	1=15-16	
(15)	2=16-17	
	3=17-18	
	4=18-19	
	5=19-20	
	6=20-21	
	7=21-22	
	8=22-23	
	9=23-24	
	10=24-25	
	11=25-26	
	12-26-27	
	13=27-28	
	14=28-29	
ETHANIM OR TISRI—	15=29-30	SEPTEMBER

Days on Jewish reckoning, 280 | 280 days, on Gentile reckoning.

According to Jewish reckoning.		According to Gentile (Western) reckoning.	
TEBETH	29 days.	DECEMBER	7 days.
SEBAT	30	JANUARY	31
ADAR	29	FEBRUARY	29
NISAN	30	MARCH	31
ZIF	29	APRIL	30
SIVAN	30	MAY	31
THAMMUZ	29	JUNE	30
AB	30	JULY	31
ELUL	29	AUGUST	31
ETHANIM	15	SEPTEMBER	29
	280		280

280 days=40 weeks—forty *sevens*, the *perfect* period of human gestation [7×5×8=280].

The Component Numbers of 280 are highly *significant* in *this connection.*

7 denotes Spiritual Perfection.
5 ,, Divine Grace.
8 ,, Resurrection, Regeneration, &c. (Ap. 10).

1st TEBETH=25th December (5 B.C.).
15th ETHANIM=29th September (4 B.C.).

From 1st TEBETH to 15th ETHANIM (inclusive)=280 days.
From 25th DECEMBER (5 B.C.) to 29th SEPTEMBER (4 B.C.)= 280 days.

1. It thus appears without the shadow of a doubt that the day assigned to the *Birth* of the Lord, viz. December 25, was the day on which He was "begotten of the Holy Ghost", i.e. by *pneuma hagion*=divine power (Matt. 1. 18, 20 marg.), and His birth took place on the 15th of *Ethanim*, September 29, in the year following, thus making beautifully clear the meaning of John 1. 14, "The Word *became flesh*" (Matt. 1. 18, 20) on 1st *Tebeth* or December 25 (5 B.C.), "and *tabernacled* (Gr. *eskēnōsen*) with us", on 15th of Ethanim or September 29 (4 B.C.).

The 15th of Ethanim (or Tisri) was the *first* day of the Feast of Tabernacles. The circumcision therefore took place on the *eighth* day of the Feast=22nd Ethanim=October 6-7 (Lev. 23. 33-43). So that these two momentous events fall into their proper place and order, and the *real reason* is made clear why the 25th of December is associated with our Lord, and was set apart by the Apostolic Church to commemorate the stupendous event of the "Word becoming flesh"—and not, as we have for so long been led to suppose, the commemoration of a pagan festival.

2. An overwhelmingly strong argument in favour of the

correctness of this view lies in the fact that the *date* of "the Festival of Michael and All Angels" has been from very early times the 29th day of September, on Gentile (Western) reckoning.

But "the Church" even then had lost sight of the reason why this date rather than any other in the Calendar should be so indissolubly associated with the great Angelic Festival.

The following expresses the almost universal knowledge or rather want of knowledge of "Christendom" on the subject: "We pass on now to consider, in the third place, the commemoration of September 29, the festival of Michaelmas, *par excellence*. It does not appear at all certain what was the *original* special idea of the commemoration of this day" (Smith's *Dict. of Chr. Antiqq.* (1893), vol. ii, p. 1177 (3)).

A reference, however, to the Table and statements above, makes the "*original* special idea" why the Festival of "Michael and All Angels" is held on September 29 abundantly clear. Our Lord was *born* on that day, the first day of the "Feast of Tabernacles" (Lev. 23. 39). This was on the *fifteenth* day of the seventh Jewish month called *Tisri*, or *Ethanim* (Ap. 51. 5), corresponding to our September 29 (of the year 4 B.C.).

The "Begetting" (*gennēsis*) Day of the Lord was announced by the Angel Gabriel. See notes on Dan. 8. 16, and Luke 1. 19.

The "Birth" Day, by "(the) Angel of the Lord", unnamed in either Matthew and Luke.

That this Angelic Being was "Michael the Archangel" (of Jude 9), and *Mīkā'ēl hassar haggādōl*—"Michael the Great Prince"—of Dan. 12. 1, seems clear for the following reason: If, "when *again* (yet future) He bringeth the First-begotten into the world, He saith, Let *all* the Angels of God worship Him" (Heb. 1. 6; quoting Ps. 97. 6)—then this must include the great Archangel Michael himself. By parity of reasoning, on the *First* "bringing" into the world of the only begotten Son, the Archangel must have been present. And the tremendous announcement to the shepherds, that the Prince of Peace (Isa. 9. 6) was on earth in the person of the Babe of Bethlehem, must therefore have been made by the same head of the heavenly host (Luke 2. 9-14). In mundane affairs, announcements of supremest importance (of kings, &c.) are invariably conveyed through the most exalted personage in the realm. The point need not be laboured.

3. The fact of the *Birth* of our Lord having been revealed to the shepherds by the Archangel Michael on the 15th of *Tisri* (or *Ethanim*), corresponding to September 29, 4 B.C.—the *first* day of the Feast of Tabernacles—must have been known to believers in the Apostolic Age. But "the mystery of iniquity" which was "already working" in Paul's day (2 Thess. 2. 7) quickly enshrouded this and the other great fact of the day of the Lord's "begetting" on the first day of the Jewish month *Tebeth* (corresponding to December 25, 5 B.C.)—as well as other events connected with His sojourn on earth,[1]—in a rising mist of obscurity in which they have ever since been lost.

The earliest allusion to December 25 (modern reckoning) as the date for the Nativity is found in the *Stromata* of Clement of Alexandria, about the beginning of the *third* century A.D. (See note 3, p. 197).[2]

That "Christmas" was a pagan festival long before the time of our Lord is beyond doubt. In Egypt Horus (or Harpocrates[3]), the son of Isis (Queen of Heaven), was born about the time of the winter solstice.[4] By the time of the early part of the fourth century A.D., the *real* reason for observing Christmas as the date for the miraculous "begetting" of Matt. 1. 18 and "the Word becoming flesh" of John 1. 14 had been lost sight of. The policy of Constantine, and his *Edict of Milan*, by establishing universal freedom of religion furthered this. When many of the followers of the old pagan systems—the vast majority of the empire, it must be remembered—adopted the Christian religion as a cult, which Constantine had made fashionable, and the "Church" became the Church of the Roman Empire, they brought in with them, among a number of other things emanating from Egypt and Babylon, the various Festival Days of the old "religions". Thus "Christmas Day," the *birthday* of the Egyptian Horus (Osiris), became gradually substituted for the real *Natalis Domini* of our blessed Saviour, viz. September 29, or *Michaelmas Day*.

4. If, however, we realize that the centre of gravity, so to speak, of what we call the Incarnation is the *Incarnation itself*—the wondrous fact of the Divine "begetting", when "the Word *became* flesh" (see notes on Matt. 1. 18 and John 1. 14)—and that this is to be associated with December 25, instead of March—as for 1,600 years Christendom has been led to believe—then "Christmas" will be seen in quite another light, and many who have hitherto been troubled with scruples concerning the day being, as they have been taught, the anniversary of a Pagan festival, will be enabled to worship on that Day without alloy of doubt, as the time when the stupendous miracle which is the foundation stone of the Christian faith, came to pass.

The "Annunciation" by the Angel Gabriel marked the *gennēsis* of Matt. 1. 18, and the first words of John 1. 14.

The announcement to the shepherds by the Archangel Michael marked the Birth of our Lord. John 1. 14 is read as though "the Word became flesh (R.V.), and dwelt among us", were one and the same thing, whereas they are *two* clauses.

The paragraph should read thus:

"And the Word became flesh;
(Gr. *ho logos sarx egeneto*.)
And tabernacled with (or among) us."
(Gr. *kai eskēnōsen en hēmin*).

The word *tabernacled* here (preserved in R.V. marg.) receives beautiful significance from the knowledge that "the Lord of Glory" was "*found* in fashion as a man", and thus *tabernacling* in human flesh. And in turn it shows in equally beautiful significance that our Lord was born on the first day of the great Jewish Feast of *Tabernacles*, viz. the 15th of Tisri, corresponding to September 29, 4 B.C. (modern reckoning).

The Circumcision of our Lord took place therefore on the *eighth* day, the last day of the Feast, the "Great Day of the Feast" of John 7. 37 ("Tabernacles" had eight days. The Feast of Unleavened Bread had seven days, and Pentecost one. See Lev. 23).

5. The main arguments *against* the Nativity having taken place in December may be set forth very simply:

(i) The extreme improbability, amounting almost to impossibility, that Mary, under such circumstances, could have undertaken a journey of about 70 miles (as the crow flies), through a hill district averaging some 3,000 feet above sea-level, in the depth of winter:

(ii) Shepherds and their flocks would not be found "abiding" (Gr. *agrauleō*) in the open fields at night in December (Tebeth), for the paramount reason that there would be no pasturage at that time. It was the custom then (as now) to withdraw the flocks during the month *Marchesvan* (Oct.-Nov.)[1] from the open districts and house them for the winter.

(iii) The Roman authorities in imposing such a "census taking" for the hated and unpopular "foreign"

[1] Notably the day of the crucifixion, &c. (see Ap. 156, 165).
[2] His statements are, however, very vague, and he mentions several dates claimed by others as correct.
[3] Osiris reincarnated.
[4] See Wilkinson's *Ancient Egyptians*, Vol. III, p.79 (Birch's ed.).

[1] It is true that the Lebanon shepherds are in the habit of keeping their flocks alive during the winter months, by cutting down branches of trees in the forests in that district, to feed the sheep on the leaves and twigs, when in autumn the pastures are dried up, and in winter, when snow covers the ground (cp. *Land and Book*, p. 204), but there is no evidence that the Bethlehem district was afforested in this manner.

tax would not have enforced the imperial decree (Luke 2. 1) at the most inconvenient and inclement season of the year, by compelling the people to enroll themselves at their respective "cities" in December. In such a case they would naturally choose the "line of least resistance", and select a time of year that would cause least friction, and interference with the habits and pursuits of the Jewish people. This would be in the autumn, when the agricultural round of the year was complete, and the people generally more or less at liberty to take advantage, as we know many did, of the opportunity of "going up" to Jerusalem for the "Feast of Tabernacles" (cp. John 7. 8-10, &c.), the crowning Feast of the Jewish year.

To take advantage of such a time would be to the Romans the simplest and most natural policy, whereas to attempt to enforce the Edict of Registration for the purposes of Imperial taxation in the depth of winter,—when travelling for such a purpose would have been deeply resented, and perhaps have brought about a revolt,—would never have been attempted by such an astute ruler as Augustus.

6. With regard to the other two "Quarter Days", June 24, March 25, these are both associated with the miraculous (Luke 1. 7) "conception" and birth of the Forerunner, as December 25 and September 29 are with our Lord's miraculous "Begetting" and Birth; and are therefore connected with "the Course of Abiah."

III.

"THE COURSE OF ABIA" (Luke 1. 5).

This was the *eighth* of the priestly courses of ministration in the Temple (1 Chron. 24. 10), and occurred, as did the others, twice in the year.

The "Courses" were changed every week, beginning each with a Sabbath. The reckoning commenced on the 22nd day of Tisri or Ethanim (Ap. 51. 5). This was the eighth and last day of the Feast of Tabernacles=the "Great Day of the Feast" (John 7. 37), and was a Sabbath (Lev. 23. 39).

The first course fell by lot to Jehoiarib, and the eighth to Abia or Abijah (1 Chron. 24. 10).

Bearing in mind that *all* the courses served together at the three Great Feasts, the dates for the two yearly "ministrations" of Abiah will be seen to fall as follows:

The first [1] ministration was from 12-18 Chisleu= December 6-12.

The second ministration was from 12-18 Sivan = June 13-19.

The announcement therefore to Zacharias in the Temple as to the conception of John the Baptist took place between 12-18 SIVAN (June 13-19), in the year 5 B.C. After finishing his "ministration", the aged priest "departed to his own house" (Luke 1. 23), which was in a city [2] in "the hill country" of Juda (verse 39).

The day following the end of the "Course of Abia" being a Sabbath (Sivan 19), he would not be able to leave Jerusalem before the 20th.

The thirty miles journey would probably occupy, for an old man, a couple of days at least. He would therefore arrive at his house on the 21st or 22nd. This leaves ample time for the miraculous "conception" of Elizabeth to take place on or about the 23rd of SIVAN [3]—which would correspond to June 23-24 of that year. The fact of the conception and *its date* would necessarily be known at the time and afterwards, and hence the 23rd SIVAN would henceforth be associated with the conception of John Baptist as the 1st TEBETH would be with that of our Lord.

But the same influences that speedily obscured and presently obliterated the real dates of our Lord's "Begetting" and Birth, were also at work with regard to those of the Forerunner, and with the same results. As soon as the true *Birth* day of Christ had been shifted from its proper date, viz. the 15th of Tisri (September 29), and a Festival Day from the Pagan Calendars substituted for it (viz. December 25), then everything else had to be altered too.

Hence "Lady Day" in association with March 25 (new style) became necessarily connected with the Annunciation. And June 24 made its appearance, as it still is in our Calendar, as the date of "the *Nativity* of John the Baptist", instead of, as it really is, the date of his miraculous conception.

The Four "Quarter Days" may therefore be set forth thus: first in the chronological order of the events with which they are associated, viz.:

The conception of John Baptist	on or about 23rd SIVAN	= June 24	in the year 5 B.C.
The *Gennēsis* (Begetting) of our Lord	" " 1st TEBETH	= December 25	" " 5 "
The birth of John Baptist	" " 4th—7th NISAN	= March 25-28	" " 4 "
The birth of our Lord	" " 15th TISRI	= September 29	" " 4 "

or, placing the two sets together naturally:—

{ The conception of John	23rd SIVAN	= June 23-24	" " 5 "
{ The birth of John	7th NISAN	= March 28-29	" " 4 "
{ The Miraculous "Begetting"	1st TEBETH	= December 25	" " 5 "
{ The NATIVITY	15th TISRI	= September 29	" " 4 "

---

[1] Reckoning of course from *Ethanim* or *Tisri*—the *First* month of the civil year. The sacred year was six months later, and began on 1st *Nisan*.

[2] The "city" is not named (possibly *Juttah*, some 30 miles to the south of Jerusalem).

[3] The conception of John the Baptist was, in view of Luke 1. 7, as miraculous as that of Isaac; but it is not necessary to insist upon the complete period of *forty sevens* (p. 198) in the case of Elizabeth. Therefore the birth of the Forerunner may have been three or four days short of the full two hundred and eighty days,—as indicated in the above table.

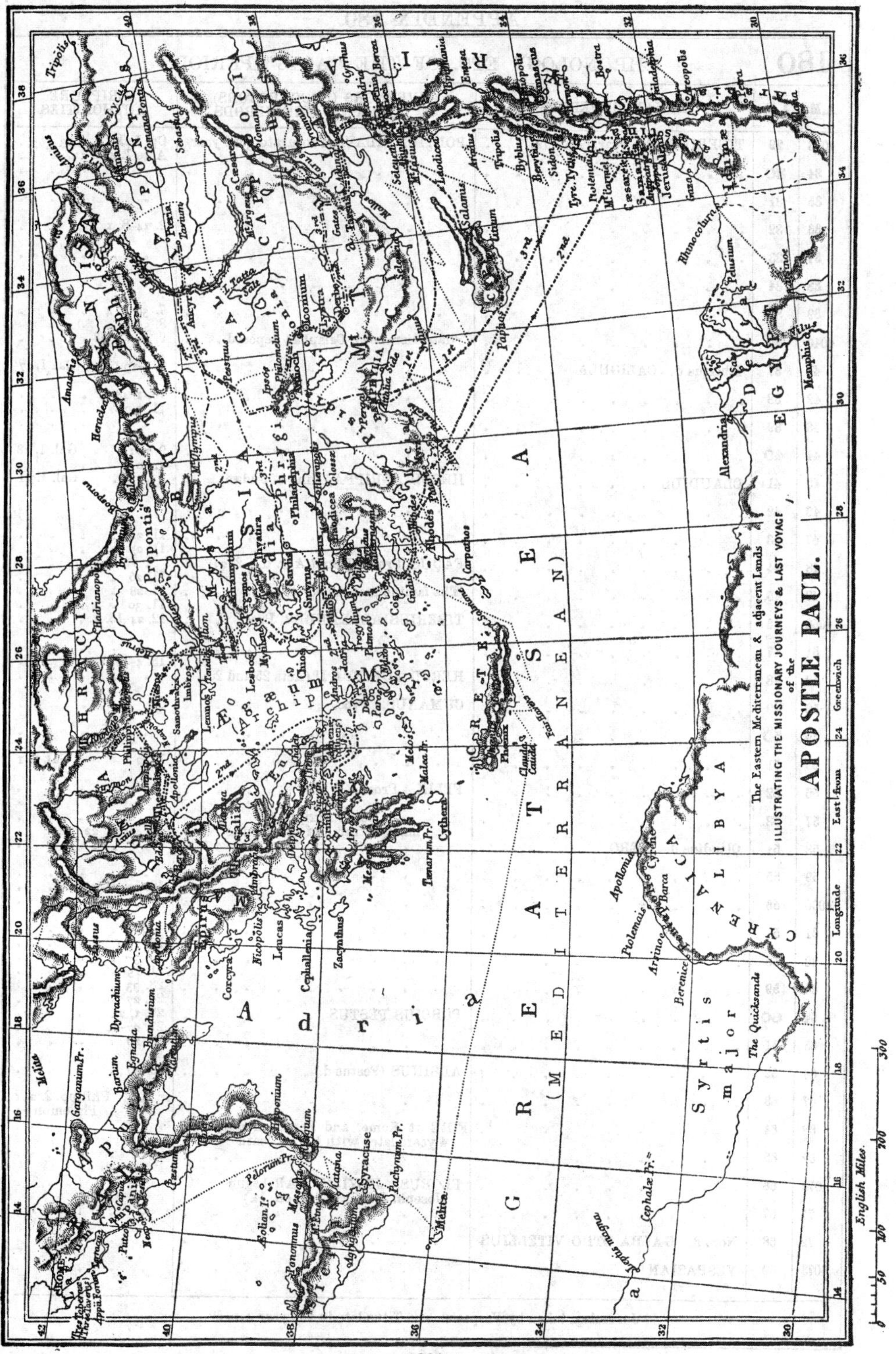
The Eastern Mediterranean & adjacent lands
ILLUSTRATING THE MISSIONARY JOURNEYS & LAST VOYAGE
of the
APOSTLE PAUL.
GREAT SEA
(MEDITERRANEAN)
Adria
Ægæum
Archipelago
CRETE
CYPRUS
LIBYA
CYRENAICA
EGYPT
Syrtis major
The Quicksands
Alexandria
Propontis
Melita
Syracuse
Antioch
Damascus
Jerusalem
Longitude East from Greenwich
English Miles

180 CHRONOLOGY ETC. OF THE "ACTS" PERIOD.

A.M.	A.D.	ROMAN EMPERORS	GOVERNORS (PROCURATORS) OF JUDÆA AND THE HERODS	SCRIPTURE AUTHORITIES
4033	29	TIBERIUS (18th year) (Ap. 179)	PONTIUS PILATE, Procurator (3rd year)	Cp. Luke 3. 1, 23 Acts 1. 4-2. 13
34	**30**			
35	31			
36	32			2. 14-8. 1
37	33			
38	34			
39	35			7. 59-8. 4 8. 5-40
4040	36		Pilate dismissed, Caiaphas deposed	9. 32-10. 48
41	37	Tiberius d. CALIGULA		9. 1-19; Gal. 1. 17
42	38			10. 1-48 11. 1-18
43	39			
44	**40**			9. 26; Gal. 1. 18 9. 30
45	41	CLAUDIUS	HEROD AGRIPPA, King of Judæa	Gal. 1. 21
46	42			
47	43			11. 22 11. 25
48	44		FADUS, Proc. Herod Agr. d. (12. 23)	11. 26
49	45		(The famine mentioned in)	11. 28 11. 30
4050	46		TIBERIUS ALEXANDER, Proc.	12. 24-13. 3
51	47			13. 4-15. 1
52	48		HEROD AGRIPPA II (Acts 25 and 26)	
53	49		CUMANUS. Proc.	
54	**50**			
55	51			15. 2; Gal. 2. 1
56	52		FELIX. Proc.	
57	53		Herod Agrippa II made Tetrarch of Trachonitis	15. 41-18. 22
58	54	Claudius d. NERO		
59	55			18. 23-20. 1
4060	56			
61	57			20. 1, 2
62	58			20. 3- 21. 15
63	59			23. 33 24. 27
64	**60**		PORCIUS FESTUS	27. 1, 2 27. 27-44
65	61			28. 16
66	62		ALBINUS (Festus d.)	28. 30
67	63			Philipp. 2. 24; Philemon 22
68	64		FIRE at Rome, and Persecution ending 4 years later with Nero's death	
69	65			
4070	66		FLORUS. JEWISH WAR begun (Joseph. J. W., Bk. II. ch. 14.)	
71	67			1 Tim. 1. 3
72	68	Nero d. GALBA OTHO VITELLIUS		
4073	69	VESPASIAN[1]		

[1] Jerusalem taken by Vespasian and Titus late in the year A.D. 69.

APPENDIX 180.

CHRONOLOGY ETC. OF THE "ACTS" PERIOD. **180**

MAIN EVENTS RECORDED IN THE "ACTS", &c.		STRUCTURE	A.D.
Christ's DEATH (April 3), RESURRECTION (April 7), ASCENSION (May 13); PENTECOST (May 23) See Ap. 156. Cp. Ap. 179, p. 198.			29
(Equipment of the Twelve for their forthcoming Ministry). (See Structure, p. 1576.)			**30**
			31
(The Ministry of Peter and John and others to the nation. In Jerusalem. (See Structures, pp. 1576-1591.)			32
			33
			34
Martyrdom of Stephen, and beginning of the DIASPORA Ministry. Philip's Mission in Samaria and results.			35
PETER'S MISSION throughout the land of Israel begins.			36
PAUL'S "CONVERSION". Goes to Arabia (Sinai? 40 days?).	Returns to Damascus. Gal. 1. 17.	B p. 1575	37
[Peter and Cornelius, ending with Peter's arraignment at Jerusalem, and result.]	PAUL escapes from ,, Acts 9. 25; 2 Cor. 11. 33.		38
	Goes to Tarsus (?) and thence in the following year "up to Jerusalem".		39
PAUL'S FIRST visit to Jerusalem "to see Peter". Afterwards "sent" to Tarsus.	{The trance in the Temple and Commission to the Gentiles} Acts 22. 17.		**40**
,, Mission in Syria and Cilicia.			41
			42
Barnabas "sent" from JERUSALEM to ANTIOCH, ,, goes to Tarsus "to seek Saul" and	(Paul's "rapture". 2 Cor. 12. 1-4) (?)		43
brings him to Antioch—where they stay for "a whole year".			44
as occurring in the days of *Claudius*.) PAUL'S SECOND visit to Jerusalem. With Barnabas.	EPISTLE OF JAMES to the *Diaspora* (?). "Relief Commission" from Antioch.		45
Return to Antioch. Mission of the Holy Ghost.	Paul and Barnabas "separated" and "sent".		46
Paul's Ministry among the *Diaspora* apart from Jerusalem and the Twelve begins from ANTIOCH to CYPRUS. Perga in Pamphylia. Antioch in Pisidia, Iconium, Lystra,	EPISTLE OF JUDE (?) (*Diaspora*).		47
Derbe and thence back to ANTIOCH. "And there they abode long time with the disciples" (14. 28).			48
			49
			50
PAUL'S THIRD visit to Jerusalem, for "the Council", with Barnabas and Titus: Ministry in association with Jerusalem and the Twelve.			51
From ANTIOCH to Cilicia, Lycaonia, Galatia.	**THE EPISTLES**		52
Philippi. Thessalonica. Berea. Athens, and CORINTH (for 18 months. 18. 11) writes	I THESSALONIANS, II THESSALONIANS, AND HEBREWS (see p. 1823).		53
"Sailed thence into Syria" (Spring 54), Ephesus (1st visit), Cæsarea JERUSALEM, FOURTH visit, and ANTIOCH (18. 18-22).		*B* p. 1575	54
"After some time there" (18. 23) visits Galatia, Phrygia, and EPHESUS (2nd visit). There stays for two years (19. 10).	JOHANNINE EPISTLES about this time (?)		55
(Public proclaiming of the kingdom ends 19. 20.)	(see p. 1870).		56
At Ephesus Paul (in the Spring of 57) writes . . . . . . After the departure from Ephesus, goes to Macedonia and writes .	I CORINTHIANS (Spring). II CORINTHIANS (Autumn).		57
Paul leaves Greece, Philippi, Miletus, Cæsarea, and goes to Jerusalem (Pentecost). FIFTH visit. Arrested.	GALATIANS (Winter). ROMANS, from Corinth (Spring).		58
Sent to Cæsarea, and the 2 years' imprisonment at Cæsarea.			59
PAUL sent to Rome by Festus (about August). Shipwrecked at Malta (Winter).	I PETER } (?) II PETER }		**60**
Arrives at ROME (Spring). PAUL'S FIRST IMPRISONMENT at ROME (A. D. 61-63).	(see p. 1855).		61
Two years, during which are written	{EPHESIANS, PHILIPPIANS, COLOSSIANS,[1] PHILEMON.		62
After his acquittal Paul goes to Macedonia (?).	ACTS published (?)		63
			64
			65
			66
From Macedonia (?) or Troas (?) Paul writes . . . . ,, Corinth (?) ,, ,,	I TIMOTHY. TITUS.		67
In PRISON at Rome ,, ,,	II TIMOTHY.		68
			69

[1] The Chronological order according to Lightfoot, *Biblical Essays* (p. 222), is Philipp., Coloss., Ephes.

181 THE DISPENSATIONAL POSITION OF THE BOOK OF THE "ACTS".

1. The original title of the Book was probably simply "Acts" (*praxeis*), as in *Codex Sinaiticus* (א), and there is no reason to doubt that it owes its human authorship to Luke, "the beloved physician" (Col. 4. 14). Tradition from very early times ascribes it to him. Eusebius (*fl.* A.D. 300) in his *Ecclesiastical History* says, "Luke . . . a physician has left us two inspired books . . . one of these is his gospel. . . . The other is his acts of the apostles which he composed not from what he had heard from others (like his gospel), but from what he had seen himself" (Bk. III, ch. 4).

2. The Book is a record of the "Acts" of the Holy Spirit through "witnesses chosen before of God" (10. 41) during the period of the final offer to the children of Israel of national restoration and blessing, on condition of national repentance and obedience. In the O.T. the offer was made by the FATHER, as Jehovah, through the prophets (Heb. 1. 1), and was rejected (cp. Zech. 7. 12–14; &c.). In the Gospels the offer was renewed *in* and *by* the SON, and was again rejected (Matt. 23. 37–39; &c.). "Acts" records the third and final presentation by the HOLY SPIRIT, and its final rejection by the Nation (28. 25–28. Rom. 11. 25, &c.). Of these "chosen witnesses" no mention is made of "works" done by any save those through Peter and John of the Twelve, and later those through Paul.

3. The Structure (p. 1575) shows that the Book consists of two main divisions (cp. the Structures of Isaiah, Jeremiah, Ezekiel, &c.), each being divided in beautiful correspondence (see detail Structures).

The FIRST portion, consisting of the first twelve chapters (after the introduction 1. 1–5), concerns the "witness" (1. 8) of the apostles in Jerusalem, Judæa, and Samaria (Ap. 180). Peter, the apostle of "the circumcision" (Gal. 2. 7), is the central figure, and this section ends with his imprisonment at Jerusalem (A.D. 44).

The SECOND division, i.e. the last sixteen chapters, carries on the "witnessing" "unto the uttermost part of the earth" (cp. 1. 8; Col. 1. 23), Paul being the chief personage (Gal. 2. 7). This division terminates with his imprisonment at Rome in A.D. 61 (Ap. 180). "Acts" was most probably published towards the end of that imprisonment, i.e. A.D. 62–63.

The period covered by the entire Book is therefore as follows:

i. From Pentecost A.D. 29 to Passover (12. 3, 4) A.D. 44;
ii. From Pentecost (?) A.D. 46 to A.D. 61.

Consecutively, from A.D. 29 to A.D. 61 = 32 years (4 × 8 = 32. Ap. 10). This must not be confounded with the whole period between the Crucifixion, the climax of the national rejection of the Lord as Messiah, and the destruction of Jerusalem by Titus, viz. from A.D. 29 to A.D. 69; that is, 40 years (Ap. 10).

4. The DISPENSATIONAL TEACHING OF "ACTS" is of profoundest import, and is significantly set forth by the Structures; cp. also Ap. 180.

In the earlier section, the "witnessing" of the Twelve, as recorded from 2. 5 to the end of chap. 12, was to "Jews and proselytes" (2. 10) alone; "unto you (Jews) first" (3. 26), &c. Their *subject* was that Jesus ("the Nazarene") IS the Messiah; cp. 2. 31, 36; 3. 18, 20; 4. 10, 26; 5. 42; 8. 5, 37 (see Note); 9. 20, 22. At Damascus, after his "Conversion", Saul (Paul) "preached (*kērussō*, Ap. 121. 1) Jesus (see Note on 9. 20) in the synagogues, that He is the Son of God", and proved "that this is very Christ", i.e. Jesus as the Messiah. There was no proclamation to Gentiles *as such* (see 11. 3). The preaching of the Word was to the Jews only (11. 19), and to the Gentile proselytes, that the crucified "Nazarene", Jesus, was in truth the Messiah (see Note on 10. 48). The duration of this witnessing was about 15 years; see above and Ap. 180. The second part of "Acts" records the apostleship of Paul, and his "witnessing", which was to Jews and Gentiles alike. He was the "chosen vessel" separated by the Holy Spirit "to bear My Name before Gentiles and Kings, and sons of Israel" (*huiōn te Israēl*, 9. 15). *His subject* was "Jesus and the resurrection" (17. 18). Not, be it marked, Jesus as Messiah, but Jesus (Saviour-God), raised from among the dead, and made the federal Head of a new race of beings by resurrection, as announced in Ps. 2. 7, with which comp. 13. 32–39, and see Notes. This "witnessing" lasted the 15–16 years (see 3 above) of the labours of Paul and those associated with him till the imprisonment in A.D. 61. And to the Jew was given priority of hearing the message (13. 5, 14, 42, 43; 14. 1; 17. 1, 10, 17; 18. 4, 7, 19, 26; 19. 8).

5. Throughout the whole period of the "Acts", the witnessing was accompanied by the miraculous gifts promised (Mark 16. 17, 18). Cp. 3. 7, 8; 5. 5, 10, 15, 16; 6. 8; 8. 6, 7, 13; 9. 33–42; 11. 28; 13. 11; 14. 8–10; 16. 18; 19. 6, 12; 20. 9–12; 28. 3–6, 8, 9. At the close these gifts ceased, as is plain from the significance of Phil. 2. 26 (A.D. 62); 1 Tim. 5. 23 (A.D. 67); 2 Tim. 4. 20 (A.D. 68). See Ap. 180. Thenceforward, the privilege of proclaiming and "witnessing" (Isa. 43. 10; 44. 8, &c.) was taken from the Jew, and "the salvation of God" (see Note on Isa. 49. 6) was "sent[1] to the Gentiles" (28. 28). The proclamation is now by witnesses taken out from among "all the Gentiles upon whom My Name is called" (15. 17), including of course the Jewish members of "the body".

6. Having now before us all the "sequence of fact" (cp. also the Structure, p. 1575, and Ap. 180), we can trace "the progress of doctrine", the development of *dispensational teaching* in Acts, as well as in the complementary "Church" Epistles of Paul, and the limitations of the strictly Hebrew Epistles (Ap. 180, and Introd. Notes to each). Our Lord's words in John 16. 12, 13, are precious, and they are precise (see Note *in loc.*). The Gospels record what the Lord "*began* to do and teach" (1. 1); after His resurrection He continued "speaking of the things pertaining to the Kingdom" (Ap. 112); and after His Ascension the teaching is carried on by the Holy Spirit, the Spirit of the truth (John 14. 16, 17, 26; 15. 26), Who was to guide (lead on) into "all the truth" (see Notes, John 16. 12, 13). During the "Acts" period, believers were guided into much truth, truth in advance of what had previously been revealed. They were instructed in much that they had been unable "to bear" before the coming of the Holy Spirit to instruct them. But not even yet had they been guided into "all the truth". This was reserved, and not permitted to be revealed, until the public proclaiming of "the kingdom" had ended, after the close of the "Acts". (See the Notes on the Epp., specially *Ephesians*, *Philippians*, *Colossians*.) Then it was, at the commencement of this present interim period during which "blindness in part is happened to Israel" (Rom. 11. 25), that "the church which is His body" (Eph. 1. 22, 23) began to be formed "to the praise of the glory of His grace" (Eph. 1. 6, and Note on 15. 14). As above stated, and as the facts show, this church did *not* begin at Pentecost as is so commonly taught and believed.

[1] Sent = sent away; Gr. *apostellō*. Implying the mission or commission employed, and the power and authority backing it (Ap. 174. 1).

182 THE LORD'S BRETHREN.

According to Matt. 13. 55, the Lord had four brothers (i. e. half-brothers, as we say), James, Joses, Simon, and Judas. He had at least three sisters also,—"and His sisters, are they not all with us?" Had there been but two, the word *all* would have been *both*.

The Lord is called Mary's "firstborn" (Matt. 1. 25 and Luke 2. 7), and the natural inference is that Mary had other children. The word *prōtotokos* is used only in these two passages and in Rom. 8. 29; Col. 1. 15, 18; Heb. 1. 6; 11. 28; 12. 23 (pl.); Rev. 1, 5, so that the meaning is easily ascertained. Had He been her *only* son, the word would have been *monogenēs*, which occurs in Luke 7. 12; 8. 42; 9. 38, of human parentage; and of the Lord, as the only-begotten of the Father, in John 1. 14, 18; 3. 16, 18; 1 John 4. 9. In Heb. 11. 17 it is used of Isaac, Abraham's only son according to the promise.

In Psalm 69, a Psalm with many predictive allusions to the Lord's earthly life (see Note on Title), verse 8 reads, "I am become a stranger unto my brethren, and an alien unto my mother's children". The Gospel history records His brethren in association with His mother. After the miracle at Cana, which they probably witnessed, we are told that "He went down to Capernaum, He, and His mother, and His brethren, and His disciples" (John 2. 12). Later on they exhibit a spirit of opposition or jealousy, for while He is speaking to the people, His brethren, accompanied by His mother, sought Him, apparently to hinder His work (Matt. 12. 46, 47; Mark 3. 31, 32; Luke 8. 19, 20). In Mark 3. 21 we read, "When His friends heard of it, they went out to lay hold on Him; for they said, He is beside Himself". The expression "His friends" (margin "kinsmen") is *hoi par' autou*, "those beside Him", and it denotes a relationship so close as to identify them with the "brethren" of *v.* 31. Again (John 7. 3–10), they showed lack of sympathy with His work, and the reason is given in *v.* 5, "For neither did His brethren believe in Him". They are not seen again till, after His resurrection, they are gathered in the upper room with the apostles, and with His mother and theirs (Acts 1. 14). Their unbelief had gone. James had become a servant of the Lord Jesus Christ (James 1. 1), through the appearance to him of the risen Saviour (1 Cor. 15. 7), and, shortly, is a "pillar" of the church in Jerusalem (Acts 12. 17; 15. 13–21; 21. 18; Gal. 1. 19; 2. 9, 12). The other brethren seem to have joined in the witness by itinerating; see 1 Cor. 9. 5.

The natural meaning of the term "His brethren", in the Scripture record, would never have been challenged, but for the desire, when corruption crept into the churches (Acts 20. 29, 30), of raising Mary from the position of "handmaid of the Lord" (Luke 1. 38) to the exalted one of *Theotokos*, mother of God, whence it was an easy step to investing her with divine honours, as being herself a goddess. And thus the way was cleared for identifying her with the great goddess of Paganism, who is the mother of a divine son, and who is yet a virgin, a deity best known by the appellation she bore in Egypt, Isis, the mother of Horus. So it was put forth that Mary had no children other than the Lord, and that His brethren and sisters were either the children of Joseph by a former wife, or the Lord's cousins, the children of Mary the wife of Cleophas. Those who maintained the former opinion asserted that Joseph was an old man when he married Mary. Of this there is not the least hint in the Gospel records. If he had older children, the right of the Lord Jesus to the throne of David would be invalidated, for the two genealogies in Matt. 1 and Luke 3 show that the regal rights were united in Joseph and Mary (Ap. 99).

With reference to Jerome's "cousin" theory, it may be stated that the word "brother" is used in Scripture, (1) in the sense of blood-relationship, as children of the same parent or parents; (2) in the wider sense of descent from a common ancestor, e.g. Acts 7. 23, 25, where Abraham is the forefather; (3) in a still wider signification of fellow-man (Matt. 7. 3–5; 18. 15); (4) to express spiritual relationship (Matt. 23. 8; 28. 10; Acts. 9. 17; Rom. 8. 29; Heb. 2. 11). In the passages where His brethren are referred to, viz. Matt. 12. 46, 47; 13. 55; Mark 3. 31; Luke 8. 19; John 7. 3, 5, 10; Acts 1. 14; 1 Cor. 9. 5; Gal. 1. 19, only the first meaning can apply. Had they been cousins, the term would have been *sungenēs*, which is used in Mark 6. 4; Luke 1. 36, 58; 2. 44; 14. 12; 21. 16; John 18. 26; Acts 10. 24; Rom. 9. 3; 16. 7, 11, 21, and is translated "kin", "kinsman", or "kinsfolk", except in Luke 1. 36, 58, where it is rendered "cousin." The Scriptures distinguish "kinsman" from "brother"; see Luke 14. 12; 21. 16. Only in Rom. 9. 3 are the two words in apposition, and there "brother" is used in the sense of fellow-Israelite (No. 2). "Brother", therefore, when used in N.T. in any sense other than that of No. 2 or of No. 3, must be restricted to signification No. 1.

183 "THIS IS THAT" (Acts 2. 16).

1. "*This is that which was spoken by the prophet Joel.*" There is nothing in the words to tell us what is "this" and what is "that". The word "this" is emphatic and the word "But", with which Peter's argument begins, sets what follows in contrast. This shows that the quotation was used to rebut the charge of drunkenness (*v.* 13).

So far from these signs and wonders being a proof that "these men" were drunken, "this", said the apostle, is "that" (same kind of thing) which Joel prophesied would take place "in the last days". Peter does not say these *were* the last days, but this (that follows) is what Joel says of those days. He does not say "then was fulfilled", nor "as it is written", but merely calls attention to what the prophet said of similar scenes yet future.

Therefore to understand what Peter really meant by "this is that", we must turn to the prophecy of Joel. And in order to understand that prophecy, we must see exactly what it is about.

Is it about the Christian Dispensation? or
The Dispensation of judgment which is to follow it? or
Is it about the Jew and the Gentile? or
Is it about the church of God?

2. The Structure on p. 1224 gives the scope of *Joel* as a whole, while that on p. 1227 gives that of the last member *B* (p. 1224) in which occur the "signs" to which Peter points in connexion with "this is that". From this it will be seen that the prophecy of Joel links up with the last clause of the "song of Moses" in Deut. 32. 43 (see Rev. 15. 3), which ends

"And (He) will be merciful unto His Land and to His People."

So Joel 2. 18 begins:

"Then will Jehovah be jealous for His Land, and pity His People."

"THIS", therefore, is "THAT". It is the subject-matter and remote context of Acts 2. 16. It concerns Jehovah's Land and Jehovah's People, and has consequently nothing to do with the church of this Dispensation. Peter calls "the house of Israel" (*v.* 36) to the very repentance spoken of in the call to repentance of Joel (1. 14—2. 17; see *A*, Structure, p. 1224).

3. But the key to the correct understanding of Peter's quotation lies in the word "afterward" of Joel 2. 28. The question is, after what? This we can learn only from Joel himself. Peter does not explain it, nor can we understand it from Peter's words alone.

The Structure (p. 1227) shows us that the whole subject of 2. 18—3. 21 is,—evil removed from the Land and the People, and blessing bestowed on both; and these are set forth alternately. In 2. 28, 29 we have spiritual blessings connected with the temporal of the previous verses, introduced thus:

> "And it shall come to pass AFTERWARD, that I will pour out My spirit upon all flesh," &c.

After what? The answer is AFTER the temporal blessings of *vv.* 23–27. It is important to note that the temporal precede the spiritual blessings. The holy spirit was not poured out on all flesh at Pentecost: only on some of those present. None of the great signs in the heavens and on the earth had been shown. No deliverance took place in Jerusalem: both Land and People were still under the Roman yoke.

4. Thus, from a careful study of the two passages, it will be seen that there is a wide divergence between the statements of apostle and prophet on the one hand, and the general belief of Christendom, which the majority hold so tenaciously, not to say acrimoniously, that "the church" was formed at Pentecost (see App. 181 and 186), on the other.

(*a*) There can be no mistake about the meaning of Joel's word "afterward". It is not the simple Heb. word *'aḥar*=after (cp. Gen. 5. 4, &c.), but the compound *'aḥarey-kēn*=after that (as Gen. 6. 4, &c.).

(*b*) It is therefore certain that the word "this" in Acts 2. 16 refers to what follows, and not to what precedes; to the future events predicted by Joel, and not to those then taking place in Jerusalem.

(*c*) As Joel speaks of no gift of tongues, "this" cannot refer to these Pentecostal tongues, the outstanding cause of all the wonder and excitement.

(*d*) None of the things detailed in *vv.* 17, 19 came to pass. "This" therefore could not be the fulfilment of Joel's prediction, as the "pouring out" was only on the apostles and those associated with them.

5. To sum up: As we have seen, there is in Acts 2. 16 no fulfilment of Joel's prophecy either expressed or implied, and Peter's argument narrows down to this, viz. that a charge of drunkenness can no more be sustained against "these" than it can be against those in the yet future scenes spoken of by Joel, when the wondrous spiritual blessings will be poured out on all flesh AFTER THAT, i.e. after all the *temporal* blessings spoken of have been bestowed upon Israel's Land and Israel's People.

184 SYNONYMOUS WORDS FOR "GRACE", ETC.

There are three nouns, two verbs, and one adjective, to be noticed here.

I. Nouns.

1. ***charis***=free, undeserved favour; occ. 156 times, rendered "grace" 130 times; "favour" 6 times; "thank", "thankworthy", &c., twelve times; "a pleasure" twice, and "acceptable", "benefit", "gift", "gracious", "joy", and "liberality", once each.

It is not found in Matthew or Mark. In Luke it occurs eight times, rendered "grace", "gracious", "favour", and "thank". John uses it four times in 1. 14, 16, 17. It occurs sixteen times in Acts, 110 times in Paul's epp., sixteen times in those of James, Peter, John, and Jude; and twice in the Revelation, at the beginning and the end of that book of judgment (1. 4; 22. 21).

2. ***charisma***= a gift of grace, a free gift. Occ. seventeen times, always of God's gifts. Rendered "gift" except in Rom. 5. 15, 16, where it is "free gift".

3. ***euprepeia***. Only in James 1. 11, meaning beauty of form, or appearance.

II. Verbs.

1. ***charizomai***=give as an act of grace; hence, forgive. Occ. twenty-three times, twelve being rendered "forgive". In the Gospels, only in Luke 7. 21 (give), *v.* 42 (frankly forgive), *v.* 43 (forgive); four times in Acts (3. 14, granted; 25. 11, 16, deliver; 27. 24, give), and sixteen times in Paul's epistles: rend. forgive, save Rom. 8. 32. 1 Cor. 2. 12. Gal. 3. 18. Phil. 1. 29; 2. 9. Philemon 22.

2. ***charitoō***=treat with grace. Only in Luke 1. 28 (highly favoured) and Eph. 1. 6 (make accepted).

III. Adjective.

chrestos=useful, serviceable, from *chraomai*, to use. Occ. seven times; "gracious" in 1 Pet. 2. 3; "easy", Matt. 11. 30; "better", Luke 5. 39; "kind", Luke 6. 35; Eph. 4. 32; "goodness", Rom. 2. 4; "good", 1 Cor. 15. 33.

(*a*) *chrēstotēs* (the noun) occ. ten times, and is transl. "goodness", "kindness", &c.

185 THE FORMULÆ OF BAPTISM IN ACTS AND THE EPISTLES.

(In relation to Matt. 28. 19, 20.)

1. To some, perplexity, and even distress, is caused by the apparent neglect of the disciples to carry out the Lord's command in Matt. 28. 19, 20, with regard to the formula of baptism. They read the express words of the risen Lord in the Gospel: then, turning to Acts and onwards, they find no single instance of, or reference to, baptism in which the Triune name of Father, Son, and Holy Spirit is employed.

2. On the contrary, from the very first, only ten days after the injunction had been given, Peter is found (Acts 2. 38) commanding all his hearers including those of the dispersion (the *diaspora*) to be baptized *in* (the texts, except T, read *en*, not *epi*, nor *eis* as in Matt. 28.19) *the name of Jesus Christ*. Acts 8. 16 (*eis*); 10. 48 (*en*); 19. 5 (*eis*), are in accord, the formula being *in* or *into* the name of the Lord, or the Lord Jesus. In the last case, whether this refers to those who heard John or Paul, or whether the baptism was that of John or Paul, the formula is the same. Rom. 6. 3,—"as many of us as were baptized into (*eis*) Christ Jesus". 1 Cor. 1. 13, 15; here baptism "in (*eis*) the name of Paul" is clearly contrasted with baptism in the name of the Lord Jesus, or Christ Jesus, which must have been used as to Crispus, Gaius, and Stephanas.

3. In all the other places where the *act* of baptism is mentioned, directly or indirectly, the formula by implication is the same. These are: Acts 8. 38; 9. 18 (and 22. 16); 16. 15, 33; 18. 8. Yet on the other hand there stands the definite command in Matt. 28. 19, 20, as to the discipling of THE NATIONS into (*eis*) the Triune name of Father, Son, and Holy Spirit.

4. The "difficulty" is *created* by non-observance of the injunction in 2 Tim. 2. 15 as to "rightly dividing the word of truth". It comes by mixing up and thus confusing the "mystery" (Ap. 193) concerning the church of God during the "times of the Gentiles" with the ordinances and observances of the "times" of Messiah (Isa. 33. 6), with which the command in Matt. 28. 19, 20 has clearly to do, as the discipling of the nations, AS NATIONS, is expressly declared. It is the commission of the Jewish ministry *at the end of this age*. There is nothing corresponding to this form of baptism in any of the foregoing passages (2), all of which are connected with individuals or families. Inasmuch as

the mystery is the great secret which was "kept secret since the world began" (Rom. 16. 25; cp. Eph. 3. 9. Col. 1. 26), it follows logically that it must not be read into the Gospels.

5. The "discipling" work of Matt. 28. 19, 20 is *national work*: its object—to bring all nations into blessing with Israel. It has nothing to do with the present dispensation and the "one baptism" (Eph. 4. 5) of this dispensation. Matt. 28. 19, 20 takes up the proclamation of the kingdom, left uncompleted in Matt. 10. 5-15, after the church has been called on high. Therefore, the baptism "in" or "into" the name of the Lord Jesus in Acts, &c., was the continuation of John's baptism for a while, i.e. during the transitional period of Acts (see App. 180, 181) until the mystery was openly revealed and fully proclaimed (see Longer Note, p. 1694). Then, the baptism of Eph. 4. 5 supervened and still maintains.

6. To hold, as some do, that the disciples had "forgotten", or were "ignorant of", or else "ignored" the express command of the Lord, is to charge those spirit-endowed men with either incompetence or insubordination! Peter and John and the rest *must* have known well the meaning and future reference of Matt. 28. 19, 20; and they knew of John's baptism also: but until "led on" into more of "all the truth", by the Holy Spirit, and until the revelation of the secret concerning the church which is His body was declared, they continued to baptize, as John had done, into the name of the Lord Jesus.

7. This explanation does no violence to the Word of God. It does not impugn the intelligence or *bona fides* of the disciples. It leaves each of the several Scriptures unscathed and in its proper place, and each as being absolute truth. What it really "touches" is tradition only and the teaching based thereon.

186 CHURCH (Gr. *EKKLĒSIA*).

1. The Greek word *ekklēsia* means *assembly*, or a gathering of *called-out ones*. It is used seventy times in the Septuagint for the Hebrew *ḳāhāl* (from which latter we have our word *call*), rendered in Sept. by *sunagōgē* and *ekklēsia*.[1] This latter word occ. in N.T. 115 times (36 in plural), and is always transl. "church" except in Acts 19. 32, 39, 41 (*assembly*).

2. *ḳāhāl* is used (1) of Israel as a People *called out* from the rest of the nations (Gen. 28. 3); (2) of the tribal council of Simeon and Levi, those *called out* from each tribe (Gen. 49. 6); (3) of an assembly of Israelites *called out* for worship or any other purpose (Deut. 18. 16; 31. 30. Josh. 8. 35. Judg. 21. 8); (4) any assembly of worshippers as a congregation (Ps. 22. 22, 25. *Ekklēsia* in Matt. 16. 18; (18. 17. 1 Cor. 14. 19, 35, &c.); (5) the equivalent *ekklēsia* of separate assemblies in different localities (Acts 5. 11; 8. 3. 1 Cor. 4. 17, &c.); (6) of the guild or "union" of Ephesian craftsmen (Acts 19. 32, 41), and *v.* 39 (the lawful assembly). Finally, the special Pauline usage of *ekklēsia* differs from all these. Other assemblies consisted of *called-out* ones from Jews, or from Gentiles (Acts 18. 22), but this new body is of *called-out* ones from both.

3. Our word "church"[2] has an equally varied usage. It is used (1) of any congregation; (2) of a particular church (England, or Rome, &c.); (3) of the ministry of a church; (4) of the building in which the congregation assembles; (5) of Church as distinct from Chapel; (6) of the church as distinct from the world, and, lastly, it is used in the Pauline sense, of the body of Christ.

4. It is of profound importance to distinguish the usage of the word in each case, else we may be reading "the church which was in the wilderness" into the Prison Epistles, although we are expressly told that there is neither Jew nor Gentile in the "church which is His body". And when our Lord said "On this rock I will build my church" (Matt. 16. 18), those who heard His words could not connect them with the "mystery" which was "hid in God" and had not then been made known to the sons of men. Confusion follows our reading what refers to Israel in the past or the future into the present dispensation. Readers are referred to the various notes in the connexions.

5. The word where qualified by other terms occurs thus:—

Church of God; Acts 20. 28. 1 Cor. 1. 2; 10. 32; 11. 16 (pl.), 22; 15. 9. 2 Cor. 1. 1. Gal. 1. 13. 1 Thess. 2. 14 (pl.). 2 Thess. 1. 4 (pl.). 1 Tim. 3. 5, 15 (c. of the living God).
Churches of Christ; Rom. 16. 16.
Church in . . house; Rom. 16. 5. 1 Cor. 16. 19. Col. 4. 15. Philem. 2.
Churches of the Gentiles; Rom. 16. 4.
Churches of Galatia; 1 Cor. 16. 1. Gal. 1. 2. Of Asia; 1 Cor. 16. 19. Of Macedonia; 2 Cor. 8. 1. Of Judæa; Gal. 1. 22. Of the Laodiceans; Col. 4. 16. Of the Thessalonians; 1 Thess. 1. 1. 2 Thess. 1. 1.
Church of the firstborn (pl.); Heb. 12. 23.
Church in Ephesus, Smyrna, &c. Rev. 2 and 3; and Churches; Rev. 22. 16.

[1] *ḳāhāl* occurs in the Old Testament 123 times; congregation eighty-six, assembly seventeen, company seventeen, and multitude three times. The Sept. uses *sunagōgē* and *ekklēsia* as practically synonymous terms. But the *sunagōgē* concerns the bringing together of the members of an *existing* society or body, excluding all others, whereas the *ekklēsia* calls and invites all men, including outsiders everywhere, to join it. *Sunagōgē* being permanently associated with Jewish worship, was dropped by the early Christians in favour of *ekklēsia* as of wider import.

[2] Is derived from the Gr. *kuriakos*, of or belonging to the Lord, house (Gr. *oikos*) being understood. It comes to us through A.S. *circe* (Scottish *kirk*).

187 THE BURYING OF THE PATRIARCHS (Acts 7. 15, 16).

It is recorded that there were two distinct purchases by Abraham and Jacob for the purpose of burying their dead: one a field with a cave (Machpelah) at the end of it, which was bought by Abraham of Ephron the Hittite for 400 shekels of silver (Gen. 23. 16-18); the other, "a parcel of a field" which was bought by Jacob of the sons of Hamor, the father of Shechem, for 100 pieces of money (Gen. 33. 18, 19).

In the former were buried Sarah (Gen. 23. 19), Abraham (Gen. 25. 9), Isaac (Gen. 49. 31), Rebekah and Leah (Gen. 49. 31), and Jacob (Gen. 50. 12, 13).

In the latter were buried Joseph (Josh. 24. 32), and the other sons of Jacob who died in Egypt (Acts 7. 16).

In Acts 7. 16 Stephen referred to these events, well known to his hearers who were seeking his life. These found nothing to stumble at in his statement that *Abraham* bought the sepulchre of the sons of Emmor (the father)[1] of Sychem, whereas Gen. 33. 18, 19 states that *Jacob* was the buyer of "a parcel of a field" from the sons of Hamor in Shechem.

The explanation probably is simple,—Abraham was a rich man: rich men often buy, if they can, "parcels" of land for some reason or other: why should not Abraham have had a second place of sepulture assured, if he so desired?

As the Hittites were eager to oblige the rich and powerful sojourner among them, in the matter of Machpelah, as we know; so he would have little difficulty in buying the parcel at Sychem from the original holders in his time. Between Abraham's death and the appearance of Jacob at Sychem, eighty-five years

[1] Almost all the texts read *en*=in, instead of *tou*=the (*father* of.

had passed (Ap. 50, pp. 51, 52). Jacob was a keen man of business, but during his long absence "abroad" the title may have lapsed, or become obscure. Hence, when he desired to resume possession of a piece of family property, so to speak, he had to pay something by way of forfeit to make good his claim. The comparatively small sum recorded strengthens this suggestion. Modern instances are familiar to us. There is no reason why it should not be so in this case. And have we never heard of two family burying-places? So here, Jacob was buried in the one, Machpelah; Joseph and his brethren in the other at Sychem.

188 "ANOTHER KING" (Acts 7. 17, 18).

(Being supplemental to Ap. 37.)

Discoveries of late years have thrown much light on ancient Egyptian life and history, as touched upon in the Bible. But so many unsolved problems and "debated questions" remain as to the dynasties and individual kings, that it is not yet possible to give any reliable "table" such as that referred to in Ap. 37.

Nevertheless, we are now able to accept definite conclusions as to the Pharaoh of the Exodus of whom Stephen spoke:

"The People grew and multiplied in Egypt, till another king arose, which knew not Joseph."

How this could be has long been a difficulty with many, but discoveries in Egypt have removed it.

If we read this passage accurately in the original we notice that the word for *another* is *heteros*, which means *another* of a *different* kind; and not *allos*, which means *another* of the *same* kind.[1] (See Ap. 124. 1 and 2.)

The word points, therefore, to the fact that it was not *another* king of the *same* dynasty, but one of a *different* dynasty altogether, and this agrees with Exod. 1. 8. The Sept. there uses *heteros* for the Hebrew word *ḥādāsh* ("new"); and *anestē* for the Heb. word *ḳūm* ("arose"), which means to stand up and, in some connexions, occupy the place of (or instead of) another. (See the kindred Chaldee word in Dan. 2. 31, 39, 44; 3. 24. For the meaning of *ḥādāsh* see Deut. 32. 17, and cp. Judg. 5. 8.)

Josephus says, "the crown being come into another family" (*Ant.* ii. 9. 1).

The discoveries now made in Egypt prove that this was the case. The mummy of this very Pharaoh is to be seen to-day in the Museum at Bulak, and it is clear that this *Rameses* was the Pharaoh of the Oppression.[1]

He was an Assyrian, and every feature of his face is seen to be quite different from the features of the Pharaoh who preceded him.

Now we can comprehend Isa. 52. 4 which has so puzzled the commentators, who were unable to understand why the two oppressions, in Egypt and by Assyria (centuries apart), should be mentioned together *in the same sentence*, as though they were almost contemporary. There was no oppression (on the lines of Egypt) in Assyria.

The discoveries in Egypt thus independently and entirely confirm the perfect accuracy of the Divine words in showing that this was so, for in Isa. 52. 4 we read:

"Thus saith Adonai Jehovah,
My People went down aforetime into Egypt to sojourn there;
And the Assyrian oppressed them without cause."

Cp. Jer. 50. 17.

[1] The force of these may be seen in Matt. 2. 12: "another way" (*allos*). Matt. 4. 21: "other two brethren" (*allos*). Gal. 1. 6, 7: "a different (*heteros*) gospel, which is not another" (*allos*). Matt. 6. 24 R.V: "hate the one and love the other" (*heteros*). Matt. 11. 3: "do we look for another" (*heteros*). Heb. 7. 11: "another priest" (*heteros*).

[1] While *Meneptah*, his son, was the Pharaoh of the Exodus.

189 APOSTLES: ELDERS: PROPHETS.

1. APOSTLES. In the Gospels the word *apostolos* (sing. and pl.) occurs only nine times as compared with sixty-nine in Acts and the Epistles, and three in Revelation. In Matthew, Mark, Luke, and Acts (except 14. 4, 14) the term is used of the Twelve chosen and commissioned by the Lord (Matt. 11. 1; Luke 6. 13) during His earthly ministry. From this office Judas fell, his place being filled later by Matthias (Acts 1. 26). In the Epistles and Revelation the context shows where the Twelve are meant.

The one occurrence in John's Gospel is in 13. 16, where it is used in the general sense of one sent forth (on some special message or errand). He Who is called *the* Apostle (Heb. 3. 1) is so constantly (presented in that Gospel as the One sent of the Father (see notes on John 14. 24; 17. 3) that other messengers are lost sight of.

Besides the Twelve there were others appointed by the Lord after His Ascension (Eph. 4. 11. Cp. 1 Cor. 12. 28). Such were Paul and Barnabas, first called so in Acts 14. 4, 14; Andronicus and Junias (Rom. 16. 7). Paul nineteen times calls himself an apostle, and argues his claim in 1 Cor. 9 and 2 Cor. 12. See also 1 Thess. 1. 1; 2. 6, where Paul associates Silvanus and Timothy with himself. Twice the word *apostolos* (besides John 13. 16 referred to above) is translated "messenger", in 2 Cor. 8. 23. Phil. 2. 25. See notes there.

2. ELDERS. "Elders" is frequently met with in the O.T. as indicating an official position, e.g. elders of the tribes, elders of the cities, elders of Midian, &c. In the Gospels and Acts the term generally refers to the Sanhedrin. The name seems to have been taken over into the Christian Church to describe the members of the Council at Jerusalem other than the apostles (Acts 11. 30; 15. 2–23), and then similar officers were appointed in local churches (Acts 14. 23; 20. 17. Tit. 1. 5). That these were identical with the "overseers" of Acts 20. 28 (Gr. *episkopoi*, rendered "bishop" in Phil. 1. 1. 1 Tim. 3. 2. Tit. 1. 7. 1 Pet. 2. 25) is clear from comparison with Acts 20. 17. 1 Tim. 5. 17. Tit. 1. 5, 7. 1 Pet. 5. 1, 2 (see notes). There were thus "business" elders and "preaching" elders. Peter and John both call themselves elders (1 Pet. 5. 1. 2 John 1. 3 John 1).

3. PROPHETS. A prophet was one who spoke for God (see Ap. 49), and this applies to those of the New Testament as well as those of the Old. It did not necessarily mean that he foretold the future, though sometimes that was done, as in the case of Agabus (Acts 11. 28; 21. 10). Prophecy was one of the gifts of the Spirit, and its chief design was to comfort, exhort (Acts 15. 32), and testify from the Scriptures for the edification of believers. Prophets are included in the gifts of 1 Cor. 12. 28. Eph. 4. 11, and directions for the orderly exercise of their gifts are given in 1 Cor. 14.

Besides Acts 13. 1, where it is impossible to distinguish between the five persons mentioned as prophets and teachers (two of them being called apostles also in the next chapter),—Judas and Silas also are called prophets in 15. 32.

190 SYNONYMOUS WORDS FOR "SERVANT", "SERVE", ETC.

I.

1. ***diakonos*** is a servant as seen in activity (cp. *diōkō*, to pursue). It occurs eight times in the Gospels (not in Luke); is twice transl. "minister" (Matt. 20. 26. Mark 10. 43); six times "servant". The other twenty-two occurrences are in Paul's epistles; transl. "minister", except Rom. 16. 1 ("servant"), and Phil. 1. 1. 1 Tim. 3. 8, 12 ("deacon"). It is not found in Acts, where the institution of the so-called deacons is recorded.

2. ***doulos*** = slave, bond-servant. There are seventy-three occ. in the Gospels, three in Acts, thirty in Paul's epistles, five in the epistles of James, 1 and 2 Peter, and Jude, and fourteen in the Revelation. It is translated "servant", except in 1 Cor. 12. 13. Gal. 3. 28. Eph. 6. 8. Col. 3. 11. Rev. 6. 15; 13. 16; 19. 18, where the rendering is "bond" or "bondman". The fem. *doulē* occ. Luke 1. 38, 48. Acts 2. 18; transl. "handmaiden"; *doulon*, "servant", occ. only in Rom. 6. 19.

3. ***hupēretēs*** means an under-rower, and is used, generally, for one in a subordinate capacity. It is transl. "officer" eleven times, "minister" five times, and "servant" four times.

4. ***leitourgos*** = one who serves an office. In O. T. used of the priests and Levites. In N. T., of God's ministers, except Phil. 2. 25 (of Epaphroditus). It occurs five times.

5. ***misthios*** and ***misthōtos*** mean hired servants (from *misthos*, pay). Occ. Luke 15. 17, 19. Mark 1. 20. John 10. 12, 13.

6. ***oiketēs*** is a household servant (*oikos*, a house), and is so rendered in Acts 10. 7. Occ. Luke 16. 13. Rom. 14. 4. 1 Peter 2. 18; "servant".

7. ***pais*** (Ap. 108. iv) means a boy, and then, like Latin *puer*, French *garçon*, and Eng. boy, it means a servant. Rendered "servant" eleven times, and should also be so transl. Acts 3. 13, 26; 4. 27, 30.

8. ***therapōn*** is an attendant, one who performs services voluntarily, whether freeman or slave. Occ. only Heb. 3. 5.

II.

1. ***diakonia*** is the service rendered by a *diakonos*. Occ. once in the Gospels (Luke 10. 40); eight times in Acts; twenty-four times in Paul's epistles, and once in the Revelation: rendered "ministry", "ministration", &c., save Acts 11. 29, where it is "relief", the result of service, and Rom. 11. 13 (office).

2. ***douleia***. Occ. five times, always transl. "bondage".

3 ***latreia***. Occ. five times, transl. "service", or "divine service".

4. ***leitourgia***. Occ. six times; transl. "ministration" (Luke 1. 23), "service" (2 Cor. 9. 12; Phil. 2. 17, 30), and "ministry" (Heb. 8. 6; 9. 21). From this comes Eng. "liturgy".

III.

1. ***diakoneō***. Occurs thirty-seven times, and is transl. "serve", "minister", &c., and twice "use the office of a deacon" (1 Tim. 3. 10, 13).

2. ***douleuō*** = to serve as a bondman. It occurs twenty-five times; transl. "serve", "do service", except John 8. 33; Acts 7. 7; Gal. 4. 9, 25; "be in bondage".

3. ***douloō*** is to enslave. Occ. eight times, twice in the active sense, Acts 7. 6; 1 Cor. 9. 19; elsewhere, in the passive (Rom. 6. 18, 22. 1 Cor. 7. 15. Gal. 4. 3. Titus 2. 3. 2 Peter 2. 19).

4. ***hupēreteō***. (Cp. I. 3, above.) Occurs only in Acts 13. 36; 20. 34; 24. 23.

5. ***latreuō***. (Cp. II. 3, above.) Occ. twenty-one times, always referring to the worship of God, save in Acts 7. 42. Transl. "serve", or "do the service", seventeen times, and "worship" four times.

6. ***leitourgeō***. (Cp. I. 4; II. 4, above). Occ. three times; Acts 13. 2. Rom. 15. 27. Heb. 10. 11, rendered "minister".

191 "JUST", "JUSTIFY", ETC.

1. ***dikaios*** = just, righteous. From *dikē*, right (see Ap. 177. 4). Occ. eighty times; forty transl. "righteous"; thirty-three "just"; five times "right"; and twice "meet". (a) In two places (Rom. 3. 8. Heb. 2. 2) "just" is the rendering of *endikos*. No other word in N. T. for "just", or "righteous".

2. ***dikaioō*** is to set forth as righteous, to justify. Occ. forty times, of which fifteen are in Romans. Always rendered "justify", except Rom. 6. 7 ("freed"), and Rev. 22. 11 ("be righteous"). The participle is transl. "justifier" in Rom. 3. 26.

3. ***dikaiosunē*** = righteousness. Occ. ninety-two times, of which thirty-six are in Romans. Always transl. "righteousness". Other words to which the same transl. is given are *dikaiōma* (see below), and *euthutēs*, which latter occ. only in Heb. 1. 8.

4. ***dikaiōma*** is a righteous ordinance, a decree (of acquittal). See Ap. 177. 4. Rendered "righteousness" in Rom. 2. 26; 5. 18; 8. 4. Rev. 19. 8; and "ordinance" in Luke 1. 6. Heb. 9. 1, 10: "judgment", Rom. 1. 32. Rev. 15. 4: "justification", Rom. 5. 16.

5. ***dikaiōsis*** = justification. Occ. only in Rom. 4. 25; 5. 18. The only other word rendered "justification" is *dikaiōma* (see 4), in Rom. 5. 16.

192 THE PAULINE EPISTLES.

A. THE CHRONOLOGICAL ORDER. (BEING SUPPLEMENTAL TO AP. 180.)

B. THE CANONICAL ORDER OF THE "CHURCH" EPISTLES.

A. The Chronological Order.

1st Group The seven earlier Letters.	I THESSALONIANS II THESSALONIANS HEBREWS I CORINTHIANS II CORINTHIANS GALATIANS ROMANS	See Ap. 180 and Introductory Notes to each Epistle.
2nd Group The Prison Letters.	PHILIPPIANS [1] PHILEMON COLOSSIANS [2] EPHESIANS [3]	See Ap. 180 and Introductory Notes to each Epistle.

[*The Hiatus between the second and third groups.* Paul's movements during some four years after his release from imprisonment (A.D. 63) are shrouded in obscurity. There is no Divine record. Various hints may, however, be gathered from Phil. 2. 24. Philemon 22. 1 Tim. 4. 13. 2 Tim. 1. 15, 18; 4. 10, 13, 20. Titus 1. 5; 3. 12, as to a journey or journeys in Asia and Europe, including most probably visits to Colosse and Ephesus, and possibly Dalmatia (Illyricum) and Spain.

Whether the desire to visit Spain (Rom. 15. 24, 28) was ever fulfilled is purely conjectural, notwithstanding a statement of Clement of Rome (Clement of Phil. 4. 3?), A.D. 91–100, in an "Epistle to Corinthians", that Paul "went to the end of the west".

Some take this to refer to Spain (and Gaul), but there is no proof; and that an inscription found in Spain recording that some "new superstition" was "got rid of" refers to Paul and his labours there, is not at all convincing. *On the other hand, the significant absence of any mention or hint of such a visit in the three closing epistles—*1 Timothy, Titus, and 2 Timothy*—can neither be overlooked nor explained away.*

The notion that Clement's words "end of the west" cover a visit to the British Isles may be dismissed in Bishop Lightfoot's words as "possessing neither evidence nor probability".]

3rd Group Pastoral Letters.	I TIMOTHY TITUS II TIMOTHY	See Ap. 180 and Introductory Notes to each Epistle.

1. From the foregoing it will be seen that the number *seven* (Ap. 10) is apparent in the grouping of the Pauline Epistles as a whole. It is equally noticeable in the *canonical* order of the *Church Epistles* (see **B** below). They divide into three groups, numbering together fourteen (two *sevens*) separate letters. The first group consists of the seven earlier epistles.[4] The second and third form another *seven* (4 + 3. See **B**. 1).

2. It may be noted (among other things) that the *seventh* in this order (Romans) and the *fourteenth* (2 Timothy) give the two unique and terrible lists of the condition and state of "the habitable world" preceding, and at the time of, the Lord's Coming at first, and preceding His Return (see notes; Rom. 1 and 2 Tim. 3). By careful study of the above table of Chronological Order, together with Ap. 180, the student will be able to elucidate for himself interesting and important problems connected with the period concerned.

B. The Canonical Order of the "Church" Epistles.

A | ROMANS (Doctrine and Instruction).
B | I and II CORINTHIANS (Reproof).
C | GALATIANS (Correction).
A | EPHESIANS (Doctrine and Instruction).
B | PHILIPPIANS (Reproof).
C | COLOSSIANS (Correction).
A | I and II THESSALONIANS (Doctrine and Instruction).

(*Note. For the details of this Interrelation see* p. 1660.)

[1, 2, 3] Order according to Bishop Lightfoot.

[4] Including *Hebrews.* The restoration of this Epistle to its proper chronological position affords a strong argument in favour of its Pauline authorship (see Introductory Notes), as without it the number of letters written by Paul would be *thirteen*, and this particular number (see Ap. 10) is inconceivable in such a connection.

1. Seven churches are addressed as such by the Holy Spirit. *Seven* is the number of spiritual perfection, the same number as the Lord Himself addresses later to the assemblies (Rev. 2 and 3) from the glory.

In these Epistles we have the perfect embodiment of the Spirit's teaching for the churches. They contain "all the truth" (John 16. 13) into which the Spirit of the Truth was to guide the Lord's people. They contain the things which the Lord could not speak on earth, for the time for it was not then. They contain the "things of Mine which He shall take and shall show unto you". The *number* of these Epistles, *seven*, is perfect. Their *order* also is perfect.

2. THAT THIS ORDER IS NOT CHRONOLOGICAL BUT TOPICAL and didactic is made clear beyond all question by the fact that the Holy Spirit has placed the Epistles written first of all (Thess.) *seventh* and last in the list. The question whether the order in which the Holy Spirit has presented these Epistles is the order in which we find them in our Bibles must, therefore, be answered by the teaching of the Spirit Himself as unfolded to us in His own Divinely perfect arrangement of the Epistles, instead of according to man's idea, which strives to evolve a doctrinal system according to the chronological sequence usually accepted.

Although the chronological sequence of the Epistles has its own wonderful lesson to impart (see **A**. 2 above), as we trace in order the gradual unfolding of the teachings of the Spirit in connection with "the progress of doctrine", from Pentecost to Paul's imprisonments, yet these other teachings are fully presented to us by our Divine Guide in the *experimental order* in which the Epistles to the seven Churches are sent out.

In all the hundreds of Greek manuscripts of the N. T. *the order of these Epistles never varies.* The general order of the books of the N. T. takes the form of groups, viz. (1) the four Gospels; (2) Acts; (3) the so-called "general"[1] Epistles; (4) the Pauline Epistles, and (5) the Apocalypse (Ap. 95). But while the order of these five groups varies in some of the manuscripts, and the Pauline Epistles vary in their position with respect to the other four groups, and while the Pauline Epistles themselves vary in their order (e.g. *Hebrews* in some cases following *Thessalonians*, see p. 1823, 5 (*e*)), the order of these seven Church Epistles is invariably the same.

3. It is ignorance of this Divinely given standard that results in the deplorable attempts to "square" the teachings of our Lord in the Gospels, which concern the kingdom of heaven (Ap. 114) and the Jewish Polity, with the teaching of Paul the apostle and bondservant of Jesus Christ in the Church Epistles. And so, when it is found that they cannot be "squared", we have the unseemly utterances and procedure of those who throw over the "Pauline doctrine", as they term it, in favour of "the teaching of Jesus", with contemptuous references to "the Hellenistic tendencies of Paul's mind", &c.; and such statements as "the Master's words must be preferred to a disciple's"; "we must get back to Jesus", and so on. All of which and similar utterances make abundantly clear the fact that the Divine teaching of the Holy Spirit, in fulfilment of the promise of the Lord in John 16. 13, is not only overlooked or not understood by some, but is deliberately ignored and rejected by others who employ them.

Any Christian who does not give earnest heed to what has been written specially for his instruction is liable thus to be led away. Every word of Scripture is *for* him and for his learning, but not every word is *about* him. But these Epistles are all about him and about the special position in which he finds himself placed with reference to the Jew and the Gentile; the old creation and the new; the "flesh" and the "spirit"; and all the various phenomena which he finds in his experience.

4. In connection with the *order* in which these "Church" Epistles come to us, we notice first of all that they are grouped in two divisions of *three* and *four* (see above, **B**). Three stand out distinct from all the others as being *treatises* rather than *epistles*, and as containing so much more *doctrinal* matter[1] as compared with that which is *epistolary*. This will be seen from the detail Structure (p. 1660) which gives the contents of each. These three are *Romans, Ephesians*, and *Thessalonians*. And the four are placed between these three in two pairs, each pair containing respectively *reproof* and *correction*, in contrast to the other three, which contain *doctrine* and *instruction* (according to 2 Tim. 3. 16).

ROMANS comes first as containing the primaries of Christian education (see Introductory Notes, p. 1661). It starts by showing *Man* (Gentile and Jew alike) as utterly ruined and helpless, lost and ungodly sinners; how the saved sinner has died together with Christ, and together with Him is risen to "newness of life"; made a son and heir of God in Him.

EPHESIANS takes up from this point, beginning not with *Man*, but with God. It reveals to us the knowledge of God and of *His purposes in Christ*. The *heading up* of all things IN Christ in "a dispensation of the fulness of times" (1. 10), and the formation of a joint-body of Jews and Gentiles as a "church" (Ap. 186), by which God's manifold ("variegated") wisdom may be made known "unto principalities and powers in the heavenlies" (3. 10).

THESSALONIANS, written first of all the Epistles, are placed in this connection last of all by the Holy Spirit. Herein is given the special revelation concerning the return of the Lord Jesus Christ. They stand last and alone, being followed by no other Church Epistle. If we have "ears to hear", this fact proclaims that,—

5. It is useless to teach Christians the truths connected with the Lord's Coming until they have learned the truths in the other Epistles. Until they know and understand from *Romans* what they are by nature, and what God has made them to be IN Christ Jesus,—sons and heirs, joint-heirs with Christ (Rom. 8. 17); until they know and understand that even now God has "blessed them with all spiritual blessing in the heavenlies IN Christ" (Eph. 1. 3), they have no place for, and no understanding of, the truths concerning His return from heaven.[2]

To sum up:—The saved sinner is shown

In ROMANS, as dead and risen with Christ:

In EPHESIANS, as seated in the heavenlies IN Christ:

In THESSALONIANS, in glory for ever with Christ.

[1] See Int. Notes to each Epistle.

[1] Lightfoot (*Biblical Essays*, p. 388) says of *Romans* and *Ephesians*: "Both alike partake of the character rather of a formal treatise than of a familiar letter."

[2] The Introductory Notes and Structure in each case show the scope of the Epistle and its teaching.

193 THE "MYSTERY".

The English word "mystery" is a transliteration of the Greek word *mustērion*,[1] which means a sacred *secret*.

It occurs in the Septuagint Version (280 B.C.) nine times as the equivalent for the Chaldee *rāz* in the Chaldee portion of "Daniel", which means to *conceal*; hence, *something concealed* that can be revealed, viz. in Dan. 2. 18, 19, 27, 28, 29, 30, 47, 47, and 4. 9.

It occurs frequently in the Apocryphal books; which, though of no use for establishing doctrine, are of great value in determining the meaning of Biblical usage of Greek words. In these books *mustērion* always means

[1] It is from *mueō* = to initiate or admit to secrets; and *mustēs* was used of the person so initiated.

the *secret* of friends, or of a king, &c.[1] See Tobit 12. 7, 11. Judith 2. 2. Wisdom 2. 22 (transl. "mysteries"); 14. 23. Ecclus. 22. 22; 27. 16, 17, 21. 2 Macc. 13. 21. (R. V.). The passage in Judith is remarkable: for Nabuchodonosor calls his captains and great men together just before entering on a campaign, and "communicated with them his secret counsel", lit. "the mystery of his will". This is exactly the same usage as in Eph. 1. 9, except that the Gr. word for will or counsel is different.[2]

By the end of the second century A.D. it was used interchangeably with *tupos* (= type), *sumbolon* (= symbol), and *parabolē* (= parable).

When we find the Greek word *mustērion* rendered *sacramentum* in the Latin Vulgate of Eph. 5. 32, it is clear that it was used as meaning a *secret sign* or *symbol*, and not in the modern meaning put upon the word "Sacrament", i.e. "holy mysteries".

It is evident to all that God has made known His will "at sundry times and in divers manners" (Heb. 1. 1, 2). He also kept certain things secret, and revealed them from time to time according to His purposes and counsels. Hence the word *mustērion* is connected with several *concealed* or *secret* things in the New Testament.

1. It was used of the *secrets of the kingdom*; which had been concealed, until the Lord revealed them to His disciples (not to the People) in Matt. 13. 10, 11. It had not before been known that the kingdom would be rejected, and that there would be a long interval between that rejection and its being set up in glory. This was concealed even from the prophets who foretold it (1 Pet. 1. 10–12).

2. In Rom. 11 it is used in connection with the duration of Israel's blindness. That blindness itself was not a secret, for it had been foretold in Isa. 6. 9, 10. But the *duration* of the blindness was kept a "secret" from Isaiah and only revealed through Paul (Rom. 11. 25).

3. It was used of a fact connected with resurrection, which had never before been made known to the sons of men.

The Lord had spoken of it to Martha (John 11. 25, 26), but though she believed it, she did not understand that to those who should be alive and remain to His Coming the Lord would be "the life", and they would "never die" (*v.* 26).

The Thessalonians who "received the word" were not left in ignorance of it (1 Thess. 4. 13), for the Lord's words in John 11. 25, 26 were explained to them.

But in 1 Cor. 15. 51 the secret was fully and plainly shown; and it was that "we shall not all sleep". Up to that moment the universal belief had been that we must all die (cp. Heb. 9. 27). Thenceforward it was revealed and made known for faith that all would not die, but that those who are alive and remain (lit. remain over) unto the Lord's Coming will not die at all (see note 1 Thess. 4. 15, and cp. Phil. 3. 14).

4. Side by side with these Divine secrets there was the secret of the [foretold] lawlessness (2 Thess. 2. 7. Cp. Dan. 12. 4). It was already working during the dispensation covered by "Acts"; and had the nation repented at the call of those "other servants" of Matt. 22. 4 (Acts 2. 38; 3. 12–26; &c.), those secret counsels of "the lawless one" and "the transgressors" would have "come to the full" (Dan. 8. 23). But now they are postponed and in abeyance until the appointed time.

5. But "the great secret" which concerns us to-day was not revealed until after the close of that dispensation covered by "Acts". (See Acts 28. 17–31 and App. 180 and 181.)

Paul was not commissioned to put in writing the "purpose" of God which was "*before* the overthrow of the world" (Ap. 146), until that dispensation was ended.

What this "great secret" was can only be learned fully from the Prison Epistles. There alone can we find the things which had been concealed and kept secret "since the world began" (Rom. 16. 25); "which in other ages was not made known unto the sons of men" (Eph. 3. 5); "which from the beginning of the world hath been hid in God" (Eph. 3. 9); "which hath been hid from ages and from generations, but now is made manifest" (Col. 1. 26), where "now" (Gr. *nun*) with the pret. = just now, recently.

The special Scriptures which describe this secret are the postscript of Rom. 16. 25, 26. Eph. 3. 1–12. Col. 1. 24–27.

The mention of "the mystery" in Rom. 16. 25, 26 has perplexed many, because the revelation of it is specifically propounded in the Epistle to the Ephesians.

Hence it has been suggested that the Epistle originally ended at Rom. 16. 24 with the *Benediction* (or even at *v.* 20 (see the marginal notes in the R. V.), and that the *ascription* (*vv.* 25–27) was added by the apostle after he reached Rome (1) in order to complete the Structure by making it correspond with the ascription in ch. 11. 33–36; and (2) to complete the *Epanodos* or *Introversion*, and thus to contrast "God's gospel", which was revealed of old by the prophets of the Old Testament and never hidden (1. 2, 3), with the mystery which was always hidden and never revealed or even mentioned until 16. 25–27. See Longer Note p. 1694.

In any case, while there is no doubt about the general order of the Epistles, the actual dates are conjectural, and rest only upon individual opinions as to the internal evidence (Ap. 180). And, after all, Rom. 16. 25–27 is not the revelation of the mystery as given in the Prison Epistles, but an ascription of glory to Him Who had at length made it manifest by prophetic writings (not "the writings of the prophets", for it is the adjective "prophetic", not the noun "prophecy" as in 2 Pet. 1. 20). *Romans* and *Ephesians* are thus brought together as the two central Epistles of the chronological groups: the one ending one group, and the other beginning the next, both being treatises rather than epistles, and both having Paul for their sole author, while in all the other Epistles he has others associated with him.

As to the great secret itself, it is certain that it cannot refer to the blessing of Gentiles in connection with Israel. This is perfectly clear from the fact that that was *never a secret*. Both blessings were made known at the very same time (Gen. 12. 3); and this well-known fact is constantly referred to in the Old Testament. See Gen. 22. 18; 26. 4; &c. Deut. 32. 8. Pss. 18. 49; 67. 1, 2; 72. 17; 117. 1. Isa. 11. 10; 49. 6. Luke 2. 32. Rom. 15. 8–12.

But the secret revealed in the Prison Epistles was never the subject of previous revelation.

In Eph. 3. 5 it is stated to be "now revealed". This cannot mean that it had been revealed before, but not in the same manner as "now"; because it is stated that it had never been revealed at all.

It concerns Gentiles; and it was "revealed unto His holy apostles [1] and prophets by the Spirit", that the Gentiles should be joint-heirs, and a joint-body,[2] and [joint] partakers of the promise in Christ through the gospel (see the Notes on Eph. 3. 5, 6).

We cannot know the whole purpose of God in keeping this concealed all through the ages; but one thing we can clearly see, viz. that had God made it known before, Israel would of necessity have had an excuse for rejecting the Messiah and His kingdom.

[1] In subsequent Revisions of the Sept., *Theodotion* (A.D. 160) uses it for the Heb. *sōd* (Job 15. 8. Ps. 25. 14. Prov. 20. 19). See Notes *in loc.*

[2] In Judith 2. 2 it is *boulē* (Ap. 102. 4), while in Eph. 1. 9 it is *thelēma* (Ap. 102. 2).

[1] These were not those of the Old Testament dispensation, but were the subjects of a promise by the Lord Himself in Matt. 23. 34. Luke 11. 49, which was fulfilled in Eph. 4. 8, 11. See the notes on these passages and Ap. 189.

[2] Greek *sussōmos*, a remarkable word occurring only here in the N. T.

As to ourselves, the question of "Who is in the secret?" does not arise. For we are not to suppose that all who do not know of it are "lost".

One thing we know, and that is: it is made known for "the obedience of faith", or for "faith-obedience" (Rom. 16. 26).

It is a *subsequent revelation;* and the question is, do we believe it and obey it by acting according to it?

Abraham had several Divine revelations made to him. From his call in Gen. 11 he was a "righteous" man. In ch. 12 he believed God concerning His promises of the future. In ch. 13 he believed God concerning the promise of the Land. But in ch. 15 God made a further revelation concerning the seed which He would give him; and it is written, "Abraham believed in the Lord, and it was counted (or imputed) unto him for righteousness".

Even so with ourselves and the subsequent revelation of the mystery in the Prison Epistles. Let us believe it, and we may be sure that it will be counted unto us for something, for some blessing, which those who refuse to believe it will lose.

194 "THE SPIRITS IN PRISON" (1 Peter 3. 19).

A correct understanding of this passage may be obtained by noting the following facts:

1. Men are never spoken of in Scripture as "spirits". Man *has* spirit, but he is not "a spirit", for a spirit hath not "flesh and bones". In this life man has "flesh and blood", a "natural" (or psychical) body. At death this spirit "returns to God Who gave it" (Ps. 31. 5. Eccles. 12. 7. Luke 23. 46. Acts 7. 59). In resurrection "God giveth it a body as it hath pleased Him" (1 Cor. 15. 38). This is no longer a "natural (or psychical) body," but "a spiritual body" (1 Cor. 15. 44).

2. Angels are "spirits", and are so called (Heb. 1.7,14).

3. In 2 Pet. 2. 4 we read of "the angels that sinned"; and in 1 Pet. 3. 19, 20 of spirits "which sometime were disobedient ... in the days of Noah". In 2 Pet. 2. 4 we are further told that these fallen angels are reserved unto judgment, and delivered into chains (i.e. bondage or "prison"). Cp. Jude 6.

4. The cause of their fall and the nature of their sin are particularly set forth by the Holy Spirit in Jude 6, 7.

a. They "left their own habitation".

b. This "habitation" is called (in Greek) *oikētērion*, which occurs again only in 2 Cor. 5. 2, where it is called our "house" (i.e. body) with which we earnestly long to be "clothed upon"; referring to the "change" which shall take place in resurrection. This is the spiritual resurrection body of 1 Cor. 15. 44.

c. This spiritual body (or *oikētērion*) is what the angels "left" (whatever that may mean, and this we do not know). The word rendered "left", here, is peculiar. It is *apoleipō* = *to leave behind*, as in 2 Tim. 4. 13, 20, where Paul uses it of "the cloke" and the "parchments" which he *left behind* at Troas, and of Trophimus whom he *left behind* at Miletum. Occ. Heb. 4. 6, 9; 10. 26. Jude 6.

d. They "kept not their first estate (*archē*)" in which they were placed when they were created.

e. The nature of their sin is clearly stated. The sin of "Sodom and Gomorrha" is declared to be "in like manner" to that of the angels; and what that sin was is described as "giving themselves over to fornication, and going after strange flesh" (Jude 6, 7). The word "strange" here denotes other, i.e. *different* (Gr. *heteros* = different in kind. See Ap. 124. 2). What this could be, and how it could be, we are not told. We are not asked to understand it, but to believe it. (See further in App. 23 and 25.)

5. In Gen. 6. 1, 2, 4 we have the historical record, which is referred to in the Epistles of Peter and Jude. There these "angels" are called "the sons of God". This expression in the Old Testament is used always of "angels", because they were not "begotten", but created, as Adam was created, and he is so called in Luke 3. 38 (cp. Gen. 5. 1). It is used of angels eight times: Gen. 6. 2,[1] 4. Job 1. 6; 2. 1; 38. 7. Ps. 29. 1 (R.V. m.); 89. 6 (R.V. m.); and Dan. 3. 25. In this last passage there is no article, and it does not mean "*the* Son of God", but "*a* son of God", i.e. an angel who was sent into the furnace (Dan. 3. 28), as one was into the den of lions (Dan. 6. 22). In one passage (Hos. 1. 10) the English expression is used of men, but there the Hebrew is different, and it refers only to what men should be "called", not to what they were.

6. Returning to 1 Pet. 3. 19, the expression "the spirits in prison" cannot be understood apart from the whole context. The passage commences with the word "For" (*v.* 17), and is introduced as the reason why "it is better, if the will of God should (so) will, to suffer for well-doing, than for evil-doing. FOR (*v.* 18) Christ also suffered for sins once (Gr. *hapax*)—a Just One for unjust ones—in order that He might bring us to God, having been put to death indeed as to [His] flesh, but made alive as to [His] spirit." This can refer only to His spiritual resurrection body (1 Cor. 15. 45). In death His body was put in the grave (or sepulchre, i.e. *Hadēs*), Acts 2. 31; but His spirit was "commended to God". Not until His spirit was reunited to the body in resurrection could He go elsewhere. And then He went not to "Gehenna", or back to *Hadēs*, but to *Tartarus* (2 Pet. 2. 4. See Ap. 131. III), where "the angels who sinned" had been "delivered into chains". To these He proclaimed His victory.

7. The word rendered "preached" is not the usual word *euangelizō* (Ap. 121. 4), but the emphatic word *kērussō* (Ap. 121. 1); which means to *proclaim as a herald*. Even so Christ *heralded* His victory over death, and the proclamation of this reached to the utmost bounds of creation.

It was "better" THEREFORE to suffer for well-doing than for evil-doing. He had suffered for well-doing. He suffered, but He had a glorious triumph. "Therefore" (runs the exhortation), "if ye suffer for righteousness' sake, happy are ye" (*v.* 14), and it concludes· "Forasmuch then as Christ suffered on our behalf as to the flesh, arm yourselves likewise with the same mind; for He that hath suffered in the flesh hath done with sin; no longer to live [our] remaining time according to men's lusts, but for God's will ... For to this end, to those also who are now dead, were the glad tidings announced, that though (Gr. *men*) they might be judged according [to the will of][2] men, in [the] flesh, yet (Gr. *de*) they might live [again] according to [the will of] God, in [the] spirit": i.e. in resurrection (1 Pet. 4. 1, 2, 6).

The above is suggested as the interpretation of the expression "the in-prison spirits", in the light of the whole of the nearer and remoter contexts.

---

[1] In the first passage (Gen. 6. 2) the Alexandrine MS. of the Septuagint has "angels" (not "sons"), showing how it was then understood.

[2] For the supply of this ellipsis see Rom. 8. 27, 28, and cp. 1 Pet. 4. 19.

195 THE DIFFERENT AGES AND DISPENSATIONS OF GOD'S DEALINGS WITH MEN.

1. God has spoken at "sundry times" as well as "in divers manners" (Heb. 1. 1). The time when He spoke to "the fathers" is distinguished from the time in which He has "spoken to us". The time in which "He spake by the prophets" stands in contrast with the time in which He spake by (His) "Son". And the "time past" is obviously distinguished from "these last days" (Heb. 1. 2). To "rightly divide the word of truth" (2 Tim. 2. 15) it is essential to regard *the times* in which the words were spoken, as well as *the times* to which they refer.

Three Greek words in the New Testament call for careful consideration. These are:

(1) *chronos*, time, duration unlimited unless defined; occ. fifty-three times and is translated "time" in thirty-two;

(2) *kairos*, a certain limited and definite portion of *chronos*, the right time or season; occ. eighty-seven times, and is rendered "time" in sixty-five passages, "season" in fifteen;

(3) *oikonomia*, meaning lit. administration of a household (Eng., economy, including the idea of stewardship); occ. eight times, trans. "dispensation" four, "stewardship" three, "edifying" once (1 Tim. 1. 4), which the R.V. rightly corrects to "dispensation", making five occ. in all of that English term.

A dispensation, administration, or arrangement, during a portion of *chronos* may, or may not, be equal to *kairos*, according as the context determines.

Nothing but confusion can arise from reading into one dispensation that which relates to another. To connect what God said and did in one dispensation with another, in which His administration was on an altogether different principle, is to ensure error. And finally, to take doctrine of late revelation and read it into the time when it was "hidden" leads to disaster.

The nations, Israel the Chosen Nation, and the church (Ap. 186) are each dealt with in distinct "times" and on distinct principles, and the doctrine relating to each must be kept distinct. When our Lord speaks (Luke 21. 24) of "the times (*kairos*) of the Gentiles", the implication is that there are times of the Jews (under Messiah, Isa. 33. 6, &c.), whatever be the contrasted elements. So that what is recorded as connected with the times of the Jews is not necessarily applicable to the times of the Gentiles. The present administration of God is in grace, not in law, judgment, or glory, and belongs to the "dispensation" (*oikonomia*) of the Mystery (Ap. 193), that secret "which hath been hid from ages and from generations, but now is made manifest to His saints" (Col. 1. 26), that secret "which in other ages was not made known unto the sons of men" (Eph. 3. 5). Hid in God from the beginning of the world (see Eph. 3. 9), it was kept secret since the world began (see Rom. 16. 25).

There is no authority for taking enactments Divinely fitted for the times of the Jews and transferring them to the present dispensation of God in grace. Similarly, the endeavour to read the precepts of the "Sermon on the Mount" (Matt. 5-7), which are the laws of the kingdom of heaven (see Ap. 114), into such church epistles as Ephesians, Philippians, Colossians, not only obscures the truth, but antagonizes one part of Scripture with another.

2. The Seven Times or Dispensations.

In the Bible seven distinct administrations are set before us. Each has its own beginning and ending; each is characterized by certain distinctive principles of God's dealings; each ends in a crisis or judgment peculiar to itself, save No. 7, which is without end. These may be tabulated thus:

1. The Edenic state of innocence.
   End—The expulsion from Eden.
2. The period "without law" (the times of ignorance, Acts 17. 30).
   End—The Flood, and the judgment on Babel.
3. The era under law.
   End—The rejection of Israel.
4. The period of grace.
   End—The "day of the Lord".
5. The epoch of judgment.
   End—The destruction of Antichrist.
6. The millennial age.
   End—The destruction of Satan, and the judgment of the great white throne.
7. The eternal state of glory.
   No End.

All seven dispensations exhibit differing characteristics which call for the close attention of the Bible student.

3. The Times of the Gentiles.

While the seven dispensations above specified are the main divisions of the long period of the Divine dealings, there is still another dispensation referred to as "the times of the Gentiles" (Luke 21. 24), a dispensation which overlaps two of the above divisions. *These* times began when Jerusalem passed under the power of Babylon (477 B.C. See Ap. 50, p. 60, and Ap. 180), and continue while Jerusalem is "trodden down of the Gentiles" (Luke 21. 24). These "times" are referred to in Rom. 11. 25, which has no reference to the completion of "the church", as is so generally believed, but relates to the fullness, or filling up, of the times of the Gentiles, the word "Gentiles" being put for *the times* which they fill up.

4. The Parenthesis of the Present Dispensation.

In the Nazareth Synagogue (Luke 4. 16-20) our Lord stood up and read from the book of the prophet Isaiah. After reading the first verse and part of the second (of ch. 61), He closed the book. Why stop there? Because the next sentence belonged, and still belongs, to a future dispensation. The acceptable "year of the Lord" had come, but "the day of vengeance of our God" has not even yet appeared. Thus did the Lord divide two dispensations. There is no mark in the Hebrew text of Isaiah 61. 2 to indicate any break, yet an interval of nearly 2,000 years separates the two clauses quoted. In this interval comes the whole of the present church dispensation, following on the years after Israel's final rejection (Acts 28. 25-28). See App. 180, 181.

196 "RECONCILE", "RECONCILIATION".

1. The word "reconcile", which our translators adopted from the Vulgate, is simply the transliteration of the Latin *reconcilio*, to bring together again, to re-unite or re-connect. The verb *to reconcile*, and its noun *reconciliation*, have, however, come to possess now merely the idea of friendship after estrangement.

2. The Greek words in the N. T. are as follow:

(*a*) *allassō*, to change, to make other (*allos*) than it is. Occ. Acts 6. 14. Rom. 1. 23. 1 Cor. 15. 51, 52. Gal. 4. 20. Heb. 1. 12. Always rendered "change".

(*b*) *diallassomai* (passive), *dia* (Ap. 104. v) and *allassō*, to be changed or altered *mutually* (the force of *dia*) from one condition to another. Occ. Matt. 5. 24.

(*c*) *katallassō*, *kata* (Ap. 104. x) and *allassō*, to change or exchange something (anything) *arbitrarily*; not as (*b*) by mutual consent, but as proceeding from *one* (the *kata* implying *from above*). Occ. Rom. 5. 10, 10. 1 Cor. 7. 11. 2 Cor. 5. 18, 19, 20: and its noun

katallagē, a change or exchange for something else. Occ. Rom. 5. 11 (atonement); 11. 15. 2 Cor. 5. 18, 19.

(*d*) *apokatallassō*; intensive form of *katallassō*, the *apo* (Ap. 104. iv) indicating that whatever is intended by (*c*) is done completely and inviolably. Occ. only in the Prison Epistles, Eph. 2. 16. Col. 1. 20, 21.

(*e*) *hilaskomai*. Occ. Luke 18. 13. Heb. 2. 17 (see notes *in loc.*) As this word means to expiate, or make atonement for sins, and is confined to mediatorial aspects and offerings, it need not here be discussed.

3. We now refer to the occ. in the connection:

(*b*) *diallassomai*, Matt. 5. 24, where is found the basic explanation of the meaning usually understood by "be reconciled", &c.; i. e. the *change* of feelings and relationships of estranged relatives; a *mutual* change of feelings *between equals* (a man and his "brother").

(*c*) *katallassō*. Rom. 5. 10, 10, &c. Here is the proper meaning of the Greek word, as clothed in its correspondent Latin dress, viz. *re-united* or *re-connected* to God. Emphasized by the last clause, "having been reconciled" (re-connected). Vital union restored by *re-connection*.

Rom. 11. 15, "the reconciling". The meaning is unmistakable; the *re-connection* of "a world" is the antithesis to the "casting away" of Israel.

1 Cor. 7. 10, 11, "be reconciled"; i. e. *connected again* with her husband. Here also the antithesis is plain.

2 Cor. 5. 18, 19, 20. These verses paraphrased read,—". . . God, Who *re-connected* (or *re-united*) us again to Himself, by means of Christ, and having given to us the ministry of the *re-connection* (*re-uniting*), to wit, that God was IN Christ *re-connecting* (*re-uniting*) a world to Himself, not reckoning (imputing) their transgressions to them; and having laid upon us (the responsibility or burden of) the message of the *re-connection*. On Christ's behalf therefore we are ambassadors . . . be ye *re-connected* (*united again*) to God." We see here, revealed in simple majesty, the sovereign grace of God in providing by virtue of "the precious blood of Christ" a means whereby the rebellious creature can be restored to the favour of the justly alienated Creator. It is not an entreaty to "forgive" and "forget" everything on man's side, but a *command* to return to God by means of the *new connection*, and by that means alone, viz. the new and living Way which God Himself provided through the death and resurrection of His Son (Acts 17. 30, 31. Heb. 10. 19, 20).

(*d*) *apokatallassō*. Occ. Eph. 2. 16. Col. 1. 20, 21. In each case the force of *apo* prefixed to *katallassō* suggests and emphasizes the perfection of the *re-connection*. So that on God's side all is complete. Here again the graciousness of God is manifest. Who MADE PEACE by virtue of the blood of Christ, and thus gave access by means of Him "by one Spirit unto the Father", to those who were far off and to those who were nigh.

4. The conclusion may be summed up thus: Christ's death upon the cross linked up again the connection with God (i) for all who are the *chosen* subjects of His grace (Eph. 1. 4), and (ii) for all who will believe and consequently *become* subjects of His grace (Rom. 10. 11-13).

197 *THE REVELATION.*

A | The King and the kingdom,[1] in promise and prophecy (*the Old Testament*):

B | The King presented, proclaimed, and rejected (*the four Gospels*):

C | Transitional. The kingdom again offered and rejected (*Acts and the earlier Epistles.* See Ap. 180 and 181):

B | The King exalted and made Head over all things to "the church which is His body". The "mystery" (*the later Pauline Epistles.* See Ap. 193). The kingdom in abeyance (Heb. 2. 8).

A | The King and the kingdom unveiled. The King enthroned. The kingdom set up. Promise and prophecy fulfilled (*The Revelation*).

[1] For further details, see Ap. 95. II and Ap. 198.

1. The Lord Jesus Christ is the one great Subject of the Word of God (cp. Luke 24. 27; John 5. 39), being the promised "Seed" of the woman (Gen. 3. 15). He is therefore the Master-key to the Divine revelation of the Word. The whole Bible is about Him directly or indirectly, and as everything centres in and around Him, apart from Him it cannot be understood.

This is set forth in the foregoing Structure, from which we see that *Genesis* and *Revelation*, "the first" and "the last" books of the Bible, are inseparably linked together. *Genesis* is "the beginning" and *Revelation* the ending of the written Word, even as the Lord, the Incarnate Word, spake of Himself (cp. 21. 6; 22. 13). *Revelation* is the complement of *Genesis*. Either without the other would be unin-

telligible. Genesis 1–2 finds its correspondence in Rev. 21–22 (see Ap. 198).

Without the first chapters of *Genesis*, *Revelation* would be an insoluble riddle, as indeed it is to those who treat the record of "the Creation" and the "Fall" as "myths" (see 2 Tim. 4. 4). Without the last chapters of the *Revelation* "the Book" would be a hopeless and heart-breaking record of the failure and doom of the Adamic race.

The Bible may be likened to a beautiful and complex girdle or belt, with a corresponding connecting clasp at each end, one the complement of the other. Do away with either, the girdle is useless, *as a girdle*. So here, *Genesis* and *Revelation* are the two clasps of the Divine Word, which link together and enclose between them in "perfection of beauty" and harmony the whole of the Scriptures in which God has been pleased to reveal His "Eternal Purpose" (Ap. 198).

2. Its Scope, &c. The key to unlock the meaning and scope of the book is found in 1. 10. "The Lord's day" = THE DAY OF THE LORD (Jehovah). (See Isa. 2. 12.) John was not in "a state of spiritual exaltation" on any particular *Sunday* at Patmos, as the result of which "he saw visions and dreamed dreams". But, as we are told, "I came to be (or found myself) by the Spirit in the day of the Lord" (cp. Ezek. 1. 1; 8. 3, &c.). He is then shown, and both sees and hears (22. 8), the things he records.

"The day of the Lord" being *yet future*, it follows that the whole book must concern the things belonging to "that day", and consequently is wholly prophecy. Though partial adumbrations of judgment may be traced in connection with affairs of past history, yet the significant, *solemn* warning here (1. 10) that the "judgments" in *Revelation* relate to the day of the Lord, "the day of vengeance" (cp. Isa. 61. 2; 63. 4, &c.), makes it clear that the book concerns the future, and the day of the unveiling (the Apocalypse) of the great "King of kings and Lord of lords" (see Ap. 198).

Its scope is further shown by its place in the Canon. The order of the separate books of the N. T. varies, but they are always formed in four *groups* that never vary chronologically. (See Ap. 95. II.)

The *Gospels* contain the prophecies of the great tribulation: *Revelation* describes it. Between, come the Scriptures of the intermediate period, *Acts* and the Epistles. Chronologically and canonically, *Revelation* follows after the Epistles, though logically in God's purpose (Eph. 3. 11) it follows the *Gospels*. Therefore we see the scope embraces the wind-up of all the affairs of time; it records the end of prophecy, the end of "the secret of God" (10. 7), the end of all "enmity towards God", and the dawn of the "ages of the ages".

3. Its Hebrew Character. The language of the book is Greek: its thoughts and idioms are Hebrew. This links it with the O. T., and shows that its great purpose is to declare God's final dealings with the *Jew* and the *Gentile* as such; and that "the church of God" of the Pauline Epistles and this dispensation (Ap. 195) has no place in *Revelation* (other than in association with its glorified Head). See Ap. 193. All the imagery of the book, Temple, Tabernacle, &c., belongs to Israel.

Again, in *Matthew* (the Hebrew Gospel) are some 92 quotations from and references to the O. T. In *Hebrews* there are 102. In *Revelation* are found no fewer than 285. This emphatically stamps its close connection with the O. T. and Israel; and it equally stamps the latest utterances of "modern scholarship", viz. that "whatever view may be taken of the indebtedness to Jewish sources, there can be no doubt that he (the writer) has produced a book which taken as a whole is profoundly Christian", as being the dicta of men who, wittingly or unwittingly, are blind to this fundamental fact of *Revelation*.

The Titles of Christ further attest its Hebrew character:

(i) "The Son of Man" (1. 13; 14. 14). Never found in the Pauline Epistles to the "churches". See Ap. 98. XVI and Ap. 99.

(ii) "The Almighty" (1. 8; &c.). See Ap. 98. IV.

(iii) "The Lord God" (3. 8 and see 22. 6). Cp. this title with Gen. 2. 4—3. 24 in connexion with "paradise".

(iv) "The First and the Last" (1. 11, 17; 2. 8; 22. 13). Never associated with "the church which is His body".

(v) "The Prince of the kings of the earth" (1. 5). Never used in connexion with "the church".

(vi) "Who is to come" (= The Coming One), 1. 4, &c. Occ. sixteen times in the Gospels, *Acts*, *Hebrews* (10. 37); *three* times in *Revelation*, and nowhere else.

(vii) "The Living One" (1. 18). A title only found in Daniel (4. 34; 12. 7) and *six* times in this book. Thus linking *Daniel* and *Revelation* in a very special manner.

4. The "Bride" and the "Wife" of 21. 9 must not be confused with the "wife" of 19. 7. The latter is Israel called out from among the nations for blessing in "the Land"; the earthly consort of "the Great King" (cp. Ps. 45; Jer. 3. 14). This "wife" (19. 7) is connected with the Millennial Jerusalem which, with the rest of the earth "that now" is, will pass away and give place to the *new* earth with the *new* Jerusalem, succeeding and replacing the former. "The bride, the Lamb's wife" of 21. 9, is still of Israel, but the Israel of the "heavenly calling" (Heb. 3. 1): all those connected with the "heavenly country" and "the city with *the foundations*" for which they "looked" (Heb. 11. 13–16); the "Jerusalem above" of Gal. 4. 26. Hence the significance of the term "bride" (*numphē*) in 21. 9.

The Israel of 19. 7 is not spoken of as bride (*numphē*), because she *has become* wife (*gunē*). Cp. the "married to you" = *am become your husband* (consummation), of Jer. 3. 14, and see the Note there relating to the "restoration" time. Here (21. 9) the term "bride" indicates clearly that the betrothal has taken place and that the marriage will be consummated when the bride shall *have come down* out of heaven. John sees her coming down (pres. part.), 21. 10.

The loose way in which *we* speak of a "bride" as not only a contracting party at the time of the marriage ceremony, but also of her after she has become wife (*gunē*), is responsible for much confusion as to the "wife" of 19. 7 and the bride-wife of 21. 9. Strictly speaking, "bride" is to be applied only to a betrothed virgin (Gr. *parthenos* = Heb. *b^ethūlāh*), when the marriage (legal) ceremony takes place. *Directly* after, she ceases to be "bride", and has become (legally) "wife", although from the forensic point of view consummation of the marriage may be delayed (cp. Matt. 1. 25, and see the Note there).

According to the Mosaic Law, a betrothed maid (Heb. *b^ethūlāh*) was *legally* a wife (*'ishshāh*), (cp. Matt. 1. 18, 20 with Deut. 22. 23, 24); hence Joseph's trouble and temptation (see Matt. 1. 20). A careful study of the terms in Matt. 1. 18-25 will afford a clue to a clearer understanding of the terms "bride" and the two "wives" of Rev. 19. 7; 21. 9 than volumes of commentary.

If the earthly millennial metropolis is real, so is this also, for both are spoken of in the same terms. And if the laying of "thy stones with fair colours" and "thy foundations with sapphires" (Isa. 54. 11) is spoken of the day when God is to be called "the God of *the whole earth*" (see *v.* 5), it must refer to the time of Isa. 65. 17; 66. 22 and Rev. 21. 1. Moreover, *laying* foundations implies a solid substratum on which to lay them, i. e. *earth*. Foundations are of no use to a city "suspended" in the air!

The same argument applies also to the "tree of life" and the "water of life". If the "river" and "trees for meat" of Ezek. 47. 1-12 are real and literal, so also are the "tree" and the "water" of life here. Again, both are spoken of in identical terms. There is no more room for "imagery" in the one case than the other. The "tree of life" lost in the paradise of *Genesis* is here seen restored to the whole earth in the day when "the God of the whole earth" will "tabernacle" with men,—(and be) "their God" (Rev. 21. 3). There is no place for "symbolism" in either case.

5. The more important Figs. of Speech are noted. These will supply helpful keys where the symbolism is not Divinely explained or indicated, and will enable the student to judge whether *Revelation* is purely Johannine "symbolic imagery", as some affirm, and a "legitimate appeal to Christian imagination"; or whether the book is, as it claims to be, a deliberate setting forth proleptically of the actual scenes and events with which God declares that His purposes concerning the heaven and the earth shall be consummated.

6. NUMBERS hold a prominent and significant place in *Revelation*. These in order are:—2 (occ. eleven times); 3 (eleven); 3½ (twice); 4 (thirty); 5 (three); 6 (twice, including 13. 18); 7 (fifty-four); 10 (nine); 12 (twenty-two); 24 (seven); 42 (twice); 144 (four); 666 (once); 1,000 (nine); 1,260 (twice); 1,600 (once); 7,000 (once); 12,000 (thirteen); 144,000 (three); 100,000,000 (once, 5. 11); 200,000,000 (once, 9. 16). Twenty-one in all (3 × 7 = 21. See Ap. 10).

Seven is thus seen to be the predominant number, occurring fifty-four times (3 × 3 × 3 × 2 = 54. Ap. 10). *Twelve* comes next—twenty-two occ. *Seven, ten,* and *twelve*, with their multiples, run throughout the book. In the Notes attention is called to other numbers of great significance. The student will thus be enabled to work out for himself many problems connected with the question of number in Scripture. Some examples are here given of word occurrences.

6 times; *Babulōn*, *basanismos* (torment), *theion* (brimstone):

7 " ; *abussos* (bottomless pit), *axios* (worthy), *basileuō* (reign), *etoimazō* (make ready), *makarios* (blessed), *prophēteia* (prophecy), *sēmeion* (sign, &c.), *hupomenē* (patience), *charagma* (mark), *Christos*:

8 " ; *Amēn*, *thusiastērion* (altar), *planaō* (deceive), *Satanas*, *sphragizō* (seal), *stephanos* (crown), *nux* (night):

9 " ; *deka* (ten), *kainos* (new), *krinō* (judge), *marturia* (testimony), *pantokratōr* (Almighty), *polemos* (battle, &c.):

10 " ; *alēthinos* (true), *eikōn* (image), *thumos* (wrath), *keras* (horn), *prosōpon* (face), *hōra* (hour), *salpizo* (to sound):

12 " ; *dunamis* (strength), *phialē* (vial):

14 " ; *astēr* (star), *Iēsous*, *doulos* (servant); &c.

The word *arnion* (lamb) occ. 29 times ("the Lamb" 28 = 4 sevens: the other occ. 13. 11). Elsewhere only in John 21. 15. *hagios* (holy) occ. 26 times according to the texts, which omit 15. 3 and 22. 6, and add 22. 21; otherwise 27 times (3 × 9, or 3 × 3 × 3): *doxa* (glory) occ. 17 times (10 + 7): *eulogia* (blessing and ascription) 3 times; *ethnos* (nations) 23 times; *nikaō* (overcome) 17 times: *drakōn* (dragon) 13 times: *plēgē* (plague, &c.) occ. 16 times (4 × 4).

Phrases occ. frequently, e. g. (i) *he that hath an ear* 7 times; *if any man hath an ear* occ. once: (ii) *third part*, 16 times: (iii) *the kings of the earth*, 9 times.

7. CONCLUSION. The "tree of life" (22. 2) and the "water of life" (*vv.* 1, 17) are seen to be the great central subjects of the new earth. No longer will there be any "curse" (*v.* 3). In place of the "Fall" we have restoration. Instead of *expulsion*—"lest he put forth his hand, and take also of the tree of life, and eat, and live for ever" (Gen. 3. 22)—is the gracious *invitation* to those who "have right to the tree of life" (*v.* 22), "Come, whosoever desireth, and let him take the water of life freely" (*v.* 17).

8. The Benediction (22. 21) not only completes the correspondence of the Structure (p. 1883), but appropriately closes the whole of the Book of God. "Grace and truth came by Jesus Christ" (John 1. 17). In this dispensation *all* is of grace. Grace now, glory hereafter (cp. Ps. 84. 11). In the time coming, with which *Revelation* is concerned, *grace* will be given to "endure to the end" (Matt. 24. 13) to all who come "out of the great tribulation" (7. 14); to all slain under antichrist "for the Word of God" (6. 9); and to all who "have the testimony of Jesus Christ" (12. 17). "*Grace, grace.*" ALL IS OF GRACE!

198 THE ETERNAL PURPOSE (Eph. 3. 11).

THE DISPENSATIONAL PLAN OF THE BIBLE.

A | THE PRIMAL CREATION. HEAVENS AND EARTH. "The world (Gr. *kosmos*) that then was." Gen. 1. 1, 2-. 2 Pet. 3. 6.

B | SATAN'S FIRST REBELLION. The earth became waste and a ruin (Heb. *tohū vā bohū*). Gen. 1. 2-. God *created* it not a ruin (Isa. 45. 18, Heb. *tohū*) nor waste ("confusion").

C | THE EARTH RESTORED AND BLESSED. "The heavens and the earth which are now." Gen. 1. -2—2. 3. 2 Pet. 3. 7.

D | SATAN ENTERS AND THE CONSEQUENCE. Gen. 3.

E | MANKIND DEALT WITH AS A WHOLE. Gen. 4—11. 26.

F | THE CHOSEN NATION CALLED AND BLESSED. Gen. 11. 27—Mal. 4. 6. (Jehovah and His kingdom rejected. Israel scattered.)

G | THE FIRST ADVENT (Micah 5. 2. Zech. 9. 9). The Four Gospels (Rom. 15. 8). The King and the kingdom proclaimed and rejected, and the King crucified.

H | THE KINGDOM RE-PROCLAIMED. Acts 3. 19, 20, &c. The church of God called and taken out, Acts 13 and on, and earlier Pauline Epistles. The kingdom again rejected and Israel again scattered.

H | THE KINGDOM POSTPONED AND IN ABEYANCE. "Not yet" (Heb. 2. 8). The later, or Prison, Epistles (Pauline). The MYSTERY revealed and proclaimed. Eph. 3. 2-11. Col. 1. 25; 2. 2, 3. 1 Tim. 3. 16. THE NEW HOPE. Phil. 3. 11, 14. Titus 2. 13. "The church which is His body" called, and taken up. Phil. 3. 11, 14.

G | THE SECOND ADVENT. "The first resurrection." The kingdom established. The King enthroned. "The day of the Lord." Matt. 24; 25. 31. Luke 19. 11-27. Isa. 2. 11-19. Joel 2; &c.

F | THE CHOSEN NATION RECALLED AND BLESSED. Rom. 11. 11-36. Acts 15. 16. Isa. 60, 61, 62. Jer. 30, 31. Zech. 12. 13, 14; &c.

E | MANKIND DEALT WITH AS A WHOLE. Joel 3. 2. Matt. 25. 31-46. Acts 15. 17. Rom. 15. 8-12. Rev. 4-19.

D | SATAN BOUND AND THE CONSEQUENCES. Rev. 20. 1-3.

C | THE EARTH RESTORED AND BLESSED. Rev. 20. 4-6. Isa. 35; &c. The Millennium.

B | SATAN'S FINAL REBELLION. Rev. 20. 7-10. Followed by the second resurrection and the judgment of the "great white throne". The destruction of "all things that offend". Rev. 20. 11-15.

A | THE NEW HEAVEN AND THE NEW EARTH. The day of God. Rev. 21, 22. 2 Pet. 3. 12, 13. Isa. 65. 17; 66. 22.

1. The above Structure shows the respective dispensations in which God has been and is dealing with the Jew, the Gentile, and the church of God (1 Cor. 10. 32). The "church which is His body" occupies the central position, and its present standing is seen to be separated from its future destiny and hope. The two rebellions of Satan also are seen to be in direct correspondence; suggesting the necessity why he must be loosed, and the loosing, for a little season (Rev. 20. 3, 7).

2. All things were created by Him "Who IS before all things and by Whom all things consist" (lit. hang together, Col. 1. 17); Who is now "upholding all things by the word of His power" (Heb. 1. 3). The Structure shows in almost pictorial form the great lesson that God sets before us from *Genesis* to *Revelation*, viz. that no created being can stand (upright) apart from Christ the Creator. Hence the necessity for a "new heaven and a new earth" wherein abideth righteousness, inhabited by a "new creation" of beings who have by grace been made "partakers of the Divine nature" (2 Pet. 1. 4).

3. Further, it will be seen that it is not God's purpose to bring in the new heaven and new earth by means of the "church". The new creation will be full of physical marvels, brought about by physical means and not "spiritual agencies". These means and their results are set before us in *Revelation*. Well may we exclaim with Paul,—**"O the depth of the riches both of the wisdom and knowledge of God! how unsearchable are His judgments, and His ways past finding out! For who hath known the mind of the Lord? or who hath been His counsellor? Or who hath first given to Him, and it shall be recompensed unto him again? For of Him, and through Him, and to Him, are all things: to WHOM BE GLORY FOR EVER. AMEN."**

GENERAL INDEX TO THE APPENDIXES

GENERAL INDEX TO THE APPENDIXES.

GENERAL INDEX TO THE APPENDIXES.

GENERAL INDEX TO THE APPENDIXES.

GENERAL INDEX TO THE APPENDIXES.

GENERAL INDEX TO THE APPENDIXES.

GENERAL INDEX TO THE APPENDIXES.

GENERAL INDEX TO THE APPENDIXES.

In Front of Saint Patrick’s Cathedral

In Front of Saint Patrick's Cathedral

A New Edition

Donald Blumberg
With an essay by Jock Reynolds

Yale University Art Gallery
New Haven

Distributed by Yale University Press
New Haven and London

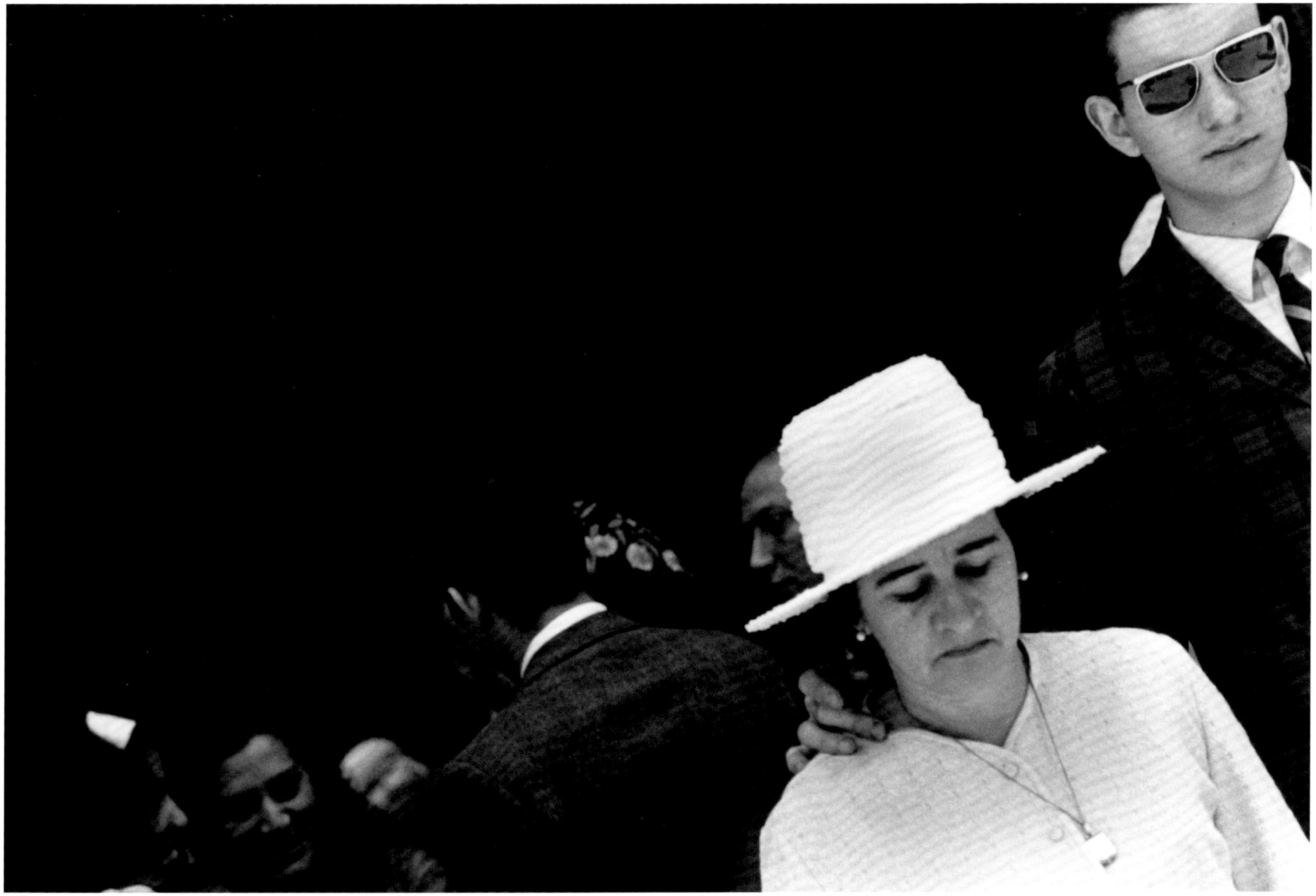

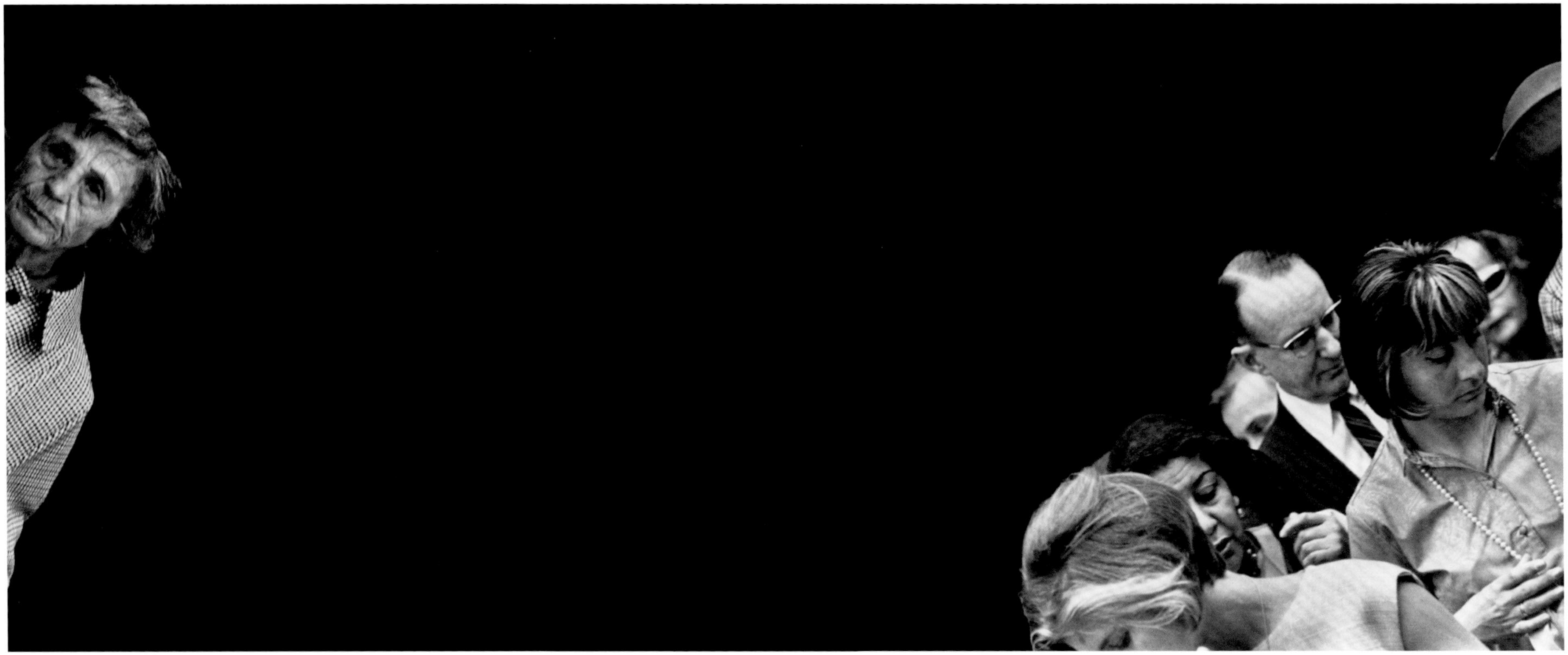

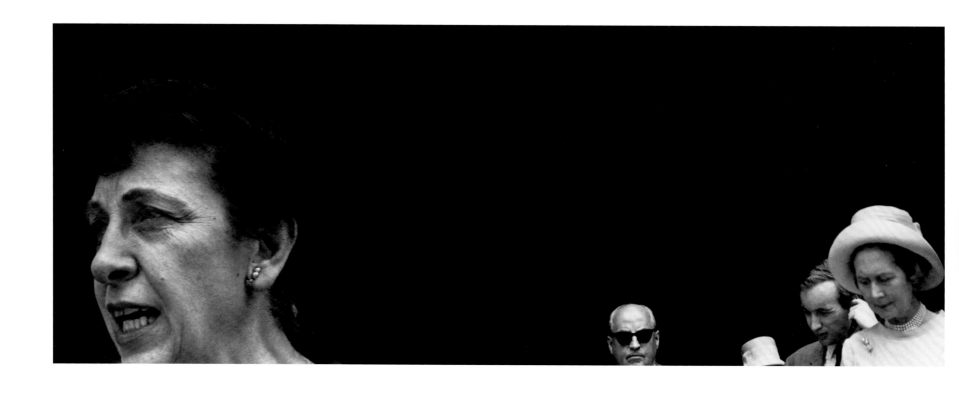

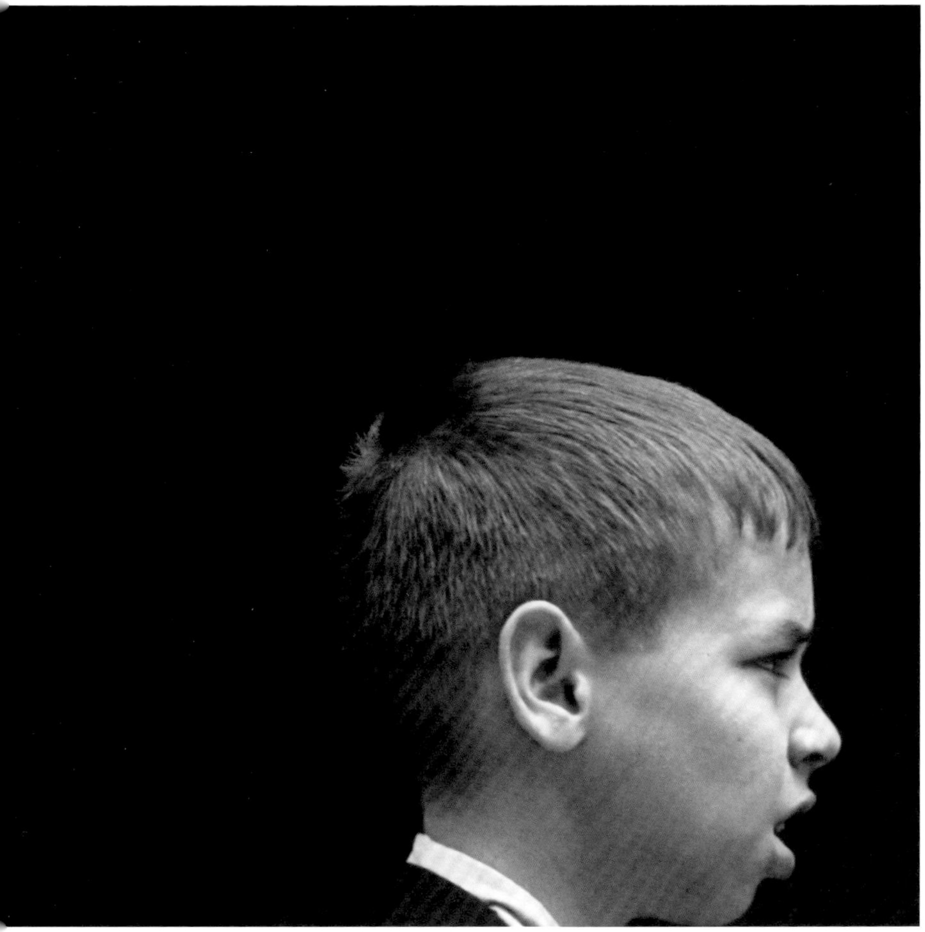

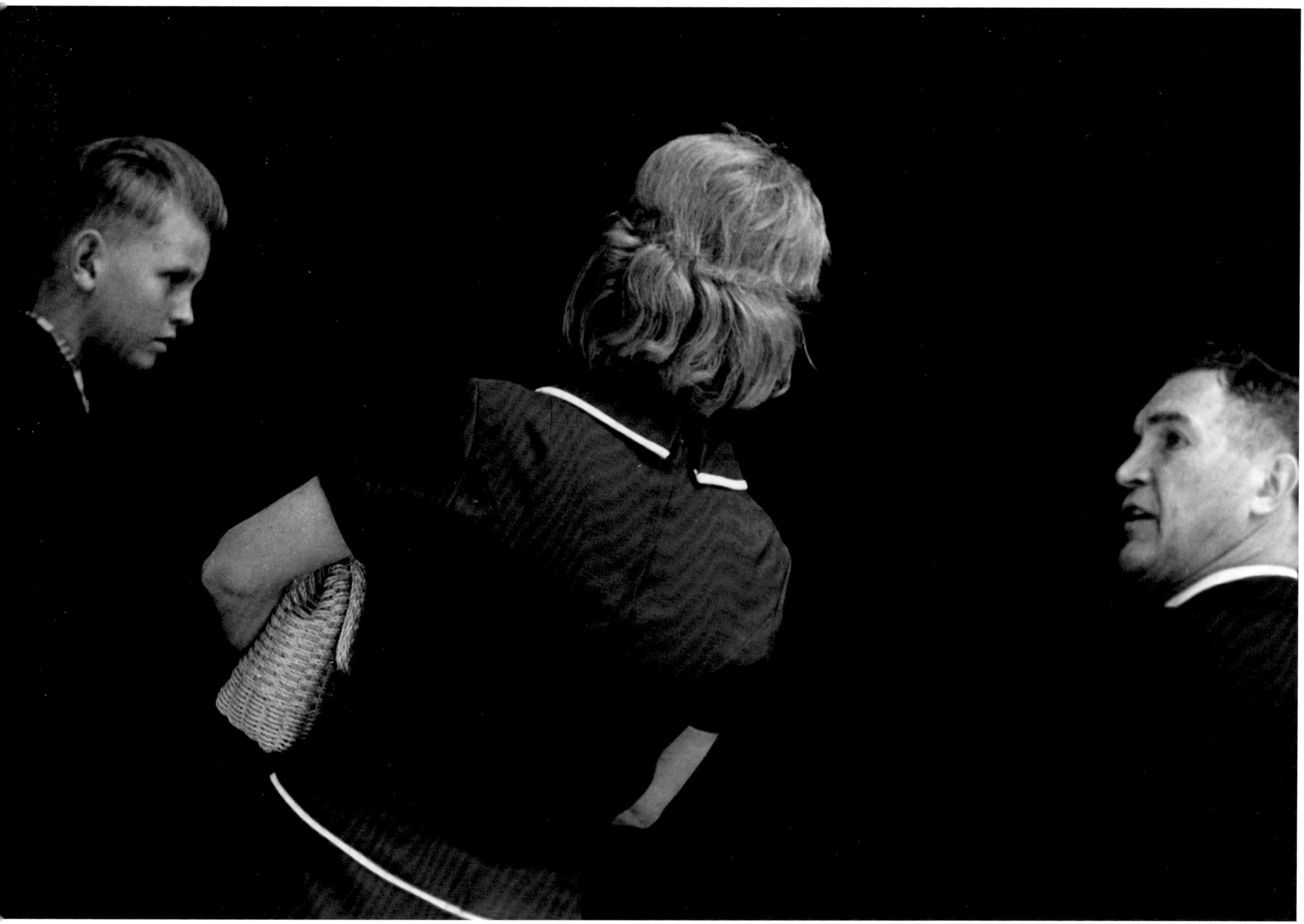

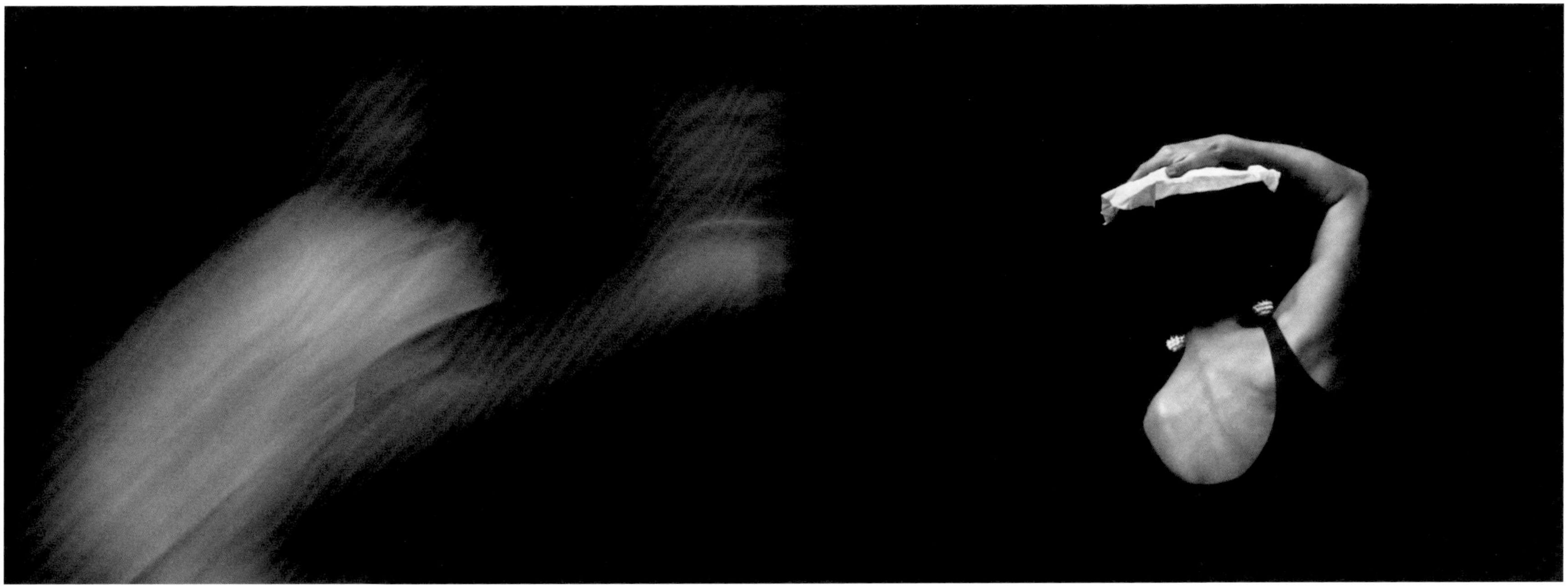

SIGHT
75¢

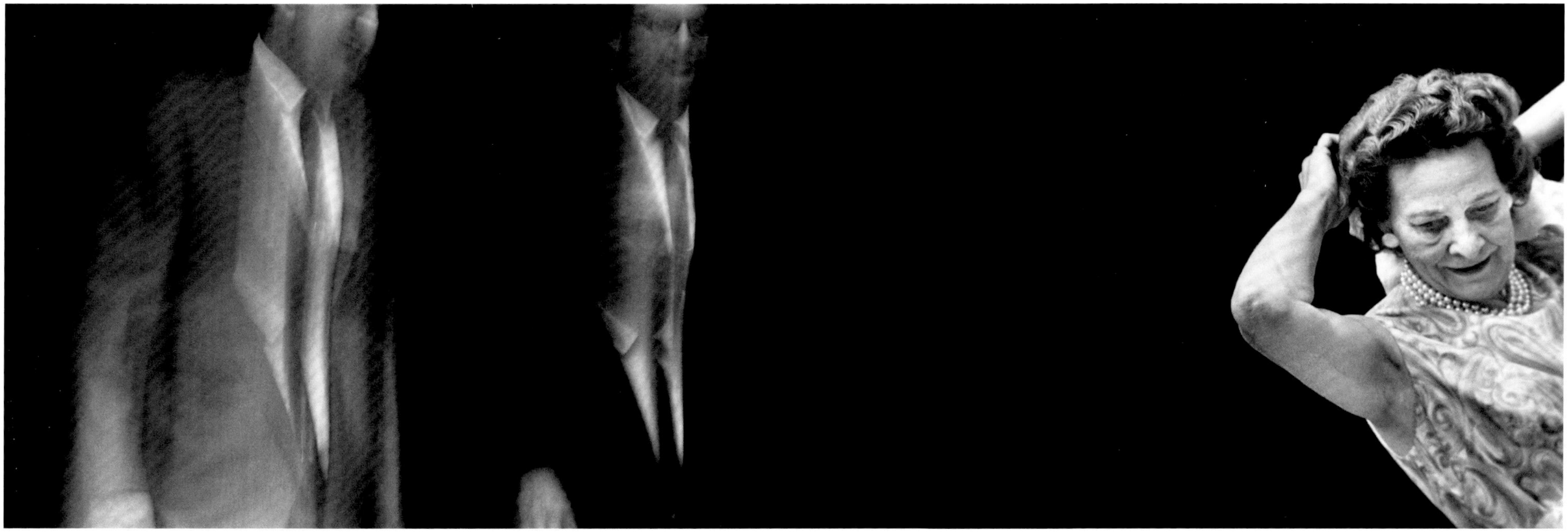

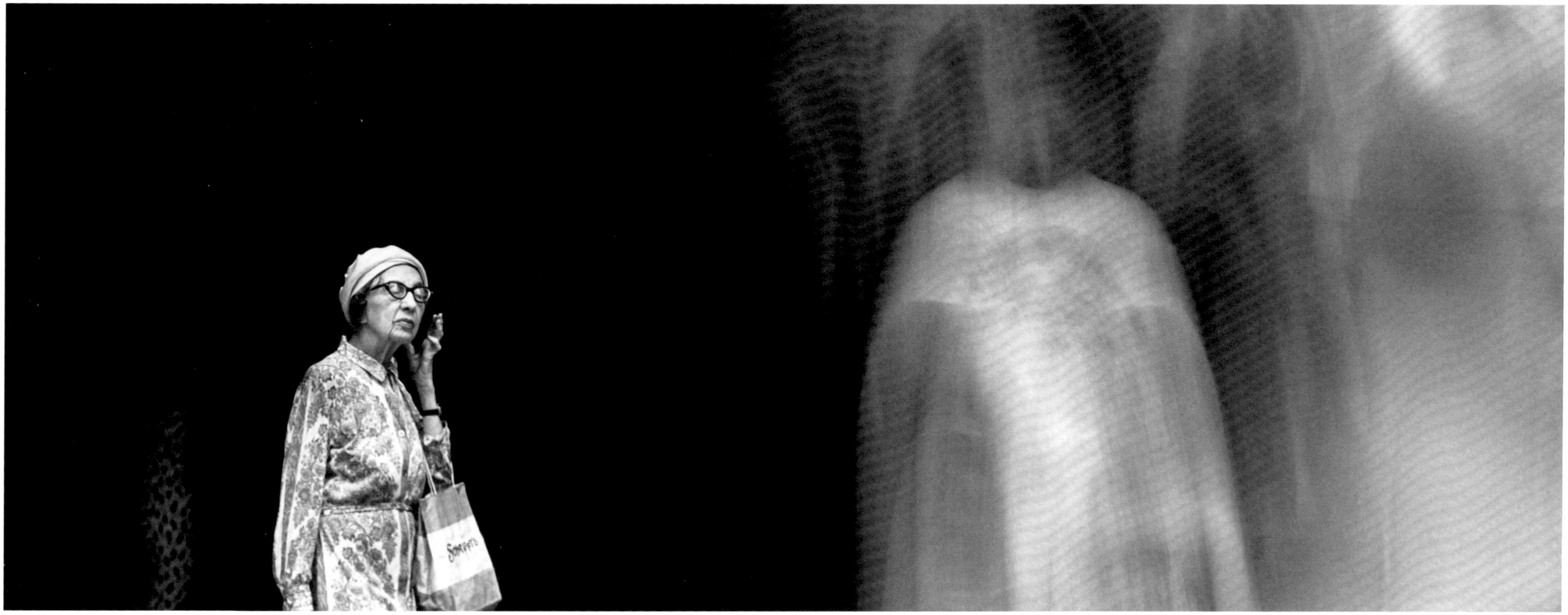

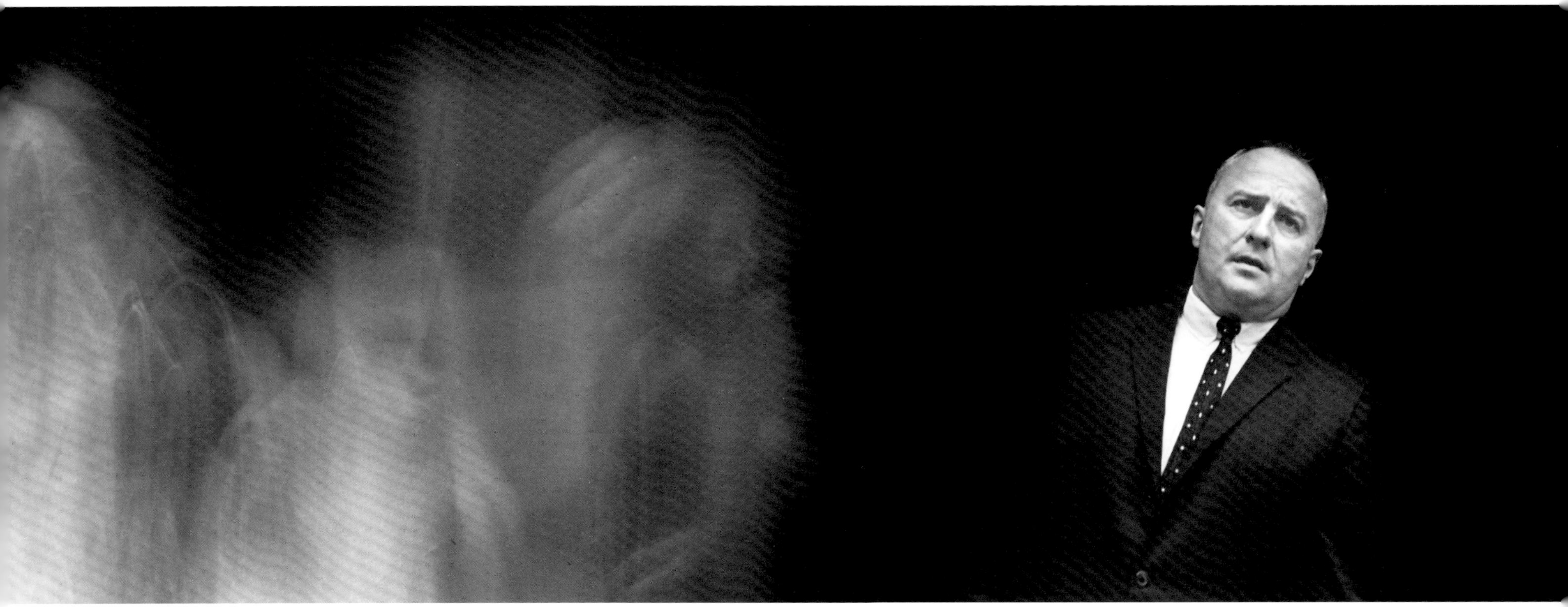

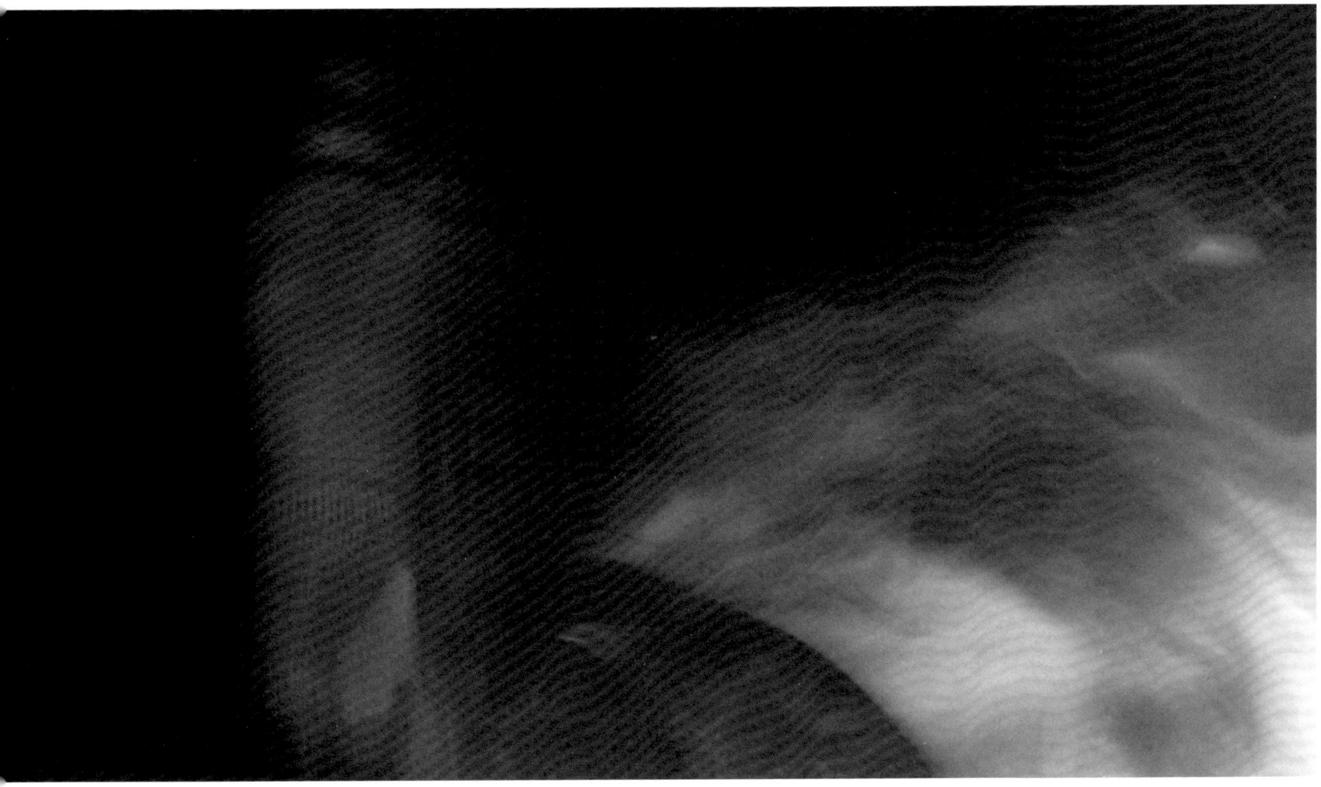

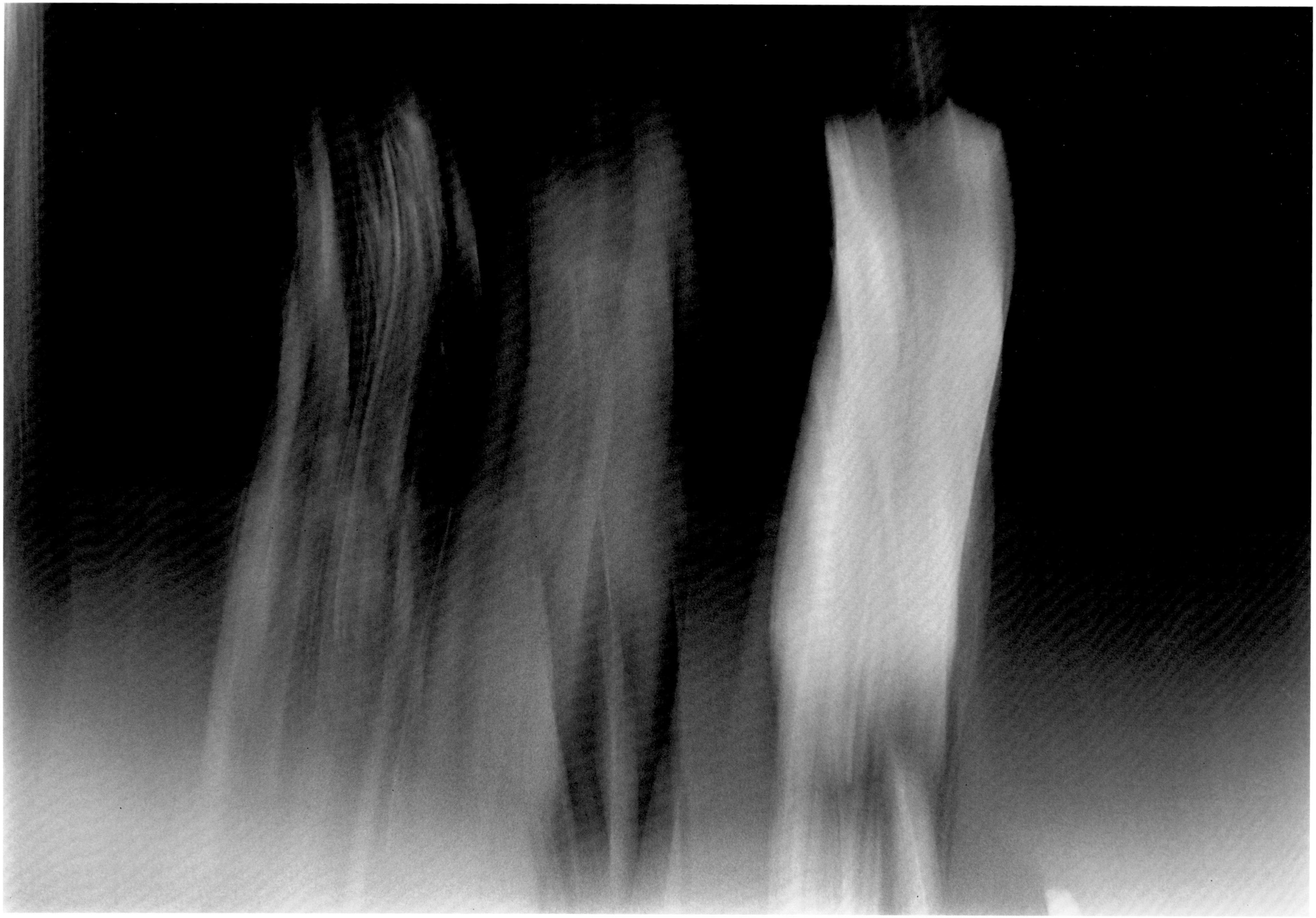

"Sharply Etched in Blackness"

Jock Reynolds

The first edition of *In Front of Saint Patrick's Cathedral*, published in 1973, drew upon a large body of photographs that Donald Blumberg began making in 1965—a set of images he came to carefully examine over time, edit, sequence, and then print as an artist's book. The original publication, long out of print, was produced with the assistance of fellow artists Nathan and Joan Lyons, cofounders of the Visual Studies Workshop in Rochester, New York. It included a concise project statement by Blumberg, a salient introduction by Nathan Lyons, and a preface by Minor White, who was at the time teaching photography at the Massachusetts Institute of Technology. Now, forty-two years later, with Blumberg's master sets having recently arrived at the Yale University Art Gallery, the time has come for this seminal artist's book to come to life again, edited anew.

Early in my directorship (1989–98) at the Addison Gallery of American Art at Phillips Academy, in Andover, Massachusetts, I was introduced to Donald Blumberg and his work by Nathan Lyons. Soon thereafter, the museum purchased several photographs by Blumberg, and I included a number of images from the first edition of *In Front of Saint Patrick's Cathedral* in the Addison's 1991 exhibition *Motion and Document, Sequence and Time: Eadweard Muybridge and Contemporary American Photography*. It was clear to me then, as well as to others who knew Blumberg as an innovative artist and outstanding educator, that he was well aware of the pioneering nineteenth-century time-motion studies that had been undertaken by Eadweard Muybridge (fig. 1), Thomas Eakins, and Étienne-Jules Marey (fig. 2). Early in Blumberg's marriage to his wife, Grace, his mother-in-law had given him a 1955 published copy of Muybridge's *Animal Locomotion*, and by the early 1960s, a strong legion of photographers and pioneering conceptual artists were already attuned to what Mel Bochner later described in an essay in *Artforum* as "The Serial Attitude." It was equally evident that Blumberg's knowledge of these early experiments with photography was linked to his keen interest in the twentieth-century media of film and television; these media opened up all manner of new camera placements, angles, exposures, and editing options—a vast array of creative possibilities,

Fig. 1.
Eadweard Muybridge, *Athletes, Twisting Summersault*, plate 106 from the series *The Attitudes of Animals in Motion*, 1881. Gelatin silver print. Addison Gallery of American Art, Phillips Academy, Andover, Massachusetts, Partial gift of The Beinecke Foundation, Inc.

many of which began to appear in his mosaic television images of the 1960s and 1970s as well as in subsequent projects.

Blumberg's career as a photographer began in the early 1960s. He had been discharged from the U.S. Army in 1957 and, shortly thereafter, abandoned a fledgling career in the sciences to commit himself to becoming a professional photographer in New York City, where he had been born and raised. He proceeded in this new endeavor with the encouragement and mentorship of the photographer Larry Fink, whom he met in New York along with a number of other young emerging photographers, many of whom shared his high regard for the work of Walker Evans, Ben Shahn, Dorothea Lange, Helen Levitt, Robert Frank, and other well-established chroniclers of American life. Their work helped fuel Blumberg's own desire to more carefully observe and record what he was experiencing day in and day out while living on Manhattan's Lower East Side. He soon became not only an artist but also an activist and educator, undertaking documentary work for a notable labor union, teaching photography classes for an inner-city youth program, and becoming a devoted participant, along with his wife, in the burgeoning civil rights movement.

I think it was likely Blumberg's awareness of both classic time-motion photography and documentary street photography that caused him, by both accident and prescient intuition, to pause one day in May 1965 and focus his attention on a procession of worshippers emerging from a service just concluded at Saint Patrick's Cathedral, in Midtown Manhattan. In Blumberg's own words:

I was photographing along Fifth Avenue on a bright day flooded with western light. I stopped on the steps in front of the open double-door portal of Saint Patrick's Cathedral to watch the churchgoers emerge from the darkened recesses into the crisp glare of the afternoon sunlight. The illuminated figures reminded me of the photographs my students made at the Saturday night dances of the Coffee Shop [a neighborhood youth program where Blumberg taught photography]. I exposed several rolls of film, developed them, made contact sheets and a selection of prints. It occurred to me that a figure could be placed randomly within the central portal's black-framed field, defying traditional horizontal and vertical visual reference points and the forces of gravity.

Fig. 2.
Étienne-Jules Marey, *Pole Vault*, ca. 1890. Chronophotography on a fixed glass-plate negative. Collège de France—Archive

Fig. 3.
Ben Shahn, *Three Men with Iron Pilaster, New York*, 1934. Gelatin silver print. Collection San Francisco Museum of Modern Art, Purchase

I returned to the cathedral steps, taking light-meter readings off highlighted flesh tones. My goal was to properly expose the emerging figures while underexposing the open portal space, throwing it into an even more intense blackness. The new prints revealed a rich, deep, creamy black surface. The highlighted figures appeared sharply etched in blackness. Some entering the margins of the frame were severed, a portion of the figure entering the black field and the remainder external to the frame, subjects for the viewer's imagination. They were evocative of the technique Ben Shahn incorporated in his early New York City figurative paintings and photographs in the 1930s [fig. 3].

While viewing the contact sheets, I found that the black lines that separate frames dissolved into the blackness of the negatives' interiors, fusing side-by-side negatives into a single image. Sometimes the effect would include the fusion of as many as three or four negatives. I returned to the cathedral steps conscious of the possibilities and began to associate image content from one frame to another. I realized that I could reincorporate the same figure at an altered relative size, change the scale of a figure that had entered one of the contiguous frames, or have a figure disappear from one frame to the next. I marked the contact sheets with a red china marker, selecting singles, doubles, and triples to print as a single image. I then had a tool-and-die maker open the 35-millimeter single-negative carrier to accommodate up to three negatives. The printing simply required setting the enlarger head to a 4 x 5–inch light spread to accommodate the multiple-negative sequence.

I returned time and again to the cathedral to work out my image possibilities and found that some of the new images were blurred, either because of long exposure or accidental camera movement. I began to create blurred images next to fixed images and eventually made a series of 20 x 24–inch images using slow shutter speeds and calculated camera movement. I had in the back of my mind the Turner paintings at the Tate, in which Turner rendered seascapes and sky in a similar visual manner.

The opportunity to review the full range of images Blumberg recorded for *In Front of Saint Patrick's Cathedral* has been a fascinating experience. We now know from carefully

examining his master sets that he took over four thousand pictures in front of the cathedral, many of which were only printed on 35-millimeter contact sheets, of which there are 112.

Appropriate to the educational mission of the Gallery, the review of this large body of work and the inquiry into how it was undertaken has been conducted by not just me but also La Tanya Autry, the Marcia Brady Tucker Fellow, and Gabriella Svenningsen, Museum Assistant, both in the Department of Modern and Contemporary Art. These talented young staff members have bridged two generations to engage an artist now entering his eightieth year—one whose ideas and work have been shared with us with a generosity that can only be described as rare. There are not many artists of the younger generation who work with cameras that record images on film, nor do many of them know what a 35-millimeter contact sheet is, nor do they print black-and-white images on gelatin-silver paper in darkrooms from negatives that they themselves have developed. New digital technologies, cameras, and software have shaken up how a photograph is regarded today, and yet Blumberg's images, as taken, printed, and presented in the first edition of *In Front of Saint Patrick's Cathedral*, still have striking visual allure. There is something poetic and compelling about the way in which Blumberg chose to portray and then blend his procession of human subjects across not just one but two or three successively shot images; when joined together, exposed, and printed, they appear mysteriously unified. The photographs are populated by people who look as though they are slipping silently in motion, across space and time and in various scales of elusive presence. Some of these worshippers even seem to defy gravity as they hover in deep blackness, coming in and out of view. The sequence of images in the book reveals an array of figures that begin to dissolve into ethereal forms of light, perhaps suggesting the manner in which souls leave their mortal bodies upon death. Engaging with this body of work again after many years, I was reminded that Goethe's oft-quoted dying words were actually not just "Mehr Licht!," or "More light!," but, when translated properly from the German, "Do open the shutter of the bedroom so that more light comes in." Donald Blumberg opened his eyes and the shutter of his camera to share an elegy of sorts in *In Front of Saint Patrick's Cathedral*, a book that remains powerful today.

When we commenced working with his master sets, Blumberg told me that he very much wanted the present edition of his book to be newly edited by someone other than himself. I asked Autry to take the lead in planning the sequencing of this expanded edition of *In Front of Saint Patrick's Cathedral*, and she quickly proposed that some of Blumberg's single-, double-, and triple-negative portraits remain presented as first published but that others be sequenced in a new order. She also suggested the addition of several never-before-printed images from Blumberg's original contact sheets and advocated that a number of the contact sheets be reproduced

at the end of this edition, to reveal a bit more about how Blumberg first set about examining, editing, and printing the images he chose to enlarge from his negatives. Autry then proceeded to pair some of Blumberg's original single-image prints, fusing them to create a number of even more extended panoramic images than appeared in the first edition. This approach has added a strong filmic sense to Blumberg's silent requiem of human figures.

Interestingly, Donald and Grace Blumberg together produced eight experimental films during the 1960s, all of which were shown at private and public screenings but never received broad distribution of any kind. They have now all been digitized for easy viewing. The earliest of these films, *Have You Been to Hamburg Lately* (1964), is an evocative impression of the German city—from nighttime to daytime—conceived and directed by Grace Blumberg, for which her husband acted as assistant cameraman. *Buffalo to New York: New York to Buffalo* (1968) is a visually syncopated single-frame travel film that the couple recorded during a round-trip car ride they took together. The two films, which will be shown at the Gallery during the presentation of the exhibition *Donald Blumberg Photographs: Selections from the Master Sets* in fall 2015, will reveal some of the innovative conceptual and visual ways in which this creative couple has explored time, light, and movement through space and place.

In addition to their experimentations with film and photography in the 1960s, Donald and Grace delved into the music scene as well. They were friends with some notable musicians of the period, including Paul Duynhouwer and Omar Clay, who improvised a jazz trombone and drum piece during a silent screening of *Have You Been to Hamburg Lately*. The music was recorded live and later added to the film as its soundtrack.

In 1966, not long after the recording of this film soundtrack, Blumberg initiated another collaboration, this time with the painter Charles Gill, with whom he was teaching in the art department at the State University of New York at Buffalo. For this project, Blumberg first exposed and developed a number of his 35-millimeter and 4 x 5–inch images on a series of large photo-linen canvases. He then mounted the carefully processed photo linens on stretcher bars and invited Gill to paint on them. Their collaboration yielded a number of successful photographic combine paintings, including one very large diptych comprising two images from *In Front of Saint Patrick's Cathedral*—bisected by a hockey stick and with painted additions by Gill. This important collaborative artwork, featured on the cover of the present publication, was the first one visitors encountered when entering the landmark 1967 exhibition *Contemporary Photographers: The Persistence of Vision*, curated by Nathan Lyons while he was the director of the George Eastman House, in Rochester, New York.

It has been a special pleasure for all of us here at the Gallery to be able to exhibit the Saint Patrick's Cathedral photographs

alongside other series by the artist, to screen films by Donald and Grace, and to have them both visit the Yale campus to discuss their work and meet with our students while Donald serves as Hayden Visiting Artist in the fall of 2015. Equally gratifying has been the opportunity to work closely with Donald to publish this new edition of *In Front of Saint Patrick's Cathedral*—putting this important series of work back into print.

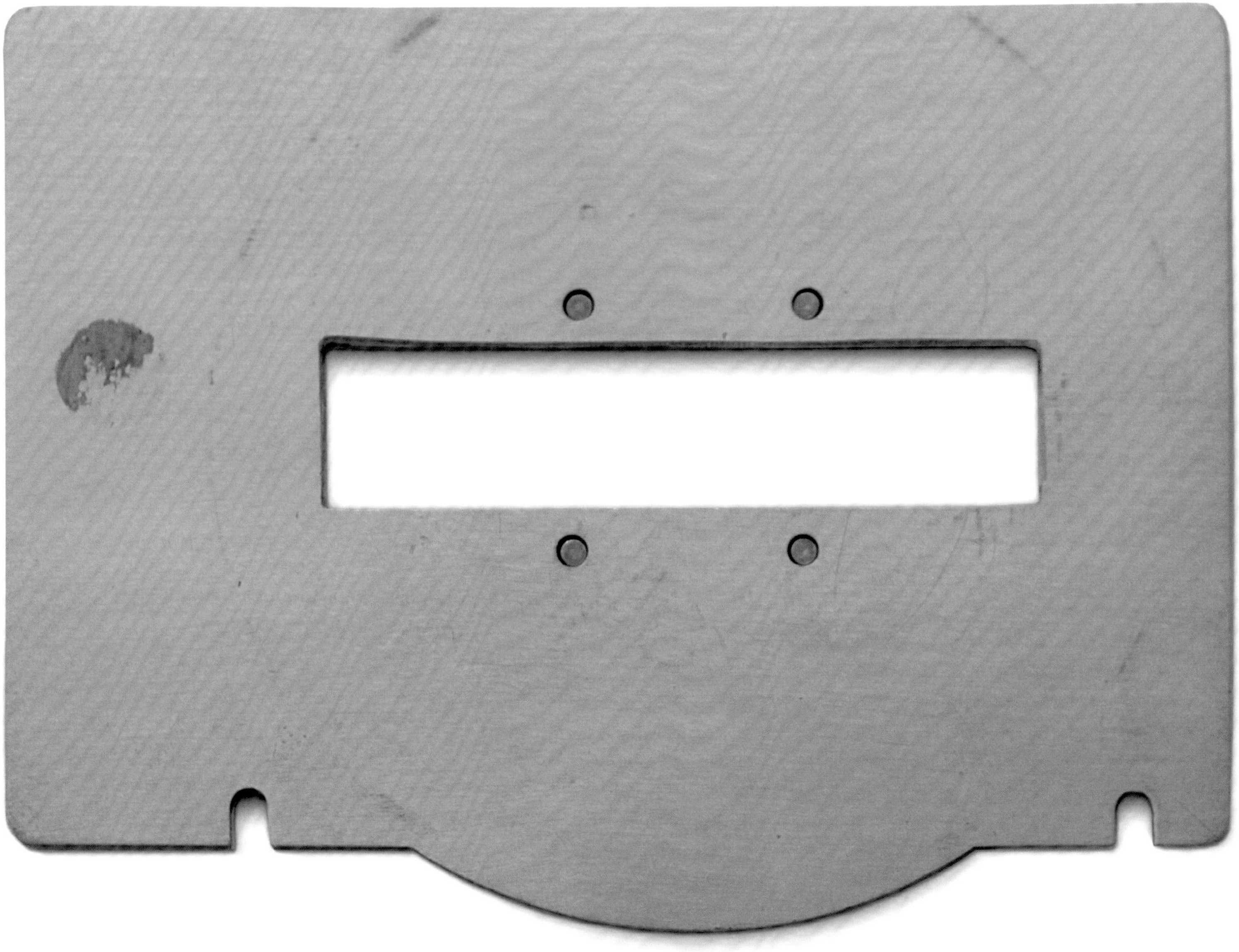

KODAK PLUS X PAN FILM
KODAK SAFETY FILM
→8
→8A
→9
→10A
→11
→12A
→2
→2A
→3A
→4
→4A
→5
→5A
→7
→7A

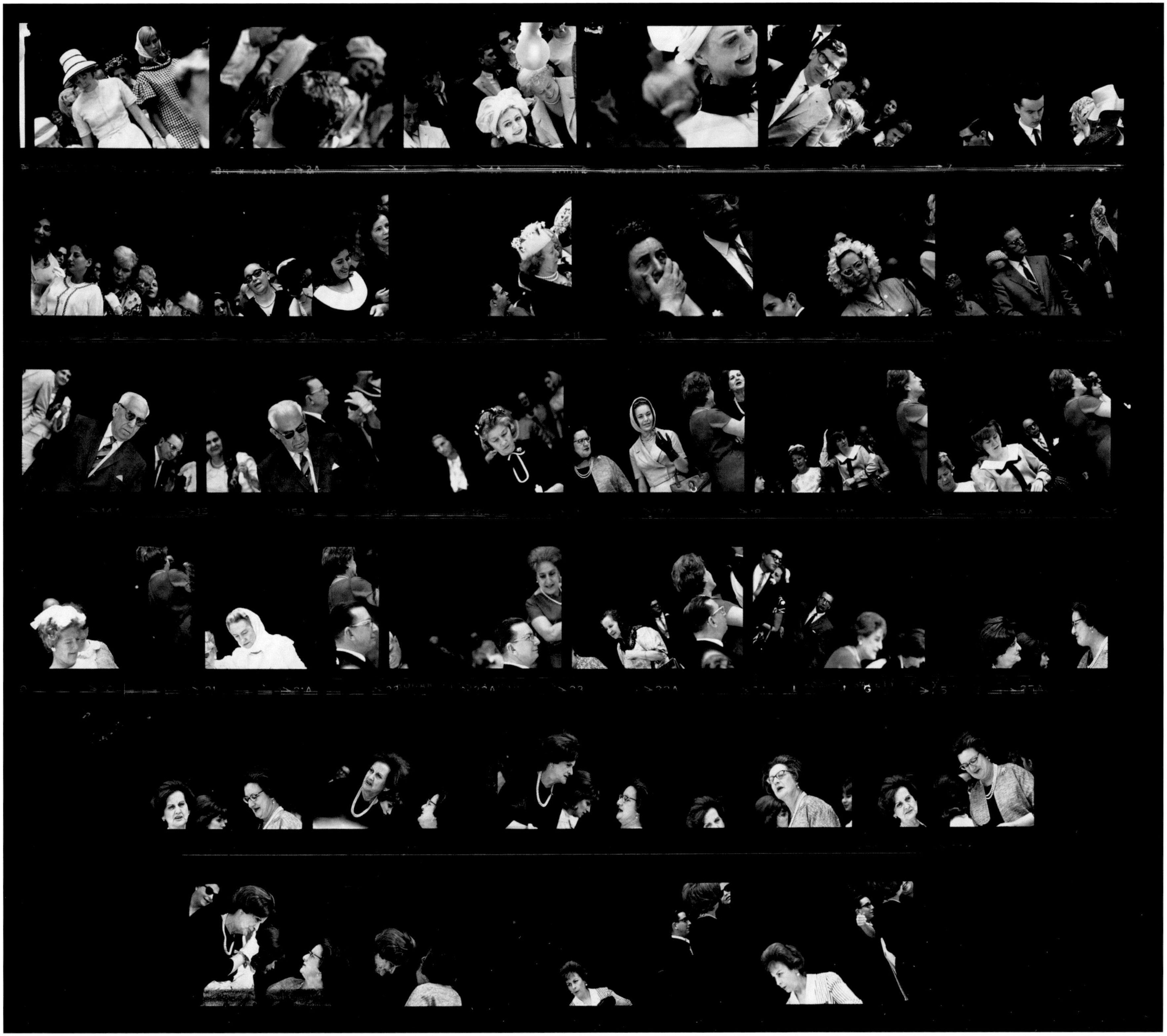

KODAK SAFETY FILM
KODAK PLUS X PAN FILM
NO
NO
NO

KODAK PLUS X PAN FILM
KODAK SAFETY FILM
KODAK
→10A →11 →11A →12 →12A →13
→25 →25A →26 →26A →27 →27A →28 →28A →29 →29A
→4 →4A →5 →5A →6 →6A →7A →8 →8A →9
→31A →32 →32A →33 →33A →34 →34A →35 →35A
→17A →18 →18A →19 →19A →20 →20A →21 →21A →22A

→32A →33 →33A →34 →34A →35 →35A →36 →36A
KODAK SAFETY FILM
KODAK PLUS X PAN FILM
→10A →11 →11A →12 →12A →13 →13A →14 →14A →15
KODAK SAFETY FILM
KODAK PLUS X PAN FILM
X PAN FILM →15A →16 →16A →17 →17A →18 →18A →19 →19A →20
KODAK SAFETY FILM
KODAK PLUS X PAN FILM
→5 →5A →6 →6A →7A →8 →8A →9 →9A →10
20A →21 →21A →22 →22A →23 →23A →24 →25 →25A →26
KODAK PLUS X PAN FILM
KODAK SAFETY FILM

21 21A 22 22A 23 23A 24
KODAK SAFETY FILM
14 14A 15 15A 16 16A 17 17A
KODAK SAFETY FILM
Yes
10 10A 11 11A 12 12A 13 13A
KODAK SAFETY FILM
KODAK PLUS X PAN FILM
KODAK SAFETY FILM
30 30A 31 31A 32 32A 33 33A 34 34A 35 35A
KODAK PLUS X PAN FILM
KODAK SAFETY FILM
KODAK PLUS X PAN FILM
6 6A 7 7A 8 8A 9 9A
KODAK SAFETY FILM
KODAK PLUS X PAN FILM

KODAK PLUS X PAN FILM
KODAK SAFETY FILM

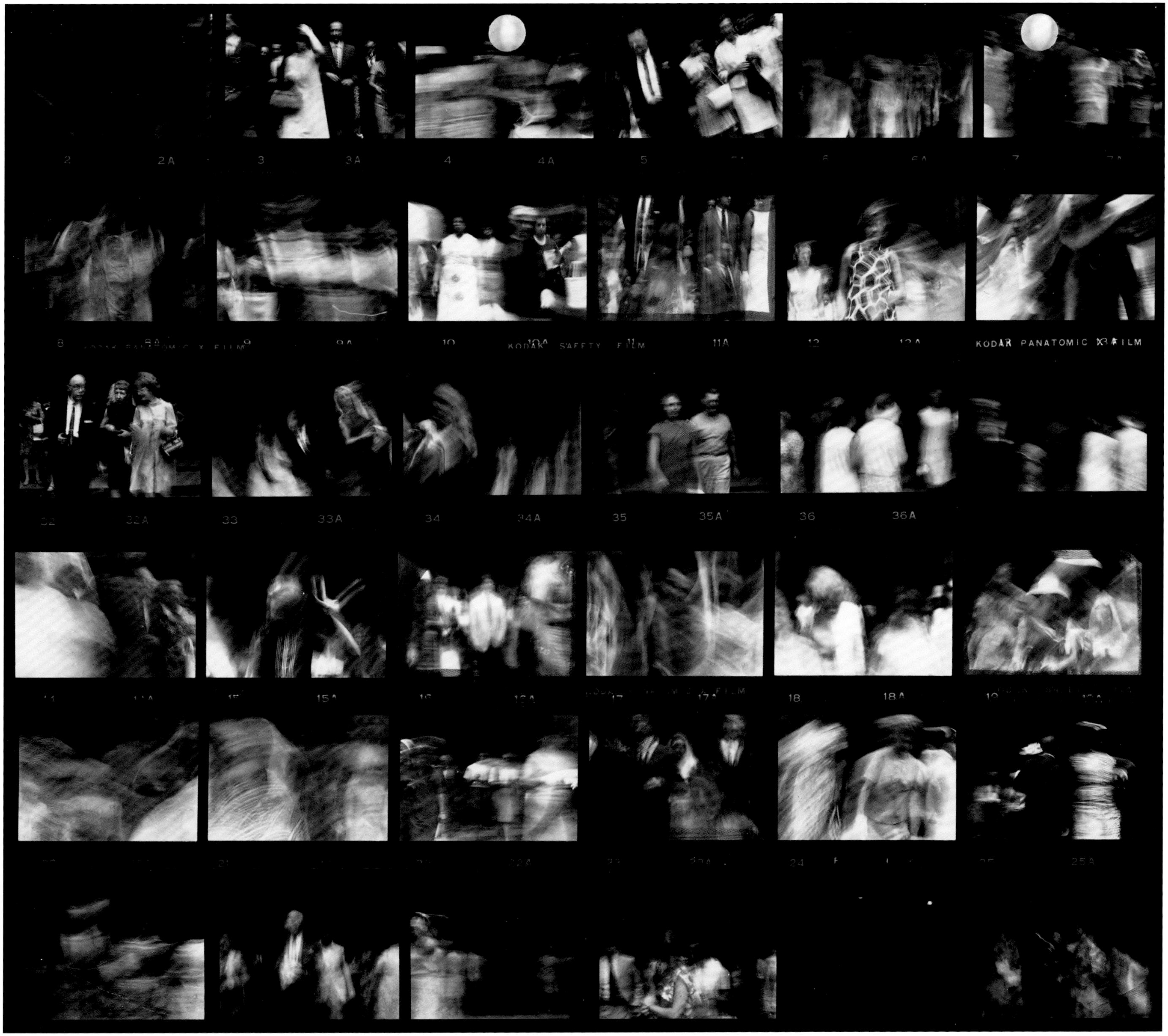
KODAK SAFETY FILM
KODAK PANATOMIC X FILM

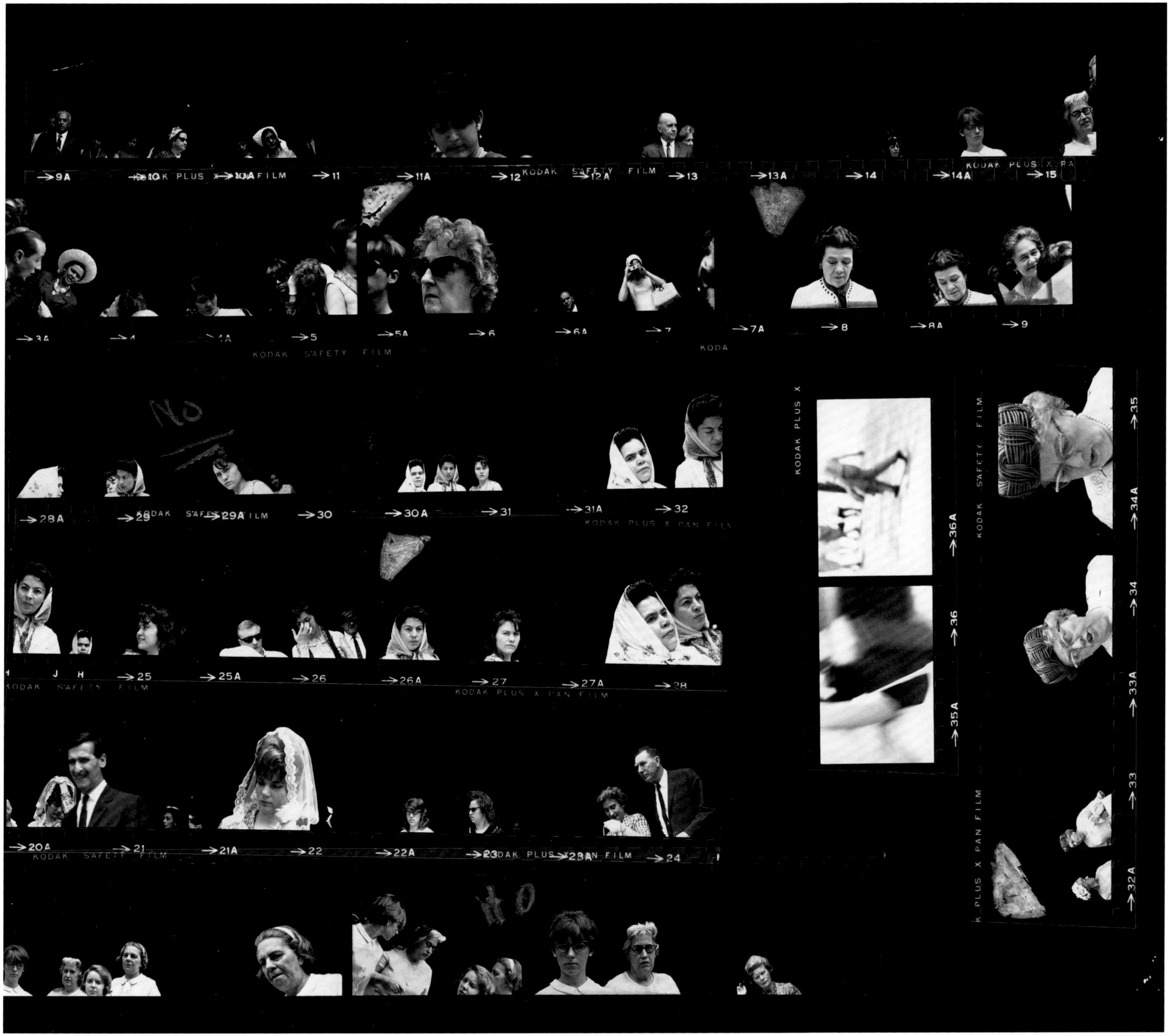
KODAK SAFETY FILM
KODAK PLUS X PAN FILM
NO
NO

KODAK PLUS X PAN FILM
KODAK SAFETY FILM
→32 →32A →33 →33A →34 →34A →35 →35A →36
→26 →26A →27 →30
→20 →20A →21 →21A →23 →25
→10 →10A →11 →11A →12
→14A →15 →15A →16 →16A →17 →17A →18 →18A →19 →19A

KODAK PLUS X PAN FILM
KODAK SAFETY FILM
NO
NO

Made possible by Eliot Nolen, B.A. 1984, and Timothy P. Bradley, B.A. 1983; Professor and Mrs. Robinson A. Grover, B.A. 1958, M.S.L. 1975; the Samuel Freeman Charitable Trust; the Janet and Simeon Braguin Fund; the Cathy M. Kaplan, B.A. 1974, Photography Endowment Fund; the James Maloney '72 Fund for Photography; and the Nitkin Family Fund for Photography.

Published in 2015 by the
Yale University Art Gallery
1111 Chapel Street
P.O. Box 208271
New Haven, CT 06520-8271
artgallery.yale.edu/publications

and distributed by
Yale University Press
302 Temple Street
P.O. Box 209040
New Haven, CT 06520-9040
yalebooks.com/art

First published in 1973 by Flower Mountain Press

Published in conjunction with the exhibition *Donald Blumberg Photographs: Selections from the Master Sets*, organized by the Yale University Art Gallery.

Yale University Art Gallery
August 21–November 22, 2015

Exhibition and publication organized by La Tanya Autry, the Marcia Brady Tucker Fellow, Department of Modern and Contemporary Art, and Jock Reynolds, the Henry J. Heinz II Director, both of the Yale University Art Gallery.

Tiffany Sprague,
Director of Publications and Editorial Services

Christopher Sleboda,
Director of Graphic Design

Project manager: Zsofia Jilling

Set in Marr Sans, 2014
Printed at GHP, West Haven, Conn.

Library of Congress Control Number: 2015943081
ISBN 978-0-300-21517-5

For Gracie again
after forty-two years
and Rachel, Sarah, and Sean
—Donald Blumberg

Cover illustration: Donald Blumberg and Charles Gill, *In Front of Saint Patrick's Cathedral Diptych Joined with a Yellow Hockey Stick* (detail), 1966. Gelatin silver print on linen with acrylic paint and a hockey stick. Yale University Art Gallery, Promised gift of Grace and Donald R. Blumberg

Frontispiece: Donald Blumberg, Untitled, from the series *In Front of Saint Patrick's Cathedral*, 1965–67. Gelatin silver print. Yale University Art Gallery, Janet and Simeon Braguin Fund. Copyright © Donald R. Blumberg

Unless otherwise noted, all photographs are from the Yale University Art Gallery, Janet and Simeon Braguin Fund, Copyright © Donald R. Blumberg. The following photographs are from the Yale University Art Gallery, Promised gift of Grace and Donald R. Blumberg, Copyright © Donald R. Blumberg: pp. 30–31, 40, 46, 53.

p. 78: Ben Shahn photograph © President and Fellows of Harvard
pp. 82–83: Photographs by Sean Collins